THE AUTHORITY SINCE 1868

THE WORLD ALMANAC

AND BOOK OF FACTS

1986

Published annually by
NEWSPAPER ENTERPRISE ASSOCIATION INC.
New York

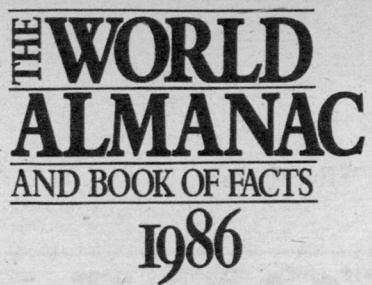

THE WORLD ALMANAC AND BOOK OF FACTS 1986

Publisher: Jane D. Flatt
Editor: Hana Umlauf Lane
Managing Editor: Mark S. Hoffman
Senior Assistant Editors: June Foley, Thomas J. McGuire

Assistant to the Publisher: Constance M. Fidler
Editorial Assistant: Carol DeMatteo
Canadian Editor: John Filion
Indexer: Deborah G. Felder
Chronology: Donald Young

Paperback cover design: Lawrence Ratzkin

The editors acknowledge with thanks the many letters of helpful comment and criticism from users of THE WORLD ALMANAC, and invite further suggestions and observations. Because of the volume of mail directed to the editorial offices, it is not possible personally to reply to each letter writer. However, every communication is read by the editors and all comments and suggestions receive careful attention. Inquiries regarding contents should be sent to: The World Almanac, 200 Park Avenue, New York, NY 10166.

THE WORLD ALMANAC is published annually in November.

THE WORLD ALMANAC does not decide wagers.

The first edition of THE WORLD ALMANAC, a 120-page volume with 12 pages of advertising, was published by the New York World in 1868, 118 years ago. Annual publication was suspended in 1876. Joseph Pulitzer, publisher of the New York World, revived THE WORLD ALMANAC in 1886 with the goal of making it a "compendium of universal knowledge." It has been published annually since then. In 1931, it was acquired by the Scripps-Howard Newspapers; until 1951, it bore the imprint of the New York World-Telegram and thereafter, until 1967, that of the New York World-Telegram and Sun. It is now published in paper and clothbound editions by Newspaper Enterprise Association, Inc., a Scripps-Howard company.

THE WORLD ALMANAC & BOOK OF FACTS 1986

Copyright© Newspaper Enterprise Association, Inc. 1985
Library of Congress Catalog Card Number 4-3781
International Standard Serial Number (ISSN) 0084-1382
Newspaper Enterprise Association, Inc. (softcover) ISBN 0-911818-94-4
Newspaper Enterprise Association Inc. (hardcover) ISBN 0-911818-95-2
Doubleday and Co., Inc. ISBN 0-385-23292-6
Ballantine Books ISBN 0-345-32659-8
Windward/W.H. Smith & Son Ltd. ISBN 0-7112-0428-4
Microfilm Edition since 1868: Bell and Howell Co.
Printed in the United States of America
The Ballantine paperback edition distributed in the United States by Ballantine Books, a division of Random House, Inc. and in Canada by Random House of Canada, Ltd.

NEWSPAPER ENTERPRISE ASSOCIATION, INC.

A division of United Media Enterprises
A Scripps Howard Company
200 Park Avenue, New York, NY 10166

1986 HIGHLIGHTS

GENERAL INDEX

3

Notable Sports Records

During 1984-85, sports fans were treated to many record-breaking performances. Here are the major accomplishments of the year.

Baseball

—Pete Rose's 4,192d hit broke Ty Cobb's 57-year-old record for most major league hits.

—Dwight Gooden, at age 20, became the youngest pitcher to win 20 major league games in a season.

—Tom Seaver became the 17th pitcher to win 300 major league games.

—Phil Niekro became the 18th pitcher to win 300 major league games.

—Rod Carew became the 16th player to collect 3,000 major league hits.

—Nolan Ryan became the first pitcher to record 4,000 strikeouts.

—Vince Coleman's 110 stolen bases set a major league rookie base stealing record.

Football

—Walter Payton broke Jimmy Brown's all-time pro football record of 12,312 career rushing yards.

—San Francisco and Miami became the first Super Bowl participants to lose their opening games the following season.

—Eric Dickerson gained 2,105 yards, breaking the NFL record for rushing yardage in a season.

—Dan Marino's 5,084 yards broke the NFL passing yardage record for a season.

—Mark Clayton's 18 touchdown receptions broke the NFL record for single-season touchdown catches.

—Art Monk broke the NFL for pass receptions in a season, with 106 catches.

—Herschel Walker's 2,411 yards set the USFL record for rushing yardage in a season.

—Eddie Robinson of Grambling College set a college football record for most coaching victories (324).

Others

—Bill Elliott collected a $1 million bonus for winning 3 of the 4 big NASCAR races.

—Mary Decker Slaney set a women's world record for the mile (4:16.71).

—Matt Biondi set a world swimming record in the 100-meter freestyle (48.95 sec.).

—Steve Cram set world records for the mile (3:34.31) and 1,500-meters (3:29.67).

—Boris Becker, at age 17, became the youngest Wimbledon champion.

—Michael Spinks became the first light heavyweight champion to win a heavyweight title.

—Isaih Thomas of the Detroit Pistons broke the NBA record for assists (1,123) in a season.

—Mark Eaton of the Utah Jazz broke the NBA record for blocked shots (456) in a season.

—Kareem Abdul-Jabbar became the NBA's all-time leading scorer (31,420 pts.).

—Scotty Bowman set the NHL record for most coaching victories (691).

—Wayne Gretzky broke the NHL record for most points (47) in a single playoff series.

—Spend a Buck won $2.6 million, including a $2 million bonus, for winning the Kentucky Derby and 3 New Jersey stakes races.

Addenda, Late News, Changes

Ambassadors (p. 624)

Joe M. Rogers was named U.S. ambassador to France replacing Evan G. Galbraith.

Awards

Nobel Prizes (pp. 346-348)

Nobel Prize in Medicine or Physiology: The Nobel Prize in medicine was awarded to two Americans, Michael S. Brown and Joseph L. Goldstein, for their 1973 discovery that cells of the human body have receptors on their surfaces that trap and absorb blood-stream particles containing cholesterol. The University of Texas scientists shared a cash award of $225,000, the highest in the 84-year history of the Nobel prizes.

Nobel Memorial Prize in Economics: Franco Modigliani, a professor at the Massachusetts Institute of Technology, won the Nobel Memorial Prize in Economic Science for his pioneering work in analyzing the behavior of household savers and the functioning of financial markets. The prize carried a cash award of about $225,000.

Nobel Prize in Physics: Klaus von Klitzing, a West German computer expert, was awarded the Nobel Prize in physics for developing an exact way of measuring electrical conductivity. He was awarded $225,000.

Nobel Prize in Chemistry: Two Americans, Herbert A. Hauptman, director of the Medical Foundation of Buffalo, and Jerome Karle, of the Naval Research Laboratory, were awarded the Nobel Prize in chemistry. Together, they developed mathematical techniques through which X-ray crystallography can be used directly to deduce the three-dimensional structure of natural substances vital to the chemistry of the human body and of drugs that can be used to treat various ailments. They shared the $225,000 award.

Nobel Peace Prize: International Physicians for the Prevention of Nuclear War was awarded the Nobel Peace Prize of about $225,000, for "spreading authoritative information and . . . creating an awareness of the catastrophic consequences of atomic warfare." The organization is based in Boston, with a branch in London.

Nobel Prize in Literature: Claude Simon, a leading exponent of the French nouveau roman—"new novel"—won the Nobel Prize in Literature, about $225,000.

Broadcasting and Theater (pp. 354-355)

Emmy Awards, by Academy of Television Arts and Sciences, for nighttime programs, 1984-85: Dramatic series: *Cagney & Lacey,* CBS; actress, drama: Tyne Daly, *Cagney and Lacey;* actor, drama: William Daniels, *St. Elsewhere,* NBC; supporting actress: Betty Thomas, *Hill Street Blues,* NBC; supporting actor: Edward James Olmos, *Miami Vice,* NBC; Comedy series: *The Cosby Show,* NBC; actress, comedy: Jane Curtin, *Kate & Allie,* CBS; actor, comedy: Robert Guillaume, *Benson,* ABC; supporting actress: Rhea Perlman, *Cheers,* NBC; supporting actor: John Larroquette, *Night Court,* NBC; Drama or comedy special: *Do You Remember Love?,* CBS; Limited series: *The Jewel in the Crown,* PBS; Variety, music, or comedy program: *Motown Returns to the Apollo,* NBC; actress, limited series or special: Joanne Woodward, *Do You Remember Love?;* actor, limited series or special: Richard Crenna, *The Rape of Richard Beck,* ABC; supporting actress, limited series or special: Kim Stanley, *Cat on a Hot Tin Roof,* PBS; supporting actor, limited series or special: Karl Malden, *Fatal Vision,* NBC; individual performance, variety or music program: George Hearn, *Sweeney Todd,* PBS.

Humanitas Prizes, for TV that enriches human values: $25,000: Hume Cronyn and Susan Cooper, *The Dollmaker;* $15,000: John Masius and Tom Fontana, *Bye, George;* $10,000: John Markus, *The Cosby Show;* $10,000, for animation in children's programming: Jeffrey Scott, *Jim Henson's Muppet Babies;* live action: Charles Purpura, *The Day the Senior Class Got Married;* news-documentary: *NBC White Paper—Vietnam—Lessons of a Lost War,* by Marvin Kalb, Anthony Potter, William Turque.

Miscellaneous (p. 355)

Astaire Dance Award, by Anglo-American Contemporary Dance Foundation, for lifetime achievement in dance: Jerome Robbins.

Country Music Association Awards: male vocalist, album: George Strait, *Does Fort Worth Ever Cross Your Mind?;* female vocalist: Reba McEntire; vocal duo: Anne Murray, Dave Loggins; vocal group: the Judds; instrumental group: Ricky Skaggs Band; song: *God Bless the U.S.A.,* Lee Greenwood; single: *Why Not Me,* the Judds; video: *All My Rowdy Friends Are Comin' Over Tonight,* Hank Williams Jr.; Horizon award: Sawyer Brown; Hall of Fame: Flatt and Scruggs; entertainer: Ricky Skaggs.

Four Freedoms Awards, by Four Freedoms Foundation, for committment to Franklin D. Roosevelt's "Four Freedoms": Four Freedoms Medal: Rep. Claude Pepper (D., Fla.); Freedom of Speech: Dr. Kenneth Clark; Freedom of Worship: Elie Wiesel; Freedom from Fear: Isidor I. Rabi; Freedom from Want: John Kenneth Galbraith.

Kennedy Center for the Performing Arts Awards: Merce Cunningham, Irene Dunne, Bob Hope, Alan Jay Lerner, Frederick Loewe, Beverly Sills.

MacArthur Foundation fellowships, for outstanding talent and creativity, $155,000 to $600,000 each over 5 years: Joan Abrahamson, painter, songwriter, organizer of Jefferson Institute; John Ashbery, poet, writer of fiction and drama, professor; John F. Benton, professor of history, specialist in medieval history; Harold Bloom, literary critic, professor; Valery Chalidze, physicist, publisher, author; William Cronon, professor of history, author; Merce Cunningham, dancer, choreographer; Jared Diamon, membrane physiologist, conservationist; Marian Wright Edelman, leading advocate for children in welfare, health, juvenile justice, family support; Morton Halperin, writer, director of American Civil Liberties Union's National Security Project; Robert M. Hayes, founder of Coalition for the Homeless; Edwin L. Hutchins, anthropologist, author; Sam Maloof, woodworker, teacher, author; Andrew McGuire, executive director of Trauma Center Foundation; Patrick Francis Noonan, founder of Conservation Resources Inc.; George F. Oster, professor, specialist in mathematical biology; Thomas G. Palaima, professor of classics, author; Peter Raven, botanist; Jane Richardson, professor, specialist in comparing and classifying protein structures and X-ray crystallography of proteins; Gregory Schopen, professor, combines philological study of inscriptions with archeological data; Franklin Stahl, professor of biology; J. Richard Steffy, professor, specialist in nautical archeology and in restoring historic ship-wrecked vessels; Ellen Stewart, producer, manager, and director of La Mama, an Off-Off Broadway theater; Paul Taylor, dancer, choreographer; Shing-Tung Yau, professor of mathematics.

Arts and Media (p. 369)

Miss Mississippi, Susan Akin, was named Miss America for 1986.

Canada (p. 700)

Quebec: Pierre Marc Johnson was elected, Sept. 29, as the leader of the Parti Québécois and as Premier of Quebec. He succeeded Premier René Lévesque, who stepped down.

Chronology (p. 906-907)

Turner abandoned his attempt to take over CBS, Aug. 7, and announced that Turner Broadcasting would buy MGM/UA Entertainment Co., a producer and distributor of films and television programs.

Arthur Walker was found guilty, Aug. 9, of espionage and conspiracy after a nonjury trial conducted in federal district court in Norfolk.

Corporate Mergers (p. 113)

R.J. Reynolds acquired Nabisco for $4.9 billion; Philip Morris acquired General Foods for $5.8 billion; General Motors acquired Hughes Aircraft for $5 billion.

Earthquakes (p. 688)

The offical death toll for the July 28, 1976 earthquake in Tangshan, China is 242,000.

Mayors (pp. 253; 255)

Atlanta: Andrew Young was reelected mayor.
There is no Bloomfield, Minn.; the correct name of the city is Bloomington.

National Defense (p. 325)

Adm. William J. Crowe Jr. was sworn in, Oct. 1, as Chairman of the Joint Chiefs of Staff. He succeeded Gen. John W. Vessey Jr. to become the 11th Chairman of the Joint Chiefs.

Nations of the World (pp. 535-621)

Bolivia: Victor Paz Estenssoro was elected president.
Egypt: Ali Lutfy was chosen prime minister replacing Kamal Hassan Ali.
Guyana: Prime Minister Desmond Hoyte became president upon the death of Linden Forbes Sampson Burnham.
Nigeria: Maj. Gen. Ibrahim Babangida became head of government in a bloodless military coup.
Panama: Vice President Eric Arturo Delvalle became president following the resignation of Nicolas Ardito Barletta.
Portugal: Anibal Cavaco Silva was elected prime minister.
Uganda: Lieut. Gen. Tito Okello became head of state following the overthrow of President Milton Obote.

Population (p. 226)

Poverty: The national poverty rate declined in 1984 by nine-tenths of a percentage point, to 14.4 percent, the largest one-year decrease in more than a decade. The total number of poor people in the U.S. declined by 1.8 million, from 35.5 million in 1983 to 33.7 million in 1984. A family of four was classified as poor if it had cash income of less than $10,609 in 1984. The overall poverty rate for black Americans declined by 1.9 percent, from 35.7 percent to 1983 to 33.8 percent in 1984. The poverty rate for whites dropped from 12.2 percent in 1983 ot 11.5 percent in 1984. The rate for Hispanics rose from 28.1 percent to 1983 to 28.4 percent in 1984. The poverty rate for families headed by women declined from 36.1 percent in 1983 to 34.5 percent in 1984. The number of people living in such families declined by 408,000, to 16.4 million, the biggest drop since 1966. Families headed by women accounted for 16 percent of all families and 48 percent of poor families in 1984. Of the 2.1 million black families below the poverty level, 1.5 million were headed by women.

United States (p. 451)

The Constitution. The proposed "D.C. Representation Amendment" became inoperative on Aug. 22 as only 16 of the required 38 states had given approval for ratification.

U.S. Population (pp. 270-271)

California: The area codes for George AFB, Ramona, and Ridgecrest should be 619, not 714.
Florida: The zip code for Belleview should be 32620, not 32506.
Iowa: The correct designation for Clear Lake City should be Clear Lake, not Clear Lake City.

U.S. Government (p. 321)

Margaret M. Heckler, Secretary of Health and Human Services, was named ambassador to Ireland.

Ten Most Dramatic Sports Events, Nov. 1984—Oct. 1985

Selected by The World Almanac Sports Staff

—Villanova Univ. upset number one ranked defending champion Georgetown Univ., 66-64, to win the NCAA basketball championship. It was the first NCAA basketball title for the Wildcats.

—Pete Rose of the Cincinnati Reds collected his 4,192d hit to break Ty Cobb's 57-year-old record for most major league hits. The historic blow was a single off Eric Show of the San Diego Padres.

—Doug Flutie threw a 64-yard touchdown pass on the final play of the game to lead Boston College to a 47-45 victory over national champion Miami Univ. Flutie's 472 passing yards in the game allowed him to become the first 10,000-yard passer in major-college history.

—Seventeen-year-old Boris Becker of West Germany became Wimbledon's youngest champion when he won the All-England men's singles title. He defeated Kevin Curren in the finals, 6-3, 6-7, 6-4.

—Eric Dickerson of the Los Angeles Rams gained 215 yards rushing against the Houston Oilers to pass O.J. Simpson's single-season NFL rushing record of 2,003 yards. Dickerson finished the season with 2,105 yards rushing.

—Steve Cram of Great Britain ran a mile in 3 minutes 34.31 seconds to set a new world record. He shaved 1.02 seconds off the previous record set by countryman Sebastian Coe in 1981.

—The Los Angeles Lakers defeated the defending champion Boston Celtics 111-100 to win the NBA championship series 4 games to 2. It was the 4th NBA championship for the Lakers.

—Dwight Gooden of the N.Y. Mets defeated the San Diego Padres 9-3, for his 20th win of the season. He became the youngest 20-game winner in major league history.

—The Kansas City Royals defeated the St. Louis Cardinals in the 1985 World Series after trailing 3 games to 1. The Royals became the 1st team to win the Series after losing the first two games at home.

—Michael Spinks won a 15-round decision over Larry Holmes to become the first light heavyweight champion to win the heavyweight title. Holmes, recognized as champion by the International Boxing Federation and most boxing fans, had hoped to equal Rocky Marciano's heavyweight record of 49 consecutive wins.

National Spelling Bee Champions

The Scripps Howard National Spelling Bee, conducted by Scripps Howard Newpapers and other leading newpapers since 1939, was instituted by the Louisville (Ky.) Courier-Journal in 1925. Children under 16 years of age and not beyond the eighth grade are eligible to compete for cash prizes at the finals, which are held annually in Washington, D.C.

In the 1985 spelldown, the runner-up missed "farrago" (mixture, confused assemblage). The winner spelled it correctly, and also the final word, "milieu" (environment, setting). **Recent winners are:**

1984 — 1. Dan Greenblatt, 13, Sterling, Va. (Loudoun Times-Mirror, Leesburg, Va.). 2. Amy McWhirter, 13, St. Joseph, Mich. (Herald Palladium, Benton Harbor/St. Joseph, Mich.). 3. Jennifer Poole, 13, Alexandria, Va. (Journal Newspapers, Wash. D.C.).

1985 — 1. Balu Natarajan, 13, Bowling Brook, Ill. (Chicago Tribune). 2. Kate Lingley, 13, Dover-Foxcroft, Me. (Maine Sunday Telegram, Portland). 3. Tanya Z. Solomon, 13, Kansas City, Mo. (The Examiner, Independence, Mo.).

The World Almanac

and Book of Facts for 1986

The Top 10 News Stories

World attention was riveted on Beirut, Lebanon, for 17 days in June while Shiite Muslim extremists held hostages seized from a TWA airliner enroute from Athens to Rome; one American was killed before all the hostages were freed.

In the wake of continued Congressional and growing international economic pressure against apartheid, U.S. Pres. Ronald Reagan ordered partial sanctions against the South African government while 11 Western European nations imposed trade, cultural and military sanctions.

Laying out improvement of the economy as his most important goal, 54-year-old Mikhail Gorbachev succeeded Konstantin Chernenko as leader of the USSR; his comparative youth and energy presaged that he would have a major influence on Soviet and world affairs for many years.

Lethal gas leaked from a Union Carbide plant in Bhopal, India, and drifted through two densely populated slum neighborhoods, bringing death to more than 2,000 persons.

Young, old and virtually all other major demographic groups gave majority support to Pres. Ronald Reagan, re-electing him in a landslide victory at age 73 as the oldest president in U.S. history.

Four Palestinian hijackers who had seized the Italian cruise ship *Achille Lauro* were intercepted in mid-flight from Cairo to Tunis by U.S. planes and forced to land on Italian territory as the U.S. disputed Egyptian handling of the affair; one American was killed by the hijackers.

Tens of thousands were made homeless and over 5,000 persons killed when a powerful earthquake sent deadly shockwaves through central and southwest Mexico, causing the heaviest devastation in Mexico City.

Ongoing coverage of and concern about the spread of AIDS was brought home to millions of Americans by the death of actor Rock Hudson, a victim of the disease.

Millions of dollars, some $70 million in all, were raised in a 17-hour "Live Aid" rock concert broadcast on radio and TV for the starving people of Africa, whose plight had attracted worldwide concern and aid throughout the year.

Plane crashes dominated the headlines, taking the lives of over 1,400 persons; in the greatest tragedy in airline history, 520 persons died in August when a Japan Air Lines Boeing 747 crashed into a mountain northwest of Tokyo.

Medical Technology in 1985: Life and Death Decisions

On September 29, 1985, the *New York Times* reported that the Massachusetts Institute of Technology had entered "a period of serious reappraisal," in response to some feeling that M.I.T. graduates were "too narrow, too technical and insufficiently concerned with social questions." Samuel J. Keyser, the new associate provost for educational programs and policy, expressed concern about "the social, political and economic implications of technological innovation." Dr. Keyser said, "I wonder if we are introducing that sufficiently—I mean the wise use of science and technology."

The wise use of science and technology was of increasing concern to many Americans in 1985. In particular, advances in medical technology and the life-and-death decisions that were the aftermath of these advances made headlines and created controversy.

"Baby Fae" Implanted with Baboon Heart

A two-week-old infant, known as "Baby Fae," became the first human to be implanted with the heart of a baboon. The child died two weeks later. Officials at Loma Linda University Medical Center in California acknowledged that they had not tried to acquire a human heart before implanting the baboon's heart. Dr. Leonard Bailey, who headed the surgical team, referred to the failure to seek a human heart donor before resorting to a baboon as "an oversight." Questions were raised as to whether physicians had adequately informed Baby Fae's parents of the risks and alternatives involved. A subsequent study by the National Institutes of Health concluded that while doctors had given the parents sufficient information, they had overstated the baby's chances for survival. Later, Dr. Bailey acknowledged that an autopsy had revealed that the baby had died because the baboon's blood type did not match hers.

Artificial Hearts Implanted

The third, fourth, and fifth Jarvik-7 artificial hearts were implanted. Murray P. Haydon, the retired auto worker who received the third Jarvik-7 heart, experienced internal bleeding and breathing problems requiring surgery, connection to a mechanical respirator, and a tracheotomy in the six weeks following the transplant.

The fourth Jarvik-7 recipient, a Swede and the first person outside the U.S. to receive an artificial heart, was named by his country's press as Leif Stenberg, Sweden's suspected "gangster king" in the 1960s and 1970s, and at the time of the transplant under indictment for tax fraud.

Jack C. Burcham, the 62-year-old retired railroad engineer who was the fifth and oldest person to receive a permanent artificial heart, died after 10 days—the shortest span yet. An autopsy revealed that large blood clots had formed outside the Jarvik-7 and cut off his blood flow by compressing a remaining part of his natural heart to which the artificial heart was attached. Dr. William C. DeVries, who had performed the transplant, acknowledged that Jack Burcham's life might have been shortened by the implant.

New Survival Record Set

Meanwhile, William J. Shroeder surpassed the survival record of 112 days set by pioneer mechanical heart recipient Dr. Barney Clark. Shroeder became the first artificial heart patient to leave the hospital when he was moved from Humana Hospital's Louisville facility to a specially equipped nearby apartment owned by the hospital. However, he was readmitted to the hospital a month later, after a CAT scan showed he had suffered a brain hemorrhage. In the May issue of *Life* magazine, William Shroeder's wife, Margaret, said she was no longer so hopeful about her husband's prospects. "I see it as more of a research experiment. The longer he lives, the more information (doctors) will get," she said. "Only for us, it's so hard sometimes."

As of late 1985, of the six people implanted with Jarvik-7 hearts, only two had not suffered strokes—Dr. Barney Clark

and Jack Burcham, both of whom had died. Dr. Claude Lenfant, director of the National Heart, Lung and Blood Institute said earlier in the year that the experience of Dr. DeVries and the Humana program had made him "extremely cautious about the future of the artificial heart."

Unsanctioned Heart Implanted

A University of Arizona surgical team, led by Dr. Jack G. Copeland, implanted a different type of artificial heart in Thomas Creighton, a dying 32-year-old man, after his body had rejected a transplanted human heart. The day after the artificial heart transplant, the man received another human heart. He died the next day, of complications from the unprecedented triple operation. The artificial heart had been tested about four times in calves, for about 12 hours, but had never been used in a human and had not been approved by the Food and Drug Administration. Dr. Copeland said the situation had been desperate, and "my conscience is clear." Reportedly, the FDA sent a letter of "mild rebuke" to the medical center for the use of the unauthorized artificial heart.

For the first time, a Jarvik-7 artificial heart was implanted temporarily, as a bridge to a human heart transplant. Michael Drummond, the 25-year-old recipient, suffered mild strokes seven days after the artificial implant and two days before the human transplant.

All these cases raised questions as to the ethics, costs, and usefulness of advances in medical technology. The same sort of questions came up before Congress and the courts.

"Right to Life" Victory

In late 1984, Congress passed and Pres. Reagan signed a bipartisan compromise bill designed to prevent child abuse. The law included provisions that would withhold federal funds from states that had not set up procedures for preventing the medical neglect of infants with life-threatening handicaps and permitting the prosecution of medical personnel who withheld treatment from such infants. Although several exceptions were cited in which lifesaving efforts could be denied, including cases when the baby was "irretrievably comatose" or would not survive even with treatment, the law said: If the child would benefit, doctors must treat it; parents would not be permitted a veto.

The action was considered a victory for "right to life" advocates and a response to the cases of "Baby Doe" and "Baby Jane Doe," severely handicapped infants born in 1982 in Bloomington, Indiana and 1984 on Long Island, New York, respectively. The federal government had gone to court to demand the medical records of these infants, after their doctors and parents had decided to withhold surgery or other medical treatment in the belief it would be futile. The federal government charged that decisions against treatment represented discrimination because of the babies' handicaps. In both cases, the courts rejected the federal demands.

On June 17, 1985, the U.S. Supreme Court agreed to decide whether federal law to protect the handicapped against discrimination also applied to the treatment of severely disabled newborn infants denied life-prolonging treatment. However, the "Baby Doe" provisions of the previously passed child-abuse bill made the high court's decision less significant.

"Right to Die" Rulings

The old, as well as the young, became the focus of controversial cases. On Dec. 27, 1984, a California appeals court ruled that a 70-year-old man who was suffering from five usually fatal diseases had the constitutional right to refuse medical treatment. William F. Bartling, who died on Nov. 6, had sought to be disconnected from the respirator that had sustained him for six months. The court ruled that the patient's right to die naturally outweighed the arguments of the Glendale Adventist Medical Center, which had maintained that medical ethics and the responsibility to preserve life prevented the hospital and the patient's physicians from removing the respirator.

On Jan. 17, 1985, the New Jersey Supreme Court ruled that all life-sustaining medical treatment, including feeding

tubes, could be withheld or withdrawn from an 84-year-old nursing home patient, Clare Conroy, who was terminally ill and had "no cognitive abilities," with the provision that this was what the patient would have wanted. The ruling came nine years after the court's landmark decision that allowed Karen Ann Quinlan to be removed from a respirator. The new decision went a step further, since removing a patient from a respirator would not necessarily cause death, but withholding or withdrawing a feeding tube would almost certainly cause death, often within a week.

The court cited several "best interest tests" to be taken before any withdrawal of life support from an incompetent patient: First, an effort must be made to determine what the patient said on the issue while competent; second, if no evidence is available, the patient's family and physicians must measure whether the burden of the patient's life would outweigh the benefits that the patient would derive from life; and third, the "unavoidable, recurring, and severe pain" of a patient's life with treatment must be such that the effect of administering life-sustaining treatment would be "inhumane."

Clare Conroy died of natural causes on Feb. 15, 1983, 13 days after the order to remove her feeding tube was issued by a N.J. Superior Court judge and stayed by the Appellate Division. The appeal was made even though the death made it moot. The decision was considered a sweeping victory for advocates of what was being called "the right to die." Although the ruling was binding only in New Jersey, it was expected to be as influential throughout the country as the ruling had been in the Karen Ann Quinlan case. Because of the latter, more than 35 states already had "brain death" laws that allowed respirators to be withdrawn when the patient no longer showed any sign of brain activity. The need for further guidelines such as the Clare Conroy ruling was expected to grow, since the nation's elderly population had reached a rate of growth twice that of other sectors of the population.

The ruling that all life-support systems could be withheld from both competent and incompetent terminally ill patients, if that was what they wanted or would have wanted, was overwhelmingly endorsed by Americans in a Gallup poll taken one week later. Across the country, 81 percent of those polled favored the decision, with only 13 percent in opposition.

However, Karen Ann Quinlan's parents, through their attorney, said that they had no intention of seeking permission to withdraw her feeding tube. On June 11, 1985, Karen Ann Quinlan died at age 31 in a nursing home in Morris Plains, New Jersey, of pulmonary failure following pneumonia. She had spent the last third of her life in a coma.

Questions Remaining

It remained unclear how the Conroy ruling would apply to younger nursing-home patients in a similar situation, or to similar patients in hospitals, or to institutionalized severely retarded individuals.

Some expressed concern that the ruling could be misinterpreted, especially because of pressure for health-care cost containment, leading doctors or health care personnel to stop treatment prematurely.

In many cases, the questions remained: Now that advances in medical technology meant that the dying process *could* be prolonged, when *should* it be prolonged? Who should live? Who should die? How should this be decided? When should it be decided? Who should decide it? What should be done in case of disagreement?

Who Should Decide?

Disagreements were dramatized in courts across the country in late 1984 and 1985. In California, Dr. Neil L. Barber and Dr. Robert J. Nejdl, who acceded to family requests to discontinue life-sustaining treatment for a severely brain-damaged comatose patient, Clarence Herbert, were charged with murder and conspiracy. The indictments were later dismissed, but doctors and nurses in many states cited the case and its costs in time, legal fees, and possible damage to reputations to support their fears of possible prosecution.

In Fairport, New York, Dr. John Kraii injected a lethal drug into an 81-year-old friend suffering from Alzheimer's

disease and severe gangrene that probably would have required the amputation of his legs. Dr. Kraii, who at age 76 still made house calls and had become a local legend for his powers of healing and acts of generosity, was arrested and charged with second-degree murder. Although townspeople rallied to his defense, sending letters of support to his family and besieging the prosecutor's office with calls and letters asking that the murder charges be dropped, the charges remained. Three weeks after his arrest, Dr. Kraii was found dead, with a suicide note.

Thomas P. Engel, a Milwaukee nurse, disconnected the life-support system of an elderly stroke victim, in accordance with the wishes of the patient's family. Mr. Engel was charged with practicing medicine without a license, pleaded no contest, and received a 20-month suspended sentence. At a Wisconsin Board of Nursing license-revocation hearing, Mr. Engel's defense involved his claim that a nurse, who knows the patient and family more intimately than a visiting doctor, can be an effective advocate of the patient's interest instead of a passive extension of the doctor's will. Mr. Engel's license was revoked for a year, after which he could be relicensed if he met certain conditions.

In Florida, Roswell Gilbert, a 75-year-old engineer, was sentenced to 25 years in prison with no chance of parole, after a jury convicted him of first-degree murder in the fatal shooting of his wife of 51 years, Emily. Mr. Gilbert used a mercy killing defense, based on his wife's having been incurably ill with Alzheimer's disease and osteoporosis. The prosecutor successfully argued that his action had been a "convenience."

Groups Made Life-and-Death Decisions

Not only individual patients, families, physicians, nurses, and judges made life-and-death decisions, groups did as well. The advice of two independent biomedical ethics committees was the basis for a Minnesota Supreme Court decision to disconnect the respirator of Rudolfo Torres, who had been comatose, with irreversible brain damage, for 16 months.

The President's Commission for the Study of Ethical Problems in Medicine found that in 1982 less than one percent of the country's hospitals had ethics committees. By 1984, the number had probably mushroomed to almost ten percent, and it was estimated that within five years virtually every American hospital would have an ethics committee. As of 1985, most committees stressed education, discussing ethical issues with hospital personnel; many committees developed hospital policies and guidelines for medical care; some advised patients, families, and doctors. However, many hospital ethics committees did not keep formal minutes because these could be used by a district attorney to prove murder conspiracy.

Still other groups who made life-and-death decisions not only met without minutes, they met out of sight. Increasingly, families, doctors, hospital administrators, and some-

times lawyers came together to decide when and how to end life-sustaining treatment in a procedure referred to as "negotiated death."

Also, "living wills," which made explicit an individual's advance directions regarding the stopping of life-sustaining procedures, were recognized in 22 states and the District of Columbia, although not necessarily followed.

Three large organizations worked for the adoption of the "right to die": The Society for the Right to Die, and Concern for Dying, both in New York City, and both off-shoots of an earlier organization, advocated passive euthanasia—allowing an individual to decide whether to live or die; the Hemlock Society, in Los Angeles, went further, maintaining that those who wanted to commit suicide should not only have medical treatment stopped on demand, but should be able to receive active assistance in dying.

Further Advances in Technology

By the end of 1985, several directions for even further advances in medical technology had come into focus. A study by a panel of experts for the National Institutes of Health had enthusiastically endorsed further research into artificial hearts. The *New York Times* reported that researchers had begun to design improvements in the Jarvik-7 artificial heart to correct a design flaw that could explain the strokes that had seriously complicated its use. A second artificial heart, developed by Dr. William S. Pierce of Penn State's Hershey Medical Center, had been approved by the FDA. According to *U.S. News and World Report*, other researchers were testing such devices as artificial skin grown in the lab; flexible, polyurethane blood vessels; an implanted, insulin-producing artificial pancreas; and an artificial eye consisting of a grid of 64 electrodes to be implanted in the brain. A panel had been named to advise the Secretary of Health and Human Services on improving the nation's organ transplant network.

In the Fall of 1985, the National Institutes of Health approved national guidelines for a revolutionary type of medical treatment—gene therapy. This would improve transplanting genes into a patient's body cells to correct an otherwise incurable disease. Although the guidelines specifically excluded any experimental treatment to produce effects that would pass from one generation to the next, this was a logical possibility for future research.

Also in the Fall of 1985, Betty Rollins, a TV news commentator, published a book called *Last Wish*. The book described the ordeal experienced by Miss Rollins when her mother, terminally ill with cancer, asked her help in committing suicide. Miss Rollins, who said her mother was her best friend, agonized over the moral and legal issues involved. Then she provided her mother with the pills she had been advised (by a physician outside the U.S.) would kill her, and sat with her husband at her mother's side while her mother swallowed the pills, thanked her, and died. The book quickly became a bestseller.

Public Concern about AIDS

Public concern about the deadly condition Acquired Immune Deficiency Syndrome (AIDS) grew during 1985 as the number of victims increased to 15,000 worldwide, with the great majority—13,074—in the United States. Fifty-one percent of those polled by the *New York Times*/CBS News, Sept. 9, ranked AIDS as the second most serious medical problem in America, behind cancer but ahead of heart disease, the country's leading cause of death.

According to the federal Centers for Disease Control in Atlanta, the overwhelming evidence was that AIDS could be spread only through intimate sexual contact, use of a contaminated hypodermic needle, transfusion of blood containing the virus, or, in the case of newborns, infection while in the womb, during birth, or from breast milk of a mother with the virus. Nevertheless, the Times/CBS poll found that about half the American people believed AIDS could be transmitted through casual contact, such as sharing a drinking glass. Federal scientists reiterated that male homosexuals and intravenous drug users remained the groups at greatest

risk. They said a few people receiving blood transfusions had also been stricken, but a test had been developed that appeared to safeguard the nation's blood supply.

The announcement in July that actor Rock Hudson, who died Oct. 2, had AIDS increased public awareness of the crisis. A House Appropriations subcommittee voted, Sept. 13, to double the suggested budget for research on AIDS and to increase funds for education and public health programs. The opening of schools in September promoted debate on whether children with AIDS should be admitted to classrooms. In Queens, New York, parents kept up to 12,000 children out of classes after a girl with AIDS received permission from the city to enroll. Smaller demonstrations and occasional legal battles occurred elsewhere. Wisconsin's largest insurance companies announced, Sept. 17, that they were considering excluding coverage of the disease, because of the rising number of health claims by AIDS victims combined with a new state law that made it difficult to determine whether policyholders had AIDS. *(continued)*

In addition, legislators throughout the U.S., on all levels of government, have adopted or proposed laws and guidelines, ranging from quarantining AIDS victims to blood tests for workers, in connection with AIDS.

The three leading federal science administrators responsible for research on AIDS sought to reassure the public, Sept. 19, saying that an "epidemic of fear" was "absolutely unnecessary." They said that the syndrome did not appear to be spreading appreciably beyond the high-risk groups and that it posed virtually no threat to school children and others who had casual contact with its victims. However, Dr. Walter Dowdle, an official at the Centers for Disease Control, said there was some concern that AIDS would, to a small degree, spread from women prostitutes who used drugs to heterosexual men.

In Hollywood, on Sept. 19, more than 2,500 people attended a fund-raiser to fight AIDS. Pres. Ronald Reagan sent a telegram declaring that his administration had made a "top priority" of halting the spread of AIDS. The World Health Organization announced, Sept. 28, that it had won the medical and financial support needed to launch a worldwide fight against AIDS. The main objective of the effort would be to coordinate research in various countries and provide a central repository for analyzing data.

June Foley

Heroes of Young America: The Sixth Annual Poll

In our sixth annual polling of high school students all across America, Eddie Murphy has taken the highest honor as "Top Hero" of Young America. Teenagers were asked to select those individuals in public life they admire most. The selection was made in 9 categories.

Students in grades 8 through 12 voted in their classrooms in selected schools across the United States. The schools, chosen to participate through The World Almanac's co-sponsoring newspapers, represented a geographic cross-section of the United States in both suburban and intercity schools.

The Top Hero Category

Eddie Murphy, who first gained fame on "Saturday Night Live" and most recently starred in the hit movie, *Beverly Hills Cop*, placed second in last year's voting for the Top Hero category. In this year's poll, he was followed, in order of ranking, by Ronald Reagan, Bill Cosby, Prince, Sylvester Stallone, Clint Eastwood, Debbie Allen, Michael Jordan, Madonna, Mary Lou Retton, Bruce Springsteen, Eddie Van Halen, and Harrison Ford.

A quick look at the other categories shows that six of the contenders for Top Hero were also winners in their individual categories.

Top Hero

Eddie Murphy, comic actor.

Movie Performers/Non-comedy

Clint Eastwood, actor, *Sudden Impact, City Heat.*
Brooke Shields, actress, model.

Television Performers/Non-comedy

Tom Selleck, actor, "Magnum, P.I."
Debbie Allen, actress, dancer, "Fame."

Comedy

Eddie Murphy, TV comic, "Saturday Night Live," *Beverly Hills Cop.*
Goldie Hawn, actress, *Private Benjamin, Protocol.*

Music and Dance

Prince, pop singer, film star, *Purple Rain.*
Madonna, pop singer.

Sports

Michael Jordan, basketball star, Chicago Bulls.
Mary Lou Retton, gymnast, 1984 Olympic gold medalist.

News and Sports Media

Andy Rooney, CBS commentator, "60 Minutes."
Barbara Walters, TV journalist, ABC News.

Artists and Writers

Stephen King, author, *Christine, Pet Sematary.*
Judy Blume, author, *Superfudge, Are You There, God. . .?*

Newsmakers

Neil Armstrong, former astronaut, the first man on the moon.
Geraldine Ferraro, 1984 vice-presidential candidate.

America's 25 Most Influential Women in 1985

The following women were chosen in a World Almanac poll by editors at daily newspapers across the U.S. First place in the balloting went to Katharine Graham, the chair of the Washington Post Company.

Arts

Judy Blume, author of novels for children and adults.
Beverly Sills, general director of the New York City Opera.

Business

Mary Kay Ash, founder and chair of Mary Kay Cosmetics.
Katharine Graham, chair of the Washington Post Co.

Education, Scholars, Scientists

Sally Ride, first U.S. woman astronaut.
Barbara Jordan, professor, former U.S. representative (D., Tex.).
Barbara Tuchman, historian and author.

Entertainment

Jane Fonda, actress, author of bestselling exercise books.
Katharine Hepburn, actress, 4-time winner of Academy Award.

Government

Elizabeth Dole, U.S. Secretary of Transportation.
Geraldine Ferraro, 1984 U.S. vice-presidential candidate.
Jeane J. Kirkpatrick, former UN ambassador.

Sandra Day O'Connor, U.S. Supreme Court justice.
Nancy Reagan, First Lady.

Media

Erma Bombeck, humorist, author of syndicated column and best-selling books.
Ellen Goodman, syndicated *Boston Globe* columnist.
Ann Landers, syndicated advice columnist.
Abigail Van Buren, syndicated advice columnist.

Social Activists

Coretta Scott King, civil rights leader.
Candy Lightner, founder, Mothers Against Drunk Drivers.
Gloria Steinem, women's rights leader, editor of *Ms* magazine.
Betty Ford, former First Lady, advocate of drug/alcohol abuse treatment.

Sports

Chris Evert Lloyd, tennis player, 6-time U.S. singles champion.
Martina Navratilova, tennis player, 6-time Wimbledon singles champion.
Mary Lou Retton, gymnast, winner of two Olympic gold medals.

OMNI Forecasts: 1987 and Beyond

When *OMNI* magazine debuted in October 1978, its editors described their creation as "the magazine of the future." Since then, *OMNI*'s unchanging focus on the future has made it one of the most widely read and influential magazines now published. Here the editors of *OMNI* offer their view of things to come.

1987

Biblical Plague Returns — American farmers, already deep in debt, watch helplessly as their crops vanish into the mouths of more than 100 billion 17-year locusts. Many in the Great Plains report total crop losses. Entomologists, still trying to undersanding the insects' periodic migrations, offer little hope of controlling them soon.

1988

Memory Drug Approved — The U.S. Food and Drug Administration okays the first practical memory booster. The drug, made from a hormone called vasopressin, does little to ease senile memory loss, but prime-of-life users report enormously better recall. Some even complain that the flood of memories interferes with work.

1989

Psychic Power Upheld — Researchers at Duke University announce that people can perform feats of mind over matter. In ten years of study, subjects have managed to alter the rate at which radioactive isotopes decay in a sealed box. Although no one has any idea about how they do it, almost everyone seems to have some of this ability. The announcement provokes a furor among scientists, but many say the experiments seem valid. No one sees any practical use for the puzzling talent.

1990

Tropical Scourge Conquered — The first human malaria vaccine reaches clinical use. Developed at New York University, the preventive is made from a gene-cloned protein found on the cell surface of the malaria parasite. It is effective against all four species that infect human beings. Malaria afflicts more than 220 million people worldwide, killing about 1 million per year in Africa alone.

1991

Food Makers Tout Sweet — Madison Avenue is pushing a new artificial sweetener based on a compound extracted from a plant called "sweet herb" by the Aztecs. The natural chemical, called hernandulcin, is 1,000 times sweeter than sugar but has a bitter aftertaste. The synthetic version, now entering soft drinks, reportedly avoids that problem. Unlike aspartame, it apparently does not enter the brain and therefore poses no risk of altered mental function or behavior.

1992

Natural Hormone Eases Hypertension — Physicians at the National Institutes of Health say a hormone produced by the heart, that resists other drugs, is ready for use in treating high blood pressure. Known as auriculin, the compound lowers blood pressure by relaxing the vessels and promoting sodium and fluid excretion. How the body coordinates these three functions was a mystery until the hormone was discovered eight years ago.

1995

Probe to Steal a Piece of the Sun — NASA scientists launch *Starprobe*, their first major space science mission in five years. After swinging past Jupiter to brake its speed, the small, conical craft will arrive at the sun early in 1999 and pass near the star's incandescent surface. *Starprobe* will take close-up pictures of the sun and map its magnetic field, but the real prize will be a small sample of the atmosphere's material for analysis. The probe will swing out to Jupiter and return every four years for further study and sampling.

1996

Cancer Studies Sabotaged — Researchers at the National Cancer Institute announce that more than 200 research projects budgeted at nearly $25 million must be re-done because suppliers sold experimenters mixed-breed mice instead of pure-breds. Similar mishaps some 15 years ago ruined cancer studies for more than five years before they were discovered.

1997

Electricity Makes High-Powered Students — A private high school in California sets up the first classroom with coils to bathe students in a pulsed electromagnetic field while they work. Tests since the 1970s have shown that pulsed fields can aid memory, or hinder it, depending on their frequency and strength. Teachers say this one helps children memorize multiplication tables and foreign-language vocabulary, but does little for tasks that demand reasoning. Similar fields have been used to heal bones, speed growth of damaged nerves, and inhibit tumors.

1999

Gene Map Nears Finish — In each cell, we carry a complete genetic plan for the human body, some 100,000 genes in all. After more than 20 years of work, scientists have almost finished mapping the sites of these hereditary factors on the chromosomes within the cell nucleus. They predict that the effort will soon yield cures for such ills as cystic fibrosis, Huntington's chorea, and many forms of cancer.

2003

Fusion Power Station Opens — The first demonstration-scale fusion generator produces its first power this year, some three years later than once forecast. Based on pioneering work at Princeton University in the 1980s, the test device can power a small city. A full-sized test facility should go on-line within ten years; two could supply all of New York City with electricity. Commercial generators will follow whenever politics allow. Cost of fusion power is only slightly more than that of an oil-fired generator, and air pollution is avoided.

2005

World Water Shortage Grows — North Africa and the Middle East are now using all the water they store from rain each year, according to the Worldwatch Institute. Future droughts there are expected to cause massive suffering. Nearing this condition are southern and eastern Europe and central and southern Asia. In the American Southwest, dependent on deep wells, falling water tables threaten permanent shortages, while the huge Ogallala aquifer, which waters the Midwest, is expected to run dry within 20 years. Pollution has made one-fourth of the world's usable water supply unfit to drink.

2019

Butlerbots Clean Up — The consumer electronics rage this year is for the new home robots. Budget models are little more than automated vacuum cleaners, but sophisticated units can set the dinner table, wash windows, make beds, and run security patrols at night. Said to be just around the corner ever since the 1980s, butlerbots were delayed because batteries held too little power for practical chores—a problem solved only three years ago. Almost half of American homes are expected to contain a robot within five years.

2050

Humanity Moves to Space — One million people now inhabit the solar system, according to astrophysicist Eric Jones, of the Los Alamos National Laboratory, in New Mexico. Most live in space stations built of material mined on the moon. Other authorities of the 1980s put the space census far lower at this time, but conceded that in the long run space dwellers will outnumber those on Earth. Jones expected them to double every 25 years and reach 1 *trillion* by the year 2550.

CONSUMER SURVIVAL KIT
Your Federal Income Tax: Facts on Filing

Who Must File

Generally, every individual under 65 years of age who resided in the United States and had a gross income of $3,430 or more during the year must file a federal income tax return. Generally, anyone 65 or older on the last day of the tax year is not required to file a return unless he or she had gross income of $4,470 or more during the year. A married couple, living together at the end of the year, both 65 or older, filing a joint return, need not file unless their gross income is $7,700 or more.

A taxpayer with gross income of less than $3,430 (or less than $4,470 if 65 or older) should file a return to claim the refund of any taxes withheld, even if he or she is listed as a dependent by another taxpayer.

If you are married, you must file a tax return if your combined gross income was $5,620 or more, provided you are eligible to file a joint return and are living together at the close of the tax year. The requirement is $6,600 if one spouse is 65 or older, and $7,700 if both of you are 65 or older. If you are married and your spouse files a separate return, or you did not share the same household at the end of the year, you must file a tax return if your gross income was $1,040 or more.

If you are a qualifying widow or widower with a dependent child, you must file a return if your gross income was $4,580 or more ($5,620 or more if you are 65 or older).

Forms to Use

A taxpayer may, at his or her election, use form 1040, form 1040A or form 1040EZ. However, those taxpayers who choose to itemize deductions must use the longer form 1040 and the 1040EZ can be used only by qualifying single taxpayers.

New Tax Changes for 1984 and After

The Tax Reform Act of 1984, signed by President Reagan on July 18, 1984, is a massive piece of legislation. Some of the changes incorporated in the Act that are most likely to affect millions of taxpayers include:

- **Net Interest Exclusion.** Beginning in 1985 individuals would have been able to exclude 15% of interest income, to the extent it exceeded certain interest deductions, up to a maximum of $450.00 per year ($900.00 for married couples filing a joint return). This interest exclusion has been repealed.

- **Earned Income Credit.** Beginning in 1985, the earned income credit is increased from 10% to 11%, thus increasing the maximum credit from $500 to $550. Further, the income range over which the credit is phased out will increase to $6,500 to $11,000 (from the present range of $6,000 to $10,000).

- **Communication Services.** The 3% excise tax imposed for local telephone service, toll telephone service and teletypewriter exchange service, which had been scheduled to expire after 1985, is extended through calendar year 1987.

- **Distilled Spirits.** The excise tax on distilled spirits is $10.50 per proof gallon. Beginning rate of tax October 1, 1985, has been increased to $12.50 per proof gallon.

- **Alimony.** Alimony is generally deductible by the payor and includible in the income of the payee. Beginning in 1985, only cash payments pursuant to a divorce or separation agreement that will terminate upon the death of the payee made between former spouses not living in the same household will qualify as alimony.

Deductions

Generally, a taxpayer may either itemize deductions or choose the zero bracket amount. For single taxpayers the zero bracket amount is $2,390. For married taxpayers filing a joint return it is $3,540. For married taxpayers filing separate returns the deduction is $1,770 each. Some taxpayers are required to itemize deductions.

Dates for Filing Returns

For individuals using the calendar year, Apr. 15 is the final date (unless it falls on a Saturday, Sunday, or a legal holiday) for filing income tax returns and paying any tax due, and for paying the first quarterly installment of the estimated tax. Other installments of estimated tax are to be paid by June 15, Sept. 15, and Jan. 15.

Instead of paying the 4th installment by Jan. 15, a final income tax return, with payment of any tax due, may be filed by Jan. 31. Farmers may file a final return by Mar. 1, with payment of any tax due, to satisfy estimated tax requirements.

Joint Return

A husband and wife may file a joint return, even if one has no income.

One provision stipulates that if one spouse dies, the survivor may compute his or her tax using joint return rates for the first two taxable years following the year of death, provided the survivor was also entitled to file a joint return with the decedent for the year of the death, and he or she furnishes over half the cost of maintaining in his or her household a home for a dependent child or stepchild. If the taxpayer remarries before the end of the taxable year, these privileges are lost but he or she is permitted to file a joint return with his or her new spouse.

Estimated Tax

Generally, if total tax exceeds withheld tax by at least $500 estimated tax installments are required from (1) single individuals, heads of a household or surviving spouses, or a married person entitled to file a joint return whose spouse does not receive wages, who expects a gross income over $20,000; (2) married individuals with over $10,000 where both spouses receive wages; (3) married individuals with over $5,000 not entitled to file a joint return; and (4) individuals whose gross income can reasonably be expected to include more than $500 from sources other than income subject to withholding.

Exemptions

Personal exemption is $1,040.

Every individual has an exemption of $1,040, to be deducted from gross income. A husband and a wife are each entitled to a $1,040 exemption. A taxpayer or spouse who is 65 or over on the last day of the year gets another exemption of $1,040. A husband or wife who is blind on the last day of the year gets another exemption of $1,040.

Exemption for dependents, over one-half of whose total support comes from the taxpayer and for whom the other dependency tests have been met, is $1,040. This applies to a child, stepchild, or adopted child as well as certain other relatives with less than $1,040 gross income; also to a child, stepchild, or adopted child of the taxpayer who is under 19 at the end of the year or was a full-time student during 5 months of the year even if the child makes $1,040 or more. A dependent can be a non-relative if a member of the taxpayer's household and living there all year.

Taxpayer gets the exemption for his child who is a student regardless of the student's age or earnings, provided the taxpayer provides over half of the student's total support. If the student gets a scholarship, this is not counted as support.

Child and Disabled Dependent Care

To qualify, a taxpayer must be employed or looking for work, and provide over one-half the cost of maintaining a household for a dependent child under 15, a dependent of any age who is mentally or physically unable to care for himself or herself; or a spouse unable to care for himself or herself.

Taxpayers may be allowed a credit based on a percentage of employment related expenses. The credit may be up to $720 if there is one qualifying dependent or spouse, and up to $1,440 for two or more. Employment related expenses are expenses that allowed the taxpayer to work (or look for work) and that are paid for household services or for the care of the qualifying dependent or spouse.

For further information consult your local IRS office or the instructional material attached to your return form.

Dividends

The first $100 in dividends can be excluded from income. A husband and wife may exclude up to $200 on their joint return. It does not matter which spouse receives the dividend income. An individual is also entitled to exclude up to $750 ($1,500 on a joint return) for certain dividends received from qualifying domestic public utilities.

The $100 ($200) dividend exclusion does not apply to dividends from tax-exempt corporations, mutual savings banks, building and loan associations, and several others.

Dividends paid in stock or in stock rights are generally exempt from tax, except: (1) when the stockholder has an option to take stock or property, or (2) when the stock distribution is disproportionate, or (3) when the distribution is in convertible preferred stock and has the same result as (2), or (4) when the distribution gives preferred stock to some common stock shareholders and common stock to other common shareholders, or (5) when the distribution is on preferred stock, except for an increase in the conversion ratio of convertible preferred stock solely to take into account a stock dividend or stock split on the stock into which the convertible preferred stock may be converted.

Deductible Medical Expenses

Expenses for medical care, not compensated for by insurance or other payment for taxpayer, spouse, and dependents, in excess of 5% of adjusted gross income are deductible. There is no limit to the maximum amount of medical expenses that can be deducted.

Medical care includes diagnosis, treatment and prevention of disease or for the purpose of affecting any structure or function of the body, and amounts paid for insurance to reimburse for hospitalization, surgical fees and other medical expenses.

Beginning in 1984 subject to certain limits, you may be able to deduct lodging expenses (but not meals) that are not provided in a hospital or similar institution, if the lodging is primarily to enable you to receive medical care.

Medical expenses for a decedent paid by his estate within one year after his death may be treated as expenses of the decedent taxpayer.

Medical and hospital benefits provided by the employer may be exempt from individual income tax.

Deductions for Contributions

Deductions up to 50% of taxpayers' adjusted gross income may be taken for contribution to most publicly supported charitable organizations, including churches or associations of churches, tax-exempt educational institutions, tax-exempt hospitals, and medical research organizations associated with a hospital. The deduction is limited to 20% for gifts of long-term capital gain appreciated property to private nonoperating foundations, and 30% for contributions to such organizations as veterans organizations, fraternal societies, and non-profit cemetery companies.

Taxpayers also are permitted to carry over for five years certain contributions, generally to publicly supported organizations, which exceed the 50% allowable deduction the year the contribution was made.

Also permissible is the deduction as a charitable contribution of unreimbursed amounts up to $50 a school month spent to maintain an elementary or high school student, other than a dependent or relative, in taxpayer's home. There must be a written agreement between you and a qualified organization.

Deductions for Interest Paid

Interest paid by the taxpayer is deductible.

To deduct interest on a debt, you must be legally liable for that debt. No deduction will be allowed for payments you make for another person if you were not legally liable to make them.

Prizes and Awards

All prizes and awards must be reported in gross income, except when received without action by the recipient and recipient is not expected to perform any future services. To be exempt, awards must be received primarily in recognition of religious, charitable, scientific, educational, artistic, literary, or civic achievement. Examples of prizes that do not have to be included in income are Nobel and Pulitzer prizes.

Deductions for Employees

An employee may use the zero bracket amount and deduct as well the following if in connection with his employment: transportation, including automobile expenses, such as gas, oil, and depreciation; however, meals and lodging are deductible as traveling expense only if the employee is away from home overnight. Commuting expenses to and from work are not deductible.

An outside salesman—a salesman who works fulltime outside the office, using the latter only for incidentals—may use the zero bracket amount and deduct all his business expenses.

Don't Forget These Changes from Prior Years

The following tax code provisions that affected prior year returns are still in effect:

• **Sale of a Home.** Two provisions, both of which apply to the sale of a principal residence only, may shield some of the gains made on the sale from taxes.

1. For those 55 or older, the tax exclusion on profit on selling a home is $125,000 on all sales made after July 20, 1981.

2. The period during which payment of income tax on the profit from selling a home can be delayed if the profit is reinvested in another principal residence in 2 years.

• **Capital Gains Tax Reduced.** The tax rate on long-term capital gains (profits from the sale of an asset such as stocks or real estate held for more than a year) decreases from a maximum of 28 percent to no more than 20 percent on sales and exchanges that took place after June 9, 1981.

• **Windfall Profit Tax Credit.** Up through 1984 royalty holders are exempt from windfall profits tax liability on up to two barrels of crude oil production per day. Beginning in 1985 and thereafter, the exemption is increased to three barrels.

• **Tougher Penalties.** In addition to the normal penalties for late filing and late payment, recent tax law changes provide new penalties for substantial understatement of tax liability and for "frivolous" tax returns. If you face the possibility of paying your taxes late, closely examine the new rules for interest rates—the IRS can charge the full prime lending rate (the rate banks often charge their best customers) on taxes paid late. Interest is now compounded daily.

An employee who is reimbursed and is required to account to his employer for his business expenses will not be required to report either the reimbursement or the expenses on his tax return. Any allowance to the employee in excess of his expenses must be included in gross income. If he claims a deduction for an excess of expenses over reimbursement he will have to report the reimbursement and claim actual expenses.

An employee who is not required to account to his employer must report on his return the total amounts of reimbursements and expenses for travel, transportation, entertainment, etc., that he incurs under a reimbursement arrangement with his employer.

The expense of moving to a new place of employment may be deducted under certain circumstances regardless of whether the taxpayer is a new or continuing employee, or whether he pays his own expenses or is reimbursed by his employer. Reimbursement must be reported as income.

Tax Credit for the Elderly and the Permanently and Totally Disabled

Subject to certain rules or exclusions, taxpayers 65 or older may claim a credit which varies according to filing status. Taxpayers should read IRS instructions carefully for full details. You may also be eligible for this credit if you are under age 65, you retired on permanent and total disability, and you received taxable disability benefits.

The credit is limited to 15% of $5,000 for single taxpayers; 15% of $5,000 for married taxpayers filing a joint return when only one taxpayer is either 65 or older or under 65 and retired on permanent and total disability; 15% of $7,500 for married taxpayers filing a joint return if both are 65 or older, or one is 65 or older and the other is under 65 and retired on permanent and total disability, or both are under 65 and both are retired on permanent and total disability; and 15% of $3,750 for a married taxpayer filing a separate return. If you are under 65 and retired on permanent and total disability and your taxable disability income is less than these amounts, the credit is limited to 15% of your taxable disability income.

Net Capital Losses

An individual taxpayer may deduct capital losses up to $3,000 against his ordinary income. However, it takes $2 of net long-term capital loss to get $1 of offset against other income. He may carry the rest over to subsequent years at the same rate, no legal limit on the number of years.

Income Averaging

Individuals with a large increase in taxable income in a particular year may be able to take advantage of income averaging provisions. Generally, a taxpayer is eligible to income average if his or her taxable income in a given year exceeds 140% if his or her average income for the prior 3 years, if the excess is more than $3,000.

Individual Income Tax Returns for 1983[1]

(money amounts are in thousands of dollars)

Size of adjusted gross income	Number of returns	Adjusted gross income less deficit	Total income tax			
			Number of returns	Percent of all returns	Amount	Average (dollars)
All returns, total	96,293,634	1,950,788,489	78,080,885	81.1	276,085,990	3,536
No adjusted gross income. . . .	935,913	−23,126,679	7,752	0.8	71,705	9,250
$1 under $1,000	2,444,289	1,429,296	203	(2)	2,532	12,473
$1,000 under $2,000	3,568,691	5,311,082	270,327	7.6	25,909	96
$2,000 under $3,000	3,705,331	9,205,762	202,524	5.5	24,023	119
$3,000 under $4,000	3,622,468	12,719,365	1,779,151	49.1	98,038	55
$4,000 under $5,000	3,512,813	15,822,052	2,352,553	67.0	309,995	132
$5,000 under $6,000	3,400,274	18,686,392	2,240,569	65.9	528,238	236
$6,000 under $7,000	3,268,248	21,232,489	2,187,842	66.9	768,879	351
$7,000 under $8,000	3,448,634	25,893,319	2,535,761	73.5	1,115,323	440
$8,000 under $9,000	3,397,156	28,878,718	2,859,006	84.2	1,480,496	518
$9,000 under $10,000	3,225,684	30,608,392	2,875,490	89.1	1,779,339	619
$10,000 under $11,000	2,993,535	31,455,073	2,831,140	94.6	2,113,973	747
$11,000 under $12,000	2,954,970	33,900,655	2,821,799	95.5	2,367,812	839
$12,000 under $13,000	2,796,023	34,939,261	2,689,978	96.2	2,665,201	991
$13,000 under $14,000	2,590,985	34,956,363,	2,513,624	97.0	2,804,273	1,116
$14,000 under $15,000	2,570,180	37,272,877	2,509,741	97.6	3,254,298	1,297
$15,000 under $16,000	2,452,781	37,991,746	2,402,418	97.9	3,457,596	1,439
$16,000 under $17,000	2,162,738	35,694,266	2,112,160	97.7	3,401,180	1,610
$17,000 under $18,000	2,242,617	39,237,993	2,211,690	98.6	3,835,402	1,734
$18,000 under $19,000	2,406,668	37,818,077	2,010,140	98.2	3,823,919	1,902
$19,000 under $20,000	1,903,124	37,098,786	1,881,764	98.9	3,832,522	2,037
$20,000 under $25,000	8,854,120	198,721,294	8,742,767	98.7	21,979,450	2,514
$25,000 under $30,000	7,348,043	201,487,885	7,294,896	99.3	24,338,804	3,336
$30,000 under $40,000	10,446,443	360,181,357	10,380,460	99.4	47,935,895	4,618
$40,000 under $50,000	5,144,573	228,169,963	5,125,908	99.6	34,843,954	6,798
$50,000 under $75,000	3,607,761	212,682,005	3,596,019	99.7	38,552,649	10,721
$75,000 under $100,000.	818,051	69,580,534	815,553	99.7	15,324,450	18,790
$100,000 under $200,000. . . .	628,471	83,250,920	627,196	99.8	22,419,509	35,746
$200,000 under $500,000. . . .	165,226	46,766,228	164,879	99.8	16,013,435	97,122
$500,000 under $1,000,000. . .	26,098	17,594,000	26,069	99.9	6,713,977	257,546
$1,000,000 or more	11,526	25,329,016	11,506	99.8	10,203,216	886,774
Taxable returns, total	78,080,885	1,900,918,500	78,080,885	100.0	276,085,990	3,536
Nontaxable returns, total	18,212,749	49,869,989	—	—	—	—

(1) Estimates. (2) Less than 0.05 percent.

Individual Income and Tax Data by State, 1983[1]

(All figures are estimates based on samples.)

State	Number of returns[2]	Adjusted gross income ($000)	Income Tax Total ($000)	Income Tax Average[3] ($)	State	Number of returns[2]	Adjusted gross income ($000)	Income Tax Total ($000)	Income Tax Average[2] ($)
United States, total[4]	96,293,634	1,950,788,489	276,085,990	3,536	Arkansas	818,332	13,389,432	1,713,141	2,666
Alabama	1,416,959	25,317,918	3,223,193	2,875	California	10,773,707	234,046,434	32,574,751	3,731
Alaska	235,486	6,193,558	1,063,124	5,442	Colorado	1,367,273	28,831,288	4,048,718	3,610
Arizona	1,204,624	23,164,833	2,995,174	3,122	Connecticut	1,486,263	35,232,996	5,707,526	4,560
					Delaware	263,758	5,620,417	791,069	3,640

(continued)

State	Number of returns[2]	Adjusted gross income ($000)	Income Tax Total ($000)	Average[3] ($)	State	Number of returns[2]	Adjusted gross income ($000)	Income Tax Total ($000)	Average[2] ($)
District of Columbia	309,902	6,572,300	1,027,206	4,061	New Hampshire	438,117	8,829,854	1,269,167	3,495
Florida	4,644,964	89,972,121	13,365,074	3,530	New Jersey	3,555,517	81,151,436	12,379,254	4,119
Georgia	2,250,999	43,018,398	5,735,300	3,156	New Mexico	550,097	9,621,874	1,274,164	3,019
Hawaii	448,016	8,731,144	1,104,344	3,036	New York	7,253,328	162,169,242	23,730,612	3,920
Idaho	361,380	6,117,673	745,377	2,603	North Carolina	2,439,599	43,347,301	5,438,038	2,763
Illinois	4,726,101	100,816,164	15,069,353	3,926	North Dakota	278,876	4,741,196	658,244	2,910
Indiana	2,173,559	41,774,770	5,750,512	3,302	Ohio	4,328,283	86,079,713	11,679,404	3,324
Iowa	1,156,727	20,999,653	2,894,955	3,100	Oklahoma	1,247,234	24,757,847	3,638,068	3,628
Kansas	992,190	19,611,667	2,844,017	3,502	Oregon	1,086,626	20,129,601	2,538,666	2,937
Kentucky	1,304,750	23,204,824	3,090,948	2,994	Pennsylvania	4,879,420	94,167,291	13,112,980	3,320
Louisiana	1,608,624	31,760,787	4,714,223	3,716	Rhode Island	415,748	7,792,034	1,027,095	3,013
Maine	473,630	7,979,505	992,198	2,611	South Carolina	1,220,503	21,497,689	2,612,077	2,686
Maryland	1,923,735	43,574,958	6,179,826	3,857	South Dakota	278,866	4,042,814	553,635	2,542
Massachusetts	2,632,976	55,676,284	8,271,674	3,757	Tennessee	1,795,982	31,920,557	4,326,902	3,034
Michigan	3,553,081	74,287,976	9,983,877	3,489	Texas	6,270,690	133,318,836	21,187,143	4,203
Minnesota	1,724,860	34,688,141	4,462,985	3,155	Utah	559,273	10,764,841	1,251,387	2,820
Mississippi	866,960	13,925,118	1,740,446	2,645	Vermont	217,373	3,751,952	475,448	2,693
Missouri	1,991,400	38,457,844	5,450,628	3,379	Virginia	2,323,758	49,465,168	6,836,717	3,548
Montana	335,256	5,545,897	735,962	2,820	Washington	1,803,079	37,409,295	5,312,640	3,614
Nebraska	664,214	11,648,548	1,619,879	3,016	West Virginia	654,614	11,883,618	1,575,761	3,048
Nevada	415,449	8,330,995	1,221,570	3,631	Wisconsin	1,946,287	36,879,071	4,690,784	2,991
					Wyoming	206,781	4,210,972	639,498	3,835

Preliminary. (2) Total returns filed include both taxable returns and returns without tax liability. (3) Average tax applies only to returns with tax liability. The number of returns with tax liability can be derived by dividing total tax by average tax. (4) Detail does not add to total which includes data for returns by U.S. citizens living abroad, U.S. citizens with APO or FPO addresses, and residents of Puerto Rico.

State Individual Income Taxes: Rates, Exemptions

Source: Tax Foundation, Inc. Data as of July 1, 1985
Footnotes at end of table.

State	Taxable income	Percentage rates	Taxable income	Percentage rates	Personal exemp.[1] Single	Married family head	Each dependent
Alabama[2]	First $1,000	2	Over $6,000	5	$1,500	$3,000	$300
	1,001-6,000	4					
Arizona[2,3]	First 1,061	2	3,184-4,244	5	1,834	3,668	1,100
	1,062-2,122	3	4,245-5,305	6			
	2,123-3,183	4	5,306-6,366	7	Over 6,366	8	
Arkansas[4]	First 2,999	1	9,000-14,999	4.5	17.50	35	6
	3,000-5,999	2.5	15,000-24,999	6	(tax credit)		
	6,000-8,999	3.5	25,000 and over	7			
California[2,3,5]	First 3,160	0	29,021-33,860	6	(tax credit)		
	3,161-9,620	1	33,861-38,660	7	40	80	13
	9,621-14,440	2	38,601-43,520	8	Over 26,601	11	
	14,441-19,260	3	43,251-48,360	9			
	19,261-24,160	4	48,361-53,200	10			
	24,161-29,020	5	Over 53,200	11			
Colorado[2,4]	First 1,420	3	8,491-9,910	6	850	1,700	850
	1,421-2,830	3.5	9,911-11,320	6.5			
	2,831-4,250	4	11,321-12,740	7	Surtax on intangible income over $15,000, 2%.		
	4,251-5,660	4.5	12,741-14,150	7.5			
	5,661-7,080	5	14,151 and over	8			
	7,081-8,490	5.5					
Connecticut	7% capital gains tax; tax on dividends earned if federal adjusted gross income is greater than or equal to $50,000; tax ranges from 6% on $50,000 through 13% on $100,000 and over.				100	200	
Delaware[2,4]	First 1,000	1.3	8,000-10,000	7.2	800	1,600	800
	1,001-2,000	1.8	10,001-15,000	7.4			
	2,001-3,000	2.7	15,001-20,000	7.6			
	3,001-4,000	3.8	20,001-25,000	7.9			
	4,001-5,000	4.7	25,001-30,000	8.5			
	5,001-6,000	5.6	30,001-40,000	9.9			
	6,001-8,000	6.5	Over 40,000	10.7			
Dist. of Col.	First 1,000	2	5,001-10,000	7	Federal exemptions.		
	1,001-2,000	3	10,001-13,000	8	Heads of households are allowed a		
	2,001-3,000	4	13,001-17,000	9	personal exemption equal to twice the		
	3,001-4,000	5	17,001-25,000	10	federal exemption.		
	4,001-5,000	6	Over 25,000	11			
Georgia[2]	First 1,000	1	5,000-6,999	4	1,500	3,000	700
	1,001-2,999	2	7,000-10,000	5			
	3,000-4,999	3	Over 10,000	6			

State	Taxable income	Percentage rates	Taxable income	Percentage rates	Personal exemp.[1] Single	Married family head	Each dependent
Hawaii[2] . . . . . . First	$1000	0	$5,001-7,000	6.5	$1,000	$2,000	$1,000
	1,001-2,000	2.25	7,001-11,000	7.5			
	2,001-3,000	3.25	11,001-21,000	8.5			
	3,001-4,000	4.5	21,001-29,000	9.5	41,001-61,000	10.5	
	4,001-5,000	5	29,001-41,000	10	Over 61,000	11	
Idaho[5] . . . . . . First	1,000	2	3,001-4,000	5.5	Federal exemptions.		
	1,001-2,000	4	4,001-5,000	6.5			
	2,001-3,000	4.5	Over 5,000	7.5			
Illinois	Total net income			2.5	1,000	2,000	1,000
Indiana . . . . . . Adjusted gross		3			1,000	*2,000	1,000

*Lesser of $1,000 or adjusted gross income of each spouse, but not less than $500.

State	Taxable income	Percentage rates	Taxable income	Percentage rates	Personal exemp.[1] Single	Married family head	Each dependent
Iowa[2,4] . . . . . . First	1,023	0.5	3,070-4,092	3.5	(tax credit) 20	40	15
	1,024-2,046	1.25	4,093-7,161	5			
	2,047-3,069	2.75	7,162-9,207	6	On up to 13% over $76,725		
Kansas[4] . . . . . . First	2,000	2	5,001-7,000	5	1,000	2,000	1,000
	2,001-3,000	3.5	7,001-10,000	6.5	20,001-25,000	8.5	
	3,001-5,000	4	10,001-20,000	7.5	Over 25,000	9.0	
Kentucky[4] . . . . . First	3,000	2	4,001-5,000	4	(tax credit)		
	3,001-4,000	3	5,001-8,000	5	20	40	20
			Over 8,000	6			
Louisiana[4,5] . . . . First 10,000		2	Over 50,000	6	4,500	9,000	1,000
	10,001-50,000	4					
Maine[2,3] . . . . . . First	4,200	1	16,701-20,800	7	1,000	2,000	1,000
	4,201-8,300	2	20,801-31,300	8			
	8,301-12,500	3	31,301-50,000	9.2			
	12,501-16,700	6	Over 50,000	10			
Maryland . . . . . First	1,000	2	2,001-3,000	4	800	1,600	800
	1,001-2,000	3	Over 3,000	5			
Massachusetts	Earned and business income:	5*			2,200	4,400	700
	Interest, divs., net capital gains:	10*	No tax on income below $7,200 for husband and wife or $4,400 for single individual. Rates shown apply above these amounts. Plus 7.5% surtax. Exemptions apply to earned income only.				
Michigan[4,6] . . . . All taxable income		5.35			1,500	3,000	1,500
Minnesota[2,3,4,6] . First	1,200	1.7	9,101-12,600	6.8	70	140	70
	1,201-1,700	2.1	12,601-17,800	8.5			
	1,701-2,700	2.3	17,801-30,800	9.3			
	2,701-5,600	3.3	Over 30,800	9.9			
	5,601-9,100	5.3					
Mississippi[3] . . . . First	5,000	3	Next 5,000	4	6,000	9,500	1,500
			Over 10,000	5			
Missouri[3,4] . . . . First	1,000	1.5	5,001- 6,000	4	1,200	2,400	400
	1,001-2,000	2	6,001- 7,000	4.5			
	2,001-3,000	2.5	7,001- 8,000	5			
	3,001-4,000	3	8,001-9,000	5.5			
	4,001-5,000	3.5	Over 9,000	6			
Montana[3,4] . . . . First	1,300	2	10,001-12,500	7	1,000	2,000	1,000
	1,301-2,500	3	12,501-17,600	8			
	2,501-5,000	4	17,601-25,100	9			
	5,001-7,500	5	25,101-43,900	10			
	7,501-10,000	6	Over 43,900	11			
Nebraska[3,4] . . . . 19% of modified federal tax liability.					Federal exemptions.		
New Hampshire	Interest and dividends (except interest on savings accounts).	5	4% commuter tax		$1,200 each income is exempt.		

State	Taxable income	Percentage rates	Taxable income	Percentage rates	Personal exemp.[1] Single	Married family head	Each Dependent
New Jersey . . .	First $20,000 Next 30,000 Over 50,000	2 2.5 3.5			$1,000	$2,000	$1,000

Commuter tax from 2% on net income up to $20,000 to 3.5% on income over $50,000. (Will cease after 12/31/90)
A taxpayer or married filing jointly with gross income of $13,000 or less is not taxable.

State	Taxable income	Percentage rates	Taxable income	Percentage rates	Single	Married family head	Each Dependent
New Mexico[2,5] . .	First 2,000 2,001-4,000 4,001-6,000 6,001-8,000 8,001-10,000 10,001-12,000 12,001-14,000 14,001-16,000 16,001-20,000	0.7 0.9 1.2 1.6 1.9 2.3 2.6 3.0 3.5	20,001-24,000 24,001-28,000 28,001-32,000 32,001-36,000 36,001-40,000 40,001-50,000 51,001-70,000 70,001-100,000 100,001-200,000 Over 200,000	3.9 4.3 4.8 5.2 5.6 6.1 6.5 6.9 7.4 7.8	Federal exemptions.		
New York.	First 1,000 1,001-3,000 3,001-5,000 5,001-7,000 7,001-9,000 9,001-11,000 11,001-13,000	2 3 4 5 6 7 8	13,001-15,000 15,001-17,000 17,001-19,000 19,001-21,000 21,001-23,000 Over 23,000	9 10 11 12 13 13.75	850 The maximum tax rate on personal service income is 9.5%.	1,700	850
North Carolina.	First 2,000 2,001-4,000 4,001-6,000	3 4 5	6,001-10,000 Over 10,000	6 7	1,100	2,200*	800

*An additional exemption of $1,100
is allowed the spouse having the lower income; joint returns are not permitted.

State	Taxable income	Percentage rates	Taxable income	Percentage rates	Single	Married family head	Each Dependent
North Dakota[4] .	First 3,000 3,001-5,000 5,001-8,000 8,000-15,000 15,001-25,000	2 3 4 5 6	25,001-35,000 35,001-50,000 Over 50,000	7 8 9	Federal exemptions.		
Ohio	First 5,000 5,001-10,000 10,001-15,000 15,001-20,000	0.903 1.805 3.61 4.513	20,001-40,000 40,001-80,000 80,001-100,000 Over 100,000	5.415 6.318 7.22 9.025	650	1,300	650
Oklahoma[2,4,6] .	First 2,000 2,001-5,000 5,001-7,500 7,501-10,000	0.5 1 2 3	10,001-12,500 12,501-15,000 Over 15,000	4 5 6	1,000	2,000	1,000
Oregon[2,3,4] . . .	First 500 501-1,000 1,001-2,000 2,001-3,000	4 5 6 7	3,001-4,000 4,001-5,000 Over 5,000	8 9 10	1,000	2,000	1,000
Pennsylvania .	2.35% of specified classes of taxable income						
Rhode Island .	23.65% of modified federal income tax liability						
South Carolina[2,4]	First 3,400 3,401-5,400 5,401-7,400 7,401-9,400	0 2 3 4	9,401-11,400 11,401-13,600 Over 13,600	5 6 7	Federal exemptions.		
Tennessee	Interest and dividends	6			Dividends from corporations, 75% of whose property is taxable in Tenn., are taxed at 4%.		
Utah[2,4]	First 1,500 1,501-3,000 3,001-4,500	2.75 3.75 4.75	4,501-6,000 6,001-7,500 Over 7,500	5.75 6.75 7.75	Federal exemptions.		
Vermont[4]	26.5% of modified federal income tax liability.						

State		Taxable Income	Percentage rates	Taxable income	Percentage rates	Personal exemp! Single	Personal exemp! Married family head	Each Dependent
Virginia	First	$3,000	2	$5,001-12,000	5	$600	$1,200	$600
		3,001-5,000	3	Over 12,000	5.75			
West Virginia[2] .	First	4,000	2.1	32,001-36,000	6.8	800	1,600	800
		4,001-8,000	2.3	36,001-40,000	7.4			
		8,001-12,000	2.8	40,001-44,000	8.2			
		12,001-16,000	3.2	44,001-52,000	9.2			
		16,001-20,000	3.5	52,001-64,000	10.5			
		20,001-24,000	4	64,001-76,000	11.6			
		24,001-28,000	5.3	76,001-120,000	12.6			
		28,001-32,000	5.9	88,001-120,000	12.9			
				Over 120,000	13			
Wisconsin[6] . . .	First	3,900	3.4	15,500-19,400	8.7	(Tax Credit)		
		3,900-7,700	5.2	19,400-25,800	9.1	20	40	20
		7,700-11,700	7.0	25,800-51,600	9.5			
		11,700-15,500	8.2	Over $51,600	10.0			

(1) Does not include exemptions or credits for age or blindness, to offset sales or property taxes paid, or for any special purpose. (2) Rates shown are for married persons filing jointly in Alabama, California, Georgia, Hawaii, Maine, Minnesota, New Mexico, Oklahoma, South Carolina, Utah, and West Virginia; separate rate schedules apply for single taxpayers and in some cases to heads of households. Rates shown for Arizona and Oregon are for single taxpayers; in the case of joint returns, the tax is twice the tax that would be due if taxable income of husband and wife were cut in half. (3) Rates and/or exemptions are subject to annual adjustment for inflation. (4) All or part of federal income tax liability is deductible in computing state income tax. (5) Community property state in which, in general, half of community income is taxed to each spouse. (6) Different rate schedules apply for taxpayers who choose to deduct Federal income tax in Minnesota and Oklahoma.

State Estate Tax Rates and Exemptions

Source: Compiled by Tax Foundation from Commerce Clearing House data

As of July 1985. *See index for state inheritance tax rates and exemptions.*

State (a)	Rates (on net estate after exemptions) (b)	Maximum rate applies above	Exemption
Alabama	Maximum federal credit (c, d)	$10,040,000	$60,000
Alaska	Maximum federal credit (c, d)	10,040,000	60,000
Arizona	Maximum federal credit (c, d)	10,000,000	60,000 (e)
Arkansas	Maximum federal credit (c, d)	10,040,000	60,000 (e)
California	Maximum federal credit (c, d)	10,040,000	60,000
Colorado	Maximum federal credit (c, d)	10,040,000	60,000
Florida	Maximum federal credit (c, d)	10,040,000	60,000
Georgia	Maximum federal credit (c, d)	10,040,000	60,000
Hawaii	Maximum federal credit (c, d)	10,040,000	60,000
Illinois	Maximum federal credit (c, d)	10,040,000	60,000
Massachusetts	5% on first $50,000 to 16%	4,000,000	30,000 (e, f)
Minnesota	9% on first $100,000 to 12% (d)	5,000,000	400,000 (e)
Mississippi	1% on first $60,000 to 16% (g)	10,000,000	175,625 (e)
Missouri	Maximum federal credit (c, d)	10,040,000	60,000
New Mexico	Maximum federal credit (c, d)	10,040,000	60,000
New York	2% on first $50,000 to 21% (g, h)	10,100,000	(e,j)
North Dakota	Maximum federal credit (c, d)	10,040,000	60,000 (e)
Ohio	2% on first $40,000 to 7% (g)	500,000	10,000 (e, j)
Oklahoma	.5% on first $10,000 to 15% (g)	10,000,000	60,000 (k, l)
Rhode Island	2% on first $25,000 to 9% (c, g)	1,000,000	25,000 (e, rn)
South Carolina	6% on first $40,000 to 8% (d, g)	100,000	120,000 (e)
Utah	Maximum federal credit (c, d)	10,040,000	60,000 (e)
Vermont	Maximum federal credit (c, d)	10,040,000	60,000 (e)
Virginia	Maximum federal credit (c, d)	10,040,000	60,000 (e)
Washington	Maximum federal credit (c, d)	10,040,000	60,000
West Virginia	Maximum federal credit (c, d)	10,040,000	60,000
Wyoming	Maximum federal credit (c, d)	10,040,000	60,000

(a) Excludes states shown in table on page 97 which levy an estate tax, in addition to their inheritance taxes, to assure full absorption of the federal credit. (b) The rates generally are in addition to graduated absolute amounts. (c) Maximum federal credit allowed under the 1954 code for state estate taxes paid is expressed as a percentage of the taxable estate (after $60,000 exemption) in excess of $40,000, plus a graduated absolute amount. In Rhode Island on net estates above $250,000. (d) A tax on nonresident estates is imposed on the proportionate share of the net estate which the property located in the state bears to the entire estate wherever situated. (e) Transfers to religious, charitable, educational, and municipal corporations generally are fully exempt. Limited in Mississippi to those located in United States or its possessions. (f) Applies to net estates above $60,000. Otherwise, exemption is equal to Massachusetts net estate. (g) An additional estate tax is imposed to assure full absorption of the federal credit. In New York, this applies only to residents. In Rhode Island on net estates above $250,000. (h) On net estate before exemption. Marital deduction is one-half of adjusted gross estate or $250,000, whichever is greater. Orphans under age 21 receive deduction. (i) The specific exemptions are $20,000 of the net estate transferred to spouse and $5,000 to lineal ancestors and descendants and certain other named relatives. The credit is variable, ranging from the full amount of tax if estate tax is $2,750 or less to $500 if estate tax is $5,000 or more. (j) Property is exempt to the extent transferred to surviving spouse, not exceeding $60,000; for a child under 18, $14,000; and for each child 18 years of age and older, $6,000. (k) An estate valued at $100 or less is exempt. (l) Exemption is a total aggregate of $175,000 for father, mother, child, and named relatives. (m) Marital deduction is $175,000 in Rhode Island. In South Carolina, marital deduction is one-half of adjusted gross estate up to $250,000.

State Government Tax Collections, 1983, and Excise Taxes, 1984

Source: U.S. Bureau of the Census

| | State Tax Collections (mil. dol.) | | | | | | | Excise Taxes[2] | | |
| | Sales and gross receipts | | | | | | | | | |
State U.S.[3]	Total[1]	Total[1]	General sales or gross receipts	Motor fuels	Alcoholic beverages and tobacco products	Individual income	Corporation net income	Motor vehicle and operator's licenses	General sales and gross receipts (percent)	Cigarettes (cents per package)	Gasoline (cents per gal.)
U.S.[3]	171,370	83,849	53,627	10,793	6,744	49,789	13,153	6,281	x	x	x
AL	2,341	1,386	660	241	157	556	134	41	[4]4 D	16.5	13
AK	2,046	75	X	37	16	2	266	16	x	8	8
AZ	2,061	1,145	845	152	66	481	160	106	[4]5 F & D	15	13
AR	1,338	707	423	133	79	388	87	74	[4]4 D	21	9.5
CA	22,260	9,953	7,767	926	399	7,649	2,554	596	[4]4.75 F & D	10	9
CO	1,743	886	623	143	61	655	56	58	[4]3 F & D	15	12
CT	2,538	1,799	1,104	159	100	179	357	89	7.5 F & D	26	15
DC[3]	1,317	424	266	23	17	351	83	20	6 F & D	13	[5]15.5
DE	639	90	x	38	17	314	30	28	x	14	11
FL	6,225	4,796	3,334	452	592	x	371	300	5 F & D	21	[5]9.7
GA	3,504	1,784	1,173	353	187	1,342	239	63	[4] [6]3	12	7.5
HI	1,151	756	601	34	27	347	22	9	[7]4	[8]23	8.5
ID	620	289	165	77	18	224	31	37	[7]4 D	9.1	14.5
IL	7,420	3,869	2,394	361	247	2,201	604	347	[4]5 F & D	12	12
IN	3,195	2,010	1,522	317	113	819	140	118	5 F & D	10.5	[5]11.1
IA	2,014	889	571	188	77	724	138	153	4 F & D	18	13
KS	1,566	728	498	115	68	531	141	73	[4] [7]3 D	16	11
KY	2,602	1,187	700	197	70	647	172	78	5 F & D	3	[5]10
LA	3,011	1,356	839	186	117	229	321	61	[4]4 F & D	16	16
ME	780	422	270	55	55	236	33	38	5 F & D	20	14
MD	3,468	1,546	865	233	98	1,459	148	92	5 F & D	13	[5]13.5
MA	5,156	1,736	1,052	250	226	2,472	661	117	[7]5 F & D	26	[5]11
MI	7,023	2,773	1,969	456	224	2,567	1,004	271	4 F & D	21	[5]15
MN	4,319	1,698	992	262	138	1,978	254	193	[4]6 F & D	18	17
MS	1,538	1,023	761	135	70	201	69	56	6 D	11	9
MO	2,640	1,388	985	194	102	885	119	123	[4]4.125 D	13	7
MT	514	107	x	49	26	152	36	26	x	16	15
NE	987	561	357	120	44	281	52	48	[4]3.5 F & D	18	[5]14.9
NV	779	669	368	67	25	x	x	33	[4] [9]5.75 F & D	15	12
NH	329	159	x	61	32	17	74	31	x	17	14
NJ	6,128	3,309	1,660	289	274	1,440	664	280	6 F & D	25	8
NM	1,163	657	477	94	32	17	62	41	[4] [7]3.75	12	[5]11
NY	16,208	5,728	3,532	437	473	8,276	1,339	337	[4]4 F & D	21	8
NC	4,028	1,764	826	379	134	1,550	307	174	[4]3 D	2	12.25
ND	526	219	146	36	17	35	31	30	4 F & D	18	13
OH	6,734	3,686	2,005	589	259	1,972	415	307	[4]5 F & D	14	[5]12
OK	2,627	801	409	128	119	651	103	188	[4] [10]3 D	18	9
OR	1,784	212	x	97	73	1,182	125	120	x	19	9
PA	8,430	4,176	2,365	558	386	2,045	830	403	6 F & D	18	12
RI	726	374	212	44	37	261	42	22	6 F & D	23	[5]13
SC	2,113	1,141	692	214	131	719	128	46	[7]5 D	7	13
SD	325	279	174	55	20	x	3	16	[4] [7]4 D	15	13
TN	2,246	1,704	1,177	283	138	52	204	119	[4] [11]5.5 D	13	10
TX	9,019	5,671	3,320	490	627	x	x	334	[4]4 F & D	18.5	5
UT	974	527	391	86	24	346	32	31	[4] [12]4.625 D	12	14
VT	358	175	67	28	24	114	25	29	[7] [13]4 D	17	13
VA	3,478	1,441	722	321	96	1,549	183	158	[4]3 D	2.5	[5]13.72
WA	4,191	3,116	2,454	241	210	x	x	136	[4] [14]6.5 F & D	23	18
WV	1,470	1,005	745	106	43	311	45	59	5 F & D	17	[5]15.35
WI	4,297	1,826	1,209	288	170	1,734	340	141	5 F & D	25	16
WY	736	242	190	37	7	x	x	36	[4] [7]3 D	8	8

(x) Not applicable. (1) Includes amounts for types of taxes not shown separately. (2) Source: Advisory Commission on Intergovernmental Relations, Washington, DC, *Significant Features of Fiscal Federalism*, annual; F = food exempt from sales tax; D = prescription drugs exempt from sales tax. (3) DC excluded from U.S. total. (4) Local sales tax rates are additional. (5) Variable tax based on wholesale price. (6) The sales tax on prescription drugs was eliminated in July 1985. (7) A sales tax credit is granted on the State income tax form. (8) Tax is 40% of wholesale price. (9) Included in a mandatory 3.75% county sales tax. (10) The 3% rate decreases to 2% in Jan. 1986. (11) The 5.5% rate decreased to 4.5% in July 1985. The sales tax on food will phase out over 3 years beginning July 1985. (12) The 4.625% rate decreases to 4.5% in July 1987. (13) The 4% rate decreases to 3% in July 1987. (14) The tax rate for the four counties bordering Oregon is 5.4%.

Average Tax Deductions, 1983

Source: Commerce Clearing House

Adjusted Gross Income	Medical Expenses	Taxes	Contributions	Interest	Adjusted Gross Income	Medical Expenses	Taxes	Contributions	Interest
$10,000–$12,000	$2,153	$1,201	$747	$2,441	$25,000–$30,000	$1,387	$2,195	$797	$3,298
$12,000–$14,000	1,870	1,197	732	2,697	$30,000–$40,000	1,405	2,690	900	3,778
$14,000–$16,000	1,482	1,331	772	2,672	$40,000–$50,000	1,872	3,437	1,113	4,679
$16,000–$18,000	1,760	1,542	773	2,663	$50,000–$75,000	2,741	4,711	1,553	6,259
$18,000–$20,000	1,416	1,539	732	2,883	$75,000–$100,000	5,900	6,833	2,697	9,187
$20,000–$25,000	1,544	1,791	734	3,016	$100,000–up	10,543	15,677	9,039	17,019

State Inheritance Tax Rates and Exemptions

Source: Compiled by Tax Foundation from Commerce Clearing House data.
July 1985

State (a)	Rates (b) (percent)			Max. rate applies above ($1,000)	Exemptions (c) ($1,000)			
	Spouse, child, or parent	Brother or sister	Other than relative		Spouse	Child or parent	Brother or sister	Other than relative
Connecticut (h)	2-8	4-10	8-14	1,000	300	50	6	1
Delaware	1-6	5-10	10-16	200	70	3	1	None
District of Columbia	1-8	5-23	5-23	1,000	5	5	1	1
Idaho	2-15	4-20	8-30	500	All	30(f)	10	10
Indiana	1-10	7-15	10-20	1,500	All	10(f)	0.5	0.1
Iowa	1-8	5-10	10-15	150	180	15(f)	None	None
Kansas	1-5	3-12.5	10-15	500	All	30	5	None
Kentucky	2-10	4-16	6-16	500	50	5	1	0.5
Louisiana	2-3	5-7	5-10	20	15(e)	15	1	0.5
Maine (q)	5-10	8-14	14-18	250(i)	50	25	1	1
Maryland (j)	1	10	10	(k)	.15(l)	.15(l)	0.15(l)	0.15(l)
Michigan	2-10 (m)	2-10 (m)	12-17 (m)	750	65(n)	10(f)	10	None
Montana	2-8	4-16	8-32	100	All	7(f)	1.0	None
Nebraska	1	1	6-18	60	All	10	10	0.5
New Hampshire	(o)	15	15	(k)	(o)	(o)	None	None
New Jersey	3-16	11-16	15-16	3,200	15	15	0.5(l)	0.5(l)
North Carolina	1-12	4-16	8-17	3,000	4.65(p)	(q)	None	None
Oregon (r)	12	12	12	(k)	None	None	None	None
Pennsylvania	6	15	15	(k)	None(s)	None(g)	None	None
South Dakota	3.75-15	4-20	6-30	100	All	30(t)	0.5	0.1
Tennessee	5.5-9.5	5.5-9.5	6.5-16	440	400(u)	400	400	50
Wisconsin	2.5-12.5	5-25	10-30	500	All	50	1	0.5

(a) In addition to an inheritance tax, all states listed also levy an estate tax, generally to assure full absorption of the federal credit. Exception is S.D.

(b) Rates generally apply to excess above graduated absolute amounts.

(c) Generally, transfers to governments or to solely charitable, educational, scientific, religious, literary, public, and other similar organizations in the U.S. are wholly exempt. Some states grant additional exemptions either for insurance, homestead, joint deposits, support allowance, disinherited minor children, orphaned, incompetent or blind children, and for previously or later taxed transfers. In many states, exemptions are deducted from the first bracket only.

(d) Adopted children generally receive the same consideration as natural children.

(e) Community property state in which, in general, either all community property to the surviving spouse is exempt, or only one-half of the community property is taxable on the death of either spouse.

(f) Exemption for child (in thousands); $50 in Iowa; and $30 in S.D.; $10 in Indiana ($5,000 per parent). Exemption for minor child is (in thousands): $50 in Idaho; $20 in Ky. In Mich. a widow receives $5,000 for every minor child to whom no property is transferred in addition to the normal exemption for a spouse; in Montana, all property is exempt.

(g) 45% between 6/30/85 and 7/1/86; after 6/30/86, no tax is imposed.

(h) On estates an additional inheritance tax equal to 30% of the basic tax is imposed. A second additional tax equal to 10% of the basic tax and the first additional tax is imposed, except on the farmland passing to a descendant.

(i) In Maine the maximum rate for any other relative applies above $150,000.

(j) Where property of a decedent subject to administration in Md. is $10,000 or less, no inheritance taxes are due.

(k) Rate applies to entire share.

(l) All real property and the first $100,000 of non-real property transferred to a spouse is exempt. For other beneficiaries, no exemption if share exceeds amount stated.

(m) There is no tax on the share of any beneficiary if the value of the share is less than $100.

(n) Spouse entitled to another $10,000 exemption.

(o) Spouses, children, parents, and adopted children in the decedent's line of succession are entirely exempt.

(p) Credit.

(q) Credits allowed on pro rata basis according to tax liability on the amount of credit unused by surviving spouse or beneficiaries.

(r) Net taxable estates are allowed an exemption of $500,000 if death occurs in 1985 or 1986; after Dec. 31, 1986, no tax is imposed.

(s) However, the $2,000 family exemption is specifically allowed as a deduction.

(t) The rates range from 3.75-7.5% for a spouse or a child and from 3-15% for parents. Parent exemption is $3,000. Spouses exempt from tax. (See (d).)

(u) There is a marital deduction equal to the greater of $250,000 or 50% of the value of the gross estate.

Federal Estate and Gift Tax

Source: Tax Foundation, Inc.

Estate Tax

As a result of the Economic Recovery Tax Act of 1981, the lifetime unified credit against combined estate and gift taxes is increased in steps from $47,000 in 1981 to $62,800 in 1982, $79,300 in 1983, $96,300 in 1984, $121,800 in 1985, $155,800 in 1986, and $192,800 in 1987. Thus, cumulative transfers exempt from estate and gift taxes are increased from $175,625 in 1981, to $225,000 in 1982, $275,000 in 1983, $325,000 in 1984, $400,000 in 1985, $500,000 in 1986, and $600,000 in 1987 and thereafter. The maximum estate and gift tax rate, which was 70 percent in 1981, is being reduced gradually to 50 percent by 1988. The schedule for 1985 is shown below.

Estate taxes are computed by applying the unified rate schedule, shown below, to the total estate minus allowable deductions, such as funeral expenses, administrative expenses, debts and charitable contributions, plus taxable gifts made after 1976. Gift taxes paid are subtracted from tax due, and credit also may be taken for state death taxes. The amount of the state tax credit is determined by the schedule shown in the table below or the actual state taxes paid, whichever is less. No state tax credit is available to an adjustable taxable estate (i.e., taxable estate minus $60,000) smaller than $40,000. Transfers to a surviving spouse are generally tax exempt.

The law provides for real property passed on to family members for use in a closely held business, such as farming, to be valued in basis of such use, rather than fair market value on basis of highest and best use. In no case may this special valuation reduce the gross estate by more than $600,000 in 1981, $700,000 in 1982, and $750,000 in 1983 and thereafter.

Generation-skipping transfers that occur after April 30, 1976, in general are now subject to taxes substantially equivalent to those that would have been imposed had the property been transferred outright to each successive generation. However, an exclusion is provided for transfers to grandchildren up to $250,000 for each child of the decedent who serves as a conduit for the transfer (not for each grandchild).

A return must be filed for the estate of every U.S. citizen or resident whose gross estate exceeds $225,000 in 1982 ($60,000 for the estate of a nonresident not a citizen). The return is due nine months after death unless an extension is granted.

Gift Tax

Any citizen or resident alien whose gifts to any one person exceed $3,000 ($10,000 after 1981) within a calender year will be liable for payment of a gift tax, at rates determined under the unified estate and gift tax schedule. Gift tax returns are filed on an annual basis and ordinarily are due by April 15 of the following year.

Gifts made by a husband and wife to a third party may be considered as having been made one-half by each, provided both spouses consent to such division.

Unified Rate Schedule for Estate and Gift Tax for 1985

If the amount with respect to which the tentative tax to be computed is:			The tentative tax is:		
Not over $10,000			18 percent of such amount.		
Over	$10,000 but not over	$20,000.	$1,800, plus 20%	of the excess over	$10,000.
Over	$20,000 but not over	$40,000.	$3,800, plus 22%	of the excess over	$20,000.
Over	$40,000 but not over	$60,000.	$8,200, plus 24%	of the excess over	$40,000.
Over	$60,000 but not over	$80,000.	$13,000, plus 26%	of the excess over	$60,000.
Over	$80,000 but not over	$100,000.	$18,200, plus 28%	of the excess over	$80,000.
Over	$100,000 but not over	$150,000.	$23,800, plus 30%	of the excess over	$100,000.
Over	$150,000 but not over	$250,000.	$38,800, plus 32%	of the excess over	$150,000.
Over	$250,000 but not over	$500,000.	$70,800, plus 34%	of the excess over	$250,000.
Over	$500,000 but not over	$750,000.	$155,800, plus 37%	of the excess over	$500,000.
Over	$750,000 but not over	$1,000,000.	$248,300, plus 39%	of the excess over	$750,000.
Over	$1,000,000 but not over	$1,250,000.	$345,800, plus 41%	of the excess over	$1,000,000.
Over	$1,250,000 but not over	$1,500,000.	$448,300, plus 43%	of the excess over	$1,250,000.
Over	$1,500,000 but not over	$2,000,000.	$555,800, plus 45%	of the excess over	$1,500,000.
Over	$2,000,000 but not over	$2,500,000.	$780,800, plus 49%	of the excess over	$2,000,000.
Over	$2,500,000 but not over	$3,000,000.	$1,025,800, plus 53%	of the excess over	$2,500,000.
Over	$3,000,000		$1,290,800, plus 55%	of the excess over	$3,000,000.
Rates remain the same for 1986 and 1987; in 1988 the top bracket is:					
	Over $2,500,000.		$1,025,800, plus 50%	of the excess over	$2,500,000

State Death Tax Credit for Estate Tax

Adjusted taxable estate from	to	Credit = +	%	Of excess over	Adjusted taxable estate from	to	Credit = +	%	Of excess over
$ 0	$ 40,000	0	0	$ 0	2,540,000	3,040,000	146,800	8.8	2,540,000
40,000	90,000	0	.8	40,000	3,040,000	3,540,000	190,800	9.6	3,040,000
90,000	140,000	400	1.6	90,000	3,540,000	4,040,000	238,800	10.4	3,540,000
140,000	240,000	1,200	2.4	140,000	4,040,000	5,040,000	290,800	11.2	4,040,000
240,000	440,000	3,600	3.2	240,000	5,040,000	6,040,000	402,800	12	5,040,000
440,000	640,000	10,000	4	440,000	6,040,000	7,040,000	522,800	12.8	6,040,000
640,000	840,000	18,000	4.8	640,000	7,040,000	8,040,000	650,800	13.6	7,040,000
840,000	1,040,000	27,600	5.6	840,000	8,040,000	9,040,000	786,800	14.4	8,040,000
1,040,000	1,540,000	38,800	6.4	1,040,000	9,040,000	10,040,000	930,800	15.2	9,040,000
1,540,000	2,040,000	70,800	7.2	1,540,000	10,040,000		1,082,800	16	10,040,000
2,040,000	2,540,000	106,800	8	2,040,000					

(1) The unified credit for estates of decedents dying during 1985 is $121,800.

City Income Tax in U.S. Cities over 50,000

Compiled by Tax Foundation from Commerce Clearing House data and other sources.

City	Rates % 1985	Orig.	Year began	City	Rates % 1985	Orig.	Year began
Cities with 500,000 or more inhabitants				Youngstown, Oh.	2.0	0.3	1948
Baltimore, Md. . . . . (50% of state tax)		1.0	1966	**Cities with 50,000 to 99,999 inhabitants**			
Cleveland, Oh.	2.0	0.5	1967	Altoona, Pa.	1.0	1.0	1948
Columbus, Oh.	2.0	0.5	1947	Bethlehem, Pa.	1.0	1.0	1957
Detroit, Mich.	3.0	1.0	1965	Chester, Pa.	2.0	1.0	1956
New York, N.Y.	.9-4.3	0.4-2.0	1966	Covington, Ky.	2.5	1.0	1956
Philadelphia, Pa.	4.96	1.5	1939	Euclid, Oh.	2.0	0.5	1967
Cities with 100,000 to 499,999 inhabitants				Gadsden, Ala.	2.0	1.0	1956
Akron, Oh.	2.0	1.0	1962	Hamilton, Oh.	1.75	0.8	1960
Allentown, Pa.	1.0	1.0	1958	Harrisburg, Pa.	1.0	1.0	1966
Birmingham, Ala.	1.0	1.0	1970	Lakewood, Oh.	1.5	1.0	1968
Canton, Oh.	2.0	0.6	1954	Lancaster, Pa.	0.5	0.5	1959
Cincinnati, Oh.	2.0	1.0	1954	Lima, Oh.	1.5	.75	1959
Dayton, Oh.	2.25	0.5	1949	Lorain, Oh.	1.5	0.5	1967
Erie, Pa.	1.0	1.0	1948	Parma, Oh.	2.0	0.5	1967
Flint, Mich.	1.0	1.0	1965	Pontiac, Mich.	1.0	1.0	1968
Grand Rapids, Mich.	1.0	1.0	1967	Reading, Pa.	1.0	1.0	1969
Kansas City, Mo.	1.0	0.5	1964	Saginaw, Mich.	1.0	1.0	1965
Lansing, Mich.	1.0	1.0	1968	Scranton, Pa.	3.5	1.0	1948
Lexington, Ky.	2.0	1.0	1952	Springfield, Oh.	2.5	1.0	1948
Louisville, Ky.¹	2.2	0.75	1948	Warren, Oh.	1.5	0.5	1952
Pittsburgh, Pa.	4.0	1.0	1954	Wilkes-Barre, Pa.	2.5	1.0	1966
St. Louis, Mo.	1.0	.25	1948	Wilmington, Del.	1.25	0.5	1970
Toledo, Oh.	2.25	1.0	1946	York, Pa.	1.5	1.0	1965

(1) Includes rates for Jefferson County and school board.

Understanding the Economy: A Glossary of Terms

Balanced Budget: The federal government budget is balanced when receipts are equal to current expenditure.

Balance of payments: The difference between all payments made to foreign countries and all payments coming in from abroad over a set period of time. A *favorable* balance exists when more payments are coming in than going out and an *unfavorable* balance exists when the reverse is true. Payments include gold, the cost of merchandise and services, interest and dividend payments, money spent by travelers, and repayment of principal on loans.

Balance of trade (trade gap): The difference between exports and imports, both in actual funds and credit. A nation's balance of trade is *favorable* when exports exceed imports and *unfavorable* when the reverse is true.

Cost of living: The cost of maintaining a particular standard of living measured in terms of purchased goods and services. The rise in the cost of living is the same as the rate of inflation.

Cost-of-living benefits: Benefits that go to those persons whose money receipts increase automatically as prices rise.

Credit crunch (liquidity crisis): The period when cash for lending to business and consumers is in short supply.

Deficit spending: The practice whereby a government goes into debt to finance some of its expenditures.

Depression: A long period of listless business activity when prices are low, unemployment is high, and purchasing power decreases sharply.

Devaluation: The official lowering of a nation's currency, decreasing its value in relations to foreign currencies.

Disposable income: Income after taxes which is available to persons for spending and saving.

Economic Growth: The steady process of increasing productive capacity of the economy, and hence of increasing national income.

Federal Reserve System: The entire banking system of the U.S., incorporating 12 Federal Reserve banks (one in each of 12 Federal Reserve districts), and 24 Federal Reserve branch banks, all national banks and state-chartered commercial banks and trust companies that have been admitted to its membership. The system greatly influences the nation's monetary and credit policies.

Full Employment: The economy is said to be at full employment when only fractional unemployment exists. That is, everyone who wishes to work at the going wage-rate for his type of labor is employed. Since it takes time to switch from one job to another, there will be at any given time a small amount of unemployment.

Gross National Product (GNP): The total dollar value of all goods that have been bought for final use and services during a year. The GNP is generally considered to be the most comprehensive measure of a nation's economic activity. The *Real* GNP is the GNP adjusted for inflation.

GNP price deflator: A statistical measure that shows changes, both up and down, in the price level of the GNP over a span of years. It covers a larger segment of the economy than is usually covered by other price indexes.

Inflation: An increase in the average level of prices; double-digit inflation occurs when the percent increase rises above 10.

Key leading indicators: A series of a dozen indicators from different segments of the economy used by the Commerce Department to foretell what will happen in the economy in the near future.

Money supply: The currency held by the public plus checking accounts in commercial banks and savings institutions.

National debt: The debt of the central government as distinguished from the debts of the political subdivisions of the nation and private business and individuals.

National debt ceiling: Limit set by Congress beyond which the national debt cannot rise. This limit is periodically raised by Congressional vote.

Per capita income: The nation's total income divided by the number of people in the nation.

Prime interest rate: The rate charged by banks on short-term loans to large commercial customers with the highest credit rating.

Producer price index (formerly the wholesale price index): A statistical measure of the change in the price of wholesale goods. It is reported for 3 different stages of the production chain: crude, intermediate, and finished goods.

Public debt: The total of the nation's debts owed by state, local, and national government. This is considered a good measure of how much of the nation's spending is financed by borrowing rather than taxation.

Recession: A mild decrease in economic activity marked by a decline in real GNP, employment, and trade, usually lasting 6 months to a year, and marked by widespread decline in many sectors of the economy. Not as severe as a depression.

Seasonal adjustment: Statistical changes made to compensate for regular fluctuations in data that are so great they tend to distort the statistics and make comparisons meaningless. For instance, seasonal adjustments are made in mid-winter for a slowdown in housing construction and for the rise in farm income in the fall after the summer crops are harvested.

Supply-side economics: The school of economic thinking which stresses the importance of the costs of production as a means of revitalizing the economy. Advocates policies that raise capital and labor output by increasing the incentives to produce.

Tax Incidence: The point at which the tax burden ultimately rests. For example, the imposition of a specific tax on a commodity may cause firms to increase the price by the amount of the tax. If consumers do not reduce their purchases of that commodity, then the entire burden of the tax will have shifted onto them.

How Much Do You Really Make?
Is Your Salary Keeping Up With Inflation?

The Consumer Price Index (CPI) is a measure of the average change in prices over time in a fixed market basket of goods and services. From Jan. 1978, the Bureau of Labor Statistics began publishing CPI's for two population groups: (1) a new CPI for All Urban Consumers (CPI-U) which covers about 80% of the total noninstitutional civilian population; and (2) a revised CPI for Urban Wage Earners and Clerical Workers (CPI-W) which represents about half the population covered by the CPI-U. The CPI-U includes, in addition to wage earners and clerical workers, groups that had been excluded from CPI coverage, such as professional, managerial, and technical workers, the self-employed, retirees and others not in the labor force.

The CPI is based on prices of food, clothing, shelter, and fuels, transportation fares, charges for doctors' and dentists' services, drugs, and the other goods and services bought for day-to-day living. The index measures price changes from a designated reference date—1967—which equals 100.0. An increase of 122%, for example, is shown as 222.0. This change can also be expressed in dollars as follows: The price of a base period "market basket" of goods and services in the CPI has risen from $10 in 1967 to $22.00.

Which Index For You?

Which index should you use to calculate the impact of inflation on your life? If your income is near the poverty level, or if you are retired on a moderate income, you should probably use the new CPI-U. Otherwise, even if you are moderately rich, the CPI-W will probably be the best indicator for you.

The CPI (W and U) emerges each month as single numbers. At the end of the year an average is computed from the monthly figures. (Averaging does away with fluctuations caused by special situations that have nothing to do with inflation.)

For example, the average CPI for 1984 was 311.1. This means that the value of goods and services, which was set at 100% in 1967, cost 211.1% more in 1984.

Changes in prices and how they affect you can be calculated by comparing the CPI of one period against another. The 1984 CPI reading of 311.1 can be compared to the 1983 reading of 298.4. Dividing by 298.4, the excess over 1 is the percentage increase for the year 1983; in this case, 4.3%.

Did your income increase by enough to keep up with this inflation? To make the comparison, dig out your old W-2 or income tax return forms, or find your old paycheck stubs. Both gross and takehome pay comparisons will be of interest to you, but take care to compare equals. Overtime pay should not be counted. Also, watch out for changes in deductions such as those for tax exemptions, credit union payments, payroll bonds, and the like. These have nothing to do with inflation and should be added back to your take home pay.

Measuring Your Paycheck

A. To compare year-to-year earnings in percent form, divide your 1984 earnings by those of 1983 and express the result as a percentage. For example, if you earned the gross wages of the average U.S. worker, your paychecks in 1983 showed about $280.70 per week as compared with $294.05 per week in 1984, an increase of 4.8%. Since prices rose by 4.3% during 1984, the average worker gained .5% in real gross income that year. You can do the same kind of calculation on your total 1983 and 1984 earnings by using your total annual income figures in place of weekly earnings figures.

B. Another way to handle the same figures takes a dollar form. For this calculation, assume your wage was $280.70 at the end of 1983. During 1984, prices increased by 4.3%. To match that price increase, your wages should have gone up to $292.77 (280.70 plus 4.3%) by the end of 1984.

While readings on a monthly basis may be misleading, you may want a rough idea of how much you are being affected by inflation right now. For example, if you had weekly earnings of $298.55 in May of 1985, compared to earnings of $291.46 in May, 1984, your income went up 2.4% (The difference, $7.09, divided by 291.46). The CPI-W went from 305.4 to 317.8 from May, 1984 to May, 1985, an increase of 4.0%. This means your increase in wages over the last 12 months was 1.6% below the increase in inflation over the same period. You can make the same calculation for any month by using the latest CPI figures as they are issued by the Department of Labor and published in your local newspaper.

Consumer Price Indexes, 1985

Source: Bureau of Labor Statistics, U.S. Labor Department

(1967=100)	April CPI-U	April CPI-W	May CPI-U	May CPI-W	June CPI-U	June CPI-W
Food, beverages	308.7	308.3	308.3	307.8	308.5	308.1
Housing	345.9	339.7	348.1	341.7	349.2	342.8
Apparel, upkeep	205.4	204.4	205.2	204.1	205.8	205.0
Transportation	322.3	324.1	321.6	323.3	321.2	322.8
Medical care	397.5	395.2	399.9	397.7	402.6	400.5
Entertainment	262.5	258.0	263.4	258.8	264.8	260.2
Other goods, services	323.0	319.1	324.3	320.2	325.9	321.5
Services	376.8	372.8	379.1	375.0	381.0	376.9
Rent, for home	112.0	101.6	113.2	102.6	113.6	102.9
Household, less rent	109.8	101.2	110.9	102.2	112.7	104.2
Transportation	333.9	329.4	334.3	329.7	335.1	330.4
Medical care	428.9	426.3	431.8	429.1	434.5	432.0
Other services	310.9	306.9	312.3	308.4	314.4	310.2
All items less food	321.2	317.6	322.3	318.5	323.1	319.2
Commodities	286.9	286.8	286.6	286.4	286.4	286.2
Commodities less food	273.4	276.2	273.1	275.7	272.8	275.3
Nondurables	292.4	293.1	293.0	293.1	293.4	294.1
Energy[1]	429.9	429.4	431.2	430.9	431.9	431.9
All items less energy[1]	312.6	308.1	313.4	308.6	314.0	309.2

(1) Excludes motor oil, coolant, and other products as of January, 1983.

Average Consumer Price Indexes

Source: Bureau of Labor Statistics, U.S. Labor Department

The Consumer Price Index (CPI-W) measures the average change in prices of goods and services purchased by urban wage earners and clerical workers. (1967 = 100). NA = Not available.

	1978 Index	%+	1979 Index	%+	1980 Index	%+	1981 Index	%+	1982 Index	%+	1983 Index	%+	1984 Index	%+
All items	195.3	7.6	217.7	11.5	247.0	13.5	273.3	10.2	288.6	6.0	298.4	3.2	311.1	4.3
Food, drink	206.2	9.7	228.7	10.9	248.7	8.7	267.8	7.7	278.5	4.0	284.7	2.2	295.1	3.7
Housing	202.6	8.6	227.5	12.3	263.2	12.3	293.2	11.4	314.7	7.3	322.0	2.3	336.5	4.5
Apparel, upkeep	159.5	3.4	166.4	4.3	177.4	6.6	186.6	5.2	190.9	2.3	195.6	2.5	200.2	2.4
Transportation	185.8	4.9	212.8	14.5	250.5	17.7	281.3	12.3	293.1	4.2	300.0	2.4	311.7	3.9
Medical care	219.4	8.4	240.1	9.4	267.2	11.3	295.1	10.4	326.9	10.8	355.1	8.6	379.5	6.9
Entertainment	176.2	5.1	187.7	6.5	203.7	8.5	219.0	7.5	232.4	6.1	242.4	4.3	255.1	5.2
Other.	183.2	6.4	196.3	7.2	213.6	8.8	233.3	9.2	257.0	10.2	286.3	11.4	307.7	7.5

Consumer Price Index by Cities

(CPI-W; 1967-100, except Anchorage and Miami)

City[1]	March 1985	April 1985	May 1985	May 1984	Percent change to May 1985 from— March 1985	April 1985
Anchorage, Alas. (10/67 = 100)	273.1	—	271.9	2.3	—.4	—
Atlanta, Ga.	—	322.3	—	—	—	—
Baltimore, Md.	320.2	—	322.3	4.2	.7	—
Boston, Mass.	312.3	—	313.2	4.1	.3	—
Buffalo, N.Y.	—	291.9	—	—	—	—
Chicago, Ill-Northwest Ind.	304.7	306.2	306.9	3.5	.7	.2
Cincinnati, Ohio-Ky.-Ind.	322.2	—	324.0	3.7	.6	—
Cleveland, Ohio	—	321.8	—	—	—	—
Dallas-Ft. Worth, Tex.	—	329.6	—	—	—	—
Denver-Boulder, Col.	350.7	—	351.9	3.2	.3	—
Detroit, Mich.	306.0	306.3	306.6	2.8	.2	.1
Honolulu-Ha.	—	300.1	—	—	—	—
Houston, Tex.	331.1	—	332.8	—	—	—
Kansas City., Mo.-Kan.	—	309.7	—	—	—	—
Los Angeles-Long Beach, Anaheim, Cal.	309.8	311.2	314.1	3.6	1.4	.9
Miami, Fla. (11/77 = 100)	171.3	—	172.2	3.0	.5	—
Milwaukee, Wis.	346.9	—	350.2	3.5	1.0	—
Minneapolis-St. Paul, Minn.-Wis.	—	329.2	—	—	—	—
New York, N.Y.-Northeast N.J.	304.2	305.1	305.8	4.9	.5	.2
Northeast Pa. (Scranton)	304.2	—	305.2	3.3	.3	—
Philadelphia, Pa.-N.J.	313.5	315.3	317.2	5.6	1.2	.6
Pittsburgh, Pa.	—	306.8	—	—	—	—
Portland, Ore.-Wash.	299.8	—	301.2	1.2	.5	—
St. Louis, Mo.-Ill.	311.0	—	313.0	5.3	.6	—
San Diego, Cal.	333.7	—	336.5	2.7	.8	—
San Francisco, Oakland, Cal.	—	326.1	—	—	—	—
Seattle-Everett, Wash.	309.0	—	308.4	1.9	—.2	—
Washington, D.C.-Md.-Va.	322.3	—	323.0	4.6	.2	—

(1) The area listed includes the entire Standard Metropolitan Statistical Area, except New York and Chicago, which include the Standard Consolidated Area.

Annual Percent Change in Productivity and Related Data, 1973-84

Source: Bureau of Labor Statistics, U.S. Labor Department

Item	1973	1974	1975	1976	1977	1978	1979	1980	1981	1982	1983	1984
Business sector:												
Output per hour of all persons	2.6	-2.4	2.2	3.3	2.4	0.5	-1.2	-0.5	1.9	0.2	2.7	3.2
Real compensation per hour .	1.6	-1.4	0.5	2.6	1.2	0.8	-1.7	-2.7	-0.9	1.9	1.1	0.0
Unit labor cost	5.3	12.1	7.3	5.1	5.1	8.0	10.7	11.0	7.3	7.9	1.6	1.0
Unit nonlabor payments. . . .	5.9	4.4	15.1	4.0	6.4	6.7	5.8	5.7	14.6	0.1	6.3	7.9
Implicit price deflator	5.5	9.5	9.8	4.7	5.6	7.5	9.0	9.3	9.6	5.3	3.0	3.2
Nonfarm business sector:												
Output per hour of all persons	2.4	-2.5	2.0	3.2	2.2	0.6	-1.5	-0.7	1.5	0.2	3.5	2.7
Real compensation per hour .	1.3	-1.4	0.4	2.2	1.0	0.8	-2.0	-2.8	-0.7	1.7	1.6	-0.1
Unit labor cost	5.0	12.2	7.5	4.7	5.2	8.0	10.7	11.1	8.0	7.7	1.4	1.4
Unit nonlabor payments. . . .	1.3	5.9	16.7	5.7	6.9	5.3	4.8	7.4	13.8	1.4	7.4	6.7
Implicit price deflator	3.8	10.2	10.3	5.1	5.7	7.1	8.8	10.0	9.8	5.7	3.2	3.1
Manufacturing:												
Output per hour of all persons	5.4	-2.4	2.9	4.5	2.5	0.9	0.7	0.2	3.1	2.1	4.3	3.5
Real compensation per hour .	0.9	-0.3	2.5	2.1	1.8	0.6	-1.4	-1.6	-0.9	2.5	0.2	-0.6
Unit labor cost	1.7	13.3	8.8	3.4	5.7	7.3	9.0	11.5	6.1	6.6	-0.8	0.1
Unit nonlabor payments. . . .	-3.3	-1.8	25.9	7.5	6.5	2.7	-2.6	-2.1	14.1	-1.0	16.5	8.9
Implicit price deflator	0.3	9.0	13.1	4.6	6.0	6.0	5.7	7.9	8.0	4.7	3.3	2.5

Consumer Price Index by Region and City Size
Source: Bureau of Labor Statistics, U.S. Labor Department

(City sizes: A=1.25 million or more; B=385,000 to 1.25 million; C=75,000 to 385,000; D=75,000 or less.)

(Dec. 1977 = 100)	CPI-U				CPI-W			
	Feb. 1985	% change, Feb. 1985 to Apr. 1985	Apr. 1985	% change, Apr. 1984 to Apr. 1985	Feb. 1985	% change, Feb. 1985 to Apr. 1985	Apr. 1985	% change, Apr. 1984 to Apr. 1985
Northeast								
Size A	165.5	0.7	166.7	3.7	162.4	0.4	163.1	4.2
Size B	171.5	1.2	173.5	4.3	169.1	1.7	169.1	3.4
Size C	175.8	1.1	177.8	4.0	177.7	.2	177.7	·4.7
Size D	170.3	2.3	174.2	4.8	172.5	1.4	172.5	4.6
North Central								
Size A	174.3	.9	175.9	3.5	172.3	1.8	172.3	3.5
Size B	169.7	1.2	171.7	2.9	170.6	3.1	170.6	4.9
Size C	166.7	1.1	168.6	3.2	166.9	2.4	166.9	3.9
Size D	168.2	.5	169.1	2.8	173.1	1.9	173.1	4.0
South								
Size A	171.0	.8	172.4	3.7	173.4	1.2	173.4	4.2
Size B	173.0	.4	173.7	3.3	172.3	1.0	172.3	4.7
Size C	171.2	.6	172.2	3.2	171.2	.1	171.2	3.7
Size D	170.1	.9	171.6	2.1	169.7	—.6	169.7	2.0
West								
Size A	173.5	.6	174.6	4.4	169.7	.7	169.7	3.3
Size B	172.0	1.4	174.4	4.6	173.3	.7	173.3	4.1
Size C	164.2	1.6	166.9	4.9	164.2	.9	164.2	4.6
Size D	170.0	.5	170.8	2.6	171.5	.4	171.5	4.8

The Northeast region includes cities from Boston to Pittsburgh; the North Central, cities from Cleveland to Grand Island, Neb. and from Minneapolis to St. Louis and Cincinnati; the South, cities from Baltimore to Dallas; the West, cities from Alamogordo, N. Mex., to Butte, Mont. Anchorage, and Honolulu.

Annual Average Purchasing Power of the Dollar
Source: Bureau of Labor Statistics, U.S. Labor Department

Obtained by dividing the index for 1967 (100.00) by the index for the given period and expressing the result in dollars and cents. Beginning 1961, wholesale prices include data for Alaska and Hawaii; beginning 1964, consumer prices include them. NA = Not available.

Year	As measured by—		Year	Wholesale prices	Consumer prices	Year	Wholesale prices	Consumer prices
	Wholesale prices	Consumer prices						
1940	$2.469	$2.381	1971	$.878	$.824	1978	$.478	$.493
1950	1.222	1.387	1972	.840	.799	1979	.463	.461
1955	1.139	1.247	1973	.744	.752	1980	.405	.406
1960	1.054	1.127	1974	.625	.677	1981	.371	367
1965	1.035	1.058	1975	.572	.620	1982	NA	.347
1968	.976	.960	1976	.546	.587	1983	NA	.285
1970	.906	.860	1977	.515	.551	1984	NA	.311

Average Weekly Earnings of Production Workers[1]
Source: Bureau of Labor Statistics, U.S. Labor Department

Year and month	Manufacturing workers						Private nonagricultural workers					
	Gross average weekly earnings		Spendable average weekly earnings[2]				Gross average weekly earnings		Spendable average weekly earnings[2]			
			Worker with no dependents		Worker with 3 dependents				Worker with no dependents		Worker with 3 dependents	
	Current dollars	1977 dollars	Current dollars	1977 dollars	Current dollars	1977 dollars	Current dollars	1977 dollars	Current dollars	1977 dollars	Current dollars	1977 dollars
1975	190.79	214.85	151.61	170.73	166.29	187.26	163.53	184.16	132.49	149.20	166.29	164.02
1976	209.32	222.92	167.83	178.73	181.32	193.10	175.45	186.85	143.30	152.61	181.32	166.00
1977	228.90	228.90	183.80	183.80	200.06	200.06	189.00	189.00	155.19	155.19	200.06	169.93
1978	249.27	231.66	197.40	183.46	214.87	199.69	203.70	189.31	165.39	153.71	214.87	167.95
1979	268.94	224.64	212.70	177.40	232.38	193.81	219.91	183.41	178.00	148.46	194.82	162.49
1980	288.62	212.64	225.79	165.90	247.01	181.49	235.10	172.74	188.82	138.74	206.40	151.65
1981	318.00	212.00	244.09	163.73	267.36	178.24	255.20	170.13	202.00	134.67	220.57	147.05
1982	330.65	207.96	—	—	—	—	266.92	167.87	—	—	—	—
1983	354.08	216.03	—	—	—	—	280.70	171.26	—	—	—	—
1984	373.63	220.43	—	—	—	—	294.05	173.48	—	—	—	—
1985 Jan.. . .	380.03	220.69	—	—	—	—	294.95	171.28	—	—	—	—
Feb.. . .	374.37	216.52	—	—	—	—	294.79	170.50	—	—	—	—
Mar.. . .	381.78	219.79	—	—	—	—	298.20	171.68	—	—	—	—
Apr.. . .	380.15	217.85	—	—	—	—	298.05	170.80	—	—	—	—
May. . . .	382.04	218.18	—	—	—	—	298.55	170.50	—	—	—	—
June . . .	385.70ᵖ	219.65ᵖ	—	—	—	—	301.82ᵖ	171.88ᵖ	—	—	—	—
July . . .	382.15ᵖ	—	—	—	—	—	301.46ᵖ	—	—	—	—	—

(1) Data relate to production workers in mining and manufacturing; to construction workers in contract construction; and to nonsupervisory workers in transportation and public utilities; wholesale and retail trade; finance, insurance, and real estate; and services. (2) Spendable average weekly earnings are based on gross average weekly earnings less the estimated amount of the worker's Federal, social security, and income taxes. Figures are no longer available after 1981. (p)—preliminary.

Interest Laws and Consumer Finance Loan Rates

Source: Revised by Christian T. Jones. Editor, Consumer Finance Law Bulletin, San Diego, Ca.

All states have laws regulating interest rates. These laws fix a legal or conventional rate which applies when there is no contract for interest. They also fix a general maximum contract rate, but there are so many exceptions that the general contract maximum actually applies only to exceptional cases. Also, federal law has preempted state limits on first home mortgages, subject to each state's right to reinstate its own law, and given depository institutions parity with other state lenders.

Legal rate of interest. The legal or conventional rate of interest applies to money obligations when no interest rate is contracted for and also to judgments. The rate is usually somewhat below the general interest rate.

General maximum contract rates. General interest laws in most states set the maximum rate between 8% and 16% per year. The general maximum is fixed by the state constitution at 5% over the Federal Reserve Discount rate in Arkansas. Loans to corporations are frequently exempted or subject to a higher maximum. In recent years, it has also been common to provide special rates for home mortgage loans and variable usury rates that are indexed to market rates.

Specific enabling acts. In many states special statutes permit industrial loan companies, second mortgage lenders, and banks to charge 1.5% a month or more. Laws regulating revolving loans, charge accounts and credit cards generally limit charges between 1.5% and 2% per month plus annual fees for credit cards. Rates for installment sales contracts in most states are somewhat higher. Credit unions may generally charge 1% to 1½% a month. Pawnbrokers' rates vary widely. Savings and loan associations, and loans insured by federal agencies, are also specially regulated. A number of states allow regulated lenders to charge any rate agreed to with the customer either for all credit or over a certain dollar amount.

Consumer finance loan statutes. Most consumer finance loan statutes are based on early models drafted by the Russell Sage Foundation (1916-42) to provide small loans to wage earners under license and other protective regulations. Since 1969 the model has frequently been the Uniform Consumer Credit Code which applies to credit sales and loans for consumer purposes. In general, licensed lenders may charge 3% a month and reduced rates for additional amounts. An add-on of 17% ($17 per $100) per year yields about 2.5% per month if paid in equal monthly installments. Discount rates produce higher yields than add-on rates of the same amount. In the table below unless otherwise stated, monthly and annual rates are based on reducing principal balances, annual add-on rates are based on the original principal for the full term, and two or more rates apply to different portions of balance or original principal.

States with consumer finance loan laws and the rates of charge as of Oct. 1, 1985:

Maximum monthly rates computed on unpaid balances, unless otherwise stated.

Ala.. . . Annual add-on: 15% to $750, 10% to $2,000, 8% over $2,000 (min. 1.5% on unpaid balances), plus 2% fee (max. $20). Higher rates for loans up to $749. Over $2,000, any agreed rate.

Alas. . . 3% to $850, 2% to $10,000, flat rate to $25,000. Over $10,000, any agreed rate.

Ariz. . . To $1,000: 3%. Over $1,000: 3% to $500, 2% to $10,000. Over $10,000, any agreed rate.

Cal.. . . 2.5% to $225, 2% to $900, 1.5% to $1,650, 1% to $5,000 (1.6% min.). Over $5,000, any agreed rate. 5% fee (max. $50) to $2,500

Colo.. . 36% per year to $630, 21% to $2,100, 15% to $25,000 (21% min.).

Conn. . Annual Add-on: 17% to $600, 11% to $5,000; 11% over $1,800 to $5,000 for certain secured loans. Any agreed rate for second mortgages.

Del.. . . Any agreed rate.

Fla.. . . 30% per year to $500, 24% to $1,000, 18% to $5,000; 18% per year on any amount over $5,000 to $25,000.

Ga.. . . 10% per year discount to 18 months, add-on to 36½ months; 8% fee to $600, 4% on excess plus $2 per month; max. $3,000. Over $3,000, any agreed rate.

Ha.. . . 3.5% to $100, 2.5% to $300; 2% on entire balance over $300 or discount rates.

Ida.. . . Any agreed rate.

Ill.. . . . Any agreed rate.

Ind.. . . 36% per year to $720, 21% to $2,400, 15% to $60,000 (21% min.).

Ia. . . . 3% to $1,000, 2% to $2,800; 1.5% to $10,000; or equivalent flat rate. Over $10,000: 21% per year.

Kan. . . 36% per year to $570, 21% to $1,900, 14.45% to $25,000 (21% min.).

Ky.. . . . 3% to $1,000, 2% to $3,000, 2% over $3,000, 2%.

La. . . . 36% per year to $1,400, 27% to $4,000, 24% to $7,000, 21% over $7,000, plus $25 fee.

Me.. . . 30% per year to $690, 21% to $1,900, 15% to $55,000 (18% min.).

Md.. . . 2.75% to $1,000, 2% to $2,000. Over $2,000, 2%.

Mass. . 23% per year plus $20 fee to $6,000; 18%.

Mich.. . 31% per year to $500, 13% to $3,000 (18% min.) for second mortgages.

Minn.. . 33% per year to $385, 19% to $38,500 (21.75% min.).

Miss.. . 36% per year to $800, 33% to $1,800, 24% to $4,500, 12% over $4,500.

Mo.. . . 2.218% to $1,200, 1.67% over $1,200, plus 5% fee (max. $15); 1.67% plus 2% for second mortgages.

Mont.. . Any agreed rate.

Neb. . . 24% per year to $1,000. 21% over, plus fee of 7% to $2,000 and 5% over (max. $500).

Nev. . . Any agreed rate.

N.H. . . 2% to $600, 1.5% to $1,500; Any agreed rate to $10,000. Any agreed rate for second mortgages.

N.J.. . . 30% per year to $5,000 or for second mortgages.

N.M. . . Any agreed rate.

N.Y. . . Any agreed rate.

N.C. . . 3% to $1,000, 1.5% to $7,500; 1.5% on entire amount to $10,000.

N.D. . . 2.5% to $250, 2% to $500, 1.75% to $750, 1.5% to $1,000; any agreed rate on entire amount over $1,000 to $30,000.

Ohio . . 28% per year to $1,000, 22% to $3,000; 25% on entire amount over $3,000; plus fee.

Okla.. . 30% per annum to $660, 21% to $2,200, 15% to $47,500. (21% min.). Special rates to $100.

Ore. . . Any agreed rate.

Pa.. . . 9.5% per year discount to 48 months, 6% for remaining time plus 2%; or 2% on unpaid balances; 1.6% for second mortgages over $5,000.

P.R. . . 24% per year.

R.I.. . . 3% to $300, 2.5% for loans between $300 and $800; 2% for larger loans to $5,000.

S.C. . . Any agreed rate.

S.D. . . Any agreed rate.

Tenn.. . Over $100, 24% per year plus fees.

Texas . Annual add-on: 18% to $900, 8% to $7,500 or formula rate (max. 24% per year on unpaid balances.)

Utah . . Any agreed rate.

Vt. . . . 2% to $1,000, 1% to $3,000 (min. 1.5%); 1.5% for second mortgages.

Va.. . . 3% to $600, 2.25% to $1,800, 1.5% to $2,800; or annual add-on of 21% to $600, 17% to $1,800, 13% to $2,800; 2% fee. Any agreed rate over $2,800 for second mortgages, plus 2% fee.

Wash. . 2.5% to $500, 1.5% to $1,000, 1% to $2,500. Over $2,500, 25% per year or discount rates.

W.Va. . 36% per year to $500, 24% to $1,500, 18% to $2,000. Over $2,000, 27% per year to $2,000, 25% to $10,000, 18% on remainder.

Wis. . . Any agreed rate, 11/1/84 to 10/31/87.

Wyo.. . 36% per year to $1,000, 21% to $25,000 (21% min.).

Shopping for Credit: Ask the Right Questions
Source: New York State Banking Department

Under federal law, all institutions that extend or arrange for the extension of consumer credit must give the borrower meaningful information about the cost of each loan. The cost must be expressed as the dollar amount of the interest or finance charge, and as the annual percentage rate computed on the amount financed.

To be sure the loan or credit agreement you are considering suits both your budget and your individual needs, shop around. And ask questions to compare and evaluate a lender's rate and services. For instance:

1. What is the annual percentage rate?
2. What is the total cost of the loan in dollars?

3. How long do you have to pay off the loan?
4. What are the number, amounts, and due dates of payments?
5. What is the cost of deferring or extending the time period of the loan?
6. What is the cost of late charges for overdue payments?
7. If you pay the loan off early, are there any prepayment penalties?
8. Does the loan have to be secured? If so, what collateral is required?
9. What is the cost of credit life or other insurance that is being offered or may be required?
10. Are there any other charges you may have to pay?

Fair Credit: What You Should Know
Source: Federal Trade Commission

Federal legislation has made it easier for you to be treated fairly in credit-related areas:

Billing. Don't let the anonymous computer get you down. The Fair Credit Billing Act states that, if you find an error in the amount of $50 or more in your credit card statement or department store revolving charge statement and you write to the company about it (on a separate sheet of paper, not the bill), the company must acknowledge your letter within 30 days and must resolve the dispute within 90 days.

Equal Credit. The Equal Credit Opportunity Act (ECOA) bans any discrimination according to sex or marital status in the granting of credit. Discrimination is also prohibited on the basis of age, race, color, religion, national origin, or receipt of public assistance payments.

However, the creditor may ask questions relating to these areas if they have bearing on your credit worthiness. The creditor does have the right to determine whether you are willing and able to repay your debts. For instance, the creditor can ask you if you are "married," "unmarried," or "separated" if, and only if, (1) you are applying jointly with your spouse; (2) your spouse will be an authorized user of the account; (3) you live in a community property state or you list assets located in a community property state. Similarly, a creditor may ask about alimony, child support, and separate maintenance if, and only if, you are depending on these as sources to establish your ability to repay your debts. In this case, the creditor may ask whether there is a court order that requires the payments or may inquire about the length of time and regularity of the payments, as well as your ex-spouse's credit history.

The ECOA also requires that if you are turned down for credit, the creditor must tell you the reason you were turned down.

Mail-Order Merchandise. By law, you have the right to receive merchandise ordered through the mail within 30 days, unless another deadline has been specified. Promises such as "one week" or "4 to 6 weeks" must be met. If either the seller's or the FTC's deadline is missed, you have the right to cancel and have all your money returned. If you run into a problem with late or non-delivery, contact the Federal Trade Commission for help.

Managing Credit: How Much Debt is Safe?
Source: Citibank

It is extremely important for consumers to keep close track of their individual use of credit and debt.

Before you make any new purchases, which involve moving income from the optional spending part of your budget to your fixed budget as a loan to be repaid, you must be sure you have those extra dollars and that you can do without them each month.

How Much Average Debt is Safe?

Once you've decided to apply for credit, you face the most-asked question about consumer debt: how much is safe?

There is no simple answer that applies to each consumer's situation. Most experts, today, avoid general rules of thumb.

Don't be misled by the percents of gross income that lenders may use to decide how much institutional risk they run in any specific application for a loan. The lending institution can use only gross income and loan-commitment averages to estimate its own average risk, and cannot know how any individual consumer will actually repay. Only you can gauge that, based on your own habits, values, and needs.

How do you determine what you can handle? To help decide, you must know at a given time how many dollars you have for optional spending, and then how many of those

dollars you can move into fixed repayments.

Here's one technique for determining how many optional dollars you have:
1. Write down your annual take-home income after deductions (for taxes, etc.) and divide by 12 to get your monthly take-home income.
2. From the monthly figure, subtract all your current monthly fixed expenses—those to which you are currently committed or must cover over the next year. Include your gasoline and car costs, other transportation, heating, utilities, food, rent, or mortgage (but no other loan repayments), real estate taxes, insurance, etc.
3. Next, total your monthly nonmortgage loan repayments and subtract them from the previous amount.

The total figure you're left with is your monthly optional spending amount. Now you must consider how comfortably you're managing with this amount. Consider that amount less the new monthly repayment. Can you still manage on the remaining amount, or should you wait until your take-home income goes up or your present debt loan goes down?

Are You Headed for Financial Trouble?

Although there is no dependable formula for determining your individual debt ratio, there are certain clear warning signals that you may have reached or have already passed it.

Consider the following signals and, if several of them describe your financial situation, it may be time to look for help.

1. Your checkbook balance is getting lower and lower each month.

2. You don't seem to be able to make it from month to month without writing overdrafts on your checking account.

3. You pay only the minimum due or even less on your charge accounts each month.

4. You have borrowed on your life insurance and see little possibility of paying it back soon.

5. Your savings account is slowly disappearing or has completely disappeared, and you're not able to put any of your regular income into savings.

6. You manage to get through each month by depending on undependable extra income like overtime or odd jobs.

7. You find yourself depending on credit cards for day-to-day living expenses and using cash advances to pay off other debts.

8. You are behind on one or more of your installment payments.

9. You don't really know how much money you owe.

10. You are receiving overdue notices or phone calls from creditors.

11. Family disputes over money are growing.

12. You occasionally juggle paying bills, paying one creditor while giving excuses to another.

13. You've had to ask creditors for extensions on due dates.

14. You've taken out loans to pay debts, or taken out a debt consolidation loan.

15. You are at or near the limit on the credit lines allowed on your credit cards.

16. When you use credit, you try to get it for the longest time period and the lowest payments without considering how much more this will cost you in interest.

17. You must borrow money to pay bills you can anticipate, like quarterly property taxes.

18. Although you regularly pay all of your debts, you are forced to continue living on credit and, as a result, your debt loan never really shrinks or is even increasing.

What can you do if you find yourself in financial trouble? The first step is to drastically cut your optional spending. Put yourself and your family on a crash tight-cash program until you can stabilize your financial situation. Also, you may need to turn some assets into cash and apply it to your debts.

If these attempts fail, get in touch with your creditors. Candidly, explain your situation. Some of them may agree to a longer repayment schedule which will insure that they get their money back and that they will keep you as a customer. You may pay more in interest, but you'll have a better credit record.

If you're still in trouble, you probably need good financial counseling.

How to Find Credit Counseling

In the U.S., there are hundreds of free volunteer-staffed credit counseling sources. Others, staffed by professionals, charge a fee.

Look up Consumer Credit Counseling in your local phone book. Call the Consumer Affairs Department of your city for referrals. Contact community-centered organizations, church, local banks, consumer finance company, credit union, labor union, or your employer's personnel department.

If you can't find a local agency, write to the Family Service Association of America (44 E. 23rd St., New York, NY 10010) or the National Foundation for Consumer Credit (1819 H Street N.W., Washington, DC 20006).

Consumer Installment Credit

Source: Federal Reserve System (estimates of amounts outstanding, millions of dollars, not seasonally adjusted)

| End of year or month | Total | By holder | | | | | | By type | | | |
		Commercial banks	Finance companies	Credit unions	Retailers	Savings-loans and other	Automobile	Mobile homes	Revolving	All others
1977	230,564	112,373	44,868	37,605	23,490	12,228	82,911	14,945	39,274	93,434
1978	273,645	136,016	54,298	44,334	25,987	13,010	101,647	15,235	48,309	108,454
1979	312,024	154,177	68,318	46,517	28,119	14,893	116,362	16,838	56,937	121,887
1980	301,379	147,013	63,226	44,041	28,697	47,100	112,260	18,785	58,506	111,828
1981	318,229	147,622	72,356	45,954	31,348	20,950	119,786	19,906	64,500	114,038
1982	334,959	152,490	78,143	47,253	32,395	24,678	126,258	22,410	69,624	116,667
1983	383,701	171,978	87,429	53,471	37,470	33,353	143,114	23,862	81,977	134,748
1984	460,500	212,391	96,747	67,858	40,913	42,591	172,589	24,556	101,555	161,800
1985, June .	497,359	231,222	105,971	73,468	37,548	49,150	192,448	25,208	104,471	175,232

Investment: A Basic Glossary

Source: Merrill, Lynch, Pierce, Fenner & Smith, Inc.

The investment possibilities in securities for you as an individual are extremely varied. If you are beginning to consider what is best for your personal needs and find the world of securities somewhat bewildering, we hope the following glossary may offer some help.

Bear Market: A market in which prices are falling.

Bond: A written promise or IOU by the issuer to repay a fixed amount of borrowed money on a specified date and to pay a set annual rate of interest in the meantime, generally at semi-annual intervals. Bonds are generally considered safe because the borrower (whether a company or the government) must make interest payments before their money is spent on anything else. Some of the most common bonds include:

Commercial Paper: An extremely short-term corporate IOU, generally due in 270 days or less. Available in face amounts of $100,000, $250,000, $500,000, $1,000,000 and combinations thereof. Yield in recent years has averaged from 12 to 17 percent.

Convertible Bond: A corporate bond (see below) which may be converted into a stated number of shares of the corporations common stock. Its price tends to fluctuate along with fluctuations in the price of the stock as well as with changes in interest rates. Average yield in recent years has ranged from 8 to 12 percent.

Corporate Bond: Evidence of debt by a corporation. Differs from a municipal bond in various ways, but particularly in taxability of interest. Considered safer than the common

or preferred stock of the same company. Yield has averaged in recent years from 12 to 17 percent.

Government Bond: An IOU of the U.S. Treasury, considered the safest security in the investment world. They are divided into two categories, those that are not marketable and those that are. *Savings Bonds* cannot be bought and sold once the original purchase is made. These include the familiar Series EE bonds. You buy them at 75 percent of their face value and when they mature, 5 years later, they will pay you back 100 percent of face value if you cash them in. Recently they have been paying about 6 percent interest compounded semiannually to maturity. Another type, Series H, are not discounted, but issued in amounts of $500, $1,000, $5,000, and $10,000 and pay their interest in semiannual checks. They pay 8 percent the first year of their 10-year life, 5.8 percent for the next 4 years, and 6 percent for the last 5 years. Marketable bonds fall into 3 categories. *Treasury Bills* are short-term U.S. obligations, maturing in 3, 6, or 12 months. They are sold at a discount of the face value, and the minimum denomination is $10,000. Yield in recent years has ranged from 7½ percent to 16½ percent. *Treasury Notes* mature in up to 10 years. Denominations range from $500, $1,000 to $5,000, $10,000 and up. In recent years the yield has ranged from 8¼ percent to 15 percent. *Treasury Bonds* mature in 10 to 30 years. The minimum investment is $1,000 and yield has ranged from 8½ to 14 percent in recent years.

Junk Bonds: Debt securities that sell at relatively low prices, because of the low credit rating of their issuers. They pay significantly higher yields than top-grade bonds to reflect their added risk. These bonds are also known as high-yielding or speculative bonds.

Mortgage-Backed Securities: Created when a bank, builder or government agency gathers together a group of mortgages and then sells bonds to other institutions and the public. The investors receive their proportionate share of the interest payments on the loans as well as the principal payments. Usually, these mortgages are guaranteed by the government, making them a fairly safe investment despite the fact that their market value does fluctuate.

Municipal Bond: Issued by governmental units such as states, cities, local taxing authorities and other agencies. Interest is exempt from U.S. — and sometimes state and local — income tax. Yield in recent years has averaged from 9 to 13 percent. *Municipal Bond Unit Investment Trusts* allow you to invest with as little as $1,000 in a portfolio of many different municipal bonds chosen by professionals. The income is paid either monthly or semiannually and is exempt from Federal income taxes.

Bull Market: A market in which prices are on the rise.

Stock: *Common Stocks* are shares of ownership in a corporation; they are the most direct way to participate in the fortunes of a company. The sometimes wide swings in the prices of this kind of stock may mean a chance for big profits (or equally big losses). *Preferred Stock* is a type of stock

on which a fixed dividend must be paid before holders of common stock are issued their share of the issuing corporation's earnings. Prices are higher and yields lower than comparable bonds and are, consequently, not the best investment for individuals. Payments are usually made quarterly. They are especially attractive to corporate investors because 85 percent of preferred dividends are tax exempt to corporations. Many high-grade preferreds currently pay about 10¼ percent to 11¼ percent interest. *Convertible Preferred Stock* can be converted into the common stock of the company that issued the preferred. This stock has the advantage of producing a higher yield than common stock and it also has appreciation potential. *Over-the-Counter Stock* is not traded on the major or regional exchanges, but rather through dealers from whom you buy directly. These stocks tend to belong to smaller companies. Prices of OTC stocks are based on the dealer's supply, what he paid for them, the demand for them, and the prices of competitive dealers. *Blue Chip* stocks are so called because they have been leading stocks for a long time. They do not show dramatic growth, but yield good dividends over time. *Growth* stocks are stocks which grow yearly by a growing percentage; they do well even in bad times.

Dow-Jones Industrial Average: A measure of stock market prices, based on the 30 leading manufacturing companies on the New York Stock Exchange.

Mutual Fund: A portfolio, or selection, of professionally bought and managed stocks in which you pool your money along with thousands of other people. A share price is based on net asset value, or the value of all the investments owned by the funds, less any debt, and divided by the total number of shares. The major advantage is less risk — it is spread out over many stocks and, if one or two do badly, the remainder may shield you from the losses. *Bond Funds* are mutual funds that deal in the bond market exclusively. *Money Market Mutual Funds* buy in the so-called "Money Market" — institutions that need to borrow large sums of money for short terms. Usually the individual investor cannot afford the denominations required in the "Money Market" (i.e. treasury bills, commercial paper, certificates of deposit), but through a money market mutual fund he can take advantage of these money makers when interest rates are high. These funds offer special checking account advantages, as you can generally write a check against your investment at any time in amounts of $500 or more. The minimum investment is generally $1,000. Average yield over recent years has been from 9 to 15 percent.

Unit Investment Trust: A portfolio of many different corporate bonds, preferred stocks, government-backed securities or utility common stocks in which you can invest with as little as $1,000. Professional managers choose the securities, arrange for safe-keeping and collect the income. You receive your pro rata share of income every month.

Year-End Assets and Liabilities of Individuals in the U.S.[1]

Source: Federal Reserve System
(billions of dollars)

	1960	1965	1970	1975	1980	1982	1983	1984
Total financial assets	1002.4	1499.8	1966.4	2611.3	4612.8	5470.5	6158.3	6721.6
Checkable deposits & curr.	91.5	107.3	137.2	190.0	283.9	336.0	376.0	402.6
Time & savings deposits	164.0	288.4	426.3	766.0	1282.2	1460.8	1659.3	1876.9
Money market fund shares	—	—	—	3.7	74.4	206.6	162.5	209.7
Securities	512.1	766.9	928.3	925.4	1600.5	1745.4	2021.7	2147.7
U.S. savings bonds	45.6	49.7	52.1	67.4	72.5	68.3	71.5	74.5
Other U.S. Treasury secur.	25.9	26.3	32.8	58.9	115.6	157.9	196.9	245.8
U.S. Govt. agency secur.	2.3	3.7	20.9	12.5	52.1	51.1	59.5	82.6
Tax-exempt obligations	30.8	36.4	46.0	68.1	89.9	132.8	173.8	206.5
Corporate & foreign bonds	10.0	9.5	36.2	60.9	58.3	45.7	45.8	49.2
Open-market paper	2.0	5.6	11.7	10.9	23.8	14.7	7.9	-.1
Mutual fund shares	17.0	35.2	46.8	43.0	63.5	89.5	129.3	162.8
Private life insurance res.	78.8	98.9	123.3	158.5	207.4	223.3	231.1	239.0
Private insured pension res.	18.9	27.3	41.0	72.3	172.0	242.9	286.4	324.8
Private noninsured pen. res.	38.1	73.6	110.4	186.6	412.7	518.1	607.8	623.3
Govt. insurance & pen. res.	40.2	60.8	95.2	154.7	283.6	371.2	437.2	495.2
Miscellaneous finan. assets	58.8	76.6	104.7	154.1	296.2	366.1	376.2	402.3

(continued)

	1960	1965	1970	1975	1980	1982	1983	1984
Total liabilities	280.5	444.9	650.2	1107.4	2069.6	2397.1	2663.7	2981.7
Mtg. debt on nonfarm homes.	137.4	214.4	290.4	482.9	967.5	1096.9	1200.1	1334.2
Other mortgage debt[2]	35.7	65.3	118.7	248.8	412.5	479.0	540.2	612.5
Consumer credit.	65.1	103.2	143.1	223.2	389.7	441.7	493.0	577.1
Security credit.	5.4	9.1	10.4	12.1	27.2	28.8	48.1	47.5
Policy loans	5.7	8.3	17.0	25.5	42.6	54.2	55.3	55.8
Other debt[2]	31.2	44.6	70.4	114.9	230.1	296.5	327.1	354.6

(1) Combined statement for households, farm business, and nonfarm noncorporate business. (2) Includes corporate farms.

Consumer Information Catalog

Source: U.S. Office of Consumer Affairs

The *Consumer Information Catalog* is a free listing of more than 200 of the best federal consumer publications. They range from booklets on financial planning to planning a diet, from learning about federal benefits to getting an education, from fixing a car to dealing effectively with consumer problems. It also lists many resources that will help you get a passport or a birth certificate, find government documents or national parks, learn your rights and stand up for them. Many of these booklets are free.

The *Consumer Information Catalog* is published quarterly by the Consumer Information Center of the U.S. General Services Administration, so you will be able to send for the most current booklets. For your free copy of the *Consumer Information Catalog*, send your name and address to: Consumer Information Catalog, Pueblo, CO 81009. Educators, libraries, and other non-profit groups who are able to distribute 25 or more copies of the *Consumer Information Catalog* on a quarterly basis should write to the same address for an application to be placed on the mailing list. Costs prevent the Consumer Information Center from maintaining a mailing list for individuals.

The booklets listed below are from the *Consumer Information Catalog*. They are available at the prices listed as of December 1, 1985. Quantities of some may be limited. Please send your name and address, the item numbers of the booklets you want, and any payment to: Consumer Information Center, Dept. MB, Pueblo, CO 81009.

Free Publications

Handbook on Child Support Enforcement. The basic steps to follow if you need child support enforcement services; tips on solving enforcement problems; and how to find help locally. 40 pp. (1985) 503P.

Student Guide—Five Federal Financial Aid Programs. Important information about five grant and loan programs for college, vocational, and technical school students. 44 pp. (1985) 508P.

Your Social Security. All about Social Security and Medicare benefits, including who gets them and how to apply. 35 pp. (1985) 510P.

Consumer Credit Handbook. How to apply for credit, what to do if you are denied, how to correct credit mistakes, and how consumer credit laws can help you. 44 pp. (1983) 513P.

Nutrition and Your Health: Dietary Guidelines for Americans. Seven dietary guidelines to help you stay healthy based on the latest nutrition research. Includes charts on desirable body weights and calorie expenditures for various exercises. 23 pp. (1985) 520P.

Sodium. What sodium does for the body and how to replace sodium intake. Fold-out poster. (1982) 523P.

The Safe Food Book: Your Kitchen Guide. Common causes and symptoms of food poisoning; what you can do to reduce the risks with specific instructions for handling meat and poultry, home canning, what to do when the freezer fails and more. 32 pp. (1985) 534P.

Some Things You Should Know About Prescription Drugs. Even prescription drugs can be dangerous; here are tips for safe use. 4 pp. (1982) 551P.

Cancer Prevention: Good News, Better News, Best News. Advice on what you can do to help protect yourself against cancer, including latest nutrition information. 20 pp. (1984) 560P.

Consumer Handbook on Adjustable Rate Mortgages. A guide to understanding the basic features, advantages and risks, and terminology associated with adjustable rate mortgages. 23 pp. (1984) 580P.

Sales of Federal Surplus Real Estate. Listing of when, where, and how surplus properties will be sold within the next three months; where to go for more information on specific pieces of property. 4 pp. Revised monthly. 581P.

Your Keys to Energy Efficiency. Tips for saving energy at home and in your car; health-related issues; state and local consumer and energy offices; and a bibliography. 20 pp. (1985) 584P.

Access Travel. Design features, facilities and services for the handicapped at 519 airport terminals in 62 countries. 40 pp. (1985) 585P.

Federal Depository Libraries. Addresses for approximately 1,400 libraries in the U.S. that maintain, or have access to, documents produced by the federal government. 40 pp. (1985) 590P.

Federal Information Centers. Lists centers across the country to contact when you need assistance from the federal government. 6 pp. (1983) 591P.

How to Choose and Use a Lawyer. Questions and answers about fees, advertising, referrals, and other legal resources. What to do when you have a problem with a lawyer. 6 pp. (1984) 592P.

Mail Order Rights. What to do about cancelled orders, unordered merchandise, unsatisfactory delays, and payment disputes. 4 pp. (1985) 593 P.

Consumer's Resource Handbook. Comprehensive guide to how to complain and get results. Lists corporate consumer representatives, private consumer organizations, and federal, state, and local government agencies with consumer responsibilities. 96 pp. (1985) 596P.

Publications for Sale

Books for Children. A descriptive listing of the best books published in 1984 for preschool through junior high school age children. 23 pp. (1985) 108P. $1.00

What Every Investor Should Know. Provides basic information for choosing investments; trading securities; safeguarding your investments; and protections guaranteed by law. Describes the different types of securities—stocks, bonds, mutual funds, Treasury notes, etc. 35 pp. (1985) 113P. $1.00.

Your Money's Worth in Foods. Guides for budgeting, menu planning, and shopping for best values. Includes tables for making cost comparisons on a variety of vegetables, fruits, and meats. 39 pp. (1984) 115P. $2.25.

Stroke. Recent research reverses some old ideas about stroke: victims can recover and it can be prevented. An overview of causes, diagnosis, treatment, and prevention. 32 pp. (1983) 125P. $1.75.

You Are Not Alone. Tips to maintain good mental health; discusses warning signals, causes and types of mental illnesses; and provides treatment information. 16 pp. (1985) 127P. $1.00.

Turning Home Equity Into Income for Older Americans. Three plans to help homeowners convert their capital into

income, with examples of how the plans work and what the costs and risks are. 15 pp. (1982) 130P. $1.25.

Tips for an Energy Efficient Apartment. Suggests ways to keep your apartment warm in winter, cool in summer, and more economical all year long. 22 pp. (1985) 133P. $1.00.

Guide and Map to the National Parks. Fold-out hightway map with lists of activities at nearly 300 parks. (1983) 146P. $1.25.

Your Trip Abroad. Practical tips on international travel, including information on customs, visas, shots, and insurance. 32 pp. (1983) 151P. $1.00.

Gasoline Engine Tune-Up. A comprehensive, illustrated guide on tune-ups, from basic inspection to ignition timing. Applies to large and small cars. 18 pp. (1983) 153P. $1.50.

We, The Americans. Facts and trends based on the 1980 census; population growth and movements, marriage, education, income, home buying, and more. 15 pp. (1984) 157P. $1.00.

Where to Write for Vital Records. How to obtain certified copies of birth, death, marriage, and divorce certificates. 20 pp. (1984) 159P. $1.50.

How to Get the Most for Your Money

Source: *Consumer's Resource Handbook.* For further information, free single copies of this publication may be obtained by writing to *Handbook*, Consumer Information Center, Pueblo, Colorado 81009.

Before Making a Purchase:

(1) Analyze what you need and what features are important to you.

(2) Compare brands. Use word-of-mouth recommendations and formal product comparison reports. Check with your local library for magazines and other publicatons containing consumer information.

(3) Compare stores. Look for a store with a good reputation and take advantage of sales.

(4) Check for any additional charges, such as delivery and service costs.

(5) Compare warranties.

(6) Read terms of contracts carefully.

(7) Check the return or exchange policy.

After Your Purchase:

(1) Follow proper use and care instructions for products.

(2) Read and understand the warranty provisions. Keep in mind that you may have additional warranty rights in your state. Check with your state or local consumer office to find out.

(3) If trouble develops, report the problem as soon as possible. Do not try to fix the product yourself as this may void the warranty.

(4) Keep a record of efforts to have your problem remedied. This record should include names of people you speak to, times, dates, and other relevant information.

(5) Send for the *Consumer's Resource Handbook* (see *Source,* above) to find out where and how to get your problem resolved.

(6) Clearly state your problem and the solution you want.

(7) Include all relevant details, along with copies of documents (proof of purchase).

(8) Briefly describe what you have done to resolve the problem.

(9) Allow each person you contact a reasonable period of time to resolve your problem before contacting another source for assistance.

Handling Your Own Complaint:

(1) Identify your problem and what you believe would be a fair settlement. Do you want your money back? Would you like the product repaired? Will an exchange do?

(2) Gather documentation regarding your complaint. Sales receipts, repair orders, warranties, cancelled checks, or contracts will back up your complaint and help the company solve your problem.

(3) Go back to where you made the purchase. Contact the person who sold you the item or performed the service. Calmly and accurately explain the problem and what action you would like taken. If that person is not helpful, ask for the supervisor or manager and repeat your complaint. A large percentage of consumer problems are resolved at this level. Chances are yours will be too.

(4) Don't give up if you are not satisfied with the response. If the company operates nationally or the product is a national brand, write a letter to the person responsible for consumer complaints at the company's headquarters. A listing of many of these companies can be found in the World Almanac's Business Directory on pages 92–98. If the company doesn't have a consumer office, direct your letter to the president of the company.

How to Write a Complaint Letter:

(1) If you have already contacted the person who sold you the product or service or the company is out of town, you will need to write a letter to pursue your complaint.

(2) If you need the president's name and the address of the company, first check in your phone directory to see if the company has a local office. If it does, call and ask for the name and address of the company's president. If there is no local listing, check *Standard & Poor's Register of Corporations, Directors and Executives.* It lists over 37,000 American business firms and can be found in most libraries.

(3) If you don't have the name of the manufacturer of the product, check your local library for the *Thomas Register.* It lists the manufacturers of thousands of products.

Basic Tips on Letter Writing:

(1) Include your name, address, and home and work phone numbers.

(2) Type your letter if possible. If it is handwritten, make sure it is neat and easy to read.

(3) Make your letter brief and to the point. Include all important facts about your purchase including the date and place where you made the purchase and any information you can give about the product or service such as serial or model numbers or specific type of service.

(4) State exactly what you want done about the problem and how long you are willing to wait to get it resolved. Be reasonable.

(5) Include all documents regarding your problems. Be sure to send COPIES, not originals.

(6) Avoid writing an angry, sarcastic, or threatening letter. The person reading your letter probably was not responsible for your problem, but may be very helpful in resolving it.

(7) Keep a copy of the letter for your records.

Canadian Consumer Associations

Automobile Protection Association

The Automobile Protection Association (APA) is a non-profit, independently-financed consumer group founded in 1969 to advise motorists on the quality of automotive products and services, to publicize and encourage legal action against what it considers dishonest or dangerous practices in the automobile industry, and to press federal and provincial governments for protective legislation. For a $25 annual fee members receive periodic APA bulletins as well as free legal consultation when needed. Accredited garage service is provided in Montreal and Toronto. Headquarters are at 292 St-Joseph West, Montreal, Quebec H2V 2N7. Branch office at 100 Granby St., Toronto, Ont. M5B 1J1.

Consumers' Association of Canada

The Consumers' Association of Canada (CAC) is a voluntary, non-profit organization founded in 1947 to represent consumer interests. It also provides members with information on consumer legislation and the results of its research and tests on consumer goods and services. The national office is at 2660 Southvale Cres., Level 3, Ottawa, Ont. K1B 5C4; branch offices are in each province and territory. CAC publishes monthly, English/French magazines, *Canadian Consumer* and *Le Consommateur Canadien* (circulation 160,000). Annual membership fee is $25.

Options for Savers

	Minimum Deposit	Maturity	Comments
Passbook savings	None	None	Low interest rate; money can be withdrawn at any time.
NOW accounts	Varies	None	Checks can be written; minimum balance may be required.
Super NOW accounts	$2,500*	None	High rate paid on readily available cash; no limit on checking.
7-to-31-day time deposits	$2,500*	7-31 days	Savings earn market yields; checking privileges; penalty for early withdrawal.
Money-market deposit accounts	$1,000*	None	Money-market rate paid on savings; six automatic monthly transfers allowed, of which three can be checks.
Certificate of deposit	Varies	Varies	Savings earn market yields; penalty for early withdrawal; no check writing.
12-month small-savers certificates	Varies	12 months	High yields for small deposits
Long-term certificates	Varies	2½ years +	Savings locked up for long time; savers can shop around for best yields. Interest compounded.
IRA certificates	Varies	Varies	Both deposits and interest income are deferred from federal income taxes until money is withdrawn; $2,000 maximum individual contribution.
Money-market mutual funds	$100- $1,000	None	Market yields paid on funds that can be withdrawn at any time; checks can be written; no federal deposit insurance.
Bond funds	Varies	None	Shares can be easily resold but lose value if interest rates rise.
Tax-exempt bond funds	Varies	None	Interest income is exempt from federal taxes; shares lose value if interest rates rise.
Stock funds	Varies	None	Small investors can diversify their holdings; shares lose value if stock prices fall.
Treasury bills	$10,000	6 months	Market yields and safety; easily sold; not subject to state and local income taxes.
U.S. savings bonds	$25	5 years	Safe; long term.
Corporate bonds	$1,000	10-30 years	Market yields plus liquidity; investment will lose value if interest rates rise.
Common stocks	—	None	Potential for dividends, long-term capital gains; risk of capital loss.
Zero-coupon bonds	$1,000 is usual minimum	6 months to 10 years +	Yields fixed for term of investment; backed by U.S. securities and sold at a deep discount; no interest is received until notes mature and are redeemed at face value.

*None if account is an IRA or Keogh Plan.

Individual Retirement Accounts

All wage earners under the age of 70 1/2 became eligible to set up their own tax-sheltered Individual Retirement Account (IRA) in 1982. Those who elect to open an IRA can choose from a wide variety of investment options offered by banks, insurance companies, credit unions, mutual funds, brokerage firms, etc. Investment in life insurance and collectibles such as gems, art works, antiques, stamps, etc. are prohibited.

What is an IRA?

An IRA is a tax-deferred investment plan that allows almost anyone who earns wages to save a portion of their income for retirement and to legally shelter that income from taxes. Each individual employee can set aside in an IRA any portion of his income up to a maximum of $2,000, or $2,250 if he or she has a non-working spouse: A married couple, when both are wage earners, can set aside $4,000. The couple may then apportion the money between them in any way they choose, so long as neither one receives more than $2,000.

A person is under no obligation to contribute the maximum $2,000 each year. In fact, if a person chooses, no yearly contribution need be made at all. The money may be invested in different kinds of investment vehicles.

Tax Advantage

The full amount that is contributed to an IRA each year is deducted from the wage earner's taxable income. No taxes are paid on the money invested or the interest it earns until the money is withdrawn from the account. It should be stressed that an IRA is not tax-free, but tax-deferred. The taxes must be paid when the money begins to be withdrawn at retirement, when the wage earner will presumably be in a much lower tax bracket and pay less tax.

Withdrawals from an IRA *may* be made without penalty in the year that a person turns 59 1/2, and *must* be made in the year that a person turns 70 1/2. Withdrawals may be made in installments over a period of years or in a single lump sum.

The minimum amount that *must* be withdrawn from an IRA at age 70 1/2 is based on a person's life expectancy, or the combined life expectancy of both spouses in the case of a married couple. Actuarial tables show that a man at age 70 1/2 has a life expectancy of 12 years; therefore, enough should be taken from his IRA in steady yearly withdrawals to empty the account in 12 years. At age 70 1/2, a woman's life expectancy is 14 years.

When a wage earner dies, the money left in an IRA goes to the named beneficiary. The beneficiary may take the money and pay tax on it, or move the money into the beneficiary's own IRA to prolong its tax-deferred status. The $2,000 ceiling does not apply in this situation, nor does it apply to persons who transfer accumulated pension benefits into an IRA.

Establishing an IRA

A person may establish an account at any time during the calendar year up until they file their tax return for that year—no later than April 15, unless an extension has been granted. To start an IRA, a person need only complete a form and provide the money, either in a single sum or in smaller contributions during the year.

While the funds in an IRA cannot be withdrawn before age 59 1/2 without a penalty, they may be moved from one investment vehicle to another. The funds may also be moved from one financial institution to another, if the wage earner is not happy with the earnings performance of the account, or as individual objectives or economic conditions change. However, this may only be done once a year.

Early Withdrawal

If a person decides to remove funds from an IRA before reaching the age of 59 1/2, the amount withdrawn is taxable that year. In addition, the person will be subject to a 10% IRS tax penalty.

Growth or Stability?

Because IRA income can be placed in a wide range of investment vehicles, individuals should give careful consideration to their objectives before committing their money.

Some may feel more comfortable with a highly stable investment with a fixed rate of return. In this case, an investor should shop around for the best rate of return.

Others may feel that they can afford to invest in stocks, corporate bonds, or a mutual fund which may fluctuate and contain an element of risk, but offer the potential for rapid growth.

By 1984, 12.8 million people (16 percent of the 80 million people who returned 1983 tax returns) had claimed an IRA deduction according to the Internal Revenue Service.

Employment and Training Services and Unemployment Insurance

Source: Employment and Training Administration, U.S. Department of Labor

Employment Service

The Federal-State Employment Service consists of the United States Employment Service and affiliated state employment services which make up the Nation's public employment service system. During fiscal year 1982, the public employment service made 4.8 million placements—4.4 million in nonagricultural and .4 million in agricultural industries. Overall, 3.0 million different individuals were placed in employment.

The employment service refers employable applicants to job openings that use their highest skills and helps the unemployed obtain services or training to make them employable. It also provides special attention to handicapped workers, migrants and seasonal farmworkers, workers who lose their jobs because of foreign trade competition, and other worker groups. Veterans receive priority services including referral to jobs and training. During fiscal year 1982, more than 408,000 veterans were placed in jobs.

Job Training

The Job Training Partnership Act (JTPA) of 1982 went into full effect on October 1, 1983, replacing the Comprehensive Employment and Training Act (CETA), with training programs focusing almost entirely on the private sector.

State governors will receive bloc grants from the Labor Department. The funds will be distributed to Service Delivery Areas—areas of 200,000 population or more where local elected officials will work with Private Industry Councils to plan and conduct training projects in local areas.

Key differences in the new act are that at least 70 cents of each training dollar must be used for direct training costs, as compared to CETA's 18 cents. (CETA wound up nine years of existence at a total cost of $58 billion with 27 million enrollees and a 15 percent placement rate for training participants.)

JTPA has provisions for the retraining and job placement of dislocated workers—persons with long attachment to the labor force who lose their jobs through plant closings and technological change, with little chance of returning to their old jobs. This program has already provided for 30,000 workers with $110 million in fiscal year 1983 and is expected to reach another 70,000 million with $223 million in FY 1984.

For the first time in the history of such programs, specific performance standards have been established and each Service Delivery Area and each state will have to match its performance to the minimum standards initially set by the Employment and Training Administration.

All in all, approximately 1 million unemployed workers are expected to be trained or assisted in obtaining employment through JTPA.

Other sections of JTPA include the Job Corps, which will enroll approximately 88,000 youth between the ages of 16 through 21 in 107 centers throughout the country for job and educational training; the summer jobs for youth program which will provide temporary summer work for nine weeks to approximately 800,000 youth; the migrant and seasonal farmworker program, which will provide job, social, and educational services to thousands of agricultural workers; and the Indian and Native American program which is expected to spend about $80 million on job and training programs, mostly on reservations.

Other National Training Programs

The Work Incentive (WIN) program for employable recipients of Aid to Families of Dependent Children has been placing approximately 350,000 persons, mostly women, in private sector jobs. The Trade Adjustment Act program for workers who have lost their jobs because of foreign trade competition assisted approximately 90,000 workers in fiscal year 1983 with 52 weeks of cash benefits and up to 26 weeks of retraining.

Unemployment Insurance

Unlike old-age and survivors insurance, entirely a federal program, the unemployment insurance program is a Federal-State system that provides insured wage earners with partial replacement of wages lost during involuntary unemployment. The program protects most workers. During calendar year 1982, an estimated 93 million workers in commerce, industry, agriculture, and government, including the armed forces, were covered under the Federal-State system. In addition, an estimated 500,000 railroad workers were insured against unemployment by the Railroad Retirement Board.

Each state, as well as the District of Columbia, Puerto Rico, and the Virgin Islands, has its own law and operates its own program. The amount and duration of the weekly benefits are determined by state laws, based on prior wages and length of employment. States are required to extend the duration of benefits when unemployment rises to and remains above specified state levels; costs of extended benefits are shared by the state and federal governments.

Under the Federal Unemployment Tax Act, as amended in 1976, the tax rate is 3.4% on the first $6,000 paid to each employee of employers with one or more employees in 20 weeks of the year or a quarterly payroll of $1,500. A credit of up to 2.7% is allowed for taxes paid under state unemployment insurance laws that meet certain criteria, leaving the federal share at 0.7% of taxable wages.

Social Security Requirement

The Social Security Act requires, as a condition of such grants, prompt payment of due benefits. The Federal Unemployment Tax Act provides safeguards for workers' right to benefits if they refuse jobs that fail to meet certain labor

standards. Through the Unemployment Insurance Service of the Employment and Training Administration, the Secretary of Labor determines whether states qualify for grants and for tax offset credit for employers.

Benefits are financed solely by employer contributions, except in Alaska, Alabama, and New Jersey, where employees also contribute. Benefits are paid through the states' public employment offices, at which unemployed workers must register for work and to which they must report regularly for referral to a possible job during the time when they are drawing weekly benefit payments. During the 1982 calendar year, $20.4 billion in benefits was paid under state unemployment insurance programs to 11.7 million beneficiaries. They received an average weekly payment of $119.34 for total unemployment for an average of 15.9 weeks.

Unemployment Insurance and Benefits

Selected unemployment insurance data by state. Calendar year 1983, state programs only.

	Insured claimants[1] (1,000)	Beneficiaries[2] (1,000)	Exhaustions[3] (1,000)	Initial claims[4] (1,000)	Benefits paid[5] (1,000)	Avg. weekly benefit for total unemployment[p]	Funds available for benefits 12-31-83[6] (millions)	Employers subject to state law (1,000)
Alabama	199	175	72	428	$182,828	$82.48	57	66
Alaska	45	43	20	77	81,720	134.40	149	14
Arizona	99	73	39	185	124,890	102.29	176	60
Arkansas	112	89	36	237	108,995	95.76	29	44
California	1,456	1,176	563	3,134	2,155,947	107.49	2,225	611
Colorado	136	108	57	222	236,902	151.55	0	80
Connecticut	147	136	35	286	229,994	127.26	51	78
Delaware	30	25	6	57	30,181	95.57	37	14
District of Columbia	30	26	15	42	74,714	147.59	2	20
Florida	264	224	100	465	296,816	97.85	910	236
Georgia	253	212	88	435	226,923	98.02	391	108
Hawaii	41	34	11	75	60,791	127.80	129	23
Idaho	47	47	26	118	68,885	117.84	19	23
Illinois	535	450	286	1,046	1,361,443	151.29	0	231
Indiana	237	199	110	537	283,645	93.05	102	93
Iowa	133	118	55	224	227,552	141.21	0	64
Kansas	90	77	45	192	154,528	131.33	160	56
Kentucky	178	138	64	361	261,692	106.95	0	64
Louisiana	242	192	121	450	595,653	158.24	0	83
Maine	62	38	26	159	65,501	107.94	24	27
Maryland	153	133	54	309	275,371	123.10	105	84
Massachusetts	270	221	83	501	429,392	122.57	545	125
Michigan	355	374	196	1,093	910,894	150.37	0	160
Minnesota	163	143	79	292	303,649	140.77	0	88
Mississippi	114	95	42	246	131,056	87.76	225	43
Missouri	228	183	80	530	242,747	93.24	56	114
Montana	36	38	17	77	58,810	128.87	7	24
Nebraska	51	48	21	92	62,471	96.00	63	40
Nevada	55	46	21	98	95,304	121.54	102	21
New Hampshire	46	41	4	68	40,607	99.22	77	25
New Jersey	406	343	172	668	688,197	125.54	190	169
New Mexico	50	39	19	92	76,475	111.83	80	30
New York	616	535	252	1,503	1,090,798	105.20	985	398
North Carolina	355	249	77	836	295,100	107.10	354	107
North Dakota	28	26	13	56	55,953	137.39	3	19
Ohio	620	396	208	1,104	989,502	142.24	0	196
Oklahoma	118	107	73	218	209,202	139.08	31	67
Oregon	143	130	53	376	246,937	122.19	135	65
Pennsylvania	692	590	256	1,717	1,594,008	150.74	0	206
Puerto Rico	123	33	18	320	93,971	65.78	34	42
Rhode Island	69	53	20	144	85,015	111.83	44	23
South Carolina	154	131	49	466	150,363	93.35	20	56
South Dakota	11	10	3	28	14,882	114.17	15	18
Tennessee	217	175	59	542	233,720	87.47	82	79
Texas	608	413	229	872	934,496	138.09	0	295
Utah	58	49	26	114	94,577	131.68	19	30
Vermont	29	24	6	55	35,810	109.84	3	15
Virginia	168	148	48	366	171,354	111.05	80	96
Virgin Islands	5	4	2	7	0	99.98	0	2
Washington	238	201	85	525	459,339	138.26	24	99
West Virginia	118	93	50	152	259,433	139.41	0	33
Wisconsin	243	228	74	548	486,952	141.30	0	101
Wyoming	44	29	15	46	74,511	139.28	7	17
TOTAL	10,923	8,907	4,180	22,792	$17,720,498	$123.59	7,747	4,880

(p.) Preliminary. (1) Claimants whose base-period earnings or whose employment — covered by the unemployment insurance program — was sufficient to make them eligible for unemployment insurance benefits as provided by state law. (2) Based on number of first payments. (3) Based on final payments. Some claimants shown, therefore, actually experienced their final week of compensable unemployment toward the end of the previous calendar year but received their final payments in the current calendar year. Similarly, some claimants who served their last week of compensable unemployment toward the end of the current calendar year did not receive their final payment in this calendar year and hence are not shown. A final week of compensable unemployment in a benefit year results in the exhaustion of benefit rights for the benefit year. Claimants who exhaust their benefit rights in one benefit year may be entitled to further benefits in the following benefit year. (4) Excludes intrastate transitional claims to reflect more nearly instances of new unemployment. Includes claims filed by interstate claimants in the Virgin Islands. (5) Adjusted for voided benefit checks and transfers under interstate combined wage plan. (6) Sum of balance in state clearing accounts, benefit payment accounts, and unemployment trust fund accounts in the U.S. Treasury.

Jobs: Job Openings to 1995 and Current Earnings

Source: Bureau of Labor Statistics, U.S. Labor Department. For more detailed information on job categories, see the Occupational Outlook Handbook, 1984-85 edition.

Occupation	Est. no. of Jobs, 1982 (000)	% Change 1982-95 (est.)	Median Weekly Earnings (dollars)[1]
Industrial			
Assemblers	1,313	20-29	246
Blue-collar worker supv.	1,200	20-29	425
Compositors	104	−6	NA
Machine tool oper.	914	20-29	330
Machinist, all-round	236	20-29	370
Photographic process workers	67	6-9	245
Printing press oper.	174	6-9	NA
Tool-and-die makers	154	20-29	435
Welders, flamecutters	490	20-29	334
Office			
Accountants	856	30-49	441
Bank officers, mgrs.	424	30-49	421
Bank tellers	539	20-29	198
Bookkeepers	1,713	6-9	239
Computer operators	580	50+	285
Computer programmers	266	50+	445
Computer systems analysts	254	50+	540
Lawyers	465	30-49	NA
Librarians	150	6-9	409
Library technicians	29	6-9	270
Personnel specialists	203	20-29	653
Postal clerks	307	−6	438
Purchasing agents	191	20-29	453
Receptionists	594	30-49	219
Secretaries	2,441	20-29	308
Shipping clerks	365	20-29	260
Stenographers	270	−6	314
Telephone operators	323	6-9	247
Typists	990	6-9	290
Service Occupations			
Barbers	115	6-9	NA
Bartenders	384	30-49	199
Correction officers	111	30-49	348
Cooks and chefs	1,200	30-49	178
Cosmetologists	519	20-29	300
Firefighters	252	6-9	350
Guards	637	30-49	174
Butchers, meatcutters	191	−6	340
Police officers	550	−6	347
Waiters and waitresses	1,770	30-49	158
Educational and related occupations			
K-6 teachers	1,366	30-49	385
Second. school teach.	1,024	6-9	405
Coll., univ. faculty	744	−6	490
Sales occupations			
Cashiers	1,570	50+	176
Insurance agent, broker	361	20-29	673
Real estate agents, brokers	337	30-49	327
Retail trade sales workers	3,367	20-29	300
Securities sales workers	78	30-49	1,153
Travel agents	62	30-49	NA
Construction occupations			
Carpenters	863	20-29	340
Constr. laborers	576	20-29	225
Electricians (constrs.)	542	30-49	430
Painters	362	20-29	295
Plumbers, pipefitters	388	30-49	420

Occupation	Est. No. of Jobs, 1982 (000)	% Change 1982-95 (est.)	Median Weekly Earnings (dollars)[1]
Roofers	102	20-29	310
Transportation occupations			
Airplane mechanics	108	6-9	414
Airplane pilots	80	20-29	1,442
Airline reser. agts.	108	6-9	445
Flight attendants	54	20-29	404
Busdrivers (local)	473	30-49	330
Truckdrivers (local)	2,400	20-29	394
Truckdrivers (long-dist.)	NA	20-29	480
Scientific and technical occupations			
Aerospace engineers	44	30-49	700
Chemical engineers	56	30-49	706
Chemists	89	20-29	635
Civil engineers	155	30-49	654
Drafters	302	6-9	365
Electrical engineers	320	50+	702
Industrial engineers	160	30-49	701
Mathematicians	11	20-29	550
Mechanical engineers	209	+50	703
Mechanics and repairers			
Appliance repairers	80	6-9	340
Automobile mechanics	844	30-49	407
Bus. machine repairers	56	50+	407
Computer serv. technicians	55	50+	430
Indust. machinery repairers	330	20-29	394
Shoe repairers	16	6-9	200
Telephone, PBX installers and repairers	134	20-29	456
TV, radio serv. technicians	80	20-29	300
Health and medical occupations			
Dentists	173	20-29	1,058
Dental assistants	153	30-49	200
Dental hygienists	69	30-49	315
Dietitians	44	30-49	477
Health serv. administrators	303	30-49	785
Medical laboratory technicians	57	30-49	331
Nurses, registered	1,312	30-49	365
Nurses, licensed practical	594	30-49	250
Operating room technicians	35	30-49	304
Pharmacists	151	20-29	463
Physical therapists	43	50+	442
Physicians, osteopaths	479	30-49	1,923
Radiologic technologists	110	30-49	372
Veterinarians	36	30-49	865
Social scientists			
Economists	30	20-29	580
Urban planners	21	6-9	539
Psychologists	83	20-29	594
Sociologists	6	20-29	594
Social service occupations			
School counselors	148	6-9	471
Social workers	345	20-29	403
Design occupations			
Architects	84	30-49	460
Interior designers	180	30-49	462
Communications occupations			
Newspaper reporters	51	20-29	380
Public relations workers	90	20-29	404

(1) No single statistic can adequately tell the great differences in earnings among workers in a particular occupation. Differences in skill and seniority, geographic variations, differing pay scales among establishments, and unionization are among the important considerations. The most important factor may be the industry in which a job is located. Unskilled workers in a high-paying industry may earn more than skilled workers in a low-paying industry.

Selected U.S. Metropolitan Areas: A Comparative Table

Sources: Personal per capita income: U.S. Dept. of Commerce, May 1985; unemployment rate: Bureau of Labor Statistics, Aug. 1985; projected growth in employment and personal income: Chase Econometrics Regional Forecasting Service, July 1985; property tax rate: District of Columbia Dept. of Finance and Revenue, 1983; crime rate: FBI Uniform Crime Reports, 1983; weather: National Oceanic and Atmospheric Administration, 1985.

	Per capita personal income 1983	% job-less June 1985[p]	Projected annual % growth in jobs 1979-1993	Projected annual % growth in income 1979-1993	Effective property tax rate per $100 1982	Per capita reported crime rates 1982 Violent	Per capita reported crime rates 1982 Property	No. of days clr.—cldy. 1984
Anaheim-Santa Ana Garden Gr., Cal.	$15,250	4.3	3.3	4.3	NA	1,185.0	15,951.0	NA
Atlanta, Ga.	12,492	5.7	3.0	4.1	2.47	719.4	6,226.8	126-138
Baltimore, Md.	12,254	5.3	1.0	2.6	.69	1,173.3	5,694.6	NA
Birmingham, Ala.	10,621	7.5	0.6	1.7	2.74	605.9	5,618.8	NA
Boston-Lowell-Brockton Lawrence-Haverhill, Mass.-N.H.	14,297	3.4[1]	2.1	3.7	7.87[1]	680.2	5,351.1	82-175[1]
Bridgeport-Stamford-Norwalk-Danbury, Ct.	18,379	6.2[2]	0.9	2.5	2.79[2]	399.8	5,442.3	NA
Buffalo, N.Y.	11,398	7.9	−0.7	0.8	NA	491.1	4,479.3	44-208
Chicago, Ill.	13,456	8.7	0.2	1.6	1.99	536.7	4,746.6	85-185
Cincinnati, Oh., Ky., Ind.	11,777	7.1	0.6	1.7	NA	481.0	4,969.4	81-204
Cleveland, Oh.	13,103	8.4	0.2	1.2	1.46	670.1	4,675.8	47-240
Columbus, Oh.	11,445	6.4	1.0	2.2	NA	555.7	6,078.4	63-208
Dallas-Ft. Worth, Tex.	14,222	5.2[3]	2.6	4.2	NA	718.0	7,329.6	144-120
Dayton, Oh.	11,395	6.9[4]	0.4	1.5	NA	613.2	5,874.7	NA
Denver-Boulder, Col.	14,504	4.7	2.5	3.5	.80[12]	596.0	7,365.0	126-113[12]
Detroit, Mich.	12,537	NA	−0.1	1.0	3.94	890.5	7,284.9	65-194
Ft. Lauderdale-Hollywood, Fla.	14,321	5.3	2.8	4.9	NA	804.4	7,317.9	NA
Hartford-New Britain-Bristol, Ct.	14,522	4.8[5]	1.4	2.4	NA	541.3	5,634.7	72-176[5]
Honolulu, Ha.	12,697	5.1	1.4	2.5	NA	273.9	6,170.4	107-67
Houston, Tex.	13,655	8.4	2.0	3.8	1.76	763.1	6,849.7	86-143
Indianapolis,Ind.	11,858	6.6	0.8	2.0	3.78	491.4	5,088.0	71-201
Kansas City, Mo.-Kan.	12,654	4.6	0.8	2.1	NA	776.3	6,120.6	118-152
Los Angeles-Long Beach, Cal.	13,417	7.7	1.3	2.6	.72[13]	1,270.0	6,902.2	170-68[13]
Louisville, Ky.-Ind.	11,507	7.7	0.3	1.6	1.23	447.0	5,224.4	81-189
Memphis, Tenn.-Ark.-Miss.	10,590	6.4	0.6	2.0	1.74	894.9	5,927.8	115-150
Miami, Fla.	12,131	8.2	1.9	3.5	NA	1,588.8	8,700.6	109-77
Milwaukee, Wis.	13,001	6.1	0.5	1.9	2.94	314.9	5,114.8	80-194
Minneapolis-St. Paul, Minn.-Wis.	13,781	4.1	1.7	2.6	2.27[10]	359.8	5,537.6	96-180
Nashville-Davidson, Tenn.	11,058	4.8[6]	1.7	2.6	NA	481.4	5,030.4	104-156[6]
Newark, N.J.	14,847	5.9	1.2	2.3	5.82	984.9	4,992.9	89-181
New Orleans, La.	11,706	11.7	1.2	2.5	1.03	1,064.3	6,493.5	79-174
New York, N.Y.-N.J.	13,808	7.0	1.1	2.5	1.66	1,633.1	6,863.6	NA
Philadelphia, Pa.-N.J.	12,700	6.9	1.0	2.4	2.70	627.8	4,309.3	86-171
Phoenix, Ariz.	11,779	4.9	3.5	4.2	.71	539.5	7,279.8	203-67
Pittsburgh, Pa.	11,920	10.5	−0.2	1.6	NA	385.2	3,841.4	49-205
Portland, Ore.-Wash.	12,268	8.0	1.0	2.4	2.10	698.2	7,236.9	65-223
Providence-Warwick-Pawtucket, R.I.	11,674	5.2[7]	0.8	2.0	3.22[7]	399.3	4,852.5	83-182[7]
Riverside-San Bernadino-Ontario, Cal.	11,188	8.3	3.0	4.3	NA	758.8	7,159.4	NA
Rochester, N.Y.	12,649	5.8	0.8	2.1	NA	384.0	5,095.3	55-204
Sacramento, Cal.	11,676	7.5	2.6	3.9	NA	640.9	7,715.5	NA
St. Louis, Mo.-Ill.	12,710	8.3	0.8	1.9	1.56	691.2	5,296.9	104-178
Salt Lake City-Ogden, Ut.	9,892	5.5	2.5	4.1	1.23[11]	349.1	6,057.6	103-164[11]
San Antonio, Tex.	10,569	7.0	3.4	4.7	NA	581.2	6,158.3	110-137
San Diego, Cal.	12,272	5.9	3.3	4.3	NA	545.3	5,535.5	154-88
San Francisco-Oakland, Cal.	17,875	5.3[8]	1.5	2.4	NA	875.4	6,899.9	183-91[8]
San Jose, Cal.	15,853	5.9	3.3	4.4	NA	431.0	6,337.3	NA
Seattle-Everett, Wash.	13,995	6.9[9]	1.8	2.8	.86[9]	495.2	6,746.7	47-221[9]
Tampa-St. Petersburg, Fla.	11,362	5.9	3.3	4.7	NA	871.9	6,274.3	127-106[14]
Washington D.C.-Md.-Va.	16,173	4.1	1.8	3.0	1.15	804.5	5,520.0	65-189

(1) Boston only; (2) Bridgeport-Milford only; (3) Dallas only; (4) Dayton-Springfield only; (5) Hartford only; (6) Nashville only; (7) Providence only; (8) San Francisco only; (9) Seattle only; (10) Minneapolis only; (11) Salt Lake City only; (12) Denver only; (13) Los Angeles only; (14) Tampa only.

Personal Computers

In 1985, the computer industry plunged into a deep and unexpected slump leading to large employee layoffs. Among those companies announcing layoffs in 1985 were: Data General, 1,300; Apple Computer, 1,200 (in addition to previous layoffs); Burroughs, 750; Texas Instruments, 1,000 (in addition to previous layoffs); Computervision, 950; and National Semiconductor, 1,300. Wang Laboratories announced 1,600 layoffs, and said it would lose money for the first time in its history. The main problem appears to be oversupply of products and overcrowding of companies into the market. Foreign competition is also seen as a major factor in the industry's setback.

In the home computer industry (a small but insignificant component of the whole computer industry), there has been a marked decrease in demand in addition to the problem of a glutted market. Sales of personal computers, which almost doubled year after year for several years, are expected to grow no more than 30 percent, and possibly not at all, in 1985.

There is a growing realization among home computer companies that they have not necessarily been satisfying their customers. Many people use their computers for only one task, rather than the multiple tasks that computer makers had envisioned and promised the public. A more fundamental problem now facing the home computer industry, is convincing the consumer of the *need* for a home computer. After the wave of growth in the late 1970's and early 1980's, the novelty of owning a home computer has worn out, and consumers are now questioning the computer's value and usefulness. Consumers have turned away from the inexpensive home computers, buying instead more powerful machines (in the $1,000 range) to be used as "personal computers" for business or educational purposes, usually at home. The cost effectiveness of a "home" computer (not a personal computer used in the home) has not been convincingly demonstrated, as many consumers still find it more efficient to maintain hand-written grocery lists, recipes, check books, etc.

The industry's turbulence is evident in the number of computer magazines that went out of business—55—compared to 35 started. The unfulfilled expectations of 1984-1985 are not seen as a deathblow for the home computer industry, but rather as an indication that the industry must reassess its products and marketplace.

Computers in Education

The number of personal computers for instructional use in public elementary and secondary schools has risen dramatically from 31,000 in 1981 to 630,000 in 1984, and is expected to double in each of the next five years, according to the National Center for Education Statistics. Despite the presence of computers in more than half the nation's schools, organizations such as the National Education Assn. claim that relatively few students actually receive any computer instruction. The equipment is primarily used for administrative purposes, or for the classes of a few isolated instructors, generally those who teach computer skills. The general failure to utilize the available computer technology seems to be the result of inadequate planning and funding, the lack of curriculum development and suitable educational software, and poor teacher training. To date, there is no national policy on integrating computers into American public education, and little cooperation or agreement on methodology among educators, government officials, and the private sector.

Some educators and social activists have voiced their concern about a widening gap in computer literacy between more affluent suburban school districts and poorer urban ones. Some have stated that federal cutbacks in aid to education have added to this discrepancy. It is argued that wealthier school districts will find the means to purchase the necessary equipment, while less affluent school districts will not, therefore perpetuating the economic status quo.

Although it is too early to draw definitive conclusions, most educators agree that computers help students with their schoolwork. Software programs offer a variety of subjects and skills, using a variety of teaching techniques. Computers can be especially helpful for slow learners who have problems with subjects that require memorization, since drill and practice are the most common types of computer exercises. Studies show that a student's attention span increases when at a computer. In addition, computers teach users how to make decisions and to think logically.

The rapid development and commercialization of the computer has caused educators, sociologists, and psychologists to become concerned with the possible adverse impact on some children. Questions being investigated about the social and emotional effects of computerization in the home and schools are strikingly similar to those raised in response to the influence of television. Studies, just beginning to be undertaken, will examine the influence of computers on child development, as well as on the quality of family life.

Transaction Services Available to PC Users

The Source. Shopping, stock trading, travel arrangements, dining, communications, sports, etc. Sign-up fee of $100 and hourly charges of $5.75 to $20.75, depending on time of day and modem running speed. Extra $20 monthly for immediate rather than delayed stock prices.

CompuServe. Communications, business and finance, computer services, shopping, education, entertainment and travel, science and medicine. Initial fee of $40 for basic service, $70 for executive service. Hourly fees from $6 to $15; surcharges for some financial data.

Delphi. Financial services, newsletters, special interest groups, general information. Membership fee is $49.95. Usage fee ranges from $6 to $16 per hour depending upon time.

Comp-U-Card. Shopping. Annual $25 fee. Accessible directly at $18 hourly weekdays, $5 in off-peak hours, or through Dow Jones News/Retrieval, CompuServe and Source at their usual hook-up fees.

Fidelity Investor's Express. Sign-up fee of $50; $15 monthly charge includes 1 hour of access time. Beyond that, $24 an hour weekdays, $6 other times. Immediate quotes cost an extra $72.50 monthly. Brokerage fees extra.

Travel-Scan. Users can reserve airline seats, hotels, rental cars; $50 sign-up fee; $19.50 an hour weekdays, $15.50 other times.

Leading Uses of Home Computers
Source: Gallup Organization

The percentage of home-computer owners surveyed who said that they used their computer for a particular task (owners were able to give multiple responses).

Use	Percent	Use	Percent
Video games	51	Word-processing	18
Business or office homework	46	Mailing lists	16
Child's learning tool	46	Information retrieval[1]	14
Adult's learning tool	42	Appointment calendar	9
Balancing checkbook or budget	37	Storing recipes	9
Business-in-home uses	27	Calorie counting	4

(1) Includes information on investing, travel and account balances, as well as paying bills by phone.

Video Cassette Recorders

Video cassette recorders (VCR's), a technology originated in the U.S. in 1961, but today dominated by Japan, continue to change the home entertainment habits of millions of Americans. The Electronic Industries Assn. estimated that 7.6 million VCR's were sold in 1984, bringing the total number in U.S. homes to 27 million.

A major reason for the VCR boom has been the steady reduction in the price of the portable recording machines—from more than $1,000 a few years ago to as low as $250 today. In 1984, there were about 15,000 video stores, as well as hundreds of grocery, drug, and other retail stores offering tapes in the U.S. In many places, the price of blank video tapes has dropped from $10 to $6 in the past year. Full length movies can now be purchased for as little as $30, while one-day rentals are available for as little as $1 or $2.

Another boom to the VCR industry was a January 1984 Supreme Court decision which established that federal copyright laws were not violated by the taping of television broadcasts at home for later viewing. This practice, called "time shifting" in the industry, has been one of the strongest selling points for VCR's. An A.C. Nielsen poll found that the average user spent 6.9 hours a week recording programs and replaying them.

The VCR is changing the way millions of Americans use their leisure time. Many families are now renting movies (and making their own popcorn) for home viewing rather than "going out" on a Saturday night. Not only have movie-going habits been affected, but weekend activities as well as vacations have been altered for those who have access to a VCR. According to the Video Marketing Newsletter, the number of tapes rented by Americans for home viewing rose from 26 million in 1980 to 304 million in 1984. In the same period, retail revenue from the rentals increased from $206 million to more than $900 million.

Top Videocassettes—Rentals

Source: Billboard Magazine
(week ending Sept. 21, 1985)

Title (Weeks on list)	Title (Weeks on list)
1. The Karate Kid (17)	9. Pinocchio (7)
2. Falcon and the Snowman (8)	10. The Mean Season (6)
3. A Soldier's Story (8)	11. Runaway (8)
4. Starman (12)	12. Stick (4)
5. Desparately Seeking Susan (2)	13. Places in the Heart (14)
6. The Flamingo Kid (10)	14. Blood Simple (4)
7. A Nightmare on Elm Street (10)	15. Into the Night (8)
8. The Terminator (22)	16. Micki & Maude

Top Videocassettes—Sales

Source: Billboard Magazine
(week ending Sept. 21, 1985)

Title (Weeks on list)	Title (Weeks on list)
1. Jane Fonda's Workout (175)	9. Star Trek III: The Search for Spock (29)
2. Prince and the Revolution (5)	10. The Jane Fonda Workout Challenge (77)
3. We Are the World, The Video Event (11)	11. Gone With the Wind (27)
4. Pinocchio (7)	12. Life with Mickey! (13)
5. Wrestlemania (13)	13. Desparately Seeking Susan (2)
6. Prime Time (42)	14. Madonna (11)
7. Wham! The Video (21)	15. Seven Brides for Seven Brothers (13)
8. Singin' in the Rain (15)	

Cable Television

After a decade of red ink, the cable television industry saw three of its services become profitable, while several others hovered near the break-even point. The three moneymakers were Nickelodeon, MTV (Music Television), and CBN Cable Network. Two reasons cited for this progress were growth in the number of cable viewers and the desire of advertising agencies to reach those viewers. At the end of 1984, about 45 percent of all Americans had access to cable television with separate channels for movies, music videos, foreign-language shows, and specialized programming devoted to religion, health, news, and sports.

Ten years ago, cable television was envisioned as a technological wonderland that would have 108 channels. It was to provide two-way services, banking, tele-shopping, home security, energy monitoring, video games, and news and sports scores on demand. However, most of these high-tech services have been delayed as the immense cost of building the cable systems, especially in the big cities, has placed a heavy debt burden on the operators.

In July 1985, a Federal appeals court panel struck down Federal Communications Commission regulations that require cable operators to carry the signals of all broadcasters within their communities. This decision suggests that cable television systems are more like newspapers than like other TV stations (strictly regulated by the F.C.C.). The constitutionality of all governmental regulation of cable programming was brought into question by this ruling. Congress explicitly approved certain types of local regulations in a 1984 act of Congress. However, it is likely that the Supreme Court will have to resolve the debate about how much First Amendment protection cable operators are entitled to, as many local governments still regulate cable systems to a significant extent. The cable industry argues that deregulation would benefit cable viewers because cable operators would be free to transmit the programs that are most in demand, rather than being required to set aside channels for local coverage, such as city council proceedings or educational programs.

Electronic Products in the Home

Source: Electronic Industries Assn./Consumer Electronics Group

(mid-1984)

Share of American households with electronic products.

Product	% of households	Product	% of households
Television	98	Console audio	18
Color TV	91	Programmable video game	24
Black & white TV	70	Video cassette recorder	13
Projection TV	1	Home computer	10
Home radio	98	Cordless telephone	9
Audio system	81	Telephone-answering device	4
Compact audio	45	Videodisc player	1
Component audio	34		

Computer Language

The following is a glossary of key words or terms that consumers should learn if they are considering buying their own personal computer.

Access: the ability to get information or use a computer or program.

Acoustic coupler: a device that allows other electronic devices to communicate by making, and also listening to sounds made over an ordinary telephone. See **Modem.**

Address: designates the location of an item of information stored in the computer's memory.

ASCII: acronym for American Standard Code for Information Interchange. A 7-bit code used to represent alphanumeric characters.

Assembly language: a machine oriented language in which mnemonics are used to represent each machine-language instruction. Each CPU has its own specific assembly language.

BASIC: a popular computer language that is used by many small and personal computer systems. It means—Beginner's All-purpose Symbolic Instruction Code.

Baud rate: serial-data transmission speed. Originally a telegraph term, expressed in terms of the number of events that take place in one second. One baud is equal to one bit per second.

Binary: refers to the base-2 number system in which the only allowable digits are 0 and 1.

Bit: short for binary digit, the smallest unit of information stored in a computer. It always has the binary value of "0" or "1."

Boot, Booting, or Bootstrap: the program, or set of commands, that gets the computer to move into action.

Bubble memory: a relatively new type of computer memory, it uses tiny magnetic "pockets" or "bubbles" to store data.

Buffer: a place to put information before further processing.

Bug: a mistake that occurs in a program within a computer or in the unit's electrical system. When a mistake is found and corrected, it's called debugging.

Bundling: the practice of selling the hardware and software as a single package.

Byte: an 8-bit sequence of binary digits. Each byte corresponds to 1 character of data, representing a single letter, number, or symbol. Bytes are the most common unit for measuring computer and disk storage capacity.

Cassette: units used to store information for mini and microcomputers. They are similar in size and shape to audio recording cassettes.

Compiler: a program that translates a high-level language, such as BASIC, into machine language.

CPU: the Central Processing Unit within the computer that executes the instructions that the user gives the system.

Chip: a term for the integrated circuit and its package which contains coded signals.

Cursor: the symbol on the computer monitor that marks the place where the operator is working.

Database: a large amount of data stored in a well organized format. A database management system is a program that allows access to the information.

Dedicated: designed for a single use.

Density: the amount of data that can be stored on one sector of one track of a disk.

Disk: a revolving plate on which information and programs are stored. See also **Floppy disk.**

Disk Drive: a peripheral machine that stores information on disks.

Documentation: user or operator instructions that come with some hardware and software and tells how to use the material.

DOS: "Disk Operating System," a collection of programs designed to facilitate the use of a disk drive and floppy disk.

Error Message: a statement by the computer indicating that the user has done something incorrectly.

File: a logical group of pieces of information labelled by a specific name; considered a single unit by the computer. It is used commonly on microcomputers and word processors.

Floppy disk: a small inexpensive disk used to record and store information. It must be used in conjunction with a disk drive.

Format: the arrangement by which information is stored.

Graphics: the pictures or illustrations in the computer program.

Hardware: the physical apparatus or "nuts and bolts" that make up a computer. It includes silicon chips, transformers, boards and wires, etc. Also used to describe various pieces of equipment including the CPU, printer, modem, CRT (cathode ray tube), etc.

Hexadecimal: refers to the base-16 number system. Machine language programs are often written in hexadecimal notation.

Interface: the hardware or software necessary to connect one device or system to another.

K: abbreviation for Kilo-byte used to denote 1,024 units of stored matter.

Language: any set of compiled, unified, or related commands or instructions that are acceptable to a computer.

Load: the actual operation of putting information and data into the computer or memory.

Menu: programs, functions or other choices displayed on the monitor for user selection.

Memory: the internal storage of information.

Microcomputer: a small, complete computer system. Most personal computers now in use are microcomputers.

Minicomputer: an intermediate computer system sized between the very small microcomputer and the large computer.

Modem: short for modulating-demodulating. An acoustic or non-acoustic coupler, used either with a telephone or on a direct-line, for transmitting information from one computer to another.

Monitor: the screen on which the material from the computer appears and can be read. Looks like a small TV screen but produces more vivid characters than a home TV.

Noise: random disturbances that degrade or disrupt data communications.

Port: a channel through which data is transferred to and from the CPU.

Printer: a computer output device that, when attached to a computer, will produce printed copy on paper.

Program: coded instructions telling a computer how to perform a specific function.

RAM: abbreviation for random-access-memory. A type of microchip, its patterns can be changed by the user and the information it generates stored on tape, disk, or in printed form.

ROM: abbreviation for read-only-memory. A type of microchip that is different from RAM in that it cannot be altered by the user.

Software: the programs, or sets of instructions, procedural rules, and, in some cases, documentation that make the computer function.

Terminal: a work station away from the main computer that allows several people to have access to a single, main computer.

User friendly: hardware or software designed to help people become familiar with their computer. Usually includes simple and easy to follow instructions.

Window: portion of a video display screen devoted to displaying specific categories of information.

Word Processor: a text–editing program or system that allows electronic writing and correcting of articles, books, etc.

Social Security Programs

Source: Social Security Administration, U.S. Department of Health and Human Services

Old-Age, Survivors, and Disability Insurance; Medicare; Supplemental Security Income

New Legislation

On October 9, 1984, President Reagan signed into law the "Social Security Benefits Reform Act of 1984" (P.L. 98-460). The most significant change made by the new legislation provides that the Social Security Administration may not terminate disability benefits on the basis that disability no longer exists unless the beneficiary has medically improved and is able to work. There are certain limited exceptions to this provision.

Social Security Benefits

Social Security benefits are based on a worker's primary insurance amount (PIA), which is related by law to the average indexed monthly earnings (AIME) on which social security contributions have been paid. The full PIA is payable to a retired worker who becomes entitled to benefits at age 65 and to an entitled disabled worker at any age. Spouses and children of retired or disabled workers and survivors of deceased workers receive set proportions of the PIA subject to a family maximum amount. The PIA is calculated by applying varying percentages to succeeding parts of the AIME. The formula is adjusted annually to reflect changes in average annual wages in the economy.

Automatic increases in Social Security benefits are initiated whenever the Consumer Price Index (CPI) of the Bureau of Labor Statistics for the third calendar quarter of a year exceeds by at least 3 percent the CPI for the base quarter, which is either the third calendar quarter of the preceding year or the quarter in which an increase was legislated by Congress. The size of the benefit increase is determined by the actual percentage rise of the CPI between the quarters measured. However, if the balance in the combined OASDI trust funds falls below a specified level, the automatic benefit increase will be based on the lesser of the increase in the CPI or the increase in average wages. If one or more benefit increases are based on the increase in average wages, a "catch up" benefit increase will be made in a subsequent year when the combined trust fund balance reaches a higher specified level.

Average monthly benefits payable to retired workers was $462.00 in April 1985. The average amount for disabled workers in that month was $470.00.

Amount of Work Required

To qualify for benefits, the worker must have worked in covered employment long enough to become insured. Just how long depends on when the worker reaches age 62 or, if earlier, when he or she dies or becomes disabled.

A person is fully insured if he or she has one quarter of coverage for every year after 1950 (or year age 21 is reached, if later) up to but not including the year in which the worker reaches age 62, dies, or becomes disabled. In 1985, a person earns one quarter of coverage for each $410 of annual earnings in covered employment, up to a maximum of 4 quarters per year.

The law permits special monthly payments under the Social Security program to certain very old persons who are not eligible for regular social security benefits since they had little or no opportunity to earn social security work credits during their working lifetime.

To get disability benefits, in addition to being fully insured, the worker must also have credit for 5 out of 10 years before he or she becomes disabled. A disabled blind worker need meet only the fully insured requirement. Persons disabled before age 31 can qualify with a briefer period of coverage. Certain survivor benefits are payable if the deceased worker had 6 quarters of coverage in the 13 quarters preceding death.

Work credit for survivors and disability benefits

Born after 1929, die or become disabled at age	Born before 1930, die or become disabled before age 62 in	Years needed
32		2½
34		3
36		3½
38		4
40		4½
42		5
44		5½
45		5¾
46		6
48		6½
50	1979	7
52	1981	7½
54	1983	8
56	1985	8½
58	1987	9
60	1989	9½
62 or older	1991 or later	10

Work Years Required

The following table shows the number of work years required to be fully insured for Old-Age or Survivors benefits, according to the year worker reaches retirement age or dies.

Work credit for retirement benefits

If you reach 62 in	Years you need	If you reach 62 in	Years you need
1974	6*	1979	7
1975	6	1981	7½
1976	6¼	1983	8
1977	6½	1987	9
1978	6¾	1991 or later	10

*For 1974 a woman needs only 5¾ years.

Contribution and benefit base

Calendar year	Base
1978	$17,700
1979	22,900
1980	25,900
1981	29,700
1982	32,400
1983	35,700
1984	37,800

Tax-rate schedule
[Percent of covered earnings]

Year	Total	OASDI	HI
	Employees and employers, each		
1979-80	6.13	5.08	1.05
1981	6.65	5.35	1.30
1982-83	6.70	5.40	1.30
1984	7.00	5.70	1.30
1985	7.05	5.70	1.35
1986-87	7.15	5.70	1.45
1988-89	7.51	6.06	1.45
1990 and after	7.65	6.20	1.45
	Self-employed		
1979-80	8.10	7.05	1.05
1981	9.30	8.00	1.30
1982-83	9.35	8.05	1.30
1984	14.00	11.40	2.60
1985	14.10	11.40	2.70
1986-87	14.30	11.40	2.90
1988-89	15.02	12.12	2.90
1990 and after	15.30	12.40	2.90

What Aged Workers Get

When a person has enough work in covered employment and reaches retirement age (currently 65 for full benefit, 62 for reduced benefit), he or she may retire and get monthly old-age benefits. The age at which unreduced benefits are payable will be increased gradually from 65 to 67 over a 21-year period beginning with workers age 62 in the year 2000; (reduced benefits will still be available as early as age 62.) If a person aged 65 or older continues to work and has earnings of more than $7,320 in 1985, $1 in benefits will be withheld for every $2 above $6,960. The annual exempt amount

for people under age 65 is $5,400 in 1985. The annual exempt amount and the monthly test are raised automatically as the general earnings level rises. The eligible worker who is 70 receives the full benefit regardless of earnings. Beginning in 1990, benefits for persons who reach the normal retirement age will be reduced $1 for each $3 of excess earnings.

For workers who reach age 65 after 1981, the worker's benefit will be raised by 3% for each year for which the worker between 65 and 70 (72 before 1984) did not receive benefits because of earnings from work or because the worker had not applied for benefits. The delayed retirement credit is 1 percent a year for workers reaching age 65 before 1982. The delayed retirement credit will gradually rise from the current 3% per year to 8% per year between the years 1990 and 2009.

Effective December 1984, the special benefit for persons aged 72 or over who do not meet the regular coverage requirements is $134.40 a month. Like the monthly benefits, these payments are subject to cost-of-living increases. The special payment is not made to persons on the public assistance or supplemental security income rolls.

Workers retiring before age 65 have their benefits permanently reduced by 5/9 of 1% for each month they receive benefits before age 65. Thus, workers entitled to benefits in the month they reach age 62 receive 80% of the PIA, while a worker retiring at age 65 receives a benefit equal to 100% of the PIA. The nearer to age 65 the worker is when he or she begins collecting a benefit, the larger the benefit will be.

Benefits for Worker's Spouse

The spouse of a worker who is getting Social Security retirement or disability payments may become entitled to a spouse's insurance benefit when he or she reaches 65 of one-half of the worker's PIA. Reduced spouse's benefits are available at age 62 (25/36 of 1% reduction for each month of entitlement before age 65). Benefits are also payable to the divorced spouse of an insured worker if he or she was married to the worker for at least 10 years.

Benefits for Children of Retired or Disabled Workers

If a retired or disabled worker has a child under 18 the child will get a benefit that is half of the worker's unreduced benefit, and so will the worker's spouse, even if he or she is under 62 if he or she is caring for an entitled child of the worker who is under 16 or who became disabled before age 22. Total benefits paid on a worker's earnings record are subject to a maximum and if the total that would be paid to a family exceeds that maximum, the individual dependents' benefits are adjusted downward. (Total benefits paid to the family of a worker who retired in January 1985 at age 65 and who always had the maximum amount of earnings creditable under Social Security can be no higher than $1,255.70.)

When entitled children reach 18, their benefits will generally stop, except that a child disabled before 22 may get a benefit as long as his or her disability meets the definition in the law. Additionally, benefits will be paid to a child until age 19 if the child is in full-time attendance at an elementary or secondary school.

Benefits may also be paid to a grandchild or stepgrandchild of a worker or of his or her spouse, in special circumstances.

What Disabled Workers Get

If a worker becomes so severely disabled that he or she is unable to work, he or she may be eligible to receive a monthly disability benefit. Benefits continue until it is determined that the individual is no longer disabled. Each beneficiary's eligibility is reviewed periodically. If the individual is still disabled when he or she reaches 65, the disability benefit becomes a retired-worker benefit.

Benefits generally like those provided for dependents of retired-worker beneficiaries may be paid to dependents of disabled beneficiaries.

Survivor Benefits

If an insured worker should die, one or more types of benefits may be payable to survivors.

1. If claiming benefits at 65, the surviving spouse will receive a benefit that is 100% of the deceased worker's PIA. The surviving spouse may choose to get the benefit as early as age 60, but the benefit is then reduced by 19/40 of 1% for each month it is paid before age 65. However, for those aged 62 and over whose spouses claimed their benefits before 65, the benefit is the reduced amount the worker would be getting if alive but not less than 82 1/2% of the worker's PIA.

Disabled widows and widowers may under certain circumstances qualify for benefits after attaining age 50 at the rate of 71.5% of the deceased worker's PIA. The widow or widower must have become totally disabled before or within 7 years after the spouse's death, the last month in which he or she received mother's or father's insurance benefits, or the last month he or she previously received surviving spouse's benefits.

2. A benefit for each child until the child reaches 18. The monthly benefit of each child of a worker who has died is three-quarters of the amount the worker would have received if he or she had lived and drawn full retirement benefits. A child with a disability that began before age 22 may receive benefits. Also, a child may receive benefits until age 19 if he or she is in full-time attendance at an elementary or secondary school.

3. A mother's or father's benefit for the widow(er), if children of the worker under 16 are in his or her care. The benefit is 75% of the PIA and he or she draws it until the youngest child reaches 16, at which time payments stop even if the child's benefit continues. They may start again when he or she is 60 unless he or she is married. If he or she marries and the marriage is ended, he or she regains benefit rights. If he or she has a disabled child beneficiary aged 16 or over in care, benefits also continue. This benefit may also be paid to the divorced spouse, if the marriage lasted for at least 10 years.

4. Dependent parents may be eligible for benefits, if they have been receiving at least half their support from the worker before his or her death, have reached age 62, and (except in certain circumstances) have not remarried since the worker's death. Each parent gets 75% of the worker's PIA; if only one parent survives the benefit is 82 1/2%.

5. A lump sum cash payment of $255. Payment is made only when there is a spouse who was living with the worker or a spouse or child eligible for immediate monthly survivor benefits.

Self-Employed

A self-employed person who has net earnings of $400 or more in a year must report such earnings for social security tax purposes. The person reports net returns from the business. Income from real estate, savings, dividends, loans, pensions or insurance policies may not be included unless they are part of the business.

A self-employed person gets a quarter of coverage for each $410 (for 1985) up to a maximum of 4 quarters of coverage. The nonfarm self-employed person must make estimated payments of his or her social security taxes, on a quarterly basis, for 1983, if combined estimated income tax and social security tax amount to at least $300.

The nonfarm self-employed have the option of reporting their earnings as 2/3 of their gross income from self-employment but not more than $1,600 a year and not less than their actual net earnings. This option can be used only if actual net earnings from self-employment income is less

OASDI	May 1985	July 1984	July 1983
Monthly beneficiaries, total (in thousands)	36,686	36,051	35,745
Aged 65 and over, total	26,227	25,754	25,301
Retired workers	19,619	19,223	18,829
Survivors and dependents . . .	6,572	6,486	6,416
Special age-72 beneficiaries. .	36	44	55
Under age 65, total	10,458	10,297	10,444
Retired workers	2,458	2,421	2,301
Disabled workers	2,621	2,574	2,588
Survivors and dependents . . .	5,379	5,303	5,555
Total monthly benefits (in millions)	$15,164	$14,292	$13,482

than $1,600 and may be used only 5 times. Also, the self-employed person must have actual net earnings of $400 or more in 2 of the 3 taxable years immediately preceding the year in which he or she uses the option.

When a person has both taxable wages and earnings from self-employment, the wages are credited for Social Security purposes first; only as much of the self-employment income as will bring total earnings up to the current taxable maximum is subject to the self-employment tax.

Farm Owners and Workers

Self-employed farmers whose gross annual earnings from farming are $2,400 or less may report ⅔ of their gross earnings instead of net earnings for social security purposes. Farmers whose gross income is over $2,400 and whose net earnings are less than $1,600 can report $1,600. Cash or crop shares received from a tenant or share farmer count if the owner participated materially in production or management. The self-employed farmer pays contributions at the same rate as other self-employed persons.

Agricultural employees. Earnings from farm work count toward benefits (1) if the employer pays $150 or more in cash during the year; or (2) if the employee works on 20 or more days for cash pay figured on a time basis. Under these rules a person gets credit for one calendar quarter for each $410 in cash pay in 1985 up to four quarters.

Foreign farm workers admitted to the United States on a temporary basis are not covered.

Household Workers

Anyone working as maid, cook, laundress, nursemaid, baby-sitter, chauffeur, gardener and at other household tasks in the house of another is covered by Social Security if he or she earns $50 or more in cash in a calendar quarter from any one employer. Room and board do not count, but carfare counts if paid in cash. The job does not have to be regular or fulltime. The employee should get a Social Security card at the social security office and show it to the employer.

The employer deducts the amount of the employee's social security tax from the worker's pay, adds an identical amount as the employer's social security tax and sends the total amount to the federal government, with the employee's social security number.

Medicare

Under Medicare, protection against the costs of hospital care is provided for Social Security and Railroad Retirement beneficiaries aged 65 and over and, for persons entitled for 24 months to receive a social security disability benefit, certain persons (and their dependents) with end-stage renal disease, and, on a voluntary basis with payment of a special premium, persons aged 65 and over not otherwise eligible for hospital benefits; all those eligible for hospital benefits may enroll for medical benefits and pay a monthly premium and so may persons aged 65 and over who are not eligible for hospital benefits.

Persons eligible for both hospital and medical insurance may choose to have their covered services provided through a Health Maintenance Organization.

Hospital insurance.—From October 1981 to September 1982, about $34.9 billion was withdrawn from the hospital insurance trust fund for hospital and related benefits.

As of January 1983, the hospital insurance program paid the cost of covered services for hospital and posthospital care as follows:

- Up to 90 days of hospital care during a benefit period (spell of illness) starting the first day that care as a bed-patient is received in a hospital or skilled-nursing facility and ending when the individual has not been a bed-patient for 60 consecutive days. For the first 60 days, the hospital insurance pays for all but the first $304 of expenses; for the 61st day to 90th day, the program pays all but $76 a day for covered services. In addition, each person has a 60-day lifetime reserve that can be used after the 90 days of hospital care in a benefit period are exhausted, and all but $152 a day of expenses during the reserve days are paid. Once used, the reserve days are not replaced. (Payment for care in a mental hospital is limited to 190 days.)
- Up to 100 days' care in a skilled-nursing facility (skilled-nursing home) in each benefit period. Hospital insurance

pays for all covered services for the first 20 days and all but $38 daily for the next 80 days. At least 3 days' hospital stay must precede these services, and the skilled-nursing facility must be entered within 14 days after leaving the hospital. (The 1972 law permits more than 14 days in certain circumstances.)
- Unlimited visits by nurses or other health workers (not doctors) from a home health agency in the 365 days after release from a hospital or extended-care facility.

Medical insurance. Aged persons can receive benefits under this supplementary program only if they sign up for them and agree to a monthly premium ($12.20 beginning July 1982 and continuing through December 1983). The Federal Government pays the rest of the cost.

About 142 million bills were reimbursed under the medical insurance program from October 1981 to September 1982 for a total of $14.9 billion. As of September 1982, about 28.2 million persons were enrolled — 2.7 million of them disabled persons under age 65.

The medical insurance program pays 80% of the reasonable charges (after the first $75 in each calendar year) for the following services:

- Physicians' and surgeons' services, whether in the doctor's office, a clinic, or hospital or at home (but physician's charges for X-ray or clinical laboratory services for hospital bed-patients are paid in full and without meeting the deductible).
- Other medical and health services, such as diagnostic tests, surgical dressings and splints, and rental or purchase of medical equipment. Services of a physical therapist in independent practice, furnished in his office or the patient's home. A hospital or extended-care facility may provide covered outpatient physical therapy services under the medical insurance program to its patients who have exhausted their hospital insurance coverage.
- Physical therapy services furnished under the supervision of a practicing hospital, clinic, skilled nursing facility, or agency.
- Certain services by podiatrists.
- All outpatient services of a participating hospital (including diagnostic tests).
- Outpatient speech pathology services, under the same requirements as physical therapy.
- Services of licensed chiropractors who meet uniform standards, but only for treatment by means of manual manipulation of the spine and treatment of subluxation of the spine demonstrated by X-ray.
- Supplies related to colostomies are considered prosthetic devices and payable under the program.
- Home health services even without a hospital stay (up to 100 visits a year) are paid up to 100%.

To get medical insurance protection, persons approaching age 65 may enroll in the 7-month period that includes 3 months before the 65th birthday, the month of the birthday, and 3 months after the birthday, but if they wish coverage to begin in the month they reach 65 they must enroll in the 3 months before their birthday. Persons not enrolling within their first enrollment period may enroll later, during the first 3 months of each year but their premium is 10% higher for each 12-month period elapsed since they first could have enrolled.

The monthly premium is deducted from the cash benefit for persons receiving Social Security, Railroad Retirement, or Civil Service retirement benefits. Income from the medical premiums and the federal matching payments are put in a Supplementary Medical Insurance Trust Fund, from which benefits and administrative expenses are paid.

Medicare card. Persons qualifying for hospital insurance under Social Security receive a health insurance card similar to cards now used by Blue Cross and other health agencies. The card indicates whether the individual has taken out medical insurance protection. It is to be shown to the hospital, skilled-nursing facility, home health agency, doctor, or whoever provides the covered services.

Payments are made only in the 50 states, Puerto Rico, the Virgin Islands, Guam, and American Samoa, except that hospital services may be provided in border areas immediately outside the U.S. if comparable services are not accessible in the U.S. for a beneficiary who becomes ill or is injured in the U.S.

Social Security Financing

Social Security is paid for by a tax on earnings (for 1985, up to $39,600; the taxable earnings base is now subject to automatic adjustment to reflect increases in average wages). The employed worker and his or her employer share the tax equally. (Cash tips count as covered wages if they amount to $20 or more in a month from one place of employment. The worker reports them to the employer, who includes them in the Social Security tax reports. The worker pays contributions on the full amount of the tips and the employer pays Social Security taxes on an amount that, when added to the employee's wages, equals the minimum wage).

The employer deducts the tax each payday and sends it, with an equal amount (the employer's share), to the District Director of Internal Revenue. (Self-employed workers pay their Social Security taxes at the time they file regular income tax forms). The collected taxes (along with revenues arising from partial taxation of the Social Security benefits of certain high-income people) are deposited in the Federal Old-Age and Survivors Insurance Trust Fund, the Federal Disability Insurance Trust Fund, and the Federal Hospital Insurance Trust Fund; they can be used only to pay benefits, the cost of rehabilitation services, and administrative expenses.

Supplemental Security Income

On Jan. 1, 1974, the Supplemental Security Income (SSI) program established by the 1972 Social Security Act amendments replaced the former federal grants to states for aid to the needy aged, blind, and disabled in the 50 states and the District of Columbia. The program provides both for federal payments based on uniform national standards and eligibility requirements and for state supplementary payments varying from state to state. The Social Security Administration administers the federal payments financed from general funds of the Treasury—and the state supplements as well, if the state elects to have its supplementary program federally administered. The states may supplement the federal payment for all recipients and must supplement it for persons otherwise adversely affected by the transition from the former public assistance programs. In April 1985, the number of persons receiving federal payments and federally administered state payments was 4,084,312 and the amount of these payments was $933.5 million.

The maximum federal SSI payment for an individual with no other countable income, living in his own household, was $325.00 in July 1985. For a couple it was $488.00.

Minimum and maximum monthly retired-worker benefits payable to individuals who retired at age 65[1]

Year of attainment of age 65[2]	Minimum benefit		Maximum benefit			
	Payable at the time of retirement	Payable effective December 1984	Payable at the time of retirement		Payable effective December 1984	
			Men[3]	Women	Men[3]	Women
1965 . . .	$44.00	$195.90	$131.70	135.90	$523.30	$540.00
1970 . . .	64.00	195.90	189.80	196.40	580.00	600.40
1980 . . .	133.90	195.90	572.00	. . .	836.40	. . .
1984 . . .	150.50	155.70	703.60	. . .	728.20	. . .

(1) Assumes retirement at beginning of year. (2) The final benefit amount payable after SMI premium or any other deductions is rounded to next lower $1 (if not already a multiple of $1). (3) Benefit for both men and women are shown in men's columns except where women's benefit appears separately.

Examples of monthly cash benefit awards for selected beneficiary families with first entitlement in 1985, effective January 1985

	Career Earnings Level		
Beneficiary Family	Low Earnings ($6,968 in 1985)	Average Earnings ($16,595 in 1985)[1]	Maximum Earnings ($39,600 in 1985)
Primary insurance amount (worker retiring at 65)	$369.50	$545.40	$717.20
Maximum family benefit (worker retiring at 65)	554.50	996.80	1,255.70
Disability maximum family benefit (worker disabled at 55)	567.60	854.10	1,111.20
Disabled worker: (worker disabled at 55)			
Worker alone	378.00	569.00	740.00
Worker, spouse, and 1 child	567.00	854.00	1,111.00
Retired worker claiming benefits at age 62:			
Worker alone[2]	302.00	455.00	591.00
Worker with spouse claiming benefits at—			
Age 65 or over	491.00	729.00	949.00
Age 62[2]	440.00	660.00	859.00
Widow or widower claiming benefits at—			
Age 65 or over[3]	369.00	548.00	717.00
Age 60	264.00	392.00	512.00
Disabled widow or widower claiming benefits at age 50-59[4]	264.00	392.00	512.00
1 surviving child	277.00	411.00	537.00
Widow or widower age 65 or over and 1 child	554.00	959.00	1,254.00
Widowed mother or father and 1 child	534.00	822.00	1,074.00
Widowed mother or father and 2 children	554.00	996.00	1,255.00

[1]Estimate. [2]Assumes maximum reduction. [3]A widow(er)'s benefit amount is limited to the amount the spouse would have been receiving if still living but not less than 82.5 percent of the PIA. [4]Effective January 1984, disabled widow(er)s claiming benefit at ages 50-59 will receive benefit equal to 71.5 percent of the PIA (based on 1983 Social Security Amendment provision).

Estimated Workers Under Social Insurance Programs
(In millions)

Employment and Coverage Status	1960	1965	1970	1975	1976	1977	1978	1979	1980	1981	1982
Total labor force[1] . .	73.1	78.5	86.2	94.9	98.1	100.6	103.7	106.0	106.9	108.4	112.7
Paid civilian population. . .	64.6	71.6	77.6	84.8	87.8	92.0	95.2	97.5	97.0	96.9	98.4
Wage and salary workers	55.3	63.6	70.8	77.6	80.6	84.3	87.2	89.2	88.4	88.5	89.5
Self-employed	9.3	8.0	6.9	7.2	7.0	7.7	8.0	8.3	8.6	8.4	8.9
Unpaid family workers . . .	1.4	1.1	.8	.7	.7	.7	.7	.6	.6	.5	.5
Unemployed	4.5	2.9	2.6	7.2	7.5	5.9	5.7	5.8	7.2	8.8	11.6
Armed Forces	2.5	2.8	3.4	2.2	2.2	2.1	2.1	2.1	2.1	2.2	2.2
Civilian population covered by:											
Public retirement programs	60.9	68.4	75.3	82.2	86.9	88.8	89.8	94.5	93.5	93.6	94.8
OASDHI[2].	55.4	62.7	69.2	75.7	80.3	82.1	83.2	87.6	86.5	86.6	87.9
Unemployment insurance	43.7	50.3	55.8	69.7	72.1	75.8	85.8	87.9	87.2	89.9	87.9
Workers compensation	44.6	52.3	59.0	68.6	70.4	74.2	74.5	77.4	79.4	79.8	77.8
Temporary disability insurance	11.3	13.0	14.6	15.7	16.2	16.7	18.0	18.1	18.4	18.4	18.1

(1) Data from U.S. Bureau of Labor Statistics and based on U.S. Bureau of the Census' Current Population Survey. (2) OASDHI = Old-age, survivors, disability, and health insurance. Excludes members of Armed Forces and railroad employees.

Social Security Trust Funds

Old-Age and Survivors Insurance Trust Fund, 1940-84

[in millions]

Calendar year	Net contrib. inc., reimbursements from gen'l rev.	Receipts — Net interest received	Cash benefit payments, rehabilitation services	Transfers to Railroad Retirement acct.	Expenditures — Admini-strative expenses	Total assets at end of year
1940	$325	$43	$35	...	$26	$2,031
1950	2,667	257	961	...	61	13,721
1960	10,866	516	10,677	$318	203	20,324
1970	30,705	1,515	28,798	579	471	32,454
1980	103,996	1,845	105,082	1,442	1,154	22,823
1981	123,301	2,060	123,804	1,585	1,307	21,490
1982	124,354	845	138,806	1,793	1,519	22,088
1983	143,878	6,706	149,215	2,251	1,534	19,672
1984[1]	167,061	2,267	157,847	2,404	1,632	27,117
Cum., 1937-84[1]	1,464,666	46,128	1,456,726	24,047	20,156	—

Disability Insurance Trust Fund, 1960-84

	Net contrib. inc., reimbursements from gen'l rev.	Net interest received	Cash benefit payments, rehabilitation services	Transfers to Railroad Retirement acct.	Admini-strative expenses	Total assets at end of year
1960	$1,010	$53	$568	$ −5	$36	$2,289
1970	4,497	277	3,085	10	164	5,614
1980	13,385	485	15,515	12	368	3,629
1981	16,906	172	17,275	29	436	3,049
1982	22,169	546	17,376	26	590	2,691
1983	19,112	1,569	17,465	28	664	—
1984[1]	16,135	1,174	17,898	22	626	3,959
Cum., 1957-84[1]	189,198	8,675	182,186	514	6,308	5,195

Hospital Insurance Trust Fund, 1970-84

[In thousands]

Fiscal year:	Net con-tribution income[1]	Receipts — Transfers from rail-road re-tirement account[2]	Reimburse ments from general revenues[3]	Net interest[4]	Expenditures — Net hospital and related service benefits[5]	Admini-strative expenses[6]	Total assets at end of period
1970	4,784,789	61,307	628,262	139,423	4,804,242	148,660	2,677,401
1975	11,296,773	126,749	529,353	614,989	10,355,390	256,134	9,870,039
1980	23,260,335	221,800	837,906	1,061,433	23,793,420	460,841	14,489,913
1981	30,445,979	246,700	800,000	1,324,834	28,909,081	305,416	18,092,929
1982	34,414,993	308,110	1,015,000	1,872,541	34,343,651	520,360	20,839,552
1983	32,906,678	308,600	—	1,631,010	38,101,524	522,228	13,719,000
1984	37,260,548	308,000	752,000	1,413,870	41,475,712	632,602	17,174,173
Cum., 1966-84	279,997,022	2,618,150	11,616,582	12,425,404	286,600,301	5,468,660	51,732,725

(1) Represents amounts appropriated (estimated tax collections with suitable subsequent adjustments) after deductions for refund of estimated amount of employee-tax overpayment; and, beginning July 1973, premiums for coverage of uninsured individuals aged 65 and over. (2) Transfers (principal only) from the railroad retirement account with respect to contributions for hospital insurance coverage of railroad workers. (3) Represents Federal Government transfers from general funds appropriations to meet costs of benefits for persons not insured for cash benefits under OASDHI or railroad retirement and for costs of benefits arising from military wage credits. (4) Interest and profit on investments after transfers of interest or reimbursed administrative expenses (see footnote 6) and interest on amounts transferred from railroad retirement account (see footnote 3). (5) Represents payment vouchers on letters of credit issued to fiscal intermediaries under sec. 1816 and direct payments to providers of services under sec. 1815 of the Social Security Act. (6) Subject to subsequent adjustment among all four Social Security trust funds for allocated cost of each operation. Fiscal year 1966 includes "tool-up" period from date of enactment of Social Security Amendments of 1965 (July 20).

Supplementary Medical Insurance Trust Fund: Status, 1970-84

[In thousands]

Fiscal year:	Premium income[1]	Receipts — Transfers from general revenues[2]	Net interest[3]	Expenditures — Net medical service benefits[4]	Admini-strative expenses[5]	Total assets at end of period
1970	$936,000	$928,151	$11,536	$1,979,287	$216,993	$57,181
1975	1,886,962	2,329,590	105,539	3,765,397	404,458	1,424,413
1980	2,927,711	6,931,713	415,510	10,143,930	593,327	4,531,591
1981	3,319,607	8,747,430	384,348	12,344,913	895,374	3,742,690
1982	3,830,558	13,323,012	473,203	14,806,214	753,255	5,809,993
1983	4,227,379	14,237,991	680,441	17,487,322	819,778	6,646,303
1984	4,907,286	16,811,010	807,162	19,472,577	899,377	8,799,305
Cum., 1967-84	39,756,834	93,716,708	3,939,578	120,172,450	8,438,459	24,998,291

(1) Represents voluntary premium payments from and in behalf of the insured aged and (beginning July 1973) disabled. (2) Represents Federal Government transfers from general funds appropriations to match aggregate premiums paid. (3) Represents interest and profit on investments, after transfers of interest on reimbursed administrative expenses (see footnote 5). (4) Represents payment vouchers on letters of credit issued to carriers under sec. 1842 of the Social Security Act. (5) Subject to subsequent adjustments among all four Social Security trust funds for allocated cost of each operation. Fiscal year 1966 includes "tool-up" period from date of enactment of Social Security Amendments of 1965 (July 30).

Tips on Cutting Energy Costs in Your Home

Source: Con Edison Conservation Services

Heating

In many homes, in areas where temperatures drop during the winter, more energy is used for heating than anything else. Conservation measures pay off in a home which is losing heat excessively. Installing the right amount of insulation, storm windows and doors, caulking and weatherstripping are important. Also consider the following advice:

- Make sure the thermostat and heating system are in good working order. An annual checkup is recommended.
- If your heating system has air filters, make sure they are clean.
- Set the thermostat no higher than 68 degrees. When no one is home, or when everyone is sleeping, the setting should be turned down to 60 degrees or lower. An automatic setback thermostat can raise and lower your home's temperature at times you specify.
- Close off and do not heat unused areas.
- Cover all air conditioner units.
- If you do not have conventional storm windows or doors, use kits to make plastic storm windows.
- Special glass fireplace doors help keep a room's heat from being drawn up the chimney when the fire is burning low. In any case, close the damper when a fireplace is not in use.
- Use the sun's heat by opening blinds and draperies on sunny days. Keep them closed at night or on cloudy days to reduce heat loss.
- Keep radiators and warm air outlets clean. Do not block them with furniture or draperies.

Water Heater

In many homes, the water heater ranks second only to the heating system in total energy consumption. It pays to keep the water heater operating efficiently, and not to waste hot water.

- Put an insulation blanket on your water heater when you go on vacation, or turn it to a minimum setting if there is danger of freezing pipes.
- If you have a dishwasher, set the water heater thermostat no higher than 140 degrees. If not, or if you have a separate water heater for baths, a setting as low as 110 degrees may be sufficient.
- Run the dishwasher and clothes washer only when you have a full load. Use warm or cold water cycles for laundry when you can.
- Take showers instead of tub baths. About half as much hot water is used for a shower.
- Install a water-saver shower head.
- Install aerators or restrictors on all your sink faucets.
- Do not leave the hot water running when rinsing dishes or shaving. Plug and partially fill the basin, or fill a pan with water.
- Use the right size water heater for your needs. An oversized unit wastes energy heating unneeded water. An undersized unit will not deliver all the hot water you want when you need it.
- When shopping for a water heater, look for the yellow-and-black federal EnergyGuide label to learn the estimated yearly energy cost of a unit.

Air Conditioning

- Clean or replace the filter in an air conditioner at the beginning of the cooling season. Then check it once a month and clean or change the filter if necessary. A dirty filter blocks the flow of air and keeps the air conditioner from doing its best job of cooling.
- Adjust the temperature control setting to provide a room temperature no lower than 78 degrees. Since most air conditioner thermostats are not marked in degrees but by words such as "cold" and "colder," use a good wall thermometer to tell which setting will provide the desired temperature.
- Close windows and doors when the air conditioner is running.
- When the outside temperature is 78 degrees or cooler, turn off the air conditioner and open windows to cool your home.
- Always keep your air conditioner turned off when you are away from home or not using the areas that it cools. An air conditioner timer can be set to turn on just before family members arrive home.
- Close draperies and shades to block out the sun's heat.
- When shopping for a new room air conditioner, look for the yellow-and-black federal EnergyGuide label to learn the Energy Efficiency Rating (EER) and the estimated yearly operating cost. The higher the EER, the less electricity will be used for a cooling job.
- Read the manufacturer's instructions and follow them closely.
- If you have a central air conditioning system, run your hands along the ducts while it is operating to check for air leaks. Repair leaks with duct tape. Make sure the duct system is properly insulated.
- On many days in the summer, a window fan can cool an apartment as effectively as an air conditioner, and it is less costly.

Refrigerators and Freezers

The refrigerator operates 24 hours a day, every day, so it is important to make sure your refrigerator is working efficiently. It is one of the biggest users of energy in the home all year round.

- Keep the condenser coils clean. The coils are on the back or at the bottom of the refrigerator. Carefully wipe, vacuum or brush the coils to remove dust and dirt at least once a year.
- Examine door gaskets and hinges regularly for air leaks. The doors should fit tightly. To check, place a piece of paper between the door and the cabinet. Close the door with normal force, then try to pull the paper straight out. There should be a slight resistance. Test all around the door, including the hinge side. If there are any places where the paper slides out easily, you need to adjust the hinges or replace the gasket, or both.
- Pause before opening your refrigerator door. Think of everything you will need before you open the door so you do not have to go back several times. When you open the door, close it quickly to keep the cool air in.
- Adjust the temperature-setting dial of the refrigerator as the manufacturer recommends. Use a thermometer to check the temperature (38 to 40 degrees is usually recommended for the refrigerator; zero degrees for the freezer). Settings that are too cold waste electricity and can ruin foods.
- If you have a manual-defrost refrigerator, do not allow the ice to build up more than $1/4$ inch thick.
- For greatest efficiency, keep your refrigerator well-stocked but allow room for air to circulate around the food.
- The freezer, on the other hand, should be packed full. If necessary, fill empty spaces with bags of ice cubes or fill milk cartons with water and freeze.

- When you are going to be away from home for a week or more, turn off and unplug the refrigerator, empty and clean it, and prop the door open.
- If you are buying a new refrigerator, look for one with a humid-dry ("power-saver") switch. This switch is used to turn off "anti-sweat" heaters in the doors to save electricity when the heaters are not needed.
- When shopping for a new refrigerator or freezer, look for the federal EnergyGuide label to help you select an efficient unit.

Cooking

There are many ways to save electricity or gas by careful use of the range or oven.

- Cook as many dishes in the oven at one time as you can instead of cooking each separately. If recipes call for slightly different temperatures, say 325, 350, and 375 degrees, pick the middle temperature of 350 to cook all 3 dishes and remove each dish as it's done.
- Don't preheat the oven unnecessarily. Usually, any food that takes more than an hour of cooking can be started in a cold oven.
- Turn off your oven or range just before the cooking is finished. The heat that is left will usually finish the cooking.
- Whenever you peek into an oven by opening a door, the temperature drops about 25 degrees. So open the oven door as little as possible.
- Use tight-fitting covers on pots and pans to retain heat and cook foods more quickly.
- Use the lowest possible heat setting to cook foods on top of the range.
- Match the pot to the size of the surface unit. Putting a small pot on a large surface unit wastes energy without cooking the food any faster.
- Adjust the flame on a gas burner so that it does not extend beyond the base of the pot. Using too high a flame wastes energy, and can be dangerous.
- On gas ranges, the flame should burn in a firm, blue cone. If the flame is not blue, the range is probably not working efficiently. Get a service representative to check it.

Lighting

There are many ways to improve your home's lighting level and save energy at the same time.

- Get all family members in the habit of turning off lights when they leave a room, even if they will be gone only for a short time.
- During the day, try to get along with as few lights as possible. Let the daylight do the work. White or lightcolored walls make a room seem brighter.
- Use bulbs of lower wattage where you don't need strong light.
- When possible, use one large bulb rather than several smaller ones. One 100-watt incandescent bulb, for example, produces more light than three 40-watt. However, never use bulbs of a higher wattage than a fixture is designed to take.
- Use three-way bulbs wherever possible and switch to a lower wattage when you do not need bright light for reading or close work.
- Buy energy-saving incandescent bulbs to replace a standard bulbs with slightly higher wattage. There's a ten percent energy cost saving, and the light output is nearly the same.
- Modern solid-state dimmer controls let you save energy by reducing your lighting level and wattage. Many are easy to install.
- Use plug-in timers to turn lights on and off automatically.
- Consider changing to fluorescent lighting, especially in kitchens, bathrooms, and work areas. Fluorescent tubes give more light at lower energy cost than incandescent bulbs with the same wattage. Plug-in fluorescent fixtures are available at hardware stores, or an electrician can install permanent fixtures. Screw-in circular fluorescent tubes are available for lamps.
- For outdoor lighting, replace standard incandescent floodlights with the new energy-saving halogen type.

Measuring Energy

Source: Energy Information Administration, U.S. Energy Dept.

The following tables of equivalents contain those figures commonly used to compare different types of energy sources and their various measurements.

Btu — a British thermal unit — the amount of heat required to raise one pound of water one degree Fahrenheit. Equivalent to 1,055 joules or about 252 gram calories. A therm is usually 100,000 Btu but is sometimes used to refer to other units.

Calorie — The amount of heat required to raise one gram of water one degree Centigrade; abbreviated cal.; equivalent to about .003968 Btu. More common is the kilogram calorie, also called a kilocalorie and abbreviated Cal. or Kcal; equivalent to about 3.97 Btu. (One Kcal is equivalent to one food calorie.)

Btu Values of Energy Sources
(These are conventional or average values, not precise equivalents.)

Coal (per 2,000 lb. ton of U.S. production):

Anthracite	=	22.9×10^6 Btu
Bituminous coal and lignite	=	22.6×10^6

Average heating value of coal used to generate electricity in 1979 was 21.4×10^6 Btu per metric ton.

Natural Gas:

Dry (per cubic foot)	=	1,028 Btu
Liquefied Natural Gas		
(Methane) (per barrel)	=	3.0×10^6

Electricity — 1 kwh = 3,412 Btu

Petroleum (per barrel):

Crude oil	=	5.80×10^6 Btu
Residual fuel oil	=	6.29×10^6
Distillate fuel oil	=	5.83×10^6
Gasoline (including aviation gas)	=	5.25×10^6
Jet fuel (kerosene)	=	5.67×10^6
Jet fuel (naphtha)	=	5.36×10^6
Kerosene	=	5.67×10^6

Nuclear — (per kilowatt hour) = 10,769

The Btu and calorie, being small amounts of energy, are usually expressed as follows when large numbers are involved.

1×10^3 Btu	= 1,000
1×10^6	= 1,000,000
1×10^9	= 1,000,000,000
1×10^{12}	= 1 trillion
1×10^{15}	= 1 quadrillion
1×10^{18}	= 1 quintillion or 1 Q unit
One Q unit	= 44.3 billion short tons of coal
	= 172.4 billion tons of oil
	= 980 trillion cubic feet of natural gas

(continued)

Other Conversion Factors

Electricity — 1 kwh
= 0.3 pounds of coal
= 0.025 gallon of crude oil
= 3.3 cubic feet of natural gas

Natural gas — 1 tcf
(trillion cubic feet)
= 45×10^6 short tons of bituminous and lignite coal produced
= 176×10^6 barrels of crude oil

Coal — 1 mstce
(million short tons of coal equivalent)
= 3.9×10^6 barrels of crude oil
= 1.7×10^6 short tons of crude oil
= 22.1×10^9 cubic feet of natural gas

Oil — 1 million short tons
(6.65×10^6 barrels)
= 4×10^9 kwh of electricity (when used to generate power)

= 12×10^9 kwh uncoverted
= 1.7×10^6 short tons of coal
= 37×10^9 cubic feet of natural gas

Approximate Conversion Factors for Oils

To convert	Barrels to metric tons	Metric tons to barrels	Barrels/ day to tons/ year	Tons/year to barrels/ day
		Multiply by:		
Crude oil[1] . .	.136	7.33	49.8	.0201
Gasoline . .	.118	8.45	43.2	.0232
Kerosene . .	.128	7.80	46.8	.0214
Diesel fuel . .	.133	7.50	48.7	.0205
Fuel oil	.149	6.70	54.5	.0184

(1) Based on world average gravity (excluding natural gas liquids).

Fuel Economy in 1986 Autos; Comparative Miles per Gallon

Source: U.S. Environmental Protection Agency

The mileage numbers and rankings below refer to testing completed through September 16, 1985. The Chevrolet Sprint ER captured the top rating with 55 miles per gallon in the city, 60 on the highway. The Honda Civic Coupe HF, which held the top spot the two previous years, bettered last year's high mark with 52 in the city, 57 on the highway. The rest of the high-rated cars, except the Ford Escort and Nissan Sentra, were various versions of a 1.0-liter three-cylinder Chevrolet Sprint and Suzuki Forsa.

Make, model, fuel[1]	Cu. in. displcmt.	Cylinders	Trans.[2]	City Mileage	Hwy. Mileage
Alfa Romeo Spider. .	120	4	m	21-28	
Audi Coupe GT	136	5	m	19-25	
Audi 4000S	109	4	m	25-30	
Audi 5000S	131	5	l	18-22	
BMW 5-Series	164	6	l	20-24	
Buick Century (d). . .	231	6	l	19-29	
Buick Electra	231	6	l	19-30	
Buick LeSabre	231	6	l	19-30	
Buick Regal	231	6	l	17-24	
Buick Riviera	231	6	l	19-30	
Buick Skyhawk	121	4	m	25-32	
Cadillac Eldorado, Seville	249	8	l	17-26	
Chevrolet Celebrity. .	151	4	m	23-31	
Chevrolet Camaro . .	305	8	l	16-26	
Chevrolet Caprice . .	307	8	l	18-25	
Chevrolet Cavalier . .	173	6	m	18-24	
Chevrolet Chevette CS	98	4	m	27-35	
Chevrolet Monte Carlo	305	8	l	17-25	
Chevrolet Sprint ER .	61	3	m	55-60	
Chrysler LeBaron. . .	135	4	a	20-24	
Chrysler New Yorker	135	4	a	20-24	
Dodge Aries.	135	4	a	23-26	
Dodge Charger.	98	4	m	24-31	
Dodge Colt	97	4	m	28-33	
Dodge Diplomat . . .	318	8	a	16-21	
Dodge 600	135	4	a	20-24	
Ford Escort	113	4	m	32-41	
Ford EXP	113	4	m	24-33	
Ford LTD	140	4	a	21-25	
Ford Mustang.	140	4	m	23-28	
Ford Tempo (d). . . .	122	4	m	36-44	
Ford Thunderbird. . .	231	6	a	19-26	
Honda Accord	119	4	m	25-30	
Honda Civic Coupe. .	91	4	m	30-33	
Honda Civic Coupe HF.	91	4	m	52-57	
Isuzu I-Mark.	90	4	m	38-42	
Isuzu Impulse	119	4	m	22-28	
Jaguar XJ	258	6	a	15-19	
Lincoln-Mercury Capri	140	4	m	23-28	
Mazda 323	98	4	m	28-34	
Mazda 626	122	4	m	26-32	
Mercedes-Benz 560SL	338	8	a	14-17	
Mercury Cougar . . .	231	6	a	19-26	
Mercury Lynx (d) . . .	122	4	m	36-43	
Mercury Mark VII. . .	302	8	l	18-26	
Mercury Marquis . . .	140	4	a	21-25	
Mitsubishi Cordia . . .	122	4	m	25-32	
Mitsubishi Mirage. . .	90	4	m	33-39	
Mitsubishi Tredia . . .	122	4	m	24-31	
Nissan 300ZX.	181	6	m	18-26	
Nissan Pulsar NX. . .	98	4	m	31-38	
Olds. Cutlass Sup. . .	307	8	l	18-25	
Oldsmobile Firenza . .	110	4	m	21-28	
Peugot 505	120	4	m	20-24	
Plymouth Colt.	90	4	m	33-39	
Plymouth Conquest .	156	4	m	19-24	
Plymouth Horizon . .	135	4	m	26-35	
Plymouth Turismo . .	135	4	m	26-35	
Pontiac Bonneville . .	305	8	l	17-25	
Pontiac Fiero	151	4	m	24-35	
Pontiac Grand Prix . .	231	6	l	19-24	
Pontiac Firebird	305	8	m	16-26	
Pontiac 1000	98	4	m	27-34	
Porsche 911	201	6	m	16-22	
Renault Alliance Convertible.	105	4	m	27-32	
Renault Fuego	132	4	l	23-31	
Rolls Royce Camargue	412	8	a	8-11	
Subaru XT.	109	4	m	25-32	
Suzuki Forsa	61	3	m	44-50	
Toyota Celica	122	4	m	23-29	
Toyota Celica Supra .	168	6	m	18-22	
Toyota Corolla	97	4	m	31-37	
Toyota Cressida . . .	168	6	m	19-24	
Toyota Tercel	89	4	m	31-38	
Volkswgn Golf (d) . .	97	4	m	37-44	
Volkswgn Jetta (d) . .	97	4	m	37-44	
Volkswgn Cabriolet .	109	4	m	24-29	
Volkswgn Scirocco. .	109	4	m	24-29	
Volvo 740/760	174	6	a	18-22	

(1) Type of fuel: (d) = diesel; all others are gasoline-powered. (2) Type of transmission: a = automatic; m = manual; l = automatic with locking torque-converter.

Removing Common Spots and Stains

By Polly Fisher, Syndicated Columnist, "Polly's Pointers," Newspaper Enterprise Association

Precaution: The following stain removal techniques are primarily intended for use on washable fabrics and surfaces, unless otherwise noted. If your fabric is labeled "dry clean only," consult a professional dry cleaner for safe treatment of the stain. Before treating any stain, be sure the remedy is safe for the fabric or finish of the stained surface. Always test the recommended cleaning solution at the recommended temperature (and this includes water, soap, and detergent) on a hidden part of the garment or other item: a seam allowance, a collar facing, a turned-under hem. While these remedies are all considered reasonably safe for most fabrics, the colorfastness of commercial dyes varies greatly. Be especially alert for any bleeding or change of color when you make your test. Above all, follow the care-label instructions and use common sense when dealing with any cleaning method. All products mentioned here can be obtained at local supermarkets, drug stores, or hardware stores.

Beverages (Alcoholic Drinks, Coffee, Fruit Juice, Soda, Tea, Wine)

When spills first occur, pour, sponge, or otherwise wet the fabric with ordinary club soda or any unflavored carbonated or sparkling water. Blot with a clean cloth, napkin, tissue, or paper towel. In most cases, this will clean up the spot without leaving any stain.

When such stains have set, stretch the stained area of fabric over a large bowl and hold it taut with a large rubber band. Then pour boiling water over the stain. If any stain remains, sponge with lemon juice. If the fabric is white, leave the lemon juice-treated fabric out in the sun to dry and bleach.

Blood

Wash fresh blood stains in cold water and a mild soap or detergent. Hand soap or dishwashing liquid is fine. Never wash blood stains with warm or hot water.

If stains have dried and set, sponge with a little hydrogen peroxide until the stain disappears.

On mattresses and other large items that are difficult to wash, spread a thick paste of cornstarch and water over the stained area. Let dry thoroughly, then vacuum off.

Candle Wax

With a dull knife, gently scrape off as much wax as possible. Sandwich the fabric between two thick layers of paper towels and iron over the spot with a hot iron. Frequently change the towels for fresh ones as the wax melts and soaks into the paper. If any colored stain remains after all wax has been removed, sponge with rubbing alcohol.

Chewing Gum

On flat, smooth fabrics, harden gum by rubbing with an ice cube, then peel gum off. If any stain remains, sponge with alcohol or dry cleaning fluid (often sold as "spot remover.")

On knits, particularly fuzzy, loose sweaters, massage vegetable shortening into the gummy area. This will loosen the gum and lift it from the fibers. Wash out with cool water and mild soap or detergent. Repeat if necessary until all gum is gone.

Chocolate

Rub with a mild detergent and warm water. If stain remains, sponge lightly with dry cleaning fluid.

Glue

To remove plastic cement, apply nail-polish remover (acetone) sparingly. This will dissolve the cement. Blot with a clean cloth. Nail-polish remover and other acetone-based products will also dissolve "super" glues. Do not use on acetates and acetate blends.

White all-purpose glue should be soaked in warm water, then sponged with ammonia. Rinse, then launder.

The glue left by price tags and labels on bottles, plastics, or almost any surface, can be easily removed by rubbing with vegetable oil and a clean cloth. Rinse or wash the oil off after removing the glue. (Not recommended for use on fabrics.)

Grease and Oil Stains

Rub fresh stains with hand soap and wash vigorously with warm water.

On fabrics that cannot be washed, sprinkle fresh grease stains liberally with cornstarch. Let set for fifteen minutes, then brush or vacuum thoroughly. The cornstarch will absorb the grease. Safe for velvets and furs if brushed out gently.

Apply waterless handcleaner to grease, oil, or tar stains. Rub in gently, then launder as usual. Place paper towels under the fabric to absorb the grease as you're working the handcleaner into the fabric.

Greying (All-Over)

Greying of fabrics may be caused by soap left in the fabric after laundering. Add one cup of white vinegar to the final rinse water of your machine's cycle. This will break up and rinse away soap buildup and soften the fabric.

Ink

Ballpoint pen ink on fabrics and vinyl can be sprayed with hairspray. The hairspray will dissolve the ink which should be blotted up and wiped away with a clean cloth or paper towels.

Sponge stains caused by printer's ink or carbon paper with rubbing alcohol, then rinse.

Mildew

Saturate light mildew stains on white and pastel fabrics with lemon juice and bleach in the sun for several hours. (Don't apply the juice to any other part of the fabric.) Launder as usual.

If mildew stains are heavy or remain after treating with lemon juice, sponge with hydrogen peroxide. Again, launder afterwards.

Paint

Dab paint spots with turpentine. When paint softens, blot up with clean paper towels. Rinse, then launder.

To remove paint from your skin, rub the spots with ordinary vegetable oil.

Perspiration

Soak stained fabric in warm white vinegar for thirty minutes, then launder as usual.

Yellowing (All-Over)

Use chlorine bleach (on cottons and other bleachable fabrics only) in laundering, according to bottle directions. Do not use chlorine bleach on nylon fabrics. Chlorine bleach can *cause* yellowing on nylon.

Restore whiteness to delicate fabrics and items that you don't want to treat with harsh chemicals by soaking in a cream of tartar solution. Add one tablespoon cream of tartar to one gallon of hot water, then soak garments overnight. Good for baby clothes, diapers, linen handkerchiefs, and delicate synthetic knits.

Life Insurance: Facts You Need to Know
Source: American Council of Insurance

For many people, one of the most important purchases they can make—and one they need to be well-informed about—is life insurance.

Most insurance companies are currently simplifying their life insurance plans in order that consumers might have a better idea of what they're really buying. In addition to making policies easier to read and understand, the companies are developing new premium payment methods to lower the financial burden of insurance purchase. Since almost one-third of all life insurance is bought by people aged 25-43, with over 60% paying more than $260 annually for insurance, such innovations as monthly payment plans (instead of annual or semi-annual, lump sum payments) are becoming common.

There are 3 basic types of insurance policies: (1) whole life—a policy that continues in effect as long as you pay the fixed premium; (2) endowment—a policy that will pay you or your beneficiary its face amount after a designated time (no longer commonly used); and (3) term—the policy pays your beneficiary the face amount if you die while the policy is in force.

Life Insurance as an Investment?

There's a good deal of controversy about the value of insurance as an investment. Whole life policies, with their fixed premiums and cash value that grows over the course of the years (that can be collected when you decide to terminate the policy or borrowed against up to the current value of the policy), are considered by many to be an effective way to protect a family financially and invest wisely. Term insurance, on the other hand, is a much less expensive type of in-

surance, and achieves much the same purpose as whole life (of course, only during the "term" of its existence). But there is no cash surrender value or borrowing privilege.

Since both current protection and a good future investment are necessary, the consumer must carefully weigh the advantages of life insurance before making a purchase.

How to Read a Life Insurance Policy

All life insurance policies, regardless of type, can be divided into 3 parts:

1. **Summary**—This is the basic agreement of the policy. It includes the name of the insured, the face amount of the policy, the beneficiary's name, and premium amount, as well as the type of policy, any riders (additions to the policy you might have bought), and whether or not the cost of the insurance has been figured on a guaranteed basis or a participating basis.

2. **Details**—Approximately 10 clauses giving the specifics of the policy's operation, such as due date of premium, value of the policy when you surrender it for either cash or a loan, the amount paid at the time of your death, and options for how your beneficiary can receive that money are included.

3. **Application**—This is a two-fold section that gives personal information about you and lets you make some decisions about how the policy will work. Among typical items covered are what happens in the event of your suicide, whether you engage in dangerous sports or occupations, what your rights are under the policy, etc.

As with any legal document, it is important to read and understand what you are purchasing. If you need further information, a good source is the American Council of Insurance, 1850 K St. N.W., Washington, DC 20006.

Stress: How Much Can Affect Your Health?

Source: Reprinted with permission from the *Journal of Psychosomatic Research,* Vol. 11, pp. 213-218, T.H. Holmes, M.D., R.H. Rahe, M.D.; The Social Readjustment Rating Scale © 1967, Pergamon Press, Ltd.

Change, both good and bad, can create stress and stress, if sufficiently severe, can lead to illness. Drs. Thomas Holmes and Richard Rahe, psychiatrists at the University of Washington in Seattle, have developed the Social Readjustment Rating Scale. In their study, they gave a point value to stressful events. The psychiatrists discovered that in 79 percent of the persons studied major illness followed the accumulation of stress-related changes totaling over 300 points in one year. The scale follows:

The Social Readjustment Rating Scale

Life Event	Value
Death of Spouse	100
Divorce	73
Marital separation from mate	65
Detention in jail or other institution	63
Death of a close family member	63
Major personal injury or illness	53
Marriage	50
Being fired at work	47
Marital reconciliation with mate	45
Retirement from work	45
Major change in the health or behavior of a family member	44
Pregnancy	40
Sexual difficulties	39
Gaining a new family member (e.g., through birth, adoption, oldster moving in, etc.)	39
Major business readjustment (e.g., merger, reorganization, bankruptcy, etc.)	39
Major change in financial state (e.g., a lot worse off or a lot better off than usual)	38
Death of a close friend	37
Changing to a different line of work	36
Major change in the number of arguments with spouse (e.g., either a lot more or a lot less than usual regarding child-rearing, personal habits, etc.)	35
Taking out a mortgage or loan for a major purchase (e.g. for a home, business, etc.)	31
Foreclosure on a mortgage or loan	30
Major change in responsibilities at work (e.g., promotion, demotion, lateral transfer)	29
Son or daughter leaving home (e.g., marriage, attending college, etc.)	29
In-law troubles	29
Outstanding personal achievement	28
Wife beginning or ceasing work outside the home	26
Beginning or ceasing formal schooling	26
Major change in living conditions (e.g., building a new home, remodeling, deterioration of home or neighborhood)	25
Revision of personal habits (dress, manners, association, etc.)	24
Troubles with the boss	23
Major change in working hours or conditions	20
Change in residence	20
Changing to a new school	20
Major change in usual type and/or amount of recreation	19
Major change in church activities (e.g., a lot more or a lot less than usual)	19
Major change in social activities (e.g., clubs, dancing, movies, visiting, etc.)	18
Taking out a mortgage or loan for a lesser purchase (e.g., for a car, TV, freezer, etc.)	17
Major change in sleeping habits (a lot more or a lot less sleep, or change in part of day when asleep)	16
Major change in number of family get-togethers (e.g., a lot more or a lot less than usual)	15
Major change in eating habits (a lot more or a lot less food intake, or very different meal hours or surroundings)	15
Vacation	13
Christmas	12
Minor violations of the law (e.g., traffic tickets, jaywalking, disturbing the peace, etc.)	11

Effects of Commonly Abused Drugs

Source: National Institute on Drug Abuse

Tobacco

Effects and dangers: Nicotine, the active ingredient in tobacco, acts as a stimulant on the heart and nervous system. When tobacco smoke is inhaled the immediate effects on the body are a faster heart beat and elevated blood pressure. These effects, however, are quickly dissipated. Tar (in the smoke) contains many carcinogens. These compounds, many of which are in polluted air but are found in vastly greater quantities in cigarette smoke, have been identified as major causes of cancer and respiratory difficulties. Even relatively young smokers can have shortness of breath, nagging cough, or develop cardiovascular and respiratory difficulties. A third principal component of cigarette smoke, carbon monoxide, is also a cause of some of the more serious health effects of smoking. Carbon monoxide can reduce the blood's ability to carry oxygen to body tissues and can promote the development of arteriosclerosis (hardening of the arteries). Long-term effects of smoking cigarettes are emphysema, chronic bronchitis, heart disease, lung cancer, and cancer in other parts of the body.

Risks during pregnancy: Women who smoke during pregnancy are more likely to have babies that weigh less, and more frequently lose their babies through stillbirth or death soon after birth.

Alcohol

Effects: Like sedatives, it is a central nervous system depressant. In small doses, it has a tranquilizing effect on most people, although it appears to stimulate others. Alcohol first acts on those parts of the brain which affect self-control and other learned behaviors; lowered self-control often leads to the aggressive behavior associated with some people who drink.

Dangers: In large doses, alcohol can dull sensation and impair muscular coordination, memory, and judgment. Taken in larger quantities over a long period time, alcohol can damage the liver and heart and can cause permanent brain damage. A large dose of alcohol, which can be as little as a pint or less of whiskey consumed at once, can interfere with the part of the brain that controls breathing. The respiratory failure which results can bring death. Delirium tremens, the most extreme manifestation of alcohol withdrawal, can also cause death. On the average, heavy drinkers shorten their life span by about 10 years.

Risks during pregnancy: Women who drink heavily during pregnancy (more than 3 ounces of alcohol per day or about 2 mixed drinks) run a higher risk than other women of delivering babies with physical, mental and behavioral abnormalities.

Dependence: Repeated drinking produces tolerance to the drug's effects and dependence. The drinker's body then needs alcohol to function. Once dependent, drinkers experience withdrawal symptoms when they stop drinking.

Marijuana ("grass", "pot", "weed")

What is it?: A common plant (*Cannabis sativa*), its chief psychoactive ingredient is delta-9-tetrahydrocannabinol, or THC. The amount of THC in the marijuana cigarette (joint) primarily determines its psychoactive potential.

Effects: Most users experience an increase in heart rate, reddening of the eyes, and dryness in the mouth and throat. Studies indicate the drug temporarily impairs short-term memory, alters sense of time, and reduces the ability to perform tasks requiring concentration, swift reactions, and coordination. Many feel that their hearing, vision, and skin sensitivity are enhanced by the drug, but these reports have not been objectively confirmed by research. Feelings of euphoria, relaxation, altered sense of body image, and bouts of exaggerated laughter are also commonly reported.

Dangers: Scientists believe marijuana can be particularly harmful to lungs because users typically inhale the filtered smoke deeply and hold it in their lungs for prolonged periods of time. Marijuana smoke has been found to have more cancer-causing agents than are found in cigarette smoke (see above). Because marijuana use increases heart rate as much as 50% and brings on chest pain in people who have a poor blood supply to the heart (and more rapidly than tobacco smoke does), doctors believe people with heart conditions or who are at high risk for heart ailments, should not use mari-

juana. Findings also suggest that regular use may reduce fertility in women and that men with marginal fertility or endocrine functioning should avoid marijuana use and that it is especially harmful during adolescence, a period of rapid physical and sexual development.

Risks during pregnancy: Research is limited, but scientists believe marijuana which crosses the placential barrier, may have a toxic effect on embryos and fetuses.

Dependence: Tolerance to marijuana, the need to take more and more of the drug over time to get the original effect, has been proven in humans and animals. Physical dependence has been demonstrated in research subjects who ingested an amount equal to smoking 10 to 20 joints a day. When the drug was discontinued, subjects experienced withdrawal symptoms—irritability, sleep disturbances, loss of appetite and weight, sweating, and stomach upset.

Bad reactions: Most commonly reported immediate adverse reaction to marijuana use is the "acute panic anxiety reaction," usually described as an exaggeration of normal marijuana effects in which intense fears of losing control and going crazy accompany severe anxiety. The symptoms often disappear in a few hours when the acute drug effects have worn off.

Hallucinogens ("psychodelics")

What are they?: Drugs which affect perception, sensation, thinking, self-awareness, and emotion.

(1) LSD (lysergic acid diethylamide), a synthetic, is converted from lysergic acid which comes from fungus (ergot).

Effects: Vary greatly according to dosage, personality of the user, and conditions under which the drug is used. Basically, it causes changes in sensation. Vision alters; users describe changes in depth perception and in the meaning of the perceived object. Illusions and hallucinations often occur. Physical reactions range from minor changes such as dilated pupils, a rise in temperature and heartbeat, or a slight increase in blood pressure, to tremors. High doses can greatly alter the state of consciousness. Heavy use of the drug may produce flashbacks, recurrences of some features of a previous LSD experience days or months after the last dose.

Dangers: After taking LSD, a person loses control over normal thought processes. Although many perceptions are pleasant, others may cause panic or may make a person believe that he or she cannot be harmed. Longer-term harmful reactions include anxiety and depression, or "breaks from reality" which may last from a few days to months. Heavy users sometimes develop signs of organic brain damage, such as impaired memory and attention span, mental confusion, and difficulty with abstract thinking. It is not known yet whether such mental changes are permanent.

(2) Mescaline: Comes from peyote cactus and its effects are similar to those of LSD.

Phencyclidine (PCP or "angel dust")

What is it?: A drug that was developed as a surgical anesthetic for humans in the late 1950s. Because of its unpleasant and unusual side effects, PCP was soon restricted to its only current legal use as a veterinary anesthetic and tranquilizer.

Effects: Vary according to dosage. Low doses may provide the usual releasing effects of many psychoactive drugs. A floaty euphoria is described, sometimes associated with a feeling of numbness (part of the drug's anesthetic effects). Increased doses produce an excited, confused intoxication, which may include muscle rigidity, loss of concentration and memory, visual disturbances, delirium, feelings of isolation, convulsions, speech impairment, violent behavior, fear of death, and changes in the user's perceptions of their bodies.

Dangers: PCP intoxication can produce violent and bizarre behavior even in people not otherwise prone to such behavior. Violent actions may be directed at themselves or others and often account for serious injuries and death. More people die from accidents caused by the erratic behavior produced by the drug than from the drug's direct effect on the body. A temporary, schizophrenic-like psychosis, which can last for days or weeks, has also occurred in users of moderate or higher doses.

Stimulants ("Uppers")

What are they?: A class of drugs which stimulate the central nervous system and produce an increase in alertness and activity.

(1) **Amphetamines** promote a feeling of alertness and increase in speech and general physical activity. Under medical supervision, the drugs are taken to control appetite.

Effects and dangers: Even small, infrequent doses can produce toxic effects in some people. Restlessness, anxiety, mood swings, panic, circulatory and cardiac disturbances, paranoid thoughts, hallucinations, convulsions, and coma have all been reported. Heavy, frequent doses can produce brain damage which results in speed disturbances and difficulty in turning thoughts into words. Death can result from injected amphetamine overdose. Long-term users often have acne resembling a measles rash; trouble with teeth, gums and nails, and dry lifeless hair. As heavy users who inject amphetamines accumulate larger amounts of the drug in their bodies, the resulting toxicity can produce amphetamine psychosis. People in this extremely suspicious, paranoid state, frequently exhibit bizarre, sometimes violent behavior.

Dependence: People with a history of sustained low-dose use quite often become dependent and feel they need the drug to get by.

(2) **Cocaine,** a very popular drug in the eighties, is a stimulant extracted from the leaves of the coca plant. It is available in many forms, the most available of which is cocaine hydrochloride. Cocaine hydrochloride is often used medically as a local anesthetic, but is also sold illegally on the street in large pieces called rocks. Street cocaine is a white, crystal-like powder that is most commonly inhaled or snorted, though some users ingest, inject, or smoke a form of the drug called freebase.

Freebase is formed by chemically converting street cocaine to a purified substance that is more suitable for smoking. Smoking freebase produces a shorter, but more intense high than other ways of using the drug. It is the most direct and rapid means of getting the drug to the brain and, because larger amounts are reaching the brain more quickly, the effects of the drug are more intense and the dangers associated with its use are greater.

Effects: The drug's usual effects are dilated pupils and increased blood pressure, heart rate, breathing rate, and body temperature. Even small doses may elicit feelings of euphoria; illusions of increased mental and physical strength and sensory awareness; and a decrease in hunger, pain, and the perceived need for sleep. Large doses significantly magnify these effects, sometimes causing irrational behavior and confusion.

Dangers: Paranoia is not an uncommon response to heavy doses. Psychosis may be triggered in users prone to mental instability. Repeated inhalation often results in nostril and nasal membrane irritation. Some regular users have reported feelings of restlessness, irritability, and anxiety. Others have experienced hallucinations of touch, sight, taste, or smell. When people stop using cocaine after taking it for a long time, they frequently become depressed. They tend to fight off this depression by taking more cocaine, just as in the up/down amphetamine cycle.

Cocaine is toxic. Although few people realize it, overdose deaths, though rare, have occurred as a result of injecting, ingesting and even snorting cocaine. The deaths are a result of seizures followed by respiratory arrest and coma, or sometimes by cardiac arrest. Other dangers associated with cocaine include the risk of infection, such as hepatitis, resulting from the use of unsterile needles and the risk of fire or explosion resulting from the use of volatile substances necessary for freebase preparation.

Dependence: Cocaine is not a narcotic; no evidence suggests that it produces a physical dependence. However, cocaine is psychologically a very dangerous, dependence-producing drug. Smoking freebase increases this risk of dependence.

(3) **Caffeine** may be the world's most popular drug. It is primarily consumed in coffee and tea, but is also found in cocoa, cola and other soft drinks, as well as in many over-the-counter medicines.

Effects: Two to four cups of coffee increase heart rate, body temperature, urine production, and gastric juice secretion. Caffeine can also raise sugar levels and cause tremors, loss of coordination, decreased appetite, and postponement of fatigue. It can interfere with the depth of sleep and the amount of dream sleep by causing more rapid eye movement (REM) sleep at first, but less than average over an entire night. Extremely high doses may cause diarrhea, sleeplessness, trembling, severe headache, and nervousness.

Dependence: A form of physical dependence may result with regular consumption. In such cases, withdrawal symptoms may occur if caffeine use is stopped or interrupted. These symptoms include headache, irritability, and fatigue. Tolerance may develop with the use of six to eight cups or more a day. A regular user of caffeine who has developed a tolerance may also develop a craving for the drug's effects.

Dangers: Poisonous doses of caffeine have occurred occasionally and have resulted in convulsions, breathing failure, and even death. However, it is almost impossible to die from drinking too much coffee or tea. The deaths that have been reported have resulted from the misuse of tablets containing caffeine.

Sedatives (Tranquilizers, sleeping pills)

What are they?: Drugs which depress the central nervous system, more appropriately called sedative-hypnotics because they include drugs which calm the nerves (the sedation effect) and produce sleep (the hypnotic effect). Of drugs in this class, barbiturates ("barbs", "downers", "reds") have the highest rate of abuse and misuse. The most commonly abused barbiturates include pentobarbital (Nembutal), secobarbital (Seconal), and amobarbital (Amytal). These all have legitimate use as sedatives or sleeping aids. Among the most commonly abused nonbarbiturate drugs are glutethimide (Doriden), meprobamate (Miltown), methyprylon (Noludar), ethchlorvynol (Placidyl), and methaqualone (Sopor, Quaalude). These are prescribed to help people sleep. Benzodiazepines, especially diazepam (Valium), prescribed to relieve anxiety, are commonly abused, and their rate of abuse and misuse is increasing.

Dangers: These can kill. Barbiturate overdose is implicated in nearly one-third of all reported drug-induced deaths. Accidental deaths may occur when a user takes an unintended larger or repeated dose of sedatives because of confusion or impairment in judgment caused by initial intake of the drug. With lesser, but still large doses, users can go into coma. Moderately large doses often produce an intoxicated stupor. Users' speech is often slurred, memory vague, and judgment impaired. Taken along with alcohol, the combination can be fatal. Tranquilizers act somewhat differently from other sedatives and are considered less hazardous. But even by themselves, or in combination with other drugs (especially alcohol and other sedatives) they can be quite dangerous.

Dependence: Potential for dependence is greatest with barbiturates, but all sedatives, tranquilizers, can be addictive. Barbiturate withdrawal is often more severe than heroin withdrawal.

Narcotics

What they are?: Drugs that relieve pain and often induce sleep. The opiates, which are narcotics, include opium and drugs derived from opium, such as morphine, codeine, and heroin. Narcotics also include certain synthetic chemicals that have a morphine-like action, such as methadone.

Which are abused?: Heroin ("junk," "smack") accounts for 90% of narcotic abuse in the U.S. Sometimes medicinal narcotics are also abused, including paregoric containing codeine, and methadone, meperidine, and morphine.

Dependence: Anyone can become heroin dependent if he or she takes the drug regularly. Although environmental stress and problems of coping have often been considered as factors that lead to heroin addiction, physicians or psychologists do not agree that some people just have an "addictive personality" and are prone to dependence. All we know for certain is that continued use of heroin causes dependence.

Dangers: Physical dangers depend on the specific drug, its source, and the way it is used. Most medical problems are caused by the uncertain dosage level, use of unsterile needles and other paraphernalia, contamination of the drug, or combination of a narcotic with other drugs, rather than by the effects of the heroin (or another narcotic) itself. The life expectancy of a heroin addict who injects the drug intravenously is significantly lower than that of one who does not. An overdose can result in death. If, for example, an addict obtains pure heroin and is not tolerant of the dose, he or she

may die minutes after injecting it. Infections from unsterile needles, solutions, syringes, cause many diseases. Serum hepatitis is common. Skin abscesses, inflammation of the veins and congestion of the lungs also occur.

Withdrawal: When a heroin-dependent person stops taking the drug, withdrawal begins within 4-6 hours after the last injection. Full-blown withdrawal symptoms—which include shaking, sweating, vomiting, a running nose and eyes, muscle aches, chills, abdominal pains, and diarrhea—begin some 12-16 hours after the last injection. The intensity of symptoms depends on the degree of dependence.

A Patient's Bill of Rights

Source: American Hospital Association, © copyright 1972.

Often, as a hospital patient, you feel you have little control over your circumstances. You do, however, have some important rights. They have been enumerated by the American Hospital Association.

1. The patient has the right to considerate and respectful care.
2. The patient has the right to obtain from his physician complete current information concerning his diagnosis, treatment, and prognosis in terms the patient can be reasonably expected to understand. When it is not medically advisable to give such information to the patient, the information should be made available to an appropriate person in his behalf. He has the right to know, by name, the physician responsible for coordinating his care.
3. The patient has the right to receive from his physician information necessary to give informed consent prior to the start of any procedure and/or treatment. Except in emergencies, such information for informed consent should include but not necessarily be limited to the specific procedure and/or treatment, the medically significant risks involved, and the probable duration of incapacitation. Where medically significant alternatives for care or treatment exist, or when the patient requests information concerning medical alternatives, the patient has the right to such information. The patient also has the right to know the name of the person responsible for the procedures and/or treatment.
4. The patient has the right to refuse treatment to the extent permitted by law and to be informed of the medical consequences of his action.
5. The patient has the right to every consideration of his privacy concerning his own medical care program. Case discussion, consultation, examination, and treatment are confidential and should be conducted discreetly. Those not directly involved in his care must have the permission of the patient to be present.
6. The patient has the right to expect that all communications and records pertaining to his care should be treated as confidential.
7. The patient has the right to expect that within its capacity a hospital must make reasonable response to the request of a patient for services. The hospital must provide evaluation, service, and/or referral as indicated by the urgency of the case. When medically permissable, a patient may be transferred to another facility only after he has received complete information and explanation concerning the need for and alternatives to such a transfer. The institution to which the patient is to be transferred must first have accepted the patient for transfer.
8. The patient has the right to obtain information as to any relationship of his hospital to other health care and education institutions insofar as this care is concerned. The patient has the right to obtain information as to the existence of any professional relationships among individuals, by name, who are treating him.
9. The patient has the right to be advised if the hospital proposes to engage in or perform human experimentation affecting his care or treatment. The patient has the right to refuse to participate in such research projects.
10. The patient has the right to expect reasonable continuity of care. He has the right to know in advance what appointment times and physicians are available and where. The patient has the right to expect that the hospital will provide a mechanism whereby he is informed by his physician of the patient's continuing health care requirements following discharge.
11. The patient has the right to examine and receive an explanation of his bill, regardless of the source of payment.
12. The patient has the right to know what hospital rules and regulations apply to his conduct as a patient.

Immunization Schedule for Children*

Source: American Academy of Pediatrics

Age	Type of Vaccination	Disease Immunized Against	Age	Type of Vaccination	Disease Immunized Against
2 months	D-T-P	Diphtheria, Tetanus (Lockjaw), Pertussis (Whooping Cough)		Mumps Vaccine[1] (Or a single injection combined vaccine for all three diseases may be given at 15 months.)	Mumps
	Oral Polio Vaccine	Polio Myelitis			
4 months	D-T-P				
	Oral Polio Vaccine				
6 months	D-T-P		18 months	D-T-P Booster	
15 months	Measles Vaccine	Measles	(2)	Oral Polio Booster	
	Rubella Vaccine[1]	German Measles	School Entry	D-T-P Booster Oral Polio Booster	

(1) Rubella or mumps vaccine alone may be given as early as 12 months. (2) The national Center for Disease Control advises immunization of children 24 months and older against Haemolphilus influenza type B, which causes the most common and serious form of meningitis in children under 5 and can also cause pneumonia, bronchitis, tonsilitis and ear infections.

*The American College of Physicians recommends that adolescents and adults consult with their physicians about further vaccinations. Those without natural infection or proper immunization against childhood diseases like measles, mumps, rubella, and poliomyelitis may be at increased risk for such disease and their complications as adults; in addition, tetanus and diphtheria should be boosted periodically; and various ages, occupations, lifestyles, environmental risks, and diseases may call for adult immunization.

Food and Nutrition

Food contains proteins, carbohydrates, fats, water, vitamins and minerals. Nutrition is the way your body takes in and uses these ingredients to maintain proper functioning. If you aren't eating foods that your body needs, you suffer from poor nutrition and, sooner or later, your health will deteriorate.

Protein

Proteins are composed of amino acids and are indispensable in the diet. They build, maintain, and repair the body. Best sources: eggs, milk, fish, meat, poultry, soybeans, nuts. High quality proteins such as eggs, meat, or fish supply all 8 amino acids needed in the diet. Low quality proteins such as nuts and grain do not.

Fats

Fats provide energy by furnishing calories to the body, and by carrying vitamins A, D, E, and K. They are the most concentrated source of energy in the diet. Best sources: butter, margarine, salad oils, nuts, cream, egg yokes, most cheeses, lard, meat.

Carbohydrates

Carbohydrates provide energy for body function and activity by supplying immediate calories. The carbohydrate group includes sugars, starches, fiber, and starchy vegetables. Best sources: grains, legumes, nuts, potatoes, fruits.

Water

Water dissolves and transports other nutrients throughout the body aiding the process of digestion, absorption, circulation, and excretion. It also helps regulate body temperature. We get water from all foods.

Vitamins

Vitamin A—promotes good eyesight and helps keep the skin and mucous membranes resistant to infection. Best sources: liver, carrots, sweet potatoes, kale, collard greens, turnips, fortified milk.

Vitamin B1 (thiamine)—prevents beriberi. Essential to carbohydrate metabolism and health of nervous system.

Vitamin B2 (riboflavin)—protects skin, mouth, eye, eyelids, and mucous membranes. Essential to protein and energy metabolism. Best sources; liver, milk, meat, poultry, broccoli, mushrooms.

Vitamin B6 (pyridoxine)—important in the regulation of the central nervous system and in protein metabolism. Best sources: whole grains, meats, nuts, brewers' yeast.

Vitamin B12 (cobalamin)—necessary for the formation of red blood cells. Best sources: liver, meat, fish, eggs, soybeans.

Niacin—maintains the health of skin, tongue, and digestive system. Best sources: poultry, peanuts, fish, organ meats, enriched flour and bread.

Other B vitamins are—biotin, choline, folic acid (folacin), inositol, PABA (para-aminobenzoic acid), and pantothenic acid.

Vitamin C (ascorbic acid)—maintains collagen, a protein necessary for the formation of skin, ligaments, and bones. It helps heal wounds and mend fractures, and aids in resisting some forms of virus and bacterial infections. Best sources: citrus fruits and juices, turnips, broccoli, Brussels sprouts, potatoes and sweet potatoes, tomatoes, cabbage.

Vitamin D—important for bone development. Best sources: sunlight, fortified milk and milk products, fish-liver oils, egg yolks, organ meats.

Vitamin E (tocopherol)—helps protect red blood cells. Best sources: vegetable oils, wheat germ, whole grains, eggs, peanuts, organ meats, margarine, green leafy vegetables.

Vitamin K—necessary for formation of prothrombin, which helps blood to clot. Also made by intestinal bacteria. Best dietary sources: green leafy vegetables, tomatoes.

Minerals

Calcium—the most abundant mineral in the body, works with phosphorus in building and maintaining bones and teeth. Best sources: milk and milk products, cheese, and blackstrap molasses.

Phosphorus—the 2d most abundant mineral, performs more functions than any other mineral, and plays a part in nearly every chemical reaction in the body. Best source: whole grains, cheese, milk.

Iron—Necessary for the formation of myoglobin, which transports oxygen to muscle tissue, and hemoglobin, which transports oxygen in the blood. Best sources: organ meats, beans, green leafy vegetables, and shellfish.

Other minerals—chromium, cobalt, copper, fluorine, iodine, magnesium, manganese, molybdenum, potassium, selenium, sodium, sulfur, and zinc.

Recommended Daily Dietary Allowances

Source: Food and Nutrition Board, National Academy of Sciences—National Research Council

The allowances are amounts of nutrients recommended as adequate for maintenance of good nutrition in almost all healthy persons in the U.S. Diets should be based on a variety of common foods in order to provide other nutrients for which human requirements have been less well defined.

Age (years)	Weight (lbs.)	Protein (grams)	Fat soluble Vitamins			Water soluble Vitamins							Minerals					
			Vitamin A[1]	Vitamin D[2]	Vitamin E[3]	Vitamin C (mg.)	Thiamin (mg.)	Riboflavin (mg.)	Niacin (mg.)[4]	Vitamin B_6 (mg.)	Folacin (micrograms)	Vitamin B_{12} (micrograms)	Calcium (mg.)	Phosphorus (mg.)	Magnesium (mg.)	Iron (mg.)	Zinc (mg.)	Iodine (micrograms)
Infants . . to 6 mos.	13 kg × 2.2		420	10	3	35	0.3	0.4	6	0.3	30	0.5	360	240	50	10	3	40
to 1 yr.	20 kg × 2.0		400	10	4	35	0.5	0.6	8	0.6	45	1.5	540	360	70	15	5	50
Children . . 1-3	29	23	400	10	5	45	0.7	0.8	9	0.9	100	2.0	800	800	150	15	10	70
4-6	44	30	500	10	6	45	0.9	1.0	11	1.3	200	2.5	800	800	200	10	10	90
7-10	62	34	700	10	7	45	1.2	1.4	16	1.6	300	3.0	800	800	250	10	10	120
Males . . . 11-14	99	45	1000	10	8	50	1.4	1.6	18	1.8	400	3.0	1200	1200	350	18	15	150
15-18	145	56	1000	10	10	60	1.4	1.7	18	2.0	400	3.0	1200	1200	400	18	15	150
19-22	154	56	1000	7.5	10	60	1.5	1.7	19	2.2	400	3.0	800	800	350	10	15	150
23-50	154	56	1000	5	10	60	1.4	1.6	18	2.2	400	3.0	800	800	350	10	15	150
51+	154	56	1000	5	10	60	1.2	1.4	16	2.2	400	3.0	800	800	350	10	15	150
Females . 11-14	101	46	800	10	8	50	1.1	1.3	15	1.8	400	3.0	1200	1200	300	18	15	150
15-18	120	46	800	10	8	60	1.1	1.3	14	2.0	400	3.0	1200	1200	300	18	15	150
19-22	120	44	800	7.5	8	60	1.1	1.3	14	2.0	400	3.0	800	800	300	18	15	150
23-50	120	44	800	5	8	60	1.0	1.2	13	2.0	400	3.0	800	800	300	18	15	150
51+	120	44	800	5	8	60	1.0	1.2	13	2.0	400	3.0	800	800	300	10	15	150
Pregnant		+30	+200	+5	+2	+20	+0.4	+0.3	+2	+0.6	+400	+1.0	+400	+400	+150	[5]	+5	+25
Lactating		+20	+400	+5	+3	+40	+0.5	+0.5	+5	+0.5	+100	+1.0	+400	+400	+150	[5]	+10	+50

(1) Retinol equivalents. (2) Micrograms of cholecalciferol. (3) Milligrams alpha-tocopherol equivalents. (4) Niacin equivalents. (5) The use of 30-60 milligrams of supplemental iron is recommended.

Nutritive Value of Food (Calories, Proteins, etc.)

Source: Home and Garden Bulletin No. 72; available from Supt. of Documents, U. S. Government Printing Office, Washington, DC 20402

Food	Measure	Grams	Food Energy (calories)	Protein (grams)	Fat (grams)	Saturated fats (grams)	Carbohydrate (grams)	Calcium (milligrams)	Iron (milligrams)	Vitamin A (I.U.)	Thiamin (milligrams)	Riboflavin (milligrams)
Dairy products												
Cheese, cheddar	1 oz.	28	115	7	9	6.1	T	204	.2	300	.01	.11
Cheese, cottage, small curd	1 cup	210	220	26	9	6.0	6	126	.3	340	.04	.34
Cheese, cream	1 oz.	28	100	2	10	6.2	1	23	.3	400	T	.06
Cheese, Swiss	1 oz.	28	105	8	8	5.0	1	272	T	240	.01	.10
Cheese, pasteurized process spread, American	1 oz.	28	82	5	6	3.8	2	159	.1	220	.01	.12
Half-and-Half	1 tbsp.	15	20	T	2	1.1	1	16	T	20	.01	.02
Cream, sour	1 tbsp.	15	25	T	3	1.6	1	14	T	90	T	.02
Milk, whole	1 cup	244	255	150	8	8	5.1	11	291	.1	310	.09
Milk, nonfat (skim)	1 cup	244	85	8	T	.3	12	302	.1	500	.09	.37
Buttermilk	1 cup	245	100	8	2	1.3	12	285	.1	60	.08	.38
Milkshake, chocolate	10.6 oz.	300	355	9	8	5.0	63	396	.9	260	.14	.67
Ice Cream, hardened	1 cup	133	270	5	14	8.9	32	176	.1	540	.05	.33
Sherbet	1 cup	193	270	2	4	2.4	59	103	.3	190	.03	.09
Yogurt, fruit-flavored	8 oz.	227	230	10	3	1.8	42	343	.2	120	.08	.40
Eggs												
Fried in butter	1	46	85	5	6	2.4	1	26	.9	290	.03	.13
Hard-cooked	1	50	80	6	6	1.7	1	28	1.0	260	.04	.14
Scrambled in butter (milk added)	1	64	95	6	7	2.8	1	47	.9	310	.04	.16
Fats & oils												
Butter	1 tbsp.	14	100	T	12	7.2	T	3	T	430	T	T
Margarine	1 tbsp.	14	100	T	12	2.1	T	3	T	470	T	T
Salad dressing, blue cheese	1 tbsp.	15	75	1	8	1.6	1	12	T	30	T	.02
Salad dressing, French	1 tbsp.	16	65	T	6	1.1	3	2	1	-	-	-
Salad dressing, Italian	1 tbsp.	15	85	T	9	1.6	1	2	T	T	T	T
Mayonnaise	1 tbsp.	14	100	T	11	2.0	T	3	.1	40	T	.01
Meat, poultry, fish												
Bluefish, baked with butter or margarine	3 oz.	85	135	22	4	-	0	25	0.6	40	.09	.08
Clams, raw, meat only	3 oz.	85	65	11	1	-	2	59	5.2	90	.08	.15
Crabmeat, white or king, canned	1 cup	135	135	24	3	.6	1	61	1.1	-	.11	.11
Fish sticks, breaded, cooked, frozen	1 oz.	28	50	5	3	-	2	3	.1	0	.01	.02
Salmon, pink, canned	3 oz.	85	120	17	5	.9	0	167	.7	60	.03	.16
Sardines, Atlantic, canned in oil	3 oz.	85	175	20	9	3.0	0	372	2.5	190	.02	.17
Shrimp, French fried	3 oz.	85	190	17	9	2.3	9	61	1.7	-	.03	.07
Tuna, canned in oil	3 oz.	85	170	24	7	1.7	0	7	1.6	70	.04	.10
Bacon, broiled or fried crisp	2 slices	15	85	4	8	2.5	T	2	.5	0	.08	.05
Ground beef, broiled, 10% fat	3 oz.	85	185	23	10	4.0	0	10	3.0	20	.08	.20
Roast beef, relatively lean	3 oz.	85	165	25	7	2.8	0	11	3.2	10	.06	.19
Beef steak, lean and fat	3 oz.	85	330	20	27	11.3	0	9	2.5	50	.05	.15
Beef & vegetable stew	1 cup	245	220	16	11	4.9	15	29	2.9	2,400	.15	.17
Lamb, chop, lean and fat	3.1 oz.	89	360	18	32	14.8	0	8	1.0	-	.11	.19
Liver, beef	3 oz.	85	195	22	9	2.5	5	9	7.5	45,390	.22	3.56
Ham, light cure, lean and fat	3 oz.	85	245	18	19	6.8	0	8	2.2	0	.40	.15
Pork, chop, lean and fat	2.7 oz.	78	305	19	25	8.9	0	9	2.7	0	.75	.22
Bologna	1 slice	28	85	3	8	3.0	T	2	.5	-	.05	.06
Frankfurter, cooked	1	56	170	7	15	5.6	1	3	.8	-	.08	.11
Sausage, pork link, cooked	1 link	13	60	2	6	2.1	T	1	.3	0	.10	.04
Veal, cutlet, braised or boiled	3 oz.	85	185	23	9	4.0	0	9	2.7	-	.06	.21
Chicken, drumstick, fried, bones removed	1.3 oz.	38	90	12	4	1.1	T	6	.9	50	.03	.15
Chicken, half broiler, broiled, bones removed	6.2 oz.	176	240	42	7	2.2	0	16	3.0	160	.09	.34
Chicken a la king	1 cup	245	470	27	34	12.7	12	127	2.5	1,130	.10	.42
Chicken potpie, baked, 1/3 of 9 in. diam. pie	1 piece	232	545	23	31	11.3	42	70	3.0	3,090	.34	.31
Fruits & products												
Apple, 2-3/4 in. diam.	1	138	80	T	1	-	20	10	.4	120	.04	.03
Applejuice	1 cup	248	120	T	T	-	30	15	1.5	-	.02	.05
Applesauce, canned, sweetened	1 cup	255	230	1	T	-	61	10	1.3	100	.05	.03
Apricots, raw	3	107	55	1	T	-	14	18	.5	2,890	.03	.04
Banana, raw	1	119	100	1	T	-	26	10	.8	230	.06	.07
Cherries, sweet, raw	10	68	45	1	T	-	12	15	.3	70	.03	.04
Fruit cocktail, canned, in heavy syrup	1 cup	255	195	1	T	-	50	23	1.0	360	.05	.03
Grapefruit, raw, medium, white	1/2	241	45	1	T	-	12	19	.5	10	.05	.02
Grapes, Thompson seedless	10	50	35	T	T	-	9	6	.2	50	.03	.02
Lemonade, frozen, diluted	1 cup	248	105	T	T	-	28	2	.1	10	.01	.02
Cantaloupe, 5-in. diam.	1/2	477	80	2	T	-	20	38	1.1	9,240	.11	.08
Orange, 2-5/8 in. diam.	1	131	65	1	T	-	16	54	.5	260	.13	.05
Orange juice, frozen, diluted	1 cup	249	120	2	T	-	29	25	.2	540	.23	.03
Peach, raw, 2-1/2 in. diam.	1	100	40	1	T	-	10	9	.5	1,330	.02	.05
Peaches, canned in syrup	1 cup	256	200	1	T	-	51	10	.8	1,100	.03	.05
Pear, raw, Bartlett, 2-1/2 in. diam.	1	164	100	1	1	-	25	13	.5	30	.03	.07
Pineapple, heavy syrup pack, crushed, chunks	1 cup	255	190	1	T	-	49	28	.8	130	.20	.05
Raisins, seedless	1 cup	145	420	4	T	-	112	90	5.1	30	.16	.12
Strawberries, whole	1 cup	149	55	1	1	-	13	31	1.5	90	.04	.10
Watermelon, 4 by 8 in. wedge	1 wedge	926	110	2	1	-	27	30	2.1	2,510	.13	.13
Grain products												
Bagel, egg	1	55	165	6	2	.5	28	9	1.2	30	.14	.10
Biscuit, 2 in. diam., from home recipe	1	28	105	2	5	1.2	13	34	.4	T	.08	.08
Bread, raisin	1 slice	25	65	2	1	.2	13	18	.6	T	.09	.06
Bread, white, enriched, soft-crumb	1 slice	25	70	2	1	.2	13	21	.6	T	.10	.06
Bread, whole wheat, soft-crumb	1 slice	28	65	3	1	.1	14	24	.8	T	.09	.03
Oatmeal or rolled oats	1 cup	240	130	5	2	.4	23	22	1.4	0	.19	.05
Bran flakes (40% bran), added sugar, salt, iron, vitamins	1 cup	35	105	4	1	-	28	19	12.4	1,650	.41	.49
Corn flakes, added sugar, salt, iron, vitamins	1 cup	25	95	2	T	-	21	•	0.6	1,180	.29	.35
Rice, puffed, added iron, thiamin, niacin	1 cup	15	60	1	T	-	13	3	.3	0	.07	.01

(continued)

(continued)

Food	Measure	Grams	Food Energy (calories)	Protein (grams)	Fat (grams)	Saturated fats (grams)	Carbohydrate (grams)	Calcium (milligrams)	Iron (milligrams)	Vitamin A (I.U.)	Thiamin (milligrams)	Riboflavin (milligrams)
Wheat, shredded, plain, 1 biscuit or 1/2 cup	1 serving	25	90	2	1	-	20	11	.9	0	.06	.03
Cake, angel food, 1/12 of cake	1	53	135	3	T	-	32	50	.2	0	.03	.08
Coffeecake, 1/6 cake	1	72	230	5	7	2.0	38	44	1.2	120	.14	.15
Cupcake, 2-1/2 in. diam., with chocolate icing	1	36	130	2	5	2.0	21	47	.4	60	.05	.06
Boston cream pie with custard filling, 1/12 of cake	1	69	210	3	6	1.9	34	46	.7	140	.09	.11
Fruitcake, dark, 1/30 of loaf	1	15	55	1	2	.5	9	11	.4	20	.02	.02
Cake, pound, 1/17 of loaf	1	33	160	2	10	2.5	16	6	.5	80	.05	.06
Brownies, with nuts, from commercial recipe	1	20	85	1	4	.9	13	9	.4	20	.03	.02
Cookies, chocolate chip, from home recipe	4	40	205	2	12	3.5	24	14	.8	40	.06	.06
Vanilla wafers	10	40	185	2	6	-	30	16	.6	50	.10	.09
Crackers, graham	2	14	55	1	1	.3	10	6	.5	0	.02	.08
Crackers, saltines	4	11	50	1	1	.3	8	2	.5	0	.05	.05
Danish pastry, round piece	1	65	275	5	15	4.7	30	33	1.2	200	.18	.19
Doughnut, cake type	1	25	100	1	5	1.2	13	10	.4	20	.05	.05
Macaroni and cheese, from home recipe	1 cup	200	430	17	22	8.9	40	362	1.8	860	.20	.40
Muffin, corn	1	40	125	3	4	1.2	19	42	.7	120	.10	.10
Noodles, enriched, cooked	1 cup	160	200	7	2	-	37	16	1.4	110	.22	.13
Pancake, plain, from home recipe	1	27	60	2	2	.5	9	27	.4	30	.06	.07
Pie, apple, 1/7 of pie	1	135	345	3	15	3.9	51	11	.9	40	.15	.11
Pie, banana cream, 1/7 of pie	1	130	285	6	12	3.8	40	86	1.0	330	.11	.22
Pie, cherry, 1/7 of pie	1	135	350	4	15	4.0	52	19	.9	590	.16	.12
Pie, lemon meringue, 1/7 of pie	1	120	305	4	12	3.7	45	17	1.0	200	.09	.12
Pie, pecan, 1/7 of pie	1	118	495	6	27	4.0	61	55	3.7	190	.26	.14
Pie, pumpkin, 1/7 of pie	1	130	275	5	15	5.4	32	66	1.0	3,210	.11	.18
Pizza, cheese, 1/8 of 12 in. diam. pie	1	60	145	6	4	1.7	22	86	1.1	230	.16	.18
Popcorn, popped, plain	1 cup	6	25	1	T	T	5	1	.2	-	-	.01
Pretzels, stick	10	3	10	T	T	-	2	1	T	0	.01	.01
Rice, white, enriched, instant, cooked	1 cup	165	180	4	T	T	40	5	1.3	0	.21	*
Rolls, enriched, brown & serve	1	26	85	2	2	.4	14	20	.5	T	.10	.06
Rolls, frankfurter & hamburger	1	40	120	3	2	.5	21	30	.8	T	.16	.10
Spaghetti with meat balls & tomato sauce, from home recipe	1 cup	248	330	19	12	3.3	39	124	3.7	1,590	.25	.30
Legumes, nuts, seeds												
Beans, Great Northern, cooked	1 cup	180	210	14	1	-	38	90	4.9	0	.25	.13
Peanuts, roasted in oil, salted	1 cup	144	840	37	72	13.7	27	107	3.0	-	.46	.19
Peanut butter	1 tbsp.	16	95	4	8	1.5	3	9	.3	-	.02	.02
Sunflower seeds	1 cup	145	810	35	69	8.2	29	174	10.3	70	2.84	.33
Sugars & sweets												
Candy, caramels	1 oz.	28	115	1	3	1.6	22	42	.4	T	.01	.05
Candy, milk chocolate	1 oz.	28	145	2	9	5.5	16	65	.3	80	.02	.10
Fudge, chocolate	1 oz.	28	115	1	3	1.3	21	22	.3	T	.01	.03
Candy, hard	1 oz.	28	110	0	T	-	28	6	.5	0	0	0
Honey	1 tbsp.	21	65	T	0	0	17	1	.1	0	T	.01
Jams & Preserves	1 tbsp.	20	55	T	T	-	14	4	.2	T	T	.01
Sugar, white, granulated	1 tbsp.	12	45	0	0	-	12	0	T	0	0	0
Vegetables												
Asparagus, canned, spears	4 spears	80	15	2	T	-	3	15	1.5	640	.05	.08
Beans, lima, thick-seeded	1 cup	170	170	10	T	-	32	34	2.9	390	.12	.09
Beans, green, from frozen, cuts	1 cup	135	35	2	T	-	8	54	.9	780	.09	.12
Beets, canned, diced or sliced	1 cup	170	65	2	T	-	15	32	1.2	30	.02	.05
Broccoli, cooked	1 stalk	180	45	6	1	-	8	158	1.4	4,500	.16	.36
Cabbage, raw, coarsely shredded or sliced	1 cup	70	15	1	T	-	4	34	.3	90	.04	.04
Carrots, raw, 7-1/2 by 1-1/8 in.	1	72	30	1	T	-	7	27	.5	7,930	.04	.04
Cauliflower, raw	1 cup	115	31	3	T	-	6	29	1.3	70	.13	.12
Celery, raw	1 stalk	40	5	T	T	-	2	16	.1	110	.01	.01
Collards, cooked	1 cup	190	65	7	1	-	10	357	1.5	14,820	.21	.38
Corn, sweet, cooked	1 ear	140	70	2	1	-	16	2	.5	310	.09	.08
Corn, cream style	1 cup	256	210	5	2	-	51	8	1.5	840	.08	.13
Cucumber, with peel	6-8 slices	28	5	T	T	-	1	7	.3	70	.01	.01
Lettuce, Iceberg, chopped	1 cup	55	5	T	T	-	2	11	.3	180	.03	.03
Mushrooms, raw	1 cup	70	20	2	T	-	3	4	.6	T	.07	.32
Onions, raw, chopped	1 cup	170	65	3	T	-	15	46	.9	T	.05	.07
Peas, frozen, cooked	1 cup	160	110	8	T	-	19	30	3.0	960	.43	.14
Potatoes, baked, peeled	1	156	145	4	T	-	33	14	1.1	T	.15	.07
Potatoes, frozen, French fried	10	50	110	2	4	1.1	17	5	.9	T	.07	.01
Potatoes, mashed, milk added	1 cup	210	135	4	2	.7	27	50	.8	40	.17	.11
Potato chips	10	20	115	1	8	2.1	10	8	.4	T	.04	.01
Potato salad	1 cup	250	250	7	7	2.0	41	80	1.5	350	.20	.18
Sauerkraut, canned	1 cup	235	40	2	T	-	9	85	1.2	120	.07	.09
Spinach, chopped, from frozen	1 cup	205	45	6	1	-	8	232	4.3	16,200	.14	.31
Squash, summer, cooked	1 cup	210	30	2	T	-	7	53	.8	820	.11	.17
Sweet potatoes, baked in skin, peeled	1	114	160	2	1	-	37	46	1.0	9,230	.10	.08
Tomatoes, raw	1	135	25	1	T	-	6	16	.6	1,110	.07	.05
Tomato catsup	1 tbsp.	15	15	T	T	-	4	3	.1	210	.01	.01
Tomato juice	1 cup	243	45	2	T	-	10	17	2.2	1,940	.12	.07
Miscellaneous												
Beer	12 fl. oz.	360	150	1	0	0	14	18	T	-	.01	.11
Gin, rum, vodka, whisky, 86 proof	1-1/2 fl. oz.	42	105	-	0	0	0	-	-	-	-	-
Wine, table	3-1/2 fl. oz.	102	85	T	0	0	4	9	.4	-	T	.01
Cola-type beverage	12 fl. oz.	369	145	0	0	0	37	-	-	0	0	0
Ginger ale	12 fl. oz	366	115	0	0	0	29	-	-	0	0	0
Gelatin dessert	1 cup	240	140	4	0	0	34	-	-	-	-	-
Mustard, prepared	1 tsp.	5	5	T	T	-	T	4	.1	-	-	-
Olives, pickled, green	4 medium	16	15	T	2	.2	T	8	.2	40	-	-
Pickles, dill, whole	1	65	5	T	T	-	1	17	.7	70	T	.01
Popsicle, 3 fl. oz.	1	95	70	0	0	0	18	0	T	0	0	0
Soup, cream of chicken, prepared with milk	1 cup	245	180	7	10	4.2	15	172	.5	610	.05	.27
Soup, cream of mushroom, prepared with milk	1 cup	245	215	7	14	5.4	16	191	.5	250	.05	.34
Soup, tomato, prepared with water	1 cup	245	90	2	3	.5	16	15	.7	1,000	.05	.05

T — Indicates trace   * — Varies by brand

Birthstones

Source: Jewelry Industry Council

Month	Ancient	Modern	Month	Ancient	Modern
January	Garnet	Garnet	July	Onyx	Ruby
February	Amethyst	Amethyst	August	Carnelian	Sardonyx or Peridot
March	Jasper	Bloodstone or Aquamarine	September	Chrysolite	Sapphire
April	Sapphire	Diamond	October	Aquamarine	Opal or Tourmaline
May	Agate	Emerald	November	Topaz	Topaz
June	Emerald	Pearl, Moonstone, or Alexandrite	December	Ruby	Turquoise or Zircon

Wedding Anniversaries

The traditional names for wedding anniversaries go back many years in social usage. As such names as wooden, crystal, silver, and golden were applied it was considered proper to present the married pair with gifts made of these products or of something related. The list of traditional gifts, with a few allowable revisions in parentheses, is presented below, followed by modern gifts in bold face.

1st-Paper, **clocks**
2d-Cotton, **china**
3d-Leather, **crystal & glass**
4th-Linen (silk), **electrical appliances**
5th-Wood, **silverware**
6th-Iron, **wood**
7th-Wool (copper), **desk sets**
8th-Bronze, **linens & lace**
9th-Pottery (china), **leather**

10th-Tin (aluminum), **diamond jewelry**
11th-Steel, **fashion jewelry, accessories**
12th-Silk, **pearls or colored gems**
13th-Lace, **textiles & furs**
14th-Ivory, **gold jewelry**
15th-Crystal, **watches**
20th-China, **platinum**
25th-Silver, **sterling silver jubliee**

30th-Pearl, **diamond**
35th-Coral (jade), **jade**
40th-Ruby, **ruby**
45th-Sapphire, **sapphire**
50th-Gold, **gold**
55th-Emerald, **emerald**
60th-Diamond, **diamond**

Canadian Marriage Information

Source: Compiled from information provided by the various provincial government departments and agencies concerned.

Marriageable age, by provinces, for both males and females with and without consent of parents or guardians. In some provinces, the court has authority, given special circumstances, to marry young couples below the minimum age. Most provinces waive the blood test requirement and the waiting period varies across the provinces.

Province	With consent		Without consent		Blood test other province		Wait for license	Wait after license
	Men	Women	Men	Women	Required	Accepted		
Newfoundland	16	16	19	19	None	None	4 days	4 days
Prince Edward Island	16	16	18	18	Yes	Yes	5 days	None
Nova Scotia	(1)	(1)	19	19	None	None	5 days	None
New Brunswick	(10)	(10)	18	18	None	None	5 days	None
Quebec	14	12	18	18	None	—	—	None
Ontario	16	16	18	18	None	—	None²	3 days
Manitoba	16	16	18	18	None	None	None	24 hours
Saskatchewan	16	16	18	18	None	None	None	24 hours
Alberta	16⁸	16⁹	18	18	Yes³	Yes⁴	None⁵	None
British Columbia	16⁶	16⁶	19	19	None	None	2 days⁷	None
Yukon Territory	15	15	19	19	None	None	None	24 hours
Northwest Territories	15	15⁹	19	19	None	None	None	None

(1) There is no statutory minimum age in the province. Anyone under the age of 19 years must have consent for marriage and no person under the age of 16 may be married without authorization of a Family Court judge and in addition must have the necessary consent of the parent or guardian. (2) Special requirements applicable to nonresidents. (3) Applies only to applicants under 60 years of age. (4) This is upon filing of negative lab report indicating blood test was taken within 14 days preceding date of application for license. (5) Exception where consent is required by mail; depending receipt of divorce documents, etc. (6) Persons under 16 years of age (no minimum age specified) may also be married if they have obtained, in addition to the usual consent from parents or guardian, an order from a judge of the Supreme or County Court in this province. (7) Including day of application, e.g., a license applied for on a Monday cannot be issued until Wednesday. (8) Under 16 allowed if pregnant or the mother of a living child. (9) Under 15 allowed if pregnant or with the written permission of the Commissioner of the NWT. (10) There is no statutory minimum age in New Brunswick; anyone under age 18 must have consent for marriage and no person under 16 may be married without authorization of a Family Court judge in adddition to the consent of a parent or guardian.

Grounds for Divorce in Canada

Source: Government of Canada Divorce Act

The grounds for divorce in Canada are the same for all the provinces and its territories. There are two categories of offense:

A. Marital Offense:
Adultery
Sodomy
Bestiality
Rape
Homosexual act
Subsequent marriage
Physical cruelty
Mental cruelty

B. Marriage breakdown by reason of:
Imprisonment for aggregate period of not less than 3 years
Imprisonment for not less than 2 years on sentence of death or sentence of 10 years or more
Addiction to alcohol
Addiction to narcotics
Whereabouts of spouse unknown
Non-consummation
Separation for not less than 3 years
Desertion by petitioner for not less than 5 years

Residence time: Domicile in Canada. Time between interlocutory and final decree: normally 3 months before final can be applied for.

Marriage Information

Source: Compiled from individual states.

Marriageable age, by states, for both males and females with and without consent of parents or guardians. In most states, the court has authority to marry young couples below the ordinary age of consent, where due regard for their morals and welfare so requires. In many states, under special circumstances, blood test and waiting period may be waived.

State	With consent		Without consent		Blood test*		Wait for	Wait after
	Men	Women	Men	Women	Required	Other state accepted	license	license
Alabama(b)	14	14	18	18	Yes	Yes	none	none
Alaska	16(m)	16(m)	18	18	No	No	3 days	none
Arizona	16(g)	16	18	18	Yes	Yes	none	none
Arkansas	17	16(h)	18	18	Yes	No	3 days	none
California	18(g)	18	18	18	Yes	Yes	none	none
Colorado	16	16	18	18	Yes	...	none	none
Connecticut	16	16(j)	18	18	Yes	Yes	4 days	none
Delaware	18	16(k)	18	18	No	No	none	24 hrs. (c)
District of Columbia	16	16	18	18	Yes	Yes	3 days	none
Florida	17	17	18	18	Yes	No	none	none
Georgia	16(g)	16(g)	18	18	Yes	Yes	none (k)	none
Hawaii	16	16	18	18	Yes	Yes	none	none
Idaho	16	16	18	18	No	No	none	none
Illinois (a)	16	16	18	18	Yes	Yes	none	1 day
Indiana	17(k)	17(k)	18	18	Yes	No	72 hours	none
Iowa	— (k)	— (k)	18	18	No	Yes	3 days	none
Kansas	— (k)	— (k)	18	18	No	No	3 days	none
Kentucky	— (k)	— (k)	18	18	Yes	No	3 days	none
Louisiana (a)	18(k)	16(h)	18	16	Yes	No	none	72 hours
Maine	16(h)	16(h)	18	18	No	No	5 days	none
Maryland	16	16	18	18	none	none	48 hours	none
Massachusetts	— (k)	— (k)	18	18	Yes	Yes	3 days	none
Michigan (a)	16	16	18	18	Yes	No	3 days	none
Minnesota	16(e)	16(e)	18	18	none	...	5 days	none
Mississippi (b)	17(l)	15(l)	21	21	Yes	...	3 days	none
Missouri	15	15	18	18	none	Yes	3 days	none
Montana	15	15	18	18	Yes	Yes	none	3 days
Nebraska	17	17	18	18	Yes	Yes	2 days	none
Nevada	16(h)	16(h)	18	18	none	none	none	none
New Hampshire (a)	14(e)	13(e)	18	18	No	No	3 days	none
New Jersey (a)	16(g)	16(g)	18	18	Yes	Yes	72 hours	none
New Mexico	16	16	18	18	Yes	Yes	none	none
New York	16	14(e)	18	18	Yes	No	none	24 hrs.(f)
North Carolina (a)	16	16	18	18	Yes	No	none	none
North Dakota (a)	16	16	18	18	Yes	...	none	none
Ohio (a)	18	16	18	18	Yes	Yes	5 days	none
Oklahoma	16	16	18	18	Yes	No	none	none
Oregon	17	17	18	18	Yes	No	3 days	none
Pennsylvania	16	16	18	18	Yes	No	3 days	none
Rhode Island (a) (b)	14	12	18	18	Yes	Yes	none	none
South Carolina	16	14	18	18	none	none	24 hrs.	none
South Dakota	16	16	18	18	No	No	none	none
Tennessee (b)	16	16	18	18	Yes	Yes	3 days	none
Texas	14(k)	14(k)	18	18	Yes	Yes	none	none
Utah	14	14	18	18	none	none	none	none
Vermont (a)	16	16	18	18	Yes	...	none	5 days
Virginia (a)	16	16	18	18	No	No	none	none
Washington	17	17	18	18	(d)	...	3 days	none
West Virginia	18	16	18	18	Yes	No	3 days	none
Wisconsin	16	16	18	18	Yes	Yes	5 days	none
Wyoming	16	16	19	19	Yes	Yes	none	none
Puerto Rico	18	16	21	21	Yes	none	none	none
Virgin Islands	16	14	18	18	none	none	8 days	none

*Many states have additional special requirements; contact individual state. (a) Special laws applicable to non-residents. (b) Special laws applicable to those under 21 years; Ala., bond required if male is under 18, female under 18. (c) 24 hours if one or both parties resident of state; 96 hours if both parties are non-residents. (d) None, but both must file affidavit. (e) Parental consent plus court's consent required. (f) As of 8/85, there is a bill on the Governor of New York's desk that would eliminate the premarital exam and reduce the 3-day waiting period to 24 hours, if passed. (g) Statute provides for obtaining license with parental or court consent with no state minimum age. (h) Under 16, with parental and court consent. (i) If either under 18, wait 3 full days. (j) If under stated age, court consent required. (k) If under 18, parental and/or court consent required. (l) Both parents' consent required for men age 17, women age 15; one parent's consent required for men 18-20 years, women ages 16-20 years. (m) Parental and court consent required if 14 or over, but under 16.

How to Obtain Birth, Marriage, Death Records

The United States government has published a series of inexpensive booklets entitled: Where to Write for Birth & Death Records; Where to Write for Marriage Records; Where to Write for Divorce Records; Where to Write for Birth and Death Records of U. S. Citizens Who were Born or Died Outside of the U. S.; Birth Certifications for Alien Children Adopted by U. S. Citizens; You May Save Time Proving Your Age and Other Birth Facts. They tell where to write to get a certified copy of an original vital record. Supt. of Documents, Government Printing Office, Washington, DC 20402.

Grounds for Divorce

Source: Compiled from individual states.

Persons contemplating divorce should study latest decisions or secure legal advice before initiating proceedings since different interpretations or exceptions in each case can change the conclusion reached.

State	Breakdown of marriage/ incompatibility	Cruelty	Desertion	Non-support	Alcohol &/or drug addiction	Felony	Impotency	Insanity[1]	Living separate and apart	Other grounds	Residence time	Time between interlocut'y and final decrees
Alabama	X	X	X	X	X	X	X	X	2 yrs.	A-B-E	6 mos.	none-M
Alaska	X	X	X	...	X	X	X	X		B-C-F	none	none
Arizona	X										90 days	none
Arkansas	...	X	X	X	X	X	X	X	3 yrs.	C-I	3 mos.	none
California[2]	X							X			6 mos.	6 mos.
Colorado[2]	X										90 days	none
Connecticut	X	X	X	X	X	X	X		18 mos.	B	1 yr.	none
Delaware	X[4]								6 mos.		6 mos.	none
Dist. of Columbia	...								6 mos.-1 yr.		6 mos.	none
Florida	X							X			6 mos.	none
Georgia	X	X	X		X	X	X	X		A-B-F	6 mos.	L
Hawaii	X								2 yrs.	K	3 mos.	none
Idaho	X	X	X	X	X	X		X	5 yrs.	H	6 wks.	none
Illinois	...	X	X		X	X	X			I-J	90 days	none
Indiana	X					X	X	X			6 mos.	none
Iowa	X										1 yr.	none-N
Kansas	X									H	60 days	none
Kentucky	X										180 days	none
Louisiana	...	X	X	X	X	X		X	1 yr.	C-J-K	12 mos.	none-N
Maine	X	X	X	X	X	X		X		H	6 mos.	none
Maryland	...	X	X			X	X	X	1-3 yrs.	D-I	1 yr.	none
Massachusetts	X	X	X	X	X	X	X		6 mos.-1 yr.		1 yr.	90 days
Michigan	X										180 days	none
Minnesota	X									K	180 days	none-O
Mississippi	X	X	X		X	X	X	X		A	6 mos.	none-P
Missouri	X[4]										90 days	none
Montana	X										90 days	none
Nebraska	X										1 yr.	6 mos.
Nevada	X							X	1 yr.		6 wks.	none
New Hampshire[3]	X	X	X		X	X		X	2 yrs.	K	1 yr.	none
New Jersey		X	X		X	X		X	18 mos.	E-K	1 yr.	none
New Mexico	X	X	X								6 mos.	none
New York	...					X			1 yr.	K	1 yr.	none
North Carolina	...						X	X	1 yr.	A-E	6 mos.	none
North Dakota	X	X	X	X	X	X	X	X		H-K	12 mos.	none
Ohio	X	X	X	X	X	X	X	X	2 yrs.	B-G-H-I	6 mos.	none
Oklahoma	X	X	X	X	X	X	X	X		A-B-G-H	6 mos.	none
Oregon[2]	X									B	6 mos.	30 days
Pennsylvania	X	X	X		X	X	X	X	3 yrs.	C-D-I	6 mos.	none
Rhode Island	X	X	X	X	X	X		X	3 yrs.		1 yr.	3 mos.
South Carolina	X	X	X	X	X				1 yr.		3 mos.	none
South Dakota	X	X	X	X	X						none	none
Tennessee	X	X	X	X	X	X				A-H-I-J-K	6 mos.	none
Texas	...	X	X	X	X	X	X		3 yrs.		6 mos.	none-O
Utah	...	X	X	X	X	X	X			K	3 mos.	3 mos.
Vermont	...	X	X	X		X		X	6 mos.		6 mos.	3 mos.
Virginia	...	X	X			X			6 mos.-1 yr.	E	6 mos.	none-P
Washington	X										none	none-R
West Virginia	X	X	X		X	X		X	1 yr.	U	1 yr.	none
Wisconsin	X							1	yr.	K	6 mos.	none-O
Wyoming	X							X	2 yrs.		60 days	none

Adultery is either grounds for divorce or evidence of irreconcilable differences and a breakdown of the marriage in all states. The plaintiff can invariably remarry in the same state where he or she procured a decree of divorce or annulment. Not so the defendant, who is barred in certain states for some offenses. After a period of time has elapsed even the offender can apply for permission.

(1) Generally 5 yrs. insanity but: permanent insanity in Ut.; incurable insanity in Col.; 1 yr. Wis.; 18 mos. Alas.; 2 yrs. Ga., Ha., Ind., Nev., N.J., Ore., Wash., Wy.; 3 yrs. Ark., Cal., Fla., Md., Minn., Miss., N.C., Tex., W. Va.; 6 yrs. Ida.; Kan: Incompability by reason of mental illness or incapacity. (2) Cal., Colo., and Ore., have procedures whereby a couple can obtain a divorce without an attorney and without appearing in court provided certain requirements are met. (3) Other grounds existing only in N.H. are: Joining a religious order disbelieving in marriage, treatment which injures health or endangers reason, wife without the state for 10 years, and wife in state 2 yrs. husband never in state and intends to become a citizen of a foreign country. (4) Provable only by fault grounds, separation for some period, generally a year, proof of marital discord or commitment for mental illness. (A) Pregnancy at marriage. (B) Fraudulent contract. (C) Indignities. (D) Consanguinity. (E) Crime against nature. (F) Mental incapacity at time of marriage. (G) Procurement of out-of-state divorce. (H) Gross neglect of duty. (I) Bigamy. (J) Attempted homicide. (K) Separation by decree in Conn.; after decree: one yr. in La., N.Y., Wis.; 18 mos. in N.H.; 2 yrs. in Ala., Ha., Minn., N.C. Tenn.; 3 yrs. in Ut.; 4 yrs. in N.J., N.D.; 5 yrs. in Md. (L) Determined by court order. (M) 60 days to remarry. (N) One yr. to remarry except Ha. one yr. with minor child; La. 90 days. (O) 6 mos. to remarry. (P) Adultery cases, remarriage in court's discretion. (Q) Plaintiff, 6 mos.; defendant 2 yrs. to remarry. (R) No remarriage if an appeal is pending. (S) Actual domicile in adultery cases. (U) Abuse and neglect of child; physical or mental injury to child. **Enoch Arden Laws.** disappearance and unknown to be alive - Conn., S.C., Va., Vt., 7 yrs. absence, Ala., Ark., N.Y. 5 yrs. (called dissolution); N.H. 2 yrs.

Note: Grounds not recognized for divorce may be recognized for separation or annulment. Local laws should be consulted.

Heart and Blood Vessel Disease

Warning Signs

Source: American Heart Association

Of Heart Attack
- Prolonged, oppressive pain or unusual discomfort in the center of the chest
- Pain may radiate to the shoulder, arm, neck or jaw
- Sweating may accompany pain or discomfort
- Nausea and vomiting may also occur
- Shortness of breath may accompany other signs

The American Heart Association advises immediate action at the onset of these symptoms. The Association points out that over half of heart attack victims die before they reach the hospital and that the average victim waits 3 hours before seeking help.

Of Stroke
- Sudden temporary weakness or numbness of face or limbs on one side of the body
- Temporary loss of speech, or trouble speaking or understanding speech
- Temporary dimness or loss of vision, particularly in one eye
- An episode of double vision
- Unexplained dizziness or unsteadiness
- Change in personality, mental ability
- New or unusual pattern of headaches

Major Risk Factors

Blood pressure—High blood pressure increases the risk of stroke, heart attack, kidney failure and congestive heart failure.

Cholesterol—More than 50% of middle-aged Americans have cholesterol levels of 200 milligrams per deciliter of blood, a level at which the risk of coronary heart disease begins to rise sharply.

Cigarettes—Cigarette smokers have more than twice the risk of heart atttacks than non-smokers. Young smokers have a higher risk for early death due to stroke.

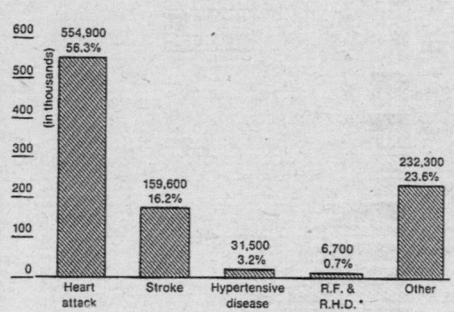

U.S. DEATHS DUE TO CARDIOVASCULAR DISEASES BY MAJOR TYPE OF DISORDER, 1982

* Rheumatic Fever and Rheumatic Heart Disease
Source: National Center for Health Statistics,
U.S. Department of Health and Human Services

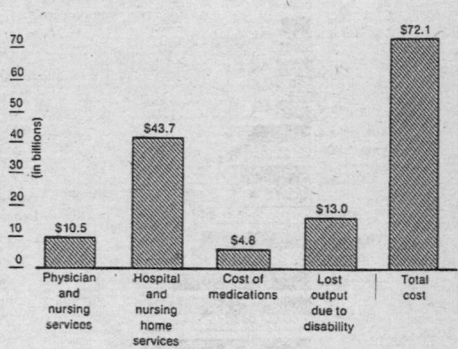

ESTIMATED ECONOMIC COSTS IN BILLIONS OF DOLLARS OF CARDIOVASCULAR DISEASES BY TYPE OF EXPENDITURE, 1985

Source: American Heart Association, Dallas, Texas

Cardiovascular Disease Statistical Summary

Cost — $72.1 billion (AHA est.) in 1985.

Prevalence — 43,500,000 Americans have one or more forms of heart and blood vessel disease.
- hypertension — 37,990,000 (more than one in 5 adults).
- coronary heart disease — 4,670,000.
- rheumatic heart disease — 2,040,000.
- stroke — 1,900,000.

Mortality — 985,040 in 1982 (nearly 50% of all deaths).
- nearly one-fifth of all persons killed by CVD are under age 65.

Congenital or inborn heart defects — 35 recognizable types of defects.
- about 25,000 babies are born every year with heart defects.
- post-natal mortality from heart defects was estimated to be 6,600 in 1982.

Heart attack — caused 554,900 deaths in 1982.

- 4,670,000 alive today have history of heart attack and/or angina pectoris.
- 350,000 a year die of heart attack before they reach hospital.
- As many as 1,500,000 Americans will have a heart attack this year and about 550,000 of them will die.

Stroke — killed 159,600 in 1982; afflicts 1,900,000.

CCU — most of the over 6,000 general hospitals in U.S. have coronary care capability.

Hypertension (high blood pressure) — 37,990,000 adults.
- easily detected and usually controllable, but only a minority have it under adequate control.

Rheumatic heart disease — 100,000 children; 1,910,000 adults.
- killed about 6,700 in 1982.

Note: 1982 mortality data are estimates based on 1982 provisional data as published by USDHHS.

Cancer Information

Source: American Cancer Society

Cancer Warnings

Site	Warning signal— see your doctor	Comment
Breast	Lump or thickening in the breast, or unusual discharge from nipple.	The leading cause of cancer death in women.
Colon and rectum	Change in bowel habits; bleeding.	Considered a highly curable disease when digital and proctoscopic examinations are included in routine checkups.
Lung	Persistent cough, or lingering respiratory ailment.	The leading cause of cancer death among men and rising mortality among women.
Oral (including pharynx)	Sore that does not heal; difficulty in swallowing.	Many more lives should be saved because the mouth is easily accessible to visual examination by physicians and dentists.
Skin	Sore that does not heal, or change in wart or mole.	Skin cancer is readily detected by observation, and diagnosed by simple biopsy.
Uterus	Unusual bleeding or discharge.	Uterine cancer mortality has declined 70% during the last 40 years with wider application of the Pap test. Postmenopausal women with abnormal bleeding should be checked.
Kidney and bladder	Urinary difficulty, bleeding.	Protective measures for workers in high-risk industries are helping to eliminate one of the important causes of these cancers.
Larynx	Hoarseness, difficulty in swallowing.	Readily curable if caught early.
Prostate	Urinary difficulty.	Occurs mainly in men over 60, the disease can be detected by palpation at regular checkup.
Stomach	Indigestion.	An 80% decline in mortality in 50 years, for reasons yet unknown.
Leukemia	Leukemia is a cancer of blood-forming tissues and is characterized by the abnormal production of immature white blood cells. Acute lymphocytic leukemia strikes mainly children and is treated by drugs which have extended life from a few months to as much as 10 years. Chronic leukemia strikes usually after age 25 and progresses less rapidly.	
Lymphomas (including multiple myeloma)	These cancers arise in the lymph system and include Hodgkin's disease and lymphosarcoma. Some patients with lymphatic cancers can lead normal lives for many years. Five-year survival rate for Hodgkin's disease increased from 25% to 54% in 20 years.	

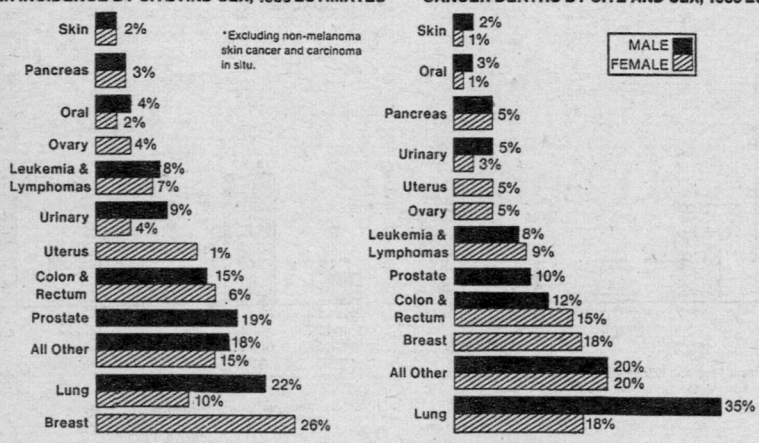

CANCER INCIDENCE BY SITE AND SEX, 1985 ESTIMATES*

*Excluding non-melanoma skin cancer and carcinoma in situ.

Site	Male	Female
Skin	2%	
Pancreas	3%	
Oral	4%	2%
Ovary		4%
Leukemia & Lymphomas	8%	7%
Urinary	9%	4%
Uterus		1%
Colon & Rectum	15%	6%
Prostate	19%	
All Other	18%	15%
Lung	22%	10%
Breast		26%

CANCER DEATHS BY SITE AND SEX, 1985 ESTIMATES

Site	Male	Female
Skin	2%	1%
Oral	3%	1%
Pancreas	5%	
Urinary	5%	3%
Uterus		5%
Ovary		5%
Leukemia & Lymphomas	8%	9%
Prostate	10%	
Colon & Rectum	12%	15%
Breast		18%
All Other	20%	20%
Lung	35%	18%

Basic First Aid

First aid experts stress that knowing what to do for an injured person until a doctor or trained person gets to an accident scene can save a life, especially in cases of stoppage of breath, severe bleeding, and shock.

People with special medical problems, such as diabetes, cardiovascular disease, epilepsy, or allergy, are also urged to wear some sort of emblem identifying it, as a safeguard against use of medication that might be injurious or fatal in an emergency. Emblems may be obtained from Medic Alert Foundation, Turlock, CA 95380.

Most accidents occur in homes. National Safety Council figures show that home accidents annually far outstrip those in other locations, such as in autos, at work, or in public places.

In all cases, get medical assistance as soon as possible.

Animal bites — Wounds should be washed with soap under running water and animal should be caught alive for rabies test.

Asphyxiation — Start mouth-to-mouth resuscitation immediately after getting patient to fresh air.

Bleeding — Elevate the wound above the heart if possible. Press hard on wound with sterile compress until bleeding stops. Send for doctor if it is severe.

Burns — If mild, with skin unbroken and no blisters, plunge into ice water until pain subsides. Apply a dry dressing if necessary. Send for physician if burn is severe. Apply sterile compresses and keep patient quiet and comfortably warm until doctor's arrival. Do not try to clean burn, or to break blisters.

Chemicals in eye — With patient lying down, pour cupfuls

of water immediately into corner of eye, letting it run to other side to remove chemicals thoroughly. Cover with sterile compress. Get medical attention immediately .

Choking — Do not use back slaps to dislodge obstruction. (See Abdominal Thrust)

Convulsions — Place person on back on bed or rug so he can't hurt himself. Loosen clothing. Turn head to side. Do not place a blunt object between the victim's teeth. If convulsions do not stop, get medical attention immediately.

Cuts (minor) — Apply mild antiseptic and sterile compress after washing with soap under warm running water.

Drowning — (See Mouth-to-Mouth Resuscitation) Artificial breathing must be started at once, before victim is out of the water, if possible. If the victim's stomach is bloated with water, put victim on stomach, place hands under stomach, and lift. If no pulse is felt, begin cardiopulmonary resuscitation. This should only be done by those professionally trained. If necessary, treat for shock. (See Shock)

Electric shock — If possible, turn off power. Don't touch victim until contact is broken; pull him from contact with electrical source using rope, wooden pole, or loop of dry cloth. Start mouth-to-mouth resuscitation if breathing has stopped.

Foreign body in eye — Touch object with moistened corner of handkerchief if it can be seen. If it cannot be seen or does not come out after a few attempts, take patient to doctor. Do not rub eye.

Fainting — If victim feels faint, lower head to knees. Lay him down with head turned to side if he becomes unconscious. Loosen clothing and open windows. Keep patient lying quietly for at least 15 minutes after he regains consciousness. Call doctor if faint lasts for more than a few minutes.

Falls — Send for physician if patient has continued pain. Cover wound with sterile dressing and stop any severe bleeding. Do not move patient unless absolutely necessary — as in case of fire — if broken bone is suspected. Keep patient warm and comfortable.

Loss of Limb — If a limb is severed, it is important to properly protect the limb so that it can possibly be reattached to the victim. After the victim is cared for, the limb should be placed in a clean plastic bag, garbage can or other suitable container. Pack ice around the limb on the OUTSIDE of the bag to keep the limb cold. Call ahead to the hospital to alert them of the situation.

Poisoning — Call doctor. Use antidote listed on label if container is found. Call local Poison Control Center if possible. Except for lye, other caustics, and petroleum products, induce vomiting unless victim is unconscious. Give milk if poision or antidote is unknown.

Shock (injury-related) — Keep the victim lying down; if uncertain as to his injuries, keep the victim flat on his back. Maintain the victim's normal body temperature; if the weather is cold or damp, place blankets or extra clothing over and under the victim; if weather is hot, provide shade.

Snakebites — Immediately get victim to a hospital. If there is mild swelling or pain, apply a consticting band 2 to 4 inches above the bite.

Stings from insects — If possible, remove stinger and apply solution of ammonia and water, or paste of baking soda. Call physician if body swells or patient collapses.

Unconsciousness — Send for doctor and place person on his back. Start resuscitation if he stops breathing. Never give food or liquids to an unconscious person.

Abdominal Thrust

The American Red Cross and the American Heart Association both agree that the recommended first aid for choking victims is the abdominal thrust, also known as the Heimlich maneuver, after its creator, Dr. Henry Heimlich. Slaps on the back are no longer advised and may even prove detrimental in an attempt to assist a choking victim.

- Get behind the victim and wrap your arms around him above his waist.
- Make a fist with one hand and place it, with the thumb knuckle pressing inward, just below the point of the "v" of the rib cage.
- Grasp the wrist with the other hand and give one or more upward thrusts or hugs.
- Start mouth-to-mouth resuscitation if breathing stops.

Mouth-to-Mouth Resuscitation

Stressing that your breath can save a life, the American Red Cross gives the following directions for mouth-to-mouth resuscitation if the victim is not breathing:

- Determine consciousness by tapping the victim on the shoulder and asking loudly, "Are you okay?"
- Tilt the victim's head back so that his chin is pointing upward. Do not press on the soft tissue under the chin, as this might obstruct the airway. If you suspect that an accident victim might have neck or back injuries, open the airway by placing the tips of your index and middle fingers on the corners of the victim's jaw to lift it forward without tilting the head.
- Place your cheek and ear close to the victim's mouth and nose. Look at the victim's chest to see if it rises and falls. Listen and feel for air to be exhaled for about 5 seconds.
- If there is no breathing, pinch the victim's nostrils shut with the .thumb and index finger of your hand that is pressing on the victim's forehead. Another way to prevent leakage of air when the lungs are inflated is to press your cheek against the victim's nose.
- Blow air into victim's mouth by taking a deep breath and then sealing your mouth tightly around the victim's mouth. Initially, give four, quick, full breaths without allowing the lungs to deflate completely between each breath.
- Watch the victim's chest to see if it rises.
- Stop blowing when the victim's chest is expanded. Raise your mouth; turn your head to the side and listen for exhalation.
- Watch the chest to see if it falls.
- Repeat the blowing cycle until the victim starts breathing.
  Note: Infants (up to one year) and children (1 to 8 years) should be administered mouth-to-mouth resuscitation as described above, except for the following:
- Do not tilt the head as far back as an adult's head.
- Both the mouth and nose of the infant should be sealed by the mouth.
- Give breaths to a child once every four seconds.
- Blow into the infants's mouth and nose once every three seconds with less pressure and volume than for a child.

Condominiums and Cooperatives

Source: U.S. Dept. of Housing and Urban Development

The condominium and the cooperative are legal forms that permit multiple ownership of a multi-family building or complex. In the United States, each form is defined by the states, so that details of laws governing condominium and cooperative formation and operation vary from place to place.

Condominium: a housing unit in a multi-family building or complex owned by an individual, who also owns a partial interest in the common areas of the building or complex.

Cooperative: a nonprofit housing corporation in which individual households own shares entitling them to live in a particular unit in a multi-family building or complex and to use the common areas and facilities of the building or complex.

Mortgages: New Alternatives to the Long-term Fixed-rate Loan

Source: Federal Home Loan Bank Board

Until quite recently the only type mortgage generally available in most parts of the country was the long-term fixed-rate mortgage. This mortgage had identical monthly payments and a term of 25 to 30 years. In the past several years, new mortgage forms have been developed, which have more flexible payment schedules and/or adjustable interest rates. These mortgages are described below.

Graduated-Payment Mortgage:

The graduated-payment mortgage (GPM) has a fixed interest rate, but the payments start out at a lower level than on a fixed-rate mortgage. The payments on a GPM increase at a known rate during the early years of the loan. On the most popular GPM plan, the payments increase at 7½ percent each year for the first 5 years of the loan. Payments on a GPM ultimately rise to a level higher than on a comparable fixed-payment mortgage.

Because the payments on a GPM start out at a low level, they may be insufficient to pay all the interest owed. That portion of the monthly interest in excess of the monthly payment is added to the loan balance. The outstanding balance on most GPM's actually increases for the first several years. This addition to the loan balance is called negative amortization.

A GPM is advantageous for a first-time homeowner who cannot, at the outset, handle the payments of a conventional loan, but hopes to be able to when his income rises.

Pledged-Account Mortgage:

The pledged-account mortgage (PAM) is a special type of GPM. On most GPM plans the low initial payments are insufficient to pay all the interest owed. On a PAM, that portion of the interest due that is not covered by the monthly payment is deducted from a savings account pledged by the borrower. A part of the borrower's down payment is used to establish the savings account which is then pledged over to the lender. Some, but not all graduated payment mortgages have the pledged account feature.

Adjustable-Rate Mortgages:

Adjustable-rate mortgages are the newest and most complex of the new mortgage forms. The common feature of adjustable-rate mortgages is that the interest rate is not fixed and will vary according to some interest rate index that is selected at the time the loan is originated. Lenders are not required to increase the interest rate on the mortgage as the index increases, but they are required to lower the interest rate if the index decreases. Adjustable-rate mortgage contracts may contain limitations on the minimum and maximum size of an interest rate change.

Depending upon a particular lender's adjustable-rate mortgage plan, a change in the interest rate may result in a change in the monthly payment, the term of the loan, the outstanding balance of the loan, or some combination of these. A number of lenders offer plans in which the interest rate can change every 3 or 6 months, but the payment changes every 3 years. Under such a plan an increase in the interest rate may mean that the monthly payment is insufficient to pay all the interest due that month. When this happens the unpaid interest will be added to the loan balance. Negative amortization can occur on adjustable-rate mortgages if payments are adjusted less frequently than the interest rate.

Graduated-Payment Adjustable-Rate Mortgage:

The graduated-payment adjustable-rate mortgage (GPARM) combines the scheduled payment increase feature of the GPM with an adjustable interest rate. All of the variations involve a deferral of some of the interest owed during the early years of the loan. Some plans have payments rising by a set amount each year for the first several years; other plans fix the low payments for the first 3 or 5 years. There are a limitless number of possible GPARM variations. Very few lenders are now offering this form of loan.

Wraparound Mortgages:

The wraparound mortgage is a technique by which a homebuyer can assume a low interest rate mortgage from the seller. Suppose a buyer needs a $50,000 mortgage and the previous owner has an assumable mortgage with a relatively low interest rate and a remaining balance of $30,000. The buyer might obtain a wraparound mortgage for $50,000. The payments to the wraparound lender must be large enough to continue to make payments on the assumed mortgage and to amortize the additional $20,000 loan. The advantage to the buyer is that the "blended" interest rate is lower than the new mortgage rates and the payments to the wraparound lender are lower than the payments on a new $50,000 mortgage at current interest rates.

Shared-Appreciation Mortgage:

A shared-appreciation mortgage (SAM) is a mortgage loan in which the borrower agrees to share the appreciation, or increase in value, of the property with the lender in return for an interest rate lower than that on a standard mortgage. SAMs have a contingent interest feature; a portion of the total interest due is contingent upon the appreciation of the property. At either the sale or transfer of the property, or the refinancing or maturity of the loan, the borrower must pay the lender a share of the appreciation of the property securing the loan. Payments on SAMs are based on a long amortization schedule, but the loan may become due at the end of 5 to 10 years.

The borrower and the lender jointly determine the size of the interest rate discount, the term of the loan, and the share of the appreciation due to the lender. The amount of appreciation is unknown at the time of origination, hence the total interest due and the effective interest rate are also uncertain. Although SAMs have a relatively low initial payment, the household's mortgage payment could increase very significantly if the lender's share of the appreciation and remaining principal balance had to be refinanced at market rate. At the current time, SAMs are offered by relatively few lenders.

Reverse Mortgages:

Reverse mortgages, often called reverse-annuity mortgages, are not financing techniques but rather a means by which elderly homeowners may convert some of their accumulated housing equity into a monthly stream of cash payments. Reverse mortgages may be structured as single-distribution or periodic distribution plans, and in some cases a single-premium annuity is purchased with the distribution. Reverse mortgages can provide significant monthly cash payments to single people over age 75. At the current time, reverse mortgages are only widely available in New Jersey.

Who Owns What: Familiar Consumer Products

The following is a list of familiar consumer products and their parent companies. If you wish to register a complaint beyond the local level, the address of the parent company can be found on pages 92-98.

Admiral appliances: Magic Chef
Ajax cleanser: Colgate-Palmolive
Allstate Insurance Co.: Sears, Roebuck
Anacin: American Home Products
Aqua Velva: Nabisco
Arrid anti-perspirant: Carter-Wallace
Baggies: Colgate-Palmolive
Ban anti-perspirant: Bristol-Myers
Bayer aspirin: Sterling Drug
Beech Aircraft: Raytheon
Benson & Hedges cigarettes; Philip Morris
Betty Crocker products: General Mills
Bolla wines: Brown-Forman
Brooks Brothers stores: Allied Stores
Budweiser beer: Anheuser-Busch
Bufferin: Bristol-Myers
Burger King restaurants: Pillsbury
Business Week magazine: McGraw-Hill
Buster Brown shoes: Brown Group
Cabbage Patch Kids dolls: Coleco
Cap'n Crunch cereal: Quaker Oats
Carrier air conditioners: United Technologies
Celeste Pizza: Quaker Oats
Chap Stick: A.H. Robins
Chef Boy-ar-dee products: American Home Products
Cheerios cereal: General Mills
Clairol hair products: Bristol-Myers
Cold Power detergent: Colgate-Palmolive
Colt 45 malt liquor: Heileman Brewing
Columbia Pictures: Coca Cola
Copenhagen snuff: U.S. Tobacco
Cover Girl cosmetics: Noxell
Cracker Jack: Borden
Crest toothpaste: Procter & Gamble
Crisco shortening: Procter & Gamble
Cycle dog food: General Foods
Dash detergent: Procter & Gamble
Del Monte foods: R.J. Reynolds
Doritos chips: PepsiCo
Drano: Bristol-Meyers
Dristan: American Home Products
Duncan Hines cookies: Procter & Gamble
Duracell batteries: Dart & Kraft
Easy-Off oven cleaner: American Home Products
Elizabeth Arden cosmetics: Eli Lilly
Esquire shoe polish: Papercraft
Ethan Allen furniture: Interco
Eveready batteries: Union Carbide
Excedrin: Bristol-Myers
Fab detergent: Colgate-Palmolive
Family Circle magazine: New York Times
Fisher Price toys: Quaker Oats
Flagg Bros. shoe stores: Genesco
Foamy shaving cream: Gillette
Folger coffee: Procter & Gamble
Formula 409 spray cleaner: Clorox
Franco-American foods: Campbell Soup
Friendly Ice Cream restaurants: Hershey Foods
Frito-Lay snacks: PepsiCo
Gatorade: Quaker Oats
Geritol: Nabisco
Gleem toothpaste: Procter & Gamble
Good Seasons salad dressing: General Foods
Green Giant vegetables: Pillsbury
Haagen-Dazs ice cream: Pillsbury
Hathaway shirts: Warnaco
Handy Wipes: Colgate-Palmolive
Harrah's resorts, casinos: Holiday
Head and Shoulders shampoo: Procter & Gamble
Hellman's mayonnaise: CPC International
Hertz car rental: RCA
Hi-C fruit drinks: Coca Cola
Ivory soap products: Procter & Gamble
Jack Daniels bourbon: Brown-Forman
Jell-o: General Foods
Jim Beam whiskey: American Brands
Ken-L-Ration pet foods: Quaker Oats
Kentucky Fried Chicken: R.J. Reynolds
Knorr soups: CPC International
Kool Aid soft drinks: General Foods
La Menu frozen dinners: Campbell Soup
Lee jeans: VF Corp.
Lenox china: Brown-Forman
Lestoil: Noxell

Life Savers candy: Nabisco
Log Cabin syrup: General Foods
Lucite paints: Clorox
Maalox: Rorer Group
Magnavox products: North American Philips
Marlboro cigarettes: Philip Morris
Maxwell House coffee: General Foods
Mazola oil: CPC International
Michelob beer: Anheuser-Busch
Miller beer: Philip Morris
Milton Bradley games: Hasbro
Minute Rice: General Foods
Nair depilatories: Carter-Wallace
NBC broadcasting: RCA
National Car Rental: Household International
Newsweek magazine: Washington Post
9-Lives cat food: H.J. Heinz
Norelco products: North American Philips
Norge appliances: Magic Chef
Noxzema skin products: Noxell
Oil of Olay: Richardson-Vicks
Ore-Ida frozen foods: H.J. Heinz
Oreo cookies: Nabisco
Oscar Mayer meats: General Foods
Pall Mall cigarettes: American Brands
Pampers: Procter & Gamble
Paper Mate pens: Gillette
Paul Masson wines: Seagram
People magazine: Time
Pepto-Bismol: Procter & Gamble
Pepperidge Farms products: Campbell Soup
Pizza Hut restaurants: PepsiCo
Planters peanuts: Nabisco
Prego spaghetti sauce: Campbell Soup
Prell shampoo: Procter & Gamble
Prince Matchabelli fragrances: Chesebrough-Pond's
Q-Tips: Chesebrough-Pond's
Radio Shack retail outlets: Tandy
Ragu foods: Chesebrough-Pond's
Ramblin root beer: Coca Cola
Red Devil paints: Insilco
Red Lobster Inns: General Mills
Right Guard deodorant: Gillette
Rise shave lathers: Carter-Wallace
Ritz crackers: Nabisco
Roy Rogers restaurants: Marriott
Samsonite luggage: Beatrice Foods
Sanka coffee: General Foods
Sea World Amusement Park: Harcourt Brace Jovanovich
San Giorgio pasta: Hershey
Sergeant's pet care products: A.H. Robins
7-Eleven stores: Southland
Seven-Up: Philip Morris
Simon & Schuster publishing: Gulf & Western
Soft and Dri deodorant: Gillette
Sports Illustrated magazine: Time
Sprite soda: Coca-Cola
Steak and Ale restaurants: Pillsbury
Sugartwin: Alberto Culver
Taco Bell restaurants: PepsiCo
Tagamet: Smithkline Beckman
Tang soft drink: General Foods
Thom McAn shoe stores: Melville
Tide detergent: Procter & Gamble
Tiparillo's: Culbro
Tropicana foods: Beatrice Foods
Tropicana hotels & casinos: Ramada Inns
Tupperware products: Dart & Kraft
Ty-D-Bol toilet cleaner: Papercraft
Tylenol: Johnson & Johnson
Ultra Brite toothpaste: Colgate-Palmolive
V-8 vegetable juice: Campbell Soup
Vanity Fair apparel: VF Corp.
Virginia Slims cigarettes: Philip Morris
Walden Book stores: K mart
Wall Street Journal: Dow Jones
Weight Watchers: H.J. Heinz
Wheaties cereal: General Mills
White Owl cigars: Culbro
White Rain shampoo: Gillette
Wizard air freshener: American Home Products
Wyler's drink mixes: Borden
Yuban coffee: General Foods

Business Directory

Listed below are major U.S. corporations, and major foreign corporations, whose operations—products and services—directly concern the American consumer. At the end of each listing is a representative sample of some of the company's products.

Should you, as a dissatisfied consumer, wish to register a complaint beyond the local level, address your correspondence to the attention of the Consumer Complaint Office of the individual company. Be as specific as possible about the dealer's name and address, purchase date or date of service, price, name and serial number (if any) of the product, and places you may have sought relief, with dates. Include copies of receipts and guarantees and/or warranties. Don't forget your name and complete address and telephone number with area code.

Company...Address...Phone Number...Chief executive officer...Business.

AMF Inc....777 Westchester Ave., White Plains, NY 10604...(914) 694-9000...W.T. York...producer bowling equip., industrial prods.

AMR Corp....PO Box 61616, Dallas/Ft. Worth Airport, TX 75261...(214) 355-1234...Albert V. Casey...Air transportation (American Airlines).

Abbott Laboratories...Abbott Park, No. Chicago, IL 60064...(312) 937-6100...R.A. Schoellhorn...health care prods.

Aetna Life & Casualty Co....151 Farmington Ave., Hartford, CT 06156...(203) 273-0123...James T. Lynn...insurance.

Alberto-Culver Co....2525 Armitage Ave., Melrose Park, IL 60160...(312) 450-3000...Leonard H. Lavin...hair care preparations, feminine hygiene products, household and grocery items.

Albertson's Inc....250 Parkchester Blvd., Boise, ID 83726...(208) 344-7441...W.E. McCain...supermarkets

Alcan Aluminium Ltd....P.O. Box 6077 Montreal, Que., Canada H3C 3A7...(514) 848-8050...D.M. Culver...aluminum producer.

Allied-Signal Inc....Box 2245R, Morristown, NJ 07960...(201) 455-2000...Edward L. Hennessy Jr....oil, gas, chemicals, fibers & plastics, electrical products, auto safety restraints.

Allied Stores Corp....1114 Ave. of the Americas, N.Y., NY 10036...(212) 764-2000...Thomas M. Macioce...dept. stores incl. Bonwit Teller; Plymouth Shops; Gertz; Garfinckel's, Stern's; Brooks Brothers.

Allis-Chalmers Corp....1205 S. 70th St., West Allis, WI 53214...(414) 475-3752...W.F. Bueche...manuf. of processing equip., electrical power equip., industrial trucks, farm machinery.

Aluminum Co. of America...1501 Alcoa Bldg., Pittsburgh, PA 15219...(412) 533-4707...C.W. Parry...mining, refining, & processing of aluminum.

Amerada Hess Corp....1185 Ave. of the Americas, N.Y., NY 10036...(212) 977-8500...P. Kramer...integrated petroleum co.

American Bakeries Co....111 E. 58th St., N.Y., NY 10022...(212) 486-9800...E.G. Bewkes, Jr....wholesale bakery goods.

American Brands, Inc....245 Park Ave., N.Y., NY 10017...(212) 880-4200...E.H. Whittemore...tobacco (Pall Mall, Lucky Strike cigarettes; Half and Half, Paleden pipe tobacco); whiskey (Jim Beam); snack foods (Sunshine Biscuits); golf equipment, office supplies, toiletries, insurance.

American Broadcasting Companies Inc....1330 Ave. of the Americas, N.Y., NY 10019...(212) 887-7777...L.H. Goldenson...broadcasting, publishing.

American Can Co....American Lane, Greenwich, CT 06836...(203) 552-2000...William S. Woodside...manuf. containers and packaging prods; financial services.

American Cyanamid Co....One Cyanamid Plaza, Wayne, NJ 07470...(201) 831-2000...G.J. Sella, Jr....medical, agricultural prods., specialty chemicals.

American Express Co....American Express Plaza, N.Y., NY 10004...(212) 323-2000...J.D. Robinson 3d...travelers checks; credit card services; insurance; investment services (Shearson Loeb Rhodes).

American Greetings Corp....10500 American Rd., Cleveland, OH 44144...(216) 252-7300...Irving I. Stone...greeting cards.

American Hoist & Derrick Co....1800 Amhoist Tower, Fourth and Peter Streets, St. Paul, MN 55102...(612) 293-4567...R.H, Nassau...heavy equip.

American Home Products Corp....685 3d Ave., N.Y., NY 10017...(212) 986-1000...J.W. Culligan...prescription drugs, household prods. (Woolite, Easy-Off oven cleaner); food (Chef Boy-ar-dee); drugs (Anacin, Dristan).

American Motors Corp....2777 Franklin Rd., Southfield, MI 48034...(313) 827-1000...J.J. Dedeurwaerder...passenger vehicles, service parts; Jeep Corp.

American Stores Co....709 East South Temple, Salt Lake City, UT 84127...(801) 539-0112...J.S. Skaggs...retail food markets, dept. & drug stores.

American Telephone & Telegraph Co....550 Madison Ave. N.Y., NY 10022...(212) 605-5500...Charles L. Brown...communications...Western Electric.

Anheuser-Busch, Inc....One Busch Place, St. Louis, MO 63118...(314) 577-2000...A.A. Busch 3d...brewing (Budweiser, Michelob, Natural Light).

Armstrong Rubber Co....500 Sargent Dr., New Haven, CT 06507...(203) 562-1161...James A. Walsh...tires.

Armstrong World Industries...W. Liberty St., Lancaster, PA 17604...(717) 397-0611...J.L. Jones...interior furnishings.

Arvin Industries, Inc....1531 13th St., Columbus, IN 47201...(812) 372-7271...J.K. Baker...auto exhaust systems, record players.

Ashland Oil, Inc....1401 Westchester Ave., Ashland, KY 41114...(606) 329-3333...J.R. Hall...petroleum refiner; chemicals, coal, insurance.

Associated Dry Goods Corp....417 5th Ave., N.Y., NY 10016...(212) 679-8700...J.H. Johnson...department stores incl. Lord & Taylor; Caldor; Loehmann's; Horne's.

Atlantic Richfield Co....515 S. Flower St., Los Angeles, CA 90071...(213) 486-3511...W.F. Keischnick...petroleum, chemicals.

Avery International Corp....150 N. Orange Grove Blvd., Pasadena, CA 91103...(213) 304-2000...Charles D. Miller...self-adhesive labels.

Avon Products, Inc....9 West 57th St., N.Y., NY 10019...(212) 546-6015...Hicks B. Waldron...cosmetics, fragrances, toiletries, jewelry.

Bally Manufacturing Corp....8700 W. Bryn Mawr Ave., Chicago, IL 60631...(312) 399-1300...R.E. Mullane...coin-operated amusement and gaming equip.; hotel-casino operator; theme park operator.

Bausch & Lomb...One Lincoln First Square, Rochester, NY 14601...(716) 338-6000...D.E. Gill...manuf. of vision care products, accessories.

Baxter Travenol Labs Inc....One Baxter Pky., Deerfield, IL. 60015...(312) 948-2000...Vernon R. Loucks, Jr....medical care prods.

Beatrice Cos. Inc....2 N. LaSalle St., Chicago, IL 60602...(302) 782-3820...James L. Dutt...foods (Tropicana, Meadow Gold, La Choy); recreational, travel (Samsonite luggage), home prods.(Stiffel Lamps).

Bell & Howell Co....5512 Old Orchard Rd., Skokie, IL 60077...(312) 470-7100...D.N. Frey...audio-visual instruments, business equip., educational & training equip.

Best Products Co....Box 26303, Richmond, VA 23260...(804) 261-2000...A.M. Lewis...catalog/showroom merchandiser.

Bethlehem Steel Corp....8th & Eaton Ave., Bethlehem, PA 18016...(215) 694-2424...D.H. Trautlein...steel & steel prods.

Bic Corporation...Wiley Street, Milford, CT 06401...(203) 783-2000...Bruno Bich...writing instruments, disposable lighters, and shavers.

Black & Decker Mfg. Co....701 E. Joppa Rd., Towson, MD 21204...(301) 583-3900...L.J. Farley...manuf. power tools.

H & R Block, Inc....4410 Main St., Kansas City, MO 64111...(816) 753-6900...Henry W. Bloch...tax preparation.

Blue Bell, Inc....335 Church St., Greensboro, NC 27420...(919) 373-3400...E.J. Bauman...manuf. western wear (Wrangler), sports and swim wear (Jantzen).

Boeing Company...7755 E. Marginal Way So., Seattle, WA 98108...(206) 655-2121...T.A. Wilson...aircraft manuf.

Boise Cascade Corp.... One Jefferson Square, Boise, ID 83728...(208) 384-6161...J.B. Fery...timber, paper, wood prod.

Borden, Inc...277 Park Ave., N.Y., NY 10172...(212) 573-4000...E.J. Sullivan...food, cheese and cheese products, snacks (Cracker Jack), beverages.

Borg-Warner Corp...200 S. Michigan Ave., Chicago, IL 60604...(312) 322-8500...J.F. Bere...air conditioning, plastics, chemicals, industrial prods., financial & protection services.

Bristol-Myers Co...345 Park Ave., N.Y., NY 10154...(212) 546-4000...Richard L. Gelb...toiletries (Ban anti-perspirant), hair items (Clairol), drugs (Bufferin, Excedrin), household prods.(Drano), infant formula (Enfamil).

Brown-Forman Distillers Corp...850 Dixie Hwy., Louisville, KY 40210...(502) 585-1100...W.L.L. Brown, Jr...distilled spirits (Jack Daniel); wines (Bolla, Cella), champagne (Korbel).

Brown Group, Inc...8400 Maryland Ave., St. Louis, MO 63166...(314) 854-4000...B.A. Brightwater, Jr...manuf. and wholesaler of women's and children's shoes (Buster Brown).

Brunswick Corp... One Brunswick Plaza, Skokie, IL 60077...(312) 470-4700...J.F. Reichert...marine, recreation prods.

Burlington Industries, Inc...3330 W. Friendly Ave., Greensboro, NC 27410...(919) 379-2000...W. A. Klopman...largest U.S. textile mfg.

Burlington Northern Inc...999 3d Ave., Seattle, WA 98104...(206) 467-3838...R.M. Bressler...rail transportation, natural resources.

Burroughs Corp... Burroughs Place, Detroit, MI 48232...(313) 972-7000...W.M. Blumenthal...business equipment.

CBS Inc...51 W. 52d St., N.Y., NY 10019...(212) 975-6075...T.H. Wyman...broadcasting, publishing, recorded music, leisure prods.

CPC International, Inc... International Plaza, Englewood Cliffs, NJ 07632...(201) 894-4000...J.W. McKee, Jr...branded food items (Hellman's; Best Foods; Mazola; Skippy; Knorr Soups), corn wet milling prods.

Campbell Soup Co... Campbell Pl., Camden, NJ 08101...(609) 342-4800...R. G. McGovern...canned soups, spaghetti (Franco-American), vegetable juice (V-8), pork and beans; pet foods, restaurants, confections; Le Menu frozen dinners; Prego spaghetti sauce; Mrs. Pauls frozen fish.

Capital Cities Communications, Inc...24 E. 51st Street, New York, NY 10022...(212) 421-9595...T.S. Murphy...operates television and radio stations, newspapers.

Carnation Co...5045 Wilshire Blvd., Los Angeles, CA 90036...(213) 932-6001...H.E. Olson...canned evaporated milk, tomato prods., pet foods (Friskies). (Acquired by Nestle in 1984).

Carter-Wallace, Inc...767 5th Ave., New York, NY 10153...(212) 758-4500...H.H. Hoyt, Jr...personal care items, anti-perspirant (Arrid), shave lathers (Rise), laxative (Carter's Pills), pet products.

Castle & Cooke, Inc... Financial Plaza of the Pacific, P.O. Box 2990, Honolulu, HI 96802...(808) 548-6611...R.D. Cook...food processing...Dole, Bumble Bee.

Caterpillar Tractor Co...100 N.E. Adams St., Peoria, IL 61629...(309) 675-1000...G.A. Schaefer...heavy duty earth-moving equip., diesel engines.

Champion International Corp...1 Champion Plaza, Stamford, CT 06921...(203) 358-7000...A.C. Sigler...forest prods.

Champion Spark Plug Co...900 Upton Ave., Toledo, OH 43661...(419) 535-2567...R.A. Stranahan, Jr...ignition devices.

Chesebrough-Pond's Inc...33 Benedict Pl., Greenwich, CT 06830...(203) 661-2000...Ralph E. Ward...cosmetics, toiletries, clothing, food prods., footwear...Adolph's; Health-Tex; Vaseline; Q-Tips; Pertussin; Prince Matchabelli; Ragu.

Chevron Corp...225 Bush St., San Francisco, CA 94104...(415) 894-7700...J.R. Grey...integrated oil co.

Chrysler Corp...1200 Lynn Townsend Dr., Detroit, MI 48231...(313) 956-5252...Lee Iacocca...cars, trucks.

Church's Fried Chicken, Inc...355A Spencer Lane, San Antonio, TX 78284...(512) 735-9392...J.D. Bamberger...fried chicken restaurants.

Citicorp...399 Park Ave., N.Y., NY 10043...(212) 559-1000...J.S. Reed...largest U.S. commercial bank.

Clorox Co...1221 Broadway, Oakland, CA 94612...(415) 271-7000...C.S. Hatch...retail consumer prods (Formula 409; Twice As Fresh; Lucite paints; Kingsford charcoal briquets).

Cluett, Peabody & Co...510 5th Ave., New York, NY 10036...(212) 930-3000...H.H. Henley, Jr...apparel (Arrow shirts; Gold Toe socks).

Coachman Industries Inc...P.O. Box 3300, Elkhart, IN 46515...(219) 262-0123...T.H. Corson...manuf. recreational vehicles.

Coca-Cola Co...310 North Ave., Atlanta, GA 30313...(404) 676-2121...R.C. Goizueta...soft drink (Coca Cola; MelloYellow; Ramblin root beer), syrups, citrus and fruit juices (Minute Maid, Hi-C), films (Columbia Pictures).

Coleco Industries, Inc...999 Quaker Lane S., Hartford, CT 06110...(203) 725-6000...A.C. Greenberg...consumer electronics, games, toys (Cabbage Patch Kids).

Coleman Co., Inc...250 N. St. Francis Ave., Wichita, KS 67202...(316) 261-3211...S. Coleman...outdoor recreation prods., heating & air conditioning equip.

Colgate-Palmolive Co...300 Park Ave., N.Y., NY 10022...(212) 310-2000...R. Mark...soaps (Palmolive; Irish Spring), detergents (Fab; Ajax; Cold Power), tooth paste (Colgate; Ultra Brite), household prods. (Baggies; Handy Wipes; Curad bandages), restaurants (Ranch House; Lum's).

Commodore International Ltd...P.O. Box N-10256, Nassau, Bahamas...(215) 431-9100...M.F. Smith...microcomputer systems, semiconductors component, consumer electronics, office equipment.

Conair Corp...11 Executive Ave., Edison, NJ 08817...(201) 287-4800...L.P. Rizzuto...health and beauty products, consumer electronic appliances.

Adolph Coors Co... East of Town, Golden, CO 80401...(303) 279-6565...W. K. Coors...brewery.

Corning Glass Works... Houghton Park, Corning, NY 14831...(607) 974-9000...J.R. Houghton...glass mfg.

Cox Communications, Inc...1400 Lake Hearn Dr., Atlanta, GA 30319...(404) 843-5126...W.A. Schwartz...broadcasting, publishing.

Crane Co...300 Park Ave., N.Y., NY 10022...(212) 980-3600...R.S. Evans...fluid & pollution controls, steel, aircraft and aerospace, building prods.

A.T. Cross Co... One Albion Rd., Lincoln, RI 02865...(401) 333-1200...B.R. Boss...writing instruments.

Crown Zellerbach Corp... One Bush St., San Francisco, CA 94104...(415) 823-5000...W.T. Creson...forest products.

Culbro Corp...387 Park Avenue South, New York, NY 10016...(212) 561-8700...E. M. Culliman...cigars (Corina; Robert Burns; White Owl; Tiparillo's), snack foods.

Dana Corp...4500 Dorr St., Toledo, OH 43697...(419) 535-4500...Gerald B. Mitchell...truck and auto parts supplies.

Dart & Kraft, Inc...2211 Sanders Rd., Northbrook, IL 60062...(312) 498-8000...J. R. Richman...food prods. (cheese, mayonnaise), direct selling (Tupperware), consumer products (Duracell batteries; West Bend appliances).

Data General Corp... Westboro, MA 01580...(617) 366-8911...E. D. deCastro...digital computers.

Dayton-Hudson Corp...777 Nicollet Mall, Minneapolis, MN 55402...(612) 370-6948...K.A. Macke...department, specialty, book stores; B. Dalton; Mervyn's; Target.

Deere & Company... John Deere Rd., Moline, IL 61265...(309) 752-8000...Robert A. Hanson...farm, industrial, and outdoor power equip.

Delta Air Lines, Inc... Hartsfield Atlanta Intl. Airport, Atlanta, GA 30320...(404) 346-6622...David C. Garrett, Jr...air transportation.

Denny's, Inc...16700 Valley View Ave., La Mirada, CA 90637...(714) 739-8100...V.O. Curtis...restaurants.

Diamond Shamrock Corp...717 North Harwood St., Dallas, TX 75201...(214) 745-2000...W.H. Bricker...energy, chemicals.

Diebold, Inc... Canton, OH 44711...(216) 489-4000...R. Mahoney...equip. for financial insts.

Digital Equipment Corp...146 Main St., Maynard, MA 01754...(617) 897-5111...Kenneth H. Olsen...computers.

Walt Disney Productions...500 S. Buena Vista St., Burbank, CA 91521...(213) 840-1000...M.D. Eisner...motion pictures, CATV, amusement parks...Disneyland, Walt Disney World, Epcot Center.

Donnelly & Sons Co...2223 Martin Luther King Drive, Chicago, IL 60616...(312) 326-8000...J.B. Schwemm...largest commercial printer.

Dow Chemical Co...2030 Dow Center, Midland, MI 48640...(517) 636-1000...P.F. Oreffice...chemicals, plastics, metals, consumer prods.

Dow Jones & Co... 22 Cortlandt St., New York, NY 10007...(212) 285-5000...W. H. Phillips...financial news service, publishing (Wall Street Journal; Barron's; Ottaway Newspapers).

Dresser Industries, Inc... 105 Elm Street, Dallas, TX 75201...(214) 746-6000...J.J. Murphy...supplier of technology and services to energy related industries.

Dun & Bradstreet Corp... 299 Park Ave., New York, NY 10171...(212) 593-6800...C.W. Moritz...business information and computer services, publishing, broadcasting.

E.I. du Pont de Nemours & Co... 1007 Market St., Wilmington, DE 19898...(302) 774-1000...E. G. Jefferson...chemicals, petroleum, consumer prods., coal.

Eastman Kodak Co... 343 State St., Rochester, NY 14650...(716) 724-4000...C.H. Chandler...photographic prods.

(Jack) Eckerd Corp... 8333 Bryan Dairy Rd., Clearwater, FL 33518...(813) 397-7461...S. Turley...drug store chain, department stores, optical & video equip. stores.

Emerson Electric Co... 8000 W. Florissant Ave., St. Louis, MO 63136...(314) 553-2197...C.F. Knight...electrical/electronics products & systems

Emery Air Freight Corp... Old Danbury Rd., Wilton, CT 06897...(203) 762-8601...John C. Emery, Jr....air freight forwarder.

Ethyl Corp... 330 S. 4th St., Richmond, VA 23217...(804) 788-5000...Floyd D. Gottwald, Jr....petroleum and industrial chemicals, plastics, aluminum.

Exxon Corp... 1251 Ave. of the Americas, N.Y., NY 10020...(212) 398-3093...C.C. Garvin Jr....world's largest oil co.

Fabergé,Inc... 1345 Ave. of the Americas, N.Y., NY 10105...(212) 581-3500...D.J. Manella...cosmetics, toiletries (Brut; Babe; Farrah Fawcett).

Fairchild Industries, Inc... Germantown, MD 20874...(301) 428-6000...E.G. Uhl...aircraft manuf.

Family Dollars Stores, Inc... 10401 Old Monroe Rd., Charlotte, NC 28212...(704)847-6961...L.E. Levine...discount variety stores.

Federal Express Corp... 2990 Airways Blvd., Memphis, TN 38194...(901) 369-3600...F.W. Smith...small package delivery service.

Federated Department Stores, Inc... 7 W. 7th St., Cincinnati, OH 45202...(513) 579-7000...H. Goldfeder...dept. stores...Abraham & Straus; Bloomingdale's; Boston Store; Burdines; Foley's; Lazarus; Rich's; Children's Place.

Fieldcrest Mills, Inc... 326 East Stadium Dr., Eden, NC 27288...(919) 623-2123...F.X. Larkin...household textile prods., rugs (Karastan, Laurelcrest).

Firestone Tire & Rubber Co... 1200 Firestone Pkwy., Akron, OH 44317...(216) 379-7000...J.J. Nevin...tires, rubber and metal prods.

Fleetwood Enterprises, Inc... 3125 Myers St., Riverside, CA 92523...(714) 351-3500...John C. Crean...mobile homes, recreational vehicles.

Fluor Corp... 3333 Michelson Dr., Irvine, CA 92730...(714) 975-2000...D.S. Tappan, Jr....engineering and construction.

Ford Motor Co... The American Rd., Dearborn, MI 48121...(313) 322-8540...D.E. Peterson...motor vehicles, Ford Tractor; Lincoln-Mercury.

Fort Howard Paper Co... 1919 S. Broadway, Green Bay; WI 54305...(414) 435-8821...P.J. Schierl...disposable paper prods.

GAF Corp... 1361 Alps Road, Wayne, NJ 07470...(201) 628-3000...S.J. Heyman...chemicals, bldg. materials.

GTE Corp... One Stamford Forum, Stamford, CT 06904...(203) 965-2000...Theodore F. Brophy...operates largest U.S. independent telephone system.

Gannett Co., Inc... P.O. Box 7858, Washington, DC 20044...(703) 276-5900...A.H. Neuharth...newspaper publishing (USA TODAY), TV stations, outdoor advertising.

Gencorp... One General St., Akron, OH 44329...(216) 798-3000...M.G. O'Neil...tires, rubber prods.

General Cinema Corp... 27 Boylston St., Chestnut Hill, MA 02167...(617) 232-8200...R. A. Smith...movie exhibitor, soft drinks (Sunkist).

General Dynamics Corp... Pierre Laclede Ctr., St. Louis, MO 63105...(314) 889-8200...D. S. Lewis...military and commercial aircraft, tactical missiles.

General Electric Co... 3135 Easton Ave., Fairfield, CT 06431...(203) 373-2431...J. F. Welch, Jr....electrical, electronic equip.

General Instruments Corp... 1775 Broadway, New York, NY 10019...(212) 708-7800...F. G. Hickey...race track betting systems, CATV, semiconductors, electronic equip.

General Mills, Inc... 9200 Wayzatta Blvd., Minneapolis, MN 55440...(612) 540-2311...H.B. Atwater Jr....foods, toys, restaurants, fashion and specialty retailing...Wheaties; Cheerios; Betty Crocker; Red Lobster Inns).

General Motors Corp... Gen. Motors Bldg., Detroit, MI 48202...(313) 556-5000...R. B. Smith...world's largest auto manuf.

Genesco Inc... Genesco Park, Nashville, TN 37202...(615) 367-7000...R.W. Hanselman...footwear and men's clothing...Hardy; Cover Girl; Jarman; Flagg Bros.; Bell Bros.; Johnston & Murphy.

Georgia-Pacific Corp... 133 Peachtree St., NE, Atlanta, GA 30303...(404) 521-4720...T.M. Hahn, Jr....building prods., pulp, paper, chemicals.

Gerber Products Co... 445 State St., Fremont, MI 49412...(616) 928-2000...C.G. Smith...baby foods, clothing, nursery accessories; life insurance.

Gillette Co... Prudential Tower Bldg., Boston, MA 02199...(617) 421-7000...Colman M. Mockler, Jr....razors, pens (Paper Mate; Flair), toiletries (Right Guard, Dri, Soft deodorants; Foamy shaving cream; Earth Born shampoo), hair products (Toni; Adorn; White Rain).

Golden Nugget, Inc... 129 Freemont St., Las Vegas, NV 89101...(702) 385-7111...Steve Wynn...operates casino-hotels.

B.F. Goodrich Company... 500 S. Main St., Akron, OH 44318...(216) 374-2632...John D. Ong...rubber, chemical, plastic prods.

Goodyear Tire & Rubber Co... 1144 E. Market St., Akron, OH 44316...(216) 794-4436...R.E. Mercer...tires, rubber prods.

Gordon Jewelry Corp... 820 Fannin St., Houston TX 77002...(713) 222-8080...A.S. Gordon...jewelry retailer.

Gould Inc... 10 Gould Center, Rolling Meadows, IL 60008...(312) 640-4000...W.T. Ylvisaker...electrical and industrial prods.

W.R. Grace & Co... Grace Plaza, 1114 Ave. of the Americas, N.Y., NY 10036...(212) 819-5500...J. Peter Grace...chemicals, natural resources, consumer prods. and services, restaurants...Channel Home Centers; Herman's World of Sporting Goods.

Great Atlantic & Pacific Tea Co... 2 Paragon Dr., Montvale, NJ 07645...(201) 573-9700...James Wood...retail food stores.

Greyhound Corp... Greyhound Tower, Phoenix, AZ 85077...(602) 248-4000...John W. Teets...bus transportation, soap (Dial), food, financial services.

Grumman Corp... 111 Stewart, Bethpage, NY 11714...(516) 575-7474...John C. Bierwirth...aerospace, truck bodies.

Gulf Corp... P.O. Box 1166, Pittsburgh, PA 15230...(412) 263-5000...J.E. Lee...production and marketing of petroleum and related products.

Gulf + Western Industries, Inc... One Gulf + Western Plaza, N.Y., NY 10023...(212) 333-7000...M.S. Davis...diversified manufacturing, financial services, consumer and food products, home furnishings, entertainment (Paramount Pictures; Madison Square Garden).

Harcourt Brace Jovanovich, Inc... 111 Fifth Avenue, New York, NY 10003...(212) 614-3000...W. Jovanovich...textbook publisher, entertainment (Sea World).

Hartmarx... 101 N. Wacker Dr., Chicago, IL 60606...(312) 372-6300...R.P. Hamilton...apparel manufacturer and retailer (Hickey-Freeman).

Hasbro Inc... 1027 Newport Ave., P.O. Box 1059, Pawtucket, R.I. 02862...(401) 726-4100...S.D. Massenfeld...toys.

Heileman (G.) Brewing Co... 100 Harborview Plaza, La Crosse, WI 54601...(608) 785-1000...R. G. Cleary...brewery (Schmidt; Blatz; Colt 45 Malt Liquor).

H.J. Heinz Co... P.O. Box 57, Pittsburgh, PA 15230...(412) 237-5757...Anthony J.F. O'Reilly...foods (Star-Kist; Ore-Ida; '57 Varieties), 9-Lives cat food, Weight Watchers.

Hershey Foods Corp... 100 Manson Rd., Hershey, PA 17033...(717) 534-4000...R.A. Zimmerman...chocolate & confectionery prods., pasta (San Giorgio); restaurants (Friendly Ice Cream).

Hewlett-Packard Co... 3000 Hanover Street, Palo Alto, CA 94304...(415) 856-1501...John A. Young...electronic instruments.

Hillenbrand Industries, Inc... Highway 46, Batesville, IN

47006...(812) 934-7000...D.A. Hillenbrand...manuf. burial
caskets, electronically operated hospital beds.
Hilton Hotels Corp....9880 Wilshire Blvd., Beverly Hills, CA
90210...(213) 278-4321...Barron Hilton...hotels, casinos.
Holiday Corp....3742 Lamar Ave., Memphis, TN 38195...(901)
364-4001...M.D. Rose...hotels, motels, casinos (Harrah's).
Honda Motor Co., LTD....1270 Ave. of the Americas, N.Y., NY
10020...(212) 765-3804...Tadashi Kume...manuf. autos,
motorcycles.
Honeywell, Inc....Honeywell Plaza, Minneapolis, MN
55408...(612) 870-5200...E.W. Spencer...industrial systems
& controls, aerospace guidance systems, information systems.
Hoover Co....101 E. Maple St., No. Canton, OH 44720...(216)
499-9200...M. R. Rawson...manuf. vacuum cleaners, washing machines, dryers.
Geo. A. Hormel & Co....501 16th Ave. N.E., Austin, MN
55912...(507) 437-5611...R.L. Knowlton...meat packaging,
pork and beef prods.
Household International Inc....2700 Sanders Rd., Prospect
Heights, IL 60070...(312) 564-5000...D.C. Clark...financial
and insurance services, merchandising, manufacturing, transportation...National Car Rental; Household Finance.
Humana, Inc....P.O. Box 1438, Louisville, KY 40201...(502)
561-2000...D. A. Jones...operates hospitals.

IC Industries, Inc....One Illinois Ctr., 111 E. Wacker Dr., Chicago, IL 60601...(312) 565-3000...William B. Johnson... diversified prods. and services...railroads, consumer products,
food, auto products.
ITT Corp....320 Park Ave., N.Y., NY 10022...(212) 752-
6000...R.V. Araskog... world's largest manuf. of telecommu-
nications equip.
Imperial Oil Ltd....111 St. Clair Ave. W., Toronto, Ont., Canada...(416) 924-4111...D.M. Ivor...Canada's largest oil co.
Insilco Corp....1000 Research Pkwy., Meriden, CT
06450...(203) 634-2000...D.J. Harper...diversified manufacturer...Red Devil Paints and Chemicals; Rolodex; Taylor Publishing; International Silver.
Intel Corp....3065 Bowers Ave., Santa Clara, CA
95051...(408) 987-8080...G. E. Moore...semiconductor
memory components.
Interco Inc....P.O. Box 8777, St. Louis, MO 63102...(314)
231-1100...H. Saligman...apparel, footwear mfg.; specialty
apparel shops, home furnishings (Ethan Allen).
International Business Machines Corp....Old Orchard Rd.,
Armonk, NY 10504...(914) 765-1900...J.F. Akers...informa-
tion-handling systems, equip., and services.
International Harvester Co....401 N. Michigan Ave., Chicago,
IL 60611...(312) 836-2000...D.D. Lennox...manuf. farm tractors and machinery, truck and construction equip.
International Paper Co....77 W. 45th St., New York, NY
10036...(212) 536-6000...J.A. Georges...paper, wood
prods.

Johnson & Johnson...One Johnson & Johnson Plaza, Brunswick, NJ 08903...(201) 524-0400...James E. Burke...surgi-
cal dressings, pharmaceuticals, health and baby prods.
Jonathan Logan, Inc....50 Terminal Rd., Secaucus, NJ
07094...Richard J. Schwartz...female apparel.
Jostens, Inc....5501 Norman Center Dr., Minneapolis, MN
55437...(612) 830-3336...H. W. Lurton...school rings, year-
books.

Kaiser Aluminum & Chemical Corp....300 Lakeside Dr., Oakland, CA 94643...(415) 271-3300...Cornell C. Maier... aluminum, chemicals.
Kaufman and Broad, Inc....11601 Wilshire Blvd., Los Angeles,
CA 90025...(213) 312-5000...Eli Broad...home builder.
Kellogg Co....235 Porter, Battle Creek, MI 49016...(616) 966-
2000...William E. LaMothe...ready to eat cereals & other
food prods....Mrs. Smith's Pie Co.; Salada Foods.
Kidde, Inc....Park 80 West-Plaza Two, Box 5555, Saddle
Brook, NJ 07622...(201) 368-9000...Fred R. Sullivan...mfgr.
safety, security, protection, industrial, commercial, consumer
and recreation prods. and services.
Kimberly-Clark Corp....N. Lake St., Neenah, WI 54956...(414)
721-2000...Darwin E. Smith...paper and lumber prods.
K mart Corp....3300 W. Big Beaver Rd., Troy, MI
48084...(313) 643-1000...B. M. Fauber...largest U.S. chain
of discount stores.
Knight-Ridder Newspapers, Inc....One Harold Plaza, Miami,
FL 33101...(305) 350-2650...A.H. Chapman, Jr...largest
U.S. newspaper co.; broadcasting, publishing.

Kroger Co....1014 Vine St., Cincinnati, OH 45201...(513) 762-
4000...Lyle Everingham...grocery chain, drugstores (Su-
peRx).
LTV Corporation...P.O. Box 225003, Dallas, TX 75265...(214)
746-7711...R.A. Hay...steel, aerospace, meat & food prods.,
shipping, energy-oriented prods.
Levi Strauss & Co....1155 Battery St., San Francisco, CA
94120...(415) 544-6000...R. D. Haas...blue denim jeans,
other apparel.
Levitz Furniture Corp....1317 NW 167th St., Miami, FL
33169...(305) 625-6421...Robert M. Elliott...furniture stores.
Libbey-Owens-Ford Co....811 Madison Ave., Toledo, OH
43695...(419) 247-4856...Don T. Mc Kone...automotive
glass and fabricated prods.
Eli Lilly & Company....307 E. McCarty St., Indianapolis, IN
46285...(317) 261-2000...Richard D. Wood...mfg. human
health and agricultural products, cosmetics (Elizabeth Arden).
The Limited, Inc....One Limited Pkwy., Columbus, OH
43216...(614) 475-4000...L.H. Wexner...women's apparel
stores...Lane Bryant.
Litton Industries, Inc....360 N. Crescent, Beverly Hills, CA
90210...(213) 859-5000...O.C. Hoch...industrial systems &
services, advanced electronic systems, electronic & electrical
prods., marine engineering, printing & publishing.
Lockheed Corp....2555 N. Hollywood Way, Burbank, CA
91520...(213) 847-6121...R.A. Anderson...commercial and
military aircraft, missiles.
Loews Corp....666 5th Ave., N.Y., NY 10019...(212) 841-
1000...Laurence A. Tisch...tobacco prods., motion picture
theaters, hotels, real estate, insurance.
Lucky Stores, Inc....6300 Clark Ave., Dublin, CA
94566...(415) 828-1000...S. D. Ritchey...supermarkets, restaurants, dept., fabric, and automotive stores.

MCA Inc....100 Universal City Plaza, Universal City, CA
91608...(213) 985-4321...Lew R. Wasserman...motion pictures, television; music publishing, mail order, novelty, and gift
merchandise.
MEI Corp....710 Marquette Ave., Minneapolis, MN
55402...(612) 339-8853...Donald E. Benson...soft drink bot-
tler, distributor.
MacMillan, Inc....866 3d Ave., New York, NY 10022...(212)
702-2000...E. P. Evans...book printing and publishing; education (Berlitz; Katharine Gibbs).
R. H. Macy & Co. Inc....151 W. 34th St., New York, NY
10001...(212) 560-3600...E. S. Finkelstein...department
stores.
Magic Chef, Inc....740 King Edward Ave., Cleveland, TN
37311...(615) 472-3371...S.B. Rymer, Jr...major household
appliances, heating and air conditioning equip., soft drink vend-
ing equip...Admiral; Norge; Gaffers & Sattler; Johnson; Dixie-
Narco; Toastmaster.
Manor Care, Inc....10750 Columbia Pike, Silver Spring, MD
20901...S. Bainum...nursing homes.
Marriott Corp....Marriott Dr., Wash., DC 20058...(301) 897-
9000...J. Willard Marriott, Jr...restaurants (Roy Rogers; Big
Boy), hotels, food services, theme parks.
Martin Marietta Corp....6801 Rockledge Dr., Bethesda, MD
20817...(301) 897-6000...T.G. Pownall...aluminum, aero-
space, chemicals.
Mary Kay Cosmetics, Inc....8787 Stemmon Freeway, Dallas,
TX 75247...(214) 630-8787...R.R. Rogers...cosmetics, toi-
letries.
Mattel, Inc....5150 Rosecrans Ave., Hawthorne, CA
90250...(213) 978-5150...A. S. Spear...toy & hobby prods.
May Department Stores Co....611 Olive Street, St. Louis, MO
63101...(314) 342-6300...D.C. Farrell...department stores
(O'Neils, Mecht, Famous Barr, Meier & Frank, Kaufman's, G.
Fox, and Strouss).
Maytag Co....403 W. 4th St. N., Newton, IA 50208...(515) 792-
7000...Daniel J. Krumm...manuf. home laundry equip.
McCormick & Co., Inc....11350 McCormick Rd., Hunt Valley,
MD 21031...(301) 667-7301...H. K. Wells...world's leading
manuf. of seasoning & flavoring prods.
McDonald's Corp....McDonald's Plaza, Oak Brook, IL
60521...(312) 887-3200...F. L. Turner...fast service restau-
rants.
McDonnell Douglas Corp....P.O. Box 516, St. Louis, MO
63131...(314) 232-0232...Sanford N. McDonnell...commer-
cial & military aircraft, space systems & missiles.
McGraw-Hill, Inc....1221 Ave. of the Americas, New York, NY
10020...(212) 512-2000...J.L. Dionne...book, magazine

publishing (Business Week), information & financial services (Standard and Poor's), TV stations.

Mead Corporation. . .Courthouse Plaza Northeast, Dayton, OH 45463. . .(513) 222-6323. . .B.R. Roberts. . .printing and writing paper, paperboard, packaging, shipping containers, pulp and lumber.

Medtronic, Inc.. . .3055 Hway 8, Minneapolis, MN 55440. . .(612) 574-4000. . .D. R. Olseth. . heart pacemakers and support systems.

Melville Corp.. . .3000 Westchester Ave., Harrison, NY 10528. . .(914) 253-8000. . .Francis C. Rooney, Jr.. . .shoe stores (Thom McAn), apparel (Marshalls); drug stores.

Merck & Co., Inc.. . .P.O. Box 2000, Rahway, NJ 07065. . .(201) 574-4000. . .P. Roy Vagelos. . .human & animal health care prods.

Merrill Lynch & Co., Inc.. . .One Liberty Plaza, N.Y., NY 10080. . .(212) 637-7455. . .W.A Schreyer. . .securities broker, financial services, real estate.

Metromedia, Inc.. . .One Harmon Plaza, Secaucus, NJ 07094. . .(201) 348-3244. . .J. W. Kluge. . .television & radio broadcasting, publishing, entertainment (Ice Capades; Harlem Globetrotters).

Milton Bradley Co.. . .111 Maple St., Springfield, MA 01105. . .(413) 525-6411. . .James J. Shea, Jr.. . .board and card games, electronic games, toys (Playskool), educational materials.

Minnesota Mining & Manuf. Co.. . .3M Center, St. Paul, MN 55144. . .(612) 733-1100. . .L.W. Lehr. . .abrasives, adhesives, building services & chemicals, electrical, health care, photographic, printing, recording materials.

Mobil Corp.. . .150 E. 42d St., N.Y., NY 10017. . .(212) 883-4242. . .Rawleigh Warner, Jr.. . .international oil co.; chemicals, dept. stores (Montgomery Ward).

Mohasco Corp.. . .57 Lyon St., Amsterdam, NY 12010. . .(518) 841-2211. . .H. J. Broner. . .interior furnishings.

Monsanto Company.. . .800 N. Lindbergh Blvd., St. Louis, MO 63166. . .(314) 694-1000. . .R. J. Mahoney. . .chemicals, plastics, agricultural prods., textiles.

Morton Thiokol, Inc.. . .110 N. Wacker Dr., Chicago, IL 60606. . .(312) 621-5200. . .Charles S. Locke. . .salt (Morton), household cleaning prods. (Fantastik; Spray 'n Wash), specialty chemicals.

Motorola, Inc.. . .1303 E. Algonquin Rd., Schaumburg, IL 60196. . .(312) 397-5000. . .R. W. Galvin. . .electronic equipment and components.

Murray Ohio Manuf. Co.. . .219 Franklin Rd., Brentwood, TN 37027. . .(615) 373-6500. . .J.N. Anderson. . .bicycles, power mowers.

NCR Corp.. . .1700 S. Patterson Blvd., Dayton, OH 45479. . .(513) 449-2000. . .Charles E. Exley, Jr.. . .business information processing systems.

National Distillers & Chemical Corp.. . .99 Park Ave., N.Y., NY 10016. . .(212) 551-0436. . .Drummond C. Bell. . .wines and liquors, chemicals, insurance. . .Almaden Vineyards.

National Semiconductor Corp.. . .2900 Semiconductor Dr., Santa Clara, CA 95051. . .(408) 721-5000. . .Charles E. Sporck. . .manuf. of semiconductors.

New York Times Co.. . .229 W. 43rd St., N.Y., NY 10036. . .(212) 556-1234. . .A. O. Sulzberger. . .newspapers, radio, CATV stations, magazines (Family Circle; Golf Digest).

North American Philips Corp.. . .100 E. 42d St., N.Y., NY 10017. . .(212) 697-3600. . .C. Bruynes. . .consumer prods., electrical, electronic prods., professional equip. . .Magnavox; Norelco.

Northrop Corp.. . .1840 Century Park E., Los Angeles, CA 90067. . .(213) 553-6262. . .Thomas V. Jones. . .aircraft, electronics, communications.

Northwest Industries, Inc.. . .6300 Sears Tower, Chicago, IL 60606. . .(312) 876-7000. . .B.W. Heineman. . .air transport.

Noxell Corp.. . .11050 York Rd., Cockeysville, MD. . .(301) 628-7300. . .G. L. Bunting, Jr.. . .toiletry, household, consumer prods. (Noxzema; Rain Tree; Lestoil; Cover Girl).

Occidental Petroleum Corp.. . .10889 Wilshire Blvd., Los Angeles, CA 90024. . .(213) 879-1700. . .Dr. Armand Hammer. .-.oil, gas, chemicals, coal.

Ogden Corp.. . .277 Park Ave., New York NY 10017. . .(212) 754-4000. . .R. E. Ablon. . .transportation, foods, metals.

Olin Corp.. . .120 Long Ridge Rd., Stamford, CT 06904. . .(203) 356-2000. . .John M. Henske. . .chemicals, metals, paper, sporting and defense ammunition.

Outboard Marine Corp.. . .100 Sea Horse Dr., Waukegan, IL 60085. . .(312) 689-6200. . .C.D. Strang. . .outboard motors,

mowers (Lawn Boy).

Owens-Corning Fiberglas Corp.. . .Fiberglas Tower, Toledo, OH 43659. . .(419) 248-8000. . .W.W. Boeschenstein. . .glass fiber and related prods.

Owens-Illinois, Inc.. . .One SeaGate, Toledo, OH 43666. . .(419) 247-5000. . .R.J. Lanigan. . .glass, corrugated, and plastic containers.

Oxford Industries, Inc.. . .222 Piedmont Ave., N.E., Atlanta, GA 30308. . .(404) 659-2424. . .J.H. Lanier. . .men's and women's apparel products.

Pan American World Airways.. . .Pan Am Bldg., 200 Park Ave., N.Y., NY 10166. . .(212) 880-1234. . .C. Edward Acker. . .air transportation.

Papercraft Corp.. . .Papercraft Park, Pittsburgh, PA 15238. . .(412) 362-8000. . .M. P. Katz. . .gift wrapping paper, ribbons, artificial Christmas trees; household products (Ty-D-Bol toilet cleaner; Esquire shoe polish).

Parker Pen Co.. . .1 Parker Place, Janesville, WI 53545. . .(608) 755-7000. . .M.F. Fromstein. . .writing instruments, recreational equip., temp. help service (Manpower, Inc.).

J.C. Penney Co.. . .1301 Ave. of the Americas, N.Y., NY 10019. . .(212) 957-4321. . .W. R. Howell, chmn.. . .dept. stores, catalog sales, food, drugs, insurance.

Pennzoil Co.. . .Pennzoil Pl., Houston, TX 77252. . .(713) 236-7876. . .J.H. Liedtke. . .Integrated oil and gas co.

Pep Boys—Manny, Moe & Jack.. . .3111 W. Allegheny Ave., Philadelphia, PA 19132. . .(215) 229-9000. . .B. Strauss. . .automotive parts and accessories, retail stores, household items, hardware, bicycles.

PepsiCo, Inc.. . .Anderson Hill Rd., Purchase, NY 10577. . .(914) 253-2000. . .D. M. Kendall. . .soft drinks, (Pepsi-Cola; Mountain Dew), snack foods (Frito-Lay; Doritos) restaurants (Pizza Hut; Taco Bell), sporting goods (Wilson), transportation (North American Van Lines).

Pfizer Inc.. . .235 E. 42d St., N.Y., NY 10017. . .(212) 573-2323. . .E.T. Pratt, Jr.. . .pharmaceutical, hospital, agricultural, chemical prods.

Philip Morris, Inc.. . .120 Park Ave., N.Y., NY 10017. . .(212) 880-5000. . .H. Maxwell. . .cigarettes (Marlboro, Benson & Hedges, Merit, Virginia Slims); beer (Miller High Life, Lite; Lowenbrau brands); soft drinks (Seven-up); specialty chemicals, paper, packaging materials, real estate; packaged foods (General Foods products).

Phillips-Van Heusen Corp.. . .1290 Ave. of the Americas, New York, NY 10104. . .(212) 541-5200. . .L. S. Phillips. . .men, boys apparel.

Pillsbury Co.. . .200 S. 6th St., Minneapolis, MN 55402. . .(612) 330-4966. . .W. H. Spoor. . .canned & frozen vegetables (Green Giant), bakery, flour mixes, ice cream (Haagen Dazs); restaurants (Burger King; Steak and Ale).

Pitney Bowes, Inc.. . .Walter H. Wheeler Dr., Stamford, CT 06904. . .(203) 356-5000. . .G. B. Harvey. . .postage meters, mail handling equip., office equipment, retail systems.

Playboy Enterprises, Inc.. . .919 N. Michigan Ave., Chicago, IL 60691. . .(312) 751-8000. . .Hugh Hefner. . .magazine publishing, night clubs, CATV.

Polaroid Corp.. . .549 Technology Sq., Cambridge, MA 02139. . .(617) 577-2000. . .W. J. McCune, Jr.. . .photographic equip., supplies and optical goods.

Ponderosa, Inc.. . .P.O. Box 578, Dayton, OH 45401. . .(513) 890-6400. . .G. S. Office, Jr.. . .steakhouse restaurants.

Prentice-Hall, Inc.. . .Sylvan Ave., Englewood, NJ 07632. . .(201) 592-2000. . .D. A. Schaefer. . .publishes college, high and elementary school textbooks.

Procter & Gamble Co.. . .301 E. 6th St., Cincinnati, OH 45202. . .(513) 562-1100. . .J. G. Smale. . .soap & detergent (Ivory; Dash; Tide; Spic and Span), shortenings (Crisco; Fluffo),toiletries (Crest and Gleem toothpastes; Prell, and Head and Shoulders shampoos), pharmaceuticals (Pepto-Bismol), Pampers disposable diapers, Folger coffee.

Purolator Courier Corp.. . .131 Morristown Road, Basking Ridge, NJ 07920. . .(201) 953-6400. . .W.H. Waltrip. . .auto equip., courier and guard services.

Quaker Oats Co.. . .Merchandise Mart Plaza, Chicago, IL 60654. . .(312) 222-7111. . .William D. Smithburg. . .foods, cereal (Life; Cap'n Crunch; Puffed Wheat; Puffed Rice), foods (Aunt Jemima; Celeste pizza; Van Camp's pork and beans; Gatorade), pet foods (Ken-L-Ration; Puss 'Boots), Fisher Price toys, Magic Pan restaurants.

Quaker State Oil Refining Corp.. . .255 Elm St., Oil City, PA 16301. . .(814) 676-7676. . .Q.E. Wood. . .refining, marketing petroleum prods., filters, mining & marketing coal.

RCA Corp....30 Rockefeller Plaza, N.Y., NY 10020...(212) 621-6000...T. F. Bradshaw...radio, television (NBC), electronics, financial services, auto rental (Hertz).

Ralston Purina Co....Checkerboard Sq., St. Louis, MO 63164...(314) 982-1000...W. R. Stritz...pet and livestock food, Jack In the Box restaurants.

Ramada Inns, Inc....3838 E. Van Buren, Phoenix, AZ 85008...(602) 273-4000...Richard Snell...hotel operation, casinos (Tropicana).

Raytheon Company....141 Spring St., Lexington, MA 02173...(617) 862-6600...Thomas L. Phillips...electronics, aviation, appliances...Amana Refrigeration; Beech Aircraft.

Revlon, Inc....767 5th Ave., N.Y., NY 10153...(212) 572-5000...Michael C. Bergerac...cosmetics, pharmaceuticals.

Reynolds Metals Co....6601 W. Broad St., Richmond, VA 23261...(804) 281-2000...D. P. Reynolds...aluminum prods.

R.J. Reynolds Industries, Inc....Reynolds Blvd., Winston-Salem, NC 27102...(919) 773-2000...J. Tylee Wilson...crude oil, petroleum, transportation, tobacco (Camels; More), food, candy, gum, and beverage prods (Del Monte and Nabisco Brand), restaurants (Kentucky Fried Chicken), toiletries (Aqua Velva), pharmaceutical prods (Geritol).

Richardson-Vicks Inc....10 Westport Rd., Wilton, CT 06897...(203) 762-2222...J.S. Scott...health and personal care prods. (NyQuil; Oil of Olay), drugs, specialty chemicals.

Rite Aid Corp....Shiremanstown, PA 17011...(717) 761-2633...A. Grass...discount drug stores.

A.H. Robins Co., Inc....1407 Cummings Dr., Richmond, VA 23261...(804) 257-2000...E.C. Robins, Jr...health care, consumer prods. (Chap Stick; Quencher), Sergeant's pet care prods.

Rockwell Intl. Corp....600 Grant St., Pittsburgh, PA 15219...(412) 565-2000...R. Anderson...aerospace, electronic, automotive prods.

Roper Corp....1905 W. Court St., Kankakee, IL 60901...(815) 937-6000...C.M. Hoover...appliances, home and lawn prods.

Rorer Group Inc....500 Virginia Dr., Ft. Washington, PA 19034...(215) 628-6000...R.E. Cawthorn...pharmaceuticals (Maalox; Ascriptin; Emetrol).

Royal Crown Cos., Inc....41 Perimeter Center East, Atlanta, GA 30346...(404) 394-6120...D.A. McMahon...soft drinks (Nehi; RC Cola; Diet Rite Cola), restaurants (Arby's), citrus prods., home furnishings.

Rubbermaid Inc....1147 Akron Rd., Wooster, OH 44691...(216) 264-6464...S. C. Gault...rubber and plastic consumer prods.

Ryder System, Inc....3600 NW 82d Ave., Miami, FL 33166...(305) 593-3726...M. A. Burns...truck leasing service.

SCM Corp....299 Park Ave., N.Y., NY 10171...(212) 752-2700...Paul H. Elicker...typewriters, appliances, food, chemicals, paper prods... Smith Corona; Proctor-Silex.

Safeway Stores, Inc....4th & Jackson Sts., Oakland, CA 94660... (415) 891-3000 ... P. A. Magowan ...retail food stores.

Santa Fe Southern Pacific Corp.,...224 S. Michigan Ave., Chicago, IL 60604...(312) 427-4900...J. J. Schmidt...railroad, real estate, construction, natural resources.

Sara Lee Corp....3 First National Plaza, Chicago, IL 60602...(312) 726-2600...J.H. Bryan, Jr...baked goods, fresh and processed meats, fresh and frozen fruits and vegetables and other packaged foods, beverages, tobacco products, hosiery, intimate apparel and knitwear; Electrolux; Fuller Brush; Hanes; Gant; Popsicle; Shasta.

Schering-Plough Corp....One Giralda Farms, Madison, NJ 07940...(201) 822-7000...R. P. Luciano...pharmaceuticals, consumer prods; radio stations.

Schlumberger Ltd....277 Park Ave., New York, NY 10172...(212) 350-9400...Jean Riboud...oilfield services, electronics, measurement and control devices.

Scott Paper Co....Scott Plaza, Phila., PA 19113...(215) 521-5000...P. E. Lippincott...paper prods.

Scovill Inc....500 Chase Pkwy., Waterbury, CT 06708...(203) 757-6061...W. F. Andrews...automotive, security, housing prods., sewing aids, small appliances (Hamilton Beach).

Seagram Co. Ltd....1430 Peel St., Montreal, Que., Canada H3A 1S9...(514) 849-5271...E.M. Bronfman...distilled spirits & wine (Crown Royal; Chivas Regal; Calvert; Wolfschmidt Vodka; Paul Masson; Christian Brothers; Gold Seal; Myer's Jamaica Rum).

G.D. Searle & Co....P.O. Box 1045, Skokie, IL 60076...(312) 982-7000...Donald Rumsfeld...pharmaceutical/consumer, medical, optical prods., vision centers.

Sears, Roebuck & Co....Sears Tower, Chicago, IL 60684...(312) 875-2500...Edward R. Telling...merchandising, insurance (Allstate), financial services (Dean Winter).

Shell Oil Co....P.O. Box 2463, Houston, TX 77001...(713) 241-4083...John F. Bookout...oil, gas, chemicals.

Sherwin-Williams Co....101 Prospect Ave. N.W., Cleveland, OH 44115...(216) 566-2000...John G. Breen...world's largest paint producer; drug stores.

Skyline Corp....2520 By-Pass Rd., Elkhart, IN 46515...(219) 294-6521...Arthur J. Decio...mfg. housing and recreational vehicles.

Smithkline Beckman Corp....One Franklin Plaza, Phila., PA 19101...(215) 751-4000...H. Wendt...pharmaceuticals, animal health prods., diagnostic instruments.

Smucker (J.M.) Co....Strawberry Lane, Orville, OH 44667...(216) 682-0015...P. H. Smucker...preserves, jams, jellies, toppings.

Snap-on Tools Corp....2801 80th St., Kenosha, WI 53141...(414) 656-5200...W. B. Rayburn...manuf. mechanic's tools, equip.

Sony Corp....Tokyo, Japan...A. Morita...manuf. televisions, radios, tape recorders, audio equip., video tape recorders.

Southland Corp....2828 N. Haskell Ave., Dallas, TX 75221...(214) 828-7011...J.P. Thompson...convenience stores (7-Eleven; Gristede's), auto parts stores.

Sperry Corp....1290 Ave. of the Americas, N.Y., NY 10104...(212) 956-2121...G. G. Probst...computers and data processing, farm, guidance & control equip.

Squibb Corp....P.O. Box 4000, Princeton, NJ 08540...(609) 921-4000...Richard M. Furlaud...drugs, confectionery, household prods...Charles of the Ritz.

A.E. Staley Manufacturing Co....2200 E. Eldorado St., Decatur, IL 62525...(217) 423-4411...Donald E. Nordlund...corn and soybean processing, consumer prods.

Standard Oil Co. (Ohio)....Midland Bldg., Cleveland, OH 44115...(216) 575-4141...Alton W. Whitehouse, Jr...oil & natural gas.

Stanley Works....1000 Stanley Drive, P.O. Box 7000, New Britain CT 06050...(203) 225-5111...D.W. Davis...hand tools, hardware, door opening equipment.

Sterling Drug Inc....90 Park Ave., N.Y., NY 10016...(212) 907-2000...J.M. Pietruski...pharmaceuticals, cosmetics & toiletries, household, proprietary prods., chemicals (Bayer Aspirin, Lysol, Dorothy Gray; Parfums Givenchy).

J.P. Stevens & Co., Inc....1185 Ave. of the Americas, N.Y., NY 10036...(212) 930-2000...W. Stevens...fabrics, carpets, other textile home furnishings.

Stop & Shop Companies, Inc....P.O. Box 369, Boston, MA 02101...(617) 770-8000...A.J. Goldberg...supermarkets, discount department stores (Bradlees and Medi Mart), The Charles B. Perkins Co. (which operates tobacco shops, Hallmark Card and Gift Shops, and Perkins/Hallmark).

Storer Communications, Inc....1200 Biscayne Blvd., Miami, FL 33261...(305) 652-9900...T. Lee...television broadcasting, CATV.

Sun Company, Inc....100 Matsonford Rd., Radnor, PA 19087...(215) 293-6000...R. McClements...petroleum.

Supermarkets General Corp....301 Blair Rd., Woodbridge, NJ 07095...(201) 499-3000...L. Lieberman...supermarkets (Pathmark); Rickel Home Centers.

Taft Broadcasting Co....1718 Young St., Cincinnati, OH 45210...(513) 721-1414...C.S. Mechem, Jr...radio, TV broadcasting, TV cartoons (Hanna-Barbera), amusement parks.

Tambrands Inc....10 Delaware Dr., Lake Success, NY 11042...(516) 437-8800...E. H. Shutt, Jr...menstrual tampons (Tampax).

Tandy Corp....1800 One Tandy Center, Fort Worth, TX 76102...(817) 390-3700...J.V. Roach...consumer electronics retailing & mfg...Radio Shack.

Teledyne, Inc....1901 Ave. of the Stars, Los Angeles, CA 90067...(213) 277-3311...H. E. Singleton...electronics, aerospace prods., industrial prods., insurance, finance.

Tenneco, Inc....P.O. Box 2511, Houston, TX 77001...(713) 757-2131...J. L. Ketelsen...oil, natural gas pipelines, construction and farm equip.

Texaco Inc...2000 Westchester Ave., White Plains, NY 10650...(914) 253-4000...K. McKinley...petroleum and petroleum prods.

Texas Instruments Inc...P.O. Box 225474, Dallas, TX 75265...(214) 238-2011...J. F. Bucy...electrical & electronics prods.

Textron, Inc...40 Westminster St., Providence, RI 02903...(401) 421-2800...Robert P. Straetz...aerospace, consumer, industrial, metal prods, consumer finance, insurance, and management services.

Tidewater Inc...1440 Canal St., New Orleans, LA 70112...(504) 568-1010...J.P. Laborde...marine equip. and services for oil industry.

Time Inc... Time & Life Bldg., New York, NY 10020...(212) 586-1212...J.R. Munro...magazine publisher (Time; Sports Illustrated; Fortune; Money; People), CATV (Home Box Office), forest prods.

Tootsie Roll Industries, Inc.,..7401 S. Cicero Ave., Chicago, IL 60629...(312) 581-6100...M.J. Gordon...candy (Tootsie Roll, Mason Dots, Mason Crows, Bonomo Turkish Taffy).

The Toro Company...811 Lyndale Ave. South, Bloomington, MN 55420...(612) 887-5900...K.B. Melrose...lawn and turf maintenance, and snow removal equipment.

Toys "R" Us...395 W. Passaic St., Rochelle Park, NJ 07662...(201) 845-5033...Charles Lazarus...toy retailer.

Transamerica Corp...600 Montgomery St., San Francisco, CA 94111...(415) 983-4180...J.R. Harvey...insurance, financial, business services (Occidental Life Ins.; Budget Rent A Car).

TransWorld Corp...605 3d Ave., N.Y., NY 10116...(212) 557-3000...L. Edwin Smart...holding co...Trans World Airlines; Hilton International; Spartan Food Systems, Century 21 real estate corp.

Travelers Corp... One Tower Sq., Hartford, CT 06115...(203) 277-0111...E. H. Budd...insurance.

Trinity Industries, Inc...2525 Stimmons Freeway, P.O. Box 10587, Dallas, TX 75207...(214) 631-4420...W.R. Wallace...manufactures variety of metal products.

TRW Inc...23555 Euclid Avenue, Cleveland, OH 44117...(216) 383-2121...R.F. Mettler...car and truck operations, electronics, and space systems.

UAL, Inc...1200 Algonquin Rd., Elk Grove Township, IL 60007...(312) 952-4000...R. J. Ferris...holding co. United Airlines, Westin Hotels.

Unilever, N.V... Museumpark, Rotterdam, The Netherlands...H.F. van der Hoven...soap, detergent, margarine, frozen food, toothpaste, tea, dried soups, ice cream (Lever Brothers, Lipton).

Union Carbide Corp... Old Ridgebury Rd., Danbury, CT 06817...(203) 794-2000...W. M. Anderson...chemicals.

Union Pacific Corp...345 Park Ave., N.Y., NY 10154...(212) 418-7800...W.S. Cook...railroad, natural resources.

Uniroyal, Inc... Middlebury, CT 06749...(203) 573-2000...Joseph P. Flannery...tires, chemical, plastic prods.

United States Gypsum Co...101 S. Wacker Dr., Chicago, IL 60606...(312) 321-4000...E. W. Duffy...largest U.S. producer of gypsum & related prods.

United States Leasing Int'l, Inc...733 Front Street, San Francisco, CA 94111...(415) 627-9000...D.E. Mundell...equipment leasing (test instruments, office products, computer peripherals, health-care equipment).

United States Shoe Corp... One Eastwood Dr., Cincinnati, OH 45227...(513) 527-7000...P. G. Barach...apparel, retailer (Casual Corner; J. Riggins), shoes (Red Cross; Joyce).

United States Steel Corp...600 Grant St., Pittsburgh, PA 15230...(412) 433-1121...David M. Roderick...largest U.S. steel co., chemicals, transportation, oil.

United States Tobacco Co...100 W. Putnam Ave., Greenwich, CT 06830...(203) 661-1100...L.F. Bantle...smokeless tobacco (Copenhagen; Skoal; Happy Days), pipes (Dr. Grabow), pipe tobacco.

United Technologies Corp... United Technologies Bldg., Hartford, CT 06101...(203) 728-7000...Harry J. Gray...aerospace, industrial prods. & services...Carrier Corp.; Otis Elevator; Pratt & Whitney, Sikorsky Aircraft.

Univar, Corp...1600 Norton Building, Seattle, WA 98504...(206) 447-5911...J.H. Wiborg...industrial and agricultural chemicals, laboratory and graphic arts products distributor, home furnishing supplies and fabrics distributors.

Universal Foods Corp...433 East Michigan Street, Milwaukee, WI 53202...(414) 271-6755...J.L. Murray...yeast products, cheese products, dehydrated seasonings, food colors and flavors, imported gourmet foods.

Upjohn Co...7000 Portage Rd., Kalamazoo, MI 49001...(616)

323-4000...R.T. Parfet, Jr...pharmaceuticals, chemicals, agricultural and health care prods.

USAIR Group, Inc...1911 Jefferson Hwy., Arlington, VA 22002...(703) 892-7000...E.I. Colodny...Air carrier of passengers, property, and mail.

VF Corp...1047 No. Park Rd., Wyomissing, PA 19610...(215) 378-1151...L.R. Pugh...apparel...Vanity Fair; Lee jeans.

Viacom Int'l Inc...1211 Avenue of the Americas, New York, NY 10036...(212) 575-5175...T.A. Elkes...Television program and feature film distributor, cable television systems operator, radio and television stations operator.

Vulcan Materials Co... One Metroplex Dr., Birmingham, AL 35209...(205) 877-3000...W.H. Blount...construction materials, chemicals, metals.

Wal-Mart Stores Inc...702 W. 8th St., Bentonville, AK 72712...(501) 273-4000...S.M. Walton...discount dept. stores.

Walgreen Co...200 Wilmot Rd., Deerfield, IL 60015...(312) 940-2500...Charles R. Walgreen 3d...retail drug chain, restaurants (Wags).

Wang Laboratories, Inc... One Industrial Ave., Lowell, MA 01851...A. Wang...word processors.

Warnaco Inc...350 Lafayette St., Bridgeport, CT 06601...(203) 579-8272...R.J. Matura...apparel...Hathaway, Puritan, Rosanna, White Stag.

Warner Communications Inc...75 Rockefeller Plaza, N.Y., NY 10019...(212) 484-8000...Steven J. Ross...filmed entertainment, records & music publishing, book publishing, CATV system, consumer prods.

Warner-Lambert Co...201 Tabor Rd., Morris Plains, NJ 07950...(201) 540-2000...J.D. Williams...health care, optical prods., candy.

Washington Post Co...1150 15th St., N.W., Washington, DC 20071...(202) 223-6000...Katharine Graham...newspapers, magazines (Newsweek), TV stations.

Weis Markets, Inc...1000 South Second Street, Sunbury, PA 17801...(717) 286-4571...S. Weis...frozen foods and grocery items.

Wendy's Intl., Inc...PO Box 256, Dublin, OH 43017...(614) 764-3100...R. L. Barney...quick service restaurants.

Western Air Lines, Inc...6060 Avion Drive, Los Angeles, CA 90045...(213) 216-3000...G. Grinstein...air carrrier of passengers, cargo, and mail.

Western Union Corp... One Lake St., Upper Saddle River, NJ 07458...(201) 825-5000...R.S. Leventhal...telecommunications.

Westinghouse Electric Corp... Westinghouse Bldg., Gateway Center, Pittsburgh, PA 15222...(412) 255-3800...D. D. Danforth...manuf. electrical, mechanical equip., radio and television stations.

West Point-Pepperell, Inc... West Point, GA 31833...(404) 645-4000...J.L. Lanier, Jr...apparel, households and industrial textiles.

Westvaco Corp...299 Park Avenue, New York, NY 10171...(212) 688-5000...D.L. Luke III...manufactures paper for graphic reproduction, communications, and packaging (largest producer of envelopes in the world).

Weyerhaeuser Co... Tacoma, WA 98477...(206) 924-2345...George H. Weyerhaeuser...manuf., distribution of forest prods.

Whirlpool Corp... Administrative Center, Benton Harbor, MI 49022...(616) 926-5000...J.D. Sparks...major home appliances.

White Consolidated Industries, Inc...11770 Berea Rd., Cleveland, OH 44111...(216) 252-3700...R.H. Holdt...major home appliances (Kelvinator, Frigidaire), industrial equip. and machinery.

Willamette Industries, Inc...3800 1st Interstate Tower, Portland, OR 97201...(503) 227-5581...William Swindells, Jr...building materials and paper prods.

Winn-Dixie Stores, Inc...5050 Edgewood Ct., Jacksonville, FL 32203...(904) 783-5000...A.D. Davis...retail grocery chain.

F.W. Woolworth Co...233 Broadway, N.Y., NY 10007...(212) 553-2000...J.W. Lynn...variety stores, shoe stores (Kinney).

Wm. Wrigley, Jr. Co...410 N. Michigan Ave., Chicago, IL 60611...(312) 644-2121...William Wrigley...chewing gum.

Xerox Corp... Stamford, CT 06904...(203) 329-8700...D, T Kearns...equip. for reproduction, reduction, and transmission of printed information.

Zale Corp...001 West Walnut Mill Lane, Irving, TX 75038...(214) 257-4000...D. Zale...jewelry retailer.

Zenith Electronics Corp...1000 Milwaukee Ave., Glenview, IL 60025...(312) 391-7000...Jerry K. Pearlman...consumer electronic prods.

ECONOMICS

U.S. Budget Receipts and Outlays—1981-1984

Source: U.S. Treasury Department, Bureau of Govt. Financial Operations
(Fiscal years end Sept. 30)
(1981 in thousands; 1982-84 in millions)

Classification	Fiscal 1981	Fiscal 1982	Fiscal 1983	Fiscal 1984
Net Receipts				
Individual income taxes	$285,550,802	$298,111	$288,938	$295,955
Corporation income taxes	61,137,136	49,207	37,022	56,893
Social insurance taxes and contributions:				
Federal old-age and survivors insurance	117,757,091	122,840	128,972	152,444
Federal disability insurance	12,418,490	20,626	18,348	15,907
Federal hospital insurance	30,360,679	34,301	35,641	40,262
Railroad retirement taxes	2,457,238	2,917	2,805	3,321
Total employment taxes and contributions. .	162,993,498	180,686	185,766	212,184
Other insurance and retirement:				
Unemployment	15,398,386	16,234	18,799	25,138
Federal employees retirement	3,908,270	4,140	4,351	4,494
Civil service retirement and disability	76,148	72	78	86
Total social insurance taxes and contributions	186,426,256	201,131	208,994	241,902
Excise taxes	40,839,143	36,311	35,300	37,361
Estate and gift taxes	6,786,537	7,991	6,053	6,010
Customs duties	8,082,808	8,854	8,655	11,370
Deposits of earnings-Federal Reserve Banks	12,833,713	15,186	14,492	15,684
All other miscellaneous receipts	955,899	976	1,109	1,281
Net Budget Receipts	$602,612,295	$617,766	600,562	666,457
Net Outlays				
Legislative Branch	$1,208,819	$1,362	$1,448	$1,584
The Judiciary	637,279	705	787	866
Executive Office of the President:				
The White House Office	21,078	20	21	16
Office of Management and Budget	35,122	37	35	37
Total Executive Office	95,635	95	94	95
Funds appropriated to the President:				
Appalachian regional development	336,795	312	264	212
Disaster relief	400,547	115	202	243
National assistance-security	3,546,682	3,052	3,677	5,034
Foreign assistance-multilateral	1,489,325	1,578	1,460	1,699
Agency for International Development	. . .	. . .	868	1,140
International Development Assistance	. . .	. . .	2,352	2,876
Total funds appropriated to the President . .	7,009,908	6,073	5,427	8,538
Agriculture Department:				
Food stamp program	11,252,902	11,014	11,839	11,561
Farmer's Home Admin	. . .	. . .	4,303	6,066
Total Agriculture Department	26,029,802	36,213	46,384	37,462
Commerce Department	2,226,045	2,045	1,929	1,892
Defense Department:				
Military personnel	36,408,884	42,341	45,523	47,655
Retired military personnel	13,729,065	14,938	15,945	16,471
Operation and maintenance	51,863,633	59,674	64,915	67,369
Procurement	35,191,231	43,271	53,624	61,879
Research and development	15,277,593	17,729	20,554	23,117
Military construction	2,458,186	2,922	3,524	3,706
Corps of Engineers and civil functions	3,124,375	2,944	2,917	3,039
Total Defense Department	159,183,160	185,821	207,945	223,877
Education Department	15,087,770	14,081	14,567	15,494
Energy Department	11,631,087	7,705	8,356	8,358
Health and Human Services Department:				
Food and Drug Administration	337,167	343	364	390
National Institutes of Health	3,603,805	3,665	3,750	4,157
Public Health Service	8,378,623	8,334	7,856	8,184
Old-age and survivors benefits	119,413,467	134,661	148,642	155,852
Social Security Administration	159,500,955	176,265	214,012	208,780
Human Development Services	5,090,101	5,104	5,344	5,896
Total Health and Human Services Dept	230,303,851	251,268	276,453	292,224
Housing and Urban Development Department	14,032,380	14,491	15,315	16,517
Interior Department	4,427,690	3,793	4,569	4,889
Justice Department:				
Federal Bureau of Investigation	691,176	737	824	916
Total Justice Department	2,682,472	2,584	2,849	3,171
Labor Department:				
Unemployment Trust Fund	18,739,096	24,282	32,655	26,089
Total Labor Department	30,083,819	30,736	38,194	24,522
State Department	1,897,364	2,185	2,267	2,428
Transportation Department	22,554,054	19,929	20,616	23,904
Treasury Department:				
Internal Revenue Service	5,033,188	5,749	6,391	6,095
Interest on the public debt	95,589,367	117,404	128,813	153,838
Total Treasury Department	92,632,962	110,521	115,248	140,864
Environmental Protection Agency	5,231,851	5,004	4,299	4,057

Classification Net Outlays (cont'd)	Fiscal 1981	Fiscal 1982	Fiscal 1983	Fiscal 1984
General Services Administration	$185,562	$229	$145	$277
National Aeronautics and Space Administration	5,421,388	6,026	6,664	7,048
Office of Personel Management	18,088,914	19,973	21,278	22,590
Small Business Administration	1,912,527	631	479	255
Veterans Administration	22,904,006	23,927	24,816	25,596
Independent agencies:				
ACTION	150,164	136	126	133
Board for International Broadcasting	88,199	83	91	105
Civil Aeronautics Board	147,151	110	78	62
Consumer Product Safety Commission	40,861	34	33	34
Corporation for Public Broadcasting	162,000	172	137	138
District of Columbia	492,231	439	427	486
Equal Employment Opportunity Commission	134,212	138	152	143
Export-Import Bank of the United States	2,066,222	1,173	578	1,068
Federal Communications Commission	80,892	80	82	87
Federal Deposit Insurance Corporation	−1,725,994	−1,440	−613	−248
Federal Emergency Management Agency	372,135	279	506	590
Federal Home Loan Bank Board	70,081	−588	−453	−561
Federal Trade Commission	70,081	68	65	66
Intragovernmental Agencies	69,152	69	55	39
Interstate Commerce Commission	74,190	11	65	56
Legal Services Corporation	324,314	259	234	271
Merit Systems Protection Board	20,569	20	24	28
National Foundation on the Arts and Humanities	314,172	298	269	302
National Labor Relations Board	114,450	119	123	130
National Science Foundation	975,009	1,099	1,055	1,198
National Transportation Safety Board	18,296	17	NA	40
Nuclear Regulatory Commission	416,844	442	515	462
Postal Service	1,343,217	707	789	877
Railroad Retirement Board	5,307,621	5,721	3,963	3,647
Securities and Exchange Commission	78,025	79	90	92
Smithsonian Institution	166,875	181	194	211
Tennessee Valley Authority	1,927,758	1,527	820	351
U.S. Information Agency	...	...	508	575
U.S. Railway Association	191,250	28	4	2
Other Independent agencies	464,643	449	327	340
Total independent agencies	35,567,788	33,110	10,350	10,977
Undistributed offsetting receipts	−30,306,097	−29,261	−35,565	−35,805
Net Budget Outlays	660,544,033	728,424	795,916	841,800
Less net receipts	602,612,295	617,766	600,562	666,457
Deficit	−$57,931,739	−$110,658	−195,354	−175,342

(NA) Not available.

U.S. Net Receipts and Outlays

Source: U.S. Treasury Department; annual statements for year ending June 30[3] (thousands of dollars)

Yearly average	Receipts	Outlays	Yearly average	Receipts	Outlays	Yearly average	Receipts	Outlays
1789-1800[1]	5,717	5,776	1871-1875	336,830	287,460	1916-1920[6]	3,483,652	8,065,333
1801-1810[2]	13,056	9,086	1876-1880	288,124	255,598	1921-1925	4,306,673	3,578,989
1811-1820[2]	21,032	23,943	1881-1885	366,961	257,691	1926-1930	4,069,138	3,182,807
1821-1830[2]	21,928	16,162	1886-1890	375,448	279,134	1931-1935[4]	2,770,973	5,214,874
1831-1840[2]	30,461	24,495	1891-1895	352,891	363,599	1936-1940[4]	4,960,614	10,192,367
1841-1850[2]	28,545	34,097	1896-1900	434,877	457,451	1941-1945[4]	25,951,137	66,037,928
1851-1860	60,237	60,163	1901-1905	559,481	535,559	1946-1950[5][7]	39,047,243	42,334,534
1861-1865	160,907	683,785	1906-1910	628,507	639,178			
1866-1870	447,301	377,642	1911-1915	710,227	720,252			

Fiscal year	Receipts	Outlays	Fiscal year	Receipts	Outlays	Fiscal year	Receipts	Outlays
1955	60,389,744	64,569,973	1973	232,191,842	246,603,359	1980	520,056,012	579,602,970
1960	77,763,460	76,539,413	1974	264,847,484	268,342,952	1981	602,612,295	660,544,033
1964	89,458,664	97,684,375	1975	281,037,466	324,641,586	1982	617,766,000	728,424,000
1965	93,071,797	96,506,904	1976	300,005,077	365,610,129	1983	600,562,000	795,916,000
1968[9]	153,675,705	172,803,186	1976 Trans[3]	81,772,766	94,472,996	1984	666,457,000	841,800,000
1970	193,843,791	194,968,258	1977[3]	356,861,331	401,896,376			
1971	188,332,129	210,652,667	1978	401,997,000	450,758,000			
1972[8]	215,262,639	238,285,907	1979	465,954,656	493,607,095			

(1) Average for period March 4, 1789, to Dec. 31, 1800. (2) Years ended Dec. 31, 1801 to 1842; average for 1841-1850 is for the period Jan. 1, 1841, to June 30, 1850. (3) Effective fiscal year 1977, fiscal year is reckoned Oct. 1-Sept. 30; transition quarter covers July 1, 1976-Sept. 30, 1976. (4) Expenditures for years 1932 through 1946 have been revised to include Government corps. (wholly owned) etc. (net). (5) Effective January 3, 1949, amounts refunded by the Government, principally for the overpayment of taxes, are being reported as deductions from total receipts rather than as expenditures. Also, effective July 1, 1948, payments to the Treasury, principally by wholly owned Government corporations for retirement of capital stock and for disposition of earnings, are excluded in reporting both budget receipts and expenditures. Neither of these changes affects the size of the budget surplus or deficit. Beginning 1931 figures in each case have been adjusted accordingly for comparative purposes. (6) Figures for 1918 through 1946 are revised to exclude statutory debt retirement (sinking fund, etc.). (7) Excludes $3 billion transferred to Foreign Economics Corporation Trust Fund, and includes $3 billion representing expenditures made from the FEC Trust Fund. (8) Effective fiscal year 1972 loan repayments and loan disbursements will be netted against expenditures and known as outlays. (9) From 1968, figures include trust funds (e.g. Social Security).

Summary of U.S. Receipts by Source and Outlays by Function

Source: U.S. Treasury Department, Financial Management Service

(in millions)

Net Receipts	Fiscal 1981	Fiscal 1982	Fiscal 1983	Fiscal 1984
Individual income taxes	$285,551	$298,111	$288,938	$295,955
Corporation income taxes	61,137	49,207	37,022	56,893
Social insurance taxes and contributions	183,086	201,132	185,766	212,184
Excise taxes	40,839	36,311	35,300	37,361
Estate and gift taxes	6,787	7,991	6,053	6,010
Customs duties	8,083	8,854	8,655	11,370
Miscellaneous receipts	13,790	16,161	15,601	16,965
Total	**$599,272**	**$617,766**	**$600,562**	**$666,457**
Net outlays				
National defense	$159,736	$187,397	$210,464	$227,405
International affairs	11,052	9,983	9,091	13,313
General science, space, and technology	6,422	7,096	7,783	8,271
Energy	10,351	4,844	4,046	2,464
Natural resources and environment	13,764	13,086	12,741	12,667
Agriculture	5,598	14,808	22,168	12,215
Commerce and housing credit	3,995	3,843	4,723	5,198
Transportation	23,312	20,589	21,358	24,705
Community and regional development	9,538	7,410	7,290	7,803
Education, training, employment and social services	30,533	25,411	25,695	26,616
Health	65,984	74,018	28,610	30,435
Income security	225,599	248,807	106,837	96,714
Social Security and Medicare	...	...	223,311	235,764
Veterans benefits and services	22,937	23,973	24,855	25,640
Administration of justice	4,720	4,648	5,082	5,616
General government	4,759	4,833	4,252	4,836
General purpose fiscal assistance	6,621	6,161	6,472	6,577
Interest	82,590	100,777	89,753	111,007
Undistributed offsetting receipts	−30,306	−29,261	−18,614	−15,454
Total	**$657,204**	**$728,424**	**$795,916**	**$841,800**

U.S. Direct Investment Abroad, Countries and Industries

Source: Bureau of Economic Analysis, U.S. Commerce Department

(millions of dollars)

	Direct investment position		Equity and intercompany account outflows (inflows (−))		Reinvested earnings		Fees and royalties		Income	
	1983	1984	1983	1984	1983	1984	1983	1984	1983	1984
All areas	226,962	233,412	4,209	6,462	9,603	10,965	6,530	6,275	21,271	23,078
Petroleum	60,330	63,319	−564	3,255	2,532	4,017	473	546	9,548	10,065
Manufacturing	90,171	93,012	1,247	−1,327	1,690	1,551	4,389	4,056	5,809	7,236
Other	76,461	77,081	3,526	4,534	5,381	5,397	1,668	1,673	5,914	5,777
Developed countries	169,975	174,057	−6	1,844	6,094	5,357	5,391	5,073	15,082	15,748
Petroleum	39,093	40,616	210	2,316	1,826	3,033	296	315	5,640	6,043
Manufacturing	71,771	72,866	928	−748	2,191	474	3,968	3,665	5,355	5,329
Other	59,111	60,575	−1,144	276	2,077	1,850	1,127	1,092	4,087	4,376
Canada	47,553	50,467	2,251	−116	3,672	2,695	1,161	991	5,165	5,500
Petroleum	10,883	11,614	443	213	949	941	32	37	1,342	1,468
Manufacturing	19,851	21,467	1,660	−309	1,921	1,314	970	762	2,646	3,090
Other	16,819	17,386	148	−20	802	440	159	192	1,177	942
Europe	102,689	103,663	−1,558	1,095	1,827	2,654	3,414	3,315	8,090	8,886
Petroleum	23,774	24,714	−106	1,561	671	2,184	205	229	3,698	4,166
Manufacturing	43,962	43,661	−473	−473	92	−674	2,528	2,475	2,088	1,864
Other	34,953	35,288	−979	7	1,064	1,144	681	611	2,304	2,856
Other	19,733	19,927	−699	865	595	8	816	766	1,827	1,362
Petroleum	4,436	4,288	−127	542	206	−92	59	50	600	409
Manufacturing	7,958	7,738	−259	34	178	−166	470	428	621	375
Other	7,339	7,901	−313	289	211	266	287	289	606	578
Developing countries	51,430	53,932	4,193	4,505	2,957	5,677	1,220	1,278	5,439	6,792
Petroleum	16,903	18,417	−704	890	158	1,015	260	308	3,184	3,523
Manufacturing	18,400	20,146	319	−580	−501	1,077	422	390	455	1,907
Other	16,127	15,369	4,578	4,195	3,300	3,585	538	580	1,800	1,362
Latin America	29,674	28,094	4,778	4,452	1,776	2,828	513	514	754	867
Petroleum	6,944	5,940	−173	547	78	−474	63	67	658	−32
Manufacturing	14,766	15,665	−25	−342	−909	537	181	143	−209	1,130
Other	7,964	6,489	4,976	4,247	2,607	2,765	269	304	305	−231
Other	21,756	25,838	−585	53	1,181	2,849	707	764	4,685	5,925
Petroleum	9,959	12,477	−531	343	80	1,489	197	241	2,526	3,555
Manufacturing	3,634	4,481	344	−238	408	540	241	247	664	777
Other	8,163	8,880	−398	−52	693	820	269	276	1,495	1,593
International	5,557	5,423	22	113	552	−69	−80	−76	749	537

Third World Debt

Source: World Bank

The following is a list of debt owed by Third World nations as of mid-1984.

Country	Dollars	Country	Dollars	Country	Dollars
Brazil	79.6 billion	Indonesia	21.8 billion	Egypt	15.5 billion
Mexico	66.7 billion	India	21.4 billion	Israel	15.1 billion
Argentina	24.6 billion	Yugoslavia	17.9 billion	Chile	15.0 billion
South Korea	23.1 billion	Turkey	15.9 billion	Venezuela	12.9 billion

U.S. Federal Budget Deficits Since 1946

(In Billions of Dollars)

Fiscal Year	President	Surplus=+ Deficit=−	% of GNP	Fiscal Year	President	Surplus=+ Deficit=−	% of GNP
1946	Truman	$15.9−	7.8%	1967	"	8.7−	1.1
1947	"	3.9+	Surplus	1968	"	25.2−	3.0
1948	"	12.0+	Surplus	1969	"	3.2+	Surplus
1949	"	0.6+	Surplus	1970	Nixon	2.8−	0.3
1950	"	3.1−	1.2	1971	"	23.0−	2.2
1951	"	6.1+	Surplus	1972	"	23.4−	2.1
1952	"	1.5−	0.4	1973	"	14.8−	1.2
1953	"	6.5−	1.8	1974	"	4.7−	0.3
1954	Eisenhower	1.2−	0.3	1975	Ford	45.2−	3.1
1955	"	3.0−	0.8	1976	"	79.4−	4.0
1956	"	4.1+	Surplus	1977	Carter	44.9−	2.4
1957	"	3.2+	Surplus	1978	"	48.8−	2.3
1958	"	2.9−	0.7	1979	"	27.7−	1.2
1959	"	12.9−	2.7	1980	"	59.6−	2.3
1960	"	0.3+	Surplus	1981	Reagan	57.9−	2.0
1961	"	3.4−	0.7	1982	"	110.6−	3.6
1962	Kennedy	7.1−	1.3	1983	"	195.4−	6.1
1963	"	4.8−	0.8	1984	"	175.3−	4.7
1964	Johnson	5.9−	1.0	1985	"	♦ 179.0−	4.6 est.
1965	"	1.6−	0.2	1986	"	171.9−est.	...
1966	"	3.8−	0.5				

Note: Fiscal year ends Sept. 30 (June 30 prior to 1977).

U.S. Balance of International Payments

Source: Bureau of Economic Analysis, U.S. Commerce Department
(millions of dollars)

	1955	1960	1965	1970	1975	1980	1982	1983	1984
Exports of goods and services . . .	19,948	28,861	41,086	65,674	155,729	342,485	350,058	333,586	362,421
Merchandise, adjusted	14,424	19,650	26,461	42,469	107,088	224,269	211,198	200,745	220,316
Transfers under U.S. military agency sales contracts	200	335	830	1,501	4,049	8,274	11,907	12,394	10,086
Receipts of income on U.S. investments abroad	2,817	4,616	7,436	11,747	25,351	72,506	84,768	78,023	87,609
Other services.	2,507	4,261	6,359	9,957	19,242	37,438	42,185	42,426	44,410
Imports of goods and services . . .	−17,795	−23,729	−32,801	−60,050	−133,000	−333,536	−349,974	−365,524	−452,539
Merchandise, adjusted	−11,527	−14,758	−21,510	−39,866	−98,185	−249,749	−247,642	−262,757	−328,597
Direct defense expenditures.	−2,901	−3,087	−2,952	−4,855	−4,795	−10,511	−12,225	−12,556	−11,651
Payments of income on foreign investments in the U.S.	−520	−1,237	−2,088	−5,516	−12,564	−42,120	−55,273	−52,621	−68,500
Other services.	−2,847	−4,646	−6,251	−9,815	−17,456	−31,158	−34,832	−37,590	−43,593
Unilateral transfers, net	−2,498	−2,308	−2,854	−3,294	−4,613	−7,077	−8,135	−8,852	−11,412
U.S. official reserve assets, net . . .	182	2,145	1,225	2,481	−849	−8,155	−4,965	−1,196	−3,131
U.S. Government assets, other than official reserve assets, net	−310	−1,100	−1,605	−1,589	−3,474	−5,162	−6,131	−5,006	−5,516
U.S. private assets, net	−1,255	−5,144	−5,335	−10,229	−35,380	−72,802	−108,122	−48,843	−11,800
Foreign official assets in the U.S., net .		1,473	134	6,908	7,027	15,497	3,672	5,795	3,424
Other foreign assets in the U.S., net . .		821	607	−550	8,643	42,615	90,775	78,526	93,895
Statistical discrepancy.	371	−1,019	−458	−219	5,917	24,982	32,821	11,513	24,660
Memoranda:									
Balance on merchandise trade . . .	2,897	4,892	4,951	2,603	8,903	−25,480	−36,444	−62,012	−108,281
Balance on goods and services . . .	2,153	5,132	8,284	5,625	22,729	8,950	84	−31,937	−90,119
Balance on goods, services, and remittances	1,556	4,496	7,238	4,067	21,011	6,604	2,549	−34,503	−93,010
Balance on current account	−345	2,824	5,431	2,331	18,116	1,873	−8,051	−40,790	−101,532

Note.—Details may not add to totals because of rounding.

Public Debt of the U.S.

Source: U.S. Treasury Department, Financial Management Service; Bureau of the Census

Fiscal year	Gross debt	Per cap.	Fiscal year	Gross debt	Per cap.	Fiscal year	Gross debt	Per cap.
1870	$2,436,453,269	$61.06	1930	$16,185,309,831	$131.51	1975	$533,188,976,772	$2,496.90
1880	2,090,908,872	41.60	1940	42,967,531,038	325.23	1980	907,701,290,900	3,969.55
1890	1,132,396,584	17.80	1950	256,087,352,351	1,688.30	1981	997,854,525,000	4,329.48
1900	1,263,416,913	16.60	1960	284,092,760,848	1,572.31	1982	1,142,035,000,000	4,862.30
1910	1,146,939,969	12.41	1965	313,818,898,984	1,612.70	1983	1,377,211,000,000	5,857.43
1920	24,299,321,467	228.23	1970	370,093,706,950	1,807.09	1984	1,572,267,000,000	6,626.57

Note: Through 1976 the fiscal year ended June 30. From 1977 on, fiscal year ends Sept. 30.

Gross National Product, National Income, and Personal Income

Source: Bureau of Economic Analysis, U.S. Commerce Department
includes Alaska and Hawaii beginning in 1960 (millions of dollars)

	1950	1960	1970	1975	1980	1984[1]
Gross national product	286,172	505,978	982,419	1,528,833	2,631,688	3,662.8
Less: Capital consumption allowances.	23,853	47,712	90,827	161,954	293,160	403.3
Equals: Net national product	262,319	458,266	894,592	1,366,879	2,338,528	3,259.6
Less: Indirect business tax and nontax liability .	23,422	45,389	94,027	139,246	213,387	304.0
Business transfer payments	778	1,974	3,983	7,599	11,677	17.6
Statistical discrepancy	2,030	−683	−2,076	7,371	2,291	−7.4
Plus: Subsidies minus current surplus of						
government enterprises	114	422	2,716	2,339	5,471	14.2
Equals: National income.	236,203	412,008	798,374	1,215,002	2,116,644	2,959.9
Less: Corporate profits and inventory						
valuation adjustment	2,272	9,760	37,549	95,902	175,429	285.7
Net interest	. . .	. . .	. . .	78,615	192,624	284.1
Contributions for social insurance	7,058	21,058	58,712	110,579	203,661	306.0
Wage accruals less disbursement	24	0	0	0	−40	.1
Plus: Government transfer payment to persons.	14,404	26,966	75,898	170,567	285,893	399.4
Personal interest income.	8,929	23,284	64,284	115,529	265,968	433.7
Dividends.	8,803	12,890	22,884	31,885	56,807	77.7
Business transfer payments	778	1,974	3,983	7,599	11,677	17.3
Equals: Personal income	226,102	399,724	801,271	2,578,622	2,165,315	3,012.1

(1) Billions of dollars.

National Income by Type of Income

(millions of dollars)

	1960	1965	1970	1975	1980	1983[1]	1984[1]
Compensation of employees	294,932	396,543	609,150	931,079	1,599,630	1,984.9	2,173.2
Wages and salaries	271,932	362,005	546,453	805,872	1,356,645	1,658.8	1,804.1
Government.	49,150	69,860	115,972	175,441	260,254	327.7	349.9
Other	222,782	292,145	430,481	630,431	1,096,391	1,331.1	1,454.2
Supplements to wages, salary	23,000	34,538	62,697	125,207	242,985	326.2	369.0
Employer contrib. for social ins. . . .	11,780	16,698	30,680	60,079	114,984	153.1	173.5
Other labor income.	11,220	17,840	32,017	65,128	128,001	173.1	195.5
Proprietors' income.	46,978	56,674	65,140	86,980	117,446	121.7	154.4
Nonfarm.	35,558	44,106	51,208	63,509	95,634	107.9	126.2
Farm.	11,420	12,568	13,932	23,471	21,812	13.8	28.2
Rental income of persons	13,758	17,117	18,644	22,426	31,515	58.3	62.5
Corp. prof., with inv. adjust.	46,580	77,096	67,891	95,902	175,429	225.2	285.7
Corp. profits before tax	48,540	75,209	71,485	120,378	234,614	203.2	235.7
Corp. profits tax liability	22,696	30,876	34,477	49,811	84,785	75.8	85.3
Corp. profits after tax	25,844	44,333	37,008	70,567	149,829	127.4	145.9
Dividends	12,890	19,120	22,884	31,885	58,589	72.9	80.5
Undistributed profits	12,954	25,213	14,124	38,682	91,240	54.5	65.4
Inventory valuation adj.	327	−1,865	−5,067	−12,432	−42,872	-11.2	-5.7
Net interest	9,760	18,529	37,549	78,615	192,624	256.6	284.1
National income	412,008	565,959	798,374	1,215,002	2,116,644	2,646.7	2,959.9

(1) Billions of dollars.

Appropriations by the Federal Government

Source: U.S. Treasury Department, Financial Management Service

Year	Appropriations	Year	Appropriations	Year	Appropriations	Year	Appropriations
1890	$395,430,284.26	1940	$13,349,202,681.73	1959	$82,055,863,758.58	1972	$247,638,104,722.57
1895	492,477,759.97	1944	118,411,173,965.24	1960	80,169,728,902.87	1973	275,554,945,383.88
1900	698,912,982.83	1945	73,067,712,071.39	1961	89,229,575,129.94	1974	311,728,034,120.95
1905	781,288,215.95	1950	52,867,672,466.21	1962	91,447,827,731.00	1975	374,124,469,875.62
1910	1,044,433,622.64	1952	127,788,153,262.97	1963	102,149,886,566.52	1977	466,559,809,964.06
1915	1,122,471,919.12	1953	94,916,821,231.67	1965	107,555,087,622.62	1978	507,782,291,489.99
1920	6,454,596,649.56	1954	74,744,844,304.88	1967	140,861,235,376.56	1979	563,960,833,788.25
1925	3,748,651,750.35	1955	54,761,172,461.58	1969	203,049,351,090.91	1980	690,391,124,920.77
1930	4,665,236,678.04	1956	63,857,731,203.86	1970	222,200,021,901.52	1981	744,409,241,781.90
1935	7,527,559,327.66	1958	77,145,934,082.25	1971	247,623,820,964.75	1984	997,031,000,000.00

Note: Through 1976 the fiscal year ended June 30. From 1977 on, fiscal year ends Sept. 30.

U.S. Customs and Internal Revenue Receipts

Source: U.S. Treasury Department, Financial Management Service

Gross. Not reduced by appropriations to Federal old-age and survivors insurance trust fund or refunds of receipts.

Fiscal year	Customs	Internal Revenue	Fiscal year	Customs	Internal Revenue	Fiscal year	Customs	Internal Revenue
1930	$587,000,903	$3,039,295,014	1955	$606,396,634	$66,288,691,586	1980	$7,481,593,000	$519,375,273,000
1935	343,353,034	3,277,690,028	1960	1,123,037,579	91,774,802,823	1981	8,523,275,124	606,799,103,000
1940	348,590,635	5,303,133,988	1965	1,477,548,820	114,428,991,753	1982	9,277,790,149	632,240,506,000
1945	354,775,542	43,902,001,929	1970	2,429,799,000	195,700,000,000	1983	9,059,594,659	627,246,793,000
1950	422,650,329	39,448,607,109	1975	3,675,532,000	293,800,000,000	1984	11,791,491,593	680,475,229,000

Note: Through 1976 the fiscal year ended June 30. From 1977 on, fiscal year ends Sept. 30.

National Income by Industry

Source: Bureau of Economic Analysis, U.S. Commerce Department
(millions of dollars)

	1960	1965	1970	1975	1980	1982	1983
Agricul., forestry, fisheries	**17,468**	**20,366**	**24,455**	**42,827**	**61,355**	**69,533**	**60,888**
Farms	16,452	18,805	22,191	39,379	54,060	61,514	52,329
Agri. services, forestry, fisheries	1,016	1,561	2,264	3,448	7,295	8,039	8,559
Mining	**5,613**	**6,013**	**7,810**	**18,149**	**38,512**	**46,473**	**39,997**
Metal mining	807	856	1,179	1,635	2,817	1,974	2,051
Coal mining	1,286	1,372	2,231	6,228	8,783	9,907	8,157
Crude petroleum, natural gas	2,606	2,670	3,099	8,075	23,289	31,291	26,457
Nonmetallic min. & quar.	914	1,115	1,301	2,211	3,623	3,301	3,332
Contract construction	**20,972**	**29,840**	**43,821**	**61,795**	**107,237**	**107,836**	**112,268**
Manufacturing	**125,448**	**170,361**	**215,388**	**312,467**	**526,514**	**549,644**	**579,863**
Nondurable goods	**51,818**	**65,416**	**88,088**	**127,942**	**214,563**	**238,274**	**250,354**
Food, kindred products	12,150	14,232	19,579	30,020	41,329	46,207	46,898
Tobacco manufactures	1,020	1,096	1,696	2,155	4,139	4,703	5,301
Textile mill products	4,484	5,872	7,525	8,754	13,387	13,478	15,440
Apparel, other fabric prod.	4,933	6,494	8,722	10,773	16,102	17,477	19,194
Paper, allied products	4,706	6,005	7,968	11,833	19,568	20,345	22,632
Printing, pub., allied industry	6,666	8,725	11,883	16,672	28,131	32,328	36,922
Chemicals, allied products	9,106	12,398	16,042	23,820	36,990	42,328	44,829
Petroleum and coal products	4,396	4,811	6,632	12,893	36,285	40,219	36,634
Rubber, misc. plastic products	2,751	3,939	5,804	8,661	14,854	16,704	18,534
Leather, leather products	1,606	1,844	2,237	2,361	3,778	4,027	3,970
Durable goods	**73,630**	**104,945**	**127,300**	**184,525**	**311,951**	**311,370**	**329,509**
Lumber, wood, except furn.	3,362	4,534	5,537	8,936	15,129	11,974	15,461
Furniture and fixtures	2,098	2,904	3,715	4,588	7,885	8,325	9,460
Stone, clay, glass products	4,620	5,654	6,891	9,858	16,424	14,410	16,588
Primary metal industries	11,066	14,491	15,757	24,231	37,554	27,975	28,622
Fabricated metal products	8,124	11,475	14,812	24,300	40,595	40,013	41,225
Machinery, except electrical	11,919	18,239	24,353	36,801	68,403	68,545	64,324
Electric and electronic equipment	10,496	14,855	20,132	26,646	49,879	53,733	57,491
Transport equip. exc. autos.	8,266	11,330	14,460	15,715	29,030	24,830	34,428
Motor vehicles and equipment.	8,399	14,455	12,086	19,045	21,863	31,519	31,570
Instruments	2,948	4,128	5,797	9,006	17,383	21,048	21,729
Misc. manufacturing	2,332	2,880	3,740	5,399	7,806	8,998	8,611
Transportation	**18,141**	**23,069**	**30,308**	**44,455**	**80,425**	**83,326**	**87,679**
Railroad	6,710	7,016	7,612	9,987	17,382	15,871	15,873
Local; interurban passenger transit	1,619	1,897	2,308	2,933	4,328	4,555	4,641
Motor freight trans., warehousing	5,886	8,396	11,830	18,935	33,044	34,929	36,714
Water transportation	1,635	1,982	2,503	3,323	5,877	6,057	5,818
Air transportation	1,370	2,636	4,358	7,062	13,290	14,317	16,395
Pipeline transportation	350	390	528	820	1,765	1,556	1,772
Transportation service	571	752	1,169	1,935	4,739	6,041	6,466
Communication	**8,228**	**11,497**	**17,600**	**27,066**	**48,181**	**59,287**	**60,080**
Telephone and telegraph	7,293	10,255	15,887	24,358	42,838	52,759	52,944
Radio broadcasting, television.	935	1,242	1,713	2,708	5,343	6,528	7,136
Electric, gas, sanitary services	**8,923**	**11,442**	**14,864**	**24,302**	**42,651**	**57,675**	**64,263**
Wholesale and retail trade	**64,737**	**84,662**	**122,213**	**194,227**	**316,630**	**358,933**	**386,363**
Wholesale trade	23,420	30,469	44,860	80,564	137,572	152,967	161,208
Retail trade	41,317	54,193	77,353	113,663	179,058	205,966	255,155
Finance, ins. and real estate	**48,608**	**63,987**	**92,625**	**140,375**	**290,851**	**355,102**	**393,955**
Banking	7,255	8,943	16,448	20,109	45,051	42,202	44,710
Credit agencies, other than banks	−1,076	−1,617	−1,981	−4,729	2,300	4,947	8,246
Security, commodity brokers	1,219	1,942	2,733	4,144	8,229	12,618	16,736
Insurance carriers.	4,816	5,880	9,269	12,751	29,278	26,655	30,092
Insurance agents, brokers, service	2,070	2,957	4,223	6,704	12,267	14,121	15,372
Real estate	33,940	45,741	61,812	100,078	195,760	250,408	273,289
Holding and other investment cos.	384	141	121	1,318	−2,034	4,151	5,510
Services	**44,648**	**64,142**	**103,304**	**168,516**	**310,008**	**387,029**	**426,636**
Hotels, other lodging places	2,114	2,964	4,659	6,952	13,826	15,799	17,381
Personal services	4,608	5,965	7,436	8,329	13,278	15,049	16,381
Misc. business services	5,091	8,399	14,051	23,928	53,027	69,119	77,860
Automobile repair, serv., garages.	1,746	2,402	3,616	5,944	11,242	12,843	13,685
Misc. repair services	1,094	1,494	2,149	3,478	6,813	7,262	7,495
Motion pictures	891	1,201	1,581	1,842	3,841	4,507	5,249
Amusement, recreation services	1,662	2,201	3,321	5,268	9,033	10,705	11,856
Medical, other health services.	10,636	15,790	29,472	54,075	99,625	130,993	144,913
Legal services.	2,695	4,197	6,691	11,828	21,310	18,065	32,514
Education services	2,419	4,145	6,688	10,014	15,438	18,514	19,750
Social Services	—	—	—	5,003	9,455	10,932	11,895
Nonprofit membership org..	4,176	5,787	8,912	11,016	15,494	29,173	31,422
Misc. professional services	3,719	5,629	9,673	15,030	31,041	37,406	40,362
Private households	3,797	3,968	5,055	5,809	6,585	7,594	7,768
Government, government enterprises	**52,707**	**75,374**	**127,421**	**199,875**	**306,343**	**364,131**	**391,653**
Federal	25,303	33,303	53,093	72,007	102,767	124,282	132,768
General Government	21,676	28,298	44,723	58,976	82,947	101,162	107,777
Government enterprises.	3,627	5,005	8,370	13,031	19,820	23,120	24,991
State & local.	27,404	42,071	74,328	127,868	2,128,707	239,849	258,885
General Government	25,470	39,294	69,964	119,641	82,947	223,746	241,398
Government enterprises.	1,934	2,777	4,364	8,227	19,820	16,103	17,487
Domestic income	**415,493**	**560,753**	**799,809**	**1,234,054**	**2,128,707**	**2,438,989**	**2,603,645**
Rest of the world.	**2,477**	**4,681**	**4,616**	**10,534**	**45,310**	**47,955**	**48,297**
All industries, total.	**417,970**	**565,434**	**804,425**	**1,244,588**	**2,174,017**	**2,486,944**	**2,651,942**

Producer Price Indexes

Source: Bureau of Labor Statistics, U.S. Labor Department

Producer Price Indexes measure average changes in prices received in primary markets of the U.S. by producers of commodities in all stages of processing.

Commodity group (1967 = 100)	Annual Avg. 1982	Annual Avg. 1984	1984 Jan.	1984 June	1985 Jan.	1985 May
All commodities	299.3	310.3	308.0	311.3	309.7	309.9
Farm products processed foods and feeds	248.9	262.4	264.4	262.8	257.6	250.6
Farm products	242.4	255.8	263.4	257.1	243.2	230.4
Processed foods and feeds	251.5	265.0	263.8	264.8	264.4	260.6
Industrial commodities	312.3	322.6	319.1	323.8	323.1	325.3
Textile products and apparel	204.6	210.0	208.2	210.2	210.3	210.7
Hides, skins, leathers, and related products	262.6	286.3	279.1	290.1	283.7	283.6
Fuels and related products and power	693.2	656.8	652.1	665.9	636.8	648.3
Chemicals and allied products	292.3	300.8	298.1	302.2	301.6	303.2
Rubber and plastic products	241.4	246.8	244.8	247.6	246.7	246.6
Lumber and wood products	284.7	307.4	309.1	307.1	304.4	307.0
Pulp, paper, and allied products	288.7	318.5	309.1	318.4	327.1	327.2
Metals and metal products	301.6	316.1	312.9	317.3	315.0	316.3
Machinery and equipment	278.8	293.1	289.7	293.1	297.9	298.8
Furniture and household durables	206.9	218.7	216.8	219.1	220.3	221.4
Nonmetallic mineral products	320.2	337.3	330.1	338.3	341.7	347.1
Transportation equipment (Dec. 1968 = 100)	249.7	262.7	261.5	262.2	266.8	268.4
Miscellaneous products	276.4	295.9	294.5	295.7	299.2	301.1

Indexes of Manufacturing, Industrial Countries

Source: Bureau of Labor Statistics, U.S. Labor Department (1977=100)

Output per hour

Country	1960	1965	1970	1975	1980	1981	1982	1983	1984[1]
United States	60.0	74.5	79.1	93.4	101.7	104.6	103.6	113.1	115.6
11 Foreign countries[2]	37.7	50.3	70.4	89.7	111.3	115.1	118.2	124.5	NA
Canada	50.4	62.9	77.0	91.2	102.3	103.1	100.3	109.0	111.9
Japan	22.0	33.1	61.4	85.3	124.5	126.3	127.6	155.2	167.4
Belgium	32.2	39.8	58.8	85.1	115.4	121.8	130.0	NA	NA
Denmark	36.4	47.4	65.3	94.4	109.8	116.0	119.5	125.6	123.6
France	39.8	51.2	70.1	87.9	112.6	114.4	122.3	129.1	135.2
West Germany	40.0	53.8	68.2	89.0	109.8	112.8	114.7	118.5	122.3
Italy	36.5	52.9	72.7	91.1	116.9	121.0	122.6	124.8	134.4
Netherlands	31.7	41.3	63.0	85.1	114.2	117.2	121.4	NA	NA
Norway	54.6	64.4	81.7	96.8	109.3	110.4	109.7	116.3	121.4
Sweden	43.0	59.4	82.0	100.5	114.4	114.5	117.9	123.9	134.9
United Kingdom	55.6	67.0	80.5	94.6	108.1	114.2	118.2	118.0	123.0

Unit Labor Costs in U.S. dollars

Country	1960	1965	1970	1975	1980	1981	1982	1983	1984[1]
United States	61.1	57.5	72.7	91.5	130.6	140.0	153.4	147.4	146.5
11 Foreign countries[2]	36.2	41.5	47.9	93.2	138.5	130.5	124.2	119.0	NA
Canada	59.3	51.0	62.0	90.3	114.9	123.5	136.9	143.6	133.0
Japan	30.2	37.4	41.3	90.4	113.8	123.8	112.0	102.7	98.4
Belgium	30.5	38.6	41.9	90.6	135.5	109.4	91.5	NA	NA
Denmark	30.1	37.0	44.5	89.8	132.6	108.8	99.3	94.6	85.7
France	40.7	49.0	48.3	100.6	151.7	134.0	122.0	114.7	103.0
West Germany	26.3	32.7	43.2	89.2	147.5	124.2	119.5	113.3	101.4
Italy	32.5	41.2	50.6	104.3	141.4	126.2	122.9	127.7	114.5
Netherlands	24.9	35.0	41.4	93.5	133.1	108.4	104.7	NA	NA
Norway	21.7	26.9	34.5	81.4	126.2	120.0	118.0	107.4	99.7
Sweden	29.6	34.9	40.5	82.9	123.2	116.4	96.7	81.2	78.0
United Kingdom	44.8	51.7	55.0	101.9	212.7	203.3	185.1	164.5	145.4

(1) Preliminary estimates. (2) Trade-weighted geometric average reflecting the relative importance of each country as a manufacturing trade competitor of the U.S.

Index of Leading Economic Indicators

Source: Bureau of Economic Analysis, U.S. Dept. of Commerce

The index of leading economic indicators, which is issued to project the economy's performance six months or a year ahead, rose four-tenths of 1 percent in July 1985. Analysts said this, along with a substantial downward revision in the increase estimated for June, suggested continued listless economic growth over the next several months.

The index is made up of twelve measurements of economic activity that tend to change direction long before the overall economy does. The volatility of the index, caused in part by the fact that many of the statistics covered do not reach the Commerce Department until weeks after the initial report, usually results in at least one revision after the initial reporting.

Two companion indexes—those of coincident and lagging indicators—rose in July by two-tenths of one percent and fell three-tenths of one percent, respectively. The coincident index reflects current economic conditions. Its components are: employees on nonagricultural payrolls; personal income less transfer payments; industrial production; and manufacturing and trade sales. The lagging index consists of items that tend to lag behind the business cycle.

At the end of July 1985, the index of leading indicators stood at 168.7, with the level in 1967 providing the base of 100. The coincident index was reported at 156.7 and the lagging index at 117.8.

Leading Indicators: Component Analysis

Components	Contribution to change June to July 1985	Components	Contribution to change June to July 1985	Components	Contribution to change June to July 1985
Average workweek of production workers in manufacturing	+0.00	Index of net business formation	+0.05	Index of stock prices	−0.13
Average weekly claims for State unemployment insurance[1]	−0.09	Contracts and orders for plant and equipment, adjusted for inflation	−0.08	Money supply: M-2, adjusted for inflation	+0.18
New orders for consumer goods and materials, adjusted for inflation	+0.03	New building permits issued	−0.03	Change in credit (business and consumer borrowing)	+0.05
Vendor performance (companies receiving slower deliveries from suppliers)	−0.00	Change in inventories on hand and on order, adjusted for inflation	NA	**Leading indicators index, percent change**	**−0.42**
		Change in sensitive materials prices	−0.09		

(1) Series is inverted in computing index; that is, a decrease in the series is considered upward movement. (NA) Not available.

State Finances

Revenues, Expenditures, Debts, Taxes, U.S. Aid, Military Contracts

For fiscal 1983 (year ending June 30, 1983, except: Alabama and Michigan, Sept. 30; New York, Mar. 31; Texas, Aug. 31.
*Military prime contracts. Taxes are State income and sales (or gross receipts) taxes, and vehicle, etc., fees.

Sources: Census Bureau, U.S. Treasury and Defense Depts.

State	Receipts (thousands)	Outlays (thousands)	Total debt (thousands)	Per cap. debt	Per cap. taxes	Per cap. U.S. aid	Military contracts (thousands)
Alabama	$5,250,162	$5,220,496	$2,339,606	$591	$591	$371	$1,127,000
Alaska	5,246,838	3,835,983	4,665,456	9,740	4,272	1,129	386,000
Arizona.	3,969,222	3,589,487	558,627	189	695	285	1,360,000
Arkansas. . . .	2,739,140	2,487,836	650,995	280	575	387	629,000
California. . . .	43,768,233	42,493,208	12,071,209	480	884	366	26,387,000
Colorado. . . .	4,202,960	4,061,778	1,150,530	367	558	337	1,007,000
Connecticut . .	4,707,166	4,427,350	5,236,226	1,669	809	379	5,132,000
Delaware. . . .	1,315,344	1,072,177	1,562,169	2,578	1,055	507	220,000
Florida	10,569,129	9,873,718	3,566,782	334	583	264	4,650,000
Georgia	6,991,699	6,563,236	1,844,100	322	611	368	2,449,000
Hawaii	2,307,762	2,178,080	2,320,186	2,268	1,125	447	639,000
Idaho	1,348,959	1,245,388	448,342	453	627	379	49,000
Illinois.	15,119,889	15,003,880	7,862,325	685	646	365	1,535,000
Indiana	6,166,425	5,843,331	1,208,419	221	583	294	2,117,000
Iowa	4,106,290	4,157,238	594,381	205	693	338	407,000
Kansas.	2,989,831	2,864,360	379,435	156	646	315	1,575,000
Kentucky. . . .	5,364,169	5,165,122	3,030,863	816	701	401	420,000
Louisiana. . . .	6,946,637	7,431,319	5,244,181	1,182	683	385	1,484,000
Maine.	1,684,821	1,671,195	1,073,016	936	681	502	405,000
Maryland. . . .	6,597,708	6,921,024	4,661,773	1,083	806	416	3,540,000
Massachusetts	9,383,415	9,332,023	7,888,009	1,368	894	503	6,328,000
Michigan . . .	16,097,094	14,789,362	4,669,139	515	774	399	1,782,000
Minnesota . . .	8,074,280	6,495,670	2,761,480	666	7,042	426	1,605,000
Mississippi . . .	3,346,255	3,132,375	908,310	357	594	426	1,840,000
Missouri	5,318,957	4,780,215	2,250,613	453	531	337	5,638,000
Montana	1,399,884	1,263,307	511,569	626	629	584	117,000
Nebraska . . .	1,880,771	1,806,700	387,355	243	618	360	163,000
Nevada.	1,696,064	1,569,977	757,067	850	875	400	159,000
New Hampshire	1,167,024	1,109,030	1,531,667	1,597	344	367	541,000
New Jersey . .	12,603,860	11,764,456	10,306,360	1,380	821	377	2,640,000
New Mexico . .	3,342,707	2,692,238	1,076,327	769	833	483	463,000
New York . . .	35,850,852	31,921,272	27,765,418	1,572	916	566	9,635,000
North Carolina.	7,661,975	7,231,826	1,622,561	267	662	309	786,000
North Dakota .	1,329,723	1,301,979	381,830	562	774	547	137,000
Ohio	17,682,400	15,900,599	6,094,837	567	627	339	3,365,000
Oklahoma . . .	4,805,124	4,772,191	1,331,290	404	795	326	612,000
Oregon.	4,695,714	4,356,448	6,589,036	2,475	670	437	181,000
Pennsylvania .	17,776,803	16,732,858	6,496,934	546	709	405	3,329,000
Rhode Island .	1,834,544	1,707,511	2,225,528	2,330	761	509	381,000
South Carolina.	4,597,759	4,229,318	3,153,922	966	647	341	400,000
South Dakota .	961,491	858,527	791,107	7,730	464	516	42,000
Tennessee. . . .	4,783,433	4,578,341	1,797,131	384	479	360	828,000
Texas.	17,400,297	15,796,490	3,028,877	793	574	242	8,229,000
Utah	2,441,901	2,303,906	1,070,279	661	602	384	722,000
Vermont	900,120	889,926	764,745	1,457	682	594	180,000
Virginia	7,539,780	6,746,574	2,666,034	480	640	800	7,072,000
Washington . .	8,352,720	7,907,602	2,527,097	588	975	357	3,986,000
West Virginia . .	3,201,658	3,046,333	1,675,680	853	748	427	122,000
Wisconsin . . .	8,544,644	7,632,876	3,210,023	670	904	401	775,000
Wyoming . . .	1,597,431	1,263,044	581,100	7,131	1,432	829	39,000
United States. Total or Average	**357,660,578**	**334,019,180**	**167,289,946**	**717**	**735**	**384**	**118,744,000**

Civilian Employment of the Federal Government

Source: Workforce Analysis and Statistics Division, U.S. Office of Personnel Management as of March 1985
(Payroll in thousands of dollars)

	All Areas		United States		Wash., D.C. MSA		Overseas	
	Employ-ment	Payroll	Employ-ment	Payroll	Employ-ment	Payroll	Employ-ment	Payroll
Total, all agencies[1]	2,983,969	7,584,448	2,839,029	7,332,626	351,351	1,052,213	144,940	261,822
Legislative branch	38,788	95,365	38,718	95,125	36,422	89,265	70	240
Congress.	19,517	43,566	19,517	43,566	19,517	43,566	—	—
Senate.	7,130	15,995	7,130	15,995	7,130	15,995	—	—
House of Representatives. . .	12,375	27,541	12,375	27,541	12,375	27,541	—	—
Comm. on Security and Coop. in Europe	12	30	12	30	12	30	—	—
Architect of the Capitol	2,209	4,290	2,209	4,290	2,209	4,290	—	—
Botanic Garden	56	121	56	121	56	121	—	—
Congressional Budget Office . .	216	695	216	695	216	695	—	—
Copyright Royalty Tribunal. . . .	7	37	7	37	7	37	—	—
General Accounting Office	5,402	14,953	5,340	14,769	3,500	9,733	62	184
Government Printing Office	5,479	13,016	5,479	13,016	5,026	12,198	—	—
Library of Congress.	5,348	17,206	5,340	17,150	5,340	17,150	8	56
Office of Technology Assessment	219	626	219	626	219	626	—	—
Prospective Payment Assessment Committee	41	108	41	108	41	108	—	—
Tax Court	294	747	294	747	291	741	—	—
Judicial branch	17,534	55,551	17,329	54,874	1,685	5,564	205	677
Supreme Court	335	699	335	699	335	699	—	—
United States Courts	17,199	54,852	16,994	54,175	1,350	4,865	205	677
Executive branch	2,927,647	7,433,532	2,782,982	7,172,627	313,244	957,384	144,665	260,905
Executive Office of the President	1,550	6,814	1,544	6,766	1,544	6,776	6	38
White House Office.	365	1,628	365	1,628	365	1,628	—	—
Office of the Vice President . .	21	110	21	110	21	110	—	—
Office of Management and Budget	583	2,815	583	2,815	583	2,815	—	—
Office of Administration	190	569	190	569	190	569	—	—
Council of Economic Advisors.	27	124	27	124	27	124	—	—
Council on Environmental Quality	12	64	12	64	12	64	—	—
Office of Policy Development .	32	160	32	160	32	160	—	—
Executive Residence.	91	283	91	283	91	283	—	—
National Security Council . . .	64	281	64	281	64	281	—	—
Office of Science and Tech. . .	21	91	21	91	21	91	—	—
Office of US Trade Representatives	144	689	138	651	138	651	6	38
Executive departments	1,777,111	4,192,395	1,654,954	3,987,106	229,636	695,601	122,157	205,289
State	25,009	54,172	8,827	24,898	7,328	21,412	16,182	29,274
Treasury.	141,965	407,943	140,941	403,447	19,217	72,817	1,024	4,496
Defense, Total	1,071,813	2,174,379	972,092	2,107,305	86,178	206,257	99,721	157,074
Department of the Army . . .	389,275	744,049	343,522	655,962	28,692	54,986	45,753	88,087
Department of the Navy. . . .	346,018	738,012	320,518	713,987	37,763	97,651	25,500	24,025
Department of the Air Force	249,738	503,139	234,326	483,718	6,367	14,420	15,412	19,421
Defense Logistics Agency . .	50,271	102,206	49,809	101,617	2,790	8,147	462	589
Other Defense Activities . .	36,511	86,973	23,917	62,021	10,566	31,053	12,594	24,952
Justice.	62,583	155,134	61,548	152,113	17,790	42,545	1,035	3,021
Interior.	73,190	164,780	72,822	163,737	9,648	26,279	368	1,043
Agriculture.	111,345	310,678	109,972	307,745	12,350	45,758	1,373	2,933
Commerce	35,616	112,514	34,781	110,460	18,614	66,094	835	2,054
Labor.	18,187	66,453	18,107	66,135	6,205	24,178	80	318
Health and Human Services .	141,135	429,251	140,269	426,572	30,444	108,372	866	2,679
Housing and Urb. Develop. . .	12,297	46,558	12,160	46,039	3,411	14,661	137	519
Transportation	62,227	196,617	61,695	194,765	9,208	29,608	532	1,852
Energy	16,596	59,010	16,593	58,989	5,808	26,795	3	21
Education	5,148	14,906	5,147	14,901	3,435	10,285	1	5
Independent agencies[2]	1,148,986	3,234,323	1,126,484	3,178,745	82,064	255,007	22,502	55,578
Environmental Protection Agency	13,493	32,160	13,474	32,113	4,697	12,535	19	47
Equal Employment Oppor. Comm.	3,245	7,925	3,245	7,925	820	1,901	—	—
Fed. Deposit Insurance Corp. . .	4,776	17,030	4,700	16,965	1,049	7,313	76	65
Federal Emergency Mgt. Agency	3,208	10,774	3,201	10,762	1,628	6,394	7	12
General Services Admin.	29,024	54,875	28,949	54,725	10,445	22,224	75	150
National Aeronautics and Space Admin.	22,147	70,269	22,139	70,228	4,710	15,091	8	41
National Labor Relations Board .	2,645	10,786	2,628	10,720	841	3,437	17	66
Nuclear Regulatory Comm. . . .	3,667	12,358	3,667	12,358	2,581	8,670	—	—
Office of Personnel Mgmt.	6,549	12,298	6,525	12,259	2,716	6,416	24	39
Panama Canal Commission . . .	8,384	21,585	14	47	5	21	8,370	21,538
Small Business Admin.	5,004	17,243	4,901	16,929	1,328	3,749	103	314
Smithsonian Summary	4,677	9,678	4,571	9,485	4,360	8,969	106	193
Tennessee Valley Authority . . .	33,168	81,265	33,618	81,265	14	51	—	—
US Information Agency	8,545	19,622	4,079	12,520	3,825	11,489	4,466	7,102
US International Development Cooperative Agency	5,215	21,610	2,395	10,638	2,373	10,508	2,820	10,972
U.S. Postal Service	728,937	2,309,948	725,860	2,300,099	18,674	68,409	3,077	9,849
Veterans Administration	243,141	458,176	240,685	454,099	6,682	20,611	2,456	4,077

(1) Excludes employees of Central Intelligence Agency, National Security Agency, and uncompensated employees; (2) Includes in totals but does not specify 61 independent agencies with fewer than 2,000 employees each.

U.S. Labor Force, Employment and Unemployment

Source: Bureau of Labor Statistics, U.S. Labor Department

(numbers in thousands; monthly data are seasonally adjusted)

Employment status	Annual averages			1985					
	1981	1983	1984	Jan.	Feb.	March	April	May	June
Civilian labor force.	108,670	111,550	113,554	114,875	115,084	115,514	115,371	115,373	114,783
Employed	100,397	100,834	105,005	106,391	106,685	107,119	106,945	106,960	106,370
Agriculture	3,368	3,383	3,321	3,320	3,340	3,362	3,428	3,312	3,138
Nonagricultural industries	97,030	97,450	101,685	103,071	103,345	103,757	103,517	103,648	103,232
Unemployed	6,137	10,717	8,539	8,484	8,399	8,390	8,426	8,413	8,413
Long term, 15 weeks & over	2,285	4,210	2,737	2,243	2,416	2,400	2,377	2,247	2,317

Unemployment rates (unemployment in each group as a percent of the groups' civilian labor force)

	1981	1983	1984	Jan.	Feb.	March	April	May	June
Total, 16 years and over	7.6	9.6	7.5	7.4	7.3	7.3	7.3	7.3	7.3
Men, 20 years and over	4.2	8.9	6.6	6.3	6.2	6.3	6.3	6.1	6.5
Women, 20 years and over	6.8	8.1	6.8	6.8	6.7	6.7	6.8	6.9	6.7
Both sexes, 16 to 19 years	19.6	22.4	18.9	18.9	18.4	18.2	17.7	18.9	18.3
White, total	6.7	8.4	6.5	6.4	6.2	6.2	6.3	6.2	6.5
Men, 20 years and over	5.6	7.9	5.7	5.5	5.4	5.4	5.5	5.2	5.8
Women, 20 years and over	5.9	6.9	5.8	5.9	5.6	5.9	5.8	5.9	5.8
Both sexes, 16 to 19 years	17.3	19.3	16.0	15.8	15.2	15.1	14.9	16.1	15.9
Black, total	15.6	19.5	15.9	14.9	16.3	15.2	15.3	15.6	14.0
Men, 20 years and over	13.5	18.1	14.3	12.7	14.4	13.3	13.6	13.6	12.2
Women, 20 years and over	13.4	16.5	13.5	12.8	13.9	12.9	13.2	13.7	12.3
Both sexes, 16 to 19 years	41.4	48.5	42.7	42.1	43.1	41.9	39.0	40.4	38.1
Married men, spouse present	4.3	6.5	4.6	4.6	4.4	4.2	4.3	4.0	4.6
Married women, spouse present	6.0	7.0	5.7	5.7	5.4	5.9	5.9	5.8	5.9
Women who maintain families	10.4	12.2	10.3	10.0	11.0	10.2	10.8	10.9	9.8
Full-time workers	7.3	9.5	7.2	7.1	7.1	6.9	6.9	6.8	6.8
Part-time workers	9.4	10.4	9.3	9.3	8.7	9.6	9.7	10.3	9.9
Nonagricultural w/s workers	7.2	9.1	7.0	6.8	6.7	6.7	6.7	6.7	6.8
Construction	15.6	18.4	14.3	13.4	13.4	13.3	13.3	10.2	13.7
Manufacturing	8.3	11.2	7.5	7.6	7.5	7.7	8.0	7.8	7.7
Durable goods	8.2	12.1	7.2	7.2	7.1	7.4	7.8	7.8	8.0
Nondurable goods	8.4	10.0	7.8	8.1	8.2	8.1	8.3	7.7	7.4
Wholesale & retail trade	8.1	10.0	8.0	7.7	7.7	7.5	7.3	7.9	7.7
Finance & service industries	5.9	7.2	5.9	5.9	5.7	5.7	5.7	6.2	5.8
Government workers	4.7	5.3	4.5	4.1	3.9	3.9	3.7	3.9	3.8

Note: Pre-1982 data have been revised to reflect 1980 census population controls.

Employed Persons by Major Occupational Groups and Sex

1984 Annual Averages	Thousands of persons			Percent distribution		
Occupational group	Both sexes	Males	Females	Both sexes	Males	Females
Total Employed	105,005	59,091	45,915	100.0	100.0	100.0
Managerial and professional specialty	24,858	14,529	10,329	23.7	24.6	22.5
Executive, administration and managerial	11,571	7,683	3,889	11.0	13.0	8.5
Professional specialty.	13,286	6,846	6,440	12.7	11.6	14.0
Technical, sales and administrative support.	32,476	11,556	20,920	30.9	19.6	45.6
Technicians and related support.	3,172	1,646	1,527	3.0	2.8	3.3
Sales occupations.	12,582	6,550	6,032	12.0	11.1	13.1
Administrative support, including clerical	16,722	3,361	13,361	15.9	5.7	29.1
Service occupations	14,151	5,545	8,607	13.5	9.4	18.7
Private household	993	38	955	.9	.1	2.1
Protective service	1,678	1,461	217	1.6	2.5	.5
Service, except private household and protective . .	11,481	4,406	7,435	10.9	6.8	16.2
Precision production, craft, and repair	13,057	11,945	1,112	12.4	20.2	2.4
Mechanics and repairers	4,376	4,244	132	4.2	7.2	.3
Construction trades	4,573	4,494	79	4.4	7.6	.2
Other precision production, craft, and repair	4,108	3,207	901	3.9	5.4	2.0
Operators, fabricators, and laborers	16,864	12,479	4,385	16.1	21.1	9.6
Machine operators, assemblers, and inspectors. . .	7,984	4,702	3,282	7.6	8.0	7.1
Transportation and material moving occupations . .	4,467	4,098	369	4.3	6.9	.8
Handlers, equipment cleaners, helpers, and laborers	4,413	3,679	734	4.2	6.2	1.6
Farming, forestry, and fishing	3,600	3,037	562	3.4	5.1	1.2

Note: Pre-1982 data have been revised to reflect 1980 census population controls.

Employment and Unemployment in the U.S.

Civilian labor force, persons 16 years of age and over (in thousands)

Year*	Employed	Unemployed	Unemployment Rate	Year*	Employed	Unemployed	Unemployment Rate
1940[1]	47,520	8,120	14.6%	1977	92,017	6,991	7.1
1950	58,918	3,288	5.0	1978	96,048	6,202	6.1
1960	65,778	3,852	5.5	1980	99,303	7,637	7.1
1965	71,088	3,366	4.5	1981	100,397	8,273	7.6
1970	78,678	4,093	4.9	1982	99,526	10,678	9.7
1975	85,846	7,929	8.5	1983	100,834	10,717	9.6
1976	88,752	7,406	7.7	1984	105,005	8,539	7.5

[1]Persons 14 years of age and over

*Early unemployment rates: 1915, 9.7; 1916, 4.8; 1917, 4.8; 1918, 1.4; 1919, 2.3; 1920, 4.0; 1921, 11.9; 1922, 7.6; 1923, 3.2; 1924, 5.5; 1925, 4.0; 1926, 1.9; 1927, 4.1; 1928, 4.4; 1929, 3.2; 1930, 8.7; 1931, 15.9; 1932, 23.6; 1933, 24.9; 1934, 21.7; 1935, 20.1; 1936, 16.9; 1937, 14.3; 1938, 19.0; 1939, 17.2.

Employment Losses and Gains

Source: Bureau of Labor Statistics, U.S. Dept. of Labor

Ten industries with the largest number of employment losses and gains since the 1980-82 recession. Since January 1980, 2.3 million manufacturing jobs have disappeared. In the same period, jobs that supply services rather than products have boomed.

Losers		Gainers	
Blast furnaces and basic steel products	245,000	Communication equipment	119,000
Construction and related machinery	145,000	Electronic components and accessories	119,000
Women's and misses' outerwear	50,000	Office and computing machines	102,000
Plastics materials and synthetics	43,000	Commercial printing	71,000
Footwear (except rubber)	42,000	Miscellaneous plastic products	71,000
Weaving mills, cotton	41,000	Guided missiles, space vehicles	68,000
Glass and glassware	38,000	Newspapers	27,000
Yarn and thread mills	32,000	Motor vehicles and equipment	24,000
Knitting mills	31,000	Periodicals	21,000
Tires and inner tubes	30,000	Miscellaneous publishing	21,000
Total job loss	**697,000**	**Total job gain**	**643,000**

Gold Reserves of Central Banks and Governments

Source: IMF, *International Financial Statistics*
(Million fine troy ounces)

Year end	All countries[1]	Int'l Monetary Fund	United States	Canada	Japan	Belgium	France	Fed. Rep. of Germany	Italy	Netherlands	Switzerland	United Kingdom
1969	1,112.90	66.00	338.83	24.92	11.81	43.40	101.34	116.56	84.46	49.16	75.49	42.06
1970	1,057.89	123.97	316.34	22.59	15.22	42.01	100.91	113.70	82.48	51.06	78.03	38.52
1971	1,028.44	135.20	291.60	22.69	19.42	44.12	100.66	116.47	82.40	54.53	83.11	22.18
1972	1,019.68	153.43	275.97	21.95	21.10	43.08	100.69	117.36	82.37	54.17	83.11	21.08
1973	1,022.24	153.43	275.97	21.95	21.11	42.17	100.91	117.61	82.48	54.33	83.20	21.01
1974	1,020.24	153.40	275.97	21.95	21.11	42.17	100.93	117.61	82.48	54.33	83.20	21.03
1975	1,018.71	153.43	274.71	21.95	21.11	42.17	100.93	117.61	82.48	54.33	83.20	21.03
1976	1,014.23	149.51	274.68	21.62	21.11	42.17	101.02	117.61	82.48	54.33	83.28	21.03
1977	1,029.19	131.57	277.55	22.01	21.62	42.45	101.67	118.30	82.91	54.63	83.28	22.23
1978	1,036.82	118.20	276.41	22.13	23.97	42.59	101.99	118.64	83.12	54.78	83.28	22.83
1979	944.44	106.83	264.60	22.18	24.23	34.21	81.92	95.25	66.71	43.97	83.28	18.25
1980	952.99	103.44	264.32	20.98	24.23	34.18	81.85	95.18	66.67	43.94	83.28	18.84
1981	953.26	103.44	264.11	20.46	24.23	34.18	81.85	95.18	66.67	43.94	83.28	19.03
1982	948.69	103.44	264.03	20.26	24.23	34.18	81.85	95.18	66.67	43.94	83.28	19.01
1983	945.27	103.44	263.39	20.17	24.23	34.18	81.85	95.18	66.67	43.94	83.28	19.01
1984	946.09	103.44	262.79	20.14	24.23	34.18	81.85	95.18	66.67	43.94	83.28	19.03

(1) Covers IMF members with reported gold holdings. For countries not listed above, see *International Financial Statistics*, a monthly publication of the International Monetary Fund.

World Gold Production

(Troy Ounces)

Year	Estimated world prod.	South Africa	Ghana	Zaire	United States	Canada	Mexico	Nicaragua	Colombia	Australia	India	Japan	Philippines	All other
1972	44,843,374	29,245,273	724,051	140,724	1,449,943	2,078,567	146,061	112,340	188,137	754,866	105,776	243,027	606,730	9,047,879
1973	43,296,755	27,494,603	722,531	133,642	1,175,750	1,954,340	132,557	85,051	215,876	554,278	105,390	188,274	572,250	9,962,213
1974	40,124,290[e]	24,388,203	[e]614,007	130,603	1,126,886	1,698,392	134,454	82,659	265,195	512,611	101,114	139,719	[e]537,615	[e]10,392,852
1975	38,476,371[e]	22,937,820	523,889	103,217	1,052,252	[e]1,653,611	[e]144,710	70,281	[e]308,864	526,821	[e]90,826	[e]143,503	[e]502,577	[e]10,418,000
1976	39,024,485[e]	[e]22,936,018	532,473	91,093	1,048,037	1,691,806	162,811	75,841	300,307	502,741	100,696	[e]137,643	501,210	10,943,809
1977	38,906,145[e]	22,501,886	480,884	80,418	1,100,347	1,733,609	212,709	65,764	[e]257,070	[e]624,270	96,902	[e]149,004	[e]558,554	[e]11,044,728
1978	38,983,019[e]	22,648,558	402,034	76,077	998,832	1,735,077	202,003	[e]73,947	[e]246,446	647,579	89,186	145,240	586,531	[e]11,131,509
1979	38,768,978[e]	[e]22,617,179	362,000	69,992	[e]964,390	1,644,265	[e]190,364	61,086	269,369	596,910	[e]84,781	127,626	[e]535,166	[e]11,245,850
1980	39,197,315	21,669,468	[e]353,000	39,963	[e]969,782	[e]1,627,477	[e]195,991	59,994	[e]510,439	547,591	78,834	[e]102,339	753,452	12,398,632
1982	43,082,814	21,355,111	331,000	62,233	1,465,666	2,081,230	214,349	54,384	472,674	866,815	71,935	104,136	834,439	15,168,822
1983[e]	44,882,480	21,847,310	280,000	147,885	1,956,400	2,363,411	198,177	46,428	438,579	983,522	70,158	100,921	812,333	15,637,356
1984[e]	46,006,698	21,904,900	260,000	80,303	2,058,784	2,614,300	205,000	34,000	735,000	1,200,000	68,600	103,519	772,931	15,969,361

(e) estimated (p) preliminary

U.S. and World Silver Production

Source: Bureau of Mines, U.S. Interior Department

Largest production of silver in the United States in 1915—74,961,075 fine ounces.

Year	United States Fine ozs.	United States Value	World Fine ozs.	Year	United States Fine ozs.	United States Value	World Fine ozs.
1930	50,748,127	$19,538,000	248,708,426	1965	39,806,033	$51,469,201	257,415,000
1935	45,924,454	33,008,000	220,704,231	1970	45,006,000	79,697,000	310,891,000
1940	69,585,734	49,483,000	275,387,000	1975	34,938,000	154,424,000	303,112,000
1945	29,063,255	20,667,200	162,000,000	1980	32,329,000	667,278,000	339,382,000
1950	43,308,739	38,291,545	203,300,000	1982	40,248,000	319,975,000	381,533,000
1955	36,469,610	33,006,839	224,000,000	1983	43,415,000	496,671,000	292,268,000
1960	36,000,000	33,305,858	241,300,000	1984[p]	44,440,000	361,773,000	398,554,000

(p) preliminary

Dow Jones Industrial Average Since 1954

	High	Year		Low		High	Year		Low
Dec. 31	404.39	1954	Jan. 11	279.87	Dec. 29	842.00	1970	May 6	631.16
Dec. 30	488.40	1955	Jan. 17	388.20	Apr. 28	950.82	1971	Nov. 23	797.97
Apr. 6	521.05	1956	Jan. 23	462.35	Dec. 11	1036.27	1972	Jan. 26	889.15
July 12	520.77	1957	Oct. 22	419.79	Jan. 11	1051.70	1973	Dec. 5	788.31
Dec. 31	583.65	1958	Feb. 25	436.89	Mar. 13	891.66	1974	Dec. 6	577.60
Dec. 31	679.36	1959	Feb. 9	574.46	July 15	881.81	1975	Jan. 2	632.04
Jan. 5	685.47	1960	Oct. 25	566.05	Sept. 21	1014.79	1976	Jan. 2	858.71
Dec. 13	734.91	1961	Jan. 3	610.25	Jan. 3	999.75	1977	Nov. 2	800.85
Jan. 3	726.01	1962	June 26	535.76	Sept. 8	907.74	1978	Feb. 28	742.12
Dec. 18	767.21	1963	Jan. 2	646.79	Oct. 5	897.61	1979	Nov. 7	796.67
Nov. 18	891.71	1964	Jan. 2	766.08	Nov. 20	1000.17	1980	Apr. 21	759.13
Dec. 31	969.26	1965	June 28	840.59	Apr. 27	1024.05	1981	Sept. 25	824.01
Feb. 9	995.15	1966	Oct. 7	744.32	Dec. 27	1070.55	1982	Aug. 12	776.92
Sept. 25	943.08	1967	Jan. 3	786.41	Nov. 29	1287.20	1983	Jan. 3	1027.04
Dec. 3	985.21	1968	Mar. 21	825.13	Jan. 6	1286.64	1984	July 24	1086.57
May 14	968.85	1969	Dec. 17	769.93	July 19	1359.54	1985*	Jan. 4	1164.96

*As of 9/15/85

Components of Dow Jones Industrial Average

Allied-Signal Corp.
Aluminum Co. of Amer.
American Brands
American Can
American Express
AT&T
Bethlehem Steel
Chevron
DuPont
Eastman Kodak

Exxon
General Electric
General Foods
General Motors
Goodyear
Inco
IBM
International Harvester
International Paper
Merck

Minn. Mining & Manuf.
Owens-Illinois
Procter & Gamble
Sears Roebuck
Texaco
Union Carbide
United Technologies
U.S. Steel
Westinghouse
Woolworth

Stocks Exchanges

N.Y. Stock Exchange Transactions and Seat Prices

Year	Yearly volumes Stock shares	Bonds par values	Year	Yearly volumes Stock shares	Bonds par values
1900	138,981,000	$579,293,000	1950	524,799,621	$1,112,425,170
1905	260,569,000	1,026,254,000	1960	766,693,818	1,346,419,750
1910	163,705,000	634,863,000	1970	2,937,359,448	4,494,864,600
1915	172,497,000	961,700,000	1975	4,693,427,000	5,178,300,000
1920	227,636,000	3,868,422,000	1979	8,155,914,000	4,087,890,000
1925	459,717,623	3,427,042,210	1980	11,352,294,000	5,190,304,000
1929	1,124,800,410	2,996,398,000	1981	11,853,740,659	5,733,071,000
1930	810,632,546	2,720,301,800	1982	16,458,036,768	7,155,443,000
1935	381,635,752	3,339,458,000	1983	21,589,576,997	7,572,315,000
1940	207,599,749	1,669,438,000	1984	23,071,031,447	6,982,291,000

A 1983 survey by the New York Stock Exchange found that 42.4 million Americans owned individual stock or stock mutual funds in U.S. corporations. The median age of these investors was 34, and 57% of them were women.

American Stock Exchange Transactions

Year	Yearly volumes Stock shares	Bonds[1] princ. amts.	Year	Yearly volumes Stock shares	Bonds[1] princ. amts.	Year	Yearly volumes Stock shares	Bonds[1] princ. amts.
1929	476,140,375	$513,551,000	1950	107,792,340	$47,549,000	1981	1,343,400,220	$301,226,000
1930	222,270,065	863,541,000	1960	286,039,982	32,670,000	1982	1,485,831,536	325,240,000
1940	42,928,337	303,902,000	1970	843,116,260	641,270,000	1983	2,081,270,000	395,190,000
1945	143,309,392	167,333,000	1980	1,626,072,625	355,723,000	1984	1,545,010,000	371,990,000

(1) corporate

NASDAQ Reports Record Volume

NASDAQ, The National Association of Securities Dealers Automated Quotations, reported turnover volume of 15.1 billion shares in 1984. This was a decline of 5% over 1983. The number of companies with shares traded in this market was about 4,000 by the end of 1984, making NASDAQ the third-largest market in the world, after the New York and Tokyo exchanges.

Federal Deposit Insurance Corporation (FDIC)

The primary purpose of the Federal Deposit Insurance Corporation (FDIC) is to insure deposits in all banks approved for insurance coverage benefits under the Federal Deposit Insurance Act. The major functions of the FDIC are to pay off depositors of insured banks closed without adequate provision having been made to pay depositors' claims, to act as receiver for all national banks placed in receivership and for state banks placed in receivership when appointed receiver by state authorities, and to prevent the continuance or development of unsafe and unsound banking practices. The FDIC's entire income consists of assessments on insured banks and income from investments; it receives no appropriations from Congress. It may borrow from the U.S. Treasury not to exceed $3 billion outstanding, but has made no such borrowings since it was organized in 1933. The FDIC surplus (Deposit Insurance Fund) as of Dec. 31, 1984 was $17.2 billion.

Federal Reserve System

The Federal Reserve System is the central bank for the United States. The system was established on December 23, 1913, originally to give the country an elastic currency, to provide facilities for discounting commercial paper, and to improve the supervision of banking. Since then, the System's responsibilities have been broadened and, through the monitoring of money and credit growth, it helps work toward sustainable economic growth and price stability.

The Federal Reserve System consists of the Board of Governors; the 12 District Reserve Banks and their branch offices; the Federal Open Market Committee; and, the member banks. Several advisory councils help the Board meet its varied responsibilities.

The hub of the System is the seven member Board of Governors in Washington. The members of the Board are appointed by the President and confirmed by the Senate, to serve 14-year terms. The President also appoints the Chairman and Vice-Chairman of the Board from among the board members for 4-year terms that may be renewed. Currently, the board members are: Paul A. Volcker, Chairman; Preston Martin, Vice Chairman; Henry C. Wallich; J. Charles Partee; Martha R. Seger; Emmett J. Rice.

The Board is the policy-making body. In addition to its policy making responsibilities, it supervises the budget and operations of the Reserve Banks, approves the appointments of their presidents and appoints 3 of each District Bank's directors, including the chairman and vice chairman of each Reserve Bank's board.

The 12 Reserve Banks and their branch offices serve as the decentralized portion of the System, carrying out day-to-day operations such as circulating currency and coin, providing fiscal agency functions and payments mechanism services. The District Banks are located in Boston, New York, Philadelphia, Cleveland, Richmond, Atlanta, Chicago, St. Louis, Minneapolis, Kansas City, Dallas and San Francisco.

The System's principal function is monetary policy, which it controls using three tools: reserve requirements, the discount rate and open market operations. Uniform reserve requirements, set by the Board, are applied to the transaction accounts and nonpersonal time deposits of all depository institutions. Responsibility for setting the discount rate (the interest rate at which depository institutions can borrow money from the Reserve Banks) is shared by the Board of Governors and the Reserve Banks. Changes in the discount rate are recommended by the individual Boards of Directors of the Reserve Banks and are subject to approval by the Board of Governors. The most important tool of monetary policy is open market operations (the purchase and sale of government securities). Responsibility for influencing the cost and availability of money and credit through the purchase and sale of government securities lies with the Federal Open Market Committee (FOMC). This committee is composed of the 7 members of the Board of Governors, the president of the Federal Reserve Bank of New York, and 4 other Federal Reserve Bank presidents, who serve on a rotating basis as voting members of the committee. The committee bases its decisions on current economic and financial developments and outlook, setting yearly growth objectives for key measures of money supply and credit. The decisions of the committee are carried out by the Domestic Trading Desk of the Federal Reserve Bank of New York.

The Federal Reserve Act prescribes a Federal Advisory Council, consisting of one member from each Federal Reserve District, elected annually by the Board of Directors of each of the 12 Federal Reserve Banks. They meet with the Federal Reserve Board at least four times a year to discuss business and financial conditions and to make advisory recommendations.

The Consumer Advisory Council is a statutory body, including both consumer and creditor representatives, which advises the Board of Governors on its implementation of consumer regulations and other consumer-related matters. Following the passage of the Monetary Control Act of 1980, the Board of Governors established the Thrift Institutions Advisory Council to provide information and views on the special needs and problems of thrift institutions. The group is comprised of representatives of mutual savings banks, savings and loan associations, and credit unions.

This piece of legislation also extended access to Federal Reserve discount and borrowing privileges and other services to all depository institutions. The act required the Federal Reserve to set a schedule of fees for its services. And, it was through this act that the Depository Institutions Deregulations Committee (DIDC) was formed to provide for the orderly elimination of the limitations on the maximum rate of interest and dividends which may be paid on deposits by commercial banks, mutual savings banks, and savings and loan associations. Congress intended that the phase-out be completed by March 31, 1986. DIDC consists of the Secretary of the Treasury, the Chairman of the Board of Governors of the Federal Reserve System, the Chairman of the Board of Directors of the Federal Deposit Insurance Corporation, the Chairman of the Federal Home Loan Bank Board, and the Chairman of the National Credit Union Administration Board, each of whom has one vote, and the Comptroller of the Currency who is a nonvoting members.

Largest Banks Outside the U.S.

Source: 500 Largest Banks in the Free World, compiled by the American Banker, New York. (Copyright 1985) Based on deposits Dec. 31, 1984, or nearest fiscal year-end.

(thousands of U.S. dollars)

Bank, country	Deposits	Bank, country	Deposits
Dai-Ichi Kangyo Bank Ltd., Tokyo, Japan	$95,096,963	Sumitomo Trust & Banking Co., Ltd., Osaka, Japan	$52,055,661
Fuji Bank, Ltd., Tokyo, Japan	90,304,209	Dresdner Bank, Frankfurt, Germany	51,960,512
Sumitomo Bank Ltd., Osaka, Japan	89,873,361	Hongkong and Shanghai Banking Corp., Hong Kong, Hong Kong	51,705,835
Mitsubishi Bank Ltd., Tokyo, Japan	87,324,124	Bank of Montreal, Canada	50,670,251
Credit Agricole Mutuel, Paris, France	84,827,843	Taiyo Kobe Bank, Ltd., Kobe, Japan	48,120,766
Banque Nationale de Paris, France	82,831,989	Lloyds Bank Plc, London, U.K.	46,870,020
Sanwa Bank Ltd., Osaka, Japan	80,928,359	Mitsui Trust & Banking Co., Ltd., Tokyo, Japan	46,481,199
Credit Lyonnais, Paris, France	77,524,868	Canadian Imperial Bank of Commerce, Toronto, Canada	45,090,906
Societe Generale, Paris, France	75,821,854	Daiwa Bank, Ltd., Osaka, Japan	44,860,497
Barclays Plc, London, U.K.	73,714,652	Union Bank of Switzerland, Zurich, Switzerland	43,530,811
Norinchukin Bank, Tokyo, Japan	73,311,156	Westdeutsche Landesbank Girozentrale, Duesseldorf, Germany	41,562,731
National Westminster Bank Plc, London, U.K.	73,266,124	Swiss Bank Corp., Basle, Switzerland	40,761,781
Industrial Bank of Japan, Ltd., Tokyo, Japan	71,222,389	Yasuda Trust & Banking Co. Ltd., Tokyo, Japan	40,465,641
Deutsche Bank, Frankfurt, Germany	67,310,193	Bank of Nova Scotia, Toronto, Canada	39,989,677
Midland Pank Plc, London, U.K.	65,427,288	Banca Nazionale del Lavoro, Rome, Italy	39,837,910
Tokai Bank Ltd., Nagoya, Japan	65,038,461	Bayerische Vereinsbank, Munich, Germany	36,938,896
Mitsui Bank Ltd., Tokyo, Japan	60,037,437	Standard Chartered Bank, London, U.K.	36,644,737
Royal Bank of Canada, Montreal, Canada	58,967,142		
Long-Term Credit Bank of Japan Ltd., Tokyo, Japan	57,603,874		
Mitsubishi Trust & Banking Corp., Tokyo, Japan	56,409,319		
Bank of Tokyo, Ltd., Japan	52,573,030		

Largest U.S. Commercial Banks

Source: Largest Commercial Banks in U.S., compiled by the American Banker, New York. (Copyright 1985) Based on deposits Dec. 31, 1984.

(thousands)

Rank	Deposits	Rank	Deposits
Bank of America NT&SA, San Francisco . . .	$88,167,000	First Fidelity Bank NA, Newark, N.J.	$5,735,478
Citibank NA, New York	79,551,000	Comerica Bank-Detroit	5,512,253
Chase Manhattan Bank NA, New York	59,399,689	Rainier National Bank, Seattle	5,469,045
Manufacturers Hanover Trust Co., New York.	45,200,916	Harris Trust & Savings Bank, Chicago.	5,465,559
Morgan Guaranty Trust Co., New York	39,995,564	Citizens & Southern National Bank, Atlanta. .	5,333,788
Chemical Bank, New York	35,068,135	Pittsburgh National Bank	5,171,956
Security Pacific National Bank, Los Angeles .	30,902,297	Philadelphia National Bank	5,145,043
Bankers Trust Co., New York.	27,882,815	MBank Dallas NA	4,953,320
First National Bank, Chicago	25,904,344	Connecticut B&T Co. NA, Hartford	4,910,666
Wells Fargo Bank NA, San Francisco	20,308,269	AmeriTrust Co. NA, Cleveland	4,850,226
Crocker National Bank, San Francisco	18,088,638	United States National Bank, Portland, Ore. .	4,848,037
Marine Midland Bank NA, Buffalo, N.Y.	15,924,063	Connecticut National Bank, Hartford.	4,795,921
Continental Illinois Nat'l B&T Co., Chicago . .	15,598,568	Fidelity Bank NA, Malvern, Pa	4,720,618
First Interstate Bank of CA, Los Angeles . . .	15,472,833	First Interstate Bank of Ariz. NA, Phoenix . .	4,706,313
Mellon Bank NA, Pittsburgh.	15,002,320	First National Bank, Minneapolis	4,683,775
First National Bank, Boston	13,069,033	Norwest Bank Minneapolis NA	4,546,009
Irving Trust Co., New York	11,145,035	First National Bank, Atlanta	4,518,912
Bank of New York	10,500,888	Manufacturers National Bank, Detroit	4,502,343
RepublicBank Dallas NA	9,758,084	United Virginia Bank, Richmond	4,473,747
Republic National Bank, New York.	8,274,088	California First Bank, San Francisco	4,433,770
National Bank of Detroit	8,091,530	Northern Trust Co., Chicago	4,399,824
Southeast Bank NA, Miami	7,589,312	Bank of Tokyo Trust Co., New York	4,370,787
Valley National Bank, Phoenix	7,415,759	Florida National Bank, Jacksonville	4,363,475
NCNB National bank of N.C., Charlotte	7,293,063	First Union National Bank, Charlotte, N.C. . . .	4,339,697
InterFirst Bank Dallas NA	7,105,781	First Interstate Bank of Oregon NA, Portland .	4,203,998
National Westminister Bank USA, New York .	7,019,218	Huntington National Bank, Columbus, Ohio. .	4,198,682
Texas Commerce Bank NA, Houston	6,775,313	Riggs National Bank, Washington, D.C.	4,173,672
Wachovia B&T Co. NA, Winston-Salem, N.C..	6,486,164	Maryland National Bank, Baltimore	4,173,161
Seattle-First National Bank	6,459,583	First Pennsylvania Bank NA, Philadelphia . . .	3,903,222
Sovran Bank NA, Richmond	6,245,413	NCNB National Bank of Florida, Tampa	3,848,812
First City National Bank, Houston	6,060,855	Bank of New England NA, Boston	3,747,904
Union Bank, Los Angeles	5,943,808	First Tennessee Bank NA, Memphis	3,648,932
European American Bank, New York	5,828,050		

Bank Suspensions and Failures

Source: Federal Deposit Insurance Corp

Year	Susp.	Closed	Year	Susp.	Closed	Year	Susp.	Closed	Year	Susp.	Closed
1929	659	—	1938	50	81	1964	7	8	1975	1	14
1930	1,352	—	1939	32	72	1965	3	9	1976	3	17
1931	2,294	—	1940	19	48	1966	1	8	1978	1	7
1932	1,456	—	1955(a)	4	5	1967	4	4	1979	3	10
1933	4,004	—	1958	3	9	1969	4	9	1980	3	10
1934	9	61	1959	3	3	1970	4	8	1981	2	10
1935	24	32	1960	1	2	1971	5	6	1982	7	42
1936	42	72	1961	5	9	1972	1	3	1983	9	48
1937	50	84	1963	2	2	1973	3	6	1984	16	79

(a) No suspensions in years 1945-1954, 1962, 1968, 1974, 1977.

All Banks in U.S.—Number, Deposits

Source: Federal Reserve System

Comprises all national banks in the United States and all state commercial banks, trust companies, mutual stock savings banks, private and industrial banks, and special types of institutions that are treated as banks by the federal bank supervisory agencies.

Year	Total all banks	Number of banks					Total deposits (millions of dollars)				
		F.R.S. members		Nonmembers			F.R.S. members		Nonmembers		
		Total	Nat'l	State	Mutual savings	Other	Total all banks	Total	Nat'l	State	Mutual savings	Other
(As of June 30)	banks	Total	Nat'l	State	ings	Other	banks	Total	Nat'l	State	ings	Other
1925.	26,479	9,538	8,066	1,472	621	18,320	51,641	32,457	19,912	12,546	7,089	12,095
1930.	23,855	8,315	7,247	1,068	604	14,936	59,828	38,069	23,235	14,834	9,117	12,642
1935.	16,047	6,410	5,425	985	569	9,068	51,149	34,938	22,477	12,461	9,830	6,381
1940.	14,955	6,398	5,164	1,234	551	8,008	70,770	51,729	33,014	18,715	10,631	8,410
1945.	14,542	6,840	5,015	1,825	539	7,163	151,033	118,378	76,534	41,844	14,413	18,242
1950.	14,674	6,885	4,971	1,914	527	7,262	163,770	122,707	82,430	40,277	19,927	21,137
1955.	14,309	6,611	4,744	1,867	525	7,173	208,850	154,670	98,636	56,034	27,310	26,870
1960.	14,006	6,217	4,542	1,675	513	7,276	249,163	179,519	116,178	63,341	35,316	34,328
1965.	14,295	6,235	4,803	1,432	504	7,556	362,611	259,743	171,528	88,215	50,980	51,889
1970.	14,167	5,805	4,638	1,167	496	7,866	502,542	346,289	254,322	91,967	69,285	86,968
1975, Dec. 31	15,108	5,787	4,741	1,046	475	8,846	896,879	590,999	447,590	143,409	110,569	195,311
1980, Dec. 31	15,145	5,422	4,425	997	460	9,263	1,333,399	843,030	651,848	191,182	150,000	340,369
1982, Dec. 31	14,934	5,632	4,580	1,052	386	8,916	1,541,015	995,230	779,110	216,120	146,524	399,261
1983, Dec. 31	14,922	5,821	4,756	1,065	366	8,735	1,686,035	1,083,149	864,495	218,654	161,543	441,343
1984, Dec. 31	14,741	5,973	4,905	1,068	267	8,501	1,758,848	1,169,910	945,028	224,882	121,559	467,379

Bank Rates on Short-term Business Loans

Source: Federal Reserve System

Percent per annum. Short-term loans mature within one year.

		Ave. 35 cities	N.Y. C.	7 Other N.E.	8 No. Cent.	7 S.E.	8 S.W.	4 West	1-9	10-99	100 to 499	500 to 999	1,000 and over
				All size loans							Size of loan in $1,000		
1967	Aug. 1-15	5.95	5.66	6.29	5.92	5.92	6.01	6.02	6.58	6.46	6.16	5.89	5.72
1970	Aug. 1-15	8.50	8.24	8.89	8.47	8.49	8.53	8.54	9.15	9.07	8.75	8.46	8.25
1974	May	11.15	11.08	11.65	11.09	10.88	10.82	11.19	10.50	11.06	11.41	11.32	11.06
1975	May	8.16	7.88	8.37	8.00	8.70	8.34	8.33	9.57	9.10	8.52	8.18	7.90
1976	Aug.	7.80	7.48	8.18	7.70	7.95	7.75	8.15	8.85	9.41	8.65	9.33	9.26
	Nov.	7.28	6.88	7.62	7.28	7.51	7.33	7.52	8.56	9.22	8.45	9.13	8.69

		All sizes	1-24	25-49	50-99	100-499	500-999	1,000 and over
				Size of loan in $1,000[1]				
1981	Feb.	19.91	19.59	19.53	19.77	20.18	20.87	19.83
	May	19.99	19.45	19.87	19.10	19.93	19.58	20.14
1982	Feb.	17.13	18.34	17.88	18.20	17.65	17.31	16.99
	May	17.11	18.51	18.56	18.06	17.77	17.98	16.94
1983	Feb.	10.20	14.44	13.57	13.40	12.71	11.59	9.81
	May	10.30	13.86	13.68	12.62	11.87	11.34	9.87
1984	Feb.	11.06	14.13	13.45	13.33	12.66	11.99	10.75
	May	12.45	14.93	14.46	14.41	13.86	13.37	12.12
1985	Feb.	10.10	14.08	13.15	12.92	12.09	11.31	9.64
	May	9.92	13.80	13.04	12.91	12.42	11.18	9.39

(1) In Feb. 1977, The Quarterly Interest Rate Survey was replaced by the Survey of Terms of Bank Lending (STBL). The STBL is conducted in the middle month of each quarter at about 340 member and nonmember banks. The regional breakdown was discontinued at that time. The last previous revision began with the survey period of Feb. 1971. It incorporated a number of technical changes in coverage, sampling, and interest rate calculations.

U.S. Industrial Corporations with Largest Sales in 1984

Source: FORTUNE Magazine

Company	Sales (thousands)	Income (or loss) (thousands)	Company	Sales (thousands)	Income (or loss) (thousands)
Exxon	$90,854,000	$5,528,000	Allied	$10,864,000	$488,000
General Motors	83,889,900	4,516,500	Unocal	10,838,000	700,400
Mobil	56,047,000	1,268,000	Eastman Kodak	10,600,000	923,000
Ford Motor	52,366,400	2,906,800	Boeing	10,354,000	787,000
Texaco	47,334,000	306,000	Westinghouse Electric	10,264,500	535,900
International Business Machines	45,937,000	6,582,000	Goodyear Tire & Rubber	10,240,800	411,000
			Philip Morris	10,137,800	888,500
E.I. du Pont de Nemours	35,915,000	1,431,000	Dart & Kraft	9,758,700	455,800
American Tel. & Tel.	33,187,500	1,369,900	McDonnell Douglas	9,662,600	325,300
General Electric	27,947,000	2,280,000	Union Carbide	9,508,000	-323,000
Standard Oil (Indiana)	26,949,000	2,183,000	Beatrice Foods	9,327,000	433,000
Chevron	26,798,000	1,534,000	Rockwell International	9,322,100	496,500
Atlantic Richfield	24,686,000	567,000	Xerox	8,971,300	490,500
Shell Oil	20,701,000	1,772,000	General Foods	8,599,754	317,105
Chrysler	19,572,700	2,380,000	PepsiCo	8,427,994	212,547
U.S. Steel	18,274,000	493,000	Amerada Hess	8,277,184	170,455
United Technologies	16,331,757	645,015	Ashland Oil	8,252,564	(172,478)
Phillips Petroleum	15,537,000	810,000	Lockheed	8,113,400	344,100
Occidental Petroleum	15,373,000	568,700	General Dynamics	7,839,000	381,700
Tenneco	14,779,000	631,000	Minnesota Mining & Manufacturing	7,705,000	773,000
Sun	14,466,000	538,000	Coca-Cola	7,363,993	628,818
ITT	14,000,988	448,046	Georgia-Pacific	7,128,000	119,000
Procter & Gamble	12,946,000	890,000	LTV	7,046,100	(378,200)
R.J. Reynolds Industries	11,902,000	1,210,000	Consolidated Foods	7,000,310	188,441
Standard Oil (Ohio)	11,692,000	1,488,000	W.R. Grace	6,727,800	195,600
Dow Chemical	11,418,000	585,000			

Largest Corporate Mergers in U.S.

(as of mid-1985)

Company	Acquirer	Dollars	Year	Company	Acquirer	Dollars	Year
Gulf Oil	Chevron	13.3 bln.	1984	Cities Service	Occidental Petroleum	4 bln.	1982
Getty Oil	Texaco	10.1 bln.	1984	Belridge Oil	Shell Oil	3.6 bln.	1979
Conoco	DuPont	7.4 bln.	1981	ABC Broadcasting	Capital Cities Comm.	3.5 bln.	1985
Marathon Oil	U.S. Steel	6.5 bln.	1981	Esmark	Beatrice Foods	2.7 bln.	1984
Superior Oil	Mobil Oil	5.7 bln.	1984	Continental Group	Kiernit-Murdock	2.7 bln.	1984
Southern Pacific	Santa Fe Railroad	5.2 bln.	1983	St. Joe Minerals	Fluor	2.6 bln.	1981
Connecticut General	INA	4.3 bln.	1981	Electronic Data Systems	General Motors	2.6 bln.	1984
Texasgulf	Elf Aquitaine	4.2 bln.	1981				

In 1984, there were 2,543 corporate mergers and acquisitions with a combined value of more than 122 billion dollars. Through May 1985, the merger pace quickened to about 11 every working day.

Average Paycheck by States in 1983

Source: Bureau of Economic Analysis, U.S. Commerce Department

State	Average 1983 Wage	One-year Gain	State	Average 1983 Wage	One-year Gain
Alabama	$15,472	5.1%	Montana	15,212	3.5
Alaska	28,720	2.9	Nebraska	14,762	5.0
Arizona	16,667	4.1	Nevada	17,118	3.9
Arkansas	14,327	5.1	New Hampshire	15,541	6.3
California	19,038	5.9	New Jersey	18,823	5.3
Colorado	18,102	4.1	New Mexico	15,922	3.5
Connecticut	18,770	6.4	New York	19,694	6.3
Delaware	18,164	3.5	North Carolina	14,676	6.1
Florida	15,543	5.1	North Dakota	15,048	2.9
Georgia	16,054	6.0	Ohio	17,920	4.5
Hawaii	16,107	4.9	Oklahoma	17,154	2.3
Idaho	15,241	4.0	Oregon	16,786	3.7
Illinois	18,708	4.1	Pennsylvania	17,161	4.3
Indiana	17,068	4.1	Rhode Island	15,397	5.9
Iowa	15,214	3.0	South Carolina	14,647	6.2
Kansas	15,915	4.2	South Dakota	13,188	3.8
Kentucky	16,020	3.4	Tennessee	15,546	5.3
Louisiana	17,342	1.6	Texas	18,133	4.2
Maine	14,130	4.9	Utah	16,511	3.8
Maryland	17,086	5.2	Vermont	14,643	6.1
Massachusetts	17,347	6.2	Virginia	16,491	5.6
Michigan	19,712	4.8	Washington	18,037	1.6
Minnesota	17,212	5.1	West Virginia	16,862	1.0
Mississippi	13,948	3.9	Wisconsin	16,376	4.5
Missouri	16,785	5.1	Wyoming	17,840	-0.8

Effective Federal Minimum Hourly Wage Rates, 1950 to 1981, and Coverage in 1983

Source: U.S. Department of Labor.

(Employee estimates as of September 1983, except as indicated. The Fair Labor Standards Act of 1938 and subsequent amendments provide for minimum wage coverage applicable to specified nonsupervisory employment categories. Exempt from coverage are executives and administrators or professionals).

Effective Date	Minimum Rates for Nonfarm Workers			Minimum rates for farm workers[4]	Sex, Race, and Industry	Nonsupervisory Employees, 1983 Subject to minimum wage rates				
	Laws prior to 1966[1]	Per-cent, avg earnings[2]	1966 and later[3]			Total (1,000)	Total (1,000)	Per-cent of total	Prior to 1966[67] (1,000)	1966 and later[367] (1,000)
Jan. 25, 1950	$.75	54	(X)	(X)	Total	77,321	60,461	78.2	43,318	17,143
Mar. 1, 1956	1.00	52	(X)	(X)	Male	41,719	32,645	78.2	24,976	7,669
Sept. 3, 1961	1.15	50	(X)	(X)	Female	35,602	27,816	78.1	18,342	9,474
Sept. 3, 1963	1.25	51	(X)	(X)	White	67,829	53,066	78.2	38,703	14,363
Feb. 1, 1967	1.40	50	$1.00	$1.00	Black and other	9,492	7,395	77.9	4,615	2,780
Feb. 1, 1968	1.60	54	1.15	1.15	Black only	8,657	6,757	78.1	4,217	2,540
Feb. 1, 1969	(5)	(5)	1.30	1.30	Private Industry	67,731	57,868	85.4	43,318	14,550
Feb. 1, 1970	(5)	(5)	1.45	(5)	Agriculture	1,620	623	38.5	—	623
Feb. 1, 1971	(5)	(5)	1.60	(5)	Mining	896	892	99.6	892	—
May 1, 1974	2.00	46	1.90	1.60	Construction	3,853	3,831	99.4	3,225	606
Jan. 1, 1975	2.10	45	2.00	1.80	Manufacturing	16,916	16,448	97.2	16,342	106
Jan. 1, 1976	2.30	46	2.20	2.00	Transp., public					
Jan. 1, 1977	(5)	(5)	2.30	2.20	utilities	4,499	4,468	99.3	4,390	78
Jan. 1, 1978	2.65	44	2.65	2.65	Wholesale trade	4,532	3,613	79.7	3,378	235
Jan. 1, 1979	2.90	45	2.90	2.90	Retail trade	13,920	11,587	83.2	6,113	5,474
Jan. 1, 1980	3.10	45	3.10	3.10	Finance, insurance,					
Jan. 1, 1981	3.35	43	3.35	3.35	real estate	4,705	3,567	75.8	3,427	140
					Service	15,163	11,790	77.8	5,551	6,239
					Private households	1,627	1,049	64.5	—	1,049
					Government[8]	9,590	2,593	27.0	—	2,593

(X) Not applicable. (1) Applies to workers covered prior to 1961 Amendments and, after Sept. 1965, to workers covered by 1961 Amendments. Rates set by 1961 Amendments were: Sept. 1961, $1.00; Sept. 1964, $1.15; and Sept. 1965, $1.25. (2) Percent of gross average hourly earnings of production workers in manufacturing. (3) Applies to workers newly covered by Amendments of 1966, 1974, and 1977, and Title IX of Education Amendments of 1972. (4) Included in coverage as of 1966, 1974, and 1977 Amendments. (5) No change in rate. (6) Currently employed workers subject to criteria in effect prior to 1966 Amendments, except workers in retail-service establishments with less than $250,000, who otherwise would have been exempt prior to the 1966 Amendments, are included if part of enterprises subject to criteria established prior to the 1966 Amendments. (7) Currently employed workers subject to provisions. (8) Federal, State, and local employees.

U.S. Currency and Coin
Source: U.S. Treasury Department (June 30, 1984)

Amounts in Circulation and Outstanding

	Amounts in circulation	Less amounts held by: United States Treasury	Less amounts held by: Federal Reserve Notes[1]	Amounts outstanding
Currency				
Federal Reserve Notes[1]	$187,637,075,048	$3,527,982	$27,727,744,624	$159,906,072,442
United States Notes	322,059,016	27,490,939	0	295,048,077
Currency No Longer Issued	273,448,105	203,353	45,451	273,199,301
Total	$188,233,062,169	$30,952,274	$27,727,744,624	$160,474,319,820
Coin[2]				
Dollars[3]	2,024,703,898	$362,346,322	$113,625,233	1,548,732,343
Fractional Coin	13,490,742,000	130,411,569	323,798,451	13,036,531,980
Total	15,515,445,898	492,757,891	437,423,684	14,585,264,323
Total currency and coin.	$203,748,508,067	$523,170,165	$28,165,213,759	$175,059,584,143

Currency in Circulation by Denominations

Denomination	Total currency in circulation	Federal Reserve Notes[1]	U.S. Notes	Currency no longer issued
1 Dollar	$3,711,519,311	$3,557,847,055	$143,481	$153,528,775
2 Dollars	700,100,832	566,989,722	133,098,066	13,044
5 Dollars	4,757,191,895	4,605,381,385	112,643,810	39,166,700
10 Dollars	11,328,418,110	11,303,055,680	5,950	25,356,480
20 Dollars	49,171,039,020	49,150,753,400	3,380	20,282,240
50 Dollars	19,905,856,950	19,894,123,200	—	11,733,750
100 Dollars	70,557,111,100	70,485,392,500	49,153,300	22,565,300
500 Dollars	156,338,000	156,146,500	—	191,500
1,000 Dollars	181,434,000	181,223,000	—	211,000
5,000 Dollars	1,830,000	1,780,000	—	50,000
10,000 Dollars	3,480,000	3,380,000	—	100,000
Fractional parts	487	—	—	487
Partial notes[4]	115	—	90	25
Total currency	**$160,474,319,820**	**$159,906,072,442**	**$295,048,077**	**$273,199,301**

Comparative Totals of Money in Circulation — Selected Dates

Date	Amounts (in millions)	Per capita[5]	Date	Amounts (in millions)	Per capita[5]	Date	Amounts (in millions)	Per capita[5]
June 30, 1984	$175,059.5[6]	$739.85	June 30, 1960	$32,064.6	$177.47	June 30, 1930	$4,522.0	$36.74[6]
June 30, 1983	162,027.1	691.74	June 30, 1955	30,229.3	182.90	June 30, 1925	4,815.2	41.56
June 30, 1981	138,080.2	600.86	June 30, 1950	27,156.3	179.03	June 30, 1920	5,467.6	51.36
June 30, 1975	81,196.4	380.08	June 30, 1945	26,746.4	191.14	June 30, 1915	3,319.6	33.01
June 30, 1970	54,351.0	265.39	June 30, 1940	7,847.5	59.40	June 30, 1910	3,148.7	34.07
June 30, 1965	39,719.8	204.14	June 30, 1935	5,567.1	43.75			

(1) Issued on and after July 1, 1929. (2) Excludes coin sold to collectors at premium prices. (3) Includes $481,781,898 in standard silver dollars. (4) Represents value of certain partial denominations not presented for redemption. (5) Based on Bureau of the Census estimates of population. (6) Highest amount to date.

The requirement for a gold reserve against U.S. notes was repealed by Public Law 90-269 approved Mar. 18, 1968. Silver certificates issued on and after July 1, 1929 became redeemable from the general fund on June 24, 1968. The amount of security after those dates has been reduced accordingly.

U.S. Money in Circulation, by Denominations
Outside Treasury and Federal Reserve Banks. (millions of dollars)
Source: U.S. Treasury Department, Financial Management Service

End of year	Total in circulation	Coin and small denomination						Large denomination currency						
		Total	Coin	$1	$2	$5	$10	$20	Total	$50	$100	$500	$1,000	$5,000	$10,000
1950	27,741	19,305	1,554	1,113	64	2,049	5,998	8,529	8,438	2,422	5,043	368	588	4	12
1960	32,869	23,521	2,427	1,533	88	2,246	6,691	10,536	9,348	2,815	5,954	249	316	3	10
1970	57,093	39,639	6,281	2,310	136	3,161	9,170	18,581	17,454	4,896	12,084	215	252	3	4
1975	86,547	54,866	8,959	2,809	135	3,841	10,777	28,344	31,681	8,157	23,139	175	204	2	4
1978	114,645	66,693	10,739	3,194	661	4,393	11,661	36,045	47,952	11,279	36,306	167	194	2	4
1979	125,600	70,693	11,658	3,308	671	4,549	11,894	38,613	54,907	12,585	41,960	164	192	2	4
1980	137,244	73,893	12,419	3,499	677	4,635	11,924	40,739	63,352	13,731	49,264	163	189	2	3

Seigniorage on Coin and Silver Bullion
Source: U.S. Treasury Department, Financial Management Service

Seigniorage is the profit from coining money; it is the difference between the monetary value of coins and their cost, including the manufacturing expense.

Fiscal year	Total		Total
Jan. 1, 1935-June 30, 1965, cumulative	$2,525,927,763.84	1979	991,909,496.55
1968	383,141,339.00[1]	1980	662,814,791.48
1970	274,217,884.01	1981	450,174,439.26
1972	580,586,683.00	1982	390,407,804.91
1974	320,706,638.49	1983	477,479,387.58
1975	660,898,070.69	1984	498,371,724.09
(1) Revised to include seigniorage on clad coins.		Cumulative Jan. 1, 1935-Sept. 30, 1984	11,890,541,452.81

United States Mint

Source: United States Mint, U.S. Treasury Department

The United States Mint was created by Act of April 2, 1792, which established our national coinage system. Initially, operations were conducted at Philadelphia, then the nation's capital. Supervision of the Mint was a function of the secretary of state, but in 1799, it became an independent agency reporting directly to the president. The Mint was made a statutory bureau of the Treasury Department in 1873, with a director appointed by the president to oversee its operations from headquarters offices in the Treasury Department at Washington, D.C.

The Mint manufactures all U.S. coins and distributes them through the Federal Reserve banks and branches. The Mint also maintains physical custody of the treasury's monetary stocks of gold and silver, moving, storing and releasing from custody as authorized. There are 6 field facilities. Mints are located in Philadelphia and Denver; the San Francisco Assay Office and San Francisco Old Mint perform coinage operations and numismatic functions; two depositories, one at Fort Knox, Ky., for the storage of gold, and the other at West Point, N.Y., where gold and silver are stored and coinage is produced by congressional authorization. A museum is maintained at the San Francisco Old Mint.

The traditional 90% silver coinage was phased out and cupronickel clad coinage introduced when the Coinage Act of 1965 removed all silver from the dime and quarter and reduced the silver content of the half dollar to 40%. In 1970, legislative action removed the remaining silver from the half dollar and in providing for the resumption of dollar coinage, directed that both denominations produced for circulation also be cupronickel clad metal. Changes in the design, weight and size of the standard silver dollar were approved by Congress in 1978, and beginning in 1979, a smaller cupronickel dollar coin bearing the likeness of Susan B. Anthony and the Apollo II moon landing was released.

A change in the composition of the cent was effected in 1982, when as an economy measure the current copper-plated zinc cent was introduced to replace the traditional 95% copper cent.

The Mint manufactures and sells bronze medals of a national character, produces numismatic coins and coin sets, and as scheduling permits, manufactures coinage for foreign governments. Recent special numismatic coinage includes congressionally authorized 90% silver half dollars marking the 250th anniversary of George Washington's birth, and 90% gold $10 coins and two 90% silver dollars dated 1983 and 1984, respectively, for the 1984 Olympic Summer Games at Los Angeles. The $10 gold coin was the first gold coin struck by the Mint in more than 50 years. Authorized by congress for release in 1985 are 3 commemorative coins for the centennial in 1986 of the Statue of Liberty. Surcharges from the cupronickel clad half dollars, 90% silver dollars and 90% gold $5 coins are to be used to restore and renovate the Statue of Liberty and immigration facilities at Ellis Island, N.Y., and ensure the continued upkeep and maintenance of these national sites.

Domestic coin production for the calendar year 1984 follows:

Domestic Coinage Executed During Calendar Year 1984

Denomination Dollars—non-silver	Philadelphia —0—	Denver —0—	West Point —0—	Total value —0—	Total Pieces —0—
Subsidiary					
Half dollars	$ 13,014,500.00	$ 13,131,079.00	-0-	$ 26,145,579.00	52,291,158
Quarter dollars	169,136,250.00	136,620,766.00	-0-	305,757,016.00	1,223,028,064
Dimes	85,666,900.00	70,480,397.60	-0-	156,147,297.60	1,561,472,976
Total subsidiary	$267,817,650.00	$220,232,242.60	-0-	$488,049,892.60	2,836,792,198
Minor					
Five-cent pieces	$ 37,338,450.00	$ 25,883,757.30	-0-	$ 63,222,207.30	1,264,444,146
One-cent pieces[1]	61,148,640.00	55,692,389.06	$20,362,150.00	137,203,179.06	13,720,317,906
Total minor,	$98,487,090.00	$ 81,576,146.36	$20,362,150.00	$200,425,386.36	14,984,762,052
Total domestic coinage	$366,304,740.00	$301,808,388.96	$20,362,150.00	$688,475,278.96	17,821,554,250

Portraits on U.S. Treasury Bills, Bonds, Notes and Savings Bonds

Denomination	Savings bonds	Treas. bills	Treas. bonds	Treas. notes
25	Washington			
50	F.D. Roosevelt		Jefferson	
75	Truman			
100	Eisenhower		Jackson	
200	Kennedy			
500	Wilson		Washington	
1,000	T. Roosevelt	H. McCulloch	Lincoln	Lincoln
5,000	McKinley	J.G. Carlisle	Monroe	Monroe
10,000	Cleveland	J. Sherman	Cleveland	Cleveland
50,000		C. Glass		
100,000		A Gallatin	Grant	Grant
1,000,000		O. Wolcott	T. Roosevelt	T. Roosevelt
100,000,000				Madison
500,000,000				McKinley

Large Denominations of U.S. Currency Discontinued

The largest denomination of United States currency now being issued is the $100 bill. Issuance of currency in denominations larger than $100 was discontinued in 1969.

As large denomination bills reach the Federal Reserve Bank they are removed from circulation.

Because some of the discontinued currency is expected to be in the hands of holders for many years, the description of the various denominations below is continued:

Amt.	Portrait	Embellishment on back	Amt.	Portrait	Embellishment on back
$ 1	Washington	Great Seal of U.S.	$ 100	Franklin	Independence Hall
2	Jefferson	Signers of Declaration	500	McKinley	Ornate denominational marking
5	Lincoln	Lincoln Memorial	1,000	Cleveland	Ornate denominational marking
10	Hamilton	U.S. Treasury	5,000	Madison	Ornate denominational marking
20	Jackson	White House	10,000	Chase	Ornate denominational marking
50	Grant	U.S. Capitol	100,000	Wilson	Ornate denominational marking

*For use only in transactions between Federal Reserve System and Treasury Department.

MANUFACTURES AND MINERALS
General Statistics for Major Industry Groups
Source: Bureau of the Census

The estimates for 1982 in the following table are based upon information extracted from a series of 443 preliminary reports issued as part of the 1982 Census of Manufactures program.

Industry	All employees		Production workers			Value added by mfr.[1] (millions)
	Number (1,000)	Payroll (millions)	Number (1,000)	Manhours (millions)	Wages (millions)	
Food and kindred products	1,493.6	26,073.7	1,048.2	2,036.1	16,409.8	80,794.7
Tobacco products	57.9	1,323.4	45.4	83.7	957.1	6,429.6
Textile mill products	720.7	9,242.4	617.7	1,117.5	6,976.2	19,463.2
Apparel, oth. textile prods.	1,188.8	12,113.9	1,007.7	1,803.3	8,826.3	25,639.9
Lumber and wood products	577.6	8,437.2	480.4	896.9	6,439.7	17,321.0
Furniture and fixtures	434.9	6,076.0	349.5	648.5	4,179.2	12,668.7
Paper and allied products	602.6	12,893.7	459.1	919.5	9,018.0	32,366.7
Printing and publishing.	1,293.5	22,687.1	712.6	1,316.1	11,287.2	49,351.6
Chemicals, allied products	866.4	20,675.0	504.1	994.9	10,463.9	80,032.3
Petroleum and coal products	151.2	4,339.2	99.2	205.0	2,612.8	26,740.3
Rubber, misc. plastics prod..	680.0	11,576.1	521.7	996.8	7,684.5	26,005.9
Leather, leather products	200.7	2,216.0	172.3	306.2	1,625.2	5,230.3
Stone, clay, glass products	530.1	10,067.9	407.5	794.5	7,153.9	24,853.9
Primary metal industries.	854.4	20,590.3	638.5	1,167.4	14,460.1	49,550.6
Fabricated metal products	1,449.7	28,106.2	1,065.8	2,057.0	18,339.3	61,558.2
Machinery, except electric	2,176.6	46,644.2	1,346.9	2,576.4	24,903.9	111,393.7
Electric, electronic equip.	1,924.7	38,713.9	1,200.9	2,274.6	19,369.9	79,720.4
Transportation equipment.	1,618.1	41,181.0	1,069.5	2,056.3	24,513.8	82,938.2
Instruments, related prods.	621.6	12,837.0	362.3	693.3	5,896.0	31,493.8
Misc. manufacturing indus.	382.3	5,641.7	280.4	522.6	3,406.3	13,953.51
Administrative and auxiliary[2]	1,286.0	38,364.4	—	—	—	—
All industries, total	**19,111.4**	**379,800.3**	**12,389.7**	**23,526.6**	**204,523.1**	**837,506.5**

(1) A new instruction for reporting inventory data was introduced for 1982. Initially, this led to some confusion in the reporting of inventories. Because of the need to evaluate these data, the 1982 value added figures, which were computed based on these inventory data, were suppressed in the preliminary report series. The final report series, which is scheduled to be issued by May 1985, will contain these figures.
(2) In addition to the employment and payroll for operating manufacturing establishments, manufacturing concerns reported separately for central administrative offices or auxiliary units (e.g., research laboratories, storage warehouses, power plants, garages, repair shops, etc.) which serve the manufacturing establishments of a company rather than the public.

Manufacturing Production Worker Statistics
Source: Bureau of Labor Statistics, U.S. Labor Department (p — preliminary)

Year		All employees	Production workers	Payroll index 1977=100	Avg. weekly earnings	Avg. hourly earnings	Avg. hrs. per wk.
1955		16,882,000	13,288,000	31.5	$75.30	$1.85	40.7
1960		16,796,000	12,586,000	35.4	89.72	2.26	39.7
1965		18,062,000	13,434,000	45.1	107.53	2.61	41.2
1970		19,367,000	14,044,000	58.6	133.33	3.35	39.8
1975		18,323,000	13,043,000	76.8	190.79	4.83	39.5
1978		20,505,000	14,734,000	113.6	249.27	6.17	40.4
1979		21,040,000	15,068,000	125.2	269.34	6.70	40.2
1980		20,285,000	14,214,000	126.8	288.62	7.27	39.7
1981		20,170,000	14,020,000	137.8	318.00	7.99	39.8
1982		18,781,000	12,742,000	130.1	330.26	8.49	38.9
1983		18,434,000	12,530,000	137.2	354.08	8.83	40.1
1984		19,412,000	13,310,000	153.6	373.63	9.18	40.7
1985	Jan.	19,403,000	13,223,000	155.3	380.03	9.43	40.3
	Feb.	19,372,000	13,187,000	152.6	374.37	9.43	39.7
	Mar.	19,399,000	13,209,000	155.8	381.78	9.45	40.4
	Apr.	19,375,000	13,182,000	154.7	381.10	9.48	40.1
	May[p]	19,409,000	13,212,000	155.9	382.04	9.48	40.3
	June[p]	19,524,000	13,310,000	158.7	385.70	9.50	40.6

Personal Consumption Expenditures for the U.S.
Source: Bureau of Economic Analysis, U.S. Commerce Department
(billions of dollars)

	1979	1980	1981	1982	1983	1984
Durable goods	213.4	214.7	235.4	245.1	279.8	318.8
Motor vehicles and parts	96.6	90.7	101.9	108.7	129.3	149.8
Furniture and household equipment	81.8	86.3	92.3	94.4	104.1	117.0
Other	35.1	37.7	41.2	42.1	46.4	51.9
Nondurable goods	600.0	668.8	730.7	757.5	801.7	856.9
Food	311.6	345.1	373.9	392.8	416.5	443.6
Clothing and shoes	99.1	104.6	114.3	118.8	127.0	140.2
Gasoline and oil	66.6	84.8	94.6	90.4	90.0	91.4
Other nondurable goods	122.8	134.3	147.9	155.6	168.2	181.7
Fuel oil and coal	16.1	18.6	20.7	20.6	21.0	21.2
Other	106.6	115.7	127.1	135.0	147.2	160.5
Services	693.7	784.5	883.0	982.2	1,074.4	1,166.1
Housing	236.0	266.2	302.0	333.8	363.3	397.9
Household operation	99.3	113.0	127.5	143.4	153.8	164.0
Electricity and gas	47.8	57.6	65.8	75.2	81.3	85.7
Other	51.5	55.4	61.7	68.2	72.5	78.3
Transportation	56.3	61.1	65.0	68.2	72.5	78.3
Other	302.0	344.3	388.5	436.8	484.8	525.9
Total personal consumption expenditures	1,507.2	1,668.1	1,849.1	1,984.9	2,155.9	2,341.8

U.S. Nonfuel Mineral Production

Source: Bureau of Mines, U.S. Interior Department

Production as measured by mine shipments, sales, or marketable production (including consumption by producers)

Metals	1983 Quantity	1983 Value (thousands)	1984 Quantity	1984 Value (thousands)
Antimony ore and concentrate ..... short tons, antimony content	838	W	557	W
Bauxite .... thousand metric tons, dried equivalent	679	$11,309	856	$15,643
Copper (recoverable content of ores, etc.) .... metric tons	1,038,098	1,751,476	1,091,284	1,608,422
Gold (recoverable content of ores, etc.). .... troy ounces	1,956,400	829,514	2,058,784	742,517
Iron ore, usable (excluding byproduct iron sinter) thousand long tons, gross weight	44,295	1,938,496	W	W
Iron oxide pigments, crude .... short tons	41,875	2,427	53,017	2,819
Lead (recoverable content of ores, etc.) .... metric tons	449,216	214,708	321,897	181,305
Manganiferous ore (5% to 35% Mn)..... short tons, gross weight	33,523	216	88,423	860
Mercury .... 76-pound flasks	25,070	W	19,048	W
Molybdenum (content of concentrate)........ thousand pounds	48,805	166,612	102,405	326,780
Nickel (content of ore and concentrate)........... short tons	—	—	14,540	W
Silver (recoverable content of ores, etc.) ... thousand troy ounces	43,415	496,671	44,440	361,773
Titanium concentrate:				
Ilmenite .... short tons, gross weight	W	W	W	W
Tungsten ore and concentrate .... thousand pounds contained W	1,016	10,528	1,173	13,409
Vanadium (recoverable in ore and concentrate) ..... short tons	2,171	30,675	1,617	24,551
Zinc (recoverable content of ores, etc.) .... metric tons	275,294	251,204	252,768	270,833
Combined value of beryllium, magnesium chloride for magnesium metal, platinum-group metals (1980), rare-earth metals, tin, titanium (rutile), zircon concentrate, and values indicated by symbol W	XX	133,220	XX	2,431,625
Total metals	XX	5,837,000	XX	5,981,000

Nonmetals (except fuels)	1983 Quantity	1983 Value	1984 Quantity	1984 Value
Abrasive stones[2] .... short tons	1,101	482	1,290	602
Asbestos................... metric tons	9,906	27,806	57,422	24,238
Barite................... do	754	29,203	775	25,445
Boron minerals................... do	1,303	439,181	1,367	456,687
Bromine................... thousand pounds	370,000	91,000	385,000	95,000
Calcium chloride................... short tons	W	W	838,000	93,000
Cement:				
Masonry................ thousand short tons	2,921	186,240	3,281	219,877
Portland................... do	67,183	3,315,690	74,376	3,810,446
Clays................... do	40,858	931,091	44,236	1,037,233
Diatomite................... do	619	114,279	627	120,926
Feldspar................... do	710,000	22,500	710,000	23,500
Fluorspar................... do	61,000	10,000	72,000	W
Garnet (abrasive)................... do	29,767	2,533	29,647	[2]2,487
Gem stones(e)...................	NA	7,425	NA	7,450
Gypsum................... thousand short tons	12,884	101,361	14,319	113,671
Helium:				
Crude................... million cubic feet	W	W	W	W
Grade-A................... do	[3]1,299	[3]45,465	1,654	62,026
Lime................... thousand short tons	14,867	757,611	15,922	811,183
Magnesium compounds................... short tons	618,227	182,495	W	W
Mica:				
Scrap................... do	140	6,479	161	7,139
Peat................... do	725	18,667	814	19,907
Perlite................... short tons	474,000	15,664	498,000	16,638
Phosphate rock................... thousand metric tons	42,573	1,021,095	49,191	1,182,244
Potassium salts......... thousand metric tons, K O equivalent	1,513	220,800	1,639	241,800
Pumice................... thousand short tons	449	4,486	502	4,929
Pyrites................... thousand metric tons	W	W	W	W
Salt................... thousand short tons	34,573	597,081	39,225	675,099
Sand and gravel (construction)................... do	655,100	1,935,000	773,900	2,244,000
Sand and gravel (industrial)................... do	26,620	335,200	29,380	377,200
Sodium sulfate (natural)................... do	423	39,425	435	40,125
Stone[4](crushed)................... do	861,608	3,327,000	[e]956,000	[3]3,755,600
Stone[4](dimension)................... do	1,090	147,843	[e]1,157	[3]154,949
Sulfur, Frasch process................... thousand metric tons	4,111	414,210	5,001	546,106
Talc and pyrophyllite................... thousand short tons	1,066	20,280	1,170	24,745
Tripoli................... short tons	111,020	649	124,482	699
Vermiculite................... thousand short tons	282	27,170	315	31,500
Combined value of aplite, asphalt (native), emery, graphite, helium (crude), iodine, kyanite, lithium minerals, magnesite, marl (greensand), olivine, sodium carbonate (natural), staurolite, wollastonite, and values indicated by symbol W...........	XX	867,486	XX	946,109
Total nonmetals	XX	15,263,000	XX	17,173,000
Grand total	XX	21,100,000	XX	25,154,000

(e) Estimate. (r) Revised. (W) Withheld to avoid disclosing company proprietary data; included in "Combined value" figures. (XX) Not applicable.
(1) Production as measured by mine shipments, sales, or marketable production (including consumption by producers).
(2) Grindstones, pulpstones, grinding pebbles, sharpening stones, and tube mill liners.
(3) Excludes output in New Mexico, withheld to avoid disclosing company proprietary data; included in nonmetals combined value figure for 1982-83.
(4) Excludes abrasive stone, bituminous limestone, bituminous sandstone; all included elsewhere in table.

Sales and Profits of Manufacturing Corporations by Industry Groups

Source: Bureau of the Census—Economic Surveys Division

(millions of dollars)

Industry Group	Sales 1Q 1984	Sales 4Q 1984	Sales 1Q 1985	Net profits after taxes 1Q 1984	Net profits after taxes 4Q 1984	Net profits after taxes 1Q 1985
All manufacturing corporations	566,089	594,019	567,565	26,663	24,337	22,587
Nondurable manufacturing corporations	301,469	306,530	294,154	14,984	12,980	13,241
Food and kindred products	72,982	75,682	72,171	2,400	2,482	1,942
Tobacco manufactures	5,830	6,581	5,695	591	930	701
Textile mill products	12,859	12,886	12,056	428	309	191
Paper and allied products	17,459	17,642	17,797	629	493	718
Printing and publishing	23,580	26,328	24,661	1,316	1,579	1,436
Chemicals and allied products	52,391	50,740	51,620	3,710	2,619	3,179
Industrial chemicals and synthetics	25,029	23,423	23,423	1,411	962	912
Drugs	7,629	7,922	8,255	1,032	999	1,088
Petroleum and coal products.	85,681	83,296	78,524	4,677	3,854	4,195
Rubber and miscellaneous plastics products	14,124	15,701	15,196	607	309	557
Other nondurable manufacturing corporations	16,562	17,675	16,433	626	406	321
Durable manufacturing corporations . .	264,620	287,489	273,411	11,679	11,357	9,346
Stone, clay and glass products . . .	11,422	12,367	11,454	161	482	113
Primary metal industries	23,653	22,520	22,701	263	-1,106	-265
Iron and steel.	13,321	12,482	12,791	44	-394	-277
Nonferrous metals.	10,332	10,038	9,910	219	-713	12
Fabricated metal products	28,367	30,858	29,295	975	1,065	889
Machinery, except electrical	48,287	53,998	48,918	2,193	3,181	1,822
Electrical and electronic equipment .	46,349	52,338	47,967	2,232	2,345	1,899
Transportation equipment.	69,941	72,788	73,835	4,148	3,729	3,234
Motor vehicles and equipment	45,010	44,297	46,329	3,202	2,612	2,202
Aircraft, guided missiles and parts. .	20,157	24,409	23,218	843	1,056	972
Instruments and related products . .	14,028	16,018	15,166	967	1,074	1,027
Other durable manufacturing corporations	22,573	26,603	24,076	740	588	617
All mining corporations.	9,927	10,587	10,600	576	-826	180
All retail trade corporations	96,657	120,950	NA	1,884	4,255	NA
All wholesale trade corporations. . . .	130,581	135,518	130,424	1,424	1,485	1,376

Retail Store Sales

Source: Bureau of the Census; U.S. Department of Commerce

(millions of dollars)

Kind of business	1983	1984
Retail trade, total	1,174,298	1,297,015
Durable goods stores, total. . . .	396,493	464,287
Automotive dealers	232,750	277,008
Motor vehicle, other miscellaneous automotive dealers.	209,923	252,624
Auto and home supply stores .	22,827	24,384
Furniture, home furnishings, equipment stores	54,689	63,581
Furniture, home furnishings stores	30,967	35,100
Household appliance, radio, and TV stores	19,673	24,034
Building materials, hardware, garden supply, and mobile home dealers.	59,669	68,703
Building materials and supply stores	42,443	49,774
Hardware stores	9,040	9,530

Kind of business	1983	1984
Nondurable goods stores, total	777,805	832,728
Apparel and accessory stores . .	60,304	66,891
Men's, boys' clothing, furnishings stores.	7,962	8,432
Women's clothing, specialty stores, furriers.	24,484	27,899
Shoe stores	9,794	10,339
Food stores	254,878	269,959
Grocery stores.	239,054	252,936
General merchandise group stores	139,386	153,642
Department stores.	116,562	129,284
Variety stores	8,624	9,067
Eating and drinking places.	114,684	124,109
Gasoline service stations	98,862	100,997
Drug stores	40,050	44,165
Liquor stores	19,014	19,494

Total retail stores sales (millions of dollars) — (1955) 183,851; (1958) 200,353; (1959) 215,413; (1960) 219,529; (1961) 218,992; (1962) 235,563; (1963) 246,666; (1964) 261,870; (1965) 284,128; (1966) 303,956; (1967) 292,956; (1968) 324,358; (1969) 346,717; (1970) 368,403; (1971) 406,234; (1972) 449,069; (1973) 509,538; (1974) 540,988; (1975) 588,146; (1976) 657,375; (1977) 725,212; (1978) 806,773; (1979) 899,116; (1980) 959,561; (1981) 1,041,327.

Employees in Non-Agricultural Establishments

Source: Bureau of Labor Statistics, U.S. Labor Department (thousands)

Annual Average by Industry Division

Year	Total	Mining	Contr./construction	Manufacturing	Trans. and public utilities	Whole., retail trade	Finance, insur., real estate	Service, miscellaneous	Government
1955	50,641	792	2,839	16,882	4,141	10,535	2,298	6,240	6,914
1960	54,189	712	2,926	16,796	4,004	11,391	2,629	7,378	8,353
1965	60,765	632	3,232	18,062	4,036	12,716	2,977	9,036	10,074
1970	70,880	623	3,588	19,367	4,515	15,040	3,645	11,548	12,554
1975	76,945	752	3,525	18,323	4,542	17,060	4,165	13,892	14,686
1980	90,406	1,027	4,346	20,285	5,146	20,310	5,160	17,890	16,241
1982	89,566	1,128	3,905	18,781	5,082	20,457	5,341	19,036	15,837
1983	90,196	952	3,948	18,434	4,954	20,881	5,468	19,694	15,870
1984	94,641	974	4,345	19,412	5,171	22,134	5,682	20,761	15,984

Offstream Water Use

Source: Geological Survey, U.S. Interior Department
(millions of gallons per day, except as noted)

1980 State	Population, in thousands	Per Capita use, fresh water in gpd	Withdrawals (includes irrigation conveyance losses)				Total, excluding reclaimed sewage	Consumptive use, fresh water
			Ground water Fresh	Saline	Surface water Fresh	Saline		
Alabama	3,890	2,700	350	1.4	10,000	73	11,000	570
Alaska.	403	550	49	0	170	0	220	35
Arizona	2,718	2,900	4,200	0	3,700	0	8,000	4,500
Arkansas	2,290	6,800	4,000	0	12,000	0	16,000	3,600
California	23,669	1,900	21,000	250	23,000	9,800	54,000	25,000
Colorado	2,889	5,400	2,800	0	13,000	0	16,000	4,000
Connecticut.	3,108	420	140	1.0	1,200	2,400	3,700	160
Delaware	595	230	82	0.3	57	1,100	1,200	11
D.C.	638	530	0.8	0	340	0	340	23
Florida.	9,740	750	3,800	42	3,600	14,000	21,000	2,400
Georgia	5,464	1,200	1,200	0	5,500	200	6,900	1,000
Hawaii.	965	1,400	800	0	510	1,200	2,500	680
Idaho	944	19,000	6,300	0	12,000	0	18,000	5,900
Illinois	11,418	1,600	930	38	17,000	0	18,000	590
Indiana	5,396	2,600	1,300	0	13,000	0	14,000	690
Iowa	2,913	1,500	760	0	3,500	0	4,300	290
Kansas	2,363	2,800	5,600	0	980	0	6,600	4,700
Kentucky	3,661	1,300	250	0	4,600	0	4,800	290
Louisiana	4,199	2,900	1,800	19	11,000	390	13,000	3,500
Maine	1,125	750	80	0	770	710	1,600	53
Maryland	4,216	270	150	0	970	6,600	7,700	100
Massachusetts	5,737	430	320	0	2,100	3,500	5,900	90
Michigan	9,258	1,600	530	420	14,000	0	15,000	460
Minnesota.	4,061	760	670	0	2,400	0	3,100	450
Mississippi	2,521	1,100	1,500	0	1,400	660	3,500	710
Missouri.	4,888	1,400	470	0	6,400	0	6,900	670
Montana.	786	14,000	260	2.1	11,000	0	11,000	2,700
Nebraska	1,570	7,700	7,200	0	4,900	0	12,000	7,600
Nevada	799	4,500	710	9.0	2,900	0	3,600	1,700
New Hampshire	921	420	65	0	320	620	1,000	17
New Jersey.	7,360	390	730	0	2,100	7,500	10,000	380
New Mexico	1,300	3,000	1,800	0.9	2,100	0	3,900	1,900
New York	17,557	450	780	12	7,200	8,600	17,000	590
North Carolina	5,874	1,400	770	0	7,300	42	8,100	760
North Dakota	652	2,000	120	0.2	1,200	0	1,300	330
Ohio	10,797	1,300	980	0	13,000	0	14,000	550
Oklahoma.	3,025	570	960	95	760	0	1,800	1,000
Oregon	2,614	2,600	1,100	0	5,700	0	6,800	3,200
Pennsylvania	11,824	1,300	1,000	0	15,000	93	16,000	920
Rhode Island	947	180	37	0	140	330	500	15
South Carolina	3,119	2,000	230	0	5,900	38	6,200	280
South Dakota	695	990	330	3.4	360	0	690	460
Tennessee	4,591	2,200	450	0	9,600	0	10,000	270
Texas	14,013	1,000	8,000	0	6,300	6,600	21,000	10,000
Utah	1,462	3,100	1,000	4.0	3,500	56	4,600	2,900
Vermont.	511	660	45	0	290	0	340	41
Virginia	5,346	1,000	390	0.2	5,200	4,100	9,700	230
Washington.	4,127	2,000	770	0	7,500	42	8,300	2,900
West Virginia	1,950	2,900	220	0	5,400	0	5,600	200
Wisconsin.	4,710	1,200	610	0	5,200	0	5,800	310
Wyoming	471	11,000	540	24	4,800	0	5,400	2,600
Puerto Rico	3,400	240	310	5.0	500	2,400	3,200	300
Virgin Islands	100	63	4.0	0	2.2	32	38	2.1
Total	229,592	1,600	88,000	930	290,000	71,000	450,000	100,000

Note: Figures may not add to totals because of independent rounding.

Canadian Pulpwood, Wood Pulp, and Newsprint

Source: Statistics Canada (thousands of metric tons)

Year	Pulpwood production[1] (1,000 cu. meters)	Wood pulp production[2] Total	Mechanical	Chemical	Wood pulp exports[3]	Newsprint production	Newsprint shipments Total	Domestic	Exports[4]
1981 . . .	52,688	19,303.7	7,630.6	11,654.3	7,433	8,947	8,917	1,041	7,877
1982 . . .	41,337	17,008.6	6,815.9	10,175.2	6,741	8,117	8,074	934	7,139
1983 . . .	43,157	19,391.3	7,816.7	11,559.8	6,806	8,486	8,440	970	7,471
1984 . . .	47,640	20,435.1	8,590.2	11,827.4	7,041	9,001	9,021	1,065	7,955

(1) Pulpwood produced for domestic use, excluding exports, but including receipts of purchased roundwood. (2) Total pulp production covers "screenings" which are already included in exports. "Screenings" are excluded throughout from mechanical and chemical pulp. (3) Customs exports. (4) Mill shipments destined for export.

Mineral Distribution, Reserves and Resources

Source: Bureau of Mines, U.S. Interior Department

Mineral	Distribution of reserves (% of world total)	Reserves[1] (million metric tons)	Resources[2]	Ratio of reserves to 1983 primary demand	Ratio of reserves to cumulative primary demand 1983-2000
Aluminum	Guinea(27) Australia(21) Brazil(11) Jamaica(9) India(5)	21,000[3]	48,000[4]	268	11.2
Chromium	Republic of South Africa(78) U.S.S.R.(12) Zimbabwe(2) Finland(2) Philippines(1)	290	39,700	97	3.9
Cobalt	Zaire(38) Cuba(29) Zambia(10) New Caledonia(6) Indonesia(5)	3.63	11	182	6.7
Columbium	Brazil(79) USSR(17) Canada(3) Nigeria(2) Zaire(1)	4	17.2	428	10
Copper	Chile(23) United States(17) Zambia(9) Zaire(8) Mexico(5)	340	2,087[5]	42	2.0
Gold	Republic of South Africa(59) USSR(16) United States(6) Canada(3) Brazil(2)	0.04	0.075	39	1.9
Iron	USSR(35) Brazil(15) Australia(14) India(7) Canada(6)	65,300	89,000	154	7.27
Lead	United States(22) Australia(17) USSR(13) Canada(13) Republic of South Africa(4)	95	1,400	32	1.6
Manganese	Republic of South Africa(41) USSR(36) Gabon(11) Australia(8) Brazil(2)	907	over 4,000	114	5.9
Nickel	Cuba(34) Canada(14) USSR(13) Indonesia(7) Republic of South Africa(5)	53	130	77	3.2
Platinum–Group Metals	Republic of South Africa(79) USSR(20)	0.03	0.10	167	8
Silver	USSR(18) Canada(15) Mexico(14) United States(12) Australia(10)	0.24	0.78	33	1.4
Tantalum	Thailand(27) USSR(17) Australia(17) Nigeria(12)	0.03	0.3	30	1.4
Titanium	Brazil(20) Republic of South Africa(14) India(12) Norway(14) Australia(9)	170[7]	700[7]	102	4.5
Vanadium	USSR(60) Republic of South Africa(20) China, People's Republic of(14) United States(4)	4	64	150	5.5
Zinc	Canada(15) United States(13) Australia(11) Republic of South Africa(6) USSR(6)	170	1,800	28	1.3

(1) Mineral Commodity Profiles-1985. Unless otherwise stated, reserves are that portion of the resources that can be economically extracted or produced at the time of determination.(2) Mineral Commodity Summaries-1985. Unless otherwise stated, resources are identified resources derived in collaboration with the U.S. Geological Survey whose location, grade, quality, and quantity are known or estimated from geologic evidence, including economic, marginally economic, and subeconomic components.(3) Bauxite. Convert to aluminum equivalent by multiplying by 0.212.(4) Includes undiscovered deposits.(5) Includes seabed deposits.(6) Includes platinum, palladium, rhodium, ruthenium, iridium, and osmium.(7) Includes ilmenite, rutile, and anatase.

U.S. Nonfuel Mineral Production—Leading States

Source: Bureau of Mines, U.S. Interior Department

State	1984 Value (thousands)	Percent of U.S. total	Principal minerals, in order of value
California	$2,003,445	8.66	Cement, boron minerals, sand and gravel (construction), stone (crushed).
Texas	1,715,407	7.41	Cement, stone (crushed), sulfur (Frasch), sand and gravel (construction).
Minnesota.	1,676,247	7.24	Iron ore, sand and gravel (construction), stone (crushed), sand and gravel (industrial).
Florida.	1,510,364	6.52	Phosphate rock, stone (crushed), cement, sand and gravel (construction).
Arizona	1,483,479	6.41	Copper, sand and gravel (construction), cement, molybdenum.
Michigan	1,408,607	6.08	Iron ore, cement, magnesium compounds, salt.
Georgia	940,492	4.06	Clays, stone (crushed), cement, stone (dimension).
Missouri.	731,897	3.16	Cement, lead, stone (crushed), lime.
Pennsylvania	708,356	3.06	Cement, stone (crushed), lime, sand and gravel (construction).
New Mexico	619,144	2.68	Copper, potassium salts, gold, cement.

U.S. Pig Iron and Steel Output

Source: American Iron and Steel Institute (net tons)

Year	Total pig iron	Pig iron and ferro-alloys	Raw steel	Year	Total pig iron	Pig iron and ferro-alloys	Raw steel
1940	46,071,666	47,398,529	66,982,686	1975	101,208,000	103,345,000	116,642,000
1945	53,223,169	54,919,029	79,701,648	1977	81,328,000	83,082,000	125,333,000
1950	64,586,907	66,400,311	96,836,075	1980	68,721,000	70,329,000	111,835,000
1955	76,857,417	79,263,865	117,036,085	1981	73,570,000	75,096,000	120,828,000
1960	66,480,648	68,566,384	99,281,601	1982	43,309,000	44,147,000	74,577,000
1965	88,184,901	90,918,040	131,461,601	1983	48,706,000	49,491,000	84,615,000
1970	91,435,000	93,851,000	131,514,000	1984	51,904,000	52,684,000	92,528,000

Steel figures include only that portion of the capacity and production of steel for castings used by foundries which were operated by companies producing steel ingots.

Value of U.S. Mineral Production

(millons of dollars)

Production as measured by mine shipments sales or marketable production.

Year[1]	Fuels	Nonmetallic	Metals	Total[2]	Year[1]	Fuels	Nonmetallic	Metals	Total[2]
1930 ...	2,500	973	501	3,980	1974 ...	40,889	8,687	5,501	55,077
1940 ...	2,662	784	752	4,198	1975 ...	47,505	9,570	5,191	62,266
1950 ...	8,689	1,882	1,351	11,862	1976 ...	52,484	10,616	6,086	69,186
1960 ...	12,142	3,868	2,022	18,032	1977 ...	59,575	11,701	5,810	77,086
1965 ...	14,047	4,933	2,544	21,524	1979 ...	NA	15,438	8,536	NA
1970 ...	20,152	5,712	3,928	29,792	1980 ...	NA	16,213	8,921	NA
1972 ...	22,061	6,482	3,642	32,185	1981 ...	NA	16,385	8,842	NA
1973 ...	24,949	7,476	4,362	36,787	1982 ...	NA	14,147	5,544	NA

(1) Excludes Alaska and Hawaii, 1930-53. (2) Data may not add to total because of rounding figures.

U.S. Copper, Lead, and Zinc Production

Source: Bureau of Mines, U.S. Interior Department

Year	Copper Mil. lbs.	Copper $1,000	Lead[1] Short tons	Lead[1] $1,000	Zinc Short tons	Zinc Mil. dol.	Year	Copper Mil. lbs.	Copper $1,000	Lead[1] Metric tons	Lead[1] $1,000	Zinc Metric tons	Zinc Mil. dol.
1950	1,823	379,122	418,809	113,078	591,454	167	1980	2,604	2,666,931	550,366	515,189	317,103	262
1960	2,286	733,708	228,899	53,562	334,101	87	1981	3,391	2,886,440	445,535	358,821	312,418	307
1965	2,703	957,028	301,147	93,959	611,153	178	1982	2,529	1,840,856	512,516	288,579	303,160	257
1970	3,439	1,984,484	571,767	178,609	534,136	164	1983	2,289	1,751,476	449,316	214,708	275,294	251
1975	2,827	1,814,763	563,783	267,230	425,792	366	1984	2,406	1,608,422	321,897	181,305	252,768	271

(1) Production from domestic ores.

Cotton, Wool, Silk, and Man-Made Fibers Production

Source: Economics, Statistics, and Cooperatives Service, U.S. Agriculture Department

Cotton and wool from reports of the Agriculture Department; silk, rayon, and non-cellulosic man-made fibers from Textile Organon, a publication of the Textile Economics Bureau, Inc.

Year	Cotton[1] U.S.	Cotton[1] World (million bales)[5]	Wool[2] U.S.	Wool[2] World (million pounds)	Silk World (mil. lbs.)	Man-made fibers[3] Cellulosic U.S.	Cellulosic World (million pounds)	Non-cellulosic[4] U.S.[4]	Non-cellulosic World[6] (million pounds)
1940	12.6	31.2	434.0	4,180	130	471.2	2,485.3	4.6	4.6
1950	10.0	30.6	249.3	4,000	42	1,259.4	3,552.8	145.9	177.4
1960	14.2	46.2	298.9	5,615	68	1,028.5	5,749.1	854.2	1,779.1
1965	14.9	55.0	224.8	5,731	72	1,527.0	7,359.4	2,062.4	4,928.9
1970	10.2	53.6	176.8	6,107	90	1,373.2	7,573.9	4,053.5	10,361.7
1975	8.3	54.0	125.5	5,911	104	749.0	6,523.2	6,432.2	17,344.6
1980	11.1	64.8	106.5	6,283	123	806.0	7,147.8	8,759.8	23,095.4
1981	15.6	70.8	110.9	6,367	126	770.1	7,063.8	9,047.0	23,869.2
1983	7.8	67.9	102.9	6,466	121	630.3	6,661.0	8,705.6	24,414.9
1984	13.0	85.8	92.9	6,539	121	620.1	6,784.2	8,865.7	26,216.6

(1) Year beginning Aug. 1. (2) Grease basis. (3) Includes filament yarn and staple and tow fiber. (4) Includes textile glass fiber. (5) 480-pound net weight bales, U.S. beginning 1960 and world beginning 1965. (6) 1966 to date, excludes Olefin.

Work Stoppages (Strikes) in the U.S.

(involving 1,000 workers or more)

Source: Bureau of Labor Statistics, U.S. Labor Department

Year	Number stoppages[1]	Workers involved[1] (thousands)	Man days idle[1] (thousands)	Year	Number stoppages[1]	Workers involved[1] (thousands)	Man days idle[1] (thousands)
1952	470	2,746	48,820	1969	412	1,576	29,397
1953	437	1,623	18,130	1970	381	2,468	52,761
1954	265	1,075	16,630	1971	298	2,516	35,538
1955	363	2,055	21,180	1972	250	975	16,764
1956	287	1,370	26,840	1973	317	1,400	16,260
1957	279	887	10,340	1974	424	1,796	31,809
1958	332	1,587	17,900	1975	235	965	17,563
1959	245	1,381	60,850	1976	231	1,519	23,962
1960	222	896	13,260	1977	298	1,212	21,258
1961	195	1,031	10,140	1978	219	1,006	23,774
1962	211	793	11,760	1979	235	1,021	20,409
1963	181	512	10,020	1980	187	795	20,844
1964	246	1,183	16,220	1981	145	729	16,908
1965	268	999	15,140	1982	96	656	9,061
1966	321	1,300	16,000	1983	81	909	17,461
1967	381	2,192	31,320	1984	62	376	8,499
1968	392	1,855	35,567				

[1]The number of stoppages and workers relate to stoppages that began in the year. Days of idleness include all stoppages in effect. Workers are counted more than once if they were involved in more than one stoppage during the year.

Labor Union Directory

Source: Bureau of Labor Statistics; World Almanac Questionnaire
(*) Independent union; all others affiliated with AFL-CIO.

Approximately 19% (17.3 million) of wage and salary workers belonged to unions in 1984. The total percentage of those who were either members or covered by unions was 22%. Both of these proportions show a decline relative to the averages for 1983.

Actors and Artistes of America, Associated (AAAA), 165 W. 46th St., New York, NY 10036; founded 1919; Frederick O'-Neal, Pres. (since 1970); no individual members, 9 National Performing Arts Unions are affiliates; 97,325 combined membership.

Actors' Equity Association, 165 W. 46th St., New York, NY 10036; founded 1913; Ellen Burstyn, Pres.; 34,000 members.

Air Line Pilots Association, 1625 Massachusetts Ave. NW, Washington, DC 20036. Henry A. Duffy, Pres.; 34,000 members.

Aluminum Brick & Glass Workers International Union (AWIU), 3362 Hollenberg Drive, Bridgeton, MO 63044; founded 1953; Lawrence A. Holley, Pres. (since 1977); 55,000 members, 415 locals.

Automobile, Aerospace & Agricultural Implement Workers of America, International Union, United (UAW), 8000 E. Jefferson Ave., Detroit, MI 48214; founded 1935; Owen Bieber, Pres. (since 1983); 1,500,000 members, 1,410 locals.

Bakery, Confectionery & Tobacco Workers International Union (BC&T), 10401 Connecticut Ave., Kensington, MD 20895; founded 1886; John DeConcini, Pres. (since 1978); 170,000 members, 200 locals.

Boilermakers, Iron Shipbuilders, Blacksmiths, Forgers and Helpers, International Brotherhood of (IBBISB/BF&H), 570 New Brotherhood Bldg., 8th and State Ave., Kansas City, KS 66101; founded 1880; Charles W. Jones, Pres. (since 1983) 125,000 members, 400 locals.

Bricklayers and Allied Craftsmen, International Union of, 815 15th St. NW, Washington, DC 20005; John T. Joyce, Pres.; 130,000 members, 565 locals.

Carpenters and Joiners of America, United Brotherhood of, 101 Constitution Ave. NW, Washington, DC 20001; founded 1881; Patrick J. Campbell, Gen. Pres.; 650,000 members, 1,800 locals.

Cement, Lime Gypsum and Allied Workers International Union, United (UCLGAWIU), 2500 Brickdale Drive, Elk Grove Village, IL 60007; founded 1939; Richard A. Northrip, Vice Pres. (since 1984); 29,500 members, 296 locals. Merged with Boilermakers (BSF) April 1, 1984.

Chemical Workers Union, International (ICWU), 1655 West Market St., Akron, OH 44313; founded 1944; Frank D. Martino, Pres. (since 1975); 70,000 members, 400 locals.

Clothing and Textile Workers Union, Amalgamated (ACTWU), 15 Union Square, New York, NY 10003; founded 1976; union founded 1914; Murray H. Finley, Pres. (since 1976); 348,000 members, 1,560 locals.

Communications Workers of America, 1925 K St. NW, Washington, DC 20006; Glenn E. Watts, Pres.; 650,000 members, 900 locals.

Distillery, Wine & Allied Workers International Union (DWU), 66 Grand Ave., Englewood, NJ 07631; founded 1940; George J. Oneto, Pres. (since 1974); 25,000 members, 67 locals.

*****Education Association, National,** 1201 16th St. NW, Washington, DC 20036; Mary H. Futrell, Pres.; 1,700,000 members, 12,000 affiliates.

*****Electrical, Radio & Machine Workers of America, United (UE),** 11 E. 51st St. New York, NY 10022; founded 1936; James Kane, Gen. Pres. (since 1981); 165,000 members, 200 locals.

Electrical Workers, International Brotherhood of (IBEW), 1125 15th St., NW, Washington, DC 20005; founded 1891; Charles H. Pillard, Int'l Pres. (since 1968); 1,000,000 members, 1,417 locals.

Electronic, Electrical, Technical, Salaried and Machine Workers, International Union of (IUE), 1126 16th St. NW, Washington, DC 20012; founded 1949; William H. Bywater, Pres. (since 1982); 180,000 members, 500 locals.

Farm Workers of America, United (UFW), La Paz, Keene, CA 93531; founded 1962; Cesar E. Chavez, Pres. (since 1973); 100,000 members.

*****Federal Employees, National Federation of (NFFE),** 1016 16th St. NW, Washington, DC 20036; founded 1917; James M. Peirce Jr., Pres. (since 1976); 52,000+ members, 487 locals.

Fire Fighters, International Association of, 1750 New York Ave. NW, Washington, DC 20006; John A. Gannon, Pres.; 172,401 members, 1,943 locals.

Firemen and Oilers, International Brotherhood of, VFW Bldg., 200 Maryland Ave. NE, Washington, DC 20002; George

J. Francisco, Pres.; 32,000 members.

Food and Commercial Workers International Union, United, (UFCW) 1775 K St., NW, Washington, DC 20006; founded 1979 following merger; William H. Wynn, Int'l Pres. (since 1977); 1.3 million members, 700 locals.

Garment Workers of America, United (UGWA), 200 Park Ave. So., New York, NY 10003; founded 1891; William O'Donnell, Gen. Pres. (since 1977); 25,000 members, 155 locals.

Glass, Pottery, Plastics & Allied Workers Intl. Union (GPPAW), 608 E. Baltimore Pike, P.O. Box 607, Media, PA 19063; founded 1842; James E. Hatfield, Int'l Pres. (since 1981); 80,000 members, 294 locals.

Glass and Ceramic Workers of North America, United, 556 E. Town St., Columbus, OH 43215; Joseph Roman, Pres.; 30,000 members, 181 locals.

Glass Workers Union, American Flint (AFGWU), 1440 So. Byrne Rd., Toledo, OH 43614; founded 1878; George M. Parker, Int'l Pres. (since 1961); 23,000 members, 167 locals.

Government Employees, American Federation of (AFGE), 1325 Massachusetts Ave. NW, Washington, DC 20005; founded 1932; Kenneth T. Blaylock, Natl. Pres. (since 1976); 225,000 members, 1,300 locals.

Grain Millers, American Federation of (AFGM), 4949 Olson Memorial Hwy., Minneapolis, MN 55422; founded 1948; Robert W. Willis, Gen. Pres.; 35,000 members, 210 locals.

Graphic Arts International Union (GAIU), 1900 L St., NW, Washington, DC 20036; founded 1882; Kenneth J. Brown, Pres. (since 1959); 120,000 members, 220 locals.

Hotel Employees and Restaurant Employees International Union, 120 E. 4th St., Cincinnati, OH 45202; Edward T. Hanley, Pres.; 400,000 members, 225 locals.

Industrial Workers of America, International Union, Allied (AIW), 3520 W. Oklahoma Ave., Milwaukee, WI 53215; founded 1935; Dominick D'Ambrosio, Intl. Pres. (since 1975); 70,000 members, 370 locals.

Iron Workers, International Association of Bridge Structural and Ornamental, 1750 New York Ave. NW, Washington, DC 20006; John H. Lyons, Pres.; 181, 647 members, 318 locals.

Laborers' International Union of North America (LIUNA), 905 16th St. NW, Washington, DC 20006; founded 1903; Angelo Fosco, Gen. Pres. (since 1976); 430,000 members, 800 locals.

Ladies Garment Workers Union, International (ILGWU), 1710 Broadway, New York, NY 10019; founded 1900; Sol C. Chaikin, Pres. (since 1975); 250,000 members, 368 locals.

Leather Goods, Plastic and Novelty Workers' Union, International, 265 W. 14th St., New York, NY 10011; Ralph Cennamo, Gen. Pres.; 40,000 members, 97 locals.

Letter Carriers, National Association of (NALC), 100 Indiana Ave. NW, Washington, DC 20001; founded 1889; Vincent R. Sombrotto, Pres. (since 1978); 268,000 members, 4,031 locals.

*****Locomotive Engineers, Brotherhood of (BLE),** 1365 Ontario Ave., Cleveland, OH 44114; founded 1863; John F. Sytsma, Pres. (since 1976); 62,888 members, 727 divisions.

Longshoremen's Association, International, 17 Battery Pl., New York, NY 10004; Thomas W. Gleason, Pres.; 76,579 members, 367 locals.

*****Longshoremen's & Warehousemen's Union, International (ILWU),** 1188 Franklin St., San Francisco, CA 94109; founded 1937; James R. Herman, Pres. (since 1977); 55,000 members, 81 locals.

Machinists and Aerospace Workers, International Association of (IAM), 1300 Connecticut Ave. NW, Washington, DC 20036; founded 1888; William W. Winpisinger, Int'l Pres.; 800,000 members, 1,610 locals.

Maintenance of Way Employes, Brotherhood of (BMWE), 12050 Woodward Ave., Detroit, MI 48203; founded 1887; O. M. Berge, Pres. (since 1978); 80,000 members, 955 locals.

Marine & Shipbuilding Workers of America, Industrial Union of (IUMSWA), 8121 Georgia Ave., Silver Springs, MD 20910; founded 1934; Arthur E. Batson Jr., Pres. (since 1982); 25,000 members, 40 locals.

Maritime Union of America, National, 346 W. 17th St., New York NY 10011; Shannon Wall, Pres.; 35,000 members.

*****Mine Workers of America, United (UMWA),** 900 15th St. NW, Washington, DC 20005; founded 1890; Richard Trumka, Int'l Pres. (since 1982); 225,000 members, 900 locals.

Molders' and Allied Workers' Union, International (IM & AWU), 1225 E. McMillan St., Cincinnati, OH 45206; founded 1859; Bernard Butsavage, Pres. (since 1983); 50,000 members, 222 locals.

Musicians of the United States and Canada, American Federation of (AF of M), 1500 Broadway, New York, NY 10036; founded 1896; Victor W. Fuentealba, Pres. (since 1978); 251,000 members, 544 locals.

Newspaper Guild, The (TNG), 1125 15th St. NW, Washington, DC; founded 1933; Charles A. Perlik Jr., Pres.5(since 1969); 32,000members, 80 locals.

Novelty & Production Workers, Intl. Union of Allied, 147-149 E. 26th St., New York, NY 10010; Julius Isaacson, Pres. 30,000 members, 18 locals.

*Nurses Association, American, 2420 Pershing Rd., Kansas City, MO 64108; Eunice Cole, Pres.; 53 constituent assns.

Office and Professional Employees International Union (OPEIU), 265 W. 14th St., New York, NY 10011; founded 1945 (AFL Charter); John Kelly, Int'l Pres. (since 1979); 135,00 members, 300 locals.

Oil, Chemical and Atomic Workers International Union (OCAW), PO Box 2812, Denver, CO 80201; Joseph M. Misbrener Pres. (since 1983); 115,000 members, 443 locals.

Operating Engineers, International Union of (IUOE), 1125 17th St. NW, Washington, DC 20036; founded 1896; Larry Dugan, Jr., Gen. Pres. (since 1985); 375,000 members, 203 locals.

Painters and Allied Trades, International Brotherhood of (IBPAT), 1750 New York Ave. NW, Washington, DC 20006; founded 1887; William A. Duval, Gen. Pres. (since 1984); 167,569 members, 709 locals.

Paperworkers International Union, United (UPIU), 702 Church St., P.O. Box 1475, Nashville, TN 37202; founded 1884; Wayne E. Glenn, Pres. (since 1978); 265,000 members, 1,250 locals.

*Plant Guard Workers of America, International Union, United (UPGWA), 25510 Kelly Rd., Roseville, MI 48066; founded 1948; James C. McGahey, Pres. (since 1948); 28,000 members, 182 locals.

Plasterers' and Cement Mason's International Association of the United States & Canada; Operative, 1125 17th St. NW, Washington, DC 20036; Melvin H. Roots, Pres.; Robert J. Holton, Secy.-Treas.; 65,000 members, 365 locals.

Plumbing and Pipe Fitting Industry of the United States and Canada, United Association of Journeymen and Apprentices of the, 901 Massachusetts Ave. NW, Washington, DC 20001; Martin Ward, Pres.; 350,000 members.

*Police, Fraternal Order of, 5613 Belair Rd., Baltimore, MD 21206; Richard A. Boyd, Pres,; 105,000 members, 1,482 affiliates.

*Postal Supervisors, National Association of, 490 L'Enfant Plaza SW, Suite 3200, Washington, DC 20024; Donald N. Ledbetter, Pres.; 37,500 members, 460 locals.

Postal Workers Union, American (APWU), 817 14th St. NW, Washington, DC 20005; founded 1971; Moe Biller, Gen. Pres. (since 1980); 320,000 members, 3,900 locals.

Printing and Graphic Communications Union, International, 1730 Rhode Island Ave. NW, Washington, DC 20036; Sol Fishko, Pres.; 110,000 members, 556 locals.

Railway, Airline and Steamship Clerks, Freight Handlers, Express and Station Employees; Brotherhood of (BRAC), 3 Research Place, Rockville, MD 20850; Richard I. Kilroy, Int'l Pres. (since 1981); 160,000 members, 750 locals.

Railway Carmen of the United States and Canada, Brotherhood (BRC of US&C), 4929 Main St., Kansas City, MO 64112; founded 1888; C.E. Wheeler, Gen. Pres. (since 1983); 72,054 members, 520 locals.

Retail, Wholesale and Department Store Union, 30 E. 29th St., New York, NY 10016; Alvin E. Heaps, Pres.; 250,000 members, 315 locals.

Roofers, Waterproofers & Allied Workers, United Union of, 1125 17th St. NW, Washington, DC 20036; Roy Johnson, Pres.; 30,000 members, 157 locals.

Rubber, Cork, Linoleum and Plastic Workers of America, United (URW), 87 South High St., Akron, OH 44308; founded 1935; Milan Stone; Int'l Pres. (since 1981); 130,000 members, 477 locals.

*Rural Letter Carriers' Association, National, Suite 100, 1448 Duke St., Alexandria, VA 22314; founded 1903; Tom W. Griffith, Pres. (since 1983); 66,000 members; state organizations, 47.

Seafarers International Union of North America (SIUNA), 5201 Auth Way, Camp Springs, MD 20746; founded 1938; Frank Drozak, Pres.; 90,000 members.

Service Employees International Union (SEIU), 1313 L St. NW, Washington, DC 20005; founded 1921; John J. Sweeney,

Pres. (since 1980); 850,000 members, 300 locals.

Sheet Metal Workers' International Association (SMWIA), 1750 New York Ave. NW, Washington, DC 20006; founded 1888; Edward J. Carlough, Gen. Pres. (since 1970); 150,000 members, 295 locals.

State, County and Municipal Employees, American Federation of, 1625 L St. NW, Washington, DC 20036; Gerald McEntee, Pres.; 1,000,000 members, 2,991 locals.

Steelworkers of America, United (USWA), 5 Gateway Center, Pittsburgh, PA 15222; founded 1936; Lynn Williams, Int'l Pres. (since 1984); 1,050,000 members, 4,200 locals.

Teachers, American Federation of (AFT), 555 New Jersey Ave. NW, Washington, DC 20001; founded 1916; Albert Shanker, Pres. (since 1974); 610,000 members, 2,200 locals.

*Teamsters, Chauffeurs, Warehousemen and Helpers of America, International Brotherhood of (IBT), 25 Louisiana Ave. NW, Washington, DC 20001; founded 1903; Jackie Presser, Gen. Pres.; 2,000,000 members, 694 locals.

Television and Radio Artists, American Federation of, 1350 Ave. of the Americas, New York, NY; founded 1937; Bill Hillman, Pres.; 60,000 members, 38 locals.

Textile Workers of America, United (UTWA), 420 Common St., Lawrence, MA 01840; founded 1901; Francis Schaufenbil, Intl. Pres. (since 1972); 50,000 members, 221 locals.

Theatrical Stage Employees and Moving Picture Operators of the United States and Canada, International Alliance of, 1515 Broadway, New York, NY 10036; Walter Diehl, Pres.; 61,471 members, 870 locals.

Transit Union, Amalgamated (ATU), 5025 Wisconsin Ave. NW, Washington, DC 20016; founded 1892; John W. Rowland, Intl. Pres. (since 1981); 160,000 members, 295 locals.

Transport Workers Union of America, 80 West End Ave., New York, NY 10023; founded 1934; John E. Lawe; Int'l Pres. (since 1985); 91,000 members, 74 locals.

Transportation Union, United (UTU), 14600 Detroit Ave., Cleveland, OH 44107; founded 1969; Fred A. Hardin, Pres. (since 1979); 120,000 members; 876 locals.

*Treasury Employees Union, National (NTEU), 1730 K St. NW, Suite 1101, Washington, DC 20006; founded 1938; Robert M. Tobias, Natl. Pres. (since 1983); 120,000 represented, 243 chapters.

Typographical Union, International (ITU), PO Box 157, Colorado Springs, CO 80901; founded 1852; Robert S. McMichen, Pres. (since 1983); 80,483 members, 491 locals.

*University Professors, American Association of (AAUP), 1012-14th St., Washington, DC 20005; founded 1915; Paul H. L. Walter, Pres.; 60,500 members, 1,300 locals.

Upholsterers' International Union of North America (UIU), 25 N. 4th St., Philadelphia, PA 19106; founded 1882; John Serembus, Pres.; 31,827 members, 133 locals.

Utility Workers Union of America (UWUA), 815 16th St. NW, Washington, DC 20006; founded 1945; James Joy Jr., Natl. Pres. (since 1980); 60,000 members, 220 locals.

Woodworkers of America, International (IWA), 1622 N. Lombard St., Portland, OR 97217; founded 1937; Keith Johnson, Intl. Pres. (since 1973); 100,000 members, 200 locals.

Canadian Unions

Source: Labour Canada

Canadian Labour Congress (CLC) (1985)

Public Employees, Canadian Union of	295,961
Government Employees, National Union of Provincial	244,992
Public Service Alliance of Canada	181,460
Steelworkers of America, United	148,000
Food and Commercial Workers, United	146,000
Automobile, Aerospace and Agricultural Implement Workers of America, International Union, United.	135,806

Confederation of National Trade Unions (CNTU) (1985)

Social Affairs Federation Inc.	93,000

Canadian Federation of Labour (CFL) (1985)

Electrical Workers, International Brotherhood	68,589

American Federation of Labour-Congress of Industrial Organizations (AFL-CIO) (1985)

Carpenters and Joiners of America, United Brotherhood of.	73,000

Independent Unions (1985)

Teamsters, Chauffeurs, Warehousemen and Helper's of America, International Brotherhood of	91,500
Teaching Congress, Quebec	89,952

ENERGY

Source: Information in this section comes from the Energy Information Administration, U.S. Dept. of Energy, unless otherwise specified.

World Nuclear Power: Current and Projected Capacities

(Net Gigawatts; as of Dec. 31, 1983)

Country[1]	1983[2]	1990[3] Low Case	1990[3] Mid-Case	1990[3] High Case	2000[3] Low Case	2000[3] Mid-Case	2000[3] High Case
OECD Countries[4]							
Belgium	3.5	5.5	5.5	5.5	7.0	7.9	9.2
Canada	7.6	12.0	12.7	12.7	16.3	18.4	21.2
Finland	2.2	2.2	2.2	2.2	2.7	3.3	4.0
France	27.2	47.5	52.6	56.4	51.8	62.4	77.5
West Germany	11.1	18.0	18.0	19.3	19.3	23.9	27.8
Italy	1.3	3.3	3.3	3.3	6.9	8.0	9.7
Japan	19.0	25.9	27.7	29.4	38.3	42.3	50.9
Netherlands	0.5	0.5	0.5	0.5	0.5	2.4	3.1
Spain	3.8	6.7	7.6	8.6	8.1	9.5	12.5
Sweden	7.3	9.4	9.4	9.4	9.6	10.2	12.5
Switzerland	1.9	2.9	2.9	2.9	2.9	3.0	4.1
United Kingdom	8.8	11.9	11.9	13.2	15.4	17.9	23.2
United States	64.4	106.6	110.8	114.0	108.1	121.8	123.0
Total OECD	158.7	252.0	265.0	277.0	287.0	332.0	384.0
Non-OECD Countries							
Argentina	0.9	0.9	0.9	1.5	1.9	2.1	2.9
Brazil	0.6	0.6	1.9	3.1	4.1	6.2	12.3
India	1.0	1.5	1.7	1.7	3.7	7.9	9.2
South Korea	1.8	5.4	5.4	7.3	7.3	8.6	12.4
Mexico	0	0	0.7	1.3	1.9	3.4	4.2
South Africa	0	1.8	1.8	1.8	2.8	3.4	6.8
Taiwan	3.1	4.9	4.9	4.9	6.0	6.7	8.5
Total Non-OECD	8.3	17.0	19.0	23.0	29.0	42.0	64.0
Total World	167.0	269.0	284.0	300.0	316.0	374.0	448.0

(1) OECD countries Austria, Greece, Portugal, and Turkey, and non-OECD countries Egypt, Israel, Pakistan, the Phillipines, and Yugosla-via have less than 1.0 current capacity and are projected for less than 5.0 in 2000, high case. (2) Total does not equal sum of components, due to independent rounding. (3) Totals are rounded to the nearest whole number. (4) OECD = Organization for Economic Cooperation and Development.

Largest Nuclear Plants in the U.S.

Plant Name	Company Name	State	Capacity (megawatts)
Sequoyah	Tennessee Valley Authority	Tennessee	1220.6
Sequoyah	Tennessee Valley Authority	Tennessee	1220.6
McGuire	Duke Power Company	No. Carolina	1220.3
McGuire	Duke Power Company	No. Carolina	1220.3
Trojan	Portland General Electric Company	Oregon	1216.0
WNP-2	Washington Public Power Supply	Washington	1200.0
La Salle	Commonwealth Edison Company	Illinois	1170.3
La Salle	Commonwealth Edison Company	Illinois	1170.3
Salem	Public Service Elec. and Gas Co.	New Jersey	1170.0
Salem	Public Service Elec. and Gas Co.	New Jersey	1170.0
Susquehanna	Pennsylvania Power & Light Co.	Pennsylvania	1152.0
Peach Bottom	Philadelphia Electric Company	Pennsylvania	1152.0
Peach Bottom	Philadelphia Electric Company	Pennsylvania	1152.0
Browns Ferry	Tennessee Valley Authority	Alabama	1152.0
Browns Ferry	Tennessee Valley Authority	Alabama	1152.0
Browns Ferry	Tennessee Valley Authority	Alabama	1152.0
Donald C. Cook	AEP: Indiana & Michigan Electric Co.	Michigan	1152.0
Donald C. Cook	AEP: Indiana & Michigan Electric Co.	Michigan	1133.3
San Onofre	Southern California Edison Company	California	1127.0
San Onofre	Southern California Edison Company	California	1127.0
Zion	Commonwealth Edison Company	Illinois	1098.0
Zion	Commonwealth Edison Company	Illinois	1098.0
Indian Point	Consolidated Edison Co. of N.Y.	New York	1013.0
Indian Point No. 3	Power Authority of the State of N.Y.	New York	1013.0
North Anna	Virginia Electric & Power Co.	Virginia	979.7
North Anna	Virginia Electric & Power Co.	Virginia	979.7
Rancho Seco	Sacramento Municipal Utility Dist.	California	963.0
Davis-Besse	Toledo Edison Company	Ohio	962.0
Three Mile Island	GPU: Metropolitan Edison Co.	Pennsylvania	961.0
V. C. Summer	South Carolina Electric & Gas Co.	So. Carolina	953.9
Arkansas Nuclear One	MID SO: Arkansas Power & Light Co.	Arkansas	942.5
Beaver Valley	Duquesne Light Company	Pennsylvania	923.4
Calvert Cliffs	Baltimore Gas & Electric Company	Maryland	918.0
Calvert Cliffs	Baltimore Gas & Electric Company	Maryland	910.7
Millstone	Northeast Nuclear Energy Co.	Connecticut	909.9
Arkansas Nuclear One	MID SO: Arkansas Power & Light Co.	Arkansas	902.5
Oconee	Duke Power Company	South Carolina	893.3
Crystal River	Florida Power Corporation	Florida	890.5
Joseph M. Farley	SO CO: Alabama Power Co.	Alabama	888.3
Joseph M. Farley	SO CO: Alabama Power Co.	Alabama	888.3
Oconee	Duke Power Company	South Carolina	886.7
Oconee	Duke Power Company	South Carolina	886.7

(continued)

Plant Name	Company Name	State	Capacity (megawatts)
James A. Fitzpatrick	Power Authority of the State of N.Y.	New York	883.0
Three Mile Island	GPU: Metropolitan Edison Co.	Pennsylvania	871.0
Brunswick	Carolina Power & Light Co.	No. Carolina	866.7
Brunswick	Carolina Power & Light Co.	No. Carolina	866.7
Maine Yankee	Maine Yankee Atomic Power Company	Maine	864.0
HGP	Washington Public Power Supply	Washington	860.0
St. Lucie	Florida Power & Light Co.	Florida	850.0
St. Lucie	Florida Power & Light Co.	Florida	850.0

Status of U.S. Nuclear Power Plants

(as of Dec. 31, 1983)

Status	# of Reactors	Net Design Capacity (Megawatts)	Status	# of Reactors	Net Design Capacity (Megawatts)
Operable			30 to 50 Percent Complete ...	4	4,600
In Commercial Operation......	76	60,200[1]	Less Than 30 Percent Complete	2	2,400
In Power Ascension.........	4	4,200	Indefinitely Deferred.........	10	11,700
Total.............	80	64,400	Reactors on Order	2	2,200
In Construction Pipeline			Total................	58	64,700
In Low-Power Testing........	3	3,400	Total...................	138	129,100
Under Construction					
More than 50 Percent Complete	37	40,400			

(1) Includes Three Mile Island 7 (819 Mwe); does not include Three Mile Island 2 or Dresden 1.

U.S. Total Energy Production by Source, 1950-1984

	Coal[1]	Petroleum[2]	NGPL[3]	Natural gas (dry)	Hydro-electric power[4]	Nuclear electric power	Total energy produced	Percent change
				Quadrillion (10^15) Btu				
1950	14.07	11.45	0.82	6.23	1.42	0	33.99	12.6
1955	12.38	14.41	1.24	9.34	1.36	0	38.74	10.2
1960	10.83	14.93	1.46	12.66	1.61	0.01	41.50	2.2
1965	13.07	16.52	1.88	15.78	2.06	0.04	49.35	3.4
1970	14.61	20.40	2.51	21.67	2.63	0.24	62.08	5.0
1975	15.00	17.73	2.37	19.64	3.15	1.90	59.87	—1.6
1980	18.60	18.25	2.25	19.91	2.90	2.74	64.76	1.5
1981	18.38	18.15	2.31	19.70	2.76	3.01	64.42	—0.5
1982	18.64	18.31	2.19	18.25	3.26	3.13	63.89	—0.8
1983	17.25	18.39	2.18	16.53	3.50	3.20	61.20	—4.2
1984p	19.70	18.59	2.37	17.75	3.39	3.55	65.51	7.0

Totals may not equal sum of parts due to independent rounding. (1) Includes bituminous, lignite, and anthracite. (2) Includes crude oil burned as fuel. (3) Natural gas plant liquids. (4) Includes industrial and utility production of hydropower. p = preliminary.

U.S. Total Energy Consumption by Source, 1950-1984

	Coal[1]	Natural gas (dry)	Petroleum	Hydro-electric power[2]	Nuclear electric power	Net imports of coal coke[3]	Total Energy consumed	Percent Change
				Quadrillion (10^15) Btu				
1950	12.36	5.97	13.32	1.44	0	—	33.09	8.6
1955	11.18	9.00	17.25	1.41	0	—0.01	38.83	10.1
1960	9.85	12.39	19.92	1.66	0.01	—0.01	43.81	3.9
1965	11.59	15.77	23.25	2.06	0.04	—0.02	52.69	4.3
1970	12.27	21.79	29.52	2.65	0.24	—0.06	66.44	3.5
1975	12.67	19.95	32.73	3.22	1.90	0.01	70.55	—2.8
1980	15.43	20.39	34.20	3.12	2.74	—0.04	75.96	—3.7
1981	15.91	19.93	31.93	3.11	3.01	—0.02	73.99	—2.6
1982	15.32	18.51	30.23	3.56	3.13	—0.02	70.84	—4.3
1983	15.90	17.36	30.05	3.87	3.20	—0.02	70.50	—0.5
1984p	17.20	18.03	31.00	3.78	3.55	—0.01	73.73	4.6

Totals may not equal sum of parts due to independent rounding. (1) Includes bituminous, lignite, and anthracite. (2) Includes crude oil burned as fuel. (3) Natural gas plant liquids. (4) Includes industrial and utility production of hydropower. p=preliminary.

U.S. Energy Imports and Exports

Quadrillion (10^15) Btu

Year	Imports	Exports	Net Imports	Year	Imports	Exports	Net Imports
1973	14.730	2.051	12.680	1979	19.616	2.871	16.745
1974	14.412	2.223	12.190	1980	15.971	3.724	12.247
1975	14.111	2.359	11.752	1981	13.974	4.329	9.644
1976	16.837	2.189	14.648	1981	12.093	4.636	7.457
1977	20.090	2.072	18.018	1982	12.024	3.719	8.306
1978	19.254	1.931	17.323	1983	12.712	3.818	8.894

Totals may not equal sum of parts due to independent rounding. Data do not include geothermal, wood, waste, wind, photovoltaic, or solar thermal energy sources except that consumed by electric utilities.

World Production of Crude Oil

(millions of barrels per day)

Year	USSR	Saudi Arabia	U.S.	All Arab OPEC Nations[1]	All OPEC Nations[2]	World Total
1973[3]	8.47	7.60	9.21	18.01	30.99	55.67
1974	9.00	8.48	8.77	17.72	30.73	55.86
1975	9.63	7.08	8.38	16.00	27.16	55.89
1976	10.14	8.58	8.14	18.58	30.74	55.31
1977	10.68	9.25	8.25	19.22	31.30	59.69
1978	11.19	8.30	8.71	18.46	29.80	60.06
1979	11.46	9.53	8.56	21.09	30.93	62.54
1980	11.77	9.90	8.60	19.05	26.89	59.54
1981	11.91	9.81	8.57	15.76	22.65	55.90
1982	12.00	6.47	8.65	11.68	18.78	53.16
1983	12.04	5.09	8.69	10.35	17.56	52.89
1984[p]	11.83	4.67	8.76	11.50	17.46	53.72

(1) Algeria, Iraq, Kuwait, Libya, Qatar, Saudi Arabia, United Arab Emirates. (2) Arab OPEC nations plus Ecuador, Gabon, Indonesia, Iran, Nigeria, Venezuela. (3) Average per day. p=preliminary.

U.S. Petroleum Imports by Source

(thousands of barrels per day)

Nation	1973	1978	1980	1981	1982	1983	1984[p]
Algeria	136	649	488	311	170	240	318
Indonesia	213	573	348	366	248	338	342
Iran	223	555	9	0	35	48	0
Libya	164	654	554	319	26	0	0
Nigeria	459	919	857	620	514	302	214
Saudi Arabia	486	1,144	1,261	1,129	552	337	322
United Arab Emirates	71	385	172	81	92	30	0
Venezuela	1,135	645	481	406	412	422	536
Other OPEC[1]	106	226	130	90	97	144	290
Total OPEC	2,993	5,751	4,300	3,323	2,146	1,862	2,023
Arab OPEC Members[2]	915	2,963	2,551	1,848	854	632	809
Bahamas	174	160	78	74	65	125	0
Canada	1,325	467	455	447	482	547	629
Neth'lands Antilles	585	229	225	197	175	189	NA
Puerto Rico	99	94	88	62	50	40	355[4]
Trinidad/Tobago	255	253	176	133	112	96	NA
Virgin Islands	329	429	388	327	316	282	[4]
Mexico	16	318	533	523	685	826	739
Other non-OPEC	465	484	491	534	627	701	1,259
Total non-OPEC	3,263	2,613	2,609	2,672	2,968	3,189	3,358
Total imports (avg.)[3]	6,256	8,363	6,909	5,995	5,113	5,051	5,381

(1) Includes Ecuador, Gabon, Iraq, Kuwait, Qatar. (2) Includes Algeria, Libya, Saudi Arabia, United Arab Emirates, Iraq, Kuwait, Qatar. (3) Imports do not add to totals because OPEC figures include petroleum transshipped through, and usually refined in, other countries and counted again as imports from those countries. (4) 1984 Puerto Rico figure includes Virgin Islands. P = preliminary.

Coal Production and Consumption in the U.S.

(million short tons)

Bituminous Coal, Lignite, and Anthracite

	Production	Domestic Consumption	Imports[1]	Exports[2]	Stocks[3]
1973	598.6	562.6	0.1	53.6	104.6
1974	610.0	558.4	2.1	60.7	96.6
1975	654.6	562.6	0.9	66.3	128.3
1976	684.9	603.8	1.2	60.1	134.7
1977	697.2	625.3	1.6	54.3	157.3
1978	670.2	625.2	3.0	40.7	145.9
1979	781.1	680.5	2.1	66.0	202.8
1980	829.7	702.7	1.2	91.7	228.4
1981	823.8	723.6	1.0	112.5	209.4
1982	838.1	706.9	0.7	106.3	232.0
1983[p]	782.1	736.7	1.3	77.8	202.6
1984	890.1	792.7	1.2	81.5	222.4

(1) Bituminous coal was the only type of coal imported during the years shown above. (2) Excludes shipments of anthracite to U.S. Armed Forces overseas (335,000 short tons in 1982). (3) Stocks held by electric utilities, coke plants, and general industry, not stocks at retail dealers consumed by residential, commercial sector. NA=Not available. P=preliminary.

Energy Consumed by U.S. Households

(quadrillion Btu)

Year	Natural Gas	Electricity	Distillate Fuel Oil and Kerosene	Liquefied Petroleum Gases	Total
1978	5.58	2.47	2.19	0.33	10.56
1979	5.31	2.42	1.71	0.31	9.74
1980	4.94	2.46	1.55	0.36	9.32
1981	5.39	2.48	1.33	0.31	9.51
1982	4.77	2.42	1.14	0.29	8.61

Household Appliance Use in the U.S.

	Million Households			Percentage of Households		
	1980	1981	1982	1980	1981	1982
Total Households	**81.6**	**83.1**	**83.8**	**100**	**100**	**100**
Type Appliances						
Electric Appliances						
Television Set (Color)	67.0	68.4	71.0	82	82	85
Television Set (B/W)	41.9	39.5	38.9	51	48	47
Clothes Washer (Automatic)	58.4	58.4	57.9	72	70	69
Clothes Washer (Wringer)	2.9	2.8	2.5	4	3	3
Range (Stove-Top or Burners)	43.8	45.2	44.7	54	54	53
Oven	48.5	48.2	49.3	59	58	59
Microwave	11.6	14.0	17.3	14	17	21
Clothes Dryer	38.3	37.5	37.9	47	45	45
Separate Freezer	21.1	31.9	31.0	38	38	37
Dishwasher	30.4	30.5	30.3	37	37	36
Humidifier	11.0	10.8	11.3	14	13	14
Dehumidifier	7.3	7.8	7.5	9	9	9
Window or Ceiling Fan	NA	NA	23.5	NA	NA	28
Whole House Cooling Fan	NA	NA	6.5	NA	NA	8
Evaporative Cooler	3.2	3.0	3.6	4	4	4
Gas Appliances						
Range (Stove-Top or Burners)	37.5	38.2	39.0	46	46	47
Oven	34.2	33.0	35.0	42	40	42
Clothes Dryer	11.8	13.1	12.2	14	16	15
Outdoor Gas Grill	7.1	7.4	9.4	9	9	11
Outdoor Gas Light	1.6	1.4	1.4	2	2	2
Swimming Pool Heater	0.4	0.4	0.3	(¹)	(¹)	(¹)
Refrigerators						
One	70.0	72.4	72.4	86	87	86
Two or More	11.5	10.5	11.1	14	13	13
None	0.2	0.2	0.2	(¹)	(¹)	(¹)
Air Conditioning (A/C)						
Central	22.2	22.4	23.3	27	27	28
Individual Room Units	24.5	26.0	25.3	30	31	30
None	34.9	34.7	35.1	43	42	42

(1) Less than 0.5%. NA=not available.

U.S. Household Motor Vehicle Use in 1983

	Census Region				Family Income					
	Northeast	North Central	South	West	Less than $10,000	$10,000 to $14,999	$15,000 to $24,999	$25,000 to 34,999	$35,000 or More	Total
Households with Vehicles (millions)	13.9	18.3	24.7	15.3	13.1	10.5	18.4	14.7	15.6	72.2
Vehicles (millions)	23.9	32.5	45.1	27.7	18.5	16.1	31.8	28.3	34.6	129.3
Miles Traveled (billions)	227	298	436	254	151	144	292	282	347	1,215
Fuel Consumed (billion gallons)										
Motor Gasoline, Leaded	5.1	8.1	11.5	7.4	5.4	4.7	9.0	6.4	6.7	32.2
Motor Gasoline, Unleaded	9.1	11.4	16.8	8.7	5.2	5.0	10.6	11.3	14.0	46.1
Diesel Oil, Other . . .	0.3	0.6	0.7	0.3	0.2	0.1	0.4	0.4	0.8	1.9
Total	14.5	20.2	29.1	16.5	10.8	9.8	20.0	18.1	21.6	80.3
Averages per Household										
Vehicles	1.7	1.8	1.8	1.8	1.4	1.5	1.7	1.9	2.2	1.8
Miles Traveled	16,324	16,299	17,689	16,541	11,559	13,682	15,897	19,252	22,167	16,830
Fuel Consumed (gallons)	1,044	1,104	1,178	1,076	830	933	1,087	1,236	1,380	1,112
Fuel Expenditures (dollars)	1,254	1,314	1,385	1,269	979	1,104	1,282	1,461	1,650	1,317
Averages per Vehicle										
Miles Traveled	9,511	9,153	9,674	9,144	8,166	8,919	9,183	9,981	10,004	9,399
Fuel Consumed (gallons)	609	620	644	595	586	608	628	641	623	621
Fuel Expenditure (dollars)	731	738	758	701	691	719	740	757	745	736
Price (dollars per gallon)										
Motor Gasoline, Leaded	1.15	1.15	1.12	1.14	1.14	1.14	1.14	1.13	1.14	1.14
Motor Gasoline, Unleaded	1.23	1.22	1.21	1.22	1.22	1.22	1.22	1.21	1.23	1.22
Diesel Oil, Other . . .	1.18	1.16	1.13	1.17	1.14	1.15	1.15	1.18	1.14	1.15
Average	1.20	1.19	1.18	1.18	1.18	1.18	1.18	1.18	1.20	1.18
Fuel Efficiency (miles per gallon) . .	15.6	14.8	15.0	15.4	13.9	14.7	14.6	15.6	16.1	15.1

U.S. Energy Expenditures by State

(1982; billions of current dollars)

Rank	State	Expenditures	Rank	State	Expenditures	Rank	State	Expenditures
1	Texas	$40.1	18	Wisconsin	8.0	35	Nebraska	3.0
2	California	38.9	19	Alabama	7.6	36	New Mexico	2.5
3	New York	26.2	20	Maryland	7.2	37	Utah	2.5
4	Ohio	20.3	21	Minnesota	7.2	38	Maine	2.4
5	Illinois	19.8	22	Washington	6.8	39	Hawaii	2.0
6	Pennsylvania	19.6	23	Kentucky	6.5	40	Nevada	1.9
7	Florida	17.0	24	Oklahoma	6.4	41	Wyoming	1.7
8	New Jersey	15.2	25	Iowa	5.8	42	Idaho	1.6
9	Michigan	14.8	26	Connecticut	5.6	43	Alaska	1.5
10	Louisiana	13.0	27	South Carolina	5.5	44	Montana	1.5
11	Indiana	10.9	28	Colorado	5.2	45	New Hampshire	1.5
12	Georgia	10.1	29	Arizona	5.0	46	North Dakota	1.5
13	North Carolina	9.8	30	Kansas	4.7	47	Rhode Island	1.4
14	Massachusetts	9.5	31	Oregon	4.5	48	South Dakota	1.3
15	Virginia	9.4	32	Mississippi	4.5	49	Delaware	1.1
16	Tennessee	8.7	33	Arkansas	4.3	50	Vermont	0.8
17	Missouri	8.6	34	West Virginia	3.5			

Major U.S. Public and Private Dams and Reservoirs

Source: Corps of Engineers, U.S. Army
Heights over 350 feet.

Height—Difference in elevation in feet, between lowest point in foundation and top of dam, exclusive of parapet or other projections. **Length**—Overall length of barrier in feet, main dam and its integral features as located between natural abutments. **Volume**—Total volume in cubic yards of all material in main dam and its appurtenant works. **Year**—Date structure was originally completed for use. (UC) Under construction subject to revision. **River**—Mainstream. **Purpose**—I-Irrigation; C-Flood Control; H-Hydroelectric; N-Navigation; S-Water Supply; R-Recreation; D-Debris Control; O-Other. **Parentheses** after name indicate type of dam as follows: (RE)-Earth; (PG)-Gravity; (ER)-Rockfill; (CB)-Buttress; (VA)-Arch; (MV)-Multi-arch; (OT)-Other.

Name of dam	State	River	Ht.	Lgth.	Vol. (1,000)	Purpose	Year
Oroville (RE)	Cal.	Feather River	756	6800	78000	RCSH	1968
Hoover (VA)	Nev.	Colorado River	726	1242	4400	IHCO	1936
Dworshak (PG)	Ida.	North Fork of Clearwater	717	3287	6450	HCR	1973
Glen Canyon (VA)	Ariz.	Colorado River	710	1560	4901	HCSR	1966
New Bullards Bar (VA)	Cal.	North Yuba River	635	2200	2600	SH	1970
New Melones (ER)	Cal.	Stanislaus River	625	1560	16000	IHCR	1979
Swift (RE)	Wash.	North Fork Lewis River	610	2100	15400	HRC	1958
Mossyrock (VA)	Wash.	Cowlitz River	606	1648	1270	HCR	1968
Shasta (PG)	Cal.	Sacramento River	602	3460	8711	ISHN	1945
Don Pedro (RE)	Cal.	Tuolumne River	568	1800	16000	H	1971
Hungry Horse (VA)	Mon.	South Fork of Flathead River	564	2115	3086	IHCN	1953
Grand Coulee (PG)	Wash.	Columbia River	550	4173	10585	IHCN	1942
Ross (VA)	Wash.	Skagit River	540	1300	900	HR	1949
Trinity (RE)	Cal.	Trinity River	537	2450	29410	IHCR	1962
Yellowtail (VA)	Mon.	Bighorn River	525	1480	1546	ICHR	1966
Cougar (ER)	Ore.	South Fork McKenzie River	519	1600	13000	HCIR	1964
Flaming Gorge (VA)	Ut.	Green River	502	1285	987	HCSR	1964
Fontana (PG)	N.C.	Little Tennessee River	480	2365	3576	H	1944
New Exchequer (ER)	Cal.	Merced River	479	1240	5169	H	1926
Little Blue Run (RE)	Penn.	Little Blue Run	400	2100	13000	—	1977
Morrow Point (VA)	Col.	Gunnison River	468	741	365	HCR	1968
Carters (ER)	Ga.	Coosawattee River	464	1950	15000	CHR	1974
Detroit (PG)	Ore.	North Santiam River	463	1580	1500	HCRI	1953
Anderson Ranch (RE)	Ida.	South Fork Boise River	456	1350	9653	IHCR	1950
Union Valley (RE)	Cal.	Silver Creek	453	1800	10000	S	1963
Round Butte (RE)	Ore.	Deschutes River	440	1450	9600	HR	1964
Pine Flat Lake (PG)	Cal.	Kings River	440	1840	2400	CIRH	1954
Jocassee (RE)	S.C.	Keowee River	435	1800	11600	H	1973
O'Shaughnessy (PG)	Cal.	Moccasin Creek	430	900	663	HS	1923
Mud Mountain (ER)	Wash.	White River	425	700	2300	C	1948
Libby (PG)	Mon.	Kootenai River	422	2890	3760	HCR	1973
Pacoima (VA)	Cal.	Pacoima Creek	420	640	226	C	1929
Owyhee (VA)	Ore.	Owyhee River	417	833	538	ICR	1932
Lower Hell Hole (ER)	Cal.	Rubicon River	410	1550	8315	SH	1966
Castaic (RE)	Cal.	Castaic Creek	410	5200	44000	IRS	1973
Mammoth Pool (RE)	Cal.	San Joaquin River	406	820	5355	HS	1960
San Gabriel No. 1 (ER)	Cal.	San Gabriel River	405	1520	10600	CS	1939
Navajo (RE)	N.M.	San Juan River	402	3648	26840	IR	1963
No name (RE)	S.C.	Jocassee River	400	1000		H	1972
Pyramid (ER)	Cal.	Piru Creek	400	1080	6952	IRSH	1973
Bath County Upper (ER,RE)	Va.	Little Bush Creek	470	2398	23544	H	1984
Brownlee (ER)	Ida.	Snake River	395	1380	6000	HCR	1958
Summersville (ER)	W.Va.	Gauley River	390	2280	13565	CRS	1965
Blue Mesa (RE, ER)	Col.	Gunnison River	390	785	3080	HCR	1966
Diablo (VA)	Wash.	Skagit River	386	1180	350	HR	1929
San Luis (RE)	Cal.	San Luis Creek	382	18500	77900	ISHR	1967
Green Peter (PG)	Ore.	Middle Santiam River	378	1517	1142	CHRI	1967
Merriman (RE)	N.Y.	Roundout Creek	375	2400	5800	S	1945
Arrowrock (VA)	Ida.	Boise River	350	1150	636	ICR	1915

Major Dams of the World

Source: T.W. Mermel, *Intl. Water Power & Dam Construction,* July, 1985.

World's Highest Dams

Rank order	Name	Country	Height above lowest foundation (m)	Rank order	Name	Country	Height above lowest foundation (m)
1	Rogun*	USSR	335	14	Mauvoisin	Switzerland	237
2	Nurek	USSR	300	14 =	Chivor	Colombia	237
3	Grand Dixence	Switzerland	285	16	Chirkei	USSR	233
4	Inguri	USSR	272	17	Oroville	USA	230
5	Boruca*	Costa Rica	267	18	Bhakra	India	226
6	Vaiont	Italy	262	18 =	El Cajón*	Honduras	226
7	Chicoasén	Mexico	261	20	Hoover	USA	221
7 =	Tehri*	India	261	21	Contra	Switzerland	220
9	Alvaro Obregon	Mexico	260	21 =	Mratinje	Yugoslavia	220
10	Kishau*	India	253	23	Dworshak	USA	219
11	Sayano-Shushensk	USSR	245	24	Glen Canyon	USA	216
12	Guavio*	Colombia	243	25	Toktogol	USSR	215
13	Mica	Canada	242				

*Planned or under construction.

World's Largest Volume Dams

Rank order	Name	Country	Dam volume m³ × 10³	Rank Order	Name	Country	Dam volume m³ × 10³
1	Chapetón*	Argentina	296,200	15	Oroville	USA	59,635
2	New Cornelia Tailings	USA	209,500	16	San Luis	USA	59,559
3	Tarbela	Pakistan	105,570	17	Nurek	USSR	58,000
4	Fort Peck	USA	96,050	18	Garrison	USA	50,845
5	Loser Usuma	Nigeria	93,000	19	Cochiti	USA	50,230
6	Atatürk*	Turkey	85,000	20	Oosterschelde	Netherlands	50,000
7	Yacyretá-Apipe*	Paraguay/Argentina	81,000	21	Tabqua (Thawra)	Syria	46,000
8	Guri*	Venezuela	77,971	22	Aswan (High)	Egypt	44,300
9	Rogun*	USSR	75,500	23	Bennett W.A.C. (Portage Mt.)	Canada	43,700
10	Oahe	USA	70,339				
11	Gardiner	Canada	65,440	24	Boruca*	Costa Rica	43,000
12	Mangla	Pakistan	65,379	25	Kiev	USSR	42,841
13	Tucurui*	Brazil	64,300				
14	Afsluitdijk	Netherlands	63,430				

*Planned or under construction.

World's Largest Capacity Reservoirs

Rank order	Name	Country	Dam volume m³ × 10⁶	Rank Order	Name	Country	Dam volume m³ × 10⁶
1	Owens Falls	Uganda	2,700,000	14	La Grande 2	Canada	61,715
2	Kahkovskaya	USSR	182,000	15	La Grande 3	Canada	60,020
3	Bratsk	USSR	169,270	16	Ust Ilim	USSR	59,300
4	Aswan (High)	Egypt	168,900	17	Volga-V.I. Lenin (Kuibyshev)	USSR	58,000
5	Kariba	Zimbabwe	160,368				
6	Akosombo	Ghana	148,000	18	São Felix	Brazil	55,200
7	Daniel Johnson	Canada	141,852	19	Caniapiscau (KA-3, KA-4 & KA-5)	Canada	53,800
8	Guri (Raul Leoni) (Final Stage)	Venezuela	138,000	20	Cerros Colorados	Argentina	53,750
9	Kama	USSR	122,000	20 =	Chapetón*	Argentina	53,750
10	Bennett W.A.C. (Portage Mt.)	Canada	74,250	22	Shintoyone	Japan	53,500
				23	Upper Wainganga*	India	50,700
11	Krasnoyarsk	USSR	73,300	24	Bukhtarma	USSR	49,800
12	Zeya	USSR	68,400	25	Atatürk*	Turkey	48,700
13	Cabora Bassa	Mozambique	63,000				

*Planned or under construction.

Production of Electricity in the U.S. by Source[1]

Includes both privately-owned and publicly-owned utilities.

(million kilowatt hours)

Amount and Percentage Produced by Source

Year	Total Production	Coal	%	Oil	%	Gas	%	Nuclear	%	Hydro	%
1975	1,917,649	852,786	44.5	289,095	15.1	299,778	15.6	172,505	9.0	300,047	15.6
1980	2,286,439	1,161,562	50.8	245,994	10.8	346,240	15.1	251,116	11.0	276,021	12.0
1981	2,294,812	1,203,203	52.4	206,421	9.0	345,777	15.1	272,674	11.9	260,684	11.4
1982	2,241,211	1,192,004	53.2	146,797	6.5	305,260	13.6	282,773	12.6	309,213	13.8
1983	2,310,285	1,259,424	54.5	144,499	6.3	274,098	11.9	293,677	12.7	332,130	14.4
1984p	2,413,000	1,341,000	—	120,000	—	297,000	—	325,000	—	321,000	—

(1) Other sources, representing less than one percent of production, include geothermal power, wood, and waste. p = preliminary.

U.S. Electricity Sales

	Commer-cial	Industrial	Resi-dential	Other[1]	Total [2]		Commer-cial	Industrial	Resi-dential	Other[1]	Total[2]
1975	403,049	687,680	588,140	68,222	1,747,091	1982	526,397	744,949	729,512	85,575	2,086,440
1980	488,156	815,067	717,495	73,732	2,094,449	1983	543,788	775,999	750,948	80,219	2,150,955
1981	514,338	825,742	722,265	84,756	2,147,101	1984[p]	579,000	842,000	780,000	82,000	2,282,000

(1) Includes sales to government, railways, street lighting authorities. (2) Totals may not equal sum of components due to independent rounding. p = preliminary.

Largest Hydroelectric Plants in U.S.

(Capacities as of Aug. 16, 1985)

Plant Name	State	Owner	Installed Capacity (KW)
Coulee Dam	Washington	USBR-Pacific NW Region	6,494,000
John Day	Oregon	USCE-North Pacific Div	2,160,000
Chf Joseph	Washington	USCE-North Pacific Div	2,069,000
LD Pump St	Michigan	Consumers Power Co	1,978,800
Moses Niag	New York	Power Authy of St of NY	1,950,000
Dalles Dam	Oregon	USCE-North Pacific Div	1,806,800
Raccoon Mt	Tennessee	Tennessee Valley Auth	1,530,000
Castaic	California	Los Angeles (city of)	1,331,000
Rocky Reach	Washington	Chelan Pub Util Dist #1	1,213,950
Helms	California	Pacific Gas & Electric	1,125,000
Glen Canyon	Arizona	USBR-Upper Colorado Reg.	1,113,748
Bonneville	Oregon	USCE-North Pacific Div	1,076,000
Blenheim G	New York	Power Authy of St of NY	1,000,000
McNary	Oregon	USCE-North Pacific Div	980,000
Moses Pr Dm	New York	Power Authy of St of NY	912,000
Northfld Mt	Massachusetts	W Massachusetts Elec Co	846,000
Wanapum	Washington	Grant Pub Util Dist #2	831,250
Little Goose	Washington	USCE-North Pacific Div	810,000
Monumental	Washington	USCE-North Pacific Div	810,000
Lwr Granite	Washington	USCE-North Pacific Div	810,000
Muddy Run	Pennsylvania	Philadelphia Elec Co	800,000
Priest Rpds	Washington	Grant Pub Util Dist #2	788,500
Wells	Washington	Douglas Pub Util Dist #1	774,300
Hoover Dam	Nevada	USBR-Lower Colorado Reg	672,500
Hoover Dam	Arizona	USBR-Lower Colorado Reg	667,500
Edward Hyatt	California	California (state of)	644,250
Boundary	Washington	Seattle (city of)	634,600
Wilson Dam	Alabama	Tennessee Valley Auth	629,840
Rock Island	Washington	Chelan Pub Util Dist #1	622,500
Jocassee	South Carolina	Duke Power Co	610,000
Ice Harbor	Washington	USCE-North Pacific Div	603,000
Bear Swamp	Massachusetts	New England Elec System	600,000
Oahe	South Dakota	USCE-Omaha District	595,000
Brownlee	Idaho	Idaho Power Co	585,400
Smith Mt	Virginia	Appalachian Power Co	547,250
Shasta Dam	California	USBR-Mid Pacific Region	535,000
Libby	Montana	USCE-North Pacific Riv.	525,000
Fairfield	South Carolina	So Carolina Elec & Gas Co	511,200
Carters	Georgia	USCE-Alt-Buf-Cart Prj	500,000

World's Largest Capacity Hydro Plants

Rank order	Country	Name	Rated capacity now (MW)	Rated capacity planned (MW)	Rank order	Country	Name	Rated capacity now (MW)	Rated capacity planned (MW)
1	Itaipú	Brazil/Paraguay	2,800	12,600	13	Cabora Bassa	Mozambique	2,000	4,000
2	Guri (Raul Leoni) (final stage)*	Venezuela	2,800	10,000	14	Rogun*	USSR		3,600
3	Tucuruí*	Brazil	3,960	8,000	15	Paulo Afonso I	Brazil	1,524	3,409
4	Grand Coulee	USA	6,494	6,494	16	Ilha Solteira	Brazil	3,200	3,200
5	Sayano-Shushensk	USSR	6,400	6,400	17	Gezhouba	P.R. of China	2,715	2,715
6	Corpus Posadas	Argentina/Paraguay		6,000	18	John Day	USA	2,160	2,700
6=	Krasnoyarsk	USSR	6,000	6,000	18=	Nurek	USSR	900	2,700
8	La Grande 2	Canada	2,000	5,328	18=	Revelstoke	Canada	900	2,700
9	Churchill Falls	Canada	5,225	5,225	21	Sao Simao	Brazil	2,680	2,680
10	Bratsk	USSR	4,500	4,500	22	Mica	Canada	1,736	2,610
10=	Ust-Ilim	USSR	3,675	4,500	23	Volgograd 22nd Congress	USSR	2,563	2,563
12	Yacyretá-Apipe*	Argentina/Paraguay	2,700	4,050	24	Itaparica*	Brazil		2,500
					25	Chicoasen	Mexico	2,400	2,400

*Planned or under construction.

ENVIRONMENT

Environmental Quality Index

Source: Copyright 1984 by the National Wildlife Federation.
Reprinted with permission from the Feb.-Mar., 1985 issue of NATIONAL WILDLIFE Magazine.

Wildlife: Overall, the situation for wildlife worsened, due to continuing habitat loss. Since the 1950s, more than 11 million acres of freshwater wetlands have been converted to cropland and urban projects. In 1984, the conversion of prairielands in Illinois reduced grassland bird species by as much as 90 percent in some areas. A 1984 Michigan appellate court's sharp limitation on the kinds of wetlands protected by the Clean Water Act meant that the situation could decline further. Conservation groups sought a Supreme Court review of the ruling.

Also, Congress failed to act on several air and water pollution control amendments that might have meant relief for various beleaguered species. In Pennsylvania, the decline of several trout species was attributed to acid rain and agricultural runoff. Levels of DDT—the pesticide banned more than a decade earlier because of its effect on wildlife—were found to be increasing again in parts of the West and along the Gulf Coast. A legal pesticide containing traces of DDT was thought to be the culprit.

The efforts of recent years did result in some favorable signs for wildlife in 1984. The bald eagle seemed to be holding its own after years of decline. Peregrine falcons hatched a brood of nestlings in Baltimore. Cleanup programs in some U.S. cities returned game fish to urban waterways. Interior Dept. Secy. William D. Clark temporarily withdrew a proposal that would permit oil and gas exploration in National Wildlife Refuges. The federal system gained new refuge lands, including 120,000 acres along North Carolina's Alligator River. And after ten years of struggle, Congress approved the addition to the nation's wilderness system of some 7 million acres of U.S. forestland habitat in 21 states.

Air: In dozens of U.S. cities, the air was found to be cleaner than 14 years earlier, when the average urban American breathed unsafe air almost 70 days a year. In 1984, that figure was cut almost in half. Further improvement was highly questionable, however, because of the unchecked spread of acid rain and dozens of toxic air pollutants suspected of causing cancer. Although most of the U.S. complied with the health standards for conventional pollutants like carbon monoxide and particulates, more than 94 million Americans lived in cities that exceeded the standard for ozone. A principal component of smog, ozone has been found to be responsible for human respiratory problems and up to $4 billion a year in crop damage.

In addition, the improved economy put other pollutants, including sulfur dioxide and nitrogen oxides, on the rise again. Changes were approved in 11 state clean air plants, permitting 13 additional factories and power plants to add 16,000 more tons of sulfur dioxide to the air annually. And there was evidence that acid rain was spreading nationwide: In one analysis of 21 states outside New England, highly acidic rain was found to fall from Pennsylvania to Florida, as well as in California, Colorado, and Texas. The EPA proposed a sharp reduction in the amount of lead allowed in gasoline because the substance was found to be harmful at lower levels than previously believed.

On the bright side, the idea that cleanup could be profitable was reinforced by a report that although air and water cleanup requirements have closed 155 plants at a cost of 33,000 jobs since 1971, the same laws will have stimulated some 524,000 new jobs by 1987.

Water: Despite efforts to clean up U.S. surface waters, the total amount of pollutants entering waters from sewage treatment plants was found to have remained approximately the same during the past decade. The number of operating sewage treatment plants increased each year, but so did the amount of water requiring treatment. Some streams, rivers, and lakes showed considerable improvement, but others were found to be slowly degrading, due to agricultural runoff, mining wastes, storm sewer overflows, air pollution, and toxic dumps.

In 1984, health officials in dozens of states warned against consuming fish from highly contaminated waters. In some areas, scientists discovered virtual epidemics of fish cancers. Elsewhere, there was increasing evidence of contamination of the aquifers supplying drinking water to half of all Americans. Evidence of groundwater pollution was found in practically every state in the nation.

Congress failed again in 1984 to give the EPA additional authority to control some sources of groundwater contamination. Further, lack of money inhibited monitoring, research, and enforcement of existing controls, with many industries found to be violating water discharge permits. The Administration agreed to fund further research into the programs of Chesapeake Bay, where runoff pollution was strangling fishery. But conservationists had to keep struggling against federal water projects that promised cheap irrigation water for the arid West and hydropower for the rest of the country, while possibly destroying wetlands and other natural areas. There was concern, too, because only six of the 738 most hazardous toxic waste dump sites were cleaned up, making toxic waste a continued threat to U.S. groundwater supplies. Finally, at least one third of all municipal sewage facilities and industrial waste dischargers continued to illegally pollute U.S. waters.

Soil: Soil erosion continued to be a problem. A summer drought in the nation's breadbasket in 1983 was followed by one of the worst winters on record. First baked by the heat, then cracked and crumbled by alternate freezing and thawing, millions of tons of the richest topsoil were taken away on winter winds. Then millions more were stripped by torrential spring rains. In the Great Plains, wind damage affected more than 12 million acres, the worst record since the 1930's Dust Bowl days. Some fields in the Mississippi Delta lost more soil in one cloudburst than nature created in a century.

Some of the land damaged by wind and water in 1984 was cropland retired in the federal payment-in-kind program of 1983. The program was designed to help conserve soil as well as reduce crop surpluses. However, at least 40 percent of the more than 80 million acres taken out of production went unplanted, therefore were not protected from weather ravages. Further, the worst erosion occurred on a small percentage of the most vulnerable lands, including fragile prairie lands in the West and steep hillsides in the Delta states. These areas were among the nearly half a million acres of highly erodible rangeland that were plowed up in the past three years by "sodbusters"—financially strapped farmers desperate to increase production. Conservationists pressed Congress to pass a bill prohibiting government agricultural subsidies to sodbusters, but no such measure was enacted.

Minerals: For the first time in four years, the nation's energy consumption seemed to rise. An ample fuel supply plus stable oil prices were important factors in reducing the Dept. of the Interior's impetus to conserve. Conservationists feared that energy complacency was on the increase, reversing a decade-long trend. Sales of cars continued to grow, while use of public transportation declined. The U.S. used 7 percent more coal than in the previous year, partly the result of greater industrial activity. The growing popularity of coal brought concern as to the future effects of increased strip mining and power-plant emissions.

On the positive side, millions of Americans were found to have been saving fuel. In 1981, only 50 percent of U.S. households set their thermostats higher than 70 degrees, compared to 85 percent in 1973. Also, Interior Dept. Secy. William Clark started a series of reforms in the federal coal-leasing program that included reviewing proposed tracts for their fair market value and eliminating environmentally sensitive areas from mining. In an out-of-court settlement, the Interior Dept. agreed to start enforcing the federal Surface Mining Act, with U.S. authorities to collect unpaid fines totalling about $150 million and denying new strip-mining permits to violators of the law. Further, the Tennessee Valley Authority abandoned four partially completed nuclear reactors at a cost of more than $2 billion. Finally, American private enterprise programs, including biomass conversion—the production of fuels such as gasahol from organic matter—contributed almost as much fuel to the country's energy pool as did hydropower.

Forests: Americans continued to grow more timber than we harvested, but the greatest surpluses seemed to be in hardwoods, which were not necessarily in the greatest demand.

There was mounting evidence that air pollution was taking a toll on the health of some trees. An estimated 25 percent decrease was found in the growth rates of some trees. A systematic and sustained decline of some species was discovered to have occurred in the past 20 to 30 years, with experts undecided as to the chief culprit—acid rain, ozone, or a combination of pollutants.

The good news: As a result of a legal decision, federal authorities were required to prepare long-range impact studies demonstrating the potential environmental effects of harvesting timber on public lands.

Quality of life: There were many minuses. A decade after the passage of the Safe Drinking Water Act, there were still no reliable safety guidelines for most of the common chemical water pollutants. After seven years of work, the EPA had tested only a handful of the active ingredients in agricultural pesticides. Eight years after Congress passed a "cradle to grave" law on hazardous waste disposal, fewer than 120 disposal sites were issued permits, with more than 4,500 remaining. It was estimated that nearly 200 million metric tons of garbage would be produced in the U.S. by the end of the decade, almost a third more than the garbage produced in 1980. The EPA also raised its estimate of toxic waste production to 71 billion gallons, or 270 million tons a year, 60 percent more than it estimated six months earlier.

Because of federal inaction, some state and local governments began to move forward on their own. Florida began an ambitious program to protect groundwater months before the EPA announced its limited program. New York State officials passed a law to trim sulfur emissions by 30 percent in a decade.

Hazardous Waste Sites

Source: Environmental Protection Agency

As of Sept., 1984 there were 538 abandoned hazardous waste sites on the EPA's "national priority list" of sites requiring remedial action for posing the gravest threats to public health and the environment; another 248 sites were proposed for addition to the list. The map shows the number of locations given priority for cleanup, by state. New Jersey has the most—85 sites. The EPA has identified almost 19,000 hazardous waste sites around the country.

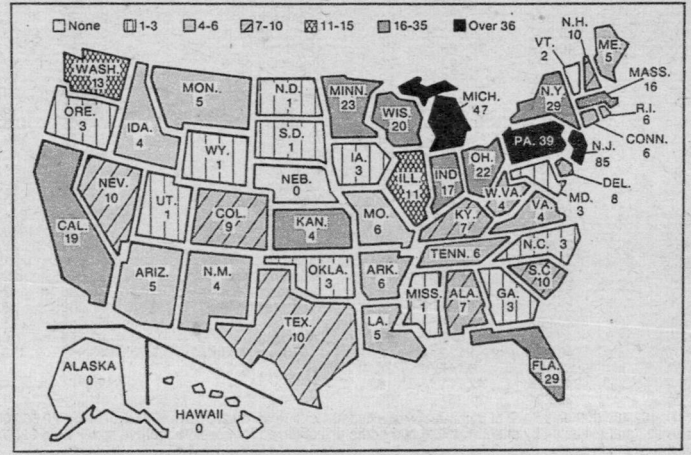

Investment for Pollution Control by U.S. Industries

Source: Bureau of Economic Analysis, U.S. Commerce Department
(billions of dollars)

New plant and equipment expenditures by U.S. nonfarm business: total and for pollution abatement

	1983[p] Total expendi-tures[1]	Pollution abatement Total	Air	Water	Solid waste	Planned 1984 Total expendi-tures[1]	Pollution abatement Total	Air	Water	Solid waste
Total nonfarm business	302.50	7.24	3.66	2.90	.68	343.57	7.64	3.79	2.85	1.00
Manufacturing	111.53	4.01	1.72	1.94	.36	129.72	4.31	1.75	2.07	.49
Durable goods	51.78	1.33	.65	.55	.13	62.78	1.62	.76	.68	.18
Primary metals[2]	6.39	.36	.19	.15	.02	7.23	.50	.26	.20	.04
Blast furnaces, steel works	2.97	.19	.08	.11	(*)	3.27	.29	.12	.16	.01
Nonferrous metals	2.44	.13	.10	.02	(*)	2.73	.17	.13	.03	.01
Fabricated metals	2.22	.03	.01	.02	.01	2.57	.05	.01	.03	(*)
Electrical machinery	10.90	.14	.04	.08	.01	13.48	.15	.04	.10	.01
Machinery, except elec.	12.35	.26	.08	.15	.04	14.73	.28	.09	.15	.04
Transportation equipment[3]	13.02	.30	.17	.10	.03	16.65	.33	.17	.13	.04
Motor vehicles	7.17	.24	.15	.07	.02	9.61	.24	.13	.09	.02
Aircraft	4.93	.05	.02	.02	.01	5.93	.08	.03	.04	.01
Stone, clay, and glass	2.45	.07	.04	.02	.01	2.81	.12	.09	.02	.02
Other durables[3]	4.45	.17	.12	.03	.01	5.30	.19	.10	.06	.03
Nondurable goods	59.75	2.68	1.06	1.39	.23	66.93	2.69	.98	1.39	.31
Food including beverage	6.60	.25	.13	.10	.02	6.76	.20	.10	.08	.02
Textiles	1.39	.03	.01	.02	(*)	1.78	.03	.01	.01	(*)
Paper	6.18	.25	.16	.07	.02	7.13	.39	.22	.10	.07
Chemicals	13.28	.57	.24	.28	.05	14.34	.55	.18	.32	.05
Petroleum	23.48	1.55	.51	.91	.12	26.51	1.50	.47	.88	.15
Rubber	1.91	.01	(*)	(*)	(*)	2.21	.01	(*)	.01	(*)
Other nondurables[4]	6.91	.04	.02	.02	.01	8.20	.02	.01	(*)	.01
Nonmanufacturing	190.97	3.23	1.94	.96	.32	213.86	3.33	2.04	.78	.50
Mining	11.83	.26	.08	.14	.05	14.34	.26	.08	.12	.07
Transportation	11.20	.06	.02	.05	(*)	12.00	.08	.02	.05	(*)
Railroad	3.92	.03	(*)	.02	(*)	4.73	.04	(*)	.03	(*)
Air	3.77	(*)	(*)	.00	.00	2.78	.01	.01	.00	.00
Other	3.50	.04	.01	.03	(*)	4.49	.04	.01	.02	(*)
Public utilities	42.00	2.77	1.78	.75	.24	44.79	2.85	1.88	.58	.39
Electric	34.99	2.69	1.74	.72	.23	35.54	2.64	1.82	.46	.37
Gas and other	7.00	.07	.04	.03	(*)	9.24	.21	.06	.12	.02
Trade and services	87.94	.10	.05	.02	.03	100.25	.12	.05	.03	.04
Communication and other[5]	38.02	.03	.02	.01	(*)	42.47	.02	.01	.01	(*)

[p] Preliminary (1) Consists of final estimates taken from the quarterly surveys of total new plant and equipment and, for 1983, plans based on the 1982 fourth-quarter survey taken in late January and February 1983. (2) Includes industries not shown separately. (3) Consists of lumber, furniture, instruments, and miscellaneous. (4) Consists of apparel, tobacco, leather, and printing-publishing. (5) Consists of communication; construction; social services and membership organizations; and forestry, fisheries, and agricultural services. *Less than $5 million.

U.S. Forest Land by State and Region

Source: Forest Service, U.S. Agriculture Department, 1979.

State or region	Land area (1,000 acres)	Area forested	Percent forested	State or region	Land area (1,000 acres)	Area forested	Percent forested
Connecticut	3,081	1,861	60	Arkansas	33,091	18,282	55
Maine	19,729	17,718	90	Florida	33,994	17,040	50
Massachusetts	5,007	2,952	59	Georgia	36,796	25,256	69
New Hampshire	5,731	5,013	87	Louisiana	28,409	14,558	51
Rhode Island	664	404	61	Mississippi	29,930	16,716	56
Vermont	5,907	4,512	76	North Carolina	30,956	20,043	65
New England	**40,119**	**32,460**	**81**	Oklahoma	43,728	8,513	19
Delaware	1,233	392	32	South Carolina	19,143	12,249	64
Maryland	6,289	2,653	42	Tennessee	26,290	13,161	50
New Jersey	4,775	1,928	40	Texas	167,283	23,279	14
New York	30,357	17,218	57	Virginia	25,286	16,417	65
Pennsylvania	28,592	16,826	59	**South**	**474,906**	**185,514**	**39**
West Virginia	15,334	11,669	76	Alaska	362,485	119,145	33
Mid Atlantic	**87,813**	**50,686**	**58**	California	99,847	40,152	48
Michigan	30,634	19,270	63	Hawaii	4,109	1,986	40
Minnesota	50,382	16,709	33	Oregon	61,356	29,810	49
North Dakota	43,939	422	1	Washington	42,456	23,181	55
South Dakota	48,381	1,702	4	**Pacific Coast**	**570,253**	**214,274**	**38**
Wisconsin	34,616	14,908	43	Arizona	72,580	18,494	25
Lake States	**207,952**	**53,011**	**25**	Colorado	66,283	22,271	34
Illinois	35,442	3,810	11	Idaho	52,676	21,726	41
Indiana	22,951	3,943	17	Montana	92,826	22,559	24
Iowa	35,634	1,561	4	Nevada	70,295	7,683	11
Kansas	52,127	1,344	3	New Mexico	77,669	18,060	23
Kentucky	25,282	12,161	48	Utah	52,505	15,557	30
Missouri	43,868	12,876	29	Wyoming	62,055	10,028	16
Nebraska	48,828	1,029	2	**Rocky Mountain**	**546,959**	**136,378**	**25**
Ohio	26,121	6,147	24				
Central	**241,425**	**42,871**	**18**	**Total U.S.**	**2,169,427**	**¹715,194**	**33**
Alabama	32,231	21,361	66				

(1) Of this total, 482,486,000 acres are of commercial quality (137 million acres are government owned); 20,664,000 acres are productive but reserved (land set aside by statute); 4,626,000 acres are deferred for possible reserve status; and 228,782,000 acres are unproductive or awaiting survey.

Major U.S. Public Zoological Parks

Source: World Almanac questionnaire, 1985; budget and attendance in millions. (A) park has not provided up-to-date data.

Zoo	Budget	Atten- dance	Acres	Species	Major Attractions
Albuquerque (A)	$2.0	0.4	50	281	Rain forest exhibit, reptile house.
Arizona-Sonora Desert Museum (Tucson)	2.5	0.45	11	300	Earth science center, Sonora Desert exhibit.
Bronx (N.Y.C.)	22.0	2.0	265	699	Wild Asia, children's zoo, World of Birds.
Brookfield (Chicago) (A)	14.5	1.8	200	500	Porpoise show, predator ecology, baboon island.
Buffalo (A)	2.3	0.4	24	234	Rhino yard, tropical gorilla exhibit, children's zoo.
Calgary (A)	6.5	0.75	220	325	Exotic vertebrates, prehistoric park, tropical conservatory.
Cincinnati	4.6	1.0	65	780	Children's Zoo, Insect World, World of Cats.
Cleveland	3.0	0.8	130	322	Birds of the World, African Plains.
Dallas (A)	2.4	0.6	50	507	Okapi, bongo antelope, Grevy's zebra.
Denver	3.2	0.95	76	356	Bird world, Bighorn and Dall sheep exhibit.
Detroit	7.8	0.8	122	397	Aviary, Penguinarium, Marine mammals.
Houston	2.5	2.6	50	708	Children's Zoo, Kipp aquarium.
Lincoln Park (Chicago) (A)	3.5	4.0	35	417	Great Ape House, farm in the zoo.
Los Angeles (A)	4.0	1.5	73	500	Koalas, white tigers, children's zoo.
Memphis	2.1	0.45	36	382	Zoo rides, aquarium, waterfowl.
Miami Metrozoo (A)	5.4	0.7	225	193	Open air paddocks, crocodile breeding program.
Milwaukee	7.9	1.3	185	625	White Bengal tiger, Great Ape Escape.
Minnesota	6.0	0.9	500	375	Whale and dolphin show, flying bird show, hands-on Zoolab.
National (Wash. D.C.) (A)	9.2	3.3	168	395	Lion/Tiger complex, Beaver Valley, giant pandas.
New Orleans (Audubon)	6.0	1.2	58	268	Asian Domain, Tropical Bird House, primates.
Oklahoma City	4.8	5.5	110	500	African plains, Patagonian cliffs, Galapagos Isl.
Philadelphia (A)	5.5	1.1	42	525	Reptiles, African plains, hummingbirds.
Phoenix	2.6	0.7	125	275	Arabian oryx herd, Orangutans, Arizona exhibit.
Riverbanks (Columbia, S.C.)	1.5	0.4	50	180	Natural habitat exhibits, rain forest exhibit.
St. Louis	9.37	2.0	83	630	Big cat country, herpetarium, primate house.
San Antonio	4.8	1.0	52	700	Antelopes, whooping crane, Children's Zoo.
San Diego	30.0	3.0	100	777	Southeast Asian bird and primate complex; koalas; Skyfari aerial tram.
San Diego (Wild Animal Park)	18.0	1.2	1,800	225	Large, mixed-species enclosures; exotic hooved stock.
San Francisco	3.3	1.0	75	260	Gorilla World, insect zoo, musk ox meadow, wolf woods.
Toledo (A)	2.9	0.5	30	352	Aquarium, greenhouse, botanical gardens, children's zoo.
Toronto (A)	9.4	1.1	710	413	Canadian Domain ride, polar bears, gorillas.
Washington Pk (Portland)	8.5	0.74	62	118	Alaska tundra exhibit, penguin colony, Cascade Stream and Pond.
Woodland Pk (Seattle)	3.3	0.8	90	305	African savanna, swamp & marsh exhibit.

Mammals: Orders and Major Families

Left column

Subclass Theria
Infraclass Placentalia

Family	Superfamily	Infraorder	Suborder	Order

Canidae:wolf, dog, jackal, fox — *Canoids have long snouts and unretractable claws.*

Ursidae:bear, giant panda
Procyonidae:coati, racoon, lesser panda — Canoidea
Mustelidae:badger, weasel, skunk, otter — Fissipedia (toe-footed)

Felidae:cat, leopard, lion, tiger, cheetah
Hyaenidae:hyena, aardwolf — Feloidea — *Feloids have retractable claws.* — *Most carnivora also eat some plants and insects.* — Carnivora
Viverridae:mongoose, civet

Otariidae:eared seals, sea lion
Odobenidae:walrus — Pinnipedia (fin-footed)
Phocidae:earless seals

Suidae:pig — Suina
Tayassuidae:peccary — Suiformes
Hippopotamidae:hippopotamus — Ancodonta

Camelidae:camel, llama — Tylopoda

Giraffidae:giraffe, okapi
Cervidae:deer, moose, reindeer, wapiti (elk) — *The artiodactyla have an even number of toes.*

Antilocapridae:prong-horn — Artiodactyla

Subfamily

Bovinae:cattle, eland, kudu, bison, yak
Hippotraginae:sable, oryx, waterbuck — Ruminantia
Acelaphinae:hartebeest, wildebeest (gnu) — Bovoidea — Family Bovidae — *All ruminants have 4-chamber stomachs and chew cuds.*
Antilopinae:gazelle, springbok, saiga
Caprinae:sheep, goat, musk ox

Family

Equidae:horse, donkey, zebra — Hippomorpha — *The perissodactyla have an odd number of toes.*

Tapiridae:tapir — Perissodactyla
Rhinocerotidae:rhinoceros — Ceratomorpha

Aplodontidae:mountain beaver
Sciuridae:chipmunk, squirrel, marmot — Sciuromorpha

Cricetidae:field mice, lemming, muskrat, hamster, gerbil
Muridae:rat, Old World mice — *Rodent suborders are distinguished by the placement of a major jaw muscle.* — Myomorpha
Heteromyidae: New World mice
Geomyidae:gopher
Dipodidae:jerboa — *Rodents are the most numerous of all mammals.* — Rodentia

Chinchillidae:chinchilla
Dasyproctidae:agouti, paca — Caviomorpha

Erethizontidae: New World porcupine

Hystricidae: Old World porcupine
Castoridae:beaver

Bats - various families — Chiroptera

Right column

Subclass Theria
Infraclass Placentalia

Family	Superfamily	Infraorder	Suborder	Order

Leporidae:rabbit, hare
Ochotonidae:pika — Lagomorpha

Manidae:pangolin — Pholidata

Erinaceidae:hedgehog
Talpidae:mole — Insectivora
Saricidae:some shrews

Dasypodidae:armadillo — Loricata
Bradypodidae:sloth — Pilosa — Edentate (toothless)
Myrmecophagidae:hairy anteater — Vermilingua

Physeteridae:sperm whale
Monodontidae:narwhal, beluga — Odontoceti (toothed)
Phocoenidae:porpoise
Delphinidae:dolphin, killer whale — Cetacea
Eschrichtiidae:gray whale
Balaenidae:right whale — Mysticeti (baleen)
Balaenopteridae:hump-back whale

Manatee, dugong — Sirenea

Elephantidae:elephant — Proboscidea

Tupaiidae:tree shrew
Lemuridae:lemur
Daubentoniidae:aye-aye — *The prosimians usually have longer snouts than anthropoids.* — Prosimii
Lorisidae:loris, potto
Tarsiidae:tarsier — Primates

Callitrichidae:marmoset
Cebidae: New World monkeys (flat-nosed)
Cercopithecidae:baboon, Old World monkeys (long-nosed, bare buttocks) — Anthropoidea
Hylobatidae:gibbon — *Most primates have opposable thumbs; all but man have opposable big toes.*
Pongidae (great apes): gorilla, chimpanzee, orangutan
Hominidae:human

Infraclass Marsupialia

Dasyuridae:mouse- and ratlike, Tasmanian devil
Notoryctidae:molelike — Dasyuroidea
Thylacinidae:wolflike — Marsupicanivora

Didelphidae: American opossums — Didelphoidea

Caenolestidae:ratlike So. America only — Paucituberculata

Peramelidae:bandicoot — Peramalina

Burramyidae:mouse- and squirrellike
Macropodidae:kangaroo, wallaby — Phalangeroidea
Petauridae:squirrellike, some Australian possums
Phalangeridae:cuscus, some Australian possums — Diprodonta

Tarsipedidae:honey possum — Tarsipedoidea

Vombatidae:wombat
Phascolarctidae:koala — Vombatoidea

Subclass Prototheria

Ornithorhynchidae:duck-billed platypus
Tachyglossidae:echidna (spiny anteater) — Monotremata

Some Endangered Species in the World

Source: U.S. Fish and Wildlife Service, U.S. Interior Department; as of July, 1984

Common name	Scientific name	Range
Mammals		
Chimpanzee*	Pan troglodytes	W. & Central Africa
African elephant*	Loxodonta africana	Africa
Asian elephant	Elephas maximas	S. Central & E. Africa
Bactrian camel	Camelus bactrianus	Mongolia, China
Saudi Arabian gazelle	Gazella dorcas saudiya	Israel, Iraq, Jordan, Syria, Arabian Peninsula
Gorilla	Gorilla gonilla	Central & W. Africa
Red kangaroo*	Macropus (=Megaleia rufus)	Australia
Leopard**	Panthera pardus	Africa, Asia
Howler monkey*	Alouatta pigra	Mexico to S. America
Giant panda	Ailuropoda melanoleuca	China
Tiger	Panthera tigris	Asia
Gray whale	Eschrichtius robustus	N. Pacific Ocean
Wild yak	Bos grunniens	China (Tibet), India
Mountain zebra	Equus zebra zebra	South Africa
Birds		
Hummingbird	Glaucisdohrni	Brazil
Indigo macaw	Anodorhynchus leari	Brazil
West African ostrich	Struthio camelus spatzi	Spanish Sahara
Golden parakeet	Aratinga guarouba	Brazil
Australian parrot	Geopsittacus occidentalis	Australia

*Threatened rather than endangered.   **Threatened in South Africa.

Some Endangered Species in North America

Source: U.S. Fish and Wildlife Service, U.S. Interior Department; as of July, 1984

Common name	Scientific name	Range
Mammals		
Virginia big-eared bat	Plecotus townsendii virginianus	U.S. (Ky., W.V., Va.)
Brown or grizzly bear	Ursus arctos horribilis	U.S. (48 conterminous states)
Eastern cougar	Felis concolor cougar	Eastern N.A.
Columbian white-tailed deer	Odocoileus virginianus leucurus	U.S. (Wash., Ore.)
San Joaquin kit fox	Vulpes macrotis mutica	U.S. (Cal.)
Ocelot	Felis pardalis	U.S. (Tex., Ariz.) C. and S. America
Florida panther*	Felis concolor coryi	U.S. (La., Ark. east to S.C., Fla.)
Utah prairie dog*	Cynomys parvidens	U.S. (Ut.)
Morro Bay kangaroo rat	Dipodomys heermanni morroensis	U.S. (Cal.)
Delmarva Peninsula fox squirrel	Sciurus niger cinereus	U.S. (DelMarVa Peninsula to SE Pa.)
Red wolf	Canis rufus	U.S. (Southeast to central Tex.)
Birds		
Masked bobwhite (quail)	Colinus virginianus ridgwayi	U.S. (Ariz.), Mexico (Sonora)
California condor	Gymnogyps californianus	U.S. (Ore., Cal.), Mexico (Baja Calif.)
Whooping crane	Grus americana	U.S. (Rky. Mntns. east to Carolinas), Canada, Mexico
Eskimo curlew	Numenius borealis	Alaska and N. Canada to Argentina
Bald eagle**	Haliaeetus leucocephalus	U.S. (most states), Canada
American peregrine falcon	Falco peregrinus anatum	Canada to Mexico
Aleutian Canada goose	Branta canadensis leucopareia	U.S. (Alaska, Cal., Ore., Wash.), Japan
Brown pelican	Pelecanus occidentalis	U.S. (Carolinas to Tex., Cal.), West Indies, C. and S. America
Attwater's greater prairie-chicken	Tympanuchus cupido attwateri	U.S. (Tex.)
Bachman's warbler (wood)	Vermivora bachmanii	U.S. (Southeastern), Cuba
Kirtland's warbler (wood)	Dendroica kirtlandii	U.S., Canada, Bahama Is.
Ivory-billed woodpecker	Campephilus principalis	U.S. (Southcentral and Southeast), Cuba
Reptiles		
American alligator**	Alligator mississippiensis	U.S. (Southeast)
American crocodile	Crocodylus acutus	U.S. (Fla.), Mexico, South and Central America, Caribbean
Island night lizard*	Xantusia (=Klauberina) riversiana	U.S. (Cal.)
Eastern indigo snake*	Drymarchon corais couperi	U.S. (Ala., Fla., Ga., Miss., S.C.)

*Threatened rather than endangered.   **Endangered except where listed as threatened.

Young of Animals Have Special Names

The young of many animals, birds and fish have come to be called by special names. A young eel, for example, is an elver. Many young animals, of course, are often referred to simply as infants, babies, younglets, or younglings.

bunny: rabbit.
calf: cattle, elephant, antelope, rhino, hippo, whale, etc.

cheeper: grouse, partridge, quail.
chick, chicken: fowl.
cockerel: rooster.

codling, sprag: codfish.
colt: horse (male).
cub: lion, bear, shark, fox, etc.

cygnet: swan.
duckling: duck.
eaglet: eagle.
elver: eel.
eyas: hawk, others.
fawn: deer.
filly: horse (female).
fingerling: fish generally.
flapper: wild fowl.
fledgling: birds generally.
foal: horse, zebra, others.
fry: fish generally.

gosling: goose.
heifer: cow.
joey: kangaroo, others.
kid: goat.
kit: fox, beaver, rabbit, cat.
kitten, kitty, catling: cats, other fur-bearers.
lamb, lambkin, cosset, hog: sheep.
leveret: hare.
nestling: birds generally.
owlet: owl.
parr, smolt, grilse: salmon.

piglet, shoat, farrow, suckling: pig.
polliwog, tadpole: frog.
poult: turkey.
pullet: hen.
pup: dog, seal, sea lion, fox.
puss, pussy: cat.
spike, blinker, tinker: mackerel.
squab: pigeon.
squeaker: pigeon, others.
whelp: dog, tiger, beasts of prey.
yearling: cattle, sheep, horse, etc.

Speeds of Animals

Source: Natural History magazine, March 1974.
Copyright © The American Museum of Natural History, 1974.

Animal	Mph	Animal	Mph	Animal	Mph
Cheetah	70	Mongolian wild ass	40	Human	27.89
Pronghorn antelope	61	Greyhound	39.35	Elephant	25
Wildebeest	50	Whippet	35.50	Black mamba snake	20
Lion	50	Rabbit (domestic)	35	Six-lined race runner	18
Thomson's gazelle	50	Mule deer	35	Wild turkey	15
Quarterhorse	47.5	Jackal	35	Squirrel	12
Elk	45	Reindeer	32	Pig (domestic)	11
Cape hunting dog	45	Giraffe	32	Chicken	9
Coyote	43	White-tailed deer	30	Spider (Tegenaria atrica)	1.17
Gray fox	42	Wart hog	30	Giant tortoise	0.17
Hyena	40	Grizzly bear	30	Three-toed sloth	0.15
Zebra	40	Cat (domestic)	30	Garden snail	0.03

Most of these measurements are for maximum speeds over approximate quarter-mile distances. Exceptions are the lion and elephant, whose speeds were clocked in the act of charging; the whippet, which was timed over a 200-yard course; the cheetah over a 100-yard distance; man for a 15-yard segment of a 100-yard run (of 13.6 seconds); and the black mamba, six-lined race runner, spider, giant tortoise, three-toed sloth, and garden snail, which were measured over various small distances.

Gestation, Longevity, and Incubation of Animals

Longevity figures were supplied by Ronald T. Reuther. They refer to animals in captivity; the potential life span of animals is rarely attained in nature. Maximum longevity figures are from the Biology Data Book, 1972. Figures on gestation and incubation are averages based on estimates by leading authorities.

Animal		Gestation (day)	Average longevity (years)	Maximun longevity (yrs., mos.)	Animal	Gestation (day)	Average longevity (years)	Maximum longevity (yrs., mos.)
Ass		365	12	35-10	Leopard	98	12	19-4
Baboon		187	20	35-7	Lion	100	15	25-1
Bear:	Black	219	18	36-10	Monkey (rhesus)	164	15	—
	Grizzly	225	25	—	Moose	240	12	—
	Polar	240	20	34-8	Mouse (meadow)	21	3	—
Beaver		122	5	20-6	Mouse (dom. white)	19	3	3-6
Buffalo (American)		278	15	—	Opossum (American)	14-17	1	—
Bactrian camel		406	12	29-5	Pig (domestic)	112	10	27
Cat (domestic)		63	12	28	Puma	90	12	19
Chimpanzee		231	20	44-6	Rabbit (domestic)	31	5	13
Chipmunk		31	6	8	Rhinoceros (black)	450	15	—
Cow		284	15	30	Rhinoceros (white)	—	20	—
Deer (white-tailed)		201	8	17-6	Sea lion (California)	350	12	28
Dog (domestic)		61	12	20	Sheep (domestic)	154	12	20
Elephant (African)		—	35	60	Squirrel (gray)	44	10	—
Elephant (Asian)		645	40	70	Tiger	105	16	26-3
Elk		250	15	26-6	Wolf (maned)	63	5	—
Fox (red)		52	7	14	Zebra (Grant's)	365	15	—
Giraffe		425	10	33-7				
Goat (domestic)		151	8	18	**Incubation time (days)**			
Gorilla		257	20	39-4	Chicken			21
Guinea pig		68	4	7-6	Duck			30
Hippopotamus		238	25	—	Goose			30
Horse		330	20	46	Pigeon			18
Kangaroo		42	7	—	Turkey			26

A Collection of Animal Collectives

The English language boasts an abundance of names to describe groups of things, particularly pairs or aggregations of animals. Some of these words have fallen into comparative disuse, but many of them are still in service, helping to enrich the vocabularies of those who like their language to be precise, who tire of hearing a group referred to as "a bunch of," or who enjoy the sound of words that aren't overworked.

band of gorillas
bed of clams, oysters
bevy of quail, swans
brace of ducks
brood of chicks
cast of hawks
cete of badgers
charm of goldfinches
chattering of choughs
cloud of gnats

clowder of cats
clutch of chicks
clutter of cats
colony of ants
congregation of plovers
covey of quail, partridge
crash of rhinoceri
cry of hounds
down of hares
drift of swine

drove of cattle, sheep
exaltation of larks
flight of birds
flock of sheep, geese
gaggle of geese
gam of whales
gang of elks
grist of bees
herd of elephants
horde of gnats

husk of hares
kindle or kendle of kittens
knot of toads
leap of leopards
leash of greyhounds, foxes
litter of pigs
mob of kangaroos
murder of crows
muster of peacocks
mute of hounds

nest of vipers	school of fish	sounder of boars, swine	troop of kangaroos,
nest, nide of pheasants	sedge or siege of cranes	span of mules	monkeys
pack of hounds, wolves	shoal of fish, pilchards	spring of teals	volery of birds
pair of horses	skein of geese	swarm of bees	watch of nightingales
pod of whales, seals	skulk of foxes	team of ducks, horses	wing of plovers
pride of lions	sleuth of bears	tribe or trip of goats	yoke of oxen

Major Venomous Animals

Snakes

Coral snake - 2 to 4 ft. long, in Americas south of Canada; bite is nearly painless; very slow onset of paralysis, difficulty breathing; mortality high without antivenin.

Rattlesnake - 2 to 8 ft. long, throughout W. Hemisphere. Rapid onset of symptoms of severe pain, swelling; mortality low, but amputation of affected limb is sometimes necessary; antivenin. Probably higher mortality rate for Mojave rattler.

Cottonmouth water moccasin - less than 5 ft. long, wetlands of southern U.S. from Virginia to Texas. Rapid onset of symptoms of severe pain, swelling; mortality low, but tissue destruction can be extensive; antivenin.

Copperhead - less than 4 ft. long, from New England to Texas; pain and swelling; very seldom fatal.

Bushmaster - up to 9 ft. long, jungles of C. and S. America; few bites occur, but mortality rate is high.

Barba Amarilla or Fer-de-lance - up to 7 ft. long, from tropical Mexico to Brazil; severe tissue damage common; moderate mortality; antivenin.

Asian pit vipers - from 2 to 5 ft. long throughout Asia; reactions and mortality vary but most bites cause tissue damage and mortality is generally low.

Sharp-nosed pit viper or One Hundred Pace Snake - up to 5 ft. long, in eastern China and Indo-China; the most toxic of Asian pit vipers; very rapid onset of swelling and tissue damage, internal bleeding; moderate mortality; antivenin.

Boomslang - under 6 ft. long, in African savannahs; rapid onset of nausea and dizziness, often followed by slight recovery and then sudden death from internal hemorrhaging; bites rare, mortality high; antivenin.

European vipers - from 1 to 3 ft. long; bleeding and tissue damage; mortality low; antivenins.

Puff adder - up to 5 ft. long, fat; south of the Sahara and throughout the Middle East; rapid large swelling, great pain, dizziness; moderate mortality often from internal bleeding; antivenin.

Gaboon viper - over 6 ft. long, fat; 2-inch fangs; south of the Sahara; massive tissue damage, internal bleeding; few recorded bites.

Saw-scaled or carpet viper - up to 2 ft. long, in dry areas from India to Africa; severe bleeding, fever; high mortality, causes more human fatalities than any other snake; antivenin.

Desert horned viper - in dry areas of Africa and western Asia; swelling and tissue damage; low mortality; antivenin.

Russell's viper or tic-palonga - over 5 ft. long, throughout Asia; internal bleeding; moderate mortality rate; bite reports common; antivenin.

Black mamba - up to 14 ft. long, fast-moving; S. and C. Africa; rapid onset of dizziness, difficulty breathing, erratic heart-beat; mortality high, nears 100% without antivenin.

Kraits - in S. Asia; rapid onset of sleepiness; numbness; up to 50% mortality even with antivenin treatment.

Common or Asian cobra - 4 to 8 ft. long, throughout S. Asia; considerable tissue damage, sometimes paralysis; mortality probably not more than 10%; antivenin.

King cobra - up to 16 ft. long, throughout S. Asia; rapid swelling, dizziness, loss of consciousness, difficulty breathing, erratic heart-beat; mortality varies sharply with amount of venom involved, most bites involve non-fatal amounts; antivenin.

Yellow or Cape cobra - 7 ft. long, in southern Africa; most toxic venom of any cobra; rapid onset of swelling, breathing and cardiac difficulties; mortality high without treatment; antivenin.

Ringhals, or spitting, cobra - 5 ft. and 7 ft. long; southern Africa; squirt venom through holes in front of fangs as a defense; venom is severely irritating and can cause blindness.

Australian brown snakes - very slow onset of symptoms of cardiac or respiratory distress; moderate mortality; antivenin.

Tiger snake - 2 to 6 ft. long, S. Australia; pain, numbness, mental disturbances with rapid onset of paralysis; may be the most deadly of all land snakes though antivenin is quite effective.

Death adder - less than 3 ft. long, Australia; rapid onset of faintness, cardiac and respiratory distress; at least 50% mortality without antivenin.

Taipan - up to 11 ft. long, in Australia and New Guinea; rapid paralysis with severe breathing difficulty; mortality nears 100% without antivenin.

Sea snakes - throughout Pacific, Indian oceans except NE Pacific; almost painless bite, variety of muscle pain, paralysis; mortality rate low, many bites are not envenomed; some antivenins.

Notes: Not all snake bites by venomous snakes are actually envenomed. Any animal bite, however, carries the danger of tetanus and anyone suffering a venomous snake bite should seek medical attention. Antivenins are not certain cures; they are only an aid in the treatment of bites. Mortality rates above are for envenomed bites; low mortality, up to 2% result in death; moderate, 2–5%; high, 5–15%. Even when the victim recovers fully, prolonged hospitalization and extensive medical procedures are usually required.

Lizards

Gila monster - up to 24 inches long with heavy body and tail, in high desert in southwest U.S. and N. Mexico; immediate severe pain followed by vomiting, thirst, difficulty swallowing, weakness approaching paralysis; no recent mortality.

Mexican beaded lizard - similar to Gila monster, Mexican west-coast; reaction and mortality rate similar to Gila monster.

Insects

Ants, bees, wasps, hornets, etc. Global distribution. Usual reaction is piercing pain in area of sting. Not directly fatal, except in cases of massive multiple stings. Many people suffer allergic reactions - swelling, rashes, partial paralysis –and a few may die within minutes from severe sensitivity to the venom (anaphylactic shock).

Spiders, scorpions

Black widow - small, round-bodied with hour-glass marking; the widow and its relatives are found around the world in tropical and temperate zones; sharp pain, weakness, clammy skin, muscular rigidity, breathing difficulty and, in small children, convulsions; low mortality; antivenin.

Brown recluse or fiddleback - small, oblong body; throughout U.S.; slow onset of pain and severe ulceration at place of bite; in severe cases fever, nausea, and stomach cramps; ulceration may last months; very low mortality.

Atrax **spiders** - several varieties, often large, in Australia; slow onset of breathing, circulation difficulties; low mortality.

Tarantulas - large, hairy spiders found around the world; American tarantulas, and probably all others, are **harmless**, though their bite may cause some pain and swelling.

Scorpions - crab-like body with stinger in tail; various sizes, many varieties throughout tropical and subtropical areas; various symptoms may include severe pain spreading from the wound, numbness, severe emotional agitation, cramps; severe reactions include vomiting, diarrhea, respiratory failure; moderate to high mortality, particularly in children; antivenins.

Sea Life

Sea wasps - jellyfish, with tentacles up to 30 ft. long, in the S. Pacific; very rapid onset of circulatory problems; high mortality largely because of speed of toxic reaction; antivenin.

Portuguese man-of-war - jellyfish-like, with tentacles up to 70 ft. long, in most warm water areas; immediate severe pain; not fatal, though shock may cause death in a rare case.

Octopi - global distribution, usually in warm waters; all varieties produce venom but only a few can cause death; rapid onset of paralysis with breathing difficulty.

Stingrays - several varieties of differing sizes, found in tropical and temperate seas and some fresh water; severe pain, rapid onset of nausea, vomiting, breathing difficulties; wound area may ulcerate, gangrene may appear; seldom fatal.

Stonefish - brownish fish which lies motionless as a rock on bottom in shallow water; throughout S. Pacific and Indian oceans; extraordinary pain, rapid paralysis; low mortality.

Cone-shells - molluscs in small, beautiful shells in the S. Pacific and Indian oceans; shoot barbs into victims; paralysis; low mortality.

American Kennel Club Registrations

Breed	Rank 1984	1984	Rank 1983	1983
Cocker Spaniels	1	94,803	1	92,836
Poodles	2	87,750	2	90,250
Labrador Retrievers	3	71,235	3	67,389
German Shepherd Dogs	4	59,450	5	65,073
Golden Retrievers	5	54,490	6	52,525
Doberman Pinschers	6	51,414	4	66,184
Beagles	7	40,052	7	39,992
Miniature Schnauzers	8	37,694	8	37,820
Shetland Sheepdogs	9	33,164	10	33,375
Dachshunds	10	33,068	9	33,514
Chow Chows	11	32,777	12	27,815
Yorkshire Terriers	12	29,342	11	26,350
Lhasa Apsos	13	27,910	13	27,087
Shih Tzu	14	25,588	14	23,308
English Springer Span.	15	21,660	15	22,626
Pomeranians	16	21,207	18	19,961
Siberian Huskies	17	20,889	16	21,237
Collies	18	19,261	17	20,789
Basset Hounds	19	18,710	19	19,042
Boxers	20	17,745	22	17,365
Pekingese	21	17,653	21	17,611
Chihuahuas	22	17,250	23	16,946
Rottweilers	23	17,193	24	13,265
Brittanys	24	17,046	20	18,433
Boston Terriers	25	12,205	25	11,855
Great Danes	26	10,403	26	11,352
Maltese	27	9,367	28	8,796
German Shorthaired Pointers	28	9,018	27	10,126
Samoyeds	29	8,032	29	7,918
West Highland White Terriers	30	7,520	31	7,540
Pugs	31	7,134	35	6,544
Bulldogs	32	7,004	34	6,943
Alaskan Malamutes	33	6,748	33	7,044
Keeshonden	34	6,359	36	6,214
Dalmatians	35	6,354	39	6,032
Airedale Terriers	36	6,169	32	7,149
Old English Sheepdogs	37	6,124	30	7,658
Cairn Terriers	38	5,892	37	6,154
Scottish Terriers	39	5,538	40	5,857
Irish Setters	40	4,553	38	6,114
Chesapeake Bay Retr.	41	4,499	42	4,512
Bichons Frises	42	4,439	47	4,038
Akitas	43	4,235	48	3,865
Weimaraners	44	4,107	41	4,578
Norwegian Elkhounds	45	3,916	43	4,308
St. Bernards	46	3,797	45	4,052
Fox Terriers (Smooth & Wire)	47	3,646	46	3,878
Afghan Hounds	48	3,225	44	4,063
Miniature Pinschers	49	2,784	51	2,554
Pembroke Welsh Corgis	50	2,768	49	2,757
Silky Terriers	51	2,567	50	2,641
Newfoundlands	52	2,297	52	2,428
Great Pyrenees	53	1,836	58	1,590
Bouviers des Flandres	54	1,827	53	1,903
Schipperkes	55	1,747	55	1,758
Vizslas	56	1,730	54	1,859
American Staffordshire Terriers	57	1,659	56	1,630
Mastiffs	58	1,548	59	1,580
Rhodesian Ridgebacks	59	1,450	57	1,614
Basenjis	60	1,421	60	1,473
English Cocker Spaniels	61	1,371	61	1,393
Borzois	62	1,344	62	1,383
Whippets	63	1,337	63	1,348
Bloodhounds	64	1,247	64	1,336
Bull Terriers	65	1,191	65	1,195
English Setters	66	1,066	70	1,012
Soft-Coated Wheaten Terriers	66	1,066	66	1,159
Bullmastiffs	68	1,050	71	997
German Wirehaired Pointers	69	1,037	69	1,098
Irish Wolfhounds	70	1,018	68	1,109
Gordon Setters	71	1,008	67	1,142
Bearded Collies	72	858	72	895
Giant Schnauzers	73	802	73	771
Papillons	74	772	78	714
Belgian Sheepdogs	75	710	80	677
Australian Cattle Dogs	76	708	79	709
Welsh Terriers	77	660	76	724
Australian Terriers	78	652	74	747
Salukis	79	642	83	649
Italian Greyhounds	80	609	85	640
Bernese Mountain Dogs	81	594	89	482
Standard Schnauzers	82	561	82	650
Kerry Blue Terriers	83	558	84	648
Tibetan Terriers	84	552	86	514
Pointers	85	439	90	434
Manchester Terriers	86	429	87	510
Belgian Tervuren	87	422	88	501
Japanese Chin	88	402	91	426
Cardigan Welsh Corgis	89	360	92	360
Flat-Coated Retrievers	90	301	98	273
Irish Terriers	91	299	104	228
Kuvaszok	92	296	95	311
Lakeland Terriers	93	289	101	239
Staffordshire Bull Terriers	94	281	102	238
Border Terriers	95	276	99	265
American Water Span.	96	268	93	339
Pulik	97	265	96	300
Briards	98	259	97	288
Bedlington Terriers	99	254	94	334
Norwich Terriers	100	248	106	216
French Bulldogs	101	240	107	201
Welsh Springer Spaniels	102	239	105	227
Greyhounds	103	222	115	125
Skye Terriers	104	204	108	186
Brussels Griffons	105	199	103	237
Komondorok	106	192	112	138
Black and Tan Coonhounds	107	191	100	240
Portuguese Water Dogs	108	182	77	721
Scottish Deerhounds	109	173	110	162
Dandie Dinmont Terriers	110	162	109	175
Norfolk Terriers	111	152	111	151
Affenpinschers	112	140	119	98
English Toy Spaniels	113	134	113	134
Pharaoh Hounds	114	130	81	673
Tibetan Spaniels	115	113	75	743
Sealyham Terriers	116	111	118	107
Irish Water Spaniels	117	105	121	79
Clumber Spaniels	118	102	114	126
Ibizan Hounds	119	98	117	109
Wirehaired Pointing Griffons	120	84	116	113
Belgian Malinois	121	74	122	64
Field Spaniels	122	61	123	53
Curly-Coated Retrievers	123	54	120	86
American Foxhounds	124	42	124	38
Otter Hounds	125	23	125	27
Sussex Spaniels	125	23	125	27
English Foxhounds	127	22	128	18
Harriers	128	19	127	26
Total Registrations:		**1,071,299**		**1,085,248**

Dogs Registered by Groups	1984	1983
Sporting breeds	289,299	287,400
Hound breeds	108,350	111,249
Working breeds	149,850	161,950
Terrier breeds	74,950	77,150
Toy breeds	135,150	128,700
Non-sporting breeds	187,450	183,450
Herding breeds	126,250	135,349

Cat Breeds

There are 27 cat breeds recognized: abyssinian, american shorthair, balinese, birman, bombay, burmese, colorpoint shorthair, egyptian mau, exotic shorthair, havana brown, himalayan, japanese bobtail, korat, leopard cat, lilac foreign shorthair, maine coon cat, manx, ocicat, oriental shorthair, persian, rex, russian blue, scottish fold, siamese, sphynx, turkish angora, wirehair shorthair.

Giant Trees of the U.S.

Source: The American Forestry Association, Washington, D.C.

There are approximately 748 different species of trees native to the continental U.S., including a few imports that have become naturalized to the extent of reproducing themselves in the wild state.

The oldest living trees in the world are reputed to be the bristlecone pines, the majority of which are found growing on the arid crags of California's White Mts. Some of them are estimated to be more than 4,600 years old. The largest known bristlecone pine is the "Patriarch," believed to be 1,500 years old. The oldest known redwoods are about 3,500 years old.

Recognition as the National Champion of each species is determined by total mass of each tree, based on this formula: the circumference in inches as measured at a point 4 1/2 feet above the ground plus the total height of the tree in feet plus 1/4 of the average crown spread in feet. Trees are compared on the basis of this formula. Trees within five points of each other are declared co-champions. The Giant Sequoia champion has the largest circumference, 83 ft. 2 in., Gallberry Holly the smallest, 5 in. Following is a small selection of the 661 trees registered with the American Forestry Assn.

(Figure in parentheses is year of most recent measurement)

Species	Height (ft.)	Location
Acacia, Koa (1969)	140	Kau, Ha.
Ailanthus, Tree-of-Heaven (1972)	64	Long Island, N.Y.
Alder, European (1982)	70	Princeton, Ill.
Apple, So. Crab (1981)	35.5	Swannanoa, N.C.
Ash, Blue (1970)	86	Danville, Ky.
Bald Cypress, Common (1981)	83	St. Francisville, La.
Basswood, Amer. (1983)	101	Grand Traverse Co., MI
Bayberry, Pacific (1972)	38	Siuslaw Natl. Forest, Ore.
Beech, American (1984)	130	Ashtabula Co., OH
Birch, River (1983)	86	Anne Arundel Co., Md.
Birch, Yellow (1983)	76	Deer Isle, Me.
Blackbead, Catclaw (1976)	88	Sarasota, Fla.
Blackhaw, Rusty (1961)	25	nr. Washington, Ark.
Bladdernut, Amer. (1972)	36	nr. Utica, Mich.
Boxelder (1976)	110	Lenawee Co., Mich.
Buckeye, Painted (1984)	144	Union County, Ga.
Buckthorn, Cascara (1977)	35	Coos County, Ore.
Buckthorn, Cascara (1977)	37	Seaside, Ore.
Buckwheat-tree (1981)	44	Wash. County, Fla.
Buffaloberry, Silver (1975)	22	Malheur Co., Ore.
Bumelia, Gum (1977)	80	Robertson Co., Tex.
Buttonbush, Common (1977)	23	nr. High Springs, Fla.
Cajeput Tree (1983)	83	Davie, FL
Camphor-tree (1977)	72	Hardee Co., Fla.
Casuarina, Horsetail (1968)	89	Olowalo, Maui, Ha.
Catalpa, Northern (1984)	98	Lansing, MI
Cedar, Port-Orford (1972)	219	Siskiyou Natl. Forest, Ore.
Cercocarpus, Birchleaf (1972)	34	Central Point, Ore.
Cherry, Black (1984)	93	Allegan Co., MI
Chestnut, American (1979)	82	Oregon City, Ore.
Chinaberry (1967)	75	Koahe, So. Kuona, Ha.
Chinkapin, Giant (1979)	75	Cottage Grove, Ore.
Chokecherry, Common (1982)	67	Ada, Mich.
Coconut (1979)	92.5	Hilo, Ha.
Coffeetree, Kentucky (1976)	110	Van Buren Co., Mich.
Cottonwood, Black (1982)	148	Rainbow Falls St. Park, Wash.
Cypress, Monterey (1975)	97	Brookings, Ore.
Dahoon (1975)	72	Osceola For., Fla.
Desert-Willow (1976)	56	Gila Co., Ariz.
Devil's-walkingstick (1982)	51	San Felasco Hammock, Fla.
Devilwood (1972)	37	Mayo, Fla.
Dogwood, Pacific (1975)	50	nr. Clatskanie, Ore.
Douglas-fir, Coast (1975)	221	Olympic Natl. Park, Wash.
Doveplum (1965)	45	Miami, Fla.
False-Mastic (1975)	70	Lignumvitae Key, Fla.
Fig, Florida Strangler (1973)	80	Old Cutler Hammock, Fla.
Fir, Noble (1972)	278	Gifford Pinchot Natl. Forest, Wash.
Gumbo-limbo (1973)	50	Homestead, Fla.
Hackberry, Common (1972)	118	Allegany Co., Mich.
Hawthorn, Scarlet (1980)	37	Clinton, New York
Hemlock, Western (1978)	195	Tillamook, Ore.
Hercules-club (1961)	38	Little Rock, Ark.
Hickory, Pignut (1972)	125	nr. Brunswick, Ga.
Holly, American (1983)	50	St. Mary's City, Md.
Honeylocust, Thornless (1976)	130	Washtenaw Co., Mich.
Hophornbeam, Eastern (1976)	73	Grand Traverse Co., Mich.
Hoptree, Common (1982)	35	Ada, Mich.
Hornbeam, American (1982)	69	Milton, N.Y.
Joshua-tree (1967)	32	San Bernardino Natl. Forest, Cal.
Juniper, Western (1983)	86	Stanislaus Natl. Forest, CA

Species	Height (ft.)	Location
Larch, Western (1980)	175	Libby, Mont.
Laurelcherry, Carolina (1972)	44	Dellwood, Fla.
Lebbek (1968)	65	Lahaina, Maui, Ha.
Lobolly-Bay (1983)	94	Ocala Natl. Forest, FL
Locust, Black (1974)	96	Dansville, N.Y.
Lysiloma, Bahama (1973)	79	Homestead, Fla.
Madrone, Pacific (1955)	79	Ettersburg, CA
Magnolia, Cucumber tree (1982)	94	North Canton, Oh.
Mangrove, Red (1975)	75	Everglades Natl. Pk., Fla.
Maple, Red (1984)	179	St. Clair Co., MI
Mesquite, Velvet (1952)	55	Coronado Natl. Forest, Ariz.
Mountain-Ash, Showy (1982)	58	nr. Gould City, Mich.
Mountain-Laurel (1981)	28	Oconee County, S.C.
Mulberry, White (1982)	55	Leavenworth, Ks.
Oak, Pin (1978)	134	Smithland, Ky.
Oak, Scarlet (1978)	150	Maud, Ala.
Osage-Orange (1969)	51	nr. Brookneal, VA
Palmetto, Cabbage (1978)	90	Highlands Hammock State Pk., Fla.
Paloverde, Blue (1976)	53	Riverside Co., Cal.
Paulownia, Royal (1969)	105	Philadelphia, Pa.
Pawpaw, Common (1981)	56	Pickens County, S.C.
Pear (1976)	57	Clawson, Mich.
Pecan (1983)	130	Warren Co., Miss.
Peppertree (1973)	47	San Juan Capistrano, Cal.
Pinckneya (1982)	32	nr. Orange Springs, Fla.
Pine, Ponderosa (1974)	223	Plumas, Cal.
Plum, American (1972)	35	Oakland Co., Mich.
Poison Sumac (1972)	20	Robin's Island, N.Y.
Pondcypress (1972)	135	nr. Newton, Ga.
Poplar, Balsam (1982)	98	South Egremont, Mass.
Possumhaw (1981)	42	Congaree Swamp, S.C.
Redbay (1972)	58	Randolph City, Ga.
Redwood, Coast (1972)	362	Humboldt Redwoods State Park, Cal.
Royalpalm, Florida (1973)	80	Homestead, Fla.
Sassafras (1972)	100	Owensboro, Ky.
Seagrape (1972)	57	Miami, Fla.
Sequoia, Giant (1975)	275	Sequoia Natl. Pk., Cal.
Serviceberry, Downy (1984)	63	Barry Co., MI
Silktree (1971)	41	Gilmer, Tex.
Silverbell, Two-wing (1982)	66.5	Ashville, S.C.
Smoketree, American (1984)	35	West Lafayette, IN
Soapberry, Western (1984)	72	Coyle, OK
Sourwood (1972)	118	nr. Robbinsville, N.C.
Sparkleberry Tree (1977)	30	Pensacola, Fla.
Spruce, Sitka (1973)	216	Seaside, Ore.
Sugarberry (1976)	78	Society Hills, S.C.
Sumac, Shining (1974)	55	Grenada Co., Miss.
Sweetleaf (1972)	55	Tallahassee, Fla.
Sycamore, Cal. (1945)	116	nr. Santa Barbara, Cal.
Tamarisk (1981)	34	Columbus, N.M.
Tesota (1972)	32	nr. Quartzsite, Ariz.
Trifoliate-Orange (1984)	14	Aiken Co., SC
Tupelo, Black (1969)	117	Harrison Co., Tex.
(1971)	139	nr. Houston, Tex.
Walnut, Cal. (1973)	116	nr. Chico, Cal.
Willow, Crack (1972)	112	nr. Utica, Mich.
Winterberry, Common (1971)	40	Wildwood, Fla.
Yaupon (1972)	45	nr. Devers, Tex.
Yellow-Poplar (1972)	124	Bedford, Va.
Yew, Pacific (1969)	60	nr. Mineral, Wash.
Yucca, Aloe (1972)	15	Lakeland, Fla.

TRADE AND TRANSPORTATION
Notable Steamships and Motorships
Source: Lloyd's Register of Shipping as of June 1985

Gross tonnage is a measurement of enclosed space (1 gross ton = 100 cu. ft.) Deadweight tonnage is the weight (in tons of 1,000 kg) of cargo, fuel, etc., which a vessel is designed to carry safely.

Oil Tankers

Name, registry	Dwght. ton.	Lgth. ft.	Bdth. ft.
Seawise Giant, Liber.	564,739	1504.0	209.0
Prairial, Fr.	555,051	1359.0	206.0
Bellamya, Fr.	553,662	1359.0	206.0
Batillus, Fr.	553,662	1358.0	206.0
Esso Atlantic, Bahamas.	516,893	1333.0	233.0
Esso Pacific, Liber.	516,423	1333.0	233.0
King Alexander, Gr.	491,120	1194.0	259.0
Nissei Maru, Jap.	484,276	1242.0	203.0
Globtik London, Liber.	483,933	1243.0	203.0
Globtik Tokyo, Liber.	483,662	1243.0	203.0
Burmah Enterprise, U.K.	457,927	1241.0	224.0
Burmah Endeavour, U.K.	457,841	1241.0	223.0
Auriga, Liber.	431,232	1236.0	226.0
Coraggio, It.	423,798	1240.0	226.0
Berge Empress, Nor.	423,700	1252.0	223.0
Berge Emperor, Nor.	423,700	1285.0	223.0
Buyuk Selcuklu, Tur.	423,639	1240.0	226.0
Esso Deutschland, W. Ger.	421,681	1240.0	226.0
Jinko Maru, Jap.	413,553	1200.0	229.0
Chevron South America, Liber.	413,158	1200.0	229.0
David Packard, Liber.	413,115	1200.0	229.0
Aiko Maru, Jap.	412,941	1200.0	229.0
Chevron No. Amer., Liber.	412,612	1200.0	229.0
World Petrobras, Liber.	411,508	1187.0	229.0
Nai Superba, It.	409,400	1253.0	207.0
Esso Japan, Liber.	406,640	1187.0	229.0
Esso Tokyo, Liber.	406,258	1187.0	229.0
U.S.T. Pacific, U.S.	404,531	1188.0	228.0
U.S.T. Atlantic, U.S.	404,531	1188.0	228.0

Bulk, Ore, Bulk Oil, & Ore Oil Carriers

Name, registry	Dwght. ton.	Lgth. ft.	Bdth. ft.
World Gala, Liber.	282,462	1109.0	179.0
Weser Ore, Liber.	278,734	1099.0	170.0
Docecanyon, Liber.	275,588	1113.0	180.0
Main Ore, Liber.	274,999	1099.0	170.0
Jose Bonifacio, Braz.	270,358	1106.0	179.0
Usa Maru, Jap.	269,110	1105.0	179.0
Castor, Liber.	268,728	1101.0	176.0
Hitachi Venture, Liber.	267,889	1063.0	180.0
Rhine Ore, Pan.	264,999	1099.0	170.0
Alkisma Alarabia, Saud. Arab.	264,591	1101.0	176.0
Licorne Atlantique, Fr.	262,596	1101.0	176.0
Hyundai Giant, S. Kor.	259,588	1,078.0	177.0
Hoegh Hill, Nor.	249,259	1069.0	170.0
World Truth, Liber.	249,223	1069.0	170.0
Hoegh Hood, Nor.	248,604	1069.0	170.0
Seiko Maru, Jap.	247,867	1069.0	170.0
Konkar Dinos, Gr.	234,752	1075.0	160.0
World Recovery, Liber.	231,054	1075.0	161.0
Berge Brioni, Nor.	227,558	1030.0	165.0
Berge Adria, Nor.	227,558	1030.0	164.0
Rimula, U.K.	227,412	1091.0	149.0
Rapana, U.K.	227,400	1091.0	149.0
Ruhr Ore, Liber.	227,086	1096.0	149.0
Konkar Theodoros, Gr.	225,162	1028.0	164.0
Red Sea, Jap.	225,010	1090.0	149.0
Chishirokawa Maru, Jap.	224,666	1033.0	164.0
Frontier Maru, Jap.	224,222	1023.0	164.0
Andros Atlas, Gr.	224,074	1061.0	158.0
Andros Antares, Liber.	223,888	1061.0	158.0
Andros Aries, Gr.	223,605	1061.0	158.0
World Lady, Liber.	219,080	1075.0	164.0
Donau Ore, Liber.	218,957	1075.0	164.0
Tantra, Cyp.	218,035	1075.0	164.0

World's Largest Passenger Ships

Name, registry	Dwght. ton.	Lgth. ft.	Bdth. ft.
Norway, Nor.	70,202	1035.0	110.0
Queen Elizabeth 2, U.K.	67,139	963.0	105.0
Canberra, U.K.	44,807	818.0	102.0
Royal Princess, U.K.	44,807	818.0	102.0
Oriana, U.K.	41,920	804.0	97.0
Rotterdam, Neth. Ant.	38,644	748.0	94.0
United States, U.S.	38,216	990.0	101.0
Song of America, Nor.	37,584	703.0	107.0
Noordam, Neth. Ant.	33,930	704.0	89.0
Nieuw Amsterdam, Neth. Ant.	33,930	704.0	89.0
Europa, W. Ger.	33,819	654.0	98.0
Eugenio C, It.	30,567	713.0	96.0

Container, Liquefied Gas, Misc. Ships

Name, registry	Dwght. ton.	Lgth. ft.	Bdth. ft.
Echigo Maru, Jap.	102,390	928.0	147.0
Banshu Maru, Jap.	102,390	928.0	146.0
Dewa Maru, Jap.	102,376	928.0	147.0
Senshu Maru, Jap.	102,330	925.0	145.0
Kotowaka Maru, Jap.	97,788	921.0	145.0
Bishu Maru, Jap.	97,395	921.0	145.0
Hoegh Gandria, Nor.	95,683	943.0	142.0
LNG Libra, U.S.	95,084	936.0	149.0
LNG Taurus, U.S.	95,084	936.0	149.0
LNG Virgo, U.S.	95,084	936.0	149.0
LNG Capricorn, U.S.	95,084	936.0	149.0
LNG Gemini, U.S.	95,084	936.0	149.0
LNG Leo, U.S.	95,084	936.0	143.0
LNG Aquarius, U.S.	95,084	936.0	143.0
LNG Aries, U.S.	95,084	936.0	149.0
Golar Spirit, Liber.	93,815	948.0	146.0
Golar Freeze, Liber.	85,158	943.0	142.0
Khannur, Liber.	84,855	961.0	136.0
Gimi, Liber.	84,855	963.0	136.0
Hilli, Liber.	84,855	961.0	136.0
Lake Charles, U.S.	83,743	936.0	149.0
Louisiana, U.S.	83,743	936.0	149.0
Mostefa Ben-Boulaid, Alger.	82,243	914.0	134.0
Rhenania, W. Ger.	80,946	941.0	137.0
LNG 564, Swed.	80,912	941.0	137.0
Bachir Chihani, Alger.	80,328	924.0	136.0
Larbi Ben M'Hidi, Alger.	80,328	924.0	136.0
Ben Franklin, Pan.	80,070	894.0	134.0
Nestor, Bermuda	78,915	902.0	138.0
Methania, Belg.	78,511	918.0	136.0
Edouard L.D., Fr.	78,212	920.0	136.0
Pollenger, U.K.	76,496	857.0	131.0
Mourad Didouche, Alger.	74,741	900.0	137.0
Ramdane Abane, Alger.	74,741	900.0	137.0
Columbia, U.S.	72,000	931.0	140.0
Southern, U.S.	69,472	948.0	135.0
Gamma, U.S.	69,472	948.0	135.0
Arzew, U.S.	69,472	948.0	135.0
Gastor, Pan.	68,246	902.0	138.0
Tenaga Dua, Malays.	68,085	920.0	136.0
Tenaga Lima, Malays.	68,085	920.0	136.0
Tenaga Empat, Malays.	68,085	920.0	136.0
Tenaga Tiga, Malays.	68,085	920.0	136.0
Tenaga Satu, Malays.	68,085	920.0	136.0
El Paso Consolidated, Liber.	66,807	920.0	136.0
Al Rawdatain, Kuw.	66,807	920.0	136.0
El Paso Paul Kayser, Liber.	66,807	920.0	136.0
Norman Lady, Liber.	63,495	818.0	131.0
Esso Westernport, Bah.	63,495	838.0	116.0
Palace Tokyo, Jap.	63,204	807.0	131.0
Kurama Maru, Jap.	59,407	949.0	105.0
Thames Maru, Jap.	58,653	949.0	105.0
Nedlloyd Dejima, Neth.	58,613	941.0	106.0
Nedlloyd Delft, Neth.	58,613	941.0	106.0
Cardigan Bay, U.K.	58,497	950.0	106.0
Kowloon Bay, U.K.	58,496	950.0	106.0
Tokyo Bay, U.K.	58,496	950.0	106.0
Liverpool Bay, U.K.	58,496	950.0	106.0
Kasuga Maru, Jap.	58,440	948.0	105.0
Frankfurt Express, W. Ger.	58,384	943.0	106.0
City of Edinburgh, U.K.	58,284	950.0	106.0
Benavon, U.K.	58,283	950.0	106.0
Benalder, U.K.	58,283	950.0	106.0
Hamburg Express, W. Ger.	58,087	943.0	106.0
Tokio Express, W. Ger.	57,995	943.0	106.0
Bremen Express, W. Ger.	57,495	949.0	106.0
Hongkong Express, W. Ger.	57,495	949.0	106.0
Korrigan, Fr.	57,304	946.0	105.0
Toyama, Nor.	57,123	949.0	105.0

Nuclear Powered Merchant Ships

Name, registry	Dwght. ton.	Lgth. ft.	Bdth. ft.
Leonid Ilich Brezhnev, USSR.	18,172	485.0	98.0
Norasia Susan, W. Ger.	16,291	564.0	77.0
Lenin, USSR.	13,366	439.0	90.0
Mutsu, Jap.	8,214	428.0	62.0

U.S. Foreign Trade with Leading Countries

Source: Office of Industry and Trade Information, U.S. Commerce Department

(millions of dollars)

Exports from the U.S. to the following areas and countries and imports into the U.S. from those areas and countries:	Exports			Imports		
	1980	1983	1984	1980	1983	1984
Total	220,705	200,538	217,888	240,834	258,048	325,726
Western Hemisphere	74,114	63,970	76,209	78,489	93,873	114,373
Canada	35,395	38,244	46,524	41,455	52,130	66,478
20 Latin American Republics	36,030	22,618	26,302	29,851	35,683	42,341
Central American Common Market	1,951	1,494	1,659	1,849	1,585	1,757
Dominican Republic	795	632	646	786	814	1,018
Panama	699	748	757	330	337	328
Bahamas	396	452	555	1,382	1,687	1,173
Jamaica	305	452	495	383	273	377
Netherlands Antilles	448	553	648	2,564	2,291	2,048
Trinidad and Tobago	680	728	601	2,378	1,318	1,360
Europe	71,372	59,590	62,207	47,849	55,243	73,307
OECD countries (excludes depend. and Yugo.)	66,654	55,261	57,486	45,952	53,468	70,626
Western Europe	67,512	55,980	58,019	46,416	53,884	71,153
European Economic Community	53,679	44,311	46,976	35,958	43,892	57,360
Belgium and Luxembourg	6,661	5,049	5,301	1,914	2,412	3,139
Denmark	863	24,953	605	725	1,067	1,418
France	7,485	5,961	6,037	5,247	6,025	8,113
Germany, Federal Republic of	10,960	8,737	9,084	11,681	12,695	16,996
Ireland	836	1,115	1,354	411	560	844
Italy	5,511	3,908	4,375	4,313	5,455	7,935
Netherlands	8,669	7,767	7,554	1,910	2,970	4,069
United Kingdom	12,694	10,621	12,210	9,755	12,470	14,492
Austria	448	371	375	388	447	714
Finland	505	413	350	439	496	782
Iceland	79	53	51	200	219	207
Norway	843	813	859	2,632	1,358	1,904
Portugal	911	1,212	961	256	280	477
Sweden	1,767	1,581	1,542	1,617	2,429	3,244
Switzerland	3,781	2,960	2,563	2,787	2,494	3,117
Greece	922	503	456	292	238	355
Spain	3,179	2,763	2,561	1,209	1,533	2,391
Turkey	540	783	1,249	175	320	433
Yugoslavia	756	572	432	446	386	478
Eastern Europe	3,860	2,891	4,188	1,433	1,359	2,154
USSR	1,513	2,003	3,284	453	347	554
Asia	60,168	63,813	64,533	78,848	91,464	120,132
Near East	11,900	13,796	11,133	17,280	7,135	8,062
Iran	23	190	162	339	1,130	700
Iraq	724	512	664	352	59	124
Israel	2,045	2,071	2,194	943	1,255	1,750
Jordan	407	436	299	3	5	4
Kuwait	886	741	636	472	130	260
Lebanon	303	484	286	33	17	7
Saudi Arabia	5,769	7,903	5,564	12,509	3,627	3,741
Syria	239	112	104	26	8	2
Japan	20,790	21,894	23,575	30,701	41,183	57,135
East and South Asia	27,478	28,123	29,825	30,867	43,146	54,935
Bangladesh	292	190	303	85	88	133
China, People's Republic of	3,755	2,173	22	1,054	2,244	3,065
China, Republic of	4,337	4,667	5,003	6,850	11,204	14,768
Hong Kong	2,686	2,564	3,062	4,736	6,394	8,266
India	1,689	1,828	1,570	1,098	2,191	2,552
Indonesia	1,545	1,466	1,216	5,183	5,285	5,462
Korea, Republic of	4,685	5,925	5,983	4,147	7,148	9,353
Malaysia	1,337	1,684	1,856	2,577	2,124	2,721
Pakistan	642	812	1,093	128	167	244
Philippines	1,999	1,807	1,766	1,730	2,001	2,430
Singapore	3,033	3,759	3,675	1,920	2,868	3,979
Thailand	1,263	1,063	1,113	816	967	1,326
Oceania	4,876	4,827	5,745	3,392	3,044	3,558
Australia	4,093	3,954	4,793	2,509	2,222	2,675
New Zealand and Samoa	599	625	712	703	737	791
Africa	9,060	8,768	8,827	32,251	14,425	14,355
Algeria	542	594	520	6,577	3,551	3,638
Botswana	. . .	4	19	. . .	3	57
Egypt	1,874	2,813	2,704	458	303	170
Gabon	48	63	36	278	657	680
Ghana	127	119	46	206	120	47
Ivory Coast	185	61	65	288	343	469
Kenya	141	69	74	54	65	64
Liberia	113	110	97	128	91	98
Libya	509	191	200	7,124	1	9
Morocco	344	440	526	35	31	34
Nigeria	1,150	864	577	10,905	3,736	2,508
South Africa, Rep. of	2,464	2,129	2,265	3,321	2,027	2,488
Sudan	143	157	136	17	19	20
Tunisia	174	216	434	60	33	3C
Zaire	155	83	82	361	366	502

U.S. Exports and Imports of Leading Commodities

Source: Office of Industry and Trade Information, U.S. Commerce Department (millions of dollars)

Commodity	Exports			Imports		
	1980	1983	1984	1980	1983	1984
Food and live animals	27,744	24,166	24,463	15,763	15,412	17,973
Cattle, except for breeding	...	...	...	228	301	279
Meat and preparations	1,293	1,191	1,208	2,346	2,034	2,034
Dairy products and eggs	255	373	368	318	403	426
Fish	915	917	850	2,612	3,594	3,671
Grains and preparations	18,079	15,123	16,076	...	...	...
Wheat, including flour	6,586	6,508	6,698	...	...	...
Rice	1,285	926	845	...	...	...
Grains and animal feed	2,878	2,802	2,226	331	483	614
Vegetables and Fruit	...	...	2,435	1,188	1,748	3,891
Sugar	...	...	...	1,988	1,047	1,258
Coffee, crude	...	...	...	3,872	2,590	3,064
Cocoa or cacao beans	...	...	...	395	349	411
Tea	...	...	...	131	132	203
Beverages and Tobacco	2,663	2,813	2,849	2,772	3,408	3,653
Alcoholic beverages	...	...	...	2,220	2,626	2,853
Tobacco, unmanufactured	2,390	1,462	1,511	422	464	625
Crude materials, inedible, except fuels	23,791	18,596	20,249	10,496	9,590	11,082
Hides and skins	694	807	1,171	88	64	70
Soybeans, oilseeds, peanuts	5,883	5,925	5,438	...	92	88
Synthetic rubber	695	543	624	...	...	...
Rubber, including latex	...	...	...	816	655	824
Lumber and rough wood	2,675	2,104	2,042	2,134	2,719	2,853
Wood pulp and pulpwood	2,454	1,916	2,144	1,725	1,609	1,883
Textile fibers and wastes	2,864	1,817	...	242	312	387
Ores and metal scrap	4,518	2,276	2,666	3,696	2,500	2,890
Mineral fuels and related mat'ls	7,982	9,500	9,311	79,058	57,952	60,980
Coal	4,523	4,115	4,219	...	...	...
Petroleum and products	2,833	4,557	4,470	73,771	52,325	55,906
Natural gas	...	...	...	5,155	5,530	4,923
Animal and vegetable oils and fats	1,946	1,459	1,922	533	495	696
Chemicals	20,740	19,751	22,336	8,583	10,779	13,697
Medicines and pharmaceuticals	1,932	2,494	2,628	508	703	931
Fertilizers, manufactured	2,265	1,267	1,815	1,104	997	1,142
Plastic materials and resins	3,884	3,732	4,050	...	...	...
Machinery and transport equip.	84,629	82,578	89,973	60,546	86,131	119,192
Machinery	55,790	54,309	60,318	31,904	46,975	68,390
Aircraft engines and parts	1,915	2,788	3,011	...	...	...
Auto engines and parts	1,688	2,082	2,410	...	...	...
Agricultural machinery	3,104	1,589	1,740	682	1,196	1,520
Tractors and parts	1,809	757	775	...	711	907
Office machines and computers	8,709	11,669	14,592	2,929	6,759	10,791
Transport equipment	28,839	28,269	29,655	28,642	39,156	50,802
Road motor vehicles and parts	14,590	14,463	17,548	24,134	46,247	46,143
Aircraft and parts except engines	12,816	12,189	10,914	1,885	2,051	3,011
Other manufactured goods	42,714	34,666	36,670	55,900	66,539	88,625
Tires and tubes	511	304	392	1,143	1,406	1,839
Wood and manufactures, exc. furniture	2,675	...	...	632	754	808
Paper and manufactures	2,831	2,553	2,620	3,587	4,215	5,571
Glassware and pottery	...	...	...	1,224	1,602	1,984
Diamonds, excl. industrial	...	...	...	2,252	2,275	2,905
Nonmetallic mineral manuf.	2,209	1,770	1,865	...	...	...
Metal manufactures	4,205	3,444	3,602	...	4,504	5,924
Pig iron and ferroalloys	3,123	1,478	1,348	...	...	...
Iron and steel-mill products	2,998	1,415	1,248	6,686	6,338	10,208
Nonferrous base metals	2,964	1,606	1,634	7,623	7,422	8,170
Textiles, other than clothing	3,632	2,368	2,382	2,493	3,225	4,531
Clothing	1,203	818	807	6,427	9,583	13,497
Footwear	...	...	...	2,808	4,010	5,034
Furniture	521	593	622	...	...	...
Scientific and photo equip., photo supplies	6,763	7,221	7,662	...	...	...
Printed matter	1,097	1,324	1,391	613	739	980
Clocks and watches	133	90	84	1,097	1,058	1,254
Toys, games, sporting goods	1,012	878	674	1,914	2,506	3,329
Artworks and antiques	...	...	...	2,672	2,017	2,467
Other transactions	8,496	7,009	10,116	7,183	7,742	9,828
Total	220,705	200,538	217,888	240,834	258,048	325,726

Value of U.S. Exports, Imports, and Merchandise Balance

Source: Office of Trade and Investment Analysis, U.S. Dept. of Commerce

(millions of dollars)

Year	Principal Census trade totals					Other Census totals		
	U.S. exports and reexports excluding military grant-aid	U.S. general imports f.a.s. transaction values[1]	U.S. merchandise balance f.a.s.[1]	U.S. general imports c.i.f.	U.S. balance exports f.a.s. imports c.i.f.	Military grant-aid shipments	Exports of domestic merchandise	Re-exports
1950	9,997	8,954	1,043	—	—	282	10,146	133
1955	14,298	11,566	2,732	—	—	1,256	15,426	128
1960	19,659	15,073	4,586	—	—	949	20,408	201
1965	26,742	21,520	5,222	—	—	779	27,178	343
1970	42,681	40,356	2,325	42,833	−152	565	42,612	634
1975	107,652	98,503	9,149	105,935	1,716	461	106,622	1,490
1980	220,626	244,871	−24,245	256,984	−36,358	156	216,668	4,115
1983	200,486	258,048[2]	−57,562	269,878	−69,392	52	195,969	4,568
1984	217,865	325,726	−107,861	341,177	−123,312	23	212,057	5,831

Note: Export values include both commercially-financed shipments and shipments under government-financed programs such as AID and PL-480. (1) Prior to 1974, imports are customs values, i.e. generally at prices in principal foreign markets. (2) In 1981 import value changes back to customers value.

U.S. Foreign Trade, by Economic Classes

(millions of dollars)

Economic class	1965	1970	1975	1980	1982	1983	1984
Exports, total	29,128	45,114	106,622	216,672	207,158	195,969	212,057
Excluding military grant-aid	—	—	106,161	216,515	207,076	195,918	212,034
Crude foods	2,587	2,748	11,804	9,695	9,077	8,969	8,330
Manufactured foods	1,590	1,921	4,221	13,197	12,618	11,936	12,810
Crude materials	2,887	4,492	10,883	18,776	15,710	15,817	16,985
Agricultural	1,942	2,524	5,747	—	—	—	—
Semimanufactures	4,114	6,866	12,815	37,312	40,545	37,059	40,627
Finished manufactures	16,008	26,563	66,379	126,518	129,208	122,188	133,305
Excluding military grant-aid	—	—	65,918	126,362	129,127	122,136	133,282
Imports, total[1]	22,293	40,748	99,305	245,262	243,952	258,048	325,726
Crude foods	2,008	2,579	3,642	7,737	7,318	7,664	8,809
Manufactured foods	1,877	3,519	5,953	10,385	9,832	10,549	12,289
Crude materials	3,709	4,126	23,570	76,380	57,704	48,293	49,264
Agricultural	864	797	1,280	2,336	2,109	2,291	2,782
Semimanufactures	4,964	7,263	17,326	34,072	33,264	39,797	48,233
Finished manufactures	8,871	22,464	46,411	112,620	135,833	151,745	207,130

(1) Customs values are shown for imports.

Total Exports and Exports Financed by Foreign Aid

(millions of dollars)

	1965	1970	1975	1980	1982	1983	1984
Exports, total	27,530	43,224	107,592	220,783	212,275	200,538	217,888
Agricultural commodities	6,306	7,349	22,097	41,757	37,011	36,456	38,231
Nonagricultural commodities	20,445	35,310	85,094	178,948	175,264	164,082	179,657
Manufactured goods (domestic)	17,439	29,343	70,950	143,971	139,738	132,427	143,148
Military grant—aid	779	565	461	156	82	52	23
Export financed under P.L.-480	1,323	1,021	1,181	1,094	956	1,043	995
Sales for foreign currency	899	276	—	—	—	—	—
Donations, including disaster relief	253	255	257	329	228	286	177
Long-term dollar credit sales	152	490	924	765	727	758	814
AID expend. for U.S. goods for export	—	—	665	673	567	580	646

Value of Principal Agricultural Exports

(millions of dollars)

Commodity	Avg. 1961-65	Avg. 1966-70	1965	1970	1975	1980	1983	1984
Wheat and wheat products	1,268	1,197	1,214	1,144	5,292	6,660	6,561	6,740
Feed grains	841	1,082	1,162	1,099	5,492	9,759	7,266	8,109
Rice	178	311	244	314	858	1,288	926	845
Fodders and feeds	179	386	278	496	987	1,126	1,230	1,183
Oilseeds and products	774	1,182	1,029	1,642	NA	9,393	8,716	8,392
Cotton, raw	639	408	495	377	991	2,864	1,817	2,441

Public Transportation Usage

Source: U.S. Bureau of the Census

(percentage of workers 16 years and older in each region or SMSA.)

	1970	1980		1970	1980		1970	1980
United States	9.0	6.4	Los Angeles	5.6	7.0	St. Louis	8.0	5.7
			San Francisco	15.5	16.4	Minneapolis	8.5	8.7
Northeast	19.1	14.2	Anaheim	0.4	2.1	Cleveland	13.4	10.6
New York	52.5	45.1	San Diego	4.3	3.3	South	5.0	3.3
Philadelphia	20.7	14.0	Denver	4.4	6.1	Washington, D.C.	16.3	15.5
Boston	19.7	15.6	North Central	6.7	4.9	Dallas	5.1	3.4
Nassau-Suffolk, N.Y.	15.5	12.5	Chicago	23.3	18.0	Houston	5.4	3.0
Pittsburgh	14.6	11.5	Detroit	7.9	3.7	Baltimore	13.8	10.3
West	4.6	5.0				Atlanta	8.4	7.6

Merchant Fleets of the World

Source: Maritime Administration, U.S. Commerce Department

Oceangoing steam and motor ships of 1,000 gross tons and over as of July 1, 1984, excludes ships operating exclusively on the Great Lakes and inland waterways and special types such as channel ships, icebreakers, cable ships, etc., and merchant ships owned by any military force. Tonnage is in thousands. Gross tonnage is a volume measurement; each cargo gross ton represents 100 cubic ft. of enclosed space. Deadweight tonnage is the carrying capacity of a ship in long tons (2,240 lbs.).

Country of registry	Total no.	Total gross tons	Dwt. tons	Freighters Num-ber	Freighters Dwt. tons	Bulk Carriers Num-ber	Bulk Carriers Dwt. tons	Tankers Num-ber	Tankers Dwt. tons
Total-All Countries . . .	25,498	393,888	661,615	14,173	125,426	5,456	219,732	5,497	314,806
United States [1]	754	15,461	23,908	418	6,402	24	1,058	275	16,160
Privately-Owned. . . .	517	13,240	21,205	228	4,274	24	1,058	259	15,825
Government-Owned. .	237	2,221	2,703	190	2,128	—	—	16	336
Algeria	63	1,296	1,906	35	281	6	127	21	1,495
Argentina.	191	2,258	3,404	101	1,086	19	774	70	1,542
Australia	82	1,866	2,916	31	380	33	1,635	18	900
Belgium.	81	2,069	3,449	33	434	33	2,393	14	607
Brazil . . . . ☆	336	5,437	8,949	182	1,577	77	4,032	74	3,336
British Colonies	335	6,830	11,167	152	1,190	151	8,049	29	1,922
*Bulgaria	114	1,201	1,781	50	338	43	885	17	538
*China (People's Rep.) .	886	8,587	12,961	609	6,111	147	4,723	119	2,056
China (Republic of) . . .	185	3,972	6,490	104	1,220	59	3,748	21	1,522
Cyprus	538	5,983	10,390	373	2,461	92	2,401	69	5,512
Denmark	261	4,678	7,560	161	1,905	17	767	80	4,885
Finland	150	1,933	3,106	73	518	34	609	40	1,971
France	307	9,206	16,075	157	1,956	47	2,935	98	11,171
*German Dem. Rep. . . .	158	1,216	1,609	132	1,083	20	456	4	67
Germany (Fed. Rep.) . .	448	5,596	8,616	329	3,295	25	1,432	89	3,859
Greece	2,296	37,440	66,023	1,020	10,918	882	29,887	358	25,094
India	374	6,131	9,955	203	2,563	122	5,100	42	2,251
Indonesia	311	1,411	2,131	231	1,238	11	222	60	616
Iran	93	1,876	3,195	45	609	27	795	21	1,791
Iraq	39	1,084	1,931	17	177	—	—	21	1,752
Italy	580	8,521	14,237	233	1,586	112	6,017	224	6,584
Japan.	1,665	36,947	60,727	685	6,599	475	23,020	499	31,092
Korea (Republic of) . . .	502	6,252	10,657	255	1,877	172	6,566	75	2,214
Kuwait	78	2,526	3,832	47	995	—	—	31	2,837
Liberia	1,962	65,600	126,263	437	5,264	787	41,568	729	79,365
Malaysia	155	1,526	2,185	106	674	18	758	28	743
Malta	156	1,338	2,019	117	1,060	33	883	4	69
Mexico	78	1,239	1,954	23	200	8	353	47	1,401
Nassau Bahamas	61	2,791	4,952	15	122	10	394	32	4,418
Netherlands	454	4,297	6,759	353	2,290	30	1,273	65	3,165
Norway.	515	17,895	31,243	127	1,486	130	9,075	236	20,613
Panama	3,431	36,724	61,093	2,118	17,651	801	25,223	478	18,012
Philippines	302	2,879	4,719	175	1,210	74	2,425	39	1,047
Poland	293	2,970	4,144	202	1,698	79	1,917	9	521
Portugal	75	1,455	2,617	45	319	6	222	22	2,068
*Romania	245	2,556	3,895	179	1,186	57	2,022	8	685
Saudi Arabia	217	4,071	6,990	120	1,507	22	856	72	4,619
Singapore	533	6,598	10,995	344	3,454	85	3,416	100	4,113
Spain	509	5,864	10,703	324	1,616	76	2,298	108	6,788
Sweden	216	3,129	4,953	118	1,314	20	573	75	3,057
Turkey	278	2,757	4,637	175	877	50	1,749	46	1,993
*USSR.	2,475	17,547	23,518	1,779	11,396	203	4,464	448	7,554
United Kingdom	642	15,295	24,494	239	2,964	123	6,364	269	15,098
Yugoslavia	263	2,631	4,039	192	1,906	57	1,753	10	372

*Source material limited. (1) Excludes 164 non-merchant type and/or Navy-owned vessels currently in the Natl. Defense Reserve Fleet.

Commerce at Principal U.S. Ports

Source: Corps of Engineers, Department of the Army (short tons per year, 1983)

Port	Total	Foreign	Port	Total	Foreign
New Orleans, La.	156,272,189	61,275,812	Lake Charles, La.	21,783,071	9,178,548
New York, N.Y.	147,307,246	46,270,614	Pascagoula, Miss.	20,327,662	11,351,918
Valdez Hrbr., Alas.	93,536,165	1,411	Port Arthur, Tex..	18,338,237	8,592,562
Houston, Tex.	88,706,519	40,631,400	Seattle, Wash..	17,583,810	8,983,938
Baton Rouge, La.	68,395,407	19,052,289	Toledo Hrbr., Ohio	17,408,794	6,852,152
Norfolk Hrbr., Va.	42,967,830	33,447,610	Boston, Mass, Port of.	17,036,478	6,020,339
Tampa Harbor, Fla.	41,434,462	20,368,734	Cincinnati, Ohio	15,963,819	0
Long Beach, Calif.	41,112,584	19,980,039	Richmond, Calif.	15,803,285	5,113,954
Corpus C. Ship. Chnl., Tex. . .	39,131,318	17,211,888	Paulsboro, N.J.	15,783,699	7,240,668
Corpus Christi, Tex.	37,455,132	16,284,888	Freeport, Tex.	15,671,990	9,121,719
Beaumont, Tex.	36,001,675	18,221,128	Detroit, Mich.	14,955,003	2,144,550
Texas City, Tex.	35,496,241	16,253,759	Huntington, W. Va.	14,824,845	0
Baltimore, Hrbr., Md.	31,574,307	21,506,962	Indiana, Ind.	14,475,365	200,015
Duluth-Supr., Minn.	30,094,178	6,136,493	Tacoma Hrbr., Wash..	14,458,374	9,569,627
Philadelphia, Pa.	29,808,414	17,070,542	Newport News, Va.	13,517,510	12,124,862
Mobile, Ala.	29,690,361	13,327,084	St. Paul, Minn.	12,141,999	0
Los Angeles, Calif.	28,034,661	12,213,215	Memphis, Tenn.	12,134,447	0
Pittsburgh, Pa.	26,482,941	0	Jacksonville, Fla.	11,760,221	4,583,857
Portland, Ore.	25,749,024	14,656,459	Everglades, Fla.	11,463,317	2,589,227
Chicago, Ill.	24,454,287	3,802,973	Cleveland, Ohio	11,359,960	3,338,317
Marcus Hook, Pa.	22,670,484	13,445,437	San Juan, P.R.	10,744,670	4,209,666
St. Louis, Metro., Mo.	22,657,947	0	Savannah, Ga..	10,610,367	8,260,097

Commerce on U.S. Inland Waterways

Source: Corps of Engineers, Department of the Army 1983

Mississippi River System and Gulf Intracoastal Waterway

Waterway	Tons
Mississippi River, Minneapolis to the Gulf	392,135,433
Mississippi River, Minneapolis to St. Louis	84,147,867
Mississippi River, St. Louis to Cairo	98,728,458
Mississippi River, Cairo to Baton Rouge	148,147,967
Mississippi River, Baton Rouge to New Orleans	281,028,362
Mississippi River, New Orleans to Gulf	236,099,317
Gulf Intracoastal Waterway	85,093,230
Mississippi River System	519,137,359

Ton-Mileage of Freight Carried on Inland Waterways

System	Ton-miles
Atlantic Coast waterways	22,493,949
Gulf Coast waterways	32,378,996
Pacific Coast waterways	13,243,942
Mississippi River System, including Ohio River and tributaries	223,042,419
Great Lakes system, U.S. commerce only	67,854,065
Total:	**359,013,371**

Important Waterways and Canals

The St. Lawrence & Great Lakes Waterway, the largest inland navigation system on the continent, extends from the Atlantic Ocean to Duluth at the western end of Lake Superior, a distance of 2,342 miles. With the deepening of channels and locks to 27 ft., ocean carriers are able to penetrate to ports in the Canadian interior and the American midwest.

The major canals are those of the St. Lawrence Great Lakes waterway — the 3 new canals of the St. Lawrence Seaway, with their 7 locks, providing navigation for vessels of 26-foot draught from Montreal to Lake Ontario; the Welland Ship Canal by-passing the Niagara River between Lake Ontario and Lake Erie with its 8 locks, and the Sault Ste. Marie Canal and lock between Lake Huron and Lake Superior. These 16 locks overcome a drop of 580 ft. from the head of the lakes to Montreal. From Montreal to Lake Ontario the former bottleneck of narrow, shallow canals and of slow passage through 22 locks has been overcome, giving faster and safer movement for larger vessels. The new locks and linking channels now accommodate all but the largest ocean-going vessels and the upper St. Lawrence and Great Lakes are open to 80% of the world's saltwater fleet.

Subsidiary Canadian canals or branches include the St. Peters Canal between Bras d'Or Lakes and the Atlantic Ocean in Nova Scotia; the St. Ours and Chambly Canals on the Richelieu River, Quebec; the Ste. Anne and Carillon Canals on the Ottawa River; the Rideau Canal between the Ottawa River and Lake Ontario, the Trent and Murrary Canals between Lake Ontario and Georgian Bay in Ontario and the St. Andrew's Canal on the Red River. The commercial value of these canals is not great but they are maintained to control water levels and permit the passage of small vessels and pleasure craft. The Canso Canal, completed 1957, permits shipping to pass through the causeway connecting Cape Breton Island with the Nova Scotia mainland.

The Welland Canal overcomes the 326-ft. drop of Niagara Falls and the rapids of the Niagara River. It has 8 locks, each 859 ft. long, 80 ft. wide and 30 ft. deep. Regulations permit ships of 730-ft. length and 75-ft. beam to transit.

Shortest Navigable Distances Between Ports

Source: Distances Between Ports. Defense Mapping Agency Hydrographic/Topographic Center

Distances shown are in nautical miles (1,852 meters or about 6,076.115 feet). To get statute miles, multiply by 1.15.

TO	FROM New York	Montreal	Colon[1]
Algiers, Algeria	3,618	3,592	4,737
Amsterdam, Netherlands	3,411	3,318	4,829
Baltimore, Md.	410	1,820	1,904
Barcelona, Spain	3,721	3,695	4,840
Boston, Mass.	378	1,309	2,136
Buenos Aires, Argentina	5,845	6,440	5,344
Cape Town, S. Africa[2]	6,789	7,115	6,425
Cherbourg, France	3,127	3,034	4,545
Cobh, Ireland	2,878	2,780	4,320
Copenhagen, Denmark	3,934	3,841	5,352
Dakar, Senegal	3,336	3,562	3,689
Galveston, Tex.	1,862	3,224	1,485
Gibraltar[3]	3,210	3,184	4,329
Glasgow, Scotland	3,324	3,231	4,742
Halifax, N.S.	593	958	2,298
Hamburg, W. Germany	3,636	3,543	5,054
Hamilton, Bermuda	697	1,621	1,644
Havana, Cuba	1,167	2,528	990
Helsinki, Finland	4,484	4,391	5,902
Istanbul, Turkey	5,006	4,980	6,125
Kingston, Jamaica	1,472	2,690	555
Lagos, Nigeria	4,870	5,130	5,033
Lisbon, Portugal	2,980	2,941	4,155
Marseille, France	3,896	3,870	5,015
Montreal, Quebec	1,516		3,190
Naples, Italy	4,185	4,159	5,304
Nassau, Bahamas	961	2,274	1,165
New Orleans, La.	1,707	3,069	1,403
New York, N.Y.		1,516	1,972
Norfolk, Va.	287	1,697	1,781
Oslo, Norway	3,888	3,795	5,306
Piraeus, Greece	4,687	4,661	5,806
Port Said, Egypt	5,119	5,093	6,238
Rio de Janeiro, Brazil	4,743	5,342	4,246
St. John's, Nfld.	1,097	1,038	2,697
San Juan, Puerto Rico	1,399	2,445	992
Southampton, England	3,156	3,063	4,514

TO	FROM San. Fran.	Vancouver	Panama[1]
Acapulco, Mexico	1,834	2,612	1,426
Anchorage, Alas.	1,892	1,347	5,127
Bombay, India	9,791	9,513	9,248
Calcutta, India	9,006	8,728	10,929
Colon, Panama[1]	3,290	4,065	44
Jakarta, Indonesia	7,657	7,413	10,570
Haiphong, Vietnam	6,657	6,358	9,806
Hong Kong	6,044	5,756	9,196
Honolulu, Hawaii	2,095	2,419	4,688
Los Angeles, Cal.	369	1,162	2,912
Manila, Philippines	6,223	5,946	9,355
Melbourne, Australia	6,966	7,342	7,916
Pusan, S. Korea	4,922	4,623	8,074
Ho Chi Min City, Vietnam	6,890	6,606	9,822
San Francisco, Cal.		812	3,246
Seattle, Wash.	796	126	4,005
Shanghai, China	5,398	5,110	8,571
Singapore	7,356	7,078	10,495
Suva, Fiji	4,760	5,183	6,312
Valparaiso, Chile	5,146	5,915	2,615
Vancouver, B.C.	812		4,021
Vladivostok, USSR	4,554	4,262	7,738
Yokohama, Japan	4,547	4,260	7,687

TO	FROM Port Said	Cape Town[2]	Singapore
Bombay, India	3,046	4,599	2,435
Calcutta, India	4,691	5,489	1,650
Dar es Salaam, Tanzania	3,129	2,369	4,041
Jakarta, Indonesia	5,276	5,184	527
Hong Kong	6,474	7,071	1,460
Kuwait	3,306	5,169	3,845
Manila, Philippines	6,355	6,952	1,341
Melbourne, Australia	7,837	6,104	3,842
Ho Chi Min City, Vietnam	5,660	6,263	646
Singapore	5,014	5,611	
Yokohama, Japan	7,906	8,503	2,892

(1) Colon on the Atlantic is 44 nautical miles from Panama (port) on the Pacific. (2) Cape Town is 35 nautical miles northwest of the Cape of Good Hope. (3) Gibraltar (port) is 24 nautical miles east of the Strait of Gibraltar.

Notable Ocean Passages by Ships

Compiled by N.R.P. Bonsor

Sailing Vessels

Date	Ship		From	To	Nautical miles	Time D. H. M	Speed (knots)
1846	Yorkshire		Liverpool	New York	3150	16. 0. 0	8.46†
1853	Northern Light		San Francisco	Boston	—	76. 6. 0	—
1854	James Baines		Boston Light	Light Rock	—	12. 6. 0	—
1854	Flying Cloud		New York	San Francisco	15091	89. 0. 0	7.07†
1868-9	Thermopylae		Liverpool	Melbourne	—	63.18.15	—
—	Red Jacket		New York	Liverpool	3150	13. 1.25	10.05†
—	Starr King		50 S. Lat	Golden Gate	—	36. 0. 0	—
—	Golden Fleece		Equator	San Francisco	—	12.12. 0	—
1905	Atlantic		Sandy Hook	England	3013	12. 4. 0	10.32

Atlantic Crossing by Passenger Steamships

Date	Ship		From	To	Nautical miles	Time D. H. M	Speed (knots)
1819 (5/22 - 6/20)	Savannah (a)	US	Savannah	Liverpool	—	29. 4. 0	—
1838 (5/7 - 5/22)	Great Western	Br	New York	Avonmouth	3218	14.15.59	9.14
1840 (8/4 - 8/14)	Britannia (b)	Br	Halifax	Liverpool	2610	9.21.44	10.98†
1854 (6/28 - 7/7)	Baltic	US	Liverpool	New York	3037	9.16.52	13.04
1856 (8/6 - 8/15)	Persia	Br	Sandy Hook	Liverpool	3046	8.23.19	14.15†
1876 (12/16-12/24)	Britannic	Br	Sandy Hook	Queenstown	2882	7.12.41	15.94
1895 (5/18 - 5/24)	Lucania	Br	Sandy Hook	Queenstown	2897	5.11.40	22.00
1898 (3/30 - 4/5)	Kaiser Wilhelm der Grosse	Ger	Needles	Sandy Hook	3120	5.20. 0	22.29
1901 (7/10 - 7/17)	Deutschland	Ger	Sandy Hook	Eddystone	3082	5.11. 5	23.51
1907 (10/6 - 10/10)	Lusitania	Br	Queenstown	Sandy Hook	2780	4.19.52	23.99
1924 (8/20 - 8/25)	Mauretania	Br	Ambrose	Cherbourg	3198	5. 1.49	26.25
1929 (/17 - 7/22)	Bremen*	Ger	Cherbourg	Ambrose	3164	4.17.42	27.83
1933 (6/27 - 7/2)	Europa	Ger	Cherbourg	Ambrose	3149	4.16.48	27.92
1933 (8/11 - 8/16)	Rex	It	Gibraltar	Ambrose	3181	4.13.58	28.92
1935 (5/30 - 6/3)	Normandie*	Fr	Bishop Rock	Ambrose	2971	4. 3. 2	29.98
1938 (8/10 - 8/14)	Queen Mary	Br	Ambrose	Bishop Rock	2938	3.20.42	31.69
1952 (7/11 - 7/15)	United States	US	Bishop Rock	Ambrose	2906	3.12.12	34.51
1952 (7/3 - 7/7)	United States* (e)	US	Ambrose	Bishop Rock	2942	3.10.40	35.59

Other Ocean Passages

Date	Ship		From	To	Nautical miles	Time D. H. M	Speed (knots)
1928 (June)	USS Lexington		San Pedro	Honolulu	2226	3. 0.36	30.66
1944 (Jul-Sep)	St. Roch (c) (Can)		Halifax	Vancouver	7295	86. 0. 0	—
1945 (7/16-7/19)	USS Indianapolis (d)		San Francisco	Oahu, Hawaii	2091	3. 2.20	28.07
1945 (11/26)	USS Lake Champlain		Gibraltar	Newport News	3360	4. 8.51	32.04
1950 (Jul-Aug)	USS Boxer		Japan	San Francisco	5000	7.18.36	26.80†
1951 (6/1-6/9)	USS Philippine Sea		Yokohama	Alameda	5000	7.13. 0	27.62†
1958 (2/25-3/4)	USS Skate (f)		Nantucket	Portland, Eng	3161	8.11. 0	15.57
1958 (3/23-3/29)	USS Skate (f)		Lizard, Eng	Nantucket	—	7. 5. 0	—
1958 (7/23-8/7)	USS Nautilus (g)		Pearl Harbor	Iceland (via N. Pole)	—	15. 0. 0	—
1960 (2/16-5/10)	USS Triton (h)		New London	Rehoboth, Del	41500	84. 0. 0	20.59†
1960 (8/15-8/20)	USS Seadragon (i)		Baffin Bay	NW Passage, Pac	850	6. 0. 0	—
1962 (10/30-11/11)	African Comet* (US)		New York	Cape Town	6786	12.16.22	22.03
1973 (8/20)	Sea-Land Exchange (k) (US)		Bishop Rock	Ambrose	2912	3.11.24	34.92
1973 (8/24)	Sea-Land Trade (US)		Kobe	Race Rock, BC	4126	5. 6. 0	32.75

† The time taken and/or distance covered is approximate and so, therefore, is the average speed.

* Maiden voyage. (a) The Savannah, a fully rigged sailing vessel with steam auxiliary (over 300 tons, 98.5 ft. long, beam 25.8 ft., depth 12.9 ft.) was launched in the East River in 1818. It was the first ship to use steam in crossing any ocean. It was supplied with engines and detachable iron paddle wheels. On its famous voyage it used steam 105 hours. (b) First Cunard liner. (c) First ship to complete NW Passage in one season. (d) Carried Hiroshima atomic bomb in World War II. (e) Set world speed record; average speed eastbound on maiden voyage 35.59 knots (about 41 m.p.h.). (f) First atomic submarine to cross Atlantic both ways submerged. (g) World's first atomic submarine also first to make undersea voyage under polar ice cap, 1,830 mi. from Point Barrow, Alaska, to Atlantic Ocean, Aug. 1-4, 1958, reaching North Pole Aug. 3. Second undersea transit of the North Pole made by submarine USS Skate Aug. 11, 1958, during trip from New London, Conn., and return. (h) World's largest submarine. Nuclear-powered Triton was submerged during nearly all its voyage around the globe. It duplicated the route of Ferdinand Magellan's circuit (1519-1522) 30,708 mi., starting from St. Paul Rocks off the NE coast of Brazil, Feb. 24-Apr. 25, 1960, then sailed to Cadiz, Spain, before returning home. (i) First underwater transit of Northwest Passage. (k) Fastest freighter crossing of Atlantic.

Fastest Scheduled Train Runs in U.S. and Canada

Source: Donald M. Steffee, figures are based on 1985 timetables

Passenger—(80 mph and over)

Railroad	Train	From	To	Dis. miles	Time min.	Speed mph.
Amtrak	Ten Metroliners	Baltimore	Wilmington	68.4	44	93.3
Amtrak	Two trains	Trenton	Newark	48.1	32	90.2
Amtrak	Metroliner 100	Baltimore	Wilmington	68.4	46	89.2
Amtrak	Four trains	Rensselear	Hudson	28.0	19	88.4
Amtrak	Three Metroliners	Newark	Philadelphia	80.5	55	87.8
Amtrak	Six trains	Wilmington	Baltimore	68.4	47	87.3
Amtrak	Five Metroliners	Wilmington	Baltimore	68.4	48	85.5
Amtrak	Metroliner 101	Metro Park	Trenton	33.9	24	84.7
Amtrak	Eight Metroliners	Newark	Philadelphia	80.5	57	84.7
Amtrak	Two Metroliners	Metro Park	Philadelphia	66.4	48	83.0
Amtrak	First State	No. Philadelphia	Newark	76.0	55	82.9
Amtrak	Colonial	Newark	Trenton	48.1	35	82.5
Amtrak	Clocker Service	Princeton Jct	Newark	38.4	28	82.3
Via Rail Canada	Three trains	Dorval	Kingston	165.8	121	82.2
Via Rail Canada	Two trains	Cornwall	Kingston	108.1	79	82.1
Amtrak	Valley Forge	Newark	No. Philadelphia	76.0	56	81.4

Railroad	Train	From	To	Dis. miles	Time min.	Speed mph.
Amtrak	Three Metroliners	Philadelphia	Metro Park	66.4	49	81.3
Amtrak	Southwest Chief	Garden City[1]	Lamar	99.9	74	81.0
Via Rail Canada	Renaissance	Kingston	Dorval	165.8	123	80.9
Amtrak	Two Metroliners	Philadelphia	Newark	80.5	60	80.5
Amtrak	Two trains	Newark	Trenton	48.1	36	80.2

Railroad	Train	From	To	Dis. miles	Time min.	Speed mph.
Freight — (62 mph and over)						
Union Pacific	BASV	North Platte	Cheyenne	225.4	205	66.0
Union Pacific	Super Van	North Platte	Cheyenne	225.4	215	62.9
Santa Fe	Seven trains	Gallup	Winslow	125.8	120	62.9
Santa Fe	No. 199	Seligman	Kingman	88.1	85	62.9

Fastest Scheduled Passenger Train Runs in Japan and European Countries

France	TGV trains (5 runs)	Paris	Macon	225.7	101	134.1
Japan	Yamabiko train	Koriyama	Omiya	113.4	53	128.4
Great Britain	High Speed Train	London	Didcot	53.1	31	102.8
West Germany	Fourteen trains	Hamm	Bielefeld	41.7	25	100.1
Italy	Rapido 908	Rome	Chiusi	91.9	64	86.1
Soviet Union	High Speed Train[2]	Moscow[1]	Leningrad	403.6[3]	299	81.0
Sweden	No. 978	Skvode	Laxa	52.2	41	76.3
Belgium	Thirty-two trains	Brussels[1]	Ghent	32.5	26	75.0

(1) Runs listed in both directions. (2) Once weekly; Thurs. from Leningrad, Fri. from Moscow. (3) Probable operating stop at Bologoye; times unavailable.

French Open Northern Section of Paris-Lyon High Speed Line

On September 25th, 1983, the northern section (Combs-la-ville to St. Florentin) of the new high speed line was opened to traffic. As a result, the distance between Paris and Lyon is further shortened to 264.7 miles and train time was cut to two hours—calling for an overall speed of 132.4 mph.

Passenger Car Production, U.S. Plants
Source: Motor Vehicle Manufacturers Association

	1983	1984	1985 5 Mos.		1983	1984	1985 5 Mos.
Concord	3	—	—	Nova	—	—	6,805
Eagle	4,068	—	—	Chevette	201,841	174,044	70,755
Renault Alliance	153,878	110,170	28,683	Cavalier	308,461	400,254	214,125
Renault Encore	42,436	82,026	18,300	Citation	86,878	104,045	28,697
Total American Motors Corp.	200,385	192,196	46,983	Camaro	193,118	230,082	102,283
Horizon	117,744	159,247	63,386	Celebrity/Malibu	244,480	280,653	125,159
Reliant	186,496	172,416	78,662	Monte Carlo	124,926	97,922	67,953
Caravelle (K)	1,999	2,100	807	Chevrolet	91,228	134,072	126,280
Caravelle (E)	3,285	21,023	22,095	Corvette	28,174	35,661	19,053
Caravelle (M)	45	2,226	1,503	**Total Chevrolet**	1,279,106	1,456,733	761,110
Gran Fury	1,255	21,263	8,445	Acadian	—	14,729	5,412
Total Plymouth	310,824	378,275	174,898	1000	48,178	25,063	9,396
Laser	23,656	70,075	24,091	Sunbird/2000	117,013	136,582	61,328
LeBaron	86,261	116,475	47,640	Fiero	29,630	114,002	50,263
LeBaron GTS	—	10,524	42,387	Phoenix	25,060	14,195	—
Fifth Avenue	19,733	116,802	50,993	Firebird	100,225	108,396	54,764
E Class	73,597	24,726	—	Grand AM	—	24,667	54,903
New Yorker (E)	31,402	65,057	32,233	6000	—	106	19,381
Total Chrysler-Plymouth	545,473	781,934	372,242	Bonneville	55,560	10,612	—
Omni	126,443	146,350	64,165	Grand Prix	41,797	9,391	—
Daytona	19,428	52,986	21,547	Pontiac	12,457	48,356	30,356
Aries	144,042	142,487	63,340	**Total Pontiac**	429,920	506,099	285,803
Dodge 400	18,478	—	—	Firenza	54,800	67,986	30,831
Dodge 600 (K)	8,104	30,280	12,833	Omega	59,966	29,288	—
Dodge 600 (E)	41,077	44,430	18,811	Calais	—	33,195	70,090
Lancer	—	8,218	31,015	Ciera	—	251,506	163,149
Diplomat	1,241	41,100	14,892	Supreme Coupe	527,391	171,720	63,216
Total Dodge	358,813	465,851	226,603	Supreme 4-Door	—	75,738	33,219
Total Chrysler Corp.	904,286	1,247,785	598,845	Oldsmobile 88	—	282,378	102,456
Ford	93,768	83,081	7,122	Oldsmobile 98	365,554	109,321	62,945
Thunderbird	186,566	146,203	90,153	Toronado	43,135	44,396	18,411
LTD	179,192	225,913	105,498	**Total Oldsmobile**	1,050,846	1,065,528	544,317
Fairmont	23,728	—	—	Skyhawk	79,169	127,327	47,905
Tempo	106,977	165,320	82,700	Skylark	112,843	110,849	40,953
Escort	290,045	341,901	139,387	Somerset	—	28,352	55,556
EXP	4,298	42,388	3,838	Century	—	227,973	111,461
Mustang	124,225	140,338	79,742	Regal	411,255	174,120	51,621
Total Ford	1,008,799	1,145,144	508,440	Le Sabre	—	178,500	61,071
Grand Marquis	90,805	89,312	4,733	Electra	249,838	87,819	41,479
Cougar	126,395	116,517	60,426	Riviera	52,503	53,093	28,808
Marquis	77,147	121,051	52,290	**Total Buick**	905,608	987,833	438,854
Zephyr	8,601	—	—	Cimarron	21,258	14,362	12,554
Topaz	31,005	46,564	25,605	Cadillac	180,654	199,542	98,923
Lynx	73,413	69,709	31,912	Eldorado	73,026	75,957	32,878
LN7	290	—	—	Seville	34,873	38,683	17,612
Capri	24,697	18,254	7,066	**Total Cadillac**	309,811	328,544	161,947
Lincoln	58,872	106,998	50,675	**Total General Motors Corp.**	3,975,291	4,344,737	2,192,031
Mark	34,143	25,601	7,854	Honda	55,335	138,572	69,596
Continental	13,513	36,105	12,541	Nissan	—	—	5,053
Total Lincoln-Mercury	538,881	630,113	253,102	Volkswagen of America	98,207	74,785	42,956
Total Ford Motor Co.	1,547,680	1,775,257	761,542	**Total Passenger Cars**	6,781,184	7,773,332	3,717,006

Motor Vehicle Registrations, Taxes, Motor Fuel, Drivers' Ages

Source: Federal Highway Adm.; National Transportation Safety Board

State, 1984	Driver's age Jan. 1, 1984 (1) Regular	(2) Juvenile	Minimum age for purchase alcoholic beverage (July 1, 1985)	Licensed drivers⁵ (1,000)	Registered autos, buses & trucks⁵ (1,000)	State gas tax per gal. cents (Apr. 1, 1985)	Motor fuel adjusted net total tax receipts $1,000⁵	Motor fuel consumption⁵ Highway 1,000 gallons	Non-highway 1,000 gallons
Alabama	16		21	2,444	3,210	13	251,702	2,236,000	40,000
Alaska	16		21	283	378	8	27,568	315,000	38,000
Arizona	16		21	2,311	2,357	13	256,820	1,716,000	38,000
Arkansas	16		21	1,713	1,428	9.5	140,899	1,447,000	27,000
California	16/18	14	21	16,995	18,870	13.5	1,152,536	12,628,000	280,000
Colorado	18	16	18/21³	2,278	2,779	12	199,521	1,613,000	97,000
Connecticut	16/18		21	2,300	2,340	15	202,132	1,460,000	26,000
Delaware	16/18		21	438	453	11	38,034	363,000	5,000
Dist. of Col.	18	16	18/21³	374	234	15.5	26,761	197,000	3,000
Florida	16		21	8,664	9,548	9.7	580,599	5,860,000	172,000
Georgia	16		21⁶	3,836	4,298	7.5	278,632	3,658,000	62,000
Hawaii	15		18	584	633	8.5	29,608	335,000	14,000
Idaho	16	14	19	661	889	14.5	74,202	498,000	27,000
Illinois	16/18		21	7,012	7,707	12	566,679	5,111,000	165,000
Indiana	16/18		21	3,558	3,844	11.1	345,280	3,074,000	72,000
Iowa	16/18	14	19	1,912	2,531	13	209,454	1,662,000	69,000
Kansas	16	14	18/21³	1,664	2,072	11	147,064	1,391,000	61,000
Kentucky	16		21	2,230	2,632	10	203,321	2,005,000	34,000
Louisiana	15/17	15	18	2,883	2,909	16	306,743	2,549,000	66,000
Maine	15/17	15	21	788	790	14	91,253	633,000	15,000
Maryland	16/18	15¾	21	2,852	3,192	13.5	294,126	2,160,000	32,000
Massachusetts	17/18	16½	21	3,668	3,868	11	277,620	2,513,000	38,000
Michigan	16/18	14	21	6,388	6,329	15	617,378	4,202,000	114,000
Minnesota	16/18	15	19	2,402	3,363	17	390,488	2,263,000	126,000
Mississippi	15		21⁶	1,850	1,565	9	137,240	1,470,000	27,000
Missouri	16		21	3,356	3,460	7	205,075	2,906,000	83,000
Montana	15/16		19	494	894	15	90,856	541,000	33,000
Nebraska	16	14	21	1,102	1,255	14.5	144,207	924,000	62,000
Nevada	16	14	21	709	755	12	170,310	572,000	21,000
New Hampshire	16/18	16	21	715	830	14	66,161	475,000	8,000
New Jersey	17	16	21	5,666	4,973	8	309,052	3,808,000	82,000
New Mexico	15/16		21	789	1,281	11	99,508	898,000	16,000
New York	17/18	16	21	9,709	8,672	8	434,403	5,457,000	164,000
North Carolina	16/18		19/21³	4,043	4,690	12	419,372	3,440,000	89,000
North Dakota	16	14	21	438	676	13	55,699	427,000	57,000
Ohio	16/18	14	21⁶	7,294	7,869	12	651,231	5,423,000	145,000
Oklahoma	16		21	2,239	2,775	10	198,357	2,187,000	54,000
Oregon	16	14	21	1,951	2,153	10	116,634	1,493,000	51,000
Pennsylvania	17/18	16	21	7,523	6,978	12	909,523	5,075,000	95,000
Rhode Island	16/18		21	607	605	13	54,559	383,000	11,000
South Carolina	16	15	21⁷	2,049	2,148	13	244,657	1,857,000	40,000
South Dakota	16	14	19/21³	484	641	13	56,298	422,657	62,000
Tennessee	16	14	21	2,984	3,649	10	265,284	2,785,000	61,000
Texas	16/18	15	21⁸	12,044	12,041	10	779,637	10,083,000	224,000
Utah	16/18		21	960	1,119	14	107,009	881,000	28,000
Vermont	18	16	18	368	386	13	38,260	287,000	7,000
Virginia	16/18		19/21³	3,800	3,985	11	439,942	3,158,000	78,000
Washington	16/18		21	2,950	3,401	16	359,845	2,182,000	56,000
West Virginia	16/18	16	19⁴	1,408	1,326	15.3	99,073	930,000	19,000
Wisconsin	16/18	14	19	3,124	3,314	16.5	355,187	2,334,000	89,000
Wyoming	16	14	19	411	512	8	40,110	481,000	31,000
Total				157,305	168,607	—	13,455,809	120,769,000	3,314,000

(1) Unrestricted operation of private passenger car. When 2 ages are shown, license is issued at lower age upon completion of approved driver education course. (2) Juvenile license issued with consent of parent or guardian. (3) Limited purchase of alcohol, such as beer, is permitted at 18 or 19. (4) Age is 21 for nonresidents. (5) Estimated. (6) Effective July 1, 1986. (7) Effective June 14,1986. (8) Effective Sept. 1, 1986.

As of July 20, 1985, Connecticut, Hawaii, Illinois, Indiana, Louisiana, Michigan, Missouri, Nebraska, New Jersey, New Mexico, New York, North Carolina, Oklahoma, and Texas have adopted seat belt laws. Seat belt bills are pending in 9 other states. Only in Idaho and Vermont has no bill been introduced.

Automobile Factory Sales

Source: Motor Vehicle Manufacturers Association, (wholesale values)

Year	Passenger cars Number	Value	Motor trucks, buses Number	Value	Total Number	Value
1900	4,192	$4,899,433	—	—	4,190	$4,899,443
1910	181,000	215,340,000	6,000	9,660,000	187,000	225,000,000
1920	1,905,560	1,809,170,963	321,789	423,249,410	2,227,349	2,232,420,373
1930	2,787,456	1,644,083,152	575,364	390,752,061	3,362,820	2,034,853,213
1940	3,717,385	2,370,654,083	754,901	567,820,414	4,472,286	2,938,474,497
1950	6,665,863	8,468,137,000	1,337,193	1,707,748,000	8,003,056	10,175,885,000
1970	6,546,817	14,630,217,000	1,692,440	4,819,752,000	8,239,257	19,449,969,000
1981	6,255,340	—	1,700,908	—	7,956,248	—
1982	5,049,184	—	1,906,455	—	6,955,639	—
1983	6,739,223	—	2,413,897	—	9,153,120	—
1984	7,621,176	—	3,075,325	—	10,696,501	—

After July 1, 1964 all tactical vehicles are excluded. Federal excise taxes are excluded in all years.

Road Mileage Between Selected U.S. Cities

	Atlanta	Boston	Chicago	Cincinnati	Cleveland	Dallas	Denver	Des Moines	Detroit	Houston
Atlanta, Ga....	....	1,037	674	440	672	795	1,398	870	699	789
Boston, Mass.. .	1,037	....	963	840	628	1,748	1,949	1,280	695	1,804
Chicago, Ill. . . .	674	963	....	287	335	917	996	327	266	1,067
Cincinnati, Oh. . .	440	840	287	....	244	920	1,164	571	259	1,029
Cleveland, Oh. . .	672	628	335	244	....	1,159	1,321	652	170	1,273
Dallas, Tex.. . .	795	1,748	917	920	1,159	....	781	684	1,143	243
Denver, Col.. . .	1,398	1,949	996	1,164	1,321	781	....	669	1,253	1,019
Detroit, Mich. . . .	699	695	266	259	170	1,143	1,253	584	....	1,265
Houston, Tex..	789	1,804	1,067	1,029	1,273	243	1,019	905	1,265	....
Indianapolis, Ind. .	493	906	181	106	294	865	1,058	465	278	987
Kansas City, Mo. .	798	1,391	499	591	779	489	600	195	743	710
Los Angeles, Cal.	2,182	2,979	2,054	2,179	2,367	1,387	1,059	1,727	2,311	1,538
Memphis, Tenn.. .	371	1,296	530	468	712	452	1,040	599	713	561
Milwaukee, Wis. .	761	1,050	87	374	422	991	1,029	361	353	1,142
Minneapolis, Minn.	1,068	1,368	405	692	740	936	841	252	671	1,157
New Orleans, La..	479	1,507	912	786	1,030	496	1,273	978	1,045	356
New York, N.Y.. .	841	206	802	647	473	1,552	1,771	1,119	637	1,608
Omaha, Neb. . . .	986	1,412	459	693	784	644	537	132	716	865
Philadelphia, Pa..	741	296	738	567	413	1,452	1,691	1,051	573	1,508
Pittsburgh, Pa..	687	561	452	287	129	1,204	1,411	763	287	1,313
Portland, Ore.. . .	2,601	3,046	2,083	2,333	2,418	2,009	1,238	1,786	2,349	2,205
St. Louis, Mo.. .	541	1,141	289	340	529	630	857	333	513	779
San Francisco . .	2,496	3,095	2,142	2,362	2,467	1,753	1,235	1,815	2,399	1,912
Seattle, Wash.. .	2,618	2,976	2,013	2,300	2,348	2,078	1,307	1,749	2,279	2,274
Tulsa, Okla.. . . .	772	1,537	683	736	925	257	681	443	909	478
Washington, D.C..	608	429	671	481	346	1,319	1,616	984	506	1,375

	Indiana-polis	Kansas City	Los Angeles	Louis-ville	Memphis	Mil-waukee	Minnea-polis	New Orleans	New York	Omaha
Atlanta, Ga.. . .	493	798	2,182	382	371	761	1,068	479	841	986
Boston, Mass.. .	906	1,391	2,979	941	1,296	1,050	1,368	1,507	206	1,412
Chicago, Ill. . . .	181	499	2,054	292	530	87	405	912	802	459
Cincinnati, Oh. . .	106	591	2,179	101	468	374	692	786	647	693
Cleveland, Oh. . .	294	779	2,367	345	712	422	740	1,030	473	784
Dallas, Tex.. .	865	489	1,387	819	452	991	936	496	1,552	644
Denver, Col.. . .	1,058	600	1,059	1,120	1,040	1,029	841	1,273	1,771	537
Detroit, Mich. . .	278	743	2,311	360	713	353	671	1,045	637	716
Houston, Tex.. . .	987	710	1,538	928	561	1,142	1,157	356	1,608	865
Indianapolis, Ind. .	....	485	2,073	111	435	268	586	796	713	587
Kansas City, Mo. .	485	....	1,589	520	451	537	447	806	1,198	201
Los Angeles, Cal.	2,073	1,589	....	2,108	1,817	2,087	1,889	1,883	2,786	1,595
Memphis, Tenn.. .	435	451	1,817	367	....	612	826	390	1,100	652
Milwaukee, Wis. .	268	537	2,087	379	612	....	332	994	889	493
Minneapolis, Minn.	586	447	1,889	697	826	332	....	1,214	1,207	357
New Orleans, La..	796	806	1,883	685	390	994	1,214	....	1,311	1,007
New York, N.Y.. .	713	1,198	2,786	748	1,100	889	1,207	1,311	....	1,251
Omaha, Neb. . . .	587	201	1,595	687	652	493	357	1,007	1,251	....
Philadelphia, Pa..	633	1,118	2,706	668	1,000	825	1,143	1,211	100	1,183
Pittsburgh, Pa..	353	838	2,426	388	752	539	857	1,070	368	895
Portland, Ore.. . .	1,227	1,809	959	2,320	2,259	2,010	1,678	2,505	2,885	1,654
St. Louis, Mo.. .	235	257	1,845	263	285	363	552	673	948	449
San Francisco . .	2,256	1,835	379	2,349	2,125	2,175	1,940	2,249	2,934	1,683
Seattle, Wash. .	2,194	1,839	1,131	2,305	2,290	1,940	1,608	2,574	2,815	1,638
Tulsa, Okla.. . .	631	248	1,452	659	401	757	695	647	1,344	387
Washington, D.C..	558	1,043	2,631	582	867	758	1,076	1,078	233	1,116

	Phila-delphia	Pitts-burgh	Port-land	St. Louis	Salt Lake City	San Fran-cisco	Seattle	Toledo	Tulsa	Washing-ton
Atlanta, Ga.. . .	741	687	2,601	541	1,878	2,496	2,618	640	772	608
Boston, Mass.. .	296	561	3,046	1,141	2,343	3,095	2,976	739	1,537	429
Chicago, Ill. . . .	738	452	2,083	289	1,390	2,142	2,013	232	683	671
Cincinnati, Oh. . .	567	287	2,333	340	1,610	2,362	2,300	200	736	481
Cleveland, Oh. . .	413	129	2,418	529	1,715	2,467	2,348	111	925	346
Dallas, Tex.. . .	1,452	1,204	2,009	630	1,242	1,753	2,078	1,084	257	1,319
Denver, Col.. . . .	1,691	1,411	1,238	857	504	1,235	1,307	1,218	681	1,616
Detroit, Mich. . .	573	287	2,349	513	1,647	2,399	2,274	59	909	506
Houston, Tex.. . .	1,508	1,313	2,205	779	1,438	1,912	2,274	1,206	478	1,375
Indianapolis, Ind. .	633	353	2,227	235	1,504	2,256	2,194	219	631	558
Kansas City, Mo. .	1,118	838	1,809	257	1,086	1,835	1,839	687	248	1,043
Los Angeles, Cal.	2,706	2,426	959	1,845	715	379	1,131	2,276	1,452	2,631
Memphis, Tenn.. .	1,000	752	2,259	285	1,535	2,125	2,290	654	401	867
Milwaukee, Wis. .	825	539	2,010	363	1,423	2,175	1,940	319	757	758
Minneapolis, Minn.	1,143	857	1,678	552	1,186	1,940	1,608	637	695	1,076
New Orleans, La..	1,211	1,070	2,505	673	1,738	2,249	2,574	986	647	1,078
New York, N.Y.. .	100	368	2,885	948	2,182	2,934	2,815	578	1,344	233
Omaha, Neb. . . .	1,183	895	1,654	449	931	1,683	1,638	681	387	1,116
Philadelphia, Pa..	....	288	2,821	868	2,114	2,866	2,751	514	1,264	133
Pittsburgh, Pa..	288	....	2,535	588	1,826	2,578	2,465	228	984	221
Portland, Ore.. . .	2,821	2,535	....	2,060	767	636	172	2,315	1,913	2,754
St. Louis, Mo.. . .	868	588	2,060	....	1,337	2,089	2,081	454	396	793
San Francisco . .	2,866	2,578	636	2,089	752	....	808	2,364	1,760	2,799
Seattle, Wash.. .	2,751	2,465	172	2,081	836	808	....	2,245	1,982	2,684
Tulsa, Okla.. . . .	1,264	984	1,913	396	1,172	1,760	1,982	850	....	1,189
Washington, D.C..	133	221	2,754	793	2,047	2,799	2,684	447	1,189	....

Memorable Manned Space Flights

Sources: National Aeronautics and Space Administration and The World Almanac.

Crew, date	Mission name	Orbits[1]	Duration	Remarks
Yuri A. Gagarin (4/12/61)	Vostok 1	1	1h 48m	First manned orbital flight.
Alan B. Shepard Jr. (5/5/61)	Mercury-Redstone 3	(2)	15m 22s	First American in space.
Virgil I. Grissom (7/21/61)	Mercury-Redstone 4	(2)	15m 37s	Spacecraft sank. Grissom rescued.
Gherman S. Titov (8/6-7/61)	Vostok 2	16	25h 18m	First space flight of more than 24 hrs.
John H. Glenn Jr. (2/20/62)	Mercury-Atlas 6	3	4h 55m 23s	First American in orbit.
M. Scott Carpenter (5/24/62)	Mercury-Atlas 7	3	4h 56m 05s	Manual retrofire error caused 250 mi. landing overshoot.
Andrian G. Nikolayev (8/11-15/62)	Vostok 3	64	94h 22m	Vostok 3 and 4 made first group flight.
Pavel R. Popovich (8/12-15/62)	Vostok 4	48	70h 57m	On first orbit it came within 3 miles of Vostok 3.
Walter M. Schirra Jr. (10/3/62)	Mercury-Atlas 8	6	9h 13m 11s	Closest splashdown to target to date (4.5 mi.).
L. Gordon Cooper (5/15-16/63)	Mercury-Atlas 9	22	34h 19m 49s	First U.S. evaluation of effects on man of one day in space.
Valery F. Bykovsky (6/14-6/19/63)	Vostok 5	81	119h 06m	Vostok 5 and 6 made 2d group flight.
Valentina V. Tereshkova (6/16-19/63)	Vostok 6	48	70h 50m	First woman in space.
Vladimir M. Komarov, Konstantin P. Feoktistov, Boris B. Yegorov (10/12/64)	Voskhod 1	16	24h 17m	First 3-man orbital flight; first without space suits.
Pavel I. Belyayev, Aleksei A. Leonov (3/18/65)	Voskhod 2	17	26h 02m	Leonov made first "space walk" (10 min.)
Virgil I. Grissom, John W. Young (3/23/65)	Gemini-Titan 3	3	4h 53m 00s	First manned spacecraft to change its orbital path.
James A. McDivitt, Edward H. White 2d, (6/3-7/65)	Gemini-Titan 4	62	97h 56m 11s	White was first American to "walk in space" (20 min.).
L. Gordon Cooper Jr., Charles Conrad Jr. (8/21-29/65)	Gemini-Titan 5	120	190h 55m 14s	First use of fuel cells for electric power; evaluated guidance and navigation system.
Frank Borman, James A. Lovell Jr. (12/4-18/65)	Gemini-Titan 7	206	330h 35m 31s	Longest duration Gemini flight
Walter M. Schirra Jr., Thomas P. Stafford (12/15-16/65)	Gemini-Titan 6-A	16	25h 51m 24s	Completed world's first space rendezvous with Gemini 7.
Neil A. Armstrong, David R. Scott (3/16-17/66)	Gemini-Titan 8	6.5	10h 41m 26s	First docking of one space vehicle with another; mission aborted, control malfunction.
John W. Young, Michael Collins (7/18-21/66)	Gemini-Titan 10	43	70h 46m 39s	First use of Agena target vehicle's propulsion systems; rendezvoused with Gemini 8.
Charles Conrad Jr., Richard F. Gordon Jr. (9/12-15/66)	Gemini-Titan 11	44	71h 17m 08s	Docked, made 2 revolutions of earth tethered; set Gemini altitude record (739.2 mi.).
James A. Lovell Jr., Edwin E. Aldrin Jr. (11/11-15/66)	Gemini-Titan 12	59	94h 34m 31s	Final Gemini mission; record 5½ hrs. of extravehicular activity.
Vladimir M. Komarov (4/23/67)	Soyuz 1	17	26h 40m	Crashed after re-entry killing Komarov.
Walter M. Schirra Jr., Donn F. Eisele, R. Walter Cunningham (10/11-22/68)	Apollo-Saturn 7	163	260h 09m 03s	First manned flight of Apollo spacecraft command-service module only.
Georgi T. Beregovoi (10/26-30/68)	Soyuz 3	64	94h 51m	Made rendezvous with unmanned Soyuz 2.
Frank Borman, James A. Lovell Jr., William A. Anders (12/21-27/68)	Apollo-Saturn 8	10[3]	147h 00m 42s	First flight to moon (command-service module only); views of lunar surface televised to earth.
Vladimir A. Shatalov (1/14-17/69)	Soyuz 4	45	71h 14m	Docked with Soyuz 5.
Boris V. Volyanov, Aleksei S. Yeliseyev, Yevgeny V. Khrunov (1/15-18/69)	Soyuz 5	46	72h 46m	Docked with Soyuz 4; Yeliseyev and Khrunov transferred to Soyuz 4.
James A. McDivitt, David R. Scott, Russell L. Schweickart (3/3-13/69)	Apollo-Saturn 9	151	241h 00m 54s	First manned flight of lunar module.

Crew, date	Mission name	Orbits[1]	Duration	Remarks
Thomas P. Stafford, Eugene A. Cernan, John W. Young (5/18-26/69). . . .	Apollo-Saturn 10	31[4]	192h 03m 23s . .	First lunar module orbit of moon.
Neil A. Armstrong, Edwin E. Aldrin Jr., Michael Collins (7/16-24/69)	Apollo-Saturn 11	30[3]	195h 18m 35s . .	First lunar landing made by Armstrong and Aldrin; collected 48.5 lbs. of soil, rock samples; lunar stay time 21 h, 36m, 21 s.
Georgi S. Shonin, Valery N. Kubasov (10/11-16/69)	Soyuz 6	79	118h 42m.	First welding of metals in space.
Anatoly V. Filipchenko, Vladislav N. Volkov, Viktor V. Gorbatko (10/12-17/69)	Soyuz 7	79	118h 41m.	Space lab construction tests made; Soyuz 6, 7 and 8 — first time 3 spacecraft 7 crew orbited earth at once.
Charles Conrad Jr., Richard F. Gordon, Alan L. Bean (11/14-24/69)	Apollo-Saturn 12	45[3]	244h 36m 25s . .	Conrad and Bean made 2d moon landing; collected 74.7 lbs. of samples, lunar stay time 31 h, 31 m.
James A. Lovell Jr., Fred W. Haise Jr., John L. Swigart Jr. (4/11-17/70)	Apollo-Saturn 13	. . .	142h 54m 41s . .	Aborted after service module oxygen tank ruptured; crew returned safely using lunar module oxygen and power.
Alan B. Shepard Jr., Stuart A. Roosa, Edgar D. Mitchell (1/31-2/9/71).	Apollo-Saturn 14	34[3]	216h 01m 57s . .	Shepard and Mitchell made 3d moon landing, collected 96 lbs. of lunar samples; lunar stay 33 h, 31 m.
Georgi T. Dobrovolsky, Vladislav N. Volkov, Viktor I. Patsayev (6/6-30/71)	Soyuz 11	360	569h 40m.	Docked with Salyut space station; and orbited in Salyut for 23 days; crew died during re-entry from loss of pressurization.
David R. Scott, Alfred M. Worden, James B. Irwin (7/26-8/7/71).	Apollo-Saturn 15	74[3]	295h 11m 53s . .	Scott and Irwin made 4th moon landing; first lunar rover use; first deep space walk; 170 lbs. of samples; 66 h, 55 m, stay.
Charles M. Duke Jr., Thomas K. Mattingly, John W. Young (4/16-27/72)	Apollo-Saturn 16	64[3]	265h 51m 05s . .	Young and Duke made 5th moon landing; collected 213 lbs. of lunar samples; lunar stay line 71 h, 2 m.
Eugene A. Cernan, Ronald E. Evans, Harrison H. Schmitt (12/7-19/72)	Apollo-Saturn 17	75[3]	301h 51m 59s . .	Cernan and Schmitt made 6th manned lunar landing; collected 243 lbs. of samples; record lunar stay of 75 h.
Charles Conrad Jr., Joseph P. Kerwin, Paul J. Weitz (5/25-6/22/73)	Skylab 1	. . .	672h 49m 49s . .	First American manned orbiting space station; made long-flights tests, crew repaired damage caused during boost.
Alan L. Bean, Jack R. Lousma, Owen K. Garriott (7/28-9/25/73)	Skylab 2	. . .	1,427h 09m 04s . .	Crew systems and operational tests, exceeded pre-mission plans for scientific activities; space walk total 13h, 44 m.
Gerald P. Carr, Edward G. Gibson, William Pogue (11/16/73-2/8/74). . .	Skylab 3	. . .	2,017h 16m 30s . .	Final Skylab mission; record space walk of 7 h, 1 m., record space walks total for a mission 22 h, 21 m.
Alexi Leonov, Valeri Kubason (7/15-7/21/75) .	Soyuz 19	96	143h 31m	
Vance Brand, Thomas P. Stafford, Donald K. Slayton (7/15-7/24/75)	Apollo 18	136	217h 30m.	U.S.-USSR joint flight. Crews linked-up in space, conducted experiments, shared meals, and held a joint news conference.
Leonid Kizim, Vladmir Solovyov, Oleg Atkov (2/9-10/2/84).	Salyut 7	. . .	237 days.	Set space endurance record.

(1) The U.S. measures orbital flights in revolutions while the Soviets use "orbits." (2) Suborbital. (3) Moon orbits in command module. (4) Moon orbits.

Fire aboard spacecraft Apollo I on the ground at Cape Kennedy, Fla. killed Virgil I. Grissom, Edward H. White and Roger B. Chaffee on Jan. 27, 1967. They were the only U.S. astronauts killed in space tests.

U.S. Space Shuttles

Name, date	Crew	Name, date	Crew
Columbia (4/12-14/81) . . .	Robert L. Crippen, John W. Young.	Challenger (4/4-9/83)	Paul Weitz, Karol Bobko, Story Musgrave, Donald Peterson.
Columbia (11/12-14/81) . .	Joe Engle, Richard Truly.	Challenger (6/18-24/83) . .	Robert L. Crippen, Norman Thagard, John Fabian, Frederick Hauck, Sally K. Ride (1st U.S. woman in space).
Columbia (3/22-30/82) . . .	Jack Lousma, C. Gordon Fullerton.		
Columbia (6-27/7-4/82) . . .	Thomas Mattingly 2d, Henry Hartsfield Jr.		
Columbia (11/11-16/82) . .	Vance Brand, Robert Overmyer, William Lenoir, Joseph Allen.	Challenger (8/30-9/5/83) . .	Richard Truly, Daniel Brandenstein, William Thornton,

U.S. Space Shuttles

Name, date	Crew	Name, date	Crew
Columbia (11/28-12/8/83) .	Guion Bluford (1st U.S. black in space), Dale Gardner. John Young, Brewster Shaw Jr., Robert Parker, Owen Garriott, Byron Lichtenberg, Ulf Merbold.	Discovery (1/24-27/85) . . .	Fisher, Joseph P. Allen, Dale A. Gardner. Thomas K. Mattingly, Loren J. Shriver, James F. Buchli, Ellison S. Onizuka, Gary E. Payton.
Challenger (2/3-11/84) . ..	Vance Brand, Robert Gibson, Ronald McNair, Bruce McCandless, Robert Stewart.	Discovery (4/12-19/85) . . .	Karol J. Bobko, Donald E. Williams, Sen. Jake Garn, Charles D. Walker, Jeffrey A. Hoffman, S.
Challenger (4/6-13/84) . . .	Robert L. Crippen, Francis R. Scobee, George D. Nelson, Terry J. Hart, James D. Van Hoften.	Challenger (4/29-5/6/85). .	David Griggs, M. Rhea Seddon. Robert F. Overmyer, Frederick D. Gregory, Don
Discovery (8/30-9/5/84) . .	Henry W. Hartsfield Jr., Michael L. Coats, Steven A. Hawley, Judith A. Resnik, Richard M. Mullane, Charles D. Walker.		L. Lind, Taylor G. Wang, Lodewijk van den Berg, Norman Thagard, William Thornton.
Challenger (10/5-13/84) . .	Robert L. Crippen, Jon A. McBride, Kathryn D. Sullivan, Sally K. Ride, Marc Garneau (first Canadian), David C. Leestma, Paul D. Scully-Power.	Challenger (7/29-8/6/85). .	Roy D. Bridges Jr., Anthony W. England, Karl G. Henize, F. Story Musgrave, C. Gordon Fullerton, Loren W. Acton, John-David F. Bartoe.
Discovery (11/8-16/84) . . .	Frederick H. Hauck, David M. Walker, Dr. Anna L.	Discovery (8/27-9/3/85) . .	John M. Lounge, James D. van Hoften, William F. Fisher, Joe H. Engle, Richard O. Covey.

Notable Around the World and Intercontinental Flights

(Certified by Federation Aeronautique Internationale)

	From/To	Miles	Time	Date
Nellie Bly	New York/New York.		72d 06h 11m	1889
George Francis Train	New York/New York.		67d 12h 03m	1890
Charles Fitzmorris.	Chicago/Chicago		60d 13h 29m	1901
J. W. Willis Sayre	Seattle/Seattle		54d 09h 42m	1903
J. Alcock-A.W. Brown (1)	Newfoundland/Ireland	1,960	16h 12m	June 14-15, 1919
Two U.S. Army airplanes.	Seattle/Seattle	26,103	35d 01h 11m	1924
Richard E. Byrd (2)	Spitsbergen/N. Pole.	1,545	15h 30m	May 9, 1926
Amundsen-Ellsworth-Nobile Expedition.	Spitsbergen/Teller, Alaska		80h	May 11-14,1926
E.S. Evans and L. Wells (N. Y.World) (3)	New York/New York	18,400	28d 14h 36m 05s	June 16-July 14, 1926
Charles Lindbergh (4).	New York/Paris.	3,610	33h 29m 30s	May 20-21, 1927
Amelia Earhart, W. Stultz, L. Gordon . .	Newfoundland/Wales.		20h 40m	June 17-18, 1928
Graf Zepppelin	Friedrichshafen, Ger./Lakehurst, N.J...	6,630	4d 15h 46m	Oct. 11-15, 1928
Graf Zeppelin	Friedrichshafen, Ger./Lakehurst, N.J. . .	21,700	20d 04h	Aug. 14-Sept. 4, 1929
Wiley Post and Harold Gatty (Monoplane Winnie Mae)	New York/New York	15,474	8d 15h 51m	July 1, 1931
C. Pangborn-H. Herndon Jr. (5)	Tokyo/Wanatchee, Wash.	4,458	41h 34m	Oct. 3-5, 1931
Amelia Earhart (6)	Newfoundland/Ireland	2,026	14h 56m	May 20-21, 1932
Wiley Post (Monoplane Winnie Mae) (7)	New York/New York	15,596	115h 36m 30s	July 15-22, 1933
Hindenburg Zeppelin	Lakehurst, N.J./Frankfort, Ger.		42h 53m	Aug. 9-11, 1936
H. R. Ekins (Scripps-Howard Newspapers in race) (Zeppelin Hindenburg to Germany air planes from Frankfurt)	Lakehurst, N.J./Lakehurst, N.J.	25,654	18d 11h 14m 33s	Sept. 30-Oct. 19, 1936
Howard Hughes and 4 assistants.	New York/New York	14,824	3d 19h 08m 10s	July 10-13, 1938
Douglas Corrigan	New York/Dublin		28h 13m	July 17-18, 1938
Mrs. Clara Adams (Pan American Clipper)	Port Washington, N.Y./ Newark, N.J.		16d 19h 04m	June 28-July 15, 1939
Globester, U.S. Air Transport Command	Wash., D.C./Wash., D.C.	23,279	149h 44m	Oct. 4, 1945
Capt. William P. Odom (A-26 Reynolds Bombshell)	New York/New York	20,000	78h 55m 12s	Apr. 12-16, 1947
America, Pan American 4-engine Lockheed Constellation (8).	New York/New York	22,219	101h 32m	June 17-30, 1947
Col. Edward Eagan	New York/New York	20,559	147h 15m	Dec. 13, 1948
USAF B-50 Lucky Lady II (Capt. James Gallagher) (9)	Ft. Worth, Tex./Ft. Worth, Tex. . . .	23,452	94h 01m	Feb. 26-Mar. 2, 1949
Col. D. Schilling, USAF (10).	England/Limestone, Me.	3,300	10h 01m	Sept. 22, 1950
C.F. Blair Jr..	Norway/Alaska	3,300	10h 29m	May 29, 1951
Two U.S. S-55	Massachusetts/Scotland	3,410	42h 30m	July 15-31, 1952
Canberra Bomber (11)	N. Ireland/Newfoundland	2,073	04h 34m	Aug. 26, 1952
	Newfoundland/N. Ireland	2,073	03h 25m	Aug. 26, 1952

(continued)

	From/To	Miles	Time	Date
Three USAF B-52 Stratofort- resses (12)	Merced, Cal./Cal.	24,325	45h 19m	Jan. 15-18, 1957
Max Conrad	Chicago/Rome	5,000	34h 03m	Mar. 5-6, 1959
USSR TU-114 (13)	Moscow/New York	5,092	11h 06m	June 28, 1959
Boeing 707-320	New York/Moscow	c.5090	08h 54m	July 23, 1959
Peter Gluckmann (solo)	San Francisco/San Francisco	22,800	29d	Aug. 22-Sept. 20, 1959
Sue Snyder	Chicago/Chicago	21,219	62h 59m	June 22-24, 1960
Max Conrad (solo)	Miami/Miami	25,946	8d 18h 35m 57s	Feb. 28-Mar. 8, 1961
Sam Miller & Louis Fodor	New York/New York		46h 28m	Aug. 3-4, 1963
Robert & Joan Wallick	Manila/Manila	23,129	05d 06h 17m 10s	June 2-7, 1966
Arthur Godfrey, Richard Merrill Fred Austin, Karl Keller	New York/New York	23,333	86h 9m 01s	June 4-7, 1966
Trevor K. Brougham	Darwin, Australia/Darwin	24,800	5d 05h 57m	Aug. 5-10, 1972
Walter H. Mullikin, Albert Frink, Lyman Watt, Frank Cassaniti, Edward Shields	New York/New York	23,137	1d 22h 50s	May 1-3,1976
Arnold Palmer	Denver/Denver	22,985	57h 25m 42s	May 17-19, 1976
Boeing 747 (14)	San Francisco/San Francisco	26,382	54h 7m 12s	Oct. 28-31, 1977
Concorde	London/Wash., D.C.	1,023 mph	03h 34m 48s	May 29, 1976
Concorde	Paris/Wash., D.C.	1,071.86 mph	03h 35m 15s	Aug. 18, 1978
Concorde	Paris/New York	1,037.50 mph	03h 30m 11s	Aug. 22, 1978

(1) Non-stop transtlantic flight. (2) Polar flight. (3) Mileage by train and auto, 4,110; by plane, 6,300; by steamship, 8,000. (4) Solo transatlantic flight in the Ryan monoplane the "Spirit of St. Louis". (5) Non-stop Pacific flight. (6) Woman's transoceanic solo flight. (7) First to fly solo around northern circumference of the world, also first to fly twice around the world. (8) Inception of regular commercial global air service. (9) First non-stop round-the-world flight, refueled 4 times in flight. (10) Non-stop jet transatlantic flight. (11) Transatlantic round trip on same day. (12) First non-stop global flight by jet planes; refueled in flight by KC-97 aerial tankers; average speed approx. 525 mph. (13) Non-stop between Moscow and New York. (14) Speed record around the world over both the earth's poles.

National Aviation Hall of Fame

The National Aviation Hall of Fame at Dayton, Oh., is dedicated to honoring the outstanding pioneers of air and space.

Allen, William M.
Armstrong, Neil A.
Arnold, Henry H. "Hap"
Atwood, John Leland

Balchen, Bernt
Baldwin, Thomas S.
Beachley, Lincoln
Beech, Olive A.
Beech, Walter H.
Bell, Alexander Graham
Bell, Lawrence D.
Boeing, William E.
Borman, Frank
Boyd, Albert
Brown, George "Scratchley"
Byrd, Richard E.

Cessna, Clyde V.
Chamberlin, Clarence D.
Chanute, Octave
Chennault, Claire L.
Cochran (Odlum), Jacqueline
Collins, Michael
Conrad Jr., Charles
Crossfield, A. Scott
Cunningham, Alfred A.
Curtiss, Glenn H.

deSeversky, Alexander P.
Doolittle, James H.
Douglas, Donald W.

Draper, Charles S.

Eaker, Ira C.
Earhart, (Putnam), Amelia
Eielson, C. Benjamin
Ellyson, Theodore G.
Ely, Eugene B.

Fairchild, Sherman M.
Fleet, Reuben H.
Fokker, Anthony H.G.
Ford, Henry
Foss, Joseph
Foulois, Benjamin D.

Gabreski, Francis S.
Glenn Jr., John H.
Goddard, George W.
Goddard, Robert H.
Goldwater, Barry M.
Gross, Robert E.
Grumman, Leroy R.
Guggenheim, Harry F.

Hegenberger, Albert F.
Heinemann, Edward H.
Hughes, Howard R.

Ingalls, David S.

Johnson, Clarence L.

Kenney, George C.

Kettering, Charles F.
Kindelberger, James H.
Knabenshue, A. Roy

Lahm, Frank P.
Langley, Samuel P.
Lear, William P. Sr.
LeMay, Curtis E.
LeVier, Anthony W.
Lindbergh, Anne M.
Lindbergh, Charles A.
Link, Edwin A.
Loening, Grover
Luke Jr., Frank

Macready, John A.
Martin, Glenn L.
Mcdonnell, James S.
Mitchell, William "Billy"
Montgomery, John J.
Moss, Sanford A.

Northrop, John K.

Patterson, William A.
Piper Sr., William T.
Post, Wiley H.

Read, Albert C.
Reeve, Robert C.
Rentschler, Frederick B.
Richardson, Holden C.

Rickenbacker, Edward V.
Rodgers, Calbraith P.
Rogers, Will
Ryan, T. Claude

Schriever, Bernard A.
Selfridge, Thomas E.
Shepard Jr., Alan B.
Sikorsky, Igor I.
Six, Robert F.
Smith, C.R.
Spaatz, Carl A.
Sperry Sr., Elmer A.
Sperry Sr., Lawrence B.
Stapp, John P.

Taylor, Charles E.
Towers, John H.
Trippe, Juan T.
Turner, Roscoe
Twining, Nathan F.

von Braun, Wernher
von Karman, Theodore
Wade, Leigh
Walden, Henry W.
Wilson, Thornton A.
Wright, Orville
Wright, Wilbur

Yeager, Charles

The Busiest U.S. Airports in 1984

Source: Federal Aviation Administration; (Total take-offs and landings)

Chicago O'Hare International	741,296	St. Louis International	395,906
Atlanta International	689,482	Boston Logan	387,422
Van Nuys	575,721	Anchorage Merrill	384,030
Los Angeles International	550,756	Oakland International	379,192
Dallas Ft. Worth Regional	524,564	Seattle Boeing	375,670
Denver Stapleton International	512,520	Newark	369,990
Santa Ana	488,540	La Guardia (N.Y. City)	365,118
Long Beach	449,208	San Jose Municipal	363,722
San Francisco	403,850	Denver Arapahoe County	362,777
Phoenix Sky Harbor	399,298	J.F. Kennedy International (N.Y. City)	356,647

International Aeronautical Records

Source: The National Aeronautic Association, 1400 Eye St. NW, Washington, DC 20005, representative in the United States of the Federation Aeronautique Internationale, certifying agency for world aviation and space records. The International Aeronautical Federation was formed in 1905 by representatives from Belgium, France, Germany, Great Britain, Spain, Italy, Switzerland, and the United States, with headquarters in Paris. Regulations for the control of official records were signed Oct. 14, 1905. World records are defined as maximum performance, regardless of class or type of aircraft used. Records to June, 1985.

World Air Records—Maximum Performance in Any Class

Speed over a straight course — 3,529.56 kph. (2,193.16 mph) — Capt. Elden W. Joersz, USAF, Lockheed SR-71; Beale AFB, Cal., July 28, 1976.
Speed over a closed circuit — 3,367.221 kph. (2,092.294 mph) — Maj. Adolphus H. Bledsoe Jr., USAF, Lockheed SR-71; Beale AFB, Cal., July 27, 1976.
Distance in a straight line — 20,168.78 kms (12,532.28 mi.) — Maj. Clyde P. Evely, USAF, Boeing B52-H; Kadena, Okinawa to Madrid, Spain, Jan. 11, 1962.
Distance over a closed circuit — 18,245.05 kms (11,336.92 mi.) — Capt. William Stevenson, USAF, Boeing B52-H; Seymour-Johnson, N.C., June 6-7, 1962.
Altitude — 37,650 meters (123,523.58 feet) — Alexander Fedotov, USSR, E-266M; Podmoskovnoye, USSR, Aug. 31, 1977.
Altitude in horizontal flight — 25,929.031 meters (85,068.997 ft.) — Capt. Robert C. Helt, USAF, Lockheed SR-71; Beale AFB, Cal., July 28, 1976.

Class K Spacecraft

Duration — 211 days, 9 hrs., 4 min., 32 sec. — Anatoly Berezovnoy & Valentin Lebedev, USSR, Salyut 7, Soyuz T5, Soyuz T7; May 13-Dec. 10, 1982.
Altitude — 377,668.9 kms (234,672.5 mi.) — Frank Borman, James A. Lovell Jr., William Anders, Apollo 8; Dec. 21-27, 1968.
Greatest mass lifted — 127,980 kgs. (282,197 lbs.) — Frank Borman, James S. Lovell Jr., William Anders, Apollo 8; Dec. 21-27, 1968.
Distance — 140,800,200 kms. (87,436,800 mi.) — Anatoly Berezovnoy & Valentin Lebedev, USSR, Salyut 7, Soyuz T5, Soyuz T7; May 13-Dec. 10, 1982.

World "Class" Records

All other records, international in scope, are termed World "Class" records and are divided into classes: airships, free balloons, airplanes, seaplanes, amphibians, gliders, and rotorplanes. Airplanes (Class C) are sub-divided into four groups: Group I — piston engine aircraft, Group II — turboprop aircraft, Group III — jet aircraft, Group IV — rocket powered aircraft. A partial listing of world records follows:

Airplanes (Class C-I, Group I—piston engine)

Distance, closed circuit — 16,104.0 kms (10,007 mi.) — Jerry Mullens; BD-2; Oklahoma City, Okla.—Jacksonville, Fla. course; Dec. 5-8, 1981.
Distance, straight line — 18,081.99 kms. (11,235.6 miles) — Cmdr. Thomas D. Davies, USN; Cmdr. Eugene P. Rankin, USN; Cmdr. Walter S. Reid, USN, and Lt. Cmdr. Ray A. Tabeling, USN; Lockheed P2V-1; from Pearce Field, Perth, Australia to Columbus, Oh., Sept. 29-Oct. 1, 1946.
Speed over 3-kilometer measured course — 803.138 kph. (499.04 mph) — Steve Hinton; P-51D; Tonopah, Nev., Aug. 14, 1979.
Speed for 100 kilometers (62.137 miles) without payload — 755.668 kph. (469.549 mph.) — Jacqueline Cochran, U.S.; North American P-51; Coachella Valley, Cal., Dec. 10, 1947.
Speed for 1,000 kilometers (621.369 miles) without payload — 693.78 kph. (431.09 mph.) — Jacqueline Cochran, U.S.; North American P-51; Santa Rosasummit, Cal. — Flagstaff, Ariz. course, May 24, 1948.
Speed for 5,000 kilometers (3,106.849 miles) without payload — 544.59 kph. (338.39 mph.) — Capt. James Bauer, USAF, Boeing B-29; Dayton, Oh., June 28, 1946.
Speed around the world — 327.73 kph (203.64 mph) — D.N. Dalton, Australia; Beechcraft Duke; Brisbane, Aust., July 20-25, 1975. Time: 5 days, 2 hours, 19 min., 57 sec.

Light Airplanes—(Class C-1.d)

Distance in a straight line — 12,341.20 kms. (7,668.48 miles) — Max Conrad, U.S.; Piper Comanche; Casablanca, Morocco to Los Angeles, June 2-4, 1959.
Speed for 100 kilometers — (62,137 miles) in a closed circuit — 519.480 kph. (322.780 mph.) — Ms. R. M. Sharpe, Great Britain; Vickers Supermarine Spitfire 5-B; Wolverhampton, June 17, 1950.

Helicopters (Class E-1)

Distance in a straight line — 3,561.55 kms. (2,213.04 miles) — Robert G. Ferry, U.S.; Hughes YOH-6A helicopter; Culver City, Cal., to Ormond Beach, Fla., Apr. 6-7, 1966.
Speed over 3-km. course — 348.971 kph. (216.839 mph.) — Byron Graham, U.S.; Sikorsky S-67 helicopter; Windsor Locks, Conn., Dec. 14, 1970.
Speed around the world —56.97 kph. (35.40 mph) — H. Ross Perot Jr.; Bell 206 L-11 Long Ranger N39112; Dallas, Tex.–Dallas, Tex.; Sept. 1-30, 1982; 29 days, 3 hrs., 8 min., 13 sec.

Gliders (Class D-I—single place)

Distance, straight line — 1,460.8 kms. (907.7 miles) — Hans Werner Grosse, West Germany; ASK12 sailplane; Luebeck to Biarritz, Apr. 25, 1972.
Altitude above sea level — 14,102 meters (46,267 feet) — Paul F. Bikle, U.S.; Sailplane Schweizer SGS-123-E; Mojave, Lancaster, Cal., Feb. 25, 1961.

Airplanes (Class C-I, Group II—Turboprop)

Distance in a straight line — 14,052.95 kms. (8,732.09 miles) — Lt. Col. Edgar L. Allison Jr., USAF, Lockheed HC-130 Hercules aircraft; Taiwan to Scott AFB, Ill.; Feb. 20, 1972.
Altitude — 15,549 meters (51,014 ft.) — Donald R. Wilson, U.S.; LTV L450F aircraft; Greenville, Tex., Mar. 27, 1972.
Speed for 1,000 kilometers (621.369 miles) without payload — 871.38 kph. (541.449 mph.) — Ivan Soukhomline, USSR; TU-114 aircraft; Sternberg, USSR; Mar. 24, 1960.
Speed for 5,000 kilometers (3,106.849 miles) without payload — 877.212 kph. (545.072 mph.) — Ivan Soukhomline, USSR; TU-114 aircraft, Sternberg, USSR; Apr. 9, 1960.

Speed over a 3-kilometer course — 1,590.45 kph (988.26 mph) — Darryl G. Greenamyer, U.S.; F-104; Tonopah, Nev., Oct. 24, 1977.
Speed for 100 kilometers in a closed circuit — 2,605 kph. (1,618.7 mph.) — Alexander Fedotov, USSR; E-266 airplane, Apr. 8, 1973.
Speed for 500 kilometers in a closed circuit — 2,981.5 kph. (1,852.61 mph.) — Mikhail Komarov, USSR; E-266 airplane, Oct. 5, 1967.
Speed for 1,000 kilometers in a closed circuit — 3,367.221 kph (2,092.294 mph) — Maj. Adolphus H. Bledsoe Jr., USAF; Lockheed SR-71; Beale AFB, Cal., July 27, 1976.
Speed for 2,000 kilometers in closed circuit — 2,012,257 kph. (1,250.42 mph.) — S. Agapov, USSR; Podmoscovnde, USSR; July 20, 1983.
Speed around the world — 825.32 kph. (512.853 mph) — Brooke Knapp, U.S., Gulfstream III; Washington, D.C., Feb. 13-15, 1984.

Balloons-Class A

Altitude — 34,668 meters (113,739.9 feet) — Cmdr. Malcolm D. Ross, USNR; Lee Lewis Memorial Winzen Research Balloon; Gulf of Mexico, May 4, 1961.
Distance —8,382.4 kms. (5,208.67 mi.) — Ben Abruzzo; Raven Experimental; Nagashima, Japan to Covello, Cal., Nov. 9-12, 1981.

Duration —137 hr., 5 min., 50 sec. — Ben Abruzzo and Maxie Anderson; Double Eagle II; Presque Isle, Maine to Miserey, France (3,107.61 mi.); Aug. 12-17, 1978.

FAI Course Records

Los Angeles to New York — 1,954.79 kph (1,214.65 mph) — Capt. Robert G. Sowers, USAF; Convair B-58 Hustler; elapsed time: 2 hrs. 58.71 sec., Mar. 5, 1962.
New York to Los Angeles — 1,741 kph (1,081.80 mph) — Capt. Robert G. Sowers, USAF; Convair B-58 Hustler; elapsed time: 2 hrs. 15 min. 50.08 sec., Mar. 5, 1962.
New York to Paris — 1,753.068 kph (1,089.36 mph) — Maj. W. R. Payne, U.S.; Convair B-58 Hustler; elapsed time: 3 hrs 19 min. 44 sec., May 26, 1961.
London to New York — 945.423 kph (587.457 mph) — Maj. Burl Davenport, USAF; Boeing KC-135; elapsed time: 5 hrs. 53 min. 12.77 sec.; June 27, 1958.
Baltimore to Moscow, USSR — 906.64 kph (563.36 mph) — Col. James B. Swindal, USAF; Boeing VC-137 (707); elapsed time: 8 hrs. 33 min. 45.4 sec., May 19, 1963.
New York to London — 2,908.026 kph (1,806.964 mph) — Maj. James V. Sullivan, USAF; Lockheed SR-71; elapsed time 1 hr. 54 min. 56.4 sec., Sept. 1, 1974.
London to Los Angeles — 2,310.353 kph (1,435.587 mph) — Capt. Harold B. Adams, USAF; Lockheed SR-71; elapsed time: 3 hrs. 47 min. 39 sec., Sept. 13, 1974.

U.S. Scheduled Airline Traffic

Source: Air Transport Association of America (thousands)

Passenger traffic	1982	1983	1984
Revenue passengers enplaned	294,102	318,638	343,264
Revenue passenger miles	259,643,870	281,829,148	304,458,727
Available seat miles	440,119,206	464,537,979	514,010,029
Cargo traffic (ton miles)	6,885,973	7,573,014	8,168,805
Freight	5,424,233	6,026,755	6,489,815
Express	57,965	66,177	62,395
U.S. Mail	1,374,572	1,449,824	1,581,331
Overall traffic and service			
Nonscheduled traffic—total ton miles	2,200,552	2,255,305	2,490,618
Total revenue ton miles—all services	35,050,938	38,011,227	41,105,321
Total available ton miles—all services	65,769,930	68,778,295	75,940,114

NASA Outlays for Research and Development

Source: U.S. Office of Management and Budget

(millions of dollars)

Year	Total outlays	Percent change	Performance Total	Space flight	Space science applications	Air transport and other	Facilities Total	Space flight	Space science applications	Air transport and other
1965	$5,093	22.1[1]	$4,562	$3,318	$1,126	$298	$531	$401	$78	$52
1966	5,933	16.5	5,361	3,819	1,120	422	572	391	63	118
1967	5,426	−8.5	5,137	3,477	1,160	500	289	172	47	70
1968	4,726	−12.9	4,599	3,028	1,061	510	127	69	29	29
1969	4,252	−10.0	4,187	2,754	893	540	65	27	21	17
1970	3,753	−11.7	3,699	2,195	963	541	54	14	21	19
1971	3,382	−9.9	3,338	1,877	926	535	44	8	6	30
1972	3,423	1.2	3,373	1,727	1,111	535	50	13	7	30
1973	3,316	−3.1	3,271	1,532	1,220	519	45	5	11	29
1974	3,256	−1.8	3,181	1,448	1,156	577	75	25	12	38
1975	3,266	.3	3,181	1,500	1,076	606	85	35	9	42
1976	3,670	12.4	3,549	1,934	969	646	121	66	11	43
1977	3,945	7.5	3,840	2,195	1,002	643	105	56	4	45
1978	3,984	1.0	3,860	2,204	964	692	124	56	8	60
1979	4,187	5.0	4,054	2,175	1,144	735	133	41	9	83
1980	4,850	15.8	4,710	2,556	1,341	813	140	38	5	97
1981	5,241	11.8	5,274	3,026	1,380	868	147	26	4	117
1982	6,035	11.3	5,926	3,526	1,454	946	109	17	3	89
1983	6,664	10.4	6,556	4,027	1,486	1,043	108	26	—	82
1984, est.	7,068	6.1	6,930	4,053	1,587	1,290	139	38	3	98

(1) Change from 1964.

AGRICULTURE

World Wheat, Rice and Corn Production, 1983

Source: UN Food and Agriculture Organization

(thousands of metric tons)

Country	Wheat	Rice	Corn	Country	Wheat	Rice	Corn
World, total	498,182	144,473	344,103	Italy	8,514	1,060	6,900
				Japan	747	12,958	2[1]
United States	66,010	4,523	106,781	Kampuchea	NA	1,700	60[1]
Afghanistan	3,750[3]	650[3]	1,000[3]	Korea, Dem. Peo. Rep.[1]	500	5,200[1]	2,500[1]
Argentina	11,700	277	8,840	Korea, Republic of	112	7,608	101
Australia	21,780	522	95	Laos	NA	1,002	39
Austria	1,415	NA	1,437	Madagascar	—	2,147	115
Bangladesh	1,095	21,700	1[1]	Malaysia	NA	2,000	9[1]
Belgium[2]	1,084[1]	NA	38[1]	Mexico	3,697	655	13,928
Brazil	2,273	7,760	18,756	Nepal	657	2,744	768
Bulgaria	3,600	72	3,101	Netherlands	1,043	NA	—
Burma	183	14,500[1]	301	New Zealand	280	NA	176[3]
Canada	26,914	NA	5,875	Pakistan	12,414	5,210	1,000[3]
Chile	800[1]	107	512[3]	Panama	NA	169[3]	68[3]
China: Mainland[1]	81,392[3]	17,218	64,135[1]	Peru	75[3]	770	583
Colombia	73[3]	1,780	867[3]	Philippines	NA	8,150	3,385
Cuba	NA	490	96[1]	Poland	5,165	NA	64
Czechoslovakia	5,820[3]	NA	710[1]	Portugal	281	100[3]	475[3]
Denmark	1,577	NA	NA	Romania	5,000[1]	50	10,500[1]
Ecuador	23[3]	222	258[3]	South Africa	1,770	3[1]	3,910
Egypt	1,996	2,440		Soviet Union	82,000[1]	2,500[1]	14,000[1]
Ethiopia	950[1]	NA	3,510[3]	Spain	4,330	223	1,788
Finland	550	NA	NA	Sri Lanka	NA	2,200	25[1]
France	24,781	32	10,143	Sweden	1,721	NA	NA
German Dem. Rep.	3,470	NA	1[3]	Switzerland	436	NA	136
Germany, Fed. Rep.	8,998	NA	934	Syria	1,612	—	70[3]
Greece	2,026	78	1,622	Thailand	NA	18,535	3,552
Hungary	4,800	40[1]	7,600[1]	Turkey	16,400	325[1]	1,375[1]
India	42,502	90,000[1]	7,300[1]	United Kingdom	10,880	NA	1[1]
Indonesia	NA	34,300	4,000[3]	Uruguay	450	332[3]	103[3]
Iran	6,669[1]	1,400[1]	55[1]	Venezuela	—	509	429
Iraq	1,000[1]	200[1]	90[1]	Vietnam	NA	14,500[1]	420[1]
Ireland	350[3]	NA	NA	Yugoslavia	5,519		10,688
Israel	335	NA	28				

(1) FAO estimate. (2) Includes Luxembourg. (3) Unofficial figure. (NA) Not available.

Wheat, Rice and Corn—Exports and Imports of 10 Leading Countries

Source: U.S Agriculture Department

(In thousands of metric tons.)

Leading Exporters	Exports			Leading Importers	Imports		
	1980	1981	1983/84*		1980	1981	1983/84*
Wheat				**Wheat**			
United States	35,756	43,909	38,860	Soviet Union	14,700	16,500	20,500
Canada	16,760	15,472	21,764	China: Mainland	12,255	13,038	9,600
France	9,889	12,785	13,969	Japan	5,682	5,633	5,857
Australia	14,876	10,552	11,600	Brazil	4,755	4,360	3,948
Argentina	4,495	3,758	9,570	Egypt	4,417	3,949	6,712
Soviet Union	1,270	1,600	500	Poland	3,466	3,448	2,155
United Kingdom	1,057	1,450	1,850	Italy	3,134	3,016	1,450
Hungary	814	1,298	1,300	Morocco	1,652	2,368	2,128
Netherlands	525	626	920	Iran	1,330	2,060	3,700
Spain	45	538	50	Korea, Rep. of	1,868	1,957	2,351
Rice				**Rice**			
Thailand	2,797	3,138	4,528	Korea, Rep. of	899	2,585	7
United States	3,054	3,133	2,129	Soviet Union	694	1,283	450
Pakistan	1,087	1,244	1,057	Nigeria	400	600	450
India	575	953	200	Indonesia	2,012	538	387
Japan	689	855	102	Iran	470	500	730
Burma	653	700	750	Saudi Arabia	356	427	530
China: Mainland	1,311	692	1,000	Hong Kong	359	360	5
Italy	577	572	402	Iraq	345	350	500
Korea, Dem. Peo. Rep.	300	300	250	Malaysia	168	342	500
Australia	457	281	370	Senegal	279	321	375
Corn				**Corn**			
United States	63,152	54,856	47,380	Soviet Union	10,000	14,630	9,500
Argentina	3,481	9,112	5,885	Japan	12,830	13,590	14,485
South Africa	3,317	4,400	0	Spain	4,532	4,830	3,460
Thailand	2,175	2,549	3,033	China: Mainland	4,405	3,261	131
France	3,181	2,355	4,723	Korea, Rep. of	2,351	3,051	3,357
Belgium-Luxembourg	1,357	1,486	1,240	Mexico	3,713	2,844	2,459
Canada	771	1,207	429	Portugal	2,624	2,644	2,105
Romania	1,000	1,000	1,000	Netherlands	3,010	2,622	2,161
Netherlands	490	459	54	Belgium-Luxembourg	2,570	2,576	2,200
Yugoslavia	273	220	1,078	Italy	2,931	2,556	1,583

*Note: Wheat 1983/84, July/June; Rice, 1984 calendar year; Corn 1983/84, Oct./Sept.

Agricultural Products — U.S. and World Production and Exports

Source: Foreign Agricultural Service, U.S. Agriculture Department

1984/85 Commodity	Unit	Production U.S.	Production World	% U.S.	Exports[1] U.S.	Exports[1] World	% U.S.
Wheat	MMT	70.6	513.9	13.7	38.1	105.6	36.1
Oats	MMT	7.5	45.3	16.6	0.02	1.8	1.1
Corn	MMT	194.5	452.2	43.0	48.9	68.5	71.4
Barley	MMT	13.0	173.2	7.5	1.3	18.8	6.9
Rice (milled basis)	MMT	4.4	318.2	1.4	1.9	11.9	16.0
Sorghum	MMT	22.0	67.1	32.8	7.0	12.2	57.4
Soybeans	MMT	50.6	90.9	55.7	16.3	24.6	66.3
Tobacco, unmfd.	MMT	0.78	6.3	12.4	0.25	1.4	17.9
Edible, Veg. Oils	MMT	6.0	43.7	13.7	1.1	14.0	7.9
Cotton (lint)	MB[2]	13.0	85.8	15.2	6.3	20.5	30.7

(1) Standard Trade Years Wheat: July-June (84/85); Oats: Oct-Sept (84/85); Corn: Oct-Sept (84/85); Barley: Oct-Sept (84/85); Rice: Aug-July (84/85); Sorghum: Oct-Sept (84/85); Soybeans: Sept-Aug (84/85); Tobacco: Jan-Dec (84); Edible Veg. Oils: Jan-Dec (85); Cotton: Aug-July (84/85). (2) Million Bales.

Grain, Hay, Potato, Cotton, Soybean, Tobacco Production

Source: Economic Research Service: U.S. Agriculture Department

1984 State	Barley 1,000 bushels	Corn, grain 1,000 bushels	Cotton lint 1,000 bales[1]	All hay 1,000 tons	Oats 1,000 bushels	Potatoes 1,000 cwt.	Soybeans 1,000 bushels	Tobacco 1,000 pounds	All wheat 1,000 bushels
Alabama	—	25,025	451	1,360	1,440	1,599	28,770	—	14,820
Alaska	—	—	—	—	—	—	—	—	—
Arizona	5,353	3,640	1,160	1,180	—	1,647	—	—	12,780
Arkansas	—	4,655	600	1,559	1,960	—	101,400	—	61,600
California	28,980	51,000	2,920	7,854	3,450	22,767	—	—	61,840
Colorado[2]	20,150	91,120	—	3,311	2,750	19,213	—	—	115,300
Connecticut[2]	—	—	—	212	—	315	—	2,868	—
Delaware	2,750	16,500	—	56	—	1,265	6,000	—	2,009
Florida	—	13,650	27	696	—	7,924	7,800	17,780	—
Georgia	—	80,770	280	1,320	3,300	—	40,000	85,800	31,150
Hawaii	—	—	—	—	—	—	—	—	—
Idaho	88,440	8,850	—	4,743	2,992	86,600	—	—	81,400
Illinois	—	1,247,160	—	3,880	10,725	636	288,640	—	70,400
Indiana	—	705,510	—	2,344	4,960	966	150,075	20,382	48,300
Iowa	—	1,444,800	—	7,850	47,360	210	264,600	—	3,500
Kansas	4,085	108,750	—	6,120	6,360	—	28,350	—	431,200
Kentucky	1,110	146,000	—	3,346	252	—	42,349	535,525	19,000
Louisiana	—	9,430	1,045	816	—	60	64,260	—	13,120
Maine[2]	—	—	—	410	2,240	21,360	—	—	—
Maryland	5,510	69,620	—	634	855	296	12,325	31,200	6,020
Massachusetts[2]	—	—	—	300	—	580	—	785	—
Michigan	2,040	220,080	—	5,285	21,700	15,100	32,130	—	45,600
Minnesota	61,750	689,080	—	8,440	—	5,455	172,920	—	120,711
Mississippi	—	4,900	4,651	1,292	78,000	—	76,800	—	25,080
Missouri	—	154,400	195	6,338	1,584	—	108,650	6,032	84,050
Montana	59,080	1,380	—	3,780	3,885	1,924	—	—	104,655
Nebraska	—	799,250	—	7,535	15,000	5,790	63,750	—	81,000
Nevada	2,574	—	—	1,346	—	3,300	—	—	1,840
New Hampshire[2]	—	—	—	201	—	—	—	—	—
New Jersey	825	11,663	—	317	336	1,828	4,123	—	1,677
New Mexico	1,500	8,850	109	1,488	—	2,639	—	—	11,960
New York	—	61,380	—	5,366	10,440	10,356	—	—	7,820
North Carolina	4,032	145,800	120	733	43,944	2,700	46,540	592,530	26,660
North Dakota	153,700	41,580	—	5,366	49,980	20,615	17,020	—	284,190
Ohio	—	460,200	—	3,795	13,200	2,784	137,605	26,752	48,400
Oklahoma	2,050	5,250	195	3,556	3,680	—	4,180	—	190,800
Oregon	17,360	6,678	—	3,112	6,600	22,680	—	—	68,945
Pennsylvania	3,640	148,500	—	5,082	15,960	5,160	5,950	22,370	8,360
Rhode Island[2]	—	—	—	23	—	598	—	—	—
South Carolina	1,560	34,866	170	529	2,320	—	29,800	106,320	14,440
South Dakota	30,345	186,260	—	8,083	86,800	1,820	31,280	—	126,038
Tennessee	—	65,550	340	2,678	235	270	48,100	158,730	21,400
Texas	2,000	144,150	4,026	5,415	8,750	4,065	11,890	—	150,000
Utah	11,607	1,888	—	2,160	871	1,728	—	—	8,199
Vermont[2]	—	—	—	938	—	63	—	—	—
Virginia	5,760	56,160	1	1,816	564	1,540	21,535	117,325	12,375
Washington	63,700	23,250	—	2,921	2,040	56,925	—	—	160,350
West Virginia	265	8,100	—	1,128	408	—	—	4,025	400
Wisconsin	2,650	344,500	—	12,770	53,760	21,350	13,950	15,744	10,018
Wyoming	10,400	6,000	—	2,195	3,220	520	—	—	8,072
Total U.S.	596,546	7,656,195	13,290	150,781	471,921	361,648	1,860,783	1,744,078	2,595,479

(1) Equiv. to 480 lbs. (2) All harvested corn acreage is for silage.

Production of Chief U.S. Crops

Source: Economics, Statistics, and Cooperatives Service: U.S. Agriculture Department

Year	Corn for grain 1,000 bushels	Oats 1,000 bushels	Barley 1,000 bushels	Sorghums for grain 1,000 bushels	All wheat 1,000 bushels	Rye 1,000 bushels	Flax-seed 1,000 bushels	Cotton lint 1,000 bales	Cotton seed 1,000 tons
1970 . .	4,152,243	915,236	416,091	683,179	1,351,558	36,840	29,416	10,192	4,068
1975 . .	5,828,961	638,960	379,162	754,354	2,126,927	15,924	15,553	8,302	3,218
1978 . .	7,267,927	581,657	454,759	731,270	1,775,524	24,065	8,614	10,856	4,269
1980 . .	6,639,396	458,792	361,135	579,343	2,380,934	15,958	7,728	11,122	4,470
1981 . .	8,118,650	509,529	473,512	875,835	2,785,357	18,187	7,289	15,646	6,397
1982 . .	8,235,101	592,630	515,935	835,083	2,764,967	19,533	10,278	11,963	4,744
1983 . .	4,174,678	476,961	508,925	487,521	2,419,824	27,116	6,903	7,771	3,076
1984 . .	7,649,995	471,921	596,546	865,856	2,595,479	32,392	7,022	12,926	5,303

Year	Tobacco 1,000 lbs.	All hay 1,000 tons	Beans dry edible 1,000 cwt.	Peas dry edible 1,000 cwt.	Peanuts 1,000 lbs.	Soy-beans 1,000 bushels	Pota-toes 1,000 cwt.	Sweet pota-toes 1,000 cwt.
1970	1,906,453	126,969	17,399	3,315	2,983,121	1,127,100	325,716	13,164
1975	2,182,304	132,397	17,442	2,731	3,846,722	1,548,344	321,978	12,891
1978	2,024,820	143,817	18,935	3,601	3,952,384	1,868,754	366,314	13,115
1980	1,786,225	130,740	26,729	3,285	2,307,762	1,797,543	303,905	10,953
1981	2,063,589	142,520	32,751	2,290	3,981,850	1,989,110	340,623	12,799
1982	1,994,494	149,241	25,563	—	3,440,255	2,190,297	355,131	14,833
1983	1,428,969	140,764	15,520	—	3,295,530	1,635,772	333,911	12,083
1984	1,744,078	150,781	20,754	—	4,427,400	1,860,783	361,648	12,990

Year	Five seed crops* 1,000 lbs.	Sugar and seed 1,000 tons	Sugar beets 1,000 tons	¹Pecans million lbs.	Al-monds million lbs.	¹Wal-nuts 1,000 tons	¹Fil-berts 1,000 tons	Oranges** 1,000 boxes	Grape-fruit** 1,000 boxes
1970	251,934	23,996	26,378	77.6	124.0	111.8	9.3	185,770	53,910
1975	161,609	28,344	29,704	246.8	186.0	199.3	12.1	237,810	61,610
1978	143,817	25,997	25,788	249.9	181.0	160.0	14.1	220,120	74,660
1980	131,070	26,963	23,502	183.5	322.0	197.0	15.4	273,630	73,200
1981	159,195	27,408	27,538	339.1	408.0	225.0	14.7	244,580	67,860
1982	—	29,770	20,894	218.6	347.0	234.0	18.8	176,690	70,550
1983	—	28,161	20,992	270.0	242.0	199.0	8.2	225,180	60,600
1984	—	28,029	22,207	232.4	587.0	213.0	13.4	169,310	52,640

*Fine seed crops include alfalfa, red clover, lespedeza, and timothy. **Crop year ending in year cited. (1) In shells.

Harvested Acreage of Principal U.S. Crops

Source: Statistical Reporting Service: U.S. Agriculture Department (thousands of acres)

State	1984	1983	1982	State	1984	1983	1982
Alabama	3,655	3,528	4,424	Nevada	596	594	585
Arizona	896	678	945	New Hampshire	112	112	112
Arkansas	8,487	7,821	9,237	New Jersey	472	455	524
California	5,740	4,839	6,185	New Mexico	1,303	1,137	1,356
Colorado	6,686	6,094	6,194	New York	4,041	3,904	4,206
Connecticut	150	142	148	North Carolina	5,398	4,692	5,725
Delaware	539	540	582	North Dakota	20,975	18,432	21,753
Florida	1,329	1,208	1,396	Ohio	10,608	9,081	10,865
Georgia	5,649	5,218	6,156	Oklahoma	8,677	7,479	10,244
Hawaii	96	99	95	Oregon	2,720	2,668	2,741
Idaho	4,835	4,490	4,746	Pennsylvania	4,546	4,316	4,610
Illinois	23,496	20,090	23,848	Rhode Island	17	18	18
Indiana	12,513	10,679	12,909	South Carolina	2,914	2,609	3,333
Iowa	24,724	19,973	25,369	South Dakota	16,270	13,558	16,003
Kansas	21,353	19,345	22,690	Tennessee	5,407	4,963	5,693
Kentucky	5,674	4,980	5,853	Texas	20,129	17,350	22,680
Louisiana	4,845	4,583	5,444	Utah	1,109	1,070	1,154
Maine	384	394	411	Vermont	537	539	538
Maryland	1,623	1,530	1,678	Virginia	3,117	2,913	3,184
Massachusetts	169	166	162	Washington	4,729	4,643	4,847
Michigan	7,730	6,220	7,410	West Virginia	769	766	774
Minnesota	20,759	17,610	21,658	Wisconsin	9,404	8,456	9,635
Mississippi	6,299	5,568	6,779	Wyoming	1,904	1,835	1,863
Missouri	14,514	12,773	14,416	*Total U.S.	335,644	293,944	349,644
Montana	9,183	8,709	9,656				
Nebraska	18,564	15,079	18,806				

Crop acreages included are corn, sorghum, oats, barley, wheat, rice, rye, soybeans, flaxseed, peanuts, sunflower, popcorn, cotton, all hay, dry edible beans, dry edible peas, potatoes, sweet potatoes, tobacco, sugarcane and sugar beets; harvested acreages for winter wheat, rye, all hay, tobacco and sugarcane are used in computing total planted acreage. *States may not add to U.S. total due to rounding.

Farms—Number and Acreage, by States

Source: Statistical Reporting Service: U.S. Dept. of Agriculture

State	Farms (1,000) 1980	Farms (1,000) 1983	Acreage (mil.) 1980	Acreage (mil.) 1983	Acreage per farm 1980	Acreage per farm 1983
U.S.	2,433	2,370	1,039	1,024	429	437
Ala.	59	54	13	12	220	222
Alaska	(z)	1	2	2	—	2,000
Ariz.	8	8	38	38	4,750	4,750
Ark.	59	56	17	16	288	286
Calif.	81	80	34	33	420	413
Colo.	27	27	36	35	1,333	1,296
Conn.	4	4	(z)	1	—	250
Del.	4	4	1	1	250	250
Fla.	39	40	13	13	333	325
Ga.	59	55	15	15	254	255
Hawaii	4	5	2	2	500	400
Idaho	24	25	15	15	625	600
Ill.	107	100	29	29	271	290
Ind.	87	84	17	17	195	202
Iowa	119	115	34	34	286	296
Kans.	75	75	48	48	640	640
Ky.	102	103	15	15	147	146
La.	37	37	10	10	270	270
Maine	8	8	2	2	250	250
Md.	18	18	3	3	167	167
Mass.	6	6	1	1	167	167
Mich.	65	64	11	11	169	172
Minn.	104	102	30	30	288	294
Miss.	55	51	15	14	273	275
Mo.	120	118	31	31	258	263
Mont.	24	24	62	61	2,583	2,542
Nebr.	65	62	48	47	738	758
Nev.	3	3	9	9	2,000	3,000
N.H.	3	3	1	1	333	333
N.J.	9	10	1	1	111	100
N. Mex.	14	14	47	46	3,357	3,286
N.Y.	47	49	9	10	191	204
N.C.	93	83	12	11	129	133
N. Dak.	40	37	42	41	1,050	1,108
Ohio	95	92	16	16	168	174
Okla.	72	73	35	34	486	466
Oreg.	35	38	18	18	514	474
Pa.	62	59	9	9	145	153
R.I.	1	1	(z)	(z)	—	—
S.C.	34	29	6	6	176	207
S. Dak.	39	37	45	45	1,154	1,216
Tenn.	96	95	14	13	146	137
Tex.	189	187	138	137	730	733
Utah	14	14	12	12	857	857
Vt.	8	8	2	2	250	250
Va.	58	58	10	10	172	172
Wash.	38	38	16	16	421	421
W. Va.	22	23	4	4	182	174
Wis.	93	88	19	18	204	205
Wyo.	9	9	35	35	3,889	3,889

(z) Less than 500 farms or 500,000 acres.

Livestock on Farms in the U.S.

Source: Statistical Reporting Service: U.S. Dept. of Agriculture (thousands)

Year (On Jan. 1)	All cattle	Milk cows	All sheep	Hogs	Horses and mules*
1890	60,014	15,000	44,518	48,130	18,054
1900	59,739	16,544	48,105	51,055	20,995
1910	58,993	19,450	50,239	48,072	24,211
1920	70,400	21,455	40,743	60,159	25,742
1925	63,373	22,575	38,543	55,770	22,569
1930	61,003	23,032	51,565	55,705	19,124
1935	68,846	26,082	51,808	39,066	16,683
1940	68,309	24,940	52,107	61,165	14,478
1945	85,573	27,770	46,520	59,373	11,950
1950	77,963	23,853	29,826	58,937	7,781
1955	96,592	23,462	31,582	50,474	4,309
1960	96,236	19,527	33,170	59,026	3,089
1965	109,000	²15,380	25,127	50,792	

Year (On Jan. 1)	All cattle	Milk cows	All sheep	Hogs
1970	112,369	12,091	20,423	³57,046
1971	114,578	11,909	19,731	³67,285
1973	121,539	11,622	17,641	³59,017
1974	127,788	11,297	16,310	³60,614
1975	132,028	11,220	14,515	³54,693
1976	127,980	11,071	13,311	²49,267
1978	116,375	10,896	12,421	³56,539
1980	111,242	10,758	12,699	³67,318
1981	114,351	10,849	12,947	³64,462
1982	115,444	10,986	12,997	³58,698
1983	115,001	11,047	12,140	³54,534
1984	113,700	11,109	11,487	³56,694
1985¹	109,801	10,819	10,443	54,043

*Discontinued in 1960. (1) Total estimated value on farms as of Jan. 1, 1985, was as follows (avg. value per head in parentheses): cattle and calves $44,147,243,000 ($402); sheep and lambs $637,880,000 ($61.10); hogs and pigs $4,053,714,000 ($75.00). (2) New series, milk cows and heifers that have calved, beginning 1965. (3) As of Dec. 1 of preceding year.

U.S. Meat and Lard Production and Consumption

Source: Economic Research Service: U.S. Agriculture Department (million lbs.)

Year	Beef Production	Beef Consumption	Veal Production	Veal Consumption	Lamb and mutton Production	Lamb and mutton Consumption	Pork (exclud. lard) Production	Pork (exclud. lard) Consumption	All meats Production	All meats Consumption	Lard Production	Lard Consumption
1940	7,175	7,257	981	981	876	873	10,044	9,701	19,076	18,812	2,288	1,901
1950	9,534	9,529	1,230	1,206	597	596	10,714	10,390	22,075	21,721	2,631	1,891
1960	14,753	15,147	1,109	1,093	768	852	13,905	13,838	30,535	30,930	2,562	1,358
1970	21,685	22,926	588	581	551	657	14,699	14,661	37,523	38,825	1,913	939
1980	21,664	23,321	400	412	318	350	16,615	16,562	38,979	40,645	1,207	540
1983	23,243	24,710	453	457	375	388	15,199	15,369	39,270	40,924	973	424
1984 prel.	23,598	24,900	495	503	379	398	15,396	15,396	39,284	41,197	939	355

Selected Indexes of Farm Inputs: 1960 to 1983

Source: U.S. Dept. of Agriculture, Economic Research Service

(1977 = 100. Inputs based on physical quantities of resources used in production.)

Input	1960	1965	1970	1975	1976	1978	1979	1980	1981	1982	1983¹
Total	98	96	97	96	99	102	105	103	102	100	95
Farm labor	207	156	126	107	103	95	93	92	90	87	79
Farm real estate²	103	102	104	97	98	100	100	101	101	101	100
Mechanical power and machinery	83	80	85	96	98	104	107	104	102	99	93
Agricultural chemicals	32	49	75	83	96	107	118	120	121	111	95
Feed, seed, and livestock purchases⁴	77	86	96	93	101	104	111	108	105	104	101
Taxes and interest	95	101	102	100	102	99	103	100	99	100	101

(1) Preliminary. (2) Includes service buildings, improvements. (3) Includes fertilizer, lime, and pesticides. (4) Includes nonfarm portion.

Average Prices Received by U.S. Farmers

Source: Statistical Reporting Service: U.S. Agriculture Department

The figures represent dollars per 100 lbs. for hogs, beef cattle, veal calves, sheep, lamb, and milk (wholesale), dollars per head for milk cows; cents per lb. for milk fat (in cream), chickens, broilers, turkeys, and wool; cents for eggs per dozen.

Weighted calendar year prices for livestock and livestock products other than wool. 1943 through 1963, wool prices are weighted on marketing year basis. The marketing year has been changed (1964) from a calendar year to a Dec.-Nov. basis for hogs, chickens, broilers and eggs.

Year	Hogs	Cattle (beef)	Calves (veal)	Sheep	Lambs	Cows (milk)	All Milk	Milk fat (in cream)	Chickens (excl. broilers)	Broilers	Turkeys	Eggs	Wool
1930	8.84	7.71	9.68	4.74	7.76	74	2.21	34.5	...	...	20.2	23.7	19.5
1940	5.39	7.56	8.83	3.95	8.10	61	1.82	28.0	13.0	17.3	15.2	18.0	28.4
1950	18.00	23.30	26.30	11.60	25.10	198	3.89	62.0	22.2	27.4	32.8	36.3	62.1
1960	15.30	20.40	22.90	5.61	17.90	223	4.21	60.5	12.2	16.9	25.4	36.1	42.0
1970	22.70	27.10	34.50	7.51	26.40	332	5.71	70.0	9.1	13.6	22.6	39.1	35.4
1975	46.10	32.20	27.20	11.30	42.10	412	8.75	71.0	9.9	26.3	34.8	54.5	44.8
1979	41.80	66.10	88.80	26.30	66.70	1,040	12.00	119.0	14.4	25.9	41.3	58.3	86.3
1980	38.00	62.40	76.80	21.30	63.60	1,190	13.05	—	11.0	27.7	41.3	56.3	88.1
1983	46.80	55.50	61.70	15.70	53.90	1,030	13.58	—	12.7	28.6	38.0	61.1	61.3
1984	47.10	57.30	59.90	16.40	60.10	895	13.46	—	15.9	33.7	48.9	72.3	79.5

The figures represent cents per lb. for cotton, apples, and peanuts; dollars per bushel for oats, wheat, corn, barley, and soybeans; dollars per 100 lbs. for rice, sorghum, and potatoes; dollars per ton for cottonseed and baled hay.

Weighted crop year prices. Crop years are as follows: apples, June-May; wheat, oats, barley, hay and potatoes, July-June; cotton, rice, peanuts and cottonseed, August-July; soybeans, September-August; and corn and sorghum grain, October-September.

Crop year	Corn	Wheat	Upland cotton[1]	Oats	Barley	Rice	Soybeans	Sorghum	Peanuts	Cotton-seed	Hay	Potatoes	Apples
1930	.598	.663	9.46	0.311	.420	1.74	1.34	1.02	5.01	22.00	11.00	1.47	...
1940	.618	.674	9.83	0.298	.393	1.80	.892	.873	3.72	21.70	9.78	.850	...
1950	1.52	2.00	39.90	0.788	1.19	5.09	2.47	1.88	10.9	86.60	21.10	1.50	...
1960	1.00	1.74	30.08	0.599	.840	4.55	2.13	1.49	10.0	42.50	21.70	2.00	2.72
1970	1.33	1.33	21.86	0.623	.973	5.17	2.85	2.04	12.8	56.40	26.10	2.21	6.52
1975	2.54	3.55	51.10	1.45	2.42	8.35	4.92	4.21	19.6	97.00	52.10	4.48	8.80
1979	2.52	3.78	62.3	1.36	2.29	10.50	6.28	4.18	20.6	121.00	59.50	3.43	15.40
1980	3.11	3.91	74.4	1.79	2.86[2]	12.80	7.57	5.25	25.1	129.00	71.00	6.55	12.1
1983	3.25	3.53	66.0	1.67	2.50	8.76	7.81	5.07	24.7	166.00	75.80	5.82	14.9
1984	2.67	3.38	58.4	1.71	2.30	8.23	5.90	4.27	.25.3	99.50	73.80	5.67	15.5

(1) Beginning 1964, 480 lb. net weight bales. (2) Series discontinued in 1980.

Grain Storage Capacity at Principal Grain Centers in U.S.

Source: Chicago Board of Trade Market Information Department
(bushels)

Cities	Capacity	Cities	Capacity
Atlantic Coast	36,800,000	Texas High Plains	76,800,000
Great Lakes		Enid	66,100,000
Toledo	57,700,000	Gulf Points	
Buffalo	8,200,000	South Mississippi	43,600,000
Chicago	48,835,000	North Texas Gulf	28,200,000
Milwaukee	9,100,000	South Texas Gulf	14,000,000
Duluth	75,800,000	Plains	
River Points		Wichita	60,300,000
Minneapolis	124,200,000	Topeka	61,600,000
Peoria	6,600,000	Salina	45,000,000
St. Louis	25,500,000	Hutchinson	42,000,000
Sioux City	11,600,000	Hastings-Grand Island	24,100,000
Omaha-Council Bluffs	35,300,000	Lincoln	39,600,000
Atchison	24,500,000	Pacific N.W.	
St. Joseph	20,600,000	Puget Sound	9,500,000
Kansas City, Mo.	72,400,000	Portland	24,900,000
Southwest		California Ports	14,300,000
Fort Worth	57,600,000		

Atlantic Coast — Albany, N.Y., Philadelphia, Pa., Baltimore, Md., Norfolk, Va. **Gulf Points** — New Orleans, Baton Rouge, Ama. Belle Chase, La., Mobile, Ala. **North Texas Gulf** — Houston, Galveston, Beaumont, Port Arthur, Texas. **South Texas Gulf** — Corpus Christi, Brownsville, Texas. **Pacific N.W.** — Seattle, Tacoma, Wash., Portland, Oreg., Columbia River **Calif. Ports** — San Francisco, Stockton, Sacramento, Los Angeles. **Texas High Plains** — Amarillo, Lubbock, Hereford, Plainview, Texas.

Consumption of Major Food Commodities per Person

Source: Economic Research Service: U.S. Agriculture Department

Commodity[1]	1982	1983	1984	Commodity[1]	1982	1983	1984
Meats	139.3	144.0	143.5	Processed:			
Beef	77.3	78.70	78.6	Canned fruit	16.0	16.0	NA
Veal	1.6	1.60	1.8	Canned juice	13.8	16.2	NA
Lamb and mutton	1.5	1.5	1.4	Frozen (including juices)	14.1	15.0	13.5
Pork	59.0	62.20	61.7	Chilled citrus juices	3.5	4.1	NA
Fish (edible weight)	12.3	13.10	13.6	Dried	2.8	2.9	NA
Poultry products:				**Vegetables:**			
Eggs	33.8	233.10	33.0	Fresh[2]	71.2	71.0	75.4
Chicken (ready-to-cook)	52.9	53.90	55.7	Canned (excluding potatoes and			
Turkey (ready-to-cook)	10.8	11.20	11.4	sweet potatoes)	45.7	45.3	NA
Dairy products:				Frozen (excluding potatoes)	10.7	11.1	NA
Cheese	20.0	20.10	21.7	Potatoes[3]	115.4	120.3	—
Condensed and evaporated milk	7.1	7.00	7.5	Sweet potatoes[3]	4.9	5.3	—
Fluid milk and cream (product weight)	242	245	245	**Grains:**			
Ice cream (product weight)	17.5	17.9	18.0	Wheat flour[4]	114	116.0	118.0
Fats and Oils—Total fat content.	58.4	59.6	58.6	Rice	11.8	9.8	NA
Butter (actual weight)	4.7	5.1	5.0	**Other:**			
Margarine (actual weight)	11.1	10.4	10.4	Coffee	7.5	7.6	7.7
Lard	4.1	1.8	2.1	Tea	.8	.7	0.7
Shortening	18.7	18.6	21.3	Cocoa	3.0	3.3	3.6
Other edible fats and oils	23.3	24.8	21.2	Peanuts (shelled)	6.7	6.5	6.9
Fruits:				Dry edible beans	6.6	6.5	NA
Fresh	83.9	87.5	86.6	Melons	NA	NA	NA
Citrus	24.0	27.7	23.0	Sugar (refined)	73.7	71.0	67.5
Noncitrus	60.0	59.8	63.6				

(1) Quantity in pounds, retail weight unless otherwise shown. Data on calendar year basis except for dried fruits, fresh citrus fruits, peanuts, and rice which are on a crop-year basis, and eggs which are on a marketing year basis. Data are as of August 1983. (2) Commercial production for sale as fresh produce. (3) Including fresh equivalent of processed. (4) White, whole wheat, and semolina flour including use in bakery products.

U.S. Egg Production

Source: Economic Research Service: U.S. Agriculture Department (millions of eggs)

State	1984	1983	1982	1981	State	1984	1983	1982	1981	State	1984	1983	1982	1981
Ala.	2,783	2,813	2,879	3,095	La.	395	417	457	510	Oh.	3,445	2,980	2,755	2,431
Alas.	13.6	15.6	8.8	6.7	Me.	1,355	1,402	1,430	1,607	Okla.	879	841	818	839
Ariz.	105	102	114	98	Md.	840	836	658	545	Ore.	641	630	620	665
Ark.	3,560	3,768	4,065	3,996	Mass.	268	265	314	321	Pa.	4,282	4,716	4,324	4,268
Cal.	8,325	8,173	8,288	8,400	Mich.	1,519	1,484	1,532	1,541	R.I.	74	62	74	88
Col.	637	619	627	552	Minn.	2,443	2,508	2,432	2,355	S.C.	1,617	1,594	1,656	1,613
Conn.	1,199	1,073	1,057	990	Miss.	1,253	1,285	1,524	1,717	S.D.	378	374	428	461
Del.	140	142	137	127	Mo.	1,357	1,352	1,456	1,448	Tenn.	744	822	884	922
Fla.	2,912	2,965	2,963	3,040	Mont.	198	193	188	174	Tex.	3,182	3,089	3,113	3,224
Ga.	4,474	4,671	5,357	5,578	Neb.	773	792	809	802	Ut.	438	456	439	459
Ha.	209.7	197.3	202.2	221.3	Nev.	2.3	1.8	1.8	1.8	Vt.	65	69	79	81
Ida.	258	240	238	228	N.H.	125	142	147	157	Va.	843	839	929	947
Ill.	876	1,004	1,158	1,262	N.J.	234	246	276	291	Wash.	1,306	1,232	1,334	1,332
Ind.	4,997	4,624	4,464	4,093	N.M.	281	287	302	347	W.Vir.	130	136	141	155
Ia.	1,769	1,827	1,985	1,920	N.Y.	1,710	1,741	1,859	1,858	Wis.	884	906	991	955
Kan.	466	481	462	416	N.C.	3,246	3,152	3,149	3,081	Wyo.	7.2	8.7	8.2	8.5
Ky.	434	457	284	509	N.D.	120	119	102	89	**Total.**	68,193	68,169	69,718	69,825

Note: The egg and chicken production year runs from Dec. 1 of the previous year through Nov. 30. (1) Included are eggs destroyed because of possible PCB contamination.

Hired Farmworkers—Workers and Earnings: 1970 to 1983

Represents persons 14 years old and over in the civilian noninstitutional population who did hired farmwork at any time during the year.

Source: Economic Research Service, U.S. Dept. of Agriculture

				Workers (1,000)						Median Earnings Per Day			
					1983								
						Duration of farmwork							
Characteristic	1970	1975	1979	Total	Under 25 days	25-74 days	75-149 days	150-249 days	250 days and over	1970	1975	1979	1983
All workers	2,488	2,638	2,652	2,595	973	491	397	386	349	$9.30	$14.80	$20.99	$25.52
White[1]	1,940	1,907	1,976	1,888	816	362	230	235	246	9.70	14.75	20.24	24.18
Black and other[1]	547	446	335	376	90	72	85	80	49	8.00	13.90	22.85	27.58
Hispanic	NA	285	320	331	66	57	83	70	55	NA	17.10	27.13	34.64
Northeast	241	227	188	191	58	36	40	26	31	9.95	14.00	16.63	28.45
Midwest	590	674	785	687	343	124	63	88	69	9.20	14.45	20.01	21.55
South	1,093	1,074	1,071	995	378	182	159	132	144	8.35	14.10	20.33	26.90
West	564	664	607	722	193	148	135	140	106	11.75	18.00	25.27	40.84
Migratory	196	188	217	226	36	52	62	49	29	NA	NA	NA	NA
Nonmigratory	2,291	2,450	2,435	2,369	937	439	335	337	320	NA	NA	NA	NA

(1) Beginning 1975, excludes persons of Hispanic origin. 1970 data not comparable with later years. (NA) Not available.

Net Income per Farm by States
Source: Economic Research Service, U.S. Agriculture Department (dollars)

State	1981	1982	1983	State	1981	1982	1983
Alabama	9,845	8,568	7,923	Nebraska	18,712	11,358	6,110
Alaska	6,513	2,126	4,507	Nevada	9,177	5,747	9,444
Arizona	45,065	15,173	12,768	New Hampshire	3,612	3,439	3,373
Arkansas	13,029	8,630	8,356	New Jersey	9,826	13,513	11,885
California	54,495	41,312	38,354	New Mexico	5,219	2,856	3,938
Colorado	16,238	11,091	17,683	New York	7,287	4,398	3,027
Connecticut	11,710	14,614	11,575	North Carolina	12,978	11,508	9,439
Delaware	26,799	31,099	42,770	North Dakota	19,775	9,983	17,377
Florida	36,289	31,954	36,322	Ohio	3,302	5,122	1,310
Georgia	9,642	11,210	10,914	Oklahoma	5,795	7,226	2,930
Hawaii	22,210	20,040	28,412	Oregon	11,417	7,932	9,777
Idaho	20,978	11,490	15,282	Pennsylvania	10,871	8,307	6,630
Illinois	17,676	8,989	-5,786	Rhode Island	4,555	5,073	1,043
Indiana	7,457	5,418	-1,490	South Carolina	4,064	4,128	-596
Iowa	17,680	7,376	-1,890	South Dakota	15,583	11,311	12,824
Kansas	11,353	12,180	7,958	Tenneesse	4,410	4,342	1,595
Kentucky	10,283	9,679	4,358	Texas	9,946	5,106	5,400
Louisiana	5,755	6,225	10,407	Utah	4,377	2,119	2,998
Maine	11,899	126	-3,404	Vermont	10,842	13,207	9,086
Maryland	12,463	11,172	9,122	Virginia	5,467	2,147	819
Massachusetts	15,649	19,033	19,362	Washington	20,894	20,239	25,963
Michigan	7,594	6,608	5,348	West Virginia	-374	-1,941	-923
Minnesota	14,325	9,627	7,132	Wisconsin	15,504	12,914	10,805
Mississippi	2,629	5,505	3,541	Wyoming	-189	-7,847	-6,764
Missouri	6,942	2,937	-509	Total. U.S.	12,722	93,018	67,913
Montana	8,142	2,325	2,153				

Note: Data based on the 1974 Census of Agriculture definition of a farm (sales of $1,000 or more).

Farm Income—Cash Receipts from Marketings
Source: Economic Research Service: U.S. Agriculture Department ($1,000)

1983 State	Crops	Livestock	Gov't pay'ts	Total	1983 State	Crops	Livestock	Gov't pay'ts	Total
Alabama	853,887	1,258,461	64,280	2,176,628	Nebraska	2,007,223	4,003,129	762,251	6,772,603
Alaska	11,074	7,504	240	18,818	Nevada	71,125	153,052	4,251	228,428
Arizona	928,120	715,510	111,402	1,755,032	New Hampshire	39,950	78,115	642	114,707
Arkansas	1,499,184	1,500,283	294,997	3,294,464	New Jersey	406,760	136,358	4,287	547,405
California	9,333,761	4,159,970	372,278	13,866,009	New Mexico	327,336	634,719	57,076	1,019,131
Colorado	926,571	2,000,417	163,970	3,090,958	New York	742,552	1,929,463	37,922	2,709,937
Connecticut	118,316	202,327	541	321,184	North Carolina	2,127,468	1,656,457	67,565	3,851,490
Delaware	139,249	315,875	3,885	459,009	North Dakota	2,028,479	662,654	578,760	3,269,893
Florida	3,332,605	992,765	13,040	4,338,410	Ohio	2,135,849	1,537,815	170,749	3,844,413
Georgia	1,604,531	1,705,568	82,240	3,392,339	Oklahoma	1,003,405	1,688,110	364,703	3,056,218
Hawaii	450,156	86,488	6,743	543,387	Oregon	1,145,071	555,044	66,786	1,766,901
Idaho	1,132,490	883,033	136,397	2,151,920	Pennsylvania	755,574	2,220,814	29,110	3,005,498
Illinois	5,849,047	2,294,569	542,745	8,686,361	Rhode Island	19,033	12,280	107	31,420
Indiana	2,180,237	1,829,205	264,619	4,274,061	South Carolina	652,591	405,348	47,613	1,105,552
Iowa	3,939,756	5,395,117	899,484	10,234,357	South Dakota	930,181	1,655,967	267,132	2,853,280
Kansas	2,201,620	3,196,060	598,239	5,996,106	Tennessee	1,023,386	906,922	68,235	1,998,543
Kentucky	1,322,886	1,475,261	60,095	2,858,242	Texas	3,448,249	5,522,150	1,127,875	10,098,274
Louisiana	1,369,516	483,190	157,649	2,010,755	Utah	145,960	432,747	19,136	597,843
Maine	153,260	259,802	2,679	415,741	Vermont	35,899	391,138	1,526	428,563
Maryland	330,503	701,951	12,571	1,045,025	Virginia	581,799	857,738	28,875	1,468,412
Massachusetts	230,859	136,089	710	367,658	Washington	2,104,329	958,680	158,995	3,222,004
Michigan	1,758,474	1,242,987	140,936	3,142,397	West Virginia	54,771	172,877	3,895	231,543
Minnesota	2,949,075	3,328,332	610,934	6,888,341	Wisconsin	1,062,484	4,140,446	160,053	5,362,983
Mississippi	1,364,511	926,608	221,089	2,512,208	Wyoming	114,742	478,145	19,658	612,545
Missouri	1,728,743	2,259,288	236,918	4,224,920	U.S.	69,516,144	69,203,192	9,294,293	148,013,629
Montana	846,939	656,364	239,410	1,742,713					

Farm-Real Estate Debt Outstanding by Lender Groups
Source: Economic Research Service, U.S. Agriculture Department

Dec. 31	Total farm-real estate debt[1] $1,000	Federal land banks[1] $1,000	Farmers Home Administration[2] $1,000	Life insurance companies[3] $1,000	All commercial banks $1,000	Other[4] $1,000
1955	9,012,016	1,480,204	412,670	2,271,784	1,275,429	3,571,929
1960	12,620,304	2,539,044	722,870	2,974,609	1,591,762	4,992,019
1965	21,186,886	4,240,227	1,497,313	4,801,677	2,607,404	8,040,265
1970	30,346,083	7,145,363	2,440,043	5,610,300	3,772,377	11,378,000
1975	49,682,502	16,029,468	3,368,747	6,726,000	6,296,286	17,262,000
1978	71,609,901	24,816,127	4,121,038	10,478,200	8,556,539	23,638,000
1979	85,598,828	29,819,634	7,110,613	12,165,300	8,623,281	27,880,000
1980	95,764,071	36,196,103	7,714,928	12,927,800	8,745,242	30,180,000
1981	105,800,514	43,825,202	8,744,181	13,073,900	8,387,232	31,770,000
1982	110,026,320	47,699,376	9,084,694	12,801,546	8,440,700	32,000,000
1983	112,621,564	48,811,040	9,452,124	12,717,600	9,320,800	32,320,000
1984	111,637,035	49,102,581	10,013,411	12,443,999	10,177,047	29,900,000

(1) Includes data for joint stock land banks and Federal Farm Mortgage Corporations. (2) Includes loans made directly by FmHA for farm ownership, soil and water loans to individuals, recreation loans to individuals, Indian tribe land acquisition, grazing associations, and irrigation drainage and soil conservation associations. Also includes loans for rural housing on farm tracts and labor housing. (3) American Council of Life Insurance. (4) Estimated by ERS, USDA.

Government Payments by Programs, by States

Source: Economic Research Service: U.S. Agriculture Department ($1,000)

1982 State	Conservation[1]	Feed grain program	Wheat program	Cotton program	Rice program	Drought & flood program	Misc. program[2]	Total
Alabama	4,167	1,651	1,478	22,511	0	0	1,630	31,437
Alaska	148	248	1	0	0	0	14	411
Arizona	1,492	823	1,183	54,733	0	0	1,216	59,447
Arkansas	3,312	6,708	9,063	36,939	61,620	0	1,703	119,345
California	4,869	4,280	9,524	86,731	23,697	0	5,400	134,501
Colorado	5,210	12,233	23,678	0	0	0	27,643	68,764
Connecticut	472	6	0	0	0	0	25	503
Delaware	182	129	51	0	0	0	350	712
Florida	3,223	1,256	158	1,271	90	0	1,495	7,493
Georgia	4,756	4,941	3,966	11,651	0	0	4,028	29,342
Hawaii	607	0	0	0	0	0	48	655
Idaho	2,626	10,724	24,372	0	0	0	13,845	51,567
Illinois	6,041	35,956	7,070	0	0	7	69,084	118,158
Indiana	3,681	21,588	3,992	0	0	0	28,283	57,544
Iowa	6,463	81,366	467	0	0	5	127,568	215,869
Kansas	5,020	93,149	94,329	3	0	0	87,763	280,264
Kentucky	4,349	4,640	2,252	0	0	0	1,676	12,917
Louisiana	3,132	1,106	889	48,787	27,731	0	1,474	83,119
Maine	1,940	94	3	0	0	0	250	2,287
Maryland	900	722	280	0	0	0	678	2,580
Massachusetts	543	11	0	0	0	0	86	640
Michigan	4,181	13,562	3,970	0	0	0	18,704	40,417
Minnesota	4,974	47,033	32,958	0	0	0	97,892	182,857
Mississippi	4,085	1,320	2,053	83,477	11,693	0	1,301	103,929
Missouri	6,536	33,256	16,794	10,499	2,284	0	10,456	79,825
Montana	3,559	18,230	66,805	0	0	0	28,322	116,916
Nebraska	3,965	97,817	19,922	0	0	7	155,767	277,478
Nevada	931	287	409	76	0	0	2,727	4,430
New Hampshire	591	2	0	0	0	0	66	659
New Jersey	485	245	146	0	0	0	200	1,076
New Mexico	2,143	7,396	6,183	8,188	0	0	8,029	31,939
New York	4,397	4,751	1,186	0	0	0	3,433	13,767
North Carolina	3,944	2,998	1,541	4,815	0	0	3,166	16,464
North Dakota	2,491	22,055	105,430	0	0	0	70,150	200,176
Ohio	4,197	19,935	6,543	0	0	0	11,723	42,398
Oklahoma	4,347	12,785	53,944	30,169	10	0	26,472	127,727
Oregon	3,558	2,612	15,838	0	0	0	8,614	30,622
Pennsylvania	3,766	1,528	334	0	0	0	1,810	7,438
Rhode Island	92	0	0	0	0	0	13	105
South Carolina	2,530	1,927	1,797	8,050	0	0	2,849	17,153
South Dakota	2,311	20,972	30,684	0	0	0	38,754	92,721
Tennessee	4,364	2,909	3,811	16,032	0	0	962	28,078
Texas	15,793	87,724	52,291	376,262	28,785	0	82,743	643,598
Utah	2,985	1,081	1,762	0	0	0	3,351	9,179
Vermont	1,126	40	0	0	0	0	454	1,620
Virginia	2,642	1,649	998	17	0	0	2,151	7,457
Washington	4,366	10,366	41,545	0	0	0	20,696	76,973
West Virginia	1,810	126	8	0	0	0	524	2,468
Wisconsin	4,467	18,536	603	0	0	0	22,857	46,463
Wyoming	1,463	542	1,907	0	0	0	6,565	10,477
Total	165,232	713,315	652,268	800,211	155,910	19	1,005,010	3,491,965

(1) Includes amounts paid under Agricultural and Conservation Programs. (2) Includes Sugar Act, National Wool Act, Milk Indemnity Program, Beekeepers Indemnity Program, Hay and Cattle Transportation Program, Cropland Adjustment Program, Forest Incentive Program, Water Bank Program, Emergency Livestock Feed Program, Great Plains and other miscellaneous programs.

Federal Food Program Costs[1]

Source: Management Information Division, Food and Nutrition Service, USDA (millions of dollars)

Fiscal year	Food stamps benefits[7]	WIC[3]	Food distribution[4] Needy persons[5]	Schools	Institutions	School lunch	Child nutrition (Cash payments) School breakfast	Child care	Summer food	Special milk	Total food costs
1977	5,058	212	44	541	18	1,570	149	125	131	150	7,998
1978	5,165	312	68	543	28	1,808	181	150	100	135	8,490
1979	6,478	429	96	745	54	1,984	231	189	109	134	10,449
1980	8,686	584	125	905	71	2,282	288	239	118	145	13,443
1981	10,630	708	158	895	78	2,381	332	335	110	101	15,728
1982	9,532[2]	756	351[6]	766	111	2,185	317	310	93	20	14,447
1983	11,155[2]	902	1,208[6]	840	158	2,406	351	351	98	18	17,487
1984[p]	10,703[2]	1,386	1,335[6]	830	199	2,506	369	364	106	17	16,480

(1) Cost data are direct federal benefits to recipients; they exclude federal administrative payments and applicable State and local contributions. (2) Excludes Puerto Rico Nutrition Assistance Program. (3) Special Supplemental Food Program for Women, Infants and Children. (4) Includes cost of commodity entitlements, cash-in-lieu of commodities and bonus foods. (5) Includes Food Distribution Program on Indian Reservations, Needy Family Program in Trust Territory, Commodity Supplemental Food Program and Nutrition Program for the Elderly. (6) Includes Temporary Emergency Food Assistance Program. (7) Average benefits per participant per month: 1970—$10.55; 1975—$21.41; 1981—$39.49; 1982—$39.05; 1983—$42.98; 1984ᵖ—$42.76. (p) Preliminary.

EDUCATION

American Colleges and Universities

General Information for the 1984-85 Academic Year

Source: Peterson's Guides

These listings include all accredited undergraduate degree-granting institutions in the United States and U.S. territories that have a total institutional enrollment of 600 or more. Four-year colleges (those that award a bachelor's as their highest undergraduate degree) are listed first, followed by two-year colleges (those that award an associate as their highest undergraduate degree).

All institutions are coeducational except those where the zip code is followed by: (1)–men only, (2)–primarily men, (3)–women only, (4)–primarily women.

Year is that of founding.

Governing official is the chief executive officer.

Institutional control: 1–independent (nonprofit), 2–independent-religious, 3–proprietary (profit making), 4–federal, 5–state, 7–commonwealth (Puerto Rico), 8–territory (U.S. territories), 9–county, 10–district, 11–city, 12–state and local, 13–state related.

Highest degree offered: B–bachelor's, M–master's, D–doctorate.

Enrollment is the total number of matriculated undergraduate and (if applicable) graduate students.

Faculty is the total number of faculty members teaching undergraduate and graduate courses.

Any data not reported are indicated as NR.

Four-Year Colleges

Name, address	Year	Governing official, control, and highest degree offered		Enrollment	Faculty
Abilene Christian U, Abilene, TX 79699	1906	Dr William J Teague	2-M	4,617	251
Academy of Aeronautics, Flushing, NY 11371 (2)	1932	Dr George W Brush	1-B	1,450	68
Academy of Art Coll, San Francisco, CA 94102	1929	Dr Donald Haight	3-M	1,800	120
Adams State Coll, Alamosa, CO 81102	1921	Dr William M Fulkerson Jr	5-M	2,116	97
Adelphi U, Garden City, NY 11530	1896	Dr Timothy W Costello	1-D	10,717	835
Adrian Coll, Adrian, MI 49221	1859	Dr Donald S Stanton	2-B	1,220	102
Alabama Agricultural and Mechanical U, Normal, AL 35762	1875	Dr, Douglas Covington	5-M	4,109	500
Alabama Christian Coll, Montgomery, AL 36193	1942	Dr Ernest A Clevenger Jr	2-B	1,723	109
Alabama State U, Montgomery, AL 36195	1874	Dr Leon Howard	5-M	3,786	251
Alaska Pacific U, Anchorage, AK 99508	1959	Dr Glenn A Olds	2-M	687	96
Albany Coll of Pharmacy of Union U, Albany, NY 12208	1881	Kenneth W Miller, Ph D	1-B	635	42
Albany State Coll, Albany, GA 31705	1903	Dr Billy C Black	5-M	1,893	138
Albion Coll, Albion, MI 49224	1835	Dr Melvin L Vulgamore	2-B	1,614	122
Albright Coll, Reading, PA 19603	1856	Dr David G Ruffer	2-B	1,361	126
Alcorn State U, Lorman, MS 39096	1871	Dr Walter Washington	5-M	2,442	162
Alderson-Broaddus Coll, Philippi, WV 26416	1871	Dr W Christian Sizemore	2-B	791	83
Alfred U, Alfred, NY 14802	1836	Dr Edward G Coll, Jr	1-D	2,423	176
Allegheny Coll, Meadville, PA 16335	1815	Dr David B Harned	2-M	1,950	171
Allentown Coll of St Francis de Sales, Center Valley, PA 18034	1962	Very Rev Daniel G Gambet	2-M	800	75
Alma Coll, Alma, MI 48801	1886	Dr Oscar E Remick	2-B	1,018	81
Alvernia Coll, Reading, PA 19607	1958	Sr M Dolorey	2-B	706	79
Alverno Coll, Milwaukee, WI 53215 (3)	1936	Joel Read	1-B	1,375	141
Amber U, Garland, TX 75041	1971	Dr Douglas W Warner	1-M	900	55
American Coll of Puerto Rico, Bayamón, PR 00619	1963	Juan B Nazario Negron	1-B	3,827	156
American International Coll, Springfield, MA 01109	1885	Dr Harry J Courniotes	1-D	2,280	123
American U, Washington, DC 20016	1893	Dr Richard Berendzen	2-D	9,129	1,069
Amherst Coll, Amherst, MA 01002	1821	Peter R Pouncey	1-B	1,543	169
Anderson Coll, Anderson, IN 46012	1917	Dr Robert A Nicholson	2-M	1,915	183
Andrews U, Berrien Springs, MI 49104	1874	Dr W Richard Lesher	2-D	3,034	240
Angelo State U, San Angelo, TX 76909	1928	Dr Lloyd Drexell Vincent	5-M	6,163	227
Anna Maria Coll for Men and Women, Paxton, MA 01612	1946	Sr Bernadette Madore	2-M	1,500	78
Antillian Coll, Mayagüez, PR 00708	1957	Dr Angel M Rodriguez	2-B	918	83
Antioch U Philadelphia, Philadelphia, PA 19130	1852	David Allen Frisby III	1-M	633	68
Appalachian State U, Boone, NC 28608	1899	Dr John E Thomas	5-M	10,043	592
Aquinas Coll, Grand Rapids, MI 49506	1886	Dr Norbert J Hruby	2-M	2,831	185
Arizona State U, Tempe, AZ 85287	1885	Dr J Russell Nelson	5-D	40,563	2,248
Arkansas Coll, Batesville, AR 72501	1872	Dr Dan C West	2-B	653	59
Arkansas State U, State University, AR 72467	1909	Dr Eugene W Smith	5-M	8,319	326
Arkansas Tech U, Russellville, AR 72801	1909	Dr Kenneth G Kersh	5-M	3,575	150
Armstrong State Coll, Savannah, GA 31406	1935	Dr Robert A Burnett	5-M	2,941	160
Art Center Coll of Design, Pasadena, CA 91103	1930	Mr Donald R Kubly	1-M	1,174	175
Asbury Coll, Wilmore, KY 40390	1890	Dr John N Oswalt	1-B	1,075	98
Ashland Coll, Ashland, OH 44805	1878	Dr Joseph Shultz	2-M	3,215	140
Assumption Coll, Worcester, MA 01609	1904	Joseph H Hagan	2-M	2,000	148
Athens State Coll, Athens, AL 35611	1822	Dr James R Chasteen	5-B	1,208	81
Atlantic Christian Coll, Wilson, NC 27893	1902	Dr James B Hemby	2-B	1,373	104
Auburn U, Auburn University, AL 36849	1856	Dr James E Martin	5-D	18,888	1,130
Auburn U at Montgomery, Montgomery, AL 36193	1967	Dr James O Williams	5-M	5,366	350
Augsburg Coll, Minneapolis, MN 55454	1869	Dr Charles S Anderson	2-B	1,375	183
Augusta Coll, Augusta, GA 30910	1925	Dr George A Christenberry	5-M	4,091	172
Augustana Coll, Rock Island, IL 61201	1860	Dr Thomas Tredway	2-B	2,193	144
Augustana Coll, Sioux Falls, SD 57197	1860	Dr William C Nelson	2-M	1,914	188
Aurora U, Aurora, IL 60506	1893	Dr Alan J Stone	2-M	1,567	88
Austin Coll, Sherman, TX 75090	1849	Dr Harry E Smith	2-M	1,181	105
Austin Peay State U, Clarksville, TN 37044	1927	Dr Robert O Riggs	5-M	5,417	257
Averett Coll, Danville, VA 24541	1859	Dr Howard W Lee	2-M	1,000	54
Avila Coll, Kansas City, MO 64145	1916	Sr Olive L Dallavis, CSJ	2-M	1,730	214
Azusa Pacific U, Azusa, CA 91702	1899	Dr Paul E Sago	2-M	2,578	156
Babson Coll, Babson Park, MA 02157	1919	Dr William R Dill	1-M	3,180	146
Baker U, Baldwin City, KS 66006	1858	Dr Ralph M Tanner	2-M	825	56
Baldwin-Wallace Coll, Berea, OH 44017	1845	Dr Neal Malicky	2-M	3,651	209

165

Name, address	Year	Governing official, control, and highest degree offered		Enrollment	Faculty
Ball State U, Muncie, IN 47306	1918	Dr John E Worthen	5-D	17,376	1,359
Baltimore Hebrew Coll, Baltimore, MD 21215	1919	Dr Leivy Smolar	1-D	637	21
Baptist Bible Coll, Springfield, MO 65803	1950	Mr A V Henderson	2-B	1,226	39
Baptist Bible Coll of Pennsylvania, Clarks Summit, PA 18411	1932	Dr Mark E Jackson	2-M	756	54
Baptist Coll at Charleston, Charleston, SC 29411	1964	Dr Jairy C Hunter Jr	2-M	1,646	101
Barat Coll, Lake Forest, IL 60045 (4)	1858	Dr Richard P Soter	2-B	668	72
Bard Coll, Annandale-on-Hudson, NY 12504	1860	Mr Leon Botstein	1-M	747	87
Barnard Coll, New York, NY 10027 (3)	1889	Ms Ellen Futter	1-B	2,250	236
Barry U, Miami Shores, FL 33161	1940	Sr Jeanne O'Laughlin	2-D	4,029	205
Bartlesville Wesleyan Coll, Bartlesville, OK 74006	1909	Dr Paul R Mills	2-B	648	70
Bates Coll, Lewiston, ME 04240	1855	Dr Thomas H Reynolds	1-B	1,435	134
Bayamón Central U, Bayamón, PR 00619	1970	Rev Vincent A M Van Rooij OP	2-M	2,873	121
Baylor Coll of Dentistry, Dallas, TX 75246 (4)	1905	Dr Richard E Bradley	1-D	665	229
Baylor U, Waco, TX 76798	1845	Dr Herbert H Reynolds	2-D	10,990	596
Beaver Coll, Glenside, PA 19038	1853	Dr Bruce L Wilson	2-M	2,146	159
Belhaven Coll, Jackson, MS 39202	1883	Dr Verne R Kennedy	2-B	875	82
Bellarmine Coll, Louisville, KY 40205	1950	Dr Eugene V Petrik	2-M	2,710	175
Bellevue Coll, Bellevue, NE 68005	1966	Dr Richard D Winchell	1-B	2,697	102
Belmont Abbey Coll, Belmont, NC 28012	1876	Dr John R Dempsey	2-B	840	68
Belmont Coll, Nashville, TN 37203	1951	Dr William E Troutt	2-B	2,125	181
Beloit Coll, Beloit, WI 53511	1846	Dr Roger H Hull	1-M	1,038	91
Bemidji State U, Bemidji, MN 56601	1919	Dr Lowell R Gillett	5-M	4,318	256
Benedict Coll, Columbia, SC 29204	1870	Dr Marshall C Grigsby	2-B	1,457	105
Benedictine Coll, Atchison, KS 66002	1859	Rev Gerard Senecal	2-B	898	92
Bentley Coll, Waltham, MA 02254	1917	Dr Gregory H Adamian	1-M	8,091	307
Berea Coll, Berea, KY 40404	1855	Dr John B Stephenson	1-B	1,554	127
Berklee Coll of Music, Boston, MA 02215	1945	Mr Lee Eliot Berk	1-B	2,425	230
Berry Coll, Mount Berry, GA 30149	1902	Dr Gloria M Shatto	1-M	1,394	113
Bethany Coll, Lindsborg, KS 67456	1881	Dr Peter J Ristuben	2-B	816	77
Bethany Coll, Bethany, WV 26032	1840	Dr Todd H Bullard	2-B	785	79
Bethany Nazarene Coll, Bethany, OK 73008	1899	Dr John A Knight	2-M	1,287	105
Bethel Coll, North Newton, KS 67117	1887	Dr Harold J Schultz	2-B	641	65
Bethel Coll, St Paul, MN 55112	1871	Dr George K Brushaber	2-B	1,861	194
Bethune-Cookman Coll, Daytona Beach, FL 32015	1904	Dr Oswald P Bronson Sr	2-B	1,708	126
Biola U, La Mirada, CA 90639	1908	Dr Clyde Cook	2-D	3,025	253
Birmingham-Southern Coll, Birmingham, AL 35254	1856	Dr Neal R Berte	1-M	1,540	93
Bishop Coll, Dallas, TX 75241	1881	Dr Wright L Lassiter Jr	2-B	1,196	71
Black Hills State Coll, Spearfish, SD 57783	1883	Dr J Gilbert Hause	5-M	2,280	104
Bloomfield Coll, Bloomfield, NJ 07003	1868	Dr Merle F Allshouse	2-B	1,600	135
Bloomsburg U of Pennsylvania, Bloomsburg, PA 17815	1839	Dr Larry W Jones	5-M	6,189	334
Bluefield State Coll, Bluefield, WV 24701	1895	Dr Jerold O Dugger	5-B	2,500	145
Bob Jones U, Greenville, SC 29614	1927	Dr Bob Jones III	2-D	4,287	332
Boise State U, Boise, ID 83725	1932	Dr John H Keiser	5-M	11,381	453
Boricua Coll, New York, NY 10032	1974	Victor G Alicea	1-B	965	104
Boston Coll, Chestnut Hill, MA 02167	1863	Rev J Donald Monan, SJ	2-D	14,210	704
Boston U, Boston, MA 02215	1839	Dr John R Silber	1-D	27,633	2,600
Bowdoin Coll, Brunswick, ME 04011	1794	Dr A LeRoy Greason	1-B	1,399	106
Bowie State Coll, Bowie, MD 20715	1865	Dr James E Lyons Sr	5-M	2,357	138
Bowling Green State U, Bowling Green, OH 43403	1910	Dr Paul J Olscamp	5-D	16,690	839
Bradley U, Peoria, IL 61625	1897	Dr Martin G Abegg	1-M	5,366	438
Brandeis U, Waltham, MA 02254	1948	Dr Evelyn E Handler	1-D	3,391	452
Brenau Professional Coll, Gainesville, GA 30501	1878	NR	1-M	1,200	150
Brenau Women's Coll, Gainesville, GA 30501 (3)	1878	Dr James T Rogers	1-B	642	86
Brescia Coll, Owensboro, KY 42301	1950	Sr George Ann Cecil	2-B	815	78
Brewton-Parker Coll, Mt Vernon, GA 30445	1904	Dr T Lynn Holmes	2-B	1,207	32
Briar Cliff Coll, Sioux City, IA 51104	1930	Dr Charles J Bensman	2-B	1,307	81
Bridgeport Engineering Inst, Bridgeport, CT 06606	1924	Dr William J Owens	1-B	869	108
Bridgewater Coll, Bridgewater, VA 22812	1880	Dr Wayne F Geisert	2-B	873	70
Bridgewater State Coll, Bridgewater, MA 02324	1840	Dr Adrian Rondileau	5-M	5,438	317
Brigham Young U, Provo, UT 84602	1875	Dr Jeffrey R Holland	2-D	26,963	1,536
Brigham Young U–Hawaii Campus, Laie, Oahu, HI 96762	1955	Dr J Elliot Cameron	2-B	1,820	116
Bristol Coll, Bristol, TN 37620	1895	Mr Ronald Cosby	3-B	612	63
Brooks Inst, Santa Barbara, CA 93108	1945	Mr Ernest H Brooks II	3-M	695	30
Brown U, Providence, RI 02912	1764	Dr Howard R Swearer	1-D	6,400	525
Bryant Coll, Smithfield, RI 02917	1863	Dr William T O'Hara	1-M	6,780	233
Bryn Mawr Coll, Bryn Mawr, PA 19010 (3)	1885	Mary Patterson McPherson	1-D	1,615	199
Bucknell U, Lewisburg, PA 17837	1846	Dr Gary A Sojka	1-M	3,438	258
Buena Vista Coll, Storm Lake, IA 50588	1891	Dr Keith G Briscoe	2-B	958	70
Butler U, Indianapolis, IN 46208	1855	Mr John G Johnson	1-M	3,861	340
Cabrini Coll, Radnor, PA 19087	1957	Sr Eileen Currie	2-M	924	75
Caldwell Coll, Caldwell, NJ 07006 (3)	1939	Sr Vivien Jennings	2-B	725	65
California Coll of Arts and Crafts, Oakland, CA 94618	1907	Neil J Hoffman	1-M	1,038	130
California Inst of Technology, Pasadena, CA 91125	1891	Dr Marvin L Goldberger	1-D	1,816	283
California Inst of the Arts, Valencia, CA 91355	1961	Mr Robert J Fitzpatrick	1-M	842	178
California Lutheran Coll, Thousand Oaks, CA 91360	1959	Dr Jerry H Miller	2-M	2,262	166
California Polytechnic State U, San Luis Obispo, San Luis Obispo, CA 93407	1901	Dr Warren J Baker	5-M	15,967	1,062
California State Coll, Bakersfield, Bakersfield, CA 93309	1970	Dr Tomas A Arciniega	5-M	3,620	213
California State Polytechnic U, Pomona, Pomona, CA 91768	1938	Dr Hugh O La Bounty	5-M	17,024	992
California State U, Chico, Chico, CA 95929	1887	Dr Robin Wilson	5-M	14,196	877
California State U, Dominguez Hills, Carson, CA 90747	1960	Dr Richard Butwell	5-M	7,927	489
California State U, Fresno, Fresno, CA 93740	1911	Dr Harold H Haak	5-M	16,454	1,083
California State U, Fullerton, Fullerton, CA 92634	1957	Dr Jewel Plummer Cobb	5-M	23,247	1,388
California State U, Hayward, Hayward, CA 94542	1957	Dr Ellis E McCune	5-M	12,072	615
California State U, Long Beach, Long Beach, CA 90840	1949	Dr Stephen Horn	5-M	31,124	1,739
California State U, Los Angeles, Los Angeles, CA 90032	1947	Dr James M Rosser	5-D	21,000	1,150
California State U, Northridge, Northridge, CA 91330	1958	Dr James Cleary	5-M	28,068	1,554
California State U, Sacramento, Sacramento, CA 95819	1947	Donald R Gerth	5-M	22,483	1,163
California State U, San Bornardino, San Bernardino, CA 92407	1962	Dr Anthony H Evans	5-M	5,847	272
California State U, Stanislaus, Turlock, CA 95380	1957	Dr Walter Olson	5-M	4,184	275
California U of Pennsylvania, California, PA 15419	1852	Dr John Pierce Watkins	5-M	4,882	305
Calumet Coll, Whiting, IN 46394	1951	Rev Louis Osterhage	2-B	1,130	82
Calvin Coll, Grand Rapids, MI 49506	1876	Dr Anthony J Diekema	2-M	3,971	255
Cameron U, Lawton, OK 73505	1927	Dr Don Davis	5-B	5,030	325

Name, address	Year	Governing official, control, and highest degree offered		Enrollment	Faculty
Campbellsville Coll, Campbellsville, KY 42718	1906	Dr W R Davenport	2-B	648	56
Campbell U, Buies Creek, NC 27506	1887	Dr Norman A Wiggins	2-D	3,500	120
Canisius Coll, Buffalo, NY 14208	1870	Rev James M Demske, SJ	1-M	4,599	271
Capital U, Columbus, OH 43209	1850	Rev Harvey Stegmoeller	2-M	2,537	192
Capitol Inst of Technology, Laurel, MD 20708	1964	Dr G William Troxler	1-B	1,045	57
Cardinal Stritch Coll, Milwaukee, WI 53217	1937	Sr M Camille Kliebhan	2-M	1,763	147
Caribbean U Coll, Bayamón, PR 00619	1969	Dr Angel E Juan-Ortega	1-B	3,595	127
Carleton Coll, Northfield, MN 55057	1866	Mr Robert H Edwards	1-B	1,845	156
Carlow Coll, Pittsburgh, PA 15213 (4)	1929	Mary Louise Fennell, RSM	2-M	1,088	133
Carnegie-Mellon U, Pittsburgh, PA 15213	1900	Dr Richard M Cyert	1-D	5,818	506
Carroll Coll, Waukesha, WI 53186	1846	Dr Robert V Cramer	2-B	1,190	114
Carroll Coll of Montana, Helena, MT 59625	1909	Dr Francis J Kerins	2-B	1,520	113
Carson-Newman Coll, Jefferson City, TN 37760	1851	Dr J Cordell Maddox	2-B	1,730	113
Carthage Coll, Kenosha, WI 53141	1847	Dr Erno J Dahl	2-M	1,503	112
Case Western Reserve U, Cleveland, OH 44106	1826	Dr David V Ragone	1-D	8,544	1,535
Castleton State Coll, Castleton, VT 05735	1787	Dr Thomas K Meier	5-M	2,200	114
Catawba Coll, Salisbury, NC 28144	1851	Dr Stephen H Wurster	2-M	961	66
Catholic U of America, Washington, DC 20064	1887	The Rev William J Byron, SJ	2-D	7,258	708
Catholic U of Puerto Rico, Ponce, PR 00732	1948	Rev F Toselló Giangiacomo	2-M	9,930	403
Catholic U of Puerto Rico, Arecibo Ctr, Arecibo, PR 00612	1964	Enilda Bobadilla de Morell	2-B	1,485	56
Catholic U of Puerto Rico, Mayagüez Ctr, Mayagüez, PR 00708	1975	Dr Willie Ocasio-Cabanas	2-B	1,224	82
Cedar Crest Coll, Allentown, PA 18104 (4)	1867	Dr Gene S Cesari	2-B	1,051	136
Cedarville Coll, Cedarville, OH 45314	1887	Dr Paul H Dixon	2-B	1,815	120
Centenary Coll, Hackettstown, NJ 07840 (3)	1867	Dr Stephanie M Bennett	1-B	1,335	67
Centenary Coll of Louisiana, Shreveport, LA 71134	1825	Dr Donald A Webb	2-M	1,288	108
Center for Creative Studies—Coll of Art & Design, Detroit, MI 48202	1926	Jerome Grove	1-B	954	182
Central Bible Coll, Springfield, MO 65803	1922	H Maurice Lednicky	2-B	906	51
Central Connecticut State U, New Britain, CT 06050	1849	Dr F Don James	5-M	13,333	641
Central Methodist Coll, Fayette, MO 65248	1854	Dr Joseph A Howell	2-B	628	62
Central Michigan U, Mount Pleasant, MI 48859	1892	Mr Arthur E Ellis	5-D	15,997	740
Central Missouri State U, Warrensburg, MO 64093	1871	Dr Eddie Elliott	5-M	8,979	491
Central New England Coll, Worcester, MA 01610	1888	Edward Paul Mattar III	1-B	1,746	137
Central State U, Edmond, OK 73034	1890	Dr Bill J Lillard	5-M	13,102	448
Central U of Iowa, Pella, IA 50219	1853	Dr Kenneth J Weller	2-B	1,548	93
Central Washington U, Ellensburg, WA 98926	1891	Dr Donald L Garrity	5-M	7,377	317
Centre Coll, Danville, KY 40422	1819	Dr Richard L Morrill	2-B	747	77
Chadron State Coll, Chadron, NE 69337	1911	Dr Edwin C Nelson	5-M	1,977	104
Chaminade U of Honolulu, Honolulu, HI 96816	1955	Rev Raymond A Roesch, SM	2-M	2,326	76
Chapman Coll, Orange, CA 92666	1861	Dr G T Smith	2-M	1,699	153
Charter Oak Coll, Hartford, CT 06106	1973	Dr Bernard Shea	5-B	782	55
Chestnut Hill Coll, Philadelphia, PA 19118 (4)	1924	Sr Matthew Anita MacDonald	2-M	1,124	95
Cheyney U of Pennsylvania, Cheyney, PA 19319	1837	Dr LeVerne McCummings	5-M	1,795	153
Chicago State U, Chicago, IL 60628	1867	Dr George E Ayers	5-M	7,404	430
Christian Brothers Coll, Memphis, TN 38104	1871	Br Theodore Drahmann	2-B	1,540	150
Christopher Newport Coll, Newport News, VA 23606	1961	Dr John E Anderson	5-B	4,268	116
Cincinnati Bible Coll, Cincinnati, OH 45204	1924	Mr Harvey C Bream Jr	2-B	937	37
The Citadel, Charleston, SC 29409 (1)	1842	Maj Gen James A Grimsley	5-M	3,001	150
City U, Bellevue, WA 98008	1973	Dr Michael A Pastore	2-M	3,000	220
City U of NY, Bernard M Baruch Coll, New York, NY 10010	1968	DR Joel Segall	12-M	15,581	800
City U of NY, Brooklyn Coll, Brooklyn, NY 11210	1930	Dr Robert Hess	12-M	14,607	1,045
City U of NY, City Coll, New York, NY 10031	1847	Bernard W Harleston	12-M	12,946	1,013
City U of NY, Coll of Staten Island, Staten Island, NY 10301	1955	Dr Edmond L Volpe	12-M	10,877	379
City U of NY, Herbert H Lehman Coll, Bronx, NY 10468	1931	Dr Leonard Lief	12-M	9,810	669
City U of NY, Hunter Coll, New York, NY 10021	1870	Dr Donna E Shalala	12-M	17,944	1,122
City U of NY, John Jay Coll of Crim Justice, New York, NY 10019	1964	Dr Gerald Lynch	12-D	6,518	447
City U of NY, Medgar Evers Coll, Brooklyn, NY 11225	1969	Dr Jay Carrington Chunn	12-B	2,813	323
City U of NY, New York City Tech Coll, Brooklyn, NY 11201	1946	Dr Ursula C Schwerin	12-B	11,608	1,170
City U of NY, Queens Coll, Flushing, NY 11367	1937	Dr William Hamovitchn	12-M	16,369	1,435
City U of NY, York Coll, Jamaica, NY 11451	1967	Mr Milton G Bassin	12-B	4,300	200
Claflin Coll, Orangeburg, SC 29115	1869	Dr Oscar A Rogers Jr	2-B	648	65
Claremont McKenna Coll, Claremont, CA 91711	1946	Mr Jack L Stark	1-B	830	105
Clarion U of Pennsylvania, Clarion, PA 16214	1867	Dr Thomas A Bond	5-M	5,888	320
Clark Coll, Atlanta, GA 30314	1869	Dr Elias Blake Jr	2-B	1,879	127
Clarke Coll, Dubuque, IA 52001	1843	Dr Meneve Dunham	2-M	922	82
Clarkson U, Potsdam, NY 13676	1896	Dr. Allan H. Clark	1-D	4,229	231
Clark U, Worcester, MA 01610	1887	Dr Richard P Traina	1-D	2,636	256
Cleary Coll, Ypsilanti, MI 48197	1883	Dr Harry Howard	1-B	970	57
Clemson U, Clemson, SC 29631	1889	NR	5-D	12,926	1,005
Cleveland State U, Cleveland, OH 44115	1964	Dr Walter B Waetjen	5-D	18,033	763
Clinch Valley Coll of the U of Virginia, Wise, VA 24293	1954	Dr Ned Moomaw	5-B	1,037	58
Coe Coll, Cedar Rapids, IA 52402	1851	Dr John E Brown	2-B	1,322	101
Colby Coll, Waterville, ME 04901	1813	William R Cotter	1-B	1,675	154
Coleman Coll, La Mesa, CA 92041	1963	Maurice F Egan	1-M	817	47
Colgate U, Hamilton, NY 13346	1819	Dr George D Langdon Jr	1-M	2,594	208
Coll for Human Services, New York, NY 10014	1964	Mrs Audrey C Cohen	1-B	600	19
Coll Misericordia, Dallas, PA 18612	1924	Dr Joseph R Fink	2-M	1,292	128
Coll of Boca Raton, Boca Raton, FL 33431	1963	Dr Donald E Ross	1-B	800	61
Coll of Charleston, Charleston, SC 29424	1770	Dr Edward Collins Jr	5-M	5,395	326
Coll of Great Falls, Great Falls, MT 59405	1932	Dr William A Shields	2-M	1,339	87
Coll of Idaho, Caldwell, ID 83605	1891	Dr Arthur H DeRosier Jr	2-M	970	104
Coll of Mount St Joseph on the Ohio, Mount St Joseph, OH 45051	1920	Sr Jean Patrice Harrington	2-M	2,135	183
Coll of Mount Saint Vincent, Riverdale, NY 10471 (4)	1847	Sr Doris Smith	1-B	1,079	74
Coll of New Rochelle, New Rochelle, NY 10801 (4)	1904	Sr Dorothy A Kelly	1-M	1,909	135
Coll of New Rochelle, New Resources Division, New Rochelle, NY 10801	1972	Sr Dorothy Ann Kelly	1-B	2,917	433
Coll of Notre Dame, Belmont, CA 94002	1851	Sr Veronica Skillin	2-M	1,130	141
Coll of Notre Dame of Maryland, Baltimore, MD 21210 (3)	1896	Sr Kathleen Feeley	2-M	1,666	79
Coll of Saint Benedict, Saint Joseph, MN 56374 (3)	1913	Sister Emmanuel Renner	2-B	1,788	143
Coll of St Catherine, St Paul, MN 55105 (3)	1905	Dr Anita Pampusch	2-M	2,458	213
Coll of Saint Elizabeth, Convent Station, NJ 07961 (4)	1899	Sr Jacqueline Burns	2-B	633	93
Coll of St Francis, Joliet, IL 60435	1920	Dr John C Orr	2-M	1,693	87
Coll of Saint Mary, Omaha, NE 68124 (4)	1923	Dr Kenneth Nielsen	2-B	1,055	114
Coll of Saint Rose, Albany, NY 12203	1920	Dr Louis C Vaccaro	1-M	2,840	194

Name, address	Year	Governing official, control, and highest degree offered	Enroll- ment	Faculty
Coll of St Scholastica, Duluth, MN 55811	1906	Dr Daniel H Pilon 2-M	1,431	127
Coll of St Thomas, St Paul, MN 55105	1885	Msgr Terrence J Murphy . . . 2-M	6,435	376
Coll of Santa Fe, Santa Fe, NM 87501	1947	Br Donald Mouton 2-M	910	90
Coll of the Holy Cross, Worcester, MA 01610	1843	Rev John E Brooks, SJ 2-B	2,580	214
Coll of the Ozarks, Clarksville, AR 72830	1834	Fritz Ehren 2-B	723	40
Coll of the Virgin Islands, Charlotte Amalie, St Thomas, VI 00802	1962	Dr Arthur A Richards 8-M	2,756	206
Coll of William and Mary, Williamsburg, VA 23185	1693	NR 5-D	6,640	504
Coll of Wooster, Wooster, OH 44691	1866	Dr Henry J Copeland 2-B	1,691	138
Colorado Coll, Colorado Springs, CO 80903	1874	Dr Gresham Riley 1-M	1,906	175
Colorado School of Mines, Golden, CO 80401	1874	Dr George S Ansell 5-D	2,734	210
Colorado State U, Fort Collins, CO 80523	1870	Dr Philip E Austin 5-D	18,094	1,158
Colorado Tech Coll, Colorado Springs, CO 80907	1965	Ms Marilyn Sullivan 3-B	600	65
Columbia Bible Coll, Columbia, SC 29230	1923	Mr J Robertson McQuilkin . . 2-M	885	49
Columbia Coll, Chicago, IL 60605	1890	Mr Mirron Alexandroff 1-M	4,791	473
Columbia Coll, Columbia, MO 65216	1851	Dr Donald B Ruthenberg . . . 2-B	652	60
Columbia Coll, New York, NY 10027	1754	NR 1-B	2,900	560
Columbia Coll, Columbia, SC 29203 (3)	1854	Dr Ralph T Mirse 2-M	1,192	77
Columbia Union Coll, Takoma Park, MD 20912	1904	Dr William A Loveless 2-B	857	94
Columbia U, School of Engineering & Applied Sci, New York, NY 10027	1864	Professor Robert A Gross . . 1-D	2,097	150
Columbia U, School of General Studies, New York, NY 10027	1947	NR 1-B	1,405	420
Columbia U, School of Nursing, New York, NY 10032 (4)	1935	NR 1-M	174	49
Columbus Coll, Columbus, GA 31993	1958	Dr Francis J Brooke 5-M	3,985	243
Columbus Coll of Art and Design, Columbus, OH 43215	1879	Mr Joseph V Canzani 1-B	963	69
Concord Coll, Athens, WV 24712	1872	Dr Meredith N Freeman . . . 5-B	2,217	116
Concordia Coll, River Forest, IL 60305	1864	Dr Eugene L Krentz 2-M	1,366	117
Concordia Coll, Moorhead, MN 56560	1891	Dr Paul J Dovre 2-B	2,467	194
Concordia Coll, St Paul, MN 55104	1893	Dr Alan F Harre 2-B	746	73
Concordia Coll Wisconsin, Mequon, WI 53092	1881	Dr R John Buuck 2-B	811	65
Concordia Teachers Coll, Seward, NE 68434	1894	Dr James H Pragman 2-M	968	101
Connecticut Coll, New London, CT 06320	1911	Dr Oakes Ames 1-M	1,911	230
Consortium of the California State U, Long Beach, CA 90815	1973	David H Elliott 5-M	2,199	267
Converse Coll, Spartanburg, SC 29301 (3)	1889	Dr Robert T Coleman Jr . . . 1-M	1,037	85
Cooper Union for the Advancement of Science & Art, New York, NY 10003	1859	Mr Bill N Lacy 1-M	1,065	182
Coppin State Coll, Baltimore, MD 21216	1900	Dr Calvin W Burnett 5-M	2,250	146
Cornell Coll, Mount Vernon, IA 52314	1853	Dr David G Marker 2-B	1,087	95
Cornell U, Ithaca, NY 14853	1865	Dr Frank H T Rhodes 1-D	17,540	1,534
Corpus Christi State U, Corpus Christi, TX 78412	1971	Dr B Alan Sugg 5-M	3,710	154
Creighton U, Omaha, NE 68178	1878	Rev Michael G Morrison, SJ . 2-D	5,913	991
Culver-Stockton Coll, Canton, MO 63435	1853	Dr Robert Brown 2-B	850	50
Cumberland Coll, Williamsburg, KY 40769	1889	Dr James Taylor 2-M	2,106	118
Cumberland Coll of Tennessee, Lebanon, TN 37087	1842	Robert N Clement 1-B	715	55
Curry Coll, Milton, MA 02186	1879	Dr William L Boyle Jr 1-M	1,396	112
Daemen Coll, Amherst, NY 14226	1947	Dr Robert S Marshall 1-B	1,623	123
Dakota State Coll, Madison, SD 57042	1881	Dr Richard J Gowen 5-B	980	72
Dallas Baptist U, Dallas, TX 75211	1965	Dr W Marvin Watson 2-M	1,551	84
Dartmouth Coll, Hanover, NH 03755	1769	Mr David T McLaughlin . . . 1-D	5,000	1,324
Davenport Coll of Business, Grand Rapids, MI 49503	1866	Donald W Maine 1-B	4,219	149
David Lipscomb Coll, Nashville, TN 37203	1891	Mr Willard Collins 2-M	2,270	142
Davidson Coll, Davidson, NC 28036	1837	Dr John W Kuykendall 2-B	1,373	117
Davis & Elkins Coll, Elkins, WV 26241	1904	Dr Dorothy I MacConkey . . 2-B	1,158	69
Defiance Coll, Defiance, OH 43512	1850	Dr Marvin Ludwig 2-B	903	64
Delaware State Coll, Dover, DE 19901	1891	Dr Luna I Mishoe 5-M	2,209	144
Delaware Valley Coll of Science & Agriculture, Doylestown, PA 18901	1896	Dr Joshua Feldstein 1-B	1,534	102
Delta State U, Cleveland, MS 38733	1925	Dr F Kent Wyatt 5-D	3,626	171
Denison U, Granville, OH 43023	1831	Dr Andrew G De Rocco . . . 1-B	2,131	188
DePaul U, Chicago, IL 60604	1898	Rev John T Richardson CM . 2-D	12,326	868
DePauw U, Greencastle, IN 46135	1837	Dr Richard F Rosser 2-M	2,381	208
Detroit Coll of Business, Dearborn, MI 48126	1962	Frank Paone 1-B	2,733	105
DeVry Inst of Technology, Phoenix, AZ 85021	1967	James Dugan 3-B	2,731	76
DeVry Inst of Technology, City of Industry, CA 91744	1983	Paul R McGuirk 3-B	1,018	40
DeVry Inst of Technology, Atlanta, GA 30341	1969	William N Weaver 3-B	1,693	82
DeVry Inst of Technology, Chicago, IL 60618	1931	Lee H Bishop 3-M	2,174	73
DeVry Inst of Technology, Lombard, IL 60148	1982	Thomas F Davisson 3-B	1,804	61
DeVry Inst of Technology, Kansas City, MO 64131	1931	Mr Charles R Levalley 3-B	1,196	44
DeVry Inst of Technology, Columbus, OH 43209	1952	Mr Richard A Czerniak . . . 3-B	2,613	86
DeVry Inst of Technology, Irving, TX 75062	1969	Mr David L Moffatt 3-B	1,287	87
Dickinson Coll, Carlisle, PA 17013	1773	Dr Samuel Alston Banks . . 2-B	1,837	145
Dickinson State Coll, Dickinson, ND 58601	1918	Dr Albert A Watrel 5-B	1,249	97
Dillard U, New Orleans, LA 70122	1869	Dr Samuel Du Bois Cook . . 2-B	1,212	101
Doane Coll, Crete, NE 68333	1872	Dr Philip R Heckman 2-B	657	59
Dominican Coll of Blauvelt, Orangeburg, NY 10962	1952	Sr Mary E O'Brien 1-B	1,643	157
Dominican Coll of San Rafael, San Rafael, CA 94901	1890	Dr Barbara K Bundy 2-M	725	135
Dordt Coll, Sioux Center, IA 51250	1955	Dr John B Hulst 2-B	1,103	82
Dowling Coll, Oakdale, NY 11769	1959	Dr Victor P Meskill 1-M	2,550	181
Drake U, Des Moines, IA 50311	1881	Dr Wilbur C Miller 1-D	5,749	343
Drew U, Madison, NJ 07940	1866	Dr Paul Hardin 1-D	2,330	210
Drexel U, Philadelphia, PA 19104	1891	Dr William S Gaither 1-D	12,566	679
Drury Coll, Springfield, MO 65802	1873	Dr John E Moore Jr 1-M	1,142	103
Duke U, Durham, NC 27706	1838	Dr H Keith H Brodie 1-D	9,285	1,442
Duquesne U, Pittsburgh, PA 15282	1878	Rev Donald S Nesti 2-D	6,516	492
Dyke Coll, Cleveland, OH 44115	1848	Dr John C Corfias 1-B	1,310	128
D'Youville Coll, Buffalo, NY 14201	1908	Sr Denise Roche 1-M	1,319	91
Earlham Coll, Richmond, IN 47374	1847	Dr Richard J Wood 2-M	1,050	104
East Carolina U, Greenville, NC 27834	1907	Dr John M Howell 5-D	13,826	902
East Central Oklahoma State U, Ada, OK 74820	1909	Dr Stanley P Wagner 5-M	4,144	178
Eastern Coll, St Davids, PA 19087	1932	Mr Robert A Seiple 2-M	937	96
Eastern Connecticut State U, Willimantic, CT 06226	1889	Dr Charles R Webb Jr 5-M	3,873	205
Eastern Illinois U, Charleston, IL 61920	1895	Dr Stanley Rives 5-M	9,908	549
Eastern Kentucky U, Richmond, KY 40475	1906	Dr Hanly Funderburk 5-M	12,357	630
Eastern Mennonite Coll, Harrisonburg, VA 22801	1917	Dr Richard C Detweiler . . . 2-B	846	78

Name, address	Year	Governing official, control, and highest degree offered	Enrollment	Faculty
Eastern Michigan U, Ypsilanti, MI 48197	1849	Dr John W Porter	5-M	20,241	833
Eastern Montana Coll, Billings, MT 59101	1927	Dr Bruce H Carpenter	5-M	4,207	236
Eastern Nazarene Coll, Quincy, MA 02170	1918	Dr Stephen W Nease	2-M	951	66
Eastern New Mexico U, Portales, NM 88130	1934	Dr Robert Matheny	5-M	3,549	200
Eastern Oregon State Coll, La Grande, OR 97850	1929	David E Gilbert	5-M	1,650	126
Eastern Washington U, Cheney, WA 99004	1882	Dr H George Frederickson	5-M	8,156	390
East Stroudsburg U of Pennsylvania, East Stroudsburg, PA 18301	1893	Dr Dennis Bell	5-M	4,235	207
East Tennessee State U, Johnson City, TN 37614	1911	Dr Ronald E Beller	5-D	9,646	568
East Texas Baptist U, Marshall, TX 75670	1912	Dr Jerry F Dawson	2-B	718	59
East Texas State U, Commerce, TX 75428	1889	Dr Charles J Austin	5-D	7,135	363
East Texas State U at Texarkana, Texarkana, TX 75501	1971	Dr John F Moss	5-M	1,283	55
Eckerd Coll, St Petersburg, FL 33733	1958	Dr Peter H Armacost	2-B	1,105	97
Edgewood Coll, Madison, WI 53711	1927	Sister Mary Ewens	2-B	809	65
Edinboro U of Pennsylvania, Edinboro, PA 16444	1857	Dr Foster F Diebold	5-M	6,053	348
Edward Waters Coll, Jacksonville, FL 32209	1866	Dr Cecil W Cone	2-B	748	72
Electronic Data Processing Coll of Puerto Rico, Hato Rey, PR 00918	1968	Dr Anibal Nieves	3-B	2,522	88
Elizabeth City State U, Elizabeth City, NC 27909	1891	Dr Jimmy R Jenkins	5-B	1,600	124
Elizabethtown Coll, Elizabethtown, PA 17022	1899	Dr Mark C Ebersole	2-B	1,788	138
Elmhurst Coll, Elmhurst, IL 60126	1871	Dr Ivan Frick	2-B	3,556	261
Elmira Coll, Elmira, NY 14901	1855	Dr Leonard T Grant	1-M	1,830	208
Elms Coll, Chicopee, MA 01013 (3)	1928	Sr Mary A Dooley	2-B	886	75
Elon Coll, Elon College, NC 27244	1889	Dr J Fred Young	2-B	2,794	149
Embry-Riddle Aeronautical U, Daytona Beach, FL 32014	1926	Eric S Doten	1-M	4,798	265
Embry-Riddle Aeronautical U, Intl Campus, Bunnell, FL 32010	1926	Charles S Williams	1-M	3,997	1,115
Embry-Riddle Aeronautical U, Prescott Campus, Prescott, AZ 86302	1978	Paul Daly	1-B	960	55
Emerson Coll, Boston, MA 02116	1880	Dr Allen E Koenig	1-M	2,287	167
Emmanuel Coll, Boston, MA 02115 (3)	1919	Sr Janet Eisner	2-M	1,146	79
Emory & Henry Coll, Emory, VA 24327	1836	Dr Charles W Sydnos Jr	2-B	770	66
Emory U, Atlanta, GA 30322	1836	Dr James T Laney	2-D	8,533	1,397
Emporia State U, Emporia, KS 66801	1863	Dr Robert Glennen	5-M	5,498	284
Evangel Coll, Springfield, MO 65802	1955	Dr Robert H Spence	2-B	1,780	115
Evergreen State Coll, Olympia, WA 98505	1967	Dr Joseph D Olander	5-M	2,826	165
Fairfield U, Fairfield, CT 06430	1942	Rev Aloysius P Kelley	2-M	5,104	355
Fairleigh Dickinson U, Florham-Madison Cmps, Madison, NJ 07940	1958	NR	1-M	4,283	231
Fairleigh Dickinson U, Rutherford Cmps, Rutherford, NJ 07070	1942	Samuel J Raphalides	1-M	3,002	203
Fairleigh Dickinson U, Teaneck-Hackensack Cmps, Teaneck, NJ 07666	1954	Dr Robert H Donaldson	1-D	6,667	699
Fairmont State Coll, Fairmont, WV 26554	1865	Dr Wendell G Hardway	5-B	5,005	312
Fashion Inst of Technology, New York, NY 10001	1944	Dr Marvin J Feldman	12-M	3,882	714
Fayetteville State U, Fayetteville, NC 28301	1867	Dr Charles Lyons Jr	5-M	2,679	175
Felician Coll, Lodi, NJ 07644 (4)	1942	Sister Theresa Mary Martin	2-B	643	73
Ferris State Coll, Big Rapids, MI 49307	1884	Dr J William Wenrich	5-D	10,540	650
Ferrum Coll, Ferrum, VA 24088	1913	Dr Joseph T Hart	2-B	1,580	95
Findlay Coll, Findlay, OH 45840	1882	Dr Kenneth E Zirkle	2-B	1,415	99
Fitchburg State Coll, Fitchburg, MA 01420	1894	Dr Vincent J Mara	5-M	6,692	525
Flagler Coll, St Augustine, FL 32084	1968	Dr William L Proctor	1-B	1,001	84
Florida Agricultural and Mechanical U, Tallahassee, FL 32307	1887	Dr Frederick Humphries	5-D	5,269	327
Florida Atlantic U, Boca Raton, FL 33431	1961	Dr Helen Popovich	5-D	8,150	593
Florida Inst of Technology, Melbourne, FL 32901	1958	Dr Jerome P Keuper	1-D	5,715	613
Florida Inst of Technology, Sch of Applied Tech, Jensen Beach, FL 33457	1972	Dr Marion Rice	1-M	731	89
Florida International U, Miami, FL 33199	1965	Dr Gregory B Wolfe	5-D	12,471	868
Florida Memorial Coll, Miami, FL 33054	1879	Dr W C Robinson	2-B	1,900	94
Florida Southern Coll, Lakeland, FL 33802	1885	Dr Robert A Davis	2-M	1,955	135
Florida State U, Tallahassee, FL 32306	1857	Dr Bernard F Sliger	5-D	19,904	1,489
Fontbonne Coll, St Louis, MO 63105	1917	Dr Meneve Dunham	2-M	952	130
Fordham U at Lincoln Center, New York, NY 10023	1841	Rev Joseph A O'Hare, SJ	2-D	6,436	898
Fordham U, Rose Hill Campus, Bronx, NY 10458	1841	Rev Joseph A O'Hare, SJ	2-D	5,904	930
Fort Hays State U, Hays, KS 67601	1902	Dr Gerald W Tomanek	5-M	5,399	236
Fort Lauderdale Coll, Fort Lauderdale, FL 33301	1940	Dr Robert Couch	3-B	860	40
Fort Lewis Coll, Durango, CO 81301	1911	Dr Bernard S Adams	5-B	3,708	158
Fort Valley State Coll, Fort Valley, GA 31030	1895	Dr Luther Burse	5-M	1,837	142
Framingham State Coll, Framingham, MA 01701	1839	Dr D Justin McCarthy	5-M	3,782	214
Francis Marion Coll, Florence, SC 29501	1970	Dr Thomas C Stanton	5-M	3,232	144
Franklin & Marshall Coll, Lancaster, PA 17604	1787	Dr James L Powell	1-B	1,981	188
Franklin Coll of Indiana, Franklin, IN 46131	1834	Mr William Bryan Martin	2-B	705	59
Franklin Pierce Coll, Rindge, NH 03461	1962	Dr Walter Peterson	1-B	998	145
Franklin U, Columbus, OH 43215	1902	Dr Frederick J Bunte	1-B	4,621	221
Freed-Hardeman Coll, Henderson, TN 38340	1869	Dr E C Gardner	2-B	1,131	93
Fresno Pacific Coll, Fresno, CA 93702	1944	Mr Richard Kriegbaum	2-M	890	63
Friends U, Wichita, KS 67213	1898	Dr Richard Felix	2-B	804	57
Frostburg State Coll, Frostburg, MD 21532	1898	Dr Nelson P Guild	5-M	3,400	185
Furman U, Greenville, SC 29613	1826	Dr John E Johns	2-M	2,650	163
Gallaudet Coll, Washington, DC 20002	1856	Dr Jerry C Lee	1-D	1,592	272
Gannon U, Erie, PA 16541	1944	Dr Joseph P Scottino	2-M	3,850	251
Gardner-Webb Coll, Boiling Springs, NC 28017	1905	Dr Craven E Williams	2-M	1,885	161
Geneva Coll, Beaver Falls, PA 15010	1848	Dr Joseph McFarland	2-B	1,290	101
George Fox Coll, Newberg, OR 97132	1891	Dr Edward F Stevens	2-B	624	73
George Mason U, Fairfax, VA 22030	1957	Dr George W Johnson	5-D	15,548	760
Georgetown Coll, Georgetown, KY 40324	1829	Dr W Morgan Patterson	2-M	1,298	122
Georgetown U, Washington, DC 20057	1789	Rev Timothy S Healy	2-D	11,989	1,555
George Washington U, Washington, DC 20052	1821	Dr Lloyd H Elliott	1-D	14,832	1,679
George Williams Coll, Downers Grove, IL 60515	1890	Mr John W Kessler	1-M	1,158	105
Georgia Coll, Milledgeville, GA 31061	1889	Dr Edwin G Speir	5-M	3,779	179
Georgia Inst of Technology, Atlanta, GA 30332	1885	Dr Joseph M Pettit	5-D	10,958	526
Georgian Court Coll, Lakewood, NJ 08701 (4)	1908	Sr Barbara Williams	2-M	1,298	124
Georgia Southern Coll, Statesboro, GA 30460	1906	Dr Dale W Lick	5-M	6,526	400
Georgia Southwestern Coll, Americus, GA 31709	1906	Dr William H Capitan	5-M	2,259	116
Georgia State U, Atlanta, GA 30303	1913	Dr Noah Langdale Jr	5-D	21,366	996

Name, address	Year	Governing official, control, and highest degree offered	Enrollment	Faculty
Gettysburg Coll, Gettysburg, PA 17325	1832	Dr Charles E Glassick ... 2-B	1,850	174
Glassboro State Coll, Glassboro, NJ 08028	1923	Dr Herman D James ... 5-M	8,900	534
Glenville State Coll, Glenville, WV 26351	1872	Dr William N Simmons ... 5-B	1,914	96
GMI Engineering & Management Inst, Flint, MI 48502	1919	Dr William B Cottingham ... 1-M	2,998	132
Golden Gate U, San Francisco, CA 94105	1901	Dr Otto W Butz ... 1-D	10,368	765
Goldey Beacom Coll, Wilmington, DE 19808	1886	Mr William R Baldt ... 1-B	1,918	97
Gonzaga U, Spokane, WA 99258	1887	Rev Bernard J Coughlin, SJ ... 2-D	3,249	280
Gordon Coll, Wenham, MA 01984	1889	Dr Richard F Gross ... 2-B	1,075	71
Goshen Coll, Goshen, IN 46526	1894	Dr Victor Stoltzfus ... 2-B	1,043	98
Goucher Coll, Baltimore, MD 21204 (3)	1885	Dr Rhoda M Dorsey ... 1-M	1,041	136
Governors State U, University Park, IL 60466	1969	Dr Leo Goodman Malamuth II ... 5-M	4,921	296
Grace Coll, Winona Lake, IN 46590	1948	Dr Homer A Kent Jr ... 2-B	846	49
Graceland Coll, Lamoni, IA 50140	1895	Dr Barbara J Higdon ... 2-B	998	82
Grambling State U, Grambling, LA 71245	1901	Dr Joseph B Johnson ... 5-M	4,767	200
Grand Canyon Coll, Phoenix, AZ 85061	1949	Dr William Williams ... 2-B	1,380	81
Grand Rapids Baptist Coll and Seminary, Grand Rapids, MI 49505	1941	Dr Charles Wagner ... 2-M	951	64
Grand Valley State Coll, Allendale, MI 49401	1960	Mr Arend D Lubbers ... 5-M	7,153	381
Grand View Coll, Des Moines, IA 50316	1896	Mr Karl F Langrock ... 2-B	1,333	99
Grantham Coll of Engineering, Los Alamitos, CA 90720	1951	D J Grantham ... 3-B	850	5
Greenville Coll, Greenville, IL 62246	1892	Dr W Richard Stephens ... 2-B	646	55
Griffin Coll, Seattle, WA 98121	1909	J Michael Griffin ... 3-B	712	75
Grinnell Coll, Grinnell, IA 50112	1846	Dr George A Drake ... 1-B	1,207	115
Grove City Coll, Grove City, PA 16127	1876	Dr Charles S MacKknzie ... 2-B	2,196	120
Guilford Coll, Greensboro, NC 27410	1837	Dr William R Rogers ... 2-B	1,132	127
Gustavus Adolphus Coll, St Peter, MN 56082	1862	Dr John S Kendall ... 2-B	2,213	207
Gwynedd-Mercy Coll, Gwynedd Valley, PA 19437 (4)	1948	Sr Isabelle Keiss ... 2-M	2,191	216
Hahnemann U, Philadelphia, PA 19102	1848	Dr Bertram S Brown ... 1-D	2,109	418
Hamilton Coll, Clinton, NY 13323	1812	Mr J Martin Carovano ... 1-B	1,639	146
Hamline U, St Paul, MN 55104	1854	Dr Charles J Graham ... 2-D	1,875	128
Hampden-Sydney Coll, Hampden-Sydney, VA 23943 (1)	1776	Dr Josiah Bunting III ... 2-B	750	73
Hampshire Coll, Amherst, MA 01002	1965	Dr Adele S Simmons ... 1-B	1,000	96
Hampton U, Hampton, VA 23668	1868	Dr William R Harvey ... 1-M	4,260	297
Hannibal-LaGrange Coll, Hannibal, MO 63401	1858	Dr Larry Lewis ... 2-B	756	50
Hanover Coll, Hanover, IN 47243	1827	Dr John E Horner ... 2-B	1,017	73
Harding U, Searcy, AR 72143	1924	Dr Clifton L Ganus Jr ... 2-M	2,828	168
Hardin-Simmons U, Abilene, TX 79698	1891	Dr Jesse C Fletcher ... 2-M	1,834	120
Harris-Stowe State Coll, St Louis, MO 63103	1857	Dr Henry Givens Jr ... 5-B	1,314	66
Hartwick Coll, Oneonta, NY 13820	1928	Dr Philip S Wilder Jr ... 1-B	1,444	127
Harvard U, Cambridge, MA 02138	1636	Mr Derek Bok ... 1-D	16,135	1,934
Hastings Coll, Hastings, NE 68901	1882	Dr Thomas J Reeves ... 2-B	811	71
Haverford Coll, Haverford, PA 19041	1833	Dr Robert B Stevens ... 1-B	1,080	109
Hawaii Pacific Coll, Honolulu, HI 96813	1966	Mr Chatt Wright ... 1-B	3,402	218
Heidelberg Coll, Tiffin, OH 44883	1850	Dr William C Cassell ... 2-B	1,022	79
Henderson State U, Arkadelphia, AR 71923	1890	Dr Martin B Garrison ... 5-M	2,625	122
Hendrix Coll, Conway, AR 72032	1876	Dr Joe B Hatcher ... 2-B	975	74
High Point Coll, High Point, NC 27262	1924	Dr Jacob C Martinson Jr ... 2-B	1,333	76
Hillsdale Coll, Hillsdale, MI 49242	1844	Dr George C Roche III ... 1-B	1,010	73
Hiram Coll, Hiram, OH 44234	1850	Dr Russel Aiuto ... 2-B	1,209	80
Hobart Coll, Geneva, NY 14456 (1)	1822	Mr Carroll Brewster ... 1-B	1,050	159
Hofstra U, Hempstead, NY 11550	1935	Dr James M Shuart ... 1-D	11,298	731
Hollins Coll, Roanoke, VA 24020 (3)	1842	Dr Paula P Brownlee ... 1-M	965	91
Holy Family Coll, Philadelphia, PA 19114	1954	Sr M Francesca ... 2-B	1,602	152
Holy Names Coll, Oakland, CA 94619	1868	Sr Lois MacGillivray ... 2-M	690	90
Hood Coll, Frederick, MD 21701 (4)	1893	Dr Martha E Church ... 2-M	1,799	157
Hope Coll, Holland, MI 49423	1851	Dr Gordon J Van Wylen ... 2-B	2,550	213
Houghton Coll, Houghton, NY 14744	1883	Dr Daniel R Chamberlain ... 2-B	1,270	89
Houston Baptist U, Houston, TX 77074	1960	Dr William H Hinton ... 2-M	3,013	154
Howard Payne U, Brownwood, TX 76801	1889	Dr Ralph A Phelps Jr ... 2-B	1,067	83
Howard U, Washington, DC 20059	1867	Dr James E Cheek ... 1-D	11,480	1,968
Humboldt State U, Arcata, CA 95521	1913	Dr Alistair W McCrone ... 5-M	6,113	488
Huntingdon Coll, Montgomery, AL 36194	1854	Dr Allen K Jackson ... 2-B	782	51
Husson Coll, Bangor, ME 04401	1898	Mr Delmont N Merrill ... 1-M	1,611	100
Idaho State U, Pocatello, ID 83209	1901	Dr Richard Bowen ... 5-D	6,068	505
Illinois Benedictine Coll, Lisle, IL 60532	1887	Dr Richard C Becker ... 2-M	2,193	127
Illinois Coll, Jacksonville, IL 62650	1829	Dr Donald C Mundinger ... 2-B	785	65
Illinois Inst of Technology, Chicago, IL 60616	1892	Dr Thomas L Martin Jr ... 1-D	5,335	485
Illinois State U, Normal, IL 61761	1857	Dr Lloyd I Watkins ... 5-D	20,134	1,064
Illinois Wesleyan U, Bloomington, IL 61702	1850	Dr Robert S Eckley ... 2-B	1,688	173
Immaculata Coll, Immaculata, PA 19345 (4)	1920	Sr Marian William ... 2-M	1,836	112
Incarnate Word Coll, San Antonio, TX 78209	1881	Sr Margaret P Slattery ... 2-M	1,350	115
Indiana Central U, Indianapolis, IN 46227	1902	Dr Gene E Sease ... 2-M	3,042	212
Indiana Inst of Technology, Fort Wayne, IN 46803	1930	Thomas F Scully ... 1-B	850	44
Indiana State U, Terre Haute, IN 47809	1865	Dr Richard D Landini ... 5-D	11,638	713
Indiana State U Evansville, Evansville, IN 47712	1965	Dr David L Rice ... 5-B	3,848	174
Indiana U at Kokomo, Kokomo, IN 46902	1945	Dr Hugh L Thompson ... 5-M	2,499	173
Indiana U at South Bend, South Bend, IN 46634	1922	Lester M Wolfson ... 5-M	5,442	294
Indiana U Bloomington, Bloomington, IN 47405	1820	Kenneth R R Gros Louis ... 5-D	32,715	1,581
Indiana U East, Richmond, IN 47374	1971	Dr Glenn A Goerke ... 5-B	1,326	105
Indiana U Northwest, Gary, IN 46408	1959	Dr Peggy G Elliott ... 5-M	5,116	269
Indiana U of Pennsylvania, Indiana, PA 15705	1875	Dr John Welty ... 5-D	12,806	723
Indiana U–Purdue U at Fort Wayne, Fort Wayne, IN 46805	1917	Edward A Nicholson ... 5-M	10,185	594
Indiana U–Purdue U at Indianapolis, Indianapolis, IN 46202	1969	Dr Glenn W Irwin Jr ... 5-D	23,546	1,922
Indiana U Southeast, New Albany, IN 47150	1941	Dr Edwin W Crooks ... 5-M	4,425	250
Inter American U of PR, Aguadilla Regional Coll, Aguadilla, PR 00603	1957	Mr Juan Colon ... 1-B	2,760	153
Inter American U of PR, Arecibo Regional Coll, Arecibo, PR 00613	1957	Dr Maria delos A Ortiz deLeon ... 1-B	3,531	228
Inter Amer U of PR, Barranquitas Regional Coll, Barranquitas, PR 00615	1957	Mr Vidal Rivera-Garcia ... 1-B	1,458	85
Inter American U of PR, Fajardo Regional Coll, Fajardo, PR 00648	1965	Mr Jose L Larrioux Suarez ... 1-B	1,861	108
Inter American U of PR, Metro Campus, Hato Rey, PR 00919	1960	Dr Rafael Cartagena ... 1-M	13,141	666

Name, address	Year	Governing official, control, and highest degree offered	Enroll-ment	Faculty
Inter American U of PR, Ponce Regional Coll, Ponce, PR 00715	1962	Mr Jose I Correa ... 1-B	2,788	155
Iona Coll, New Rochelle, NY 10801	1940	Br John G Driscoll ... 1-M	6,154	386
Iowa State U, Ames, IA 50011	1858	Dr W Robert Parks ... 5-D	26,321	2,063
Iowa Wesleyan Coll, Mount Pleasant, IA 52641	1842	Dr Jerry Richards ... 2-B	652	51
Ithaca Coll, Ithaca, NY 14850	1892	Dr James J Whalen ... 1-M	5,493	470
ITT Tech Inst, Fort Wayne, IN 46825	1967	Dr Jack J Bainter ... 3-B	1,252	38
ITT Tech Inst, Indianapolis, IN 46268	1970	Marvin L Copes ... 3-B	1,400	35
ITT Tech Inst, Portland, OR 97266	1971	Coy D Ritchie ... 3-B	830	28
Jackson State U, Jackson, MS 39217	1877	Dr James A Hefner ... 5-D	6,088	353
Jacksonville State U, Jacksonville, AL 36265	1883	Dr Theron E Montgomery ... 5-M	6,385	529
Jacksonville U, Jacksonville, FL 32211	1934	Dr Frances B Kinne ... 1-M	2,117	173
James Madison U, Harrisonburg, VA 22807	1908	Dr Ronald E Carrier ... 5-M	9,320	542
Jersey City State Coll, Jersey City, NJ 07305	1927	Dr William J Maxwell ... 5-M	7,003	469
John Brown U, Siloam Springs, AR 72761	1919	Dr John E Brown III ... 2-B	831	57
John Carroll U, University Heights, OH 44118	1886	Rev Thomas P O'Malley ... 2-M	3,900	223
John F Kennedy U, Orinda, CA 94563	1964	Dr Robert M Fisher ... 1-D	1,894	262
Johns Hopkins U, Baltimore, MD 21218	1876	Dr Steven Muller ... 1-D	3,397	398
Johnson & Wales Coll, Providence, RI 02903	1914	Dr Morris J Gaebe ... 1-B	4,750	125
Johnson C Smith U, Charlotte, NC 28216	1867	Mack L Davidson ... 2-B	1,278	94
Johnson State Coll, Johnson, VT 05656	1828	Mr Eric R Gilbertson ... 5-M	1,349	101
Jones Coll, Jacksonville, FL 32211	1918	James M Patch ... 1-B	1,572	63
Jordan Coll, Cedar Springs, MI 49319	1967	DeWayne A Coxon ... 2-B	1,703	144
Juilliard School, New York, NY 10023	1905	Dr Joseph W Polisi ... 1-D	874	220
Juniata Coll, Huntingdon, PA 16652	1876	Dr Frederick M Binder ... 1-B	1,214	90
Kalamazoo Coll, Kalamazoo, MI 49007	1833	Dr David Breneman ... 1-B	1,110	96
Kansas Newman Coll, Wichita, KS 67213	1933	Dr Robert J Giroux ... 2-B	891	72
Kansas State U, Manhattan, KS 66506	1863	Dr Duane C Acker ... 5-D	18,089	1,544
Kean Coll of New Jersey, Union, NJ 07083	1855	Dr Nathan Weiss ... 5-M	12,760	705
Kearney State Coll, Kearney, NE 68849	1903	Dr William R Nester ... 5-M	8,392	342
Keene State Coll, Keene, NH 03431	1909	Dr Barbara J Seelye ... 5-M	2,861	194
Kendall School of Design, Grand Rapids, MI 49503	1928	Dr Phyllis I Danielson ... 1-B	687	61
Kennesaw Coll, Marietta, GA 30061	1966	Dr Betty L Siegel ... 5-B	5,828	196
Kent State U, Kent, OH 44242	1910	Dr Michael Schwartz ... 5-D	20,066	1,035
Kentucky State U, Frankfort, KY 40601	1886	Dr Raymond M Burse ... 13-M	2,066	140
Kentucky Wesleyan Coll, Owensboro, KY 42301	1858	Dr Luther W White ... 2-B	850	85
Kenyon Coll, Gambier, OH 43022	1824	Dr Philip H Jordan Jr ... 1-B	1,440	120
King's Coll, Briarcliff Manor, NY 10510	1938	Dr Robert A Cook ... 2-B	709	68
King's Coll, Wilkes-Barre, PA 18711	1946	Rev James Lackenmier ... 2-B	2,271	151
Knox Coll, Galesburg, IL 61401	1837	Dr John P McCall ... 1-B	910	86
Kutztown U of Pennsylvania, Kutztown, PA 19530	1866	Dr Lawrence M Stratton ... 5-M	6,014	303
Lafayette Coll, Easton, PA 18042	1826	Dr David W Ellis ... 2-B	2,031	206
LaGrange Coll, LaGrange, GA 30240	1831	Dr Walter Y Murphy ... 2-M	947	62
Lake Erie Coll, Painesville, OH 44077 (4)	1859	Dr Marilyn S Jones ... 1-M	1,020	78
Lake Forest Coll, Lake Forest, IL 60045	1857	Dr Eugene Hotchkiss III ... 1-M	1,107	93
Lake Superior State Coll, Sault Sainte Marie, MI 49783	1946	Dr Kenneth F Light ... 5-M	2,783	145
Lamar U, Beaumont, TX 77710	1923	Dr Bill C Franklin ... 5-D	15,835	571
Lambuth Coll, Jackson, TN 38301	1843	Dr Harry W Gilmer ... 2-B	800	80
Lander Coll, Greenwood, SC 29646	1872	Dr Larry A Jackson ... 5-M	2,281	122
Lane Coll, Jackson, TN 38301	1882	Dr Herman Stone ... 2-B	691	47
Langston U, Langston, OK 73050	1897	Dr Ernest L Holloway ... 5-B	2,004	201
Laredo State U, Laredo, TX 78040	1969	Dr Manuel Pacheco ... 5-M	923	57
La Roche Coll, Pittsburgh, PA 15237	1963	Sr Margaret Huber ... 2-B	1,760	110
La Salle U, Philadelphia, PA 19141	1863	Br Patrick Ellis ... 2-M	6,879	294
Lawrence Inst of Technology, Southfield, MI 48075	1932	Dr Richard E Marburger ... 1-B	6,101	303
Lawrence U, Appleton, WI 54912	1847	Dr Richard Warch ... 1-B	1,080	115
Lebanon Valley Coll, Annville, PA 17003	1866	Dr Arthur L Peterson ... 2-B	950	90
Lee Coll, Cleveland, TN 37311	1918	Dr R Lamar Vest ... 2-B	1,154	70
Lehigh U, Bethlehem, PA 18015	1865	Dr Peter Likins ... 1-D	6,277	422
Le Moyne Coll, Syracuse, NY 13214	1946	Rev Frank R Haig, SJ ... 2-B	1,890	176
LeMoyne-Owen Coll, Memphis, TN 38126	1870	Dr Walter L Walker ... 2-B	1,000	77
Lenoir-Rhyne Coll, Hickory, NC 28603	1891	Dr John E Trainer, Jr ... 2-M	1,475	112
Lesley Coll, Cambridge, MA 02238 (3)	1909	Robert D Lewis ... 1-M	1,558	334
LeTourneau Coll, Longview, TX 75607 (2)	1946	Mr Richard Berry ... 2-B	906	72
Lewis and Clark Coll, Portland, OR 97219	1867	Mr James A Gardner ... 2-M	3,012	214
Lewis-Clark State Coll, Lewiston, ID 83501	1894	Dr Lee A Vickers ... 5-B	1,500	120
Lewis U, Romeoville, IL 60441	1932	Br David Delahanty, FSC ... 2-M	2,820	174
Liberty U, Lynchburg, VA 24506	1971	Dr A Pierre Guillermin ... 2-M	4,566	210
Limestone Coll, Gaffney, SC 29340	1845	Dr William J Briggs ... 1-B	1,400	50
Lincoln Memorial U, Harrogate, TN 37752	1897	Dr Gary J Burchett ... 1-M	1,425	100
Lincoln U, Jefferson City, MO 65102	1866	Dr Thomas Miller Jenkins ... 5-M	2,951	169
Lincoln U, Lincoln University, PA 19352	1854	Dr Herman R Branson ... 13-M	1,250	88
Lindenwood Coll, St Charles, MO 63301	1827	Dr James I Spainhower ... 1-M	1,755	119
Linfield Coll, McMinnville, OR 97128	1849	Dr Charles U Walker ... 2-M	1,136	104
Livingstone Coll, Salisbury, NC 28144	1879	Dr William H Greene ... 2-B	743	77
Livingston U, Livingston, AL 35470	1835	Dr Asa N Green ... 5-M	1,500	85
Lock Haven U of Pennsylvania, Lock Haven, PA 17745	1870	Dr Craig Dean Willis ... 5-B	2,624	170
Logan Coll of Chiropractic, Chesterfield, MO 63017	1935	Dr Beatrice B Hagen ... 2-D	633	62
Loma Linda U, Riverside, CA 92515	1915	Dr R Dale McCune ... 2-D	4,610	1,870
Long Island U, Brooklyn Campus, Brooklyn, NY 11201	1926	Dr David J Steinberg ... 1-D	5,795	406
Long Island U, C W Post Campus, Greenvale, NY 11548	1954	Dr Edward J Cook ... 1-M	12,460	705
Long Island U, Southampton Campus, Southampton, NY 11968	1963	Dr David J Steinberg ... 1-M	1,288	112
Longwood Coll, Farmville, VA 23901	1839	Dr Janet D Greenwood ... 5-M	2,719	166
Loras Coll, Dubuque, IA 52004	1839	Dr Pasquale Di Pasquale Jr ... 2-M	2,003	125
Loretto Heights Coll, Denver, CO 80236	1918	Dr Thomas K Craine ... 1-B	800	90
Louisiana Coll, Pineville, LA 71359	1906	Dr Robert L Lynn ... 2-B	1,067	93
Louisiana State U and A&M Coll, Baton Rouge, LA 70803	1860	Dr James H Wharton ... 5-D	29,497	1,282
Louisiana State U in Shreveport, Shreveport, LA 71115	1965	Dr E Grady Bogue ... 5-M	4,625	196
Louisiana Tech U, Ruston, LA 71272	1894	Dr F Jay Taylor ... 5-D	10,908	487
Lourdes Coll, Sylvania, OH 43560	1958	Sr Ann Francis Klimkowski, OSF ... 2-B	812	38
Loyola Coll, Baltimore, MD 21210	1852	Rev Joseph A Sellinger ... 2-M	5,738	288
Loyola Marymount U, Los Angeles, CA 90045	1911	Rev James N Loughran, SJ ... 2-D	6,410	359
Loyola U, New Orleans, New Orleans, LA 70118	1912	Rev James C Carter, SJ ... 2-M	4,873	309

Name, address	Year	Governing official, control, and highest degree offered		Enroll-ment	Faculty
Loyola U of Chicago, Chicago, IL 60611	1870	Rev Raymond C Baumhart, SJ	2-D	14,217	1,322
Lubbock Christian Coll, Lubbock, TX 79407	1957	Dr Steven S Lemley	2-B	1,000	97
Luther Coll, Decorah, IA 52101	1861	Dr H George Anderson	2-B	2,137	163
Lycoming Coll, Williamsport, PA 17701	1812	Dr Frederick E Blumer	2-B	1,286	75
Lynchburg Coll, Lynchburg, VA 24501	1903	Dr George N Rainsford	2-M	2,150	158
Lyndon State Coll, Lyndonville, VT 05851	1911	Dr Clive C Veri	5-M	1,014	86
Macalester Coll, St Paul, MN 55105	1874	Dr Robert M Gavin Jr	2-B	1,696	149
MacMurray Coll, Jacksonville, IL 62650	1846	Dr B G Stephens	2-B	607	65
Madonna Coll, Livonia, MI 48150	1947	Sr Mary Francilene	2-M	3,886	216
Maharishi International U, Fairfield, IA 52556	1971	Dr Bevan Morris	1-D	755	105
Maine Maritime Academy, Castine, ME 04420	1941	Rear Adm Edward A Rodgers	5-M	627	52
Malone Coll, Canton, OH 44709	1892	Dr Gordon R Werkema	2-B	919	70
Manchester Coll, North Manchester, IN 46962	1889	Dr A Blair Helman	2-M	1,027	82
Manhattan Coll, Riverdale, NY 10471	1853	Br J Stephen Sullivan, FSC	1-M	4,737	415
Manhattan School of Music, New York, NY 10027	1917	Mr John O Crosby	1-D	614	158
Manhattanville Coll, Purchase, NY 10577	1841	Dr Marcia Savage	1-M	1,300	170
Mankato State U, Mankato, MN 56001	1867	Dr Margaret R Preska	5-M	12,367	620
Mansfield U of Pennsylvania, Mansfield, PA 16933	1857	Mr Rod C Ketcher	5-M	3,120	205
Marian Coll, Indianapolis, IN 46222	1851	Dr Louis C Gatto	2-B	1,044	100
Marietta Coll, Marietta, OH 45750	1835	Dr Sherrill Cleland	1-M	1,150	116
Marion Coll, Marion, IN 46953	1920	Dr James P Hill Jr	2-M	1,083	88
Marist Coll, Poughkeepsie, NY 12601	1949	Dr Dennis J Murray	1-M	3,427	120
Marquette U, Milwaukee, WI 53233	1881	Rev John P Raynor, SJ	2-D	11,690	929
Marshall U, Huntington, WV 25701	1837	Dr Dale F Nitzschke	5-D	11,323	514
Mars Hill Coll, Mars Hill, NC 28754	1856	Dr Fred B Bentley	2-B	1,357	92
Mary Baldwin Coll, Staunton, VA 24401 (3)	1842	Dr Cynthia Tyson	2-B	832	78
Mary Coll, Bismarck, ND 58501	1959	Sr Thomas Welder	2-M	1,127	76
Marycrest Coll, Davenport, IA 52804	1939	Dr A Lynn Bryant	2-M	1,485	90
Marygrove Coll, Detroit, MI 48221	1910	Dr John E Shay Jr	2-M	1,017	56
Maryland Inst, Coll of Art, Baltimore, MD 21217	1826	Mr Fred Lazarus	1-M	846	90
Marylhurst Coll for Lifelong Learning, Marylhurst, OR 97036	1893	Nancy A Wilgenbusch	1-M	892	147
Marymount Coll, Tarrytown, NY 10591 (4)	1907	Sr Brigid Driscoll	1-B	961	128
Marymount Coll of Kansas, Salina, KS 67402	1922	Dr John Murry	2-B	675	66
Marymount Coll of Virginia, Arlington, VA 22207 (4)	1950	Sr M Majella Berg	2-M	2,068	188
Marymount Manhattan Coll, New York, NY 10021 (4)	1936	Sr Colette Mahoney	1-B	1,894	187
Maryville Coll, Maryville, TN 37801	1819	Dr Wayne W Anderson	2-B	600	55
Maryville Coll–Saint Louis, St Louis, MO 63141	1872	Dr Claudius H Pritchard Jr	1-M	2,247	155
Mary Washington Coll, Fredericksburg, VA 22401	1908	Dr William M Anderson Jr	5-M	3,029	169
Marywood Coll, Scranton, PA 18509	1915	Sr M Coleman Nee	2-M	3,100	198
Massachusetts Coll of Art, Boston, MA 02115	1873	Mr John F Nolan	5-M	1,088	107
Mass Coll of Pharm & Allied Health Sciences, Boston, MA 02115	1823	Dr Raymond A Gosselin	1-D	1,092	61
Massachusetts Inst of Technology, Cambridge, MA 02139	1861	Dr Paul E Gray	1-D	9,577	1,700
Massachusetts Maritime Academy, Buzzards Bay, MA 02532 (2)	1891	Rear Adm John F Aylmer	5-B	800	74
Mayville State Coll, Mayville, ND 58257	1889	Dr James A Schobel	5-B	728	59
McKendree Coll, Lebanon, IL 62254	1828	Dr Gerrit J TenBrink	2-B	1,138	50
McMurry Coll, Abilene, TX 79697	1923	Dr Thomas K Kim	2-B	1,525	121
McNeese State U, Lake Charles, LA 70609	1939	Dr Jack V Doland	5-M	7,981	331
Medaille Coll, Buffalo, NY 14214	1875	Dr Leo R Downey	1-B	787	62
Medical Coll of Georgia, Augusta, GA 30912	1828	Dr Jesse L Steinfeld	5-D	1,756	679
Memphis State U, Memphis, TN 38152	1912	Dr Thomas G Carpenter	5-D	21,295	922
Menlo Coll, Atherton, CA 94025	1927	Dr Richard F O'Brien	1-B	645	65
Mercer U, Macon, GA 31207	1833	Dr R Kirby Godsey	2-D	2,219	128
Mercer U Atlanta, Atlanta, GA 30341	1968	Dr R Kirby Godsey	2-M	1,975	101
Mercy Coll, Dobbs Ferry, NY 10522	1951	Dr Merle Kling	1-M	9,040	600
Mercy Coll of Detroit, Detroit, MI 48219	1941	Maureen A Fay, OP	2-M	2,459	202
Mercyhurst Coll, Erie, PA 16546	1926	Dr William P Garvey	2-M	1,627	110
Meredith Coll, Raleigh, NC 27607 (3)	1891	Dr John E Weems	2-M	1,507	129
Merrimack Coll, North Andover, MA 01845	1947	Rev John E Deegan, OSA	2-B	2,132	144
Mesa Coll, Grand Junction, CO 81502	1925	Dr John U Tomlinson	5-B	4,621	155
Messiah Coll, Grantham, PA 17027	1909	Dr D Ray Hostetter	2-B	1,761	113
Methodist Coll, Fayetteville, NC 28301	1956	Dr M Elton Hendricks	2-B	764	52
Metropolitan State Coll, Denver, CO 80204	1965	Dr Paul J Magelli	5-B	14,423	679
Metropolitan State U, St Paul, MN 55101	1971	Dr Reatha Clark King	5-M	3,666	481
Miami U, Oxford, OH 45056	1809	Dr Paul G Pearson	5-M	15,154	803
Michigan State U, East Lansing, MI 48824	1855	Dr Cecil Mackey	5-D	40,272	2,494
Michigan Technological U, Houghton, MI 49931	1885	Dr Dale F Stein	5-D	6,935	398
Mid-America Nazarene Coll, Olathe, KS 66061	1966	Dr R Curtis Smith	2-B	1,115	72
Middlebury Coll, Middlebury, VT 05753	1800	Dr Olin C Robison	1-D	1,900	189
Middle Tennessee State U, Murfreesboro, TN 37132	1911	Dr Sam H Ingram	5-D	11,369	520
Midland Lutheran Coll, Fremont, NE 68025	1883	Dr Carl L Hansen	2-B	848	90
Midwestern State U, Wichita Falls, TX 76308	1922	Dr Louis J Rodriguez	5-M	4,907	186
Miles Coll, Birmingham, AL 35208	1905	Dr W Clyde Williams	2-D	687	80
Millersville U of Pennsylvania, Millersville, PA 17551	1854	Dr Joseph A Caputo	5-M	6,583	338
Milligan Coll, Milligan College, TN 37682	1866	Dr Marshall J Leggett	2-B	640	71
Millikin U, Decatur, IL 62522	1901	Dr J Roger Miller	2-B	1,605	132
Millsaps Coll, Jackson, MS 39210	1890	Dr George M Harmon	2-M	1,301	96
Mills Coll, Oakland, CA 94613 (3)	1852	Dr Mary S Metz	1-M	938	153
Milwaukee School of Engineering, Milwaukee, WI 53201 (2)	1903	Mr Robert R Spitzer	1-M	2,650	98
Minot State Coll, Minot, ND 58701	1913	Dr Gordon B Olson	5-M	3,117	170
Mississippi Coll, Clinton, MS 39058	1826	Dr Lewis Nobles	2-M	3,061	155
Mississippi State U, Mississippi State, MS 39762	1878	Dr James D McComas	5-D	11,720	864
Mississippi U for Women, Columbus, MS 39701 (4)	1884	Dr James W Strobel	5-M	2,259	144
Mississippi Valley State U, Itta Bena, MS 38941	1946	Dr Joe L Boyer	5-M	2,396	147
Missouri Southern State Coll, Joplin, MO 64801	1937	Dr Julio Leon	5-B	4,323	193
Missouri Western State Coll, St Joseph, MO 64507	1915	Janet Gorman Murphy	5-B	4,077	204
Mobile Coll, Mobile, AL 36613	1961	Dr Michael A Magnoli	2-M	889	74
Molloy Coll, Rockville Centre, NY 11570	1955	Dr Janet A Fitzgerald, OP	2-B	1,656	174
Monmouth Coll, Monmouth, IL 61462	1853	Dr Bruce Haywood	2-B	645	69
Monmouth Coll, West Long Branch, NJ 07764	1933	Dr Samuel H Magill	1-M	4,225	279
Montana Coll of Mineral Science and Technology, Butte, MT 59701	1893	Dr Fred W De Money	5-M	2,128	154
Montana State U, Bozeman, MT 59717	1893	Dr William J Tietz	5-D	11,035	661
Montclair State Coll, Upper Montclair, NJ 07043	1908	Dr Donald E Walters	5-M	14,374	757
Moody Bible Inst, Chicago, IL 60610	1886	Dr George Sweeting	2-B	1,358	98

Name, address	Year	Governing official, control, and highest degree offered	Enrollment	Faculty
Moorhead State U, Moorhead, MN 56560	1887	Dr Roland Dille 5-M	7,481	337
Moravian Coll, Bethlehem, PA 18018	1742	Dr Herman E Collier Jr 1-M	1,273	135
Morehead State U, Morehead, KY 40351	1922	Dr Herb F Reinhard 5-M	6,204	341
Morehouse Coll, Atlanta, GA 30314 (1)	1867	Dr Hugh M Gloster 1-B	2,056	133
Morgan State U, Baltimore, MD 21239	1867	Dr Earl Richardson 5-D	4,351	295
Morningside Coll, Sioux City, IA 51106	1894	Dr Miles Tommeraasen 2-M	1,217	94
Morris Brown Coll, Atlanta, GA 30314	1881	Dr Calvert H Smith 2-B	1,083	84
Morris Coll, Sumter, SC 29150	1908	Dr Luns C Richardson 2-B	600	44
Mount Holyoke Coll, South Hadley, MA 01075 (3)	1837	Mrs Elizabeth Topham Kennan 1-M	1,976	230
Mount Ida Coll, Newton Centre, MA 02159 (4)	1899	Dr Bryan E Carlson 1-B	824	85
Mount Marty Coll, Yankton, SD 57078	1936	NR 2-M	612	71
Mount Mary Coll, Milwaukee, WI 53222 (3)	1913	Sr Ellen Lorenz 2-M	1,290	121
Mount Mercy Coll, Cedar Rapids, IA 52402	1928	Dr Thomas R Feld 2-B	1,287	81
Mount Saint Mary Coll, Newburgh, NY 12550	1930	Sr Ann Sakac 1-M	1,131	90
Mount St Mary's Coll, Los Angeles, CA 90049 (4)	1925	Sr Magdalen Coughlin 2-M	1,222	145
Mount Saint Mary's Coll, Emmitsburg, MD 21727	1808	Dr Robert J Wickenheiser .. 2-M	1,625	103
Mount Union Coll, Alliance, OH 44601	1846	Dr G Benjamin Lantz Jr ... 2-B	1,000	90
Mount Vernon Nazarene Coll, Mount Vernon, OH 43050	1968	Dr William J Prince 2-B	1,065	72
Muhlenberg Coll, Allentown, PA 18104	1848	Dr Jonathan C Messerli ... 2-B	1,471	140
Multnomah School of the Bible, Portland, OR 97220	1936	Dr Joseph C Aldrich 2-M	682	45
Mundelein Coll, Chicago, IL 60660 (4)	1930	Dr John Richert 2-M	1,200	89
Murray State U, Murray, KY 42071	1922	Dr Kala M Stroup 5-M	7,394	381
Muskingum Coll, New Concord, OH 43762	1837	Dr Arthur J De Jong 2-B	1,036	88
National Coll, Rapid City, SD 57709	1941	Mr John W Hauer 3-B	914	55
National Coll of Chiropractic, Lombard, IL 60148	1906	Dr Lee E Arnold 1-D	908	86
National Coll of Education, Evanston, IL 60201	1886	Dr Orley R Herron 1-D	1,699	118
National U, San Diego, CA 92108	1971	Dr David Chigos 1-M	8,735	782
Nazareth Coll in Kalamazoo, Nazareth, MI 49074	1924	Dr Patrick B Smith 2-M	821	88
Nazareth Coll of Rochester, Rochester, NY 14610	1924	Dr Rose Marie Beston ... 1-M	1,674	151
Nebraska Wesleyan U, Lincoln, NE 68504	1887	Dr John W White Jr 2-B	1,365	113
Neumann Coll, Aston, PA 19014	1965	Sr M Margarella O'Neill .. 2-M	863	85
Newberry Coll, Newberry, SC 29108	1831	NR 2-B	630	76
New Coll of California, San Francisco, CA 94110	1971	Ms Mildred Henry 1-M	800	35
New England Coll, Henniker, NH 03242	1946	William R O'Connell, Jr .. 1-M	1,082	83
New England Conservatory of Music, Boston, MA 02115	1867	Laurence Lesser 1-M	738	158
New England Inst of Technology, Providence, RI 02907 (2)	1940	Dr Richard I Gouse 1-B	1,471	69
New Hampshire Coll, Manchester, NH 03104	1932	Mr Edward M Shapiro ... 1-M	3,543	79
New Jersey Inst of Technology, Newark, NJ 07102	1881	Dr Saul K Fenster 13-D	7,235	421
New Mexico Highlands U, Las Vegas, NM 87701	1893	Dr John Aragon 5-M	2,105	135
New Mexico Inst of Mining and Technology, Socorro, NM 87801	1889	Dr Laurence H Lattman ... 5-D	1,236	94
New Mexico State U, Las Cruces, NM 88003	1888	Dr James E Halligan 5-D	12,786	712
New School for Social Research, E Lang Coll, New York, NY 10011	1919	Jonathan F Fanton 1-B	150	25
New School for Social Research, Senior Coll, New York, NY 10011	1919	NR 1-B	120	2,000
New York Inst of Technology, Old Westbury, NY 11568	1955	NR 1-M	13,078	1,064
New York School of Interior Design, New York, NY 10022	1916	Mr Arthur Satz 1-B	783	75
New York U, New York, NY 10003	1831	Dr John Brademas 1-D	33,221	5,422
Niagara U, Niagara University, NY 14109	1856	Rev Donald J Harrington C M 1-M	3,526	232
Nicholls State U, Thibodaux, LA 70310	1948	Dr Donald J Ayo 5-M	7,429	324
Nichols Coll, Dudley, MA 01570	1815	Dr Lowell C Smith 1-M	918	40
Norfolk State U, Norfolk, VA 23504	1935	Dr Harrison B Wilson ... 5-M	7,300	410
North Adams State Coll, North Adams, MA 01247	1894	Dr Catherine Tisinger ... 5-M	2,500	190
North Carolina A&T State U, Greensboro, NC 27411	1891	Dr Edward B Fort 5-M	5,397	386
North Carolina Central U, Durham, NC 27707	1910	Leroy T Walker 5-M	5,002	379
North Carolina State U at Raleigh, Raleigh, NC 27695	1862	Dr Bruce R Poulton 5-D	23,600	1,606
North Carolina Wesleyan Coll, Rocky Mount, NC 27801	1956	Dr S Bruce Petteway ... 2-B	1,141	47
North Central Bible Coll, Minneapolis, MN 55404	1930	Dr Don H Argue 2-B	1,130	44
North Central Coll, Naperville, IL 60566	1861	Mr Gael D Swing 2-B	1,656	115
North Dakota State U, Fargo, ND 58105	1890	Dr Laurel D Loftsgard ... 5-D	9,453	510
Northeastern Illinois U, Chicago, IL 60625	1961	Dr Ronald Williams 5-M	10,075	465
Northeastern Oklahoma State U, Tahlequah, OK 74464	1846	Dr W Roger Webb 5-D	7,318	350
Northeastern U, Boston, MA 02115	1898	Dr Kenneth Ryder 1-D	36,219	2,785
Northeast Louisiana U, Monroe, LA 71209	1931	Dr Dwight D Vines 5-M	11,558	444
Northeast Missouri State U, Kirksville, MO 63501	1867	Dr Charles J McClain ... 5-M	6,875	291
Northern Arizona U, Flagstaff, AZ 86011	1899	Dr Eugene M Hughes ... 5-D	11,826	489
Northern Illinois U, De Kalb, IL 60115	1895	Dr Clyde J Wingfield ... 5-D	23,689	1,230
Northern Kentucky U, Highland Heights, KY 41076	1968	Dr Leon E Boothe 5-M	8,879	480
Northern Michigan U, Marquette, MI 49855	1899	Dr James B Appleberry .. 5-M	7,869	309
Northern Montana Coll, Havre, MT 59501	1929	Dr James Erickson 5-M	1,811	120
Northern State Coll, Aberdeen, SD 57401	1901	Dr Terence Brown 5-M	2,718	118
North Georgia Coll, Dahlonega, GA 30597	1873	Dr John H Owen 5-M	1,979	114
North Park Coll, Chicago, IL 60625	1891	Dr Lloyd H Ahlem 2-B	1,103	105
Northrop U, Inglewood, CA 90306	1942	Dr B J Shell 1-D	1,522	175
North Texas State U, Denton, TX 76203	1890	Dr Alfred F Hurley 5-D	21,414	830
Northwest Coll of the Assemblies of God, Kirkland, WA 98033	1934	Dr D V Hurst 2-B	690	50
Northwestern Coll, Orange City, IA 51041	1882	Dr James E Bultman ... 2-B	900	71
Northwestern Coll, Roseville, MN 55113	1902	Dr Donald Ericksen ... 2-B	994	87
Northwestern Oklahoma State U, Alva, OK 73717	1897	Dr Joe J Struckle 5-M	1,817	85
Northwestern State U of Louisiana, Natchitoches, LA 71497	1884	Dr Joseph J Orze 5-M	6,178	257
Northwestern U, Evanston, IL 60201	1851	Dr Arnold R Weber 1-D	15,985	1,629
Northwest Missouri State U, Maryville, MO 64468	1905	Dr Dean L Hubbard 5-M	5,000	238
Northwest Nazarene Coll, Nampa, ID 83651	1913	A Gordon Wetmore 2-M	1,007	77
Northwood Inst, Midland, MI 48640	1959	Dr David E Fry 1-B	1,900	80
Norwich U, The Military Coll of Vermont, Northfield, VT 05663 (2)	1819	Lt Gen W Russell Todd .. 1-M	1,586	162
Norwich U, Vermont Coll, Montpelier, VT 05602	1834	John R Turner 1-M	802	56
Notre Dame Coll, Manchester, NH 03104 (4)	1950	Sr Carol Descoteaux, CSC . 2-M	741	70
Notre Dame Coll of Ohio, Cleveland, OH 44121 (3)	1922	Sr Mary Martha 2-B	741	74
Nova U, Fort Lauderdale, FL 33314	1964	Dr Abraham S Fischler .. 1-D	6,159	403
Nyack Coll, Nyack, NY 10960	1882	Dr David L Rambo 2-M	874	89
Oakland City Coll, Oakland City, IN 47660	1885	Dr James W Murray 2-M	734	57
Oakland U, Rochester, MI 48063	1957	Dr Joseph E Champagne . 5-D	11,971	575

Name, address	Year	Governing official, control, and highest degree offered		Enrollment	Faculty
Oakwood Coll, Huntsville, AL 35896	1896	Dr Calvin B Rock	2-B	1,331	108
Oberlin Coll, Oberlin, OH 44074	1833	Dr S Frederick Starr	1-M	2,801	227
Occidental Coll, Los Angeles, CA 90041	1887	Dr Richard C Gilman	1-M	1,586	134
Oglala Lakota Coll, Kyle, SD 57752	1970	Mr Elgin Badwound	12-B	752	93
Oglethorpe U, Atlanta, GA 30319	1835	Dr Manning M Pattillo Jr	1-M	1,029	55
Ohio Dominican Coll, Columbus, OH 43219	1911	Sr Mary Andrew Matesich	2-B	1,053	81
Ohio Northern U, Ada, OH 45810	1871	Dr De Bow Freed	2-D	2,445	188
Ohio State U, Columbus, OH 43210	1870	Dr Edward Jennings	5-D	52,434	3,262
Ohio State U–Lima Campus, Lima, OH 45804	1960	Dr James S Biddle	5-B	939	34
Ohio State U–Mansfield Campus, Mansfield, OH 44906	1958	Dr David W Kramer	5-B	1,089	36
Ohio State U–Marion Campus, Marion, OH 43302	1957	Dr Francis E Hazard	5-B	795	25
Ohio State U–Newark Campus, Newark, OH 43055	1957	Dr Julius S Greenstein	5-B	935	27
Ohio U, Athens, OH 45701	1804	Dr Charles J Ping	5-D	14,897	778
Ohio U–Belmont, St Clairsville, OH 43950	1967	Dr James W Newton	5-B	1,000	76
Ohio U–Chillicothe, Chillicothe, OH 45601	1946	Dr Ann Jones	5-B	1,186	75
Ohio U–Ironton, Ironton, OH 45638	1956	Mr Bill Dingus	5-B	1,012	80
Ohio U–Lancaster, Lancaster, OH 43130	1968	Dr Raymond Wilkes	5-M	1,592	113
Ohio U–Zanesville, Zanesville, OH 43701	1946	Dr Craig D Laubenthal	5-B	904	61
Ohio Wesleyan U, Delaware, OH 43015	1842	Dr David L Warren	2-B	1,571	183
Oklahoma Baptist U, Shawnee, OK 74801	1910	Dr Bob R Agee	2-B	1,590	134
Oklahoma Christian Coll, Oklahoma City, OK 73111	1950	Dr Terry Johnson	2-B	1,539	78
Oklahoma City U, Oklahoma City, OK 73106	1904	Dr Jerald C Walker	2-M	3,231	201
Oklahoma Panhandle State U, Goodwell, OK 73939	1909	Mr Thomas L Palmer	5-B	1,230	62
Oklahoma State U, Stillwater, OK 74078	1890	Dr Lawrence L Boger	5-D	21,931	1,071
Old Dominion U, Norfolk, VA 23508	1930	Dr Joseph M Marchello	5-D	14,966	717
Olivet Coll, Olivet, MI 49076	1844	Dr Donald A Morris	2-B	683	58
Olivet Nazarene Coll, Kankakee, IL 60901	1907	Dr Leslie A Parrott	2-M	1,771	110
Oral Roberts U, Tulsa, OK 74171	1963	Mr G Oral Roberts	2-D	4,615	385
Oregon Inst of Technology, Klamath Falls, OR 97601	1947	Larry J Blake	5-B	2,818	193
Oregon State U, Corvallis, OR 97331	1868	Dr John V Byrne	5-D	15,624	1,623
Orlando Coll, Orlando, FL 32810	1918	Mrs Ovida B Kirby	1-B	906	38
Otis Art Inst of Parsons School of Design, Los Angeles, CA 90057	1917	Michael J Piltas	1-M	710	138
Otterbein Coll, Westerville, OH 43081	1847	Dr C Brent DeVore	2-B	1,656	112
Ouachita Baptist U, Arkadelphia, AR 71923	1885	Dr Daniel R Grant	2-M	1,401	101
Our Lady of Holy Cross Coll, New Orleans, LA 70114	1916	Sr Mary Charles Clement	2-M	621	70
Our Lady of the Lake U of San Antonio, San Antonio, TX 78285	1911	Sr Elizabeth Anne Sueltenfuss	2-M	1,684	95
Pace U, New York, NY 10038	1906	Dr Edward J Mortola	1-D	10,198	588
Pace U, Pleasantville/Briarcliff Campus, Pleasantville, NY 10570	1963	Dr Frank S Falcone	1-M	3,793	418
Pace U, White Plains Campus, White Plains, NY 10603	1923	Dr Frank S Falcone	1-M	3,609	159
Pacific Lutheran U, Tacoma, WA 98447	1890	Dr William O Rieke	2-M	3,694	291
Pacific Union Coll, Angwin, CA 94508	1882	Dr D Malcolm Maxwell	2-M	1,403	103
Pacific U, Forest Grove, OR 97116	1849	Dr Robert F Duvall	1-D	1,061	98
Paine Coll, Augusta, GA 30910	1882	Dr William H Harris	2-B	721	54
Palm Beach Atlantic Coll, West Palm Beach, FL 33401	1968	Dr Claude Rhea	2-B	950	84
Pan American U, Edinburg, TX 78539	1927	Dr Miguel A Nevarez	5-M	10,057	415
Park Coll, Parkville, MO 64152	1875	Dr Harold L Condit	2-M	888	40
Parks Coll of Saint Louis U, Cahokia, IL 62206	1927	Dr Paul A Whelan	2-B	1,130	57
Parsons School of Design, New York, NY 10011	1896	Jonathan F Fanton	1-M	1,670	235
Pembroke State U, Pembroke, NC 28372	1887	Dr Paul R Givens	5-M	2,197	136
Penna State U Behrend Coll, Erie, PA 16563	1926	Dr John M Lilley	13-M	1,989	124
Penna State U Capitol Campus, Middletown, PA 17057	1966	Dr Ruth Leventhal	13-M	2,595	149
Penna State U U Park Campus, University Park, PA 16802	1855	Dr Bryce Jordan	13-D	34,401	1,782
Pepperdine U, Malibu, CA 90265	1937	Dr Howard A White	2-D	3,279	243
Pepperdine U, Pepperdine Plaza, Los Angeles, CA 90034	1937	Dr David Davenport	2-D	3,613	196
Peru State Coll, Peru, NE 68421	1867	Dr Jerry L Gallentine	5-M	1,453	70
Pfeiffer Coll, Misenheimer, NC 28109	1885	Dr Cameron P West	2-B	811	80
Philadelphia Coll of Art, Philadelphia, PA 19102	1876	Peter Solmssen	1-M	1,659	234
Philadelphia Coll of Pharmacy and Science, Philadelphia, PA 19104	1821	Dr Allen Misher	1-D	1,111	149
Philadelphia Coll of Textiles and Science, Philadelphia, PA 19144	1884	Dr James P Gallagher	1-M	2,746	111
Phillips U, Enid, OK 73702	1906	Dr Joe Jones	2-D	1,150	105
Pittsburg State U, Pittsburg, KS 66762	1903	Dr Donald W Wilson	5-M	4,927	267
Pitzer Coll, Claremont, CA 91711	1963	Dr Frank L Ellsworth	1-B	740	78
Plymouth State Coll of the U System of NH, Plymouth, NH 03264	1871	Dr William J Farrell	5-M	3,400	189
Point Loma Nazarene Coll, San Diego, CA 92106	1902	Dr Jim L Bond	2-M	1,917	137
Point Park Coll, Pittsburgh, PA 15222	1960	Dr John V Hopkins	1-M	2,594	151
Polytechnic Inst of NY, Brooklyn Campus, Brooklyn, NY 11201	1854	Dr George Bugliarello	1-D	3,181	385
Polytechnic Inst of NY, Farmingdale Campus, Farmingdale, NY 11735	1887	Dr James J Conti	1-D	1,397	385
Pomona Coll, Claremont, CA 91711	1887	Dr David Alexander	1-B	1,358	159
Portland State U, Portland, OR 97207	1946	Dr Joseph C Blumel	5-D	14,390	679
Post Coll, Waterbury, CT 06708	1890	Dr Douglas R Picht	1-B	1,507	58
Prairie View A&M U, Prairie View, TX 77446	1878	Dr Percy A Pierre	5-M	4,436	297
Pratt Inst, Brooklyn, NY 11205	1887	Mr Richardson Pratt Jr	1-M	3,518	438
Presbyterian Coll, Clinton, SC 29325	1880	Dr Kenneth B Orr	2-B	914	64
Princeton U, Princeton, NJ 08544	1756	William G Bowen	1-D	5,990	738
Principia Coll, Elsah, IL 62028	1910	Mr John E G Boyman	2-B	722	67
Providence Coll, Providence, RI 02918	1917	The Rev John F Cunningham	2-D	6,156	245
Purdue U, West Lafayette, IN 47907	1869	Dr Steven C Beering	5-D	31,457	3,100
Purdue U Calumet, Hammond, IN 46323	1951	Mr Richard J Combs	5-M	7,442	389
Purdue U North Central, Westville, IN 46391	1967	Dr Dale W Alspaugh	5-B	2,616	151
Queens Coll, Charlotte, NC 28274 (4)	1857	Dr Billy O Wireman	2-M	1,230	146
Quincy Coll, Quincy, IL 62301	1860	Rev James Toal	2-M	1,502	96
Quinnipiac Coll, Hamden, CT 06518	1929	Dr Richard A Terry	1-M	2,388	330
Radford U, Radford, VA 24142	1910	Dr Donald N Dedmon	5-M	6,806	341
Ramapo Coll of New Jersey, Mahwah, NJ 07430	1969	Dr Robert A Scott	5-B	3,961	209
Randolph-Macon Coll, Ashland, VA 23005	1830	Dr Ladell Payne	2-B	964	100
Randolph-Macon Woman's Coll, Lynchburg, VA 24503 (3)	1891	Dr Robert Atwood Spivey	2-B	750	83

Name, address	Year	Governing official, control, and highest degree offered		Enroll-ment	Faculty
Reed Coll, Portland, OR 97202	1910	Mr Paul E Bragdon	1-M	1,087	104
Regis Coll, Denver, CO 80221	1877	Rev David M Clarke, SJ	2-M	1,220	95
Regis Coll, Weston, MA 02193 (3)	1927	Sr Therese Higgins	2-M	1,180	106
Rensselaer Polytechnic Inst, Troy, NY 12180	1824	Dr Daniel Berg	1-D	6,595	638
Rhode Island Coll, Providence, RI 02908	1854	Dr John Nazarian	5-M	9,178	506
Rhode Island School of Design, Providence, RI 02903	1877	Dr Thomas F Schutte	1-M	1,792	199
Rhodes Coll, Memphis, TN 38112	1848	Dr James H Daughdrill Jr	2-B	1,024	109
Rice U, Houston, TX 77251	1891	Dr George Rupp	1-D	3,813	421
Rider Coll, Lawrenceville, NJ 08648	1865	Dr Frank N Elliott	1-M	5,349	285
Rio Grande Coll/Comm Coll, Rio Grande, OH 45674	1876	Dr Clodus R Smith	1-B	1,607	92
Ripon Coll, Ripon, WI 54971	1851	Dr William R Stott Jr	1-B	868	94
Rivier Coll, Nashua, NH 03060 (4)	1933	Sr Jeanne Perreault	2-M	2,280	173
Roanoke Coll, Salem, VA 24153	1842	Dr Norman D Fintel	2-B	1,462	91
Robert Morris Coll, Coraopolis, PA 15108	1921	Dr Charles L Sewall	1-M	5,714	233
Roberts Wesleyan Coll, Rochester, NY 14624	1866	Dr William C Crothers	2-B	680	92
Rochester Inst of Technology, Rochester, NY 14623	1829	Dr M Richard Rose	1-M	15,231	1,241
Rockford Coll, Rockford, IL 61108	1847	Dr Norman L Stewart	1-M	1,419	141
Rockhurst Coll, Kansas City, MO 64110	1910	Rev Robert F Weiss, SJ	2-M	2,697	179
Roger Williams Coll, Bristol, RI 02809	1948	Mr William H Rizzini	1-B	2,300	120
Rollins Coll, Winter Park, FL 32789	1885	Dr Thaddeus Seymour	1-M	1,625	141
Roosevelt U, Chicago, IL 60605	1945	Dr Rolf A Weil	1-M	6,061	481
Rosary Coll, River Forest, IL 60305	1848	Sr Jean Murray	2-M	1,655	134
Rose-Hulman Inst of Technology, Terre Haute, IN 47803 (1)	1874	Dr Samuel F Hulbert	1-M	1,329	96
Rosemont Coll, Rosemont, PA 19010 (3)	1921	Dr Dorothy McKenna Brown	2-B	619	85
Rush U, Chicago, IL 60612	1969	Dr Leo M Henikoff	1-D	1,105	825
Russell Sage Coll, Troy, NY 12180 (3)	1916	Dr William F Kahl	1-M	1,459	133
Rust Coll, Holly Springs, MS 38635	1866	Dr William A McMillan	2-B	870	40
Rutgers U, Camden Coll of Arts and Sciences, Camden, NJ 08102	1950	Walter K Gordon	5-B	2,632	165
Rutgers U, Coll of Engineering, New Brunswick, NJ 08903	1864	Dr Ellis Dill	5-B	2,727	114
Rutgers U, Coll of Nursing, Newark, NJ 07102 (4)	1956	Norman Samuels	5-B	508	53
Rutgers U, Coll of Pharmacy, New Brunswick, NJ 08903	1927	John Louis Colaizzi	5-B	711	33
Rutgers U, Cook Coll, New Brunswick, NJ 08903	1921	Dr Stephen J Kleinschuster	5-B	3,096	118
Rutgers U, Douglass Coll, New Brunswick, NJ 08903 (3)	1918	Dr Mary S Hartman	5-B	3,345	NR
Rutgers U, Livingston Coll, New Brunswick, NJ 08903	1969	Dr W Robert Jenkins	5-B	3,510	NR
Rutgers U, Mason Gross School of the Arts, New Brunswick, NJ 08903	1976	John Bettenbender	5-M	645	91
Rutgers U, Newark Coll of Arts and Sciences, Newark, NJ 07102	1946	Norman Samuels	5-B	3,648	244
Rutgers U, Rutgers Coll, New Brunswick, NJ 08903	1766	NR	5-B	8,270	NR
Rutgers U, U Coll–Camden, Camden, NJ 08102	1934	NR	5-B	1,069	49
Rutgers U, U Coll–Newark, Newark, NJ 07102	1934	Norman Samuels	5-B	1,753	40
Rutgers U, U Coll–New Brunswick, New Brunswick, NJ 08903	1934	Dr Barbara E Kovach	5-B	3,411	NR
Sacred Heart U, Bridgeport, CT 06606	1963	Dr Thomas P Melady	2-M	5,972	333
Saginaw Valley State Coll, University Center, MI 48710	1963	Dr Jack M Ryder	5-M	4,858	245
St Ambrose Coll, Davenport, IA 52803	1882	Dr William J Bakrow	2-M	2,236	144
St Andrews Presbyterian Coll, Laurinburg, NC 28352	1958	Mr Alvin P Perkinson	2-B	737	58
Saint Anselm Coll, Manchester, NH 03102	1889	Br Joachim W Froehlich	2-B	1,653	160
Saint Augustine's Coll, Raleigh, NC 27611	1867	Dr Prezell R Robinson	2-B	1,716	75
St Bonaventure U, St Bonaventure, NY 14778	1854	Very Rev Mathias Doyle	2-M	2,647	198
St Cloud State U, St Cloud, MN 56301	1869	Dr Brendan McDonald	5-M	10,927	658
St Edward's U, Austin, TX 78704	1885	Dr Patricia Hayes	2-M	2,557	141
Saint Francis Coll, Fort Wayne, IN 46808	1890	Sr M JoEllen Scheetz	2-M	1,310	90
St Francis Coll, Brooklyn, NY 11201	1858	Br Donald Sullivan, OSF	2-B	2,423	129
Saint Francis Coll, Loretto, PA 15940	1847	Rev Christian R Oravec	2-M	1,600	87
St John Fisher Coll, Rochester, NY 14618	1948	Rev Patrick O Braden	1-M	1,954	182
Saint John's U, Collegeville, MN 56321 (1)	1857	Fr Hilary Thimmesh, OSB	2-M	2,024	158
St John's U, Jamaica, NY 11439	1870	Very Rev Joseph T Cahill, CM	2-D	19,123	930
Saint Joseph Coll, West Hartford, CT 06117 (3)	1932	Dr M Paton Ryan, RSM	2-M	1,216	123
Saint Joseph's Coll, Rensselaer, IN 47978	1889	Fr Charles Banet	2-M	983	67
St Joseph's Coll, Brooklyn, NY 11205	1916	Sr George A O'Connor	1-B	925	113
St Joseph's Coll, Suffolk Campus, Patchogue, NY 11772	1916	S George Aquin O'Connor	1-B	1,397	110
Saint Joseph's U, Philadelphia, PA 19131	1851	Rev Donald I Maclean	2-M	5,966	191
St Lawrence U, Canton, NY 13617	1856	Dr W Lawrence Gulick	1-M	2,338	186
Saint Leo Coll, Saint Leo, FL 33574	1889	Dr Thomas B Southard	2-B	1,119	91
St Louis Coll of Pharmacy, St Louis, MO 63110	1864	Dr Sumner M Robinson	1-B	685	43
Saint Louis U, St Louis, MO 63103	1818	Rev Thomas R Fitzgerald	2-D	10,170	2,504
Saint Mary Coll, Leavenworth, KS 66048 (4)	1923	Sr M Janet McGilley	2-B	1,038	87
Saint Mary of the Plains Coll, Dodge City, KS 67801	1952	Dr Michael J McCarthy	2-B	705	87
Saint Mary-of-the-Woods Coll, Saint Mary-of-the-Woods, IN 47876 (3)	1840	Barbara Doherty, SP	2-B	670	85
Saint Mary's Coll, Notre Dame, IN 46556 (4)	1844	NR	2-B	1,753	177
Saint Mary's Coll, Winona, MN 55987	1912	Br Louis DeThomasis, FSC	2-M	1,480	102
Saint Mary's Coll of California, Moraga, CA 94575	1863	Br Mel Anderson	2-M	2,850	174
St Mary's Coll of Maryland, St Mary's City, MD 20686	1839	Dr Edward T Lewis	5-B	1,302	109
Mary's U of San Antonio, San Antonio, TX 78284	1852	Rev David J Paul SM	2-D	3,296	193
Saint Michael's Coll, Winooski, VT 05404	1904	Dr Paul J Reiss	2-M	1,969	131
St Norbert Coll, De Pere, WI 54115	1898	Dr Thomas A Manion	2-B	1,747	123
St Olaf Coll, Northfield, MN 55057	1874	Dr Melvin George	2-B	3,023	327
St Paul Bible Coll, Bible College, MN 55375	1916	Dr L John Eagen	2-B	638	45
Saint Paul's Coll, Lawrenceville, VA 23868	1888	Dr S Dallas Simmons	2-B	701	49
Saint Peter's Coll, Jersey City, NJ 07306	1872	Rev Edward Glynn, SJ	2-M	2,730	315
St Thomas Aquinas Coll, Sparkill, NY 10976	1958	Dr Donald T McNelis	1-B	1,572	67
St Thomas U, Miami, FL 33054	1961	Rev Patrick H O'Neill	2-D	2,800	268
Saint Vincent Coll, Latrobe, PA 15650	1846	Rev John F Murtha OSB	2-B	978	90
Saint Xavier Coll, Chicago, IL 60655	1847	R Champagne	2-M	2,367	160
Salem Coll, Winston-Salem, NC 27108 (3)	1772	Dr Thomas V Litzenburg Jr	2-M	601	71
Salem Coll, Salem, WV 26426	1888	Dr Ronald E Ohl	1-M	1,296	68
Salem State Coll, Salem, MA 01970	1854	Dr James T Amsler	5-M	8,654	297
Salisbury State Coll, Salisbury, MD 21801	1925	Dr Thomas A Bellavance	5-M	4,506	243
Salve Regina–The Newport Coll, Newport, RI 02840	1934	Sr M Lucille McKillop	2-M	2,120	216
Samford U, Birmingham, AL 35229	1841	Dr Thomas E Corts	2-M	4,007	291
Sam Houston State U, Huntsville, TX 77341	1879	Dr Elliott T Bowers	5-D	10,492	428
San Diego State U, San Diego, CA 92182	1897	Dr Thomas B Day	5-D	33,611	1,935
San Francisco Art Inst, San Francisco, CA 94133	1871	Dr Stephen J Goldstine	1-M	641	70

Name, address	Year	Governing official, control, and highest degree offered		Enrollment	Faculty
San Francisco State U, San Francisco, CA 94132	1899	Dr Chia-Wei Woo	5-M	24,170	1,907
Sangamon State U, Springfield, IL 62708	1969	Dr Durward Long	5-M	3,027	194
San Jose State U, San Jose, CA 95192	1857	Dr Gail Fullerton	5-M	24,843	1,674
Sarah Lawrence Coll, Bronxville, NY 10708	1926	Dr Alice Stone Ilchman	1-M	943	150
Savannah Coll of Art and Design, Savannah, GA 31401	1976	Richard G Rowan	1-M	811	64
Savannah State Coll, Savannah, GA 31404	1890	Dr Wendell G Rayburn	5-M	2,010	150
School for International Training, Brattleboro, VT 05301	1964	Dr John Middleton	1-M	656	35
Sch for Lifelong Learning of the U System of NH, Durham, NH 03824	1972	Dr Alvin L Hall	12-B	1,450	301
School of the Art Inst of Chicago, Chicago, IL 60603	1866	Mr Neil J Hoffman	1-M	1,297	168
School of the Museum of Fine Arts, Boston, MA 02115	1948	Bruce K MacDonald	1-M	646	65
School of the Ozarks, Point Lookout, MO 65726	1906	Dr Stephen G Jennings	1-B	1,236	93
School of Visual Arts, New York, NY 10010	1947	David Rhodes	3-M	2,346	647
Scripps Coll, Claremont, CA 91711 (3)	1926	Dr John H Chandler	1-B	625	86
Seattle Pacific U, Seattle, WA 98119	1891	Rev Msgr John J Strynkowski	2-M	2,935	188
Seattle U, Seattle, WA 98122	1891	Rev William J Sullivan	2-D	4,653	306
Seton Hall U, South Orange, NJ 07079	1856	Msgr John J Petillo	2-D	7,939	801
Seton Hill Coll, Greensburg, PA 15601 (3)	1882	Eileen Farrell	2-B	870	81
Shaw U, Raleigh, NC 27611	1865	Dr Stanley H Smith	2-B	1,922	83
Shenandoah Coll and Conservatory, Winchester, VA 22601	1875	Dr James A Davis	2-M	932	128
Shepherd Coll, Shepherdstown, WV 25443	1871	Dr James A Butcher	5-B	3,534	184
Shippensburg U of Pennsylvania, Shippensburg, PA 17257	1871	Dr Anthony F Ceddia	5-M	6,136	316
Shorter Coll, Rome, GA 30161	1873	Dr George Balentine	2-B	730	55
Siena Coll, Loudonville, NY 12211	1938	Fr Hugh F Hines	2-B	3,473	206
Siena Heights Coll, Adrian, MI 49221	1919	Sr Cathleen Real CHM	2-M	1,483	113
Simmons Coll, Boston, MA 02115 (3)	1899	William J Holmes	1-D	3,138	276
Simpson Coll, Indianola, IA 50125	1860	Dr Robert E McBride	2-B	1,224	70
Sioux Falls Coll, Sioux Falls, SD 57105	1883	Dr Owen P Halleen	2-M	886	60
Skidmore Coll, Saratoga Springs, NY 12866	1922	Dr Joseph C Palamountain Jr	1-B	2,142	228
Slippery Rock U of Pennsylvania, Slippery Rock, PA 16057	1889	Dr Robert Aebersold	5-M	6,479	347
Smith Coll, Northampton, MA 01063 (3)	1871	Mrs Mary Maples Dunn	1-D	2,684	284
Sonoma State U, Rohnert Park, CA 94928	1961	Dr David W Benson	5-M	5,360	373
South Carolina State Coll, Orangeburg, SC 29117	1896	Dr M Maceo Nance Jr	5-M	4,195	228
South Dakota School of Mines and Technology, Rapid City, SD 57701	1885	Dr Richard A Schleusener	5-D	2,583	132
South Dakota State U, Brookings, SD 57007	1881	Dr Robert T Wagner	5-D	6,940	401
Southeastern Coll of the Assemblies of God, Lakeland, FL 33801	1935	Dr James Hennesy	2-B	1,028	50
Southeastern Louisiana U, Hammond, LA 70402	1925	Dr J Larry Crain	5-M	8,992	294
Southeastern Massachusetts U, North Dartmouth, MA 02747	1895	Dr John R Brazil	5-M	5,708	365
Southeastern Oklahoma State U, Durant, OK 74701	1909	Dr Leon Hibbs	5-M	3,925	166
Southeastern U, Washington, DC 20024	1879	Dr W Robert Higgins	1-M	955	150
Southeast Missouri State U, Cape Girardeau, MO 63701	1873	Dr Bill W Stacy	5-M	9,189	475
Southern Arkansas U, Magnolia, AR 71753	1909	Dr Harold T Brinson	5-M	2,136	112
Southern California Coll, Costa Mesa, CA 92626	1920	Mr Wayne E Kraiss	2-M	917	75
Southern Coll of Seventh-Day Adventists, Collegedale, TN 37315	1892	Dr John Wagner	2-B	1,622	144
Southern Connecticut State U, New Haven, CT 06515	1893	Mr Michael J Adanti	5-M	10,329	657
Southern Illinois U at Carbondale, Carbondale, IL 62901	1869	Dr Albert Somit	5-D	22,874	1,478
Southern Illinois U at Edwardsville, Edwardsville, IL 62026	1957	Earl E Lazerson	5-D	10,247	650
Southern Methodist U, Dallas, TX 75275	1911	Dr L Donald Shields	1-D	9,265	637
Southern Oregon State Coll, Ashland, OR 97520	1926	Dr Natale Sicuro	5-M	4,433	240
Southern Tech Inst, Marietta, GA 30060	1948	Dr Stephen R Cheshier	5-B	3,606	175
Southern U and A&M Coll, Baton Rouge, LA 70813	1880	Dr James J Prestage	5-M	13,200	486
Southern U in New Orleans, New Orleans, LA 70126	1959	Dr Emmett W Bashful	5-M	3,200	180
Southern Utah State Coll, Cedar City, UT 84720	1897	Dr Gerald R Sherratt	5-M	2,642	115
Southwest Baptist U, Bolivar, MO 65613	1878	Dr James L Sells	2-B	1,750	99
Southwestern Adventist Coll, Keene, TX 76059	1894	Dr Marvin E Anderson	2-B	683	68
Southwestern Oklahoma State U, Weatherford, OK 73096	1903	Dr Leonard G Campbell	5-M	4,965	218
Southwestern U, Georgetown, TX 78626	1840	Dr Roy B Shilling Jr	2-B	1,001	85
Southwest Missouri State U, Springfield, MO 65804	1905	Dr Marshall Gordon	5-M	15,121	697
Southwest State U, Marshall, MN 56258	1963	Robert L Carothers	5-B	2,234	108
Southwest Texas State U, San Marcos, TX 78666	1899	Mr Robert L Hardesty	5-M	19,202	843
Spalding U, Louisville, KY 40203	1814	Sr Eileen Egan J D Ph D	2-D	1,368	101
Spelman Coll, Atlanta, GA 30314 (3)	1881	Dr Donald M Stewart	1-B	1,642	127
Spring Arbor Coll, Spring Arbor, MI 49283	1873	Dr Kenneth H Coffman	2-B	684	67
Springfield Coll, Springfield, MA 01109	1885	Dr Frank S Falcone	1-D	2,358	175
Spring Garden Coll, Philadelphia, PA 19119	1851	Dr Daniel N DeLucca	1-B	1,450	110
Spring Hill Coll, Mobile, AL 36608	1830	Very Rev Paul S Tipton, SJ	2-M	1,000	86
Stanford U, Stanford, CA 94305	1891	Dr Donald Kennedy	1-D	13,261	1,263
State U of NY A&T Coll at Farmingdale, Farmingdale, NY 11735	1912	Dr Frank A Cipriani	5-B	5,795	404
State U of NY at Albany, Albany, NY 12222	1844	Vincent I O'Leary	5-D	16,000	915
State U of NY at Binghamton, Binghamton, NY 13901	1946	Mr Clifford D Clark	5-D	10,788	686
State U of NY at Buffalo, Amherst, NY 14260	1846	Dr Steven B Sample	5-D	26,160	1,853
State U of NY at Stony Brook, Stony Brook, NY 11794	1957	Dr John H Marburger III	5-D	14,676	1,369
State U of NY Coll at Brockport, Brockport, NY 14420	1867	Dr John Van de Wetering	5-M	5,907	455
State U of NY Coll at Buffalo, Buffalo, NY 14222	1871	Dr D Bruce Johnstone	5-M	11,548	546
State U of NY Coll at Cortland, Cortland, NY 13045	1868	Dr James M Clark	5-M	6,430	347
State U of NY Coll at Fredonia, Fredonia, NY 14063	1867	Dr Robert MacVittie	5-M	4,985	238
State U of NY Coll at Geneseo, Geneseo, NY 14454	1867	Dr Edward B Jakubauskas	5-M	5,282	284
State U of NY Coll at New Paltz, New Paltz, NY 12561	1828	Dr Alice Chandler	5-M	7,344	391
State U of NY Coll at Old Westbury, Old Westbury, NY 11568	1968	Dr Clyde J Wingfield	5-B	3,797	143
State U of NY Coll at Oneonta, Oneonta, NY 13820	1889	Dr Clifford J Craven	5-M	5,884	357
State U of NY Coll at Oswego, Oswego, NY 13126	1861	Dr Virginia L Radley	5-M	7,697	408
State U of NY Coll at Plattsburgh, Plattsburgh, NY 12901	1889	Dr Joseph C Burke	5-M	5,624	370
State U of NY Coll at Potsdam, Potsdam, NY 13676	1816	Dr Humphrey Tonkin	5-M	4,146	255
State U of NY Coll at Purchase, Purchase, NY 10577	1967	Dr Sheldon Grebstein	5-M	2,264	179
State U of NY Coll of Envir Sci & Forestry, Syracuse, NY 13210	1911	Dr Ross S Whaley	5-D	1,037	125
State U of NY Coll of Technology at Utica/Rome, Utica, NY 13502	1973	Dr Peter J Cayan	5-M	2,189	138
State U of NY Downstate Medical Center, Brooklyn, NY 11203	1858	Dr Donald J Scherl	5-D	1,320	43
State U of NY Empire State Coll, Saratoga Springs, NY 12866	1971	NR	5-M	5,377	269

Name, address	Year	Governing official, control, and highest degree offered		Enrollment	Faculty
State U of NY Maritime Coll, Bronx, NY 10465	1874	Rear Adm Sheldon H Kinney	5-M	1,060	70
State U of NY Upstate Medical Center, Syracuse, NY 13210	1950	Dr John Bernard Henry	5-D	865	233
Stephen F Austin State U, Nacogdoches, TX 75962	1923	Dr William R Johnson	5-D	12,600	517
Stephens Coll, Columbia, MO 65215 (3)	1833	Dr Patsy H Sampson	1-B	1,047	110
Stetson U, DeLand, FL 32720	1883	Dr Pope A Duncan	2-M	2,795	138
Stevens Inst of Technology, Hoboken, NJ 07030	1870	Dr Kenneth C Rogers	1-D	3,323	240
Stillman Coll, Tuscaloosa, AL 35403	1876	Dr Cordell Wynn	2-B	808	34
Stockton State Coll, Pomona, NJ 08240	1971	Ms Vera King Farris	5-B	4,776	215
Stonehill Coll, North Easton, MA 02357	1948	Rev Bartley MacPhaidin	2-B	1,709	132
Strayer Coll, Washington, DC 20005	1898	Charles E Palmer Jr	3-B	1,323	75
Suffolk U, Boston, MA 02114	1906	Dr Daniel H Perlman	1-M	6,203	282
Sul Ross State U, Alpine, TX 79832	1917	Dr Jack W Humphries	5-M	2,241	122
Susquehanna U, Selinsgrove, PA 17870	1858	Dr Joel L Cunningham	2-B	1,456	130
Swarthmore Coll, Swarthmore, PA 19081	1864	Dr David W Fraser	1-B	1,327	150
Sweet Briar Coll, Sweet Briar, VA 24595 (3)	1901	Dr Nenah E Fry	1-B	732	87
Syracuse U, Syracuse, NY 13210	1870	Dr Melvin A Eggers	1-D	21,288	1,233
Tampa Coll, Tampa, FL 33614	1890	Mr Donald C Jones	1-M	1,601	65
Tarkio Coll, Tarkio, MO 64491	1883	Dr Roy McIntosh	2-B	605	40
Tarleton State U, Stephenville, TX 76402	1899	Dr Barry B Thompson	5-M	4,800	166
Taylor U, Upland, IN 46989	1846	NR	1-B	1,473	105
Temple U, Philadelphia, PA 19122	1884	Mr Peter J Liacouras	13-D	30,559	2,564
Temple U, Ambler Campus, Ambler, PA 19002	1910	Dr Walter J Gershenfeld	13-D	4,061	347
Tennessee State U, Nashville, TN 37203	1912	Dr Frederick S Humphries	5-D	7,651	479
Tennessee Technological U, Cookeville, TN 38505	1915	Dr Arliss L Roaden	5-D	7,494	400
Tennessee Temple U, Chattanooga, TN 37404	1946	Dr Lee E Roberson	2-D	2,496	143
Texas A&I U, Kingsville, TX 78363	1925	Dr Billy J Franklin	5-D	5,508	226
Texas A&M U, College Station, TX 77843	1876	Dr Frank E Vandiver	5-D	36,827	2,218
Texas Christian U, Fort Worth, TX 76129	1873	Dr William Tucker	2-D	6,747	519
Texas Lutheran Coll, Seguin, TX 78155	1891	Dr Charles H Oestreich	2-B	1,014	78
Texas Southern U, Houston, TX 77004	1947	Dr Leonard H O Spearman	5-D	8,914	600
Texas Tech U, Lubbock, TX 79409	1923	Lauro F Cavazos	5-D	23,433	1,647
Texas Wesleyan Coll, Fort Worth, TX 76105	1891	Dr Jerry G Bawcom	2-M	1,286	113
Texas Woman's U, Denton, TX 76204 (4)	1901	Dr Mary Evelyn Blagg Huey	5-D	8,259	673
Thiel Coll, Greenville, PA 16125	1866	Dr Louis T Almen	2-B	809	83
Thomas A Edison State Coll, Trenton, NJ 08625	1972	George A Pruitt	5-B	4,112	0
Thomas Coll, Waterville, ME 04901	1894	Dr Paul G Jenson	1-M	832	45
Thomas Jefferson U, Philadelphia, PA 19107	1824	Dr Lewis W Bluemle Jr	1-D	1,434	73
Thomas More Coll, Crestview Hills, KY 41017	1921	Dr Thomas A Coffey	2-B	1,319	117
Toccoa Falls Coll, Toccoa Falls, GA 30598	1907	Dr Paul L Alford	2-B	642	49
Tougaloo Coll, Tougaloo, MS 39174	1869	Dr J Herman Blake	2-B	698	86
Touro Coll, New York, NY 10036	1971	Dr Bernard Lander	1-D	3,430	215
Towson State U, Towson, MD 21204	1866	Dr Hoke L Smith	5-M	15,106	866
Transylvania U, Lexington, KY 40508	1780	Dr Charles L Shearer	2-B	782	72
Trenton State Coll, Trenton, NJ 08625	1855	Dr Harold Eickhoff	5-M	8,806	485
Trevecca Nazarene Coll, Nashville, TN 37203	1901	Dr Homer J Adams	2-M	927	104
Trinity Coll, Hartford, CT 06106	1823	James F English Jr	1-M	2,082	158
Trinity Coll, Washington, DC 20017 (3)	1897	Sr Donna M Jurick	2-M	771	82
Trinity Coll, Burlington, VT 05401 (4)	1925	Sr Janice Ryan	2-B	950	70
Trinity U, San Antonio, TX 78284	1869	Dr Ronald K Calgaard	2-M	2,925	283
Tri-State U, Angola, IN 46703	1884	Dr Beaumont Davison	1-B	973	76
Troy State U, Troy, AL 36082	1887	Dr Ralph W Adams	5-M	3,568	175
Troy State U at Dothan/Fort Rucker, Dothan, AL 36303	1962	Mr Robert Paul	5-M	1,498	76
Troy State U in Montgomery, Montgomery, AL 36195	1957	Dr Millard E Elrod	5-M	2,096	142
Tufts U, Medford, MA 02155	1852	Dr Jean Mayer	1-D	7,379	445
Tulane U, New Orleans, LA 70118	1834	Dr Eamon M Kelly	1-D	10,232	1,030
Tulane U, Newcomb Coll, New Orleans, LA 70118 (3)	1886	Dr Eamon M Kelly	1-B	1,737	147
Tuskegee U, Tuskegee, AL 36088	1881	Dr Benjamin F Payton	1-D	3,387	337
Union Coll, Barbourville, KY 40906	1879	Dr Jack C Phillips	2-M	887	71
Union Coll, Lincoln, NE 68506	1891	Benjamin R Wygal	2-B	900	109
Union Coll, Schenectady, NY 12308	1795	Dr John S Morris	1-D	2,575	197
Union for Experimenting Colleges and Universities, Cincinnati, OH 45201	1964	NR	1-D	620	66
Union U, Jackson, TN 38305	1825	Dr Robert E Craig	2-B	1,458	91
United States Air Force Academy, Colorado Springs, CO 80840	1954	LT Gen Winfield W Scott Jr	4-B	4,535	566
United States Coast Guard Academy, New London, CT 06320	1876	Rear Adm E Nelson Jr	4-B	776	114
United States International U, San Diego, CA 92131	1952	Dr William C Rust	1-D	3,605	323
United States Merchant Marine Academy, Kings Point, NY 11024	1943	Rear Adm Thomas A King	4-B	1,001	80
United States Military Academy, West Point, NY 10996	1802	Lt Gen W W Scott Jr	4-B	4,553	538
United States Naval Academy, Annapolis, MD 21402	1845	R Adm Charles R Larson	4-B	4,500	569
Universidad del Turabo, Gurabo, PR 00658	1972	NR	1-M	6,800	190
Universidad Politécnica de Puerto Rico, Hato Rey, PR 00918	1974	Ernesto Vazquez-Torres	1-B	1,218	61
U of Akron, Akron, OH 44325	1870	William V Muse	5-D	26,566	1,488
U of Alabama, University, AL 35486	1831	Dr Joab L Thomas	5-D	15,145	919
U of Alabama at Birmingham, Birmingham, AL 35294	1966	Dr S Richardson Hill	5-D	14,200	1,648
U of Alabama in Huntsville, Huntsville, AL 35899	1950	Dr John C Wright	5-D	5,908	431
U of Alaska, Anchorage, Anchorage, AK 99508	1976	Dr David L Outcalt	5-M	4,208	230
U of Alaska, Fairbanks, Fairbanks, AK 99701	1917	Dr Donald O'Dowd	5-D	4,669	429
U of Alaska–Juneau, Juneau, AK 99801	1972	Dr Michael E Paradise	5-M	2,315	131
U of Albuquerque, Albuquerque, NM 87140	1920	Rev Alfred McBride	2-B	1,200	148
U of Arizona, Tucson, AZ 85721	1885	Dr Henry Koffler	5-D	30,306	1,652
U of Arkansas, Fayetteville, AR 72701	1871	Dr Willard B Gatewood Jr	5-D	13,982	843
U of Arkansas at Little Rock, Little Rock, AR 72204	1927	Dr James H Young	5-M	10,236	643
U of Arkansas at Monticello, Monticello, AR 71655	1909	Dr Fred J Taylor	5-B	1,915	107
U of Arkansas at Pine Bluff, Pine Bluff, AR 71601	1873	Dr Lloyd V Hackley	5-B	2,640	158
U of Arkansas for Medical Sciences, Little Rock, AR 72205	1879	Dr Harry P Ward	5-D	1,365	628
U of Baltimore, Baltimore, MD 21201	1925	Dr H Mebane Turner	5-M	5,177	266
U of Bridgeport, Bridgeport, CT 06601	1927	Dr Leland Miles	1-D	5,954	523
U of California, Berkeley, Berkeley, CA 94720	1868	Mr Ira Michael Heyman	5-D	30,008	3,800
U of California, Davis, Davis, CA 95616	1906	Dr James H Meyer	5-D	19,542	1,474
U of California, Irvine, Irvine, CA 92717	1960	Dr Jack W Peltason	5-D	12,684	805
U of California, Los Angeles, Los Angeles, CA 90024	1919	Charles E Young	5-D	34,503	3,200

Name, address	Year	Governing official, control, and highest degree offered	Enroll-ment	Faculty
U of California, Riverside, Riverside, CA 92521	1954	Dr Theodore L Hullar ... 5-D	4,855	375
U of California, San Diego, La Jolla, CA 92093	1964	Dr William C Atkinson ... 5-D	13,950	947
U of California, San Francisco, San Francisco, CA 94143	1864	Dr Francis A Socy ... 5-D	3,632	2,538
U of California, Santa Barbara, Santa Barbara, CA 93106	1891	Dr Robert A Huttenback ... 5-D	16,936	1,100
U of California, Santa Cruz, Santa Cruz, CA 95064	1965	Dr Robert L Sinsheimer ... 5-D	7,137	640
U of Central Arkansas, Conway, AR 72032	1907	Dr Jefferson D Farris Jr ... 5-M	6,584	290
U of Central Florida, Orlando, FL 32816	1963	Dr Trevor Calbourn ... 5-D	15,846	658
U of Charleston, Charleston, WV 25304	1888	Dr Richard Breslin ... 1-M	1,130	133
U of Chicago, Chicago, IL 60637	1890	Dr Hanna Holborn Gray ... 1-D	8,118	1,121
U of Cincinnati, Cincinnati, OH 45221	1819	Dr Henry Winkler ... 5-D	35,249	2,850
U of Colorado at Boulder, Boulder, CO 80309	1876	Harrison Shull ... 5-D	22,285	1,151
U of Colorado at Colorado Springs, Colorado Springs, CO 80933	1965	Dr Neal F Lane ... 5-M	5,446	935
U of Colorado at Denver, Denver, CO 80202	1912	Mr Dwayne Nuzum ... 5-D	10,790	349
U of Colorado Health Sciences Center, Denver, CO 80262	1883	Dr John Conger ... 5-D	1,338	3,234
U of Connecticut, Storrs, CT 06268	1881	Dr John T Casteen III ... 5-D	17,110	1,244
U of Dallas, Irving, TX 75061	1956	Dr Robert F Sasseen ... 2-D	2,465	166
U of Dayton, Dayton, OH 45469	1850	Br Raymond L Fitz, SM ... 2-D	10,555	678
U of Delaware, Newark, DE 19716	1743	Dr E Arthur Trabant ... 13-D	15,770	920
U of Denver, Denver, CO 80208	1864	Dr Dwight Smith ... 1-D	7,875	486
U of Detroit, Detroit, MI 48221	1877	Rev Robert A Mitchell, SJ ... 2-D	6,125	425
U of Dubuque, Dubuque, IA 52001	1852	Dr Walter F Peterson ... 2-D	1,198	77
U of Evansville, Evansville, IN 47702	1854	Dr Wallace B Graves ... 2-M	4,208	262
U of Florida, Gainesville, FL 32611	1853	Mr Marshall M Criser ... 5-D	35,496	3,405
U of Georgia, Athens, GA 30602	1785	Dr Frederick C Davison ... 5-D	25,230	1,895
U of Guam, Mangilao, GU 96913	1952	Dr Jose Q Cruz ... 8-M	2,568	210
U of Hartford, West Hartford, CT 06117	1877	Mr Stephen J Trachtenberg ... 1-D	7,613	620
U of Hawaii at Hilo, Hilo, HI 96720	1970	Dr Stephen R Mitchell ... 5-B	3,234	251
U of Hawaii at Manoa, Honolulu, HI 96822	1907	Richard S Kosaki ... 5-D	20,023	1,615
U of Health Scis/Chicago Med School, North Chicago, IL 60064	1912	Mr Herman M Finch ... 1-D	825	284
U of Houston–Clear Lake, Houston, TX 77058	1971	Dr Thomas M Stauffer ... 5-M	6,392	226
U of Houston–Downtown, Houston, TX 77002	1974	Dr Alexander F Schilt ... 5-B	7,339	310
U of Houston–U Park, Houston, TX 77004	1927	Dr Richard L Van Horn ... 5-D	31,095	2,710
U of Idaho, Moscow, ID 83843	1889	Dr Richard D Gibb ... 5-D	8,970	589
U of Illinois at Chicago, Chicago, IL 60680	1965	Dr Donald N Langenberg ... 5-D	24,067	1,238
U of Illinois at Urbana-Champaign, Urbana, IL 61801	1867	Dr Thomas E Everhart ... 5-D	34,760	2,561
U of Iowa, Iowa City, IA 52242	1847	James O Freedman ... 5-D	29,712	1,634
U of Kansas, Lawrence, KS 66045	1866	Gene A Budig ... 5-D	24,436	1,143
U of Kansas Coll of Health Sciences & Hospital, Kansas City, KS 66103	1905	D Kay Clawson, MD ... 5-D	2,458	649
U of Kentucky, Lexington, KY 40536	1865	Otis A Singletary ... 5-D	21,300	1,842
U of La Verne, La Verne, CA 91750	1891	Dr Stephen Morgan ... 1-D	2,240	439
U of Louisville, Louisville, KY 40292	1798	Dr Donald C Swain ... 5-D	19,794	1,363
U of Lowell, Lowell, MA 01854	1894	Dr William T Hogan ... 5-D	15,794	782
U of Maine at Augusta, Augusta, ME 04330	1965	Dr Byron Skinner ... 5-B	3,368	238
U of Maine at Farmington, Farmington, ME 04938	1864	Dr Judith A Sturnick ... 5-B	2,140	143
U of Maine at Fort Kent, Fort Kent, ME 04743	1878	Dr Richard J Spath ... 5-B	678	30
U of Maine at Machias, Machias, ME 04654	1909	Mr Frederic A Reynolds ... 5-B	836	42
U of Maine at Orono, Orono, ME 04469	1865	Dr Arthur M Johnson ... 5-D	11,180	510
U of Maine at Presque Isle, Presque Isle, ME 04769	1903	Dr Constance H Carlson ... 5-B	1,210	90
U of Mary Hardin-Baylor, Belton, TX 76513	1845	Dr Bobby E Parker ... 2-M	1,178	74
U of Maryland at Baltimore, Baltimore, MD 21201	1807	Dr Edward N Brandt Jr ... 5-D	4,633	1,223
U of Maryland Baltimore County, Catonsville, MD 21228	1963	Dr John W Dorsey ... 5-D	8,153	503
U of Maryland Coll Park, College Park, MD 20742	1856	Dr John B Slaughter ... 5-D	38,307	2,346
U of Maryland Eastern Shore, Princess Anne, MD 21853	1886	Dr William P Hytche ... 5-D	1,230	94
U of Maryland U Coll, College Park, MD 20742	1947	Dr John B Slaughter ... 5-M	11,640	675
U of Massachusetts at Amherst, Amherst, MA 01003	1863	Joseph Duffey ... 5-D	25,838	1,465
U of Massachusetts at Boston, Boston, MA 02125	1965	Dr Robert A Corrigan ... 5-D	11,725	594
U of Miami, Coral Gables, FL 33124	1925	Dr Edward T Foote II ... 1-D	13,708	1,640
U of Michigan, Ann Arbor, MI 48109	1817	Dr Harold T Shapiro ... 5-D	34,347	2,768
U of Michigan–Dearborn, Dearborn, MI 48128	1959	Dr William A Jenkins ... 5-M	5,525	311
U of Michigan–Flint, Flint, MI 48502	1956	Dr Clinton B Jones ... 5-M	5,596	236
U of Minnesota, Duluth, Duluth, MN 55812	1948	Dr Robert L Heller ... 5-M	7,461	426
U of Minnesota, Morris, Morris, MN 56267	1959	Dr John Q Imholte ... 5-B	1,665	130
U of Minnesota, Twin Cities Campus, Minneapolis, MN 55455	1851	Dr C Peter Magrath ... 5-D	44,659	5,800
U of Mississippi, University, MS 38677	1844	Dr R Gerald Turner ... 5-D	8,715	574
U of Mississippi Medical Center, Jackson, MS 39216	1955	Dr Norman C Nelson ... 5-D	1,737	529
U of Missouri–Columbia, Columbia, MO 65211	1839	Dr Barbara S Uehling ... 5-D	23,410	2,485
U of Missouri–Kansas City, Kansas City, MO 64110	1933	Dr George A Russell ... 5-D	11,464	1,033
U of Missouri–Rolla, Rolla, MO 65401	1870	Dr Joseph M Marchello ... 5-D	6,967	333
U of Missouri–St Louis, St Louis, MO 63121	1963	Dr Arnold B Grobman ... 5-D	11,233	669
U of Montana, Missoula, MT 59812	1893	Dr Neil S Bucklew ... 5-D	9,213	487
U of Montevallo, Montevallo, AL 35115	1896	Dr James F Vickrey Jr ... 5-M	2,782	170
U of Nebraska at Omaha, Omaha, NE 68182	1908	Dr Del D Weber ... 5-M	14,037	502
U of Nebraska–Lincoln, Lincoln, NE 68588	1869	Dr Martin A Massengale ... 5-D	24,228	1,025
U of Nebraska Medical Center, Omaha, NE 68105	1869	Dr Charles E Andrews ... 5-D	2,495	602
U of Nevada, Las Vegas, Las Vegas, NV 89154	1957	Dr Robert Maxson ... 5-D	10,989	451
U of Nevada Reno, Reno, NV 89557	1874	Dr Joseph N Crowley ... 5-D	8,862	430
U of New England, Biddeford, ME 04005	1939	Charles W Ford, PhD ... 1-D	750	49
U of New Hampshire, Durham, NH 03824	1866	Dr Gordon A Haaland ... 5-D	10,500	639
U of New Haven, West Haven, CT 06516	1920	Dr Phillip S Kaplan ... 1-D	7,043	430
U of New Mexico, Albuquerque, NM 87131	1889	Dr Tom J Farer ... 5-D	24,309	1,118
U of New Orleans, New Orleans, LA 70148	1958	Dr Cooper R Mackin ... 5-D	16,660	669
U of North Alabama, Florence, AL 35632	1872	Dr Robert M Guillot ... 5-M	5,197	225
U of North Carolina at Asheville, Asheville, NC 28814	1927	Dr David G Brown ... 5-B	2,651	182
U of North Carolina at Chapel Hill, Chapel Hill, NC 27514	1795	Christopher C Fordham III ... 5-D	21,612	2,301
U of North Carolina at Charlotte, Charlotte, NC 28223	1946	Dr Elbert K Fretwell Jr ... 5-M	10,459	689
U of North Carolina at Greensboro, Greensboro, NC 27412	1891	Dr William E Moran ... 5-D	10,090	627
U of North Carolina at Wilmington, Wilmington, NC 28403	1947	Dr William H Wagoner ... 5-M	5,566	315
U of North Dakota, Grand Forks, ND 58202	1883	Dr Thomas J Clifford ... 5-D	11,060	650
U of Northern Colorado, Greeley, CO 80639	1890	Dr Robert C Dickeson ... 5-D	9,287	550
U of Northern Iowa, Cedar Falls, IA 50614	1876	Dr Constantine W Curris ... 5-D	11,161	720
U of North Florida, Jacksonville, FL 32216	1965	Dr Curtis L McCray ... 5-M	5,651	200
U of Notre Dame, Notre Dame, IN 46556	1842	Rev Theodore M Hesburgh ... 2-D	9,500	820
U of Oklahoma, Norman, OK 73019	1890	Martin C Jischke ... 5-D	19,931	882

Name, address	Year	Governing official, control, and highest degree offered	Enroll- ment	Faculty
U of Oklahoma Health Sciences Center, Oklahoma City, OK 73190	1890	Dr Clayton Rich 5-D	3,308	690
U of Oregon, Eugene, OR 97403	1876	Paul Olum 5-D	15,840	1,287
U of Osteopathic Medicine and Health Sciences, Des Moines, IA 50312	1898	Dr J Leonard Azneer 1-D	945	70
U of Pennsylvania, Philadelphia, PA 19104	1740	Dr F Sheldon Hackney 1-D	22,000	2,500
U of Phoenix, Phoenix, AZ 85004	1976	Harold J O'Donnell 3-M	4,997	537
U of Pittsburgh, Pittsburgh, PA 15260	1787	Dr Wesley W Posvar 13-D	29,197	2,765
U of Pittsburgh at Bradford, Bradford, PA 16701	1963	Dr Richard E McDowell . .13-B	1,100	59
U of Pittsburgh at Greensburg, Greensburg, PA 15601	1963	Dr George F Chambers . . .13-B	1,475	57
U of Pittsburgh at Johnstown, Johnstown, PA 15904	1927	Dr Frank H Blackington III . .13-B	3,223	133
U of Portland, Portland, OR 97203	1901	Rev Thomas C Oddo 2-M	2,861	176
U of Puerto Rico, Arecibo Tech U Coll, Arecibo, PR 00613	1967	Marcos Morell 7-B	3,589	175
U of Puerto Rico, Cayey U Coll, Cayey, PR 00633	1967	Prof Jose L Monserrate-Vila . 7-B	3,420	139
U of Puerto Rico, Humacao U Coll, Humacao, PR 00661	1962	Dr Lillian C Morales 7-B	3,447	238
U of Puerto Rico, Mayagüez, Mayagüez, PR 00708	1911	Prof Salvador E Alemany . . . 7-D	8,808	553
U of Puerto Rico Medical Sciences Campus, San Juan, PR 00936	1950	Dr Norman Maldonado 7-D	3,151	671
U of Puerto Rico, Ponce Tech U Coll, Ponce, PR 00732	1970	Mrs Ruth Fortuno de Calzada . 7-B	1,892	118
U of Puerto Rico, Río Piedras, Río Piedras, PR 00931	1903	Antonio-Miro Montilla 7-D	18,864	1,102
U of Puget Sound, Tacoma, WA 98416	1888	Dr Philip Monford Phibbs . . 2-M	2,951	183
U of Redlands, Redlands, CA 92374	1907	Dr Douglas R Moore 1-M	1,224	184
U of Rhode Island, Kingston, RI 02881	1892	Dr Edward D Eddy 5-D	10,535	738
U of Richmond, Richmond, VA 23173	1830	Dr E Bruce Heilman 2-M	4,300	364
U of Rochester, Rochester, NY 14627	1850	G Dennis O'Brien 1-D	7,649	660
U of St Thomas, Houston, TX 77006	1947	William J Young, CSB 2-D	1,964	197
U of San Diego, San Diego, CA 92110	1949	Dr Author E Hughes 2-D	5,222	326
U of San Francisco, San Francisco, CA 94117	1855	Rev John J Lo Schiavo, SJ . . 2-D	5,554	449
U of Santa Clara, Santa Clara, CA 95053	1851	Rev William J Rewak, SJ . . . 2-D	7,448	457
U of Science and Arts of Oklahoma, Chickasha, OK 73018	1908	Dr Roy Troutt 5-B	1,187	68
U of Scranton, Scranton, PA 18510	1888	Rev J A Panuska, SJ 2-M	4,685	287
U of South Alabama, Mobile, AL 36688	1964	Dr Frederick P Whiddon . . . 5-D	9,342	587
U of South Carolina, Columbia, SC 29208	1801	Dr James B Holderman 5-D	23,301	1,247
U of South Carolina at Aiken, Aiken, SC 29801	1961	Dr Robert E Alexander 5-B	1,936	148
U of South Carolina at Spartanburg, Spartanburg, SC 29303	1967	Dr Olin B Sansbury Jr 5-B	2,610	170
U of South Carolina–Coastal Carolina Coll, Conway, SC 29526	1954	Dr Fred W Hicks 5-B	2,631	174
U of South Dakota, Vermillion, SD 57069	1862	Dr Joseph M McFadden . . . 5-D	5,758	380
U of Southern California, Los Angeles, CA 90089	1880	Dr James H Zumberge 1-D	26,621	2,441
U of Southern Colorado, Pueblo, CO 81001	1933	Dr Robert Shirley 5-M	4,802	264
U of Southern Maine, Portland, ME 04103	1878	Dr Robert L Woodbury 5-M	8,700	607
U of Southern Mississippi, Hattiesburg, MS 39406	1910	Dr Aubrey K Lucus 5-D	11,169	646
U of South Florida, Tampa, FL 33620	1956	Dr John Lott Brown 5-D	27,815	1,089
U of Southwestern Louisiana, Lafayette, LA 70504	1898	Dr Ray P Authement 5-D	16,350	667
U of Steubenville, Steubenville, OH 43952	1946	Rev Michael Scanlan 2-M	946	66
U of Tampa, Tampa, FL 33606	1931	Dr Richard D Cheshire 1-M	2,047	173
U of Tennessee at Chattanooga, Chattanooga, TN 37402	1886	Dr Frederick N Obear 5-M	7,474	415
U of Tennessee at Martin, Martin, TN 38238	1927	Dr Charles E Smith 5-M	5,400	255
U of Tennessee Ctr for the Health Scis, Memphis, TN 38163	1911	James C Hunt 5-D	1,988	686
U of Tennessee, Knoxville, Knoxville, TN 37996	1794	Dr Jack E Reese 5-D	25,392	1,502
U of Texas at Arlington, Arlington, TX 76019	1895	Dr Wendell H Nedderman . . 5-D	23,397	1,269
U of Texas at Austin, Austin, TX 78712	1883	Dr Peter T Flawn 5-D	47,973	2,337
U of Texas at Dallas, Richardson, TX 75083	1969	Dr Robert H Rutford 5-D	7,442	393
U of Texas at El Paso, El Paso, TX 79968	1913	Dr Haskell M Monroe 5-D	15,322	640
U of Texas at San Antonio, San Antonio, TX 78285	1969	Dr James W Wagener 5-M	12,612	579
U of Texas at Tyler, Tyler, TX 75701	1972	Dr George F Hamm 5-M	3,546	212
U of Texas Health Sci Ctr at Dallas, Dallas, TX 75235	1972	Dr Charles C Sprague 5-D	1,398	263
U of Texas Health Sci Ctr at Houston, Houston, TX 77225	1943	Dr Roger J Bulger 5-D	2,792	874
U of Texas Health Sci Ctr at San Antonio, San Antonio, TX 78284	1976	Dr John Howe 5-M	647	64
U of Texas Medical Branch at Galveston, Galveston, TX 77550	1891	Dr William C Levin 5-D	1,728	450
U of Texas of the Permian Basin, Odessa, TX 79762	1973	Dr Duane M Leach 5-M	2,003	102
U of the District of Columbia, Washington, DC 20008	1976	Mr Lisle C Carter Jr 10-M	12,870	905
U of the Pacific, Stockton, CA 95211	1851	Dr Stanley E McCaffrey . . . 1-D	5,863	331
U of the Sacred Heart, Santurce, PR 00914	1939	Dr Pedro Gonzalez Ramos . . 2-B	8,019	351
U of the South, Sewanee, TN 37375	1858	Dr Robert M Ayres Jr 2-D	1,158	116
U of the State of New York, Regents Coll Degrees, Albany, NY 12230	1970	NR 5-B	15,000	NR
U of Toledo, Toledo, OH 43606	1872	Dr James D McComas 5-D	21,039	1,194
U of Tulsa, Tulsa, OK 74104	1894	Dr J Paschal Twyman 2-D	5,452	473
U of Utah, Salt Lake City, UT 84112	1850	Dr Chase N Peterson 5-D	24,600	2,734
U of Vermont, Burlington, VT 05405	1791	Dr Lattie F Coor 5-D	8,860	877
U of Virginia, Charlottesville, VA 22903	1819	Robert M O'Neil 13-D	16,379	1,579
U of Washington, Seattle, WA 98195	1861	William P Gerberding 5-D	26,380	2,600
U of West Florida, Pensacola, FL 32514	1963	Dr James A Robinson 5-M	6,031	342
U of Wisconsin–Eau Claire, Eau Claire, WI 54701	1916	Dr Larry Schnack 5-M	10,757	572
U of Wisconsin–Green Bay, Green Bay, WI 54302	1968	Dr Edward W Weidner 5-M	4,906	247
U of Wisconsin–La Crosse, La Crosse, WI 54601	1909	Dr Noel J Richards 5-M	9,800	380
U of Wisconsin–Madison, Madison, WI 53706	1848	Dr Irving Shain 5-D	44,218	2,269
U of Wisconsin–Milwaukee, Milwaukee, WI 53201	1956	Dr Frank E Horton 5-D	26,464	1,258
U of Wisconsin–Oshkosh, Oshkosh, WI 54901	1871	Dr Edward M Penson 5-M	11,200	600
U of Wisconsin–Parkside, Kenosha, WI 53141	1968	Dr Mary Elizabeth Shutler . . 5-M	5,600	280
U of Wisconsin–Platteville, Platteville, WI 53818	1866	Dr William W Chmurny . . . 5-M	5,305	244
U of Wisconsin–River Falls, River Falls, WI 54022	1874	NR 5-M	5,287	279
U of Wisconsin–Stevens Point, Stevens Point, WI 54481	1894	Dr Philip R Marshall 5-M	9,050	544
U of Wisconsin–Stout, Menomonie, WI 54751	1893	Dr Robert S Swanson 5-M	7,385	383
U of Wisconsin–Superior, Superior, WI 54880	1893	Dr Karl W Meyer 5-M	2,096	144
U of Wisconsin–Whitewater, Whitewater, WI 53190	1868	Dr James R Connor 5-M	10,737	636
U of Wyoming, Laramie, WY 82071	1886	Dr Donald L Veal 5-D	10,075	868
Upper Iowa U, Fayette, IA 52142	1857	Dr James R Rocheleau 1-B	714	47
Upsala Coll, East Orange, NJ 07019	1893	Dr Rodney Felder 2-M	1,418	140
Ursinus Coll, Collegeville, PA 19426	1869	Dr Richard P Richter 2-B	1,149	103
Ursuline Coll, Pepper Pike, OH 44124 (4)	1871	Sr Mary Kenan Dulzer 2-M	1,563	113
Utah State U, Logan, UT 84322	1888	Dr Stanford Cazier 5-D	11,544	504
Utica Coll of Syracuse U, Utica, NY 13502	1946	Dr Lansing G Baker 1-B	1,372	175

Name, address	Year	Governing official, control, and highest degree offered	Enrollment	Faculty
Valdosta State Coll, Valdosta, GA 31698	1906	Dr Hugh C Bailey ... 5-M	6,095	245
Valley City State Coll, Valley City, ND 58072	1890	Dr Charles B House Jr ... 5-B	1,046	66
Valley Forge Christian Coll, Phoenixville, PA 19460	1938	Wesley W Smith ... 2-B	601	25
Valparaiso U, Valparaiso, IN 46383	1859	Dr Robert V Schnabel ... 2-D	3,616	366
Vanderbilt U, Nashville, TN 37240	1873	Mr Joe B Wyatt ... 1-D	8,983	1,995
Vassar Coll, Poughkeepsie, NY 12601	1861	Virginia B Smith ... 1-M	2,198	245
Villa Julie Coll, Stevenson, MD 21153	1952	Ms Carolyn Manuszak ... 1-B	1,039	128
Villa Maria Coll, Erie, PA 16505 (4)	1925	Sr M Lawreace Antoun ... 2-B	688	72
Villanova U, Villanova, PA 19085	1842	Rev John M Driscoll, OSA ... 2-D	11,190	572
Virginia Commonwealth U, Richmond, VA 23284	1838	Dr Edmund F Ackell ... 5-D	19,984	1,876
Virginia Military Inst, Lexington, VA 24450 (1)	1839	Gen Sam S Walker ... 5-B	1,338	98
Virginia Polytechnic Inst and State U, Blacksburg, VA 24061	1872	Dr William E Lavery ... 13-D	21,455	1,943
Virginia State U, Petersburg, VA 23803	1882	Dr Wilbert Greenfield ... 5-M	3,474	263
Virginia Union U, Richmond, VA 23220	1865	Mrs Carolyn W Daughtry ... 2-M	1,333	102
Virginia Wesleyan Coll, Norfolk, VA 23502	1960	Dr Lambuth M Clarke ... 2-B	974	85
Viterbo Coll, La Crosse, WI 54601	1890	Dr Robert E Gibbons ... 2-B	1,092	106
Wabash Coll, Crawfordsville, IN 47933 (1)	1832	Dr Lewis S Salter ... 1-B	814	75
Wagner Coll, Staten Island, NY 10301	1883	Dr Sam Frank ... 1-M	2,030	216
Wake Forest U, Winston-Salem, NC 27109	1834	Dr Thomas K Hearn Jr ... 2-D	4,961	1,160
Walla Walla Coll, College Place, WA 99324	1892	Dr Jack Bergman ... 2-M	1,661	140
Walsh Coll, Canton, OH 44720	1958	Br Francis Blouin ... 2-B	1,225	102
Walsh Coll of Accountancy & Business Admin, Troy, MI 48007	1922	Dr Jeffery W Barry ... 1-M	2,052	90
Wartburg Coll, Waverly, IA 50677	1852	Dr Robert Vogel ... 2-B	1,200	86
Washburn U of Topeka, Topeka, KS 66621	1865	Dr John L Green Jr ... 11-D	7,088	258
Washington and Jefferson Coll, Washington, PA 15301	1781	Dr Howard J Burnett ... 1-B	1,030	97
Washington and Lee U, Lexington, VA 24450 (1)	1749	Dr John D Wilson ... 1-D	1,694	142
Washington Coll, Chestertown, MD 21620	1782	Mr Douglass Cater ... 1-M	820	73
Washington State U, Pullman, WA 99164	1892	Dr Samuel Smith ... 5-D	16,459	1,017
Washington U, St Louis, MO 63130	1853	Dr William H Danforth ... 1-D	10,709	2,590
Wayland Baptist U, Plainview, TX 79072	1908	Dr David L Jester ... 2-M	1,809	148
Waynesburg Coll, Waynesburg, PA 15370	1849	Dr J Thomas Mills Jr ... 2-M	824	64
Wayne State Coll, Wayne, NE 68787	1910	Dr Ed Elliott ... 5-M	2,836	126
Wayne State U, Detroit, MI 48202	1868	Dr David Adamany ... 5-D	29,070	2,148
Weber State Coll, Ogden, UT 84408	1889	Dr Rodney H Brady ... 5-M	10,198	560
Webster U, St Louis, MO 63119	1915	Dr Leigh Gerdine ... 1-M	5,715	231
Wellesley Coll, Wellesley, MA 02181 (3)	1875	Dr Nannerl Keohane ... 1-B	2,296	308
Wentworth Inst of Technology, Boston, MA 02115	1904	Dr Edward T Kirkpatrick ... 1-B	3,400	173
Wesleyan U, Middletown, CT 06457	1831	Dr Colin Campbell ... 1-D	3,075	314
Wesley Coll, Dover, DE 19901	1873	Dr Reed M Stewart ... 2-B	1,541	77
West Chester U of Pennsylvania, West Chester, PA 19383	1871	Dr Kenneth L Perrin ... 5-M	9,528	534
West Coast U, Los Angeles, CA 90020	1909	Dr Robert M L Baker Jr ... 1-M	1,400	250
Western Carolina U, Cullowhee, NC 28723	1889	Dr Myron L Coulter ... 5-M	6,131	364
Western Connecticut State U, Danbury, CT 06810	1903	Dr Stephen Feldman ... 5-M	5,908	220
Western Illinois U, Macomb, IL 61455	1899	Dr Leslie F Malpass ... 5-M	11,751	693
Western International U, Phoenix, AZ 85021	1978	Ronald C. Bauer ... 1-M	721	50
Western Kentucky U, Bowling Green, KY 42101	1906	Dr Donald W Zacharias ... 5-M	11,771	631
Western Maryland Coll, Westminster, MD 21157	1867	Dr Robert H Chambers ... 1-M	1,765	139
Western Michigan U, Kalamazoo, MI 49008	1903	Dr John T Bernhard ... 5-D	20,383	1,160
Western Montana Coll, Dillon, MT 59725	1893	Dr Douglas Treadway ... 5-M	980	52
Western New England Coll, Springfield, MA 01119	1919	Dr Beverly W Miller ... 1-D	4,620	200
Western New Mexico U, Silver City, NM 88061	1893	Dr Mervyn L Cadwallader ... 5-M	1,843	75
Western Oregon State Coll, Monmouth, OR 97361	1856	Richard S Meyers ... 5-M	2,488	185
Western State Coll of Colorado, Gunnison, CO 81230	1911	Dr Richard Laughlin ... 5-M	2,646	134
Western State U Coll of Law of Orange County, Fullerton, CA 92631	1966	NR ... 3-D	1,561	54
Western State U Coll of Law of San Diego, San Diego, CA 92110	1969	Mr William B Lawless ... 3-D	624	32
Western Washington U, Bellingham, WA 98225	1893	Dr G Robert Ross ... 5-M	9,144	527
Westfield State Coll, Westfield, MA 01086	1838	Dr Francis J Pilecki ... 5-M	3,355	201
West Georgia Coll, Carrollton, GA 30118	1933	Dr Maurice K Townsend ... 5-M	6,250	278
West Liberty State Coll, West Liberty, WV 26074	1837	Dr Clyde Campbell ... 5-B	2,524	173
Westminster Coll, Fulton, MO 65251	1851	Dr J Harvey Saunders ... 2-B	600	60
Westminster Coll, New Wilmington, PA 16172	1852	Dr Phillip A Lewis ... 2-M	1,344	118
Westminster Coll of Salt Lake City, Salt Lake City, UT 84105	1875	Charles H Dick ... 1-M	1,234	79
Westmont Coll, Santa Barbara, CA 93108	1940	Dr David K Winter ... 2-B	1,208	95
West Texas State U, Canyon, TX 79016	1909	Dr Ed Roach ... 5-M	6,474	365
West Virginia Inst of Technology, Montgomery, WV 25136	1895	Dr Leonard C Nelson ... 5-M	3,222	199
West Virginia State Coll, Institute, WV 25112	1891	Dr Thomas W Cole Jr ... 5-B	4,315	179
West Virginia U, Morgantown, WV 26506	1867	Dr Diane L Reinhard ... 5-D	19,071	2,346
West Virginia Wesleyan Coll, Buckhannon, WV 26201	1890	Dr Hugh A Latimer ... 2-M	1,392	111
Wheaton Coll, Wheaton, IL 60187	1860	Dr J Richard Chase ... 2-M	2,571	239
Wheaton Coll, Norton, MA 02766 (3)	1834	Alice F Emerson ... 1-B	1,100	126
Wheeling Coll, Wheeling, WV 26003	1954	Fr Thomas S Acker, SJ ... 2-M	1,088	87
Wheelock Coll, Boston, MA 02215 (4)	1888	Dr Daniel S Cheever Jr ... 1-M	668	88
Whitman Coll, Walla Walla, WA 99362	1859	Mr Robert A Skotheim ... 1-B	1,218	113
Whittier Coll, Whittier, CA 90608	1887	Dr Eugene S Mills ... 2-M	1,762	106
Whitworth Coll, Spokane, WA 99251	1890	Dr Robert H Mounce ... 2-M	1,764	90
Wichita State U, Wichita, KS 67208	1895	Dr Warren B Armstrong ... 5-D	17,021	703
Widener U, Delaware Campus, Wilmington, DE 19803	1965	Robert J Bruce ... 1-D	2,803	139
Widener U, Pennsylvania Campus, Chester, PA 19013	1821	Mr Robert J Bruce ... 1-D	5,750	202
Wilberforce U, Wilberforce, OH 45384	1856	Dr Yvonne Walker-Taylor ... 2-B	810	71
Wilkes Coll, Wilkes-Barre, PA 18766	1933	Dr Christopher N Breiseth ... 1-M	2,808	198
Willamette U, Salem, OR 97301	1842	Dr Jerry E Hudson ... 2-D	1,855	191
William Carey Coll, Hattiesburg, MS 39401	1906	Dr James R Noonkester ... 2-M	1,746	110
William Jewell Coll, Liberty, MO 64068	1849	Dr J Gordon Kingsley ... 2-B	1,421	173
William Paterson Coll of New Jersey, Wayne, NJ 07470	1855	Dr Arnold Speertan ... 5-M	10,023	577
Williams Coll, Williamstown, MA 01267	1793	Dr Francis C Oakley ... 1-M	2,075	232
William Smith Coll, Geneva, NY 14456 (3)	1908	NR ... 1-B	750	143
William Woods Coll, Fulton, MO 65251 (3)	1870	Dr John M Bartholomy ... 2-B	729	68
Wilmington Coll, New Castle, DE 19720	1967	Dr Audrey K Doberstein ... 1-M	1,060	79
Wilmington Coll of Ohio, Wilmington, OH 45177	1870	Neil Thorburn ... 2-B	832	59
Wingate Coll, Wingate, NC 28174	1895	Dr Paul R Corts ... 2-B	1,500	78
Winona State U, Winona, MN 55987	1858	Dr Thomae Stark ... 5-M	5,300	270
Winston-Salem State U, Winston-Salem, NC 27110	1892	Dr Cleon F Thompson Jr ... 5-B	2,370	145
Winthrop Coll, Rock Hill, SC 29733	1886	Mr Philip Lader ... 5-M	5,055	321

Name, address	Year	Governing official, control, and highest degree offered	Enroll-ment	Faculty
Wittenberg U, Springfield, OH 45501	1845	Dr William A Kinnison ... 2-B	2,140	174
Wofford Coll, Spartanburg, SC 29301	1854	Dr Joab M Lesesne ... 2-B	1,052	73
Woodbury U, Los Angeles, CA 90017	1884	Dr Wayne Miller ... 1-M	951	79
Worcester Polytechnic Inst, Worcester, MA 01609	1865	Dr Edmund T Cranch ... 1-D	3,592	323
Worcester State Coll, Worcester, MA 01602	1874	Dr Philip D Vairo ... 5-M	4,700	171
Wright State U, Dayton, OH 45435	1964	Dr Robert J Kegerreis ... 5-D	15,517	875
Xavier U, Cincinnati, OH 45207	1831	Rev Charles L Currie, SJ ... 2-M	6,850	343
Xavier U of Louisiana, New Orleans, LA 70125	1925	Dr Norman C Francis ... 2-M	2,090	159
Yale U, New Haven, CT 06520	1701	A Bartlett Giamatti ... 1-D	10,920	1,766
Yeshiva U, New York, NY 10033	1886	Dr Norman Lamm ... 1-D	4,146	2,769
York Coll of Pennsylvania, York, PA 17405	1787	Dr Robert V Iosue ... 1-M	4,570	230
Youngstown State U, Youngstown, OH 44555	1908	Dr Neil D Humphrey ... 5-M	15,254	798

Two-Year Colleges

The highest undergraduate degree offered for all two-year colleges is the associate degree.

Name, address	Year	Governing official, control	Enroll-ment	Faculty
Abraham Baldwin Agricultural Coll, Tifton, GA 31793	1933	Dr Stanley R Anderson ... 5	2,000	140
Adirondack Comm Coll, Glens Falls, NY 12801	1960	Dr Gordon C Blank ... 12	2,878	147
Aiken Tech Coll, Aiken, SC 29802	1972	Dr Paul L Blowers ... 12	1,066	111
Aims Comm Coll, Greeley, CO 80632	1967	Dr George R Conger ... 10	6,656	649
Alabama Tech Coll, East Gadsden, AL 35999	1925	Mr Robert W Howard ... 5	739	52
Alexander City State Jr Coll, Alexander City, AL 35010	1965	Dr W Byron Causey ... 5	1,098	88
Alexandria Area Vocational Tech Inst, Alexandria, MN 56308	1961	Frank Starke ... 5	1,560	114
Allan Hancock Coll, Santa Maria, CA 93454	1920	Dr Gary R Edelbrock ... 12	6,672	290
Allegany Comm Coll, Cumberland, MD 21502	1961	Dr Donald L Alexander ... 12	2,134	137
Allen County Comm Coll, Iola, KS 66749	1923	Dr Paul Hines ... 9	1,941	92
Allentown Business School, Allentown, PA 18101	1869	Mrs Patricia O Richards ... 3	900	18
Alpena Comm Coll, Alpena, MI 49707	1952	Dr Charles R Donnelly ... 12	1,918	122
Amarillo Coll, Amarillo, TX 79178	1929	Dr H D Yarbrough ... 12	6,394	321
American Academy of Art, Chicago, IL 60604	1923	Mr Clinton E Frank ... 3	853	26
American Inst of Business, Des Moines, IA 50321	1921	Keith Fenton ... 1	1,062	51
American River Coll, Sacramento, CA 95841	1955	Queen Randall ... 10	20,502	523
American Samoa Comm Coll, Pago Pago, AS 96799	1969	Dr Eneliko Sofai ... 8	845	65
Anchorage Comm Coll, Anchorage, AK 99508	1954	NR ... 9	9,656	605
Anderson Coll, Anderson, SC 29621	1911	Dr Mark L Hopkins ... 2	994	57
Angelina Coll, Lufkin, TX 75902	1968	Dr Jack W Huggins ... 12	2,440	141
Anne Arundel Comm Coll, Arnold, MD 21012	1961	Dr Thomas E Florestano ... 12	8,894	532
Anoka-Ramsey Comm Coll, Coon Rapids, MN 55433	1965	Dr Neil Christenson ... 5	3,708	137
Antelope Valley Coll, Lancaster, CA 93534	1929	Dr C W Stine ... 5	6,888	250
Arapahoe Comm Coll, Littleton, CO 80120	1965	Dr James F Weber ... 5	6,200	354
Arizona Western Coll, Yuma, AZ 85364	1962	Dr James R Carruthers ... 5	3,929	260
Arkansas State U–Beebe Branch, Beebe, AR 72012	1927	Mr William H Owen Jr ... 5	753	60
Art Inst of Atlanta, Atlanta, GA 30326	1949	Gerald A Murphy ... 3	746	50
Art Inst of Fort Lauderdale, Fort Lauderdale, FL 33316	1968	Mr Mark K Wheeler ... 3	1,167	66
Art Inst of Philadelphia, Philadelphia, PA 19103	1966	Edward R D'Allessio ... 3	1,300	66
Art Inst of Pittsburgh, Pittsburgh, PA 15222	1921	John R Knepper ... 3	1,961	74
Asheville-Buncombe Tech Coll, Asheville, NC 28801	1959	Mr Harvey L Haynes ... 5	2,619	260
Asnuntuck Comm Coll, Enfield, CT 06082	1972	Dr Daniel R McLaughlin ... 5	1,710	37
Atlanta Jr Coll, Atlanta, GA 30310	1974	Dr Edwin A Thompson ... 5	1,460	91
Atlantic Comm Coll, Mays Landing, NJ 08330	1966	Mr Ronald W Bush ... 9	4,200	190
Austin Comm Coll, Austin, MN 55912	1940	Mr James Flannery ... 5	987	69
Austin Comm Coll, Austin, TX 78768	1972	NR ... 10	16,674	802
Bailey Tech School, St Louis, MO 63108 (2)	1936	NR ... 3	792	26
Baker Coll of Business, Flint, MI 48507	1911	Mr Edward J Kurtz ... 1	2,424	76
Bakersfield Coll, Bakersfield, CA 93305	1913	Dr Richard Wright ... 12	10,242	437
Barstow Coll, Barstow, CA 92311	1962	Dr Edwin Spear ... 12	1,485	75
Barton County Comm Coll, Great Bend, KS 67530	1969	Dr Jimmie L Downing ... 12	2,640	121
Bay de Noc Comm Coll, Escanaba, MI 49829	1963	Mr Dwight E Link ... 9	1,806	94
Bay Path Jr Coll, Longmeadow, MA 01106 (3)	1897	Dr Jeanette T Wright ... 1	660	35
Beaufort County Comm Coll, Washington, NC 27889	1968	Mr James P Blanton ... 5	1,086	72
Beaufort Tech Coll, Beaufort, SC 29902	1972	Mr George W Goldsmith Jr ... 5	1,029	150
Becker Jr Coll–Worcester Campus, Worcester, MA 01609	1887	Mr Lloyd H Van Buskirk ... 1	734	45
Beckley Coll, Beckley, WV 25802	1933	Dr John W Saunders ... 1	1,663	66
Bee County Coll, Beeville, TX 78102	1965	Dr Norman Wallace ... 9	2,240	121
Belleville Area Coll, Belleville, IL 62221	1946	Dr Bruce R Wisore ... 10	12,480	597
Bellevue Comm Coll, Bellevue, WA 98007	1966	Dr Paul N Thompson ... 5	6,556	386
Belmont Tech Coll, St Clairsville, OH 43950	1971	Dr Paul R Ohm ... 5	1,300	75
Bergen Comm Coll, Paramus, NJ 07652	1965	Dr Jose Lopez-Isa ... 9	11,000	562
Berkeley School, Little Falls, NJ 07424 (4)	1931	Jack R Jones ... 3	715	32
Berkeley School, New York, NY 10017 (4)	1945	Dr John E Clow ... 3	703	33
Berkshire Comm Coll, Pittsfield, MA 01201	1960	Dr Jonathan M Daube ... 5	2,089	125
Bessemer State Tech Coll, Bessemer, AL 35021	1966	Dr W. Michael Bailey ... 5	2,000	198
Big Bend Comm Coll, Moses Lake, WA 98837	1962	Dr Peter D DeVries ... 5	1,943	159
Bismarck Jr Coll, Bismarck, ND 58501	1939	Dr Kermit Lidstrom ... 5	2,406	109
Black Hawk Coll–East Campus, Kewanee, IL 61443	1967	Dr Ronald F Williams ... 12	1,250	66
Black Hawk Coll–Quad-Cities Campus, Moline, IL 61265	1946	Dr Richard J Puffer ... 12	5,272	215
Blackhawk Tech Inst, Janesville, WI 53547	1968	Mr O L Johnson ... 10	2,299	174
Blair Jr Coll, Colorado Springs, CO 80915	1897	NR ... 1	717	43
Blinn Coll, Brenham, TX 77833	1883	Dr James H Atkinson ... 12	3,499	123
Blue Mountain Comm Coll, Pendleton, OR 97801	1962	Mr Ronald L Daniels ... 9	2,061	152
Blue Ridge Comm Coll, Weyers Cave, VA 24486	1965	Dr James A Armstrong ... 5	2,064	102
Blue Ridge Tech Coll, Flat Rock, NC 28731	1969	Dr William D Killian ... 12	1,041	76
Bossier Parish Comm Coll, Bossier City, LA 71111	1967	NR ... 12	1,706	65
Bowling Green Jr Coll of Business, Bowling Green, KY 42101	1966	Timothy E Johnson ... 3	601	24
Bowling Green State U–Firelands Coll, Huron, OH 44839	1968	Dr William R McGraw ... 5	1,136	62
Brainerd Comm Coll, Brainerd, MN 56401	1938	Sally Jane Ihne ... 5	653	44
Brazosport Coll, Lake Jackson, TX 77566	1948	Dr Wilbur A Bass ... 12	3,609	200
Brevard Coll, Brevard, NC 28712	1853	Dr Jacob C Martinson Jr ... 2	685	68
Brevard Comm Coll, Cocoa, FL 32922	1960	Dr Maxwell C King ... 5	11,109	818
Brewer State Jr Coll, Fayette, AL 35555	1969	Dr Tommy M Boothe ... 5	676	29
Bristol Comm Coll, Fall River, MA 02720	1965	Ms Eileen Farley ... 5	2,636	159

Name, address	Year	Governing official, control	Enrollment	Faculty
Brookdale Comm Coll, Lincroft, NJ 07738	1967	Dr B A Barringer	9	11,048	438
Brookhaven Coll, Farmers Branch, TX 75234	1978	Dr Patsy J Fulton	9	6,954	344
Brooks Coll, Long Beach, CA 90804	1971	Mr Steve Sotraidis	3	840	60
Broome Comm Coll, Binghamton, NY 13902	1946	Dr Donald W Beattie	2	6,406	563
Broward Comm Coll, Fort Lauderdale, FL 33301	1960	Dr A Hugh Adams	5	27,363	842
Brunswick Jr Coll, Brunswick, GA 31520	1961	Dr John W Teel	5	1,243	64
Bryant and Stratton Business Inst, Buffalo, NY 14202	1854	Mr Francis J Gustina Jr	3	2,033	182
Bryant and Stratton Business Inst, Rochester, NY 14604 (4)	1973	Paul Hossenlopp	3	850	31
Bryant and Stratton Powelson Business Inst, Syracuse, NY 13202	1926	Barbara Balto	3	1,046	31
Bucks County Comm Coll, Newtown, PA 18940	1964	Dr Charles E Rollins	9	9,681	389
Bunker Hill Comm Coll, Boston, MA 02129	1973	Harold E Shively	5	3,829	160
Burlington County Coll, Pemberton, NJ 08068	1966	Dr Harmon B Pierce	9	5,835	245
Butler County Comm Coll, El Dorado, KS 67042	1927	Dr Carl L Heinrich	12	3,279	200
Butler County Comm Coll, Butler, PA 16001	1965	Dr Thomas Ten Hoeve Jr	9	1,250	85
Butte Coll, Oroville, CA 95965	1966	Dr Wendell L Reeder	5	6,200	330
Caldwell Comm Coll and Tech Inst, Hudson, NC 28638	1964	Dr Eric B McKeithan	5	2,160	129
Camden County Coll, Blackwood, NJ 08012	1967	Dr Otto R Mauke	12	8,148	327
Cañada Coll, Redwood City, CA 94061	1968	D Robert Stiff	10	7,195	270
Cape Cod Comm Coll, West Barnstable, MA 02668	1961	Dr James F Hall	5	1,876	135
Cape Fear Tech Inst, Wilmington, NC 28401	1959	Mr Malcolm J McLeod	5	1,900	67
Carl Sandburg Coll, Galesburg, IL 61401	1967	Dr Jack W Fuller	12	1,120	117
Carteret Tech Coll, Morehead City, NC 28557	1963	Dr Donald W Bryant	5	1,057	58
Casper Coll, Casper, WY 82601	1945	Dr Lloyd H Loftin	10	1,832	190
Catawba Valley Tech Coll, Hickory, NC 28601	1960	Mr Robert E Paap	12	2,339	144
Catonsville Comm Coll, Catonsville, MD 21228	1957	Dr John M Kingsmore	9	9,793	506
Cayuga County Comm Coll, Auburn, NY 13021	1953	Dr Helena Howe	12	3,270	144
Cazenovia Coll, Cazenovia, NY 13035	1824	Dr Stephen M Schneeweiss	1	801	80
Cecil Comm Coll, North East, MD 21901	1968	Dr Robert L Gell	9	1,494	97
Cedar Valley Coll, Lancaster, TX 75134	1977	Dr Floyd S Elkins	9	2,237	105
Central Arizona Coll, Coolidge, AZ 85228	1961	Dr James M Kraby	5	3,477	211
Central Carolina Tech Coll, Sanford, NC 27330	1962	Dr Marvin R Joyner	12	1,936	207
Central City Business Inst, Syracuse, NY 13203	1904	Mr Donald J Nelli	3	737	57
Central Comm Coll–Grand Island Campus, Grand Island, NE 68802	1976	Larry L Keller	12	1,181	45
Central Comm Coll–Hastings Campus, Hastings, NE 68901	1966	Dr Carl Rolf	12	1,306	158
Central Comm Coll–Platte Campus, Columbus, NE 68601	1968	Dr Jerry A Lee	12	1,314	54
Central Florida Comm Coll, Ocala, FL 32670	1957	Dr Henry E Goodlett	12	2,852	110
Centralia Coll, Centralia, WA 98531	1925	Dr Jerry Young	5	3,248	270
Central Ohio Tech Coll, Newark, OH 43055	1971	Dr Julius S Greenstein	5	1,306	84
Central Oregon Comm Coll, Bend, OR 97701	1949	Dr Frederick H Boyle	10	2,003	142
Central Pennsylvania Business School, Summerdale, PA 17093	1922	Bart A Milano	3	722	43
Central Piedmont Comm Coll, Charlotte, NC 28235	1963	Dr Richard H Hagemeyer	12	15,761	1,111
Central Texas Coll, Killeen, TX 76541	1967	Dr Luis M Morton	12	5,777	212
Central Virginia Comm Coll, Lynchburg, VA 24502	1966	Dr J E Merritt	5	3,839	142
Central Wyoming Coll, Riverton, WY 82501	1966	Dr Edward L Donovan	12	1,192	68
Cerritos Coll, Norwalk, CA 90650	1956	Dr Wilford Michael	12	18,498	600
Cerro Coso Comm Coll, Ridgecrest, CA 93555	1973	Dr Raymond McCue	5	3,299	125
Chabot Coll, Hayward, CA 94545	1961	Dr William J Moore	5	18,986	1,000
Chamberlayne Jr Coll, Boston, MA 02116	1892	Mr Matthew J Malloy	1	850	55
Champlain Coll, Burlington, VT 05402	1878	Dr Robert A Skiff	1	1,277	74
Charles County Comm Coll, La Plata, MD 20646	1958	Dr John Sine	12	4,462	247
Charles Stewart Mott Comm Coll, Flint, MI 48503	1923	Mr David G Moore	9	11,158	404
Chattahoochee Valley State Comm Coll, Phenix City, AL 36867	1974	Dr James E Owen	5	1,395	73
Chattanooga State Tech Comm Coll, Chattanooga, TN 37406	1965	Dr Charles W Branch	5	5,247	158
Chemeketa Comm Coll, Salem, OR 97309	1955	William Segura	12	10,945	670
Chesapeake Coll, Wye Mills, MD 21679	1967	Dr Robert C Schleiger	12	2,005	126
Chesterfield-Marlboro Tech Coll, Cheraw, SC 29520	1967	Dr Ronald W Hampton	12	608	47
Chipola Jr Coll, Marianna, FL 32446	1947	Dr James R Richburg	5	1,425	71
Chowan Coll, Murfreesboro, NC 27855	1848	Dr Bruce E Whitaker	2	911	71
Cincinnati Tech Coll, Cincinnati, OH 45223	1966	Mr Frederick B Schlimm	5	3,920	205
Cisco Jr Coll, Cisco, TX 76437	1940	Dr Henry E McCullough	12	1,774	113
Citrus Coll, Azusa, CA 91702	1915	Dr Louis Zellers	9	8,936	523
City Coll of San Francisco, San Francisco, CA 94112	1935	Mr Harry W Frustuck	12	23,283	1,072
City Colls of Chicago, Chicago City-Wide Coll, Chicago, IL 60601	1975	Mark Warden	12	7,841	418
City Colls of Chicago, Harry S Truman Coll, Chicago, IL 60640	1956	Dr Wallace B Appelson	12	11,151	436
City Colls of Chicago, Kennedy-King Coll, Chicago, IL 60621	1935	Dr Ewen M Akin	12	8,081	375
City Colls of Chicago, Loop Coll, Chicago, IL 60601	1962	Dr Bernice Miller	12	8,798	292
City Colls of Chicago, Malcolm X Coll, Chicago, IL 60612	1911	Mr James C Griggs	12	6,437	369
City Colls of Chicago, Olive-Harvey Coll, Chicago, IL 60628	1970	Mr Homer D Franklin	12	7,893	292
City Colls of Chicago, Richard J Daley Coll, Chicago, IL 60652	1960	Dr William P Conway	12	10,502	346
City Colls of Chicago, Wilbur Wright Coll, Chicago, IL 60634	1934	Mr Ernest V Clements	12	9,032	335
City U of NY, Borough of Manhattan Comm Coll, New York, NY 10007	1963	Dr Joshua L Smith	12	12,215	933
City U of NY, Bronx Comm Coll, Bronx, NY 10453	1959	Dr Roscoe C Brown	12	7,095	426
City U of NY, Fiorello H LaGuardia Comm Coll, Long Island City, NY 11101	1971	Dr Joseph Shenker	12	7,000	368
City U of NY, Hostos Comm Coll, Bronx, NY 10451	1968	Dr Flora M Edwards	12	4,200	192
City U of NY, Kingsborough Comm Coll, Brooklyn, NY 11235	1963	Dr Leon M Goldstein	12	8,102	775
City U of NY, Queensborough Comm Coll, Bayside, NY 11364	1958	Dr Kurt R Schmeller	12	13,176	719
Clackamas Comm Coll, Oregon City, OR 97045	1966	Dr John S Keyser	9	4,332	353
Clarendon Coll, Clarendon, TX 79226	1898	Mr Kenneth D Vaughan	5	759	32
Clark Coll, Vancouver, WA 98663	1933	Dr Earl P Johnson	5	7,500	300
Clark County Comm Coll, North Las Vegas, NV 89030	1971	Dr Paul Meacham	5	9,935	465
Clark Tech Coll, Springfield, OH 45501	1962	George H Robertson	5	2,399	166
Clatsop Comm Coll, Astoria, OR 97103	1958	Mr Philip L Bainer	5	2,465	164
Clayton Jr Coll, Morrow, GA 30260	1969	Dr Harry S Downs	5	3,060	140
Cleveland Inst of Electronics, Cleveland, OH 44114 (2)	1934	NR	3	1,650	63

Name, address	Year	Governing official, control	Enroll-ment	Faculty
Cleveland State Comm Coll, Cleveland, TN 37320	1967	Dr L Quentin Lane 5	3,124	141
Cleveland Tech Coll, Shelby, NC 28150	1965	Dr James B Petty 5	1,257	83
Clinton Comm Coll, Clinton, IA 52732	1946	Dr Charles Spence 5	1,015	58
Clinton Comm Coll, Plattsburgh, NY 12901	1969	Dr Alfred Light 12	1,586	103
Cloud County Comm Coll, Concordia, KS 66901	1965	Dr James P Ihrig 12	2,082	208
Coastal Carolina Comm Coll, Jacksonville, NC 28540	1964	Dr James L Henderson Jr 12	3,073	122
Coastline Comm Coll, Fountain Valley, CA 92708	1976	Dr William M Vega 12	15,013	634
Cochise Coll, Douglas, AZ 85607	1962	Mr Dan W Rehurek 12	4,194	299
Coffeyville Comm Coll, Coffeyville, KS 67337	1923	Gilmer K Nellis 12	1,650	50
Coll of Alameda, Alameda, CA 94501	1970	Donald R Hongisto 12	4,900	122
Coll of DuPage, Glen Ellyn, IL 60137	1966	Dr Harold D McAninch 12	22,524	1,167
Coll of Eastern Utah, Price, UT 84501	1937	Dr James R Randolph 5	1,134	65
Coll of Lake County, Grayslake, IL 60030	1967	Dr John O Hunter 12	12,284	552
Coll of Southern Idaho, Twin Falls, ID 83301	1964	Mr Gerald R Meyerhoeffer . . . 12	2,658	124
Coll of the Albemarle, Elizabeth City, NC 27909	1960	Dr Parker Chesson Jr 5	1,487	98
Coll of the Canyons, Valencia, CA 91355	1969	Ramon F La Grandeur 12	3,535	85
Coll of the Desert, Palm Desert, CA 92260	1959	Dr F D Stout 12	9,940	373
Coll of the Mainland, Texas City, TX 77591	1967	Mr Larry L Stanley 12	2,901	182
Coll of the Sequoias, Visalia, CA 93277	1925	Dr Ivan C Crookshanks 12	7,239	160
Coll of the Siskiyous, Weed, CA 96094	1957	Dr Eugene Schumacher 12	3,400	141
Colorado Inst of Art, Denver, CO 80203	1952	NR 3	1,150	48
Colorado Mountain Coll, Spring Valley Campus, Glenwood Springs, CO 81601	1965	Dr Gordon L Snowbarger 10	690	57
Columbia Basin Coll, Pasco, WA 99301	1955	Dr Fred L Esvelt 5	5,000	310
Columbia Coll, Columbia, CA 95310	1968	Dr Dean Cunningham 12	2,736	92
Columbia-Greene Comm Coll, Hudson, NY 12534	1969	Dr Robert K Luther 12	770	59
Columbia Jr Coll of Business, Columbia, SC 29203	1935	Mr Michael Gorman 3	604	32
Columbia State Comm Coll, Columbia, TN 38401	1966	Dr Paul Sands 5	2,557	105
Columbus Tech Inst, Columbus, OH 43216	1963	Dr Harold M Nestor 5	8,559	557
Comm Coll of Allegheny County Allegheny Cmps, Pittsburgh, PA 15212	1966	Dr Julius R Brown 9	7,750	455
Comm Coll of Allegheny County Boyce Cmps, Monroeville, PA 15146	1966	Dr Carl A Di Sibio 12	4,810	110
Comm Coll of Allegheny County Coll Center–North, Pittsburgh, PA 15237	1972	Dr Fred F Bartok 12	3,469	196
Comm Coll of Baltimore, Baltimore, MD 21215	1947	Mr Charles G Tildon Jr 12	7,516	446
Comm Coll of Beaver County, Monaca, PA 15061	1966	Dr Terry L Dicianna 5	2,200	87
Comm Coll of Philadelphia, Philadelphia, PA 19130	1964	Dr Judith S Eaton 12	11,115	659
Comm Coll of Rhode Island, Flanagan Cmps, Lincoln, RI 02865	1964	Edward J Liston 5	2,978	179
Comm Coll of Rhode Island, Knight Cmps, Warwick, RI 02886	1964	Mr Edward Liston 5	4,183	519
Comm Coll of the Air Force, Maxwell Air Force Base, AL 36112	1972	Col Rodney V Cox Jr 4	215,782	9,345
Comm Coll of the Finger Lakes, Canandaigua, NY 14424	1965	Dr Charles J Meder 12	1,500	193
Comm Coll of Vermont, Waterbury, VT 05676	1970	Mr Ken Kalb 5	866	326
Compton Comm Coll, Compton, CA 90221	1927	Mrs Jean Larson 12	3,979	338
Condie Jr Coll of Business and Technology, Campbell, CA 95008	1968	Mr Wayne P Wilson 3	600	30
Connors State Coll, Warner, OK 74469	1908	Dr Carl O Westbrook 5	1,352	62
Contra Costa Coll, San Pablo, CA 94806	1948	Dr H Rex Craig 12	7,059	281
Control Data Inst, Anaheim, CA 92801	1965	D E Scherer 3	675	18
Cooke County Coll, Gainesville, TX 76240	1924	Dr Alton Laird 9	1,687	93
Copiah-Lincoln Jr Coll, Wesson, MS 39191	1928	Dr Billy B Thames 10	1,278	94
Corning Comm Coll, Corning, NY 14830	1956	Dr Donald H Hangen 12	2,773	142
Cosumnes River Coll, Sacramento, CA 95823	1970	Dr Marc E Hall 10	5,303	194
County Coll of Morris, Randolph, NJ 07869	1968	Dr Sherman H Masten 9	11,000	494
Cowley County Comm Coll, Arkansas City, KS 67005	1922	Dr Gwendel Nelson 9	1,679	82
Crafton Hills Coll, Yucaipa, CA 92399	1972	Dr Donald L Singer 12	3,267	139
Craven Comm Coll, New Bern, NC 28560	1965	Dr Thurman E Brock 5	1,816	137
Crowder Coll, Neosho, MO 64850	1963	Dr Dell Reed 12	1,214	70
Cuesta Coll, San Luis Obispo, CA 93403	1964	Dr Frank R Martinez 10	5,875	248
Culinary Inst of America, Hyde Park, NY 12538	1946	Mr Ferdinand E Metz 1	1,800	94
Cumberland County Coll, Vineland, NJ 08360	1963	Dr Philip S Phelon 12	2,336	94
Cuyahoga Comm Coll, Eastern Campus, Warrensville Township, OH 44122	1971	Dr David C Mitchell 9	5,474	215
Cuyahoga Comm Coll, Metropolitan Campus, Cleveland, OH 44115	1969	Dr Curtis F Jefferson 12	7,570	391
Cuyahoga Comm Coll, Western Campus, Parma, OH 44130	1966	Mr Ronald M Sobel 12	12,058	418
Cuyamaca Coll, El Cajon, CA 92020	1978	Dr Samuel M Ciccati 5	2,332	109
Cypress Coll, Cypress, CA 90630	1966	Dr Jack Scott 12	12,868	375
Dabney S Lancaster Comm Coll, Clifton Forge, VA 24422	1964	Dr John F Backels 5	1,224	79
Dalton Jr Coll, Dalton, GA 30720	1963	Dr Derrell C Roberts 5	1,616	70
Danville Area Comm Coll, Danville, IL 61832	1946	Dr Ronald K Lingle 5	2,803	139
Danville Comm Coll, Danville, VA 24541	1967	Dr Walter S Delany 5	2,023	112
Davidson County Comm Coll, Lexington, NC 27293	1958	Dr J Bryan Brooks 5	2,166	111
Dawson Comm Coll, Glendive, MT 59330	1940	Mr Donald H Kettner 12	761	32
Daytona Beach Comm Coll, Daytona Beach, FL 32015	1958	Dr Charles H Polk 5	7,271	696
Dean Jr Coll, Franklin, MA 02038	1865	Mr Richard E Crockford 1	1,084	82
De Anza Coll, Cupertino, CA 95014	1967	Dr A Robert Dehart 12	26,262	855
DeKalb Comm Coll, Clarkston, GA 30021	1964	Dr Marvin M Cole 9	18,537	819
Delaware County Comm Coll, Media, PA 19063	1967	Dr Richard D De Cosmo 10	7,254	498
Delaware Tech & Comm Coll, Southern Cmps, Georgetown, DE 19947	1967	Mr Jack Owens 5	1,548	128
Delaware Tech & Comm Coll, Stanton/Wilmington Cmps, Newark, DE 19702	1968	Mr John H Jones 5	3,825	248
Delaware Tech & Comm Coll, Terry Cmps, Dover, DE 19901	1972	Dr William C Pfeifer 5	1,296	52
Delgado Comm Coll, New Orleans, LA 70119	1921	Dr Harry J Boyer 5	8,081	493
Del Mar Coll, Corpus Christi, TX 78404	1935	Dr Edwin Biggerstaff 12	8,400	407
Delta Coll, University Center, MI 48710	1961	Mr Donald J Carlyon 9	9,790	603
Denmark Tech Coll, Denmark, SC 29042	1948	Dr John W Henry Jr 5	684	44
Denver Auraria Comm Coll, Denver, CO 80204	1970	Dr Myer L Titus 5	2,180	293
Denver Inst of Technology, Denver, CO 80221 (2)	1953	R Wade Murphree 3	875	43
Des Moines Area Comm Coll, Ankeny, IA 50021	1966	Dr Joseph Borgen 12	8,056	362
District One Tech Inst, Eau Claire, WI 54701	1912	Mr Norbert K Wurtzel 10	3,037	175
Dixie Coll, St George, UT 84770	1912	Dr Alton L Wade 5	1,904	73

Name, address	Year	Governing official, control	Enroll-ment	Faculty
Dodge City Comm Coll, Dodge City, KS 67801	1935	Mr Gay Dahn ... 9	1,363	100
Donnelly Coll, Kansas City, KS 66102	1949	Rev Raymond J Davern ... 2	779	48
Draughon's Jr Coll, Savannah, GA 31406	1899	Mr John T South III ... 3	709	48
Draughons Jr Coll, Knoxville, TN 37919	1903	NR ... 3	1,031	39
Dundalk Comm Coll, Baltimore, MD 21222	1970	Dr Philip R Day Jr ... 9	3,203	184
Durham Tech Inst, Durham, NC 27703	1963	Dr Phail Wynn Jr ... 5	3,811	120
Dutchess Comm Coll, Poughkeepsie, NY 12601	1957	Dr Jerry Lee ... 12	5,863	458
Dyersburg State Comm Coll, Dyersburg, TN 38024	1969	Dr Karen A Bowyer ... 5	1,618	94
East Arkansas Comm Coll, Forrest City, AR 72335	1974	Dr Bob C Burns ... 5	1,202	69
East Central Coll, Union, MO 63084	1968	Dr Donald D Shook ... 10	2,300	120
East Central Jr Coll, Decatur, MS 39327	1928	Mr Charles V Wright ... 12	842	58
Eastern Arizona Coll, Thatcher, AZ 85552	1888	Mr Gherald L Hoopes Jr ... 12	1,521	246
Eastern New Mexico U–Roswell, Roswell, NM 88201	1958	Dr Loyd R Hughes ... 5	1,285	70
Eastern Oklahoma State Coll, Wilburton, OK 74578	1907	Dr James M Miller ... 5	1,907	60
Eastern Wyoming Coll, Torrington, WY 82240	1948	Mr Guido Smith ... 12	1,267	53
Eastfield Coll, Mesquite, TX 75150	1970	Mrs Eleanor Ott ... 12	8,866	316
Edgecombe Tech Coll, Tarboro, NC 27886	1968	Mr Charles B McIntyre ... 12	1,250	68
Edison Comm Coll, Fort Myers, FL 33907	1962	Dr David G Robinson ... 12	5,455	218
Edison State Comm Coll, Piqua, OH 45356	1973	Dr Conrad W Burchill ... 5	2,374	136
Edmonds Comm Coll, Lynnwood, WA 98036	1967	Mr Thomas C Nielsen ... 12	6,944	262
El Centro Coll, Dallas, TX 75202	1966	Dr Ruth G Shaw ... 9	5,543	308
Elgin Comm Coll, Elgin, IL 60120	1949	Dr Searle Charles ... 12	6,033	364
Elizabeth Seton Coll, Yonkers, NY 10701	1960	Sr Mary Ellen Brosnan ... 1	1,354	101
Ellsworth Comm Coll, Iowa Falls, IA 50126	1890	Duane R Lloyd ... 12	925	53
El Paso Comm Coll, El Paso, TX 79998	1969	Dr Robert E Shepack ... 9	14,000	695
El Reno Jr Coll, El Reno, OK 73036	1938	Dr Bill S Cole ... 12	1,659	84
Endicott Coll, Beverly, MA 01915 (3)	1939	Dr Carol A Hawkes ... 1	750	75
Enterprise State Jr Coll, Enterprise, AL 36331	1965	Dr J D Talmadge ... 5	2,076	96
Erie Comm Coll, City Campus, Buffalo, NY 14203	1971	Dr John R Birkholz ... 12	2,596	103
Erie Comm Coll, North Campus, Buffalo, NY 14221	1946	Dr John R Birkholz ... 12	5,572	378
Erie Comm Coll, South Campus, Orchard Park, NY 14127	1974	Mr Vincent Rolletta ... 12	3,144	103
Essex Agricultural and Tech Inst, Hathorne, MA 01937	1912	Mr Raymond F Potter ... 9	700	29
Essex Comm Coll, Baltimore, MD 21237	1957	Dr John E Ravekes ... 12	9,861	484
Essex County Coll, Newark, NJ 07102	1966	Dr Zachary Yamba ... 9	5,816	329
Everett Comm Coll, Everett, WA 98201	1941	Mr Robert Drewel ... 5	6,371	310
Evergreen Valley Coll, San Jose, CA 95135	1975	Dr Gerald H Strelitz ... 12	6,607	212
Fairleigh Dickinson U, Edward Williams Coll, Hackensack, NJ 07601	1964	Kenneth T Vehrkens ... 1	1,062	54
Fashion Inst–Design/Merchandising, LA Campus, Los Angeles, CA 90017	1969	Ms Tonian Hohberg ... 3	2,309	144
Fayetteville Tech Inst, Fayetteville, NC 28303	1961	Dr Craig Allen ... 5	5,538	285
Feather River Coll, Quincy, CA 95971	1968	Dr Joseph Brennan ... 10	841	59
Fergus Falls Comm Coll, Fergus Falls, MN 56537	1960	Mr Dan F True ... 5	680	44
Fisher Jr Coll, Boston, MA 02116 (3)	1903	Dr Scott A' Fisher ... 1	650	45
Flathead Valley Comm Coll, Kalispell, MT 59901	1967	Dr Howard L Fryett PhD ... 12	1,956	127
Florence-Darlington Tech Coll, Florence, SC 29501	1963	Mr Fred C Fore ... 5	1,986	178
Florida Keys Comm Coll, Key West, FL 33040	1965	Dr William A Seeker ... 5	752	76
Foothill Coll, Los Altos Hills, CA 94022	1958	Dr Robert M Gavin Jr ... 12	14,026	376
Forsyth Tech Inst, Winston-Salem, NC 27103	1964	Dr Bob H Greene ... 5	3,085	193
Fort Scott Comm Coll, Fort Scott, KS 66701	1919	Mr Richard D Hedges ... 5	1,295	72
Fox Valley Tech Inst, Appleton, WI 54913	1967	Dr Stanley J Spanbauer ... 12	4,760	700
Frank Phillips Coll, Borger, TX 79007	1948	Dr Andy Hicks ... 12	1,010	86
Frederick Comm Coll, Frederick, MD 21701	1957	Dr Jack Kussmaul ... 12	3,150	225
Fresno City Coll, Fresno, CA 93741	1910	Dr Clyde C McCully ... 10	13,188	378
Front Range Comm Coll, Westminster, CO 80030	1968	Dr Donald R Mankenberg ... 5	5,449	337
Fullerton Coll, Fullerton, CA 92634	1913	Dr Philip W Borst ... 12	16,652	602
Fulton-Montgomery Comm Coll, Johnstown, NY 12095	1964	Mr John G Boshart ... 12	1,827	100
Gadsden State Jr Coll, Gadsden, AL 35999	1965	Dr James D McEwen ... 5	2,990	147
Gainesville Jr Coll, Gainesville, GA 30503	1964	Dr J Foster Watkins ... 5	1,744	75
Galveston Coll, Galveston, TX 77550	1967	John E Pickelman ... 12	1,976	124
Garden City Comm Coll, Garden City, KS 67846	1919	Dr Thomas F Saffell ... 10	1,260	93
Garland County Comm Coll, Hot Springs, AR 71913	1973	Dr Gerald R Fisher ... 12	1,536	97
Gateway Tech Inst, Kenosha, WI 53141	1912	Dr Keith W Stoehr ... 12	9,000	293
Gavilan Coll, Gilroy, CA 95020	1919	Dr Rudolph Melone ... 12	2,822	164
Genesee Comm Coll, Batavia, NY 14020	1966	Dr Stuart Steiner ... 12	2,637	155
George Corley Wallace State Comm Coll, Selma, AL 36701	1966	Dr Charles L Byrd ... 5	1,368	50
George C Wallace State Comm Coll, Dothan, AL 36303	1949	Dr Nathan L Hodges ... 5	2,885	128
Germanna Comm Coll, Locust Grove, VA 22508	1970	Dr Marshall W Smith ... 5	1,784	94
Glendale Comm Coll, Glendale, AZ 85302	1965	Dr John R Waltrip ... 12	13,013	475
Glendale Comm Coll, Glendale, CA 91208	1927	Dr H Rex Craig ... 12	11,294	397
Glen Oaks Comm Coll, Centreville, MI 49032	1965	Dr Philip G Ward ... 12	1,213	129
Gloucester County Coll, Sewell, NJ 08080	1967	Dr Gary L Reddig ... 5	3,565	143
Gogebic Comm Coll, Ironwood, MI 49938	1932	Dr C Robert Bennett ... 12	1,517	59
Golden West Coll, Huntington Beach, CA 92647	1966	Dr Lee A Stevens ... 5	16,000	648
Gordon Jr Coll, Barnesville, GA 30204	1852	Dr Jerry M Williamson ... 5	1,510	81
Grand Rapids Jr Coll, Grand Rapids, MI 49503	1914	Mr Richard Calkins ... 11	8,900	440
Grays Harbor Coll, Aberdeen, WA 98520	1930	Dr Joseph A Malik ... 5	1,099	135
Grayson County Coll, Denison, TX 75020	1964	Dr Jim M Williams ... 12	4,637	201
Greater Hartford Comm Coll, Hartford, CT 06105	1967	Dr Arthur C Banks Jr ... 5	3,655	72
Greater New Haven State Tech Coll, North Haven, CT 06473	1977	Edmund L Sobolewski ... 5	1,300	78
Greenfield Comm Coll, Greenfield, MA 01301	1962	Dr Theodore L Provo ... 5	1,501	92
Greenville Tech Coll, Greenville, SC 29606	1962	Dr Thomas E Barton Jr ... 5	6,614	377
Grossmont Coll, El Cajon, CA 92020	1961	Dr Ivan L Jones ... 12	13,524	474
Guam Comm Coll, Guam Main Facility, GU 96921	1977	Peter R Nelson ... 8	617	207
Guilford Tech Comm Coll, Jamestown, NC 27282	1958	Dr Ray Needham ... 5	4,745	244
Gulf Coast Comm Coll, Panama City, FL 32401	1957	Dr Lawrence W Tyree ... 5	4,000	184
Hagerstown Jr Coll, Hagerstown, MD 21740	1946	Dr Atlee C Kepler ... 9	2,497	153
Halifax Comm Coll, Weldon, NC 27890	1967	Dr Phillip W Taylor ... 12	1,008	68
Harcum Jr Coll, Bryn Mawr, PA 19010 (4)	1915	Dr Norma F Furst ... 1	860	71
Hardbarger Jr Coll of Business, Raleigh, NC 27602	1924	NR ... 3	733	32
Harford Comm Coll, Bel Air, MD 21014	1957	Dr Alfred C O'Connell ... 12	4,285	231
Harrisburg Area Comm Coll, Harrisburg, PA 17110	1964	Dr Kenneth B Woodbury Jr ... 12	6,866	283
Harry M Ayers State Tech Coll, Anniston, AL 36202	1966	Mr Pierce C Cain ... 5	624	38

Name, address	Year	Governing official, control	Enrollment	Faculty
Hartford State Tech Coll, Hartford, CT 06106	1946	Mr Kenneth E DeRego 5	1,802	51
Hartnell Coll, Salinas, CA 93901	1920	Dr James R Hardt 10	8,270	239
Haskell Indian Jr Coll, Lawrence, KS 66044	1884	Dr Gerald E Gipp 4	925	65
Hawkeye Inst of Technology, Waterloo, IA 50704	1967	Dr John E Hawse 12	1,948	144
Haywood Tech Coll, Clyde, NC 28721	1964	Mr Joseph H Nanney 12	957	68
Heald Coll, Business Division, San Francisco, CA 94103	1863	NR 1	750	20
Henderson County Jr Coll, Athens, TX 75751	1946	Dr William C Campion 12	3,690	154
Henry Ford Comm Coll, Dearborn, MI 48128	1938	Dr Stuart M Bundy 10	16,117	744
Herkimer County Comm Coll, Herkimer, NY 13350	1966	Mr Robert McLaughlin 12	2,011	88
Hesser Coll, Manchester, NH 03101	1900	Kenneth W Galeucia 3	1,983	143
Highland Comm Coll, Freeport, IL 61032	1962	Dr Joseph C Piland 10	2,945	103
Highland Comm Coll, Highland, KS 66035	1858	Dr Bill R Spencer 5	1,266	59
Highland Park Comm Coll, Highland Park, MI 48203	1918	Dr Chrystine R Shack 12	2,416	112
Highline Comm Coll, Midway, WA 98032	1961	Dr Shirley B Gordon 5	8,500	426
Hilbert Coll, Hamburg, NY 14075	1957	Sr Edmunette Paczesny 1	705	66
Hill Jr Coll, Hillsboro, TX 76645	1923	Dr W R Auvenshine 10	1,501	55
Hillsborough Comm Coll, Tampa, FL 33622	1968	Dr Barbara D Holmes 5	12,644	678
Hiwassee Coll, Madisonville, TN 37354	1849	Dr Curtis Schofield 2	655	32
Hocking Tech Coll, Nelsonville, OH 45764	1968	Dr John J Light 5	4,100	210
Holyoke Comm Coll, Holyoke, MA 01040	1946	Mr David M Bartley 5	3,021	203
Housatonic Comm Coll, Bridgeport, CT 06608	1966	Dr Vincent S Darnowski 5	2,386	94
Houston Comm Coll System, Houston, TX 77007	1971	Dr J B Whiteley 12	25,118	1,186
Howard Coll at Big Spring, Big Spring, TX 79720	1945	Dr Bob E Riley 12	1,167	99
Howard Comm Coll, Columbia, MD 21044	1966	Dr Dwight A Burrill 12	3,534	208
Hudson County Comm Coll, Jersey City, NJ 07306	1974	Mr Walter N Sheil 12	3,544	187
Hudson Valley Comm Coll, Troy, NY 12180	1953	Dr Joseph J Bulmer 12	8,174	366
Huertas Business Coll, Caguas, PR 00625	1945	Ruben Lopez 3	684	28
Hutchinson Comm Coll, Hutchinson, KS 67501	1928	Dr James H Stringer 12	3,567	239
ICM School of Business, Pittsburgh, PA 15222	1963	Wayne R Zanardelli 3	1,000	44
ICS Center for Degree Studies, Scranton, PA 18515	1975	Mr David Crowther 3	6,000	40
Illinois Central Coll, East Peoria, IL 61635	1967	Dr Leon H Perley 12	12,908	596
Illinois East Comm Colls, Frontier Comm Coll, Fairfield, IL 62837	1976	Richard Mason 12	3,853	436
Illinois East Comm Colls, Lincoln Trail Coll, Robinson, IL 62454	1969	Dr Richard L Behrendt 12	1,514	234
Illinois East Comm Colls, Olney Central Coll, Olney, IL 62450	1960	Dr Stephen J. Kridelbaugh . . . 12	2,449	368
Illinois East Comm Colls, Wabash Valley Coll, Mount Carmel, IL 62863	1960	Dr Curtis Murton 12	2,354	240
Illinois Valley Comm Coll, Oglesby, IL 61348	1924	Dr Alfred E Wisgoski 10	4,150	184
Imperial Valley Coll, Imperial, CA 92251	1922	Dr John A DePaoli 12	4,456	210
Independence Comm Coll, Independence, KS 67301	1925	Mr M Leon Foster 10	930	59
Indiana Vocational Tech Coll–Central Indiana, Indianapolis, IN 46202	1963	Dr Meredith L Carter 5	2,684	236
Indiana Vocational Tech Coll–Columbus, Columbus, IN 47203	1963	Mr Harvey Poling 5	1,891	108
Indiana Vocational Tech Coll–Eastcentral, Muncie, IN 47302	1968	Mr Richard L Davidson 5	1,918	116
Indiana Vocational Tech Coll–Kokomo, Kokomo, IN 46901	1968	Mr James B Lansinger 5	1,415	111
Indiana Vocational Tech Coll–Lafayette, Lafayette, IN 47903	1968	Dr Thomas E Reckard 5	1,343	83
Indiana Vocational Tech Coll–Northcentral, South Bend, IN 46619	1968	Dr Carl F Lutz 5	2,407	118
Indiana Vocational Tech Coll–Northeast, Fort Wayne, IN 46805	1969	Mr Jon L Rupright 5	3,402	141
Indiana Vocational Tech Coll–Northwest, Gary, IN 46409	1963	Mr Mearle R Donica 5	3,637	125
Indiana Vocational Tech Coll–Southcentral, Sellersburg, IN 47172	1968	Mr Carl F Scott 5	1,388	83
Indiana Vocational Tech Coll–Southeast, Madison, IN 47250	1963	NR 5	729	74
Indiana Vocational Tech Coll–Southwest, Evansville, IN 47710	1963	Dr H Victor Baldi 5	2,103	98
Indiana Vocational Tech Coll–Wabash Valley, Terre Haute, IN 47802	1966	Mr Sam Borden 5	1,784	80
Indiana Vocational Tech Coll–Whitewater, Richmond, IN 47374	1963	Dr Judith A Redwine 5	1,085	89
Indian Hills Comm Coll, Ottumwa, IA 52501	1966	Dr Lyle A Hellyer 12	2,212	68
Indian River Comm Coll, Fort Pierce, FL 33450	1960	Dr Herman A Heise 5	6,750	200
Instituto Comercial de Puerto Rico Jr Coll, Hato Rey, PR 00919	1946	Atty Enrique Pineiro 3	1,653	85
Inter American U of PR, Guayama Regional Coll, Guayama, PR 00654	1958	Mr Pablo I Rivera Diaz 1	1,374	100
Interboro Inst, New York, NY 10019	1888	Mr Mischa Lazoff 3	900	40
International Academy of Merchandising and Design, Chicago, IL 60654	1977	Clem Stein Jr 3	608	81
Inver Hills Comm Coll, Inver Grove Heights, MN 55075	1969	Dr Patrick A Roche 5	3,694	236
Iowa Central Comm Coll, Fort Dodge, IA 50501	1966	Dr Harvey D Martin 12	2,889	103
Iowa Lakes Comm Coll, North Attendance Ctr, Estherville, IA 51334	1967	Mr Richard H Blacker 12	722	30
Iowa Lakes Comm Coll, South Attendance Ctr, Emmetsburg, IA 50536	1967	Mr Richard H Blacker 12	978	42
Iowa Western Comm Coll, Council Bluffs, IA 51502	1966	Dr Robert D Looft 10	2,864	172
Isothermal Comm Coll, Spindale, NC 28160	1965	Dr Ben E Fountain Jr 5	2,435	164
Itasca Comm Coll, Grand Rapids, MN 55744	1922	Dr Lawrence N Dukes 5	1,100	110
Itawamba Jr Coll, Fulton, MS 38843	1947	Dr W O Benjamin 12	2,385	178
ITS Career Inst, Miami, FL 33137	1976	NR 3	685	27
ITT Business Inst, Indianapolis, IN 46268	1970	NR 3	1,300	13
Jackson Comm Coll, Jackson, MI 49201	1928	Dr Clyde LeTarte 9	7,000	358
Jackson State Comm Coll, Jackson, TN 38301	1967	Dr James A Hefner 5	2,738	122
James H Faulkner State Jr Coll, Bay Minette, AL 36507	1965	Dr Gary L Branch 5	1,710	85
James Sprunt Tech Coll, Kenansville, NC 28349	1964	Dr Carl D Price 5	743	58
Jamestown Comm Coll, Jamestown, NY 14701	1950	Mr Paul A Benke 12	3,947	229
Jefferson Coll, Hillsboro, MO 63050	1963	Dr B Ray Henry 12	3,023	123
Jefferson Comm Coll, Watertown, NY 13601	1961	Mr John T Henderson 12	1,750	108
Jefferson Davis State Jr Coll, Brewton, AL 36427	1965	Mr George R McCormick 5	819	47
Jefferson State Jr Coll, Birmingham, AL 35215	1965	Dr Judy M Merritt 5	6,030	279
Jefferson Tech Coll, Steubenville, OH 43952	1965	Dr Edward L Florak 12	1,449	92
John A Logan Coll, Carterville, IL 62918	1967	Harold R O'Neil 12	2,415	67
John C Calhoun State Comm Coll, Decatur, AL 35602	1965	Dr James R Chasteen 5	5,482	266

Name, address	Year	Governing official, control	Enrollment	Faculty
John M Patterson State Tech Coll, Montgomery, AL 36116	1962	Mr J L Taunton ... 5	900	51
Johnson County Comm Coll, Overland Park, KS 66210	1967	Dr Charles J Carlsen ... 12	8,080	343
Johnston Tech Coll, Smithfield, NC 27577	1969	Dr John L Tart ... 5	1,663	125
John Tyler Comm Coll, Chester, VA 23831	1967	Dr Freddie W Nicholas ... 12	3,914	184
John Wood Comm Coll, Quincy, IL 62301	1974	Dr Paul R Heath ... 10	3,884	102
Joliet Jr Coll, Joliet, IL 60436	1901	NR ... 12	9,845	600
Jones County Jr Coll, Ellisville, MS 39437	1928	Dr T Terrell Tisdale ... 12	2,443	125
J Sargeant Reynolds Comm Coll, Richmond, VA 23241	1972	Dr S A Burnette ... 5	9,500	612
Jr Coll of Albany, Albany, NY 12208	1957	Dr William F Kahl ... 1	1,113	96
Kalamazoo Valley Comm Coll, Kalamazoo, MI 49009	1966	Dr Marilyn J Schlack ... 12	8,773	246
Kankakee Comm Coll, Kankakee, IL 60901	1966	Dr Lilburn H Horton Jr ... 12	3,300	109
Kansas City Kansas Comm Coll, Kansas City, KS 66112	1923	Dr Alton L Davies ... 9	3,772	236
Kansas Tech Inst, Salina, KS 67401	1965	Mr Thomas F Creech ... 5	629	45
Kaskaskia Coll, Centralia, IL 62801	1966	Dr Bruce G Stahl ... 12	3,185	95
Kellogg Comm Coll, Battle Creek, MI 49016	1956	Dr Richard F Whitmore ... 12	6,055	200
Kent State U, Ashtabula Campus, Ashtabula, OH 44004	1958	Mr Paul A Reichert ... 5	873	65
Kent State U, East Liverpool Campus, East Liverpool, OH 43920	1967	Mr Richard Q King ... 5	645	50
Kent State U, Stark Campus, Canton, OH 44720	1967	Dr William G Bittle ... 5	1,723	98
Kent State U, Trumbull Campus, Warren, OH 44483	1910	Dr Dennis L Smith ... 5	1,605	87
Kent State U, Tuscarawas Campus, New Philadelphia, OH 44663	1962	Harold D Shade ... 5	956	51
Keystone Jr Coll, La Plume, PA 18440	1868	Dr Louis V Wilcox Jr ... 1	743	103
Kilgore Coll, Kilgore, TX 75662	1935	Dr Stewart H McLaurin ... 12	4,469	160
King's River Comm Coll, Reedley, CA 93654	1926	Dr Abel Sykes Jr ... 12	3,123	174
Kirkwood Comm Coll, Cedar Rapids, IA 52406	1966	Dr Bill F Stewart ... 12	6,340	401
Kirtland Comm Coll, Roscommon, MI 48653	1966	Mr Raymond D Homer ... 12	1,333	99
Kishwaukee Coll, Malta, IL 60150	1967	Dr Norman L Jenkins ... 12	3,444	175
Labouré Coll, Boston, MA 02124	1971	Sr Maureen St Charles ... 2	714	57
Lackawanna Jr Coll, Scranton, PA 18505	1894	Dr John X McConkey ... 1	1,061	66
Lake City Comm Coll, Lake City, FL 32055	1962	Dr Charles M Greene ... 5	1,946	170
Lake Land Coll, Mattoon, IL 61938	1966	Dr David V Schultz ... 12	3,389	285
Lakeland Comm Coll, Mentor, OH 44060	1967	Dr James Catanzaro ... 12	9,209	435
Lake Michigan Coll, Benton Harbor, MI 49022	1946	Dr Anne E Mulder ... 10	3,200	304
Lake Region Comm Coll, Devils Lake, ND 58301	1941	Dr William L Taylor ... 12	810	53
Lakeshore Tech Inst, Cleveland, WI 53015	1967	Mr Frederick J Nierode ... 12	3,500	121
Lake-Sumter Comm Coll, Leesburg, FL 32788	1961	Dr Robert S Palinchak ... 12	1,745	114
Lake Tahoe Comm Coll, South Lake Tahoe, CA 95702	1975	Dr James W Duke ... 12	1,494	82
Lane Comm Coll, Eugene, OR 97405	1964	Dr Eldon G Schafer ... 12	6,944	343
Laney Coll, Oakland, CA 94607	1953	Dr Lawrence A Davis ... 5	11,687	329
Lansing Comm Coll, Lansing, MI 48901	1957	Dr Philip J Gannon ... 12	20,407	1,000
Laramie County Comm Coll, Cheyenne, WY 82007	1968	Dr Harlan L Heglar ... 9	3,352	162
Laredo Jr Coll, Laredo, TX 78040	1946	Dr Domingo Arechiga ... 12	3,100	160
Lasell Jr Coll, Newton, MA 02166 (3)	1851	Dr Peter T Mitchell ... 1	650	77
Lassen Coll, Susanville, CA 96130	1925	Dr Warren Sorenson ... 12	1,907	200
Latter-Day Saints Business Coll, Salt Lake City, UT 84111	1886	Mr R F Kirkham ... 2	968	38
Lawson State Comm Coll, Birmingham, AL 35221	1965	Dr Jesse J Lewis ... 5	1,552	58
Lees-McRae Coll, Banner Elk, NC 28604	1900	Dr Bradford L Crain ... 2	710	40
Lehigh County Comm Coll, Schnecksville, PA 18078	1967	Dr Robert L Barthlow ... 12	3,468	120
Lenoir Comm Coll, Kinston, NC 28502	1960	Dr Jesse L McDaniel ... 5	1,978	105
Lewis and Clark Comm Coll, Godfrey, IL 62035	1970	Mr J Neil Admire ... 10	4,743	300
Lewis Coll of Business, Detroit, MI 48235	1929	Dr Marjorie Harris ... 1	656	32
Lima Tech Coll, Lima, OH 45804	1971	Dr James S Biddle ... 12	1,885	130
Lincoln Land Comm Coll, Springfield, IL 62708	1967	Dr Robert L Poorman ... 10	6,646	391
Long Beach City Coll, Long Beach, CA 90808	1927	Dr John T McCuen ... 5	23,525	1,320
Longview Comm Coll, Lee's Summit, MO 64063	1969	Mr Aldo W Leker ... 10	5,225	254
Lorain County Comm Coll, Elyria, OH 44035	1963	Dr Omar L Olson ... 12	6,448	320
Lord Fairfax Comm Coll, Middletown, VA 22645	1969	Dr William H McCoy ... 12	1,726	66
Los Angeles City Coll, Los Angeles, CA 90029	1929	Dr Stelle Feuers ... 10	16,800	750
Los Angeles Harbor Coll, Wilmington, CA 90744	1949	Mr James L Heinselman ... 12	7,988	275
Los Angeles Mission Coll, San Fernando, CA 91340	1974	Mr Lowell J Erickson ... 12	4,376	127
Los Angeles Pierce Coll, Woodland Hills, CA 91371	1947	Dr Herbert W Ravetch ... 12	19,286	499
Los Angeles Southwest Coll, Los Angeles, CA 90047	1967	Dr Walter C McIntosh ... 12	4,500	195
Los Angeles Trade-Tech Coll, Los Angeles, CA 90015	1925	Mr Thomas L Stevens Jr ... 10	18,500	802
Los Angeles Valley Coll, Van Nuys, CA 91401	1949	Dr Mary E Lee ... 12	17,973	583
Louisburg Coll, Louisburg, NC 27549	1787	Dr J Allen Norris Jr ... 2	700	45
Louisiana State U at Alexandria, Alexandria, LA 71302	1960	Dr James W Firnberg ... 5	1,985	95
Louisiana State U at Eunice, Eunice, LA 70535	1967	Dr Anthony Mumphrey ... 5	1,650	87
Lower Columbia Coll, Longview, WA 98632	1934	Dr Vernon R Pickett ... 5	4,079	150
Lurleen B Wallace State Jr Coll, Andalusia, AL 36420	1969	Dr William H McWhorter ... 5	774	49
Luzerne County Comm Coll, Nanticoke, PA 18634	1966	Thomas J Moran ... 9	4,259	274
MacCormac Jr Coll, Chicago, IL 60604	1904	Mr Gordon C Borchardt ... 1	715	50
Macomb Comm Coll, Warren, MI 48093	1954	Mr Albert L Lorenzo ... 10	30,100	815
Macon Jr Coll, Macon, GA 31297	1968	Dr S Aaron Hyatt ... 5	2,819	101
Madison Area Tech Coll, Madison, WI 53703	1911	Mr Norman P Mitby ... 10	8,712	350
Manatee Comm Coll, Bradenton, FL 33507	1957	Dr Stephen J Korcheck ... 5	6,025	245
Manchester Comm Coll, Manchester, CT 06040	1963	Dr William E Vincent ... 5	5,200	200
Maple Woods Comm Coll, Kansas City, MO 64156	1969	Dr Stephen R Brainard ... 12	2,513	122
Maria Coll, Albany, NY 12208	1958	Sr Laureen Fitzgerald ... 1	1,217	76
Maria Regina Coll, Syracuse, NY 13208 (3)	1961	Sr Stella Maris Zuccolillo ... 2	632	41
Maricopa Tech Comm Coll, Phoenix, AZ 85034	1968	Dr Charles A Green ... 5	2,877	164
Marion Tech Coll, Marion, OH 43302	1971	Dr John Richard Bryson ... 13	1,362	86
Marshalltown Comm Coll, Marshalltown, IA 50158	1927	Dr Paul Kegel ... 10	1,183	96
Martin Comm Coll, Williamston, NC 27892	1968	Dr W Travis Martin ... 5	844	57
Mary Holmes Coll, West Point, MS 39773	1892	Dr Joseph A Gore ... 2	704	28
Marymount Palos Verdes Coll, Rancho Palos Verdes, CA 90274	1968	Dr Thomas D Wood ... 2	622	70
Massachusetts Bay Comm Coll, Wellesley Hills, MA 02181	1961	Mr Roger A Van Winkle ... 5	4,203	148
Massasoit Comm Coll, Brockton, MA 02402	1966	Dr Gerard F Burke ... 5	3,105	138
Mattatuck Comm Coll, Waterbury, CT 06708	1967	Dr Richard L Sanders ... 5	3,584	148
Mayland Tech Coll, Spruce Pine, NC 28777	1971	Dr O M Blake ... 12	646	51
McCook Comm Coll, McCook, NE 69001	1926	Dr Harold Deselms ... 12	841	55
McDowell Tech Coll, Marion, NC 28752	1966	Dr Robert M Boggs ... 5	602	39
McHenry County Coll, Crystal Lake, IL 60014	1967	Mr Robert C Bartlett ... 12	3,329	143
McLennan Comm Coll, Waco, TX 76708	1965	Dr Wilbur A Ball ... 9	4,632	214

Name, address	Year	Governing official, control	Enroll-ment	Faculty
Mendocino Coll, Ukiah, CA 95482	1973	Dr Leroy R Lowery	12	3,285	160
Merced Coll, Merced, CA 95340	1962	Dr Tom K Harris Jr	12	6,119	418
Mercer County Comm Coll, Trenton, NJ 08690	1966	Mr John P Hanley	9	5,631	315
Meridian Jr Coll, Meridian, MS 39305	1937	Dr William F Scaggs	12	2,539	151
Merritt Coll, Oakland, CA 94619	1953	Ms Norma J Tucker	12	6,100	325
Mesabi Comm Coll, Virginia, MN 55792	1918	Richard Kohlase		1,137	35
Mesa Comm Coll, Mesa, AZ 85202	1965	Dr Wallace A Simpson	12	14,915	151
Metropolitan Tech Comm Coll, Omaha, NE 68103	1974	Dr J Richard Gilliland	12	5,745	345
Miami-Dade Comm Coll, Miami, FL 33176	1960	Dr Robert H McCabe	12	41,427	1,936
Miami-Jacobs Jr Coll of Business, Dayton, OH 45401	1860	Dr Charles G Campbell	3	610	34
Miami U–Hamilton Campus, Hamilton, OH 45011	1968	Dr Harriet Taylor	5	1,778	51
Miami U–Middletown Campus, Middletown, OH 45042	1966	Dr C Eugene Bennett	5	1,718	143
Middle Georgia Coll, Cochran, GA 31014	1884	Dr Louis C Alderman Jr	5	1,327	100
Middlesex Comm Coll, Middletown, CT 06457	1966	Mr Robert A Chapman	5	2,900	75
Middlesex Comm Coll, Bedford, MA 01730	1970	Dr James E Houlihan Jr	5	2,250	100
Middlesex County Coll, Edison, NJ 08818	1964	Dr Rose M Channing	9	11,197	620
Midland Coll, Midland, TX 79705	1969	Dr Jess H Parrish	12	3,502	189
Midlands Tech Coll, Columbia, SC 29202	1974	Dr James R Morris	12	4,980	330
Mid Michigan Comm Coll, Harrison, MI 48625	1965	Dr Eugene F Schorzmann	12	1,966	84
Mid-Plains Comm Coll, North Platte, NE 69101	1965	Mr Kenneth L Aten	10	1,720	74
Miles Comm Coll, Miles City, MT 59301	1939	Dr Judson H Flower	12	867	60
Milwaukee Area Tech Coll, Milwaukee, WI 53203	1912	Dr Rus F Slicker	10	16,991	1,629
Mineral Area Coll, Flat River, MO 63601	1922	Dr Dixie Kohn	10	1,675	70
Minneapolis Comm Coll, Minneapolis, MN 55403	1965	Earl W Bowman	5	2,919	161
MiraCosta Coll, Oceanside, CA 92056	1934	Dr H Deon Holt	5	7,796	320
Mission Coll, Santa Clara, CA 95054	1977	Dr G Mellanderellander	12	7,967	375
Mississippi County Comm Coll, Blytheville, AR 72315	1975	Dr John P Sullins	5	1,214	65
Mississippi Delta Jr Coll, Moorhead, MS 38761	1926	Dr J T Hall	10	1,442	110
Miss Gulf Coast Jr Coll, Jackson County Cmps, Gautier, MS 39553	1965	Mr Curtis L Davis	10	1,875	122
Miss Gulf Coast Jr Coll, Jefferson Davis Cmps, Gulfport, MS 39501	1965	Mr Glen W Cadle	12	2,900	165
Miss Gulf Coast Jr Coll, Perkinston Cmps, Perkinston, MS 39573	1925	Dr Clyde E Strickland	12	932	58
Mitchell Coll, New London, CT 06320	1938	Dr Robert C Weller	1	920	38
Mitchell Comm Coll, Statesville, NC 28677	1852	Dr Charles C Poindexter	5	1,453	76
Moberly Area Jr Coll, Moberly, MO 65270	1927	Dr Andrew Komar Jr	12	1,178	68
Modesto Jr Coll, Modesto, CA 95350	1921	Dr Louis E Zellers	12	7,980	412
Mohave Comm Coll, Kingman, AZ 86401	1971	Dr Charles W Hall	5	3,211	178
Mohawk Valley Comm Coll, Utica, NY 13501	1946	Dr Michael I Schafer	5	7,400	427
Mohegan Comm Coll, Norwich, CT 06360	1969	Ms Myrna R Miller	5	2,023	86
Monroe Comm Coll, Rochester, NY 14623	1961	Dr Peter A Spina	12	11,479	547
Monroe County Comm Coll, Monroe, MI 48161	1964	Dr Ronald Campbell	9	2,880	98
Montcalm Comm Coll, Sidney, MI 48885	1965	Dr Donald C Burns	12	1,363	96
Monterey Peninsula Coll, Monterey, CA 93940	1947	Mr Max R Tadlock	5	7,500	315
Montgomery Coll–Germantown Campus, Germantown, MD 20874	1975	Dr Stanley M Dahlman	12	2,554	88
Montgomery Coll–Rockville Campus, Rockville, MD 20850	1965	Dr Antoinette P Hastings	12	12,682	540
Montgomery Coll–Takoma Park Campus, Takoma Park, MD 20912	1946	Dr O Robert Brown Jr	12	4,650	196
Montgomery County Comm Coll, Blue Bell, PA 19422	1964	Dr Edmond A Watters III	9	7,993	347
Moorpark Coll, Moorpark, CA 93021	1967	Dr W Ray Hearon	9	9,250	290
Moraine Park Tech Inst, Fond du Lac, WI 54935	1967	Dr John J Shanahan	12	3,011	301
Moraine Valley Comm Coll, Palos Hills, IL 60465	1967	Dr Fred Gaskin	12	13,990	571
Morgan Comm Coll, Fort Morgan, CO 80701	1967	Larry D Carter	12	662	77
Morton Coll, Cicero, IL 60650	1924	Dr Robert V Moriarty	12	2,843	168
Motlow State Comm Coll, Tullahoma, TN 37388	1969	Dr Harry D Wagner	12	2,427	128
Mountain Empire Comm Coll, Big Stone Gap, VA 24219	1972	Dr Victor Ficker	5	2,700	90
Mountain View Coll, Dallas, TX 75211	1970	Dr William H Jordan	12	5,891	245
Mt Hood Comm Coll, Gresham, OR 97030	1966	Dr R Stephen Nicholson	12	8,214	566
Mt San Antonio Coll, Walnut, CA 91789	1946	Dr John D Randall	10	21,885	681
Mt San Jacinto Coll, San Jacinto, CA 92383	1963	Dr Dennis M Mayer	12	2,840	156
Mount Wachusett Comm Coll, Gardner, MA 01440	1963	Dr Arthur F Haley	5	1,750	92
Murray State Coll, Tishomingo, OK 73460	1908	Dr Clyde R Kindell	5	1,463	60
Muscatine Comm Coll, Muscatine, IA 52761	1929	Dr Lee J Betts	5	860	45
Muskegon Business Coll, Muskegon, MI 49442	1888	Mr Robert D Jewell	1	1,464	50
Muskegon Comm Coll, Muskegon, MI 49442	1926	Dr John G Thompson	12	5,000	195
Napa Valley Coll, Napa, CA 94558	1940	Dr William H Feddersen	12	5,631	294
Nash Tech Coll, Rocky Mount, NC 27804	1968	Dr J Reid Parrott Jr	5	1,407	90
Nashville State Tech Inst, Nashville, TN 37209	1970	Dr Howard J Lawrence	5	5,341	200
Nassau Comm Coll, Garden City, NY 11530	1959	Dr Sean A Fanelli	12	21,132	1,307
National Ed Ctr–Bauder Coll Campus, Fort Lauderdale, FL 33334 (4)	1964	Erik Brumme	3	825	28
National Ed Ctr–Brown Inst Campus, Minneapolis, MN 55406	1946	Bill Johnson	3	1,500	64
National Ed Ctr–Spartan Sch of Aeronaut Campus, Tulsa, OK 74158 (2)	1928	William A Orth	3	1,821	84
National Ed Ctr–Tampa Tech Inst Campus, Tampa, FL 33610	1948	NR	3	1,885	67
National Ed Ctr–Thompson Inst Campus, Harrisburg, PA 17111	1934	Sherman D Harlow	3	633	37
National Ed Ctr–Vale Tech Inst Campus, Blairsville, PA 15717	1947	E Ray Buhler	3	700	21
National Tech Schools, Los Angeles, CA 90037 (2)	1905	R Parma	3	922	68
Navajo Comm Coll, Tsaile, AZ 86556	1968	Mr Dean Jackson	4	1,457	117
Navarro Coll, Corsicana, TX 75110	1946	Dr Kenneth P Walker	12	2,359	118
Nebraska Western Coll, Scottsbluff, NE 69361	1926	Dr John N Harms	12	1,615	72
Neosho County Comm Coll, Chanute, KS 66720	1936	Dr J C Sanders	12	1,043	83
Newbury Jr Coll, Boston, MA 02115	1962	Mr Edward J Tassinari	1	1,325	72
New Hampshire Tech Inst, Concord, NH 03301	1964	Dr David E Larrabee Sr	5	754	81
New Mexico Jr Coll, Hobbs, NM 88240	1965	Dr Robert A Anderson Jr	12	2,570	96
New Mexico State U–Alamogordo, Alamogordo, NM 88310	1958	Dr Charles R Reidlinger	12	1,391	68
New Mexico State U–Carlsbad, Carlsbad, NM 88220	1950	Dr Shelton W Marlow	5	950	55
New River Comm Coll, Dublin, VA 24084	1969	Dr H Randall Edwards	5	1,080	168
Niagara County Comm Coll, Sanborn, NY 14132	1962	Dr Donald J Donato	12	4,518	238
Nicolet Coll and Tech Inst, Rhinelander, WI 54501	1968	Dr Richard J Brown	12	1,185	92
Normandale Comm Coll, Bloomington, MN 55431	1968	Mr Dale A Lorenz	5	6,500	190

Name, address	Year	Governing official, control	Enroll-ment	Faculty
Northampton County Area Comm Coll, Bethlehem, PA 18017	1967	Dr Robert J Kopecek 12	4,168	221
North Arkansas Comm Coll, Harrison, AR 72601	1974	Dr Bill Baker 12	881	75
North Central Michigan Coll, Petoskey, MI 49770	1958	Mr Alfred D Shankland 9	1,692	92
North Central Tech Coll, Mansfield, OH 44906	1961	Dr Byron E Kee 5	1,872	113
North Central Tech Inst, Wausau, WI 54401	1912	Dr Donald Hagen 10	3,700	139
North Country Comm Coll, Saranac Lake, NY 12983	1967	David W Petty 12	1,687	227
North Dakota State School of Science, Wahpeton, ND 58075	1903	Dr Clair T Blikre 5	2,932	174
Northeast Alabama State Jr Coll, Rainsville, AL 35986	1963	Dr Charles M Pendley 5	1,004	63
Northeastern Jr Coll, Sterling, CO 80751	1941	Dr Marvin W Weiss 12	1,590	72
Northeastern Oklahoma A&M Coll, Miami, OK 74354	1919	Dr Bobby R Wright 5	2,865	110
Northeast Iowa Tech Inst–South Center, Peosta, IA 52068	1970	Mr James L Arneson 12	625	49
Northeast Mississippi Jr Coll, Booneville, MS 38829	1948	Mr Harold T White 10	2,300	145
Northeast Tech Comm Coll, Norfolk, NE 68701	1973	Dr Robert P Cox 12	2,405	117
Northern Essex Comm Coll, Haverhill, MA 01830	1960	Dr John R Dimitry 5	6,110	527
Northern Nevada Comm Coll, Elko, NV 89801	1967	Dr William J Berg 5	1,746	125
Northern New Mexico Comm Coll, Española, NM 87532	1909	Mr Frank A Serrano III 5	1,008	97
Northern Virginia Comm Coll, Annandale, VA 22003	1965	Dr Richard J Ernst 5	35,067	1,422
North Florida Jr Coll, Madison, FL 32340	1958	Dr Robert Ramsay 5	840	128
North Harris County Coll, Houston, TX 77073	1972	Dr Joe A Airola 12	10,954	460
North Hennepin Comm Coll, Minneapolis, MN 55445	1966	Dr John Helling 5	4,555	175
North Idaho Coll, Coeur d'Alene, ID 83814	1933	Mr Barry G Schuler 12	2,274	152
North Iowa Area Comm Coll, Mason City, IA 50401	1918	Dr David Buettner 12	2,096	173
North Lake Coll, Irving, TX 75038	1977	Dr James F Horton Jr 9	5,334	206
Northland Comm Coll, Thief River Falls, MN 56701	1965	Dr T A Easton 5	694	33
Northland Pioneer Coll, Holbrook, AZ 86025	1974	Dr Marvin L Vasher 12	4,535	340
North Seattle Comm Coll, Seattle, WA 98103	1970	Dr Cecil Baxter Jr 5	6,624	229
North Shore Comm Coll, Beverly, MA 01915	1965	Dr George Traicoff 5	2,737	120
Northwest Alabama State Jr Coll, Phil Campbell, AL 35581	1961	Dr Charles W Britnell 5	1,086	72
Northwest Comm Coll, Powell, WY 82435	1946	Dr Sinclair Orendorff 12	1,013	140
Northwestern Business Coll–Tech Center, Lima, OH 45805	1920	Mr Loren R Jarvis 3	710	70
Northwestern Connecticut Comm Coll, Winsted, CT 06098	1965	Dr Regina M Duffy 5	2,343	63
Northwestern Electronics Inst, Columbia Heights, MN 55421	1930	David Arneson 1	1,090	60
Northwestern Michigan Coll, Traverse City, MI 49684	1951	Dr George T Miller 12	3,223	123
Northwest Tech Coll, Archbold, OH 43502	1968	Dr James O Miller 5	939	79
Norwalk Comm Coll, Norwalk, CT 06854	1961	Dr William H Schwab 5	3,383	105
Norwalk State Tech Coll, Norwalk, CT 06856	1961	Dr William M Krummel 5	801	100
Oakland Comm Coll, Bloomfield Hills, MI 48013	1964	Mr Robert F Roelofs 12	26,934	642
Oakton Comm Coll, Des Plaines, IL 60016	1969	Dr William A Koehnline 10	8,871	392
Ocean County Coll, Toms River, NJ 08753	1964	Dr Milton Shaw 9	5,712	225
Odessa Coll, Odessa, TX 79762	1946	Dr Philip T Speegle 12	5,145	265
Ohlone Coll, Fremont, CA 94539	1967	Dr Peter Blomerley 12	7,501	300
Oklahoma City Comm Coll, Oklahoma City, OK 73159	1969	Dr Donald L Newport 5	7,709	235
Oklahoma State U Sch of Tech Training, Okmulgee, OK 74447	1946	Dr Robert Klabenes 5	3,551	160
Oklahoma State U Tech Inst, Oklahoma City, OK 73107	1961	Dr Philip P Chandler 5	2,925	159
Olympic Coll, Bremerton, WA 98310	1946	Dr Henry M Milander 5	6,399	337
Onondaga Comm Coll, Syracuse, NY 13215	1962	Dr Bruce H Leslie 12	7,262	520
Orangeburg-Calhoun Tech Coll, Orangeburg, SC 29115	1968	Mr M Rudolph Groomes 12	1,311	177
Orange Coast Coll, Costa Mesa, CA 92626	1947	Mr S Arthur Martinez 12	22,691	877
Orange County Comm Coll, Middletown, NY 10940	1950	Dr Mary M Norman 12	5,245	260
Otero Jr Coll, La Junta, CO 81050	1941	Dr W L McDivitt 5	651	52
Owens Tech Coll, Toledo, OH 43699	1966	Dr Jacob H See 5	4,535	370
Oxnard Coll, Oxnard, CA 93033	1975	Mr Edward W Robings 9	4,662	255
Palm Beach Jr Coll, Lake Worth, FL 33461	1933	Dr Edward M Eissey 5	11,637	467
Palomar Coll, San Marcos, CA 92069	1946	Dr Omar H Scheidt 12	15,491	651
Panola Jr Coll, Carthage, TX 75633	1947	Dr Gary McDaniel 12	1,370	56
Paris Jr Coll, Paris, TX 75460	1924	Dr Dennis F Michaelis 12	2,186	128
Parkersburg Comm Coll, Parkersburg, WV 26101	1971	Dr Eldon L Miller 5	2,954	166
Parks Coll, Denver, CO 80221	1895	Dr Morgan Landry 3	767	44
Pasadena City Coll, Pasadena, CA 91106	1924	Dr John W Casey 10	18,132	684
Pasco-Hernando Comm Coll, Dade City, FL 33525	1972	Dr Milton O Jones 5	2,881	181
Passaic County Comm Coll, Paterson, NJ 07509	1968	NR 9	2,987	189
Patrick Henry Comm Coll, Martinsville, VA 24115	1962	Dr Max F Wingett 5	1,630	63
Patrick Henry State Jr Coll, Monroeville, AL 36460	1965	Mr James R Allen 5	671	32
Paul D Camp Comm Coll, Franklin, VA 23851	1971	Dr Michael B McCall 5	1,165	65
Paul Smith's Coll, Paul Smiths, NY 12970	1937	Harry K Miller Jr 1	891	80
Pearl River Jr Coll, Poplarville, MS 39470	1909	Mr Marvin R White 12	1,715	107
Peirce Jr Coll, Philadelphia, PA 19102	1865	Dr Raymond C Lewin 1	1,642	81
Peninsula Coll, Port Angeles, WA 98362	1961	Dr Paul G Cornaby 5	768	118
Pennco Tech, Bristol, PA 19007	1961	John Hobyak 3	750	65
Penna State U Altoona Campus, Altoona, PA 16603	1929	Dr James A Duplass 13	2,081	90
Penna State U Beaver Campus, Monaca, PA 15061	1964	David B Otto 13	1,142	60
Penna State U Berks Campus, Reading, PA 19608	1924	Dr Frederick H Gaige 13	1,092	55
Penna State U Delaware County Campus, Media, PA 19063	1966	John D Vairo 13	1,504	78
Penna State U DuBois Campus, DuBois, PA 15801	1935	Dr Jacqueline Schoch 13	868	41
Penna State U Fayette Campus, Uniontown, PA 15401	1934	Dr Albert Skomra 13	835	39
Penna State U Hazelton Campus, Hazelton, PA 18201	1934	Dr William J David 13	1,105	53
Penna State U McKeesport Campus, McKeesport, PA 15132	1947	Dr Charles R Bursey 13	1,449	62
Penna State U Mont Alto Campus, Mont Alto, PA 17237	1929	Vernon L Shockley 13	797	42
Penna State U New Kensington Campus, New Kensington, PA 15068	1958	Dr Robert D Arbuckle 13	1,270	71
Penna State U Ogontz Campus, Abington, PA 19001	1950	Dr Robert A Bernoff 13	3,492	114
Penna State U Schuylkill Campus, Schuylkill Haven, PA 17972	1934	Dr Wayne Lammie 13	951	42
Penna State U Shenango Valley Campus, Sharon, PA 16146	1965	Dr Vincent De Sanctis 13	1,067	34
Penna State U Wilkes-Barre Campus, Lehman, PA 18627	1916	Dr James H Ryan 13	686	50
Penna State U Worthington Scranton Campus, Dunmore, PA 18512	1923	Dr James D Gallagher 13	1,202	70
Penna State U York Campus, York, PA 17403	1926	Mr Edward M Elias 13	1,111	58
Penn Valley Comm Coll, Kansas City, MO 64111	1969	Mr Andrew V Stevenson 10	5,129	'08
Pensacola Jr Coll, Pensacola, FL 32504	1948	Dr Horace E Hartsell 5	7,163	909
Phillips Coll, Gulfport, MS 39501	1927	NR 3	645	33

Name, address	Year	Governing official, control	Enrollment	Faculty
Phillips County Comm Coll, Helena, AR 72342	1965	Dr John W Easley ... 12	1,476	90
Phillips Jr Coll, New Orleans, LA 70121	1970	Jessy Adams ... 3	1,100	51
Phoenix Coll, Phoenix, AZ 85013	1920	Dr William E Berry ... 12	12,000	503
Piedmont Tech Coll, Roxboro, NC 27573	1970	Dr Edward W Cox ... 5	681	56
Piedmont Tech Coll, Greenwood, SC 29648	1966	Dr Lex D Walters ... 5	1,580	175
Piedmont Virginia Comm Coll, Charlottesville, VA 22901	1972	Dr George B Vaughan ... 5	3,644	160
Pikes Peak Comm Coll, Colorado Springs, CO 80906	1969	Dr Monique Amerman ... 5	5,545	264
Pima Comm Coll, Tucson, AZ 85702	1966	Dr S James Manilla ... 5	20,882	1,002
Pitt Comm Coll, Greenville, NC 27835	1961	Dr Charles E Russell ... 12	2,710	110
Pittsburgh Inst of Aeronautics, Pittsburgh, PA 15236 (2)	1929	Ivan D Livi ... 1	600	28
Polk Comm Coll, Winter Haven, FL 33880	1964	Dr Maryly VanLeer Peck ... 5	4,600	182
Porterville Coll, Porterville, CA 93257	1927	Dr Paul D Alcantra ... 5	1,983	174
Portland Comm Coll, Portland, OR 97219	1961	Dr John H Anthony ... 12	18,286	1,737
Potomac State Coll of West Virginia U, Keyser, WV 26726	1901	Dr James L McBee Jr ... 5	1,063	64
Prairie State Coll, Chicago Heights, IL 60411	1958	Dr Richard C Creal ... 12	5,073	410
Prince George's Comm Coll, Largo, MD 20772	1958	Dr Robert I Bickford ... 9	14,083	645
Pueblo Comm Coll, Pueblo, CO 81004	1979	Dr Tony Zeiss ... 5	1,299	156
Puerto Rico Jr Coll, Rio Piedras, PR 00928	1949	Mr Domingo E Mrrero ... 1	4,405	366
Quincy Jr Coll, Quincy, MA 02169	1958	Dr O Clayton Johnson ... 11	1,225	173
Quinebaug Valley Comm Coll, Danielson, CT 06239	1971	Dr Robert E Miller ... 5	1,131	47
Quinsigamond Comm Coll, Worcester, MA 01606	1963	Dr Clifford S Peterson ... 5	2,662	188
Ramirez Coll of Business and Technology, Hato Rey, PR 00918	1922	NR ... 3	1,316	73
Randolph Tech Coll, Asheboro, NC 27203	1962	Mr Merton H Branson ... 5	1,144	55
Ranger Jr Coll, Ranger, TX 76470	1926	Dr Jack M Elsom ... 13	800	55
Rappahannock Comm Coll, Glenns, VA 23149	1970	Dr John H Upton ... 12	1,347	59
Reading Area Comm Coll, Reading, PA 19603	1971	Dr Lewis W Ogle ... 10	1,384	73
Red Rocks Comm Coll, Golden, CO 80401	1967	Dr Richard E Wilson ... 5	5,141	211
Rend Lake Coll, Ina, IL 62846	1967	Dr Harry J Braun ... 5	3,724	180
RETS Electronic Inst, Birmingham, AL 35234	1974	Gene Smythe ... 3	809	18
Richard Bland Coll, Petersburg, VA 23805	1961	Dr Clarence Maze Jr ... 5	1,026	46
Richland Coll, Dallas, TX 75243	1972	Dr Stephen Mittelstet ... 12	13,350	570
Richland Comm Coll, Decatur, IL 62526	1971	Mr John M Kirk ... 10	3,263	159
Richmond Tech Coll, Hamlet, NC 28345	1964	R Kenneth Melvin ... 5	983	111
Ricks Coll, Rexburg, ID 83440	1888	Dr Bruce C Hafen ... 2	6,318	302
Rio Hondo Comm Coll, Whittier, CA 90608	1960	Herbert M Sussman ... 12	10,872	347
Riverside City Coll, Riverside, CA 92506	1916	Dr Charles A Kane ... 12	13,809	544
Roane State Comm Coll, Harriman, TN 37748	1971	Dr Cuyler A Dunbar ... 5	3,587	115
Roanoke-Chowan Tech Coll, Ahoskie, NC 27910	1967	Dr David W Sink Jr ... 5	710	59
Robert Morris Coll, Carthage Campus, Carthage, IL 62321	1965	Richard D Pickett ... 1	650	30
Robert Morris Coll, Chicago Campus, Chicago, IL 60601	1965	Richard D Pickett ... 1	1,602	46
Rochester Comm Coll, Rochester, MN 55904	1915	Dr Geraldine A Evans ... 5	3,158	160
Rockingham Comm Coll, Wentworth, NC 27375	1964	Dr N J Owens Jr ... 5	1,729	138
Rockland Comm Coll, Suffern, NY 10901	1959	Dr F Thomas Clark ... 12	8,149	328
Rock Valley Coll, Rockford, IL 61101	1964	Dr Karl J Jacobs ... 10	8,606	555
Rogers State Coll, Claremore, OK 74017	1909	Dr Richard H Mosier ... 5	2,669	121
Rogue Comm Coll, Grants Pass, OR 97527	1971	Dr Howard D Sims ... 12	2,842	267
Rose State Coll, Midwest City, OK 73110	1971	Dr Joe T Packnett ... 12	9,250	272
Rowan Tech Coll, Salisbury, NC 28144	1963	Dr Richard L Brownell ... 5	2,100	130
Roxbury Comm Coll, Boston, MA 02115	1973	Mrs Brunetta R Wolfman ... 5	1,200	41
Sacramento City Coll, Sacramento, CA 95822	1916	Dr Carl Christian Andersen ... 12	13,213	450
Saddleback Comm Coll, Mission Viejo, CA 92692	1967	Dr William O Jay ... 12	24,800	725
Saint Augustine Coll, Chicago, IL 60640	1980	Fr Carlos A Plazas, PhD ... 2	774	71
St Bernard Parish Comm Coll, Chalmette, LA 70043	1967	Dr Elizabeth Zimmerman ... 12	633	27
St Johns River Comm Coll, Palatka, FL 32077	1958	Dr R L McLendon Jr ... 5	1,463	96
St Louis Comm Coll at Florissant Valley, St Louis, MO 63135	1963	Dr David Harris ... 10	11,297	241
St Louis Comm Coll at Forest Park, St Louis, MO 63110	1962	Dr Vernon O Crawley ... 10	8,801	371
St Louis Comm Coll at Meramec, Kirkwood, MO 63122	1963	Dr Ralph R Doty ... 10	12,666	388
Saint Mary's Coll of O'Fallon, O'Fallon, MO 63366	1921	Sr Elizabeth Weiman ... 2	644	51
St Mary's Jr Coll, Minneapolis, MN 55454 (4)	1964	Sr Anne Joachim Moore ... 2	824	90
St Petersburg Jr Coll, St Petersburg, FL 33733	1927	Dr Carl M Kuttler Jr ... 12	15,865	555
St Philip's Coll, San Antonio, TX 78203	1898	Dr Kay M Moore ... 10	6,920	464
Salem Comm Coll, Carneys Point, NJ 08069	1971	Dr William Wenzel ... 9	1,177	73
Sampson Tech Coll, Clinton, NC 28328	1965	Dr Clifton W Paderick ... 12	876	66
San Antonio Coll, San Antonio, TX 78284	1925	Dr Max Castillo ... 12	22,397	964
San Bernardino Valley Coll, San Bernardino, CA 92403	1926	Dr Arthur M Jensen ... 12	11,061	511
Sandhills Comm Coll, Carthage, NC 28327	1963	Dr Raymond A Stone ... 12	1,937	105
San Diego City Coll, San Diego, CA 92101	1914	Dr Allen J Repashy ... 12	12,300	768
San Diego Mesa Coll, San Diego, CA 92111	1962	Dr Allen Brooks ... 10	19,000	890
San Diego Miramar Coll, San Diego, CA 92126	1969	Dr George F Yee ... 12	5,276	303
San Jacinto Coll–North Campus, Houston, TX 77049	1974	Dr Edwin E Lehr ... 12	3,578	165
San Jacinto Coll–South Campus, Houston, TX 77089	1979	Dr Parker Williams ... 12	3,791	147
San Joaquin Delta Coll, Stockton, CA 95207	1935	Mr Lawrence A DeRicco ... 10	14,205	534
San Jose City Coll, San Jose, CA 95126	1921	Mr Richard C Casey ... 10	10,508	431
San Juan Coll, Farmington, NM 87401	1958	Dr James C Henderson ... 9	2,360	170
Santa Ana Coll, Santa Ana, CA 92706	1915	Dr Robert D Jensen ... 10	20,225	860
Santa Barbara City Coll, Santa Barbara, CA 93109	1908	Dr Peter R MacDougall ... 12	9,975	444
Santa Fe Comm Coll, Gainesville, FL 32601	1966	Mr Alan J Robertson ... 12	7,296	419
Santa Monica Coll, Santa Monica, CA 90405	1929	Dr Richard L Moore ... 12	22,111	743
Santa Rosa Jr Coll, Santa Rosa, CA 95401	1918	Dr Roy Mikalson ... 12	20,178	670
Sauk Valley Coll, Dixon, IL 61021	1965	Dr Hal Garner ... 10	3,489	180
Schenectady County Comm Coll, Schenectady, NY 12305	1968	Dr Wright L Lassiter Jr ... 12	1,904	169
Schoolcraft Coll, Livonia, MI 48152	1961	Dr Richard W McDowell ... 10	8,304	350
Scott Comm Coll, Bettendorf, IA 52722	1966	John T Blong ... 12	2,587	138
S D Bishop State Jr Coll, Mobile, AL 36690	1965	Dr Yvonne Kennedy ... 12	1,587	51
Seattle Central Comm Coll, Seattle, WA 98122	1966	Dr Ernest Martinez ... 12	8,269	384
Seminole Comm Coll, Sanford, FL 32771	1966	Dr Earl S Weldon ... 12	4,692	309
Seminole Jr Coll, Seminole, OK 74868	1931	Gregory G Fitch ... 5	1,437	67
Seward County Comm Coll, Liberal, KS 67901	1969	Dr James E Hooper ... 5	1,501	105
Shawnee Coll, Ullin, IL 62992	1967	Dr Loren E Klaus ... 12	2,550	219
Shawnee State Comm Coll, Portsmouth, OH 45662	1975	Frank C Taylor ... 5	1,910	167
Shelby State Comm Coll, Memphis, TN 38104	1970	Dr Raymond C Bowen ... 5	4,675	248
Shelton State Comm Coll, Tuscaloosa, AL 35404	1979	Dr Leo Sumner ... 5	2,898	31
Sheridan Coll, Sheridan, WY 82801	1948	Dr Gordon A Ward ... 12	1,215	133

Name, address	Year	Governing official, control	Enrollment	Faculty
Shoreline Comm Coll, Seattle, WA 98133	1964	Dr Ronald E Bell 5	5,866	285
Sierra Coll, Rocklin, CA 95677	1914	Dr Gerald C Angove 5	8,667	317
Sinclair Comm Coll, Dayton, OH 45402	1887	Dr David H Ponitz 12	17,253	805
Skagit Valley Coll, Mount Vernon, WA 98273	1926	Dr James M Ford 5	1,939	258
Skyline Coll, San Bruno, CA 94066	1969	Mr Gus J Petropoulos 9	7,063	268
Snead State Jr Coll, Boaz, AL 35957	1935	Dr William H Osborn 5	1,116	49
Snow Coll, Ephraim, UT 84627	1888	Dr Steven D Bennion 5	1,328	60
Solano Comm Coll, Suisun City, CA 94585	1945	Dr Marjorie K Blaha 5	7,541	343
Somerset County Coll, Somerville, NJ 08876	1965	Dr S Charles Irace 9	4,870	195
South Central Comm Coll, New Haven, CT 06511	1968	Dr Richard M Turner III . . . 5	2,244	110
Southeast Comm Coll, Lincoln Campus, Lincoln, NE 68520	1973	Dr Jack Huck 10	3,562	567
Southeast Comm Coll, Milford Campus, Milford, NE 68405	1941	Dr Thomas Stone 10	945	120
Southeastern Comm Coll, Whiteville, NC 28472	1964	Dr Dan W Moore 5	1,714	95
Southeastern Comm Coll, North Campus, West Burlington, IA 52655	1968	Mr Carlton W Callison 12	1,700	135
Southeastern Illinois Coll, Harrisburg, IL 62946	1960	Dr Harry W Abell 5	2,900	183
Southern Arkansas U–El Dorado Branch, El Dorado, AR 71730	1975	Dr Ben Whitfield 5	640	41
Southern Arkansas U Tech, East Camden, AR 71701	1968	Dr George J Brown 5	683	43
Southern Jr Coll of Business, Birmingham, AL 35203	1969	NR 3	984	38
Southern Maine Vocational-Tech Inst, South Portland, ME 04106	1946	Dr Wayne H Ross 5	1,330	144
Southern Ohio Coll, Cincinnati Campus, Cincinnati, OH 45237	1927	Mr Elmer Smith 3	1,300	75
Southern Ohio Coll, Northeast Campus, Akron, OH 44312	1968	Wayne F Mullis 3	712	60
Southern State Comm Coll, Hillsboro, OH 45133	1975	Dr Lewis C Miller 5	1,334	119
Southern Union State Jr Coll, Wadley, AL 36276	1922	Dr L Ray Jones 5	1,801	106
Southern U, Shreveport-Bossier City Campus, Shreveport, LA 71107	1964	Mr Leonard C Barnes 5	621	51
Southern West Virginia Comm Coll, Logan, WV 25601	1971	Dr Gregory D Adkins 5	2,454	127
South Florida Comm Coll, Avon Park, FL 33825	1966	Dr Catherine P Cornelius . . 5	1,000	40
South Georgia Coll, Douglas, GA 31533	1906	Dr Edward D Jackson Jr . . . 5	1,059	58
South Mountain Comm Coll, Phoenix, AZ 85040	1979	Raul Cardenas 5	1,242	120
South Plains Coll, Levelland, TX 79336	1958	Dr Marvin L Baker 12	3,672	206
South Puget Sound Comm Coll, Olympia, WA 98502	1970	Dr Kenneth Minnaert 5	3,412	175
South Seattle Comm Coll, Seattle, WA 98106	1970	Mr Jerry M Brockey 5	4,764	234
Southside Virginia Comm Coll, Alberta, VA 23821	1969	Dr John J Cavan 5	1,512	106
Southwestern Baptist Theological Seminary, Fort Worth, TX 76122	1908	Dr Russell H Dilday Jr 2	4,296	180
Southwestern Coll, Chula Vista, CA 92010	1961	Dr Jewell E Stindt 12	10,324	393
Southwestern Comm Coll, Creston, IA 50801	1966	Dr Richard L Byerly 5	677	48
Southwestern Michigan Coll, Dowagiac, MI 49047	1964	Mr David C Briegel 12	3,000	170
Southwestern Oregon Comm Coll, Coos Bay, OR 97420	1961	Mr Jack E Brookins 12	4,207	240
Southwestern Tech Coll, Sylva, NC 28779	1964	Dr Norman K Myers 5	1,215	134
Southwest Mississippi Jr Coll, Summit, MS 39666	1918	Mr Horace C Holmes 10	1,142	53
Southwest State Tech Coll, Mobile, AL 36605	1954	Mr Donald S Jefferies 5	894	46
Southwest Texas Jr Coll, Uvalde, TX 78801	1946	Dr Jimmy Goodson 12	2,583	135
Southwest Virginia Comm Coll, Richlands, VA 24641	1968	Dr Charles R King 5	3,650	170
Southwest Wisconsin Vocational-Tech Inst, Fennimore, WI 53809	1967	Mr Ronald H Anderson . . . 12	1,261	117
Spartanburg Methodist Coll, Spartanburg, SC 29301	1911	Dr George D Fields 2	1,050	76
Spartanburg Tech Coll, Spartanburg, SC 29303	1961	Dr Joe D Gault 5	1,853	180
Spokane Comm Coll, Spokane, WA 99207	1963	Dr Donald E Bressler 5	5,258	262
Spokane Falls Comm Coll, Spokane, WA 99204	1967	Mrs Phyllis Everest 5	4,944	307
Spoon River Coll, Canton, IL 61520	1959	Robert N Rue 5	2,362	135
Springfield Tech Comm Coll, Springfield, MA 01105	1967	Andrew M Scibelli 5	3,505	189
Stanly Tech Coll, Albemarle, NC 28001	1971	Dr Charles H Byrd 5	909	65
Stark Tech Coll, Canton, OH 44720	1970	Dr John J Mc Grath 12	3,421	188
State Comm Coll of East St Louis, East St Louis, IL 62201	1969	Rogers Conner 5	1,490	88
State Fair Comm Coll, Sedalia, MO 65301	1966	Dr Marvin Fielding 10	1,528	113
State Tech Inst at Memphis, Memphis, TN 38134	1967	Dr Charles Temple 5	6,780	422
State U of NY A&T Coll at Alfred, Alfred, NY 14802	1908	Dr David H Huntington 5	3,980	225
State U of NY A&T Coll at Canton, Canton, NY 13617	1906	Dr Earl W MacArthur 5	2,326	122
State U of NY A&T Coll at Cobleskill, Cobleskill, NY 12043	1916	Dr Walton A Brown 5	2,642	143
State U of NY A&T Coll at Delhi, Delhi, NY 13753	1913	Mr Seldon M Kruger 5	2,389	135
State U of NY A&T Coll at Morrisville, Morrisville, NY 13408	1908	Dr Donald G Butcher 5	3,054	150
Stautzenberger Coll, Toledo, OH 43623	1923	Larry Mitchell & George Hawes 3	1,900	142
Stenotype Inst, New York, NY 10019	1937	NR 3	602	29
Stevens Henager Coll, Ogden, UT 84401	1891	Dr Frank Johnson 3	730	43
Suffolk County Comm Coll-Ammerman Campus, Selden, NY 11784	1962	Mr Robert T Kreiling 12	12,566	435
Suffolk County Comm Coll-Eastern Campus, Riverhead, NY 11901	1977	R David Cox 12	2,123	38
Suffolk County Comm Coll-Western Campus, Brentwood, NY 11717	1974	Saluatore J LaLima 12	5,407	259
Sullivan County Comm Coll, Loch Sheldrake, NY 12759	1962	Dr John F Walter 12	1,670	96
Sullivan Jr Coll of Business, Louisville, KY 40232	1864	David P Higley 3	1,617	67
Sumter Area Tech Coll, Sumter, SC 29150	1963	Dr James L Hudgins 5	1,738	231
Suomi Coll, Hancock, MI 49930	1896	Rev Ralph J Jalkanen 2	681	43
Surry Comm Coll, Dobson, NC 27017	1965	Dr Swanson Richards 5	2,715	75
Tacoma Comm Coll, Tacoma, WA 98465	1965	Dr Carleton Opgard 5	4,512	303
Taft Coll, Taft, CA 93268	1922	Dr David Cothrun 5	979	70
Tallahassee Comm Coll, Tallahassee, FL 32304	1966	Dr James H Hinson Jr 12	4,885	203
Tarrant County Jr Coll, Fort Worth, TX 76102	1967	Dr Joe B Rushing 12	26,369	996
Taylor Business Inst, New York, NY 10119	1961	Mr William N Wildish 3	1,500	87
Tech Career Institutes, New York, NY 10001	1974	George Leelike 3	2,300	90
Tech Coll of Alamance, Haw River, NC 27258	1959	Dr W Ronold McCarter 5	2,325	128
Temple Jr Coll, Temple, TX 76501	1926	Dr Marvin R Felder 10	2,400	104
Terra Tech Coll, Fremont, OH 43420	1968	Dr Richard M Simon 5	2,305	110
Texarkana Comm Coll, Texarkana, TX 75501	1927	Dr Carl M Nelson 12	3,586	200
Texas Southmost Coll, Brownsville, TX 78520	1926	Dr Albert A Besteiro 10	4,776	200
Texas State Tech Inst-Amarillo Cmps, Amarillo, TX 79111	1970	Mr Ronald DeSpain 5	1,118	89
Texas State Tech Inst-Harlingen Cmps, Harlingen, TX 78550	1967	Mr J Gilbert Leal 5	2,081	128
Texas State Tech Inst-Waco Cmps, Waco, TX 76705	1965	Dr Jack E Tompkins 5	4,561	319
Thames Valley State Tech Coll, Norwich, CT 06360	1963	Mr Raymond J Wodatch . . . 5	750	45

Name, address	Year	Governing official, control	Enrollment	Faculty
Thomas Nelson Comm Coll, Hampton, VA 23670	1968	Dr Thomas S Kubala .5	6,151	276
Thornton Comm Coll, South Holland, IL 60473	1927	Dr James L Evanko .5	8,200	327
Three Rivers Comm Coll, Poplar Bluff, MO 63901	1966	Dr Jack L Bottenfield .5	1,537	62
Tidewater Comm Coll, Chesapeake Campus, Chesapeake, VA 23320	1968	Dr George B Pass .5	2,043	103
Tidewater Comm Coll, Frederick Campus, Portsmouth, VA 23703	1968	Dr George B Pass .5	4,424	200
Tidewater Comm Coll, Virginia Beach Campus, Virginia Beach, VA 23456	1968	Dr George B Pass .5	8,508	390
Tompkins Cortland Comm Coll, Dryden, NY 13053	1968	Hushang Bahar .5	2,868	100
Treasure Valley Comm Coll, Ontario, OR 97914	1962	Glenn Mayle .12	1,500	70
Trenholm State Tech Coll, Montgomery, AL 36108	1965	Mr Tad McClammy .5	891	60
Trenton Jr Coll, Trenton, MO 64683	1925	Robert M Webb .10	608	59
Tri-Cities State Tech Inst, Blountville, TN 37617	1966	H James Owen .5	1,733	120
Tri-County Comm Coll, Murphy, NC 28906	1964	Mr Vincent W Crisp .5	724	47
Tri-County Tech Coll, Pendleton, SC 29670	1962	Dr Don C Garrison .5	2,405	267
Trident Tech Coll, Charleston, SC 29411	1964	Dr William A Orth .12	4,785	586
Trinidad State Jr Coll, Trinidad, CO 81082	1925	Dr Thomas E Sullivan .5	1,784	115
Triton Coll, River Grove, IL 60171	1964	Daniel F Moriarty .5	15,720	710
Trocaire Coll, Buffalo, NY 14220	1958	Sr Mary Carmina Coppola .1	1,040	79
Truckee Meadows Comm Coll, Reno, NV 89512	1971	V James Eardley .5	7,555	373
Tulsa Jr Coll, Tulsa, OK 74135	1968	Dr Alfred M Philips .5	15,153	650
Tunxis Comm Coll, Farmington, CT 06032	1969	Dr Eduardo Marti .5	1,528	98
Tyler Jr Coll, Tyler, TX 75711	1926	Dr Raymond M Hawkins .12	6,988	352
Ulster County Comm Coll, Stone Ridge, NY 12484	1962	Mr Robert T Brown .12	3,200	201
Umpqua Comm Coll, Roseburg, OR 97470	1964	Dr Bud Hakanson .12	1,650	250
Union County Coll, Cranford, NJ 07016	1933	Dr Derek Nunney .12	8,571	402
United Electronics Inst, Tampa, FL 33607 (2)	1967	George E Glenn .3	1,029	24
U of Akron, Wayne General and Tech Coll, Orrville, OH 44667	1972	Dr William V Muse .5	900	113
U of Alaska, Islands Comm Coll, Sitka, AK 99835	1962	Dr Jerry L Harris .5	886	61
U of Alaska, Kenai Peninsula Comm Coll, Soldotna, AK 99669	1964	Dr Les Vierra .5	1,580	79
U of Alaska, Ketchikan Comm Coll, Ketchikan, AK 99901	1954	John C Menzie .5	860	77
U of Alaska, Kodiak Comm Coll, Kodiak, AK 99615	1968	Ms Carolyn Floyd .5	1,115	53
U of Alaska, Matanuska-Susitna Comm Coll, Palmer, AK 99645	1958	Mr Alvin S Okeson .5	1,311	93
U of Alaska, Tanana Valley Comm Coll, Fairbanks, AK 99701	1974	Michael Metty .5	2,192	140
U of Cincinnati, R Walters Gen and Tech Coll, Cincinnati, OH 45236	1967	Dr Ernest G Muntz .5	3,200	100
U of Hawaii–Honolulu Comm Coll, Honolulu, HI 96817	1920	Dr Peter R Kessinger .5	4,549	245
U of Hawaii–Kapiolani Comm Coll, Honolulu, HI 96814	1946	Mr John F Morton .5	5,264	198
U of Hawaii–Kauai Comm Coll, Lihue, HI 96766	1965	Mr David Iha .5	1,159	64
U of Hawaii–Leeward Comm Coll, Pearl City, HI 96782	1968	Dr Melvyn K Sakaguchi .5	5,753	238
U of Hawaii–Maui Comm Coll, Kahului, HI 96732	1967	Ms Alma Cooper .5	2,087	106
U of Hawaii–Windward Comm Coll, Kaneohe, HI 96744	1972	Dr Peter T Dyer .5	1,363	73
U of Kentucky, Ashland Comm Coll, Ashland, KY 41101	1937	Mr Robert L Goodpaster .5	1,997	93
U of Kentucky, Elizabethtown Comm Coll, Elizabethtown, KY 42701	1964	Dr James S Owen .5	2,096	91
U of Kentucky, Hazard Comm Coll, Hazard, KY 41701	1968	Dr J M Jolly .5	629	39
U of Kentucky, Henderson Comm Coll, Henderson, KY 42420	1963	Dr Marshall Arnold .5	1,448	55
U of Kentucky, Hopkinsville Comm Coll, Hopkinsville, KY 42240	1965	Dr Thomas L Riley .5	1,116	64
U of Kentucky, Lexington Comm Coll, Lexington, KY 40506	1965	Dr Sharon B Jaggard .5	2,570	190
U of Kentucky, Madisonville Comm Coll, Madisonville, KY 42431	1968	Dr Arthur D Stumpf .5	1,417	84
U of Kentucky, Maysville Comm Coll, Maysville, KY 41056	1967	Dr Harry K Benson .5	654	35
U of Kentucky, Paducah Comm Coll, Paducah, KY 42001	1932	Dr Donald J Clemens .5	1,761	73
U of Kentucky, Prestonsburg Comm Coll, Prestonsburg, KY 41653	1964	Dr Henry A Campbell Jr .5	1,267	43
U of Kentucky, Somerset Comm Coll, Somerset, KY 42501	1965	Dr Roscoe D Kelley .5	1,153	77
U of Kentucky, Southeast Comm Coll, Cumberland, KY 40823	1960	Dr Vivian B Blevins .5	726	67
U of Minnesota Tech Coll, Crookston, Crookston, MN 56716	1966	Dr Donald G Sargeant .5	1,145	80
U of Minnesota Tech Coll, Waseca, Waseca, MN 56093	1971	Dr Edward C Frederick .5	719	76
U of New Mexico–Gallup Branch, Gallup, NM 87301	1968	Dr John M Phillips .5	1,491	100
U of New Mexico–Los Alamos Branch, Los Alamos, NM 87544	1980	NR .5	800	103
U of New Mexico–Valencia Branch, Belen, NM 87002	1981	NR .5	760	54
U of North Dakota–Williston, Williston, ND 58801	1957	Dr Garvin L Stevens .5	666	50
U of Puerto Rico, Aguadilla Regional Coll, Ramey, PR 00604	1972	Mrs Ruth Burgos-Sasscer .7	1,518	73
U of Puerto Rico, Carolina Regional Coll, Carolina, PR 00630	1974	Gilberto Moreno-Rodriguez .7	1,436	76
U of South Carolina at Beaufort, Beaufort, SC 29902	1959	Dr Ron Tuttle .5	838	56
U of South Carolina at Lancaster, Lancaster, SC 29720	1959	Mr John R Arnold .5	847	44
U of South Carolina at Sumter, Sumter, SC 29150	1966	Mr J C Anderson Jr .5	1,155	44
U of Wisconsin Center–Fond du Lac, Fond du Lac, WI 54935	1966	Willard J Henken .5	609	42
U of Wisconsin Center–Fox Valley, Menasha, WI 54952	1933	Dr Rue C Johnson .5	1,175	53
U of Wisconsin Center–Marathon County, Wausau, WI 54401	1933	Dr Stephen R Portch .5	1,201	70
U of Wisconsin Center–Rock County, Janesville, WI 53545	1966	Dr Thomas W Walterman .5	1,000	36
U of Wisconsin Center–Sheboygan County, Sheboygan, WI 53081	1933	Dr Kenneth M Bailey .5	702	42
U of Wisconsin Center–Washington County, West Bend, WI 53095	1968	Dr Robert Thompson .5	754	41
U of Wisconsin Center–Waukesha County, Waukesha, WI 53186	1966	Dr Mary S Knudten .5	2,200	90
Utah Tech Coll at Provo, Provo, UT 84603	1941	Dr J Marvin Higbee .5	5,593	300
Utah Tech Coll at Salt Lake City, Salt Lake City, UT 84131	1948	Dr Orville D Carnahan .5	8,289	205
Valencia Comm Coll, Orlando, FL 32802	1967	Dr Paul C Gianini Jr .5	11,432	663
Vance-Granville Comm Coll, Henderson, NC 27536	1969	Dr Ben F Currin .5	1,370	85

Name, address	Year	Governing official, control	Enroll-ment	Faculty
Ventura Coll, Ventura, CA 93003	1925	Dr Richard A Glenn 12	12,000	576
Vermont Tech Coll, Randolph Center, VT 05061	1957	Dr Robert G Clarke 5	688	65
Vernon Regional Jr Coll, Vernon, TX 76384	1972	Dr Jim M Williams 12	1,800	103
Victoria Coll, Victoria, TX 77901	1925	Dr Roland E Bing 9	2,990	120
Victor Valley Coll, Victorville, CA 92392	1960	Dr Howard B Larsen 5	4,600	135
Villa Maria Coll of Buffalo, Buffalo, NY 14225	1960	Sr Marcella Marla Garus 2	650	55
Vincennes U, Vincennes, IN 47591	1801	Dr Phillip M Summers 5	4,896	182
Virginia Highlands Comm Coll, Abingdon, VA 24210	1967	Dr N DeWitt Moore Jr 5	1,595	95
Virginia Western Comm Coll, Roanoke, VA 24038	1966	Dr Charles L Downs 5	4,000	218
Volunteer State Comm Coll, Gallatin, TN 37066	1970	Dr Hal R Ramer 5	3,323	190
Wake Tech Coll, Raleigh, NC 27603	1958	Dr Bruce I Howell 12	4,332	203
Walker Coll, Jasper, AL 35501	1938	Dr David Rowland 1	714	36
Wallace State Comm Coll, Hanceville, AL 35077	1966	Dr James C Bailey 5	2,543	133
Walla Walla Comm Coll, Walla Walla, WA 99362	1967	Dr Steven L VanAusdle 5	4,400	252
Walters State Comm Coll, Morristown, TN 37814	1970	Dr Jack E Campbell 5	4,023	220
Washington Tech Coll, Marietta, OH 45750	1971	Dr Donald R Neff 5	621	71
Waterbury State Tech Coll, Waterbury, CT 06708	1964	Mr Charles A Ekstrom 5	1,902	104
Watterson Coll, Louisville, KY 40218	1962	Dr James E Seitz 3	840	75
Waubonsee Comm Coll, Sugar Grove, IL 60554	1966	Dr John J Swalec 10	5,773	306
Waukesha County Tech Inst, Pewaukee, WI 53072	1923	Dr Richard T Anderson 12	5,710	765
Wayne Comm Coll, Goldsboro, NC 27530	1957	Dr Clyde A Erwin Jr 12	2,003	130
Wayne County Comm Coll, Detroit, MI 48226	1967	Dr Thomas F Waters 12	12,083	507
Weatherford Coll, Weatherford, TX 76086	1869	Dr E W Mince 5	1,702	74
Wenatchee Valley Coll, Wenatchee, WA 98801	1939	Dr James R Davis 12	2,929	190
Westark Comm Coll, Fort Smith, AR 72913	1928	Mr Joel R Stubblefield 12	3,733	140
Westchester Business Inst, White Plains, NY 10602	1915	Ernest H Sutkowski 3	729	29
Westchester Comm Coll, Valhalla, NY 10595	1946	Dr Joseph N Hankin 12	7,763	394
Western Nebraska Tech Coll, Sidney, NE 69162	1965	Gary Lund 12	710	31
Western Nevada Comm Coll, Carson City, NV 89701	1971	Dr Anthony D Calabro 5	3,256	126
Western Oklahoma State Coll, Altus, OK 73521	1926	Dr W C Burris 5	1,984	66
Western Piedmont Comm Coll, Morganton, NC 28655	1964	Dr Jim A Richardson 5	2,055	99
Western Texas Coll, Snyder, TX 79549	1969	Dr Don Newbury 12	1,319	75
Western Wisconsin Tech Inst, La Crosse, WI 54601	1911	Mr Charles G Richardson 10	2,200	883
Western Wyoming Comm Coll, Rock Springs, WY 82901	1959	Dr Bert S Slafter 12	1,869	81
West Hills Coll, Coalinga, CA 93210	1932	Mr Joseph M Conte 5	2,400	185
West Los Angeles Coll, Culver City, CA 90230	1969	Dr M J Fujimoto 12	7,300	289
Westmoreland County Comm Coll, Youngwood, PA 15697	1970	Dr Norman P Shea 9	3,496	170
West Shore Comm Coll, Scottville, MI 49454	1967	Dr William M Anderson 10	1,078	67
West Valley Coll, Saratoga, CA 95070	1963	Dr Dale A Johnston 12	12,800	500
West Virginia Northern Comm Coll, Wheeling, WV 26003	1972	Dr Daniel B Crowder 5	3,540	170
Wharton County Jr Coll, Wharton, TX 77488	1946	Dr Elbert C Hutchins 12	2,526	139
Wilkes Comm Coll, Wilkesboro, NC 28697	1965	Dr David E Daniel 5	2,935	178
William Rainey Harper Coll, Palatine, IL 60067	1965	Mr James J McGrath 12	14,000	500
Williamsport Area Comm Coll, Williamsport, PA 17701	1965	Dr Robert Breuder 12	4,084	259
Willmar Comm Coll, Willmar, MN 56201	1961	Dr John W Torgelson 5	897	58
Wilson County Tech Inst, Wilson, NC 27893	1958	Dr Frank L Eagles 5	1,369	59
Wisconsin Indianhead Tech Inst, Rice Lake Cmps, Rice Lake, WI 54868	1941	NR 10	1,317	47
Wisconsin Indianhead Tech Inst, Superior Cmps, Superior, WI 54880	1912	Richard Parish 10	678	43
Wor-Wic Tech Comm Coll, Salisbury, MD 21801	1976	Dr Arnold H Maner 12	856	80
Wright State U, Western Ohio Branch Campus, Celina, OH 45822	1969	Dr Thomas A Knapke 5	950	59
Wytheville Comm Coll, Wytheville, VA 24382	1967	Dr William F Snyder 5	1,700	96
Yakima Valley Comm Coll, Yakima, WA 98907	1928	Dr Terrance R Brown 5	4,703	261
Yavapai Coll, Prescott, AZ 86301	1966	Dr Paul Walker 12	5,203	363
York Tech Coll, Rock Hill, SC 29730	1961	Dr Baxter Hood 12	2,070	111
Youngstown Coll of Business & Prof Drafting, Youngstown, OH 44501	1967	Michael L Thompson 3	697	38
Yuba Coll, Marysville, CA 95901	1927	Dr Patricia L Wirth 12	7,683	267

Tuition and College Costs 1985-86

Based on the Peterson's Guides Annual Survey of Undergraduate Institutions, the average cost of tuition, mandatory fees, and college room and board at four-year private colleges is $7971. The average cost at four-year public colleges is $3621 for area residents and $5489 for nonresidents. Two-year public colleges are the least expensive group of institutions and have an average cost of $2594 for resident students and $3855 for nonresidents.

The most expensive institutions, including tuition, mandatory fees, and college room and board, are Bennington College ($15,810); Sarah Lawrence College ($15,435); Barnard College ($15,276); Massachusetts Institute of Technology ($15,230); Harvard University ($15,100); Yale University ($15,020); Columbia University, School of Nursing ($15,005); Tufts University ($14,983); Princeton University ($14,940); and Dartmouth College ($14,919). Bennington College has the highest tuition of all undergraduate institutions ($12,780). The least expensive institutions are the U.S. service academies, which are all free.

Bachelor's Degrees Conferred, 1981-82

Source: National Center for Education Statistics, U.S. Dept. of Education

Major field of study	Degrees conferred	Major field of study	Degrees conferred	Major field of study	Degrees conferred
All Fields	952,998	Engineering	80,005	Mathematics	11,599
Agc. & Natural Resources	21,029	Fine & Applied Arts	40,422	Military Sciences	283
Architecture & Envir. Design	9,728	Foreign Languages	9,841	Physical Sciences	24,052
Area Studies	2,509	Health Professions	63,653	Psychology	41,031
Biological Sciences	41,639	Home Economics	17,872	Public Affairs & Services	34,428
Bus. & Management	215,817	Law	846	Social Sciences	99,898
Communications	34,222	Letters (English, Philosophy, etc.)	40,693	Theology	5,998
Computer & Info. Sciences	20,267			Interdisciplinary	35,796
Education	101,063	Library Science	307		

Canadian Colleges and Universities

Source: Statistics Canada

Each institution listed has an enrollment of at least 600 students of college grade. Enrollment and faculty include all branches and campuses for the academic year 1984-85. Number of full-time teachers is the total number of individuals on teaching staff. Governing official is the president unless otherwise designated. All institutions are co-educational. Indented colleges are degree-granting affiliates.

Name	Location	Established	Governing Official	Students	Teachers
Acadia Univ.	Wolfville, N.S.	1838	G.R.C. Perkin	3,256	220
Alberta, Univ. of	Edmonton, Alta.	1906	Dr. W. Criew	22,914	1,674
Bishop's Univ.	Lennoxville, Qué.	1843	G.I.H. Nicholl	953	80'
Brandon Univ.	Brandon, Man.	1899	Dr. E. Taylor	1,482	129
British Columbia, Univ. of	Vancouver, B.C.	1908	Dr. K.G. Pederson	21,803	2,041
Brock Univ.	St. Catharines, Ont.	1964	A.J. Earp	3,945	242
Calgary, Univ.	Calgary, Alta.	1945	N.E. Wagner	14,572	1,178
Carleton Univ.	Ottawa, Ont.	1942	W. Beckel	10,341	624
Concordia Univ.	Montréal, Qué.	1974	P. Kenniff, Rector	12,387	700'
Dalhousie Univ.	Halifax, N.S.	1818	W.A. Mackay	7,810	872
Guelph, Univ. of	Guelph, Ont.	1964	Dr. B.C. Matthews	10,775	788
Lakehead Univ.	Thunder Bay, Ont.	1965	Dr. R.G. Rosehart	3,539	257
Laurentian Univ.	Sudbury, Ont.	1960	Dr. J.S. Daniel	3,100	284
Laval, Univ. de	Québec, Qué.	1852	J.-G. Paquet, Rector	19,933	1,390'
Lethbridge, Univ. of	Lethbridge, Alta.	1967	J. Woods	2,426	191
Manitoba, Univ. of	Winnipeg, Man.	1877	A. Naimark	15,983	1,285
McGill Univ.	Montréal, Qué.	1821	D. Johnston	17,983	1,370'
McMaster Univ.	Hamilton, Ont.	1887	A.A. Lee	11,495	964
Memorial Univ.	St. John's, Nfld.	1925	L. Harris	8,027	852
Moncton, Univ. de	Moncton, N.B.	1963	G. Finn	3,203	300
Montréal, Univ. de	Montréal, Qué.	1920	P. Lacoste, Rector	15,577	1,450'
École Polytechnique	Montréal, Qué.	1865	J.B. Lavigueur	3,350	200'
Hautes Études Commerciales	Montréal, Qué.	1907	B. Nadeau	1,676	130'
Mount Allison Univ.	Sackville, N.B.	1840	G.R. MacLean	1,625	145
Mount St. Vincent Univ.	Halifax, N.S.	1925	M. Fulton	1,786	124
New Brunswick, Univ. of	Fredericton, N.B.	1785	J. Downey	7,540	564
Ottawa, Univ. of	Ottawa, Ont.	1848	Dr. A. D'Ionio	13,023	999
Prince Edward Island, Univ. of	Charlottetown, P.E.I.	1969	P. Meincke	1,676	114
Québec, Univ. de	Ste. Foy, Qué.	1969	G. Boulet	23,748	1,440'
Queen's Univ.	Kingston, Ont.	1841	D.C. Smith	11,350	928
Regina, Univ. of	Regina, Sask.	1974	L.I. Barber	4,441	377
Royal Military Coll. of Canada	Kingston, Ont.	1876	J.B. Piant	828	169
Ryerson Polytechnical Inst.	Toronto, Ont.	1948	B. Segal	8,765	660
St. Francis Xavier Univ.	Antigonish, N.S.	1853	G.A. Mackinnon, Rev.	2,430	155
Cape Breton, College of	Sidney, N.S.	1974	Dr. W. Reid	1,195	64
St. Mary's Univ.	Halifax, N.S.	1802	K.L. Ozmon	3,131	173
St. Thomas Univ.	Fredericton, N.B.	1934	G.W. Martin	1,197	62
Saskatchewan, Univ. of	Saskatoon, Sask.	1907	L.F. Kirstjanson	11,975	1,071
Sherbrooke, Univ. de	Sherbrooke, Qué.	1954	C. Hamel	7,993	640'
Simon Fraser Univ.	Burnaby, B.C.	1965	W.G. Saywell	7,057	505
Technical Univ. of Nova Scotia	Halifax, N.S.	1907	J.C. Callaghan	1,093	95
Toronto, Univ. of	Toronto, Ont.	1827	G.E. Connell	34,939	2,491
Ontario Inst. for Studies in Education	Toronto, Ont.	1965	B.J. Shapiro	614	138
Trent Univ.	Petersborough, Ont.	1963	D.F. Theall	2,858	179
Trinity Western Coll.	Langley, B.C.	1969	R.N. Snider	646	33
Victoria, Univ. of	Victoria, B.C.	1963	H.E. Petch	7,192	554
Waterloo, Univ. of	Waterloo, Ont.	1957	D. Wright	15,818	779
Western Ontario, Univ. of	London, Ont.	1878	A.K. Adington	17,516	1,392
Huron College	London, Ont.	1863	Dr. J.A. Trentman	684	37
King's College	London, Ont.	1855	J.D. Morgan	1,375	49
Wilfrid Laurer, Univ. of	Waterloo, Ont.	1973	J.A. Weir	4,488	229
Windsor, Univ. of	Windsor, Ont.	1857	Dr. R. Lanni	8,396	515
Winnipeg, Univ. of	Winnipeg, Man.	1871	R. Farquhar	2,436	209
York Univ.	Downsview, Ont.	1959	H.W. Arthurs	14,766	1,044

(1) Estimated.

High School Dropouts: 1970 to 1983

Source: U.S. Bureau of the Census

Age and Race	Number of dropouts (1,000)					Percent of population				
	1970	1975	1980	1982	1983	1970	1975	1980	1982	1983
Total dropouts .	4,670	4,974	5,212	5,160	5,025	12.2	11.5	12.0	11.8	11.7
16–17 years	617	715	709	556	494	8.0	8.6	8.8	7.3	6.8
18–21 years	2,138	2,557	2,578	2,646	2,419	16.4	16.3	15.8	16.3	15.3
22–24 years	1,770	1,553	1,798	1,854	1,991	18.7	14.5	15.2	14.6	15.7
White[1]	3,577	3,861	4,169	4,080	3,950	10.8	10.5	11.3	11.2	11.0
16–17 years	485	594	619	478	424	7.3	8.4	9.2	7.6	7.1
18–21 years	1,618	1,980	2,032	2,056	1,897	14.3	14.7	14.7	15.2	14.4
22–24 years	1,356	1,169	1,416	1,467	1,531	16.3	12.6	14.0	13.7	14.3
Black[1]	1,047	1,024	934	937	918	22.2	18.5	16.0	15.5	15.3
16–17 years	125	116	80	66	62	12.8	10.2	6.9	6.0	5.8
18–21 years	500	540	486	519	436	30.5	27.0	23.0	23.0	19.5
22–24 years	397	337	346	332	396	37.8	27.8	24.0	20.5	24.3

(1) Includes other age and race groups not shown separately.

Scholastic Aptitude Test (SAT) Scores and Characteristics of College Bound Seniors: 1967 to 1983

Source: College Entrance Examination Board

(For school year ending in year shown)

Type of Test and Characteristic	Unit	1967	1970	1975	1976	1977	1978	1979	1980	1981	1982	1983
Test Scores[1]												
Verbal, total[1]	Point	466	460	434	431	429	429	427	424	424	426	425
Male	Point	463	459	437	433	431	433	431	428	430	431	430
Female	Point	468	461	431	430	427	425	423	420	418	421	420
Math, total[2]	Point	492	488	472	472	470	468	467	466	466	467	468
Male	Point	514	509	495	497	497	494	493	491	492	493	493
Female	Point	467	465	449	446	445	444	443	443	443	443	445
Participants												
Total	1,000	NA	NA	996	1,000	979	989	992	992	994	989	963
Male	Percent	NA	NA	49.9	49.5	48.9	48.4	48.3	48.2	48.0	48.1	48.2
White	Percent	NA	NA	86.0	85.0	83.9	83.0	82.9	82.1	81.9	81.7	81.1
Black	Percent	NA	NA	7.9	8.2	8.8	9.0	8.9	9.1	9.0	8.9	8.8
Obtaining scores[1] of—600 or above:												
Verbal	Percent	NA	NA	7.9	8.0	8.0	7.9	7.7	7.2	7.0	7.1	6.9
Math	Percent	NA	NA	15.6	16.3	16.1	15.8	15.0	15.1	14.4	15.3	15.9
Below 400:												
Verbal	Percent	NA	NA	37.8	39.7	39.1	39.8	40.7	41.8	41.6	40.2	41.1
Math	Percent	NA	NA	28.5	29.1	29.7	29.8	29.9	30.2	29.5	29.5	30.1

(NA) Not available. (1) Minimum score, 200; maximum score, 800. (2) 1967 and 1970 are estimates based on total number of persons taking SAT.

American College Testing (ACT) Program Scores and Characteristics of College-Bound Students: 1970 to 1984

Source: The American College Testing Program

Data for academic year ending in year shown. Test scores and characteristics of college-bound students based on sample.

Type of Test and Characteristic	Unit	1970	1975	1977	1978	1979	1980	1981	1982	1983	1984
Test Scores[1]											
Composite	Point	19.9	18.6	18.4	18.5	18.6	18.5	18.5	18.4	18.3	18.5
Male	Point	20.3	19.5	19.2	19.3	19.3	19.3	19.3	19.2	19.1	19.3
Female	Point	19.4	17.8	17.8	17.8	17.9	17.9	17.8	17.8	17.6	17.9
English	Point	18.5	17.7	17.7	17.9	17.9	17.9	17.8	17.9	17.8	18.1
Male	Point	17.6	17.1	17.0	17.4	17.4	17.3	17.3	17.3	17.3	17.5
Female	Point	19.4	18.3	18.2	18.3	18.4	18.3	18.2	18.4	18.2	18.6
Math	Point	20.0	17.6	17.4	17.5	17.5	17.4	17.3	17.2	16.9	17.3
Male	Point	21.1	19.3	18.9	19.1	19.1	18.9	18.9	18.6	18.4	18.6
Female	Point	18.8	16.2	16.1	16.2	16.2	16.2	16.0	16.0	15.7	16.1
Social Studies	Point	19.7	17.4	17.3	17.1	17.2	17.2	17.2	17.3	17.1	17.3
Male	Point	20.3	18.7	18.5	18.0	18.1	18.2	18.3	18.1	18.0	18.1
Female	Point	19.0	16.4	16.5	16.4	16.4	16.4	16.4	16.6	16.4	16.5
Natural Science	Point	20.8	21.1	20.9	20.9	21.1	21.1	21.0	20.8	20.9	21.0
Male	Point	21.6	22.4	22.3	22.3	22.3	22.4	22.3	22.2	22.4	22.4
Female	Point	20.0	20.0	19.6	19.8	20.2	20.0	20.0	19.7	19.6	19.9
Participants											
Total	1,000	788	714	744	770	780	822	836	805	835	849
Male	Percent	52	46	45	45	45	45	45	45	46	46
White	Percent	(NA)	77	76	76	84	83	83	83	82	82
Black	Percent	4	7	7	7	8	8	8	8	9	9
Obtaining composite scores of—											
26 or above	Percent	14	14	13	13	13	13	13	13	13	13
15 or below	Percent	21	33	34	34	33	33	33	34	35	33

(NA) Not available. (1) Minimum score, 1; maximum score, 36.

Current Languages Other Than English Spoken at Home: 1980

Source: U.S. Bureau of the Census

Current Language Spoken	Persons 5 to 17 years old		Persons 18 yrs. old and over		Current Language Spoken	Persons 5 to 17 years old		Persons 18 yrs. old and over	
	Total (1,000)	Difficulty with English[1] (percent)	Total (1,000)	Difficulty with English[1] (percent)		Total (1,000)	Difficulty with English[1] (percent)	Total (1,000)	Difficulty with English[1] (percent)
Total persons	47,494	x	162,753	x	Greek	66	5.2	336	17.0
Speaking a language other than English	4,568	14.0	18,492	19.4	Philippine languages	63	8.9	411	9.4
Spanish	2,952	15.4	8,164	27.6	Portuguese	68	10.3	284	31.6
Italian	147	5.4	1,471	14.0	Japanese	34	18.7	303	19.6
French	223	6.8	1,328	7.2	Korean	60	17.0	207	32.4
German	192	6.2	1,395	4.7	Vietnamese	64	36.0	130	38.7
Polish	41	5.7	780	10.6	All other	544	12.3	3,167	11.2
Chinese	114	20.9	516	31.6					

-(x) Not applicable. (1) Persons reported as speaking English "not well" or "not at all."

Educational Attainment by Age, Race, and Sex

Source: U.S. Bureau of the Census unpublished data as of March, 1984 (Number of persons in thousands)

Race, age, and sex	Years of school completed					Percent			
	All persons	Less than high school, 4 years	High school, 4 years	College, 1 to 3 years	College, 4 years or more	Less than high school 4 years	High school, 4 years	College, 1 to 3 years	College, 4 years or more
March 1984									
All races									
18 to 24 years	28,678	6,214	12,948	7,582	1,935	21.7	45.1	26.4	6.7
25 years and over	140,794	37,577	54,073	22,282	26,862	26.7	38.4	15.8	19.1
25 to 34 years	40,173	5,416	16,431	8,555	9,771	13.5	40.9	21.3	24.3
35 to 44 years	30,058	5,030	11,855	5,576	7,596	16.7	39.4	18.6	25.3
45 to 54 years	22,240	5,777	9,435	3,124	3,904	26.0	42.4	14.0	17.6
55 to 64 years	22,033	7,606	8,795	2,524	3,109	34.5	39.9	11.5	14.1
65 years and over	26,291	13,746	7,558	2,503	2,483	52.3	28.7	9.5	9.4
Male, 25 years and over	66,350	17,470	22,990	10,679	15,211	26.3	34.6	16.1	22.9
Female, 25 years and over	74,444	20,106	31,083	11,603	11,651	27.0	41.8	15.6	15.7
White									
18 to 24 years	23,939	4,910	10,845	6,431	1,753	20.5	45.3	26.9	7.3
25 years and over	123,103	30,817	48,177	19,794	24,316	25.0	39.1	16.1	19.8
25 to 34 years	34,211	4,213	13,896	7,376	8,726	12.3	40.6	21.6	25.5
35 to 44 years	26,012	3,937	10,417	4,867	6,791	15.1	40.0	18.7	26.1
45 to 54 years	19,408	4,615	8,466	2,787	3,540	23.8	43.6	14.4	18.2
55 to 64 years	19,701	6,209	8,210	2,380	2,901	31.5	41.7	12.1	14.7
65 years and over	23,771	11,842	7,187	2,385	2,356	49.8	30.2	10.0	9.9
Male, 25 years and over	58,476	14,410	20,530	9,557	13,979	24.6	35.1	16.3	23.9
Female, 25 years and over	64,627	16,407	27,647	10,237	10,337	25.4	42.8	15.8	16.0
Black									
18 to 24 years	3,919	1,109	1,813	893	102	28.3	46.3	22.8	2.6
25 years and over	14,369	5,960	4,926	1,989	1,495	41.5	34.3	13.8	10.4
25 to 34 years	4,805	1,034	2,195	949	629	21.5	45.7	19.8	13.1
35 to 44 years	3,134	949	1,200	566	419	30.3	38.3	18.1	13.4
45 to 54 years	2,286	1,030	783	265	208	45.1	34.3	11.6	9.1
55 to 64 years	1,953	1,238	456	111	149	63.4	23.3	5.7	7.6
65 years and over	2,191	1,709	292	100	90	78.0	13.3	4.6	4.1
Male, 25 years and over	6,334	2,721	2,081	871	662	43.0	32.9	13.8	10.5
Female, 25 years and over	8,035	3,240	2,845	1,118	833	40.3	35.4	13.9	10.4
Spanish Origin[1]									
18 to 24 years	2,019	898	722	359	41	44.5	35.8	17.8	2.0
25 years and over	7,269	3,848	1,984	843	593	52.9	27.3	11.6	8.2
25 to 34 years	2,745	1,156	877	437	276	42.1	31.9	15.9	10.1
35 to 44 years	1,806	854	539	244	168	47.3	29.8	13.5	9.3
45 to 54 years	1,235	736	317	96	86	59.6	25.7	7.8	7.0
55 to 64 years	838	564	188	50	37	67.3	22.4	6.0	4.4
65 years and over	645.	538	63	16	26	83.4	9.8	2.5	4.0
Male, 25 years and over	3,388	1,741	889	438	321	51.4	26.2	12.9	9.5
Female, 25 years and over	3,880	2,108	1,095	406	272	54.3	28.2	10.5	7.0

[1] Persons of Spanish origin may be of any race.

112 Years of Public Schools

	1869-70	1899-1900	1909-10	1919-20	1929-30	1939-40	1949-50	1959-60	1969-70	1980-81
Pupils and teachers (thousands)										
Total U.S. population	39,818	75,995	90,492	104,512	121,770	130,880	148,665	179,323	203,212	227,156
Population 5-17 years of age	12,055	21,573	24,009	27,556	31,417	30,150	30,168	43,881	52,490	47,120
Percent aged 5-17 years	30.3	28.4	26.5	26.4	25.8	23.0	20.3	24.5	25.8	20.8
Enrollment (thousands)										
Elementary and secondary	6,872	15,503	17,814	21,578	25,678	25,434	25,111	36,087	45,619	40,987
Percent pop. 5-17 enrolled	57.0	71.9	74.2	78.3	81.7	84.4	83.2	82.2	86.9	86.8
Percent in high schools	1.2	3.3	5.1	10.2	17.1	26.0	22.7	23.5	28.5	32.5
High school graduates	...	62	111	231	592	1,143	1,063	1,627	2,589	2,725
Average school term (in days)	132.2	144.3	157.5	161.9	172.7	175.0	177.9	178.0	178.9	178.2
Total instructional staff	...	...	...	678	880	912	962	1,464	2,253	2,452
Teachers, librarians: Men	78	127	110	93	140	195	195	402	691	774[4]
Women	123	296	413	565	703	681	719	985	1,440	1,536[4]
Percent men	38.7	29.9	21.1	14.1	16.6	22.2	21.3	29.0	33.4	33.5[4]
Revenue & expenditures (millions)										
Total revenue	...	$219	$433	$970	$2,088	$2,260	$5,437	$14,746	$40,267	$105,949
Total expenditures	$63	214	426	1,036	2,316	2,344	5,837	15,613[1]	40,683	103,586
Current elem. and secondary	...	179	356	861	1,843	1,941	4,687	12,329	34,218	94,321
Capital outlay	...	35	69	153	370	257	1,014	2,661	4,659	6,739
Interest on school debt	...	...	...	18	92	130	100	489	1,171	1,865
Other	...	...	...	3	9	13	35	132	636	662
Salaries and pupil cost					(Data in unadjusted dollars)					
Average annual teacher salary[2]	$189	$325	$485	$2,130	$3,869	$3,894	$5,928	$8,213	$10,917	$18,404[4]
Expenditure per capita total pop.	1.59	2.83	4.71	24.24	51.85	48.40	77.34	138.21	247.23	456.01
Current expenditure per pupil ADA[3]	...	16.67	27.85	130.41	236.25	238.05	411.29	595.50	1,007.65	2,487.29

(1) Because of a modification of the scope, "current expenditures for elementary and secondary schools" data for 1959-60 and later years are not entirely comparable with data for prior years. (2) Includes supervisors, principals, teachers and other non-supervisory instructional staff. (3) "ADA" means average daily attendance in elementary and secondary day schools. (4) Estimated.

Fall Enrollment and Teachers in Full-time Day Schools
Elementary and Secondary Day Schools, Fall 1983
Source: National Center for Education Statistics, U.S. Education Dept.

	Local school districts Total	Operating	Enrollment Total	Pupils per teacher	Classroom teachers	Instruc- tional aides	Expendi- ture per pupil
United States.	15,747	15,398	39,327,797	18.5	2,125,756	278,119	2,948
Alabama	128	128	721,901	20.3	35,619	2,930	2,177
Alaska	53	53	92,918	16.2	5,747	978	7,325
Arizona	221	202	503,228	19.2	26,268	3,700	2,524
Arkansas	367	364	432,120	18.2	23,696	2,131	1,971
California	1,030	1,027	4,089,017	23.5	174,290	47,639	2,733
Colorado	181	181	542,196	19.1	28,421	3,490	3,171
Connecticut	165	165	477,585	14.8	32,317	NA	3,636
Delaware	19	17	91,406	16.8	5,429	579	3,456
District of Columbia	1	1	88,843	16.0	5,569	534	4,260
Florida	67	67	1,495,543	17.6	85,028	14,677	2,680
Georgia	187	187	1,050,859	18.6	56,491	9,100	2,169
Hawaii	1	1	162,241	23.2	7,007	785	3,239
Idaho	115	114	206,352	21.0	9,847	819	2,052
Illinois	1,009	1,007	1,853,316	18.1	102,130	9,186	3,100
Indiana	305	304	984,384	19.5	50,509	6,172	2,414
Iowa	439	437	497,287	15.6	31,779	2,626	3,095
Kansas	385	304	405,222	15.5	26,096	2,204	3,058
Kentucky	180	100	647,414	19.9	32,458	2,758	2,100
Louisiana	66	66	782,434	18.6	42,179	6,501	2,739
Maine	282	230	209,753	15.5	13,492	1,960	2,458
Maryland	24	24	683,491	18.3	37,275	4,770	3,445
Massachusetts	404	346	878,844	15.5	56,873	6,095	3,378
Michigan	574	573	1,735,881	21.7	79,982	9,987	3,307
Minnesota	437	435	705,242	17.9	39,392	6,193	3,085
Mississippi	154	153	467,744	18.7	24,955	3,951	1,849
Missouri	545	544	795,453	17.0	46,761	3,347	2,468
Montana	561	551	153,646	16.2	9,479	1,109	3,289
Nebraska	994	930	266,998	15.2	17,548	2,043	2,984
Nevada	17	17	150,442	20.4	7,366	0	2,613
New Hampshire	169	158	159,030	16.2	9,821	1,363	2,750
New Jersey	604	581	1,147,571	15.6	73,593	4,811	4,007
New Mexico	89	89	269,711	18.6	14,532	2,099	2,901
New York	720	713	2,674,818	18.4	145,647	19,078	4,686
North Carolina	142	141	1,089,606	19.8	55,126	16,011	2,162
North Dakota	321	288	117,213	16.6	7,067	661	2,853
Ohio	616	614	1,827,300	18.9	96,927	6,116	2,676
Oklahoma	615	615	591,389	16.9	34,999	3,317	2,805
Oregon	309	307	447,109	18.3	24,409	3,557	3,504
Pennsylvania	500	500	1,737,952	17.0	102,207	9,110	3,329
Rhode Island	40	40	136,180	15.4	8,848	884	3,570
South Carolina	92	92	604,553	18.7	32,323	4,027	2,017
South Dakota	195	187	123,060	14.7	8,355	1,040	2,486
Tennessee	143	141	822,057	20.9	39,409	4,018	2,027
Texas	1,075	1,072	2,989,796	17.5	170,629	23,580	2,731
Utah	40	40	379,065	24.2	15,650	1,624	2,013
Vermont	273	245	90,416	14.5	6,242	1,065	3,051
Virginia	138	134	966,110	17.1	56,388	7,384	2,620
Washington	299	298	736,239	21.2	34,757	3,876	3,211
West Virginia	55	55	371,251	16.5	22,503	2,705	2,764
Wisconsin	432	431	774,646	17.1	45,311	4,727	3,237
Wyoming	49	49	100,965	14.4	7,010	882	4,045

Federal Funds for Education, 1984
Source: National Center for Education Statistics, U.S. Department of Education

Federal funds obligated for major programs administered by the Dept. of Education (thousands of dollars).

Total	$17,044,773	assistance	7,478,401
Elementary-secondary education.	4,294,269	Educational opportunity grants	3,561,209
Grants for the disadvantaged	3,501,383	Work study	561,322
Special programs.	549,117	Direct student loans	191,962
Bilingual education	173,051	Guaranteed student loans	3,130,939
Indian education	70,718	Other student assistance programs . . .	32,969
School asst.—federally affected areas .	608,791	Direct aid to postsecondary institutions	311,221
Maintenance and operation	555,300	Aid to minority and developing institutions	132,081
Construction.	28,491	Special programs for the disadvantaged.	164,740
Disaster assistance.	25,000	Cooperative education	14,400
Education for the handicapped	2,416,799	Higher education facilities	216,893
State grant programs	1,082,180	College housing loans	138,863
Early childhood education	53,164	Other higher education programs	82,410
Special centers, projects, and research .	54,871	International education and foreign	
Captioned films and media services . . .	14,609	languages.	30,800
Personnel training	55,540	Fund for improvement of postsecondary	
Handicapped rehab. service and res. . .	1,157,044	education	11,710
Vocational education and adult		Public library services	107,895
programs	954,320	Payments to special institutions	221,892
Basic programs.	689,324	Departmental accounts.	351,882
Adult education, grants to States	99,755	Educational research and improvement .	57,165
Postsecondary student financial		Departmental management account . . .	293,351

Preprimary School Enrollment of Children 3 to 5 Years Old: 1968 to 1983

Source: U.S. Bureau of the Census

Civilian noninstitutional population. Includes public and non-public nursery school and kindergarten programs. Excludes year olds enrolled in elementary school.

	Number of children (1,000)								Enrollment rate		
	1968	1970	1975	1979	1980	1981	1982	1983	1968	1970	1983
Population, 3–5 years old .	11,895	10,877	10,183	9,119	9,284	9,644	9,873	10,252			
Total Enrolled[1]	3,925	4,075	4,954	4,664	4,878	4,936	5,105	5,385	33.0	37.5	52.5
Nursery	816	1,093	1,745	1,862	1,982	2,055	2,151	2,347	6.9	10.0	22.9
Kindergarten	3,110	2,982	3,209	2,802	2,896	2,881	2,954	3,038	26.1	27.4	29.6
White.	3,309	3,414	4,105	3,786	3,994	4,038	4,165	4,430	33.2	37.8	53.1
Black.	553	585	731	738	725	725	769	758	31.2	34.9	48.8
Spanish origin[3]	NA	NA	NA	289	370	399	368	406	NA	NA	42.7
3 years old	317	454	683	746	857	891	928	1,005	8.3	13.0	28.1
4 years old	911	1,003	1,418	1,393	1,423	1,442	1,496	1,619	22.8	27.9	47.4
5 years old	2,698	2,617	2,852	2,525	2,598	2,604	2,681	2,762	65.9	69.2	84.6
Labor Force Status of Mother											
All races:[2] With mother in											
labor force[4]	1,217	1,345	2,168	2,353	2,480	2,515	2,629	2,853	33.2	38.8	55.3
3 and 4 years old . . .	456	526	973	1,139	1,252	1,204	1,268	1,453	18.9	23.5	41.3
5 years old	761	818	1,195	1,214	1,229	1,311	1,360	1,399	60.6	66.6	85.0
Married, spouse present	1,015	1,131	1,733	1,922	1,976	1,999	2,095	2,296	32.9	39.5	55.8
Other marital status. .	200	214	435	431	504	517	534	556	34.9	36.0	53.3
Employed	1,134	1,246	1,948	2,158	2,256	2,264	2,302	2,578	33.6	39.3	56.4
Full-time	778	770	1,236	1,416	1,445	1,444	1,361	1,655	34.1	38.6	55.9
Mother not in labor force .	2,642	2,694	2,704	2,196	2,266	2,254	2,340	2,378	32.8	37.0	49.7

(NA) Not available. (1) Includes children with mothers whose labor force status is unknown and children with no mother present in household, not shown separately. (2) Includes other races not shown separately. (3) Person of Spanish origin may be of any race. (4) Includes children with mothers who are unemployed, not shown separately.

Public and Private School Enrollment

According to the National Education Association (NEA), the nation's public schools enroll 12.8 percent fewer students today than a decade ago, but the number of teachers and school administrators declined less than 1 percent in that period. There are now 2.1 million classroom teachers, earning an average of $23,546. In the fall of 1974, more than 45.1 million children were enrolled in the public schools compared to 39.3 million in the fall of 1984.

While there are about 25,000 fewer classroom teachers now than in the 1974-75 school year, the NEA report, "Estimates of School Statistics, 1984-85," stated that the rest of the instructional staff, including librarians, guidance counselors, and aides, has grown. One possible reason for the disproportion between enrollment and the number of teachers may be that many schools have reduced class size and have hired additional teachers for handicapped students and other special needs.

At the same time that public schools were losing students, private school enrollment was increasing dramatically. The National Center for Education Statistics reported that one in every eight American children now attend schools outside the public system. It is estimated that 5.7 million, or 12.6 percent, of the 45.2 million students in all U.S. elementary and secondary schools in the fall of 1983 were in 27,700 private schools. Between 1980 and 1983, Catholic parochial school enrollment fell by 5 percent, whereas other religious schools reported an increase of 22 percent, and nonsectarian private schools has an increase of 36 percent. The pupil-teacher ratio was 18.6 to 1 in public schools in 1983, and 16.9 to 1 in private schools.

Public Libraries

Source: World Almanac questionnaire (1985)

First figure in parentheses denotes number of branches-2d figure indicates number of bookmobiles. (*) indicates county library system; (†) indicates state library system; (C) Canadian dollars; (A) library has not provided up-to-date information.

City	No. bound volumes	Circulation	Cost of operation
Akron, Oh.* (18-2)	1,200,677	1,953,376	$ 4,991,407
Albuquerque, N.M. (8-2)(A)	NA	1,630,000	2,568,716
Atlanta, Ga.* (25-0)	1,600,000	2,183,274	9,452,587
Austin, Tex. (16-0)	887,002	2,124,421	6,499,624
Baton Rouge, La.* (10-0)	493,506	1,640,686	2,631,607
Boston, Mass. (25-2)(A)	4,916,277	1,454,414	11,500,000
Buffalo, N.Y.* (52-3)	3,425,918	6,228,129	12,343,977
Cincinnati, Oh.* (40-2)	3,413,334	6,592,469	16,020,795
Cleveland, Oh. (31-1)	2,483,283	4,102,968	17,800,000
Columbus, Oh.* (21-1)	1,353,261	4,320,000	11,500,000
Dallas, Tex. (18-0)	1,777,073	3,874,425	14,847,539
Dayton, Oh.* (19-1)	1,344,584	5,012,236	9,040,820
Denver, Col. (21-1)	1,177,785	2,570,396	11,398,400
Des Moines, Ia. (5-2)	548,244	1,218,816	2,437,592
Detroit, Mich. (25-4)	2,446,111	1,441,476	14,690,093
El Paso, Tex. (12-0)	1,060,000	1,200,000	3,500,000
Ft. Worth, Tex. (8-0)(A)	798,608	1,650,930	3,784,161
Honolulu, Ha. (47-7)	442,482	517,066	12,400,000
Indianapolis, Ind.* (22-2)	1,476,674	3,988,952	11,265,372
Jacksonville, Fla.* (11-1)(A)	1,013,497	2,026,528	3,808,000
Kansas City, Mo. (14-0)	1,346,364	875,040	5,091,058
Long Beach, Cal. (12-0)(A)	709,815	1,986,085	7,501,378
Los Angeles, Cal. (62-5)	5,107,313	10,538,792	22,928,548
Louisville, Ky.* (A-2)	1,410,381	3,031,941	6,400,000
Memphis, Tenn.* (22-2)	1,535,556	2,500,000	8,726,456
Miami, Fla.* (25-6)(A)	2,000,000	3,700,000	7,000,000
Minneapolis, Minn. (14-0)	1,691,597	2,595,421	11,700,000
Mobile, Ala. (5-1)	371,657	766,420	2,433,475
Nashville, Tenn.* (15-2)	581,276	1,699,291	5,000,000
New Haven, Conn. (8-0)(A)	550,000	450,000	1,600,000
New Orleans, La. (11-0)(A)	802,934	1,176,304	3,735,693
New York (resrch)	7,271,592	780,171	3,737,693
N.Y.C. brches (82-2)(A)	3,450,969	8,107,362	
Brooklyn* (58-0)(A)	3,885,530	6,970,799	18,759,885
Queens* (59-0)(A)	4,260,930	6,877,351	25,434,000
Norfolk, Va. (11-1)	748,684	964,340	3,310,823
Okla. City, Okla.* (13-5)	600,000	2,350,000	7,376,199
Oakland, Calif. (17-3)	778,753	1,633,352	5,868,967
Omaha, Neb. (9-0)	561,028	1,690,478	3,652,008
Philadelphia, Pa. (51-0)	3,038,638	5,205,332	22,379,832
Phoenix, Ariz. (9-1)	1,332,400	4,137,000	8,794,000
Pittsburgh, Pa. (21-3)(A)	1,907,373	2,837,534	8,539,756
Portland, Ore.* (14-2)	1,178,703	3,237,547	5,526,054
Richmond, Va. (7-2)	696,966	961,000	2,771,504
Rochester, N.Y. (11-2)	959,207	1,457,210	
St. Louis, Mo. (13-2)	1,457,314	1,101,640	6,416,180
St. Paul, Minn. (11-1)	656,679	1,942,816	4,640,703
San Antonio, Tex.* (13-3)(A)	1,200,000	2,217,603	6,672,424
San Diego, Cal. (30-1)(A)	1,733,387	4,191,538	7,391,165
San Francisco, Cal. (26-1)(A)	1,749,129	2,470,091	9,146,080
San Jose, Cal. (17-1)(A)	1,250,000	2,800,000	5,800,000
Syracuse, N.Y.* (8-1)	509,386	1,189,319	5,655,999
Tucson, Ariz.* (15-2)	760,000	3,900,000	7,876,000
Tulsa, Okla. (20-1)	600,000	2,000,000	7,000,000
Wash. D.C. (26-1)	1,354,564	1,724,846	13,003,000
Wichita, Kan. (10-0)	854,046	1,224,426	2,853,098
Yonkers, N.Y. (3-1)	230,347	849,529	3,486,634

The Principal Languages of the World

Source: Sidney S. Culbert, Guthrie Hall NI-25 — University of Washington

Total number of speakers of languages spoken by at least one million persons (midyear 1985)

Language	Millions	Language	Millions	Language	Millions
Achinese (Indonesia)	2	Ilocano (Philippines)	4	Pedi (see Sotho, Northern)	
Afrikaans (S. Africa)	9	Iloko (see Ilocano)		Persian (Iran, Afghanistan)	30
Albanian	4	Indonesian (see Malay-Indonesian)		Polish	40
Amharic (Ethiopia)	10	Italian	63	Portuguese	161
Arabic	171			Provencal (Southern France)	4
Armenian	4	Japanese	121	Punjabi[1] (India; Pakistan)	70
Assamese[1] (India)	15	Javanese	50	Pushtu (mainly Afghanistan)	20
Aymara (Bolivia; Peru)	2				
Azerbaijani (USSR; Iran)	8	Kamba (E. Africa)	1	Quechua (S. America)	7
		Kanarese (see Kannada)			
Bahasa (see Malay-Indonesian)		Kannada[1] (India)	37	Romanian	24
Balinese	3	Kanuri (W. and Central Africa)	3	Ruanda (S. Central Africa)	7
Baluchi (Pakistan; Iran)	3	Kashmiri[1]	3	Rundi (S. Central Africa)	5
Batak (Indonesia)	2	Kazakh (USSR)	6	Russian (Great Russian only)	282
Bemba (S. Central Africa)	2	Khalkha (Mongolia)	2		
Bengali[1] (Bangladesh; India)	166	Khmer (Kampuchea)	6	Samar-Leyte (Philippines)	2
Berber[2] (N. Africa)		Kikongo (see Kongo)		Sango (Central Africa)	2
Bhili (India)	4	Kikuyu (or Gekoyo)(Kenya)	3	Santali (India)	4
Bikol (Philippines)	2	Kimbundu (see Mbundu-Kimbundu)		Sepedi (see Sotho, Northern)	
Bisaya (see Cebuano, Panay-Hiligaynon,		Kirghiz (USSR)	2	Serbo-Croatian (Yugoslavia)	20
and Samar-Leyte)		Kituba (Congo River)	3	Shan (Burma)	2
Bugi (Indonesia)	3	Kongo (Congo River)	3	Shona (S.E. Africa)	5
Bulgarian	9	Konkani (India)	2	Siamese (see Thai)	
Burmese	28	Korean	64	Sindhi[1] (India; Pakistan)	11
Buyi (China)	1	Kurdish (S.W. of Caspian Sea)	8	Sinhalese (Sri Lanka)	12
Byelorussian (mainly USSR)	9	Kurukh (or Oraon)(India)	1	Slovak	5
				Slovene (Yugoslavia)	2
Cambodian (see Khmer)		Lao[5] (Laos, Asia)	3	Somali (E. Africa)	5
Canarese (see Kannada)		Latvian (or Lettish)	2	Sotho, Northern (S. Africa)	2
Cantonese (China)	58	Lingala (see Ngala)		Sotho, Southern (S. Africa)	3
Catalan (Spain; France; Andorra)	6	Lithuanian	3	Spanish	285
Cebuano (Philippines)	9	Luba-Lulua (Zaire)	3	Sundanese (Indonesia)	17
Chinese[2]		Luganda (see Ganda)		Swahili (E. Africa)	37
Chuang[7] (China)		Luhya (or Luhia)(Kenya)	1	Swedish	9
Chuvash (USSR)	2	Luo (Kenya)	2		
Czech	12	Luri (Iran)	2	Tagalog (Philippines)	30
				Tajiki (USSR)	4
Danish	5	Macedonian (Yugoslavia)	2	Tamil[1] (India; Sri Lanka)	61
Dayak (Borneo)	1	Madurese (Indonesia)	9	Tatar (or Kazan-Turkic)(USSR)	7
Dutch (see Netherlandish)		Makua (S.E. Africa)	3	Telugu[1] (India)	61
		Malagasy (Madagascar)	10	Thai[5]	43
Edo (W. Africa)	1	Malay-Indonesian	125	Thonga (S.E. Africa)	1
Efik	3	Malayalam[1] (India)	32	Tibetan	6
English	415	Malinke-Bambara-Dyula (Africa)	8	Tigrinya (Ethiopia)	4
Esperanto	1	Mandarin (China)	771	Tiv (E. Central Nigeria)	2
Estonian	1	Marathi[1] (India)	60	Tong (China)	1
Ewe (W. Africa)	3	Mazandarani (Iran)	2	Tswana (S. Africa)	3
		Mbundu (Umbundu group)(S.Angola)	3	Tulu (India)	1
Fang-Bulu (W. Africa)	3	Mbundu (Kimbundu group)(Angola)	2	Turkish	50
Finnish	5	Mende (Sierra Leone)	1	Turkoman (USSR)	2
Flemish (see Netherlandish)		Meo (see Miao)		Twi-Fante (or Akan)(W.Africa)	6
French	112	Miao (and Meo)(S.E.Asia)	4		
Fula (W. Africa)	10	Min (China)	44	Uighur (Sinkiang, China)	6
		Minankabau (Indonesia)	4	Ukrainian (mainly USSR)	42
Galician (Spain)	3	Moldavian (inc. with Romanian)		Umbundu (see Mbundu-Umbundu)	
Galla (see Oromo)		Mongolian (see Khalkha)		Urdu[1] (Pakistan; India)	80
Ganda (or Luganda)(E. Africa)	3	Mordvin (USSR)	1	Uzbek (USSR)	10
Georgian (USSR)	3	Moré (see Mossi)			
German	118	Mossi (or Moré)(W. Africa)	3	Vietnamese	50
Gilaki (Iran)	2			Visayan (see Cebuano, Panay-	
Gondi (India)	2	Ndongo (see Mbundu-Kimbundu)		Hiligaynon, and Samar-Leyte)	
Greek	11	Nepali (Nepal; India)	11		
Guarani (mainly Paraguay)	3	Netherlandish (Dutch and Flemish)	20	White Russian (see Byelorussian)	
Gujarati[1] (India)	35	Ngala (or Lingala)(Africa)	3	Wolof (W. Africa)	3
		Norwegian	5	Wu (China)	56
Hakka (China)	25	Nyamwezi-Sukuma (S.E. Africa)	2		
Hani (S.E. Asia)	1	Nyanja (S.E. Africa)	3	Xhosa (S. Africa)	6
Hausa (W. and Central Africa)	28				
Hebrew	3	Oraon (see Kurukh)		Yao (S.E. Asia)	1
Hindi[1,4]	287	Oriya[1] (India)	28	Yi (China)	5
Hindustani[4]		Oromo (Ethiopia)	8	Yiddish[6]	
Hungarian (or Magyar)	14			Yoruba (W. Africa)	16
		Panay-Hiligaynon (Philippines)	4		
Ibibio (see Efik)		Panjabi (see Punjabi)		Zhuang[7] (China)	
Ibo (or Igbo)(W. Africa)	14	Pashto (see Pushtu)		Zulu (S. Africa)	7
Ijaw (W. Africa)	2				

(1) One of the fifteen languages of the Constitution of India. (2) Here considered a group of dialects. (3) See Mandarin, Cantonese, Wu, Min and Hakka. The "national language" (Guoyu) or "common speech" (Putonghua) is a standardized form of Mandarin as spoken in the area of Peking. (4) Hindi and Urdu are essentially the same language, Hindustani. As the official language of India it is written in the Devanagari script and called Hindi. As the official language of Pakistan it is written in a modified Arabic script and called Urdu. (5) Thai includes Central, Southwestern, Northern and Northeastern Thai. The distinction between Northeastern Thai and Lao is political rather than linguistic. (6) Yiddish is usually considered a variant of German, though it has its own standard grammar, dictionaries, a highly developed literature, and is written in Hebrew characters. (7) A group of Thai-like dialects with about 11 million speakers.

PRESIDENTIAL ELECTIONS

Popular and Electoral Vote, 1980 and 1984

Source: News Election Service

States	1980 Electoral Vote Carter	1980 Electoral Vote Reagan	Democrat Carter	Republican Reagan	Indep. Anderson	1984 Electoral Vote Mondale	1984 Electoral Vote Reagan	Democrat Mondale	Republican Reagan
Ala. . . .	0	9	636,730	654,192	16,481	0	9	551,899	872,849
Alas. . .	0	3	41,842	86,112	11,156	0	3	62,007	138,377
Ariz. . .	0	6	246,843	529,688	76,952	0	7	333,854	681,416
Ark. . .	0	6	398,041	403,164	22,468	0	6	338,646	534,774
Cal. . . .	0	45	3,083,652	4,524,835	739,832	0	47	3,815,947	5,305,410
Col. . . .	0	7	368,009	652,264	130,633	0	8	454,975	821,817
Conn. . .	0	8	541,732	677,210	171,807	0	8	569,597	890,877
Del. . . .	0	3	105,754	111,252	16,288	0	3	101,656	152,190
D.C. . . .	3	0	130,231	23,313	16,131	3	0	180,408	29,009
Fla. . . .	0	17	1,419,475	2,046,951	189,692	0	21	1,448,344	2,728,775
Ga. . . .	12	0	890,733	654,168	36,055	12	0	706,628	1,068,722
Ha. . . .	4	0	135,879	130,112	32,021	0	4	147,098	184,934
Ida. . . .	0	4	110,192	290,699	27,058	0	4	108,510	297,523
Ill.	0	26	1,981,413	2,358,094	346,754	0	24	2,086,499	2,707,103
Ind. . . .	0	13	844,197	1,255,656	111,639	0	12	841,481	1,377,230
Ia.	0	8	508,672	676,026	115,633	0	8	605,620	703,088
Kan. . .	0	7	326,150	566,812	68,231	0	7	332,471	674,646
Ky. . . .	0	9	617,417	635,274	31,127	0	9	536,756	815,345
La. . . .	0	10	708,453	792,853	26,345	0	10	651,586	1,037,299
Me. . . .	0	4	220,974	238,522	53,327	0	4	214,515	336,500
Md. . . .	10	0	726,161	680,606	119,537	0	10	787,935	879,918
Mass. . .	0	14	1,053,802	1,056,223	382,539	0	13	1,239,606	1,310,936
Mich. . .	0	21	1,661,532	1,915,225	275,223	0	20	1,529,638	2,251,571
Minn. . .	10	0	954,173	873,268	174,997	10	0	1,036,364	1,032,603
Miss. . .	0	7	429,281	441,089	12,036	0	7	352,192	582,377
Mo. . . .	0	12	931,182	1,074,181	77,920	0	11	848,583	1,274,188
Mon. . .	0	4	118,032	206,814	29,281	0	4	146,742	232,450
Neb. . .	0	5	166,424	419,214	44,854	0	5	187,475	459,135
Nev. . .	0	3	66,666	155,017	17,651	0	4	91,655	188,770
N.H. . .	0	4	108,864	221,705	49,693	0	4	120,377	267,051
N.J. . . .	0	17	1,147,364	1,546,557	234,632	0	16	1,261,323	1,933,630
N.M. . .	0	4	167,826	250,779	29,459	0	5	201,769	307,101
N.Y. . . .	0	41	2,728,372	2,893,831	467,801	0	36	3,119,609	3,664,763
N.C. . . .	0	13	875,635	915,018	52,800	0	13	824,287	1,346,481
N.D. . . .	0	3	79,189	193,695	23,640	0	3	104,429	200,336
Oh. . . .	0	25	1,352,414	2,206,545	254,472	0	23	1,825,440	2,678,559
Okla. . .	0	8	402,026	695,570	38,284	0	8	385,080	861,530
Ore. . . .	0	6	456,890	571,044	112,389	0	7	536,479	685,700
Pa. . . .	0	27	1,933,540	2,261,872	292,921	0	25	2,228,131	2,584,323
R.I. . . .	4	0	198,342	154,393	59,819	0	4	197,106	212,080
S.C. . . .	0	8	428,220	439,277	13,868	0	8	344,459	615,539
S.D. . . .	0	4	103,855	198,343	21,431	0	3	116,113	200,267
Tenn. . .	0	10	783,051	787,361	35,991	0	11	711,714	990,212
Tex. . . .	0	26	1,881,147	2,510,705	111,613	0	29	1,949,276	3,433,428
Ut. . . .	0	4	124,266	439,687	30,284	0	5	155,369	469,105
Vt. . . .	0	3	81,952	94,628	31,761	0	3	95,730	135,865
Va. . . .	0	12	752,174	989,609	95,418	0	12	796,250	1,337,078
Wash. .	0	9	650,193	865,244	185,073	0	10	798,352	1,051,670
W.Va. . .	6	0	367,462	334,206	31,691	0	6	328,125	405,483
Wis. . . .	0	11	981,584	1,088,845	160,657	0	11	995,740	1,198,584
Wyo. . .	0	3	49,427	110,700	12,072	0	3	53,370	133,241
Total . .	49	489	35,481,435	43,899,248	5,719,437	13	525	37,457,215	54,281,858

Presidential Election Returns by Counties

All results are official. Results for New England states are for selected cities or towns due to unavailability of county results. Totals are always statewide.

Source: News Election Service

Alabama

County	Carter 1980 (D)	Reagan 1980 (R)	Anderson 1980 (I)	Mondale 1984 (D)	Reagan 1984 (R)
Autauga	4,295	6,292	125	3,386	6,350
Baldwin	8,448	18,652	414	7,272	24,964
Barbour	4,458	4,171	65	4,591	5,459
Bibb	3,097	2,491	22	2,167	3,487
Blount	5,656	6,819	75	3,738	8,508
Bullock	3,960	1,446	29	3,537	1,697
Butler	4,156	3,810	59	3,641	4,941
Calhoun	17,017	17,475	433	12,752	23,291
Chambers	6,649	4,864	122	5,302	8,024
Cherokee	3,764	2,482	63	3,029	3,225
Chilton	4,706	6,615	60	3,924	8,243
Choctaw	3,680	2,859	22	3,373	3,960
Clarke	5,249	5,059	55	4,452	6,282
Clay	2,858	2,764	34	1,456	3,432
Cleburne	2,050	2,389	34	1,238	3,259
Coffee	6,140	6,760	189	4,370	10,558
Colbert	12,550	6,619	209	11,008	9,530
Conecuh	3,102	2,948	29	2,737	3,538
Coosa	2,383	1,714	19	1,781	2,585
Covington	6,305	7,014	110	3,812	9,944
Crenshaw	2,704	2,478	39	1,904	3,261
Cullman	11,525	10,212	228	7,989	14,782
Dale	4,936	7,247	134	3,215	10,319
Dallas	9,770	7,647	131	10,955	9,585
DeKalb	8,820	9,673	107	7,212	12,098
Elmore	5,947	8,688	171	4,198	11,694
Escambia	5,148	6,513	87	3,853	8,694
Etowah	20,790	16,177	358	19,074	19,243
Fayette	3,389	3,315	47	2,533	4,654
Franklin	6,136	4,448	51	4,601	5,304
Geneva	4,703	4,747	67	2,330	6,308
Greene	3,474	1,034	16	3,675	1,361
Hale	3,583	2,074	56	3,289	2,691
Henry	2,973	2,813	18	2,231	3,952
Houston	7,848	14,884	184	6,488	20,834
Jackson	8,776	4,897	156	7,635	6,730
Jefferson	113,069	132,612	3,509	107,506	158,362
Lamar	3,396	2,778	16	1,910	3,943
Lauderdale	15,379	10,467	431	12,907	15,354
Lawrence	6,112	2,456	64	4,866	4,466
Lee	9,606	10,982	643	9,077	16,757
Limestone	8,180	4,574	183	5,410	8,423
Lowndes	3,577	1,524	15	3,567	1,629
Macon	7,028	1,259	36	7,857	1,543
Madison	30,469	30,604	2,246	26,889	50,428
Marengo	5,178	4,048	35	4,811	5,261
Marion	5,450	5,182	61	3,918	6,771
Marshall	10,854	8,159	283	7,704	12,330
Mobile	46,180	67,515	1,333	47,252	81,923
Monroe	4,262	4,615	43	3,725	5,917
Montgomery	28,018	35,745	985	31,206	43,328
Morgan	14,703	13,214	457	11,324	24,103
Perry	4,208	2,262	28	3,731	2,600
Pickens	4,504	3,582	61	3,586	4,685
Pike	4,417	5,220	83	3,541	6,231
Randolph	3,378	3,279	58	2,439	4,940
Russell	8,123	4,485	137	7,610	6,654
St. Clair	5,236	7,768	121	4,000	10,408
Shelby	7,396	14,957	407	5,884	21,858
Sumter	5,015	2,104	45	4,478	2,493
Talladega	10,159	9,902	140	8,490	14,067
Tallapoosa	7,260	5,958	96	4,458	9,045
Tuscaloosa	19,103	19,750	789	16,066	28,075
Walker	13,616	8,795	82	10,591	12,852
Washington	3,520	3,045	24	3,081	4,434
Wilcox	4,951	2,280	13	2,663	2,337
Winston	3,368	4,981	39	2,624	6,845
Totals	636,730	654,192	16,481	551,899	872,849

Alabama Vote Since 1936

1936, Roosevelt, Dem., 238,195; Landon, Rep., 35,358; Colvin, Proh., 719; Browder, Com., 679; Lemke, Union, 549; Thomas, Soc., 242.

1940, Roosevelt, Dem., 250,726; Willkie, Rep., 42,174; Babson, Proh., 698; Browder, Com., 509; Thomas, Soc., 100.

1944, Roosevelt, Dem., 198,918; Dewey, Rep., 44,540; Watson, Proh., 1,095; Thomas, Soc., 190.

1948, Thurmond, States' Rights, 171,443; Dewey, Rep., 40,930; Wallace, Prog., 1,522; Watson, Proh., 1,085.

1952, Eisenhower, Rep., 149,231; Stevenson, Dem., 275,075; Hamblen, Proh., 1,814.

1956, Stevenson, Dem., 290,844; Eisenhower, Rep. 195,694; Independent electors, 20,323.

1960, Kennedy, Dem., 324,050; Nixon, Rep., 237,981; Faubus, States' Rights, 4,367; Decker, Proh., 2,106; King, Afro-Americans, 1,485; scattering, 236.

1964, Dem. 209,848 (electors unpledged); Goldwater, Rep., 479,085; scattering, 105.

1968, Nixon, Rep., 146,923; Humphrey, Dem., 196,579; Wallace, 3d party, 691,425; Munn, Proh., 4,022.

1972, Nixon, Rep., 728,701; McGovern, Dem., 219,108 plus 37,815 Natl. Demo. Party of Alabama; Schmitz, Conservative, 11,918; Munn., Proh., 8,551.

1976, Carter, Dem., 659,170; Ford, Rep., 504,070; Maddox, Am. Ind., 9,198; Bubar, Proh., 6,669; Hall, Com., 1,954; MacBride, Libertarian, 1,481.

1980, Reagan, Rep., 654,192; Carter, Dem., 636,730; Anderson, Independent, 16,481; Rarick, Amer. Ind., 15,010; Clark, Libertarian, 13,318; Bubar, Statesman, 1,743; Hall, Com., 1,629; DeBerry, Soc. Work., 1,303; McReynolds, Socialist, 1,006; Commoner, Citizens, 517.

1984, Reagan, Rep., 872,849; Mondale, Dem., 551,899; Bergland, Libertarian, 9,504.

Alaska

Election District	Carter 1980 (D)	Reagan 1980 (R)	Anderson 1980 (I)	Mondale 1984 (D)	Reagan 1984 (R)
No. 1	1,772	3,473	440	2,937	5,256
No. 2	1,256	1,612	329	1,857	2,645
No. 3	1,354	2,019	346	1,561	2,540
No. 4	3,899	5,345	1,282	5,293	7,322
No. 5	973	2,847	288	2,896	8,188
No. 6	1,316	5,008	402	1,261	2,883
No. 7	2,620	4,311	676	1,539	4,363
No. 8	2,860	7,432	737	2,752	8,603
No. 9	1,164	2,363	342	3,186	8,361
No. 10	2,778	7,659	849	3,034	7,634
No. 11	3,308	9,741	1,016	2,621	5,176
No. 12	2,456	7,450	829	4,063	5,348
No. 13	1,806	6,170	479	2,616	6,106
No. 14	844	1,473	254	2,843	7,465
No. 15	710	832	213	2,749	8,993
No. 16	1,083	869	204	2,935	9,942
No. 17	1,623	720	280	1,014	3,793
No. 18	1,327	769	193	967	4,858
No. 19	1,168	2,255	267	1,905	3,880
No. 20	5,310	11,673	1,304	2,914	6,538
No. 21	1,022	1,010	223	2,433	3,629
No. 22	1,193	1,081	202	1,319	2,075
No. 23	—	—	—	1,546	2,165
No. 24	—	—	—	1,473	2,321
No. 25	—	—	—	1,825	2,004
No. 26	—	—	—	1,216	3,019
No. 27	—	—	—	1,252	3,270
Totals	41,842	86,112	11,155	62,007	138,377

Alaska Vote Since 1960

1960, Kennedy, Dem., 29,809; Nixon, Rep. 30,953.

1964, Johnson, Dem., 44,329; Goldwater, Rep., 22,930.

1968, Nixon, Rep., 37,600; Humphrey, Dem., 35,411; Wallace, 3d party, 10,024.

1972, Nixon, Rep., 55,349; McGovern, Dem., 32,967; Schmitz, American, 6,903.

1976, Carter, Dem., 44,058; Ford, Rep., 71,555; MacBride, Libertarian, 6,785.

1980, Reagan, Rep., 86,112; Carter, Dem., 41,842; Clark, Libertarian, 18,479; Anderson, Ind., 11,155; Write-in, 857.

1984, Reagan, Rep., 138,377; Mondale, Dem., 62,007; Bergland, Libertarian, 6,378.

Arizona

County	Carter 1980 (D)	Reagan 1980 (R)	Anderson 1980 (I)	Mondale 1984 (D)	Reagan 1984 (R)
Apache	3,917	5,991	495	7,277	5,638
Cochise	7,028	13,351	1,656	9,671	16,405
Coconino	7,832	14,613	2,815	11,528	17,581

......	5,068	7,405	656	6,509	8,543	Izard........	2,750	2,266	160	2,346	2,726

County	1980					County					
....	5,068	7,405	656	6,509	8,543	Izard........	2,750	2,266	160	2,346	2,726
n......	2,801	4,765	268	3,080	5,247	Jackson......	4,651	3,191	174	4,038	3,901
lee......	2,043	1,537	150	1,963	1,801	Jefferson......	17,292	10,697	802	18,082	14,514
az......	—	—	—	1,502	2,757	Johnson......	3,709	3,619	187	3,056	4,720
copa.....	119,752	316,287	38,975	154,833	411,902	Lafayette......	1,947	1,756	47	1,695	2,290
nave......	4,900	13,809	978	7,436	17,364	Lawrence......	3,547	3,245	117	2,594	4,039
navajo......	5,110	10,790	710	8,017	11,379	Lee..........	3,103	1,711	47	2,541	2,101
ma......	64,418	93,055	25,294	91,585	123,830	Lincoln......	2,517	1,243	56	2,406	1,860
inal......	9,207	12,195	1,346	11,923	16,464	Little River.....	2,631	2,272	41	2,090	3,155
Santa Cruz....	2,089	2,674	482	2,463	3,855	Logan........	4,098	4,511	166	3,206	5,663
Yavapai......	6,664	19,823	1,754	9,609	24,802	Lonoke......	5,605	5,619	246	4,636	8,425
Yuma......	6,014	13,393	1,373	6,458	13,848	Madison......	2,434	3,180	126	2,133	3,516
Totals	246,843	529,688	76,952	333,854	681,416	Marion......	2,046	3,059	160	1,945	3,545
						Miller......	5,996	6,770	105	4,686	8,302
						Mississippi.....	8,908	7,170	234	7,548	10,180
						Monroe......	2,686	2,027	82	2,413	2,508
						Montgomery....	1,878	1,585	86	1,497	2,221
						Nevada......	2,631	1,697	50	1,783	2,352
						Newton......	1,436	2,423	100	1,414	2,749
						Ouachita......	7,152	4,329	248	5,858	6,700
						Perry......	1,606	1,459	73	1,404	2,047
						Phillips......	6,642	4,270	163	5,946	4,686
						Pike......	2,094	1,916	58	1,443	2,665
						Poinsett......	4,894	4,040	153	3,906	5,622
						Polk........	2,617	3,993	139	2,101	5,181
						Pope........	6,364	7,217	471	5,082	10,667
						Prairie......	1,928	1,855	64	1,437	2,407
						Pulaski......	54,839	52,125	4,657	54,237	77,651
						Randolph......	3,070	2,579	125	2,507	3,188
						St. Francis.....	5,816	4,485	132	4,866	5,378
						Saline......	10,368	8,330	643	5,977	11,709
						Scott........	2,236	2,228	92	1,609	3,066
						Searcy......	1,536	2,459	101	1,313	2,819
						Sebastian.....	10,141	23,403	1,023	8,688	27,595
						Sevier......	2,854	2,502	97	1,942	3,302
						Sharp........	2,774	3,420	160	2,492	4,392
						Stone........	1,968	1,793	133	1,654	2,325
						Union........	6,852	9,401	313	6,208	12,333
						Van Buren......	2,968	3,090	153	2,529	4,060
						Washington...	12,276	20,788	1,737	11,319	24,993
						White........	8,750	8,079	309	6,603	12,566
						Woodruff......	2,452	1,204	74	2,055	1,675
						Yell........	3,702	3,187	181	2,679	4,051
						Totals	398,041	403,164	22,468	338,646	534,774

Arizona Vote Since 1936

1936, Roosevelt, Dem., 86,722; Landon, Rep., 33,433; Lemke, Union, 3,307; Colvin, Proh., 384; Thomas, Soc., 317.

1940, Roosevelt, Dem., 95,267; Willkie, Rep., 54,030; Babson, Proh., 742.

1944, Roosevelt, Dem., 80,926; Dewey, Rep., 56,287; Watson, Proh., 421.

1948, Truman, Dem., 95,251; Dewey, Rep., 77,597; Wallace, Prog., 3,310; Watson, Proh., 786; Teichert, Soc. Labor, 121.

1952, Eisenhower, Rep., 152,042; Stevenson, Dem., 108,528.

1956, Eisenhower, Rep., 176,990; Stevenson, Dem., 112,880; Andrews, Ind. 303.

1960, Kennedy, Dem., 176,781; Nixon, Rep., 221,241; Hass, Soc. Labor, 469.

1964, Johnson, Dem., 237,753; Goldwater, Rep., 242,535; Hass, Soc. Labor, 482.

1968, Nixon, Rep., 266,721; Humphrey, Dem., 170,514; Wallace, 3d party, 46,573; McCarthy, New Party, 2,751; Halstead, Soc. Worker, 85; Cleaver, Peace and Freedom, 217; Blomen, Soc. Labor, 75.

1972, Nixon, Rep., 402,812; McGovern, Dem., 198,540; Schmitz, Amer., 21,208; Soc. Workers, 30,945. (Due to ballot peculiarities in 3 counties (particularly Pima), thousands of voters cast ballots for the Socialist Workers Party *and* one of the major candidates. Court ordered both votes counted as official.

1976, Carter, Dem., 295,602; Ford, Rep., 418,642; McCarthy, Ind., 19,229; MacBride, Libertarian, 7,647; Camejo, Soc. Workers, 928; Anderson, Amer., 564; Maddox, Am. Ind., 85.

1980, Reagan, Rep., 529,688; Carter, Dem., 246,843; Anderson, Ind., 76,952; Clark, Libertarian, 18,784; De Berry, Soc. Workers, 1,100; Commoner, Citizens, 551; Hall, Com., 25; Griswold, Workers World, 2.

1984, Reagan, Rep., 681,416; Mondale, Dem., 333,854; Bergland, Libertarian, 10,585.

Arkansas

	1980			1984	
County	Carter (D)	Reagan (R)	Anderson (I)	Mondale (D)	Reagan (R)
Arkansas.....	4,303	3,409	193	3,153	4,804
Ashley.......	4,552	3,960	130	3,373	5,675
Baxter......	4,789	9,684	494	4,528	10,870
Benton......	9,231	18,830	1,018	7,306	24,296
Boone.......	4,576	6,778	429	3,356	7,961
Bradley......	3,139	1,650	66	2,313	2,690
Calhoun.....	1,438	896	52	1,058	1,474
Carroll......	2,977	4,273	298	2,263	5,041
Chicot.......	3,445	2,239	26	3,407	2,502
Clark........	6,122	2,743	215	4,638	4,185
Clay........	3,985	3,091	121	3,279	3,767
Cleburne.....	4,021	4,042	204	3,172	5,769
Cleveland	1,856	1,124	36	1,378	1,773
Columbia.....	4,445	5,259	107	3,680	6,526
Conway......	4,698	4,145	232	3,742	5,049
Craighead.....	9,231	11,010	708	8,035	14,047
Crawford.....	3,948	8,542	245	3,071	9,551
Crittenden	7,022	6,248	185	6,520	6,663
Cross.......	3,471	2,895	89	2,701	3,917
Dallas.......	2,838	1,596	74	2,035	2,361
Desha.......	3,748	2,057	77	2,918	2,696
Drew.......	3,757	2,272	117	2,638	3,407
Faulkner......	8,528	7,544	769	7,169	11,595
Franklin......	2,716	3,448	197	2,399	4,382
Fulton......	2,037	2,101	83	1,864	2,329
Garland......	12,515	15,739	1,042	11,484	21,213
Grant	3,078	2,007	102	2,148	3,167
Greene......	5,996	4,514	219	4,730	6,179
Hempstead....	4,671	3,852	72	3,327	4,904
Hot Spring	6,897	3,561	244	5,836	5,629
Howard......	2,564	2,386	63	1,746	3,079
Independence ...	5,683	5,076	276	4,415	7,428

Arkansas Vote Since 1936

1936, Roosevelt, Dem. 146,765; Landon, Rep., 32,039; Thomas, Soc., 446; Browder, Com., 164; Lemke, Union, 4.

1940, Roosevelt, Dem., 158,622; Willkie, Rep., 42,121; Babson, Proh., 793; Thomas, Soc., 305.

1944, Roosevelt, Dem., 148,965; Dewey, Rep., 63,551; Thomas, Soc. 438.

1948, Truman, Dem., 149,659; Dewey, Rep., 50,959; Thurmond, States' Rights, 40,068; Thomas, Soc., 1,037; Wallace, Prog., 751; Watson, Proh., 1.

1952, Eisenhower, Rep., 177,155; Stevenson, Dem., 226,300; Hamblen, Proh., 886; MacArthur, Christian Nationalist, 458; Hass, Soc. Labor, 1.

1956, Stevenson, Dem., 213,277; Eisenhower, Rep., 186,287; Andrews, Ind., 7,008.

1960, Kennedy, Dem., 215,049; Nixon, Rep., 184,508; Nat'l. States' Rights, 28,952.

1964, Johnson, Dem., 314,197; Goldwater, Rep., 243,264; Kasper, Nat'l. States Rights, 2,965.

1968, Nixon, Rep., 189,062; Humphrey, Dem., 184,901; Wallace, 3d party, 235,627.

1972, Nixon, Rep., 445,751; McGovern, Dem., 198,899; Schmitz, Amer. , 3,016.

1976, Carter, Dem., 498,604; Ford, Rep., 267,903; McCarthy, Ind., 639; Anderson, Amer., 389.

1980, Reagan, Rep., 403,164; Carter, Dem., 398,041; Anderson, Ind., 22,468; Clark, Libertarian, 8,970; Commoner, Citizens, 2,345; Bubar, Statesman, 1,350; Hall, Comm., 1,244.

1984, Reagan, Rep., 534,774; Mondale, Dem., 338,646; Bergland, Libertarian, 2,220.

California

	1980			1984	
County	Carter (D)	Reagan (R)	Anderson (I)	Mondale (D)	Reagan (R)
Alameda	201,720	158,531	40,834	279,281	190,029
Alpine........	133	254	50	194	264
Amador......	3,191	5,401	788	4,166	6,970
Butte........	19,520	38,188	6,108	25,126	44,836
Calaveras.....	3,076	6,054	776	3,919	7,339
Colusa.......	1,605	2,897	325	1,715	3,362
Contra Costa...	107,398	144,112	28,209	137,941	167,797
Del Norte......	2,338	4,016	486	2,693	3,989

County	Carter (D)	Reagan (R)	Anderson (I)	Mondale (D)	Reagan (R)
El Dorado	10,765	21,238	3,287	13,969	26,900
Fresno	65,254	82,515	10,727	83,416	101,156
Glenn	2,227	5,386	537	2,480	5,994
Humboldt	17,113	24,047	5,440	24,870	27,495
Imperial	7,961	12,068	1,203	8,231	13,816
Inyo	2,080	5,201	515	2,348	5,811
Kern	41,097	72,842	5,799	44,523	85,872
Kings	7,299	10,531	901	7,317	13,357
Lake	5,978	8,934	1,157	8,292	10,291
Lassen	2,941	4,464	543	3,253	5,338
Los Angeles	979,830	1,224,533	175,882	1,114,578	1,370,813
Madera	7,783	10,599	1,013	8,701	13,853
Marin	39,231	49,678	13,805	56,796	55,845
Mariposa	1,889	3,082	458	2,121	3,571
Mendocino	10,784	12,432	2,747	14,172	16,107
Merced	15,886	18,043	2,316	16,875	25,003
Modoc	1,046	2,579	293	1,219	2,995
Mono	865	2,132	302	944	2,630
Monterey	29,086	47,452	8,008	39,676	54,440
Napa	14,898	23,632	4,218	18,234	25,715
Nevada	7,605	15,207	2,235	10,941	19,440
Orange	176,704	529,797	55,299	200,477	615,099
Placer	17,311	28,179	4,356	20,527	36,565
Plumas	2,911	4,182	783	3,709	5,079
Riverside	76,650	145,642	16,362	99,853	178,397
Sacramento	130,031	153,721	29,655	153,450	197,957
San Benito	2,749	4,054	552	3,454	5,530
San Bernardino	91,790	172,957	19,106	114,710	217,556
San Diego	195,410	459,510	67,491	251,134	487,362
San Francisco	133,184	80,967	29,365	190,396	88,683
San Joaquin	41,551	64,718	8,416	53,441	81,084
San Luis Obispo	20,508	38,631	8,407	26,626	48,331
San Mateo	87,335	116,491	27,985	120,853	133,912
Santa Barbara	40,650	69,629	14,786	49,505	85,458
Santa Clara	166,995	229,048	65,481	224,032	280,425
Santa Cruz	32,346	37,347	10,590	47,240	39,862
Shasta	15,364	27,547	3,220	19,178	32,854
Sierra	651	855	156	781	1,078
Siskiyou	5,664	9,531	1,269	7,130	10,544
Solano	30,952	40,919	6,713	41,435	50,867
Sonoma	45,596	60,722	14,068	69,383	74,014
Stanislaus	33,683	41,595	7,134	36,599	54,085
Sutter	5,103	11,778	1,089	5,526	14,425
Tehama	4,832	9,140	1,014	6,511	11,536
Trinity	1,734	3,048	506	2,204	3,525
Tulare	25,155	41,317	3,244	27,707	50,262
Tuolumne	5,449	8,810	1,390	7,212	10,376
Ventura	56,311	114,930	14,887	64,623	146,647
Yolo	21,527	19,603	6,669	25,264	23,604
Yuba	4,896	7,942	878	4,996	9,265
Totals	3,083,661	4,524,858	739,833	3,815,947	5,305,410

California Vote Since 1936

1936, Roosevelt, Dem., 1,766,836; Landon, Rep., 836,431; Colvin, Proh., 12,917; Thomas, Soc., 11,325; Browder, Com., 10,877.

1940, Roosevelt, Dem., 1,877,618; Willkie, Rep., 1,351,419; Thomas, Prog., 16,506; Browder, Com., 13,586; Babson, Proh., 9,400.

1944, Roosevelt, Dem., 1,988,564; Dewey, Rep., 1,512,965; Watson, Proh., 14,770; Thomas, Soc., 3,923; Teichert, Soc. Labor, 327.

1948, Truman, Dem., 1,913,134; Dewey, Rep., 1,895,269; Wallace, Prog., 190,381; Watson, Proh., 16,926; Thomas, Soc., 3,459; Thurmond, States' Rights, 1,228; Teichert, Soc. Labor, 195; Dobbs, Soc. Workers, 133.

1952, Eisenhower, Rep., 2,897,310; Stevenson, Dem., 2,197,548; Hallinan, Prog., 24,106; Hamblen, Proh., 15,653; MacArthur, (Tenny Ticket) 3,326; (Kellems Ticket) 178; Hass, Soc. Labor, 273; Hoopes, Soc., 206; scattered, 3,249.

1956, Eisenhower, Rep., 3,027,668; Stevenson, Dem., 2,420,136; Holtwick, Proh., 11,119; Andrews, Constitution, 6,087; Hass, Soc. Labor, 300; Hoopes, Soc., 123; Dobbs, Soc. Workers, 96; Smith, Christian Nat'l., 8.

1960, Kennedy, Dem., 3,224,099; Nixon, Rep., 3,259,722; Decker, Proh., 21,706; Hass, Soc. Labor, 1,051.

1964, Johnson, Dem., 4,171,877; Goldwater, Rep., 2,879,108; Hass, Soc. Labor, 489; DeBerry, Soc. Worker, 378; Munn, Proh., 305; Hensley, Universal, 19.

1968, Nixon, Rep., 3,467,664; Humphrey, Dem., 3,244,318; Wallace, 3d party, 487,270; Peace and Freedom party, 27,707; McCarthy, Alternative, 20,721; Gregory, write-in, 3,230; Mitchell, Com., 260; Munn, Proh., 59; Blomen, Soc. Labor, 341; Soeters, Defense, 17.

1972, Nixon, Rep., 4,602,096; McGovern, Dem., 3,475,847; Schmitz, Amer., 232,554; Spock, Peace and Freedom, 55,167; Hall, Com., 373; Hospers, Libertarian, 980; Munn, Proh., 53; Fisher, Soc. Labor, 197; Jenness, Workers, 574; Green, Universal, 21.

1976, Carter, Dem., 3,742,284; Ford, Rep., 3,882,244; Ma Bride, Libertarian, 56,388; Maddox, Am. Ind., 51,09 Wright, People's, 41,731; Camejo, Soc. Workers, 17,259 Hall, Com., 12,766; write-in, McCarthy, 58,412; other write-in, 4,935.

1980, Reagan, Rep. 4,524,858; Carter, Dem., 3,083,661; Anderson, Ind., 739,833; Clark, Libertarian, 148,434; Commoner, Ind. 61,063; Smith, Peace & Freedom, 18,116; Rarick, Amer. Ind., 9,856.

1984, Reagan, Rep. 5,305,410; Mondale, Dem., 3,815,947; Bergland, Libertarian, 48,400.

Colorado

County	1980 Carter (D)	Reagan (R)	Anderson (I)	1984 Mondale (D)	Reagan (R)
Adams	31,357	42,916	8,342	35,285	55,092
Alamosa	1,821	2,601	289	1,720	2,953
Arapahoe	30,148	79,594	15,329	39,891	107,556
Archuleta	532	1,252	83	584	1,557
Baca	551	1,999	106	580	1,903
Bent	894	1,206	164	859	1,314
Boulder	28,422	40,698	13,712	42,195	53,535
Chaffee	1,583	3,327	432	1,779	3,680
Cheyenne	322	816	76	307	892
Clear Creek	837	1,784	402	1,089	2,151
Conejos	1,503	1,597	90	1,553	1,669
Costilla	1,036	489	38	997	621
Crowley	472	926	57	517	993
Custer	231	674	59	241	832
Delta	2,348	6,179	455	2,835	6,678
Denver	85,903	88,398	28,610	110,200	105,096
Dolores	157	615	32	173	667
Douglas	2,108	8,126	1,058	3,011	12,249
Eagle	1,608	3,061	906	2,032	4,500
Elbert	698	2,107	238	802	2,605
El Paso	27,463	66,199	7,886	28,185	88,377
Fremont	3,952	7,162	731	3,895	8,250
Garfield	2,639	5,416	978	3,076	7,111
Gilpin	441	694	175	634	896
Grand	820	2,133	413	1,017	2,865
Gunnison	1,297	2,756	704	1,424	3,100
Hinsdale	76	232	13	98	310
Huerfano	1,574	1,258	146	1,602	1,581
Jackson	283	673	80	191	722
Jefferson	41,525	97,008	19,530	53,700	124,496
Kiowa	331	754	61	265	850
Kit Carson	790	2,622	185	778	2,762
Lake	1,213	1,375	289	1,324	1,364
La Plata	3,034	7,291	1,537	4,040	8,719
Larimer	17,072	36,240	8,887	23,896	49,883
Las Animas	4,117	2,917	278	3,670	2,992
Lincoln	602	1,535	175	587	1,661
Logan	2,332	5,238	588	2,155	5,883
Mesa	7,549	22,686	2,004	9,938	23,736
Mineral	125	271	41	117	333
Moffat	1,079	3,344	329	1,228	3,630
Montezuma	1,467	4,120	275	1,665	4,753
Montrose	2,232	6,685	635	2,864	7,162
Morgan	2,246	5,209	693	2,331	6,097
Otero	3,294	4,801	572	3,005	5,373
Ouray	237	813	129	366	914
Park	674	1,623	293	782	2,041
Philips	640	1,488	193	651	1,689
Pitkin	1,760	2,153	1,128	2,293	3,117
Prowers	1,669	3,115	340	1,467	3,501
Pueblo	21,874	20,770	3,102	27,126	24,634
Rio Blanco	462	1,971	143	484	2,131
Rio Grande	1,370	2,844	185	1,104	3,122
Routt	1,944	3,574	920	2,051	4,239
Saguache	893	1,124	71	867	1,201
San Juan	146	268	94	183	320
San Miguel	651	774	297	654	833
Sedgwick	438	1,151	100	429	1,146
Summit	1,285	2,027	845	1,588	3,253
Teller	802	2,457	322	1,043	3,460
Washington	568	2,007	160	568	2,080
Weld	11,433	23,901	4,309	13,863	31,293
Yuma	1,043	3,220	319	1,121	3,394
Total	367,973	652,264	130,633	454,975	821,817

Colorado Vote Since 1936

1936, Roosevelt, Dem., 295,081; Landon, Rep., 181,267; Lemke, Union, 9,962; Thomas, Soc., 1,593; Browder, Com., 497; Aiken, Soc. Labor, 336.

1940, Roosevelt, Dem., 265,554; Willkie, Rep., 279,576; Thomas, Soc., 1,899; Babson, Proh., 1,597; Browder, Com., 378.

Roosevelt, Dem., 234,331; Dewey, Rep., 268,731; ...omas, Soc., 1,977.

..., Truman, Dem., 267,288; Dewey, Rep., 239,714; ...vallace, Prog., 6,115; Thomas, Soc., 1,678; Dobbs, Soc. Workers, 228; Teichert, Soc. Labor, 214.

...952, Eisenhower, Rep., 379,782; Stevenson, Dem., 245,504; MacArthur, Constitution, 2,181; Hallinan, Prog., 1,919; Hoopes, Soc., 365; Hass, Soc. Labor, 352.

1956, Eisenhower, Rep., 394,479; Stevenson, Dem., 263,997; Hass, Soc. Lab., 3,308; Andrews, Ind., 759; Hoopes, Soc., 531.

1960, Kennedy, Dem., 330,629; Nixon, Rep., 402,242; Hass, Soc. Labor, 2,803; Dobbs, Soc. Workers, 572.

1964, Johnson, Dem., 476,024; Goldwater, Rep., 296,767; Hass, Soc. Labor, 302; DeBerry, Soc. Worker, 2,537; Munn, Proh., 1,356.

1968, Nixon, Rep., 409,345; Humphrey, Dem., 335,174; Wallace, 3d party, 60,813; Blomen, Soc. Labor, 3,016; Gregory, New-party, 1,393; Munn, Proh., 275; Halstead, Soc. Worker, 235.

1972, Nixon, Rep., 597,189; McGovern, Dem., 329,980; Fisher, Soc. Labor, 4,361; Hospers, Libertarian, 1,111; Hall, Com., 432; Jenness, Soc. Workers, 555; Munn, Proh., 467; Schmitz, Amer., 17,269; Spock, Peoples, 2,403.

1976, Carter, Dem., 460,353; Ford, Rep., 584,367; McCarthy, Ind., 26,107; MacBride, Libertarian, 5,330; Bubar, Proh., 2,882.

1980, Reagan, Rep., 652,264; Carter, Dem., 367,973; Anderson, Ind., 130,633; Clark, Libertarian, 25,744; Commoner, Citizens, 5,614; Bubar, Statesman, 1,180; Pulley, Socialist, 520; Hall, Com., 487.

1984, Reagan, Rep., 821,817; Mondale, Dem., 454,975; Bergland, Libertarian, 11,257.

Connecticut

City	1980 Carter (D)	Reagan (R)	Anderson (I)	1984 Mondale (D)	Reagan (R)
Bridgeport	23,505	19,185	2,793	24,332	24,256
Hartford	27,657	8,138	3,441	29,327	11,621
New Britain	15,649	10,292	3,203	14,608	13,723
New Haven	26,648	14,388	3,930	32,518	16,483
Norwalk	11,785	16,696	3,284	12,509	22,447
Stamford	17,633	23,250	4,669	19,432	29,167
Waterbury	17,992	19,461	3,853	18,217	24,764
West Hartford	14,662	16,590	6,807	16,882	20,517
Totals	541,732	677,210	171,807	569,597	890,877

Connecticut Vote Since 1936

1936, Roosevelt, Dem., 382,129; Landon, Rep., 278,685; Lemke, Union, 21,805; Thomas, Soc., 5,683; Browder, Com., 1,193.

1940, Roosevelt, Dem., 417,621; Willkie, Rep., 361,021; Browder, Com., 1,091; Aiken, Soc. Labor, 971; Willkie, Union, 798.

1944, Roosevelt, Dem., 435,146; Dewey, Rep., 390,527; Thomas, Soc., 5,097; Teichert, Soc. Labor, 1,220.

1948, Truman, Dem., 423,297; Dewey, Rep., 437,754; Wallace, Prog., 13,713; Thomas, Soc., 6,964; Teichert, Soc. Labor, 1,184; Dobbs, Soc. Workers, 606.

1952, Eisenhower, Rep., 611,012; Stevenson, Dem., 481,649; Hoopes, Soc., 2,244; Hallinan, Peoples, 1,466; Hass, Soc. Labor, 535; write-in, 5.

1956, Eisenhower, Rep., 711,837; Stevenson, Dem., 405,079; scattered, 205.

1960, Kennedy, Dem., 657,055; Nixon, Rep., 565,813.

1964, Johnson, Dem., 826,269; Goldwater, Rep., 390,996; scattered, 1,313.

1968, Nixon, Rep., 556,721; Humphrey, Dem., 621,561; Wallace, 3d party, 76,650; scattered, 1,300.

1972, Nixon, Rep., 810,763; McGovern, Dem., 555,498; Schmitz, Amer., 17,239; scattered, 777.

1976, Carter, Dem., 647,895; Ford, Rep., 719,261; Maddox, George Wallace Party, 7,101; LaRouche, U.S. Labor, 1,789.

1980, Reagan, Rep., 677,210; Carter, Dem., 541,732; Anderson, Ind., 171,807; Clark, Libertarian, 8,570; Commoner, Citizens, 6,130; scattered, 836.

1984, Reagan, Rep., 890,877; Mondale, Dem., 569,597.

Delaware

County	1980 Carter (D)	Reagan (R)	Anderson (I)	1984 Mondale (D)	Reagan (R)
Kent	12,884	14,882	1,831	11,789	21,531
New Castle	76,897	76,898	12,828	76,238	102,322
Sussex	15,973	19,472	1,629	13,629	28,337
Totals	105,754	111,252	16,288	101,656	152,190

Delaware Vote Since 1936

1936, Roosevelt, Dem., 69,702; Landon, Rep. 54,014; Lemke, Union, 442; Thomas, Soc., 179; Browder, Com., 52.

1940, Roosevelt, Dem., 74,559; Willkie, Rep., 61,440; Babson, Proh., 220; Thomas, Soc., 115.

1944, Roosevelt, Dem., 68,166; Dewey, Rep., 56,747; Watson, Proh., 294; Thomas, Soc., 154.

1948, Truman, Dem., 67,813; Dewey, Rep., 69,688; Wallace, Prog., 1,050; Watson, Proh., 343; Thomas, Soc., 250; Teichert, Soc. Labor, 29.

1952, Eisenhower, Rep., 90,059; Stevenson, Dem., 83,315; Hass, Soc. Labor, 242; Hamblen, Proh., 234; Hallinan, Prog., 155; Hoopes, Soc., 20.

1956, Eisenhower, Rep., 98,057; Stevenson, Dem., 79,421; Oltwick, Proh., 400; Hass, Soc. Labor, 110.

1960, Kennedy, Dem., 99,590; Nixon, Rep., 96,373; Faubus, States' Rights, 354; Decker, Proh., 284; Hass, Soc. Labor, 82.

1964, Johnson, Dem., 122,704; Goldwater, Rep., 78,078; Hass, Soc. Labor, 113; Munn, Proh., 425.

1968, Nixon, Rep., 96,714; Humphrey, Dem., 89,194; Wallace, 3d party, 28,459.

1972, Nixon, Rep., 140,357; McGovern, Dem., 92,283; Schmitz, Amer., 2,638; Munn, Proh., 238.

1976, Carter, Dem., 122,596; Ford, Rep., 109,831; McCarthy, non-partisan, 2,437; Anderson, Amer., 645; LaRouche, U.S. Labor, 136; Bubar, Proh., 103; Levin, Soc. Labor, 86.

1980, Reagan, Rep., 111,252; Carter, Dem., 105,754; Anderson, Ind., 16,288; Clark, Libertarian, 1,974; Greaves, American, 400.

1984, Reagan, Rep., 152,190; Mondale, Dem., 101,656; Bergland, Libertarian, 268.

District of Columbia

County	1980 Carter (D)	Reagan (R)	Anderson (I)	1984 Mondale (D)	Reagan (R)
Totals	130,231	23,313	16,131	180,408	29,009

District of Columbia Vote Since 1964

1964, Johnson, Dem., 169,796; Goldwater, Rep., 28,801.

1968, Nixon, Rep., 31,012; Humphrey, Dem., 139,566.

1972, Nixon, Rep., 35,226; McGovern, Dem., 127,627; Reed, Soc. Workers, 316; Hall, Com., 252.

1976, Carter, Dem., 137,818; Ford, Rep., 27,873; Camejo, Soc. Workers, 545; MacBride, Libertarian, 274; Hall, Com., 219; LaRouche, U.S. Labor, 157.

1980, Reagan, Rep., 23,313; Carter, Dem., 130,231; Anderson, Ind., 16,131; Commoner, Citizens, 1,826; Clark, Libertarian, 1,104; Hall, Com., 369; De Berry, Soc. Work., 173; Griswold, Workers World, 52; write-ins, 690.

1984, Mondale, Dem., 180,408; Reagan, Rep., 29,009; Bergland, Libertarian, 279.

Florida

County	1980 Carter (D)	Reagan (R)	Anderson (I)	1984 Mondale (D)	Reagan (R)
Alachua	26,817	19,771	4,167	26,551	30,582
Baker	2,606	2,271	56	1,381	3,485
Bay	12,338	20,815	720	9,381	29,322
Bradford	3,340	2,771	89	2,341	4,128
Brevard	38,915	69,228	5,820	36,963	102,339
Broward	146,322	229,693	31,553	194,542	254,501
Calhoun	2,295	1,504	52	1,312	2,493
Charlotte	9,750	20,433	1,204	11,303	27,464
Citrus	9,148	14,276	784	10,463	20,754
Clay	7,589	15,497	679	5,488	21,545
Collier	7,735	23,878	1,675	9,065	33,603
Columbia	5,677	5,638	246	4,261	8,807
Dade	210,683	265,550	44,723	223,793	324,216
De Soto	2,709	3,340	155	2,302	4,822

County				
Dixie	2,007	1,098	45	1,224	2,204
Duval	90,330	98,389	5,153 ·	77,459	128,653
Escambia	33,378	51,443	2,595	26,798	66,638
Flagler	2,494	2,876	153	2,999	4,907
Franklin	1,772	1,500	53	1,089	2,218
Gadsden	8,207	3,708	201	7,359	5,605
Gilchrist	1,625	1,089	55	1,051	2,056
Glades	1,203	1,096	61	1,070	1,987
Gulf	2,680	2,116	56	1,783	3,573
Hamilton	1,921	1,301	40	1,401	1,921
Hardee	2,597	2,595	83	1,536	3,957
Hendry	2,540	2,696	130	2,018	4,524
Hernando	8,835	12,099	852	12,204	21,273
Highlands	6,685	11,914	531	7,217	16,465
Hillsborough	88,221	106,080	8,939	86,189	157,827
Holmes	2,767	3,208	68	1,231	4,547
Indian River	7,748	15,545	1,184 ·	8,731	23,694
Jackson	7,549	6,331	158	4,956	9,086
Jefferson	2,366	1,621	96	2,055	2,244
Lafayette	1,034	795	22	862	1,513
Lake	13,121	26,775	1,240	12,215	35,304
Lee	28,007	60,717	4,191	30,011	85,006
Leon	28,420	24,840	3,181	29,654	36,301
Levy	4,170	3,203	175	3,103	5,561
Liberty	1,111	895	24	649	1,409
Madison	3,129	2,275	65	2,101	2,816
Manatee	21,660	40,506	2,921	20,887	55,775
Marion	15,362	23,668	1,173	16,221	37,796
Martin	8,078	20,493	1,317	8,976	28,897
Monroe	7,875	11,546	1,914	7,771	16,316
Nassau	5,051	5,414	178	3,483	8,033
Okaloosa	10,738	27,665	1,080	7,289	36,963
Okeechobee	3,226	2,778	156	2,226	4,447
Orange	48,732	87,375	5,389	48,737	122,007
Osceola	6,594	10,839	560	6,627	16,344
Palm Beach	91,932	143,491	15,178	116,071	186,755
Pasco	34,045	50,080	3,565	40,961	66,609
Pinellas	138,307	185,482	17,789	128,547	240,535
Polk	43,291	59,600	2,618	35,505	84,174
Putnam	8,898	8,258	410	7,821	11,424
St. Johns	6,879	11,179	546	6,652	16,493
St. Lucie	10,341	18,107	1,109	13,039	28,189
Santa Rosa	6,964	13,802	606	4,646	21,237
Sarasota	25,557	67,946	4,773	30,512	67,713
Seminole	17,431	39,970	2,451	17,789	56,229
Sumter	4,378	3,666	141	3,460	6,252
Suwannee	4,345	3,894	135	2,788	6,079
Taylor	2,955	2,772	78	1,728	4,030
Union	1,235	1,120	45	761	1,804
Volusia	44,476	52,598	3,296	43,811	68,317
Wakulla	2,078	2,014	111	1,469	3,087
Walton	4,323	4,651	194	2,500	7,117
Washington	3,095	3,222	92	1,916	4,603
Totals	1,419,475	2,046,951	189,692	1,448,344	2,728,775

Florida Vote Since 1936

1936, Roosevelt, Dem., 249,117; Landon, Rep., 78,248.

1940, Roosevelt, Dem., 359,334; Willkie, Rep., 126,158.

1944, Roosevelt, Dem., 339,377; Dewey, Rep., 143,215.

1948, Truman, Dem., 281,988; Dewey, Rep., 194,280; Thurmond, States' Rights, 89,755; Wallace, Prog., 11,620.

1952, Eisenhower, Rep., 544,036; Stevenson, Dem., 444,950; scattered, 351.

1956, Eisenhower, Rep., 643,849; Stevenson, Dem., 480,371.

1960, Kennedy, Dem., 748,700; Nixon, Rep., 795,476.

1964, Johnson, Dem., 948,540; Goldwater, Rep., 905,941.

1968, Nixon, Rep., 886,804; Humphrey, Dem., 676,794; Wallace, 3d party, 624,207.

1972, Nixon, Rep., 1,857,759; McGovern, Dem., 718,117; scattered, 7,407.

1976, Carter, Dem., 1,636,000; Ford, Rep., 1,469,531; McCarthy, Ind., 23,643; Anderson, Amer., 21,325.

1980, Reagan, Rep., 2,046,951; Carter, Dem., 1,419,475; Anderson, Ind., 189,692; Clark, Libertarian, 30,524; write-ins, 285.

1984, Reagan, Rep., 2,728,775; Mondale, Dem., 1,448,344.

Georgia

	1980			1984	
County	Carter (D)	Reagan (R)	Anderson (I)	Mondale (D)	Reagan (R)
Appling	2,985	1,961	41	1,958	2,929
Atkinson	1,449	747	16	901	944
Bacon	1,622	1,427	32	1,010	1,778
Baker	1,035	510	11	691	675
Baldwin	4,368	3,639	230	3,853	5,717
Banks	2,091	746	18	1,063	1,549
Barrow	3,876	2,284	99	2,367	4,123
Bartow	7,490	3,135	135	4,780	7,104
Ben Hill	2,544	1,459	41	1,859	2,313
Berrien	2,869	1,487	24	1,670	2,395
Bibb	31,770	15,175	848	26,427	24,170
Bleckley	2,014	1,261	47	1,465	1,912

County				
Brantley	2,066	882	17	1,517	
Brooks	2,230	1,546	39	1,661	
Bryan	1,966	1,212	51	1,398	2,
Bulloch	4,921	3,750	160	3,644	6,
Burke	3,047	1,871	56	3,127	3,1
Butts	2,574	1,210	38	1,820	2,1
Calhoun	1,414	652	16	1,077	77
Camden	2,924	1,439	62	2,164	2,841
Candler	1,358	1,030	24	1,014	1,497
Carroll	8,202	5,815	294	5,590	11,436
Catoosa	4,921	5,962	121	3,089	7,908
Charlton	1,469	779	26	1,111	1,868
Chatham	28,635	26,499	1,244	28,271	38,482
Chattahoochee	476	256	16	428	459
Chattooga	4,279	1,946	61	2,576	2,953
Cherokee	6,020	5,250	230	3,499	11,146
Clarke	10,519	8,094	1,060	10,132	11,503
Clay	909	316	9	750	419
Clayton	17,540	19,160	923	11,763	31,553
Clinch	1,325	513	18	625	862
Cobb	39,157	51,977	3,229	28,414	97,429
Coffee	4,038	2,499	58	2,633	4,200
Colquitt	5,353	3,593	80	3,208	5,815
Columbia	5,335	6,293	248	3,727	12,294
Cook	2,461	1,186	25	1,510	1,860
Coweta	5,697	4,480	161	3,650	7,981
Crawford	1,673	642	35	1,423	1,298
Crisp	3,403	1,861	54	2,128	2,895
Dade	1,735	2,114	62	1,150	2,750
Dawson	1,072	729	23	643	1,322
Decatur	3,242	2,919	54	2,656	4,134
DeKalb	82,743	74,904	7,241	77,329	104,697
Dodge	4,635	1,719	56	2,513	2,765
Dooly	2,364	1,083	31	1,726	1,435
Dougherty	13,430	12,726	326	12,904	16,920
Douglas	6,807	6,945	304	4,371	12,428
Early	2,110	1,538	23	1,494	2,239
Echols	515	259	8	227	453
Effingham	2,783	2,528	38	2,055	4,266
Elbert	4,014	1,967	50	2,670	3,366
Emanuel	3,971	2,199	45	2,458	3,920
Evans	1,456	1,090	20	1,193	1,601
Fannin	2,526	3,196	61	1,965	4,159
Fayette	3,798	6,351	272	2,861	12,575
Floyd	13,710	9,220	398	8,873	15,437
Forsyth	4,325	3,157	160	2,275	6,841
Franklin	3,528	1,387	30	1,838	2,549
Fulton	118,748	64,909	6,738	125,567	95,149
Gilmer	2,246	2,170	72	1,234	2,972
Glascock	614	510	7	317	827
Glynn	7,540	7,214	296	6,574	11,724
Gordon	5,199	3,107	141	2,607	5,566
Grady	3,023	2,018	56	2,261	3,886
Greene	2,571	961	29	1,992	1,599
Gwinnett	21,958	27,185	1,497	14,139	54,749
Habersham	4,394	2,224	100	2,125	4,647
Hall	12,124	7,760	463	7,421	15,076
Hancock	2,205	573	23	2,109	644
Haralson	3,606	2,229	71	1,938	3,945
Harris	2,807	2,001	100	2,096	3,138
Hart	4,539	1,577	59	2,496	2,842
Heard	1,348	875	35	810	1,492
Henry	5,635	5,326	163	4,096	9,142
Houston	10,915	9,005	536 ·	9,226	14,255
Irwin	1,555	1,056	11	905	1,330
Jackson	4,591	2,209	107	2,717	4,202
Jasper	1,546	879	38	1,122	1,431
Jeff Davis	2,059	1,191	40	1,380	2,233
Jefferson	3,305	1,605	44	2,816	2,999
Jenkins	1,632	824	24	1,108	1,399
Johnson	1,854	1,123	29	1,199	1,733
Jones	3,239	1,828	112	2,781	3,401
Lamar	2,453	1,298	42	1,605	2,198
Lanier	1,116	470	9	741	852
Laurens	7,860	4,392	147	5,471	7,181
Lee	1,670	1,942	26	1,284	2,972
Liberty	3,099	1,507	49	2,803	3,229
Lincoln	1,617	806	10	1,115	1,357
Long	1,202	514	23	816	1,099
Lowndes	5,989	6,622	214	6,167	10,437
Lumpkin	1,951	1,024	83	1,110	1,991
McDuffie	2,667	1,928	59	2,006	3,284
McIntosh	2,104	876	38	1,796	1,512
Macon	3,025	694	39	2,521	1,515
Madison	2,980	2,330	59	1,690	3,768
Marion	1,174	567	16	951	846
Meriwether	3,876	1,838	59	2,664	3,195
Miller	1,127	900	19	526	1,348
Mitchell	3,566	2,231	40	2,791	2,737
Monroe	2,542	1,242	43	2,189	2,420
Montgomery	1,663	948	23	950	1,365
Morgan	2,276	1,323	57	1,714	2,301
Murray	3,094	1,538	42	1,649	3,521
Muscogee	23,272	15,203	811	20,835	23,816
Newton	5,611	3,205	150	3,389	5,810
Oconee	2,141	2,065	106	1,467	3,471
Oglethorpe	1,611	1,187	44	1,238	2,122
Paulding	4,686	2,845	97	2,621	6,048
Peach	3,415	1,642	68	3,369	2,652
Pickens	2,358	1,612	73	1,329	2,801

	1980 Carter (D)	Reagan (R)	Anderson (I)	1984 Mondale (D)	Reagan (R)
...e........	1,918	1,027	21	1,501	1,978
....	1,755	1,271	45	1,203	1,855
...k.....	5,421	2,949	116	3,262	5,435
...aski......	1,997	1,153	54	1,440	1,509
...tnam......	1,951	1,166	35	1,336	1,830
Quitman......	589	240	2	490	361
Rabun....	2,327	1,070	67	1,267	2,191
Randolph......	1,861	879	1	1,454	1,578
Richmond.....	24,104	19,619	887	21,208	29,869
Rockdale......	4,395	5,300	219	3,291	10,121
Schley......	613	453	9	403	614
Screven......	2,117	1,490	36	1,747	2,583
Seminole......	1,794	1,117	16	1,350	1,636
Spalding......	7,176	4,809	248	4,878	8,571
Stephens......	4,529	2,045	69	2,272	4,057
Stewart......	1,440	611	23	1,308	805
Sumter......	4,956	2,657	103	3,725	4,607
Talbot......	1,635	572	20	1,494	778
Taliaferro......	670	270	8	550	318
Tattnall......	2,864	2,082	37	1,954	3,641
Taylor......	1,845	815	19	1,340	1,292
Telfair......	2,700	1,173	41	2,049	1,980
Terrell......	2,010	1,378	21	1,598	1,744
Thomas......	5,695	4,294	117	4,039	6,427
Tift......	4,572	3,280	99	2,736	4,429
Toombs......	3,255	2,835	68	2,385	4,470
Towns......	1,510	1,475	57	1,007	1,960
Treutlen......	1,307	668	21	843	1,086
Troup......	7,716	5,398	191	5,272	9,340
Turner......	1,990	898	16	1,270	1,329
Twiggs......	2,213	747	8	1,755	1,143
Union......	1,700	1,546	43	1,112	1,914
Upson......	4,713	2,788	77	2,943	4,803
Walker......	6,809	7,088	171	5,000	10,734
Walton......	4,525	2,618	112	2,481	4,995
Ware......	6,307	3,715	77	4,435	5,547
Warren......	1,517	779	20	1,258	1,087
Washington......	3,452	1,822	60	3,034	2,887
Wayne......	3,843	2,213	52	2,434	3,698
Webster......	608	312	8	534	402
Wheeler......	1,599	550	28	774	833
White......	2,017	1,175	58	1,090	2,369
Whitfield......	9,691	6,404	229	5,284	11,957
Wilcox......	1,780	827	13	1,212	1,218
Wilkes......	2,350	1,212	31	1,586	1,837
Wilkinson......	2,365	1,116	31	2,102	1,756
Worth......	2,567	2,076	35	1,685	2,910
Totals......	890,955	654,168	36,055	706,628	1,068,722

Georgia Vote Since 1936

1936, Roosevelt, Dem., 255,364; Landon, Rep., 36,942; Colvin, Proh., 660; Lemke, Union, 141; Thomas, Soc., 68.

1940, Roosevelt, Dem., 265,194; Willkie, Rep., 23,934; Ind. Dem., 22,428; total, 46,362; Babson, Proh., 983.

1944, Roosevelt, Dem., 268,187; Dewey, Rep., 56,506; Watson, Proh., 36.

1948, Truman, Dem., 254,646; Dewey, Rep., 76,691; Thurmond, States' Rights, 85,055; Wallace, Prog., 1,636; Watson, Proh., 732.

1952, Eisenhower, Rep., 198,979; Stevenson, Dem., 456,823; Liberty Party, 1.

1956, Stevenson, Dem., 444,388; Eisenhower, Rep., 222,778; Andrews, Ind., write-in, 1,754.

1960, Kennedy, Dem., 458,638; Nixon, Rep., 274,472; write-in, 239.

1964, Johnson, Dem., 522,557; Goldwater, Rep., 616,600.

1968, Nixon, Rep., 380,111; Humphrey, Dem., 334,440; Wallace, 3d party, 535,550; write-in, 162.

1972, Nixon, Rep., 881,496; McGovern, Dem., 289,529; Schmitz, Amer., 2,288; scattered.

1976, Carter, Dem., 979,409; Ford, Rep., 483,743; write-in, 4,306.

1980, Reagan, Rep., 654,168; Carter, Dem., 890,955; Anderson, Ind., 36,055; Clark, Libertarian, 15,627.

1984, Reagan, Rep., 1,068,722; Mondale, Dem., 706,628.

Hawaii

County	1980 Carter (D)	Reagan (R)	Anderson (I)	1984 Mondale (D)	Reagan (R)
Hawaii.......	17,630	14,247	3,091	17,866	20,707
Kauai......	9,081	5,883	1,352	8,862	9,249
Maui......	12,674	10,359	2,237	12,966	14,720
Oahu.........	96,472	99,596	25,331	107,404	140,258
Absentees....	22	27	10	NA	NA
Totals.......	135,879	130,112	32,021	147,098	184,934

Hawaii Vote Since 1960

1960, Kennedy, Dem., 92,410; Nixon, Rep., 92,295.

1964, Johnson, Dem., 163,249; Goldwater, Rep., 44,022.

1968, Nixon, Rep., 91,425; Humphrey, Dem., 141,324; Wallace, 3d party, 3,469.

1972, Nixon, Rep., 168,865; McGovern, Dem., 101,409.

1976, Carter, Dem., 147,375; Ford, Rep., 140,003; MacBride, Libertarian, 3,923.

1980, Reagan, Rep., 130,112; Carter, Dem., 135,879; Anderson, Ind., 32,021; Clark, Libertarian, 3,269; Commoner, Citizens, 1,548; Hall, Com., 458.

1984, Reagan, Rep., 184,934; Mondale, Dem., 147,098; Bergland, Libertarian, 2,167.

Idaho

County	1980 Carter (D)	Reagan (R)	Anderson (I)	1984 Mondale (D)	Reagan (R)
Ada.........	21,324	55,205	7,987	21,760	60,036
Adams......	590	1,189	88	540	1,381
Bannock......	8,639	18,477	1,896	9,399	18,742
Bear Lake......	508	2,941	63	481	2,760
Benewah......	1,361	2,111	286	1,447	2,039
Bingham......	2,933	11,781	489	3,064	11,900
Blaine......	1,840	2,716	775	1,971	3,603
Boise......	518	1,134	86	436	1,249
Bonner......	4,060	6,727	880	4,628	6,689
Bonneville......	5,052	24,715	1,355	4,877	24,392
Boundary......	1,087	2,088	225	1,158	2,159
Butte......	424	1,275	35	429	1,245
Camas......	145	360	16	123	364
Canyon......	9,172	24,375	1,798	7,527	24,613
Caribou......	481	3,234	106	535	3,032
Cassia......	1,369	6,511	212	1,036	6,503
Clark......	87	379	11	59	353
Clearwater......	1,699	2,178	291	1,608	2,176
Custer......	398	1,398	64	461	1,653
Elmore......	1,760	3,994	311	1,458	4,595
Franklin......	511	3,669	61	439	3,261
Fremont......	926	4,167	108	818	4,006
Gem......	1,613	3,766	218	1,607	3,644
Gooding......	1,461	3,897	218	1,247	3,819
Idaho......	2,078	4,425	409	1,996	4,219
Jefferson......	833	5,860	135	743	5,770
Jerome......	1,368	4,962	178	1,284	4,913
Kootenai......	7,521	17,022	1,808	9,004	17,330
Latah......	5,037	6,967	2,465	5,571	7,709
Lemhi......	794	2,646	167	852	2,810
Lewis......	774	1,088	160	648	1,000
Lincoln......	462	1,294	83	386	1,211
Madison......	728	6,555	64	483	6,798
Minidoka......	1,689	6,035	260	1,398	5,938
Nez Perce......	6,565	7,495	1,344	5,981	8,153
Oneida......	434	1,461	50	360	1,528
Owyhee......	732	2,257	93	574	2,141
Payette......	1,828	4,508	253	1,410	4,605
Power......	727	2,235	119	678	2,298
Shoshone......	3,102	3,994	407	3,033	3,156
Teton......	360	1,227	67	370	1,242
Twin Falls......	4,835	17,425	976	4,567	16,974
Valley......	926	2,041	245	945	2,299
Washington......	1,421	2,915	172	1,119	3,015
Totals.......	110,192	290,699	27,058	108,510	297,523

Idaho Vote Since 1936

1936, Roosevelt, Dem., 125,683; Landon, Rep., 66,256; Lemke, Union, 7,684.

1940, Roosevelt, Dem., 127,842; Willkie, Rep., 106,553; Thomas, Soc., 497; Browder, Com., 276.

1944, Roosevelt, Dem., 107,399; Dewey, Rep., 100,137; Watson, Proh., 503; Thomas, Soc., 282.

1948, Truman, Dem., 107,370; Dewey, Rep., 101,514; Wallace, Prog., 4,972; Watson, Proh., 628; Thomas, Soc., 332.

1952, Eisenhower, Rep., 180,707; Stevenson, Dem., 95,081; Hallinan, Prog., 443; write-in, 23.

1956, Eisenhower, Rep., 166,979; Stevenson, Dem., 105,868; Andrews, Ind., 126; write-in, 16.

1960, Kennedy, Dem., 138,853; Nixon, Rep., 161,597.

1964, Johnson, Dem., 148,920; Goldwater, Rep., 143,557.

1968, Nixon, Rep., 165,369; Humphrey, Dem., 89,273; Wallace, 3d party, 36,541.

1972, Nixon, Rep., 199,384; McGovern, Dem., 80,826; Schmitz, Amer., 28,869; Spock, Peoples, 903.

1976, Carter, Dem., 126,549; Ford, Rep., 204,151; Maddox, Amer., 5,935; MacBride, Libertarian, 3,558; LaRouche, U.S. Labor, 739.

1980, Reagan, Rep., 290,699; Carter, Dem., 110,192; Anderson, Ind., 27,058; Clark, Libertarian, 8,425; Rarick, Amer., 1,057.

1984, Reagan, Rep., 297,523; Mondale, Dem., 108,510; Bergland, Libertarian, 2,823.

Illinois

County	1980 Carter (D)	Reagan (R)	Anderson (I)	1984 Mondale (D)	Reagan (R)
Adams	10,606	19,842	1,202	10,336	20,225
Alexander	2,925	2,650	74	2,872	2,574
Bond	2,834	4,398	244	2,870	4,240
Boone	3,175	6,697	1,578	3,717	7,536
Brown	950	1,660	59	959	1,478
Bureau	5,753	11,484	1,093	6,925	11,741
Calhoun	1,208	1,591	76	1,443	1,648
Carroll	2,214	5,084	705	2,398	5,237
Cass	2,543	3,965	199	2,937	3,435
Champaign	21,017	33,329	9,972	27,266	39,224
Christian	6,625	8,770	499	7,541	8,534
Clark	2,855	5,476	243	3,032	5,318
Clay	2,587	4,447	187	2,524	4,562
Clinton	4,470	8,500	528	4,628	9,233
Coles	6,743	11,994	1,726	7,156	14,044
Cook	1,124,584	856,574	149,712	1,112,641	1,055,558
Crawford	3,372	5,894	341	3,130	6,261
Cumberland	1,892	3,159	190	1,733	3,002
DeKalb	8,913	16,370	4,526	10,942	20,294
DeWitt	2,262	4,648	368	2,352	4,534
Douglas	2,564	5,330	344	2,686	5,691
DuPage	68,991	182,308	29,810	71,430	227,141
Edgar	3,394	6,639	400	3,241	6,821
Edwards	1,041	2,556	118	1,057	2,778
Effingham	4,229	9,104	393	3,841	9,617
Fayette	3,614	6,523	229	3,844	6,607
Ford	1,803	5,024	328	1,763	4,871
Franklin	9,425	9,731	558	10,667	9,656
Fulton	7,481	10,316	838	9,131	9,147
Gallatin	1,678	1,700	78	2,164	1,939
Greene	2,607	4,224	220	2,563	4,057
Grundy	3,970	8,397	701	4,671	9,595
Hamilton	1,990	3,254	171	2,251	3,074
Hancock	3,522	6,597	383	3,713	6,251
Hardin	1,314	1,721	56	1,205	1,689
Henderson	1,609	2,443	143	1,969	2,289
Henry	7,977	14,506	1,440	10,679	14,504
Iroquois	3,362	11,247	592	3,300	11,327
Jackson	10,291	10,505	2,526	12,105	13,609
Jasper	1,846	3,548	157	1,750	3,673
Jefferson	6,761	8,972	506	7,200	9,642
Jersey	3,324	5,266	314	3,762	5,146
JoDaviess	2,678	5,186	983	3,348	5,877
Johnson	1,586	3,201	84	1,647	3,424
Kane	29,015	64,106	9,179	31,875	72,655
Kankakee	14,626	23,810	1,802	15,246	23,807
Kendall	3,143	10,028	979	3,789	10,872
Knox	8,749	14,907	2,069	12,027	14,974
Lake	48,287	96,350	17,726	53,947	118,401
LaSalle	16,818	27,323	3,041	20,532	27,388
Lawrence	3,030	4,453	293	2,924	4,686
Lee	3,170	11,373	781	3,919	11,178
Livingston	4,111	11,544	980	4,567	12,291
Logan	3,916	9,681	650	4,052	9,932
McDonough	4,093	8,995	1,230	4,561	9,383
McHenry	14,540	40,045	5,871	14,420	47,282
McLean	13,587	30,096	4,961	15,880	32,221
Macon	22,325	28,298	2,804	25,463	30,457
Macoupin	9,116	12,131	901	10,502	12,282
Madison	43,860	51,160	4,206	48,352	57,021
Marion	6,990	10,969	587	7,599	11,300
Marshall	1,903	4,349	336	2,386	4,060
Mason	2,680	4,644	267	3,354	4,109
Massac	2,821	4,284	124	3,194	3,827
Menard	1,589	3,622	274	1,826	3,925
Mercer	3,361	5,144	540	3,982	4,907
Monroe	3,121	6,315	405	3,256	6,936
Montgomery	5,721	8,947	611	6,360	8,191
Morgan	5,483	10,406	900	5,361	10,683
Moultrie	2,332	3,495	280	2,458	3,593
Ogle	4,067	12,533	2,042	4,803	13,503
Peoria	28,276	47,815	6,169	36,530	45,607
Perry	4,337	5,886	319	4,584	5,852
Piatt	2,421	4,897	447	2,640	5,050
Pike	3,695	5,301	303	3,965	5,295
Pope	880	1,501	58	940	1,545
Pulaski	1,955	2,083	49	1,724	1,923
Putnam	1,158	1,959	235	1,487	1,912
Randolph	6,052	8,810	514	6,355	9,415
Richland	2,463	5,241	358	2,182	5,665
Rock Island	30,045	34,768	5,818	40,208	35,121
St. Clair	50,046	46,063	3,879	52,294	51,046
Saline	5,683	7,157	321	6,038	7,176
Sangamon	29,354	49,372	5,439	34,059	54,086
Schuyler	1,445	2,799	155	1,533	2,515
Scott	941	1,990	80	943	1,976
Shelby	3,988	6,441	381	4,317	6,372
Stark	806	2,358	147	1,072	2,228
Stephenson	6,195	10,779	3,145	6,723	14,237
Tazewell	16,924	35,481	3,206	23,095	33,782
Union	3,781	4,289	291	3,815	4,721
Vermilion	14,498	22,579	2,110	16,530	22,932
Wabash	1,975	3,571	230	1,795	3,6
Warren	2,756	5,667	489	3,318	5,8
Washington	2,158	5,354	205	2,363	5,1
Wayne	3,258	6,013	222	2,621	6,29
White	3,463	5,279	274	3,457	5,500
Whiteside	7,191	17,389	1,242	11,226	16,743
Will	41,975	69,310	7,855	45,193	78,684
Williamson	10,779	14,451	793	11,614	14,930
Winnebago	32,384	48,825	22,596	44,629	64,203
Woodford	3,552	10,791	711	4,425	10,758
Totals	1,981,413	2,358,049	346,754	2,086,499	2,707,103

Illinois Vote Since 1936

1936, Roosevelt, Dem., 2,282,999; Landon, Rep., 1,570,393; Lemke, Union, 89,439; Thomas, Soc., 7,530; Colvin, Proh., 3,439; Aiken, Soc. Labor, 1,921.

1940, Roosevelt, Dem., 2,149,934; Willkie, Rep., 2,047,240; Thomas, Soc., 10,914; Babson, Proh., 9,190.

1944, Roosevelt, Dem., 2,079,479; Dewey, Rep., 1,939,314; Teichert, Soc. Labor, 9,677; Watson, Proh., 7,411; Thomas, Soc., 180.

1948, Truman, Dem., 1,994,715; Dewey, Rep., 1,961,103; Watson, Proh., 11,959; Thomas, Soc., 11,522; Teichert, Soc. Labor, 3,118.

1952, Eisenhower, Rep., 2,457,327; Stevenson, Dem., 2,013,920; Hass, Soc. Labor, 9,363; write-in, 448.

1956, Eisenhower, Rep., 2,623,327; Stevenson, Dem., 1,775,682; Hass, Soc. Labor, 8,342; write-in, 56.

1960, Kennedy, Dem., 2,377,846; Nixon, Rep., 2,368,988; Hass, Soc. Labor, 10,560; write-in, 15.

1964, Johnson, Dem., 2,796,833; Goldwater, Rep., 1,905,946; write-in, 62.

1968, Nixon, Rep., 2,174,774; Humphrey, Dem., 2,039,814; Wallace, 3d party, 390,958; Blomen, Soc. Labor, 13,878; write-in, 325.

1972, Nixon, Rep. 2,788,179; McGovern, Dem., 1,913,472; Fisher, Soc. Labor, 12,344; Schmitz, Amer., 2,471; Hall, Com., 4,541; others, 2,229.

1976, Carter, Dem., 2,271,295; Ford, Rep., 2,364,269; McCarthy, Ind., 55,939; Hall, Com., 9,250; MacBride, Libertarian, 8,057; Camejo, Soc. Workers, 3,615; Levin, Soc. Labor, 2,422; LaRouche, U.S. Labor, 2,018; write-in, 1,968.

1980, Reagan, Rep., 2,358,049; Carter, Dem., 1,981,413; Anderson, Ind., 346,754; Clark, Libertarian, 38,939; Commoner, Citizens, 10,692; Hall, Com., 9,711; Griswold, Workers World, 2,257; DeBerry, Socialist Workers, 1,302; write-ins, 604.

1984, Reagan, Rep., 2,707,103; Mondale, Dem., 2,086,499; Bergland, Libertarian, 10,086.

Indiana

County	1980 Carter (D)	Reagan (R)	Anderson (I)	1984 Mondale (D)	Reagan (R)
Adams	4,673	6,368	767	3,923	7,958
Allen	37,765	68,524	10,368	38,462	75,505
Bartholomew	9,260	15,801	1,604	8,075	18,704
Benton	1,520	3,189	197	1,357	3,281
Blackford	2,431	3,168	258	2,395	3,787
Boone	4,535	10,484	681	3,982	11,790
Brown	2,014	2,884	237	2,657	3,517
Carroll	2,966	5,262	338	2,774	5,528
Cass	5,839	11,500	695	5,521	12,355
Clark	14,137	15,508	1,102	14,138	19,419
Clay	4,363	6,980	311	3,707	6,957
Clinton	5,258	8,150	427	4,329	8,969
Crawford	2,130	2,554	124	2,256	2,633
Daviess	4,057	7,022	345	3,545	7,721
Dearborn	5,135	7,467	464	4,920	9,149
Decatur	3,646	5,819	377	2,766	6,551
Dekalb	4,911	7,866	883	4,617	8,769
Delaware	20,923	26,342	2,743	19,791	30,092
Dubois	6,700	6,775	578	5,423	9,391
Elkhart	14,883	30,081	3,256	13,240	34,621
Fayette	4,304	6,004	293	4,122	7,142
Floyd	11,543	12,456	1,047	10,616	15,466
Fountain	2,845	5,298	280	2,897	5,450
Franklin	2,834	4,551	234	2,225	5,202
Fulton	2,786	5,458	349	2,527	6,057
Gibson	6,834	7,643	591	7,082	8,618
Grant	10,390	19,078	1,043	9,986	20,482
Greene	6,027	7,452	299	5,267	8,438
Hamilton	7,036	26,218	1,736	6,364	30,254
Hancock	5,124	12,093	746	4,550	12,880
Harrison	4,865	6,297	341	4,634	7,255
Hendricks	7,412	19,366	1,048	6,659	21,307
Henry	7,626	12,724	552	7,064	11,926

	1980 Carter (D)	Reagan (R)	Anderson (I)	1984 Mondale (D)	Reagan (R)
Howard	12,916	21,272	1,325	10,458	22,386
Huntington	5,415	9,497	824	4,598	10,805
Jackson	6,425	6,903	430	5,163	9,879
Jasper	2,544	6,316	283	2,821	6,537
Jay	3,256	5,351	484	3,174	5,975
Jefferson	5,496	6,831	477	4,952	7,482
Jennings	3,931	5,498	281	3,264	6,356
Johnson	8,445	20,018	1,348	7,715	23,482
Knox	7,829	10,083	617	6,417	10,872
Kosciusko	5,684	15,633	1,164	4,877	17,560
LaGrange	2,095	4,259	377	1,884	4,772
Lake	101,145	95,408	8,275	117,984	94,870
LaPorte	15,387	22,424	2,080	15,904	23,346
Lawrence	5,826	10,846	380	5,608	11,440
Madison	23,554	35,582	2,389	22,254	36,510
Marion	126,103	168,680	15,709	130,185	184,880
Marshall	5,113	10,209	836	4,931	11,100
Martin	2,479	3,082	149	1,937	3,363
Miami	4,927	8,672	508	4,224	9,551
Monroe	13,316	18,233	3,921	14,719	21,772
Montgomery	4,158	9,936	622	3,626	11,119
Morgan	5,439	13,321	498	4,627	14,884
Newton	1,649	3,850	194	1,596	3,560
Noble	4,721	7,624	749	4,237	8,459
Ohio	1,074	1,264	57	1,068	1,503
Orange	3,228	5,073	181	2,571	5,909
Owen	2,325	3,632	188	2,082	4,204
Parke	2,432	4,595	194	2,205	5,052
Perry	4,540	4,350	448	4,760	4,785
Pike	3,346	3,343	190	3,231	3,689
Porter	12,869	30,055	3,061	17,862	32,505
Posey	4,465	6,096	667	4,452	6,472
Pulaski	2,092	3,916	175	2,008	4,167
Putnam	3,996	7,090	501	3,392	7,820
Randolph	4,025	7,762	426	3,805	7,793
Ripley	4,022	5,770	303	3,336	7,143
Rush	2,388	4,829	224	2,307	5,429
St. Joseph	44,218	50,607	6,962	47,513	54,404
Scott	3,694	3,432	139	3,460	4,110
Shelby	5,861	10,496	614	5,357	11,056
Spencer	4,153	5,284	196	4,005	5,816
Starke	3,615	5,035	297	3,674	5,104
Steuben	2,606	5,670	602	2,441	6,424
Sullivan	4,335	4,465	212	4,006	4,771
Switzerland	1,704	1,584	38	1,484	1,857
Tippecanoe	14,636	27,569	5,141	15,789	29,706
Tipton	2,547	5,150	285	2,328	5,687
Union	898	1,766	92	816	1,970
Vanderburgh	29,930	36,248	4,150	31,049	40,994
Vermillion	3,793	4,195	269	3,666	4,428
Vigo	19,261	24,133	2,484	18,429	26,259
Wabash	4,620	8,738	797	4,077	9,862
Warren	1,287	2,665	145	1,309	2,825
Warrick	6,845	8,681	890	6,345	10,202
Washington	3,683	5,234	191	3,334	5,874
Wayne	9,593	16,981	1,174	10,173	18,955
Wells	3,760	5,864	717	3,274	7,579
White	3,247	6,999	466	3,157	7,279
Whitley	4,497	7,146	928	3,690	7,763
Totals	844,197	1,255,656	111,639	841,481	1,377,230

Indiana Vote Since 1936

1936, Roosevelt, Dem., 943,974; Landon, Rep., 691,570; Lemke, Union, 19,407; Thomas, Soc., 3,856; Browder, Com., 1,090.

1940, Roosevelt, Dem., 874,063; Willkie, Rep., 899,466; Babson, Proh., 6,437; Thomas, Soc., 2,075; Aiken, Soc. Labor, 706.

1944, Roosevelt, Dem., 781,403; Dewey, Rep., 875,891; Watson, Proh., 12,574; Thomas, Soc., 2,223.

1948, Truman, Dem., 807,833; Dewey, Rep., 821,079; Watson, Proh., 14,711; Wallace, Prog., 9,649; Thomas, Soc., 2,179; Teichert, Soc. Labor, 763.

1952, Eisenhower, Rep., 1,136,259; Stevenson, Dem., 801,530; Hamblen, Proh., 15,335; Hallinan, Prog., 1,222; Hass, Soc. Labor, 979.

1956, Eisenhower, Rep., 1,182,811; Stevenson, Dem., 783,908; Holtwick, Proh., 6,554; Hass, Soc. Labor, 1,334.

1960, Kennedy, Dem., 952,358; Nixon, Rep., 1,175,120; Decker, Proh., 6,746; Hass, Soc. Labor, 1,136.

1964, Johnson, Dem., 1,170,848; Goldwater, Rep., 911,118; Munn, Proh., 8,266; Hass, Soc. Labor, 1,374.

1968, Nixon, Rep., 1,067,885; Humphrey, Dem., 806,659; Wallace, 3d party, 243,108; Munn, Proh., 4,616; Halstead, Soc. Worker, 1,293; Gregory, write-in, 36.

1972, Nixon, Rep., 1,405,154; McGovern, Dem., 708,568; Reed, Soc. Workers, 5,575; Fisher, Soc. Labor, 1,688; Spock, Peace & Freedom, 4,544.

1976, Carter, Dem., 1,014,714; Ford, Rep., 1,185,958; Anderson, Amer., 14,048; Camejo, Soc. Workers, 5,695; LaRouche, U.S. Labor, 1,947.

1980 Reagan, Rep., 1,255,656; Carter, Dem., 844,197; Anderson, Ind., 111,639; Clark, Libertarian, 19,627; Commoner, Citizens, 4,852; Greaves, American, 4,750; Hall, Com., 702; DeBerry, Soc., 610.

1984 Reagan, Rep., 1,377,230; Mondale, Dem., 841,481; Bergland, Libertarian, 6,741.

Iowa

County	1980 Carter (D)	Reagan (R)	Anderson (I)	1984 Mondale (D)	Reagan (R)
Adair	1,454	2,821	356	1,979	2,615
Adams	940	1,779	214	1,221	1,706
Allamakee	2,170	4,000	343	2,282	3,997
Appanoose	2,769	3,544	353	3,289	3,412
Audubon	1,546	2,523	251	1,854	2,306
Benton	4,223	5,329	948	4,993	5,566
Black Hawk	27,443	29,627	5,847	31,467	32,262
Boone	5,126	5,732	1,081	6,485	5,746
Bremer	3,527	6,706	970	4,084	6,895
Buchanan	3,605	5,041	689	4,129	4,965
Buena Vista	3,468	5,272	771	4,109	5,193
Butler	1,990	4,730	392	2,323	4,570
Calhoun	2,150	3,633	407	2,541	3,311
Carroll	3,885	5,017	736	4,960	5,021
Cass	2,176	5,391	475	2,417	5,053
Cedar	2,589	4,398	697	3,086	4,617
Cerro Gordo	9,363	11,189	2,024	11,570	11,214
Cherokee	2,719	4,087	599	3,349	4,046
Chickasaw	2,935	3,929	500	3,186	3,661
Clarke	1,614	2,417	310	2,030	2,262
Clay	3,179	4,479	991	3,774	4,450
Clayton	3,297	5,115	669	3,446	5,029
Clinton	9,698	13,025	2,140	11,240	13,914
Crawford	2,500	4,883	509	3,396	4,552
Dallas	5,310	6,296	1,200	6,564	6,080
Davis	1,689	2,003	200	2,187	1,956
Decatur	2,048	2,212	318	2,098	2,104
Delaware	2,671	4,316	727	3,158	4,769
Des Moines	9,977	9,158	1,041	11,173	9,559
Dickinson	2,620	4,028	687	3,025	4,064
Dubuque	18,689	18,649	3,708	21,876	19,239
Emmet	2,153	3,062	446	2,746	2,946
Fayette	4,377	6,374	647	4,677	6,505
Floyd	3,634	4,665	728	4,154	4,341
Franklin	1,920	3,290	406	2,349	3,129
Fremont	1,203	2,693	191	1,426	2,686
Greene	2,210	3,154	510	2,831	2,579
Grundy	1,869	4,644	440	1,915	4,527
Guthrie	1,866	3,214	384	2,517	2,783
Hamilton	2,741	4,745	679	3,330	4,279
Hancock	1,918	3,681	462	2,539	3,362
Hardin	3,757	5,329	730	4,477	5,195
Harrison	2,152	4,502	311	2,495	4,352
Henry	3,317	4,430	629	3,377	4,516
Howard	2,214	2,975	336	2,135	2,718
Humboldt	1,840	3,575	394	2,406	3,396
Ida	1,235	2,825	254	1,559	2,618
Iowa	2,606	4,153	667	2,815	4,352
Jackson	3,518	4,479	622	4,400	4,811
Jasper	7,258	8,286	1,221	8,023	8,576
Jefferson	2,577	4,099	505	2,961	4,727
Johnson	20,122	13,642	8,101	26,000	18,677
Jones	3,521	4,506	759	3,825	4,907
Keokuk	2,390	3,145	369	2,649	2,913
Kossuth	3,810	5,568	775	4,838	4,872
Lee	8,204	8,793	1,047	8,912	8,756
Linn	31,950	36,254	8,773	38,528	41,061
Louisa	1,700	2,530	291	1,927	2,623
Lucas	1,989	2,593	291	2,422	2,630
Lyon	1,431	4,349	375	1,401	4,178
Madison	2,496	3,320	505	3,067	3,168
Mahaska	3,968	5,650	603	4,107	6,086
Marion	5,490	6,665	1,232	6,313	7,259
Marshall	7,114	10,707	1,541	8,809	10,839
Mills	1,244	3,581	281	1,434	3,994
Mitchell	2,040	3,401	361	2,531	3,144
Monona	1,660	3,268	275	2,159	2,746
Monroe	1,866	2,003	216	2,342	1,927
Montgomery	1,556	4,115	301	1,661	4,224
Muscatine	5,597	7,829	1,522	5,986	9,069
O'Brien	2,210	4,937	536	2,479	5,008
Osceola	1,051	2,177	234	1,146	2,285
Page	1,772	5,618	356	1,914	5,876
Palo Alto	2,463	3,025	412	3,018	2,715
Plymouth	2,965	6,515	756	3,464	6,482
Pocahontas	1,959	3,194	397	2,481	2,627
Polk	61,984	64,156	15,819	75,413	71,413
Pottawattamie	10,709	20,222	1,870	12,329	21,527
Poweshiek	3,529	4,598	821	4,103	4,715
Ringgold	1,150	1,884	191	1,593	1,512
Sac	1,976	3,725	467	2,363	3,298
Scott	26,391	34,701	5,760	32,550	38,034
Shelby	1,892	4,147	372	2,291	4,200
Sioux	2,698	10,768	610	2,585	11,665
Story	13,529	15,829	7,252	18,277	19,804
Tama	3,049	4,840	593	4,061	4,882

Taylor	1,226	2,715	240	1,499	2,496
Union	2,182	3,372	368	2,875	3,583
Van Buren	1,311	2,142	183	1,606	2,138
Wapello	8,923	7,475	1,050	10,545	7,008
Warren	6,610	7,360	1,369	8,171	8,277
Washington	2,877	3,967	703	3,079	4,613
Wayne	1,627	2,221	218	1,927	2,061
Webster	9,001	10,438	1,386	9,930	9,619
Winnebago	2,208	3,808	417	2,669	3,616
Winneshiek	3,201	5,033	938	3,724	5,277
Woodbury	15,930	23,553	3,184	18,951	23,002
Worth	1,721	2,247	301	2,263	1,985
Wright	2,645	3,936	497	2,980	3,675
Totals	508,672	676,026	115,633	605,620	703,088

Iowa Vote Since 1936

1936, Roosevelt, Dem., 621,756; Landon, Rep., 487,977; Lemke, Union, 29,687; Thomas, Soc., 1,373; Colvin, Proh., 1,182; Browder, Com., 506; Aiken, Soc. Labor, 252.

1940, Roosevelt, Dem., 578,800; Willkie, Rep., 632,370; Babson, Proh., 2,284; Browder, Com., 1,524; Aiken, Soc. Labor, 452.

1944, Roosevelt, Dem., 499,876; Dewey, Rep., 547,267; Watson, Proh., 3,752; Thomas, Soc., 1,511; Teichert, Soc. Labor, 193.

1948, Truman, Dem., 522,380; Dewey, Rep., 494,018; Wallace, Prog., 12,125; Teichert, Soc. Labor, 4,274; Watson, Proh., 3,382; Thomas, Soc., 1,829; Dobbs, Soc. Workers, 26.

1952, Eisenhower, Rep., 808,906; Stevenson, Dem., 451,513; Hallinan, Prog., 5,085; Hamblen, Proh., 2,882; Hoopes, Soc., 219; Hass, Soc. Labor, 139; scattering 29.

1956, Eisenhower, Rep., 729,187; Stevenson, Dem., 501,858; Andrews (A.C.P. of Iowa), 3,202; Hoopes, Soc., 192; Hass, Soc. Labor, 125.

1960, Kennedy, Dem., 550,565; Nixon, Rep., 722,381; Hass, Soc. Labor, 230; write-in, 634.

1964, Johnson, Dem., 733,030; Goldwater, Rep., 449,148; Hass, Soc. Labor, 182; DeBerry, Soc. Worker, 159; Munn, Proh., 1,902.

1968, Nixon, Rep., 619,106; Humphrey, Dem., 476,699; Wallace, 3d party, 66,422; Munn, Proh., 362; Halstead, Soc. Worker, 3,377; Cleaver, Peace and Freedom, 1,332; Blomen, Soc. Labor, 241.

1972, Nixon, Rep., 706,207; McGovern, Dem., 496,206; Schmitz, Amer., 22,056; Jenness, Soc. Workers, 488; Fisher, Soc. Labor, 195; Hall, Com. 272; Green, Universal, 199; scattered, 321.

1976, Carter, Dem., 619,931; Ford, Rep., 632,863; McCarthy, Ind., 20,051; Anderson, Amer., 3,040; MacBride, Libertarian, 1,452.

1980, Reagan, Rep., 676,026; Carter, Dem., 508,672; Anderson, Ind., 115,633; Clark, Libertarian, 13,123; Commoner, Citizens, 2,273; McReynolds, Socialist, 534; Hall Com., 298; DeBerry, Soc. Work., 244; Greaves, American, 189; Bubar, Statesman, 150; scattering, 519.

1984, Reagan, Rep., 703,088; Mondale, Dem., 605,620; Bergland, Libertarian, 1,844.

Kansas

County	1980 Carter (D)	Reagan (R)	Anderson (I)	1984 Mondale (D)	Reagan (R)
Allen	2,009	3,811	380	1,779	4,266
Anderson	1,170	2,363	184	1,155	2,462
Atchison	3,063	4,084	345	2,641	4,536
Barber	914	1,872	168	805	2,111
Barton	3,663	9,147	793	3,111	10,234
Bourbon	2,605	4,263	251	2,174	4,856
Brown	1,370	3,598	286	1,303	3,894
Butler	6,875	10,210	1,015	6,352	12,920
Chase	413	1,073	92	393	1,162
Chautauqua	543	1,566	57	497	1,688
Cherokee	3,969	5,296	282	3,663	5,081
Cheyenne	358	1,330	81	356	1,442
Clark	430	901	67	324	1,075
Clay	932	3,449	217	919	3,559
Cloud	1,793	3,581	344	1,878	3,856
Coffey	938	2,491	128	1,037	3,063
Comanche	393	877	50	285	993
Cowley	5,474	8,749	866	5,153	9,930
Crawford	7,658	8,058	847	6,722	9,518
Decatur	443	1,642	125	467	1,769
Dickinson	2,108	5,654	469	2,168	6,487
Doniphan	1,001	2,523	146	962	2,818
Douglas	9,360	14,106	4,770	12,877	18,804
Edwards	616	1,409	127	606	1,352

Elk	482	1,280	54	452	1,301
Ellis	3,940	5,634	923	3,457	7,509
Ellsworth	886	2,155	167	905	2,353
Finney	2,689	4,831	531	2,398	6,943
Ford	3,194	5,686	622	2,914	6,738
Franklin	2,726	5,525	432	2,524	6,283
Geary	2,357	3,534	332	2,301	4,475
Gove	396	1,263	91	426	1,310
Graham	473	1,450	98	480	1,423
Grant	683	1,711	150	615	2,043
Gray	583	1,310	123	514	1,580
Greeley	235	600	85	227	699
Greenwood	1,241	2,685	170	1,173	2,900
Hamilton	402	889	66	408	1,037
Harper	990	2,254	182	893	2,696
Harvey	4,173	7,045	1,356	4,599	8,507
Haskell	374	1,014	84	281	1,151
Hodgeman	339	831	69	306	939
Jackson	1,537	3,211	234	1,667	3,464
Jefferson	1,776	4,046	364	1,990	4,524
Jewell	578	2,074	153	583	1,992
Johnson	33,210	78,048	10,947	37,782	101,042
Kearny	375	924	62	321	1,214
Kingman	1,133	2,610	286	1,047	2,826
Kiowa	438	1,433	88	361	1,537
Labette	3,947	5,244	588	3,631	6,542
Lane	321	924	100	282	1,008
Leavenworth	6,354	9,157	955	6,583	11,018
Lincoln	528	1,685	96	551	1,723
Linn	1,157	2,407	103	1,152	2,794
Logan	358	1,261	66	331	1,235
Lyon	4,680	8,431	1,216	4,188	9,796
McPherson	3,340	6,843	1,222	3,185	8,630
Marion	1,569	3,960	488	1,633	4,407
Marshall	1,555	4,127	330	1,813	4,097
Meade	482	1,618	121	491	1,804
Miami	3,071	4,740	368	3,076	5,877
Mitchell	876	2,821	197	919	3,036
Montgomery	5,282	10,656	488	4,933	12,023
Morris	810	1,933	166	820	2,240
Morton	414	1,157	71	322	1,353
Nemaha	1,600	3,546	243	1,761	3,653
Neosho	2,923	4,613	432	2,679	4,968
Ness	615	1,657	136	539	1,779
Norton	666	2,625	151	611	2,515
Osage	2,088	3,617	330	2,072	4,288
Osborne	620	2,188	125	686	2,171
Ottawa	630	2,118	150	698	2,343
Pawnee	1,184	2,170	281	1,092	2,570
Phillips	748	2,731	143	626	2,810
Pottawatomie	1,724	3,895	444	1,798	4,596
Pratt	1,369	2,866	329	1,253	3,240
Rawlins	427	1,524	87	412	1,625
Reno	9,615	13,804	2,225	9,229	16,621
Republic	850	3,031	183	966	2,974
Rice	1,847	3,211	426	1,559	3,598
Riley	5,224	8,904	2,443	5,974	11,306
Rooks	725	2,275	144	699	2,604
Rush	557	1,840	144	718	1,758
Russell	910	3,241	229	1,055	3,673
Saline	6,382	12,758	1,706	6,527	15,242
Scott	456	1,829	99	427	2,017
Sedgwick	55,105	75,317	10,222	55,060	95,972
Seward	1,460	4,385	250	1,198	5,047
Shawnee	24,852	36,290	5,524	26,307	43,435
Sheridan	391	1,202	68	429	1,274
Sherman	779	2,315	215	714	2,702
Smith	779	2,415	183	684	2,330
Stafford	872	1,865	184	844	2,062
Stanton	231	672	62	205	783
Stevens	478	1,502	67	386	1,862
Summer	3,761	6,038	486	3,713	6,942
Thomas	1,045	2,789	269	887	3,106
Trego	523	1,340	138	598	1,491
Wabaunsee	853	2,255	173	805	2,276
Wallace	167	811	36	152	838
Washington	784	3,058	195	889	2,979
Wichita	303	880	60	232	916
Wilson	1,205	3,328	208	1,343	3,660
Woodson	646	1,435	89	596	1,408
Wyandotte	32,763	23,012	3,018	35,887	27,267
Totals	326,150	566,812	68,231	332,471	674,646

Kansas Vote Since 1936

1936, Roosevelt, Dem., 464,520; Landon, Rep., 397,727; Thomas, Soc., 2,766; Lemke, Union, 494.

1940, Roosevelt, Dem., 364,725; Willkie, Rep., 489,169; Babson, Proh., 4,056; Thomas, Soc., 2,347.

1944, Roosevelt, Dem., 287,458; Dewey, Rep., 442,096; Watson, Proh., 2,609; Thomas, Soc., 1,613.

1948, Truman, Dem., 351,902; Dewey, Rep., 423,039; Watson, Proh., 6,468; Wallace, Prog., 4,603; Thomas, Soc., 2,807.

1952, Eisenhower, Rep., 616,302; Stevenson, Dem., 273,296; Hamblen, Proh., 6,038; Hoopes, Soc., 530.

1956, Eisenhower, Rep., 566,878; Stevenson, Dem., 296,317; Holtwick, Proh., 3,048.

), Kennedy, Dem., 363,213; Nixon, Rep., 561,474; Decker, Proh., 4,138.

64, Johnson, Dem., 464,028; Goldwater, Rep., 386,579; Munn, Proh., 5,393; Hass, Soc. Labor, 1,901.

968, Nixon, Rep., 478,674; Humphrey, Dem., 302,996; Wallace, 3d, 88,921; Munn, Proh., 2,192.

1972, Nixon, Rep., 619,812; McGovern, Dem., 270,287; Schmitz, Cons., 21,808; Munn, Proh., 4,188.

1976, Carter, Dem., 430,421; Ford, Rep., 502,752; McCarthy, Ind., 13,185; Anderson, Amer., 4,724; MacBride, Libertarian, 3,242; Maddox, Cons., 2,118; Bubar, Proh., 1,403.

1980, Reagan, Rep., 566,812; Carter, Dem., 326,150; Anderson, Ind., 68,231; Clark, Libertarian, 14,470; Shelton, American, 1,555; Hall, Com., 967; Bubar, Statesman, 821; Rarick, Conservative, 789.

1984, Reagan, Rep., 674,646; Mondale, Dem., 332,471; Bergland, Libertarian, 3,585.

Kentucky

County	1980 Carter (D)	1980 Reagan (R)	Anderson (I)	1984 Mondale (D)	1984 Reagan (R)
Adair	2,285	4,051	53	1,812	4,500
Allen	2,010	3,186	54	1,521	3,427
Anderson	2,567	2,052	90	1,717	3,425
Ballard	2,583	1,190	23	2,002	1,663
Barren	5,285	6,405	164	4,503	7,717
Bath	2,174	1,463	47	1,781	2,020
Bell	6,362	5,433	150	5,490	7,249
Boone	5,374	8,263	383	4,853	12,690
Bourbon	3,641	2,475	153	2,649	3,836
Boyd	10,702	10,367	496	9,601	10,925
Boyle	4,429	3,848	254	3,378	5,675
Bracken	1,420	1,154	36	1,136	1,812
Breathitt	3,916	1,532	68	3,435	2,855
Breckinridge	3,163	3,629	72	2,669	4,432
Bullitt	5,884	6,364	202	5,005	9,556
Butler	1,274	3,129	28	1,055	3,121
Caldwell	2,924	2,609	66	2,427	3,162
Calloway	6,809	4,498	318	5,028	6,442
Campbell	11,059	16,743	943	9,068	21,473
Carlisle	1,542	975	8	1,277	1,308
Carroll	2,127	1,076	82	1,564	1,824
Carter	3,782	3,934	86	3,985	4,656
Casey	1,298	4,239	38	1,122	4,356
Christian	7,048	8,209	190	5,432	10,708
Clark	5,071	4,302	242	3,595	6,130
Clay	2,121	4,594	37	1,634	4,772
Clinton	1,000	3,539	34	838	3,459
Crittenden	1,508	2,219	28	1,483	2,167
Cumberland	821	2,216	27	766	2,729
Daviess	14,902	14,643	752	13,347	19,495
Edmonson	1,252	2,913	28	1,200	3,001
Elliott	1,668	551	15	1,683	601
Estill	1,965	2,818	45	1,593	3,512
Fayette	30,511	35,349	4,933	28,961	51,993
Fleming	2,051	2,189	54	1,616	2,824
Floyd	10,975	4,179	171	10,259	5,218
Franklin	11,193	6,455	610	7,790	11,057
Fulton	2,016	1,462	31	1,534	1,780
Gallatin	988	684	20	1,042	1,042
Garrard	1,774	2,585	62	1,566	3,284
Grant	2,272	1,779	76	1,685	2,840
Graves	6,999	6,556	135	6,759	7,287
Grayson	2,788	5,084	78	2,200	5,524
Green	1,758	2,775	39	1,611	3,210
Greenup	7,126	6,857	220	6,923	7,451
Hancock	1,530	1,367	52	1,287	1,967
Hardin	8,339	9,779	452	6,329	14,293
Harlan	8,798	5,460	131	7,663	6,959
Harrison	3,319	2,184	107	2,405	3,467
Hart	3,005	3,129	42	2,278	3,065
Henderson	8,082	5,074	354	6,795	7,389
Henry	2,999	1,723	69	2,279	2,802
Hickman	1,456	1,143	28	1,049	1,380
Hopkins	8,810	6,238	213	6,743	9,368
Jackson	702	3,379	29	542	3,806
Jefferson	125,844	127,254	9,686	20,034	52,241
Jessamine	3,310	4,809	278	2,379	7,081
Johnson	3,142	5,039	96	3,078	5,225
Kenton	17,907	25,965	1,583	14,642	34,304
Knott	5,405	1,602	25	4,487	1,728
Knox	3,543	5,539	113	2,932	5,730
Larue	2,183	2,000	43	1,514	2,873
Laurel	3,969	8,868	114	3,267	9,621
Lawrence	2,362	2,564	32	2,223	2,713
Lee	1,017	1,650	41	768	1,862
Leslie	1,327	3,536	40	1,075	3,385
Letcher	4,280	3,426	78	4,153	3,676
Lewis	1,543	2,802	34	1,484	3,445
Lincoln	2,991	3,034	58	2,498	3,996
Livingston	2,287	1,670	30	2,007	1,866
Logan	4,264	3,366	85	3,347	4,889
Lyon	1,496	968	26	1,272	969
McCracken	13,365	10,281	369	12,535	12,903
McCreary	1,377	3,786	40	1,609	4,028
McLean	2,147	1,497	44	1,917	1,942
Madison	8,208	8,437	739	6,509	11,309
Magoffin	2,986	2,265	25	2,942	2,343
Marion	3,577	2,126	87	2,835	3,305
Marshall	6,231	4,403	96	5,725	5,152
Martin	1,567	2,793	51	1,471	3,248
Mason	3,181	2,926	127	2,663	2,751
Meade	3,205	2,740	90	2,503	3,820
Menifee	966	547	11	956	785
Mercer	3,528	3,275	92	2,516	4,592
Metcalfe	1,628	2,013	39	1,575	2,349
Monroe	1,156	4,592	47	1,052	4,670
Montgomery	3,391	2,869	117	2,490	3,864
Morgan	2,698	1,450	31	2,481	1,834
Muhlenberg	6,616	4,893	148	6,157	6,094
Nelson	5,514	3,349	162	4,199	6,044
Nicholas	1,349	915	56	1,107	1,535
Ohio	3,486	5,272	103	3,253	5,119
Oldham	3,487	5,586	351	2,857	8,112
Owen	2,323	944	43	1,575	1,735
Owsley	437	1,250	7	375	1,466
Pendleton	1,992	1,757	69	1,529	2,767
Perry	6,031	4,226	72	5,258	5,218
Pike	14,878	10,550	204	15,817	11,869
Powell	2,006	1,716	33	1,575	2,269
Pulaski	6,570	12,970	257	4,384	14,434
Robertson	562	416	14	467	567
Rockcastle	1,345	3,543	37	1,089	4,328
Rowan	2,975	2,758	191	2,748	3,698
Russell	1,693	3,804	29	1,448	4,476
Scott	3,531	2,868	197	2,606	4,461
Shelby	4,429	3,423	178	3,326	5,390
Simpson	2,713	2,020	59	2,140	3,073
Spencer	1,216	935	27	910	1,456
Taylor	3,400	4,243	84	3,286	5,932
Todd	1,956	1,945	44	1,505	2,364
Trigg	2,619	1,913	56	1,905	2,512
Trimble	1,478	824	49	1,088	1,389
Union	3,479	1,847	68	3,090	2,524
Warren	9,643	12,184	602	7,937	16,167
Washington	2,147	2,008	43	1,786	2,804
Wayne	2,673	3,972	50	2,277	4,449
Webster	3,506	1,939	52	3,042	2,504
Whitley	3,889	7,007	125	3,575	7,851
Wolfe	1,814	951	19	1,394	1,257
Woodford	3,122	3,105	213	2,280	4,746
Totals	616,417	635,274	31,127	536,756	815,345

Kentucky Vote Since 1936

1936, Roosevelt, Dem., 541,944; Landon, Rep., 369,702; Lemke, Union, 12,501; Colvin, Proh., 929; Thomas, Soc., 627; Aiken, Soc. Labor, 294; Browder, Com., 204.

1940, Roosevelt, Dem., 557,222; Willkie, Rep., 410,384; Babson, Proh., 1,443; Thomas, Soc., 1,014.

1944, Roosevelt, Dem., 472,589; Dewey, Rep., 392,448; Watson, Proh., 2,023; Thomas, Soc., 535; Teichert, Soc. Labor, 326.

1948, Truman, Dem., 466,756; Dewey, Rep., 341,210; Thurmond, States' Rights, 10,411; Wallace, Prog., 1,567; Thomas, Soc., 1,284; Watson, Proh., 1,245; Teichert, Soc. Labor, 185.

1952, Eisenhower, Rep., 495,029; Stevenson, Dem., 495,729; Hamblen, Proh., 1,161; Hass, Soc. Labor, 893; Hallinan, Proh., 336.

1956, Eisenhower, Rep., 572,192; Stevenson, Dem., 476,453; Byrd, States' Rights, 2,657; Holtwick, Proh., 2,145; Hass, Soc. Labor, 358.

1960, Kennedy, Dem., 521,855; Nixon, Rep., 602,607.

1964, Johnson, Dem., 669,659; Goldwater, Rep., 372,977; John Kasper, Nat'l. States Rights, 3,469.

1968, Nixon, Rep., 462,411; Humphrey, Dem., 397,547; Wallace, 3d p., 193,098; Halstead, Soc. Worker, 2,843.

1972, Nixon, Rep., 676,446; McGovern, Dem., 371,159; Schmitz, Amer., 17,627; Jenness, Soc. Workers, 685; Hall, Com., 464; Spock, Peoples, 1,118.

1976, Carter, Dem., 615,717; Ford, Rep., 531,852; Anderson, Amer., 8,308; McCarthy, Ind., 6,837; Maddox, Amer. Ind., 2,328; MacBride, Libertarian, 814.

1980, Reagan, Rep., 635,274; Carter, Dem., 616,417; Anderson, Ind., 31,127; Clark, Libertarian, 5,531; McCormack, Respect For Life, 4,233; Commoner, Citizens, 1,304; Pulley, Socialist, 393; Hall, Com., 348.

1984, Reagan, Rep., 815,345; Mondale, Dem., 536,756.

Louisiana

Parish	1980 Carter (D)	Reagan (R)	Anderson (I)	1984 Mondale (D)	Reagan (R)
Acadia	9,948	11,533	416	9,262	14,906
Allen	6,057	3,328	110	4,842	4,474
Ascension	12,381	7,238	286	11,048	11,945
Assumption	4,679	4,001	153	4,660	5,433
Avoyelles	7,174	8,216	190	6,808	9,402
Beauregard	5,556	5,250	163	4,199	7,353
Bienville	4,123	3,508	51	3,530	4,587
Bossier	9,377	16,515	327	7,006	22,638
Caddo	36,422	51,202	1,128	35,727	63,429
Calcasieu	35,446	27,600	1,259	33,214	35,566
Caldwell	1,786	2,653	43	1,348	3,341
Cameron	2,221	1,449	82	1,608	2,265
Catahoula	2,414	2,942	38	1,649	3,640
Claiborne	3,443	3,538	53	2,788	4,349
Concordia	3,956	4,933	52	3,332	6,177
DeSoto	5,861	4,349	49	4,642	5,989
E. Baton Rouge	57,442	71,063	3,312	56,673	95,704
East Carroll	2,283	1,867	24	2,089	1,974
East Feliciana	4,033	2,650	53	4,122	4,166
Evangeline	6,722	7,412	160	6,981	8,680
Franklin	4,177	5,301	65	2,937	6,708
Grant	3,290	3,611	77	2,588	5,334
Iberia	9,681	14,273	410	10,170	17,727
Iberville	9,361	4,463	172	8,587	6,455
Jackson	3,609	3,923	56	2,568	5,034
Jefferson	50,870	99,403	3,578	41,183	123,997
Jefferson Davis	6,140	5,667	201	5,962	8,296
Lafayette	19,694	31,429	1,263	19,265	44,344
Lafourche	14,222	14,951	675	10,186	20,930
LaSalle	2,665	3,792	61	1,318	5,404
Lincoln	5,598	7,515	177	5,432	9,087
Livingston	11,319	10,666	287	8,913	17,465
Madison	3,264	2,531	16	2,906	2,849
Morehouse	4,856	7,254	65	4,829	8,585
Natchitoches	7,102	6,668	158	5,806	8,836
Orleans	106,858	74,302	4,246	119,478	86,316
Ouachita	16,306	29,799	495	15,525	37,270
Plaquemines	4,318	5,489	154	3,261	7,655
Pointe Coupee	6,395	3,667	105	6,732	5,477
Rapides	19,436	25,576	530	16,121	32,879
Red River	2,776	2,147	29	1,958	3,060
Richland	3,745	4,772	48	2,918	5,980
Sabine	5,100	4,265	74	2,980	6,295
St. Bernard	11,367	19,410	616	8,076	24,428
St. Charles	7,898	6,779	283	6,784	10,185
St. Helena	3,183	1,531	42	2,956	2,366
St. James	6,206	3,429	113	5,989	4,627
St. John The Baptist	7,647	5,819	261	7,646	9,093
St. Landry	17,125	14,940	332	17,950	19,055
St. Martin	7,760	6,701	281	8,589	9,698
St. Mary	10,506	10,378	339	9,411	15,275
St. Tammany	14,161	27,214	872	11,719	38,664
Tangipahoa	15,272	15,187	491	12,799	19,580
Tensas	2,046	1,645	25	1,628	1,956
Terrebonne	10,804	16,644	559	9,640	23,696
Union	3,841	5,130	60	2,916	6,585
Vermilion	9,743	10,481	473	9,033	12,721
Vernon	7,198	5,869	167	4,076	9,035
Washington	10,413	8,681	170	7,680	11,185
Webster	8,568	8,865	118	6,509	12,055
W. Baton Rouge	4,739	2,828	117	4,631	4,189
West Carroll	2,118	3,430	38	1,474	3,874
West Feliciana	2,341	1,237	40	2,296	2,097
Winn	3,411	3,944	57	2,633	4,934
Totals	708,453	792,853	26,345	651,586	1,037,299

Louisiana Vote Since 1936

1936, Roosevelt, Dem., 292,894; Landon, Rep., 36,791.

1940, Roosevelt, Dem., 319,751; Willkie, Rep., 52,446.

1944, Roosevelt, Dem., 281,564; Dewey, Rep., 67,750.

1948, Thurmond, States' Rights, 204,290; Truman, Dem., 136,344; Dewey, Rep., 72,657; Wallace, Prog., 3,035.

1952, Eisenhower, Rep., 306,925; Stevenson, Dem., 345,027.

1956, Eisenhower, Rep., 329,047; Stevenson, Dem., 243,977; Andrews, States' Rights, 44,520.

1960, Kennedy, Dem., 407,339; Nixon, Rep., 230,890; States' Rights (unpledged) 169,572.

1964, Johnson, Dem., 387,068; Goldwater, Rep., 509,225.

1968, Nixon, Rep., 257,535; Humphrey, Dem., 309,615; Wallace, 3d party, 530,300.

1972, Nixon, Rep., 686,852; McGovern, Dem., 298,142; Schmitz, Amer., 52,099; Jenness, Soc. Workers, 14,398.

1976, Carter, Dem., 661,365; Ford, Rep., 587,446; Maddox, Amer., 10,058; Hall, Com., 7,417; McCarthy, Ind., 6,588; MacBride, Libertarian, 3,325.

1980, Reagan, Rep., 792,853; Carter, Dem., 708,453; Anderson, Ind., 26,345; Rarick, Amer. Ind., 10,333; Clark, Libertarian, 8,240; Commoner, Citizens, 1,584; DeBerry, Work., 783.

1984, Reagan, Rep., 1,037,299; Mondale, Dem., 651,5?; Bergland, Libertarian, 1,876.

Maine

City	1980 Carter (D)	Reagan (R)	Anderson (I)	1984 Mondale (D)	Reagan (R)
Auburn	5,071	4,886	1,136	4,430	6,994
Augusta	4,470	4,271	1,262	4,451	5,995
Bangor	6,032	6,082	1,562	6,155	8,389
Bath	2,173	2,005	398	1,714	2,899
Biddeford	5,788	2,738	888	5,489	4,147
Brewer	1,767	2,526	435	1,461	3,093
Gardiner	1,325	1,265	415	1,216	1,942
Lewiston	11,365	6,205	1,875	9,853	9,480
Old Town	2,454	1,480	466	2,217	2,087
Portland	14,815	9,122	3,325	17,543	13,315
Rockland	1,140	1,366	292	1,051	2,169
Saco	3,240	2,583	695	3,094	3,761
Sanford	4,020	3,124	695	3,517	4,578
South Portland	5,371	4,519	1,280	5,377	6,653
Waterville	4,125	2,952	877	4,075	3,873
Westbrook	3,882	2,952	693	3,345	4,456
Totals	220,974	238,522	53,327	214,515	336,500

Maine Vote Since 1936

1936, Landon, Rep., 168,823; Roosevelt, Dem., 126,333; Lemke, Union, 7,581; Thomas, Soc., 783; Colvin, Proh., 334; Browder, Com., 257; Aiken, Soc. Labor, 129.

1940, Roosevelt, Dem., 156,478; Willkie, Rep., 165,951; Browder, Com., 411.

1944, Roosevelt, Dem., 140,631; Dewey, Rep., 155,434; Teichert, Soc. Labor, 335.

1948, Truman, Dem., 111,916; Dewey, Rep., 150,234; Wallace, Prog., 1,884; Thomas, Soc., 547; Teichert, Soc. Labor, 206.

1952, Eisenhower, Rep., 232,353; Stevenson, Dem., 118,806; Hallinan, Prog., 332; Hass, Soc. Labor, 156; Hoopes, Soc., 138; scattered, 1.

1956, Eisenhower, Rep., 249,238; Stevenson, Dem., 102,468.

1960, Kennedy, Dem., 181,159; Nixon, Rep., 240,608.

1964, Johnson, Dem., 262,264; Goldwater, Rep., 118,701.

1968, Nixon, Rep., 169,254; Humphrey, Dem., 217,312; Wallace, 3d party, 6,370.

1972, Nixon, Rep., 256,458; McGovern, Dem., 160,584; scattered, 229.

1976, Carter, Dem., 232,279; Ford, Rep., 236,320; McCarthy, Ind., 10,874; Bubar, Proh., 3,495.

1980, Reagan, Rep., 238,522; Carter, Dem., 220,974; Anderson, Ind., 53,327; Clark, Libertarian, 5,119; Commoner, Citizens, 4,394; Hall, Com., 591; write-ins, 84.

1984, Reagan, Rep., 336,500; Mondale, Dem., 214,515.

Maryland

County	1980 Carter (D)	Reagan (R)	Anderson (I)	1984 Mondale (D)	Reagan (R)
Allegany	12,167	17,512	1,486	11,143	19,763
Anne Arundel	50,780	69,443	10,020	47,565	94,171
Baltimore	121,280	132,490	23,096	106,908	171,929
Calvert	4,745	5,440	590	5,455	8,303
Caroline	2,833	3,582	291	2,198	4,876
Carroll	10,393	19,859	2,243	8,898	27,230
Cecil	7,937	9,673	1,037	6,681	13,111
Charles	8,887	11,807	1,153	10,264	16,132
Dorchester	4,908	5,160	360	3,160	6,699
Frederick	13,629	22,033	2,891	13,411	29,606
Garrett	2,708	5,475	270	2,386	7,011
Harford	20,042	26,713	3,761	17,193	37,382
Howard	20,702	24,272	6,028	23,713	35,641
Kent	2,986	2,889		2,390	3,897
Montgomery	105,822	125,511	32,730	146,036	146,924
Prince George's	98,757	78,977	14,574	136,063	95,121
Queen Anne's	3,820	4,749	480	2,938	6,784
St. Mary's	6,773	8,267	892	6,420	11,201
Somerset	3,342	3,312	215	2,439	4,508
Talbot	3,995	6,044	570	3,198	8,028
Washington	14,118	22,901	1,689	13,329	27,118
Wicomico	9,431	11,229	1,092	8,160	16,124
Worcester	4,195	5,362	586	3,770	8,208
BALTIMORE CITY	191,911	57,902	13,112	202,277	80,120
Totals	726,161	680,606	119,537	787,935	879,918

Maryland Vote Since 1936

1936, Roosevelt, Dem., 389,612; Landon, Rep., 231,435; Thomas, Soc., 1,629; Aiken, Soc. Labor, 1,305; Browder, Com., 915.

1940, Roosevelt, Dem., 384,546; Willkie, Rep., 269,534; Thomas, Soc., 4,093; Browder, Com., 1,274; Aiken, Soc. Labor, 657.

1944, Roosevelt, Dem., 315,490; Dewey, Rep., 292,949.

1948, Truman, Dem., 286,521; Dewey, Rep., 294,814; Wallace, Prog., 9,983; Thomas, Soc., 2,941; Thurmond, States' Rights, 2,476; Wright, write-in, 2,294.

1952, Eisenhower, Rep., 499,424; Stevenson, Dem., 395,337; Hallinan, Prog., 7,313.

1956, Eisenhower, Rep., 559,738; Stevenson, Dem., 372,613.

1960, Kennedy, Dem., 565,800; Nixon, Rep., 489,538.

1964, Johnson, Dem., 730,912; Goldwater, Rep., 385,495; write-in, 50.

1968, Nixon, Rep., 517,995; Humphrey, Dem., 538,310; Wallace, 3d party, 178,734.

1972, Nixon, Rep., 829,305; McGovern, Dem., 505,781; Schmitz, Amer., 18,726.

1976, Carter, Dem., 759,612; Ford, Rep., 672,661.

1980, Reagan, Rep., 680,606; Carter, Dem., 726,161; Anderson, Ind., 119,537; Clark, Libertarian, 14,192.

1984, Reagan, Rep., 879,918; Mondale, Dem., 787,935; Bergland, Libertarian, 5,721.

Massachusetts

| City | 1980 | | | 1984 | |
	Carter (D)	Reagan (R)	Anderson (I)	Mondale (D)	Reagan (R)
Boston	95,133	58,656	22,577	131,745	75,311
Brockton	12,751	15,350	4,633	14,130	17,161
Cambridge	24,337	7,952	6,694	32,582	10,007
Fall River	19,644	9,958	3,694	20,722	11,463
Framingham	12,275	11,979	4,940	14,368	15,074
Lawrence	12,145	8,020	2,341	10,986	9,877
Lowell	16,353	12,568	3,791	15,042	16,834
Lynn	15,777	11,966	3,911	17,103	14,445
New Bedford	18,014	13,217	3,843	22,070	13,147
Newton	20,173	15,621	7,778	27,343	16,184
Quincy	17,977	18,038	5,328	18,971	20,123
Somerville	16,931	9,533	4,143	21,065	11,318
Springfield	26,414	17,694	6,327	29,376	21,431
Worcester	31,146	23,305	8,411	32,525	27,348
Totals	1,053,802	1,057,631	382,539	1,239,606	1,310,936

Massachusetts Vote Since 1936

1936, Roosevelt, Dem., 942,716; Landon, Rep., 768,613; Lemke, Union, 118,639; Thomas, Soc., 5,111; Browder, Com., 2,930; Aiken, Soc. Labor, 1,305; Colvin, Proh., 1,032.

1940, Roosevelt, Dem., 1,076,522; Willkie, Rep., 939,700; Thomas, Soc., 4,091; Browder, Com., 3,806; Aiken, Soc. Labor, 1,492; Babson, Proh., 1,370.

1944, Roosevelt, Dem., 1,035,296; Dewey, Rep., 921,350; Teichert, Soc. Labor, 2,780; Watson, Proh., 973.

1948, Truman, Dem., 1,151,788; Dewey, Rep., 909,370; Wallace, Prog., 38,157; Teichert, Soc. Labor, 5,535; Watson, Proh., 1,663.

1952, Eisenhower, Rep., 1,292,325; Stevenson, Dem., 1,083,525; Hallinan, Prog., 4,636; Hass, Soc. Labor, 1,957; Hamblen, Proh., 886; scattered, 69; blanks, 41,150.

1956, Eisenhower, Rep., 1,393,197; Stevenson, Dem., 948,190; Hass, Soc. Labor, 5,573; Holtwick, Proh., 1,205; others, 341.

1960, Kennedy, Dem., 1,487,174; Nixon, Rep., 976,750; Hass, Soc. Labor, 3,892; Decker, Proh., 1,633; others, 31; blank and void, 26,024.

1964, Johnson, Dem., 1,786,422; Goldwater, Rep., 549,727; Hass, Soc. Labor, 4,755; Munn, Proh., 3,735; scattered, 159; blank, 48,104.

1968, Nixon, Rep., 766,844; Humphrey, Dem., 1,469,218; Wallace, 3d party, 87,088; Blomen, Soc. Labor, 6,180; Munn, Proh., 2,369; scattered, 53; blanks, 25,394.

1972, Nixon, Rep., 1,112,078; McGovern, Dem., 1,332,540; Jenness, Soc. Workers, 10,600; Fisher, Soc. Labor, 129; Schmitz, Amer., 2,877; Spock, Peoples, 101; Hall, Com., 46; Hospers, Libertarian, 43; scattered, 342.

1976, Carter, Dem., 1,429,475; Ford, Rep., 1,030,276; McCarthy, Ind., 65,637; Camejo, Soc. Workers, 8,138; An-

derson, Amer., 7,555; La Rouche, U.S. Labor, 4,922; MacBride, Libertarian, 135.

1980, Reagan, Rep., 1,057,631; Carter, Dem., 1,053,802; Anderson, Ind., 382,539; Clark, Libertarian, 22,038; DeBerry, Soc. Workers, 3,735; Commoner, Citizens, 2,056; McReynolds, Socialist, 62; Bubar, Statesman, 34; Griswold, Workers World, 19; scattered, 2,382.

1984, Reagan, Rep., 1,310,936; Mondale, Dem., 1,239,936.

Michigan

| County | 1980 | | | 1984 | |
	Carter (D)	Reagan (R)	Anderson (I)	Mondale (D)	Reagan (R)
Alcona	1,857	2,905	247	1,616	3,223
Alger	2,242	2,059	263	2,018	2,175
Allegan	9,877	20,560	1,984	8,389	23,762
Alpena	5,834	6,901	913	5,136	8,212
Antrim	2,909	4,706	602	2,507	5,726
Arenac	2,547	3,436	333	2,436	3,483
Baraga	1,609	2,046	201	1,818	1,965
Barry	6,857	12,006	1,399	5,898	14,245
Bay	24,517	25,331	3,886	22,597	26,198
Benzie	1,842	3,054	455	1,866	3,590
Berrien	22,152	41,458	3,422	21,228	43,160
Branch	4,635	10,224	1,102	3,860	11,004
Calhoun	23,022	30,912	4,468	20,313	34,470
Cass	7,058	11,206	1,156	6,634	11,647
Charlevoix	3,741	5,053	816	3,175	6,355
Cheboygan	3,938	5,221	638	3,358	6,053
Chippewa	5,268	7,059	951	4,575	8,135
Clare	4,164	5,719	663	3,764	6,587
Clinton	7,539	14,968	1,736	6,226	17,387
Crawford	1,826	2,652	390	1,558	3,303
Delta	8,475	8,146	849	7,934	8,952
Dickinson	5,694	6,614	596	5,614	6,880
Eaton	12,742	22,927	3,533	10,290	27,720
Emmet	3,724	5,930	1,134	3,254	7,760
Genesee	90,393	78,572	12,274	89,491	92,943
Gladwin	3,733	4,509	463	3,368	5,401
Gogebic	5,254	4,388	493	5,554	4,006
Grand Traverse	7,150	14,484	2,568	7,271	18,036
Gratiot	4,916	9,294	1,193	4,000	10,456
Hillsdale	4,375	10,951	882	3,616	12,063
Houghton	6,858	7,926	1,423	6,434	8,652
Huron	4,434	10,553	976	3,966	11,073
Ingham	48,278	56,777	17,139	46,411	68,753
Ionia	7,039	12,040	1,539	5,735	14,162
Iosco	4,255	6,680	739	3,850	7,907
Iron	3,742	3,507	371	3,559	3,468
Isabella	7,293	10,407	2,511	6,435	12,215
Jackson	23,685	33,749	4,165	18,340	40,133
Kalamazoo	34,528	48,669	10,833	32,460	58,327
Kalkaska	1,807	2,802	260	1,595	3,623
Kent	72,790	112,604	17,913	66,238	137,417
Keweenaw	570	583	87	628	599
Lake	2,041	1,730	187	1,845	2,125
Lapeer	9,671	15,996	1,868	7,800	19,222
Leelanau	2,346	4,585	839	2,498	5,356
Lenawee	12,935	20,366	2,230	11,012	22,409
Livingston	12,626	25,012	3,247	10,720	31,846
Luce	992	1,659	177	833	1,715
Mackinac	2,262	3,021	415	1,949	3,627
Macomb	120,125	154,155	18,975	97,816	194,300
Manistee	4,164	5,662	699	3,917	6,328
Marquette	13,312	13,181	2,481	14,074	14,196
Mason	4,134	7,137	825	3,803	8,202
Mecosta	5,228	7,754	1,322	4,048	9,023
Menominee	4,962	6,170	452	4,425	6,618
Midland	12,019	17,828	3,152	10,769	21,521
Missaukee	1,563	3,221	230	1,256	3,970
Monroe	20,578	25,612	3,111	19,617	29,419
Montcalm	6,708	10,822	1,309	5,491	13,109
Montmorency	1,654	2,400	195	1,387	2,913
Muskegon	26,645	36,512	4,094	25,247	39,355
Newaygo	5,236	8,918	850	4,496	10,636
Oakland	164,869	253,211	38,273	150,286	306,050
Oceana	3,386	5,465	570	2,865	6,405
Ogemaw	3,426	4,169	425	3,132	4,901
Ontonagon	2,375	2,569	237	2,350	2,464
Osceola	2,650	4,902	466	2,127	5,923
Oscoda	1,325	1,915	183	951	2,239
Otsego	2,666	3,771	493	2,117	4,639
Ottawa	18,435	51,217	4,903	15,000	60,142
Presque Isle	2,952	3,486	382	2,481	4,207
Roscommon	3,763	5,280	508	3,359	6,419
Saginaw	41,650	45,233	5,677	38,420	51,495
St. Clair	20,410	31,021	3,592	16,998	36,114
St. Joseph	6,318	13,631	1,283	5,795	15,405
Sanilac	4,898	12,158	863	4,126	12,627
Schoolcraft	1,964	2,097	243	1,920	2,139
Shiawassee	11,985	15,756	2,121	9,514	18,756
Tuscola	7,632	13,306	1,266	6,212	14,698
Van Buren	9,248	14,451	1,691	8,853	16,426
Washtenaw	51,013	48,599	13,463	55,084	58,736
Wayne	522,024	315,532	43,608	496,632	357,391

Wexford	4,173	6,027	752	3,398	7,279
Totals	1,661,532	1,915,225	275,223	1,529,638	2,251,571

Michigan Vote Since 1936

1936, Roosevelt, Dem., 1,016,794; Landon, Rep., 699,733; Lemke, Union, 75,795; Thomas, Soc., 8,208; Browder, Com., 3,384; Aiken, Soc. Labor, 600; Colvin, Proh., 579.

1940, Roosevelt, Dem., 1,032,991; Willkie, Rep., 1,039,917; Thomas, Soc., 7,593; Browder, Com., 2,834; Babson, Proh., 1,795; Aiken, Soc. Labor, 795.

1944, Roosevelt, Dem., 1,106,899; Dewey, Rep., 1,084,423; Watson, Proh., 6,503; Thomas, Soc., 4,598; Smith, America First, 1,530; Teichert, Soc. Labor, 1,264.

1948, Truman, Dem., 1,003,448; Dewey, Rep., 1,038,595; Wallace, Prog., 46,515; Watson, Proh., 13,052; Thomas, Soc. 6,063; Teichert, Soc. Labor, 1,263; Dobbs, Soc. Workers, 672.

1952, Eisenhower, Rep., 1,551,529; Stevenson, Dem., 1,230,657; Hamblen, Proh., 10,331; Hallinan, Prog., 3,922; Hass, Soc. Labor, 1,495; Dobbs, Soc. Workers, 655; scattered, 3.

1956, Eisenhower, Rep., 1,713,647; Stevenson, Dem., 1,359,898; Holtwick, Proh., 6,923.

1960, Kennedy, Dem., 1,687,269; Nixon, Rep., 1,620,428; Dobbs, Soc. Workers, 4,347; Decker, Proh., 2,029; Daly, Tax Cut, 1,767; Hass, Soc. Labor, 1,718; Ind. American, 539.

1964, Johnson, Dem., 2,136,615; Goldwater, Rep., 1,060,152; DeBerry, Soc. Workers, 3,817; Hass, Soc. Labor, 1,704; Proh. (no candidate listed), 699, scattering, 145.

1968, Nixon, Rep., 1,370,665; Humphrey, Dem., 1,593,082; Wallace, 3d party, 331,968; Halstead, Soc. Worker, 4,099; Blomen, Soc. Labor, 1,762; Cleaver, New Politics, 4,585; Munn, Proh., 60; scattering, 29.

1972, Nixon, Rep., 1,961,721; McGovern, Dem., 1,459,435; Schmitz, Amer., 63,321; Fisher, Soc. Labor, 2,437; Jenness, Soc. Workers, 1,603; Hall, Com., 1,210.

1976, Carter, Dem., 1,696,714; Ford, Rep., 1,893,742; McCarthy, Ind., 47,905; MacBride, Libertarian, 5,406; Wright, People's, 3,504, Camejo, Soc. Workers, 1,804; LaRouche, U.S. Labor, 1,366; Levin, Soc. Labor, 1,148; scattering, 2,160.

1980, Reagan, Rep., 1,915,225; Carter, Dem., 1,661,532; Anderson, Ind., 275,223; Clark, Libertarian, 41,597; Commoner, Citizens, 11,930; Hall, Com., 3,262; Griswold, Workers World, 30; Greaves, American, 21; Bubar, Statesman, 9.

1984, Reagan, Rep., 2,251,571; Mondale, Dem., 1,529,638; Bergland, Libertarian, 10,055.

Minnesota

	1980			1984	
County	Carter (D)	Reagan (R)	Anderson (I)	Mondale (D)	Reagan (R)
Aitkin	3,677	3,396	380	3,943	3,422
Anoka	45,532	33,100	6,828	50,305	46,578
Becker	5,221	6,848	866	5,456	7,553
Beltrami	7,432	6,481	1,254	7,481	7,414
Benton	5,272	5,513	646	4,922	6,830
Big Stone	1,814	1,950	249	1,994	1,821
Blue Earth	10,930	11,966	2,698	11,877	14,298
Brown	4,915	8,051	842	4,469	8,399
Carlton	8,822	4,760	883	9,189	4,877
Carver	6,621	9,909	1,496	6,725	11,963
Cass	4,717	6,119	434	4,773	6,619
Chippewa	3,164	4,252	532	3,047	3,964
Chisago	6,240	5,017	939	6,683	6,279
Clay	8,940	10,447	2,773	10,294	11,565
Clearwater....	1,955	1,919	185	1,917	2,066
Cook	871	1,174	182	1,129	1,219
Cottonwood ...	2,958	4,258	535	3,073	4,275
Crow Wing	9,323	10,844	1,046	8,719	11,362
Dakota	43,433	40,708	8,588	49,125	55,119
Dodge	2,698	3,900	367	2,786	4,428
Douglas	5,530	7,778	844	5,444	9,005
Faribault	3,620	6,206	525	3,993	5,690
Fillmore	4,010	6,452	650	4,351	6,342
Freeborn	8,212	8,475	808	9,338	8,413
Goodhue	8,586	9,929	1,964	8,679	11,171
Grant	1,822	2,054	333	1,867	2,111
Hennepin	239,592	194,998	56,390	272,401	253,921
Houston	3,218	5,582	477	3,512	5,645
Hubbard	2,840	4,172	365	2,806	4,621
Isanti	5,457	4,400	641	5,378	5,660
Itasca	12,138	8,368	1,080	11,455	9,306
Jackson	3,062	3,391	463	3,437	3,131
Kanabec	2,654	2,500	269	2,660	3,027
Kandiyohi.....	8,038	8,480	1,244	8,402	9,539
Kittson	1,407	1,875	243	1,610	1,716
Koochiching ...	4,181	3,433	496	4,238	3,466
LacQuiParle ...	2,457	2,981	334	2,685	2,731
Lake	3,864	2,414	443	4,468	2,003
Lake O'Woods...	763	1,052	128	824	1,094
Le Sueur	5,161	5,478	731	5,070	6,033
Lincoln	1,640	2,122	295	1,827	1,905
Lyon	5,626	5,852	1,129	5,389	7,170
McLeod	4,987	7,819	852	4,864	8,728
Mahnomen....	1,175	1,275	153	1,241	1,328
Marshall......	2,636	3,638	397	2,705	3,433
Martin........	4,301	7,057	751	4,673	7,308
Meeker	4,238	5,032	668	4,156	5,511
Mille Lacs	4,443	3,860	550	4,011	4,307
Morrison	6,930	6,296	559	6,225	7,556
Mower	10,538	7,908	1,465	12,498	8,054
Murray	2,714	3,004	359	2,741	2,780
Nicollet	5,400	6,436	1,519	5,789	7,472
Nobles	4,703	4,706	657	4,619	4,876
Norman	2,253	2,192	369	2,202	2,152
Olmsted	13,983	22,704	3,638	16,335	28,129
Otter Tail	9,108	15,091	1,538	9,714	15,664
Pennington ...	3,101	3,715	472	2,913	3,536
Pine	5,121	3,899	467	5,223	4,493
Pipestone.....	2,392	3,207	561	2,391	3,043
Polk	7,151	9,036	1,207	7,033	8,617
Pope	2,527	3,159	354	2,757	3,064
Ramsey	124,774	78,860	23,222	141,623	95,667
Red Lake	1,318	1,223	116	1,294	1,184
Redwood	2,952	5,993	548	2,957	6,020
Renville	4,058	5,544	653	3,972	5,571
Rice	9,531	8,168	2,414	10,880	10,456
Rock	2,089	3,164	397	2,188	2,971
Roseau	2,616	3,358	259	2,319	3,445
St. Louis	69,403	33,407	8,719	77,683	34,162
Scott	9,115	9,018	1,475	9,452	12,573
Sherburne	6,229	6,035	985	6,140	7,738
Sibley	2,521	4,460	509	2,761	4,638
Stearns	21,862	24,888	3,555	20,944	30,216
Steele	5,095	7,805	1,087	5,060	8,780
Stevens	2,559	3,283	524	2,451	3,251
Swift	3,245	2,943	511	3,531	2,893
Todd	4,975	6,451	451	4,657	6,585
Traverse	1,258	1,574	159	1,325	1,399
Wabasha	3,712	4,886	549	3,872	5,299
Wadena	2,635	4,089	265	2,454	4,306
Waseca	3,535	4,801	777	3,527	5,509
Washington ...	25,634	22,718	5,050	28,527	29,046
Watonwan	2,442	3,629	415	2,425	3,526
Wilkin	1,496	2,224	318	1,410	2,367
Winona	9,814	10,332	1,780	9,577	11,981
Wright	12,383	12,293	1,692	12,486	15,399
Yellow Med	2,833	4,004	456	3,018	3,819
Totals	954,173	873,268	174,997	1,036,364	1,032,603

Minnesota Vote Since 1936

1936, Roosevelt, Dem., 698,811; Landon, Rep., 350,461; Lemke, Union, 74,296; Thomas, Soc., 2,872; Browder, Com., 2,574; Aiken, Soc. Labor, 961.

1940, Roosevelt, Dem., 644,196; Willkie, Rep., 596,274; Thomas, Soc., 5,454; Browder, Com., 2,711; Aiken, Ind., 2,553.

1944, Roosevelt, Dem., 589,864; Dewey, Rep., 527,416; Thomas, Soc., 5,073; Teichert, Ind. Gov't., 3,176.

1948, Truman, Dem., 692,966; Dewey, Rep., 483,617; Wallace, Prog., 27,866; Thomas, Soc., 4,646; Teichert, Soc. Labor, 2,525; Dobbs, Soc. Workers, 606.

1952, Eisenhower, Rep., 763,211; Stevenson, Dem., 608,458; Hallinan, Prog., 2,666; Hass, Soc. Labor, 2,383; Hamblen, Proh., 2,147; Dobbs, Soc. Workers, 618.

1956, Eisenhower, Rep., 719,302; Stevenson, Dem., 617,525; Hass, Soc. Labor (Ind. Gov.), 2,080; Dobbs, Soc. Workers, 1,098.

1960, Kennedy, Dem., 779,933; Nixon, Rep., 757,915; Dobbs, Soc. Workers, 3,077; Industrial Gov., 962.

1964, Johnson, Dem., 991,117; Goldwater, Rep., 559,624; DeBerry, Soc. Workers, 1,177; Hass, Industrial Gov., 2,544.

1968, Nixon, Rep., 658,643; Humphrey, Dem., 857,738; Wallace, 3d party, 68,931; scattered, 2,443; Halstead, Soc. Worker, 808; Blomen, Ind. Gov't., 285; Mitchell, Com., 415; Cleaver, Peace, 935; McCarthy, write-in, 585; scattered, 170.

1972, Nixon, Rep., 898,269; McGovern, Dem., 802,346; Schmitz, Amer., 31,407; Spock, Peoples, 2,805; Fisher, Soc. Labor, 4,261; Jenness, Soc. Workers, 940; Hall, Com., 662; scattered, 962.

6, Carter, Dem., 1,070,440; Ford, Rep., 819,395; McCarthy, Ind., 35,490; Anderson, Amer., 13,592; Camejo, Soc. Workers, 4,149; MacBride, Libertarian, 3,529; Hall, Com., 1,092.

980, Reagan, Rep., 873, 268; Carter, Dem., 954,173; Anderson, Ind., 174,997; Clark, Libertarian, 31,593; Commoner, Citizens, 8,406; Hall, Com., 1,117; DeBerry, Soc. Workers, 711; Griswold, Workers World, 698; McReynolds, Socialist, 536; write-ins, 281.

1984, Mondale, Dem., 1,036,364; Reagan, Rep., 1,032,603; Bergland, Libertarian, 2,996.

Mississippi

County	1980 Carter (D)	Reagan (R)	Anderson (I)	1984 Mondale (D)	Reagan (R)
Adams	7,226	7,523	151	7,849	9,440
Alcorn	6,242	5,196	898	4,862	7,203
Amite	3,229	2,653	43	2,569	3,463
Attala	4,117	3,975	71	3,327	4,870
Benton	2,094	1,254	35	1,715	1,737
Bolivar	8,839	5,148	280	8,769	6,939
Calhoun	3,295	2,579	64	1,749	3,579
Carroll	2,037	2,153	22	1,462	2,823
Chickasaw	3,622	2,540	71	2,329	3,605
Choctaw	1,729	1,927	26	1,166	2,491
Claiborne	3,032	1,129	22	3,179	1,294
Clarke	3,303	3,303	41	2,262	4,551
Clay	4,275	3,439	124	4,046	4,112
Coahoma	7,030	4,592	256	6,839	5,759
Copiah	5,517	4,461	76	4,591	5,806
Covington	2,956	3,471	39	2,219	4,165
DeSoto	6,344	9,655	237	4,369	12,576
Forrest	8,274	12,656	275	6,786	15,719
Franklin	2,040	2,026	23	1,494	2,564
George	2,757	3,052	64	1,655	4,346
Greene	1,740	1,772	23	1,297	2,744
Grenada	4,182	3,993	59	3,325	5,181
Hancock	3,544	5,088	159	2,630	7,662
Harrison	16,318	25,175	822	12,495	33,995
Hinds	39,369	48,135	1,414	42,373	56,953
Holmes	5,463	2,693	57	5,461	3,102
Humphreys	2,970	1,841	68	2,596	2,309
Issaquena	598	349	5	501	512
Itawamba	4,852	2,906	57	2,674	4,587
Jackson	12,226	22,498	653	8,821	29,585
Jasper	3,813	2,781	34	3,104	3,727
Jefferson	2,871	751	41	3,049	856
Jefferson Davis	3,831	2,280	24	2,644	2,884
Jones	11,117	12,900	155	7,298	17,586
Kemper	2,601	1,822	12	2,089	2,354
Lafayette	4,887	4,366	243	3,646	6,006
Lamar	3,005	5,395	84	1,964	7,929
Lauderdale	9,918	14,727	784	7,534	18,807
Lawrence	2,692	2,781	49	2,274	3,970
Leake	4,033	3,624	40	2,845	4,663
Lee	10,047	8,326	321	6,208	13,312
Leflore	7,496	5,798	166	7,443	7,550
Lincoln	5,213	7,286	75	4,458	8,898
Lowndes	6,187	9,973	140	6,078	12,049
Madison	7,621	6,024	276	8,002	9,298
Marion	5,366	5,218	62	3,757	7,355
Marshall	7,153	3,455	121	5,845	4,389
Monroe	6,998	4,793	177	4,437	7,387
Montgomery	2,730	2,479	42	1,881	3,093
Neshoba	3,872	5,165	72	2,630	6,715
Newton	3,455	4,317	86	2,127	5,911
Noxubee	3,434	1,970	47	2,928	2,123
Oktibbeha	6,039	6,300	258	5,097	7,574
Panola	6,179	4,219	149	5,465	5,850
Pearl River	5,028	6,822	161	3,085	9,978
Perry	1,957	2,255	25	1,415	3,098
Pike	6,694	6,661	129	6,137	8,254
Pontotoc	4,499	3,198	58	2,434	5,182
Prentiss	4,832	3,264	40	2,897	4,821
Quitman	2,925	1,691	83	2,343	2,198
Rankin	8,047	16,650	296	5,874	22,393
Scott	4,043	4,645	72	3,274	5,763
Sharkey	1,957	996	28	1,723	1,487
Simpson	4,015	5,190	70	2,894	5,983
Smith	2,474	3,772	46	1,573	5,116
Stone	1,821	1,888	53	1,185	2,980
Sunflower	5,035	3,728	82	4,913	5,178
Tallahatchie	3,467	2,183	45	2,725	2,901
Tate	3,692	3,343	80	2,846	4,677
Tippah	3,878	3,338	118	2,566	4,706
Tishomingo	4,595	2,489	79	2,879	3,527
Tunica	2,198	954	24	1,621	1,109
Union	5,001	3,545	94	2,766	5,837
Walthall	2,960	2,703	34	2,219	3,305
Warren	7,489	10,151	274	8,054	12,959
Washington	10,722	8,978	186	10,617	12,454
Wayne	3,494	3,844	26	2,818	5,000
Webster	2,178	2,386	75	1,397	3,390
Wilkinson	2,981	1,442	25	2,627	1,722
Winston	4,416	3,998	65	3,543	5,192
Yalobusha	3,432	2,224	78	2,337	2,934
Yazoo	5,468	4,819	99	5,037	6,275
Totals	429,281	441,089	12,036	352,192	582,377

Mississippi Vote Since 1936

1936, Roosevelt, Dem., 157,318; Landon, Rep., Howard faction, 2,760; Rowlands faction, 1,675 total 4,435; Thomas, Soc., 329.

1940, Roosevelt, Dem., 168,252; Willkie, Ind. Rep., 4,550; Rep., 2,814; total, 7,364; Thomas, Soc., 103.

1944, Roosevelt, Dem., 158,515; Dewey, Rep., 3,742; Reg. Dem., 9,964; Ind. Rep., 7,859.

1948, Thurmond, States' Rights, 167,538; Truman, Dem., 19,384; Dewey, Rep., 5,043; Wallace, Prog., 225.

1952, Eisenhower, Ind. vote pledged to Rep. candidate, 112,966; Stevenson, Dem., 172,566.

1956, Stevenson, Dem., 144,498; Eisenhower, Rep., 56,372; Black and Tan Grand Old Party, 4,313; total, 60,685; Byrd, Ind., 42,966.

1960, Democratic unpledged electors, 116,248; Kennedy, Dem., 108,362; Nixon, Rep., 73,561. Mississippi's victorious slate of 8 unpledged Democratic electors cast their votes for Sen. Harry F. Byrd (D-Va.).

1964, Johnson, Dem., 52,618; Goldwater, Rep., 356,528.

1968, Nixon, Rep., 88,516; Humphrey, Dem., 150,644; Wallace, 3d party, 415,349.

1972, Nixon, Rep., 505,125; McGovern, Dem., 126,782; Schmitz, Amer., 11,598; Jenness, Soc. Workers, 2,458.

1976, Carter, Dem., 381,309; Ford, Rep., 366,846; Anderson, Amer., 6,678; McCarthy, Ind., 4,074; Maddox, Ind., 4,049; Camejo, Soc. Workers, 2,805; MacBride, Libertarian, 2,609.

1980, Reagan, Rep., 441,089; Carter, Dem., 429,281; Anderson, Ind., 12,036; Clark, Libertarian, 5,465; Griswold, Workers World, 2,402; Pulley, Soc. Worker, 2,347.

1984, Reagan, Rep., 582,377; Mondale, Dem., 352,192; Bergland, Libertarian, 2,336.

Missouri

County	1980 Carter (D)	Reagan (R)	Anderson (I)	1984 Mondale (D)	Reagan (R)
Adair	3,507	5,513	414	3,119	6,430
Andrew	2,575	3,690	245	2,457	4,252
Atchison	1,273	2,096	151	1,219	2,277
Audrain	5,168	6,347	233	4,662	7,261
Barry	4,193	7,038	150	3,483	7,683
Barton	1,901	3,337	115	1,348	3,996
Bates	3,297	4,061	114	2,889	4,223
Benton	2,241	3,451	126	2,251	3,805
Bollinger	2,160	2,863	35	1,923	2,778
Boone	18,527	16,313	3,519	19,364	26,600
Buchanan	16,967	16,551	1,301	15,369	19,735
Butler	5,605	8,342	181	4,699	8,712
Caldwell	1,541	2,551	108	1,382	2,678
Callaway	5,560	6,755	420	4,327	8,262
Camden	3,416	6,541	218	3,088	8,057
Cape Girardeau	8,625	14,861	873	7,346	17,404
Carroll	2,130	3,291	130	1,980	3,495
Carter	1,087	1,218	37	916	1,402
Cass	8,198	10,105	667	7,517	14,456
Cedar	1,703	3,469	86	1,440	3,539
Chariton	2,250	2,641	63	2,244	2,744
Christian	3,502	6,487	205	3,223	7,634
Clark	1,494	2,042	56	1,627	2,068
Clay	24,250	28,521	2,782	22,586	36,529
Clinton	3,001	3,599	184	2,778	4,226
Cole	9,210	16,373	691	6,702	20,366
Cooper	2,687	3,996	130	2,219	4,603
Crawford	2,710	4,081	170	2,610	4,716
Dade	1,283	2,410	61	1,100	2,600
Dallas	2,011	3,297	114	1,902	3,577
Daviess	1,770	2,125	61	1,526	2,414
DeKalb	1,677	2,062	111	1,464	2,188
Dent	2,528	3,477	86	2,544	3,490
Douglas	1,677	3,440	93	1,536	3,662
Dunklin	6,120	5,253	128	4,967	6,092
Franklin	10,480	15,210	863	8,319	18,669
Gasconade	1,550	4,481	136	1,130	4,678
Gentry	1,720	2,005	117	1,600	2,047
Greene	30,498	43,116	3,261	27,965	57,250
Grundy	2,064	2,890	110	1,861	3,156
Harrison	1,732	2,734	140	1,649	2,844
Henry	4,648	4,807	238	3,741	5,419
Hickory	1,248	1,893	52	1,212	2,190
Holt	1,119	1,993	59	1,026	2,087
Howard	2,243	2,179	114	2,014	2,360
Howell	4,472	7,149	211	3,767	8,204
Iron	2,226	2,205	94	2,023	2,326
Jackson	135,805	106,156	12,260	135,067	132,271
Jasper	11,953	21,664	785	9,259	23,066

County				
Jefferson	24,042	28,546	1,753	20,026	34,525
Johnson	5,441	6,449	571	4,238	8,413
Knox	1,187	1,475	36	1,097	1,513
Laclede	3,443	5,642	153	2,665	6,406
Lafayette	5,792	7,271	339	4,848	8,581
Lawrence	4,670	7,921	184	3,720	8,370
Lewis	2,314	2,350	102	1,977	2,438
Lincoln	4,110	4,963	182	3,290	6,137
Linn	3,467	3,585	139	3,112	3,822
Livingston	3,368	3,654	205	2,699	4,090
McDonald	2,485	4,114	124	2,109	4,521
Macon	3,578	4,430	135	3,037	4,542
Madison	2,231	2,618	70	1,862	2,808
Maries	1,732	1,985	39	1,388	2,267
Marion	5,890	6,036	192	4,666	6,831
Mercer	821	1,266	54	875	1,229
Miller	2,469	5,560	115	2,054	6,706
Mississippi	3,040	2,459	64	2,524	2,502
Moniteau	2,284	3,430	98	1,614	4,197
Monroe	2,445	2,026	53	1,992	2,163
Montgomery	2,007	3,061	124	1,668	3,261
Morgan	2,460	3,577	114	2,169	4,392
New Madrid	4,171	4,041	64	3,776	4,323
Newton	5,621	10,515	341	4,623	11,709
Nodaway	4,257	4,544	414	3,615	5,471
Oregon	2,326	1,523	26	2,026	1,979
Osage	2,045	3,679	72	1,343	4,381
Ozark	1,242	2,434	63	1,110	2,614
Pemiscot	4,140	3,519	52	3,293	3,733
Perry	2,416	5,053	178	1,837	4,493
Pettis	6,475	8,833	435	5,413	10,991
Phelps	5,470	7,366	620	5,074	9,012
Pike	3,454	3,932	158	3,313	3,933
Platte	7,342	10,092	1,107	7,668	12,859
Polk	3,336	4,842	135	2,819	5,467
Pulaski	3,707	3,998	128	2,865	5,330
Putnam	871	1,722	44	797	1,540
Ralls	2,069	1,968	75	2,011	2,067
Randolph	4,884	5,141	213	4,471	5,735
Ray	4,518	4,064	215	3,979	4,875
Reynolds	1,919	1,271	44	2,026	1,330
Ripley	2,156	2,524	61	1,883	2,927
St. Charles	20,668	36,050	2,494	17,617	47,784
St. Clair	1,706	2,419	60	1,655	2,667
St. Francois	7,495	8,914	397	7,137	9,792
Ste. Genevieve	3,324	2,768	151	2,723	3,245
St. Louis	192,796	263,518	25,032	173,144	307,684
Saline	4,943	5,218	353	4,281	6,042
Schuyler	1,114	1,386	48	1,141	1,250
Scotland	1,200	1,592	63	1,075	1,485
Scott	6,854	8,227	203	5,569	8,727
Shannon	1,818	1,523	44	1,580	1,779
Shelby	1,849	2,151	60	1,573	2,243
Stoddard	5,128	6,199	132	4,294	6,701
Stone	2,210	4,760	180	2,119	5,706
Sullivan	1,824	2,412	76	1,784	2,306
Taney	3,389	6,230	195	2,912	7,082
Texas	4,261	4,879	125	3,662	5,591
Vernon	3,704	4,391	285	2,984	5,181
Warren	2,132	4,366	192	1,964	5,150
Washington	2,873	3,439	89	2,987	3,755
Wayne	2,549	2,823	44	2,363	2,867
Webster	3,409	5,121	149	2,982	5,529
Worth	760	833	47	734	921
Wright	2,182	4,451	56	1,973	4,687
ST. LOUIS CITY	113,697	50,333	5,656	112,318	61,020
Totals	931,182	1,074,181	77,920	848,583	1,274,188

Missouri Vote Since 1936

1936, Roosevelt, Dem., 1,111,403; Landon, Rep., 697,891; Lemke, Union, 14,630; Thomas, Soc., 3,454; Colvin, Proh., 908; Browder, Com., 417; Aiken, Soc. Labor, 292.

1940, Roosevelt, Dem., 958,476; Willkie, Rep., 871,009; Thomas, Soc., 2,226; Babson, Proh., 1,809; Aiken, Soc. Labor, 209.

1944, Roosevelt, Dem., 807,357; Dewey, Rep., 761,175; Thomas, Soc., 1,750; Watson, Proh., 1,175; Teichert, Soc. Labor, 221.

1948, Truman, Dem., 917,315; Dewey, Rep., 655,039; Wallace, Prog., 3,998; Thomas, Soc., 2,222.

1952, Eisenhower, Rep., 959,429; Stevenson, Dem., 929,830; Hallinan, Prog., 987; Hamblen, Proh., 885; MacArthur, Christian Nationalist, 302; America First, 233; Hoopes, Soc., 227; Hass, Soc. Labor, 169.

1956, Stevenson, Dem., 918,273; Eisenhower, Rep., 914,299.

1960, Kennedy, Dem., 972,201; Nixon, Rep., 962,221.

1964, Johnson, Dem., 1,164,344; Goldwater, Rep., 653,535.

1968, Nixon, Rep., 811,932; Humphrey, Dem., 791,444; Wallace, 3d party, 206,126.

1972, Nixon, Rep., 1,154,058; McGovern, Dem., 698,531.

1976, Carter, Dem., 999,163; Ford, Rep., 928,808; McCarthy, Ind., 24,329.

1980, Reagan, Rep., 1,074,181; Carter, Dem., 931,182; Anderson, Ind., 77,920; Clark, Libertarian, 14,422; DeBerry, Soc. Workers, 1,515; Commoner, Citizens, 573; write-in, 31.

1984, Reagan, Rep., 1,274,188; Mondale, Dem., 848,583.

Montana

	1980			1984	
County	Carter (D)	Reagan (R)	Anderson (I)	Mondale (D)	Reagan (R)
Beaverhead	842	2,955	205	942	3,044
Big Horn	1,644	1,730	308	2,681	2,390
Blaine	1,107	1,686	163	1,229	1,736
Broadwater	401	1,052	69	458	1,345
Carbon	1,468	2,471	331	1,657	2,877
Carter	237	766	37	194	823
Cascade	11,105	17,664	2,655	14,252	19,846
Chouteau	853	2,448	216	896	2,425
Custer	1,822	3,533	369	1,982	3,879
Daniels	483	1,086	77	473	984
Dawson	1,543	3,045	424	1,776	3,468
Deer Lodge	3,077	1,905	474	3,539	1,901
Fallon	512	1,286	94	569	1,237
Fergus	1,840	4,455	388	1,804	4,585
Flathead	6,349	15,102	1,621	8,310	17,012
Gallatin	5,747	12,738	2,432	8,163	15,643
Garfield	169	760	29	134	770
Glacier	1,394	2,283	297	2,167	2,228
Golden Valley	155	362	28	211	384
Granite	439	811	76	417	880
Hill	2,875	4,448	604	3,657	4,635
Jefferson	1,055	1,841	216	1,324	2,226
Judith Basin	480	1,030	93	483	1,050
Lake	2,615	5,083	573	3,473	5,754
Lewis & Clark	6,815	12,128	1,793	8,768	13,569
Liberty	283	672	71	323	895
Lincoln	2,422	4,202	485	2,959	4,080
Madison	676	2,220	174	708	2,308
McCone	349	1,000	86	459	1,015
Meagher	247	689	41	283	771
Mineral	660	800	138	718	943
Missoula	13,115	16,161	3,847	16,540	19,777
Musselshell	784	1,279	106	781	1,541
Park	1,663	3,929	459	2,387	4,115
Petroleum	90	225	15	86	258
Phillips	745	1,723	146	787	1,934
Pondera	897	2,270	207	1,039	2,239
Powder River	336	985	94	346	1,066
Powell	883	1,770	198	1,066	1,877
Prairie	283	580	57	289	693
Ravalli	3,063	7,268	743	3,825	8,161
Richland	1,252	3,348	343	1,382	3,847
Roosevelt	1,504	2,298	304	1,962	2,431
Rosebud	1,167	1,875	265	1,920	2,413
Sanders	1,395	2,194	291	1,654	2,467
Sheridan	955	1,658	247	1,087	1,774
Silver Bow	9,721	7,301	1,752	11,095	6,637
Stillwater	919	1,828	181	1,100	2,118
Sweet Grass	440	1,169	98	378	1,417
Teton	902	2,415	186	1,102	2,257
Toole	634	2,000	154	789	1,949
Treasure	181	321	34	209	353
Valley	1,567	3,242	264	1,849	3,123
Wheatland	381	742	88	407	753
Wibaux	219	450	45	216	423
Yellowstone	15,272	27,332	4,590	19,437	34,124
Totals	118,032	206,814	29,281	146,742	232,450

Montana Vote Since 1936

1936, Roosevelt, Dem., 159,690; Landon, Rep., 63,598; Lemke, Union, 5,549; Thomas, Soc., 1,066; Browder, Com., 385; Colvin, Proh., 224.

1940, Roosevelt, Dem., 145,698; Willkie, Rep., 99,579; Thomas, Soc., 1,443; Babson, Proh., 664; Browder, Com., 489.

1944, Roosevelt, Dem., 112,556; Dewey, Rep., 93,163; Thomas, Soc., 1,296; Watson, Proh., 340.

1948, Truman, Dem., 119,071; Dewey, Rep., 96,770; Wallace, Prog., 7,313; Thomas, Soc., 695; Watson, Proh., 429.

1952, Eisenhower, Rep., 157,394; Stevenson, Dem., 106,213; Hallinan, Prog., 723; Hamblen, Proh., 548; Hoopes, Soc., 159.

1956, Eisenhower, Rep., 154,933; Stevenson, Dem., 116,238.

1960, Kennedy, Dem., 134,891; Nixon, Rep., 141,841; Decker, Proh., 456; Dobbs, Soc. Workers, 391.

1964, Johnson, Dem., 164,246; Goldwater, Rep., 113,032; Kasper, Nat'l States Rights, 519; Munn, Proh., 499; DeBerry, Soc. Worker, 332.

968, Nixon, Rep., 138,835; Humphrey, Dem., 114,117;
Wallace, 3d party, 20,015; Halstead, Soc. Worker, 457;
Munn, Proh., 510; Caton, New Reform, 470.

1972, Nixon, Rep., 183,976; McGovern, Dem., 120,197;
Schmitz, Amer., 13,430.

1976, Carter, Dem., 149,259; Ford, Rep., 173,703; Anderson, Amer., 5,772.

1980, Reagan, Rep., 206,814; Carter, Dem., 118,032; Anderson, Ind., 29,281; Clark, Libertarian, 9,825.

1984, Reagan, Rep., 232,450; Mondale, Dem., 146,742;
Bergland, Libertarian, 5,185.

Nebraska

County	Carter (D) 1980	Reagan (R)	Anderson (I)	Mondale (D) 1984	Reagan (R)
Adams	3,361	8,469	879	2,940	9,092
Antelope	659	3,192	150	697	3,222
Arthur	55	242	9	33	248
Banner	33	481	14	58	457
Blaine	63	361	15	48	363
Boone	769	2,598	176	690	2,508
Box Butte	1,206	3,898	307	1,471	4,011
Boyd	376	1,261	62	308	1,173
Brown	341	1,614	105	312	1,513
Buffalo	3,162	9,764	1,028	3,083	11,343
Burt	814	2,806	232	1,054	2,645
Butler	1,112	2,596	159	1,192	2,555
Cass	2,007	5,180	487	2,495	5,451
Cedar	1,265	3,257	273	1,201	3,298
Chase	324	1,593	91	367	1,687
Cherry	469	2,517	105	463	2,720
Cheyenne	776	3,073	196	857	3,159
Clay	840	2,739	190	811	2,919
Colfax	892	3,259	230	981	2,998
Cuming	803	3,999	266	779	3,931
Custer	1,011	4,562	285	1,090	4,749
Dakota	1,928	3,165	317	2,510	3,467
Dawes	703	3,281	228	864	3,325
Dawson	1,462	6,687	357	1,487	6,878
Deuel	192	943	63	198	961
Dixon	822	2,328	200	985	2,154
Dodge	3,556	9,514	988	4,259	10,167
Douglas	51,504	96,741	13,198	58,867	112,557
Dundy	192	1,135	55	225	992
Fillmore	1,025	2,435	221	1,009	2,474
Franklin	441	1,672	109	522	1,597
Frontier	259	1,345	84	258	1,351
Furnas	536	2,483	113	579	2,363
Gage	2,258	6,072	722	2,699	6,102
Garden	202	1,297	63	180	1,158
Garfield	238	811	42	196	899
Gosper	181	783	47	201	802
Grant	76	373	13	51	404
Greeley	495	1,028	78	485	948
Hall	4,391	12,063	981	4,615	13,082
Hamilton	777	3,199	245	840	3,417
Harlan	486	1,690	109	493	1,692
Hayes	82	617	21	100	591
Hitchcock	328	1,471	115	341	1,391
Holt	1,016	4,488	243	893	4,611
Hooker	63	386	18	55	433
Howard	788	1,969	170	887	1,899
Jefferson	1,125	3,090	297	1,366	3,114
Johnson	623	1,716	180	821	1,536
Kearney	726	2,510	227	726	2,505
Keith	710	3,373	199	631	3,423
Keya Paha	130	524	27	126	505
Kimball	385	1,615	97	339	1,732
Knox	1,057	3,404	245	1,149	3,364
Lancaster	27,040	38,630	9,221	32,780	48,627
Lincoln	3,762	9,631	841	4,483	10,692
Logan	71	442	17	66	445
Loup	74	368	21	79	323
McPherson	49	285	5	57	295
Madison	1,924	9,715	552	1,755	9,786
Merrick	712	2,710	212	818	2,696
Morrill	512	1,887	96	463	1,888
Nance	561	1,439	100	524	1,391
Nemaha	929	2,693	221	1,004	2,752
Nuckolls	899	2,180	159	947	2,132
Otoe	1,471	4,611	391	1,868	4,679
Pawnee	431	1,418	122	552	1,306
Perkins	313	1,338	81	307	1,418
Phelps	734	3,465	192	739	3,739
Pierce	517	2,935	155	545	3,016
Platte	2,385	8,781	546	2,057	10,035
Polk	538	2,206	149	610	2,149
Red Willow	892	4,019	254	1,022	4,101
Richardson	1,350	3,634	264	1,422	3,634
Rock	145	855	39	147	873
Saline	1,908	2,934	480	2,385	2,941
Sarpy	5,678	15,523	1,685	6,831	20,155
Saunders	2,034	5,222	516	2,467	5,217
Scotts Bluff	2,851	9,485	677	3,060	10,676
Seward	1,799	3,525	533	1,905	3,969
Sheridan	369	2,747	121	377	2,661
Sherman	576	1,253	116	701	1,144
Sioux	120	759	32	121	732
Stanton	361	1,942	118	410	2,080
Thayer	925	2,514	178	946	2,578
Thomas	65	306	26	73	298
Thurston	724	1,454	140	1,077	1,410
Valley	654	2,100	124	739	2,052
Washington	1,445	4,560	356	1,561	5,163
Wayne	733	2,844	300	833	3,075
Webster	547	1,676	138	645	1,694
Wheeler	93	371	22	97	365
York	1,118	5,065	323	1,114	5,012
Totals	166,424	419,214	44,854	187,475	459,135

Nebraska Vote Since 1936

1936, Roosevelt, Dem., 347,454; Landon, Rep., 248,731; Lemke, Union, 12,847.

1940, Roosevelt, Dem., 263,677; Willkie, Rep., 352,201.

1944, Roosevelt, Dem., 233,246; Dewey, Rep., 329,880.

1948, Truman, Dem., 224,165; Dewey, Rep., 264,774.

1952, Eisenhower, Rep., 421,603; Stevenson Dem., 188,057.

1956, Eisenhower, Rep., 378,108; Stevenson, Dem., 199,029.

1960, Kennedy, Dem., 232,542; Nixon, Rep., 380,553.

1964, Johnson, Dem., 307,307; Goldwater, Rep., 276,847.

1968, Nixon, Rep., 321,163; Humphrey, Dem., 170,784; Wallace, 3d party, 44,904.

1972, Nixon, Rep., 406,298; McGovern, Dem., 169,991; scattered 817.

1976, Carter, Dem., 233,287; Ford, Rep., 359,219; McCarthy, Ind., 9,383; Maddox, Amer. Ind., 3,378; MacBride, Libertarian, 1,476.

1980, Reagan, Rep., 419,214; Carter, Dem., 166,424; Anderson, Ind., 44,854; Clark, Libertarian, 9,041.

1984, Reagan, Rep., 459,135; Mondale, Dem., 187,475; Bergland, Libertarian, 2,075.

Nevada

County	Carter (D) 1980	Reagan (R)	Anderson (I)	Mondale (D) 1984	Reagan (R)
Churchill	1,055	3,841	257	1,304	4,479
Clark	38,313	76,194	8,702	53,386	94,133
Douglas	1,352	5,254	511	1,877	6,385
Elko	1,296	4,393	301	1,566	5,110
Esmeralda	110	311	29	158	453
Eureka	103	430	13	124	439
Humboldt	684	1,950	128	862	2,498
Lander	361	935	64	301	1,222
Lincoln	396	1,087	38	397	1,175
Lyon	1,288	3,709	271	1,673	4,370
Mineral	631	1,628	147	766	1,645
Nye	973	2,387	204	1,269	3,573
Pershing	311	877	60	333	956
Storey	222	460	62	252	570
Washoe	15,621	41,276	5,705	22,321	50,418
White Pine	1,181	1,895	195	1,276	1,917
CARSON CITY	2,769	8,389	964	3,790	9,477
Totals	66,666	155,017	17,651	91,655	186,770

Nevada Vote Since 1936

1936, Roosevelt, Dem., 31,925; Landon, Rep., 11,923.

1940, Roosevelt, Dem., 31,945; Willkie, Rep., 21,229.

1944, Roosevelt, Dem., 29,623; Dewey, Rep., 24,611.

1948, Truman, Dem., 31,291; Dewey, Rep., 29,357; Wallace, Prog., 1,469.

1952, Eisenhower, Rep., 50,502; Stevenson, Dem., 31,688.

1956, Eisenhower, Rep., 56,049; Stevenson, Dem., 40,640.

1960, Kennedy, Dem., 54,880; Nixon, Rep., 52,387.

1964, Johnson, Dem., 79,339; Goldwater, Rep., 56,094.

1968, Nixon, Rep., 73,188; Humphrey, Dem., 60,598; Wallace, 3d party, 20,432.

1972, Nixon, Rep., 115,750; McGovern, Dem. 66,016.

1976, Carter Dem., 92,479; Ford, Rep., 101,273; MacBride, Libertarian, 1,519; Maddox, Amer. Ind., 1,497; scattered 5,108.

1980, Reagan, Rep., 155,017; Carter, Dem., 66,666; Anderson, Ind., 17,651; Clark, Libertarian, 4,358.

1984, Reagan, Rep., 108,770; Mondale, Dem., 91,655; Bergland, Libertarian, 2,292.

New Hampshire

City	1980 Carter (D)	Reagan (R)	Anderson (I)	1984 Mondale (D)	Reagan (R)
Berlin City	2,202	2,847	347	1,863	3,261
Claremont	2,171	2,365	506	2,006	2,868
Concord	4,330	6,092	2,204	5,172	7,190
Dover	3,344	4,497	1,517	3,826	5,397
Keene	2,875	4,317	1,650	3,238	4,975
Laconia	1,635	3,529	628	1,552	4,151
Manchester	10,919	23,557	3,178	10,283	24,780
Nashua	9,156	13,874	3,391	9,305	16,961
Portsmith	3,666	4,023	1,467	4,418	4,967
Rochester	2,566	4,495	650	2,622	5,457
Totals	108,864	221,705	49,693	120,377	267,051

New Hampshire Vote Since 1936

1936, Roosevelt, Dem., 108,640; Landon, Rep., 104,642; Lemke, Union, 4,819; Browder, Com., 193.

1940, Roosevelt, Dem., 125,292; Willkie, Rep., 110,127.

1944, Roosevelt, Dem., 119,663; Dewey, Rep., 109,916; Thomas, Soc., 46.

1948, Truman, Dem., 107,995; Dewey, Rep., 121,299; Wallace, Prog., 1,970; Thomas, Soc., 86; Teichert, Soc. Labor, 83; Thurmond, States' Rights, 7.

1952, Eisenhower, Rep., 166,287; Stevenson, Dem., 106,663.

1956, Eisenhower, Rep., 176,519; Stevenson, Dem., 90,364; Andrews, Const., 111.

1960, Kennedy, Dem., 137,772; Nixon, Rep., 157,989.

1964, Johnson, Dem., 182,065; Goldwater, Rep., 104,029.

1968, Nixon, Rep., 154,903; Humphrey, Dem., 130,589; Wallace, 3d party, 11,173; New Party, 421; Halstead, Soc. Worker, 104.

1972, Nixon, Rep., 213,724; McGovern, Dem., 116,435; Schmitz, Amer., 3,386; Jenness, Soc. Workers, 368; scattered, 142.

1976, Carter, Dem., 147,645; Ford, Rep., 185,935; McCarthy, Ind., 4,095; MacBride, Libertarian, 936; Reagan, write-in, 388; La Rouche, U.S. Labor, 186; Camejo, Soc. Workers, 161; Levin, Soc. Labor, 66; scattered, 215.

1980, Reagan, Rep., 221,705; Carter, Dem., 108,864; Anderson, Ind., 49,693; Clark, Libertarian, 2,067; Commoner, Citizens, 1,325; Hall, Com., 729; Griswold, Workers World, 76; DeBerry, Soc. Workers, 72; scattered, 68.

1984, Reagan, Rep., 267,051; Mondale, Dem., 120,377; Bergland, Libertarian, 735.

New Jersey

County	1980 Carter (D)	Reagan (R)	Anderson (I)	1984 Mondale (D)	Reagan (R)
Atlantic	31,286	37,973	5,582	33,240	49,158
Bergen	139,474	232,043	38,242	155,039	268,507
Burlington	50,083	68,415	11,314	57,467	89,815
Camden	80,033	87,939	16,125	90,233	109,749
Cape May	12,708	22,729	2,550	13,378	28,768
Cumberland	19,356	23,242	3,253	21,141	29,398
Essex	145,281	117,222	21,271	173,295	136,798
Gloucester	29,804	40,306	7,533	32,702	54,041
Hudson	95,622	91,207	8,941	94,304	112,834
Hunterdon	10,029	21,403	3,610	10,972	29,737
Mercer	60,888	53,450	12,117	66,398	71,195
Middlesex	97,304	122,354	17,463	104,905	160,221
Monmouth	71,328	120,173	17,444	79,382	152,595
Morris	48,965	105,260	17,181	53,201	137,719
Ocean	46,923	98,433	10,073	51,012	124,391
Passaic	61,486	82,531	9,385	69,590	101,951
Salem	10,209	13,000	1,800	8,935	17,368
Somerset	29,470	52,591	8,346	31,924	66,303
Sussex	10,531	27,063	3,988	11,502	35,880
Union	86,074	112,288	15,586	92,056	135,446
Warren	10,510	16,935	2,828	10,647	21,938
Totals	1,147,364	1,546,557	234,632	1,261,323	1,933,630

New Jersey Vote Since 1936

1936, Roosevelt, Dem., 1,083,549; Landon, Rep., 719,421; Lemke, Union, 9,405; Thomas, Soc., 3,895; Browder, Com., 1,590; Colvin, Proh., 916; Aiken, Soc. Labor, 346.

1940, Roosevelt, Dem., 1,016,404; Willkie, Rep., 944,876; Browder, Com., 8,814; Thomas, Soc., 2,823; Babson, Proh., 851; Aiken, Soc. Labor, 446.

1944, Roosevelt, Dem., 987,874; Dewey, Rep., 961,335; Teichert, Soc. Labor, 6,939; Watson, Nat'l. Proh., 4,255; Thomas, Soc., 3,385.

1948, Truman, Dem., 895,455; Dewey, Rep., 981,124; Wallace, Prog., 42,683; Watson, Proh., 10,593; Thomas,

Soc., 10,521; Dobbs, Soc. Workers, 5,825; Teichert, Soc. Labor, 3,354.

1952, Eisenhower, Rep., 1,373,613; Stevenson, Dem., 1,015,902; Hoopes, Soc., 8,593; Hass, Soc. Labor, 5,815; Hallinan, Prog., 5,589; Krajewski, Poor Man's, 4,203; Dobbs, Soc. Workers, 3,850; Hamblen, Proh., 989.

1956, Eisenhower, Rep., 1,606,942; Stevenson Dem., 850,337; Holtwick, Proh., 9,147; Hass, Soc. Labor, 6,736; Andrews, Conservative, 5,317; Dobbs, Soc. Workers, 4,004; Krajewski, American Third Party, 1,829.

1960, Kennedy, Dem., 1,385,415; Nixon, Rep., 1,363,324; Dobbs, Soc. Workers, 11,402; Lee, Conservative, 8,708; Hass, Soc. Labor, 4,262.

1964, Johnson, Dem., 1,867,671; Goldwater, Rep., 963,843; DeBerry, Soc. Workers, 8,181; Hass, Soc. Labor, 7,075.

1968, Nixon, Rep., 1,325,467; Humphrey, Dem., 1,264,206; Wallace, 3d party, 262,187; Halstead, Soc. Worker, 8,667; Gregory, Peace Freedom, 8,084; Blomen, Soc. Labor, 6,784.

1972, Nixon, Rep., 1,845,502; McGovern, Dem., 1,102,211; Schmitz, Amer., 34,378; Spock, Peoples, 5,355; Fisher, Soc. Labor, 4,544; Jenness, Soc. Workers, 2,233; Mahalchik, Amer. First, 1,743; Hall, Com., 1,263.

1976, Carter, Dem., 1,444,653; Ford, Rep., 1,509,688; McCarthy, Ind., 32,717; MacBride, Libertarian, 9,449; Maddox, Amer., 7,716; Levin, Soc. Labor, 8,686; Hall, Com., 1,662; LaRouche, U.S. Labor, 1,650; Camejo, Soc. Workers, 1,184; Wright, People's, 1,044; Bubar, Proh., 554; Zeidler, Soc., 469.

1980, Reagan, Rep., 1,546,557; Carter, Dem., 1,147,364; Anderson, Ind., 234,632; Clark, Libertarian, 20,652; Commoner, Citizens, 8,203; McCormack, Right to Life, 3,927; Lynen, Middle Class, 3,694; Hall, Com., 2,555; Pulley, Soc. Workers, 2,198; McReynolds, Soc., 1,973; Gahres, Down With Lawyers, 1,718; Griswold, Workers World, 1,288; Wendelken, Ind., 923.

1984, Reagan, Rep., 1,933,630; Mondale, Dem., 1,261,323; Bergland, Libertarian, 6,416.

New Mexico

County	1980 Carter (D)	Reagan (R)	Anderson (I)	1984 Mondale (D)	Reagan (R)
Bernalillo	54,841	83,956	15,118	67,789	104,694
Catron	466	906	40	418	970
Chaves	5,350	12,502	543	5,332	15,248
Cibola				3,140	3,578
Colfax	2,266	2,537	199	2,435	2,994
Curry	3,622	8,132	183	3,108	9,188
De Baca	484	655	14	386	756
Dona Ana	10,839	15,539	1,863	13,878	22,153
Eddy	7,028	9,817	326	7,364	11,810
Grant	4,600	4,628	349	5,755	4,979
Guadalupe	980	1,065	58	946	990
Harding	225	356	14	224	401
Hidalgo	840	1,059	59	860	1,282
Lea	5,006	10,727	298	4,558	14,569
Lincoln	1,127	3,009	172	1,134	3,992
Los Alamos	2,368	5,460	1,388	2,859	6,882
Luna	2,443	3,636	157	2,557	4,145
McKinley	4,869	7,329	498	7,915	6,557
Mora	1,274	1,037	44	1,235	1,017
Otero	4,111	7,210	478	4,167	9,751
Quay	1,422	2,499	58	1,368	2,842
Rio Arriba	6,245	3,794	379	6,938	4,116
Roosevelt	2,240	3,950	208	1,696	4,598
Sandoval	4,740	6,762	789	7,080	9,005
San Juan	6,705	15,579	741	8,963	18,690
San Miguel	4,514	3,292	416	5,227	3,485
Santa Fe	12,658	12,361	3,123	18,262	15,886
Sierra	1,169	2,222	117	1,335	2,663
Socorro	2,226	2,685	387	2,541	3,403
Taos	4,346	3,584	482	5,144	4,154
Torrance	1,261	1,907	101	1,274	2,326
Union	675	1,407	32	488	1,503
Valencia	6,886	11,177	825	5,393	8,474
Totals	167,826	250,779	29,459	201,769	307,101

New Mexico Vote Since 1936

1936, Roosevelt, Dem., 105,838; Landon, Rep., 61,710; Lemke, Union, 942; Thomas, Soc., 343; Browder, Com., 43.

1940, Roosevelt, Dem., 103,699; Willkie, Rep., 79,315.

1944, Roosevelt, Dem., 81,389; Dewey, Rep., 70,688; Watson, Proh., 148.

1948, Truman, Dem., 105,464; Dewey, Rep., 80,303; Wallace, Prog., 1,037; Watson, Proh., 127; Thomas, Soc., 83; Teichert, Soc. Labor, 49.

1952, Eisenhower, Rep., 132,170; Stevenson, Dem., 105,661; Hamblen, Proh., 297; Hallinan, Ind. Prog., 225; MacArthur, Christian National, 220; Hass, Soc. Labor, 35.

1956, Eisenhower, Rep., 146,788; Stevenson, Dem., 106,098; Holtwick, Proh., 607; Andrews, Ind., 364; Hass, Soc. Labor, 69.

1960, Kennedy, Dem., 156,027; Nixon, Rep., 153,733; Decker, Proh., 777; Hass, Soc. Labor, 570.

1964, Johnson, Dem., 194,017; Goldwater, Rep., 131,838; Hass, Soc. Labor, 1,217; Munn, Proh., 543.

1968, Nixon, Rep., 169,692; Humphrey, Dem., 130,081; Wallace, 3d party, 25,737; Chavez, 1,519; Halstead, Soc. Worker, 252.

1972, Nixon, Rep., 235,606; McGovern, Dem., 141,084; Schmitz, Amer., 8,767; Jenness, Soc. Workers, 474.

1976, Carter, Dem., 201,148; Ford, Rep., 211,419; Camejo, Soc. Workers, 2,462; MacBride, Libertarian, 1,110; Zeidler, Soc., 240; Bubar, Proh., 211.

1980, Reagan, Rep., 250,779; Carter, Dem., 167,826; Anderson, Ind., 29,459; Clark, Libertarian, 4,365; Commoner, Citizens, 2,202; Bubar, Statesman, 1,281; Pulley, Soc. Worker, 325.

1984, Reagan, Rep., 307,101; Mondale, Dem., 201,769; Bergland, Libertarian, 4,459.

New York

County	1980 Carter (D)	Reagan (R-C**)	Anderson (L)	1984 Mondale (D)	Reagan (R)
Albany	74,429	52,354	14,563	75,447	74,542
Allegany	5,879	10,423	973	4,720	14,527
Bronx	181,090	86,843	11,286	223,112	109,308
Broome	37,013	39,275	11,388	37,658	58,109
Cattaraugus	12,917	17,222	1,848	10,194	24,162
Cayuga	11,708	17,945	2,539	12,207	21,451
Chautauqua	22,871	30,081	4,699	22,986	39,597
Chemung	14,565	19,674	2,465	14,638	24,909
Chenango	6,917	10,400	1,908	6,343	14,254
Clinton	11,498	13,120	1,904	10,804	19,549
Columbia	9,500	13,946	2,204	8,960	18,814
Cortland	6,176	9,885	1,603	6,438	13,691
Delaware	6,333	10,609	1,865	5,745	14,002
Dutchess	28,616	53,616	8,824	32,867	70,324
Erie	215,263	169,209	29,580	237,631	222,882
Essex	6,443	9,025	1,213	5,119	12,114
Franklin	7,281	7,620	1,182	6,400	10,617
Fulton	8,105	11,448	1,566	7,644	14,887
Genesee	10,677	11,650	1,651	8,549	16,582
Greene	6,488	11,286	1,538	5,858	14,150
Hamilton	925	2,038	176	737	2,637
Herkimer	11,497	14,105	1,830	10,346	18,827
Jefferson	13,271	16,455	2,834	10,960	23,445
Kings	288,893	200,306	24,541	368,518	230,084
Lewis	3,973	4,937	716	2,757	7,069
Livingston	9,030	11,193	1,694	7,399	16,389
Madison	7,843	13,369	2,122	8,291	17,568
Monroe	142,423	128,615	29,118	132,109	182,696
Montgomery	9,645	11,917	2,080	9,044	14,398
Nassau	207,602	333,567	44,758	240,697	392,017
New York	275,742	115,911	38,597	379,521	144,281
Niagara	40,405	38,760	6,014	41,368	51,289
Oneida	44,292	51,968	6,929	42,603	65,377
Onondaga	73,453	97,887	18,805	81,777	121,857
Ontario	14,477	17,036	3,147	12,844	24,507
Orange	30,022	51,268	7,656	32,663	69,413
Orleans	5,767	7,536	977	4,429	10,453
Oswego	15,343	22,816	3,333	14,437	31,481
Otsego	8,795	11,814	2,874	9,582	16,777
Putnam	8,691	20,193	2,340	9,473	25,707
Queens	269,147	251,333	32,566	328,379	285,477
Rensselaer	29,880	32,005	6,443	26,755	43,892
Richmond	37,306	64,885	7,055	44,345	83,187
Rockland	35,277	59,068	8,709	44,687	70,020
St. Lawrence	17,006	18,437	3,544	15,963	26,062
Saratoga	23,641	34,184	6,201	22,166	47,394
Schenectady	29,932	32,003	7,146	30,612	42,808
Schoharie	4,715	6,382	940	3,996	8,692
Schuyler	2,514	3,838	476	2,422	5,207
Seneca	5,010	7,174	1,205	4,825	9,420
Steuben	12,826	22,418	2,257	10,471	28,848
Suffolk	149,945	256,294	34,743	171,295	335,485
Sullivan	9,553	15,089	2,095	10,475	18,037
Tioga	6,690	10,291	1,851	5,860	14,856
Tompkins	11,970	12,448	4,081	19,357	18,255
Ulster	22,179	36,709	5,995	26,445	47,372
Warren	6,971	13,264	1,766	5,886	17,616
Washington	7,144	12,835	1,501	5,909	16,580
Wayne	12,590	16,498	2,623	9,700	24,171
Westchester	130,136	198,552	30,119	160,225	229,005
Wyoming	5,234	8,108	855	4,381	11,199
Yates	2,828	4,694	690	2,670	6,367
Totals	2,728,372	2,893,831	467,801	3,119,609	3,664,763

New York Vote Since 1936

1936, Roosevelt, Dem., 3,018,298; American Lab., 274,924; total 3,293,222; Landon, Rep., 2,180,670; Thomas, Soc., 86,879; Browder, Com., 35,609.

1940, Roosevelt, Dem., 2,834,500; American Lab., 417,418; total, 3,251,918; Willkie, Rep., 3,027,478; Thomas, Soc., 18,950; Babson, Proh., 3,250.

1944, Roosevelt, Dem., 2,478,598; American Lab., 496,405; Liberal, 329,325; total, 3,304,238; Dewey, Rep., 2,987,647; Teichert, Ind. Gov't., 14,352; Thomas, Soc., 10,553.

1948, Truman, Dem., 2,557,642; Liberal, 222,562; total, 2,780,204; Dewey, Rep., 2,841,163; Wallace, Amer. Lab., 509,559; Thomas, Soc., 40,879; Teichert, Ind. Gov't., 2,729; Dobbs, Soc. Workers, 2,675.

1952, Eisenhower, Rep., 3,952,815; Stevenson, Dem., 2,687,890, Liberal, 416,711; total, 3,104,601; Hallinan, American Lab., 64,211; Hoopes, Soc., 2,664; Dobbs, Soc. Workers, 2,212; Hass, Ind. Gov't., 1,560; scattering, 178; blank and void, 87,813.

1956, Eisenhower, Rep., 4,340,340; Stevenson, Dem., 2,458,212; Liberal, 292,557; total, 2,750,769; write-in votes for Andrews, 1,027; Werdel, 492; Hass, 150; Hoopes, 82; others, 476.

1960, Kennedy, Dem., 3,423,909; Liberal, 406,176; total, 3,830,085; Nixon, Rep., 3,446,419; Dobbs, Soc. Workers, 14,319; scattering, 256; blank and void, 88,896.

1964, Johnson, Dem., 4,913,156; Goldwater, Rep., 2,243,559; Hass, Soc. Labor, 6,085; DeBerry, Soc. Workers, 3,215; scattering, 188; blank and void, 151,383.

1968, Nixon, Rep., 3,007,932; Humphrey, Dem., 3,378,470; Wallace, 3d party, 358,864; Blomen, Soc. Labor, 8,432; Halstead, Soc. Worker, 11,851; Gregory, Freedom and Peace, 24,517; blank, void, and scattering, 171,624.

1972, Nixon, Rep., 3,824,642; Conservative, 368,136; McGovern, Dem., 2,767,956; Liberal, 183,128; Reed, Soc. Workers, 7,797; Fisher, Soc. Labor, 4,530; Hall, Com., 5,641; blank, void, or scattered, 161,641.

1976, Carter, Dem., 3,389,558; Ford, Rep., 3,100,791; MacBride, Libertarian, 12,197; Hall, Com., 10,270; Camejo, Soc. Workers, 6,996; LaRouche, U.S. Labor, 5,413; void, or scattered, 143,037.

1980, Reagan, Rep., 2,893,831; Carter, Dem., 2,728,372; Anderson, Lib., 467,801; Clark, Libertarian, 52,648; McCormack, Right To Life, 24,159; Commoner, Citizens, 23,186; Hall, Com., 7,414; DeBerry, Soc. Workers, 2,068; Griswold, Workers World, 1,416; scattering, 1,064.

1984, Reagan, Rep., 3,664,763; Mondale, Dem., 3,119,609; Bergland, Libertarian, 11,949.

North Carolina

County	1980 Carter (D)	Reagan (R)	Anderson (I)	1984 Mondale (D)	Reagan (R)
Alamance	15,042	18,077	760	11,230	26,063
Alexander	4,546	6,376	137	3,581	8,502
Alleghany	2,198	1,995	91	2,013	2,589
Anson	4,973	1,968	111	5,015	3,719
Ashe	4,461	5,643	154	4,009	6,611
Avery	1,527	3,480	147	1,159	4,702
Beaufort	6,024	6,773	186	5,987	9,284
Bertie	3,863	1,695	45	3,953	2,879
Bladen	6,104	2,745	64	5,064	4,701
Brunswick	6,761	5,897	265	6,774	9,673
Buncombe	24,837	26,124	2,153	23,337	37,698
Burke	11,680	12,956	558	10,353	18,766
Cabarrus	9,768	15,143	562	8,477	22,528
Caldwell	8,738	12,965	440	7,311	17,024
Camden	1,212	813	45	1,075	1,282
Carteret	6,485	7,733	460	5,882	11,637
Caswell	3,529	2,156	66	4,157	3,992
Catawba	13,873	22,873	866	11,700	31,476
Chatham	7,144	5,414	481	7,458	8,595
Cherokee	3,114	3,849	80	2,776	4,894
Chowan	2,146	1,424	71	1,736	2,171
Clay	1,324	2,136	53	1,340	2,259
Cleveland	12,219	10,828	333	10,288	17,095
Columbus	10,212	5,522	148	8,728	9,150
Craven	7,781	8,554	356	7,166	12,893

Cumberland	22,073	21,540	1,261	22,614	31,602
Currituck	1,980	1,668	97	1,668	2,885
Dare	2,497	2,794	260	1,839	4,738
Davidson	14,579	22,794	679	11,469	30,471
Davie	3,289	6,302	223	2,911	8,201
Duplin	7,524	5,403	109	6,830	7,708
Durham	24,969	19,276	3,052	32,244	29,185
Edgecombe	7,945	5,916	148	10,545	9,635
Forsyth	38,870	42,389	2,897	36,814	59,208
Franklin	5,427	3,508	104	4,766	5,984
Gaston	19,016	25,139	823	14,142	39,167
Gates	2,435	957	61	2,225	1,694
Graham	1,608	1,961	36	1,494	2,514
Granville	5,556	3,513	133	5,217	6,302
Greene	2,835	2,221	34	2,772	3,195
Guilford	44,516	53,291	4,019	46,027	73,096
Halifax	8,364	6,033	180	9,278	8,832
Harnett	8,791	7,284	165	7,106	11,198
Haywood	9,814	7,217	349	7,958	10,146
Henderson	7,578	13,573	901	7,222	19,369
Hertford	4,102	1,854	80	4,498	3,176
Hoke	3,376	1,168	56	3,214	2,449
Hyde	1,221	807	37	1,004	1,195
Iredell	12,067	14,926	624	9,999	23,641
Jackson	4,857	4,140	246	4,367	5,582
Johnston	9,601	10,444	271	7,833	16,210
Jones	2,198	1,401	18	2,025	2,062
Lee	5,426	4,847	251	3,925	8,198
Lenoir	7,546	9,832	263	8,556	13,321
Lincoln	7,796	9,009	299	5,996	12,621
McDowell	4,703	5,680	175	4,076	7,639
Macon	4,105	4,727	153	3,570	6,661
Madison	3,202	2,629	108	2,988	3,666
Martin	4,750	2,564	81	3,870	4,266
Mecklenburg	66,995	68,384	6,560	63,190	106,754
Mitchell	1,765	4,322	146	1,286	4,737
Montgomery	4,129	3,587	99	3,831	5,109
Moore	8,084	10,158	563	7,063	14,681
Nash	8,184	11,043	293	8,588	17,295
New Hanover . . .	13,670	17,243	1,114	12,591	23,771
Northampton	4,933	1,847	62	5,094	3,198
Onslow	7,371	8,861	400	5,713	13,928
Orange	15,226	9,261	3,364	20,564	15,585
Pamlico	2,224	1,504	48	2,152	2,554
Pasquotank	4,128	3,340	179	3,854	4,646
Pender	4,382	3,018	103	4,354	5,079
Perquimans	1,560	1,210	63	1,441	1,939
Person	4,111	3,281	104	3,528	5,854
Pitt	12,590	12,816	827	13,481	18,983
Polk	2,375	3,021	160	2,169	4,046
Randolph	10,107	19,881	563	7,511	25,759
Richmond	7,416	3,911	224	7,494	6,807
Robeson	17,618	6,982	331	15,257	12,947
Rockingham	11,708	11,205	463	10,605	17,895
Rowan	11,671	18,566	707	10,643	25,207
Rutherford	8,315	8,363	203	6,862	11,369
Sampson	9,090	8,097	308	9,115	10,665
Scotland	4,446	2,133	155	4,028	4,077
Stanly	7,784	9,734	248	6,138	13,116
Stokes	5,764	7,275	151	4,950	9,515
Surry	6,987	10,065	256	7,188	13,340
Swain	1,987	1,457	70	2,000	2,012
Transylvania	4,008	4,826	274	3,733	6,956
Tyrrell	887	466	14	807	774
Union	10,073	9,012	487	7,048	16,885
Vance	5,415	4,217	101	5,880	6,836
Wake	49,003	49,768	5,455	50,323	81,251
Warren	3,750	1,582	74	3,946	2,664
Washington	3,008	1,943	68	3,114	2,731
Watauga	5,022	6,149	645	5,163	9,370
Wayne	9,586	12,860	322	10,011	17,961
Wilkes	8,184	14,462	282	6,852	18,670
Wilson	8,042	8,329	243	8,343	12,243
Yadkin	3,850	7,530	136	3,075	8,976
Yancey	4,010	3,363	110	3,651	4,296
Totals	**875,635**	**915,018**	**52,800**	**824,287**	**1,346,481**

North Carolina Vote Since 1936

1936, Roosevelt, Dem., 616,141; Landon, Rep., 223,283; Thomas, Soc., 21; Browder, Com., 11; Lemke, Union 2.

1940, Roosevelt, Dem., 609,015; Willkie, Rep., 213,633.

1944, Roosevelt, Dem., 527,399; Dewey, Rep., 263,155.

1948, Truman, Dem., 459,070; Dewey, Rep., 258,572; Thurmond, States' Rights, 69,652; Wallace, Prog., 3,915.

1952, Eisenhower, Rep., 558,107; Stevenson, Dem., 652,803.

1956, Eisenhower, Rep., 575,062; Stevenson, Dem., 590,530.

1960, Kennedy, Dem., 713,136; Nixon, Rep., 655,420.

1964, Johnson, Dem., 800,139; Goldwater Rep., 624,844.

1968, Nixon, Rep., 627,192; Humphrey, Dem., 464,113; Wallace, 3d party, 496,188.

1972, Nixon, Rep., 1,054,889; McGovern, Dem., 438,705; Schmitz, Amer., 25,018.

1976, Dem., 927,365; Ford, Rep., 741,960; Anderson, Amer., 5,607; MacBride, Libertarian, 2,219; LaRouche, U.S. Labor, 755.

1980, Reagan, Rep., 915,018; Carter, Dem., 875,635; Anderson, Ind., 52,800; Clark, Libertarian, 9,677; Commoner, Citizens, 2,287; DeBerry, Soc. Workers, 416.

1984, Reagan, Rep., 1,346,481; Mondale, Dem., 824,287; Bergland, Libertarian, 3,794.

North Dakota

	1980			1984	
County	Carter (D)	Reagan (R)	Anderson (I)	Mondale (D)	Reagan (R)
Adams	470	1,334	107	530	1,343
Barnes	2,128	4,392	705	2,507	4,348
Benson	1,119	2,149	262	1,599	1,729
Billings	122	524	33	133	505
Bottineau	1,090	3,394	267	1,279	3,356
Bowman	454	1,507	142	562	1,559
Burke	418	1,442	82	543	1,298
Burleigh	6,129	18,437	2,109	8,781	19,913
Cass	13,562	23,886	5,421	18,054	29,221
Cavalier	1,105	2,582	238	1,110	2,661
Dickey	917	2,455	161	1,051	2,460
Divide	509	1,267	109	626	1,165
Dunn	532	1,706	115	716	1,583
Eddy	539	1,153	145	796	1,049
Emmons	502	2,369	132	620	1,885
Foster	586	1,534	152	765	1,422
Golden Valley . . .	259	1,006	62	325	964
Grand Forks	6,997	14,257	2,932	10,050	15,898
Grant	317	1,891	110	507	1,607
Griggs	636	1,342	158	828	1,254
Hettinger	434	1,699	104	524	1,646
Kidder	325	1,474	85	506	1,240
La Moure	850	2,136	254	1,086	1,978
Logan	283	1,474	69	401	1,222
McHenry	939	2,922	190	1,283	2,485
McIntosh	308	2,471	72	427	2,047
McKenzie	867	2,265	182	974	2,610
McLean	1,613	4,234	318	2,062	3,673
Mercer	1,209	3,224	204	1,729	3,705
Morton	2,861	7,659	742	3,996	7,146
Mountrail	1,183	2,165	182	1,565	1,959
Nelson	726	1,611	226	1,026	1,445
Oliver	270	966	55	419	915
Pembina	1,239	3,101	303	1,367	2,895
Pierce	517	2,273	168	691	1,883
Ramsey	1,607	4,078	514	2,304	4,150
Ransom	974	1,883	237	1,222	1,706
Renville	570	1,154	98	592	1,163
Richland	2,698	5,711	750	3,047	5,980
Rolette	1,660	1,599	265	2,179	1,479
Sargent	1,048	1,565	174	1,295	1,385
Sheridan	208	1,326	65	306	1,075
Sioux	383	620	72	655	442
Slope	128	462	45	174	419
Stark	2,016	6,312	512	2,759	7,641
Steele	617	997	229	781	941
Stutsman	2,573	6,545	960	3,495	6,591
Towner	568	1,375	152	789	1,242
Traill	1,428	3,092	512	1,580	3,037
Walsh	1,850	4,468	485	2,264	4,347
Ward	5,554	14,997	1,234	7,336	16,077
Wells	746	2,660	148	1,036	2,426
Williams	2,545	6,530	592	3,177	8,166
Totals	**79,189**	**193,695**	**23,640**	**104,429**	**200,336**

North Dakota Vote Since 1936

1936, Roosevelt, Dem., 163,148; Landon, Rep., 72,751; Lemke, Union, 36,708; Thomas, Soc., 552; Browder, Com., 360; Colvin, Proh., 197.

1940, Roosevelt, Dem., 124,036; Willkie, Rep., 154,590; Thomas, Soc., 1,279; Knutson, Com., 545; Babson, Proh., 325.

1944, Roosevelt, Dem., 100,144; Dewey, Rep., 118,535; Thomas, Soc., 943, Watson, Proh., 549.

1948, Truman, Dem., 95,812; Dewey, Rep., 115,139; Wallace, Prog., 8,391; Thomas, Soc., 1,000, Thurmond, States' Rights, 374.

1952, Eisenhower, Rep., 191,712; Stevenson, Dem., 76,694; MacArthur, Christian Nationalist, 1,075; Hallinan, Prog., 344; Hamblen, Proh., 302.

1956, Eisenhower, Rep., 156,766; Stevenson, Dem., 96,742; Andrews, Amer., 483.

1960, Kennedy, Dem., 123,963; Nixon, Rep., 154,310; Dobbs, Soc. Workers, 158.

64, Johnson, Dem., 149,784; Goldwater, Rep., 108,207; DeBerry, Soc. Worker, 224; Munn, Proh., 174.

968, Nixon, Rep., 138,669; Humphrey, Dem., 94,769; Wallace, 3d party, 14,244; Halstead, Soc. Worker, 128; Munn, Prohibition, 38; Troxell, Ind., 34.

1972, Nixon, Rep., 174,109; McGovern, Dem., 100,384; Jenness, Soc. Workers, 288; Hall, Com., 87; Schmitz, Amer., 5,646.

1976, Carter, Dem., 136,078; Ford, Rep., 153,470; Anderson, Amer., 3,698; McCarthy, Ind., 2,952; Maddox, Amer. Ind., 269; MacBride, Libertarian, 256; scattering, 371.

1980, Reagan, Rep., 193,695; Carter, Dem., 79,189; Anderson, Ind., 23,640; Clark, Libertarian, 3,743; Commoner, Libertarian, 429; McLain, Nat'l People's League, 296; Greaves, American, 235; Hall, Com., 93; DeBerry, Soc. Workers, 89; McReynolds, Soc., 82; Bubar, Statesman, 54.

1984, Reagan, Rep., 200,336; Mondale, Dem., 104,429; Bergland, Libertarian, 703.

Ohio

County	1980 Carter (D)	1980 Reagan (R)	Anderson (I)	1984 Mondale (D)	1984 Reagan (R)
Adams	4,161	5,336	303	3,534	6,113
Allen	13,140	29,070	1,439	12,176	33,506
Ashland	5,142	11,691	1,128	4,786	14,339
Ashtabula	17,363	19,847	2,481	19,344	21,669
Athens	9,514	8,170	1,544	10,201	11,548
Auglaize	5,022	11,537	785	4,102	14,766
Belmont	16,653	13,601	1,432	19,458	15,170
Brown	4,706	6,065	339	4,067	8,221
Butler	31,796	61,231	4,717	27,700	76,216
Carroll	3,476	5,806	406	3,771	6,703
Champaign	4,109	7,356	596	3,544	9,935
Clark	22,630	27,237	3,414	21,154	35,831
Clermont	13,199	26,674	1,697	11,713	35,316
Clinton	3,967	7,675	608	3,332	9,603
Columbiana	17,459	20,798	2,320	20,155	24,552
Coshocton	4,725	8,359	525	4,392	9,842
Crawford	6,058	12,424	915	4,932	14,682
Cuyahoga	307,448	254,883	40,750	362,626	284,094
Darke	7,635	12,773	1,198	5,904	16,379
Defiance	5,096	9,358	896	5,004	10,951
Delaware	6,417	14,740	1,278	5,773	19,050
Erie	12,343	15,628	1,908	13,508	19,174
Fairfield	13,144	24,096	1,689	9,817	30,843
Fayette	2,610	5,827	327	2,126	6,838
Franklin	143,932	200,948	21,269	131,530	250,360
Fulton	3,972	9,519	1,026	4,217	11,412
Gallia	4,406	6,469	401	4,251	8,194
Geauga	9,542	17,762	2,359	9,954	22,369
Greene	20,068	24,922	3,160	17,129	34,267
Guernsey	5,121	8,180	604	4,967	10,252
Hamilton	129,114	206,979	17,898	140,350	246,288
Hancock	6,843	18,264	1,467	5,758	22,169
Hardin	3,863	7,457	528	3,813	8,722
Harrison	2,848	3,639	331	3,370	4,276
Henry	3,059	7,584	691	2,779	9,317
Highland	4,363	7,359	454	3,784	9,000
Hocking	3,765	4,588	312	3,280	6,071
Holmes	2,094	3,860	329	1,737	5,146
Huron	6,537	11,173	1,110	6,609	14,388
Jackson	4,409	5,902	274	4,369	7,411
Jefferson	20,382	15,777	1,797	22,832	17,105
Knox	6,586	10,384	987	5,730	14,062
Lake	35,246	43,485	5,925	36,711	54,587
Lawrence	11,366	13,799	813	11,431	14,973
Licking	17,208	28,425	2,419	13,995	37,560
Logan	4,319	9,727	718	3,645	12,230
Lorain	40,919	51,034	7,324	52,970	57,379
Lucas	85,341	86,653	16,636	97,293	100,285
Madison	3,565	7,166	438	2,928	8,979
Mahoning	63,677	50,153	9,490	76,514	53,424
Marion	9,419	14,605	1,255	8,827	17,392
Medina	13,573	24,723	2,965	15,897	30,690
Meigs	3,827	4,911	294	3,549	6,307
Mercer	5,505	8,673	941	4,422	11,542
Miami	12,893	19,928	2,429	9,695	26,300
Monroe	3,168	2,870	266	3,611	3,302
Montgomery	105,110	101,443	13,817	94,016	137,053
Morgan	1,875	3,236	156	1,868	3,994
Morrow	3,239	6,179	383	2,839	8,116
Muskingum	12,584	17,921	1,329	10,037	21,621
Noble	1,944	3,025	208	1,777	3,853
Ottawa	6,753	8,641	1,281	7,053	10,920
Paulding	2,778	4,971	550	2,811	5,545
Perry	4,383	5,725	369	3,581	7,548
Pickaway	5,052	9,269	515	4,110	11,342
Pike	4,938	4,426	257	4,895	6,318
Portage	20,570	22,829	3,798	21,719	29,536
Preble	5,416	8,376	687	4,198	11,065
Putnam	3,742	9,752	533	3,194	11,936
Richland	18,253	29,213	2,586	16,141	35,299
Ross	9,355	13,251	812	8,020	17,015
Sandusky	8,482	13,420	1,851	8,564	17,214
Scioto	15,552	15,881	816	14,120	18,818
Seneca	7,303	14,172	1,415	7,905	16,520
Shelby	6,425	8,988	895	4,315	13,509
Stark	59,005	87,769	8,030	65,157	98,434
Summit	102,459	92,299	15,002	109,569	115,637
Trumbull	44,366	41,056	6,281	56,902	45,623
Tuscarawas	12,117	15,708	1,779	13,149	19,366
Union	3,038	7,576	421	2,579	9,336
Van Wert	4,070	7,866	741	3,338	9,570
Vinton	2,381	2,484	138	1,990	3,041
Warren	11,306	22,430	1,348	9,031	29,848
Washington	7,935	14,310	1,121	7,920	16,529
Wayne	12,129	18,962	2,313	11,323	24,415
Williams	4,015	9,146	872	3,624	10,804
Wood	14,139	23,311	4,156	15,907	29,750
Wyandot	2,757	5,786	407	2,342	7,204
Totals	1,752,414	2,206,545	254,472	1,825,440	2,678,559

Ohio Vote Since 1936

1936, Roosevelt, Dem., 1,747,122; Landon, Rep., 1,127,709; Lemke, Union, 132,212; Browder, Com., 5,251; Thomas, Soc., 117; Aiken, Soc. Labor, 14.

1940, Roosevelt, Dem., 1,733,139; Willkie, Rep., 1,586,773.

1944, Roosevelt, Dem., 1,570,763; Dewey, Rep., 1,582,293.

1948, Truman, Dem., 1,452,791; Dewey, Rep., 1,445,684; Wallace, Prog., 37,596.

1952, Eisenhower, Rep., 2,100,391; Stevenson, Dem., 1,600,367.

1956, Eisenhower, Rep., 2,262,610; Stevenson, Dem., 1,439,655.

1960, Kennedy, Dem., 1,944,248; Nixon, Rep., 2,217,611.

1964, Johnson, Dem., 2,498,331; Goldwater, Rep., 1,470,865.

1968, Nixon, Rep., 1,791,014; Humphrey, Dem., 1,700,586; Wallace, 3d party, 467,495; Gregory, 372; Munn, Proh., 19; Blomen, Soc. Labor, 120; Halstead, Soc. Worker, 69; Mitchell, Com., 23.

1972, Nixon, Rep., 2,441,827; McGovern, Dem., 1,558,889; Fisher, Soc. Labor, 7,107; Hall, Com., 6,437; Schmitz, Amer., 80,067; Wallace, Ind., 460.

1976, Carter, Dem., 2,011,621; Ford, Rep., 2,000,505; McCarthy, Ind., 58,258; Maddox, Amer. Ind., 15,529; MacBride, Libertarian, 8,961; Hall, Com., 7,817; Camejo, Soc. Workers, 4,717; LaRouche, U.S. Labor, 4,335; scattered, 130.

1980, Reagan, Rep., 2,206,545; Carter, Dem., 1,752,414; Anderson, Ind., 254,472; Clark, Libertarian, 49,033; Commoner, Citizens, 8,564; Hall, Com., 4,729; Congress, Ind. 4,029; Griswold, Workers World, 3,790; Bubar, Statesman, 27.

1984, Reagan, Rep., 2,678,559; Mondale, Dem., 1,825,440; Bergland, Libertarian, 5,886.

Oklahoma

County	1980 Carter (D)	1980 Reagan (R)	Anderson (I)	1984 Mondale (D)	1984 Reagan (R)
Adair	2,761	3,429	107	2,266	4,423
Alfalfa	899	2,528	86	866	2,715
Atoka	2,505	1,613	66	2,047	2,361
Beaver	696	2,430	58	536	2,689
Beckham	3,298	3,637	123	2,601	5,005
Blaine	1,399	3,708	103	1,484	4,037
Bryan	6,410	3,980	129	5,475	6,246
Caddo	4,695	5,945	232	4,463	6,811
Canadian	4,889	15,272	642	5,245	20,929
Carter	6,509	9,262	258	6,161	11,578
Cherokee	5,215	5,594	362	5,307	7,614
Choctaw	3,507	2,394	73	2,801	3,155
Cimarron	373	1,404	23	359	1,420
Cleveland	14,536	31,176	3,910	16,512	42,806
Coal	1,442	926	47	1,284	1,259
Comanche	9,972	16,609	1000	8,890	21,382
Cotton	1,410	1,702	63	1,264	1,796
Craig	2,801	2,956	156	2,515	3,629
Creek	7,339	11,749	460	7,465	15,011
Custer	3,008	6,469	290	2,700	8,191
Delaware	4,244	5,302	177	3,789	6,690
Dewey	826	1,943	70	664	2,098
Ellis	561	1,908	54	562	1,881
Garfield	5,718	17,989	846	5,730	19,642
Garvin	5,033	5,520	210	4,215	7,505
Grady	5,330	8,131	351	4,846	11,042
Grant	927	2,411	84	825	2,470
Greer	1,492	1,535	48	1,220	1,664
Harmon	961	676	21	785	1,009

County					
Harper	517	1,652	40	373	1,748
Haskell	2,874	2,024	65	2,535	2,417
Hughes	3,211	2,170	85	2,901	2,663
Jackson	4,031	4,327	144	2,996	5,773
Jefferson	1,812	1,440	55	1,496	1,656
Johnston	2,066	1,701	57	1,820	2,195
Kay	6,449	15,004	665	6,044	16,731
Kingfisher	1,282	4,962	122	1,125	5,528
Kiowa	2,372	2,636	88	2,016	2,951
Latimer	2,105	1,737	71	1,858	2,210
Le Flore	6,668	6,807	174	5,990	8,604
Lincoln	3,231	6,064	204	3,020	8,088
Logan	3,246	6,311	259	3,551	8,356
Love	1,578	1,449	31	1,359	1,833
McClain	2,990	4,284	185	2,549	6,056
McCurtain	5,953	5,189	149	3,994	6,381
McIntosh	3,654	2,925	118	3,479	3,646
Major	584	3,059	62	619	3,385
Marshall	2,157	1,961	52	2,039	2,488
Mayes	5,344	6,633	256	5,154	8,585
Murray	2,384	2,494	126	2,229	3,073
Muskogee	13,341	11,511	633	12,343	14,652
Noble	1,398	3,663	124	1,238	4,018
Nowata	1,694	2,640	75	1,687	3,030
Okfuskee	2,177	2,126	58	1,684	2,443
Oklahoma	58,765	139,538	9,190	60,235	159,974
Okmulgee	7,236	6,652	286	7,380	8,704
Osage	5,687	8,044	363	6,095	10,083
Ottawa	6,143	6,362	317	5,781	7,666
Pawnee	2,020	3,902	161	2,165	4,699
Payne	7,466	15,955	1,812	7,653	20,811
Pittsburg	8,292	7,062	339	6,860	9,778
Pontotoc	5,942	6,232	335	5,526	8,301
Pottawatomie	8,526	12,466	625	6,966	16,143
Pushmataha	2,666	1,989	65	2,079	2,499
Roger Mills	877	1,221	50	680	1,550
Rogers	6,399	11,581	461	6,013	16,137
Seminole	4,726	5,067	224	3,957	6,009
Sequoyah	4,983	5,987	178	4,202	7,042
Stephens	7,191	10,199	310	6,359	12,871
Texas	1,451	5,503	93	1,033	5,968
Tillman	2,144	2,450	69	1,674	2,637
Tulsa	53,438	124,643	7,802	58,274	159,549
Wagoner	5,235	8,969	369	5,271	12,534
Washington	5,854	16,563	851	5,476	19,043
Washita	2,044	3,206	71	1,547	3,847
Woods	1,364	3,592	191	1,231	3,741
Woodward	1,703	5,318	175	1,647	6,376
Totals	402,026	695,570	38,284	385,080	861,530

Oklahoma Vote Since 1936

1936, Roosevelt, Dem., 501,069; Landon, Rep., 245,122; Thomas, Soc., 2,221; Colvin, Proh., 1,328.

1940, Roosevelt, Dem., 474,313; Willkie, Rep., 348,872; Babson, Proh., 3,027.

1944, Roosevelt, Dem., 401,549; Dewey, Rep., 319,424; Watson, Proh., 1,663.

1948, Truman, Dem., 452,782; Dewey, Rep., 268,817.

1952, Eisenhower, Rep., 518,045; Stevenson, Dem., 430,939.

1956, Eisenhower, Rep., 473,769; Stevenson, Dem., 385,581.

1960, Kennedy, Dem., 370,111; Nixon, Rep., 533,039.

1964, Johnson, Dem., 519,834; Goldwater, Rep. 412,665.

1968, Nixon, Rep., 449,697; Humphrey, Dem., 301,658; Wallace, 3d party, 191,731.

1972, Nixon, Rep. 759,025; McGovern, Dem., 247,147; Schmitz, Amer., 23,728.

1976, Carter, Dem., 532,442; Ford, Rep., 545,708; McCarthy, Ind., 14,101.

1980, Reagan, Rep., 695,570; Carter, Dem., 402,026; Anderson, Ind., 38,284; Clark, Libertarian, 13,828.

1984, Reagan, Rep., 861,530; Mondale, Dem., 385,080; Bergland, Libertarian, 9,066.

Oregon

	1980			1984	
County	Carter (D)	Reagan (R)	Anderson (I)	Mondale (D)	Reagan (R)
Baker	2,515	4,747	487	2,591	5,204
Benton	13,150	14,982	4,950	16,073	17,836
Clackamas	40,462	54,111	11,386	47,254	68,830
Clatsop	6,482	6,124	1,854	7,525	7,522
Columbia	7,124	6,623	1,158	8,219	7,811
Coos	11,817	13,041	2,428	13,582	13,637
Crook	2,162	3,113	435	2,268	3,773
Curry	2,656	4,910	652	3,423	5,363
Deschutes	9,641	15,184	2,909	11,671	19,323
Douglas	12,554	23,101	2,529	14,609	25,243
Gilliam	394	622	85	369	700
Grant	1,274	2,519	273	1,344	1,003
Harney	1,110	2,313	255	1,004	2,197
Hood River	2,924	3,450	500	3,022	4,531
Jackson	19,903	32,879	4,019	22,230	37,895
Jefferson	1,654	1,025	431	1,920	3,283

County					
Josephine	7,116	16,827	1,401	8,539	19,4..
Klamath	7,371	16,060	1,427	7,575	17,68.
Lake	1,147	2,234	201	1,184	2,46.
Lane	52,240	54,750	12,076	63,999	61,493
Lincoln	7,009	7,637	1,637	8,637	9,110
Linn	13,516	18,943	2,823	16,161	23,463
Malheur	2,937	7,705	472	2,611	8,441
Marion	32,134	42,191	8,755	36,440	54,535
Morrow	1,077	1,728	239	1,254	2,130
Multnomah	120,487	101,606	27,572	144,179	119,932
Polk	7,833	10,006	2,025	8,709	12,678
Sherman	389	677	62	398	828
Tillamook	4,521	4,123	931	4,988	5,267
Umatilla	7,382	12,950	1,531	8,246	14,211
Union	3,677	6,514	763	4,134	6,645
Wallowa	995	2,485	216	1,204	2,619
Wasco	4,336	4,703	819	5,526	6,905
Washington	37,915	57,165	13,076	44,602	75,877
Wheeler	282	442	62	253	504
Yamhill	8,694	12,054	1,919	9,450	15,797
Totals	456,890	571,044	112,389	536,479	685,700

Oregon Vote Since 1936

1936, Roosevelt, Dem., 266,733; Landon, Rep., 122,706; Lemke, Union, 21,831; Thomas, Soc., 2,143; Aiken, Soc. Labor, 500; Browder, Com., 104; Colvin, Proh., 4.

1940, Roosevelt, Dem., 258,415; Willkie, Rep., 219,555; Aiken, Soc. Labor, 2,487; Thomas, Soc., 398; Browder, Com., 191; Babson, Proh., 154.

1944, Roosevelt, Dem., 248,635; Dewey, Rep., 225,365; Thomas, Soc., 3,785; Watson, Proh., 2,362.

1948, Truman, Dem., 243,147; Dewey, Rep., 260,904; Wallace, Prog., 14,978; Thomas, Soc., 5,051.

1952, Eisenhower, Rep., 420,815; Stevenson, Dem., 270,579; Hallinan, Ind., 3,665.

1956, Eisenhower, Rep., 406,393; Stevenson, Dem., 329,204.

1960, Kennedy, Dem., 367,402; Nixon, Rep., 408,060.

1964, Johnson, Dem., 501,017; Goldwater, Rep., 282,779; write-in, 2,509.

1968, Nixon, Rep., 408,433; Humphrey, Dem., 358,866; Wallace, 3d party, 49,683; write-in, McCarthy, 1,496; N. Rockefeller, 69; others, 1,075.

1972, Nixon, Rep., 486,686; McGovern, Dem., 392,760; Schmitz, Amer., 46,211; write-in, 2,289.

1976, Carter, Dem., 490,407; Ford, Rep., 492,120; McCarthy, Ind., 40,207; write-in, 7,142.

1980, Reagan, Rep., 571,044; Carter, Dem., 456,890; Anderson, Ind., 112,389; Clark, Libertarian, 25,838; Commoner, Citizens, 13,642; scattered, 1,713.

1984, Reagan, Rep., 658,700; Mondale, Dem., 536,479.

Pennsylvania

	1980			1984	
County	Carter (D)	Reagan (R)	Anderson (I)	Mondale (D)	Reagan (R)
Adams	7,266	13,760	1,139	7,289	16,786
Allegheny	297,464	271,850	38,710	372,576	284,692
Armstrong	12,718	12,955	1,153	14,525	13,709
Beaver	43,955	30,496	4,549	54,765	32,052
Bedford	4,950	10,930	416	5,424	13,085
Berks	36,449	60,576	8,863	37,849	74,605
Blair	15,014	28,931	2,011	15,651	30,104
Bradford	6,439	13,139	1,068	5,474	14,808
Bucks	59,120	100,536	18,107	74,568	130,119
Butler	19,711	28,821	3,453	24,735	31,676
Cambria	36,121	33,072	2,398	39,865	32,173
Cameron	1,112	1,795	92	990	2,031
Carbon	8,009	10,042	956	8,836	10,701
Centre	15,987	20,605	5,247	16,194	27,802
Chester	34,307	73,046	10,911	38,870	92,221
Clarion	5,472	8,812	678	5,407	9,836
Clearfield	11,647	15,299	944	11,963	18,653
Clinton	4,842	6,288	733	4,525	6,678
Columbia	9,449	12,426	1,197	8,254	14,402
Crawford	11,778	16,552	2,095	12,792	20,181
Cumberland	19,789	41,152	5,437	21,374	49,282
Dauphin	27,252	44,039	6,034	33,576	54,330
Delaware	88,314	143,262	20,907	98,207	161,7.1
Elk	5,898	7,175	472	5,4..	9,470
Erie	45,946	48,918	6,349	52,471	55,860
Fayette	27,963	19,252	1,1..	35,098	21,314
Forest	819	1,1..	93	839	1,468
Franklin	12,0..	22,716	1,724	11,480	27,243
Fulton	1,340	2,740	107	1,309	3,254
Greene	8,193	5,336	450	9,365	6,376
Huntingdon	5,094	8,140	567	4,430	10,220
Indiana	13,828	15,607	1,708	15,791	18,845
Jefferson	6,296	9,628	687	5,950	11,334
Juniata	2,696	4,189	280	2,624	5,059
Lackawanna	45,257	44,242	4,209	45,851	48,132
Lancaster	30,026	79,963	7,442	31,308	99,090

County	Carter (D)	Reagan (R)	Anderson (I)	Mondale (D)	Reagan (R)
Lawrence	19,506	18,404	1,908	23,981	19,277
Lebanon	8,281	24,495	2,314	10,520	27,008
Lehigh	34,827	50,782	8,977	41,089	61,799
Luzerne	59,976	67,822	4,947	58,482	69,169
Lycoming	14,609	23,415	2,034	13,147	28,498
McKean	5,064	9,229	661	4,818	10,963
Mercer	19,716	22,372	3,247	24,658	24,211
Mifflin	5,226	7,541	578	5,178	9,106
Monroe	7,551	12,357	1,967	8,193	16,109
Montgomery	84,289	156,996	26,133	99,741	181,426
Montour	2,272	3,399	375	2,055	4,174
Northampton	31,920	35,787	6,823	37,979	44,648
Northumberland	13,750	20,608	1,515	13,748	22,109
Perry	3,681	8,026	717	3,692	9,365
Philadelphia	421,253	244,108	42,967	501,369	267,178
Pike	2,132	5,249	452	2,503	6,343
Potter	2,299	4,073	225	1,789	5,164
Schuylkill	24,968	36,273	3,079	25,758	37,330
Snyder	2,418	7,634	451	2,383	8,968
Somerset	11,695	17,729	815	13,900	19,502
Sullivan	1,074	1,676	130	952	1,926
Susquehanna	4,660	8,994	786	4,471	10,566
Tioga	4,273	8,770	664	4,060	10,532
Union	2,687	6,798	628	2,747	7,792
Venango	7,800	11,547	1,015	9,114	13,507
Warren	5,560	9,165	922	6,244	10,838
Washington	45,295	32,532	3,413	50,911	34,782
Wayne	3,375	8,468	496	3,155	10,061
Westmoreland	68,627	63,140	5,985	79,906	71,377
Wyoming	2,766	5,919	384	2,518	7,230
York	33,406	61,098	5,779	33,359	75,020
Totals	1,937,540	2,261,872	292,921	2,228,131	2,584,323

Pennsylvania Vote Since 1936

1936, Roosevelt, Dem., 2,353,788; Landon, Rep., 1,690,300; Lemke, Royal Oak, 67,467; Thomas, Soc., 14,375; Colvin, Proh., 6,691; Browder, Com., 4,060; Aiken, Ind. Lab., 1,424.

1940, Roosevelt, Dem., 2,171,035; Willkie, Rep., 1,889,848; Thomas, Soc., 10,967; Browder, Com., 4,519; Aiken, Ind. Gov., 1,518.

1944, Roosevelt, Dem., 1,940,479; Dewey, Rep., 1,835,054; Thomas, Soc., 11,721; Watson, Proh., 5,750; Teichert, Ind. Gov., 1,789.

1948, Truman, Dem., 1,752,426; Dewey, Rep., 1,902,197; Wallace, Prog., 55,161; Thomas, Soc., 11,325; Watson, Proh., 10,338; Dobbs, Militant Workers, 2,133; Teichert, Ind. Gov., 1,461.

1952, Eisenhower, Rep., 2,415,789; Stevenson, Dem., 2,146,269; Hamblen, Proh., 8,771; Hallinan, Prog., 4,200; Hoopes, Soc., 2,684; Dobbs, Militant Workers, 1,502; Hass, Ind. Gov., 1,347; scattered, 155.

1956, Eisenhower, Rep., 2,585,252; Stevenson, Dem., 1,981,769; Hass, Soc. Labor, 7,447; Dobbs, Militant Workers, 2,035.

1960, Kennedy, Dem., 2,556,282; Nixon, Rep., 2,439,956; Hass, Soc. Labor, 7,185; Dobbs, Soc. Workers, 2,678; scattering, 440.

1964, Johnson, Dem., 3,130,954; Goldwater, Rep., 1,673,657; DeBerry, Soc. Workers, 10,456; Hass, Soc. Labor, 5,092; scattering, 2,531.

1968, Nixon, Rep., 2,090,017; Humphrey, Dem., 2,259,405; Wallace, 3d party, 378,582; Blomen, Soc. Labor, 4,977; Halstead, Soc. Workers, 4,862; Gregory, 7,821; others, 2,264.

1972, Nixon, Rep., 2,714,521; McGovern, Dem., 1,796,951; Schmitz, Amer., 70,593; Jenness, Soc. Workers, 4,639; Hall, Com., 2,686; others, 2,715.

1976, Carter, Dem., 2,328,677; Ford, Rep., 2,205,604; McCarthy, Ind., 50,584; Maddox, Constitution, 25,344; Camejo, Soc. Workers, 3,009; LaRouche, U.S. Labor, 2,744; Hall, Com., 1,891; others, 2,934.

1980, Reagan, Rep., 2,261,872; Carter, Dem., 1,937,540; Anderson, Ind., 292,921; Clark, Libertarian, 33,263; DeBerry, Soc. Workers, 20,291; Commoner, Consumer, 10,430; Hall, Com., 5,184.

1984, Reagan, Rep., 2,584,323; Mondale, Dem., 2,228,131; Bergland, Libertarian, 6,982.

Rhode Island

	1980			1984	
City	Carter (D)	Reagan (R)	Anderson (I)	Mondale (D)	Reagan (R)
Cranston	17,293	14,781	5,420	17,742	19,517
East Providence	11,440	7,566	3,094	11,064	10,332
Pawtucket	14,455	8,402	3,644	14,109	12,460
Providence	36,249	16,689	7,932	35,751	19,748
Warwick	18,424	15,890	6,498	19,278	22,276
Totals	198,342	154,793	59,819	197,106	212,080

Rhode Island Vote Since 1936

1936, Roosevelt, Dem., 165,238; Landon, Rep., 125,031; Lemke, Union, 19,569; Aiken, Soc. Labor, 929; Browder, Com., 411.

1940, Roosevelt, Dem., 182,182; Willkie, Rep., 138,653; Browder, Com., 239; Babson, Proh., 74.

1944, Roosevelt, Dem., 175,356; Dewey, Rep., 123,487; Watson, Proh., 433.

1948, Truman, Dem., 188,736; Dewey, Rep., 135,787; Wallace, Prog., 2,619; Thomas, Soc., 429; Teichert, Soc. Labor, 131.

1952, Eisenhower, Rep., 210,935; Stevenson, Dem., 203,293; Hallinan, Prog., 187; Hass, Soc. Labor, 83.

1956, Eisenhower, Rep., 225,819; Stevenson, Dem., 161,790.

1960, Kennedy, Dem., 258,032; Nixon, Rep., 147,502.

1964, Johnson, Dem., 315,463; Goldwater, Rep., 74,615.

1968, Nixon, Rep., 122,359; Humphrey, Dem., 246,518; Wallace, 3d party, 15,678; Halstead, Soc. Worker, 383.

1972, Nixon, Rep., 220,383; McGovern, Dem., 194,645; Jenness, Soc. Workers, 729.

1976, Carter, Dem., 227,636; Ford, Rep., 181,249; MacBride, Libertarian, 715; Camejo, Soc. Workers, 462; Hall, Com., 334; Levin, Soc. Labor, 188.

1980, Reagan, Rep., 154,793; Carter, Dem., 198,342; Anderson, Ind., 59,819; Clark, Libertarian, 2,458; Hall, Com., 218; McReynolds, Socialist, 170; DeBerry, Soc. Worker, 90; Griswold, Workers World, 77.

1984, Reagan, Rep., 212,080; Mondale, Dem., 197,106; Bergland, Libertarian, 277.

South Carolina

	1980			1984	
County	Carter (D)	Reagan (R)	Anderson (I)	Mondale (D)	Reagan (R)
Abbeville	4,049	2,261	111	3,051	3,798
Aiken	13,014	18,568	601	9,872	25,872
Allendale	2,775	1,181	18	2,170	1,570
Anderson	18,796	15,666	474	10,324	24,123
Bamberg	3,294	2,098	18	2,892	2,908
Barnwell	3,399	3,228	64	2,811	4,346
Beaufort	7,415	8,620	513	7,347	13,668
Berkeley	9,850	12,790	17	7,380	16,972
Calhoun	2,043	1,767	31	2,315	2,742
Charleston	32,744	44,006	2,213	29,470	53,779
Cherokee	6,891	5,378	86	4,101	6,655
Chester	5,145	3,104	87	3,559	4,441
Chesterfield	6,393	3,477	65	4,593	5,451
Clarendon	5,980	4,158	28	5,591	5,102
Colleton	5,745	4,719	58	4,910	6,200
Darlington	9,009	8,289	219	7,456	11,100
Dillon	4,518	3,384	59	3,360	4,646
Dorchester	7,237	10,893	140	7,037	15,289
Edgefield	3,465	2,415	30	3,227	3,224
Fairfield	4,153	2,098	37	4,117	3,147
Florence	16,391	17,069	348	14,639	22,753
Georgetown	6,701	5,151	148	6,392	7,370
Greenville	32,135	46,168	1,600	24,137	66,766
Greenwood	9,283	7,287	230	6,339	10,887
Hampton	4,329	2,217	35	3,736	3,464
Horry	13,885	14,322	530	8,940	20,396
Jasper	3,316	1,617	33	3,753	3,102
Kershaw	5,103	6,652	145	4,323	8,822
Lancaster	8,282	6,409	331	5,804	10,383
Laurens	7,858	6,034	129	5,312	9,729
Lee	4,816	2,952	18	3,912	3,548
Lexington	12,334	28,313	762	8,828	38,628
McCormick	5,378	2,585	52	1,526	1,186
Marion	1,774	797	22	5,043	4,698
Marlboro	5,377	3,318	80	4,294	3,951
Newberry	4,825	5,568	80	3,790	7,176
Oconee	7,677	5,652	188	3,333	8,625
Orangeburg	16,178	11,313	141	15,121	14,286
Pickens	7,789	9,574	402	4,481	15,155
Richland	33,298	35,843	1,808	32,212	46,773
Saluda	2,649	2,451	38	1,962	3,515
Spartanburg	27,238	26,820	933	20,130	41,553
Sumter	9,205	10,655	250	9,566	12,909
Union	6,274	4,035	93	4,424	6,331
Williamsburg	8,135	5,110	64	7,586	6,492
York	12,075	11,265	539	9,273	20,008
Totals	428,220	439,277	13,868	344,459	615,539

South Carolina Vote Since 1936

1936, Roosevelt, Dem., 113,791; Landon, Rep., Tolbert faction 953, Hambright faction 693, total, 1,646.

1940, Roosevelt, Dem., 95,470; Willkie, Rep., 1,727.

1944, Roosevelt, Dem., 90,601; Dewey, Rep., 4,547; Southern Democrats, 7,799; Watson, Proh., 365; Rep. Tolbert faction, 63.

1948, Thurmond, States' Rights, 102,607; Truman, Dem., 34,423; Dewey, Rep., 5,386; Wallace, Prog., 154; Thomas, Soc., 1.

1952, Eisenhower ran on two tickets. Under state law vote cast for two Eisenhower slates of electors could not be combined. Eisenhower, Ind., 158,289; Rep., 9,793; total, 168,082; Stevenson, Dem., 173,004; Hamblen, Proh., 1.

1956, Stevenson, Dem., 136,372; Byrd, Ind., 88,509; Eisenhower, Rep., 75,700; Andrews, Ind., 2.

1960, Kennedy, Dem., 198,129; Nixon, Rep., 188,558; write-in, 1.

1964, Johnson, Dem., 215,700; Goldwater, Rep., 309,048; write-ins: Nixon, 1, Wallace, 5; Powell, 1; Thurmond, 1.

1968, Nixon, Rep., 254,062; Humphrey, Dem., 197,486; Wallace, 3d party, 215,430.

1972, Nixon, Rep., 477,044; McGovern, Dem., 184,559, United Citizens, 2,265; Schmitz, Amer., 10,075; write-in, 17.

1976, Carter, Dem., 450,807; Ford, Rep., 346,149; Anderson, Amer., 2,996; Maddox, Amer. Ind., 1,950; write-in, 681.

1980, Reagan, Rep., 439,277; Carter, Dem., 428,220; Anderson, Ind., 13,868; Clark, Libertarian, 4,807; Rarick, Amer. Ind., 2,086.

1984, Reagan, Rep., 615,539; Mondale, Dem., 344,459; Bergland, Libertarian, 4,359.

South Dakota

County	1980 Carter (D)	Reagan (R)	Anderson (I)	1984 Mondale (D)	Reagan (R)
Aurora	709	1,251	125	840	1,029
Beadle	3,521	5,921	545	3,523	5,876
Bennett	350	919	42	453	856
Bon Homme	1,191	2,794	214	1,408	2,478
Brookings	3,934	5,727	1,169	4,089	6,679
Brown	6,050	10,550	1,143	6,852	10,541
Brule	925	1,674	153	961	1,578
Buffalo	147	272	26	236	253
Butte	843	2,850	150	784	2,865
Campbell	182	1,271	39	214	1,035
Chas. Mix	1,741	2,608	203	1,879	2,660
Clark	774	1,963	151	960	1,748
Clay	2,271	3,004	906	2,711	3,057
Codington	3,353	5,903	638	3,528	6,108
Corson	522	1,233	82	792	955
Custer	708	2,057	129	858	2,183
Davison	3,107	4,743	568	3,248	4,783
Day	1,720	2,507	259	1,932	2,150
Deuel	891	1,657	169	941	1,537
Dewey	600	1,045	109	772	941
Douglas	508	1,855	91	536	1,713
Edmunds	883	1,881	125	1,007	1,553
Fall River	982	2,831	184	1,135	2,748
Faulk	520	1,300	110	579	1,124
Grant	1,602	2,691	254	1,606	2,738
Gregory	883	2,283	121	780	1,777
Haakon	255	1,162	38	237	1,168
Hamlin	903	1,885	197	963	1,782
Hand	803	2,066	159	846	2,030
Hanson	598	1,015	93	625	898
Harding	205	727	28	186	723
Hughes	1,751	4,652	554	2,072	4,985
Hutchinson	1,145	3,789	228	1,237	3,372
Hyde	273	864	60	350	797
Jackson	354	929	50	365	903
Jerauld	595	1,018	103	542	1,012
Jones	189	689	37	206	689
Kingsbury	1,132	2,376	258	1,249	2,121
Lake	2,207	3,093	504	2,367	3,027
Lawrence	2,259	5,306	574	2,565	5,949
Lincoln	2,261	3,848	524	2,626	3,988
Lyman	486	1,256	106	478	1,120
McCook	1,223	2,014	269	1,448	1,902
McPherson	287	2,056	54	418	1,813
Marshall	1,120	1,710	147	1,111	1,529
Meade	1,721	5,349	342	2,093	5,908
Mellette	279	624	46	303	616
Miner	833	1,172	148	960	1,004
Minnehaha	20,008	26,260	4,658	23,042	29,908
Moody	1,364	1,807	279	1,586	1,633
Pennington	7,121	18,991	1,650	8,224	21,947
Perkins	595	1,931	93	114	1,686
Potter	436	1,633	91	482	1,551
Roberts	1,829	2,904	235	2,063	2,767
Sanborn	628	1,178	107	611	1,080
Shannon	1,132	438	91	1,489	324
Spink	1,572	2,915	294	1,680	2,627
Stanley	339	892	55	351	942
Sully	220	852	60	266	836
Todd	972	803	112	1,022	679
Tripp	947	2,669	130	935	2,483
Turner	1,369	3,343	281	1,486	3,086
Union	1,830	2,788	359	2,221	2,431
Walworth	753	2,675	139	779	2,396
Yankton	2,698	5,355	553	2,932	5,161
Ziebach	246	523	30	359	429
Totals	103,855	198,343	21,431	116,113	200,267

South Dakota Vote Since 1936

1936, Roosevelt, Dem., 160,137; Landon, Rep., 125,977; Lemke, Union, 10,338.

1940, Roosevelt, Dem., 131,862; Willkie, Rep., 177,065.

1944, Roosevelt, Dem., 96,711; Dewey, Rep., 135,365.

1948, Truman, Dem., 117,653; Dewey, Rep., 129,651; Wallace, Prog., 2,801.

1952, Eisenhower, Rep., 203,857; Stevenson, Dem., 90,426.

1956, Eisenhower, Rep., 171,569; Stevenson, Dem., 122,288.

1960, Kennedy, Dem., 128,070; Nixon, Rep., 178,417.

1964, Johnson, Dem., 163,010; Goldwater, Rep., 130,108.

1968, Nixon, Rep., 149,841; Humphrey, Dem., 118,023; Wallace, 3d party, 13,400.

1972, Nixon, Rep., 166,476; McGovern, Dem., 139,945; Jenness, Soc. Workers, 994.

1976, Carter, Dem., 147,068; Ford, Rep., 151,505; MacBride, Libertarian, 1,619; Hall, Com., 318; Camejo, Soc. Workers, 168.

1980, Reagan, Rep., 198,343; Carter, Dem., 103,855; Anderson, Ind., 21,431; Clark, Libertarian, 3,824; Pulley, Soc. Workers, 250.

1984, Reagan, Rep., 200,267; Mondale, Dem., 116,113.

Tennessee

County	1980 Carter (D)	Reagan (R)	Anderson (I)	1984 Mondale (D)	Reagan (R)
Anderson	10,194	14,235	1,161	10,415	16,783
Bedford	5,987	3,377	159	4,499	4,699
Benton	3,811	2,281	71	3,398	2,481
Bledsoe	1,585	1,970	26	1,316	1,950
Blount	9,412	17,959	620	9,188	20,525
Bradley	7,638	11,869	316	6,085	16,322
Campbell	4,752	5,537	120	4,692	5,685
Cannon	2,351	1,403	41	1,846	1,669
Carroll	5,277	5,681	125	4,568	6,017
Carter	6,006	11,648	326	4,642	13,153
Cheatham	3,771	2,296	90	3,007	4,109
Chester	2,123	2,751	52	1,854	2,793
Claiborne	2,844	4,289	94	2,870	4,474
Clay	1,376	1,344	27	1,281	1,338
Cocke	2,139	6,802	139	2,068	6,665
Coffee	7,612	5,454	239	5,691	7,695
Crockett	2,422	2,117	27	1,937	2,479
Cumberland	3,775	6,354	227	3,605	7,083
Davidson	103,741	65,772	4,834	89,498	98,115
Decatur	2,139	2,095	35	2,031	2,390
De Kalb	2,948	1,841	48	2,645	2,337
Dickson	6,622	3,636	157	5,809	5,846
Dyer	5,713	5,475	158	3,991	6,610
Fayette	4,141	2,944	75	3,634	3,733
Fentress	1,543	2,493	49	1,755	2,922
Franklin	6,760	3,995	251	5,846	5,705
Gibson	9,829	6,792	227	8,334	9,484
Giles	4,653	2,757	85	3,812	3,875
Grainger	1,495	3,254	66	1,565	3,212
Greene	5,822	10,704	338	4,763	13,215
Grundy	2,837	1,139	33	2,596	1,396
Hamblen	5,890	9,741	336	4,922	11,144
Hamilton	41,913	57,575	2,087	41,449	69,626
Hancock	704	1,734	32	619	1,491
Hardeman	4,153	2,931	73	3,797	3,712
Hardin	3,164	4,152	76	3,051	4,632
Hawkins	5,283	7,836	310	4,802	9,863
Haywood	3,445	2,435	49	3,308	2,839
Henderson	2,702	5,108	78	2,426	5,318
Henry	6,601	4,299	200	5,407	5,376
Hickman	3,225	1,903	78	2,941	2,370
Houston	1,757	738	31	1,716	882
Humphreys	3,974	1,001	74	3,668	2,249
Jackson	2,001	995	27	2,894	1,544
Jefferson	3,180	6,944	201	3,185	7,721
Johnson	1,141	3,716	66	999	3,853
Knox	45,634	66,153	4,801	43,448	76,965
Lake	1,718	823	11	1,191	878
Lauderdale	4,318	2,818	73	3,506	3,566
Lawrence	6,082	6,532	212	5,458	6,034
Lewis	2,190	1,076	33	1,556	1,733
Lincoln	5,387	2,856	119	4,103	3,982

County	Carter (D)	Reagan (R)	Anderson (I)	Mondale (D)	Reagan (R)	County	Carter (D)	Reagan (R)	Anderson (I)	Mondale (D)	Reagan (R)
Loudon	3,699	6,382	235	3,227	7,113	Archer	1,444	1,804	30	1,089	2,487
McMinn	5,460	7,825	200	5,141	9,604	Armstrong	333	709	9	238	791
McNairy	3,801	4,603	76	3,825	4,776	Atascosa	3,980	4,364	93	3,547	5,279
Macon	1,947	2,925	65	1,747	3,330	Austin	1,893	3,734	87	1,941	4,872
Madison	12,986	13,667	363	12,006	17,819	Bailey	800	1,809	26	684	1,888
Marion	4,623	3,902	93	3,942	4,337	Bandera	894	2,373	64	771	3,152
Marshall	4,277	2,282	78	2,935	3,416	Bastrop	4,716	3,768	205	4,744	6,439
Maury	7,957	6,637	225	6,950	9,008	Baylor	1,183	1,098	14	1,019	1,314
Meigs	999	1,278	31	1,012	1,575	Bee	3,606	4,171	125	3,659	5,377
Monroe	4,612	6,246	125	4,223	6,665	Bell	15,823	20,729	934	13,322	31,117
Montgomery	11,573	8,503	490	9,939	13,228	Bexar	137,729	159,578	9,467	136,947	203,319
Moore	993	551	34	808	863	Blanco	794	1,434	52	700	1,957
Morgan	2,094	2,653	70	2,121	2,903	Borden	131	279	3	140	325
Obion	5,766	5,397	138	4,769	6,384	Bosque	2,431	2,908	62	2,046	3,923
Overton	3,343	1,869	38	2,749	2,054	Bowie	11,339	13,942	244	10,077	18,244
Perry	1,401	783	32	1,316	948	Brazoria	18,253	27,614	1,205	18,609	39,166
Pickett	758	1,319	12	706	1,246	Brazos	9,856	17,798	1,453	12,348	34,733
Polk	2,470	2,414	45	2,112	2,785	Brewster	1,271	1,496	89	1,462	2,066
Putnam	8,084	6,235	342	7,443	8,999	Briscoe	561	562	13	471	538
Rhea	3,070	4,689	93	2,804	5,692	Brooks	2,488	780	43	2,702	896
Roane	6,473	11,096	481	6,623	11,882	Brown	4,867	6,515	102	4,070	8,468
Robertson	7,381	3,560	127	5,756	5,445	Burleson	2,615	1,943	33	2,578	3,076
Rutherford	15,213	11,208	703	11,618	19,503	Burnet	3,711	4,033	132	2,983	5,895
Scott	1,724	3,014	63	1,810	3,107	Caldwell	3,155	2,879	112	3,401	4,315
Sequatchie	1,509	1,512	23	1,238	1,785	Calhoun	3,034	3,312	136	2,586	4,434
Sevier	3,450	10,576	338	3,384	12,517	Callahan	2,002	2,284	29	1,305	3,538
Shelby	159,240	140,157	7,180	16,625	70,500	Cameron	23,200	22,041	801	26,394	29,545
Smith	3,674	1,755	69	3,258	2,393	Camp	2,052	1,531	19	1,917	2,238
Stewart	2,274	985	42	2,174	1,285	Carson	1,006	1,888	26	826	2,412
Sullivan	22,341	25,963	1,874	16,925	36,516	Cass	5,578	4,993	60	5,053	6,677
Sumner	14,150	11,876	540	11,535	18,442	Castro	1,199	1,955	44	1,009	2,026
Tipton	4,934	4,339	109	3,895	5,945	Chambers	2,517	3,140	96	2,632	4,322
Trousdale	1,674	629	30	1,142	781	Cherokee	5,726	5,629	92	4,494	8,187
Unicoi	1,880	3,828	97	1,696	4,249	Childress	1,222	1,443	33	900	1,574
Union	1,435	2,453	45	1,495	2,447	Clay	2,233	1,824	40	1,844	2,569
Van Buren	886	499	11	810	718	Cochran	513	1,064	23	557	1,117
Warren	6,021	3,680	148	4,813	4,801	Coke	838	708	10	532	1,060
Washington	11,599	17,457	934	9,452	21,762	Coleman	1,719	2,228	33	1,420	2,790
Wayne	1,633	3,418	78	1,534	3,332	Collin	15,187	36,559	1,559	13,604	61,095
Weakley	5,910	5,668	136	4,752	6,480	Collingsworth	798	1,020	18	742	1,396
White	3,415	2,100	64	3,033	2,895	Colorado	2,377	3,520	58	2,428	4,528
Williamson	8,815	11,597	551	6,929	17,975	Comal	3,554	9,758	324	4,179	13,452
Wilson	11,248	7,535	380	8,433	12,858	Comanche	2,550	1,977	40	2,248	2,678
Totals	783,051	787,761	35,991	711,714	990,212	Concho	702	700	8	580	821

Tennessee Vote Since 1936

1936, Roosevelt, Dem., 327,083; Landon, Rep., 146,516; Thomas, Soc., 685; Colvin, Proh., 632; Browder, Com., 319; Lemke, Union, 296.

1940, Roosevelt, Dem., 351,601; Willkie, Rep., 169,153; Babson, Proh., 1,606; Thomas, Soc., 463.

1944, Roosevelt, Dem., 308,707; Dewey, Rep., 200,311; Watson, Proh., 882; Thomas, Soc., 892.

1948, Truman, Dem., 270,402; Dewey, Rep., 202,914; Thurmond, States' Rights, 73,815; Wallace, Prog., 1,864; Thomas, Soc., 1,288.

1952, Eisenhower, Rep., 446,147; Stevenson, Dem., 443,710; Hamblen, Proh., 1,432; Hallinan, Prog., 885; MacArthur, Christian Nationalist, 379.

1956, Eisenhower, Rep., 462,288; Stevenson, Dem., 456,507; Andrews, Ind., 19,820; Holtwick, Proh., 789.

1960, Kennedy, Dem., 481,453; Nixon, Rep., 556,577; Faubus, States' Rights, 11,304; Decker, Proh., 2,458.

1964, Johnson, Dem. 635,047; Goldwater, Rep., 508,965; write-in, 34.

1968, Nixon, Rep., 472,592; Humphrey, Dem., 351,233; Wallace, 3d party, 424,792.

1972, Nixon, Rep., 813,147; McGovern, Dem., 357,293; Schmitz, Amer., 30,373; write-in, 369.

1976, Carter, Dem., 825,879; Ford, Rep., 633,969; Anderson, Amer., 5,769; McCarthy, Ind., 5,004; Maddox, Am. Ind., 2,303; MacBride, Libertarian, 1,375; Hall, Com., 547; LaRouche, U.S. Labor, 512; Bubar, Proh., 442; Miller, Ind., 316; write-in, 230.

1980, Reagan, Rep., 787,761; Carter, Dem., 783,051; Anderson, Ind., 35,991; Clark, Libertarian, 7,116; Commoner, Citizens, 1,112; Bubar, Statesman, 521; McReynolds, Socialist, 519; Hall, Com., 503; DeBerry, Soc. Worker, 490; Griswold, Workers World, 400; write-ins, 152.

1984, Reagan, Rep., 990,212; Mondale, Dem., 711,714; Bergland, Libertarian, 3,072.

Texas

	1980			1984	
County	Carter (D)	Reagan (R)	Anderson (I)	Mondale (D)	Reagan (R)
Anderson	5,163	5,970	137	4,747	8,634
Andrews	1,155	2,800	39	820	3,918
Angelina	10,140	9,900	232	9,054	14,685
Aransas	1,800	3,081	134	1,696	4,352

(continued, right column)

County	Carter (D)	Reagan (R)	Anderson (I)	Mondale (D)	Reagan (R)
Cooke	3,842	6,760	129	3,278	8,260
Coryell	4,097	5,494	228	3,113	9,056
Cottle	732	511	9	623	507
Crane	607	1,310	23	392	1,473
Crockett	595	885	10	589	1,094
Crosby	1,408	1,361	17	1,212	1,376
Culberson	423	541	7	407	509
Dallam	632	965	33	496	1,594
Dallas	190,459	306,682	14,271	203,592	405,444
Dawson	1,867	3,267	55	1,781	3,685
Deaf Smith	1,666	4,073	77	1,485	4,762
Delta	1,347	767	18	973	1,024
Denton	17,381	29,908	1,953	16,772	52,865
DeWitt	2,044	3,450	66	1,882	4,401
Dickens	912	554	13	692	594
Dimmit	2,102	1,173	25	2,546	1,338
Donley	751	1,106	22	529	1,297
Duval	3,706	1,012	28	3,748	1,201
Eastland	3,346	3,442	37	2,522	4,841
Ector	9,069	26,188	636	8,913	31,228
Edwards	237	575	11	159	626
Ellis	9,219	10,046	214	8,029	16,973
El Paso	40,082	53,276	5,096	51,917	66,114
Erath	4,156	3,981	92	3,234	6,122
Falls	3,328	2,606	51	2,834	3,133
Fannin	5,284	3,196	74	4,399	4,692
Fayette	2,590	4,104	77	2,379	5,711
Fisher	1,564	838	23	1,384	965
Floyd	1,477	2,043	24	1,023	2,092
Foard	617	349	7	448	472
Fort Bend	11,583	25,366	1,005	18,729	41,370
Franklin	1,487	1,105	14	1,104	1,836
Freestone	2,739	2,468	33	2,489	3,624
Frio	2,849	1,753	47	2,656	2,003
Gaines	1,182	2,390	46	797	2,714
Galveston	30,778	29,527	1,955	36,092	40,262
Garza	677	1,188	22	521	1,219
Gillespie	1,170	4,736	90	1,137	5,496
Glasscock	116	416	2	128	403
Goliad	1,081	1,170	22	836	1,540
Gonzales	2,896	2,931	61	2,196	3,962
Gray	2,786	7,187	103	2,003	8,955
Grayson	13,807	16,811	532	11,803	22,554
Gregg	10,219	23,399	311	10,700	29,697
Grimes	2,440	2,087	42	2,370	3,365
Guadalupe	5,049	9,901	407	5,060	14,382
Hale	3,610	7,277	123	3,202	7,670
Hall	1,057	1,141	13	984	1,058
Hamilton	1,526	1,683	30	1,130	2,118
Hansford	518	2,046	17	259	2,213
Hardeman	1,174	1,056	28	927	1,238
Hardin	7,358	6,087	200	6,782	8,380
Harris	274,061	416,555	22,917	334,135	536,029
Harrison	7,746	9,328	125	7,773	12,618
Hartley	470	1,248	28	356	1,419
Haskell	1,951	1,447	22	1,434	1,701
Hays	6,013	6,517	590	6,663	12,467

County					
Hemphill	592	1,152	21	413	1,650
Henderson	8,199	7,903	134	7,302	12,725
Hidalgo	34,542	25,808	1,063	44,147	35,059
Hill	4,688	4,113	73	3,420	5,344
Hockley	2,447	4,599	90	2,044	5,462
Hood	3,001	3,755	109	3,063	6,817
Hopkins	4,344	3,834	93	3,707	5,772
Houston	4,181	2,889	47	3,275	4,542
Howard	4,451	6,658	158	4,115	7,519
Hudspeth	394	471	14	362	557
Hunt	8,773	9,283	327	6,971	14,303
Hutchinson	2,935	7,439	170	2,052	9,078
Irion	239	427	2	199	619
Jack	1,349	1,482	29	945	1,825
Jackson	1,826	2,540	66	1,804	3,661
Jasper	5,707	4,396	98	5,787	5,965
Jeff Davis	300	409	10	299	511
Jefferson	45,642	36,763	1,664	54,846	45,124
Jim Hogg	1,437	535	23	1,703	608
Jim Wells	7,267	4,606	102	7,795	5,896
Johnson	10,542	11,411	333	9,148	18,254
Jones	3,043	2,765	45	2,343	4,017
Karnes	2,284	2,719	52	1,802	3,068
Kaufman	6,266	5,852	110	5,554	9,343
Kendall	1,075	3,890	88	938	4,568
Kenedy	106	76	2	110	96
Kent	351	339	0	253	332
Kerr	3,387	9,090	259	3,102	11,829
Kimble	608	1,011	22	442	1,333
King	55	144	5	53	141
Kinney	472	543	23	486	774
Kleberg	5,125	4,608	231	4,924	5,712
Knox	1,163	783	17	921	1,027
Lamar	7,176	6,094	148	5,504	9,273
Lamb	2,132	3,723	51	1,919	3,892
Lampasas	1,979	2,323	56	1,356	3,285
LaSalle	1,442	773	19	1,504	1,007
Lavaca	2,678	3,254	54	2,464	5,058
Lee	1,581	1,803	59	1,659	2,967
Leon	2,190	1,821	19	1,821	3,207
Liberty	6,810	6,470	163	6,292	10,504
Limestone	3,403	2,835	45	3,228	4,063
Lipscomb	338	1,343	28	241	1,461
Live Oak	1,380	2,193	32	1,260	2,481
Llano	2,130	2,866	72	1,894	4,042
Loving	22	50	0	16	57
Lubbock	18,732	46,711	1,952	18,793	57,151
Lynn	1,236	1,603	28	1,009	1,617
McCulloch	1,750	1,572	24	1,433	2,060
McLennan	26,305	31,968	964	23,206	42,232
McMullen	122	271	4	61	337
Madison	1,583	1,389	32	1,384	2,158
Marion	2,015	1,666	28	2,111	2,336
Martin	605	1,093	15	512	1,218
Mason	630	966	17	570	1,168
Matagorda	4,585	5,545	146	5,201	8,452
Maverick	2,932	1,370	39	3,063	1,783
Medina	3,034	4,742	84	3,053	5,737
Menard	489	548	11	394	725
Midland	6,839	25,027	586	7,214	33,706
Milam	4,230	3,251	111	3,734	4,384
Mills	1,028	985	24	688	1,262
Mitchell	1,446	1,455	12	1,332	2,007
Montague	3,233	3,143	59	2,602	4,406
Montgomery	12,593	26,237	819	13,293	41,230
Moore	1,743	3,736	67	1,129	4,649
Morris	3,105	2,133	27	2,925	2,778
Motley	341	573	7	282	533
Nacogdoches	5,981	8,626	422	5,694	13,063
Navarro	5,988	5,400	126	5,672	7,816
Newton	3,284	1,379	24	3,296	2,123
Nolan	2,796	2,781	87	2,524	3,608
Nueces	43,424	40,586	2,045	46,721	54,333
Ochiltree	594	3,032	52	419	3,492
Oldham	290	557	9	226	762
Orange	14,928	12,389	395	16,816	15,386
Palo Pinto	4,244	4,068	98	3,349	5,701
Panola	3,637	4,022	58	3,179	5,676
Parker	7,336	8,505	189	6,050	13,647
Parmer	707	2,640	30	567	2,524
Pecos	1,602	2,723	37	1,596	3,451
Polk	4,213	3,771	80	3,898	5,987
Potter	9,633	16,327	545	8,365	20,396
Presidio	1,039	723	22	992	837
Rains	1,174	813	18	1,027	1,560
Randall	7,323	23,136	677	6,044	30,249
Reagan	414	917	14	243	1,079
Real	603	832	14	360	1,004
Red River	3,501	2,225	31	2,518	2,979
Reeves	2,138	2,315	52	2,396	2,461
Refugio	2,224	1,944	57	1,559	2,421
Roberts	150	482	4	106	539
Robertson	3,572	1,661	33	3,339	2,663
Rockwall	1,985	4,036	113	1,639	6,688
Runnels	1,648	2,532	36	1,179	2,968
Rusk	5,582	8,705	116	4,599	11,081
Sabine	1,983	1,387	15	1,940	2,045
San Augustine	1,674	1,397	14	1,583	1,937
San Jacinto	2,370	1,726	42	2,466	3,174
San Patricio	8,627	8,326	280	8,838	11,074
San Saba	1,405	948	23	1,070	1,566
Schleicher	444	672	6	326	854
Scurry	2,003	3,745	53	1,564	5,028
Shackelford	606	959	9	415	1,181
Shelby	4,215	3,500	71	3,610	4,863
Sherman	286	1,128	28	246	1,269
Smith	14,838	28,236	414	15,227	40,740
Somervell	1,015	792	21	635	1,422
Starr	4,782	1,389	50	5,047	1,658
Stephens	1,372	2,161	34	1,046	2,898
Sterling	218	364	2	129	577
Stonewall	719	488	6	643	599
Sutton	485	1,000	13	465	1,251
Swisher	1,854	1,450	50	1,642	1,611
Tarrant	121,058	173,466	7,818	120,147	248,050
Taylor	13,245	22,961	620	9,628	34,444
Terrell	260	411	14	289	407
Terry	1,945	3,178	45	1,535	3,181
Throckmorton	455	444	7	388	586
Titus	3,872	3,747	44	3,631	5,069
Tom Green	9,892	16,555	661	8,981	23,847
Travis	75,028	73,151	9,796	94,124	124,944
Trinity	2,510	1,503	32	2,115	2,599
Tyler	3,540	2,545	70	3,119	3,638
Upshur	4,894	4,836	78	4,614	7,325
Upton	485	1,169	13	380	1,603
Uvalde	2,402	3,887	62	2,482	4,790
Val Verde	4,116	5,055	145	3,857	5,909
Van Zandt	5,707	5,495	78	4,506	8,474
Victoria	7,382	13,392	347	7,037	18,787
Walker	4,869	5,657	274	4,263	8,809
Waller	3,329	3,019	76	3,828	4,116
Ward	1,405	2,912	50	1,188	3,474
Washington	2,518	4,821	95	2,483	6,506
Webb	11,856	5,421	242	12,308	8,582
Wharton	5,138	6,598	160	5,072	8,495
Wheeler	1,090	1,626	16	805	2,251
Wichita	17,857	22,884	847	16,009	28,932
Wilbarger	2,347	3,031	53	2,011	3,644
Willacy	3,047	1,995	38	3,037	2,340
Williamson	10,408	15,035	946	9,911	25,774
Wilson	3,097	3,443	73	2,829	4,588
Winkler	1,021	2,160	35	752	2,213
Wise	4,674	4,350	108	3,856	6,958
Wood	4,033	4,515	74	3,449	7,144
Yoakum	715	1,937	28	456	2,204
Young	2,740	4,153	84	2,203	5,282
Zapata	1,218	874	19	1,577	1,214
Zavala	2,621	831	69	2,937	924
Totals	1,881,147	2,510,705	111,613	1,949,276	3,433,428

Texas Vote Since 1936

1936, Roosevelt, Dem., 734,485; Landon, Rep., 103,874; Lemke, Union, 3,281; Thomas, Soc., 1,075; Colvin, Proh., 514; Browder, Com., 253.

1940, Roosevelt, Dem., 840,151; Willkie, Rep., 199,152; Babson, Proh., 925; Thomas, Soc., 728; Browder, Com., 212.

1944, Roosevelt, Dem., 821,605; Dewey, Rep., 191,425; Texas Regulars, 135,439; Watson, Proh., 1,017; Thomas, Soc., 594; America First, 250.

1948, Truman, Dem., 750,700; Dewey, Rep., 282,240; Thurmond, States' Rights, 106,909; Wallace, Prog., 3,764; Watson, Proh., 2,758; Thomas, Soc., 874.

1952, Eisenhower, Rep., 1,102,878; Stevenson, Dem., 969,228; Hamblen, Proh., 1,983; MacArthur, Christian Nationalist, 833; MacArthur, Constitution, 730; Hallinan, Prog., 294.

1956, Eisenhower, Rep., 1,080,619; Stevenson, Dem., 859,958; Andrews, Ind., 14,591.

1960, Kennedy, Dem., 1,167,932; Nixon, Rep., 1,121,699; Sullivan, Constitution, 18,169; Decker, Proh., 3,870; write-in, 15.

1964, Johnson, Dem., 1,663,185; Goldwater, Rep., 958,566; Lightburn, Constitution, 5,060.

1968, Nixon, Rep., 1,227,844; Humphrey, Dem., 1,266,804; Wallace, 3d party, 584,269; write-in, 489.

1972, Nixon, Rep., 2,298,896; McGovern, Dem., 1,154,289; Schmitz, Amer., 6,039; Jenness, Soc. Workers, 8,664; others, 3,393.

1976, Carter, Dem., 2,082,319; Ford, Rep., 1,953,300; McCarthy, Ind., 20,118; Anderson, Amer., 11,442; Camejo, Soc. Workers, 1,723; write-in, 2,982.

1980, Reagan, Rep., 2,510,705; Carter, Dem., 1,881,147; Anderson, Ind., 111,613; Clark, Libertarian, 37,643; write-in, 528.

Reagan, Rep., 3,433,428; Mondale, Dem., 1,949,276.

Utah

County	1980 Carter (D)	Reagan (R)	Anderson (I)	1984 Mondale (D)	Reagan (R)
...ver	621	1,477	43	708	1,516
. Elder	2,142	12,500	306	1,983	13,243
...che	3,639	20,251	1,494	4,123	22,127
...arbon	4,317	4,320	309	4,357	4,393
...aggett	109	290	10	227	296
Davis	9,065	45,695	2,253	11,727	49,863
Duchesne	854	3,827	87	746	4,437
Emery	1,315	3,076	90	1,326	3,081
Garfield	375	1,578	50	315	1,609
Grand	703	2,362	205	876	2,463
Iron	1,242	6,207	240	1,342	6,856
Juab	720	1,872	51	917	1,902
Kane	256	1,492	59	294	1,710
Millard	795	3,620	72	1,192	4,345
Morgan	373	1,985	42	481	1,934
Piute	157	551	3	151	606
Rich	143	762	18	131	797
Salt Lake	58,472	169,411	19,547	78,488	183,536
San Juan	763	2,774	72	1,145	2,598
Sanpete	1,260	5,143	112	1,227	5,507
Sevier	1,112	5,614	117	1,072	5,736
Summit	1,184	3,330	480	1,539	4,093
Tooele	3,132	6,024	391	3,584	6,478
Uintah	1,049	6,045	155	1,186	7,337
Utah	12,166	71,859	1,264	14,801	72,284
Wasatch	994	2,799	113	1,015	2,789
Washington	1,678	10,181	185	1,846	12,049
Wayne	226	835	15	224	930
Weber	15,404	43,807	2,501	18,346	44,590
Totals	124,266	439,687	30,284	155,369	469,105

Utah Vote Since 1936

1936, Roosevelt, Dem., 150,246; Landon, Rep., 64,555; Lemke, Union, 1,121; Thomas, Soc., 432; Browder, Com., 280; Colvin, Proh., 43.

1940, Roosevelt, Dem., 154,277; Willkie, Rep., 93,151; Thomas, Soc., 200; Browder, Com., 191.

1944, Roosevelt, Dem., 150,088; Dewey, Rep., 97,891; Thomas, Soc., 340.

1948, Truman, Dem., 149,151; Dewey, Rep., 124,402; Wallace, Prog., 2,679; Dobbs, Soc. Workers, 73.

1952, Eisenhower, Rep., 194,190; Stevenson, Dem., 135,364.

1956, Eisenhower, Rep., 215,631; Stevenson, Dem., 118,364.

1960, Kennedy, Dem., 169,248; Nixon, Rep., 205,361; Dobbs, Soc. Workers, 100.

1964, Johnson, Dem., 219,628; Goldwater, Rep., 181,785.

1968, Nixon, Rep., 238,728; Humphrey, Dem., 156,665; Wallace, 3d party, 26,906; Halstead, Soc. Worker, 89; Peace and Freedom, 180.

1972, Nixon, Rep., 323,643; McGovern, Dem., 126,284; Schmitz, Amer., 28,549.

1976, Carter, Dem., 182,110; Ford, Rep., 337,908; Anderson, Amer., 13,304; McCarthy, Ind., 3,907; MacBride, Libertarian, 2,438; Maddox, Am. Ind., 1,162; Camejo, Soc. Workers, 268; Hall, Com., 121.

1980, Reagan, Rep., 439,687; Carter, Dem., 124,266; Anderson, Ind., 30,284; Clark, Libertarian, 7,226; Commoner, Citizens, 1,009; Greaves, American, 965; Rarick, Amer. Ind., 522; Hall, Com., 139; DeBerry, Soc. Worker, 124.

1984, Reagan, Rep., 469,105; Mondale, Dem., 155,369; Bergland, Libertarian, 2,447.

Vermont

City	1980 Carter (D)	Reagan (R)	Anderson (I)	1984 Mondale (D)	Reagan (R)
Barre City	1,857	1,603	461	1,903	2,195
Bennington	2,528	2,059	828	2,879	3,237
Brattleboro	1,877	1,890	1,021	2,741	2,645
Burlington	6,752	4,506	2,796	10,080	7,857
Montpelier	1,575	1,824	656	2,120	2,257
Rutland City	3,284	2,921	991	3,298	3,970
St. Albans City	1,395	1,381	299	1,346	1,748
St. Johnsbury	1,055	1,918	300	915	2,152
South Burlington	2,044	2,324	1,025	2,728	3,443
Winooski	1,425	686	251	1,361	1,264
Totals	81,891	94,598	31,760	95,730	135,865

Vermont Vote Since 1936

1936, Landon, Rep., 81,023; Roosevelt, Dem., 62,124; Browder, Com., 405.

1940, Roosevelt, Dem., 64,269; Willkie, Rep., 78,371; Browder, Com., 411.

1944, Roosevelt, Dem., 53,820; Dewey, Rep., 71,527.

1948, Truman, Dem., 45,557; Dewey, Rep., 75,926; Wallace, Prog., 1,279; Thomas, Soc., 585.

1952, Eisenhower, Rep., 109,717; Stevenson, Dem., 43,355; Hallinan, Prog., 282; Hoopes, Soc., 185.

1956, Eisenhower, Rep., 110,390; Stevenson, Dem., 42,549; scattered, 39.

1960, Kennedy, Dem., 69,186; Nixon, Rep., 98,131.

1964, Johnson, Dem., 107,674; Goldwater, Rep., 54,868.

1968, Nixon, Rep., 85,142; Humphrey, Dem., 70,255; Wallace, 3d party, 5,104; Halstead, Soc. Worker, 295; Gregory, New Party, 579.

1972, Nixon, Rep., 117,149; McGovern, Dem., 68,174; Spock, Liberty Union, 1,010; Jenness, Soc. Workers, 296; scattered, 318.

1976, Carter, Dem., 77,798; Carter, Ind. Vermonter, 991; Ford, Rep., 100,387; McCarthy, Ind., 4,001; Camejo, Soc. Workers, 430; LaRouche, U.S. Labor, 196; scattered, 99.

1980, Reagan, Rep., 94,598; Carter, Dem., 81,891; Anderson, Ind., 31,760; Commoner, Citizens, 2,316; Clark, Libertarian, 1,900; McReynolds, Liberty Union, 136; Hall, Com. 118; DeBerry, Soc. Worker, 75; scattering, 413.

1984, Reagan, Rep., 135,865; Mondale, Dem., 95,730; Bergland, Libertarian, 1,002.

Virginia

County	1980 Carter (D)	Reagan (R)	Anderson (I)	1984 Mondale (D)	Reagan (R)
Accomack	4,872	5,371	292	4,355	8,047
Albemarle	7,293	10,424	1,435	7,982	14,455
Alleghany	2,411	2,185	116	1,932	3,067
Amelia	1,643	1,969	52	1,432	2,336
Amherst	3,476	5,088	208	3,409	7,004
Appomattox	1,492	2,548	85	1,498	3,386
Arlington	26,502	30,854	8,042	37,031	34,848
Augusta	5,202	11,011	539	3,899	15,308
Bath	999	921	70	727	1,434
Bedford	4,721	6,608	336	4,754	10,371
Bland	1,002	1,278	35	667	1,812
Botetourt	3,698	4,408	329	3,243	5,959
Brunswick	3,430	2,310	70	3,040	2,950
Buchanan	5,768	4,554	95	7,828	5,053
Buckingham	1,933	1,864	77	1,879	2,627
Campbell	4,473	9,592	396	4,380	13,388
Caroline	2,924	2,071	116	3,111	2,949
Carroll	3,437	5,905	183	2,914	7,056
Charles City	1,564	506	39	1,776	776
Charlotte	2,108	2,322	59	1,811	2,999
Chesterfield	13,060	37,908	2,182	13,739	54,896
Clarke	1,156	1,876	177	1,215	2,529
Craig	946	768	41	845	1,173
Culpeper	2,519	4,312	231	2,255	5,596
Cumberland	1,355	1,515	51	1,237	2,027
Dickenson	4,177	3,687	77	4,848	3,921
Dinwiddie	3,475	3,369	107	3,485	4,547
Essex	1,280	1,581	76	1,300	2,120
Fairfax	73,734	137,620	24,605	107,295	183,181
Fauquier	4,119	6,782	548	4,056	10,319
Floyd	1,642	2,447	131	1,599	3,431
Fluvanna	1,424	1,605	108	1,332	2,247
Franklin	5,685	4,993	304	4,903	7,684
Frederick	2,948	7,293	455	2,671	9,542
Giles	3,627	2,978	211	3,047	4,340
Gloucester	3,138	4,261	354	2,830	7,109
Goochland	2,290	2,423	113	2,178	3,404
Grayson	2,875	3,494	106	2,319	4,508
Greene	925	1,702	105	760	2,216
Greensville	2,142	1,583	39	2,352	2,304
Halifax	4,528	5,088	125	4,231	6,726
Hanover	5,383	14,262	589	4,831	18,800
Henrico	21,023	50,505	2,956	21,336	63,864
Henry	8,800	8,258	355	6,976	12,693
Highland	487	751	25	398	997
Isle of Wight	3,951	3,526	197	3,650	5,664
James City	3,068	4,289	551	3,486	7,104
King George	1,318	1,784	185	1,450	2,356
King and Queen	1,128	949	43	1,201	1,449
King William	1,446	2,036	80	1,448	2,803
Lancaster	1,567	2,780	106	1,559	3,416
Lee	4,758	4,417	137	5,085	5,365
Loudoun	6,694	12,076	1,312	8,227	17,765
Louisa	2,809	2,633	160	2,703	3,789
Lunenburg	1,958	2,045	59	1,754	2,713
Madison	1,351	1,959	156	1,302	2,723
Mathews	1,300	2,204	148	1,106	2,868
Mecklenburg	3,790	4,853	142	3,438	6,777
Middlesex	1,395	1,810	90	1,206	2,612
Montgomery	7,455	8,222	1,400	7,202	12,428
Nelson	2,410	1,866	143	2,021	2,777
New Kent	1,204	1,739	68	1,204	2,679
Northampton	2,363	2,165	114	2,226	2,906

County					
Northumberland..	1,551	2,598	109	1,407	3,166
Nottoway......	2,593	2,813	113	2,296	3,418
Orange.......	2,420	3,381	241	2,285	4,483
Page........	2,607	4,297	161	2,437	5,021
Patrick.......	2,382	3,436	105	1,908	4,703
Pittsylvania...	7,653	12,022	250	7,791	15,743
Powhatan.....	1,484	2,933	98	1,381	3,921
Prince Edward...	2,553	2,774	137	2,589	3,454
Prince George..	2,310	3,389	130	2,136	4,999
Prince William ..	12,787	23,061	2,676	15,631	34,992
Pulaski......	5,769	5,747	343	4,364	8,242
Rappahannock...	1,055	1,179	99	999	1,696
Richmond.....	854	1,567	49	830	1,869
Roanoke......	12,114	17,182	1,286	10,569	23,348
Rockbridge....	2,475	2,784	296	2,098	4,057
Rockingham....	5,294	11,397	771	4,220	13,480
Russell......	5,764	4,778	125	6,760	5,738
Scott	4,314	4,744	153	3,904	5,804
Shenandoah ...	3,137	7,517	385	2,771	9,048
Smyth........	5,335	6,033	224	4,102	8,593
Southampton...	3,347	2,997	163	3,300	4,669
Spotsylvania ...	4,039	5,385	464	4,012	8,207
Stafford.......	4,211	7,106	623	4,429	10,283
Surry	1,756	962	63	1,875	1,462
Sussex	2,447	1,664	86	2,408	2,183
Tazewell	7,003	7,021	225	8,014	9,645
Warren	2,597	3,861	297	2,551	5,016
Washington ...	6,390	8,402	382	5,573	12,132
Westmoreland..	2,271	2,510	133	2,363	3,219
Wise	6,779	5,767	258	7,303	7,909
Wythe.......	3,677	4,758	164	2,996	6,773
York........	4,532	6,744	723	4,063	10,214
City					
Alexandria	17,134	17,865	4,546	23,552	21,166
Bedford.......	1,149	1,145	75	997	1,553
Bristol.......	2,889	3,432	160	2,429	5,012
Buena Vista ..	1,031	942	59	724	1,335
Charlottesville..	6,866	5,907	1,377	7,317	6,947
Chesapeake....	17,155	17,888	1,189	16,740	27,542
Clifton Forge.	1,012	716	68	895	965
Colonial Heights...	1,692	5,012	219	1,218	6,387
Covington	1,813	1,187	101	1,391	1,722
Danville......	6,138	10,665	296	5,846	12,141
Emporia	855	988	41	807	1,252
Fairfax	2,614	4,475	800	3,263	6,234
Falls Church....	1,703	2,485	497	2,398	2,684
Franklin......	1,324	1,045	62	1,537	1,561
Fredericksburg..	2,174	2,502	245	2,439	3,500
Galax	1,061	1,188	31	814	1,548
Hampton	18,517	17,023	1,598	18,180	25,537
Harrisonburg...	1,896	3,388	403	2,384	5,221
Hopewell	3,102	4,423	178	2,564	5,661
Lexington.....	963	956	129	946	1,197
Lynchburg.....	7,783	15,245	854	8,542	17,447
Manassas	1,565	3,009	318	1,824	4,615
Manassas Park ..	447	729	52	375	975
Martinsville....	3,337	3,433	162	2,942	4,234
Newport News..	22,066	22,423	2,068	21,834	33,614
Norfolk.......	35,118	27,506	3,333	38,913	36,360
Norton	762	572	42	842	806
Petersburg....	7,931	5,001	254	9,248	5,753
Poquoson	877	2,338	158	647	3,667
Portsmouth....	20,900	13,660	1,124	21,623	18,940
Radford......	2,225	1,964	233	1,781	2,855
Richmond.....	47,975	34,629	3,502	49,408	38,754
Roanoke	18,139	15,164	1,350	17,300	19,008
Salem.......	4,091	4,862	359	3,347	6,419
South Boston ..	971	1,615	51	974	1,899
Staunton	2,658	4,819	311	2,012	6,137
Suffolk	9,064	7,179	360	8,842	10,128
Virginia Beach ..	24,895	47,936	4,830	24,703	72,571
Waynesboro ...	1,926	3,697	255	1,579	4,465
Williamsburg...	1,199	1,344	340	1,469	1,913
Winchester....	2,006	4,240	320	2,064	5,055
Total	752,174	989,609	95,418	796,250	1,337,078

Virginia Vote Since 1936

1936, Roosevelt, Dem., 234,980; Landon, Rep., 98,366; Colvin, Proh., 594; Thomas, Soc., 313; Lemke, Union, 233; Browder, Com., 98.

1940, Roosevelt, Dem., 235,961; Willkie, Rep., 109,363; Babson, Proh., 882; Thomas, Soc., 282; Browder, Com., 71; Aiken, Soc. Labor, 48.

1944, Roosevelt, Dem., 242,276; Dewey, Rep., 145,243; Watson, Proh., 459; Thomas, Soc., 417; Teichert, Soc. Labor, 90.

1948, Truman, Dem., 200,786; Dewey, Rep., 172,070; Thurmond, States' Rights, 43,393; Wallace, Prog., 2,047; Thomas, Soc., 726; Teichert, Soc. Labor, 234.

1952, Eisenhower, Rep., 349,037; Stevenson, Dem., 268,677; Hass, Soc. Labor, 1,160; Hoopes, Social Dem., 504; Hallinan, Prog., 311.

1956, Eisenhower, Rep., 386,459; Stevenson, Dem., 267,760; Andrews, States' Rights 11,964; Hoopes, Soc. Dem., 444; Hass, Soc. Labor, 351.

1960, Kennedy, Dem., 362,327; Nixon, Rep., 4C[...] Coiner, Conservative, 4,204; Hass, Soc. Labor, 397.

1964, Johnson, Dem., 558,038; Goldwater, Rep., 481[...] Hass, Soc. Labor, 2,895.

1968, Nixon, Rep., 590,319; Humphrey, Dem., 442,3[...] Wallace, 3d party, *320,272; Blomen, Soc. Labor, 4,6[...] Munn, Proh., 601; Gregory, Peace and Freedom, 1,680.

*10,561 votes for Wallace were omitted in the count.

1972, Nixon, Rep., 988,493; McGovern, Dem., 438,887, Schmitz, Amer., 19,721; Fisher, Soc. Labor, 9,918.

1976, Carter, Dem., 813,896; Ford, Rep., 836,554; Camejo, Soc. Workers, 17,802; Anderson, Amer., 16,686; LaRouche, U.S. Labor, 7,508; MacBride, Libertarian, 4,648.

1980, Reagan, Rep., 989,609; Carter, Dem., 752,174; Anderson, Ind., 95,418; Commoner, Citizens, 14,024; Clark, Libertarian, 12,821; DeBerry, Soc. Worker, 1,986.

1984, Reagan, Rep., 1,337,078; Mondale, Dem., 796,250.

Washington

	1980			1984	
County	Carter (D)	Reagan (R)	Anderson (I)	Mondale (D)	Reagan (R)
Adams	1,223	3,248	255	1,311	3,449
Asotin	2,724	3,275	539	3,042	3,876
Benton	11,561	28,728	3,301	13,784	32,307
Chelan	6,483	11,299	1,608	6,978	13,667
Clallam	8,029	11,515	2,172	9,701	13,605
Clark	30,584	33,223	6,445	35,248	40,681
Columbia	587	1,349	119	673	1,404
Cowlitz	12,560	13,154	2,336	15,361	14,858
Douglas	2,833	5,171	564	3,127	6,443
Ferry	802	1,108	127	935	1,232
Franklin	3,719	7,327	699	4,328	7,724
Garfield	509	875	122	493	913
Grant	5,673	11,152	1,091	6,298	12,888
Grays Harbor ...	11,290	10,226	3,267	14,050	11,286
Island	5,422	10,926	1,800	6,850	13,548
Jefferson	3,279	3,645	876	4,602	4,543
King	235,046	272,567	76,119	289,620	332,987
Kitsap	20,893	29,420	8,525	29,681	36,101
Kittitas	4,075	5,359	1,066	4,830	6,580
Klickitat	2,596	3,113	423	2,712	3,910
Lewis	6,962	13,636	1,603	7,634	15,846
Lincoln	1,597	3,324	357	1,671	3,474
Mason	5,241	6,745	1,353	7,007	8,410
Okanogan ..	4,634	6,460	1,030	5,330	7,476
Pacific	3,727	3,132	945	4,679	3,613
Pend Oreille ...	1,399	2,136	221	1,655	2,374
Pierce	64,444	90,247	18,345	79,498	112,877
San Juan ...	1,666	2,363	728	2,514	2,900
Skagit	11,299	15,520	2,854	13,947	18,840
Skamania ..	1,373	1,416	218	1,552	1,736
Snohomish ..	52,003	66,153	14,465	66,728	90,362
Spokane ...	49,263	78,096	11,258	59,620	88,043
Stevens	3,584	7,094	601	4,304	8,211
Thurston ...	20,508	26,369	5,993	26,840	34,442
Wahkiakum ..	751	828	148	930	776
Walla Walla ..	5,825	11,223	1,591	6,804	12,361
Whatcom	18,430	21,371	4,906	22,670	27,228
Whitman	5,726	8,636	2,331	6,621	10,021
Yakima	21,873	33,815	4,672	24,724	40,678
Totals	650,193	865,244	185,073	798,352	1,051,570

Washington Vote Since 1936

1936, Roosevelt, Dem., 459,579; Landon, Rep., 206,892; Lemke, Union, 17,463; Thomas, Soc., 3,496; Browder, Com., 1,907; Pelisy, Christian, 1,598; Colvin, Proh., 1,041; Aiken, Soc. Labor, 362.

1940, Roosevelt, Dem., 462,145; Willkie, Rep., 322,123; Thomas, Soc., 4,586; Browder, Com., 2,626; Babson, Proh., 1,686; Aiken, Soc. Labor, 667.

1944, Roosevelt, Dem., 486,774; Dewey, Rep., 361,689; Thomas, Soc., 3,824; Watson, Proh., 2,396; Teichert, Soc. Labor, 1,645.

1948, Truman, Dem., 476,165; Dewey, Rep., 386,315; Wallace, Prog., 31,692; Watson, Proh., 6,117; Thomas, Soc., 3,534; Teichert, Soc. Labor, 1,133; Dobbs, Soc. Workers, 103.

1952, Eisenhower, Rep., 599,107; Stevenson, Dem., 492,845; MacArthur, Christian Nationalist, 7,290; Hallinan, Prog., 2,460; Hass, Soc. Labor, 633; Hoopes, Soc., 254; Dobbs, Soc. Workers, 119.

1956, Eisenhower, Rep., 620,430; Stevenson, Dem., 523,002; Hass, Soc. Labor, 7,457.

, Kennedy, Dem., 599,298; Nixon, Rep., 629,273; Hass, Soc. Labor, 10,895; Curtis, Constitution, 1,401; Dobbs, Soc. Workers, 705.

'64, Johnson, Dem., 779,699; Goldwater, Rep., 470,366; Hass, Soc. Labor, 7,772; DeBerry, Freedom Soc., 537.

'968, Nixon, Rep., 588,510; Humphrey, Dem., 616,037; Wallace, 3d party, 96,990; Blomen, Soc. Labor, 488; Cleaver, Peace and Freedom, 1,609; Halstead, Soc. Worker, 270; Mitchell, Free Ballot, 377.

1972, Nixon, Rep., 837,135; McGovern, Dem., 568,334; Schmitz, Amer., 58,906; Spock, Ind., 2,644; Fisher, Soc. Labor, 1,102; Jenness, Soc. Worker, 623; Hall, Com., 566; Hospers, Libertarian, 1,537.

1976, Carter, Dem., 717,323; Ford, Rep., 777,732; McCarthy, Ind., 36,986; Maddox, Amer. Ind., 8,585; Anderson, Amer., 5,046; McBride, Libertarian, 2,643; Camejo, Soc. Workers, 905; LaRouche, U.S. Labor, 903; Hall, Com., 817; Levin, Soc. Labor, 713; Zeidler, Soc., 358.

1980, Reagan, Rep., 865,244; Carter, Dem., 650,193; Anderson, Ind., 185,073; Clark, Libertarian, 29,213; Commoner, Citizens, 9,403; DeBerry, Soc. Worker, 1,137; McReynolds, Socialist, 956; Hall, Com., 834; Griswold, Workers World, 341.

1984, Reagan, Rep., 1,051,670; Mondale, Dem., 798,352; Bergland, Libertarian, 8,844.

West Virginia

County	1980 Carter (D)	Reagan (R)	Anderson (I)	1984 Mondale (D)	Reagan (R)
Barbour	3,451	3,311	292	3,108	3,877
Berkeley	6,783	9,955	625	6,181	12,887
Boone	7,515	4,164	268	7,121	4,656
Braxton	3,795	2,403	173	3,350	2,902
Brooke	6,430	4,622	634	6,636	4,819
Cabell	17,732	19,482	2,146	15,513	21,815
Calhoun	1,717	1,606	92	1,473	1,765
Clay	2,185	1,452	102	2,117	1,667
Doddridge	1,043	1,886	120	836	2,343
Fayette	13,175	5,784	725	11,650	7,360
Gilmer	1,854	1,452	153	1,494	1,953
Grant	1,041	3,452	87	828	3,715
Greenbrier	7,128	6,221	546	5,599	7,337
Hampshire	2,522	2,879	157	2,102	4,065
Hancock	8,784	6,610	917	8,708	7,326
Hardy	2,050	2,329	99	1,641	2,938
Harrison	18,813	14,251	1,339	14,969	19,400
Jackson	4,120	6,041	362	4,147	7,117
Jefferson	4,679	4,454	572	4,216	5,884
Kanawha	42,829	42,604	5,838	37,832	51,499
Lewis	3,455	3,747	359	2,693	5,297
Lincoln	5,317	4,009	128	5,467	4,405
Logan	12,024	4,945	381	10,892	6,425
McDowell	9,822	3,862	216	8,546	4,284
Marion	14,189	10,952	1,171	13,833	13,106
Marshall	7,832	7,252	725	7,947	8,615
Mason	5,683	6,040	312	5,701	6,648
Mercer	11,604	12,273	563	9,164	13,910
Mineral	4,671	6,125	386	3,832	7,291
Mingo	9,328	3,716	208	8,434	4,275
Monongalia	12,883	11,972	2,745	13,236	14,972
Monroe	2,877	2,999	166	2,333	3,612
Morgan	1,594	2,833	172	1,457	3,469
Nicholas	5,265	3,885	322	4,588	4,656
Ohio	10,973	11,414	1,334	10,163	13,447
Pendleton	1,724	1,677	80	1,464	2,047
Pleasants	1,494	1,852	84	1,458	2,255
Pocahontas	2,170	2,011	150	1,903	2,479
Preston	4,317	5,828	515	4,054	6,955
Putnam	6,409	7,561	632	5,208	9,238
Raleigh	16,955	10,713	1,046	14,442	14,571
Randolph	5,937	4,374	518	4,839	6,100
Ritchie	1,450	3,081	128	1,231	3,355
Roane	2,498	3,219	164	2,468	3,751
Summers	3,114	2,456	201	2,670	2,975
Taylor	3,216	3,010	233	2,754	4,007
Tucker	1,862	1,798	153	1,766	2,240
Tyler	1,482	2,707	163	1,395	3,170
Upshur	2,867	4,751	415	2,468	5,951
Wayne	8,687	7,541	441	8,378	8,811
Webster	2,578	1,262	117	2,355	1,585
Wetzel	4,035	3,588	327	3,549	4,626
Wirt	1,058	1,176	44	868	1,450
Wood	13,622	20,080	1,536	11,357	24,821
Wyoming	6,624	4,537	299	5,691	5,379
Totals	367,462	334,206	31,691	328,125	405,483

West Virginia Vote Since 1936

1936, Roosevelt, Dem., 502,582; Landon, Rep., 325,358; Colvin, Prog., 1,173; Thomas, Soc., 832.

1940, Roosevelt, Dem., 495,662; Willkie, Rep., 372,414.

1944, Roosevelt, Dem., 392,777; Dewey, Rep., 322,819.

1948, Truman, Dem., 429,188; Dewey, Rep., 316,251; Wallace, Prog., 3,311.

1952, Eisenhower, Rep., 419,970; Stevenson, Dem., 453,578.

1956, Eisenhower, Rep., 449,297; Stevenson, Dem., 381,534.

1960, Kennedy, Dem., 441,786; Nixon, Rep., 395,995.

1964, Johnson, Dem., 538,087; Goldwater, Rep., 253,953.

1968, Nixon, Rep., 307,555; Humphrey, Dem., 374,091; Wallace, 3d party, 72,560.

1972, Nixon, Rep., 484,964; McGovern, Dem., 277,435.

1976, Carter, Dem., 435,864; Ford, Rep., 314,726.

1980, Reagan, Rep., 334,206; Carter, Dem., 367,462; Anderson, Ind., 31,691; Clark, Libertarian, 4,356.

1984, Reagan, Rep., 405,483; Mondale, Dem., 328,125.

Wisconsin

County	1980 Carter (D)	Reagan (R)	Anderson (I)	1984 Mondale (D)	Reagan (R)
Adams	2,773	3,304	318	2,713	3,644
Ashland	4,469	3,262	685	4,680	3,517
Barron	8,654	8,791	863	8,060	9,587
Bayfield	3,705	3,278	554	4,034	3,474
Brown	29,796	47,067	4,680	30,208	51,186
Buffalo	3,276	3,569	404	2,921	3,325
Burnet	3,200	3,027	393	3,328	3,528
Calumet	5,036	7,885	1,064	4,735	8,969
Chippewa	9,836	10,531	1,160	10,200	10,983
Clark	6,091	7,921	679	5,647	8,098
Columbia	8,715	10,478	1,373	8,124	11,658
Crawford	3,392	3,934	371	3,435	4,411
Dane	85,609	57,545	19,772	94,638	74,009
Dodge	11,966	19,435	1,709	11,052	20,455
Door	4,961	7,170	655	3,915	8,264
Douglas	11,703	7,258	1,728	14,290	7,066
Dunn	7,743	7,428	1,565	7,709	8,472
Eau Claire	17,602	17,304	3,486	19,344	20,394
Florence	943	1,187	86	870	1,227
Fond duLac	15,293	24,196	2,191	13,982	26,067
Forest	2,402	2,070	141	2,213	2,296
Grant	8,406	13,298	1,690	7,890	13,427
Green	5,336	7,714	947	4,367	7,826
Green Lake	2,851	5,868	368	2,441	6,198
Iowa	4,154	4,068	546	3,842	4,982
Iron	1,941	1,811	219	1,967	1,667
Jackson	3,629	4,327	413	3,427	4,383
Jefferson	11,335	16,174	1,925	10,766	17,779
Juneau	3,884	5,591	463	3,151	5,627
Kenosha	26,738	24,481	3,602	29,233	26,112
Kewaunee	3,706	5,577	318	3,444	5,705
La Crosse	17,304	23,427	3,652	17,787	25,717
La Fayette	3,598	4,421	450	2,959	4,582
Langlade	4,498	4,866	369	3,675	5,828
Lincoln	5,438	6,473	630	5,352	6,681
Manitowoc	17,330	16,591	2,014	17,249	19,635
Marathon	23,261	25,866	3,257	20,126	27,077
Marinette	7,718	10,444	683	6,798	11,449
Marquette	2,180	3,166	270	2,031	3,404
Menominee	544	302	57	832	392
Milwaukee	240,174	183,450	34,281	259,134	196,259
Monroe	6,521	8,136	780	5,564	8,225
Oconto	5,352	8,292	440	5,286	8,713
Oneida	7,008	8,602	832	6,416	9,782
Outagamie	21,284	31,500	5,735	19,769	36,765
Ozaukee	10,779	21,371	2,463	10,763	23,696
Pepin	1,673	1,541	183	1,629	1,555
Pierce	7,312	6,209	1,752	7,285	7,611
Polk	7,607	7,207	1,102	8,033	8,101
Portage	16,443	10,465	2,851	14,399	13,603
Price	3,595	4,026	394	3,479	4,286
Racine	33,565	39,683	5,167	36,953	42,085
Richland	3,413	4,601	413	2,844	4,857
Rock	24,740	30,960	4,408	26,430	32,483
Rusk	3,584	3,704	340	3,843	4,061
St. Croix	10,203	9,265	1,867	10,126	11,365
Sauk	8,456	9,992	1,405	7,157	11,067
Sawyer	3,065	3,548	323	2,981	3,911
Shawano	5,410	9,922	652	5,469	10,635
Sheboygan	20,974	23,036	3,859	21,111	26,343
Taylor	3,739	4,596	403	3,271	4,918
Trempealeau	5,390	5,992	558	5,405	6,007
Vernon	5,501	6,528	494	5,051	6,488
Vilas	3,293	6,034	421	2,940	5,963
Walworth	11,344	19,194	2,581	9,876	20,590
Washburn	3,172	3,193	355	3,188	3,847
Washington	12,944	23,213	2,654	12,966	25,278
Waukesha	46,612	81,059	9,778	47,308	92,415
Waupaca	6,401	12,568	1,072	5,894	13,097
Waushara	2,987	5,576	335	2,782	5,768
Winnebago	24,203	34,286	4,779	22,791	39,014
Wood	13,804	17,987	2,010	12,118	20,525
Totals	981,584	1,088,845	160,657	995,740	1,198,584

Wisconsin Vote Since 1936

1936, Roosevelt, Dem., 802,984; Landon, Rep., 380,828; Lemke, Union, 60,297; Thomas, Soc., 10,626; Browder, Com., 2,197; Colvin, Proh., 1,071; Aiken, Soc. Labor, 557.

1940, Roosevelt, Dem., 704,821; Willkie, Rep., 679,260; Thomas, Soc., 15,071; Browder, Com., 2,394; Babson, Proh., 2,148; Aiken, Soc. Labor, 1,882.

1944, Roosevelt, Dem., 650,413; Dewey, Rep., 674,532; Thomas, Soc., 13,205; Teichert, Soc. Labor, 1,002.

1948, Truman, Dem., 647,310; Dewey, Rep., 590,959; Wallace, Prog., 25,282; Thomas, Soc., 12,547; Teichert, Soc. Labor, 399; Dobbs, Soc. Workers, 303.

1952, Eisenhower, Rep., 979,744; Stevenson, Dem., 622,175; Hallinan, Ind., 2,174; Dobbs, Ind., 1,350; Hoopes, Ind., 1,157; Hass, Ind., 770.

1956, Eisenhower, Rep., 954,844; Stevenson, Dem., 586,768; Andrews, Ind., 6,918; Hoopes, Soc., 754; Hass, Soc. Labor, 710; Dobbs, Soc. Workers, 564.

1960, Kennedy, Dem., 830,805; Nixon, Rep., 895,175; Dobbs, Soc. Workers, 1,792; Hass, Soc. Labor, 1,310.

1964, Johnson, Dem., 1,050,424; Goldwater, Rep., 638,495; DeBerry, Soc. Worker, 1,692; Hass, Soc. Labor, 1,204.

1968, Nixon, Rep., 809,997; Humphrey, Dem., 748,804; Wallace, 3d party, 127,835; Blomen, Soc. Labor, 1,338; Halstead, Soc. Worker, 1,222; scattered, 2,342.

1972 Nixon, Rep., 989,430; McGovern, Dem., 810,174; Schmitz, Amer., 47,525; Spock, Ind., 2,701; Fisher, Soc. Labor, 998; Hall, Com., 663; Reed, Ind., 506; scattered, 893.

1976, Carter, Dem., 1,040,232; Ford, Rep., 1,004,987; McCarthy, Ind., 34,943; Maddox, Amer. Ind., 8,552; Zeidler, Soc., 4,298; MacBride, Libertarian, 3,814; Camejo, Soc. Workers, 1,691; Wright, People's, 943; Hall, Com., 749; LaRouche, U.S. Lab., 738; Levin, Soc. Labor, 389; scattered, 2,839.

1980, Reagan, Rep., 1,088,845; Carter, Dem., 981,584; Anderson, Ind., 160,657; Clark, Libertarian, 29,135; Commoner, Citizens, 7,767; Rarick, Constitution, 1,519; McReynolds, Socialist, 808; Hall, Com., 772; Griswold, Workers World, 414; DeBerry, Soc. Workers, 383; scattering, 1,337.

1984, Reagan, Rep., 1,198,584; Mondale, Dem., 995,740; Bergland, Libertarian, 4,883.

Wyoming

| | 1980 | | | 1984 | |
County	Carter (D)	Reagan (R)	Anderson (I)	Mondale (D)	Reagan (R)
Albany	3,772	5,830	1,630	4,708	7,452
Big Horn	1,212	3,709	209	1,175	4,019
Campbell	1,400	5,613	460	1,525	8,387
Carbon	2,272	4,337	493	2,295	4,557
Converse	922	2,987	215	929	3,542
Crook	413	1,909	70	450	2,286
Fremont	3,307	9,077	731	3,969	9,885
Goshen	1,373	3,572	269	1,364	3,776
Hot Springs	745	1,602	136	672	1,943
Johnson	635	2,291	139	558	2,634
Laramie	9,512	15,361	2,225	10,110	19,348
Lincoln	1,063	3,412	120	1,021	3,854
Natrona	7,111	16,801	1,768	7,598	18,488
Niobrara	270	1,075	38	239	1,098
Park	1,718	6,435	496	1,965	7,994
Platte	1,555	2,642	262	1,232	2,813
Sheridan	3,034	5,649	641	3,648	7,460
Sublette	357	1,538	139	389	1,976
Sweetwater	4,728	6,265	826	5,230	8,308
Teton	1,361	3,004	664	1,565	3,487
Uinta	1,138	2,738	189	1,276	4,075
Washakie	945	2,634	230	970	3,245
Weston	583	2,219	122	482	2,614
Totals	49,427	110,700	12,072	53,370	133,241

Wyoming Vote Since 1936

1936, Roosevelt, Dem., 62,624; Landon, Rep., 38,739; Lemke, Union, 1,653; Thomas, Soc., 200; Browder, Com., 91; Colvin, Proh., 75.

1940, Roosevelt, Dem., 59,287; Willkie, Rep., 52,633; Babson, Proh., 172; Thomas, Soc., 148.

1944, Roosevelt, Dem., 49,419; Dewey, Rep., 51,921.

1948, Truman, Dem., 52,354; Dewey, Rep., 47,947; Wallace, Prog., 931; Thomas, Soc., 137; Teichert, Soc. Labor, 56.

1952, Eisenhower, Rep., 81,047; Stevenson, Dem., 47,934; Hamblen, Proh., 194; Hoopes, Soc., 40; Haas, Soc. Labor, 36.

1956, Eisenhower, Rep., 74,573; Stevenson, Dem., 49,554.

1960, Kennedy, Dem., 63,331; Nixon, Rep., 77,451.

1964, Johnson, Dem., 80,718; Goldwater, Rep., 61,998.

1968, Nixon, Rep., 70,927; Humphrey, Dem., 45,173; Wallace, 3d party, 11,105.

1972, Nixon, Rep., 100,464; McGovern, Dem., 44,358; Schmitz, Amer., 748.

1976, Carter, Dem., 62,239; Ford, Rep., 92,717; McCarthy, Ind., 624; Reagan, Ind., 307; Anderson, Amer., 290; MacBride, Libertarian, 89; Brown, Ind., 47; Maddox, Amer. Ind., 30.

1980, Reagan, Rep., 110,700; Carter, Dem., 49,427; Anderson, Ind., 12,072; Clark, Libertarian, 4,514.

1984, Reagan, Rep., 133,241; Mondale, Dem., 53,370; Bergland, Libertarian, 2,357.

Law on Succession to the Presidency

If by reason of death, resignation, removal from office, inability, or failure to qualify there is neither a president nor vice president to discharge the powers and duties of the office of president, then the speaker of the House of Representatives shall upon his resignation as speaker and as representative, act as president. The same rule shall apply in the case of the death, resignation, removal from office, or inability of an individual acting as president.

If at the time when a speaker is to begin the discharge of the powers and duties of the office of president there is no speaker, or the speaker fails to qualify as acting president, then the president pro tempore of the Senate, upon his resignation as president pro tempore and as senator, shall act as president.

An individual acting as president shall continue to act until the expiration of the then current presidential term, except that (1) if his discharge of the powers and duties of the office is founded in whole or in part in the failure of both the president-elect and the vice president-elect to qualify, then he shall act only until a president or vice president qualifies, and (2) if his discharge of the powers and duties of the office is founded in whole or in part on the inability of the president or vice president, then he shall act only until the removal of the disability of one of such individuals.

If, by reason of death, resignation, removal from office, or failure to qualify, there is no president pro tempore to act as president, then the officer of the United States who is highest on the following list, and who is not under any disability to discharge the powers and duties of president shall act as president; the secretaries of state, treasury, defense, attorney general, secretaries of interior, agriculture, commerce, labor, health and human services, housing and urban development, transportation, energy, education.

(Legislation approved July 18, 1947; amended Sept. 9, 1965, Oct. 15, 1966, Aug. 4, 1977, and Sept. 27, 1979. (See also Constitutional Amendment XXV.)

Voting for President

Source: Federal Election Commission; Commission for Study of American Electorate

Candidates	Voter Participation (% of voting-age population)	Candidates	Voter Participation (% of voting-age population)
932 Roosevelt-Hoover	52.4	1960 Kennedy-Nixon	62.8
1936 Roosevelt-Landon	56.0	1964 Johnson-Goldwater	61.9
1940 Roosevelt-Wilkie	58.9	1968 Humphrey-Nixon	60.9
1944 Roosevelt-Dewey	56.0	1972 McGovern-Nixon	55.2
1948 Truman-Dewey	51.1	1976 Carter-Ford	53.5
1952 Stevenson-Eisenhower	61.6	1980 Carter-Reagan	54.0
1956 Stevenson-Eisenhower	59.3	1984 Mondale-Reagan	53.3

Americans voted in record numbers in the 1984 Presidential election, according to a state-by-state tabulation of votes compiled by the Federal Election Commission.

The report, which is based on official counts provided to the FEC by voting authorities of each of the 50 states and the District of Columbia, shows 92,652,842 votes were cast for the President out of the 1984 estimated voting age population of 173,936,000. The votes went to 17 Presidential candidates plus write-ins.

In 1980, there were 86,495,678 votes cast for 21 Presidential candidates appearing on various state ballots, plus write-ins.

Because of the variety of state laws governing registration, there is no official record of total registered voters in the United States. Estimated voting age population figures, upon which the FEC bases its statistics, are provided each year by the Bureau of the Census.

Also, because the FEC figures are obtained from official state election sources, the counts are based on individual state definitions of a valid vote cast and counted for a candidate.

Participation in National Elections, 1964 to 1982, and by Population Characteristics, 1982

Source: U.S. Bureau of the Census

Year and Characteristics	Persons of voting age (mil.)	Persons reporting they registered Total (mil.)	Persons reporting they registered Percent	Persons reporting they voted Total (mil.)	Persons reporting they voted Percent	Persons reporting they did not vote Total[1] (mil.)	Persons reporting they did not vote Registered (mil.)	Persons reporting they did not vote Not registered[1] Number (mil.)	Persons reporting they did not vote Not registered[1] Percent	Percent of voting age population not a citizen
1964	110.6	NA	NA	76.7	69.3	33.9	NA	NA	NA	NA
1966	112.8	79.3	70.3	62.5	55.4	50.3	16.8	33.1	29.3	2.0
1968	116.5	86.6	74.3	79.0	67.8	37.6	7.6	30.0	25.7	2.3
1970	120.7	82.2	68.1	65.9	54.6	54.8	16.3	38.5	31.9	2.5
1972	136.2	98.5	72.3	85.8	63.0	50.4	12.7	37.7	27.7	2.6
1974	141.3	87.9	62.2	63.2	44.7	78.1	24.7	53.4	37.8	2.8
1976	146.5	97.8	66.7	86.7	59.2	59.9	11.1	48.8	33.3	3.0
1978	151.6	94.9	62.6	69.6	45.9	82.1	25.3	56.8	37.4	3.5
1980	157.1	105.0	66.9	93.1	59.2	64.0	12.0	52.1	33.1	4.0
1982, total[2]	165.5	106.0	64.1	80.3	48.5	85.2	25.7	59.5	35.9	4.3
Male	78.0	49.7	63.7	38.0	48.7	40.0	11.7	28.3	36.3	4.2
Female	87.4	56.3	64.4	42.3	48.4	45.2	14.0	31.2	35.6	4.3
White	143.6	94.2	65.6	71.7	49.9	71.9	22.5	49.4	34.4	3.4
Black	17.6	10.4	59.1	7.6	43.0	10.0	2.8	7.2	40.9	3.2
Spanish origin[3]	8.8	3.1	35.3	2.2	25.3	6.5	.9	5.7	64.7	31.8
18-20 yr. old	12.1	4.2	35.0	2.4	19.8	9.7	1.8	7.9	65.0	5.2
21-24 yr. old	16.7	8.0	47.8	4.7	28.4	12.0	3.3	8.7	52.2	4.7
25-34 yr. old	38.8	22.1	57.1	15.7	40.4	23.1	6.5	16.6	42.9	5.6
35-44 yr. old	28.1	19.0	67.5	14.7	52.2	13.5	4.3	9.1	32.5	5.3
45-64 yr. old	44.2	33.4	75.6	27.5	62.2	16.7	5.9	10.8	24.4	3.1
65 yr. and over	25.6	19.2	75.2	15.3	59.9	10.3	3.9	6.4	24.8	2.3
Median age (yr.)	40.4	44.8	x	47.0	x	34.1	38.0	33.1	x	x
Region										
Northeast	36.4	22.7	62.5	18.1	49.8	18.3	4.6	13.6	37.5	4.8
Midwest	41.9	29.8	71.1	22.9	54.7	19.0	6.9	12.1	28.9	1.9
South	55.4	34.2	61.7	23.1	41.8	32.2	11.0	21.2	38.3	3.0
West	31.9	19.3	60.6	16.2	50.7	15.7	3.2	12.5	39.4	9.0
Metropolitan	113.1	70.8	62.6	54.6	48.3	58.5	16.2	42.3	37.4	5.6
In central cities	46.8	28.3	60.4	22.1	47.2	24.7	6.2	18.5	39.6	7.1
Outside central cities	66.2	42.4	64.1	32.5	49.1	33.7	10.0	23.8	35.9	4.5
Nonmetropolitan	52.4	35.2	67.2	25.7	49.1	26.7	9.5	17.2	32.8	1.5
School years completed										
8 yr. or less	22.4	11.7	52.3	8.0	35.7	14.4	3.7	10.7	47.7	10.6
High school:										
1-3 yr.	22.3	11.9	53.3	8.4	37.7	13.9	3.5	10.4	46.7	3.5
4 yr.	65.2	41.0	62.9	30.7	47.1	34.5	10.3	24.2	37.1	3.0
College:										
1-3 yr.	28.8	20.1	70.0	15.3	53.3	13.4	4.8	8.6	30.0	3.0
4 yr. or more	26.9	21.3	79.4	17.9	66.5	9.0	3.5	5.5	20.6	4.1

(NA) Not available. (x) Not applicable. (1) Includes do not know and not reported. (2) Includes characteristics not shown separately. (3) Persons of Spanish origin may be of any race.

Major Parties' Popular and Electoral Vote for President

(F) Federalist; (D) Democrat; (R) Republican; (DR) Democrat Republican; (NR) National Republican;
(W) Whig; (P) People's; (PR) Progressive; (SR) States' Rights; (LR) Liberal Republican; Asterisk (*)—See notes.

Year	President elected	Popular	Elec.	Losing candidate	Popular	Elec
1789	George Washington (F)	Unknown	69	No opposition.	—	—
1792	George Washington (F)	Unknown	132	No opposition.	—	—
1796	John Adams (F).	Unknown	71	Thomas Jefferson (DR)	Unknown	68
1800*	Thomas Jefferson (DR) . . .	Unknown	73	Aaron Burr (DR)	Unknown	73
1804	Thomas Jefferson (DR) . . .	Unknown	162	Charles Pinckney (F)	Unknown	14
1808	James Madison (DR).	Unknown	122	Charles Pinckney (F)	Unknown	47
1812	James Madison (DR).	Unknown	128	DeWitt Clinton (F)	Unknown	89
1816	James Monroe (DR)	Unknown	183	Rufus King (F)	Unknown	34
1820	James Monroe (DR)	Unknown	231	John Quincy Adams (DR). . . .	Unknown	1
1824*	John Quincy Adams (DR) . . .	105,321	84	Andrew Jackson (DR)	155,872	99
				Henry Clay (DR)	46,587	37
				William H. Crawford (DR)	44,282	41
1828	Andrew Jackson (D)	647,231	178	John Quincy Adams (NR)	509,097	83
1832	Andrew Jackson (D)	687,502	219	Henry Clay (NR)	530,189	49
1836	Martin Van Buren (D)	762,678	170	William H. Harrison (W)	548,007	73
1840	William H. Harrison (W)	1,275,017	234	Martin Van Buren (D)	1,128,702	60
1844	James K. Polk (D)	1,337,243	170	Henry Clay (W).	1,299,068	105
1848	Zachary Taylor (W).	1,360,101	163	Lewis Cass (D)	1,220,544	127
1852	Franklin Pierce (D)	1,601,474	254	Winfield Scott (W)	1,386,578	42
1856	James C. Buchanan (D)	1,927,995	174	John C. Fremont (R)	1,391,555	114
1860	Abraham Lincoln (R)	1,866,352	180	Stephen A. Douglas (D)	1,375,157	12
				John C. Breckinridge (D)	845,763	72
				John Bell (Const. Union)	589,581	39
1864	Abraham Lincoln (R)	2,216,067	212	George McClellan (D)	1,808,725	21
1868	Ulysses S. Grant (R)	3,015,071	214	Horatio Seymour (D)	2,709,615	80
1872*	Ulysses S. Grant (R)	3,597,070	286	Horace Greeley (D-LR)	2,834,079	—
1876*	Rutherford B. Hayes (R). . . .	4,033,950	185	Samuel J. Tilden (D)	4,284,757	184
1880	James A. Garfield (R)	4,449,053	214	Winfield S. Hancock (D).	4,442,030	155
1884	Grover Cleveland (D)	4,911,017	219	James G. Blaine (R)	4,848,334	182
1888*	Benjamin Harrison (R)	5,444,337	233	Grover Cleveland (D)	5,540,050	168
1892	Grover Cleveland (D)	5,554,414	277	Benjamin Harrison (R)	5,190,802	145
				James Weaver (P)	1,027,329	22
1896	William McKinley (R)	7,035,638	271	William J. Bryan (D-P)	6,467,946	176
1900	William McKinley (R)	7,219,530	292	William J. Bryan (D)	6,358,071	155
1904	Theodore Roosevelt (R)	7,628,834	336	Alton B. Parker (D)	5,084,491	140
1908	William H. Taft (R)	7,679,006	321	William J. Bryan (D)	6,409,106	162
1912	Woodrow Wilson (D)	6,286,214	435	Theodore Roosevelt (PR)	4,216,020	88
				William H. Taft (R)	3,483,922	8
1916	Woodrow Wilson (D)	9,129,606	277	Charles E. Hughes (R).	8,538,221	254
1920	Warren G. Harding (R)	16,152,200	404	James M. Cox (D)	9,147,353	127
1924	Calvin Coolidge (R)	15,725,016	382	John W. Davis (D)	8,385,586	136
				Robert M. LaFollette (PR)	4,822,856	13
1928	Herbert Hoover (R)	21,392,190	444	Alfred E. Smith (D).	15,016,443	87
1932	Franklin D. Roosevelt (D) . . .	22,821,857	472	Herbert Hoover (R)	15,761,841	59
				Norman Thomas (Socialist) . . .	884,781	—
1936	Franklin D. Roosevelt (D) . . .	27,751,597	523	Alfred Landon (R)	16,679,583	8
1940	Franklin D. Roosevelt (D) . . .	27,243,466	449	Wendell Willkie (R)	22,304,755	82
1944	Franklin D. Roosevelt (D) . . .	25,602,505	432	Thomas E. Dewey (R)	22,006,278	99
1948	Harry S Truman (D)	24,105,812	303	Thomas E. Dewey (R)	21,970,065	189
				J. Strom Thurmond (SR)	1,169,021	39
				Henry A. Wallace (PR)	1,157,172	—
1952	Dwight D. Eisenhower (R) . . .	33,936,252	442	Adlai E. Stevenson (D)	27,314,992	89
1956*	Dwight D. Eisenhower (R) . . .	35,585,316	457	Adlai E. Stevenson (D)	26,031,322	73
1960*	John F. Kennedy (D)	34,227,096	303	Richard M. Nixon (R).	34,108,546	219
1964	Lyndon B. Johnson (D).	43,126,506	486	Barry M. Goldwater (R)	27,176,799	52
1968	Richard M. Nixon (R)	31,785,480	301	Hubert H. Humphrey (D)	31,275,166	191
				George C. Wallace (3d party) . .	9,906,473	46
1972*	Richard M. Nixon (R)	47,165,234	520	George S. McGovern (D)	29,170,774	17
1976*	Jimmy Carter (D)	40,828,929	297	Gerald R. Ford (R)	39,148,940	240
1980	Ronald Reagan (R)	43,899,248	489	Jimmy Carter (D).	35,481,435	49
				John B. Anderson (independent)	5,719,437	—
1984	Ronald Reagan (R)	54,455,075	525	Walter F. Mondale (D)	37,577,185	13

1800—Elected by House of Representatives because of tied electoral vote.

1824—Elected by House of Representatives. No candidate polled a majority. In 1824, the Democrat Republicans had become a loose coalition of competing political groups. By 1828, the supporters of Jackson were known as Democrats, and the J.Q. Adams and Henry Clay supporters as National Republicans.

1872—Greeley died Nov. 29, 1872. His electoral votes were split among 4 individuals.

1876—Fla., La., Ore., and S. C. election returns were disputed. Congress in joint session (Mar. 2, 1877) declared Hayes and Wheeler elected President and Vice-President.

1888—Cleveland had more votes than Harrison but the 233 electoral votes cast for Harrison against the 168 for Cleveland elected Harrison president.

1956—Democrats elected 74 electors but one from Alabama refused to vote for Stevenson.

1960—Sen. Harry F. Byrd (D-Va.) received 15 electoral votes.

1972—John Hospers of Cal. and Theodora Nathan of Ore. received one vote from an elector of Virginia.

1976—Ronald Reagan of Cal. received one vote from an elector of Washington.

Electoral Votes for President

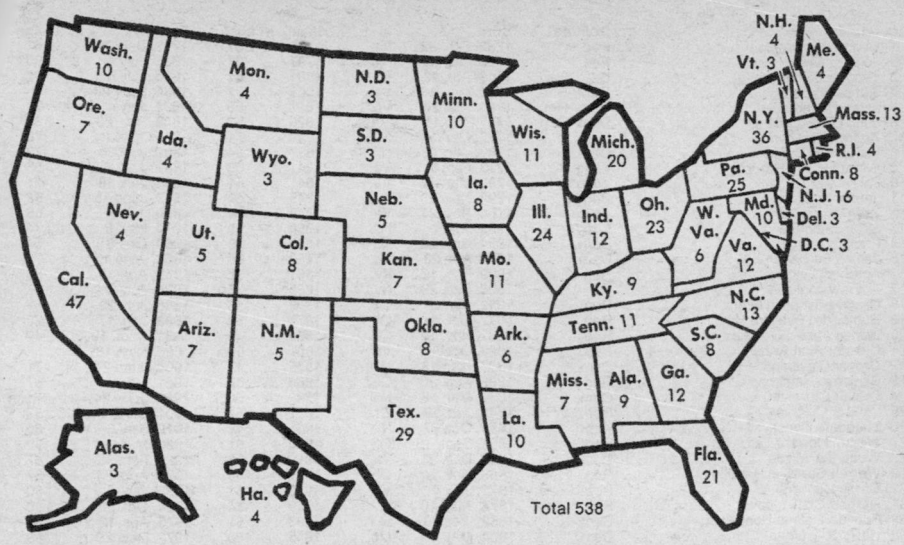

Total 538

Voter Turnout in Presidential Elections
Source: Committee for the Study of the American Electorate

National average of voting age population that voted: 1960—63.1; 1964—61.9; 1968—60.6; 1972—55.2; 1976—53.5; 1980—52.6; 1984—53.3. The sharp drop in 1972 reflects the expansion of eligibility with the enfranchisement of 18 to 21 year olds.

	1984 Registered voters voting	1980 Voting age population voting	1980 Voting age population voting		1984 Registered voters voting	1980 Voting age population voting	1980 Voting age population voting		1984 Registered voters voting	1980 Voting age population voting	1980 Voting age population voting
Ala.	61.5%	50.2%	48.7%	Ky.	67.7	50.7	49.9	N.D.	n/a	62.9	64.7
Alas.	68.0	60.2	57.4	La.	75.5	54.2	53.1	Oh.	71.8	58.2	55.4
Ariz.	70.1	46.6	44.5	Me.	68.2	65.2	64.6	Okla.	64.4	51.2	52.2
Ark.	69.8	52.2	51.5	Md.	74.4	51.4	50.0	Ore.	76.2	62.6	61.3
Cal.	72.7	49.9	49.0	Mass.	78.7	57.9	59.0	Pa.	78.2	53.9	51.9
Col.	80.0	54.8	55.8	Mich.	64.6	58.2	59.9	R.I.	75.7	56.0	58.7
Conn.	81.2	61.0	61.0	Minn.	72.1	68.5	70.0	S.C.	69.4	40.6	40.4
Del.	81.1	55.7	54.7	Miss.	56.4	52.0	51.8	S.D.	71.8	63.8	67.3
D.C.	76.9	43.8	35.5	Mo.	71.5	57.7	58.7	Tenn.	66.4	49.3	48.7
Fla.	75.0	49.0	48.7	Mon.	73.0	65.0	65.0	Tex.	68.3	47.0	44.9
Ga.	65.0	42.2	41.2	Neb.	72.2	56.1	56.7	Ut.	74.9	60.5	64.4
Ha.	80.2	44.5	43.6	Nev.	80.4	41.6	41.2	Vt.	72.8	60.0	57.6
Ida.	70.6	60.4	67.8	N.H.	71.5	53.9	57.2	Va.	84.1	51.1	47.6
Ill.	74.5	57.3	57.7	N.J.	79.0	56.9	54.9	Wash.	76.3	58.5	57.4
Ind.	73.1	56.3	57.6	N.M.	79.0	51.6	50.8	W.Va.	71.8	51.3	52.8
Ia.	76.3	62.3	62.8	N.Y.	75.3	51.1	48.0	Wis.	n/a	63.4	67.4
Kan.	79.1	57.0	56.7	N.C.	66.5	47.7	43.4	Wy.	78.8	51.8	53.2
n/a—not available.											

Party Nominees for President and Vice President
Asterisk (•) denotes winning ticket

Year	Democratic President	Democratic Vice President	Republican President	Republican Vice President
1920	James M. Cox	Franklin D. Roosevelt	Warren G. Harding*	Calvin Coolidge
1924	John W. Davis	Charles W. Bryan	Calvin Coolidge*	Charles G. Dawes
1928	Alfred E. Smith	Joseph T. Robinson	Herbert Hoover*	Charles Curtis
1932	Franklin D. Roosevelt*	John N. Garner	Herbert Hoover	Charles Curtis
1936	Franklin D. Roosevelt*	John N. Garner	Alfred M. Landon	Frank Knox
1940	Franklin D. Roosevelt*	Henry A. Wallace	Wendell L. Willkie	Charles McNary
1944	Franklin D. Roosevelt*	Harry S. Truman	Thomas E. Dewey	John W. Bricker
1948	Harry S. Truman*	Alben W. Barkley	Thomas E. Dewey	Earl Warren
1952	Adlai E. Stevenson	John J. Sparkman	Dwight D. Eisenhower*	Richard M. Nixon
1956	Adlai E. Stevenson	Estes Kefauver	Dwight D. Eisenhower*	Richard M. Nixon
1960	John F. Kennedy*	Lyndon B. Johnson	Richard M. Nixon	Henry Cabot Lodge
1964	Lyndon B. Johnson*	Hubert H. Humphrey	Barry M. Goldwater	William E. Miller
1968	Hubert H. Humphrey	Edmund S. Muskie	Richard M. Nixon*	Spiro T. Agnew
1972	George S. McGovern	R. Sargent Shriver Jr.	Richard M. Nixon*	Spiro T. Agnew
1976	Jimmy Carter*	Walter F. Mondale	Gerald R. Ford	Robert J. Dole
1980	Jimmy Carter	Walter F. Mondale	Ronald Reagan*	George Bush
1984	Walter F. Mondale	Geraldine Ferraro	Ronald Reagan*	George Bush

Presidents of the U.S.

No.	Name	Politics	Born	in	Inaug.	at age	Died	at age
1	George Washington	Fed.	1732, Feb. 22	Va.	1789	57	1799, Dec. 14	67
2	John Adams	Fed.	1735, Oct. 30	Mass.	1797	61	1826, July 4	90
3	Thomas Jefferson	Dem.-Rep.	1743, Apr. 13	Va.	1801	57	1826, July 4	83
4	James Madison	Dem.-Rep.	1751, Mar. 16	Va.	1809	57	1836, June 28	85
5	James Monroe	Dem.-Rep.	1758, Apr. 28	Va.	1817	58	1831, July 4	73
6	John Quincy Adams	Dem.-Rep.	1767, July 11	Mass.	1825	57	1848, Feb. 23	80
7	Andrew Jackson	Dem.	1767, Mar. 15	S.C.	1829	61	1845, June 8	78
8	Martin Van Buren	Dem.	1782, Dec. 5	N.Y.	1837	54	1862, July 24	79
9	William Henry Harrison	Whig	1773, Feb. 9	Va.	1841	68	1841, Apr. 4	68
10	John Tyler	Whig	1790, Mar. 29	Va.	1841	51	1862, Jan. 18	71
11	James Knox Polk	Dem.	1795, Nov. 2	N.C.	1845	49	1849, June 15	53
12	Zachary Taylor	Whig	1784, Nov. 24	Va.	1849	64	1850, July 9	65
13	Millard Fillmore	Whig	1800, Jan. 7	N.Y.	1850	50	1874, Mar. 8	74
14	Franklin Pierce	Dem.	1804, Nov. 23	N.H.	1853	48	1869, Oct. 8	64
15	James Buchanan	Dem.	1791, Apr. 23	Pa.	1857	65	1868, June 1	77
16	Abraham Lincoln	Rep.	1809, Feb. 12	Ky.	1861	52	1865, Apr. 15	56
17	Andrew Johnson	(1)	1808, Dec. 29	N.C.	1865	56	1875, July 31	66
18	Ulysses Simpson Grant	Rep.	1822, Apr. 27	Oh.	1869	46	1885, July 23	63
19	Rutherford Birchard Hayes	Rep.	1822, Oct. 4	Oh.	1877	54	1893, Jan. 17	70
20	James Abram Garfield	Rep.	1831, Nov. 19	Oh.	1881	49	1881, Sept. 19	49
21	Chester Alan Arthur	Rep.	1829, Oct. 5	Vt.	1881	50	1886, Nov. 18	57
22	Grover Cleveland	Dem.	1837, Mar. 18	N.J.	1885	47	1908, June 24	71
23	Benjamin Harrison	Rep.	1833, Aug. 20	Oh.	1889	55	1901, Mar. 13	67
24	Grover Cleveland	Dem.	1837, Mar. 18	N.J.	1893	55	1908, June 24	71
25	William McKinley	Rep.	1843, Jan. 29	Oh.	1897	54	1901, Sept. 14	58
26	Theodore Roosevelt	Rep.	1858, Oct. 27	N.Y.	1901	42	1919, Jan. 6	60
27	William Howard Taft	Rep.	1857, Sept. 15	Oh.	1909	51	1930, Mar. 8	72
28	Woodrow Wilson	Dem.	1856, Dec. 28	Va.	1913	56	1924, Feb. 3	67
29	Warren Gamaliel Harding	Rep.	1865, Nov. 2	Oh.	1921	55	1923, Aug. 2	57
30	Calvin Coolidge	Rep.	1872, July 4	Vt.	1923	51	1933, Jan. 5	60
31	Herbert Clark Hoover	Rep.	1874, Aug. 10	Ia.	1929	54	1964, Oct. 20	90
32	Franklin Delano Roosevelt	Dem.	1882, Jan. 30	N.Y.	1933	51	1945, Apr. 12	63
33	Harry S. Truman	Dem.	1884, May 8	Mo.	1945	60	1972, Dec. 26	88
34	Dwight David Eisenhower	Rep.	1890, Oct. 14	Tex.	1953	62	1969, Mar. 28	78
35	John Fitzgerald Kennedy	Dem.	1917, May 29	Mass.	1961	43	1963, Nov. 22	46
36	Lyndon Baines Johnson	Dem.	1908, Aug. 27	Tex.	1963	55	1973, Jan. 22	64
37	Richard Milhous Nixon (2)	Rep.	1913, Jan. 9	Cal.	1969	56		
38	Gerald Rudolph Ford	Rep.	1913, July 14	Neb.	1974	61		
39	Jimmy (James Earl) Carter	Dem.	1924, Oct. 1	Ga.	1977	52		
40	Ronald Reagan	Rep.	1911, Feb. 6	Ill.	1981	69		

(1) Andrew Johnson — a Democrat, nominated vice president by Republicans and elected with Lincoln on National Union ticket. (2) Resigned Aug. 9, 1974.

Presidents, Vice Presidents, Congresses

	President	Service		Vice President	Congress
1	George Washington	Apr. 30, 1789—Mar. 3, 1797	1	John Adams	1, 2, 3, 4
2	John Adams	Mar. 4, 1797—Mar. 3, 1801	2	Thomas Jefferson	5, 6
3	Thomas Jefferson	Mar. 4, 1801—Mar. 3, 1805	3	Aaron Burr	7, 8
	"	Mar. 4, 1805—Mar. 3, 1809	4	George Clinton	9, 10
4	James Madison	Mar. 4, 1809—Mar. 3, 1813		"(1)	11, 12
	"	Mar. 4, 1813—Mar. 3, 1817	5	Elbridge Gerry (2)	13, 14
5	James Monroe	Mar. 4, 1817—Mar. 3, 1825	6	Daniel D. Tompkins	15, 16, 17, 18
6	John Quincy Adams	Mar. 4, 1825—Mar. 3, 1829	7	John C. Calhoun	19, 20
7	Andrew Jackson	Mar. 4, 1829—Mar. 3, 1833		"(3)	21, 22
	"	Mar. 4, 1833—Mar. 3, 1837	8	Martin Van Buren	23, 24
8	Martin Van Buren	Mar. 4, 1837—Mar. 3, 1841	9	Richard M. Johnson	25, 26
9	William Henry Harrison (4)	Mar. 4, 1841—Apr. 4, 1841	10	John Tyler	27
10	John Tyler	Apr. 6, 1841—Mar. 3, 1845			27, 28
11	James K. Polk	Mar. 4, 1845—Mar. 3, 1849	11	George M. Dallas	29, 30
12	Zachary Taylor (4)	Mar. 5, 1849—July 9, 1850	12	Millard Fillmore	31
13	Millard Fillmore	July 10, 1850—Mar. 3, 1853			31, 32
14	Franklin Pierce	Mar. 4, 1853—Mar. 3, 1857	13	William R. King (5)	33, 34
15	James Buchanan	Mar. 4, 1857—Mar. 3, 1861	14	John C. Breckinridge	35, 36
16	Abraham Lincoln	Mar. 4, 1861—Mar. 3, 1865	15	Hannibal Hamlin	37, 38
	"(4)	Mar. 4, 1865—Apr. 15, 1865	16	Andrew Johnson	39
17	Andrew Johnson	Apr. 15, 1865—Mar. 3, 1869			39, 40
18	Ulysses S. Grant	Mar. 4, 1869—Mar. 3, 1873	17	Schuyler Colfax	41, 42
	"	Mar. 4, 1873—Mar. 3, 1877	18	Henry Wilson (6)	43, 44
19	Rutherford B. Hayes	Mar. 4, 1877—Mar. 3, 1881	19	William A. Wheeler	45, 46
20	James A. Garfield (4)	Mar. 4, 1881—Sept. 19, 1881	20	Chester A. Arthur	47
21	Chester A. Arthur	Sept. 20, 1881—Mar. 3, 1885			47, 48
22	Grover Cleveland (7)	Mar. 4, 1885—Mar. 3, 1889	21	Thomas A. Hendricks (8)	49, 50
23	Benjamin Harrison	Mar. 4, 1889—Mar. 3, 1893	22	Levi P. Morton	51, 52
24	Grover Cleveland (7)	Mar. 4, 1893—Mar. 3, 1897	23	Adlai E. Stevenson	53, 54
25	William McKinley	Mar. 4, 1897—Mar. 3, 1901	24	Garret A. Hobart (9)	55, 56
	"(4)	Mar. 4, 1901—Sept. 14, 1901	25	Theodore Roosevelt	57
26	Theodore Roosevelt	Sept. 14, 1901—Mar. 3, 1905			57, 58
	"	Mar. 4, 1905—Mar. 3, 1909	26	Charles W. Fairbanks	59, 60

President	Service	Vice President	Congress
27 William H. Taft	Mar. 4, 1909—Mar. 3, 1913	27 James S. Sherman (10)	61, 62
28 Woodrow Wilson	Mar. 4, 1913—Mar. 3, 1921	28 Thomas R. Marshall	63, 64, 65, 66
29 Warren G. Harding (4)	Mar. 4, 1921—Aug. 2, 1923	29 Calvin Coolidge	67
30 Calvin Coolidge	Aug. 3, 1923—Mar. 3, 1925		68
"	Mar. 4, 1925—Mar. 3, 1929	30 Charles G. Dawes	69, 70
31 Herbert C. Hoover	Mar. 4, 1929—Mar. 3, 1933	31 Charles Curtis	71, 72
32 Franklin D. Roosevelt (16)	Mar. 4, 1933—Jan. 20, 1941	32 John N. Garner	73, 74, 75, 76
"	Jan. 20, 1941—Jan. 20, 1945	33 Henry A. Wallace	77, 78
"(4)	Jan. 20, 1945—Apr. 12, 1945	34 Harry S. Truman	79
33 Harry S. Truman	Apr. 12, 1945—Jan. 20, 1949		79, 80
"	Jan. 20, 1949—Jan. 20, 1953	35 Alben W. Barkley	81, 82
34 Dwight D. Eisenhower	Jan. 20, 1953—Jan. 20, 1961	36 Richard M. Nixon	83, 84, 85, 86
35 John F. Kennedy (4)	Jan. 20, 1961—Nov. 22, 1963	37 Lyndon B. Johnson	87, 88
36 Lyndon B. Johnson	Nov. 22, 1963—Jan. 20, 1965		88
"	Jan. 20, 1965—Jan. 20, 1969	38 Hubert H. Humphrey	89, 90
37 Richard M. Nixon	Jan. 20, 1969—Jan. 20, 1973	39 Spiro T. Agnew (11)	91, 92, 93
"(12)	Jan. 20, 1973—Aug. 9, 1974	40 Gerald R. Ford (13)	93
38 Gerald R. Ford (14)	Aug. 9, 1974—Jan. 20, 1977	41 Nelson A. Rockefeller (15)	93, 94
39 Jimmy (James Earl) Carter	Jan. 20, 1977—Jan. 20, 1981	42 Walter F. Mondale	95, 96
40 Ronald Reagan	Jan. 20, 1981—	43 George Bush	97, 98, 99

(1) Died Apr. 20, 1812. (2) Died Nov. 23, 1814. (3) Resigned Dec. 28, 1832, to become U.S. Senator. (4) Died in office. (5) Died Apr. 18, 1853. (6) Died Nov. 22, 1875. (7) Terms not consecutive. (8) Died Nov. 25, 1885. (9) Died Nov. 21, 1899. (10) Died Oct. 30, 1912. (11) Resigned Oct. 10, 1973. (12) Resigned Aug. 9, 1974. (13) First non-elected vice president, chosen under 25th Amendment procedure. (14) First non-elected president. (15) 2d non-elected vice president. (16) First president to be inaugurated under 20th Amendment, Jan. 20, 1937.

Vice Presidents of the U.S.

The numerals given vice presidents do not coincide with those given presidents, because some presidents had none and some had more than one.

	Name	Birthplace	Year	Home	Inaug.	Politics	Place of death	Year	Age
1	John Adams	Quincy, Mass.	1735	Mass. . .	1789	Fed.	Quincy, Mass.	1826	90
2	Thomas Jefferson	Shadwell, Va.	1743	Va. . . .	1797	Dem.-Rep.	Monticello, Va.	1826	83
3	Aaron Burr	Newark, N.J.	1756	N.Y. . .	1801	Dem.-Rep.	Staten Island, N.Y. . . .	1836	80
4	George Clinton	Ulster Co., N.Y.	1739	N.Y. . .	1805	Dem.-Rep.	Washington, D.C. . . .	1812	73
5	Elbridge Gerry	Marblehead, Mass. . .	1744	Mass. . .	1813	Dem.-Rep.	Washington, D.C. . . .	1814	70
6	Daniel D. Tompkins . . .	Scarsdale, N.Y.	1774	N.Y. . .	1817	Dem.-Rep.	Staten Island, N.Y. . . .	1825	51
7	John C. Calhoun (1) . . .	Abbeville, S.C.	1782	S.C. . .	1825	Dem.-Rep.	Washington, D.C. . . .	1850	68
8	Martin Van Buren	Kinderhook, N.Y.	1782	N.Y. . .	1833	Dem. . . .	Kinderhook, N.Y. . . .	1862	79
9	Richard M. Johnson . . .	Louisville, Ky.	1780	Ky. . . .	1837	Dem. . . .	Frankfort, Ky.	1850	70
10	John Tyler	Greenway, Va.	1790	Va. . . .	1841	Whig . . .	Richmond, Va.	1862	71
11	George M. Dallas	Philadelphia, Pa.	1792	Pa. . . .	1845	Dem. . . .	Philadelphia, Pa.	1864	72
12	Millard Fillmore	Summerhill, N.Y.	1800	N.Y. . .	1849	Whig . . .	Buffalo, N.Y.	1874	74
13	William R. King	Sampson Co., N.C. . .	1786	Ala. . .	1853	Dem. . . .	Dallas Co., Ala.	1853	67
14	John C. Breckinridge . .	Lexington, Ky.	1821	Ky. . . .	1857	Dem. . . .	Lexington, Ky.	1875	54
15	Hannibal Hamlin	Paris, Me.	1809	Me. . . .	1861	Rep. . . .	Bangor, Me.	1891	81
16	Andrew Johnson	Raleigh, N.C.	1808	Tenn. . .	1865	(2)	Carter Co., Tenn.	1875	66
17	Schuyler Colfax	New York, N.Y.	1823	Ind. . .	1869	Rep. . . .	Mankato, Minn.	1885	62
18	Henry Wilson	Farmington, N.H.	1812	Mass. . .	1873	Rep. . . .	Washington, D.C. . . .	1875	63
19	William A. Wheeler . . .	Malone, N.Y.	1819	N.Y. . .	1877	Rep. . . .	Malone, N.Y.	1887	68
20	Chester A. Arthur	Fairfield, Vt.	1829	N.Y. . .	1881	Rep. . . .	New York, N.Y.	1886	57
21	Thomas A. Hendricks . .	Muskingum Co., Oh. . .	1819	Ind. . .	1885	Dem. . . .	Indianapolis, Ind.	1885	66
22	Levi P. Morton	Shoreham, Vt.	1824	N.Y. . .	1889	Rep. . . .	Rhinebeck, N.Y.	1920	96
23	Adlai E. Stevenson (3) . .	Christian Co., Ky. . . .	1835	Ill. . . .	1893	Dem. . . .	Chicago, Ill.	1914	78
24	Garret A. Hobart	Long Branch, N.J. . . .	1844	N.J. . .	1897	Rep. . . .	Paterson, N.J.	1899	55
25	Theodore Roosevelt . . .	New York, N.Y.	1858	N.Y. . .	1901	Rep. . . .	Oyster Bay, N.Y.	1919	60
26	Charles W. Fairbanks . .	Unionville Centre, Oh. .	1852	Ind. . .	1905	Rep. . . .	Indianapolis, Ind.	1918	66
27	James S. Sherman . . .	Utica, N.Y.	1855	N.Y. . .	1909	Rep. . . .	Utica, N.Y.	1912	57
28	Thomas R. Marshall . . .	N. Manchester, Ind. . .	1854	Ind. . .	1913	Dem. . . .	Washington, D.C. . . .	1925	71
29	Calvin Coolidge	Plymouth, Vt.	1872	Mass. . .	1921	Rep. . . .	Northampton, Mass. . .	1933	60
30	Charles G. Dawes	Marietta, Oh.	1865	Ill. . . .	1925	Rep. . . .	Evanston, Ill.	1951	85
31	Charles Curtis	Topeka, Kan.	1860	Kan. . .	1929	Rep. . . .	Washington, D.C. . . .	1936	76
32	John Nance Garner . . .	Red River Co., Tex. . .	1868	Tex. . .	1933	Dem. . . .	Uvalde, Tex.	1967	98
33	Henry Agard Wallace . .	Adair County, Ia.	1888	Iowa . .	1941	Dem. . . .	Danbury, Conn.	1965	77
34	Harry S. Truman	Lamar, Mo.	1884	Mo. . . .	1945	Dem. . . .	Kansas City, Mo.	1972	88
35	Alben W. Barkley	Graves County, Ky. . .	1877	Ky. . . .	1949	Dem. . . .	Lexington, Va.	1956	78
36	Richard M. Nixon	Yorba Linda, Cal. . . .	1913	Cal. . .	1953	Rep. . . .			
37	Lyndon B. Johnson . . .	Johnson City, Tex. . . .	1908	Tex. . .	1961	Dem. . . .	San Antonio, Tex. . . .	1973	64
38	Hubert H. Humphrey . .	Wallace, S.D.	1911	Minn. . .	1965	Dem. . . .	Waverly, Minn.	1978	66
39	Spiro T. Agnew	Baltimore, Md.	1918	Md. . . .	1969	Rep. . . .			
40	Gerald R. Ford	Omaha, Neb.	1913	Mich. . .	1973	Rep. . . .			
41	Nelson A. Rockefeller . .	Bar Harbor, Me.	1908	N.Y. . .	1974	Rep. . . .	New York, N.Y.	1979	70
42	Walter F. Mondale	Ceylon, Minn.	1928	Minn. . .	1977	Dem. . . .			
43	George Bush	Milton, Mass.	1924	Tex. . .	1981	Rep. . . .			

(1) John C. Calhoun resigned Dec. 28, 1832, having been elected to the Senate to fill a vacancy. (2) Andrew Johnson — a Democrat nominated by Republicans and elected with Lincoln on the National Union Ticket. (3) Adlai E. Stevenson, 23d vice president, was grandfather of Democratic candidate for president, 1952 and 1956.

The Continental Congress: Meetings, Presidents

Meeting places	Dates of meetings	Congress presidents	Date elected
Philadelphia	Sept. 5 to Oct. 26, 1774	Peyton Randolph, Va. (1)	Sept. 5, 1774
"		Henry Middleton, S.C.	Oct. 22, 1774
Philadelphia	May 10, 1775 to Dec. 12, 1776	Peyton Randolph, Va.	May 10, 1775
		John Hancock, Mass.	May 24, 1775
Baltimore	Dec. 20, 1776 to Mar. 4, 1777	"	
Philadelphia	Mar. 5 to Sept. 18, 1777	"	
Lancaster, Pa.	Sept. 27, 1777 (one day)	"	
York, Pa.	Sept. 30, 1777 to June 27, 1778	Henry Laurens, S.C.	Nov. 1, 1777(4)
Philadelphia	July 2, 1778 to June 21, 1783	John Jay, N.Y.	Dec. 10, 1778
"	"	Samuel Huntington, Conn.	Sept. 28, 1779
"	"	Thomas McKean, Del.	July 10, 1781
"	"	John Hanson, Md. (2)	Nov. 5, 1781
"	"	Elias Boudinot, N.J.	Nov. 4, 1782
Princeton, N.J.	June 30 to Nov. 4, 1783	Thomas Mifflin, Pa.	Nov. 3, 1783
Annapolis, Md.	Nov. 26, 1783 to June 3, 1784		
Trenton, N.J.	Nov. 1 to Dec. 24, 1784	Richard Henry Lee, Va.	Nov. 30, 1784
New York City	Jan. 11 to Nov. 4, 1785		
"	Nov. 7, 1785 to Nov. 3, 1786	John Hancock, Mass. (3)	Nov. 23, 1785
"		Nathaniel Gorham, Mass.	June 6, 1786
"	Nov. 6, 1786 to Oct. 30, 1787	Arthur St. Clair, Pa.	Feb. 2, 1787
"	Nov. 5, 1787 to Oct. 21, 1788	Cyrus Griffin, Va.	Jan. 22, 1788
"	Nov. 3, 1788 to Mar. 2, 1789		

(1) Resigned Oct. 22, 1774. (2) Titled "President of the United States in Congress Assembled," John Hanson is considered by some to be the first U.S. President as he was the first to serve under the Articles of Confederation. He was, however, little more than presiding officer of the Congress, which retained full executive power. He could be considered the head of government, but not head of state. (3) Resigned May 29, 1786, without serving, because of illness. (4) Articles of Confederation agreed upon, Nov. 15, 1777; last ratification from Maryland, Mar. 1, 1781.

Cabinets of the U. S.

Secretaries of State

The Department of Foreign Affairs was created by act of Congress July 27, 1789, and the name changed to Department of State on Sept. 15.

President	Secretary	Home	Apptd.	President	Secretary	Home	Apptd.
Washington	Thomas Jefferson.	Va. . . .	1789	"	Thomas F. Bayard	Del. . . .	1885
"	Edmund Randolph	"	1794	Harrison, B. . .	"	"	1889
"	Timothy Pickering	Pa. . . .	1795	"	James G. Blaine.	Me.	1889
Adams, J. . . .	"	"	1797	"	John W. Foster	Ind. . . .	1892
"	John Marshall	Va. . . .	1800	Cleveland	Walter Q. Gresham	Ill. . . .	1893
Jefferson . . .	James Madison	"	1801	"	Richard Olney	Mass. . .	1895
Madison	Robert Smith	Md. . . .	1809	McKinley	"	"	1897
"	James Monroe	Va. . . .	1811	"	John Sherman.	Oh.	1897
Monroe	John Quincy Adams	Mass. . .	1817	"	William R. Day.	"	1898
Adams, J.Q. . .	Henry Clay	Ky. . . .	1825	"	John Hay.	D.C. . . .	1898
Jackson	Martin Van Buren	N.Y. . .	1829	Roosevelt, T. . .	"	"	1901
"	Edward Livingston	La. . . .	1831	"	Elihu Root	N.Y. . . .	1905
"	Louis McLane	Del. . . .	1833	"	Robert Bacon	"	1909
"	John Forsyth	Ga. . . .	1834	Taft	"	"	1909
Van Buren . . .	"	"	1837	"	Philander C. Knox.	Pa. . . .	1909
Harrison, W.H. .	Daniel Webster	Mass. . .	1841	Wilson	"	"	1913
Tyler	"	"	1841	"	William J. Bryan.	Neb. . . .	1913
"	Abel P. Upshur	Va. . . .	1843	"	Robert Lansing	N.Y. . . .	1915
"	John C. Calhoun	S.C. . . .	1844	"	Bainbridge Colby	"	1920
Polk	"	"	1845	Harding.	Charles E. Hughes	"	1921
"	James Buchanan	Pa. . . .	1845	Coolidge	"	"	1923
Taylor.	"	"	1849	"	Frank B. Kellogg	Minn. . . .	1925
"	John M. Clayton.	Del. . . .	1849	Hoover	"	"	1929
Fillmore.	"	"	1850	"	Henry L. Stimson	N.Y. . . .	1929
"	Daniel Webster	Mass. . .	1850	Roosevelt, F.D.	Cordell Hull	Tenn. . .	1933
"	Edward Everett	"	1852	"	E.R. Stettinius Jr.	Va. . . .	1944
Pierce.	William L. Marcy	N.Y. . . .	1853	Truman	"	"	1945
Buchanan . . .	"	"	1857	"	James F. Byrnes	S.C. . . .	1945
"	Lewis Cass	Mich. . .	1857	"	George C. Marshall.	Pa. . . .	1947
"	Jeremiah S. Black	Pa. . . .	1860	"	Dean G. Acheson	Conn. . .	1949
Lincoln	"	"	1861	Eisenhower	John Foster Dulles	N.Y. . . .	1953
"	William H. Seward	N.Y. . .	1861	"	Christian A. Herter	Mass. . .	1959
Johnson, A. . .	"	"	1865	Kennedy . . .	Dean Rusk.	N.Y. . . .	1961
Grant	Elihu B. Washburne. . . .	Ill. . . .	1869	Johnson, L.B. .	"	"	1963
"	Hamilton Fish	N.Y. . . .	1869	Nixon	William P. Rogers	N.Y. . . .	1969
Hayes.	"	"	1877	"	Henry A. Kissinger	D.C. . . .	1973
"	William M. Evarts	"	1877	Ford.	"	"	1974
Garfield.	"	"	1881	Carter.	Cyrus R. Vance	N.Y. . . .	1977
"	James G. Blaine.	Me. . . .	1881	"	Edmund S. Muskie	Me.	1980
Arthur.	"	"	1881	Reagan	Alexander M. Haig Jr. . . .	Conn. . .	1981
"	F.T. Frelinghuysen	N.J.	1881	"	George P. Shultz	Cal. . . .	1982
Cleveland . . .	"	"	1885				

Secretaries of the Treasury

The Treasury Department was organized by act of Congress Sept. 2, 1789.

President	Secretary	Home	Apptd.	President	Secretary	Home	Apptd.
Washington	Alexander Hamilton	N.Y.	1789	Arthur	Charles J. Folger	N.Y.	1881
"	Oliver Wolcott	Conn.	1795	"	Walter Q. Gresham	Ind.	1884
Adams, J.	"	"	1797	"	Hugh McCulloch	"	1884
"	Samuel Dexter	Mass.	1801	Cleveland	Daniel Manning	N.Y.	1885
Jefferson	"	"	1801	Cleveland	Charles S. Fairchild	"	1887
"	Albert Gallatin	Pa.	1801	Harrison, B.	William Windom	Minn.	1889
Madison	"	Pa.	1809	"	Charles Foster	Oh.	1891
"	George W. Campbell	Tenn.	1814	Cleveland	John G. Carlisle	Ky.	1893
"	Alexander J. Dallas	Pa.	1814	McKinley	Lyman J. Gage	Ill.	1897
"	William H. Crawford	Ga.	1816	Roosevelt, T.	"	"	1901
Monroe	"	"	1817	"	Leslie M. Shaw	Ia.	1902
Adams, J.Q.	Richard Rush	Pa.	1825	"	George B. Cortelyou	N.Y.	1907
Jackson	Samuel D. Ingham	"	1829	Taft	Franklin MacVeagh	Ill.	1909
"	Louis McLane	Del.	1831	Wilson	William G. McAdoo	N.Y.	1913
"	William J. Duane	Pa.	1833	"	Carter Glass	Va.	1918
"	Roger B. Taney	Md.	1833	"	David F. Houston	Mo.	1920
"	Levi Woodbury	N.H.	1834	Harding	Andrew W. Mellon	Pa.	1921
Van Buren	"	"	1837	Coolidge	"	"	1923
Harrison, W.H.	Thomas Ewing	Oh.	1841	Hoover	"	"	1929
Tyler	"	"	1841	"	Ogden L. Mills	N.Y.	1932
"	Walter Forward	Pa.	1841	Roosevelt, F.D.	William H. Woodin	"	1933
"	John C. Spencer	N.Y.	1843	"	Henry Morgenthau, Jr.	"	1934
Tyler	George M. Bibb	Ky.	1844	Truman	Fred M. Vinson	Ky.	1945
Polk	Robert J. Walker	Miss.	1845	"	John W. Snyder	Mo.	1946
Taylor	William M. Meredith	Pa.	1849	Eisenhower	George M. Humphrey	Oh.	1953
Fillmore	Thomas Corwin	Oh.	1850	"	Robert B. Anderson	Conn.	1957
Pierce	James Guthrie	Ky.	1853	Kennedy	C. Douglas Dillon	N.J.	1961
Buchanan	Howell Cobb	Ga.	1857	Johnson, L.B.	"	"	1963
"	Phillip F. Thomas	Md.	1860	"	Henry H. Fowler	Va.	1965
"	John A. Dix	N.Y.	1861	"	Joseph W. Barr	Ind.	1968
Lincoln	Salmon P. Chase	Oh.	1861	Nixon	David M. Kennedy	Ill.	1969
"	William P. Fessenden	Me.	1864	"	John B. Connally	Tex.	1971
"	Hugh McCulloch	Ind.	1865	"	George P. Shultz	Ill.	1972
Johnson, A.	"	"	1865	"	William E. Simon	N.J.	1974
Grant	George S. Boutwell	Mass.	1869	Ford	"	"	1974
"	William A. Richardson	Mass.	1873	Carter	W. Michael Blumenthal	Mich.	1977
"	Benjamin H. Bristow	Ky.	1874	"	G. William Miller	R.I.	1979
"	Lot M. Morrill	Me.	1876	Reagan	Donald T. Regan	N.Y.	1981
Hayes	John Sherman	Oh.	1877	"	James A Baker 3d	Tex.	1985
Garfield	William Windom	Minn.	1881				

Secretaries of Defense

The Department of Defense, originally designated the National Military Establishment, was created Sept. 18, 1947. It is headed by the secretary of defense, who is a member of the president's cabinet.

The departments of the army, of the navy, and of the air force function within the Department of Defense, and their respective secretaries are no longer members of the president's cabinet.

President	Secretary	Home	Apptd.	President	Secretary	Home	Apptd.
Truman	James V. Forrestal	N.Y.	1947	"	Clark M. Clifford	Md.	1968
"	Louis A. Johnson	W.Va.	1949	Nixon	Melvin R. Laird	Wis.	1969
"	George C. Marshall	Pa.	1950	"	Elliot L. Richardson	Mass.	1973
"	Robert A. Lovett	N.Y.	1951	"	James R. Schlesinger	Va.	1973
Eisenhower	Charles E. Wilson	Mich.	1953	Ford	"	"	1974
"	Neil H. McElroy	Oh.	1957	"	Donald H. Rumsfeld	Ill.	1975
"	Thomas S. Gates Jr.	Pa.	1959	Carter	Harold Brown	Cal.	1977
Kennedy	Robert S. McNamara	Mich.	1961	Reagan	Caspar W. Weinberger	Cal.	1981
Johnson, L.B.	Robert S. McNamara	Mich.	1963				

Secretaries of War

The War (and Navy) Department was created by act of Congress Aug. 7, 1789, and Gen. Henry Knox was commissioned secretary of war under that act Sept. 12, 1789.

President	Secretary	Home	Apptd.	President	Secretary	Home	Apptd.
Washington	Henry Knox	Mass.	1789	Tyler	John Bell	Tenn	1841
"	Timothy Pickering	Pa.	1795	Tyler	John C. Spencer	N.Y.	1841
"	James McHenry	Md.	1796	"	James M. Porter	Pa.	1843
Adams, J.	"	"	1797	"	William Wilkins	"	1844
"	Samuel Dexter	Mass.	1800	Polk	William L. Marcy	N.Y.	1845
Jefferson	Henry Dearborn	"	1801	Taylor	George W. Crawford	Ga.	1849
Madison	William Eustis	Mass.	1809	Fillmore	Charles M. Conrad	La.	1850
"	John Armstrong	N.Y.	1813	Pierce	Jefferson Davis	Miss.	1853
Madison	James Monroe	Va.	1814	Buchanan	John B. Floyd	Va.	1857
"	William H. Crawford	Ga.	1815	"	Joseph Holt	Ky.	1861
Monroe	John C. Calhoun	S.C.	1817	Lincoln	Simon Cameron	Pa.	1861
Adams, J.Q.	James Barbour	Va.	1825	"	Edwin M. Stanton	Pa.	1862
"	Peter B. Porter	N.Y.	1828	Johnson, A.	"	"	1865
Jackson	John H. Eaton	Tenn.	1829	"	John M. Schofield	Ill.	1868
"	Lewis Cass	Oh.	1831	Grant	John A. Rawlins	Ill.	1869
"	Benjamin F. Butler	N.Y.	1837	"	William T. Sherman	Oh.	1869
Van Buren	Joel R. Poinsett	S.C.	1837	"	William W. Belknap	Ia.	1869
Harrison, W.H.	John Bell	Tenn.	1841	"	Alphonso Taft	Oh.	1876

President	Secretary	Home	Apptd.	President	Secretary	Home	Apptd.
Grant	James D. Cameron	Pa.	1876	Taft	Jacob M. Dickinson	Tenn.	1909
Hayes	George W. McCrary	Ia.	1877	"	Henry L. Stimson	N.Y.	1911
"	Alexander Ramsey	Minn.	1879	Wilson	Lindley M. Garrison	N.J.	1913
Garfield	Robert T. Lincoln	Ill.	1881	"	Newton D. Baker	Oh.	1916
Arthur	"	"	1881	Harding	John W. Weeks	Mass.	1921
Cleveland	William C. Endicott	Mass.	1885	Coolidge	"	"	1923
Harrison, B.	Redfield Proctor	Vt.	1889	"	Dwight F. Davis	Mo.	1925
"	Stephen B. Elkins	W.Va.	1891	Hoover	James W. Good	Ill.	1929
Cleveland	Daniel S. Lamont	N.Y.	1893	Hoover	Patrick J. Hurley	Okla.	1929
McKinley	Russel A. Alger	Mich.	1897	Roosevelt, F.D.	George H. Dern	Ut.	1933
"	Elihu Root	N.Y.	1899	"	Harry H. Woodring	Kan.	1937
Roosevelt, T.	"	"	1901	Roosevelt, F.D.	Henry L. Stimson	N.Y.	1940
"	William H. Taft	Oh.	1904	Truman	Robert P. Patterson	N.Y.	1945
"	Luke E. Wright	Tenn.	1908	"	*Kenneth C. Royall	N.C.	1947

Secretaries of the Navy
The Navy Department was created by act of Congress Apr. 30, 1798.

President	Secretary	Home	Apptd.	President	Secretary	Home	Apptd.
Adams, J.	Benjamin Stoddert	Md.	1798	Lincoln	Gideon Welles	Conn.	1861
Jefferson	"	"	1801	Johnson, A.	"	"	1865
"	Robert Smith	"	1801	Grant	Adolph E. Borie	Pa.	1869
Madison	Paul Hamilton	S.C.	1809	"	George M. Robeson	N.J.	1869
"	William Jones	Pa.	1813	Hayes	Richard W. Thompson	Ind.	1877
"	Benjamin Williams Crowninshield	Mass.	1814	"	Nathan Goff Jr.	W.Va.	1881
Monroe	"	"	1817	Garfield	William H. Hunt	La.	1881
"	Smith Thompson	N.Y.	1818	Arthur	William E. Chandler	N.H.	1882
"	Samuel L. Southard	N.J.	1823	Cleveland	William C. Whitney	N.Y.	1885
Adams, J.Q.	"	"	1825	Harrison, B.	Benjamin F. Tracy	N.Y.	1889
Jackson	John Branch	N.C.	1829	Cleveland	Hilary A. Herbert	Ala.	1893
"	Levi Woodbury	N.H.	1831	McKinley	John D. Long	Mass.	1897
"	Mahlon Dickerson	N.J.	1834	Roosevelt, T.	"	"	1901
Van Buren	"	"	1837	"	William H. Moody	"	1902
"	James K. Paulding	N.Y.	1838	"	Paul Morton	Ill.	1904
Harrison, W.H.	George E. Badger	N.C.	1841	"	Charles J. Bonaparte	Md.	1905
Tyler	"	"	1841	"	Victor H. Metcalf	Cal.	1906
"	Abel P. Upshur	Va.	1841	"	Truman H. Newberry	Mich.	*1908
"	David Henshaw	Mass.	1843	Taft	George von L. Meyer	Mass.	1909
"	Thomas W. Gilmer	Va.	1844	Wilson	Josephus Daniels	N.C.	1913
"	John Y. Mason	"	1844	Harding	Edwin Denby	Mich.	1921
Polk	George Bancroft	Mass.	1845	Coolidge	"	"	1923
"	John Y. Mason	Va.	1846	"	Curtis D. Wilbur	Cal.	1924
Taylor	William B. Preston	"	1849	Hoover	Charles Francis Adams	Mass.	1929
Fillmore	William A. Graham	N.C.	1850	Roosevelt, F.D.	Claude A. Swanson	Va.	1933
"	John P. Kennedy	Md.	1852	"	Charles Edison	N.J.	1940
Pierce	James C. Dobbin	N.C.	1853	"	Frank Knox	Ill.	1940
Buchanan	Isaac Toucey	Conn.	1857	"	*James V. Forrestal	N.Y.	1944
				Truman	"	"	1945

*Last members of Cabinet. The War Department became the Department of the Army and it and the Navy Department became branches of the Department of Defense, created Sept. 18, 1947.

Attorneys General
The office of attorney general was organized by act of Congress Sept. 24, 1789. The Department of Justice was created June 22, 1870.

President	Attorney General	Home	Apptd.	President	Attorney General	Home	Apptd.
Washington	Edmund Randolph	Va.	1789	Lincoln	Edward Bates	Mo.	1861
"	William Bradford	Pa.	1794	"	James Speed	Ky.	1864
"	Charles Lee	Va.	1795	Johnson, A.	"	"	1865
Adams, J.	"	"	1797	"	Henry Stanbery	Oh.	1866
Jefferson	Levi Lincoln	Mass.	1801	"	William M. Evarts	N.Y.	1868
"	John Breckenridge	Ky.	1805	Grant	Ebenezer R. Hoar	Mass.	1869
"	Caesar A. Rodney	Del.	1807	"	Amos T. Akerman	Ga.	1870
Madison	"	"	1809	"	George H. Williams	Ore.	1871
"	William Pinkney	Md.	1811	"	Edwards Pierrepont	N.Y.	1875
"	Richard Rush	Pa.	1814	"	Alphonso Taft	Oh.	1876
Monroe	"	"	1817	Hayes	Charles Devens	Mass.	1877
"	William Wirt	Va.	1817	Garfield	Wayne MacVeagh	Pa.	1881
Adams, J.Q.	"	"	1825	Arthur	Benjamin H. Brewster	"	1881
Jackson	John M. Berrien	Ga.	1829	Cleveland	Augustus Garland	Ark.	1885
"	Roger B. Taney	Md.	1831	Harrison, B.	William H. H. Miller	Ind.	1889
"	Benjamin F. Butler	N.Y.	1833	Cleveland	Richard Olney	Mass.	1893
Van Buren	"	"	1837	"	Judson Harmon	Oh.	1895
"	Felix Grundy	Tenn.	1838	McKinley	Joseph McKenna	Cal.	1897
"	Henry D. Gilpin	Pa.	1840	"	John W. Griggs	N.J.	1898
Harrison, W.H.	John J. Crittenden	Ky.	1841	"	Philander C. Knox	Pa.	1901
Tyler	"	"	1841	Roosevelt, T.	"	"	1901
"	Hugh S. Legare	S.C.	1841	"	William H. Moody	Mass.	1904
"	John Nelson	Md.	1843	"	Charles J. Bonaparte	Md.	1906
Polk	John Y. Mason	Va.	1845	Taft	George W. Wickersham	N.Y.	1909
"	Nathan Clifford	Me.	1846	Wilson	J.C. McReynolds	Tenn.	1913
"	Isaac Toucey	Conn.	1848	"	Thomas W. Gregory	Tex.	1914
Taylor	Reverdy Johnson	Md.	1849	"	A. Mitchell Palmer	Pa.	1919
Fillmore	John J. Crittenden	Ky.	1850	Harding	Harry M. Daugherty	Oh.	1921
Pierce	Caleb Cushing	Mass.	1853	Coolidge	"	"	1923
Buchanan	Jeremiah S. Black	Pa.	1857	"	Harlan F. Stone	N.Y.	1924
"	Edwin M. Stanton	Pa.	1860	"	John G. Sargent	Vt.	1925

President	Attorney General	Home	Apptd.	President	Attorney General	Home	Apptd.
Hoover	William D. Mitchell	Minn.	1929	Johnson, L.B.	N. de B. Katzenbach	Ill.	1964
Roosevelt, F.D.	Homer S. Cummings	Conn.	1933	"	Ramsey Clark	Tex.	1967
"	Frank Murphy	Mich.	1939	Nixon	John N. Mitchell	N.Y.	1969
"	Robert H. Jackson	N.Y.	1940	"	Richard G. Kleindienst	Ariz.	1972
"	Francis Biddle	Pa.	1941	"	Elliot L. Richardson	Mass.	1973
Truman	Thomas C. Clark	Tex.	1945	"	William B. Saxbe	Oh.	1974
"	J. Howard McGrath	R.I.	1949	Ford	"	"	1974
"	J.P. McGranery	Pa.	1952	"	Edward H. Levi	Ill.	1975
Eisenhower	Herbert Brownell Jr.	N.Y.	1953	Carter	Griffin B. Bell	Ga.	1977
"	William P. Rogers	Md.	1957	"	Benjamin R. Civiletti	Md.	1979
Kennedy	Robert F. Kennedy	Mass.	1961	Reagan	William French Smith	Cal.	1981
Johnson, L.B.	"	"	1963	"	Edwin Meese 3d	Cal.	1985

Secretaries of the Interior
The Department of Interior was created by act of Congress Mar. 3, 1849

President	Secretary	Home	Apptd.	President	Secretary	Home	Apptd.
Taylor	Thomas Ewing	Oh.	1849	"	Walter L. Fisher	Ill.	1911
Fillmore	Thomas M. T. McKennan	Pa.	1850	Wilson	Franklin K. Lane	Cal.	1913
Fillmore	Alex H. H. Stuart	Va.	1850	"	John B. Payne	Ill.	1920
Pierce	Robert McClelland	Mich.	1853	Harding	Albert B. Fall	N.M.	1921
Buchanan	Jacob Thompson	Miss.	1857	"	Hubert Work	Col.	1923
Lincoln	Caleb B. Smith	Ind.	1861	Coolidge	"	"	1923
"	John P. Usher	"	1863	"	Roy O. West	Ill.	1929
Johnson, A.	"	"	1865	Hoover	Ray Lyman Wilbur	Cal.	1929
"	James Harlan	Ia.	1865	Roosevelt, F.D.	Harold L. Ickes	Ill.	1933
"	Orville H. Browning	Ill.	1866	Truman	"	"	1945
Grant	Jacob D. Cox	Oh.	1869	"	Julius A. Krug	Wis.	1946
"	Columbus Delano	"	1870	"	Oscar L. Chapman	Col.	1949
"	Zachariah Chandler	Mich.	1875	Eisenhower	Douglas McKay	Ore.	1953
Hayes	Carl Schurz	Mo.	1877	"	Fred A Seaton	Neb.	1956
Garfield	Samuel J. Kirkwood	Ia.	1881	Kennedy	Stewart L. Udall	Ariz.	1961
Arthur	Henry M. Teller	Col.	1882	Johnson, L.B.	"	"	1963
Cleveland	Lucius Q.C. Lamar	Miss.	1885	Nixon	Walter J. Hickel	Alas.	1969
"	William F. Vilas	Wis.	1888	"	Rogers C.B. Morton	Md.	1971
Harrison, B.	John W. Noble	Mo.	1889	Ford	"	"	1974
Cleveland	Hoke Smith	Ga.	1893	"	Stanley K. Hathaway	Wyo.	1975
"	David R. Francis	Mo.	1896	"	Thomas S. Kleppe	N.D.	1975
McKinley	Cornelius N. Bliss	N.Y.	1897	Carter	Cecil D. Andrus	Ida.	1977
"	Ethan A. Hitchcock	Mo.	1898	Reagan	James G. Watt	Col.	1981
Roosevelt, T.	"	"	1901	"	William P. Clarke	Cal.	1983
"	James R. Garfield	Oh.	1907	"	Donald P. Hodel	Ore.	1985
Taft	Richard A. Ballinger	Wash.	1909				

Secretaries of Agriculture
The Department of Agriculture was created by act of Congress May 15, 1862. On Feb. 8, 1889, its commissioner was renamed secretary of agriculture and became a member of the cabinet.

President	Secretary	Home	Apptd.	President	Secretary	Home	Apptd.
Cleveland	Norman J. Colman	Mo.	1889	Roosevelt, F.D.	Henry A. Wallace	Ia.	1933
Harrison, B.	Jeremiah M. Rusk	Wis.	1889	"	Claude R. Wickard	Ind.	1940
Cleveland	J. Sterling Morton	Neb.	1893	Truman	Clinton P. Anderson	N.M.	1945
McKinley	James Wilson	Ia.	1897	"	Charles F. Brannan	Col.	1948
Roosevelt, T.	"	"	1901	Eisenhower	Ezra Taft Benson	Ut.	1953
Taft	"	"	1909	Kennedy	Orville L. Freeman	Minn.	1961
Wilson	David F. Houston	Mo.	1913	Johnson, L.B.	"	"	1963
"	Edwin T. Meredith	Ia.	1920	Nixon	Clifford M. Hardin	Ind.	1969
Harding	Henry C. Wallace	Ia.	1921	"	Earl L. Butz	Ind.	1971
Coolidge	"	"	1923	Ford	"	"	1974
"	Howard M. Gore	W.Va.	1924	"	John A. Knebel	Va.	1976
"	William M. Jardine	Kan.	1925	Carter	Bob Bergland	Minn.	1977
Hoover	Arthur M. Hyde	Mo.	1929	Reagan	John R. Block	Ill.	1981

Secretaries of Commerce and Labor
The Department of Commerce and Labor, created by Congress Feb. 14, 1903, was divided by Congress Mar. 4, 1913, into separate departments of Commerce and Labor. The secretary of each was made a cabinet member.

President	Secretary	Home	Apptd.	President	Secretary	Home	Apptd.
Secretaries of Commerce and Labor				Eisenhower	Martin P. Durkin	Ill.	1953
Roosevelt, T.	George B. Cortelyou	N.Y.	1903	"	James P. Mitchell	N.J.	1953
"	Victor H. Metcalf	Cal.	1904	Kennedy	Arthur J. Goldberg	Ill.	1961
"	Oscar S. Straus	N.Y.	1906	"	W. Willard Wirtz	Ill.	1962
Taft	Charles Nagel	Mo.	1909	Johnson, L.B.	"	Ill.	1963
Secretaries of Labor				Nixon	George P. Shultz	Ill.	1969
Wilson	William B. Wilson	Pa.	1913	"	James D. Hodgson	Cal.	1970
Harding	James J. Davis	Pa.	1921	"	Peter J. Brennan	N.Y.	1973
Coolidge	"	"	1923	Ford	"	"	1974
Hoover	"	"	1929	"	John T. Dunlop	Cal.	1975
"	William N. Doak	Va.	1930	"	W.J. Usery Jr.	Ga.	1976
Roosevelt, F.D.	Frances Perkins	N.Y.	1933	Carter	F. Ray Marshall	Tex.	1977
Truman	L.B. Schwellenbach	Wash.	1945	Reagan	Raymond J. Donovan	N.J.	1981
"	Maurice J. Tobin	Mass.	1949	"	William E. Brock	Tenn.	1985

President	Secretary	Home	Apptd.
	Secretaries of Commerce		
Wilson	William C. Redfield	N.Y.	1913
"	Joshua W. Alexander	Mo.	1919
Harding	Herbert C. Hoover	Cal.	1921
Coolidge	"	"	1923
"	William F. Whiting	Mass.	1928
Hoover	Robert P. Lamont	Ill.	1929
"	Roy D. Chapin	Mich.	1932
Roosevelt, F.D.	Daniel C. Roper	S.C.	1933
"	Harry L. Hopkins	N.Y.	1939
"	Jesse Jones	Tex.	1940
"	Henry A. Wallace	Ia.	1945
Truman	"	"	1945
"	W. Averell Harriman	N.Y.	1947
"	Charles Sawyer	Oh.	1948
Eisenhower	Sinclair Weeks	Mass.	1953
Eisenhower	Lewis L. Strauss	N.Y.	1958
"	Frederick H. Mueller	Mich.	1959
Kennedy	Luther H. Hodges	N.C.	1961
Johnson, L.B.	"	"	1963
"	John T. Connor	N.J.	1965
"	Alex B. Trowbridge	N.J.	1967
"	Cyrus R. Smith	N.Y.	1968
Nixon	Maurice H. Stans	Minn.	1969
"	Peter G. Peterson	Ill.	1972
"	Frederick B. Dent	S.C.	1973
Ford	"	"	1974
"	Rogers C.B. Morton	Md.	1975
"	Elliot L. Richardson	Mass.	1975
Carter	Juanita M. Kreps	N.C.	1977
"	Philip M. Klutznick	Ill.	1979
Reagan	Malcolm Baldrige	Conn.	1981

Secretaries of Education, and Health and Human Services

The Department of Health, Education and Welfare, created by Congress Apr. 11, 1953, was divided by Congress Sept. 27, 1979, into separate departments of Education, and Health and Human Services. The secretary of each is a cabinet member.

President	Secretary	Home	Apptd.
	Secretaries of Health, Education, and Welfare		
Eisenhower	Oveta Culp Hobby	Tex.	1953
"	Marion B. Folsom	N.Y.	1955
"	Arthur S. Flemming	Oh.	1958
Kennedy	Abraham A. Ribicoff	Conn.	1961
"	Anthony J. Celebrezze	Oh.	1962
Johnson, L.B.	"	"	1963
"	John W. Gardner	N.Y.	1965
Johnson, L.B.	Wilbur J. Cohen	Mich.	1968
Nixon	Robert H. Finch	Cal.	1969
"	Elliot L. Richardson	Mass.	1970
"	Caspar W. Weinberger	Cal.	1973
Ford	"	"	1974
"	Forrest D. Mathews	Ala.	1975
Carter	Joseph A. Califano, Jr.	D.C.	1977
"	Patricia Roberts Harris	D.C.	1979
	Secretaries of Health and Human Services		
Carter	Patricia Roberts Harris	D.C.	1979
Reagan	Richard S. Schweiker	Pa.	1981
"	Margaret M. Heckler	Mass.	1983
	Secretaries of Education		
Carter	Shirley Hufstedler	Cal.	1979
Reagan	Terrel Bell	Ut.	1981
"	William J. Bennett	N.Y.	1985

Secretaries of Housing and Urban Development

The Department of Housing and Urban Development was created by act of Congress Sept. 9, 1965.

President	Secretary	Home	Apptd.
Johnson, L.B.	Robert C. Weaver	Wash.	1966
"	Robert C. Wood	Mass.	1969
Nixon	George W. Romney	Mich.	1969
"	James T. Lynn	Oh.	1973
Ford	"	"	1974
"	Carla Anderson Hills	Cal.	1975
Carter	Patricia Roberts Harris	D.C.	1977
"	Moon Landrieu	La.	1979
Reagan	Samuel R. Pierce Jr.	N.Y.	1981

Secretaries of Transportation

The Department of Transportation was created by act of Congress Oct. 15, 1966.

President	Secretary	Home	Apptd.
Johnson, L.B.	Alan S. Boyd	Fla.	1966
Nixon	John A. Volpe	Mass.	1969
"	Claude S. Brinegar	Cal.	1973
Ford	Claude S. Brinegar	Cal.	1974
"	William T. Coleman Jr.	Pa.	1975
Carter	Brock Adams	Wash.	1977
"	Neil E. Goldschmidt	Ore.	1979
Reagan	Andrew L. Lewis Jr.	Pa.	1981
"	Elizabeth Hanford Dole	Kan.	1983

Secretaries of Energy

The Department of Energy was created by federal law Aug. 4, 1977.

President	Secretary	Home	Apptd.
Carter	James R. Schlesinger	Va.	1977
"	Charles Duncan Jr.	Wyo.	1979
Reagan	James B. Edwards	S.C.	1981
"	Donald P. Hodel	Ore.	1982
"	John S. Herrington	Cal.	1985

Burial Places of the Presidents

Washington	Mt. Vernon, Va.
J. Adams	Quincy, Mass.
Jefferson	Charlottesville, Va.
Madison	Montpelier Station, Va.
Monroe	Richmond, Va.
J.Q. Adams	Quincy, Mass.
Jackson	Nashville, Tenn.
Van Buren	Kinderhook, N.Y.
W.H. Harrison	North Bend, Oh.
Tyler	Richmond, Va.
Polk	Nashville, Tenn.
Taylor	Louisville, Ky.
Fillmore	Buffalo, N.Y.
Pierce	Concord, N.H.
Buchanan	Lancaster, Pa.
Lincoln	Springfield, Ill.
A. Johnson	Greeneville, Tenn.
Grant	New York City
Hayes	Fremont, Oh.
Garfield	Cleveland, Oh.
Arthur	Albany, N.Y.
Cleveland	Princeton, N.J.
B. Harrison	Indianapolis, Ind.
McKinley	Canton, Oh.
T. Roosevelt	Oyster Bay, N.Y.
Taft	Arlington Nat'l. Cem'y.
Wilson	Washington Cathedral
Harding	Marion, Oh.
Coolidge	Plymouth, Vt.
Hoover	West Branch, Ia.
F.D. Roosevelt	Hyde Park, N.Y.
Truman	Independence, Mo.
Eisenhower	Abilene, Kan.
Kennedy	Arlington Nat'l. Cem'y.
L.B. Johnson	Stonewall, Tex.

Presidents Pro Tempore of the Senate

Until 1890, presidents "pro tem" were named "for the occasion only." Beginning with that year, they have served "until the Senate otherwise ordered." Sen. John J. Ingalls, chosen under the old rule in 1887, was again elected, under the new rule, in 1890. Party designations are D, Democrat; R, Republican.

Name	Party	State	Elected	Name	Party	State	Elected
John J. Ingalls	R	Kan.	Apr. 3, 1890	Key Pittman	D	Nev.	Mar. 9, 1933
Charles F. Manderson	R	Neb.	Mar. 2, 1891	William H. King	D	Ut.	Nov. 19, 1940
Isham G. Harris	D	Tenn.	Mar. 22, 1893	Pat Harrison	D	Miss.	Jan. 6, 1941
Matt W. Ransom	D	N.C.	Jan. 7, 1895	Carter Glass	D	Va.	July 10, 1941
Isham G. Harris	D	Tenn.	Jan. 10, 1895	Kenneth McKellar	D	Tenn.	Jan. 6, 1945
William P. Frye	R	Me.	Feb. 7, 1896	Arthur H. Vandenberg	R	Mich.	Jan. 4, 1947
Charles Curtis	R	Kan.	Dec. 4, 1911	Kenneth McKellar	D	Tenn.	Jan. 3, 1949
Augustus O. Bacon	D	Ga.	Jan. 15, 1912	Styles Bridges	R	N.H.	Jan. 3, 1953
Jacob H. Gallinger	R	N.H.	Feb. 12, 1912	Walter F. George	D	Ga.	Jan. 5, 1955
Henry Cabot Lodge	R	Mass.	Mar. 25, 1912	Carl Hayden	D	Ariz.	Jan. 3, 1957
Frank R. Brandegee	R	Conn.	May 25, 1912	Richard B. Russell	D	Ga.	Jan. 3, 1969
James P. Clarke	D	Ark.	Mar. 23, 1915	Allen J. Ellender	D	La.	Jan. 22, 1971
Willard Saulsbury	D	Del.	Dec. 14, 1916	James O. Eastland	D	Miss.	July 28, 1972
Albert B. Cummins	R	Ia.	May 19, 1919	Warren G. Magnuson	D	Wash.	Jan. 23, 1979
George H. Moses	R	N.H.	Mar. 6, 1925	Strom Thurmond	R	S.C.	Jan. 5, 1981

Speakers of the House of Representatives

Party designations: A, American; D, Democratic; DR, Democratic Republican; F, Federalist; R, Republican; W, Whig. *Served only one day.

Name	Party	State	Tenure	Name	Party	State	Tenure
Frederick Muhlenberg	F	Pa.	1789-1791	Schuyler Colfax	R	Ind.	1863-1869
Jonathan Trumbull	F	Conn.	1791-1793	*Theodore M. Pomeroy	R	N.Y.	1869-1869
Frederick Muhlenberg	F	Pa.	1793-1795	James G. Blaine	R	Me.	1869-1875
Jonathan Dayton	F	N.J.	1795-1799	Michael C. Kerr	D	Ind.	1875-1876
Theodore Sedgwick	F	Mass.	1799-1801	Samuel J. Randall	D	Pa.	1876-1881
Nathaniel Macon	DR	N.C.	1801-1807	Joseph W. Keifer	R	Oh.	1881-1883
Joseph B. Varnum	DR	Mass.	1807-1811	John G. Carlisle	D	Ky.	1883-1889
Henry Clay	DR	Ky.	1811-1814	Thomas B. Reed	R	Me.	1889-1891
Langdon Cheves	DR	S.C.	1814-1815	Charles F. Crisp	D	Ga.	1891-1895
Henry Clay	DR	Ky.	1815-1820	Thomas B. Reed	R	Me.	1895-1899
John W. Taylor	DR	N.Y.	1820-1821	David B. Henderson	R	Ia.	1899-1903
Philip P. Barbour	DR	Va.	1821-1823	Joseph G. Cannon	R	Ill.	1903-1911
Henry Clay	DR	Ky.	1823-1825	Champ Clark	D	Mo.	1911-1919
John W. Taylor	D	N.Y.	1825-1827	Frederick H. Gillett	R	Mass.	1919-1925
Andrew Stevenson	D	Va.	1827-1834	Nicholas Longworth	R	Oh.	1925-1931
John Bell	D	Tenn.	1834-1835	John N. Garner	D	Tex.	1931-1933
James K. Polk	D	Tenn.	1835-1839	Henry T. Rainey	D	Ill.	1933-1935
Robert M. T. Hunter	D	Va.	1839-1841	Joseph W. Byrns	D	Tenn.	1935-1936
John White	W	Ky.	1841-1843	William B. Bankhead	D	Ala.	1936-1940
John W. Jones	D	Va.	1843-1845	Sam Rayburn	D	Tex.	1940-1947
John W. Davis	D	Ind.	1845-1847	Joseph W. Martin Jr.	R	Mass.	1947-1949
Robert C. Winthrop	W	Mass.	1847-1849	Sam Rayburn	D	Tex.	1949-1953
Howell Cobb	D	Ga.	1849-1851	Joseph W. Martin Jr.	R	Mass.	1953-1955
Linn Boyd	D	Ky.	1851-1855	Sam Rayburn	D	Tex.	1955-1961
Nathaniel P. Banks	A	Mass.	1856-1857	John W. McCormack	D	Mass.	1962-1971
James L. Orr	D	S.C.	1857-1859	Carl Albert	D	Okla.	1971-1977
William Pennington	R	N.J.	1860-1861	Thomas P. O'Neill Jr.	D	Mass.	1977-
Galusha A. Grow	R	Pa.	1861-1863				

National Political Parties

As of mid-1985

Republican Party

National Headquarters—310 First St., SE, Washington, DC 20003.
Chairman—Frank J. Fahrenkopf Jr.
Co-Chairman—Betty Heitman.
Vice Chairmen—Bernard M. Shanley, Shelia Roberge, Jack Londen, Martha Moore, Peter Secchia, Nelda Barton, Ernest Angelo Jr., Jennifer Dunn.
Secretary—Kit Mehrtens.
Treasurer—William J. McManus.

General Counsel—Roger Allan Moore.

Democratic Party

National Headquarters—430 South Capitol St., SE, Washington, DC 20003.
Chairman—Paul G. Kirk Jr.
Vice Chairpersons—Roland Burris, Polly Baca, Lynn Cutler.
Secretary—Dorothy V. Bush.
Treasurer—Sharon Pratt Dixon.
Finance Chairman—vacant.

Other Major Political Organizations

American Independent Party
(P.O. Box 427, Lemon Grove, CA 92045)
National Chairman—Eileen M. Shearer.
Treasurer—Lon L. Laymon.

American Party of the United States
(P.O. Box 120, Pigeon Forge, TN 37863)
National Chairman—Delmar Dennis.
Secretary—Doris Feimer.
Treasurer—Lynn McKnight.

Americans For Democratic Action
(1411 K St. NW, Washington, DC 20005)
President—Barney Frank.
National Director—Ann F. Lewis.
Chairperson Exec. Comm.—Marvin Rich.

Comm. on Political Education, AFL-CIO
(AFL-CIO Building, 815 16th St., Wash., DC 20006)
Chairman—Lane Kirkland.
Secretary-Treasurer—Thomas R. Donahue.

Communist Party U.S.A.
(235 W. 23d St., New York, NY 10011)
National Chairman—Henry Winston.
General Secretary—Gus Hall.

Conservative Party of the State of N.Y.
(45 E. 29th St., New York, NY 10016)
Chairman—J. Daniel Mahoney.
Executive Director—Serphin R. Maltese.
Secretary—John J. Flynn.
Treasurer—James E. O'Doherty.

Liberal Party of New York State
(1560 Broadway, New York, NY 10036)
Chairman—Donald S. Harrington.
Treasurer—Alan A. Bailey.
Secretary—James F. Notaro.

Libertarian National Committee
(7887 Katy Freeway #385, Houston, TX 77024.)
Chair—Paul Grant.
Vice-Chair—Mary Gingell.
Secretary—Heide Hartmann-Davis.
National Director—Honey Lanham.

National Unity Party
(2433 18th St. NW, Washington, DC 20009)
Chair—John B. Anderson.
Vice-Chair—Grace Pierce.
Secretary—Anne Lee.

Prohibition National Committee
(P.O. Box 2635, Denver, CO 80201)
National Chairman—Earl F. Dodge.
National Secretary—Rayford G. Feather.

Socialist Party USA
(7109 N. Glenwood Ave. #704, Chicago, IL 60626)
Co-Chairs—Margaret Feigin, William Shakalis.
Secretary—Rick Kissell.

Socialist Labor Party
In Minnesota: Industrial Gov't. Party
(914 Industrial Ave., Palo Alto, CA 94303)
National Secretary—Robert Bills.
Financial Secretary—Genevieve Gunderson.

Socialist Workers Party
(14 Charles Lane, New York, NY 10014)
National Secretary—Jack Barnes.

America's Third Parties

Since 1860, there have been only 4 presidential elections in which all third parties together polled more than 10% of the vote: the Populists (James Baird Weaver) in 1892, the National Progressives (Theodore Roosevelt) in 1912, the La Follette Progressives in 1924, and George Wallace's American Party in 1968. In 1948, the combined third parties (Henry Wallace's Progressives, Strom Thurmond's States'

Rights party or Dixiecrats, Prohibition, Socialists, and others) received only 5.75% of the vote. In most elections since 1860, fewer than one vote in 20 has been cast for a third party. The only successful third party in American history was the Republican Party in the election of Abraham Lincoln in 1860.

Notable Third Parties

Party	Presidential nominee	Election	Issues	Strength in
Anti-Masonic	William Wirt	1832	Against secret societies and oaths	Pa., Vt.
Liberty	James G. Birney	1844	Anti-slavery	North
Free Soil	Martin Van Buren	1848	Anti-slavery	New York, Ohio
American (Know Nothing)	Millard Fillmore	1856	Anti-immigrant	Northeast, South
Greenback	Peter Cooper	1876	For "cheap money,"	
Greenback	James B. Weaver	1880	labor rights	National
Prohibition	John P. St. John	1884	Anti-liquor	National
Populist	James B. Weaver	1892	For "cheap money," end of national banks	South, West
Socialist	Eugene V. Debs	1900-20	For public ownership	National
Progressive (Bull Moose)	Theodore Roosevelt	1912	Against high tariffs	Midwest, West
Progressive	Robert M. LaFollette	1924	Farmer & labor rights	Midwest, West
Socialist	Norman Thomas	1928-48	Liberal reforms	National
Union	William Lemke	1936	Anti "New Deal"	National
States' Rights	Strom Thurmond	1948	For segregation	South
Progressive	Henry Wallace	1948	Anti-cold war	New York, California
American Independent	George Wallace	1968	For states' rights	South
American	John G. Schmitz	1972	For "law and order"	Far West, Oh., La.
None (Independent)	John B. Anderson	1980	A 3d choice	National

The Electoral College

The president and the vice president of the United States are the only elective federal officials not elected by direct vote of the people. They are elected by the members of the Electoral College, an institution that has survived since the founding of the nation despite repeated attempts in Congress to alter or abolish it. In the elections of 1824, 1876 and 1888 the presidential candidate receiving the largest popular vote failed to win a majority of the electoral votes.

On presidential election day, the first Tuesday after the first Monday in November of every 4th year, each state chooses as many electors as it has senators and representatives in Congress. In 1964, for the first time, as provided by the 23d Amendment to the Constitution, the District of Columbia voted for 3 electors. Thus, with 100 senators and 435 representatives, there are 538 members of the Electoral College, with a majority of 270 electoral votes needed to elect the president and vice president.

Political parties customarily nominate their lists of electors at their respective state conventions. An elector cannot be a member of Congress or any person holding federal office.

Some states print the names of the candidates for president and vice president at the top of the November ballot

while others list only the names of the electors. In either case, the electors of the party receiving the highest vote are elected. The electors meet on the first Monday after the 2d Wednesday in December in their respective state capitals or in some other place prescribed by state legislatures. By longestablished custom they vote for their party nominees, although the Constitution does not require them to do so. All of the state's electoral votes are then awarded to the winners. The only Constitutional requirement is that at least one of the persons each elector votes for shall not be an inhabitant of that elector's home state.

Certified and sealed lists of the votes of the electors in each state are mailed to the president of the U.S. Senate. He opens them in the presence of the members of the Senate and House of Representatives in a joint session held on Jan. 6 (the next day if that falls on a Sunday), and the electoral votes of all the states are then counted. If no candidate for president has a majority, the House of Representatives chooses a president from among the 3 highest candidates, with all representatives from each state combining to cast one vote for that state. If no candidate for vice president has a majority, the Senate chooses from the top 2, with the senators voting as individuals.

CONGRESS

The Ninety-Ninth Congress
With 1984 Election Results

The Senate

Terms are for 6 years and end Jan. 3 of the year preceding name. Annual salary $75,100. To be eligible for the U.S. Senate a person must be at least 30 years of age, a citizen of the United States for at least 9 years, and a resident of the state from which he is chosen. The Congress must meet annually on Jan. 3, unless it has, by law, appointed a different day.

Senate officials (99th Congress): President Pro Tempore Strom Thurmond; Majority Leader Robert J. Dole; Majority Whip Alan Simpson; Minority Leader Robert C. Byrd; Minority Whip Alan Cranston.

Rep., 55; Dem., 45; Total, 100. *Incumbent. Bold face denotes winner.

Official Returns (Source: News Election Service)

Term ends	Senator (Party, home)	1984 Election
	Alabama	
1987	Jeremiah Denton* (R, Mobile)	
1991	**Howell Heflin*** (D, Tuscumbia)	860,535
	Albert Lee Smith (R, Birmingham) . .	498,508
	Alaska	
1987	Frank Murkowski* (R, Anchorage)	
1991	**Ted Stevens*** (R, Anchorage)	146,919
	John E. Havelock (D, Anchorage). . .	58,804
	Arizona	
1987	Barry M. Goldwater* (R, Scottsdale)	
1989	Dennis DeConcini* (D, Tuscon)	
	Arkansas	
1987	Dale Bumpers* (D, Charleston)	
1991	**David Pryor*** (D, Little Rock)	502,341
	Ed Bethune (R, Searcy)	373,615
	California	
1987	Alan Cranston* (D, Palm Springs)	
1989	Pete Wilson (R, San Diego)	
	Colorado	
1987	Gary Hart* (D, Denver)	
1991	**William L. Armstrong*** (R, Aurora) .	833,821
	Nancy Dick (D, Aspen)	449,327
	Connecticut	
1987	Christopher J. Dodd* (D, Norwich)	
1989	Lowell P. Weicker Jr.* (R, Mystic)	
	Delaware	
1989	William V. Roth Jr.* (R, Wilmington)	
1991	**Joseph R. Biden Jr.*** (D, Wilmington)	147,831
	John M. Burris (R, Milford)	98,101
	Florida	
1987	Paula Hawkins* (R, Winter Park)	
1989	Lawton Chiles* (D, Holmes Beach)	
	Georgia	
1987	Mack Mattingly* (R, St. Simons Is.)	
1991	**Sam Nunn*** (D, Perry)	1,344,104
	Mike Hicks (R, Riverdale)	337,196
	Hawaii	
1987	Daniel K. Inouye* (D, Honolulu)	
1989	Spark M. Matsunaga* (D, Honolulu)	
	Idaho	
1987	Steven D. Symms* (R, Boise)	
1991	**James A. McClure***(R, McCall) . . .	293,193
	Peter Busch (D, Lewiston)	105,591
	Illinois	
1987	Alan J. Dixon* (D, Belleville)	
1991	**Paul Simon** (D, Makanda).	2,397,165
	Charles H. Percy* (R, Wilmette) . . .	2,308,039
	Indiana	
1987	Dan Quayle* (R, Huntington)	
1989	Richard G. Lugar* (R, Indianapolis)	
	Iowa	
1987	Charles E. Grassley* (R, New Hartford)	
1991	**Tom Harkin** (D, Cumming)	716,883
	Roger W. Jepsen* (R, Eldridge). . . .	564,381
	Kansas	
1987	Robert J. Dole* (R, Russell)	
1991	**Nancy Landon Kassebaum*** (R, Wichita)	755,681
	James Maher (D, Overland Pk.) . . .	210,816
	Kentucky	
1987	Wendell H. Ford* (D, Owensboro)	
1991	**Mitch McConnell** (R, Louisville) . . .	638,518
	Walter D. Huddleston* (D, Elizabethtown)	636,236
	Louisiana	
1987	Russell B. Long* (D, Baton Rouge)	
1991	**J. Bennett Johnston*** (D, Shreveport)	Unopposed
	Maine	
1989	George J. Mitchell* (D, Waterville)	
1991	**William S. Cohen*** (R, Bangor). . . .	404,414
	Elizabeth Mitchell (D, Vassalboro) . .	142,626
	Maryland	
1987	Charles McC. Mathias Jr.* (R, Frederick)	
1989	Paul S. Sarbanes* (D, Baltimore)	
	Massachusetts	
1989	Edward M. Kennedy* (D, Barnstable)	
1991	**John Kerry** (D, Boston)	1,392,981
	Raymond Shamie (R, Walpole)	1,136,806
	Michigan	
1989	Donald W. Riegle Jr.* (D, Flint)	
1991	**Carl Levin*** (D, Detroit)	1,915,831
	Jack Lousma (R, Ann Arbor)	1,745,302
	Minnesota	
1989	David Durenberger* (R, Minneapolis)	
1991	**Rudolph E. Boschwitz*** (R, Wayzata).	1,199,926
	Joan Growe (D, Minneapolis)	852,844
	Mississippi	
1989	John C. Stennis* (D, DeKalb)	
1991	**Thad Cochran*** (R, Jackson).	580,314
	William F. Winter (D, Jackson)	371,926
	Missouri	
1987	Thomas F. Eagleton* (D, St. Louis)	
1989	John C. Danforth* (R, Newburg)	
	Montana	
1987	John Melcher* (D, Forsyth)	
1991	**Max Baucus*** (D, Helena).	215,704
	Chuck Cozzens (R, Billings)	154,308
	Nebraska	
1989	Edward Zorinsky* (D, Omaha)	
1991	**J. James Exon*** (D, Lincoln)	332,217
	Nancy Hoch (R, Nebraska City). . . .	307,147
	Nevada	
1987	Paul Laxalt* (R, Carson City)	
1989	Chic Hecht (R, Las Vegas)	
	New Hampshire	
1987	Warren Rudman* (R, Nashua)	
1991	**Gordon J. Humphrey*** (R, Chichester).	225,828
	Norman D'Amours (D, Manchester) .	157,447

241

Term ends	Senator (Party, home)	1984 Election
	New Jersey	
1989	Frank R. Lautenburg (D, Montclair)	
1991	**Bill Bradley*** (D, Denville).	1,986,644
	Mary Mochary (R, Montclair)	1,080,096
	New Mexico	
1989	Jeff Bingaman (D, Santa Fe)	
1991	**Pete V. Domenici*** (R, Albuquerque)	361,371
	Judith A. Pratt (D, Albuquerque) . . .	141,253
	New York	
1987	Alfonse M. D'Amato* (R, C, RTL, Island Park)	
1989	Daniel Patrick Moynihan* (D, Oneonta)	
	North Carolina	
1987	John P. East* (R, Greenville)	
1991	**Jesse Helms*** (R, Raleigh)	1,156,768
	James B. Hunt (D, Lucama)	1,070,488
	North Dakota	
1987	Mark Andrews* (R, Mapleton)	
1989	Quentin N. Burdick* (D, Fargo)	
	Ohio	
1987	John Glenn* (D, Grandview Hts.)	
1989	Howard M. Metzenbaum* (D, Lyndhurst)	
	Oklahoma	
1987	Don Nickles* (R, Ponca City)	
1991	**David Boren*** (D, Seminole)	906,131
	Bill Crozier (R, Minco)	280,638
	Oregon	
1987	Bob Packwood* (R, Lake Oswego)	
1991	**Mark O. Hatfield*** (R, Portland) . . .	808,152
	Margie Hendriksen (D, Eugene). . . .	406,122
	Pennsylvania	
1987	Arlen Specter* (R, Philadelphia)	
1989	John Heinz* (R, Pittsburgh)	
	Rhode Island	
1989	John H. Chafee* (R, Warwick)	
1991	**Claiborne deB. Pell*** (D, Newport) .	286,780
	Barbara M. Leonard (R, Providence).	108,492
	South Carolina	
1987	Ernest Fritz Hollings* (D, Columbia)	
1991	**Strom Thurmond*** (R, Aiken).	644,815
	Melvin Purvis (D, Florence)	306,982

Term ends	Senator (Party, home)	1984 Election
	South Dakota	
1987	James Abdnor* (R, Mitchell)	
1991	**Larry Pressler*** (R, Humboldt)	235,176
	George V. Cunningham (D, Watertown)	80,537
	Tennessee	
1989	James R. Sasser* (D, Nashville)	
1991	**Albert Gore Jr.** (D, Carthage)	1,000,607
	Victor Ashe (R, Knoxville)	557,016
	Texas	
1989	Lloyd Bentsen* (D, Houston)	
1991	**Phil Gramm** (R, Bryan)	3,111,348
	Lloyd Doggett (D, Austin)	2,202,557
	Utah	
1987	Jake Garn* (R, Salt Lake City)	
1989	Orrin G. Hatch* (R, Salt Lake City)	
	Vermont	
1987	Patrick J. Leahy* (D, Burlington)	
1989	Robert T. Stafford* (R, Rutland)	
	Virginia	
1989	Paul S. Trible Jr. (R, Newport News)	
1991	**John William Warner*** (R, Richmond)	1,406,194
	Edythe C. Harrison (D, Norfolk)	601,142
	Washington	
1987	Slade Gorton* (R, Olympia)	
1989	Daniel J. Evans* (R, Olympia)	
	West Virginia	
1989	Robert C. Byrd* (D, Sophia)	
1991	**Jay Rockefeller** (D, Charleston) . . .	374,233
	John R. Raese (R, Morgantown) . . .	344,680
	Wisconsin	
1987	Robert W. Kasten Jr.* (R, Thiensville)	
1989	William Proxmire* (D, Madison)	
	Wyoming	
1989	Malcolm Wallop* (R, Big Horn)	
1991	**Alan Kooi Simpson*** (R, Cody) . . .	146,373
	Victor A. Ryan (D, Laramie)	40,525

The House of Representatives

Members' terms to Jan. 3, 1987. Annual salary $75,100; house speaker $97,900. To be eligible for membership, a person must be at least 25, a U.S. citizen for at least 7 years, and a resident of the state from which he or she is chosen.

House Officials (99th Congress): Speaker Thomas P. O'Neill; Majority Leader James Wright; Majority Whip Thomas S. Foley; Minority Leader Robert H. Michel; Minority Whip Trent Lott.

C-Conservative; Com-Communist; COP-Concerns of People; D-Democrat; I-Independent; L-Liberal; Libert- Libertarian; PF-Peace and Freedom; PBP-People Before Profits; R-Republican; RTL-Right to Life; SW-Socialist Workers.

Dem., 253, Rep., 182. Total 435. *Incumbent. Bold face denotes winner.

Official Returns (Source: News Election Service)

Dist.	Representative (Party, Home)	1984 Election
	Alabama	
1.	**Sonny Callahan** (R, Mobile)	102,479
	Frank McWright (D, Mobile)	98,455
2.	**William L. Dickinson*** (R, Montgomery)	118,153
	Larry Lee (D, Montgomery)	75,506
3.	**Bill Nichols*** (D, Sylacauga)	120,357
	Mark Thornton (Libert., Auburn). . . .	4,745
4.	**Tom Bevel*** (D, Jasper).	Unopposed
5.	**Ronnie G. Flippo*** (D, Florence) . . .	140,542
	D. M. Samsil (Libert., Birmingham) . .	6,033

Dist.	Representative (Party, Home)	1984 Election
6.	**Ben Erdreich** (D, Birmingham)	130,973
	J. T. Waggoner (R, Birmingham) . . .	87,550
7.	**Richard C. Shelby*** (D, Tuscaloosa)	135,834
	Charles Ewing (Libert., Birmingham) .	4,498
	Alaska At Large	
	Don Young* (R, Fort Yukon)	113,582
	Pegge Begich (D, Anchorage)	86,052
	Arizona	
1.	**John McCain** (R, Tompe)	162,418
	Harry W. Braun III (D, Tempe)	45,609

Dist.	Representative (Party, Home)	1984 Election
2.	Morris K. Udall* (D, Tucson)	106,332
	Lorenzo Torrez (PBP, Tucson)	14,869
3.	Bob Stump* (R, Tolleson)	156,686
	Bob Schuster (D, Kingman)	57,748
4.	Eldon Rudd* (R, Scottsdale)	Unopposed
5.	Jim Kolbe (R, Tucson)	116,075
	Jim McNulty (R, Tucson)	109,871

Arkansas

Dist.	Representative (Party, Home)	1984 Election
1.	Bill Alexander* (D, Osceola)	Unopposed
2.	Tommy Robinson (D, Little Rock)	103,165
	M. Petty (R, Little Rock)	90,841
3.	John Paul Hammerschmidt* (R, Harrison)	Unopposed
4.	Beryl Anthony Jr.* (D, El Dorado)	Unopposed

California

Dist.	Representative (Party, Home)	1984 Election
1.	Douglas H. Bosco (D, Santa Rosa)	153,422
	David Redick (R, Fulton)	92,676
2.	Gene Chappie* (R, Chico)	156,758
	Harry Cozad (D, Chico)	68,930
3.	Robert T. Matsui* (D, Sacramento)	Unopposed
4.	Vic Fazio* (D, Woodland)	127,133
	Roger Canfield (R, Sacramento)	75,522
5.	Sala Burton* (D, San Francisco)	137,763
	Tom Spinosa (R, San Francisco)	45,178
6.	Barbara Boxer* (D, San Rafael)	159,727
	Douglas Bindcrup (R, Mill Valley)	69,518
7.	George Miller* (D, Martinez)	154,846
	Rosemary Thakar (R, Alamo)	76,877
8.	Ronald V. Dellums* (D, Oakland)	142,349
	Charles Conner (R, Oakland)	92,913
9.	Fortney H. (Pete) Stark* (D, Hayward)	135,316
	J. T. Eager Beaver (R, San Leandro)	50,711
10.	Don Edwards* (D, San Jose)	100,368
	Robert P. Herriott (R, Milpitas)	55,238
11.	Tom Lantos* (D, Burlingame)	146,131
	John Hickey (R, Redwood City)	59,125
12.	Ed Zschau* (R, Los Altos)	150,144
	Martin Carnoy (D, Menlo Pk.)	88,368
13.	Norman Y. Mineta* (D, San Jose)	136,936
	John D. Williams (R, San Jose)	69,180
14.	Norm Shumway* (R, Stockton)	175,631
	Ruth "Paula" Carlson (D, Penryn)	57,263
15.	Tony Coelho* (D, Merced)	106,518
	Carol Harner (R, Mariposa)	53,078
16.	Leon E. Panetta* (D, Carmel Valley)	149,252
	Patricia Smith Ramsey (R, Carmel)	58,385
17.	Charles "Chip" Pashayan Jr.* (R, Fresno)	125,346
	Simon Lakritz (D, Hanford)	47,138
18.	Richard H. Lehman* (D, Sanger)	125,178
	Dale L. Ewen (R, Groveland)	60,808
19.	Robert J. Lagomarsino* (R, Ventura)	146,161
	James C. Carey Jr. (D, Santa Barbara)	67,938
20.	William M. Thomas* (R, Bakersfield)	142,186
	Mike LeSage (D, Paso Robles)	58,233
21.	Bobbi Fiedler* (R, Chatsworth)	168,765
	Charlie Davis (D, Thousand Oaks)	60,655
22.	Carlos J. Moorhead* (R, Glendale)	178,782
	Michael B. Yauch (Libert., Pasadena)	30,988
23.	Anthony C. Beilenson* (D, Los Angeles)	136,110
	Claude Parrish (R, Los Angeles)	80,523
24.	Henry A. Waxman* (D, Los Angeles)	93,811
	Jerry Zerg (R, Los Angeles)	48,751
25.	Edward R. Roybal* (D, Los Angeles)	71,756
	Roy D. Bloxom (R, Los Angeles)	23,717
26.	Howard L. Berman* (D, Panorama City)	113,722
	Miriam Ojeda (R, Mission Hills)	66,896
27.	Mel Levine* (D, Santa Monica)	101,922
	Robert B. Scribner (R, Pacific Palisades)	83,719
28.	Julian C. Dixon* (D, Inglewood)	109,753
	Beatrice M. Jett (R, Los Angeles)	32,225

Dist.	Representative (Party, Home)	1984 Election
29.	Augustus F. "Gus" Hawkins* (D, Los Angeles)	106,494
	Echo Y. Gotto (R, Los Angeles)	16,289
30.	Matthew G. "Marty" Martinez (D, Montebello)	62,837
	Richard Gomez (R, Montebello)	52,205
31.	Mervyn M. Dymally (D, Compton)	97,972
	Henry C. Minturn (R, Hawthorne)	40,440
32.	Glenn M. Anderson* (D, Hawthorne)	99,472
	Roger E. Fiola (R, Downey)	59,860
33.	David Dreier* (R, Covina)	142,951
	Claire K. McDonald (D, Claremont)	52,925
34.	Esteban E. Torres (D, Norwalk)	85,033
	Paul R. Jackson (R, Pico Rivera)	56,786
35.	Jerry Lewis* (R, Apple Valley)	176,477
	Kevin Akin (P&F, Riverside)	29,990
36.	George E. Brown Jr.* (D, Colton)	103,076
	John Paul Stark (R, San Bernardino)	78,904
37.	Al McCandless (R, Palm Desert)	146,196
	David E. "Dave" Skinner (D, Riverside)	83,932
38.	Robert K. Dornan (R, Buena Park)	84,131
	Jerry M. Patterson (D, Santa Ana)	71,288
39.	William E. Dannemeyer* (R, Fullerton)	170,250
	Robert E. Ward (D, Fullerton)	53,546
40.	Robert E. Badham* (R, Newport Beach)	158,455
	Carol Ann Bradford (D, Newport Beach)	84,622
41.	Bill Lowery* (R, San Diego)	156,554
	Robert Simmons (D, San Diego)	83,552
42.	Dan Lungren* (R, Long Beach)	171,142
	Mary Lou Brophy (D, Seal Beach)	58,161
43.	Ron Packard (R, Carlsbad)	159,315
	Lois E. Humphreys (D, Carlsbad)	49,525
44.	Jim Bates* (D, San Diego)	97,467
	Neill Campbell (R, San Diego)	38,961
45.	Duncan Hunter* (R, El Cajon)	145,014
	David W. Guthrie (D, San Diego)	44,420

Colorado

Dist.	Representative (Party, Home)	1984 Election
1.	Patricia Schroeder* (D, Denver)	126,348
	Mary Downs (R, Denver)	73,933
2.	Timothy E. Wirth* (D, Boulder)	118,580
	Michael J. Norton (R, Lakewood)	101,488
3.	Mike Strang (R, Carbondale)	122,669
	W. Mitchell (D, Crested Butte)	90,063
4.	Hank Brown* (R, Greeley)	146,469
	Mary Fagan Bates (D, Ft. Collins)	56,462
5.	Ken Kramer* (R, Colorado Springs)	163,654
	William Geffen (D, Colorado Springs)	44,588
6.	Daniel Schaefer* (R, Lakewood)	171,427
	John Heckman (COP, Lakewood)	20,333

Connecticut

Dist.	Representative (Party, Home)	1984 Election
1.	Barbara B. Kennelly* (D, Hartford)	147,748
	Herschel A. Klein (R, Windsor)	90,823
2.	Samuel Gejdenson* (D, Bozrah)	124,110
	Roberta F. Koontz (R, Coventry)	103,119
3.	Bruce A. Morrison (D, Hamden)	129,230
	Lawrence J. DeNardis* (R, Hamden)	115,939
4.	Stewart B. McKinney* (R, Westport)	165,644
	John M. Orman (D, Fairfield)	69,666
5.	John G. Rowland (R, Waterbury)	130,700
	William R. Ratchford (D, Danbury)	109,425
6.	Nancy L. Johnson* (R, New Britain)	155,422
	Arthur House (D, E. Granby)	87,489

Delaware At Large

		1984 Election
Thomas R. Carper (D, New Castle)		142,070
Elise du Pont (R, Dover)		100,650

Florida

Dist.	Representative (Party, Home)	1984 Election
1.	Earl Hutto* (D, Panama City)	Unopposed
2.	Don Fuqua* (D, Altha)	Unopposed
3.	Charles E. Bennett* (D, Jacksonville)	Unopposed

Dist.	Representative (Party, Home)	1984 Election
4.	**Bill Chappell*** (D, Daytona Beach) .	**134,651**
	Alton Starling (R, Jacksonville)	73,158
5.	**Bill McCollum*** (R, Altamonte Springs).	**Unopposed**
6.	**Kenneth H. "Buddy" MacKay*** (D, Ocala).	**Unopposed**
7.	**Sam Gibbons*** (D, Tampa)	**100,358**
	Michael Kavouklis (R, Tampa)	70,238
8.	**C. W. Bill Young*** (R, Madeira Beach)	**184,504**
	Robert Kent (D, Treasure Island) . . .	45,383
9.	**Michael Bilirakis*** (R, Palm Harbor).	**191,315**
	Jack Wilson (D, Clearwater)	52,138
10.	**Andy Ireland*** (R, Winter Haven) . .	**126,143**
	Patricia M. Glass (D, Sarasota). . . .	77,601
11.	**Bill Nelson*** (D, Melbourne)	**145,665**
	Rob Quartel (R, Orlando)	95,006
12.	**Tom Lewis*** (R, North Palm Beach) .	**Unopposed**
13.	**Connie Mack*** (R, Cape Coral) . . .	**Unopposed**
14.	**Daniel A. Mica*** (D, Boynton Beach).	**153,921**
	Don Ross (R, Boca Raton)	123,897
15.	**Clay Shaw Jr.*** (R, Fort Lauderdale)	**128,043**
	Bill Humphrey (D, Oakland Park). . . .	66,811
16.	**Larry Smith*** (D, Hollywood)	**108,388**
	Tom Bush (R, Ft. Lauderdale).	83,887
17.	**William Lehman*** (D, Biscayne Park)	**Unopposed**
18.	**Claude Pepper*** (D, Miami). ✓	**76,362**
	Ricardo Nunez (R, Coral Gables). . . .	49,784
19.	**Dante B. Fascell*** (D, Miami).	**115,577**
	Bill Flanagan (R, Coral Gables). . . .	64,253

Georgia

1.	**Lindsay Thomas*** (D, Screven) . . .	**126,082**
	Erie Lee Downing (R, Savannah) . . .	28,460
2.	**Charles Hatcher*** (D, Albany)	**Unopposed**
3.	**Richard Ray** (D, Perry)	**111,061**
	Mitchell Cantu (R, Columbus).	25,410
4.	**Patrick Swindall*** (R, Dunwoody) . .	**120,456**
	Elliott H. Levitas (D, Atlanta)	106,376
5.	**Wyche Fowler Jr.*** (D, Atlanta) . . .	**Unopposed**
6.	**Newt Gingrich*** (R, Jonesboro) . . .	**116,655**
	Gerald Johnson (D, Carrollton) . . .	52,061
7.	**George Darden*** (D, Marietta)	**106,586**
	Bill Bronson (R, Marietta)	86,431
8.	**J. Roy Rowland** (D, Dublin).	**Unopposed**
9.	**Ed Jenkins*** (D, Jasper)	**109,422**
	Frank Cofer (R, Hoschton)	52,731
10.	**Doug Barnard Jr.*** (D, Augusta). . . .	**Unopposed**

Hawaii

1.	**Cecil (Cec) Heftel*** (D, Honolulu) . .	**114,834**
	Willard Beard (R, Honolulu).	20,572
2.	**Daniel K. Akaka*** (D, Honolulu) . . .	**112,340**
	A. D. (Al) Shipley (R, Kailua)	19,981

Idaho

1.	**Larry E. Craig*** (R, Midvale)	**139,085**
	Bill Heller (D, Coeve d'Alene).	63,591
2.	**Richard Stallings** (D, Rexburg) . . .	**101,266**
	George Hansen* (R, Pocatello). . . .	101,133

Illinois

1.	**Charles Hayes*** (D, Chicago)	**177,438**
	Eddie L. Warren (SW, Chicago). . . .	8,096
2.	**Gus Savage*** (D, Chicago)	**155,349**
	Dale Harman (R, Chicago)	31,865
3.	**Marty Russo*** (D, South Holland) . .	**143,363**
	Richard D. Murphy (R, Chicago) . . .	79,218
4.	**George M. O'Brien*** (R, Joliet). . . .	**121,744**
	Dennis Marlow (D, Calumet City). . .	68,547
5.	**William O. Lipinski*** (D, Chicago) . .	**106,597**
	John Paczkowski (R, Chicago)	61,109
6.	**Henry J. Hyde*** (R, Bensenville). . .	**157,370**
	Robert Renshaw (D, Lombard)	52,189
7.	**Cardiss Collins*** (D, Chicago)	**135,493**
	James Bevel (R, Chicago).	37,411
8.	**Dan Rostenkowski*** (D, Chicago). . .	**114,385**
	Spiro F. Georgeson (R, Chicago). . . .	46,030
9.	**Sidney R. Yates*** (D, Chicago). . . .	**144,879**
	Herbert Sohn (R, Skokie)	69,613

Dist.	Representative (Party, Home)	1984 Election
10.	**John E. Porter*** (R, Winnetka)	**153,330**
	Ruth Braver (D, Highland Park). . . .	57,809
11.	**Frank Annunzio*** (D, Chicago). . . .	**138,171**
	Charles Teusch (R, Chicago)	82,518
12.	**Philip M. Crane*** (R, Mt. Prospect). .	**159,582**
	Edward LaFlamme (D, Round Lake Beach)	45,537
13.	**Harris Fawell*** (R, Naperville)	**157,603**
	Michael Donahue (R, Naperville) . . .	77,623
14.	**John Grotberg*** (R, St. Charles) . . .	**135,967**
	Dan McGrath (D, Ottawa)	82,756
15.	**Edward R. Madigan*** (R, Lincoln) . .	**149,096**
	John Hoffman (D, Bloomington). . . .	54,516
16.	**Lynn Martin*** (R, Rockford).	**127,684**
	Carl R. Schwerdtfeger (D, Elizabeth).	90,850
17.	**Lane Evans*** (D, Rock Island)	**128,273**
	Kenneth G. McMillan (R, Bushnell) . .	98,069
18.	**Robert H. Michel*** (R, Peoria)	**136,183**
	Gerald Bradley (D, Bloomington) . . .	86,884
19.	**Terry Bruce** (D, Olney)	**117,643**
	Daniel B. Crane (R, Danville)	107,463
20.	**Richard J. Durbin*** (D, Springfield) . .	**145,092**
	Dick Austin (R, Springfield)	91,728
21.	**Melvin Price*** (D, East St. Louis). . .	**127,046**
	Robert H. Gaffner (R, Greenville). . . .	84,148
22.	**Ken Gray** (D, W. Frankfort).	**116,952**
	Randy Patchett (R, Marion)	115,775

Indiana

1.	**Peter Visclosky** (D, Merrillville)	**147,035**
	Joe Grendhik (R, Whiting)	59,986
2.	**Philip R. Sharp*** (D, Muncie)	**118,965**
	Ken Mackenzie (R, Muncie)	103,061
3.	**John Hiler*** (R, LaPorte)	**115,139**
	Michael Barnes (D, South Bend) . . .	103,961
4.	**Dan R. Coats*** (R, Fort Wayne) . . .	**129,674**
	Michael Barnard (D, Fort Wayne) . . .	82,053
5.	**Elwood Hillis*** (R, Kokomo)	**143,560**
	Allen B. Maxwell (D, Kokomo)	66,631
6.	**Dan Burton*** (R, Indianapolis). . . .	**178,814**
	Howard Campbell (D, Indianapolis). . .	65,772
7.	**John T. Myers*** (R, Covington)	**147,787**
	Arthur E. Smith (D, Lafayette).	69,097
8.	**Richard McIntyre** (R, Bedford). . . .	**116,490**
	Francis X. McCloskey (D, Bloomington)	116,456
9.	**Lee H. Hamilton*** (D, Nashville)	**137,018**
	Floyd E. Coates (R, Lexington)	72,652
10.	**Andrew Jacobs Jr.*** (D, Indianapolis)	**115,274**
	Joseph P. Watkins (R, Indianapolis) .	79,342

Iowa

1.	**Jim Leach*** (R, Davenport).	**131,182**
	Kevin Ready (D, Bettendorf)	65,293
2.	**Thomas J. Tauke*** (R, Dubuque) . .	**136,893**
	Joe Welch (D, Dubuque).	77,335
3.	**Cooper Evans*** (R, Grundy Center).	**133,737**
	Joe Johnston (D, Tiffin)	86,574
4.	**Neal Smith*** (D, Altoona)	**136,922**
	Bob Lockart (R, Des Moines)	88,717
5.	**James Lightfoot** (R, Shenandoah) .	**104,632**
	Jerry Fitzgerald (D, Ft. Dodge)	101,435
6.	**Berkley Bedell*** (D, Okoboji).	**127,706**
	Darrel Rensink (R, Sioux Center). . .	78,182

Kansas

1.	**Pat Roberts*** (R, Dodge City)	**158,954**
	Darrell Ringer (D, Quinter)	48,986
2.	**Jim Slattery** (D, Topeka)	**112,448**
	James Van Slyke (R, Topeka)	72,223
3.	**Jan Meyers** (R, Overland Park) . . .	**116,060**
	Jack Reardan (D, Kansas City). . . .	84,838
4.	**Dan Glickman*** (D, Wichita)	**138,319**
	William Krause (R, Wichita).	47,355
5.	**Bob Whittaker*** (R, Augusta)	**143,957**
	John Barnes (D, Cherryvale)	49,296

Dist.	Representative (Party, Home)	1984 Election

Kentucky

Dist.	Representative (Party, Home)	1984 Election
1.	**Carroll Hubbard Jr.*** (D, Mayfield)	**Unopposed**
2.	**William H. Natcher*** (D, Bowling Green)	**93,042**
	Timothy Morrison (R, Philpot)	56,700
3.	**Romano L. Mazzoli*** (D, Louisville)	**145,680**
	Susanne Warner (R, Louisville)	68,185
4.	**Gene Snyder*** (R, Brownsboro Farm)	**108,398**
	Patrick Mulloy (D, Louisville)	93,640
5.	**Harold Rogers*** (R, Somerset)	**125,164**
	Sherman McIntosh (D, Williamsburg)	39,783
6.	**Larry J. Hopkins*** (R, Lexington)	**126,525**
	Jerry Hammond (D, Versailles)	49,657
7.	**Carl C. Perkins*** (D, Leburn)	**122,679**
	Aubrey Russel* (R, Ashland)	43,890

Louisiana

Dist.	Representative (Party, Home)
1.	**Bob Livingston*** (R, Metairie)
2.	**Lindy (Mrs. Hale) Boggs*** (D, New Orleans)
3.	**W.J. "Billy" Tauzin** (D, Thibodaux)
4.	**Buddy Roemer** (D, Bossier City)
5.	**Jerry Huckaby*** (D, Ringgold)
6.	**W. Henson Moore*** (R, Baton Rouge)
7.	**John B. Breaux*** (D, Crowley)
8.	**Cathy Long*** (D, Alexandria)

In Louisiana, all candidates of all parties run against each other in an open primary. All candidates who receive more than 50 percent of the primary vote run unopposed in the general election. If no candidate wins a majority, the top two finishers regardless of party oppose each other in a November runoff. This year, all eight incumbents won majorities in the primary and thus were elected to Congress.

Maine

Dist.	Representative (Party, Home)	1984 Election
1.	**John R. McKernan Jr.*** (R, Cumberland)	**182,785**
	Barry Hobbins (D, Saco)	104,972
2.	**Olympia J. Snowe*** (R, Auburn)	**192,166**
	Chipman Bull (D, Presque Isle)	57,347

Maryland

Dist.	Representative (Party, Home)	1984 Election
1.	**Roy Dyson*** (D, Great Mills)	**96,673**
	Harley Williams (R, Elkton)	68,865
2.	**Helen D. Bentley** (R, Lutherville)	**111,517**
	Clarence D. Long* (D, Ruxton)	105,571
3.	**Barbara A. Mikulski*** (D, Baltimore)	**133,189**
	Ross Pierpont (R, Baltimore)	59,493
4.	**Marjorie S. Holt*** (R, Severna Park)	**114,430**
	Howard Greenebaum (D, Arnold)	58,312
5.	**Steny H. Hoyer*** (D, Berkshire)	**116,310**
	John Ritchie (R, Laurel)	44,839
6.	**Beverly B. Byron*** (D, Frederick)	**123,383**
	Robin Ficker (R, Potomac)	66,056
7.	**Parren J. Mitchell*** (D, Baltimore)	**Unopposed**
8.	**Michael D. Barnes*** (D, Kensington)	**181,947**
	Albert Ceccone (R, Chevy Chase)	70,715

Massachusetts

Dist.	Representative (Party, Home)	1984 Election
1.	**Silvio O. Conte*** (R, Pittsfield)	**162,646**
	Mary Wentworth (D, Amherst)	60,372
2.	**Edward P. Boland*** (D, Springfield)	**132,693**
	Thomas P. Swank (R, West Brookfield)	60,463
3.	**Joseph D. Early*** (D, Worcester)	**148,461**
	Kenneth Redding (R, Uxbridge)	71,765
4.	**Barney Frank*** (D, Newton)	**172,903**
	Jim Forte (R, Newton)	60,121
5.	**Chester Atkins** (D, Concord)	**120,008**
	Greg Hyatt (R, Methuen)	104,912
6.	**Nicholas Mavroules*** (D, Peabody)	**168,662**
	Frederick Leber (R, Manchester)	63,363
7.	**Edward J. Markey*** (D, Malden)	**167,211**
	Lester Ralph (R, Reading)	66,930
8.	**Thomas P. O'Neill Jr.*** (D, Cambridge)	**179,617**
	Laura Ross (Com., Boston)	15,810
9.	**John Joseph Moakley*** (D, Boston)	**Unopposed**
10.	**Gerry E. Studds*** (D, Cohasset)	**143,062**
	Lew Crompton (R, Plymouth)	113,745
11.	**Brian J. Donnelly*** (D, Boston)	**Unopposed**

Michigan

Dist.	Representative (Party, Home)	1984 Election
1.	**John Conyers Jr.*** (D, Detroit)	**152,432**
	Edward Mack (R, Detroit)	17,393
2.	**Carl D. Pursell*** (R, Plymouth)	**140,688**
	Mike McCauley (D, Plymouth)	62,374
3.	**Howard Wolpe*** (D, Lansing)	**106,505**
	Jackie McGregor (R, Lansing)	94,714
4.	**Mark D. Siljander*** (R, Three Rivers)	**127,907**
	Charles Rodebaugh (D, Vicksburg)	63,159
5.	**Paul Henry** (R, Grand Rapids)	**140,131**
	Gary McInerney (D, Grand Rapids)	85,232
6.	**Bob Carr*** (D, East Lansing)	**106,705**
	Tom Ritter (R, Clarkston)	95,113
7.	**Dale E. Kildee*** (D, Flint)	**Unopposed**
8.	**Bob Traxler*** (D, Bay City)	**126,161**
	John Heussner (R, Marlette)	69,683
9.	**Guy Vander Jagt*** (R, Luther)	**150,885**
	Mike Senger (D, Traverse City)	61,233
10.	**Bill Schuette** (R, Sanford)	**104,950**
	Donald Joseph Albosta* (D, St. Charles)	103,636
11.	**Robert W. Davis*** (R, Gaylord)	**126,992**
	Tom Stewart (D, Harbor Springs)	89,640
12.	**David E. Bonior*** (D, Mt. Clemens)	**113,772**
	Eugene Tyza (R, Mt. Clemens)	79,824
13.	**George W. Crockett Jr.*** (D, Detroit)	**132,222**
	Robert Murphy (R, Detroit)	20,416
14.	**Dennis M. Hertel*** (D, Detroit)	**113,610**
	John Lauve (R, Grosse Pte. Woods)	77,427
15.	**William D. Ford*** (D, Taylor)	**98,973**
	Gerald Carlson (R, Wayne)	66,172
16.	**John D. Dingell*** (D, Trenton)	**121,463**
	Frank Grzywacki (R, Monroe)	68,116
17.	**Sander Levin*** (D, Southfield)	**Unopposed**
18.	**William S. Broomfield*** (R, Birmingham)	**186,505**
	Vivian Smargon (D, Franklin)	46,191

Minnesota

Dist.	Representative (Party, Home)	1984 Election
1.	**Timothy J. Penny*** (D, New Richland)	**140,095**
	Keith Spicer (R, Rochester)	105,723
2.	**Vin Weber*** (R, Slayton)	**153,308**
	Todd Lundquist (D, No. Mankato)	89,770
3.	**Bill Frenzel*** (R, Golden Valley)	**207,819**
	David Peterson (D, Golden Valley)	76,132
4.	**Bruce F. Vento*** (D, St. Paul)	**167,678**
	Mary Jane Rachner (R, St. Paul)	57,450
5.	**Martin Olav Sabo*** (D, Minneapolis)	**165,075**
	Richard Weiblen (R, Minneapolis)	62,642
6.	**Gerry Sikorski*** (D, Stillwater)	**154,603**
	Patrick Trueman (R, Buffalo)	101,058
7.	**Arlan Stangeland*** (R, Barnesville)	**135,087**
	Collin Peterson (D, Detroit Lakes)	101,720
8.	**James L. Oberstar*** (D, Duluth)	**165,727**
	Dave Rueof (R, Aitkin)	79,181

Mississippi

Dist.	Representative (Party, Home)	1984 Election
1.	**Jamie L. Whitten*** (D, Charleston)	**136,530**
	John Hargett (I., Tupelo)	17,991
2.	**Webb Franklin*** (R, Greenwood)	**92,392**
	Robert G. Clark (D, Greenville)	89,154
3.	**G. V. (Sonny) Montgomery*** (D, Meridian)	**Unopposed**
4.	**Wayne Dowdy*** (D, McComb)	**113,635**
	David Armstrong (R, Natchez)	91,797
5.	**Trent Lott*** (R, Pascagoula)	**142,637**
	Arlon (Blackie) Coate (D, Ocean Springs)	25,840

Missouri

Dist.	Representative (Party, Home)	1984 Election
1.	**William (Bill) Clay*** (D, St. Louis)	**147,436**
	Eric Rathbone (R, St. Louis)	68,538
2.	**Robert A. Young*** (D, Maryland Heights)	**139,123**
	Jack Buechner (R, Kirkwood)	127,710
3.	**Richard A. Gephardt*** (D, St. Louis)	**Unopposed**

Dist.	Representative (Party, Home)	1984 Election		Dist.	Representative (Party, Home)	1984 Election
4.	Ike Skelton* (D, Lexington).	150,624			**New York**	
	Carl Russell (R, Russelville). . . .	74,434		1.	William Carney* (R, C, RTL Haup-	
5.	Alan Wheat* (D, Kansas City) . . .	150,675			pauge)	107,029
	Jim Kenworthy (R, Kansas City) . .	72,477			George Hochbrueckner (D)	94,551
6.	E. Thomas Coleman* (R, Kansas			2.	Thomas J. Downey* (D, I, West Islip)	97,648
	City)	150,996			Paul Aniboli (R, I, Amityville).	80,855
	Kenneth Hensley (D, Gallatin). . . .	81,917		3.	Robert J. Mrazek* (D, Huntington) .	120,191
7.	Gene Taylor* (R, Sarcoxie)	164,586			Robert Quinn (R, C, Locust Valley).	112,909
	Ken Young (D, Point Lookout). . . .	71,867		4.	Norman F. Lent* (R, C, Baldwin) . .	154,875
8.	Bill Emerson* (R, Cape Girardeau) .	134,186			Sheldon Englehart (D, L, Oceanside)	65,678
	Bill Blue (D, Rolla)	70,922		5.	Raymond J. McGrath* (R, C, Valley	
9.	Harold L. Volkmer* (D, Hannibal) . .	123,588			Stream)	138,560
	Carrie Francke (R, Columbia).	110,100			Michael D'Innocenzo (D, Uniondale) .	78,429
	Montana			6.	Joseph P. Addabbo* (D, L, Ozone	
1.	Pat Williams* (D, Helena)	126,998			Park)	120,098
	Gary Carlson (R, Hamilton)	61,794			Philip Veltre (R, C, RTL, Queens). . .	25,040
2.	Ron Marlenee* (R, Great Falls) . . .	116,932		7.	Gary Ackerman* (D, L, Queens) . . .	97,674
	Chet Blaylock (D, Laurel)	60,445			Gustave Reifenkugel (R, C, Queens).	43,370
	Nebraska			8.	James H. Scheuer* (D, L, Queens) .	104,558
1.	Douglas K. Bereuter* (R, Utica). . .	158,836			Bob Brandofino (R, C, So. Ozone) . .	62,015
	Monica Bauer (D, Crete).	55,508		9.	Thomas Manton* (D, Queens). . . .	71,420
2.	Hal Daub* (R, Omaha).	139,384			Serphin Maltese (R, C, RTL, Queens)	63,910
	Thomas Cavanaugh (D, Omaha). . .	75,210		10.	Charles E. Schumer* (D, L, Brook-	
3.	Virginia Smith* (R, Chappell). . . .	183,901			lyn)	115,867
	Tom Vickers (D, Farnham)	36,899			John H. Fox (R, C, Brooklyn)	42,009
	Nevada			11.	Edolphus Towns* (D, L, Brooklyn) .	81,002
1.	Harry Reid* (D, Las Vegas)	73,242			Nathaniel Hendricks (R, Brooklyn) . .	12,494
	Peggy Cavnar (R, Las Vegas)	55,391		12.	Major R. Owens* (D, L, Brooklyn). .	82,047
2.	Barbara Vucanovich* (R, Reno) . . .	99,775			Joseph Caesar (R, C, RTL, Brooklyn)	8,609
	Andy Barbano (D, Reno).	36,130		13.	Stephen J. Solarz* (D, L, Brooklyn).	82,610
	New Hampshire				Yehuda Levin (R, C, RTL, Brooklyn) .	42,737
1.	Robert C. Smith (R, Tuftonboro). . .	111,627		14.	Guy V. Molinari* (R, C, RTL, Staten	
	Dudley Dudley (D, Durham)	76,854			Island).	117,041
2.	Judd Gregg* (R, Greenfield)	138,975			Kevin Sheehy (D, Staten Island) . . .	49,776
	Larry Converse (D, Claremont). . . .	42,257		15.	Bill Green* (R, Manhattan)	107,644
	New Jersey				Andrew Stein (D, Mahattan).	84,404
1.	James J. Florio* (D, Pine Hill)	152,125		16.	Charles B. Rangel (D, R, Manhattan)	117,759
	Fred Busch (R, Clementon)	58,800			Michael T. Berns (C, Manhattan) . . .	2,541
2.	William J. Hughes* (D, Ocean City).	133,120		17.	Ted Weiss* (D, L, Manhattan)	162,489
	Ray Massie (R, Brigantine)	77,231			Kenneth Katzman (R, Bronx)	33,316
3.	James J. Howard* (D, Spring Lake			18.	Robert Garcia* (D, L, Bronx).	85,960
	Heights)	122,291			Curtis Johnson (R, Bronx)	8,970
	Brian Kennedy (R, Bradley Beach) . .	105,028		19.	Mario Biaggi* (D, R, L, Bronx)	155,067
4.	Christopher H. Smith* (R, Hamilton				Alice Farrell (C, Bronx).	8,472
	Square)	139,295		20.	Joe Dioguardi (R, C, Scarsdale). . . .	106,958
	James Hedden (D, Trenton).	87,908			Orel Teicher (D, White Plains)	102,842
5.	Marge Roukema* (R, Ridgewood) . .	171,979		21.	Hamilton Fish Jr.* (R, C, Millbrook) .	160,053
	Rose Brunetto (D, Ridgewood)	69,666			Lawrence Grunberger (D, Peekskill) .	44,274
6.	Bernard J. Dwyer* (D, Edison) . . .	118,532		22.	Benjamin A. Gilman* (R, Middlet-	
	Dennis Adams (R, Edison).	90,862			own)	144,278
7.	Matthew J. Rinaldo* (R, Union) . . .	165,685			Bruce Levine (D, L, Spring Valley) . .	57,934
	John Feely (D, Roselle Park)	56,798		23.	Samuel S. Stratton* (D, Schenec-	
8.	Robert A. Roe* (D, Pompton Lakes)	118,793			tady).	188,144
	Marguerite Page (R, Passaic).	69,973			Frank Wicks (R, Nuclear Freeze,	
9.	Robert G. Torricelli* (D, Hacken-				Schenectady)	53,060
	sack)	149,493		24.	Gerald B. H. Solomon* (R, C, RTL,	
	Neil Romano (R, Englewood Cliffs). .	89,166			Glen Falls)	164,019
10.	Peter W. Rodino Jr.* (D, Newark). .	111,244			Edward Bloch (D, Latham)	60,188
	Howard Berkeley (R, Irvington)	21,712		25.	Sherwood L. Boehlert* (R, Utica). .	140,256
11.	Dean Gallo (R, Morris Plains).	133,662			James Ball (D, Meridale).	52,434
	Joseph G. Minish* (D, West Orange).	106,038		26.	David O'B. Martin* (R, C, Canton) .	131,257
12.	Jim Courter* (R, Hackettstown) . . .	148,042			Bernard Lammers (D, Canton)	54,663
	Peter Bearse (D, Princeton)	78,167		27.	George C. Wortley* (R, C, Fayette-	
13.	Jim Saxton (R, Bordentown)	141,136			ville)	122,215
	Jim Smith (D, Mt. Holly)	89,307			Tom Buckel (D, L, Syracuse)	93,601
14.	Frank J. Guarini* (D, Jersey City) . .	115,117		28.	Matthew F. McHugh* (D, Ithaca). . .	123,334
	Edward Magee (R, Jersey City) . . .	58,265			Connie Cook (R, Ithaca)	90,324
	New Mexico			29.	Frank Horton* (R, Rochester)	138,362
1.	Manuel Lujan Jr.* (R, Albuquerque).	115,808			James R. Toole (D, Rochester)	48,301
	Ted Asbury (D, Albuquerque)	60,598		30.	Fred Eckert (R, C, Stafford)	119,844
2.	Joe Skeen* (R, Picacho)	116,006			Doug Call (D, Stafford)	100,066
	Peter York (D, Roswell)	40,063		31.	Jack F. Kemp* (R, C, Hamburg). . .	168,332
3.	Bill Richardson* (D, Santa Fe) . . .	100,470			Peter Martinelli (D, L, Amherst) . . .	56,156
	Lour Gallegos (R, Sena).	62,351		32.	John J. LaFalce* (D, L, Kenmore). .	140,179
					Anthony Murty (R, C, RTL, Niagara	
					Falls)	61,797

Dist.	Representative (Party, Home)	1984 Election
33.	**Henry J. Nowak*** (D, L, Buffalo) . . .	**155,198**
	David Lewandowski (R, C, RTL, Depew)	44,880
34.	**Stanley N. Lundine*** (D, Jamestown)	**110,902**
	Jill Emery (R, C, Geneseo)	91,016

North Carolina

Dist.	Representative (Party, Home)	1984 Election
1.	**Walter B. Jones*** (D, Farmville) . . .	**122,815**
	Herbert Lee (R, Greenville)	60,153
2.	**I.T. "Tim" Valentine Jr.*** (D, Nashville)	**122,292**
	Frank Hill, Jr. (D, Durham).	58,312
3.	**Charles O. Whitley*** (D, Mt. Olive)	**100,185**
	Danny Moody (R, Fuquay-Varina) . .	56,096
4.	**William Cobey Jr.** (R, Chapel Hill). .	**117,436**
	Ike Andrews* (D, Cary)	114,462
5.	**Stephen L. Neal*** (D, Winston-Salem)	**109,831**
	Stuart Epperson (R, Winston-Salem).	106,599
6.	**J. Howard Coble** (R, Greensboro). .	**102,925**
	Charles Robin Britt* (D, Greensboro)	100,263
7.	**Charles Rose*** (D, Fayetteville). . . .	**92,157**
	Tommy Rhodes (R, Wilmington) . . .	63,625
8.	**W. G. (Bill) Hefner*** (D, Concord). .	**99,731**
	Harris D. Blake (R, Pinehurst). . . .	96,354
9.	**Alex McMillan** (R, Charlotte)	**109,420**
	David Martin (D, Charlotte)	109,099
10.	**James T. Broyhill*** (R, Lenoir)	**142,873**
	Ted Poovey (D, Granite Falls).	51,860
11.	**William M. (Bill) Hendon** (R, Asheville)	**112,598**
	James McClure Clarke* (D, Fairview)	108,284

North Dakota At Large

Dist.	Representative (Party, Home)	1984 Election
	Byron L. Dorgan* (D, Bismarck). . .	**242,968**
	Lois Altenburg (R, Fargo)	65,761

Ohio

Dist.	Representative (Party, Home)	1984 Election
1.	**Thomas A. Luken*** (D, Cincinnati) . .	**121,577**
	Norm Murdock (R, Cincinnati).	88,859
2.	**Bill Gradison*** (R, Cincinnati).	**149,856**
	Thomas Porter (D, Cincinnati).	68,597
3.	**Tony P. Hall*** (D, Dayton).	**Unopposed**
4.	**Michael Oxley*** (R, Findlay)	**162,199**
	William Sutton (D, St. Marys)	47,018
5.	**Delbert L. Latta*** (R, Bowling Green)	**132,582**
	James R. Sherck (D, Fremont City) .	78,809
6.	**Bob McEwen*** (R, Hillsboro)	**150,101**
	Bob Smith (D, Portsmouth)	52,727
7.	**Michael Dewine*** (R, Cedarville) . . .	**147,885**
	Donald E. Scott (D, St. Paris)	40,621
8.	**Thomas N. Kindness*** (R, Hamilton)	**155,200**
	John Francis (D, Greenville).	46,673
9.	**Marcy Kaptur*** (D, Toledo)	**117,985**
	Frank Venner (R, Toledo)	93,210
10.	**Clarence E. Miller*** (R, Lancaster). .	**149,337**
	John M. Buchanan (D, Newark). . . .	55,172
11.	**Dennis E. Eckart*** (D, Mentor)	**133,096**
	Dean Beagle (R, Farmdale)	66,278
12.	**John R. Kasich*** (R, Columbus)	**148,899**
	Richard Sloan (D, Columbus)	65,215
13.	**Donald J. Pease*** (D, Oberlin)	**131,923**
	William Schaffner (R, Brunswick) . . .	59,610
14.	**John F. Seiberling*** (D, Akron)	**155,729**
	Jean Bender (R, Akron)	62,366
15.	**Chalmers P. Wylie*** (R, Columbus) .	**148,311**
	Duane Jager (D, Columbus).	58,870
16.	**Ralph Regula*** (R, Navarre)	**152,399**
	James Gwin (D, Canton).	58,048
17.	**James Traficant*** (D, Poland)	**123,014**
	Lyle Williams* (R, Warren)	105,449
18.	**Douglas Applegate*** (D, Steubenville)	**155,759**
	Kenneth Burt Jr. (R, E. Liverpool). . .	49,356
19.	**Edward F. Feighan** (D, Lakewood) . .	**139,605**
	Matt Hatchadorian (R, Highland Heights).	107,957
20.	**Mary Rose Oakar*** (D, Cleveland). .	**Unopposed**

Dist.	Representative (Party, Home)	1984 Election
21.	**Louis Stokes*** (D, Warrensville Hts.)	**165,247**
	Robert Woodall (R, Cleveland)	29,500

Oklahoma

Dist.	Representative (Party, Home)	1984 Election
1.	**James R. Jones*** (D, Tulsa)	**113,919**
	Frank Keating (R, Tulsa).	103,098
2.	**Mike Synar*** (D, Muskogee).	**148,124**
	Gary Rice (R, Broken Arrow)	51,889
3.	**Wes Watkins*** (D, Ada).	**137,964**
	Patrick M. Miller (R, Snow).	39,454
4.	**Dave McCurdy*** (D, Norman)	**109,447**
	Jerry Smith (R, Lindsay).	60,844
5.	**Mickey Edwards*** (R, Oklahoma City).	**135,167**
	Alan Greeson (D, Guthrie).	39,089
6.	**Glenn English*** (D, Cordell)	**96,994**
	Craig Dodd (R, Enid).	67,601

Oregon

Dist.	Representative (Party, Home)	1984 Election
1.	**Les AuCoin*** (D, Portland)	**138,393**
	Bill Moshofsky (R, Portland).	122,247
2.	**Bob Smith*** (R, Burns).	**132,649**
	Larryann Willis (D, Vale).	100,152
3.	**Ron Wyden*** (D, Portland)	**173,438**
	Drew Davis (R, Lake Oswego)	66,394
4.	**James Weaver*** (D, Eugene).	**134,190**
	Bruce Long (R, Roseburg).	96,487
5.	**Denny Smith*** (R, Salem)	**130,424**
	J. Ruth McFarland (D, Boring).	108,919

Pennsylvania

Dist.	Representative (Party, Home)	1984 Election
1.	**Thomas M. Foglietta*** (D, Philadelphia).	**148,123**
	Carmine DiBiase (R, Philadelphia) . .	49,559
2.	**William H. Gray III*** (D, Philadelphia)	**200,484**
	Ronald Sharper (R, Philadelphia). . .	18,224
3.	**Robert A. Borski*** (D, Philadelphia)	**152,598**
	Flora Becker (R, Philadelphia).	85,358
4.	**Joseph P. Kolter*** (D, New Brighton)	**114,040**
	Jim Kunder (R, Beaver Falls)	86,769
5.	**Richard T. Schulze*** (R, Paoli). . . .	**141,965**
	Louis Fanti (D, Coatesville).	53,586
6.	**Gus Yatron*** (D, Reading)	**Unopposed**
7.	**Robert W. Edgar*** (D, Springfield) . .	**124,458**
	Curt Weldon (R, Aston)	124,046
8.	**Peter H. Kostmayer*** (D, New Hope)	**112,648**
	Dave Christian (R, Washington Crossing).	108,696
9.	**Bud Shuster*** (R, Everett).	**118,437**
	Nancy Kulp (D, Port Royal)	59,549
10.	**Joseph M. McDade*** (R, Clarks Summit).	**150,166**
	Gene Basalyga (D, Olyphant).	44,572
11.	**Paul Kanjorski** (D, Nanticoke)	**108,430**
	Bob Hudock (R, Hazleton).	76,692
12.	**John P. Murtha*** (D, Johnstown). . . .	**134,384**
	Thomas Fullard (R, Acme)	57,446
13.	**Lawrence Coughlin*** (R, Villanova) .	**133,948**
	Joseph Hoeffel (D, Abington)	104,756
14.	**William J. Coyne*** (D, Pittsburgh) . .	**163,818**
	John R. Clark (Pittsburgh)	42,616
15.	**Don Ritter*** (R, Allentown)	**110,338**
	Jane Wells-Schooley (D, Allentown) .	79,490
16.	**Robert S. Walker*** (R, E. Petersburg)	**138,477**
	Martin Bard (D, Manheim)	39,515
17.	**George W. Gekas*** (R, Harrisburg) . .	**129,716**
	Steven Anderson (D, Williamsport) . .	48,935
18.	**Doug Walgren*** (D, Pittsburgh)	**149,628**
	John Maxwell (R, Mt. Lebanon)	87,521
19.	**William F. Goodling*** (R, York)	**141,196**
	John Rahrig (D, Orrtanna).	44,117
20.	**Joseph M. Gaydos*** (D, McKeesport)	**158,751**
	Daniel Lloyd (R, Homestead)	50,247
21.	**Thomas J. Ridge*** (R, Erie)	**125,730**
	Jim Young (D, Edinboro).	65,594
22.	**Austin J. Murphy*** (D, Charleroi). . .	**153,514**
	Nancy Pryor (R, Washington).	39,752
23.	**William F. Clinger Jr.*** (R, Warren) . .	**94,952**
	William Wachob (D, State College). .	88,957

Dist.	Representative (Party, Home)	1984 Election
	Rhode Island	
1.	**Fernand J. St Germain*** (D, Woonsocket)	**130,585**
	Alfred Rego (R, Bristol)	59,926
2.	**Claudine Schneider*** (R, Narragansett)	**135,151**
	Richard Sinapi (D, Warwick)	64,357
	South Carolina	
1.	**Thomas F. Hartnett*** (R, Charleston)	**103,288**
	Ed Pendarvis (D, Charleston)	64,022
2.	**Floyd Spence*** (R, Lexington)	**108,085**
	Ken Mosely (D, Orangeburg)	63,932
3.	**Butler Derrick*** (D, Edgefield)	**88,917**
	Clarence Taylor (R, Seneca)	61,739
4.	**Carroll A. Campbell Jr.*** (R, Fountain Inn)	**105,139**
	Jeff Smith (D, Greer)	57,854
5.	**John Spratt** (D, York)	**98,513**
	Linda Blevins (Libert., Kings Creek)	4,185
6.	**Robert M. Tallon Jr.** (D, Florence)	**97,329**
	Lois Eargle (R, Florence)	63,005
	South Dakota At Large	
1.	**Thomas A. Daschle*** (D, Aberdeen)	**181,401**
	Dale Bell (R, Spearfish)	134,821
	Tennessee	
1.	**James H. Quillen*** (R, Kingsport)	**Unopposed**
2.	**John J. Duncan*** (R, Knoxville)	**132,604**
	John Bowen (D, Knoxville)	38,846
3.	**Marilyn Lloyd*** (D, Chattanooga)	**99,465**
	John Davis (R, Harriman)	90,216
4.	**Jim Cooper*** (D, Shelbyville)	**93,848**
	James Seigneur (R, Shelbyville)	31,011
5.	**Bill Boner*** (D, Nashville)	**Unopposed**
6.	**Bart Gordon** (D, Murfreesboro)	**103,989**
	Joe Simpkins (R, Franklin)	61,559
7.	**Don Sundquist*** (R, Memphis)	**Unopposed**
8.	**Ed Jones*** (D, Yorkville)	**Unopposed**
9.	**Harold E. Ford*** (D, Memphis)	**133,428**
	William Thompson Jr. (R, Memphis)	53,064
	Texas	
1.	**Sam B. Hall Jr.*** (D, Marshall)	**Unopposed**
2.	**Charles Wilson*** (D, Lufkin)	**113,225**
	Louis Dugas (R, Orange)	77,842
3.	**Steve Bartlett*** (R, Dallas)	**228,819**
	James Westbrook (D, Dallas)	46,890
4.	**Ralph M. Hall*** (D, Rockwall)	**120,749**
	Thomas Blow (R, Tyler)	87,553
5.	**John Bryant*** (D, Dallas)	**Unopposed**
6.	**Joe Barton** (R, Ennis)	**131,482**
	Dan Kubiak (D, College Station)	100,799
7.	**Bill Archer*** (R, Houston)	**213,480**
	Billy Willibey (D, Houston)	32,835
8.	**Jack Fields*** (R, Humble)	**113,031**
	Don Buford (D, Houston)	62,072
9.	**Jack Brooks*** (D, Beaumont)	**120,559**
	Jim Mahan (R, Galveston)	84,306
10.	**J. J. "Jake" Pickle*** (D, Austin)	**Unopposed**
11.	**Marvin Leath*** (D, Waco)	**Unopposed**
12.	**Jim Wright*** (D, Fort Worth)	**Unopposed**
13.	**Beau Boulter*** (R, Amarillo)	**107,600**
	Jack Hightower* (D, Vernon)	95,367
14.	**Mac Sweeney*** (R, Victoria)	**104,181**
	William N. "Bill" Patman* (D, Ganado)	98,885
15.	**E. "Kika" de la Garza*** (D, Mission)	**Unopposed**
16.	**Ronald Coleman*** (D, El Paso)	**76,375**
	Jack Hammond (R, El Paso)	56,589
17.	**Charles W. Stenholm*** (D, Stamford)	**Unopposed**
18.	**Mickey Leland*** (D, Houston)	**109,626**
	Glen E. Beaman (R, Houston)	26,400
19.	**Larry Combest** (R, Lubbock)	**102,805**
	Don Richards (D, Lubbock)	74,044
20.	**Henry B. Gonzalez*** (D, San Antonio)	**Unopposed**

Dist.	Representative (Party, Home)	1984 Election
21.	**Tom Loeffler*** (R, Hunt)	**199,909**
	Joe Sullivan (D, San Antonio)	48,039
22.	**Tom DeLay** (R, Sugar Land)	**125,225**
	Douglas Williams (D, Missouri City)	66,495
23.	**Albert Bustamente** (D, San Antonio)	**Unopposed**
24.	**Martin Frost*** (D, Dallas)	**105,210**
	Robert Burk (R, Irving)	71,703
25.	**Mike Andrews*** (D, Houston)	**113,946**
	Jerry Patterson (R, Houston)	63,974
26.	**Dick Armey** (R, Denton)	**126,641**
	Tom Vandergriff* (D, Arlington)	120,451
27.	**Solomon P. Ortiz*** (D, Corpus Christi)	**105,516**
	Richard Moore (R, Corpus Christi)	60,283
	Utah	
1.	**James V. Hansen*** (R, Farmington)	**142,952**
	Milton Abrams (D, Logan)	56,619
2.	**Dave Monson** (R, Salt Lake City)	**105,540**
	Frances Farley (D, Salt Lake City)	105,044
3.	**Howard C. Nielson*** (R, Provo)	**138,918**
	Bruce Baird (D, Murray)	46,560
	Vermont At Large	
1.	**James M. Jeffords*** (R, Montpelier)	**148,025**
	Anthony Pollina (D, Montpelier)	60,360
	Virginia	
1.	**Herbert Bateman*** (R, Newport News)	**118,085**
	John J. McGlennon (D, Williamsburg)	79,577
2.	**G. William Whitehurst*** (R, Norfolk)	**Unopposed**
3.	**Thomas J. Bliley Jr.*** (R, Richmond)	**169,987**
	Roger L. Coffey (I., Richmond)	28,556
4.	**Norman Sisisky*** (D, Petersburg)	**Unopposed**
5.	**Dan Daniel*** (D, Danville)	**Unopposed**
6.	**James Olin*** (D, Roanoke)	**105,207**
	Ray Garland (R, Roanoke)	91,344
7.	**French Slaughter*** (R, Culpepper)	**109,110**
	Lewis Costello (D, Winchester)	77,624
8.	**Stan Parris*** (R, Woodbridge)	**125,015**
	Richard Saslaw (D, Annandale)	97,250
9.	**Frederick Boucher*** (D, Abingdon)	**102,446**
	Jefferson Stafford (R, Pearisburg)	94,510
10.	**Frank R. Wolf*** (R, Falls Church)	**158,528**
	John Flannery (D, Arlington)	95,074
	Washington	
1.	**John Miller*** (R, Seattle)	**147,926**
	Brock Evans (D, Seattle)	115,001
2.	**Al Swift*** (D, Bellingham)	**142,065**
	Jim Klauder (R, Eastsound)	93,472
3.	**Don Bonker*** (D, Vancouver)	**150,432**
	Herb Elder (R, Olympia)	61,219
4.	**Sid Morrison*** (R, Zillah)	**150,322**
	Mark Epperson (D, Golendale)	47,158
5.	**Thomas S. Foley*** (D, Spokane)	**154,988**
	Jack Hebner (R, Spokane)	67,438
6.	**Norman D. Dicks*** (D, Bremerton)	**124,367**
	Mike Lonergan (R, Tacoma)	60,721
7.	**Mike Lowry*** (D, Renton)	**174,560**
	Bob Dorse (R, Seattle)	71,576
8.	**Rodney Chandler*** (R, Redmond)	**146,891**
	Bob Lamson (D, Mercer Island)	88,379
	West Virginia	
1.	**Alan B. Mollohan*** (D, Fairmont)	**104,639**
	Jim Altmeyer (R, Wheeling)	87,622
2.	**Harley O. Staggers Jr.*** (D, Keyser)	**100,345**
	Cleve Benedict (R, Lewisburg)	78,936
3.	**Bob Wise*** (D, Charleston)	**125,306**
	Peggy Miller (R, So. Charleston)	59,128
4.	**Nick J. Rahall II *** (D, Beckley)	**98,919**
	Jess Shumate (R, Beckley)	49,474
	Wisconsin	
1.	**Les Aspin*** (D, East Troy)	**127,184**
	Peter N. Jansson (R, Racine)	99,080

Dist.	Representative (Party, Home)	1984 Election	Dist.	Representative (Party, Home)	1984 Election
2.	Robert Kastenmeier* (D, Sun Prairie)	159,987		**Wyoming At Large**	
				Richard B. Cheney* (R, Casper)	138,234
	Albert Wiley (R, Stoughton)	91,345		Hugh McFadden (D, Laramie)	45,857
3.	Steven Gunderson* (R, Osseo)	160,437		**Non-Voting Delegates**	
	Charles Dahl (D, Viroqua)	74,253		**District of Columbia**	
4.	Gerry Kleczka (D, Milwaukee)	158,722		Walter E. Fauntroy* (D)	
	Robert Nolan (R, So. Milwaukee)	78,056		**Guam**	
5.	Jim Moody* (D, Milwaukee)	175,243		Antonio Borja Won Pat* (D, Agana)	
	William C. Breihan (SW, Milwaukee)	3,364		Ben Garrido Blaz (R, Agana)	
6.	Thomas E. Petri* (R, Fond du Lac)	170,271		**Virgin Islands**	
	David Iaquinta (D, Oshkosh)	54,266		Ron de Lugo (D, St. Croix)	
7.	David R. Obey* (D, Wausau)	146,131		Janet Watlington (I, Charlotte Amalie)	
	Mark Michaelson (R, Marshfield)	92,507		**American Samoa**	
8.	Toby Roth* (R, Appleton)	161,005		Fofo I. F. Sunia (D, Pago Pago)	
	Paul Willems (D, Green Bay)	73,090		Aumoeulogo Salanoa Soli (I, Pago Pago)	
9.	F. James Sensenbrenner Jr.* (R, Menomonee Falls)	180,247		**Puerto Rico**	
	John Krause (D, Germantown)	64,157		Nelson Famadas (D, Hato Rey)	

Top Congressional Fund-Raisers

Source: Federal Election Commission

Senate	Total	Political Action Committees	House	Total	Political Action Committees
Jesse Helms (R-N.C.)	$16,522,266	$ 840,530	Andrew Stein[1] (D-N.Y.)	$ 1,780,130	$12,700
Jay Rockefeller (D-W. Va.)	12,093,549	533,322	James R. Jones (D-Okla.)	1,419,585	662,861
James B. Hunt[1] (D-N.C.)	10,063,502	833,046	William S. Green (R-N.Y.)	1,143,653	100,597
Philip W. Gramm (R-Tex.)	9,804,902	1,326,875	Robert K. Dornan (R-Cal.)	1,046,909	86,082
Lloyd A. Doggett[1] (D-Tex.)	6,032,864	802,607	Ronald V. Dellums (D-Cal.)	951,097	51,021
Rudolph Boschwitz (R-Minn.)	5,983,410	998,793	Jack M. Fields (R-Tex.)	945,280	345,216
Charles H. Percy[1] (R-Ill.)	5,331,736	1,084,988	Bruce A. Morrison (D-Conn.)	929,192	357,565
Paul Simon (D-Ill.)	4,586,036	897,395	Tommy F. Robinson (D-Ark.)	921,486	20,550
Bill Bradley (D-N.J.)	4,317,423	662,421	Joseph P. Addabbo (D-N.Y.)	898,556	324,521
Raymond Shamie[1] (R-Mass.)	4,196,521	(2)	Robert W. Edgar (D-Pa.)	880,767	282,828
Carl Levin (D-Mich.)	3,517,444	707,653	Stan Parris (R-Va.)	865,985	269,083
Albert Gore (D-Tenn.)	3,166,007	782,948	Robert P. Quinn[1] (R-N.Y.)	861,034	(3)
William L. Armstrong (R-Col.)	3,105,821	800,156	Chester G. Atkins (D-Mass.)	858,658	(3)
Thomas Harkin (D-Ia.)	2,848,763	770,202	Les AuCoin (D-Ore.)	856,055	399,545
John W. Warner (R-Va.)	2,830,558	691,998	Lindy Boggs (D-La.)	796,527	297,584

(1) Lost 1984 election. (2) Less than $82,000. (3) Less than $231,000.

Political Action Committees

Source: Federal Election Commission

Political-action committees that reported the highest outlays during 1983-84.

National Conservative PAC	$19,332,000	National Committee to Preserve Social Security	$2,400,526
Fund for a Conservative Majority	5,451,498	National Committee for an Effective Congress	2,381,384
National Congressional Club	5,222,378	Campaign for Prosperity	2,186,144
Realtors Political Action Committee	3,874,782	National Education Associaton	2,177,756
National Rifle Assn. Political Victory Fund	3,774,796	National PAC	2,154,447
Republican Majority Fund	3,531,125	United Auto Workers	2,131,847
American Medical Association	3,513,763	Associated Milk Producers, Inc.	1,997,805
Ruff Political Action Committee	3,499,272	United Food and Commercial Workers	1,933,898
Fund for a Democratic Majority	2,955,393	Machinists Non-Partisan Political League	1,865,697
Citizens for the Republic	2,754,549	National Association of Home Builders	1,846,987

Foreign Lobby Expenditures

Source: U.S. Department of Justice

Outlays on U.S. lobbying activities as officially reported in 1984.

1.	Japan	$14,294,000	6.	Indonesia	$5,290,000
2.	Canada	7,531,000	7.	Scotland	3,504,000
3.	W. Germany	6,362,000	8.	Korea	3,221,000
4.	U.S.S.R.	5,469,000	9.	Saudi Arabia	3,209,000
5.	Ireland	5,438,000	10.	France	3,204,000

Political Divisions of the U.S. Senate and House of Representatives
From 1859 (36th Cong.) to 1985-1987 (99th Cong.)
Source: Clerk of the House of Representatives; Secretary of the Senate

Congress	Years	Senate					House of Representatives				
		Number of Senators	Democrats	Republicans	Other parties	Vacant	Number of Representatives	Democrats	Republicans	Other parties	Vacant
36th. . . .	1859-61	66	38	26	2		237	101	113	23	
37th. . . .	1861-63	50	11	31	7	1	178	42	106	28	2
38th. . . .	1863-65	51	12	39			183	80	103		
39th. . . .	1865-67	52	10	42			191	46	145		
40th. . . .	1867-69	53	11	42			193	49	143		1
41st. . . .	1869-71	74	11	61		2	243	73	170		
42d	1871-73	74	17	57			243	104	139		
43d	1873-75	74	19	54		1	293	88	203		2
44th. . . .	1875-77	76	29	46		1	293	181	107	3	2
45th. . . .	1877-79	76	36	39	1		293	156	137		
46th. . . .	1879-81	76	43	33			293	150	128	14	1
47th. . . .	1881-83	76	37	37	2		293	130	152	11	
48th. . . .	1883-85	76	36	40			325	200	119	6	
49th. . . .	1885-87	76	34	41		1	325	182	140	2	1
50th. . . .	1887-89	76	37	39			325	170	151	4	
51st. . . .	1889-91	84	37	47			330	156	173	1	
52d	1891-93	88	39	47	2		333	231	88	14	
53d	1893-95	88	44	38	3	3	356	220	126	10	
54th. . . .	1895-97	88	39	44	5		357	104	246	7	
55th. . . .	1897-99	90	34	46	10		357	134	206	16	1
56th. . . .	1899-1901	90	26	53	11		357	163	185	9	
57th. . . .	1901-03	90	29	56	3	2	357	153	198	5	1
58th. . . .	1903-05	90	32	58			386	178	207		1
59th. . . .	1905-07	90	32	58			386	136	250		
60th. . . .	1907-09	92	29	61		2	386	164	222		
61st. . . .	1909-11	92	32	59		1	391	172	219		
62d	1911-13	92	42	49		1	391	228	162	1	
63d	1913-15	96	51	44	1		435	290	127	18	
64th. . . .	1915-17	96	56	39	1		435	231	193	8	3
65th. . . .	1917-19	96	53	42	1		435	210	216	9	
66th. . . .	1919-21	96	47	48	1		435	191	237	7	
67th. . . .	1921-23	96	37	59			435	132	300	1	2
68th. . . .	1923-25	96	43	51	2		435	207	225	3	
69th. . . .	1925-27	96	40	54	1	1	435	183	247	5	
70th. . . .	1927-29	96	47	48	1		435	195	237	3	
71st. . . .	1929-31	96	39	56	1		435	163	267	1	4
72d	1931-33	96	47	48	1		435	[2]216	218	1	
73d	1933-35	96	59	36	1		435	313	117	5	
74th. . . .	1935-37	96	69	25	2		435	322	103	10	
75th. . . .	1937-39	96	75	17	4		435	333	89	13	
76th. . . .	1939-41	96	69	23	4		435	262	169	4	
77th. . . .	1941-43	96	66	28	2		435	267	162	6	
78th. . . .	1943-45	96	57	38	1		435	222	209	4	
79th. . . .	1945-47	96	57	38	1		435	243	190	2	
80th. . . .	1947-49	96	45	51			435	188	246	1	
81st. . . .	1949-51	96	54	42			435	263	171	1	
82d	1951-53	96	48	47	1		435	234	199	2	
83d	1953-55	96	46	48	2		435	213	221	1	
84th. . . .	1955-57	96	48	47	1		435	232	203		
85th. . . .	1957-59	96	49	47			435	234	201		
86th. . . .	1959-61	98	64	34			[3]436	283	153		
87th. . . .	1961-63	100	64	36			[4]437	262	175		
88th. . . .	1963-65	100	67	33			435	258	176		1
89th. . . .	1965-67	100	68	32			435	295	140		
90th. . . .	1967-69	100	64	36			435	248	187		
91st. . . .	1969-71	100	58	42			435	243	192		
92d	1971-73	100	54	44	2		435	255	180		
93d	1973-75	100	56	42	2		435	242	192	1	
94th. . . .	1975-77	100	61	37	2		435	291	144		
95th. . . .	1977-79	100	61	38	1		435	292	143		
96th. . . .	1979-81	100	58	41	1		435	277	158		
97th. . . .	1981-83	100	46	53	1		435	242	190		3
98th. . . .	1983-85	100	46	54			435	269	166		
99th. . . .	1985-87	100	47	53			435	253	182		

(1) Democrats organized House with help of other parties. (2) Democrats organized House due to Republican deaths. (3) Proclamation declaring Alaska a State issued Jan. 3, 1959. (4) Proclamation declaring Hawaii a State issued Aug. 21, 1959.

Senate Standing Committees
(Preliminary: as of May 1. 1985)

Agriculture, Nutrition, and Forestry
Chairman: Jesse Helms, N.C.
Ranking Dem.: Edward Zorinsky, Neb.
Appropriations
Chairman: Mark O. Hatfield, Ore.
Ranking Dem.: John C. Stennis, Miss.
Armed Services
Chairman: Barry Goldwater, Ariz.
Ranking Dem.: Sam Nunn, Ga.
Banking, Housing, and Urban Affairs
Chairman: Jake Garn, Utah
Ranking Dem.: William Proxmire, Wis.
Budget
Chairman: Pete V. Domenici, N.M.
Ranking Dem.: Lawton Chiles, Fla.
Commerce, Science, and Transportation
Chairman: John C. Danforth, Mo.
Ranking Dem.: Ernest F. Hollings, S.C.
Energy and Natural Resources
Chairman: James A. McClure, Idaho
Ranking Dem.: J. Bennett Johnston, La.
Environment and Public Works
Chairman: Robert T. Stafford, Vt.
Ranking Dem.: Lloyd Bentsen, Tex.
Finance
Chairman: Bob Packwood, Ore.
Ranking Dem.: Russell B. Long, La.
Foreign Relations
Chairman: Richard G. Lugar, Ind.
Ranking Dem.: Claiborne Pell, R.I.
Governmental Affairs
Chairman: William V. Roth, Del.
Ranking Dem.: Thomas F. Eagleton, Mo.
Judiciary
Chairman: Strom Thurmond, S.C.
Ranking Dem.: Joseph R. Biden, Del.
Labor and Human Resources
Chairman: Orrin G. Hatch, Utah
Ranking Dem.: Edward M. Kennedy, Mass.
Rules and Administration
Chairman: Charles McC. Mathias, Jr., Md.
Ranking Dem.: Wendell H. Ford, Ky.
Small Business
Chairman: Lowell P. Weicker Jr., Conn.
Ranking Dem.: Dale Bumpers, Ark.
Veterans' Affairs
Chairman: Frank H. Murkowski, Alas.
Ranking Dem.: Alan Cranston, Calif.

Senate Select and Special Committees

Aging
Chairman: John Heinz, Pa.
Ranking Dem.: John Glenn, Ohio
Ethics
Chairman: Warren Rudman, N.H.
Ranking Dem.: Howell Heflin, Ala.
Indian Affairs
Chairman: Mark Andrews, N.D.
Ranking Dem.: John Melcher, Mont.
Intelligence
Chairman: David Durenberger, Minn.
Ranking Dem.: Patrick J. Leahy, Vt.

Joint Committees of Congress

Economic Committee
Chairman: Rep. David R. Obey (D), Wis.
V. Chairman: Sen. James Abdnor (R), S. Dak.
Committee on the Library
Chairman: Rep. Frank Annunzio (D), Ill.
V. Chairman: Sen. Charles McC. Mathias, Jr. (R), Md.
Committee on Printing
Chairman: Sen. Charles McC. Mathias, Jr. (R), Md.
V. Chairman: Rep. Frank Annunzio (D), Ill.
Committee on Taxation
Chairman: Rep. Dan Rostenkowski (D), Ill.
V. Chairman: Sen. Bob Packwood (R), Ore.

House Standing Committees
(As of Apr. 25, 1985)

Agriculture
Chairman: E de la Garza, Tex.
Ranking Rep.: Edward R. Madigan, Ill.
Appropriations
Chairman: Jamie L. Whitten, Miss.
Ranking Rep.: Silvio O. Conte, Mass.
Armed Services
Chairman: Les Aspin, Wis.
Ranking Rep.: William L. Dickinson, Ala.
Banking, Finance, and Urban Affairs
Chairman: Fernand J. St. Germain, R.I.
Ranking Rep.: Chalmers P. Wylie, Ohio
Budget
Chairman: William H. Gray III, Pa.
Ranking Rep.: Delbert L. Latta, Ohio
District of Columbia
Chairman: Ronald V. Dellums, Calif.
Ranking Rep.: Stewart B. McKinney, Conn.
Education and Labor
Chairman: Augustus F. Hawkins, Calif.
Ranking Rep.: James M. Jeffords, Vt.
Energy and Commerce
Chairman: John D. Dingell, Mich.
Ranking Rep.: James T. Broyhill, N.C.
Foreign Affairs
Chairman: Dante B. Fascell, Fla.
Ranking Rep.: William S. Broomfield, Mich.
Government Operations
Chairman: Jack Brooks, Tex.
Ranking Rep.: Frank Horton, N.Y.
House Administration
Chairman: Frank Annunzio, Ill.
Ranking Rep.: Bill Frenzel, Minn.
Interior and Insular Affairs
Chairman: Morris K. Udall, Ariz.
Ranking Rep.: Don Young, Alas.
Judiciary
Chairman: Peter W. Rodino, Jr., N.J.
Ranking Rep.: Hamilton Fish, Jr., N.Y.
Merchant Marine and Fisheries
Chairman: Walter B. Jones, N.C.
Ranking Rep.: Norman F. Lent, N.Y.
Post Office and Civil Service
Chairman: William D. Ford, Mich.
Ranking Rep.: Gene Taylor, Mo.
Public Works and Transportation
Chairman: James J. Howard, N.J.
Ranking Rep.: Gene Snyder, Ky.
Rules
Chairman: Claude Pepper, Fla.
Ranking Rep.: James H. Quillen, Tenn.
Science and Technology
Chairman: Don Fuqua, Fla.
Ranking Rep.: Manuel Lujan, Jr., N. Mex.
Small Business
Chairman: Parren J. Mitchell, Md.
Ranking Rep.: Joseph M. McDade, Pa.
Standards of Official Conduct
Chairman: Julian C. Dixon, Calif.
Ranking Rep.: Floyd Spence, S.C.
Veterans' Affairs
Chairman: G.V. Montgomery, Miss.
Ranking Rep.: John Paul Hammerschmidt, Ark.
Ways and Means
Chairman: Dan Rostenkowski, Ill.
Ranking Rep.: John J. Duncan, Tenn.

House Select Committees

Aging
Chairman: Edward R. Roybal, Calif.
Ranking Rep.: Matthew J. Rinaldo, N.J.
Children, Youth, and Families
Chairman: George Miller, Calif.
Ranking Rep.: Dan Coats, Md.
Hunger
Chairman: Mickey Leland, Tex.
Ranking Rep.: Marge Roukema, N.J.

(continued)

Intelligence
Chairman: Lee H. Hamilton, Ind.
Ranking Rep.: Bob Stump, Ariz.

Narcotics Abuse and Control
Chairman: Charles B. Rangel, N.Y.
Ranking Rep.: Benjamin A. Gilman, N.Y.

Governors of States and Possessions

As of mid-1985

State	Capital	Governor	Party	Term years	Term expires	Annual salary
Alabama	Montgomery	George C. Wallace	Dem.	4	Jan. 1987	$63,838
Alaska	Juneau	William Sheffield	Dem.	4	Dec. 1986	81,648
Arizona	Phoenix	Bruce Babbitt	Dem.	4	Jan. 1987	62,500
Arkansas	Little Rock	Bill Clinton	Dem.	2	Jan. 1987	35,000
California	Sacramento	George Deukmejian	Rep.	4	Jan. 1987	85,000
Colorado	Denver	Richard D. Lamm	Dem.	4	Jan. 1987	60,000
Connecticut	Hartford	William A. O'Neill	Dem.	4	Jan. 1987	65,000
Delaware	Dover	Michael N. Castle	Rep.	4	Jan. 1989	70,000
Florida	Tallahassee	Robert Graham	Dem.	4	Jan. 1987	69,550
Georgia	Atlanta	Joe Frank Harris	Dem.	4	Jan. 1987	79,358
Hawaii	Honolulu	George R. Ariyoshi	Dem.	4	Dec. 1986	59,400
Idaho	Boise	John V. Evans	Dem.	4	Jan. 1987	50,000
Illinois	Springfield	James R. Thompson	Rep.	4	Jan. 1987	58,000
Indiana	Indianapolis	Robert D. Orr	Rep.	4	Jan. 1989	66,000
Iowa	Des Moines	Terry Branstad	Rep.	4	Jan. 1987	64,000
Kansas	Topeka	John Carlin	Dem.	4	Jan. 1987	65,000
Kentucky	Frankfort	Martha L. Collins	Dem.	4	Dec. 1987	60,000
Louisiana	Baton Rouge	Edwin W. Edwards	Dem.	4	May 1988	73,440
Maine	Augusta	Joseph E. Brennan	Dem.	4	Jan. 1987	35,000
Maryland	Annapolis	Harry Hughes	Dem.	4	Jan. 1987	75,000
Massachusetts	Boston	Michael S. Dukakis	Dem.	4	Jan. 1987	75,000
Michigan	Lansing	James J. Blanchard	Dem.	4	Jan. 1987	81,900
Minnesota	St. Paul	Rudy Perpich	Dem.	4	Jan. 1987	84,560
Mississippi	Jackson	William A. Allain	Dem.	4	Jan. 1988	63,000
Missouri	Jefferson City	John D. Ashcroft	Rep.	4	Jan. 1989	75,000
Montana	Helena	Ted Schwinden	Dem.	4	Jan. 1989	48,923
Nebraska	Lincoln	Robert Kerrey	Dem.	4	Jan. 1987	40,000
Nevada	Carson City	Richard Bryan	Dem.	4	Jan. 1987	65,000
New Hampshire	Concord	John H. Sununu	Rep.	2	Jan. 1987	59,885
New Jersey	Trenton	Thomas H. Kean	Rep.	4	Jan. 1986	85,000
New Mexico	Santa Fe	Toney Anaya	Dem.	4	Jan. 1987	60,000
New York	Albany	Mario Cuomo	Dem.	4	Jan. 1987	100,000
North Carolina	Raleigh	James G. Martin	Rep.	4	Jan. 1989	90,516
North Dakota	Bismarck	George A. Sinner	Dem.	4	Jan. 1989	65,000
Ohio	Columbus	Richard F. Celeste	Dem.	4	Jan. 1987	65,000
Oklahoma	Oklahoma City	George Nigh	Dem.	4	Jan. 1987	70,000
Oregon	Salem	Victor Atiyeh	Rep.	4	Jan. 1987	55,423
Pennsylvania	Harrisburg	Dick Thornburgh	Rep.	4	Jan. 1987	85,000
Rhode Island	Providence	Edward DiPrete	Rep.	2	Jan. 1987	49,500
South Carolina	Columbia	Richard W. Riley	Dem.	4	Jan. 1987	60,000
South Dakota	Pierre	William J. Janklow	Rep.	4	Jan. 1987	53,000
Tennessee	Nashville	Lamar Alexander	Rep.	4	Jan. 1987	68,220
Texas	Austin	Mark White Jr.	Dem.	4	Jan. 1987	90,700
Utah	Salt Lake City	Norman Bangerter	Rep.	4	Jan. 1989	60,000
Vermont	Montpelier	Madeleine Kunin	Dem.	2	Jan. 1987	50,000
Virginia	Richmond	Charles S. Robb	Dem.	4	Jan. 1986	75,000
Washington	Olympia	Booth Gardner	Dem.	4	Jan. 1989	63,000
West Virginia	Charleston	Arch A. Moore	Rep.	4	Jan. 1989	72,000
Wisconsin	Madison	Anthony S. Earl	Dem.	4	Jan. 1987	75,337
Wyoming	Cheyenne	Ed Herschler	Dem.	4	Jan. 1987	70,000
Amer. Samoa	Pago Pago	Peter Coleman	Rep.	4	Jan. 1989	—
Guam	Agana	Ricardo Bordallo	Dem.	4	Jan. 1989	50,000
Puerto Rico	San Juan	Rafael Hernandez Colon	P.D.	4	Jan. 1989	36,200
Virgin Islands	Charlotte Amalie	Juan Luis	Ind.	4	Jan. 1987	52,000

Number of Governors, by Political Party Affiliation: 1960 to 1984

Source: National Governors' Association

[Reflects results of elections in previous year and holdover incumbents]

Year	Democratic	Republican	Year	Democratic	Republican	Independent	Year	Democratic	Republican	Independent
1960	34	16	1969	20	30	—	1977	37	12	1
1962	34	16	1970	18	32	—	1978	37	12	1
1963	34	16	1971	29	21	—	1979	32	18	—
1964	34	16	1972	30	20	—	1980	31	19	—
1965	33	17	1973	31	19	—	1981	27	23	—
1966	33	17	1974	32	18	—	1982	27	23	—
1967	25	25	1975	36	13	1	1983	34	16	—
1968	24	26	1976	36	13	1	1984	35	15	—

Mayors and City Managers of Larger North American Cities

As of mid-1985

*Asterisk before name denotes city manager. All others are mayors. For mayors, dates are those of next election; for city managers, they are dates of appointment.

D, Democrat; R, Republican; N-P, Non-Partisan

City	Name	Term	City	Name	Term
Abilene, Tex.	David Stubbeman, N-P	1987, Apr.	Bryan, Tex.	*Ernest R. Clark	1979, Feb.
Abington, Pa.	*Albert Herrmann	1978, May	Buffalo, N.Y.	James D. Griffin, D	1985, Nov.
Akron, Oh.	Thomas C. Sawyer, D	1987, Nov.	Burbank, Cal.	*Bud Ovrom	1985, June
Alameda, Cal.	Anne B. Diament, N-P	1987, May.	Burlington, Vt.	Bernard Sanders, N-P	1987, Mar.
Albany, Ga.	*Carl Leavy	1980, Feb.	Calumet City, Ill.	Robert C. Stefaniak, D	1989, Apr.
Albany, N.Y.	Thomas M. Whalen,3d,D	1985, Nov.	Cambridge, Mass.	*Robert Healy,	1974, May
Albuquerque, N.M.	Harry Kinney, N-P	1985, Oct.	Camden, N.J.	Melvin Primas Jr., D.	1989, May
Alexandria, La.	John K. Snyder, D	1986, Sept.	Canton, Oh.	Sam Purses, D.	1987, Nov.
Alexandria, Va.	*Douglas Harman	1975, Nov.	Cape Girardeau, Mo.	*Gary A. Eide	1981, Mar.
Alhambra, Cal.	*Kevin J. Murphy.	1983, May	Carson, Cal.	*Raymond Meador	1982, May
Allen Park, Mich.	Frank J. Lada, D.	1985, Nov.	Casper, Wyo.	*Joseph Minner, Act.	1985, Mar.
Allentown, Pa.	Joseph S. Daddona, D	1985, Nov.	Cedar Rapids, Ia.	Donald J. Canney, N-P	1985, Nov.
Altoona, Pa.	David Jannetta, D	1987, Nov.	Champaign, Ill.	*Steven C. Carter	1985, Feb.
Amarillo, Tex.	*John Ward	1983, June	Charleston, S.C.	Joseph P. Riley Jr., D	1987, Nov.
Ames, Ia.	*Steven L. Schainker	1982, Oct.	Charleston, W. Va.	James E. Roark, R	1987, Apr.
Anaheim, Cal.	*William O. Talley	1976, July	Charlotte, N.C.	Harvey Gantt, D	1985, Nov.
Anchorage, Alas.	Tony Knowles, N-P	1986, Oct.	Charlottesville, Va.	*Cole Hendrix	1970, Jan.
Anderson, Ind.	Thomas McMahan, R	1987, Nov.	Chattanooga, Tenn.	Gene Roberts, R	1987, Mar.
Anderson, S.C.	*Richard Burnette	1976, Sept.	Chesapeake, Va.	*John T. Maxwell	1978, Sept.
Ann Arbor, Mich.	*Godfrey Collins	1982, Dec.	Chester, Pa.	Joseph Battle, R.	1987, Nov.
Appleton, Wis.	Dorothy Johnson, N-P	1988, Apr.	Cheyenne, Wyo.	Donald Erickson, R	1988, Nov.
Arcadia, Cal.	*George J. Watts	1981, Feb.	Chicago, Ill.	Harold Washington, D	1987, Apr.
Athens, Ga.	Lauren Coile, D	1985, Nov.	Chicago Hts., Ill.	Charles Panici, R	1987, Apr.
Arlington, Mass.	*Donald R. Marquis	1966, Nov.	Chicopee, Mass.	Richard S. Lak, D	1985, Nov.
Arlington, Tex.	*William Kirchhoff	1984, Oct.	Chino, Cal.	Larry Walker, N-P	1988, Nov.
Arlington Hts., Ill.	James Ryan, N-P	1989, Apr.	Chula Vista, Cal.	*John Goss	1983, Jan.
Arvada, Col.	*Craig Kocian	1977, Mar.	Cincinnati, Oh.	*Sylvester Murray	1979, Sept.
Asheville, N.C.	*Neal Creighton	1984, Oct.	Clearwater, Fla.	*Anthony Shoemaker	1977, June
Athens, Ga.	Lauren Coile, D	1985, Nov.	Cleveland, Oh.	George Voinovich, R	1985, Nov.
Atlanta, Ga.	Andrew Young, D	1985, Nov.	Cleveland Hgts., Oh.	*Robert Downey	1985, Jan.
Atlantic City, N.J.	James L. Usry, R	1986, May	Clifton, N.J.	*Joseph J. Lynn	1982, Sept.
Auburn, N.Y.	*Bruce Clifford.	1966, Aug.	Col. Spgs., Col.	*George H. Fellows	1966, July
Augusta, Ga.	Charles Devaney, D.	1987, Oct.	Columbia, Mo.	*vacant	
Aurora, Col.	*James Griesemer	1984, Jan.	Columbia, S.C.	*Graydon V. Olive Jr.	1970, Mar.
Aurora, Ill.	David L. Pierce, N-P	1989, Apr.	Columbus, Ga.	J. W. Feighner, N-P	1986, Nov.
Austin, Tex.	*Jorge Carrasco	1984, Mar.	Columbus, Oh.	Dana Rinehart, R	1988, Nov.
Bakersfield, Cal.	*George Caravalho	1984, Aug	Commerce, Cal.	*Robert Hinderliter	1973, Aug.
Baldwin Park, Cal.	*Ralph Webb	1981, Apr.	Compton, Cal.	*Laventa Montgomery	1983, Apr.
Baltimore, Md.	William Schaefer, D	1987, Nov.	Concord, Cal.	*F.A. Stewart	1960, Apr.
Bangor, Me.	*John W. Flynn	1977, Feb.	Coon Rapids., Minn.	*Richard Thistle	1979, July
Baton Rouge, La.	Pat Screen, D	1988, Nov.	Coral Gables, Fla.	*Donald E. Leburn	1982, Mar.
Battle Creek, Mich.	*Gordon Jaeger	1976, Mar.	Corpus Christi, Tex.	*Edward A. Martin	1982, Mar.
Bay City, Mich.	*David D. Barnes	1979, May	Corvallis, Ore.	*Gary F. Pokorny	1978, Nov.
Bayonne, N.J.	Dennis P. Collins, D	1986, May	Costa Mesa, Cal.	*Fred Sorsabel	1970, Nov.
Baytown, Tex.	*Fritz Lanham	1972, May	Council Bluffs, Ia.	*Michael G. Miller	1978, Aug.
Beaumont, Tex.	*Karl Nollenberger	1983, June	Covington, Ky.	Tom Behan, N-P	1987, Nov.
Belleville, Ill.	Richard Brauer, N-P	1989, Apr.	Cranston, R.I.	Michael Traficante, R	1986, Nov.
Bellevue, Wash.	*Phillip Kushlaw	1985, Feb.	Crystal, Minn.	*John Irving	1963, Jan.
Bellflower, Cal.	John Ansdell, D	1986, Apr.	Culver City, Cal.	*Dale Jones	1967, Sept.
Beloit, Wis.	*H. Herbert Holt	1971, Mar.	Cuyahoga Falls, Oh.	Robert Quirk, D	1985, Nov.
Berkeley, Cal.	*Daniel Boggan Jr.	1982, Jan.	Dallas, Tex.	*Charles S. Anderson	1981, Oct.
Bessemer, Ala.	Ed Porter, N-P	1986, July	Daly City, Cal.	*David R. Rowe	1969, Sept.
Bethlehem, Pa.	Paul M. Marcincin, D	1985, Nov.	Danbury, Conn.	James Dyer, D.	1985, Nov.
Beverly Hills, Cal.	*Edward Kreins	1979, Oct.	Danville, Va.	*Charles Church	1981, June
Billings, Mont.	*Al Thelen	1979, Nov.	Davenport, Ia.	Charles Peart, R.	1985, Nov.
Biloxi, Miss.	Gerald Blessey, D.	1989, May	Dayton, Oh.	*Richard Helwig	1984, June
Binghamton, N.Y.	Juanita M. Crabb, D	1985, Nov.	Daytona Bch., Fla.	*Howard D. Tipton	1978, Oct.
Birmingham, Ala.	Richard Arrington Jr., D	1987, Oct.	Dearborn, Mich.	John O'Reilly, N-P	1985, Nov.
Bismarck, N.D.	Bus Leary, D	1986, Apr.	Dearborn Hts., Mich.	Wesley Tennant, D	1985, Nov.
Bloomfield, Minn.	*John Pidgeon	1967, Dec.	Decatur, Ala.	Bill Dukes, D	1988, July
Bloomfield, N.J.	John W. Kinder, R	1986, Nov.	Decatur, Ill.	*Leslie T. Allen	1972, Sept.
Bloomington, Ill.	Jesse Smart, R	1989, Apr.	Denton, Tex.	*G. C. Hartung.	1977, Sept.
Bloomington, Ind.	Tomilea Allison, D	1987, Nov.	Denver, Col.	Federico Pena, D	1987, May
Bloomington, Minn.	*John Pidgeon	1967, Sept.	Des Moines, Ia.	*Cy Carney, act.	1985, Feb.
Boca Raton, Fla.	*James Rutherford	1984, Apr.	Des Plaines, Ill.	John Seitz, R.	1989, Apr.
Boise, Ida.	Dick Eardley, N-P	1985, Nov.	Detroit, Mich.	Coleman A. Young, N-P	1987, Nov.
Bossier City, La.	Don E. Jones, D	1989, Apr.	Dover, Del.	Crawford J. Carroll, N-P	1986, Apr.
Boston, Mass.	Raymond L. Flynn, D	1987 Nov.	Downers Grove, Ill.	*James R. Griesemer.	1972, Sept.
Boulder, Col.	*James W. Piper	1984, May	Downey, Cal.	*Robert Ovrom	1983, May
Bowie, Md.	*G. Charles Moore	1976, Aug.	Dubuque, Ia.	*W. Kenneth Gearhart	1979, Aug.
Bowling Green, Ky.	*Charles W. Coates.	1977, Feb.	Duluth, Minn.	John Fedo, N-P	1987, Nov.
Bridgeport, Conn.	Leonard Paoletta, R.	1985, Nov.	Durham, N.C.	*Orville Powell	1983, Mar.
Bristol, Conn.	John Leone, D	1985, Nov.	E. Chicago, Ind.	Robert A. Pastrick, D	1987, Nov.
Brockton, Mass.	Carl Pitaro, D	1985, Nov.	E. Cleveland, Oh.	*Frank Wise	1979, Jan.
Brooklyn Center, Minn.	*Gerald G. Splinter	1977, Oct.	E. Hartford, Conn.	George Dagon, D	1985, Nov.
Brownsville, Tex.	*Kenneth Lieck	1981, Apr.	E. Lansing, Mich.	*Thomas Dority	1984, Nov.
			E. Orange, N.J.	Thomas H. Cooke Jr., D	1985, Nov.

City	Name	Term	City	Name	Term
E. Providence, R. I.	*Peter J. Witschen	1985, Mar.	Holyoke, Mass.	Ernest Proulx, D	1985, Nov.
Eau Claire, Wis.	*Eric Anderson	1984, Jan.	Honolulu, Ha.	Frank Fasi, R	1988, Nov.
Edina, Minn.	*Kenneth Rosland	1977, Nov.	Hot Springs, Ark.	Jim Randall, N-P	1986, Nov.
Edison, N.J.	Anthony Yelencsics, D	1985, Nov.	Houston, Tex.	Kathryn Whitmire, N-P	1985, Nov.
El Cajon, Cal.	*Robert Acker	1982, July	Huntington, W. Va.	*Stephen Williams	1984, July
El Monte, Cal.	Don McMillen, R	1986, Apr.	Huntington Beach, Cal.	*Charles Thompson	1981, Oct.
El Paso, Tex.	Johnathan W. Rogers, N-P	1987, Apr.	Huntsville, Ala.	Joe W. Davis, N-P	1988, July
Elgin, Ill.	*Robert Malm	1984, May	Hutchinson, Kan.	*George Pyle	1967, Sept.
Elizabeth, N.J.	Thomas G. Dunn, D	1988, Nov.	Idaho Falls, Ida.	Thomas Campbell, N-P	1985, Nov.
Elkhart, Ind.	James Perron, D	1987, Nov.	Independence, Mo.	Barbara Potts, N-P	1986, Apr.
Elmhurst, Ill.	Robert Quinn, N-P	1989, Apr.	Indianapolis, Ind.	William Hudnut, R	1987, Nov.
Elmira, N.Y.	*John Gridley	1983, Jan.	Inglewood, Cal.	*Paul Eckles	1975, Nov.
Elyria, Oh.	Michael Keys, D	1987, Nov.	Inkster, Mich.	*Gregory Knowles	1984, June
Enfield, Conn.	*Robert J. Mulready	1983, Feb.	Iowa City, Ia.	*Neal Berlin	1975, Feb.
Enid, Okla.	*Lyle Smith	1979, Feb.	Irving, Tex.	*Jack Huffman	1974, Jan.
Erie, Pa.	Louis J. Tullio, D	1985, Nov.	Irvington, N.J.	Anthony T. Blasi, D	1986, May
Escondido, Cal.	*Vernon Hazen	1982, July	Jackson, Mich.	*S.W. McAllister Jr.	1974, Mar.
Euclid, Oh.	Anthony Giunta, D	1987, Nov.	Jackson, Miss.	Dale Danks, D	1989, May
Eugene, Ore.	*Michael Gleason	1981, Jan.	Jackson, Tenn.	Bob Conger, D	1987, June
Evanston, Ill.	*Joel Asprooth	1981, Mar.	Jacksonville, Fla.	Jake Godbold, D	1987, May
Evansville, Ind.	Michael Vandeveer, D	1987, Nov.	Jamestown, N.Y.	Steve Carlson, D	1985, Nov.
Everett, Mass.	Edward Connolly, D	1985, Nov.	Janesville, Wis.	*Philip L. Deaton	1976, Mar.
Everett, Wash.	William Moore, N-P	1985, Nov.	Jefferson City, Mo.	George Hartsfield, D	1987, Apr.
Fairborn, Oh.	*William Burns	1977, Feb.	Jersey City, N.J.	Anthony Cucci	1989, June
Fairfield, Cal.	*B. Gale Wilson	1956, Mar.	Johnson City, Tenn.	*John G. Campbell	1984, June
Fair Lawn, N.J.	*Joseph Garger	1979, Oct.	Johnstown, Pa.	Herbert Pfuhl Jr., R	1985, Nov.
Fall River, Mass.	Carlton Viveiros, D	1985, Nov.	Joliet, Ill.	*Paul A. Flynn	1984, Sept.
Fargo, N.D.	Jon Lindgren, D	1986, Apr.	Joplin, Mo.	*Stribling Boynton	1983, Oct.
Farmington Hills, Mich.	*William M. Costick	1981, Jan.	Kalamazoo, Mich.	*Sheryl Sculley	1984, Apr.
Fayetteville, Ark.	*Donald Grimes	1972, Apr.	Kansas City, Kan.	John Reardon, D	1987, Mar.
Fayetteville, N.C.	*John P. Smith	1981, Jan.	Kansas City, Mo.	*David Olson	1984, Nov.
Fitchburg, Mass.	Bernard Chartrand, D	1985, Nov.	Kenosha, Wis.	John Bilotti, D	1988, Apr.
Flagstaff, Ariz.	*Frank Abeyta	1981, Jan.	Kettering, Oh.	*Robert Walker	1982, Oct.
Flint, Mich.	James Sharp Jr., N-P	1987, Nov.	Key West, Fla.	*Joel L. Koford	1982, Oct.
Florissant, Mo.	James J. Eagan, N-P	1987, Apr.	Killeen, Tex.	*Robert M. Hopkins	1982, Apr.
Fond du Lac, Wis.	*Daniel Thompson	1983, Dec.	Knoxville, Tenn.	Kyle C. Testerman, N-P	1987, Nov.
Ft. Collins, Col.	*John Arnold	1977, Oct.	Kokomo, Ind.	Stephen Daily, D	1987, Nov.
Ft. Lauderdale, Fla.	*Constance Hoffmann	1980, Oct.	LaCrosse, Wis.	Patrick Zielke, N-P	1989, Apr.
Ft. Lee, N.J.	Nicholas Corbiscello, R	1987, Nov.	La Habra, Cal.	*Lee Risner	1970, Nov.
Ft. Smith, Ark.	*William Faught	1981, July	La Mesa, Cal.	*Ronald Bradley	1980, May
Ft. Wayne, Ind.	Win Moses, D	1987, Nov.	La Mirada, Cal.	*Gary K. Sloan	1980, Nov.
Ft. Worth, Tex.	*Douglas Harman	1985, Mar.	Lafayette, Ind.	James Riehle, D	1987, Nov.
Fountain Valley, Cal.	*Judy Kelsey	1984, May	Lafayette, La.	Dud Lastrapes, R	1988, May
Fremont, Cal.	*Charles Kent McClain	1981, May	Lake Charles, La.	Edward S. Watson D	1989, June
Fresno, Cal.	*Robert Christofferson	1983, Nov.	Lakeland, Fla.	*Robert V. Youkey	1960, Jan.
Fullerton, Cal.	*William C. Winter	1979, Oct.	Lakewood, Cal.	*Howard L. Chambers	1976, June
Gadsden, Ala.	Steve Means, D	1986, July	Lakewood, Col.	*Richard Robinson	1985, Jan.
Gainesville, Fla.	*W.D. Higginbotham Jr.	1984, Sept.	Lakewood, Oh.	Anthony Sinagra, R	1987, Nov.
Galesburg, Ill.	*Lawrence Asaro	1979, Sept.	Lancaster, Pa.	Arthur E. Morris, R	1985, Nov.
Galveston, Tex.	*Stephen Huffman	1980, Apr.	Lansing, Mich.	Terry John McKane, N-P	1985, Nov.
Gardena, Cal.	*Kenneth Landau	1985, Apr.	Laredo, Tex.	*Marvin Townsend	1982, June
Garden Grove, Cal.	*Delbert L. Powers	1980, July	Largo, Fla.	*D. Russell Barr	1979, Dec.
Garfield Hts., Oh.	Thomas Longo, D	1985, Nov.	Las Cruces, N.M.	*Dana Miller	1983, Feb.
Garland, Tex.	*James K. Spore	1985, Mar.	Las Vegas, Nev.	William Briare, N-P	1987, June
Gary, Ind.	Richard G. Hatcher, D	1987, Nov.	Lawrence, Kan.	*Buford M. Watson Jr.	1970, Jan.
Gastonia, N.C.	*Gary Hicks	1973, Dec.	Lawrence, Mass.	John J. Buckley, D	1985, Nov.
Glendale, Ariz.	*Martin Vanacour	1985, Mar.	Lawton, Okla.	Wayne Gilley, N-P	1987, May
Glendale, Cal.	*James M. Rez	1983, Dec.	Lewiston, Me.	*Lucien Gosselin	1980, July
Grand Forks, N.D.	H.C. Wessman, R	1988, Apr.	Lexington, Ky.	Scotty Baesler, D	1985, Nov.
Grand Island, Neb.	Bill Wright, N-P	1986, Nov.	Lima, Oh.	Harry Moyer, N-P	1985, Nov.
Gr. Prairie, Tex.	*Bob Blodgett	1984, July	Lincoln, Neb.	Roland Luedtke, R	1987, Apr.
Gr. Rapids, Mich.	*G. Stevens Bernard	1981, Dec.	Linden, N.J.	*George Hudak, D	1986, Nov.
Great Falls, Mont.	*G. Allen Johnson	1981, Jan.	Little Rock, Ark.	*Susan B. Fleming	1983, May
Greeley, Col.	*Peter Morrell	1973, Dec.	Livermore, Cal.	*Leland Horner	1978, Oct.
Green Bay, Wis.	Samuel Halloin, N-P	1987, Apr.	Lombard, Ill.	*William Lichter	1985, Jan.
Greensboro, N.C.	*T.Z. Osborne	1973, Feb.	Long Beach, Cal.	*John Dever	1977, Jan.
Greenville, Miss.	William Burnley Jr., D	1987, Oct.	Long Beach, N.Y.	*Edwin Eaton	1979, June
Greenville, S.C.	*John Dullea	1971, Oct.	Longmont, Col.	*William Swenson, N-P	1983, Nov.
Greenwich, Conn.	Roger Pierson, D, first selectman	1985, Nov.	Longview, Tex.	*C. Ray Jackson	1980, Apr.
Gulfport, Miss.	Leroy Urie, D	1989, May	Lorain, Oh.	Alex Olejko, D	1987, Nov.
Hackensack, N.J.	*Joseph J. Squillace	1964, Oct.	Los Angeles, Cal.	Thomas Bradley, N-P	1989, June
Hagerstown, Md.	*William Breichner	1983, Aug.	Louisville, Ky.	Harvey Sloane, D	1985, Nov.
Hamden, Conn.	Peter Villano, D	1985, Nov.	Lowell, Mass.	*B. Joseph Tully	1979, June
Hamilton, Oh.	*J.P. Becker	1984, Dec.	L. Merion, Pa.	*Thomas B. Fulweiler	1968, Jan.
Hammond, Ind.	Thomas McDermott, R	1987, Nov.	Lubbock, Tex.	*Larry Cunningham	1976, Sept.
Hampton, Va.	*Thomas Miller	1981, Mar.	Lynchburg, Va.	*E. Allen Culverhouse	1979, June
Harlingen, Tex.	*G.D. Sotelo	1981, July	Lynn, Mass.	Antonio J. Marino, D	1985, Nov.
Harrisburg, Pa.	Stephen Reed, D	1985, Nov.	Lynwood, Cal.	*Charles Gomez	1982, Mar.
Hartford, Conn.	Thirman L. Milner, D	1985, Nov.	Macon, Ga.	George Israel, R	1987, Nov.
Harvey, Ill.	David Johnson, N-P	1987, Apr.	Madison, Wis.	F.T. Sensenbrenner Jr., D	1989, Apr.
Haverhill, Mass.	William H. Ryan, R	1985, Nov.	Malden, Mass.	Thomas Fallon, D	1985, Nov.
Hawthorne, Cal.	*R. Kenneth Jue	1977, Jan.	Manchester, Conn.	Barbara Weinberg, D	1985, Nov.
Hayward, Cal.	*Donald Blubaugh	1979, Nov.	Manchester, N.H.	Robert Shaw, R	1985, Nov.
Hialeah, Fla.	Raul Martinez, D	1985, Nov.	Manitowoc, Wis.	Anthony V. Dufek, D	1987, Apr.
High Point, N.C.	*H. Lewis Price	1983, July	Mansfield, Oh.	Edward Meehan, R	1987, Nov.
Hoboken, N.J.	Thomas F. Vezzetti, D	1989, May	Marion, Oh.	Ronald Malone, D	1987, Nov.
Hollywood, Fla.	*James Chandler	1976, Nov.	McAllen, Tex.	Othal Brand, R	1989, Apr.

City	Name	Term	City	Name	Term
McKeesport, Pa.	Lou Washowich, D	1987, Nov.	Pasadena, Tex.	John Ray Harrison	1988, Apr.
Medford, Mass.	*John Ghiloni	1982	Passaic, N.J.	Joseph Lipari, N-P	1989, May
Melbourne, Fla.	*Samuel Halter	1978, July	Paterson, N.J.	Frank X. Graves Jr., D	1986, May
Memphis, Tenn.	Richard C. Hackett, N-P	1987, Nov.	Pawtucket, R.I.	Henry Kinch, D	1985, Nov.
Mentor, Oh.	*Edward Podojil	1977, Nov.	Peabody, Mass.	Peter Torigian, D	1985, Nov.
Meriden, Conn.	*Eugene Moody	1985, June	Pekin, Ill.	Willard Birkmeier, D	1987, Apr.
Meridian, Miss.	*Wallace Heggie	1984, June	Pensacola, Fla.	*Steve Garman	1978, May
Mesa, Ariz.	*C.K. Luster	1979, June	Peoria, Ill.	*James B. Daken	1979, Jan.
Mesquite, Tex.	*C.K. Duggins	1976, Feb.	Perth Amboy, N.J.	George J. Otlowski, D	1988, May
Miami, Fla.	*Sergio Pereira	1985, Apr.	Philadelphia, Pa.	W. Wilson Goode, D	1987, Nov.
Miami Beach, Fla.	*Rob Parkins	1982, Apr.	Phoenix, Ariz.	Terry Goddard, N-P	1985, Nov.
Middletown, Conn.	Sebastian Garafalo, R	1985, Nov.	Pico Rivera, Cal.	*Dennis Courtemarche	1984, Nov.
Middletown, Conn.	*vacant		Pine Bluff, Ark	Carolyn Robinson, D	1988, Nov.
Midland, Tex.	G. Thane Akins, R	1986, Apr.	Pittsburgh, Pa.	Richard S. Caliguiri, D	1985, Nov.
Midwest City, Okla.	Dave Herbert, D	1986, Mar.	Pittsfield, Mass.	Charles Smith, N-P	1985, Nov.
Milford, Conn.	Alberta Jagoe, D	1985, Nov.	Plainfield, N.J.	Everett C. Lattimore, D	1985, Nov.
Milwaukee, Wis.	Henry W. Maier, D	1988, Apr.	Plano, Tex.	*Robert Woodruff Jr.	1985, Jan.
Minneapolis, Minn.	Donald Fraser, D	1985, Nov.	Pocatello, Ida.	*Charles W. Moss.	1970, Sept.
Minnetonka, Minn.	*James F. Miller.	1980, Jan.	Pomona, Cal.	*Ora E. Lampman.	1978, July
Minot, N.D.	Charles Reiten, R	1986, Apr.	Pompano Beach, Fla.	*James Soderlund	1984, Sept.
Mobile, Ala.	Arthur Outlaw, N-P	1989, July	Pontiac, Mich.	Wallace Holland, N-P	1985, Nov.
Modesto, Cal.	*Garth Lipsky	1977, Jan.	Port Arthur, Tex.	*George Dibrell	1962, Oct.
Monroe, La.	Robert Powell, D	1988, Apr.	Port Huron, Mich.	*Gerald R. Bouchard	1965, June
Montclair, N.J.	*Bertrand Kendall	1980, Sept.	Portage, Mich.	*Donald Ziemke	1974, Aug.
Montebello, Cal.	*Joseph Goeden	1980, May	Portland, Me.	*Stephen Honey.	1980, Sept.
Monterey Park, Cal.	*Lloyd de Llamas	1976, Sept.	Portland, Ore.	Bud Clark, N-P	1988, Nov.
Montgomery, Ala.	Emory Folmar, R	1987, Nov.	Portsmouth, Oh.	*Barry Feldman	1977, Jan.
Mt. Lebanon, Pa.	*James Cain	1982, Apr.	Portsmouth, Va.	*George Hanbury	1982, June
Mt. Prospect, Ill.	*Terrance Burghard.	1978, Nov.	Poughkeepsie, N.Y.	*William J. Theysohn	1982, Mar.
Mt. Vernon, N.Y.	Thomas E. Sharpe, D	1987, Nov.	Prichard, Ala.	John W. Smith, R	1988, July
Mountain View, Cal.	*Bruce Liedstrand.	1976, June	Providence, R.I.	Joseph Paolino Jr., D	1986, Nov.
Muncie, Ind.	James Carey, D	1987, Nov.	Provo, Ut.	Jim Ferguson, D	1985, Nov.
Muskegon, Mich.	*Robert Hagemann	1983, Sept.	Pueblo, Col.	*John Bramble.	1984, Apr.
Muskogee, Okla.	*Walter Beckham	1984, Feb.	Quincy, Ill.	Verne Hagstrom, D	1989, Apr.
Napa, Cal.	*vacant		Quincy, Mass.	Francis X. McCauley, R.	1985, Nov.
Naperville, Ill.	*George Smith.	1978, June	Racine, Wis.	Stephen Olson, N-P	1987, Apr.
Nashua, N.H.	James Donchess, D.	1987, Nov.	Raleigh, N.C.	*Dempsey Benton.	1983, Dec.
Nashville, Tenn.	Richard Fulton, D	1987, Aug.	Rapid City, S.D.	Arthur La Croix, R.	1987, May
National City, Cal.	*Tom McCabe	1979, Feb.	Reading, Pa.	Karen Miller, D.	1987, Nov.
New Bedford, Mass.	Brian Lawler, D	1985, Oct.	Redding, Cal.	*Robert E. Courtney	1982, Dec.
New Britain, Conn.	William J. McNamara, D	1985, Nov.	Redlands, Cal.	*John E. Holmes	1983, Apr.
New Brunswick, N.J.	John Lynch, D	1986, Nov.	Redondo Beach, Cal.	*Timothy Casey	1981, Nov.
New Castle, Pa.	Dale W. Yoho, R	1987, Nov.	Redwood City, Cal.	*James M. Smith	1982, Feb.
New Haven, Conn.	Biagio DiLieto, D.	1985, Nov.	Reno, Nev.	*Chris Cherches.	1980, Nov.
New London, Conn.	*C.F. Driscoll.	1969, May	Revere, Mass.	George V. Colella, D	1985, Nov.
New Orleans, La.	Ernest Morial, D.	1986, Feb.	Richardson, Tex.	Martha Ritter, R	1987, Apr.
New Rochelle, N.Y.	*C. Samuel Kissinger	1975, Apr.	Richfield, Minn.	*John Cartwright	1983, Oct.
New York, N.Y.	Edward Koch, D	1985, Nov.	Richmond, Cal.	*James M. Fales Jr.	1983, May
Newark, N.J.	Kenneth Gibson, D	1986, May	Richmond, Ind.	Frank Waltermann, D	1987, Nov.
Newark, Oh.	William Moore, R	1987, Nov.	Richmond, Va.	*Manuel Deese	1979, Jan.
Newport, R.I.	*John Connors Jr.	1981, Mar.	Riverside, Cal.	*Douglas Weiford	1980, Mar.
Newport Beach, Cal.	*Robert L. Wynn.	1971, Aug.	Roanoke, Va.	Noel Taylor, R.	1988, May
Newport News, Va.	*Robert T. Williams	1981, Feb.	Rochester, Minn.	*Steven Kvenvold	1979, June
Newton, Mass.	Theodore Mann, R	1985, Nov.	Rochester, N.Y.	*Peter Korn	1980, Mar.
Niagara Falls, N.Y.	*Nicholas Merchelos	1984, June	Rock Hill, S.C.	*Joe Lanford.	1979, July
Norfolk, Va.	*Julian Hirst	1976, Apr.	Rockford, Ill.	John McNamara, D	1989, Apr.
Norman, Okla.	*James D. Crosby	1976, Feb.	Rockville, Md.	Viola Hovsepian, N-P	1985, Nov.
Norristown, Pa.	John Marberger, R	1985, Nov.	Rome, N.Y.	Carl Eilenberg, R	1987, Nov.
North Charleston, S.C.	John Bourne Jr., R	1986, May	Rosemead, Cal.	*Frank Tripepi	1974, Oct.
North Las Vegas,	*Michael Dyal	1982, May	Roseville, Mich.	*Thomas Van Damme	1983, Dec.
No. Little Rock, Ark.	Terry Hartwick, D	1988, May	Roseville, Minn.	*James Andre	1974, May
Norwalk, Cal.	*Ray Gibbs.	1984, Feb.	Roswell, N.M.	*James Whitford Jr.	1982, Aug.
Norwalk, Conn.	William Collins, D	1985, Nov.	Royal Oak, Mich.	*William Baldridge.	1975, Sept.
Norwich, Conn.	*Charles Whitty	1973, Feb.	Sacramento, Cal.	*Walter Slipe.	1976, Mar.
Novato, Cal.	*Phillip J. Brown	1974, May	Saginaw, Mich.	*Thomas Dalton	1978, Nov.
Oak Lawn, Ill.	Ernest Kolb, R	1989, Apr.	St. Clair Shores, Mich.	*Roy Stype.	1982, May
Oak Park, Ill.	*Ralph De Santis	1980, July	St. Cloud, Minn.	Robert Huston, N-P	1989, Nov.
Oak Ridge, Tenn.	*M. Lyle Lacy 3d	1980, Dec.	St. Joseph, Mo.	*Hal Kooistra	1983, Sept.
Oakland, Cal.	*Henry L. Gardner	1981, June	St. Louis, Mo.	Vincent Schoemehl, D	1989, Apr.
Oceanside, Cal.	*Suzanne Foucault	1982, Nov.	St. Louis Park, Minn.	*James Brimeyer	1980, Aug.
Odessa, Tex.	*John Harrison	1982, Aug.	St. Paul, Minn.	George Latimer, D	1985, Nov.
Ogden, Ut.	Robert A. Madsen, N-P	1985, Nov.	St. Petersburg, Fla.	*Alan Harvey	1980, Mar.
Oklahoma City, Okla.	*Scott Johnson	1981, Dec.	Salem, Mass.	Anthony V. Salvo, D	1985, Nov.
Omaha, Neb.	Michael Boyle, D	1989, May	Salem, Ore.	*Russ Abolt	1982, Jan.
Ontario, Cal.	R.E. Ellingwood, N-P	1986, Apr.	Salina, Kan.	*Rufus L. Nye	1979, May
Orange, Cal.	*J. William Little	1984, Jan.	Salinas, Cal.	James B. Barnes, R.	1987, June
Orange, N.J.	Paul Monacelli, D	1988, July	Salt Lake City, Ut.	Ted Wilson, N-P	1987, Nov.
Orlando, Fla.	Bill Frederick, D	1988, Sept.	San Angelo, Tex.	*Stephen Brown.	1982, May
Oshkosh, Wis.	*W. O. Frueh.	1976, Aug.	San Antonio, Tex.	*Louis J. Fox.	1982, Jan.
Overland Park, Kan.	*Donald Pipes	1977, June	San Bernardino, Cal.	Evlyn Wilcox, N-P	1989, Mar.
Owensboro, Ky.	*Max Rhoads	1983, July	San Bruno, Cal.	*Gerald Minford	1971, Dec.
Oxnard, Cal.	*James Frandsen.	1984, Aug.	San Diego, Cal.	*Ray Blair Jr.	1978, May
Pacifica, Cal.	*David Finigan	1981, May	San Francisco, Cal.	Dianne Feinstein, D	1987, Nov.
Palm Springs, Cal.	*Norman R. King	1979, Dec.	San Jose, Cal.	*Gerald Newfarmer.	1983, July
Palo Alto, Cal.	*William Zaner.	1979, Sept.	San Leandro, Cal.	*Lee Riordan.	1976, Apr.
Park Ridge, Ill.	*George E. Hagman	1984, July	San Mateo, Cal.	*Richard Delong.	1976, Sept.
Parkersburg, W. Va.	Pat S. Pappas, R	1985, Nov.	San Rafael, Cal.	*vacant	
Parma, Oh.	John Petruska	1987, Nov.	Sandusky, Oh.	*Frank Link.	1972, Jan.
Pasadena, Cal.	*Donald F. McIntyre.	1973, June	Sandy, Ut.	Lawrence P. Smith, R.	1985, Nov.

City	Name	Term
Santa Ana, Cal.	*A. J. Wilson	1980, July
Santa Barbara, Cal.	*Richard Thomas	1977, Jan.
Santa Clara, Cal.	*Donald Von Raesfeld	1962, Feb.
Santa Cruz, Cal.	*Richard Wilson	1981, June
Santa Fe, N.M.	Louis Montano, D	1986, Mar.
Santa Maria, Cal.	*Robert Grogan	1963, Jan.
Santa Monica, Cal.	*John Jalili	1984, Dec.
Santa Rosa, Cal.	Kenneth Blackman	1969, July
Sarasota, Fla.	*Kenneth Thompson	1950, Feb.
Savannah, Ga.	*Arthur A. Mendonsa	1962, July
Schenectady, N.Y.	Karen Johnson, D	1987, Nov.
Scottsdale, Ariz.	*Roy Pederson	1980, Mar.
Scranton, Pa.	James McNulty, D	1985, Nov.
Seattle, Wash.	Charles Royer, D	1985, Nov.
Shaker Heights, Oh.	Stephen Alfred, N-P	1987, Nov.
Sheboygan, Wis.	Richard Schneider, N-P	1989, Apr.
Shreveport, La.	John Hussey, D	1986, Sept.
Simi Valley, Cal.	*Lin Koester	1979, Sept.
Sioux City, la.	*J.R. Castner	1982, Sept.
Sioux Falls, S.D.	Joe Cooper, R	1989, Apr.
Skokie, Ill.	*Robert Eppley	1979, Jan.
Somerville, Mass.	Eugene Brune, D	1985, Nov.
South Bend, Ind.	Roger Parent, D	1987, Nov.
South Gate, Cal.	Herbert Cranton, N-P	1986, Apr.
Southfield, Mich.	*Robert Block	1985, Jan.
Sparks, Nev.	*Patricia Thompson	1983,Sept.
Spartanburg, S.C.	*Wayne Bowers	1984, Sept.
Spokane, Wash.	*Terry Novak	1978, July
Springfield, Ill.	J. Michael Houston, R	1987, Apr.
Springfield, Mass	Richard Neal	1985, Nov.
Springfield, Mo.	*Don G. Busch	1971, Oct.
Springfield, Oh.	*Thomas Bay	1978, Sept.
Springfield, Ore.	*Steven Burkett	1980, Feb.
Stamford, Conn.	Thom Seriana, D	1985, Nov.
Sterling Hts., Mich.	*Barry Feldman	1982, Nov.
Stillwater, Okla.	*Carl Weinaug	1983, Apr.
Stockton, Cal.	*S.E. Griffith	1984, Dec.
Stratford, Conn.	*Ronald Owens	1984, July
Suffolk, Va.	*John Rowe Jr.	1981, Mar.
Sunnyvale, Cal.	*Thomas Lewcock	1980, Apr.
Syracuse, N.Y.	Lee Alexander, D	1985, Nov.
Tacoma, Wash.	*Erling O. Mork	1975, June
Tallahassee, Fla.	*Daniel A. Kleman	1974, Aug.
Tampa, Fla.	Bob Martinez, N-P	1987, Mar.
Taunton, Mass.	Richard Johnson, D	1985, Nov.
Taylor, Mich.	Cameron Priebe, D	1985, Nov.
Teaneck, N.J.	*Werner H. Schmid	1959, Mar.
Tempe, Ariz.	Harry E. Mitchell, D	1986, Mar.
Temple, Tex.	*Barney Knight	1978, Dec.
Terre Haute, Ind.	P. Pete Chalos, D	1987, Nov.
Thornton, Col.	Margaret Carpenter, N-P	1987, Nov.
Thousand Oaks, Cal.	*Grant Brimhall	1978, Jan.
Titusville, Fla.	*Norman Hickey	1974, June
Toledo, Oh.	*C.E. Riser	1985, May
Topeka, Kan.	Douglas Wright, N-P	1989, Apr.
Torrance, Cal.	*Leroy J. Jackson	1983, Jan.
Trenton, N.J.	Arthur Holland, N-P	1986, May
Troy, Mich.	*Frank Gerstenecker	1970, Feb.
Troy, N.Y.	*John P. Buckley	1972, June
Tucson, Ariz.	*Joel Valdez	1974, May
Tulsa, Okla.	Terry Young	1986, Apr.
Tuscaloosa, Ala.	Alvin DuPont, D	1989, July
Tyler, Tex.	*Gary Gwyn	1982, Nov.
Union City, N.J.	William Musto, D	1986, May
Univ. City, Mo.	*Frank Ollendorff	1980, Mar.
Upland, Cal.	*S. Lee Travers	1974, June
Upper Arlington, Oh.	*Richard King	1984, Aug.
Urbana, Ill.	Jeffrey Markland, R	1989, Apr.
Utica, N.Y.	Louis La Polla, R	1985, Nov.
Vallejo, Cal.	*Ted McDonell	1979, Jan.
Vancouver, Wash.	*Paul Grattet	1980, Aug.
Victoria, Tex.	*James J. Miller	1980, June
Vineland, N.J.	James E. Romano, R	1988, May
Virginia Beach, Va.	*Thomas Muelhenbeck	1982, June
Waco, Tex.	*David F. Smith Jr.	1971, Sept.
Walnut Creek, Cal.	*Thomas Dunne	1972, May
Waltham, Mass.	Arthur J. Clark, N-P	1985, Nov.
Warren, Mich.	James Randlett, N-P	1985, Nov.
Warren, Oh.	Daniel Sferra, D	1987, Nov.
Warwick, R.I.	Francis X. Flaherty, D	1986, Nov.
Wash, D.C.	Marion Barry, D	1987, Nov.

City	Name	Term
Waterbury, Conn.	Edward Bergin, D	1985, Nov.
Waterloo, la.	Delman L. Bowers, R	1985, Nov.
Waukegan, Ill.	Robert Sabonjian, R	1989, Apr.
Waukesha, Wis.	Paul Keenan, N-P	1986, Apr.
Wausau, Wis.	John Kannenberg, N-P	1988, Apr.
Wauwatosa, Wis.	James Brundahl, N-P	1988, Apr.
W. Covina, Cal.	*Herman Fast	1976, Aug.
W. Hartford, Conn.	*vacant	
W. Haven, Conn.	Lawrence Minichino, R	1985, Nov.
W. New York, N.J.	Anthony DeFino, D	1987, May
W. Orange, N.J.	Samuel Spina, D	1986, May
W. Palm Beach, Fla.	*Richard Simmons	1969, Nov.
Westland, Mich.	Charles Pickering Jr., N-P	1985, Nov.
Westminster, Cal.	*Chris Christiansen	1983, June
Westminster, Col.	*Bill Christopher	1978, June
Wheaton, Ill.	*Donald Rose	1980, Nov.
Wheeling, W. Va.	*F. Wayne Barte	1979, Nov.
White Plains, N.Y.	Alfred Del Vecchio, R	1985, Nov.
Whittier, Cal.	*Tom Mauk	1980, Sept.
Wichita, Kan.	Robert Finch, act.	1985, Apr.
Wichita Falls, Tex.	*James Berzina	1983, June
Wilkes-Barre, Pa.	Thomas McLaughlin, D	1987, Nov.
Williamsport, Pa.	Stephen Lucasi, R	1987, Nov.
Wilmington, Del.	Daniel Frawley, D	1988, Nov.
Wilmington, N.C.	*William B. Farris	1983, May
Winston-Salem, N.C.	*Bryce A. Stuart	1980, Jan.
Woonsocket, R.I.	Gaston Ayotte Jr., D	1985, Nov.
Worcester, Mass.	*William Mulford	1985, Feb.
Wyoming, Mich.	*James Sheeran	1979, July
Yakima, Wash.	*Richard Zais Jr.	1979, Jan.
Yonkers, N.Y.	*Rodney H. Irwin	1984, Feb.
York, Pa.	William Althaus, R	1985, Nov.
Youngstown, Oh.	George Vukovich, D	1985, Nov.
Yuma, Ariz.	Philip Clark, R	1985, Dec.
Zanesville, Oh.	Donald Lewis Mason, R	1987, Nov.

Canadian Cities

(as of Aug. 15, 1985)

City	Name	Term
Calgary, Alta.	Ralph Klein	1986, Oct.
Charlottetown, P.E.I.	Frank Moran	1986, Nov.
Edmonton, Alta.	Laurence Decore	1986, Oct.
Fredericton, N.B.	Elbridge Wilkins	1986, May
Guelph, Ont.	Norman Jary	1985, Nov.
Halifax, N.S.	Ronald Wallace	1985, Oct.
Hamilton, Ont.	Robert Morrow	1985, Nov.
Hull, Que.	Michel Legere	1985, Nov.
Kingston, Ont.	John Gerretsen	1985, Nov.
Kitchener, Ont.	Domenic P. D. Cardillo	1985, Nov.
London, Ont.	Al Gleeson	1985, Nov.
Mississauga, Ont.	Hazel McCallion	1985, Nov.
Moncton, N.B.	J. S. Rideout	1986, May
Montreal, Que.	Jean Drapeau	1985, Nov.
North York, Ont.	Mel Lastman	1985, Nov.
Oshawa, Ont.	Ailan Pilkey	1985, Nov.
Ottawa, Ont.	Mrs. Marion Dewar	1985, Nov.
Peterborough, Ont.	Robert J. Barker	1985, Nov.
Quebec, Que.	Jean Pelletier	1985, Nov.
Regina, Sask.	Larry Schneider	1985, Oct.
Saint John, N.B.	Elsie Wayne	1986, May
St. John's, Nfld.	John Murphy	1985, Nov.
Saskatoon, Sask.	Clifford Wright	1985, Oct.
Sherbrooke, Que.	Jacques O'Bready	1985, Nov.
Sudbury, Ont.	Peter Wong	1985, Nov.
Toronto, Ont.	Art Eggleton	1985, Nov.
Vancouver, B.C.	Michael Harcourt	1986, Nov.
Victoria, B.C.	Peter Pollen	1985, Nov.
Waterloo, Ont.	Mrs. Marjorie Carroll	1985, Nov.
Windsor, Ont.	Mrs. Elizabeth Kishkon	1985, Nov.
Winnipeg, Man.	Bill Norrie	1986, Nov.

UNITED STATES POPULATION

Changing Population Patterns

By John G. Keane
Director, U.S. Bureau of the Census

On January 1, 1985, the estimated resident population was 237.2 million people, a 4.7 percent increase over the 1980 census count of 226.5 million.

The South and West had about 90 percent of the growth from April 1, 1980 to July 1, 1984. Population increased 8.3 percent in the West, 6.9 percent in the South, 0.4 percent in the Midwest, and 1.2 percent in the Northeast. Alaska led the fastest growing states with a 24.4 percent gain, followed by Nevada, Utah, Florida, Texas, Arizona, Colorado, New Mexico, Oklahoma and Wyoming.

Rapid reversals also were evident; in 1983-1984, the energy-producing states of Oklahoma, Wyoming and West Virginia were estimated to have lost population.

Reversing a trend that appeared in the 1970s, the metropolitan areas are growing faster than the rest of the country. Estimates show that the population grew 2.4 percent, or 4 million, from 1980 to 1982 in metropolitan areas, and 1.9 percent, or 1 million, in nonmetropolitan areas. While the annual rate for metropolitan growth remained at about 1 percent, the annual nonmetro rate fell from 1.3 percent in the 1970s to just 0.8 percent.

A recent report on national population projections suggests that the country will continue to grow more slowly and will virtually cease growing halfway through the 21st century. These projections assume a small rise in childbearing, steady increases in life expectancy, and net legal immigration that will remain at recent levels.

An Aging Nation

Meanwhile, the nation's population under age five in 1983 was the largest in 15 years. An estimated 17.8 million children under five were reported in 1983, up 9 percent since the 1980 census. With the rate of childbearing nearly stable, the under-five growth rate is attributed almost entirely to an increase in the number of women in their prime childbearing years.

Among the various population groups, the fastest growth was among 35 to 44 years olds. This group increased by 14.8 percent in 1980-83 to 29.5 million and will continue to grow the fastest for some time. The sharpest decline, 9.9 percent, was among 14 to 17 years olds.

Overall, the nation's population continues to age. The median age in 1983 was 30.9 years, an all-time high. It is projected to continue upward to 36.3 in 2000, to 40.8 in 2030, and to 42.8 years by 2080. Life expectancy is projected to increase from 74.3 years in 1982, to 76.7 years in 2000, and 81 years in 2080.

On an economic note, the ratio of the working-age population—those 18 to 64—to the retirement age population soon will begin an unprecedented decline. The nation had 5.3 people of working age in 1982 for every person 65 or older. The ratio is projected to drop to 4.7 in 2000, to 2.7 in 2030, and to 2.4 in 2080.

Households and Family Income

More American women are delaying childbirth until their thirties. The birth rate among women 30 to 34 years old showed an increase between 1980 and 1983, from 60 to 69 births per 1,000 women, while no other age group recorded a significant change.

Mothers between 30 and 44 years old were more likely than younger mothers to have completed at least one year of college, live in families with at least $25,000 annual income, and, if employed, hold professional jobs.

The Bureau reported that in March 1984, the nation had 85.4 million households, 1.5 million more than a year earlier. The increase was about the same as in the 1970s, but sharply higher than the 391,000 recorded during the 1982-83 recession.

Families accounted for 73 percent of all households, just slightly lower than in 1980. One out of every four households added since 1980 was a family with no husband present. In 1984, there were 50.1 million family households with married couples, 9.9 million with female householders (no husband present), and 2 million with male householders (no wife present). The average number of people per household fell to a new low of 2.71 in 1984, resuming a decline that began in the mid-1960s.

In looking at the economic aspects of family households, a Census Bureau study found that in 1981, wives were the main breadwinners among 6 million couples, or 12 percent of all couples. The wife was the sole provider for about two million of these couples. While the study found that wives who outearned their husbands, in general, were highly educated—25 percent had four or more years of college—the wife often became the primary breadwinner because of the husband's employment difficulties.

The latest data released by the Bureau showed that full-time working couples earned an average of $34,560 in 1981. Wives working full-time averaged $13,070 compared with $23,800 for husbands. And the study found that 55 percent of all working wives had at least one child under age 18.

Household income after taxes averaged $18,910 in 1982, a gain of 1.7 percent over 1981 after adjustment for inflation. The increase in after-tax income followed a 2.6 percent decline between 1980 and 1981. The report attributed the gain to the federal income tax reductions resulting from the Economic Recovery Tax Act of 1981, since there was little change in household income before taxes. The study found that for the three out of four households that paid a federal income tax, the average tax was $4,270.

Real median family income in 1983 increased 1.6 pecent over the 1982 figure to $24,580, the first increase in four years. The growth in family income reversed declines in the three previous years, the largest being a 5.5 percent drop in 1979-80.

Over 35 Million Live in Poverty

The poverty rate of 15.2 percent was not significantly changed from 1982, but there was some evidence of an increase in total persons in poverty—35.3 million in 1983 compared with 34.4 million in 1982. The average unemployment rate in 1983 was 9.6 percent, about the same as the previous year.

During the year, the Bureau issued estimates of the number of people in poverty if one were to include the value of selected noncash benefits. When dollar values are assigned to noncash benefits such as food stamps, school lunches, public housing, Medicaid, and Medicare, estimates of the poverty population are lower than the offical figures.

The valuation of noncash benefits would lower the poverty estimates by a greater extent for groups most likely to receive the benefits. These groups include blacks, the elderly, and persons in female-maintained families. The largest relative reduction occurs for persons 65 years and over, since nearly all of them are covered by Medicare.

Survey of Income and Program Participation

During the year, the Bureau published the first results from the Survey of Income and Program Participation (SIPP), which collects monthly information on income, labor force, experience, and participation in major government programs. The first report presents average monthly data for the third quarter of 1983, and showed that about 30 percent of the 224.3 million people living in non-farm households took part in programs ranging from Social Security to assistance programs such as Medicaid and food stamps.

The two largest means-tested programs (in which recipients must demonstrate some level of need) were food stamps, for 18.7 million people, and Medicaid, covering 17.5 million persons. The two largest programs (which are not means-tested) are Social Security, whose benefits went to 31.7 million persons, and Medicare, which covered some 26.7 million.

Foreign-Born Residents

The Bureau counted just over 14 million foreign-born residents in the 1980 census, an increase of 4.4 million from 1970.

Of the recent arrivals, 1.3 came from Latin America and 1.2 million from Asia. More than half the newcomers from

Latin America arrived from Mexico. The Bureau found 2,199,221 residents of the U.S. who were born in Mexico. A distant second on the list of homelands was Germany (849,384 residents), followed by Canada, Italy, and Cuba. Most residents born in Vietnam (231,120), Laos (54,881), and Cambodia (20,175) arrived in the U.S. from 1975 to 1980, as was the case for one-third of the residents born in Mexico.

For the first time in a census, Asian Indians were counted as a separate group. They numbered 387,223, or 11.2 percent of the total Asian population.

The census found that 25 Asian and Pacific Islander groups were primarily concentrated in the West, although there were substantial numbers in New York and New Jersey.

The 1980 census data concerning people born in 163 countries indicated that the foreign-born are similar to native-born Americans in regard to college education and professional occupations. About 16 percent of each group 25 years and over were college graduates. And about 12 percent of employed persons in each group were in professional positions.

Median household income for the foreign-born was $14,588 compared with $17,010 for the U.S.-born. However, there were sharp variations by country of birth, such as India, $25,644; Iran, $11,344; and Nigeria, $6,927.

1990 Census

The Census Bureau already is laying the foundation for the 1990 decennial census, which will mark the 200th anniversary of the Nation's first census. Test censuses have been completed in two cities, and additional ones will be conducted in other areas during the next few years.

The Census Bureau is trying out a number of innovations, including increased automation, improved management and training of temporary workers, specific techniques for achieving the most complete counts possible, and public information programs tailored to specific groups.

At the same time, census planners face the problem of balancing the growing needs of an information-hungry society with the demands involved in acquiring more information.

Readers with suggestions and comments about the 1990 census may write Peter A. Bounpane, Assistant Director for Demographic Censuses, Bureau fo the Census, Room 3049-3, Washington, D.C. 20233.

Resident Population by Sex, Race, Residence, and Median Age: 1790 to 1982

Source: U.S. Bureau of the Census (thousands, except as indicated)

Date	Sex Male	Sex Female	Race White	Race Black Number	Race Black Percent	Race Other	Residence Urban	Residence Rural	Median Age (years) All races	Median Age (years) White	Median Age (years) Black
Conterminous U.S.[1]											
1790 (Aug. 2)...	NA	NA	3,172	757	19.3	NA	202	3,728	NA	NA	NA
1810 (Aug. 6)...	NA	NA	5,862	1,378	19.0	NA	525	6,714	NA	16.0	NA
1820 (Aug. 7)...	4,897	4,742	7,867	1,772	18.4	NA	693	8,945	16.7	16.5	17.2
1840 (June 1)...	8,689	8,381	14,196	2,874	16.8	NA	1,845	15,224	17.8	17.9	17.3
1860 (June 1)...	16,085	15,358	26,923	4,442	14.1	79	6,217	25,227	19.4	19.7	17.7
1870 (June 1)...	19,494	19,065	33,589	4,880	12.7	89	9,902	28,656	20.2	20.4	18.5
1880 (June 1)...	25,519	24,637	43,403	6,581	13.1	172	14,130	36,026	20.9	21.4	18.0
1890 (June 1)...	32,237	30,711	55,101	7,489	11.9	358	22,106	40,841	22.0	22.5	17.8
1900 (June 1)...	38,816	37,178	66,809	8,834	11.6	351	30,160	45,835	22.9	23.4	19.4
1920 (Jan. 1)...	53,900	51,810	94,821	10,463	9.9	427	54,158	51,553	25.3	25.6	22.3
1930 (Apr. 1)...	62,137	60,638	110,287	11,891	9.7	597	68,955	53,820	26.4	26.9	23.5
1940 (Apr. 1)...	66,062	65,608	118,215	12,866	9.8	589	74,424	57,246	29.0	29.5	25.3
United States											
1950 (Apr. 1)...	75,187	76,139	135,150	15,045	9.9	1,131	96,847	54,479	30.2	30.7	26.2
1960 (Apr. 1)...	88,331	90,992	158,832	18,872	10.5	1,620	125,269	54,054	29.5	30.3	23.5
1970 (Apr. 1)[2]..	98,926	104,309	178,098	22,581	11.1	2,557	149,325	53,887	28.0	28.9	22.4
1980 (Apr. 1)[3]..	110,053	116,493	194,811	26,631	11.8	5,104	167,051	59,495	30.0	30.9	24.9
1981 (July 1, est)	111,444	117,904	196,664	27,153	11.8	5,530	NA	NA	30.3	31.2	25.2
1982 (July 1, est)	112,498	119,035	198,108	27,589	11.9	5,837	NA	NA	30.6	31.5	25.5

(NA) Not available. (1) Excludes Alaska and Hawaii. (2) The revised 1970 resident population count is 203,302,031, which incorporates changes due to errors found after tabulations were completed. The race and sex data shown here reflect the official 1970 census count while the residence data come from the tabulated count. (3) The race data shown for April 1, 1980 have been modified.

Projections of the Total Population by Sex and Age: 1985 to 2000

Source: U.S. Bureau of the Census (thousands)

Sex and age	Lowest series[1] 1985	Lowest series[1] 1990	Lowest series[1] 2000	Middle series 1985	Middle series 1990	Middle series 2000	Highest series 1985	Highest series 1990	Highest series 2000
Total population	237,366	245,507	255,638	238,648	249,731	267,990	240,364	254,686	282,339
Male..............	115,515	119,455	124,349	116,124	121,498	130,379	116,953	123,904	137,372
Under 5 years old ...	9,221	8,957	7,639	9,453	9,831	9,024	9,711	10,576	10,528
5–17 years old.....	22,595	22,707	22,966	22,671	23,077	25,465	22,815	23,603	27,903
18–24 years old	14,522	12,992	12,284	14,587	13,115	12,523	14,661	13,291	12,910
25–44 years old	36,544	40,248	39,417	36,680	40,594	40,194	36,950	41,234	41,594
45–64 years old	21,202	22,056	28,871	21,259	22,230	29,439	21,319	22,411	30,124
65 years old and over..	11,430	12,497	13,172	11,473	12,652	13,734	11,497	12,790	14,313
Female	121,851	126,053	131,289	122,525	128,234	137,611	123,411	130,782	144,966
Under 5 years old	8,790	8,538	7,284	9,009	9,369	8,601	9,259	10,083	10,036
5–17 years old.....	21,609	21,700	21,928	21,681	22,045	24,298	21,818	22,554	26,637
18–24 years old	14,050	12,516	11,819	14,127	12,663	12,067	14,238	12,868	12,479
25–44 years old	36,937	40,352	39,007	37,099	40,758	39,912	37,379	41,464	41,476
45–64 years old	23,333	24,059	30,881	23,408	24,251	31,434	23,478	24,434	32,030
65 years old and over..	17,132	18,889	20,369	17,200	19,147	21,302	17,241	19,379	22,309

(1) For the series shown the following assumptions were made about fertility (ultimate lifetime births per woman), mortality (life expectancy in 2050), and immigration (yearly net immigration). Lowest series: 1.6 births per woman, 76.7 years, and 250,000 net immigration. Middle series: 1.9 births per woman, 79.6 years, and 450,000 net immigration. Highest series: 2.3 births per woman, 83.3 years, and 750,000 net immigration. Zero migration series: 1.9 births per woman and 76.9 years.

Congressional Apportionment

	1980	1970		1980	1970		1980	1970		1980	1970		1980	1970
Ala..	7	7	Ida..	2	2	Minn..	8	8	N.D..	1	1	Vt...	1	1
Alas..	1	1	Ill...	22	24	Miss..	5	5	Oh..	21	23	Va...	10	10
Ariz.	5	4	Ind..	10	11	Mo..	9	10	Okla.	6	6	Wash..	8	7
Ark..	4	4	Ia...	6	6	Mon..	2	2	Ore..	5	4	W. Va.	4	4
Cal..	45	43	Kan..	5	5	Neb..	3	3	Pa..	23	25	Wis...	9	9
Col..	6	5	Ky...	7	7	Nev..	2	1	R.I...	2	2	Wy...	1	1
Conn..	6	6	La...	8	8	N.H..	2	2	S.C..	6	6			
Del..	1	1	Me..	2	2	N.J..	14	15	S.D..	1	2	Totals.	435	435
Fla...	19	15	Md...	8	8	N.M..	3	2	Tenn..	9	8			
Ga...	10	10	Mass..	11	12	N.Y...	34	39	Tex...	27	24			
Ha...	2	2	Mich..	18	19	N.C...	11	11	Ut...	3	2			

The chief reason the Constitution provided for a census of the population every 10 years was to give a basis for apportionment of representatives among the states. This apportionment largely determines the number of electoral votes allotted to each state.

The number of representatives of each state in Congress is determined by the state's population, but each state is entitled to one representative regardless of population. A Congressional apportionment has been made after each decennial census except that of 1920.

Under provisions of a law that became effective Nov. 15, 1941, apportionment of representatives is made by the method of equal proportions. In the application of this method, the apportionment is made so that the average population per representative has the least possible variation between one state and any other. The first House of Representatives, in 1789, had 65 members, as provided by the Constitution. As the population grew, the number of representatives was increased but the total membership has been fixed at 435 since the apportionment based on the 1910 census.

U.S. Area and Population: 1790 to 1980

Source: U.S. Bureau of the Census

	Area (square miles)			Population			
Census date	Gross	Land	Water	Number	Per sq. mile of land	Increase over preceding census Number	%
1980 (Apr. 1).........	3,618,770	3,539,289	79,481	226,545,805	64.0	23,243,774	11.4
1970 (Apr. 1).........	3,618,770	3,536,855	81,915	203,302,031	57.5	23,978,856	13.4
1960 (Apr. 1).........	3,618,770	3,540,911	77,859	179,323,175	50.6	27,997,377	18.5
1950 (Apr. 1).........	3,618,770	3,552,206	66,564	151,325,798	42.6	19,161,229	14.5
1940 (Apr. 1).........	3,618,770	3,554,608	64,162	132,164,569	37.2	8,961,945	7.3
1930 (Apr. 1).........	3,618,770	3,551,608	67,162	123,202,624	34.7	17,181,087	16.2
1920 (Jan. 1).........	3,618,770	3,546,931	71,839	106,021,537	29.9	13,793,041	15.0
1910 (Apr. 15)........	3,618,770	3,547,045	71,725	92,228,496	26.0	16,016,328	21.0
1900 (June 1)	3,618,770	3,547,314	71,456	76,212,168	21.5	13,232,402	21.0
1890 (June 1)	3,612,299	3,540,705	71,594	62,979,766	17.8	12,790,557	25.5
1880 (June 1)	3,612,299	3,540,705	71,594	50,189,209	14.2	11,630,838	30.2
1870 (June 1)	3,612,299	3,540,705	71,594	38,558,371	10.9	7,115,050	22.6
1860 (June 1)	3,021,295	2,969,640	51,655	31,443,321	10.6	8,251,445	35.6
1850 (June 1)	2,991,655	2,940,042	51,613	23,191,876	7.9	6,122,423	35.9
1840 (June 1)	1,792,552	1,749,462	43,090	17,069,453	9.8	4,203,433	32.7
1830 (June 1)	1,792,552	1,749,462	43,090	12,866,020	7.4	3,227,567	33.5
1820 (June 1)	1,792,552	1,749,462	43,090	9,638,453	5.5	2,398,572	33.1
1810 (Aug. 6)	1,722,685	1,681,828	40,857	7,239,881	4.3	1,931,398	36.4
1800 (Aug. 4)	891,364	864,746	26,618	5,308,483	6.1	1,379,269	35.1
1790 (Aug. 2)	891,364	864,746	26,618	3,929,214	4.5	—	—

NOTE: Percent changes are computed on basis of change in population since preceding census date, and period covered therefore is not always exactly 10 years.

Population density figures given for various years represent the area within the boundaries of the United States which was under the jurisdiction on date in question, including in some cases considerable areas not organized or settled and not covered by the census. In 1870, for example, Alaska was not covered by the census.

Revised figure of 39,818,449 for the 1870 population includes adjustments for undernumeration in the Southern states. On the basis of the revised figure, the population increased by 8,375,128, or 26.6 percent between 1860 and 1870, and by 10,370,760, or 26.1 percent between 1870 and 1880.

Black and Hispanic Population by States

Source: U.S. Bureau of the Census (1980)

	Black	Hispanic		Black	Hispanic		Black	Hispanic
Ala......	996,335	33,299	La......	1,238,241	99,134	Okla.	204,674	57,419
Alas......	13,643	9,507	Me......	3,128	5,005	Ore......	37,060	65,847
Ariz......	74,977	440,701	Md.	958,150	64,746	Pa........	1,046,810	153,961
Ark......	373,768	17,904	Mass.....	221,279	141,043	R.I.......	27,584	19,707
Cal......	1,819,281	4,544,331	Mich.	1,199,023	162,440	S.C......	948,623	33,426
Col......	101,703	339,717	Minn.	53,344	32,123	S.D......	2,144	4,023
Conn.....	217,433	124,499	Miss......	887,206	24,731	Tenn.....	725,942	34,077
Del......	95,845	9,661	Mo......	514,276	51,653	Tex......	1,710,175	2,985,824
D.C......	448,906	17,679	Mon......	1,786	9,974	Ut.......	9,225	60,302
Fla......	1,342,688	858,158	Neb......	48,390	28,025	Vt.......	1,135	3,304
Ga......	1,465,181	61,260	Nev......	50,999	53,879	Va.......	1,008,668	79,868
Ha......	17,364	71,263	N.H......	3,990	5,587	Wash.....	105,574	120,016
Ida......	2,716	36,615	N.J......	925,066	491,883	W.Va.....	65,051	12,707
Ill........	1,675,398	635,602	N.M......	24,020	477,222	Wis......	182,592	62,972
Ind......	414,785	87,047	N.Y......	2,402,006	1,659,300	Wy.......	3,364	24,499
Ia.......	41,700	25,536	N.C......	1,318,857	56,667	Total	26,495,025	14,608,673
Kan......	126,127	63,339	N.D......	2,568	3,902			
Ky.......	259,477	27,406	Oh.......	1,076,748	119,883			

U.S. Population by Official

(Members of the Armed Forces overseas or

State	1790	1800	1810	1820	1830	1840	1850	1860	1870	1880
Ala. . .	....	1,250	9,046	127,901	309,527	590,756	771,623	964,201	996,992	1,262,505
Alas.. .	....	....	....	....	....	....	....	....	....	33,426
Ariz.. .	....	....	....	....	....	....	....	....	9,658	40,440
Ark. . .	....	....	1,062	14,273	30,388	97,574	209,897	435,450	484,471	802,525
Cal. . .	....	....	....	....	....	....	92,597	379,994	560,247	864,694
Col. . .	....	....	....	....	....	....	....	34,277	39,864	194,327
Conn. .	237,946	251,002	261,942	275,248	297,675	309,978	370,792	460,147	537,454	622,700
Del. . .	59,096	64,273	72,674	72,749	76,748	78,085	91,532	112,216	125,015	146,608
D.C. . .	....	8,144	15,471	23,336	30,261	33,745	51,687	75,080	131,700	177,624
Fla. . .	....	....	....	....	34,730	54,477	87,445	140,424	187,748	269,493
Ga.. .	82,548	162,686	252,433	340,989	516,823	691,392	906,185	1,057,286	1,184,109	1,542,180
Ha.. .	....	....	....	....	....	....	....	....	....	....
Ida. . .	....	....	....	....	....	....	....	....	14,999	32,610
Ill. . . .	....	....	12,282	55,211	157,445	476,183	851,470	1,711,951	2,539,891	3,077,871
Ind. . .	....	5,641	24,520	147,178	343,031	685,866	988,416	1,350,428	1,680,637	1,978,301
Ia. . .	....	....	....	....	....	43,112	192,214	674,913	1,194,020	1,624,615
Kan.. .	....	....	....	....	....	....	....	107,206	364,399	996,096
Ky. . .	73,677	220,955	406,511	564,317	687,917	779,828	982,405	1,155,684	1,321,011	1,648,690
La. . .	....	....	76,556	153,407	215,739	352,411	517,762	708,002	726,915	939,946
Me. . .	96,540	151,719	228,705	298,335	399,455	501,793	583,169	628,279	626,915	648,936
Md.. .	319,728	341,548	380,546	407,350	447,040	470,019	583,034	687,049	780,894	934,943
Mass. .	378,787	422,845	472,040	523,287	610,408	737,699	994,514	1,231,066	1,457,351	1,783,085
Mich.. .	....	....	4,762	8,896	31,639	212,267	397,654	749,113	1,184,059	1,636,937
Minn.. .	....	....	....	....	....	....	6,077	172,023	439,706	780,773
Miss.. .	....	7,600	31,306	75,448	136,621	375,651	606,526	791,305	827,922	1,131,597
Mo. . .	....	....	19,783	66,586	140,455	383,702	682,044	1,182,012	1,721,295	2,168,380
Mon.. .	....	....	....	....	....	....	....	....	20,595	39,159
Neb.. .	....	....	....	....	....	....	....	28,841	122,993	452,402
Nev.. .	....	....	....	....	....	....	....	6,857	42,491	62,266
N.H. . .	141,885	183,858	214,460	244,161	269,328	284,574	317,976	326,073	318,300	346,991
N.J. . .	184,139	211,149	245,562	277,575	320,823	373,306	489,555	672,035	906,096	1,131,116
N.M.. .	....	....	....	....	....	....	61,547	93,516	91,874	119,565
N.Y.. .	340,120	589,051	959,049	1,372,812	1,918,608	2,428,921	3,097,394	3,880,735	4,382,759	5,082,871
N.C.. .	393,751	478,103	555,500	638,829	737,987	753,419	869,039	992,622	1,071,361	1,399,750
N.D.. .	....	....	....	....	....	....	....	....	*2,405	36,909
Oh. . .	....	45,365	230,760	581,434	937,903	1,519,467	1,980,329	2,339,511	2,665,260	3,198,062
Okla. . .	....	....	....	....	....	....	....	....	....	....
Ore. . .	....	....	....	....	....	....	12,093	52,465	90,923	174,768
Pa. . .	434,373	602,365	810,091	1,049,458	1,348,233	1,724,033	2,311,786	2,906,215	3,521,951	4,282,891
R.I. . .	68,825	69,122	76,931	83,059	97,199	108,830	147,545	174,620	217,353	276,531
S.C. . .	249,073	345,591	415,115	502,741	581,185	594,398	668,507	703,708	705,606	995,577
S.D.. .	....	....	....	....	....	....	....	*4,837	*11,776	98,268
Tenn. .	35,691	105,602	261,727	422,823	681,904	829,210	1,002,717	1,109,801	1,258,520	1,542,359
Tex.. .	....	....	....	....	....	....	212,592	604,215	818,579	1,591,749
Ut. . . .	....	....	....	....	....	....	11,380	40,273	86,786	143,963
Vt. . .	85,425	154,465	217,895	235,981	280,652	291,948	314,120	315,098	330,551	332,286
Va.. .	691,737	807,557	877,683	938,261	1,044,054	1,025,227	1,119,348	1,219,630	1,225,163	1,512,565
Wash.. .	....	....	....	....	....	....	1,201	11,594	23,955	75,116
W. Va.. .	55,873	78,592	105,469	136,808	176,924	224,537	302,313	376,688	442,014	618,457
Wis. . .	....	....	....	....	....	30,945	305,391	775,881	1,054,670	1,315,497
Wy.. .	....	....	....	....	....	....	....	....	9,118	20,789
U.S.. .	3,929,214	5,308,483	7,239,881	9,638,453	12,860,702	17,063,353	23,191,876	31,443,321	38,558,371	50,189,209

Note: Where possible, population shown is that of 1980 area of state.
*1860 figure is for Dakota Territory; 1870 figures are for parts of Dakota Territory. (1) U.S. total includes persons (5,318 in 1830 and 6,100 in 1840) on public ships in the service of the United States not credited to any region, division, or state.

Density of Population by States

(Per square mile, land area only)

State	1920	1960	1970	1980	State	1920	1960	1970	1980	State	1920	1960	1970	1980
Ala.. .	45.8	64.2	67.9	76.6	La.. .	39.6	72.2	81.0	94.5	Oh.. .	141.4	236.6	260.0	263.3
Alas.*	0.1	0.4	0.5	0.7	Me.. .	25.7	31.3	32.1	36.3	Okla..	29.2	33.8	37.2	44.1
Ariz.. .	2.9	11.5	15.6	23.9	Md.. .	145.8	313.5	396.6	428.7	Ore..	8.2	18.4	21.7	27.4
Ark.. .	33.4	34.2	37.0	43.9	Mass..	479.2	657.3	727.0	733.3	Pa.. .	194.5	251.4	262.3	264.3
Cal.. .	22.0	100.4	127.6	151.4	Mich..	63.8	137.7	156.2	162.6	R.I.. .	566.4	819.3	902.5	897.8
Col.. .	9.1	16.9	21.3	27.9	Minn..	29.5	43.1	48.0	51.2	S.C.. .	55.2	78.7	85.7	103.4
Conn..	286.4	520.6	623.6	637.8	Miss..	38.6	46.0	46.9	53.4	S.D.. .	8.3	9.0	8.8	9.1
Del.. .	113.5	225.2	276.5	307.6	Mo.. .	49.5	62.6	67.8	71.3	Tenn..	56.1	86.2	94.9	111.6
D. C..	7,292.9	12,523.9	12,401.8	10,132.3	Mon.. .	3.8	4.6	4.8	5.4	Tex.. .	17.8	36.4	42.7	54.3
Fla.. .	17.7	91.5	125.5	180.0	Neb.. .	16.9	18.4	19.4	20.5	Ut.. .	5.5	10.8	12.9	17.8
Ga.. .	49.3	67.8	79.0	94.1	Nev.. .	.7	2.6	4.4	7.3	Vt.. .	38.6	42.0	47.9	55.2
Ha.*	39.9	98.5	119.6	150.1	N. H..	49.1	67.2	81.7	102.4	Va.. .	57.4	99.6	116.9	134.7
Ida.. .	5.2	8.1	8.6	11.5	N. J..	420.0	805.5	953.1	986.2	Wash..	20.3	42.8	51.2	62.1
Ill.. . .	115.7	180.4	199.4	205.3	N. M..	2.9	7.8	8.4	10.7	W. Va..	60.9	77.2	72.5	80.8
Ind.. .	81.3	128.8	143.9	152.8	N. Y..	217.9	350.6	381.3	370.6	Wis.. .	47.6	72.6	81.1	86.5
Ia.. .	43.2	49.2	50.5	52.1	N. C..	52.5	93.2	104.1	120.4	Wy.. .	2.0	3.4	3.4	4.9
Kan.. .	21.6	26.6	27.5	28.9	N. D..	9.2	9.1	8.9	9.4					
Ky.. .	60.1	76.2	81.2	92.3						U.S. .	*29.9	50.6	57.4	64.0

*For purposes of comparison, Alaska and Hawaii included in above tabulation for 1920, even though not states then.

Census from 1790 to 1980

other U.S. nationals overseas are not included.

1890	1900	1910	1920	1930	1940	1950	1960	1970	1980[1]
1,513,401	1,828,697	2,138,093	2,348,174	2,646,248	2,832,961	3,061,743	3,266,740	3,444,354	3,893,046
32,052	63,592	64,356	55,036	59,278	72,524	128,643	226,167	302,583	401,851
88,243	122,931	204,354	334,162	435,573	499,261	749,587	1,302,161	1,775,399	2,718,425
1,126,211	1,311,564	1,574,449	1,752,204	1,854,482	1,949,387	1,909,511	1,786,272	1,923,322	2,286,414
1,213,398	1,485,053	2,377,549	3,426,861	5,677,251	6,907,387	10,586,223	15,717,204	19,971,069	23,668,049
413,249	539,700	799,024	939,629	1,035,791	1,123,296	1,325,089	1,753,947	2,209,596	2,889,735
746,258	908,420	1,114,756	1,380,631	1,606,903	1,709,242	2,007,280	2,535,234	3,032,217	3,107,564
168,493	184,735	202,322	223,003	238,380	266,505	318,085	446,292	548,104	594,338
230,392	278,718	331,069	437,571	486,869	663,091	802,178	763,956	756,668	638,432
391,422	528,542	752,619	968,470	1,468,211	1,897,414	2,771,305	4,951,560	6,791,418	9,747,197
1,837,353	2,216,331	2,609,121	2,895,832	2,908,506	3,123,723	3,444,578	3,943,116	4,587,930	5,462,982
....	154,001	191,874	255,881	368,300	422,770	499,794	632,772	769,913	964,691
88,548	161,772	325,594	431,866	445,032	524,873	588,637	667,191	713,015	944,127
3,826,352	4,821,550	5,638,591	6,485,280	7,630,654	7,897,241	8,712,176	10,081,158	11,110,285	11,427,409
2,192,404	2,516,462	2,700,876	2,930,390	3,238,503	3,427,796	3,934,224	4,662,498	5,195,392	5,490,212
1,912,297	2,231,853	2,224,771	2,404,021	2,470,939	2,538,268	2,621,073	2,757,537	2,825,368	2,913,808
1,428,108	1,470,495	1,690,949	1,769,257	1,880,999	1,801,028	1,905,299	2,178,611	2,249,071	2,364,236
1,858,635	2,147,174	2,289,905	2,416,630	2,614,589	2,845,627	2,944,806	3,038,156	3,220,711	3,660,380
1,118,588	1,381,625	1,656,388	1,798,509	2,101,593	2,363,880	2,683,516	3,257,022	3,644,637	4,206,116
661,086	694,466	742,371	768,014	797,423	847,226	913,774	969,265	993,722	1,125,043
1,042,390	1,188,044	1,295,346	1,449,661	1,631,526	1,821,244	2,343,001	3,100,689	3,923,897	4,216,941
2,238,947	2,805,346	3,366,416	3,852,356	4,249,614	4,316,721	4,690,514	5,148,578	5,689,170	5,737,093
2,093,890	2,420,982	2,810,173	3,668,412	4,842,325	5,256,106	6,371,766	7,823,194	8,881,826	9,262,044
1,310,283	1,751,394	2,075,708	2,387,125	2,563,953	2,792,300	2,982,483	3,413,864	3,806,103	4,075,970
1,289,600	1,551,270	1,797,114	1,790,618	2,009,821	2,183,796	2,178,914	2,178,141	2,216,994	2,520,698
2,679,185	3,106,665	3,293,335	3,404,055	3,629,367	3,784,664	3,954,653	4,319,813	4,677,623	4,916,766
142,924	243,329	376,053	548,889	537,606	559,456	591,024	674,767	694,409	786,690
1,062,656	1,066,300	1,192,214	1,296,372	1,377,963	1,315,834	1,325,510	1,411,330	1,485,333	1,569,825
47,355	42,335	81,875	77,407	91,058	110,247	160,083	285,278	488,738	800,508
376,530	411,588	430,572	443,083	465,293	491,524	533,242	606,921	737,681	920,610
1,444,933	1,883,669	2,537,167	3,155,900	4,041,334	4,160,165	4,835,329	6,066,782	7,171,112	7,365,011
160,282	195,310	327,301	360,350	423,317	531,818	681,187	951,023	1,017,055	1,303,302
6,003,174	7,268,894	9,113,614	10,385,227	12,588,066	13,479,142	14,830,192	16,782,304	18,241,391	17,558,165
1,617,949	1,893,810	2,206,287	2,559,123	3,170,276	3,571,623	4,061,929	4,556,155	5,084,411	5,881,462
190,983	319,146	577,056	646,872	680,845	641,935	619,636	632,446	617,792	652,717
3,672,329	4,157,545	4,767,121	5,759,394	6,646,697	6,907,612	7,946,627	9,706,397	10,657,423	10,797,603
258,657	790,391	1,657,155	2,028,283	2,396,040	2,336,434	2,233,351	2,328,284	2,559,463	3,025,487
317,704	413,536	672,765	783,389	953,786	1,089,684	1,521,341	1,768,687	2,091,533	2,633,156
5,258,113	6,302,115	7,665,111	8,720,017	9,631,350	9,900,180	10,498,012	11,319,366	11,800,766	11,864,720
345,506	428,556	542,610	604,397	687,497	713,346	791,896	859,488	949,723	947,154
1,151,149	1,340,316	1,515,400	1,683,724	1,738,765	1,899,804	2,117,027	2,382,594	2,590,713	3,122,717
348,600	401,570	583,888	636,547	692,849	642,961	652,740	680,514	666,257	690,768
1,767,518	2,020,616	2,184,789	2,337,885	2,616,556	2,915,841	3,291,718	3,567,089	3,926,018	4,591,120
2,235,527	3,048,710	3,896,542	4,663,228	5,824,715	6,414,824	7,711,194	9,579,677	11,198,655	14,227,770
210,779	276,749	373,351	449,396	507,847	550,310	688,862	890,627	1,059,273	1,461,037
332,422	343,641	355,956	352,428	359,611	359,231	377,747	389,881	444,732	511,456
1,655,980	1,854,184	2,061,612	2,309,187	2,421,851	2,677,773	3,318,680	3,966,949	4,651,448	5,346,797
357,232	518,103	1,141,990	1,356,621	1,563,396	1,736,191	2,378,963	2,853,214	3,413,244	4,132,353
762,794	958,800	1,221,119	1,463,701	1,729,205	1,901,974	2,005,552	1,860,421	1,744,237	1,950,186
1,693,330	2,069,042	2,333,860	2,632,067	2,939,006	3,137,587	3,434,575	3,951,777	4,417,821	4,705,642
62,555	92,531	145,965	194,402	225,565	250,742	290,529	330,066	332,416	469,557
62,979,766	76,212,168	92,228,496	106,021,537	123,202,624	132,164,569	151,325,798	179,323,175	203,302,031	226,549,448

U.S. Center of Population, 1790-1980

Center of Population is that point which may be considered as center of population gravity of the U.S. or that point upon which the U.S. would balance if it were a rigid plane without weight and the population distributed thereon with each individual being assumed to have equal weight and to exert an influence on a central point proportional to his distance from that point.

Year	N. Lat.		W.Long.		Approximate location
1790	39 16	30	76 11	12	23 miles east of Baltimore, Md.
1800	39 16	6	76 56	30	18 miles west of Baltimore, Md.
1810	39 11	30	77 37	12	40 miles northwest by west of Washington, D.C. (in Va.)
1820	39 5	42	78 33	0[1]	16 miles east of Moorefield, W. Va.[1]
1830	38 57	54	79 16	54	19 miles west-southwest of Moorefield, W. Va.[1]
1840	39 2	0	80 18	0	16 miles south of Clarksburg, W. Va.[1]
1850	38 59	0	81 19	0	23 miles southeast of Parkersburg, W. Va.[1]
1860	39 0	24	82 48	48	20 miles south by east of Chillicothe, Oh.
1870	39 12	0	83 35	42	48 miles east by north of Cincinnati, Oh.
1880	39 4	8	84 39	40	8 miles west by south of Cincinnati, Oh. (in Ky.)
1890	39 11	56	85 32	53	20 miles east of Columbus, Ind.
1900	39 9	36	85 48	54	6 miles southeast of Columbus, Ind.
1910	39 10	12	86 32	20	In the city of Bloomington, Ind.
1920	39 10	21	86 43	15	8 miles south-southeast of Spencer, Owen County, Ind.
1930	39 3	45	87 8	6	3 miles northeast of Linton, Greene County, Ind.
1940	38 56	54	87 22	35	2 miles southeast by east of Carlisle, Sullivan County, Ind.
1950 (Inc. Alaska & Hawaii)	38 48	15	88 22	8	3 miles northeast of Louisville, Clay County, Ill.
1960	38 35	58	89 12	35	6 1/2 miles northwest of Centralia, Ill.
1970	38 27	47	89 42	22	5 miles east southeast of Mascoutah, St. Clair County, Ill.
1980	38 8	13	90 34	26	1/4 mile west of DeSoto, Mo.

(1) West Virginia was set off from Virginia Dec. 31, 1862, and admitted as a state June 20, 1863.

Metropolitan Statistical Areas: 1980 and 1970
Source: U.S. Bureau of the Census
(MSAs over 275,000 listed by 1980 population)

By current standards, an area qualifies for recognition as a Metropolitan Statistical Area (MSA) in one of two ways: if there is a city of at least 50,000 population; or a Census Bureau-defined urbanized area of at least 50,000 with a total metropolitan population of at least 100,000 (75,000 in New England). In addition to the county containing the main city, an MSA also includes other counties having strong economic and social ties to the central county. If an area has more than one million population and meets certain other specified requirements, it now is termed a Consolidated Metropolitan Statistical Area (CMSA). MSAs are defined by the Office of Management and Budget as of June 30, 1983.

MSA	Population 1980	1970	Percent Change 1970 to 1980
New York-Northern New Jersey-Long Island, NY-NJ-CT CMSA	17,539,344	18,192,819	−3.6
Los Angeles-Anaheim-Riverside, CA CMSA	11,497,568	9,980,859	15.2
Chicago-Gary-Lake County, IL-IN-WI CMSA	7,937,326	7,778,948	2.0
Philadelphia-Wilmington-Trenton, PA-NJ-DE-MD CMSA	5,680,768	5,749,093	−1.2
San Francisco-Oakland-San Jose, CA CMSA	5,367,925	4,754,366	12.9
Detroit-Ann Arbor, MI CMSA	4,752,820	4,788,369	−0.7
Boston-Lawrence-Salem, MA CMSA	3,971,736	3,939,029	0.8
Washington, DC-MD-VA	3,250,822	3,040,307	6.9
Houston-Galveston-Brazoria, TX CMSA	3,101,293	2,169,128	43.0
Dallas-Fort Worth, TX CMSA	2,930,516	2,351,568	24.6
Cleveland-Akron-Lorain, OH CMSA	2,834,062	2,999,811	−5.5
Miami-Fort Lauderdale, FL CMSA	2,643,981	1,887,892	40.0
Pittsburgh-Beaver Valley, PA CMSA	2,423,311	2,556,029	−5.2
St. Louis-East St. Louis-Alton, MO-IL CMSA	2,376,998	2,429,376	−2.2
Baltimore, MD	2,199,531	2,089,438	5.3
Atlanta, GA.	2,138,231	1,684,200	27.0
Minneapolis-St. Paul, MN-WI.	2,137,133	1,981,951	7.8
Seattle-Tacoma, WA CMSA.	2,093,112	1,836,949	13.9
San Diego, CA.	1,861,846	1,357,854	37.1
Cincinnati-Hamilton, OH-KY-IN CMSA	1,660,278	1,613,414	2.9
Denver-Boulder, CO CMSA	1,618,461	1,238,273	30.7
Tampa-St. Petersburg, FL	1,613,603	1,105,553	46.0
Milwaukee-Racine, WI CMSA	1,570,275	1,574,722	−0.3
Phoenix, AZ	1,509,052	971,228	55.4
Kansas City, MO-Kansas City, KS CMSA	1,433,458	1,373,146	4.4
Portland-Vancouver, OR-WA CMSA	1,297,926	1,047,343	23.9
New Orleans, LA	1,256,256	1,099,833	14.2
Columbus, OH.	1,243,833	1,149,432	8.2
Buffalo-Niagara Falls, NY CMSA	1,242,826	1,349,211	−7.9
Indianapolis, IN	1,166,575	1,111,352	5.0
Norfolk-Virginia Beach-Newport News, VA	1,160,311	1,058,764	9.6
Sacramento, CA	1,099,814	847,626	29.8
Providence-Pawtucket-Fall River, RI-MA CMSA	1,083,139	1,065,417	1.7
San Antonio, TX	1,071,954	888,179	20.7
Hartford-New Britain-Middletown, CT CMSA	1,013,508	999,842	1.4
Charlotte-Gastonia-Rock Hill, NC-SC.	971,391	840,347	15.6
Rochester, NY.	971,230	961,516	1.0
Louisville, KY-IN.	956,756	906,752	5.5
Dayton-Springfield, OH.	942,083	974,927	−3.4
Memphis, TN-AR-MS	913,472	834,103	9.5
Salt Lake City-Ogden, UT	910,222	683,913	33.1
Birmingham, AL	883,946	794,083	11.3
Oklahoma City, OK	860,969	718,737	19.8
Greensboro-Winston-Salem-High Point, NC	851,851	742,984	14.7
Nashville, TN.	850,505	699,271	21.6
Albany-Schenectady-Troy, NY	835,880	811,113	3.1
Honolulu, HI	762,565	630,528	20.9
Richmond-Petersburg, VA.	761,311	676,351	12.6
Scranton-Wilkes-Barre, PA.	728,796	696,078	4.7
Jacksonville, FL	722,252	612,585	17.9
Orlando, FL	700,055	453,270	54.4
Tulsa, OK	657,173	525,852	25.0
Syracuse, NY	642,971	636,596	1.0
Allentown-Bethlehem, PA-NJ	635,481	594,382	6.9
Toledo, OH.	616,864	606,344	1.7
Grand Rapids, MI	601,680	539,225	11.6
Omaha, NE-IA	585,122	555,956	5.2
West Palm Beach-Boca Raton-Delray Beach, FL.	576,863	348,993	65.3
Greenville-Spartanburg, SC	569,066	473,454	20.2
Knoxville, TN.	565,970	476,538	18.8
Raleigh-Durham, NC	561,222	446,074	25.8
Harrisburg-Lebanon-Carlisle, PA	555,158	510,170	8.8
Austin, TX	536,688	360,463	48.9
Tucson, AZ.	531,443	351,667	51.1
Youngstown-Warren, OH.	531,350	537,124	−1.1
Springfield, MA	515,259	528,072	−2.4
Fresno, CA.	514,621	413,329	24.5
New Haven-Meriden, CT	500,474	488,732	2.4
Baton Rouge, LA	494,151	375,628	31.6
El Paso, TX	479,899	359,291	33.6
Little Rock-North Little Rock, AR	474,484	381,123	24.5
Las Vegas, NV.	463,087	273,288	69.5
Flint, MI.	450,449	445,589	1.1
Mobile, AL	443,536	376,690	17.7
Johnson City-Kingsport-Bristol, TN-VA	433,638	373,591	16.1
Charleston, SC	430,462	336,036	28.1
Chattanooga, TN-GA	426,540	370,857	15.0
Saginaw-Bay City-Midland, MI	421,518	400,851	5.2
Lansing-East Lansing, MI.	419,750	378,423	10.9
Albuquerque, NM	419,700	315,774	32.9
Wichita, KS.	411,313	389,352	5.6
Columbia, SC	410,088	322,880	27.0
Canton, OH	404,421	393,789	2.7
Bakersfield, CA	403,089	330,234	22.1
Worcester, MA	402,918	399,682	0.8
Davenport-Rock Island-Moline, IA-IL.	383,958	362,638	5.9
York, PA	381,255	329,540	15.7
Beaumont-Port Arthur, TX	375,497	347,568	8.0
Des Moines, IA	367,561	339,647	8.2
Peoria, IL.	365,864	341,979	7.0
Lancaster, PA	362,346	320,079	13.2
Jackson, MS.	362,038	288,643	25.4
Fort Wayne, IN	354,156	334,687	5.8
Stockton, CA.	347,342	291,073	19.3
Augusta, GA-SC.	345,918	291,063	18.8
Spokane, WA	341,835	287,487	18.9
Huntington-Ashland, WV-KY-OH	336,410	306,785	9.7
Shreveport, LA	333,079	296,061	12.5
Corpus Christi, TX.	326,228	284,832	14.5
Madison, WI	323,545	290,272	11.5
Lakeland-Winter Haven, FL	321,652	228,515	40.8
Utica-Rome, NY	320,180	340,477	−6.0
Lexington-Fayette, KY	317,629	266,701	19.1
Reading, PA	312,509	296,382	5.4
Colorado Springs, CO	309,424	235,972	31.1
Santa Barbara-Santa Maria-Lompoc, CA.	298,694	264,324	13.0
Appleton-Oshkosh-Neenah, WI	291,369	276,948	5.2
Salinas-Seaside-Monterey, CA	290,444	247,450	17.4
Pensacola, FL	289,782	243,075	19.2
McAllen-Edinburg-Mission, TX	283,229	181,535	56.0
Erie, PA.	279,780	263,654	6.1
Rockford, IL	279,514	272,063	2.7
Atlantic City, NJ	276,385	234,597	17.8
Evansville, IN-KY	276,252	254,515	8.5
Eugene-Springfield, OR	275,226	215,401	27.8

Population of U.S. Cities
Source: U.S. Bureau of the Census (100 most populated cities ranked by July 1, 1982 estimates)

Rank	City	1982	1980	1970	1960	1950	1900	1850
1	New York, N.Y.	7,086,096	7,071,639	7,895,563	7,781,984	7,891,957	3,437,202	696,115
2	Los Angeles, Cal.	3,022,247	2,966,850	2,811,801	2,479,015	1,970,358	102,479	1,610
3	Chicago, Ill.	2,997,155	3,005,072	3,369,357	3,550,404	3,620,962	1,698,575	29,963
4	Houston, Tex.	1,725,617	1,595,138	1,233,535	938,219	596,163	44,633	2,396
5	Philadelphia, Pa.	1,665,382	1,688,210	1,949,996	2,002,512	2,071,605	1,293,697	121,376
6	Detroit, Mich.	1,138,717	1,203,339	1,514,063	1,670,144	1,849,568	285,704	21,019
7	Dallas, Tex.	943,848	904,078	844,401	679,684	434,462	42,638	...
8	San Diego, Cal.	915,956	875,538	697,471	573,224	334,387	17,700	...
9	Phoenix, Ariz.	824,230	789,704	584,303	439,170	106,818	5,544	...
10	San Antonio, Tex.	819,021	785,880	654,153	587,718	408,442	53,321	3,488
11	Honolulu, Ha.[1]	781,899	762,874	630,58	294,194	248,034	39,306	...
12	Baltimore, Md.	774,113	786,775	905,787	939,024	949,708	508,957	169,054
13	Indianapolis, Ind.	707,655	700,807	736,856	476,258	427,173	169,164	8,091
14	San Francisco, Cal.	691,637	678,974	715,674	740,316	775,357	342,782	34,776
15	San Jose, Cal.	659,181	629,442	459,913	204,196	95,280	21,500	...
16	Memphis, Tenn.	645,760	646,356	623,988	497,524	396,000	102,320	8,841
17	Washington, D.C.	633,425	638,333	756,668	763,956	802,178	278,718	40,001
18	Milwaukee, Wis.	631,509	636,212	717,372	741,324	637,392	285,315	20,061
19	Columbus, Oh.	570,588	564,871	540,025	471,316	375,901	125,560	17,882
20	New Orleans, La.	564,561	557,515	593,471	627,525	570,445	287,104	116,375
21	Boston, Mass.	560,847	562,994	641,071	697,197	801,444	560,892	136,881
22	Cleveland, Oh.	558,869	573,822	750,879	876,050	914,808	381,768	17,034
23	Jacksonville, Fla.	556,370	540,920	504,265	201,030	204,517	28,429	1,045
24	Denver, Col.	505,563	492,365	514,678	493,887	415,786	133,859	...
25	Seattle, Wash.	490,077	493,846	530,831	557,087	467,591	80,671	...
26	Nashville-Davidson, Tenn.	455,252	455,651	426,029	170,874	174,307	80,865	10,165
27	Kansas City, Mo.	445,222	448,159	507,330	475,539	456,622	163,752	...
28	El Paso, Tex.	445,071	425,259	322,261	276,687	130,485	15,906	...
29	St. Louis, Mo.	437,354	453,085	622,236	750,026	856,796	575,238	77,860
30	Atlanta, Ga.	428,153	425,022	495,039	487,455	331,314	89,872	2,572
31	Oklahoma City, Okla.	427,714	403,213	368,164	324,253	243,504	10,037	...
32	Pittsburgh, Pa.	414,936	423,938	520,089	604,332	676,806	321,616	46,601
33	Fort Worth, Tex.	401,402	385,164	393,455	356,268	278,778	26,688	...
34	Miami, Fla.	382,726	346,865	334,859	291,688	249,276	1,681	...
35	Cincinnati, Oh.	380,118	385,457	453,514	502,550	503,998	325,902	115,435
36	Tulsa, Okla.	375,300	360,919	330,350	261,685	182,740	1,390	...
37	Long Beach, Cal.	371,426	361,334	358,879	344,168	250,767	2,252	...
38	Minneapolis, Minn.	369,161	370,951	434,400	482,872	521,718	202,718	...
39	Austin, Tex.	368,135	345,496	253,539	186,545	132,459	22,258	629
40	Portland, Ore.	367,530	366,383	379,967	372,676	373,628	90,426	...
41	Baton Rouge, La.	361,572	346,029	165,921	152,419	125,629	11,269	3,905
42	Tucson, Ariz.	352,455	330,537	262,933	212,892	45,454	7,531	...
43	Toledo, Oh.	350,565	354,635	383,062	318,003	303,616	131,822	3,829
44	Buffalo, N.Y.	348,035	357,870	462,768	532,759	580,132	352,387	42,261
45	Oakland, Cal.	344,652	339,337	361,561	367,548	384,575	66,960	...
46	Albuquerque, N.M.	341,978	331,767	244,501	201,189	96,815	6,238	...
47	Omaha, Neb.	328,557	314,255	346,929	301,598	251,17	102,555	...
48	Charlotte, N.C.	323,972	314,447	241,420	201,564	134,042	18,091	1,065
49	Newark, N.J.	320,512	329,248	381,930	405,220	438,776	246,070	38,894
50	Louisville, Ky.	293,531	298,451	361,706	390,639	369,129	204,731	43,194
51	Wichita, Kan.	288,723	279,272	276,554	254,698	168,279	24,671	...
52	Birmingham, Ala.	283,239	284,413	300,910	340,887	326,037	38,415	...
53	Sacramento, Cal.	288,597	275,741	257,105	191,667	137,572	29,282	6,820
54	Virginia Beach, Va.	282,588	262,199	172,106	8,091	5,390	...	...
55	Tampa, Fla.	276,413	271,523	277,714	274,970	124,681	15,839	...
56	St. Paul, Minn.	270,443	270,230	309,866	313,411	311,349	163,065	1,112
57	Norfolk, Va.	266,874	266,979	307,951	304,869	213,513	46,624	14,326
58	Corpus Christi, Tex.	246,081	231,999	204,525	167,690	108,287	4,703	...
59	Fresno, Cal.	244,623	218,202	165,655	133,929	91,669	12,470	...
60	Rochester, N.Y.	244,094	241,741	295,011	318,611	332,488	162,608	36,403
61	St. Petersburg, Fla.	241,214	238,647	216,159	181,298	96,738	1,575	...
62	Colorado Springs, Col.	231,699	215,150	135,517	70,194	45,472	21,085	...
63	Akron, Oh.	231,659	237,177	275,425	290,351	274,605	42,728	3,266
64	Anaheim, Cal.	226,467	219,311	166,408	104,184	14,556	1,456	...
65	Jersey City, N.J.	222,881	223,532	260,350	276,101	299,017	206,433	6,856
66	Richmond, Va.	218,237	219,214	249,332	219,958	230,310	85,050	27,570
67	Santa Ana, Cal.	217,219	203,713	155,710	100,350	45,533	4,933	...
68	Shreveport, La.	210,881	205,820	182,064	164,372	127,206	16,013	1,728
69	Lexington-Fayette, Ky.	207,668	204,165	108,137	62,810	55,534	26,369	8,159
70	Mobile, Ala.	204,586	200,452	190,026	194,856	129,009	38,469	20,515
71	Jackson, Miss.	204,195	202,895	153,968	144,422	98,271	7,816	1,881
72	Anchorage, Alas.	194,675	174,431	48,081	44,237	11,254	...	...
73	Yonkers, N.Y.	192,342	195,351	204,297	190,634	152,798	47,931	...
74	Des Moines, Ia.	191,506	191,003	201,404	208,982	177,965	62,139	...
75	Dayton, Oh.	188,499	203,371	243,023	262,332	243,872	85,333	10,977
76	Aurora, Col.	184,372	158,588	74,974	48,548	11,421	202	...
77	Arlington, Tex.	182,975	160,113	90,229	44,775	7,692	1,079	...
78	Grand Rapids, Mich.	182,774	181,843	197,649	177,313	176,515	87,565	2,686
79	Montgomery, Ala.	182,406	177,857	133,386	134,393	106,525	30,346	8,728
80	Las Vegas, Nev.	179,587	164,674	125,787	64,405	24,624	...	...
81	Lincoln, Neb.	177,340	171,932	149,518	128,521	98,884	40,169	...
82	Lubbock, Tex.	176,588	173,979	149,101	126,691	71,747	...	...
83	Huntington Beach, Cal.	176,314	170,505	115,960	11,492	5,237	...	...
84	Knoxville, Tenn.	175,298	175,030	174,587	111,827	124,769	32,637	2,076
85	Columbus, Ga.	174,348	169,441	155,028	116,779	79,611	17,614	9,621

Rank	City	1982	1980	1970	1960	1950	1900	1850
86	Riverside, Cal.	174,023	170,876	140,089	84,332	46,764	7,973	...
87	Madison, Wis.	172,640	170,616	171,809	126,706	96,056	19,164	1,525
88	Spokane, Wash.	171,903	171,300	170,516	181,608	161,721	36,848	...
89	Mesa, Ariz.	171,695	152,453	63,049	33,772	16,790	722	...
90	Chattanooga, Tenn.	168,016	169,565	119,923	130,009	131,041	30,154	...
91	Little Rock, Ark.	167,974	158,461	132,483	107,813	102,213	38,307	2,167
92	Fort Wayne, Ind.	167,633	172,196	178,269	161,776	133,607	45,115	4,282
93	Syracuse, N.Y.	166,187	170,105	197,297	216,038	220,583	108,374	22,271
94	Salt Lake City, Ut.	163,859	163,033	175,885	189,454	182,121	53,531	...
95	Kansas City, Kans.	162,211	161,087	168,213	121,901	129,553	51,418	...
96	Stockton, Cal.	161,815	149,779	109,963	86,321	70,853	17,506	...
97	Tacoma, Wash.	161,351	158,501	154,407	147,979	143,673	37,714	...
98	Worcester, Mass.	161,049	161,799	176,572	186,587	203,486	118,421	17,049
99	Greensboro, N.C.	157,337	155,642	144,076	119,574	74,389	10,035	...
100	Warren, Mich.	156,131	161,134	179,260	89,246	727	350	...

City Population by Race and Spanish Origin

Source: U.S. Bureau of the Census

This table presents a summary of the final 1980 census population counts for cities over 250,000, classified by race and Spanish origin. Counts of the population by race as well as Spanish origin in this table are provisional.

	Total	White	Black	Am.Indian Eskimo & Aleut.	Asian & Pacific Islander[1]	Other	Spanish origin[2]
Albuquerque, NM	331,767	268,731	8,361	7,341	3,162	44,172	112,084
Atlanta, GA	425,022	137,878	282,912	422	2,000	1,810	5,842
Austin, TX	345,496	261,166	42,118	1,003	3,642	37,567	64,766
Baltimore, MD	786,775	345,113	431,151	2,108	4,949	3,454	7,641
Birmingham, AL	284,413	124,730	158,223	185	793	482	2,227
Boston, MA	562,994	393,937	126,229	1,302	15,150	26,376	36,068
Buffalo, NY	357,870	252,365	95,116	2,383	1,322	6,684	9,499
Charlotte, NC	314,447	211,980	97,627	1,039	2,367	1,434	3,418
Chicago, IL	3,005,072	1,490,217	1,197,000	6,072	69,191	242,592	422,061
Cincinnati, OH	385,457	251,144	130,467	425	2,216	1,205	2,988
Cleveland, OH	573,822	307,264	251,347	1,094	3,384	10,733	17,772
Columbus, OH	564,871	430,678	124,880	924	4,714	3,675	4,651
Dallas, TX	904,078	555,270	265,594	3,732	7,678	71,804	111,082
Denver, CO	492,365	367,344	59,252	3,847	7,007	53,946	91,937
Detroit, MI	1,203,339	413,730	758,939	3,420	6,621	20,629	28,970
El Paso, TX	425,259	249,214	13,466	1,251	3,544	157,784	265,819
Fort Worth, TX	385,164	265,428	87,723	1,227	2,340	28,423	48,696
Honolulu, HI (county)	762,874	252,293	16,831	2,182	456,873	34,695	54,777
Houston,TX	1,595,138	977,530	440,257	3,228	32,898	140,173	281,224
Indianapolis, IN	700,807	540,294	152,626	994	3,792	3,101	6,145
Jacksonville, FL	540,920	394,734	137,324	1,198	5,240	2,402	9,775
Kansas City, MO	448,159	312,836	122,699	1,622	3,499	7,503	14,703
Long Beach, CA	361,334	269,953	40,732	2,982	19,609	28,058	50,700
Los Angeles, CA	2,966,850	1,816,683	505,208	16,595	196,024	432,253	815,989
Louisville, KY	298,451	212,102	84,080	336	931	1,002	2,005
Memphis, TN	646,356	333,789	307,702	530	2,701	1,634	5,225
Miami, FL	346,865	231,069	87,110	329	1,861	26,562	194,087
Milwaukee, WI	636,212	466,620	146,940	5,018	3,600	14,034	26,111
Minneapolis, MN	370,951	323,832	38,433	8,932	4,104	5,650	4,684
Nashville-Davidson, TN	455,651	344,886	105,942	529	2,202	2,092	3,627
New Orleans, LA	557,515	236,967	308,136	524	7,332	4,523	19,219
New York, NY	7,071,639	4,293,695	1,784,124	11,824	231,505	749,882	1,405,957
Newark, NJ	329,248	101,417	191,743	551	2,366	33,171	61,254
Norfolk, VA	266,979	162,300	93,987	885	7,149	2,658	6,074
Oakland, CA	339,337	129,690	159,234	2,199	26,341	21,824	32,491
Oklahoma City, OK	403,213	322,374	58,702	10,405	4,167	7,565	11,295
Omaha, NE	314,255	266,070	37,852	1,792	1,734	4,233	7,304
Philadelphia, PA	1,688,210	983,084	638,878	2,325	17,764	46,159	63,570
Phoenix, AZ	789,704	642,059	37,682	10,771	6,979	67,420	115,572
Pittsburgh, PA	423,938	316,694	101,813	482	2,596	2,353	3,196
Portland, OR	366,383	316,993	27,734	3,526	10,636	7,494	7,807
Sacramento, CA	275,741	186,477	36,866	3,322	24,017	25,059	39,160
St. Louis, MO	453,085	242,576	206,386	642	1,696	1,785	5,531
St. Paul, MN	270,230	243,226	13,305	2,538	2,695	8,466	7,864
San Antonio, TX	785,880	617,636	57,654	1,782	5,086	103,252	421,774
San Diego, CA	875,538	666,829	77,700	5,065	57,207	68,703	130,610
San Francisco, CA	678,974	395,082	86,414	3,548	147,426	46,504	83,373
San Jose, CA	629,442	470,013	29,157	4,826	52,448	80,106	140,574
Seattle, WA	493,846	392,766	46,755	6,253	36,613	11,459	12,646
Tampa, FL	271,523	200,741	63,835	545	1,903	4,499	35,982
Toledo, OH	354,635	283,920	61,750	661	1,653	6,651	10,667
Tucson, AZ	330,537	270,186	12,301	4,341	3,523	40,184	82,189
Tulsa, OK	360,919	298,114	42,594	13,740	2,813	3,658	6,189
Virginia Beach, VA	262,199	226,788	26,291	633	6,570	1,917	5,160
Washington, DC	638,333	171,796	448,229	1,031	6,635	9,960	17,652
Wichita, KA	279,272	235,818	30,200	2,579	3,895	6,780	9,902

(1) Excludes other Asian and Pacific Islander groups identified in sample tabulations.
(2) Persons of Spanish origin may be of any race.

Immigration by Country of Last Residence 1820-1984

Source: U.S. Immigration and Naturalization Service (thousands)

Country	Total 1820-1984	Total 1961-1970	Total 1971-1980	1979	1980[10]	1981[10]	1982[10]	1983[10]	1984	Percent 1820-1984	Percent 1961-1970	Percent 1971-1980
All countries*..	51,951	3,321.7	4,493.3	460.3	530.6	596.6	594.1	559.8	543.9	100.0	100.0	100.0
Europe	36,605	1,123.4	800.3	64.2	72.1	66.7	69.2	58.9	69.9	70.5	33.8	17.8
Austria[1]	4,323	20.6	9.5	0.5	0.4	0.4	0.3	0.4	0.4	8.3	.6	.2
Hungary.......		5.4	6.6	0.5	0.8	0.6	0.6	0.6	0.5		.2	.1
Belgium.......	206	9.2	5.1	0.6	0.4	0.5	0.6	0.5	0.8	.4	.3	.1
Czechoslovakia ..	143	3.3	6.1	0.5	1.1	0.8	1.0	0.9	0.7	.3	.1	.1
Denmark	368	9.2	4.4	0.4	0.5	0.5	0.5	0.5	0.5	.7	.3	.1
Finland	36	4.2	2.7	0.3	0.4	0.3	0.3	0.3	0.2	.1	.1	.1
France	764	45.2	24.6	2.9	1.9	1.7	2.0	2.1	3.3	1.5	1.4	5.
Germany[1]......	7,021	190.8	74.5	7.2	6.6	6.6	6.7	7.2	9.4	13.5	5.7	1.7
Great Britain[2]	5,025	214.5	137.4	15.5	15.5	15.0	14.5	14.8	16.5	9.7	6.5	3.1
Greece	680	86.0	92.4	5.9	4.7	4.4	3.5	3.0	3.3	1.3	2.6	2.1
Ireland........	4,696	37.5	11.6	0.8	1.0	0.9	0.9	1.1	1.1	9.0	1.1	.3
Italy	5,323	214.1	129.4	6.0	5.5	4.7	3.6	3.2	6.3	10.2	6.4	2.9
Netherlands	367	30.6	10.7	1.2	1.2	1.0	1.1	1.2	1.3	.7	.9	.2
Norway	859	15.5	3.9	0.4	0.4	0.3	0.3	0.4	0.4	1.7	.5	.1
Poland[1]	548	53.5	37.2	3.9	4.7	5.0	5.9	6.4	7.2	1.1	1.6	.8
Portugal.......	478	76.1	101.7	7.1	8.4	7.0	3.5	3.2	3.8	.9	2.3	2.3
Spain	272	44.7	39.3	3.3	1.9	1.7	1.6	1.5	2.2	.5	1.3	.9
Sweden........	1,278	17.1	6.6	0.8	0.8	0.8	0.9	0.9	1.1	2.5	.5	.1
Switzerland.....	353	18.5	8.4	0.8	0.7	0.6	0.6	0.7	0.8	.7	.6	.2
USSR[1,3]........	3,419	2.3	38.9	1.9	10.5	9.2	15.5	5.2	3.3	6.6	.1	.9
Yugoslavia	123	20.4	30.6	1.9	2.1	2.0	1.4	1.4	1.4	.2	.6	.7
Other Europe....	323	4.7	18.7	1.8	2.6	2.7	3.9	2.6	3.4	.6	.1	.4
Asia	4,377	427.8	1,588.2	183.0	236.1	264.3	313.3	277.7	247.8	8.4	12.9	35.3
China[4]........	703	34.8	124.4	12.3	27.7	25.8	37.0	42.5	29.1	1.4	1.0	2.8
Hong Kong	231	75.0	113.4	16.8	3.9	4.1	5.0	5.9	12.3	.4	2.3	2.5
India.........	[5]298	27.2	164.0	18.6	22.6	21.5	21.7	25.5	23.6	.6	.8	3.6
Iran	102	10.3	45.3	8.3	10.4	11.1	10.3	11.2	11.1	.2	.3	1.0
Israel	[5]107	29.6	37.7	4.3	3.5	3.5	3.4	3.2	4.1	.2	.9	.8
Japan	[5]432	40.0	49.6	4.5	4.2	3.9	3.9	4.1	4.5	.8	1.2	1.1
Jordan	56	11.7	27.3	3.2	3.3	3.8	2.9	2.7	2.2	.1	.4	.6
Korea	439	34.5	267.7	28.7	32.3	32.7	31.7	33.3	32.5	.9	1.0	6.0
Lebanon	76	15.2	41.4	4.8	4.1	4.0	3.5	2.9	3.0	.1	.5	.9
Philippines	[5,6]651	98.4	355.0	40.8	42.3	43.8	45.1	41.5	47.0	1.3	3.0	7.9
Turkey	399	10.1	13.3	1.3	2.2	2.8	2.9	2.3	1.7	.8	.3	.3
Vietnam.......	[7]370	4.3	172.8	19.1	43.5	55.6	72.6	37.6	25.8	.7	.1	3.8
Other Asia	516	36.7	176.4	20.3	36.1	51.7	73.3	65.0	50.9	1.0	.1	3.9
America........	10,305	1,716.4	1,982.8	197.1	204.5	246.3	193.5	204.6	208.1	19.8	51.7	44.1
Argentina......	[8]108	49.7	30.0	3.1	2.8	2.2	2.1	2.0	2.3	.2	1.5	.7
Brazil	[8]67	29.3	18.0	1.8	1.6	1.6	1.5	1.5	2.2	.1	.9	.4
Canada.......	4,188	413.3	169.8	20.2	13.6	11.2	10.8	11.4	15.7	8.1	12.4	3.8
Colombia......	[8]207	72.0	77.3	10.5	11.3	10.3	8.6	9.7	10.9	.4	2.2	1.7
Cuba	[9]588	208.5	264.8	14.0	15.1	10.9	8.2	9.0	5.7	1.1	6.3	5.9
Dominican Rep. ..	[8]333	93.3	148.0	17.5	17.2	18.2	17.5	22.1	23.2	.6	2.8	3.3
Ecuador.......	[8]114	36.8	50.1	4.4	6.1	5.1	4.1	4.2	4.2	.2	1.1	1.1
El Salvador.....	[8]89	15.0	34.5	4.5	6.1	8.2	7.1	8.6	8.8	.1	.5	.8
Guatemala	[8]64	15.9	26.0	2.6	3.8	3.9	3.6	4.1	4.0	.1	.5	.6
Haiti	[8]129	34.5	56.3	6.1	6.5	6.7	8.8	8.4	9.6	.2	1.0	1.3
Honduras	[8]52	15.7	17.4	2.5	2.6	2.4	3.2	3.6	3.4	.1	.5	.4
Mexico	2,507	453.9	640.4	52.5	56.7	101.3	56.1	59.1	57.8	4.8	13.7	14.3
Panama.......	[8]68	19.4	23.4	3.5	3.6	4.6	3.3	2.5	3.2	.1	.6	.5
Peru.........	[8]73	19.1	29.1	4.0	4.0	4.7	4.2	4.4	4.3	.1	.6	.6
West Indies.....	1,064	133.9	271.9	33.5	34.5	37.5	32.9	33.8	29.9	2.0	4.0	6.1
Other America...	654	106.2	125.9	16.4	19.0	17.5	21.5	20.2	22.9	1.3	3.2	2.8
Africa	215	29.0	80.7	11.2	14.0	15.0	14.3	15.1	13.6	.4	.9	1.8
Australia and New Zealand.......	131	19.6	23.8	2.5	2.2	1.9	2.0	1.9	2.3	.2	.6	.5
Other Oceania....	318	5.7	17.4	2.4	1.7	2.3	1.8	1.7	1.9	.6	.2	.4
Unknown or Not Reported	0.3	—	—	—	—	—	—	—	0.3			

* Figures may not add to total due to rounding. (1) 1938-1945, Austria included with Germany; 1899-1919, Poland included with Austria-Hungary, Germany, and USSR. (2) Beginning 1952, includes data for United Kingdom not specified, formerly included with "Other Europe". (3) Europe and Asia. (4) Beginning 1957, includes Taiwan. (5) Prior to 1951, included with "Other Asia". (6) Prior to 1951, Philippines included with "All other". (7) Prior to 1953, data for Vietnam not available. (8) Prior to 1951, included with "Other America". (9) Prior to 1951, included with "West Indies". (10) Data on immigration by country of last residence for 1980–1983 are not available; data based on country of birth.

Poverty by Family Status, Sex, and Race

Source: U.S. Bureau of the Census, Current Population Reports
By thousands

	1983 No.[1]	1983 %[2]	1982 No.[1]	1982 %[2]	1979 No.[1]	1979 %[2]	1978 No.[1]	1978 %[2]
Total poor	35,266	15.2	34,398	15.0	26,072	11.7	24,497	11.4
In families	27,804	13.8	27,349	13.6	19,964	10.2	19,062	10.0
Head	7,641	12.3	7,512	12.2	5,461	9.2	5,280	9.1
Related children	13,326	21.7	13,139	21.3	9,993	16.0	9,722	15.7
Other relatives	6,837	8.8	6,698	8.7	4,509	6.1	4,059	5.7
Unrelated individuals	6,832	23.4	6,458	23.1	5,743	21.9	5,435	22.1
In female-head families	12,020	40.2	11,701	40.6	10,563	34.9	9,269	35.6
Head	3,557	36.0	3,434	36.3	2,816	30.4	2,654	31.4
Related children	6,709	55.4	6,696	56.0	4,358	48.6	5,687	50.6
Other relatives	1,755	22.1	1,571	21.2	3,389	16.9	928	14.6
Unrelated female individuals	4,213	26.2	4,110	26.6	1,972	26.0	3,611	26.0
In male-head families	15,784	9.2	15,649	9.1	9,400	6.3	9,793	5.9
Head	4,084	7.8	4,079	7.9	2,645	5.5	2,626	5.3
Related children	6,617	13.4	6,443	13.0	5,635	8.5	4,035	7.9
Other relatives	5,083	7.3	5,127	7.3	1,120	5.1	3,131	4.8
Unrelated male individuals	2,619	19.9	2,347	18.8	3,771	16.9	1,824	17.1
Total white poor	23,074	12.1	23,517	12.0	17,214	9.0	16,259	8.7
In families	18,249	10.1	18,015	10.6	12,495	7.4	12,050	7.3
Head	5,223	9.7	5,118	9.6	3,581	6.9	3,523	6.9
Female	1,920	28.3	1,813	27.9	1,350	22.3	1,391	23.5
Related children	8,456	16.9	8,282	16.5	5,909	11.4	5,674	11.0
Other relatives	4,590	6.8	4,615	6.9	3,006	4.7	2,852	4.5
Unrelated individuals	5,291	20.9	5,041	20.7	4,452	19.7	4,209	19.8
Total black poor	9,885	35.7	9,697	35.6	8,050	31.0	7,625	30.6
In families	8,381	34.7	8,355	34.9	6,800	30.0	6,493	29.5
Head	2,162	32.4	2,158	33.0	1,722	27.8	1,622	27.5
Female	1,545	53.8	1,535	56.2	1,234	49.4	1,208	50.6
Related children	4,258	46.3	4,388	47.3	3,745	40.8	3,781	41.2
Other relatives	1,961	23.7	1,809	22.2	1,333	18.2	1,094	15.7
Unrelated individuals	1,334	40.8	1,229	40.3	1,168	37.3	1,132	38.6

[1] Beginning in 1979, total includes members of unrelated subfamilies not shown separately. For earlier years, unrelated subfamily members are included in the "in family " category.
[2] Percent of total population in that general category who fell below poverty level. For example, of all black female heads of households in 1978, 50.6% were poor.

Poverty Level by Family Size 1982, 1983

By thousands

	1983	1982		1983	1982
1 persons	$ 5,061	$ 4,901	3 persons	$ 7,983	$ 7,693
Under 65 years	5,180	5,019	4 persons	10,178	9,862
65 years and over	4,775	4,626	5 persons	12,049	11,684
2 persons	6,483	6,281	6 persons	13,630	13,207
Householder under 65 years	6,697	6,487	7 persons	15,500	15,036
Householder 65 years and			8 persons	17,170	16,719
over	6,023	5,836	9 persons or more	20,310	19,698

Income Distribution by Population Fifths

Families, 1983 Race	Top income of each fifth Lowest	Second	Third	Fourth	Top 5%	Percent distribution of total income Lowest fifth	Second fifth	Third fifth	Fourth fifth	Highest fifth	Top 5%
Total	$11,629	$20,060	$29,204	$41,824	$67,326	4.7	11.1	17.1	24.4	42.7	15.8
White	12,878	21,288	30,255	42,915	69,342	5.2	11.5	17.2	24.2	42.0	15.8
Black and other	6,206	12,000	20,120	32,011	52,712	3.6	8.8	15.6	25.3	46.8	17.0
Black	5,915	11,025	18,300	29,100	47,610	3.7	9.0	15.9	25.5	45.9	16.0
Region											
Northeast	$12,580	$22,000	$31,325	$43,887	$70,226	4.8	11.5	17.6	24.6	41.6	15.0
North Central	12,000	20,484	29,200	41,000	64,200	4.8	11.5	17.4	24.3	41.9	15.6
South	10,600	18,220	27,200	39,922	65,500	4.5	10.6	16.6	24.3	43.9	16.6
West	12,306	21,000	30,100	43,862	70,000	4.9	11.2	17.1	24.5	42.4	15.5

Persons Below Poverty Level, 1959-1983

Year	Number Below Poverty Level (mil.) All races[1]	White	Black	Spanish origin[2]	Percent Below Poverty Level All races[1]	White	Black	Spanish origin[2]	Average income cutoffs for non-farm family of 4[3] at poverty level
1960	39.9	28.3	NA	NA	22.2	17.8	NA	NA	3,022
1965	33.2	22.5	NA	NA	17.3	13.3	NA	NA	3,223
1970	25.4	17.5	7.5	NA	12.6	9.9	33.5	NA	3,968
1975	25.9	17.8	7.5	3.0	12.3	9.7	31.3	26.9	5,500
1980[4]	29.3	19.7	8.6	3.5	13.0	10.2	32.5	25.7	8,414
1981[4]	31.8	21.6	9.2	3.7	14.0	11.1	34.2	26.5	9,287
1982[4]	34.4	23.5	9.7	4.3	15.0	12.0	35.6	29.9	9,862
1983[4]	35.3	23.9	9.8	4.2	15.2	12.1	35.7	28.4	10,178

NA = Not Available. (1) Includes other races not shown separately. (2) Persons of Spanish origin may be of any race. (3) Beginning in 1981, income cutoffs for nonfarm families are applied to both farm and nonfarm families. (4) Data based on revised poverty definition.

Aid to Families with Dependent Children

Source: Office of Research and Statistics, Social Security Administration
(thousands)

1983 State	Total Assistance Payments	Ave. Monthly Caseload	Ave. Monthly Recipients	Ave. Payment Per Family	Ave. Payment Per Person
Alabama	$73,168	55,022	154,547	$110.82	$39.45
Alaska	30,039	4,644	11,026	538.99	227.04
Arizona	62,513	24,163	67,463	215.60	77.22
Arkansas	34,460	22,455	63,761	127.89	45.04
California	2,986,330	538,848	1,579,695	461.84	157.54
Colorado	99,017	29,208	85,194	282.51	96.85
Connecticut	217,422	43,903	127,980	412.70	141.57
Delaware	27,236	9,576	26,505	237.00	85.63
Dist. of Columbia	80,073	23,838	62,362	279.92	107.00
Florida	239,576	103,344	281,308	193.19	70.97
Georgia	189,307	89,168	239,945	176.92	65.75
Hawaii	86,414	17,719	54,607	406.40	131.87
Idaho	21,434	6,960	18,944	256.62	94.28
Illinois	824,339	237,123	734,882	289.70	93.48
Indiana	145,694	57,070	164,546	212.74	73.79
Iowa	144,761	37,164	103,263	324.60	116.82
Kansas	91,050	24,769	72,228	306.33	105.05
Kentucky	126,737	57,545	152,487	183.53	69.26
Lousiana	133,196	65,944	200,306	168.32	55.41
Maine	63,377	17,029	48,925	310.14	107.95
Maryland	224,514	70,429	192,364	265.65	97.26
Massachusetts	416,357	91,483	256,431	379.27	135.31
Michigan	1,132,177	240,069	751,634	393.00	125.52
Minnesota	257,723	47,718	138,661	450.08	154.89
Mississippi	56,595	51,814	151,177	91.02	31.20
Missouri	187,202	64,799	181,495	240.75	85.95
Montana	23,714	6,536	17,951	302.34	110.09
Nebraska	54,328	14,213	40,956	318.54	110.54
Nevada	10,868	4,685	12,971	193.33	69.82
New Hampshire	23,689	7,024	18,947	281.05	104.19
New Jersey	497,916	132,595	397,082	312.93	104.49
New Mexico	43,261	17,626	48,031	204.53	75.06
New York	1,737,668	360,372	1,089,780	401.82	132.88
North Carolina	152,964	69,647	174,245	183.02	73.16
North Dakota	14,891	4,009	10,957	309.56	113.25
Ohio	652,861	211,418	634,440	257.33	85.75
Oklahoma	77,065	25,027	72,264	256.61	88.87
Oregon	100,065	27,622	73,638	301.69	113.24
Pennsylvania	733,780	194,097	579,399	315.04	105.54
Rhode Island	67,559	15,938	45,159	353.24	124.67
South Carolina	75,846	49,569	134,145	127.51	47.12
South Dakota	17,573	5,995	16,746	244.26	87.45
Tennessee	81,190	58,367	152,625	115.92	44.33
Texas	156,266	102,266	307,045	127.34	42.41
Utah	53,916	12,892	38,050	348.50	118.08
Vermont	36,479	7,280	21,389	417.58	142.12
Virginia	168,523	60,449	160,809	232.32	87.33
Washington	261,579	54,539	144,868	399.68	150.47
West Virginia	56,607	28,395	79,400	166.13	59.41
Wisconsin	457,114	87,799	266,390	450.95	148.63
Wyoming	11,181	2,954	7,679	315.40	121.34
Guam	4,224	1,500	5,410	234.66	65.07
Puerto Rico	63,976	54,795	183,385	97.30	29.07
Virgin Islands	2,995	1,301	3,748	191.93	66.60
Total	$13,606,809	3,650,713	10,659,245	$310.60	$106.38

Welfare Recipients and Payments, 1955-1982

Category		1955, Dec.	1965, Dec.	1970, Dec.	1975, Dec. (b)	1980, Dec.	1981, Dec.	1982, Dec.
Old age:	Recipients	2,538,000	2,087,000	2,082,000	2,333,685	1,807,776	1,678,090	1,548,741
	Total amt.	$127,003,000	$131,674,000	$161,642,000	$217,002,000	$221,303,000	$231,274,000	$225,637,000
	Avg. amt.	$50.05	$63.10	$77.65	$92.99	$128.20	$137.81	$145.69
	(a)Avg. real $	$62.41	$66.75	$66.78	$57.65	$49.56	$49.03	$49.89
AFDC:	Recipients	2,192,000	4,396,000	9,659,000	11,389,000	11,101,556	10,612,943	10,503,918
	Total amt.	$51,472,000	$144,355,000	$485,877,000	$824,648,000	$1,105,777,000	$1,109,068,000	$1,101,149,000
	Avg. amt.	$23.50	$32.85	$50.30	$72.40	$99.61	$103.09	$104.83
	(a)Avg. real $	$29.30	$34.76	$43.26	$44.89	$38.55	$36.62	$35.85
Blind:	Recipients	104,000	85,100	81,000	75,315	78,401	78,570	77,356
	Total amt.	$5,803,000	$6,922,000	$8,446,000	$11,220,000	$16,381,000	$17,891,000	$18,689,000
	Avg. amt.	$55.55	$81.35	$104.35	$148.97	$213.23	$227.70	$241.60
	(a)Avg. real $	$69.27	$86.07	$89.74	$92.36	$82.42	$81.00	$82.73
Disabled:	Recipients	241,000	557,000	935,000	1,950,625	2,255,840	2,262,215	2,231,493
	Total amt.	$11,750,000	$37,035,000	$91,325,000	$279,073,000	$444,322,000	$485,235,000	$511,114,000
	Avg. amt.	$48.75	$66.50	$97.65	$143.07	$197.90	$214.49	$229.04
	(a)Avg. real $	$60.79	$70.36	$83.98	$88.70	$76.50	$79.36	$78.44

(a) Dollar amounts adjusted to represent actual purchasing power in terms of average value of dollar during 1967. (b) Administration of the public assistance programs of Old-age Assistance, Aid to the Blind, and Aid to the Disabled was transferred to the Social Security Administration by Public Law 92-603 effective 1/1/74.

U.S. Places of 5,000 or More Population—With ZIP and Area Codes

Source: U.S. Bureau of the Census; U.S. Postal Service; N.Y. Telephone Co.

The listings below show the official urban population of the United States. "Urban population" is defined as all persons living in (a) places of 5,000 inhabitants or more, incorporated as cities, villages, boroughs (except Alaska), and towns (except in New England, New York, New Jersey, Pennsylvania and Wisconsin), but excluding those persons living in the rural portions of extended cities; (b) unincorporated places of 5,000 inhabitants or more; and (c) other territory, incorporated or unincorporated, included in urbanized areas.

The non-urban portion of an extended city contains one or more areas, each at least 5 square miles in extent and with a population density of less than 100 persons per square mile. The area or areas constitute at least 25 percent of the legal city's land area of a total of 25 square miles or more.

In New England, New York, New Jersey, Pennsylvania, and Wisconsin, minor civil divisions called "towns" often include rural areas and one or more urban areas. Only the urban areas of these "towns" are included here, except in the case of New England where entire town populations, which may include some rural population, are shown; these towns are indicated by italics. Boroughs in Alaska may contain one or more urban areas which are included here. Population in Hawaii is counted by county subdivisions.

(u) means place is unincorporated.

The ZIP Code of each place appears before the name of that place, if it is obtainable. Telephone Area Code appears in parentheses after the name of the state or, if a state has more than one number, after the name of the place.

CAUTION—Where an asterisk (*) appears before the ZIP Code, ask your local postmaster for the correct ZIP Code for a specific address within the place listed.

ZIP code	Place	1980	1970
	Alabama (205)		
35007	Alabaster.	7,079	2,642
35950	Albertville	12,039	9,963
35010	Alexander City.	13,807	12,358
36420	Andalusia	10,415	10,092
36201	Anniston	29,135	31,533
35016	Arab	5,967	4,399
35611	Athens	14,558	14,360
36502	Atmore	8,789	8,293
35954	Attalla	7,737	7,510
36830	Auburn	28,471	22,767
36507	Bay Minette	7,455	6,727
35020	Bessemer	31,729	33,428
*35203	Birmingham	284,413	300,910
35957	Boaz	7,151	5,635
36426	Brewton	6,680	6,747
35020	Brighton	5,308	2,277
35215	Center Point(u)	23,317	15,675
36611	Chickasaw	7,402	8,447
35044	Childersburg	5,084	4,831
35045	Clanton.	5,832	5,868
35055	Cullman	13,084	12,601
35601	Decatur.	42,002	38,044
36732	Demopolis	7,678	7,651
36301	Dothan	48,750	36,733
36330	Enterprise	18,033	15,591
36027	Eufaula.	12,097	9,102
35064	Fairfield.	13,242	14,369
36532	Fairhope.	7,286	5,720
35555	Fayette	5,287	4,568
35630	Florence	37,029	34,031
35214	Forestdale(u)	10,814	6,091
35967	Fort Payne.	11,485	8,435
36360	Fort Rucker(u).	8,932	14,242
35068	Fultondale	6,217	5,163
*35901	Gadsden	47,565	53,928
35071	Gardendale	8,005	6,537
36037	Greenville	7,807	8,033
35976	Guntersville	7,041	6,491
35565	Haleyville	5,306	4,190
35640	Hartselle	8,858	7,355
35209	Homewood	21,271	21,245
35226	Hoover	15,064	688
35020	Hueytown	13,452	7,095
*35804	Huntsville	142,513	139,282
35210	Irondale	6,521	3,166
36545	Jackson	6,073	5,957
36265	Jacksonville	9,735	7,715
35501	Jasper	11,894	10,798
36863	Lanett	8,959	6,908
35094	Leeds.	8,638	6,991
35228	Midfield.	6,182	6,621
*36601	Mobile	200,452	190,026
36460	Monroeville	5,674	4,846
*36104	Montgomery	178,157	133,386
35223	Mountain Brook	17,400	19,474
35660	Muscle Shoals.	8,911	6,907
35476	Northport.	14,291	9,435
36801	Opelika	21,896	19,027
36467	Opp.	7,204	6,493
36203	Oxford	8,939	4,361
36360	Ozark.	13,188	13,555
35124	Pelham.	6,759	931
35125	Pell City	6,616	5,602
36867	Phenix City.	26,928	25,281
36272	Piedmont	5,544	5,063
35127	Pleasant Grove	7,102	5,090
36067	Prattville	18,647	13,116
36610	Prichard	39,541	41,578
35901	Rainbow City	6,299	3,099
35809	Redstone Arsenal(u) . . .	5,728	....
36274	Roanoke	5,896	5,251
35653	Russellville.	8,195	7,814
36201	Saks(u).	11,118	....
36571	Saraland	9,833	7,840
35768	Scottsboro.	14,758	9,324
36701	Selma	26,684	27,379
36701	Selmont-West Selmont(u)	5,255	2,270
35660	Sheffield	11,903	13,115
35901	Southside	5,141	983
35150	Sylacauga	12,708	12,255
35160	Talladega	19,128	17,662
35217	Tarrant City	8,148	6,835
36582	Theodore(u)	6,392	....
36619	Tillman's Corner(u)	15,941	....
36081	Troy.	13,124	11,482
35401	Tuscaloosa	75,143	65,773
35674	Tuscumbia.	9,137	8,828
36083	Tuskegee	12,716	11,028
35216	Vestavia Hills	15,733	12,250
36201	West End-Cobb(u)	5,189	5,515
	Alaska (907)		
*99502	Anchorage.	173,017	48,081
99702	Eielson AFB(u)	5,232	6,149
99701	Fairbanks	22,645	14,771
99801	Juneau	19,528	6,050
99611	Kenai Peninsula borough. . . .	25,282	16,586
99901	Ketchikan	7,198	6,994
99835	Sitka	7,803	3,370
	Arizona (602)		
85321	Ajo(u).	5,189	5,881
85220	Apache Junction	9,935	2,443
85323	Avondale.	8,134	6,626
85603	Bisbee	7,154	8,328
86430	Bullhead City-Riviera(u) .	10,364	....
85222	Casa Grande	14,971	10,536
85224	Chandler.	29,673	13,763
85228	Coolidge	6,851	5,314
85707	Davis-Monthan AFB(u)	6,279	....
85607	Douglas	13,058	12,462
85205	Dreamland-VeldaRose(u)	5,969	....
85231	Eloy.	6,240	5,381
86001	Flagstaff	34,641	26,117
85613	Fort Huachuca(u)	NA	6,659
85234	Gilbert	5,717	1,971
*85301	Glendale	96,988	36,228
85501	Globe.	6,886	7,333
85614	Green Valley(u)	7,999	....
86025	Holbrook	5,785	4,759
86401	Kingman	9,257	7,312
86403	Lake Havasu City	15,737	4,111
85301	Luke(u)	NA	5,047
*85201	Mesa.	152,453	63,049
85621	Nogales	15,683	8,946
86040	Page(u).	NA	1,439
85253	Paradise Valley	10,832	6,637
85345	Peoria	12,307	4,792
*85026	Phoenix.	764,911	584,303
86301	Prescott	20,055	13,631
85546	Safford	7,010	5,493

ZIP code	Place	1980	1970
85631	San Manuel(u).	5,443	....
*85251	Scottsdale	88,622	67,823
85635	Sierra Vista	25,968	6,689
85350	Somerton	5,761	2,225
85713	South Tucson	6,554	6,220
85351	Sun City(u).	40,505	13,670
*85282	Tempe	106,919	63,550
86045	Tuba City(u)	5,045	....
*85726	Tucson	330,537	262,933
85364	West Yuma(u).	NA	5,552
86047	Winslow	7,921	8,066
85364	Yuma.	42,481	29,007

Arkansas (501)

71923	Arkadelphia	10,005	9,841
72501	Batesville.	8,447	7,209
72015	Benton	17,437	16,499
72712	Bentonville	8,756	5,508
72315	Blytheville	24,314	24,752
71701	Camden	15,356	15,147
72830	Clarksville	5,237	4,616
72032	Conway	20,375	15,510
71635	Crossett	6,706	6,191
71639	Dumas	6,091	4,600
71730	El Dorado	26,685	25,283
72701	Fayetteville	36,604	30,729
71742	Fordyce	5,175	4,837
72335	Forrest City	13,803	12,521
72901	Fort Smith	71,384	62,802
72601	Harrison	9,567	7,239
72342	Helena	9,598	10,415
71801	Hope	10,290	8,830
71901	Hot Springs	35,166	35,631
72076	Jacksonville	27,589	19,832
72401	Jonesboro	31,530	27,050
*72201	Little Rock	158,915	132,483
71753	Magnolia	11,909	11,303
72104	Malvern	10,163	8,739
72360	Marianna	6,220	6,196
71654	McGehee	5,671	4,683
71953	Mena	5,154	4,530
71655	Monticello	8,259	5,085
72110	Morrilton	7,355	6,814
72653	Mountain Home	7,447	3,936
72112	Newport	8,339	7,725
*72114	North Little Rock	64,388	60,040
72370	Osceola	8,881	7,892
72450	Paragould	15,214	10,639
71601	Pine Bluff	56,576	57,389
72455	Pocahontas	5,995	4,544
72756	Rogers	17,429	11,050
72801	Russellville.	14,000	11,750
72143	Searcy	13,612	9,040
72116	Sherwood	10,423	2,754
72761	Siloam Springs	7,940	6,009
72764	Springdale	23,458	16,783
72160	Stuttgart	10,941	10,477
75501	Texarkana	21,459	21,682
72472	Trumann	6,395	6,023
72956	Van Buren	12,020	8,373
71671	Warren	7,646	6,433
72390	West Helena.	11,367	11,007
72301	West Memphis	28,138	26,070
72396	Wynne	7,805	6,696

California

94501	Alameda	(415)	63,852	70,968
94507	Alamo(u)	(415)	8,505	14,059
94706	Albany	(415)	15,130	15,561
*91802	Alhambra	(818)	64,767	62,125
90249	Alondra Park(u)	(213)	12,096	12,193
92001	Alpine(u)	(619)	5,368	1,570
91001	Altadena(u)	(818)	40,510	42,415
95116	Alum Rock(u)	(408)	17,471	18,355
94590	American Canyon(u)	(707)	5,712	....
*92803	Anaheim	(714)	219,494	166,408
96007	Anderson	(916)	7,381	5,492
94509	Antioch	(415)	43,559	28,060
92307	Apple Valley(u)	(714)	14,305	6,702
95003	Aptos(u)	(408)	7,039	8,704
91006	Arcadia	(818)	45,993	45,138
95521	Arcata	(707)	12,849	8,985
95825	Arden-Arcade(u)	(916)	87,570	82,492
93420	Arroyo Grande	(805)	11,290	7,454
90701	Artesia	(213)	14,301	14,757
93203	Arvin	(805)	6,863	5,199
94577	Ashland(u)	(415)	13,893	14,810
93422	Atascadero	(805)	15,930	10,290
94025	Atherton	(415)	7,797	8,085
95301	Atwater.	(209)	17,530	11,640
95603	Auburn	(916)	7,540	6,570
92505	August(u)	(209)	5,445	6,293
91746	Avocado Heights(u).	(213)	11,721	9,810
91702	Azusa	(818)	29,380	25,217
*93302	Bakersfield.	(805)	105,611	69,515
91706	Baldwin Park	(818)	50,554	47,285

92220	Banning	(714)	14,020	12,034
92311	Barstow	(619)	17,690	17,442
93402	Baywood-Los Osos(u)	(805)	10,933	3,487
95903	Beale AFB East(u)	(916)	6,329	7,029
92223	Beaumont	(714)	6,818	5,484
90201	Bell	(213)	25,450	21,836
90706	Bellflower	(213)	53,441	52,334
90201	Bell Gardens	(213)	34,117	29,308
94002	Belmont	(415)	24,505	23,538
94510	Benicia	(707)	15,376	7,349
95005	Ben Lomond(u)	(408)	7,238	2,793
*94704	Berkeley	(415)	103,328	114,091
*90213	Beverly Hills	(213)	32,646	33,416
92314	Big Bear(u)	(714)	11,151	5,268
92316	Bloomington(u)	(714)	6,674	11,957
92225	Blythe	(619)	6,805	7,047
92002	Bonita(u)	(714)	6,257	....
95006	Boulder Creek(u)	(408)	5,662	1,806
92227	Brawley	(619)	14,946	13,746
92621	Brea	(714)	27,913	18,447
95605	Broderick-Bryte(u)	(916)	10,194	12,782
*90620	Buena Park	(714)	64,165	63,646
*91505	Burbank	(818)	84,625	88,871
94010	Burlingame	(415)	26,173	27,320
92231	Calexico	(714)	14,412	10,625
93725	Calwa(u)	(209)	6,640	5,191
93010	Camarillo	(805)	37,732	19,219
93010	Camarillo Heights(u)	(805)	6,341	5,892
95682	Cameron Park(u)	(916)	5,607	....
95008	Campbell	(408)	26,910	23,797
91351	Canyon Country(u)	(805)	15,728	....
92055	Camp Pendleton South(u)	(714)	7,952	13,692
92624	Capistrano Beach(u)	(714)	6,168	4,149
95010	Capitola	(408)	9,095	5,080
92007	Cardiff-by-the-Sea(u).	(714)	10,054	5,724
92008	Carlsbad	(619)	35,490	14,944
95608	Carmichael(u)	(916)	43,108	37,625
93013	Carpinteria.	(805)	10,835	6,982
90744	Carson	(213)	81,221	71,150
92077	Casa De Oro-Mt. Helix(u)	(714)	19,651	....
92010	Castle Park-Otay(u)	(714)	21,049	15,445
94546	Castro Valley(u)	(415)	44,011	44,760
95307	Ceres.	(209)	13,281	6,029
90701	Cerritos	(213)	52,756	15,856
91724	Charter Oak(u)	(213)	6,840	....
94541	Cherryland(u)	(415)	9,425	9,969
92223	Cherry Valley(u)	(714)	5,012	3,165
95926	Chico	(916)	26,716	19,580
95926	Chico North(u).	(916)	11,739	6,656
95926	Chico West(u)	(916)	6,378	4,787
91710	Chino.	(714)	40,165	20,411
93610	Chowchilla.	(209)	5,122	4,349
*92010	Chula Vista	(619)	83,927	67,901
95610	Citrus(u)	(916)	12,450	....
95610	Citrus Heights(u)	(916)	85,911	21,760
91711	Claremont	(714)	31,028	24,776
93612	Clovis.	(209)	33,021	13,856
92236	Coachella	(714)	9,129	8,353
93210	Coalinga	(209)	6,593	6,161
92324	Colton	(714)	27,419	20,016
90022	Commerce.	(213)	10,509	10,635
*90220	Compton.	(213)	81,230	78,547
*94520	Concord	(415)	103,763	85,164
93212	Corcoran.	(209)	6,454	5,249
91720	Corona	(714)	37,791	27,519
92118	Coronado	(619)	18,790	20,020
94925	Corte Madera	(415)	8,074	8,464
*92626	Costa Mesa	(714)	82,291	72,660
	Country Club(u)	(209)	9,585	....
*91722	Covina	(818)	32,746	30,395
92325	Crestline(u)	(714)	6,715	....
90201	Cudahy.	(213)	18,275	16,998
90230	Culver City.	(213)	38,139	34,451
95014	Cupertino.	(408)	34,297	17,895
90630	Cypress	(714)	40,391	31,569
*94017	Daly City.	(415)	78,519	66,922
94526	Danville(u).	(415)	26,446	....
92629	Dana Point(u)	(714)	10,602	4,745
95616	Davis	(916)	36,640	23,488
90250	Del Aire(u)	(213)	8,487	11,930
93215	Delano	(805)	16,491	14,559
92014	Del Mar	(619)	5,017	3,956
92240	Desert Hot Springs	(619)	5,941	2,738
91765	Diamond Bar(u)	(714)	28,045	10,576
93618	Dinuba	(209)	9,907	7,917
95620	Dixon	(916)	7,541	4,432
*90241	Downey	(213)	82,602	88,573
91010	Duarte	(818)	16,766	14,981
94566	Dublin(u).	(415)	13,496	13,641
90220	East Compton(u)	(213)	6,435	5,853
92343	East Hemet(u).	(714)	14,712	8,598
90638	East La Mirada(u).	(213)	9,688	12,339
90022	East Los Angeles(u)	(213)	110,017	104,881
94303	East Palo Alto	(415)	18,191	18,727
93257	East Porterville(u).	(209)	5,218	4,042
92508	Edgemont(u).	(714)	5,215	....
93523	Edwards AFB(u)	(805)	8,554	10,331
*92020	El Cajon	(619)	73,892	52,273
92243	El Centro.	(619)	23,996	19,272
94530	El Cerrito.	(415)	22,731	25,190
95624	Elk Grove(u).	(916)	10,959	3,721

ZIP code	Place	1980	1970
*91734	El Monte	(818)	79,494	69,892
93446	El Paso de Robles	(213)	9,163	7,168
93300	El Rio(u)	(805)	5,074	6,173
90245	El Segundo	(213)	13,752	15,620
94803	El Sobrante(u)	(415)	10,535	....
92630	El Toro(u)	(714)	38,153	8,654
92709	El Toro Station(u)	(714)	7,632	6,970
92024	Encinitas(u)	(619)	10,796	5,375
*92025	Escondido	(619)	62,480	36,792
95501	Eureka	(707)	24,153	24,337
93221	Exeter	(209)	5,619	4,475
94930	Fairfax	(415)	7,391	7,661
94533	Fairfield	(707)	58,099	44,146
95628	Fair Oaks(u)	(916)	20,235	11,256
92028	Fallbrook(u)	(619)	14,041	6,945
93223	Farmersville	(209)	5,544	3,456
93015	Fillmore	(805)	9,602	6,285
90001	Florence-Graham(u)	(213)	48,662	42,900
95828	Florin(u)	(916)	16,523	9,646
95630	Folsom	(916)	11,003	5,810
92335	Fontana	(714)	36,804	20,673
95841	Foothill Farms(u)	(916)	13,700	....
95437	Fort Bragg	(707)	5,019	4,455
95540	Fortuna	(707)	7,591	4,203
94404	Foster City	(415)	23,287	9,522
92708	Fountain Valley	(714)	55,080	31,886
95019	Freedom(u)	(408)	6,416	5,563
*94536	Fremont	(415)	131,945	100,869
*93706	Fresno	(209)	217,491	165,655
*92631	Fullerton	(714)	102,246	85,987
95632	Galt	(209)	5,514	3,200
*90247	Gardena	(213)	45,165	41,021
95205	Garden Acres(u)	(213)	7,361	7,870
*92640	Garden Grove	(714)	123,351	121,155
92392	George AFB(u)	(714)	7,061	7,404
95020	Gilroy	(408)	21,641	12,684
92509	Glen Avon(u)	(714)	8,444	5,759
*91209	Glendale	(818)	139,060	132,664
91740	Glendora	(818)	38,500	32,143
92324	Grand Terrace	(714)	8,498	5,901
95945	Grass Valley	(916)	6,697	5,149
93308	Greenacres(u)	(805)	5,381	2,116
93433	Grover City	(805)	8,827	5,939
91745	Hacienda Heights	(213)	49,422	35,969
94019	Half Moon Bay	(415)	7,282	4,023
93230	Hanford	(209)	20,958	15,179
90716	Hawaiian Gardens	(213)	10,548	9,052
90250	Hawthorne	(213)	56,437	53,304
*94544	Hayward	(415)	93,585	93,058
95448	Healdsburg	(707)	7,217	5,438
92343	Hemet	(714)	23,531	12,252
94547	Hercules	(415)	5,963	252
90254	Hermosa Beach	(213)	18,070	17,412
92345	Hesperia(u)	(714)	13,540	4,592
92346	Highland(u)	(714)	10,908	12,669
94010	Hillsborough	(415)	10,372	8,753
95023	Hollister	(408)	11,488	7,663
91720	Home Gardens(u)	(714)	5,783	5,116
*92647	Huntington Beach	(714)	170,505	115,960
90255	Huntington Park	(213)	45,932	33,744
92032	Imperial Beach	(619)	22,689	20,244
92201	Indio	(619)	21,611	14,459
*90306	Inglewood	(213)	94,162	89,985
*92711	Irvine	(714)	62,134	7,381
94707	Kensington(u)	(415)	5,342	5,823
93930	King City	(408)	5,495	3,717
93631	Kingsburg	(209)	5,115	3,843
91011	La Canada-Flintridge	(818)	20,153	20,714
91214	La Crescenta-Montrose(u)	(213)	16,531	19,620
90045	Ladera Heights(u)	(213)	6,647	6,079
94549	Lafayette	(415)	20,837	20,484
*92651	Laguna Beach	(714)	17,858	14,550
92653	Laguna Hills(u)	(714)	33,600	13,676
92677	Laguna Niguel(u)	(714)	12,237	4,644
90631	La Habra	(213)	45,232	41,350
92352	Lake Arrowhead(u)	(714)	6,272	2,682
92040	Lakeside(u)	(714)	23,921	11,991
92330	Lake Elsinore	(714)	5,982	3,530
*90714	Lakewood	(213)	74,654	83,025
92041	La Mesa	(619)	50,342	39,178
90638	La Mirada	(213)	40,986	30,808
93241	Lamont(u)	(805)	9,616	7,007
93534	Lancaster	(805)	48,027	32,728
90624	La Palma	(213)	15,663	9,687
91747	La Puente	(818)	30,882	31,092
	La Riviera(u)	(916)	10,906	....
94939	Larkspur	(415)	11,064	10,487
91750	La Verne	(714)	23,508	12,965
90260	Lawndale	(213)	23,460	24,825
92045	Lemon Grove	(619)	20,780	19,794
93245	Lemoore	(209)	8,832	4,219
93245	Lemoore Station(u)	(209)	5,888	9,210
90304	Lennox(u)	(213)	18,445	16,121
92024	Leucadia(u)	(714)	9,478	....
95207	Lincoln Village(u)	(916)	6,476	6,111
95901	Linda(u)	(916)	10,225	7,112
93247	Lindsay	(209)	6,936	5,206
95062	Live Oak(u) (Santa Cruz)	(916)	11,482	6,443
94550	Livermore	(415)	48,349	37,703
95334	Livingston	(209)	5,326	2,588
95240	Lodi	(209)	35,221	28,691
92354	Loma Linda	(714)	10,694	7,651
90717	Lomita	(213)	17,191	19,784
93436	Lompoc	(805)	26,267	25,284
*90801	Long Beach	(213)	361,355	358,879
90720	Los Alamitos	(213)	11,529	11,346
94022	Los Altos	(415)	25,769	25,062
94022	Los Altos Hills	(415)	7,421	6,871
*90052	Los Angeles	(818)	2,968,579	2,811,801
93635	Los Banos	(209)	10,341	9,188
95030	Los Gatos	(408)	26,593	22,613
94903	Lucas Valley-Marinwood(u)	(415)	6,409	....
90262	Lynwood	(213)	48,409	43,354
93637	Madera	(209)	21,732	16,044
90266	Manhattan Beach	(213)	31,542	35,352
95336	Manteca	(209)	24,925	13,845
93933	Marina	(408)	20,647	8,343
90291	Marina Del Rey(u)	(213)	8,065	....
94553	Martinez	(415)	22,582	16,506
95901	Marysville	(916)	9,898	9,353
95655	Mather AFB(u)	(916)	5,245	7,027
91016	Mayflower Village(u)	(213)	5,017	....
90270	Maywood	(213)	21,810	16,996
93250	Mc Farland	(805)	5,151	4,177
95521	McKinleyville(u)	(707)	7,772	....
93023	Meiners Oaks-Mira Monte(u)	(805)	9,512	7,025
93640	Mendota	(209)	5,038	2,705
94025	Menlo Park	(415)	26,438	26,826
95340	Merced	(209)	36,423	22,670
94030	Millbrae	(415)	20,058	20,920
94941	Mill Valley	(415)	12,967	12,942
95035	Milpitas	(408)	37,820	26,561
91752	Mira Loma(u)	(714)	8,707	8,482
92675	Mission Viejo(u)	(714)	48,384	11,933
*95350	Modesto	(209)	106,963	61,712
91016	Monrovia	(818)	30,531	30,562
91763	Montclair	(714)	22,628	22,546
90640	Montebello	(213)	52,929	42,807
93940	Monterey	(408)	27,558	26,302
91754	Monterey Park	(818)	54,338	49,166
94556	Moraga	(415)	15,014	14,205
95037	Morgan Hill	(408)	17,060	5,579
93442	Morro Bay	(805)	9,064	7,109
*94042	Mountain View	(415)	58,655	54,132
92405	Muscoy(u)	(714)	6,188	7,091
94558	Napa	(707)	50,879	36,103
92050	National City	(619)	48,772	43,184
94560	Newark	(415)	32,126	27,153
91321	Newhall(u)	(805)	12,029	9,651
*92660	Newport Beach	(714)	63,475	49,582
93444	Nipomo(u)	(805)	5,247	3,642
91760	Norco	(714)	19,732	14,511
95603	North Auburn(u)	(916)	7,619	....
94025	North Fair Oaks(u)	(415)	10,294	9,740
95660	North Highlands(u)	(916)	37,825	31,854
90650	Norwalk	(213)	84,901	90,164
94947	Novato	(415)	43,916	31,006
95361	Oakdale	(209)	8,474	6,594
*94615	Oakland	(415)	339,288	361,561
92054	Oceanside	(714)	76,698	40,494
93308	Oildale(u)	(805)	23,382	20,879
93023	Ojai	(805)	6,816	5,591
95961	Olivehurst(u)	(916)	8,929	8,100
*91761	Ontario	(714)	88,820	64,118
95060	Opal Cliffs(u)	(408)	5,041	5,425
*92667	Orange	(714)	91,450	77,365
95662	Orangevale(u)	(916)	20,585	16,493
94563	Orinda (u)	(415)	16,825	6,790
95965	Oroville	(916)	8,683	7,536
93030	Oxnard	(805)	108,195	71,225
94044	Pacifica	(415)	36,866	36,020
93950	Pacific Grove	(408)	15,755	13,505
93550	Palmdale	(805)	12,277	8,511
92260	Palm Desert	(619)	11,801	6,171
92262	Palm Springs	(619)	32,359	20,936
94302	Palo Alto	(415)	55,225	56,040
90274	Palos Verdes Estates	(213)	14,376	13,631
95969	Paradise	(916)	22,571	14,539
90723	Paramount	(213)	36,407	34,734
95823	Parkway-Sacramento So.(u)	(916)	26,815	28,574
*91109	Pasadena	(818)	118,072	112,951
92370	Perris	(714)	6,740	4,228
94952	Petaluma	(707)	33,834	24,870
90660	Pico Rivera	(213)	53,387	54,170
94611	Piedmont	(415)	10,498	10,917
94564	Pinole	(415)	14,253	13,266
93449	Pismo Beach	(805)	5,364	4,043
94565	Pittsburg	(415)	33,465	21,423
92670	Placentia	(714)	35,041	21,948
95667	Placerville	(916)	6,739	5,416
94523	Pleasant Hill	(415)	25,547	24,610
94566	Pleasanton	(415)	35,160	18,328
91766	Pomona	(714)	92,742	87,384
93257	Porterville	(209)	19,707	12,602
93041	Port Hueneme	(805)	17,803	14,295
92064	Poway(u)	(619)	32,263	9,422
93534	Quartz Hill(u)	(213)	7,421	4,935
92065	Ramona(u)	(714)	8,173	3,554
95670	Rancho Cordova(u)	(916)	42,881	30,451
91730	Rancho Cucamonga	(714)	55,250	19,484

ZIP code	Place		1980	1970
92270	Rancho Mirage	(714)	6,281	2,767
90274	Rancho Palos Verdes	(213)	35,227	33,285
96080	Red Bluff	(916)	9,490	7,676
96001	Redding	(916)	42,103	16,659
92373	Redlands	(714)	43,619	36,355
*90277	Redondo Beach	(213)	57,102	57,451
*94064	Redwood City	(415)	54,965	55,686
93654	Reedley	(209)	11,071	8,131
92376	Rialto	(714)	37,862	28,370
*94802	Richmond	(415)	74,676	79,043
93555	Ridgecrest	(714)	15,929	7,629
95003	Rio Del Mar(u)	(408)	7,067	
95673	Rio Linda(u)	(916)	7,359	7,524
95367	Riverbank	(209)	5,695	3,949
*92502	Riverside	(714)	170,591	140,089
95677	Rocklin	(916)	7,344	3,039
94572	Rodeo(u)	(415)	8,286	5,356
94928	Rohnert Park	(707)	22,965	6,133
90274	Rolling Hills Estates	(213)	9,412	6,735
95401	Roseland(u)	(707)	7,915	5,105
91770	Rosemead	(818)	42,604	40,972
95826	Rosemont(u)	(916)	18,888	
95678	Roseville	(916)	24,347	18,221
90720	Rossmoor(u)	(213)	10,457	12,922
91745	Rowland Heights(u)	(213)	28,252	16,881
92509	Rubidoux(u)	(714)	16,763	13,969
*95813	Sacramento	(916)	275,741	257,105
93901	Salinas	(408)	80,479	58,896
94960	San Anselmo	(415)	12,067	13,031
*92403	San Bernardino	(714)	118,794	106,869
94066	San Bruno	(415)	35,417	36,254
...	San Buenaventura (*see* Ventura)	(805)		
94070	San Carlos	(415)	24,710	26,053
92672	San Clemente	(714)	27,325	17,063
*92109	San Diego	(619)	875,504	697,471
91773	San Dimas	(714)	24,014	15,692
*91340	San Fernando	(818)	17,731	16,571
*94101	San Francisco	(415)	678,974	715,674
91776	San Gabriel	(818)	30,072	29,336
93657	Sanger	(209)	12,558	10,088
92383	San Jacinto	(714)	7,098	4,385
95101	San Jose	(408)	629,400	459,913
92375	San Juan Capistrano	(714)	18,959	3,781
94577	San Leandro	(415)	63,952	68,698
94580	San Lorenzo(u)	(415)	20,545	24,633
93401	San Luis Obispo	(805)	34,252	28,036
92069	San Marcos	(619)	17,479	3,896
91108	San Marino	(213)	13,307	14,177
*94402	San Mateo	(415)	77,640	78,991
94806	San Pablo	(415)	19,750	21,461
*94901	San Rafael	(415)	44,700	38,977
94583	San Ramon(u)	(415)	22,356	4,084
*92711	Santa Ana	(714)	204,023	155,710
*93102	Santa Barbara	(805)	74,542	70,215
*95050	Santa Clara	(408)	87,700	86,118
95060	Santa Cruz	(408)	41,483	32,076
90670	Santa Fe Springs	(213)	14,559	14,750
93454	Santa Maria	(805)	39,685	32,749
*90406	Santa Monica	(213)	88,314	88,289
93060	Santa Paula	(805)	20,658	18,001
*95402	Santa Rosa	(707)	83,205	50,006
92071	Santee(u)	(619)	47,080	21,107
95070	Saratoga	(408)	29,261	26,810
91350	Saugus-Bouquet Canyon(u)	(805)	16,283	
94965	Sausalito	(415)	7,090	6,158
95066	Scotts Valley	(408)	6,891	3,621
90740	Seal Beach	(213)	25,975	24,441
93955	Seaside	(408)	36,567	36,883
95472	Sebastopol	(707)	5,500	3,993
93662	Selma	(209)	10,942	7,459
93263	Shafter	(805)	7,010	5,327
91024	Sierra Madre	(818)	10,837	12,140
90806	Signal Hill	(213)	5,734	5,588
93065	Simi Valley	(805)	77,500	59,832
92075	Solana Beach(u)	(714)	13,047	5,023
93960	Soledad	(408)	5,928	4,222
95476	Sonoma	(707)	6,054	4,259
95073	Soquel(u)	(408)	6,212	5,795
91733	South El Monte	(213)	16,623	13,443
90280	South Gate	(213)	66,784	56,909
92677	South Laguna(u)	(714)	6,013	2,556
95705	South Lake Tahoe	(916)	20,681	12,921
95350	South Modesto(u)	(209)	12,492	7,889
95965	South Oroville(u)	(916)	7,246	4,111
91030	South Pasadena	(818)	22,681	22,979
94080	South San Francisco	(415)	49,393	46,646
91770	South San Gabriel(u)	(213)	5,421	5,051
91744	South San Jose Hills(u)	(213)	16,049	12,386
90605	South Whittier(u)	(213)	43,815	46,641
95991	South Yuba(u)	(916)	7,530	5,352
*92077	Spring Valley(u)	(714)	40,191	29,742
94305	Stanford(u)	(415)	11,045	8,691
90680	Stanton	(714)	21,144	18,186
*95204	Stockton	(209)	149,779	109,963
94585	Suisun City	(707)	11,087	2,917
92381	Sun City(u)	(714)	8,460	5,519
92388	Sunnymead(u)	(714)	11,554	6,708
*94086	Sunnyvale	(408)	106,618	95,976
96130	Susanville	(916)	6,520	6,608
93268	Taft	(805)	5,316	4,285
94806	Tara Hills-Montalvin Manor(u)	(415)	9,471	....
94941	Tamalpais-Homestead Valley(u)	(415)	8,511	....
91780	Temple City	(818)	28,972	31,034
*91360	Thousand Oaks	(805)	77,797	35,873
94920	Tiburon	(415)	6,685	6,209
*90510	Torrance	(213)	131,497	134,968
95396	Tracy	(209)	18,428	14,724
93274	Tulare	(209)	22,530	16,235
95380	Turlock	(209)	26,291	13,992
92680	Tustin	(714)	32,248	22,313
92705	Tustin-Foothills(u)	(714)	26,174	26,699
92277	Twentynine Palms(u)	(619)	7,465	5,667
92278	Twentynine Palms Base(u)	(619)	7,079	5,647
95482	Ukiah	(707)	12,035	10,095
94587	Union City	(415)	39,406	14,724
91786	Upland	(714)	47,647	32,551
95688	Vacaville	(707)	43,367	21,690
91355	Valencia(u)	(805)	12,163	4,243
91744	Valinda(u)	(213)	18,700	18,837
94590	Vallejo	(707)	80,188	71,710
92343	Valle Vista(u)	(714)	5,474	....
93437	Vandenberg AFB(u)	(805)	8,136	13,193
93436	Vandenberg Village(u)	(805)	5,839	....
*93001	Ventura	(805)	73,774	57,964
92392	Victorville	(619)	14,220	10,845
90043	View Park-Windsor Hills(u)	(213)	12,101	12,268
92667	Villa Park	(714)	7,137	2,723
94553	Vine Hill-Pacheco(u)	(415)	6,129	....
93277	Visalia	(209)	49,729	27,130
92083	Vista	(619)	35,834	24,688
91789	Walnut	(714)	9,978	5,992
*94596	Walnut Creek	(415)	54,410	39,844
94596	Walnut Creek West(u)	(415)	5,893	8,330
90255	Walnut Park(u)	(213)	11,811	8,925
93280	Wasco	(805)	9,613	8,269
95076	Watsonville	(408)	23,662	14,719
90044	West Athens(u)	(213)	8,531	13,311
90502	West Carson(u)	(213)	17,997	15,501
90247	West Compton(u)	(213)	5,907	5,748
*91793	West Covina	(818)	80,292	68,034
90069	West Hollywood	(213)	35,703	34,622
92683	Westminster	(714)	71,133	60,076
95351	West Modesto(u)	(209)	NA	6,135
90047	Westmont(u)	(213)	27,916	29,310
94565	West Pittsburg(u)	(415)	8,773	5,969
91746	West Puente Valley(u)	(213)	20,445	20,733
95691	West Sacramento(u)	(916)	10,875	12,002
*90606	West Whittier-Los Nietos(u)	(213)	20,962	20,845
*90605	Whittier	(213)	68,558	72,863
90222	Willowbrook(u)	(213)	30,645	28,705
93286	Woodlake	(209)	5,375	3,371
95695	Woodland	(916)	30,235	20,677
94062	Woodside	(415)	5,291	4,734
92686	Yorba Linda	(714)	28,254	11,856
96097	Yreka City	(916)	5,916	5,394
95991	Yuba City	(916)	18,736	13,986
92399	Yucaipa(u)	(714)	23,345	19,284
92284	Yucca Valley(u)	(619)	8,294	3,893

Colorado (303)

ZIP code	Place	1980	1970
80840	Air Force Academy	8,655	....
81101	Alamosa	6,830	6,985
80401	Applewood(u)	12,040	8,214
*80001	Arvada	84,576	49,844
80010	Aurora	158,588	74,974
*80302	Boulder	76,685	66,870
80601	Brighton	12,773	8,309
80020	Broomfield	20,730	7,261
81212	Canon City	13,037	9,206
.....	Castlewood	16,413	....
80110	Cherry Hills Village	5,127	4,605
81220	Cimarron Hills	6,597	....
81520	Clifton	5,223	....
*80901	Colorado Springs	215,105	135,517
80120	Columbine	23,523	....
80022	Commerce City	16,234	17,407
81321	Cortez	7,095	6,032
81625	Craig	8,133	4,205
*80202	Denver	492,686	514,678
80022	Derby(u)	8,578	10,206
81301	Durango	11,649	10,333
80110	Englewood	30,021	33,695
80620	Evans	5,063	2,570
80439	Evergreen	6,376	2,321
80221	Federal Heights	7,846	1,502
80913	Fort Carson(u)	13,219	19,399
80521	Fort Collins	64,632	43,337
80701	Fort Morgan	8,768	7,594
80017	Fountain	8,324	3,515
80401	Golden	12,237	9,817
81501	Grand Junction	27,956	20,170
80631	Greeley	53,006	38,902
80110	Greenwood Village	5,729	3,095
80501	Gunbarrel	5,172	....
81230	Gunnison	5,785	4,613

ZIP code	Place	1980	1970
.....	Ken Caryl	10,661	....
80026	Lafayette.	8,985	3,498
81050	La Junta	8,338	8,205
80215	Lakewood	113,808	92,743
81052	Lamar	7,713	7,797
80120	Littleton.	28,631	26,466
80120	Littleton Southeast(u).	33,029	22,899
80501	Longmont	42,942	23,209
80027	Louisville	5,593	2,409
80537	Loveland	30,215	16,220
81401	Montrose.	8,722	6,496
80233	Northglenn.	29,847	27,785
*81003	Pueblo	101,686	97,774
80911	Security-Widefield(u)	18,768	15,297
80110	Sheridan	5,377	4,787
80221	Sherrelwood(u)	17,629	18,868
80122	Southglenn.	37,767	....
80477	Steamboat Springs	5,098	2,340
80751	Sterling	11,385	10,636
80906	Stratmoor	5,519	....
80229	Thornton	40,343	13,326
81082	Trinidad.	9,663	9,901
80229	Welby(u)	9,668	6,875
80030	Westminster	50,211	19,512
80221	Westminster East(u)	6,002	7,576
80033	Wheat Ridge.	30,293	29,778

Connecticut (203)

See Note on Page 268

ZIP code	Place	1980	1970
06401	Ansonia	19,039	21,160
06001	Avon	11,201	8,352
06037	Berlin.	15,121	14,149
06801	Bethel	16,004	10,945
06002	Bloomfield	18,608	18,301
06405	Branford	23,363	20,444
*06602	Bridgeport	142,546	156,542
06010	Bristol.	57,370	55,487
06804	Brookfield	12,872	9,688
06013	Burlington	5,660	4,070
06234	Brooklyn	5,691	4,965
06019	Canton	7,635	6,868
06410	Cheshire	21,788	19,051
06413	Clinton	11,195	10,267
06415	Colchester	7,761	6,603
06340	Conning Towers-Nautilus Park(u) .	9,665	9,791
06238	Coventry	8,895	8,140
06416	Cromwell.	10,265	7,400
06810	Danbury	60,470	50,781
06820	Darien	18,892	20,336
06418	Derby	12,346	12,599
06422	Durham	5,143	4,489
06423	East Haddam	5,621	4,676
06424	East Hampton	8,572	7,078
06108	East Hartford	52,563	57,583
06512	East Haven	25,028	25,120
06333	East Lyme	13,870	11,399
06425	Easton	5,962	4,885
06016	East Windsor	8,925	8,513
06029	Ellington	9,711	7,707
06082	Enfield	42,695	46,189
06426	Essex.	5,078	4,911
06430	Fairfield.	54,849	56,487
06032	Farmington.	16,407	14,390
06033	Glastonbury	24,327	20,651
06035	Granby	7,956	6,150
06830	Greenwich	59,578	59,755
06351	Griswold	8,967	7,763
06340	Groton	41,062	38,244
06340	Groton Borough	10,086	8,933
06437	Guilford.	17,375	12,033
06438	Haddam	6,383	4,934
06514	Hamden	51,071	49,357
*06101	Hartford	136,392	158,017
06082	Hazardville(u)	5,436	....
06248	Hebron	5,453	3,815
06037	Kensington(u)	7,502	....
06239	Killingly	14,519	13,573
06339	Ledyard	13,735	14,837
06759	Litchfield	7,605	7,399
06443	Madison	14,031	9,768
06040	Manchester	49,761	47,994
06250	Mansfield	20,634	19,994
06450	Meriden	57,118	55,959
06762	Middlebury	5,995	5,542
06457	Middletown.	39,040	36,924
06460	Milford	50,898	50,858
06468	Monroe	14,010	12,047
06353	Montville	16,455	15,662
06770	Naugatuck	26,456	23,034
*06050	New Britain	73,840	83,441
06840	New Canaan	17,931	17,451
06810	New Fairfield	11,260	6,991
*06510	New Haven	126,089	137,707
06111	Newington	28,841	26,037
06320	New London	28,842	31,630
06776	New Milford	19,420	14,601

ZIP code	Place	1980	1970
06470	Newtown.	19,107	16,942
06471	North Branford	11,554	10,778
06473	North Haven.	22,080	22,194
06856	Norwalk	77,767	79,288
06360	Norwich	38,074	41,739
06779	Oakville(u)	8,737	....
06371	Old Lyme	5,159	4,964
06475	Old Saybrook	9,287	8,468
06477	Orange.	13,237	13,524
06483	Oxford	6,634	4,480
02891	Pawcatuck(u)	5,216	5,255
06374	Plainfield	12,774	11,957
06062	Plainville	16,401	16,733
06782	Plymouth.	10,732	10,321
06480	Portland	8,383	8,812
06712	Prospect	6,807	6,543
06260	Putnam.	6,855	6,918
.....	Putnam.	8,580	8,598
06875	Redding	7,272	5,590
06877	Ridgefield Center(u)	6,066	5,878
.....	Ridgefield	20,120	18,188
06067	Rocky Hill	14,559	11,103
06483	Seymour.	13,434	12,776
06484	Shelton.	31,314	27,165
06082	Sherwood Manor(u)	6,303	....
06070	Simsbury.	21,161	17,475
06071	Somers.	8,473	6,893
06488	Southbury	14,156	7,852
06489	Southington	36,879	30,946
06074	South Windsor.	17,198	15,553
06082	Southwood Acres(u)	9,779	....
06075	Stafford	9,268	8,680
*06904	Stamford	102,466	108,798
06378	Stonington	16,220	15,940
06268	Storrs(u)	11,394	10,691
06430	Stratfield-Brooklawn(u). . . .	8,890	....
06497	Stratford.	50,541	49,775
06078	Suffield.	9,294	8,634
06786	Terryville(u)	5,234	....
06787	Thomaston.	6,272	6,233
06277	Thompson	8,141	7,580
06084	Tolland	9,694	7,857
06790	Torrington	30,987	31,952
06611	Trumbull	32,989	31,394
06060	Vernon	27,974	27,237
06492	Wallingford.	37,274	35,714
*06701	Waterbury	103,266	108,033
06385	Waterford	17,843	17,227
06795	Watertown.	19,489	18,610
06498	Westbrook	5,216	3,820
06107	West Hartford	61,301	68,031
06516	West Haven	53,184	52,851
06880	Weston	8,284	7,417
06880	Westport.	25,290	27,318
06109	Wethersfield	26,013	26,662
06226	Willimantic	14,652	14,402
06897	Wilton.	15,351	13,572
06094	Winchester.	10,841	11,106
06280	Windham	21,062	19,626
06095	Windsor	25,204	22,502
06096	Windsor Locks	12,190	15,080
06098	Winsted	8,092	8,954
06716	Wolcott.	13,008	12,495
06525	Woodbridge	7,761	7,673
06798	Woodbury	6,942	5,869
06281	Woodstock.	5,117	4,311

Delaware (302)

ZIP code	Place	1980	1970
19711	Brookside(u)	15,255	7,856
19703	Claymont(u)	10,022	6,584
19901	Dover.	23,507	17,488
19802	Edgemoor(u).	7,397	....
19805	Elsmere	6,493	8,415
19963	Milford	5,366	5,314
19711	Newark.	25,247	21,298
19973	Seaford	5,256	5,537
19804	Stanton(u)	5,495	....
19803	Talleyville(u)	6,880	....
19899	Wilmington	70,195	80,386
19720	Wilmington Manor —Chelsea—Leedom	9,233	10,134

District of Columbia (202)

ZIP code	Place	1980	1970
*20013	Washington	638,432	756,668

Florida

ZIP code	Place		1980	1970
32701	Altamonte Springs	(305)	21,105	4,391
32703	Apopka.	(305)	6,019	4,045
33821	Arcadia.	(813)	6,002	5,658
32233	Atlantic Beach	(904)	7,847	6,132
33823	Auburndale	(813)	6,501	5,386
.....	Aventura(u)	(305)	10,162	....
33825	Avon Park	(813)	8,026	6,712
32807	Azalea Park(u)	(305)	8,304	7,367
33830	Bartow	(813)	14,780	12,891
.....	Bay Crest(u).	(813)	5,927	....

ZIP code	Place	1980	1970
....	Bayonet Point(u) (813)	16,455	....
33542	Bay Pines(u) (813)	5,757	....
33505	Bayshore Gardens(u) (813)	14,945	9,255
33589	Beacon Square(u) (813)	6,513	2,927
32073	Bellair-Meadowbrook Terrace(u) (904)	12,144	....
33430	Belle Glade (305)	16,535	15,949
32506	Belleview(u) (904)	15,439	916
32661	Beverly Hills(u) (904)	5,024	....
33432	Boca Raton (305)	49,447	28,506
33923	Bonita Springs(u) (813)	5,435	1,932
33435	Boynton Beach (305)	35,624	18,115
*33506	Bradenton (813)	30,228	21,040
33511	Brandon(u). (813)	41,826	12,749
32525	Brent(u) (904)	21,872	....
33314	Broadview Park(u) (305)	6,022	6,049
33313	Broadview-Pompano Park(u) (305)	5,256	....
33512	Brooksville. (904)	5,582	4,060
33311	Browardale(u) (305)	7,571	17,444
33142	Browns Village(u) (305)	NA	23,442
33142	Brownsville(u). (305)	18,058	....
33054	Bunche Park(u) (305)	NA	5,773
32401	Callaway. (904)	7,154	3,240
32920	Cape Canaveral. (305)	5,733	4,258
33904	Cape Coral (813)	32,103	11,470
33055	Carol City(u). (305)	47,349	27,361
32707	Casselberry. (305)	15,037	9,438
33401	Century Village(u). (305)	10,619	2,679
32324	Chattahoochee (904)	5,332	7,944
*33515	Clearwater. (813)	85,450	52,074
32711	Clermont. (904)	5,461	3,661
33440	Clewiston (813)	5,219	3,896
32922	Cocoa (305)	16,096	16,110
32931	Cocoa Beach (305)	10,926	9,952
32922	Cocoa West(u) (305)	6,432	5,779
33066	Coconut Creek (305)	6,288	1,359
33060	Collier City(u) (305)	7135	....
33064	Collier Manor-Cresthaven(u) (305)	7,045	7,202
33801	Combee Settlement(u).. (813)	5,400	4,963
32809	Conway(u). (305)	23,940	8,642
33314	Cooper City (305)	10,140	2,535
33134	Coral Gables (305)	43,241	42,494
33065	Coral Springs (305)	37,349	1,489
....	Coral Terrace(u) (305)	22,702	....
32536	Crestview (904)	7,617	7,952
33803	Crystal Lake(u) (813)	6,827	6,227
33157	Cutler(u). (305)	15,593	....
33157	Cutler Ridge(u) (305)	20,886	17,441
33880	Cypress Gardens(u) (813)	8,043	3,757
....	Cypress Lake(u) (813)	8,721	....
33004	Dania. (305)	11,796	9,013
33314	Davie. (305)	20,515	5,859
*32015	Daytona Beach (904)	54,176	45,327
33441	Deerfield Beach. (305)	39,193	16,662
32433	DeFuniak Springs. (904)	5,563	4,966
32720	De Land (904)	15,354	11,641
33444	Delray Beach (305)	34,329	19,915
33617	Del Rio(u) (813)	7,409	....
32725	Deltona(u) (904)	15,710	4,868
33528	Dunedin (813)	30,203	17,639
33610	East Lake-Orient Park (u) (813)	5,612	5,697
33940	East Naples(u) (813)	12,127	6,152
32032	Edgewater (904)	6,726	3,348
32542	Eglin AFB(u). (904)	7,574	7,769
33614	Egypt Lake(u) (813)	11,932	7,556
33531	Elfers(u) (813)	11,396	....
33533	Englewood(u) (813)	10,242	5,108
32504	Ensley(u) (904)	14,422	....
32726	Eustis. (904)	9,453	6,722
32804	Fairview Shores(u) (305)	10,174	....
32034	Fernandina Beach (904)	7,224	6,955
32730	Fern Park(u) (305)	8,890	....
32504	Ferry Pass(u) (904)	16,910	....
33030	Florida City (305)	6,174	5,133
32751	Forest City(u) (305)	6,819	....
*33310	Fort Lauderdale (305)	153,256	139,590
33841	Fort Meade (813)	5,546	4,374
*33920	Fort Myers (813)	36,638	27,351
33931	Fort Myers Beach(u) (813)	5,753	4,305
33450	Fort Pierce. (305)	33,802	29,721
33452	Fort Pierce NW(u) (305)	5,929	3,269
32548	Fort Walton Beach (904)	20,829	19,994
*32601	Gainesville. (904)	81,371	64,510
33801	Gibsonia(u) (813)	5,011	....
32960	Gifford(u). (305)	6,240	5,772
....	Gladeview(u) (305)	18,919	....
33143	Glenvar Heights(u) (305)	13,216	....
33055	Golden Glades(u) (305)	23,154	....
32733	Goldenrod(u). (305)	13,681	....
32560	Gonzalez(u) (904)	6,084	....
32503	Goulding(u) (904)	5,352	....
33170	Goulds(u) (305)	7,078	6,690
33463	Greenacres City. (305)	8,780	1,731
32561	Gulf Breeze (904)	5,478	4,190
33581	Gulf Gate Estates(u) (813)	9,248	5,874
33737	Gulfport (813)	11,180	9,976
33844	Haines City (813)	10,799	8,956
33009	Hallandale (305)	36,517	23,849
*33010	Hialeah. (305)	145,254	102,452
33455	Hobe Sound(u) (305)	6,822	2,029
32805	Holden Heights(u). (305)	13,840	6,206
33590	Holiday(u) (813)	18,392	....
32017	Holly Hill (904)	9,953	8,191
*33022	Hollywood (305)	117,188	106,873
33030	Homestead (305)	20,668	13,674
33030	Homestead Base(u) (305)	7,594	8,257
33568	Hudson(u) (813)	5,799	2,278
33934	Immokalee(u) (813)	11,038	3,764
32937	Indian Harbour Beach (305)	5,967	5,371
33880	Inwood(u) (813)	6,668	....
33162	Ives Estates(u) (305)	12,623	....
*32201	Jacksonville (904)	540,898	504,265
32250	Jacksonville Beach (904)	15,462	12,779
33568	Jasmine Estates(u) (813)	11,995	2,967
33457	Jensen Beach(u) (305)	6,639	....
33458	Jupiter (305)	9,868	3,136
....	Kendale Lakes(u) (305)	32,769	....
33156	Kendall(u) (305)	73,758	35,497
....	Kendall Green(u) (305)	6,768	....
33149	Key Biscayne(u). (305)	6,313	....
33037	Key Largo(u) (305)	7,447	2,866
33040	Key West (305)	24,292	29,312
32303	Killearn(u) (904)	8,700	....
....	Kings Point(u) (305)	8,724	....
32741	Kissimmee. (305)	15,487	7,119
33618	Lake Carroll(u) (305)	13,012	5,577
32055	Lake City. (904)	9,257	10,575
*33802	Lakeland (813)	47,406	42,803
33801	Lakeland Highlands(u) (813)	10,426	....
....	Lake Lorraine(u) (813)	5,427	....
33054	Lake Lucerne(u) (305)	9,762	....
33612	Lake Magdalene(u) (813)	13,331	9,266
33403	Lake Park (305)	6,909	6,993
....	Lakeside(u) (305)	10,534	....
33853	Lake Wales (813)	8,466	8,240
33460	Lake Worth (305)	27,048	23,714
33460	Lantana (305)	8,048	7,126
33540	Largo(u) (813)	58,977	24,230
33313	Lauderdale Lakes. (305)	25,426	10,577
33313	Lauderhill (305)	37,271	8,465
33545	Laurel(u) (813)	6,368	....
33717	Lealman(u) (813)	19,873	....
32748	Leesburg. (904)	13,191	11,869
33936	Lehigh Acres(u) (813)	9,604	4,394
33033	Leisure City(u). (305)	17,905	....
33614	Leto(u) (813)	9,003	8,458
33064	Lighthouse Point (305)	11,488	9,071
....	Lindgren Acres(u). (305)	11,986	....
32060	Live Oak (904)	6,732	6,830
32810	Lockhart(u) (305)	10,571	5,809
33548	Longboat Key (813)	8,221	2,850
32750	Longwood (305)	10,029	3,203
33549	Lutz(u) (813)	5,555	....
32444	Lynn Haven (904)	6,239	4,044
32751	Maitland (305)	8,763	7,157
33550	Mango-Seffner(u) (813)	6,493	....
33050	Marathon(u) (305)	7,568	4,397
33063	Margate (305)	35,900	8,867
32446	Marianna (904)	7,074	7,282
*32901	Melbourne (305)	46,536	40,236
33314	Melrose Park(u). (904)	5,725	6,111
33561	Memphis(u) (813)	5,501	3,207
32952	Merritt Island(u) (305)	30,708	29,233
*33152	Miami. (305)	346,931	334,859
33139	Miami Beach. (305)	96,298	87,072
33023	Miami Gardens —Utopia-Carver(u) (305)	9,025	....
33014	Miami Lakes(u) (305)	9,809	....
33153	Miami Shores(u) (305)	9,244	9,425
33166	Miami Springs (305)	12,350	13,279
32570	Milton. (904)	7,206	5,360
32754	Mims(u) (305)	7,583	8,309
33023	Miramar (305)	32,813	23,997
32757	Mount Dora (904)	5,883	4,646
32506	Myrtle Grove(u) (904)	14,238	16,186
33940	Naples (813)	17,581	12,042
33940	Naples Park(u) (813)	5,438	1,522
33032	Naranja-Princeton(u) (305)	10,381	....
32233	Neptune Beach (904)	5,248	4,281
33552	New Port Richey (813)	11,196	6,098
33552	New Port Richey East(u) (813)	6,627	2,758
32069	New Smyrna Beach (904)	13,557	10,580
32578	Niceville (904)	8,543	4,155
33169	Norland(u) (305)	19,471	....
33308	North Andrews Gardens(u) (305)	8,967	7,082
33903	North Fort Myers(u) (813)	22,808	8,798
33068	North Lauderdale (305)	18,653	1,213
33161	North Miami (305)	42,566	34,767
33160	North Miami Beach (305)	36,481	30,544
33940	North Naples(u) (813)	7,950	3,201
33408	North Palm Beach (305)	11,344	9,035
33596	North Port (813)	6,205	2,244
33169	Norwood(u) (305)	NA	14,973
33308	Oakland Park (305)	22,944	16,261
33860	Oak Ridge(u) (305)	15,477	....
32670	Ocala. (904)	37,170	22,583
32548	Ocean City(u) (904)	5,582	5,267
32761	Ocoee (813)	7,803	3,937
33163	Oius(u) (305)	17,344	....
33165	Olympia Heights(u) (305)	33,112	....

ZIP code	Place		1980	1970
33558	Oneco(u)	(813)	6,417	3,246
33054	Opa-Locka	(305)	14,460	11,902
33054	Opa-Locka North(u)	(305)	5,721	....
32073	Orange Park	(904)	8,766	5,019
*32802	Orlando	(305)	128,394	99,006
32811	Orlovista(u)	(305)	6,474	....
32074	Ormond Beach	(904)	21,438	14,063
32074	Ormond By-The-Sea(u)	(904)	7,665	6,002
32570	Pace(u)	(904)	5,006	1,776
33476	Pahokee	(305)	6,346	5,663
32077	Palatka	(904)	10,175	9,444
33505	Palma Sola(u)	(813)	5,297	1,745
32905	Palm Bay	(305)	18,560	7,176
33480	Palm Beach	(305)	9,729	9,086
33403	Palm Beach Gardens	(305)	14,407	6,102
33561	Palmetto	(813)	8,637	7,422
33157	Palmetto Estates(u)	(305)	11,116	....
33563	Palm Harbor(u)	(813)	5,215	....
33619	Palm River-Clair Mel(u)	(813)	14,447	8,536
33460	Palm Springs	(305)	8,166	4,340
33012	Palm Springs North(u)	(305)	5,838	....
32401	Panama City	(904)	33,346	32,096
33866	Pembroke Park	(305)	5,326	2,949
33023	Pembroke Pines	(305)	35,776	15,496
32502	Pensacola	(904)	57,619	59,507
33157	Perrine(u)	(305)	16,129	10,257
32347	Perry	(904)	8,254	7,701
32809	Pine Castle(u)	(305)	9,992	....
32808	Pine Hills(u)	(305)	35,771	13,882
33565	Pinellas Park	(813)	32,811	22,287
33168	Pinewood(u)	(305)	16,216	....
33566	Plant City	(813)	17,064	15,451
33314	Plantation	(305)	48,653	23,523
*33060	Pompano Beach	(305)	52,618	38,587
33064	Pompano Beach Highlands(u)	(305)	16,154	5,014
33950	Port Charlotte(u)	(813)	25,730	10,769
32019	Port Orange	(904)	18,756	3,761
33452	Port St. Lucie	(305)	14,690	330
*33950	Punta Gorda	(813)	6,797	3,879
32351	Quincy	(904)	8,591	8,334
33156	Richmond Heights(u)	(305)	8,577	6,663
33312	Riverland (u)	(305)	5,919	5,512
33404	Riviera Beach	(305)	26,596	21,401
33314	Rock Island(u)	(813)	5,022	....
32955	Rockledge	(305)	11,877	10,523
33570	Ruskin(u)	(813)	5,117	2,414
33572	Safety Harbor	(813)	6,461	3,103
32084	St. Augustine	(904)	11,985	12,352
32769	St. Cloud	(305)	7,840	5,041
*33730	St. Petersburg	(813)	236,893	216,159
33706	St. Petersburg Beach	(813)	9,354	8,024
33508	Samoset(u)	(813)	5,747	4,070
33432	Sandalfoot Cove(u)	(305)	5,299	....
32771	Sanford	(305)	23,176	17,393
*33578	Sarasota	(813)	48,868	40,237
33577	Sarasota Springs(u)	(813)	13,860	4,405
32937	Satellite Beach	(305)	9,163	6,558
....	Scott Lake(u)	(305)	14,154	....
33870	Sebring	(813)	8,736	7,223
33578	Siesta Key(u)	(813)	7,010	4,460
32809	Sky Lake(u)	(305)	6,692	....
32703	South Apopka(u)	(305)	5,687	2,293
33505	South Bradenton(u)	(813)	14,297	....
32021	South Daytona	(904)	9,608	4,979
33512	Southgate(u)	(813)	7,322	6,885
33143	South Miami	(305)	10,895	11,780
33157	South Miami Heights(u)	(305)	23,559	10,395
32937	South Patrick Shores(u)	(305)	9,816	10,313
33595	South Venice(u)	(813)	8,075	4,680
32401	Springfield	(904)	7,220	5,949
33512	Spring Hill(u)	(813)	6,468	....
32091	Starke	(904)	5,306	4,848
33494	Stuart	(305)	9,467	4,820
33570	Sun City Center(u)	(813)	5,605	2,143
33160	Sunny Isles(u)	(305)	12,564	....
33304	Sunrise	(305)	39,681	7,403
33139	Sunset(u)	(305)	13,531	....
33144	Sweetwater	(305)	8,067	3,357
33614	Sweetwater Creek(u)	(813)	NA	19,453
*32303	Tallahassee	(904)	81,548	72,624
33313	Tamarac	(305)	29,142	5,193
33144	Tamiami(u)	(305)	17,607	....
*33602	Tampa	(813)	271,577	277,714
....	Tanglewood(u)	(813)	8,229	....
33589	Tarpon Springs	(813)	13,251	7,118
33617	Temple Terrace	(813)	11,097	7,347
33905	Tice(u)	(813)	6,645	7,254
32780	Titusville	(305)	31,910	30,515
32505	Town 'n' Country(u)	(904)	37,834	....
33740	Treasure Island	(813)	6,316	6,120
32807	Union Park(u)	(305)	19,175	2,595
33620	University (Hillsborough)(u)	(813)	24,514	10,039
32580	Valparaiso	(904)	6,142	6,504
33595	Venice	(813)	12,153	6,648
33595	Venice Gardens(u)	(813)	6,568	....
32960	Vero Beach	(305)	16,176	11,908
32960	Vero Beach South(u)	(305)	12,636	7,330
33901	Villas(u)	(813)	8,724	....
32507	Warrington(u)	(904)	15,792	15,848
33314	Washington Park(u)	(305)	7,240	....
32703	Wekiva Springs(u)	(305)	13,386	....
33505	West Bradenton(u)	(813)	NA	6,162
33155	Westchester(u)	(305)	29,272	....
32446	West End(u)	(904)	NA	5,289
33138	West Little River(u)	(305)	32,492	....
32901	West Melbourne	(305)	5,078	3,050
33144	West Miami	(305)	6,076	5,494
*33401	West Palm Beach	(305)	62,530	57,375
32505	West Pensacola(u)	(904)	24,371	20,924
33168	Westview(u)	(305)	9,102	....
33880	West Winter Haven(u)	(813)	NA	7,716
33165	Westwood Lakes(u)	(305)	11,478	12,811
33305	Wilton Manors	(305)	12,742	10,948
33803	Winston(u)	(813)	9,315	4,505
32787	Winter Garden	(305)	6,789	5,153
33880	Winter Haven	(813)	21,119	16,136
32708	Winter Park	(305)	22,314	21,895
32707	Winter Springs	(305)	10,475	1,161
32548	Wright(u)	(904)	13,011	....
33599	Zephyrhills	(813)	5,742	3,369

Georgia

ZIP code	Place		1980	1970
31620	Adel	(912)	5,592	4,972
*31701	Albany	(912)	74,425	72,623
31709	Americus	(912)	16,120	16,091
*30601	Athens	(404)	42,549	44,342
*30304	Atlanta	(404)	425,022	495,039
*30901	Augusta	(404)	47,532	59,864
31717	Bainbridge	(912)	10,553	10,887
30032	Belvedere Park(u)	(404)	17,766	....
31723	Blakely	(912)	5,880	5,267
30518	Brunswick	(912)	17,605	19,585
30518	Buford	(404)	6,578	4,640
31728	Cairo	(912)	8,777	8,061
30701	Calhoun	(404)	5,335	4,748
31730	Camilla	(912)	5,414	4,987
30032	Candler-McAfee(u)	(404)	27,006	....
30117	Carrollton	(404)	14,078	13,520
30120	Cartersville	(404)	9,247	10,138
30125	Cedartown	(404)	8,619	9,253
30341	Chamblee	(404)	7,137	9,127
31014	Cochran	(912)	5,121	5,161
30337	College Park	(404)	24,632	18,203
*31902	Columbus	(404)	169,441	155,028
30027	Conley(u)	(404)	6,033	....
30207	Conyers	(404)	6,567	4,809
31015	Cordele	(912)	11,184	10,733
30209	Covington	(404)	10,586	10,267
30720	Dalton	(404)	20,581	18,872
31742	Dawson	(912)	5,699	5,383
*30030	Decatur	(404)	18,404	21,943
31520	Dock Junction(u)	(912)	6,189	6,009
30340	Doraville	(404)	7,414	9,157
31533	Douglas	(912)	10,980	10,195
30134	Douglasville	(404)	7,641	5,472
30333	Druid Hills(u)	(404)	12,700	....
31021	Dublin	(912)	16,083	15,143
30338	Dunwoody(u)	(404)	17,768	....
31023	Eastman	(912)	5,330	5,416
30344	East Point	(404)	37,486	39,315
30635	Elberton	(404)	5,686	6,438
30060	Fair Oaks(u)	(404)	8,486	....
30535	Fairview(u)	(404)	6,558	....
31750	Fitzgerald	(912)	10,187	8,187
30050	Forest Park	(404)	18,782	19,994
31905	Fort Benning South(u)	(404)	15,074	27,495
30905	Fort Gordon(u)	(404)	14,069	15,589
30741	Fort Oglethorpe	(404)	5,443	3,869
31313	Fort Stewart(u)	(912)	15,031	4,467
31030	Fort Valley	(912)	9,000	9,251
30501	Gainesville	(404)	15,280	15,459
31408	Garden City	(912)	6,895	5,790
30316	Gresham Park(u)	(404)	6,232	....
30223	Griffin	(404)	20,728	22,734
30354	Hapeville	(404)	6,166	9,567
31313	Hinesville	(912)	11,309	4,115
31545	Jesup	(912)	9,418	9,091
30144	Kennesaw	(404)	5,095	3,548
30728	La Fayette	(404)	6,517	6,044
30240	La Grange	(404)	24,204	23,301
30245	Lawrenceville	(404)	8,928	5,207
30057	Lithia Springs(u)	(404)	9,145	....
31059	Mableton(u)	(404)	25,111	....
*31201	Macon	(912)	116,860	122,423
30060	Marietta	(404)	30,821	27,216
30907	Martinez(u)	(404)	16,472	....
31034	Midway-Hardwick(u)	(912)	8,977	14,047
31061	Milledgeville	(912)	12,176	11,601
30655	Monroe	(404)	8,854	6,071
31768	Moultrie	(912)	15,105	14,400
30075	Mountain Park(u)	(404)	9,425	268
30263	Newnan	(404)	11,449	11,205
30319	North Atlanta(u)	(404)	30,521	....
30033	North Decatur(u)	(404)	11,830	....
30033	North Druid Hills(u)	(404)	12,438	....
30032	Panthersville(u)	(404)	11,366	....
30269	Peachtree City	(404)	6,429	793
31069	Perry	(912)	9,453	7,771
31643	Quitman	(912)	5,188	4,818

ZIP code	Place		1980	1970
*30274	Riverdale.	(404)	7,121	2,521
30161	Rome.	(404)	29,928	30,759
30075	Roswell	(404)	23,337	5,430
31522	St. Simons(u)	(912)	6,566	5,346
31082	Sandersville	(912)	6,137	5,546
30328	Sandy Springs(u)	(404)	46,877	....
*31401	Savannah	(912)	141,654	118,349
30079	Scottdale(u)	(404)	8,770	....
30080	Smyrna.	(404)	20,312	19,157
30278	Snellville	(404)	8,514	1,990
30901	South Augusta(u)	(404)	51,072	....
30458	Statesboro.	(912)	14,866	14,616
30401	Swainsboro	(912)	7,602	7,325
31791	Sylvester.	(912)	5,860	4,226
30286	Thomaston.	(404)	9,682	10,024
31792	Thomasville	(912)	18,463	18,155
30824	Thomson.	(404)	7,001	6,503
31794	Tifton.	(912)	13,749	12,179
30577	Toccoa.	(404)	8,869	6,971
30084	Tucker(u)	(404)	25,399	....
31601	Valdosta.	(912)	37,596	32,303
30474	Vidalia.	(912)	10,393	9,507
31093	Warner Robins	(912)	39,893	33,491
31501	Waycross	(912)	19,371	18,996
30830	Waynesboro.	(404)	5,760	5,530
30901	West Augusta(u)	(404)	24,242	....
31410	Wilmington Island(u)	(912)	7,546	3,284
30680	Winder	(404)	6,705	6,605

Hawaii (808)

See Note on Page 268

ZIP code	Place	1980	1970
96706	Ewa.	190,037	132,299
96720	Hilo.	37,017	28,412
*96815	Honolulu.	365,048	324,871
96732	Kahului.	13,026	8,287
96749	Keaau-Mountain View	7,055	3,802
96752	Kekaha-Waimea.	5,256	4,159
96753	Kihei	6,035	1,636
.....	Koolauloa	14,195	10,562
.....	Koolaupoko	109,373	92,219
96790	Kula.	5,077	2,124
96761	Lahaina.	10,284	5,524
96768	Makawao-Paia	10,361	5,788
.....	North Kona.	13,748	4,832
96781	Papaikou-Wailea	5,261	5,503
.....	South Kona	5,914	4,004
96786	Wahiawa.	41,562	37,329
96791	Waialua.	9,849	9,171
96792	Waianae	32,810	24,077
96703	Wailua-Anahola	6,030	3,599
96793	Wailuku.	10,674	9,084

Idaho (208)

ZIP code	Place	1980	1970
83221	Blackfoot.	10,065	8,716
*83708	Boise City	102,249	74,990
83318	Burley.	8,761	8,279
83605	Caldwell	17,699	14,219
83201	Chubbuck	7,052	2,924
83814	Coeur D'Alene.	19,913	16,228
83401	Idaho Falls.	39,734	35,776
83338	Jerome.	6,891	4,183
83501	Lewiston	27,986	26,068
83642	Meridian	6,658	2,616
83843	Moscow	16,513	14,146
83647	Mountain Home	7,540	6,451
83648	Mountain Home AFB(u)	6,403	6,038
83651	Nampa.	25,112	20,768
83661	Payette.	5,448	4,521
83201	Pocatello.	46,340	40,036
83854	Post Falls	5,736	2,371
83440	Rexburg	11,559	8,272
83350	Rupert	5,476	4,563
83301	Twin Falls	26,209	21,914

Illinois

ZIP code	Place		1980	1970
60101	Addison	(312)	29,826	24,482
60102	Algonquin	(312)	5,834	3,515
60658	Alsip	(312)	17,134	11,608
62002	Alton	(618)	34,171	39,700
62906	Anna	(618)	5,408	4,766
*60004	Arlington Heights	(312)	66,116	65,058
*60507	Aurora	(312)	81,293	74,389
60010	Barrington	(312)	9,029	8,581
60103	Bartlett	(312)	13,254	3,501
61607	Bartonville	(309)	6,110	7,221
60510	Batavia.	(312)	12,574	9,060
62618	Beardstown	(217)	6,338	6,222
*62220	Belleville	(618)	42,150	41,223
60104	Bellwood.	(312)	19,811	22,096
61008	Belvidere.	(815)	15,176	14,061
60106	Bensenville	(312)	16,106	12,956
62812	Benton	(618)	7,778	6,833
60162	Berkeley	(312)	5,467	6,152
60402	Berwyn.	(312)	46,849	52,502
62010	Bethalto	(618)	8,630	7,074
60108	Bloomingdale	(312)	12,659	2,974
61701	Bloomington.	(309)	44,189	39,992
60406	Blue Island.	(312)	21,855	22,629
60439	Bolingbrook.	(312)	37,261	7,651
60538	Boulder Hill(u)	(312)	9,333	....
60914	Bourbonnais.	(815)	13,280	5,909
60915	Bradley.	(815)	11,015	9,881
60455	Bridgeview.	(312)	14,155	12,506
60153	Broadview.	(312)	8,618	9,623
60513	Brookfield	(312)	19,395	20,284
60090	Buffalo Grove	(312)	22,230	12,333
60459	Burbank.	(312)	28,462	26,726
62206	Cahokia.	(618)	18,904	20,649
62914	Cairo.	(618)	5,931	6,277
60409	Calumet City	(312)	39,673	33,107
60643	Calumet Park	(312)	8,788	10,069
61520	Canton.	(309)	14,626	14,217
62901	Carbondale.	(618)	26,414	22,816
62626	Carlinville	(217)	5,439	5,675
62821	Carmi.	(618)	6,107	6,033
60187	Carol Stream	(312)	15,472	4,434
60110	Carpentersville	(312)	23,272	24,059
60013	Cary.	(312)	6,640	4,358
62801	Centralia.	(618)	15,126	15,966
62206	Centreville.	(618)	9,747	11,378
61820	Champaign.	(217)	58,267	56,837
61920	Charleston.	(217)	19,355	16,421
62629	Chatham.	(217)	5,597	2,788
62233	Chester	(618)	8,027	5,310
*60607	Chicago	(312)	3,005,072	3,369,357
60411	Chicago Heights	(312)	37,026	40,900
60415	Chicago Ridge.	(312)	13,473	9,187
61523	Chillicothe.	(309)	6,176	6,052
60650	Cicero	(312)	61,232	67,058
60514	Clarendon Hills	(312)	6,857	6,750
61727	Clinton.	(217)	8,014	7,581
62234	Collinsville.	(618)	19,613	18,224
60477	Country Club Hills	(312)	14,676	6,920
60525	Countryside.	(312)	6,242	2,864
60435	Crest Hill.	(815)	9,252	7,460
60445	Crestwood.	(312)	10,712	5,770
60417	Crete.	(312)	5,417	4,656
61611	Creve Coeur.	(309)	6,851	6,440
60014	Crystal Lake.	(815)	18,590	14,541
61832	Danville	(217)	38,985	42,570
60559	Darien.	(312)	14,968	7,789
*62521	Decatur	(217)	93,939	90,397
60015	Deerfield.	(312)	17,432	18,876
60115	De Kalb	(815)	33,157	32,949
*60016	Des Plaines.	(312)	53,568	57,239
61021	Dixon.	(815)	15,710	18,147
60419	Dolton.	(312)	24,766	25,990
60515	Downers Grove.	(312)	42,691	32,544
62832	Du Quoin.	(618)	6,594	6,691
62024	East Alton.	(618)	7,096	7,309
60411	East Chicago Heights	(312)	5,347	5,000
61244	East Moline.	(309)	20,907	20,956
61611	East Peoria.	(309)	22,385	18,671
*62201	East St. Louis.	(618)	55,200	70,169
62025	Edwardsville.	(618)	12,460	11,070
62401	Effingham	(217)	11,270	9,458
62930	Eldorado.	(618)	5,198	3,876
60120	Elgin.	(312)	63,668	55,691
60007	Elk Grove Village	(312)	28,679	20,346
60126	Elmhurst.	(312)	44,251	46,392
60635	Elmwood Park.	(312)	24,016	26,160
*60204	Evanston.	(312)	73,706	80,113
60642	Evergreen Park.	(312)	22,260	25,921
62837	Fairfield.	(618)	5,954	5,897
62208	Fairview Heights.	(618)	12,414	10,050
62839	Flora.	(618)	5,379	5,283
60422	Flossmoor.	(312)	8,423	7,846
60130	Forest Park.	(312)	15,177	15,472
60020	Fox Lake.	(312)	6,831	4,511
60131	Franklin Park.	(312)	17,507	20,348
61032	Freeport.	(815)	26,406	27,736
60030	Gages Lake-Wildwood(u)	(312)	5,648	5,337
61401	Galesburg.	(309)	35,305	36,290
61254	Geneseo.	(309)	6,373	5,840
60134	Geneva.	(312)	9,881	9,049
62034	Glen Carbon.	(618)	5,197	1,897
60022	Glencoe.	(312)	9,200	10,542
60137	Glendale Heights.	(618)	23,163	11,406
60137	Glen Ellyn.	(312)	23,743	21,909
60025	Glenview.	(312)	30,842	24,880
60425	Glenwood.	(312)	10,538	7,416
62040	Granite City.	(618)	36,815	40,685
60030	Grayslake.	(312)	5,260	4,907
62246	Greenville.	(618)	5,271	4,631
60031	Gurnee.	(312)	7,179	2,738
60103	Hanover Park.	(312)	28,719	11,735
62946	Harrisburg.	(618)	9,322	9,535
60033	Harvard.	(815)	5,126	5,177
60426	Harvey.	(312)	35,810	34,636
60656	Harwood Heights.	(312)	8,228	9,060
60429	Hazel Crest.	(312)	13,973	10,329
62948	Herrin.	(618)	10,708	9,623
60457	Hickory Hills.	(312)	13,778	13,176
62249	Highland.	(618)	7,122	5,981

ZIP code	Place		1980	1970
60035	Highland Park	(312)	30,599	32,263
60040	Highwood	(312)	5,455	4,973
60162	Hillside	(312)	8,270	8,888
60521	Hinsdale	(312)	16,726	15,918
60172	Hoffman Estates	(312)	38,258	22,238
60456	Hometown	(312)	5,324	6,729
60430	Homewood	(312)	19,724	18,871
60942	Hoopeston	(217)	6,411	6,461
60143	Itasca	(312)	7,948	4,638
62650	Jacksonville	(217)	20,284	20,553
62052	Jerseyville	(618)	7,506	7,446
*60431	Joliet	(815)	77,956	78,827
60458	Justice	(312)	10,552	9,473
60901	Kankakee	(815)	29,633	30,944
61443	Kewanee	(309)	14,508	15,762
60525	La Grange	(312)	15,693	17,814
60525	La Grange Park	(312)	13,359	15,459
60045	Lake Forest	(312)	15,245	15,642
60102	Lake in the Hills	(312)	5,651	3,240
60047	Lake Zurich	(312)	8,225	4,082
60438	Lansing	(312)	29,039	25,805
61301	La Salle	(815)	10,347	10,736
62439	Lawrenceville	(618)	5,652	5,863
60439	Lemont	(312)	5,640	5,080
60048	Libertyville	(312)	16,520	11,684
62656	Lincoln	(217)	16,327	17,582
60645	Lincolnwood	(312)	11,921	12,929
60046	Lindenhurst	(312)	6,220	3,141
60532	Lisle	(312)	13,638	5,329
62056	Litchfield	(217)	7,204	7,190
60441	Lockport	(815)	9,192	9,861
60148	Lombard	(312)	36,879	34,043
61111	Loves Park	(815)	13,192	12,390
60534	Lyons	(312)	9,925	11,124
61455	Macomb	(309)	19,632	19,643
62060	Madison	(618)	5,301	7,042
62959	Marion	(618)	14,031	11,724
60426	Markham	(312)	15,172	15,987
60443	Matteson	(312)	10,223	4,741
61938	Mattoon	(217)	19,293	19,681
60153	Maywood	(312)	27,998	29,019
60050	McHenry	(815)	10,737	6,772
*60160	Melrose Park	(312)	20,735	22,716
61342	Mendota	(815)	7,134	6,902
62960	Metropolis	(618)	7,171	6,940
60445	Midlothian	(312)	14,274	14,422
61264	Milan	(309)	6,371	4,873
61265	Moline	(309)	46,407	46,237
61462	Monmouth	(309)	10,706	11,022
60450	Morris	(815)	8,833	8,194
61550	Morton	(309)	14,178	10,811
60053	Morton Grove	(312)	23,747	26,369
62863	Mount Carmel	(618)	8,908	8,096
60056	Mount Prospect	(312)	52,634	34,995
62864	Mount Vernon	(618)	16,995	16,270
60060	Mundelein	(312)	17,053	16,128
62966	Murphysboro	(618)	9,866	10,013
60540	Naperville	(312)	42,601	22,794
60451	New Lenox	(815)	5,792	2,855
60648	Niles	(312)	30,363	31,432
61761	Normal	(309)	35,672	26,396
60656	Norridge	(312)	16,483	17,113
60542	North Aurora	(312)	5,205	4,833
60062	Northbrook	(312)	30,735	25,422
60064	North Chicago	(312)	38,774	47,275
60164	Northlake	(312)	12,166	14,191
61111	North Park(u)	(815)	15,806	15,679
60546	North Riverside	(312)	6,764	8,097
60521	Oak Brook	(312)	6,676	4,164
60452	Oak Forest	(312)	26,096	19,271
*60454	Oak Lawn	(312)	60,590	60,305
*60301	Oak Park	(312)	54,887	62,511
62269	O'Fallon	(618)	12,173	7,268
62450	Olney	(618)	9,026	8,974
60462	Orland Park	(312)	23,045	6,391
61350	Ottawa	(815)	18,166	18,716
60067	Palatine	(312)	32,176	26,050
60463	Palos Heights	(312)	11,096	8,544
60465	Palos Hills	(312)	16,654	6,629
62557	Pana	(217)	6,040	6,326
61944	Paris	(217)	9,885	9,971
60466	Park Forest	(312)	26,222	30,638
60466	Park Forest South	(312)	6,245	1,748
60068	Park Ridge	(312)	38,704	42,614
61554	Pekin	(309)	33,967	31,375
*61601	Peoria	(309)	124,160	126,963
61614	Peoria Heights	(309)	7,453	7,943
61354	Peru	(815)	10,886	11,772
61764	Pontiac	(815)	11,227	10,595
61356	Princeton	(815)	7,342	6,959
60070	Prospect Heights	(312)	11,823	13,333
62301	Quincy	(217)	42,352	45,288
61866	Rantoul	(217)	20,161	25,562
60471	Richton Park	(312)	9,403	2,558
60627	Riverdale	(312)	13,233	15,806
60305	River Forest	(312)	12,392	13,402
60171	River Grove	(312)	10,368	11,465
60546	Riverside	(312)	9,236	10,357
60472	Robbins	(312)	8,119	9,641

ZIP code	Place		1980	1970
62454	Robinson	(618)	7,285	7,178
61068	Rochelle	(815)	8,982	8,594
61071	Rock Falls	(815)	10,624	10,287
*61125	Rockford	(815)	139,712	147,370
61201	Rock Island	(309)	46,821	50,166
60008	Rolling Meadows	(312)	20,167	19,178
60441	Romeoville	(815)	15,519	12,888
60172	Roselle	(312)	17,034	6,207
62024	Rosewood Heights(u)	(217)	5,085	3,391
60073	Round Lake Beach	(312)	12,921	5,717
60174	St. Charles	(312)	17,492	12,945
62881	Salem	(618)	7,813	6,187
60548	Sandwich	(815)	5,365	5,056
60411	Sauk Village	(312)	10,906	7,479
60172	Schaumburg	(312)	53,355	18,531
60176	Schiller Park	(312)	11,458	12,712
62225	Scott AFB(u)	(618)	8,648	7,871
62565	Shelbyville	(217)	5,259	4,887
61282	Silvis	(309)	7,130	5,907
60076	Skokie	(312)	60,278	68,322
60177	South Elgin	(312)	5,970	4,289
60473	South Holland	(312)	24,977	23,931
*62703	Springfield	(217)	100,054	91,753
61362	Spring Valley	(815)	5,822	5,605
60475	Steger	(312)	9,269	8,104
61081	Sterling	(815)	16,273	16,113
60402	Stickney	(312)	5,893	6,601
60103	Streamwood	(312)	23,456	18,176
61364	Streator	(815)	14,795	15,600
60501	Summit	(312)	10,110	11,569
62221	Swansea	(618)	5,347	5,482
60178	Sycamore	(815)	9,219	7,843
62568	Taylorville	(217)	11,386	10,644
60477	Tinley Park	(312)	26,178	12,572
61801	Urbana	(217)	35,978	33,976
62471	Vandalia	(618)	5,338	5,160
60061	Vernon Hills	(312)	9,827	1,056
60181	Villa Park	(312)	23,155	25,891
60555	Warrenville	(312)	7,519	3,281
61571	Washington	(309)	10,364	6,790
62204	Washington Park	(618)	8,223	9,524
60970	Watseka	(815)	5,543	5,294
60084	Wauconda	(312)	5,688	5,460
60085	Waukegan	(312)	67,653	65,134
60153	Westchester	(312)	17,730	20,033
60185	West Chicago	(312)	12,550	9,988
60558	Western Springs	(312)	12,876	13,029
62896	West Frankfort	(618)	9,437	8,854
60559	Westmont	(312)	17,353	8,832
61604	West Peoria(u)	(309)	5,219	6,873
60187	Wheaton	(312)	43,043	31,138
60090	Wheeling	(312)	23,266	13,243
60091	Wilmette	(312)	28,221	32,134
60093	Winnetka	(312)	12,772	14,131
60096	Winthrop Harbor	(312)	5,427	4,794
60097	Wonder Lake(u)	(312)	5,917	4,806
60191	Wood Dale	(312)	11,251	8,831
60515	Woodridge	(312)	21,763	11,028
62095	Wood River	(618)	12,446	13,186
60098	Woodstock	(815)	11,725	10,226
60482	Worth	(312)	11,592	11,999
60099	Zion	(312)	17,865	17,268

Indiana

ZIP code	Place		1980	1970
46001	Alexandria	(317)	6,028	5,600
46011	Anderson	(317)	64,695	70,787
46703	Angola	(219)	5,486	5,117
46706	Auburn	(219)	8,122	7,388
47421	Bedford	(812)	14,410	13,087
46107	Beech Grove	(317)	13,196	13,559
47401	Bloomington	(812)	51,646	43,262
46714	Bluffton	(219)	8,705	8,297
47601	Boonville	(812)	6,300	5,736
47834	Brazil	(812)	7,852	8,163
46112	Brownsburg	(317)	6,242	5,751
46032	Carmel	(317)	18,272	6,691
46303	Cedar Lake	(219)	8,754	7,589
47111	Charlestown	(812)	5,596	5,933
46304	Chesterton	(219)	8,531	6,177
47130	Clarksville	(812)	15,164	13,298
47842	Clinton	(317)	5,267	5,340
47725	Columbia City	(219)	5,091	4,911
47201	Columbus	(812)	30,292	26,457
47331	Connersville	(317)	17,023	17,604
47933	Crawfordsville	(317)	13,325	13,842
46307	Crown Point	(219)	16,455	10,931
46733	Decatur	(219)	8,649	8,445
46226	Dunlap(u)	(219)	5,397	
46311	Dyer	(219)	9,555	4,906
46312	East Chicago	(219)	39,786	46,982
46514	Elkhart	(219)	41,305	43,152
46036	Elwood	(317)	10,867	11,196
47708	Evansville	(812)	130,496	138,764
*46802	Fort Wayne	(219)	172,391	178,269
46041	Frankfort	(317)	15,168	14,956
46131	Franklin	(317)	11,563	11,477
*46401	Gary	(219)	151,968	175,415
46933	Gas City	(317)	6,370	5,742
46526	Goshen	(219)	19,665	17,871
46135	Greencastle	(317)	8,403	8,852

ZIP code	Place		1980	1970
46140	Greenfield	(317)	11,299	9,986
47240	Greensburg	(812)	9,254	8,620
46142	Greenwood	(317)	19,327	11,869
46319	Griffith	(219)	17,026	18,168
*46320	Hammond	(219)	93,714	107,983
47348	Hartford City	(317)	7,622	8,207
46322	Highland	(219)	25,935	24,947
46342	Hobart	(219)	22,987	21,485
47542	Huntingburg	(812)	5,376	4,794
46750	Huntington	(219)	16,202	16,217
*46206	Indianapolis	(317)	700,807	736,856
47546	Jasper	(812)	9,097	8,641
47130	Jeffersonville	(812)	21,220	20,008
46755	Kendallville	(219)	7,299	6,838
46901	Kokomo	(317)	47,808	44,042
*47901	Lafayette	(317)	43,011	44,955
46405	Lake Station	(219)	15,087	9,858
46350	La Porte	(219)	21,796	22,140
46226	Lawrence	(317)	25,591	16,353
46052	Lebanon	(317)	11,456	9,766
47441	Linton	(812)	6,315	5,450
46947	Logansport	(219)	17,731	19,255
46356	Lowell	(219)	5,827	3,839
47250	Madison	(812)	12,472	13,081
46952	Marion	(317)	35,874	39,607
46151	Martinsville	(317)	11,311	9,723
46410	Merrillville	(219)	27,677	15,918
46360	Michigan City	(219)	36,850	39,369
46544	Mishawaka	(219)	40,224	36,060
47960	Monticello	(219)	5,162	4,869
46158	Mooresville	(317)	5,349	5,800
47620	Mount Vernon	(812)	7,656	6,770
*47302	Muncie	(317)	77,216	69,082
46321	Munster	(219)	20,671	16,514
47150	New Albany	(812)	37,103	38,402
47362	New Castle	(317)	20,056	21,215
46774	New Haven	(219)	6,714	5,346
46060	Noblesville	(317)	12,253	7,548
46962	North Manchester	(219)	5,998	5,791
47265	North Vernon	(812)	5,768	4,582
47130	Oak Park(u)	(812)	5,871	....
46970	Peru	(317)	13,764	14,139
46168	Plainfield	(317)	9,191	8,211
46563	Plymouth	(219)	7,693	7,661
46368	Portage	(219)	27,409	19,127
47371	Portland	(219)	7,074	7,115
47670	Princeton	(812)	8,976	7,431
47374	Richmond	(317)	41,349	43,999
46975	Rochester	(219)	5,050	4,631
46173	Rushville	(317)	6,113	6,686
47167	Salem	(812)	5,290	5,041
46375	Schererville	(219)	13,209	3,663
47170	Scottsburg	(812)	5,068	4,791
47274	Seymour	(812)	15,050	13,352
46176	Shelbyville	(317)	14,989	15,094
*46624	South Bend	(219)	109,727	125,580
46383	South Haven(u)	(219)	6,679	....
46224	Speedway	(317)	12,641	14,523
47586	Tell City	(812)	8,704	7,933
*47808	Terre Haute	(812)	61,125	70,335
46072	Tipton	(317)	5,004	5,313
46383	Valparaiso	(219)	22,247	20,020
47591	Vincennes	(812)	20,857	19,867
46992	Wabash	(219)	12,985	13,379
46580	Warsaw	(219)	10,647	7,506
47501	Washington	(812)	11,325	11,358
*47906	West Lafayette	(317)	21,247	19,157
46394	Whiting	(219)	5,630	7,054
47394	Winchester	(317)	5,659	5,493

Iowa

ZIP code	Place		1980	1970
50511	Algona	(515)	6,289	6,032
50009	Altoona	(515)	5,764	2,883
50010	Ames	(515)	45,775	39,505
50021	Ankeny	(515)	15,429	9,151
50022	Atlantic	(712)	7,789	7,306
52722	Bettendorf	(319)	27,381	22,126
50036	Boone	(515)	12,602	12,468
52601	Burlington	(319)	29,529	32,366
51401	Carroll	(712)	9,705	8,716
50613	Cedar Falls	(319)	36,322	29,597
*52401	Cedar Rapids	(319)	110,243	110,642
52544	Centerville	(515)	6,558	6,531
50049	Chariton	(515)	5,116	5,009
50616	Charles City	(515)	8,778	9,268
51012	Cherokee	(712)	7,004	7,272
51632	Clarinda	(712)	5,458	5,420
50428	Clear Lake City	(515)	7,458	6,430
52732	Clinton	(319)	32,828	34,719
50053	Clive	(515)	5,906	3,005
52240	Coralville	(319)	7,687	6,130
51501	Council Bluffs	(712)	56,449	60,348
50801	Creston	(515)	8,429	8,234
*52802	Davenport	(319)	103,264	98,469
52101	Decorah	(319)	7,991	7,237
51442	Denison	(712)	6,675	6,218
*50318	Des Moines	(515)	191,003	201,404
52001	Dubuque	(319)	62,374	62,309
51334	Estherville	(712)	7,518	8,108
52556	Fairfield	(515)	9,428	8,715
50501	Fort Dodge	(515)	29,423	31,263
52627	Fort Madison	(319)	13,520	13,996
51534	Glenwood	(712)	5,280	4,421
50112	Grinnell	(515)	8,868	8,402
51537	Harlan	(712)	5,357	5,049
50644	Independence	(319)	6,392	5,910
50125	Indianola	(515)	10,843	8,852
52240	Iowa City	(319)	50,508	46,850
50126	Iowa Falls	(515)	6,174	6,454
52632	Keokuk	(319)	13,536	14,631
50138	Knoxville	(515)	8,143	7,755
51031	Le Mars	(712)	8,276	8,159
52060	Maquoketa	(319)	6,313	5,677
52302	Marion	(319)	19,474	18,028
50158	Marshalltown	(515)	26,938	26,219
50401	Mason City	(515)	30,144	30,379
52641	Mount Pleasant	(319)	7,322	7,007
52761	Muscatine	(319)	23,467	22,405
50201	Nevada	(515)	5,912	4,952
50208	Newton	(515)	15,292	15,619
50662	Oelwein	(319)	7,564	7,735
52577	Oskaloosa	(515)	10,629	11,224
52501	Ottumwa	(515)	27,381	29,610
50219	Pella	(515)	8,349	6,668
50220	Perry	(515)	7,053	6,906
51566	Red Oak	(712)	6,810	6,210
51201	Sheldon	(712)	5,003	4,535
51601	Shenandoah	(712)	6,274	5,968
*51301	Sioux City	(712)	82,003	85,925
51301	Spencer	(712)	11,726	10,278
50588	Storm Lake	(712)	8,814	8,591
50322	Urbandale	(515)	17,869	14,434
52349	Vinton	(319)	5,040	4,845
52353	Washington	(319)	6,584	6,317
*50701	Waterloo	(319)	75,985	75,533
50677	Waverly	(319)	8,444	7,205
50595	Webster City	(515)	8,572	8,488
50265	West Des Moines	(515)	21,894	16,441
50311	Windsor Heights	(515)	5,632	6,303

Kansas

ZIP code	Place		1980	1970
67410	Abilene	(913)	6,572	6,661
67005	Arkansas City	(316)	13,201	13,216
66002	Atchison	(913)	11,407	12,565
67010	Augusta	(316)	6,968	5,977
66012	Bonner Springs	(913)	6,266	3,884
66720	Chanute	(316)	10,506	10,341
67337	Coffeyville	(316)	15,185	15,116
67701	Colby	(913)	5,544	4,658
66901	Concordia	(913)	6,847	7,221
67037	Derby	(316)	9,786	7,947
67801	Dodge City	(316)	18,001	14,127
67042	El Dorado	(316)	11,555	12,308
66801	Emporia	(316)	25,287	23,327
66442	Fort Riley North(u)	(913)	16,086	12,469
66701	Fort Scott	(316)	8,893	8,967
67846	Garden City	(316)	18,256	14,790
67735	Goodland	(913)	5,708	5,510
67530	Great Bend	(316)	16,608	16,133
67601	Hays	(913)	16,301	15,396
67060	Haysville	(316)	8,006	6,531
67501	Hutchinson	(316)	40,284	36,885
67301	Independence	(316)	10,598	10,347
66749	Iola	(316)	6,938	6,493
66441	Junction City	(913)	19,305	19,018
*66110	Kansas City	(913)	161,148	168,213
66043	Lansing	(913)	5,307	3,797
66044	Lawrence	(913)	52,738	45,698
66048	Leavenworth	(913)	33,656	25,147
66206	Leawood	(913)	13,360	10,645
66215	Lenexa	(913)	18,639	5,549
67901	Liberal	(316)	14,911	13,862
67640	McPherson	(316)	11,753	10,851
66502	Manhattan	(913)	32,644	27,575
66203	Merriam	(913)	10,794	10,955
66222	Mission	(913)	8,643	8,125
67114	Newton	(316)	16,332	15,439
66061	Olathe	(913)	37,258	17,917
66067	Ottawa	(913)	11,016	11,036
66204	Overland Park	(913)	81,784	77,934
67357	Parsons	(316)	12,898	13,015
66762	Pittsburg	(316)	18,770	20,171
66208	Prairie Village	(913)	24,657	28,378
67124	Pratt	(316)	6,885	6,736
66203	Roeland Park	(913)	7,962	9,760
67665	Russell	(316)	5,427	5,371
67401	Salina	(913)	41,843	37,714
*66203	Shawnee	(913)	29,653	20,946
*66603	Topeka	(913)	118,690	125,011
67152	Wellington	(316)	8,212	8,072
*67202	Wichita	(316)	279,835	276,554
67156	Winfield	(316)	10,736	11,405

Kentucky

ZIP code	Place		1980	1970
41101	Ashland	(606)	27,064	29,245
40004	Bardstown	(502)	6,155	5,816

ZIP code	Place		1980	1970
41073	Bellevue	(606)	7,678	8,847
40403	Berea	(606)	8,226	6,956
42101	Bowling Green	(502)	40,450	36,705
40218	Buechel(u)	(502)	6,912	5,359
42718	Campbellsville	(502)	8,715	7,598
42330	Central City	(502)	5,250	5,450
40701	Corbin	(606)	8,075	7,474
*41011	Covington	(606)	49,585	52,535
41031	Cynthiana	(606)	5,881	6,356
40422	Danville	(606)	12,942	11,542
41074	Dayton	(606)	6,979	8,751
41017	Edgewood	(606)	7,243	4,139
42701	Elizabethtown	(502)	15,380	11,748
41018	Eismere	(606)	7,203	5,161
41018	Erlanger	(606)	14,466	12,676
40118	Fairdale(u)	(502)	7,315	....
40291	Fern Creek(u)	(502)	16,866	....
41139	Flatwoods	(606)	8,354	7,380
41042	Florence	(606)	15,586	11,661
42223	Fort Campbell North(u)	(502)	17,211	13,616
40121	Fort Knox(u)	(502)	31,035	37,608
41017	Fort Mitchell	(606)	7,294	6,982
41075	Fort Thomas	(606)	16,012	16,338
40601	Frankfort	(502)	25,973	21,902
42134	Franklin	(502)	7,738	6,553
40324	Georgetown	(502)	10,972	8,629
42141	Glasgow	(502)	12,958	11,301
40330	Harrodsburg	(606)	7,265	6,741
41701	Hazard	(606)	5,429	5,459
42420	Henderson	(502)	24,834	22,976
40228	Highview(u)	(502)	13,286	....
40229	Hillview	(502)	5,196	....
42240	Hopkinsville	(502)	27,318	21,395
41051	Independence	(606)	7,998	1,715
40299	Jeffersontown	(502)	15,795	9,701
40342	Lawrenceburg	(502)	5,167	3,579
40033	Lebanon	(502)	6,590	5,528
*40511	Lexington-Fayette	(606)	204,165	108,137
*40201	Louisville	(502)	298,694	361,706
42431	Madisonville	(502)	16,979	15,332
42066	Mayfield	(502)	10,705	10,724
41056	Maysville	(606)	7,983	7,411
40965	Middlesborough	(606)	12,251	11,878
42633	Monticello	(606)	5,677	3,618
40351	Morehead	(606)	7,789	7,191
40353	Mount Sterling	(606)	5,820	5,083
42071	Murray	(502)	14,248	13,537
40218	Newburg(u)	(502)	24,612	....
*41071	Newport	(606)	21,587	25,998
40356	Nicholasville	(606)	10,400	5,829
40219	Okolona(u)	(502)	20,039	17,643
42301	Owensboro	(502)	54,450	50,329
42001	Paducah	(502)	29,315	31,627
40361	Paris	(606)	7,935	7,823
40258	Pleasure Ridge Park(u)	(502)	27,332	28,566
42445	Princeton	(502)	7,073	6,292
40160	Radcliff	(502)	14,519	8,426
40475	Richmond	(606)	21,705	16,861
42276	Russellville	(502)	7,520	6,456
40207	St. Matthews	(502)	13,519	13,152
40065	Shelbyville	(502)	5,308	4,182
40216	Shively	(502)	16,645	19,139
42501	Somerset	(606)	10,649	10,436
40272	Valley Station(u)	(502)	24,474	24,471
40383	Versailles	(606)	6,427	5,679
41101	Westwood(u)	(606)	5,973	777
40769	Williamsburg	(606)	5,560	3,687
40391	Winchester	(606)	15,216	13,402

Louisiana

ZIP code	Place		1980	1970
70510	Abbeville	(318)	12,391	10,996
71301	Alexandria	(318)	51,565	41,811
70032	Arabi(u)	(504)	10,248	....
70094	Avondale(u)	(504)	6,699	....
70714	Baker	(504)	12,865	8,281
71220	Bastrop	(318)	15,527	14,713
*70821	Baton Rouge	(504)	220,394	165,921
70360	Bayou Cane(u)	(504)	15,723	9,077
70380	Bayou Vista(u)	(504)	5,805	5,121
70037	Belle Chasse(u)	(504)	5,412	....
70427	Bogalusa	(504)	16,976	18,412
71110	Bossier City	(318)	49,969	43,769
70517	Breaux Bridge	(318)	5,922	4,942
	Broadmoor(u)	(318)	7,051	....
71291	Brownsville-Bawcomville(u)	(318)	7,252	....
71322	Bunkie	(318)	5,364	5,395
70043	Chalmette(u)	(504)	33,847	....
71291	Claiborne(u)	(318)	6,278	....
70433	Covington	(504)	7,892	7,170
70526	Crowley	(318)	16,036	16,104
70345	Cut Off(u)	(504)	5,049	....
70726	Denham Springs	(504)	8,412	6,752
70634	De Ridder	(318)	11,057	8,030
70346	Donaldsonville	(318)	7,901	7,367
70072	Estelle(u)	(504)	12,724	....
70535	Eunice	(318)	12,479	11,390
70538	Franklin	(318)	9,584	9,325
70354	Galliano(u)	(504)	5,159	....
70737	Gonzales	(504)	7,287	4,512
70053	Gretna	(504)	20,615	24,875
70401	Hammond	(504)	15,226	12,487
70123	Harahan	(504)	11,384	13,037
70058	Harvey(u)	(504)	22,709	6,347
70360	Houma	(504)	32,602	30,922
70544	Jeanerette	(318)	6,511	6,322
70121	Jefferson(u)	(504)	15,550	16,489
70546	Jennings	(318)	12,401	11,783
71251	Jonesboro	(318)	5,061	5,072
70548	Kaplan	(318)	5,016	5,540
70062	Kenner	(504)	66,382	29,858
70445	Lacombe(u)	(504)	5,146	....
70501	Lafayette	(318)	80,584	68,908
70601	Lake Charles	(318)	75,051	77,998
71254	Lake Providence	(318)	6,361	6,183
70068	Laplace(u)	(504)	16,112	5,953
70373	Larose(u)	(504)	5,234	4,267
71446	Leesville	(318)	9,054	8,928
70123	Little Farms(u)	(504)	NA	15,713
70448	Mandeville	(504)	6,076	2,571
71052	Mansfield	(318)	6,485	6,432
71351	Marksville	(318)	5,113	4,519
70072	Marrero(u)	(504)	36,548	29,015
*70004	Metairie(u)	(504)	164,160	136,477
71055	Minden	(318)	15,074	13,996
71201	Monroe	(318)	57,597	56,374
70380	Morgan City	(504)	16,114	16,586
70601	Moss Bluff(u)	(318)	7,004	....
71457	Natchitoches	(318)	16,664	15,974
70560	New Iberia	(318)	32,766	30,147
*70113	New Orleans	(504)	557,927	593,471
71463	Oakdale	(318)	7,155	7,301
70570	Opelousas	(318)	18,903	20,387
71360	Pineville	(318)	12,034	8,951
70764	Plaquemine	(504)	7,521	7,739
70454	Ponchatoula	(504)	5,469	4,545
70767	Port Allen	(504)	6,114	5,728
70085	Poydras(u)	(504)	5,722	....
70601	Prien(u)	(318)	6,224	....
70394	Raceland(u)	(504)	6,302	4,880
70578	Rayne	(318)	9,066	9,510
70084	Reserve(u)	(504)	7,288	6,381
70123	River Ridge(u)	(504)	17,146	....
71270	Ruston	(318)	20,585	17,365
70582	St. Martinville	(318)	7,965	7,153
70807	Scotlandville(u)	(504)	15,113	22,599
*71102	Shreveport	(318)	205,815	182,064
70458	Slidell	(504)	26,718	16,101
71459	South Fort Polk(u)	(318)	12,498	15,600
71075	Springhill	(318)	6,516	6,496
70663	Sulphur	(318)	19,709	14,959
71282	Tallulah	(318)	11,341	9,643
71285	Terrytown(u)	(504)	23,548	13,382
70301	Thibodaux	(504)	15,810	15,028
70053	Timberlane(u)	(504)	11,579	....
71373	Vidalia	(318)	5,936	5,538
70586	Ville Platte	(318)	9,201	9,692
70092	Violet(u)	(504)	11,678	....
70094	Waggaman(u)	(504)	9,004	....
70669	Westlake	(318)	5,246	4,082
71291	West Monroe	(318)	14,993	14,868
70094	Westwego	(504)	12,663	11,402
71483	Winnfield	(318)	7,311	7,142
71295	Winnsboro	(318)	5,921	5,349
70791	Zachary	(504)	7,297	4,964

Maine (207)

See Note Page 268

ZIP code	Place	1980	1970
04210	Auburn	23,128	24,151
04330	Augusta	21,819	21,945
04401	Bangor	31,643	33,168
04530	Bath	10,246	9,679
04915	Belfast	6,243	5,957
04005	Biddeford	19,638	19,983
04412	Brewer	9,017	9,300
04011	Brunswick Center(u)	10,990	10,867
04011	Brunswick	17,366	16,195
04093	Buxton	5,775	3,135
04107	Cape Elizabeth	7,838	7,873
04736	Caribou	9,916	10,419
04021	Cumberland	5,284	4,096
04605	Ellsworth	5,179	4,603
04937	Fairfield	6,113	5,684
04105	Falmouth	6,853	6,291
04938	Farmington	6,730	5,657
04032	Freeport	5,863	4,781
04345	Gardiner	6,485	6,685
04038	Gorham	10,101	7,839
04444	Hampden	5,250	4,693
04730	Houlton Center(u)	5,730	6,760
04730	Houlton	6,766	8,111
04239	Jay	5,080	3,954
04043	Kennebunk	6,621	5,646
03904	Kittery Center(u)	5,465	7,363
03904	Kittery	9,314	11,028
04240	Lewiston	40,481	41,779

ZIP code	Place	1980	1970
04750	*Limestone*	8,719	10,360
04457	*Lincoln*	5,066	4,759
04250	*Lisbon*	8,769	6,544
04750	Loring(u)	6,572	7,881
04756	*Madawaska*	5,282	5,585
04462	Millinocket Center(u)	7,567	7,558
04462	*Millinocket*	7,567	7,742
04062	North Windham(u)	5,492	....
04963	*Oakland*	5,162	3,535
04064	Old Orchard Beach Ctr.(u).	6,023	5,273
04064	*Old Orchard Beach.*	6,291	5,404
04468	Old Town	8,422	8,741
04473	Orono Center(u)	9,891	9,146
04473	*Orono*	10,578	9,989
*04101	*Portland*	61,572	65,116
04769	Presque Isle	11,172	11,452
04841	Rockland.	7,919	8,505
04276	Rumford Compact(u).	6,256	6,198
04276	*Rumford*	8,240	9,363
04072	Saco	12,921	11,678
04073	Sanford Center(u)	10,268	10,457
04073	*Sanford.*	18,020	15,812
04074	*Scarborough.*	11,347	7,845
04976	Skowhegan Center(u)	6,517	6,571
04976	*Skowhegan*	8,098	7,601
04106	South Portland	22,712	23,267
04084	*Standish*	5,946	3,122
04086	*Topsham.*	6,431	5,022
04901	Waterville	17,779	18,192
04090	*Wells*	8,211	4,448
04092	Westbrook	14,976	14,444
04082	*Windham.*	11,282	6,593
04901	Winslow Center(u)	5,903	5,389
04901	*Winslow*	8,057	7,299
04364	*Winthrop.*	5,889	4,335
04096	*Yarmouth*	6,585	4,854
03909	*York*	8,465	5,690

Maryland (301)

ZIP code	Place	1980	1970
21001	Aberdeen	11,533	7,403
21005	Aberdeen Proving Ground(u)	5,772	7,403
20783	Adelphi(u)	12,530	....
20331	Andrews(u)	10,064	6,418
*21401	Annapolis	31,740	30,095
21227	Arbutus(u)	20,163	22,745
21012	Arnold(u)	12,285	....
20906	Aspen Hill(u)	47,455	16,887
*21233	Baltimore.	786,741	905,787
21014	Bel Air	7,814	6,307
21050	Bel Air North(u)	5,043	....
21014	Bel Air South(u)	8,461	....
20705	Beltsville(u)	12,760	8,912
20815	Bethesda(u)	63,022	71,621
20710	Bladensburg	7,691	7,977
20715	Bowie.	33,695	35,028
21225	Brooklyn Park(u)	11,508	....
20731	Cabin John-Brookmont(u)	5,135	....
20619	California(u)	5,770	....
21613	Cambridge	11,703	11,595
20748	Camp Springs(u)	16,118	22,776
21401	Cape St. Clair(u)	6,022	....
20027	Carmody Hills-Pepper Mill(u)	5,571	6,245
21234	Carney(u)	21,488	....
21228	Catonsville(u).	33,208	54,812
20785	Cheverly	5,751	6,808
20815	Chevy Chase(u).	12,232	16,424
20783	Chillum(u)	32,775	35,656
20735	Clinton(u).	16,438	....
20904	Cloverly(u).	5,153	....
21030	Cockeysville(u)	17,013	....
20904	Colesville(u)	14,359	9,455
20740	College Park.	23,614	26,156
21043	Columbia(u).	52,518	8,815
20027	Coral Hills(u).	11,602	9,058
21114	Crofton(u)	12,009	4,478
21502	Cumberland .	25,933	29,724
20747	District Heights	6,799	7,846
20785	Dodge Park(u).	5,275	....
21222	Dundalk(u).	71,293	85,377
21601	Easton.	7,536	6,809
20849	East Riverdale(u)	14,117	....
21219	Edgemere(u).	9,078	10,352
21040	Edgewood .	19,455	8,551
21921	Elkton.	6,468	5,362
*21043	Ellicott(u).	21,784	9,435
21221	Essex(u)	39,614	38,193
20904	Fairland(u)	5,154	....
21047	Fallston(u)	5,572	....
21061	Ferndale(u)	4,314	9,929
21050	Forestville(u)	16,401	16,188
20755	Fort Meade(u)	14,083	16,699
21701	Frederick.	27,557	23,641
	Friendly(u)	8,848	....
21532	Frostburg.	7,715	7,327
20877	Gaithersburg.	26,424	8,344
20874	Germantown(u)	9,721	....

ZIP code	Place	1980	1970
....	Glassmanor(u)	7,751	....
21061	Glen Burnie(u).	37,263	38,608
20769	Glenn Dale(u)	5,106	....
20771	Goddard(u)	6,147	....
20770	Greenbelt	16,000	18,199
21122	Green Haven(u)	6,577	....
21740	Hagerstown	34,132	35,862
21740	Halfway(u).	8,659	6,106
21204	Hampton(u)	5,220	....
21078	Havre De Grace.	8,763	9,791
20903	Hillandale(u)	9,686	....
20031	Hillcrest Heights.	17,021	24,037
*20780	Hyattsville	12,709	14,998
21085	Joppatowne(u)	11,348	9,092
20785	Kentland(u)	8,596	9,649
20870	Kettering(u)	6,972	....
21122	Lake Shore(u)	10,181	....
20785	Landover(u)	5,374	5,597
20787	Langley Park(u)	14,038	11,564
20706	Lanham-Seabrook(u)	15,814	13,244
21227	Lansdowne-Baltimore Highlands(u)	16,759	17,770
	Largo(u)	5,557	....
20810	Laurel	12,103	10,525
21502	La Vale-Narrows Park(u).	5,523	3,971
20653	Lexington Pk.(u).	10,361	9,136
21090	Linthicum(u)	7,457	9,775
21207	Lochearn(u)	26,908	....
21037	Londontowne(u).	6,052	3,864
21093	Lutherville-Timonium(u).	17,854	24,055
20031	Marlow Heights(u)	5,824	....
20810	Maryland City(u)	6,949	7,102
	Mays Chapel(u).	5,213	....
21220	Middle River(u)	26,756	19,935
	Milford Mill(u)	20,354	....
20879	Montgomery Village(u)	18,725	....
20822	Mount Rainier	7,361	8,180
21402	Naval Academy(u)	5,367	....
20784	New Carrollton	12,632	14,870
20014	North Bethesda(u)	22,671	....
20795	North Kensington(u)	9,039	....
20810	North Laurel(u)	6,093	....
21113	Odenton(u).	13,270	5,989
20832	Olney(u)	13,026	2,138
21206	Overlea(u)	12,965	13,124
21117	Owings Mills(u)	9,526	7,360
20745	Oxon Hill(u)	36,267	11,974
20785	Palmer Park(u)	7,986	8,172
21234	Parkville	35,159	33,589
21122	Pasadena(u).	7,439	....
21128	Perry Hall(u)	13,455	5,446
21208	Pikesville(u)	22,555	25,395
20854	Potomac(u)	40,402	....
21227	Pumphrey(u).	5,666	6,425
20760	Quince Orchard(u)	5,107	....
21133	Randallstown(u)	25,927	33,683
	Redland(u)	10,759	....
21136	Reisterstown(u)	19,385	12,568
21122	Riviera Beach(u)	8,812	7,464
*20850	Rockville(u)	43,811	42,739
21237	Rosedale(u)	19,956	19,417
21221	Rossville(u)	6,646	....
20601	St. Charles(u)	13,921	....
21801	Salisbury.	16,429	15,252
20027	Seat Pleasant	5,217	7,217
21740	Security(u)	29,453	....
21144	Severn(u)	20,147	....
21146	Severna Park	21,253	16,358
*20907	Silver Spring(u)	72,893	77,411
21061	South Gate(u)	24,185	9,356
20795	South Kensington(u)	9,344	10,289
20810	South Laurel(u)	18,034	13,345
20023	Suitland-Silver Hills(u)	32,164	30,355
20912	Takoma Park	16,231	18,507
	Tantallon(u)	9,945	....
20748	Temple Hills(u)	6,630	....
21204	Towson(u)	51,083	77,768
20601	Waldorf(u)	9,782	7,368
20028	Walker Mill(u)	10,651	7,103
21157	Westminster	8,808	7,207
20902	Wheaton Glenmont(u)	48,598	66,280
20903	White Oak(u)	13,700	19,769
20695	White Plains(u)	5,167	....
21207	Woodlawn(u)	5,306	....

Massachusetts

See Note on Page 268

ZIP code	Place		1980	1970
02351	*Abington*	(617)	13,517	12,334
01720	*Acton.*	(617)	17,544	14,770
02743	*Acushnet.*	(617)	8,704	7,767
01220	Adams Center(u)	(413)	6,857	11,256
	Adams.	(413)	10,381	11,772
01001	*Agawam.*	(413)	26,271	21,717
01913	Amesbury Center(u)	(617)	12,236	10,088
	Amesbury	(617)	13,971	11,388
01002	Amherst Center	(413)	17,773	17,926
	Amherst	(413)	33,229	26,331
01810	*Andover*	(617)	26,370	23,695
02174	*Arlington*	(617)	48,219	53,524
01721	*Ashland*	(617)	9,165	8,882

ZIP code	Place		1980	1970
01331	Athol Center(u)	(617)	8,708	9,723
.....	Athol	(617)	10,634	11,185
02703	Attleboro	(617)	34,196	32,907
01501	Auburn	(617)	14,845	15,347
02322	Avon	(617)	5,026	5,295
*01432	Ayer	(617)	6,993	8,325
02630	Barnstable	(617)	30,898	19,842
01730	Bedford	(617)	13,067	13,513
01007	Belchertown	(413)	8,339	5,936
02019	Bellingham	(617)	14,300	13,967
02178	Belmont	(617)	26,100	28,285
01915	Beverly	(617)	37,655	38,348
01821	Billerica	(617)	36,727	31,648
01504	Blackstone	(617)	6,570	6,566
*02109	Boston	(617)	562,994	641,071
02532	Bourne	(617)	13,874	12,636
01921	Boxford	(617)	5,374	4,032
02184	Braintree	(617)	36,337	35,050
02631	Brewster	(617)	5,226	1,790
02324	Bridgewater	(617)	17,202	12,911
*02403	Brockton	(617)	95,172	89,040
02146	Brookline	(617)	55,062	58,689
01803	Burlington	(617)	23,486	21,980
*02138	Cambridge	(617)	95,322	100,361
02021	Canton	(617)	18,182	17,100
02330	Carver	(617)	6,988	2,420
01507	Charlton	(617)	6,719	4,654
02633	Chatham	(617)	6,071	4,554
01824	Chelmsford	(617)	31,174	31,432
02150	Chelsea	(617)	25,431	30,625
*01021	Chicopee	(413)	55,112	66,676
01510	Clinton	(617)	12,771	13,383
01778	Cochituate(u)	(617)	6,126	.....
02025	Cohasset	(617)	7,174	6,954
01742	Concord	(617)	16,293	16,148
01226	Dalton	(413)	6,797	7,505
01923	Danvers	(617)	24,100	26,151
02714	Dartmouth	(617)	23,966	18,800
02026	Dedham	(617)	25,298	26,938
02638	Dennis	(617)	12,360	6,454
02715	Dighton	(617)	5,352	4,667
01826	Dracut	(617)	21,249	18,214
01570	Dudley	(617)	8,717	8,087
02332	Duxbury	(617)	11,807	7,636
02333	East Bridgewater	(617)	9,945	8,347
02536	East Falmouth(u)	(617)	5,181	2,971
01027	Easthampton	(413)	15,580	13,012
01028	East Longmeadow	(413)	12,905	13,029
02334	Easton	(617)	16,623	12,157
01249	Everett	(617)	37,195	42,485
02719	Fairhaven	(617)	15,759	16,332
*02722	Fall River	(617)	92,574	96,898
*02540	Falmouth Center(u)	(617)	5,720	5,806
.....	Falmouth	(617)	23,640	15,942
01420	Fitchburg	(617)	39,580	43,343
01433	Fort Devens(u)	(617)	9,546	12,915
02035	Foxborough	(617)	14,148	14,218
01701	Framingham	(617)	65,113	64,048
02038	Franklin Center(u)	(617)	9,296	8,863
.....	Franklin	(617)	18,217	17,830
02702	Freetown	(617)	7,058	4,270
01440	Gardner	(617)	17,900	19,748
01833	Georgetown	(617)	5,687	5,290
01930	Gloucester	(617)	27,768	27,941
01519	Grafton	(617)	11,238	11,659
01033	Granby	(413)	5,380	5,473
01230	Great Barrington	(413)	7,405	7,537
01301	Greenfield Center(u)	(413)	14,198	14,642
.....	Greenfield	(413)	18,436	18,116
01450	Groton	(617)	6,154	5,109
01834	Groveland	(617)	5,040	5,382
02338	Halifax	(617)	5,513	3,537
01936	Hamilton	(617)	6,960	6,373
02339	Hanover	(617)	11,358	10,107
02341	Hanson	(617)	8,617	7,148
01451	Harvard	(617)	12,170	12,494
02645	Harwich	(617)	8,971	5,892
01830	Haverhill	(617)	46,865	46,120
02043	Hingham	(617)	20,339	18,845
02343	Holbrook	(617)	11,140	11,775
01520	Holden	(617)	13,336	12,564
01746	Holliston	(617)	12,622	12,069
01040	Holyoke	(413)	44,678	50,112
01748	Hopkinton	(617)	7,114	5,981
01749	Hudson Center(u)	(617)	14,156	14,283
.....	Hudson	(617)	16,408	16,084
02045	Hull	(617)	9,714	9,961
02601	Hyannis(u)	(617)	9,118	6,847
01938	Ipswich	(617)	NA	5,022
.....	Ipswich	(617)	11,158	10,750
02364	Kingston	(617)	7,362	5,999
02346	Lakeville	(617)	5,931	4,376
01523	Lancaster	(617)	6,334	6,095
*01842	Lawrence	(617)	63,175	66,915
01238	Lee	(413)	6,247	6,426
01524	Leicester	(617)	9,446	9,140
01240	Lenox	(413)	6,523	5,804
01453	Leominster	(617)	34,508	32,939
02173	Lexington	(617)	29,479	31,886
01773	Lincoln	(617)	7,098	7,567
01460	Littleton	(617)	6,970	6,380
01106	Longmeadow	(413)	16,301	15,630
*01853	Lowell	(617)	92,418	94,239
01056	Ludlow	(413)	18,150	17,580
01462	Lunenburg	(617)	8,405	7,419
*01901	Lynn	(617)	78,471	90,294
01940	Lynnfield	(617)	11,267	10,826
02148	Malden	(617)	53,386	56,127
01944	Manchester	(617)	5,424	5,151
02048	Mansfield	(617)	13,453	9,939
01945	Marblehead	(617)	20,126	21,295
01752	Marlborough	(617)	30,617	27,936
02050	Marshfield	(617)	20,916	15,223
02739	Mattapoisett	(617)	5,597	4,500
01754	Maynard	(617)	9,590	9,710
02052	Medfield	(617)	10,220	9,821
02155	Medford	(617)	58,076	64,397
02053	Medway	(617)	8,447	7,938
02176	Melrose	(617)	30,055	33,180
01844	Methuen	(617)	36,701	35,456
02346	Middleborough Center(u)	(617)	7,012	6,259
.....	Middleborough	(617)	16,404	13,607
01757	Milford Center(u)	(617)	NA	13,740
.....	Milford	(617)	23,390	19,352
01527	Millbury	(617)	11,808	11,987
02054	Millis	(617)	6,908	5,686
02186	Milton	(617)	25,860	27,190
01057	Monson	(413)	7,315	7,355
01351	Montague	(413)	8,011	8,451
02554	Nantucket	(617)	5,087	3,774
01760	Natick	(617)	29,461	31,057
02192	Needham	(617)	27,901	29,748
*02741	New Bedford	(617)	98,478	101,777
01950	Newburyport	(617)	15,900	15,807
02158	Newton	(617)	83,622	91,263
02056	Norfolk	(617)	6,363	4,656
01247	North Adams	(413)	18,063	19,195
01002	North Amherst(u)	(413)	5,616	2,854
01060	Northampton	(413)	29,286	29,664
01845	North Andover	(617)	20,129	16,284
*02760	North Attleborough	(617)	21,095	18,665
01532	Northborough	(617)	10,568	9,218
01534	Northbridge	(617)	12,246	11,795
01864	North Reading	(617)	11,455	11,264
02060	North Scituate(u)	(617)	5,221	5,507
02766	Norton	(617)	12,690	9,487
02061	Norwell	(617)	9,182	7,796
02062	Norwood	(617)	29,711	30,815
01364	Orange	(617)	6,844	6,104
02653	Orleans	(617)	5,306	3,055
01253	Otis(u)	(413)	NA	5,596
01540	Oxford Center(u)	(617)	6,369	6,109
.....	Oxford	(617)	11,680	10,345
01069	Palmer	(413)	11,389	11,680
01960	Peabody	(617)	45,976	48,080
02359	Pembroke	(617)	13,487	11,193
01463	Pepperell	(617)	8,061	5,887
01866	Pinehurst(u)	(617)	6,588	.....
01201	Pittsfield	(413)	51,974	57,020
02062	Plainville	(617)	5,857	4,953
*02360	Plymouth Center(u)	(617)	7,232	6,940
.....	Plymouth	(617)	35,913	18,606
02169	Quincy	(617)	84,743	87,966
02368	Randolph	(617)	28,218	27,035
02767	Raynham	(617)	9,085	6,705
01867	Reading	(617)	22,678	22,539
02769	Rehoboth	(617)	7,570	6,512
02151	Revere	(617)	42,423	43,159
02370	Rockland	(617)	15,695	15,674
01966	Rockport	(617)	6,345	5,636
01970	Salem	(617)	38,276	40,556
01950	Salisbury	(617)	5,973	4,179
02563	Sandwich	(617)	8,727	5,239
01906	Saugus	(617)	24,746	25,110
02066	Scituate	(617)	17,317	16,973
02771	Seekonk	(617)	12,269	11,116
02067	Sharon	(617)	13,601	12,367
01464	Shirley	(617)	5,124	4,909
01545	Shrewsbury	(617)	22,674	19,196
02725	Somerset	(617)	18,813	18,088
02143	Somerville	(617)	77,372	88,779
01772	Southborough	(617)	6,193	5,798
01550	Southbridge Center(u)	(617)	12,882	14,261
.....	Southbridge	(617)	16,665	17,057
01075	South Hadley	(413)	16,399	17,033
01077	Southwick	(413)	7,382	6,330
02664	South Yarmouth(u)	(617)	7,525	5,380
01562	Spencer Center	(617)	6,350	5,895
.....	Spencer	(617)	10,774	8,779
01938	Springfield	(413)	152,319	163,905
01564	Sterling	(617)	5,440	4,247
02180	Stoneham	(617)	21,424	20,725
02072	Stoughton	(617)	26,710	23,459
01775	Stow	(617)	5,144	3,984
01566	Sturbridge	(617)	5,976	4,878
01776	Sudbury	(617)	14,027	13,506
01527	Sutton	(617)	5,855	4,590
01907	Swampscott	(617)	13,837	13,578
02777	Swansea	(617)	15,461	12,640
02780	Taunton	(617)	45,001	43,756

ZIP code	Place		1980	1980
01468	Templeton	(617)	6,070	5,863
01876	Tewksbury	(617)	24,635	22,755
01983	Topsfield	(617)	5,709	5,225
01469	Townsend	(617)	7,201	4,281
01376	Turners Falls(u)	(413)	NA	5,168
01879	Tyngsborough	(617)	5,683	4,204
01569	Uxbridge	(617)	8,374	8,253
01880	Wakefield	(617)	24,895	25,402
02081	Walpole	(617)	18,859	18,149
02154	Waltham	(617)	58,200	61,582
01082	Ware Center(u)	(413)	6,806	6,509
.....	Ware	(413)	8,953	8,187
02571	Wareham	(617)	18,457	11,492
02172	Watertown	(617)	34,384	39,307
01778	Wayland	(617)	12,170	13,461
01570	Webster Center(u)	(617)	11,175	12,432
.....	Webster	(617)	14,480	14,917
02181	Wellesley	(617)	27,209	28,051
01581	Westborough	(617)	13,619	12,594
01583	West Boylston	(617)	6,204	6,369
02379	West Bridgewater	(617)	6,359	6,070
01742	West Concord(u)	(617)	5,331	----
01085	Westfield	(413)	36,465	31,433
01886	Westford	(617)	13,434	10,368
01473	Westminster	(617)	5,139	4,273
02193	Weston	(617)	11,169	10,870
02790	Westport	(617)	13,763	9,791
01089	West Springfield	(413)	27,042	28,461
02090	Westwood	(617)	13,212	12,570
02188	Weymouth	(617)	55,601	54,610
01588	Whitinsville(u)	(617)	5,379	5,210
02382	Whitman	(617)	13,534	13,059
01095	Wilbraham	(413)	12,053	11,984
01267	Williamstown	(413)	8,741	8,454
01887	Wilmington	(617)	17,471	17,102
01475	Winchendon	(617)	7,019	6,635
01890	Winchester	(617)	20,701	22,269
02152	Winthrop	(617)	19,294	20,335
01801	Woburn	(617)	36,626	37,406
*01613	Worcester	(617)	161,799	176,572
02093	Wrentham	(617)	7,580	7,315
02675	Yarmouth	(617)	18,449	12,033

Michigan

ZIP code	Place		1980	1980
49221	Adrian	(517)	21,276	20,382
49224	Albion	(517)	11,059	12,112
48101	Allen Park	(313)	34,196	40,747
48801	Alma	(517)	9,652	9,611
49707	Alpena	(517)	12,214	13,805
*48106	Ann Arbor	(313)	107,969	100,035
48063	Avon(u)	(313)	40,779	----
*49016	Battle Creek	(616)	35,724	38,931
48706	Bay City	(517)	41,593	49,449
48505	Beecher(u)	(313)	17,178	----
48809	Belding	(616)	5,634	5,121
49022	Benton Harbor	(616)	14,707	16,481
49022	Benton Heights(u)	(616)	6,787	----
48072	Berkley	(313)	18,637	21,879
48009	Beverly Hills	(313)	11,598	13,598
49307	Big Rapids	(616)	14,361	11,995
*48012	Birmingham	(313)	21,689	26,170
48013	Bloomfield(u)	(313)	42,870	----
48107	Buchanan	(616)	5,142	4,645
*48502	Burton	(313)	29,976	32,540
49601	Cadillac	(616)	10,199	9,990
48724	Carrollton(u)	(517)	7,482	7,300
48015	Center Line	(313)	9,293	10,379
48813	Charlotte	(517)	8,251	8,244
49721	Cheboygan	(616)	5,106	5,553
48017	Clawson	(313)	15,103	17,617
48043	Clinton(u)	(313)	72,400	1,677
49036	Coldwater	(517)	9,461	9,155
49321	Comstock Park(u)	(616)	5,506	5,766
49508	Cutlerville(u)	(616)	8,256	6,267
48423	Davison	(313)	6,087	5,259
*48120	Dearborn	(313)	90,660	104,199
48127	Dearborn Heights	(313)	67,706	80,069
*48233	Detroit	(313)	1,203,368	1,514,063
49047	Dowagiac	(616)	6,307	6,583
48021	East Detroit	(313)	38,280	45,920
49506	East Grand Rapids	(616)	10,914	12,565
48823	East Lansing	(517)	48,309	47,540
49001	Eastwood(u)	(517)	7,186	9,682
48229	Ecorse	(313)	14,447	17,515
49829	Escanaba	(906)	14,355	15,368
49022	Fair Plain(u)	(616)	8,289	3,680
48024	Farmington	(313)	11,022	10,329
48024	Farmington Hills	(313)	58,056	48,694
48430	Fenton	(313)	8,098	8,284
48220	Ferndale	(313)	26,227	30,850
48134	Flat Rock	(313)	6,853	5,643
*48502	Flint	(313)	159,611	193,317
48433	Flushing	(313)	8,624	7,190
48026	Fraser	(313)	14,560	11,868
48135	Garden City	(313)	35,640	41,864
48439	Grand Blanc	(313)	6,848	5,132
49417	Grand Haven	(616)	11,763	11,844
48837	Grand Ledge	(517)	6,920	6,032
*49501	Grand Rapids	(616)	181,843	197,649
49418	Grandville	(616)	12,412	10,764
48838	Greenville	(616)	8,019	7,493
48138	Grosse Ile(u)	(313)	9,320	8,306
48236	Grosse Pointe	(313)	5,901	6,637
48236	Grosse Pointe Farms	(313)	10,551	11,701
48236	Grosse Pointe Park	(313)	13,562	15,641
48236	Grosse Pointe Woods	(313)	18,886	21,878
48212	Hamtramck	(313)	21,300	26,783
49930	Hancock	(906)	5,122	4,820
48236	Harper Woods	(313)	16,361	20,186
48625	Harrison(u)	(517)	23,649	----
48840	Haslett(u)	(517)	7,025	----
49058	Hastings	(616)	6,418	6,501
48030	Hazel Park	(313)	20,914	23,784
48203	Highland Park	(313)	27,909	35,444
49242	Hillsdale	(517)	7,432	7,728
49423	Holland	(616)	26,281	26,479
48842	Holt(u)	(517)	10,097	6,980
49931	Houghton	(906)	7,512	6,067
48843	Howell	(517)	6,976	5,224
48070	Huntington Woods	(313)	6,937	8,536
48141	Inkster	(313)	35,190	38,595
48846	Ionia	(616)	5,920	6,361
49801	Iron Mountain	(906)	8,341	8,702
49938	Ironwood	(906)	7,741	8,711
49849	Ishpeming	(906)	7,538	8,245
*49201	Jackson	(517)	39,739	45,484
49428	Jenison(u)	(616)	16,330	11,266
*49001	Kalamazoo	(616)	79,722	85,555
49508	Kentwood	(616)	30,438	20,310
49801	Kingsford	(906)	5,290	5,276
49643	K.I. Sawyer(u)	(906)	7,345	8,224
49015	Lakeview(u)	(517)	13,345	11,391
48144	Lambertville(u)	(313)	6,341	5,711
*48924	Lansing	(517)	130,414	131,403
48446	Lapeer	(313)	6,225	6,314
48146	Lincoln Park	(313)	45,105	52,984
*48150	Livonia	(313)	104,814	110,109
49431	Ludington	(616)	8,937	9,021
48071	Madison Heights	(313)	35,375	38,599
49660	Manistee	(616)	7,665	7,723
49855	Marquette	(906)	23,288	21,967
49068	Marshall	(616)	7,201	7,253
48040	Marysville	(313)	7,345	5,610
48854	Mason	(517)	6,019	5,468
48122	Melvindale	(313)	12,322	13,862
49858	Menominee	(906)	10,099	10,748
49254	Michigan Center(u)	(517)	5,244	----
48640	Midland	(517)	37,269	35,176
48042	Milford	(313)	5,041	4,699
48161	Monroe	(313)	23,531	23,894
48043	Mount Clemens	(313)	18,991	20,476
48858	Mount Pleasant	(517)	23,746	20,524
*49440	Muskegon	(616)	40,823	44,631
49444	Muskegon Heights	(616)	14,611	17,304
49866	Negaunee	(906)	5,189	5,248
48047	New Baltimore	(313)	5,439	4,132
49120	Niles	(616)	13,115	12,988
.....	Northview(u)	.....	11,662	----
48167	Northville	(313)	5,698	5,400
49441	Norton Shores	(616)	22,025	22,271
48050	Novi	(313)	22,525	9,668
48237	Oak Park	(313)	31,537	36,762
48864	Okemos(u)	(517)	8,882	7,770
48867	Owosso	(517)	16,455	17,179
49770	Petoskey	(616)	6,097	6,342
48170	Plymouth	(313)	9,986	11,758
*48053	Pontiac	(313)	76,715	85,279
49081	Portage	(616)	38,157	33,590
48060	Port Huron	(313)	33,981	35,794
48239	Redford(u)	(313)	58,441	----
48218	River Rouge	(313)	12,912	15,947
48192	Riverview	(313)	14,569	11,342
48063	Rochester	(313)	7,203	7,054
48174	Romulus	(313)	24,857	22,879
48066	Roseville	(313)	54,311	60,529
*48068	Royal Oak	(313)	70,893	86,238
*48605	Saginaw	(517)	77,508	91,849
*48083	St. Clair Shores	(313)	76,210	88,093
48879	St. Johns	(517)	7,376	6,672
49085	St. Joseph	(616)	9,622	11,042
48176	Saline	(313)	6,483	4,811
49783	Sault Ste. Marie	(906)	14,448	15,136
*48075	Southfield	(313)	75,568	69,285
48195	Southgate	(313)	32,058	33,909
49090	South Haven	(616)	5,943	6,471
48178	South Lyon	(313)	5,214	2,675
49015	Springfield	(616)	5,917	3,994
*48078	Sterling Heights	(313)	108,999	61,365
49091	Sturgis	(616)	9,468	9,295
48473	Swartz Creek	(313)	5,013	4,928
48180	Taylor	(313)	77,568	70,020
49286	Tecumseh	(517)	7,320	7,120
49093	Three Rivers	(616)	7,015	7,355
49684	Traverse City	(616)	15,516	18,048
48183	Trenton	(313)	22,762	24,127
48084	Troy	(313)	67,102	39,419
48087	Utica	(313)	5,282	3,504
49504	Walker	(616)	15,088	11,492

ZIP code	Place		1980	1970
*48089	Warren	(313)	161,134	179,260
48095	Waterford(u)	(313)	64,250	....
48184	Wayne	(313)	21,159	21,054
48033	West Bloomfield(u)	(313)	41,962	....
48185	Westland	(313)	84,603	86,749
49007	Westwood(u)	(616)	8,519	9,143
48019	White Lake-Seven Harbors(u)	(313)	7,557	....
48096	Wixom	(313)	6,705	2,010
48183	Woodhaven	(313)	10,902	3,566
48753	Wurtsmith(u)	(517)	5,166	6,932
*48192	Wyandotte	(313)	34,006	41,061
49509	Wyoming	(616)	59,616	56,560
48197	Ypsilanti	(313)	24,031	29,538

Minnesota

56007	Albert Lea	(507)	19,190	19,418
56308	Alexandria	(612)	7,608	6,973
55303	Andover	(612)	9,387	....
55303	Anoka	(612)	15,634	13,298
55068	Apple Valley	(612)	21,818	8,502
55112	Arden Hills	(612)	8,012	5,149
55912	Austin	(507)	23,020	26,210
56601	Bemidji	(218)	10,949	11,490
55433	Blaine	(612)	28,558	20,573
55420	Bloomington	(612)	81,831	81,970
56401	Brainerd	(218)	11,489	11,667
55429	Brooklyn Center	(612)	31,230	35,173
55429	Brooklyn Park	(612)	43,332	26,230
55337	Burnsville	(612)	35,674	19,940
55316	Champlin	(612)	9,006	2,275
55317	Chanhassen	(612)	6,359	4,879
55318	Chaska	(612)	8,346	4,352
55719	Chisholm	(218)	5,930	5,913
55720	Cloquet	(218)	11,142	8,699
55421	Columbia Heights	(612)	20,029	23,997
55433	Coon Rapids	(612)	35,826	30,505
55016	Cottage Grove	(612)	18,994	13,419
56716	Crookston	(218)	8,628	8,312
55428	Crystal	(612)	25,543	30,925
56501	Detroit Lakes	(218)	7,105	5,797
*55806	Duluth	(218)	92,811	100,578
55121	Eagan	(612)	20,532	10,398
55005	East Bethel	(612)	6,626	2,586
56721	East Grand Forks	(218)	8,537	7,607
55343	Eden Prairie	(612)	16,263	6,938
55424	Edina	(612)	46,073	44,046
55330	Elk River	(612)	6,785	2,252
55734	Eveleth	(218)	5,042	4,721
56031	Fairmont	(507)	11,506	10,751
55113	Falcon Heights	(507)	5,291	5,530
55021	Faribault	(507)	16,241	16,595
56537	Fergus Falls	(218)	12,519	12,443
55421	Fridley	(612)	30,228	29,233
55427	Golden Valley	(612)	22,775	24,246
55744	Grand Rapids	(218)	7,934	7,247
55303	Ham Lake	(612)	7,832	3,327
55033	Hastings	(612)	12,827	12,195
55811	Hermantown	(218)	6,759	....
55746	Hibbing	(218)	21,193	16,104
55343	Hopkins	(612)	15,336	13,428
55350	Hutchinson	(612)	9,244	8,031
55649	International Falls	(218)	5,611	6,439
55075	Inver Grove Heights	(612)	17,171	12,148
55042	Lake Elmo	(612)	5,296	3,565
55044	Lakeville	(612)	14,790	7,556
55355	Litchfield	(612)	5,904	5,262
55110	Little Canada	(612)	7,102	3,481
56345	Little Falls	(612)	7,250	7,467
56001	Mankato	(507)	28,646	30,895
55369	Maple Grove	(612)	20,525	6,275
55109	Maplewood	(612)	26,990	25,186
56258	Marshall	(507)	11,161	9,886
55118	Mendota Heights	(612)	7,288	6,565
*55401	Minneapolis	(612)	370,951	434,400
55343	Minnetonka	(612)	38,683	35,776
56265	Montevideo	(612)	5,845	5,661
56560	Moorhead	(218)	29,998	29,687
56267	Morris	(612)	5,367	5,366
55364	Mound	(612)	9,280	7,572
55112	Mounds View	(612)	12,593	10,599
55112	New Brighton	(612)	23,269	19,507
54428	New Hope	(612)	23,087	23,180
56073	New Ulm	(507)	13,755	13,051
55057	Northfield	(507)	12,562	10,235
56001	North Mankato	(507)	9,145	7,347
55109	North St. Paul	(612)	11,921	11,950
55119	Oakdale	(612)	12,123	7,795
55323	Orono	(612)	6,845	6,787
55060	Owatonna	(507)	18,632	15,341
55427	Plymouth	(612)	31,615	18,077
55372	Prior Lake	(612)	7,284	1,114
55303	Ramsey	(612)	10,093	....
55066	Red Wing	(612)	13,736	10,441
56283	Redwood Falls	(507)	5,210	4,774
55423	Richfield	(612)	37,851	47,231
55422	Robbinsdale	(612)	14,422	16,845
55901	Rochester	(507)	57,906	53,766

55068	Rosemount	(612)	5,083	1,337
55113	Roseville	(612)	35,820	34,438
55418	St. Anthony	(612)	7,981	9,239
56301	St. Cloud	(612)	42,566	39,691
55426	St. Louis Park	(612)	42,931	48,883
*55101	St. Paul	(612)	270,230	309,866
56082	St. Peter	(507)	9,056	8,339
56379	Sauk Rapids	(612)	5,793	5,051
55379	Shakopee	(612)	9,941	6,876
55112	Shoreview	(612)	17,300	10,978
55075	South St. Paul	(612)	21,235	25,016
55432	Spring Lake Park	(612)	6,477	6,417
55082	Stillwater	(612)	12,290	10,191
56701	Thief River Falls	(218)	9,105	8,618
55110	Vadnais Heights	(612)	5,111	3,411
55792	Virginia	(218)	11,056	12,450
56093	Waseca	(507)	8,219	6,789
55118	West St. Paul	(612)	18,527	18,802
55110	White Bear Lake	(612)	22,538	23,313
56201	Willmar	(612)	15,895	12,869
55987	Winona	(507)	25,075	26,438
55119	Woodbury	(612)	10,297	6,184
56187	Worthington	(507)	10,243	9,916

Mississippi (601)

39730	Aberdeen	7,184	6,507
38821	Amory	7,307	7,236
38606	Batesville	5,162	3,796
39520	Bay St. Louis	7,850	6,752
*39530	Biloxi	49,311	48,486
38829	Booneville	6,199	5,895
39042	Brandon	9,626	2,685
39601	Brookhaven	10,800	10,700
39046	Canton	11,116	10,503
38614	Clarksdale	21,137	21,673
38732	Cleveland	14,524	13,327
39056	Clinton	14,660	7,289
39429	Columbia	7,733	7,587
39701	Columbus	27,503	25,795
38834	Corinth	13,180	11,581
39532	D'Iberville(u)	13,369	7,288
39552	Escatawpa(u)	5,367	1,579
39074	Forest	5,229	4,085
39553	Gautier(u)	8,917	2,087
38701	Greenville	40,613	39,648
38930	Greenwood	20,115	22,400
38901	Grenada	12,641	9,944
39501	Gulfport	39,676	40,791
39401	Hattiesburg	40,829	38,277
38635	Holly Springs	7,285	5,728
38751	Indianola	8,050	8,947
*39205	Jackson	202,895	153,968
39090	Kosciusko	7,415	7,266
39440	Laurel	21,897	24,145
38756	Leland	6,667	6,000
39560	Long Beach	14,199	6,170
39339	Louisville	7,323	6,626
39648	McComb	12,331	11,851
39301	Meridian	46,577	45,083
39563	Moss Point	18,998	19,321
39120	Natchez	22,209	19,704
38652	New Albany	7,072	6,426
39501	North Gulfport(u)	6,660	6,996
39560	North Long Beach(u)	7,063	....
39564	Ocean Springs	14,504	9,160
39567	Orange Grove(u)	13,476	....
38655	Oxford	9,882	8,519
39567	Pascagoula	29,318	27,264
39571	Pass Christian	5,014	2,979
39208	Pearl	18,602	9,623
39465	Petal	8,476	6,986
39350	Philadelphia	6,434	6,274
39466	Picayune	10,361	9,760
39157	Ridgeland	5,461	1,650
38668	Senatobia	5,013	4,247
38671	Southaven(u)	16,071	8,931
39759	Starkville	16,139	11,369
38801	Tupelo	23,905	20,471
39180	Vicksburg	25,434	25,478
39367	Waynesboro	5,349	4,368
39773	West Point	8,811	8,714
38967	Winona	6,177	5,521
39194	Yazoo City	12,092	11,688

Missouri

63123	Affton(u)	(314)	23,181	24,264
63010	Arnold	(314)	19,141	17,381
65605	Aurora	(417)	6,437	5,359
63011	Ballwin	(314)	12,750	10,656
63137	Bellefontaine Neighbors	(314)	12,082	14,084
64012	Belton	(816)	12,708	12,270
63134	Berkeley	(314)	15,922	19,743
63031	Black Jack	(314)	5,293	4,145
64015	Blue Springs	(816)	25,936	6,779
65613	Bolivar	(417)	5,919	4,769
65233	Boonville	(816)	6,959	7,514
63114	Breckenridge Hills	(816)	5,666	7,011
63144	Brentwood	(314)	8,209	11,248
63044	Bridgeton	(314)	18,445	19,992

ZIP code	Place		1980	1970
64628	Brookfield	(816)	5,555	5,491
63701	Cape Girardeau	(314)	34,361	31,282
64836	Carthage	(417)	11,104	11,035
63830	Caruthersville	(314)	7,958	7,350
63834	Charleston	(314)	5,230	5,131
64601	Chillicothe	(816)	9,089	9,519
63105	Clayton	(314)	14,306	16,100
64735	Clinton	(816)	8,366	7,504
65201	Columbia	(314)	62,061	58,812
63128	Concord(u)	(314)	20,896	21,217
63126	Crestwood	(314)	12,815	15,123
63141	Creve Coeur.	(314)	11,743	8,967
63136	Dellwood.	(314)	6,200	7,137
63020	De Soto	(314)	5,993	5,984
63131	Des Peres	(314)	7,953	5,333
63841	Dexter	(314)	7,043	6,024
63011	Ellisville	(314)	6,233	4,681
64024	Excelsior Springs	(816)	10,424	9,411
63640	Farmington	(314)	8,270	6,590
63135	Ferguson.	(314)	24,549	28,759
63028	Festus	(314)	7,574	7,530
*63033	Florissant	(314)	55,721	65,908
65473	Fort Leonard Wood(u)	(314)	21,262	33,799
65251	Fulton	(314)	11,046	12,248
64118	Gladstone	(816)	24,990	23,422
63122	Glendale	(314)	6,035	6,981
64030	Grandview	(816)	24,561	17,456
63401	Hannibal	(314)	18,811	18,609
64701	Harrisonville	(816)	6,372	5,052
*63042	Hazelwood.	(314)	13,098	14,082
*64051	Independence	(816)	111,797	111,630
63755	Jackson	(314)	7,827	5,896
65101	Jefferson City	(314)	33,619	32,407
63136	Jennings	(314)	16,934	19,379
64801	Joplin	(417)	39,023	39,256
*64108	Kansas City	(816)	448,028	507,330
63857	Kennett.	(314)	10,145	10,090
63501	Kirksville	(816)	17,167	15,560
63122	Kirkwood	(314)	27,987	31,679
63124	Ladue	(314)	9,369	10,306
65536	Lebanon	(417)	9,507	8,616
64063	Lee's Summit	(816)	28,741	16,230
63125	Lemay(u)	(314)	35,424	40,529
64067	Lexington	(816)	5,063	5,388
64068	Liberty	(816)	16,251	13,704
63552	Macon	(816)	5,680	5,301
63863	Malden	(314)	6,096	5,374
63011	Manchester	(314)	6,351	5,031
63143	Maplewood	(314)	10,960	12,785
65340	Marshall	(816)	12,781	12,051
63043	Maryland Heights(u)	(314)	5,676	8,805
64468	Maryville	(816)	9,558	9,970
65265	Mexico	(314)	12,276	11,807
65270	Moberly	(816)	13,418	12,988
65708	Monett	(417)	6,148	5,937
63026	Murphy(u)	(314)	8,121	....
64850	Neosho	(417)	9,493	7,517
64772	Nevada	(417)	9,044	9,736
63121	Normandy	(314)	5,174	6,236
63121	Northwoods	(314)	5,831	4,607
63366	O'Fallon	(314)	8,654	7,018
63124	Olivette.	(314)	7,952	9,156
63114	Overland	(314)	19,620	24,819
63775	Perryville	(314)	7,343	5,149
63120	Pine Lawn	(314)	6,570	5,745
63901	Poplar Bluff	(314)	17,139	16,653
64133	Raytown	(816)	31,831	33,306
64085	Richmond	(816)	5,499	4,948
63117	Richmond Heights	(314)	11,516	13,802
63124	Rock Hill	(314)	5,702	6,815
65401	Rolla	(314)	13,303	13,571
63074	St. Ann	(314)	15,523	18,215
63301	St. Charles.	(314)	37,379	31,834
63114	St. John	(314)	7,854	8,960
*64501	St. Joseph	(816)	76,691	72,748
*63155	St. Louis	(314)	452,801	622,236
63376	St. Peters	(314)	15,700	486
63126	Sappington(u)	(314)	11,388	10,603
65301	Sedalia	(816)	20,927	22,847
63119	Shrewsbury	(314)	5,077	5,896
63801	Sikeston	(314)	17,431	14,699
63138	Spanish Lake(u).	(314)	20,632	15,647
*65801	Springfield	(314)	133,116	120,096
63080	Sullivan.	(314)	5,461	5,111
64683	Trenton	(816)	6,811	6,063
63084	Union	(314)	5,506	5,183
63130	University City	(314)	42,690	47,527
64093	Warrensburg	(816)	13,807	13,125
63090	Washington	(314)	9,251	8,499
64870	Webb City	(417)	7,309	6,923
63119	Webster Groves	(314)	23,097	27,457
65775	West Plains	(417)	7,741	6,693

Montana (406)

59711	Anaconda-Deer Lodge County . .		12,518	9,771
*59101	Billings		66,842	61,581
59101	Billings Heights(u).		8,480	....

59715	Bozeman.		21,645	18,670
59701	Butte-Silver Bow		37,205	23,368
59330	Glendive		5,978	6,305
*59401	Great Falls		56,725	60,091
59501	Havre		10,891	10,558
59601	Helena		23,938	22,730
59901	Kalispell		10,689	10,526
59044	Laurel		5,481	4,454
59457	Lewistown		7,104	6,437
59047	Livingston		6,994	6,883
59402	Malmstrom AFB(u)		6,675	8,374
59301	Miles City		9,602	9,023
59801	Missoula		33,351	29,497
59801	Missoula South(u)		5,557	4,886
59801	Orchard Homes(u)		10,837	....
59270	Sidney		5,726	4,543

Nebraska

69301	Alliance	(308)	9,920	6,862
68310	Beatrice	(402)	12,891	12,389
68005	Bellevue	(402)	21,813	21,953
68008	Blair	(402)	6,418	6,106
69337	Chadron	(308)	5,933	5,921
68601	Columbus	(402)	17,328	15,471
68355	Falls City	(402)	5,374	5,444
68025	Fremont	(402)	23,979	22,962
69341	Gering	(308)	7,760	5,639
68801	Grand Island.	(308)	33,180	32,358
68901	Hastings	(402)	23,045	23,580
68949	Holdrege	(308)	5,624	5,635
68847	Kearney	(308)	21,158	19,181
68128	La Vista	(402)	9,588	4,858
68850	Lexington	(308)	6,898	5,654
*68501	Lincoln	(402)	171,932	149,518
69001	McCook	(308)	8,404	8,285
68410	Nebraska City	(402)	7,127	7,441
68701	Norfolk	(402)	19,449	16,607
69101	North Platte	(308)	24,509	19,447
68113	Offutt AFB West(u)	(402)	8,787	8,445
69153	Ogallala	(308)	5,638	4,976
*68108	Omaha	(402)	313,939	346,929
68046	Papillion	(402)	6,399	5,606
68048	Plattsmouth	(402)	6,295	6,371
68127	Ralston.	(402)	5,143	4,731
69361	Scottsbluff	(308)	14,156	14,507
68434	Seward	(402)	5,713	5,294
69162	Sidney	(308)	6,010	6,403
68776	South Sioux City	(402)	9,339	7,920
68787	Wayne	(402)	5,240	5,379
68467	York	(402)	7,723	6,778

Nevada (702)

89005	Boulder City		9,590	5,223
89701	Carson City		32,022	15,468
89112	East Las Vegas(u)		6,449	6,501
89801	Elko		8,758	7,621
89015	Henderson		24,363	16,395
89450	Incline Village-Crystal Bay(u) . .		6,225	....
*89114	Las Vegas		164,674	125,787
89110	Nellis AFB(u)		6,205	6,449
89030	North Las Vegas		42,739	46,067
89109	Paradise(u)		84,818	24,477
*89501	Reno		100,756	72,863
89431	Sparks		40,780	24,187
89110	Sunrise Manor(u)		44,155	9,684
89431	Sun Valley(u)		8,822	2,414
89109	Vegas Creek(u)		NA	8,970
89101	Winchester(u)		19,728	13,981

New Hampshire (603)

See note on page 268

03031	Amherst		8,243	4,605
03102	Bedford		9,481	5,859
03570	Berlin		13,084	15,256
03743	Claremont		14,557	14,221
03301	Concord		30,400	30,022
03818	Conway		7,158	4,865
03038	Derry Compact(u).		12,248	6,090
.....	Derry.		18,875	11,712
03820	Dover		22,377	20,850
03824	Durham Compact(u)		8,448	7,221
.....	Durham		10,652	8,869
03833	Exeter Compact(u)		8,947	6,439
.....	Exeter		11,024	8,892
03235	Franklin		7,901	7,292
03045	Goffstown		11,315	9,284
03842	Hampton Compact(u)		6,779	5,407
.....	Hampton		10,493	8,011
03755	Hanover Compact(u)		6,861	6,147
.....	Hanover		9,119	8,494
03106	Hooksett		7,303	5,564
03061	Hudson		14,022	10,638
03431	Keene		21,449	20,467
03246	Laconia		15,575	14,888
03766	Lebanon		11,134	9,725

ZIP code	Place	1980	1970
03516	Littleton	5,558	5,290
03053	Londonderry	13,598	5,346
*03101	Manchester	90,936	87,754
03054	Merrimack	15,406	8,595
03055	Milford	8,685	6,622
03060	Nashua	67,865	55,820
03773	Newport	6,229	5,899
03076	Pelham	8,090	5,408
03865	Plaistow	5,609	4,712
03801	Portsmouth	26,254	25,717
03077	Raymond	5,453	3,003
03867	Rochester	21,560	17,938
03079	Salem	24,124	20,142
03874	Seabrook	5,917	3,053
03878	Somersworth	10,350	9,026
03087	Windham	5,664	3,008

New Jersey

ZIP code	Place	1980	1970
07747	Aberdeen(u) (201)	17,235	....
08201	Absecon (609)	6,859	6,094
07401	Allendale (201)	5,901	6,240
07712	Asbury Park (201)	17,015	16,533
*08401	Atlantic City (609)	40,199	47,859
08106	Audubon (609)	9,533	10,802
08007	Barrington (609)	7,418	8,409
07002	Bayonne (201)	65,047	72,743
08722	Beachwood (201)	7,687	4,390
07109	Belleville (201)	35,367	37,629
08031	Bellmawr (609)	13,721	15,618
07719	Belmar (201)	6,771	5,782
07621	Bergenfield (201)	25,568	29,000
07922	Berkeley Hts. Twp. (201)	12,549	13,078
08009	Berlin (609)	5,786	4,997
07924	Bernardsville (201)	6,715	6,652
08012	Blackwood(u) (609)	5,219	....
07003	Bloomfield (201)	47,792	52,029
07403	Bloomingdale (201)	7,867	7,797
07603	Bogota (201)	8,344	8,960
07005	Boonton (201)	8,620	9,261
08805	Bound Brook (201)	9,710	10,450
08723	Brick Twp (201)	53,629	35,057
08302	Bridgeton (609)	18,795	20,435
08203	Brigantine (609)	8,318	6,741
08015	Browns Mills(u) (609)	10,568	7,144
07828	Budd Lake (201)	6,523	....
08016	Burlington (609)	10,246	12,010
07405	Butler (201)	7,616	7,051
07006	Caldwell (201)	7,624	8,677
*08101	Camden (609)	84,910	102,551
08701	Candlewood(u) (201)	6,750	5,629
07072	Carlstadt (201)	6,166	6,724
08069	Carney's Point (609)	7,574	....
07008	Carteret (201)	20,598	23,137
07009	Cedar Grove Twp. (201)	12,600	15,582
07928	Chatham (201)	8,537	9,566
*08002	Cherry Hill Twp. (609)	68,785	64,395
08077	Cinnaminson Twp. (609)	16,072	16,962
07066	Clark Twp. (201)	16,699	18,829
08312	Clayton (609)	6,013	5,193
08021	Clementon (609)	5,764	4,492
07010	Cliffside Park (201)	21,464	18,891
07721	Cliffwood-Cliffwood Beach(u) (201)	NA	7,056
*07015	Clifton (201)	74,388	82,437
07624	Closter (201)	8,164	8,604
08108	Collingswood (609)	15,838	17,422
07016	Cranford Twp. (201)	24,573	27,391
07626	Cresskill (201)	7,609	8,298
	Crestwood Village (201)	7,965	....
08075	Delran Twp. (609)	14,811	10,065
07834	Denville Twp. (201)	14,380	14,045
08096	Deptford Twp. (609)	23,473	24,232
07801	Dover (201)	14,681	15,039
07628	Dumont (201)	18,334	20,155
08812	Dunellen (201)	6,593	7,072
08816	East Brunswick Twp. (201)	37,711	34,166
07936	East Hanover (201)	9,319	....
*07019	East Orange (201)	77,878	75,471
07073	East Rutherford (201)	7,849	8,536
08520	East Windsor Twp. (609)	21,041	11,736
07724	Eatontown (201)	12,703	14,619
08010	Edgewater Park (609)	9,273	....
08817	Edison Twp. (201)	70,193	67,120
*07201	Elizabeth (201)	106,201	112,654
07407	Elmwood Park (201)	18,377	20,511
07630	Emerson (201)	7,793	8,428
*07631	Englewood (201)	23,701	24,985
07632	Englewood Cliffs (201)	5,698	5,938
08053	Evesham Twp. (609)	21,659	13,477
08618	Ewing Twp. (609)	34,842	32,831
07006	Fairfield (201)	7,987	6,731
07701	Fair Haven (201)	5,679	6,142
07410	Fair Lawn (201)	32,229	38,040
07022	Fairview (201)	10,519	10,698
07023	Fanwood (201)	7,767	8,920
08518	Florence-Roebling(u) (609)	7,677	7,551
07932	Florham Park (201)	9,359	9,373
08640	Fort Dix(u) (609)	14,297	26,290
07024	Fort Lee (201)	32,449	30,631
07417	Franklin Lakes (201)	8,769	7,550
07728	Freehold (201)	10,020	10,545
07026	Garfield (201)	26,803	30,797
08753	Gilford Park (201)	6,528	4,007
08028	Glassboro (609)	14,574	12,938
08029	Glendora (609)	5,632	....
07028	Glen Ridge (201)	7,855	8,518
07452	Glen Rock (201)	11,497	13,011
08030	Gloucester City (609)	13,121	14,707
	Gordon's Corner (201)	6,320	....
07093	Guttenberg (201)	7,340	5,754
*07602	Hackensack (201)	36,039	36,008
07840	Hackettstown (201)	8,850	9,472
08108	Haddon Twp. (609)	15,875	18,192
08033	Haddonfield (609)	12,337	13,118
08035	Haddon Heights (609)	8,361	9,365
07508	Haledon (201)	6,607	6,767
08037	Hammonton (609)	12,298	11,464
07981	Hanover Twp. (201)	11,846	10,700
07029	Harrison (201)	12,242	11,811
07604	Hasbrouck Heights (201)	12,166	13,651
07506	Hawthorne (201)	18,200	19,173
07730	Hazlet Twp. (201)	23,013	22,239
06904	Highland Park (201)	13,396	14,385
07732	Highlands (201)	5,187	3,916
07642	Hillsdale (201)	10,495	11,768
07205	Hillside Twp. (201)	21,440	21,636
07030	Hoboken (201)	42,460	45,380
08753	Holiday City-Berkeley (201)	9,019	....
07843	Hopatcong (201)	15,531	9,052
08560	Hopewell Twp. (Mercer) (609)	10,893	10,030
07111	Irvington (201)	61,493	59,743
08527	Jackson Twp. (201)	25,644	18,276
*07303	Jersey City (201)	223,532	260,350
07734	Keansburg (201)	10,613	9,720
07032	Kearny (201)	35,735	37,585
08824	Kendall Park(u) (201)	7,419	7,412
07033	Kenilworth (201)	8,221	9,165
07735	Keyport (201)	7,413	7,205
07405	Kinnelon (201)	7,770	7,600
07034	Lake Hiawatha(u) (201)	NA	11,389
07871	Lake Mohawk(u) (201)	8,498	6,262
07054	Lake Parsippany(u) (201)	NA	7,488
08701	Lakewood(u) (201)	22,863	17,874
08879	Laurence Harbor(u) (201)	6,737	6,715
07605	Leonia (201)	8,027	8,847
07035	Lincoln Park (201)	8,806	9,034
07036	Linden (201)	37,836	41,409
08021	Lindenwold (609)	18,196	12,199
08221	Linwood (609)	6,144	6,159
07424	Little Falls Twp. (201)	11,496	11,727
07643	Little Ferry (201)	9,399	9,064
07739	Little Silver (201)	5,548	6,010
07039	Livingston Twp. (201)	28,040	30,127
07644	Lodi (201)	23,956	25,163
07740	Long Branch (201)	29,819	31,774
07071	Lyndhurst Twp. (201)	20,326	22,729
07940	Madison (201)	15,357	16,710
08859	Madison Park (201)	7,447	....
07430	Mahwah Twp. (201)	12,127	10,800
08736	Manasquan (201)	5,354	4,971
08835	Manville (201)	11,278	13,029
08052	Maple Shade Twp. (609)	20,525	16,464
07040	Maplewood Twp. (201)	22,950	24,932
08402	Margate City (609)	9,179	10,576
08746	Marlboro Twp. (201)	17,560	12,273
08053	Marlton(u) (609)	9,411	10,180
07747	Matawan (201)	8,837	9,136
07607	Maywood (201)	9,895	11,087
08641	McGuire AFB(u) (609)	7,853	10,933
06619	Mercerville-Hamilton Sq.(u) (609)	25,446	24,465
08840	Metuchen (201)	13,762	16,031
08846	Middlesex (201)	13,480	15,038
07748	Middletown Twp. (201)	61,615	54,623
07432	Midland park. (201)	7,381	8,159
07041	Milburn Twp. (201)	19,543	21,089
08850	Milltown (201)	7,136	6,470
08332	Millville (609)	24,815	21,366
08094	Monroe Twp. (Gloucester) (609)	21,639	14,071
*07042	Montclair (201)	38,321	44,043
07645	Montvale (201)	7,318	7,327
07045	Montville Twp. (201)	14,290	11,846
08057	Moorestown-Lenola(u) (609)	13,695	14,179
07950	Morris Plains (201)	5,305	5,540
07960	Morristown (201)	16,614	17,662
07092	Mountainside (201)	7,118	7,520
08060	Mount Holly Twp. (609)	10,818	12,713
07753	Neptune Twp. (201)	28,366	27,863
07753	Neptune City (201)	5,276	5,502
*07102	Newark (201)	329,248	381,930
*08901	New Brunswick (201)	41,442	41,885
08511	New Hanover (201)	14,248	27,410
07646	New Milford (201)	16,876	19,149
07974	New Providence (201)	12,426	13,796
07860	Newton (201)	7,748	7,297
07032	North Arlington (201)	16,587	18,096
07047	North Bergen Twp. (201)	47,019	47,751
08902	North Brunswick Twp. (201)	22,220	16,691
07006	North Caldwell (201)	5,832	6,733
08225	Northfield (609)	7,795	8,646
07508	North Haledon (201)	8,177	7,614

ZIP code	Place		1980	1970
07060	North Plainfield	(201)	19,108	21,796
07647	Northvale	(201)	5,046	5,177
07110	Nutley	(201)	28,998	31,913
07755	Oakhurst(u)	(201)	NA	5,558
07436	Oakland	(201)	13,443	14,420
08226	Ocean City	(609)	13,949	10,575
07757	Oceanport	(201)	5,888	7,503
08758	Ocean Twp	(201)	23,570	—
08857	Old Bridge	(201)	21,815	25,176
08857	Old Bridge Twp	(201)	51,515	48,715
07649	Oradell	(201)	8,656	8,903
*07050	Orange	(201)	31,136	32,566
08650	Palisades Park	(201)	13,732	13,351
08065	Palmyra	(609)	7,085	6,969
07652	Paramus	(201)	26,474	28,381
07656	Park Ridge	(201)	8,515	8,709
07054	Parsippany-Troy Hills.	(201)	49,868	—
*07055	Passaic	(201)	52,463	55,124
*07510	Paterson	(201)	137,970	144,824
08066	Paulsboro	(609)	6,944	8,084
08110	Pennsauken Twp..	(609)	33,775	36,394
08069	Penns Grove	(609)	5,760	5,727
08070	Pennsville Center(u)	(609)	12,467	11,014
07440	Pequannock Twp..	(201)	13,776	14,350
*08861	Perth Amboy	(201)	38,951	38,798
08865	Phillipsburg	(201)	16,647	17,849
08021	Pine Hill	(201)	8,684	5,132
08854	Piscataway Twp.	(201)	42,223	36,418
08071	Pitman	(609)	9,744	10,257
*07061	Plainfield	(201)	45,555	46,862
08232	Pleasantville	(609)	13,435	14,007
08742	Point Pleasant	(201)	17,747	15,968
08742	Point Pleasant Beach.	(201)	5,415	4,882
07442	Pompton Lakes	(201)	10,660	11,397
08540	Princeton.	(609)	12,035	12,311
08540	Princeton North(u)	(609)	NA	5,488
07508	Prospect Park	(201)	5,142	5,176
*07065	Rahway	(201)	26,723	29,114
08057	Ramblewood(u)	(609)	6,475	5,556
07446	Ramsey	(201)	12,899	12,571
07869	Randolph Twp.	(201)	17,828	13,296
08869	Raritan	(201)	6,128	6,691
07701	Red Bank	(201)	12,031	12,847
07657	Ridgefield	(201)	10,294	11,308
07660	Ridgefield Park	(201)	12,738	13,990
*07451	Ridgewood.	(201)	25,208	27,547
07456	Ringwood	(201)	12,625	10,393
07661	River Edge.	(201)	11,111	12,850
08075	Riverside Twp.	(609)	7,941	8,591
07675	River Vale.	(201)	9,489	—
07726	Robertsville	(201)	8,461	—
07662	Rochell Park Twp.	(201)	5,603	6,380
07866	Rockaway	(201)	6,852	6,363
07068	Roseland.	(201)	5,330	4,453
07203	Roselle.	(201)	20,641	22,585
07204	Roselle Park.	(201)	13,377	14,277
07760	Rumson.	(201)	7,623	7,421
08078	Runnemede	(609)	9,461	10,475
*07070	Rutherford	(201)	19,068	20,802
07662	Saddle Brook Twp.	(201)	14,084	15,910
08079	Salem	(609)	6,959	7,648
08872	Sayreville	(201)	29,969	32,508
07076	Scotch Plains Twp.	(201)	20,774	22,279
07094	Secaucus	(201)	13,719	13,228
08753	Silverton	(201)	7,236	—
08083	Somerdale.	(609)	5,900	6,510
08873	Somerset	(201)	21,731	—
08244	Somers Point	(609)	10,330	7,919
08876	Somerville.	(201)	11,973	13,652
08879	South Amboy	(201)	8,322	9,338
07079	South Orange Vill. Twp.	(201)	15,864	—
07080	South Plainfield	(201)	20,521	21,142
08882	South River	(201)	14,361	15,428
07871	Sparta Twp.	(201)	13,333	10,819
08884	Spotswood.	(201)	7,840	7,891
07081	Springfield Twp.	(201)	13,955	15,740
07762	Spring Lake Heights	(201)	5,424	4,602
08084	Stratford	(609)	8,005	9,801
07747	Strathmore(u)	(609)	NA	7,674
07876	Succasunna-Kenvil	(201)	10,931	—
07901	Summit.	(201)	21,071	23,620
07666	Teaneck Twp.	(201)	39,007	42,355
07670	Tenafly.	(201)	13,552	14,827
07724	Tinton Falls	(201)	7,740	8,395
08753	Toms River(u)	(201)	7,465	7,303
07512	Totowa.	(201)	11,448	11,580
*08608	Trenton.	(609)	92,124	104,786
08520	Twin Rivers	(609)	7,742	—
07083	Union Twp..	(201)	50,184	53,077
07735	Union Beach.	(201)	6,354	6,472
07087	Union City	(201)	55,593	57,305
07458	Upper Saddle River.	(201)	7,958	7,949
08406	Ventnor City.	(609)	11,704	10,385
07044	Verona.	(201)	14,166	15,067
08251	Villas.	(609)	5,909	3,155
08360	Vineland.	(609)	53,753	47,399
07463	Waldwick.	(201)	10,802	12,313
07057	Wallington.	(201)	10,741	10,284
07465	Wanaque.	(201)	10,025	8,636
07882	Washington	(201)	6,429	5,943
07675	Washington Twp. (Bergen).	(201)	9,550	10,577
07060	Watchung	(201)	5,290	4,750
07470	Wayne Twp.	(201)	46,474	49,141
07087	Weehawken Twp..	(201)	13,168	13,383
07006	West Caldwell.	(201)	11,407	11,913
*07091	Westfield.	(201)	30,447	33,720
07728	West Freehold.	(201)	9,929	—
07764	West Long Branch	(201)	7,380	6,845
07480	West Milford Twp..	(201)	22,750	17,304
07093	West New York	(201)	39,194	40,627
07052	West Orange	(201)	39,510	43,715
07424	West Paterson	(201)	11,293	11,692
07675	Westwood	(201)	10,714	11,105
07885	Wharton	(201)	5,485	5,535
08610	White Horse	(609)	10,098	—
07886	White Meadow Lake(u).	(201)	8,429	8,499
08094	Williamstown	(609)	5,768	4,075
08046	Willingboro Twp.	(609)	39,912	43,386
08095	Winslow Twp.	(609)	20,034	11,202
07095	Woodbridge Twp.	(201)	90,074	98,944
08096	Woodbury	(609)	10,353	12,408
07675	Woodcliff Lake	(201)	5,644	5,506
07075	Wood-Ridge.	(201)	7,929	8,311
07481	Wyckoff Twp.	(201)	15,500	16,039
08620	Yardville-Groveville.	(609)	9,414	—
.....	Yorketown	(201)	5,330	—

New Mexico (505)

ZIP code	Place	1980	1970
88310	Alamogordo	24,024	23,035
*87101	Albuquerque.	332,336	244,501
88210	Artesia	10,385	10,315
87410	Aztec	5,512	3,354
87002	Belen	5,617	4,823
88101	Cannon(u)	NA	5,461
88220	Carlsbad	25,496	21,297
88101	Clovis	31,194	28,495
88030	Deming	9,964	8,343
87532	Espanola	6,803	4,528
87401	Farmington.	30,729	21,979
87301	Gallup	18,167	14,596
87020	Grants	11,451	8,768
88240	Hobbs	28,794	26,025
88330	Holloman AFB(u)	7,245	6,001
88001	Las Cruces	45,086	37,857
87701	Las Vegas	14,322	7,528
87544	Los Alamos(u)	11,039	11,310
88260	Lovington.	9,727	8,915
87107	North Valley(u)	13,006	10,366
87114	Paradise Hills	5,096	—
88130	Portales	9,940	10,554
87740	Raton.	8,225	6,962
87124	Rio Rancho Estates.	9,985	—
88201	Roswell.	39,676	33,908
87115	Sandia(u).	5,288	6,867
87501	Santa Fe	49,160	41,167
87420	Shiprock	7,237	—
88061	Silver City	9,887	8,557
87801	Socorro	7,576	5,849
87105	South Valley(u)	38,916	29,389
87901	Truth or Consequences	5,219	4,656
88401	Tucumcari	6,765	7,189
87544	White Rock	6,560	3,861
87327	Zuni Pueblo	5,551	3,958

New York

ZIP code	Place		1980	1970
*12207	Albany	(518)	101,727	115,781
11507	Albertson(u)	(516)	5,561	6,825
11701	Amityville.	(516)	9,076	9,794
12010	Amsterdam	(518)	21,872	25,524
12603	Arlington(u)	(914)	11,305	11,203
13021	Auburn.	(315)	32,548	34,599
*11702	Babylon	(516)	12,388	12,897
11510	Baldwin(u)	(516)	31,630	34,525
13027	Baldwinsville	(315)	6,446	6,298
14020	Batavia	(716)	16,703	17,338
14810	Bath	(607)	6,042	6,053
13088	Bayberry-Lynelle Meadows(u).	(315)	14,813	—
11705	Bayport(u)	(516)	9,282	8,232
11706	Bay Shore(u)	(516)	10,784	11,119
11709	Bayville.	(516)	7,034	6,147
12508	Beacon.	(914)	12,937	13,255
11710	Bellmore(u)	(516)	18,106	18,431
11714	Bethpage(u)	(516)	16,840	18,555
*13902	Binghamton	(607)	55,860	64,123
10913	Blauvelt(u)	(914)	NA	5,426
11716	Bohemia(u)	(516)	9,308	8,926
11717	Brentwood(u)	(516)	44,321	28,327
10510	Briarcliff Manor	(914)	7,115	6,521
14610	Brighton	(716)	35,776	—
14420	Brockport	(716)	9,776	7,878
10708	Bronxville	(914)	6,267	6,674
*14240	Buffalo	(716)	357,870	462,768
14424	Canandaigua	(716)	10,419	10,488

ZIP code	Place		1980	1970
13617	Canton	(315)	7,055	6,398
11514	Carle Place(u)	(516)	5,470	6,326
11516	Cedarhurst	(516)	6,162	6,941
11720	Centereach(u)	(516)	30,136	9,427
11934	Center Moriches(u)	(516)	5,703	3,802
11721	Centerport(u)	(516)	6,576	....
11722	Central Islip(u)	(516)	19,734	36,391
14225	Cheektowaga(u)	(716)	92,145	....
12065	Clifton Park	(518)	23,989	14,867
12043	Cobleskill	(518)	5,272	4,368
12047	Cohoes	(518)	18,144	18,653
11724	Cold Spring Harbor(u)	(516)	5,336	5,509
12205	Colonie	(518)	8,869	8,701
11725	Commack(u)	(516)	34,719	24,138
10920	Congers(u)	(914)	7,123	5,928
11726	Copiague(u)	(516)	20,132	19,632
11727	Coram(u)	(516)	24,752	....
14830	Corning	(607)	12,953	15,792
13045	Cortland	(607)	20,138	19,621
10520	Croton-on-Hudson	(914)	6,889	7,523
11729	Deer Park(u)	(516)	30,394	32,274
12054	Delmar(u)	(518)	8,423	....
14043	Depew	(716)	19,819	22,158
13214	DeWitt(u)	(315)	9,024	10,032
11746	Dix Hills(u)	(516)	26,693	10,050
10522	Dobbs Ferry	(914)	10,053	10,353
14048	Dunkirk	(716)	15,310	16,855
14052	East Aurora	(716)	6,803	7,033
10709	Eastchester(u)	(914)	20,305	23,750
11735	East Farmingdale(u)	(516)	5,522	....
12302	East Glenville(u)	(518)	6,537	5,898
11746	East Half Hollow Hills(u)	(516)	NA	9,691
11576	East Hills	(516)	7,160	8,624
11730	East Islip(u)	(516)	13,852	6,861
11758	East Massapequa(u)	(516)	13,987	15,926
11554	East Meadow(u)	(516)	39,317	46,290
11743	East Neck(u)	(516)	NA	5,221
11731	East Northport(u)	(516)	20,187	12,392
11772	East Patchogue(u)	(516)	18,139	8,092
14445	East Rochester	(716)	7,596	8,347
11518	East Rockaway	(516)	10,917	11,795
13902	East Vestal(u)	(607)	NA	10,472
*14901	Elmira	(607)	35,327	39,945
11003	Elmont(u)	(516)	27,592	29,363
11731	Elwood(u)	(516)	11,847	15,031
13760	Endicott	(607)	14,457	16,556
13760	Endwell(u)	(607)	13,745	15,999
13219	Fairmount(u)	(315)	13,415	15,317
14450	Fairport	(716)	5,970	6,474
12601	Fairview(u)	(914)	5,852	8,517
11735	Farmingdale	(516)	7,946	9,297
11738	Farmingville(u)	(516)	13,398	....
*11001	Floral Park	(516)	16,805	18,466
11768	Fort Salonga(u)	(516)	9,550	....
11010	Franklin Square(u)	(516)	29,051	32,156
14063	Fredonia	(716)	11,126	10,326
11520	Freeport	(516)	38,272	40,374
13069	Fulton	(315)	13,312	14,003
11530	Garden City	(516)	22,927	25,373
11040	Garden City Park(u)	(516)	7,712	7,488
14624	Gates-North Gates(u)	(716)	15,244	....
14454	Geneseo	(716)	6,746	5,714
14456	Geneva	(315)	15,133	16,793
11542	Glen Cove	(516)	24,618	25,770
12801	Glens Falls	(518)	15,897	17,222
12801	Glens Falls North(u)	(518)	6,956	NA
12078	Gloversville	(518)	17,836	19,677
*11022	Great Neck	(516)	9,168	10,798
11020	Great Neck Plaza	(516)	5,604	6,043
14616	Greece(u)	(716)	16,177	....
11740	Greenlawn(u)	(516)	13,869	8,493
12083	Greenville(u)	(518)	8,706	....
11746	Half Hollow Hills(u)	(516)	NA	12,081
14075	Hamburg	(716)	10,582	10,215
11946	Hampton Bays(u)	(516)	7,256	1,862
14221	Harris Hill(u)	(716)	5,087	....
10528	Harrison	(914)	23,046	21,544
10530	Hartsdale(u)	(914)	10,216	12,226
10706	Hastings-on-Hudson	(914)	8,573	9,479
11787	Hauppauge(u)	(516)	20,960	13,957
10927	Haverstraw	(914)	8,800	8,198
10532	Hawthorne(u)	(914)	5,010	....
*11551	Hempstead	(516)	40,404	39,411
13350	Herkimer	(315)	8,383	8,960
11040	Herricks(u)	(516)	8,123	9,112
11557	Hewlett(u)	(516)	6,986	6,796
*11802	Hicksville(u)	(516)	43,245	49,820
10977	Hillcrest(u)	(914)	5,733	5,357
11741	Holbrook(u)	(516)	24,382	....
11742	Holtsville(u)	(516)	13,515	....
14843	Hornell	(607)	10,234	12,144
14845	Horseheads	(607)	7,348	7,989
12534	Hudson	(518)	7,986	8,940
12839	Hudson Falls	(518)	7,419	7,917
11743	Huntington(u)	(516)	21,727	12,601
11746	Huntington Station(u)	(516)	28,769	28,817
13357	Ilion	(315)	9,450	9,808
11696	Inwood(u)	(516)	8,228	8,433
14617	Irondequoit(u)	(716)	57,648	....
10533	Irvington	(914)	5,774	5,878
11751	Islip(u)	(516)	13,438	7,692
11752	Islip Terrace(u)	(516)	5,588	....
14850	Ithaca	(607)	28,732	26,226
14701	Jamestown	(716)	35,775	39,795
10535	Jefferson Valley-Yorktown(u)	(914)	13,380	9,008
11753	Jericho(u)	(516)	12,739	14,010
13790	Johnson City	(607)	17,126	18,025
12095	Johnstown	(518)	9,360	10,045
14217	Kenmore	(716)	18,474	20,980
11754	Kings Park(u)	(516)	16,131	5,555
11024	Kings Point	(516)	5,234	5,614
12401	Kingston	(914)	24,481	25,544
14218	Lackawanna	(716)	22,701	28,657
10512	Lake Carmel(u)	(914)	7,295	4,796
11755	Lake Grove	(516)	9,692	8,133
11779	Lake Ronkonkoma(u)	(516)	38,336	7,284
11552	Lakeview(u)	(516)	5,276	5,471
14086	Lancaster	(716)	13,056	13,365
10538	Larchmont	(914)	6,308	7,203
12110	Latham(u)	(518)	11,182	9,661
11559	Lawrence	(516)	6,175	6,566
11756	Levittown(u)	(516)	57,045	65,440
11757	Lindenhurst	(516)	26,919	28,359
13365	Little Falls	(315)	6,156	7,629
14094	Lockport	(716)	24,844	25,399
11791	Locust Grove(u)	(516)	9,670	11,626
11561	Long Beach	(516)	34,073	33,127
12211	Loudonville(u)	(518)	11,480	9,299
11563	Lynbrook	(516)	20,424	23,151
13208	Lyncourt(u)	(315)	5,129	....
10541	Mahopac(u)	(914)	7,681	5,265
12953	Malone	(518)	7,668	8,048
11565	Malverne	(516)	9,262	10,036
10543	Mamaroneck	(914)	17,616	18,909
11030	Manhasset(u)	(516)	8,485	8,541
13104	Manlius	(315)	5,241	4,295
11050	Manorhaven	(516)	5,384	5,488
11758	Massapequa(u)	(516)	24,454	26,821
11762	Massapequa Park	(516)	19,779	22,112
13662	Massena	(315)	12,851	14,042
11950	Mastic(u)	(516)	10,413	....
11951	Mastic Beach(u)	(516)	8,318	4,870
13211	Mattydale(u)	(315)	7,511	8,292
12118	Mechanicville	(518)	5,500	6,247
11763	Medford(u)	(516)	20,418	....
14103	Medina	(716)	6,392	6,415
11746	Melville(u)	(516)	8,139	6,641
11566	Merrick(u)	(516)	24,478	25,904
11953	Middle Island(u)	(516)	5,703	....
10940	Middletown	(914)	21,454	22,607
11764	Miller Place(u)	(516)	7,877	....
11501	Mineola	(516)	20,757	21,845
10950	Monroe	(914)	5,996	4,439
10952	Monsey(u)	(914)	12,380	8,797
12701	Monticello	(914)	6,306	5,991
10549	Mt. Kisco	(914)	8,025	8,172
11766	Mount Sinai(u)	(516)	6,591	....
*10551	Mount Vernon	(914)	66,713	72,788
12590	Myers Corner(u)	(914)	5,180	2,826
10954	Nanuet(u)	(914)	12,578	10,447
11767	Nesconset(u)	(516)	10,706	10,048
14513	Newark	(315)	10,017	11,644
12550	Newburgh	(914)	23,438	26,219
11590	New Cassel(u)	(516)	9,635	8,721
10956	New City(u)	(914)	35,859	27,344
11040	New Hyde Park	(516)	9,801	10,116
*10802	New Rochelle	(914)	70,794	75,385
*12550	New Windsor Center(u)	(914)	7,812	8,803
*10001	New York	(212)	7,071,639	7,895,563
*10451	Bronx	(212)	1,168,972	1,471,701
*11201	Brooklyn	(718)	2,230,936	2,602,102
*10001	Manhattan	(212)	1,428,285	1,539,233
*(Q)	Queens	(718)	1,891,325	1,987,174

(Q) There are 4 P.O.s for Queens: 11101 for L.I. City; 11690 Far Rockaway; 11351 Flushing; and 11431 Jamaica.

ZIP code	Place		1980	1970
*10314	Staten Island	(718)	352,121	295,443
14301	Niagara(u)	(716)	9,648	....
*14302	Niagara Falls	(716)	71,384	85,615
12309	Niskayuna(u)	(518)	5,223	6,186
11701	North Amityville(u)	(516)	13,140	11,936
11703	North Babylon(u)	(516)	19,019	39,526
11706	North Bay Shore(u)	(516)	35,020	....
11710	North Bellmore(u)	(516)	20,630	22,893
11713	North Bellport(u)	(516)	7,432	5,903
11752	North Great River(u)	(516)	11,416	12,080
11757	North Lindenhurst(u)	(516)	11,511	11,117
11758	North Massapequa(u)	(516)	21,385	23,123
11566	North Merrick(u)	(516)	12,848	13,650
11040	North New Hyde Park(u)	(516)	15,114	18,154
11772	North Patchogue(u)	(516)	7,126	5,232
11768	Northport	(516)	7,651	7,494
13212	North Syracuse	(315)	7,970	8,687
10591	North Tarrytown	(914)	7,994	8,334
14120	North Tonawanda	(716)	35,760	36,012
11580	North Valley Stream(u)	(516)	14,530	14,881
11793	North Wantagh(u)	(516)	12,677	15,053
13815	Norwich	(607)	8,082	8,843
10960	Nyack	(914)	6,428	6,659
11769	Oakdale(u)	(516)	8,090	7,334

ZIP code	Census Division		1980	1970
11572	Oceanside(u)	(516)	33,639	35,372
13669	Ogdensburg	(315)	12,375	14,554
11804	Old Bethpage(u)	(516)	6,215	7,084
14760	Olean	(716)	18,207	19,169
13421	Oneida	(315)	10,810	11,658
13820	Oneonta	(607)	14,933	16,030
12550	Orange Lake(u)	(914)	5,120	4,348
10562	Ossining	(914)	20,196	21,659
13126	Oswego	(315)	19,793	20,913
11771	Oyster Bay(u)	(516)	6,497	6,822
11772	Patchogue	(516)	11,291	11,582
10965	Pearl River(u)	(914)	15,893	17,146
10566	Peekskill	(914)	18,236	19,283
10803	Pelham	(914)	6,848	2,076
10803	Pelham Manor	(914)	6,130	6,673
14827	Penn Yan	(315)	5,242	5,293
13212	Pitcher Hill	(315)	5,063	....
11714	Plainedge(u)	(516)	9,629	10,759
11803	Plainview(u)	(516)	28,037	31,695
12901	Plattsburgh	(518)	21,057	18,715
12903	Plattsburgh AFB(u)	(518)	5,905	7,078
10570	Pleasantville	(914)	6,749	7,110
10573	Port Chester	(914)	23,565	25,803
11777	Port Jefferson	(516)	6,731	5,515
11776	Port Jefferson Station(u)	(516)	17,009	7,403
12771	Port Jervis	(914)	8,699	8,852
11050	Port Washington(u)	(516)	14,521	15,923
13676	Potsdam	(315)	10,635	10,303
*12601	Poughkeepsie	(914)	29,757	32,029
12603	Red Oaks Mill(u)	(914)	5,236	3,919
12144	Rensselaer	(518)	9,047	10,136
11961	Ridge(u)	(516)	8,977	....
11901	Riverhead(u)	(516)	6,339	7,585
11901	Riverside-Flanders(u)	(516)	5,400	....
*14603	Rochester	(716)	241,741	295,011
*11570	Rockville Centre	(516)	25,412	27,444
11778	Rocky Point(u)	(516)	7,012	....
12205	Roessleville(u)	(518)	11,685	5,476
13440	Rome	(315)	43,826	50,148
11575	Roosevelt(u)	(516)	14,109	15,008
11577	Roslyn Heights(u)	(516)	6,546	7,242
12303	Rotterdam(u)	(518)	22,933	25,214
10580	Rye	(914)	15,083	15,869
11780	St. James(u)	(516)	12,122	10,500
14779	Salamanca	(716)	6,890	7,877
12983	Saranac Lake	(518)	5,578	6,086
12866	Saratoga Springs	(518)	23,906	18,845
11782	Sayville(u)	(516)	12,013	11,680
10583	Scarsdale	(914)	17,650	19,229
*12301	Schenectady	(518)	67,972	77,958
10940	Scotchtown(u)	(914)	7,352	2,119
12302	Scotia	(518)	7,280	7,370
11579	Sea Cliff	(516)	5,364	5,890
11783	Seaford(u)	(516)	16,117	17,379
11784	Selden(u)	(516)	17,259	11,613
13148	Seneca Falls	(315)	7,466	7,794
11733	Setauket-East Setauket(u)	(516)	10,176	6,857
11967	Shirley(u)	(516)	18,072	6,280
11787	Smithtown(u)	(516)	30,906	....
13209	Solvay	(315)	7,140	8,280
11789	South Beach(u)	(516)	8,071	....
11735	South Farmingdale(u)	(516)	16,439	20,464
14850	South Hill(u)	(607)	5,276	....
11746	South Huntington(u)	(516)	14,854	9,115
14904	Southport(u)	(607)	8,329	8,685
11587	South Valley Stream(u)	(516)	5,462	6,595
11590	South Westbury(u)	(516)	9,732	10,978
10977	Spring Valley	(914)	20,537	18,112
11790	Stony Brook(u)	(516)	16,155	6,391
10980	Stony Point(u)	(914)	6,686	8,270
10901	Suffern	(914)	10,794	8,273
11791	Syosset(u)	(516)	9,818	10,084
*13201	Syracuse	(315)	170,105	197,297
10983	Tappan(u)	(914)	8,267	7,424
10591	Tarrytown	(914)	10,648	11,115
10594	Thornwood(u)	(914)	7,197	6,874
14150	Tonawanda	(716)	18,693	21,898
*12180	Troy	(518)	56,638	62,918
10707	Tuckahoe	(914)	6,076	6,236
11553	Uniondale(u)	(516)	20,016	22,077
*13503	Utica	(315)	75,632	91,373
10989	Valley Cottage(u)	(914)	8,214	6,007
*11580	Valley Stream	(516)	35,769	40,413
10901	Viola(u)	(914)	5,340	5,136
12586	Walden	(914)	5,659	5,277
11793	Wantagh(u)	(516)	19,817	21,783
12590	Wappingers Falls	(914)	5,110	5,607
13165	Waterloo	(315)	5,403	5,418
13601	Watertown	(315)	27,861	30,787
12189	Watervliet	(518)	11,354	12,404
14580	Webster	(716)	5,499	5,037
14895	Wellsville	(716)	5,769	5,815
11758	West Amityville(u)	(516)	6,623	6,424
11704	West Babylon(u)	(516)	41,699	12,893
11706	West Bay Shore(u)	(516)	5,118	....
11590	Westbury	(516)	13,871	15,362
14905	West Elmira(u)	(607)	5,485	5,901
12801	West Glens Falls(u)	(518)	5,331	3,363
10993	West Haverstraw	(914)	9,181	8,558
11552	West Hempstead(u)	(516)	18,536	20,375
11743	West Hills(u)	(516)	6,071	....
11795	West Islip(u)	(516)	29,533	17,374
12203	Westmere(u)	(518)	6,881	6,364
10994	West Nyack(u)	(914)	8,553	5,510
10996	West Point(u)	(914)	8,105	....
11796	West Sayville(u)	(516)	8,185	7,386
14224	West Seneca(u)	(716)	51,210	....
13219	Westvale(u)	(315)	6,169	7,253
*10602	White Plains	(914)	46,999	50,346
14221	Williamsville	(716)	6,217	6,878
11596	Williston Park	(516)	8,216	9,154
11797	Woodbury(u)	(516)	7,043	....
11598	Woodmere(u)	(516)	17,205	19,831
11798	Wyandach(u)	(516)	13,215	15,716
*10701	Yonkers	(914)	195,351	204,297
10598	Yorktown Heights(u)	(914)	7,696	6,805

North Carolina

ZIP code	Census Division		1980	1970
28001	Albemarle	(704)	15,110	11,126
27263	Archdale	(919)	5,326	4,874
27203	Asheboro	(919)	15,252	10,797
*28801	Asheville	(704)	54,022	57,820
28303	Bonnie Doone(u)	(919)	5,950	....
28607	Boone	(704)	10,191	8,754
28712	Brevard	(704)	5,323	5,243
27215	Burlington	(919)	37,266	35,930
28542	Camp Le Jeune(u)	(919)	30,764	34,549
27510	Carrboro	(919)	7,517	5,058
27511	Cary	(919)	21,612	7,640
27514	Chapel Hill	(919)	32,421	26,199
*28202	Charlotte	(704)	315,474	241,420
27012	Clemmons(u)	(919)	7,401	....
28328	Clinton	(919)	7,552	7,157
28025	Concord	(704)	16,942	18,464
28334	Dunn	(919)	8,962	8,302
*27701	Durham	(919)	100,538	95,438
28379	East Rockingham(u)	(919)	5,190	2,858
27288	Eden	(919)	15,672	15,871
27932	Edenton	(919)	5,264	4,956
27909	Elizabeth City	(919)	13,784	14,381
28728	Enka(u)	(704)	5,567	....
*28302	Fayetteville	(919)	59,507	53,510
28043	Forest City	(704)	7,688	7,179
28307	Fort Bragg(u)	(919)	37,834	46,995
27529	Garner	(919)	9,556	4,923
28052	Gastonia	(704)	47,333	47,322
27530	Goldsboro	(919)	31,871	26,960
27253	Graham	(919)	8,415	8,172
*27420	Greensboro	(919)	155,642	144,076
27834	Greenville	(919)	35,740	29,063
28532	Havelock	(919)	17,718	3,012
27536	Henderson	(919)	13,522	13,896
28739	Hendersonville	(704)	6,862	6,443
28601	Hickory	(704)	20,757	20,569
*27260	High Point	(919)	63,479	63,229
28348	Hope Mills	(919)	5,412	1,866
28540	Jacksonville	(919)	18,237	16,289
28081	Kannapolis(u)	(704)	34,564	36,293
27284	Kernersville	(919)	5,875	4,815
27021	King(u)	(919)	8,757	1,033
	Kings Grant(u)	(919)	6,652	....
28086	Kings Mountain	(704)	9,080	8,465
28501	Kinston	(919)	25,234	23,020
28352	Laurinburg	(919)	11,480	8,859
28645	Lenoir	(704)	13,748	14,705
27292	Lexington	(704)	15,711	17,205
28358	Lumberton	(919)	18,340	16,961
28212	Mint Hill	(704)	9,830	....
28110	Monroe	(704)	12,639	11,282
28115	Mooresville	(704)	8,575	8,808
28655	Morganton	(704)	13,763	13,625
27030	Mount Airy	(919)	6,862	7,325
28560	New Bern	(919)	14,557	14,660
27604	New Hope (Wake)(u)	(919)	6,768	....
	New Hope (Wayne)(u)	(919)	6,685	....
28540	New River Station(u)	(919)	5,401	....
28658	Newton	(704)	7,624	7,857
28012	North Belmont(u)	(704)	10,762	10,672
27565	Oxford	(919)	7,580	7,178
	Piney Green-White Oak(u)	(919)	6,058	....
*27611	Raleigh	(919)	149,771	122,830
27320	Reidsville	(919)	12,492	13,636
27870	Roanoke Rapids	(919)	14,702	13,508
28379	Rockingham	(919)	8,300	5,852
27801	Rocky Mount	(919)	41,526	34,284
27573	Roxboro	(919)	7,532	5,370
28601	St. Stephens(u)	(704)	10,797	....
28144	Salisbury	(704)	22,677	22,515
27330	Sanford	(919)	14,773	11,716
28150	Shelby	(704)	15,310	16,328
27577	Smithfield	(919)	7,288	6,677
28387	Southern Pines	(919)	8,620	5,937
28390	Spring Lake	(919)	6,273	3,968
27045	Stanleyville(u)	(919)	5,039	2,362
28677	Statesville	(704)	18,622	20,007
28778	Swannanoa(u)	(704)	5,586	1,966
27886	Tarboro	(919)	8,741	9,425
27360	Thomasville	(919)	14,144	15,230

ZIP code	Place		1980	1970
27370	Trinity(u)	(919)	6,726	....
27689	Washington	(919)	8,418	8,961
28786	Waynesville	(704)	6,765	6,488
28025	West Concord(u)	(704)	5,859	5,347
28472	Whiteville	(919)	5,565	4,195
27892	Williamston	(919)	6,159	6,570
28401	Wilmington	(010)	44,000	46,169
27893	Wilson	(919)	34,424	29,347
*27102	Winston-Salem	(919)	131,885	133,683

North Dakota (701)

58501	Bismarck		44,485	34,703
58301	Devils Lake		7,442	7,078
58601	Dickinson		15,924	12,405
58102	Fargo		61,308	53,365
58237	Grafton		5,293	5,946
58201	Grand Forks(u)		43,765	39,008
58201	Grand Forks AFB(u)		9,390	10,474
58401	Jamestown		16,280	15,385
58554	Mandan		15,513	11,093
58701	Minot		32,843	32,290
58701	Minot AFB(u)		9,880	12,077
58072	Valley City		7,774	7,843
58075	Wahpeton		9,064	7,076
58078	West Fargo		10,099	5,161
58801	Williston		13,336	11,280

Ohio

45810	Ada	(419)	5,669	5,309
*44309	Akron	(216)	237,177	275,425
44601	Alliance	(216)	24,315	26,547
44001	Amherst	(216)	10,638	9,902
44805	Ashland	(419)	20,326	19,872
44004	Ashtabula	(216)	23,449	24,313
45701	Athens	(614)	19,743	24,168
44202	Aurora	(216)	8,177	6,549
44515	Austintown(u)	(216)	33,636	29,393
44011	Avon	(216)	7,241	7,214
44012	Avon Lake	(216)	13,222	12,261
44203	Barberton	(216)	29,751	33,052
44140	Bay Village	(216)	17,846	18,163
44122	Beachwood	(216)	9,983	9,631
45385	Beavercreek	(513)	31,589	...
44146	Bedford	(216)	15,056	17,552
44146	Bedford Heights	(216)	13,214	13,063
43906	Bellaire	(614)	8,241	9,655
45305	Bellbrook	(513)	5,174	1,268
43311	Bellefontaine	(513)	11,888	11,255
44811	Bellevue	(419)	8,187	8,604
45714	Belpre	(614)	7,193	7,189
44017	Berea	(216)	19,567	22,465
43209	Bexley	(614)	13,405	14,888
43004	Blacklick Estates(u)	(614)	11,223	8,351
45242	Blue Ash	(513)	9,510	8,324
44512	Boardman(u)	(216)	39,161	30,852
43402	Bowling Green	(419)	25,728	14,656
44141	Brecksville	(216)	10,132	9,137
45231	Brentwood(u)	(513)	5,508	....
45211	Bridgetown(u)	(513)	11,460	13,352
44141	Broadview Heights	(216)	10,920	11,463
44144	Brooklyn	(216)	12,342	13,142
44142	Brook Park	(216)	26,195	30,774
44212	Brunswick	(216)	27,689	15,852
43506	Bryan	(419)	7,879	7,008
44820	Bucyrus	(419)	13,433	13,111
43725	Cambridge	(614)	13,573	13,656
44405	Campbell	(216)	11,619	12,577
44406	Canfield	(216)	5,535	4,997
*44711	Canton	(216)	93,077	110,053
45822	Celina	(419)	9,137	8,072
45459	Centerville	(513)	18,886	10,333
45211	Cheviot	(513)	9,888	11,135
45601	Chillicothe	(614)	23,420	24,842
*45234	Cincinnati	(513)	385,409	453,514
43113	Circleville	(614)	11,700	11,687
*44101	Cleveland	(216)	573,822	750,879
44118	Cleveland Heights	(216)	56,438	60,767
43410	Clyde	(419)	5,489	5,503
*43216	Columbus	(614)	565,032	540,025
44030	Conneaut	(216)	13,835	14,552
44410	Cortland	(216)	5,011	2,525
43812	Coshocton	(614)	13,405	13,747
45238	Covedale(u)	(513)	5,830	6,639
44827	Crestline	(419)	5,406	5,965
*44222	Cuyahoga Falls	(216)	43,710	49,815
*45401	Dayton	(513)	193,536	243,023
45236	Deer Park	(513)	6,745	7,415
43512	Defiance	(419)	16,810	16,281
43015	Delaware	(614)	18,780	15,008
45238	Delhi Hills(u)	(513)	27,647	....
45833	Delphos	(419)	7,314	7,608
44622	Dover	(216)	11,526	11,516
44112	East Cleveland	(216)	36,957	39,600
44094	Eastlake	(216)	22,104	19,690

43920	East Liverpool	(216)	16,687	20,020
44413	East Palestine	(216)	5,306	5,604
44320	Eaton	(513)	6,839	6,020
*44035	Elyria	(216)	57,504	53,427
45322	Englewood	(513)	11,329	7,885
44117	Euclid	(216)	59,999	71,552
45324	Fairborn	(513)	29,702	32,267
45014	Fairfield	(513)	30,777	14,680
44313	Fairlawn	(216)	6,100	6,102
44126	Fairview Park	(216)	19,311	21,699
45840	Findlay	(419)	35,594	35,800
45405	Forest Park	(513)	18,566	15,139
45426	Fort McKinley(u)	(513)	10,161	11,536
44830	Fostoria	(419)	15,743	16,037
45005	Franklin	(513)	10,711	10,075
43420	Fremont	(419)	17,834	18,490
43230	Gahanna	(614)	18,001	12,400
44833	Galion	(419)	12,391	13,123
45631	Gallipolis	(614)	5,578	7,490
44125	Garfield Heights	(216)	33,380	41,417
44041	Geneva	(216)	6,655	6,449
45327	Germantown	(513)	5,015	4,088
44420	Girard	(216)	12,517	14,119
43212	Grandview Heights	(614)	7,420	8,460
45123	Greenfield	(513)	5,150	4,780
45331	Greenville	(513)	12,999	12,380
45239	Groesbeck(u)	(513)	9,594	....
43123	Grove City	(614)	16,793	13,911
*45012	Hamilton	(513)	63,189	67,865
45030	Harrison	(513)	5,855	4,408
43055	Heath	(614)	6,969	6,768
44124	Highland Heights	(216)	5,739	5,926
43026	Hilliard	(614)	8,131	8,369
45133	Hillsboro	(513)	6,356	5,584
44484	Howland(u)	(216)	7,441	....
44425	Hubbard	(216)	9,245	8,583
45424	Huber Heights(u)	(513)	31,731	18,943
43081	Huber Ridge(u)	(614)	5,835	....
44839	Huron	(419)	7,123	6,896
44131	Independence	(216)	8,165	7,034
45638	Ironton	(614)	14,290	15,030
45640	Jackson	(614)	6,675	6,843
44240	Kent	(216)	26,164	28,183
43326	Kenton	(419)	8,605	8,315
45236	Kenwood(u)	(513)	9,928	15,789
45429	Kettering	(513)	61,186	71,864
44094	Kirtland	(216)	5,969	5,530
44107	Lakewood	(216)	61,963	70,173
43130	Lancaster	(614)	34,953	32,911
45036	Lebanon	(513)	9,636	7,934
*45802	Lima	(419)	47,827	53,734
45215	Lincoln Heights	(513)	5,259	6,099
43228	Lincoln Village(u)	(614)	10,548	11,215
43138	Logan	(614)	6,557	6,269
43140	London	(614)	6,958	6,481
*44052	Lorain	(216)	75,416	78,185
44641	Louisville	(216)	7,996	6,298
45140	Loveland	(513)	9,106	7,126
44124	Lyndhurst	(216)	18,092	19,749
44056	Macedonia	(216)	6,571	6,375
45243	Madeira	(513)	9,341	6,713
*44901	Mansfield	(419)	53,927	55,047
44137	Maple Heights	(216)	29,735	34,093
45750	Marietta	(614)	16,467	16,861
43302	Marion	(614)	37,040	38,646
43935	Martins Ferry	(614)	9,331	10,757
43040	Marysville	(513)	7,414	5,744
45040	Mason	(513)	8,692	5,677
44646	Massillon	(216)	30,557	32,539
45537	Maumee	(419)	15,747	15,937
44124	Mayfield Heights	(216)	21,550	22,139
44256	Medina	(216)	15,268	10,913
44060	Mentor	(216)	42,065	36,912
44060	Mentor-on-the-Lake	(216)	7,919	6,517
45342	Miamisburg	(513)	15,304	14,797
44130	Middleburg Heights	(216)	16,218	12,367
45042	Middletown	(513)	43,719	48,767
45042	Middletown South(u)	(513)	5,260	....
45150	Milford	(513)	5,232	4,828
45239	Monfort Heights(u)	(513)	9,745	....
45242	Montgomery	(513)	10,084	5,683
45439	Moraine	(513)	5,325	4,898
45231	Mount Healthy	(513)	7,562	7,446
43050	Mount Vernon	(614)	14,380	13,373
43545	Napoleon	(419)	8,614	7,791
43055	Newark	(614)	41,200	41,836
45344	New Carlisle	(513)	6,498	6,112
43764	New Lexington	(614)	5,179	4,921
44663	New Philadelphia	(216)	16,883	15,184
44446	Niles	(216)	23,088	21,581
45239	Northbrook(u)	(513)	8,357	....
44720	North Canton	(216)	14,228	15,228
45239	North College Hill	(513)	10,990	12,363
44057	North Madison(u)	(216)	8,741	6,882
44070	North Olmsted	(216)	36,486	34,861
45502	Northridge(u) (Clark)	(513)	5,559	12
45414	Northridge(u) (Montgomery)	(513)	9,720	10,084
44039	North Ridgeville	(216)	21,522	13,152
44133	North Royalton	(216)	17,671	12,807
.....	Northview(u)	(513)	9,973	....
43619	Northwood	(419)	5,495	4,222

ZIP code	Place		1980	1970
44203	Norton	(216)	12,242	12,308
44857	Norwalk	(419)	14,358	13,386
45212	Norwood	(513)	26,342	30,420
45873	Oakwood	(419)	9,372	10,095
44074	Oberlin	(216)	8,660	8,761
44138	Olmsted Falls	(216)	5,868	2,504
43616	Oregon	(419)	18,675	16,563
44667	Orrville	(216)	7,511	7,408
45431	Overlook-Page Manor(u)	(513)	14,825	19,719
45056	Oxford	(513)	17,655	15,868
44077	Painesville	(216)	16,391	16,536
45344	Park Layne(u)	(513)	5,372	....
44129	Parma	(216)	92,548	100,216
44130	Parma Heights	(216)	23,112	27,192
44124	Pepper Pike	(216)	6,177	5,382
44646	Perry Heights(u)	(216)	9,206	....
43551	Perrysburg	(419)	10,215	7,693
45356	Piqua	(513)	20,480	20,741
45069	Pisgah(u)	(513)	15,660	....
44319	Portage Lakes(u)	(216)	11,310	....
43452	Port Clinton	(419)	7,223	7,202
45662	Portsmouth	(614)	25,943	27,633
44266	Ravenna	(216)	11,987	11,780
45215	Reading	(513)	12,879	14,617
43068	Reynoldsburg	(614)	20,661	13,921
44143	Richmond Heights	(213)	10,095	9,220
44270	Rittman	(216)	6,063	6,308
44116	Rocky River	(216)	21,084	22,958
43460	Rossford	(419)	5,978	5,302
45217	St. Bernard	(513)	5,396	6,131
43950	St. Clairsville	(614)	5,452	4,754
45885	St. Marys	(419)	8,414	7,699
44460	Salem	(216)	12,869	14,186
44870	Sandusky	(419)	31,360	32,674
44870	Sandusky South(u)	(419)	6,548	8,501
44672	Sebring	(216)	5,078	4,954
44131	Seven Hills	(216)	13,650	12,700
44120	Shaker Heights	(216)	32,487	36,306
45241	Sharonville	(513)	10,108	11,393
44054	Sheffield Lake	(216)	10,484	8,734
44875	Shelby	(419)	9,703	9,847
45415	Shiloh(u)	(419)	11,735	11,368
45365	Sidney	(513)	17,657	16,332
45236	Silverton	(513)	6,172	6,588
44139	Solon	(216)	14,341	11,147
44121	South Euclid	(216)	25,713	29,579
45246	Springdale	(216)	10,111	8,127
*45501	Springfield	(513)	72,563	81,941
43952	Steubenville	(614)	26,400	30,771
44224	Stow	(216)	25,303	20,061
44240	Streetsboro	(216)	9,055	7,966
44136	Strongsville	(216)	28,577	15,182
44471	Struthers	(216)	13,624	15,343
43560	Sylvania	(419)	15,527	12,031
44278	Tallmadge	(216)	15,269	15,274
45243	The Village of Indian Hill	(513)	5,521	5,651
44883	Tiffin	(419)	19,549	21,596
45371	Tipp City	(513)	5,595	5,090
*43601	Toledo	(419)	354,635	383,062
43964	Toronto	(614)	6,934	7,705
45067	Trenton	(513)	6,401	5,278
45426	Trotwood	(513)	7,802	6,997
45373	Troy	(513)	19,086	17,186
44087	Twinsburg	(216)	7,632	6,432
44683	Uhrichsville	(614)	6,130	5,731
45322	Union	(513)	5,219	3,654
44118	University Heights	(216)	15,401	17,055
43221	Upper Arlington	(614)	35,648	38,727
43351	Upper Sandusky	(419)	5,967	5,645
43078	Urbana	(513)	10,762	11,237
45377	Vandalia	(513)	13,161	10,796
45891	Van Wert	(419)	11,035	11,320
44089	Vermilion	(216)	11,012	9,872
44281	Wadsworth	(216)	15,166	13,142
45895	Wapakoneta	(419)	8,402	7,324
*44481	Warren	(216)	56,629	63,494
44122	Warrensville Heights	(216)	16,565	18,925
43160	Washington	(513)	12,682	12,495
43567	Wauseon	(419)	6,173	4,932
45692	Wellston	(614)	6,016	5,410
43968	Wellsville	(216)	5,095	5,891
45449	West Carrollton	(513)	13,148	10,748
43081	Westerville	(614)	23,414	12,530
44145	Westlake	(216)	19,483	15,689
43213	Whitehall	(614)	21,299	25,263
45239	White Oak(u)	(513)	9,563	....
44092	Wickliffe	(216)	16,790	20,632
44890	Willard	(419)	5,674	5,510
44094	Willoughby	(216)	19,329	18,634
44094	Willoughby Hills	(216)	8,612	5,969
44094	Willowick	(216)	17,834	21,237
45177	Wilmington	(513)	10,431	10,051
45459	Woodbourne-Hyde Park(u)	(513)	8,826	....
44691	Wooster	(216)	19,289	18,703
43085	Worthington	(614)	15,016	15,326
45215	Wyoming	(513)	8,282	9,089
45385	Xenia	(513)	24,653	25,373
*44501	Youngstown	(216)	115,511	140,909
43701	Zanesville	(614)	28,655	33,045

Oklahoma

ZIP code	Place		1980	1970
74820	Ada	(405)	15,902	14,859
73521	Altus	(405)	23,101	23,302
73717	Alva	(405)	6,416	7,440
73005	Anadarko	(405)	6,378	6,682
73401	Ardmore	(405)	23,689	20,881
74003	Bartlesville	(918)	34,568	29,683
73008	Bethany	(405)	22,038	22,694
74008	Bixby	(918)	6,969	3,973
74631	Blackwell	(405)	8,400	8,645
74728	Broken Arrow	(918)	35,761	11,018
73018	Chickasha	(405)	15,828	14,194
73020	Choctaw	(405)	7,520	4,750
74017	Claremore	(918)	12,085	9,084
73601	Clinton	(405)	8,796	8,513
74023	Cushing	(918)	7,720	7,529
73115	Del City	(405)	28,523	27,133
73533	Duncan	(405)	22,517	19,718
74701	Durant	(405)	11,972	11,118
73034	Edmond	(405)	34,637	16,633
73644	Elk City	(405)	9,579	7,323
73036	El Reno	(405)	15,486	14,510
73701	Enid	(405)	50,363	44,986
73503	Fort Sill(u)	(405)	15,924	21,217
73542	Frederick	(405)	6,153	6,132
73044	Guthrie	(405)	10,312	9,575
73942	Guymon	(405)	8,492	7,674
74437	Henryetta	(918)	6,432	6,430
74848	Holdenville	(405)	5,469	5,181
74743	Hugo	(405)	7,172	6,585
74745	Idabel	(405)	7,622	5,946
74037	Jenks	(918)	5,876	2,685
73501	Lawton	(405)	80,054	74,470
73055	Marlow	(405)	5,017	3,995
74501	McAlester	(918)	17,255	18,802
74354	Miami	(918)	14,237	13,880
73110	Midwest City	(405)	49,559	48,212
73060	Moore	(405)	35,063	18,761
74401	Muskogee	(918)	40,011	37,331
73064	Mustang	(405)	7,496	2,637
73069	Norman	(405)	68,020	52,117
*73125	Oklahoma City	(405)	404,014	368,164
74447	Okmulgee	(918)	16,263	15,180
74055	Owasso	(918)	6,149	3,491
73075	Pauls Valley	(405)	5,664	5,769
73077	Perry	(405)	5,796	5,341
74601	Ponca City	(405)	26,238	25,940
74953	Poteau	(918)	7,089	5,500
74361	Pryor Creek	(918)	8,483	7,057
74955	Sallisaw	(918)	6,403	4,888
74063	Sand Springs	(918)	13,121	10,565
74066	Sapulpa	(918)	15,853	15,159
74868	Seminole	(405)	8,590	7,878
74801	Shawnee	(405)	26,506	25,075
74074	Stillwater	(405)	38,268	31,126
73086	Sulphur	(405)	5,516	5,158
74464	Tahlequah	(918)	9,708	9,254
74873	Tecumseh	(405)	5,123	4,451
73120	The Village	(405)	11,114	13,695
*74101	Tulsa	(918)	360,919	330,350
74156	Turley(u)	(918)	6,336	....
74301	Vinita	(918)	6,740	5,847
74467	Wagoner	(918)	6,191	4,959
73132	Warr Acres	(405)	9,940	9,887
73096	Weatherford	(405)	9,640	7,959
74884	Wewoka	(405)	5,472	5,284
73801	Woodward	(405)	13,781	9,563
73099	Yukon	(405)	17,112	8,411

Oregon (503)

ZIP code	Place	1980	1970
97321	Albany	26,511	18,181
97005	Aloha(u)	28,353	....
97601	Altamont(u)	19,805	15,746
97520	Ashland	14,943	12,342
97103	Astoria	9,998	10,244
97814	Baker	9,471	9,354
97005	Beaverton	31,926	18,577
97701	Bend	17,263	13,710
97013	Canby	7,659	3,813
97225	Cedar Hills(u)	9,619	....
	Centennial(u)	22,118	....
97502	Central Point	6,357	4,004
97420	Coos Bay	14,424	13,466
97330	Corvallis	40,960	35,056
97424	Cottage Grove	7,148	6,004
	Cully(u)	10,569	....
97338	Dallas	8,530	6,361
97266	Errol Heights(u)	10,487	....
*97401	Eugene	105,664	79,028
97116	Forest Grove	11,499	8,275
97301	Four Corners(u)	11,331	5,823
97223	Garden Home-Whitford(u)	6,926	....
97027	Gladstone	9,500	6,254
97526	Grants Pass	14,997	12,455
97030	Gresham	33,005	10,030
97303	Hayesville(u)	9,213	5,518
97230	Hazelwood(u)	25,541	....
97838	Hermiston	9,408	4,893

ZIP code	Place	1980	1970
97123	Hillsboro	27,664	14,675
97303	Keizer(u)	18,592	11,445
97601	Klamath Falls	16,661	15,775
97850	La Grande	11,354	9,645
97034	Lake Oswego	22,527	14,615
97355	Lebanon	10,413	6,636
97367	Lincoln City	5,469	4,198
97128	McMinnville	14,080	10,125
97501	Medford	39,603	28,973
97223	Metzger(u)	5,544	....
97862	Milton-Freewater	5,086	4,105
97222	Milwaukie	17,931	16,444
97361	Monmouth	5,594	5,237
97132	Newberg	10,394	6,507
97365	Newport	7,519	5,188
97459	North Bend	9,779	8,553
....	North Springfield(u)	6,140	....
97268	Oak Grove(u)	11,640	....
97914	Ontario	8,814	6,523
97045	Oregon City	14,673	9,176
97220	Parkrose(u)	21,108	....
97801	Pendleton	14,521	13,197
*97208	Portland	368,148	379,967
97236	Powellhurst(u)	20,132	....
97754	Prineville	5,276	4,101
97225	Raleigh Hills(u)	6,517	....
97756	Redmond	6,452	3,721
97404	River Road(u)	10,370	....
97470	Roseburg	16,644	14,461
97051	St. Helens	7,064	6,212
*97301	Salem	89,233	68,725
97138	Seaside	5,193	4,402
97381	Silverton	5,168	4,301
97477	Springfield	41,621	26,874
97386	Sweet Home	6,921	3,799
97058	The Dalles	10,820	10,423
97223	Tigard	14,799	6,499
97060	Troutdale	5,908	1,661
97062	Tualatin	7,483	750
97068	West Linn	11,358	7,091
97225	West Slope(u)	5,364	....
97501	White City(u)	5,445	....
97233	Wilkes-Rockwood(u)	23,216	....
97071	Woodburn	11,196	7,495

Pennsylvania

ZIP code	Place		1980	1970
19001	Abington Township(u)	(215)	59,084	63,625
15001	Aliquippa	(412)	17,094	22,277
*18101	Allentown	(215)	103,758	109,871
*16603	Altoona	(814)	57,078	63,115
19002	Ambler	(215)	6,628	7,800
15003	Ambridge	(412)	9,575	11,324
18403	Archbald	(717)	6,295	6,118
19003	Ardmore(u)	(215)	NA	5,131
15068	Arnold	(412)	6,853	8,174
19014	Aston Township(u)	(215)	14,530	13,704
15202	Avalon	(412)	6,240	7,010
15005	Baden	(412)	5,318	5,536
19004	Bala-Cynwyd(u)	(215)	NA	6,483
15234	Baldwin	(412)	24,714	26,729
18013	Bangor	(215)	5,006	5,425
15009	Beaver	(412)	5,441	6,100
15010	Beaver Falls	(412)	12,525	14,635
16823	Bellefonte	(814)	6,300	6,828
15202	Bellevue	(412)	10,128	11,586
19020	Bensalem Township(u)	(215)	52,399	33,038
18603	Berwick	(717)	12,189	12,274
15102	Bethel Park	(412)	34,755	34,758
*18016	Bethlehem	(215)	70,419	72,686
18447	Blakely	(717)	7,438	6,391
17815	Bloomsburg	(717)	11,717	11,652
15104	Braddock	(412)	5,634	8,795
16701	Bradford	(814)	11,211	12,672
15227	Brentwood	(412)	11,859	13,732
15017	Bridgeville	(412)	6,154	6,717
19007	Bristol	(215)	10,867	12,085
19007	Bristol Twp(u)	(215)	58,733	67,498
19015	Brookhaven	(215)	7,912	7,370
16001	Butler	(412)	17,026	18,691
15419	California	(412)	5,703	6,635
17011	Camp Hill	(717)	8,422	9,931
15317	Canonsburg	(412)	10,459	11,439
18407	Carbondale	(717)	11,255	12,478
17013	Carlisle	(717)	18,314	18,079
15106	Carnegie	(412)	10,099	10,864
15108	Carnot-Moon(u)	(412)	11,102	13,093
15234	Castle Shannon	(412)	10,164	12,036
18032	Catasauqua	(215)	7,944	5,702
17201	Chambersburg	(717)	16,174	17,315
15022	Charleroi	(412)	5,717	6,723
19012	Cheltenham Twp(u)	(215)	35,509	40,238
*19003	Chester	(215)	45,794	56,331
19013	Chester Twp(u)	(215)	5,687	5,708
15025	Clairton	(412)	12,188	15,051
16214	Clarion	(814)	6,198	6,095
18411	Clarks Summit	(717)	5,272	5,376
16830	Clearfield	(814)	7,580	8,176
19018	Clifton Heights	(215)	7,320	8,348
19320	Coatesville	(215)	10,698	12,331
19023	Collingdale	(215)	9,539	10,605
17512	Columbia	(717)	10,466	11,237
15425	Connellsville	(412)	10,319	11,643
19428	Conshohocken	(215)	8,591	10,195
15108	Coraopolis	(412)	7,308	8,435
16407	Corry	(814)	7,149	7,435
15205	Crafton	(412)	7,623	8,233
17821	Danville	(717)	5,239	6,176
19023	Darby	(215)	11,513	13,729
19036	Darby Twp(u)	(215)	12,264	.....
19333	Devon-Berwyn(u)	(215)	5,246	.....
18519	Dickson City	(717)	6,699	7,698
15033	Donora	(412)	7,524	8,825
15216	Dormont	(412)	11,275	12,856
19335	Downingtown	(215)	7,650	7,437
18901	Doylestown	(215)	8,717	8,270
15801	Du Bois	(814)	9,290	10,112
18512	Dunmore	(717)	16,781	18,168
15110	Duquesne	(412)	10,094	11,410
18642	Duryea	(717)	5,415	5,264
19401	East Norriton(u)	(215)	12,711	.....
18042	Easton	(215)	26,027	29,450
18301	East Stroudsburg	(717)	8,039	7,894
15005	Economy	(412)	9,538	7,176
16412	Edinboro	(814)	6,324	4,871
18704	Edwardsville	(717)	5,729	5,633
17022	Elizabethtown	(717)	8,233	8,072
16117	Ellwood City	(412)	9,998	10,857
18049	Emmaus	(215)	11,001	11,511
17522	Ephrata	(717)	11,095	9,662
*16501	Erie	(814)	119,123	129,265
18643	Exeter	(717)	5,493	4,670
19054	Falls Twp(u)	(215)	36,083	35,830
16121	Farrell	(412)	8,645	11,000
19032	Folcroft	(215)	8,231	9,610
15221	Forest Hills	(412)	8,198	9,561
18704	Forty Fort	(717)	5,590	6,114
15238	Fox Chapel	(412)	5,049	4,684
17931	Frackville	(717)	5,308	5,445
16323	Franklin	(814)	8,146	8,629
15143	Franklin Park	(412)	6,135	5,310
18052	Fullerton(u)	(215)	8,055	7,908
17325	Gettysburg	(717)	7,194	7,275
15045	Glassport	(412)	6,242	7,450
19036	Glenolden	(215)	7,633	8,697
15601	Greensburg	(412)	17,558	17,077
15220	Green Tree	(412)	5,722	6,441
16125	Greenville	(412)	7,730	8,704
16127	Grove City	(412)	8,162	8,312
17331	Hanover	(717)	14,890	15,623
*17105	Harrisburg	(717)	53,264	68,061
19040	Hatboro	(215)	7,579	8,880
19083	Haverford Twp(u)	(215)	52,349	55,132
18201	Hazleton	(717)	27,318	30,426
18055	Hellertown	(215)	6,025	6,615
17033	Hershey(u)	(717)	13,249	7,407
18042	Highland Park (Northampton)(u)	(717)	5,922	5,500
16648	Hollidaysburg	(814)	5,892	6,262
16001	Homeacre-Lyndora(u)	(412)	8,333	8,415
15120	Homestead	(412)	5,092	6,309
18431	Honesdale	(717)	5,128	5,224
19044	Horsham(u)	(215)	9,900	.....
17036	Hummelstown	(717)	6,159	4,723
16652	Huntingdon	(814)	7,042	6,987
15701	Indiana	(412)	16,051	16,100
15644	Jeannette	(412)	13,106	15,209
15344	Jefferson	(412)	8,643	8,512
18229	Jim Thorpe	(717)	5,263	5,456
*15901	Johnstown	(814)	35,496	42,476
15108	Kennedy Twp(u)	(412)	7,159	6,859
18704	Kingston	(717)	15,681	18,325
16201	Kittanning	(412)	5,432	6,231
*17604	Lancaster	(717)	54,725	57,690
19446	Lansdale	(215)	16,526	18,451
19050	Lansdowne	(215)	11,891	14,090
15650	Latrobe	(412)	10,799	11,749
17042	Lebanon	(717)	25,711	28,572
18235	Lehighton	(717)	5,826	6,095
17837	Lewisburg	(717)	5,407	5,718
17044	Lewistown	(717)	9,830	11,098
17543	Lititz	(717)	7,590	7,072
17745	Lock Haven	(717)	9,617	11,427
15068	Lower Burrell	(412)	13,200	13,654
19003	Lower Merion Twp(u)	(215)	59,651	63,392
19006	Lower Moreland Twp(u)	(215)	12,472	11,746
19047	Lower Southampton Twp(u)	(215)	18,305	17,578
19008	Marple Twp(u)	(215)	23,642	25,040
15237	McCandless Twp(u)	(412)	26,250	22,404
*15134	McKeesport	(412)	31,012	37,977
15136	McKees Rocks	(412)	8,742	11,901
17948	Mahanoy City	(717)	6,167	7,257
17545	Manheim	(717)	5,015	5,434
16335	Meadville	(814)	15,544	16,573
17055	Mechanicsburg	(717)	9,487	9,385
*19063	Media	(215)	6,119	6,444
17057	Middletown (Dauphin)	(717)	10,122	9,080
18017	Middletown (Northampton)(u)	(215)	5,801	

ZIP code	Place		1980	1970
17057	Middletown Twp			
	(Delaware)(u)	(215)	12,463	12,878
17551	Millersville	(717)	7,668	6,396
17847	Milton	(717)	6,730	7,723
17954	Minersville	(717)	5,635	6,012
15061	Monaca	(412)	7,661	7,486
15062	Monessen	(412)	11,928	15,216
15063	Monongahela	(412)	5,950	7,113
15146	Monroeville	(412)	30,977	29,011
17754	Montoursville	(717)	5,403	5,985
18507	Moosic	(717)	6,068	4,646
19067	Morrisville	(215)	9,845	11,309
17851	Mount Carmel	(717)	8,190	9,317
17552	Mount Joy	(717)	5,680	5,041
15666	Mount Pleasant	(412)	5,354	5,895
15228	Mount Lebanon(u)	(412)	34,414	39,157
15120	Munhall	(412)	14,535	16,574
15668	Murrysville	(412)	16,036	12,661
18634	Nanticoke	(717)	13,044	14,638
18064	Nazareth	(215)	5,443	5,815
	Nether Providence Twp(u)	(215)	12,730	13,644
15066	New Brighton	(412)	7,364	7,637
*16101	New Castle	(412)	33,621	38,559
17070	New Cumberland	(717)	8,051	9,803
15068	New Kensington	(412)	17,660	20,312
*19401	Norristown	(215)	34,684	38,169
18067	Northampton	(215)	8,240	8,389
15104	North Braddock	(412)	8,711	10,838
15137	North Versailles(u)	(412)	13,294	....
16421	Northwest Harbor-Creek(u)	(814)	7,485	....
19074	Norwood	(215)	6,647	7,229
15139	Oakmont	(412)	7,039	7,550
16301	Oil City	(814)	13,881	15,033
18518	Old Forge	(717)	9,304	9,522
18447	Olyphant	(717)	5,204	5,422
18071	Palmerton	(215)	5,455	5,620
17078	Palmyra	(717)	7,228	7,615
19301	Paoli(u)	(215)	6,698	5,835
17331	Parkville(u)	(717)	5,009	5,120
15235	Penn Hills(u)	(412)	57,632	....
18944	Perkasie	(215)	5,241	5,451
*19104	Philadelphia	(215)	1,688,210	1,949,996
19460	Phoenixville	(215)	14,165	14,823
*15219	Pittsburgh	(412)	423,959	520,089
*18640	Pittston	(717)	9,930	11,113
18705	Plains(u)	(717)	5,455	6,606
15236	Pleasant Hills	(412)	9,604	10,409
15239	Pium	(412)	25,390	21,932
18651	Plymouth	(717)	7,605	9,536
19462	Plymouth Twp(u)	(215)	17,168	16,876
15133	Port Vue	(412)	5,316	5,862
19464	Pottstown	(215)	22,729	25,355
17901	Pottsville	(717)	18,195	19,715
19076	Prospect Park	(215)	6,593	7,250
15767	Punxsutawney	(814)	7,479	7,792
18951	Quakertown	(215)	8,867	7,276
19087	Radnor Twp(u)	(215)	27,676	27,459
*19603	Reading	(215)	78,686	87,643
17356	Red Lion	(717)	5,824	5,645
18954	Richboro(u)	(215)	5,141	....
15853	Ridgway	(814)	5,604	6,022
19078	Ridley Park	(215)	7,889	9,025
19033	Ridley Twp(u)	(215)	33,771	39,085
15237	Ross Twp(u)	(412)	35,102	32,892
15857	St. Marys	(814)	6,417	7,470
18840	Sayre	(717)	6,951	7,473
17972	Schuylkill Haven	(717)	5,977	6,125
15683	Scottdale	(412)	5,833	5,818
15106	Scott Twp(u)	(412)	20,413	21,856
*18503	Scranton	(717)	88,117	102,696
17870	Selinsgrove	(717)	5,227	5,116
15116	Shaler Twp(u)	(412)	33,712	33,369
17872	Shamokin	(717)	10,357	11,719
16146	Sharon	(412)	19,057	22,653
19079	Sharon Hill	(215)	6,221	7,464
16150	Sharpsville	(412)	5,375	6,126
17976	Shenandoah	(717)	7,589	8,287
19607	Shillington	(215)	5,601	6,249
17404	Shiloh(u)	(717)	5,315	....
17257	Shippensburg	(717)	5,261	6,536
15501	Somerset	(814)	6,474	6,269
18964	Souderton	(215)	6,657	6,366
17701	South Williamsport		6,581	7,153
19064	Springfield(u)	(215)	25,326	....
19118	Springfield Twp(u)	(215)	20,344	22,394
16801	State College	(814)	36,130	32,833
17113	Steelton	(717)	6,484	8,556
15136	Stowe Twp(u)	(412)	9,202	10,119
18360	Stroudsburg	(717)	5,148	5,451
16323	Sugar Creek	(814)	5,954	5,944
17801	Sunbury	(717)	12,292	13,025
19081	Swarthmore	(215)	5,950	6,156
17111	Swatara Twp(u)	(717)	18,796	17,178
15218	Swissvale	(412)	11,345	13,819
18704	Swoyersville	(717)	5,795	6,786
18252	Tamaqua	(717)	8,843	9,246
15084	Tarentum	(412)	6,419	7,379
18517	Taylor	(717)	7,246	6,977
16354	Titusville	(814)	6,884	7,331

ZIP code	Place		1980	1970
19401	Trooper(u)	(215)	7,370	....
15145	Turtle Creek	(412)	6,959	8,308
16686	Tyrone	(814)	6,346	7,072
15401	Uniontown	(412)	14,510	16,282
19061	Upper Chichester Twp(u)	(215)	14,377	11,414
19082	Upper Darby(u)	(215)	84,054	95,910
19034	Upper Dublin Twp(u)	(215)	22,348	19,449
19406	Upper Merion Twp(u)	(215)	26,138	23,699
19090	Upper Moreland Twp(u)	(215)	25,874	24,866
19063	Upper Providence Twp(u)	(215)	9,477	9,234
15241	Upper St. Clair(u)	(412)	19,023	....
19006	Upper Southampton Twp(u)	(215)	15,806	13,936
15690	Vandergrift	(412)	6,823	7,889
18974	Warminster(u)	(215)	35,543	....
16365	Warren	(814)	12,146	12,998
15301	Washington	(412)	18,363	19,827
17268	Waynesboro	(717)	9,726	10,011
	Weigelstown(u)	(717)	5,213	....
19380	West Chester	(215)	17,435	19,301
19380	West Goshen(u)	(215)	7,998	....
15122	West Mifflin	(412)	26,322	28,070
19401	West Norriton(u)	(215)	14,034	....
15905	Westmont	(814)	6,113	6,673
18643	West Pittston	(717)	5,980	7,074
15229	West View	(412)	7,648	8,312
15052	Whitehall	(215)	15,143	16,450
19428	Whitemarsh Twp(u)	(215)	15,101	15,886
15131	White Oak	(717)	9,480	9,304
*18701	Wilkes-Barre	(717)	51,551	58,856
15221	Wilkinsburg	(412)	23,669	26,780
15145	Wilkins Twp(u)	(412)	8,472	8,749
17701	Williamsport	(717)	33,401	37,918
15025	Wilson	(412)	7,564	8,406
15963	Windber	(814)	5,585	6,332
19610	Wyomissing	(215)	6,551	7,136
19050	Yeadon	(215)	11,727	12,136
*17405	York	(717)	44,619	50,335

Rhode Island (401)

See Note on Page 268

		1980	1970
02806	Barrington	16,174	17,554
02809	Bristol	20,128	17,860
02830	Burrillville	13,164	10,087
02863	Central Falls	16,995	18,716
02816	Coventry	27,065	22,947
02910	Cranston	71,992	74,287
02864	Cumberland	27,069	26,605
02864	Cumberland Hill(u)	5,421	....
02818	East Greenwich	10,211	9,577
02914	East Providence	50,980	48,207
02814	Glocester	7,550	5,160
02828	Greenville(u)	7,576	....
02833	Hopkinton	6,406	5,392
02919	Johnston	24,907	22,037
02881	Kingston(u)	5,479	5,601
02865	Lincoln	16,949	16,182
02840	Middletown	17,216	29,290
02882	Narragansett	12,088	7,138
02840	Newport	29,259	34,562
02843	Newport East(u)	11,030	10,285
02852	North Kingstown	21,938	29,793
02908	North Providence	29,188	24,337
02876	North Smithfield	9,972	9,349
*02860	Pawtucket	71,204	76,984
02871	Portsmouth	14,257	12,521
*02904	Providence	156,804	179,116
02857	Scituate	8,405	7,489
02917	Smithfield	16,886	13,468
02879	South Kingstown	20,414	16,913
02878	Tiverton	13,526	12,559
02864	Valley Falls(u)	10,892	....
*02880	Wakefield-Peacedale(u)	6,474	6,331
02885	Warren	10,640	10,523
*02887	Warwick	87,123	83,694
02891	Westerly	18,580	17,248
02891	Westerly Center(u)	14,093	13,654
02893	West Warwick	27,026	24,323
02895	Woonsocket	45,914	46,820

South Carolina (803)

		1980	1970
29620	Abbeville	5,863	5,515
29801	Aiken	14,978	13,436
29621	Anderson	27,546	27,556
29407	Avondale-Moorland(u)	5,355	5,236
29812	Barnwell	5,572	4,439
29902	Beaufort	8,634	9,434
29627	Belton	5,312	5,257
29841	Belvedere(u)	6,859	....
29512	Bennettsville	8,774	7,468
29611	Berea(u)	13,164	7,186
	Brookdale(u)	6,123	....
29020	Camden	7,462	8,532
29209	Capitol View(u)	9,962	....
29033	Cayce	11,701	9,967
*29401	Charleston	69,779	66,945
29404	Charleston Base(u)	NA	6,238

ZIP code	Place	1980	1970
29408	Charleston Yard(u)	NA	13,565
29520	Cheraw	5,654	5,627
29706	Chester	6,820	7,045
29631	Clemson	8,118	6,690
29325	Clinton	8,596	8,130
*29201	Columbia	101,229	113,542
29526	Conway	10,240	8,151
29532	Darlington	7,989	6,990
29204	Dentsville(u)	13,579	....
29536	Dillon	7,042	6,391
29405	Dorchester Terrace-Brentwood(u)	7,862	....
29601	Dunean(u)	5,146	1,266
29640	Easley	14,264	11,175
29501	Florence	29,842	25,997
29206	Forest Acres	6,062	6,808
29340	Gaffney	13,453	13,131
29605	Gantt(u)	13,719	11,386
29440	Georgetown	10,144	10,449
29445	Goose Creek	17,811	3,825
*29602	Greenville	58,242	61,436
29203	Greenview(u)	5,515	....
29646	Greenwood	21,613	21,069
29651	Greer	10,525	10,642
29410	Hanahan	13,224	9,118
29550	Hartsville	7,631	8,017
29928	Hilton Head Island(u)	11,344	....
29621	Homeland Park(u)	6,720	....
29412	James Island(u)	24,124	....
29456	Ladson(u)	13,246	....
29560	Lake City	5,636	6,247
29720	Lancaster	9,703	9,186
29902	Laurel Bay(u)	5,238	....
29360	Laurens	10,587	10,298
29571	Marion	7,700	7,435
29662	Mauldin	8,143	3,797
29464	Mount Pleasant	14,464	6,879
29574	Mullins	6,068	6,006
29577	Myrtle Beach	18,758	9,035
29108	Newberry	9,866	9,218
29841	North Augusta	13,593	12,883
29406	North Charleston	62,504	21,211
.....	North Trenholm(u)	10,962	....
29565	Oak Grove(u)	7,092	....
29115	Orangeburg	14,933	13,252
29905	Parris Island(u)	7,752	8,868
29483	Pinehurst-Sheppard Park(u)	6,956	1,711
29730	Rock Hill	35,327	33,846
29407	St. Andrews (Charleston)(u)	9,908	9,202
29210	St. Andrews (Richland)(u)	20,245	....
29609	Sans Souci(u)	8,393	....
29678	Seneca	7,436	6,573
.....	Seven Oaks(u)	16,604	....
29152	Shaw AFB(u)	6,939	5,819
29681	Simpsonville	9,037	3,308
.....	South Sumter(u)	7,096	....
*29301	Spartanburg	43,826	44,546
29483	Summerville	6,492	3,839
29150	Sumter	24,921	24,555
29687	Taylors(u)	15,801	6,831
29379	Union	10,523	10,775
29205	Valencia Heights(u)	5,328	....
29607	Wade-Hampton(u)	20,180	17,152
29488	Walterboro	6,036	6,257
29405	Wando Woods(u)	5,266	....
29611	Welcome(u)	6,922	....
29169	West Columbia	10,409	7,838
29206	Woodfield(u)	9,588	....
29388	Woodruff	5,171	4,690
29745	York	6,412	5,081

South Dakota (605)

57401	Aberdeen	25,851	26,476
57006	Brookings	14,951	13,717
57350	Huron	13,000	14,299
57042	Madison	6,210	6,315
57301	Mitchell	13,916	13,425
57501	Pierre	11,973	9,699
57701	Rapid City	46,492	43,836
*57101	Sioux Falls	81,343	72,488
57785	Sturgis	5,184	4,536
57069	Vermillion	9,582	9,128
57201	Watertown	15,649	13,388
57078	Yankton	12,011	11,919

Tennessee

37701	Alcoa	(615)	6,870	7,739
37303	Athens	(615)	12,080	11,790
38134	Bartlett	(901)	17,170	1,150
37660	Bloomingdale(u)	(615)	12,088	3,120
38008	Bolivar	(901)	6,597	6,674
37027	Brentwood	(615)	9,431	4,099
37620	Bristol	(615)	23,986	20,064
38012	Brownsville	(901)	9,307	7,011
*37401	Chattanooga	(615)	169,728	119,923
37040	Clarksville	(615)	54,777	31,719

37311	Cleveland	(615)	26,415	21,446
37716	Clinton	(615)	5,245	4,794
38017	Collierville	(901)	7,839	3,651
37663	Colonial Heights(u)	(615)	6,744	3,027
38401	Columbia	(615)	26,571	21,471
37922	Concord (Knox)(u)	(615)	8,569	....
38501	Cookeville	(615)	20,350	14,403
38019	Covington	(901)	6,065	5,801
38555	Crossville	(615)	6,394	5,381
37321	Dayton	(615)	5,913	4,361
37055	Dickson	(615)	7,040	5,665
38024	Dyersburg	(901)	15,856	14,523
37801	Eagleton Village(u)	(615)	5,331	5,345
37412	East Ridge	(615)	21,236	21,799
37643	Elizabethton	(615)	12,431	12,269
37334	Fayetteville	(615)	7,559	7,691
37064	Franklin	(615)	12,407	9,497
37066	Gallatin	(615)	17,191	13,253
38138	Germantown	(901)	21,482	3,474
37072	Goodlettsville	(615)	8,327	6,168
37075	Greater Hendersonville(u)	(615)	25,029	11,996
37743	Greeneville	(615)	14,097	13,722
37918	Halls(u)	(615)	10,363	....
37748	Harriman	(615)	8,303	8,734
37341	Harrison(u)	(615)	6,206	....
37075	Hendersonville	(615)	26,561	412
38343	Humboldt	(901)	10,209	10,066
38301	Jackson	(901)	49,258	39,996
37760	Jefferson City	(615)	5,612	5,124
37601	Johnson City	(615)	39,753	33,770
*37662	Kingsport	(615)	32,027	31,938
*37901	Knoxville	(615)	175,045	174,587
37766	La Follette	(615)	8,176	6,902
37086	LaVergne	(615)	5,495	5,220
38464	Lawrenceburg	(615)	10,175	8,889
37087	Lebanon	(615)	11,872	12,492
37771	Lenoir City	(615)	5,180	5,324
37091	Lewisburg	(615)	8,760	7,207
38351	Lexington	(901)	5,934	5,024
37665	Lynn Garden(u)	(615)	7,213	....
38201	McKenzie	(901)	5,405	4,873
37110	McMinnville	(615)	10,683	10,662
37355	Manchester	(615)	7,250	6,208
38237	Martin	(901)	8,898	7,781
37801	Maryville	(615)	17,480	13,808
*38101	Memphis	(901)	646,174	623,988
37343	Middle Valley(u)	(615)	11,420	....
38358	Milan	(901)	8,083	7,313
38053	Millington	(901)	20,236	21,177
37814	Morristown	(615)	19,570	20,318
37130	Murfreesboro	(615)	32,845	26,360
*37202	Nashville-Davidson	(615)	455,651	**426,029
37821	Newport	(615)	7,580	7,328
37830	Oak Ridge	(615)	27,662	28,319
38242	Paris	(901)	10,728	9,892
37849	Powell(u)	(615)	7,220	....
38478	Pulaski	(615)	7,184	6,989
37415	Red Bank White Oak	(615)	13,129	12,715
38063	Ripley	(901)	6,366	4,794
37854	Rockwood	(615)	5,767	5,259
38372	Savannah	(901)	6,992	5,576
37160	Shelbyville	(615)	13,530	12,262
37377	Signal Mountain	(615)	5,818	4,839
37167	Smyrna	(615)	8,839	5,698
37379	Soddy-Daisy	(615)	8,388	7,569
37172	Springfield	(615)	10,814	9,720
37363	Summit (Hamilton)(u)	(615)	8,345	....
37388	Tullahoma	(615)	15,800	15,311
38261	Union City	(901)	10,436	11,925
37398	Winchester	(615)	5,821	5,256

**Comprises the Metropolitan Government of Nashville and Davidson County.

Texas

*79604	Abilene	(915)	98,315	89,653
75001	Addison	(214)	5,553	593
78516	Alamo	(512)	5,831	4,291
78209	Alamo Heights	(512)	6,252	6,933
77039	Aldine(u)	(713)	12,623	....
78332	Alice	(512)	20,961	20,121
75002	Allen	(214)	8,314	1,940
79830	Alpine	(915)	5,465	5,971
77511	Alvin	(713)	16,515	10,671
*79105	Amarillo	(806)	149,230	127,010
79714	Andrews	(915)	11,061	8,625
77515	Angleton	(409)	13,929	9,906
78336	Aransas Pass	(512)	7,173	5,813
*76010	Arlington	(817)	160,123	90,229
75751	Athens	(214)	10,197	9,582
75551	Atlanta	(214)	6,272	5,007
*78710	Austin	(512)	345,890	253,539
76020	Azle	(817)	5,822	4,493
75149	Balch Springs	(214)	13,746	10,464
77414	Bay City	(409)	17,837	13,445
77520	Baytown	(713)	56,923	43,980
*77704	Beaumont	(409)	118,102	117,548
76021	Bedford	(817)	20,821	10,049
78102	Beeville	(512)	14,574	13,506
77401	Bellaire	(713)	14,950	19,009

ZIP code	Place		1980	1970
76704	Bellmead	(817)	7,569	7,698
76513	Belton	(817)	10,660	8,696
76126	Benbrook	(817)	13,579	8,169
79720	Big Spring	(915)	24,804	28,735
75418	Bonham	(214)	7,338	7,698
79007	Borger	(806)	15,837	14,195
76230	Bowie	(817)	5,610	5,185
76825	Brady	(915)	5,969	5,557
76024	Breckenridge	(817)	6,921	5,944
77833	Brenham	(409)	10,966	8,922
77611	Bridge City	(713)	7,667	8,164
79316	Brownfield	(806)	10,387	9,647
78520	Brownsville	(512)	84,997	52,522
76801	Brownwood	(915)	19,203	17,368
77801	Bryan	(409)	44,337	33,719
76354	Burkburnett	(817)	10,668	9,230
76028	Burleson	(817)	11,734	7,713
76520	Cameron	(817)	5,721	5,546
79015	Canyon	(806)	10,724	8,333
78834	Carrizo Springs	(512)	6,886	5,374
75006	Carrollton	(214)	40,591	13,855
75633	Carthage	(214)	6,447	5,392
75104	Cedar Hill	(214)	6,849	2,610
75935	Center	(409)	5,827	4,989
	Champions(u)	(713)	14,692	....
77530	Channelview(u)	(713)	17,471	....
79201	Childress	(817)	5,817	5,408
76033	Cleburne	(817)	19,218	16,015
77327	Cleveland	(713)	5,977	5,627
77015	Clover Leaf(u)	(713)	17,317	....
77531	Clute	(409)	9,577	6,023
76834	Coleman	(915)	5,960	5,608
77840	College Station	(409)	37,272	17,676
76034	Colleyville	(817)	6,700	3,342
79512	Colorado City	(915)	5,405	5,227
75428	Commerce	(214)	8,136	9,534
77301	Conroe	(409)	18,034	11,969
78109	Converse	(512)	5,150	1,383
76522	Copperas Cove	(817)	19,469	10,818
*78408	Corpus Christi	(512)	231,134	204,525
75110	Corsicana	(214)	21,712	19,972
75835	Crockett	(713)	7,405	6,616
76036	Crowley	(817)	5,852	2,662
78839	Crystal City	(512)	8,334	8,104
77954	Cuero	(512)	7,124	6,956
79022	Dalhart	(806)	6,854	5,705
*75260	Dallas	(214)	904,599	844,401
77536	Deer Park	(713)	22,648	12,773
78840	Del Rio	(512)	30,034	21,330
75020	Denison	(214)	23,884	24,923
76201	Denton	(817)	48,063	39,874
75115	De Soto	(214)	15,538	6,617
75941	Diboll	(713)	5,227	3,557
77539	Dickinson	(713)	7,505	10,776
79027	Dimmitt	(806)	5,019	4,327
78537	Donna	(512)	9,952	7,365
79029	Dumas	(806)	12,194	9,771
75116	Duncanville	(214)	27,781	14,105
78852	Eagle Pass	(512)	21,407	15,364
78539	Edinburg	(512)	24,075	17,163
77957	Edna	(512)	5,650	5,332
77437	El Campo	(619)	10,462	9,332
79910	El Paso	(915)	425,259	322,261
78543	Elsa	(512)	5,061	4,400
75119	Ennis	(214)	12,110	11,046
76039	Euless	(817)	24,002	19,316
76140	Everman	(817)	5,387	4,570
78355	Falfurrias	(512)	6,103	6,355
75234	Farmers Branch	(214)	24,863	27,492
76119	Forest Hill	(817)	11,684	8,236
79906	Fort Bliss(u)	(915)	12,687	13,288
76544	Fort Hood(u)	(817)	31,250	32,597
79735	Fort Stockton	(915)	8,688	8,283
76101	Fort Worth	(817)	385,141	393,455
78624	Fredericksburg	(512)	6,412	5,326
77541	Freeport	(409)	13,444	11,997
77546	Friendswood	(713)	10,719	5,675
76240	Gainesville	(817)	14,081	13,830
77547	Galena Park	(713)	9,879	10,479
77550	Galveston	(409)	61,902	61,809
*75040	Garland	(214)	138,857	81,437
76528	Gatesville	(817)	6,260	4,683
78626	Georgetown	(512)	9,468	6,395
75644	Gilmer	(214)	5,167	4,196
75647	Gladewater	(214)	6,548	5,574
78629	Gonzales	(512)	7,152	5,854
76046	Graham	(817)	9,055	7,477
75050	Grand Prairie	(214)	71,462	50,904
76051	Grapevine	(817)	11,801	7,049
75401	Greenville	(214)	22,161	22,043
77619	Groves	(713)	17,090	18,067
76117	Haltom City	(817)	29,014	28,127
76541	Harker Heights	(817)	7,345	4,216
78550	Harlingen	(512)	43,543	33,503
77859	Hearne	(713)	5,418	4,982
75652	Henderson	(214)	11,473	10,187
79045	Hereford	(806)	15,853	13,414
76643	Hewitt	(817)	5,247	569
75205	Highland Park	(214)	8,909	10,133
77562	Highlands	(713)	6,467	3,462
76645	Hillsboro	(817)	7,397	7,224
77563	Hitchcock	(713)	6,103	5,565
78861	Hondo	(512)	6,057	5,487
*77013	Houston	(713)	1,594,086	1,233,535
77338	Humble	(713)	6,729	3,272
77340	Huntsville	(409)	23,936	17,610
76053	Hurst	(817)	31,420	27,215
78362	Ingleside	(512)	5,436	3,763
76367	Iowa Park	(817)	6,184	5,796
*75061	Irving	(214)	109,943	97,260
77029	Jacinto City	(713)	8,953	9,563
75766	Jacksonville	(214)	12,264	9,734
75951	Jasper	(409)	6,959	6,251
77450	Katy	(713)	5,660	2,923
79745	Kermit	(915)	8,015	7,884
78028	Kerrville	(512)	15,276	12,672
75662	Kilgore	(214)	11,331	9,495
76541	Killeen	(817)	46,296	35,507
78363	Kingsville	(512)	28,808	28,915
......	Kingwood	(713)	16,261	....
78219	Kirby	(512)	6,435	3,238
78236	Lackland AFB(u)	(512)	14,459	19,141
77566	Lake Jackson	(409)	19,102	13,376
77568	La Marque	(409)	15,372	16,131
79631	Lamesa	(806)	11,790	11,559
76550	Lampasas	(512)	6,165	5,922
75146	Lancaster	(214)	14,807	10,522
77571	La Porte	(713)	14,062	7,149
78040	Laredo	(512)	91,449	69,024
77573	League City	(713)	16,578	10,818
78238	Leon Valley	(512)	9,088	2,487
79336	Levelland	(806)	13,809	11,445
75067	Lewisville	(214)	24,273	9,264
77575	Liberty	(713)	7,945	5,591
79339	Littlefield	(806)	7,409	6,738
78233	Live Oak	(512)	8,183	2,779
78644	Lockhart	(512)	7,953	6,489
75601	Longview	(214)	62,762	45,547
*79408	Lubbock	(806)	173,979	149,101
75901	Lufkin	(409)	28,562	23,049
78648	Luling	(512)	5,039	4,719
78501	McAllen	(512)	67,042	37,636
75069	McKinney	(214)	16,249	15,193
76063	Mansfield	(817)	8,092	3,658
76661	Marlin	(817)	7,099	6,351
75670	Marshall	(214)	24,921	22,937
76368	Mathis	(512)	5,667	5,351
79570	Mercedes	(512)	11,851	9,355
75149	Mesquite	(214)	67,053	55,131
76667	Mexia	(817)	7,094	5,943
79701	Midland	(915)	70,525	59,463
76067	Mineral Wells	(817)	14,468	18,411
78572	Mission	(512)	22,653	13,043
77459	Missouri City	(713)	24,423	4,136
79756	Monahans	(915)	8,397	8,333
75455	Mount Pleasant	(214)	11,003	9,459
75961	Nacogdoches	(409)	27,149	22,544
77868	Navasota	(409)	5,971	5,111
77627	Nederland	(409)	16,855	16,810
78130	New Braunfels	(512)	22,402	17,859
76118	North Richland Hills	(817)	30,592	16,514
*79760	Odessa	(915)	90,027	78,380
77630	Orange	(409)	23,628	24,457
75801	Palestine	(214)	15,948	14,525
79065	Pampa	(806)	21,396	21,726
75460	Paris	(214)	25,498	23,441
*77501	Pasadena	(713)	112,560	89,957
77581	Pearland	(713)	13,248	6,444
78061	Pearsall	(512)	7,383	5,545
79772	Pecos	(915)	12,855	12,682
79070	Perryton	(806)	7,991	7,810
78577	Pharr	(512)	21,381	15,829
79072	Plainview	(806)	22,187	19,096
75074	Plano	(214)	72,331	17,872
78064	Pleasanton	(512)	6,346	5,407
77640	Port Arthur	(409)	61,195	57,371
78374	Portland	(512)	12,023	7,302
77979	Port Lavaca	(512)	10,911	10,491
77651	Port Neches	(713)	13,944	10,894
78580	Raymondville	(512)	9,493	7,987
75080	Richardson	(214)	72,496	48,405
76118	Richland Hills	(817)	7,977	8,865
77469	Richmond	(713)	9,692	5,777
78582	Rio Grande City(u)	(512)	8,930	5,676
77019	River Oaks	(817)	6,890	8,193
76017	Robinson	(817)	6,074	3,807
78380	Robstown	(512)	12,100	11,227
76567	Rockdale	(512)	5,611	4,655
75087	Rockwall	(512)	5,939	3,121
77471	Rosenberg	(713)	17,840	12,098
78664	Round Rock	(512)	12,740	2,811
75088	Rowlett	(214)	7,522	2,243
76179	Saginaw	(817)	5,736	2,382
76901	San Angelo	(915)	73,240	63,884
*78284	San Antonio	(512)	785,940	654,153
78586	San Benito	(512)	17,988	15,176
78384	San Diego	(512)	5,225	4,490
78589	San Juan	(512)	7,608	5,070
78666	San Marcos	(512)	23,420	18,860
77550	Santa Fe	(713)	5,413	...

ZIP code	Place	1980	1970
78154	Schertz . . . . (512)	7,262	4,061
75159	Seagoville . . . . (214)	7,304	4,390
78155	Seguin . . . . (512)	17,854	15,934
79360	Seminole . . . . (915)	6,080	5,007
75090	Sherman . . . . (214)	30,413	29,061
77656	Silsbee . . . . (713)	7,684	7,271
78387	Sinton . . . . (512)	6,044	5,563
79364	Slaton . . . . (806)	6,804	6,583
79549	Snyder . . . . (915)	12,705	11,171
77587	South Houston . . . . . . (713)	13,293	11,527
76401	Stephenville . . . . (817)	11,881	9,277
77478	Sugar Land . . . . (713)	8,826	3,318
75482	Sulphur Springs . . . . . (214)	12,804	10,642
79556	Sweetwater . . . . (915)	12,242	12,020
76574	Taylor . . . . (512)	10,619	9,616
76501	Temple . . . . (817)	42,354	33,431
75160	Terrell . . . . (214)	13,269	14,182
75501	Texarkana . . . . (214)	31,271	30,497
77590	Texas City . . . . (409)	41,201	38,908
75056	The Colony . . . . (214)	11,586	....
77380	The Woodlands . . . . . . (713)	8,443	....
79088	Tulia . . . . (806)	5,033	5,294
75701	Tyler . . . . (214)	70,508	57,770
78148	Universal City . . . . . . (512)	10,720	7,613
76308	University Park . . . . . . (214)	22,254	23,498
78801	Uvalde . . . . (512)	14,178	10,764
76384	Vernon . . . . (817)	12,695	11,454
77901	Victoria . . . . (512)	50,695	41,349
77662	Vidor . . . . (713)	11,834	9,738
*76701	Waco . . . . (817)	101,261	95,326
76148	Watauga . . . . (817)	10,284	3,778
75165	Waxahachie . . . . (214)	14,624	13,452
76086	Weatherford . . . . (817)	12,049	11,750
78596	Weslaco . . . . (512)	19,331	15,313
77005	West University Place . . (713)	12,010	13,317
77488	Wharton . . . . (713)	9,033	7,881
76108	White Settlement . . . . . (817)	13,508	13,449
*76307	Wichita Falls . . . . (817)	94,201	96,265
78239	Windcrest . . . . (512)	5,332	3,371
76710	Woodway . . . . (817)	7,091	4,819
77995	Yoakum . . . . (512)	6,148	5,755

Utah (801)

84003	American Fork	12,417	7,713
84118	Bennion(u)	9,632	....
84010	Bountiful	32,877	27,751
84302	Brigham City	15,596	14,007
84720	Cedar City	10,972	8,946
84014	Centerville	8,069	3,268
84015	Clearfield	17,982	13,316
84015	Clinton	5,777	1,768
84121	Cottonwood(u)	11,554	8,431
84121	Cottonwood Heights(u) . . .	22,665	....
84020	Draper	5,530	....
84109	East Millcreek(u)	24,150	26,579
84106	Granite Park(u)	5,554	9,573
84117	Holladay(u)	22,189	23,014
84037	Kaysville	9,811	6,192
84118	Kearns(u)	21,353	17,247
84041	Layton	22,862	13,603
84043	Lehi	6,848	4,659
84321	Logan	26,844	22,333
84044	Magna(u)	13,138	5,509
84047	Midvale	10,144	7,840
84532	Moab	5,333	4,793
84117	Mount Olympus(u)	6,068	5,909
84107	Murray	25,750	21,206
84404	North Ogden	9,309	5,257
84054	North Salt Lake	5,548	2,143
*84401	Ogden	64,407	69,478
84057	Orem	52,399	25,729
84651	Payson	8,246	4,501
84062	Pleasant Grove	10,669	5,327
84501	Price	9,086	6,218
84601	Provo	74,111	53,131
84701	Richfield	5,482	4,471
84065	Riverton	7,032	2,820
84067	Roy	19,694	14,356
84770	St. George	11,350	7,097
*84101	Salt Lake City	163,034	175,885
84070	Sandy City	52,210	6,438
84121	South Cottonwood(u)	11,117	....
84065	South Jordan	7,492	2,942
84403	South Ogden	11,366	9,991
84115	South Salt Lake	10,413	7,810
84660	Spanish Fork	9,825	7,284
84663	Springville	12,101	8,790
84015	Sunset	5,733	6,268
84107	Taylorsville(u)	17,448	....
84074	Tooele	14,335	12,539
84047	Union-East Midvale(u) . . .	9,663	....
84010	Val Verda(u)	6,422	....
84078	Vernal	6,600	3,908
84403	Washington Terrace	8,212	7,241
84084	West Jordan	27,325	4,221
84119	West Valley(u)	72,299	....
84070	White City(u)	7,180	6,402

Vermont (802)

See Note on Page 268

05641	Barre	9,824	10,209
......	*Barre*	7,090	6,509
05201	*Bennington*	15,815	14,586
......	Bennington(u)	9,349	7,950
05301	Brattleboro Center(u) . . .	8,596	9,055
......	*Brattleboro*	11,886	12,239
05401	Burlington	37,712	38,633
05446	*Colchester*	12,629	8,776
05451	*Essex*	14,392	10,951
05452	Essex Junction	7,033	6,511
05753	*Middlebury*	7,574	6,532
05602	Montpelier	8,241	8,609
05701	Rutland	18,436	19,293
05478	St. Albans	7,308	8,082
05819	St. Johnsbury	7,938	8,409
05401	*South Burlington*	10,679	10,032
05156	Springfield Center(u) . . .	5,603	5,632
......	*Springfield*	10,190	10,063
05404	Winooski	6,318	7,309

Virginia

*22313	Alexandria . . . . (703)	103,217	110,927
22003	Annandale(u) . . . . . . (703)	49,524	27,405
*22210	Arlington(u) . . . . (703)	152,599	174,284
22041	Bailey's Crossroads(u) . . (703)	12,564	7,295
24523	Bedford . . . . (703)	5,991	6,011
22307	Belle Haven(u) . . . . . (703)	6,520	....
23234	Bellwood(u) . . . . (804)	6,439	....
23234	Bensley(u) . . . . (804)	5,299	....
24060	Blacksburg . . . . (703)	30,638	9,384
24605	Bluefield . . . . (703)	5,946	5,286
23235	Bon Air(u) . . . . (804)	16,224	10,771
24201	Bristol . . . . (703)	19,042	14,857
24416	Buena Vista . . . . (703)	6,717	6,425
22015	Burke(u) . . . . (703)	33,835	....
24018	Cave Spring(u) . . . . . (703)	21,682	....
22020	Centreville(u) . . . . . . (703)	7,473	....
23227	Chamberlayne(u) . . . . (804)	5,136	....
22021	Chantilly(u) . . . . (703)	12,259	....
*22906	Charlottesville . . . . . . (804)	45,010	38,880
*23320	Chesapeake . . . . . . (804)	114,226	89,580
23831	Chester(u) . . . . (804)	11,728	5,556
24073	Christiansburg . . . . . . (703)	10,345	7,857
24422	Clifton Forge . . . . . . (703)	5,046	5,501
24078	Collinsville(u) . . . . . . (703)	7,517	6,015
23834	Colonial Heights . . . . (804)	16,509	15,097
24426	Covington . . . . (703)	9,063	10,060
22701	Culpeper . . . . (703)	6,621	6,056
22191	Dale City(u) . . . . (703)	33,127	13,857
24541	Danville . . . . (804)	45,642	46,391
23228	Dumbarton(u) . . . . . . (804)	8,149	....
22027	Dunn Loring(u) . . . . . (804)	6,077	....
23222	East Highland Park(u) . . (804)	11,797	....
22030	Fairfax . . . . (703)	19,390	22,727
*22046	Falls Church . . . . (703)	9,515	10,772
23901	Farmville . . . . (804)	6,067	4,331
22060	Fort Belvoir(u) . . . . . . (703)	7,726	14,591
22308	Fort Hunt(u) . . . . (703)	14,294	10,415
23801	Fort Lee(u) . . . . (804)	9,784	12,435
22310	Franconia(u) . . . . . . (703)	8,476	....
23851	Franklin . . . . (804)	7,308	6,880
22401	Fredericksburg . . . . . (703)	15,322	14,450
22630	Front Royal . . . . (703)	11,126	8,211
24333	Galax . . . . (703)	6,524	6,278
23060	Glen Allen(u) . . . . . . (804)	6,202	....
23062	Gloucester Point(u) . . . (804)	5,841	....
22306	Groveton(u) . . . . (703)	18,860	11,761
*23660	Hampton . . . . (804)	122,617	120,779
22801	Harrisonburg . . . . . . (703)	19,671	14,605
22070	Herndon . . . . (703)	11,449	4,301
23075	Highland Springs(u) . . . (804)	12,146	7,345
24019	Hollins(u) . . . . (703)	12,187	....
23860	Hopewell . . . . (804)	23,397	23,471
22303	Huntington(u) . . . . . . (703)	5,813	5,559
22306	Hybla Valley(u) . . . . . (703)	15,533	....
22043	Idylwood(u) . . . . (703)	11,982	....
22042	Jefferson(u) . . . . (804)	24,342	25,432
22041	Lake Barcroft(u) . . . . . (703)	8,725	11,605
22191	Lake Ridge(u) . . . . . . (703)	11,072	....
23228	Lakeside(u) . . . . (804)	12,289	11,137
23060	Laurel(u) . . . . (804)	10,569	....
22075	Leesburg . . . . (703)	8,357	4,821
24450	Lexington . . . . (703)	7,292	7,597
22312	Lincolnia(u) . . . . (703)	10,350	10,355
22079	Lorton(u) . . . . (703)	5,813	....
*24505	Lynchburg . . . . (804)	66,743	54,083
24572	Madison Heights(u) . . . (804)	14,146	....
22110	Manassas . . . . (703)	15,438	9,164
22110	Manassas Park . . . . . (703)	6,524	6,844
22030	Mantua(u) . . . . (703)	6,523	6,911
24354	Marion . . . . (703)	7,287	8,158
24112	Martinsville . . . . (703)	18,149	19,653
22101	McLean(u) . . . . (703)	35,664	17,698
23111	Mechanicsville(u) . . . . (804)	9,269	5,189
22116	Merrifield(u) . . . . (703)	7,525	....

ZIP code	Place		1980	1970
23231	Montrose(u)	(804)	5,349	
22121	Mount Vernon(u)	(703)	24,058	....
22122	Newington(u)	(703)	8,313	
*23607	Newport News	(804)	144,903	138,177
*23501	Norfolk	(804)	266,979	307,951
22151	North Springfield(u)	(703)	9,538	8,631
22124	Oakton(u)	(703)	19,150	....
23803	Petersburg	(804)	41,055	36,103
22043	Pimmit Hills(u)	(703)	6,658	....
23662	Poquoson	(804)	8,726	5,441
*23705	Portsmouth	(804)	104,577	110,963
24301	Pulaski	(703)	10,106	10,279
22134	Quantico Station(u)	(703)	7,121	6,213
24141	Radford	(703)	13,225	11,596
22090	Reston(u)	(703)	36,407	5,723
24641	Richlands	(703)	5,796	4,843
23232	Richmond	(804)	219,214	249,332
*24001	Roanoke	(703)	100,427	92,115
22310	Rose Hill(u)	(703)	11,926	14,492
24153	Salem	(703)	23,958	21,982
22044	Seven Corners(u)	(703)	6,058	5,590
24592	South Boston	(804)	7,093	6,889
*22150	Springfield	(703)	21,435	11,613
24401	Staunton	(703)	21,857	24,504
22170	Sterling Park(u)	(703)	16,080	8,321
23434	Suffolk	(804)	47,621	9,858
22170	Sugarland Run(u)	(703)	6,258	....
24502	Timberlake(u)	(804)	9,697	....
23229	Tuckahoe(u)	(804)	39,888	....
22101	Tysons Corner(u)	(703)	10,065	....
22180	Vienna	(703)	15,469	17,146
24179	Vinton	(703)	8,027	6,347
*23458	Virginia Beach	(804)	262,199	172,106
22980	Waynesboro	(703)	15,329	16,707
22110	West Gate(u)	(703)	7,119	....
22152	West Springfield(u)	(703)	25,012	14,143
23185	Williamsburg	(804)	9,870	9,069
22601	Winchester	(703)	20,217	14,643
24592	Wolf Trap(u)	(804)	9,875	....
22191	Woodbridge(u)	(703)	24,004	25,412
24382	Wytheville	(703)	7,135	6,069

Washington

ZIP code	Place		1980	1970
98520	Aberdeen	(206)	18,739	18,489
98036	Alderwood Manor(u) . . .	(206)	16,524	....
98221	Anacortes	(206)	9,013	7,701
98002	Auburn	(206)	26,417	21,653
*98009	Bellevue	(206)	73,903	61,196
98225	Bellingham	(206)	45,794	39,375
98390	Bonney Lake	(206)	5,328	2,700
98011	Bothell	(206)	7,943	5,420
....	Boulevard Park(u)	(206)	8,382	....
98310	Bremerton	(206)	36,208	35,307
98178	Bryn Mawr-Skyway(u) . .	(206)	11,754	....
98166	Burien(u)	(206)	23,189	....
98607	Camas	(206)	5,681	5,790
98055	Cascade-Fairwood(u) . . .	(206)	16,939	....
98531	Centralia	(206)	10,809	10,054
98532	Chehalis	(206)	6,100	5,727
99004	Cheney	(509)	7,630	6,358
99403	Clarkston	(509)	6,903	6,312
99324	College Place	(509)	5,771	4,510
98188	Des Moines	(206)	7,378	3,951
99213	Dishman(u)	(509)	10,169	9,079
....	Dumas Bay-Twin Lakes(u) . .	(206)	14,535	....
98004	Eastgate(u)	(206)	8,341	....
....	East Renton Highlands(u) . .	(206)	12,033	....
98001	East Wenatchee Bench(u) .	(509)	11,410	2,446
98020	Edmonds	(206)	27,526	23,684
98926	Ellensburg	(509)	11,752	13,568
98022	Enumclaw	(206)	5,427	4,703
98823	Ephrata	(509)	5,359	5,255
99210	Esperance(u)	(509)	11,120	....
*98201	Everett	(206)	54,413	53,622
99011	Fairchild AFB(u)	(509)	5,353	6,754
98201	Fairmont-Intercity(u) . . .	(206)	6,997	....
98055	Fairwood(u)	(206)	5,337	....
98466	Fircrest	(206)	5,477	5,651
98433	Fort Lewis(u)	(206)	23,761	38,054
98930	Grandview	(509)	5,615	3,605
98660	Hazel Dell(u)	(206)	15,386	....
98550	Hoquiam	(206)	9,719	10,466
98011	Inglewood(u)	(206)	12,467	....
98027	Issaquah	(206)	5,536	4,313
98033	Juanita(u)	(206)	17,232	....
98626	Kelso	(206)	11,129	10,296
98028	Kenmore(u)	(206)	7,281	....
99336	Kennewick	(509)	34,397	15,212
98031	Kent	(206)	22,961	17,711
98033	Kingsgate(u)	(206)	12,652	....
98033	Kirkland	(206)	18,785	14,970
98503	Lacey	(206)	13,940	9,696
98155	Lake Forest North(u) . . .	(206)	7,995	....
....	Lakeland North(u)	(206)	11,451	....
....	Lakeland South(u)	(206)	5,225	....

ZIP code	Place		1980	1970
....	Lake Stickney(u)	(206)	6,135	....
98499	Lakes District(u)	(206)	54,533	48,195
98632	Longview	(206)	31,052	28,373
98036	Lynnwood	(206)	21,937	17,381
....	Martha Lake(u)	(206)	7,022	....
98270	Marysville	(206)	5,080	4,343
98438	McChord AFB(u)	(206)	5,746	6,515
98040	Mercer Island	(206)	21,522	19,047
98837	Moses Lake	(509)	10,629	10,310
98043	Mountlake Terrace	(206)	16,534	16,600
98273	Mount Vernon	(206)	13,009	8,804
98006	Newport Hills(u)	(206)	12,245	....
98155	North City-Ridgecrest(u) . .	(206)	13,551	....
....	North Hill(u)	(206)	10,170	....
98270	North Marysville(u)	(206)	15,159	....
98277	Oak Harbor	(206)	12,271	9,167
*98501	Olympia	(206)	27,447	23,296
99214	Opportunity(u)	(509)	21,241	16,604
98662	Orchards(u)	(206)	8,828	....
98444	Parkland(u)	(206)	23,355	21,012
99301	Pasco	(509)	18,428	13,920
98362	Port Angeles	(206)	17,311	16,367
98368	Port Townsend	(206)	6,067	5,241
....	Poverty Bay(u)	(206)	8,353	....
99163	Pullman	(509)	23,579	20,509
98371	Puyallup	(206)	18,251	14,742
98052	Redmond	(206)	23,318	11,020
98055	Renton	(206)	31,031	25,878
99352	Richland	(509)	33,578	26,290
98160	Richmond Beach-Innis Arden(u)	(206)	6,700	....
98113	Richmond Highlands(u) . .	(206)	24,463	....
98188	Riverton(u)	(206)	14,182	....
98033	Rose Hill(u)	(206)	7,616	....
*98109	Seattle	(206)	493,846	530,831
98284	Sedro Woolley	(206)	6,110	4,598
98584	Shelton	(206)	7,629	6,515
98155	Sheridan Beach(u)	(206)	6,873	....
98201	Silver Lake-Fircrest(u) . . .	(206)	10,299	....
98290	Snohomish	(206)	5,294	5,174
98387	Spanaway(u)	(206)	8,868	5,768
*99210	Spokane	(509)	171,300	170,516
98944	Sunnyside	(509)	9,225	6,751
*98402	Tacoma	(206)	158,501	154,407
98501	Tanglewilde-Thompson Place(u) .		5,910	3,423
98948	Toppenish	(509)	6,517	5,744
99268	Town and Country(u) . . .	(509)	5,578	6,484
98502	Tumwater	(206)	6,705	5,373
98406	University Place(u)	(206)	20,381	13,230
....	Valley Ridge(u)	(206)	17,961	....
*98660	Vancouver	(206)	42,834	41,859
99037	Veradale(u)	(509)	7,256	....
99362	Walla Walla	(509)	25,618	23,619
98801	Wenatchee	(206)	17,257	16,912
98003	West Federal Way(u) . . .	(206)	16,872	....
99301	West Pasco(u)	(509)	6,210	....
98166	White Center-Shorewood(u) .	(206)	19,362	....
*98901	Yakima	(509)	49,826	45,588
98188	Zenith-Saltwater(u)	(206)	8,982	....

West Virginia (304)

ZIP code	Place		1980	1970
25801	Beckley		20,492	19,884
24701	Bluefield		16,060	15,921
26330	Bridgeport		6,604	4,777
26201	Buckhannon		6,820	7,261
*25301	Charleston		63,968	71,505
26301	Clarksburg		22,371	24,864
25064	Dunbar		9,285	9,151
26241	Elkins		8,536	8,287
26554	Fairmont		23,863	26,093
26354	Grafton		6,845	6,433
*25701	Huntington		63,684	74,315
26726	Keyser		6,569	6,586
25401	Martinsburg		13,063	14,626
26505	Morgantown		27,605	29,431
26041	Moundsville		12,419	13,560
26155	New Martinsville		7,109	6,528
25143	Nitro		8,074	8,019
25901	Oak Hill		7,120	4,738
26101	Parkersburg		39,946	44,208
25550	Point Pleasant		5,682	6,122
24740	Princeton		7,538	7,253
25177	St. Albans		12,402	14,356
25303	South Charleston		15,968	16,333
26105	Vienna		11,618	11,549
26062	Weirton		25,371	27,131
26452	Weston		6,250	7,323
26003	Wheeling		43,070	48,188
25661	Williamson		5,219	5,831

Wisconsin

ZIP code	Place		1980	1970
54301	Allouez(u)	(414)	14,882	13,753
54409	Antigo	(715)	8,653	9,005
54911	Appleton	(414)	58,913	56,377
54806	Ashland	(715)	9,115	9,615

ZIP code	Place		1980	1970
54304	Ashwaubenon	(414)	14,486	9,323
53913	Baraboo	(608)	8,081	7,931
53916	Beaver Dam	(414)	14,149	14,265
53511	Beloit	(608)	35,207	35,729
53511	Beloit North(u)	(608)	5,457	....
54923	Berlin	(414)	5,478	5,338
53005	Brookfield	(414)	34,035	31,761
53209	Brown Deer	(414)	12,921	12,582
53105	Burlington	(414)	8,385	7,479
53012	Cedarburg	(414)	9,005	7,697
54729	Chippewa Falls	(715)	11,845	12,351
53110	Cudahy	(414)	19,547	22,078
53115	Delavan	(414)	5,684	5,526
54115	De Pere	(414)	14,892	13,309
54701	Eau Claire	(715)	51,509	44,619
53122	Elm Grove	(414)	6,735	7,201
54935	Fond Du Lac	(414)	35,863	35,515
53538	Fort Atkinson	(414)	9,785	9,164
53217	Fox Point	(414)	7,649	7,939
53132	Franklin	(414)	16,871	12,247
53022	Germantown	(414)	10,729	6,974
53209	Glendale	(414)	13,882	13,426
53024	Grafton	(414)	8,381	5,998
*54305	Green Bay	(414)	87,899	87,809
53129	Greendale	(414)	16,928	15,089
53220	Greenfield	(414)	31,353	24,424
53130	Hales Corners	(414)	7,110	7,771
53027	Hartford	(414)	7,159	6,499
53029	Hartland	(414)	5,559	2,763
54303	Howard	(414)	8,240	4,911
54016	Hudson	(715)	5,434	5,049
53545	Janesville	(608)	51,071	46,426
53549	Jefferson	(414)	5,647	5,429
54130	Kaukauna	(414)	11,310	11,308
53140	Kenosha	(414)	77,685	78,805
54136	Kimberly	(414)	5,881	6,131
54601	La Crosse	(608)	48,347	50,286
53147	Lake Geneva	(414)	5,612	4,890
54140	Little Chute	(414)	7,907	5,522
*53701	Madison	(608)	170,616	171,809
54220	Manitowoc	(414)	32,547	33,430
54143	Marinette	(715)	11,965	12,696
54449	Marshfield	(715)	18,290	15,619
54952	Menasha	(414)	14,728	14,836
53051	Menomonee Falls	(414)	27,845	31,697
54751	Menomonie	(715)	12,769	11,112
53092	Mequon	(414)	16,193	12,150
54452	Merrill	(715)	9,578	9,502
53562	Middleton	(608)	11,851	8,246
*53203	Milwaukee	(414)	636,297	717,372
53716	Monona	(608)	8,809	10,420
53566	Monroe	(608)	10,027	8,654
53150	Muskego	(414)	15,277	11,573
54956	Neenah	(414)	23,272	22,902
53151	New Berlin	(414)	30,529	26,910
54961	New London	(414)	6,210	5,801
53154	Oak Creek	(414)	16,932	13,928
53066	Oconomowoc	(414)	9,909	8,741

ZIP code	Place		1980	1970
54650	Onalaska	(608)	9,249	4,909
54901	Oshkosh	(414)	49,678	53,082
53818	Platteville	(608)	9,580	9,599
54467	Plover	(715)	5,310	....
53073	Plymouth	(414)	6,027	5,810
53901	Portage	(608)	7,896	7,821
53074	Port Washington	(414)	8,612	8,752
53821	Prairie du Chien	(608)	5,859	5,540
*53401	Racine	(414)	85,725	95,162
53959	Reedsburg	(608)	5,038	4,585
54501	Rhinelander	(715)	7,873	8,218
54868	Rice Lake	(715)	7,691	7,278
54971	Ripon	(414)	7,111	7,053
54022	River Falls	(715)	9,019	7,238
53207	St. Francis	(414)	10,095	10,489
54166	Shawano	(715)	7,013	6,488
53081	Sheboygan	(414)	48,085	48,484
53085	Sheboygan Falls	(414)	5,253	4,771
53211	Shorewood	(414)	14,327	15,576
53172	South Milwaukee	(414)	21,069	23,297
54656	Sparta	(608)	6,934	6,258
54481	Stevens Point	(715)	22,970	23,479
53589	Stoughton	(608)	7,589	6,096
54235	Sturgeon Bay	(414)	8,847	6,776
53590	Sun Prairie	(608)	12,931	9,935
54880	Superior	(715)	29,571	32,237
54660	Tomah	(608)	7,204	5,647
54241	Two Rivers	(414)	13,354	13,732
53094	Watertown	(414)	18,113	15,683
53186	Waukesha	(414)	50,365	39,695
53963	Waupun	(414)	8,132	7,946
54401	Wausau	(715)	32,426	32,806
54401	Wausau West Rib Mt.(u)	(715)	6,005	....
53213	Wauwatosa	(414)	51,308	58,676
53214	West Allis	(414)	63,982	71,649
53095	West Bend	(414)	21,484	16,555
54476	Weston(u)	(715)	8,775	3,375
53217	Whitefish Bay	(414)	14,930	17,402
53190	Whitewater	(414)	11,520	12,038
54494	Wisconsin Rapids	(715)	17,995	18,587

Wyoming (307)

ZIP code	Place	1980	1970
82601	Casper	51,016	39,361
82001	Cheyenne	47,283	41,254
82414	Cody	6,599	5,161
82633	Douglas	6,030	2,677
82930	Evanston	6,265	4,462
82716	Gillette	12,134	7,194
82335	Green River	12,807	4,196
82520	Lander	9,126	7,125
82070	Laramie	24,410	23,143
82435	Powell	5,310	4,807
82301	Rawlins	11,547	7,855
82501	Riverton	9,562	7,995
82901	Rock Springs	19,458	11,657
82801	Sheridan	15,146	10,856
82240	Torrington	5,441	4,237
82201	Wheatland	5,816	2,498
82401	Worland	6,391	5,055

Census and Areas of Counties and States

Source: U.S. Bureau of the Census
With names of county seats or court houses

Population figures listed below are final counts in the 1980 census, conducted on Apr. 1, 1980, and updated in March 1985, for all counties and states. Figures are subject to change pending the outcome of various lawsuits dealing with the census counts.

Alabama

(67 counties, 50,767 sq. mi. land; pop., 3,894,046)

County	Pop.	County seat or court house	Land area sq. mi.
Autauga	32,259	Prattville	597
Baldwin	78,440	Bay Minette	1,589
Barbour	24,756	Clayton	884
Bibb	15,723	Centreville	625
Blount	36,459	Oneonta	643
Bullock	10,596	Union Springs	625
Butler	21,680	Greenville	779
Calhoun	116,936	Anniston	611
Chambers	39,191	Lafayette	596
Cherokee	18,760	Centre	553
Chilton	30,612	Clanton	695
Choctaw	16,839	Butler	909
Clarke	27,702	Grove Hill	1,230
Clay	13,703	Ashland	605
Cleburne	12,595	Heflin	561
Coffee	38,533	Elba	680
Colbert	54,519	Tuscumbia	589
Conecuh	15,884	Evergreen	854
Coosa	11,377	Rockford	657
Covington	36,850	Andalusia	1,038
Crenshaw	14,110	Luverne	611
Cullman	61,642	Cullman	738
Dale	47,821	Ozark	561
Dallas	53,981	Selma	975
De Kalb	53,658	Fort Payne	778

County	Pop.	County seat	Pop.
Elmore	43,390	Wetumpka	622
Escambia	38,392	Brewton	951
Etowah	103,057	Gadsden	542
Fayette	18,809	Fayette	630
Franklin	28,350	Russellville	643
Geneva	24,253	Geneva	578
Greene	11,021	Eutaw	631
Hale	15,604	Greensboro	661
Henry	15,302	Abbeville	557
Houston	74,632	Dothan	577
Jackson	51,407	Scottsboro	1,070
Jefferson	671,392	Birmingham	1,119
Lamar	16,453	Vernon	605
Lauderdale	80,504	Florence	661
Lawrence	30,170	Moulton	693
Lee	76,283	Opelika	609
Limestone	46,005	Athens	559
Lowndes	13,253	Hayneville	714
Macon	26,829	Tuskegee	614
Madison	196,966	Huntsville	806
Marengo	25,047	Linden	982
Marion	30,041	Hamilton	743
Marshall	65,622	Guntersville	567
Mobile	364,379	Mobile	1,238
Monroe	22,651	Monroeville	1,019
Montgomery	197,038	Montgomery	793
Morgan	90,231	Decatur	575
Perry	15,012	Marion	718
Pickens	21,481	Carrollton	890
Pike	28,050	Troy	672
Randolph	20,075	Wedowee	584

County	Pop.	County Seat or court house	Land area sq. mi.
Russell	47,356	Phenix City	634
St. Clair	41,205	Ashville & Pell City	646
Shelby	66,298	Columbiana	800
Sumter	16,908	Livingston	907
Talladega	73,826	Talladega	753
Tallapoosa	38,766	Dadeville	701
Tuscaloosa	137,473	Tuscaloosa	1,336
Walker	68,660	Jasper	804
Washington	16,821	Chatom	1,081
Wilcox	14,755	Camden	883
Winston	21,953	Double Springs	613

Alaska
(23 divisions, 570,833 sq. mi. land; pop., 401,851)

Census area	Pop.	Land area sq. mi.
Aleutian Islands	7,768	10,890
Anchorage Borough	173,017	1,732

Census division	Pop.	Land area sq. mi.
Bethel	10,999	36,104
Bristol Bay Borough	1,094	531
Dillingham	4,616	46,042
Fairbanks North Star Borough	53,983	7,404
Haines Borough	1,680	2,374
Juneau Borough	19,528	2,626
Kenai Peninsula Borough	25,282	16,056
Ketchikan Gateway Borough	11,316	1,242
Kobuk	4,831	31,593
Kodiak Island Borough	9,939	4,796
Matanuska-Susitna Borough	17,766	24,502
Nome	6,537	23,871
North Slope Borough	4,199	90,955
Prince of Wales-Outer Ketchikan	3,822	7,660
Sitka Borough	7,803	2,938
Skagway-Yakutat-Angoon	3,478	13,229
Southeast Fairbanks	5,770	24,169
Valdez-Cordova	8,348	39,229
Wade Hampton	4,665	17,816
Wrangell-Petersburg	6,167	5,965
Yukon-Koyukuk	7,873	159,099

Arizona
(14 counties, 113,508 sq. mi. land; pop. 2,718,425)

County	Pop.	County seat or court house	Land area sq. mi.
Apache	52,083	Saint Johns	11,211
Cochise	86,717	Bisbee	6,218
Coconino	74,947	Flagstaff	18,608
Gila	37,080	Globe	4,752
Graham	22,862	Safford	4,630
Greenlee	11,406	Clifton	1,837
La Paz	12,487	Parker	4,430
Maricopa	1,509,262	Phoenix	9,127
Mohave	55,693	Kingman	13,285
Navajo	67,709	Holbrook	9,955
Pima	531,263	Tucson	9,187
Pinal	90,918	Florence	5,343
Santa Cruz	20,459	Nogales	1,238
Yavapai	68,145	Prescott	8,123
Yuma	90,554	Yuma	9,994

Arkansas
(75 counties, 52,078 sq. mi. land; pop. 2,286,357)

County	Pop.	County seat or court house	Land area sq. mi.
Arkansas	24,175	DeWitt & Stuttgart	1,006
Ashley	26,538	Hamburg	934
Baxter	27,409	Mountain Home	546
Benton	78,115	Bentonville	843
Boone	26,067	Harrison	584
Bradley	13,803	Warren	654
Calhoun	6,079	Hampton	628
Carroll	16,203	Berryville and Eureka Sp.	634
Chicot	17,793	Lake Village	649
Clark	23,326	Arkadelphia	867
Clay	20,616	Corning; Piggott	641
Cleburne	16,909	Heber Springs	551
Cleveland	7,868	Rison	599
Columbia	26,644	Magnolia	767
Conway	19,505	Morrilton	558
Craighead	63,218	Jonesboro and Lake City	713
Crawford	36,892	Van Buren	594
Crittenden	49,097	Marion	599
Cross	20,434	Wynne	622
Dallas	10,515	Fordyce	668
Desha	19,760	Arkansas City	746
Drew	17,910	Monticello	831
Faulkner	46,192	Conway	645
Franklin	14,705	Charleston and Ozark	609
Fulton	9,975	Salem	616
Garland	69,916	Hot Spgs. Nat'l Pk.	657
Grant	13,008	Sheridan	633
Greene	30,744	Paragould	579
Hempstead	23,635	Hope	725
Hot Spring	26,819	Malvern	615
Howard	13,459	Nashville	574
Independence	30,147	Batesville	763
Izard	10,768	Melbourne	581
Jackson	21,646	Newport	633
Jefferson	90,718	Pine Bluff	882
Johnson	17,423	Clarksville	676
Lafayette	10,213	Lewisville	518
Lawrence	18,447	Walnut Ridge	589
Lee	15,539	Marianna	602
Lincoln	13,369	Star City	562
Little River	13,952	Ashdown	516
Logan	20,144	Booneville & Paris	717
Lonoke	34,518	Lonoke	783
Madison	11,373	Huntsville	837
Marion	11,334	Yellville	587
Miller	37,766	Texarkana	619
Mississippi	59,517	Blytheville and Osceola	896
Monroe	14,052	Clarendon	609
Montgomery	7,771	Mount Ida	774
Nevada	11,097	Prescott	620
Newton	7,756	Jasper	823
Ouachita	30,541	Camden	737
Perry	7,266	Perryville	550
Phillips	34,772	Helena	685
Pike	10,373	Murfreesboro	598
Poinsett	27,032	Harrisburg	762
Polk	17,007	Mena	860
Pope	38,964	Russellville	820
Prairie	10,140	Des Arc and De Valls Bluff	656
Pulaski	340,597	Little Rock	767
Randolph	16,834	Pocahontas	656
St. Francis	30,858	Forrest City	638
Saline	53,156	Benton	725
Scott	9,685	Waldron	896
Searcy	8,847	Marshall	668
Sebastian	94,930	Fort Smith; Greenwood	535
Sevier	14,060	De Queen	560
Sharp	14,607	Ash Flat	606
Stone	9,022	Mountain View	606
Union	49,988	El Dorado	1,053
Van Buren	13,357	Clinton	709
Washington	99,735	Fayetteville	951
White	50,835	Searcy	1,040
Woodruff	11,222	Augusta	592
Yell	17,026	Danville and Dardanelle	930

California
(58 counties, 156,299 sq. mi. land; pop. 23,667,947)

County	Pop.	County seat or court house	Land area sq. mi.
Alameda	1,105,379	Oakland	736
Alpine	1,097	Markleeville	738
Amador	19,314	Jackson	589
Butte	143,851	Oroville	1,646
Calaveras	20,710	San Andreas	1,021
Colusa	12,791	Colusa	1,152
Contra Costa	656,331	Martinez	730
Del Norte	18,217	Crescent City	1,007
El Dorado	85,812	Placerville	1,715
Fresno	515,013	Fresno	5,978
Glenn	21,350	Willows	1,319
Humboldt	108,525	Eureka	3,579
Imperial	92,110	El Centro	4,173
Inyo	17,895	Independence	10,223
Kern	403,089	Bakersfield	8,130
Kings	73,738	Hanford	1,392
Lake	36,366	Lakeport	1,262
Lassen	21,661	Susanville	4,553
Los Angeles	7,477,421	Los Angeles	4,070
Madera	63,116	Madera	2,145
Marin	222,592	San Rafael	523
Mariposa	11,108	Mariposa	1,456
Mendocino	66,738	Ukiah	3,512
Merced	134,558	Merced	1,944
Modoc	8,610	Alturas	4,064
Mono	8,577	Bridgeport	3,018
Monterey	290,444	Salinas	3,303
Napa	99,199	Napa	744
Nevada	51,645	Nevada City	960
Orange	1,932,921	Santa Ana	798
Placer	117,247	Auburn	1,416
Plumas	17,340	Quincy	2,573
Riverside	663,199	Riverside	7,214
Sacramento	783,381	Sacramento	971
San Benito	25,005	Hollister	1,388
San Bernardino	893,157	San Bernardino	20,064
San Diego	1,861,846	San Diego	4,212
San Francisco	678,974	San Francisco	46
San Joaquin	347,342	Stockton	1,415
San Luis Obispo	155,345	San Luis Obispo	3,308
San Mateo	588,164	Redwood City	447
Santa Barbara	298,660	Santa Barbara	2,748
Santa Clara	1,295,071	San Jose	1,293
Santa Cruz	188,141	Santa Cruz	446
Shasta	115,613	Redding	3,786
Sierra	3,073	Downieville	959
Siskiyou	39,732	Yreka	6,281
Solano	235,203	Fairfield	834
Sonoma	299,827	Santa Rosa	1,604
Stanislaus	265,902	Modesto	1,506
Sutter	52,246	Yuba City	602
Tehama	38,888	Red Bluff	2,953
Trinity	11,858	Weaverville	3,190

County	Pop.	County seat or court house	Land area sq. mi.
Tulare	245,751	Visalia	4,808
Tuolumne	33,920	Sonora	2,234
Ventura	529,899	Ventura	1,862
Yolo	113,374	Woodland	1,014
Yuba	49,733	Marysville	040

Colorado
(63 counties, 103,595 sq. mi. land; pop. 2,889,735)

County	Pop.	County seat or court house	Land area sq. mi.
Adams	245,944	Brighton	1,235
Alamosa	11,799	Alamosa	719
Arapahoe	293,300	Littleton	800
Archuleta	3,664	Pagosa Springs	1,353
Baca	5,419	Springfield	2,554
Bent	5,945	Las Animas	1,517
Boulder	189,625	Boulder	742
Chaffee	13,227	Salida	1,008
Cheyenne	2,153	Cheyenne Wells	1,783
Clear Creek	7,308	Georgetown	396
Conejos	7,794	Conejos	1,284
Costilla	3,071	San Luis	1,227
Crowley	2,988	Ordway	790
Custer	1,528	Westcliffe	740
Delta	21,225	Delta	1,141
Denver	492,365	Denver	111
Dolores	1,658	Dove Creek	1,064
Douglas	25,153	Castle Rock	841
Eagle	13,171	Eagle	1,690
Elbert	6,850	Kiowa	1,851
El Paso	309,424	Colorado Springs	2,129
Fremont	28,676	Canon City	1,538
Garfield	22,514	Glenwood Springs	2,952
Gilpin	2,441	Central City	149
Grand	7,475	Hot Sulphur Springs	1,854
Gunnison	10,689	Gunnison	3,238
Hinsdale	467	Lake City	1,115
Huerfano	6,440	Walsenburg	1,584
Jackson	1,863	Walden	1,614
Jefferson	371,741	Golden	768
Kiowa	1,936	Eads	1,758
Kit Carson	7,599	Burlington	2,160
Lake	8,830	Leadville	379
La Plata	27,195	Durango	1,692
Larimer	149,184	Fort Collins	2,604
Las Anima	14,897	Trinidad	4,771
Lincoln	4,663	Hugo	2,586
Logan	19,800	Sterling	1,818
Mesa	81,530	Grand Junction	3,309
Mineral	804	Creede	877
Moffat	13,133	Craig	4,732
Montezuma	16,510	Cortez	2,038
Montrose	24,352	Montrose	2,240
Morgan	22,513	Fort Morgan	1,276
Otero	22,567	LaJunta	1,247
Ouray	1,925	Ouray	542
Park	5,333	Fairplay	2,192
Phillips	4,542	Holyoke	688
Pitkin	10,338	Aspen	968
Prowers	13,070	Lamar	1,629
Pueblo	125,972	Pueblo	2,377
Rio Blanco	6,255	Meeker	3,222
Rio Grande	10,511	Del Norte	913
Routt	13,404	Steamboat Springs	2,367
Saguache	3,935	Saguache	3,167
San Juan	833	Silverton	388
San Miguel	3,192	Telluride	1,287
Sedgwick	3,266	Julesburg	540
Summit	8,848	Breckenridge	607
Teller	8,034	Cripple Creek	559
Washington	5,304	Akron	2,520
Weld	123,438	Greeley	3,990
Yuma	9,682	Wray	2,365

Connecticut
(8 counties, 4,872 sq. mi. land; pop. 3,107,564)

County	Pop.	County seat or court house	Land area sq. mi.
Fairfield	807,143	Bridgeport	632
Hartford	807,766	Hartford	739
Litchfield	156,769	Litchfield	921
Middlesex	129,017	Middletown	373
New Haven	761,325	New Haven	610
New London	238,409	Norwich	669
Tolland	114,823	Rockville	412
Windham	92,312	Putnam	515

Delaware
(3 counties, 1,932 sq. mi. land; pop. 594,338)

County	Pop.	County seat or court house	Land area sq. mi.
Kent	98,219	Dover	595
New Castle	399,002	Wilmington	396
Sussex	98,004	Georgetown	942

District of Columbia
(63 sq. mi. land; pop. 638,432)

Florida
(67 counties, 54,153 sq. mi. land; pop. 9,747,063)

County	Pop.	County seat or court house	Land area sq. mi.
Alachua	151,369	Gainesville	901
Baker	15,289	Macclenny	585
Bay	97,740	Panama City	758
Bradford	20,023	Starke	293
Brevard	272,959	Titusville	995
Broward	1,018,257	Fort Lauderdale	1,211
Calhoun	9,294	Blountstown	568
Charlotte	59,115	Punta Gorda	690
Citrus	54,703	Inverness	629
Clay	67,052	Green Cove Spgs.	592
Collier	85,791	Naples	1,994
Columbia	35,399	Lake City	796
Dade	1,625,611	Miami	1,955
De Soto	19,039	Arcadia	636
Dixie	7,751	Cross City	701
Duval	570,981	Jacksonville	776
Escambia	233,794	Pensacola	660
Flagler	10,913	Bunnell	491
Franklin	7,661	Apalachicola	545
Gadsden	41,674	Quincy	518
Gilchrist	5,767	Trenton	354
Glades	5,992	Moore Haven	763
Gulf	10,658	Port St. Joe	559
Hamilton	8,761	Jasper	517
Hardee	20,357	Wauchula	637
Hendry	18,599	La Belle	1,163
Hernando	44,469	Brooksville	477
Highlands	47,526	Sebring	1,029
Hillsborough	646,939	Tampa	1,053
Holmes	14,723	Bonifay	488
Indian River	59,896	Vero Beach	497
Jackson	39,154	Marianna	942
Jefferson	10,703	Monticello	609
Lafayette	4,035	Mayo	545
Lake	104,870	Tavares	954
Lee	205,266	Fort Myers	803
Leon	148,655	Tallahassee	676
Levy	19,870	Bronson	1,100
Liberty	4,260	Bristol	837
Madison	14,894	Madison	710
Manatee	148,445	Bradenton	747
Marion	122,488	Ocala	1,610
Martin	64,014	Stuart	555
Monroe	63,098	Key West	1,034
Nassau	32,894	Fernandina Beach	649
Okaloosa	109,920	Crestview	936
Okeechobee	20,264	Okeechobee	770
Orange	470,865	Orlando	910
Osceola	49,287	Kissimmee	1,350
Palm Beach	576,758	West Palm Beach	1,993
Pasco	193,661	Dade City	738
Pinellas	728,409	Clearwater	280
Polk	321,652	Bartow	1,823
Putnam	50,549	Palatka	733
St. Johns	51,303	Saint Augustine	617
St. Lucie	87,182	Fort Pierce	581
Santa Rosa	55,988	Milton	1,024
Sarasota	202,251	Sarasota	573
Seminole	179,752	Sanford	298
Sumter	24,272	Bushnell	561
Suwannee	22,287	Live Oak	690
Taylor	16,532	Perry	1,058
Union	10,166	Lake Butler	246
Volusia	258,762	De Land	1,113
Wakulla	10,887	Crawfordville	601
Walton	21,300	De Funiak Springs	1,066
Washington	14,509	Chipley	590

Georgia
(159 counties, 58,056 sq. mi. land; pop. 5,462,892)

County	Pop.	County seat or court house	Land area sq. mi.
Appling	15,565	Baxley	510
Atkinson	6,141	Pearson	344
Bacon	9,379	Alma	286
Baker	3,808	Newton	347
Baldwin	34,686	Milledgeville	257
Banks	8,702	Homer	234
Barrow	21,293	Winder	163
Bartow	40,760	Cartersville	456
Ben Hill	16,000	Fitzgerald	254
Berrien	13,525	Nashville	456
Bibb	151,085	Macon	253
Bleckley	10,767	Cochran	219
Brantley	8,701	Nahunta	445
Brooks	15,255	Quitman	491
Bryan	10,175	Pembroke	441
Bulloch	35,785	Statesboro	678
Burke	19,349	Waynesboro	833
Butts	13,665	Jackson	187
Calhoun	5,717	Morgan	284
Camden	13,371	Woodbine	649
Candler	7,518	Metter	248
Carroll	56,346	Carrollton	501
Catoosa	36,991	Ringgold	162
Charlton	7,343	Folkston	780
Chatham	202,226	Savannah	443
Chattahoochee	21,732	Cusseta	250
Chattooga	21,856	Summerville	313
Cherokee	51,699	Canton	424
Clarke	74,498	Athens	122
Clay	3,553	Fort Gaines	196
Clayton	150,357	Jonesboro	148
Clinch	6,660	Homerville	821
Cobb	297,694	Marietta	343
Coffee	26,894	Douglas	602
Colquitt	35,376	Moultrie	557

County	Pop.	County seat or court house	Land area sq. mi.
Columbia	40,118	Appling	290
Cook	13,490	Adel	233
Coweta	39,268	Newnan	444
Crawford	7,684	Knoxville	328
Crisp	19,489	Cordele	275
Dade	12,318	Trenton	176
Dawson	4,774	Dawsonville	210
Decatur	25,495	Bainbridge	586
De Kalb	483,024	Decatur	270
Dodge	16,955	Eastman	504
Dooly	10,826	Vienna	397
Dougherty	100,710	Albany	330
Douglas	54,573	Douglasville	203
Early	13,158	Blakely	516
Echols	2,297	Statenville	421
Effingham	18,327	Springfield	482
Elbert	18,758	Elberton	367
Emanuel	20,795	Swainsboro	688
Evans	8,428	Claxton	186
Fannin	14,748	Blue Ridge	384
Fayette	29,043	Fayetteville	199
Floyd	79,800	Rome	519
Forsyth	27,958	Cumming	226
Franklin	15,185	Carnesville	264
Fulton	589,904	Atlanta	534
Gilmer	11,110	Ellijay	427
Glascock	2,382	Gibson	144
Glynn	54,981	Brunswick	412
Gordon	30,070	Calhoun	355
Grady	19,845	Cairo	459
Greene	11,391	Greensboro	389
Gwinnett	166,808	Lawrenceville	435
Habersham	25,020	Clarkesville	278
Hall	75,649	Gainesville	379
Hancock	9,466	Sparta	470
Haralson	18,422	Buchanan	283
Harris	15,464	Hamilton	464
Hart	18,585	Hartwell	230
Heard	6,520	Franklin	292
Henry	36,309	McDonough	321
Houston	77,605	Perry	380
Irwin	8,988	Ocilla	362
Jackson	25,343	Jefferson	342
Jasper	7,553	Monticello	371
Jeff Davis	11,473	Hazlehurst	335
Jefferson	18,403	Louisville	529
Jenkins	8,841	Millen	353
Johnson	8,660	Wrightsville	306
Jones	16,579	Gray	394
Lamar	12,215	Barnesville	186
Lanier	5,654	Lakeland	194
Laurens	36,990	Dublin	816
Lee	11,684	Leesburg	358
Liberty	37,583	Hinesville	517
Lincoln	6,949	Lincolnton	196
Long	4,524	Ludowici	402
Lowndes	67,972	Valdosta	507
Lumpkin	10,762	Dahlonega	287
McDuffie	18,546	Thomson	256
McIntosh	8,046	Darien	425
Macon	14,003	Oglethorpe	404
Madison	17,747	Danielsville	285
Marion	5,297	Buena Vista	366
Meriwether	21,229	Greenville	506
Miller	7,038	Colquitt	284
Mitchell	21,114	Camilla	512
Monroe	14,610	Forsyth	397
Montgomery	7,011	Mount Vernon	244
Morgan	11,572	Madison	349
Murray	19,685	Chatsworth	345
Muscogee	170,108	Columbus	218
Newton	34,489	Covington	277
Oconee	12,427	Watkinsville	186
Oglethorpe	8,929	Lexington	442
Paulding	26,042	Dallas	312
Peach	19,151	Fort Valley	152
Pickens	11,652	Jasper	232
Pierce	11,897	Blackshear	344
Pike	8,937	Zebulon	219
Polk	32,382	Cedartown	311
Pulaski	8,950	Hawkinsville	249
Putnam	10,295	Eatonton	344
Quitman	2,357	Georgetown	146
Rabun	10,466	Clayton	370
Randolph	9,599	Cuthbert	431
Richmond	181,629	Augusta	326
Rockdale	36,747	Conyers	132
Schley	3,433	Ellaville	169
Screven	14,043	Sylvania	655
Seminole	9,057	Donalsonville	225
Spalding	47,899	Griffin	199
Stephens	21,761	Toccoa	177
Stewart	5,896	Lumpkin	452
Sumter	29,360	Americus	489
Talbot	6,536	Talbotton	395
Taliaferro	2,032	Crawfordville	196
Tattnall	18,134	Reidsville	484
Taylor	7,902	Butler	382
Telfair	11,445	McRae	444
Terrell	12,017	Dawson	337
Thomas	38,098	Thomasville	551
Tift	32,862	Tifton	268
Toombs	22,592	Lyons	371
Towns	5,638	Hiawassee	165
Treutlen	6,087	Soperton	202
Troup	50,003	La Grange	414
Turner	9,510	Ashburn	289
Twiggs	9,354	Jeffersonville	362
Union	9,390	Blairsville	320
Upson	25,998	Thomaston	326
Walker	56,470	La Fayette	446
Walton	31,211	Monroe	330
Ware	37,180	Waycross	907
Warren	6,583	Warrenton	286
Washington	18,842	Sandersville	684
Wayne	20,750	Jesup	647
Webster	2,341	Preston	210
Wheeler	5,155	Alamo	299
White	10,120	Cleveland	242
Whitfield	65,775	Dalton	291
Wilcox	7,682	Abbeville	382
Wilkes	10,951	Washington	470
Wilkinson	10,368	Irwinton	451
Worth	18,064	Sylvester	575

Hawaii
(4 counties, 6,425 sq. mi. land; pop. 964,691)

County	Pop.	County seat or court house	Land area sq. mi.
Hawaii	92,053	Hilo	4,034
Honolulu	762,874	Honolulu	596
Kauai	39,082	Lihue	620
Maui*	70,991	Wailuku	1,175

*Includes population of Kalawao County (146).

Idaho
(44 counties, 82,412 sq. mi. land; pop. 944,127)

County	Pop.	County seat or court house	Land area sq. mi.
Ada	173,125	Boise	1,052
Adams	3,347	Council	1,362
Bannock	65,421	Pocatello	1,112
Bear Lake	6,931	Paris	990
Benewah	8,292	Saint Maries	784
Bingham	36,489	Blackfoot	2,096
Blaine	9,841	Hailey	2,634
Boise	2,999	Idaho City	1,901
Bonner	24,163	Sandpoint	1,726
Bonneville	65,980	Idaho Falls	1,840
Boundary	7,289	Bonners Ferry	1,268
Butte	3,342	Arco	2,236
Camas	818	Fairfield	1,071
Canyon	83,756	Caldwell	584
Caribou	8,695	Soda Springs	1,763
Cassia	19,427	Burley	2,560
Clark	798	Dubois	1,763
Clearwater	10,390	Orofino	2,236
Custer	3,385	Challis	4,927
Elmore	21,565	Mountain Home	3,071
Franklin	8,895	Preston	664
Fremont	10,813	Saint Anthony	1,852
Gem	11,972	Emmett	558
Gooding	11,874	Gooding	728
Idaho	14,769	Grangeville	8,497
Jefferson	15,304	Rigby	1,093
Jerome	14,840	Jerome	601
Kootenai	59,770	Coeur d'Alene	1,240
Latah	28,749	Moscow	1,077
Lemhi	7,460	Salmon	4,564
Lewis	4,118	Nezperce	478
Lincoln	3,436	Shoshone	1,205
Madison	19,480	Rexburg	468
Minidoka	19,718	Rupert	757
Nez Perce	33,220	Lewiston	845
Oneida	3,258	Malad City	1,200
Owyhee	8,272	Murphy	7,643
Payette	15,825	Payette	405
Power	6,844	American Falls	1,403
Shoshone	19,226	Wallace	2,641
Teton	2,897	Driggs	448
Twin Falls	52,927	Twin Falls	1,944
Valley	5,604	Cascade	3,670
Washington	8,803	Weiser	1,454

Illinois
(102 counties, 55,645 sq. mi. land; pop. 11,427,409)

County	Pop.	County seat or court house	Land area sq. mi.
Adams	71,622	Quincy	852
Alexander	12,264	Cairo	236
Bond	16,224	Greenville	377
Boone	28,630	Belvidere	282
Brown	5,411	Mount Sterling	306
Bureau	39,114	Princeton	869
Calhoun	5,867	Hardin	250
Carroll	18,779	Mount Carroll	444
Cass	15,084	Virginia	374
Champaign	168,392	Urbana	998
Christian	36,446	Taylorville	710
Clark	16,913	Marshall	506
Clay	15,283	Louisville	469
Clinton	32,617	Carlyle	472
Coles	52,992	Charleston	509

County	Pop.	County seat or court house	Land area sq. mi.
Cook	5,253,628	Chicago	958
Crawford	20,818	Robinson	446
Cumberland	11,062	Toledo	346
De Kalb	74,628	Sycamore	634
De Witt	18,108	Clinton	397
Douglas	10,774	Tuscola	417
Du Page	658,858	Wheaton	337
Edgar	21,725	Paris	623
Edwards	7,961	Albion	223
Effingham	30,944	Effingham	478
Fayette	22,167	Vandalia	709
Ford	15,265	Paxton	486
Franklin	43,201	Benton	414
Fulton	43,687	Lewiston	871
Gallatin	7,590	Shawneetown	325
Greene	16,661	Carrollton	543
Grundy	30,582	Morris	423
Hamilton	9,172	McLeansboro	436
Hancock	23,877	Carthage	796
Hardin	5,383	Elizabethtown	181
Henderson	9,114	Oquawka	373
Henry	57,968	Cambridge	824
Iroquois	32,976	Watseka	1,118
Jackson	61,649	Murphysboro	590
Jasper	11,318	Newton	496
Jefferson	36,558	Mount Vernon	570
Jersey	20,538	Jerseyville	373
Jo Daviess	23,520	Galena	603
Johnson	9,624	Vienna	346
Kane	278,405	Geneva	524
Kankakee	102,926	Kankakee	679
Kendall	37,202	Yorkville	322
Knox	61,607	Galesburg	720
Lake	440,388	Waukegan	454
La Salle	109,139	Ottawa	1,139
Lawrence	17,807	Lawrenceville	374
Lee	36,328	Dixon	725
Livingston	41,381	Pontiac	1,046
Logan	31,802	Lincoln	619
McDonough	37,236	Macomb	590
McHenry	147,724	Woodstock	606
McLean	119,149	Bloomington	1,185
Macon	131,375	Decatur	581
Macoupin	49,384	Carlinville	865
Madison	247,661	Edwardsville	728
Marion	43,523	Salem	573
Marshall	14,479	Lacon	388
Mason	19,492	Havana	536
Massac	14,990	Metropolis	241
Menard	11,700	Petersburg	315
Mercer	19,286	Aledo	559
Monroe	20,117	Waterloo	388
Montgomery	31,686	Hillsboro	705
Morgan	37,502	Jacksonville	568
Moultrie	14,546	Sullivan	325
Ogle	46,338	Oregon	759
Peoria	200,466	Peoria	621
Perry	21,714	Pinckneyville	443
Piatt	16,581	Monticello	439
Pike	18,896	Pittsfield	830
Pope	4,404	Golconda	374
Pulaski	8,840	Mound City	203
Putnam	6,085	Hennepin	160
Randolph	35,566	Chester	583
Richland	17,587	Olney	360
Rock Island	166,759	Rock Island	423
St. Clair	265,469	Belleville	672
Saline	27,360	Harrisburg	385
Sangamon	176,070	Springfield	866
Schuyler	8,365	Rushville	436
Scott	6,142	Winchester	251
Shelby	23,923	Shelbyville	747
Stark	7,389	Toulon	288
Stephenson	49,536	Freeport	564
Tazewell	132,078	Pekin	650
Union	16,851	Jonesboro	414
Vermilion	95,222	Danville	900
Wabash	13,713	Mt. Carmel	224
Warren	21,943	Monmouth	543
Washington	15,472	Nashville	563
Wayne	18,059	Fairfield	715
White	17,864	Carmi	497
Whiteside	65,970	Morrison	682
Will	324,460	Joliet	844
Williamson	56,538	Marion	427
Winnebago	250,884	Rockford	516
Woodford	33,320	Eureka	527

Indiana
(92 counties; 35,932 sq. mi. land; pop. 5,490,212)

Adams	29,619	Decatur	340
Allen	294,335	Fort Wayne	659
Bartholomew	65,088	Columbus	409
Benton	10,218	Fowler	407
Blackford	15,570	Hartford City	166
Boone	36,446	Lebanon	423
Brown	12,377	Nashville	312
Carroll	19,722	Delphi	372
Cass	40,936	Logansport	414
Clark	88,838	Jeffersonville	376
Clay	24,862	Brazil	360
Clinton	31,545	Frankfort	405
Crawford	9,820	English	307
Daviess	27,836	Washington	432
Dearborn	34,291	Lawrenceburg	307
Decatur	23,841	Greensburg	373
DeKalb	33,606	Auburn	364
Delaware	128,587	Muncie	392
Dubois	34,238	Jasper	429
Elkhart	137,330	Goshen	466
Fayette	28,272	Connersville	215
Floyd	61,205	New Albany	150
Fountain	19,033	Covington	398
Franklin	19,612	Brookville	385
Fulton	19,335	Rochester	369
Gibson	33,156	Princeton	490
Grant	80,934	Marion	415
Greene	30,416	Bloomfield	546
Hamilton	82,381	Noblesville	398
Hancock	43,939	Greenfield	307
Harrison	27,276	Corydon	486
Hendricks	69,804	Danville	409
Henry	53,336	New Castle	394
Howard	86,896	Kokomo	293
Huntington	35,596	Huntington	366
Jackson	36,523	Brownstown	513
Jasper	26,138	Rensselaer	561
Jay	23,239	Portland	384
Jefferson	30,419	Madison	363
Jennings	22,854	Vernon	378
Johnson	77,240	Franklin	321
Knox	41,838	Vincennes	520
Kosciusko	59,555	Warsaw	540
Lagrange	25,550	Lagrange	380
Lake	522,917	Crown Point	501
La Porte	108,632	La Porte	600
Lawrence	42,472	Bedford	452
Madison	139,336	Anderson	453
Marion	765,233	Indianapolis	396
Marshall	39,155	Plymouth	444
Martin	11,001	Shoals	339
Miami	39,820	Peru	369
Monroe	98,387	Bloomington	385
Montgomery	35,501	Crawfordsville	505
Morgan	51,999	Martinsville	409
Newton	14,844	Kentland	401
Noble	35,443	Albion	413
Ohio	5,114	Rising Sun	87
Orange	18,677	Paoli	408
Owen	15,840	Spencer	386
Parke	16,372	Rockville	444
Perry	19,346	Cannelton	382
Pike	13,465	Petersburg	341
Porter	119,816	Valparaiso	418
Posey	26,414	Mount Vernon	409
Pulaski	13,258	Winamac	435
Putnam	29,163	Greencastle	482
Randolph	29,997	Winchester	454
Ripley	24,398	Versailles	447
Rush	19,604	Rushville	408
St. Joseph	241,617	South Bend	459
Scott	20,422	Scottsburg	191
Shelby	39,887	Shelbyville	413
Spencer	19,361	Rockport	400
Starke	21,997	Knox	309
Steuben	24,694	Angola	308
Sullivan	21,107	Sullivan	452
Switzerland	7,153	Vevay	223
Tippecanoe	121,702	Lafayette	502
Tipton	16,819	Tipton	260
Union	6,860	Liberty	162
Vanderburgh	167,515	Evansville	236
Vermillion	18,229	Newport	260
Vigo	112,385	Terre Haute	405
Wabash	36,640	Wabash	398
Warren	8,976	Williamsport	366
Warrick	41,474	Boonville	391
Washington	21,932	Salem	516
Wayne	76,058	Richmond	404
Wells	25,401	Bluffton	370
White	23,867	Monticello	506
Whitley	26,215	Columbia City	336

Iowa
(99 counties; 55,965 sq. mi. land; pop. 2,913,387)

Adair	9,509	Greenfield	570
Adams	5,731	Corning	425
Allamakee	15,108	Waukon	633
Appanoose	15,511	Centerville	498
Audubon	8,559	Audubon	444
Benton	23,649	Vinton	718
Black Hawk	137,961	Waterloo	573
Boone	26,184	Boone	573
Bremer	24,820	Waverly	439
Buchanan	22,900	Independence	572
Buena Vista	20,774	Storm Lake	575
Butler	17,668	Allison	582
Calhoun	13,542	Rockwell City	571

County	Pop.	County seat or court house	Land area sq. mi.
Carroll.	22,951	Carroll.	570
Cass.	16,932	Atlantic.	565
Cedar.	18,635	Tipton.	582
Cerro Gordo.	48,458	Mason City.	569
Cherokee.	16,238	Cherokee.	577
Chickasaw.	15,437	New Hampton.	505
Clarke.	8,612	Osceola.	431
Clay.	19,576	Spencer.	569
Clayton.	21,098	Elkader.	779
Clinton.	57,122	Clinton.	695
Crawford.	18,935	Denison.	714
Dallas.	29,513	Adel.	591
Davis.	9,104	Bloomfield.	504
Decatur.	9,794	Leon.	535
Delaware.	18,933	Manchester.	578
Des Moines.	46,203	Burlington.	414
Dickinson.	15,629	Spirit Lake.	381
Dubuque.	93,745	Dubuque.	607
Emmet.	13,336	Estherville.	394
Fayette.	25,488	West Union.	731
Floyd.	19,597	Charles City.	501
Franklin.	13,036	Hampton.	583
Fremont.	9,401	Sidney.	515
Greene.	12,119	Jefferson.	571
Grundy.	14,366	Grundy Center.	501
Guthrie.	11,983	Guthrie Center.	590
Hamilton.	17,862	Webster City.	576
Hancock.	13,833	Garner.	571
Hardin.	21,776	Eldora.	569
Harrison.	16,348	Logan.	697
Henry.	18,890	Mount Pleasant.	436
Howard.	11,114	Cresco.	473
Humboldt.	12,246	Dakota City.	436
Ida.	8,908	Ida Grove.	432
Iowa.	15,429	Marengo.	587
Jackson.	22,503	Maquoketa.	638
Jasper.	36,425	Newton.	731
Jefferson.	16,316	Fairfield.	440
Johnson.	81,717	Iowa City.	614
Jones.	20,401	Anamosa.	576
Keokuk.	12,921	Sigourney.	580
Kossuth.	21,891	Algona.	974
Lee.	43,106	Fort Madison and Keokuk.	522
Linn.	169,775	Cedar Rapids.	724
Louisa.	12,055	Wapello.	402
Lucas.	10,313	Chariton.	432
Lyon.	12,896	Rock Rapids.	588
Madison.	12,597	Winterset.	563
Mahaska.	22,507	Oskaloosa.	571
Marion.	29,669	Knoxville.	560
Marshall.	41,652	Marshalltown.	573
Mills.	13,406	Glenwood.	439
Mitchell.	12,329	Osage.	470
Monona.	11,692	Onawa.	697
Monroe.	9,209	Albia.	434
Montgomery.	13,413	Red Oak.	424
Muscatine.	40,436	Muscatine.	442
O'Brien.	16,972	Primghar.	574
Osceola.	8,371	Sibley.	399
Page.	19,063	Clarinda.	535
Palo Alto.	12,721	Emmetsburg.	562
Plymouth.	24,743	Le Mars.	864
Pocahontas.	11,369	Pocahontas.	577
Polk.	303,170	Des Moines.	582
Pottawattamie.	86,500	Council Bluffs.	953
Poweshiek.	19,306	Montezuma.	585
Ringgold.	6,112	Mount Ayr.	535
Sac.	14,118	Sac City.	576
Scott.	160,022	Davenport.	459
Shelby.	15,043	Harlan.	591
Sioux.	30,813	Orange City.	769
Story.	72,326	Nevada.	574
Tama.	19,533	Toledo.	721
Taylor.	8,353	Bedford.	537
Union.	13,858	Creston.	426
Van Buren.	8,626	Keosauqua.	484
Wapello.	40,241	Ottumwa.	434
Warren.	34,878	Indianola.	573
Washington.	20,141	Washington.	570
Wayne.	8,199	Corydon.	526
Webster.	45,953	Fort Dodge.	718
Winnebago.	13,010	Forest City.	401
Winneshiek.	21,876	Decorah.	690
Woodbury.	100,884	Sioux City.	873
Worth.	9,075	Northwood.	401
Wright.	16,319	Clarion.	579

Kansas

(105 counties, 81,778 sq. mi. land; pop. 2,364,236)

County	Pop.	County seat or court house	Land area sq. mi.
Allen.	15,654	Iola.	505
Anderson.	8,749	Garnett.	584
Atchison.	18,397	Atchison.	431
Barber.	6,548	Medicine Lodge.	1,136
Barton.	31,343	Great Bend.	895
Bourbon.	15,969	Fort Scott.	638
Brown.	11,955	Hiawatha.	572
Butler.	44,782	El Dorado.	1,443
Chase.	3,309	Cottonwood Falls.	777
Chautauqua.	5,016	Sedan.	644
Cherokee.	22,304	Columbus.	590
Cheyenne.	3,678	Saint Francis.	1,021
Clark.	2,599	Ashland.	975
Clay.	9,802	Clay Center.	632
Cloud.	12,494	Concordia.	718
Coffey.	9,370	Burlington.	615
Comanche.	2,554	Coldwater.	789
Cowley.	36,824	Winfield.	1,128
Crawford.	37,916	Girard.	595
Decatur.	4,509	Oberlin.	894
Dickinson.	20,175	Abilene.	852
Doniphan.	9,268	Troy.	388
Douglas.	67,640	Lawrence.	461
Edwards.	4,271	Kinsley.	620
Elk.	3,918	Howard.	650
Ellis.	26,098	Hays.	900
Ellsworth.	6,640	Ellsworth.	717
Finney.	23,825	Garden City.	1,302
Ford.	24,315	Dodge City.	1,099
Franklin.	21,813	Ottawa.	577
Geary.	29,852	Junction City.	384
Gove.	3,726	Gove.	1,072
Graham.	3,995	Hill City.	898
Grant.	6,977	Ulysses.	575
Gray.	5,138	Cimarron.	868
Greeley.	1,845	Tribune.	778
Greenwood.	8,764	Eureka.	1,135
Hamilton.	2,514	Syracuse.	998
Harper.	7,778	Anthony.	802
Harvey.	30,531	Newton.	540
Haskell.	3,814	Sublette.	578
Hodgeman.	2,269	Jetmore.	860
Jackson.	11,644	Holton.	658
Jefferson.	15,207	Oskaloosa.	535
Jewell.	5,241	Mankato.	910
Johnson.	270,269	Olathe.	478
Kearny.	3,435	Lakin.	868
Kingman.	8,960	Kingman.	865
Kiowa.	4,046	Greensburg.	723
Labette.	25,682	Oswego.	653
Lane.	2,472	Dighton.	717
Leavenworth.	54,809	Leavenworth.	463
Lincoln.	4,145	Lincoln.	720
Linn.	8,234	Mound City.	601
Logan.	3,478	Oakley.	1,073
Lyon.	35,108	Emporia.	844
McPherson.	26,855	McPherson.	900
Marion.	13,522	Marion.	944
Marshall.	12,720	Marysville.	878
Meade.	4,788	Meade.	979
Miami.	21,618	Paola.	590
Mitchell.	8,117	Beloit.	717
Montgomery.	42,281	Independence.	646
Morris.	6,419	Council Grove.	693
Morton.	3,454	Elkhart.	731
Nemaha.	11,211	Seneca.	719
Neosho.	18,967	Erie.	576
Ness.	4,498	Ness City.	1,074
Norton.	6,689	Norton.	873
Osage.	15,319	Lyndon.	695
Osborne.	5,959	Osborne.	882
Ottawa.	5,971	Minneapolis.	721
Pawnee.	8,065	Larned.	755
Phillips.	7,406	Phillipsburg.	887
Pottawatomie.	14,782	Westmoreland.	828
Pratt.	10,275	Pratt.	735
Rawlins.	4,105	Atwood.	1,069
Reno.	64,983	Hutchinson.	1,259
Republic.	7,569	Belleville.	719
Rice.	11,900	Lyons.	728
Riley.	63,505	Manhattan.	593
Rooks.	7,006	Stockton.	888
Rush.	4,516	LaCrosse.	718
Russell.	8,868	Russell.	869
Saline.	48,905	Salina.	721
Scott.	5,782	Scott City.	718
Sedgwick.	367,088	Wichita.	1,007
Seward.	17,071	Liberal.	640
Shawnee.	154,916	Topeka.	549
Sheridan.	3,544	Hoxie.	896
Sherman.	7,759	Goodland.	1,057
Smith.	5,947	Smith Center.	897
Stafford.	5,539	Saint John.	788
Stanton.	2,339	Johnson.	681
Stevens.	4,736	Hugoton.	727
Sumner.	24,928	Wellington.	1,183
Thomas.	8,451	Colby.	1,075
Trego.	4,165	Wakeeney.	890
Wabaunsee.	6,867	Alma.	797
Wallace.	2,045	Sharon Springs.	914
Washington.	8,543	Washington.	898
Wichita.	3,041	Leoti.	719
Wilson.	12,128	Fredonia.	575
Woodson.	4,600	Yates Center.	498
Wyandotte.	172,335	Kansas City.	149

Kentucky

(120 counties, 39,669 sq. mi. land; pop. 3,660,330)

County	Pop.	County seat or court house	Land area sq. mi.
Adair.	15,233	Columbia.	407

County	Pop.	County seat or court house	Land area sq. mi.
Allen	14,128	Scottsville	338
Anderson	12,567	Lawrenceburg	204
Ballard	6,798	Wickliffe	254
Barren	34,009	Glasgow	482
Bath	10,025	Owingsville	277
Bell	34,330	Pineville	361
Boone	45,842	Burlington	246
Bourbon	19,405	Paris	292
Boyd	55,513	Catlettsburg	160
Boyle	25,066	Danville	182
Bracken	7,738	Brooksville	203
Breathitt	17,004	Jackson	495
Breckinridge	16,861	Hardinsburg	565
Bullitt	43,346	Shepherdsville	300
Butler	11,064	Morgantown	431
Caldwell	13,473	Princeton	347
Calloway	30,031	Murray	386
Campbell	83,317	Alexandria	152
Carlisle	5,487	Bardwell	191
Carroll	9,270	Carrollton	130
Carter	25,060	Grayson	407
Casey	14,818	Liberty	445
Christian	66,878	Hopkinsville	722
Clark	28,322	Winchester	255
Clay	22,752	Manchester	471
Clinton	9,321	Albany	196
Crittenden	9,207	Marion	360
Cumberland	7,289	Burkesville	304
Daviess	85,949	Owensboro	463
Edmonson	9,962	Brownsville	302
Elliott	6,908	Sandy Hook	234
Estill	14,495	Irvine	256
Fayette	204,165	Lexington	285
Fleming	12,323	Flemingsburg	351
Floyd	48,764	Prestonsburg	393
Franklin	41,830	Frankfort	212
Fulton	8,971	Hickman	211
Gallatin	4,842	Warsaw	99
Garrard	10,853	Lancaster	232
Grant	13,308	Williamstown	259
Graves	34,049	Mayfield	557
Grayson	20,854	Leitchfield	493
Green	11,043	Greensburg	289
Greenup	39,132	Greenup	347
Hancock	7,742	Hawesville	189
Hardin	88,917	Elizabethtown	629
Harlan	41,889	Harlan	468
Harrison	15,166	Cynthiana	310
Hart	15,402	Munfordville	412
Henderson	40,849	Henderson	438
Henry	12,740	New Castle	291
Hickman	6,065	Clinton	245
Hopkins	46,174	Madisonville	552
Jackson	11,996	McKee	346
Jefferson	684,638	Louisville	386
Jessamine	26,065	Nicholasville	174
Johnson	24,432	Paintsville	264
Kenton	137,058	Independence	163
Knott	17,940	Hindman	352
Knox	30,239	Barbourville	388
Larue	11,983	Hodgenville	263
Laurel	38,982	London	434
Lawrence	14,121	Louisa	420
Lee	7,754	Beattyville	211
Leslie	14,882	Hyden	402
Letcher	30,687	Whitesburg	339
Lewis	14,545	Vanceburg	484
Lincoln	19,053	Stanford	337
Livingston	9,219	Smithland	312
Logan	24,138	Russellville	556
Lyon	6,490	Eddyville	209
McCracken	61,310	Paducah	251
McCreary	15,634	Whitley City	427
McLean	10,090	Calhoun	256
Madison	53,352	Richmond	443
Magoffin	13,515	Salyersville	310
Marion	17,910	Lebanon	347
Marshall	25,637	Benton	304
Martin	13,925	Inez	230
Mason	17,760	Maysville	241
Meade	22,854	Brandenburg	306
Menifee	5,117	Frenchburg	203
Mercer	19,011	Harrodsburg	250
Metcalfe	9,484	Edmonton	291
Monroe	12,353	Tompkinsville	331
Montgomery	20,046	Mount Sterling	199
Morgan	12,103	West Liberty	382
Muhlenberg	32,238	Greenville	478
Nelson	27,584	Bardstown	424
Nicholas	7,157	Carlisle	197
Ohio	21,765	Hartford	596
Oldham	28,094	La Grange	190
Owen	8,924	Owenton	354
Owsley	5,709	Booneville	198
Pendleton	10,989	Falmouth	281
Perry	33,763	Hazard	341
Pike	81,123	Pikeville	785
Powell	11,101	Stanton	180
Pulaski	45,803	Somerset	660
Robertson	2,270	Mount Olivet	100
Rockcastle	13,973	Mount Vernon	318
Rowan	19,049	Morehead	282
Russell	13,708	Jamestown	250
Scott	21,813	Georgetown	286
Shelby	23,328	Shelbyville	385
Simpson	14,673	Franklin	236
Spencer	5,929	Taylorsville	192
Taylor	21,178	Campbellsville	270
Todd	11,874	Elkton	377
Trigg	9,384	Cadiz	421
Trimble	6,253	Bedford	148
Union	17,821	Morganfield	341
Warren	71,828	Bowling Green	548
Washington	10,764	Springfield	301
Wayne	17,022	Monticello	446
Webster	14,832	Dixon	336
Whitley	33,396	Williamsburg	443
Wolfe	6,698	Campton	223
Woodford	17,778	Versailles	192

Louisiana

(64 parishes, 44,521 sq. mi. land; pop. 4,206,116)

Parish	Pop.	Parish seat	Land area sq. mi.
Acadia	56,427	Crowley	657
Allen	21,408	Oberlin	765
Ascension	50,068	Donaldsville	296
Assumption	22,084	Napoleonville	342
Avoyelles	41,393	Marksville	846
Beauregard	29,692	De Ridder	1,163
Bienville	16,387	Arcadia	816
Bossier	80,721	Benton	845
Caddo	252,437	Shreveport	894
Calcasieu	167,048	Lake Charles	1,082
Caldwell	10,761	Columbia	541
Cameron	9,336	Cameron	1,417
Catahoula	12,287	Harrisonburg	732
Claiborne	17,095	Homer	765
Concordia	22,981	Vidalia	717
De Soto	25,664	Mansfield	880
East Baton Rouge	366,164	Baton Rouge	458
East Carroll	11,772	Lake Providence	426
East Feliciana	19,015	Clinton	455
Evangeline	33,343	Ville Platte	667
Franklin	24,141	Winnsboro	635
Grant	16,703	Colfax	653
Iberia	63,752	New Iberia	589
Iberville	32,159	Plaquemine	638
Jackson	17,321	Jonesboro	579
Jefferson	454,592	Gretna	348
Jefferson Davis	32,168	Jennings	655
Lafayette	150,017	Lafayette	270
Lafourche	82,483	Thibodaux	1,141
La Salle	17,004	Jena	638
Lincoln	39,763	Ruston	472
Livingston	58,655	Livingston	661
Madison	15,682	Tallulah	631
Morehouse	34,803	Bastrop	807
Natchitoches	39,863	Natchitoches	1,264
Orleans	557,927	New Orleans	199
Ouachita	139,241	Monroe	627
Plaquemines	26,049	Pointe a la Hache	1,035
Pointe Coupee	24,045	New Roads	566
Rapides	135,282	Alexandria	1,341
Red River	10,433	Coushatta	394
Richland	22,187	Rayville	563
Sabine	25,280	Many	855
St. Bernard	64,097	Chalmette	486
St. Charles	37,259	Hahnville	286
St. Helena	9,827	Greensburg	409
St. James	21,495	Convent	248
St. John The Baptist	31,924	Edgard	213
St. Landry	84,128	Opelousas	936
St. Martin	40,214	Saint Martinville	749
St. Mary	64,395	Franklin	613
St. Tammany	110,554	Covington	873
Tangipahoa	80,698	Amite	783
Tensas	8,525	Saint Joseph	623
Terrebonne	94,393	Houma	1,367
Union	21,167	Farmerville	884
Vermilion	48,458	Abbeville	1,205
Vernon	53,475	Leesville	1,332
Washington	44,207	Franklinton	676
Webster	43,631	Minden	602
West Baton Rouge	19,086	Port Allen	194
West Carroll	12,922	Oak Grove	360
West Feliciana	12,186	Saint Francisville	406
Winn	17,253	Winnfield	953

Maine

(16 counties, 30,995 sq. mi. land; pop. 1,125,043)

County	Pop.	County seat	Land area sq. mi.
Androscoggin	99,509	Auburn	477
Aroostook	91,344	Houlton	6,721
Cumberland	215,789	Portland	876
Franklin	27,447	Farmington	1,699
Hancock	41,781	Ellsworth	1,537
Kennebec	109,889	Augusta	876
Knox	32,941	Rockland	370
Lincoln	25,691	Wiscasset	458
Oxford	49,043	South Paris	2,053

County	Pop.	County seat or court house	Land area sq. mi.
Penobscot	137,015	Bangor	3,430
Piscataquis	17,634	Dover-Foxcroft	3,986
Sagadahoc	28,795	Bath	257
Somerset	45,049	Skowhegan	3,930
Waldo	28,414	Belfast	730
Washington	34,963	Machias	2,586
York	139,739	Alfred	1,008

Maryland
(23 cos., 1 ind. city, 9,837 sq. mi. land; pop. 4,216,941)

County	Pop.	County seat or court house	Land area sq. mi.
Allegany	80,548	Cumberland	421
Anne Arundel	370,775	Annapolis	418
Baltimore	655,615	Towson	598
Calvert	34,638	Prince Frederick	213
Caroline	23,143	Denton	321
Carroll	96,356	Westminster	452
Cecil	60,430	Elkton	360
Charles	72,751	La Plata	452
Dorchester	30,623	Cambridge	593
Frederick	114,263	Frederick	663
Garrett	26,498	Oakland	657
Harford	145,930	Bel Air	448
Howard	118,572	Ellicott City	251
Kent	16,695	Chestertown	278
Montgomery	579,053	Rockville	495
Prince Georges	665,071	Upper Marlboro	487
Queen Annes	25,508	Centreville	372
St. Mary's	59,895	Leonardtown	373
Somerset	19,188	Princess Anne	338
Talbot	25,604	Easton	259
Washington	113,086	Hagerstown	455
Wicomico	64,540	Salisbury	379
Worcester	30,889	Snow Hill	475
Independent City			
Baltimore	786,775		80

Massachusetts
(14 counties; 7,824 sq. mi. land; pop. 5,737,093)

County	Pop.	County seat or court house	Land area sq. mi.
Barnstable	147,925	Barnstable	400
Berkshire	145,110	Pittsfield	929
Bristol	474,641	Taunton	557
Dukes	8,942	Edgartown	102
Essex	633,688	Salem	495
Franklin	64,317	Greenfield	702
Hampden	443,018	Springfield	618
Hampshire	138,813	Northampton	528
Middlesex	1,367,034	Cambridge	822
Nantucket	5,087	Nantucket	47
Norfolk	606,587	Dedham	400
Plymouth	405,437	Plymouth	655
Suffolk	650,142	Boston	57
Worcester	646,352	Worcester	1,513

Michigan
(83 counties; 56,954 sq. mi. land; pop. 9,262,044)

County	Pop.	County seat or court house	Land area sq. mi.
Alcona	9,740	Harrisville	679
Alger	9,225	Munising	912
Allegan	81,555	Allegan	832
Alpena	32,315	Alpena	567
Antrim	16,194	Bellaire	480
Arenac	14,706	Standish	367
Baraga	8,484	L'Anse	901
Barry	45,781	Hastings	560
Bay	119,881	Bay City	447
Benzie	11,205	Beulah	322
Berrien	171,276	Saint Joseph	576
Branch	40,188	Coldwater	508
Calhoun	141,579	Marshall	712
Cass	49,499	Cassopolis	496
Charlevoix	19,907	Charlevoix	421
Cheboygan	20,649	Cheboygan	720
Chippewa	29,029	Sault Sainte Marie	1,590
Clare	23,822	Harrison	570
Clinton	55,893	Saint Johns	573
Crawford	9,465	Grayling	559
Delta	38,947	Escanaba	1,173
Dickinson	25,341	Iron Mountain	770
Eaton	88,337	Charlotte	579
Emmet	22,992	Petoskey	468
Genesee	450,449	Flint	642
Gladwin	19,957	Gladwin	505
Gogebic	19,686	Bessemer	1,105
Grand Traverse	54,899	Traverse City	466
Gratiot	40,448	Ithaca	570
Hillsdale	42,071	Hillsdale	603
Houghton	37,872	Houghton	1,014
Huron	36,459	Bad Axe	830
Ingham	272,437	Mason	560
Ionia	51,815	Ionia	577
Iosco	28,349	Tawas City	546
Iron	13,635	Crystal Falls	1,163
Isabella	54,110	Mount Pleasant	577
Jackson	151,495	Jackson	705
Kalamazoo	212,378	Kalamazoo	562
Kalkaska	10,952	Kalkaska	563
Kent	444,506	Grand Rapids	862
Keweenaw	1,963	Eagle River	543
Lake	7,711	Baldwin	568
Lapeer	70,038	Lapeer	658
Leelanau	14,007	Leland	341
Lenawee	89,948	Adrian	753
Livingston	100,289	Howell	574
Luce	6,659	Newberry	904
Mackinac	10,178	Saint Ignace	1,025
Macomb	694,600	Mount Clemens	482
Manistee	23,019	Manistee	543
Marquette	74,101	Marquette	1,821
Mason	26,365	Ludington	494
Mecosta	36,961	Big Rapids	560
Menominee	26,201	Menominee	1,045
Midland	73,578	Midland	525
Missaukee	10,009	Lake City	565
Monroe	134,659	Monroe	557
Montcalm	47,555	Stanton	713
Montmorency	7,492	Atlanta	550
Muskegon	157,589	Muskegon	507
Newaygo	34,917	White Cloud	847
Oakland	1,011,793	Pontiac	875
Oceana	22,002	Hart	541
Ogemaw	16,436	West Branch	570
Ontonagon	9,861	Ontonagon	1,311
Osceola	18,928	Reed City	569
Oscoda	6,858	Mio	568
Otsego	14,993	Gaylord	516
Ottawa	157,174	Grand Haven	567
Presque Isle	14,267	Rogers City	656
Roscommon	16,374	Roscommon	528
Saginaw	226,059	Saginaw	815
St. Clair	138,802	Port Huron	734
St. Joseph	56,083	Centreville	503
Sanilac	40,789	Sandusky	964
Schoolcraft	8,575	Manistique	1,173
Shiawassee	71,140	Corunna	540
Tuscola	56,961	Caro	812
Van Buren	66,814	Paw Paw	611
Washtenaw	264,740	Ann Arbor	710
Wayne	2,337,843	Detroit	615
Wexford	25,102	Cadillac	566

Minnesota
(87 counties; 79,548 sq. mi. land; pop. 4,075,970)

County	Pop.	County seat or court house	Land area sq. mi.
Aitkin	13,404	Aitkin	1,834
Anoka	195,998	Anoka	430
Becker	29,336	Detroit Lakes	1,312
Beltrami	30,982	Bemidji	2,507
Benton	25,187	Foley	408
Big Stone	7,716	Ortonville	504
Blue Earth	52,314	Mankato	749
Brown	28,645	New Ulm	610
Carlton	29,936	Carlton	864
Carver	37,046	Chaska	351
Cass	21,050	Walker	2,033
Chippewa	14,941	Montevideo	584
Chisago	25,717	Center City	417
Clay	49,327	Moorhead	1,049
Clearwater	8,761	Bagley	999
Cook	4,092	Grand Marais	1,412
Cottonwood	14,854	Windom	640
Crow Wing	41,722	Brainerd	1,008
Dakota	194,111	Hastings	574
Dodge	14,773	Mantorville	439
Douglas	27,839	Alexandria	643
Faribault	19,714	Blue Earth	714
Fillmore	21,930	Preston	862
Freeborn	36,329	Albert Lea	705
Goodhue	38,749	Red Wind	763
Grant	7,171	Elbow Lake	547
Hennepin	941,411	Minneapolis	541
Houston	19,617	Caledonia	564
Hubbard	14,098	Park Rapids	936
Isanti	23,600	Cambridge	440
Itasca	43,006	Grand Rapids	2,661
Jackson	13,690	Jackson	699
Kanabec	12,161	Mora	527
Kandiyohi	36,763	Willmar	784
Kittson	6,672	Hallock	1,104
Koochiching	17,571	International Falls	3,108
Lac qui Parle	10,592	Madison	772
Lake	13,043	Two Harbors	2,053
Lake of the Woods	3,764	Baudette	1,296
Le Sueur	23,434	Le Center	446
Lincoln	8,207	Ivanhoe	538
Lyon	25,207	Marshall	714
McLeod	29,657	Glencoe	489
Mahnomen	5,535	Mahnomen	559
Marshall	13,027	Warren	1,760
Martin	24,687	Fairmont	706
Meeker	20,594	Litchfield	624
Mille Lacs	18,430	Milaca	578
Morrison	29,311	Little Falls	1,124
Mower	40,390	Austin	711
Murray	11,507	Slayton	702
Nicollet	26,929	Saint Peter	440
Nobles	21,840	Worthington	714
Norman	9,379	Ada	877
Olmsted	91,971	Rochester	655
Otter Tail	51,937	Fergus Falls	1,973

County	Pop.	County seat or court house	Land area sq. mi.
Pennington	15,258	Thief River Falls	618
Pine	19,871	Pine City	1,421
Pipestone	11,690	Pipestone	466
Polk	34,844	Crookston	1,982
Pope	11,657	Glenwood	668
Ramsey	459,784	Saint Paul	154
Red Lake	5,471	Red Lake Falls	433
Redwood	19,341	Redwood Falls	882
Renville	20,401	Olivia	984
Rice	46,087	Faribault	501
Rock	10,703	Luverne	483
Roseau	12,574	Roseau	1,677
St. Louis	222,229	Duluth	6,125
Scott	43,784	Shakopee	357
Sherburne	29,908	Elk River	435
Sibley	15,448	Gaylord	593
Stearns	108,161	Saint Cloud	1,338
Steele	30,328	Owatonna	431
Stevens	11,322	Morris	560
Swift	12,920	Benson	743
Todd	24,991	Long Prairie	941
Traverse	5,542	Wheaton	575
Wabasha	19,335	Wabasha	537
Wadena	14,192	Wadena	538
Waseca	18,448	Waseca	422
Washington	113,571	Stillwater	390
Watonwan	12,361	Saint James	435
Wilkin	8,382	Breckenridge	751
Winona	46,256	Winona	630
Wright	58,962	Buffalo	672
Yellow Medicine	13,653	Granite Falls	758

Mississippi

(82 counties, 47,233 sq. mi. land; pop. 2,520,698)

County	Pop.	County seat	Land area
Adams	38,071	Natchez	456
Alcorn	33,036	Corinth	401
Amite	13,369	Liberty	732
Attala	19,665	Kosciusko	737
Benton	8,153	Ashland	407
Bolivar	45,965	Cleveland & Rosedale	892
Calhoun	15,664	Pittsboro	573
Carroll	9,776	Carrollton & Vaiden	634
Chickasaw	17,851	Houston & Okolona	503
Choctaw	8,996	Ackerman	420
Claiborne	12,279	Port Gibson	494
Clarke	16,945	Quitman	692
Clay	21,082	West Point	415
Coahoma	36,918	Clarksdale	559
Copiah	26,503	Hazlehurst	779
Covington	15,927	Collins	416
De Soto	53,930	Hernando	483
Forrest	66,018	Hattiesburg	469
Franklin	8,208	Meadville	566
George	15,297	Lucedale	483
Greene	9,827	Leakesville	718
Grenada	21,043	Grenada	421
Hancock	24,496	Bay Saint Louis	478
Harrison	157,665	Gulfport	581
Hinds	250,998	Jackson & Raymond	875
Holmes	22,970	Lexington	759
Humphreys	13,931	Belzoni	430
Issaquena	2,513	Mayersville	406
Itawamba	20,518	Fulton	540
Jackson	118,015	Pascagoula	731
Jasper	17,265	Bat Springs & Paulding	678
Jefferson	9,181	Fayette	523
Jefferson Davis	13,846	Prentiss	409
Jones	61,912	Ellisville & Laurel	696
Kemper	10,148	De Kalb	766
Lafayette	31,030	Oxford	669
Lamar	23,821	Purvis	499
Lauderdale	77,285	Meridian	705
Lawrence	12,518	Monticello	435
Leake	18,790	Carthage	584
Lee	57,061	Tupelo	451
Leflore	41,525	Greenwood	605
Lincoln	30,174	Brookhaven	587
Lowndes	57,304	Columbus	517
Madison	41,613	Canton	718
Marion	25,708	Columbia	548
Marshall	29,296	Holly Springs	709
Monroe	36,404	Aberdeen	772
Montgomery	13,366	Winona	408
Neshoba	23,789	Philadelphia	572
Newton	19,967	Decatur	580
Noxubee	13,212	Macon	698
Oktibbeha	36,018	Starkville	459
Panola	28,164	Batesville & Sardis	694
Pearl River	33,795	Poplarville	818
Perry	9,864	New Augusta	651
Pike	36,173	Magnolia	410
Pontotoc	20,918	Pontotoc	499
Prentiss	24,025	Booneville	418
Quitman	12,636	Marks	406
Rankin	69,427	Brandon	782
Scott	24,556	Forest	610
Sharkey	7,964	Rolling Fork	435
Simpson	23,441	Mendenhall	591
Smith	15,077	Raleigh	635
Stone	9,716	Wiggins	446
Sunflower	34,844	Indianola	706
Tallahatchie	17,157	Charleston & Sumner	651
Tate	20,119	Senatobia	406
Tippah	18,739	Ripley	458
Tishomingo	18,434	Iuka	434
Tunica	9,652	Tunica	460
Union	21,741	New Albany	416
Walthall	13,761	Tylertown	404
Warren	51,627	Vicksburg	596
Washington	72,344	Greenville	733
Wayne	19,135	Waynesboro	813
Webster	10,300	Walthall	424
Wilkinson	10,021	Woodville	678
Winston	19,474	Louisville	610
Yalobusha	13,183	Coffeeville & Water Valley	478
Yazoo	27,349	Yazoo City	933

Missouri

(114 cos., 1 ind. city, 68,945 sq. mi. land; pop. 4,916,766)

County	Pop.	County seat	Land area
Adair	24,870	Kirksville	567
Andrew	13,980	Savannah	435
Atchison	8,605	Rockport	542
Audrain	26,458	Mexico	697
Barry	24,408	Cassville	773
Barton	11,292	Lamar	596
Bates	15,873	Butler	849
Benton	12,183	Warsaw	729
Bollinger	10,301	Marble Hill	621
Boone	100,376	Columbia	687
Buchanan	87,888	Saint Joseph	409
Butler	37,693	Poplar Bluff	698
Caldwell	8,660	Kingston	430
Callaway	32,252	Fulton	842
Camden	19,963	Camdenton	641
Cape Girardeau	58,837	Jackson	577
Carroll	12,131	Carrollton	695
Carter	5,428	Van Buren	509
Cass	51,029	Harrisonville	701
Cedar	11,894	Stockton	470
Chariton	10,489	Keytesville	758
Christian	22,402	Ozark	564
Clark	8,493	Kahoka	507
Clay	136,488	Liberty	403
Clinton	15,916	Plattsburg	423
Cole	56,663	Jefferson City	392
Cooper	14,643	Boonville	567
Crawford	18,300	Steelville	744
Dade	7,383	Greenfield	491
Dallas	12,096	Buffalo	543
Daviess	8,905	Gallatin	568
De Kalb	8,222	Maysville	425
Dent	14,517	Salem	755
Douglas	11,594	Ava	814
Dunklin	36,324	Kennett	547
Franklin	71,233	Union	922
Gasconade	13,181	Hermann	521
Gentry	7,887	Albany	493
Greene	185,302	Springfield	677
Grundy	11,959	Trenton	437
Harrison	9,890	Bethany	725
Henry	19,672	Clinton	729
Hickory	6,367	Hermitage	379
Holt	6,882	Oregon	457
Howard	10,008	Fayette	465
Howell	28,807	West Plains	928
Iron	11,084	Ironton	552
Jackson	629,180	Independence	611
Jasper	86,958	Carthage	641
Jefferson	146,814	Hillsboro	661
Johnson	39,059	Warrensburg	834
Knox	5,508	Edina	507
Laclede	24,323	Lebanon	768
Lafayette	29,931	Lexington	632
Lawrence	28,973	Mount Vernon	613
Lewis	10,901	Monticello	509
Lincoln	22,193	Troy	627
Linn	15,495	Linneus	620
Livingston	15,739	Chillicothe	537
McDonald	14,917	Pineville	540
Macon	16,313	Macon	797
Madison	10,725	Fredericktown	497
Maries	7,551	Vienna	528
Marion	28,638	Palmyra	438
Mercer	4,685	Princeton	454
Miller	18,539	Tuscumbia	593
Mississippi	15,726	Charleston	410
Moniteau	12,068	California	417
Monroe	9,716	Paris	670
Montgomery	11,537	Montgomery City	540
Morgan	13,807	Versailles	594
New Madrid	22,945	New Madrid	658
Newton	40,555	Neosho	627
Nodaway	21,996	Maryville	875
Oregon	10,238	Alton	792
Osage	12,014	Linn	606
Ozark	7,961	Gainesville	731
Pemiscot	24,987	Caruthersville	517
Perry	16,784	Perryville	473

County	Pop.	County seat or court house	Land area sq. mi.
Pettis	36,378	Sedalia	686
Phelps	33,633	Rolla	674
Pike	17,568	Bowling Green	673
Platte	46,341	Platte City	421
Polk	18,822	Bolivar	636
Pulaski	42,011	Waynesville	550
Putnam	6,092	Unionville	520
Ralls	8,984	New London	482
Randolph	25,460	Huntsville	477
Ray	21,378	Richmond	568
Reynolds	7,230	Centerville	809
Ripley	12,458	Doniphan	631
St. Charles	143,455	St. Charles	558
St. Clair	8,622	Osceola	699
St. Francois	42,600	Farmington	451
St. Louis	974,180	Clayton	506
Ste. Genevieve	15,180	Ste. Genevieve	504
Saline	24,913	Marshall	755
Schuyler	4,979	Lancaster	309
Scotland	5,415	Memphis	438
Scott	39,647	Benton	423
Shannon	7,885	Eminence	1,004
Shelby	7,826	Shelbyville	501
Stoddard	29,009	Bloomfield	815
Stone	15,587	Galena	451
Sullivan	7,434	Milan	651
Taney	20,467	Forsyth	608
Texas	21,070	Houston	1,180
Vernon	19,806	Nevada	837
Warren	14,900	Warrenton	429
Washington	17,983	Potosi	762
Wayne	11,277	Greenville	762
Webster	20,414	Marshfield	594
Worth	3,008	Grant City	266
Wright	16,188	Hartville	682
Independent City			
St. Louis	453,085	....	61

Montana

(57 counties, 145,388 sq. mi. land; pop., 786,690)

County	Pop.	County seat	Land area sq. mi.
Beaverhead	8,186	Dillon	5,529
Big Horn	11,096	Hardin	4,983
Blaine	6,999	Chinook	4,257
Broadwater	3,267	Townsend	1,189
Carbon	8,099	Red Lodge	2,056
Carter	1,799	Ekalaka	3,342
Cascade	80,696	Great Falls	2,699
Chouteau	6,092	Fort Benton	3,987
Custer	13,109	Miles City	3,776
Daniels	2,835	Scobey	1,427
Dawson	11,805	Glendive	2,374
Deer Lodge	12,518	Anaconda	740
Fallon	3,763	Baker	1,623
Fergus	13,076	Lewistown	4,340
Flathead	51,966	Kalispell	5,112
Gallatin	42,865	Bozeman	2,510
Garfield	1,656	Jordan	4,491
Glacier	10,628	Cut Bank	2,994
Golden Valley	1,026	Ryegate	1,172
Granite	2,700	Philipsburg	1,729
Hill	17,985	Havre	2,897
Jefferson	7,029	Boulder	1,657
Judith Basin	2,646	Stanford	1,871
Lake	19,056	Polson	1,445
Lewis & Clark	43,039	Helena	3,461
Liberty	2,329	Chester	1,426
Lincoln	17,752	Libby	3,616
McCone	2,702	Circle	2,626
Madison	5,448	Virginia City	3,590
Meagher	2,154	White Sulphur Springs	2,392
Mineral	3,675	Superior	1,216
Missoula	76,016	Missoula	2,582
Musselshell	4,428	Roundup	1,871
Park	12,869	Livingston	1,665
Petroleum	655	Winnett	1,652
Phillips	5,367	Malta	5,130
Pondera	6,731	Conrad	1,632
Powder River	2,520	Broadus	3,288
Powell	6,958	Deer Lodge	2,329
Prairie	1,836	Terry	1,732
Ravalli	22,493	Hamilton	2,384
Richland	12,243	Sidney	2,081
Roosevelt	10,467	Wolf Point	2,357
Rosebud	9,899	Forsyth	5,019
Sanders	8,675	Thompson Falls	2,749
Sheridan	5,414	Plentywood	1,681
Silver Bow	38,092	Butte	718
Stillwater	5,598	Columbus	1,793
Sweet Grass	3,216	Big Timber	1,903
Teton	6,491	Choteau	2,275
Toole	5,559	Shelby	1,931
Treasure	981	Hysham	975
Valley	10,250	Glasgow	4,936
Wheatland	2,359	Harlowton	1,419
Wibaux	1,476	Wibaux	888
Yellowstone	108,035	Billings	2,624

Nebraska

(93 counties, 76,644 sq. mi. land; pop., 1,569,825)

County	Pop.	County seat	Land area sq. mi.
Adams	30,656	Hastings	564
Antelope	8,675	Neligh	859
Arthur	513	Arthur	711
Banner	918	Harrisburg	747
Blaine	867	Brewster	714
Boone	7,391	Albion	687
Box Butte	13,696	Alliance	1,077
Boyd	3,331	Butte	532
Brown	4,377	Ainsworth	1,214
Buffalo	34,797	Kearney	945
Burt	8,813	Tekamah	486
Butler	9,330	David City	584
Cass	20,297	Plattsmouth	557
Cedar	10,852	Hartington	740
Chase	4,758	Imperial	894
Cherry	6,758	Valentine	5,961
Cheyenne	10,057	Sidney	1,196
Clay	8,106	Clay Center	574
Colfax	9,890	Schuyler	410
Cuming	11,664	West Point	575
Custer	13,877	Broken Bow	2,571
Dakota	16,573	Dakota City	258
Dawes	9,609	Chadron	1,397
Dawson	22,162	Lexington	982
Deuel	2,462	Chappell	437
Dixon	7,137	Ponca	474
Dodge	35,847	Fremont	534
Douglas	397,884	Omaha	333
Dundy	2,861	Benkelman	920
Fillmore	7,920	Geneva	576
Franklin	4,377	Franklin	576
Frontier	3,647	Stockville	976
Furnas	6,486	Beaver City	721
Gage	24,456	Beatrice	858
Garden	2,802	Oshkosh	1,680
Garfield	2,363	Burwell	570
Gosper	2,140	Elwood	461
Grant	877	Hyannis	775
Greeley	3,462	Greeley	570
Hall	47,690	Grand Island	537
Hamilton	9,301	Aurora	543
Harlan	4,292	Alma	555
Hayes	1,356	Hayes Center	713
Hitchcock	4,079	Trenton	709
Holt	13,552	O'Neil	2,406
Hooker	990	Mullen	721
Howard	6,773	Saint Paul	564
Jefferson	9,817	Fairbury	575
Johnson	5,285	Tecumseh	377
Kearney	7,053	Minden	519
Keith	9,364	Ogallala	1,039
Keya Paha	1,301	Springview	769
Kimball	4,882	Kimball	952
Knox	11,457	Center	1,105
Lancaster	192,884	Lincoln	839
Lincoln	36,455	North Platte	2,525
Logan	983	Stapleton	571
Loup	859	Taylor	574
McPherson	593	Tryon	859
Madison	31,382	Madison	575
Merrick	8,945	Central City	478
Morrill	6,085	Bridgeport	1,405
Nance	4,740	Fullerton	439
Nemaha	8,367	Auburn	409
Nuckolls	6,726	Nelson	576
Otoe	15,183	Nebraska City	615
Pawnee	3,937	Pawnee City	433
Perkins	3,637	Grant	885
Phelps	9,769	Holdrege	540
Pierce	8,481	Pierce	575
Platte	28,852	Columbus	669
Polk	6,320	Osceola	437
Red Willow	12,615	McCook	718
Richardson	11,315	Falls City	553
Rock	2,383	Bassett	1,003
Saline	13,131	Wilber	575
Sarpy	86,015	Papillion	238
Saunders	18,716	Wahoo	753
Scotts Bluff	38,344	Gering	725
Seward	15,789	Seward	575
Sheridan	7,544	Rushville	2,453
Sherman	4,226	Loup City	564
Sioux	1,845	Harrison	2,070
Stanton	6,549	Stanton	431
Thayer	7,582	Hebron	575
Thomas	973	Thedford	713
Thurston	7,186	Pender	391
Valley	5,633	Ord	567
Washington	15,508	Blair	386
Wayne	9,858	Wayne	443
Webster	4,858	Red Cloud	575
Wheeler	1,060	Bartlett	575
York	14,798	York	576

Nevada

(16 cos., 1 ind. city, 109,894 sq. mi. land; pop., 800,508)

County	Pop.	County seat	Land area sq. mi.
Churchill	13,917	Fallon	4,990
Clark	461,816	Las Vegas	7,881

County	Pop.	County seat or court house	Land area sq. mi.
Douglas	19,421	Minden	708
Elko	17,269	Elko	17,135
Esmeralda	777	Goldfield	3,587
Eureka	1,198	Eureka	4,175
Humboldt	9,449	Winnemucca	9,698
Lander	4,082	Austin	5,515
Lincoln	3,732	Pioche	10,635
Lyon	13,594	Yerington	2,007
Mineral	6,217	Hawthorne	3,744
Nye	9,048	Tonopah	18,155
Pershing	3,408	Lovelock	6,036
Storey	1,459	Virginia City	264
Washoe	193,623	Reno	6,317
White Pine	8,167	Ely	8,902
Independent City			
Carson City	32,022	Carson City	146

New Hampshire
(10 counties, 8,993 sq. mi. land; pop., 920,610)

County	Pop.	Seat	Land
Belknap	42,884	Laconia	404
Carroll	27,931	Ossipee	933
Cheshire	62,116	Keene	711
Coos	35,147	Lancaster	1,804
Grafton	65,806	Woodsville	1,719
Hillsborough	276,608	Nashua	876
Merrimack	98,302	Concord	936
Rockingham	190,345	Exeter	699
Strafford	85,408	Dover	370
Sullivan	36,063	Newport	540

New Jersey
(21 counties, 7,468 sq. mi. land; pop., 7,365,011)

County	Pop.	Seat	Land
Atlantic	194,119	Mays Landing	568
Bergen	845,385	Hackensack	237
Burlington	362,542	Mount Holly	808
Camden	471,650	Camden	223
Cape May	82,266	Cape May Court House	263
Cumberland	132,866	Bridgeton	498
Essex	851,304	Newark	127
Gloucester	199,917	Woodbury	327
Hudson	556,972	Jersey City	46
Hunterdon	87,361	Flemington	426
Mercer	307,863	Trenton	227
Middlesex	595,893	New Brunswick	316
Monmouth	503,173	Freehold	472
Morris	407,630	Morristown	470
Ocean	346,038	Toms River	641
Passaic	447,585	Paterson	187
Salem	64,676	Salem	338
Somerset	203,129	Somerville	305
Sussex	116,119	Newton	526
Union	504,094	Elizabeth	103
Warren	84,429	Belvidere	359

New Mexico
(32 counties, 121,335 sq. mi. land; pop., 1,303,302)

County	Pop.	Seat	Land
Bernalillo	420,261	Albuquerque	1,169
Catron	2,720	Reserve	6,929
Chaves	51,103	Roswell	6,066
Colfax	13,706	Raton	3,762
Curry	42,019	Clovis	1,408
De Baca	2,454	Fort Sumner	2,323
Dona Ana	96,340	Las Cruces	3,819
Eddy	47,855	Carlsbad	4,184
Grant	26,204	Silver City	3,969
Guadalupe	4,496	Santa Rosa	3,092
Harding	1,090	Mosquero	2,122
Hidalgo	6,049	Lordsburg	3,445
Lea	55,634	Lovington	4,389
Lincoln	10,997	Carrizozo	4,832
Los Alamos	17,599	Los Alamos	109
Luna	15,585	Deming	2,965
McKinley	56,536	Gallup	5,442
Mora	4,205	Mora	1,930
Otero	44,665	Alamogordo	6,626
Quay	10,577	Tucumcari	2,874
Rio Arriba	29,282	Tierra Amarilla	5,856
Roosevelt	15,695	Portales	2,453
Sandoval	34,400	Bernalillo	3,707
San Juan	80,833	Aztec	5,521
San Miguel	22,751	Las Vegas	4,709
Santa Fe	75,519	Santa Fe	1,905
Sierra	8,454	Truth or Consequences	4,178
Socorro	12,969	Socorro	6,625
Taos	18,862	Taos	2,204
Torrance	7,491	Estancia	3,335
Union	4,725	Clayton	3,830
Valencia	60,853	Los Lunas	5,616

New York
(62 counties, 47,377 sq. mi. land; pop., 17,558,165)

County	Pop.	Seat	Land
Albany	285,909	Albany	524
Allegany	51,742	Belmont	1,032
Bronx	1,168,972	Bronx	42
Broome	213,648	Binghamton	712
Cattaraugus	85,697	Little Valley	1,306
Cayuga	79,894	Auburn	695
Chautauqua	146,925	Mayville	1,064
Chemung	97,656	Elmira	411
Chenango	49,344	Norwich	897
Clinton	80,750	Plattsburgh	1,043
Columbia	59,487	Hudson	638
Cortland	48,820	Cortland	500
Delaware	46,824	Delhi	1,440
Dutchess	245,055	Poughkeepsie	804
Erie	1,015,472	Buffalo	1,046
Essex	36,176	Elizabethtown	1,806
Franklin	44,929	Malone	1,642
Fulton	55,153	Johnstown	497
Genesee	59,400	Batavia	495
Greene	40,861	Catskill	648
Hamilton	5,034	Lake Pleasant	1,721
Herkimer	66,714	Herkimer	1,416
Jefferson	88,151	Watertown	1,273
Kings	2,231,028	Brooklyn	70
Lewis	25,035	Lowville	1,283
Livingston	57,006	Geneseo	633
Madison	65,150	Wampsville	656
Monroe	702,238	Rochester	663
Montgomery	53,439	Fonda	404
Nassau	1,321,582	Mineola	287
New York	1,428,285	New York	22
Niagara	227,354	Lockport	526
Oneida	253,466	Utica	1,219
Onondaga	463,920	Syracuse	784
Ontario	88,909	Canandaigua	644
Orange	259,603	Goshen	826
Orleans	38,496	Albion	391
Oswego	113,901	Oswego	954
Otsego	59,075	Cooperstown	1,004
Putnam	77,193	Carmel	231
Queens	1,891,325	Jamaica	109
Rensselaer	151,966	Troy	655
Richmond	352,029	Saint George	59
Rockland	259,530	New City	175
St. Lawrence	114,347	Canton	2,728
Saratoga	153,759	Ballston Spa	810
Schenectady	149,946	Schenectady	206
Schoharie	29,710	Schoharie	624
Schuyler	17,686	Watkins Glen	329
Seneca	33,733	Ovid & Waterloo	327
Steuben	99,217	Bath	1,396
Suffolk	1,284,231	Riverhead	911
Sullivan	65,155	Monticello	976
Tioga	49,812	Owego	519
Tompkins	87,085	Ithaca	477
Ulster	158,158	Kingston	1,131
Warren	54,854	Lake George	882
Washington	54,795	Hudson Falls	836
Wayne	84,581	Lyons	605
Westchester	866,599	White Plains	438
Wyoming	39,895	Warsaw	595
Yates	21,459	Penn Yan	339

North Carolina
(100 counties, 48,843 sq. mi. land; pop., 5,880,965)

County	Pop.	Seat	Land
Alamance	99,136	Graham	433
Alexander	24,999	Taylorsville	259
Alleghany	9,587	Sparta	235
Anson	25,562	Wadesboro	533
Ashe	22,325	Jefferson	426
Avery	14,409	Newland	247
Beaufort	40,266	Washington	826
Bertie	21,024	Windsor	701
Bladen	30,448	Elizabethtown	879
Brunswick	35,767	Southport	860
Buncombe	160,934	Asheville	659
Burke	72,504	Morganton	504
Cabarrus	85,895	Concord	364
Caldwell	67,746	Lenoir	471
Camden	5,829	Camden	240
Carteret	41,092	Beaufort	526
Caswell	20,705	Yanceyville	428
Catawba	105,208	Newton	396
Chatham	33,415	Pittsboro	708
Cherokee	18,933	Murphy	452
Chowan	12,558	Edenton	182
Clay	6,619	Hayesville	214
Cleveland	83,435	Shelby	468
Columbus	51,037	Whiteville	938
Craven	71,043	New Bern	701
Cumberland	247,160	Fayetteville	657
Currituck	11,089	Currituck	256
Dare	13,377	Manteo	391
Davidson	113,162	Lexington	548
Davie	24,599	Mocksville	267
Duplin	40,952	Kenansville	819
Durham	152,785	Durham	298
Edgecombe	55,988	Tarboro	506
Forsyth	243,704	Winston-Salem	412
Franklin	30,055	Louisburg	494
Gaston	162,568	Gastonia	357
Gates	8,875	Gatesville	338
Graham	7,217	Robbinsville	289
Granville	33,995	Oxford	534
Greene	16,117	Snow Hill	266

County	Pop.	County seat or court house	Land area sq. mi.
Guilford	317,154	Greensboro	651
Halifax	55,076	Halifax	724
Harnett	59,570	Lillington	601
Haywood	46,495	Waynesville	555
Henderson	58,580	Hendersonville	374
Hertford	23,368	Winton	356
Hoke	20,383	Raeford	391
Hyde	5,873	Swanquarter	624
Iredell	82,538	Statesville	574
Jackson	25,811	Sylva	491
Johnston	70,599	Smithfield	795
Jones	9,705	Trenton	470
Lee	36,718	Sanford	259
Lenoir	59,819	Kinston	402
Lincoln	42,372	Lincolnton	298
McDowell	35,135	Marion	437
Macon	20,178	Franklin	517
Madison	16,827	Marshall	451
Martin	25,948	Williamston	461
Mecklenburg	404,270	Charlotte	528
Mitchell	14,428	Bakersville	222
Montgomery	22,469	Troy	490
Moore	50,505	Carthage	701
Nash	67,153	Nashville	540
New Hanover	103,471	Wilmington	185
Northampton	22,195	Jackson	538
Onslow	112,784	Jacksonville	763
Orange	77,055	Hillsboro	400
Pamlico	10,398	Bayboro	341
Pasquotank	28,462	Elizabeth City	228
Pender	22,262	Burgaw	875
Perquimans	9,486	Hertford	246
Person	29,164	Roxboro	398
Pitt	83,651	Greenville	657
Polk	12,984	Columbus	238
Randolph	91,300	Asheboro	789
Richmond	45,481	Rockingham	477
Robeson	101,577	Lumberton	949
Rockingham	83,426	Wentworth	569
Rowan	99,186	Salisbury	519
Rutherford	53,787	Rutherfordton	568
Sampson	49,687	Clinton	947
Scotland	32,273	Laurinburg	319
Stanly	48,517	Albemarle	396
Stokes	33,086	Danbury	452
Surry	59,449	Dobson	539
Swain	10,283	Bryson City	526
Transylvania	23,417	Brevard	378
Tyrrell	3,975	Columbia	407
Union	70,436	Monroe	639
Vance	36,748	Henderson	249
Wake	301,429	Raleigh	854
Warren	16,232	Warrenton	427
Washington	14,801	Plymouth	332
Watauga	31,678	Boone	314
Wayne	97,054	Goldsboro	554
Wilkes	58,657	Wilkesboro	752
Wilson	63,132	Wilson	374
Yadkin	28,439	Yadkinville	336
Yancey	14,934	Burnsville	314

North Dakota

(53 counties, 69,300 sq. mi. land; pop., 652,717)

County	Pop.	County seat or court house	Land area sq. mi.
Adams	3,584	Hettinger	988
Barnes	13,960	Valley City	1,498
Benson	7,944	Minnewaukan	1,412
Billings	1,138	Medora	1,152
Bottineau	9,338	Bottineau	1,668
Bowman	4,229	Bowman	1,162
Burke	3,822	Bowbells	1,118
Burleigh	54,811	Bismarck	1,618
Cass	88,247	Fargo	1,767
Cavalier	7,636	Langdon	1,507
Dickey	7,207	Ellendale	1,139
Divide	3,494	Crosby	1,288
Dunn	4,627	Manning	1,993
Eddy	3,554	New Rockford	634
Emmons	5,877	Linton	1,499
Foster	4,611	Carrington	640
Golden Valley	2,391	Beach	1,003
Grand Forks	66,100	Grand Forks	1,440
Grant	4,274	Carson	1,660
Griggs	3,714	Cooperstown	708
Hettinger	4,275	Mott	1,133
Kidder	3,833	Steele	1,362
La Moure	6,473	La Moure	1,150
Logan	3,493	Napoleon	1,000
McHenry	7,858	Towner	1,887
McIntosh	4,800	Ashley	984
McKenzie	7,132	Watford City	2,754
McLean	12,288	Washburn	2,065
Mercer	9,378	Stanton	1,044
Morton	25,177	Mandan	1,921
Mountrail	7,679	Stanley	1,837
Nelson	5,233	Lakota	991
Oliver	2,495	Center	723
Pembina	10,399	Cavalier	1,120
Pierce	6,166	Rugby	1,037
Ramsey	13,048	Devils Lake	1,241
Ransom	6,698	Lisbon	862
Renville	3,608	Mohall	874
Richland	19,207	Wahpeton	1,436
Rolette	12,177	Rolla	914
Sargent	5,512	Forman	857
Sheridan	2,819	McClusky	989
Sioux	3,620	Fort Yates	1,099
Slope	1,157	Amidon	1,219
Stark	23,697	Dickinson	1,338
Steele	3,106	Finley	713
Stutsman	24,154	Jamestown	2,263
Towner	4,052	Cando	1,035
Traill	9,624	Hillsboro	861
Walsh	15,371	Grafton	1,290
Ward	58,392	Minot	2,041
Wells	6,979	Fessenden	1,288
Williams	22,237	Williston	2,074

Ohio

(88 counties, 41,004 sq. mi. land; pop., 10,797,603)

County	Pop.	County seat or court house	Land area sq. mi.
Adams	24,328	West Union	586
Allen	112,241	Lima	405
Ashland	46,178	Ashland	424
Ashtabula	104,215	Jefferson	703
Athens	56,399	Athens	508
Auglaize	42,554	Wapakoneta	398
Belmont	82,569	Saint Clairsville	537
Brown	31,920	Georgetown	493
Butler	258,787	Hamilton	470
Carroll	25,598	Carrollton	393
Champaign	33,649	Urbana	429
Clark	150,236	Springfield	398
Clermont	128,483	Batavia	456
Clinton	34,603	Wilmington	410
Columbiana	113,572	Lisbon	534
Coshocton	36,024	Coshocton	566
Crawford	50,075	Bucyrus	403
Cuyahoga	1,498,295	Cleveland	459
Darke	55,096	Greenville	600
Defiance	39,987	Defiance	414
Delaware	53,840	Delaware	443
Erie	79,655	Sandusky	264
Fairfield	93,678	Lancaster	506
Fayette	27,467	Washington C. H.	405
Franklin	869,126	Columbus	543
Fulton	37,751	Wauseon	407
Gallia	30,098	Gallipolis	471
Geauga	74,474	Chardon	408
Greene	129,769	Xenia	416
Guernsey	42,024	Cambridge	522
Hamilton	873,203	Cincinnati	412
Hancock	64,581	Findlay	532
Hardin	32,719	Kenton	471
Harrison	18,152	Cadiz	400
Henry	28,383	Napoleon	415
Highland	33,477	Hillsboro	553
Hocking	24,304	Logan	423
Holmes	29,416	Millersburg	424
Huron	54,608	Norwalk	494
Jackson	30,592	Jackson	420
Jefferson	91,564	Steubenville	410
Knox	46,309	Mount Vernon	529
Lake	212,801	Painesville	231
Lawrence	63,849	Ironton	457
Licking	120,981	Newark	686
Logan	39,155	Bellefontaine	458
Lorain	274,909	Elyria	495
Lucas	471,741	Toledo	341
Madison	33,004	London	467
Mahoning	289,487	Youngstown	417
Marion	67,974	Marion	403
Medina	113,150	Medina	422
Meigs	23,641	Pomeroy	432
Mercer	38,334	Celina	457
Miami	90,381	Troy	410
Monroe	17,382	Woodsfield	457
Montgomery	571,697	Dayton	458
Morgan	14,241	McConnelsville	420
Morrow	26,480	Mount Gilead	406
Muskingum	83,340	Zanesville	654
Noble	11,310	Caldwell	399
Ottawa	40,076	Port Clinton	253
Paulding	21,302	Paulding	419
Perry	31,032	New Lexington	412
Pickaway	43,662	Circleville	503
Pike	22,802	Waverly	443
Portage	135,856	Ravenna	493
Preble	38,223	Eaton	426
Putnam	32,991	Ottawa	484
Richland	131,205	Mansfield	497
Ross	65,004	Chillicothe	692
Sandusky	63,267	Fremont	409
Scioto	84,545	Portsmouth	613
Seneca	61,901	Tiffin	553
Shelby	43,089	Sidney	409
Stark	378,823	Canton	574
Summit	524,472	Akron	412
Trumbull	241,863	Warren	612
Tuscarawas	84,614	New Philadelphia	570

County	Pop.	County seat or court house	Land area sq. mi.
Union	29,536	Marysville	437
Van Wert	30,458	Van Wert	410
Vinton	11,584	McArthur	414
Warren	99,276	Lebanon	403
Washington	64,266	Marietta	640
Wayne	97,408	Wooster	557
Williams	36,369	Bryan	422
Wood	107,372	Bowling Green	619
Wyandot	22,651	Upper Sandusky	406

Oklahoma

(77 counties, 68,655 sq. mi. land; pop., 3,025,487)

County	Pop.	County seat	Land area sq. mi.
Adair	18,575	Stillwell	577
Alfalfa	7,077	Cherokee	864
Atoka	12,748	Atoka	980
Beaver	6,806	Beaver	1,808
Beckham	19,243	Sayre	904
Blaine	13,443	Watonga	920
Bryan	30,535	Durant	902
Caddo	30,905	Anadarko	1,286
Canadian	56,452	El Reno	901
Carter	43,610	Ardmore	828
Cherokee	30,684	Tahlequah	748
Choctaw	17,203	Hugo	762
Cimarron	3,648	Boise City	1,842
Cleveland	133,173	Norman	529
Coal	6,041	Coalgate	520
Comanche	112,456	Lawton	1,076
Cotton	7,338	Walters	656
Craig	15,014	Vinita	763
Creek	59,210	Sapulpa	930
Custer	25,995	Arapaho	981
Delaware	23,946	Jay	720
Dewey	5,922	Taloga	1,007
Ellis	5,596	Arnett	1,232
Garfield	62,820	Enid	1,060
Garvin	27,856	Pauls Valley	813
Grady	39,490	Chickasha	1,106
Grant	6,518	Medford	1,004
Greer	6,877	Mangum	638
Harmon	4,519	Hollis	537
Harper	4,715	Buffalo	1,039
Haskell	11,010	Stigler	570
Hughes	14,338	Holdenville	805
Jackson	30,356	Altus	817
Jefferson	8,294	Waurika	769
Johnston	10,356	Tishomingo	639
Kay	49,852	Newkirk	921
Kingfisher	14,187	Kingfisher	906
Kiowa	12,711	Hobart	1,019
Latimer	9,840	Wilburton	728
Le Flore	40,698	Poteau	1,585
Lincoln	26,601	Chandler	964
Logan	26,881	Guthrie	748
Love	7,469	Marietta	519
McClain	20,291	Purcell	582
McCurtain	36,151	Idabel	1,826
McIntosh	15,495	Eufaula	599
Major	8,772	Fairview	958
Marshall	10,550	Madill	372
Mayes	32,261	Pryor	644
Murray	12,147	Sulphur	420
Muskogee	67,033	Muskogee	815
Noble	11,573	Perry	736
Nowata	11,486	Nowata	540
Okfuskee	11,125	Okemah	628
Oklahoma	568,933	Oklahoma City	708
Okmulgee	39,169	Okmulgee	698
Osage	39,327	Pawhuska	2,265
Ottawa	32,870	Miami	465
Pawnee	15,310	Pawnee	551
Payne	62,435	Stillwater	691
Pittsburg	40,524	McAlester	1,251
Pontotoc	32,598	Ada	717
Pottawatomie	55,239	Shawnee	783
Pushmataha	11,773	Antlers	1,417
Roger Mills	4,799	Cheyenne	1,146
Rogers	46,436	Claremore	683
Seminole	27,465	Wewoka	639
Sequoyah	30,749	Sallisaw	678
Stephens	43,419	Duncan	884
Texas	17,727	Guymon	2,040
Tillman	12,398	Frederick	904
Tulsa	470,593	Tulsa	572
Wagoner	41,801	Wagoner	559
Washington	48,113	Bartlesville	423
Washita	13,798	Cordell	1,006
Woods	10,923	Alva	1,291
Woodward	21,172	Woodward	1,242

Oregon

(36 counties, 96,184 sq. mi. land; pop., 2,633,156)

County	Pop.	County seat	Land area sq. mi.
Baker	16,134	Baker	3,072
Benton	68,211	Corvallis	679
Clackamas	241,911	Oregon City	1,870
Clatsop	32,489	Astoria	805
Columbia	35,646	Saint Helens	651
Coos	64,047	Coquille	1,606
Crook	13,091	Prineville	2,984
Curry	16,992	Gold Beach	1,629
Deschutes	62,142	Bend	3,025
Douglas	93,748	Roseburg	5,044
Gilliam	2,057	Condon	1,213
Grant	8,210	Canyon City	4,525
Harney	8,314	Burns	10,174
Hood River	15,835	Hood River	521
Jackson	132,456	Medford	2,767
Jefferson	11,599	Madras	1,789
Josephine	58,820	Grants Pass	1,640
Klamath	59,117	Klamath Falls	5,954
Lake	7,532	Lakeview	8,251
Lane	275,226	Eugene	4,562
Lincoln	35,264	Newport	980
Linn	89,495	Albany	2,296
Malheur	26,896	Vale	9,861
Marion	204,692	Salem	1,184
Morrow	7,519	Heppner	2,044
Multnomah	562,647	Portland	431
Polk	45,203	Dallas	741
Sherman	2,172	Moro	827
Tillamook	21,164	Tillamook	1,101
Umatilla	58,861	Pendleton	3,218
Union	23,921	La Grande	2,035
Wallowa	7,273	Enterprise	3,150
Wasco	21,732	The Dalles	2,384
Washington	245,860	Hillsboro	725
Wheeler	1,513	Fossil	1,713
Yamhill	55,332	McMinnville	715

Pennsylvania

(67 counties, 44,888 sq. mi. land; pop., 11,864,720)

County	Pop.	County seat	Land area sq. mi.
Adams	68,292	Gettysburg	521
Allegheny	1,450,195	Pittsburgh	727
Armstrong	77,768	Kittanning	646
Beaver	204,441	Beaver	436
Bedford	46,784	Bedford	1,017
Berks	312,509	Reading	861
Blair	136,621	Hollidaysburg	527
Bradford	62,919	Towanda	1,152
Bucks	479,180	Doylestown	610
Butler	147,912	Butler	789
Cambria	183,263	Ebensburg	691
Cameron	6,674	Emporium	398
Carbon	53,285	Jim Thorpe	384
Centre	112,760	Bellefonte	1,106
Chester	316,660	West Chester	758
Clarion	43,362	Clarion	607
Clearfield	83,578	Clearfield	1,149
Clinton	38,971	Lock Haven	891
Columbia	61,967	Bloomsburg	486
Crawford	88,869	Meadville	1,011
Cumberland	179,625	Carlisle	547
Dauphin	232,317	Harrisburg	528
Delaware	555,029	Media	184
Elk	38,338	Ridgeway	830
Erie	279,780	Erie	804
Fayette	160,395	Uniontown	794
Forest	5,072	Tionesta	428
Franklin	113,629	Chambersburg	774
Fulton	12,842	McConnellsburg	438
Greene	40,355	Waynesburg	577
Huntingdon	42,253	Huntingdon	877
Indiana	92,281	Indiana	829
Jefferson	48,303	Brookville	657
Juniata	19,188	Mifflintown	392
Lackawanna	227,908	Scranton	461
Lancaster	362,346	Lancaster	952
Lawrence	107,150	New Castle	363
Lebanon	109,829	Lebanon	363
Lehigh	273,582	Allentown	348
Luzerne	343,079	Wilkes-Barre	891
Lycoming	118,416	Williamsport	1,237
McKean	50,635	Smethport	979
Mercer	128,299	Mercer	672
Mifflin	46,908	Lewistown	413
Monroe	69,409	Stroudsburg	609
Montgomery	643,371	Norristown	486
Montour	16,675	Danville	131
Northampton	225,418	Easton	376
Northumberland	100,381	Sunbury	461
Perry	35,718	New Bloomfield	557
Philadelphia	1,688,210	Philadelphia	136
Pike	18,271	Milford	550
Potter	17,726	Coudersport	1,081
Schuylkill	160,630	Pottsville	782
Snyder	33,584	Middleburg	329
Somerset	81,243	Somerset	1,073
Sullivan	6,349	Laporte	451
Susquehanna	37,876	Montrose	826
Tioga	40,973	Wellsboro	1,131
Union	32,870	Lewisburg	317
Venango	64,444	Franklin	679
Warren	47,449	Warren	885
Washington	217,074	Washington	958
Wayne	35,237	Honesdale	731
Westmoreland	392,184	Greensburg	1,033
Wyoming	26,433	Tunkhannock	399
York	312,963	York	906

County	Pop.	County seat or court house	Land area sq. mi.

Rhode Island
(5 counties, 1,055 sq. mi. land; pop., 947,154)

County	Pop.	County seat or court house	Land area sq. mi.
Bristol	46,942	Bristol	26
Kent	154,163	East Greenwich	172
Newport	81,383	Newport	107
Providence	571,349	Providence	416
Washington	93,317	West Kingston	333

South Carolina
(46 counties, 30,203 sq. mi. land; pop., 3,122,717)

County	Pop.	County seat or court house	Land area sq. mi.
Abbeville	22,627	Abbeville	508
Aiken	105,630	Aiken	1,092
Allendale	10,700	Allendale	413
Anderson	133,235	Anderson	718
Bamberg	18,118	Bamberg	395
Barnwell	19,868	Barnwell	558
Beaufort	65,364	Beaufort	579
Berkeley	94,745	Moncks Corner	1,108
Calhoun	12,206	Saint Matthews	380
Charleston	276,573	Charleston	938
Cherokee	40,983	Gaffney	396
Chester	30,148	Chester	580
Chesterfield	38,161	Chesterfield	802
Clarendon	27,464	Manning	602
Colleton	31,676	Walterboro	1,052
Darlington	62,717	Darlington	563
Dillon	31,083	Dillon	406
Dorchester	59,028	Saint George	575
Edgefield	17,528	Edgefield	490
Fairfield	20,700	Winnsboro	685
Florence	110,163	Florence	804
Georgetown	42,461	Georgetown	822
Greenville	287,895	Greenville	795
Greenwood	57,847	Greenwood	451
Hampton	18,159	Hampton	561
Horry	101,419	Conway	1,143
Jasper	14,504	Ridgeland	655
Kershaw	39,015	Camden	723
Lancaster	53,361	Lancaster	552
Laurens	52,214	Laurens	712
Lee	18,929	Bishopville	411
Lexington	140,353	Lexington	707
McCormick	7,797	McCormick	350
Marion	34,179	Marion	493
Marlboro	31,634	Bennettsville	483
Newberry	31,111	Newberry	634
Oconee	48,611	Walhalla	629
Orangeburg	82,276	Orangeburg	1,111
Pickens	79,292	Pickens	499
Richland	269,600	Columbia	762
Saluda	16,136	Saluda	456
Spartanburg	203,023	Spartanburg	814
Sumter	88,243	Sumter	665
Union	30,764	Union	515
Williamsburg	38,226	Kingstree	934
York	106,720	York	685

South Dakota
(67 counties, 75,952 sq. mi. land; pop., 690,768)

County	Pop.	County seat or court house	Land area sq. mi.
Aurora	3,628	Plankinton	707
Beadle	19,195	Huron	1,259
Bennett	3,236	Martin	1,182
Bon Homme	8,059	Tyndall	552
Brookings	24,332	Brookings	795
Brown	36,962	Aberdeen	1,722
Brule	5,245	Chamberlain	815
Buffalo	1,795	Gannvalley	475
Butte	8,372	Belle Fourche	2,251
Campbell	2,243	Mound City	732
Charles Mix	9,680	Lake Andes	1,090
Clark	4,894	Clark	953
Clay	13,135	Vermillion	409
Codington	20,885	Watertown	694
Corson	5,196	McIntosh	2,467
Custer	6,000	Custer	1,559
Davison	17,820	Mitchell	436
Day	8,133	Webster	1,022
Deuel	5,289	Clear Lake	631
Dewey	5,366	Timber Lake	2,310
Douglas	4,181	Armour	434
Edmunds	5,159	Ipswich	1,149
Fall River	8,439	Hot Springs	1,740
Faulk	3,327	Faulkton	1,004
Grant	9,013	Milbank	681
Gregory	6,015	Burke	1,013
Haakon	2,794	Philip	1,822
Hamlin	5,261	Hayti	512
Hand	4,948	Miller	1,437
Hanson	3,415	Alexandria	433
Harding	1,700	Buffalo	2,678
Hughes	14,220	Pierre	757
Hutchinson	9,350	Olivet	816
Hyde	2,069	Highmore	860
Jackson	3,437	Kadoka	1,872
Jerauld	2,929	Wessington Spgs	530
Jones	1,463	Murdo	971
Kingsbury	6,679	De Smet	824
Lake	10,724	Madison	560
Lawrence	18,339	Deadwood	800
Lincoln	13,942	Canton	578
Lyman	3,864	Kennebec	1,679
McCook	6,444	Salem	576
McPherson	4,027	Leola	1,148
Marshall	5,404	Britton	848
Meade	20,717	Sturgis	3,481
Mellette	2,249	White River	1,311
Miner	3,739	Howard	570
Minnehaha	109,435	Sioux Falls	810
Moody	6,692	Flandreau	520
Pennington	70,133	Rapid City	2,783
Perkins	4,700	Bison	2,884
Potter	3,674	Gettysburg	869
Roberts	10,911	Sisseton	1,102
Sanborn	3,213	Woonsocket	569
Shannon	11,323	(Attached to Fall River)	2,094
Spink	9,201	Redfield	1,505
Stanley	2,533	Fort Pierre	1,431
Sully	1,990	Onida	972
Todd	7,328	(Attached to Tripp)	1,388
Tripp	7,268	Winner	1,618
Turner	9,255	Parker	617
Union	10,938	Elk Point	453
Walworth	7,011	Selby	707
Washabaugh	—	(Attached to Jackson)	—
Yankton	18,952	Yankton	518
Ziebach	2,308	Dupree	1,969

Tennessee
(95 counties, 41,155 sq. mi. land; pop., 4,591,120)

County	Pop.	County seat or court house	Land area sq. mi.
Anderson	67,346	Clinton	339
Bedford	27,916	Shelbyville	475
Benton	14,901	Camden	392
Bledsoe	9,478	Pikeville	407
Blount	77,770	Maryville	558
Bradley	67,547	Cleveland	327
Campbell	34,841	Jacksboro	479
Cannon	10,234	Woodbury	266
Carroll	28,285	Huntingdon	600
Carter	50,205	Elizabethton	341
Cheatham	21,616	Ashland City	304
Chester	12,727	Henderson	289
Claiborne	24,595	Tazewell	432
Clay	7,676	Celina	227
Cocke	28,792	Newport	432
Coffee	38,311	Manchester	428
Crockett	14,941	Alamo	266
Cumberland	28,676	Crossville	682
Davidson	477,811	Nashville	501
Decatur	10,857	Decaturville	330
De Kalb	13,589	Smithville	291
Dickson	30,037	Charlotte	491
Dyer	34,663	Dyersburg	520
Fayette	25,305	Somerville	705
Fentress	14,826	Jamestown	498
Franklin	31,983	Winchester	543
Gibson	49,467	Trenton	602
Giles	24,625	Pulaski	610
Grainger	16,751	Rutledge	273
Greene	54,406	Greeneville	619
Grundy	13,787	Altamont	361
Hamblen	49,300	Morristown	116
Hamilton	287,740	Chattanooga	539
Hancock	6,887	Sneedville	223
Hardeman	23,873	Bolivar	670
Hardin	22,280	Savannah	578
Hawkins	43,751	Rogersville	486
Haywood	20,318	Brownsville	534
Henderson	21,390	Lexington	520
Henry	28,656	Paris	560
Hickman	15,151	Centerville	610
Houston	6,871	Erin	200
Humphreys	15,957	Waverly	528
Jackson	9,398	Gainesboro	308
Jefferson	31,284	Dandridge	265
Johnson	13,745	Mountain City	297
Knox	319,694	Knoxville	506
Lake	7,455	Tiptonville	169
Lauderdale	24,555	Ripley	474
Lawrence	34,110	Lawrenceburg	617
Lewis	9,700	Hohenwald	282
Lincoln	26,483	Fayetteville	571
Loudon	28,553	Loudon	235
McMinn	41,878	Athens	429
McNairy	22,525	Selmer	562
Macon	15,700	Lafayette	307
Madison	74,546	Jackson	558
Marion	24,416	Jasper	512
Marshall	19,698	Lewisburg	376
Maury	51,095	Columbia	616
Meigs	7,431	Decatur	189
Monroe	28,700	Madisonville	648
Montgomery	83,342	Clarksville	539
Moore	4,510	Lynchburg	129
Morgan	16,604	Wartburg	523
Obion	32,781	Union City	550
Overton	17,575	Livingston	433
Perry	6,111	Linden	412
Pickett	4,358	Byrdstown	159

County	Pop.	County seat or court house	Land area sq. mi.
Polk	13,602	Benton	438
Putnam	47,601	Cookeville	399
Rhea	24,235	Dayton	309
Roane	48,425	Kingston	357
Robertson	37,021	Springfield	476
Rutherford	84,058	Murfreesboro	606
Scott	19,259	Huntsville	528
Sequatchie	8,605	Dunlap	266
Sevier	41,418	Sevierville	590
Shelby	777,113	Memphis	772
Smith	14,935	Carthage	313
Stewart	8,665	Dover	454
Sullivan	143,968	Blountville	415
Sumner	85,790	Gallatin	529
Tipton	32,747	Covington	454
Trousdale	6,137	Hartsville	114
Unicoi	16,362	Erwin	186
Union	11,707	Maynardville	218
Van Buren	4,728	Spencer	273
Warren	32,653	McMinnville	431
Washington	88,755	Jonesboro	326
Wayne	13,946	Waynesboro	734
Weakley	32,896	Dresden	581
White	19,567	Sparta	373
Williamson	58,108	Franklin	584
Wilson	56,064	Lebanon	570

Texas

(254 counties, 262,017 sq. mi. land; pop., 14,227,799)

County	Pop.	County seat or court house	Land area sq. mi.
Anderson	38,381	Palestine	1,077
Andrews	13,323	Andrews	1,501
Angelina	64,172	Lufkin	807
Aransas	14,260	Rockport	280
Archer	7,266	Archer City	907
Armstrong	1,994	Claude	909
Atascosa	25,055	Jourdanton	1,218
Austin	17,726	Bellville	656
Bailey	8,168	Muleshoe	826
Bandera	7,084	Bandera	793
Bastrop	24,726	Bastrop	895
Baylor	4,919	Seymour	862
Bee	26,030	Beeville	880
Bell	157,820	Belton	1,055
Bexar	988,971	San Antonio	1,248
Blanco	4,681	Johnson City	714
Borden	859	Gail	900
Bosque	13,401	Meridian	989
Bowie	75,301	Boston	891
Brazoria	169,587	Angleton	1,407
Brazos	93,588	Bryan	589
Brewster	7,573	Alpine	6,169
Briscoe	2,579	Silverton	887
Brooks	8,428	Falfurrias	942
Brown	33,057	Brownwood	936
Burleson	12,313	Caldwell	669
Burnet	17,803	Burnet	994
Caldwell	23,637	Lockhart	546
Calhoun	19,574	Port Lavaca	540
Callahan	10,992	Baird	899
Cameron	209,680	Brownsville	906
Camp	9,275	Pittsburg	203
Carson	6,672	Panhandle	924
Cass	29,430	Linden	937
Castro	10,556	Dimmitt	899
Chambers	18,538	Anahuac	616
Cherokee	38,127	Rusk	1,052
Childress	6,950	Childress	707
Clay	9,582	Henrietta	1,086
Cochran	4,825	Morton	775
Coke	3,196	Robert Lee	908
Coleman	10,439	Coleman	1,277
Collin	144,490	McKinney	851
Collingsworth	4,648	Wellington	909
Colorado	18,823	Columbus	965
Comal	36,446	New Braunfels	555
Comanche	12,617	Comanche	930
Concho	2,915	Paint Rock	992
Cooke	27,656	Gainesville	893
Coryell	56,767	Gatesville	1,057
Cottle	2,947	Paducah	895
Crane	4,600	Crane	782
Crockett	4,608	4,588 Ozona	2,806
Crosby	8,859	Crosbyton	899
Culberson	3,315	Van Horn	3,815
Dallam	6,531	Dalhart	1,505
Dallas	1,556,419	Dallas	880
Dawson	16,184	Lamesa	903
Deaf Smith	21,165	Hereford	1,497
Delta	4,839	Cooper	278
Denton	143,126	Denton	911
Dewitt	18,903	Cuero	910
Dickens	3,539	Dickens	907
Dimmit	11,367	Carrizo Springs	1,307
Donley	4,075	Clarendon	929
Duval	12,517	San Diego	1,795
Eastland	19,480	Eastland	924
Ector	115,374	Odessa	903
Edwards	2,033	Rocksprings	2,121
Ellis	59,743	Waxahachie	939
El Paso	479,899	El Paso	1,014
Erath	22,560	Stephenville	1,080
Falls	17,946	Marlin	770
Fannin	24,285	Bonham	895
Fayette	18,832	La Grange	950
Fisher	5,891	Roby	897
Floyd	9,834	Floydada	992
Foard	2,158	Crowell	703
Fort Bend	130,962	Richmond	876
Franklin	6,893	Mount Vernon	294
Freestone	14,830	Fairfield	888
Frio	13,785	Pearsall	1,133
Gaines	13,150	Seminole	1,504
Galveston	195,738	Galveston	399
Garza	5,336	Post	895
Gillespie	13,532	Fredericksburg	1,061
Glasscock	1,304	Garden City	900
Goliad	5,193	Goliad	859
Gonzales	16,949	Gonzales	1,068
Gray	26,386	Pampa	921
Grayson	89,796	Sherman	934
Gregg	99,495	Longview	273
Grimes	13,580	Anderson	799
Guadalupe	46,708	Seguin	713
Hale	37,592	Plainview	1,005
Hall	5,594	Memphis	877
Hamilton	8,297	Hamilton	836
Hansford	6,209	Spearman	921
Hardeman	6,368	Quanah	688
Hardin	40,721	Kountze	898
Harris	2,409,544	Houston	1,734
Harrison	52,265	Marshall	908
Hartley	3,987	Channing	1,462
Haskell	7,725	Haskell	901
Hays	40,594	San Marcos	678
Hemphill	5,304	Canadian	903
Henderson	42,606	Athens	888
Hidalgo	283,323	Edinburg	1,569
Hill	25,024	Hillsboro	968
Hockley	23,230	Levelland	908
Hood	17,714	Granbury	425
Hopkins	25,247	Sulphur Springs	789
Houston	22,299	Crockett	1,234
Howard	33,142	Big Spring	901
Hudspeth	2,728	Sierra Blanca	4,567
Hunt	55,248	Greenville	840
Hutchinson	26,304	Stinnett	872
Irion	1,386	Mertzon	1,052
Jack	7,408	Jacksboro	920
Jackson	13,352	Edna	844
Jasper	30,781	Jasper	921
Jeff Davis	1,647	Fort Davis	2,257
Jefferson	250,938	Beaumont	937
Jim Hogg	5,168	Hebbronville	1,136
Jim Wells	36,498	Alice	867
Johnson	67,649	Cleburne	730
Jones	17,268	Anson	931
Karnes	13,593	Karnes City	753
Kaufman	39,038	Kaufman	788
Kendall	10,635	Boerne	663
Kenedy	543	Sarita	1,389
Kent	1,145	Jayton	878
Kerr	28,780	Kerrville	1,107
Kimble	4,063	Junction	1,250
King	425	Guthrie	914
Kinney	2,279	Brackettville	1,359
Kleberg	33,358	Kingsville	853
Knox	5,329	Benjamin	845
Lamar	42,156	Paris	919
Lamb	18,669	Littlefield	1,013
Lampasas	12,005	Lampasas	714
La Salle	5,514	Cotulla	1,517
Lavaca	19,004	Hallettsville	971
Lee	10,952	Giddings	631
Leon	9,594	Centerville	1,079
Liberty	47,088	Liberty	1,174
Limestone	20,224	Groesbeck	930
Lipscomb	3,766	Lipscomb	933
Live Oak	9,606	George West	1,057
Llano	10,144	Llano	939
Loving	91	Mentone	670
Lubbock	211,651	Lubbock	900
Lynn	8,605	Tahoka	888
McCulloch	8,735	Brady	1,071
McLennan	170,755	Waco	1,031
McMullen	789	Tilden	1,163
Madison	10,649	Madisonville	472
Marion	10,360	Jefferson	385
Martin	4,684	Staton	914
Mason	3,683	Mason	934
Matagorda	37,828	Bay City	1,127
Maverick	31,398	Eagle Pass	1,280
Medina	23,164	Hondo	1,331
Menard	2,346	Menard	902
Midland	82,636	Midland	902
Milam	22,732	Cameron	1,019
Mills	4,477	Goldthwaite	748
Mitchell	9,088	Colorado City	912
Montague	17,410	Montague	928
Montgomery	127,222	Conroe	1,047

County	Pop.	County seat or court house	Land area sq. mi.
Moore	16,575	Dumas	905
Morris	14,629	Daingerfield	256
Motley	1,950	Matador	959
Nacogdoches	46,786	Nacogdoches	939
Navarro	35,323	Corsicana	1,068
Newton	13,254	Newton	935
Nolan	17,359	Sweetwater	915
Nueces	268,215	Corpus Christi	847
Ochiltree	9,588	Perryton	919
Oldham	2,283	Vega	1,485
Orange	83,838	Orange	362
Palo Pinto	24,062	Palo Pinto	949
Panola	20,724	Carthage	812
Parker	44,609	Weatherford	902
Parmer	11,038	Farwell	885
Pecos	14,618	Fort Stockton	4,777
Polk	24,407	Livingston	1,061
Potter	98,637	Amarillo	902
Presidio	5,188	Marfa	3,857
Rains	4,839	Emory	243
Randall	75,062	Canyon	917
Reagan	4,135	Big Lake	1,173
Real	2,469	Leakey	697
Red River	16,101	Clarksville	1,054
Reeves	15,801	Pecos	2,626
Refugio	9,289	Refugio	771
Roberts	1,187	Miami	915
Robertson	14,653	Franklin	864
Rockwall	14,528	Rockwall	128
Runnels	11,872	Ballinger	1,056
Rusk	41,382	Henderson	932
Sabine	8,702	Hemphill	486
San Augustine	8,785	San Augustine	524
San Jacinto	11,434	Coldspring	572
San Patricio	58,013	Sinton	693
San Saba	5,841	San Saba	1,136
Schleicher	2,820	Eldorado	1,309
Scurry	18,192	Snyder	900
Shackelford	3,915	Albany	915
Shelby	23,084	Center	791
Sherman	3,174	Stratford	923
Smith	128,366	Tyler	932
Somervell	4,154	Glen Rose	188
Starr	27,266	Rio Grande City	1,226
Stephens	9,926	Breckenridge	894
Sterling	1,206	Sterling City	923
Stonewall	2,406	Aspermont	925
Sutton	5,130	5,120 Sonora	1,455
Swisher	9,723	Tulia	902
Tarrant	860,880	Fort Worth	868
Taylor	110,932	Abilene	917
Terrell	1,595	Sanderson	2,357
Terry	14,581	Brownfield	887
Throckmorton	2,053	Throckmorton	912
Titus	21,442	Mount Pleasant	412
Tom Green	84,784	San Angelo	1,515
Travis	419,335	Austin	989
Trinity	9,450	Groveton	692
Tyler	16,223	Woodville	922
Upshur	28,595	Gilmer	587
Upton	4,619	Rankin	1,243
Uvalde	22,441	Uvalde	1,564
Val Verde	35,910	Del Rio	3,150
Van Zandt	31,426	Canton	855
Victoria	68,807	Victoria	887
Walker	41,789	Huntsville	786
Waller	19,798	Hempstead	514
Ward	13,976	Monahans	836
Washington	21,998	Brenham	610
Webb	99,258	Laredo	3,362
Wharton	40,242	Wharton	1,086
Wheeler	7,137	Wheeler	904
Wichita	121,082	Wichita Falls	606
Wilbarger	15,931	Vernon	947
Willacy	17,495	Raymondville	589
Williamson	76,521	Georgetown	1,137
Wilson	16,756	Floresville	807
Winkler	9,944	Kermit	840
Wise	26,525	Decatur	902
Wood	24,697	Quitman	689
Yoakum	8,299	Plains	800
Young	19,001	Graham	919
Zapata	6,628	Zapata	999
Zavala	11,666	Crystal City	1,298

Utah

(29 counties, 82,073 sq. mi. land; pop. 1,461,037)

County	Pop.	County seat	Land area
Beaver	4,378	Beaver	2,586
Box Elder	33,222	Brigham City	5,614
Cache	57,176	Logan	1,171
Carbon	22,179	Price	1,479
Daggett	769	Manila	699
Davis	146,540	Farmington	299
Duchesne	12,565	Duchesne	3,233
Emery	11,451	Castle Dale	4,449
Garfield	3,673	Panguitch	5,148
Grand	8,241	Moab	3,689
Iron	17,349	Parowan	3,301

Juab	5,530	Nephi	3,396
Kane	4,024	Kanab	3,898
Millard	8,970	Fillmore	6,818
Morgan	4,917	Morgan	603
Piute	1,329	Junction	759
Rich	2,100	Randolph	1,034
Salt Lake	619,066	Salt Lake City	756
San Juan	12,253	Monticello	7,725
Sanpete	14,620	Manti	1,587
Sevier	14,727	Richfield	1,910
Summit	10,198	Coalville	1,865
Tooele	26,033	Tooele	6,919
Uintah	20,506	Vernal	4,479
Utah	218,106	Provo	2,018
Wasatch	8,523	Heber City	1,191
Washington	26,065	Saint George	2,422
Wayne	1,911	Loa	2,461
Weber	144,616	Ogden	566

Vermont

(14 counties, 9,273 sq. mi. land; pop. 511,456)

County	Pop.	County seat	Land area
Addison	29,406	Middlebury	773
Bennington	33,345	Bennington	677
Caledonia	25,808	Saint Johnsbury	651
Chittenden	115,534	Burlington	540
Essex	6,313	Guildhall	666
Franklin	34,788	Saint Albans	649
Grand Isle	4,613	North Hero	89
Lamoille	16,767	Hyde Park	461
Orange	22,739	Chelsea	690
Orleans	23,440	Newport	697
Rutland	58,347	Rutland	932
Washington	52,393	Montpelier	690
Windham	36,933	Newfane	787
Windsor	51,030	Woodstock	972

Virginia

(95 cos., 41 ind. cities, 39,704 sq. mi. land; pop. 5,346,797)

County	Pop.	County seat	Land area
Accomack	31,268	Accomac	476
Albemarle	50,689	Charlottesville	725
Alleghany	14,333	Covington	446
Amelia	8,405	Amelia, C.H.	357
Amherst	29,122	Amherst	479
Appomattox	11,971	Appomattox	336
Arlington	152,599	Arlington	26
Augusta	53,732	Staunton	989
Bath	5,860	Warm Springs	538
Bedford	34,927	Bedford	747
Bland	6,349	Bland	359
Botetourt	23,270	Fincastle	545
Brunswick	15,632	Lawrenceville	563
Buchanan	37,989	Grundy	504
Buckingham	11,751	Buckingham	583
Campbell	45,424	Rustburg	505
Caroline	17,904	Bowling Green	535
Carroll	27,270	Hillsville	478
Charles City	6,692	Charles City	181
Charlotte	12,266	Charlotte Courthouse	477
Chesterfield	141,372	Chesterfield	434
Clarke	9,965	Berryville	178
Craig	3,948	New Castle	330
Culpeper	22,620	Culpeper	382
Cumberland	7,881	Cumberland	300
Dickenson	19,806	Clintwood	331
Dinwiddie	22,602	Dinwiddie	507
Essex	8,864	Tappahannock	263
Fairfax	596,901	Fairfax	394
Fauquier	35,889	Warrenton	651
Floyd	11,563	Floyd	381
Fluvanna	10,244	Palmyra	290
Franklin	35,740	Rocky Mount	683
Frederick	34,150	Winchester	415
Giles	17,810	Pearisburg	362
Gloucester	20,107	Gloucester	225
Goochland	11,761	Goochland	281
Grayson	16,579	Independence	446
Greene	7,625	Stanardsville	157
Greensville	10,903	Emporia	300
Halifax	30,418	Halifax	816
Hanover	50,398	Hanover	467
Henrico	180,735	Richmond	238
Henry	57,654	Martinsville	382
Highland	2,937	Monterey	416
Isle of Wight	21,603	Isle of Wight	319
James City	22,763	Williamsburg	153
King and Queen	5,968	King and Queen	317
King George	10,543	King George	180
King William	9,327	King William	278
Lancaster	10,129	Lancaster	133
Lee	25,956	Jonesville	437
Loudoun	57,427	Leesburg	521
Louisa	17,825	Louisa	497
Lunenburg	12,124	Lunenburg	432
Madison	10,232	Madison	322
Mathews	7,995	Mathews	87
Mecklenburg	29,444	Boydton	616
Middlesex	7,719	Saluda	134
Montgomery	63,516	Christiansburg	390
Nelson	12,204	Lovingston	474
New Kent	8,781	New Kent	213

County	Pop.	County seat or court house	Land area sq. mi.
Northampton	14,625	Eastville	226
Northumberland	9,828	Heathsville	185
Nottoway	14,666	Nottoway	316
Orange	17,827	Orange	342
Page	19,401	Luray	313
Patrick	17,585	Stuart	481
Pittsylvania	66,147	Chatham	995
Powhatan	13,062	Powhatan	261
Prince Edward	16,456	Farmville	354
Prince George	25,733	Prince George	266
Prince William	144,703	Manassas	339
Pulaski	35,229	Pulaski	318
Rappahannock	6,093	Washington	267
Richmond	6,952	Warsaw	193
Roanoke	72,945	Salem	251
Rockbridge	17,911	Lexington	603
Rockingham	57,038	Harrisonburg	865
Russell	31,761	Lebanon	479
Scott	25,068	Gate City	535
Shenandoah	27,559	Woodstock	512
Smyth	33,345	Marion	452
Southampton	18,731	Courtland	603
Spotsylvania	34,435	Spotsylvania	404
Stafford	40,470	Stafford	271
Surry	6,046	Surry	281
Sussex	10,874	Sussex	491
Tazewell	50,511	Tazewell	520
Warren	21,200	Front Royal	217
Washington	46,487	Abingdon	562
Westmoreland	14,041	Montross	227
Wise	43,863	Wise	405
Wythe	25,522	Wytheville	465
York	35,463	Yorktown	113

Independent cities

City	Pop.	Land area sq. mi.
Alexandria	103,217	15
Bedford	5,991	7
Bristol	19,042	12
Buena Vista	6,717	3
Charlottesville	45,010	10
Chesapeake	114,226	340
Clifton Forge	5,046	3
Colonial Heights	16,509	8
Covington	9,063	4
Danville	45,642	17
Emporia	4,840	2
Fairfax	19,390	6
Falls Church	9,515	2
l,1 Franklin	7,308	4
Fredericksburg	15,322	6
Galax	6,524	8
Hampton	122,617	51
Harrisonburg	19,671	6
Hopewell	23,397	10
Lexington	7,292	2
Lynchburg	66,743	50
Manassas	15,438	8
Manassas Park	6,524	2
Martinsville	18,149	11
Newport News	144,903	65
Norfolk	266,979	53
Norton	4,757	7
Petersburg	41,055	23
Poquoson	8,726	17
Portsmouth	104,577	30
Radford	13,225	7
Richmond	219,214	60
Roanoke	100,427	43
Salem	23,958	14
South Boston	7,093	6
Staunton	21,857	9
Suffolk	47,621	409
Virginia Beach	262,199	256
Waynesboro	15,329	8
Williamsburg	9,870	5
Winchester	20,217	9

Washington

(39 counties, 66,511 sq. mi. land; pop., 4,132,353)

County	Pop.	County seat	Land area sq. mi.
Adams	13,267	Ritzville	1,921
Asotin	16,823	Asotin	635
Benton	109,444	Prosser	1,715
Chelan	45,061	Wenatchee	2,916
Clallam	51,648	Port Angeles	1,753
Clark	192,227	Vancouver	627
Columbia	4,057	Dayton	865
Cowlitz	79,548	Kelso	1,140
Douglas	22,144	Waterville	1,817
Ferry	5,811	Republic	2,200
Franklin	35,025	Pasco	1,243
Garfield	2,468	Pomeroy	706
Grant	48,522	Ephrata	2,660
Grays Harbor	66,314	Montesano	1,918
Island	44,048	Coupeville	208
Jefferson	15,965	Port Townsend	1,805
King	1,269,898	Seattle	2,128
Kitsap	146,609	Port Orchard	393
Kittitas	24,877	Ellensburg	2,308
Klickitat	15,822	Goldendale	1,880
Lewis	55,279	Chehalis	2,409
Lincoln	9,604	Davenport	2,310
Mason	31,184	Shelton	961
Okanogan	30,663	Okanogan	5,281
Pacific	17,237	South Bend	908
Pend Oreille	8,580	Newport	1,400
Pierce	485,667	Tacoma	1,675
San Juan	7,838	Friday Harbor	179
Skagit	64,138	Mount Vernon	1,735
Skamania	7,919	Stevenson	1,672
Snohomish	337,016	Everett	2,098
Spokane	341,835	Spokane	1,762
Stevens	28,979	Colville	2,470
Thurston	124,264	Olympia	727
Wahkiakum	3,832	Cathlamet	261
Walla Walla	47,435	Walla Walla	1,261
Whatcom	106,701	Bellingham	2,125
Whitman	40,103	Colfax	2,151
Yakima	172,508	Yakima	4,287

West Virginia

(55 counties, 24,119 sq. mi. land; pop., 1,950,186)

County	Pop.	County seat	Land area sq. mi.
Barbour	16,639	Philippi	343
Berkeley	46,775	Martinsburg	321
Boone	30,447	Madison	503
Braxton	13,894	Sutton	513
Brooke	31,117	Wellsburg	90
Cabell	106,835	Huntington	282
Calhoun	8,250	Grantsville	280
Clay	11,265	Clay	346
Doddridge	7,433	West Union	321
Fayette	57,863	Fayetteville	667
Gilmer	8,334	Glenville	340
Grant	10,210	Petersburg	480
Greenbrier	37,665	Lewisburg	1,025
Hampshire	14,867	Romney	644
Hancock	41,053	New Cumberland	84
Hardy	10,030	Moorefield	585
Harrison	77,710	Clarksburg	417
Jackson	25,794	Ripley	464
Jefferson	30,302	Charles Town	209
Kanawha	231,414	Charleston	901
Lewis	18,813	Weston	389
Lincoln	23,675	Hamlin	439
Logan	50,679	Logan	456
McDowell	49,899	Welch	535
Marion	65,789	Fairmont	312
Marshall	41,608	Moundsville	305
Mason	27,045	Point Pleasant	433
Mercer	73,870	Princeton	420
Mineral	27,234	Keyser	329
Mingo	37,336	Williamson	424
Monongalia	75,024	Morgantown	363
Monroe	12,873	Union	473
Morgan	10,711	Berkeley Springs	230
Nicholas	28,126	Summersville	650
Ohio	61,389	Wheeling	106
Pendleton	7,910	Franklin	698
Pleasants	8,236	St. Marys	131
Pocahontas	9,919	Marlinton	942
Preston	30,460	Kingwood	651
Putnam	38,181	Winfield	346
Raleigh	86,821	Beckley	608
Randolph	28,734	Elkins	1,040
Ritchie	11,442	Harrisville	454
Roane	15,952	Spencer	484
Summers	15,875	Hinton	353
Taylor	16,584	Grafton	174
Tucker	8,675	Parsons	421
Tyler	11,320	Middlebourne	258
Upshur	23,427	Buckhannon	355
Wayne	46,021	Wayne	508
Webster	12,245	Webster Springs	556
Wetzel	21,874	New Martinsville	359
Wirt	4,922	Elizabeth	235
Wood	93,627	Parkersburg	367
Wyoming	35,993	Pineville	502

Wisconsin

(72 counties, 54,426 sq. mi. land; pop., 4,705,642)

County	Pop.	County seat	Land area sq. mi.
Adams	13,457	Friendship	648
Ashland	16,783	Ashland	1,048
Barron	38,730	Barron	865
Bayfield	13,822	Washburn	1,462
Brown	175,280	Green Bay	524
Buffalo	14,309	Alma	699
Burnett	12,340	Grantsburg	818
Calumet	30,867	Chilton	326
Chippewa	51,702	Chippewa Falls	1,017
Clark	32,910	Neillsville	1,218
Columbia	43,222	Portage	771
Crawford	16,556	Prairie du Chien	566
Dane	323,545	Madison	1,205
Dodge	74,747	Juneau	887
Door	25,029	Sturgeon Bay	492
Douglas	44,421	Superior	1,305
Dunn	34,314	Menomonie	853
Eau Claire	78,805	Eau Claire	638
Florence	4,172	Florence	486

County	Pop.	County seat or court house	Land area sq. ml.
Fond Du Lac	88,952	Fond du Lac	725
Forest	9,044	Crandon	1,011
Grant	51,736	Lancaster	1,144
Green	30,012	Monroe	583
Green Lake	18,370	Green Lake	357
Iowa	19,802	Dodgeville	760
Iron	6,730	Hurley	751
Jackson	16,831	Black River Falls	998
Jefferson	66,152	Jefferson	562
Juneau	21,037	Mauston	774
Kenosha	123,137	Kenosha	273
Kewaunee	19,539	Kewaunee	343
La Crosse	91,056	La Crosse	457
Lafayette	17,412	Darlington	634
Langlade	19,978	Antigo	873
Lincoln	26,311	Merrill	886
Manitowoc	82,918	Manitowoc	594
Marathon	111,270	Wausau	1,559
Marinette	39,314	Marinette	1,395
Marquette	11,672	Montello	455
Menominee	3,373	Keshena	359
Milwaukee	964,988	Milwaukee	241
Monroe	35,074	Sparta	904
Oconto	28,947	Oconto	1,002
Oneida	31,216	Rhinelander	1,130
Outagamie	128,730	Appleton	642
Ozaukee	66,981	Port Washington	235
Pepin	7,477	Durand	231
Pierce	31,149	Ellsworth	577
Polk	32,351	Balsam Lake	919
Portage	57,420	Stevens Point	810
Price	15,788	Phillips	1,256
Racine	173,132	Racine	335
Richland	17,476	Richland Center	585
Rock	139,420	Janesville	723
Rusk	15,589	Ladysmith	913
St. Croix	43,872	Hudson	723
Sauk	43,469	Baraboo	838

	Pop.		
Sawyer	12,843	Hayward	1,255
Shawano	35,928	Shawano	897
Sheboygan	100,935	Sheboygan	515
Taylor	18,817	Medford	975
Trempealeau	26,158	Whitehall	736
Vernon	25,642	Viroqua	808
Vilas	16,535	Eagle River	867
Walworth	71,507	Elkhorn	556
Washburn	13,174	Shell Lake	815
Washington	84,848	West Bend	430
Waukesha	280,203	Waukesha	554
Waupaca	42,831	Waupaca	754
Waushara	18,526	Wautoma	628
Winnebago	131,772	Oshkosh	449
Wood	72,799	Wisconsin Rapids	801

Wyoming

(23 counties, 96,989 sq. mi. land; pop., 469,557)

County	Pop.	County seat	Land area sq. ml.
Albany	29,062	Laramie	4,268
Big Horn	11,896	Basin	3,139
Campbell	24,367	Gillette	4,796
Carbon	21,896	Rawlins	7,877
Converse	14,069	Douglas	4,271
Crook	5,308	Sundance	2,855
Fremont	40,251	Lander	9,181
Goshen	12,040	Torrington	2,186
Hot Springs	5,710	Thermopolis	2,005
Johnson	6,700	Buffalo	4,166
Laramie	68,649	Cheyenne	2,684
Lincoln	12,177	Kemmerer	4,070
Natrona	71,856	Casper	5,347
Niobrara	2,924	Lusk	2,684
Park	21,639	Cody	6,936
Platte	11,975	Wheatland	2,023
Sheridan	25,048	Sheridan	2,532
Sublette	4,548	Pinedale	4,872
Sweetwater	41,723	Green River	10,352
Teton	9,355	Jackson	4,011
Uinta	13,021	Evanston	2,085
Washakie	9,496	Worland	2,243
Weston	7,106	Newcastle	2,402

Population of Outlying Areas

Source: U.S. Bureau of the Census
Population figures are final counts from the census conducted on Apr. 1, 1980.

Puerto Rico

ZIP code	Municipios	Pop.	Land area sq. mile	ZIP code	Municipios	Pop.	Land area sq. mile	ZIP code	Municipios	Pop.	Land area sq. mile
00601	Adjuntas	18,786	67	00650	Florida	7,232	10	00720	Orocovis	19,332	64
00602	Aguada	31,567	31	00653	Guanica	18,799	37	00723	Patillas	17,774	47
00603	Aguadilla	54,606	37	00654	Guayama	40,183	65	00724	Penuelas	19,116	45
00607	Aguas Buenas	22,429	30	00656	Guayanilla	21,050	42	00731	Ponce	189,046	117
00609	Aibonito	22,167	31	00657	Guaynabo	80,742	27	00742	Quebradillas	19,728	23
00610	Anasco	23,274	40	00658	Gurabo	23,574	28	00743	Rincon	11,788	14
00612	Arecibo	86,766	127	00659	Hatillo	28,958	42	00745	Rio Grande	34,283	62
00615	Arroyo	17,014	15	00660	Hormigueros	14,030	11	00747	Sabana Grande	20,207	36
00617	Barceloneta	18,942	24	00661	Humacao	46,134	45	00751	Salinas	26,438	71
00618	Barranquitas	21,639	34	00662	Isabela	37,435	56	00753	San German	32,922	54
00619	Bayamon	196,206	45	00664	Jayuya	14,722	44	*00936	San Juan	434,849	47
00623	Cabo Rojo	34,045	72	00665	Juana Diaz	43,505	61	00754	San Lorenzo	32,428	53
00625	Caguas	117,959	59	00666	Juncos	25,397	27	00755	San Sebastian	35,690	71
00627	Camuy	24,884	47	00667	Lajas	21,236	60	00757	Santa Isabel	19,854	35
00629	Canovanas	31,880	33	00669	Lares	26,743	62	00758	Toa Alta	31,910	28
00630	Carolina	165,954	48	00670	Las Marias	8,747	46	00759	Toa Baja	78,246	24
00632	Catano	26,243	6	00671	Las Piedras	22,412	34	00760	Trujillo Alto	51,389	21
00633	Cayey	41,099	52	00672	Loiza	20,867	21	00761	Utuado	34,505	115
00635	Ceiba	14,944	27	00673	Luquillo	14,895	26	00762	Vega Alta	28,696	28
00638	Ciales	16,211	67	00701	Manati	36,562	46	00763	Vega Baja	47,115	48
00639	Cidra	28,365	36	00706	Maricao	6,737	37	00765	Vieques	7,662	53
00640	Coamo	30,822	78	00707	Maunabo	11,813	21	00766	Villalba	20,734	37
00642	Comerio	18,212	29	00708	Mayaguez	96,193	77	00767	Yabucoa	31,425	55
00643	Corozal	28,221	43	00716	Moca	29,185	50	00768	Yauco	37,742	69
00645	Culebra	1,265	13	00717	Morovis	21,142	39	Total		3,196,520	3,459
00646	Dorado	25,511	24	00718	Naguabo	20,617	52				
00648	Fajardo	32,087	31	00719	Naranjito	23,633	28				

ZIP code	Area	Pop.	Land area sq. mile	ZIP code	Area	Pop.	Land area sq. mile	ZIP code	Area	Pop.	Land area sq. mile
	American Samoa				Mongmong-Toto-Maite	5,245	2	00820	Christiansted	2,904	
96799	American Samoa	32,297	77		Piti	2,866	7	00840	Frederiksted	1,046	
				96915	Santa Rita	9,183	17	Total		96,569	132
	Guam				Sinajana	2,485	1				
96910	Agana	896	1		Talofofo	2,006	17		**Trust Territory of Pacific Islands**		
	Agana Hts	3,284	1	96911	Tamuning	13,580	6				
96915	Agat	3,999	10		Umatac	732	6		Kosrae	NA	42
	Asan	2,034	6		Yigo	10,359	35		Marshall Islands	NA	70
96913	Barrigada	7,756	9	96914	Yona	4,228	20		Palau	NA	192
	Chalan-Pago-Ordot	3,120	6		Total	105,979	209		Ponape	NA	176
96912	Dededo	23,644	30						Truk	NA	49
96916	Inarajan	2,059	19		**Virgin Islands**				Yap	NA	46
	Mangilao	6,840	10		St. Croix	49,725	80		Total	NA	533
96916	Merizo	1,663	6		St. John	2,472	20				
					St. Thomas	44,372	32		**No. Mariana Islands**	16,758	184
				00801	Charlotte Amalie	11,671					

UNITED STATES GOVERNMENT

The Reagan Administration

As of mid-1985

Terms of office of the president and vice president, from Jan. 20, 1985 to Jan. 20, 1989. No person may be elected president of the United States for more than two 4-year terms.

President — Ronald Reagan of California receives salary of $200,000 a year taxable; in addition an expense allowance of $50,000 to assist in defraying expenses resulting from his official duties. Also there may be expended not exceeding $100,000, nontaxable, a year for travel expenses and $20,000 for official entertainment available for allocation within the Executive Office of the President. Congress has provided lifetime pensions of $69,630 a year, free mailing privileges, free office space, and up to $96,000 a year for office help for former Presidents except for the first 30 month period during which a former President is entitled to staff assistance for which an amount up to $150,000 a year may be paid, and $20,000 annually for their widows.

Vice President — George Bush of Texas receives salary of $91,000 a year and $10,000 for expenses, all of which is taxable.

For succession to presidency, see Succession in Index.

The Cabinet

(Salary: $80,100 per annum)
Secretary of State — George P. Shultz, Cal.
Secretary of Treasury — James A. Baker 3d, Tex.
Secretary of Defense — Caspar W. Weinberger, Cal.
Attorney General — Edwin Meese 3d, Cal.
Secretary of Interior — William P. Clark, Cal.
Secretary of Agriculture — Donald P. Hodel, Ore.
Secretary of Commerce — Malcolm Baldrige, Conn.
Secretary of Labor — William E. Brock, Tenn.
Secretary of Health and Human Services — Margaret M. Heckler, Mass.
Secretary of Housing and Urban Development — Samuel R. Pierce Jr., N.Y.
Secretary of Transportation — Elizabeth Hanford Dole, Kan.
Secretary of Energy — John S. Herrington, Cal.
Secretary of Education — William J. Bennett, N.Y.

The White House Staff

1600 Pennsylvania Ave. NW 20500
Chief of Staff — Donald T. Regan.
Assistants to the President
  Press Secy. — James S. Brady.
  Counsel to the President — Fred F. Fielding.
  Deputy Press Secy. — Larry Speakes.
  Legislative Strategy Coordinator — Max L. Friedesdorf.
  Political & Governmental — Edward Rollins.
  Communications Director — Patrick J. Buchanan.
  Special Support Services — Edward V. Hickey Jr.
  Legislative Affairs — M. B. Oglesby.
  National Security Affairs — Robert C. McFarlane.
  Policy Development — John A. Svahn.

Executive Agencies

Council of Economic Advisers — Beryl Sprinkel.
Central Intelligence Agency — William J. Casey, dir.
Office of Management and Budget — James C. Miller 3d., dir.
U.S. Trade Representative — Clayton Yeutter.
Office of Administration — John F. W. Rogers, dir.
Office of Science and Technology Policy — George A. Keyworth 2d, dir.
Council on Environmental Quality — A. Alan Hill, chmn.

Department of State

2201 C St. NW 20520
Secretary of State — George P. Shultz.
Deputy Secretary — John C. Whitehead.
Under Sec. for Political Affairs — Michael Armacost.
Under Sec. for Security Assistance, Science and Technology — William Schneider.
Under Sec. for Economic Affairs — W. Allen Wallis.
Under Secretary for Management — Ronald I. Spiers.
Legal Advisor — Judge Abraham Sofaer.
Assistant Secretaries for:
  Administration — Robert E. Lamb.
  African Affairs — Chester Crocker.
  Congressional Relations — William L. Ball 3d.
  East Asian & Pacific Affairs — Paul Wolfowitz.
  Economic & Business Affairs — Douglas W. McMinn.
  European & Canadian Affairs — Richard Burt.
  Human Rights & Humanitarian Affairs — vacant.
  Inter-American Affairs — Elliot Abrams.
  International Organization Affairs — Alan Keys.
  Near-Eastern & S. Asian Affairs — Richard W. Murphy.
  Public Affairs — Bernard Kalb.
  Oceans, International Environmental & Scientific Affairs — John Negroponte.
Consular Affairs — Joan M. Clark.
Intl. Narcotics Matters — Jon R. Thomas.
Chief of Protocol — Selwa Roosevelt.
Dir. General, Foreign Service & Dir. of Personnel — George. S. Vest.
Dir. of Intelligence & Research — Morton Abramowitz.
Dir. of Politico-Military Affairs — John T. Chain Jr.
Dir. of Refugee Programs — James Purcell Jr.
Inspector General — William Harrop.
Policy Planning Staff — Peter Rodman.
Related Agencies:
  Arms Control & Disarmament Agency — Kenneth Adelman, dir.
  U.S. Information Agency — Charles Z. Wick, dir.
  Agency for International Development — M. Peter McPherson.
U.S. Rep. to the UN — Gen. Vernon Walters.

Treasury Department

1500 Pennsylvania Ave. NW 20220
Secretary of the Treasury — James A. Baker 3d.
Deputy Sec. of the Treasury — Richard Darman.
Under Sec. for Monetary Affairs — vacant.
General Counsel — vacant.
Assistant Secretaries: — John Walker, John Chapoton, Manuel Johnson, Carole Dineen, Margaret Tutwiler, John Rogers, Ronald Pearlman, David Mulford, Bruce Thompson, Thomas Dawson.
Bureaus:
  Comptroller of the Currency — vacant.
  Customs — William von Raab.
  Engraving & Printing — Robert J. Leuver, dir.
  Government Financial Operations — William E. Douglas, comm.
  Internal Revenue Service — Roscoe Egger, comm.
  Mint — Donna Pope, dir.
  Public Debt — W. M. Gregg, comm.
  Treasurer of the U.S. — Katherine Ortega.
  U.S. Secret Service — John R. Simpson, dir.

Department of Defense
The Pentagon 20301
Secretary of Defense — Caspar W. Weinberger.
Deputy Secretary — William H. Taft IV.
Asst. to the Secy. & Deputy Secy. of Defense — Marybel Batjer.
Executive Secretariat — Col. David R. Brown.
Under Secy. for Research & Engineering — vacant.
Under Secy. for Policy — Fred C. Ikle.
Asst. Secretaries of Defense:
  Atomic Energy — Richard Wagner.
  Command Control Communications & Intelligence — David C. Latham.
  Comptroller — Robert W. Helm.
  Health Affairs — Dr. William Mayer.
  International Security Affairs — Richard L. Armitage.
  International Security Policy — Richard N. Perle.
  Legislative Affairs — Russell A. Rourke.
  Manpower, Installations & Logistics — Lawrence J. Korb.
  Public Affairs — Michael I. Burch.
  Research & Technology — Robert S. Cooper.
  Reserve Affairs — James H. Webb.
Intelligence Oversight — Werner E. Michel.
Chairman, Joint Chiefs of Staff —Gen. William J. Crowe Jr.
General Counsel — Chapman B. Cox.

Department of the Army
The Pentagon 20301
Secretary of the Army — John O. Marsh Jr.
Under Secretary — James R. Ambrose.
Assistant Secretaries for:
  Civil Works — Robert K. Dawson.
  Installations & Logistics — John W. Shannon.
  Financial Management — Pat Hillier.
  Research, Development and Acquisition — Jay R. Sculley.
  Manpower & Reserve Affairs — Delbert L. Spurlock Jr.
Chief of Public Affairs — Charles D. Bussey.
Chief of Staff — Gen. John A. Wickham Jr.
Adjutant General — Gen. Robert M. Joyce.
Inspector General — Lt. Gen. Richard G. Trefry.
Deputy Chiefs of Staff:
  Logistics — Lt. Gen. Benjamin F. Register.
  Operations & Plans — Lt. Gen. F. K. Mahaffey.
  Research, Development, Acquisition — Lt. Gen. Louis C. Wagner Jr.
  Personnel — Lt. Gen. Robert M. Elton.
Commanders:
  U.S. Army Materiel Command — Gen. Richard H. Thompson.
  U.S. Army Forces Command — Gen. Robert W. Sennewald.
  U.S. Army Training and Doctrine Command — Gen. William R. Richardson.
  First U.S. Army — Lt. Gen. Charles D. Franklin.
  Second U.S. Army — Lt. Gen. Charles P. Graham.
  Third U.S. Army — Lt. Gen. Theodore G. Jones Jr.
  Fourth U.S. Army — Lt. Gen. Edward C. Peter 2d.
  Fifth U.S. Army — Lt. Gen. Louis Menetry.
  Sixth U.S. Army — Lt. Gen. Robert Arter.
  U.S. Army Europe & Seventh U.S. Army — Gen. Glen K. Otis.
  U.S. Forces Korea & Eighth U.S. Army — Gen. William J. Livsey.
  Military Dist. of Washington — Maj. Gen. John L. Ballantyne 3d.

Department of the Navy
The Pentagon 20350
Secretary of the Navy — John Lehman.
Under Secretary — James F. Goodrich.
Assistant Secretaries for:
Financial Management — Robert H. Conn.
Manpower, Reserve Affairs — Chase Untermeyer.

Research, Engineering & Systems — Melvyn Paisley.
  Shipbuilding & Logistics — vacant.
Judge Advocate General — RADM Thomas E. Flynn.
Chief of Naval Operations — ADM James D. Watkins.
Chief of Information — COMO Jack A. Garrow.
Naval Military Personnel Command — RADM David L. Harlow.
Military Sealift Command — VADM William H. Rowden.
Chief of Naval Personnel — VADM William P. Lawrence.
Commanders, Naval Bases:
  Philadelphia — RADM James W. Austin.
  Norfolk — RADM Jackson K. Parker.
  Charleston — RADM Don G. Primeau.
  San Diego — COMO Bruce R. Boland.
  Seattle — RADM Laverne S. Severance Jr.
  Pearl Harbor — RADM Henry F. Boyle Jr.
  Naval District Washington — COMO John W. Adams.

U.S. Marine Corps:
(Arlington Annex 20380)
Commandant — Gen. Paul X. Kelly.
  Asst. Commandant — Gen. John K. Davis.
  Chief of Staff — Lt. Gen. D'Wayne Gray.

Department of the Air Force
The Pentagon 20330
Secretary of the Air Force — Verne Orr.
Under Secretary — Edward C. Aldridge Jr.
Assistant Secretaries for:
  Financial Management — Richard E. Carver.
  Research, Development & Logistics — Dr. Thomas E. Cooper.
  Manpower, Reserve Affairs & Installations — Tidal W. McCoy.
Public Affairs — Col. Michael P. McRaney.
Director of Space Systems — Brig. Gen. Thomas S. Moorman Jr.
Chief of Staff — Gen. Charles A. Gabriel.
Inspector General — Lt. Gen. Monroe W. Hatch Jr.
Deputy Chiefs of Staff:
  Logistics & Engineering — Lt. Gen. Leo Marquez.
  Programs & Resources — Lt. Gen. Charles J. Cunningham Jr.
  Manpower & Personnel — Lt. Gen. Duane H. Cassidy.
  Research, Development & Acquisition — Lt. Gen. Robert D. Russ.
  Plans & Operations — Lt. Gen. David L. Nichols.
Major Air Commands:
  AF Logistics Command — Gen. Earl T. O'Loughlin.
  AF Systems Command — Gen. Lawrence A. Skantze.
  Strategic Air Command — Gen. Larry D. Welch.
  Tactical Air Command — Lt. Gen. Robert D. Russ.
  Alaskan Air Command — Lt. Gen. Bruce K. Brown.
  Pacific Air Forces — Gen. Robert W. Bazley.
  USAF Europe — Gen. Charles L. Donnelly Jr.
  Electronic Security Command — Brig. Gen. Paul H. Martin.
  AF Communications Command — Maj. Gen. Gerald L. Prather.
  Air Training & Command — Gen. Andrew P. Iosue.
  Military Airlift Command — Gen. Thomas M. Ryan Jr.
  Space Command — Gen. Robert T. Herres.

Department of Justice
Constitution Ave. & 10th St. NW 20530
Attorney General — Edwin Meese 3d.
Deputy Attorney General — D. Lowell Jensen.
Legal Policy — James M. Spears, act.
Legal Counsel — Ralph W. Tarr, act.
Intelligence Policy & Review — Mary Lawton.
Professional Responsibility —Michael E. Shaheen Jr.
Solicitor General — Charles Fried, act.
Associate Attorney General — vacant.
Antitrust Division — Charles F. Rule.
Civil Division — Richard Willard.

Civil Rights Division — vacant.
Criminal Division — Stephen Trott.
Drug Enforcement Admin. — John C. Lawn, act.
Justice Management Division — W. Lawrence Wallace, act.
Land & Natural Resources Division — F. Henry Habicht 3d.
Office of Legislative & Ingovernmental Affairs — Philip D. Brady, act.
Tax Division — Glenn L. Archer Jr.
Fed. Bureau of Investigation — William H. Webster, dir.
Exec. Off. for Immigration Review — David L. Milhollan, chmn.
Bureau of Prisons — Norman A. Carlson, dir.
Comm. Relations Service — Gilbert Pompa, dir.
Office of Justice Programs — Lois H. Harrington.
Exec. Off. for U.S. Trustees — Thomas Stanton, dir.
Exec. Off. for U.S. Attorneys — William P. Tyson, dir.
Office of Public Affairs — Terry H. Eastland.
Immigration and Naturalization Service — Alan C. Nelson, comm.
Pardon Attorney — D. C. Stephenson.
U.S. Parole Commission — Benjamin Baer, chmn.
U.S. Marshalls Service — Stanley Morris, dir.

Department of the Interior

C St. between 18th & 19th Sts. NW 20240
Secretary of the Interior — Donald P. Hodel.
Under Secretary — Ann D. McLaughlin.
Assistant Secretaries for:
    Fish, Wildlife and Parks — J. Craig Potter, act.
    Water & Science — Robert Broadbent.
    Land & Minerals Management — Steven Griles, act.
    Policy, Budget, and Administration — vacant.
    Indian Affairs — John Fritz, act.
    Territorial & Intl. Affairs — Richard Montoya.
Bureau of Land Management — Bob Burford, dir.
Bureau of Mines — Robert C. Horton, dir.
Bureau of Reclamation — Robert A. Olson, act. comm.
Fish & Wildlife Service — Robert A. Jantzen, dir.
Geological Survey — Dallas L. Peck, dir.
National Park Service — William Penn Mott.
Public Affairs — David Prosperi.
Office of Congressional and Legislative Affairs — Roger Brown.
Solicitor — Frank K. Richardson.

Department of Agriculture

The Mall, 12th & 14th Sts. 20250
Secretary of Agriculture — John R. Block.
Deputy Secretary — John R. Norton.
Executive Assistant — Randy Russell.
Administration — John Franke Jr.
Internat. Affairs & Commodity Programs — Daniel Amstutz.
Food & Consumer Services — Mary C. Jarratt.
Marketing & Inspection Services — Karen Darling, act.
Small Community & Rural Development — Frank Naylor Jr.
Economics — Robert L. Thompson.
Governmental & Public Affairs — Wilmer D. Mizell.
Natural Resources & Environment — Peter C. Myers.
General Counsel — Daniel Oliver.
Science & Education — Orville G. Bentley.
Inspector General — John V. Graziano.

Department of Commerce

14th St. between Constitution & E St. NW 20230
Secretary of Commerce — Malcolm Baldrige.
Deputy Secretary — Clarence J. Brown.
Congressional Affairs — Paul A. Vander Myde.
Inspector General — Sherman M. Funk.
General Counsel — Douglas A. Riggs.
Productivity, Technology & Innovation — D. Bruce Merrifield.

Administration — Katherine M. Bulow.
Bureau of the Census — John G. Keane, dir.
Bureau of Economic Analysis — Allan H. Young, act.
Under Secy. for International Trade — Lionel H. Olmer
Under Secy. for Econ. Affairs — Sidney L. Jones.
Natl. Oceanic & Atmospheric Admin. — Anthony Calio, act.
Natl. Technical Info. Service — Joseph F. Caponio.
Economic Develop. Admin. — Paul Batemen, act.
Natl. Bureau of Standards — Ernest Ambler, dir.
Minority Business Development Agency — James H. Richardson.
Natl. Telecomm. & Information Admin. — David G. Marley, dir.
U.S. Travel & Tourism Adm. — Donna F. Tuttle.
Patent & Trademark Office — Donald Quigg, act.
Public Affairs — B. Jay Cooper, dir.

Department of Labor

200 Constitution Ave. NW 20210
Secretary of Labor — William E. Brock.
Under Secretary — Ford B. Ford.
Chief of Staff — Dennis E. Whitfield.
Assistant Secretaries for:
    Administration and Management — Thomas C. Komarek.
    Mine Safety & Health — David A. Zegeer.
    Occupational Safety & Health — Robert A. Rowland.
    Policy — Michael Baroody.
    Labor Management Relations — Steven Schlossberg.
    Veteran's Employment — Donald E. Shasteen.
Solicitor of Labor — Francis X. Lilly.
Comm. of Labor Statistics — Janet Norwood.
Dep. Under Secy. for Employment Standards — Susan R. Meisinger.
Dep. Under Secy. for Internatl. Affairs — Robert W. Searby.
Dep. Under Secy. for Congressional Affairs — William J. Maroni.
Office of Information & Public Affairs — Vernon Louviere.
dir. of Women's Bureau — Lenora Cole-Alexander.
Inspector General — J. Brian Hyland.

Department of Health and Human Services

200 Independence Ave. SW 20201
Secretary of HHS — Margaret M. Heckler.
Under Secretary — Charles D. Baker.
Assistant Secretaries for:
    Management and Budget — John J. O'Shaughnessy.
    Public Affairs — Stephanie Lee Miller.
    Health — James O. Mason, act.
    Planning and Evaluation — Robert B. Helms, act.
    Human Development Services — Dorcas Hardy.
    Legislation — Lawrence DeNardis, act.
    Personnel Administration — Thomas McFee.
General Counsel — Jerry Coleman, act.
Inspector General — Richard P. Kusserow.
Civil Rights — Betty Lou Dotson.
Health Care Financing Admin. — Carolyn Davis, adm.

Department of Housing and Urban Development

451 7th St. SW 20410
Secretary of Housing & Urban Development — Samuel R. Pierce Jr.
Under Secretary — Lee L. Verstandig.
Assistant Secretaries for:
    Administration — Judith L. Tardy.
    Community Planning & Development — Alfred C. Moran.
    Fair Housing & Equal Opportunity — Antonio Monroig.
    Housing & Federal Housing Commissioner — vacant.
    Legislation & Congressional Relations — Stephen May.
    Policy Development & Research — June Koch.
    Public Affairs — Jayne Gallagher, dir.
    Public & Indian Housing — Warren T. Lindquist.

President, Govt. Natl. Mortgage Assn. — vacant.
International Affairs — Theodore Britton Jr.
Labor Relations — Justin Logsdon, act.
Small & Disadvantaged Business Utilization — Bernice Williams.
General Counsel — John J. Knapp.
Inspector General — Paul Adams.

Department of Transportation

400 7th St. SW 20590

Secretary of Transportation — Elizabeth Hanford Dole.
Deputy Secretary — James H. Burnley 4th.
Assistant Secretaries — Matthew V. Scocozza (Policy and International Affairs); Donald Derman (Budget and Programs); John H. Seymour (Administration); Jennifer Hillings (Public Affairs); Rebecca C. Range (Governmental Affairs).
National Highway Traffic Safety Admin. — Diane K. Steed.
U. S. Coast Guard Commandant — Adm. James Gracey.
Federal Aviation Admin. — Donald D. Engen.
Federal Highway Admin. — Ray Barnhart.
Federal Railroad Admin. — John Riley.
Maritime Admin. — Harold E. Shear.
Urban Mass Transportation Admin. — Ralph L. Stanley.
Research & Special Programs Admin. — Cindy Douglass.
Saint Lawrence Seaway Development Corp. — James L. Emery.

Department of Energy

1000 Independence Ave. SW 20585

Secretary of Energy — John S. Herrington.
Deputy Secy. — Danny J. Boggs.
Under Secretary — Joseph Salgado.
General Counsel — J. Michael Farrell.

Assistant Secretaries — Martha Hesse Dolan (Management & Administration); Theodore Garrish, act. (Congressional, Intergovernmental & Public Affairs); Jan W. Mares (International Affairs & Energy Emergencies); vacant (Nuclear Energy); Jan W. Mares (Policy Safety & Environment); William W. Hoover (Defense Programs); William A. Vaughan (Fossil Energy); Donna Fitzpatrick (Conservation & Renewable Energy).
Federal Energy Regulatory Comm. — Raymond J. O'Connor.
Inspector General — James R. Richards.
Energy Information Adm. — Helmut A. Merklein, adm.
Office of Energy Research — Alvin Trivelpiece, dir.
Office of Civilian Radioactive Waste Management — Ben Rusche, dir.

Department of Education

Wash., D.C. 20202

Secretary of Education — William J. Bennett.
Under Secretary — Gary Bauer.
Deputy Under Secretaries — A. Wayne Roberts, Linda Combs.
General Counsel — Maureen Corcoran.
Assistant Secretaries:
Legislation & Public Affairs — Anne Graham.
Elementary and Secondary Education — Lawrence Davenport.
Postsecondary Education — vacant.
Educational Research and Improvement — vacant.
Adult & Vocational Education — Robert Worthington.
Special Education and Rehabilitative Services — Madeline Will.
Civil Rights — Harry M. Singleton.
Bilingual & Minority Languages — Carol P. Whitten.
Regions — George Y. Ouster.

Judiciary of the U.S.

Data as of Jan. 1985

Justices of the United States Supreme Court

The Supreme Court comprises the chief justice of the United States and 8 associate justices, all appointed by the president with advice and consent of the Senate. Salaries: chief justice $104,700 annually, associate justice $100,600.

Name; apptd from Chief Justices in italics	Term	Service Yrs.	Born	Died	Name; apptd from Chief Justices in italics	Term	Service Yrs.	Born	Died
John Jay, N. Y.	1789-1795	5	1745	1829	Noah H. Swayne, Oh.	1862-1881	18	1804	1884
John Rutledge, S. C.	1789-1791	1	1739	1800	Samuel F. Miller, Ia.	1862-1890	28	1816	1890
William Cushing, Mass.	1789-1810	20	1732	1810	David Davis, Ill.	1862-1877	14	1815	1886
James Wilson, Pa.	1789-1798	8	1742	1798	Stephen J. Field, Cal.	1863-1897	34	1816	1899
John Blair, Va.	1789-1796	6	1732	1800	Salmon P. Chase, Oh.	1864-1873	8	1808	1873
James Iredell, N. C.	1790-1799	9	1751	1799	William Strong, Pa.	1870-1880	10	1808	1895
Thomas Johnson, Md.	1791-1793	1	1732	1819	Joseph P. Bradley, N. J.	1870-1892	21	1813	1892
William Paterson, N. J.	1793-1806	13	1745	1806	Ward Hunt, N. Y.	1872-1882	9	1810	1886
John Rutledge, S.C.	1795(a)	—	1739	1800	Morrison R. Waite, Oh.	1874-1888	14	1816	1888
Samuel Chase, Md.	1796-1811	15	1741	1811	John M. Harlan, Ky.	1877-1911	34	1833	1911
Oliver Ellsworth, Conn.	1796-1800	4	1745	1807	William B. Woods, Ga.	1880-1887	6	1824	1887
Bushrod Washington, Va.	1798-1829	31	1762	1829	Stanley Matthews, Oh.	1881-1889	7	1824	1889
Alfred Moore, N. C.	1799-1804	4	1755	1810	Horace Gray, Mass.	1881-1902	20	1828	1902
John Marshall, Va.	1801-1835	34	1755	1835	Samuel Blatchford, N. Y.	1882-1893	11	1820	1893
William Johnson, S. C.	1804-1834	30	1771	1834	Lucius Q. C. Lamar, Miss.	1888-1893	5	1825	1893
Henry B. Livingston, N. Y.	1806-1823	16	1757	1823	Melville W. Fuller, Ill.	1888-1910	21	1833	1910
Thomas Todd, Ky.	1807-1826	18	1765	1826	David J. Brewer, Kan.	1889-1910	20	1837	1910
Joseph Story, Mass.	1811-1845	33	1779	1845	Henry B. Brown, Mich.	1890-1906	15	1836	1913
Gabriel Duval, Md.	1811-1835	22	1752	1844	George Shiras Jr., Pa.	1892-1903	10	1832	1924
Smith Thompson, N. Y.	1823-1843	20	1768	1843	Howell E. Jackson, Tenn.	1893-1895	2	1832	1895
Robert Trimble, Ky.	1826-1828	2	1777	1828	Edward D. White, La.	1894-1910	16	1845	1921
John McLean, Oh.	1829-1861	32	1785	1861	Rufus W. Peckham, N. Y.	1895-1909	13	1838	1909
Henry Baldwin, Pa.	1830-1844	14	1780	1844	Joseph McKenna, Cal.	1898-1925	26	1843	1926
James M. Wayne, Ga.	1835-1867	32	1790	1867	Oliver W. Holmes, Mass.	1902-1932	29	1841	1935
Roger B. Taney, Md.	1836-1864	28	1777	1864	William R. Day, Oh.	1903-1922	19	1849	1923
Philip P. Barbour, Va.	1836-1841	4	1783	1841	William H. Moody, Mass.	1906-1910	3	1853	1917
John Catron, Tenn.	1837-1865	28	1786	1865	Horace H. Lurton, Tenn.	1909-1914	4	1844	1914
John McKinley, Ala.	1837-1852	15	1780	1852	Charles E. Hughes, N. Y.	1910-1916	5	1862	1948
Peter V. Daniel, Va.	1841-1860	19	1784	1860	Willis Van Devanter, Wy.	1910-1937	26	1859	1941
Samuel Nelson, N. Y.	1845-1872	27	1792	1873	Joseph R. Lamar, Ga.	1910-1916	5	1857	1916
Levi Woodbury, N. H.	1845-1851	5	1789	1851	Edward D. White, La.	1910-1921	10	1845	1921
Robert C. Grier, Pa.	1846-1870	23	1794	1870	Mahlon Pitney, N. J.	1912-1922	10	1858	1924
Benjamin R. Curtis, Mass.	1851-1857	6	1809	1874	James C. McReynolds, Tenn.	1914-1941	26	1862	1946
John A. Campbell, Ala.	1853-1861	8	1811	1889	Louis D. Brandeis, Mass.	1916-1939	22	1856	1941
Nathan Clifford, Me.	1858-1881	23	1803	1881	John H. Clarke, Oh.	1916-1922	5	1857	1945
					William H. Taft, Conn.	1921-1930	8	1857	1930

Name; apptd from	Service Term	Yrs.	Born	Died
George Sutherland, Ut....	1922-1938	15	1862	1942
Pierce Butler, Minn.....	1922-1939	16	1866	1939
Edward T. Sanford, Tenn..	1923-1930	7	1865	1930
Harlan F. Stone, N. Y. . .	1925-1941	16	1872	1946
Charles E. Hughes, N. Y. .	1930-1941	11	1862	1948
Owen J. Roberts, Pa....	1930-1945	15	1875	1955
Benjamin N. Cardozo, N.Y.	1932-1938	6	1870	1938
Hugo L. Black, Ala.....	1937-1971	34	1886	1971
Stanley F. Reed, Ky....	1938-1957	19	1884	1980
Felix Frankfurter, Mass. . .	1939-1962	23	1882	1965
William O. Douglas, Conn. .	1939-1975	36	1898	1980
Frank Murphy, Mich. . . .	1940-1949	9	1890	1949
Harlan F. Stone, N. Y. . .	1941-1946	5	1872	1946
James F. Byrnes, S. C. . .	1941-1942	1	1879	1972
Robert H. Jackson, N. Y. . .	1941-1954	12	1892	1954
Wiley B. Rutledge, Ia. . . .	1943-1949	6	1894	1949
Harold H. Burton, Oh. . . .	1945-1958	13	1888	1964
Fred M. Vinson, Ky.	1946-1953	7	1890	1953
Tom C. Clark, Tex.	1949-1967	18	1899	1977
Sherman Minton, Ind. . . .	1949-1956	7	1890	1965
Earl Warren, Cal.	1953-1969	16	1891	1974
John Marshall Harlan, N. Y.	1955-1971	16	1899	1971
William J. Brennan Jr., N. J.	1956	—	1906	—
Charles E. Whittaker, Mo.	1957-1962	5	1901	1973
Potter Stewart, Oh.	1958-1981	23	1915	—
Byron R. White, Col. . . .	1962	—	1917	—
Arthur J. Goldberg, III. . . .	1962-1965	3	1908	—
Abe Fortas, Tenn.	1965-1969	4	1910	1982
Thurgood Marshall, N.Y. . .	1967	—	1908	—
Warren E. Burger, Va. . .	1969	—	1907	—
Harry A. Blackmun, Minn. .	1970	—	1908	—
Lewis F. Powell Jr., Va. . .	1972	—	1907	—
William H. Rehnquist, Ariz. .	1972	—	1924	—
John Paul Stevens, III. . . .	1975	—	1920	—
Sandra Day O'Connor, Ariz.	1981	—	1930	—

(a) Rejected Dec. 15, 1795.

U.S. Court of International Trade

New York, NY 10007 (Salaries, $76,000)
Chief Judge — Edward D. Re.
Judges — Paul P. Rao, Morgan Ford, James L. Watson, Gregory W. Carman, Jane A. Restani, Dominick L. DiCarlo.

U.S. Tax Court

Washington DC 20217 (Salaries, $76,000)
Chief Judge — Harry A. Dawson Jr.
Judges — William M. Fay, Charles R. Simpson, Samuel B. Sterrett, William A. Goffe, Darrell D. Wiles, Richard C. Wilbur, Herbert L. Chabot, Arthur L. Nims 3d, Edna G. Parker, C. Moxley Featherston, Jules J. Korner 3d, Meade Whitaker, Mary Ann Cohen, Perry Shields, Charles E. Clapp 2d, Lapsley W. Hamblen Jr., Stephen J. Swift.

U.S. Courts of Appeals

(Salaries, $80,400. CJ means Chief Judge)

Federal District — Howard T. Markey, CJ; Daniel M. Friedman, Giles S. Rich, Oscar H. Davis, Phillip B. Baldwin, Shiro Kashiwa, Marion T. Bennett, Jack R. Miller, Edward S. Smith, Helen W. Nies; Pauline Newman, Jean G. Bissel; Clerk's Office, Washington, DC 20439.

District of Columbia — Spottswood W. Robinson 3d, CJ; J. Skelly Wright, Edward Allen Tamm, George E. MacKinnon, Malcolm Richard Wilkey, Patricia M. Wald, Abner J. Mikva, Harry T. Edwards, Ruth Bader Ginsburg, Robert H. Bork, Antonin Scalia, Kenneth W. Starr; Clerk's Office, Washington, DC 20001.

First Circuit (Me., Mass., N.H., R.I., Puerto Rico) — Levin H. Campbell, CJ; Frank M. Coffin, Hugh H. Bownes, Stephen Breyer; Clerk's Office, Boston, MA 02109.

Second Circuit (Conn., N.Y., Vt.) — Wilfred Feinberg, CJ; Irving R. Kaufman, James L. Oakes, Ellsworth Van Graafeiland, Thomas J. Meskill, Jon O. Newman, Amalya Lyle Kearse, Richard J. Cardamone, Lawrence W. Pierce, Ralph K. Winter Jr., George C. Pratt; Clerk's Office, New York, NY 10007.

Third Circuit (Del., N.J., Pa., Virgin Is.) — Ruggero J. Aldisert, CJ; Collins J. Seitz, Arlin M. Adams, John J. Gibbons, James Hunter 3d, Joseph F. Weis Jr., Leonard I. Garth, A. Leon Higginbotham Jr., Dolores K. Sloviter, Edward R. Becker; Clerk's Office, Philadelphia, PA 19106.

Fourth Circuit (Md., N.C., S.C., Va., W.Va.) — Harrison L. Winter, CJ; Kenneth K. Hall, Donald Stuart Russell, H. Emory Widener Jr., James D. Phillips Jr., Francis D. Murnaghan Jr., James M. Sprouse, Sam J. Ervin 3d, Robert F. Chapman, James H. Wilkinson 3d; Clerk's Office, Richmond, VA 23219.

Fifth Circuit (La., Miss., Tex.) — Charles Clark, CJ; Thomas G. Gee, Alvin B. Rubin, Thomas M. Reavley, Henry A. Politz, Carolyn D. Randall, Samuel D. Johnson, Albert Tate Jr., Jerre S. Williams, William L. Garwood, E. Grady Jolly, Patrick E. Higginbotham, W. Eugene Davis, Robert M. Hill; Clerk's Office, New Orleans, LA 70130.

Sixth Circuit (Ky., Mich., Ohio, Tenn.) — Pierce Lively, CJ; Albert J. Engel, George Clifton Edwards, Gilbert S. Merritt, Damon J. Keith, Boyce F. Martin Jr., Nathaniel R. Jones, Leroy J. Contie Jr., Robert B. Krupansky, Harry W. Wellford; Clerk's Office, Cincinnati, OH 45202.

Seventh Circuit (Ill., Ind., Wis.) — Walter J. Cummings, CJ; Harlington Wood Jr., William J. Bauer, Richard D. Cudahy, Richard A. Posner, Jesse E. Eschbach, John L. Coffey, Joel M. Flaum; Clerk's Office, Chicago, IL 60604.

Eighth Circuit (Ark., Ia., Minn., Mo., Neb., N.D., S.D.) — Donald P. Lay, CJ; Gerald W. Heaney, Myron H. Bright, Donald R. Ross, Theodore McMillian, Richard S. Arnold, John R. Gibson, George C. Fagg, Pasco M. Bowman 2d; Clerk's Office, St. Louis, MO 63101.

Ninth Circuit (Alaska, Ariz., Cal., Ha., Ida., Mont., Nev., Ore., Wash., Guam, N. Mariana Islands) — James R. Browning, CJ; Herbert Y. C. Choy, J. Clifford Wallace, Alfred T. Goodwin, Anthony M. Kennedy, J. Blaine Anderson, Procter Hug Jr., Thomas Tang, Joseph T. Sneed, Jerome Farris, Betty B. Fletcher, Mary M. Schroeder, Otto R. Skopil Jr., Harry Pregerson, Arthur L. Alarcon, Cecil F. Poole, Warren J. Ferguson, Dorothy W. Nelson, William C. Canby Jr., Robert Boochever, William A. Norris, Stephen Reinhardt, Robert R. Beezer; Clerk's Office, San Francisco, CA 94101.

Tenth Circuit (Col., Kan., N.M., Okla., Ut., Wy.) — Oliver Seth, CJ; William J. Holloway Jr., James E. Barrett, William E. Doyle, Monroe G. McKay, James K. Logan, Stephanie K. Seymour; Clerk's Office, Denver, CO 80294.

Eleventh Circuit (Ala. Fla., Ga.) — John C. Godbold, CJ; Paul H. Roney, Gerald B. Tjoflat, James C. Hill, Peter T. Fay, Robert S. Vance, Phyllis A. Kravitch, Frank M. Johnson Jr., Albert J. Henderson, Joseph W. Hatchett, R. Lanier Anderson 3d, Thomas C. Clark; Clerk's Office, Atlanta GA 30303.

Temporary Emergency Court of Appeals — J. Skelly Wright, CJ; Clerk's Office, Washington, DC 20001 .

U.S. District Courts

(Salaries, $76,000. CJ means Chief Judge)

Alabama — **Northern:** Sam C. Pointer Jr., CJ; James Hughes Hancock, J. Foy Guin Jr., Robert B. Probst, E. B. Haltom Jr., U. W. Clemon, William M. Acker Jr.; Clerk's Office, Birmingham 35203. **Middle:** Robert E. Varner, CJ; Truman M. Hobbs, Myron H. Thompson; Clerk's Office, Montgomery 36101. **Southern:** William Brevard Hand, CJ; Emmett R. Cox; Clerk's Office, Mobile 36601.

Alaska — James M. Fitzgerald, CJ; H. Russel Holland; Clerk's Office, Anchorage 99513.

Arizona — C. A. Muecke, CJ; Vlademar A. Cordova, Richard M. Bilby, Charles L. Hardy, Alfredo C. Marquez, Earl H. Carroll, William D. Browning, Paul G. Rosenblat; Clerk's Office, Phoenix 85025.

Arkansas — **Eastern:** Garnett Thomas Eisele, CJ; Elsijane Trimble Roy, William Ray Overton, Henry Woods, George Howard Jr.; Clerk's Office, Little Rock 72203. **Western:** H. Franklin Waters, CJ; Elsijane Trimble Roy, George Howard Jr.; Clerk's Office, Fort Smith 72902.

California — **Northern:** Robert F. Peckham, CJ; Lloyd H. Burke, Samuel Conti, Spencer M. Williams, William H. Orrick Jr., William W. Schwarzer, William A. Ingram, Robert P. Aguilar, Thelton E. Henderson, Marilyn H. Patel, Eugene F. Lynch, John P. Vukasin Jr.; Clerk's Office, San Francisco 94102. **Eastern:** Lawrence K. Karlton, CJ; Milton L. Schwartz, Edward Dean Price, Raul A. Ramirez, Robert E. Coyle, Edward J. Garcia; Clerk's Office, Sacramento 95814. **Central:** Manuel L. Real, CJ; Wm. Matthew Byrne Jr., Robert M. Takasugi, Laughlin E. Waters, Mariana R. Pfaelzer, Terry J. Hatter Jr., A. Wallace Tashima, Consuelo Bland Marshall, David V. Kenyon, Cynthia H. Hall, Richard A. Gadbois, Edward Rafeedie, Pamela A. Rymer, Harry L. Hupp, Alicemarie H. Stotler, James M. Ideman, William J. Rea; Clerk's

Office, Los Angeles 90012. **Southern:** Gordon Thompson Jr., CJ; Leland C. Nielsen, William B. Enright, Judith N. Keep, Earl B. Gilliam, J. Lawrence Irving, Rudi M. Brewster; Clerk's Office, San Diego 92189.

Colorado — Sherman G. Finesilver, CJ; Richard P. Matsch, John L. Kane, Jim R. Carrigan, Zita L. Weinshienk, John P. Moore; Clerk's Office, Denver 80294.

Connecticut — T. F. Gilroy Daly, CJ; Ellen B. Burns, Warren W. Eginton, Jose A. Cabranes, Peter C. Dorsey; Clerk's Office, New Haven 06510.

Delaware — Walter K. Stapleton, CJ; Murray M. Schwartz, Joseph J. Longobardi; Clerk's Office, Wilmington 19801.

District of Columbia — Aubrey E. Robinson Jr., CJ; Gerhard A. Gesell, John H. Pratt, Barrington D. Parker, Charles R. Richey, Thomas A. Flannery, Louis F. Oberdorfer, Harold H. Greene, John Garrett Penn, Joyce Hens Green, Norma H. Johnson, Thomas P. Jackson, Thomas F. Hogan, Stanley S. Harris; Clerk's Office, Washington DC 20001.

Florida — **Northern:** William H. Stafford Jr. CJ; Maurice M. Paul, C. Roger Vinson; Clerk's Office, Tallahassee 32301. **Middle:** William Terrell Hodges, CJ; Howard W. Melton, John A. Reed Jr., George C. Carr, Susan H. Black, William J. Castagna; John H. Moore 2d, Elizabeth A. Kovachevich, George K. Sharp; Clerk's Office, Jacksonville 32201. **Southern:** James Lawrence King, CJ; Joe Eaton, Norman C. Roettger Jr.; Sidney M. Aronovitz, William H. Hoeveler, Jose A. Gonzalez, James W. Kehoe, Eugene P. Spellman, Edward B. Davis, James C. Paine, Alcee L. Hastings, Lenore C. Nesbitt; Clerk's Office, Miami 33101.

Georgia — **Northern:** Charles A. Moye Jr., CJ; William C.O'-Kelley, Richard C. Freeman, Harold L. Murphy, Marvin H. Shoob, G. Ernest Tidwell, Orinda Dale Evans, Robert L. Vining Jr., Robert H. Hall, Harold T. Ward, J. Owen Forrester; Clerk's Office, Atlanta 30335. **Middle:** Wilbur D. Owens Jr., CJ; J. Robert Elliott; Clerk's Office, Macon 31202. **Southern:** Anthony A. Alaimo, CJ; B. Avant Edenfield, Dudley H. Bowen Jr.; Clerk's Office, Savannah 31412.

Hawaii — Samuel P. King, CJ; Harold M. Fong; Clerk's Office, Honolulu 96850.

Idaho — Marion J. Callister, CJ; Harold L. Ryan; Clerk's Office; Boise, 83724.

Illinois — **Northern:** Frank J. McGarr, CJ; Thomas R. McMillen, Prentice H. Marshall, John F. Grady, George N. Leighton, Nicholas J. Bua, Stanley J. Roszkowski, James B. Moran, Marvin E. Aspen, Milton I. Shadur, Charles P. Kocoras, Susan Getzendanner, John A. Nordberg, William T. Hart, Paul E. Plunkett; Clerk's Office, Chicago 60604. **Central:** J. Waldo Ackerman, CJ; Michael M. Mihm, Harold A. Baker; Clerk's Office, Peoria 61602. **Southern:** James L. Foreman, CJ; William L. Beatty; Clerk's Office, Benton 62812.

Indiana — **Northern:** Allen Sharp, CJ; William C. Lee, James T. Moody, Michael S. Kanne; Clerk's Office, South Bend 46601. **Southern:** James E. Noland, CJ; William R. Steckler, S. Hugh Dillin, Gene E. Brooks, Sarah E. Barker; Clerk's Office, Indianapolis 46204.

Iowa — **Northern:** Edward J. McManus, CJ; Donald E. O'-Brien; Clerk's Office, Cedar Rapids 52407. **Southern:** William C. Stuart, CJ; Donald E. O'Brien, Harold D. Vietor; Clerk's Office, Des Moines 50309.

Kansas — Earl E. O'Connor, CJ; Richard Dean Rogers, Dale E. Saffels, Patrick F. Kelly, Sam A. Crow; Clerk's Office, Wichita 67202.

Kentucky — **Eastern:** Eugene E. Siler Jr., CJ; Scott Reed, William Bertelsman, G. Wix Unthank, Henry R. Wilhoit Jr.; Clerk's Office, Lexington 40586. **Western:** Charles M. Allen, CJ; Eugene E. Siler Jr., Edward H. Johnstone, Thomas A. Ballantine; Clerk's Office, Louisville 40202.

Louisiana — **Eastern:** Frederick J. R. Heebe, CJ; Charles Schwartz Jr., Morley L. Sear, Adrian A. Duplantier, Robert F. Collins, George Arceneaux Jr., Veronica D. Wicker, Patrick E. Carr, Peter Beer, A J. McNamara, Henry A. Mentz Jr., Martin Feldman; Clerk's Office, New Orleans 70130. **Middle:** John V. Parker, CJ; Frank J. Polozola; Clerk's Office, Baton Rouge 70801. **Western:** Tom Stagg, CJ; Nauman S. Scott, Earl Ernest Veron, John M. Shaw, John M. Duhe Jr.; Clerk's Office, Shreveport 71101.

Maine — Conrad K. Cyr, CJ; Gene Carter; Clerk's Office, Portland 04112.

Maryland — Frank A. Kaufman, CJ; Alexander Harvey 2d, James R. Miller Jr., Joseph H. Young, Herbert F. Murray, Joseph C. Howard, Norman P. Ramsey, William E. Black Jr., John R. Hargrove; Clerk's Office, Baltimore 21201.

Massachusetts — Andrew A. Caffrey, CJ; W. Arthur Garrity Jr., Frank H. Freedman, Joseph L. Tauro, Walter Jay Skinner, A. David Mazzone, Robert E. Keeton, John J. McNaught, Rya W. Zobel, David S. Nelson; Clerk's Office, Boston 02109:

Michigan — **Eastern:** John Feikens, CJ; Philip Pratt, Robert E. DeMascio, Charles W. Joiner, James Harvey, James P. Churchill, Ralph B. Guy Jr., Julian A. Cook, Stewart A. Newblatt, Avern Cohn, Anna Diggs Taylor, Horace W. Gilmore, George E. Woods; Clerk's Office, Detroit 48226. **Western:** Wendell A. Miles, CJ; Douglas W. Hillman, Benjamin F. Gibson, Richard A. Enslen; Clerk's Office, Grand Rapids 49503.

Minnesota — Miles W. Lord, CJ; Donald D. Alsop, Harry H. MacLaughlin, Robert G. Renner, Diana E. Murphy, Paul A. Magnuson; Clerk's Office, St. Paul 55101.

Mississippi — **Northern:** L. T. Senter Jr., CJ; Neal Biggers; Clerk's Office, Oxford 38655. **Southern:** Walter L. Nixon Jr., CJ; William H. Barbour Jr., Tom S. Lee; Clerk's Office, Jackson 39205.

Missouri — **Eastern:** John F. Nangle, CJ; Edward D. Filippine, William L. Hungate, Clyde S. Cahill Jr., Stephen N. Limbaugh; Clerk's Office, St. Louis 63101. **Western:** Russell G. Clark, CJ; Harold Sachs, Scott O. Wright, Joseph E. Stevens Jr., D. Brook Bartlett, Ross T. Roberts; Clerk's Office, Kansas City 64106.

Montana — James F. Battin, CJ; Paul G. Hatfield; Clerk's Office, Billings 59101.

Nebraska — Warren K. Urbom, CJ; Clarence A. Beam, Albert G. Schatz; Clerk's Office, Omaha 68101.

Nevada — Harry E. Claiborne, CJ; Edward C. Reed Jr., Lloyd D. George; Clerk's Office, Las Vegas 89101.

New Hampshire — Shane Devine, CJ; Martin F. Loughlin; Clerk's Office, Concord 03301.

New Jersey — Clarkson S. Fisher, CJ; Frederick B. Lacey, Herbert J. Stern, John F. Gerry, Stanley S. Brotman, Anne E. Thompson, D. R. Debevoise, H. Lee Sarokin, Harold A. Ackerman, John W. Bissell, Maryanne Trump Barry; Clerk's Office, Newark 07102.

New Mexico — Howard C. Bratton, CJ; Santiago E. Campos, Juan G. Burciaga, Bobby R. Baldock; Clerk's Office, Albuquerque 87103.

New York — **Northern:** Howard G. Munson, CJ; Neal P. McCurn, Roger J. Miner; Clerk's Office, Albany 12201. **Eastern:** Jack B. Weinstein, CJ; Mark A. Costantino, Thomas C. Platt Jr., Henry Bramwell, Charles P. Sifton, Eugene H. Nickerson, Joseph M. McLaughlin, Israel Leo Glasser, Frank X. Altimari, Leonard D. Wexler; Clerk's Office, Brooklyn 11201. **Southern:** Constance Baker Motley, CJ; David N. Edelstein, Edward Weinfeld, Lee P. Gagliardi, Charles L. Brieant, Whitman Knapp, Charles E. Stewart Jr., Thomas P. Griesa, Robert L. Carter, Robert J. Ward, Kevin Thomas Duffy, William C. Conner, Richard Owen, Leonard B. Sand, Mary Johnson Lowe, Gerard L. Goettel, Charles S. Haight Jr., Vincent L. Broderick, Pierre N. Leval, Robert W. Sweet, Abraham D. Sofaer, John E. Sprizzo, Shirley Wohl Kram, John F. Keenan, Peter K. Leisure; Clerk's Office N. Y. City 10007. **Western:** John T. Curtin, CJ; John T. Elfvin, Michael A. Telesca; Clerk's Office, Buffalo 14202.

North Carolina — **Eastern:** W. Earl Britt, CJ; James C. Fox, Terrence W. Boyle; Clerk's Office, Raleigh 27611. **Middle:** Hiram H. Ward, CJ; Frank W. Bullock Jr., Richard C. Erwin; Clerk's Office, Greensboro 27402. **Western:** Robert D. Potter, CJ; Woodrow Wilson Jones, James B. McMillan; Clerk's Office Asheville 28802.

North Dakota — Paul Benson, CJ; Bruce M. Van Sickle; Clerk's Office, Bismarck 58501.

Ohio — **Northern:** Frank J. Battisti, CJ; Thomas D. Lambros, Nicholas J. Walinski, John M. Manos, George W. White, Ann Aldrich, Alvin I. Krenzler, John W. Potter, David D. Dowd Jr., Sam H. Bell; Clerk's Office, Cleveland 44114. **Southern:** Carl B. Rubin, CJ; Joseph P. Kinneary, Robert M. Duncan, John D. Holschuh, Walter H. Rice, S. Arthur Spiegel; Clerk's Office, Columbus 43215.

Oklahoma — **Northern:** H. Dale Cook, CJ; James O. Ellison, Thomas R. Brett, David L. Russell; Clerk's Office, Tulsa 74103. **Eastern:** Frank H. Shey, CJ; H. Dale Cook, David L. Russell; Clerk's Office, Muskogee 74401. **Western:** Luther B. Eubanks, CJ; H. Dale Cook, Ralph G. Thompson, Lee R. West, David L. Russell; Clerk's Office, Oklahoma City 73102.

Oregon — James M. Burns, CJ; Robert C. Belloni, Owen M. Panner, James A. Redden, Helen J. Frye, Edward Leavy; Clerk's Office, Portland 97205.

Pennsylvania — **Eastern:** Alfred L. Luongo, CJ; John P. Fullam, Charles R. Weiner, Daniel H. Huyett 3d, Donald W. VanArtsdalen, J. William Ditter Jr., Clarence C. Newcomer, Clifford Scott Green, Louis Charles Bechtle, Joseph L. McGlynn Jr., Edward N. Cahn, Louis H. Pollak, Norma L. Shapiro, James T.

Giles, James McGirr Kelly, Thomas N. O'Neill Jr., Marvin Katz; Clerk's Office, Philadelphia 19106. **Middle:** William J. Nealon Jr., CJ; Richard P. Conaboy, Sylvia H. Rambo, William W. Caldwell; Clerk's Office, Scranton 18501. **Western:** Hubert I. Teitelbaum, CJ; Gerald J. Weber, Barron P. McCune, Maurice B. Cohill Jr., Paul A. Simmons, Gustave Diamond, Donald E. Ziegler, Alan N. Bloch, Glenn E. Mencer, Carol Los Mansmann; Clerk's Office, Pittsburgh 15230.￿

Rhode Island — Francis J. Boyle, CJ; Bruce M. Selya; Clerk's Office, Providence 02903

South Carolina — Charles E. Simons Jr., CJ; Solomon Blatt Jr., C. Weston Houck, Falcon B. Hawkins, Matthew J. Perry Jr., George R. Anderson Jr., William W. Wilkins Jr., Clyde H. Hamilton; Clerk's Office, Columbia 29202.

South Dakota — Andrew A. Bogue, CJ; Donald J. Porter, John Bailey Jones; Clerk's Office, Sioux Falls 57102.

Tennessee — **Eastern:** H. Theodore Milburn, CJ; Robert L. Taylor, Thomas G. Hull; Clerk's Office, Knoxville 37901. **Middle:** L. Clure Morton, CJ, Thomas A. Wiseman Jr, John T. Nixon; Clerk's Office, Nashville 37203. **Western:** Robert M. McRae Jr., CJ; Odell Horton, Julia S. Gibbons; Clerk's Office, Memphis 38103.

Texas — **Northern:** Halbert O. Woodward, CJ; Eldon B. Mahon, Robert W. Porter, Mary Lou Robinson, Barefoot Sanders, David O. Belew Jr., Jerry Buchmeyer, A. Joe Fish; Clerk's Office, Dallas 75242. **Southern:** John V. Singleton Jr., CJ; Carl O. Bue Jr., Robert O'Conor Jr., Ross N. Sterling, Norman W. Black, James De Anda, George E. Cire, Gabrielle K. McDonald, George P. Kazen, Hugh Gibson, Filemon B. Vela, Hayden W. Head Jr., Ricardo H. Hinojosa; Clerk's Office, Houston 77208. **Eastern:** William Wayne Justice, CJ; William M. Steger, Robert M. Parker; Clerk's Office, Beaumont 77701. **Western:** William S. Sessions, CJ; Lucius D. Bunton 3d, Harry Lee Hudspeth, Hipolito F. Garcia, James R. Nowlin; Clerk's Office, San Antonio 78206.

Utah — Aldon J. Anderson, CJ; Bruce S. Jenkins, David K. Winder; Clerk's Office, Salt Lake City 84110.

Vermont — Albert W. Coffrin, CJ; Franklin S. Billings Jr.; Clerk's Office, Burlington 05402.

Virginia — **Eastern:** John A. MacKenzie, CJ; Robert R. Merhige Jr., Albert V. Bryan Jr., D. Dortch Warriner, J. Calvitt Clarke, Richard L. Williams, James C. Cacheris, Robert G. Doumar; Clerk's Office, Norfolk 23510. **Western:** James C. Turk, CJ; Glen M. Williams, James H. Michael Jr., Jackson L. Kiser; Clerk's Office, Roanoke 24006.

Washington — **Eastern:** Robert J. McNichols, CJ; Justin L. Quackenbush; Clerk's Office, Spokane 99210. **Western:** Walter T. McGovern, CJ; Donald S. Voorhees, Jack E. Tanner, Barbara J. Rothstein, John C. Coughenour; Clerk's Office, Seattle 98104.

West Virginia — **Northern:** Robert Earl Maxwell, CJ; William M. Kidd; Clerk's Office, Elkins 26241. **Southern:** Charles H. Haden 2d, CJ; Robert J. Staker, John T. Copenhaver Jr., Elizabeth V. Hallanan; Clerk's Office, Charleston 25329.

Wisconsin — **Eastern:** John W. Reynolds, CJ; Robert W. Warren, Terence T. Evans, Thomas J. Curran; Clerk's Office, Milwaukee 53202. **Western:** Barbara B. Crabb, CJ; John C. Shabaz; Clerk's Office, Madison 53701.

Wyoming — Clarence A. Brimmer; Clerk's Office, Cheyenne 82001.

U.S. Territorial District Courts

Guam — Cristobal C. Duenas; Clerk's Office, Agana 96910.

Puerto Rico — Juan R. Torruella, CJ; Juan M. Perez-Gimenez, Gilberto Gierbolini-Ortiz, Carman Consuelo Cerezo, Jaime Pieras Jr., Raymond L. Acosta, Hector M. Laffitte; Clerk's Office, San Juan 00904.

Virgin Islands — Almeric L. Christian, CJ; David V. O'Brien; Clerk's Office, Charlotte Amalie, St. Thomas 00801.

State Officials, Salaries, Party Membership

As of mid-1985

Alabama

Governor — George C. Wallace, D., $68,838.
Lt. Gov. — Bill Baxley, D., $95 per legislative day, plus annual salary of $600 per month plus $1,500 per month for expenses.
Sec. of State — Don Siegelman, D., $32,940.
Atty. Gen. — Charles Graddick, D., $58,000.
Treasurer — Mrs. Annie Laurie Gunter, D., $45,000.
Legislature: meets annually the 3d Tuesday in Apr. (first year of term of office, first Tuesday in Feb. (2d and 3d years), 2d Tuesday in Jan. (4th year) at Montgomery. Members receive $600 per month, plus $95 per day during legislative sessions, and mileage of 10c per mile.
Senate — Dem., 28; Rep., 4; ind. 3. Total, 35.
House — Dem., 87; Rep., 11; ind. 6.; 1 vacancy. Total, 105.

Alaska

Governor — William Sheffield, D., $81,648.
Lt. Gov. — Stephen McAlpine, D., $76,188.
Atty. General — Norman Gorsuch, D., $73,620.
Legislature: meets annually in January at Juneau, for 120 days with a 10-day extension possible upon ⅔ vote. First session in odd years. Members receive $46,800 per year plus $4,000 for postage, personal stationery, and other expenses.
Senate — Dem., 9; Rep., 11. Total, 20.
House — Dem., 21; Rep., 18; Libertarians, 1. Total, 40.

Arizona

Governor — Bruce Babbitt, D., $62,500.
Sec. of State — Rose Mofford, D., $35,000.
Atty. Gen. — Bob Corbin, R., $56,250.
Treasurer — Clark Dierks, R., $37,500.
Legislature: meets annually in January at Phoenix. Each member receives an annual salary of $15,000.
Senate — Dem., 12; Rep., 18. Total, 30.
House — Dem., 22; Rep., 38. Total, 60.

Arkansas

Governor — Bill Clinton, D., $35,000.
Lt. Gov. — Winston Bryant, D., $14,000.
Sec. of State — W. J. "Bill" McCuen, D., $22,500.
Atty. Gen. — Steve Clark, D., $26,500.
Treasurer — Jimmie Lou Fisher, D., $22,500.
General Assembly: meets odd years in January at Little Rock. Members receive $7,500 per year, $50 a day while in regular session, plus 20½c a mile travel expense.
Senate — Dem., 31; Rep., 4. Total, 35.
House — Dem., 91; Rep., 9. Total, 100.

California

Governor — George Deukmejian, R., $85,000.
Lt. Gov. — Leo T. McCarthy, D., $72,500.
Sec. of State — March Fong Eu, D., $72,500.
Controller — Kenneth Cory, D., $72,500.
Atty. Gen. — John Van de Kamp, D., $77,500.
Treasurer — Jesse M. Unruh, D., $72,500.
Legislature: meets at Sacramento; regular sessions commence on the first Monday in Dec. of every even-numbered year; each session lasts 2 years. Members receive $33,732 per year plus mileage and $65 per diem.
Senate — Dem., 25; Rep., 15. Total, 40.
Assembly — Dem., 47; Rep., 33. Total, 80.

Colorado

Governor — Richard D. Lamm, D., $60,000.
Lt. Gov. — Nancy Dick, D., $32,500.
Secy. of State — Natalie Meyer, R., $32,500.
Atty. Gen. — Duane Woodard, R., $40,000.
Treasurer — Roy Romer, D., $32,500.
General Assembly: meets annually in January at Denver. Members receive $14,000 annually.
Senate — Dem., 11; Rep., 24. Total, 35.
House — Dem., 17; Rep., 48. Total, 65.

Connecticut

Governor — William A. O'Neill, D., $65,000.
Lt. Gov. — Joseph J. Fauliso, D., $40,000.
Sec. of State — Julia H. Tashjian, D., $35,000.
Treasurer — Henry E. Parker, D., $35,000.
Comptroller — J. Edward Caldwell, D., $35,000.
Atty. Gen. — Joseph I. Liberman, D., $50,000.
General Assembly: meets annually odd years in January and even years in February at Hartford. Salary $26,000 per 2-year term plus $3,500 per year for expenses, plus travel allowance.
Senate — Dem., 12; Rep., 24. Total, 36.
House — Dem., 66; Rep., 85. Total, 151.

Delaware

Governor — Michael N. Castle, R., $70,000.
Lt. Gov. — S. B. Wood, D., $30,000.
Sec. of State — Michael Harkins, R., $50,000.
Atty. Gen. — Charles Oberly 3d, D., $52,320.
Treasurer — Janet C. Rzewnicki, R., $33,960.
General Assembly: meets annually at Dover from the 2d Tuesday in January to midnight June 30. Members receive $20,000 base salary.

Senate — Dem., 13; Rep., 8. Total, 21.
House — Dem., 19; Rep., 22. Total, 41.

Florida

Governor — Robert Graham, D., $69,550.
Lt. Gov. — Wayne Mixon, D., $60,455.
Sec. of State — George Firestone, D., $59,385.
Comptroller — Gerald Lewis, D., $59,385.
Atty. Gen. — Jim Smith, D., $59,385.
Treasurer — Bill Gunter, D., $59,385.
Legislature: meets annually at Tallahassee. Members receive $12,000 per year plus expense allowance while on official business.
Senate — Dem., 32; Rep., 8. Total, 40.
House — Dem., 77; Rep., 43. Total, 120.

Georgia

Governor — Joe Frank Harris, D., $79,358.
Lt. Gov. — Zell Miller, D., $45,000.
Sec. of State — Max Cleland, D., $60,500.
Comptroller General — Johnnie L. Caldwell, D., $60,000.
Atty. Gen. — Michael J. Bowers, $62,000.
General Assembly: meets annually at Atlanta. Members receive $10,000 per year. During session $59 per day for expenses.
Senate — Dem., 47; Rep., 9. Total, 56.
House — Dem., 154; Rep., 26. Total, 180.

Hawaii

Governor — George R. Ariyoshi, D., $59,400.
Lt. Gov. — John Waihee, D., $53,460.
Atty. Gen. — Michael A. Lilly, act., $50,490.
Comptroller — Hideo Murakami, $50,490.
Dir. of Budget & Finance — Jensen S. L. Hee, $50,490.
Legislature: meets annually on 3d Wednesday in January at Honolulu. Members receive $15,600 per year plus expenses.
Senate — Dem., 21. Rep., 4. Total, 25.
House — Dem., 40. Rep., 11. Total, 51.

Idaho

Governor — John V. Evans, D., $50,000.
Lt. Gov. — David H. Leroy, R., $14,000.
Sec. of State — Pete T. Cenarrusa, R., $37,500.
Treasurer — Marjorie Ruth Moon, D., $37,500.
Atty. Gen. — Jim Jones, R., $42,000.
Legislature: meets annually on the Monday after the first day in January at Boise. Members receive $4,200 per year, plus $25 per day when authorized, plus travel allowances.
Senate — Dem., 14; Rep., 28. Total, 42.
House — Dem., 17; Rep., 67. Total, 84.

Illinois

Governor — James R. Thompson, R., $58,000.
Lt. Gov. — George H. Ryan, R., $45,500.
Sec. of State — Jim Edgar, R., $50,500.
Comptroller — Roland W. Burris, D., $48,000.
Atty. Gen. — Neil F. Hartigan, D., $50,500.
Treasurer — James H. Donnewald, D., $48,000.
General Assembly: meets annually in January at Springfield. Members receive $30,250 per annum.
Senate — Dem., 31; Rep., 28. Total, 59.
House — Dem., 61; Rep., 57. Total, 118.

Indiana

Governor — Robert D. Orr, R., $66,000 plus discretionary expenses.
Lt. Gov. — John M. Mutz, R., $51,000 plus discretionary expenses.
Sec. of State — Edwin J. Simcox, R., $46,000.
Atty. Gen. — Linley E. Pearson, R., $51,000.
Treasurer — Julian Ridlen, R., $46,000.
General Assembly: meets annually in January. Members receive $11,600 per year plus $65 per day while in session, $15 per day while not in session.
Senate — Dem., 20; Rep., 30. Total, 50.
House — Dem., 39; Rep., 61. Total, 100.

Iowa

Governor — Terry Branstad, R., $64,000 plus $5,724 expenses.
Lt. Gov. — Robert Anderson, D., $21,900 plus personal expenses and travel allowances at same rate as for a senator.
Sec. of State — Mary Jane Odell, R., $41,000.
Atty. Gen. — Tom Miller, D., $54,000.
Treasurer — Michael L. Fitzgerald, D., $41,000.
General Assembly: meets annually in January at Des Moines. Members receive $14,600 annually plus maximum expense allowance of $40 per day for first 120 days of first session, and first 100 days of 2d session; mileage expenses at 24c a mile.
Senate — Dem., 28; Rep., 22. Total, 50.
House — Dem., 60; Rep., 40. Total, 100.

Kansas

Governor — John Carlin, D., $65,000.
Lt. Gov. — Tom Docking. D., $16,436 plus $1,875 for expenses.
Sec. of State — Jack H. Brier, R., $50,000.
Atty. Gen. — Robert T. Stephan, R., $57,500.
Treasurer — Joan Finney, D., $50,000.
Legislature: meets annually in January at Topeka. Members receive $49 a day plus $50 a day expenses while in session, plus $600 per month while not in session.
Senate — Dem., 16; Rep., 24. Total, 40.
House — Dem., 49; Rep., 76. Total, 125.

Kentucky

Governor — Martha L. Collins, D., $60,000.
Lt. Gov. — Steve Beshear, D., $52,028.
Sec. of State — Drexell R. Davis, D., $52,028.
Atty. Gen. — Dave Armstrong, D., $52,028.
Treasurer — Francis J. Mills, D., $52,028.
Auditor — Mary A. Tobin. D., $52,028.
General Assembly: meets even years in January at Frankfort. Members receive $100 per day and $100 per day during session and $950 per month for expenses for interim.
Senate — Dem., 28; Rep., 10. Total, 38.
House — Dem., 74; Rep., 26. Total, 100.

Louisiana

Governor — Edwin W. Edwards, D., $73,440.
Lt. Gov. — Robert L. Freeman, D., $63,367.
Sec. of State — James H. Brown, D., $60,169.
Atty. Gen. — William J. Guste Jr., D., $60,169.
Treasurer — Mary Evelyn Parker, D., $60,169.
Legislature: meets annually for 60 legislative days commencing on 3d Monday in April. Members receive $75 per day and mileage at 21c a mile for 13 round trips, plus $1,400 per month expense allowance.
Senate — Dem., 37; Rep., 2. Total, 39.
House — Dem., 89; Rep., 16. Total, 105.

Maine

Governor — Joseph E. Brennan, D., $35,000.
Sec. of State — Rodney Quinn, D., $39,915.
Atty. Gen. — James Tierney, D., $45,489.
Treasurer — Samuel Shapiro, D., $36,296.
Legislature: meets biennially in January at Augusta. Members receive $7,500 for regular sessions, $4,000 for special session plus expenses; presiding officers receive 50% more.
Senate — Dem., 24; Rep., 11. Total, 35.
House — Dem., 85; Rep., 66. Total, 151.

Maryland

Governor — Harry Hughes, D., $75,000.
Lt. Gov. — J. Joseph Curran Jr., D., $62,500.
Comptroller — Louis L. Goldstein, D., $62,500.
Atty. Gen. — Stephen H. Sachs, D., $62,500.
Sec. of State — Lorraine Sheehan, D., $45,000.
Treasurer — William S. James, D., $62,500.
General Assembly: meets 90 days annually on the 2d Wednesday in January at Annapolis. Members receive $21,000 per year.
Senate — Dem., 41; Rep., 6. Total, 47.
House — Dem., 124; Rep., 17. Total, 141.

Massachusetts

Governor — Michael S. Dukakis, D., $75,000.
Lt. Gov. — vacant, $60,000.
Sec. of State — Michael Joseph Connolly, D., $60,000.
Atty. Gen. — Francis X. Bellotti, D., $65,000.
Treasurer — Robert Q. Crane, D., $60,000.
Auditor — John J. Finnegan, D., $60,000.
General Court (Legislature): meets each January in Boston. Salaries $30,000 per annum.
Senate — Dem., 32; Rep., 8. Total, 40.
House — Dem., 126; Rep., 34. Total, 160.

Michigan

Governor — James J. Blanchard, D., $81,900.
Lt. Gov. — Martha W. Griffiths, D., $56,175.
Sec. of State — Richard H. Austin, D., $75,000.
Atty. Gen. — Frank J. Kelley, D., $75,000.
Treasurer — Robert A. Bowman, N-P, $62,500.
Legislature: meets annually in January at Lansing. Members receive $34,860 per year, plus $6,700 expense allowance.
Senate — Dem., 18; Rep., 20. Total, 38.
House — Dem., 57; Rep., 52; 1 vacancy. Total, 110.

Minnesota

Governor — Rudy Perpich, DFL, $84,560.
Lt. Gov. — Marlene Johnson, DFL, $46,510.
Sec. of State — Joan Anderson Growe, DFL., $46,510.
Atty. Gen. — Hubert H. Humphrey 3d, DFL., $66,060.

Treasurer — Robert W. Mattson, DFL., $44,000.
Auditor — Arne H. Carlson, IR, $50,740.
Legislature: meets for a total of 120 days within every 2 years at St. Paul. Members receive $18,500 per year, plus expense allowance during session.
Senate — DFL., 42; IR, 25. Total, 67.
House — DFL., 65; IR, 69. Total, 134.
(DFL means Democratic-Farmer-Labor. IR means Independent Republican.)

Mississippi

Governor — William A. Allain, D., $63,000.
Lt. Gov. — Brad Dye, D., $34,000 per regular legislative session, plus expense allowance.
Sec. of State — Dick Molpus, D., $45,000.
Atty. Gen. — Edwin L. Pittman, D., $51,000.
Treasurer — William J. Cole 3d, D., $45,000.
Legislature: meets annually at Jackson. Members receive $10,100 per regular session plus travel allowance, and $500 per month while not in session.
Senate — Dem., 49; Rep., 3. Total, 52.
House — Dem., 117; Rep., 5. Total, 122.

Missouri

Governor — John D. Ashcroft, R., $75,000.
Lt. Gov. — Harriett Woods, D., $45,000.
Sec. of State — Roy D. Blunt, R., $60,000.
Atty. Gen. — William L. Webster, R., $60,000.
Treasurer — Wendell Bailey, R., $60,000.
State Auditor — Margaret Kelly, R., $60,000.
General Assembly: meets annually in Jefferson City on the first Wednesday after first Monday in January; adjournment in off-numbered years by June 30, in even-numbered years by May 15. Members receive $18,078 annually.
Senate — Dem., 21; Rep., 13. Total, 34.
House — Dem., 108; Rep., 55. Total, 163.

Montana

Governor — Ted Schwinden, D., $48,923.
Lt. Gov. — George Turman, D., $35,031.
Sec. of State — Jim Waltermire, R., $32,326.
Atty. Gen. — Mike Greely, D., $44,620.
Legislative Assembly: meets odd years in January at Helena. Members receive $50.02 per legislative day plus $45 per day for expenses while in session.
Senate — Dem., 28; Rep., 22. Total, 50.
House — Dem., 50; Rep., 50. Total, 100.

Nebraska

Governor — Robert Kerrey, D., $40,000.
Lt. Gov. — Donald F. McGinley, D., $32,000.
Sec. of State — Allen J. Beermann, R., $32,000.
Atty. Gen. — Robert Spire, R., $39,500.
Treasurer — Kay Orr, R., $32,000.
Legislature: meets annually in January at Lincoln. Members receive salary of $4,800 annually plus travelling expenses for one round trip to and from session.
Unicameral body composed of 49 members who are elected on a nonpartisan ballot and are classed as senators.

Nevada

Governor — Richard Bryan, D., $65,000.
Lt. Gov. — Robert Cashell, R., $10,500 plus $104 per day when acting as governor and president of the Senate during legislative sessions.
Sec. of State — William D. Swackhamer, D., $42,500.
Comptroller — Darrel Daines, R., $41,000.
Atty. Gen. — Brian McKay, R., $52,500.
Treasurer — Patty Cafferata, R., $41,000.
Legislature: meets odd years in January at Carson City. Members receive $104 per day for 60 days (20 days for special sessions), plus per diem of $50 per day for entire length of session. Travel allowance of 20c per mile.
Senate — Dem., 13; Rep., 8. Total, 21.
Assembly — Rep., 25; Dem., 17. Total, 42.

New Hampshire

Governor — John H. Sununu, R., $59,885.
Sec. of State — William M. Gardner, D., $42,064.
Atty. Gen. — Stephen E. Merrill, $53,460.
Treasurer — Georgie A. Thomas, R., $32,794.
General Court (Legislature): meets odd years in January at Concord. Members receive $200; presiding officers $250.
Senate — Dem., 9; Rep., 14; 1 vacancy. Total, 24.
House — Rep., 234; Dem., 158; 2 ind., 6 vacancies. Total, 400.

New Jersey

Governor — Thomas H. Kean, R., $85,000.
Sec. of State — Jane Burgio, R., $66,000.
Atty. Gen. — Irwin I. Kimmelman, R., $70,000.

Treasurer — Michael M. Horn, R., $70,000.
Legislature: meets throughout the year at Trenton. Members receive $25,000 per year, except president of Senate and speaker of Assembly who receive 1/3 more.
Senate — Dem., 23; Rep., 17. Total, 40.
Assembly — Dem., 44; Rep. 36. Total, 80.

New Mexico

Governor — Toney Anaya, D., $60,000.
Lt. Gov. — Mike Runnels, D., $38,500. Acting governor, $150 per day.
Sec. of State — Clara Jones, D., $38,500.
Atty. Gen. — Paul G. Bardacke, D., $44,000.
Treasurer — Earl Edward Hartley, D., $38,500.
Legislature: meets in January at Sante Fe; odd years for 60 days, even years for 30 days. Members receive $75 per day while in session.
Senate — Dem., 21; Rep., 21. Total, 42.
House — Dem., 44; Rep., 26. Total, 70.

New York

Governor — Mario M. Cuomo, D., $100,000.
Lt. Gov. — vacant., $85,000.
Sec. of State — Gail S. Shaffer, D., $72,100.
Comptroller — Edward V. Regan, R., $85,000.
Atty. Gen. — Robert Abrams, D., $85,000.
Legislature: meets annually in January at Albany. Members receive $43,000 per year.
Senate — Dem., 26; Rep., 35. Total, 61.
Assembly — Dem., 94; Rep., 56. Total, 150.

North Carolina

Governor — James G. Martin, D., $90,516 plus $11,500 per year expenses.
Lt. Gov. — Robert B. Jordan 3d, D., $55,368 per year, plus $11,500 per year expense allowance.
Sec. of State — Thad Eure, D., $55,368
Atty. Gen. — Lacy Thornberg, D., $55,368.
Treasurer — Harlan E. Boyles, D., $55,368.
General Assembly: meets odd years in January at Raleigh. Members receive $8,400 annual salary and $2,508 annual expense allowance, plus $60 per diem subsistence and travel allowance while in session.
Senate — Dem., 38; Rep., 12. Total, 50.
House — Dem., 82; Rep., 38. Total, 120.

North Dakota

Governor — George A. Sinner, D., $65,000.
Lt. Gov. — Ruth Meiers, D., $50,000.
Sec. of State — Ben Meier, R., $46,000.
Atty. Gen. — Nicholas Spaeth, D., $52,000.
Treasurer — Robert Hanson, D., $46,000.
Legislative Assembly: meets odd years in January at Bismarck. Members receive $90 per day expenses during session and $180 per month when not in session.
Senate — Dem., 24; Rep., 29. Total, 53.
House — Dem., 41; Rep., 65. Total, 106.

Ohio

Governor — Richard F. Celeste, D., $65,000.
Lt. Gov. — Myrl H. Shoemaker, D., $35,000.
Sec. of State — Sherrod Brown, D., $50,000.
Atty. Gen. — Anthony J. Celebrezze Jr., D., $50,000.
Treasurer — Mary Ellen Withrow, D., $50,000.
Auditor — Thomas E. Ferguson, D., $50,000.
General Assembly: meets odd years at Columbus on first Monday in January for the 1st session, and no later than Mar. 15th of the following year for the 2d session. Members receive $30,152 per annum.
Senate — Dem., 15; Rep., 18. Total, 33.
House — Dem., 59; Rep., 40. Total, 99.

Oklahoma

Governor — George Nigh, D., $70,000.
Lt. Gov. — Spencer T. Bernard, D., $40,000.
Sec. of State — Jeannette B. Edmondson, D., $37,000.
Atty. Gen. — Mike Turpen, D., $55,000.
Treasurer — Leo Winters, D., $50,000.
Legislature: meets annually in January at Oklahoma City. Members receive $20,000 annually.
Senate — Dem., 34; Rep., 14. Total, 48.
House — Dem., 69; Rep., 32. Total, 101.

Oregon

Governor — Victor Atiyeh, R., $55,423, plus $500 monthly expenses.
Sec. of State — Barbara Roberts, D., $42,864.
Atty. Gen. — David B. Frohnmayer, R., $53,308.
Treasurer — Bill Rutherford, R., $45,619.

Legislative Assembly: meets odd years in January at Salem. Members receive $700 monthly and $44 expenses per day while in session; $300 per month while not in session.
Senate — Dem., 18; Rep., 12. Total, 30.
House — Dem., 34; Rep., 26. Total, 60.

Pennsylvania

Governor — Dick Thornburgh, R., $85,000.
Lt. Gov. — William W. Scranton 3d, R., $57,500.
Sec. of the Commonwealth — William R. Davis, R., $48,000.
Atty. Gen. — Leroy S. Zimmerman, R., $65,000.
Treasurer — R. Budd Dwyer, R., $58,000.
General Assembly — convenes annually in January at Harrisburg. Members receive $35,000 per year plus expenses.
Senate — Dem., 23; Rep., 27. Total, 50.
House — Dem., 103; Rep., 100. Total, 203.

Rhode Island

Governor — Edward DiPrete, R., $49,500.
Lt. Gov. — Richard A. Licht, D., $35,500.
Sec. of State — Susan Farmer, R., $35,500.
Atty. Gen. — Arlene N. Violet, R., $41,875.
Treasurer — Roger N. Begin, D., $35,500.
General Assembly: meets annually in January at Providence. Members receive $5 per day for 60 days, and travel allowance of 8c per mile.
Senate — Dem., 38; Rep., 12. Total, 50.
House — Dem., 77; Rep., 22; 1 Ind. Total, 100.

South Carolina

Governor — Richard W. Riley, D., $60,000.
Lt. Gov. — Michael Daniel, D., $35,000.
Sec. of State — John T. Campbell, D., $55,000.
Comptroller Gen. — Earle E. Morris Jr., D., $55,000.
Atty. Gen. — T.T. Medlock, D., $55,000.
Treasurer — G.L. Patterson Jr., D., $55,000.
General Assembly: meets annually in January at Columbia. Members receive $10,000 per year and expense allowance of $68 per day, plus travel and postage allowance.
Senate — Dem., 36; Rep., 10. Total, 46.
House — Dem. 96; Rep., 27; 1 vacancy. Total, 124.

South Dakota

Governor — William J. Janklow, R., $53,000.
Lt. Gov. — Lowell C. Hansen 2d, R., $7,375 plus $75 per day during legislative session.
Sec. of State — Alice Kundert, R., $36,000.
Treasurer — David Volk, R., $36,000.
Atty. Gen. — Mark Meierhenry, R., $45,000.
Auditor — Vernon Larson, R., $36,000.
Legislature: meets annually in January at Pierre. Members receive $3,200 for 40-day session in odd-numbered years, and $2,800 for 35-day session in even-numbered years, plus $75 per legislative day.
Senate — Dem., 10; Rep., 25. Total, 35.
House — Dem., 13; Rep., 57. Total, 70.

Tennessee

Governor — Lamar Alexander, R., $68,220.
Lt. Gov. — John S. Wilder, D., $12,500.
Sec. of State — Gentry Crowell, D., $59,500.
Comptroller — William Snodgrass, D., $59,500.
Atty. Gen. — Michael Cody, D., $65,650.
General Assembly: meets annually in January at Nashville. Members receive $12,500 yearly plus $71.00 expenses for each day in session.
Senate — Dem., 23; Rep., 10. Total, 33.
House — Dem., 62; Rep., 37. Total, 99.

Texas

Governor — Mark White Jr., D., $90,700.
Lt. Gov. — Bill Hobby, D., $7,200, plus living quarters. Governor's salary when acting as governor.
Sec. of State — Myra A. McDaniel, D., $62,400.
Comptroller — Bob Bullock, D., $70,400.
Atty. Gen. — Jim Mattox, D., $70,400.
Treasurer — Ann W. Richards, D., $70,400.
Legislature: meets odd years in January at Austin. Members receive annual salary not exceeding $7,200, per diem while in session, and travel allowance.
Senate — Dem., 25; Rep., 6. Total, 31.
House — Dem., 97; Rep., 53. Total, 150.

Utah

Governor — Norman Bangerter, R., $60,000.
Lt. Gov. — W. Val Oveson, R., $50,000.
Atty. Gen. — David L. Wilkinson, R., $49,000.
Treasurer — Edward T. Alter, D., $45,500.
Legislature: convenes for 60 days on 2d Monday in January

each year; members receive $25 per day, $15 daily expenses, and mileage.
Senate — Dem., 6; Rep., 23. Total, 29.
House — Dem., 14; Rep., 61. Total, 75.

Vermont

Governor — Madeleine M. Kunin, D., $50,000.
Lt. Gov. — Peter Smith, R., $25,000.
Sec. of State — James H. Douglas, R., $35,000.
Atty. Gen. — Jeffrey Amestoy, R., $45,000.
Treasurer — Emory Hebard, R., $35,000.
Auditor of Accounts — Alexander V. Acebo, R., $35,000.
General Assembly: meets odd years in January at Montpelier. Members receive $285 weekly while in session, with a limit of $11,000 for a regular session and $57 per day for special session, plus specified expenses.
Senate — Dem., 18; Rep., 12. Total, 30.
House — Dem., 72; Rep., 77; 1 Ind. Total, 150.

Virginia

Governor — Charles S. Robb, D., $75,000.
Lt. Gov. — Richard J. Davis, D., $20,000.
Atty. Gen. — Gerald L. Baliles, D., $56,000.
Sec. of the Commonwealth — Laurie Naismith, D., $36,410.
Treasurer — C. J. Boehm, $60,632.
General Assembly: meets annually in January at Richmond. Members receive $11,000 annually plus expense and mileage allowances.
Senate — Dem., 32; Rep., 8. Total, 40.
House — Dem., 65; Rep., 34; Ind., 1. Total, 100.

Washington

Governor — Booth Gardner, R., $63,000.
Lt. Gov. — John A. Cherberg, D., $28,600.
Sec. of State — Ralph Munro, R., $31,000.
Atty. Gen. — Ken Eikenberry, R., $47,100.
Treasurer — Robert S. O'Brien, D., $37,200.
Legislature: meets annually in January at Olympia. Members receive $14,800 annually plus per diem of $50 per diem and 10¢ per mile while in session, and $50 per diem for attending meetings during interim.
Senate — Dem., 27; Rep., 22. Total, 49.
House — Dem., 53; Rep., 45. Total, 98.

West Virginia

Governor — Arch A. Moore Jr., R., $72,000
Sec. of State — Ken Hechler, D., $43,200.
Atty. Gen. — Charlie Brown, D., $50,400.
Treasurer — A. James Manchin, D., $50,400.
Comm. of Agric. — Gus R. Douglass, D., $46,800.
Auditor — Glen B. Gainer Jr., D., $46,800.
Legislature: meets annually in January at Charleston. Members receive $5,136.
Senate — Dem., 30; Rep., 4. Total, 34.
House — Dem., 73; Rep., 27. Total, 100.

Wisconsin

Governor — Anthony S. Earl, D., $75,337.
Lt. Gov. — James T. Flynn, D., $41,390.
Sec. of State — Douglas La Follette, D., $37,334.
Treasurer — Charles P. Smith, D., $37,334.
Atty. Gen. — Bronson C. La Follette, D., $58,139.
Superintendent of Public Instruction — Herbert J. Grover, $60,149.
Legislature: meets in January at Madison. Members receive $27,202 annually plus $41.63 per day expenses.
Senate — Dem., 19; Rep., 14. Total, 33.
Assembly — Dem., 52; Rep., 47. Total, 99.

Wyoming

Governor — Ed Herschler, D., $70,000.
Sec. of State — Thyra Thomson, R., $52,500.
Atty. Gen. — A.G. McClintock., $52,500.
Treasurer — Stan Smith, R., $52,500.
Legislature: meets odd years in January, even years in February, at Cheyenne. Members receive $75 per day while in session, plus $60 per day for expenses.
Senate — Dem., 11; Rep., 19. Total, 30.
House — Dem., 18; Rep. 46. Total, 64.

Puerto Rico

Governor — Rafael Hernández-Cólon.
Secretary of State — Héctor Luis Acevedo.
Secy. of Justice — Héctor Rivera-Cruz.
These officials belong to the Popular Democratic Party.
Legislature: composed of a Senate of 27 members and a House of Representatives of 51 members. Majority of the members of both chambers belongs to the Popular Democratic Party. They meet annually on the 2d Monday in January at San Juan.

U.S. Government Independent Agencies

Source: National Archives & Records Administration
Address: Washington, DC. Location and ZIP codes of agencies in parentheses; as of mid-1985.

ACTION — Donna M. Alvarado, dir. (806 Connecticut Ave., NW, 20525).

Administrative Conference of the United States — Loren A. Smith, chmn. (2120 L St., NW, 20037).

African Development Foundation — Leonard H. Robinson Jr., pres. (1724 Massachusetts Ave. NW, 20036).

American Battle Monuments Commission — vacancy, chmn. (5127 Pulaski Bldg., 20314).

Appalachian Regional Commission — Winifred A. Pizzano, federal co-chmn.; Gov. Harry R. Hughes of Md., states co-chmn. (1666 Connecticut Ave. NW, 20235).

Board for International Broadcasting — Frank Shakespeare, chmn. (1201 Connecticut Ave., 20005).

Central Intelligence Agency — William J. Casey, dir. (Wash., DC 20505).

Commission on Civil Rights — Clarence M. Pendleton Jr., chmn. (1121 Vermont Ave. NW, 20425).

Commission of Fine Arts — J. Carter Brown, chmn. (708 Jackson Pl. NW, 20006).

Commodity Futures Trading Commission — Susan M. Phillips, chmn. (2033 K St. NW, 20581).

Consumer Product Safety Commission — Terrence M. Scanlon, chmn. (1111 18th St. NW, 20207).

Environmental Protection Agency — Lee M. Thomas, adm. (401 M St., SW, 20460).

Equal Employment Opportunity Commission — Clarence Thomas, chmn. (2401 E St., NW, 20507).

Export-Import Bank of the United States — William H. Draper 3d, pres. and chmn. (811 Vermont Ave. NW, 20571).

Farm Credit Administration — William D. Wampler, chmn., Federal Farm Credit Board (1501 Farm Credit Drive, McLean, VA 22102).

Federal Communications Commission — Mark S. Fowler, chmn. (1919 M St. NW, 20554).

Federal Deposit Insurance Corporation — William M. Isaac, chmn. (550 17th St. NW, 20429).

Federal Election Commission — John Warren McGarry, chmn. (1325 K St. NW, 20463).

Federal Emergency Management Agency — Louis O. Giuffrida, dir. (500 C St. SW, 20472).

Federal Home Loan Bank Board — Edwin J. Gray, chmn. (1700 G St. NW, 20552).

Federal Labor Relations Authority — vacancy, chmn. (500 C St. SW, 20424).

Federal Maritime Commission — Alan Green Jr., chmn. (1100 L St. NW, 20573).

Federal Mediation and Conciliation Service — Kay McMurray, dir. (2100 K St. NW, 20427).

Federal Reserve System — Chairman, board of governors: Paul A. Volcker. (20th St. & Constitution Ave. NW, 20551).

Federal Trade Commission — James C. Miller 3d, chmn. (Pennsylvania Ave. at 6th St. NW, 20580).

General Accounting Office — Comptroller General of the U.S.; Charles A. Bowsher (441 G St. NW, 20548).

General Services Administration — Dwight A. Ink, act. adm. (18th & F Sts. NW, 20405).

Government Printing Office — Public printer: Ralph E. Kennickell Jr. (North Capitol and H Sts. NW, 20401).

Inter-American Foundation — Victor Blanco, chmn. (1515 Wilson Blvd., Rosslyn, VA 22209).

Interstate Commerce Commission — Reese H. Taylor Jr., chmn. (12th St. and Constitution Ave. NW, 20423).

Library of Congress — Daniel J. Boorstin, librarian (10 First St. SE, 20540).

Merit Systems Protection Board — Herbert E. Ellingwood, chmn. (1120 Vermont Ave. NW, 20419).

National Aeronautics and Space Administration — James M. Beggs, adm. (400 Maryland Ave., SW 20546).

National Archives & Records Administration — Frank G. Burke, act. archivist (7th & Pennsylvania Ave. NW, 20408).

National Capital Planning Commission — Glen T. Urquhart, chmn. (1325 G St. NW, 20576).

National Credit Union Administration — vacancy, chmn. (1776 G St. NW, 20456).

National Foundation on the Arts and the Humanities — Frank Hodsoll, chmn. (arts) 1100 Pennsylvania Ave. NW, 20506; John Agresto, act. chmn. (humanities) same address. Institute of Museum Services: Susan E. Phillips, dir., same address.

National Labor Relations Board — Donald L. Dotson, chmn. (1717 Pennsylvania Ave. NW, 20570).

National Mediation Board — Walter C. Wallace, chmn. (1425 K St. NW, 20572).

National Science Foundation — Roland W. Schmitt, chmn., National Science Board (1800 G St. NW, 20550).

National Transportation Safety Board — James E. Burnett, chmn. (800 Independence Ave. SW, 20594).

Nuclear Regulatory Commission — Nunzio J. Pallidino, chmn. (1717 H St. NW, 20555).

Occupational Safety and Health Review Commission — E. Ross Buckley, chmn. (1825 K St. NW, 20006).

Office of Personnel Management — Loretta Cornelius, act. dir., (1900 E St. NW, 20415).

Overseas Private Investment Corporation — Craig A. Nalen, pres. & CEO (1129 20th St. NW, 20527).

Panama Canal Commission — Dennis P. McAuliffe, adm. (in Panama); Michael Rhode Jr., secy. (in Washington: 425 13th St., NW 20004).

Peace Corps — Loret Miller Ruppe, dir. (806 Connecticut Ave. NW, 20526).

Pennsylvania Avenue Development Corporation — Henry A. Berliner, chmn., board of directors (425 13th St. NW, 20004).

Pension Benefit Guaranty Corporation — David M. Walker, exec. dir. (2020 K St. NW, 20006).

Postal Rate Commission — Janet D. Steiger, chmn. (2000 L St. NW, 20268).

Railroad Retirement Board — Robert A. Gielow, chmn. (Rm. 630, 425 13th St. NW, 20004), Main Office (844 Rush St., Chicago, IL 60611).

Securities and Exchange Commission — John S.R. Shad, chmn. (450 5th St. NW, 20549).

Selective Service System — Thomas K. Turnage, dir. (National Headquarters, 20435).

Small Business Administration — James C. Sanders, adm. (1441 L St. NW, 20416).

Smithsonian Institution — S. Dillon Ripley, secy. (1000 Jefferson Dr. SW, 20560).

Tennessee Valley Authority — Chairman, board of directors: C.H. Dean Jr. (400 W. Summit Hill Dr., Knoxville, TN 37902 and Capitol Hill Office Bldg., 412 1st St. SE, Washington, DC 20444).

United States Arms Control & Disarmament Agency — Kenneth L. Adelman, dir. (320 21st St. NW 20451).

United States Information Agency — Charles Z. Wick, dir. (400 C St. SW, 20547).

United States International Development Cooperation Agency — M. Peter McPherson, act. dir. (320 21st St. NW, 20523).

United States International Trade Commission — Paula Stern, chairwoman (701 E St. NW, 20436).

United States Postal Service — Paul N. Carlin, postmaster general (475 L'Enfant Plaza West SW, 20260).

Veterans Administration — Harry N. Walters, adm. (810 Vermont Ave. NW, 20420).

NATIONAL DEFENSE

Data as of July, 1985

Chairman, Joint Chiefs of Staff
John W. Vessey Jr. (USA)

The Joint Chiefs of Staff consists of the Chairman of the Joint Chiefs of Staff; the Chief of Staff, U.S. Army; the Chief of Naval Operations; the Chief of Staff, U.S. Air Force; and the Commandant of the Marine Corps.

Army

Chief of Staff—John A. Wickham, Jr.
Generals

	Date of Rank
Galvin, John R.	Feb. 25, 1985
Kingston, Robert C.	Nov. 6, 1984
Livsey, William J.	May 3, 1984
Mahaffey, Fred	June 17, 1985
Otis, Glenn K.	Aug. 1, 1981
Richardson, William R.	Feb. 28, 1983
Robinson, Roscoe, Jr.	Aug. 30, 1982
Rogers, Bernard W.	Nov. 7, 1974
Sennewald, Robert W.	May 24, 1982
Thompson, Richard H.	June 29, 1984
Thurman, Maxwell R.	June 23, 1983
Vessey, John W., Jr.	Nov. 1, 1976
Wickham, John A., Jr.	July 10, 1979

Air Force

Chief of Staff—Charles A. Gabriel
Generals

Bazley, Robert W.	Nov. 1, 1984
Dalton, James E.	Aug. 1, 1983
Davis, Bennie L.	Apr. 1, 1979
Donnelly, Charles L., Jr.	Nov. 1, 1984
Gabriel, Charles A.	Aug. 1, 1980
Herres, Robert T.	Aug. 1, 1984
Iosue, Andrew P.	July 1, 1983
Lawson, Richard L.	July 1, 1980
O'Loughlin, Earl T.	Nov. 1, 1984
Ryan, Thomas M., Jr.	July 31, 1981
Skantze, Lawrence A.	Oct. 6, 1983
Welch, Larry D.	Aug. 1, 1984

Navy

Chief of Naval Operations
Admiral James D. Watkins (submariner)
Admirals

Baggett, Lee, Jr.	May 30, 1985
Crowe, William J., Jr. (submariner)	May 30, 1980
Foley, Sylvester R., Jr. (aviator)	May 28, 1982
Hays, Ronald J. (aviator)	April 29, 1983
McDonald, Wesley L. (aviator)	Oct. 1, 1982
McKee, Kinnaird R. (submariner)	Mar. 2, 1982
Small, William N. (aviator)	July 1, 1981
Watkins, James D. (submariner)	Sept. 18, 1979

Marine Corps

Corps Commandant, with rank of General
Paul X. Kelley . . . . July 1, 1983

Asst. Commandant, with rank of General
John K. Davis. . . . . July 1, 1983

Chief of Staff, with rank of Lt. Gen.
D'Wayne Gray . . . . May 20, 1983

Coast Guard

Commandant, with rank of Admiral
James S. Gracey. . . . . May 27, 1982

Vice Commandant, with rank of Vice Admiral
Benedict Stabile. . . . . May 21, 1982

United States Unified and Specified Commands

Atlantic Command—Admiral Wesley L. McDonald, USN
HQ Aerospace Defense Command—General Robert T. Herres, USAF
U.S. European Command—General Bernard W. Rogers, USA
Pacific Command—Admiral William J. Crowe, USN
U.S. Southern Command—General John R. Galvin, USA
Strategic Air Command—General Larry D. Welch, USAF

U.S. Central Command—Lt. Gen. Robert C. Kingston, USA
U.S. Readiness Command—General W.A. Nutting, USA
Military Air Lift Command—General Thomas M. Ryan, Jr., USAF
Military Sea Lift Command—Vice Admiral William H. Rowden, USN

North Atlantic Treaty Organization International Commands

Supr. Allied Commander, Europe (SACEUR)—Gen. Bernard W. Rogers, USA
Deputy SACEUR—Air Ch. Marshal Sir Peter Terry (UK),
C-in-C SACEUR—Gen. H. J. Mack, Army (Germany)
C-in-C Allied Forces, Northern Europe—Gen. Sir Richard Lawson (UK)
C-in-C Allied Forces, Central Europe—Gen. Leopold Chalupa, Army (Germany)
C-in-C Allied Forces, Southern Europe—Adm. L. Baggett,

USN
Supr. Allied Commander Atlantic (SACLANT)—Adm. Wesley L. McDonald, USN
Deputy SACLANT—R. Adm. K. E. Moranville, USN
Commander Strike Force South—V. Adm. F. B. Kelso II, USN
Allied Commander in Chief, Channel—Adm. William D.M. Staveley, (UK)

Principal U.S. Military Training Centers
Army

Name, P.O. address	Zip	Nearest city	Name, P.O. address	Zip	Nearest city
Aberdeen Proving Ground, MD	21005	Aberdeen	Fort Jackson, SC	29207	Columbia
Carlisle Barracks, PA	17013	Carlisle	Fort Knox, KY	40121	Louisville
Fort Belvoir, VA	22060	Alexandria	Fort Leavenworth, KS	66027	Leavenworth
Fort Benning, GA	31905	Columbus	Fort Lee, VA	23801	Petersburg
Fort Bliss, TX	79916	El Paso	Fort McClellan, AL	36205	Anniston
Fort Bragg, NC	28307	Fayetteville	Fort Monmouth, NJ	07703	Red Bank
Fort Devens, MA	01433	Ayer	Fort Rucker, AL	36362	Dothan
Fort Dix, NJ	08640	Trenton	Fort Sill, OK	73503	Lawton
Fort Eustis, VA	23604	Newport News	Fort Leonard Wood, MO	65473	Rolla
			National Training Center	92311	Ft. Irwin
Fort Gordon, GA	30905	Augusta	Redstone Arsenal, AL	35809	Huntsville
Fort Benjamin Harrison, IN	46216	Indianapolis	The Judge Advocate		Charlottes-
Fort Sam Houston, TX	78234	San Antonio	General School, VA	22901	ville
Fort Huachuca, AZ	85613	Sierra Vista			

Navy Recruit Training Centers

Great Lakes, IL	60088	North Chicago	Orlando, FL	32813	Orlando
San Diego, CA	92133	San Diego			

Major Marine Corps Facilities

Name, P.O. address	Zip	Nearest city	Name, P.O. address	Zip	Nearest city
MCB Camp Lejeune, NC	28542	Jacksonville	MCAS Iwakuni, Japan.	FPO Seattle	Iwakuni
MCB Camp Pendleton, CA . . .	92055	Oceanside		98764	
MCB Camp Butler, Okinawa	FPO Seattle	Futenma,	MCAS Kaneohe Bay,		
	98773	Okinawa	Oahu, HI.	FPO San Francisco	Kailua
MCAGCC Twentynine Palms, CA	92278	Palm Springs		96615	
MCDEC Quantico, VA	22134	Quantico	MCAS (Helo) Futenma,		
MCRD Parris Island, SC.	29905	Beaufort	Okinawa FPO Seattle	98764	Futenma
MCRD San Diego, CA.	92140	San Diego	MCAS Beaufort, SC	29902	Beaufort
MCAS Cherry Point, NC.	28533	Cherry Point	MCAS Yuma, AZ	85364	Yuma
MCAS El Toro (Santa Ana), CA .	92709	Santa Ana	MCMWTC Bridgeport, CA.	93517	Bridgeport
MCAS (Helo) Tustin, CA.	92780	Santa Ana	MCLB Albany, GA	31704	Albany
MCAS (Helo) New River, NC . .	28540	Jacksonville	MCLB Barstow, CA.	92311	Barstow

MCB = Marine Corps Base. MCDEC = Marine Corps Development & Education Command. MCAS = Marine Corps Air Station. Helo = Helicopter. MCAGCC = Marine Corps Air-Ground Combat Center. MCMWTC = Marine Corps Mountain Warfare Training Center. MCLB = Marine Corps Logistics Base.

Air Force

Chanute AFB, IL	61868	Rantoul	Mather AFB, CA	95655	Sacramento
Columbus AFB, MS	39701	Columbus	Maxwell AFB, AL.	36112	Montgomery
Goodfellow AFB, TX	76903	San Angelo	Randolph AFB, TX	78150	San Antonio
Gunter AFS, AL.	36114	Montgomery	Reese AFB, TX	79489	Lubbock
Keesler AFB, MS	39534	Biloxi	Sheppard AFB, TX	76311	Wichita Falls
Lackland AFB, TX	78236	San Antonio	Vance AFB, OK.	73702	Enid
Laughlin AFB, TX.	78843	Del Rio	Williams AFB, AZ	85224	Phoenix
Lowry AFB, CO.	80230	Denver			

Personal Salutes and Honors

The United States national salute, 21 guns, is also the salute to a national flag. The independence of the United States is commemorated by the salute to the union — one gun for each state — fired at noon on July 4 at all military posts provided with suitable artillery.

A 21-gun salute on arrival and departure, with 4 ruffles and flourishes, is rendered to the President of the United States, to an ex-President and to a President-elect. The national anthem or *Hail to the Chief*, as appropriate, is played for the President, and the national anthem for the others. A 21-gun salute on arrival and departure with 4 ruffles and flourishes, also is rendered to the sovereign or chief of state of a foreign country or a member of a reigning royal family; the national anthem of his or her country is played. The music is considered an inseparable part of the salute and will immediately follow the ruffles and flourishes without pause.

Rank	Salute—guns Arrive—Leave		Ruffles, flour- ishes	Music
Vice President of United States.	19		4	Hail Columbia
Speaker of the House	19		4	March
American or foreign ambassador.	19		4	Nat. anthem of official
Premier or prime minister	19		4	Nat. anthem of official
Secretary of Defense, Army, Navy or Air Force	19	19	4	March
Other Cabinet members, Senate President pro tempore, Governor, or Chief Justice of U.S.	19		4	March
Chairman, Joint Chiefs of Staff.	19	19	4	
Army Chief of Staff, Chief of Naval Operations, Air Force Chief of Staff, Marine Commandant	19	19	4	General's or Admiral's March
General of the Army, General of the Air Force, Fleet Admiral. . . .	19	19	4	
Generals, Admirals	17	17	4	
Assistant Secretaries of Defense, Army, Navy or Air Force	17	17	4	March
Chairman of a Committee of Congress	17		4	March

Other salutes (on arrival only) include 15 guns for American envoys or ministers and foreign envoys or ministers accredited to the United States; 15 guns for a lieutenant general or vice admiral; 13 guns for a major general or rear admiral (upper half); 13 guns for American ministers resident and ministers resident accredited to the U.S.; 11 guns for a brigadier general or rear admiral (lower half); 11 guns for American charges d'affaires and like officials accredited to U.S.; and 11 guns for consuls general accredited to U.S.

Military Units, U.S. Army and Air Force

Army units. Squad. In infantry usually ten men under a staff sergeant. **Platoon.** In infantry 4 squads under a lieutenant. **Company.** Headquarters section and 4 platoons under a captain. (Company in the artillery is a battery; in the cavalry, a troop.) **Battalion.** Hdqts. and 4 or more companies under a lieutenant colonel. (Battalion size unit in the cavalry is a squadron.) **Brigade.** Hdqts. and 3 or more battalions under a colonel. **Division.** Hdqts. and 3 brigades with artillery, combat support, and combat service support units under a major general. **Army Corps.** Two or more divisions with corps troops under a lieutenant general. **Field Army.** Hdqts. and two or more corps with field Army troops under a general.

Air Force Units. Flight. Numerically designated flights are the lowest level unit in the Air Force. They are used primarily where there is a need for small mission elements to be incorporated into an organized unit. **Squadron.** A squadron is the basic unit in the Air Force. It is used to designate the mission units in operational commands. **Group.** The group is a flexible unit composed of two or more squadrons whose functions may be either tactical, support or administrative in nature. **Wing.** An operational wing normally has two or more assigned mission squadrons in an area such as combat, flying training or airlift. **Air Division.** The organization of the air division may be similar to that of the numbered air force, though on a much smaller scale. Functions are usually limited to operations and logistics. **Numbered Air Forces.** Normally an operationally oriented agency, the numbered air force is designed for the control of two or more air divisions or units of comparable strength. It is a flexible organization and may be of any size. Its wings may be assigned to air divisions or directly under the numbered air force. **Major Command.** A major subdivision of the Air Force that is assigned a major segment of the USAF mission.

U.S. Army Insignia and Chevrons

Source: Department of the Army

| Grade | Insignia | Non-commissioned Officers |

General of the Armies

General John J. Pershing, the only person to have held this rank, was authorized to prescribe his own insignia, but never wore in excess of four stars. The rank originally was established by Congress for George Washington in 1799, and he was promoted to the rank by joint resolution of Congress, approved by Pres. Ford Oct. 19, 1976.

General of Army... Five silver stars fastened together in a circle and the coat of arms of the United States in gold color metal with shield and crest enameled.

General . . . . Four silver stars
Lieutenant General . . . . . Three silver stars
Major General . . . . Two silver stars
Brigadier General . . . . . . One silver star
Colonel . . . . Silver eagle
Lieutenant Colonel . . . . . Silver oak leaf
Major. . . . . Gold oak leaf
Captain . . . . Two silver bars
First Lieutenant . . . . One silver bar
Second Lieutenant . . . . . . One gold bar

Warrant officers

Grade Four—Silver bar with 4 enamel black bands.
Grade Three—Silver bar with 3 enamel black bands.
Grade Two—Silver bar with 2 enamel black bands.
Grade One—Silver bar with 1 enamel black band.

Sergeant Major of the Army (E-9). Same as Command Sergeant Major (below) but with 2 stars. Also wears distinctive red and white shield on lapel.

Command Sergeant Major (E-9). Three chevrons above three arcs with a 5-pointed star with a wreath around the star between the chevrons and arcs.

Sergeant Major (E-9). Three chevrons above three arcs with a five-pointed star between the chevrons and arcs.

First Sergeant (E-8). Three chevrons above three arcs with a lozenge between the chevrons and arcs.

Master Sergeant (E-8). Three chevrons above three arcs.

Platoon Sergeant or Sergeant First Class (E-7). Three chevrons above two arcs.

Staff Sergeant (E-6). Three chevrons above one arc.

Sergeant (E-5). Three chevrons.

Corporal (E-4). Two chevrons.

Specialists

Specialist Seven (E-7). Three arcs above the eagle device.

Specialist Six (E-6). Two arcs above the eagle device.

Specialist Five (E-5). One arc above the eagle device.

Specialist Four (E-4). Eagle device only.

Other enlisted

Private First Class (E-3). One chevron above one arc.

Private (E-2). One chevron.

Private (E-1). None.

U.S. Army

Source: Department of the Army

Army Military Personnel on Active Duty[1]

June 30[2]	Total strength	Commissioned officers			Warrant officers		Enlisted personnel		
		Total	Male	Female[3]	Male[4]	Female	Total	Male	Female
1940	267,767	17,563	16,624	939	763	—	249,441	249,441	
1942	3,074,184	203,137	190,662	12,475	3,285	—	2,867,762	2,867,762	
1943	6,993,102	557,657	521,435	36,222	21,919	0	6,413,526	6,358,200	55,325
1944	7,992,868	740,077	692,351	47,726	36,893	10	7,215,888	7,144,601	71,287
1945	8,266,373	835,403	772,511	62,892	56,216	44	7,374,710	7,283,930	90,780
1946	1,889,690	257,300	240,643	16,657	9,826	18	1,622,546	1,605,847	16,699
1950	591,487	67,784	63,375	4,409	4,760	22	518,921	512,370	6,551
1955	1,107,606	111,347	106,173	5,174	10,552	48	985,659	977,943	7,716
1960	871,348	91,056	86,832	4,224	10,141	39	770,112	761,833	8,279
1965	967,049	101,812	98,029	3,783	10,285	23	854,929	846,409	8,520
1969	1,509,637	148,836	143,699	5,137	23,734	20	1,337,047	1,316,326	10,721
1970	1,319,735	143,704	138,469	5,235	23,005	13	1,153,013	1,141,537	11,476
1975	781,316	89,756	85,184	4,572	13,214	22	678,324	640,621	37,703
1978 (May 31)	772,202	96,553	90,749	5,804	13,160	57	662,432	614,961	47,471
1980 (Mar. 31)	762,739	83,117	76,237	6,880	13,093	103	666,426	608,223	58,203
1982 (Mar.)	788,026	87,874	79,379	8,495	14,058	143	685,951	618,783	67,168
1983 (Mar.)	774,704	89,012	80,091	8,921	14,481	178	674,033	606,956	67,077
1984 (Mar.)	774,935	90,393	81,046	9,347	14,971	198	669,373	602,702	66,671
1985 (Mar.)	778,639	91,986	81,996	9,990	15,109	256	671,288	609,917	67,371

(1) Represents strength of the active Army, including Philippine Scouts, retired Regular Army personnel on extended active duty, and National Guard and Reserve personnel on extended active duty; excludes U.S. Military Academy cadets, contract surgeons, and National Guard and Reserve personnel not on extended active duty.

(2) Data for 1940 to 1947 include personnel in the Army Air Forces and its predecessors (Air Service and Air Corps).

(3) Includes: women doctors, dentists, and Medical Service Corps officers for 1946 and subsequent years, women in the Army Nurse Corps for all years, and the Women's Army Corps and Women's Medical Specialists Corps (dieticians, physical therapists, and occupational specialists) for 1943 and subsequent years.

(4) Act of Congress approved April 27, 1926, directed the appointment as warrant officers of field clerks still in active service. Includes flight officers as follows: 1943, 5,700; 1944, 13,615; 1945, 31,117; 1946, 2,580.

The Federal Service Academies

U.S. Military Academy, West Point, N.Y. Founded 1802. Awards B.S. degree and Army commission for a 5-year service obligation. For admissions information, write Admissions Office, USMA, West Point, NY 10996.

U.S. Naval Academy, Annapolis, Md. Founded 1845. Awards B.S. degree and Navy or Marine Corps commission for a 5-year service obligation. For admissions information, write Dean of Admissions, Naval Academy, Annapolis, MD 21402.

U.S. Air Force Academy, Colorado Springs, Colo. Founded 1954. Awards B.S. degree and Air Force commission for a 5-year service obligation. For admissions information, write Registrar, U.S. Air Force Academy, CO 80840.

U.S. Coast Guard Academy, New London, Conn. Founded 1876. Awards B.S. degree and Coast Guard commission for a 5-year service obligation. For admissions information, write Director of Admissions, Coast Guard Academy, New London, CT 06320.

U.S. Merchant Marine Academy, Kings Point, N.Y. Founded 1943. Awards B.S. degree, a license as a deck, engineer, or dual officer, and a U.S. Naval Reserve commission. Service obligations vary according to options taken by the graduate. For admissions information, write Admission Office, U.S. Merchant Marine Academy, Kings Point, NY 11024.

U.S. Navy Insignia

Source: Department of the Navy

Navy

Stripes and corps device are of gold embroidery.

Stripes

Fleet Admiral . . . . . 1 two inch with 4 one-half inch.
Admiral . . . . 1 two inch with 3 one-half inch.
Vice Admiral. . . . . . 1 two inch with 2 one-half inch.
Rear Admiral . . . . . 1 two inch with 1 one-half inch.
Commodore . . . . . . 1 two inch.
Captain. . . . . 4 one-half inch.
Commander . . . . . 3 one-half inch.
Lieut. Commander . . 2 one-half inch, with 1 one-quarter inch between.
Lieutenant . . . . . . 2 one-half inch.
Lieutenant (j.g.) . . . . 1 one-half inch with one-quarter inch above.
Ensign . . . . 1 one-half inch.
Warrant Officers—One 1/2" broken with 1/2" intervals of blue as follows:
  Warrant Officer W-4—1 break
  Warrant Officer W-3—2 breaks, 2" apart

Warrant Officer W-2—3 breaks, 2" apart
The breaks are symmetrically centered on outer face of the sleeve.
Enlisted personnel (non-Commissioned petty officers). . .A rating badge worn on the upper left arm, consisting of a spread eagle, appropriate number of chevrons, and centered specialty mark.

Marine Corps

Marine Corps and Army officer insignia are similar. Marine Corps and Army enlisted insignia, although basically similar, differ in color, design, and fewer Marine Corps subdivisions. The Marine Corps' distinctive cap and collar ornament is a combination of the American eagle, globe, and anchor.

Coast Guard

Coast Guard insignia follow Navy custom, with certain minor changes such as the officer cap insignia. The Coast Guard shield is worn on both sleeves of officers and on the right sleeve of all enlisted personnel.

U.S. Navy Personnel on Active Duty

June 30	Officers[1]	Nurses	Enlisted[2]	Off. Cand.	Total
1940	13,162	442	144,824	2,569	160,997
1945	320,293	11,086	2,988,207	61,231	3,380,817
1950	42,687	1,964	331,860	5,037	381,538
1960	67,456	2,103	544,040	4,385	617,984
1970	78,488	2,273	605,899	6,000	692,660
1980	63,100	—	464,100	—	527,200
1984 (Jan.)	70,075	—	494,767	—	564,842
1985 (Jan.)	70,291	—	500,810	—	571,101

(1) Nurses are included after 1973. (2) Officer candidates are included after 1973.

Marine Corps Personnel On Active Duty

Yr.	Officers	Enl.	Total	Yr.	Officers	Enl.	Total	Yr.	Officers	Enl.	Total
1955 . .	18,417	186,753	205,170	1965 . . .	17,258	172,955	190,213	1980. . .	18,198	170,271	188,469
1960 . .	16,203	154,418	170,621	1970 . . .	24,941	234,796	259,737	1984 (est.)	20,000	174,000	197,000

Armed Services Senior Enlisted Adviser

The U.S. Army, Navy and Air Force in 1966-67 each created a new position of senior enlisted adviser whose primary job is to represent the point of view of his services' enlisted men and women on matters of welfare, morale, and any problems concerning enlisted personnel. The senior adviser will have direct access to the military chief of his branch of service and policy-making bodies.

The senior enlisted adviser for each Dept. is:
  Army—Sgt. Major of the Army Glen E. Morrell.
  Navy—Master Chief Petty Officer of the Navy William H. Plackett.
  Air Force—Chief Master Sgt. of the AF Sam E. Parish.
  Marines—Sgt. Major of the Marine Corps Robert E. Cleary.

Veteran Population

Source: Veterans Administration

	March 1985
Veterans in civil life, end of month — Total	27,947,000
War Veterans — Total	22,617,000
Vietnam Era — Total	8,275,000
And service in Korean Conflict.	644,000
No service in Korean Conflict.	7,631,000
Korean Conflict — Total	5,208,000
And service in WW II.	1,011,000
No service in WW II	4,197,000
World War II	10,560,000
World War I	228,000
Spanish-American War	18
Peacetime Veterans — Total	5,330,000
Post-Vietnam Era	1,902,000
Peacetime service between Korean Conflict and Vietnam Era only	3,030,000
Peacetime Service — other	397,000

Compensation and Pension Case Payments

Fiscal year	Living veteran cases No.	Deceased veteran cases No.	Total cases No.	Total disbursement Dollars	Fiscal year	Living veteran cases No.	Deceased veteran cases No.	Total cases No.	Total disbursement Dollars
1890 . . .	415,654	122,290	537,944	106,093,850	1965 . . .	3,204,275	1,277,009	4,481,284	3,901,598,010
1900 . . .	752,510	241,019	993,529	138,462,130	1970 . . .	3,127,338	1,487,176	4,614,514	5,113,649,490
1910 . . .	602,622	318,461	921,083	159,974,056	1975 . . .	3,226,701	1,628,146	4,854,847	7,600,000,000
1920 . . .	419,627	349,916	769,543	316,418,029	1979 . . .	3,240,283	1,529,206	4,769,489	10,324,258,000
1930 . . .	542,610	298,223	840,833	418,432,808	1980 . . .	3,195,395	1,450,785	4,646,180	11,045,412,000
1940 . . .	610,122	239,176	849,298	429,138,465	1981 . . .	3,154,030	1,381,280	4,535,310	12,225,027,341
1950 . . .	2,368,238	658,123	3,026,361	2,009,462,298	1982 . . .	3,099,109	1,307,710	4,406,819	13,134,689,000
1955 . . .	2,668,786	808,303	3,477,089	2,634,292,537	1983 . . .	3,043,968	1,241,807	4,285,775	13,699,777,000
1960 . . .	3,008,935	950,802	3,959,737	3,314,761,383	1984 . . .	2,980,406	1,143,007	4,123,413	13,749,617,000

USAF and Air Reserve Forces Personnel by Categories

Category	FY '81	FY '82	FY '83	FY '84	FY '85	FY '86¹
Air Force Military						
Officers	99,000	102,000	104,600	106,200	108,200	109,600
Airmen	467,000	476,000	483,000	486,400	489,500	497,400
Cadets	4,000	4,000	4,500	4,500	4,400	4,400
Total, Air Force Military	570,000	582,000	592,100	597,100	602,100	611,500
Career Reenlistments	43,000	44,400	43,500	38,000	44,600	50,700
Rate	86%	90%	92%	90%	90%	90%
First-Term Reenlistments	19,900	27,100	31,100	24,700	23,900	21,200
Rate	43%	57%	66%	62%	59%	54%
Civilian Personnel						
Direct Hire (including Technicians)	233,000	235,500	230,000	239,800	242,800	252,495
Indirect Hire—Foreign Nationals	13,000	13,000	13,000	13,000	13,600	14,319
Total, Civilian Personnel	246,000	248,500	243,000	252,800	256,400	266,814
Total, Military and Civilian¹	816,000	830,500	835,100	849,900	858,500	878,314
Technicians (including above as Direct Hire Civilians)						
AFRES Technicians	7,600	7,748	7,984	7,634	8,305	9,042
ANG Technicians	21,829	21,834	21,949	22,160	22,401	22,792
Air Reserve Forces						
Air National Guard, Selected Reserve	98,000	100,700	102,200	104,104	105,690	110,859
Air Force Reserve, Paid	62,000	64,500	67,227	70,318	74,829	77,400
Air Force Reserve, Nonpaid	44,000	43,000	42,864	40,000	40,000	40,000
Total, Ready Reserve	202,000	208,200	212,291	214,422	220,519	228,259
Standby	37,000	33,000	28,939	29,121	28,600	29,000
Total, Air Reserve Forces³	239,000	241,200	241,230	243,543	249,119	257,259

Note: Totals may not add due to rounding. (1) President's Budget Request. (2) FY '81-84 are actual figures; FY '85-86 are estimates; excludes nonchargeable personnel. (3) Excludes Retired Air Force Reserve.

U.S. Air Force Personnel Strength: 1907–1986

Year	Strength	Year	Strength	Year	Strength	Year	Strength
1907	3	1927	10,078	1947	305,827	1967	897,426
1908	13	1928	10,549	1948	387,730	1968	904,759
1909	27	1929	12,131	1949	419,347	1969	862,062
1910	11	1930	13,531	1950	411,277	1970	791,078
1911	23	1931	14,780	1951	788,381	1971	755,107
1912	51	1932	15,028	1952	973,474	1972	725,635
1913	114	1933	15,099	1953	977,593	1973	690,999
1914	122	1934	15,861	1954	947,918	1974	643,795
1915	208	1935	16,247	1955	959,946	1975	612,551
1916	311	1936	17,233	1956	909,958	1976	585,207
1917	1,218	1937	19,147	1957	919,835	1977	570,479
1918	195,023	1938	21,089	1958	871,156	1978	569,491
1919	25,603	1939	23,455	1959	840,028	1979	559,450
1920	9,050	1940	51,165	1960	814,213	1980	557,969
1921	11,649	1941	152,125	1961	820,490	1981	570,302
1922	9,642	1942	764,415	1962	883,330	1982	582,845
1923	9,441	1943	2,197,114	1963	868,644	1983	592,044
1924	10,547	1944	2,372,292	1964	855,802	1984	597,125¹
1925	9,670	1945	2,282,259	1965	823,633	1985	602,070¹
1926	9,674	1946	455,515	1966	886,350	1986	611,500¹

(1) Programmed.

Women in the Armed Forces

Women in the Army, Navy, Air Force, Marines, and Coast Guard are all fully integrated with male personnel. Expansion of military women's programs began in the Department of Defense in fiscal year 1973.

Although women are prohibited by law and directives based on law from serving in combat positions, policy changes in the Department of Defense have made possible the assignment of women to almost all other career fields. Career progression for women is now comparable to that for male personnel. Women are routinely assigned to overseas locations formerly closed to female personnel. Women are in command of activities and units that have missions other than administration of women.

Admission of women to the service academies began in the fall of 1976. The academies provide single-track education, allowing only for minor variations in the cadet program based on physiological differences between men and women.

Army — Information: Chief, Office of Public Affairs, Dept. of Army, Wash., DC 20310; 77,123 women, 69,921 enlisted women, 9,956 women commissioned officers, 246 women warrant officers.

Army Nurse Corps — Brig. Gen. Connie L. Slewitzke, Chief Army Nurse Corps, Office of the Surgeon General, Dept. of Army, Wash., DC 20310.

Navy — Information: Chief of Information, Dept. of Navy, Wash., DC 20350-1200; 6,764 women officers; 43,092 enlisted women.

Navy Nurse Corps — Como. Mary J. Nielubowicz, Dir., Navy Nurse Corps, Dept. of Navy, Wash., DC 20372-2000; 2,179 women officers; 778 men.

Air Force — Information: Office of Public Affairs, Dept. of the Air Force, Wash., DC 20330; 11,274 women officers; 55,760 enlisted women.

Air Force Nurse Corps — Brig. Gen. Diann A. Hale, Chief, Air Force Nurse Corps, Office of the Surgeon Gen., USAF, Bolling AFB, Wash., DC 20332.

Marine Corps — Information: Commandant of the Marine Corps (Code PA), Headquarters, Marine Corps, Wash., DC 20380; 652 women officers; 8,935 enlisted women.

Coast Guard — Information: Commandant (G-BPA), U.S. Coast Guard, 2100 Second St., SW, Wash., DC 20593; 163 women commissioned officers; 1 woman warrant officer; 2,039 enlisted women.

Monthly Pay Scale of
Effective

Commissioned Officers

Pay grade	Army rank	Navy rank	Under 2	2	3	4	6	8
	Rank or pay grade					Cumulative years of service		
O-10[1]	General*	Admiral	$5,069.40	$5,247.00	$5,247.90	$5,247.90	$5,247.90	$5,449.20
O-9	Lieutenant General . .	Vice Admiral	4,493.10	4,619.70	4,708.80	4,708.80	4,700.80	4,828.50
O-8	Major General	Rear Admiral	4,069.50	4,191.30	4,290.90	4,290.00	4,290.90	4,610.70
O-7	Brigadier General . . .	Commodore	3,381.60	3,611.40	3,611.40	3,611.40	3,773.10	3,773.10
O-6	Colonel	Captain	2,506.20	2,753.70	2,934.00	2,934.00	2,934.00	2,934.00
O-5	Lieutenant Colonel . .	Commander	2,004.60	2,354.10	2,516.40	2,516.40	2,516.40	2,516.40
O-4	Major	Lieutenant Comdr. . .	1,689.60	2,057.40	2,194.80	2,235.30	2,235.30	2,334.30
O-3	Captain	Lieutenant	1,570.20	1,755.30	1,876.50	2,076.30	2,175.60	2,254.20
O-2	First Lieutenant	Lieutenant (J.G.) . . .	1,369.20	1,495.20	1,796.10	1,856.70	1,895.70	1,895.70
O-1	Second Lieutenant . . .	Ensign	1,188.60	1,237.50	1,495.20	1,495.20	1,495.20	1,495.20
Commissioned officers with over 4 years active duty as an enlisted member or warrant officer								
O-3E	Captain	Lieutenant	0.00	0.00	0.00	2,076.30	2,175.60	2,254.20
O-2E	First Lieutenant	Lieutenant (J.G.) . . .	0.00	0.00	0.00	1,856.70	1,895.70	1,955.70
O-1E	Second Lieutenant . . .	Ensign	0.00	0.00	0.00	1,495.20	1,597.20	1,656.00

Warrant Officers

W-4	Chief Warrant	Comm. Warrant	1,599.60	1,716.00	1,716.00	1,755.30	1,835.10	1,916.10
W-3	Chief Warrant	Comm. Warrant	1,453.80	1,577.10	1,577.10	1,597.20	1,616.10	1,734.30
W-2	Chief Warrant	Comm. Warrant	1,273.50	1,377.60	1,377.60	1,417.80	1,495.20	1,577.10
W-1	Warrant Officer	Warrant Officer	1,061.10	1,216.50	1,216.50	1,317.90	1,377.60	1,436.70

Enlisted Personnel[2]

E-9[3]	Sergeant Major** . . .	Master C.P.O.	0.00	0.00	0.00	0.00	0.00	0.00
E-8[3]	Master Sergeant	Senior C.P.O.	0.00	0.00	0.00	0.00	0.00	1,568.60
E-7	Sgt. 1st Class	Chief Petty Officer	1,089.60	1,176.00	1,219.80	1,262.40	1,385.60	1,347.00
E-6	Staff Sergeant	Petty Officer 1st Class . .	937.20	1,021.80	1,064.40	1,109.70	1,150.80	1,192.80
E-5	Sergeant	Petty Officer 2nd Cl. . . .	822.60	895.50	938.70	979.80	1,044.00	1,086.30
E-4	Corporal	Petty Officer 3rd Cl. . . .	767.40	810.30	857.70	924.60	960.90	960.90
E-3	Private 1st Class. . . .	Seaman	723.00	762.30	793.20	824.70	824.70	824.70
E-2	Private	Seaman Apprentice. . . .	695.40	695.40	695.40	695.40	695.40	695.40
E-1 > 4 Private		Seaman Recruit.	620.40	620.40	620.40	620.40	620.40	620.40
E-1 < 4. . . .			573.60	573.60	573.60	573.60	573.60	573.60

The pay scale also applies to: Coast Guard and Marine Corps, National Oceanic and Atmospheric Administration, Public Health Service, National Guard, and the Organized Reserves.

*Basic pay is limited to $5,724 by Level V of the Executive Schedule and further limited by Sec. 101C, P.L. 96-86 to $4,176.00 max. Four star General or Admiral—personal money allowances of $2,200 per annum, or $4,000 if Chief of Staff of the Army, Chief of Staff of the Air Force, Chief of Naval Operations, Commandant of the Marine Corps, or Commandant of the Coast Guard. Three star General or Admiral—personal money allowance of $500 per annum.

**A new title of Chief Master Sergeant created in 1965 rates E-9 classification.

(1) While serving as Chairman of Joint Chiefs of Staff, Chief of Staff of the Army, Chief of Naval Operations, Chief of Staff of the Air Forces, or Commandant of the Marine Corps, basic pay for this grade is $6,988.50 regardless of years of service.

(2) Air Force enlisted personnel pay grades: E-9, Chief Master Sergeant; E-8, Sr. Master Sergeant; E-7, Master Sergeant; E-6, Technical Sergeant; E-5, Staff Sergeant; E-4, Sergeant; E-3, Airman 1st Class; E-2, Airman; E-1, Basic Airman.

Marine Corps enlisted ranks are as follows: E-9, Sergeant Major and Master Gunnery Sergeant; E-8, First Sergeant and Master Sergeant: E-7, Gunnery Sergeant; E-6, Staff Sergeant; E-5, Sergeant; E-4, Corporal; E-3, Lance Corporal; E-2, Private, First Class Marine; E-1, Private.

Marine Corps and Air Force officer ranks are same as Army.

(3) While serving as Sergeant Major of the Army, Master Chief Petty Officer of the Navy, Chief Master Sergeant of the Air Force, or Sergeant Major of the Marine Corps, basic pay for this grade is $2,692.50 regardless of years of service.

U.S. Military Personnel Strengths—Worldwide

(As of Sept. 30, 1984)

Source: U.S. Department of Defense

U.S. Territory & Special		**East Asia & Pacific**	**121,299**	Cuba (Guantanamo)	**2,347**
Locations	**1,627,427**	Japan	45,761	Afloat	4,787
Continental U.S.	1,318,968	Rep. of Korea	40,785	**Antarctica**	**65**
Hawaii	47,648	Philippines	15,319	**Eastern Europe**	**179**
Guam	9,175	Afloat	18,338	U.S.S.R.	51
Afloat	168,462	**Africa, Near East & South Asia**	**16,997**	**Total Foreign Countries**	**510,730**
Western & Southern Europe	**351,683**	British Indian Ocean Terr.	1,253	Ashore[2]	449,470
W. Germany[1]	253,722	Egypt	1,048	Afloat	61,260
United Kingdom[1]	28,823	Saudi Arabia	537		
Italy[1]	14,809	Afloat	13,353	**Total Worldwide**	**2,138,157**
Spain[1]	9,436	**Western Hemisphere**	**20,094**	Ashore[2]	1,908,435
Afloat	24,782	Panama	9,354	Afloat	229,722

(1) European NATO. (2) Includes temporarily shore-based.

the Uniformed Services
January 1985

Commissioned Officers

| Cumulative years of service | | | | | | | | Monthly basic allowances for quarters rates | | |
10	12	14	16	18	20	22	26	Without dependents — Full Rate	Partial Rate	With Dependents
$5,449.20	$5,866.20	$5,866.20	$6,285.90	$6,285.90	$6,706.50	$6,706.50	$7,124.70	$537.30	$50.70	$660.90
4,828.50	5,029.50	5,029.50	5,449.20	5,449.20	5,866.20	5,866.20	6,285.90	537.30	50.70	660.90
4,610.70	4,828.50	4,828.50	5,029.50	5,247.90	5,449.20	5,667.60	5,667.60	537.30	50.70	660.90
3,992.10	3,992.10	4,191.30	4,610.70	4,927.50	4,927.50	4,927.50	4,927.50	537.30	50.70	660.90
2,934.00	2,934.00	3,033.60	3,513.30	3,603.00	3,773.10	3,992.10	4,329.60	493.20	39.60	599.40
2,592.90	2,732.10	2,915.10	3,133.20	3,133.20	3,413.40	3,532.50	3,532.50	465.30	33.00	552.30
2,493.30	2,633.70	2,753.70	2,874.60	2,954.10	2,954.10	2,954.10	2,954.10	426.60	26.70	504.90
2,375.70	2,493.30	2,554.40	2,544.80	2,544.80	2,544.80	2,554.40	2,544.80	345.30	22.20	420.90
1,895.70	1,895.70	1,895.70	1,895.70	1,895.70	1,895.70	1,895.70	1,895.70	278.10	17.70	360.90
1,495.20	1,495.20	1,495.20	1,495.20	1,495.20	1,495.20	1,495.20	1,495.20	238.50	13.20	323.70
2,375.30	2,493.30	2,592.90	2,592.90	2,592.90	2,592.90	2,592.90	2,592.90			
2,057.90	2,136.90	2,194.80	2,194.80	2,194.80	2,194.80	2,194.80	2,194.80			
1,176.00	1,775.70	1,856.70	1,856.70	1,856.70	1,856.70	1,856.70	1,856.70			

Warrant Officers

10	12	14	16	18	20	22	26	Full Rate	Partial Rate	With Dependents
1,996.50	2,136.00	2,235.30	2,313.90	2,375.70	2,452.50	2,534.70	2,732.10	391.20	25.20	453.90
1,835.10	1,895.70	1,955.70	2,014.20	2,076.30	2,157.00	2,235.30	2,313.90	330.30	20.70	405.90
1,636.80	1,696.80	1,755.30	1,816.80	1,876.50	1,935.90	2,014.20	2,104.20	297.00	15.90	379.50
1,495.20	1,557.30	1,616.10	1,675.80	1,734.30	1,796.10	1,796.10	1,796.10	251.40	13.80	330.90

Enlisted Personnel

10	12	14	16	18	20	22	26	Full Rate	Partial Rate	With Dependents
1,869.60	1,902.90	1,945.80	1,990.50	2,034.90	2,074.50	2,183.70	2,395.80	315.30	18.60	429.90
1,605.00	1,647.00	1,690.20	1,734.60	1,774.80	1,818.30	1,925.10	2,139.90	292.20	15.30	400.50
1,390.20	1,433.40	1,498.20	1,540.80	1,584.00	1,604.70	1,712.40	1,925.10	249.30	12.00	372.60
1,236.60	1,300.20	1,314.00	1,384.20	1,405.20	1,405.20	1,405.20	1,405.20	221.40	9.90	337.80
1,129.80	1,171.20	1,192.80	1,192.80	1,192.80	1,192.80	1,192.80	1,192.80	204.90	8.70	300.30
960.90	960.90	960.90	960.90	960.90	960.90	960.90	960.90	177.60	8.10	259.50
824.70	824.70	824.70	824.70	824.70	824.70	824.70	824.70	172.50	7.80	238.50
695.40	695.40	695.40	695.40	695.40	695.40	695.40	695.40	146.40	7.20	238.50
620.40	620.40	620.40	620.40	620.40	620.40	620.40	620.40	133.50	6.90	238.50
573.60	573.60	573.60	573.60	573.60	573.60	573.60				

Basic Allowance for Subsistence

This allowance, the quarters allowance, and any other allowance are not subject to income tax.

Officers — Subsistence (food) is paid to all officers regardless of rank $106.18/month
Enlisted members: When on leave or authorized to mess separately $5.06/day
When rations in kind are not available. $5.72/day
When assigned to duty under emergency conditions where
no government messing facilities are available $7.57/day

Family Separation Allowance

Under certain conditions of family separation of more than 30 days, a member in Pay Grades E-4 (with over 4 years' service) and above will be allowed $30 a month in addition to any other allowances to which he is entitled. When separated from family and required to maintain a home for his family and one for himself, the member is entitled to an additional monthly basic allowance for quarters at the "without dependents" rate for his grade.

The Medal of Honor

The Medal of Honor is the highest military award for bravery that can be given to any individual in the United States. The first Army Medals were awarded on March 25, 1863, and the first Navy Medals went to sailors and Marines on April 3, 1863.

The Medal of Honor, established by Joint Resolution of Congress, 12 July 1862 (amended by Act of 9 July 1918 and Act of 25 July 1963) is awarded in the name of Congress to a person who, while a member of the Armed Forces, distinguishes himself conspicuously by gallantry and intrepidity at the risk of his life above and beyond the call of duty while engaged in an action against any enemy of the United States; while engaged in military operations involving conflict with an opposing foreign force; or while serving with friendly foreign forces engaged in an armed conflict against an opposing armed force in which the United States is not a belligerent party. The deed performed must have been one of personal bravery or self-sacrifice so conspicuous as to clearly distinguish the individual above his comrades and must have involved risk of life. Incontestable proof of the performance of service is exacted and each recommendation for award of this decoration is considered on the standard of extraordinary merit.

Prior to World War I, the 2,625 Army Medal of Honor awards up to that time were reviewed to determine which past awards met new stringent criteria. The Army removed 911 names from the list, most of them former members of a volunteer infantry group during the Civil War who had been induced to extend their enlistments when they were promised the Medal.

Since that review Medals of Honor have been awarded in the following numbers:

World War I 123   Korean War 131
World War II 433   Vietnam (to date) 239

Major U.S. Weapons Systems Cost Data

Source: DMS, Inc., Greenwich, Conn., as of June 10, 1985
(millions of dollars)

Designation	Total production	Total cost	Designation	Total production	Total cost
Aircraft			**Ships**		
General Dynamics F-16	2,795	56,843	CG-47 (DDG-47)	5	27,381
Grumman E-2C	127	5,921	CVN-72/73	2	7,131
Grumman F-14A	899	37,870	DDG-51	29	18,479
Hughes AH-64	675	9,102	FFG-7	62	9,804
Lockheed C-5B	50	8,426	SSN-688	64	31,614
McDonnell Douglas C-17A	210-225	37,855	SSN-21	1	3,875
McDonnell Douglas F-15	1,376	39,062	TAO	17	3,190
McDonnell Douglas F-18	1,050	42,898	Trident II Sub	16	16,062
Rockwell International B-1B	100	28,204	**Vehicles**		
Sikorsky UH-60A	1,118	6,625	FVS (MICV)	1,142	11,312
Missiles			M-1	6,958	20,125
AMRAAM	24,504	9,438	**Electronics**		
Patriot (Fire Unit)	205	12,704	CONUS-OTH/B	15	2,432
Peacekeeper	243	21,647	DSCS-III	56	2,032
Phoenix (AIM-54C)	7,249	7,327	DSP	5	6,268
Trident	790	37,481	TMLS	140	103
Tomahawk	4,068	13,791			

Strategic Nuclear Armaments: U.S. and USSR

Source: International Institute for Strategic Services, London, England

United States

		Range[2] (km)	Estimated warhead yield[3]	Deployed (July 1985)
Land-based missiles[1]				
ICBM	Titan 2	15,000	9 MT	26
	Minuteman 2	11,300	1-2 MT	450
	Minuteman 3	13,000	3x170 KT	550
Sea-based missiles				
SLBM (nuclear subs)	Poseidon C3	4,600	10x50 KT	304
	Trident C4	7,400	8x100 KT	312

		Range[3] (km)	Weapons load (lb)	Deployed (July 1985)
Aircraft[8]				
Long-range	B-52G	12,000	70,000	90
	B-52H	16,000	70,000	90
Medium-range	FB-111A	4,700	37,500	56
Strike aircraft:	F-4-E	2,200	16,000	(96)[11]
land-based	F-111E/F	4,700	28,000	(150)[11]
Strike aircraft:	A-6E	3,200	18,000	(60)[11]
carrier-based	A-7E	2,800	20,000	(144)[11]

Soviet Union

		Range[2] (km)	Estimated warhead yield[3]	Deployed (July 1985)
Land-based missiles[1]				
ICBM	SS-11 Sego	10,500	1 MT[4]	520
	SS-13 Savage	10,000	1x750 KT	60
	SS-17	10,000	4x200 KT[5]	150
	SS-18	10,000	1x20 MT[6]	308
	SS-19	10,000	6x550 KT	360
Sea-based missiles				
SLBM (nuclear subs)	SS-N-5-Serb	1,400	1x1 MT	39
	SS-N-6-Sawfly	3,000	1x1 MT[7]	336
	SS-N-8	7,800	1x1 MT[8]	292
	SS-N-17	3,900	1x1 MT	12
	SS-N-18	6,500	7x200 KT MIRV	224
	SS-N-20	8,300	9x200 MIRV	60

		Range[10] (km)	Weapons load (lb)	Deployed (July 1985)
Aircraft[9]				
	Tu-95 Bear	12,800	40,000	105
	Mya-4 Bison	11,200	20,000	45
	Tu-16 Badger	4,800	20,000	442
	Tu-22-Blinder	4,000	12,000	160
	Tu22M-26 Backfire	8,000	17,500	230
	Su-7 Fitter A	1,400	5,500	130
	MiG-21 Fishbed L	1,100	2,000	130
	MiG-27 Flogger D J	1,400	7,500	750
	Su-17 Fitter D/H	1,800	11,000	1,000
	Su-24 Fencer	4,000	8,000	250

(1) ICBM = intercontinental ballistic missile; SLBM = submarine-launched ballistic missile. (2) Operation range depends upon the payload carried; use of maximum payload may reduce missile range by up to 25%. (3) MT = megaton range = 1,000,000 tons of TNT equivalent or over; KT = kiloton range = 1,000 tons of TNT equivalent or more, but less than 1 MT. (4) Some 420 SS-11 missiles carry 3x100 to 300 KT warheads. (5) Some SS-17 carry 1x3.6 MT warheads. (6) Three SS-18 warhead variants: 10x500 KT, 8x900KT. (7) SS-N-6, 1x1 MT or 2x200 KT MIRV warheads. (8) 85-N-8 variant; 1x800 KT to 9,000 KA. (9) All aircraft listed are dual-capable and many, especially in the categories of strike aircraft, would be more likely to carry conventional than nuclear weapons. (10) Theoretical maximum range, with internal fuel only, at optimum altitude and speed. Ranges for strike aircraft assume no weapons load. Especially in the case of strike aircraft, therefore, range falls sharply for flights at lower altitude, at higher speed, or with full weapons load. (11) Figures in parentheses are estimates of Europe-based systems only.

World Arms Exporters and Importers, 1982

(millions of constant 1981 dollars)

Source: U.S. Arms Control and Disarmament Agency, *World Military Expenditures and Arms Transfers.*

World, total[1] 34,424	Czechoslovakia 235	Cuba 919	Libya 2,263
Suppliers	German Dem. Rep. . . . 542	Ecuador. 216	Morocco 245
China 943	Germany, Fed. Rep. of . 462	Egypt 1,980	Nicaragua 94
Czechoslovakia 801	Japan 565	Ethiopia 273	Pakistan. 415
France 3,018	Poland 235	Greece 349	Peru 264
Germany, Fed. Rep. of . 683	Soviet Union 919	India 1,131	Saudi Arabia 2,452
Poland 542	United Kingdom 471	Iran 1,226	Spain 443
Soviet Union 10,281	United States. 405	Iraq 4,056	Sudan 160
United Kingdom 1,886	**Developing[1]** 28,190	Israel 943	Syria 2,169
United States. 8,961	Algeria 1,037	Jordan 778	Turkey 396
Recipient Countries	Angola 330	Korea, Dem. Peo. Rep. . 254	Venezuela 226
Developed[1] 6,234	Argentina 282	Korea, Rep. 358	Vietnam, Soc. Rep. . . . 754
Canada 235	Chile. 264	Kuwait. 122	Yemen (Arab Rep.) . . . 226

(1) Includes countries not shown separately.

Casualties in Principal Wars of the U.S.

Data on Revolutionary War casualties is from **The Toll of Independence**, Howard H. Peckham, ed., U. of Chicago Press, 1974. Data prior to World War I are based on incomplete records in many cases. Casualty data are confined to dead and wounded personnel and therefore exclude personnel captured or missing in action who were subsequently returned to military control. Dash (—) indicates information is not available.

Wars	Branch of service	Number serving	Casualties			
			Battle deaths	Other deaths	Wounds not mortal[8]	Total
Revolutionary War	Total	—	6,824	18,500	8,445	33,769
1775-1783	Army	184,000	5,992	—	7,988	13,980
	Navy &	to	—	—	—	—
	Marines	250,000	832	—	457	1,289
War of 1812	Total	²286,730	2,260	—	4,505	6,765
1812-1815	Army	—	1,950	—	4,000	5,950
	Navy	—	265	—	439	704
	Marines	—	45	—	66	111
Mexican War	Total	²78,718	1,733	11,550	4,152	17,435
1846-1848	Army	—	1,721	11,500	4,102	17,373
	Navy	—	1	—	3	4
	Marines	—	11	—	47	58
Civil War	Total	²2,213,363	140,414	224,097	281,881	646,392
(Union forces only)	Army	2,128,948	138,154	221,374	280,040	639,568
1861-1865	Navy	—	2,112	2,411	1,710	6,233
	Marines	84,415	148	312	131	591
Confederate forces	Total	—	74,524	59,297	—	133,821
(estimate)[1]	Army	600,000	—	—	—	—
1863-1866	Navy	to	—	—	—	—
	Marines	1,500,000	—	—	—	—
Spanish-American	Total	306,760	385	2,061	1,662	4,108
War	Army[4]	280,564	369	2,061	1,594	4,024
1898	Navy	22,875	10	0	47	57
	Marines	3,321	6	0	21	27
World War I	Total	4,743,826	53,513	63,195	204,002	320,710
April 6, 1917-	Army[5]	4,057,101	50,510	55,868	193,663	300,041
Nov. 11, 1918	Navy	599,051	431	6,856	819	8,106
	Marines	78,839	2,461	390	9,520	12,371
	Coast Gd.	8,835	111	81	—	192
World War II	Total	16,353,659	292,131	115,185	670,846	1,078,162
Dec. 7, 1941-	Army[6]	11,260,000	234,874	83,400	565,861	884,135
Dec. 31, 1946[2]	Navy[7]	4,183,466	36,950	25,664	37,778	100,392
	Marines	669,100	19,733	4,778	67,207	91,718
	Coast Gd.	241,093	574	1,343	—	1,917
Korean War	Total	5,764,143	33,629	20,617	103,284	157,530
June 25, 1950-	Army	2,834,000	27,704	9,429	77,596	114,729
July 27, 1953[3]	Navy	1,177,000	458	4,043	1,576	6,077
	Marines	424,000	4,267	1,261	23,744	29,272
	Air Force	1,285,000	1,200	5,884	368	7,452
	Coast Gd.	44,143	—	—	—	—
Vietnam (preliminary)[10]	Total	8,744,000	47,321	10,700	153,303	211,324
Aug. 4, 1964-	Army	4,368,000	30,899	7,271	96,802	134,972
Jan. 27, 1973	Navy	1,842,000	1,606	913	4,178	6,697
	Marines	794,000	13,073	1,748	51,392	66,213
	Air Force	1,740,000	1,738	766	931	3,435
	Coast Gd.	—	5	2	—	7

(1) Authoritative statistics for the Confederate Forces are not available. An estimated 26,000-31,000 Confederate personnel died in Union prisons.
(2) Data are for the period Dec. 1, 1941 through Dec. 31, 1946 when hostilities were officially terminated by Presidential Proclamation, but few battle deaths or wounds not mortal were incurred after the Japanese acceptance of Allied peace terms on Aug. 14, 1945. Numbers serving from Dec. 1, 1941-Aug. 31, 1945 were: Total—14,903,213; Army—10,420,000; Navy—3,883,520; and Marine Corps—599,693.
(3) Tentative final data based upon information available as of Sept. 30, 1954, at which time 24 persons were still carried as missing in action.
(4) Number serving covers the period April 21-Aug. 13, 1898, while dead and wounded data are for the period May 1-Aug. 31, 1898. Active hostilities ceased on Aug. 13, 1898, but ratifications of the treaty of peace were not exchanged between the United States and Spain until April 11, 1899.
(5) Includes Air Service Battle deaths and wounds not mortal include casualties suffered by American forces in Northern Russia to Aug. 25, 1919 and in Siberia to April 1, 1920. Other deaths covered the period April 1, 1917-Dec. 31, 1918.
(6) Includes Army Air Forces.
(7) Battle deaths and wounds not mortal include casualties incurred in Oct. 1941 due to hostile action.
(8) Marine Corps data for World War II, the Spanish-American War and prior wars represent the number of individuals wounded, whereas all other data in this column represent the total number (incidence) of wounds.
(9) As reported by the Commissioner of Pensions in his Annual Report for Fiscal Year 1903.
(10) Number serving covers the period Aug. 4 1964-Jan. 27, 1973 (date of ceasefire). Number of casualties incurred in connection with the conflict in Vietnam from Jan. 1, 1961-Sept. 30, 1977. Includes casualties incurred in Mayaguez Incident. Wounds not mortal exclude 150,375 persons not requiring hospital care.

Nuclear Arms Treaties and Negotiations: An Historical Overview

Aug. 4, 1963—Nuclear Test Ban Treaty, signed in Moscow by the U.S., USSR, and Great Britain, prohibited testing of nuclear weapons in space, above ground, and under water.

1966—Outer Space Treaty banned the introduction of nuclear weapons into space.

1968—Non-proliferation of Nuclear Weapons Treaty, with U.S., USSR, and Great Britain as major signers, limited the spread of military nuclear technology by agreement not to assist nonnuclear nations in getting or making nuclear weapons.

March 26, 1972—SALT I (Strategic Arms Limitations Talks) agreement, in negotiation since Nov. 17, 1969, signed in Moscow by U.S. and USSR. In the area of defensive nuclear weapons, the treaty limited antiballistic missiles to 2 sites of 100 antiballistic missile launchers in each country (amended in 1974 to one site in each country). The treaty also imposed a 5-year freeze on testing and deployment of intercontinental ballistic missiles and submarine-launched ballistic missiles (U.S.: 1,054 ICBMs and 656 SLBMs; USSR: 1,400 ICBMs and 950 SLBMs). An interim short-term agreement putting a ceiling on numbers of offensive nuclear weapons was also signed. SALT I was in effect until Oct. 3, 1977.

July 3, 1974—Protocol on antiballistic missile systems and a treaty and protocol on limiting underground testing of nuclear weapons was signed by U.S. and USSR in Moscow.

Nov. 24, 1974—Vladivostok Agreement announced establishing the framework for a more comprehensive agreement on offensive nuclear arms, setting the guidelines of a second SALT treaty.

Sept. 1977—U.S. and USSR agreed to continue to abide by SALT I, despite its expiration date.

June 18, 1979—SALT II, signed in Vienna by the U.S. and USSR, constrained offensive nuclear weapons, limiting each side to 2,400 missile launchers and heavy bombers with that ceiling to apply until Jan. 1, 1985. The treaty also set a combined total of 1,320 ICBMs and SLBMs with multiple warheads on each side. Although approved by the U.S. Senate Foreign Relations Committee, the treaty never reached the Senate floor because Pres. Jimmy Carter withdrew his support for the treaty following the December 1979 invasion of Afghanistan by Soviet troops.

Nov. 18, 1981—U.S. Pres. Ronald Reagan proposed his controversial "zero option" to cancel deployment of new U.S. intermediate-range missiles in Western Europe in return for Soviet dismantling of comparable forces (600 SS-20, SS-4, and SS-5 missiles already stationed in the European part of its territory).

Nov. 30, 1981—Geneva talks on limiting intermediate nuclear forces based in and around Europe began.

May 9, 1982—U.S. Pres. Ronald Reagan proposed 2-step plan for strategic arms reductions and announced that he had proposed to the USSR that START (Strategic Arms Reduction Talks) begin in June.

May 18, 1982—Soviet Pres. Leonid Brezhnev rejected Reagan's plan as one-sided, but responded positively to the call for arms reduction talks.

June 29, 1982—START (Strategic Arms Reduction Talks) began in Geneva.

1985—Disarmament talks between the U.S. and the USSR began in Geneva, Switzerland on March 12. The first two rounds of these talks were unproductive. On June 10, Pres. Reagan decided to continue to honor fully the unratified 1979 Strategic Arms Limitation Treaty.

(*For events after Aug. 1, 1985, see Index and Chronology of the Year's Events.*)

Estimates of Total Dollar Costs of American Wars

(In millions of dollars, except percent)

Source: *The Military Budget and National Economic Priorities,* revised and updated by James L. Clayton, Univ. of Utah.

Item	World War II	Vietnam Conflict	Korean Conflict	World War I	Civil War: Union	Civil War: Confederacy	Spanish American War	American Revolution	War of 1812	Mexican War
Original increment, direct costs:[1]										
Current dollars	360,000	140,600	50,000	32,700	2,300	1,000	270	100-140	87	82
Constant (1967) dollars .	816,300	148,800	69,300	100,000	8,500	3,700	1,100	400-680	170	300
Percent 1 year's GNP . .	188	14	15	43	74	123	2	104	14	4
Service-connected veterans' benefits[2]	69,634	15,497	12,447	14,098	3,289	—	2,111	28	20	26
Interest, pmts. on war loans[3]	220,000	[5]	[5]	11,000	1,200	[5]	60	20	14	10
Current cost to 1983[4] . .	649,600	156,100	62,400	57,800	6,800	[5]	2,441	170	120	120

(1) Figures are rounded and taken from Claudia D. Goldin, *Encyclopedia of American Economic History.* (2) Total cost to Oct. 1, 1982. For World War I and later wars, benefits are actual service-connected figures from 1981 *Annual Report* of Veterans Administration. For earlier wars, service-connected veterans' benefits are estimated at 40 percent of total, the approximate ratio of service-connected to total benefits since World War I. (3) Total cost to 1983. Interest payments are a very rough approximation based on the percentage of the original costs of each war financed by money creation and debt, the difference between the level of public debt at the beginning of the war and at its end, and the approximate time required to pay off the war debts. (4) Figures are rounded estimates. (5) Unknown.

Armed Forces Personnel—Number and Rate, 1982

Source: U.S. Arms Control Disarmament Agency, *World Military Expenditures and Arms Transfers.*

(Number (1,000), Rate per 1,000 population)

Armed forces refer to active-duty military personnel, including paramilitary forces where those forces resemble regular units in their organization, equipment, training or mission. Reserve forces are not included.

	Number	Rate		Number	Rate		Number	Rate
United States	2,108	9.1	Greece	186	19.0	Poland	429	11.9
Argentina	175	6.0	India	1,120	1.6	Romania	237	10.5
Brazil	460	3.6	Indonesia	270	1.7	Soviet Union	4,400	16.3
Bulgaria	175	19.7	Iran	470	11.4	Spain	353	9.3
China	4,490	4.3	Iraq	450	32.1	Syria	290	30.9
Taiwan	504	27.2	Israel	180	46.2	Thailand	241	4.8
Cuba	230	23.5	Italy	391	6.9	Turkey	638	13.3
Czechoslovakia	213	13.8	Japan	241	2.0	United Kingdom	322	5.8
Egypt	447	10.0	Korea, Dem. People's Rep. of	710	38.0	Vietnam	1,200	21.5
France	485	8.9	Korea, Rep. of	600	14.7	Yugoslavia	247	10.9
German Dem. Rep. . . .	233	14.0	Nigeria	132	1.6			
Germany, Fed. Rep. . .	480	7.8	Pakistan	478	5.2			

RELIGIOUS INFORMATION

Census of Religious Groups in the U.S.

Source: 1985 Yearbook of American and Canadian Churches

The 1985 Yearbook of American and Canadian Churches reported a total of 140,816,385 members of religious groups in the U.S.—60.1 percent of the population; membership rose slightly less than one percent from the previous year, ending a long decline in membership in mainline denominations.

Comparisons of membership statistics from group to group are not necessarily meaningful. Membership definitions vary —e.g., Roman Catholics count members from infancy, but some Protestant groups count only "adult" members, usually 13 years or older; some groups compile data carefully, but others estimate; not all groups report annually.

The number of churches appear in parentheses. Asterisk (*) indicates church declines to publish membership figures; (**) indicates figures date from 1976 or earlier.

Group	Members
Adventist churches:	
Advent Christian Ch. (364)	29,838
Primitive Advent Christian Ch. (10)	546
Seventh-day Adventists (3,907)	623,563
American Rescue Workers (20)	2,700
Anglican Orthodox Church (40)	6,000
Baha'i Faith (1,650)	100,000
Baptist churches:	
Amer. Baptist Assn. (1,641)	225,000
Amer. Baptist Chs. in U.S.A. (5,851)	1,637,099
Baptist General Conference (732)	128,913
Baptist Missionary Assn. of America (1,411)	234,142
Conservative Baptist Assn. of America (1,140)	225,000
Duck River (and Kindred) Assn. of Baptists (85)	**8,632
Free Will Baptists (2,480)	226,422
Gen. Assn. of General Baptists (860)	75,133
Gen. Assn. of Regular Baptist Chs. (1,571)	300,839
Natl. Baptist Convention of America (11,398)	**2,668,799
Natl. Baptist Convention, U.S.A. (26,000)	**5,500,000
Natl. Primitive Baptist Convention (606)	**250,000
No. Amer. Baptist Conference (260)	43,286
Seventh Day Baptist General Conference (63)	5,008
Southern Baptist Convention (34,464)	14,178,051
Brethren (German Baptists):	
Brethren Ch. (Ashland, Ohio) (124)	14,410
Christian Congregation (La Follette, IN) (1,429)	101,351
Ch. of the Brethren (1,067)	164,680
Old German Baptist Brethren (52)	5,254
Brethren, River:	
Brethren in Christ Ch. (172)	15,058
Buddhist Churches of America (100)	70,000
Christadelphians (850)	**15,800
The Christian and Missionary Alliance (1,532).	215,857
Christian Catholic Church (4)	2,500
Christian Church (Disciples of Christ) (4,608)..	1,145,918
Christian Churches and Churches of Christ (5,502)	1,043,642
Christian Methodist Episcopal Church (2,340)..	718,922
Christian Nation Church U.S.A. (5)	226
Christian Union (114)	6,000
Churches of Christ (13,056)	1,600,000
Churches of Christ in Christian Union (251)	11,954
Churches of God:	
Chs. of God, General Conference (352)	34,424
Ch. of God (Anderson, Ind.) (2,286)	182,190
Ch. of God (Seventh Day), Denver, Col. (125)..	5,249
Church of Christ, Scientist (3,000)	*
Church of God by Faith (105)	**4,500
Church of the Nazarene (4,931)	507,574
Conservative Congregational Christian Conference (148)	26,765
Eastern Orthodox churches:	
Albanian Orth. Diocese of America (10)	5,250
American Carpatho-Russian Orth. Greek Catholic Ch. (70)	**100,000
Antiochian Orth. Christian Archdiocese of No. Amer. (120)	280,000
Diocese of the Armenian Ch. of America (66)	**450,000
Bulgarian Eastern Orth. Ch. (13)	**86,000
Coptic Orthodox Ch. (29)	100,000
Greek Orth. Archdiocese of N. and S. America (535)	1,950,000
Orthodox Ch. in America (440)	1,000,000
Patriarchal Parishes of the Russian Orth. Ch. in the U.S.A. (41)	**51,500
Romanian Orth. Episcopate of America (35)	41,000
Serbian Eastern Orth. Ch. (68)	97,123
Syrian Orth. Ch. of Antioch (Archdiocese of the U.S.A. and Canada) (13)	30,000
Ukrainian Orth. Ch. of America (Ecumenical Patriarchate) (30)	25,000

Group	Members
Ukrainian Orthodox Church in the U.S.A. (107) .	**87,745
The Episcopal Church in the U.S.A. (7,387)	2,794,690
American Ethical Union (Ethical Culture Movement) (26).	4,000
Evangelical Church of North America (143)	13,088
Evangelical Congregational Church (160)	38,432
The Evangelical Covenant Church of America (554)	82,943
Evangelical Free Church of America (900)	146,000
Evangelical associations:	
Apostolic Christian Chs. of America (83)	22,450
Apostolic Christian Ch. (Nazarean) (46)	2,864
Christian Congregation (1,429)	101,351
Friends:	
Evangelical Friends Alliance (217)	24,095
Friends General Conference (233)	**26,184
Friends United Meeting (534)	58,371
Grace Gospel Fellowship (47)	4,250
Independent Fundamental Churches of America (1,019).	120,446
Jehovah's Witnesses (7,921)	649,697
Jewish organizations:	
Union of Amer. Hebrew Congregations (Reformed) (791)	1,370,000
Union of Orthodox Jewish Congregations of America (1,700)	1,000,000
United Synagogue of America (Conservative) (800)	1,250,000
Latter-day Saints:	
Ch. of Jesus Christ (Bickertonites) (53)	2,654
Ch. of Jesus Christ of Latter-day Saints (Mormon) (8,017)	3,602,000
Reorganized Ch. of Jesus Christ of Latter Day Saints (1,059)	192,830
Lutheran churches:	
American Lutheran Ch. (4,905)	2,343,412
Ch. of the Lutheran Brethren of America (109)	10,997
Ch. of the Lutheran Confession (66)	8,898
Assn. of Evangelical Lutheran Chs. (272)	110,934
Evangelical Lutheran Synod (111)	20,556
Assn. of Free Lutheran Congregations (148)...	17,484
Latvian Evangelical Lutheran Church in America (62)	14,160
Lutheran Ch. in America (5,815)	2,925,008
Lutheran Ch.-Missouri Synod (5,829)	2,630,947
Protestant Conference (Lutheran) (10)	960
Wisconsin Evangelical Lutheran Synod (1,193)	414,199
Mennonite churches:	
Beachy Amish Mennonite Chs. (81)	5,388
Evangelical Mennonite Ch. (24)	3,857
General Conference of Mennonite Brethren Chs. (124)	17,065
The General Conference Mennonite Ch. (218)	36,644
Hutterian Brethren (213)	37,000
Mennonite Ch. (1,201)	110,294
Old Order Amish Ch. (598)	34,000
Old Order (Wisler) Mennonite Ch. (38)	9,731
Methodist churches:	
African Methodist Episcopal Ch. (6,200)	2,210,000
African Methodist Episcopal Zion Ch. (6,023)	1,134,179
Evangelical Methodist Ch. (139)	**10,502
Free Methodist Ch. of North America (1,012)	70,657
Fundamental Methodist Ch. (14)	700
Primitive Methodist Ch., U.S.A. (87)	9,978
Reformed Methodist Union Episcopal Ch. (18)	3,800
Southern Methodist Ch. (152)	7,300
United Methodist Ch. (38,181)	9,405,164
Moravian churches:	
Moravian Ch. (Unitas Fratrum), Northern Province (99)	32,895

Group	Members	Group	Members
Moravian Ch. in America (Unitas Fratrum),		**Presbyterian churches:**	
Southern Province (55)	21,726	Associate Reformed Presbyterian Ch. (Gen.	
Unity of the Brethren (32)	**6,142	Synod) (170)	35,934
Muslims	**2,000,000+**	Cumberland Presbyterian Ch. (878)	99,887
New Apostolic Church of North America (432) .	31,623	Orthodox Presbyterian Ch. (166)	17,304
North American Old Roman Catholic Church		Presbyterian Ch. in America (825)	155,988
(130)	62,380	Presbyterian Ch. (U.S.A.) (11,596)	3,122,213
Old Catholic churches:		Reformed Presbyterian Ch. of No. Amer. (67). .	4,836
Christ Catholic Ch. (6)	1,358	**Reformed churches:**	
Mariavite Old Cath. Ch. Province of North		Christian Reformed Ch. in N. America (639) . . .	213,659
America (166).	357,927	Hungarian Reformed Ch. in America (31)	11,000
No. Amer. Old Roman Cath. Ch. (Schweikert)		Protestant Reformed Chs. in America (21). . . .	4,544
(130).	62,380	Reformed Ch. in America (920)	344,520
Pentecostal churches:		Reformed Ch. in the U.S. (30)	3,710
Apostolic Faith (45)	4,100	**The Roman Catholic Church (24,260)**	52,392,934
Assemblies of God (10,386)	1,992,754	**The Salvation Army (1,061)**	428,046
Bible Church of Christ (6)	4,350	**The Schwenkfelder Church (5)**	3,001
Bible Way Church of Our Lord Jesus Christ		**Social Brethren (40)**	**1,784
World Wide (350).	**30,000	**Natl. Spiritualist Assn. of Churches (164).**	**5,168
Church of God (Cleveland, Tenn.) (5,410)	493,904	**Gen. Convention, The Swedenborgian**	
Church of God of Prophecy (2,040).	74,384	Church (39)	1,820
Congregational Holiness Ch. (174)	8,347	**Unitarian Universalist Assn. (945)**	169,168
Gen. Council, Christian Ch. of No. Amer. (101) .	12,500	**United Brethren:**	
Intl. Ch. of the Foursquare Gospel (113)	164,688	Ch. of the United Brethren in Christ (256)	26,869
Open Bible Standard Chs. (290)	46,351	United Christian Ch. (11)	430
Pentecostal Assemblies of the World (550) . . .	**4,500	**United Church of Christ (6,427)**	1,701,513
Pentecostal Church of God (1,120).	89,559	**Universal Fellowship of Metropolitan**	
United Pentecostal Ch. Intl. (3,300)	465,000	Community Chs. (200)	33,500
Pentecostal Free-Will Baptist Ch. (217)	10,627	**Vedanta Society (13)**	1,000
Plymouth Brethren (1,100)	98,000	**Volunteers of America (607)**	36,634
Polish Natl. Catholic Church of America (162). .	**282,411	**The Wesleyan Church (1,722).**	107,672

Religious Population of the World

Source: The 1985 Encyclopaedia Britannica Book of the Year

Religion	N. America[1]	S. America	Europe[2]	Asia[3]	Africa	Oceania[4]	Totals
Total Christian. . . .	260,924,600	197,642,000	334,467,100	103,740,700	147,400,400	18,781,100	1,062,955,900
Roman Catholic .	142,433,400	186,660,800	178,000,400	57,300,100	57,950,100	5,230,600	627,575,400
Eastern Orthodox	5,650,600	351,200	45,100,000	2,340,000	8,800,200	390,100	62,632,100
Protestant[5]. . . .	112,840,600	10,630,000	111,366,700	44,100,600	80,650,100	13,160,400	372,748,400
Jewish	7,610,700	738,600	4,110,200	4,290,700	229,400	73,900	17,053,500
Muslim[6]	1,580,900	405,100	20,200,600	378,100,100	153,220,400	87,000	553,594,100
Zoroastrian	2,700	2,600	14,000	228,200	1,100	1,000	249,600
Shinto	45,000	—	—	32,000,000	—	—	32,045,000
Taoist	32,000	13,000	13,500	20,000,000	800	2,900	20,062,200
Confucian	99,000	58,000	440,000	157,500,000	2,000	18,000	158,117,000
Buddhist	330,000	240,000	240,000	248,770,100	15,000	23,700	249,618,800
Hindu.	310,000	635,000	440,000	458,600,000	850,000	325,000	461,160,000
Totals.	270,934,900	199,734,300	359,925,400	1,403,229,800	301,719,100	19,312,600	2,554,856,100
Population[7]. . . .	395,365,000	262,963,000	766,325,000	2,777,385,000	536,589,000	24,458,000	4,763,085,000

(1) Includes Central America and West Indies. (2) Includes communist countries where it is difficult to determine religious affiliation. (3) Includes areas in which persons have traditionally enrolled in several religions, as well as China, with an official communist establishment. (4) Includes Australia, New Zealand, and islands of the South Pacific. (5) Protestant figures outside Europe usually include "full members" (adults) rather than all baptized persons and are not comparable to those of ethnic religions or churches counting all adherents. (6) According to the Islamic Center, Wash., D.C., there are 1 billion Muslims worldwide. (7) United Nations data, midyear 1984.

National Council of Churches of Christ

The National Council of the Churches of Christ in the U.S.A. is a cooperative agency of 31 Protestant, Orthodox and Anglican churches which seeks to advance programs and policies of mutual interest to its members. The NCCC was formed in 1950 by the merger of 14 inter-denominational agencies. The Council's member churches now have an aggregate membership totaling approximately 40 million. The NCCC is not a governing body and has no control over the policies or operations of any church belonging to it. The work of the Council is divided into 3 divisions: Church and Society; Education and Ministry; Overseas Ministries; and 5 commissions — Faith and Order; Regional and Local Ecumenism; Communication; Stewardship; Justice and Liberation. The chief administrative officer of the NCCC is the Rev. Arie R. Brouwer, 475 Riverside Drive, N.Y., NY 10115.

Headquarters, Leaders of U.S. Religious Groups

See Associations and Societies section for religious organizations. (year organized in parentheses)

Adventist churches:

Advent Christian Church (1854) — Pres., Glennon Balser; exec. v.p., David H. Northrup, Box 23152, Charlotte, NC 28212.

Primitive Advent Christian Church — Pres., Elza Moss; sec., Hugh W. Good, 395 Frame Rd., Elkview, WV 25071.

Seventh-day Adventists (1863) — Pres., Neal C. Wilson; sec., G. Ralph Thompson, 6840 Eastern Ave. NW, Wash., DC 20012.

Baha'i Faith — Chpsn., Judge James E. Nelson; sec., Robert Henderson, 536 Sheridan Rd., Wilmette, IL 60091.

Baptist churches:

American Baptist Assn. (1905) — Pres., Dr. J. C. James; rec. clk., W E. Norris, 4605 N. State Line, Texarkana, TX 75503.

American Baptist Churches in the U.S.A. (1907) — Pres., Mrs. Margaret Prine; gen. sec., Rev. Dr. Robert C. Campbell, Valley Forge, PA 19481.

Baptist General Conference (1879) — Gen. sec., Dr. Warren Magnuson, 2002 S. Arlington Heights Rd., Arlington Heights, IL 60005.

Baptist Missionary Assn. of America (formerly **North American Baptist Assn.**) (1950) — Pres., Rev. Kenny L. Digby, rec. sec., Rev. Ralph Cottrell, Box 2866, Texarkana, AR 75501.

Conservative Baptist Assn. of America (1947) — Gen. Dir., Dr. Russell A. Shive, Box 66, Wheaton, IL 60189.

Free Will Baptists (1727) — Mod., Rev. Bobby Jackson; exec. sec., Dr. Melvin Worthington, Box 1088, Nashville, TN 37202.

General Assn. of General Baptists (1823) — Exec. sec., Rev. Glen Spence, 100 Stinson Dr., Poplar Bluff, MO 63901.

General Assn. of Regular Baptist Churches (1932) — Chpsn., Dr. Ernest Pickering; natl. rep., Dr. Paul N. Tassell, 1300 N. Meacham Rd., Schaumburg, IL 60195.

Natl. Baptist Convention, U.S.A. (1880) — Pres., Dr. T.J. Jemison; gen. sec., W. Franklyn Richardson, 52 S. 6th Ave., Mt. Vernon, NY 10550.

North American Baptist Conference (1865) — Mod., Rev. Eugene Kern; exec. dir., Dr. John Binder, 1 S. 210 Summit Ave., Oakbrook Terrace, IL 60181.

Southern Baptist Convention (1845) — Pres., Charles F. Stanley, exec. sec., exec. sec.-treas., Dr. Harold C. Bennett, 901 Commerce, Nashville, TN 37203.

United Free Will Baptist Church (1870) — Vice-Mod., Rev. O.L. Williams; chpsn. exec. bd., Rev. W. F. Cox, Kingston College, 1101 University St., Kinston, NC 28501.

Brethren in Christ Church (1798) — Mod., Bishop Owen H. Alderfer; gen. sec., Dr. R. Donald Shafer, P.O. Box 245, Upland, CA 91785.

Brethren (German Baptists):

Brethren Church (Ashland, Oh.) (1882) — Dir., Sterling Ward, 524 College Ave., Ashland, OH 44805.

Church of the Brethren (1719) — Mod., James F. Meyer; gen. sec., Robert Neff, 1451 Dundee Ave., Elgin, IL 60120.

Buddhist Churches of America (1899) — Bishop, Rt. Rev. Selgen H. Yamaoka, 1710 Octavia St., San Francisco, CA 94109.

Calvary Grace Christian Church of Faith (1898) — Intl. gen. supt., Col. Herman Keck Jr., U.S. Box 4266, Norton AFB, San Bernardino, CA 92409.

The Christian and Missionary Alliance (1887) — Pres., Dr. Louis L. King; sec., Dr. Elwood N. Nielsen, 350 N. Highland Ave., Nyack, NY 10960.

Christian Church (Disciples of Christ) (1809) — Gen. minister and pres., Dr. Kenneth L. Teegarden, 222 S. Downey Ave., Box 1986, Indianapolis, IN 46206.

The Christian Congregation (1887) — Gen. supt., Rev. Ora Wilbert Eads, 804 W. Hemlock St., LaFollette, TN 37766.

Christian Methodist Episcopal Church (1870) — Adm. Coord., Rev. Tyrone T. Davis; sec., Rev. Edgar L. Wade, P. O. Box 3403, Memphis, TN 38101.

Churches of Christ in Christian Union (1909) — Gen. supt., Rev. Robert Kline; gen. sec., Rev. Robert Barth, Box, 30, Circleville, OH 43113.

Churches of God:

Churches of God, General Conference (1825) — Admin., Dr. Richard E. Wilkin, Box 926, Findlay, OH 45839.

Church of God (Anderson, Ind.) (1880) — Chpsn., Samuel G. Hines; exec. sec., Paul A. Tanner, Box 2420, Anderson, IN 46018.

Church of Christ, Scientist (1879) — Pres., Zadie Hatfield; clerk, Beulah M. Roegge, Christian Science Center, Boston, MA 02115.

Church of the Nazarene (1908) — Gen. sec., B. Edgar Johnson, 6401 The Paseo, Kansas City, MO 64131.

National Association of Congregational Christian Churches (1955) — Mod., Dr. Robert J. L. Williams; exec. sec., Dr. A. Ray Appelquist, Box 1620, Oak Creek, WI 53154.

Eastern Orthodox churches:

Antiochian Orthodox Christian Archdiocese of North America (formerly **Syrian Antiochian Orthodox Archdiocese**) (1894) — Primate, Metropolitan Archbishop Philip (Saliba); aux., Archbishop Michael (Shaheen), Bishop Antoun (Khouri), 358 Mountain Rd., Englewood, NJ 07631.

Diocese of the Armenian Church of America (1889) — Primate, His Eminence Archbishop Torkom Manoogian; sec., Dr. Arra Avakian, 6149 N. 9th, Fresno, CA 93710.

Coptic Orthodox Ch. —. Correspnt., Archpriest Fr. Gabriel Abdelsayed, 427 West Side Ave., Jersey City, NJ 07304.

Greek Orthodox Archdiocese of North and South America (1864) — Primate, Archbishop Iakovos; sec., Peter Kourides, 8-10 E. 79th St., N.Y., NY 10021.

Orthodox Church in America (formerly **Russian Orthodox Greek Catholic Church of North America**) (1792) — Primate, Metropolitan Theodosius; chancellor, V. Rev. Daniel Hubiak, P.O. Box 675, Syosset, NY 11791.

Romanian Orthodox Episcopate of America (1929) — Aux. Bishop, Nathaniel (Popp); sec., Rev. Fr. Richard J. Grabowski, 3256 Warren Rd., Cleveland, OH 44111.

Serbian Eastern Orthodox Church for the U.S.A. and Canada — Bishops, Rt. Rev. Bishop Firmilian, Rt. Rev. Bishop Gregory; Bishop Christophor; St. Sava Monastery, Box 519, Libertyville, IL 60048.

Syrian Orthodox Church of Antioch, Archdiocese of the U.S.A. and Canada (1957) — Primate, Archbishop MarAthanasius Y. Samuel; gen. sec., Very Rev. Chorepiscopus John Meno, 45 Fairmount Ave., Hackensack, NJ 07601.

Ukrainian Orthodox Church in America (Ecumenical Patriarchate) (1928) — Primate, Most Rev. Metropolitan Andrei Kuschak; aux., Most Rev. Bishop Nicholas Smisko, 90-34 139th St., Jamaica, NY 11435.

Ukrainian Orthodox Church in the U.S.A. (1919) — Metropolitan, Most Rev. Mstyslav S. Skrypnyk, Box 495, South Bound Brook, NJ 08880.

The Episcopal Church (1789) — Presiding bishop, Most Rev. John M. Allin; sec., Rt. Rev. Scott Field Bailey, Box 6885, San Antonio, TX 78209.

The Evangelical Covenant Church (1885) — Pres., Dr. Milton B. Engebretson; sec., Rev. Clifford Bjorklund, 5101 N. Francisco Ave., Chicago, IL 60625.

Friends:

Evangelical Friends Alliance (1965) — Pres., Maurice A. Roberts, 2018 Maple, Wichita, KS 67213.

Friends General Conference (1900) — Clk., George N. Webb; gen. sec., Lloyd Lee Wilson, 1520B Race St., Phila., PA 19102.

Friends United Meeting (formerly **Five Years Meeting of Friends**) (1902) — Presiding clerk, Richard Whitehead, 101 Quaker Hill Dr., Richmond, IN 47374.

Independent Fundamental Churches of America (1930) — Pres., Dr. Leslie Madison, 10101 E. 147th St., Kansas City, MO 64149.

Federation of Islamic Assns. in U.S. and Canada — 300 E. 44th St., N.Y., NY 10017.

Jehovah's Witnesses (1879) — Watch Tower Pres., Frederick W. Franz, 25 Columbia Heights, Brooklyn, NY 11201.

Jewish congregations:

Union of American Hebrew Congregations (Reform) — Pres., Rabbi Alexander M. Schindler, 838 5th Ave., N.Y., NY 10021.

Union of Orthodox Jewish Congregations of America — Pres., Julius Berman, 116 E. 27th St., N.Y., NY 10016.

United Synagogue of America (Conservative) — Pres., Marshall Wolke, exec. v.p., Rabbi Benjamin Z. Kreitman, 155 5th Ave., N.Y., NY 10010.

Latter-day Saints:

The Church of Jesus Christ of Latter-day Saints (Mormon) (1830) — Pres., Spencer W. Kimball, 50 E. North Temple St., Salt Lake City, UT 84150.

Reorganized Church of Jesus Christ of Latter Day Saints (1830) — Pres., Wallace B. Smith, The Auditorium, P.O. Box 1059, Independence, MO 64051.

Lutheran churches:

The American Lutheran Church (1961) — Pres., Dr. David W. Preus; gen. sec., Dr. Kathryn E. Baerwald, 422 S. 5th St., Minneapolis, MN 55415.

Church of the Lutheran Brethren of America (1900) — Pres., Rev. Everald H. Strom; sec., Rev. George Aase, 1007 Westside Dr., Box 655, Fergus Falls, MN 56537.

Church of the Lutheran Confession (1961) — Pres., Rev. Daniel Fleischer; sec., Rev. Paul F. Nolting, 3956 Persimmon Dr., Apt. 104, Fairfax, VA 22013.

Assn. of Evangelical Lutheran Churches (1976) — Bishop, Dr. William H. Kohn; exec. sec., Doctor Elwyn Ewald, 12015 Manchester Rd., St. Louis, MO 63131.

Evangelical Lutheran Synod (1853) — Pres., Rev. George Orvick; sec., Rev. Alf Merseth, 106 13th St. S., Northwood, IA 50459.

Assn. of Free Lutheran Congregations (1962) — Bishop, Dr. Will Herzfeld, exec. sec., Dr. Elwyn Ewald, 12015 Manchester Rd., St. Louis, MO 63131.

Lutheran Church in America (1962) — Bishop, Rev. James R. Crumley Jr.; sec., Rev. Reuben T. Swanson, 231 Madison Ave., N.Y. NY 10016.

Lutheran Church — Missouri Synod (1847) — Pres., Dr. Ralph Bohlmann; sec., Dr. Walter L. Rosin, 1333 S. Kirkwood, St. Louis, MO 63122.

Wisconsin Evangelical Lutheran Synod (1850) — Pres., Rev. Carl H. Mischke; sec., Prof. David Worgull, 1201 W. Tulsa, Chandler, AZ 85224.

Mennonite churches:

The General Conference Mennonite Church (1860) — Pres. Jacob Tilitzky; gen. sec., Norma Weins, 722 Main, Newton, KS 67114.

Mennonite Church (1690) — Mod., Myron S. Augsberger, 528 E. Madison St., Lombard, IL 60148.

Methodist churches:

African Methodist Episcopal Zion Church (1796) — Sr. Bishop, William M. Smith; sec., Bishop Charles H. Foggie, 1200 Windermere Dr., Pittsburgh, PA 15218.

Evangelical Methodist Church (1946) — Gen. supt., John F. Kunkle; gen. sec., Rev. R.D. Driggers, 3000 W. Kellogg Dr., Wichita, KS 67213.

Free Methodist Church of North America (1860) — Bishops R. Andrews, D. Bastian, W. Cryderman, E. Parsons, C. Van Valin, gen. conf. sec., C.T. Denbo, 999 College Ave., Winona Lake, IN 46590.

The United Methodist Church (1968) — Pres. Counc. of Bishops, Bishop James S. Thomas, sec., gen. conf., Faith Richardson, 168 Mt. Vernon St., Newtonville, MA 02160.

Universal Fellowship of Metropolitan Community Churches — Mod., Rev. Elder Troy D. Perry; clerk, Rev. Elder Nancy L. Wilson, 5300 Santa Monica Blvd., Los Angeles, CA 90029.

Moravian Church (Unitas Fratum) (1740) **Northern Province** — Pres., The Rt. Rev. Wilbur Behrend, 69 W. Church St., Box 1245, Bethlehem, PA 18018. **Southern Province** — Pres., Rev. Graham H. Rights, 459 S. Church St., Winston-Salem, NC 27108.

Old Catholic churches:

Mariavite Old Catholic Church-Province of North America (1932) — Prime bishop, Most Rev. Robert R.J.M. Zaborowski O.M., D.D., 2803 10th St., Wyandotte, MI 48192.

North American Old Roman Catholic Church (1915) — Archbishop, Most Rev. J.E. Schweikert, 4200 N. Kedvale Ave., Chicago, IL 60641.

Pentecostal churches:

Assemblies of God (1914) — Gen. supt., Thomas F. Zimmerman; gen. sec., Joseph R. Flower, 1445 Boonville Ave., Springfield, MO 65802.

Bible Way Church of Our Lord Jesus Christ World Wide (1927) — Presiding bishop, Smallwood E. Williams; gen. sec., Bishop Christal T. Hairston, 16 Fells St., Richmond VA 23222.

Gen. Council, Christian Church of No. America (1948) — Gen. overseer; Rev. Guy Bonigiovani; gen. sec.-treas., Rev. John H. King, Box 141-A, RD #1, Rt. 18 & Rutledge Rd., Transfer, PA 16154.

The Church of God (1903) — Gen. overseer, Bishop Voy M. Bullen; gen. sec.-treas., Betty Bullen, 2504 Arrow Wood Dr. SE, Huntsville, AL 35803.

Church of God (Cleveland, Tenn.) (1886) — Gen. overseer, C. C. Thomas; gen. sec., Robert Hart, Keith St. at 25th NW, Cleveland, TN 37311.

International Church of the Foursquare Gospel (1927) — Pres., Dr. Rolf K. McPherson; sec., Dr. Leland B. Edwards, 1100 Glendale Blvd., Los Angeles, CA 90026.

National Gay Pentecostal Alliance (1980) — Pres., Rev. Wm. H. Carey, P.O. Box 1391, Schenctady, NY 12301.

Open Bible Standard Churches (1919) — Gen. supt., Ray E. Smith; sec.-treas., Patrick L. Bowlin, 2020 Bell Ave., Des Moines, IA 50315.

Pentecostal Church of God (1919) — Gen. supt., Dr. Roy M. Chappell; gen. sec.-treas., Rev. Ronald R. Minor, 211 Main St., Joplin, MO 64801.

United Pentecostal Church International (1945) — Gen. supt., Rev. Nathaniel A. Urshan; gen. sec.-treas., Rev. C. M. Becton, 8855 Dunn Rd., Hazelwood, MO 63042.

Pentecostal Free Will Baptist Church (1959) — Gen. supt., Dr. Herbert Carter; gen. sec., Rev. Don Sauls, Box 1568, Dunn, NC 28334.

Presbyterian churches:

Cumberland Presbyterian Church (1810) — Mod., C. Ray Dobbins, stated clerk, T.V. Warnick, 1978 Union Ave., Memphis, TN 38104.

The Orthodox Presbyterian Church (1936) — Mod. Richard B. Gaffin, Jr.; stated clerk, John P. Galbraith, 7401 Old York Rd., Phila., PA 19126.

Presbyterian Church in America (1973) — Mod., James M. Baird; stated clerk, Rev. Morton H. Smith, P.O. Box 1428, Decatur, GA 30031.

Presbyterian Church in the U.S.A. (1984) — Mod., Harriet Nelson; stated clerk, Rev. James E. Andrews, 475 Riverside Dr., N.Y. NY, 10115.

Reformed Presbyterian Church of No. America (1871) — Mod., Rev. Paul E. Faris, P.O. Box 126-B, Lisbon, NY 13658.

Reformed churches:

Christian Reformed Church in North America (1857) — Stated clerk, Rev. Leonard J. Hoffman, 2850 Kalamazoo Ave., SE, Grand Rapids, MI 49560.

Reformed Church in America (1628) — Pres., William C. Brownson; gen. sec., Edwin G. Mulder, 475 Riverside Dr., N.Y., NY 10115.

Reformed Episcopal Church (1873) — Pres., Rev. Theophilus J. Herter; sec., Rev. Dale H. Crouthamel, 14 Culberson Rd., Basking Ridge, NJ 07920.

Roman Catholic Church — National Conference of Catholic Bishops. Pres., Archbishop James W. Malone; sec., Bishop Thomas C. Kelly, 1312 Massachusetts Ave. NW, Wash., DC 20005.

The Salvation Army (1880) — Natl. cmdr., Commissioner Norman S. Marshall; natl. chief sec., Col. James Osborne, 799 Bloomfield Ave., Verona, NJ 07044.

Sikh (1972) — Chief adm., Siri Singh Sahib, Harbhajan Singh Khalsa Yogiji; sec. gen., Mukhia Sardarni Sahiba, Sardarni Premka Kaur Khalsa, 1649 S. Robertson Blvd., Los Angeles, CA 90035.

Unitarian Universalist Assn. (1961) — Pres., Dr. O. Eugene Pickett; sec., Donald W. Male, 25 Beacon St., Boston, MA 02108.

United Brethren in Christ (1789) — Chpsn., Bishop C. Ray Miller; 302 Lake St., Huntington, IN 46750.

United Church of Christ (1957) — Pres., Rev. Avery D. Post; sec., Rev. Carol Joyce Brun, 105 Madison Ave., N.Y., NY 10016.

Volunteers of America (1896) — Pres., Raymond C. Tremont; 3813 N. Causeway Blvd., Metairie, LA 70002.

The Wesleyan Church (1968) — Gen. supts., Drs. J. D. Abbott, O.D. Emery, R. W. McIntyre, Earle L. Wilson; gen. sec., Rev. Ronald R. Brannon, Box 2000, Marion, IN 46953.

Headquarters of Religious Groups in Canada

(year organized in parentheses)

Anglican Church of Canada (creation of General Synod 1893) - Primate, Most Rev. E.W. Scott; 600 Jarvis St., Toronto, Ont. M4Y 2J6.

Apostolic Church in Canada - H.O. 27 Castlefield Ave., Toronto, Ont. M4R 1G3; Pres., Rev. D.S. Morris, 685 Park St. South, Peterborough, Ont. K9J 3S9.

Baha'is of Canada, The National Spiritual Assembly of the (1949) - Gen. Sec. Douglas Martin, 7200 Leslie St., Thornhill, Ont. L3T 2A1.

Bible Holiness Movement, The (1949) - Pres., Evangelist Wesley H. Wakefield, Box 223, Stn. A, Vancouver, B.C. V6C 2M3.

Canadian Baptist Federation - Pres., Mrs. Shirley Bentall; Gen. Sec.-Treas., Dr. Richard C. Coffin, 219 St. George St., Toronto, Ont. M5R 2M2

Canadian Council of Churches, The (1938) - Gen. Sec., Rev. Donald W. Anderson, 40 St. Clair Ave. E., Suite 201, Toronto, Ont. M4T 1M9.

Canadian Jewish Congress (1919) - Pres., Milton Harris; Exec. Vice-Pres., Alan Rose; 1590 Avenue Docteur Penfield, Montreal, Que. H3G 1C5.

Christian and Missionary Alliance in Canada, The (1889) - Pres., Dr. M.P. Sylvester, Box 7900, Stn. B, Willowdale, Ont. M2K 2R6.

Christian Church (Disciples of Christ) (All Canada Committee formed 1922) - Exec. Min. W. Ray Miles 39 Arkell Rd., R.R. 2, Guelph, Ont. N1H 6H8.

Christian Science in Canada - Mr. J. Don Fulton, 339 Bloor St. W., Ste. 214, Toronto, Ont. M5S 1W7.

Church of Jesus Christ of Latter-Day Saints (Mormons) (1830) - Pres. Calgary Stake, R.H. Walker, 930 Prospect Ave. S.W., Calgary Alta. T2T 0W5; Pres. Edmonton Stake, Donald D. Salmon, 11619 48 Ave.., Edmonton, Alta. T6H 0E7; Pres. Toronto Stake, James L. Kirschbaum, 5 Edenbrook Hill, Islington, Ont. M9A 3Z5; Pres. Vancouver Stake, R.W. Komm, 1384 Chartwell Dr., West Vancouver, B.C. V7S 2R5.

Church of the Nazarene (1902) - Dist. Superintendent of Canada Central District, Rev. Lorne MacMillan, 38 Riverhead Dr., Rexdale, Ont. M9W 4G6; Chairman of Exec. Board, Rev. Alexander Ardrey, 2236 Capitol Hill Cres. N.W., Calgary, Alta. T2M 4B9.

Fellowship of Evangelical Baptist Churches in Canada (1953) - Gen. Sec. Dr. Roy W. Lawson, 74 Sheppard Ave. W., Willowdale, Ont. M2N 1M3.

Free Methodist Church in Canada (1880) - Pres., Bishop D.N. Bastian, 4315 Village Centre Cres., Mississauga, Ont. L4Z 1S2.

Greek Orthodox Church in Canada - His Grace Bishop Sotirios, 27 Teddington Park Ave., Toronto, Ont. M4N 2C4.

Jehovah's Witnesses (Branch Office estab. in Winnipeg 1918) - Branch Coordinator, Mr. Kenneth A. Little, Watch Tower Bible and Tract Society of Canada, Box 4100, Georgetown, Ont. L7G 4Y4.

Lutheran Council in Canada (a joint body of **The Evangelical Lutheran Church of Canada, Lutheran Church-Canada,** and **Lutheran Church in America - Canada Section**) - Pres., Dr. Roger Nostbakken; Exec. Dir. W.A. Schultz, 500-365 Hargrave St., Winnipeg, Man. R3B 2K3.

Mennonite Brethren Churches of North America, Canadian Conference (inc. 1945) - Mod. John Redekop, 298 Ferndale Place, Waterloo, Ont. N2J 3X9.

Mennonites in Canada, Conference of (1903) - Chairman, Jake Fransen, 600 Shaftesbury Blvd., Winnipeg, Man. R3P 0M4.

Pentecostal Assemblies of Canada, The (inc. 1919) - Gen. Supt., Rev. James MacKnight, 10 Overlea Blvd., Toronto, Ont. M4H 1A5.

Presbyterian Church in Canada, The (1875) - Gen. Sec. of the Administrative Council, Dr. Earle F. Roberts, 50 Wynford Dr., Don Mills, Ont. M3C 1J7.

Religious Society of Friends (Quakers), (Canadian Yearly Meeting of the Religious Society of Friends formed 1955) - Presiding Clerk, Donald Laitin, 60 Lowther Ave., Toronto, Ont. M5R 1C7.

Reorganized Church of Jesus Christ of Latter-Day Saints (Canada) (1830) - Ont. Region Pres., Donald H. Comer; Bishop of Canada and Ont. Region, D. Frank Silverthorn, 390 Speedvale Ave. E., Guelph, Ont. N1E 1N5.

Roman Catholic Church in Canada - Canadian Conference of Catholic Bishops, 90 Parent Ave., Ottawa, Ont. K1N 7B1.

Salvation Army, The (1882) - Commissioner Arthur R. Pitcher, P.O. Box 4021, Postal Station A, Toronto, Ont. M5W 2B1.

Seventh-day Adventist Church in Canada - Pres., J.W. Wilson; Sec. G.E. Maxson; 1148 King St. E., Oshawa, Ont. L1H 1H8.

Ukrainian Greek Orthodox Church in Canada (1918) - Primate, His Eminence, Most Rev. Archbishop Wasyly (Fedak), 9 St. Johns Ave., Winnipeg, Man. R2W 1G8.

Union of Spiritual Communities of Christ (Orthodox Doukhobors in Canada) (1938) - Administrator, S.W. Babakaiff; Honorary Chmn. of the Exec. Comm., John J. Verigin, Box 760, Grand Forks, B.C. V0H 1H0.

Unitarian Council, Canadian (1961) - Pres., Mrs. Ruth Patrick; Admin. Sec. Mrs. Thelma Peters, 175 St. Clair Ave. W., Toronto, Ont. M4V 1P7.

United Church of Canada, The (1925) - Mod. Rt. Rev. Robert F. Smith; Sec. of General Council, Rev. Philip A. Cline, 85 St. Clair Ave. E., Toronto, Ont. M4T 1M8.

Episcopal Church Calendar and Liturgical Colors

White—from Christmas Day through the First Sunday after Epiphany; Maundy Thursday (as an alternative to crimson at the Eucharist); from the Vigil of Easter to the Day of Pentecost (Whitsunday); Trinity Sunday; Feasts of the Lord (except Holy Cross Day); the Confession of St. Peter; the Conversion of St. Paul; St. Joseph; St. Mary Magdalene; St. Mary the Virgin; St. Michael and All Angels; All Saint's Day; St. John the Evangelist; memorials of other saints who were not martyred; Independence Day and Thanksgiving Day; weddings and funerals. **Red**.—the Day of Pentecost; Holy Cross Day; feasts of apostles and evangelists (except those listed above); feasts and memorials of martyrs (including Holy Innocents' Day). **Violet**—Advent and Lent. **Crimson** (dark red)—Holy Week. **Green**—the seasons after Epiphany and after Pentecost. **Black**—optional alternative for funerals. Alternative colors used in some churches: **Blue**—Advent; **Lenten White**—Ash Wednesday to Palm Sunday.

Days, etc.	1985	1986	1987	1988	1989
Golden Number	10	11	12	13	14
Sunday Letter	F	E	D	CB	A
Sundays after Epiphany	6	5	8	6	5
Ash Wednesday	Feb. 20	Feb. 12	Mar. 4	Feb. 17	Feb. 8
First Sunday in Lent	Feb. 24	Feb. 16	Mar. 8	Feb. 21	Feb. 12
Passion/Palm Sunday	Mar. 31	Mar. 23	Apr. 12	Mar. 27	Mar. 19
Good Friday	Apr. 5	Mar. 28	Apr. 17	Apr. 1	Mar. 24
Easter Day	Apr. 7	Mar. 30	Apr. 19	Apr. 3	Mar. 26
Ascension Day	May 16	May 8	May 28	May 12	May 4
The Day of Pentecost	May 26	May 18	June 7	May 22	May 14
Trinity Sunday	June 2	May 25	June 14	May 29	May 21
Numbered Proper of 2 Pentecost	#5	#4	#7	#5	#3
First Sunday of Advent	Dec. 1	Nov. 30	Nov. 29	Nov. 27	Dec. 3

In the Episcopal Church the days of fasting are Ash Wednesday and Good Friday. Other days of special devotion (abstinence) are the 40 days of Lent and all Fridays of the year, except those in Christmas and Easter seasons and any Feasts of the Lord which occur on a Friday or during Lent. Ember Days (optional) are days of prayer for the Church's ministry. They fall on the Wednesday, Friday, and Saturday after the first Sunday in Lent, the Day of Pentecost, Holy Cross Day, and the Third Sunday of Advent. Rogation Days (also optional) are the three days before Ascension Day, and are days of prayer for God's blessing on the crops, on commerce and industry, and for the conservation of the earth's resources.

Jewish Holy Days, Festivals, and Fasts

	1985 (5744-45)		1986 (5745-46)		1987 (5746-47)		1988 (5747-48)		1989 (5748-49)	
Tu B'Shvat	Feb.	6 Wed	Jan.	25 Sat	Feb.	14 Sat	Feb.	3 Wed	Jan.	21 Sat
Ta'anis Esther (Fast of Esther)	Mar.	6 Wed	Mar.	24 Mon	Mar.	12 Thu*	Mar.	2 Wed	Mar.	20 Mon
Purim	Mar.	7 Thu	Mar.	25 Tue	Mar.	15 Sun	Mar.	3 Thu	Mar.	21 Tue
Passover	April	6 Sat	April	24 Thu	April	14 Tue	April	2 Sat	April	20 Thu
. . . .	April	13 Sat	May	1 Thu	April	21 Tue	April	9 Sat	April	27 Thu
Lag B'Omer.	May	9 Thu	May	27 Tue	May	17 Sun	May	5 Thu	May	23 Tue
Shavuot	May	26 Sun	June	13 Fri	June	3 Wed	May	27 Sun	June	9 Fri
. . . .	May	27 Mon	June	14 Sat	June	4 Thu	May	28 Mon	June	10 Sat
Fast of the 17th Day of Tammuz . . .	July	7 Sun*	July	24 Thu	July	14 Tue	July	3 Sun	July	20 Thu
Fast of the 9th Day of AV	July	28 Sun*	Aug.	14 Thu	Aug.	4 Tue	July	24 Sun	Aug.	10 Thu
Rosh Hashanah	Sep.	16 Mon	Oct.	4 Sat	Sep.	24 Thu	Sep.	12 Mon	Sep.	30 Sat
. . . .	Sep.	17 Tue	Oct.	5 Sun	Sep.	25 Fri	Sep.	13 Tue	Oct.	1 Sun
Fast of Gedalya	Sep.	18 Wed	Oct.	6 Mon	Sep.	27 Sun*	Sep.	14 Wed	Oct.	2 Mon
Yom Kippur	Sep.	25 Wed	Oct.	13 Mon	Oct.	3 Sat	Sep.	21 Wed	Oct.	9 Mon
Sukkot	Sep.	30 Mon	Oct.	18 Sat	Oct.	8 Thu	Sep.	26 Mon	Oct.	14 Sat
. . . .	Oct.	6 Sun	Oct.	24 Fri	Oct.	14 Wed	Oct.	2 Sun	Oct.	20 Fri
Shmini Atzeret	Oct.	7 Mon	Oct.	25 Sat	Oct.	15 Thu	Oct.	3 Mon	Oct.	21 Sat
. . . .	Oct.	8 Tue	Oct.	26 Sun	Oct.	16 Fri	Oct.	4 Tue	Oct.	22 Sun
Chanukah	Dec.	8 Sun	Dec.	27 Sat	Dec.	16 Wed	Dec.	4 Sun	Dec.	23 Sat
. . . .	Dec.	15 Sun	Jan.	3 Sat	Dec.	23 Wed	Dec.	11 Sun	Dec.	30 Sat
Fast of the 10th of Tevet	Dec.	22 Sun	Jan.	11 Sat	Dec.	31 Thu	Dec.	18 Sun	Jan.	7 Sun

The months of the Jewish year are: 1) Tishri; 2) Cheshvan (also Marcheshvan); 3) Kislev; 4) Tebet (also Tebeth); 5) Shebat (also Shebhat); 6) Adar; 6a) Adar Sheni (II) added in leap years; 7) Nisan; 8) Iyar; 9) Sivan; 10) Tammuz; 11) Av (also Abh); 12) Elul. All Jewish holy days, etc., begin at sunset on the day previous.
*Date changed to avoid Sabbath.

Greek Orthodox Church Calendar, 1986

Date		Holy Days	Date		Holy Days
Jan.	1	Circumcision of Jesus Christ; feast day of St. Basil	*June	22	Sunday of Pentecost
Jan.	6	Epiphany: Baptism of Jesus Christ - Sanctification of the Waters	June	29	Feast day of Sts. Peter and Paul
			June	30	Feast day of the Twelve Apostles of Jesus Christ
Jan.	7	Feast day of St. John the Baptist	Aug.	6	Transfiguration of Jesus Christ
Jan.	30	Feast day of the Three Hierarchs: St. Basil the Great, St. Gregory the Theologian, and St. John Chrysostom	Aug.	15	Dormition of the Virgin Mary
			Aug.	29	Beheading of St. John the Baptist
			Sept.	1	Beginning of the Church Year
Feb.	2	Presentation of Jesus Christ in the Temple	Sept.	14	Adoration of the Holy Cross
Mar.	17	Easter Lent begins	Oct.	23	Feast day of St. James
Mar.	23	Sunday of Orthodoxy (1st. Sunday of Lent)	Oct.	26	Feast day of St. Demetrios the Martyr
Mar.	25	Annunciation of the Virgin Mary	Nov.	15	Christmas Lent begins
Apr.	27	Palm Sunday	Nov.	21	Presentation of the Virgin Mary
Apr. 27-May 4		Holy Week	Nov.	30	Feast day of St. Andrew the Apostle
May	2	Holy (Good) Friday: Burial of Jesus Christ	Dec.	6	Feast day of St. Nicholas, Bishop of Myra
May	4	Easter Sunday: Resurrection of Jesus Christ	Dec.	25	Christmas Day; Nativity of Jesus Christ
*Apr.	23	Feast of St. George			
May	21	Feast day of Sts. Constantine and Helen			
June	12	Ascension of Jesus Christ			

*Movable holy days dependent upon the date of Easter. (The feast day of St. George is normally celebrated Apr. 23. If this day arrives during Lent, it is then celebrated the day after Easter.) The Greek Orthodox Church celebrates holy days in accordance with the Gregorian Calendar. Some Eastern Orthodox Churches still adhere to the Julian Calendar and observe the holy days (with the exception of the Easter cycle) 13 days later.

Islamic (Muslim) Calendar 1985-1986

The Islamic Calendar is a lunar reckoning from the year of the *hegira*, 622 A.D., when Muhammed moved from Mecca to Medina. It runs in cycles of 30 years, of which the 2d, 5th, 7th, 10th, 13th, 16th, 18th, 21st, 24th, 26th, and 29th are leap years; 1406 is the 26th year of the cycle. Common years have 354 days, leap years 355, the extra day being added to the last month, Zu'lhijjah. Except for this case, the 12 months beginning with Muharram have alternately 30 and 29 days.

Year	Name of month	Month begins	Year	Name of month	Month begins
1406	Muharram (New Year)	Sept. 16, 1985	1406	Rajab	Mar. 12, 1986
1406	Safar.	Oct. 16, 1985	1406	Shaban	Apr. 11, 1986
1406	Rabia I	Nov. 14, 1985	1406	Ramadan*.	May 10, 1986
1406	Rabia II	Dec. 14, 1985	1406	Shawwai.	June 9, 1986
1406	Jumada I	Jan. 12, 1986	1406	Zu'lkadah	July 8, 1986
1406	Jumada II	Feb. 11, 1986	1406	Zu'lhijjah.	Aug. 7, 1986

* The date on which Ramadan begins may vary from the calendar date. It actually starts only after the new moon is sighted from the Naval Observatory in Cairo.

Date of Paschal Full Moon, 1900-2199

The Golden Number, used in determining the date of Easter, is greater by unity (one) than the remainder obtained upon dividing the given year by 19. For example, when dividing 1986 by 19, one obtains a remainder of 10. Adding 11 gives 21 as the Golden Number for the year 1986. From the table then the date of the Paschal Full Moon is Mar. 25, 1986. Since this is a Tuesday, Easter is celebrated on the next Sunday, Mar. 30.

Golden Number	Date	Golden Number	Date	Golden Number	Date	Golden Number	Date
1	Apr. 14	6	Apr. 18	11	Mar. 25	16	Mar. 30
2	Apr. 3	7	Apr. 8	12	Apr. 13	17	Apr. 17
3	Mar. 23	8	Mar. 28	13	Apr. 2	18	Apr. 7
4	Apr. 11	9	Apr. 16	14	Mar. 22	19	Mar. 27
5	Mar. 31	10	Apr. 5	15	Apr. 10		

The Major World Religions

Buddhism

Founded: About 525 BC, reportedly near Benares, India.
Founder: Gautama Siddhartha (ca. 563-480), the Buddha, who achieved enlightenment through intense meditation.
Sacred Texts: The *Tripitaka*, a collection of the Buddha's teachings, rules of monastic life, and philosophical commentaries on the teachings; also a vast body of Buddhist teachings and commentaries, many of which are called *sutras.*
Organization: The basic institution is the *sangha* or monastic order through which the traditions are passed to each generation. Monastic life tends to be democratic and anti-authoritarian. Large lay organizations have developed in some sects.
Practice: Varies widely according to the sect and ranges from austere meditation to magical chanting and elaborate temple rites. Many practices, such as exorcism of devils, reflect pre-Buddhist beliefs.
Divisions: A wide variety of sects grouped into 3 primary branches: Therevada (sole survivor of the ancient Hinayana schools) which emphasizes the importance of pure thought and deed; Mahayana, which includes Zen and Soka-gakkai, ranges from philosophical schools to belief in the saving grace of higher beings or ritual practices, and to practical meditative disciplines; and Tantrism, an unusual combination of belief in ritual magic and sophisticated philosophy.
Location: Throughout Asia, from Ceylon to Japan. Zen and Soka-gakkai have several thousand adherents in the U.S.
Beliefs: Life is misery and decay, and there is no ultimate reality in it or behind it. The cycle of endless birth and rebirth continues because of desire and attachment to the unreal "self". Right meditation and deeds will end the cycle and achieve Nirvana, the Void, nothingness.

Hinduism

Founded: Ca. 1500 BC by Aryan invaders of India where their Vedic religion intermixed with the practices and beliefs of the natives.
Sacred texts: The *Veda*, including the *Upanishads*, a collection of rituals and mythological and philosophical commentaries; a vast number of epic stories about gods, heroes and saints, including the *Bhagavadgita*, a part of the *Mahabharata*, and the *Ramayana;* and a great variety of other literature.
Organization: None, strictly speaking. Generally, rituals should be performed or assisted by Brahmins, the priestly caste, but in practice simpler rituals can be performed by anyone. Brahmins are the final judges of ritual purity, the vital element in Hindu life. Temples and religious organizations are usually presided over by Brahmins.
Practice: A variety of private rituals, primarily passage rites (eg. initiation, marriage, death, etc.) and daily devotions, and a similar variety of public rites in temples. Of the latter, the *puja*, a ceremonial dinner for a god, is the most common.
Divisions: There is no concept of orthodoxy in Hinduism, which presents a bewildering variety of sects, most of them devoted to the worship of one of the many gods. The 3 major living traditions are those devoted to the gods Vishnu and Shiva and to the goddess Shakti; each of them divided into further sub-sects. Numerous folk beliefs and practices, often in amalgamation with the above groups, exist side-by-side with sophisticated philosophical schools and exotic cults.
Location: Confined to India, except for the missionary work of Vedanta, the Krishna Consciousness society, and individual *gurus* (teachers) in the West.
Beliefs: There is only one divine principle; the many gods are only aspects of that unity. Life in all its forms is an aspect of the divine, but it appears as a separation from the divine, a meaningless cycle of birth and rebirth (*samsara*) determined by the purity or impurity of past deeds (*karma*). To improve one's *karma* or escape *samsara* by pure acts, thought, and/or devotion is the aim of every Hindu.

Islam (submission)

Founded: 622 AD in Medina, Arabian peninsula.

Founder: Mohammed (ca. 570-632), the Prophet, as a result of visions.
Sacred texts: *Koran*, the words of God, delivered to Mohammed by the angel Gabriel; *Hadith*, collections of the sayings of the Prophet.
Organization: Theoretically the state and religious community are one, administered by a caliph. In practice, Islam is a loose collection of congregations united by a very conservative tradition. Islam is basically egalitarian and non-authoritarian.
Practice: Every Moslem is supposed to make the profession of faith ("There is no god but Allah . . ."), pray 5 times a day, give a regular portion of his goods to charity, fast during the day in the month of Ramadan, and make at least one pilgrimage to Mecca if possible. Additionally saints' days are celebrated and pilgrimages made to shrines.
Divisions: The 2 major sects of Islam are the Sunni (orthodox) and the Shi'ah. The Shi'ah believe in 12 *imams*, perfect teachers, who still guide the faithful from Paradise. Shi'ah practice tends toward the ecstatic, while the Sunni is staid and simple. The Shi'ah sect affirms man's free will; the Sunni is deterministic. The mystic tradition in Islam is Sufism. A Sufi adept believes he has acquired a special inner knowledge direct from Allah.
Location: From the west coast of Africa to the Philippines across a broad band that includes Tanzania, southern USSR and western China, India, Malaysia and Indonesia. Islam has perhaps 100,000 adherents among American blacks.
Beliefs: Strictly monotheistic. God is creator of the universe, omnipotent, just, and merciful. Man is God's highest creation, but limited and sinful. He is misled by Satan, a prideful angel. God gave the *Koran* to Mohammed to guide men to the truth. Those who repent and sincerely submit to God return to a state of sinlessness. In the end, the sinless go to Paradise, a place of physical and spiritual pleasure, and the wicked burn in Hell.

Judaism

Founded: About 1300 BCE.
Founder: Abrahm is regarded as the founding patriarch, but the Torah of Moses is the basic source of the teachings.
Sacred Texts: The five books of Moses constitute the written Torah. Special sanctity is also assigned other writings of the Hebrew Bible—the teachings of oral Torah are recorded in the Talmud, the Midrash, and various commentaries.
Organization: Originally theocratic, Judaism has evolved a congregational polity. The basic institution is the local synagogue, operated by the congregation and led by a rabbi of their choice. Chief Rabbis in France and Great Britain have authority only over those who accept it; in Israel, the 2 Chief Rabbis have civil authority in family law.
Practice: Among traditional practitioners, almost all areas of life are governed by strict religious discipline. Sabbath and holidays are marked by special observances, and attendance at public worship is regarded as especially important then. The chief annual observances are Passover, celebrating the liberation of the Israelites from Egypt and marked by the ritual Seder meal in the home, and the 10 days from Rosh Hashana (New Year) to Yom Kippur (Day of Atonement), a period of fasting and penitence.
Divisions: Judaism is an unbroken spectrum from ultra conservative to ultra liberal, largely reflecting different points of view regarding the binding character of the prohibitions and duties—particularly the dietary and Sabbath observations—prescribed in the daily life of the Jew.
Location: Almost worldwide, with concentrations in Israel and the U.S.
Beliefs: Strictly monotheistic. God is the creator and absolute ruler of the universe. Men are free to choose to rebel against God's rule. God established a particular relationship with the Hebrew people: by obeying a divine law God gave them they would be a special witness to God's mercy and justice. The emphasis in Judaism is on ethical behavior (and, among the traditional, careful ritual obedience) as the true worship of God.

Major Christian Denominations:

Italics indicate that area which, generally speaking, most

Denomination	Origins	Organization	Authority	Special rites
Baptists	In radical Reformation objections to infant baptism, demands for church-state separation; John Smyth, English Separatist in 1609; Roger Williams, 1638, Providence, R.I.	Congregational, *i.e.*, each local church is autonomous.	Scripture; some Baptists, particularly in the South, interpret the Bible literally.	Baptism, after about age 12, by total immersion; Lord's Supper.
Church of Christ (Disciples)	Among evangelical Presbyterians in Ky. (1804) and Penn. (1809), in distress over Protestant factionalism and decline of fervor. Organized 1832.	Congregational.	*"Where the Scriptures speak, we speak; where the Scriptures are silent, we are silent."*	Adult baptism, Lord's Supper (weekly).
Episcopalians	Henry VIII separated English Catholic Church from Rome, 1534, for political reasons. Protestant Episcopal Church in U.S. founded 1789.	*Bishops, in apostolic succession, are elected by diocesan representatives; part of Anglican Communion, symbolically headed by Archbishop of Canterbury.*	Scripture as interpreted by tradition, esp. *39 Articles* (1563); not dogmatic. Tri-annual convention of bishops, priests, and laymen.	Infant baptism, Holy Communion, others. Sacrament is symbolic, but has real spiritual effect.
Lutherans	Martin Luther in Wittenberg, Germany, 1517, objected to Catholic doctrine of salvation by merit and sale of indulgences; break complete by 1519.	Varies from congregational to episcopal; in U.S. a combination of regional synods and congregational polities is most common.	*Scripture, and tradition as spelled out in Augsburg Confession (1530) and other creeds. These confessions of faith are binding although interpretations vary.*	Infant baptism, Lord's Supper. Christ's true body and blood present "in, with, and under the bread and wine."
Methodists	Rev. John Wesley began movement, 1738, within Church of England. First U.S. denomination Baltimore, 1784.	Conference and superintendent system. *In United Methodist Church, general superintendents are bishops—not a priestly order, only an office—who are elected for life.*	Scripture as interpreted by tradition, reason, and experience.	Baptism of infants or adults, Lord's Supper commanded. Other rites, inc. marriage, ordination, solemnize personal commitments.
Mormons	In visions of the Angel Moroni by Joseph Smith, 1827, in New York, in which he received a new revelation on golden tablets: *The Book of Mormon.*	Theocratic; all male adults are in priesthood which culminates in Council of 12 Apostles and 1st Presidency (1st President, 2 counselors).	*The Bible, Book of Mormon and other revelations to Smith, and certain pronouncements of the 1st Presidency.*	Adult baptism, laying on of hands (which confers the gift of the Holy Spirit), Lord's Supper. Temple rites: baptism for the dead, marriage for eternity, others.
Orthodox	Original Christian proselytizing in 1st century; broke with Rome, 1054, after centuries of doctrinal disputes and diverging traditions.	Synods of bishops in autonomous, usually national, churches elect a patriarch, archbishop or metropolitan. These men, as a group, are the heads of the church.	Scripture, tradition, and the first 7 church councils up to Nicaea II in 787. Bishops in council have authority in doctrine and policy.	Seven sacraments: infant baptism and anointing, Eucharist (both bread and wine), ordination, penance, anointing of the sick, marriage.
Pentecostal	In Topeka, Kansas (1901), and Los Angeles (1906) in reaction to loss of evangelical fervor among Methodists and other denominations.	Originally a movement, not a formal organization, Pentecostalism now has a variety of organized forms and continues also as a movement.	Scripture, individual charismatic leaders, the teachings of the Holy Spirit.	*Spirit baptism, esp. as shown in "speaking in tongues"; healing and sometimes exorcism; adult baptism, Lord's Supper.*
Presbyterians	In Calvinist Reformation in 1500s; differed with Lutherans over sacraments, church government. John Knox founded Scotch Presbyterian church about 1560.	*Highly structured representational system of ministers and laypersons (presbyters) in local, regional and national bodies. (synods).*	Scripture.	Infant baptism, Lord's Supper; bread and wine symbolize Christ's spiritual presence.
Roman Catholics	Traditionally, by Jesus who named St. Peter the 1st Vicar; historically, in early Christian proselytizing and the conversion of imperial Rome in the 4th century.	Hierarchy with supreme power vested in Pope elected by cardinals. Councils of Bishops advise on matters of doctrine and policy.	*The Pope, when speaking for the whole church in matters of faith and morals, and tradition, which is partly recorded in scripture and expressed in church councils.*	Seven sacraments: baptism, contrition and penance, confirmation, Eucharist, marriage, ordination, and anointing of the sick (unction).
United Church of Christ	*By ecumenical union, 1957, of Congregationalists and Evangelical & Reformed, representing both Calvinist and Lutheran traditions.*	Congregational; a General Synod, representative of all congregations, sets general policy.	Scripture.	Infant baptism, Lord's Supper.

How Do They Differ?

distinguishes that denomination from any other.

Practice	Ethics	Doctrine	Other	Denomination
Worship style varies from staid to evangelistic. Extensive missionary activity.	Usually opposed to alcohol and tobacco; sometimes tends toward a perfectionist ethical standard.	*No creed; true church is of believers only, who are all equal.*	Since no authority can stand between the believer and God, the Baptists are strong supporters of church-state separation.	Baptists
Tries to avoid any rite or doctrine not explicitly part of the 1st century church. Some congregations may reject instrumental music.	Some tendency toward perfectionism; increasing interest in social action programs.	Simple New Testament faith; avoids any elaboration not firmly based on Scripture.	Highly tolerant in doctrinal and religious matters; strongly supportive of scholarly education.	Church of Christ (Disciples)
Formal, based on *Book of Common Prayer* (1549); services range from austerely simple to highly elaborate.	Tolerant; sometimes permissive; some social action programs.	*Apostles' Creed* is basic; otherwise, considerable variation ranges from rationalist and liberal to acceptance of most Roman Catholic dogma.	Strongly ecumenical, holding talks with all other branches of Christendom.	Episcopalians
Relatively simple formal liturgy with emphasis on the sermon.	Generally, conservative in personal and social ethics; doctrine of "2 kingdoms" (worldly and holy) supports conservatism in secular affairs.	Salvation by faith alone through grace. Lutheranism has made major contributions to Protestant theology.	Though still somewhat divided along ethnic lines (German, Swede, etc.), main divisions are between fundamentalists and liberals.	Lutherans
Worship style varies widely by denomination, local church, geography.	Originally pietist and perfectionist; always strong social activist elements.	No distinctive theological development; 25 Articles abriged from Church of England's 39 not binding.	In 1968, United Methodist Church joined pioneer English- and German-speaking groups. UMs leaders in ecumenical movement.	Methodists
Staid service with hymns, sermon. Secret temple ceremonies may be more elaborate. Strong missionary activity.	Temperance; strict tithing. Combine a strong work ethic with communal self-reliance.	God is a material being; he created the universe out of pre-existing matter; all persons can be saved and many will become divine. Most other beliefs are traditionally Christian.	Mormons regard mainline churches as apostate, corrupt. Reorganized Church (founded 1860) rejects most Mormon doctrine and practice except Book of Mormon.	Mormons
Elaborate liturgy, usually in the vernacular, though extremely traditional. The liturgy is the essence of Orthodoxy. Veneration of icons.	Tolerant; very little social action; divorce, remarriage permitted in some cases. Priests need not be celibate; bishops are.	Emphasis on Christ's resurrection, rather than crucifixion; the Holy Spirit proceeds from God the Father only.	Orthodox Church in America, originally under Patriarch of Moscow, was granted autonomy in 1970. Greek Orthodox do not recognize this autonomy.	Orthodox
Loosely structured service with rousing hymns and sermons, culminating in spirit baptism.	Usually, emphasis on perfectionism with varying degrees of tolerance.	Simple traditional beliefs, usually Protestant, with emphasis on the immediate presence of God in the Holy Spirit	Once confined to lower-class "holy rollers," Pentecostalism now appears in mainline churches and has established middle-class congregations.	Pentecostal
A simple, sober service in which the sermon is central.	Traditionally, a tendency toward strictness with firm church- and self-discipline; otherwise tolerant.	Emphasizes the sovereignty and justice of God; no longer doctrinaire.	While traces of belief in predestination (that God has foreordained salvation for the "elect") remain, this idea is no longer a central element in Presbyterianism.	Presbyterians
Relatively elaborate ritual; wide variety of public and private rites, eg., rosary recitation, processions, novenas.	Theoretically very strict; tolerant in practice on most issues. Divorce and remarriage not accepted. Celibate clergy, except in Eastern rite.	Highly elaborated. Salvation by merit gained through faith. Unusual development of doctrines surrounding Mary. Dogmatic.	Roman Catholicism is presently in a period of relatively rapid change as a result of Vatican Councils I and II.	Roman Catholics
Usually simple services with emphasis on the sermon.	Tolerant; some social action emphasis.	Standard Protestant; *Statement of Faith* (1959) is not binding.	The 2 main churches in the 1957 union represented earlier unions with small groups of almost every Protestant denomination.	United Church of Christ

Roman Catholic Hierarchy

Source: Apostolic Nunciature, Washington, D.C.; as of May, 1985

Supreme Pontiff

At the head of the Roman Catholic Church is the Supreme Pontiff, Pope John Paul II, Karol Wojtyla, born at Wadowice (Krakow), Poland, May 18, 1920; ordained priest Nov. 1, 1946; promoted to Archbishop of Krakow Jan. 13, 1964; proclaimed Cardinal June 26, 1967; elected pope as successor of Pope John Paul I Oct. 16, 1978; solemn commencement as pope Oct. 22, 1978.

College of Cardinals

Members of the Sacred College of Cardinals are chosen by the Pope to be his chief assistants and advisors in the administration of the church. Among their duties is the election of the Pope when the Holy See becomes vacant. The title of cardinal is a high honor, but it does not represent any increase in the powers of holy orders.

Name	Office	Nationality	Year Named Cardinal
Alfrink, Bernard		Dutch	1960
Antonelli, Ferdinando		Italian	1973
Aponte Martinez, Luis	Archbishop of San Juan	American	1973
Aramburu, Juan	Archbishop of Buenos Aires	Argentinian	1976
Arinze, Francis A.	Acting Pres. of Secretariat for Non-Christians	Italian	1985
Arns, Paulo	Archbishop of Sao Paulo	Brazilian	1973
Bafile, Corrado		Italian	1976
Baggio, Sebastiano	Pres. of Pontifical Commission for Vatican City	Italian	1969
Ballestrero, Anastasio A.	Archbishop of Turin	Italian	1979
Baum, William	Prefect of Congregation for Catholic Ed.	American	1976
Beras-Rojas, Octavio		Dominican	1976
Bernardin, Joseph Louis	Archbishop of Chicago	American	1983
Bertoli, Paolo	Chamberlain of Holy Roman Church	Italian	1969
Biffi, Giacomo	Acting Pres. of Secretariat for Non-Christians	Italian	1985
Brandao Vilela, Avelar	Archbishop of Sao Salvador da Bahia	Brazilian	1973
Bueno y Monreal, Jose		Spanish	1958
Caprio, Giuseppe	Pres. of Administration of Patrimony of Holy See	Italian	1979
Carberry, John		American	1969
Carpino, Francesco		Italian	1967
Carter, Gerald E.	Archbishop of Toronto	Canadian	1979
Casaroli, Agostino	Secretary of State to His Holiness	Italian	1979
Casoria, Giuseppe		Italian	1983
Cè, Marco	Patriarch of Venice	Italian	1979
Ciappi, O.P., Mario Luigi	Pro-Theologian of Pontifical Household	Italian	1977
Civardi, Ernesto		Italian	1979
Colombo, Giovanni		Italian	1965
Confalonieri, Carlo	Dean of Sacred College	Italian	1958
Cooray, Thomas B.		Ceylonese	1965
Cordeiro, Joseph	Archbishop of Karachi	Pakistani	1973
Corripio Ahumada, Ernesto	Archbishop of Mexico City	Mexican	1979
Dadaglio, Luigi		Italian	1985
Danneels, Godfried	Archbishop of Malines-Brussels	Belgian	1983
Darmojuwono, Justinus	Archbishop of Semarang	Indonesian	1967
de Araujo Sales, Eugenio	Archbishop of St. Sebastian	Brazilian	1969
Dearden, John		American	1969
Decourtray, Albert		French	1985
de Furstenberg, Maximilian		Belgian	1967
Deskur, Andrzej	Archbishop of Poland, Pres. Emeritus of Pontif. Commission for Social Communications	Polish	1985
Duval, Leon-Etienne	Archbishop of Algiers	Algerian	1965
Ekandem, Dominic	Bishop of Ikote Ekpene	Nigerian	1976
Enrique y Tarancon, Vicente		Spanish	1969
Etchegaray, Roger	Pres. of Justicia et Pax	French	1979
Flahiff, George		Canadian	1969
Florit, Ermenegildo		Italian	1965
Freeman, James	Archbishop of Sydney	Australian	1973
Gagnon, Edouard	Act. Pres. of Pontifical Council for the Family	Canadian	1985
Gantin, Bernardin	Prefect of Congregation for the Bishops	Benin	1977
Garrone, Gabriel-Marie		French	1967
Glemp, Josef	Archbishop of Warsaw, Gniezno	Polish	1983
Goicoechea, Angel Suguia	Archbishop of Madrid	Spanish	1985
Gonzalez Martin, Marcelo	Archbishop of Toledo	Spanish	1973
Gouyon, Paul	Archbishop of Rennes	French	1969
Gray, Gordon		Scottish	1969
Guerri, Sergio		Italian	1969
Gulbinowicz, Henryk Roman	Archbishop of Wroclaw	Polish	1985
Guyot, Jean		French	1973
Hamer, Jean Jerome	Act. Prefect of Congregation of Religious and Secular Institutes	Italian	1985
Hoffner, Joseph	Archbishop of Cologne	German	1969
Hume, George Basil	Archbishop of Westminster	English	1976
Innocenti, Antonio	Apostolic Nuncio to Spain	Italian	1985
Jubany Arnau, Narciso	Archbishop of Barcelona	Spanish	1973
Khoraiche, Anthony Peter	Patriarch of Maronites	Lebanese	1983
Kim, Stephan Sou Hwan	Archbishop of Seoul	Korean	1969
Kitbunchu, Michael	Archbishop of Bangkok	Thai	1983
König, Franz	Archbishop of Vienna	Austrian	1958
Krol, John	Archbishop of Philadelphia	American	1967
Kuharic, Franjo	Archbishop of Zagreb	Yugoslavian	1983
Landazuri, Ricketts Juan	Archbishop of Lima	Peruvian	1962
Lara, Rosario Jose Castillo	Archbishop of Venezuela	Venezuelan	1985

Name	Office	Nationality	Year Named Cardinal
Larrain, Juan Francisco Fresno	Archbishop of Santiago	Chilean	1985
Law, Bernard F.	Archbishop of Boston	American	1985
Lebrun-Moratinos, Jose Ali	Archbishop of Caracas	Venezuelan	1983
Léger, Paul		Canadian	1953
Lékai, Laszlo	Archbishop of Esztergom	Hungarian	1976
Lopez-Trujillo, Alphonso	Archbishop of Medellin	Colombian	1983
Lorscheider, Aloisio	Archbishop of Fortaleza	Brazilian	1976
Lourdusamy, Simon D.	Archbishop of India; Secy. of Propaganda Fide	Indian	1985
deLubac, Henri	Priest of the Society of Jesus, Province of France.	French	1983
Lubachivsky, Myroslav Ivan	Primate of Ukranian Catholic Church	Ukrainian	1985
Lustiger, Jean-Marie	Archbishop of Paris	French	1983
Macharski, Franciszek	Archbishop of Cracow	Polish	1979
Malula, Joseph	Archbishop of Kinshasa	Congolese	1969
Manning, Timothy	Archbiship of Los Angeles	American	1973
Martini, Carlo Maria	Archbishop of Milan	Italian	1983
Marty, Francois		French	1969
Maurer, Jose	Archbishop of Sucre	Bolivian	1967
Mayer, Augustin	Archbishop of W. Germany; Act. Prefect for Congregation for Sacraments & Divine Cult	W. German	1985
McCann, Owen	Archbishop of Cape Town	S. African	1965
Meisner, Joachim	Bishop of Berlin	German	1983
Miranda y Gomez, Miguel		Mexican	1969
Munoz Duque, Anibal	Archbishop of Bogota	Colombian	1973
Munoz Vega, Paolo	Archbishop of Quito	Ecuadorian	1969
Nasalli Rocca di Corneliano, Mario		Italian	1969
Nasimento, Alexandre do	Archbishop of Lubango	Angolan	1983
Nsubuga, Emmanuel	Archbishop of Kampala	Ugandan	1976
Obando y Bravo	Archbishop of Managua	Nicaraguan	1985
O'Boyle, Patrick		American	1967
Oddi, Silvio	Prefect of Congregation of the Clergy	Italian	1969
O'Connor, John J.	Archbishop of New York	American	1985
O'Fiaich, Tomás	Archbishop of Armagh, Primate for all Ireland	Irish	1979
Otunga, Maurice	Archbishop of Nairobi	Kenyan	1973
Palazzini, Pietro	Prefect for Congregation for Causes of Saints	Italian	1973
Pappalardo, Salvatore	Archbishop of Palermo	Italian	1973
Parecattil, Joseph	Archbishop of Ernakulam	Indian	1969
Parente, Pietro		Italian	1967
Paupini, Giuseppe		Italian	1969
Pavan, Pietro		Italian	1985
Pellegrino, Michele		Italian	1967
Picachy, Lawrence	Archbishop of Calcutta	Indian	1976
Piovanelli, Silvano		Italian	1985
Pironio, Eduardo	Pres. of Pontifical Council on the Laity	Argentian	1976
Poletti, Ugo	Vicar General of His Holiness for City of Rome	Italian	1973
Poma, Antonio		Italian	1969
Poupard, Paul	Archbishop of France; Pres. of Pontif. Executive Commission for Culture	French	1985
Primatesta, Raul Francisco	Archbishop of Cordoba	Argentinian	1973
Ratzinger, Joseph	Prefect of Congregation for Doctrine of the Faith	German	1977
Razafimahatratra, Victor	Archbishop of Tananarive	Madagascan	1976
Ribeiro, Antonio	Patriarch of Lisbon	Portuguese	1973
Righi-Lambertini, Egano		Italian	1979
Rossi, Agnelo		Brazilian	1965
Rossi, Opilio		Italian	1976
Roy, Maurice		Canadian	1983
Rubin, Wladyslaw	Prefect of Congregation for Oriental Churches	Polish	1979
Rugambwa, Laurean	Archbishop of Dar-es-Salaam	Tanzanian	1960
Sabattani, Aurelio	Prefect of Supreme Tribunal of Apostolic Signatura	Italian	1983
Salazar Lopez, Jose	Archbishop of Guadalajara	Mexican	1973
Satowaki, Joseph A.	Archbishop of Nagasaki	Japanese	1979
Scherer, Alfredo		Brazilian	1969
Sensi, Giuseppe		Italian	1976
Sidarouss, Stephanos	Coptic Patriarch of Alexandria	Egyptian	1965
Silva Henriquez, Raul		Chilean	1962
Simonis, Adrianus J.	Archbishop of Utrecht	Dutch	1985
Sin, Jaime	Archbishop of Manila	Filipino	1976
Siri, Giuseppe	Archbishop of Genoa	Italian	1953
Stickler, Alfons	Archbishop of Austria, Act. Head Librarian and Archivist	Austrian	1985
Suenens, Leo		Belgian	1962
Taofinu'u, Pio	Bishop, Samoa, Tokelau	Samoan	1973
Thiandoum, Hyacinthe	Archbishop of Dakar	Senegalese	1976
Tomasek, Frantisek	Archbishop of Prague	Czech	1976
Tomko, Jozef	Archbishop of Czechoslovakia; Secy. General of Vatican Synod of Bishops	Czech	1985
Trinh Van Can, Joseph-Marie	Archbishop of Hanoi	Vietnamese	1979
Tzadua, Paulos	Archbishop of Addis Ababa	Ethiopian	1985
Ursi, Corrado	Archbishop of Naples	Italian	1967
Vanchon, Louis-Albert	Archbishop of Quebec	Canadian	1985
Vaivods, Julijans	Apostolic Administration of Riga and Liepaja	Latvian	1964
Vidal, Ricardo	Archbishop of Cebu	Filipino	1985
Vilela, Avelar	Archbishop of Sao Salvador	Brazilian	1973
Volk, Hermann		German	1973
Wetter, Frederich	Archbishop of Munich, Freising	German	1985
Willebrands, John	Pres. of Secretariat for Union of Christians	Dutch	1969
Williams, Thomas	Archbishop of Wellington	New Zealander	1983
Yago, Bernard	Archbishop of Abidjan, Ivory Coast	Ivorian	1960
Zoungrana, Paul	Archbishop of Ougadougou	Burkina B	1965

AWARDS — MEDALS — PRIZES

The Alfred B. Nobel Prize Winners

Alfred B. Nobel, inventor of dynamite, bequeathed $9,000,000, the interest to be distributed yearly to those who had most benefited mankind in physics, chemistry, medicine-physiology, literature, and peace. The first Nobel Memorial Prize in Economics was awarded in 1969. No awards given for years omitted. In 1984, each prize was worth approximately $190,000.

Physics

1984 Carlo Rubbia, Italian, Simon van der Meere, Dutch
1983 Subrahmanyan Chandrasekhar, William A. Fowler, both U.S.
1982 Kenneth G. Wilson, U.S.
1981 Nicolass Boembergen, Arthur Schlawlow, both U.S.; Kai M. Siegbahn, Swedish
1980 James W. Cronin, Val L. Fitch, both U.S.
1979 Steven Weinberg, Sheldon L. Glashow, both U.S.; Abdus Salam, Pakistani
1978 Pyotr Kapitsa, USSR; Arno Penzias, Robert Wilson, both U.S.
1977 John H. Van Vleck, Philip W. Anderson, both U.S.; Nevill F. Mott, British
1976 Burton Richter, U.S. Samuel C.C. Ting, U.S.
1975 James Rainwater, U.S. Ben Mottelson, U.S.-Danish, Aage Bohr, Danish
1974 Martin Ryle, British Antony Hewish, British
1973 Ivar Giaever, U.S. Leo Esaki, Japan Brian D. Josephson, British
1972 John Bardeen, U.S. Leon N. Cooper, U.S. John R. Schrieffer, U.S.
1971 Dennis Gabor, British
1970 Louis Neel, French Hannes Alfven, Swedish
1969 Murray Gell-Mann, U.S.
1968 Luis W. Alvarez, U.S.
1967 Hans A. Bethe, U.S.
1966 Alfred Kastler, French
1965 Richard P. Feynman, U.S. Julian S. Schwinger, U.S. Shinichiro Tomonaga, Japanese
1964 Nikolai G. Basov USSR

Aleksander M. Prochorov, USSR Charles H. Townes, U.S.
1963 Maria Goeppert-Mayer, U.S. J. Hans D. Jensen, German Eugene P. Wigner, U.S.
1962 Lev. D. Landau, USSR
1961 Robert Hofstadter, U.S. Rudolf L. Mossbauer, German
1960 Donald A. Glaser, U.S.
1959 Owen Chamberlain, U.S. Emilio G. Segre, U.S.
1958 Pavel Cherenkov, Ilya Frank, Igor Y. Tamm, all USSR
1957 Tsung-dao Lee, Chen Ning Yang, both U.S.
1956 John Bardeen, U.S. Walter H. Brattain, U.S. William Shockley, U.S.
1955 Polykarp Kusch, U.S. Willis E. Lamb, U.S.
1954 Max Born, British Walter Bothe, German
1953 Frits Zernike, Dutch
1952 Felix Bloch, U.S. Edward M. Purcell, U.S.
1951 Sir John D. Cockroft, British Ernest T. S. Walton, Irish
1950 Cecil F. Powell, British
1949 Hideki Yukawa, Japanese
1948 Patrick M. S. Blackett, British
1947 Sir Edward V. Appleton, British
1946 Percy Williams Bridgman, U.S.
1945 Wolfgang Pauli, U.S.
1944 Isidor Isaac Rabi, U.S.
1943 Otto Stern, U.S.
1939 Ernest O. Lawrence, U.S.
1938 Enrico Fermi, U.S.
1937 Clinton J. Davisson, U.S. Sir George P. Thomson, British
1936 Carl D. Anderson, U.S. Victor F. Hess, Austrian
1935 Sir James Chadwick, British

1933 Paul A. M. Dirac, British Erwin Schrodinger, Austrian
1932 Werner Heisenberg, German
1930 Sir Chandrasekhara V. Raman, Indian
1929 Prince Louis-Victor de Broglie, French
1928 Owen W. Richardson, British
1927 Arthur H. Compton, U.S. Charles T. R. Wilson, British
1926 Jean B. Perrin, French
1925 James Franck, Gustav Hertz, both German
1924 Karl M. G. Siegbahn, Swedish
1923 Robert A. Millikan, U.S.
1922 Niels Bohr, Danish
1921 Albert Einstein, Ger.-U.S.
1920 Charles E. Guillaume, French
1919 Johannes Stark, German
1918 Max K. E. L. Planck, German
1917 Charles G. Barkla, British
1915 Sir William H. Bragg, British Sir William L. Bragg, British
1914 Max von Laue, German
1913 Heike Kamerlingh-Onnes, Dutch
1912 Nils G. Dalen, Swedish
1911 Wilhelm Wien, German
1910 Johannes D. van der Waals, Dutch
1909 Carl F. Braun, German Guglielmo Marconi, Italian
1908 Gabriel Lippmann, French
1907 Albert A. Michelson, U.S.
1906 Sir Joseph J. Thomson, British
1905 Philipp E. A. von Lenard, Ger.
1904 John W. Strutt, Lord Rayleigh, British
1903 Antoine Henri Becquerel, French Marie Curie, Polish-French Pierre Curie, French
1902 Hendrik A. Lorentz, Pieter Zeeman, both Dutch
1901 Wilhelm C. Roentgen, German

Chemistry

1984 Bruce Merrifield, U.S.
1983 Henry Taube, Canadian
1982 Aaron Klug, S. African
1981 Kenichi Fukui, Japan., Roald Hoffmann, U.S.
1980 Paul Berg, U.S.; Walter Gilbert, U.S., Frederick Sanger, U.K.
1979 Herbert C. Brown, U.S. George Wittig, German
1978 Peter Mitchell, British
1977 Ilya Prigogine, Belgian
1976 William N. Lipscomb, U.S.
1975 John Cornforth, Austral.-Brit., Vladimir Prelog, Yugo.-Switz.
1974 Paul J. Flory, U.S.
1973 Ernst Otto Fischer, W. German Geoffrey Wilkinson, British
1972 Christian B. Anfinsen, U.S. Stanford Moore, U.S. William H. Stein, U.S.
1971 Gerhard Herzberg, Canadian
1970 Luis F. Leloir, Arg.
1969 Derek H. R. Barton, British Odd Hassel, Norwegian
1968 Lars Onsager, U.S.
1967 Manfred Eigen, German Ronald G. W. Norrish, British George Porter, British
1966 Robert S. Mulliken, U.S.
1965 Robert B. Woodward, U.S.
1964 Dorothy C. Hodgkin, British
1963 Giulio Natta, Italian Karl Ziegler, German

1962 John C. Kendrew, British Max F. Perutz, British
1961 Melvin Calvin, U.S.
1960 Willard F. Libby, U.S.
1959 Jaroslav Heyrovsky, Czech
1958 Frederick Sanger, British
1957 Sir Alexander R. Todd, British
1956 Sir Cyril N. Hinshelwood, British Nikolai N. Semenov, USSR
1955 Vincent du Vigneaud, U.S.
1954 Linus C. Pauling, U.S.
1953 Hermann Staudinger, German
1952 Archer J. P. Martin, British Richard L. M. Synge, British
1951 Edwin M. McMillan, U.S. Glenn T. Seaborg, U.S.
1950 Kurt Alder, German Otto P. H. Diels, German
1949 William F. Giauque, U.S.
1948 Arne W. K. Tiselius, Swedish
1947 Sir Robert Robinson, British
1946 James B. Sumner, John H. Northrop, Wendell M. Stanley, all U.S.
1945 Artturi I. Virtanen, Finnish
1944 Otto Hahn, German
1943 Georg de Hevesy, Hungarian
1939 Adolf F. J. Butenandt, German Leopold Ruzicka, Swiss
1938 Richard Kuhn, German
1937 Walter N. Haworth, British Paul Karrer, Swiss
1936 Peter J. W. Debye, Dutch
1935 Frederic Joliot-Curie, French

Irene Joliot-Curie, French
1934 Harold C. Urey, U.S.
1932 Irving Langmuir, U.S.
1931 Friedrich Bergius, German Karl Bosch, German
1930 Hans Fischer, German
1929 Sir Arthur Harden, British Hans von Euler-Chelpin, Swed.
1928 Adolf O. R. Windaus, German
1927 Heinrich O. Wieland, German
1926 Theodor Svedberg, Swedish
1925 Richard A. Zsigmondy, German
1923 Fritz Pregl, Austrian
1922 Francis W. Aston, British
1921 Frederick Soddy, British
1920 Walther H. Nernst, German
1918 Fritz Haber, German
1915 Richard M. Willstatter, German
1914 Theodore W. Richards, U.S.
1913 Alfred Werner, Swiss
1912 Victor Grignard, French Paul Sabatier, French
1911 Marie Curie, Polish-French
1910 Otto Wallach, German
1909 Wilhelm Ostwald, German
1908 Ernest Rutherford, British
1907 Eduard Buchner, German
1906 Henri Moissan, French
1905 Adolf von Baeyer, German
1904 Sir William Ramsay, British
1903 Svante A. Arrhenius, Swedish
1902 Emil Fischer, German
1901 Jacobus H. van't Hoff, Dutch

Physiology or Medicine

1984 Cesar Milstein, Brit.-Argentina; Georges J. F. Koehler, German; Niels K. Jerne, Brit.-Danish
1983 Barbara McClintock, U.S.
1982 Sune Bergstrom, Bengt Samuelsson, both Swedish; John R. Vane, British.
1981 Roger W. Sperry, David H. Hubel, Tosten N. Wiesel, all U.S.
1980 Baruj Benacerraf, George Snell, both U.S.; Jean Dausset, France
1979 Alian M. Cormack, U.S. Geoffrey N. Hounsfield, British
1978 Daniel Nathans, Hamilton O. Smith, both U.S.; Werner Arber, Swiss
1977 Rosalyn S. Yalow, Roger C.L. Guillemin, Andrew V. Schally, all U.S.
1976 Baruch S. Blumberg, U.S. Daniel Carleton Gajdusek, U.S.
1975 David Baltimore, Howard Temin, both U.S.; Renato Dulbecco, Ital.-U.S.
1974 Albert Claude, Lux.-U.S.; George Emil Palade, Rom.-U.S.; Christian Rene de Duve, Belg.
1973 Karl von Frisch, Ger.; Konrad Lorenz, Ger.-Austrian; Nikolaas Tinbergen, Brit.
1972 Gerald M. Edelman, U.S. Rodney R. Porter, British
1971 Earl W. Sutherland Jr., U.S.
1970 Julius Axelrod, U.S. Sir Bernard Katz, British Ulf von Euler, Swedish
1969 Max Delbruck, Alfred D. Hershey, Salvador Luria, all U.S.
1968 Robert W. Holley, H. Gobind Khorana, Marshall W. Nirenberg, all U.S.
1967 Ragnar Granit, Swedish Haldan Keffer Hartline, U.S. George Wald, U.S.
1966 Charles B. Huggins,

Francis Peyton Rous, both U.S.
1965 Francois Jacob, Andre Lwoff, Jacques Monod, all French
1964 Konrad E. Bloch, U.S. Feodor Lynen, German
1963 Sir John C. Eccles, Australian Alan L. Hodgkin, British Andrew F. Huxley, British
1962 Francis H. C. Crick, British James D. Watson, U.S. Maurice H. F. Wilkins, British
1961 Georg von Bekesy, U.S.
1960 Sir F. MacFarlane Burnet, Australian Peter B. Medawar, British
1959 Arthur Kornberg, U.S. Severo Ochoa, U.S.
1958 George W. Beadle, U.S. Edward L. Tatum, U.S. Joshua Lederberg, U.S.
1957 Daniel Bovet, Italian
1956 Andre F. Cournand, U.S. Werner Forssmann, German Dickinson W. Richards, Jr., U.S.
1955 Alex H. T. Theorell, Swedish
1954 John F. Enders, Frederick C. Robbins, Thomas H. Weller, all U.S.
1953 Hans A. Krebs, British Fritz A. Lipmann, U.S.
1952 Selman A. Waksman, U.S.
1951 Max Theiler, U.S.
1950 Philip S. Hench, Edward C. Kendall, both U.S. Tadeus Reichstein, Swiss
1949 Walter R. Hess, Swiss Antonio Moniz, Portuguese
1948 Paul H. Müller, Swiss
1947 Carl F. Cori, Gerty T. Cori, both U.S. Bernardo A. Houssay, Arg.
1946 Hermann J. Muller, U.S.
1945 Ernst B. Chain, British Sir Alexander Fleming, British Sir Howard W. Florey, British
1944 Joseph Erlanger, U.S.

Herbert S. Gasser, U.S.
1943 Henrik C. P. Dam, Danish Edward A. Doisy, U.S.
1939 Gerhard Domagk, German
1938 Corneille J. F. Heymans, Belg.
1937 Albert Szent-Gyorgyi, Hung.-U.S.
1936 Sir Henry H. Dale, British Otto Loewi, U.S.
1935 Hans Spemann, German
1934 George R. Minot, Wm. P. Murphy, G. H. Whipple, all U.S.
1933 Thomas H. Morgan, U.S.
1932 Edgar D. Adrian, British Sir Charles S. Sherrington, Brit.
1931 Otto H. Warburg, German
1930 Karl Landsteiner, U.S.
1929 Christiaan Eijkman, Dutch Sir Frederick G. Hopkins, British
1928 Charles J. H. Nicolle, French
1927 Julius Wagner-Jauregg, Aus.
1926 Johannes A. G. Fibiger, Danish
1924 Willem Einthoven, Dutch
1923 Frederick G. Banting, Canadian John J. R. Macleod, Scottish
1922 Archibald V. Hill, British Otto F. Meyerhof, German
1920 Schack A. S. Krogh, Danish
1919 Jules Bordet, Belgian
1914 Robert Barany, Austrian
1913 Charles R. Richet, French
1912 Alexis Carrel, French
1911 Allvar Gullstrand, Swedish
1910 Albrecht Kossel, German
1909 Emil T. Kocher, Swiss
1908 Paul Ehrlich, German Elie Metchnikoff, French
1907 Charles L. A. Laveran, French
1906 Camillo Golgi, Italian Santiago Ramon y Cajal, Sp.
1905 Robert Koch, German
1904 Ivan P. Pavlov, Russian
1903 Niels R. Finsen, Danish
1902 Sir Ronald Ross, British
1901 Emil A. von Behring, German

Literature

1984 Jaroslav Siefert, Czech.
1983 William Golding, British
1982 Gabriel Garcia Marquez, Colombian-Mex.
1981 Elias Cenetti, Bulgarian-British
1980 Czeslaw Milosz, Polish-U.S.
1979 Odysseus Elytis, Greek
1978 Isaac Bashevis Singer, U.S. (Yiddish)
1977 Vicente Aleixandre, Spanish
1976 Saul Bellow, U.S.
1975 Eugenio Montale, Ital.
1974 Eyvind Johnson, Harry Edmund Martinson, both Swedish
1973 Patrick White, Australian
1972 Heinrich Boll, W. German
1971 Pablo Neruda, Chilean
1970 Aleksandr I. Solzhenitsyn, Russ.
1969 Samuel Beckett, Irish
1968 Yasunari Kawabata, Japanese
1967 Miguel Angel Asturias, Guate.
1966 Samuel Joseph Agnon, Israeli Nelly Sachs, Swedish
1965 Mikhail Sholokhov, Russian
1964 Jean Paul Sartre, French (Prize declined)
1963 Giorgos Seferis, Greek
1962 John Steinbeck, U.S.
1961 Ivo Andric, Yugoslavian

1960 Saint-John Perse, French
1959 Salvatore Quasimodo, Italian
1958 Boris L. Pasternak, Russian (Prize declined)
1957 Albert Camus, French
1956 Juan Ramon Jimenez, Puerto Rican-Span.
1955 Halldor K. Laxness, Icelandic
1954 Ernest Hemingway, U.S.
1953 Sir Winston Churchill, British
1952 Francois Mauriac, French
1951 Par F. Lagerkvist, Swedish
1950 Bertrand Russell, British
1949 William Faulkner, U.S.
1948 T.S. Eliot, British
1947 Andre Gide, French
1946 Hermann Hesse, Swiss
1945 Gabriela Mistral, Chilean
1944 Johannes V. Jensen, Danish
1939 Frans E. Sillanpaa, Finnish
1938 Pearl S. Buck, U.S.
1937 Roger Martin du Gard, French
1936 Eugene O'Neill, U.S.
1934 Luigi Pirandello, Italian
1933 Ivan A. Bunin, French
1932 John Galsworthy, British
1931 Erik A. Karlfeldt, Swedish
1930 Sinclair Lewis, U.S.
1929 Thomas Mann, German

1928 Sigrid Undset, Norwegian
1927 Henri Bergson, French
1926 Grazia Deledda, Italian
1925 George Bernard Shaw, British
1924 Wladyslaw S. Reymont, Polish
1923 William Butler Yeats, Irish
1922 Jacinto Benavente, Spanish
1921 Anatole France, French
1920 Knut Hamsun, Norwegian
1919 Carl F. G. Spitteler, Swiss
1917 Karl A. Gjellerup, Danish Henrik Pontoppidan, Danish
1916 Verner von Heidenstam, Swed.
1915 Romain Rolland, French
1913 Rabindranath Tagore, Indian
1912 Gerhart Hauptmann, German
1911 Maurice Maeterlinck, Belgian
1910 Paul J. L. Heyse, German
1909 Selma Lagerlof, Swedish
1908 Rudolf C. Eucken, German
1907 Rudyard Kipling, British
1906 Giosue Carducci, Italian
1905 Henryk Sienkiewicz, Polish
1904 Frederic Mistral, French Jose Echegaray, Spanish
1903 Bjornsterne Bjornson, Norw.
1902 Theodor Mommsen, German
1901 Rene F. A Sully Prudhomme, French

Nobel Memorial Prize in Economics

1984 Richard Stone, Brit.
1983 Gerard Debreu, Fr.-U.S.
1982 George J. Stigler, U.S.
1981 James Tobin, U.S.
1980 Lawrence R. Klein, U.S.
1979 Theodore W. Schultz, U.S., Sir Arthur Lewis, British
1978 Herbert A. Simon, U.S.

1977 Bertil Ohlin, Swedish James E. Meade, British
1976 Milton Friedman, U.S.
1975 Tjalling Koopmans, Dutch-U.S., Leonid Kantorovich, USSR
1974 Gunnar Myrdal, Swed., Friedrich A. von Hayek, Austrian
1973 Wassily Leontief, U.S.

1972 Kenneth J. Arrow, U.S. John R. Hicks, British
1971 Simon Kuznets, U.S.
1970 Paul A. Samuelson, U.S.
1969 Ragnar Frisch, Norwegian Jan Tinbergen, Dutch

Peace

1984 Bishop Desmond Tutu, So. African	1959 Philip J. Noel-Baker, British	Gustav Stresemann, German
1983 Lech Walesa, Polish	1958 Georges Pire, Belgian	1925 Sir J. Austen Chamberlain, Brit.
1982 Alva Myrdal, Swedish; Alfonso	1957 Lester B. Pearson, Canadian	Charles G. Dawes, U.S.
Garcia Robles, Mexican	1954 Office of the UN High	1922 Fridtjof Nansen, Norwegian
1981 Office of U.N. High Commissioner	Commissioner for Refugees	1921 Karl H. Branting, Swedish
for Refugees	1953 George C. Marshall, U.S.	Christian L. Lange, Norwegian
1980 Adolfo Perez Esquivel, Argentine	1952 Albert Schweitzer, French	1920 Leon V.A. Bourgeois, French
1979 Mother Teresa of Calcutta,	1951 Leon Jouhaux, French	1919 Woodrow Wilson, U.S.
Albanian-Indian	1950 Ralph J. Bunche, U.S.	1917 International Red Cross
1978 Anwar Sadat, Egyptian	1949 Lord John Boyd Orr of Brechin	1913 Henri La Fontaine, Belgian
Menachem Begin, Israeli	Mearns, British	1912 Elihu Root, U.S.
1977 Amnesty International	1947 Friends Service Council, Brit.	1911 Tobias M.C. Asser, Dutch
1976 Mairead Corrigan, Betty Williams,	Amer. Friends Service Com.	Alfred H. Fried, Austrian
N. Irish	1946 Emily G. Balch,	1910 Permanent Intl. Peace Bureau
1975 Andrei Sakharov, USSR	John R. Mott, both U.S.	1909 Auguste M. F. Beernaert, Belg.
1974 Eisaku Sato, Japanese, Sean	1945 Cordell Hull, U.S.	Paul H. B. B. d'Estournelles de
MacBride, Irish	1944 International Red Cross	Constant, French
1973 Henry Kissinger, U.S.	1938 Nansen International Office	1908 Klas P. Arnoldson, Swedish
Le Duc Tho, N. Vietnamese	for Refugees	Fredrik Bajer, Danish
(Tho declined)	1937 Viscount Cecil of Chelwood, Brit.	1907 Ernesto T. Moneta, Italian
1971 Willy Brandt, W. German	1936 Carlos de Saavedra Lamas, Arg.	Louis Renault, French
1970 Norman E. Borlaug, U.S.	1935 Carl von Ossietzky, German	1906 Theodore Roosevelt, U.S.
1969 Intl. Labor Organization	1934 Arthur Henderson, British	1905 Baroness Bertha von Suttner,
1968 Rene Cassin, French	1933 Sir Norman Angell, British	Austrian
1965 U.N. Children's Fund (UNICEF)	1931 Jane Addams, U.S.	1904 Institute of International Law
1964 Martin Luther King Jr., U.S.	Nicholas Murray Butler, U.S.	1903 Sir William R. Cremer, British
1963 International Red Cross,	1930 Nathan Soderblom, Swedish	1902 Elie Ducommun,
League of Red Cross Societies	1929 Frank B. Kellogg, U.S.	Charles A. Gobat, both Swiss
1962 Linus C. Pauling, U.S.	1927 Ferdinand E. Buisson, French	1901 Jean H. Dunant, Swiss
1961 Dag Hammarskjold, Swedish	Ludwig Quidde, German	Frederic Passy, French
1960 Albert J. Luthuli, South African	1926 Aristide Briand, French	

Pulitzer Prizes in Journalism, Letters, and Music

The Pulitzer Prizes were endowed by Joseph Pulitzer (1847-1911), publisher of The World, New York, N.Y., in a bequest to Columbia University, New York, N.Y., and are awarded annually by the president of the university on recommendation of the Pulitzer Prize Board for work done during the preceding year. The administrator is Robert C. Christopher of Columbia Univ. All prizes are $1,000 (originally $500) in each category, except Meritorious Public Service for which a gold medal is given.

Journalism

Meritorious Public Service

For distinguished and meritorious public service by a United States newspaper.

1918—New York Times. Also special award to Minna Lewinson and Henry Beetle Hough.
1919—Milwaukee Journal.
1921—Boston Post.
1922—New York World.
1923—Memphis (Tenn.) Commercial Appeal.
1924—New York World.
1926—Enquirer-Sun, Columbus, Ga.
1927—Canton (Oh.) Daily News.
1928—Indianapolis Times.
1929—Evening World, New York.
1931—Atlanta (Ga.) Constitution
1932—Indianapolis (Ind.) News.
1933—New York World-Telegram.
1934—Medford (Ore.) Mail-Tribune.
1935—Sacramento (Cal.) Bee.
1936—Cedar Rapids (Ia.) Gazette.
1937—St. Louis Post-Dispatch.
1938—Bismarck (N.D.) Tribune.
1939—Miami (Fla.) Daily News.
1940—Waterbury (Conn.) Republican and American.
1941—St. Louis Post-Dispatch.
1942—Los Angeles Times.
1943—Omaha World Herald.
1944—New York Times.
1945—Detroit Free Press.
1946—Scranton (Pa.) Times.
1947—Baltimore Sun.
1948—St. Louis Post-Dispatch.
1949—Nebraska State Journal.
1950—Chicago Daily News; St. Louis Post-Dispatch.
1951—Miami (Fla.) Herald and Brooklyn Eagle.
1952—St. Louis Post-Dispatch.
1953—Whiteville (N.C.) News Reporter; Tabor City (N.C.) Tribune.
1954—Newsday (Long Island, N.Y.)
1955—Columbus (Ga.) Ledger and Sunday Ledger-Enquirer.
1956—Watsonville (Cal.) Register-Pajaronian.
1957—Chicago Daily News.
1958—Arkansas Gazette, Little Rock.
1959—Utica (N.Y.) Observer-Dispatch and Utica Daily Press.
1960—Los Angeles Times.
1961—Amarillo (Tex.) Globe-Times.
1962—Panama City (Fla.) News-Herald.
1963—Chicago Daily News.
1964—St. Petersburg (Fla.) Times.

1965—Hutchinson (Kan.) News.
1966—Boston Globe.
1967—The Louisville Courier-Journal; The Milwaukee Journal.
1968—Riverside (Cal.) Press-Enterprise.
1969—Los Angeles Times.
1970—Newsday (Long Island, N.Y.).
1971—Winston Salem (N.C.) Journal & Sentinel.
1972—New York Times.
1973—Washington Post.
1974—Newsday (Long Island, N.Y.).
1975—Boston Globe.
1976—Anchorage Daily News.
1977—Lufkin (Tex.) News.
1978—Philadelphia Inquirer.
1979—Point Reyes (Cal.) Light.
1980—Gannett News Service.
1981—Charlotte (N.C.) Observer.
1982—Detroit News.
1983—Jackson (Miss.) Clarion-Ledger.
1984—Los Angeles Times.
1985—Ft. Worth (Tex.) Star-Telegram.

Reporting

This category originally embraced all fields, local, national, and international. Later separate categories were created for the different fields of reporting.

1917—Herbert Bayard Swope, New York World.
1918—Harold A. Littledale, New York Evening Post.
1920—John J. Leary, Jr., New York World.
1921—Louis Seibold, New York World.
1922—Kirke L. Simpson, Associated Press.
1923—Alva Johnston, New York Times.
1924—Magner White, San Diego Sun.
1925—James W. Mulroy and Alvin H. Goldstein, Chicago Daily News.
1926—William Burke Miller, Louisville Courier-Journal.
1927—John T. Rogers, St. Louis Post-Dispatch.
1929—Paul Y. Anderson, St. Louis Post-Dispatch.
1930—Russell D. Owens, New York Times. Also $500 to W.O. Dapping, Auburn (N.Y.) Citizen.
1931—A.B. MacDonald, Kansas City (Mo.) Star.
1932—W.C. Richards, D.D. Martin, J.S. Pooler, F.D. Webb, J.N.W. Sloan, Detroit Free Press.
1933—Francis A. Jamieson, Associated Press.
1934—Royce Brier, San Francisco Chronicle.
1935—William H. Taylor, New York Herald Tribune.
1936—Lauren D. Lyman, New York Times.
1937—John J. O'Neill, N. Y. Herald Tribune; William L. Laurence, N.Y Times; Howard W. Blakeslee, A. P.; Gobind Behari Lal, University Service; and David Dietz, Scripps-Howard Newspapers

1938—Raymond Sprigle, Pittsburgh Post-Gazette.
1939—Thomas L. Stokes, Scripps-Howard Newspaper Alliance.
1940—S. Burton Heath, New York World-Telegram.
1941—Westbrook Pegler, New York World-Telegram.
1942—Stanton Delaplane, San Francisco Chronicle.
1943—George Weller, Chicago Daily News.
1944—Paul Schoenstein, N.Y. Journal-American.
1945—Jack S. McDowell, San Francisco Call-Bulletin.
1946—William L. Laurence, New York Times.
1947—Frederick Woltman, N.Y. World-Telegram.
1948—George E. Goodwin, Atlanta Journal.
1949—Malcolm Johnson, New York Sun.
1950—Meyer Berger, New York Times.
1951—Edward S. Montgomery, San Francisco Examiner.
1952—Geo. de Carvalho, San Francisco Chronicle.

(1) General or Spot; (2) Special or Investigative

1953—(1) Providence (R.I.) Journal and Evening Bulletin; (2) Edward J. Mowery, N.Y. World-Telegram & Sun.
1954—(1) Vicksburg (Miss.) Sunday Post-Herald; (2) Alvin Scott McCoy, Kansas City (Mo.) Star.
1955—(1) Mrs. Caro Brown, Alice (Tex.) Daily Echo; (2) Roland K. Towery, Cuero (Tex.) Record.
1956—(1) Lee Hills, Detroit Free Press; (2) Arthur Daley, New York Times.
1957—(1) Salt Lake Tribune, Salt Lake City, Ut.; (2) Wallace Turner and William Lambert, Portland Oregonian.
1958—(1) Fargo, (N.D.) Forum; (2) George Beveridge, Evening Star, Washington, D.C.
1959—(1) Mary Lou Werner, Washington Evening Star; (2) John Harold Brislin, Scranton (Pa.) Tribune, and The Scrantonian.
1960—(1) Jack Nelson, Atlanta Constitution; (2) Miriam Ottenberg, Washington Evening Star.
1961—(1) Sanche de Gramont, N.Y. Herald Tribune; (2) Edgar May, Buffalo Evening News.
1962—(1) Robert D. Mullins, Deseret News, Salt Lake City; (2) George Bliss, Chicago Tribune.
1963—(1) Shared by Sylvan Fox, William Longgood, and Anthony Shannon, N.Y. World-Telegram & Sun; (2) Oscar Griffin, Jr., Pecos (Tex.) Independent and Enterprise.

(1) General Reporting; (2) Special Reporting.

1964—(1) Norman C. Miller, Wall Street Journal; (2) Shared by James V. Magee, Albert V. Gaudiosi, and Frederick A. Meyer, Philadelphia Bulletin.
1965—(1) Melvin H. Ruder, Hungry Horse News (Columbia Falls, Mon.); (2) Gene Goltz, Houston Post.
1966—(1) Los Angeles Times Staff; (2) John A. Frasca, Tampa (Fla.) Tribune.
1967—(1) Robert V. Cox, Chambersburg (Pa.) Public Opinion; (2) Gene Miller, Miami Herald.
1968—Detroit Free Press Staff; (2) J. Anthony Lukas, N.Y. Times.
1969—(1) John Fetterman, Louisville Courier-Journal and Times; (2) Albert L. Delugach, St. Louis Globe Democrat, and Denny Walsh, Life.
1970—(1) Thomas Fitzpatrick, Chicago Sun-Times; (2) Harold Eugene Martin, Montgomery Advertiser & Alabama Journal.
1971—(1) Akron Beacon Journal Staff; (2) William Hugh Jones, Chicago Tribune.
1972—(1) Richard Cooper and John Machacek, Rochester Times-Union; (2) Timothy Leland, Gerard M. O'Neill, Stephen A. Kurkjian and Anne De Santis, Boston Globe.
1973—(1) Chicago Tribune; (2) Sun Newspapers of Omaha.
1974—(1) Hugh F. Hough, Arthur M. Petacque, Chicago Sun-Times; (2) William Sherman, N.Y. Daily News.
1975—(1) Xenia (Oh.) Daily Gazette; (2) Indianapolis Star.
1976—(1) Gene Miller, Miami Herald; (2) Chicago Tribune.
1977—(1) Margo Huston, Milwaukee Journal; (2) Acel Moore, Wendell Rawls Jr., Philadelphia Inquirer.
1978—(1) Richard Whitt, Louisville Courier-Journal; (2) Anthony R. Dolan, Stamford (Conn.) Advocate.
1979—(1) San Diego (Cal.) Evening Tribune; (2) Gilbert M. Gaul, Elliot G. Jaspin, Pottsville (Pa.) Republican.
1980—(1) Philadelphia Inquirer; (2) Stephen A. Kurkjian, Alexander B. Hawes Jr., Nils Bruzelius, Joan Vennochi, Robert M. Porterfield, Boston Globe.
1981—(1) Longview (Wash.) Daily News staff; (2) Clark Hallas and Robert B. Lowe, Arizona Daily Star.
1982—(1) Kansas City Star, Kansas City Times; (2) Paul Henderson, Seattle Times.
1983—(1) Fort Wayne (Ind.) News-Sentinel; (2) Loretta Tofani, Washington Post.
1984—(1) Newsday (N.Y.); (2) Boston Globe.
1985—(1) Thomas Turcol, Virginian-Pilot and Ledger-Star, Norfolk, Va.; (2) William K. Marimow, Philadelphia Inquirer.

Criticism or Commentary

(1) Criticism; (2) Commentary

1970—(1) Ada Louise Huxtable, N.Y. Times; (2) Marquis W. Childs, St. Louis Post-Dispatch.
1971—(1) Harold C. Schonberg, N.Y. Times; (2) William A. Caldwell, The Record, Hackensack, N.J.
1972—(1) Frank Peters Jr., St. Louis Post-Dispatch; (2) Mike Royko, Chicago Daily News.
1973—(1) Ronald Powers, Chicago Sun-Times; (2) David S. Broder, Washington Post.
1974—(1) Emily Genauer, Newsday, (N.Y.); (2) Edwin A. Roberts, Jr., National Observer.
1975—(1) Roger Ebert, Chicago Sun Times; (2) Mary McGrory, Washington Star.
1976—(1) Alan M. Kriegsman, Washington Post; (2) Walter W. (Red) Smith, N.Y. Times.

1977—(1) William McPherson, Washington Post; (2) George F. Will, Wash. Post Writers Group.
1978—(1) Walter Kerr, New York Times; (2) William Safire, New York Times.
1979—(1) Paul Gapp, Chicago Tribune; (2) Russell Baker, New York Times.
1980—(1) William A. Henry III, Boston Globe; (2) Ellen Goodman, Boston Globe.
1981—(1) Jonathan Yardley, Washington Star; (2) Dave Anderson, New York Times.
1982—(1) Martin Bernheimer, Los Angeles Times; (2) Art Buchwald, Los Angeles Times Syndicate.
1983—(1) Manuela Hoelterhoff, Wall St. Journal; (2) Claude Sitton, Raleigh (N.C.) News & Observer.
1984—Paul Goldberger, New York Times; (2) Vermont Royster, Wall St. Journal
1985—(1) Howard Rosenberg, Los Angeles Times; (2) Murray Kempton, Newsday (N.Y.).

National Reporting

1942—Louis Stark, New York Times.
1944—Dewey L. Fleming, Baltimore Sun.
1945—James B. Reston, New York Times.
1946—Edward A. Harris, St. Louis Post-Dispatch.
1947—Edward T. Folliard, Washington Post.
1948—Bert Andrews, New York Herald Tribune; Nat S. Finney, Minneapolis Tribune.
1949—Charles P. Trussell, New York Times.
1950—Edwin O. Guthman, Seattle Times.
1952—Anthony Leviero, New York Times.
1953—Don Whitehead, Associated Press.
1954—Richard Wilson, Des Moines Register.
1955—Anthony Lewis, Washington Daily News.
1956—Charles L. Bartlett, Chattanooga Times.
1957—James Reston, New York Times.
1958—Relman Morin, AP; Clark Mollenhoff, Des Moines Register & Tribune.
1959—Howard Van Smith, Miami (Fla.) News.
1960—Vance Trimble, Scripps-Howard, Washington, D.C.
1961—Edward R. Cony, Wall Street Journal.
1962—Nathan G. Caldwell and Gene S. Graham, Nashville Tennessean.
1963—Anthony Lewis, New York Times.
1964—Merriman Smith, UPI.
1965—Louis M. Kohlmeier, Wall Street Journal.
1966—Haynes Johnson, Washington Evening Star.
1967—Monroe Karmin and Stanley Penn, Wall Street Journal.
1968—Howard James, Christian Science Monitor; Nathan K. Kotz, Des Moines Register.
1969—Robert Cahn, Christian Science Monitor.
1970—William J. Eaton, Chicago Daily News.
1971—Lucinda Franks & Thomas Powers, UPI.
1972—Jack Anderson, United Features.
1973—Robert Boyd and Clark Hoyt, Knight Newspapers.
1974—James R. Polk, Washington Star-News; Jack White, Providence Journal-Bulletin.
1975—Donald L. Barlett and James B. Steele, Philadelphia Inquirer.
1976—James Risser, Des Moines Register.
1977—Walter Mears, Associated Press.
1978—Gaylord D. Shaw, Los Angeles Times.
1979—James Risser, Des Moines Register.
1980—Charles Stafford, Bette Swenson Orsini, St. Petersburg (Fla.) Times.
1981—John M. Crewdson, New York Times.
1982—Rick Atkinson, Kansas City Times.
1983—Boston Globe.
1984—John Noble Wilford, New York Times.
1985—Thomas J. Knudson, Des Moines (Ia.) Register.

International Reporting

1942—Laurence Edmund Allen, Associated Press.
1943—Ira Wolfert, No. Am. Newspaper Alliance.
1944—Daniel DeLuce, Associated Press.
1945—Mark S. Watson, Baltimore Sun.
1946—Homer W. Bigart, New York Herald Tribune.
1947—Eddy Gilmore, Associated Press.
1948—Paul W. Ward, Baltimore Sun.
1949—Price Day, Baltimore Sun.
1950—Edmund Stevens, Christian Science Monitor.
1951—Keyes Beech and Fred Sparks, Chicago Daily News; Homer Bigart and Marguerite Higgins, New York Herald Tribune; Relman Morin and Don Whitehead, AP.
1952—John M. Hightower, Associated Press.
1953—Austin C. Wehrwein, Milwaukee Journal.
1954—Jim G. Lucas, Scripps-Howard Newspapers.
1955—Harrison Salisbury, New York Times.
1956—William Randolph Hearst, Jr., Frank Conniff, Hearst Newspapers; Kingsbury Smith, INS.
1957—Russell Jones, United Press.
1958—New York Times.
1959—Joseph Martin and Philip Santora, N.Y. News.
1960—A.M. Rosenthal, New York Times.
1961—Lynn Heinzerling, Associated Press.
1962—Walter Lippmann, N.Y. Herald Tribune Synd.
1963—Hal Hendrix, Miami (Fla.) News.
1964—Malcolm W. Browne, AP; David Halberstam, N.Y. Times.
1965—J.A. Livingston, Philadelphia Bulletin.
1966—Peter Arnett, AP.
1967—R. John Hughes, Christian Science Monitor.
1968—Alfred Friendly, Washington Post.
1969—William Tuohy, L.A. Times.

1970—Seymour M. Hersh, Dispatch News Service.
1971—Jimmie Lee Hoagland, Washington Post.
1972—Peter R. Kann, Wall Street Journal.
1973—Max Frankel, N.Y. Times.
1974—Hedrick Smith, N.Y. Times.
1975—William Mullen and Ovie Carter, Chicago Tribune.
1976—Sydney H. Schanberg, N.Y. Times.
1978—Henry Kamm, N.Y. Times.
1979—Richard Ben Cramer, Philadelphia Inquirer.
1980—Joel Brinkley, Jay Mather, Louisville (Ky.) Courier-Journal.
1981—Shirley Christian, Miami Herald.
1982—John Darnton, New York Times.
1983—Thomas L. Friedman, New York Times; Loren Jenkins, Washington Post.
1984—Karen Elliot House, Wall St. Journal
1985—Josh Friedman, Dennis Bell, Ozler Muhammad, Newsday (N.Y.).

Correspondence

For Washington or foreign correspondence. Category was merged with those in national and international reporting in 1948.
1929—Paul Scott Mowrer, Chicago Daily News.
1930—Leland Stowe, New York Herald Tribune.
1931—H.R. Knickerbocker, Philadelphia Public Ledger and New York Evening Post.
1932—Walter Duranty, New York Times, and Charles G. Ross, St. Louis Post-Dispatch.
1933—Edgar Ansel Mowrer, Chicago Daily News.
1934—Frederick T. Birchall, New York Times.
1935—Arthur Krock, New York Times.
1936—Wilfred C. Barber, Chicago Tribune.
1937—Anne O'Hare McCormick, New York Times.
1938—Arthur Krock, New York Times.
1939—Louis P. Lochner, Associated Press.
1940—Otto D. Tolischus, New York Times.
1941—Bronze plaque to commemorate work of American correspondents on war fronts.
1942—Carlos P. Romulo, Philippines Herald.
1943—Hanson W. Baldwin, New York Times.
1944—Ernest Taylor Pyle, Scripps-Howard Newspaper Alliance.
1945—Harold V. (Hal) Boyle, Associated Press.
1946—Arnaldo Cortesi, New York Times.
1947—Brooks Atkinson, New York Times.

Editorial Writing

1917—New York Tribune.
1918—Louisville (Ky.) Courier-Journal.
1920—Harvey E. Newbranch, Omaha Evening World-Herald.
1922—Frank M. O'Brien, New York Herald.
1923—William Allen White, Emporia Gazette.
1924—Frank Buxton, Boston Herald. Special Prize. Frank I. Cobb, New York World.
1925—Robert Lathan, Charleston (S.C.) News and Courier.
1926—Edward M. Kingsbury, N. Y. Times.
1927—F. Lauriston Bullard, Boston Herald.
1928—Grover C. Hall, Montgomery Advertiser.
1929—Louis Isaac Jaffe, Norfolk Virginian-Pilot.
1931—Chas. Ryckman, Fremont (Neb.) Tribune.
1933—Kansas City (Mo.) Star
1934—E. P. Chase, Atlantic (Ia.) News Telegraph.
1936—Felix Morley, Washington Post. George B. Parker, Scripps-Howard Newspapers.
1937—John W. Owens, Baltimore Sun.
1938—W.W. Waymack. Des Moines (Ia.) Register and Tribune.
1939—Ronald G. Callvert, Portland Oregonian.
1940—Bart Howard, St. Louis Post-Dispatch.
1941—Reuben Maury, Daily News, N.Y.
1942—Geoffrey Parsons, New York Herald Tribune.
1943—Forrest W. Seymour, Des Moines (Ia.) Register and Tribune.
1944—Henry J. Haskell, Kansas City (Mo.) Star.
1945—George W. Potter, Providence (R.I.) Journal-Bulletin.
1946—Hodding Carter, Greenville (Miss.) Delta Democrat-Times.
1947—William H. Grimes, Wall Street Journal.
1948—Virginius Dabney, Richmond (Va.) Times-Dispatch.
1949—John H. Crider, Boston (Mass.) Herald, Herbert Elliston, Washington Post.
1950—Carl M. Saunders, Jackson (Mich.) Citizen-Patriot.
1951—William H. Fitzpatrick, New Orleans States.
1952—Louis LaCoss, St. Louis Globe Democrat.
1953—Vermont C. Royster, Wall Street Journal.
1954—Don Murray, Boston Herald.
1955—Royce Howes, Detroit Free Press.
1956—Lauren K. Soth, Des Moines (Ia.) Register and Tribune.
1957—Buford Boone, Tuscaloosa (Ala.) News.
1958—Harry S. Ashmore, Arkansas Gazette.
1959—Ralph McGill, Atlanta Constitution.
1960—Lenoir Chambers, Norfolk Virginian-Pilot.
1961—William J. Dorvillier, San Juan (Puerto Rico) Star.
1962—Thomas M. Storke, Santa Barbara (Cal.) News-Press.
1963—Ira B. Harkey, Jr., Pascagoula (Miss.) Chronicle.
1964—Hazel Brannon Smith, Lexington (Miss.) Advertiser.
1965—John R. Harrison, The Gainesville (Fla.) Sun.
1966—Robert Lasch, St. Louis Post-Dispatch.
1967—Eugene C. Patterson, Atlanta Constitution.
1968—John S. Knight, Knight Newspapers.
1969—Paul Greenberg, Pine Bluff (Ark.) Commercial.
1970—Philip L. Geyelin, Washington Post.
1971—Horance G. Davis, Jr., Gainesville (Fla.) Sun.
1972—John Strohmeyer, Bethlehem (Pa.) Globe-Times.

1973—Roger B. Linscott, Berkshire Eagle, Pittsfield, Mass.
1974—F. Gilman Spencer, Trenton (N.J.) Trentonian.
1975—John D. Maurice, Charleston (W. Va.) Daily Mail.
1976—Philip Kerby, Los Angeles Times.
1977—Warren L. Lerude, Foster Church, and Norman F. Cardoza, Reno (Nev.) Evening Gazette and Nevada State Journal.
1978—Meg Greenfield, Washington Post.
1979—Edwin M. Yoder, Washington Star.
1980—Robert L. Bartley, Wall Street Journal.
1982—Jack Rosenthal, New York Times.
1983—Editorial board, Miami Herald.
1984—Albert Scardino, Georgia Gazette
1985—Richard Aregood, Philadelphia Daily News.

Editorial Cartooning

1922—Rollin Kirby, New York World.
1924—Jay N. Darling, Des Moines Register.
1925—Rollin Kirby, New York World.
1926—D. R. Fitzpatrick, St. Louis Post-Dispatch.
1927—Nelson Harding, Brooklyn Eagle.
1928—Nelson Harding, Brooklyn Eagle.
1929—Rollin Kirby, New York World.
1930—Charles Macauley, Brooklyn Eagle.
1931—Edmund Duffy, Baltimore Sun.
1932—John T. McCutcheon, Chicago Tribune.
1933—H. M. Talburt, Washington Daily News.
1934—Edmund Duffy, Baltimore Sun.
1935—Ross A. Lewis, Milwaukee Journal.
1937—C. D. Batchelor, New York Daily News.
1938—Vaughn Shoemaker, Chicago Daily News.
1939—Charles G. Werner, Daily Oklahoman.
1940—Edmund Duffy, Baltimore Sun.
1941—Jacob Burck, Chicago Times.
1942—Herbert L. Block, Newspaper Enterprise Assn.
1943—Jay N. Darling, Des Moines Register.
1944—Clifford K. Berryman, Washington Star.
1945—Bill Mauldin, United Feature Syndicate.
1946—Bruce Alexander Russell, Los Angeles Times.
1947—Vaughn Shoemaker, Chicago Daily News.
1948—Reuben L. (Rube) Goldberg, N. Y. Sun.
1949—Lute Pease, Newark (N.J.) Evening News.
1950—James T. Berryman, Washington Star.
1951—Reginald W. Manning, Arizona Republic.
1952—Fred L. Packer, New York Mirror.
1953—Edward D. Kuekes, Cleveland Plain Dealer.
1954—Herbert L. Block, Washington Post & Times-Herald.
1955—Daniel R. Fitzpatrick, St. Louis Post-Dispatch.
1956—Robert York, Louisville (Ky.) Times.
1957—Tom Little, Nashville Tennessean.
1958—Bruce M. Shanks, Buffalo Evening News.
1959—Bill Mauldin, St. Louis Post-Dispatch.
1961—Carey Orr, Chicago Tribune.
1962—Edmund S. Valtman, Hartford Times.
1963—Frank Miller, Des Moines Register.
1964—Paul Conrad, Denver Post.
1966—Don Wright, Miami News.
1967—Patrick B. Oliphant, Denver Post.
1968—Eugene Gray Payne, Charlotte Observer.
1969—John Fischetti, Chicago Daily News.
1970—Thomas F. Darcy, Newsday.
1971—Paul Conrad, L. A. Times.
1972—Jeffrey K. MacNelly, Richmond News-Leader.
1974—Paul Szep, Boston Globe.
1975—Garry Trudeau, Universal Press Syndicate.
1976—Tony Auth, Philadelphia Inquirer.
1977—Paul Szep, Boston Globe.
1978—Jeffrey K. MacNelly, Richmond News Leader.
1979—Herbert L. Block, Washington Post.
1980—Don Wright, Miami (Fla.) News.
1981—Mike Peters, Dayton (Oh.) Daily News.
1982—Ben Sargent, Austin American-Statesman.
1983—Richard Lochner, Chicago Tribune.
1984—Paul Conrad, Los Angeles Times.
1985—Jeffrey K. MacNelly, Chicago Tribune.

Spot News Photography

1942—Milton Brooks, Detroit News.
1943—Frank Noel, Associated Press.
1944—Frank Filan, AP; Earl L. Bunker, Omaha World-Herald.
1945—Joe Rosenthal, Associated Press, for photograph of planting American flag on Iwo Jima.
1947—Arnold Hardy, amateur, Atlanta, Ga.
1948—Frank Cushing, Boston Traveler.
1949—Nathaniel Fein, New York Herald Tribune.
1950—Bill Crouch, Oakland (Cal.) Tribune.
1951—Max Desfor, Associated Press.
1952—John Robinson and Don Ultang, Des Moines Register and Tribune.
1953—William M. Gallagher, Flint (Mich.) Journal.
1954—Mrs. Walter M. Schau, amateur.
1955—John L. Gaunt, Jr., Los Angeles Times.
1956—New York Daily News.
1957—Harry A. Trask, Boston Traveler.
1958—William C. Beall, Washington Daily News.
1959—William Seaman, Minneapolis Star.
1960—Andrew Lopez, UPI.
1961—Yasushi Nagao, Mainichi Newspapers, Tokyo.
1962—Paul Vathis, Associated Press.
1963—Hector Rondon, La Republica, Caracas, Venezuela.

1964—Robert H. Jackson, Dallas Times-Herald.
1965—Horst Faas, Associated Press.
1966—Kyoichi Sawada, UPI.
1967—Jack R. Thornell, Associated Press.
1968—Rocco Morabito, Jacksonville Journal.
1969—Edward Adams, AP.
1970—Steve Starr, AP.
1971—John Paul Filo, Valley Daily News & Daily Dispatch of Tarentum & New Kensington, Pa.
1972—Horst Faas and Michel Laurent, AP.
1973—Huynh Cong Ut, AP.
1974—Anthony K. Roberts, AP.
1975—Gerald H. Gay, Seattle Times.
1976—Stanley Forman, Boston Herald American.
1977—Neal Ulevich, Associated Press; Stanley Forman, Boston Herald American.
1978—John H. Blair, UPI.
1979—Thomas J. Kelly III, Pottstown (Pa.) Mercury.
1980—UPI.
1981—Larry C. Price, Ft. Worth (Tex.) Star-Telegram.
1982—Ron Edmonds, Associated Press.
1983—Bill Foley, AP.
1984—Stan Grossfeld, Boston Globe.
1985—The Register, Santa Ana, Calif.

Feature Photography

1968—Toshio Sakai, UPI.
1969—Moneta Sleet Jr., Ebony.
1970—Dallas Kinney, Palm Beach Post.
1971—Jack Dykinga, Chicago Sun-Times.
1972—Dave Kennerly, UPI.
1973—Brian Lanker, Topeka Capitol-Journal.
1974—Slava Veder, AP.
1975—Matthew Lewis, Washington Post.
1976—Louisville Courier-Journal and Louisville Times.
1977—Robin Hood, Chattanooga News-Free Press.
1978—J. Ross Baughman, AP.
1979—Staff Photographers, Boston Herald American.
1980—Erwin H. Hagler, Dallas Times-Herald.
1981—Taro M. Yamasaki, Detroit Free Press.
1982—John H. White, Chicago Sun-Times.
1983—James B. Dickman, Dallas Times-Herald.

Fiction

For fiction in book form by an American author, preferably dealing with American life.
1918—Ernest Poole, His Family.
1919—Booth Tarkington, The Magnificent Ambersons.
1921—Edith Wharton, The Age of Innocence.
1922—Booth Tarkington, Alice Adams.
1923—Willa Cather, One of Ours.
1924—Margaret Wilson, The Able McLaughlins.
1925—Edna Ferber, So Big.
1926—Sinclair Lewis, Arrowsmith. (Refused prize.)
1927—Louis Bromfield, Early Autumn.
1928—Thornton Wilder, Bridge of San Luis Rey.
1929—Julia M. Peterkin, Scarlet Sister Mary.
1930—Oliver LaFarge, Laughing Boy.
1931—Margaret Ayer Barnes, Years of Grace.
1932—Pearl S. Buck, The Good Earth.
1933—T. S. Stribling, The Store.
1934—Caroline Miller, Lamb in His Bosom.
1935—Josephine W. Johnson, Now in November.
1936—Harold L. Davis, Honey in the Horn.
1937—Margaret Mitchell, Gone with the Wind.
1938—John P. Marquand, The Late George Apley.
1939—Marjorie Kinnan Rawlings, The Yearling.
1940—John Steinbeck, The Grapes of Wrath.
1942—Ellen Glasgow, In This Our Life.
1943—Upton Sinclair, Dragon's Teeth.
1944—Martin Flavin, Journey in the Dark.
1945—John Hersey, A Bell for Adano.
1947—Robert Penn Warren, All the King's Men.
1948—James A Michener, Tales of the South Pacific.
1949—James Gould Cozzens, Guard of Honor.
1950—A. B. Guthrie Jr., The Way West.
1951—Conrad Richter, The Town.
1952—Herman Wouk, The Caine Mutiny.
1953—Ernest Hemingway, The Old Man and the Sea.
1955—William Faulkner, A Fable.
1956—MacKinlay Kantor, Andersonville.
1958—James Agee, A Death in the Family.
1959—Robert Lewis Taylor, The Travels of Jaimie McPheeters.
1960—Allen Drury, Advise and Consent.
1961—Harper Lee, To Kill a Mockingbird.
1962—Edwin O'Connor, The Edge of Sadness.
1963—William Faulkner, The Reivers.
1965—Shirley Ann Grau, The Keepers of the House.
1966—Katherine Anne Porter, Collected Stories of Katherine Anne Porter.
1967—Bernard Malamud, The Fixer.
1968—William Styron, The Confessions of Nat Turner.
1969—N. Scott Momaday, House Made of Dawn.
1970—Jean Stafford, Collected Stories.
1972—Wallace Stegner, Angle of Repose.
1973—Eudora Welty, The Optimist's Daughter.
1975—Michael Shaara, The Killer Angels.
1976—Saul Bellow, Humboldt's Gift.

1984—Anthony Suad, Denver Post.
1985—Stan Grossfeld, Boston Globe; Larry C. Price, Philadelphia Inquirer.

Special Citation

1938—Edmonton (Alberta) Journal, bronze plaque.
1941—New York Times.
1944—Byron Price and Mrs. William Allen White. Also to Richard Rodgers and Oscar Hammerstein 2d, for musical, Oklahoma!
1945—Press cartographers for war maps.
1947—(Pulitzer centennial year.) Columbia Univ. and the Graduate School of Journalism, and St. Louis Post-Dispatch.
1948—Dr. Frank Diehl Fackenthal.
1951—Cyrus L. Sulzberger, New York Times.
1952—Max Kase, New York Journal-American, Kansas City Star.
1953—The New York Times; Lester Markel.
1957—Kenneth Roberts, for his historical novels.
1958—Walter Lippmann, New York Herald Tribune.
1960—Garrett Mattingly, for The Armada.
1961—American Heritage Picture History of the Civil War.
1964—The Gannett Newspapers.
1973—James T. Flexner, for biography of George Washington.
1976—John Hohenberg, for services to American journalism.
1977—Alex Haley, for Roots.
1978—Richard Lee Strout, Christian Science Monitor and New Republic. —E.B. White.
1984—Theodore Geisel ("Dr. Seuss").
1985—William Schuman, composer, educational leader.

Feature Writing

1979—Jon D. Franklin, Baltimore Evening Sun.
1980—Madeleine Blais, Miami Herald Tropic Magazine.
1981—Teresa Carpenter, Village Voice, New York City.
1982—Saul Pett, Associated Press.
1984—Peter M. Rinearson, Seattle Times.
1985—Alice Steinbach, Baltimore Sun.

Explanatory Journalism

1985—Jon Franklin, Baltimore Evening Star.

Specialized Reporting

1985—Randall Savage, Jackie Crosby, Macon (Ga.) Telegraph and News.

Letters

1978—James Alan McPherson, Elbow Room.
1979—John Cheever, The Stories of John Cheever.
1980—Norman Mailer, The Executioner's Song.
1981—John Kennedy Toole, A Confederacy of Dunces.
1982—John Updike, Rabbit is Rich.
1983—Alice Walker, The Color Purple.
1984—William Kennedy, Ironweed.
1985—Alison Lurie, Foreign Affairs.

Drama

For an American play, preferably original and dealing with American life.
1918—Jesse Lynch Williams, Why Marry?
1920—Eugene O'Neill, Beyond the Horizon.
1921—Zona Gale, Miss Lulu Bett.
1922—Eugene O'Neill, Anna Christie.
1923—Owen Davis, Icebound.
1924—Hatcher Hughes, Hell-Bent for Heaven.
1925—Sidney Howard, They Knew What They Wanted.
1926—George Kelly, Craig's Wife.
1927—Paul Green, In Abraham's Bosom.
1928—Eugene O'Neill, Strange Interlude.
1929—Elmer Rice, Street Scene.
1930—Marc Connelly, The Green Pastures.
1931—Susan Glaspell, Alison's House.
1932—George S. Kaufman, Morrie Ryskind and Ira Gershwin, Of Thee I Sing.
1933—Maxwell Anderson, Both Your Houses.
1934—Sidney Kingsley, Men in White.
1935—Zoe Akins, The Old Maid.
1936—Robert E. Sherwood, Idiot's Delight.
1937—George S. Kaufman and Moss Hart, You Can't Take It With You.
1938—Thornton Wilder, Our Town.
1939—Robert E. Sherwood, Abe Lincoln in Illinois.
1940—William Saroyan, The Time of Your Life.
1941—Robert E. Sherwood, There Shall Be No Night.
1943—Thornton Wilder, The Skin of Our Teeth.
1945—Mary Chase, Harvey.
1946—Russel Crouse and Howard Lindsay, State of the Union.
1948—Tennessee Williams, A Streetcar Named Desire.
1949—Arthur Miller, Death of a Salesman.
1950—Richard Rodgers, Oscar Hammerstein 2d, and Joshua Logan, South Pacific.
1952—Joseph Kramm, The Shrike.
1953—William Inge, Picnic.
1954—John Patrick, Teahouse of the August Moon.
1955—Tennessee Williams, Cat on a Hot Tin Roof.
1956—Frances Goodrich and Albert Hackett, The Diary of Anne Frank.
1957—Eugene O'Neill, Long Day's Journey Into Night.
1958—Ketti Frings, Look Homeward, Angel.
1959—Archibald MacLeish, J. B.
1960—George Abbott, Jerome Weidman, Sheldon Harnick and Jerry Bock, Fiorello.
1961—Tad Mosel, All the Way Home.

1962—Frank Loesser and Abe Burrows, How To Succeed In Business Without Really Trying.
1965—Frank D. Gilroy, The Subject Was Roses.
1967—Edward Albee, A Delicate Balance.
1969—Howard Sackler, The Great White Hope.
1970—Charles Gordone, No Place to Be Somebody.
1971—Paul Zindel, The Effect of Gamma Rays on Man-in-the-Moon Marigolds.
1973—Jason Miller, That Championship Season.
1975—Edward Albee, Seascape.
1976—Michael Bennett, James Kirkwood, Nicholas Dante, Marvin Hamlisch, Edward Kleban, A Chorus Line.
1977—Michael Cristofer, The Shadow Box.
1978—Donald L. Coburn, The Gin Game.
1979—Sam Shepard, Buried Child.
1980—Lanford Wilson, Talley's Folly.
1981—Beth Henley, Crimes of the Heart.
1982—Charles Fuller, A Soldier's Play.
1983—Marsha Norman, 'night, Mother.
1984—David Mamet, Glengarry Glen Ross.
1985—Stephen Sondheim, James Lapine, Sunday in the Park with George.

History

For a book on the history of the United States.

1917—J. J. Jusserand, With Americans of Past and Present Days.
1918—James Ford Rhodes, History of the Civil War.
1920—Justin H. Smith, The War with Mexico.
1921—William Sowden Sims, The Victory at Sea.
1922—James Truslow Adams, The Founding of New England.
1923—Charles Warren, The Supreme Court in United States History.
1924—Charles Howard McIlwain, The American Revolution: A Constitutional Interpretation.
1925—Frederick L. Paxton, A History of the American Frontier.
1926—Edward Channing, A History of the U.S.
1927—Samuel Flagg Bemis, Pinckney's Treaty.
1928—Vernon Louis Parrington, Main Currents in American Thought.
1929—Fred A. Shannon, The Organization and Administration of the Union Army, 1861-65.
1930—Claude H. Van Tyne, The War of Independence.
1931—Bernadotte E. Schmitt, The Coming of the War, 1914.
1932—Gen. John J. Pershing, My Experiences in the World War.
1933—Frederick J. Turner, The Significance of Sections in American History.
1934—Herbert Agar, The People's Choice.
1935—Charles McLean Andrews, The Colonial Period of American History.
1936—Andrew C. McLaughlin, The Constitutional History of the United States.
1937—Van Wyck Brooks, The Flowering of New England.
1938—Paul Herman Buck, The Road to Reunion, 1865-1900.
1939—Frank Luther Mott, A History of American Magazines.
1940—Carl Sandburg, Abraham Lincoln: The War Years.
1941—Marcus Lee Hansen, The Atlantic Migration, 1607-1860.
1942—Margaret Leech, Reveille in Washington.
1943—Esther Forbes, Paul Revere and the World He Lived In.
1944—Merle Curti, The Growth of American Thought.
1945—Stephen Bonsal, Unfinished Business.
1946—Arthur M. Schlesinger Jr., The Age of Jackson.
1947—James Phinney Baxter 3d, Scientists Against Time.
1948—Bernard De Voto, Across the Wide Missouri.
1949—Roy F. Nichols, The Disruption of American Democracy.
1950—O. W. Larkin, Art and Life in America.
1951—R. Carlyle Buley, The Old Northwest: Pioneer Period 1815-1840.
1952—Oscar Handlin, The Uprooted.
1953—George Dangerfield, The Era of Good Feelings.
1954—Bruce Catton, A Stillness at Appomattox.
1955—Paul Horgan, Great River: The Rio Grande in North American History.
1956—Richard Hofstadter, The Age of Reform.
1957—George F. Kennan, Russia Leaves the War.
1958—Bray Hammond, Banks and Politics in America—From the Revolution to the Civil War.
1959—Leonard D. White and Jean Schneider, The Republican Era; 1869-1901.
1960—Margaret Leech, In the Days of McKinley.
1961—Herbert Feis, Between War and Peace: The Potsdam Conference.
1962—Lawrence H. Gibson, The Triumphant Empire: Thunderclouds Gather in the West.
1963—Constance McLaughlin Green, Washington: Village and Capital, 1800-1878.
1964—Sumner Chilton Powell, Puritan Village: The Formation of A New England Town.
1965—Irwin Unger, The Greenback Era.
1966—Perry Miller, Life of the Mind in America.
1967—William H. Goetzmann, Exploration and Empire: the Explorer and Scientist in the Winning of the American West.
1968—Bernard Bailyn, The Ideological Origins of the American Revolution.
1969—Leonard W. Levy, Origin of the Fifth Amendment.
1970—Dean Acheson, Present at the Creation: My Years in the State Department.
1971—James McGregor Burns, Roosevelt: The Soldier of Freedom.
1972—Carl N. Degler, Neither Black Nor White.
1973—Michael Kammen, People of Paradox: An Inquiry Concerning the Origins of American Civilization.
1974—Daniel J. Boorstin, The Americans: The Democratic Experience.
1975—Dumas Malone, Jefferson and His Time.
1976—Paul Horgan, Lamy of Santa Fe.
1977—David M. Potter, The Impending Crisis.

1978—Alfred D. Chandler, Jr., The Visible Hand: The Managerial Revolution in American Business.
1979—Don E. Fehrenbacher, The Dred Scott Case: Its Significance in American Law and Politics.
1980—Leon F. Litwack, Been in the Storm So Long.
1981—Lawrence A. Cremin, American Education: The National Experience, 1783-1876.
1982—C. Vann Woodward, ed., Mary Chestnut's Civil War.
1983—Rhys L. Issac, The Transformation of Virginia, 1740-1790.
1985—Thomas K. McCraw, Prophets of Regulation.

Biography or Autobiography

For a distinguished biography or autobiography by an American author.

1917—Laura E. Richards and Maude Howe Elliott, assisted by Florence Howe Hall, Julia Ward Howe.
1918—William Cabell Bruce, Benjamin Franklin, Self-Revealed.
1919—Henry Adams, The Education of Henry Adams.
1920—Albert J. Beveridge, The Life of John Marshall.
1921—Edward Bok, The Americanization of Edward Bok.
1922—Hamlin Garland, A Daughter of the Middle Border.
1923—Burton J. Hendrick, The Life and Letters of Walter H. Page.
1924—Michael Pupin, From Immigrant to Inventor.
1925—M. A. DeWolfe Howe, Barrett Wendell and His Letters.
1926—Harvey Cushing, Life of Sir William Osler.
1927—Emory Holloway, Whitman: An Interpretation in Narrative.
1928—Charles Edward Russell, The American Orchestra and Theodore Thomas.
1929—Burton J. Hendrick, The Training of an American: The Earlier Life and Letters of Walter H. Page.
1930—Marquis James, The Raven (Sam Houston).
1931—Henry James, Charles W. Eliot.
1932—Henry F. Pringle, Theodore Roosevelt.
1933—Allan Nevins, Grover Cleveland.
1934—Tyler Dennett, John Hay.
1935—Douglas Southall Freeman, R. E. Lee
1936—Ralph Barton Perry, The Thought and Character of William James.
1937—Allan Nevins, Hamilton Fish: The Inner History of the Grant Administration.
1938—Divided between Odell Shepard, Pedlar's Progress; Marquis James, Andrew Jackson.
1939—Carl Van Doren, Benjamin Franklin.
1940—Ray Stannard Baker, Woodrow Wilson, Life and Letters.
1941—Ola Elizabeth Winslow, Jonathan Edwards.
1942—Forrest Wilson, Crusader in Crinoline.
1943—Samuel Eliot Morison, Admiral of the Ocean Sea (Columbus).
1944—Carleton Mabee, The American Leonardo: The Life of Samuel F. B. Morse.
1945—Russell Blaine Nye, George Bancroft; Brahmin Rebel.
1946—Linny Marsh Wolfe, Son of the Wilderness.
1947—William Allen White, The Autobiography of William Allen White.
1948—Margaret Clapp, Forgotten First Citizen: John Bigelow.
1949—Robert E. Sherwood, Roosevelt and Hopkins.
1950—Samuel Flag Bemis, John Quincy Adams and the Foundations of American Foreign Policy.
1951—Margaret Louise Coit, John C. Calhoun: American Portrait.
1952—Merlo J. Pusey, Charles Evans Hughes.
1953—David J. Mays, Edmund Pendleton, 1721-1803.
1954—Charles A. Lindbergh, The Spirit of St. Louis.
1955—William S. White, The Taft Story.
1956—Talbot F. Hamlin, Benjamin Henry Latrobe.
1957—John F. Kennedy, Profiles in Courage.
1958—Douglas Southall Freeman (decd. 1953), George Washington, Vols. I-VI: John Alexander Carroll and Mary Wells Ashworth, Vol. VII.
1959—Arthur Walworth, Woodrow Wilson: American Prophet.
1960—Samuel Eliot Morison, John Paul Jones.
1961—David Donald, Charles Sumner and The Coming of the Civil War.
1963—Leon Edel, Henry James: Vol. II. The Conquest of London, 1870-1881; Vol. III, The Middle Years, 1881-1895.
1964—Walter Jackson Bate, John Keats.
1965—Ernest Samuels, Henry Adams.
1966—Arthur M. Schlesinger Jr., A Thousand Days.
1967—Justin Kaplan, Mr. Clemens and Mark Twain.
1968—George F. Kennan, Memoirs (1925-1950).
1969—B. L. Reid, The Man from New York: John Quinn and his Friends.
1970—T. Harry Williams, Huey Long.
1971—Lawrence Thompson, Robert Frost: The Years of Triumph, 1915-1938.
1972—Joseph P. Lash, Eleanor and Franklin.
1973—W. A. Swanberg, Luce and His Empire.
1974—Louis Sheaffer, O'Neill, Son and Artist.
1975—Robert A. Caro, The Power Broker: Robert Moses and the Fall of New York.
1976—R.W.B. Lewis, Edith Wharton: A Biography.
1977—John E. Mack, A Prince of Our Disorder, The Life of T.E. Lawrence.
1978—Walter Jackson Bate, Samuel Johnson.
1979—Leonard Baker, Days of Sorrow and Pain: Leo Baeck and the Berlin Jews.
1980—Edmund Morris, The Rise of Theodore Roosevelt.
1981—Robert K. Massie, Peter the Great: His Life and World.
1982—William S. McFeely, Grant: A Biography.
1983—Russell Baker, Growing Up.
1984—Louis R. Harlan, Booker T. Washington.
1985—Kenneth Silverman, The Life and Times of Cotton Mather.

American Poetry

Before this prize was established in 1922, awards were made from

American Poetry

Before this prize was established in 1922, awards were made from provided by the Poetry Society: 1918—Love Songs, by Sara Teasdale. 1919—Old Road to Paradise, by Margaret Widemer; Corn Husk, by Carl Sandburg.
1922—Edwin Arlington Robinson, Collected Poems.
1923—Edna St. Vincent Millay, The Ballad of the Harp-Weaver; A Few Figs from Thistles; Eight Sonnets in American Poetry, 1922; A Miscellany.
1924—Robert Frost, New Hampshire: A Poem with Notes and Grace Notes.
1925—Edwin Arlington Robinson, The Man Who Died Twice.
1926—Amy Lowell, What's O'Clock.
1927—Leonora Speyer, Fiddler's Farewell.
1928—Edwin Arlington Robinson, Tristram.
1929—Stephen Vincent Benet, John Brown's Body.
1930—Conrad Aiken, Selected Poems.
1931—Robert Frost, Collected Poems.
1932—George Dillon, The Flowering Stone.
1933—Archibald MacLeish, Conquistador.
1934—Robert Hillyer, Collected Verse.
1935—Audrey Wurdemann, Bright Ambush.
1936—Robert P. Tristram Coffin, Strange Holiness.
1937—Robert Frost, A Further Range.
1938—Marya Zaturenska, Cold Morning Sky.
1939—John Gould Fletcher, Selected Poems.
1940—Mark Van Doren, Collected Poems.
1941—Leonard Bacon, Sunderland Capture.
1942—William Rose Benet, The Dust Which Is God.
1943—Robert Frost, A Witness Tree.
1944—Stephen Vincent Benet, Western Star.
1945—Karl Shapiro, V-Letter and Other Poems.
1947—Robert Lowell, Lord Weary's Castle.
1948—W. H. Auden, The Age of Anxiety.
1949—Peter Viereck, Terror and Decorum.
1950—Gwendolyn Brooks, Annie Allen.
1951—Carl Sandburg, Complete Poems.
1952—Marianne Moore, Collected Poems.
1953—Archibald MacLeish, Collected Poems.
1954—Theodore Roethke, The Waking.
1955—Wallace Stevens, Collected Poems.
1956—Elizabeth Bishop, Poems, North and South.
1957—Richard Wilbur, Things of This World.
1958—Robert Penn Warren, Promises: Poems 1954-1956.
1959—Stanley Kunitz, Selected Poems 1928-1958.
1960—W. D. Snodgrass, Heart's Needle.
1961—Phyllis McGinley, Times Three: Selected Verse from Three Decades.
1962—Alan Dugan, Poems.
1963—William Carlos Williams, Pictures From Breughel.
1964—Louis Simpson, At the End of the Open Road.

1965—John Berryman, 77 Dream Songs.
1966—Richard Eberhart, Selected Poems.
1967—Anne Sexton, Live or Die.
1968—Anthony Hecht, The Hard Hours.
1969—George Oppen, Of Being Numerous.
1970—Richard Howard, Untitled Subjects.
1971—William S. Merwin, The Carrier of Ladders.
1972—James Wright, Collected Poems.
1973—Maxine Winokur Kumin, Up Country.
1975—Gary Snyder, Turtle Island.
1976—John Ashbery, Self-Portrait in a Convex Mirror.
1977—James Merrill, Divine Comedies.
1978—Howard Nemerov, Collected Poems.
1979—Robert Penn Warren, Now and Then: Poems 1976-1978.
1980—Donald Justice, Selected Poems.
1981—James Schuyler, The Morning of the Poem.
1982—Sylvia Plath, The Collected Poems.
1983—Galway Kinnell, Selected Poems.
1984—Mary Oliver, American Primitive.
1985—Carolyn Kizer, Yin.

General Non-Fiction

1962—Theodore H. White, The Making of the President 1960.
1963—Barbara W. Tuchman, The Guns of August.
1964—Richard Hofstadter, Anti-Intellectualism in American Life.
1965—Howard Mumford Jones, O Strange New World.
1966—Edwin Way Teale, Wandering Through Winter.
1967—David Brion Davis, The Problem of Slavery in Western Culture.
1968—Will and Ariel Durant, Rousseau and Revolution.
1969—Norman Mailer, The Armies of the Night; and Rene Jules Dubos, So Human an Animal: How We Are Shaped by Surroundings and Events.
1970—Eric H. Erikson, Gandhi's Truth.
1971—John Toland, The Rising Sun.
1972—Barbara W. Tuchman, Stilwell and the American Experience in China, 1911-1945.
1973—Frances FitzGerald, Fire in the Lake: The Vietnamese and the Americans in Vietnam; and Robert Coles, Children of Crisis, Volumes II and III.
1974—Ernest Becker, The Denial of Death.
1975—Annie Dillard, Pilgrim at Tinker Creek.
1976—Robert N. Butler, Why Survive? Being Old in America.
1977—William W. Warner, Beautiful Swimmers.
1978—Carl Sagan, The Dragons of Eden.
1979—Edward O. Wilson, On Human Nature.
1980—Douglas R. Hofstadter, Gödel, Escher, Bach: An Eternal Golden Braid.
1981—Carl E. Schorske, Fin-de-Siecle Vienna: Politics and Culture.
1982—Tracy Kidder, The Soul of a New Machine.
1983—Susan Sheehan, Is There No Place on Earth for Me?
1984—Paul Starr, Social Transformation of American Medicine.
1985—Studs Terkel, The Good War.

Music

For composition by an American (before 1977, by a composer resident in the U.S.), in the larger forms of chamber, orchestra or choral music or for an operatic work including ballet. A special posthumous award was granted in 1976 to Scott Joplin.
1943—William Schuman, Secular Cantata No. 2, A Free Song.
1944—Howard Hanson, Symphony No. 4, Op. 34.
1945—Aaron Copland, Appalachian Spring.
1946—Leo Sowerby, The Canticle of the Sun.
1947—Charles E. Ives, Symphony No. 3.
1948—Walter Piston, Symphony No. 3.
1949—Virgil Thomson, Louisiana Story.
1950—Gian-Carlo Menotti, The Consul.
1951—Douglas Moore, Giants in the Earth.
1952—Gail Kubik, Symphony Concertante.
1954—Quincy Porter, Concerto for Two Pianos and Orchestra.
1955—Gian-Carlo Menotti, The Saint of Bleecker Street.
1956—Ernest Toch, Symphony No. 3.
1957—Norman Dello Joio, Meditations on Ecclesiastes.
1958—Samuel Barber, Vanessa.
1959—John La Montaine, Concerto for Piano and Orchestra.
1960—Elliott Carter, Second String Quartet.
1961—Walter Piston, Symphony No. 7.

1962—Robert Ward, The Crucible.
1963—Samuel Barber, Piano Concerto No. 1.
1966—Leslie Bassett, Variations for Orchestra.
1967—Leon Kirchner, Quartet No. 3.
1968—George Crumb, Echoes of Time and The River.
1969—Karel Husa, String Quartet No. 3.
1970—Charles W. Wuorinen, Time's Encomium.
1971—Mario Davidovsky, Synchronisms No. 6.
1972—Jacob Druckman, Windows.
1973—Elliott Carter, String Quartet No. 3.
1974—Donald Martino, Notturno. (Special citation) Roger Sessions.
1975—Dominick Argento, From the Diary of Virginia Woolf.
1976—Ned Rorem, Air Music.
1977—Richard Wernick, Visions of Terror and Wonder.
1978—Michael Colgrass, Deja Vu for Percussion and Orchestra.
1979—Joseph Schwantner, Aftertones of Infinity.
1980—David Del Tredici, In Memory of a Summer Day.
1982—Roger Sessions, Concerto For Orchestra. (Special Citation) Milton Babbitt.
1983—Ellen T. Zwilich, Three Movements for Orchestra.
1984—Bernard Rands, Canti del Sole.
1985—Stephen Albert, Symphony, RiverRun.

Special Awards

Awarded in 1985 unless otherwise noted.

Books, Allied Arts

American Academy and Institute of Arts and Letters: poetry gold medal: Robert Penn Warren; distinguished service: Sen. Claiborne Pell; special citation: William Shawn; Rome fellowship: Oscar Hijuelos; Bynner poetry prize, $1,500: J.D. McClatchy; Kaufman first fiction prize, $2,500: Louise Erdrich; merit award, $5,000: Richard Stern; Rosenthal Foundation fiction award, $5,000: Janet Kaufman; Stein fiction award, $5,000: George W.S. Trow; Vursell award, $5,000: Harriet Doerr; Zabel criticism award, $2,500: Stanley Cavell; special literature awards, $5,000 each: Alan Dugan, Maria Irene Fornes, George Garrett, Carolyn Kizer, Gilbert Sorrentino, Paul West, John Williams, Paul Zimmer.

American Book Awards, by Assn. of Amer. Publishers, $10,000 each: first fiction: Harriet Doerr, Stones for Ibarra; fiction: Ellen Gilchrist, Victory Over Japan; non-fiction: Robert V. Remini, Andrew Jackson and the Course of American Democracy, 1833-1845, Vol. III.

Bancroft Prizes in History, by Columbia Univ., $4,000 each: Suzanne Lebstock, The Free Women of Petersburg; Kenneth Silverman, The Live and Times of Cotton Mather.

Bennett Award, by Hudson Review, $15,000: Anthony Powell.

Caldecott Medal, by American Library Assn., for children's book illustration: Trina Schart Hyman, St. George

and the Dragon, retold by Margaret Hodges.

Children's Book Council, honor citation: Beverly Cleary.

Bollingen Prize in Poetry, by Yale Univ. Library, $2,500 each: John Ashbery, Fred Chappell.

Golden Kite Awards, by Soc. of Children's Book Writers: fiction: Belinda Hurmence, *Tancy;* non-fiction: James C. Giblin, *Walls;* illustration: Don Wood, *The Napping House.*

Goethe Medal, by Goethe House: Helen Wolff, publisher.

Harcourt Award, for biography and memoirs, by Columbia Univ., $10,000: Ernst Pawel, *The Nightmare of Reason.*

Hemingway Foundation Award, for first fiction: Josephine Humphreys, *Dreams of Sleep.*

Ingersoll Prizes, $15,000 each: Eliot award, for creative writing: Anthony Powell; Weaver award, for letters: Russell Kirk.

Iowa School of Letters Award, for short fiction: Susan M. Dodd, *Old Wives' Tales.*

Jewish Museum Prizes, $1,500: Smilen fiction award: Saul Bellow, *Him With His Foot in His Mouth and Other Stories;* biography: Primo Levi, *The Periodic Table;* social and political analysis: Benjamin Pinkus, *The Soviet Government and the Jews, 1948-1967;* history: Naomi W. Cohen, *Encounter with Emancipation;* religious thought: Rachel Biale, *Women and Jewish Law;* translation: Seymour Feldman, *The Wars of the Lord, Book One;* nonfiction: Lucjan Dobroszycki, *The Chronicle of the Lodz Ghetto, 1941-1944;* juvenile: Rabbi Kenneth Roseman, *The Melting Pot;* art: Avram Kampf, *Jewish Experience in the Art of the 20th Century;* special award: Nahum N. Glatzer; Weizmann National Memorial.

Kennedy Memorial Book Award, by Arthur Schlesinger Jr., $2,500: Raymond Bonner, *Weakness and Deceit.*

Mitchell Prizes, for art books: art history, $10,000: Graham Reynolds, *The Later Paintings and Drawings of John Constable;* first book, $2,000: Elizabeth Johns, *Thomas Eakins;* criticism, $3,000: John Russell.

National Book Critics Circle Awards: fiction: Louise Erdrich, *Love Medicine;* biography: Joseph Frank, *Dostoyevsky, The Years of Ordeal, 1850-1859;* criticism: Robert Hass, *Twentieth Century Pleasures;* nonfiction: Freeman Dyson, *Weapons and Hope;* poetry: Sharon Olds, *The Dead and the Living;* reviewing citation: Alida Becker; Sandroff/Nl board award for distinguished contribution: Library America.

Newberry Medal, by American Library Assn., for ch dren's book: Robin McKinley, *The Hero and the Crown.*

New York Times Best Illustrated Children's Books: Trin Schart Hyman, *St. George and the Dragon,* retold by Marga ret Hodges; Bert Kitchen, *Animal Alphabet;* Roy Gerard, Sir *Cedric;* Maurice Sendak, *Nutcracker,* by E.T.A. Hoffmann; Chris Van Allsburg, *The Mysteries of Harris Burdick;* Margot Tomes, *If There Were Dreams to Sell,* by Barbara Lalicki; Thomas Locker, *Where the River Begins;* Don Wood, *The Napping House,* by Audrey Wood; Charles Mikolaycak, *Babushka;* Warwick Hutton, *Jonah and the Great Fish.*

New Voice Award, by Quality Paperback Book Club, $5,000: Susan Kenney, *In Another Country.*

O'Dell Award for Historical Fiction, $5,000: Avi, *The Fighting Ground.*

PEN Awards: Faulkner fiction award, $5,000: Tobias Wolff, *The Barracks Thief;* Klein editing award: Jonathan Galassi; publisher citation: Robert Gottlieb.

Phi Beta Kappa Awards, $2,500 each: Gauss award, for scholarship and criticism: Irvin Ehrenpreis, *Swift,* Vol. III; contribution by scientist to culture: George Greenstein, *Frozen Star;* study of man's intellectual and cultural condition: David G. Roskies, *Against the Apocalypse.*

Poe Awards, by Mystery Writers of America: novel: Ross Thomas, *Briarpatch;* first novel: R.D. Rosen, *Strike Three, You're Dead;* paperback original: Warren Murphy and Molly Cochran, *Grandmaster;* fact crime: Mike Weiss, *Double Play;* critical: Jon L. Breen, *Novel Verdicts;* juvenile novel: Phyllis Reynolds Naylor, *Night Cry;* grandmaster: Dorothy Salisbury Davis.

Present Tense Award, by American Jewish Committee, $250 each: David S. Wyman, *The Abandonment of the Jews;* Primo Levi, *The Periodic Table,* Raymond Rosenthal, translator; A. B. Yenoshua, *A Late Divorce;* Samuel Heilman, *The Gate Behind the Wall;* Roman Vishniac, *A Vanished World.*

Regina Medal, by Catholic Library Assn., for lifetime dedication to children's literature: Jean Fritz.

Journalism Awards

Amer. Assn. for the Advancement of Science—Westinghouse Science Writing Awards, $5,000: Hill Williams, *Seattle Times;* Byron G. Spice, *Albuquerque Journal;* James T. Trefil, *Smithsonian* magazine.

Broun Awards, for concern for the underdog (1984), $1,000: Don Rodricks, *Baltimore Evening Sun.*

Catholic Press Assn. Award, for contribution to Catholic journalism: Ethel M. Gintoft, *Milwaukee Catholic-Herald.*

Clapper Award, for reporting on national govt. (1984), $2,000: Greg Gordon, UPI; Mark Rohner, Dennis Camie, Gannett News Service.

Kennedy Awards, for problems of disadvantaged (1984), $7,000: George Getschow, *Wall Street Journal;* cartoons: Doug Marlette, *Charlotte Observer;* photography: April Saul, *Philadelphia Inquirer.*

National Journalism Awards, by Scripps-Howard Foundation, $27,000: Schulz award, for promising cartoonist: Richard Orin; Pyle award, for human interest writing: Bill McClellan, *St. Louis Post-Dispatch;* Meeman award, for conservation journalism: James Risser, *Des Moines Register; Advertiser,* Montgomery, AL; Stone award, for editorials: Albert (Hap) Cawood, *Dayton Daily News;* Howard award, for public service, newspaper: *Hartford Courant;* Scripps award, for service to 1st Amendment: *Riverside* (CA) *Press-Enterprise; Hartford Courant.*

National Press Club Awards, for hometown reporting, $1,000: Margaret Freivogel, William Freivogel, Jo Mannies, *St. Louis Post-Dispatch;* Dennis Camire, Mark Rohner, Gannet New Service.

Penney-Missouri Newspaper Awards, for lifestyle reporting, by J.C. Penney Co. and Univ. of Missouri (1984), $14,250: Don Myers, *Rocky Mountain News;* Greta Tilley, *Greensboro* (NC) *News and Record;* Janet Rogers Phillips, *Greenville* (SC) *Piedmont;* Nancy Erikson, *The* (Everett, WA) *Herald;* Cyndi Meagher, *Seattle Times;* Christie Gray, *Hillsboro* (OR) *Argus; Village Voice; Newsday.*

Pictures of the Year, by Canon USA, Natl. Press Photographers Assn., Univ. of Missouri, $12,000: newspaper: Steve Ringman, *San Francisco Chronicle;* magazine: James Nachtwey, Black Star, *Time* magazine; photo essay: Mary Ellen Mark, Archive Agency, *Life* magazine.

Reuben Awards, by National Cartoonists Society: cartoonist of the year: Brant Parker, "The Wizard of Id"; advertising and illustration: Arnold Roth; animation: Nancy Beiman; comic books: Kurt Schaffenberger; editorial (tie): Pat Oliphant, Don Wright; humor strip: Dik Browne, "Hagar the Horrible"; magazine gags: Don Orehek, *Playboy;* special features: Kevin McVey; sports: Bill Gallo, N.Y. *Daily News;* story strip: John Cullen Murphy, "Prince Valiant"; syndicated panel: Bob Thaves, "Frank & Ernest."

Sigma Delta Chi Distinguished Service Awards, by Society of Professional Journalists (1984): David Ashenfelter, John Castine, *Detroit Free Press;* Louis J. Salome, Betsy Wileford, Ellis Berger, *Miami News;* Michael Himowitz, *Baltimore Evening Sun;* William Branigin, *Washington Post;* Rich Lipski, UPI; Rob Lawlor, *Philadelphia Daily News; Philadelphia Inquirer; Philadelphia* magazine; *Memphis* magazine.

Broadcasting and Theater Awards

Children's Book Council, honor citation for communications: Fred Rogers, *Mister Rogers' Neighborhood.*

Derwent Awards, for most promising Broadway actors, $1,000 each: Bill Sadler, "Biloxi Blues"; Joanna Gleason, "Joe Egg."

duPont-Columbia Univ. Broadcast Journalism Awards: KCTS-TV and Face to Face Productions, Seattle; KRON-TV, San Francisco; WBBM-TV, Chicago; John Camp and WBRZ-TV, Baton Rouge, LA; WMAQ-TV, Chicago; WSMV-TV, Nashville, TN; WTCN-TV, Minneapolis; Na-

tional Public Radio; Richard Threlkeld, Status Reports on *CBS Evening News; 60 Minutes; NBC News Overnight;* special independent production: Jon Alpert and NBC News.

Emmy Awards, by Academy of Television Arts and Sciences, for nighttime programs (1983–84): Dramatic series: *Hill Street Blues;* actor: Tom Selleck, *Magnum, P.I.;* actress: Tyne Daly, *Cagney and Lacey;* supporting actor: Bruce Weitz, *Hill Street Blues;* supporting actress: Alfre Woodard, *Hill Street Blues;* directing: Corey Allen, *Hill Street Blues;* writing: *St. Elsewhere.* Comedy series: *Cheers;* actor: John Ritter, *Three's Company;* actress: Jane Curtin, *Kate & Allie;* supporting actor: Pat Harrington, *One Day at a Time;* actress: Rhea Perlman, *Cheers;* directing: Bill Persky, *Kate & Allie;* writing: David Angell, *Cheers.* Limited series: *Concealed Enemies;* actor: Laurence Olivier, *Laurence Olivier's King Lear;* actress: Jane Fonda, *The Dollmaker;* supporting actor: Art Carney, *Terrible Joe Moran;* supporting actress: Roxanna Zal, *Something About Amelia;* directing: Jeff Bleckner, *Concealed Enemies;* writing: William Hanley, *Something About Amelia;* drama special: *Something About Amelia.* Variety, music, or comedy program: *The Sixth Annual Kennedy Center Honors;* directing: Dwight Hemion, *Here's Television Entertainment;* writing: *Late Night with David Letterman.* Children's program: *He Makes Me Feel Like Dancin'.* Animated program: *Garfield on the Town.* Informational special: *America Remembers John F. Kennedy;* series: *A Walk through the 20th Century with Bill Moyers.* Classical program: *Placido Domingo Celebrates Seville.*

Humanitas Prizes, by Human Family Institute, for affirmation of human dignity: $25,000: John Pielmeier, *Choices of the Heart;* $15,000: Peter Silverman, Steven Bochco, Jeffrey Lewis, David Milch, *Hill Street Blues;* $10,000: Gary David Goldberg, Ruth Bennett, *Family Ties.*

Kennedy Awards, for broadcast journalism on disadvantaged, $7,000 (1984): grand prize: WMAQ-TV, Chicago; WMAQ Radio, Chicago.

Nathan Ward, for dramatic criticism, $5,000: Bonnie Marranca, *Performing Arts Journal.*

National Journalism Awards, by Scripps-Howard Foundation, for broadcasting: overall: KOMO-TV, Seattle, WA; radio: WRAL-FM, Raleigh, NC; TV: KTLA, Los Angeles.

N.Y. Drama Critics Circle Award, $1,000: play: August Wilson, "Ma Rainey's Black Bottom."

Sigma Delta Chi Awards, by Soc. of Professional Journalists (1984): Howard Berkes, National Public Radio; WMAQ-AM, Chicago; Gene Slaymaker, WTLC-FM, Indianapolis; Peter Arnett, Cable News Network; WSMV-TV, Nashville; Pat Polillo, KYW-TV, Philadelphia; Sig Mickelson, former head, Radio Free Europe and Radio Liberty.

Television Academy Hall of Fame: Carol Burnett, Sid Caesar, Walter Cronkite, Rod Serling, Ed Sullivan, Sylvester (Pat) Weaver, the Hallmark Hall of Fame series.

Tonys (Antoinette Perry Awards), for broadway theater: Play: "Biloxi Blues"; actress: Stockard Channing, "Joe Egg"; actor: Derek Jacobi, "Much Ado About Nothing"; featured actress: Judith Ivey, "Hurlyburly"; featured actor: Barry Miller, "Biloxi Blues"; director: Gene Saks, "Biloxi Blues." Musical: "Big River"; featured actress: Leilani Jones, "Grind"; featured actor: Ron Richardson, "Big River"; director: Des McAnuff, "Big River"; score: Roger Miller, "Big River." Revival: "Joe Egg." Sets: Heidi Landesman, "Big River"; costumes: Florence Klotz, "Grind"; lighting: Richard Riddell, "Big River." Special awards: Yul Brynner; N.Y. State Arts Council; regional theater: Steppenwolf Theater, Chicago; Langner award for liifetime achievement: Edwin Lester.

Miscellaneous Awards

American Academy and Institute of Arts and Letters: music gold medal: Leonard Bernstein; Berliawsky award, $5,000: Group for Contemporary Music; Hinrichsen award: Louis S. Karchin; Ives fellowship, $10,000: Thomas Oboe Lee; Rosenthal Foundation painting award, $5,000: David Kapp; Brunner architecture prize, $1,000: William Pedersen, Arthur May; special art awards, $5,000 each: James Bohary, Kim Jones, Scott Pfaffman, George Sugarman, Estaban Vicente; special music awards: Gheorghe Costinescu, Donald J. Erb, John Stewart McLellan, Ezra Sims.

American Dance Festival Award, by Samuel H. Scripps, for choreographer's life achievement, $25,000: Alwain Nikolais.

Children's Book Council, honor citation: J. Larry Brown.

Congressional Gold Medal of Achievement: Elie Wiesel.

Dance Magazine Awards: Richard Cragun, Frederic Franklin, Heather Watts, Walter Sorell, Charles (Honi) Coles.

International Center for Photography Awards: master of photography: Andre Kertesz; photography in art: David Hockney; emerging photographer: Masaalo Miyazawa; news photography: Alberto Venzago; photography in publishing: Robert Delpire; advertising photography: Sarah Moon.

Kennedy Center Honors, for lifetime achievement in the arts: Lena Horne, Danny Kaye, Gian Carlo Menotti, Arthur Miller, Isaac Stern.

Lasker Medical Research Awards, $14,000: Cesar Milstein, Georges J.F. Kohler, Michael Potter; clinical contribution: Paul C. Lauterbur; public service: Henry J. Heimlich.

MacArthur Fellows, $176,000 to $300,000: Shelley Bernstein, Peter Bickel, William Drayton Jr., Sidney Drell, Mitchell Feigenbaum, Michael Freeman, Curtis Hames Sr.,

Shirley Brice Heath, Bette Howland, Bill Irwin, Fritz John, Gallway Kinnel, Henry Krays, Peter Matthews, Beumont Newhall, Roger Payne, Edward Roberts, Elliot Sperling, Frank J. Sulloway, Alar Toomre, Amos Tversky, John Kirk Train Varnedoe, Bret Wallach, Arthur T. Winfree, Billie Jean Young.

National Medal of Arts, for contribution to American culture: Elliott Carter, Ralph Ellison, Jose Ferrer, Martha Graham, Louise Nevelson, Leontyne Price, George O' Keeffe, Dorothy Chandler, Lincoln Kirstein, Paul Mellon, Alice Tully, Hallmark cards.

National Medal of Science: Howard L. Bachrach, Paul Berg, Wendell L. Roelofs, Berta Schnarrer, Roald Hoffman, George C. Pimentel, Richard N. Zare, William R. Hewlett, George M. Low, John G. Trump, Herman H. Goldstine, I.M. Singer, E. Margaret Burbridge, Maurice Goldhaber, Helmut E. Lansberg, Walter H. Munk, Frederick Reines, Bruno B. Rossi, K. Robert Schrieffer.

Pritzker Architecture Prize, for career: Hans Hollein.

Songwriters Hall of Fame, by National Academy of Popular Music: Gene De Paul and Don Raye, Saul Chaplin, Kris Kristofferson, Jerry Leiber and Mike Stoller, Charles Strouse, Fred Rose, Carolyn Leigh; Mercer award: Alan Jay Lerner; lifetime achievement: John Hammond.

Wonder Woman Awards, for achieving women over 40, $7,500 each: Roosevelt award: Rosa L. Parks; Sister Elaine Roulet, Clara Hale, Jill Halverson, Clementine Barthold, Meridel LeSueur, Ruth M. Rothstein, Dr. Marion Moses, Jeanne Wakatusi Houston, Josephine Lutz, Juana Maria Bordas, Ignatia Broker, Barbara Reynolds, Kathleen Barry, Maria Gutierrez Spencer.

Motion Picture Academy Awards (Oscars)

1927-28

Actor: Emil Jannings, *The Way of All Flesh.*
Actress: Janet Gaynor, *Seventh Heaven.*
Director: Frank Borzage, *Seventh Heaven;* Lewis Milestone, *Two Arabian Knights.*
Picture: *Wings,* Paramount.

1928-29

Actor: Warner Baxter, *In Old Arizona.*
Actress: Mary Pickford, *Coquette.*
Director: Frank Lloyd, *The Divine Lady.*
Picture: *Broadway Melody,* MGM.

1929-30

Actor: George Arliss, *Disraeli.*
Actress: Norma Shearer, *The Divorcee.*
Director: Lewis Milestone, *All Quiet on the Western Front.*
Picture: *All Quiet on the Western Front,* Univ.

1930-31

Actor: Lionel Barrymore, *Free Soul.*
Actress: Marie Dressler, *Min and Bill.*
Director: Norman Taurog, *Skippy.*
Picture: *Cimarron,* RKO.

1931-32
Actor: Fredric March, *Dr. Jekyll and Mr. Hyde;* Wallace Beery, *The Champ* (tie).
Actress: Helen Hayes, *Sin of Madelon Claudet.*
Director: Frank Borzage, *Bad Girl.*
Picture: *Grand Hotel,* MGM.
Special: Walt Disney, *Mickey Mouse.*

1932-33
Actor: Charles Laughton, *Private Life of Henry VIII.*
Actress: Katharine Hepburn, *Morning Glory.*
Director: Frank Lloyd, *Cavalcade.*
Picture: *Cavalcade,* Fox.

1934
Actor: Clark Gable, *It Happened One Night.*
Actress: Claudette Colbert, same.
Director: Frank Capra, *It Happened One Night.*
Picture: *It Happened One Night,* Columbia.

1935
Actor: Victor McLaglen, *The Informer.*
Actress: Bette Davis, *Dangerous.*
Director: John Ford, *The Informer.*
Picture: *Mutiny on the Bounty,* MGM.

1936
Actor: Paul Muni, *Story of Louis Pasteur.*
Actress: Luise Rainer, *The Great Ziegfeld.*
Sup. Actor: Walter Brennan, *Come and Get It.*
Sup. Actress: Gale Sondergaard, *Anthony Adverse.*
Director: Frank Capra, *Mr. Deeds Goes to Town.*
Picture: *The Great Ziegfeld,* MGM.

1937
Actor: Spencer Tracy, *Captains Courageous.*
Actress: Luise Rainer, *The Good Earth.*
Sup. Actor: Joseph Schildkraut, *Life of Emile Zola.*
Sup. Actress: Alice Brady, *In Old Chicago.*
Director: Leo McCarey, *The Awful Truth.*
Picture: *Life of Emile Zola,* Warner.

1938
Actor: Spencer Tracy, *Boys Town.*
Actress: Bette Davis, *Jezebel.*
Sup. Actor: Walter Brennan, *Kentucky.*
Sup. Actress: Fay Bainter, *Jezebel.*
Director: Frank Capra, *You Can't Take It With You.*
Picture: *You Can't Take It With You,* Columbia.

1939
Actor: Robert Donat, *Goodbye Mr. Chips.*
Actress: Vivien Leigh, *Gone With the Wind.*
Sup. Actor: Thomas Mitchell, *Stage Coach.*
Sup. Actress: Hattie McDaniel, *Gone With the Wind.*
Director: Victor Fleming, *Gone With the Wind.*
Picture: *Gone With the Wind,* Selznick International.

1940
Actor: James Stewart, *The Philadelphia Story.*
Actress: Ginger Rogers, *Kitty Foyle.*
Sup. Actor: Walter Brennan, *The Westerner.*
Sup. Actress: Jane Darwell, *The Grapes of Wrath.*
Director: John Ford, *The Grapes of Wrath.*
Picture: *Rebecca,* Selznick International.

1941
Actor: Gary Cooper, *Sergeant York.*
Actress: Joan Fontaine, *Suspicion.*
Sup. Actor: Donald Crisp, *How Green Was My Valley.*
Sup. Actress: Mary Astor, *The Great Lie.*
Director: John Ford, *How Green Was My Valley.*
Picture: *How Green Was My Valley,* 20th Cent.-Fox.

1942
Actor: James Cagney, *Yankee Doodle Dandy.*
Actress: Greer Garson, *Mrs. Miniver.*
Sup. Actor: Van Heflin, *Johnny Eager.*
Sup. Actress: Teresa Wright, *Mrs. Miniver.*
Director: William Wyler, *Mrs. Miniver.*
Picture: *Mrs. Miniver,* MGM.

1943
Actor: Paul Lukas, *Watch on the Rhine.*
Actress: Jennifer Jones, *The Song of Bernadette.*
Sup. Actor: Charles Coburn, *The More the Merrier.*
Sup. Actress: Katina Paxinou, *For Whom the Bell Tolls.*
Director: Michael Curtiz, *Casablanca.*
Picture: *Casablanca,* Warner.

1944
Actor: Bing Crosby, *Going My Way.*
Actress: Ingrid Bergman, *Gaslight.*
Sup. Actor: Barry Fitzgerald, *Going My Way.*
Sup. Actress: Ethel Barrymore, *None But the Lonely Heart.*
Director: Leo McCarey, *Going My Way.*
Picture: *Going My Way,* Paramount.

1945
Actor: Ray Milland, *The Lost Weekend.*
Actress: Joan Crawford, *Mildred Pierce.*
Sup. Actor: James Dunn, *A Tree Grows in Brooklyn.*
Sup. Actress: Anne Revere, *National Velvet.*
Director: Billy Wilder, *The Lost Weekend.*
Picture: *The Lost Weekend,* Paramount.

1946
Actor: Fredric March, *Best Years of Our Lives.*
Actress: Olivia de Havilland, *To Each His Own.*
Sup. Actor: Harold Russell, *The Best Years of Our Lives.*
Sup. Actress: Anne Baxter, *The Razor's Edge.*
Director: William Wyler, *The Best Years of Our Lives.*
Picture: *The Best Years of Our Lives,* Goldwyn, RKO.

1947
Actor: Ronald Colman, *A Double Life.*
Actress: Loretta Young, *The Farmer's Daughter.*
Sup. Actor: Edmund Gwenn, *Miracle on 34th Street.*
Sup. Actress: Celeste Holm, *Gentleman's Agreement.*
Director: Elia Kazan, *Gentleman's Agreement.*
Picture: *Gentleman's Agreement,* 20th Cent.-Fox.

1948
Actor: Laurence Olivier, *Hamlet.*
Actress: Jane Wyman, *Johnny Belinda.*
Sup. Actor: Walter Huston, *Treasure of Sierra Madre.*
Sup. Actress: Claire Trevor, *Key Largo.*
Director: John Huston, *Treasure of Sierra Madre.*
Picture: *Hamlet,* Two Cities Film, Universal International.

1949
Actor: Broderick Crawford, *All the King's Men.*
Actress: Olivia de Havilland, *The Heiress.*
Sup. Actor: Dean Jagger, *Twelve O'Clock High.*
Sup. Actress: Mercedes McCambridge, *All the King's Men.*
Director: Joseph L. Mankiewicz, *Letter to Three Wives.*
Picture: *All the King's Men,* Columbia.

1950
Actor: Jose Ferrer, *Cyrano de Bergerac.*
Actress: Judy Holliday, *Born Yesterday.*
Sup. Actor: George Sanders, *All About Eve.*
Sup. Actress: Josephine Hull, *Harvey.*
Director: Joseph L. Mankiewicz, *All About Eve.*
Picture: *All About Eve,* 20th Century-Fox.

1951
Actor: Humphrey Bogart, *The African Queen.*
Actress: Vivien Leigh, *A Streetcar Named Desire.*
Sup. Actor: Karl Malden, *A Streetcar Named Desire.*
Sup. Actress: Kim Hunter, *A Streetcar Named Desire.*
Director: George Stevens, *A Place in the Sun.*
Picture: *An American in Paris,* MGM.

1952
Actor: Gary Cooper, *High Noon.*
Actress: Shirley Booth, *Come Back, Little Sheba.*
Sup. Actor: Anthony Quinn, *Viva Zapata!*
Sup. Actress: Gloria Grahame, *The Bad and the Beautiful.*
Director: John Ford, *The Quiet Man.*
Picture: *Greatest Show on Earth,* C.B. DeMille, Paramount.

1953
Actor: William Holden, *Stalag 17.*
Actress: Audrey Hepburn, *Roman Holiday.*
Sup. Actor: Frank Sinatra, *From Here to Eternity.*
Sup. Actress: Donna Reed, *From Here to Eternity.*
Director: Fred Zinnemann, *From Here to Eternity.*
Picture: *From Here to Eternity,* Columbia.

1954
Actor: Marlon Brando, *On the Waterfront.*
Actress: Grace Kelly, *The Country Girl.*
Sup. Actor: Edmond O'Brien, *The Barefoot Contessa.*
Sup. Actress: Eva Marie Saint, *On the Waterfront.*
Director: Elia Kazan, *On the Waterfront.*
Picture: *On the Waterfront,* Horizon-American, Colum.

1955
Actor: Ernest Borgnine, *Marty.*
Actress: Anna Magnani, *The Rose Tattoo.*
Sup. Actor: Jack Lemmon, *Mister Roberts.*
Sup. Actress: Jo Van Fleet, *East of Eden.*
Director: Delbert Mann, *Marty.*
Picture: *Marty,* Hecht and Lancaster's Steven Prods., U.A.

1956
Actor: Yul Brynner, *The King and I.*
Actress: Ingrid Bergman, *Anastasia.*
Sup. Actor: Anthony Quinn, *Lust for Life.*
Sup. Actress: Dorothy Malone, *Written on the Wind.*
Director: George Stevens, *Giant.*
Picture: *Around the World in 80 Days,* Michael Todd, U.A.

1957
Actor: Alec Guinness, *The Bridge on the River Kwai.*
Actress: Joanne Woodward, *The Three Faces of Eve.*
Sup. Actor: Red Buttons, *Sayonara.*
Sup. Actress: Miyoshi Umeki, *Sayonara.*
Director: David Lean, *The Bridge on the River Kwai.*
Picture: *The Bridge on the River Kwai,* Columbia.

1958
or: David Niven, *Separate Tables.*
tress: Susan Hayward, *I Want to Live.*
.p. Actor: Burl Ives, *The Big Country.*
.up. Actress: Wendy Hiller, *Separate Tables.*
Director: Vincente Minnelli, *Gigi.*
Picture: *Gigi*, Arthur Freed Production, MGM.

1959
Actor: Charlton Heston, *Ben-Hur.*
Actress: Simone Signoret, *Room at the Top.*
Sup. Actor: Hugh Griffin, *Ben-Hur.*
Sup. Actress: Shelley Winters, *Diary of Anne Frank.*
Director: William Wyler, *Ben-Hur.*
Picture: *Ben-Hur*, MGM.

1960
Actor: Burt Lancaster, *Elmer Gantry.*
Actress: Elizabeth Taylor, *Butterfield 8.*
Sup. Actor: Peter Ustinov, *Spartacus.*
Sup. Actress: Shirley Jones, *Elmer Gantry.*
Director: Billy Wilder, *The Apartment.*
Picture: *The Apartment*, Mirisch Co., U.A.

1961
Actor: Maximilian Schell, *Judgment at Nuremberg.*
Actress: Sophia Loren, *Two Women.*
Sup. Actor: George Chakiris, *West Side Story.*
Sup. Actress: Rita Moreno, *West Side Story.*
Director: Jerome Robbins, Robert Wise, *West Side Story.*
Picture: *West Side Story*, United Artists.

1962
Actor: Gregory Peck, *To Kill a Mockingbird.*
Actress: Anne Bancroft, *The Miracle Worker.*
Sup. Actor: Ed Begley, *Sweet Bird of Youth.*
Sup. Actress: Patty Duke, *The Miracle Worker.*
Director: David Lean, *Lawrence of Arabia.*
Picture: *Lawrence of Arabia*, Columbia.

1963
Actor: Sidney Poitier, *Lilies of the Field.*
Actress: Patricia Neal, *Hud.*
Sup. Actor: Melvyn Douglas, *Hud.*
Sup. Actress: Margaret Rutherford, *The V.I.P.s.*
Director: Tony Richardson, *Tom Jones.*
Picture: *Tom Jones*, Woodfall Prod., UA-Lopert Pictures.

1964
Actor: Rex Harrison, *My Fair Lady.*
Actress: Julie Andrews, *Mary Poppins.*
Sup. Actor: Peter Ustinov, *Topkapi.*
Sup. Actress: Lila Kedrova, *Zorba the Greek.*
Director: George Cukor, *My Fair Lady.*
Picture: *My Fair Lady*, Warner Bros.

1965
Actor: Lee Marvin, *Cat Ballou.*
Actress: Julie Christie, *Darling.*
Sup. Actor: Martin Balsam, *A Thousand Clowns.*
Sup. Actress: Shelley Winters, *A Patch of Blue.*
Director: Robert Wise, *The Sound of Music.*
Picture: *The Sound of Music*, 20th Century-Fox.

1966
Actor: Paul Scofield, *A Man for All Seasons.*
Actress: Elizabeth Taylor, *Who's Afraid of Virginia Woolf?*
Sup. Actor: Walter Matthau, *The Fortune Cookie.*
Sup. Actress: Sandy Dennis, *Who's Afraid of Virginia Woolf?*
Director: Fred Zinnemann, *A Man for All Seasons.*
Picture: *A Man for All Seasons*, Columbia.

1967
Actor: Rod Steiger, *In the Heat of the Night.*
Actress: Katharine Hepburn, *Guess Who's Coming to Dinner.*
Sup. Actor: George Kennedy, *Cool Hand Luke.*
Sup. Actress: Estelle Parsons, *Bonnie and Clyde.*
Director: Mike Nichols, *The Graduate.*
Picture: *In the Heat of the Night.*

1968
Actor: Cliff Robertson, *Charly.*
Actress: Katharine Hepburn, *The Lion in Winter;* Barbra Streisand, *Funny Girl* (tie).
Sup. Actor: Jack Albertson, *The Subject Was Roses.*
Sup. Actress: Ruth Gordon, *Rosemary's Baby.*
Director: Sir Carol Reed, *Oliver!*
Picture: *Oliver!*

1969
Actor: John Wayne, *True Grit.*
Actress: Maggie Smith, *The Prime of Miss Jean Brodie.*
Sup. Actor: Gig Young, *They Shoot Horses, Don't They?*
Sup. Actress: Goldie Hawn, *Cactus Flower.*
Director: John Schlesinger, *Midnight Cowboy.*
Picture: *Midnight Cowboy.*

1970
Actor: George C. Scott, *Patton* (refused).
Actress: Glenda Jackson, *Women in Love.*

Sup. Actor: John Mills, *Ryan's Daughter.*
Sup. Actress: Helen Hayes, *Airport.*
Director: Franklin Schaffner, *Patton.*
Picture: *Patton.*

1971
Actor: Gene Hackman, *The French Connection.*
Actress: Jane Fonda, *Klute.*
Sup. Actor: Ben Johnson, *The Last Picture Show.*
Sup. Actress: Cloris Leachman, *The Last Picture Show.*
Director: William Friedkin, *The French Connection.*
Picture: *The French Connection.*

1972
Actor: Marlon Brando, *The Godfather* (refused).
Actress: Liza Minnelli, *Cabaret.*
Sup. Actor: Joel Grey, *Cabaret.*
Sup. Actress: Eileen Heckart, *Butterflies are Free.*
Director: Bob Fosse, *Cabaret.*
Picture: *The Godfather.*

1973
Actor: Jack Lemmon, *Save the Tiger.*
Actress: Glenda Jackson, *A Touch of Class.*
Sup. Actor: John Houseman, *The Paper Chase.*
Sup. Actress: Tatum O'Neal, *Paper Moon.*
Director: George Roy Hill, *The Sting.*
Picture: *The Sting.*

1974
Actor: Art Carney, *Harry and Tonto.*
Actress: Ellen Burstyn, *Alice Doesn't Live Here Anymore.*
Sup. Actor: Robert DeNiro, *The Godfather, Part II.*
Sup. Actress: Ingrid Bergman, *Murder on the Orient Express.*
Director: Francis Ford Coppola, *The Godfather, Part II.*
Picture: *The Godfather, Part II.*

1975
Actor: Jack Nicholson, *One Flew Over the Cuckoo's Nest.*
Actress: Louise Fletcher, *One Flew Over the Cuckoo's Nest.*
Sup. Actor: George Burns, *The Sunshine Boys.*
Sup. Actress: Lee Grant, *Shampoo.*
Director: Milos Forman, *One Flew Over the Cuckoo's Nest.*
Picture: *One Flew Over the Cuckoo's Nest.*

1976
Actor: Peter Finch, *Network.*
Actress: Faye Dunaway, *Network.*
Sup. Actor: Jason Robards, *All the President's Men.*
Sup. Actress: Beatrice Straight, *Network.*
Director: John G. Avildsen, *Rocky.*
Picture: *Rocky.*

1977
Actor: Richard Dreyfuss, *The Goodbye Girl.*
Actress: Diane Keaton, *Annie Hall.*
Sup. Actor: Jason Robards, *Julia.*
Sup. Actress: Vanessa Redgrave, *Julia.*
Director: Woody Allen, *Annie Hall.*
Picture: *Annie Hall.*

1978
Actor: Jon Voight, *Coming Home.*
Actress: Jane Fonda, *Coming Home.*
Sup. Actor: Christopher Walken, *The Deer Hunter.*
Sup. Actress: Maggie Smith, *California Suite.*
Director: Michael Cimino, *The Deer Hunter.*
Picture: *The Deer Hunter.*

1979
Actor: Dustin Hoffman, *Kramer vs. Kramer.*
Actress: Sally Field, *Norma Rae.*
Sup. Actor: Melvyn Douglas, *Being There.*
Sup. Actress: Meryl Streep, *Kramer vs. Kramer.*
Director: Robert Benton, *Kramer vs. Kramer.*
Picture: *Kramer vs. Kramer.*

1980
Actor: Robert De Niro, *Raging Bull.*
Actress: Sissy Spacek, *Coal Miner's Daughter.*
Sup. Actor: Timothy Hutton, *Ordinary People.*
Sup. Actress: Mary Steenburgen, *Melvin & Howard.*
Director: Robert Redford, *Ordinary People.*
Picture: *Ordinary People.*

1981
Actor: Henry Fonda, *On Golden Pond.*
Actress: Katharine Hepburn, *On Golden Pond.*
Sup. Actor: John Gielgud, *Arthur.*
Sup. Actress: Maureen Stapleton, *Reds.*
Director: Warren Beatty, *Reds.*
Picture: *Chariots of Fire.*

1982
Actor: Ben Kingsley, *Gandhi.*
Actress: Meryl Streep, *Sophie's Choice.*
Sup. Actor: Louis Gossett, Jr., *An Officer and a Gentleman.*
Sup. Actress: Jessica Lange, *Tootsie.*
Director: Richard Attenborough, *Gandhi.*
Picture: *Gandhi.*
Foreign Film: *Volver A Empezar.*

Screenplay (original): John Briley, *Gandhi.*
(adapted): Costa-Gavras, Donald Stewart, *Missing.*
Editing: John Bloom, *Gandhi.*
Cinematography: Billy Williams, Ronnie Taylor, *Gandhi.*
Score (original): John Williams, *E.T.: The Extra-Terrestrial.*
Song: "Up Where We Belong," *An Officer and a Gentleman.*
Art Direction: Stuart Craig, Bob Lang, *Gandhi.*
Costumes: John Mollo, Bhanu Athaiya, *Gandhi.*
Sound: Buzz Knudson, Robert Glass, Con Digirolamo,
Gene Cantamessa, *E.T.: The Extra-Terrestrial.*
Honorary Oscar: Mickey Rooney.

1983
Actor: Robert Duvall, *Tender Mercies.*
Actress: Shirley MacLaine, *Terms of Endearment.*
Supporting Actor: Jack Nicholson, *Terms of Endearment.*
Supporting Actress: Linda Hunt, *The Year of Living Dangerously.*
Director: James L. Brooks, *Terms of Endearment.*
Picture: *Terms of Endearment.*
Foreign Film: *Fanny and Alexander,* Sweden.
Original Song: "Flashdance. . .What a Feeling," *Flashdance.*
Original Screenplay: Horton Foote, *Tender Mercies.*
Screenplay Adaptation: James L. Brooks, *Terms of Endearment.*
Cinematography: Sven Nykvist, *Fanny and Alexander.*
Original Score: Bill Conti, *The Right Stuff.*
Original Song Score or Adaptation Score: Michel Legrand and
Alan and Marilyn Bergman, *Yentl.*
Art Director: *Fanny and Alexander.*
Costume Design: *Fanny and Alexander.*
Documentary Feature: *He Makes Me Feel Like Dancin'.*
Documentary Short: *Flamenco at 5:15.*
Editing: *The Right Stuff.*
Animated Short: *Sundae in New York.*
Live Action Short: *Boys and Girls.*
Sound: *The Right Stuff.*
Sound Effects Editing: *The Right Stuff.*

Honorary: Hal Roach.
Jean Hersholt Humanitarian: M.J. Frankovich.

1984
Picture: *Amadeus.*
Actor: F. Murray Abraham, *Amadeus.*
Actress: Sally Field, *Places in the Heart.*
Supporting Actor: Haing S. Ngor, *The Killing Fields.*
Supporting Actress: Peggy Ashcroft, *A Passage to India.*
Director: Milos Forman, *Amadeus.*
Foreign Film: *Dangerous Moves,* Switzerland.
Original Song: "I Just Called to Say I Love You," Stevie Wonder,
The Woman in Red.
Original Screenplay: Robert Benton, *Places in the Heart.*
Screenplay Adaptation: Peter Shaffer, *Amadeus.*
Cinematography: Chris Menges, *The Killing Fields.*
Original Score: Maurice Jarre, *A Passage to India.*
Original Song Score or Adaptation Score: Prince, *Purple Rain.*
Art Direction: Patrizia Von Brandenstein, Karel Cerny, *Amadeus.*
Costume Design: Theodore Pistek, *Amadeus.*
Documentary Feature: *The Times of Harvey Milk.*
Documentary Short Subject: *The Stone Carvers.*
Film Editing: Jim Clark, *The Killing Fields.*
Animated Short Film: *Charade.*
Live Action Short Film: *Up.*
Sound: Mark Berger, Tom Scott, Todd Boekelheide, Chris Newman, *Amadeus.*
Visual Effects: Dennis Muren, Michael McAlister, Lorne Peterson,
George Gibbs, *Indiana Jones and the Temple of Doom.*
Makeup: Paul LeBlanc, Dick Smith, *Amadeus.*
Jean Hersholt Award: David Wolper, producer.
Special Achievement, Sound Effects Editing: Kay Rose, *The River.*
Gordon E. Sawyer Technical Award: Linwood G. Dunn, special
effects cameraman.
Honorary Awards: James Stewart; National Endowment for the
Arts.

Genie (Canadian Film) Awards
Source: Academy of Canadian Cinema
(To qualify, films must be Canadian-made; actors and actresses must be Canadian citizens or landed immigrants starring in a Canadian film. Awards apply
to films released the previous year.)

1982
Actor: Nick Mancuso, Ticket to Heaven
Actress: Margot Kidder, Heartaches
Picture: Ticket to Heaven

1983
Actor: Donald Sutherland, Threshold
Actress: Rae Dawn Chong, Quest For Fire
Picture: The Grey Fox

1984
Actor: Eric Fryer, The Terry Fox Story
Actress: Martha Henry, The Wars
Picture: The Terry Fox Story

1985
Actor: Gabriel Arcand, Le crime d'ovide Plouffe
Actress: Louise Marleau, La femme de l'hotel
Picture: The Bay Boy

The Governor General's Literary Awards

Canada's most prestigious literary awards, instituted in 1937 by the Canadian Authors Association with the agreement of then Governor General John
Buchan (Lord Tweedsmuir), a novelist. The awards, now administered by the Canada Council, include a $5,000 cash prize.

English	French

1983

Fiction: Shakespeare's Dog, Leon Rooke
Non-fiction: Byng fo Vimy: General and
Governor General, Jeffery Williams
Poetry: Settlements, David Donnell
Drama: Quiet in the Land, Anne Chislett

Laura Laur, Suzanne Jacob
Le contrôle social du crime, Maurice Cusson

Un goût de sel, Suzanne Paradis
Syncope, René Gingras

1984

Fiction: The Engineer of Human Souls, Josef Skvorecky
Non-fiction: The Private Capital: Ambition and Love
in the Age of MacDonald and Laurier, Sandra Gwyn
Poetry: Celestial Navigation, Paulette Jiles
Drama: White Biting Dog, Judith Thompson

Agonie, Jacques Brault
Le XXe Siècle: Histoire du Catholicisme
Québécois, Nicole Gagnon
Double Impression, Nicole Brossard
Ne blamez jamais les bedouins, René-Daniel Dubois

The Spingarn Medal

The Spingarn Medal has been awarded annually since 1914 by the National Association for the Advancement of Colored People for the
highest achievement by a black American.

1946 Dr. Percy L. Julian	1958 Edward Kennedy (Duke) Ellington	1971 Gordon Parks
1947 Channing H. Tobias	1959 Langston Hughes	1972 Wilson C. Riles
1948 Ralph J. Bunche	1960 Kenneth B. Clark	1973 Damon Keith
1949 Charles Hamilton Houston	1961 Robert C. Weaver	1974 Henry (Hank) Aaron
1950 Mabel Keaton Staupers	1962 Medgar Wiley Evers	1975 Alvin Ailey
1951 Harry T. Moore	1963 Roy Wilkins	1976 Alex Haley
1952 Paul R. Williams	1964 Leontyne Price	1977 Andrew Young
1953 Theodore K. Lawless	1965 John H. Johnson	1978 Mrs. Rosa L. Parks
1954 Carl Murphy	1966 Edward W. Brooke	1979 Dr. Rayford W. Logan
1955 Jack Roosevelt Robinson	1967 Sammy Davis Jr.	1980 Coleman Young
1956 Martin Luther King Jr.	1968 Clarence M. Mitchell Jr.	1981 Dr. Benjamin Elijah Mays
1957 Mrs. Daisy Bates and the Little	1969 Jacob Lawrence	1982 Lena Horne
Rock Nine	1970 Leon Howard Sullivan	1983 Thomas Bradley

ARTS AND MEDIA

Notable New York Theater Openings, 1984-85 Season

A Day in the Death of Joe Egg, revival of the Peter Nichols play; with Jim Dale and Stockard Channing.

After the Fall, revival of the 1964 Arthur Miller drama; with Frank Langella and Dianne Wiest.

Alone Together, play by Lawrence Roman; with Janis Paige and Kevin McCarthy.

Aren't We All, revival of the 1923 Frederick Lonsdale comedy; with Rex Harrison, Claudette Colbert, Jeremy Brett, and Lynn Redgrave.

Arms and the Man, revival of George Bernard Shaw's 1894 comedy; with Kevin Kline, Raul Julia, and Glenne Headly.

As Is, play by William M. Hoffman; with Jonathan Hogan and Jonathan Hadary.

Big River, musical by Roger Miller based on Mark Twain's *Huckleberry Finn;* with Daniel H. Jenkins, Ron Richardson, Rene Auberjonois, and Bob Gunton.

Biloxi Blues, comedy by Neil Simon; with Matthew Broderick, Barry Miller and Bill Sadler.

Cyrano de Bergerac, the Royal Shakespeare Company's production of the Edmond Rostand classic; with Derek Jacobi and Sinead Cusack.

Dancing in the End Zone, play by Bill C. Davis; with Matt Salinger, Pat Carroll, Laurence Luckinbill, and Dorothy Lyman.

Digby, romantic comedy by Joseph Dougherty, with Anthony Heald and Roxanne Hart.

Doubles, comedy by David Wiltse; with Ron Leibman, Tony Roberts, John Cullum, and Austin Pendleton.

Grind, musical by Larry Grossman and Ellen Fitzhugh; with Ben Vereen, Leilani Jones, Stubby Kaye, and Carol Woods.

Harrigan 'n Hart, musical about 19th-century vaudeville. Period songs by Edward Harrigan and David Braham; new music by Max Showaltar; with Harry Groener, Mark Hamill, and Christine Ebersole.

Home Front, play by James Duff; with Carroll O'Connor and Frances Sternhagen.

I'm Not Rappaport, play by Herb Gardner; with Judd Hirsch and Cleavon Little.

In Celebration, play by David Storey; with Malcolm McDowell, Frank Grimes, and Robert Symonds.

La Boheme, pop, English-language version of the Puccini opera; with Linda Ronstadt, Gary Morris, Patty Cohenour, and David Carroll.

Leader of the Pack, musical featuring 1960s pop music; with Dinah Manoff, Darlene Love, and Patrick Cassidy.

Ma Rainey's Black Bottom, drama by August Wilson;

with Charles S. Dutton and Theresa Merritt.

Mayor, cabaret musical by Charles Strouse based on the memoirs of New York City mayor Edward Koch; with Lenny Wolpe.

Much Ado About Nothing, the Royal Shakespeare Company's production of the Shakespeare comedy; with Derek Jacobi and Sinead Cusack.

Pack of Lies, play by Hugh Whitemore; with Rosemary Harris, Patrick McGoohan, and Dana Ivey.

Rat in the Skull, play by Ron Hutchinson; with Brian Cox and Colum Convey.

Requiem For a Heavyweight, Rod Serling's stage version of his 1956 television drama; with John Lithgow, George Segal, and Maria Tucci.

Salonika, play by Louise Page; with Jessica Tandy, Elizabeth Wilson, and Maxwell Caulfield.

Singin' in the Rain, stage version of the classic Hollywood musical; with Don Correia, Mary D'Arcy, and Peter Slutsker.

Strange Interlude, revival of the 1928 Eugene O'Neill drama; with Glenda Jackson, Tom Aldredge, Edward Petherbridge, and Brian Cox.

Take Me Along, revival of the 1959 Bob Merrill musical; with Robert Nichols, Kurt Knudson, and Beth Fowler.

The King and I, revival of the Rodgers and Hammerstein 2d musical classic; with Yul Brynner and Mary Beth Peil.

The Loves of Anatol, adaptation by Ellis Rabb and Nicholas Martin from the works of Arthur Schnitzler; with Stephen Collins, Philip Bosco, and Michael Learned.

The Marriage of Bette and Boo, play by Christopher Durang; with Joan Allen, Richard B. Shull, and Graham Beckel.

The Octette Bridge Club, play by P.J. Barry; with Nancy Marchand, Lois de Banzie, Peggy Cass, and Ann Pitoniak.

The Odd Couple, female version of Neil Simon's comedy classic; with Rita Moreno and Sally Struthers.

The Three Musketeers, revival of the 1928 Rudolf Friml musical; with Liz Callaway, Michael Praed, and Marianne Tatum.

The Vienna Notes, play by Richard Nelson; with James Noble, Mia Dillon, and Lois Smith.

Tom and Viv, play by Michael Hastings about the first marriage of T.S. Eliot; with Edward Herrmann and Julie Covington.

Tracers, play by David Berry about the Vietnam War; with Vincent Caristi and Richard Chaves.

Virginia, play by Edna O'Brien based on the writings of Virginia Woolf; with Kate Nelligan.

Record Long Run Broadway Plays

*Chorus Line	4,117	Born Yesterday	1,642	The King and I	1,246
*Oh, Calcutta (revival)	3,909	Ain't Misbehavin'	1,604	Cactus Flower	1,234
Grease	3,388	Best Little Whorehouse in Texas	1,584	Sleuth	1,222
Fiddler on the Roof	3,242	Mary, Mary	1,572	"1776"	1,217
Life With Father	3,224	Evita	1,567	Equus	1,209
Tobacco Road	3,182	Voice of the Turtle	1,557	Sugar Babies	1,208
Hello Dolly	2,844	Barefoot in the Park	1,530	Guys and Dolls	1,200
My Fair Lady	2,717	Mame	1,508	Torch Song Trilogy	1,166
Annie	2,377	*Dreamgirls	1,466	Cabaret	1,165
Man of La Mancha	2,328	Same Time, Next Year	1,453	Mister Roberts	1,157
Abie's Irish Rose	2,327	Arsenic and Old Lace	1,444	Amadeus	1,155
Oklahoma!	2,212	The Sound of Music	1,443	*Cats	1,145
*42d Street	2,017	How To Succeed in Business		Annie Get Your Gun	1,147
Pippin	1,994	Without Really Trying	1,417	Seven Year Itch	1,141
South Pacific	1,925	Hellzapoppin	1,404	Butterflies Are Free	1,128
Magic Show	1,920	The Music Man	1,375	Pins and Needles	1,108
Deathtrap	1,792	Funny Girl	1,348	Plaza Suite	1,097
Gemini	1,788	Mumenschanz	1,326	They're Playing Our Song	1,082
Harvey	1,775	Oh! Calcutta! (original)	1,314	Kiss Me Kate	1,070
Dancin'	1,774	Angel Street	1,295	Don't Bother Me, I Can't Cope	1,065
Hair	1,750	Lightnin'	1,291	Pajama Game	1,065
The Wiz	1,672	Promises, Promises	1,281	Shenandoah	1,050

*Still Running July 1, 1985

Major Movies of the Year (Aug. 1984 to July 1985)

Movie	Stars	Director
A Passage to India	Victor Banerjee, Peggy Ashcroft, Alec Guinness, James Fox	David Lean
A Soldier's Story	Howard Rollins Jr., Adolph Caesar, Patti LaBelle	Norman Jewison
A View to a Kill	Roger Moore, Grace Jones, Tanya Roberts, Christopher Walken	John Glen
All of Me	Steve Martin, Lily Tomlin	Carl Reiner
Amadeus	F. Murray Abraham, Tom Hulce, Elizabeth Berridge	Milos Forman
Back to the Future	Michael J. Fox, Lea Thompson, Christopher Lloyd	Robert Zerneckis
Beverly Hills Cop	Eddie Murphy, Lisa Eilbacher	Martin Brest
Birdy	Matthew Modine, Nicholas Cage	Alan Parker
Body Double	Craig Wasson, Melanie Griffith	Brian DePalma
Bolero	Bo Derek, George Kennedy	John Derek
Brewster's Millions	Richard Pryor, Lonette McKee, John Candy	Walter Hill
Carmen	Placido Domingo, Julia Migenes-Johnson, Ruggero Raimondi	Francesco Rosi
Cat's Eye	Drew Barrymore, James Woods, Alan King, Candy Clark	Lewis Teague
City Heat	Clint Eastwood, Burt Reynolds	Richard Benjamin
Cocoon	Don Ameche, Hume Cronyn, Jessica Tandy, Wilford Brimley	Ron Howard
Code of Silence	Chuck Norris, Henry Silva	Andy Davis
Country	Jessica Lange, Sam Shepard	Richard Pearce
Crimes of Passion	Kathleen Turner, Anthony Perkins	Ken Russell
D.A.R.Y.L.	Mary Beth Hurt, Michael McKeon, Barret Oliver	Simon Wincer
Desparately Seeking Susan	Rosanna Arquette, Madonna, Mark Blum	Susan Seidelmann
Falling in Love	Robert De Niro, Meryl Streep	Ulu Grosbard
First Born	Teri Garr, Peter Weller, Christopher Collet	Michael Apted
Flamingo Kid	Matt Dillon, Hector Elizondo, Richard Crenna	Garry Marshall
Fletch	Chevy Chase, Joe Don Baker, Tim Matheson	Michael Ritchie
Garbo Talks	Anne Bancroft, Carrie Fisher	Sidney Lumet
Give My Regards to Broad Street	Paul McCartney, Linda McCartney, Ringo Starr	Peter Webb
Grace Quigley	Katherine Hepburn, Nick Nolte	Anthony Harvey
Heaven Help Us	Andrew McCarthy, Mary Stuart, John Heard, Donald Sutherland	Michael Dinner
Into the Night	Jeff Goldblum, Michelle Pfeiffer, Irene Papas	John Landis
Irreconcilable Differences	Shelley Long, Ryan O'Neal, Drew Barrymore	Charles Shyer
Johnny Dangerously	Michael Keaton, Joe Piscopo, Marilu Henner, Maureen Stapleton	Amy Heckerling
Ladyhawk	Matthew Broderick, Michelle Pfeiffer, John Wood	Richard Donner
Little Treasure	Ted Danson, Margot Kidder, Burt Lancaster	Alan Sharp
Lost in America	Albert Brooks, Julie Hagerty	Albert Brooks
Mad Max Beyond Thunderdome	Mel Gibson, Tina Turner	G. Miller, G. Ogilvie
Maria's Lovers	Nastassia Kinski, John Savage, Robert Mitchum	Andrei Konchalovsky
Mask	Cher, Sam Elliott, Eric Stoltz	Peter Bogdanovich
Mass Appeal	Jack Lemmon, Zeljko Ivanek, Charles Durning	Glenn Jordan
Micki & Maude	Dudley Moore, Amy Irving, Ann Reinking	Blake Edwards
Mrs. Soffel	Diane Keaton, Mel Gibson	Gillian Armstrong
1984	John Hurt, Richard Burton, Suzanna Hamilton	Michael Radford
Oh God! You Devil	George Burns, Ted Wass, Ron Silver	Paul Bogart
Pale Rider	Clint Eastwood, Michael Moriarty, Carrie Snodgress	Clint Eastwood
Paris, Texas	Harry Dean Stanton, Nastassia Kinski, Dean Stockwell	Wim Wenders
Perfect	John Travolta, Jamie Lee Curtis, Marilu Henner, Laraine Newman	James Bridges
Places in the Heart	Sally Field, Lindsay Crouse, John Malkovich	Robert Benton
Police Academy 2	Steve Guttenberg, Michael Winslow, Bubba Smith, Howard Hesseman	Jerry Paris
Prizzi's Honor	Jack Nicholson, Kathleen Turner	John Huston
Protocol	Goldie Hawn, Chris Sarandon	Herbert Ross
Rambo First Blood Part II	Sylvester Stallone, Richard Crenna	George P. Cosmatos
Return to Oz	Nicol Williamson, Fairuza Balk, Jean Marsh	Walter Murch
Runaway	Tom Selleck, Cynthia Rhodes, Kirstie Alley	Michael Crichton
St. Elmo's Fire	Emilio Estevez, Rob Lowe, Demi Moore, Ally Sheedy	Joel Schumacher
Silverado	Kevin Kline, Scott Glenn, Kevin Costner	Lawrence Kasden
Starman	Jeff Bridges, Karen Allen	John Carpenter
Stick	Burt Reynolds, George Segal, Candice Bergen, Charles Durning	Burt Reynolds
Supergirl	Faye Dunaway, Helen Slater, Peter Cook, Peter O'Toole	Jeannot Szwarc
Sylvester	Richard Farnsworth, Melissa Gilbert	Tim Hunter
Teachers	Nick Nolte, JoBeth Williams, Judd Hirsch	Arthur Hiller
The Breakfast Club	Emilio Estevez, Molly Ringwald, Ally Sheedy, Anthony Michael Hall	John Hughes
The Cotton Club	Richard Gere, Diane Lane, Gregory Hines, Lonette McKee	Francis Coppola
The Falcon and the Snowman	Timothy Hutton, Sean Penn	John Schlesinger
The Goonies	Sean Astin, Josh Brolin, Jeff Cohen	Richard Donner
The Killing Fields	Sam Waterston, Haing S. Ngor, Craig T. Nelson	Roland Joffe
The Little Drummer Girl	Diane Keaton, Klaus Kinski	George Roy Hill
The Mean Season	Kurt Russell, Mariel Hemingway	Phillip Borsos
The Purple Rose of Cairo	Mia Farrow, Jeff Daniels	Woody Allen
The Razor's Edge	Bill Murray, Catherine Hicks, Theresa Russell	John Byrum
The Return of the Soldier	Glenda Jackson, Julie Christie, Ann-Margret, Alan Bates	Alan Bridges
The River	Mel Gibson, Sissy Spacek	Mark Rydell
The Shooting Party	James Mason, Edward Fox	Alan Bridges
The Terminator	Arnold Schwartzenegger, Linda Hamilton	James Cameron
The Wild Duck	Liv Ullmann, Jeremy Irons	Henry Safran
Turk 182	Timothy Hutton, Robert Urich, Robert Culp	Bob Clark
2010	Roy Schieder, John Lithgow, Keir Dullea	Peter Hyams
Witness	Harrison Ford, Kelly McGillis, Alexander Gudunov	Peter Weir

Best-Selling Books of 1984-85

Listed according to position and frequency of citation on best seller reports from June 1984 through May 1985. Numbers in parentheses show rank on top ten list for calendar year 1984, according to Publishers Weekly.

Hardcover Fiction

1. ". . . And Ladies of the Club," Helen Hooven Santmyer (3)
2. The Talisman, Stephen King and Peter Straub (2)
3. The Fourth Protocol, Frederick Forsyth (6)
4. If Tomorrow Comes, Sidney Sheldon
5. Lincoln, Gore Vidal (4)
6. The Aquitaine Progression, Robert Ludlum (1) (tie) Love and War, John Jakes (7)
7. First Among Equals, Jeffrey Archer
8. Full Circle, Danielle Steel (10)
9. The Life and Hard Times of Heidi Abramowitz, Joan Rivers (tie) The Sicilian, Mario Puzo
10. Family Album, Danielle Steel
11. So Long, and Thanks for All the Fish, Douglas Adams
12. Thinner, Richard Bachman (Stephen King)
13. The Haj, Leon Uris (9)
14. Glitz, Elmore Leonard
15. The Walking Drum, Louis L'Amour
16. The Butter Battle Book, Dr. Seuss (5)
17. Deep Six, Clive Cussler
18. Strong Medicine, Arthur Hailey
19. Nutcracker, E.T.A. Hoffman, il. Maurice Sendak
20. The Hunt for Red October, Tom Clancey

Hardcover General Nonfiction

1. Loving Each Other, Leo Buscaglia (2)
2. Iacocca: An Autobiography, Lee Iacocca with William Novak (1)
3. Pieces of My Mind, Andrew A. Rooney (4)
4. The Bridge Across Forever, Richard Bach (10)
5. The Kennedys: An American Drama, Peter Collier and David Horowitz (7)
6. Moses the Kitten, James Herriot (5)
7. Wired, Bob Woodward (6)
8. The Good War, Studs Terkel (8)
9. The Nightmare Years, 1930-1940, William L. Shirer
10. Breaking with Moscow, Arkady N. Schevchenko
11. One Writer's Beginnings, Eudora Welty (6)
12. The Fire from Within, Carlos Castaneda
13. Citizen Hughes, Michael Drosnin
14. Hey, Wait a Minute (I Wrote a Book!), John Madden with Dave Anderson
15. Son of the Morning Star, Evan S. Connell
16. Dr. Burns' Prescription for Happiness, George Burns
17. First Lady from Plains, Rosalynn Carter
18. Motherhood: The Second Oldest Profession, Erma Bombeck (3)
19. Good Morning, Merry Sunshine, Bob Greene (tie) The Rest of Us, Stephen Birmingham (tie) The Courage to Change, Dennis Wholey
20. Past Imperfect, Joan Collins

Hardcover How-to, Advice and Others

1. What They Don't Teach You at Harvard Business School, Mark H. McCormack (4)
2. Eat to Win, Robert Haas (1)
3. Weight Watchers' Quick Start Program Cookbook, Jean Nidetch
4. The One Minute Sales Person, Spencer Johnson and Larry Wilson
5. Webster's 9th New Collegiate Dictionary (2)

6. Chef Paul Prudhomme's Louisiana Kitchen, Paul Prudhomme (5)
7. Webster's II: New Riverside University Dictionary
8. Zig Ziglar's Secrets of Closing the Sale, Zig Ziglar
9. Webster's New World Dictionary, 2nd College Edition
10. The Frugal Gourmet, Jeff Smith

Paperback Fiction

1. Changes, Danielle Steel (7)
2. The Robots of Dawn, Isaac Asimov
3. Pet Sematary, Stephen King (3)
4. Thurston House, Danielle Steel (4)
5. Hollywood Wives, Jackie Collins (5)
6. The Aquitaine Progression, Robert Ludlum
7. Almost Paradise, Susan Isaacs (tie) Poland, James A. Michener
8. Dune, Frank Herbert
9. Come Love a Stranger, Kathleen E. Woodiwiss
10. August, Judith Rossner
11. The Auerbach Will, Stephen Birmingham
12. The Name of the Rose, Umberto Eco (8)
13. Descent from Xanadu, Harold Robbins
14. One Police Plaza, William J. Cauitz
15. Bowdrie's Law, Louis L'Amour
16. Lord of the Dance, Andrew M. Greeley (tie) Smart Women, Judy Blume
17. The Wicked Day, Mary Stewart
18. One More Sunday, John D. MacDonald
19. Indiana Jones and the Temple of Doom, James Zahn
20. Everything and More, Jacqueline Briskin

Paperback General Nonfiction

1. In Search of Excellence, Thomas J. Peters and Robert H. Waterman Jr. (2)
2. The Road Less Traveled, M. Scott Peck (7)
3. Fatal Vision, Joe McGinnis (3)
4. Living, Loving & Learning, Leo Buscaglia (8)
5. Lines and Shadows, Joseph Wambaugh
6. On Wings of Eagles, Ken Follett
7. Out on a Limb, Shirley MacLaine (5)
8. Megatrends, John Naisbitt (1)
9. Mafia Princess, Antoinette Giancana and Thomas C. Renner
10. Wired, Bob Woodward
11. The Peter Pan Syndrome, Dan Kiley
12. Past Imperfect, Joan Collins
13. Chickenhawk, Robert Mason (tie) Knock Wood, Candice Bergen
14. Coroner, Thomas T. Noguchi with Joseph DiMona (tie) Growing Up, Russell Baker
15. The Falcon and the Snowman, Robert Lindsay

Paperback How-to, Advice and Others

1. The One Minute Manager, Kenneth Blanchard and Spencer Johnson (1)
2. Rand McNally Road Atlas: U.S., Canada, Mexico (2)
3. Eat to Win, Robert Haas
4. Garfield Loses His Feet, Jim Davis
5. Sniglets, Rich Hall and Friends (5)
6. In Search of the Far Side, Gary Larson
7. Fit Or Fat? Covert Bailey
8. The World Almanac and Book of Facts 1985

(continued)

9. The Far Side Gallery, Gary Larson
10. J.F. Lasser's Your Income Tax
11. 'Toons for Our Times, Berke Breathed (4)
12. No More Secrets for Me, Oralee Wachter

   (tie) The Arthur Young Tax Guide 1985
13. The Old Farmer's 1985 Almanac
14. Breakdancing, Mr. Fresh and the Supreme Rockers
15. Blanche Knott's Truly Tasteless Jokes

Book Buyers

Source: Gallup Organization

During any 3-month period of 1984, approximately 6 in 10 adults (61%) reported purchasing at least one book. This table shows the percentage of adults who **purchased 5 or more books in a 3 month period.**

	%		%		%
All adults	24	50 and older	16	$10,000–19,999	22
Male	23	College graduate	38	Under $10,000	16
Female	26	High school graduate	20	**Region**	
Age		Less than high school graduate	10	East	24
18–24 yrs.	30	**Annual household income**		Midwest	23
25–34 yrs.	30	$30,0000 and over	35	South	24
35–49 yrs.	30	$20,000–29,999	26	West	29

Recordings

The Recording Industry Association of America, Inc. confers Gold Record Awards on single records that sell one million units, Platinum Awards to those selling two million, Gold Awards to albums and their tape equivalents that sell 500,000 units, Platinum Awards to those selling one million. Platinum Album Awards, Platinum and Gold Single Awards in 1984 follow:

Artists and Recording Titles

Albums, Platinum

Alabama; *Roll On.*
David Bowie; *Tonight.*
The Cars; *Heartbeat City.*
Chicago; *Chicago 17.*
Culture Club; *Waking Up with the House on Fire.*
Neil Diamond; *12 Greatest Hits, Vol. II.*
Duran Duran; *Seven and the Ragged Tiger.*
Eurythmics; *Touch.*
The Fixx; *Reach the Beach.*
Merle Haggard and Willie Nelson; *Poncho & Lefty.*
Hall and Oates; *Big Bam Boom.*
The Honeydrippers; *Volume I.*
Billy Idol; *Rebel Yell.*
Julio Iglesias; *Julio.*
Julio Iglesias; *1100 Bel Air Place.*
The Jacksons; *Victory.*
Chaka Khan; *I Feel for You.*
Kiss; *Animalize.*
Cyndi Lauper; *She's So Unusual.*
Huey Lewis and the News; *Sports.*
Madonna; *Madonna.*
Paul McCartney; *Pipes of Peace.*
Motley Curie; *Shout at the Devil.*
Olivia Newton-John, John Travolta; *Two of a Kind* (soundtrack).
Night Ranger; *Midnight Madness.*
Steve Perry; *Street Talk.*
Robert Plant; *The Principle of Moments.*
Pointer Sisters; *Break Out.*
Police; *Outlandos D'Amour.*
The Pretenders; *Learning to Crawl.*
Prince and the Revolution; *Purple Rain* (soundtrack).
Quiet Riot; *Condition Critical.*
Ratt; *Out of the Cellar.*
Kenny Rogers; *What About Me.*
Kenny Rogers and Dolly Parton; *Once Upon a Christmas.*
The Rolling Stones; *Undercover.*
Rush; *Grace Under Pressure.*
Scorpions; *Blackout.*
Scorpions; *Love at First Sting.*
Soundtrack; *The Big Chill.*
Soundtrack; *Footloose.*
Soundtrack; *Breakin'.*
Soundtrack; *Ghostbusters.*

Soundtrack; *Eddie & the Cruisers.*
Soundtrack; *The Woman in Red.*
Rick Springfield; *Hard to Hold.*
Bruce Springsteen; *Born in the U.S.A.*
Billy Squier; *Signs of Life.*
Barbra Streisand; *Yentl* (soundtrack).
Thirty-Eight Special (.38); *Tour De Force.*
Thompson Twins; *Into the Gap.*
Tina Turner; *Private Dancer.*
Twisted Sister; *Stay Hungry.*
Van Halen; *1984.*
Wham!; *Make It Big.*
Hank Williams Jr.; *Hank Williams Jr.'s Biggest Hits.*
Yes; *90125.*
ZZ Top; *Deguello.*

Singles, Platinum

Prince; *When Doves Cry.*
Various; *Star Wars.*

Singles, Gold

Band Aid; *Do They Know It's Christmas?*
Phil Collins; *Against All Odds* (Take a Look at Me Now).
Culture Club; *Karma Chameleon.*
Julio Iglesias and Willie Nelson; *To All the Girls I've Loved Before.*
The Jacksons; *State of Shock.*
Billy Joel; *Uptown Girl.*
Chaka Khan; *I Feel For You.*
Cyndi Lauper; *Girls Just Want to Have Fun.*
Kenny Loggins; *Footloose.*
Nena; *99 Luft Balloons.*
Billy Ocean; *Caribbean Queen.*
Ray Parker Jr.; *Ghostbusters.*
Prince; *Let's Go Crazy.*
Prince & the Revolution; *Purple Rain.*
Lionel Richie; *Hello.*
Rockwell; *Somebody's Watching Me.*
Shannon; *Let the Music Play.*
Tina Turner; *What's Love Got to Do With It.*
Van Halen; *Jump.*
Various; *The Jungle Book.*
Various; *Robin Hood.*
Various; *Rescuers.*
Wham!; *Wake Me Up Before You Go-Go.*
Deniece Williams; *Let's Hear It for the Boy.*
Stevie Wonder; *I Just Called to Say I Love You.*

Grammy Awards

Source: National Academy of Recording Arts & Sciences

1961
Record: Henry Mancini, *Moon River.*
Album: Judy Garland, *Judy At Carnegie Hall.*
Male vocalist: Jack Jones, *Lollipops and Roses.*
Female vocalist: Judy Garland, *Judy at Carnegie Hall* (album).
Group: Lambert, Hendricks and Ross, *High Flying.*

1962
Record: Tony Bennett, *I Left My Heart in San Francisco.*
Album: Vaughn Meader, *The First Family.*
Male vocalist: Tony Bennett, *I Left My Heart in San Francisco.*
Female vocalist: Ella Fitzgerald, *Ella Swings Brightly with Nelson Riddle* (album).
Group: Peter, Paul and Mary, *If I Had a Hammer.*

1963
Record: Henry Mancini, *The Days of Wine and Roses.*
Album: *The Barbra Streisand Album.*
Male vocalist: Jack Jones, *Wives and Lovers.*
Female vocalist: *The Barbra Streisand Album.*
Group: Peter, Paul and Mary, *Blowin' in the Wind.*

1964
Record: Stan Getz and Astrud Gilberto, *The Girl From Ipanema.*
Album: *Getz/Gilberto.*
Male vocalist: Louis Armstrong, *Hello, Dolly!*
Female vocalist: Barbra Streisand, *People.*
Group: The Beatles, *A Hard Day's Night.*

1965
Record: Herb Alpert, *A Taste Of Honey.*
Album: Frank Sinatra, *September of My Years.*
Male vocalist: Frank Sinatra, *It Was a Very Good Year.*
Female vocalist: Barbra Streisand, *My Name is Barbra* (album).
Group: Anita Kerr Singers, *We Dig Mancini* (album).

1966
Record: Frank Sinatra, *Strangers in the Night.*
Album: Frank Sinatra, *A Man and His Music.*
Male vocalist: Frank Sinatra, *Strangers in the Night.*
Female vocalist: Eydie Gorme, *If He Walked Into My Life.*
Group: Anita Kerr Singers, *A Man and A Woman.*

1967
Record: 5th Dimension, *Up, Up and Away.*
Album: The Beatles, *Sgt. Pepper's Lonely Hearts Club Band.*
Male vocalist: Glen Campbell, *By the Time I Get to Phoenix.*
Female vocalist: Bobbie Gentry, *Ode to Billie Joe.*
Group: 5th Dimension, *Up, Up and Away.*

1968
Record: Simon & Garfunkel, *Mrs. Robinson.*
Album: Glen Campbell, *By the Time I Get to Phoenix.*
Male pop vocalist: Jose Feliciano, *Light My Fire.*
Female pop vocalist: Dionne Warwick, *Do You Know the Way to San Jose.*
Pop group: Simon & Garfunkel, *Mrs. Robinson.*

1969
Record: 5th Dimension, *Aquarius/Let the Sunshine In.*
Album: *Blood, Sweat and Tears.*
Male pop vocalist: Harry Nilsson, *Everybody's Talkin'.*
Female pop vocalist: Peggy Lee, *Is That All There Is.*
Pop group: 5th Dimension, *Aquarius/Let the Sunshine In.*

1970
Record: Simon & Garfunkel, *Bridge Over Troubled Waters.*
Album: *Bridge Over Troubled Waters.*
Male pop vocalist: Ray Stevens, *Everything is Beautiful.*
Female pop vocalist: Dionne Warwick, *I'll Never Fall in Love Again.*
Pop group: The Carpenters, *Close to You.*

1971
Record: Carole King, *It's Too Late.*
Album: Carole King, *Tapestry.*
Male pop vocalist: James Taylor, *You've Got a Friend.*
Female pop vocalist: Carole King, *Tapestry* (album).
Pop group: The Carpenters *(album).*

1972
Record: Roberta Flack, *The First Time Ever I Saw Your Face.*
Album: *The Concert For Bangla Desh.*
Male pop vocalist: Harry Nilsson, *Without You.*
Female pop vocalist: Helen Reddy, *I Am Woman.*
Pop group: Roberta Flack, Donny Hathaway, *Where is the Love.*

1973
Record: Roberta Flack, *Killing Me Softly with His Song.*
Album: Stevie Wonder, *Innervisions.*
Male pop vocalist: Stevie Wonder, *You Are the Sunshine of My Life.*
Female pop vocalist: Roberta Flack, *Killing Me Softly with His Song.*
Pop group: Gladys Knight & The Pips, *Neither One of Us (Wants to Be the First to Say Goodbye).*

1974
Record: Olivia Newton-John, *I Honestly Love You.*
Album: Stevie Wonder, *Fulfillingness' First Finale.*
Male pop vocalist: Stevie Wonder, *Fulfillingness' First Finale* (album).
Female pop vocalist: Olivia Newton-John, *I Honestly Love You.*
Pop group: Paul McCartney & Wings, *Band on the Run.*

1975
Record: Captain & Tennille, *Love Will Keep Us Together.*
Album: Paul Simon, *Still Crazy After All These Years.*
Male pop vocalist: Paul Simon, *Still Crazy After All These Years* (album).
Female pop vocalist: Janis Ian, *At Seventeen.*
Pop group: Eagles, *Lyin' Eyes.*

1976
Record: George Benson, *This Masquerade.*
Album: Stevie Wonder, *Songs in the Key of Life.*
Male pop vocalist: Stevie Wonder, *Songs in the Key of Life* (album).
Female pop vocalist: Linda Ronstadt, *Hasten Down the Wind* (album).
Pop group: Chicago, *If You Leave Me Now.*

1977
Record: Eagles, *Hotel California.*
Album: Fleetwood Mac, *Rumours.*
Male pop vocalist: James Taylor, *Handy Man.*
Female pop vocalist: Barbra Streisand, *Evergreen.*
Pop group: Bee Gees, *How Deep is Your Love.*

1978
Record: Billy Joel, *Just the Way You Are.*
Album: Bee Gees, *Saturday Night Fever.*
Male pop vocalist: Barry Manilow, *Copacabana.*
Female pop vocalist: Anne Murray, *You Needed Me.*
Pop group: Bee Gees, *Saturday Night Fever* (album).

1979
Record: The Doobie Brothers, *What a Fool Believes.*
Album: Billy Joel, *52nd Street.*
Male pop vocalist: Billy Joel, *52nd Street* (album).
Female pop vocalist: Dionne Warwick, *I'll Never Love This Way Again.*
Pop group: The Doobie Brothers, *Minute by Minute* (album).

1980
Record: Christopher Cross, *Sailing.*
Album: Christopher Cross, *Christopher Cross.*
Male pop vocalist: Kenny Loggins, *This Is It.*
Female pop vocalist: Bette Midler, *The Rose.*
Pop group: Barbra Streisand & Barry Gibb, *Guilty* (album).

1981
Record: Kim Carnes, *Bette Davis Eyes.*
Album: John Lennon, Yoko Ono, *Double Fantasy.*
Male pop vocalist: Al Jarreau, *Breaking Away* (album).
Female pop vocalist: Lena Horne, *Lena Horne: The Lady and Her Music,* Live on Broadway (album).
Pop group: Manhattan Transfer, *Boy from New York City.*

1982
Record: Toto, *Rosanna.*
Album: Toto, *Toto IV.*
Male pop vocalist: Lionel Richie, *Truly.*
Female pop vocalist: Melissa Manchester, *You Should See How She Talks About You.*
Pop Group: Joe Cocker & Jennifer Warnes, *Up Where We Belong.*

1983
Record: Michael Jackson, *Beat It.*
Album: Michael Jackson, *Thriller.*
Male pop vocalist: Michael Jackson, *Thriller.*
Female pop vocalist: Irene Cara, *Flashdance.*
Pop group: Police, *Every Breath You Take.*

1984
Record: Tina Turner, *What's Love Got to Do With It.*
Album: Lionel Richie, *Can't Slow Down.*
Male pop vocalist: Phil Collins, *Against All Odds.*
Female pop vocalist: Tina Turner, *What's Love Got to Do With It.*
Pop group: Pointer Sisters, *Jump.*
Song: Tina Turner, *What's Love Got to Do With It.*
New Artist: Cyndi Lauper.
Male rock vocalist: Bruce Springsteen, *Dancing in the Dark.*
Female rock vocalist: Tina Turner, *Better Be Good to Me.*
Rock group: Prince and the Revolution, *Purple Rain.*
Male rhythm and blues vocalist: Billy Ocean, *Caribbean Queen.*
Female rhythm and blues vocalist: Chaka Khan, *I Feel for You.*

Selected U.S. Daily Newspaper Circulation

Source: Audit Bureau of Circulations' FAS-FAX Report of average paid circulation for 6 months to Mar. 31, 1985.

Newspaper	Daily	Sunday
Akron Beacon Journal (e)	162,409	233,511
Albuquerque Journal (m)	96,391	137,897
Albuquerque Tribune (e)	44,776	
Allentown Call (m)	*130,996	169,046
Asbury Park Press (e)	127,984	189,140
Atlanta Constitution (m)	*235,044	595,625
Atlanta Journal (e)	*185,112	
Austin American-Statesman (m&e)	*167,307	200,183
Baltimore News-American (e)	*101,076	141,608
Baltimore Sun (m&e)	349,901	414,330
Baton Rouge Advocate (m)	85,123	139,359
Bergen Co. (N.J.) Record (e)	*†156,954	†225,520
Birmingham News (e)	*169,251	212,273
Birmingham Post-Herald (m)	*61,200	146,904
Boston Globe (m)	*510,567	802,891
Boston Herald (m)	*368,027	308,823
Bristol Herald-Courier (m)	*35,960	41,937
Bristol Virginia-Tennessean (e)	*7,196	
Brockton Enterprise (e)	*59,501	62,194
Buffalo News (m&e)	*317,750	373,071
Camden (N.J.) Courier-Post (e)	*†109,388	†98,488
Cedar Rapids-Marion Gazette (m)	69,725	80,238
Charlotte News (e)	*39,981	
Charlotte Observer (m)	187,180	259,029
Chicago Sun-Times (m)	*639,187	690,904
Chicago Tribune (m&e)	*775,664	1,165,605
Christian Science Monitor (m)	*151,122	
Cincinnati Enquirer (m)	190,072	308,545
Cincinnati Post (e)	127,142	
Cleveland Plain Dealer (m)	*464,251	542,682
Columbia, S.C. State (m)	113,832	147,929
Columbia, S.C. Record (e)	30,864	
Columbus, Ga. Enquirer (m)	*34,637	67,651
Columbus, Ga. Ledger (e)	*25,924	
Columbus, O. Citizen-Journal (m)	119,150	
Columbus, O. Dispatch (m)	204,705	366,626
Dallas News (m)	368,683	476,004
Dallas Times Herald (m&e)	241,055	345,932
Davenport-Bettendorf Quad. City Times (m&e)	62,529	84,778
Dayton Journal-Herald (m)	103,014	
Dayton News (e)	115,912	233,509
Denver Post (e)	215,625	345,097
Denver: Rocky Mountain News (m)	329,381	385,807
Des Moines Register (m)	235,231	382,604
Detroit Free Press (m)	*646,476	778,178
Detroit News (m&e)	*666,949	884,763
Flint Journal (e)	*109,876	119,182
Ft. Myers News-Press (m)	80,599	96,452
Ft. Worth Star-Telegram (m&e)	121,691	272,384
Fresno Bee (m)	†139,969	†165,497
Gary Post-Tribune (e)	75,680	91,102
Grand Rapids Press (e)	132,823	172,090
Hartford Courant (m)	218,775	296,275
Honolulu Advertiser (m)	88,963	
Honolulu Star-Bulletin (e)	109,332	199,340
Indianapolis News (e)	†130,290	
Indianapolis Star (m)	227,556	393,427
Jacksonville Journal (e)	42,018	
Jacksonville: Fla. Times Union (m)	*162,011	218,919
Kansas City Star (e)	*230,722	402,417
Kansas City Times (m)	280,196	
Knoxville News-Sentinel (e)	94,596	162,425
Little Rock: Ark. Gazette (m)	129,848	164,393
Long Island, N.Y.: Newsday (e)	*542,073	611,403
Los Angeles Herald-Examiner (m)	*237,424	213,898
Los Angeles Times (m)	*1,069,564	1,332,138
Louisville Courier-Journal (m)	175,266	331,686
Louisville Times (e)	133,661	
Madison, Wis. State Journal (m)	77,346	140,313
Miami Herald (m)	464,745	559,886
Milwaukee Journal (e)	301,772	527,065
Milwaukee Sentinel (m)	184,967	
Minneapolis Star Tribune (m)	*383,657	596,181
Nashville Banner (e)	70,279	
Nashville Tennessean (m)	123,909	249,473
Newark Star-Ledger (m)	*†434,804	†661,037
New Haven Register (e)	90,534	139,766
New Haven Journal-Courier (m)	*37,657	
New Orleans Times-Picayune/States-Item (m&e)	*278,888	343,421
New York News (m)	1,390,955	1,773,676
New York Post (m&e)	*901,313	
New York Times (m)	*1,013,211	1,623,562
Norfolk Ledger-Star (e)	†87,377	
Norfolk Virginian-Pilot (m)	†141,370	†224,453
Oakland Tribune (e)	*150,336	156,944
Omaha World-Herald (m&e)	221,919	283,708
Orange Co. (Cal.) Register (m&e)	*285,821	326,038
Orlando Sentinel (m&e)	*245,194	309,078
Peoria Journal Star (m&e)	100,987	115,953
Philadelphia Inquirer (m)	*519,621	1,011,837
Philadelphia News (e)	*284,253	
Phoenix Gazette (e)	†125,021	
Phoenix Republic (m)	†325,677	†499,917
Pittsburgh Post Gazette (m)	*174,982	
Pittsburgh Press (e)	*247,784	594,025
Portland, Me. Press-Herald (m)	58,682	
Portland Oregonian (m&e)	*309,395	408,126
Providence Bulletin (e)	*125,321	
Providence Journal (m)	*84,866	255,425
Raleigh News & Observer (m)	†135,187	†179,032
Raleigh Times (e)	†35,141	
Richmond News Leader (e)	113,619	
Richmond Times Dispatch (m)	140,217	234,993
Rochester Democrat-Chronicle (m)	*129,317	252,443
Rochester Times-Union (e)	*101,583	
Sacramento Bee (m)	230,160	263,763
Sacramento Union (m)	102,317	101,182
St. Louis Globe-Democrat (m)	*201,418	182,608
St. Louis Post-Dispatch (e)	*273,784	495,111
St. Paul Dispatch (e)	*86,271	
St. Paul Pioneer Press (m)	*111,732	244,914
St. Petersburg Independent (e)	38,085	
St. Petersburg Times (m)	287,700	370,283
Salt Lake City Tribune (m)	110,274	132,107
San Diego Union (m)	†231,306	†368,285
San Diego Tribune (e)	†122,590	
San Francisco Examiner (e)	151,758	
San Francisco Chronicle (m)	*554,979	717,426
San Jose Mercury/News (m)	*259,059	309,527
Sarasota Herald-Tribune (m)	119,276	140,961
Seattle Post-Intelligencer (m)	*196,996	
Seattle Times (e)	*227,844	477,307
Shreveport Times (m)	*77,148	109,705
Sioux City Journal (m)	55,077	48,456
South Bend Tribune (e)	100,165	124,125
Spokane Chronicle (e)	47,046	
Spokane Spokesman-Review (m)	81,858	139,877
Springfield, Ill. State Journal-Register (m)	68,724	71,760
Springfield, Mass. Union (m)	70,957	
Springfield, Mass. News (e)	68,882	
Syracuse Herald-Journal (e)	103,598	231,731
Syracuse Post-Standard (m)	82,730	
Tacoma News Tribune (e)	106,499	117,547
Tampa Tribune (m&e)	225,748	297,802
Toledo Blade (e)	163,194	219,072
Tucson Daily Star (m)	80,384	150,059
Tulsa Tribune (e)	†79,188	
Tulsa World (m)	†136,592	†233,611
USA Today (m)	1,162,606	
Wall St. Journal (m) (total)	*1,990,025	
Washington, D.C. Post (m)	*771,253	1,065,782
Waterloo-Cedar Falls-Evansdale Courier (e)	50,974	48,456
West Palm Beach Post (m)	*113,976	181,184
West Palm Beach Times (e)	*26,304	
Wichita Eagle-Beacon (m)	125,661	190,582
Winston-Salem Journal (m)	*74,292	98,509
Winston-Salem Sentinel (e)	*31,136	
Worcester Telegram (m)	†56,197	†126,115
Worcester Gazette (e)	†85,133	
Youngstown Vindicator (e)	†98,541	†151,653

(m) morning; (e) evening; *Mon-Fri. average; † 3 months.

Circulation of Leading U.S. Magazines

Source: Audit Bureau of Circulations' FAS-FAX Report

General magazines, exclusive of groups and comics. Based on total average paid circulation during the 6 months prior to Dec. 31, 1984.

Magazine	Circulation	Magazine	Circulation	Magazine	Circulation
Reader's Digest	17,866,798	Bon Appetit	1,300,887	The Homeowner	660,549
TV Guide	17,115,233	Discovery	1,264,710	Games	660,028
Modern Maturity	10,770,688	The Dial	1,256,676	GQ (Gentleman's	
National Geographic	10,392,548	Golf Digest	1,225,397	Quarterly)	642,156
Better Homes & Gardens	8,058,839	Vogue	1,218,742	Flower & Garden	637,054
Family Circle	6,920,333	Mademoiselle	1,211,080	Catholic Digest	620,530
Woman's Day	6,517,684	Self	1,066,181	Colonial Homes	607,389
McCall's	6,311,011	Health	1,022,064	Playgirl	606,041
Good Housekeeping	5,184,559	Consumer's Digest	1,021,229	Home	602,634
Ladies' Home Journal	5,058,538	New Woman	1,014,244	Architectural Digest	600,928
Time	4,619,777	'Teen	1,011,482	Grit	594,769
National Enquirer	4,512,689	Discover	977,526	Stereo Review	581,114
Playboy	4,217,324	National Examiner	967,448	House & Garden	574,915
Redbook	4,009,584	Yankee	959,827	Personal Computing	565,944
Penthouse	3,771,404	Travel & Leisure	941,246	Food & Wine	557,067
The Star	3,213,728	Scouting	936,272	Inc	551,390
Newsweek	3,012,746	Sport	932,546	Working Mother	519,979
People	2,840,775	Weekly World News	917,307	Sports Afield	518,010
Cosmopolitan	2,826,282	Popular Photography	905,171	Shape	517,727
Prevention	2,821,501	Workbench	881,833	Guns & Ammo	512,823
Sports Illustrated	2,637,751	Car & Driver	881,285	Crafts	507,952
American Legion	2,503,017	House Beautiful	867,736	Tennis	503,838
Glamour	2,288,988	Hot Rod	865,609	The New Yorker	500,746
Southern Living	2,253,569	Nation's Business	865,590	Natural History	500,099
Smithsonian	2,135,953	Rolling Stone	860,991	Gallery	494,980
U.S. News & World Report	2,071,241	Weight Watchers	852,275	Rotarian	480,876
Field & Stream	2,002,883	Psychology Today	850,845	Ms	475,628
V.F.W. Magazine	1,942,265	Omni	842,282	Circus	470,363
Popular Science	1,803,994	Jet	842,172	National Lampoon	451,096
The Workbasket	1,762,060	Soap Opera Digest	840,732	Capper's Weekly	445,553
The Globe	1,750,819	Michigan Living	815,235	New York Magazine	439,958
Seventeen	1,744,435	Signature	812,547	Car Craft	432,771
Ebony	1,705,455	Jr. Scholastic	792,626	Ski	432,393
Parents	1,694,236	Young Miss	786,314	Skiing Magazine	432,058
Popular Mechanics	1,640,503	Golf	778,798	Muscle & Fitness	431,479
The Elks Magazine	1,624,033	Motor Trend	778,171	Atlanta Magazine	427,170
Mechanics Illustrated	1,582,147	Business Week	776,046	Endless Vacation	421,277
1001 Home Ideas	1,546,479	Road & Track	741,614	Cycle	421,233
True Story	1,542,478	Harper's Bazaar	737,430	Westways	415,100
Adventure Road	1,531,010	Creative Ideas for Living	732,127	Coed	413,698
Outdoor Life	1,514,660	Modern Photography	727,389	High Fidelity	408,343
Motorland	1,509,337	New Shelter	726,574	Bassmaster Magazine	402,191
Money	1,505,964	National News	725,934	Byte Magazine	394,986
The American Hunter	1,464,993	Forbes	725,727	World Tennis	386,377
The American Rifleman	1,457,148	Metropolitan Home	719,522	Family Computing	383,048
Life	1,445,124	Science 84	718,657	Video Review	380,309
Boy's Life	1,410,415	Saturday Evening Post	711,635	Audubon	378,810
Sunset	1,390,791	Fortune	710,141	Cycle World	350,208
Changing Times	1,383,513	Working Woman	702,460	High Society	346,104
Organic Gardening	1,378,628	Esquire	700,340	Bride's	342,349
Women's World	1,346,159	The Sporting News	675,743	Cheri	340,686
Country Living	1,319,823	Gourmet	664,501		

Selected Canadian Daily Newspaper Circulation

Source: Audit Bureau of Circulations' FAS-FAX Report; average paid circulation for 6 months ending Mar. 31, 1985.

Newspaper	Daily	Saturday	Newspaper	Daily	Saturday
Calgary Sun. (m)	*72,253	82,958	Regina Leader Post (e)	72,441	
Calgary Herald (e)	142,284	114,165	St. Catharines Standard (e)	42,470	
Edmonton Journal (e)	171,753	**147,232	Saint John Telegraph-Journal (m)	33,365	64,654
Edmonton Sun	*77,843	105,534	Saint John Times Globe (e)	*32,822	
Halifax Chronicle-Herald (m)	78,759		Saskatoon Star-Phoenix (e)	61,180	
Halifax Mail-Star (e)	58,589		Sudbury Star (e)	26,355	
Hamilton Spectator (e)	144,091		Sydney: Cape Breton Post (e)	31,676	
Kitchener-Waterloo Record (e)	77,046		Toronto Globe and Mail (m)	*316,763	
Montreal Gazette (m)	198,559	272,498	Toronto Star (m & e)	*519,154	826,856
Montreal: La Presse (m)	201,721	313,954	Toronto Sun (m)	*252,119	456,036
Montreal: Le Devoir (m)	33,300	35,149	Trois Rivieres Nouvelliste (m)	54,529	
Montreal: Le Journal de Montreal (m)	320,886	357,286	Vancouver Province (m)	*162,154	202,841
Ottawa Citizen (m & e)	*189,448	240,826	Vancouver Sun (e)	240,907	288,321
Ottawa: Le Droit (e)	43,976	49,487	Windsor Star (e)	86,489	
Quebec: Le Journal de Quebec (m)	105,791	106,678	Winnipeg Free Press (e)	179,949	246,530
Quebec: Le Soleil (e)	122,374	144,889			

(m) Morning; (e) Evening; * Based on Monday to Friday average; **Sunday.

Average Television Viewing Time

Source: A.C. Nielsen estimates, Nov. 1984 (hours: minutes, per week)

		Total	Mon.-Fri. 10am-4:30pm	Mon.-Fri. 4:30pm-7:30pm	Mon.-Sun. 8-11pm	Sat. 7am-1pm	Mon.-Fri. 11:30pm-1am
Avg. all persons		30:38	4:33	4:38	8:58	:58	1:05
Women	Total 18+	35:19	6:38	5:08	10:30	:40	1:20
	18-24	27:28	5:55	3:43	7:30	:40	1:16
	55+	42:07	8:21	7:10	12:06	:53	1:53
Men	Total 18+	29:04	2:53	3:59	9:02	:50	1:23
	18-24	19:46	2:32	2:32	5:20	:26	1:13
	55+	37:11	4:31	6:10	11:00	:54	1:26
Teens	Female	21:37	2:30	4:23	7:04	1:14	:18
	Male	23:19	1:38	3:59	8:02	1:20	:30
Children	2-5	28:20	7:03	4:52	4:16	2:14	:07
	6-11	26:34	2:56	5:22	6:40	2:29	:08

America's Favorite Television Programs

Source: A.C. Nielsen
(Percent of TV Households and Persons in TV households)

Network Programs (November 1984)

(Nielsen Average Audience Estimates)

	TV House-holds	Women	Men	Teens	Chil-dren
Dallas	25.6	23.0	13.6		
Dynasty	24.6	22.7	14.5		
60 Minutes	23.9	18.1	17.6		
NBC Monday Night Movie	23.0	19.5	12.6	17.3	
Simon & Simon	20.9	16.8	12.8		
A Team	20.6	15.3	15.2		
Falcon Crest	20.5	18.6		14.7	
ABC Sunday Night Movie	20.1	15.5	16.5	20.4	16.2
Bill Cosby Show	20.1	17.5		22.7	18.5
Hotel	19.4	18.0			
Magnum, P.I.	19.1	14.8	13.4		
Knots Landing	18.9	17.0			
NBC Sunday Night Movie	18.8	15.6			
Murder, She Wrote	18.6	16.0			
Family Ties	18.4	15.6		21.6	17.3
NFL Football Game 2-NBC			16.1		
NFL Monday Night Football			15.3		
Hill Street Blues			14.2		
CBS NFL Football Game 1			14.2		
CBS NFL Football-Game 2			13.6		
Hardcastle and McCormick			13.6	12.2	
Fall Guy			12.7		
Diff'rent Strokes-Sat				19.0	19.5
TV Bloopers & Prac. Jokes			18.3		
Gimme A Break			17.5	18.3	
V			16.3	17.9	
Knight Rider			15.7	24.2	
Facts Of Life			14.8		
Cheers			14.2		
It's Your Move			13.3		
Who's the Boss			11.9		
Smurfs III					23.9

	TV House-holds	Women	Men	Teens	Chil-dren
Alvin & The Chipmunks					22.2
Smurfs II					21.1
Muppet Babies					18.2
Kidd Video					15.0
Turbo Teen					14.7
Smurfs I					14.5
Dungeons & Dragons					14.4

Syndicated Programs (Nov. 1984)*

(Average Ratings for Total U.S.)

	TV house-holds	Women	Men	Teens	Chil-dren
Wheel of Fortune	16.4	13.8	9.9	6.7	7.0
M*A*S*H	10.0	6.6	6.7	6.2	4.3
Three's Company	9.6	6.0	4.8	10.8	9.0
Entertainment Tonight	8.7	6.6	5.1	3.3	2.5
Family Feud	8.4	6.8	4.7	3.6	3.5
PM Magazine	8.2	6.1	5.0	3.3	2.9
Hee Haw	7.9	6.0	5.6	2.4	3.2
People's Court	7.8	6.0	4.4	2.7	1.7
Jeffersons	7.7	5.3	3.8	7.6	6.1
Diff'rent Strokes	7.6	4.1	2.8	11.3	12.3
Fight Back	7.6	5.6	4.7	3.4	2.3
Jeopardy	7.0	5.7	3.4	2.8	2.3
Benson	7.0	4.7	3.5	6.2	5.7
Dance Fever	6.6	4.9	3.5	4.9	5.1
Name That Tune	6.5	5.3	3.4	2.7	2.0
Solid Gold Orig.	6.2	4.4	3.5	6.6	5.8
Taxi	6.0	3.7	3.7	3.4	2.6
2 Close for Comfort	6.0	4.2	3.1	4.9	4.2
Barney Miller	5.9	3.9	3.6	2.5	2.1
Phil Donahue	5.9	4.6	2.1	0.4	0.5

*Programs that cleared in 20+ Markets.

Network TV Program Ratings

Source: A. C. Nielsen, November, 1984

Program or type	TV Households Rating %	TV Households No. (000)	Men (18+)	Women (18+)	Teens 12-17	Children 2-11
Today (7:30-8:00)	4.4	3,740	1,770	2,670	80	440
Morning (7:30-8:00)	3.5	2,970	1,270	1,750	60	50
Good Morning Am. (7:30-8:00)	5.0	4,250	1,530	3,400	160	480
Daytime Drama (Soaps)	6.1	5,160	1,190	4,660	310	530
Quiz & Aud. Participation	5.0	4,260	1,300	3,360	150	570
All 10am-4:30pm	4.5	3,860	1,180	3,090	160	540
Evening Informational	11.9	10,080	6,090	7,690	620	1,050
General Drama	17.4	14,810	7,430	13,480	1,530	1,460
Susp. & Mystery	14.6	12,370	7,570	9,940	1,480	1,540
Sit. Comedy	15.0	12,770	6,370	10,630	2,300	3,040
Feature Film	17.7	15,000	9,330	12,560	2,770	2,630
All 7-11pm Regular	16.2	13,720	8,170	11,210	2,010	2,310

All-time Top Television Programs

Source: A.C. Nielsen estimates

Program	Date	Network	Households	Program	Date	Network	Households
M*A*S*H Special	2/28/83	CBS	50,150,000	Super Bowl XV	1/25/81	NBC	34,540,000
Dallas	11/21/80	CBS	41,470,000	Super Bowl XII	1/15/78	CBS	34,410,000
Super Bowl XVII	1/30/83	NBC	40,480,000	Winds of War	2/13/83	ABC	34,150,000
Super Bowl XVI	1/24/82	CBS	40,020,000	Gone With The Wind	11/7/76	NBC	33,960,000
Super Bowl XIX	1/20/85	ABC	39,390,000	Gone With The Wind	11/8/76	NBC	33,750,000
Super Bowl XVIII	1/22/84	CBS	38,800,000	Winds of War	2/7/83	ABC	33,490,000
The Day After	11/20/83	ABC	38,550,000	Thorn Birds	3/27/83	ABC	32,900,000
Roots	1/30/77	ABC	36,380,000	Roots	1/28/77	ABC	32,680,000
Thorn Birds	3/29/83	ABC	35,990,000	Winds of War	2/6/83	ABC	32,570,000
Thorn Birds	3/30/83	ABC	35,900,000	Roots	1/27/77	ABC	32,540,000
Thorn Birds	3/28/83	ABC	35,400,000	Winds of War	2/9/83	ABC	32,490,000
Super Bowl XIV	1/20/80	CBS	35,330,000	Winds of War	2/8/83	ABC	32,240,000
Super Bowl XIII	1/21/79	NBC	35,090,000	Roots	1/25/77	ABC	31,900,000
CBS NFC Championship Game	1/10/82	CBS	34,960,000	World Series Game 7	10/20/82	NBC	31,820,000
				Academy Awards	4/11/83	ABC	31,650,000
				Super Bowl XI	1/9/77	NBC	31,610,000

U.S. Television Sets and Stations Received

Set Ownership
(Nielsen est. as of Jan. 1, 1985)

Total TV homes	86,530,000	
(98% of U.S. homes own at least one TV set)		
Homes with:		
Color TV sets	77,700,000	91%
B&W only	8,490,000	10
2 or more sets	48,200,000	57
One set	38,200,000	45
Cable (Feb. 1985)	38,018,100	44.6

Number of Stations
(FCC, Jan. 1, 1985)

Commercial	862
Educational	287
Total	1,149

Stations Receivable
(Nielsen, Sept. 1984)

% of TV homes receiving:

1-4 stations	4%
5	4
6	7
7	10
8	11
9	12
10	10
11+	42%

Total TV Households—84.9 million, 18+ women—88,570; 18+ men—79,860; teens 12-17 21,070; children 2-11 32,870

Television Network Addresses and Phone Numbers

American Broadcasting Company (ABC)
1330 Avenue of Americas
New York, NY 10019
(212) 887-7777

CBS, Inc.
51 W. 52nd St.
New York, NY 10019
(212) 975-4321

National Broadcasting Company (NBC)
30 Rockefeller Plaza
New York, NY 10112
(212) 664-4444

Westinghouse Broadcasting (Group W)
90 Park Ave.
New York, NY 10016
(212) 883-6100

Metromedia
205 E. 67 St.
New York, NY 10021
(212) 734-1000

Public Broadcasting Service (PBS)
609 Fifth Ave.
New York, NY 10017
(212) 753-7373

Canadian Broadcasting Corp. (CBC)
1500 Bronson Ave.
Ottawa, Ontario, Canada K1G 3J5
(613) 724-1200

Symphony Orchestras of the U.S.

Source: American Symphony Orchestra League (as of Dec. 1984)

Classifications are based on annual incomes or budgets of orchestras.

Major Symphony Orchestras	Principal Conductor	Regional Orchestras	Principal Conductor
Atlanta Symphony	Robert Shaw	Charlotte Symphony	Leo Driehuys
Baltimore Symphony	David Zinman	Colorado Springs Symphony	Charles A. Ansbacher
Boston Symphony	Seiji Ozawa	Columbus Symphony	Christian Badea
Buffalo Philharmonic	Julius Rudel	Dayton Philharmonic	Charles Wendelken-Wilson
Chicago Symphony	Sir Georg Solti	Florida Orchestra (Tampa)	Irwin Hoffman
Cincinnati Symphony	Michael Gielen	Florida Symphony (Orlando)	Sidney Rothstein
Cleveland Orchestra	Christoph von Dohnanyi	Fort Worth Symphony	John Giordano
Dallas Symphony	Eduardo Mata	Grand Rapids Symphony	Semyon Bychkov
Denver Symphony	Gaetano Delogu	Hartford Symphony	Daniel Parker
Detroit Symphony	Michael Krajewski	Honolulu Symphony	Donald Johanos
Houston Symphony	Sergiu Comissiona	Jacksonville Symphony	Roger Nierenberg
Indianapolis Symphony	John Nelson	Long Beach Symphony	Murry Sidlin
Los Angeles Philharmonic	Andre Previn	Los Angeles Chamber Orchestra	Gerard Schwarz
Milwaukee Symphony	Lukas Foss	Louisville Orchestra	Lawrence L. Smith
Minnesota Orchestra (Minneapolis)	Clyn Dee Barrus	Memphis Symphony	Alan Balter
National Symphony (D.C.)	Mstislav Rostropovich	Nashville Symphony	Kenneth Schermerhorn
New Orleans Philharmonic-		New Haven Symphony	Murry Sidlin
Symphony	Dean Angeles	New Jersey Symphony (Newark)	George Manahan
New York Philharmonic	Zubin Mehta	New Mexico Symphony (Albuquerque)	vacant
Oregon Symphony (Portland)	James DePreist	North Carolina Symphony (Raleigh)	Gerhardt Zimmerman
Philadelphia Orchestra	Riccardo Muti	Oakland Symphony	Richard Buckley
Pittsburgh Symphony	Lorin Maazel	Oklahoma Symphony (Oklahoma	
Rochester Philharmonic	David Zinman	City)	Luis Herrera de la Fuente
St. Louis Symphony	Leonard Slatkin	Omaha Symphony	Bruce Hangen
St. Paul Chamber Orchestra	Pinchas Zukerman	Phoenix Symphony	Theo Alcantara
San Antonio Symphony	Lawrence Leighton Smith	Puerto Rico Symphony (Santurce)	John Barnett
San Diego Symphony	David Atherton	Richmond Symphony	Jacques Houtmann
San Francisco Symphony	Edo de Waart	Sacramento Symphony	Carter Nice
Seattle Symphony	Gerard Schwarz	San Jose Symphony	George Cleve
Syracuse Symphony	Christopher Keene	Spokane Symphony	Gunther Schuller
Utah Symphony	Joseph Silverstein	Springfield Symphony	John E. Ferritto
		Toledo Symphony	Yuval Zaliouk
Regional Orchestras	**Principal Conductor**	Tulsa Philharmonic	Bernard Rubenstein
Alabama Symphony (Birmingham)	Amerigo Marino	Virginia Symphony (Norfolk)	Richard Williams
American Symphony (NY)	John Maucer	Wichita Symphony	Michael Palmer
Austin Symphony	Sung Kwak		

Metropolitan Orchestras

Akron Symphony OH
Albany Symphony NY
Amarillo Symphony TX
American Composers Orchestra NY
Anchorage Symphony AK
Arkansas Symphony AR
B.C. Pops, Inc. NY
Baton Rouge Symphony LA
Binghampton Symphony & Choral Society NY
Boise Philharmonic ID
Brevard Symphony FL
Brooklyn Philharmonic Symphony NY
Cabrillo Music Festival CA
Canton Symphony OH
Cedar Rapids Symphony IA
Charleston Symphony SC
Charleston Symphony WV
Chattanooga Symphony TN
Chautauqua Symphony NY
Colorado Music Festival CO
Concerto Soloists of Philadelphia PA
Corpus Christi Symphony TX
Delaware Symphony DE
Des Moines Symphony IA
Duluth-Superior Symphony MN
Eastern Philharmonic NC
El Paso Symphony TX
Erie Philharmonic PA
Eugene Symphony OR
Evansville Philharmonic IN
Fairfax Symphony VA

Flint Symphony MI
Florida Chamber Orchestra FL
Florida West Coast Symphony FL
Fort Wayne Philharmonic IN
Fresno Philharmonic CA
Glendale Symphony CA
Greensboro Symphony NC
Handel and Hayden Society MA
Harrisburg Symphony PA
Houston Pops TX
Hudson Valley Philharmonic NY
Illinois (Orchestra of) IL
Jackson Symphony MS
Kalamazoo Symphony MI
Knoxville Symphony TN
Lake Forest Symphony IL
Lansing Symphony MI
Lexington Philharmonic KY
Lincoln Symphony NE
Little Orchestra Society of New York NY
Lubbock Symphony TX
Madison Symphony WI
Marin Symphony CA
Miami Symphony (Greater) FL
Midland-Odessa Symphony & Chorale TX
Monterey County Symphony CA
Music of the Baroque IL
New England (Chamber Orchestra of) CT
New Hampshire Symphony NH

Northeastern Pennsylvania Philharmonic PA
Ohio Chamber Orchestra OH
Orange County Pacific Symphony CA
Orchestra da Camera NY
Pasadena Symphony CA
Philharmonia Virtuosi NY
Portland Symphony ME
Queens Symphony NY
Regina Symphony SK
Rhode Island Philharmonic RI
Rochester Symphony MN
Saginaw Symphony MI
Santa Barbara Symphony CA
Santa Rosa Symphony CA
Savannah Symphony GA
Shreveport Symphony LA
South Bend Symphony IN
South Dakota Symphony SD
Stockton Symphony CA
Tacoma Symphony WA
Tri-City Symphony IA
Tucson Symphony AZ
Vermont Symphony VT
Westchester (County Symphony of) NY
Wheeling Symphony WV
White Plains Symphony NY
Winston-Salem Symphony NC
Y Chamber Symphony NY
Youngstown Symphony OH

U.S. and Canadian Opera Companies with Budgets of $500,000 or More

Source: Central Opera Service, New York, N.Y.; Apr. 1985

Anchorage Civic Opera; Elvera Yoth, art. dir.
Arizona Opera Co. (Tucson); Glynn Ross, gen. dir.
Long Beach Civic Light Opera (Calif.); Harvey Waggoner, exec. dir.
Los Angeles Opera Theater; Henry Hort, art. dir.
San Diego Civic Light Opera; Leon Drew, gen mgr.
San Diego Opera Assn.; Ian Campbell, gen. mgr.
San Francisco Opera; Terence McEwen, gen. dir.
San Francisco Opera Center; Christine Bullin, mgr.
Western Opera Theater (San Francisco); Terence McEwen, gen. dir.
Central City Opera (Denver); Daniel Rule, gen. mgr.
Opera Colorado (Denver); Nathaniel Merrill, art. dir.
Connecticut Opera (Hartford); George Osborne, gen. dir.
Washington Opera (D.C.); Martin Feinstein, gen. dir.
Greater Miami Opera Assn.; Robert Herman, gen. mgr.
Palm Beach Opera; Anton Guadagno, art. dir.
Hawaii Opera Theatre; Bebe Freitas, art. dir.
Chicago Opera Theatre; Alan Stone, art. dir.
Lyric Opera of Chicago; Ardis Krainik, gen. mgr.
Indianapolis Opera Co.; Robert Driver, art. dir.
Music Theatre of Wichita; John Holly, prod. dir.
Des Moines Metro Opera; Robert Larsen, art. dir.
Kentucky Opera Assn. (Louisville); Thomson Smillie, gen. dir.
New Orleans Opera Assn.; Arthur Cosenza, gen. dir.
Baltimore Opera Co.; Jay Holbrook, gen. mgr.
Boston Lyric Opera; John Balme, mus. dir.
Opera Company of Boston; Sarah Caldwell, art. dir.
Michigan Opera Theatre (Detroit); David DiChiera, gen. dir.
Children's Theatre Co. (Minneapolis); Sarah Lawless, exec. dir.
Minnesota Opera Co. (St. Paul); Edward Corn, exec. prod.
Lyric Opera of Kansas City (Missouri); Russell Patterson, gen. dir. & art. dir.
Opera Theatre of St. Louis (Missouri); Richard Gaddes, gen. dir.
St. Louis Municipal Theatre; Edward Greenberg, exec. prod.
New Jersey State Opera (Newark); Alfredo Silipigni, art. dir.
Santa Fe Opera (New Mexico); John Crosby, gen. dir.

Lake George Opera Festival (Glens Falls, N.Y.); Paulette Haupt-Nolen, gen. dir.
Artpark/Natural Heritage Trust (Lewiston, N.Y.); Joanne Allison, exec. dir.
Syracuse Opera; Robert Diver, gen. dir.
Light Opera of Manhattan; Judith O'Sullivan, gen. mgr.
Metropolitan Opera Assn. (New York City); Bruce Crawford, gen. mgr.
New York City Opera; Beverly Sills, gen. dir.
New York City Opera Natl. Co.; Nancy Kelly, adm.
Charlotte Opera Assn. (No. Carolina); Bruce Chalmers, gen. dir.
Cincinnati Opera Assn.; James deBlasis, gen. mgr.
Cleveland Opera; David Bamberger, gen. mgr. & art. dir.
Lyric Theatre of Oklahoma (Oklahoma City); Clyde Rader, mng. dir.
Tulsa Opera (Oklahoma); Edward Purrington, gen. dir.
Portland Opera Assn. (Oregon); Robert Bailey, exec. dir.
Opera Company of Philadelphia; Margaret Anne Everitt, gen. dir.
Pittsburgh Opera Co.; Tito Capobiano, gen. dir.
Spoleto Festival USA (Charleston, So. Carolina); Philip Semark, gen. mgr.
Dallas Opera; Plato Karayanis, gen. dir.
Fort Worth Opera; Dwight Bowes, gen. dir.
Houston Grand Opera Assn.; R. David Gockley, gen. dir.
Texas Opera Theater (Houston); M. Jane Weaver, gen. mgr.
Theatre Under the Stars (Houston); Ange Finn, gen. mgr.
Pioneer Memorial Theatre (Salt Lake City); Keith Engar, exec. dir.
Utah Opera Company (Salt Lake City); Glade Peterson, gen. dir.
Virginia Opera (Norfolk); Peter Mark, gen. dir.
Seattle Opera Assn.; Speight Jenkins, gen. dir.
Florentine Opera of Milwaukee; John Gage, gen. mgr.
Calgary Opera Assn.; Brian Hanson, gen. mgr.
Edmonton Opera Assn.; Robert Hallanan, mgr.
Vancouver Opera; Brian McMaster, art. dir.
Manitoba Opera Assn.; Irving Guttman, art. dir.
Canadian Opera Co. (Toronto); Lotfi Mansouri, gen. dir.
L'Opera de Montreal; Jean-Paul Jeannotte, art. dir.

Miss America Winners

1921	Margaret Gorman, Washington, D.C.	1958	Marilyn Van Derbur, Denver, Colorado
1922-23	Mary Campbell, Columbus, Ohio	1959	Mary Ann Mobley, Brandon, Mississippi
1924	Ruth Malcolmson, Philadelphia, Pennsylvania	1960	Lynda Lee Mead, Natchez, Mississippi
1925	Fay Lamphier, Oakland, California	1961	Nancy Fleming, Montague, Michigan
1926	Norma Smallwood, Tulsa, Oklahoma	1962	Maria Fletcher, Asheville, North Carolina
1927	Lois Delaner, Joliet, Illinois	1963	Jacquelyn Mayer, Sandusky, Ohio
1933	Marion Bergeron, West Haven, Connecticut	1964	Donna Axum, El Dorado, Arkansas
1935	Henrietta Leaver, Pittsburgh, Pennsylvania	1965	Vonda Kay Van Dyke, Phoenix, Arizona
1936	Rose Coyle, Philadelphia, Pennsylvania	1966	Deborah Irene Bryant, Overland Park, Kansas
1937	Bette Cooper, Bertrand Island, New Jersey	1967	Jane Anne Jayroe, Laverne, Oklahoma
1938	Marilyn Meseke, Marion, Ohio	1968	Debra Dene Barnes, Moran, Kansas
1939	Patricia Donnelly, Detroit, Michigan	1969	Judith Anne Ford, Belvidere, Illinois
1940	Frances Marie Burke, Philadelphia, Pennsylvania	1970	Pamela Anne Eldred, Birmingham, Michigan
1941	Rosemary LaPlanche, Los Angeles, California	1971	Phyllis Ann George, Denton, Texas
1942	Jo-Caroll Dennison, Tyler, Texas	1972	Laurie Lea Schaefer, Columbus, Ohio
1943	Jean Bartel, Los Angeles, California	1973	Terry Anne Meeuwsen, DePere, Wisconsin
1944	Venus Ramey, Washington, D.C.	1974	Rebecca Ann King, Denver, Colorado
1945	Bess Myerson, New York City, N.Y.	1975	Shirley Cothran, Fort Worth, Texas
1946	Marilyn Buferd, Los Angeles, California	1976	Tawney Elaine Godin, Yonkers, N.Y.
1947	Barbara Walker, Memphis, Tennessee	1977	Dorothy Kathleen Benham, Edina, Minnesota
1948	BeBe Shopp, Hopkins, Minnesota	1978	Susan Perkins, Columbus, Ohio
1949	Jacque Mercer, Litchfield, Arizona	1979	Kylene Baker, Galax, Virginia
1951	Yolande Betbeze, Mobile, Alabama	1980	Cheryl Prewitt, Ackerman, Mississippi
1952	Coleen Kay Hutchins, Salt Lake City, Utah	1981	Susan Powell, Elk City, Oklahoma
1953	Neva Jane Langley, Macon, Georgia	1982	Elizabeth Ward, Russellville, Arkansas
1954	Evelyn Margaret Ay, Ephrata, Pennsylvania	1983	Debra Maffett, Anaheim, California
1955	Lee Meriwether, San Francisco, California	1984	Vanessa Williams, Milwood, New York*
1956	Sharon Ritchie, Denver, Colorado		Suzette Charles, Mays Landing, New Jersey
1957	Marian McKnight, Manning, South Carolina	1985	Sharlene Wells, Salt Lake City, Utah

*Resigned July 23, 1984.

50 Leading U.S. Advertisers, 1983

Source: Advertising Age, Sept. 14, 1984; copyright © Crain Communications Inc. 1984.

Rank	Company	U.S. Ad Costs (000)	U.S. Sales (000)	Ads as % sales
	Electronics			
29	RCA Corp.	$212,300	$ 8,010,000	2.7
32	General Electric	196,507	17,649,000	1.1
40	Tandy Corp.	156,728	2,354,000	6.7
	Automobiles			
4	General Motors Corp.	595,129	66,160,000	0.9
7	Ford Motor Corp.	479,060	33,000,000	1.5
27	Chrysler Corp.	230,020	11,642,100	2.0
	Chemicals			
45	American Cyanamid Co.	142,400	2,388,662	6.0
	Communications, Entertainment			
25	Warner Communications	251,050	2,715,940	9.2
39	CBS Inc.	167,711	3,900,000	4.3
	Food			
3	Beatrice Cos.	602,775	NA	NA
10	General Foods Corp.	386,134	6,407,500	6.0
11	Nabisco Brands Inc.	367,530	3,655,600	10.1
16	McDonald's Corp.	311,378	7,069,000	4.4
21	Ralston Purina Co.	285,667	3,848,600	7.4
23	General Mills	268,690	6,905,300	3.0
30	Dart & Kraft	210,279	2,555,368	7.9
31	H.J. Heinz Co.	202,400	5,100,000	5.3
33	Consolidated Foods	195,858	5,195,752	3.0
34	Pillsbury Co.	190,944	4,160,000	4.6
37	Kellogg Co.	176,307	1,560,000	11.3
42	Quaker Oats Co.	148,442	1,623,500	9.1
	Retail Chains			
2	Sears, Roebuck & Co.	732,500	32,637,000	2.2
9	K mart Corp.	400,000	17,785,700	2.2
19	J.C. Penney Co.	292,451	11,565,000	2.5
	Soaps, Cleansers			
1	Procter & Gamble	773,618	9,554,000	8.1
15	Unilever U.S. Inc.	324,866	2,808,000	12.2
24	Colgate-Palmolive Co.	268,000	2,200,000	12.2
	Soft drinks			
12	PepsiCo Inc.	356,400	6,714,000	5.3
22	Coca-Cola Co.	282,150	4,071,400	6.9
	Telephone service, equipment			
8	American T & T	463,096	67,648,000	0.7
49	International T & T	134,229	12,430,000	1.1
	Tobacco			
5	R.J. Reynolds Industries	593,350	10,769,000	5.5
6	Philip Morris	527,482	9,303,100	5.7
43	Batus	146,076	6,064,000	2.4
48	Loews Corp.	135,115	5,260,075	2.6
	Toiletries, Cosmetics, Drugs			
13	Warner Lambert Co.	343,553	1,822,000	18.9
14	American Home Products	333,485	3,482,300	9.6
17	Johnson & Johnson	295,329	3,600,000	8.2
26	Bristol-Myers Co.	235,000	2,889,300	8.1
35	Gillette Co.	185,604	1,020,000	18.2
38	Sterling Drug	171,828	703,433	24.4
41	Richardson-Vicks	150,814	667,134	22.6
46	Chesebrough-Pond's	141,325	1,310,242	10.8
50	Beecham Group	134,126	2,800,000	4.8
	Wine, Beer, Liquor			
20	Anheuser-Busch Cos.	290,616	6,658,500	4.4
	Miscellaneous			
18	Mobil Corp.	294,932	23,900,000	1.2
28	U.S. Government	228,857	NA	NA
36	Mattel Inc.	179,935	840,000	21.4
44	Gulf & Western	145,500	3,443,000	4.2
47	Eastman Kodak Co.	141,319	6,435,000	2.2

30 Top U.S. Advertisers: Expenditures by Type of Media

Source: Advertising Age, Sept. 14, 1984; copyright © Crain Communications Inc., 1984.

Rank	Company	News- papers	General magazines	Spot TV	Net. TV	Spot Radio	Net. Radio	Out- door
				% of Total Dollars				
1	Procter & Gamble Co.	—	5.2	29.6	47.4	0.4	0.2	—
2	Sears, Roebuck & Co.	—	4.6	31.2	19.8	0.7	1.5	—
3	Beatrice Cos.	2.9	7.3	7.6	14.7	—	—	0.7
4	General Motors Corp.	14.9	15.0	—	33.8	4.9	1.6	0.7
5	R.J. Reynolds Industries	18.9	26.1	6.7	—	—	—	15.0
6	Philip Morris Inc.	12.4	26.6	9.6	24.3	4.3	—	10.5
7	Ford Motor Co.	10.4	16.8	7.9	36.0	2.7	1.5	—
8	American Telephone & Telegraph	15.5	13.2	8.9	31.7	6.0	2.1	—
9	K Mart Corp.	—	2.7	2.5	5.9	1.2	—	—
10	General Foods Corp.	1.0	8.6	18.9	44.0	0.6	0.4	—
11	Nabisco Brands	1.6	2.5	6.0	22.3	—	1.3	—
12	PepsiCo Inc.	1.7	1.1	34.2	20.8	4.0	—	0.5
13	Warner-Lambert Co.	0.4	2.1	11.5	21.7	0.5	2.3	—
14	American Home Products Corp.	0.5	6.4	9.6	48.4	0.6	0.2	—
15	Unilever U.S.	1.5	4.0	17.2	34.0	—	—	—
16	McDonald's Corp.	—		33.7	26.0	0.7	—	1.4
17	Johnson & Johnson	0.7	7.9	3.1	44.5	—	0.5	—
18	Mobil Corp.	2.4	1.3	7.1	2.4	0.8	—	—
19	J.C. Penney Co.	—	3.7	6.2	10.9	—	—	—
20	Anheuser-Busch Cos.	1.4	3.8	20.4	40.1	14.0	2.4	1.4
21	Ralston Purina Co.	1.1	5.1	12.5	33.0	3.1	—	—
22	Coca-Cola Co.	2.1	3.0	25.0	34.0	2.9	—	1.2
23	General Mills	2.1	9.5	42.0	37.3	2.3	0.8	—
24	Colgate-Palmolive Co.	0.3	3.2	11.0	22.4	1.5	—	—
25	Warner Communications	6.3	10.2	11.0	33.6	0.9	—	—
26	Bristol-Myers Co.	0.6	12.1	4.3	51.5	0.8	0.7	—
27	Chrysler Corp.	13.8	19.5	8.1	36.6	7.2	1.2	—
28	U.S. Government	2.3	11.1	7.1	13.1	2.5	4.1	0.6
29	RCA Corp.	14.9	16.6	4.9	11.4	1.7	1.6	—
30	Dart & Kraft	3.4	15.8	20.2	41.6	0.9	1.5	—

NOTED PERSONALITIES
Widely Known Americans of the Present

Statesmen, authors of nonfiction, military men, and other prominent persons not listed in other categories.

Name (Birthplace)	Birthdate	Name (Birthplace)	Birthdate
Abel, I. W. (Magnolia, Oh.)	8/11/08	Fraser, Douglas A. (Glasgow, Scotland)	12/18/16
Abzug, Bella (New York, N.Y.)	7/24/20	Friedan, Betty (Peoria, Ill.)	2/4/21
Albert, Carl (McAlester, Okla.)	5/10/08	Friedman, Milton (Brooklyn, N.Y.)	7/31/12
Aldrin, Edwin E. Jr. "Buzz" (Glen Ridge, N.J.)	1/20/30	Fulbright, J. William (Sumner, Mo.)	4/9/05
Alsop, Joseph W. Jr. (Avon, Conn.)	10/11/10	Galbraith, John Kenneth (Ontario, Can.)	10/15/08
Arledge, Roone (Forest Hills, N.Y.)	7/8/31	George, Phyllis (Denton, Tex.)	6/25/49
Armstrong, William L. (Fremont, Neb.)	1937	Gephardt, Richard (St. Louis, Mo.)	1/31/41
Anderson, Jack (Long Beach, Cal.)	10/19/22	Gifford, Frank (Santa Monica, Cal.)	8/16/30
Armstrong, Neil (Wapakoneta, Oh.)	8/5/30	Ginsberg, Allen (Paterson, N.J.)	6/3/21
Bailey, F. Lee (Waltham, Mass.)	6/10/33	Glenn, John (Cambridge, Oh.)	7/18/21
Baker, Howard (Huntsville, Tenn.)	11/15/25	Goldberg, Arthur J. (Chicago, Ill.)	8/8/08
Baker, James A. (Houston, Tex.)	4/28/30	Goldwater, Barry M. (Phoenix, Ariz.)	1/1/09
Baker, Russell (Loudoun Co., Va.)	8/14/25	Goodman, Ellen (Newton, Mass.)	4/11/41
Belli, Melvin (Sonora, Cal.)	7/29/07	Graham, Billy (Charlotte, N.C.)	11/7/18
Bentsen, Lloyd (Mission, Tex.)	2/11/21	Graham, Katharine (New York, N.Y.)	6/16/17
Bernstein, Carl (Washington, DC)	2/14/44	Greenspan, Alan (New York, N.Y.)	3/6/26
Blackmun, Harry (Nashville, Ill.)	11/12/08	Gumble, Bryant (New Orleans, La.)	9/29/48
Blass, Bill (Ft. Wayne, Ind.)	6/22/22	Haig, Alexander (Philadelphia, Pa.)	12/2/24
Bok, Derek (Ardmore, Pa.)	3/22/30	Hammar, Armand (New York, N.Y.)	5/21/98
Bombeck, Erma (Dauton, Oh.)	2/21/27	Harriman, W. Averell (New York, N.Y.)	11/15/91
Bond, Julian (Nashville, Tenn.)	1/14/40	Hart, Gary (Ottawa, Kan.)	11/28/37
Borman, Frank (Gary, Ind.)	3/14/28	Hartman, David (Pawtucket, R.I.)	5/19/35
Borstin, Daniel (Atlanta, Ga.)	10/1/14	Hatch, Orrin (Homestead, Pa.)	3/22/34
Bradlee, Ben (Boston, Mass.)	8/26/21	Hatfield, Mark O. (Dallas, Ore.)	7/12/22
Bradley, Bill (Crystal City, Mo.)	7/28/43	Hawkins, Paula (Salt Lake City, Ut.)	1/24/27
Bradley, Ed (Philadelphia, Pa.)	6/22/41	Heckler, Margaret M. (Flushing, N.Y.)	6/21/31
Bradley, Thomas (Calvert, Tex.)	12/29/17	Hefner, Hugh (Chicago, Ill.)	4/9/26
Brennan, William J. (Newark, N.J.)	4/25/06	Heller, Walter (Buffalo, N.Y.)	8/27/15
Breslin, Jimmy (Jamaica, N.Y.)	10/17/30	Helms, Jesse (Monroe, N.C.)	10/18/21
Brinkley, David (Wilmington, N.C.)	7/10/20	Hershey, Lenore (New York, N.Y.)	3/20/20
Brock, William (Chattanooga, Tenn.)	11/23/30	Hesburgh, Theodore (Syracuse, N.Y.)	5/25/17
Brokaw, Tom (Webster, S. Dak.)	2/6/40	Hiss, Alger (Baltimore, Md.)	11/11/04
Brown, Edmund G. Jr. (San Francisco, Cal.)	4/7/38	Hodel, Donald P. (Portland, Ore.)	5/23/35
Brown, Helen Gurley (Green Forest, Ark.)	2/18/22	Hollings, Ernest (Charleston, S.C.)	1/1/22
Brzezinski, Zbigniew (Warsaw, Poland)	3/28/28	Iacocca, Lee A. (Allentown, Pa.)	10/15/24
Buchwald, Art (Mt. Vernon, N.Y.)	10/20/25	Inouye, Daniel (Honolulu, Ha.)	9/7/24
Buckley, William F. (New York, N.Y.)	11/24/25	Jackson, Jesse (Greenville, N.C.)	10/8/41
Bumpers, Dale (Charleston, Ark.)	8/12/25	Javits, Jacob K. (New York, N.Y.)	5/18/04
Burger, Warren (St. Paul, Minn.)	9/17/07	Jennings, Peter (Toronto, Ont.)	8/29/38
Burns, Arthur F. (Stanislau, Aust.)	4/27/04	Johnson, Lady Bird (Karnack, Tex.)	12/22/12
Bush, George (Milton, Mass.)	6/12/24	Jordan, Barbara (Houston, Tex.)	2/21/36
Byrd, Robert (N. Wilkesboro, N.C.)	11/20/17	Kael, Pauline (Petaluma, Calif.)	6/19/19
Calderone, Dr. Mary (New York, N.Y.)	7/1/04	Kemp, Jack (Los Angeles, Cal.)	7/13/35
Carter, Jimmy (Plains, Ga.)	10/1/24	Kennedy, Edward M. (Brookline, Mass.)	2/22/32
Carter, Rosalynn (Plains, Ga.)	8/18/27	Kennedy, Rose (Boston, Mass.)	7/22/90
Casey, William J. (Queens, N.Y.)	3/13/13	Kerr, Walter (Evanston, Ill.)	7/8/13
Chancellor, John (Chicago, Ill.)	7/14/27	King, Coretta (Mrs. Martin L.) (Marion, Ala.)	4/27/27
Chavez, Cesar (Yuma, Ariz.)	3/31/27	Kirkland, Lane (Camden, S.C.)	3/12/22
Child, Julia (Pasadena, Cal.)	8/15/12	Kirkpatrick, Jeane (Duncan, Okla.)	11/19/26
Chisholm, Shirley (Brooklyn, N.Y.)	11/30/24	Kissinger, Henry (Fuerth, Germany)	5/27/23
Chung, Connie (Washington, D.C.)	8/20/46	Klein, Calvin (New York, N.Y.)	11/19/42
Cisneros, Henry (San Antonio, Tex.)	6/11/47	Koch, Edward I. (New York, N.Y.)	12/12/24
Claiborne, Craig (Sunflower, Miss.)	9/4/20	Koppel, Ted (Lancashire, Eng.)	2/8/40
Clark, William (Dallas, Tex.)	12/11/30	Landers, Ann (Sioux City, Ia.)	7/4/18
Collins, Martha (Shelby Cty, Ky.)	12/7/36	Landon, Alfred (West Middlesex, Pa.)	9/9/87
Commager, Henry Steele (Pittsburgh, Pa.)	10/25/02	Lauren, Ralph (Bronx, N.Y.)	10/14/39
Cooney, Joan Ganz (Phoenix, Ariz.)	10/30/29	Laxalt, Paul (Reno, Nev.)	8/2/22
Cosell, Howard (Winston-Salem, N.C.)	1920	Lindbergh, Anne Morrow (Englewood, N.J.)	1906
Cousins, Norman (Union Hill, N.J.)	6/24/12	Long, Russell B. (Shreveport, La.)	11/3/18
Cranston, Alan (Palo Alto, Cal.)	6/19/14	Luce, Clare Boothe (New York, N.Y.)	4/10/03
Crist, Judith (New York, N.Y.)	5/22/22	Manchester, William (Attleboro, Mass.)	4/1/22
Cronkite, Walter (St. Joseph, Mo.)	11/4/16	Mansfield, Mike (New York, N.Y.)	3/16/03
Cuomo, Mario (Queens, N.Y.)	6/15/32	Marshall, Thurgood (Baltimore, Md.)	7/2/08
Curtis, Charlotte (Chicago, Ill.)	1929	McCarthy, Eugene (Watkins, Minn.)	3/29/16
Deaver, Michael K. (Bakersfield, Cal.)	4/11/38	McGovern, George (Avon, S.D.)	7/19/22
Dodd, Christopher (Willimantic, Conn.)	5/27/44	McNamara, Robert S. (San Francisco, Cal.)	6/9/16
Dole, Elizabeth (Salisbury, N.C.)	7/29/36	Meese, Edwin (Oakland, Cal.)	12/2/31
Dole, Robert (Russell, Kan.)	7/22/23	Meredith, Don (Mt. Vernon, Tex.)	4/10/38
Domenici, Pete (Albuquerque, N.M.)	5/7/32	Metzenbaum, Howard (Cleveland, Oh.)	6/4/17
Donaldson, Sam (El Paso, Tex.)	3/11/34	Michel, Robert H. (Peoria, Ill.)	3/2/23
Doolittle, James H. (Alameda, Cal.)	12/14/96	Mondale, Walter (Ceylon, Minn.)	1/5/28
Ephron, Nora (New York, N.Y.)	5/19/41	Moynihan, Daniel P. (Tulsa, Okla.)	3/16/27
Falwell, Jerry (Lynchburg, Va.)	8/11/33	Mudd, Roger (Washington, D.C.)	2/9/28
Feinstein, Dianne (San Francisco, Cal.)	6/22/33	Muskie, Edmund (Rumford, Me.)	3/28/14
Feldstein, Martin (New York, N.Y.)	11/25/39	Nader, Ralph (Winsted, Conn.)	2/27/34
Fenwick, Millicent (New York, N.Y.)	2/25/10	Nixon, Pat (Ely, Nev.)	3/16/12
Ferraro, Geraldine (Newburgh, N.Y.)	8/26/35	Nixon, Richard (Yorba Linda, Cal.)	1/9/13
Foley, Thomas S. (Spokane, Wash.)	3/6/29	Nizer, Louis (London, England)	2/6/02
Ford, Betty (Chicago, Ill.)	4/8/18	Norton, Eleanor Holmes (Washington, D.C.)	6/13/37
Ford, Gerald R. (Omaha, Neb.)	7/14/13	Nunn, Sam (Perry, Ga.)	9/8/38

Name (Birthplace)	Birthdate	Name (Birthplace)	Birthdate
O'Connor, Sandra Day (nr. Duncan, Ariz.)	3/26/30	Smith, Margaret Chase (Skowhegan, Me.)	12/14/97
Ogilvy, David (W. Horsley, Eng.)	6/23/11	Spock, Benjamin (New Haven, Conn.)	5/2/03
Onassis, Jacqueline (Southampton, N.Y.)	7/28/29	Stahl, Leslie (Lynn, Mass.)	12/16/41
O'Neill, Thomas P. (Cambridge, Mass.)	12/9/12	Stassen, Harold (West St. Paul, Minn.)	4/13/07
Paley, William S. (Chicago, Ill.)	9/28/01	Steinbrenner, George (Rocky River, Oh.)	7/4/30
Pauley, Jane (Indianapolis, Ind.)	10/31/50	Steinem, Gloria (Toledo, Oh.)	3/25/34
Pauling, Linus (Portland, Ore.)	2/28/01	Stennis, John (Kamper City, Miss.)	8/3/01
Peale, Norman Vincent (Bowersville, Oh.)	5/31/98	Stevens, John Paul (Chicago, Ill.)	4/20/20
Pepper, Claude (Dudleyville, Ala.)	9/8/00	Stockman, David (Ft. Hood, Tex.)	11/10/46
Porter, Sylvia (Patchogue, N.Y.)	6/18/13	Sulzberger, Arthur Ochs (New York, N.Y.)	2/5/26
Powell, Lewis F. (Suffolk, Va.)	9/19/07	Taft, Robert Jr. (Cincinnati, Oh.)	2/26/17
Proxmire, William (Lake Forest, Ill.)	1/11/15	Terkel, Studs (New York, N.Y.)	5/16/12
Quinn, Jane Bryant (Niagara Falls, N.Y.)	2/5/39	Thomas, Helen (Winchester, Ky.)	8/4/20
Rather, Dan (Wharton, Tex.)	10/31/31	Thurmond, J. Strom (Edgefield, S.C.)	12/5/02
Reagan, Nancy (New York, N.Y.)	7/6/23	Tinker, Grant (Stamford, Conn.)	1/11/26
Reagan, Ronald (Tampico, Ill.)	2/6/11	Tower, John (Houston, Tex.)	9/29/25
Reasoner, Harry (Dakota City, Ia.)	4/17/23	Trillin, Calvin (Kansas City, Mo.)	12/5/35
Regan, Donald T. (Cambridge, Mass.)	12/21/18	Truman, Margaret (Independence, Mo.)	2/17/24
Rehnquist, William (Milwaukee, Wis.)	10/1/24	Trump, Donald (New York, N.Y.)	1946
Reston, James (Clydebank, Scotland)	11/3/09	Tuchman, Barbara (New York, N.Y.)	1/30/12
Richardson, Elliot L. (Boston, Mass.)	7/20/20	Turner, Ted (Cincinnati, Oh.)	1938
Rickover, Hyman (Makowa, Poland)	1/27/00	Udall, Morris K. (St. Johns, Ariz.)	6/15/22
Ride, Sally K. (Encino, Calif.)	1952	Ueberroth, Peter (Chicago, Ill.)	9/2/37
Roberts, Oral (nr. Ada, Okla.)	1/24/18	Van Buren, Abigail (Sioux City, Ia.)	7/4/18
Rockefeller, David (New York, N.Y.)	6/12/15	Vance, Cyrus R. (Clarksburg, W. Va.)	3/27/17
Rockefeller, John D. 4th "Jay" (New York, N.Y.)	6/18/37	Vanderbilt, Gloria (New York, N.Y.)	2/20/24
Rockefeller, Laurance S. (New York, N.Y.)	5/26/10	Veeck, Bill (Chicago, Ill.)	2/9/14
Rodino, Peter (Newark, N.J.)	6/7/09	Volcker, Paul A. (Cape May, N.J.)	9/5/27
Rooney, Andy (Albany, N.Y.)	1/14/19	Wallace, George (Clio, Ala.)	8/25/19
Ruckelshaus, William D. (Indianapolis, Ind.)	7/24/32	Wallace, Mike (Brookline, Mass.)	5/9/18
Rusk, Dean (Cherokee Co., Ga.)	2/9/09	Walters, Barbara (Boston, Mass.)	9/25/31
Safer, Morley (Toronto, Ontario)	11/8/31	Warhol, Andy (Pittsburgh, Pa.)	—
Safire, William (New York, N.Y.)	12/17/29	Washington, Harold (Chicago, Ill.)	4/15/22
Sagan, Carl (New York, N.Y.)	11/9/34	Watt, James G. (Lusk., Wyo.)	1/31/38
Salk, Jonas (New York, N.Y.)	10/28/14	Webster, William H. (St. Louis, Mo.)	3/6/24
Salk, Lee (New York, N.Y.)	12/27/26	Weicker, Lowell (Paris, France)	5/16/31
Sawyer, Diane (Glasgow, Ky.)	12/22/45	Weinberger, Caspar (San Francisco, Cal.)	8/18/17
Schlafly, Phyllis (St. Louis, Mo.)	8/15/24	Westmoreland, William (Spartanburg, S.C.)	3/26/14
Schlesinger, Arthur Jr. (Columbus, Oh.)	10/15/17	White, E.B. (Mt. Vernon, N.Y.)	7/11/99
Schroeder, Patricia (Portland, Ore.)	7/30/40	White, Theodore (Boston, Mass.)	5/6/15
Schuller, Robert (Alton, Ia.)	9/16/26	Wicker, Tom (Hamlet, N.C.)	6/18/26
Seaborg, Glenn T. (Ishpeming, Mich.)	4/19/12	Williams, Edward Bennett (Hartford, Conn.)	5/31/20
Sevareid, Eric (Velva, N.D.)	11/26/12	Wolfe, Tom (Richmond, Va.)	3/2/31
Shanker, Albert (New York, N.Y.)	9/14/28	Woodcock, Leonard (Providence, R.I.)	2/15/11
Shirer, William L. (Chicago, Ill.)	2/23/04	Woodruff, Judy (Tulsa, Okla.)	11/20/46
Shriver, R. Sargent (Westminster, Md.)	11/9/15	Woodward, Robert (Geneva, Ill.)	3/26/43
Shultz, George P. (New York, N.Y.)	12/13/20	Wright, James C. Jr. (Ft. Worth, Tex.)	12/22/22
Silverstein, Shel (Chicago, Ill.)	1932	Young, Andrew (New Orleans, La.)	3/12/32
Smeal, Eleanor (Ashtabula, Oh.)	7/30/39	Young, Coleman (Tuscaloosa, Ala.)	5/24/18
Smith, Howard K. (Ferriday, La.)	5/12/14		

Noted Black Americans

Names of black athletes and entertainers are not included here as they are listed elsewhere in The World Almanac.

The Rev. Dr. Ralph David Abernathy, b. 1926, organizer, 1957, and president, 1968, of the Southern Christian Leadership Conference.

Crispus Attucks, c. 1723-1770, agitator led group that precipitated the "Boston Massacre," Mar. 5, 1770.

James Baldwin, b. 1924, author, playwright; *The Fire Next Time, Blues for Mister Charlie, Just Above My Head.*

Benjamin Banneker, 1731-1806, inventor, astronomer, mathematician, and gazeteer; served on commission that surveyed and laid out Washington, D. C.

Imamu Amiri Baraka, b. LeRoi Jones, 1934, poet, playwright.

James P. Beckwourth, 1798-c. 1867, western fur-trader, scout, after whom Beckwourth Pass in northern California is named.

Dr. Mary McCleod Bethune, 1875-1955, adviser to presidents F. D. Roosevelt and Truman; division administrator, National Youth Administration, 1935; founder, president of Bethune-Cookman College.

Henry Blair, 19th century, obtained patents (believed the first issued to a black) for a corn-planter, 1834, and for a cotton-planter, 1836.

Julian Bond, b. 1940, civil rights leader first elected to the Georgia state legislature, 1965; helped found Student Nonviolent Coordinating Committee.

Edward Bouchet, 1852-1918, first black to earn a Ph.D., Yale, 1876, at a U. S. university; first black elected to Phi Beta Kappa.

Thomas Bradley, b. 1917, elected mayor of Los Angeles, 1973.

Andrew F. Brimmer, b. 1926, first black member, 1966, Federal Reserve Board.

Edward W. Brooke, b. 1919, attorney general, 1962, of Massachusetts; first black elected to U. S. Senate, 1967, since 19th century Reconstruction.

Gwendolyn Brooks, b. 1917, poet, novelist; first black to win a Pulitzer Prize, 1950, for *Annie Allen.*

William Wells Brown, 1815-1884, novelist, dramatist; first American black to publish a novel.

Dr. Ralph Bunche, 1904-1971, first black to win the Nobel Peace Prize, 1950; undersecretary of the UN, 1950.

George E. Carruthers, b. 1940, physicist developed the Apollo 16 lunar surface ultraviolet camera/spectograph.

George Washington Carver, 1861-1943, botanist, chemurgist, and educator; his extensive experiments in soil building and plant diseases revolutionized the economy of the South.

Charles Waddell Chestnutt, 1858-1932, author known primarily for his short stories, including *The Conjure Woman.*

Shirley Chisholm, b. 1924, first black woman elected to House of Representatives, Brooklyn, N.Y., 1968.

Countee Cullen, 1903-1946, poet; won many literary prizes.

Lt. Gen. Benjamin O. Davis Jr., b. 1912, West Point, 1936, first black Air Force general, 1954.

Brig. Gen. Benjamin O. Davis Sr., 1877-1970, first black general, 1940, in U. S. Army.

William L. Dawson, 1886-1970, Illinois congressman, first black chairman of a major House of Representatives committee.

Isaiah Dorman, 19th century, U. S. Army interpreter, killed with Custer, 1876, at Battle of the Little Big Horn.

Aaron Douglas, 1900-1979, painter; called father of black American art.

Frederick Douglass, 1817-1895, author, editor, orator, diplomat; edited the abolitionist weekly, The North Star, in Rochester, N. Y.; U.S. minister and consul general to Haiti.

Dr. Charles Richard Drew, 1904-1950, pioneer in development of blood banks; director of American Red Cross blood donor project in World War II.

William Edward Burghardt Du Bois, 1868-1963, historian, sociologist; a founder of the National Association for the Advancement of Colored People (NAACP), 1909, and founder of its magazine The Crisis; author, *The Souls of Black Folk.*

Paul Laurence Dunbar, 1872-1906, poet, novelist; won fame with *Lyrics of Lowly Life,* 1896.

Jean Baptiste Point du Sable, c. 1750-1818, pioneer trader and first settler of Chicago, 1779.

Ralph Ellison, b. 1914, novelist, winner of 1952 National Book Award, for *Invisible Man.*

Estevanico, explorer led Spanish expedition of 1538 into the American Southwest.

James Farmer, b. 1920, a founder of the Congress of Racial Equality, 1942; asst. secretary, Dept. of HEW, 1969.

Henry O. Flipper, 1856-1940, first black to graduate, 1877, from West Point.

Charles Fuller, b. 1939, Pulitzer Prize-winning playwright; *A Soldier's Play.*

Marcus Garvey, 1887-1940, founded Universal Negro Improvement Assn., 1911.

Kenneth Gibson, b. 1932, elected Newark, N.J., mayor, 1970.

Charles Gordone, b. 1925, won 1970 Pulitzer Prize in Drama, with *No Place to Be Somebody.*

Vice Adm. Samuel L. Gravely Jr. b. 1922, first black admiral, 1971, served in World War II, Korea, and Vietnam; commander, Third Fleet.

Alex Haley, b. 1921, Pulitzer Prize-winning author; *Roots, The Autobiography of Malcolm X.*

Jupiter Hammon, c. 1720-1800, poet; the first black American to have his works published, 1761.

Lorraine Hansberry, 1930-1965, playwright; won N. Y. Drama Critics Circle Award, 1959, with *Raisin in the Sun.*

Patricia Roberts Harris, 1924-1985, U. S. ambassador to Luxembourg, 1965-67, secretary; Dept. of HUD, 1977-1979, Dept. of H.H.S., 1979-1981.

William H. Hastie, 1904-1976 first black federal judge, appointed 1937; governor of Virgin Islands, 1946-49; judge, U.S. Circuit Court of Appeals, 1949.

Matthew A. Henson, 1866-1955, member of Peary's 1909 expedition to the North Pole; placed U.S. flag at the Pole.

Dr. William A. Hinton, 1883-1959, developed the Hinton and Davies-Hinton tests for detection of syphilis; first black professor, 1949, at Harvard Medical School.

Benjamin L. Hooks, b. 1925, first black member, 1972-1979, Federal Communications Comm.; exec. dir., 1977, NAACP.

Langston Hughes, 1902-1967, poet; story, song lyric author.

The Rev. Jesse Jackson, b. 1941, national director, Operation Bread Basket; campaigned for Democratic presidential nomination, 1984.

Maynard Jackson, b. 1938, elected mayor of Atlanta, 1973.

Gen. Daniel James Jr. 1920-1978, first black 4-star general, 1975; Commander, North American Air Defense Command.

Pvt. Henry Johnson, 1897-1929, the first American decorated by France in World War I with the Croix de Guerre.

James Weldon Johnson, 1871-1938, poet, lyricist, novelist; first black admitted to Florida bar; U.S. consul in Venezuela and Nicaragua.

Barbara Jordan, b. 1936, former congresswoman from Texas; member, House Judiciary Committee.

Vernon E. Jordan, b. 1935, exec. dir. Natl. Urban League, 1972.

Ernest E. Just, 1883-1941, marine biologist, studied egg development; author, *Biology of Cell Surfaces,* 1941.

The Rev. Dr. Martin Luther King Jr., 1929-1968, led 382-day, Montgomery, Ala., boycott that brought 1956 U.S. Supreme Court decision holding segregation on buses unconstitutional; founder, president of the Southern Christian Leadership Conference, 1957; won Nobel Peace Prize, 1964.

Lewis H. Latimer, 1848-1928, associate of Edison; supervised installation of first electric street lighting in N.Y.C.

Malcolm X, 1925-1965, leading spokesman for black pride, founded, 1963, Organization of Afro-American Unity.

Thurgood Marshall, b. 1908, first black U.S. solicitor general 1965; first black justice of the U. S. Supreme Court, 1967; as a lawyer led the legal battery that won the historic decision from the Supreme Court declaring racial segregation of public schools unconstitutional, 1954.

Jan Matzeliger, 1852-1889, invented lasting machine, patented 1883, which revolutionized the shoe industry.

Benjamin Mays, 1895-1984, educator, civil rights leader; headed Morehouse College, 1940-1967.

Wade H. McCree Jr., b. 1920, solicitor general of the U.S.

Donald E. McHenry, b. 1936, U.S. ambassador to the United Nations, 1979-1981.

Dorie Miller, 1919-1943, Navy hero of Pearl Harbor attack; awarded the Navy Cross.

Ernest N. Morial, b. 1929, elected first black mayor of New Orleans, 1977.

Toni Morrison, novelist; *Song of Solomon, Tar Baby.*

Willard Motley, 1912-1965, novelist; *Knock on Any Door.*

Elijah Muhammad, 1897-1975, founded Black Muslims, 1931.

Pedro Alonzo Nino, navigator of the Nina, one of Columbus' 3 ships on his first voyage of discovery to the New World, 1492.

Adam Clayton Powell, 1908-1972, early civil rights leader, congressman, 1945-1969; chairman, House Committee on Education and Labor, 1960-1967.

Joseph H. Rainey, 1832-1887, first black elected to House of Representatives, 1869, from South Carolina.

A. Philip Randolph, 1889-1979, organized the Brotherhood of Sleeping Car Porters, 1925; organizer of 1941 and 1963 March on Washington movements; vice president, AFL-CIO.

Charles Rangel, b. 1930, congressman from N.Y.C., 1970; chairman, Congressional Black Caucus.

Hiram R. Revels, 1822-1901, first black U.S. senator, elected in Mississippi, served 1870-1871.

Wilson C. Riles, b. 1917, elected, 1970, California State Superintendent of Public Instruction.

Norbert Rillieux, 1806-1894; invented a vacuum pan evaporator, 1846, revolutionizing the sugar-refining industry.

Paul Robeson, 1898-1976, actor and concert singer, graduated 1st in class at Rutgers, 1918, Phi Beta Kappa; grad. Columbia Univ. law school, 1923; associated with communist causes.

Carl T. Rowan, b. 1925, prize-winning journalist; director of the U.S. Information Agency, 1964, the first black to sit on the National Security Council; U. S. ambassador to Finland, 1963.

John B. Russwurm, 1799-1851, with **Samuel E. Cornish,** 1793-1858, founded, 1827, the nation's first black newspaper, Freedom's Journal, in N.Y.C.

Bayard Rustin, b. 1910, organizer of the 1963 March on Washington; executive director, A. Philip Randolph Institute.

Peter Salem, at the Battle of Bunker Hill, June 17, 1775, shot and killed British commander Maj. John Pitcairn.

Ntozake Shange, b. Paulette Williams, 1948, writer, *For Colored Girls Who Have Considered Suicide/When the Rainbow is Enuf.*

Bishop Stephen Spottswood, 1897-1974, board chairman of NAACP from 1966.

Willard Townsend, 1895-1957, organized the United Transport Service Employees, 1935 (redcaps, etc.); vice pres. AFL-CIO.

Sojourner Truth, 1797-1883, born Isabella Baumfree; preacher, abolitionist; raised funds for Union in Civil War; worked for black educational opportunities.

Harriet Tubman, 1823-1913, Underground Railroad conductor served as nurse and spy for Union Army in the Civil War.

Nat Turner, 1800-1831, leader of the most significant of over 200 slave revolts in U.S. history, in Southampton, Va.; he and 16 others were hanged.

Alice Walker, b. 1944, novelist, author of best-selling and award-winning *The Color Purple.*

Booker T. Washington, 1856-1915, founder, 1881, and first president of Tuskegee Institute; author, *Up From Slavery.*

Dr. Robert C. Weaver, b. 1907, first black member of the U.S. Cabinet, secretary, Dept. of HUD, 1966.

Phillis Wheatley, c. 1753-1784, poet; 2d American woman and first black woman to have her works published, 1770.

Walter White, 1893-1955, exec. secretary, NAACP, 1931-1955.

Roy Wilkins, 1901-1981, exec. director, NAACP, 1955-1977.

Dr. Daniel Hale Williams, 1858-1931, performed one of first 2 open-heart operations, 1893; founded Provident, Chicago's first Negro hospital; first black elected a fellow of the American College of Surgeons.

Granville T. Woods, 1856-1910, invented the third-rail system now used in subways, a complex railway telegraph device that helped reduce train accidents, and an automatic air brake.

Dr. Carter G. Woodson, 1875-1950, historian; founded Assn. for the Study of Negro Life and History, 1915, and Journal of Negro History, 1916.

Richard Wright, 1908-1960, novelist; *Native Son, Black Boy.*

Frank Yerby, b. 1916, first best-selling American black novelist; *The Foxes of Harrow, Vixen.*

Andrew Young, b. 1932, civil rights leader, congressman from Georgia, U.S. ambassador to the United Nations, 1977-79.

Whitney M. Young Jr., 1921-1971, exec. director, 1961, National Urban League; author, lecturer, newspaper columnist.

About 5,000 blacks served in the Continental Army during the **American Revolution,** mostly in integrated units, some in all-black combat units. Some 200,000 blacks served in the Union Army during the **Civil War;** 38,000 gave their lives; 22 won the Medal of Honor, the nation's highest award. Of 367,000 blacks in the armed forces during **World War I,** 100,000 served in France. More than 1,000,000 blacks served in the armed forces during **World War II;** all-black fighter and combat AAF units and infantry divisions gave distinguished service. In 1954 the policy of all-black units was finally abolished. Of 274,937 blacks who served in the armed forces during the **Vietnam War** (1965-1974), 5,681 were killed in combat.

As of Jan., 1984, there were 255 black mayors, 2,480 members of municipal governing bodies, 518 county officers, 4 state administrators, 385 state legislators, and 21 U.S. representatives. There are now 5,247 blacks holding elected office in the U.S. and Virgin Islands, an increase of 1.7% over the previous year, according to a survey by the Joint Center for Political Studies, Washington, D.C.,

Notable American Fiction Writers and Playwrights

Name (Birthplace)	Birthdate	Name (Birthplace)	Birthdate
Albee, Edward (Washington, D.C.)	3/12/28	LeGuin, Ursula (Berkeley, Cal.)	10/21/29
Anderson, Robert (New York, N.Y.)	4/28/17	Leonard, Elmore (New Orleans)	10/11/25
Asimov, Isaac (Petrovichi, Russia)	1/2/20	Levin, Ira (New York, N.Y.)	8/27/29
Auchincloss, Louis (Lawrence, N.Y.)	9/27/17	Ludlum, Robert (New York, N.Y.)	5/25/27
Baldwin, James (New York, N.Y.)	8/2/24	MacDonald, John D. (Sharon, Pa.)	7/24/16
Barth, John (Cambridge, Md.)	5/27/30	MacInnes, Helen (Glasgow, Scotland)	10/7/07
Barthelme, Donald (Philadelphia, Pa.)	1931	Mailer, Norman (Long Branch, N.J.)	1/31/23
Beattie, Ann (Washington, D.C.)	9/7/47	Malamud, Bernard (Brooklyn, N.Y.)	4/26/14
Bellow, Saul (Quebec, Canada)	7/10/15	Mamet, David (Chicago, Ill.)	11/30/47
Benchley, Peter (New York, N.Y.)	5/8/40	McCarthy, Mary (Seattle, Wash.)	6/21/12
Blume, Judy (Elizabeth, N.J.)	2/12/38	McMurtry, Larry (Wichita Falls, Tex.)	6/3/36
Bradbury, Ray (Waukegan, Ill.)	8/22/20	Michener, James A. (New York, N.Y.)	2/3/07
Brooks, Gwendolyn (Topeka, Kan.)	6/7/17	Miller, Arthur (New York, N.Y.)	10/17/15
Burrows, Abe (New York, N.Y.)	12/18/10	Morris, Wright (Central City, Neb.)	1/6/10
Caldwell, Erskine (Coweta Co., Ga.)	12/17/03	Morrison, Toni (Lorain, Oh.)	—
Caldwell, Taylor (London, England)	1900	Oates, Joyce Carol (Lockport, N.Y.)	6/16/38
Calisher, Hortense (New York, N.Y.)	12/20/11	Ozick, Cynthia (New York, N.Y.)	4/17/28
Carver, Raymond (Clatskanie, Ore.)	5/25/38	Paley, Grace (New York, N.Y.)	12/11/22
Clavell, James (England)	10/10/24	Percy, Walker (Birmingham, Ala.)	5/28/16
Cleary, Beverly (McMinnville, Ore.)		Potok, Chaim (New York, N.Y.)	2/17/29
Crews, Harry (Alma, Ga.)	6/6/35	Puzo, Mario (New York, N.Y.)	10/15/20
Crichton, Michael (Chicago, Ill.)	10/23/42	Pynchon, Thomas (Glen Cove, N.Y.)	5/8/37
De Vries, Peter (Chicago, Ill.)	2/27/10	Rabe, David (Dubuque, Ia.)	3/10/40
Dickey, James (Atlanta, Ga.)	2/2/23	Reed, Ishmael (Chattanooga, Tenn.)	2/22/38
Didion, Joan (Sacramento, Cal.)	12/5/34	Robbins, Harold (New York, N.Y.)	5/21/12
Doctorow, E. L. (New York, N.Y.)	1/6/31	Rogers, Rosemary (Panadora, Ceylon)	12/7/32
Drury, Allen (Houston, Tex.)	9/2/18	Roth, Henry (Austria-Hungary)	2/8/06
Dunne, John Gregory (Hartford, Conn.)	5/25/32	Roth, Philip (Newark, N.J.)	3/19/33
Elkin, Stanley (New York, N.Y.)	5/11/30	Salinger, J. D. (New York, N.Y.)	1/1/19
Ellison, Ralph (Oklahoma City, Okla.)	3/1/14	Sanders, Lawrence (New York, N.Y.)	1920
Fast, Howard (New York, N.Y.)	11/11/14	Scarry, Richard (Boston, Mass.)	6/5/19
Gaddis, William (New York, N.Y.)	1922	Schisgal, Murray (New York, N.Y.)	11/25/26
Geisel, Theodore ("Dr. Seuss,"		Schulberg, Budd (New York, N.Y.)	3/27/14
Springfield, Mass.)	3/2/04	Segal, Erich (Brooklyn, N.Y.)	6/16/37
Gibson, William (New York, N.Y.)	11/13/14	Sendak, Maurice (New York, N.Y.)	6/10/28
Gilroy, Frank (New York, N.Y.)	10/13/25	Shepard, Sam (Ft. Sheridan, Fla.)	11/5/42
Godwin, Gail (Birmingham, Ala.)	6/18/37	Simon, Neil (New York, N.Y.)	7/4/27
Goldman, William (Chicago, Ill.)	8/12/31	Singer, Isaac Bashevis (Radzymin, Poland)	7/14/04
Grau, Shirley Ann (New Orleans, La.)	7/8/29	Slaughter, Frank (Washington, D.C.)	2/25/08
Hailey, Arthur (Luton, England)	4/5/20	Spillane, Mickey (Brooklyn, N.Y.)	3/9/18
Haley, Alex (Ithaca, N.Y.)	8/11/21	Stegner, Wallace (Lake Mills, Ia.)	2/18/09
Hawkes, John (Stamford, Conn.)	8/17/25	Stone, Irving (San Francisco, Cal.)	7/14/03
Heinlein, Robert (Butler, Mon.)	7/7/07	Styron, William (Newport News, Va.)	6/11/25
Heller, Joseph (Brooklyn, N.Y.)	5/1/23	Theroux, Paul (Medford, Mass.)	4/10/41
Hellman, Lillian (New Orleans, La.)	6/20/07	Tyler, Anne (Minneapolis, Minn.)	10/25/41
Helprin, Mark (New York, N.Y.)	6/28/47		
Hersey, John (Tientsin, China)	6/17/14	Updike, John (Shillington, Pa.)	3/18/32
Himes, Chester (Jefferson City, Mo.)	7/29/09	Uris, Leon (Baltimore, Md.)	8/3/24
Irving, John (Exeter, N.H.)	3/2/42	Vidal, Gore (West Point, N.Y.)	10/3/25
		Vonnegut, Kurt Jr. (Indianapolis, Ind.)	11/11/22
Jaffe, Rona (New York, N.Y.)	6/12/32	Walker, Alice (Eatonton, Ga.)	1944
Jong, Erica (New York, N.Y.)	3/26/42	Wallace, Irving (Chicago, Ill.)	3/18/16
Kennedy, William (Albany, N.Y.)	1/16/28	Wambaugh, Joseph (East Pittsburgh, Pa.)	1/22/37
Kerr, Jean (Scranton, Pa.)	7/?/23	Warren, Robert Penn (Guthrie, Ky.)	4/24/05
Kesey, Ken (La Junta, Col.)	9/17/35	Welty, Eudora (Jackson, Miss.)	4/13/09
King, Stephen (Portland, Me.)	9/21/47	Wilson, Lanford (Lebanon, Mo.)	4/13/37
Kingsley, Sidney (New York, N.Y.)	10/22/06	Willingham, Calder (Atlanta, Ga.)	12/23/22
Knowles, John (Fairmont, W. Va.)	9/16/26	Wouk, Herman (New York, N.Y.)	5/27/15
Kosinski, Jerzy (Lódz, Poland)	6/14/33	Yerby, Frank (Augusta, Ga.)	9/5/16
L'Amour, Louis (Jamestown, N.D.)	—	Zindel, Paul (New York, N.Y.)	5/15/36
Lee, Harper (Alabama)	1926		

American Architects and Some of Their Achievements

Max Abramovitz, b. 1908, Avery Fisher Hall, Lincoln Center, N.Y.C.

Henry Bacon, 1866-1924, Lincoln Memorial.

Pietro Belluschi, b. 1899, Juilliard School of Music, Lincoln Center, N.Y.C.

Marcel Breuer, 1902-1981, Whitney Museum of American Art, N.Y.C. (with Hamilton Smith).

Charles Bulfinch, 1763-1844, State House, Boston; Capitol, Wash. D.C., (part).

Daniel H. Burnham, 1846-1912, Union Station, Wash. D.C.; Flatiron, N.Y.C.

Ralph Adams Cram, 1863-1942, Cathedral of St. John the Divine, N.Y.C.; U.S. Military Academy (part).

R. Buckminster Fuller, b. 1895, U.S. Pavilion, Expo 67, Montreal (geodesic domes).

Cass Gilbert, 1859-1934, Custom House, Woolworth Bldg., N.Y.C.; Supreme Court bldg., Wash., D.C.

Bertram G. Goodhue, 1869-1924, Capitol, Lincoln, Neb.; St. Thomas, St. Bartholomew, N.Y.C.

Walter Gropius, 1883-1969, Pan Am Building, N.Y.C. (with Pietro Belluschi).

Peter Harrison, 1716-1775, Touro Synagogue, Redwood Library, Newport, R.I.

Wallace K. Harrison, 1895-1981, Metropolitan Opera House, Lincoln Center, N.Y.C.

Thomas Hastings, 1860-1929, Public Library, Frick Mansion, N.Y.C.

James Hoban, 1762-1831, The White House.

William Holabird, 1854-1923, Crerar Library, City Hall, Chicago.

Raymond Hood, 1881-1934, Rockefeller Center, N.Y.C. (part); Daily News, N.Y.C.; Tribune, Chicago.

Richard M. Hunt, 1827-1895, Metropolitan Museum, N.Y.C. (part); Natl. Observatory, Wash., D.C.

William Le Baron Jenney, 1832-1907, Home Insurance, Chicago (demolished 1931).

Philip C. Johnson, b. 1906, N.Y. State Theater, Lincoln Center, N.Y.C.

Albert Kahn, 1869-1942, Athletic Club Bldg., General Motors Bldg., Detroit.

Louis Kahn, 1901-1974, Salk Laboratory, La Jolla, Cal.; Yale Art Gallery.

Christopher Grant LaFarge, 1862-1938, Roman Catholic Chapel, West Point.

Benjamin H. Latrobe, 1764-1820, U.S. Capitol (part).

William Lescaze, 1896-1969, Philadelphia Savings Fund Society; Borg-Warner Bldg., Chicago.

Charles F. McKim, 1847-1909, Public Library, Boston, Columbia Univ., N.Y.C.

Charles M. McKim, b. 1920, KUHT-TV Transmitter Building, Houston; Lutheran Church of the Redeemer, Houston.

Ludwig Mies van der Rohe, 1886-1969, Seagram Building, N.Y.C. (with Philip C. Johnson); National Gallery, Berlin.

Robert Mills, 1781-1855, Washington Monument.

Richard J. Neutra, 1892-1970, Mathematics Park, Princeton; Orange Co. Courthouse, Santa Ana, Cal.

Gyo Obata, b. 1923, Natl. Air & Space Mus., Smithsonian Institution; Dallas-Ft. Worth Airport.

Frederick L. Olmsted, 1822-1903, Central Park, N.Y.C.; Fairmount Park, Philadelphia.

Ieoh Ming Pei, b. 1917, National Center for Atmospheric Research, Boulder, Col.

William Pereira, b. 1909, Cape Canaveral; Transamerica Bldg., San Francisco.

John Russell Pope, 1874-1937, National Gallery.

John Portman, b. 1924, Peachtree Center, Atlanta.

James Renwick Jr., 1818-1895, Grace Church, St. Patrick's Cathedral, N.Y.C.; Smithsonian, Corcoran Galleries, Wash., D.C.

Henry H. Richardson, 1838-1886, Trinity Church, Boston.

Kevin Roche, b. 1922, Oakland Cal. Museum; Fine Arts Center, U. of Mass.

James Gamble Rogers, 1867-1947, Columbia-Presbyterian Medical Center, N.Y.C.; Northwestern Univ., Chicago.

John Wellborn Root, 1887-1963, Palmolive Building, Chicago; Hotel Statler, Washington; Hotel Tamanaco, Caracas.

Paul Rudolph, b. 1918, Jewitt Art Center, Wellesley College; Art & Architecture Bldg., Yale.

Eero Saarinen, 1910-1961, Gateway to the West Arch, St. Louis; Trans World Flight Center, N.Y.C.

Louis Skidmore, 1897-1962, AEC town site, Oak Ridge, Tenn.; Terrace Plaza Hotel, Cincinnati.

Clarence S. Stein, 1882-1975, Temple Emanu-El, N.Y.C.

Edward Durell Stone, 1902-1978, U.S. Embassy, New Delhi, India; (H. Hartford) Gallery of Modern Art, N.Y.C.

Louis H. Sullivan, 1856-1924, Auditorium, Chicago.

Richard Upjohn, 1802-1878, Trinity Church, N.Y.C.

Ralph T. Walker, 1889-1973, N.Y. Telephone Hdqrs., N.Y.C.; IBM Research Lab., Poughkeepsie, N.Y.

Roland A. Wank, 1898-1970, Cincinnati Union Terminal; head architect TVA, 1933-44.

Stanford White, 1853-1906, Washington Arch; first Madison Square Garden, N.Y.C.

Frank Lloyd Wright, 1867 or 1869-1959, Imperial Hotel, Tokyo; Guggenheim Museum, N.Y.C.

William Wurster, 1895-1973, Ghirardelli Sq., San Francisco; Cowell College, U. Cal., Berkeley.

Minoru Yamasaki, b. 1912, World Trade Center, N.Y.C.

Noted American Cartoonists

Charles Addams, b. 1912, noted for macabre cartoons.

Peter Arno, 1904-1968, noted for urban characterizations.

George Baker, 1915-1975, The Sad Sack.

C. C. Beck, b. 1910, Captain Marvel.

Herb Block (Herblock), b. 1909, leading political cartoonist.

Clare Briggs, 1875-1930, Mr. & Mrs.

Dik Browne, b. 1917, Hi & Lois, Hagar the Horrible.

Ernie Bushmiller, 1905-1982, Nancy.

Milton Caniff, b. 1907, Terry & the Pirates; Steve Canyon.

Al Capp, 1909-1979, Li'l Abner.

Paul Conrad, 1924, political cartoonist.

Roy Crane, 1901-1977, Captain Easy; Buz Sawyer.

Robert Crumb, b. 1943, "Underground" cartoonist.

Jay N. Darling (Ding), 1876-1962, political cartoonist.

Jim Davis, b. 1945, Garfield.

Billy DeBeck, 1890-1942, Barney Google.

Rudolph Dirks, 1877-1968, The Katzenjammer Kids.

Walt Disney, 1901-1966, producer of animated cartoons created Mickey Mouse & Donald Duck.

Jules Feiffer, b. 1929, satirical *Village Voice* cartoonist.

Bud Fisher, 1884-1954, Mutt & Jeff.

Ham Fisher, 1900-1955, Joe Palooka.

James Montgomery Flagg, 1877-1960, illustrator created the famous Uncle Sam recruiting poster during WWI.

Hal Foster, 1892-1982, Tarzan; Prince Valiant.

Fontaine Fox, 1884-1964, Toonerville Folks.

Rube Goldberg, 1883-1970, Boob McNutt.

Chester Gould, 1900-1985, Dick Tracy.

Harold Gray, 1894-1968, Little Orphan Annie.

Johnny Hart, b. 1931, BC, Wizard of Id.

Jimmy Hatlo, 1898-1963, Little Iodine.

John Held Jr., 1889-1958, "Jazz Age" cartoonist.

George Herriman, 1881-1944, Krazy Kat.

Harry Hershfield, 1885-1974, Able the Agent.

Burne Hogarth, b. 1911, Tarzan.

Helen Hokinson, 1900-1949, satirized clubwomen.

Walt Kelly, 1913-1973, Pogo.

Hank Ketcham, b. 1920, Dennis the Menace.

Ted Key, b. 1912, Hazel.

Frank King, 1883-1969, Gasoline Alley.

Jack Kirby, b. 1917, Captain America.

Rollin Kirby, 1875-1952, political cartoonist.

Walter Lantz, b. 1900, Woody Woodpecker.

Stan Lee, b. 1922, Spiderman, Incredible Hulk.

Bill Mauldin, b. 1921, depicted squalid life of the G.I. in WWII.

Jeff MacNelly, b. 1947, political cartoonist, and strip Shoe.

Winsor McCay, 1872-1934, Little Nemo.

John T. McCutcheon, 1870-1949, midwestern rural life.

George McManus, 1884-1954, Bringing Up Father (Maggie & Jiggs).

Dale Messick, b. 1906, Brenda Starr.

Bob Montana, 1920-1975, Archie.

Dick Moores, b. 1909, Gasoline Alley.

Willard Mullin, 1902-1978, sports cartoonist; created Dodgers "Bum" and Mets "Kid".

Russel Myers, b. 1938, Broom Hilda.

Thomas Nast, 1840-1902, political cartoonist; created the Democratic donkey and Republican elephant.

Pat Oliphant, b. 1935, political cartoonist.

Frederick Burr Opper, 1857-1937, Happy Hooligan.

Richard Outcault, 1863-1928, Yellow Kid; Buster Brown.

Mike Peters, b. 1943, editorial cartoonist.

Alex Raymond, 1909-1956, Flash Gordon; Jungle Jim.

Charles Schulz, b. 1922, Peanuts.

Elzie C. Segar, 1894-1938, Popeye.

Sydney Smith, 1887-1935, The Gumps.

Otto Soglow, 1900-1975, Little King; Canyon Kiddies.

James Swinnerton, 1875-1974, Little Jimmy.

James Thurber, 1894-1961, *New Yorker* cartoonist.

Garry Trudeau, b. 1948, Doonesbury.

Mort Walker, b. 1923, Beetle Bailey.

Russ Westover, 1887-1966, Tillie the Toiler.

Frank Willard, 1893-1958, Moon Mullins.

J. R. Williams, 1888-1957, The Willets Family; Out Our Way.

Gahan Wilson, b. 1930, cartoonist of the macabre.

Tom Wilson, b. 1931, Ziggy.

Art Young, 1866-1943, political radical and satirist.

Chic Young, 1901-1973, Blondie.

Noted Political Leaders of the Past

(U.S. presidents and most vice presidents, Supreme Court justices, signers of Declaration of Independence, listed elsewhere.)

Abu Bakr, 573-634, Mohammedan leader, first caliph, chosen successor to Mohammed.

Dean Acheson, 1893-1971, (U.S.) secretary of state, chief architect of cold war foreign policy.

Samuel Adams, 1722-1803, (U.S.) patriot, Boston Tea Party firebrand.

Konrad Adenauer, 1876-1967, (G.) West German chancellor.

Emilio Aguinaldo, 1869-1964, (Philip.) revolutionary, fought against Spain and the U.S.

Akbar, 1542-1605, greatest Mogul emperor of India.

Salvador Allende Gossens, 1908-1973, (Chil.) president, advocate of democratic socialism.

Herbert H. Asquith, 1852-1928, (Br.) Liberal prime minister, instituted an advanced program of social reform.

Atahualpa, ?-1533, Inca (ruling chief) of Peru.

Kemal Atatürk, 1881-1938, (Turk.) founded modern Turkey.

Clement Attlee, 1883-1967, (Br.) Labour party leader, prime minister, enacted national health, nationalized many industries.

Stephen F. Austin, 1793-1836, (U.S.) led Texas colonization.

Mikhail Bakunin, 1814-1876, (R.) revolutionary, leading exponent of anarchism.

Arthur J. Balfour, 1848-1930, (Br.) as foreign secretary under Lloyd George issued Balfour Declaration expressing official British approval of Zionism.

Bernard M. Baruch, 1870-1965, (U.S.) financier, gvt. adviser.

Fulgencio Batista y Zaldívar, 1901-1973, (Cub.) dictator overthrown by Castro.

Lord Beaverbrook, 1879-1964, (Br.) financier, statesman, newspaper owner.

Eduard Benes, 1884-1948, (Czech.) president during interwar and post-WW II eras.

David Ben-Gurion, 1886-1973, (Isr.) first premier of Israel.

Thomas Hart Benton, 1782-1858, (U.S.) Missouri senator, championed agrarian interests and westward expansion.

Lavrenti Beria, 1899-1953, (USSR) Communist leader prominent in political purges under Stalin.

Aneurin Bevan, 1897-1960, (Br.) Labour party leader.

Ernest Bevin, 1881-1951, (Br.) Labour party leader, foreign minister, helped lay foundation for NATO.

Otto von Bismarck, 1815-1898, (G.) statesman known as the Iron Chancellor, uniter of Germany, 1870.

James G. Blaine, 1830-1893, (U.S.) Republican politician, diplomat, influential in launching Pan-American movement.

Léon Blum, 1872-1950, (F.) socialist leader, writer, headed first Popular Front government.

Simón Bolívar, 1783-1830, (Venez.) South American revolutionary who liberated much of the continent from Spanish rule.

William E. Borah, 1865-1940, (U.S.) isolationist senator, instrumental in blocking U.S. membership in League of Nations and the World Court.

Cesare Borgia, 1476-1507, (It.) soldier, politician, an outstanding figure of the Italian Renaissance.

Leonid Brezhnev, 1906-1982, (USSR) leader of the Soviet Union, 1964-82.

Aristide Briand, 1862-1932, (F.) foreign minister, chief architect of Locarno Pact and anti-war Kellogg-Briand Pact.

William Jennings Bryan, 1860-1925, (U.S.) Democratic, populist leader, orator, 3 times lost race for presidency.

Nikolai Bukharin, 1888-1938, (USSR) communist leader.

William C. Bullitt, 1891-1967, (U.S.) diplomat, first ambassador to USSR, ambassador to France.

Ralph Bunche, 1904-1971, (U.S.) a founder and key diplomat of United Nations for more than 20 years.

John C. Calhoun, 1782-1850, (U.S.) political leader, champion of states' rights and a symbol of the Old South.

Robert Castlereagh, 1769-1822, (Br.) foreign secy, guided Grand Alliance against Napoleon.

Camillo Benso Cavour, 1810-1861, (It.) statesman, largely responsible for uniting Italy under the House of Savoy.

Austen Chamberlain, 1863-1937, (Br.) Conservative party leader, largely responsible for Locarno Pact of 1925.

Neville Chamberlain, 1869-1940, (Br.) Conservative prime minister whose appeasement of Hitler led to Munich Pact.

Salmon P. Chase, 1808-1873, (U.S.) public official, abolitionist, jurist, 6th Supreme Court chief justice.

Chiang Kai-shek, 1887-1975, (Chin.) Nationalist Chinese president whose govt. was driven from mainland to Taiwan.

Chou En-lai, 1898-1976, (Chin.) diplomat, prime minister, a leading figure of the Chinese Communist party.

Winston Churchill, 1874-1965, (Br.) prime minister, soldier, author, guided Britain through WW II.

Galeazzo Ciano, 1903-1944, (It.) fascist foreign minister, helped create Rome-Berlin Axis, executed by Mussolini.

Henry Clay, 1777-1852, (U.S.) "The Great Compromiser," one of most influential pre-Civil War political leaders.

Georges Clemenceau, 1841-1929, (F.) twice premier, Wilson's chief antagonist at Paris Peace Conference after WW I.

DeWitt Clinton, 1769-1828, (U.S.) political leader, responsible for promoting idea of the Erie Canal.

Robert Clive, 1725-1774, (Br.) first administrator of Bengal, laid foundation for British Empire in India.

Jean Baptiste Colbert, 1619-1683, (F.) statesman, influential under Louis XIV, created the French navy.

Oliver Cromwell, 1599-1658, (Br.) Lord Protector of England, led parliamentary forces during Civil War.

Curzon of Kedleston, 1859-1925, (Br.) viceroy of India, foreign secretary, major force in dealing with post-WW I problems in Europe and Far East.

Édouard Daladier, 1884-1970, (F.) radical socialist politician, arrested by Vichy, interned by Germans until liberation in 1945.

Georges Danton, 1759-1794, (F.) a leading figure in the French Revolution.

Jefferson Davis, 1808-1889, (U.S.) president of the Confederate States of America.

Charles G. Dawes, 1865-1951, (U.S.) statesman, banker, advanced Dawes Plan to stabilize post-WW I German finances.

Alcide De Gasperi, 1881-1954, (It.) premier, founder of the Christian Democratic party.

Charles DeGaulle, 1890-1970, (F.) general, statesman, and first president of the Fifth Republic.

Eamon De Valera, 1882-1975, (Ir.-U.S.) statesman, led fight for Irish independence.

Thomas E. Dewey, 1902-1971, (U.S.) New York governor, twice loser in try for presidency.

Ngo Dinh Diem, 1901-1963, (Viet.) South Vietnamese president, assassinated in government take-over.

Everett M. Dirksen, 1896-1969, (U.S.) Senate Republican minority leader, orator.

Benjamin Disraeli, 1804-1881, (Br.) prime minister, considered founder of modern Conservative party.

Engelbert Dollfuss, 1892-1934, (Aus.) chancellor, assassinated by Austrian Nazis.

Andrea Doria, 1466-1560, (It.) Genoese admiral, statesman, called "Father of Peace" and "Liberator of Genoa."

Stephen A. Douglas, 1813-1861, (U.S.) Democratic leader, orator, opposed Lincoln for the presidency.

John Foster Dulles, 1888-1959, (U.S.) secretary of state under Eisenhower, cold war policy maker.

Friedrich Ebert, 1871-1925, (G.) Social Democratic movement leader, instrumental in bringing about Weimar constitution.

Sir Anthony Eden, 1897-1977, (Br.) foreign secretary, prime minister during Suez invasion of 1956.

Ludwig Erhard, 1897-1977, (G.) economist, West German chancellor, led nation's economic rise after WW II.

Hamilton Fish, 1808-1893, (U.S.) secretary of state, successfully mediated disputes with Great Britain, Latin America.

James V. Forrestal, 1892-1949, (U.S.) secretary of navy, first secretary of defense.

Francisco Franco, 1892-1975, (Sp.) leader of rebel forces during Spanish Civil War and dictator of Spain.

Benjamin Franklin, 1706-1790, (U.S.) printer, publisher, author, inventor, scientist, diplomat.

Louis de Frontenac, 1620-1698, (F.) governor of New France (Canada); encouraged explorations, fought Iroquois.

Hugh Gaitskell, 1906-1963, (Br.) Labour party leader, major force in reversing its stand for unilateral disarmament.

Albert Gallatin, 1761-1849, (U.S.) secretary of treasury who was instrumental in negotiating end of War of 1812.

Léon Gambetta, 1838-1882, (F.) statesman, politician, one of the founders of the Third Republic.

Indira Gandhi, 1902-1984, (Ind.) succeeded father, Jawaharlal Nehru, as prime minister, assassinated.

Mohandas K. Gandhi, 1869-1948, (Ind.) political leader, ascetic, led nationalist movement against British rule.

Giuseppe Garibaldi, 1807-1882, (It.) patriot, soldier, a leading figure in the Risorgimento, the Italian unification movement.

Genghis Khan, c. 1167-1227, brilliant Mongol conqueror, ruler of vast Asian empire.

William E. Gladstone, 1809-1898, (Br.) prime minister 4 times, dominant force of Liberal party from 1868 to 1894.

Paul Joseph Goebbels, 1897-1945, (G.) Nazi propagandist, master of mass psychology.

Klement Gottwald, 1896-1953, (Czech.) communist leader ushered communism into his country.

Che (Ernesto) Guevara, 1928-1967, (Arg.) guerilla leader, prominent in Cuban revolution, killed in Bolivia.

Haile Selassie, 1891-1975, (Eth.) emperor, maintained monarchy through invasion, occupation, internal resistance.

Alexander Hamilton, 1755-1804, (U.S.) first treasury secretary, champion of strong central government.

Dag Hammarskjold, 1905-1961, (Swed.) statesman, UN secretary general.

John Hancock, 1737-1793, (U.S.) revolutionary leader, first signer of Declaration of Independence.

John Hay, 1838-1905, (U.S.) secretary of state, primarily associated with Open Door Policy toward China.

Patrick Henry, 1736-1799, (U.S.) major revolutionary figure, remarkable orator.

Édouard Herriot, 1872-1957, (F.) Radical Socialist leader, twice premier, president of National Assembly.

Theodor Herzl, 1860-1904, (Aus.) founder of modern Zionism.

Heinrich Himmler, 1900-1945, (G.) chief of Nazi SS and Gestapo, primarily responsible for the Holocaust.

Paul von Hindenburg, 1847-1934, (G.) field marshal, president.

Adolf Hitler, 1889-1945, (G.) dictator, founder of National Socialism.

Ho Chi Minh, 1890-1969, (Viet.) North Vietnamese president, Vietnamese Communist leader, national hero.

Harry L. Hopkins, 1890-1946, (U.S.) New Deal administrator, closest adviser to FDR during WW II.

Edward M. House, 1858-1938, (U.S.) diplomat, confidential adviser to Woodrow Wilson.

Samuel Houston, 1793-1863, (U.S.) leader of struggle to win control of Texas from Mexico.

Cordell Hull, 1871-1955, (U.S.) secretary of state, initiated reciprocal trade to lower tariffs, helped organize UN.

Hubert H. Humphrey, 1911-1978, (U.S.) Minnesota Democrat, senator, vice president, spent 32 years in public service.

Ibn Saud, c. 1888-1953, (S. Arab.) founder of Saudi Arabia and its first king.

Benito Juarez, 1806-1872, (Mex.) rallied countrymen against foreign threats, sought to create democratic, federal republic.

Frank B. Kellogg, 1856-1937, (U.S.) secretary of state, negotiated Kellogg-Briand Pact to outlaw war.

Robert F. Kennedy, 1925-1968, (U.S.) attorney general, senator, assassinated while seeking presidential nomination.

Aleksandr Kerensky, 1881-1970, (R.) revolutionary, served as premier after Feb. 1917 revolution until Bolshevik overthrow.

Nikita Khrushchev, 1894-1971, (USSR) premier, first secretary of Communist party, initiated de-Stalinization.

Lajos Kossuth, 1802-1894, (Hung.) principal figure in 1848 Hungarian revolution.

Pyotr Kropotkin, 1842-1921, (R.) anarchist, championed the peasants but opposed Bolshevism.

Kublai Khan, c. 1215-1294, Mongol emperor, founder of Yüan dynasty in China.

Béla Kun, 1886-c.1939, (Hung.) communist dictator, member of 3d International, tried to foment worldwide revolution.

Robert M. LaFollette, 1855-1925, (U.S.) Wisconsin public official, leader of progressive movement.

Pierre Laval, 1883-1945, (F.) politician, Vichy foreign minister, executed for treason.

Andrew Bonar Law, 1858-1923, (Br.) Conservative party politician, led opposition to Irish home rule.

Vladimir Ilyich Lenin (Ulyanov), 1870-1924, (USSR) revolutionary, founder of Bolshevism, Soviet leader 1917-1924.

Ferdinand de Lesseps, 1805-1894, (F.) diplomat, engineer, conceived idea of Suez Canal.

Liu Shoa-ch'i, c.1898-1974, (Chin.) communist leader, fell from grace during "cultural revolution."

Maxim Litvinov, 1876-1951, (USSR) revolutionary, commissar of foreign affairs, favored cooperation with Western powers.

David Lloyd George, 1863-1945, (Br.) Liberal party prime minister, laid foundations for modern welfare state.

Henry Cabot Lodge, 1850-1924, (U.S.) Republican senator, led opposition to participation in League of Nations.

Huey P. Long, 1893-1935, (U.S.) Louisiana political demagogue, governor, assassinated.

Rosa Luxemburg, 1871-1919, (G.) revolutionary, leader of the German Social Democratic party and Spartacus party.

J. Ramsay MacDonald, 1866-1937, (Br.) first Labour party prime minister of Great Britain.

Joseph R. McCarthy, 1908-1957, (U.S.) senator notorious for his witch hunt for communists in the government.

Makarios III, 1913-1977, (Cypr.) Greek Orthodox archbishop, first president of Cyprus.

Malcolm X (Malcolm Little), 1925-1965, (U.S.) black separatist leader, assassinated.

Mao Tse-tung, 1893-1976, (Chin.) chief Chinese Marxist theorist, soldier, led Chinese revolution establishing his nation as an important communist state.

Jean Paul Marat, 1743-1793, (F.) revolutionary, politician, identified with radical Jacobins, assassinated.

José Martí, 1853-1895, (Cub.) patriot, poet, leader of Cuban struggle for independence.

Jan Masaryk, 1886-1948, (Czech.) foreign minister, died by mysterious suicide following communist coup.

Thomas G. Masaryk, 1850-1937, (Czech.) statesman, philosopher, first president of Czechoslovak Republic.

Jules Mazarin, 1602-1661, (F.) cardinal, statesman, prime minister under Louis XIII and queen regent Anne of Austria.

Tom Mboya, 1930-1969, (Kenyan) political leader, instrumental in securing independence for his country.

Cosimo I de' Medici, 1519-1574, (It.) Duke of Florence, grand duke of Tuscany.

Lorenzo de' Medici, the Magnificent, 1449-1492, (It.) merchant prince, a towering figure in Italian Renaissance.

Catherine de Medicis, 1519-1589, (F.) queen consort of Henry II, regent of France, influential in Catholic-Huguenot wars.

Golda Meir, 1898-1979, (Isr.) prime minister, 1969-74.

Klemens W.N.L. Metternich, 1773-1859, (Aus.) statesman, arbiter of post-Napoleonic Europe.

Anastas Mikoyan, 1895-1978, (USSR) prominent Soviet leader from 1917; president 1964-65.

Guy Mollet, 1905-1975, (F.) social politician, resistance leader.

Henry Morgenthau Jr., 1891-1967, (U.S.) secretary of treasury, raised funds to finance New Deal and U.S. WW II activities.

Gouverneur Morris, 1752-1816, (U.S.) statesman, diplomat, financial expert who helped plan decimal coinage system.

Wayne Morse, 1900-1974, (U.S.) senator, long-time critic of Vietnam War.

Muhammad Ali, 1769?-1849, (Egypt), pasha, founder of dynasty that encouraged emergence of modern Egyptian state.

Benito Mussolini, 1883-1945, (It.) dictator and leader of the Italian fascist state.

Imre Nagy, c. 1895-1958, (Hung.) communist premier, assassinated after Soviets crushed 1956 uprising.

Gamel Abdel Nasser, 1918-1970, (Egypt.) leader of Arab unification, second Egyptian president.

Jawaharlal Nehru, 1889-1964, (Ind.) prime minister, guided India through its early years of independence.

Kwame Nkrumah, 1909-1972, (Ghan.) dictatorial prime minister, deposed in 1966.

Frederick North, 1732-1792, (Br.) prime minister, his inept policies led to loss of American colonies.

Daniel O'Connell, 1775-1847, (Ir.) political leader, known as The Liberator.

Omar, c.581-644, Mohammedan leader, 2d caliph, led Islam to become an imperial power.

Ignance Paderewski, 1860-1941, (Pol.) statesman, pianist, composer, briefly prime minister, an ardent patriot.

Viscount Palmerston, 1784-1865, (Br.) Whig-Liberal prime minister, foreign minister, embodied British nationalism.

George Papandreou, 1888-1968, (Gk.) Republican politician, served three times as prime minister.

Franz von Papen, 1879-1969, (G.) politician, played major role in overthrow of Weimar Republic and rise of Hitler.

Charles Stewart Parnell, 1864-1891, (Ir.) nationalist leader, "uncrowned king of Ireland."

Lester Pearson, 1897-1972, (Can.) diplomat, Liberal party leader, prime minister.

Robert Peel, 1788-1850, (Br.) reformist prime minister, founder of Conservative party.

Juan Perón, 1895-1974, (Arg.) president, dictator.

Joseph Pilsudski, 1867-1935, (Pol.) statesman, instrumental in re-establishing Polish state in the 20th century.

Charles Pinckney, 1757-1824, (U.S.) founding father, his Pinckney plan was largely incorporated into constitution.

William Pitt, the Elder, 1708-1778, (Br.) statesman, called the "Great Commoner," transformed Britain into imperial power.

William Pitt, the Younger, 1759-1806, (Br.) prime minister during French Revolutionary wars.

Georgi Plekhanov, 1857-1918, (R.) revolutionary, social philosopher, called "father of Russian Marxism."

Raymond Poincaré, 1860-1934, (F.) 9th president of the Republic, advocated harsh punishment of Germany after WW I.

Georges Pompidou, 1911-1974, (F.) Gaullist political leader, president from 1969 to 1974.

Grigori Potemkin, 1739-1791, (R.) field marshal, favorite of Catherine II.

Edmund Randolph, 1753-1813, (U.S.) attorney, prominent in drafting, ratification of constitution.

John Randolph, 1773-1833, (U.S.) southern planter, strong advocate of states' rights.

Jeannette Rankin, 1880-1973, (U.S.) pacifist, first woman member of U.S. Congress.

Walter Rathenau, 1867-1922, (G.) industrialist, social theorist, statesman.

Sam Rayburn, 1882-1961, (U.S.) Democratic leader, representative for 47 years, House speaker for 17.

Paul Reynaud, 1878-1966, (F.) statesman, premier in 1940 at the time of France's defeat by Germany.

Syngman Rhee, 1875-1965, (Kor.) first president of the Republic of Korea.

Cecil Rhodes, 1853-1902, (Br.) imperialist, industrial magnate, established Rhodes scholarships in his will.

Cardinal de Richelieu, 1585-1642, (F.) statesman, known as "red eminence," chief minister to Loius XIII.

Maximilien Robespierre, 1758-1794, (F.) leading figure of French Revolution, responsible for much of Reign of Terror.

Nelson Rockefeller, 1908-1979, (U.S.) Republican gov. of N.Y., 1959-73; U.S. vice president, 1974-77.

Eleanor Roosevelt, 1884-1962, (U.S.) humanitarian, United Nations diplomat.

Elihu Root, 1845-1937, (U.S.) lawyer, statesman, diplomat, leading Republican supporter of the League of Nations.

John Russell, 1792-1878, (Br.) Liberal prime minister during the Irish potato famine.

Anwar el-Sadat, 1918-1981, (Egypt) president, 1970-1981, promoted peace with Israel.

Antônio de O. Salazar, 1899-1970, (Port.) statesman, long-time dictator.

José de San Martin, 1778-1850, South American revolutionary, protector of Peru.

Eisaku Sato, 1901-1975, (Jap.) prime minister, presided over Japan's post-WW II emergence as major world power.

Philipp Scheidemann, 1865-1939, (G.) Social Democratic leader, first chancellor of the German republic.

Robert Schuman, 1886-1963, (F.) statesman, founded European Coal and Steel Community.

Carl Schurz, 1829-1906, (U.S.) German-American political leader, journalist, orator, dedicated reformer.

Kurt Schuschnigg, 1897-1977, (Aus.) chancellor, unsuccessful in stopping his country's annexation by Germany.

William H. Seward, 1801-1872, (U.S.) anti-slavery activist, as Lincoln's secretary of state purchased Alaska.

Carlo Sforza, 1872-1952, (It.) foreign minister, anti-fascist.

Alfred E. Smith, 1873-1944, (U.S.) New York Democratic governor, first Roman Catholic to run for presidency.

Jan C. Smuts, 1870-1950, (S.Af.) statesman, philosopher, soldier, prime minister.

Paul Henri Spaak, 1899-1972, (Belg.) statesman, socialist leader.

Joseph Stalin, 1879-1953, (USSR) Soviet dictator, 1924-53.

Edwin M. Stanton, 1814-1869, (U.S.) Lincoln's secretary of war during the Civil War.

Edward R. Stettinius Jr., 1900-1949, (U.S.) industrialist, secretary of state who coordinated aid to WW II allies.

Adlai E. Stevenson, 1900-1865, (U.S.) Democratic leader, diplomat, Illinois governor, presidential candidate.

Henry L. Stimson, 1867-1950, (U.S.) statesman, served in 5 administrations, influenced foreign policy in 1930s and 1940s.

Gustav Stresemann, 1878-1929, (G.) chancellor, foreign minister, dedicated to regaining friendship for post-WW I Germany.

Sukarno, 1901-1970, (Indon.) dictatorial first president of the Indonesian republic.

Sun Yat-sen, 1866-1925, (Chin.) revolutionary, leader of Kuomintang, regarded as the father of modern China.

Robert A. Taft, 1889-1953, (U.S.) conservative Senate leader, called "Mr. Republican."

Charles de Talleyrand, 1754-1838, (F.) statesman, diplomat, the major force of the Congress of Vienna of 1814-15.

U Thant, 1909-1974 (Bur.) statesman, UN secretary-general.

Norman M. Thomas, 1884-1968, (U.S.) social reformer, 6 times unsuccessful Socialist party presidential candidate.

Josip Broz Tito, 1892-1980, (Yug.) president of Yugoslavia from 1953, World War II guerrilla chief, postwar rival of Stalin, leader of 3d world movement.

Palmiro Togliatti, 1893-1964, (It.) major leader of Italian Communist party.

Hideki Tojo, 1885-1948, (Jap.) statesman, soldier, prime minister during most of WW II.

François Toussaint L'Ouverture, c. 1744-1803, (Hait.) patriot, martyr, thwarted French colonial aims.

Leon Trotsky, 1879-1940, (USSR) revolutionary, founded Red Army, expelled from party in conflict with Stalin.

Rafael L. Trujillo Molina, 1891-1961, (Dom.) absolute dictator, assassinated.

Moise K. Tshombe, 1919-1969, (Cong.) politician, president of secessionist Katanga, premier of Republic of Congo (Zaire).

William M. Tweed, 1823-1878, (U.S.) politician, absolute leader of Tammany Hall, NYC's Democratic political machine.

Walter Ulbricht, 1893-1973, (G.) communist leader of German Democratic Republic.

Arthur H. Vandenberg, 1884-1951, (U.S.) senator, proponent of anti-communist bipartisan foreign policy after WW II.

Eleutherios Venizelos, 1864-1936, (Gk.) most prominent Greek statesman in early 20th century; expanded territory.

Hendrik F. Verwoerd, 1901-1966, (S.Af.) prime minister, rigorously applied apartheid policy despite protest.

Robert Walpole, 1676-1745, (Br.) statesman, generally considered Britain's first prime minister.

Daniel Webster, 1782-1852, (U.S.) orator, politician, advocate of business interests during Jacksonian agrarianism.

Chaim Weizmann, 1874-1952, Zionist leader, scientist, first Israeli president.

Wendell L. Wilkie, 1892-1944, (U.S.) Republican who tried to unseat FDR when he ran for his 3d term.

Emiliano Zapata, c. 1879-1919, (Mex.) revolutionary, major influence on modern Mexico.

Notable Military and Naval Leaders of the Past

Creighton Abrams, 1914-1974, (U.S.) commanded forces in Vietnam, 1968-72.

Harold Alexander, 1891-1969, (Br.) led Allied invasion of Italy, 1943.

Ethan Allen, 1738-1789, (U.S.) headed Green Mountain Boys; captured Ft. Ticonderoga, 1775.

Edmund Allenby, 1861-1936, (Br.) in Boer War, WW1; led Egyptian expeditionary force, 1917-18.

Benedict Arnold, 1741-1801, (U.S.) victorious at Saratoga; tried to betray West Point to British.

Henry "Hap" Arnold, 1886-1950, (U.S.) commanded Army Air Force in WW2.

Petr Bagration, 1765-1812, (R.) hero of Napoleonic wars.

John Barry, 1745-1803, (U.S.) won numerous sea battles during revolution.

Pierre Beauregard, 1818-1893, (U.S.) Confederate general ordered bombardment of Ft. Sumter that began the Civil War.

Gebhard v. Blücher, 1742-1819, (G.) helped defeat Napoleon at Waterloo.

Napoleon Bonaparte, 1769-1821, (F.) defeated Russia and Austria at Austerlitz, 1805; invaded Russia, 1812; defeated at Waterloo, 1815.

Edward Braddock, 1695-1755, (Br.) commanded forces in French and Indian War.

Omar N. Bradley, 1893-1981, (U.S.) headed U.S. ground troops in Normandy invasion, 1944.

John Burgoyne, 1722-1792, (Br.) defeated at Saratoga.

Claire Chennault, 1890-1958, (U.S.) headed Flying Tigers in WW2.

Mark Clark, 1896-1984, (U.S.) led forces in WW2 and Korean War.

Karl v. Clausewitz, 1780-1831, (G.) wrote books on military theory.

Henry Clinton, 1738-1795, (Br.) commander of forces in America, 1778-81.

Lucius D. Clay, 1897-1978, (U.S.) led Berlin airlift, 1948-49.

Charles Cornwallis, 1738-1805, (Br.) victorious at Brandywine, 1777; surrendered at Yorktown.

Crazy Horse, 1849-1877, (U.S.) Sioux war chief victorious at Little Big Horn.

George A. Custer, 1839-1876, (U.S.) defeated and killed at Little Big Horn.

Moshe Dayan, 1915-1981, (Isr.) directed campaigns in the 1967, 1973 wars.

Stephen Decatur, 1779-1820, (U.S.) naval hero of Barbary wars, War of 1812.

Anton Denikin, 1872-1947, (R.) led White forces in Russian civil war.

George Dewey, 1837-1917, (U.S.) destroyed Spanish fleet at Manila, 1898.

Hugh C. Dowding, 1883-1970, (Br.) headed RAF, 1936-40.

Jubal Early, 1816-1894, (U.S.) Confederate general led raid on Washington, 1864.

Dwight D. Eisenhower, 1890-1969, (U.S.) commanded Allied forces in Europe, WW2.

David Farragut, 1801-1870, (U.S.) Union admiral captured New Orleans, Mobile Bay.

Ferdinand Foch, 1851-1929, (F.) headed victorious Allied armies, 1918.

Nathan Bedford Forrest, 1821-1877, (U.S.) Confederate general led cavalry raids against Union supply lines.

Frederick the Great, 1712-1786, (G.) led Prussia in The Seven Years War.

Nathanael Greene, 1742-1786, (U.S.) defeated British in Southern campaign, 1780-81.

Charles G. Gordon, 1833-1885, (Br.) led forces in China; killed at Khartoum.

Horatio Gates, 1728-1806, (U.S.) commanded army at Saratoga.

Ulysses S. Grant, 1822-1885, (U.S.) headed Union army, 1864-65; forced Lee's surrender, 1865.

Heinz Guderian, 1888-1953, (G.) tank theorist led panzer forces in Poland, France, Russia.

Douglas Haig, 1861-1928, (Br.) led British armies in France, 1915-18.

William F. Halsey, 1882-1959, (U.S.) defeated Japanese fleet at Leyte Gulf, 1944.

Sir Arthur Travers Harris, 1895-1984, (Br.) led Britain's WWII bomber command.

Richard Howe, 1726-1799, (Br.) commanded navy in America, 1776-78; first of June victory against French, 1794.

William Howe, 1729-1814, (Br.) commanded forces in America, 1776-78.

Isaac Hull, 1773-1843, (U.S.) sunk British frigate Guerriere, 1812.

Thomas (Stonewall) Jackson, 1824-1863, (U.S.) Confederate general led forces in the Shenandoah Valley campaign.

Joseph Joffre, 1852-1931, (F.) headed Allied armies, won Battle of the Marne, 1914.

Battle of the Marne, 1914.

John Paul Jones, 1747-1792, (U.S.) raided British coast; commanded Bonhomme Richard in victory over Serapis, 1779.

Stephen Kearny, 1794-1848, (U.S.) headed Army of the West in Mexican War.

Ernest J. King, 1878-1956, (U.S.) chief naval strategist in WW2.

Horatio H. Kitchener, 1850-1916, (Br.) led forces in Boer War; victorious at Khartoum; organized army in WW1.

Lavrenti Kornilov, . 1870-1918, (R.) Commander-in-Chief, 1917; led counter-revolutionary march on Petrograd.

Thaddeus Kosciusko, 1746-1817, (P.) aided American cause in revolution.

Mikhail Kutuzov, 1745-1813, (R.) fought French at Borodino, 1812; abandoned Moscow; forced French retreat.

Marquis de Lafayette, 1757-1834, (F.) aided American cause in the revolution.

Thomas E. Lawrence (of Arabia), 1888-1935, (Br.) organized revolt of Arabs against Turks in WW1.

Henry (Light-Horse Harry) Lee, 1756-1818, (U.S.) cavalry officer in revolution.

Robert E. Lee, 1807-1870, (U.S.) Confederate general defeated at Gettysburg; surrendered to Grant, 1865.

James Longstreet, 1821-1904, (U.S.) aided Lee at Gettysburg.

Douglas MacArthur, 1880-1964, (U.S.) commanded forces in SW Pacific in WW2; headed occupation forces in Japan, 1945-50; UN commander in Korean War.

Francis Marion, 1733-1795, (U.S.) led guerrilla actions in S.C. during revolution.

Duke of Marlborough, 1650-1722, (Br.) led forces against Louis XIV in War of the Spanish Sucession.

George C. Marshall, 1880-1959, (U.S.) chief of staff in WW2; authored Marshall Plan.

George B. McClellan, 1826-1885, (U.S.) Union general commanded Army of the Potomac, 1861-62.

George Meade, 1815-1872, (U.S.) commanded Union forces at Gettysburg.

Billy Mitchell, 1879-1936, (U.S.) air-power advocate; court-martialed for insubordination, later vindicated.

Helmuth v. Moltke, 1800-1891; (G.) victorious in Austro-Prussian, Franco-Prussian wars.

Louis de Montcalm, 1712-1759, (F.) headed troops in Canada; defeated at Quebec, 1759.

Bernard Law Montgomery, 1887-1976, (Br.) stopped German offensive at Alamein, 1942; helped plan Normandy invasion.

Daniel Morgan, 1736-1802, (U.S.) victorious at Cowpens, 1781.

Louis Mountbatten, 1900-1979, (Br.) Supreme Allied Commander of SE Asia, 1943-46.

Joachim Murat, 1767-1815, (F.) leader of cavalry at Marengo, 1800; Austerlitz, 1805; and Jena, 1806.

Horatio Nelson, 1758-1805, (Br.) naval commander destroyed French fleet at Trafalgar.

Michel Ney, 1769-1815, (F.) commanded forces in Switzerland, Austria, Russia; defeated at Waterloo.

Chester Nimitz, 1885-1966, (U.S.) commander of naval forces in Pacific in WW2.

George S. Patton, 1885-1945, (U.S.) led assault on Sicily, 1943; headed 3d Army invasion of German-occupied Europe.

Oliver Perry, 1785-1819, (U.S.) won Battle of Lake Erie in War of 1812.

John Pershing, 1860-1948, (U.S.) commanded Mexican border campaign, 1916; American expeditionary forces in WW1.

Henri Philippe Pétain, 1856-1951, (F.) defended Verdun, 1916; headed Vichy government in WW2.

George E. Pickett, 1825-1875, (U.S.) Confederate general famed for "charge" at Gettysburg.

Erwin Rommel, 1891-1944, (G.) headed Afrika Korps.

Karl v. Rundstedt, 1875-1953, (G.) supreme commander in West, 1943-45.

Aleksandr Samsonov, 1859-1914, (R.) led invasion of E. Prussia, defeated at Tannenberg, 1914.

Winfield Scott, 1786-1866, (U.S.) hero of War of 1812; headed forces in Mexican war, took Mexico City.

Philip Sheridan, 1831-1888, (U.S.) Union cavalry officer headed Army of the Shenandoah, 1864-65.

William T. Sherman, 1820-1891, (U.S.) Union general sacked Atlanta during "march to the sea," 1864.

Carl Spaatz, 1891-1974, (U.S.) directed strategic bombing against Germany, later Japan, in WW2.

Raymond Spruance, 1886-1969, (U.S.) victorious at Midway Island, 1942.

Joseph W. Stilwell, 1883-1946, (U.S.) headed forces in the China, Burma, India theater in WW2.

J.E.B. Stuart, 1833-1864, (U.S.) Confederate cavalry commander.

George H. Thomas, 1816-1870, (U.S.) saved Union army at Chattanooga, 1863; victorious at Nashville, 1864.

Semyon Timoshenko, 1895-1970, (USSR) defended Moscow, Stalingrad; led winter offensive, 1942-43.

Alfred v. Tirpitz, 1849-1930, (G.) responsible for submarine blockade in WW1.

Jonathan M. Wainwright, 1883-1953, (U.S.) forced to surrender on Corregidor, 1942.

George Washington, 1732-1799, (U.S.) led Continental army, 1775-83.

Archibald Wavell, 1883-1950, (Br.) commanded forces in N. and E. Africa, and SE Asia in WW2.

Anthony Wayne, 1745-1796, (U.S.) captured Stony Point, 1779; defeated Indians at Fallen Timbers, 1794.

Duke of Wellington, 1769-1852, (Br.) defeated Napoleon at Waterloo.

James Wolfe, 1727-1759, (Br.) captured Quebec from French, 1759.

Georgi Zhukov, 1895-1974, (USSR) defended Moscow, 1941; led assault on Berlin.

Poets Laureate of England

There is no authentic record of the origin of the office of Poet Laureate of England. According to Warton, there was a Versificator Regis, or King's Poet, in the reign of Henry III (1216-1272), and he was paid 100 shillings a year. Geoffrey Chaucer (1340-1400) assumed the title of Poet Laureate, and in 1389 got a royal grant of a yearly allowance of wine. In the reign of Edward IV (1461-1483), John Kay held the post. Under Henry VII (1485-1509), Andrew Bernard was the Poet Laureate, and was succeeded under Henry VIII (1509-1547) by John Skelton. Next came Edmund Spenser, who died in 1599; then Samuel Daniel, appointed 1599, and then Ben Jonson, 1619. Sir William D'Avenant was appointed in 1637. He was a godson of William Shakespeare.

Others were John Dryden, 1670; Thomas Shadwell, 1688; Nahum Tate, 1692; Nicholas Rowe, 1715; the Rev. Laurence Eusden, 1718; Colley Cibber, 1730; William Whitehead, 1757, on the refusal of Gray; Rev. Thomas Warton, 1785, on the refusal of Mason; Henry J. Pye, 1790; Robert Southey, 1813, on the refusal of Sir Walter Scott; William Wordsworth, 1843; Alfred, Lord Tennyson, 1850; Alfred Austin, 1896; Robert Bridges, 1913; John Masefield, 1930; Cecil Day Lewis, 1967; Sir John Betjeman, 1972-1984; Ted Hughes, 1984-.

Noted Writers of the Past

Henry Adams, 1838-1918, (U.S.) historian, philosopher. *The Education of Henry Adams.*

George Ade, 1866-1944, (U.S.) humorist. *Fables in Slang.*

Conrad Aiken, 1889-1973, (U.S.) poet, critic.

Louisa May Alcott, 1832-1888, (U.S.) novelist. *Little Women.*

Sholom Aleichem, 1859-1916. (R.) Yiddish writer. *Tevye's Daughter, The Great Fair.*

Horatio Alger, 1832-1899, (U.S.) "rags-to-riches" books.

Hans Christian Anderson, 1805-1875, (Den.) author of fairy tales. *The Princess and the Pea, The Ugly Duckling.*

Maxwell Anderson, 1888-1959, (U.S.) playwright. *What Price Glory?, High Tor, Winterset, Key Largo.*

Sherwood Anderson, 1876-1941, (U.S.) author. *Winesburg, Ohio.*

Matthew Arnold, 1822-1888, (Br.) poet, critic. "Thrysis," "Dover Beach."

Jane Austen, 1775-1817, (Br.) novelist. *Pride and Prejudice, Sense and Sensibility, Emma, Mansfield Park.*

Isaac Babel, 1894-1941, (R.) short-story writer, playwright. *Odessa Tales, Red Cavalry.*

Enid Bagnold, 1890-1981, (Br.) playwright, novelist. *National Velvet.*

James M. Barrie, 1860-1937, (Br.) playwright, novelist. *Peter Pan, Dear Brutus, What Every Woman Knows.*

Honoré de Balzac, 1799-1850, (Fr.) novelist. *Le Père Goriot, Cousine Bette, Eugénie Grandet, The Human Comedy.*

Charles Baudelaire, 1821-1867, (Fr.) symbolist poet. *Les Fleurs du Mal.*

L. Frank Baum, 1856-1919, (U.S.) children's author. *Wizard of Oz* series.

Brendan Behan, 1923-1964, (Ir.) playwright. *The Quare Fellow, The Hostage, Borstal Boy.*

Robert Benchley, 1889-1945, (U.S.) humorist. *From Bed to Worse, My Ten Years in a Quandary.*

Stephen Vincent Benét, 1898-1943, (U.S.) poet, novelist. *John Brown's Body.*

John Berryman, 1914-1972, (U.S.) poet. *Homage to Mistress Bradstreet.*

Ambrose Bierce, 1842-1914, (U.S.) short-story writer, journalist. *In the Midst of Life, The Devil's Dictionary.*

William Blake, 1757-1827, (Br.) poet, mystic, artist. *Songs of Innocence, Songs of Experience.*

Giovanni Boccaccio, 1313-1375, (It.) poet, storyteller. *Decameron, Filostrato.*

James Boswell, 1740-1795, (Sc.) author. *The Life of Samuel Johnson.*

Anne Bradstreet, c. 1612-1672, (U.S.) poet. *The Tenth Muse Lately Sprung Up in America.*

Bertolt Brecht, 1898-1956, (G.) dramatist, poet. *The Threepenny Opera, Mother Courage and Her Children.*

Charlotte Brontë, 1816-1855, (Br.) novelist. *Jane Eyre.*

Emily Brontë, 1818-1848, (Br.) novelist. *Wuthering Heights.*

Elizabeth Barrett Browning, 1806-1861, (Br.) poet. *Sonnets from the Portuguese.*

Robert Browning, 1812-1889, (Br.) poet. *"My Last Duchess," "Soliloquy of the Spanish Cloister."*

Pearl Buck, 1892-1973, (U.S.) novelist. *The Good Earth.*

Mikhail Bulgakov, 1891-1940, (R.) novelist, playwright. *The Heart of a Dog, The Master and Margarita.*

John Bunyan, 1628-1688, (Br.) writer. *Pilgrim's Progress.*

Robert Burns, 1759-1796, (Sc.) poet. *"Flow Gently, Sweet Afton," "My Heart's in the Highlands," "Auld Lang Syne."*

Edgar Rice Burroughs, 1875-1950, (U.S.) novelist. *Tarzan of the Apes.*

George Gordon Lord Byron, 1788-1824, (Br.) poet. *Don Juan, Childe Harold.*

Albert Camus, 1913-1960, (F.) novelist. *The Plague, The Stranger, Caligula, The Fall.*

Lewis Carroll, 1832-1898, (Br.) writer, mathematician. *Alice's Adventures in Wonderland, Through the Looking Glass.*

Karel Capek, 1890-1938, (Czech.) playwright, novelist, essayist. *R.U.R. (Rossum's Universal Robots).*

Giacomo Casanova, 1725-1798, (It.) Venetian adventurer, author, world famous for his memoirs.

Willa Cather, 1876-1947, (U.S.) novelist, essayist. *O Pioneers!, My Antonia.*

Miguel de Cervantes Saavedra, 1547-1616, (Sp.) novelist, dramatist, poet. *Don Quixote de la Mancha.*

Raymond Chandler, 1888-1959, (U.S.) writer of detective fiction. Philip Marlowe series.

Geoffrey Chaucer, c. 1340-1400, (Br.) poet. *The Canterbury Tales.*

John Cheevers, 1912-1983, (U.S.) short story writer, novelist. *The Wapshot Scandal.*

Anton Chekhov, 1860-1904, (R.) short-story writer, dramatist. *Uncle Vanya, The Cherry Orchard, The Three Sisters.*

G.K. Chesterton, 1874-1936, (Br.) author, Fr. Brown series.

Agatha Christie, 1891-1976, (Br.) mystery writer. *And Then There Were None, Murder on the Orient Express.*

Jean Cocteau, 1889-1963, (F.) writer, visual artist, filmmaker. *The Beauty and the Beast, Enfants Terribles.*

Samuel Taylor Coleridge, 1772-1834, (Br.) poet, man of letters. *"Kubla Khan," "The Rime of the Ancient Mariner."*

Sidonie Colette, 1873-1954, (F.) novelist. *Claudine, Gigi.*

Joseph Conrad, 1857-1924, (Br.) novelist. *Lord Jim, Heart of Darkness, The Nigger of the Narcissus.*

James Fenimore Cooper, 1789-1851, (U.S.) novelist. *Leather-Stocking Tales.*

Pierre Corneille, 1606-1684, (F.) Dramatist. *Medeé, Le Cid, Horace, Cinna, Polyeucte.*

Hart Crane, 1899-1932, (U.S.) poet. *"The Bridge."*

Stephen Crane, 1871-1900, (U.S.) novelist. *The Red Badge of Courage.*

e.e. cummings, 1894-1962, (U.S.) poet. *Tulips and Chimneys.*

Gabriele D'Annunzio, 1863-1938, (It.) poet, novelist, dramatist. *The Child of Pleasure, The Intruder, The Victim.*

Dante Alighieri, 1265-1321, (It.) poet. *The Divine Comedy.*

Daniel Defoe, 1660-1731, (Br.) writer. *Robinson Crusoe, Moll Flanders, Journal of the Plague Year.*

Charles Dickens, 1812-1870, (Br.) novelist. *David Copperfield, Oliver Twist, Great Expectations, The Pickwick Papers.*

Emily Dickinson, 1830-1886, (U.S.) poet.

Isak Dinesen (Karen Blixen), 1885-1962, (Dan.) author. *Out of Africa, Seven Gothic Tales, Winter's Tales.*

John Donne, 1573-1631, (Br.) poet. *Songs and Sonnets, Holy Sonnets, "Death Be Not Proud."*

John Dos Passos, 1896-1970, (U.S.) author. *U.S.A.*

Fyodor Dostoyevsky, 1821-1881, (R.) author. *Crime and Punishment, The Brothers Karamazov, The Possessed.*

Arthur Conan Doyle, 1859-1930, (Br.) author, created Sherlock Holmes.

Theodore Dreiser, 1871-1945, (U.S.) novelist. *An American Tragedy, Sister Carrie.*

John Dryden, 1631-1700, (Br.) poet, dramatist, critic. *Fables, Ancient and Modern.*

Alexandre Dumas, 1802-1870, (F.) novelist, dramatist. *The Three Musketeers, The Count of Monte Cristo.*

Alexandre Dumas (fils), 1824-1895, (F.) dramatist, novelist. *La Dame aux camélias, Le Demi-Monde.*

Ilya G. Ehrenburg, 1891-1967, (R.) novelist, journalist. *The Thaw.*

George Eliot, 1819-1880, (Br.) novelist. *Adam Bede, Silas Marner, The Mill on the Floss.*

T.S. Eliot, 1888-1965, (Br.) poet, critic. *The Waste Land,* "The Love Song of J. Alfred Prufrock," *Murder in the Cathedral.*

Ralph Waldo Emerson, 1803-1882, (U.S.) poet, essayist. "The Concord Hymn," "Brahma," "The Rhodora."

James T. Farrell, 1904-1979, (U.S.) novelist. Studs Lonigan trilogy.

William Faulkner, 1897-1962, (U.S.) novelist. *Sanctuary, Light in August, The Sound and the Fury, Absalom, Absalom!*

Edna Ferber, 1885-1968, (U.S.) novelist, dramatist. *Show Boat, Saratoga Trunk, Giant, Dinner at Eight.*

Henry Fielding, 1707-1754, (Br.) novelist. *Tom Jones.*

F. Scott Fitzgerald, 1896-1940, (U.S.) short-story writer, novelist. *The Great Gatsby, Tender is the Night.*

Gustave Flaubert, 1821-1880, (F.) novelist. *Madame Bovary.*

C.S. Forester, 1899-1966, (Br.) novelist. Horatio Hornblower series.

E.M. Forster, 1879-1970, (Br.) novelist. *A Passage to India, Where Angels Fear to Tread, Maurice.*

Anatole France, 1844-1924, (F.) writer. *Penguin Island, My Friend's Book, Le Crime de Sylvestre Bonnard.*

Robert Frost, 1874-1963, (U.S.) poet. "Birches," "Fire and Ice," "Stopping by Woods on a Snowy Evening."

John Galsworthy, 1867-1933, (Br.) novelist, dramatist. *The Forsyte Saga, A Modern Comedy.*

Erle Stanley Gardner, 1889-1970, (U.S.) author, lawyer. Perry Mason series.

André Gide, 1869-1951, (F.) writer, *The Immoralist, The Pastoral Symphony, Strait is the Gate.*

Jean Giraudoux, 1882-1944, (F.) novelist, dramatist. *Electra, The Madwoman of Chaillot, Ondine, Tiger at the Gate.*

Johann W. von Goethe, 1749-1832, (G.) poet, dramatist, novelist. *Faust.*

Nikolai Gogol, 1809-1852, (R.) short-story writer, dramatist, novelist. *Dead Souls, The Inspector General.*

Oliver Goldsmith, 1730?-1774, (Br.-Ir.) writer. *The Vicar of Wakefield, She Stoops to Conquer.*

Maxim Gorky, 1868-1936, (R.) writer, founder of Soviet realism. *Mother, The Lower Depths.*

Thomas Gray, 1716-1771, (Br.) poet. "Elegy Written in a Country Churchyard."

Zane Grey, 1875-1939, (U.S.) writer of western stories.

Jakob Grimm, 1785-1863, (G.) philologist, folklorist. *German Methodology, Grimm's Fairy Tales.*

Wilhelm Grimm, 1786-1859, (G.) philologist, folklorist. *Grimm's Fairy Tales.*

Edgar A. Guest, 1881-1959, (U.S.) poet. *A Heap of Livin!*

Dashiell Hammett, 1894-1961, (U.S.) writer of detective fiction, created Sam Spade.

Thomas Hardy, 1840-1928, (Br.) novelist, poet. *The Return of the Native, Tess of the D'Urbervilles, Jude the Obscure.*

Joel Chandler Harris, 1848-1908, (U.S.) short-story writer. Uncle Remus series.

Moss Hart, 1904-1961, (U.S.) playwright. *Once in a Lifetime, You Can't Take It With You.*

Bret Harte, 1836-1902, (U.S.) short-story writer, poet. *The Luck of Roaring Camp.*

Jaroslav Hasek, 1883-1923, (Czech.) writer. *The Good Soldier Schweik.*

Nathaniel Hawthorne, 1804-1864, (U.S.) novelist, short story writer. *The Scarlet Letter, The House of the Seven Gables.*

Heinrich Heine, 1797-1856, (G.) poet. *Book of Songs.*

Lillian Hellman, 1907-1984, (U.S.) playwright, author of memoirs. *"The Little Foxes," An Unfinished Woman.*

Ernest Hemingway, 1899-1961, (U.S.) novelist, short-story writer. *A Farewell to Arms, For Whom the Bell Tolls.*

O. Henry (W.S. Porter), 1862-1910, (U.S.) short-story writer. "The Gift of the Magi."

Hermann Hesse, 1877-1962, (G.) novelist, poet. *Death and the Lover, Steppenwolf, Siddhartha.*

Oliver Wendell Holmes, 1809-1894, (U.S.) poet, novelist. *The Autocrat of the Breakfast-Table.*

Alfred E. Housman, 1859-1936, (Br.) poet. *A Shropshire Lad.*

William Dean Howells, 1837-1920, (U.S.) novelist, critic,

dean of late 19th century American letters.

Langston Hughes, 1902-1967, (U.S.) poet, playwright. *The Weary Blues, One-Way Ticket, Shakespeare in Harlem.*

Victor Hugo, 1802-1885, (F.) poet, dramatist, novelist. *Notre Dame de Paris, Les Misérables.*

Aldous Huxley 1894-1963, (Br.) author. *Point Counter Point, Brave New World.*

Henrik Ibsen, 1828-1906, (Nor.) dramatist, poet. *A Doll's House, Ghosts, The Wild Duck, Hedda Gabler.*

William Inge, 1913-1973, (U.S.) playwright. *Come Back Little Sheba, Bus Stop, The Dark at the Top of the Stairs, Picnic.*

Washington Irving, 1783-1859, (U.S.) essayist, author. "Rip Van Winkle," "The Legend of Sleepy Hollow."

Shirley Jackson, 1919-1965, (U.S.) writer. *The Lottery.*

Henry James, 1843-1916, (U.S.) novelist, critic. *Washington Square, Portrait of a Lady, The American.*

Robinson Jeffers, 1887-1962, (U.S.) poet, dramatist. *Tamar and Other Poems, Medea.*

Samuel Johnson, 1709-1784, (Br.) author, scholar, critic. *Dictionary of the English Language.*

Ben Jonson, 1572-1637, (Br.) dramatist, poet. *Volpone.*

James Joyce, 1882-1941, (Ir.) novelist. *Ulysses, A Portrait of the Artist as a Young Man, Finnegans Wake.*

Franz Kafka, 1883-1924, (G.) novelist, short-story writer. *The Trial, Amerika, The Castle.*

George S. Kaufman, 1889-1961, (U.S.) playwright. *The Man Who Came to Dinner, You Can't Take It With You, Stage Door.*

Nikos Kazantzakis, 1883?-1957, (Gk.) novelist. *Zorba the Greek, A Greek Passion.*

John Keats, 1795-1821, (Br.) poet. *On a Grecian Urn, La Belle Dame Sans Merci.*

Joyce Kilmer, 1886-1918, (U.S.) poet, "Trees."

Rudyard Kipling, 1865-1936, (Br.) author, poet. "The White Man's Burden," "Gunga Din," *The Jungle Book.*

Jean de la Fontaine, 1621-1695, (F.) poet. *Fables choisies.*

Pär Lagerkvist, 1891-1974, (Swed.) poet, dramatist, novelist. *Barabbas, The Sybil.*

Selma Lagerlöf, 1858-1940, (Swed.) novelist. *Jerusalem, The Ring of the Lowenskolds.*

Alphonse de Lamartine, 1790-1869, (F.) poet, novelist, statesman. *Méditations poétiques.*

Charles Lamb, 1775-1834, (Br.) essayist. *Specimens of English Dramatic Poets, Essays of Elia.*

Giuseppe di Lampedusa, 1896-1957, (It.) novelist. *The Leopard.*

Ring Lardner, 1885-1933, (U.S.) short story writer, humorist. *You Know Me, Al.*

D. H. Lawrence, 1885-1930, (Br.) novelist. *Women in Love, Lady Chatterley's Lover, Sons and Lovers.*

Mikhail Lermontov, 1814-1841, (R.) novelist, poet. "Demon," *Hero of Our Time.*

Alain-René Lesage, 1668-1747, (F.) novelist. *Gil Blas de Santillane.*

Gotthold Lessing, 1729-1781, (G.) dramatist, philosopher, critic. *Miss Sara Sampson, Minna von Barnhelm.*

Sinclair Lewis, 1885-1951, (U.S.) novelist, playwright. *Babbitt, Arrowsmith, Dodsworth, Main Street.*

Vachel Lindsay, 1879-1931, (U.S.) poet. *General William Booth Enters into Heaven, The Congo.*

Hugh Lofting, 1886-1947, (Br.) Dr. Doolittle series.

Jack London, 1876-1916, (U.S.) novelist, journalist. *Call of the Wild, The Sea-Wolf.*

Henry Wadsworth Longfellow, 1807-1882, (U.S.) poet. *Evangeline, The Song of Hiawatha.*

Amy Lowell, 1874-1925, (U.S.) poet, critic. *A Dome of Many-Colored Glass,* "Patterns," "Lilacs."

James Russell Lowell, 1819-1891, (U.S.) poet, editor. *Poems, The Bigelow Papers.*

Robert Lowell, 1917-1977, (U.S.) poet. "Lord Weary's Castle," "For the Union Dead."

Emil Ludwig, 1881-1948, (G.) biographer. *Goethe, Beethoven, Napoleon, Bismarck.*

Niccolò Machiavelli, 1469-1527, (It.) author, statesman. *The Prince, Discourses on Livy.*

Stéphane Mallarmé, 1842-1898, (F.) poet. *The Afternoon of a Faun.*

Thomas Malory, ?-1471, (Br.) writer. *Morte d'Arthur.*

Andre Malraux, 1901-1976, (F.) novelist. *Man's Fate, The Voices of Silence.*

Osip Mandelstam, 1891-1938, (R.) Acmeist poet.

Thomas Mann, 1875-1955, (G.) novelist, essayist. *Buddenbrooks, Death in Venice, The Magic Mountain.*

Katherine Mansfield, 1888-1923, (Br.) short story writer. *Bliss, The Garden Party.*

Christopher Marlowe, 1564-1593, (Br.) dramatist, poet. *Tamburlaine the Great, Dr. Faustus, The Jew of Malta.*

John Masefield, 1878-1967, (Br.) poet. "Sea Fever," "Cargoes," *Salt Water Ballads.*

Edgar Lee Masters, 1869-1950, (U.S.) poet, biographer.

Spoon River Anthology.

W. Somerset Maugham, 1874-1965, (Br.) author. *Of Human Bondage, The Razor's Edge, The Moon and Sixpence.*

Guy de Maupassant, 1850-1893, (F.) novelist, short-story writer. *A Life, Bel-Ami,* "The Necklace."

François Mauriac, 1885-1970, (F.) novelist, dramatist. *Viper's Tangle, The Kiss to the Leper.*

Vladimir Mayakovsky, 1893-1930, (R.) poet, dramatist. *The Cloud in Trousers.*

Carson McCullers, 1917-1967, (U.S.) novelist. *The Heart is a Lonely Hunter, Member of the Wedding.*

Herman Melville, 1819-1891, (U.S.) novelist, poet. *Moby Dick, Typee, Billy Budd, Omoo.*

H.L. Mencken, 1880-1956, (U.S.) author, critic, editor. *Prejudices, The American Language.*

George Meredith, 1828-1909, (Br.) novelist, poet. *The Ordeal of Richard Feverel, The Egoist.*

Prosper Mérimée, 1803-1870, (F.) author. *Carmen.*

Edna St. Vincent Millay, 1892-1950, (U.S.) poet. *The Harp Weaver and Other Poems, A Few Figs from Thistles.*

A.A. Milne, 1882-1956, (Br.) author. *Winnie-the-Pooh.*

John Milton, 1608-1674, (Br.) poet. *Paradise Lost.*

Gabriela Mistral, 1889-1957, (Chil.) poet. *Sonnets of Death, Desolación, Tala, Lagar.*

Margaret Mitchell, 1900-1949, (U.S.) novelist. *Gone With the Wind.*

Jean Baptiste Molière, 1622-1673, (F.) dramatist. *Le Tartuffe, Le Misanthrope, Le Bourgeois Gentilhomme.*

Ferenc Molnár, 1878-1952, (Hung.) dramatist, novelist. *Liliom, The Guardsman, The Swan.*

Michel de Montaigne, 1533-1592, (F.) essayist. *Essais.*

Eugenio Montale, 1896-1981, (It.) poet.

Clement C. Moore, 1779-1863, (U.S.) poet, educator. "A Visit from Saint Nicholas."

Marianne Moore, 1887-1972, (U.S.) poet. *O to Be a Dragon.*

Thomas More, 1478-1535, (Br.) author. *Utopia.*

H.H. Munro (Saki), 1870-1916, (Br.) author. *Reginald, The Chronicles of Clovis, Beasts and Super-Beasts.*

Alfred de Musset, 1810-1857, (F.) poet, dramatist. *Confession d'un enfant du siècle.*

Vladimir Nabokov, 1899-1977, (U.S.) author. *Lolita, Ada.*

Ogden Nash, 1902-1971, (U.S.) poet. *Hard Lines, I'm a Stranger Here Myself, The Private Dining Room.*

Pablo Neruda, 1904-1973, (Chil.) poet. *Twenty Love Poems and One Song of Despair, Toward the Splendid City.*

Sean O'Casey, 1884-1964, (Ir.) dramatist. *Juno and the Paycock, The Plough and the Stars.*

Flannery O'Connor, 1925-1964, (U.S.) novelist, short story writer. *Wise Blood,* "A Good Man Is Hard to Find."

Clifford Odets, 1906-1963, (U.S.) playwright. *Waiting for Lefty, Awake and Sing, Golden Boy, The Country Girl.*

John O'Hara, 1905-1970, (U.S.) novelist. *Butterfield 8, From the Terrace, Appointment in Samarra.*

Omar Khayyam, c. 1028-1122, (Per.) poet. *Rubaiyat.*

Eugene O'Neill, 1888-1953, (U.S.) playwright. *Emperor Jones, Anna Christie, Long Day's Journey into Night, Desire Under the Elms, Mourning Becomes Electra.*

George Orwell, 1903-1950, (Br.) novelist, essayist. *Animal Farm, Nineteen Eighty-Four.*

Thomas (Tom) Paine, 1737-1809, (U.S.) author, political theorist. *Common Sense.*

Dorothy Parker, 1893-1967, (U.S.) poet, short-story writer. *Enough Rope, Laments for the Living.*

Boris Pasternak, 1890-1960, (R.) poet, novelist. *Doctor Zhivago, My Sister, Life.*

Samuel Pepys, 1633-1703, (Br.) public official, author of the greatest diary in the English language.

S. J. Perelman, 1904-1979, (U.S.) humorist. *The Road to Miltown, Under the Spreading Atrophy.*

Francesco Petrarca, 1304-1374, (It.) poet, humanist. *Africa, Trionfi, Canzoniere, On Solitude.*

Luigi Pirandello, 1867-1936, (It.) novelist, dramatist. *Six Characters in Search of an Author.*

Edgar Allan Poe, 1809-1849, (U.S.) poet, short-story writer, critic. "Annabel Lee," "The Raven," "The Purloined Letter."

Alexander Pope, 1688-1744, (Br.) poet. *The Rape of the Lock, An Essay on Man.*

Katherine Anne Porter, 1890-1980, (U.S.) novelist, short story writer. *Ship of Fools.*

Ezra Pound, 1885-1972, (U.S.) poet. *Cantos.*

Marcel Proust, 1871-1922, (F.) novelist. *A la recherche du temps perdu (Remembrance of Things Past).*

Aleksandr Pushkin, 1799-1837, (R.) poet, prose writer. *Boris Godunov, Eugene Onegin, The Bronze Horseman.*

François Rabelais, 1495-1553, (F.) writer, physician. *Gargantua, Pantagruel.*

Jean Racine, 1639-1699, (F.) dramatist. *Andromaque, Phèdre, Bérénice, Britannicus.*

Erich Maria Remarque, 1898-1970, (Ger.-U.S.) novelist. *All*

Samuel Richardson, 1689-1761, (Br.) novelist. *Clarissa Harlowe, Pamela; or, Virtue Rewarded.*

James Whitcomb Riley, 1849-1916, (U.S.) poet. "When the Frost is on the Pumpkin," "Little Orphant Annie."

Rainer Maria Rilke, 1875-1926, (G.) poet. *Life and Songs, Divine Elegies, Sonnets to Orpheus.*

Arthur Rimbaud, 1854-1891, (F.) *A Season in Hell,* "Le Bateau ivre."

Edwin Arlington Robinson, 1869-1935, (U.S.) poet. "Richard Cory," "Miniver Cheevy."

Theodore Roethke, 1908-1963, (U.S.) poet. *Open House, The Waking, The Far Field.*

Romain Rolland, 1866-1944, (F.) novelist, biographer. *Jean-Christophe.*

Pierre de Ronsard, 1524-1585, (F.) poet. *Sonnets pour Hélène.*

Edmond Rostand, 1868-1918, (F.) poet, dramatist. *Cyrano de Bergerac.*

Damon Runyon, 1880-1946, (U.S.) short-story writer, journalist. *Guys and Dolls, Blue Plate Special.*

John Ruskin, 1819-1900, (Br.) critic, social theorist. *Modern Painters, The Seven Lamps of Architecture.*

Antoine de Saint-Exupery, 1900-1944, (F.) writer, aviator. *Wind, Sand and Stars, Le Petit Prince.*

George Sand, 1804-1876, (F.) novelist. *Consuelo, The Haunted Pool, Les Maitres sonneurs.*

Carl Sandburg, 1878-1967, (U.S.) poet. *Chicago Poems, Smoke and Steel, Harvest Poems.*

George Santayana, 1863-1952, (U.S.) poet, essayist, philosopher. *The Sense of Beauty, The Realms of Being.*

William Saroyan, 1908-1981, (U.S.) playwright, novelist. *The Time of Your Life, The Human Comedy.*

Friedrich von Schiller, 1759-1805, (G.) dramatist, poet, historian. *Don Carlos, Maria Stuart, Wilhelm Tell.*

Sir Walter Scott, 1771-1832, (Sc.) novelist, poet. *Ivanhoe, Rob Roy, The Bride of Lammermoor.*

William Shakespeare, 1564-1616, (Br.) dramatist, poet. *Romeo and Juliet, Hamlet, King Lear, The Merchant of Venice.*

George Bernard Shaw, 1856-1950, (Ir.) playwright, critic. *St. Joan, Pygmalion, Major Barbara, Man and Superman.*

Mary Wollstonecraft Shelley, 1797-1851, (Br.) author. *Frankenstein.*

Percy Bysshe Shelley, 1792-1822, (Br.) poet. *Prometheus Unbound, Adonais,* "Ode to the West Wind," "To a Skylark."

Richard B. Sheridan, 1751-1816, (Br.) dramatist. *The Rivals, School for Scandal.*

Robert Sherwood, 1896-1955, (U.S.) playwright. *The Petrified Forest, Abe Lincoln in Illinois, Reunion in Vienna.*

Mikhail Sholokhov, 1906-1984 (U.S.S.R.) author, 1965 Nobel laureate. *And Quiet Flows the Don.*

Upton Sinclair, 1878-1968, (U.S.) novelist. *The Jungle.*

Edmund Spenser, 1552-1599, (Br.) poet. *The Faerie Queen.*

Christina Stead, 1903-1983 (Austral.) novelist, short-story writer. *The Man Who Loved Children.*

Richard Steele, 1672-1729, (Br.) essayist, playwright, began the Tatler and Spectator. *The Conscious Lovers.*

Lincoln Steffens, 1866-1936, (U.S.) editor, author. *The Shame of the Cities.*

Gertrude Stein, 1874-1946, (U.S.) author. *Three Lives.*

John Steinbeck, 1902-1968, (U.S.) novelist. *Grapes of Wrath, Of Mice and Men, Winter of Our Discontent.*

Stendhal (Marie Henri Beyle), 1783-1842, (F.) poet, novelist. *The Red and the Black, The Charterhouse of Parma.*

Laurence Sterne, 1713-1768, (Br.) novelist. *Tristram Shandy.*

Wallace Stevens, 1879-1955, (U.S.) poet. *Harmonium, The Man With the Blue Guitar, Transport to Summer.*

Robert Louis Stevenson, 1850-1894, (Br.) novelist, poet, essayist. *Treasure Island, A Child's Garden of Verses.*

Rex Stout, 1886-1975, (U.S.) novelist, created Nero Wolfe.

Harriet Beecher Stowe, 1811-1896, (U.S.) novelist. *Uncle Tom's Cabin.*

Lytton Strachey, 1880-1932, (Br.) biographer, critic. *Eminent Victorians, Queen Victoria, Elizabeth and Essex.*

August Strindberg, 1849-1912, (Swed.) dramatist, novelist. *The Father, Miss Julie, The Creditors.*

Jonathan Swift, 1667-1745, (Br.) author. *Gulliver's Travels.*

Algernon C. Swinburne, 1837-1909, (Br.) poet, critic. *Songs Before Sunrise.*

John M. Synge, 1871-1909, (Ir.) poet, dramatist. *Riders to the Sea, The Playboy of the Western World.*

Rabindranath Tagore, 1861-1941, (Ind.), author, poet. *Sadhana, The Realization of Life, Gitanjali.*

Booth Tarkington, 1869-1946, (U.S.) novelist. *Seventeen, Alice Adams, Penrod.*

Sara Teasdale, 1884-1933, (U.S.) poet. *Helen of Troy and Other Poems, Rivers to the Sea, Flame and Shadow.*

Alfred Lord Tennyson, 1809-1892, (Br.) poet. *Idylls of the King, In Memoriam,* "The Charge of the Light Brigade."

William Makepeace Thackeray, 1811-1863, (Br.) novelist. *Vanity Fair.*

Dylan Thomas, 1914-1953, (Welsh) poet. *Under Milk Wood, A Child's Christmas in Wales.*

James Thurber, 1894-1961, (U.S.) humorist, artist. *The New Yorker, The Owl in the Attic, Thurber Carnival.*

J.R.R. Tolkien, 1892-1973, (Br.) author. *The Hobbit, Lord of the Rings.*

Lev Tolstoy, 1828-1910, (R.) novelist. *War and Peace, Anna Karenina.*

Anthony Trollope, 1815-1882, (Br.) novelist. *The Warden, Barchester Towers,* The Palliser novels.

Ivan Turgenev, 1818-1883, (R.) novelist, short-story writer. *Fathers and Sons, First Love, A Month in the Country.*

Mark Twain (Samuel Clemens), 1835-1910, (U.S.) novelist, humorist. *The Adventures of Huckleberry Finn, Tom Sawyer.*

Sigrid Undset, 1881-1949, (Nor.) novelist, poet. *Kristin Lavransdatter.*

Paul Valéry, 1871-1945, (F.) poet, critic. *La Jeune Parque, The Graveyard by the Sea.*

Jules Verne, 1828-1905, (F.) novelist, originator of modern science fiction. *Twenty Thousand Leagues Under the Sea.*

François Villon, 1431-1463?, (F.) poet. *Le petit et le Grand Testament.*

Evelyn Waugh, 1903-1966, (Br.) satirist. *The Loved One.*

H.G. Wells, 1866-1946, (Br.) author. *The Time Machine, The Invisible Man, The War of the Worlds.*

Rebecca West, 1893-1983 (Br.) author. *Black Lamb and Grey Falcon.*

Edith Wharton, 1862-1937, (U.S.) novelist. *The Age of Innocence, The House of Mirth.*

T.H. White, 1906-1964, (Br.) author. *The Once and Future King.*

Walt Whitman, 1819-1892, (U.S.) poet. *Leaves of Grass.*

John Greenleaf Whittier, 1807-1892, (U.S.) poet, journalist. *Snow-bound.*

Oscar Wilde, 1854-1900, (Ir.) author, wit. *The Picture of Dorian Gray, The Importance of Being Earnest.*

Thornton Wilder, 1897-1975, (U.S.) playwright. *Our Town, The Skin of Our Teeth, The Matchmaker.*

Tennessee Williams, 1912-1983 (U.S.) playwright. *A Streetcar Named Desire, Cat on a Hot Tin Roof, The Glass Menagerie.*

William Carlos Williams, 1883-1963, (U.S.) poet, physician. *Tempers, Al Que Quiere!, Paterson.*

Edmund Wilson, 1895-1972, (U.S.) author, literary and social critic. *Axel's Castle, To the Finland Station.*

P.G. Wodehouse, 1881-1975, (U.S.) poet, dramatist. The "Jeeves" novels, *Anything Goes.*

Thomas Wolfe, 1900-1938, (U.S.) novelist. *Look Homeward, Angel, You Can't Go Home Again, Of Time and the River.*

Virginia Woolf, 1882-1941, (Br.) novelist, essayist. *Mrs. Dalloway, To the Lighthouse, The Waves.*

William Wordsworth, 1770-1850, (Br.) poet. "Tintern Abbey," "Ode: Intimations of Immortality."

William Butler Yeats, 1865-1939, (Ir.) poet, playwright. *The Wild Swans at Coole, The Tower, Last Poems.*

Émile Zola, 1840-1902, (F.) novelist. *Nana, The Dram Shop.*

Noted Artists and Sculptors of the Past

Artists are painters unless otherwise indicated.

Washington Allston, 1779-1843, landscapist. *Belshazzar's Feast.*

Albrecht Altdorfer, 1480-1538, landscapist. *Battle of Alexander.*

Andrea del Sarto, 1486-1530, frescoes. *Madonna of the Harpies.*

Fra Angelico, c. 1400-1455, Renaissance muralist. *Madonna of the Linen Drapers' Guild.*

Alexandr Archipenko, 1887-1964, sculptor. *Boxing Match, Medranos.*

John James Audubon, 1785-1851, *Birds of America.*

Hans Baldung Grien, 1484-1545, *Todentanz.*

Ernst Barlach, 1870-1938, Expressionist sculptor. *Man Drawing a Sword.*

Frederic-Auguste Bartholdi, 1834-1904, *Liberty Enlightening the World, Lion of Belfort.*

Fra Bartolommeo, 1472-1517, *Vision of St. Bernard.*

Aubrey Beardsley, 1872-1898, illustrator. *Salome, Lysistrata.*

Max Beckmann, 1884-1950, Expressionist. *The Descent from the Cross.*

Gentile Bellini, 1426-1507, Renaissance. Procession in St. Mark's Square.

Giovanni Bellini, 1428-1516, St. Francis in Ecstasy.

Jacopo Bellini, 1400-1470, Crucifixion.

George Wesley Bellows, 1882-1925, sports artist. Stag at Sharkey's.

Thomas Hart Benton, 1889-1975, American regionalist. Threshing Wheat, Arts of the West.

Gianlorenzo Bernini, 1598-1680, Baroque sculpture. The Assumption.

Albert Bierstadt, 1830-1902, landscapist. The Rocky Mountains, Mount Corcoran.

George Caleb Bingham, 1811-1879, Fur Traders Descending the Missouri.

William Blake, 1752-1827, engraver. Book of Job, Songs of Innocence, Songs of Experience.

Rosa Bonheur, 1822-1899, The Horse Fair.

Pierre Bonnard, 1867-1947, intimist. The Breakfast Room.

Paul-Emile Borduas, 1905-1960, Abstractionist. Leeward of the Island, Enchanted Shields.

Gutzon Borglum, 1871-1941, sculptor. Mt. Rushmore Memorial.

Hieronymus Bosch, 1450-1516, religious allegories. The Crowning with Thorns.

Sandro Botticelli, 1444-1510, Renaissance. Birth of Venus.

Constantin Brancusi, 1876-1957, Nonobjective sculptor. Flying Turtle, The Kiss.

Georges Braque, 1882-1963, Cubist. Violin and Palette.

Pieter Bruegel the Elder, c. 1525-1569, The Peasant Dance.

Pieter Bruegel the Younger, 1564-1638, Village Fair, The Crucifixion.

Edward Burne-Jones, 1833-1898, Pre-Raphaelite artist-craftsman. The Mirror of Venus.

Alexander Calder, 1898-1976, sculptor. Lobster Trap and Fish Tail.

Michelangelo Merisi da Caravaggio, 1573-1610, Baroque. The Supper at Emmaus.

Emily Carr, 1871-1945, landscapist. Blunden Harbour, Big Raven.

Carlo Carra, 1881-1966, Metaphysical school. Lot's Daughters.

Mary Cassatt, 1845-1926, Impressionist. Woman Bathing.

George Catlin, 1796-1872, American Indian life. Gallery of Indians.

Benvenuto Cellini, 1500-1571, Mannerist sculptor, goldsmith. Perseus.

Paul Cezanne, 1839-1906, Card Players, Mont-Sainte-Victoire with Large Pine Trees.

Marc Chagall, 1898-1985, Jewish life and folklore. I and the Village.

Jean Simeon Chardin, 1699-1779, still lifes. The Kiss, The Grace.

Frederic Church, 1826-1900, Hudson River school. Niagara, Andes of Ecuador.

Cimabue, 1240-1302, Byzantine mosaicist. Madonna Enthroned with St. Francis.

Claude Lorrain, 1600-1682, ideal-landscapist. The Enchanted Castle.

Thomas Cole, 1801-1848, Hudson River school. The Ox-Bow.

John Constable, 1776-1837, landscapist. Salisbury Cathedral from the Bishop's Grounds.

John Singleton Copley, 1738-1815, portraitist. Samuel Adams, Watson and the Shark.

Lovis Corinth, 1858-1925, Expressionist. Apocalypse.

Jean-Baptiste-Camille Corot, 1796-1875, landscapist. Souvenir de Mortefontaine, Pastorale.

Correggio, 1494-1534, Renaissance muralist. Mystic Marriages of St. Catherine.

Gustave Courbet, 1819-1877, Realist. The Artist's Studio.

Lucas Cranach the Elder, 1472-1553, Protestant Reformation portraitist. Luther.

Nathaniel Currier, 1813-1888, and **James M. Ives**, 1824-1895, lithographers. A Midnight Race on the Mississippi.

Honore Daumier, 1808-1879, caricaturist. The Third-Class Carriage.

Jacques-Louis David, 1748-1825, Neoclassicist. The Oath of the Horatii.

Arthur Davies, 1862-1928, Romantic landscapist. Unicorns.

Edgar Degas, 1834-1917, The Ballet Class.

Eugene Delacroix, Co. 1400-1455, Romantic. Massacre at Chios.

Paul Delaroche, 1797-1856, historical themes. Children of Edward IV.

Luca Della Robbia, 1400-1482, Renaissance terracotta artist. Cantoria (singing gallery), Florence cathedral.

Donatello, 1386-1466, Renaissance sculptor. David, Gattamelata.

Jean Dubuffet, 1902-1985, painter, sculptor, printmaker. Group of Four Trees.

Marcel Duchamp, 1887-1968, Nude Descending a Staircase.

Raoul Dufy, 1877-1953, Fauvist. Chateau and Horses.

Asher Brown Durand, 1796-1886, Hudson River school. Kindred Spirits.

Albrecht Durer, 1471-1528, Renaissance engraver, woodcuts. St. Jerome in His Study, Melancholia I, Apocalypse.

Anthony van Dyck, 1599-1641, Baroque portraitist. Portrait of Charles I Hunting.

Thomas Eakins, 1844-1916, Realist. The Gross Clinic.

Jacob Epstein, 1880-1959, religious and allegorical sculptor. Genesis, Ecce Homo.

Jan van Eyck, 1380-1441, naturalistic panels. Adoration of the Lamb.

Anselm Feuerbach, 1829-1880, Romantic Classicism. Judgement of Paris, Iphigenia.

John Bernard Flannagan, 1895-1942, animal sculptor. Triumph of the Egg.

Jean-Honore Fragonard, 1732-1806, Rococo. The Swing.

Daniel Chester French, 1850-1931, The Minute Man of Concord; seated Lincoln, Lincoln Memorial, Washington, D.C.

Caspar David Friedrich, 1774-1840, Romantic landscapes. Man and Woman Gazing at the Moon.

Thomas Gainsborough, 1727-1788, portraitist. The Blue Boy.

Paul Gauguin, 1848-1903, Post-impressionist. The Tahitians.

Lorenzo Ghiberti, 1378-1455, Renaissance sculptor. Gates of Paradise baptistry doors, Florence.

Alberto Giacometti, 1901-1966, attenuated sculptures of solitary figures. Man Pointing.

Giorgione, c. 1477-1510, Renaissance. The Tempest.

Giotto di Bondone, 1267-1337, Renaissance. Presentation of Christ in the Temple.

Francois Girardon, 1628-1715, Baroque sculptor of classical themes. Apollo Tended by the Nymphs.

Vincent van Gogh, 1853-1890, The Starry Night, L'Arlesienne.

Arshile Gorky, 1905-1948, Surrealist. The Liver is the Cock's Comb.

Francisco de Goya y Lucientes, 1746-1828, The Naked Maja, The Disasters of War (etchings).

El Greco, 1541-1614, View of Toledo.

Horatio Greenough, 1805-1852, Neo-classical sculptor. George Washington.

Matthias Grünewald, 1480-1528, mystical religious themes. The Resurrection.

Frans Hals, c. 1580-1666, portraitist. Laughing Cavalier, Gypsy Girl.

Childe Hassam, 1859-1935, Impressionist. Southwest Wind.

Edward Hicks, 1780-1849, folk painter. The Peaceable Kingdom.

Hans Hofmann, 1880-1966, early Abstract Expressionist. Spring. The Gate.

William Hogarth, 1697-1764, caricaturist. The Rake's Progress.

Katsushika Hokusai, 1760-1849, printmaker. Crabs.

Hans Holbein the Elder, 1460-1524, late Gothic. Presentation of Christ in the Temple.

Hans Holbein the Younger, 1497-1543, portraitist. Henry VIII.

Winslow Homer, 1836-1910, marine themes. Marine Coast, High Cliff.

Edward Hopper, 1882-1967, realistic urban scenes. Sunlight in a Cafeteria.

Jean-Auguste-Dominique Ingres, 1780-1867, Classicist. Valpincon Bather.

George Inness, 1825-1894, luminous landscapist. Delaware Water Gap.

Vasily Kandinsky, 1866-1944, Abstractionist. Capricious Forms.

Paul Klee, 1879-1940, Abstractionist. Twittering Machine.

Oscar Kokoschka, 1886-1980, Expressionist. View of Prague.

Kathe Kollwitz, 1867-1945, printmaker, social justice themes. The Peasant War.

Gaston Lachaise, 1882-1935, figurative sculptor. Standing Woman.

John La Farge, 1835-1910, muralist. Red and White Peonies.

Fernand Leger, 1881-1955, machine art. The Cyclists.

Leonardo da Vinci, 1452-1519, Mona Lisa, Last Supper, The Annunciation.

Emanuel Leutze, 1816-1868, historical themes. Washington Crossing the Delaware.

Jacques Lipchitz, 1891-1973, Cubist sculptor. Harpist.

Filippino Lippi, 1457-1504, Renaissance. The Vision of St. Bernard.

Fra Filippo Lippi, 1406-1469, Renaissance. Coronation of the Virgin.

Morris Louis, 1912-1962, abstract expressionist. Signa,

Stripos.

Aristide Maillol, 1861-1944, sculptor. The Mediterranean.

Edouard Manet, 1832-1883, forerunner of Impressionism. Luncheon on the Grass, Olympia.

Andrea Mantegna, 1431-1506, Renaissance frescoes. Triumph of Caesar.

Franz Marc, 1880-1916, Expressionist. Blue Horses.

John Marin, 1870-1953, expressionist seascapes. Maine Island.

Reginald Marsh, 1898-1954, satirical artist. Tattoo and Haircut.

Masaccio, 1401-1428, Renaissance. The Tribute Money.

Henri Matisse, 1869-1954, Fauvist. Woman with the Hat.

Michelangelo Buonarroti, 1475-1564, Pieta, David, Moses, The Last Judgment, Sistine Ceiling.

Carl Milles, 1875-1955, expressive rhythmic sculptor. Playing Bears.

Jean-Francois Millet, 1814-1875, painter of peasant subjects. The Gleaners, The Man with a Hoe.

David Milne, 1882-1953, landscapist. Boston Corner, Berkshire Hills.

Amedeo Modigliani, 1884-1920, Reclining Nude.

Piet Mondrian, 1872-1944, Abstractionist. Composition.

Claude Monet, 1840-1926, Impressionist. The Bridge at Argenteuil, Haystacks.

Gustave Moreau, 1826-1898, Symbolist. The Apparition, Dance of Salome.

James Wilson Morrice, 1865-1924, landscapist. The Ferry, Quebec, Venice, Looking Over the Lagoon.

Grandma Moses, 1860-1961, folk painter. Out for the Christmas Trees.

Edvard Munch, 1863-1944, Expressionist. The Cry.

Bartolome Murillo, 1618-1682, Baroque religious artist. Vision of St. Anthony. The Two Trinities.

Barnett Newman, 1905-1970, Abstract Expressionist. Stations of the Cross.

Jose Clemente Orozco, 1883-1949, frescoes. House of Tears.

Charles Willson Peale, 1741-1827, American Revolutionary portraitist. Washington, Franklin, Jefferson, John Adams.

Rembrandt Peale, 1778-1860, portraitist. Thomas Jefferson.

Pietro Perugino, 1446-1523, Renaissance. Delivery of the Keys to St. Peter.

Pablo Picasso, 1881-1973, Guernica, Dove, Head of a Woman.

Piero della Francesca, c. 1415-1492, Renaissance. Duke of Urbino, Flagellation of Christ.

Camille Pissarro, 1830-1903, Impressionist. Morning Sunlight.

Jackson Pollock, 1912-1956, Abstract Expressionist. Autumn Rhythm.

Nicolas Poussin, 1594-1665, Baroque pictorial classicism. St. John on Patmos.

Maurice B. Prendergast, c. 1860-1924, Post-impressionist water colorist. Umbrellas in the Rain.

Pierre-Paul Prud'hon, 1758-1823, Romanticist. Crime pursued by Vengeance and Justice.

Pierre Cecile Puvis de Chavannes, 1824-1898, muralist. The Poor Fisherman.

Raphael Sanzio, 1483-1520, Renaissance. Disputa, School of Athens, Sistine Madonna.

Man Ray, 1890-1976, Dadaist. Observing Time, The Lovers.

Odilon Redon, 1840-1916, Symbolist lithographer. In the Dream.

Rembrandt van Rijn, 1606-1669, The Bridal Couple, The Night Watch.

Frederic Remington, 1861-1909, painter, sculptor, portrayer of the American West. Bronco Buster.

Pierre-Auguste Renoir, 1841-1919, Impressionist. The Luncheon of the Boating Party.

Ilya Repin, 1844-1918, historical canvases. Zaporozhye Cossacks.

Joshua Reynolds, 1723-1792, portraitist. Mrs. Siddons as the Tragic Muse.

Diego Rivera, 1886-1957, frescoes. The Fecund Earth.

Norman Rockwell, 1894-1978, illustrator. Saturday Evening Post covers.

Auguste Rodin, 1840-1917, sculptor. The Thinker, The Burghers of Calais.

Mark Rothko, 1903-1970, Abstract Expressionist. Light, Earth and Blue.

Georges Rouault, 1871-1958, Expressionist. The Old King.

Henri Rousseau, 1844-1910, primitive exotic themes. The Snake Charmer.

Theodore Rousseau, 1812-1867, landscapist. Under the Birches, Evening.

Peter Paul Rubens, 1577-1640, Baroque. Mystic Marriage of St. Catherine.

Andrey Rublyov, 1370-1430, icon painter. Old Testament Trinity.

Jacob van Ruisdael, c. 1628-1682, landscapist. Jewish Cemetery.

Salomon van Ruysdael, c. 1600-1670, landscapist. River with Ferry-Boat.

Albert Pinkham Ryder, 1847-1917, seascapes and allegories. Toilers of the Sea.

Augustus Saint-Gaudens, 1848-1907, memorial statues. Farragut, Mrs. Henry Adams (Grief).

Andrea Sansovino, 1460-1529, Renaissance sculptor. Baptism of Christ.

Jacopo Sansovino, 1486-1570, Renaissance sculptor. St. John the Baptist.

John Singer Sargent, 1856-1925, Edwardian society portraitist. The Wyndham Sisters, Madam X.

Johann Gottfried Schadow, 1764-1850, monumental sculptor. Quadriga, Brandenburg Gate.

Georges Seurat, 1859-1891, Pointillist. Sunday Afternoon on the Island of Grande Jatte.

Gino Severini, 1883-1966, Futurist and Cubist. Dynamic Hieroglyph of the Bal Tabarin.

Ben Shahn, 1898-1969, social and political themes. Sacco and Vanzetti series, Seurat's Lunch, Handball.

Charles Sheeler, 1883-1965, Abstractionist. Upper Deck.

David Alfaro Siqueiros, 1896-1974, political muralist. March of Humanity.

John F. Sloan, 1871-1951, depictions of New York City. Wake of the Ferry.

David Smith, 1906-1965, welded metal sculpture. Hudson River Landscape, Zig, Cubi series.

Gilbert Stuart, 1755-1828, portraitist. George Washington.

Thomas Sully, 1783-1872, portraitist. Col. Thomas Handasyd Perkins, The Passage of the Delaware.

Yves Tanguy, 1900-1955, Surrealist. Rose of the Four Winds.

Thomas J. Thomson, 1877-1918, landscapist. Spring Ice.

Giovanni Battista Tiepolo, 1696-1770, Rococo frescoes. The Crucifixion.

Jacopo Tintoretto, 1518-1594, Mannerist. The Last Supper.

Titian, c. 1485-1576, Renaissance. Venus and the Lute Player, The Bacchanal.

Henri de Toulouse-Lautrec, 1864-1901, At the Moulin Rouge.

John Trumbull, 1756-1843, historical themes. The Declaration of Independence.

Joseph Mallord William Turner, 1775-1851, Romantic landscapist. Snow Storm.

Paolo Uccello, 1397-1475, Gothic-Renaissance. The Rout of San Romano.

Maurice Utrillo, 1883-1955, Impressionist. Sacre-Coeur de Montmartre.

John Vanderlyn, 1775-1852, Neo-classicist. Ariadne Asleep on the Island of Naxos.

Diego Velazquez, 1599-1660, Baroque. Las Meninas, Portrait of Juan de Pareja.

Jan Vermeer, 1632-1675, interior genre subjects. Young Woman with a Water Jug.

Paolo Veronese, 1528-1588, devotional themes, vastly peopled canvases. The Temptation of St. Anthony.

Andrea del Verrocchio, 1435-1488, Florentine sculptor. Colleoni.

Maurice de Vlaminck, 1876-1958, Fauvist landscapist. The Storm.

Antoine Watteau, 1684-1721, Rococo painter of "scenes of gallantry". The Embarkation for Cythera.

George Frederic Watts, 1817-1904, painter and sculptor of grandiose allegorical themes. Hope, Physical Energy.

Benjamin West, 1738-1820, realistic historical themes. Death of General Wolfe.

James Abbott McNeill Whistler, 1834-1903, Arrangement in Grey and Black, No. 1: The Artist's Mother.

Archibald M. Willard, 1836-1918, The Spirit of '76.

Grant Wood, 1891-1942, Midwestern regionalist. American Gothic, Daughters of Revolution.

Ossip Zadkine, 1890-1967, School of Paris sculptor. The Destroyed City, Musicians, Christ.

Noted Philosophers and Religionists of the Past

Lyman Abbott, 1835-1922, (U.S.) clergyman, reformer; advocate of Christian Socialism.

Pierre Abelard, 1079-1142, (F.) philosopher, theologian, and teacher, used dialectic method to support Christian dogma.

Felix Adler, 1851-1933, (U.S.) German-born founder of the Ethical Culture Society.

St. Augustine, 354-430, Latin bishop considered the founder of formalized Christian theology.

Averroes, 1126-1198, (Sp.) Islamic philosopher.

Roger Bacon, c.1214-1294, (Br.) philosopher and scientist.

Karl Barth, 1886-1968, (Sw.) theologian, a leading force in 20th-century Protestantism.

St. Benedict, c.480-547, (It.) founded the Benedictines.

Jeremy Bentham, 1748-1832, (Br.) philosopher, reformer, founder of Utilitarianism.

Henri Bergson, 1859-1941, (F.) philosopher of evolution.

George Berkeley, 1685-1753, (Ir.) philosopher, churchman.

John Biddle, 1615-1662, (Br.) founder of English Unitarianism.

Jakob Boehme, 1575-1624, (G.) theosophist and mystic.

William Brewster, 1567-1644, (Br.) headed Pilgrims, signed Mayflower Compact.

Emil Brunner, 1889-1966, (Sw.) theologian.

Giordano Bruno, 1548-1600, (It.) philosopher.

Martin Buber, 1878-1965, (G.) Jewish philosopher, theologian, wrote *I and Thou.*

Buddha (Siddhartha Gautama), c.563-c.483 BC, (Ind.) philosopher, founded Buddhism.

John Calvin, 1509-1564, (F.) theologian, a key figure in the Protestant Reformation.

Rudolph Carnap, 1891-1970, (U.S.) German-born philosopher, a founder of logical positivism.

William Ellery Channing, 1780-1842, (U.S.) clergyman, early spokesman for Unitarianism.

Auguste Comte, 1798-1857, (F.) philosopher, the founder of positivism.

Confucius, 551-479 BC, (Chin.) founder of Confucianism.

John Cotton, 1584-1652, (Br.) Puritan theologian.

Thomas Cranmer, 1489-1556, (Br.) churchman, wrote much of *Book of Common Prayer;* promoter of English Reformation.

René Descartes, 1596-1650, (F.) philosopher, mathematician.

John Dewey, 1859-1952, (U.S.) philosopher, educator; helped inaugurate the progressive education movement.

Denis Diderot, 1713-1784, (F.) philosopher, creator of first modern encyclopedia.

Mary Baker Eddy, 1821-1910, (U.S.) founder of Christian Science.

Jonathan Edwards, 1703-1758, (U.S.) preacher, theologian.

(Desiderius) Erasmus, c.1466-1536, (Du.) Renaissance humanist.

Johann Fichte, 1762-1814, (G.) philosopher, the first of the Transcendental Idealists.

George Fox, 1624-1691, (Br.) founder of Society of Friends.

St. Francis of Assisi, 1182-1226, (It.) founded Franciscans.

al Ghazali, 1058-1111, Islamic philosopher.

Georg W. Hegel, 1770-1831, (G.) Idealist philosopher.

Martin Heidegger, 1889-1976, (G.) existentialist philosopher, affected fields ranging from physics to literary criticism.

Johann G. Herder, 1744-1803, (G.) philosopher, cultural historian; a founder of German Romanticism.

David Hume, 1711-1776, (Sc.) philosopher, historian.

Jan Hus, 1369-1415, (Czech.) religious reformer.

Edmund Husserl, 1859-1938, (G.) philosopher, founded the Phenomenological movement.

Thomas Huxley, 1825-1895, (Br.) philosopher, educator.

Ignatius of Loyola, 1491-1556, (Sp.) founder of the Jesuits.

William Inge, 1860-1954, (Br.) theologian, explored the mystic aspects of Christianity.

William James, 1842-1910, (U.S.) philosopher, psychologist; advanced theory of the pragmatic nature of truth.

Karl Jaspers, 1883-1969, (G.) existentialist philosopher.

Immanuel Kant, 1724-1804, (G.) metaphysician, preeminent founder of modern critical philosophy.

Soren Kierkegaard, 1813-1855, (Den.) philosopher, considered the father of Existentialism.

John Knox, 1505-1572, (Sc.) leader of the Protestant Reformation in Scotland.

Lao-Tzu, 604-531 BC, (Chin.) philosopher, considered the founder of the Taoist religion.

Gottfried von Leibniz, 1646-1716, (G.) philosopher, mathematician.

Martin Luther, 1483-1546, (G.) leader of the Protestant Reformation, founded Lutheran church.

Maimonides, 1135-1204, (Sp.) Jewish philosopher.

Jacques Maritain, 1882-1973, (F.) Neo-Thomist philosopher.

Cotton Mather, 1663-1728, (U.S.) defender of orthodox Puritanism; founded Yale, 1703.

Aimee Semple McPherson, 1890-1944, (U.S.) evangelist.

Philipp Melanchthon, 1497-1560, (G.) theologian, humanist; an important voice in the Reformation.

Mohammed, c.570-632, Arab prophet of the religion of Islam.

Dwight Moody, 1837-1899, (U.S.) evangelist.

George E. Moore, 1873-1958, (Br.) ethical theorist.

Elijah Muhammad, 1897-1975, (U.S.) leader of the Black Muslim sect.

Heinrich Muhlenberg, 1711-1787, (G.) organized the Lutheran Church in America.

John H. Newman, 1801-1890, (Br.) Roman Catholic cardinal, led Oxford Movement.

Reinhold Niebuhr, 1892-1971, (U.S.) Protestant theologian, social and political critic.

Friedrich Nietzsche, 1844-1900, (G.) moral philosopher.

Blaise Pascal, 1623-1662, (F.) philosopher and mathematician.

St. Patrick, c.389-c.461, brought Christianity to Ireland.

St. Paul, ?-c.67, a founder of the Christian religion.

Charles S. Peirce, 1839-1914, (U.S.) philosopher, logician; originated concept of Pragmatism, 1878.

Josiah Royce 1855-1916, (U.S.) Idealist philosopher.

Charles T. Russell, 1852-1916, (U.S.) founder of Jehovah's Witnesses.

Fredrich von Schelling, 1775-1854, (G.) philosopher.

Friedrich Schleiermacher, 1768-1834, (G.) theologian, a founder of modern Protestant theology.

Arthur Schopenhauer, 1788-1860, (G.) philosopher.

Joseph Smith, 1805-1844, (U.S.) founded Latter Day Saints (Mormon) movement, 1830.

Herbert Spencer, 1820-1903, (Br.) philosopher of evolution.

Baruch Spinoza, 1632-1677, (Du.) rationalist philosopher.

Billy Sunday, 1862-1935, (U.S.) evangelist.

Daisetz Teitaro Suzuki, 1870-1966, (Jap.) Buddhist scholar.

Emanuel Swedenborg, 1688-1722, (Swed.) philosopher, mystic.

Thomas à Becket, 1118-1170, (Br.) archbishop of Canterbury, opposed Henry II.

Thomas à Kempis, c.1380-1471, (G.) theologian probably wrote *Imitation of Christ.*

Thomas Aquinas, 1225-1274, (It.) theologian, philosopher.

Paul Tillich, 1886-1965, (U.S.) German-born philosopher and theologian.

John Wesley, 1703-1791, (Br.) theologian, evangelist; founded Methodism.

Alfred North Whitehead, 1861-1947, (Br.) philosopher, mathematician.

William of Occam, c.1285-c.1349 (Br.) philosopher.

Roger Williams, c.1603-1683, (U.S.) clergyman, championed religious freedom and separation of church and state.

Ludwig Wittgenstein, 1889-1951, (Aus.) philosopher.

John Wycliffe, 1320-1384, (Br.) theologian, reformer.

Brigham Young, 1801-1877, (U.S.) Mormon leader, colonized Utah.

Huldrych Zwingli, 1484-1531, (Sw.) theologian, led Swiss Protestant Reformation.

Noted Social Reformers and Educators of the Past

Jane Addams, 1860-1935, (U.S.) co-founder of Hull House; won Nobel Peace Prize, 1931.

Susan B. Anthony, 1820-1906, (U.S.) a leader in temperance, anti-slavery, and women's suffrage movements.

Henry Barnard, 1811-1900, (U.S.) public school reformer.

Thomas Barnardo, 1845-1905, (Br.) social reformer, pioneered in the care of destitute children.

Clara Barton, 1821-1912, (U.S.) organizer of the American Red Cross.

Henry Ward Beecher, 1813-1887, (U.S.) clergyman, abolitionist.

Amelia Bloomer, 1818-1894, (U.S.) social reformer, women's rights advocate.

William Booth, 1829-1912, (Br.) founded the Salvation Army.

Nicholas Murray Butler, 1862-1947, (U.S.) educator headed Columbia Univ., 1902-45; won Nobel Peace Prize, 1931.

Frances X. (Mother) Cabrini, 1850-1917, (U.S.) Italian-born nun founded charitable institutions; first American canonized.

Carrie Chapman Catt, 1859-1947, (U.S.) suffragette, helped win passage of the 19th amendment.

Dorothy Day, 1897-1980, (U.S.) founder of Catholic Worker Movement.

Eugene V. Debs, 1855-1926, (U.S.) labor leader, led Pullman strike, 1894; 4-time Socialist presidential candidate.

Melvil Dewey, 1851-1931, (U.S.) devised decimal system of library-book classification.

Dorothea Dix, 1802-1887, (U.S.) crusader for humane care of mentally ill.

Frederick Douglass, 1817-1895, (U.S.) abolitionist.

W.E.B. DuBois, 1868-1963, (U.S.) Negro-rights leader, educator, and writer.

William Lloyd Garrison, 1805-1879, (U.S.) abolitionist, re-

former.

Giovanni Gentile, 1875-1944, (It.) philosopher, educator; reformed Italian educational system.

Samuel Gompers, 1850-1924, (U.S.) labor leader; a founder and president of AFL.

William Green, 1873-1952, (U.S.) president of AFL, 1924-52.

Sidney Hillman, 1887-1946, (U.S.) labor leader, helped organize CIO.

Samuel G. Howe, 1801-1876, (U.S.) social reformer, changed public attitudes toward the handicapped.

Helen Keller, 1880-1968, (U.S.) crusader for better treatment for the handicapped.

Martin Luther King Jr., 1929-1968, (U.S.) civil rights leader; won Nobel Peace Prize, 1964.

John L. Lewis, 1880-1969, (U.S.) labor leader, headed United Mine Workers, 1920-60.

Horace Mann, 1796-1859, (U.S.) pioneered modern public school system.

William H. McGuffey, 1800-1873, (U.S.) author of *Reader,* the mainstay of 19th century U.S. public education.

Alexander Meiklejohn, 1872-1964, (U.S.) British-born educator, championed academic freedom and experimental curricula.

Lucretia Mott, 1793-1880, (U.S.) reformer, pioneer feminist.

Philip Murray, 1886-1952, (U.S.) Scotch-born labor leader.

Florence Nightingale, 1820-1910, (Br.) founder of modern nursing.

Emmeline Pankhurst, 1858-1928, (Br.) woman suffragist.

Elizabeth P. Peabody, 1804-1894, (U.S.) education pioneer, founded 1st kindergarten in U.S., 1860.

Walter Reuther, 1907-1970, (U.S.) labor leader, headed UAW.

Jacob Riis, 1849-1914, (U.S.) crusader for urban reforms.

Margaret Sanger, 1883-1966, (U.S.) social reformer, pioneered the birth control movement.

Elizabeth Seton, 1774-1821, (U.S.) established parochial school education in U.S.

Earl of Shaftesbury (A.A. Cooper), 1801-1885, (Br.) social reformer.

Elizabeth Cady Stanton, 1815-1902, (U.S.) women's suffrage pioneer.

Lucy Stone, 1818-1893, (U.S.) feminist, abolitionist.

Harriet Tubman, c.1820-1913, (U.S.) abolitionist, ran Underground Railroad.

Booker T. Washington, 1856-1915, (U.S.) educator, reformer; championed vocational training for blacks.

Walter F. White, 1893-1955, (U.S.) headed NAACP, 1931-55.

William Wilberforce, 1759-1833, (Br.) social reformer, prominent in struggle to abolish the slave trade.

Emma Hart Willard, 1787-1870, (U.S.) pioneered higher education for women.

Frances E. Willard, 1839-1898, (U.S.) temperance, woman's rights leader.

Whitney M. Young Jr., 1921-1971, (U.S.) civil rights leader, headed National Urban League, 1961-71.

Noted Historians, Economists, and Social Scientists of the Past

Brooks Adams, 1848-1927, (U.S.) historian, political theoretician.

Francis Bacon, 1561-1626, (Br.) philosopher, essayist, and statesman.

George Bancroft, 1800-1891, (U.S.) historian, wrote 10-volume *History of the United States.*

Charles A. Beard, 1874-1948, (U.S.) historian, attacked motives of the Founding Fathers.

Bede (the Venerable), c.673-735, (Br.) scholar, historian.

Ruth Benedict, 1887-1948, (U.S.) anthropologist, studied Indian tribes of the Southwest.

Louis Blanc, 1811-1882, (F.) Socialist leader and historian whose ideas were a link between utopian and Marxist socialism.

Franz Boas, 1858-1942, (G.) German-born anthropologist, studied American Indians.

Van Wyck Brooks, 1886-1963, (U.S.) cultural historian, critic.

Edmund Burke, 1729-1797, (Ir.) British parliamentarian and political philosopher; influenced many Federalists.

Thomas Carlyle, 1795-1881, (Sc.) philosopher, historian, and critic.

Edward Channing, 1856-1931, (U.S.) historian wrote 6-volume *A History of the United States.*

John R. Commons, 1862-1945, (U.S.) economist, labor historian.

Benedetto Croce, 1866-1952, (It.) philosopher, statesman, and historian.

Bernard A. De Voto, 1897-1955, (U.S.) historian, won Pulitzer prize in 1948 for *Across the Wide Missouri.*

Ariel Durant, 1898-1981, (U.S.) historian, collaborated with husband on 11-volume *The Story of Civilization.*

Will Durant, 1885-1981, (U.S.) historian. *The Story of Civilization, The Story of Philosophy.*

Emile Durkheim, 1858-1917, (F.) a founder of modern sociology.

Friedrich Engels, 1820-1895, (G.) political writer, with Marx wrote the *Communist Manifesto.*

Irving Fisher, 1867-1947, (U.S.) economist, contributed to the development of modern monetary theory.

John Fiske, 1842-1901, (U.S.) historian and lecturer, popularized Darwinian theory of evolution.

Charles Fourier, 1772-1837, (F.) utopian socialist.

Henry George, 1839-1897, (U.S.) economist, reformer, led single-tax movement.

Edward Gibbon, 1737-1794, (Br.) historian, wrote *The History of the Decline and Fall of the Roman Empire.*

Francesco Guicciardini, 1483-1540, (It.) historian, wrote *Storia d'Italia,* principal historical work of the 16th-century.

Alvin Hansen, 1887-1975, (U.S.) economist.

Thomas Hobbes, 1588-1679, (Br.) social philosopher.

Richard Hofstadter, 1916-1970, (U.S.) historian, wrote *The Age of Reform.*

John Maynard Keynes, 1883-1946, (Br.) economist, principal advocate of deficit spending.

Alfred L. Kroeber, 1876-1960, (U.S.) cultural anthropologist, studied Indians of North and South America.

James L. Laughlin, 1850-1933, (U.S.) economist, helped establish Federal Reserve System.

Lucien Lévy-Bruhl, 1857-1939, (F.) philosopher, studied the psychology of primitive societies.

Kurt Lewin, 1890-1947, (U.S.) German-born psychologist, studied human motivation and group dynamics.

John Locke, 1632-1704, (Br.) political philosopher.

Thomas B. Macauley, 1800-1859, (Br.) historian, statesman.

Bronislaw Malinowski, 1884-1942, (Pol.) anthropologist, considered the father of social anthropology.

Thomas R. Malthus, 1766-1834, (Br.) economist, famed for *Essay on the Principle of Population.*

Karl Mannheim, 1893-1947, (Hung.) sociologist, historian.

Karl Marx, 1818-1883, (G.) political philosopher, proponent of modern communism.

Giuseppe Mazzini, 1805-1872, (It.) political philosopher.

George H. Mead, 1863-1931, (U.S.) philosopher and social psychologist.

Margaret Mead, 1901-1978, (U.S.) cultural anthropologist, popularized field.

James Mill, 1773-1836, (Sc.) philosopher, historian, and economist; a proponent of Utilitarianism.

John Stuart Mill, 1806-1873, (Br.) philosopher, political economist.

Perry G. Miller, 1905-1963, (U.S.) historian, interpreted 17th-century New England.

Theodor Mommsen, 1817-1903, (G.) historian, wrote *The History of Rome.*

Charles-Louis Montesquieu, 1689-1755, (F.) social philosopher.

Samuel Eliot Morison, 1887-1976, (U.S.) historian, chronicled voyages of early explorers.

Allan Nevins, 1890-1971, (U.S.) historian, biographer; twice won Pulitzer prize.

Jose Ortega y Gasset, 1883-1955, (Sp.) philosopher and humanist; advocated control by an elite.

Robert Owen, 1771-1858, (Br.) political philosopher, reformer.

Vilfredo Pareto, 1848-1923, (It.) economist, sociologist.

Francis Parkman, 1823-1893, (U.S.) historian, wrote 8-volume *France and England in North America, 1851-92.*

Marco Polo, c.1254-1324, (It.) narrated an account of his travels to China.

William Prescott, 1796-1859, (U.S.) early American historian.

Pierre Joseph Proudhon, 1809-1865, (F.) social theorist, regarded as the father of anarchism.

Francois Quesnay, 1694-1774, (F.) economic theorist, demonstrated circular flow of economic activity through society.

David Ricardo, 1772-1823, (Br.) economic theorist, advocated free international trade.

James H. Robinson, 1863-1936, (U.S.) historian, educator.

Jean-Jacques Rousseau, 1712-1778, (F.) social philosopher, author.

Hjalmar Schacht, 1877-1970, (G.) economist.

Joseph Schumpeter, 1883-1950, (U.S.) Czech.-born economist, championed big business, capitalism.

Albert Schweitzer, 1875-1965, (Alsatian) social philosopher, theologian, and humanitarian.

George Simmel, 1858-1918, (G.) sociologist, philosopher.

Adam Smith, 1723-1790, (Br.) economist, advocated laissez-faire economy and free trade.

Jared Sparks, 1789-1866, (U.S.) historian, among first to do research from original documents.

Oswald Spengler, 1880-1936, (G.) philosopher and historian, wrote *The Decline of the West.*

William G. Sumner, 1840-1910, (U.S.) social scientist, economist; championed laissez-faire economy, Social Darwinism.

Hippolyte Taine, 1828-1893, (F.) historian.

Frank W. Taussig, 1859-1940, (U.S.) economist, educator.

Alexis de Tocqueville, 1805-1859, (F.) political scientist, historian.

Francis E. Townsend, 1867-1960, (U.S.) author of old-age pension plan.

Arnold Toynbee, 1889-1975, (Br.) historian, wrote 10-volume *A Study of History.*

Heinrich von Treitschke, 1834-1896, (G.) historian, political

writer.

George Trevelyan, 1838-1928, (Br.) historian, statesman.

Frederick J. Turner, 1861-1932, (U.S.) historian, educator.

Thorstein B. Veblen, 1857-1929, (U.S.) economist, social philosopher.

Giovanni Vico, 1668-1744, (It.) historian, philosopher.

Voltaire (F.M. Arouet), 1694-1778, (F.) philosopher, historian, and poet.

Izaak Walton, 1593-1683, (Br.) author, wrote first biographical works in English literature.

Sidney J., 1859-1947, and wife **Beatrice,** 1858-1943, **Webb** (Br.) leading figures in Fabian Society and British Labour Party.

Walter P. Webb, 1888-1963, (U.S.) historian of the West.

Max Weber, 1864-1920, (G.) sociologist.

Noted Scientists of the Past

Howard H. Aiken, 1900-1973, (U.S.) mathematician, credited with designing forerunner of digital computer.

Albertus Magnus, 1193-1280, (G.) theologian, philosopher, scientist, established medieval Christian study of natural science.

Andre-Marie Ampère, 1775-1836, (F.) scientist known for contributions to electrodynamics.

Amedeo Avogadro, 1776-1856, (It.) chemist, physicist, advanced important theories on properties of gases.

A.C. Becquerel, 1788-1878, (F.) physicist, pioneer in electrochemical science.

A.H. Becquerel, 1852-1908, (F.) physicist, discovered radioactivity in uranium.

Alexander Graham Bell, 1847-1922, (U.S.) inventor, first to patent and commercially exploit the telephone, 1876.

Daniel Bernoulli, 1700-1782, (Swiss) mathematician, advanced kinetic theory of gases and fluids.

Jöns Jakob Berzelius, 1779-1848, (Swed.) chemist, developed modern chemical symbols and formulas.

Henry Bessemer, 1813-1898, (Br.) engineer, invented Bessemer steel-making process.

Louis Blériot, 1872-1936, (F.) engineer, pioneer aviator, invented and constructed monoplanes.

Niels Bohr, 1885-1962, (Dan.) physicist, leading figure in the development of quantum theory.

Max Born, 1882-1970, (G.) physicist known for research in quantum mechanics.

Robert Bunsen, 1811-1899, (G.) chemist, invented Bunsen burner.

Luther Burbank, 1849-1926, (U.S.) plant breeder whose work developed plant breeding into a modern science.

Vannevar Bush, 1890-1974, (U.S.) electrical engineer, developed differential analyzer, first electronic analogue computer.

Alexis Carrel, 1873-1944, (F.) surgeon, biologist, developed methods of suturing blood vessels and transplanting organs.

George Washington Carver, 1860?-1943, (U.S.) agricultural chemist, experimenter, benefactor of South, a black hero.

Henry Cavendish, 1731-1810, (Br.) chemist, physicist, discovered hydrogen.

James Chadwick, 1891-1974, (Br.) physicist, discovered the neutron.

Jean M. Charcot, 1825-1893, (F.) neurologist known for work on hysteria, hypnotism, sclerosis.

Albert Claude, 1899-1983, (Belg.) a founder of modern cell biology.

John D. Cockcroft, 1897-1967, (Br.) nuclear physicist, constructed first atomic particle accelerator with E.T.S. Walton.

William Crookes, 1832-1919, (Br.) physicist, chemist, discovered thallium, invented a cathode-ray tube, radiometer.

Marie Curie, 1867-1934, (Pol.-F.) physical chemist known for work on radium and its compounds.

Pierre Curie, 1859-1906, (F.) physical chemist known for work with his wife on radioactivity.

Gottlieb Daimler, 1834-1900, (G.) engineer, inventor, pioneer automobile manufacturer.

John Dalton, 1766-1844, (Br.) chemist, physicist, formulated atomic theory, made first table of atomic weights.

Charles Darwin, 1809-1882, (Br.) naturalist, established theory of organic evolution.

Humphry Davy, 1778-1829, (Br.) chemist, research in electrochemistry led to isolation of potassium, sodium, calcium, barium, boron, magnesium, and strontium.

Lee De Forest, 1873-1961, (U.S.) inventor, pioneer in development of wireless telegraphy, sound pictures, television.

Max Delbruck, 1907-1981, (U.S.) pioneer in modern molecular genetics.

Rudolf Diesel, 1858-1913, (G.) mechanical engineer, patented Diesel engine.

Thomas Dooley, 1927-1961, (U.S.) "jungle doctor," noted for efforts to supply medical aid to underdeveloped countries.

Christian Doppler, 1803-1853, (Aus.) physicist, demon-

strated Doppler effect (change in energy wavelengths caused by motion).

Thomas A. Edison, 1847-1931, (U.S.) inventor, held over 1,000 patents, including incandescent electric lamp, phonograph.

Paul Ehrlich, 1854-1915, (G.) bacteriologist, pioneer in modern immunology and bacteriology.

Albert Einstein, 1879-1955, (U.S.) theoretical physicist, known for formulation of relativity theory.

Leonhard Euler, 1707-1783, (Swiss) mathematician, physicist, authored first calculus book.

Gabriel Fahrenheit, 1686-1736, (G.) physicist, introduced Fahrenheit scale for thermometers.

Michael Faraday, 1791-1867, (Br.) chemist, physicist, known for work in field of electricity.

Pierre de Fermat, 1601-1665, (F.) mathematician, discovered analytic geometry, founded modern theory of numbers and calculus of probabilities.

Enrico Fermi, 1901-1954, (It.) physicist, one of chief architects of the nuclear age.

Galileo Ferraris, 1847-1897, (It.) physicist, electrical engineer, discovered principle of rotary magnetic field.

Camille Flammarion, 1842-1925, (F.) astronomer, popularized study of astronomy.

Alexander Fleming, 1881-1955, (Br.) bacteriologist, discovered penicillin.

Jean B.J. Fourier, 1768-1830, (F.) mathematician, discovered theorem governing periodic oscillation.

James Franck, 1882-1964, (G.) physicist, proved value of quantum theory.

Sigmund Freud, 1856-1939, (Aus.) psychiatrist, founder of psychoanalysis.

Galileo Galilei, 1564-1642, (It.) astronomer, physicist, a founder of the experimental method.

Luigi Galvani, 1737-1798, (It.) physician, physicist, known as founder of galvanism.

Carl Friedrich Gauss, 1777-1855, (G.) mathematician, astronomer, physicist, made important contributions to almost every field of physical science, founded a number of new fields.

Joseph Gay-Lussac, 1778-1850, (F.) chemist, physicist, investigated behavior of gases, discovered law of combining volumes.

Josiah W. Gibbs, 1839-1903, (U.S.) theoretical physicist, chemist, founded chemical thermodynamics.

Robert H. Goddard, 1882-1945 (U.S.) physicist, father of modern rocketry.

George W. Goethals, 1858-1928, (U.S.) army engineer, built the Panama Canal.

William C. Gorgas, 1854-1920, (U.S.) sanitarian, U.S. army surgeon-general, his work to prevent yellow fever, malaria helped insure construction of Panama Canal.

Ernest Haeckel, 1834-1919, (G.) zoologist, evolutionist, a strong proponent of Darwin.

Otto Hahn, 1879-1968, (G.) chemist, worked on atomic fission.

J.B.S. Haldane, 1892-1964, (Sc.) scientist, known for work as geneticist and application of mathematics to science.

James Hall, 1761-1832, (Br.) geologist, chemist, founded experimental geology, geochemistry.

Edmund Halley, 1656-1742, (Br.) astronomer, calculated the orbits of many planets.

William Harvey, 1578-1657, (Br.) physician, anatomist, discovered circulation of the blood.

Hermann v. Helmholtz, 1821-1894, (G.) physicist, anatomist, physiologist, made fundamental contributions to physiology, optics, electrodynamics, mathematics, meteorology.

William Herschel, 1738-1822, (Br.) astronomer, discovered Uranus.

Heinrich Hertz, 1857-1894, (G.) physicist, his discoveries led to wireless telegraphy.

David Hilbert, 1862-1943, (G.) mathematician, formulated

first satisfactory set of axioms for modern Euclidean geometry.

Edwin P. Hubble, 1889-1953, (U.S.) astronomer, produced first observational evidence of expanding universe.

Alexander v. Humboldt, 1769-1859, (G.) explorer, naturalist, propagator of earth sciences, originated ecology, geophysics.

Julian Huxley, 1887-1975, (Br.) biologist, a gifted exponent and philosopher of science.

Edward Jenner, 1749-1823, (Br.) physician, discovered vaccination.

William Jenner, 1815-1898, (Br.) physician, pathological anatomist.

Frederic Joliot-Curie, 1900-1958, (F.) physicist, with his wife continued work of Curies on radioactivity.

Irene Joliot-Curie, 1897-1956, (F.) physicist, continued work of Curies in radioactivity.

James P. Joule, 1818-1889, (Br.) physicist, determined relationship between heat and mechanical energy (conservation of energy).

Carl Jung, 1875-1961, (Sw.) psychiatrist, founder of analytical psychology.

Wm. Thomson Kelvin, 1824-1907, (Br.) mathematician, physicist, known for work on heat and electricity.

Sister Elizabeth Kenny, 1886-1952, (Austral.) nurse, developed method of treatment for polio.

Johannes Kepler, 1571-1630, (G.) astronomer, discovered important laws of planetary motion.

Joseph Lagrange, 1736-1813, (F.) geometer, astronomer, worked in all fields of analysis, and number theory, and analytical and celestial mechanics.

Jean B. Lamarck, 1744-1829, (F.) naturalist, forerunner of Darwin in evolutionary theory.

Irving Langmuir, 1881-1957, (U.S.) physical chemist, his studies of molecular films on solid and liquid surfaces opened new fields in colloid research and biochemistry.

Pierre S. Laplace, 1749-1827, (F.) astronomer, physicist, put forth nebular hypothesis of origin of solar system.

Antoine Lavoisier, 1743-1794, (F.) chemist, founder of modern chemistry.

Ernest O. Lawrence, 1901-1958, (U.S.) physicist, invented the cyclotron.

Louis Leakey, 1903-1972, (Br.) anthropologist, discovered important fossils, remains of early hominids.

Anton van Leeuwenhoek, 1632-1723, (Du.) microscopist, father of microbiology.

Gottfried Wilhelm Leibniz, 1646-1716, (G.) mathematician, developed theories of differential and integral calculus.

Justus von Liebig, 1803-1873, (G.) chemist, established quantitative organic chemical analysis.

Joseph Lister, 1827-1912, (Br.) pioneer of antiseptic surgery.

Percival Lowell, 1855-1916, (U.S.) astronomer, predicted the existence of Pluto.

Guglielmo Marconi, 1874-1937, (It.) physicist, known for his development of wireless telegraphy.

James Clerk Maxwell, 1831-1879, (Sc.) physicist, known especially for his work in electricity and magnetism.

Maria Goeppert Mayer, 1906-1972, (G.-U.S.) physicist, independently developed theory of structure of atomic nuclei.

Lise Meitner, 1878-1968, (Aus.) physicist whose work contributed to the development of the atomic bomb.

Gregor J. Mendel, 1822-1884, (Aus.) botanist, known for his experimental work on heredity.

Franz Mesmer, 1734-1815, (G.) physician, developed theory of animal magnetism.

Albert A. Michelson, 1852-1931, (U.S.) physicist, established speed of light as a fundamental constant.

Robert A. Millikan, 1868-1953, (U.S.) physicist, noted for study of elementary electronic charge and photoelectric effect.

Thomas Hunt Morgan, 1866-1945, (U.S.) geneticist, embryologist, established chromosome theory of heredity.

Isaac Newton, 1642-1727, (Br.) natural philosopher, mathematician, discovered law of gravitation, laws of motion.

J. Robert Oppenheimer, 1904-1967, (U.S.) physicist, director of Los Alamos during development of the atomic bomb.

Wilhelm Ostwald, 1853-1932, (G.) physical chemist, philosopher, chief founder of physical chemistry.

Louis Pasteur, 1822-1895, (F.) chemist, originated process of pasteurization.

Max Planck, 1858-1947, (G.) physicist, originated and developed quantum theory.

Henri Poincaré, 1854-1912, (F.) mathematician, physicist, influenced cosmology, relativity, and topology.

Joseph Priestley, 1733-1804, (Br.) chemist, one of the discoverers of oxygen.

Walter S. Reed, 1851-1902, (U.S.) army pathologist, bacteriologist, proved mosquitos transmit yellow fever.

Bernhard Riemann, 1826-1866, (G.) mathematician, contributed to development of calculus, complex variable theory, and mathematical physics.

Wilhelm Roentgen, 1845-1923, (G.) physicist, discovered X-rays.

Bertrand Russell, 1872-1970, (Br.) logician, philosopher, one of the founders of modern logic, wrote *Principia Mathematica*.

Ernest Rutherford, 1871-1937, (Br.) physicist, discovered the atomic nucleus.

Giovanni Schiaparelli, 1835-1910, (It.) astronomer, hypothesized canals on the surface of Mars.

Angelo Secchi, 1818-1878, (It.) astronomer, pioneer in classifying stars by their spectra.

Harlow Shapley, 1885-1972, (U.S.) astronomer, noted for his studies of the galaxy.

Charles P. Steinmetz, 1865-1923, (G.-U.S.) electrical engineer, developed basic ideas on alternating current systems.

Leo Szilard, 1898-1964, (U.S.) physicist, helped create first sustained nuclear reaction.

Nikola Tesla, 1856-1943, (Croatia-U.S.) electrical engineer, contributed to most developments in electronics.

Rudolf Virchow, 1821-1902, (G.) pathologist, a founder of cellular pathology.

Alessandro Volta, 1745-1827, (It.) physicist, pioneer in electricity.

Alfred Russell Wallace, 1823-1913, (Br.) naturalist, proposed concept of evolution similar to Darwin.

August v. Wasserman, 1866-1925, (G.) bacteriologist, discovered reaction used as test for syphilis.

James E. Watt, 1736-1819, (Sc.) mechanical engineer, inventor, invented modern steam condensing engine.

Alfred L. Wegener, 1880-1930, (G.) meteorologist, geophysicist, postulated theory of continental drift.

Norbert Wiener, 1894-1964, (U.S.) mathematician, founder of the science of cybernetics.

Ferdinand v. Zeppelin, 1838-1917 (G.) soldier, aeronaut, airship designer.

Noted Business Leaders, Industrialists, and Philanthropists of the Past

Elizabeth Arden (F.N. Graham), 1884-1966, (U.S.) Canadian-born businesswoman founded and headed cosmetics empire.

Philip D. Armour, 1832-1901, (U.S.) industrialist, streamlined meat packing.

John Jacob Astor, 1763-1848, (U.S.) German-born fur trader, banker, real estate magnate; at death, richest in U.S.

Francis W. Ayer, 1848-1923, (U.S.) ad industry pioneer.

August Belmont, 1816-1890, (U.S.) German-born financier.

James B. (Diamond Jim) Brady, 1856-1917, (U.S.) financier, philanthropist, legendary bon vivant.

Adolphus Busch, 1839-1913, (U.S.) German-born businessman, established brewery empire.

Asa Candler, 1851-1929, (U.S.) founded Coca-Cola Co.

Andrew Carnegie, 1835-1919, (U.S.) Scots-born industrialist, founded U.S. Steel; financed over 2,800 libraries.

William Colgate, 1783-1857, (U.S.) British-born businessman, philanthropist; founded soap-making empire.

Jay Cooke, 1821-1905, (U.S.) financier, sold $1 billion in Union bonds during Civil War.

Peter Cooper, 1791-1883, (U.S.) industrialist, inventor, philanthropist.

Ezra Cornell, 1807-1874, (U.S.) businessman, philanthropist; headed Western Union, established univ.

Erastus Corning, 1794-1872, (U.S.) financier, headed N.Y. Central.

Charles Crocker, 1822-1888, (U.S.) railroad builder, financier.

Samuel Cunard, 1787-1865, (Can.) pioneered trans-Atlantic steam navigation.

Marcus Daly, 1841-1900, (U.S.) Irish-born copper magnate.

Walt Disney, 1901-1966, (U.S.) pioneer in cinema animation, built entertainment empire.

Herbert H. Dow, 1866-1930, (U.S.) Canadian-born founder of chemical co.

James Duke, 1856-1925, (U.S.) founded American Tobacco, Duke Univ.

Eleuthere I. du Pont, 1771-1834, (U.S.) French-born gunpowder manufacturer; founded one of world's largest business empires.

Thomas C. Durant, 1820-1885, (U.S.) railroad official, financier.

William C. Durant, 1861-1947, (U.S.) industrialist, formed General Motors.

George Eastman, 1854-1932, (U.S.) inventor, manufacturer of photographic equipment.

Marshall Field, 1834-1906, (U.S.) merchant, founded Chicago's largest department store.

Harvey Firestone, 1868-1938, (U.S.) industrialist, founded tire co.

Henry M. Flagler, 1830-1913, (U.S.) financier, helped form

Standard Oil; developed Florida as resort state.

Henry Ford, 1863-1947, (U.S.) auto maker, developed first popular low-priced car.

Henry C. Frick, 1849-1919, (U.S.) industrialist, helped organize U.S. Steel.

Jakob Fugger (Jakob the Rich), 1459-1525, (G.) headed leading banking house, trading concern, in 16th-century Europe.

Alfred C. Fuller, 1885-1973, (U.S.) Canadian-born businessman, founded brush co.

Elbert H. Gary, 1846-1927, (U.S.) U.S. Steel head, 1903-27.

Amadeo P. Giannini, 1870-1949, (U.S.) founded Bank of America.

Stephen Girard, 1750-1831, (U.S.) French-born financier, philanthropist; richest man in U.S. at his death.

Jean Paul Getty, 1892-1976, (U.S.) founded oil empire.

Jay Gould, 1836-1892, (U.S.) railroad magnate, financier, speculator.

Hetty Green, 1834-1916, (U.S.) financier, the "witch of Wall St."; richest woman in U.S in her day.

William Gregg, 1800-1867, (U.S.) launched textile industry in the South.

Meyer Guggenheim, 1828-1905, (U.S.) Swiss-born merchant, philanthropist; built merchandising, mining empires.

Edward H. Harriman, 1848-1909, (U.S.) railroad financier, administrator; headed Union Pacific.

William Randolph Hearst, 1863-1951, (U.S.) a dominant figure in American journalism; built vast publishing empire.

Henry J. Heinz, 1844-1919, (U.S.) founded food empire.

James J. Hill, 1838-1916, (U.S.) Canadian-born railroad magnate, financier; founded Great Northern Railway.

Conrad N. Hilton, 1888-1979, (U.S.) intl. hotel chain founder.

Howard Hughes, 1905-1976, (U.S.) industrialist, financier, movie maker.

H.L. Hunt, 1889-1974, (U.S.) oil magnate.

Collis P. Huntington, 1821-1900, (U.S.) railroad magnate.

Henry E. Huntington, 1850-1927, (U.S.) railroad builder, philanthropist.

Howard Johnson, 1896-1972, (U.S.) founded restaurant chain.

Henry J. Kaiser, 1882-1967, (U.S.) industrialist, built empire in steel, aluminum.

Minor C. Keith, 1848-1929, (U.S.) railroad magnate; founded United Fruit Co.

Will K. Kellogg, 1860-1951, (U.S.) businessman, philanthropist, founded breakfast food co.

Richard King, 1825-1885, (U.S.) cattleman, founded half-million acre King Ranch in Texas.

William S. Knudsen, 1879-1948, (U.S.) Danish-born auto industry executive.

Samuel H. Kress, 1863-1955, (U.S.) businessman, art collector, philanthropist; founded "dime store" chain.

Ray A. Kroc, 1902-1984, (U.S.) builder of McDonald's fast food empire; owner, San Diego Padres baseball team.

Alfred Krupp, 1812-1887, (G.) armaments magnate.

Albert Lasker, 1880-1952, (U.S.) businessman, philanthropist.

Thomas Lipton, 1850-1931, (Ir.) merchant, built tea empire.

James McGill, 1744-1813, (Can.) Scots-born fur trader, founded univ.

Andrew W. Mellon, 1855-1937, (U.S.) financier, industrialist; benefactor of National Gallery of Art.

Charles E. Merrill, 1885-1956, (U.S.) financier, developed firm of Merrill Lynch.

John Pierpont Morgan, 1837-1913, (U.S.) most powerful figure in finance and industry at the turn-of-the-century.

Malcolm Muir, 1885-1979, (U.S.) created *Business Week* magazine; headed *Newsweek*, 1937-61.

Samuel Newhouse, 1895-1979, (U.S.) publishing and broadcasting magnate, built communications empire.

Aristotle Onassis, 1900-1975, (Gr.) shipping magnate.

George Peabody, 1795-1869, (U.S.) merchant, financier, philanthropist.

James C. Penney, 1875-1971, (U.S.) businessman, developed department store chain.

William C. Procter, 1862-1934, (U.S.) headed soap co.

John D. Rockefeller, 1839-1937, (U.S.) industrialist, established Standard Oil; became world's wealthiest person.

John D. Rockefeller Jr., 1874-1960, (U.S.) philanthropist, established foundation; provided land for United Nations.

Meyer A. Rothschild, 1743-1812, (G.) founded international banking house.

Thomas Fortune Ryan, 1851-1928, (U.S.) financier, dominated N.Y. City public transportation; helped found American Tobacco.

Russell Sage, 1816-1906, (U.S.) financier.

David Sarnoff, 1891-1971, (U.S.) broadcasting pioneer, established first radio network, NBC.

Richard W. Sears, 1863-1914, (U.S.) founded mail-order co.

(Ernst) Werner von Siemens, 1816-1892, (G.) industrialist, inventor.

Alfred P. Sloan, 1875-1966, (U.S.) industrialist, philanthropist; headed General Motors.

A. Leland Stanford, 1824-1893, (U.S.) railroad official, philanthropist; founded univ.

Nathan Strauss, 1848-1931, (U.S.) German-born merchant, philanthropist; headed Macy's.

Levi Strauss, c.1829-1902, (U.S.) pants manufacturer.

Clement Studebaker, 1831-1901, (U.S.) wagon, carriage manufacturer.

Gustavus Swift, 1839-1903, (U.S.) pioneer meat-packer; promoted refrigerated railroad cars.

Gerard Swope, 1872-1957, (U.S.) industrialist, economist; headed General Electric.

James Walter Thompson, 1847-1928, (U.S.) ad executive.

Theodore N. Vail, 1845-1920, (U.S.) organized Bell Telephone system, headed ATT.

Cornelius Vanderbilt, 1794-1877, (U.S.) financier, established steamship, railroad empires.

Henry Villard, 1835-1900, (U.S.) German-born railroad executive, financier.

Charles R. Walgreen, 1873-1939, (U.S.) founded drugstore chain.

DeWitt Wallace, 1890-1981, (U.S.) and **Lila Wallace,** 1890-1984, (U.S.) co-founders of *Reader's Digest* magazine, philanthropists.

John Wanamaker, 1838-1922, (U.S.) pioneered department-store merchandising.

Aaron Montgomery Ward, 1843-1913, (U.S.) established first mail-order firm.

Thomas J. Watson, 1874-1956, (U.S.) headed IBM, 1924-49.

John Hay Whitney, 1905-1982, (U.S.) publisher, sportsman, philanthropist.

Charles E. Wilson, 1890-1961, (U.S.) auto industry executive; public official.

Frank W. Woolworth, 1852-1919, (U.S.) created 5 & 10 chain.

William Wrigley Jr., 1861-1932, (U.S.) founded chewing gum co.

Composers of the Western World

Carl Philipp Emanuel Bach, 1714-1788, (G.) Prussian and Wurtembergian Sonatas.

Johann Christian Bach, 1735-1782, (G.) Concertos; sonatas.

Johann Sebastian Bach, 1685-1750, (G.) St. Matthew Passion, The Well-Tempered Clavichord.

Samuel Barber, 1910-1981, (U.S.) Adagio for Strings, Vanessa.

Bela Bartok, 1881-1945, (Hung.) Concerto for Orchestra, The Miraculous Mandarin.

Ludwig Van Beethoven, 1770-1827, (G.) Concertos (Emperor); sonatas (Moonlight, Pastorale, Pathetique); symphonies (Eroica).

Vincenzo Bellini, 1801-1835, (It.) La Sonnambula, Norma, I Puritani.

Alban Berg, 1885-1935, (Aus.) Wozzeck, Lulu.

Hector Berlioz, 1803-1869, (F.) Damnation of Faust, Symphonie Fantastique, Requiem.

Leonard Bernstein, b. 1918, (U.S.) Jeremiah, West Side Story.

Georges Bizet, 1838-1875, (F.) Carmen, Pearl Fishers.

Ernest Bloch, 1880-1959, (Swiss) Schelomo, Voice in the Wilderness, Sacred Service.

Luigi Boccherini, 1743-1805, (It.) Cello Concerto in B Flat, Symphony in C.

Alexander Borodin, 1833-1887, (R.) Prince Igor, In the Steppes of Central Asia.

Johannes Brahms, 1833-1897, (G.) Liebeslieder Waltzes, Rhapsody in E Flat Major, Opus 119 for Piano, Academic Festival Overture; symphonies; quartets.

Benjamin Britten, 1913-1976, (Br.) Peter Grimes, Turn of the Screw, Ceremony of Carols, War Requiem.

Anton Bruckner, 1824-1896, (Aus.) Symphonies (Romantic), Intermezzo for String Quintet.

Ferruccio Busoni, 1866-1924, (It.) Doctor Faust, Comedy Overture.

Dietrich Buxtehude, 1637-1707, (D.) Cantatas, trio sonatas.

William Byrd, 1543-1623, (Br.) Masses, sacred songs.

(Alexis-) Emmanuel Chabrier, 1841-1894, (Fr.) Le Roi Malgre Lui, Espana.

Gustave Charpentier, 1860-1956, (F.) Louise.

Frederic Chopin, 1810-1849, (P.) Polonaises, mazurkas, waltzes, etudes, nocturnes. Polonaise No. 6 in A Flat Major (Heroic); sonatas.

Aaron Copland, b. 1900, (U.S.) Appalachian Spring.

(Achille-) Claude Debussy, 1862-1918, (F.) Pelleas et Melisande, La Mer, Prelude to the Afternoon of a Faun.

C.P. Leo Delibes, 1836-1891, (F.) Lakme, Coppelia, Sylvia.

Norman Dello Joio, b. 1913, (U.S.), Triumph of St. Joan, Psalm of David.

Gaetano Donizetti, 1797-1848, (It.) Elixir of Love, Lucia Di Lammermoor, Daughter of the Regiment.

Paul Dukas, 1865-1935, (Fr.) Sorcerer's Apprentice.

Antonin Dvorak, 1841-1904, (C.) Symphony in E Minor (From the New World).

Edward Elgar, 1857-1934, (Br.) Pomp and Circumstance.

Manuel de Falla, 1876-1946, (Sp.) La Vide Breve, El Amor Brujo.

Gabriel Faure, 1845-1924, (Fr.) Requiem, Ballade.

Friedrich von Flotow, 1812-1883, (G.) Martha.

Cesar Franck, 1822-1890, (Belg.) D Minor Symphony.

George Gershwin, 1898-1937, (U.S.) Rhapsody in Blue, American in Paris, Porgy and Bess.

Umberto Giordano, 1867-1948, (It.) Andrea Chenier.

Alexander K. Glazunoff, 1865-1936, (R.) Symphonies, Stenka Razin.

Mikhail Glinka, 1804-1857, (R.) Ruslan and Ludmilla.

Christoph W. Gluck, 1714-1787, (G.) Alceste, Iphigenie en Tauride.

Charles Gounod, 1818-1893, (F.) Faust, Romeo and Juliet.

Edvard Grieg, 1843-1907, (Nor.) Peer Gynt Suite, Concerto in A Minor.

George Frederick Handel, 1685-1759, (G., Br.) Messiah, Xerxes, Berenice.

Howard Hanson, 1896-1981, (U.S.) Symphonies No. 1 (Nordic) and 2 (Romantic).

Roy Harris, 1898-1979, (U.S.) Symphonies, Amer. Portraits.

Joseph Haydn, 1732-1809, (Aus.) Symphonies (Clock); oratorios; chamber music.

Paul Hindemith, 1895-1963, (U.S.) Mathis Der Maler.

Gustav Holst, 1874-1934, (Br.) The Planets.

Arthur Honegger, 1892-1955, (Swiss) Judith, Le Roi David, Pacific 231.

Alan Hovhaness, b. 1911, (U.S.) Symphonies, Magnificat.

Engelbert Humperdinck, 1854-1921, (G.) Hansel and Gretel.

Charles Ives, 1874-1954, (U.S.) Third Symphony.

Aram Khachaturian, 1903-1978, (R.) Gayane (ballet), symphonies.

Zoltan Kodaly, 1882-1967, (Hung.) Hary Janos, Psalmus Hungaricus.

Fritz Kreisler, 1875-1962, (Aus.) Caprice Viennois, Tambourin Chinois.

Rodolphe Kreutzer, 1766-1831, (F.) 40 etudes for violin.

Edouard V.A. Lalo, 1823-1892, (F.) Symphonie Espagnole.

Ruggiero Leoncavallo, 1857-1919, (It.) Pagliacci.

Franz Liszt, 1811-1886, (Hung.) 20 Hungarian rhapsodies; symphonic poems.

Edward MacDowell, 1861-1908, (U.S.) To a Wild Rose.

Gustav Mahler, 1860-1911, (Aus.) Lied von der Erde.

Pietro Mascagni, 1863-1945, (It.) Cavalleria Rusticana.

Jules Massenet, 1842-1912, (F.) Manon, Le Cid, Thais.

Felix Mendelssohn, 1809-1847, (G.) Midsummer Night's Dream, Songs Without Words.

Gian-Carlo Menotti, b. 1911, (It.-U.S.) The Medium, The Consul, Amahl and the Night Visitors.

Giacomo Meyerbeer, 1791-1864, (G.) Robert le Diable, Les Huguenots.

Claudio Monteverdi, 1567-1643, (It.) Opera; masses; madrigals.

Wolfgang Amadeus Mozart, 1756-1791, (Aus.) Magic Flute, Marriage of Figaro; concertos; symphonies, etc.

Modest Moussorgsky, 1835-1881, (R.) Boris Godunov, Pictures at an Exhibition.

Jacques Offenbach, 1819-1880, (F.) Tales of Hoffmann.

Carl Orff, 1895-1982, (G.) Carmina Burana.

Ignace Paderewski, 1860-1941, (P.) Minuet in G.

Giovanni P. da Palestrina, c. 1525-1594, (It.) Masses; madrigals.

Amilcare Ponchielli, 1834-1886, (It.) La Gioconda.

Francis Poulenc, 1899-1963, (F.) Dialogues des Carmelites.

Serge Prokofiev, 1891-1953, (R.) Love for Three Oranges, Lt. Kije, Peter and the Wolf.

Giacomo Puccini, 1858-1924, (It.) La Boheme, Manon Lescaut, Tosca, Madame Butterfly.

Sergei Rachmaninov, 1873-1943, (R.) 24 preludes, E concerti, 4 symphonies. Prelude in C Sharp Minor.

Maurice Ravel, 1875-1937, (Fr.) Bolero, Daphnis et Chloe, Rapsodie Espagnole.

Nikolai Rimsky-Korsakov, 1844-1908, (R.) Golden Cockerel, Capriccio Espagnol, Scheherazade, Russian Easter Overture.

Gioacchino Rossini, 1792-1868, (It.) Barber of Seville, Semiramide, William Tell.

Chas. Camille Saint-Saens, 1835-1921, (F.) Samson and Delilah, Danse Macabre.

Alessandro Scarlatti, 1660-1725, (It.) Cantatas; concertos.

Domenico Scarlatti, 1685-1757, (It.) Harpsichord sonatas.

Arnold Schoenberg, 1874-1951, (Aus.) Pelleas and Melisande, Transfigured Night, De Profundis.

Franz Schubert, 1797-1828, (A.) Lieder; symphonies (Unfinished); overtures (Rosamunde).

William Schuman, b. 1910, (U.S.) Credendum, New England Triptych.

Robert Schumann, 1810-1856, (G.) Symphonies, songs.

Aleksandr Scriabin, 1872-1915, (R.) Prometheus.

Dimitri Shostakovich, 1906-1975, (R.) Symphonies, Lady Macbeth of Mzensk, The Nose.

Jean Sibelius, 1865-1957, (Finn.) Finlandia, Karelia.

Bedrich Smetana, 1824-1884, (Cz.). The Bartered Bride.

Karlheinz Stockhausen, b. 1928, (G.) Kontrapunkte, Kontakte.

Richard Strauss, 1864-1949, (G.) Salome, Elektra, Der Rosenkavalier, Thus Spake Zarathustra.

Igor F. Stravinsky, 1882-1971, (R.-U.S.) Oedipus Rex, Le Sacre du Printemps, Petrushka.

Peter I. Tchaikovsky, 1840-1893, (R.) Nutcracker Suite, Swan Lake, Eugene Onegin.

Ambroise Thomas, 1811-1896, (F.) Mignon.

Virgil Thomson, b. 1896, (U.S.) Opera, ballet; Four Saints in Three Acts.

Ralph Vaughan Williams, 1872-1958, (Br.) Job, London Symphony, Symphony No. 7 (Antartica).

Giuseppe Verdi, 1813-1901, (It.) Aida, Rigoletto, Don Carlo, Il Trovatore, La Traviata, Falstaff, Macbeth.

Heitor Villa-Lobos, 1887-1959, (Brazil) Choros.

Antonio Vivaldi, 1678-1741, (It.) Concerti, The Four Seasons.

Richard Wagner, 1813-1883, (G.) Rienzi, Tannhauser, Lohengrin, Tristan und Isolde.

Carl Maria von Weber, 1786-1826, (G.) Der Freischutz.

Composers of Operettas, Musicals, and Popular Music

Richard Adler, b. 1921, (U.S.) *Pajama Game; Damn Yankees.*

Milton Ager, 1893-1979, (U.S.) I Wonder What's Become of Sally; Hard Hearted Hannah; Ain't She Sweet?

Leroy Anderson, 1908-1975, (U.S.) Syncopated Clock; Blue Tango; Sleigh Ride.

Harold Arlen, b. 1905, (U.S.) Stormy Weather; Over the Rainbow; Blues in the Night; That Old Black Magic.

Burt Bacharach, b. 1928, (U.S.) Raindrops Keep Fallin' on My Head; Walk on By; What the World Needs Now is Love.

Ernest Ball, 1878-1927, (U.S.) Mother Machree; When Irish Eyes Are Smiling.

Irving Berlin, b. 1888, (U.S.) *This is the Army; Annie Get Your Gun; Call Me Madam;* God Bless America; White Christmas.

Eubie Blake, 1883-1983, (U.S.) *Shuffle Along;* I'm Just Wild about Harry.

Jerry Bock, b. 1928, (U.S.) *Mr. Wonderful; Fiorello; Fiddler on the Roof; The Rothschilds.*

Carrie Jacobs Bond, 1862-1946, (U.S.) I Love You Truly.

Nacio Herb Brown, 1896-1964, (U.S.) Singing in the Rain; You Were Meant for Me; All I Do Is Dream of You.

Hoagy Carmichael, 1899-1981, (U.S.) Stardust; Georgia on My Mind; Old Buttermilk Sky.

George M. Cohan, 1878-1942, (U.S.) Give My Regards to Broadway; You're A Grand Old Flag; Over There.

Noel Coward, 1899-1973 (Br.) *Bitter Sweet;* Mad Dogs and Englishmen; Mad About the Boy.

Walter Donaldson, 1893-1947, (U.S.) My Buddy; Carolina in the Morning; You're Driving Me Crazy; Makin' Whoopee.

Vernon Duke, 1903-1969, (U.S.) April in Paris.

Gus Edwards, 1879-1945, (U.S.) School Days; By the Light of the Silvery Moon; In My Merry Oldsmobile.

Sherman Edwards, b. 1919, (U.S.) See You in September; Wonderful! Wonderful!

Sammy Fain, b. 1902, Wedding Bells Are Breaking Up That Old Gang of Mine; Let a Smile Be Your Umbrella.

Fred Fisher, 1875-1942, (U.S.) Peg O' My Heart; Chicago; Dardanella.

Stephen Collins Foster, 1826-1864, (U.S.) My Old Kentucky Home; Old Folks At Home.

Rudolf Friml, 1879-1972, (naturalized U.S.) *The Firefly; Rose Marie; Vagabond King; Bird of Paradise.*

John Gay, 1685-1732, (Br.) *The Beggar's Opera.*

Edwin F. Goldman, 1878-1956, (U.S.) marches.

Percy Grainger, 1882-1961, (Br.) Country Gardens.

John Green, b. 1908, (U.S.) Body and Soul; Out of Nowhere;

I Cover the Waterfront.

Ferde Grofe, 1892-1972, (U.S.) *Grand Canyon Suite.*

W. C. Handy, 1873-1958, (U.S.) *St. Louis Blues.*

Ray Henderson, 1896-1970, (U.S.) *George White's Scandals;* That Old Gang of Mine; Five Foot Two, Eyes of Blue.

Victor Herbert, 1859-1924, (Ir.-U.S.) *Mlle. Modiste; Babes in Toyland; The Red Mill; Naughty Marietta; Sweethearts.*

Jerry Herman, b. 1932, (U.S.) *Milk and Honey; Hello Dolly; Mame; Dear World.*

Al Hoffman, 1902-1960, (U.S.) Heartaches, Mairzy Doats.

Scott Joplin, 1868-1917, (U.S.) *Treemonisha.*

John Kander, b. 1927, (U.S.) *Cabaret; Chicago; Funny Lady.*

Jerome Kern, 1885-1945, (U.S.) *Sally; Sunny; Show Boat; Cat and the Fiddle; Music in the Air; Roberta.*

Burton Lane, b. 1912, (U.S.) *Three's a Crowd; Finian's Rainbow; On A Clear Day You Can See Forever.*

Franz Lehar, 1870-1948, (Hung.) *Merry Widow.*

Mitch Leigh, b. 1928, (U.S.) *Man of La Mancha.*

John Lennon, 1940-1980, (Br.) Hard Day's Night, I Want to Hold Your Hand.

Frank Loesser, 1910-1969, (U.S.) *Guys and Dolls; Where's Charley?; The Most Happy Fella; How to Succeed . . . .*

Frederick Loewe, b. 1901, (Aust.-U.S.) *The Day Before Spring; Brigadoon; Paint Your Wagon; My Fair Lady; Camelot.*

Henry Mancini, b. 1924, (U.S.) Moon River; Days of Wine and Roses; Pink Panther Theme.

Paul McCartney, b. 1942, (Br.) Michelle, Hey Jude, And I Love Her, Yesterday.

Jimmy McHugh, 1894-1969, (U.S.) I Can't Give You Anything But Love; I Feel a Song Coming On.

Joseph Meyer, b. 1894, (U.S.) If You Knew Susie; California, Here I Come; Crazy Rhythm.

Chauncey Olcott, 1860-1932, (U.S.) Mother Machree; My Wild Irish Rose.

Cole Porter, 1893-1964, (U.S.) *Anything Goes; Jubilee; Du-Barry Was a Lady; Panama Hattie; Mexican Hayride; Kiss Me Kate; Can Can; Silk Stockings.*

Andre Previn, b. 1929, (U.S.) *Coco.*

Richard Rodgers, 1902-1979, (U.S.) *Garrick Gaieties; Connecticut Yankee; America's Sweetheart; On Your Toes; Babes in Arms; The Boys from Syracuse; Oklahoma!; Carousel; South Pacific; The King and I; Flower Drum Song; The Sound of Music.*

Sigmund Romberg, 1887-1951, (Hung.) *Maytime; The Student Prince; Desert Song; Blossom Time.*

Harold Rome, b. 1908, (U.S.) *Pins and Needles; Call Me Mister; Wish You Were Here; Fanny; Destry Rides Again.*

Vincent Rose, b. 1880-1944, (U.S.) Avalon; Whispering; Blueberry Hill.

Harry Ruby, 1895-1974, (U.S.) Three Little Words; Who's Sorry Now?

Arthur Schwartz, 1900-1984, (U.S.) *The Band Wagon; Inside U.S.A.; A Tree Grows in Brooklyn.*

Stephen Sondheim, b. 1930, (U.S.) *A Little Night Music; Company, Sunday in the Park with George.*

John Philip Sousa, 1854-1932, (U.S.) *El Capitan;* Stars and Stripes Forever.

Oskar Straus, 1870-1954, (Aus.) *Chocolate Soldier.*

Johann Strauss, 1825-1899, (Aus.) *Gypsy Baron; Die Fledermaus;* waltzes: Blue Danube, Artist's Life.

Charles Strouse, b. 1928, (U.S.) *Bye Bye, Birdie; All American; Golden Boy; Applause; Annie.*

Jule Styne, b. 1905, (b. London-U.S.) *Gentlemen Prefer Blondes; Bells Are Ringing; Gypsy; Funny Girl.*

Arthur S. Sullivan, 1842-1900, (Br.) *H.M.S. Pinafore, Pirates of Penzance; The Mikado.*

Deems Taylor, 1885-1966, (U.S.) *Peter Ibbetson.*

Egbert van Alstyne, 1882-1951, (U.S.) In the Shade of the Old Apple Tree; Memories; Pretty Baby.

James Van Heusen, b. 1913, (U.S.) Moonlight Becomes You; Swinging on a Star.

Albert von Tilzer, 1878-1956, (U.S.) I'll Be With You in Apple Blossom Time; Take Me Out to the Ball Game.

Harry von Tilzer, 1872-1946, (U.S.) Only a Bird in a Gilded Cage; On a Sunday Afternoon.

Harry Warren, 1893-1981, (U.S.) You're My Everything; We're in the Money; I Only Have Eyes for You; September in the Rain.

Kurt Weill, 1900-1950, (G.-U.S.) *Threepenny Opera; Lady in the Dark; Knickerbocker Holiday; One Touch of Venus.*

Percy Wenrich, 1887-1952, (U.S.) When You Wore a Tulip; Moonlight Bay; Put On Your Old Gray Bonnet.

Richard A. Whiting, 1891-1938, (U.S.) Till We Meet Again; Sleepytime Gal; Beyond the Blue Horizon.

Meredith Willson, 1902-1984, (U.S.) *The Music Man.*

Vincent Youmans, 1898-1946, (U.S.) *Two Little Girls in Blue; Wildflower; No, No, Nanette; Hit the Deck; Rainbow; Smiles.*

Lyricists

Sammy Cahn, b. 1913, (U.S.) High Hopes; Love and Marriage; The Second Time Around.

Betty Comden, b. 1919 (U.S.) and **Adolph Green,** b. 1915 (U.S.) The Party's Over; Just in Time; New York, New York.

Buddy De Sylva, 1895-1950, (U.S.) When Day is Done; Look for the Silver Lining; April Showers.

Hal David, b. 1921 (U.S.) What the World Needs Now Is Love.

Howard Dietz, b. 1896, (U.S.) Dancing in the Dark; You and the Night and the Music.

Al Dubin, 1891-1945, (U.S.) Tiptoe Through the Tulips; Anniversary Waltz; Lullaby of Broadway.

Dorothy Fields, 1905-1974, (U.S.) On the Sunny Side of the Street; Don't Blame Me; The Way You Look Tonight.

Ira Gershwin, 1896-1983, (U.S.) The Man I Love; Fascinating Rhythm; S'Wonderful; Embraceable You.

Wm. S. Gilbert, 1836-1911, (Br.) *The Mikado; H.M.S. Pinafore.*

Oscar Hammerstein II, 1895-1960, (U.S.) Ol' Man River; *Oklahoma; Carousel.*

E. Y. (Yip) Harburg, 1898-1981, (U.S.) Brother, Can You Spare a Dime; April in Paris; Over the Rainbow.

Lorenz Hart, 1895-1943, (U.S.) Isn't It Romantic; Blue Moon; Lover; Manhattan; My Funny Valentine.

DuBose Heyward, 1885-1940, (U.S.) Summertime; A Woman Is A Sometime Thing.

Gus Kahn, 1886-1941, (U.S.) Memories; Ain't We Got Fun.

Johnny Mercer, 1909-1976, (U.S.) Blues in the Night; Come Rain or Come Shine; Laura; That Old Black Magic.

Jack Norworth, 1879-1959, (U.S.) Take Me Out to the Ball Game; Shine On Harvest Moon.

Jack Yellen, b. 1892, (U.S.) Down by the O-Hi-O; Ain't She Sweet; Happy Days Are Here Again.

Noted Jazz Artists

Jazz has been called America's only completely unique contribution to Western culture. The following individuals have made major contributions in this field:

Julian "Cannonball" Adderley, 1928-1975: alto sax.

Louis "Satchmo" Armstrong, 1900-1971: trumpet, singer; originated the "scat" vocal.

Mildred Bailey, 1907-1951: blues singer.

Chet Baker, b. 1929: trumpet.

Count Basie, 1904-1984: orchestra leader, piano.

Sidney Bechet, 1897-1950: early innovator, soprano sax.

Bix Beiderbecke, 1903-1931: cornet, piano, composer.

Bunny Berrigan, 1909-1942: trumpet, singer.

Barney Bigard, b. 1906: clarinet.

Art Blakey, b. 1919: drums, leader.

Jimmy Blanton, 1921-1942: bass.

Charles "Buddy" Bolden, 1868-1931: cornet; formed the first jazz band in the 1890s.

Big Bill Broonzy, 1893-1958: blues singer, guitar.

Clifford Brown, 1930-1956: trumpet.

Ray Brown, b. 1926: bass.

Dave Brubeck, b. 1920: piano, combo leader.

Harry Carney, 1910-1974: baritone sax.

Benny Carter, b. 1907: alto sax, trumpet, clarinet.

Sidney Catlett, 1910-1951: drums.

Charlie Christian, 1919-1942: guitar.

Kenny Clarke, 1914-1985: pioneer of modern drums.

Buck Clayton, b. 1911: trumpet, arranger.

Al Cohn, b. 1925: tenor sax, composer.

Cozy Cole, 1909-1981: drums.

Ornette Coleman, b. 1930: saxophone; unorthodox style.

John Coltrane, 1926-1967: tenor sax innovator.

Eddie Condon, 1904-1973: guitar, band leader; promoter of Dixieland.

Chick Corea, b. 1941: pianist, composer.

Miles Davis, b. 1926: trumpet; pioneer of cool jazz.

Tadd Dameron, 1917-1965: piano, composer.

Wild Bill Davison, b. 1906: cornet, leader; prominent in early Chicago jazz.

Buddy De Franco, b. 1933: clarinet.

Paul Desmond, 1924-1977: alto sax.

Vic Dickenson, 1906-1984: trombone, composer.

Warren "Baby" Dodds, 1898-1959: Dixieland drummer.
Johnny Dodds, 1892-1940: clarinet.
Jimmy Dorsey, 1904-1957: clarinet, alto sax; band leader.
Tommy Dorsey, 1905-1956: trombone; band leader.
Roy Eldridge, b. 1911: trumpet, drums, singer.
Duke Ellington, 1899-1974: piano, band leader, composer.
Bill Evans, 1929-1980: piano.
Gil Evans, b. 1912: composer, arranger, piano.
Ella Fitzgerald, b. 1918: singer.
"Red" Garland, 1923-1984; piano.
Erroll Garner, 1921-1977: piano, composer, "Misty."
Stan Getz, b. 1927: tenor sax.
Dizzy Gillespie, b. 1917: trumpet, composer; bop developer.
Benny Goodman, b. 1909: clarinet, band and combo leader.
Dexter Gordon, b. 1923: tenor sax; bop-derived style.
Stephane Grappelli, b. 1908: violin.
Bobby Hackett, 1915-1976: trumpet, cornet.
Lionel Hampton, b. 1913: vibes, drums, piano, combo leader.
Herbie Hancock, b. 1940: piano, composer.
W. C. Handy, 1873-1958: composer, "St. Louis Blues."
Coleman Hawkins, 1904-1969: tenor sax; 1939 recording of "Body and Soul", a classic.
Roy Haynes, b. 1926: drums.
Fletcher Henderson, 1898-1952: orchestra leader, arranger; pioneered jazz and dance bands of the 30s.
Woody Herman, b. 1913: clarinet, alto sax, band leader.
Jay C. Higginbotham, 1906-1973: trombone.
Earl "Fatha" Hines, 1905-1983: piano, songwriter.
Johnny Hodges, 1906-1971: alto sax.
Billie Holiday, 1915-1959: blues singer, "Strange Fruit."
Sam "Lightnin' " Hopkins, 1912-1982: blues singer, guitar.
Mahalia Jackson, 1911-1972: gospel singer.
Milt Jackson, b. 1923: vibes, piano, guitar.
Illinois Jacquet, b. 1922: tenor sax.
Keith Jarrett, b. 1945: technically phenomenal pianist.
Blind Lemon Jefferson, 1897-1930: blues singer, guitar.
Bunk Johnson, 1879-1949: cornet, trumpet.
James P. Johnson, 1891-1955: piano, composer.
J. J. Johnson, b. 1924: trombone, composer.
Jo Jones, b. 1911: drums.
Philly Joe Jones, 1923: drums.
Quincy Jones, b. 1933: arranger.
Thad Jones, b. 1923: trumpet, cornet.
Scott Joplin, 1868-1917: composer; "Maple Leaf Rag."
Stan Kenton, 1912-1979: orchestra leader, composer, piano.
Barney Kessel, b. 1923: guitar.
Lee Konitz, b. 1927: alto sax.
Gene Krupa, 1909-1973: drums, band and combo leader.
Scott LaFaro, 1936-1961: bass.
Huddie Ledbetter (Leadbelly), 1888-1949: blues singer, guitar.
John Lewis, b. 1920: composer, piano, combo leader.
Jimmie Lunceford, 1902-1947: band leader, sax.
Herbie Mann, b. 1930: flute.
Wynton Marsalis, b. 1961: trumpet.
Jimmy McPartland, b. 1907: trumpet.
Marian McPartland, b. 1920: piano.
Glenn Miller, 1904-1944: trombone, dance band leader.
Charles Mingus, 1922-1979: bass, composer, combo leader.
Thelonious Monk, 1920-1982: piano, composer, combo leader; a developer of bop.
Wes Montgomery, 1925-1968: guitar.
"Jelly Roll" Morton, 1885-1941: composer, piano, singer.
Bennie Moten, 1894-1935: piano; an early organizer of large jazz orchestras.
Gerry Mulligan, b. 1927: baritone sax, arranger, leader.

Turk Murphy, b. 1915: trombone, band leader.
Theodore "Fats" Navarro, 1923-1950: trumpet.
Red Nichols, 1905-1965: cornet, combo leader.
Red Norvo, b. 1908: vibes, band leader.
Anita O'Day, b. 1919: singer.
King Oliver, 1885-1938: cornet, band leader; teacher of Louis Armstrong.
Kid Ory, 1886-1973: trombone, "Muskrat Ramble".
Charlie "Bird" Parker, 1920-1955: alto sax, composer; rated by many as the greatest jazz improviser.
Art Pepper, 1925-1983: alto sax.
Oscar Peterson, b. 1925: piano, composer, combo leader.
Oscar Pettiford, 1922-1960: a leading bassist in the bop era.
Bud Powell, 1924-1966: piano; modern jazz pioneer.
Sun Ra, b. 1915?: big band leader, pianist, composer.
Gertrude "Ma" Rainey, 1886-1939: blues singer.
Don Redman, 1900-1964: composer, arranger; pioneer in the evolution of the large orchestra.
Django Reinhardt, 1910-1953: guitar; Belgian gypsy, first European to influence American jazz.
Buddy Rich, b. 1917: drums, band leader.
Max Roach, b. 1925: drums.
Sonny Rollins, b. 1929: tenor sax.
Frank Rosolino, 1926-1978: trombone.
Jimmy Rushing, 1903-1972: blues singer.
George Russell, b. 1923: composer, piano.
Pee Wee Russell, 1906-1969: clarinet.
Artie Shaw, b. 1910: clarinet, combo leader.
George Shearing, b. 1919: piano, composer, "Lullaby of Birdland."
Horace Silver, b. 1928: piano, combo leader.
Zoot Sims, 1925-1985: tenor, alto sax; clarinet.
Zutty Singleton, 1898-1975: Dixieland drummer.
Bessie Smith, 1894-1937: blues singer.
Clarence "Pinetop" Smith, 1904-1929: piano, singer; pioneer of boogie woogie.
Willie "The Lion" Smith, 1897-1973: stride style pianist.
Muggsy Spanier, 1906-1967: cornet, band leader.
Billy Strayhorn, 1915-67: composer, piano.
Sonny Stitt, 1924-1982: alto, tenor sax.
Art Tatum, 1910-1956: piano; technical virtuoso.
Billy Taylor, b. 1921: piano, composer.
Cecil Taylor, b. 1933: piano, composer.
Jack Teagarden, 1905-1964: trombone, singer.
Dave Tough, 1908-1948: drums.
Lennie Tristano, 1919-1978: piano, composer.
Joe Turner, b. 1911: blues singer.
Joe Turner, b. 1907: stride piano.
McCoy Tyner, b. 1938: piano, composer.
Sarah Vaughan, b. 1924: singer.
Joe Venuti, 1904-1978: first great jazz violinist.
Thomas "Fats" Waller, 1904-1943: piano, singer, composer. "Ain't Misbehavin' ".
Dinah Washington, 1924-1963: singer.
Chick Webb, 1902-1939: band leader, drums.
Ben Webster, b. 1909: tenor sax.
Paul Whiteman, 1890-1967: orchestra leader; a major figure in the introduction of jazz to a large audience.
Charles "Cootie" Williams, b. 1908: trumpet, band leader.
Mary Lou Williams, 1914-1981: piano, composer.
Teddy Wilson, b. 1912: piano, composer.
Kai Winding, 1922-1983: trombone, composer.
Jimmy Yancey, 1894-1951: piano.
Lester "Pres" Young, 1909-1959: tenor sax, composer: a bop pioneer.

Rock & Roll Notables

For more than a quarter of a century, rock & roll has been an important force in American popular culture. The following individuals or groups have made a significant impact. Next to each is an associated single record or record album.

Adam and the Ants: "Goody Two Shoes"
Alabama: "Tennessee River"
The Allman Brothers Band: "Ramblin' Man"
America: "A Horse With No Name"
The Animals: "House of the Rising Sun"
Paul Anka: "Lonely Boy"
The Association: "Cherish"
Frankie Avalon: "Venus"
The Band: "The Weight"
The Beach Boys: "Surfin' U.S.A."
The Beatles: "Hey Jude"
The Bee Gees: "Stayin' Alive"
Pat Benatar: "Hit Me With Your Best Shot"
Chuck Berry: "Johnny B. Goode"
The Big Bopper: "Chantilly Lace"
Blind Faith: "Can't Find My Way Home"

Blondie: "Heart of Glass"
Blood, Sweat and Tears: "Spinning Wheel"
Gary "U.S." Bonds: "Quarter to Three"
Booker T. and the MGs: "Green Onions"
David Bowie: "Let's Dance"
James Brown: "Papa's Got a Brand New Bag"
Jackson Browne: "Doctor My Eyes"
Buffalo Springfield: "For What It's Worth"
Canned Heat: "Going Up the Country"
The Cars: "Shake It Up"
Ray Charles: "Georgia on My Mind"
Chubby Checker: "The Twist"
Chicago: "Hard Habit to Break"
Eric Clapton: "Layla"
The Clash: "Rock the Casbah"
The Coasters: "Yakety Yak"

Phil Collins: "Against All Odds"
Sam Cooke: "You Send Me"
Alice Cooper: "School's Out"
Elvis Costello: "Allison"
John Cougar Mellencamp: "Hurt So Good"
Cream: "Sunshine of Your Love"
Credence Clearwater Revival: "Proud Mary"
Crosby, Stills, Nash and Young: "Suite: Judy Blue Eyes"
The Crystals: "Da Doo Ron Ron"
Culture Club: *Colour by Numbers*
Danny and the Juniors: "At the Hop"
Spencer Davis Group: "Gimme Some Lovin' "
Def Leppard: "Photograph"
Bo Diddley: "Who Do You Love?"
Dion and the Belmonts: "A Teenager in Love"
Fats Domino: "Blueberry Hill"
The Doobie Brothers: "What a Fool Believes"
The Doors: "Light My Fire"
The Drifters: "Save the Last Dance for Me"
Duran Duran: "Hungry Like the Wolf"
Bob Dylan: "Like a Rolling Stone"
The Eagles: "Hotel California"
Earth, Wind and Fire: "Shining Star"
Emerson, Lake and Palmer: "From the Beginning"
The Eurythmics: "Sweet Dreams (Are Made of This)"
Everly Brothers: "Wake Up Little Susie"
Jose Feliciano: "Light My Fire"
The Five Satins: "In the Still of the Night"
Fleetwood Mac: *Rumours*
Dan Fogelberg: "Missing You"
The Four Seasons: "Sherry"
The Four Tops: "I Can't Help Myself"
Aretha Franklin: "Respect"
Marvin Gaye: "I Heard It through the Grapevine"
The J. Geils Band: *Freeze-Frame*
Grand Funk Railroad: "We're an American Band"
The Grateful Dead: "Truckin' "
Bill Haley and the Comets: "Rock Around the Clock"
Hall and Oates: "Rich Girl"
Jimi Hendrix: *Are You Experienced?*
Buddy Holly and the Crickets: "That'll Be the Day"
Janis Ian: "At Seventeen"
The Isley Brothers: "It's Your Thing"
The Jackson 5/The Jacksons: "ABC"
Michael Jackson: "Beat It"
Jay and the Americans: "This Magic Moment"
The Jefferson Airplane/Jefferson Starship: "White Rabbit"
Jethro Tull: *Aqualung*
Joan Jett: "I Love Rock' n' Roll"
Billy Joel: "Uptown Girl"
Elton John: "Sad Songs"
Janis Joplin: "Me and Bobby McGee"
Chaka Khan: "I Feel for You"
Carole King: *Tapestry*
Kiss: "Rock' n' Roll All Night"
Gladys Knight and the Pips: "Midnight Train to Georgia"
Cyndi Lauper: "Girls Just Want to Have Fun"
Led Zeppelin: "Stairway to Heaven"
Brenda Lee: "I'm Sorry"
Jerry Lee Lewis: "Whole Lotta Shakin' Going On"
Little Anthony and the Imperials: "Tears on My Pillow"
Little Richard: "Tutti Frutti"
Lovin Spoonful: "Do You Believe in Magic?"
Frankie Lymon: "Why Do Fools Fall in Love?"
Lynyrd Skynyrd: "Sweet Home Alabama"
Madonna: "Material Girl"
The Mamas and the Papas: "Monday, Monday"
Bob Marley: "Roots, Rock, Reggae"
Martha and the Vandellas: "Dancin' in the Streets"
The Marvelettes: "Please Mr. Postman"

Meat Loaf: "Paradise by the Dashboard Light"
Men at Work: "Who Can It Be Now?"
Steve Miller Band: "Abracadabra"
Joni Mitchell: "Big Yellow Taxi"
The Monkees: "I'm a Believer"
Moody Blues: "Nights in White Satin"
Rick Nelson: "Hello Mary Lou"
Roy Orbison: "Oh Pretty Woman"
Ozzy Osbourne: "You Can't Kill Rock 'n' Roll"
Steve Perry: "Oh Sherry"
Pink Floyd: *Dark Side of the Moon*
Poco: *Deliverin'*
The Police: "Every Breath You Take"
Iggy Pop: "Lust for Life"
Elvis Presley: "Love Me Tender"
The Pretenders: *Learning to Crawl*
Lloyd Price: "Stagger Lee"
Prince: "Purple Rain"
Procul Harum: "A Whiter Shade of Pale"
Gary Puckett and the Union Gap: "Young Girl"
Queen: "Bohemian Rhapsody"
The Ramones: "Rockaway Beach"
The Rascals: "Good Lovin' "
Otis Redding: "The Dock of the Bay"
Lou Reed: "Walk on the Wild Side"
REO Speedwagon: "Keep on Lovin' You"
Righteous Brothers: "You've Lost that Lovin' Feeling"
Johnny Rivers: "Poor Side of Town"
Smokey Robinson and the Miracles: "Ooh Baby Baby"
The Rolling Stones: "Satisfaction"
The Ronettes: "Be My Baby"
Linda Ronstadt: "You're No Good"
Todd Rundgren: "Hello It's Me"
Sam and Dave: "Soul Man"
Santana: "Black Magic Woman"
Neil Sedaka: "Breaking Up is Hard to Do"
Bob Seger: "Nighmoves"
The Sex Pistols: "God Save the Queen"
Del Shannon: "Runaway"
The Shirelles: "Soldier Boy"
Simon and Garfunkel: "Bridge Over Troubled Water"
Carly Simon: "You're So Vain"
Sly and the Family Stone: "Everyday People"
Patti Smith: "Because the Night"
Southside Johnny and the Asbury Jukes: *This Time*
Dusty Springfield: "You Don't Have to Say You Love Me"
Bruce Springsteen: "Born in the U.S.A."
Steely Dan: "Rikki Don't Lose That Number"
Steppenwolf: "Born to Be Wild"
Cat Stevens: "Wild World"
Rod Stewart: "Maggie Mae"
Donna Summer: "Bad Girls"
The Supremes: "Stop! In the Name of Love"
Talking Heads: "Burning Down the House"
James Taylor: "You've Got a Friend"
The Temptations: "My Girl"
Three Dog Night: "Joy to the World"
Traffic: "Feelin' Alright"
Tina Turner: "What's Love Got to Do with It?"
The Turtles: "Happy Together"
Van Halen: "Jump"
Dionne Warwick: "I'll Never Fall in Love Again"
Mary Wells: "My Guy"
The Who: "My Generation"
Jackie Wilson: "That's Why"
Stevie Wonder: "You Are the Sunshine of My Life"
The Yardbirds: "For Your Love"
Yes: "Owner of a Lonely Heart"
Frank Zappa/Mothers of Invention: *Sheik Yerbouti*

Entertainment Personalities — Where and When Born

Actors, Actresses, Dancers, Musicians, Producers, Radio-TV Performers, Singers

Name	Birthplace	Born	Name	Birthplace	Born
Abbado, Claudio	Milan, Italy	6/26/33	Adams, Maud	Lulea, Sweden	2/12/45
Abbott, George	Forestville, N.Y.	6/25/87	Adler, Larry	Baltimore, Md.	2/10/14
Abel, Walter	St. Paul, Minn.	6/6/98	Agutter, Jenny	London, England	12/20/52
Abraham, F. Murray	El Paso, Tex.	1940	Aherne, Brian	Worcestershire, England.	5/2/02
Acuff, Roy	Maynardville, Tenn.	9/15/03	Ailey, Alvin	Rogers, Tex.	1/5/31
Adams, Don	New York, N.Y.	4/19/26	Aimee, Anouk	Paris, France	4/27/32
Adams, Edie	Kingston, Pa.	4/16/29	Akins, Claude	Nelson, Ga.	5/25/18
Adams, Joey	New York, N.Y.	1/6/11	Albanese, Licia	Bari, Italy	7/22/13
Adams, Julie	Waterloo, Ia.	10/17/28	Alberghetti, Anna Maria.	Pesaro, Italy	5/15/36
Adams, Mason	New York, N.Y.	2/26/19	Albert, Eddie	Rock Island, Ill.	4/22/08

Name	Birthplace	Born
Albert, Edward	Los Angeles, Cal.	2/20/51
Albright, Lola	Akron, Oh.	7/20/24
Alda, Alan	New York, N.Y.	1/28/36
Alda, Robert	New York, N.Y.	2/26/14
Alexander, Jane	Boston, Mass.	10/28/39
Allen, Debbie	Houston, Tex.	1/16/-
Allen, Karen	Carrollton, Ill.	10/5/51
Allen, Mel	Birmingham, Ala.	2/14/13
Allen, Nancy	New York, N.Y.	6/24/50
Allen, Peter	Tenterfield, Australia	2/10/44
Allen, Steve	New York, N.Y.	12/26/21
Allen, Woody	Brooklyn, N.Y.	12/1/35
Allison, Fran	LaPorte City, Ia.	—
Allman, Gregg	Nashville, Tenn.	12/7/47
Allyson, June	Lucerne, N.Y.	10/7/17
Alpert, Herb	Los Angeles, Cal.	3/31/35
Altman, Robert	Kansas City, Mo.	2/20/25
Ameche, Don	Kenosha, Wis.	5/31/08
Ames, Ed	Boston, Mass.	7/9/27
Ames, Leon	Portland, Ind.	1/20/03
Amos, John	Newark, N.J.	12/27/39
Amsterdam, Morey	Chicago, Ill.	12/14/14
Anderson, Harry	Newport, R.I.	10/14/-
Anderson, Ian	Dunfermline, Scotland	8/10/47
Anderson, Judith	Adelaide, Australia	2/10/98
Anderson, Loni	St. Paul, Minn.	8/7/44
Anderson, Lynn	Grand Forks, N.D.	9/26/47
Anderson, Marian	Philadelphia, Pa.	2/17/02
Anderson, Melissa Sue	Berkeley, Cal.	9/26/62
Anderson, Richard	Long Branch, N.J.	8/8/26
Andersson, Bibi	Stockholm, Sweden	11/11/35
Andress, Ursula	Switzerland	3/19/36
Andrews, Dana	Collins, Miss.	1/1/09
Andrews, Julie	Walton, England	10/1/35
Andrews, Maxene	Minneapolis, Minn.	1/3/18
Andrews, Patty	Minneapolis, Minn.	2/16/20
Anka, Paul	Ottawa, Ont.	7/30/41
Ann-Margret	Stockholm, Sweden	4/28/41
Ant, Adam	London, England	11/3/54
Arden, Eve	Mill Valley, Cal.	4/30/12
Arkin, Alan	New York, N.Y.	3/26/34
Arnaz, Desi	Santiago, Cuba	3/2/17
Arnaz, Desi Jr.	Los Angeles, Cal.	1/19/53
Arnaz, Lucie	Hollywood, Cal.	7/17/51
Arness, James	Minneapolis, Minn.	5/26/23
Arnold, Eddy	Henderson, Tenn.	5/15/18
Arrau, Claudio	Chillau, Chile	2/6/03
Arroyo, Martina	New York, N.Y.	2/2/37
Arthur, Beatrice	New York, N.Y.	5/13/23
Arthur, Jean	New York, N.Y.	10/17/08
Ashcroft, Peggy	England	1907
Ashley, Elizabeth	Ocala, Fla.	8/30/41
Asner, Ed	Kansas City, Mo.	11/15/29
Astaire, Fred	Omaha, Neb.	5/10/99
Astin, John	Baltimore, Md.	3/30/30
Astor, Mary	Quincy, Ill.	5/3/06
Atkins, Chet	Luttrell, Tenn.	6/20/24
Attenborough, Richard	Cambridge, England	8/29/23
Auberjonois, Rene	New York, N.Y.	6/1/40
Aumont, Jean-Pierre	Paris, France	1/5/11
Autry, Gene	Tioga, Tex.	9/29/11
Avalon, Frankie	Philadelphia, Pa.	9/8/40
Ayers-Allen, Phylicia	Houston, Tex.	6/17/-
Aykroyd, Dan	Ottawa, Ont.	7/1/52
Ayres, Lew	Minneapolis, Minn.	12/28/08
Aznavour, Charles	Paris, France	5/22/24
Bacall, Lauren	New York, N.Y.	9/16/24
Bach, Catherine	Warren, Oh.	3/1/54
Backus, Jim	Cleveland, Oh.	2/25/13
Baddeley, Hermione	Shropshire, England	11/13/06
Baez, Joan	Staten Island, N.Y.	1/9/41
Bailey, Pearl	Newport News, Va.	3/29/18
Bain, Conrad	Lethbridge, Alta.	2/4/23
Baio, Scott	Brooklyn, N.Y.	9/22/61
Baird, Bil	Grand Island, Neb.	8/15/04
Baker, Carroll	Johnstown, Pa.	5/28/31
Baker, Joe Don	Groesbeck, Tex.	2/12/36
Baker, Kenny	Monrovia, Cal.	9/30/12
Ball, Lucille	Jamestown, N.Y.	8/6/11
Ballard, Kaye	Cleveland, Oh.	11/20/26
Balsam, Martin	New York, N.Y.	11/4/19
Bancroft, Anne	New York, N.Y.	9/17/31
Barber, Red	Columbus, Miss.	2/17/08
Bardot, Brigitte	Paris, France	9/28/34
Bari, Lynn	Roanoke, Va.	12/18/17
Barker, Bob	Darrington, Wash.	12/12/23
Barnes, Priscilla	Ft. Dix, N.J.	12/7/56

Name	Birthplace	Born
Barrault, Jean-Louis	Vesinet, France	9/8/10
Barrie, Barbara	Chicago, Ill.	5/23/31
Barrie, Mona	London, England	12/18/09
Barry, Gene	New York, N.Y.	6/4/22
Bartholomew, Freddie	London, England	3/28/24
Bartok, Eva	Budapest, Hungary	6/18/29
Baryshnikov, Mikhail	Riga, Latvia	1/28/48
Basinger, Kim	Athens, Ga.	12/8/53
Bassey, Shirley	Cardiff, Wales	1/8/37
Bates, Alan	Allestree, England	2/17/34
Baxter, Anne	Michigan City, Ind.	5/7/23
Baxter-Birney, Meredith	Los Angeles, Cal.	6/21/47
Beal, John	Joplin, Mo.	8/13/09
Bean, Orson	Burlington, Vt.	7/22/28
Beatty, Ned	Louisville, Ky.	7/6/37
Beatty, Robert	Hamilton, Ont.	10/19/09
Beatty, Warren	Richmond, Va.	3/30/37
Bedelia, Bonnie	New York, N.Y.	3/25/48
Bee Gees		
Gibb, Barry	Manchester, England	9/1/46
Gibb, Robin	" "	12/22/49
Gibb, Maurice	" "	12/22/49
Beery, Noah Jr.	New York, N.Y.	8/10/16
Belafonte, Harry	New York, N.Y.	3/1/27
Belafonte-Harper, Shari	New York, N.Y.	9/22/-
Bel Geddes, Barbara	New York, N.Y.	10/31/22
Bellamy, Ralph	Chicago, Ill.	6/17/04
Belmondo, Jean-Paul	Neuilly-sur-Seine, France	4/9/33
Benatar, Pat	Brooklyn, N.Y.	1/10/53
Benedict, Dirk	Helena, Mont.	3/1/45
Benjamin, Richard	New York, N.Y.	5/22/38
Bennett, Joan	Palisades, N.J.	2/27/10
Bennett, Michael	Buffalo, N.Y.	4/8/43
Bennett, Tony	New York, N.Y.	8/3/26
Benson, George	Pittsburgh, Pa.	3/22/43
Benson, Robby	Dallas, Tex.	1/21/55
Bentley, John	Warwickshire, England	12/2/16
Beradino, John	Los Angeles, Cal.	5/1/17
Bergen, Candice	Beverly Hills, Cal.	5/9/46
Bergen, Polly	Knoxville, Tenn.	7/4/30
Bergerac, Jacques	Biarritz, France	5/26/27
Bergman, Ingmar	Uppsala, Sweden	7/14/18
Bergner, Elisabeth	Vienna, Austria	8/22/00
Berle, Milton	New York, N.Y.	7/12/08
Berlinger, Warren	Brooklyn, N.Y.	8/31/37
Berman, Lazar	Leningrad, USSR	2/26/30
Berman, Shelley	Chicago, Ill.	2/3/26
Bernardi, Herschel	New York, N.Y.	10/20/23
Bernstein, Leonard	Lawrence, Mass.	8/25/18
Berry, Chuck	San Jose, Cal.	1/15/26
Berry, Ken	Moline, Ill.	—
Bertinelli, Valerie	Wilmington, Del.	4/23/60
Bikel, Theodore	Vienna, Austria	5/2/24
Birney, David	Washington, D.C.	4/23/39
Bishop, Joey	Bronx, N.Y.	2/3/18
Bisoglio, Val	New York, N.Y.	5/7/26
Bisset, Jacqueline	Weybridge, England	9/13/46
Bixby, Bill	San Francisco, Cal.	1/22/34
Black, Karen	Park Ridge, Ill.	7/1/42
Blackstone Jr., Harry	Three Rivers, Mich.	6/30/34
Blaine, Vivian	Newark, N.J.	11/21/23
Blair, Linda	St. Louis, Mo.	1/22/59
Blake, Amanda	Buffalo, N.Y.	2/20/31
Blake, Robert	Nutley, N.J.	9/18/34
Blanc, Mel	San Francisco, Cal.	5/30/08
Bloom, Claire	London, England	2/15/31
Blyth, Ann	Mt. Kisco, N.Y.	8/16/28
Bogarde, Dirk	London, England	3/28/20
Bogdanovich, Peter	Kingston, N.Y.	7/30/39
Bolger, Ray	Dorchester, Mass.	1/10/04
Bonet, Lisa	San Francisco, Cal.	11/16/67
Bono, Sonny	Detroit, Mich.	2/16/40
Booke, Sorrell	Buffalo, N.Y.	1/4/30
Boone, Debby	Hackensack, N.J.	9/22/56
Boone, Pat	Jacksonville, Fla.	6/1/34
Booth, Shirley	New York, N.Y.	8/30/07
Borge, Victor	Copenhagen, Denmark	1/3/09
Borgnine, Ernest	Hamden, Conn.	1/24/17
Bosley, Tom	Chicago, Ill.	10/1/27
Bossom, Barbara	Charleroi, Pa.	11/1/39
Bottoms, Joseph	Santa Barbara, Cal.	4/22/54
Bottoms, Timothy	Santa Barbara, Cal.	8/30/51
Bowie, David	London, England	1/8/47
Boxleitner, Bruce	Elgin, Ill.	5/12/50
Boyle, Peter	Philadelphia, Pa.	10/18/33
Bracken, Eddie	New York, N.Y.	2/7/20
Brand, Neville	Kewanee, Ill.	8/13/21
Brando, Marlon	Omaha, Neb.	4/3/24

Name	Birthplace	Born	Name	Birthplace	Born
Brazzi, Rossano	Bologna, Italy	9/18/16	Cavallaro, Carmen	New York, N.Y.	5/6/13
Brendel, Alfred	Wiesenberg, Austria	1/5/31	Cavett, Dick	Gibbon, Neb.	11/19/36
Brennan, Eileen	Los Angeles, Cal.	9/3/35	Chamberlain, Richard	Beverly Hills, Cal.	3/31/35
Brenner, David	Philadelphia, Pa.	1945	Champion, Marge	Los Angeles, Cal.	9/2/23
Brewer, Teresa	Toledo, Oh.	5/7/32	Channing, Carol	Seattle, Wash.	1/31/23
Brian, David	New York, N.Y.	8/5/14	Channing, Stockard	New York, N.Y.	2/13/44
Bridges, Beau	Hollywood, Cal.	12/9/41	Chaplin, Geraldine	Santa Monica, Cal.	7/31/44
Bridges, Jeff	Los Angeles, Cal.	12/4/49	Chaplin, Sydney	Beverly Hills, Cal.	3/31/26
Bridges, Lloyd	San Leandro, Cal.	1/15/13	Charisse, Cyd	Amarillo, Tex.	3/8/21
Bridges, Todd	San Francisco, Cal.	5/27/65	Charles, Ray	Albany, Ga.	9/23/30
Brolin, James	Los Angeles, Cal.	7/18/42	Charo	Murcia, Spain	1/15/51
Bronson, Charles	Scooptown, Pa.	11/3/22	Chase, Chevy	New York, N.Y.	10/8/43
Brooks, Albert	Beverly Hills, Cal.	1947	Checker, Chubby	Philadelphia, Pa.	10/3/41
Brooks, Louise	Cherryvale, Kan.	11/14/05	Cher	El Centro, Cal.	5/20/46
Brooks, Mel	New York, N.Y.	6/28/26	Chong, Thomas	Edmonton, Alta.	5/24/38
Brooks, Stephen	Columbus, Oh.	1942	Christie, Julie	Assam, India	4/14/41
Brosnan, Pierce	Co. Meath, Ireland	5/16/52	Christopher, William	Evanston, Ill.	10/20/32
Brown, James	Pulaski, Tenn.	6/17/28	Christy, June	Springfield, Ill.	11/20/25
Brown, Jim	St. Simons Island, Ga.	2/17/36	Clapton, Eric	Surrey, England	3/30/45
Brown, Les	Reinerton, Pa.	3/14/12	Clark, Dane	New York, N.Y.	2/18/15
Brown, Ray	Pittsburgh, Pa.	10/13/26	Clark, Dick	Mt. Vernon, N.Y.	11/30/29
Browne, Roscoe Lee	Woodbury, N.J.	1925	Clark, Petula	Ewell, Surrey, England.	11/15/32
Bruce, Carol	Great Neck, N.Y.	11/15/19	Clark, Roy	Meherrin, Va.	4/5/33
Bryant, Anita	Barnsdall, Okla.	3/25/40	Clark, Susan	Sarnia, Ont.	3/8/44
Brynner, Yul	Sakhalin, Japan	7/11/20	Clayburgh, Jill	New York, N.Y.	4/30/44
Bujold, Genevieve	Montreal, Que.	7/1/42	Clary, Robert	Paris, France	3/1/26
Bumbry, Grace	St. Louis, Mo.	1/4/37	Cliburn, Van	Shreveport, La.	7/12/34
Burghoff, Gary	Bristol, Conn.	5/24/-	Clooney, Rosemary	Maysville, Ky.	5/23/28
Burke, Paul	New Orleans, La.	7/21/26	Close, Glenn	Greenwich, Conn.	1947
Burnett, Carol	San Antonio, Tex.	4/26/36	Coburn, James	Laurel, Neb.	8/31/28
Burns, George	New York, N.Y.	1/20/96	Coca, Imogene	Philadelphia, Pa.	11/18/08
Burr, Raymond	New Westminster, B.C.	5/21/17	Coco, James	New York, N.Y.	3/21/30
Burstyn, Ellen	Detroit, Mich.	12/7/32	Cohen, Myron	Grodno, Poland	1902
Burton, LaVar	Landsthul, W. Germany	2/16/57	Cohn, Mindy	Los Angeles, Cal.	5/20/66
Bushell, Anthony	Kent, England	5/19/04	Colbert, Claudette	Paris, France	9/18/05
Busey, Gary	Goose Creek, Tex.	6/29/44	Cole, Natalie	Los Angeles, Cal.	2/6/50
Buttons, Red	New York, N.Y.	2/5/19	Coleman, Dabney	Austin, Tex.	1/3/32
Buzzi, Ruth	Westerly, R.I.	7/24/36	Coleman, Gary	Zion, Ill.	2/8/68
Caan, James	New York, N.Y.	3/26/39	Collins, Dorothy	Windsor, Ont.	11/18/26
Caballe, Montserrat	Barcelona, Spain	4/12/33	Collins, Joan	London, England	5/23/33
Caesar, Sid	Yonkers, N.Y.	9/8/22	Collins, Judy	Seattle, Wash.	5/1/39
Cagney, James	New York, N.Y.	7/17/99	Colonna, Jerry	Boston, Mass.	9/17/04
Caine, Michael	London, England	3/14/33	Comden, Betty	Brooklyn, N.Y.	5/3/19
Caldwell, Sarah	Maryville, Mo.	3/6/24	Como, Perry	Canonsburg, Pa.	5/18/12
Caldwell, Zoe	Melbourne, Australia	9/14/33	Compton, Forrest	Reading, Pa.	9/15/25
Calhoun, Rory	Los Angeles, Cal.	8/8/22	Conklin, Peggy	Dobbs Ferry, N.Y.	11/2/10
Callas, Charlie	Brooklyn, N.Y.	12/20/-	Conner, Nadine	Compton, Cal.	2/20/13
Calloway, Cab	Rochester, N.Y.	12/25/07	Connery, Sean	Edinburgh, Scotland	8/25/30
Campbell, Glen	Billstown, Ark.	4/22/36	Conniff, Ray	Attleboro, Mass.	11/6/16
Cannon, Dyan	Tacoma, Wash.	1/4/37	Connors, Chuck	Brooklyn, N.Y.	4/10/21
Cantrell, Lana	Sydney, Australia	8/7/43	Connors, Mike	Fresno, Cal.	8/15/25
Capra, Frank	Palermo, Italy	5/18/97	Conrad, Robert	Chicago, Ill.	3/1/35
Cara, Irene	New York, N.Y.	3/18/59	Constantine, Michael	Reading, Pa.	5/22/27
Carey, Macdonald	Sioux City, Ia.	3/15/13	Conti, Tom	Paisley, Scotland	11/22/41
Carey, Phil	Hackensack, N.J.	7/15/25	Convy, Bert	St. Louis, Mo.	6/23/33
Carey, Ron	Newark, N.J.	12/11/35	Conway, Tim	Willoughby, Oh.	12/15/33
Cariou, Len	Winnipeg, Canada	9/30/39	Cook, Barbara	Atlanta, Ga.	10/25/27
Carle, Frankie	Providence, R.I.	3/25/03	Cook, Peter	Torquay, England.	11/17/37
Carlin, George	New York, N.Y.	5/12/37	Cooke, Alistair	England	11/20/08
Carlisle, Kitty	New Orleans, La	9/3/15	Coolidge, Rita	Nashville, Tenn.	5/1/45
Carmen, Eric	Cleveland, Oh.	8/11/49	Cooper, Alice	Detroit, Mich.	2/4/48
Carmichael, Ian	Hull, England	6/18/20	Cooper, Jackie	Los Angeles, Cal.	9/15/22
Carpenter, John	Carthage, N.Y.	1/16/48	Coppola, Francis	Detroit, Mich.	4/7/39
Carney, Art	Mt. Vernon, N.Y.	11/4/18	Corby, Ellen	Racine, Wis.	6/3/13
Carnovsky, Morris	St. Louis, Mo.	9/5/97	Cord, Alex	New York, N.Y.	8/3/31
Caron, Leslie	Boulogne, France.	7/1/31	Corelli, Franco	Ancona, Italy	4/8/23
Carr, Vikki	El Paso, Tex.	7/19/41	Corey, Jeff	New York, N.Y.	8/10/14
Carradine, David	Hollywood, Cal.	10/8/36	Cosby, Bill	Philadelphia, Pa.	7/12/37
Carradine, John	New York, N.Y.	2/5/06	Costello, Elvis	London, England	8/25/54
Carradine, Keith	San Mateo, Cal.	8/8/49	Cotten, Joseph	Petersburg, Va.	5/15/05
Carreras, Jose	Barcelona, Spain	12/5/47	Courtenay, Tom	Hull, England	2/25/37
Carroll, Diahann	Bronx, N.Y.	7/17/35	Craddock, Crash	Greensboro, N.C.	6/16/40
Carroll, Madeleine	W. Bromwich, England.	2/26/06	Crain, Jeanne	Barstow, Cal.	5/25/25
Carroll, Pat	Shreveport, La.	5/5/27	Crawford, Broderick	Philadelphia, Pa.	12/9/11
Carson, Johnny	Corning, Ia.	10/23/25	Crenna, Richard	Los Angeles, Cal.	11/30/27
Carter, Jack	New York, N.Y.	6/24/23	Cronyn, Hume	London, Ont.	7/18/11
Carter, June	Maces Spring, Va.	6/23/29	Crosby, Bob	Spokane, Wash.	8/25/13
Carter, Lynda	Phoenix, Ariz.	7/24/51	Crosby, Cathy Lee	Los Angeles, Cal.	12/2/-
Carter, Nell	Birmingham, Ala.	9/13/48	Crosby, David	Los Angeles, Cal.	8/14/41
Casadesus, Gaby	Marseilles, France	1902	Crosby, Kathryn	Houston, Tex.	11/25/33
Cash, Johnny	Kingsland, Ark.	2/26/32	Crosby, Norm	Boston, Mass.	1/15/27
Cass, Peggy	Boston, Mass.	5/21/24	Cross, Christopher	San Antonio, Tex.	5/3/51
Cassavetes, John	New York, N.Y.	12/9/29	Crothers, Scatman	Terre Haute, Ind.	5/23/10
Cassidy, David	New York, N.Y.	4/12/50	Crystal, Billy	Long Beach, N.Y.	3/14/47
Cassidy, Shaun	Los Angeles, Cal.	9/27/58	Cugat, Xavier	Barcelona, Spain	1/1/00
Castellano, Richard	New York, N.Y.	9/4/33	Cullen, Bill	Pittsburgh, Pa.	2/18/20
Caulfield, Joan	West Orange, N.J.	6/1/22			

Name	Birthplace	Born
Cullum, John	Knoxville, Tenn.	3/2/30
Culp, Robert	Oakland, Cal.	8/16/30
Cummings, Constance	Seattle, Wash.	5/15/10
Cummings, Robert	Joplin, Mo.	6/9/10
Curtin, Jane	Cambridge, Mass.	9/6/47
Curtin, Phyllis	Clarksburg, W.Va.	12/3/30
Curtis, Jamie Lee	Los Angeles, Cal.	11/22/58
Curtis, Keene	Salt Lake City, Ut.	2/15/23
Curtis, Ken	Lamar, Col.	7/2/16
Curtis, Tony	New York, N.Y.	6/3/25
Cusack, Cyril	Durban, S. Africa	11/26/10
Cushing, Peter	Surrey, England	5/26/13
Dahl, Arlene	Minneapolis, Minn.	8/11/28
Dale, Jim	Rothwell, England	8/15/35
Dalton, Abby	Las Vegas, Nev.	8/15/35
Daly, John	Johannesburg, S. Africa	2/20/14
Daly, Tyne	Madison, Wis.	2/21/47
Damone, Vic	Brooklyn, N.Y.	6/12/28
Dangerfield, Rodney	Babylon, N.Y.	1922
Daniels, Charlie	Wilmingham, N.C.	10/28/36
Daniels, William	Brooklyn, N.Y.	3/31/27
Danilova, Alexandra	Peterhof, Russia	11/20/07
Danner, Blythe	Philadelphia, Pa.	2/3/43
Danson, Ted	San Diego, Cal.	12/29/-
Danza, Tony	New York, N.Y.	4/21/-
Darby, Kim	Hollywood, Cal.	7/8/48
Darcel, Denise	Paris, France	9/8/25
Darren, James	Philadelphia, Pa.	6/8/36
Da Silva, Howard	Cleveland, Oh.	5/4/09
Davidson, John	Pittsburgh, Pa.	12/13/41
Davis, Ann B.	Schenectady, N.Y.	5/5/26
Davis, Bette	Lowell, Mass.	4/5/08
Davis, Clifton	Chicago, Ill.	10/4/45
Davis, Geena	Ware, Mass.	1957
Davis, Judy	Perth, Australia	1956
Davis, Mac	Lubbock, Tex.	1/21/42
Davis, Ossie	Cogdell, Ga.	12/18/17
Davis, Sammy Jr.	New York, N.Y.	12/8/25
Davis, Skeeter	Dry Ridge, Ky.	12/30/31
Dawber, Pam	Detroit, Mich.	10/18/51
Dawn, Hazel	Ogden, Ut.	3/23/98
Dawson, Richard	Hampshire, England	11/20/32
Day, Dennis	New York, N.Y.	5/21/17
Day, Doris	Cincinnati, Oh.	4/3/24
Day, Laraine	Roosevelt, Ut.	10/13/20
Dean, Jimmy	Plainview, Tex.	8/10/28
De Camp, Rosemary	Prescott, Ariz.	11/14/10
DeCarlo, Yvonne	Vancouver, B.C.	9/1/22
Dee, Frances	Los Angeles, Cal.	11/26/07
Dee, Ruby	Cleveland, Oh.	10/27/23
Dee, Sandra	Bayonne, N.J.	4/29/42
Defore, Don	Cedar Rapids, Ia.	8/25/17
DeHaven, Gloria	Los Angeles, Cal.	7/23/25
de Havilland, Olivia	Tokyo, Japan	7/1/16
De Niro, Robert	New York, N.Y.	8/17/45
Dell, Gabriel	Barbados, BWI	10/7/19
Della Chiesa, Vivienne	Chicago, Ill.	10/9/20
Delon, Alain	Sceaux, France	11/8/35
DeLuise, Dom	Brooklyn, N.Y.	8/1/33
De Mille, Agnes	New York, N.Y.	1905
Deneuve, Catherine	Paris, France	10/22/43
Denning, Richard	Poughkeepsie, N.Y.	3/27/14
Dennis, Sandy	Hastings, Neb.	4/27/37
Denver, Bob	New Rochelle, N.Y.	1935
Denver, John	Roswell, N.M.	12/31/43
DePalma, Brian	Newark, N.J.	9/11/40
Derek, Bo	Long Beach, Cal.	11/20/56
Derek, John	Hollywood, Cal.	8/12/26
Dern, Bruce	Chicago, Ill.	6/4/36
Desmond, Johnny	Detroit, Mich.	11/14/21
Devane, William	Albany, N.Y.	9/5/37
DeVito, Danny	Neptune, N.J.	11/17/44
Dewhurst, Colleen	Montreal, Que.	6/3/26
DeWitt, Joyce	Wheeling, W.Va.	4/23/49
Dey, Susan	Pekin, Ill.	12/10/52
Diamond, Neil	Brooklyn, N.Y.	1/24/41
Dickinson, Angie	Kulm, N.D.	9/30/31
Dierkop, Charles	La Crosse, Wis.	9/11/36
Dietrich, Marlene	Berlin, Germany	12/27/01
Diller, Phyllis	Lima, Oh.	7/17/17
Dillman, Bradford	San Francisco, Cal.	4/14/30
Dillon, Matt	Westchester Co., N.Y.	2/18/64
Dixon, Ivan	New York, N.Y.	4/6/31
Domingo, Placido	Madrid, Spain	1/21/41
Domino, Fats	New Orleans, La.	2/26/28
Donahue, Phil	Cleveland, Oh.	12/21/35
Donahue, Troy	New York, N.Y.	1/27/36

Name	Birthplace	Born
Donald, James	Aberdeen, Scotland	5/18/17
Donovan	Glasgow, Scotland	5/10/43
Douglas, Kirk	Amsterdam, N.Y.	12/9/18
Douglas, Michael	New Brunswick, N.J.	9/25/44
Douglas, Mike	Chicago, Ill.	8/11/25
Down, Leslie-Ann	London, England	3/17/54
Downey, Morton	Wallingford, Conn.	11/14/01
Downs, Hugh	Akron, Oh.	2/14/21
Doyle, David	Lincoln, Neb.	12/1/29
Dragon, Daryl	Los Angeles, Cal.	8/27/42
Drake, Alfred	Bronx, N.Y.	10/7/14
Drew, Ellen	Kansas City, Mo.	11/23/15
Dreyfuss, Richard	Brooklyn, N.Y.	10/29/47
Dru, Joanne	Logan, W.Va.	1/31/23
Duchin, Peter	New York, N.Y.	7/28/37
Duff, Howard	Bremerton, Wash.	11/24/17
Duffy, Patrick	Townsend, Mont.	3/17/49
Dufour, Val	New Orleans, La.	2/5/27
Duke, Patty	New York, N.Y.	12/14/46
Dullea, Keir	Cleveland, Oh.	5/30/36
Dunaway, Faye	Bascom, Fla.	1/14/41
Duncan, Sandy	Henderson, Tex.	2/20/46
Duncan, Todd	Danville, Ky.	2/12/00
Duncan, Vivian	Los Angeles, Cal.	6/17/02
Dunham, Katherine	Joliet, Ill.	6/22/10
Dunne, Irene	Louisville, Ky.	12/20/04
Dunnock, Mildred	Baltimore, Md.	1/25/04
Durbin, Deanna	Winnipeg, Man.	12/4/21
Durning, Charles	Highland Falls, N.Y.	2/28/23
Dussault, Nancy	Pensacola, Fla.	6/30/36
Duvall, Robert	San Diego, Cal.	1/5/31
Duvall, Shelley	Houston, Tex.	1949
Dylan, Bob	Duluth, Minn.	5/24/41
Easton, Sheena	Glascow, Scotland	4/27/59
Eastwood, Clint	San Francisco, Cal.	5/31/30
Ebsen, Buddy	Belleville, Ill.	4/2/08
Eckstine, Billy	Pittsburgh, Pa.	7/8/14
Edelman, Herb.	Brooklyn, N.Y.	11/5/33
Eden, Barbara	Tucson, Ariz.	8/23/34
Edwards, Blake	Tulsa, Okla.	7/26/22
Edwards, Ralph	Merino, Col.	6/13/13
Edwards, Vincent	Brooklyn, N.Y.	7/7/28
Egan, Richard	San Francisco, Cal.	7/29/23
Eggar, Samantha	London, England	3/5/39
Eichhorn, Lisa	Reading, Pa.	2/4/52
Ekberg, Anita	Malmo, Sweden	9/29/31
Ekland, Britt	Stockholm, Sweden	10/6/42
Elam, Jack	Miami, Ariz.	11/13/16
Eldridge, Florence	Brooklyn, N.Y.	9/5/01
Elgart, Larry	New London, Conn.	3/20/22
Elgart, Les	New Haven, Conn.	1918
Elliott, Bob	Boston, Mass.	3/26/23
Elliott, Sam	Sacramento, Cal.	8/9/44
Erickson, Leif	Alameda, Cal.	10/27/11
Estrada, Erik	New York, N.Y.	3/16/49
Evans, Dale	Uvalde, Tex.	10/31/12
Evans, Gene	Holbrook, Ariz.	7/11/24
Evans, Linda	Hartford, Conn.	11/18/42
Evans, Maurice	Dorchester, England	6/3/01
Evans, Robert	New York, N.Y.	6/29/30
Everett, Chad	South Bend, Ind.	6/11/37
Everly, Don	Brownie, Ky.	2/1/37
Everly, Phil	Brownie, Ky.	1/19/38
Ewell, Tom	Owensboro, Ky.	4/29/09
Fabares, Shelley	Santa Monica, Cal.	1/19/42
Fabian (Forte)	Philadelphia, Pa.	2/6/43
Fabray, Nanette	San Diego, Cal.	10/27/20
Fairbanks, Douglas Jr.	New York, N.Y.	12/9/09
Fairchild, Morgan	Dallas, Tex.	2/3/50
Falana, Lola	Philadelphia, Pa.	9/11/46
Falk, Peter	New York, N.Y.	9/16/27
Farentino, James	Brooklyn, N.Y.	2/24/38
Fargo, Donna	Mt. Airy, N.C.	11/10/49
Farr, Jamie	Toledo, Oh.	7/1/36
Farrell, Charles	Onset Bay, Mass.	1901
Farrell, Eileen	Willimantic, Conn.	2/13/20
Farrell, Mike	St. Paul, Minn.	2/6/39
Farrow, Mia	Los Angeles, Cal.	2/9/45
Fawcett, Farrah	Corpus Christi, Tex.	2/2/47
Faye, Alice	New York, N.Y.	5/5/15
Feld, Fritz	Berlin, Germany	10/15/00
Feldon, Barbara	Pittsburgh, Pa.	3/12/41
Feldsuh, Tovah	New York, N.Y.	12/27/52
Feliciano, Jose	Lares, Puerto Rico	9/10/45
Fell, Norman	Philadelphia, Pa.	3/24/25
Fellini, Federico	Rimini, Italy	1/20/20

Name	Birthplace	Born	Name	Birthplace	Born
Fellows, Edith	Boston, Mass.	5/20/23	Gennaro, Peter	Metairie, La.	1924
Fender, Freddy	San Benito, Tex.	6/4/37	Gentry, Bobbie	Chickasaw Co., Miss.	7/27/44
Ferrer, Jose	Santurce, P.R.	1/8/12	George, Phyllis	Denton, Tex.	6/25/49
Ferrer, Mel	Elberon, N.J.	8/25/17	Gerard, Gil	Little Rock, Ark.	1/23/43
Ferrigno, Lou	Brooklyn, N.Y.	11/9/52	Gere, Richard	Philadelphia, Pa.	8/31/49
Fetchit, Stepin	Key West, Fla.	5/30/02	Ghostley, Alice	Eve, Mo.	8/14/26
Field, Sally	Pasadena, Cal.	11/6/46	Giannini, Giancarlo	Spezia, Italy	8/1/42
Fields, Kim	Los Angeles, Cal.	5/12/69	Gibb, Andy	Manchester, England.	3/5/58
Finney, Albert	Salford, England	5/9/36	Gibbs, Marla	Chicago, Ill.	6/14/31
Firkusny, Rudolf	Napajedla, Czechoslova-kia	2/11/12	Gibson, Henry	Germantown, Pa.	9/21/35
			Gibson, Mel	New York, N.Y.	1956
Firth, Peter	Yorkshire, England	10/27/53	Gielgud, John	London, England	4/14/04
Fischer-Dieskau, Dietrich	Berlin, Germany	5/28/25	Gilbert, Melissa	Los Angeles, Cal.	5/8/64
Fisher, Carrie	Beverly Hills, Cal.	10/21/56	Gilberto, Astrud	Salvador, Brazil.	3/30/40
Fisher, Eddie	Philadelphia, Pa.	8/10/28	Gilford, Jack	New York, N.Y.	7/25/07
Fitzgerald, Ella	Newport News, Va.	4/25/18	Gillette, Anita.	Baltimore, Md.	8/16/36
Fitzgerald, Geraldine	Dublin, Ireland.	11/24/13	Gilley, Mickey	Natchez, Miss.	3/9/36
Flack, Roberta	Black Mountain, N.C.	2/10/39	Gingold, Hermione	London, England	12/9/97
Flanders, Ed	Minneapolis, Minn.	12/29/34	Ginty, Robert.	New York, N.Y.	11/14/48
Fleming, Rhonda	Hollywood, Cal.	8/10/23	Gish, Lillian.	Springfield, Oh.	10/14/96
Fletcher, Louise	Birmingham, Ala.	1936	Glaser, Paul Michael	Cambridge, Mass.	3/25/43
Foch, Nina	Leyden, Netherlands	4/20/24	Glass, Ron	Evansville, Ind.	7/10/45
Fogelberg, Dan	Peoria, Ill.	8/13/51	Gleason, Jackie	Brooklyn, N.Y..	2/26/16
Fonda, Jane	New York, N.Y.	12/21/37	Gless, Sharon	Los Angeles, Cal..	5/31/43
Fonda, Peter	New York, N.Y.	2/23/40	Gobel, George.	Chicago, Ill.	5/20/19
Fontaine, Joan	Tokyo, Japan	10/22/17	Godard, Jean Luc	Paris, France	12/3/30
Fonteyn, Margot	Reigate, England	5/18/19	Goddard, Paulette	Great Neck, N.Y.	6/3/11
Ford (Tenn.), Ernie	Bristol, Tenn.	2/13/19	Godunov, Alexander	Sakhalin Is., USSR	11/28/49
Ford, Glenn	Quebec, Canada	5/1/16	Goldblum, Jeff	Pittsburgh, Pa.	1953
Ford, Harrison	Chicago, Ill.	7/13/42	Goldsboro, Bobby	Marianna, Fla..	1/11/41
Ford, Ruth	Brookhaven, Miss.	1920	Goodman, Benny	Chicago, Ill.	5/30/09
Forrest, Steve	Huntsville, Tex.	9/29/24	Goodman, Dody	Columbus, Oh.	10/28/29
Forsythe, Henderson	Macon, Mo.	9/11/17	Gordon, Gale	New York, N.Y.	2/2/06
Forsythe, John	Penns Grove, N.J.	1/29/18	Gordon, Ruth	Wollaston, Mass.	10/30/96
Fosse, Bob	Chicago, Ill.	6/23/27	Gorin, Igor	Ukraine, Russia	10/26/09
Foster, Jodie	Los Angeles, Cal..	11/19/62	Gorman, Cliff.	New York, N.Y.	10/13/36
Fox, James	London, England	5/19/39	Gorme, Eydie	Bronx, N.Y.	8/16/32
Fox, Michael J.	Edmonton, Alta.	6/9/61	Gorshin, Frank.	Pittsburgh, Pa.	4/5/34
Foxx, Redd.	St. Louis, Mo.	12/9/22	Gossett Jr., Louis	Brooklyn, N.Y..	5/27/36
Frampton, Peter	Kent, England.	4/22/50	Gould, Elliott	Brooklyn, N.Y.	8/29/38
Francescatti, Zino	Marseilles, France	8/9/05	Gould, Harold	Schenectady, N.Y.	12/10/23
Franciosa, Anthony	New York, N.Y.	10/25/28	Gould, Morton	Richmond Hill, N.Y..	12/10/13
Francis, Anne	Ossining, N.Y..	9/16/32	Goulding, Ray	Lowell, Mass.	3/20/22
Francis, Arlene	Boston, Mass.	10/20/08	Goulet, Robert.	Lawrence, Mass.	11/26/33
Francis, Connie	Newark, N.J.	12/12/38	Gowdy, Curt	Green River, Wyo.	7/31/19
Francis, Genie	Los Angeles, Cal..	5/26/62	Graham, Martha	Pittsburgh, Pa.	5/11/94
Franciscus, James	Clayton, Mo..	1/31/34	Graham, Virginia	Chicago, Ill.	7/4/12
Frankenheimer, John	Malba, N.Y.	2/19/30	Grandy, Fred.	Sioux City, Ia.	6/29/-
Franklin, Aretha	Memphis, Tenn.	3/25/42	Granger, Farley	San Jose, Cal.	7/1/25
Franklin, Bonnie	Santa Monica, Cal.	1/6/44	Granger, Stewart	London, England	5/6/13
Franklin, Joe	New York, N.Y.	1929	Granville, Bonita	New York, N.Y.	2/2/23
Frann, Mary	St. Louis, Mo.	2/27/43	Grant, Cary	Bristol, England.	1/18/04
Freberg, Stan	Pasadena, Cal.	8/7/26	Grant, Lee	New York, N.Y.	10/31/31
Freed, Bert.	New York, N.Y.	11/3/19	Graves, Peter	Minneapolis, Minn.	3/18/26
Freeman Jr., Al	San Antonio, Tex..	3/21/34	Gray, Coleen	Staplehurst, Neb.	10/23/22
French, Victor	Santa Barbara, Cal.	12/4/34	Gray, Linda.	Santa Monica, Cal.	9/12/40
Frick, Mr. (G. Werner).	Basel, Switzerland	4/21/15	Grayson, Kathryn	Winston-Salem, N.C..	2/9/23
Friedkin, William.	Chicago, Ill.	8/29/39	Graziano, Rocky	New York, N.Y.	6/7/22
Frost, David	Tenterden, England	4/7/39	Greco, Buddy	Philadelphia, Pa.	8/14/26
Frye, David.	Brooklyn, N.Y..	1934	Greco, Jose	Abruzzi, Italy	12/23/18
Funicello, Annette	Utica, N.Y..	10/22/42	Green, Adolph	New York, N.Y.	12/2/15
Funt, Allen	New York, N.Y.	9/16/14	Green, Al	Forest City, Ark.	4/13/46
			Greene, Lorne	Ottawa, Ont.	2/12/15
Gabel, Martin	Philadelphia, Pa.	6/19/12	Greenwood, Joan	London, England	3/4/21
Gabriel, John.	Niagara Falls, N.Y.	5/25/-	Gregory, Cynthia	Los Angeles, Cal..	7/8/46
Gabor, Eva.	Hungary	1921	Gregory, Dick	St. Louis, Mo.	10/12/32
Gabor, Zsa Zsa	Hungary	—	Gregory, James	Bronx, N.Y.	12/23/11
Gail, Max	Detroit, Mich.	4/5/43	Grey, Joel	Cleveland, Oh.	4/11/32
Galloway, Don	Brooksville, Ky.	7/27/37	Griffin, Merv	San Mateo, Cal.	7/6/25
Galway, James	Belfast, Ireland	12/8/39	Griffith, Andy	Mount Airy, N.C.	6/1/26
Garagiola, Joe	St. Louis, Mo.	2/12/26	Grimes, Tammy	Lynn, Mass.	1/30/36
Garbo, Greta.	Stockholm, Sweden	9/18/05	Grizzard, George	Roanoke Rapids, N.C..	4/1/28
Gardenia, Vincent	Naples, Italy	1/7/22	Grodin, Charles	Pittsburgh, Pa.	4/21/35
Gardner, Ava	Smithfield, N.C.	12/24/22	Groh, David	New York, N.Y.	5/2/41
Garfunkel, Art	New York, N.Y.	10/13/41	Grosbard, Ulu	Antwerp, Belgium.	1/19/29
Garland, Beverly	Santa Cruz, Cal.	10/17/29	Gross, Mary	Chicago, Ill.	3/25/53
Garner, James	Norman, Okla.	4/7/28	Gross, Michael.	Chicago, Ill.	6/21/-
Garrett, Betty	St. Joseph, Mo.	5/23/19	Guardino, Harry	New York, N.Y.	12/23/25
Garrett, Leif	Hollywood, Cal.	11/8/61	Guillaume, Robert.	St. Louis, Mo.	11/30/-
Garson, Greer	Co. Down, N. Ireland	9/29/08	Guinness, Alec.	London, England	4/2/14
Gatlin, Larry	Seminole, Tex.	5/2/48	Gunn, Moses.	St. Louis, Mo.	10/2/29
Gavin, John	Los Angeles, Cal..	4/8/32	Guthrie, Arlo	New York, N.Y.	7/10/47
Gayle, Crystal	Paintsville, Ky.	1/9/51	Gwynne, Fred	New York, N.Y.	7/10/26
Gaynor, Janet	Philadelphia, Pa.	10/6/06			
Gaynor, Mitzi	Chicago, Ill.	9/4/31	Hackett, Buddy	Brooklyn, N.Y..	8/31/24
Gazzara, Ben	New York, N.Y.	8/28/30	Hackman, Gene	San Bernardino, Cal..	1/30/30
Geary, Anthony	Coalsville, Ut.	5/29/47	Hagen, Uta.	Gottingen, Germany	6/12/19
Gedda, Nicolai	Stockholm, Sweden	7/11/25	Haggard, Merle	Bakersfield, Cal.	4/6/37

Name	Birthplace	Born	Name	Birthplace	Born
Haggerty, Dan	Hollywood, Cal.	11/19/41	Hopper, Dennis	Dodge City, Kan.	5/17/36
Hagman, Larry	Ft. Worth, Tex.	9/21/31	Horne, Lena	Brooklyn, N.Y.	6/30/17
Haid, Charles	San Francisco, Cal.	6/2/43	Horne, Marilyn	Bradford, Pa.	1/16/34
Hale, Barbara	DeKalb, Ill.	4/18/22	Horowitz, Vladimir	Kiev, Russia	10/1/04
Hall, Daryl	Pottstown, Pa.	10/11/49	Horsley, Lee	Muleshoe, Tex.	5/15/55
Hall, Huntz	New York, N.Y.	1920	Horton, Robert	Los Angeles, Cal.	7/29/24
Hall, Monty	Winnipeg, Man.	8/25/23	Houseman, John	Bucharest, Romania	9/22/02
Hall, Tom T.	Olive Hill, Ky.	5/25/36	Howard, Ken	El Centro, Cal.	3/28/44
Hamel, Veronica	Philadelphia, Pa.	11/20/43	Howard, Ron	Duncan, Okla.	3/1/54
Hamill, Mark	Oakland, Cal.	9/25/52	Howard, Trevor	Kent, England	9/29/16
Hamilton, George	Memphis, Tenn.	8/12/39	Howes, Sally Ann	London, England	7/20/34
Hampshire, Susan	London, England	5/12/42	Hudson, Rock	Winnetka, Ill.	11/17/25
Hampton, Lionel	Birmingham, Ala.	4/12/13	Hughes, Barnard	Bedford Hills, N.Y.	7/16/15
Hancock, Herbie	Chicago, Ill.	4/12/40	Hulce, Tom	White Water, Wis.	1953
Harmon, Mark	Burbank, Cal.	9/2/51	Humperdinck, Engelbert	Madras, India	5/3/36
Harper, Valerie	Suffern, N.Y.	8/22/40	Hunt, Lois	York, Pa.	11/26/25
Harrington, Pat Jr.	New York, N.Y.	8/13/29	Hunter, Kim	Detroit, Mich.	11/12/22
Harris, Barbara	Evanston, Ill.	7/25/35	Hunter, Ross	Cleveland, Oh.	5/6/26
Harris, Emmylou	Birmingham, Ala.	4/2/47	Hunter, Tab	New York, N.Y.	7/11/31
Harris, Julie	Grosse Pte. Park, Mich.	12/2/25	Hurt, John	Chesterfield, England	1/22/40
Harris, Phil	Linton, Ind.	6/24/06	Hurt, William	Washington, D.C.	3/20/50
Harris, Richard	Co. Limerick, Ireland	10/1/33	Hussey, Olivia	Buenos Aires, Argentina	4/17/51
Harris, Rosemary	Ashby, England	9/19/30	Hussey, Ruth	Providence, R.I.	10/30/17
Harrison, George	Liverpool, England	2/25/43	Huston, John	Nevada, Mo.	8/5/06
Harrison, Gregory	Avalon, Cal.	5/31/50	Hutchinson, Josephine	Seattle, Wash.	10/12/09
Harrison, Rex	Huyton, England	3/5/08	Hutton, Betty	Battle Creek, Mich.	2/26/21
Harry, Deborah	Miami, Fla.	7/1/45	Hutton, Lauren	Charleston, S.C.	1944
Hartley, Mariette	New York, N.Y.	6/21/40	Hutton, Timothy	Malibu, Cal.	8/16/61
Hartman, David	Pawtucket, R.I.	5/19/35	Hyde-White, Wilfrid	Gloucester, England	5/12/03
Hartman, Lisa	Houston, Tex.	—	Hyman, Earle	Rocky Mount, N.C.	11/11/26
Harwood, Dorian	Dayton, Oh.	8/6/-	Ian, Janis	New York, N.Y.	4/7/51
Hasselhoff, David	Baltimore, Md.	7/17/52	Iglesias, Julio	Spain	9/23/43
Hasso, Signe	Stockholm, Sweden	8/15/18	Ireland, Jill	London, England	4/24/36
Haver, June	Rock Island, Ill.	6/10/26	Ireland, John	Vancouver, B.C.	1/30/15
Havoc, June	Vancouver, B.C.	11/8/16	Irons, Jeremy	Cowes, England	9/19/48
Hawn, Goldie	Washington, D.C.	11/21/45	Irving, Amy	Palo Alto, Cal.	9/10/53
Hayden, Melissa	Toronto, Ont.	4/25/23	Irving, George S.	Springfield, Mass.	11/1/22
Hayden, Sterling	Montclair, N.J.	3/26/16	Ives, Burl	Hunt Township, Ill.	6/14/09
Hayes, Helen	Washington, D.C.	10/10/00	Jackson, Anne	Allegheny, Pa.	9/3/26
Hayes, Isaac	Covington, Tenn.	8/20/42	Jackson, Glenda	Liverpool, England	5/9/38
Hayes, Peter Lind	San Francisco, Cal.	6/25/15	Jackson, Jermaine	Gary, Ind.	12/11/54
Hays, Robert	Bethesda, Md.	7/24/47	Jackson, Kate	Birmingham, Ala.	10/29/48
Hayworth, Rita	New York, N.Y.	10/17/18	Jackson, Michael	Gary, Ind.	8/29/58
Healy, Mary	New Orleans, La.	4/14/18	Jacobi, Derek	London, England	10/22/38
Heatherton, Joey	Rockville Centre, N.Y.	9/14/44	Jaeckel, Richard	Long Beach, Cal.	10/10/26
Heckart, Eileen	Columbus, Oh.	3/29/19	Jagger, Dean	Columbus Grove, Oh.	11/7/05
Heifetz, Jascha	Vilna, Lithuania	2/2/01	Jagger, Mick	Dartford, England	7/26/43
Helmond, Katherine	Galveston, Tex.	7/5/34	James, Dennis	Jersey City, N.J.	8/24/17
Helpmann, Robert	Mt. Gambier, Australia	4/9/09	Janis, Conrad	New York, N.Y.	2/11/28
Hemingway, Margaux	Portland, Ore.	1955	Jarreau, Al	Milwaukee, Wis	3/12/40
Hemingway, Mariel	Portland, Ore.	—	Jeanmaire, Renee	Paris, France	4/29/24
Hemmings, David	Guildford, England	11/2/41	Jeffreys, Anne	Goldsboro, N.C.	1/26/23
Hemsley, Sherman	Philadelphia, Pa.	2/1/38	Jeffries, Fran	San Jose, Cal.	1939
Henderson, Florence	Dale, Ind.	2/14/34	Jenner, Bruce	Mt. Kisco, N.Y.	10/28/49
Henderson, Skitch	Halstad, Minn.	1/27/18	Jennings, Waylon	Littlefield, Tex.	6/15/37
Henner, Marilu	Chicago, Ill.	4/6/52	Jepson, Helen	Titusville, Pa.	11/28/07
Henning, Doug	Ft. Garry, Man., Canada	5/3/47	Jett, Joan	Philadelphia, Pa.	9/22/60
Henreid, Paul	Trieste, Austria	1/10/08	Jillian, Ann	Cambridge, Mass.	1/29/51
Hensley, Pamela	Los Angeles, Cal.	10/3/50	Joel, Billy	Bronx, N.Y.	5/9/49
Henson, Jim	Greenville, Miss.	9/24/36	John, Elton	Middlesex, England	3/25/47
Hepburn, Audrey	Brussels, Belgium	5/4/29	Johns, Glynis	Durban, S. Africa	10/5/23
Hepburn, Katharine	Hartford, Conn.	11/8/09	Johnson, Arte	Benton Harbor, Mich.	1/20/29
Herrmann, Edward	Washington, D.C.	7/21/43	Johnson, Ben	Foeaker, Okla.	6/13/18
Hesseman, Howard	Lebanon, Ore.	2/27/40	Johnson, Van	Newport, R.I.	8/25/16
Heston, Charlton	Evanston, Ill.	10/4/23	Jones, Allan	Scranton, Pa.	10/14/08
Higgins, Joel	Bloomington, Ill.	9/28/-	Jones, Chris	Jackson, Tenn.	8/18/41
Hildegarde	Adell, Wis.	2/1/06	Jones, Dean	Morgan City, Ala.	1/25/35
Hill, Arthur	Melfort, Sask.	8/1/22	Jones, George	Saratoga, Tex.	9/12/31
Hill, Benny	Southampton, England	1/21/25	Jones, Grace	Spanishtown, Jamaica	5/19/52
Hill, George Roy	Minneapolis, Minn.	12/20/22	Jones, Grandpa	Niagara, Ky.	10/20/13
Hiller, Wendy	Stockport, England	8/15/12	Jones, Henry	Philadelphia, Pa.	8/1/12
Hillerman, John	Denison, Tex.	12/30/32	Jones, Jack	Hollywood, Cal.	1/14/38
Hines, Gregory	New York, N.Y.	2/14/46	Jones, James Earl	Tate Co., Miss.	1/17/31
Hines, Jerome	Hollywood, Cal.	11/8/21	Jones, Jennifer	Tulsa, Okla.	3/2/19
Hingle, Pat	Denver, Col.	7/19/24	Jones, Shirley	Smithton, Pa.	3/31/34
Hirsch, Judd	Bronx, N.Y.	3/15/35	Jones, Tom	Pontypridd, Wales	6/7/40
Hirt, Al	New Orleans, La.	11/7/22	Jones, Tommy Lee	San Saba, Tex.	9/15/46
Ho, Don	Kakaako, Oahu, Ha.	8/13/30	Jourdan, Louis	Marseilles, France	6/19/21
Hoffman, Dustin	Los Angeles, Cal.	8/8/37	Julia, Raul	San Juan, P.R.	3/9/40
Holbrook, Hal	Cleveland, Oh.	2/17/25	Jurado, Katy	Guadalajara, Mexico	1/16/24
Holder, Geoffrey	Trinidad	8/1/30	Kahn, Madeline	Boston, Mass.	9/29/42
Holliday, Polly	Jasper, Ala.	7/2/37	Kanaly, Steve	Burbank, Cal.	3/14/46
Holliman, Earl	Delhi, La.	9/11/28	Kane, Carol	Cleveland, Oh.	6/18/52
Holloway, Sterling	Cedartown, Ga.	1/4/05	Kaplan, Gabe	Brooklyn, N.Y.	3/31/45
Holm, Celeste	New York, N.Y.	4/29/19	Karras, Alex	Gary, Ind.	7/15/35
Hooks, Robert	Washington, D.C.	4/18/37	Kavner, Judy	Los Angeles, Cal.	9/7/51
Hope, Bob	London, England	5/29/03	Kaye, Danny	Brooklyn, N.Y.	1/18/13
Hopkins, Anthony	Wales	12/31/37			

Name	Birthplace	Born	Name	Birthplace	Born
Kaye, Sammy	Lakewood, Oh.	3/13/13	Lean, David	Croydon, England	3/25/08
Kazan, Elia	Constantinople, Turkey	9/7/09	Lear, Norman	New Haven, Conn.	7/27/22
Kazan, Lainie	New York, N.Y.	5/15/42	Learned, Michael	Washington, D.C.	4/9/39
Keach, Stacy	Savannah, Ga.	6/2/41	Lederer, Francis	Prague, Czechoslovakia	11/6/06
Keaton, Diane	Santa Ana, Cal.	1/5/46	Lee, Brenda	Atlanta, Ga.	12/11/44
Keel, Howard	Gillespie, Ill.	4/13/17	Lee, Christopher	London, England	5/27/22
Keeler, Ruby	Halifax, N.S.	8/25/10	Lee, Michele	Los Angeles, Cal.	6/24/42
Keeshan, Bob	Lynbrook, N.Y.	6/27/27	Lee, Peggy	Jamestown, N.D.	5/26/20
Keitel, Harvey	Brooklyn, N.Y.	1947	Le Gallienne, Eva	London, England	1/11/99
Keith, Brian	Bayonne, N.J.	11/14/21	Legrand, Michel	Paris, France	2/24/32
Keith, David	Knoxville, Tenn.	1954	Leibman, Ron	New York, N.Y.	10/11/37
Keller, Marthe	Basel, Switzerland	1945	Leigh, Janet	Merced, Cal.	7/6/27
Kellerman, Sally	Long Beach, Cal.	6/2/37	Leinsdorf, Erich	Vienna, Austria	2/4/12
Kelley, DeForrest	Atlanta, Ga.	1/20/20	Lemmon, Jack	Boston, Mass.	2/8/25
Kelly, Gene	Pittsburgh, Pa.	8/23/12	Lennon, Dianne	Los Angeles, Cal.	12/1/39
Kelly, Jack	Astoria, N.Y.	9/16/27	Lennon, Janet	Culver City, Cal.	11/15/46
Kelly, Nancy	Lowell, Mass.	3/25/21	Lennon, Kathy	Santa Monica, Cal.	8/22/42
Kennedy, Arthur	Worcester, Mass.	2/17/14	Lennon, Peggy	Los Angeles, Cal.	4/8/41
Kennedy, George	New York, N.Y.	2/18/26	Leonard, Sheldon	New York, N.Y.	2/22/07
Kennedy, Jayne	Washington, D.C.	11/27/51	Leontovich, Eugenie	Moscow, Russia	3/21/00
Kennedy, Mimi	Rochester, N.Y.	9/25/49	LeRoy, Mervyn	San Francisco, Cal.	10/15/00
Kent, Allegra	Los Angeles, Cal.	8/11/37	Leslie, Joan	Detroit, Mich.	1/26/25
Kercheval, Ken	Wolcottville, Ind.	7/15/35	Lester, Jerry	Chicago, Ill.	1911
Kerr, Deborah	Helensburgh, Scotland.	9/30/21	Letterman, David	Indianapolis, Ind.	4/12/47
Kerr, John	New York, N.Y.	11/15/31	Levine, James	Cincinnati, Oh.	6/23/43
Khan, Chaka	Great Lakes, Ill.	3/23/53	Lewis, Emmanuel	New York, N.Y.	3/9/71
Kidd, Michael	New York, N.Y.	8/12/25	Lewis, Jerry	Newark, N.J.	3/16/26
Kidder, Margot	Yellowknife, N.W.T.	10/17/48	Lewis, Jerry Lee	Ferriday, La.	9/29/35
Kiley, Richard	Chicago, Ill.	3/31/22	Lewis, Shari	New York, N.Y.	1/17/34
King, Alan	Brooklyn, N.Y.	12/26/27	Liberace	West Allis, Wis.	5/16/19
King, B. B.	Itta Bena, Miss.	9/16/25	Lightfoot, Gordon	Orillia, Ont.	11/17/38
King, Carole	Brooklyn, N.Y.	2/9/42	Lillie, Beatrice	Toronto, Ont.	5/29/94
King, Perry	Alliance, Oh.	4/30/-	Linden, Hal	New York, N.Y.	3/20/31
King, Wayne	Savannah, Ga.	2/16/01	Lindfors, Viveca	Uppsala, Sweden.	12/29/20
Kingsley, Ben	Yorkshire, England	12/31/43	Lindsey, Mort	Newark, N.J.	3/21/23
Kinski, Klaus	Berlin, Germany	1926	Linkletter, Art	Saskatchewan, Canada	7/17/12
Kinski, Nastassia	Berlin, Germany	1/24/60	Lithgow, John	Rochester, N.Y.	10/19/45
Kirby, Durward	Covington, Ky.	8/24/12	Little, Cleavon	Chickasha, Okla.	6/1/39
Kirkland, Gelsey	Bethlehem, Pa.	12/29/52	Little, Rich	Ottawa, Ont.	11/26/38
Kirsten, Dorothy	Montclair, N.J.	7/6/19	Little Richard	Macon, Ga.	1935
Kitt, Eartha	North, S.C.	1/26/28	Lloyd, Christopher	Stamford, Conn.	10/22/38
Klein, Robert	New York, N.Y.	2/8/42	Locke, Sondra	Shelbyville, Tenn.	5/28/47
Klemperer, Werner	Cologne, Germany	3/22/20	Lockhart, June	New York, N.Y.	6/25/25
Kline, Kevin	St. Louis, Mo.	10/24/47	Locklear, Heather	Los Angeles, Cal.	9/25/-
Klugman, Jack	Philadelphia, Pa.	4/27/22	Lockwood, Margaret	Karachi, India	9/15/16
Knight, Gladys	Atlanta, Ga.	5/28/44	Loder, John	London, England	1898
Knight, Ted	Terryville, Conn.	12/7/23	Logan, Joshua	Texarkana, Tex.	10/5/08
Knotts, Don	Morgantown, W. Va.	7/21/24	Loggia, Robert	New York, N.Y.	1/3/30
Knox, Alexander	Strathroy, Ont., Canada	1/16/07	Loggins, Kenny	Everett, Wash.	1/7/48
Kopell, Bernie	New York, N.Y.	6/21/33	Lollobrigida, Gina	Subiaco, Italy	7/4/28
Korman, Harvey	Chicago, Ill.	2/15/27	Lom, Herbert	Prague, Czechoslovakia	1917
Kotto, Yaphet	New York, N.Y.	11/15/37	London, Julie	Santa Rosa, Cal.	9/26/26
Kramer, Stanley	New York, N.Y.	9/29/13	Long, Shelley	Ft. Wayne, Ind.	8/23/49
Kristofferson, Kris	Brownsville, Tex.	6/22/36	Lopez, Priscilla	New York, N.Y.	2/26/48
Kubelik, Rafael	Bychori, Czechoslovakia.	6/29/14	Lopez, Trini	Dallas, Tex.	5/15/37
Kubrick, Stanley	Bronx, N.Y.	7/26/28	Lord, Jack	New York, N.Y.	—
Kulp, Nancy	Harrisburg, Pa.	8/28/21	Loren, Sophia	Rome, Italy	9/20/34
Kurtz, Swoozie	Omaha, Neb.	9/6/44	Loring, Gloria	New York, N.Y.	12/10/46
Kyser, Kay	Rocky Mount, N.C.	6/18/05	Loudon, Dorothy	Boston, Mass.	9/17/33
			Louise, Tina	New York, N.Y.	3/11/34
Ladd, Cheryl	Huron, S.D.	7/12/51	Love, Bessie	Midland, Tex.	9/10/98
Laine, Frankie	Chicago, Ill.	3/30/13	Loy, Myrna	Helena, Mon.	8/2/05
Lamarr, Hedy	Vienna, Austria	9/11/15	Lucas, George	Modesto, Cal.	5/14/44
Lamas, Lorenzo	Los Angeles, Cal.	1/20/58	Luckinbill, Laurence	Ft. Smith, Ark.	11/21/34
Lamb, Gil	Minneapolis, Minn.	6/14/06	Ludwig, Christa	Berlin, Germany	3/16/28
Lamour, Dorothy	New Orleans, La.	12/10/14	Luke, Keye	Canton, China.	1904
Lancaster, Burt	New York, N.Y.	11/2/13	Lumet, Sidney	Philadelphia, Pa.	6/25/24
Lanchester, Elsa	London, England	10/28/02	Lund, John	Rochester, N.Y.	1913
Landau, Martin	Brooklyn, N.Y.	1934	Lupino, Ida	London, England	2/4/18
Landesberg, Steve	New York, N.Y.	11/23/-	LuPone, Patti	Northport, N.Y.	4/21/49
Landon, Michael	Forest Hills, N.Y.	—	Lynley, Carol	New York, N.Y.	2/13/42
Lane, Abbe	Brooklyn, N.Y.	12/14/32	Lynn, Jeffrey	Auburn, Mass.	2/16/09
Lane, Priscilla	Indianola, Ia.	6/12/17	Lynn, Loretta	Butcher Hollow, Ky.	4/14/35
Lange, Hope	Redding Ridge, Conn.	11/28/31	Lyon, Sue	Davenport, Ia.	7/10/46
Lange, Jessica	Cloquet, Minn.	4/20/49			
Langella, Frank	Bayonne, N.J.	1/1/46	Maazel, Lorin	Paris, France	3/6/30
Langford, Frances	Lakeland, Fla.	4/4/13	MacArthur, James	Los Angeles, Cal.	12/8/37
Lansbury, Angela	London, England	10/16/25	MacGraw, Ali	Pound Ridge, N.Y.	4/1/39
Lansing, Robert	San Diego, Cal.	6/5/29	MacKenzie, Gisele	Winnipeg, Man.	1/10/27
Laredo, Ruth	Detroit, Mich.	11/20/37	MacLaine, Shirley	Richmond, Va.	4/24/34
Lasser, Louise	New York, N.Y.	4/11/39	MacLeod, Gavin	Mt. Kisco, N.Y.	2/28/30
Lauper, Cyndy	New York, N.Y.	6/30/53	MacMurray, Fred	Kankakee, Ill.	8/30/08
Laurie, Piper	Detroit, Mich.	1/22/32	MacNeil, Cornell	Minneapolis, Minn.	9/24/22
Lavin, Linda	Portland, Me.	10/15/37	MacRae, Gordon	East Orange, N.J.	3/12/21
Lawrence, Carol	Melrose Park, Ill.	9/5/34	Macy, Bill	Revere, Mass.	5/18/22
Lawrence, Steve	Brooklyn, N.Y.	7/8/35	Madden, John	Austin, Minn.	4/10/36
Lawrence, Vicki	Inglewood, Cal.	3/26/49	Madonna (Ciccone)	Bay City, Mich.	1960
Leachman, Cloris	Des Moines, Ia.	4/4/26	Majors, Lee	Wyandotte, Mich.	4/23/40

Name	Birthplace	Born
Makarova, Natalia	Leningrad, USSR	11/21/40
Malbin, Elaine	New York, N.Y.	5/24/32
Malden, Karl	Chicago, Ill.	3/22/13
Malfitano, Catherine	New York, N.Y.	4/18/48
Malle, Louis	Thumeries, France	10/30/32
Malone, Dorothy	Chicago, Ill.	1/30/25
Manchester, Melissa	Bronx, N.Y.	2/15/51
Mancini, Henry	Cleveland, Oh.	4/16/24
Mandrell, Barbara	Houston, Tex.	12/25/48
Mangione, Chuck	Rochester, N.Y.	11/29/40
Manilow, Barry	New York, N.Y.	6/17/46
Mann, Herbie	New York, N.Y.	4/16/30
Marceau, Marcel	Strasbourg, France	3/22/23
Marchand, Nancy	Buffalo, N.Y.	6/19/28
Margo	Mexico City, Mexico	5/10/18
Margolin, Janet	New York, N.Y.	1943
Marin, Cheech	Los Angeles, Cal.	7/13/46
Markova, Alicia	London, England	12/1/10
Marriner, Neville	Lincoln, England	4/15/24
Marsh, Jean	London, England	7/1/34
Marshall, E. G.	Owatonna, Minn.	6/18/10
Marshall, Penny	New York, N.Y.	10/15/43
Marshall, Peter	Huntington, W.Va.	3/30/-
Martens, Peter	Copenhagen, Denmark	10/27/46
Martin, Dean	Steubenville, Oh.	6/17/17
Martin, Dick	Detroit, Mich.	1/30/23
Martin, Mary	Weatherford, Tex.	12/1/13
Martin, Pamela Sue	Westport, Conn.	1/5/54
Martin, Steve	Waco, Tex.	1945
Martin, Tony	San Francisco, Cal.	12/25/13
Martino, Al	Philadelphia, Pa.	10/7/27
Marvin, Lee	New York, N.Y.	2/19/24
Mason, Jackie	Sheboygan, Wis.	1931
Mason, Marsha	St. Louis, Mo.	4/3/42
Mason, Pamela	London, England	3/10/22
Mastroianni, Marcello	Rome, Italy	9/28/24
Matheson, Tim	Glendale, Cal.	12/31/47
Mathis, Johnny	San Francisco, Cal.	9/30/35
Matthau, Walter	New York, N.Y.	10/1/20
Mature, Victor	Louisville, Ky.	1/29/16
May, Elaine	Philadelphia, Pa.	4/21/32
Mayo, Virginia	St. Louis, Mo.	11/30/20
Mazurki, Mike	Austria	12/25/09
Mazursky, Paul	Brooklyn, N.Y.	4/25/30
McArdle, Andrea	Philadelphia, Pa.	11/5/63
McBride, Patricia	Teaneck, N.J.	8/23/42
McCallum, David	Glasgow, Scotland	9/19/33
McCambridge, Mercedes	Joliet, Ill.	3/17/18
McCarthy, Kevin	Seattle, Wash.	2/15/14
McCartney, Paul	Liverpool, England	6/18/42
McClure, Doug	Glendale, Cal.	5/11/38
McCoo, Marilyn	Jersey City, N.J.	9/30/43
McCord, Kent	Los Angeles, Cal.	9/26/42
McCrea, Joel	Los Angeles, Cal.	11/5/05
McDowall, Roddy	London, England	9/17/28
McDowell, Malcolm	Leeds, England	6/19/43
McFarland, Spanky	Dallas, Tex.	10/2/28
McGavin, Darren	San Joaquin, Cal.	5/7/22
McGee, Fibber	Peoria, Ill.	11/6/96
McGoohan, Patrick	New York, N.Y.	3/19/28
McGovern, Maureen	Youngstown, Oh.	7/27/49
McGuire, Dorothy	Omaha, Neb.	6/14/19
McIntire, John	Spokane, Wash.	6/27/07
McKechnie, Donna	Pontiac, Mich.	11/16/42
McKellen, Ian	Burnley, England	5/25/39
McKenna, Siobhan	Belfast, Ireland	5/24/22
McKeon, Nancy	Westbury, N.Y.	4/4/-
McLean, Don	New Rochelle, N.Y.	10/2/45
McLerie, Allyn	Grand Mere, Que.	12/1/26
McMahon, Ed	Detroit, Mich.	3/6/23
McNair, Barbara	Racine, Wis.	3/4/39
McNichol, Jimmy	Los Angeles, Cal.	7/2/61
McNichol, Kristy	Los Angeles, Cal.	9/11/62
McQueen, Butterfly	Tampa, Fla.	1/7/11
McRaney, Gerald	Collins, Miss.	8/19/-
Meadows, Audrey	Wu Chang, China.	1924
Meadows, Jayne	Wu Chang, China.	9/27/26
Meara, Anne	New York, N.Y.	9/20/29
Meeker, Ralph	Minneapolis, Minn.	11/21/20
Mehta, Zubin	Bombay, India.	4/29/36
Melanie	New York, N.Y.	1/3/47
Mendes, Sergio	Nitero, Brazil	2/11/41
Menuhin, Yehudi	New York, N.Y.	4/22/16
Mercouri, Melina	Athens, Greece	10/18/25
Meredith, Burgess	Cleveland, Oh.	11/16/08
Merkel, Una	Covington, Ky.	12/10/03
Merrick, David	Hong Kong	11/27/12

Name	Birthplace	Born
Merrill, Dina	New York, N.Y.	12/9/25
Merrill, Gary	Hartford, Conn.	8/2/15
Merrill, Robert	Brooklyn, N.Y.	6/4/19
Messina, Jim	Maywood, Cal.	12/5/47
Michaelson, Kari	New York, N.Y.	11/3/61
Midler, Bette	Paterson, N.J.	12/1/45
Milanov, Zinka	Zagreb, Yugoslavia.	5/17/08
Miles, Joanna	Nice, France	3/6/40
Miles, Sarah	Ingatestone, England.	12/31/41
Miles, Vera	near Boise City, Okla.	8/23/30
Milland, Ray	Neath, Wales	1/3/08
Miller, Ann	Houston, Tex.	4/12/23
Miller, Jason	New York, N.Y.	4/22/39
Miller, Mitch	Rochester, N.Y.	7/4/11
Miller, Roger	Ft. Worth, Tex.	1/2/36
Mills, Donna	Chicago, Ill.	12/11/47
Mills, Hayley	London, England	4/18/46
Mills, John	Suffolk, England	2/22/08
Mills, Juliet	London, England	11/21/41
Mills Brothers:		
Mills, Herbert	Piqua, Oh.	4/12/12
Mills, Donald	Piqua, Oh.	4/29/15
Milner, Martin	Detroit, Mich.	12/28/31
Milnes, Sherrill	Downers Grove, Ill.	1/10/35
Milsap, Ronnie	Robinsville, N.C.	1/16/43
Milstein, Nathan	Odessa, Russia.	12/31/04
Mimieux, Yvette	Hollywood, Cal.	1/8/42
Minnelli, Liza	Los Angeles, Cal.	3/12/46
Mitchell, Cameron	Dallastown, Pa.	11/4/18
Mitchell, James	Sacramento, Cal.	2/29/20
Mitchell, Joni	McLeod, Alta.	11/7/43
Mitchum, Robert	Bridgeport, Conn.	8/6/17
Moffat, Donald	Plymouth, England	12/26/30
Moffo, Anna	Wayne, Pa.	6/27/34
Molinaro, Al	Kenosha, Wis.	6/24/19
Montalban, Ricardo	Mexico City, Mexico	11/25/20
Montand, Yves	Monsumagno, Italy	10/13/21
Montgomery, Elizabeth	Hollywood, Cal.	4/15/33
Montgomery, George	Brady, Mon.	8/29/16
Moody, Ron	London, England	1/8/24
Moore, Clayton	Chicago, Ill.	9/14/14
Moore, Constance	Sioux City, Ia.	1/18/22
Moore, Dudley	London, England	4/19/35
Moore, Garry	Baltimore, Md.	1/31/15
Moore, Mary Tyler	Brooklyn, N.Y.	12/29/37
Moore, Melba	New York, N.Y.	10/29/45
Moore, Roger	London, England	10/14/27
Moore, Terry	Los Angeles, Cal.	1/1/32
Moran, Erin	Los Angeles, Cal.	10/18/61
Moreau, Jeanne	Paris, France	1/23/28
Moreno, Rita	Humacao, P.R.	12/11/31
Morgan, Dennis	Prentice, Wis.	12/10/10
Morgan, Harry	Detroit, Mich.	4/10/15
Morgan, Henry	New York, N.Y.	3/31/15
Morgan, Jane	Boston, Mass.	1920
Morgan, Jaye P.	Mancos, Col.	12/3/31
Morgana, Nina	Buffalo, N.Y.	11/15/95
Moriarty, Michael	Detroit, Mich.	4/5/41
Morini, Erika	Vienna, Austria	1/5/10
Morley, Robert	Wiltshire, England	5/26/08
Morris, Greg	Cleveland, Oh.	9/27/34
Morris, Howard	New York, N.Y.	9/4/25
Morse, Robert	Newton, Mass.	5/18/31
Mulhare, Edward	Ireland	4/8/23
Mull, Martin	Chicago, Ill.	8/18/43
Mulligan, Richard	New York, N.Y.	11/13/32
Munsel, Patrice	Spokane, Wash.	5/14/25
Murphy, Ben	Jonesboro, Ark.	3/6/42
Murphy, Eddie	Brooklyn, N.Y.	4/3/61
Murphy, George	New Haven, Conn.	7/4/02
Murphy, Michael	Los Angeles, Cal.	5/5/38
Murray, Anne	Springhill, Nova Scotia.	6/20/45
Murray, Arthur	New York, N.Y.	4/4/95
Murray, Bill	Evanston, Ill.	9/21/50
Murray, Don	Hollywood, Cal.	7/31/29
Murray, Kathryn	Jersey City, N.J.	9/15/06
Murray, Ken	New York, N.Y.	7/14/03
Musante, Tony	Bridgeport, Conn.	6/30/36
Musburger, Brent	Portland, Ore.	5/26/39
Nabors, Jim	Sylacauga, Ala.	6/12/33
Nash, Graham	Blackpool, England.	1942
Natwick, Mildred	Baltimore, Md.	6/19/08
Neal, Patricia	Packard, Ky.	1/20/26
Neff, Hildegarde	Ulm, Germany	12/28/25
Negri, Pola	Lipno, Poland	1899
Neligan, Kate	London, Ontario	3/16/51
Nelson, Barry	San Francisco, Cal.	4/16/20

Name	Birthplace	Born
Nelson, David	New York, N.Y.	10/24/36
Nelson, Ed	New Orleans, La.	12/21/28
Nelson, Gene	Seattle, Wash.	3/24/20
Nelson, Harriet (Hilliard)	Des Moines, Ia.	7/18/14
Nelson, Rick	Teaneck, N.J.	5/8/40
Nelson, Willie	Abbott, Tex.	4/30/33
Nero, Peter	New York, N.Y.	5/22/34
Newhart, Bob	Oak Park, Ill.	9/5/29
Newley, Anthony	Hackney, England	9/24/31
Newman, Barry	Boston, Mass.	11/7/38
Newman, Loraine	Los Angeles, Cal.	3/2/-
Newman, Paul	Cleveland, Oh.	1/26/25
Newman, Phyllis	Jersey City, N.J.	3/19/35
Newman, Randy	Los Angeles, Cal.	11/28/43
Newton, Wayne	Norfolk, Va.	4/3/42
Newton-John, Olivia	Cambridge, England	9/26/48
Nichols, Mike	Berlin, Germany	11/6/31
Nicholson, Jack	Neptune, N.J.	4/28/37
Nicks, Stevie	California	5/26/48
Nielsen, Leslie	Regina, Sask.	2/11/26
Nilsson, Birgit	Karup, Sweden	5/17/18
Nimoy, Leonard	Boston, Mass.	3/26/31
Noble, James	Dallas, Tex.	3/5/22
Nolan, Lloyd	San Francisco, Cal.	8/11/02
Nolte, Nick	Omaha, Neb.	2/8/40
Norman, Jessye	Augusta, Ga.	9/15/45
Norris, Chuck	Ryan, Okla.	1942
North, Sheree	Los Angeles, Cal.	1/17/33
Norton-Taylor, Judy	Santa Monica, Cal.	1/29/58
Novak, Kim	Chicago, Ill.	2/18/33
Novello, Don	Ashabula, Oh.	1/1/43
Nureyev, Rudolf	Russia	3/17/38
Oates, John	New York, N.Y.	4/7/48
O'Brian, Hugh	Rochester, N.Y.	4/19/30
O'Brien, Margaret	San Diego, Cal.	1/15/37
O'Connell, Helen	Lima, Oh.	1920
O'Connor, Carroll	New York, N.Y.	8/2/24
O'Connor, Donald	Chicago, Ill.	8/28/25
Odetta	Birmingham, Ala.	12/31/30
O'Hara, Maureen	Dublin, Ireland	8/17/21
O'Herlihy, Dan	Wexford, Ireland	5/1/19
Olivier, Laurence	Dorking, England	5/22/07
Olsen, Merlin	Logan, Ut.	9/15/40
O'Neal, Patrick	Ocala, Fla.	9/26/27
O'Neal, Ryan	Los Angeles, Cal.	4/20/41
O'Neal, Tatum	Los Angeles, Cal.	11/5/63
O'Neill, Jennifer	Brazil	2/20/49
Opatoshu, David	New York, N.Y.	1/30/18
Orbach, Jerry	New York, N.Y.	10/20/35
Orlando, Tony	New York, N.Y.	4/3/44
Osbourne, Ozzy	Birmingham, England.	12/3/48
Osmond, Donny	Ogden, Ut.	12/9/57
Osmond, Marie	Ogden, Ut.	10/13/59
O'Sullivan, Maureen	Boyle, Ireland	5/17/11
O'Toole, Annette	Houston, Tex.	4/1/52
O'Toole, Peter	Connemara, Ireland	8/2/32
Owens, Buck	Sherman, Tex.	8/12/29
Owens, Gary	Mitchell, S.D.	5/10/36
Ozawa, Seiji	Shenyang, China	9/1/35
Paar, Jack	Canton, Oh.	5/1/18
Pacino, Al	New York, N.Y.	4/25/40
Page, Geraldine	Kirksville, Mo.	11/22/24
Page, LaWanda	Cleveland, Oh.	10/19/20
Page, Patti	Claremore, Okla.	11/8/27
Paige, Janis	Tacoma, Wash.	9/16/22
Palance, Jack	Lattimer, Pa.	2/18/20
Palmer, Betsy	East Chicago, Ind.	11/1/29
Palmer, Lilli	Posen, Germany	5/24/14
Papas, Irene	Greece	1926
Papp, Joseph	Brooklyn, N.Y.	6/22/21
Parker, Eleanor	Cedarville, Oh.	6/26/22
Parker, Fess	Ft. Worth, Tex.	8/16/25
Parker, Jameson	Baltimore, Md.	11/18/50
Parker, Jean	Deer Lodge, Mon.	1916
Parks, Bert	Atlanta, Ga.	12/30/14
Parsons, Estelle	Lynn, Mass.	11/20/27
Parton, Dolly	Sevierville, Tenn.	1/19/46
Pasternak, Joseph	Hungary	9/19/01
Patane, Giuseppe	Napoli, Italy	1/1/32
Patinkin, Mandy	Chicago, Ill.	11/30/52
Patterson, Lorna	Whittier, Cal.	7/1/56
Paulsen, Pat	South Bend, Wash.	—
Pavarotti, Luciano	Modena, Italy	10/12/35
Paycheck, Johnny	Greenville, Oh.	5/31/41
Payne, John	Roanoke, Va.	5/23/12
Pearl, Minnie	Centerville, Tenn.	10/25/12
Peck, Gregory	La Jolla, Cal.	4/5/16

Name	Birthplace	Born
Pendergrass, Teddy	Philadelphia, Pa.	3/26/50
Penn, Arthur	Philadelphia, Pa.	9/27/22
Penn, Sean	Santa Monica, Cal.	1961
Peppard, George	Detroit, Mich.	10/1/28
Perkins, Anthony	New York, N.Y.	4/4/32
Perlman, Itzhak	Tel Aviv, Israel	8/31/45
Perlman, Rhea	Brooklyn, N.Y.	3/31/-
Perrine, Valerie	Galveston, Tex.	9/3/43
Persoff, Nehemiah	Jerusalem, Palestine	8/14/20
Peters, Bernadette	New York, N.Y.	2/28/48
Peters, Brock	New York, N.Y.	7/2/27
Peters, Jean	Canton, Oh.	10/15/26
Peters, Roberta	New York, N.Y.	5/4/30
Petit, Pascale	Paris, France	2/27/38
Phillips, MacKenzie	Alexandria, Va.	11/10/59
Phillips, Michelle	Long Beach, Cal.	4/6/44
Piazza, Marguerite	New Orleans, La.	5/6/26
Picon, Molly	New York, N.Y.	6/1/98
Piscopo, Joe	Passaic, N.J.	6/17/51
Plato, Dana	Maywood, Cal.	11/7/64
Pleasence, Donald	Worksop, England	10/5/19
Pleshette, Suzanne	New York, N.Y.	1/31/37
Plowright, Joan	Brigg, England	10/28/29
Plummer, Christopher.	Toronto, Ont.	12/13/29
Poitier, Sidney	Miami, Fla.	2/20/27
Polanski, Roman	Paris, France	8/18/33
Ponti, Carlo	Milan, Italy	12/11/13
Poston, Tom	Columbus, Oh.	10/17/21
Powell, Jane	Portland, Ore.	4/1/28
Powers, Stefanie	Hollywood, Cal.	11/12/43
Preminger, Otto	Vienna, Austria	12/5/06
Prentiss, Paula	San Antonio, Tex.	3/4/39
Presley, Priscilla	New York, N.Y.	5/24/45
Preston, Billy	Houston, Tex.	9/9/46
Preston, Robert	Newton, Mass.	6/8/18
Previn, Andre	Berlin, Germany	4/6/29
Price, Leontyne	Laurel, Miss.	2/10/27
Price, Ray	Perryville, Tex.	1/12/26
Price, Vincent	St. Louis, Mo.	5/27/11
Pride, Charlie	Sledge, Miss.	3/18/39
Prince (Rogers Nelson)	Minneapolis, Minn.	6/7/60
Principal, Victoria	Japan	1/30/50
Prowse, Juliet	Bombay, India.	9/25/37
Pryor, Richard	Peoria, Ill.	12/1/40
Pyle, Denver	Bethune, Col.	5/11/20
Quaid, Dennis	Houston, Tex.	4/9/54
Quaid, Randy	Houston, Tex.	1953
Quayle, Anthony.	Lancashire, England	9/7/13
Quillan, Eddie	Philadelphia, Pa.	3/31/07
Quinlan, Kathleen	Pasadena, Cal.	11/19/54
Quinn, Anthony	Chihuahua, Mexico	4/21/15
Rabb, Ellis	Memphis, Tenn.	6/20/30
Rabbitt, Eddie	Brooklyn, N.Y.	11/27/41
Radner, Gilda	Detroit, Mich.	6/28/46
Rae, Charlotte	Milwaukee, Wis.	4/22/26
Raffin, Deborah	Los Angeles, Cal.	3/13/53
Rainer, Luise	Vienna, Austria	1/12/10
Raines, Ella	Snoqualmie Falls, Wash.	8/6/21
Raitt, John	Santa Ana, Cal.	1/19/17
Ralston, Esther	Bar Harbor, Me.	9/19/02
Ralston, Vera Hruba	Prague, Czechoslovakia.	6/12/21
Rampal, Jean-Pierre	Marseilles, France	1/7/22
Randall, Tony	Tulsa, Okla.	2/26/20
Ratzenberger, John	Bridgeport, Conn.	4/6/-
Rawls, Lou	Chicago, Ill.	12/1/36
Ray, Aldo	Pen Argyl, Pa.	9/25/26
Ray, Gene Anthony	New York, N.Y.	5/24/-
Ray, Johnnie	Dallas, Ore.	1/10/27
Rayburn, Gene	Christopher, Ill.	12/22/17
Raye, Martha	Butte, Mon.	8/27/16
Raymond, Gene	New York, N.Y.	8/13/08
Reddy, Helen	Melbourne, Australia	10/25/41
Redford, Robert	Santa Monica, Cal.	8/18/37
Redgrave, Lynn	London, England	3/8/43
Redgrave, Vanessa	London, England	1/30/37
Reed, Donna	Denison, Ia.	1/27/21
Reed, Jerry	Atlanta, Ga.	3/20/37
Reed, Oliver	London, England	2/13/38
Reed, Rex	Ft. Worth, Tex.	10/2/38
Reed, Robert	Highland Park, Ill.	10/19/32
Reese, Della	Detroit, Mich.	7/6/31
Reeve, Christopher	New York, N.Y.	9/25/52
Reeves, Dell	Sparta, N.C.	7/14/33
Regan, Phil	Brooklyn, N.Y.	5/28/06
Reid, Kate	London, England	11/4/30
Reid, Tim	Norfolk, Va.	12/19/44

Name	Birthplace	Born
Reilly, Charles Nelson	New York, N.Y.	1/13/31
Reiner, Carl	Bronx, N.Y.	3/20/22
Reiner, Rob	Bronx, N.Y.	3/6/45
Reinking, Ann	Seattle, Wash.	11/10/49
Remick, Lee	Boston, Mass.	12/14/35
Resnik, Regina	New York, N.Y.	8/30/24
Rey, Alejandro	Buenos Aires, Argentina	2/8/30
Reynolds, Burt	Waycross, Ga.	2/11/36
Reynolds, Debbie	El Paso, Tex.	4/1/32
Reynolds, Marjorie	Buhl, Ida.	8/12/21
Rich, Charlie	Forest City, Ark.	12/14/32
Rich, Irene	Buffalo, N.Y.	10/13/97
Richard, Keith	Kent, England	12/18/43
Richardson, Tony	Shipley, England	6/5/28
Richie, Lionel	Tuskegee, Ala.	6/20/50
Rickles, Don	New York, N.Y.	5/8/26
Riddle, Nelson	Hackensack, N.J.	6/1/21
Rigg, Diana	Doncaster, England	7/20/38
Ringwald, Molly	Los Angeles, Cal.	1968
Ritter, John	Burbank, Cal.	9/17/48
Ritz, Harry	Newark, N.J.	1906
Ritz, Jimmy	Newark, N.J.	1903
Rivera, Chita	Washington, D.C.	1/23/33
Rivers, Joan	Brooklyn, N.Y.	6/8/33
Robards, Jason Jr.	Chicago, Ill.	7/26/22
Robbins, Jerome	New York, N.Y.	10/11/18
Roberts, Doris	St. Louis, Mo.	11/4/30
Roberts, Pernell	Waycross, Ga.	5/18/30
Roberts, Tony	New York, N.Y.	10/22/39
Robertson, Cliff	La Jolla, Cal.	9/9/25
Robertson, Dale	Oklahoma City, Okla.	7/14/23
Robinson, Smokey	Detroit, Mich.	2/19/40
Rodgers, Jimmie	Camas, Wash.	1933
Rodriquez, Johnny	Sabinal, Tex.	12/10/51
Rogers, Chas. (Buddy)	Olathe, Kan.	8/13/04
Rogers, Ginger	Independence, Mo.	7/16/11
Rogers, Kenny	Houston, Tex.	8/21/38
Rogers, Roy	Cincinnati, Oh.	11/5/12
Rogers, Wayne	Birmingham, Ala.	4/7/33
Roland, Gilbert	Juarez, Mexico	12/11/05
Rolle, Esther	Pompano Beach, Fla.	11/8/33
Romero, Cesar	New York, N.Y.	2/15/07
Ronstadt, Linda	Tucson, Ariz.	7/15/46
Rooney, Mickey	Brooklyn, N.Y.	9/23/20
Rose, George	Bicester, England	2/19/20
Rose Marie	New York, N.Y.	8/15/25
Ross, Diana	Detroit, Mich.	3/26/44
Ross, Katharine	Hollywood, Cal.	1/29/43
Ross, Lanny	Seattle, Wash.	1/19/06
Ross, Marion	Albert Lea, Minn.	10/25/28
Rostropovich, Mstislav	Baku USSR	3/12/27
Roth, David Lee	Bloomingtonm, Ind.	10/10/55
Rowan, Dan	Beggs, Okla.	7/2/22
Rowlands, Gena	Cambria, Wis.	6/19/36
Rubin, Benny	Boston, Mass.	1899
Rubenstein, John	Los Angeles, Cal.	12/8/46
Rudolf, Max	Frankfurt, Germany	6/15/02
Rule, Janice	Norwood, Oh.	8/15/31
Rush, Barbara	Denver, Col.	1/4/30
Russell, Jane	Bemidji, Minn.	6/21/21
Russell, Ken	Southampton, England.	7/3/27
Russell, Kurt	Springfield, Mass.	3/17/51
Russell, Mark	Buffalo, N.Y.	8/23/32
Russell, Nipsey	Atlanta, Ga.	10/13/24
Rutherford, Ann	Toronto, Ont.	11/2/20
Ryan, Peggy	Long Beach, Cal.	8/28/24
Rydell, Bobby	Philadelphia, Pa.	4/26/42
Sahl, Mort	Montreal, Que.	5/11/27
Saint, Eva Marie	Newark, N.J.	7/4/22
St. James, Susan	Los Angeles, Cal.	8/14/46
St. John, Jill	Los Angeles, Cal.	8/19/40
Sainte-Marie, Buffy	Maine	2/20/41
Saks, Gene	New York, N.Y.	11/8/21
Sales, Soupy	Franklinton, N.C.	1/8/26
Sandy, Gary	Dayton, Oh.	12/25/45
Sanford, Isabel	New York, N.Y.	8/29/17
Santana, Carlos	Mexico	7/20/47
Sarandon, Chris	Beckley, W.Va.	7/24/42
Sarandon, Susan	New York, N.Y.	10/4/46
Sarnoff, Dorothy	New York, N.Y.	5/25/17
Sarrazin, Michael	Quebec City, Que.	5/22/40
Savalas, Telly	Garden City, N.Y.	1/21/24
Saxon, John	Brooklyn, N.Y.	8/5/35
Sayao, Bidu	Rio de Janeiro, Brazil	5/11/02
Sayer, Leo	Sussex, England	5/21/48
Scaggs, Boz	Dallas, Tex.	6/8/44
Schallert, William	Los Angeles, Cal.	7/6/22

Name	Birthplace	Born
Scheider, Roy	Orange, N.J.	11/10/35
Schell, Maria	Vienna, Austria	1/15/26
Schell, Maximilian	Vienna, Austria	12/8/30
Schell, Ronnie	Richmond, Cal.	12/23/31
Schenkel, Chris	Bippus, Ind.	1924
Schnabel, Stefan	Berlin, Germany	2/2/12
Schneider, Alexander	Vilna, Poland	10/21/08
Schneider, John	Mt. Kisco, N.Y.	4/8/54
Schreiber, Avery	Chicago, Ill.	1935
Schroder, Ricky	Staten Island, N.Y.	4/13/70
Schwartzenegger, Arnold	Braz, Austria	7/30/47
Schwarzkopf, Elisabeth	Jarotschin, Poland	12/9/15
Scofield, Paul	Hurst, Pierpont, England.	1/21/22
Scorsese, Martin	New York, N.Y.	11/17/42
Scott, George C.	Wise, Va.	10/18/27
Scott, Lizabeth	Scranton, Pa.	9/29/22
Scott, Martha	Jamesport, Mo.	9/22/14
Scott, Randolph	Orange Co., Va.	1/23/03
Scotto, Renata	Savona, Italy	2/24/35
Scully, Vin	New York, N.Y.	11/29/27
Sebastian, John	New York N.Y.	3/17/44
Sedaka, Neil	New York, N.Y.	3/13/39
Seeger, Pete	New York, N.Y.	5/3/19
Segal, George	Great Neck, N.Y.	2/13/34
Segal, Vivienne	Philadelphia, Pa.	4/19/97
Segovia, Andres	Linares, Spain.	2/18/94
Selleca, Connie	New York, N.Y.	5/25/-
Selleck, Tom	Detroit, Mich.	1/29/45
Serkin, Rudolf	Eger, Austria	3/28/03
Severinsen, Doc	Arlington, Ore.	7/7/27
Seymour, Jane	Middlesex, England.	2/15/51
Shackelford, Ted	Oklahoma City, Okla.	6/23/46
Shankar, Ravi	India	4/7/20
Sharif, Omar	Alexandria, Egypt.	4/10/32
Shatner, William	Montreal, Que.	3/22/31
Shaw, Robert	Red Bluff, Cal.	4/30/16
Shawn, Dick	Buffalo, N.Y.	12/1/29
Shearer, Moira	Scotland	1/17/26
Sheedy, Ally	New York, N.Y.	1962
Sheen, Martin	Dayton, Oh.	8/3/40
Sheldon, Jack	Jacksonville, Fla.	1931
Shelley, Carole	London, England	8/16/39
Shepard, Sam	Ft. Sheridan, Ill.	11/5/43
Shepherd, Cybill	Memphis, Tenn.	2/18/50
Shera, Mark	Bayonne, N.J.	7/10/49
Sherwood, Roberta	St. Louis, Mo.	1913
Shields, Brooke	New York, N.Y.	5/31/65
Shire, Talia	New York, N.Y.	4/25/46
Shirley, Ann	New York, N.Y.	4/17/18
Shore, Dinah	Winchester, Tenn.	3/1/17
Short, Bobby	Danville, Ill.	9/15/24
Sidney, Sylvia	New York, N.Y.	8/8/10
Siepi, Cesare	Milan, Italy.	2/10/23
Signoret, Simone	Wiesbaden, Germany	3/25/21
Sikking, James B.	Los Angeles, Cal.	3/5/-
Sills, Beverly	Brooklyn, N.Y.	5/25/29
Silvers, Phil.	Brooklyn, N.Y.	5/11/12
Simmons, Gene	Haifa, Israel	8/25/49
Simmons, Jean	London, England	1/31/29
Simon, Carly	New York, N.Y.	6/25/45
Simon, Paul	Newark, N.J.	—
Simone, Nina	Tyron, N.C.	2/21/33
Sinatra, Frank	Hoboken, N.J.	12/12/15
Sinatra, Nancy	Jersey City, N.J.	6/8/40
Singer, Lori	Corpus Christie, Tex.	5/6/-
Singer, Marc	Vancouver, B.C.	—
Skelton, Red (Richard)	Vincennes, Ind.	7/18/13
Skerritt, Tom	Detroit, Mich.	8/25/33
Slick, Grace	Chicago, Ill.	10/30/39
Smith, Alexis	Penticton, B.C.	6/8/21
Smith, Buffalo Bob	Buffalo, N.Y.	11/27/17
Smith, Connie	Elkhart, Ind.	8/14/41
Smith, Jaclyn	Houston, Tex.	10/26/48
Smith, Kate	Greenville, Va.	5/1/07
Smith, Keely	Norfolk, Va.	3/9/35
Smith, Maggie	Ilford, England.	12/28/34
Smith, Roger	South Gate, Cal.	12/18/32
Smothers, Dick	New York, N.Y.	11/20/39
Smothers, Tom	New York, N.Y.	2/2/37
Snodgress, Carrie	Park Ridge, Ill.	10/27/45
Snow, Hank	Nova Scotia, Canada	5/9/14
Snyder, Jimmy "Greek"	Steubenville, Oh.	9/9/19
Snyder, Tom	Milwaukee, Wis.	5/12/36
Solti, Georg	Budapest, Hungary.	10/21/12
Somers, Suzanne	San Bruno, Cal.	10/16/46
Somes, Michael	nr. Stroud, England.	9/28/17

Name	Birthplace	Born
Sommer, Elke	Berlin, Germany	11/5/41
Sorvino, Paul	Brooklyn, N.Y.	1939
Sothern, Ann	Valley City, N.D.	1/22/12
Soul, David	Chicago, Ill.	8/28/43
Spacek, Sissy	Quitman, Tex.	12/25/49
Spano, Joe	San Francisco, Cal.	7/7/-
Spielberg, Steven	Cincinnati, Oh.	12/18/47
Springfield, Dusty	London, England	4/16/39
Springfield, Rick	Sydney, Australia	8/23/49
Springsteen, Bruce	Freehold, N.J.	9/23/49
Stack, Robert	Los Angeles, Cal.	1/13/19
Stafford, Jo	Coalinga, Cal.	11/12/18
Stallone, Sylvester	New York, N.Y.	7/6/46
Stamp, Terence	Stepney, England	7/22/39
Stander, Lionel	New York, N.Y.	1/11/08
Stang, Arnold	Chelsea, Mass.	9/28/25
Stanley, Kim	Tularosa, N.M.	2/11/25
Stanwyck, Barbara	Brooklyn, N.Y.	7/16/07
Stapleton, Jean	New York, N.Y.	1/19/23
Stapleton, Maureen	Troy, N.Y.	6/21/25
Starr, Kay	Dougherty, Okla.	7/21/22
Starr, Ringo	Liverpool, England	7/7/40
Steber, Eleanor	Wheeling, W. Va.	7/17/16
Steenburgen, Mary	Newport, Ark.	—
Steiger, Rod	W. Hampton, N.Y.	4/14/25
Steinberg, David	Winnipeg, Man.	8/9/42
Stephens, James	Mt. Kisco, N.Y.	5/18/51
Sterling, Jan	New York, N.Y.	4/3/23
Sterling, Robert	New Castle, Pa.	11/13/17
Stern, Isaac	Kreminiecz, Russia	7/21/20
Sternhagen, Frances	Washington, D.C.	1/13/30
Stevens, Andrew	Memphis, Tenn.	6/10/55
Stevens, Cat	London, England	7/21/48
Stevens, Connie	Brooklyn, N.Y.	8/8/38
Stevens, Kaye	E. Cleveland, Oh.	7/21/35
Stevens, Rise	New York, N.Y.	6/11/13
Stevens, Stella	Yazoo City, Miss.	10/1/36
Stevens, Warren	Clark's Summit, Pa.	11/2/19
Stevenson, McLean	Normal, Ill.	11/14/29
Stevenson, Parker	Philadelphia, Pa.	6/4/53
Stewart, James	Indiana, Pa.	5/20/08
Stewart, Rod	London, England	1/10/45
Stickney, Dorothy	Dickinson, N.D.	6/21/00
Stiers, David Ogden	Peoria, Ill.	10/31/42
Stiller, Jerry	New York, N.Y.	6/8/29
Stills, Stephen	Dallas, Tex.	1/3/45
Sting (G. Sumner)	Newcastle, England	10/2/51
Stockwell, Dean	Hollywood, Cal.	3/5/36
Storch, Larry	New York, N.Y.	1/8/25
Storm, Gale	Bloomington, Tex.	4/5/21
Straight, Beatrice	Old Westbury, N.Y.	8/2/18
Strasberg, Susan	New York, N.Y.	5/22/38
Strasser, Robin	New York, N.Y.	5/7/45
Stratas, Teresa	Toronto, Ont.	5/26/38
Strauss, Peter	New York, N.Y.	2/20/47
Streep, Meryl	Summit, N.J.	1949
Streisand, Barbra	Brooklyn, N.Y.	4/24/42
Stritch, Elaine	Detroit, Mich.	2/2/26
Struthers, Sally	Portland, Ore.	7/28/48
Stuarti, Enzo	Rome, Italy	3/3/25
Sullivan, Barry	New York, N.Y.	8/29/12
Sullivan, Susan	New York, N.Y.	11/18/43
Sullivan, Tom	Boston, Mass.	3/27/47
Sumac, Yma	Ichocan, Peru	9/10/27
Summer, Donna	Boston, Mass.	12/31/48
Susskind, David	New York, N.Y.	12/19/20
Sutherland, Donald	St. John, New Brunswick	7/17/34
Sutherland, Joan	Sydney, Australia	11/7/26
Suzuki, Pat	Cressey, Cal	1931
Sweet, Blanche	Chicago, Ill.	6/18/95
Swenson, Inga	Omaha, Neb.	12/29/34
Swit, Loretta	Passaic, N.J.	11/4/37
Mr. T (Lawrence Tero)	Chicago, Ill.	5/21/52
Talbot, Lyle	Pittsburgh, Pa.	2/8/02
Tallchief, Maria	Fairfax, Okla.	1/24/25
Tandy, Jessica	London, England	6/7/09
Tarkenton, Fran	Richmond, Va.	2/3/40
Tayback, Vic	New York, N.Y.	1/6/29
Taylor, Elizabeth	London, England	2/27/32
Taylor, James	Boston, Mass.	3/12/48
Taylor, Kent	Nashua, Ia.	5/11/07
Taylor, Rod	Sydney, Australia	1/11/29
Te Kanawa, Kiri	Gisborne, New Zealand	3/6/44
Tebaldi, Renata	Pesaro, Italy	2/1/22
Temple, Shirley	Santa Monica, Cal.	4/23/28
Tennille, Toni	Montgomery, Ala.	5/8/43
Terris, Norma	Columbus, Kan.	1904
Terry-Thomas	London, England	7/14/11
Tharp, Twyla	Portland, Ind.	7/1/41
Thaxter, Phyllis	Portland, Me.	11/20/21
Thinnes, Roy	Chicago, Ill.	4/6/38
Thomas, B.J.	Houston, Tex.	8/7/42
Thomas, Betty	St. Louis, Mo.	7/27/47
Thomas, Danny	Deerfield, Mich.	1/6/14
Thomas, Heather	Greenwich, Conn.	9/8/57
Thomas, Marlo	Detroit, Mich.	11/21/43
Thomas, Richard	New York, N.Y.	6/13/51
Thompson, Marshall	Peoria, Ill.	11/27/26
Thompson, Sada	Des Moines, Ia.	9/27/29
Thulin, Ingrid	Sweden	1/27/29
Tiegs, Cheryl	Minnesota	9/27/47
Tierney, Gene	Brooklyn, N.Y.	11/20/20
Tillis, Mel	Tampa, Fla.	8/8/32
Tillstrom, Burr	Chicago, Ill.	10/13/17
Tilton, Charlene	San Diego, Cal.	12/1/58
Tiny Tim	New York, N.Y.	4/12/25
Todd, Richard	Dublin, Ireland	6/11/19
Tomlin, Lily	Detroit, Mich.	9/1/39
Tomlinson, David	Scotland	5/7/17
Toomey, Regis	Pittsburgh, Pa.	8/13/02
Torme, Mel	Chicago, Ill.	9/13/25
Torn, Rip	Temple, Tex.	2/6/31
Tracy, Arthur	Russia	6/25/03
Travanti, Daniel J.	Kenosha, Wis.	3/7/40
Travers, Mary	Louisville, Ky.	11/9/36
Travolta, John	Englewood, N.J.	2/18/54
Trevor, Claire	New York, N.Y.	3/8/09
Troyanos, Tatiana	New York, N.Y.	9/12/38
Tucker, Forrest	Plainfield, Ind.	2/12/19
Tucker, Tanya	Seminole, Tex.	10/10/58
Tune, Tommy	Wichita Falls, Tex.	2/28/39
Turner, Ike	Clarksdale, Miss.	11/5/31
Turner, Lana	Wallace, Ida.	2/8/20
Turner, Tina	Brownsville, Tex.	11/25/41
Tushingham, Rita	Liverpool, England	3/14/42
Twiggy (Leslie Hornby)	London, England	9/19/49
Twitty, Conway	Friar's Point, Miss.	9/1/33
Tyson, Cicely	New York, N.Y.	12/19/33
Uggams, Leslie	New York, N.Y.	5/25/43
Ullmann, Liv	Tokyo, Japan	12/16/39
Urich, Robert	Toronto, Oh.	12/19/47
Ustinov, Peter	London, England	4/16/21
Vaccaro, Brenda	Brooklyn, N.Y.	11/18/39
Vale, Jerry	New York, N.Y.	7/8/31
Valente, Caterina	Paris, France	1/14/32
Valentine, Karen	Santa Rosa, Cal.	5/25/47
Vallee, Rudy	Island Pond, Vt.	7/28/01
Valli, Frankie	Newark, N.J.	5/3/37
Van Ark, Joan	New York, N.Y.	6/16/46
Van Cleef, Lee	Somerville, N.J.	1/9/25
Van Devere, Trish	Tenafly, N.J.	1945
Van Doren, Mamie	Rowena, S.D.	2/6/33
Van Dyke, Dick	West Plains, Mo.	12/13/25
Van Dyke, Jerry	Danville, Ill.	7/27/32
Van Fleet, Jo	Oakland, Cal.	12/30/19
Van Pallandt, Nina	Copenhagen, Denmark	7/15/32
Van Patten, Dick	New York, N.Y.	12/9/28
Vaughan, Sarah	Newark, N.J.	3/27/24
Vaughn, Robert	New York, N.Y.	11/22/32
Venuta, Benay	San Francisco, Cal.	1/27/11
Verdon, Gwen	Los Angeles, Cal.	1/13/25
Vereen, Ben	Miami, Fla.	10/10/46
Verrett, Shirley	New Orleans, La.	5/31/31
Vickers, Jon	Prince Albert, Sask.	10/26/26
Vigoda, Abe	New York, N.Y.	2/24/21
Villechaize, Herve	Paris, France	4/23/43
Villella, Edward	Long Island, N.Y.	10/1/36
Vincent, Jan-Michael	Denver, Col.	7/15/44
Vinson, Helen	Beaumont, Tex.	9/17/07
Vinton, Bobby	Canonsburg, Pa.	4/16/35
Voight, Jon	Yonkers, N.Y.	12/29/38
Von Stade, Frederica	Somerville, N.J.	6/1/45
Von Sydow, Max	Lund, Sweden	4/10/29
Voorhees, Donald	Allentown, Pa.	7/26/03
Waggoner, Lyle	Kansas City, Kan.	4/13/35
Wagner, Lindsay	Los Angeles, Cal.	6/22/49
Wagner, Robert	Detroit, Mich.	2/10/30
Wagoner, Porter	West Plains, Mo.	8/12/27
Wain, Bea	Bronx, N.Y.	4/30/17
Waite, Ralph	White Plains, N.Y.	6/22/29
Walden, Robert	New York, N.Y.	9/25/43
Walken, Christopher	New York, N.Y.	3/31/43
Walker, Clint	Hartford, Ill.	5/30/27
Walker, Nancy	Philadelphia, Pa.	5/10/21
Wallach, Eli	Brooklyn, N.Y.	12/7/15
Wallis, Hal	Chicago, Ill.	9/14/99
Walston, Ray	Laurel, Miss.	12/2/14
Walter, Jessica	New York, N.Y.	1/31/44

Name	Birthplace	Born	Name	Birthplace	Born
Wanamaker, Sam	Chicago, Ill.	6/14/19	Wilson, Demond	Valdosta, Ga.	—
Ward, Simon	London, England	10/19/41	Wilson, Dolores	Philadelphia, Pa.	1929
Warden, Jack	Newark, N.J.	9/18/20	Wilson, Flip	Jersey City, N.J.	12/8/33
Warfield, William	W. Helena, Ark.	1/22/20	Wilson, Nancy	Chillicothe, Oh.	2/20/37
Warhol, Andy	Pittsburgh, Pa.	8/6/27	Winchell, Paul	New York, N.Y.	12/21/22
Warren, Michael	So. Bend, Ind.	3/5/46	Windom, William	New York, N.Y.	9/28/23
Warwick, Dionne	E. Orange, N.J.	12/12/41	Winfield, Paul	Los Angeles, Cal.	5/22/41
Waterson, Sam	Cambridge, Mass.	11/15/40	Winger, Debra	Columbus, Oh.	5/16/55
Watson, Mills	Oakland, Cal.	7/10/40	Winkler, Henry	New York, N.Y.	10/30/45
Watts, Andre	Nuremberg, Germany	6/20/46	Winters, Jonathan	Dayton, Oh.	11/11/25
Wayne, David	Traverse City, Mich.	1/30/14	Winters, Shelley	St. Louis, Mo.	8/18/22
Weaver, Dennis	Joplin, Mo.	6/4/24	Wiseman, Joseph	Montreal, Que.	5/15/18
Weaver, Fritz	Pittsburgh, Pa.	1/19/26	Withers, Jane	Atlanta, Ga.	4/12/27
Weaver, Sigourney	Los Angeles, Cal.	10/8/49	Wonder, Stevie	Saginaw, Mich.	5/13/50
Welch, Raquel	Chicago, Ill.	9/5/42	Woodward, Joanne	Thomasville, Ga.	2/27/30
Weld, Tuesday	New York, N.Y.	8/27/43	Wopat, Tom	Lodi, Wis.	9/9/51
Welk, Lawrence	nr. Strasburg, N.D.	3/11/03	Worth, Irene	Nebraska	6/23/16
Welles, Orson	Kenosha, Wis.	5/6/15	Wray, Fay	Alberta, Canada	9/10/07
Wells, Kitty	Nashville, Tenn.	8/30/19	Wright, Martha	Seattle, Wash.	3/23/26
Wendt, George	Chicago, Ill.	10/17/48	Wright, Teresa	New York, N.Y.	10/27/18
Whelchel, Lisa	Ft. Worth, Tex.	5/29/63	Wrightson, Earl	Baltimore, Md.	1916
White, Barry	Galveston, Tex.	9/12/44	Wyatt, Jane	Campgaw, N.J.	8/10/11
White, Betty	Oak Park, Ill.	1/17/24	Wyman, Jane	St. Joseph, Mo.	1/4/14
White, Jesse	Buffalo, N.Y.	1/3/19	Wynette, Tammy	Red Bay, Ala.	5/5/42
Whiting, Margaret	Detroit, Mich.	7/22/24	Wynn, Keenan	New York, N.Y.	7/27/16
Whitmore, James	White Plains, N.Y.	10/1/21	Wynter, Dana	London, England	6/8/30
Widmark, Richard	Sunrise, Minn.	12/26/14			
Wilcox, Larry	San Diego, Cal.	8/8/47	Yarborough, Glenn	Milwaukee, Wis.	1/12/30
Wilde, Cornel	New York, N.Y.	10/13/18	Yarrow, Peter	New York, N.Y.	5/31/38
Wilder, Billy	Vienna, Austria	6/22/06	York, Dick	Ft. Wayne, Ind.	9/4/28
Wilder, Gene	Milwaukee, Wis.	6/11/35	York, Michael	Fulmer, England	3/27/42
Williams, Andy	Wall Lake, Ia.	12/3/30	York, Susannah	London, England	1/9/41
Williams, Billy Dee	New York, N.Y.	4/6/38	Young, Alan	Northumberland, England	11/19/19
Williams, Cindy	Van Nuys, Cal.	8/22/47	Young, Burt	New York, N.Y.	4/30/40
Williams, Emlyn	Mostyn, Wales	11/26/05	Young, Loretta	Salt Lake City, Ut.	1/6/13
Williams, Esther	Los Angeles, Cal.	8/8/23	Young, Neil	Toronto, Ont.	11/12/45
Williams Jr., Hank	Shreveport, La.	5/26/49	Young, Robert	Chicago, Ill.	2/22/07
Williams, Joe	Cordele, Ga.	12/12/18	Youngman, Henny	Liverpool, England	1906
Williams, JoBeth	Houston, Tex.	1953			
Williams, Paul	Omaha, Neb.	9/19/40	Zappa, Frank	Baltimore, Md.	12/21/40
Williams, Robin	Chicago, Ill.	7/21/52	Zeffirelli, Franco	Florence, Italy	2/12/23
Williams, Roger	Omaha, Neb.	1926	Zimbalist, Efrem Jr.	New York, N.Y.	11/30/23
Williams, Treat	Rowayton, Conn.	—	Zimbalist, Stephanie	New York, N.Y.	10/6/56
Williamson, Nicol	Hamilton, Scotland	9/14/38	Zmed, Adrian	Chicago, Ill.	3/14/-
			Zukerman, Pinchas	Tel Aviv, Israel	7/16/48

Entertainment Personalities of the Past

Born	Died	Name	Born	Died	Name	Born	Died	Name
1895	1974	Abbott, Bud	1810	1891	Barnum, Phineas T.	1900	1943	Bledsoe, Jules
1872	1953	Adams, Maude	1912	1978	Barrie, Wendy	1928	1972	Blocker, Dan
1855	1926	Adler, Jacob P.	1879	1959	Barrymore, Ethel	1909	1979	Blondell, Joan
1898	1933	Adoree, Renee	1882	1942	Barrymore, John	1888	1959	Blore, Eric
1909	1964	Albertson, Frank	1878	1954	Barrymore, Lionel	1901	1975	Blue, Ben
1910	1981	Albertson, Jack	1848	1905	Barrymore, Maurice	1899	1957	Bogart, Humphrey
1885	1952	Alda, Frances	1897	1963	Barthelmess, Richard	1880	1965	Boland, Mary
1894	1956	Allen, Fred	1890	1962	Barton, James	1897	1969	Boles, John
1906	1964	Allen, Gracie	1919	1984	Basehart, Richard	1903	1960	Bond, Ward
1883	1950	Allgood, Sara	1904	1984	Basie, Count	1892	1981	Bondi, Beulah
1886	1954	Anderson, John Murray	1873	1951	Bauer, Harold	1917	1981	Boone, Richard
1915	1967	Andrews, Laverne	1893	1951	Baxter, Warner	1833	1893	Booth, Edwin
1933	1971	Angeli, Pier	1880	1928	Bayes, Nora	1796	1852	Booth, Junius Brutus
1876	1958	Anglin, Margaret	1904	1965	Beatty, Clyde	1894	1953	Bordoni, Irene
1887	1933	Arbuckle, Fatty (Roscoe)	1904	1962	Beavers, Louise	1888	1960	Bori, Lucrezia
1900	1976	Arlen, Richard	1884	1946	Beery, Noah	1905	1965	Bow, Clara
1868	1946	Arliss, George	1889	1949	Beery, Wallace	1874	1946	Bowes, Maj. Edward
1888	1945	Armetta, Henry	1901	1970	Begley, Ed	1928	1977	Boyd, Stephen
1900	1971	Armstrong, Louis	1854	1931	Belasco, David	1898	1972	Boyd, William
1890	1956	Arnold, Edward	1949	1982	Belushi, John	1899	1978	Boyer, Charles
1905	1974	Arquette, Cliff	1906	1968	Benaderet, Bea	1893	1939	Brady, Alice
1885	1946	Atwill, Lionel	1906	1964	Bendix, William	1871	1936	Breese, Edmund
1845	1930	Auer, Leopold	1904	1965	Bennett, Constance	1898	1964	Brendel, El
1905	1967	Auer, Mischa	1873	1944	Bennett, Richard	1894	1974	Brennan, Walter
1900	1972	Austin, Gene	1894	1974	Benny, Jack	1904	1979	Brent, George
1898	1940	Ayres, Agnes	1924	1970	Benzell, Mimi	1875	1948	Brian, Donald
			1899	1966	Berg, Gertrude	1891	1951	Brice, Fanny
1864	1922	Bacon, Frank	1903	1978	Bergen, Edgar	1891	1959	Broderick, Helen
1891	1968	Bainter, Fay	1915	1982	Bergman, Ingrid	1904	1951	Bromberg, J. Edward
1895	1957	Baker, Belle	1895	1976	Berkeley, Busby	1892	1973	Brown, Joe E.
1906	1975	Baker, Josephine	1863	1927	Bernard, Sam	1926	1966	Bruce, Lenny
1898	1963	Baker, Phil	1844	1923	Bernhardt, Sarah	1895	1953	Bruce, Nigel
1904	1983	Balanchine, George	1893	1943	Bernie, Ben	1910	1982	Bruce, Virginia
1882	1956	Bancroft, George	1889	1967	Bickford, Charles	1903	1979	Buchanan, Edgar
1903	1968	Bankhead, Tallulah	1911	1960	Bjoerling, Jussi	1891	1957	Buchanan, Jack
1890	1952	Banks, Leslie	1898	1973	Blackmer, Sidney	1885	1957	Buck, Gene
1890	1955	Bara, Theda	1882	1951	Blaney, Charles E.	1938	1982	Buono, Victor

Born	Died	Name
1885	1970	Burke, Billie
1912	1967	Burnette, Smiley
1896	1956	Burns, Bob
1902	1971	Burns, David
1882	1941	Burr, Henry
1925	1984	Burton, Richard
1897	1946	Busch, Mae
1883	1966	Bushman, Francis X.
1896	1946	Butterworth, Charles
1893	1971	Byington, Spring
1905	1972	Cabot, Bruce
1918	1977	Cabot, Sebastian
1895	1956	Calhern, Louis
1923	1977	Callas, Maria
1853	1942	Calve, Emma
1933	1976	Cambridge, Godfrey
1865	1940	Campbell, Mrs. Patrick
1892	1964	Cantor, Eddie
1878	1947	Carey, Harry
1950	1983	Carpenter, Karen
1880	1961	Carrillo, Leo
1892	1972	Carroll, Leo G.
1905	1965	Carroll, Nancy
1910	1963	Carson, Jack
1862	1937	Carter, Mrs. Leslie
1873	1921	Caruso, Enrico
1876	1973	Casals, Pablo
1927	1976	Cassidy, Jack
1893	1969	Castle, Irene
1887	1918	Castle, Vernon
1889	1960	Catlett, Walter
1887	1950	Cavanaugh, Hobart
1873	1938	Chaliapin, Feodor
1921	1980	Champion, Gower
1918	1961	Chandler, Jeff
1883	1930	Chaney, Lon
1905	1973	Chaney Jr., Lon
1889	1977	Chaplin, Charles
1893	1940	Chase, Charlie
1893	1961	Chatterton, Ruth
1888	1972	Chevalier, Maurice
1888	1960	Clark, Bobby
1914	1968	Clark, Fred
1887	1950	Clayton, Lou
1920	1966	Clift, Montgomery
1932	1963	Cline, Patsy
1900	1937	Clive, Colin
1892	1967	Clyde, Andy
1911	1976	Cobb, Lee J.
1877	1961	Coburn, Charles
1887	1934	Cody, Lew
1878	1942	Cohan, George M.
1919	1965	Cole, Nat (King)
1878	1955	Collier, Constance
1890	1965	Collins, Ray
1891	1958	Colman, Ronald
1908	1934	Columbo, Russ
1907	1944	Compton, Betty
1887	1940	Connolly, Walter
1915	1982	Conried, Hans
1855	1909	Conried, Henrich
1914	1975	Conte, Richard
1914	1984	Coogan, Jackie
1901	1961	Cooper, Gary
1891	1971	Cooper, Gladys
1896	1973	Cooper, Melville
1914	1968	Corey, Wendell
1893	1974	Cornell, Katherine
1890	1972	Correll, Charles (Andy)
1905	1979	Costello, Dolores
1904	1957	Costello, Helene
1908	1959	Costello, Lou
1877	1950	Costello, Maurice
1899	1973	Coward, Noel
1890	1950	Cowl, Jane
1924	1973	Cox, Wally
1908	1983	Crabbe, Buster
1847	1924	Crabtree, Lotta
1928	1978	Crane, Bob
1875	1945	Craven, Frank
1908	1977	Crawford, Joan
1916	1944	Cregar, Laird
1880	1942	Crews, Laura Hope
1880	1974	Crisp, Donald
1942	1973	Croce, Jim
1910	1960	Cromwell, Richard
1903	1977	Crosby, Bing
1897	1975	Cross, Milton
1878	1968	Currie, Finlay
1816	1876	Cushman, Charlotte
1917	1978	Dailey, Dan
1899	1981	Chief Dan George
1923	1965	Dandridge, Dorothy
1869	1941	Danforth, William
1894	1963	Daniell, Henry
1901	1971	Daniels, Bebe
1860	1935	Daniels, Frank
1936	1973	Darin, Bobby
1921	1965	Darnell, Linda
1879	1967	Darwell, Jane
1866	1949	Davenport, Harry
1897	1961	Davies, Marion
1907	1961	Davis, Joan
1931	1955	Dean, James
1881	1950	DeCordoba, Pedro
1905	1968	Dekker, Albert
1908	1983	Del Rio, Dolores
1881	1959	DeMille, Cecil B.
1891	1967	Denny, Reginald
1901	1974	DeSica, Vittorio
1905	1977	Devine, Andy
1942	1972	De Wilde, Brandon
1907	1974	De Wolfe, Billy
1865	1950	De Wolfe, Elsie
1879	1947	Digges, Dudley
1901	1966	Disney, Walt
1894	1949	Dix, Richard
1856	1924	Dockstader, Lew
1892	1941	Dolly, Jennie
1892	1970	Dolly, Rosie
1905	1958	Donat, Robert
1903	1972	Donlevy, Brian
1901	1981	Douglas, Melvyn
1907	1959	Douglas, Paul
—	1980	Dragonette, Jessica
1889	1956	Draper, Ruth
1881	1965	Dresser, Louise
1869	1934	Dressler, Marie
1820	1897	Drew, Mrs. John
1853	1927	Drew, John (son)
1909	1951	Duchin, Eddy
1890	1965	Dumont, Margaret
1878	1927	Duncan, Isadora
1905	1967	Dunn, James
1893	1980	Durante, Jimmy
1907	1968	Duryea, Dan
1858	1924	Duse, Eleanora
1894	1929	Eagels, Jeanne
1896	1930	Eames, Clare
1865	1952	Eames, Emma
1901	1967	Eddy, Nelson
1897	1971	Edwards, Cliff
1879	1945	Edwards, Gus
1899	1974	Ellington, Duke
1941	1974	Elliot, Cass
1871	1940	Elliott, Maxine
1891	1967	Elman, Mischa
1881	1951	Errol, Leon
1903	1967	Erwin, Stuart
1888	1976	Evans, Edith
1913	1967	Evelyn, Judith
1883	1939	Fairbanks, Douglas
1915	1970	Farmer, Frances
1870	1929	Farnum, Dustin
1876	1953	Farnum, William
1882	1967	Farrar, Geraldine
1904	1971	Farrell, Glenda
1868	1940	Faversham, William
1861	1939	Fawcett, George
1897	1961	Fay, Frank
1895	1962	Fazenda, Louise
1933	1982	Feldman, Marty
1894	1979	Fiedler, Arthur
1918	1973	Field, Betty
1898	1979	Fields, Gracie
1867	1941	Fields, Lew
1879	1946	Fields, W.C.
1931	1978	Fields, Totie
1916	1977	Finch, Peter
1865	1932	Fiske, Minnie Maddern
1888	1961	Fitzgerald, Barry
1895	1962	Flagstad, Kirsten
1900	1971	Flippen, Jay C.
1909	1959	Flynn, Errol
1925	1974	Flynn, Joe
1880	1942	Fokine, Michel
1910	1968	Foley, Red
1905	1982	Fonda, Henry
1920	1978	Fontaine, Frank
1887	1983	Fontanne, Lynn
1853	1937	Forbes-Robertson, J.
1895	1973	Ford, John
1901	1976	Ford, Paul
1899	1966	Ford, Wallace
1806	1872	Forrest, Edwin
1902	1970	Foster, Preston
1857	1928	Foy, Eddie
1903	1968	Francis, Kay
1893	1966	Frawley, William
1885	1938	Frederick, Pauline
1870	1955	Friganza, Trixie
1890	1958	Frisco, Joe
1860	1915	Frohman, Charles
1851	1940	Frohman, Daniel
1885	1947	Fyffe, Will
1901	1960	Gable, Clark
1889	1963	Galli-Curci, Amelita
1877	1967	Garden, Mary
1913	1952	Garfield, John
1922	1969	Garland, Judy
1893	1963	Gaxton, William
1939	1984	Gaye, Marvin
1902	1978	Geer, Will
1904	1954	George, Gladys
1892	1962	Gibson, Hoot
1890	1957	Gigli, Beniamino
1894	1971	Gilbert, Billy
1899	1936	Gilbert, John
1855	1937	Gillette, William
1867	1943	Gillmore, Frank
1879	1939	Gilpin, Charles
1898	1968	Gish, Dorothy
1886	1959	Gleason, James
1884	1938	Gluck, Alma
1903	1983	Godfrey, Arthur
1874	1955	Golden, John
1882	1974	Goldwyn, Samuel
1917	1969	Gorcey, Leo
1884	1940	Gordon, C. Henry
1899	1982	Gosden, Freeman (Amos)
1869	1944	Gottschalk, Ferdinand
1829	1869	Gottschalk, Louis
1916	1973	Grable, Betty
1929	1981	Grahame, Gloria
1901	1959	Gray, Gilda
1879	1954	Greenstreet, Sydney
1893	1978	Greenwood, Charlotte
1874	1948	Griffith, David Wark
1912	1967	Guthrie, Woody
1875	1959	Gwenn, Edmund
1888	1942	Hackett, Charles
1902	1958	Hackett, Raymond
1870	1943	Haines, Robert T.
1892	1950	Hale, Alan
1927	1981	Haley, Bill
1899	1979	Haley, Jack
1902	1985	Hamilton, Margaret
1847	1919	Hammerstein, Oscar
1879	1955	Hampden, Walter
1924	1964	Haney, Carol
1893	1964	Hardwicke, Sir Cedric
1892	1957	Hardy, Oliver
1883	1939	Hare, T.E. (Ernie)
1911	1937	Harlow, Jean
1872	1946	Harned, Virginia
1844	1911	Harrigan, Edward
1870	1946	Hart, William S.
1907	1955	Hartman, Grace
1928	1973	Harvey, Laurence
1910	1973	Hawkins, Jack
1890	1973	Hayakawa, Sessue
1885	1969	Hayes, Gabby
1918	1980	Haymes, Dick
1902	1971	Hayward, Leland
1917	1975	Hayward, Susan
1896	1937	Healy, Ted
1910	1971	Heflin, Van

Born	Died	Name
1874	1948	Niblo, Fred
1890	1950	Nijinsky, Vaslav
1893	1974	Nilsson, Anna Q.
1898	1930	Normand, Mabel
1879	1959	Norworth, Jack
1905	1968	Novarro, Ramon
1893	1951	Novello, Ivor
1903	1978	Oakie, Jack
1860	1926	Oakley, Annie
1911	1979	Oberon, Merle
1915	1985	O'Brien, Edmund
1899	1983	O'Brien, Pat
1908	1981	O'Connell, Arthur
1898	1943	O'Connell, Hugh
1880	1959	O'Connor, Una
1878	1945	O'Hara, Fiske
1908	1968	O'Keefe, Dennis
1880	1938	Oland, Warner
1860	1932	Olcott, Chauncey
1883	1942	Oliver, Edna May
1892	1963	Olsen, Ole
1849	1920	O'Neill, James
1899	1985	Ormandy, Eugene
1876	1949	Ouspenskaya, Maria
1887	1972	Owen, Reginald
1860	1941	Paderewski, Ignace
1889	1954	Pallette, Eugene
1894	1958	Pangborn, Franklin
1914	1975	Parks, Larry
1881	1940	Pasternack, Josef A.
1837	1908	Pastor, Tony
1843	1919	Patti, Adelina
1840	1889	Patti, Carlotta
1885	1931	Pavlova, Anna
1900	1973	Paxinou, Katina
1904	1984	Peerce, Jan
1885	1950	Pemberton, Brock
1899	1967	Pendleton, Nat
1905	1941	Penner, Joe
1892	1937	Perkins, Osgood
1893	1956	Peters, Brandon
1915	1963	Piaf, Edith
1893	1979	Pickford, Mary
1897	1984	Pidgeon, Walter
1892	1957	Pinza, Ezio
1898	1963	Pitts, Zasu
1904	1976	Pons, Lily
1897	1981	Ponselle, Rosa
1903	1969	Portman, Eric
1904	1963	Powell, Dick
1912	1982	Powell, Eleanor
1892	1984	Powell, William
1913	1958	Power, Tyrone
1872	1935	Powers, Eugene
1935	1977	Presley, Elvis
1856	1919	Primrose, George
1954	1977	Prinze, Freddie
1879	1956	Prouty, Jed
1871	1942	Pryor, Arthur
1895	1980	Raft, George
1890	1967	Rains, Claude
1889	1970	Rambeau, Marjorie
1900	1947	Rankin, Arthur
1892	1967	Rathbone, Basil
1897	1960	Ratoff, Gregory
1883	1953	Rawlinson, Herbert
1891	1943	Ray, Charles
1941	1967	Redding, Otis
1908	1985	Redgrave, Michael
1914	1959	Reeves, George
1923	1964	Reeves, Jim
1860	1916	Rehan, Ada
1892	1923	Reid, Wallace
1873	1943	Reinhardt, Max
1909	1971	Rennie, Michael
1902	1983	Richardson, Ralph
1870	1940	Richman, Charles
1895	1972	Richman, Harry
1872	1961	Ring, Blanche
1898	1977	Ritchard, Cyril
1907	1974	Ritter, Tex
1905	1969	Ritter, Thelma
1903	1966	Ritz, Al
1925	1982	Robbins, Marty
1898	1976	Robeson, Paul

Born	Died	Name
1878	1949	Robinson, Bill
1893	1973	Robinson, Edward G.
1865	1942	Robson, May
1905	1977	Rochester (E. Anderson)
1897	1933	Rodgers, Jimmy
1894	1958	Rodzinsky, Artur
1879	1935	Rogers, Will
1897	1937	Roland, Ruth
1880	1962	Rooney, Pat
1899	1966	Rose, Billy
1910	1980	Roth, Lillian
1882	1936	Rothafel, S. L. (Roxy)
1887	1982	Rubinstein, Artur
1878	1953	Ruffo, Titta
1892	1970	Ruggles, Charles
1864	1936	Russell, Annie
1924	1961	Russell, Gail
1861	1922	Russell, Lillian
1911	1976	Russell, Rosalind
1892	1972	Rutherford, Margaret
1902	1973	Ryan, Irene
1909	1973	Ryan, Robert
1924	1963	Sabu (Dastagir)
1877	1968	St. Denis, Ruth
1884	1955	Sakall, S.Z.
1885	1936	Sale (Chic), Charles
1906	1972	Sanders, George
1934	1973	Sands, Diana
1896	1960	Savo, Jimmy
1879	1954	Scheff, Fritzi
1892	1930	Schenck, Joe
1895	1964	Schildkraut, Joseph
1865	1930	Schildkraut, Rudolph
1889	1965	Schipa, Tito
1882	1951	Schnabel, Artur
1938	1982	Schneider, Romy
1910	1949	Schumann, Henrietta
1861	1936	Schumann-Heink, E.
1866	1945	Scott, Cyril
1914	1965	Scott, Zachary
1843	1896	Scott-Siddons, Mrs.
1938	1979	Seberg, Jean
1892	1974	Seeley, Blossom
1925	1980	Sellers, Peter
1902	1965	Selznick, David O.
1858	1935	Sembrich, Marcella
1880	1960	Sennett, Mack
1881	1951	Shattuck, Arthur
1860	1929	Shaw, Mary
1927	1978	Shaw, Robert
1891	1972	Shawn, Ted
1868	1949	Shean, Al
1902	1983	Shearer, Norma
1915	1967	Sheridan, Ann
1885	1934	Sherman, Lowell
1918	1970	Shriner, Herb
1875	1953	Shubert, Lee
1755	1831	Siddons, Mrs. Sarah
1882	1930	Sills, Milton
1900	1976	Sim, Alastair
1878	1946	Sis Hopkins (Melville)
1891	1934	Skelly, Hal
1858	1942	Skinner, Otis
1870	1952	Skipworth, Alison
1863	1948	Smith, C. Aubrey
1917	1979	Soo, Jack
1826	1881	Sothern, Edward A.
1859	1933	Sothern, Edward H.
1884	1957	Sothern, Harry
1854	1932	Sousa, John Philip
1884	1957	Sparks, Ned
1876	1948	Speaks, Oley
1890	1970	Spitalny, Phil
1873	1937	Standing, Guy
1900	1941	Stephenson, James
1883	1939	Sterling, Ford
1882	1928	Stevens, Emily A.
1934	1970	Stevens, Inger
1896	1961	Stewart, Anita
1882	1977	Stokowski, Leopold
1873	1959	Stone, Fred
1879	1953	Stone, Lewis
1904	1980	Stone, Milburn
1898	1959	Sturges, Preston
1911	1960	Sullavan, Margaret
1902	1974	Sullivan, Ed
1903	1956	Sullivan, Francis L.

Born	Died	Name
1892	1946	Summerville, Slim
1899	1983	Swanson, Gloria
1904	1969	Swarthout, Gladys
1893	1957	Talmadge, Norma
1900	1972	Tamiroff, Akim
1878	1947	Tanguay, Eva
1899	1934	Tashman, Lilyan
1885	1966	Taylor, Deems
1899	1958	Taylor, Estelle
1887	1946	Taylor, Laurette
1911	1969	Taylor, Robert
1878	1938	Tearle, Conway
1884	1953	Tearle, Godfrey
1892	1937	Tell, Alma
1864	1942	Tempest, Marie
1910	1963	Templeton, Alec
1847	1928	Terry, Ellen
1871	1940	Tetrazzini, Luisa
1899	1936	Thalberg, Irving
1857	1914	Thomas, Brandon
1892	1960	Thomas, John Charles
1882	1976	Thorndike, Sybil
		(Three Stooges)
1902	1975	Fine, Larry
1906	1952	Howard, Curly
1897	1975	Howard, Moe
1869	1936	Thurston, Howard
1896	1960	Tibbett, Lawrence
1887	1940	Tinney, Frank
1909	1958	Todd, Michael
1906	1935	Todd, Thelma
1874	1947	Toler, Sidney
1905	1968	Tone, Franchot
1867	1957	Toscanini, Arturo
1898	1968	Tracy, Lee
1900	1967	Tracy, Spencer
1903	1972	Traubel, Helen
1894	1975	Treacher, Arthur
1853	1917	Tree, Herbert Beerbohm
1889	1973	Truex, Ernest
1932	1984	Truffaut, Francois
1915	1975	Tucker, Richard
1884	1966	Tucker, Sophie
1874	1940	Turpin, Ben
1908	1959	Twelvetrees, Helen
1894	1970	Ulric, Lenore
1933	1975	Ure, Mary
1895	1926	Valentino, Rudolph
1870	1950	Van, Billy B.
1912	1979	Vance, Vivian
1893	1943	Veidt, Conrad
1926	1981	Vera-Ellen
1885	1957	Von Stroheim, Erich
1906	1981	Von Zell, Harry
1887	1969	Walburn, Raymond
1874	1946	Waldron, Charles D.
1904	1966	Walker, June
1914	1951	Walker, Robert
1898	1983	Wallenstein, Alfred
1887	1980	Walsh, Raoul
1876	1962	Walter, Bruno
1878	1936	Walthall, Henry B.
1872	1952	Ward, Fannie
1866	1951	Warfield, David
1876	1958	Warner, H. B.
1878	1964	Warwick, Robert
1924	1963	Washington, Dinah
1900	1977	Waters, Ethel
1867	1945	Watson, Billy
1907	1979	Wayne, John
1896	1966	Webb, Clifton
1920	1982	Webb, Jack
1867	1942	Weber, Joe
1905	1973	Webster, Margaret
1896	1975	Wellman, William
1922	1984	Werner, Oskar
1892	1980	West, Mae
1895	1968	Wheeler, Bert
1889	1938	White, Pearl
1891	1967	Whiteman, Paul
1865	1948	Whitty, Dame May
1912	1979	Wilding, Michael
1895	1948	William, Warren
1877	1922	Williams, Bert

Born	Died	Name	Born	Died	Name	Born	Died	Name
1867	1918	Williams, Evan	1907	1961	Wong, Anna May	1890	1960	Young, Clara Kimball
1923	1953	Williams, Hank	1938	1981	Wood, Natalie	1917	1978	Young, Gig
1905	1975	Wills, Bob	1892	1978	Wood, Peggy	1887	1953	Young, Roland
1902	1978	Wills, Chill	1888	1963	Woolley, Monty			
1917	1972	Wilson, Marie	1881	1956	Wycherly, Margaret	1902	1979	Zanuck, Darryl F.
1884	1969	Winninger, Charles	1902	1981	Wyler, William	1869	1932	Ziegfeld, Florenz
1904	1959	Withers, Grant	1886	1966	Wynn, Ed	1873	1976	Zukor, Adolph
1881	1931	Wolheim, Louis	1906	1964	Wynyard, Diana			

The Theater Hall of Fame

The Theater Hall of Fame was created to honor those who have made outstanding contributions to the New York theater. Members are elected annually by the nation's drama critics and drama editors.

George Abbott
Maude Adams
Viola Adams
Edward Albee
Ira Aldridge
Winthrop Ames
Judith Anderson
Maxwell Anderson
Robert Anderson
Margaret Anglin
Harold Arlen
George Arliss
Boris Aronson
Fred & Adele Astaire
Brooks Atkinson
Tallulah Bankhead
Philip Barry
Ethel Barrymore
John Barrymore
Lionel Barrymore
Nora Bayes
S. N. Behrman
David Belasco
Norman Bel Geddes
Richard Bennett
Irving Berlin
Sarah Bernhardt
Leonard Bernstein
Kermit Bloomgarden
Ray Bolger
Edwin Booth
Junius Brutus Booth
Shirley Booth
Alice Brady
Fannie Brice
Peter Brook
John Mason Brown
Billie Burke
Abe Burrows
Richard Burton
Mrs. Patrick Campbell
Eddie Cantor
Morris Carnovsky
Mrs. Leslie Carter
Gower Champion
Carol Channing
Ruth Chatterton
Ina Claire
Bobby Clark
Harold Clurman
Lee J. Cobb
George M. Cohan
Constance Collier
Betty Comden & Adolph Green
Marc Connelly
Katharine Cornell
Noel Coward
Jane Cowl
Cheryl Crawford
Hume Cronyn
Russel Crouse
Charlotte Cushman
Augustin Daly
Alfred de Liagre, Jr.
Agnes DeMille
Colleen Dewhurst
Howard Dietz & Arthur Schwartz
Dudley Digges
Melvyn Douglas
Alfred Drake
Marie Dressler
Mrs. John Drew
John Drew
Mildred Dunnock
Eleanora Duse
Jeanne Eagles
Florence Eldridge
Lehman Engel
Maurice Evans
Jose Ferrer
W. C. Fields

Minnie Maddern Fiske
Cylde Fitch
Henry Fonda
Lynn Fontanne
Edwin Forrest
Bob Fosse
Rudolf Friml
Charles Frohman
Grace George
George & Ira Gershwin
John Gielgud
William Gillette
Lillian Gish
John Golden
Ruth Gordon
Charlotte Greenwood
Tyrone Guthrie
Uta Hagen
Oscar Hammerstein II
Walter Hampden
Otto Harbach
E. Y. "Yip" Harburg
Harrigan & Hart
Jed Harris
Julie Harris
Sam H. Harris
Rex Harrison
Lorenz Hart
Moss Hart
Helen Hayes
Lillian Hellman
Katharine Hepburn
Victor Herbert
Raymond Hitchcock
Arthur Hopkins
De Wolf Hopper
John Houseman
Leslie Howard
Sidney Howard
Willie & Eugene Howard
Henry Hull
Walter Huston
William Inge
Elsie Janis
Joseph Jefferson
Al Jolson
James Earl Jones
Robert Edmond Jones
Garson Kanin
George S. Kaufman
Elia Kazan
George Kelly
Jerome Kern
Walter Kerr
Michael Kidd
Sidney Kingsley
Bert Lahr
Lawrence Langner
Lillie Langtry
Angela Lansbury
Arthur Laurents
Gertrude Lawrence
Eva Le Gallienne
Lotte Lenya
Alan Jay Lerner
Sam Levene
Beatrice Lillie
Howard Lindsay
Frank Loesser
Frederick Loewe
Joshua Logan
Pauline Lord
Alfred Lunt
Ben Hecht & Charles MacArthur
Rouben Mamoulian
Richard Mansfield
Robert B. Mantell
Frederich March
Julia Marlowe
Mary Martin

Helen Menken
Burgess Meredith
Ethel Merman
David Merrick
Jo Mielziner
Arthur Miller
Henry Miller
Marilyn Miller
Helena Modjeska
Ferenc Molnar
Victor Moore
Zero Mostel
Paul Muni
Tharon Musser
George Jean Nathan
Nazimova
Clifford Odets
Donald Oenslager
Laurence Olivier
Eugene O'Neill
Geraldine Page
Osgood Perkins
Molly Picon
Cole Porter
Robert Preston
Harold Prince
Jose Quintero
Ada Rehan
Elmer Rice
Ralph Richardson
Jason Robards
Jerome Robbins
Paul Robeson
Richard Rodgers
Will Rogers
Sigmund Romberg
Lillian Russell
William Saroyan
Alan Schneider
Robert E. Sherwood
Lee & J. J. Shubert
Herman Shumlin
Neil Simon
Lee Simonson
Otis Skinner
Oliver Smith
Stephen Sondheim
E. A. Sothern
E. H. Sothern
Kim Stanley
Maureen Stapleton
Dorothy Stickney
Fred Stone
Lee Strasberg
Jule Styne
Margaret Sullavan
Jessica Tandy
Laurette Taylor
Ellen Terry
Gwen Verdon
James & Lester Wallack
David Warfield
Ethel Waters
Clifton Webb
Margaret Webster
Robert Whitehead
Weber & Fields
Kurt Weill
Orson Welles
Mae West
Thornton Wilder
Bert Williams
Tennessee Williams
P. G. Wodehouse
Peggy Wood
Irene Worth
Ed Wynn
Vincent Youmans
Stark Young
Florenz Ziegfeld

Original Names of Selected Entertainers

Edie Adams: Elizabeth Edith Enke
Eddie Albert: Edward Albert Heimberger
Alan Alda: Alphonso D'Abruzzo
Fred Allen: John Sullivan
Woody Allen: Allen Konigsberg
Julie Andrews: Julia Wells
Eve Arden: Eunice Quedens
Beatrice Arthur: Bernice Frankel
Jean Arthur: Gladys Greene
Fred Astaire: Frederick Austerlitz
Lauren Bacall: Betty Joan Perske
Anne Bancroft: Anna Maria Italiano
Brigitte Bardot: Camille Javal
Pat Benatar: Patricia Andrejewski
Tony Bennett: Anthony Benedetto
Busby Berkeley: William Berkeley Enos
Jack Benny: Benjamin Kubelsky
Robert Blake: Michael Gubitosi
Victor Borge: Borge Rosenbaum
Fanny Brice: Fanny Borach
Charles Bronson: Charles Buchinski
Mel Brooks: Melvin Kaminsky
George Burns: Nathan Birnbaum
Ellen Burstyn: Edna Gilhooley
Richard Burton: Richard Jenkins
Red Buttons: Aaron Chwatt
Michael Caine: Maurice Micklewhite
Maria Callas: Maria Kalogeropoulos
Diahann Carroll: Carol Diahann Johnson
Cyd Charisse: Tula Finklea
Cher: Cherilyn Sarkisian
Claudette Colbert: Lily Chauchoin
Michael Connors: Kreker Ohanian
Robert Conrad: Conrad Robert Falk
Howard Cosell: Howard Cohen
Alice Cooper: Vincent Furnier
Elvis Costello: Declan Patrick McManus
Joan Crawford: Lucille Le Sueur
Tony Curtis: Bernard Schwartz
Vic Damone: Vito Farinola
Rodney Dangerfield: Jacob Cohen
Bobby Darin: Walden Waldo Cassotto
Doris Day: Doris von Kappelhoff
Yvonne De Carlo: Peggy Middleton
Sandra Dee: Alexandra Zuck
John Denver: Henry John Deutschendorf Jr.
Bo Derek: Cathleen Collins
John Derek: Derek Harris
Angie Dickinson: Angeline Brown
Melvyn Douglas: Melvyn Hesselberg
Bob Dylan: Robert Zimmerman
Barbara Eden: Barbara Huffman
Ron Ely: Ronald Pierce
Chad Everett: Raymond Cramton
Douglas Fairbanks: Douglas Ullman
Morgan Fairchild: Patsy McClenny
Alice Faye: Ann Leppert
W.C. Fields: William Claude Dukenfield
Peter Finch: William Mitchell
Joan Fontaine: Joan de Havilland
John Forsythe: John Freund
Redd Foxx : John Sanford
Anthony Franciosa: Anthony Papaleo
Arlene Francis: Arlene Kazanjian
Connie Francis: Concetta Franconero
Greta Garbo: Greta Gustafsson
Judy Garland: Frances Gumm
James Garner: James Baumgardner
Bobbie Gentry: Roberta Streeter
Stewart Granger: James Stewart
Cary Grant: Archibald Leach
Joel Grey: Joe Katz
Buddy Hackett: Leonard Hacker
Jean Harlow: Harlean Carpentier
Helen Hayes: Helen Brown
Susan Hayward: Edythe Marriner
Rita Hayworth: Margarita Cansino
William Holden: William Beedle
Billie Holiday: Eleanora Fagan
Judy Holliday: Judith Tuvim
Harry Houdini: Ehrich Weiss
Leslie Howard: Leslie Stainer
Rock Hudson: Roy Scherer Jr. (later Fitzgerald)
Engelbert Humperdinck: Arnold Dorsey
Kim Hunter: Janet Cole
Betty Hutton: Betty Thornberg
David Janssen: David Meyer

Elton John: Reginald Dwight
Jennifer Jones: Phyllis Isley
Tom Jones: Thomas Woodward
Louis Jourdan: Louis Gendre
Boris Karloff: William Henry Pratt
Diane Keaton: Diane Hall
Carole King: Carole Klein
Ted Knight: Tadeus Wladyslaw Konopka
Cheryl Ladd: Cheryl Stoppelmoor
Veronica Lake: Constance Ockleman
Michael Landon: Eugene Orowitz
Mario Lanza: Alfredo Cocozza
Stan Laurel: Arthur Jefferson
Steve Lawrence: Sidney Leibowitz
Gypsy Rose Lee: Rose Louise Hovick
Peggy Lee: Norma Egstrom
Janet Leigh: Jeanette Morrison
Vivian Leigh: Vivien Hartley
Jerry Lewis: Joseph Levitch
Hal Linden: Harold Lipshitz
Jack Lord: John Joseph Ryan
Sophia Loren: Sophia Scicoloni
Peter Lorre: Laszio Lowenstein
Myrna Loy: Myrna Williams
Shirley MacLaine: Shirley Beaty
Lee Majors: Harvey Lee Yeary 2d
Karl Malden: Malden Sekulovich
Jayne Mansfield: Vera Jane Palmer
Fredric March: Frederick Bickel
Dean Martin: Dino Crocetti
Tony Martin: Alvin Morris
Walter Matthau: Walter Matuschanskayasky
Ethel Merman: Ethel Zimmerman
Ray Milland: Reginald Truscott-Jones
Ann Miller: Lucille Collier
Marilyn Monroe: Norma Jean Mortenson, (later) Baker
Yves Montand: Ivo Levi
Garry Moore: Thomas Garrison Morfit
Harry Morgan: Harry Bratsburg
Mike Nichols: Michael Igor Peschowsky
Sheree North: Dawn Bethel
Hugh O'Brian: Hugh Krampke
Maureen O'Hara: Maureen Fitzsimmons
Jack Palance: Walter Palanuik
Lilli Palmer: Lilli Peiser
Bert Parks: Bert Jacobson
Minnie Pearl: Sarah Ophelia Cannon
Bernadette Peters: Bernadette Lazzaro
Mary Pickford: Gladys Smith
Stephanie Powers: Stefania Federkiewcz
Robert Preston: Robert Preston Meservey
Tony Randall: Leonard Rosenberg
Della Reese: Delloreese Patricia Early
Joan Rivers: Joan Sandra Molinsky
Ginger Rogers: Virginia McMath
Roy Rogers: Leonard Slye
Mickey Rooney: Joe Yule Jr.
Lillian Russell: Helen Leonard
Susan St. James: Susan Miller
Randolph Scott: Randolph Crance
Jane Seymour: Joyce Frankenberg
Omar Sharif: Michael Shalhoub
Martin Sheen: Ramon Estevez
Beverly Sills: Belle Silverman
Suzanne Somers: Suzanne Mahoney
Ann Sothern: Harriette Lake
Barbara Stanwyck: Ruby Stevens
Jean Stapleton: Jeanne Murray
Ringo Starr: Richard Starkey
Connie Stevens: Concetta Ingolia
Donna Summers: LaDonna Gaines
Robert Taylor: Spangler Arlington Brugh
Danny Thomas: Amos Jacobs
Sophie Tucker: Sophia Kalish
Conway Twitty: Harold Lloyd Jenkins
Rudolph Valentino: Rudolpho D'Antonguolla
Frankie Valli: Frank Castelluccio
Nancy Walker: Myrtle Swoyer
David Wayne: Wayne McMeekan
John Wayne: Marion Morrison
Raquel Welch: Raquel Tejada
Gene Wilder: Jerome Silberman
Shelly Winters: Shirley Schrift
Stevie Wonder: Stevland Morris
Natalie Wood: Natasha Gurdin
Jane Wyman: Sarah Jane Fulks
Gig Young: Byron Barr

ASSOCIATIONS AND SOCIETIES

Source: World Almanac questionnaire

Arranged according to key words in titles. Founding year of organization in parentheses; last figure after ZIP code indicates membership.

Aaron Burr Assn. (1946), R.D. #1, Route 33, Box 429, Hightstown-Freehold, Hightstown, NJ 08520; 500.

Abortion Federation, Natl. (1977), 900 Pennsylvania Ave. SE, Washington, DC 20003; 270 institutions.

Abortion Rights Action League, Natl. (1969), 1424 K St. NW, Wash., DC 20005; 150,000.

Accountants, Amer. Institute of Certified Public (1887), 1211 Ave. of the Americas, N.Y., NY 10036; 190,000.

Accountants, Natl. Assn. of (1919), 10 Paragon Dr., Box 433, Montvale, NJ 07645; 95,000.

Accountants, Natl. Soc. of for Cooperatives (1935), 6320 Augusta Dr., Springfield, VA 22151; 2,300.

Accountants, Natl. Society of Public (1945), 1010 N. Fairfax St., Alexandria, VA 22314.

Acoustical Society of America (1929), 335 E. 45 St., N.Y., NY 10017; 5,700.

Actors' Equity Assn. (1913), 165 W. 46 St., N.Y., NY 10036.

Actors' Fund of America (1882), 1501 Broadway, N.Y., NY 10036; 3,500.

Actuaries, American Academy of (1965), 1835 K St. NW, Wash., DC 20006; 6,400.

Actuaries, Society of (1949), 500 Park Blvd., Itasca, IL 60143; 9,500.

Adirondack Mountain Club (1922), 172 Ridge St., Glens Falls, NY 12801; 11,000.

Advertisers, Assn. of Natl. (1910), 155 E. 44th St., N.Y., NY 10017; 450 cos.

Advertising Agencies, Amer. Assn. of (1917), 666 Third Ave., N.Y., NY 10017; 600 agencies.

Aeronautic Assn. of USA, Inc., Natl. (1922), 1400 Eye St. NW, #550, Wash., DC 20005; 5,000.

Aeronautics and Astronautics, Amer. Institute of (1963), 1633 Broadway, N.Y., NY 10019; 37,000.

Aerospace Industries Assn. of America (1919), 1725 De Sales St. NW, Wash., DC 20036; 51 cos.

Aerospace Medical Assn. (1923), Washington Natl. Airport, Wash., DC 20001; 4,000.

Afro-American Life and History, Assn. for the Study of (1915), 1401 14th St. NW, Wash., DC 20005; 2,000.

Aging Assn., Amer. (1970), Univ. of Nebraska Medical Center, 42d & Dewey Ave., Omaha, NE 68105; 500.

Agnostics, Soc. of Evangelical (1975), Box 515, Auberry, CA 93602; 950.

Agricultural Chemicals Assn., Natl. (1933), 1155 15th St. NW, Wash., DC 20005; 125 cos.

Agricultural Economics Assn., Amer. (1910), Dept. of Economics, Iowa State Univ., Ames, IA 50011; 4,750.

Agricultural History Society (1919), 1301 New York Ave. NW, Wash., DC 20250; 1,400.

Agronomy, Amer. Society of (1907), 677 S. Segoe Rd., Madison, WI 53711; 12,446.

Aircraft Assn., Experimental (1953), 11311 W. Forest Home Ave., Franklin, WI 53132; 70,000.

Aircraft Owners and Pilots Assn. (1939), 421 Aviation Way, Frederick, MD 21701; 265,000.

Air Force Assn. (1946), 1501 Lee Hwy., Arlington, VA 22209-1198; 200,000.

Air Force Sergeants Assn. (1961), P.O. Box 31050, Temple Hills, MD 20748.

Air Line Employees Assn. (1952), 5600 S. Central Ave., Chicago, IL 60638; 10,000.

Air Line Pilots Assn. (1931), 1625 Massachusetts Ave. NW, Wash., DC 20036; 33,000.

Air Pollution Control Assn. (1906), P.O. Box 2861, Pittsburgh, PA 15230; 7,600.

Air Transport Assn. of America (1936), 1709 New York Ave. NW, Wash., DC 20006; 32 airlines.

Alcohol Problems, Amer. Council on (1895), 2908 Patricia Dr., Des Moines, IA 50322.

Alcoholics Anonymous (1935), 468 Park Ave. So., N.Y., NY 10016; 1,000,000+.

Alcoholism, Natl. Council on (1944), 12 W. 21st St., N.Y., NY 10010; 200 affiliates.

All-Terrain Vehicle Owners Assn., Natl. (1972) P.O. Box 1272, Bensalem, PA 19020; 1,207.

Allergy and Immunology, Amer. Academy of (1943), 611 E. Wells St., Milwaukee, WI 53202; 3,600.

Alpine Club, Amer. (1902), 113 E. 90th St., N.Y., NY 10028.

Altrusa Intl. (1917), 8 S. Michigan Ave., Chicago, IL 60603.

Amer. Feder. of Labor & Congress of Industrial Organizations (AFL-CIO) (1955, by merging Amer. Feder. of Labor estab. 1881 and Congress of Industrial Organizations estab. 1935), 815 16th St. NW, Wash., DC 20006; 15,000,000.

Amer. Field Service (1947), 313 E. 43d St., N.Y., NY 10017.

Amer. Indian Affairs, Assn. on (1923), 95 Madison Ave., N.Y., NY 10016; 50,000.

American Legion, The (1919), 700 N. Pennsylvania St., Indianapolis, IN 46204; 2.6 mln. American Legion Auxiliary (1921), 777 N. Meridian St., Indianapolis, IN 46204; 950,000.

Amer. States, Organization of (1948), General Secretariat, Wash., DC 20006; 28 countries.

Amer. Veterans of World War II, Korea & Vietnam (AMVETS), (1944), 4647 Forbes Blvd., Lanham, MD 20706; 200,000. AMVETS Auxiliary (1947), Saco Rd., Old Orchard Beach, ME 04064; 60,000.

Amnesty Intl. (1961), 304 W. 58th St., N.Y., NY 10019.

Amputation Foundation, Natl. (1919), 12-45 150th St., Whitestone, NY 11357; 2,000.

Andersonville, Natl. Soc. of (1976), 10 Church St., Andersonville, GA 31711.

Animal Protection Institute of America (1968), 6130 Freeport Blvd., Sacramento, CA 95822; 180,000.

Animal Welfare Institute (1951), P.O. Box 3650, Wash., DC 20007; 8,000.

Animals, Amer. Society for Prevention of Cruelty to (ASPCA) (1866), 441 E. 92d St., N.Y., NY 10028; 75,000.

Animals, Friends of (1957), One Pine St., Neptune, NJ 07753; 125,000.

Animals, The Fund for (1967), 140 W. 57th St., N.Y., NY 10019; 172,000.

Anthropological Assn., Amer. (1902), 1703 New Hampshire Ave. NW, Wash., DC 20009; 10,000.

Antiquarian Society, Amer. (1812), 185 Salisbury St., Worcester, MA 01609; 451.

Anti-Vivisection Society, Amer. (1883), Suite 204, Noble Plaza, 801 Old York Rd., Jenkintown, PA 19046; 10,000+.

Appalachian Mountain Club (1876), 5 Joy St., Boston, MA 02108; 35,000.

Appalachian Trail Conference (1925), Box 807, Harpers Ferry, WV 25425; 19,000.

Appraisers, Amer. Society of (1936), P.O. Box 17265, Wash., DC 20041; 5,000.

Arab Americans, Natl. Assn. of (1972), 2033 M St. NW, Wash., DC 20036.

Arbitration Assn., Amer. (1926), 140 W. 51st St., N.Y., NY 10020; 5,000.

Arboriculture, Intl. Society of (1924), 5 Lincoln Sq., Urbana, IL 61801; 4,000.

Archaeological Institute of America (1879), P.O. Box 1901, Kenmore Station, Boston, MA 02215; 10,000.

Archaeology, Institute of Nautical (1973), Texas A & M University, Drawer AU, College Station, TX 77840; 650.

Archery, Assn., Natl. (1879), 1750 E. Boulder St., Colorado Springs, CO 80909; 3,100.

Architects, Amer. Institute of (1857), 1735 New York Ave. NW, Wash., DC 20006; 41,000.

Architectural Historians, Society of (1940), 1700 Walnut St., Phila., PA 19103; 4,200.

Archivists, Society of Amer. (1936), 330 S. Wells St., Suite 810, Chicago, IL 60606; 4,000.

Armed Forces Communications and Electronics Assn. (1946), 5641 Burke Centre Pkwy., Burke, VA 22152; 30,000.

Army, Assn. of the United States (1950), 2425 Wilson Blvd., Arlington, VA 22201; 159,000.

Arts, Action & Consciousness, Comprehensive (1958), P.O. Box 188, Monticello, GA 31064.

Arts, Amer. Council for the (1960), 570 7th Ave., N.Y., NY 10018; 4,000.

Arts, Amer. Federation of (1909), 41 E. 65th St., N.Y., NY 10021; 1,400.

Arts, Associated Councils of the (1969), 570 Seventh Ave., N.Y., NY 10018; 2,000.

Arts, Natl. Endowment for the (1965), 2401 E. St. NW, Wash., DC 20506.

Arts and Letters, Amer. Academy and Institute of (1898), 633 W. 155th St., N.Y., NY 10032; 245.

Arts and Letters, Natl. Society of (1944), 9915 Litzsinger Rd., St. Louis, MO 63124; 1,600.

Arts & Psychology, Assn. for the (1976), P.O. Box 160371, Sacramento, CA 95816.

Arts & Sciences, Amer. Academy of (1780), Norton's Woods, 136 Irving St., Cambridge, MA 02138; 2,800.

Assistance League, Natl. (1935), 5627 Fernwood Ave., Los Angeles, CA 90038; 16,000.

Astrologers, Amer. Federation of (1938), 6535 S. Rural Rd., Tempe, AZ 85282; 5,000.

Astronautical Society, Amer. (1953), 6060 Duke St., Alexandria, VA 22304; l,000.

Astronomical Society, Amer. (1899), 1816 Jefferson Pl. NW, Wash., DC 20036; 4,100.

Atheist Assn. (1925), Box 2832, San Diego, CA 92112.

Atheists, Amer. (1963), 2210 Hancock Dr., Austin, TX 78756.

Athletic Associations, Natl. Federation of State H. S. (1920), 11724 Plaza Circle, Box 20626, Kansas City, MO 64195.

Athletic Union of the U.S., Amateur (1888), 3400 W. 86th St., Indianapolis, IN 46268.

Athletics Congress/USA, The (1979), P.O. Box 120, 155 W. Washington St., Suite 220, Indianapolis, IN 46206; 250,000.

Auctioneers Assn., Natl. (1949), 8880 Ballentine, Overland Park, KS 66214; 6,100.

Audubon Society, Natl. (1905), 950 Third Ave., N.Y., NY 10022; 400,000.

Authors and Composers, Amer. Guild of (1931), 40 W. 57th St., N.Y., NY 10019; 3,000.

Authors League of America (1912), 234 W. 44th St., N.Y., NY 10036; 13,000.

Autism, Natl. Society for Children and Adults with, (1965), 1234 Massachusetts Ave. NW, Wash., DC 20005; 16,000.

Autograph Collectors Club, Universal (1965), P.O. Box 467, Rockville Centre, NY 11571-0467; 2,200.

Automobile Assn., Amer. (1902), 8111 Gatehouse Rd., Falls Church, VA 22047; 25 million+.

Automobile Club, Natl. (1924), One Market Plaza, San Francisco, CA 94105; 316,000.

Automobile Club of America, Antique (1935), 501 W. Governor Rd., Hershey, PA 17033; 48,000.

Automobile Dealers Assn., Natl. (1917), 8400 Westpark Dr., McLean, VA 22102; 19,500.

Automobile License Plate Collectors' Assn. (1954), P.O. Box 712, Weston, W. VA 26452.

Automotive Booster Clubs Intl. (1921), 501 W. Algonquin Rd., Arlington Heights, IL 60005; 2,856.

Automotive Hall of Fame (1939), P.O. Box 1727, Midland, MI 48641-1727.

Automotive Organization Team (1939), P.O. Box 1742, Midland, MI 48640; 3,000.

Avon Collectors, Inc., Natl. Assn. of (1971), P.O. Box 398, New Lenox, IL 60451; 15,000.

B-24 Liberator Club, Intl. (1968), P.O. Box 841, San Diego, CA 92112; 12,000.

Backpackers' Assn., Intl. (1973), P.O. Box 85, Lincoln Center, ME 04458; 22,861.

Badminton Assn., U.S. (1937), P.O. Box 456, Waterford, MI 48095; 1,500.

Bald-Headed Men of America (1973), P.O. Box 1466, Morehead Pl., Morehead City, N.C. 28557-1466; 12,500.

Ballplayers of Amer., Assn. of Professional (1924), 12062 Valley View St., #211, Garden Grove, CA 92645; 10,000.

Bankers Assn., Amer. (1875), 1120 Connecticut Ave. NW, Wash., DC 20036.

Bankers Assn. of America, Independent (1930), 1625 Massachusetts Ave. NW, Suite 202, Wash. DC 20036; 7,000 banks.

Banks, Natl. Assn. of Mutual Savings (1920), 200 Park Ave., N.Y., NY 10166; 435 banks.

Bar Assn., Amer. (1878), 1155 E. 60th St., Chicago, IL 60637; 300,000.

Bar Assn., Federal (1920), 1815 H St. NW, Wash., DC 20006; 15,000.

Barbershop Quartet Singing in Amer., Soc. for Preservation & Encouragement of (1938), 6315 Third Ave., Kenosha, WI 53140-5199; 38,000.

Baseball Congress, Amer. Amateur (1935), 215 E. Green, Marshall, WI 49068; 7,657 teams.

Baseball Congress, Natl. (1931), 338 S. Sycamore, Wichita, KS 67213.

Baseball Players of America, Assn. of Pro. (1924), 12062 Valley View St., Garden Grove, CA 92645.

Baseball Research, Society for Amer. (1971), P.O. Box 1010, Cooperstown, NY 13326.

Basketball Assn., Natl. (1946), 645 5th Ave., N.Y., NY 10022; 22 teams.

Baton Twirling Assn. of America & Abroad, Intl. (1967), Box 234, Waldwick, NJ 07463; 1,500.

Battleship Assn., Amer. (1963), P.O. Box 11247, San Diego, CA 92111; 1,100.

Beer Can Collectors of America (1970), 747 Merus Ct., Fenton, MO 63026; 5,000.

Bertrand Russell Soc., The (1974), RD 1, Box 409, Coopersburg, PA 18036; 300.

Beta Gamma Sigma (1913), 605 Old Ballas, Suite 220, St. Louis, MO 63141; 200,000.

Beta Sigma Phi (1931), P.O. Box 8500, Kansas City, MO 64114; 250,000.

Bible Society, Amer. (1816), 1865 Broadway, N.Y., NY 10023; 500,000.

Biblical Literature, Society of (1880), 2201 S. University Blvd., Denver, CO 80210; 5,000.

Bibliographical Society of America (1904), P.O. Box 397, Grand Central Sta., N.Y., NY 10163; 1,300.

Bide-A-Wee Home Assn. (1903), 410 E. 38th St., N.Y., NY 10016; 8,600.

Big Brothers/Big Sisters of America (1903), 117 S. 17th St., Suite 1200, Phila., PA 19103; 80,000.

Biological Chemists, Amer. Society of (1906), 9650 Rockville Pike, Bethesda, MD 20814; 6,302.

Biological Sciences, Amer. Institute of (1947), 1401 Wilson Blvd., Arlington, VA 22209; 12,500.

Birding Assn., Amer. (1969), 618 Lavaca, Austin, TX 78701; 8,500.

Blind, Amer. Council of the (1961) 1211 Connecticut Ave. NW, Suite 506, Wash., DC 20036; 20,000.

Blind, Amer. Foundation for the (1921), 15 W. 16th St., N.Y., NY 10011.

Blind, Natl. Federation of the (1940), 1629 K St., NW, Wash., DC 20006; 50,000.

Blind & Visually Handicpd., Natl. Accred. Cncl. for Agencies Serving (1967), 79 Madison Ave., N.Y., NY 10016.

Blindness, Natl. Society to Prevent (1908), 79 Madison Ave., N.Y., NY 10016.

Blindness, Research to Prevent (1960), 598 Madison Ave., N.Y., NY 10022; 3,300.

Blizzard Club, January 12th, 1888, (1940), 1201 Lincoln Mall, #611, Lincoln, NE 68508; 45.

Blue Cross Assn. (1948), 676 St. Clair, Chicago, IL 60611.

Blue Shield Plans, Natl. Assn. of (1946), 676 St. Clair, Chicago, IL 60611; 69 plans.

Blueberry Council, No. Amer. (1965), P.O. Box 166, Marmora, NJ 08223; 35 organizations.

Bluebird Society, No. Amer. (1978), Box 6295, Silver Spring, MD 20906-0295; 5,000.

B'nai B'rith Intl. (1843), 1640 Rhode Island Ave. NW, Wash., DC 20036; 500,000.

Boat Assn., Amer. Power (1903), 17640 E. Nine Mile Rd., E. Detroit, MI 48021; 5,000.

Boat Club, Chris Craft Antique (1974), 217 S. Adams St., Tallahassee, FL 32301; 1,300.

Boat Owners Assn. of the U.S. (1971), 880 S. Pickett St., Alexandria, VA 22304; 115,000.

Bookplate Collectors and Designers, Amer. Soc. of (1922), 605 N. Stoneman Ave. #F, Alhambra, CA 91801; 200.

Booksellers Assn., Amer. (1900), 122 E. 42d St., N.Y., NY 10168; 5,400.

Botanical Gardens & Arboreta, Amer. Assn. of (1971), P.O. Box 206, Swarthmore, PA 19081; 900.

Bottle Clubs, Federation of Historical (1969), 5001 Queen Ave. N., Minneapolis, MN 55430; 120 clubs.

Bowling Congress, Amer. (1895), 5301 S. 76th St., Greendale, WI 53129; 3.7 mln.

Boys' Brigades of America, United (1893), P.O. Box 8406, Baltimore, MD 21234; 150.

Boys' Clubs of America (1906), 771 First Ave., N.Y., NY 10017; 1,000,000+.

Boy Scouts of America (1910), 1325 Walnut Hill Lane, Irving, TX 75038-3096; 4.5 mln.

Brick Institute of America (1934), 1750 Old Meadow Rd., McLean, VA 22102; 100 cos.

Bridge, Tunnel and Turnpike Assn., Intl. (1932), 2120 L St., Suite 305, Wash., DC 20037; 215 agencies.

Brith Sholom (1905), 3939 Conshohocken Ave., Philadelphia, PA 19131; 6,000.

Broadcasters, Natl. Assn. of (1923), 1771 N St. NW, Wash., DC 20036; 4,500.

Burroughs Bibliophiles, The (1960), 454 Elaine Dr., Pittsburgh, PA 15236; 238.

Bus Assn., Amer. (1926), 1025 Connecticut Ave. NW, Wash., DC 20036; 700.

Business Bureaus, Council of Better (1970), 1515 Wilson Blvd., Arlington, VA 22209.

Business Clubs, Natl. Assn. of Amer. (1922), 3315 No. Main St., High Point, NC 27262; 6,562.

Business Communication Assn., Amer. (1935), Univ. of Illinois, English Bldg., 608 S. Wright St., Urbana, IL 61801; 2,400.

Business Communicators, Intl. Assn. of (1970), 870 Market St., Suite 928, San Francisco, CA 94102; 7,000+.

Business Education Assn., Natl. (1946), 1906 Association Dr., Reston, VA 22091; 18,000.

Business Real Estate & Law Assn., Amer. (1923), Dept. of Legal Studies, Univ. of Georgia, Athens, GA 30602; 1,050+.

Business-Professional Advertising Assn. (1922), 205 E. 42d St., N.Y., NY 10017; 4,500.

Button Society, Natl. (1938), 2733 Juno Pl., Akron, OH 44313.

Byron Society, The (1971 England, 1973 in U.S.), 259 New Jersey Ave., Collingswood, NJ 08108; 300.

CARE (Cooperative For American Relief Everywhere) (1945), 660 First Ave., N.Y., NY 10016.

CORE (Congress of Racial Equality) (1942), 1916-38 Park Ave., N.Y., NY 10037.

Campers & Hikers Assn., Natl. (1954), 7172 Transit Rd., Buffalo, NY 14221.

Camp Fire (1910), 4601 Madison Ave., Kansas City, MO 64112; 350,000.

Campers & Hikers Assn., Inc. (1954), 7172 Transit Rd., Buffalo, NY 14221; 30,000.

Camping Assn., Amer. (1910), Bradford Woods, Martinsville, IN 46151; 5,300.

Cancer Council, United (1959), 650 E. Carmel Dr., Suite 340, Carmel, IN 46032; 50 agencies.

Cancer Society, Amer. (1913), 90 Park Ave., N.Y., NY 10017; 257.

Canoe Assn., U.S. (1968), 617 South 94, Milwaukee, WI 53214; 1,500.

Carillonneurs in North America, Guild of (1936), 3718 Settle Rd., Cincinnati, OH 45227; 441.

Carnegie Hero Fund Commission (1904), 606 Oliver Bldg., Pittsburgh, PA 15222.

Cartoonists Society, Natl. (1946), 9 Ebony Ct., Brooklyn, NY 11229; 450.

Cat Fanciers' Assn. (1906), 1309 Allaire Ave., Ocean, NJ 07712; 530.

Catholic Bishops, Natl. Conference of/U.S. Cath. Conference (1966), 1312 Massachusetts Ave. NW, Wash., DC 20005.

Catholic Charities, Natl. Conference of (1910), 1346 Connecticut Ave. NW, Wash., DC 20036; 3,000.

Catholic Church Extension Society of the U.S.A. (1905), 35 E. Wacker Dr., Chicago, IL 60601; 60,000.

Catholic Daughters of the Americas (1903), 10 W. 71st St., N.Y., NY 10023; 165,000.

Catholic Educational Assn., Natl. (1904), 1077-30th St. NW, Suite 100, Wash, DC 20007; 15,000.

Catholic Historical Soc., Amer. (1884), 263 S. Fourth St., Philadelphia, PA 19106; 825.

Catholic Library Assn. (1921), 461 W. Lancaster Ave., Haverford, PA 19041; 1,518.

Catholic Press Assn. of U.S. and Canada (1911), 119 N. Park Ave., Rockville Centre, NY 11570; 575.

Catholic Rural Life Conference, Natl. (1923), 4625 NW Beaver Dr., Des Moines, IA 50310; 3,000.

Catholic War Veterans of the U.S.A. (1935), 2 Massachusetts Ave. NW, Wash., DC 20001; 35,000.

Cemetery Assn., Amer. (1887), 5201 Leesburg Pike, Falls Church, VA 22041; 2,300.

Ceramic Society, Amer. (1899), 65 Ceramic Dr., Columbus, OH 43214; 9,594.

Cerebral Palsy Assns., United (1949), 66 E. 34th St., N.Y., NY 10016.

Chamber of Commerce of the U.S.A. (1912), 1615 H St. NW, Wash., DC 20062; 200,000.

Chamber Music Players, Amateur (1947), 633 E St., NW, Wash., DC 20004.

Chaplain's Assn., Intl. (1962), U.S. Box 4266, Norton Air Force Base, CA 92409; 500.

Chaplain's Assn., Natl. (1900), 717 Hitching Post Dr., Pigeon Forge, TN 37863; 5,452.

Chaplains Assn. of the U.S.A., Military (1930), 6216 Baltimore Ave., P.O. Box 645, Riverdale, MD 20737; 1,575.

Checker Federation, Amer., (1948), 3475 Belmont Ave., Baton Rouge, LA 70808; 1,100.

Chemical Manufacturers Assn. (1872), 2501 M St. NW, Wash., DC 20037; 200 companies.

Chemical Society, Amer. (1876), 1155 16th St. NW, Wash., DC 20036; 125,000.

Chemistry, Amer. Assn. for Clinical (1948), 1725 K St. NW, Wash., DC 20006; 6,247.

Chemists, Amer. Institute of (1923), 7315 Wisconsin Ave., Wash., DC 20814; 4,800.

Chemists, Amer. Soc. of Biological (1906), 9650 Rockville Pike, Bethesda, MD 20814; 5,891.

Chemists and Chemical Engineers, Assn. of Consulting (1928), 50 E. 41st St., N.Y., NY 10017; 125.

Chemists Assn., Manufacturing (1872), 1001 Connecticut Ave. NW, Wash., DC 20036.

Chess Federation, U.S. (1939), 186 Rte. 9W, New Windsor, NY 12550; 53,827.

Chess League of Amer., Correspondence (1897), Box 363, Decatur, IL 62525; 1,500.

Child Welfare League of America (1920), 67 Irving Pl., N.Y., NY 10003; 350 agencies.

Childbirth Without Pain Education Assn. (1959), 20134 Snowden, Detroit, MI 48235; 3,000.

Childhood Education Intl., Assn. for (1896), 11141 Georgia Ave., Suite 200, Wheaton, MD 20902; 10,088.

Children of the Amer. Revolution, Natl. Society (1895), 1776 D St. NW, Wash., DC 20006; 12,000+.

Children's Aid Society (1853), 105 E. 22d St., N.Y., NY 10010; 1,207.

Children's Book Council (1945), 67 Irving Pl., N.Y., NY 10003; 65 publishing houses.

Chiropractic Assn., Amer. (1963), 1916 Wilson Blvd., Arlington, VA 22201; 18,700.

Chiropractors Assn., Intl. (1926), 1901 L St. NW, Wash., DC 20036; 6,000.

Christian Culture Society (1972), P.O. Box 325, Kokomo, IN 46901; 16,009.

Christian Endeavor, Intl. Society of (1881), 1221 E. Broad St., Columbus, OH 43216.

Christian Laity Counseling Board (1970), 5901 Plainfield Dr., Charlotte, NC 28215; 38,000,000.

Christians and Jews, Natl. Conference of (1928), 43 W. 57th St., N.Y., NY 10019.

Church Business Administration, Natl. Assn. of (1956), Suite 324, 7001 Grapevine Hwy., Ft. Worth, TX 76118; 1,050.

Churches, U.S. Conference for the World Council of (1948), 475 Riverside Dr., N.Y., NY 10115; 27 churches.

Church Women United in the U.S.A. (1941), 475 Riverside Dr., N.Y., NY 10027; 2,000.

Cincinnati, Society of the (1783), 2118 Massachusetts Ave. NW, Wash., DC 20008; 3,200.

Circulation Managers Assn., Intl. (1889), 11600 Sunrise Valley Dr., Reston, VA 22091; 1,400.

Circus Fans Assn. of America (1926), 4 Center Dr., Camp Hill, PA 17011; 2,800.

Cities, Natl. League of (1924), 1301 Pennsylvania Ave. NW, Wash., DC 20004; 15,000 cities.

Citizens Band Radio Patrol (1977), 1100 NE 125th St., N. Miami, FL 33161; 35,000.

City Management Assn., Intl. (1914), 1120 G St. NW, Wash., DC 20005; 7,240.

Civil Air Patrol, (1941), Maxwell AFB, AL 36112; 66,000.

Civil Engineers, Amer. Society of (1852), 345 E. 47th St., N.Y., NY 10017; 88,000.

Civil Liberties Union, Amer. (1920), 132 W. 43rd St., N.Y. NY 10036; 200,000.

Civil War Round Table of New York (1951), 820 Carleton Rd., Westfield, NJ 07090; 135.

Civitan Internatl. (1920), 1401 52 St. S., Birmingham, AL 35213; 37,907.

Classical League, Amer. (1947), Miami Univ., Oxford, OH 45056; 3,000.

Clergy, Academy of Parish (1968), 12604 Britton Dr., Cleveland, OH 44120; 450.

Clinical Pastoral Education, Assn. for (1967), 1549 Clairmont Rd., Decatur, GA 30033; 3,900.

Clinical Pathologists, Amer. Society of (1922), 2100 W. Harrison St., Chicago, IL 60612; 34,000.

Coal Association, Natl. (1917), 1130 17th St. NW, Wash., DC 20036; 200+ companies.

Collectors Assn., Amer. (1939), Box 35106, Minneapolis, MN 55435; 2,908.

College Athletic Assn., Natl. Junior (1938), 12 E. Second St., P.O. Box 1586, Hutchinson, KS 67504-1586; 1,000.

College Athletic Conference, Eastern (1938), 1311 Craigville Beach Rd., P.O. Box 3, Centerville, MA 02632; 239 colleges.

College Board, The (1900), 45 Columbus Ave., N.Y., NY 10023; 2,550 institutions.

College Music Society (1958), 1444 Fifteenth St., Boulder, CO 80302; 5,500.

College Physical Education Assn. for Men, Natl. (1897), 108 Cooke Hall, Univ. of Minnesota, Minneapolis, MN 55455.

College Placement Council (1956), 62 E. Highland Ave., Bethlehem, PA 18017; 2,500.

Colleges, Amer. Assn. of Community and Jr. (1920), One Dupont Circle, Wash., DC 20036; 1,280 institutions.

Colleges, Assn. of Amer. (1915), 1818 R St. NW, Wash., DC 20009; 560 institutions.

Colleges and Universities, Assn. of Intl. (1973), l301 S. Noland Rd., Independence, MO 64055; 11,000+.

Collegiate Athletic Assn., Natl. (1906), 6299 Nall, Mission, KS 66202; 983.

Collegiate Schools of Business, Amer. Assembly of (1916), 11500 Olive Blvd., St. Louis, MO 63141; 650 schools.

Colonial Dames of Amer. (1890), 421 E. 61 St., N.Y., NY 10021.

Colonial Dames XVII Century, Natl. Society (1915), 1300 New Hampshire Ave. NW, Wash., DC 20036; 13,500.

Colonial Wars, General Society of (1891), 840 Woodbine Ave., Glendale, OH 45246; 4,160.

Commercial Law League of America (1895), 222 W. Adams St., Chicago, IL 60606; 6,000.

Commercial Travelers of America, Order of United (1888), 632 N. Park St., Columbus, OH 43215; 186,000.

Common Cause (1970), 2030 M St. NW, Wash., DC 20036.

Community Cultural Center Assoc., Amer. (1978), 19 Foothills Dr., Pompton Plains, NJ 07444.

Composers/USA, Natl. Assn. of (1929), P.O. Box 29652, Barrington Sta., Los Angeles, CA 90049; 550.

Composers, Authors & Publishers, Amer. Society of (ASCAP) (1914), One Lincoln Plaza, N.Y., NY 10023; 24,000.

Computing Machinery, Assn. for (1947), 11 W. 42nd St., N.Y., NY 10036; 55,000.

Concrete Institute, Amer. (1904), 22400 W. Seven Mile Rd., Detroit, MI 48219; 18,000.

Conscientious Objection, Central Committee for (1948), 2208 South St., Phila., PA 19146.

Conservation Corps Alumni, Natl. Assn. of Civilian (1977), 7245 Arlington Blvd., Falls Church, VA 22042; 11,420.

Conservation Engineers, Assn. of (1961), Missouri Dept. of Conservation, P.O. Box 180, Jefferson City, MO 65076.

Conservation Foundation (1948), 1717 Massachusetts Ave. NW, Wash., DC 20036.

Constantian Society, The (1970), 123 Orr Rd., Pittsburgh, PA 15241; 500.

Construction Industry Manufacturers Assn. (1909), 111 E. Wisconsin Ave., Milwaukee, WI 53202; 165 companies.

Construction Specifications Institute (1948), 601 Madison St., Alexandria, VA 22314.

Consumer Credit Assn., Intl. (1912), 243 N. Lindbergh, St. Louis, MO 63141; 20,000.

Consumer Federation of America (1968), 1314 14th St. NW, Wash., DC 20005; 200+.

Consumer Interests, Amer. Council on (1953), 240 Stanley Hall, Univ. of Missouri, Columbia, MO 65211; 1,800.

Consumer Protection Institute (1970), 5901 Plainfield Dr., Charlotte, NC 28215.

Consumers League, Natl. (1899), 600 Madison Ave. SW, Suite 202, W. Wing, Wash., DC 20024.

Consumers Union of the U.S. (1936), 256 Washington St., Mount Vernon, NY 10553; 3.4 mln.

Contract Bridge League, Amer. (1927), 2200 Democrat Rd., Memphis, TN 38116; 200,000.

Contract Management Assn., Natl. (1959), 6728 Old McLean Village Dr., McLean, VA 22101; 16,000+.

Contractors of Amer., General (1918), 1957 E St. NW, Wash., DC 20036; 30,000.

Cooperative League of the U.S.A. (1916), 1828 L St. NW, Wash., DC 20036; 176 co-ops.

Correctional Assn., Amer. (1870), 4321 Hartwick Rd., Suite L-208, College Park, MD 20740; 13,500.

Correctional Officers, Amer. Assn. of (1979), Criminal Justice Dept., Northern Michigan Univ., Marquette, MI 49855.

Cosmopolitan Intl. (1914), P.O. Box 4588, Overland Park, KS 66204.

Cotton Council of America, Natl. (1938), 1918 North Parkway, Memphis, TN 38112; 295.

Counseling and Development, Amer. Assn. for (1952), 5999 Stevenson Ave., Alexandria, VA 22304; 43,814.

Counselors and Family Therapists, Natl. Academy of (1972), 225 Jericho Turnpike, Suite 4, Floral Park, NY 11001; 900.

Country Music Assn. (1958), P.O. Box 22299, Nashville, TN 37202; 6,300.

Creative Children and Adults, Natl. Assn. for (1974), 8080 Springvalley Dr., Cincinnati, OH 45236; 1,500.

Credit Management, Nat. Assn. of (1896), 475 Park Ave. So., N.Y., NY 10016; 45,000.

Credit Union Natl. Assn. (1934), P.O.Box 431, Madison, WI 53701; 52 leagues.

Crime and Delinquency, Natl. Council on (1907), 760 Market St., Suite 433, San Francisco, CA 94102; 2,500.

Criminal Investigators Assn., Natl. (1984), P.O. Box 15350, Chevy Chase, MD 20815; 1,400.

Criminology, Amer. Society of (1940), 1314 Kinnear Rd., Columbus, OH 43212; 1,850.

Crop Science Society of America (1955), 677 S. Segoe Rd., Madison, WI 53711; 5,540.

Cross-Examination Debate Assn. (1971), California State Univ.-Northridge, Northridge, CA 91330.

Cryptogram Assn., Amer. (1929) 4 Hawthorne Dr., Cherry Hill, NJ 08003; 1,100.

Customs Brokers & Forwarders Assn. of Amer. (1897), 1 World Trade Center, Suite 1109, N.Y., NY 10048; 450.

Cyprus, Sovereign Order of (1192, 1964 in U.S.), 853 Seventh Ave., N.Y., NY 10019; 464.

Dairy Council, Natl. (1915), 6300 N. River Rd., Rosemont, IL 60018; 600.

Dairy and Food Industries Supply Assn. (1919), 6245 Executive Blvd., Rockville, MD 20852; 594.

Dairylea Cooperative (1919), 831 James St., Syracuse, NY13203; 4,000.

Daughters of the American Revolution, Natl. Society, (1890), 1776 D St. NW, Wash., DC 20006; 214,000.

Daughters of the Confederacy, United (1894), 328 N. Blvd., Richmond, VA 23220; 26,000.

Daughters of 1812, Natl. Society, U.S. (1892), 1461 Rhode Island Ave. NW, Wash., DC 20005; 4,300.

Daughters of Union Veterans of the Civil War (1885), 503 S. Walnut St., Springfield, IL 62704; 6,000.

Deaf, Alexander Graham Bell Assn. for the (1890), 3417 Volta Pl. NW, Wash., DC 20007; 5,466.

Deaf, Natl. Assn. of the (1880), 814 Thayer Ave., Silver Spring, MD 20910; 18,000.

Defense Preparedness Assn., Amer. (1919), 1700 N. Moore St., Arlington, VA 22209; 45,000.

Delta Kappa Gamma Society Intl. (1929), 416 W. 12th St., Austin, TX 78701; 157,000.

Deltiologists of America (1960), 10 Felton Ave., Ridley Park, PA 19078; 750.

Democratic Natl. Committee (1848), 1625 Massachusetts Ave. NW, Wash., DC 20036; 378.

Democratic Socialists of Amer. (1982), 853 Broadway, Suite 801, New York, NY 10003; 6,000.

DeMolay, Intl. Council, Order of (1919), 10200 N. Executive Hills Blvd., Kansas City, MO 64153.

Dental Assn., Amer. (1859), 211 E. Chicago Ave., Chicago, IL 60611; 145,000.

Descendants of the Colonial Clergy, Society of the (1933), 30 Leewood Rd., Wellesley, MA 02181; 1,400.

Descendants of the Signers of the Declaration of Independence (1907), 1300 Locust St., Phila., PA 19107; 937.

Descendants of Washington's Army at Valley Forge, Society of (1976), P.O. Box 915, Valley Forge, PA 19482-0915; 500.

Desert Protective Council (1955), 3648 Mt. Vernon, Riverside CA 92507; 400+.

Diabetes Assn., Amer. (1940), 2 Park Ave., N.Y., NY 10016.

Dialect Society, Amer. (1889), MacMurray College, Jacksonville, IL 62650; 525.

Dietetic Assn., Amer. (1917), 430 N. Michigan Ave., Chicago, IL 60611; 49,419.

Ding-A-Ling Club, Natl. (1971), 3930-D Montclair Rd., Birmingham, AL 35213; 2,055.

Direct Marketing Assn. (1917), 6 E. 43d St., N.Y., NY 10017; 5,149 companies.

Directors Guild of America (1936), 7950 Sunset Blvd., Los Angeles, CA 90046; 7,000.

Disability Examiners, Natl. Assn. of (1964), P.O. Box 44237, Indianapolis, IN 46244; 1,800.

Disabled Amer. Veterans (1921), P.O. Box 14301, Cincinnati, OH 45214; 850,000.

Discount Club, Neighborhood (1985), 11015 Cumpston St., N. Hollywood, CA 91601; 8,500.

Divorce Reform, U.S. (1961), P.O. Box 243, Kenwood, CA 95452; 6,000.

Dowsers, Amer. Society of (1961), P.O. Box 24, Danville, VT 05828; 3,500.

Dozenal Soc. of America (1944), Math Dept., Nassau Community College, Garden City, NY 11530.

Dracula Society, Count (1962), 334 W. 54th St., Los Angeles, CA 90037; 1,000.

Drug, Chemical and Allied Trades Assn. (1890), 42-40 Bell Blvd., Suite 604, Bayside, NY 11361; 500 companies.

Ducks Unlimited (1937), One Waterfowl Way at Gilmer Rd., Long Grove, IL 60014; 565,000.

Dulcimer Assn., Southern Appalachian (1973), 5313 Quincy Ave., Birmingham, AL 35208; 138.

Dutch Settlers Soc. of Albany (1924), Box 163, R.D. 2, Troy, NY 12182; 277.

Earth, Friends of the (1969), 1045 Sansome St., San Francisco, CA 94111; 31,000.

Easter Seal Society, Natl. (1919), 2023 W. Ogden Ave., Chicago, IL 60612.

Eastern Star, Order of the (1876), 1618 New Hampshire Ave. NW, Wash., DC 20009; 2,500,000.

Economic Assn., Amer. (1885), 1313 21st Ave. So., Nashville, TN 37212; 20,422.

Economic Development, Committee for (1942), 1700 K St. NW, Washington, DC 20006.

Edison Electric Institute (1933), 1111 19th St. NW, Wash., DC 20036; 185 companies.

Education, Amer. Assn. for Adult and Continuing (1982), 1201 16th St. NW, Wash., DC 20036; 4,000.

Education, Amer. Council on (1918), One Dupont Circle NW, Wash., DC 20036; 1,605 schools.

Education, Amer. Soc. for Engineering (1893), 11 Dupont Circle NW, Suite 200, Washington, DC 20036; 10,000.

Education, Council for Advancement & Support of (1974), 11 Dupont Circle NW, Wash., DC 20036; 2,500 schools.

Education, Council for Basic (1956), 725 15th St. NW, Wash., DC 20005; 3,500.

Education, Institute of Intl. (1919), 809 United Nations Plaza, N.Y., NY 10017.

Education, Natl. Committee for Citizens in (1973), 410 Wilde Lake Village Green, Columbia, MD 21044; 410.

Education, Natl. Society for the Study of (1902), 5835 Kimbark Ave., Chicago, IL 60637; 4,500.

Education, Society for the Advancement of (1939), 1860 Broadway, N.Y., NY 10023; 3,000.

Education Assn., Natl. (1857), 1201 16th St. NW, Wash., DC 20036; 1,700,000.

Education Society, Comparative and Intl. (1956), Univ. of S. California, Univ. Park, Los Angeles, CA 90089; 2,500.

Education of Young Children, Natl. Assn. for the (1926), 1834 Connecticut Ave. NW, Wash., DC 20009; 40,000.

Educational Exchange, Council on Intl. (1947), 205 E. 42d St., N.Y., NY 10017; 162 organizations.

Educational Research Assn., Amer. (1916), 1230 17th St. NW, Wash., DC 20036; 14,000.

Electrical and Electronics Engineers, Institute of (1884), 345 E. 47th St., N.Y., NY 10017; 234,875.

Electrical Manufacturers Assn., Natl. (1926), 2101 L St. NW, Wash., DC 20037; 560 companies.

Electrochemical Society (1902), 10 S. Main St., Pennington, NJ 08534; 5,000.

Electronic Industries Assn. (1924), 2001 Eye St. NW, Wash., DC 20006; 1,000+ companies.

Electronics, Sales & Service Dealers Assn., Natl. (1963), 2708 W. Berry, Ft. Worth, TX 76109; 1,522.

Electronics Technicians, Intl. Society of Certified (1970), 2708 W. Berry, Ft. Worth, TX 76109; 1,078.

Electroplaters' Society, Amer. (1909), 1201 Louisiana Ave., Winter Park, FL 32789; 8,695.

Elks of the U.S.A., Benevolent and Protective Order of (1868), 2750 N. Lake View Ave., Chicago, IL 60614; 1,630,000.

Emergency Medical Technicians, Natl. Assn. of (1975), P.O. Box 334, Newton Highlands, MA 02161; 10,000.

Energy, Intl. Assn. for Hydrogen (1974), P.O. Box 24866, Coral Gables, FL 33124; 1,500.

Engine and Boat Manufacturers, Natl. Assn. of (1904), 401 N. Michigan Ave., Chicago, IL 60611.

Engineering, Natl. Academy of (1964), 2101 Constitution Ave. NW, Wash., DC 20418; 1,107.

Engineering, Soc. for the Advancement of Material & Process (1944), P.O. Box 2459, Covina, CA 91722.

Engineering Societies, Amer. Assn. of (1979), 345 E. 47th St., N.Y., NY 10017; 38 societies.

Engineering Society of N. America, Illuminating (1907), 345 E. 47th St., N.Y., NY 10017; 8,773.

Engineering Technicians, Amer. Society of Certified (1964), 10401 Holmes Rd., Kansas City, MO 64131; 5,000.

Engineering Trustees, United (1904), 345 E. 47th St., N.Y., NY 10017.

Engineers, Amer. Soc. of Agricultural (1907), 2950 Niles Rd., St. Joseph, MI 49085; 12,000.

Engineers, Amer. Inst. of Chemical (1908), 345 E. 47th St., N.Y., N.Y. 10017; 55,000.

Engineers, Amer. Institute of Mining, Metallurgical and Petroleum (1871), 345 E. 47th St., N.Y., NY 10017.

Engineers, Amer. Society of Lubrication (1944), 838 Busse Hwy., Park Ridge, IL 60068; 3,200.

Engineers, Amer. Soc. of Plumbing (1964), 15233 Ventura Blvd., #811, Sherman Oaks, CA 91403; 4,500.

Engineers, Amer. Soc. of Safety (1911), 850 Busse Hwy., Park Ridge, IL 60068; 20,000.

Engineers, Assn. of Energy (1977), 4025 Pleasantdale Rd., Suite 340, Atlanta, GA 30340; 5,400.

Engineers, Inst. of Industrial (1948), 25 Technology Park, Atlanta, GA 30092; 43,000.

Engineers, Inst. of Transportation (1930), Suite 410, 525 School St. NW, Wash., DC 20024.

Engineers, Natl. Society of Professional (1934), 1420 King St., Alexandria, VA 22314; 75,000.

Engineers, Soc. of Fire Protection (1950), 60 Batterymarch St., Boston, MA 02110; 3,251.

Engineers, Soc. of Logistics (1966), 303 Williams Ave., Suite 922, Huntsville, AL 35801; 8,500.

Engineers, Soc. of Manufacturing (1932), P.O. Box 930, Dearborn, MI 48121; 72,000.

Engineers, Society of Plastics (1942), 14 Fairfield Dr., Brookfield Ctr., CT 06805; 25,500.

English Assn., College (1939), English Dept., Nazareth College, 4245 East Ave., Rochester, NY 14610; 1,600.

English-Speaking Union of the U.S. (1921), 16 E. 69th St., N.Y., NY 10021; 30,000.

Entomological Society of America (1889), 4603 Calvert Rd., College Park, MD 20740; 8,500.

Epigraphic Society, Inc., The (1974), 6625 Bamburgh Dr., San Diego, CA 92117; 1,050.

Esperanto League for North America (1952), P.O. Box 1129, El Cerrito, CA 94530; 700.

Exchange Club, Natl. (1911), 3050 Central Ave., Toledo, OH 43606; 46,000.

Experiment in Internatl. Living (1932), Kipling Rd., Brattleboro, VT 05301; 64,000.

Fairs & Expositions, Intl. Assn. of (1919), P.O. Box 985, Springfield, MO 65801; 1,500.

Family Life, Natl. Alliance for, Inc. (1973), Ste. 4, 225 Jericho Tpk., Floral Park, NY 11001; 499.

Family Relations, Natl. Council on (1980), 1910 W. Country Rd. B, Suite 147, St. Paul, MN 55113.

Family Service Assn. of America (1911), 44 E. 23d St., N.Y., NY 10010; 280 agencies.

Farm Bureau Federation, Amer. (1919), 225 Touhy Ave., Park Ridge, IL 60068; 3.3 mln.

Farmer Cooperatives, Natl. Council of (1929), 1800 Massachusetts Ave. NW, Wash., DC 20036; 121 co-ops.

Farmers of America, Future (1928), 5632 Mt. Vernon Memorial Hwy., Alexandria, VA 22309; 460,000.

Farmers Educational and Co-Operative Union of America (1902), 12025 E. 45th Ave., Denver, CO 80251; 300,000.

Fat Americans, Natl. Assn. to Aid (NAAFA) (1969), P.O. Box 43, Bellerose, NY 11426; 1,500.

Federal Employees, Natl. Federation of (1917), 1016 16th St. NW, Wash., DC 20036; 150,000.

Federal Employees Veterans Assn. (1953), P.O. Box 183, Merion Sta., PA 19066; 896.

Feminists for Life of America (1972), 811 E. 47th St., Kansas City, MO 64110; 1,000.

Fencers League of America, Amateur (1893), 601 Curtis St., Albany, CA 94706; 8,000.

Film Library Assn., Educational (1943), 45 John St., N.Y., NY 10038; 1,563.

Financial Analysts Federation (1945), 1633 Broadway, N.Y., NY 10019; 15,137.

Financial Executives Institute (1931), 10 Madison Ave., P.O. Box 1938, Morristown, NJ 07960, 12,700

Financiers, Intl. Soc. of (1979), 399 Laurel St., Suite 6, San Carlos, CA 94070; 250+.

Fire Chiefs, Intl. Assn. of (1873), 1329 18th St. NW, Wash., DC 20036; 8,947.

Fire Marshals Assn. of No. America (1906), Capital Gallery, Suite #1220, 1110 Vermont Ave., NW, Wash., DC 20005.

Fire Protection Assn., Natl. (1896), Batterymarch Park, Quincy MA 02269; 32,500.

Fish Assn., Intl. Game (1939), 3000 E. Las Olas Blvd., Ft. Lauderdale, FL 33316; 25,000.

Fishes, Soc. for the Protection of Old (1967), School of Fisheries, Univ. of Washington, Seattle, WA 98195; 250.

Fishing Institute, Sport (1949), 1010 Massachusetts Ave. NW, Wash., DC 20005; 110 companies.

Fishing Tackle Manufacturers Assn., Amer. (1933), 2625 Clearbrook Dr., Arlington Heights, IL 60005; 450 organizations.

Florida Dental Hygienists' Assn., Inc. (1925), 217 S. Adams St., Tallahassee, FL 32301; 1,567.

Fluid Power Society (1959), 3333 N. Mayfair Rd., Milwaukee, WI 53222; 2,500.

Food Processing Machinery and Supplies Assn. (1885), 1828 L St. NW, Wash., DC 20036; 475 organizations.

Food Processors Assn., Natl. (1907), 1133 20th St. NW, Wash., DC 20036.

Food Society, Living (1983), 5227 Corteen Pl., N. Hollywood, CA 91607; 1,200.

Football Assn., U.S. Touch and Flag (1976), 2705 Normandy Dr., Youngstown, OH 44511; 20,000.

Footwear Industries Assn., Amer. (1869), 1611 N. Kent St., Arlington, VA 22209; 260.

Foreign Policy Assn. (1918), 205 Lexington Ave., N.Y., NY 10016.

Foreign Relations, Council on (1921), 58 E. 68th St., N.Y., NY 10021; 2,031.

Foreign Student Affairs, Natl. Assn. for (1948), 1860 19th St. NW, Wash., DC 20009; 5,200.

Foreign Study, Amer. Institute for (1964), 102 Greenwich Ave., Greenwich, CT 06830; 300,000.

Foreign Trade Council, Inc., Natl. (1914), 100 E. 42d St., N.Y., NY 10017; 550+ companies.

Forensic Sciences, Amer. Academy of (1948), 225 S. Academy Blvd., Colorado Springs, CO 80910; 2,500.

Forest Institute, Amer. (1932), 1619 Massachusetts Ave. NW, Wash., DC 20036; 60 companies.

Forest Products Assn., Natl. (1902), 1619 Massachusetts Ave. NW, Wash., DC 20036; 2,500 companies.

Forest Products Research Society (1947), 2801 Marshall Ct., Madison, WI 53705; 3,285.

Foresters, Society of Amer. (1900), 5400 Grosvenor La., Bethesda, MD 20814; 21,000

Forestry Assn., Amer. (1875), 1319 18th St. NW, Wash., DC 20036; 55,000.

Fortean Organization, Intl. (1966), P.O. Box 367, Arlington, VA 22210; 700.

Foundrymen's Society, Amer. (1896), Golf & Wolf Rds., Des Plaines, IL 60016; 14,200.

4-H Clubs (1901-1905), Extension Service, U.S. Dept of Agriculture, Wash., DC 20250; 5,800,000.

Franklin D. Roosevelt Philatelic Society (1963), 154 Laguna Ct., St. Augustine Shores, FL 32086; 432.

Freedom, Young Americans for (1960), Box 1002, Woodland Rd. Sterling, VA 22170; 80,000.

Freedoms Foundation at Valley Forge (1949), Valley Forge, PA 19481; 9,000.

Friedreich's Ataxia Group in America (1969), P.O. Box 11116, Oakland, CA 94611; 2,100.

French Institute (1911), 22 E. 60th St., N.Y., NY 10022.

French-Amer. Chamber of Commerce in the U.S. (1896), 1350 Ave. of the Americas, N.Y, NY 10019; 2,491.

Friends Service Committee, Amer. (1917), 1501 Cherry St., Phila., PA 19102.

Frisbee Assn., Intl. (1967), 900 E. El Monte, San Gabriel, CA 91776; 110,000.

Funeral and Memorial Societies, Continental Assn. of (1963), 2001 S. St. NW, Suite 530, Washington, DC 20009.

GASP (Group Against Smokers' Pollution) (1971), P.O. Box 632, College Park, MD 20740; 200 chapters.

Gamblers Anonymous (1957), 1543 W. Olympic, Suite 533, Los Angeles, CA 90015; 10,600.

Game Collectors Assn., American (1985), P.O. Box 1179, Great Neck, N.Y. 11023; 75.

Garden Club of Amer. (1913), 598 Madison Ave., N.Y., NY 10022.

Garden Clubs, Natl. Council of State (1929), 4401 Magnolia Ave., St. Louis, MO 63110; 310,047.

Garden Clubs of America, Men's (1932), 5560 Merle Hay Rd., Johnston, IA 50323; 9,000.

Gas Appliance Manufacturers Assn. (1935), 1901 N. Ft. Myer Dr., Arlington, VA 22209; 240 companies.

Gas Assn., Amer. (1918), 1515 Wilson Blvd., Arlington, VA 22209; 300 cos.

Gay Academic Union (1973), P.O. Box 82123, San Diego, CA 92138; 1,100.

Gay Task Force, Natl. (1973), 80 Fifth Ave., Suite 1601, N.Y., NY 10011; 10,000.

Genealogical Society, Natl. (1903), 4527 17th St. N., Arlington, VA 22207-2363; 7,000.

Genetic Assn., Amer. (1903), 818 18th St. NW, Wash., DC 20006; 1,600.

Geographers, Assn. of Amer. (1904), 1710 16th St. NW, Wash., DC 20009; 5,500.

Geographic Education, Natl. Council for (1915), Western Illinois Univ., Macomb, IL 61455; 3,500.

Geographic Society, Natl. (1888), Washington, DC 20036.

Geographical Society, Amer. (1851), 156 Fifth Ave., Suite 600, N.Y., NY 10010; 700.

Geolinguistics, Amer. Society of (1964), Bronx Community College, 120 E. 181st St., Bronx, NY 10453; 100.

Geological Institute, Amer. (1948), 4220 King St., Alexandria, VA 22302; 17 societies.

Geological Society of America (1888), 3300 Penrose Pl., P.O. Box 9140, Boulder, CO 80301; 13,386.

Geologists, Assn. of Engineering (1963), P.O. Box 1068, Brentwood, TN 37027; 3,000.

Geologists, Amer. Assn. of Petroleum (1917), 1444 S. Boulder, Tulsa, OK 74119; 43,933.

Geophysicists, Society of Exploration (1930), P.O. Box 3098, Tulsa, OK 74101; 18,000.

George S. Patton, Jr. Historical Society (1970), 11307 Vela Dr., San Diego, CA 92126.

Geriatrics Society, Amer. (1942), 10 Columbus Circle, N.Y., NY 10019; 5,000.

Gideons Intl. (1899), 2900 Lebanon Rd., Nashville, TN 37214; 86,195.

Gifted Children, Amer. Assn. for (1946), 15 Gramercy Park, N.Y., NY 10016.

Gifted Children, Natl. Assn. for (1954), 5100 N. Edgewood Dr., St. Paul, MN 55112; 5,000.

Girls Clubs of America (1945), 205 Lexington Ave., N.Y., NY 10016; 240 centers.

Girl Scouts of the U.S.A. (1912), 830 Third Ave., N.Y., NY 10022; 2,888,000.

Gladiolus Council, No. Amer. (1945), 9338 Manzanita Dr., Sun City, AZ 85373; 1,350.

Goat Assn., American Dairy (1904), 209 W. Main St., Spindale, NC 28160; 18,500.

Gold Star Mothers, Amer. (1928), 2128 Leroy Pl. NW, Wash., DC 20008; 5,793.

Golf Association, U.S. (1894), Golf House, Far Hills, NJ 07931; 5,400 clubs.

Goose Island Bird & Girl Watching Society (1960), 301 Arthur Ave., Park Ridge, IL 60068; 947.

Gospel Music Assn. (1964), 38 Music Square W., Nashville, TN 37203; 3,000.

Government Finance Officers Assn. (1906), 180 N. Michigan Ave., Suite 800, Chicago, IL 60601; 9,207.

Government Funding of Social Services, Greater Wash. Organizations for (1981), 6612 Virginia View Ct. NW, Wash., DC 20816; 23 organizations.

Governmental Research Assn. (1914), One Federal St., Boston, MA 02110; 275.

Graduate Schools in the U.S., Council of (1961), One Dupont Circle NW, Wash., DC 20036; 365 institutions.

Grandmother Clubs of America, Natl. Federation of (1938), 203 N. Wabash Ave., Chicago, IL 60601; 14,000.

Grange, Natl. (1867), 1616 H St. NW, Wash., DC 20006.

Graphic Artists, Society of Amer. (1915), 32 Union Sq., 1214, N.Y., NY 10003; 250.

Graphic Arts, Amer. Institute of (1914), 1059 Third Ave., N.Y., NY 10021; 2,200.

Gray Panthers (1970), 3700 Chestnut, Phila., PA 19103; 70,000.

Greek-Amer. War Veterans in America, Natl. Legion of (1938), 739 W. 186th St., N.Y., NY 10033; 11.

Green Mountain Club, The (1910), 43 State St., Box 889, Montpelier, VT 05602; 4,200.

Grocers, Natl. Assn. of (1893), 1825 Samuel Morse Dr., Reston, VA 22090.

Grocery Manufacturers of America (1908), 1010 Wisconsin Ave., Wash., DC 20007; 130 companies.

Guide Dog Foundation for the Blind (1946), 371 Jericho Tpke., Smithtown, NY 11787; 2,500.

Gyro Intl. (1912), 1096 Mentor Ave., Painesville, OH 44077.

HIAS (Hebrew Immigrant Aid Society) (1880), 200 Park Ave. S, N.Y., NY 10003; 12,000.

Hadassah, the Women's Zionist Organization of America (1912), 50 W. 58th St., N.Y., NY 10019; 370,000.

Hairdressers and Cosmetologists Assn., Natl. (1921), 3510 Olive St., St. Louis, MO 63103; 50,406.

Handball Assn., U.S. (1951), 930 N. Benton Ave., Tucson, AZ 85711.

Handgun, Intl. Metallic Silhouette Assn. (1976), Box 1609, 1409 Benton, Idaho Falls, ID 83401.

Handicapped, Federation of the (1935), 211 W. 14th St., N.Y., NY 10011; 650.

Handicapped, Natl. Assn. of the Physically (1958), 76 Elm St., London, OH 43140; 650.

Hang Gliding Assn., U.S. (1971), P.O. Box 66306, Los Angeles, CA 90066.

Health Council, Natl. (1920), 70 W. 40th St., N.Y., NY 10018.

Health Insurance Assn. of America (1956), 1850 K St. NW, Wash., DC 20006; 335 companies.

Health Insurance Institute (1956), 1850 K St. NW, Wash., DC; 325 companies.

Health, Physical Education, Recreation and Dance, Amer. Alliance for (1885), 1900 Association Dr., Reston, VA 22091.

Hearing Aid Society, Natl. (1951), 20361 Middlebelt Rd., Livonia, MI 48152; 3,600.

Hearing and Speech Action, Natl. Assn. for (1919), 10801 Rockville Pike, Rockville, MD 20852.

Heart Assn., Amer. (1924), 7320 Greenville Ave., Dallas TX 75231; 144,000.

Hearts, Mended (1955), 7320 Greenville Ave., Dallas TX 75231; 16,000.

Heating, Refrigerating & Air Conditioning Engineers, Amer. Soc. of (1894), 1791 Tullie Circle NE, Atlanta, GA 30329.

Helicopter Assn. Intl. (1948), 1110 Vermont Ave. NW, Wash., DC 20005; 840 companies.

Helicopter Society, Amer. (1943), 217 N. Washington St., Alexandria VA 22314; 6,600.

Hemispheric Affairs, Council on (1975), 1612 20th St. NW, Wash., DC 20009; 250.

High School Assns., Natl. Federation of State (1920), 11724 Plaza Circle, Kansas City, MO 64195; 51.

High Twelve Internatl. (1921), 3663 Lindell Blvd., Suite 260, St. Louis, MO 63108; 29,450.

Historians, Organization of Amer. (1907), 112 N. Bryan St., Bloomington, IN 47401; 12,000.

Historical Assn., Amer. (1884), 400 A St. SE, Wash., DC 20003; 15,500.

Historic Preservation, Natl. Trust for (1949), 1785 Massachusetts Ave. NW, Wash., DC 20036; 140,000.

Hockey Assn. of the U.S., Amateur (1937), 2997 Broadmoor Valley Rd., Colorado Springs, CO 80906; 200,000.

Holy Cross of Jerusalem, Order of (1965), 853 Seventh Ave., N.Y., NY 10019; 2,019.

Home Builders, Natl. Assn. of (1942), 15th & M Sts. NW, Wash., DC 20005; 104,000+ firms.

Home Economics Assn., Amer. (1909), 2010 Massachusetts Ave. NW, Wash., DC 20020; 30,000.

Homemakers of America, Future (1945), 1910 Association Dr., Reston, VA 22091.

Homemakers Council, Natl. Extension (1936), Route 2, Box 3070, Vale, OR 97918; 500,000.

Horatio Alger Soc. (1961), 4907 Allison Dr., Lansing, MI 48910.

Horse Protection Assn., Amer. (1966), 1902 T St. NW, Wash., DC 20009; 15,000.

Horse Show Assn. of America Ltd., Natl. (1883), One Penn Plaza, Rm. 4501, N.Y., NY 10001.

Horse Shows Assn., Amer. (1917), 598 Madison Ave., N.Y., NY 10022; 25,000.

Hospital Association, Amer. (1899), 840 N. Lake Shore Dr., Chicago, IL 60611; 40,000.

Hospital Public Relations, Amer. Society for (1965), 840 N. Lake Shore Dr., Chicago, IL 60611; 2,000.

Hotel & Motel Assn., Amer. (1910), 888 Seventh Ave., N.Y., NY 10019; 8,200 hotels & motels.

Hot Rod Assn., Natl. (1951), 10639 Riverside Dr., N. Hollywood, CA 91602; 40,000.

Humane Society of the U.S. (1954), 2100 L St. NW, Wash., DC 20037; 200,000.

Humanics Foundation, Amer. (1948), 4601 Madison Ave., Kansas City, MO 64112; 2,000.

Humanities, Natl. Endowment for the (1965), 806 15th St. NW, Wash., DC 20506.

Human Rights and Social Justice, Americans for (1977), P.O. Box 6258, Ft. Worth, TX 76115; 3,400.

Hydrogen Energy, Intl. Assn. for (1974), 219 McArthur Hall, P.O. Box 248266, Coral Gables, FL 33124; 2,500.

Iceland Veterans (1950), 2101 Walnut St., Phila., PA 19103.

Idaho, U.S.S.(BB-42) Assn. (1957), P.O. Box 11247, San Diego, CA 92111; 1,000.

Identification, Intl. Assn. for (1915), P.O. Box 90259, Columbia, SC 29290; 2,500.

Illustrators, Society of (1901), 128 E. 63 St., N.Y., NY 10021; 920.

Indian Rights Assn. (1882), 1505 Race St., Phila., PA 19102.

Industrial Democracy, League for (1905), 275 Seventh Ave., N.Y., NY 10001; 1,500.

Industrial Engineers, Amer. Institute of (1948), 25 Technology Park, Norcross, GA 30092; 35,000.

Industrial Health Foundation (1935), 34 Penn Circle West, Pittsburgh, PA 15206; 170 companies.

Industrial Security, Amer. Soc. for (1955), 1655 N. Ft. Myer Dr., Suite 1200, Arlington, VA 22209; 20,000.

Information, Freedom of, Center (1958), P.O. Box 858, Columbia, MO 65205.

Information and Image Management, Assn. for (1942), 1100 Wayne Ave., Silver Spring, MD 20910; 8,000.

Information Industry Assn. (1968), 316 Pennsylvania Ave. SE, Suite 502, Wash., DC 20003; 350 companies.

Information Managers, Associated (1978), 1776 E. Jefferson St., Rockville, MD 20852; 1,000.

Insurance Assn., Amer. (1964), 85 John St., N.Y., NY 10038; 174 companies.

Insurance Seminars, Intl. (1964), P.O. Box J, University, AL 35486; 5,000.

Intelligence Officers, Assn. of Former (1975), 6723 Whittier Ave., Suite 303A, McLean, VA 22101; 3,500.

Intercollegiate Athletics, Natl. Assn. of (1940), 1221 Baltimore Ave., Kansas City, MO 64105; 517 schools.

Interior Designers, Amer. Society of (1975), 1430 Broadway, N.Y., NY 10018; 23,000.

Inventors, Amer. Assn. of (1975), 6562 E. Curtis Rd., Bridgeport, MI 48722; 3,961.

Investors, Natl. Assn. of (1951), 1515 E. Eleven Mile Rd., Royal Oak, MI 48067; 110,000.

Investment Clubs, Natl. Assn. of (1951), 1515 E. Eleven Mile Rd., Royal Oak, MI 48067; 65,000.

Irish-American Cultural Inst. (1962), 683 Osceola Ave., St. Paul, MN 55105; 79,700.

Iron Castings Society (1897), 455 State St., Des Plaines, IL 60016; 151 firms.

Iron and Steel Engineers, Assn. of (1907), Three Gateway Center, Suite 2350, Pittsburgh, PA 15222; 11,856.

Iron and Steel Institute, Amer. (1908), 1000 16th St. NW, Wash., DC 20036; 1,313.

Italian Historical Society of America (1949), 111 Columbia Heights, Bklyn., NY 11201; 2,477.

Italy-America Chamber of Commerce (1887), 350 Fifth Ave., N.Y., NY 10118; 650.

Izaak Walton League of America, The (1922), 1701 Ft. Myer Dr., Arlington, VA 22209; 50,000.

JAPOS Study Group (1974), 154 Laguna Ct., St. Augustine Shores, FL 32084; 276.

Jamestowne Society (1936), P.O. Box 14523, Richmond, VA 23221; 2,430.

Jane Austen Society of N. Amer. (1979), P.O. Box 252, Wayne, PA 19087; 1,750.

Japanese Amer. Citizens League (1929), 1765 Sutter St., San Francisco, CA 94115; 30,000.

Jaycees, U.S. (1920), 4 W. 21st St., Tulsa, OK 74104.

Jewish Appeal, United (1939), 1290 Ave. of the Americas, N.Y., NY 10019.

Jewish Center Workers, Assn. of (1918), 15 E. 26th St., N.Y., NY 10010.

Jewish Committee, Amer. (1906), 165 E. 56th St., N.Y., NY 10022; 40,000.

Jewish Congress, Amer. (1918), 15 E. 84th St., N.Y., NY 10028; 50,000.

Jewish Federations, Council of (1932), 575 Lexington Ave., N.Y., NY 10022; 200 agencies.

Jewish Historical Society, Amer. (1892), 2 Thornton Rd., Waltham, MA 02154; 3,750.

Jewish War Veterans of the U.S.A. (1896), 1811 R St. NW, Wash., DC 20009; 100,000.

Jewish Welfare Bd. Natl. (1917), 15 E. 26th St., N.Y., NY 10010.

Jewish Women, Natl. Council of (1893), 15 E. 26th St., N.Y., NY 10010; 100,000.

Job's Daughters, Internatl. Order of (1921), 119 S. 19th St., Rm. 402, Omaha, NE 68102; 60,000.

Jockey Club (1894), 380 Madison Ave., N.Y., NY 10017; 90.

Jogging Assn., Natl. (1968), 2420 K St. NW, Wash., DC 20037; 35,000.

John Birch Society (1958), 395 Concord Ave., Belmont, MA 02178; 50,000.

Joseph Diseases Foundation, Intl. (1977), P.O. Box 2550, Livermore, CA 94550; 3,800.

Journalists, Society of Professional (Sigma Delta Chi) (1909), 840 N. Lake Shore Dr., Suite 801, Chicago, IL 60611.

Journalists and Authors, Amer. Society of (1948), 1501 Broadway, Suite 1907, N.Y., NY 10036; 715.

Judaism, Amer. Council for (1943), 298 Fifth Ave., N.Y., NY 10001; 20,000.

Judicature Society, Amer. (1913), 25 E. Washington, Chicago, IL 60602; 30,000.

Juggler's Assn., Intl. (1947), 203 Crosby Ave., Kenmore, NY 12417; 3,000.

Junior Achievement (1919), 550 Summer St., Stamford, CT 06901; 300,000.

Junior Auxiliaries, Natl. Assn. of (1941), 255 S. Poplar, P.O. Box 1873, Greenville, MS 38701; 7,294.

Junior Colleges, Amer. Assn. of Community and (1920), One Dupont Circle NW, Wash., DC 20036; 900.

Junior Leagues, Assn. of (1921), 825 Third Ave., N.Y., NY 10022; 140,000+.

Kennel Club, Amer. (1884), 51 Madison Ave., N.Y., NY 10010; 438 clubs.

Kiwanis Intl. (1915), 3636 Woodview, Indianapolis, IN 46268.

Knights of Columbus (1882), One Columbus Plaza, New Haven, CT 06507; 1.4 mln.

Knights Templar U.S.A., Grand Encampment (1816), 14 E. Jackson Blvd., Suite 1700, Chicago, IL 60604; 340,000.

Krishna Consciousness, Intl. Soc. for (1966), 3764 Watseka Ave., Los Angeles, CA 90034; 2,000,000.

Labor, Amer. Federation of and Congress of Industrial Organizations (1955), 815 16th St. NW, Wash., DC 20006.

La Leche League Intl. (1956), 9616 Minneapolis, Franklin Park, IL 60131; 50,000.

Lambs, The (1874), 3 W. 51st St., N.Y., NY 10019; 400.

Landscape Architects, Amer. Society of (1899), 1733 Connecticut Ave., NW, Wash., DC 20009; 7,000.

Law, Amer. Society of Intl. (1906), 2223 Massachusetts Ave. NW, Wash., DC 20008; 4,000.

Law Enforcement Officers Assn., Amer. (1966), 1000 Connecticut Ave. NW, Suite 9, Wash., DC 20036; 50,000.

Law Libraries, Amer. Assn. of (1904), 53 W. Jackson Blvd., Chicago, IL 60604; 3,600.

Law and Social Policy, Center for (1969), 1751 N St. NW, Wash., DC 20036.

Learned Societies, Amer. Council of (1919), 228 E. 45th St., N.Y., NY 10017; 44 societies.

Lefthanders, League of (1975), P.O. Box 89, New Milford, NJ 07646; 500.

Lefthanders Intl. (1975), 3601 SW 29th St., Topeka, KS 66614; 8,000.

Legal Administrators, Assn. of (1971), 1800 Pickwick Ave., Glenview, IL 60025; 3,000.

Legion of Valor of the U.S.A. (1890), 548 Bellemeade, Gretna, LA 70053; 750.

Leif Ericson Society (1962), Box 301, Chicago, IL 60690-0301; 1,200.

Leprosy Missions, Amer. (1906), One Broadway, Elmwood Park, NJ 07407.

Lesbian & Gay Academic Union (1979), P.O. Box 82123, San Diego, CA 92138; 3,500.

Leukemia Society of America (1949), 733 Third Ave., N.Y., NY 10017.

Lewis Carroll Society of N. America (1974), 617 Rockford Rd., Silver Spring, MD 20902; 300.

Liberty Lobby (1955), 300 Independence Ave. SE, Wash., DC 20003; 33,000.

Libraries Assn., Special (1909), 235 Park Ave. So., N.Y., NY 10003; 11,750.

Library Assn., Amer. (1876), 50 E. Huron St., Chicago, IL 60611; 40,000.

Library Assn., Medical (1898), 919 N. Michigan Ave., Chicago, IL 60611; 5,100.

Library and Information Assns., Council of Natl. (1942), 461 W. Lancaster Ave., Haverford, PA 19041; 21.

Life, Americans United for (1971), 343 S. Dearborn, Chicago, IL 60604.

Life Insurance, Amer. Council of (1976), 1850 K St. NW, Wash., DC 20006; 570 firms.

Life Office Management Assn. (1924), 100 Colony Sq., Atlanta, GA 30361; 700+companies.

Life Underwriters, Amer. Soc. of Certified (1929), 270 Bryn Mawr Ave., Byrn Mawr, PA 19010; 28,000.

Life Underwriters, Natl. Assn. of (1890), 1922 F St. NW, Wash., DC 20006; 120,000.

Lighter-Than-Air Society (1952), 1800 Triplett Blvd., Akron, OH 44306; 1,200.

Lions Clubs, Intl. Assn. of (1917), 300 22d St., Oak Brook, IL 60570; 1,332,000.

Literacy Volunteers of America (1962), 404 Oak St., Syracuse, NY 13203.

Little League Baseball (1939), P.O. Box 3485, Williamsport, PA 17701; 15,640 leagues.

Little People of America (1957), Box 633, San Bruno, CA 94066; 4,000.

London Club (1975), P.O. Box 4527, Topeka, KS 66604.

Lung Assn., Amer. (1904), 1740 Broadway, N.Y., NY 10019.

Lutheran Education Assn. (1942), 7400 Augusta St., River Forest, IL 60305; 3,750.

Magazine Publishers Assn. (1919), 575 Lexington Ave., N.Y., NY 10022; 200 publishers.

Magicians, Intl. Brotherhood of (1926), 28 N. Main St., Kenton, OH 43326; 10,500.

Magicians, Society of Amer. (1902), 325 Maple St., Lynn, MA 01904; 5,100.

Male Nurse Assn., Natl. (1971), Rush Univ., 1725 W. Harrison St., Chicago, IL 60612; 1,400.

Man Watchers, Inc. (1974), 8033 Sunset, L.A., CA 90046.

Management Assn., Amer. (1923), 135 W. 50th St., N.Y., NY 10020; 80,000.

Management Consultants, Institute of (1968), 19 W. 44th St., N.Y., NY 10036; 1,500.

Management Consulting Firms, Assn. of (1929), 230 Park Ave., N.Y., NY 10169; 57 firms.

Manufacturers, Natl. Assn. of (1897), 1776 F St. NW, Wash., DC 20006; 13,000 companies.

Manufacturers' Agents Natl. Assn. (1947), P.O. Box 3467, Laguna Hills, CA 92654; 8,500.

March of Dimes Birth Defects Foundation (1938), 1275 Mamaroneck Ave., White Plains, NY 10605.

Marijuana Laws, Natl. Organization for the Reform of (NORML) (1970), 2001 S St., #640, Wash., DC 20009; 8,000.

Marine Corps League (1937), 956 N. Monroe St., Arlington, VA 22201; 30,000.

Marine Manufacturers Assn., Natl. (1904), 401 N. Michigan Ave., Chicago, IL 60611; 760 companies.

Marine Surveyors, Natl. Assn. of (1960), 86 Windsor Gate Dr., N. Hills, NY 11040; 404.

Marine Technology Society (1963), 2000 Florida Ave. NW, #500, Wash., DC 20009; 3,000.

Marketing Assn., Amer. (1937), 250 S. Wacker Dr., Chicago, IL 60606; 40,105.

Masonic Relief Assn. of U.S. and Canada (1885), 32613 Seidel Dr., Burlington, WS 53105; 14,700.

Masonic Service Assn. of the U.S. (1919), 8120 Fenton St., Silver Spring, MD 20910; 43 Grand Lodges.

Masons, Ancient and Accepted Scottish Rite, Southern Jurisdiction, Supreme Council (1801), 1733 16th St. NW, Wash., DC 20009; 641,785.

Masons, Supreme Council 33°, Ancient and Accepted Scottish Rite, Northern Masonic Jurisdiction (1813), 33 Marrett Rd., Lexington, MA 02173; 475,885.

Masons, Royal Arch, General Grand Chapter (1797), 1084 New Circle Rd. NE, Lexington, KY 40505; 336,280.

Mathematical Assn. of America (1915), 1225 Connecticut Ave. NW, Wash., DC 20036; 18,500.

Mathematical Society, Amer. (1888), P.O. Box 6248, Providence, RI 02940; 21,500.

Mathematical Statistics, Institute of (1935), 3401 Investment Blvd., 6, Hayward, CA 94545; 3,000.

Mathematics, Society for Industrial and Applied (1952), 117 S. 17th St., Phila., PA 19103-5052; 5,500.

Mayflower Descendants, General Society of (1897), 4 Winslow St., Plymouth, MA 02361; 21,000.

Mayors, U.S. Conference of (1932), 1620 Eye St. NW, Wash., DC 20006; 840 cities.

Mechanical Engineers, Amer. Society of (1880), 345 E. 47th St., N.Y., NY 10017; 114,922.

Mechanics, Amer. Academy of (1969), Dept. of Civil Engineering, Northwestern Univ., Evanston, IL 60201; 1,200.

Mechanics, State Council of VA Jr. Order of Amer. (1853), 170 Railway Rd., Grafton, VA; 1,200.

Medical Assn., Amer. (1847), 535 N. Dearborn St., Chicago, IL 60610.

Medical Assn., Natl. (1895), 1012 Tenth St. NW, Wash., DC 20001; 13,500+.

Medical Record Assn., Amer. (1928), 875 N. Michigan Ave., Chicago, IL 60611; 25,000.

Medical Technicians, Natl. Assn. of Emergency (1975), 621 Main St., Waltham, MA 02154; 12,000.

Medieval Academy of America (1925), 1430 Massachusetts Ave., Cambridge, MA 02138; 5,400.

Medical Technologists, Amer. College of (1942), 5608 Lane, Raytown, MO 64133; 368.

Mega Society, The (1982), 439 W. 50th St., N.Y., NY 10019.

Mensa, Amer. (1960), 1701 W. 3d St., Brooklyn, NY 11223.

Mental Health Assn., Natl. (1909), 1021 Prince St., Alexandria, VA 22314; 1 mln.

Mental Health Program Directors, Natl. Assn. of State (1963), 1001 3d St. SW, Wash., DC 20024; 54.

Merchant Marine Library Assn., Amer. (1921), One World Trade Center, Suite 2601, N.Y., NY 10048; 1,100.

Merchant Marine Veterans, Amer. (1984), 905 Cape Coral Pkwy., Cape Coral, FL 33904; 895.

Merchant Marine Veterans of WWII, U.S. (1944), 1712 Harbor Way, Seal Beach, CA 90740; 6,742.

Merchants Assn., Natl. Retail (1911), 100 W. 31st St., N.Y., NY 10001; 45,000.

Metal Finishers, Natl. Assn. of (1955), 111 E. Wacker Dr., Chicago, IL 60601; 1,086.

Metallurgy Institute, Amer. Powder (1959), 105 College Rd. East, Princeton, NJ 08540; 2,300.

Metal Powder Industries Federation (1946), 105 College Rd. East, Princeton, NJ 08540; 260 cos.

Metals, Amer. Society for (1913), Metals Park, OH 44073.

Meteorological Society, Amer. (1919), 45 Beacon St., Boston, MA 02108; 10,000.

Metric Assn., U.S. (1916), 10245 Andasol Ave., Northridge, CA 91325; 3,500.

Microbiology, Amer. Society for (1899), 1913 Eye St. NW, Wash. DC 20006; 32,000.

Micrographics Assn., Natl. (1942), 8719 Colesville Rd., Silver Spring, MD 20910; 9,000.

Mideast Educational and Training Services, America-, (1951), 1717 Massachusetts Ave. NW, Wash., DC 20036.

Military Order of the Loyal Legion of the U.S.A. (1865), 1805 Pine St., Phila., PA 19103; 1,200.

Military Order of the Purple Heart of the USA (1932), 5413-B Backlick Rd., Springfield, VA 22151; 15,000.

Military Order of the World Wars (1920), 435 N. Lee St., Alexandria, VA 22314; 17,000+.

Mining and Metallurgical Society of America (1908), 275 Madison Ave., N.Y., NY 10016; 295.

Ministerial Assn., Amer. (1929), 2210 Wilshire Blvd., Suite 582, Santa Monica, CA 90403.

Model Railroad Assn., Natl. (1935), 4121 Cromwell Rd., Chattanooga, TN 37421; 25,000.

Modern Language Assn. of America (1883), 62 Fifth Ave., N.Y., NY 10011; 26,000.

Modern Language Teachers Assns., Natl. Federation of (1916), Gannon Univ., Erie, PA 16541.

Moose, Loyal Order of (1888), Mooseheart, IL 60539; 1,303,173.

Mothers, American (1933), 301 Park Ave., N.Y., NY 10022.

Mothers-in-Law Club Intl. (1970), 420 Adelberg Ln., Cedarhurst, NY 11516; 5,000.

Mothers of Twins Clubs, Natl. Organization of (1960), 5402 Amberwood Ln., Rockville, MD 20853; 8,000.

Motion Picture Arts & Sciences, Academy of (1927), 8949 Wilshire Blvd., Beverly Hills, CA 90211; 4,500.

Motion Pictures, Natl. Board of Review of (1909), P.O. Box 589, Lenox Hill Sta., N.Y., NY 10021.

Motion Picture & Television Engineers, Society of (1916), 862 Scarsdale Ave., Scarsdale, NY 10583; 9,604.

Motor Vehicle Administrators, Amer. Assn. of (1933), 1201 Connecticut Ave. NW, Wash., DC 20036; 2,000.

Motor Vehicle Manufacturers Assn. (1900), 300 New Center Building, Detroit, MI 48202; 10 companies.

Motorcyclist Assn., Amer. (1924), 33 Collegeview, Westerville, OH 43081; 133,000.

Multiple Sclerosis Society, Natl. (1946), 205 E. 42d St., N.Y., NY 10017; 321,000.

Municipal Finance Officers Assn. (1906), 180 N. Michigan Ave., Suite 800, Chicago, IL 60601.

Municipal League, Natl. (1894), 55 W. 44th St., N.Y., NY 10036; 3,000.

Muscular Dystrophy Assn. (1950), 810 Seventh Ave., N.Y., NY 10019.

Museums, Amer. Assn. of (1906), 1055 Thomas Jefferson St. NW, Wash., DC 20007; 8,900.

Music Center, Amer. (1940), 250 W. 54th St., N.Y., NY 10019; 1,200.

Music Conference, Amer. (1947), 1000 Skokie Blvd., Wilmette, IL 60091; 400.

Music Council, Natl. (1940), 10 Columbus Circle, N.Y., NY 10019; 50+ organizations.

Music Educators Natl. Conference (1907), 1902 Association Dr., Reston, VA 22090; 55,000.

Musicians, Amer. Federation of (1896), 1500 Broadway, N.Y., NY 10036; 330,000.

Musicological Society, Amer. (1934), 201 S. 34th St., Phila., PA 19104, 3,500.

Music Publishers' Assn., Natl. (1917), 205 E. 42nd St., N.Y., NY 10017; 350.

Music Scholarship Assn., Amer. (1956), 1826 Carew Tower, Cincinnati, OH 45202; 2,500.

Music Teachers Natl. Assn. (1876), 2113 Carew Tower, Cincinnati, OH 45202; 23,000.

Muzzle Loading Rifle Assn., Natl. (1933), P.O. Box 67, Friendship, IN 47021; 26,000.

NAACP (Natl. Assn. for the Advancement of Colored People) (1909), 186 Remsen St., Brooklyn, NY 11201.

Name Assn., Amer. (1953), 7 E. 14th St., N.Y., NY 10003; 1,000.

Narcolepsy and Cataplexy Foundation of Amer. (1975), 1410 York Ave., Suite 2D, N.Y. NY 10021; 3,982.

Narcolepsy Assoc., Amer. (1975), 1139 Bush St., Suite D, San Carlos, CA 94070; 3,000.

National Guard Assn. of the U.S. (1878), One Massachusetts Ave. NW, Wash., DC 20001; 54,000.

Nationalities Service, Amer. Council for (1919), 20 W. 40th St., N.Y., NY 10018; 34 agencies.

Naturalists, Assn. of Interpretive (1961), 6700 Needwood Rd., Derwood, MD 20855; 1,200.

Natural Science for Youth Foundation (1961), 763 Silvermine Rd., New Canaan, CT 06840; 400.

Nature Conservancy (1951), 1800 N. Kent St., Arlington, VA 22209; 245,000.

Navajo Code Talkers Assn. (1971), Red Rock State Park, P.O. Box 328, Church Rock, NM 87311; 90.

Naval Architects & Marine Engineers, Society of (1893), One World Trade Center, Suite 1369, N.Y., NY 10048; 13,487.

Naval Engineers, Amer. Society of (1888), 1452 Duke St., Alexandria, VA 22203; 7,600.

Naval Institute, U.S. (1873), U.S. Naval Academy, Annapolis, MD 21402; 90,000.

Naval Reserve Assn. (1954), 110 N. Royal St., Suite 307, Alexandria, VA 22314; 23,000.

Navigation, Institute of (1945), 815 15th St. NW, Suite 832, Wash., DC 20005; 2,500.

Navy Club of the U.S.A. Auxiliary (1941), 418 W. Pontiac St., Ft. Wayne, IN 46807; 1,000.

Navy League of the U.S. (1902), 2300 Wilson Blvd., Arlington, VA 22201; 49,675.

Needlework Guild of America (1885), 1342 E. Lincoln Hwy., Langhorne, PA 19047; 150,000.

Negro College Fund, United (1944), 500 E. 62d St., N.Y., NY 10021; 42 institutions.

Neurofibromatosis Foundation, Natl. (1978), 70 W. 40th St., N.Y., NY 10018; 10,000.

Newspaper Editors, Amer. Society of (1922), P.O. Box 17004, Washington, DC 20041; 897.

Newspaper Promotion Assn., Intl. (1930), 11600 Sunrise Valley Dr., Reston, VA 22091; 1,500.

Newspaper Publishers Assn., Amer. (1887), 11600 Sunrise Valley Dr., Reston, VA 22091; 1,400 newspapers.

Ninety-Nines (Intl. Organization of Women Pilots) (1929), P.O. Box 59965; Will Rogers Airport, Oklahoma City, OK 73159.

Non-Commissioned Officers Assn. (1960), 10635 IH 35 No., San Antonio, TX 78233; 182,000.

Northern Cross Society (1983), Northern Cross Ranch, P.O. Box 4527, Topeka, KS 66604; 400+.

Notaries, Amer. Society of (1965), 918 16th St. NW, Wash., DC 20006; 21,825.

Nuclear Society, Amer. (1954), 555 N. Kensington Ave., La Grange Park, IL 60525; 14,000.

Numismatic Assn., Amer. (1891), 818 N. Cascade Ave., Colorado Springs, CO 80903; 35,000.

Numismatic Society, Amer. (1858), Broadway at 155th St., N.Y., NY 10032; 2,219.

Nurse Education and Service, Natl. Assn. for Practical (1941), 254 W. 31st St., N.Y., NY 10001; 25,000.

Nurses' Assn., Amer. (1896), 2420 Pershing Rd., Kansas City, MO 64108.

Nursing, Amer. Assembly for Men in (1971), Rush Univ., 600 S. Paulina, Chicago, IL 60617; 1,590.

Nursing, Natl. League for (1952), 10 Columbus Circle, N.Y., NY 10019; 20,000.

Nutrition, Amer. Institute of (1928), 9650 Rockville Pike, Bethesda, MD 20814; 2,200.

ORT Federation, Amer. (Org. for Rehabilitation through Training) (1925), 817 Broadway, N.Y., NY 10014; 20,000.

Odd Fellows, Sovereign Grand Lodge Independent Order of (1819), 422 N. Trade St., Winston Salem, NC 27101.

Old Crows, Assn. of (1964), 2300 9th St. S., Arlington, VA 22204; 18,000.

Olympic Committee, U.S. (1920), 1759 E. Boulder St., Colorado Springs, CO 80909; 60 organizations.

Optical Society of America (1916), 1816 Jefferson Pl. NW, Wash., DC 20036; 8,828.

Optimist Intl. (1919), 4494 Lindell Blvd., St. Louis, MO 63108.

Optometric Assn., Amer. (1898), 243 N. Lindbergh Blvd., St. Louis, MO 63141; 23,304.

Oral and Maxillofacial Surgeons, Amer. Assn. of (1918), 211 E. Chicago Ave., Chicago, IL 60611; 4,611.

Organists, Amer. Guild of (1896), 815 Second Ave., Suite 318, N.Y., NY 10017; 21,000.

Oriental Society, Amer. (1842), 329 Sterling Memorial Library, Yale Sta., New Haven, CT 06520; 1,600.

Ornithologists' Union, Amer. (1883), c/o National Museum of Natural History, Smithsonian, Wash., DC 20560; 4,500.

Osteopathic Assn., Amer. (1897), 212 E. Ohio St., Chicago, IL 60611; 15,894.

Ostomy Assn., United (1962), 2001 W. Beverly Blvd., Los Angeles, CA 90057; 45,000.

Outlaw and Lawman History, Assn. for (1974), Univ. of Wyoming, Box 3334, Laramie, WY 82071; 470.

Overeaters Anonymous (1960), 2190 W. 190th St., Torrance, CA 90504; 85,000.

Over-the-Counter Cos., Natl. Assn. of (1973), 1735 K St. NW, Washington, DC 20006; 500+.

PTA (Parent-Teacher Assn.), Natl. (1897), 700 N. Rush St., Chicago, IL 60611; 5.3 mln.

Paleontological Research Institution (1932), 1259 Trumansburg Rd., Ithaca, NY 14850; 700+.

Paper Converters Assn. (1934), 1133 15th St. NW, Wash., DC 20005.

Paper Industry, Technical Assn. of the Pulp and (1916), P.O. Box 105113, Atlanta, GA 30348; 24,000.

Paper Institute, Amer. (1966), 260 Madison Ave., N.Y., NY 10016; 170 companies.

Parasitologists, Amer. Society of (1924), 1041 New Hampshire St., Box 368, Lawrence, KS 66044; 1,500.

Parents Without Partners (1958), 7910 Woodmont Ave. NW, Wash., DC 20014; 200,000.

Parkinson's Disease Foundation (1957), 650 W. 168th St., N.Y., NY 10032; 40,000.

Parliamentarians, Amer. Institute of (1958), 124 W. Washington Blvd. Ft. Wayne, IN 46802; 1,300.

Parliamentarians, Natl. Assn. of (1930), 3706 Broadway, Suite 300, Kansas City, MO 64111; 4,500.

Parliamentary Law, Intl. Organization of Professionals in (1977), 3611 Victoria Ave., L.A., CA 90016; 300.

Pasta Assn., Natl. (1904), 1901 N. Ft. Myer Dr., Suite 307, Arlington, VA 22209.

Pathologists, Amer. Assn. of (1976), 9650 Rockville Pike, Bethesda, MD 20814; 2,400.

Patriotism, Natl. Committee for Responsible (1967), P.O. Box 665, Grand Central Sta., N.Y., NY 10163; 175.

Pearl Harbor History Associates (1958), P.O. Box 205, Sperryville, VA 22740.

Pedestrian Tolls, Committee for (1979), P.O. Box 283, Phillipsburg, NJ 08865.

P.E.N. Amer. Center (1922), 47 Fifth Ave., N.Y., NY 10003.

Pen Women, Natl. League of Amer. (1897), 1300 17th St. NW, Wash., DC 20036; 6,000.

Pennsylvania Society of New York (1899), 80 N. Main St., Sellersville, PA 18960; 2,150.

Pension Actuaries, Amer. Society of (1966), 1413 K St. NW, Wash., DC 20015.

P.E.O (Philanthropic Educational Organization) Sisterhood (1869), 3700 Grand Ave., Des Moines, IA 50312; 223,000.

Personnel Administration, Amer. Society for (1948), 606 N. Washington St., Alexandria, VA 22314; 33,000.

Petroleum Equipment Inst. (1951), 3739 E. 31st St., Tulsa, OK 74114; 1,050.

Petroleum Geologists, Amer. Assn. of (1917), Box 979, 1444 S. Boulder, Tulsa, OK 74101; 33,000.

Petroleum Institute, Amer. (1919), 1220 L St. NW, Wash., DC 20005; 6,000.

Petroleum Landmen, Amer. Assn. of (1955), 2408 Continental Life Bldg., Fort Worth, TX 76102; 6,200.

Pharmaceutical Assn., Amer. (1852), 2215 Constitution Ave. NW, Wash., DC 20037; 50,000.

Philatelic Society, Amer. (1886), P.O. Box 8000, State College, PA 16803; 53,372.

Philately Assn., Graphics (1975), 1450 Parkchester Rd., Bronx, NY 10462; 160.

Philaticians, Society of (1972), 154 Laguna Ct., St. Augustine Shores, FL 33086; 308.

Philological Assn., Amer. (1869), 617 Hamilton Hall, Columbia Univ., N.Y., NY 10027; 2,500.

Philosophical Assn., Amer. (1900), Univ. of Delaware, Newark, DE 19716; 6,500.

Philosophical Enquiry, Intl. Society for (1974), P.O. Box 3282, Kingsport, TN 37664; 360.

Philosophical Society, Amer. (1743), 104 S. 5th St., Phila., PA 19106; 650.

Photogrammetry, Amer. Society of (1934), 210 Little Falls St., Falls Church, VA 22046; 8,000.

Photographers of America, Professional (1880), 1090 Executive Way, Des Plaines, IL 60018; 14,000.

Photographic Society of Amer. (1934), 2005 Walnut St., Phila. PA 19103; 14,000.

Physical Therapy Assn., Amer. (1921), 1111 N. Fairfax St., Alexandria, VA 22314; 37,000.

Physicians, Amer. Academy of Family (1947), 1740 W. 92nd St., Kansas City, MO 64114; 57,000.

Physics, Amer. Inst. of (1931), 335 E. 45th St., N.Y., NY 10017.

Physiological Society, Amer. (1887), 9650 Rockville Pike, Bethesda, MD 20814.

Phytopathological Soc., The Amer. (1908), 3340 Pilot Knob Rd., St. Paul, MN 55121; 4,000.

Pilgrim Society (I820), 75 Court St., Plymouth, MA 02360; 850.

Pilgrims of the U.S. (1903), 74 Trinity Pl., N.Y., NY 10006; 1,000.

Pilot Club Intl. (1921), 244 College St., Macon, GA 31213; 21,000.

Pioneer Women, The Women's Labor Zionist Organization of America (1925), 200 Madison Ave., N.Y., NY 10021

Planetary Society (1979), 110 S. Euclid Ave., Pasadena, CA 91109; 110,000.

Planned Parenthood Federation of America (1916), 810 Seventh Ave., N.Y., NY 10019; 191 affiliates.

Planning Assn., Amer. (1917), 1976 Massachusetts Ave. NW, Wash., DC 10019; 190 affiliates.

Plastic Modelers Society, Intl. (1965), P.O. Box 480, Denver, CO 80201; 7,221.

Plastics Industry, Society of (1937), 355 Lexington Ave., N.Y., NY 10017; 1,200 companies.

Platform Assn., Intl. (1831), 2564 Berkshire Rd., Cleveland Heights, OH 44106; 5,000.

Podiatry Assn., Amer. (1912), 20 Chevy Chase Circle NW, Wash., DC 20015; 8,400.

Poetry Day Committee, Natl. (1947), 1110 N. Venetian Dr., Miami, FL 33139; 17,000.

Poetry Society of America (1910), 15 Gramercy Park, N.Y., NY 10003; 1,400.

Poets, Academy of Amer. (1934), 177 E. 87th St., N.Y., NY 10128; 3,000+.

Polar Society, Amer. (1934), 98-20 62d Dr., Apt. 7H, Rego Park, NY 11374; 2,143.

Police, Amer. Federation of (1966), 1100 NE 125 St., N. Miami, FL 33161; 47,000.

Police, Internatl. Assn. of Chiefs of (1893), 13 Firstfield Rd., Gaithersburg, MD 20878; 13,600.

Police Reserve Officers Assn., Natl. (1967), 609 W. Main St., Louisville, KY 40202; 11,000.

Polish Army Veterans Assn. of America (1921), 19 Irving Pl., N.Y., NY 10003; 9,762.

Polish Cultural Society of America (1940), 41 John St., N.Y., NY 10038; 101,921.

Polish Legion of American Veterans (1921), 3024 N. Laramie Ave., Chicago, IL 60641; 13,000.

Political Items Collectors, Amer. (1945), P.O. Box 340339, San Antonio, TX 78234.

Political Science, Academy of (1880), 2852 Broadway, N.Y., NY 10025; 12,000.

Political Science Assn., Amer. (1903), 1527 New Hampshire Ave. NW, Wash., DC 20036; 12,500.

Political & Social Science, Amer. Academy of (1889), 3937 Chestnut St., Phila., PA 19104; 4,900.

Pollution Control, Internatl. Assn. for (1970), 1625 Eye St. NW, Wash. DC 20006; 500.

Polo Assn., U.S. (1890), 1301 W. 22d St., Oak Brook, IL 60521; 2,400.

Population Assn. of America (1931), 806 15th St. NW, Wash., DC 20005; 2,600.

Portuguese Continental Union of the U.S.A. (1925), 899 Boylston St., Boston, MA 02115; 8,171.

Postmasters of the U.S., Natl. Assn. of (1898), 4212 King St., Arlington, VA 22302; 43,000.

Postmasters of the U.S., Natl. League of (1904), 1023 N. Royal St., Alexandria, VA 22314-1569; 21,000.

Poultry Science Assn. (1908), 309 W. Clark, Champaign, IL 61820; 1,900.

Power Boat Assn., Amer. (1903), 17640 E. Nine Mile Rd., E. Detroit, MI 48021; 4,500.

Precancel Collectors, Natl. Assn. of (1950), 5121 Park Blvd., Wildwood, NJ 08260; 8,500.

Press, Associated (1848), 50 Rockefeller Plaza, N.Y., NY 10020; 1,365 newspapers & 3,600 breadcast stations.

Press Club, Natl. (1908), Natl. Press Bldg., Wash., DC 20045; 4,104.

Press Intl., United (1907), 1400 I St. NW, Wash. DC 20005.

Press and Radio Club (1948), P.O. Box 7023, Montgomery, AL 36107; 717.

Press Women, Natl. Federation of (1937), 1105 Main St., Blue Springs, MD 64015; 5,000.

Printing Industries of America (1887), 1730 N. Lynn St., Arlington, VA 22209; 12,000 companies.

Procrastinators' Club of America (1956), 1111 Broad-Locust Bldg., Phila., PA 19102; 4,400.

Propeller Club of the U.S. (1927), 1030 15th St. NW, Suite 430, Wash., DC 20005; 17,000.

Psychiatric Assn., Amer. (1844), 1400 K St. NW, Wash., DC 20005; 27,000.

Psychical Research, Amer. Society for (1885), 5 W. 73d St., N.Y., NY 10023; 2,200.

Psychoanalytic Assn., Amer. (1911), One E. 57th St., N.Y., NY 10022; 2,700.

Psychological Assn., Amer. (1892), 1200 17th St. NW, Wash., DC 20036; 60,000.

Psychological Assn. for Psychoanalysis, Natl. (1948), 150 W. 13th St., N.Y., NY 10011; 290.

Psychological Minorities, Society for the Aid of (1953), 42-25 Hampton St., Elmhurst, NY 11373; 528.

Psychotherapy Assn., Amer. Group (1942), 1995 Broadway, N.Y., NY 10023; 3,000.

Public Health Assn., Amer. (1972), 1015 15th St. NW, Wash., DC 20005; 30,000.

Public Relations Soc. of Amer. (1947), 845 Third Ave., N.Y., NY 10022.

Publishers, Assn. of Amer. (1970), One Park Ave., N.Y., NY 10016; 330 publishing houses.

Puppeteers of Amer. (1937), 5 Cricklewood Path, Pasadena, CA 91107; 2,100.

Quality Control, Amer. Society for (1946), 230 W. Wells St., Milwaukee, WI 53203; 43,000.

Quota Internatl. (1919), 1828 L St. NW, Suite 908, Wash., DC 20036.

Rabbinical Alliance of America (1944), 156 5th Ave., N.Y., NY 10010; 502.

Rabbinical Assembly (1900), 3080 Broadway, N.Y., NY 10027.

Rabbis, Central Conference of Amer. (1889), 21 E. 40th St., N.Y., NY 10016; 1,410.

Radio, The Natl. Assn. of Business and Educational (1965), 1330 New Hampshire Ave. NW, Suite 122, Wash., DC 20036; 10,000.

Radio Clubs, Assn. of N. American (1964), 1500 Bunbury Dr., Whittier, CA 90601; 18 organizations.

Radio Union, Intl. Amateur (1925), P.O. Box AAA, Newington, CT 06111; 121 societies.

Radio and TV Society, Intl. (1939), 420 Lexington Ave., N.Y., NY 10170; 1,800.

Radio Relay League, Amer. (1914), 225 Main St., Newington, CT 06111; 150,000+.

Railroad Passengers, Natl. Assn. of (1967), 417 New Jersey Ave. SE, Wash., DC 20003; 11,500.

Railroads, Assn. of Amer. (1934), 1920 L St. NW, Wash., DC 20036; 450.

Railway Historical Society, Natl. (1935), P.O. Box 58153, Phila., PA 19102; 12,000.

Railway Progress Institute (1908), 700 N. Fairfax St., Alexandria, VA 22314; 152 companies.

Range Management, Society for (1948), 2760 W. 5th Ave., Denver, CO 80204; 5,400.

Rape, Feminist Alliance Against (1974), P.O. Box 21033, Wash., DC 20009.

Real Estate Appraisers, Natl. Assn. of (1967), 853 Broadway, N.Y., NY 10003; 1,000.

Real Estate Investment Trusts, Natl. Assn. of (1961), 1101 17th St. NW, Wash., DC 20036; 300 associates.

Rebekah Assemblies, Intl. Assn. of (1916), P.O. Box 153, Minneapolis, KS 67467; 294,142.

Reconciliation, Fellowship of (1914), 523 N. Broadway, Nyack, NY 10960; 32,000.

Recording Industry Assn. of America (1951), 888 7th Ave., N.Y., NY 10101; 60.

Records Managers & Administrators, Assn. of (1975), 4200 Somerset Dr., Suite 215, Prairie Village, KS 66208; 8,000.

Recreation and Park Assn., Natl. (1965), 3101 Park Ctr. Dr., 12th Fl., Alexandria, VA 22302.

Red Cross, Amer. Natl. (1881), 17th & D Sts. NW, Wash., DC 20006; 2,963 chapters.

Red Men, Improved Order of (1765), 1525 West Ave., P.O. Box 683, Waco, TX 76703; 45,000.

Redwoods League, Save-the- (1918), 114 Sansome St., San Francisco, CA 94104; 43,000.

Reed Organ Society, Inc. (1981), The Musical Museum, Deansboro, NY 13328; 550.

Regional Plan Assn. (1929), 1040 Ave. of the Americas, N.Y., NY 10018; 1,200.

Rehabilitation Assn., Natl. (1925), 633 S. Washington St., Alexandria, VA 22314.

Religion, Amer. Academy of (1909), Dept. of Religion, Syracuse Univ., Syracuse, NY 13210; 4,000.

Religion, Freedom from Foundation (1978), 30 W. Mifflin St., Suite 312, Madison, WI 53701; 1,900+.

Remodeling Industry, Natl. Assn. of the (1956), 1901 N. Moore St., Suite 808, Arlington, VA 22209.

Renaissance Society of America (1948), 1161 Amsterdam Ave., N.Y., NY 10027; 2,858.

Reserve Officers Assn. of the U.S. (1922), One Constitution Ave., NE, Wash., DC 20002; 123,500.

Restaurant Assn., Natl. (1019), 311 First St. NW, Wash., DC 20001; 10,000.

Retarded Citizens of the U.S., Assn. for (1950), 2501 Ave. J, Arlington, TX 76006; 160,000+.

Retired Credit Union People, Natl. Assn. for (1978), P.O. Box 391, 5910 Mineral Pt. Rd., Madison, WI 53701; 67,000.

Retired Federal Employees, Natl. Assn. of (1921), 1533 New Hampshire Ave. NW, Wash., DC 20008; 491,770.

Retired Officers Assn. (1929), 201 N. Washington St., Alexandria, VA 22314; 339,570.

Retired Persons, Amer. Assn. of (1958), 1909 K St. NW, Wash., DC 20049; 18 mln.

Retired Teachers Assn., Natl. (1947), 1909 K St. NW, Wash., DC 20049; 540,000.

Retreads (of World War I & II) (1947), 40-07 154th St., Flushing, NY 11354; 1,000.

Revolver Assn., U.S. (1900), 96 W. Union St., Ashland, MA 01721; 1,400.

Reye's Syndrome Foundation, Natl. (1974), 426 N. Lewis, Bryan, OH 43506; 10,000.

Richard III Society (1964), P.O. Box 217, Sea Cliff, NY 11579; 600.

Rifle Assn., Natl. (1871), 1600 Rhode Island Ave. NW, Wash., DC 20036; 3 mln.

Road & Transportation Builders' Assn., Amer. (1902), 525 School St. SW, Wash., DC 20024; 4,500.

Rodeo Cowboys Assn., Professional (1936), 101 Pro Rodeo Dr., Colorado Springs, CO 80919; 10,000.

Roller Skating, U.S. Amateur Confederation of (1971), 7700 A St., Lincoln, NE 68501; 35,000.

Roller Skating Rink Operators Assn. (1937), 7700 A St., Lincoln, NE 68501; 1,800.

Rose Society, Amer. (1899), P.O. Box 30,000, Shreveport, LA 71130; 25,000.

Rosicrucians, Soc. of (1909), 321 W. 101st St., N.Y., NY 10025.

Rotary Intl. (1905), 1600 Ridge Ave., Evanston, IL 60201.

Running and Fitness Assn., Amer. (1968), 2420 K St. NW, Wash, DC 20037; 35,000.

Ruritan Natl. (1928), Ruritan Natl. Rd., Dublin, VA 24084.

Safety and Fairness Everywhere, Natl. Assn. Taunting (1980), P.O. Box 5743A, Montecito, CA 93150; 11,080.

Safety Council, Natl. (1913), 444 N. Michigan Ave., Chicago, IL 60611; 12,000.

Sailors, Tin Can (1976), Battleship Cove, Fall River, MA 02726; 4,500.

St. Andrew the Apostle, The Soc. of (1983), Route 3, Sylvester, WV 25193; 450.

St. Dennis of Zante, Sovereign Greek Order of (1096; 1953 in U.S.), 739 W. 186th St., N.Y., NY 10033; 911.

St. George the Martyr, Knightly Assn. of (1980), State Route #3, Sylvester, WV 25193; 15,000.

St. Luke the Physician, Order of (1880), 2210 Wilshire Blvd., Suite 582, Santa Monica, CA 90403; 720.

St. Paul, Natl. Guild of (1937), 601 Hill 'n Dale, Lexington, KY 40503; 13,652.

Salespersons, Natl. Assn. of Professional (1970), P.O. Box 76461, Atlanta, GA 30358; 35,000.

Salt Institute (1914), 206 N. Washington St., Alexandria, VA 22314; 30 companies.

Samuel Butler Society (1978), Chaplain Library, Williams College, P.O. Box 426, Williamstown, MA 01267; 100.

Sane Nuclear Policy, Committee for a (1957), 711 G St. SE, Wash., DC 20003; 130,000.

Savings & Loan League, Natl. (1943), 1101 15th St. NW, Wash., DC 20005; 300 associations.

School Administrators, Amer. Assn. of (1865), 1801 N. Moore St., Arlington, VA 22209; 17,500.

School Boards Assn., Natl. (1940), 1680 Duke St., Alexandria, VA 22314; 52 boards.

School Counselor Assn., Amer. (1953), 5999 Stevenson Ave., Alexandria, VA 22304; 9,138.

Schools of Art, Natl. Assn. of (also: **School of Art and Design, School of Dance, Music, and Theater**) (1944), 11250 Roger Bacon Dr., #5, Reston, VA 22090.

Schools & Colleges, Amer. Council on (1927), P.O. Box 219, Lomita, CA 90717-0219.

Science, Amer. Assn. for the Advancement of (1848), 1515 Massachusetts Ave. NW, Wash., DC 20005; 136,020.

Science Service (1921), 1719 N St. NW, Wash., DC 20036.

Science Teachers Assn., Natl. (1944), 1742 Connecticut Ave. NW, Wash., DC 20009; 19,272.

Science Writers, Natl. Assn. of (1004), P.O. Box 294, Greenlawn, NY 11740; 1,175.

Sciences, Natl. Academy of (1863), 2101 Constitution Ave. NW, Wash., DC 20418; 1,415.

Scientists, Federation of Amer. (1946), 307 Massachusetts Ave. NE, Wash., DC 20002; 7,000.

Screen Actors Guild (1933), 7750 Sunset Blvd., Hollywood, CA 90046; 54,000.

Sculpture Soc., Natl. (1893), 15 E. 26th St., N.Y., NY 10010.

Seamen's Service, United (1942), One World Trade Ctr., Suite 2601, N.Y., NY 10048.

2d Air Division Assn. (1947), 1 Jeffrey's Neck Rd., Ipswich, MA 01938; 4,186.

Secondary School Principals, Natl. Assn. of (1916), 1904 Association Dr., Reston, VA 22091; 35,000.

Secretaries, Natl. Assn. of Legal (1950), 3005 E. Skelly Dr., Tulsa, OK 74105; 19,000.

Secularists of America, United (1947), 1301 E. Ventura Blvd. #36, Oxnard, CA 93030.

Securities Industry Assn. (1972), 120 Broadway, N.Y., NY 10271; 514 firms.

Semantics, Institute of General (1938), Office of the Director, 3029 Eastern Ave., Baltimore, MD 21224; 500.

Separation of Church & State, Americans United for (1947), 8120 Fenton St., Silver Spring, MD 20910; 50,000.

Sertoma Internatl. (1912), 1912 E. Meyer Blvd., Kansas City, MO 64132; 35,000.

Sex Information & Education Council of the U.S. (SIECUS) (1964), 80 5th Ave., N.Y., NY 10011; 3,200.

Shakespeare Assn. of America (1973), Box 6328, Vanderbilt Sta., Nashville, TN 37235; 650.

Shemya WWII Veterans Assn. (1983), 3926 Old Gentilly Rd., P.O. Box 26093, New Orleans, LA 70186; 60.

Sheriff's Assn., Natl. (1940), 1250 Connecticut Ave. NW, Wash., DC 20036; 45,000.

Shipbuilders Council of America (1920), 1110 Vermont Ave. NW, Wash., DC 20005; 74 organizations.

Ship Society, World (1946), 3319 Sweet Dr., Lafayette, CA 94549; 4,300.

Ships in Bottles Assn. of Amer. (1982), P.O. Box 550, Coronado, CA 92118; 200.

Shoe Retailers Assn., Natl. (1913), 1414 Ave. of the Americas, N.Y., NY 10016; 4,000.

Shore & Beach Preservation Assn., Amer. (1926), 412 O'Brien Hall, Univ. of California, Berkeley, CA 94720; 1,100.

Shrine, Ancient Arabic Order of the Nobles of the Mystic (1872), 2900 Rocky Pt. Dr., Tampa, FL 33607; 1,000,000.

Shut-Ins, Natl. Society for (1970), 237 Franklin St., Reading, PA 19602; 300.

Sierra Club (1892), 530 Bush St., San Francisco, CA 94108.

Signalmen, Society of (1971), P.O. Box 11247, San Diego, CA 92111; 400.

Silurians, Soc. of the (1924), 45 John St., N.Y., NY 10038.

Skating Union of the U.S., Amateur (1928), 4423 W. Deming Pl., Chicago, IL 60639; 2,000.

Skeet Shooting Assn., Natl. (1946), P.O. Box 28188, San Antonio, TX 78228; 15,500.

Ski Assn., U.S. (1904), 1750 E. Boulder St., Colorado Springs, CO 80909.

Small Business, Amer. Federation of (1938), 407 S. Dearborn St., Chicago, IL 60605; 25,000.

Small Business Assn., Natl. (1937), 1604 K St. NW, Wash., DC 20006; 50,000.

Smoking & Health, Natl. Clearinghouse for (1965), Center for Disease Control, 1600 Clifton Road NE, Atlanta, GA 30333.

Soaring Society of America (1932), P.O. Box 66071, Los Angeles, CA 90066-0071; 16,000.

Soccer Federation, U.S. (1913), 350 Fifth Ave., N.Y., NY 10001; 700,000.

Social Biology, Society for the Study of (1926), Medical Dept., Brookhaven Natl. Laboratory, Upton, NY 11973; 415.

Social Sciences, Natl. Institute of (1899), 1133 Broadway, Suite 824, N.Y., NY 10010; 800.

Social Service, Intl., Amer. Branch (1923), 20 W. 40th St., N.Y., NY 10018.

Social Work Education, Council on (1952), 111 8th Ave., N.Y., NY 10017; 4,500.

Social Workers, Natl. Assn. of (1955), 7981 Eastern Ave., Silver Spring, MD 20910; 100,000.

Sociological Assn., Amer. (1905), 1722 N St. NW, Wash., DC 20036; 12,000.

Softball Assn. of America, Amateur (1933), 2801 N.E. 50th St., Oklahoma City, OK 73111; 4.5 mln.

Softball League, Cinderella (1958), P.O. Box 1411, Corning, NY 14830.

Soft Drink Assn., Natl. (1919), 1101 16th St. NW, Wash., DC 20036; 1,800.

Soil Conservation Society of America (1945), 7515 N.E. Ankeny Rd., Ankeny, IA 50021; 13,000.

Soil Science Society of America (1936), 677 S. Segoe Rd., Madison, WI 53711; 6,540.

Sojourners, Natl. (1921), 8301 E. Boulevard Dr., Alexandria, VA 22308; 9,200.

Soldier's, Sailor's and Airmen's Club (1919), 283 Lexington Ave., N.Y., NY 10016.

Songwriters Guild, The (1931), 276 Fifth Ave., N.Y., NY 10001; 3,000.

Sons of the Amer. Legion (1932), Box 1055, Indianapolis, IN 46206; 59,577.

Sons of the American Revolution, Natl. Society of (1889), 1000 S. 4th, Louisville, KY 40203; 23,500.

Sons of Confederate Veterans (1896), Southern Station, Box 5164, Hattiesburg, MS 39406; 7,300.

Sons of the Desert (1965), P.O. Box 8341, Universal City, CA 91608; 3,000.

Sons of Norway (1895), 1455 W. Lake St., Minneapolis, MN 55408; 105,429.

Sons of Poland, Assn. of the (1903), 591 Summit Ave., Jersey City, NJ 07306; 10,000.

Sons of St. Patrick, Society of the Friendly (1784), 80 Wall St., N.Y., NY 10005; 1,000.

Sons of Sherman's March to the Sea (1966), 1725 Farmers Ave., Tempe, AZ 85281; 582.

Sons of Union Veterans of the Civil War (1881), P.O. Box 24, Gettysburg, PA 17325; 3,500.

Soroptimist Intl. of the Americas (1921), 1616 Walnut St., Phila., PA 19103; 40,000.

Southern Christian Leadership Conference (1957), 334 Auburn Ave. NE, Atlanta, GA 30303; 1 mln.

Southern Regional Council (1944), 75 Marietta St. NW, Atlanta, GA 30303; 120.

Space Education Assoc., U.S. (1973), 746 Turnpike Rd., Elizabethtown, PA 17022; 1,000.

Spanish War Veterans, United (1899), P.O. Box 1915, Washington, DC 20013; 10.

Speech Communication Assn. (1914), 5105 Backlick Rd., Annandale, VA 22003; 5,300.

Speech-Language-Hearing Assn., Amer. (1925), 10801 Rockville Pike, Rockville, MD 20852.

Speleological Society, Natl. (1941), 2813 Cave Ave., Huntsville, AL 35810; 6,200.

Sports Car Club of America (1944), 6750 S. Emporia, Englewood, CO 80112; 24,000.

Sports Club, Indoor (1930), 1145 Highland St., Napoleon, OH 43545.

Standards Institute, Amer. Natl. (1918), 1430 Broadway, N.Y., NY 10018; 1,000.

State Communities Aid Assn. (1872), 105 E. 22d St., N.Y., NY 10010; 75.

State Governments, Council of (1933), P.O. Box 11910, Iron Works Pike, Lexington, KY 40578; 50 states.

State & Local History, Amer. Assn. for (1940), 172 Second Ave. N., Nashville, TN 37201; 7,700.

Statistical Assn., Amer. (1839), 806 15th St. NW, Wash., DC 20005; 15,000.

Steamship Historical Society of America (1935), 414 Pelton Ave., Staten Island, NY 10310; 3,461.

Steel Construction, Amer. Institute of (1921), 400 N. Michigan Ave., Chicago, IL 60611; 350.

Sterilization, Assn. for Voluntary (1943), 122 E. 42nd St., N.Y., NY 10168; 2,600.

Stock Car Auto Racing, Natl. Assn. for (NASCAR) (1948), 1801 Speedway Blvd., Daytona Beach, FL 32015; 17,000.

Stock Exchange, Amer. (1911), 86 Trinity Pl., N.Y., NY 10006; 871.

Stock Exchange, N.Y. (1792), 11 Wall St., N.Y., NY 10005.

Stock Exchange, Phila. (1790), 1900 Market St., Phila., PA 19103.

Structural Stability Research Council (1944), Fritz Engineering Laboratory No. 13, Lehigh Univ., Bethlehem, PA 18015.

Student Assn., U.S. (1947), 11 Dupont Circle, Suite 130, Wash., DC 20036.

Student Councils, Natl. Assn. of (1931), 1904 Association Dr., Reston, VA 22091; 200,000.

Student Consumer Protection Council, Natl. (1972), Villanova Univ., Villanova, PA 19085; 50.

Stuttering Project, Natl. (1977), 1269 7th Ave., San Francisco, CA 94122; 1,600.

Sudden Infant Death Syndrome Foundation, Inc., Natl. (1962), 8240 Professional Pl., Landover, MA 20785.

Sugar Brokers Assn., Natl. (1893), 1 World Trade Center N.Y., NY 10047; 120.

Sunbathing Assn., Amer. (1932), 1703 N. Main St., Kissimmee, FL 32743-3396; 30,000.

Sunday League (1933), 279 Highland Ave., Newark, NJ 07104; 25,000.

Surgeons, Amer. College of (1913), 55 E. Erie St., Chicago IL 60611; 47,636.

Surgeons, Intl. College of (1935), 1516 N. Lake Shore Dr., Chicago IL 60610; 15,000.

Surgeons of the U.S., Assn. of Military (1903), 10605 Concord St., Kensington, MD 20895; 13,000.

Surveying & Mapping, Amer. Congress on (1941), 210 Little Falls, Falls Church, VA 22046; 10,500.

Symphony Orchestra League, Amer. (1942), 633 E St. NW, Wash., DC 20004.

Systems Management, Assn. for (1947), 24587 Bagley Rd., Cleveland, OH 44138; 8,500.

Table Tennis Assn., U.S. (1933), Olympic House, 1750 E. Boulder, Colorado Springs, CO 80909; 6,000.

Tailhook Assn., The (1957), P.O. Box 40, Bonita, CA 92000; 8,100+.

Tall Buildings and Urban Habitat, Council on (1969), Bldg. 13, Lehigh Univ., Bethlehem, PA 18015; 2,400.

Tattoo Club of America (1976), 822 Ave. of the Americas, N.Y., NY 10001; 10,000.

Tax Accountants, Natl. Assn. of Enrolled Federal (1960), 6108 N. Harding Ave., Chicago, IL 60659; 500.

Tax Administrators, Federation of (1937), 444 N. Capitol St. NW, Wash., DC 20001; 50 agencies.

Tax Assn.-Natl. Tax Institute of America (1907), 21 E. State St., Columbus, OH 43215; 2,000.

Tax Foundation, Inc. (1937), 1 Thomas Circle NW, Wash., DC 20005; 1,000.

Taxpayers Against Unfair Taxes (1971), 11015 Cumpston St., N. Hollywood, CA 91601; 34,000.

Taxpayers Union, Natl. (1969), 713 Maryland Ave., NE, Washington, DC 20002; 110,000.

Tea Assn. of the U.S.A. (1899), 230 Park Ave., N.Y., NY 10169; 300.

Teachers, Amer. String Assn. (1954), UGA Sta. Box 2066, Athens, GA 30612; 5,550+.

Teachers of English, Natl. Council of (1911), 1111 Kenyon Rd., Urbana, IL 61801; 90,000.

Teachers of English to Speakers of Other Languages (1966), 201 DC Transit Bldg., Georgetown Univ., Wash., DC 20057; 10,700.

Teachers of French, Amer. Assn. of (1927), 57 E. Armory Ave., Champaign, IL 61820; 10,000.

Teachers of German, American Assn. of (1928), 523 Building, Suite 201, Route 38, Cherry Hill, NJ 08034; 7,000+.

Teachers of Mathematics, Natl. Council of (1920), 1906 Association Dr., Reston, VA 22091; 60,000.

Teachers of Singing, Natl. Assn. of (1944), New York Univ., 35 W. 4th St., #778, N.Y., NY 10003.

Teachers of Spanish & Portuguese, Amer. Assn. of (1917), P.O. Box 6349, Mississippi State Univ., Mississippi State, MS 39762-6349; 11,000+.

Telephone Pioneers of Amer. (1911), 195 Broadway, N.Y., NY 10007; 577,000.

Television Arts & Sciences, Natl. Academy of (1947), 110 W. 57th St., N.Y., NY 10019.

Television Bureau of Advertising (1954), 485 Lexington Ave., N.Y., NY 10017.

Television & Radio Artists, Amer. Federation of (1937), 1350 Ave. of the Americas, N.Y., NY 10019; 66,000.

Telluride Assn. (1910), 217 West Ave., Ithaca, NY 14850.

Tennis Assn., U.S. (1881), 51 E. 42d St., N.Y., NY 10017.

Tesla Memorial Soc., Inc. (1979), 453 Martin Rd. Lackawanna, NY 14218; 3,300.

Testing & Materials, Amer. Society for (1898), 1916 Race St., Phila., PA 19103; 30,000.

Textile Assn., Northern (1854), 211 Congress St., Boston, MA 02110.

Textile Manufacturers Institute, Amer. (1949), 1101 Connecticut Ave. NW, Suite 300, Wash., DC 20036.

Theatre Assn., Amer. (1936), 1010 Wisconsin Ave. NW, Suite 620, Wash., DC 20007; 7,200.

Theatre Organ Society, Amer. (1955), 1930-301 Encinitas Rd., San Marcos, CA 92069; 6,000.

Theodore Roosevelt Assn. (1919), P.O. Box 720, Oyster Bay, NY 11771; 1,200.

Theological Library Assn., Amer. (1947), 5600 S. Woodlawn Ave., Chicago, IL 60637; 502.

Theological Schools in the U.S. and Canada, Assn. of (1918), 42 E. National Rd., P.O. Box 130, Vandalia, OH 45377.

Theosophical Society (1875), P.O. Box 270, 1926 N. Main St., Wheaton, IL 60187; 5,339.

Thoreau Society (1941), 156 Belknap St., Concord, MA 01742; 1,000.

Thoroughbred Racing Assns. of No. America (1942), 3000 Marcus Ave., Lake Success, NY 11042; 50 racetracks.

Titanic Historical Society (1963), P.O. Box 53, Indian Orchard, MA 01151; 2,500.

Toastmasters Intl. (1924), 2200 N. Grand Ave., Santa Ana, CA 92701; 103,000.

Toastmistress Clubs, Intl. (1938), 2519 Woodland Dr., Anaheim, CA 92801; 25,000.

Topical Assn., Amer. (1949), P.O. Box 630, Johnstown, PA 15907; 10,000.

Torch Clubs, Internatl. Assn. of (1924), 435 N. Michigan Ave., #1717, Chicago, IL 60611; 3,700.

Toy Manufacturers of America (1916), 200 Fifth Ave., N.Y., NY 10010; 250.

Trade Relations Council of the U.S. (1885), 1001 Connecticut Ave. NW, Wash., DC 20036; 50 companies.

Traffic and Transportation, Amer. Society of (1946), 1816 Norris Pl. #4, Louisville, KY 40205; 2,400.

Trail Association, North Country (1980), 2780 Mundy Ave., White Cloud, MI 49349; 200+.

Training Corps, Amer. (1960), 107-12 Jamaica Ave., Richmond Hill, NY 11418; 60.

Transit Assn., Amer. Public (1974), 1225 Connecticut Ave. NW, Wash., DC 20036; 750.

Translators Assn., Amer. (1959), 109 Croton Ave., Ossining, NY 10562; 2,000+.

Transportation and Logistics, Inc., Amer. Society of (1946), P.O. Box 33095, Louisville, KY 40232; 2,300.

Trapshooting Assn., Amateur (1900), 601 W. National Rd. Vandalia, OH 45377; 80,000+.

Travel Agents, Amer. Society of (1931), 4400 MacArthur Blvd. NW, Wash., DC 20007.

Travel Industry Assn. of America (1965), 1899 L St. NW, Wash., DC 20036; 1,600.

Travelers Protective Assn. of America (1890), 3755 Lindell Blvd., St. Louis, MO 63108; 204,000.

Trilateral Commission (1973), 345 E. 46th, N.Y., NY 10017.

Triple Nine Society (1979), 2119 College St., Cedar Falls, IA 50613; 400.

Trucking Assn., Amer. (1933), 1616 P St. NW, Wash., DC.

True Sisters, United Order (1846), 212 Fifth Ave., N.Y., NY 10010; 12,000.

Tuberous Sclerosis Assn. of Amer. (1970), P.O. Box 44, Rockland, MA 02370; 2,500.

UFOs, Natl. Investigation Committee on (1956), 7970 Woodman Ave., Van Nuys, CA 91402.

UNICEF, U.S. Committee for (1947), 331 E. 38th St., N.Y., NY 10016.

USO (United Service Organizations) (1941), 1146 19th St. NW, Wash., DC 20036.

Underwriters, Amer. Soc. of Chartered Life (1927), 270 Bryn Mawr Ave., Bryn Mawr, PA 19010; 30,000.

Underwriters, Soc. of Chartered Property and Casualty (1944), Kahler Hall, 720 Providence Rd., Malvern, PA 19355; 15,000.

Uniformed Services, Natl. Assn. for (1968), 5535 Hempstead Way, Springfield, VA 22151; 25,000.

United Nations Assn. of the U.S.A. (1923, as League of Nations Assn.) 300 E. 42d St., N.Y., NY 10017; 25,000.

U.S., Amer. Assn. for the Study of in World Affairs (1948), 3813 Annandale Rd., Annandale, VA 22003; 1,500.

United Way of America (1918), 801 N. Fairfax St., Alexandria, VA 22309; 1,200.

Universities, Assn. of Amer. (1900), One Dupont Circle NW, Wash., DC 20036; 53 institutions.

Universities & Colleges, Assn. of Governing Bds. of (1921), One Dupont Circle NW, Wash., DC 20036; 1,000 boards.

University Extension Assn., Natl. (1915), One Dupont Circle, Suite 360, NW, Wash., DC 20036; 1,200.

University Foundation, Intl. (1973), 1301 S. Noland Rd., Independence, MO 64055; 10,500+.

University Professors, Amer. Assn. of (1915), One Dupont Circle, Suite 500, NW, Wash., DC 20036; 70,000.

University Professors for Academic Order (1970), 635 SW 4th St., Corvallis, OR 97333; 500.

University Women, Amer. Assn. of (1881), 2401 Virginia Ave. NW, Wash., DC 20037; 193,000.

Urban Coalition, Natl. (1968), 1120 G St. NW, Suite 900, Wash., DC 20005; 42 affiliates.

Urban League, Natl. (1910), 500 E. 62d St., N.Y., NY 10020.

Utility Commissioners, Natl. Assn. of Regulatory (1889), P.O. Box 684, Wash., DC 20044; 366.

Valley Forge, Society of the Descendants of Washington's Army at (1976) P.O. Box 915, Valley Forge, PA 19481.

Vampire Research Center (1972), P.O. Box 252, Elmhurst, N.Y. 11373; 30.

Variety Clubs Intl. (1928), 58 W. 58th St., N.Y., NY 10019.

VASA Order of America (1896), 65 Bryant Rd., Cranston, R.I. 02910; 35,000.

Ventriloquists, No. Amer. Assn. of (1940), 800 W. Littleton Blvd., Littleton, CO 80160; 1,750.

Ventriloquists, Soc. of Amer. (1976), 414 Oak St., Baltimore, OH 43105; 1,000.

Veterans Assn., Blinded (1945), 1735 DeSales St. NW, Wash., DC 20036; 6,000.

Veterans Assn., China-Burma-India (1947), 750 N. Lincoln Memorial Dr., Milwaukee, WI 53201; 3,221+.

Veterans Committee, Amer. (1944), 1346 Connecticut Ave. NW, Wash., DC 20036; 25,000.

Veterans of Foreign Wars of the U.S. (1899) **& Ladies Auxiliary** (1914), 406 W. 34th St., Kansas City, MO 64111.

Veterans of World War I (1958), 801 N. Fairfax St., Alexandria, VA 22314; 140,000.

Veterinary Medical Assn., Amer. (1863), 930 N. Meacham Rd., Schaumburg, IL 60196; 36,636.

Victorian Society in America (1966), 219 S. Sixth St., Phila., PA 19106; 4,088.

Vivisection Society, The Amer. Anti- (1883), 801 Old York Rd., Jenkintown, PA 19046; 10,000+.

Vocational Assn., Amer. (1925), 2020 N. 14th St., Arlington, VA 22201; 56,000.

Volleyball Assn., U.S. (1928), 1750 E. Boulder, Colorado Springs, CO 80909; 25,000.

Walking Assn. (1976), 4113 Lee Hwy., Arlington, VA 22207.

Walking Society Amer. (1980), P.O. Box 1315, Beverly Hills, CA 90213; 103,185.

War of 1812, General Society of the (1814), Wisconsin Ave. and Woodley Rd., NW, Wash., DC 20016.

War Mothers, Amer. (1917), 2615 Woodley Pl. NW, Wash., DC 20008; 7,000.

Warrant and Warrant Officers' Assn., Chief, U.S. Coast Guard (1929), 492 L'Enfant Plaza E., SW, Wash., DC 20024.

Washington, DC Area Trucking Assn. (1933), 2200 Mill Rd., Alexandria, VA 22314; 110 companies.

Watch & Clock Collectors, Natl. Assn. of (1943), 514 Poplar St., Columbia, PA 17512; 32,200.

Watercolor Soc., American (1866), 47 Fifth Ave., N.Y., NY 10003.

Water Pollution Control Federation (1928), 2626 Pennsylvania Ave. NW, Wash., DC 20037; 30,000.

Water Resources Assn., Amer. (1964), 5410 Grosvenor Ln., Suite 220, Bethesda, MD 20814; 2,750.

Water Ski Assn., Amer. (1939), P.O. Box 191, Winter Haven, FL 33882; 18,000.

Water Well Assn., Natl. (1948), 500 W. Wilson Bridge Rd., Worthington, OH 43085; 8,400.

Water Works Assn., Amer. (1881), 6666 W. Quincy Ave., Denver, CO 80235; 36,500.

Watts Family Assn. (1969), 12401 Burton St., N. Hollywood, CA 91605; 12 branches.

Weather Modification Assn. (1969), P.O. Box 8116, Fresno, CA 93727; 250.

Welding Society, Amer. (1919), 550 N.W. LeJeune Rd., Miami, FL 33126; 32,000.

Wheelchair Athletic Assn., Natl. (1958), Nassau Community College, Garden City, NY 11530; 2,000+.

Wilderness Society (1935), 1400 Eye St. NW, Wash., DC 20005; 130,000.

Wild Horse Organized Assistance (WHOA!) (1971), 140 Greenstone Dr., Reno, NV 89512; 10,000.

Wildlife, Defenders of (1947), 1244 19th St. NW, Wash., DC, 20036; 63,000.

Wildlife Federation, Natl. (1936), 1412 16th St. NW, Wash., DC 20036; 4.2 mln.

Wildlife Foundation, No. Amer. (1911), 1101-14th St. NW, Suite 725, Wash., DC 20005.

Wildlife Fund, World (1961), 1601 Connecticut Ave. NW, Wash., DC 20009; 85,000.

Wildlife Management Institute (1911), 1101-14th St., Suite 725, NW, Wash., DC 20005.

William Penn Assn. (1886), 709 Brighton Rd., Pittsburgh, PA 15233; 90,000.

Wilsonian Club (1920), 1331 Parkside Dr., Riverside, CA 92506; 150.

Wireless Pioneers, Society of (1968), 3366—15 Mendocino Ave., Santa Rosa, CA 95401; 5,427.

Wizard of Oz Club, Intl. (1957), Box 95, Kinderhook, IL 62345; 1,925.

Women, Natl. Assn. of Bank (1921), 500 No. Michigan Ave., Chicago, IL 60611; 30,000.

Women, Natl. Organization for (NOW) (1966), 1401 New York Ave. NW, Wash., DC 20005; 200,000.

Women, Rural Amer. (1977), 1522 K St. NW, Wash., DC 20005.

Women Artists, Natl. Assn. of (1889), 41 Union Sq., N.Y., NY 10003; 700.

Women Engineers, Society of (1950), 345 E. 47th St., N.Y., NY 10017; 12,500.

Women in Communications (1909), P.O. Box 9561, Austin, TX 78766.

Women in Radio and TV, Inc. (1951), 1321 Connecticut Ave. NW, Washington, DC 20036; 3,000.

Women Geographers, Society of (1925), 1619 New Hampshire Ave. NW, Wash., DC 20009; 500.

Women Marines Assn. (1960), 1008 Scenic View Dr., College Pl., WA 99324; 2,500.

Women Strike for Peace (1961), 145 S. 13th St., Phila., PA 19107; 9,000.

Women of the U.S., Natl. Council of (1888), 777 U.N. Plaza, N.Y., NY 10017; 27 organizations.

Women Voters of the U.S., League of (1920), 1730 M St. NW, Wash., DC 20036; 110,000.

Women World War Veterans (1919), 237 Madison Ave., N.Y., NY 10016; 85,000.

Women's Army Corps Veterans Assn. (1946), 1409 E. Euclid Ave., Arlington Heights, IL 60004; 2,400.

Women's Assn., Amer. Business (1949), 9100 Ward Pkwy., P.O. Box 8728, Kansas City, MO 64114; 112,000.

Women's Christian Temperance Union, Natl. (1874), 1730 Chicago Ave., Evanston, IL 60201.

Women's Clubs, General Federation of (1890), 1734 N St. NW., Wash. DC, 20036; 500,000.

Women's Clubs, Natl. Federation of Business & Professional (1919), 2012 Massachusetts Ave. NW, Wash., DC 20036, 150,000.

Women's Educational & Industrial Union (1877), 356 Boylston St., Boston, MA 02116; 3,000.

Women's Intl. League for Peace & Freedom (1915), 1213 Race St., Phila., PA 19107; 9,000.

Women's Legal Defense Fund (1971), 2000 P St. NW, Suite 400, Washington, DC 20036; 1,300.

Women's Overseas Service League (1921), P.O. Box 39058, Friendship Sta., Wash., DC 20016; 1,500.

Woodmen of America, Modern (1883), Mississippi River at 17th St., Rock Island, IL 61201; 384,294.

Woodmen of the World (1890), 1450 Speer Blvd., Denver, CO 80204; 28,954.

Woodmen of the World Life Ins. Soc. (1890), 1700 Farnam St., Omaha, NE 68102; 958,800.

Wool Growers Assn., Natl. (1865), 425 13th St., Rm. 548, Wash., DC 20004; 24 state assns.

Workmen's Circle (1900), 45 E. 33d St., N.Y., NY 10016.

World Future Society (1967), 4916 St. Elmo Ave., Bethesda, MD 20814; 28,000.

World Health, Amer. Assn. for (1951), 515 22nd St. NW, Wash., DC 20037.

World Health, U.S. Committee for (1951), 777 United Nations Plaza, N.Y., NY 10017; 2,017.

World Peace, International Assn. of Educators for (1969), P.O. Box 3282, Blue Spring Station, Huntsville, AL 35810-0282; 18,000.

Writers of America, Western (1953), 1052 Meridian Rd., Victor, MT 59875; 449.

Writers Assn. of America, Outdoor (1927), 3101 W. Peoria Ave., Suite A-207, Phoenix, AZ 85029.

Writers Guild of America, West (1954), 8955 Beverly Blvd., Los Angeles, CA 90048; 6,000.

Yeoman F. Natl. (1936), 223 El Camino Real, Vallejo, CA 94590; 800.

Young Americans for Freedom (1960), Woodland Rd., Sterling, VA 22170; 55,000.

Young Men's Christian Assns. of the U.S.A., (1851), 101 N. Wacker Dr., Chicago, IL 60606; 13 mln.

YM-YMHAs of Greater New York, Associated (1957), 130 E. 59th St., N.Y., NY 10020; 55,100.

Young Women's Christian Assn. of the U.S.A. (1906), 726 Broadway, N.Y., NY 10003; 1.6 mln.

Young Engineers & Scientists of America Foundation, Inc. (1959), P.O. Box 9066, Phoenix, AZ 85068; 260 chapters.

Youth, Allied (1936), 1556 Wisconsin Ave., Wash., DC 20007.

Youth Hostels, American (1934), 1332 Eye St. NW, Suite 800, Wash., DC 20005; 100,000.

Zero Population Growth (1968), 1346 Connecticut Ave. NW, Wash., DC 20036; 15,000.

Ziegfeld Club (1936), 593 Park Ave., N.Y., NY 10021; 303.

Zionist Organization of America (1897), 4 E. 34th St., N.Y., NY 10016; 130,000.

Zonta Intl. (1919), 35 E. Wacker Dr., Chicago, IL 60601.

Zoological Parks & Aquariums, Amer. Assn. of (1924), Oglebay Park, Wheeling, WV 26003; 4,400.

Zoologists, Amer. Society of (1890), Box 2739, California Lutheran College, Thousand Oaks, CA 91360; 4,500.

BIOGRAPHIES OF U.S. PRESIDENTS

George Washington

George Washington, first president, was born Feb. 22, 1732 (Feb. 11, 1731, old style), the son of Augustine Washington and Mary Ball, at Wakefield on Pope's Creek, Westmoreland Co., Va. His early childhood was spent on the Ferry farm, near Fredericksburg. His father died when George was 11. He studied mathematics and surveying and when 16 went to live with his half brother Lawrence, who built and named Mount Vernon. George surveyed the lands of William Fairfax in the Shenandoah Valley, keeping a diary. He accompanied Lawrence to Barbados, West Indies, contracted small pox, and was deeply scarred. Lawrence died in 1752 and George acquired his property by inheritance. He valued land and when he died owned 70,000 acres in Virginia and 40,000 acres in what is now West Virginia.

Washington's military service began in 1753 when Gov. Dinwiddie of Virginia sent him on missions deep into Ohio country. He clashed with the French and had to surrender Fort Necessity July 3, 1754. He was an aide to Braddock and at his side when the army was ambushed and defeated on a march to Ft. Duquesne, July 9, 1755. He helped take Fort Duquesne from the French in 1758.

After his marriage to Martha Dandridge Custis, a widow, in 1759, Washington managed his family estate at Mount Vernon. Although not at first for independence, he opposed British exactions and took charge of the Virginia troops before war broke out. He was made commander-in-chief by the Continental Congress June 15, 1775.

The successful issue of a war filled with hardships was due to his leadership. He was resourceful, a stern disciplinarian, and the one strong, dependable force for unity. He favored a federal government and became chairman of the Constitutional Convention of 1787. He helped get the Constitution ratified and was unanimously elected president by the electoral college and inaugurated, Apr. 30, 1789, on the balcony of New York's Federal Hall.

He was reelected 1792, but refused to consider a 3d term and retired to Mount Vernon. He suffered acute laryngitis after a ride in snow and rain around his estate, was bled profusely, and died Dec. 14, 1799.

John Adams

John Adams, 2d president, Federalist, was born in Braintree (Quincy), Mass., Oct. 30, 1735 (Oct. 19, o. s.), the son of John Adams, a farmer, and Susanna Boylston. He was a great-grandson of Henry Adams who came from England in 1636. He was graduated from Harvard, 1755, taught school, studied law. In 1765 he argued against taxation without representation before the royal governor. In 1770 he defended the British soldiers who fired on civilians in the "Boston Massacre." He was a delegate to the first Continental Congress, and signed the Declaration of Independence. He was a commissioner to France, 1778, with Benjamin Franklin and Arthur Lee; won recognition of the U.S. by The Hague, 1782; was first American minister to England, 1785-1788, and was elected vice president, 1788 and 1792.

In 1796 Adams was chosen president by the electors. Intense antagonism to America by France caused agitation for war, led by Alexander Hamilton. Adams, breaking with Hamilton, opposed war.

To fight alien influence and muzzle criticism Adams supported the Alien and Sedition laws of 1798, which led to his defeat for reelection. He died July 4, 1826, on the same day as Jefferson (the 50th anniversary of the Declaration of Independence).

Thomas Jefferson

Thomas Jefferson, 3d president, was born Apr. 13, 1743 (Apr. 2, o. s.), at Shadwell, Va., the son of Peter Jefferson, a civil engineer of Welsh descent who raised tobacco, and Jane Randolph. His father died when he was 14, leaving him 2,750 acres and his slaves. Jefferson attended the College of

William and Mary, 1760-1762, read classics in Greek and Latin and played the violin. In 1769 he was elected to the House of Burgesses. In 1770 he began building Monticello, near Charlottesville. He was a member of the Virginia Committee of Correspondence and the Continental Congress. Named a member of the committee to draw up a Declaration of Independence, he wrote the basic draft. He was a member of the Virginia House of Delegates, 1776-79, elected governor to succeed Patrick Henry, 1779, reelected 1780, resigned June 1781, amid charges of ineffectual military preparation. During his term he wrote the statute on religious freedom. In the Continental Congress, 1783, he drew up an ordinance for the Northwest Territory, forbidding slavery after 1800; its terms were put into the Ordinance of 1787. He was sent to Paris with Benjamin Franklin and John Adams to negotiate commercial treaties, 1784; made minister to France, 1785.

Washington appointed him secretary of state, 1789. Jefferson's strong faith in the consent of the governed, as opposed to executive control favored by Hamilton, secretary of the treasury, often led to conflict: Dec. 31, 1793, he resigned. He was the Republican candidate for president in 1796; beaten by John Adams, he became vice president. In 1800, Jefferson and Aaron Burr received equal electoral college votes for president. The House of Representatives elected Jefferson. Major events of his administration were the Louisiana Purchase, 1803, and the Lewis and Clark Expedition. He established the Univ. of Virginia and designed its buildings. He died July 4, 1826, on the same day as John Adams.

James Madison

James Madison, 4th president, Republican, was born Mar. 16, 1751 (Mar. 5, 1750, o. s.) at Port Conway, King George Co., Va., eldest son of James Madison and Eleanor Rose Conway. Madison was graduated from Princeton, 1771; studied theology, 1772; sat in the Virginia Constitutional Convention, 1776. He was a member of the Continental Congress. He was chief recorder at the Constitutional Convention in 1787, and supported ratification in the Federalist Papers, written with Alexander Hamilton and John Jay. He was elected to the House of Representatives in 1789, helped frame the Bill of Rights and fought the Alien and Sedition Acts. He became Jefferson's secretary of state, 1801.

Elected president in 1808, Madison was a "strict constructionist," opposed to the free interpretation of the Constitution by the Federalists. He was reelected in 1812 by the votes of the agrarian South and recently admitted western states. Caught between British and French maritime restrictions, the U.S. drifted into war, declared June 18, 1812. The war ended in a stalemate. He retired in 1817 to his estate at Montpelier. There he edited his famous papers on the Constitutional Convention. He became rector of the Univ. of Virginia, 1826. He died June 28, 1836.

James Monroe

James Monroe, 5th president, Republican, was born Apr. 28, 1758, in Westmoreland Co., Va., the son of Spence Monroe and Eliza Jones, who were of Scottish and Welsh descent, respectively. He attended the College of William and Mary, fought in the 3d Virginia Regiment at White Plains, Brandywine, Monmouth, and was wounded at Trenton. He studied law with Thomas Jefferson, 1780, was a member of the Virginia House of Delegates and of Congress, 1783-86. He opposed ratification of the Constitution because it lacked a bill of rights; was U.S. senator, 1790; minister to France, 1794-96; governor of Virginia, 1799-1802, and 1811. Jefferson sent him to France as minister, 1803. He helped R. Livingston negotiate the Louisiana Purchase, 1803. He ran against Madison for president in 1808. He was elected to the Virginia Assembly, 1810-1811; was secretary of state under Madison, 1811-1817.

In 1816 Monroe was elected president; in 1820 reelected

with all but one electoral college vote. Monroe's administration became the "Era of Good Feeling." He obtained Florida from Spain; settled boundaries with Canada, and eliminated border forts. He supported the anti-slavery position that led to the Missouri Compromise. His most significant contribution was the "Monroe Doctrine," which became a cornerstone of U.S. foreign policy. Monroe retired to Oak Hill, Va. Financial problems forced him to sell his property. He moved to New York City to live with a daughter. He died there July 4, 1831.

John Quincy Adams

John Quincy Adams, 6th president, independent Federalist, was born July 11, 1767, at Braintree (Quincy), Mass., the son of John and Abigail Adams. His father was the 2d president. He was educated in Paris, Leyden, and Harvard, graduating in 1787. He served as American minister in various European capitals, and helped draft the War of 1812 peace treaty. He was U.S. Senator, 1803-08. President Monroe made him secretary of state, 1817, and he negotiated the cession of the Floridas from Spain, supported exclusion of slavery in the Missouri Compromise, and helped formulate the Monroe Doctrine. In 1824 he was elected president by the House after he failed to win an electoral college majority. His expansion of executive powers was strongly opposed and he was beaten in 1828 by Jackson. In 1831 he entered Congress and served 17 years with distinction. He opposed slavery, the annexation of Texas, and the Mexican War. He helped establish the Smithsonian Institution. He had a stroke in the House and died in the Speaker's Room, Feb. 23, 1848.

Andrew Jackson

Andrew Jackson, 7th president, was a Jeffersonian-Republican, later a Democrat. He was born in the Waxhaws district, New Lancaster Co., S.C., Mar. 15, 1767, the posthumous son of Andrew Jackson and Elizabeth Hutchinson, who were Irish immigrants. At 13, he joined the militia in the Revolution and was captured.

He read law in Salisbury, N.C., moved to Nashville, Tenn., speculated in land, married, and practiced law. In 1796 he helped draft the constitution of Tennessee and for a year occupied its one seat in Congress. He was in the Senate in 1797, and again in 1823. He defeated the Creek Indians at Horseshoe Bend, Ala., 1814. With 6,000 backwoods fighters he defeated Packenham's 12,000 British troops at the Chalmette, outside New Orleans, Jan. 8, 1815. In 1818 he briefly invaded Spanish Florida to quell Seminoles and outlaws who harassed frontier settlements. In 1824 he ran for president against John Quincy Adams and had the most popular and electoral votes but not a majority; the election was decided by the House, which chose Adams. In 1828 he defeated Adams, carrying the West and South. He was a noisy debater and a duelist and introduced rotation in office called the "spoils system." Suspicious of privilege, he ruined the Bank of the United States by depositing federal funds with state banks. Though "Let the people rule" was his slogan, he at times supported strict constructionist policies against the expansionist West. He killed the Congressional caucus for nominating presidential candidates and substituted the national convention, 1832. When South Carolina refused to collect imports under his protective tariff he ordered army and naval forces to Charleston. Jackson recognized the Republic of Texas, 1836. He died at the Hermitage, June 8, 1845.

Martin Van Buren

Martin Van Buren, 8th president, Democrat, was born Dec. 5, 1782, at Kinderhook, N.Y., the son of Abraham Van Buren, a Dutch farmer, and Mary Hoes. He was surrogate of Columbia County, N.Y., state senator and attorney general. He was U.S. Senator 1821, reelected, 1827, elected governor of New York, 1828. He helped swing eastern support to Jackson in 1828 and was his secretary of state 1829-31. In 1832 he was elected vice president. He was a

consummate politician, known as "the little magician," who influenced Jackson's policies. In 1836 he defeated William Henry Harrison for president and took office as the Panic of 1837 initiated a 5-year nationwide depression. He inaugurated the independent treasury system. His refusal to spend land revenues led to his defeat by Harrison in 1840. He lost the Democratic nomination of 1844 to Polk. In 1848 he ran for president on the Free Soil ticket and lost. He died July 24, 1862, at Kinderhook.

William Henry Harrison

William Henry Harrison, 9th president, Whig, who served only 31 days, was born in Berkeley, Charles City Co., Va., Feb. 9, 1773, the 3d son of Benjamin Harrison, signer of the Declaration of Independence. He attended Hampden Sydney College. He was secretary of the Northwest Territory, 1798; its delegate in Congress, 1799; first governor of Indiana Territory, 1800; and superintendent of Indian affairs. With 900 men he routed Tecumseh's Indians at Tippecanoe, Nov. 7, 1811. A major general, he defeated British and Indians at Battle of the Thames, Oct. 5, 1813. He served in Congress, 1816-19; Senate, 1825-28. In 1840, when 68, he was elected president with a "log cabin and hard cider" slogan. He caught pneumonia during the inauguration and died Apr. 4, 1841.

John Tyler

John Tyler, 10th president, independent Whig, was born Mar. 29, 1790, in Greenway, Charles City Co., Va., son of John Tyler and Mary Armistead. His father was governor of Virginia, 1808-11. Tyler was graduated from William and Mary, 1807; member of the House of Delegates, 1811; in congress, 1816-21; in Virginia legislature, 1823-25; governor of Virginia, 1825-26; U.S. senator, 1827-36. In 1840 he was elected vice president and, on Harrison's death, succeeded him. He favored pre-emption, allowing settlers to get government land; rejected a national bank bill and thus alienated most Whig supporters; refused to honor the spoils system. He signed the resolution annexing Texas, Mar. 1, 1845. He accepted renomination, 1844, but withdrew before election. In 1861, he chaired an unsuccessful Washington conference called to avert civil war. After its failure he supported secession, sat in the provisional Confederate Congress, became a member of the Confederate House, but died, Jan. 18, 1862, before it met.

James Knox Polk

James Knox Polk, 11th president, Democrat, was born in Mecklenburg Co., N.C., Nov. 2, 1795, the son of Samuel Polk, farmer and surveyor of Scotch-Irish descent, and Jane Knox. He graduated from the Univ. of North Carolina, 1818; member of the Tennessee state legislature, 1823-25. He served in Congress 1825-39 and as speaker 1835-39. He was governor of Tennessee 1839-41, but was defeated 1841 and 1843. In 1844, when both Clay and Van Buren announced opposition to annexing Texas, the Democrats made Polk the first dark horse nominee because he demanded control of all Oregon and annexation of Texas. Polk reestablished the independent treasury system originated by Van Buren. His expansionist policy was opposed by Clay, Webster, Calhoun; he sent troops under Zachary Taylor to the Mexican border and, when Mexicans attacked, declared war existed. The Mexican war ended with the annexation of California and much of the Southwest as part of America's "manifest destiny." He compromised on the Oregon boundary ("54-40 or fight!") by accepting the 49th parallel and giving Vancouver to the British. Polk died in Nashville, June 15, 1849.

Zachary Taylor

Zachary Taylor, 12th president, Whig, who served only 16 months, was born Nov. 24, 1784, in Orange Co., Va., the son of Richard Taylor, later collector of the port of Louisville, Ky., and Sarah Strother. Taylor was commissioned first lieutenant, 1808; fought in the War of 1812; the Black

Hawk War, 1832; and the second Seminole War, 1837. He was called Old Rough and Ready. He settled on a plantation near Baton Rouge, La. In 1845 Polk sent him with an army to the Rio Grande. When the Mexicans attacked him, Polk declared war. Taylor was successful at Palo Alto and Resaca de la Palma, 1846; occupied Monterrey. Polk made him major general but sent many of his troops to Gen. Winfield Scott. Outnumbered 4-1, he defeated Santa Anna at Buena Vista, 1847. A national hero, he received the Whig nomination in 1848, and was elected president. He resumed the spoils system and though once a slave-holder worked to have California admitted as a free state. He died in office July 9, 1850.

Millard Fillmore

Millard Fillmore, 13th president, Whig, was born Jan. 7, 1800, in Cayuga Co., N.Y., the son of Nathaniel Fillmore and Phoebe Miller. He taught school and studied law; admitted to the bar, 1823. He was a member of the state assembly, 1829-32; in Congress, 1833-35 and again 1837-43. He opposed the entrance of Texas as slave territory and voted for a protective tariff. In 1844 he was defeated for governor of New York. In 1848 he was elected vice president and succeeded as president July 10, 1850, after Taylor's death. Fillmore favored the Compromise of 1850 and signed the Fugitive Slave Law. His policies pleased neither expansionists nor slave-holders and he was not renominated in 1852. In 1856 he was nominated by the American (Know-Nothing) party and accepted by the Whigs, but defeated by Buchanan. He died in Buffalo, Mar. 8, 1874.

Franklin Pierce

Franklin Pierce, 14th president, Democrat, was born in Hillsboro, N. H., Nov. 23, 1804, the son of Benjamin Pierce, veteran of the Revolution and governor of New Hampshire, 1827. He graduated from Bowdoin, 1824. A lawyer, he served in the state legislature 1829-33; in Congress, supporting Jackson, 1833-37; U.S. senator, 1837-42. He enlisted in the Mexican War, became brigadier general under Gen. Winfield Scott. In 1852 Pierce was nominated on the 49th ballot over Lewis Cass, Stephen A. Douglas, and James Buchanan, and defeated Gen. Scott, Whig. Though against slavery, Pierce was influenced by Southern pro-slavery men. He ignored the Ostend Manifesto that the U.S. either buy or take Cuba. He approved the Kansas-Nebraska Act, leaving slavery to popular vote ("squatter sovereignty"), 1854. He signed a reciprocity treaty with Canada and approved the Gadsden Purchase from Mexico, 1853. Denied renomination by the Democrats, he spent most of his remaining years in Concord, N.H., where he died Oct. 8, 1869.

James Buchanan

James Buchanan, 15th president, Federalist, later Democrat, was born of Scottish descent near Mercersburg, Pa., Apr. 23, 1791. He graduated from Dickinson, 1809; was a volunteer in the War of 1812; member, Pennsylvania legislature, 1814-16; Congress, 1820-31; Jackson's minister to Russia, 1831-33; U.S. senator 1834-45. As Polk's secretary of state, 1845-49, he ended the Oregon dispute with Britain, supported the Mexican War and annexation of Texas. As minister to Britain, 1853, he signed the Ostend Manifesto. Nominated by Democrats, he was elected, 1856, over John C. Fremont (Republican) and Millard Fillmore (American Know-Nothing and Whig tickets). On slavery he favored popular sovereignty and choice by state constitutions; he accepted the pro-slavery Dred Scott decision as binding. He denied the right of states to secede. A strict constructionist, he desired to keep peace and found no authority for using force. He died at Wheatland, near Lancaster, Pa., June 1, 1868.

Abraham Lincoln

Abraham Lincoln, 16th president, Republican, was born Feb. 12, 1809, in a log cabin on a farm then in Hardin Co.,

Ky., now in Larue. He was the son of Thomas Lincoln, a carpenter, and Nancy Hanks.

The Lincolns moved to Spencer Co., Ind., near Gentryville, when Abe was 7. Nancy died 1818, and his father married Mrs. Sarah Bush Johnston, 1819; she had a favorable influence on Abe. In 1830 the family moved to Macon Co., Ill. Lincoln lost election to the Illinois General Assembly, 1832, but later won 4 times, beginning in 1834. He enlisted in the militia for the Black Hawk War, 1832. In New Salem he ran a store, surveyed land, and was postmaster.

In 1837 Lincoln was admitted to the bar and became partner in a Springfield, Ill., law office. He was elected to Congress, 1847-49. He opposed the Mexican War. He supported Zachary Taylor, 1848. He opposed the Kansas-Nebraska Act and extension of slavery, 1854. He failed, in his bid for the Senate, 1855. He supported John C. Fremont, 1856.

In 1858 Lincoln had Republican support in the Illinois legislature for the Senate but was defeated by Stephen A. Douglas, Dem., who had sponsored the Kansas-Nebraska Act.

Lincoln was nominated for president by the Republican party on an anti-slavery platform, 1860. He ran against Douglas, a northern Democrat; John C. Breckinridge, southern pro-slavery Democrat; John Bell, Constitutional Union party. When he won the election, South Carolina seceded from the Union Dec. 20, 1860, followed in 1861 by 10 Southern states.

The Civil War erupted when Fort Sumter was attacked Apr. 12, 1861. On Sept. 22, 1862, 5 days after the battle of Antietam, he announced that slaves in territory then in rebellion would be free Jan. 1, 1863, date of the Emancipation Proclamation, His speeches, including his Gettysburg and Inaugural addresses, are remembered for their eloquence.

Lincoln was reelected, 1864, over Gen. George B. McClellan, Democrat. Lee surrendered Apr. 9, 1865. On Apr. 14, Lincoln was shot by actor John Wilkes Booth in Ford's Theatre, Washington. He died the next day.

Andrew Johnson

Andrew Johnson, 17th president, Democrat, was born in Raleigh, N.C., Dec. 29, 1808, the son of Jacob Johnson, porter at an inn and church sexton, and Mary McDonough. He was apprenticed to a tailor but ran away and eventually settled in Greeneville, Tenn. He became an alderman, 1828; mayor, 1830; state representative and senator, 1835-43; member of Congress, 1843-53; governor of Tennessee, 1853-57; U.S. senator, 1857-62. He supported John C. Breckinridge against Lincoln in 1860. He had held slaves, but opposed secession and tried to prevent his home state, Tennessee, from seceding. In Mar. 1862, Lincoln appointed him military governor of occupied Tennessee. In 1864 he was nominated for vice president with Lincoln on the National Union ticket to win Democratic support. He succeeded Lincoln as president April 15, 1865. In a controversy with Congress over the president's power over the South, he proclaimed, May 26, 1865, an amnesty to all Confederates except certain leaders if they would ratify the 13th Amendment abolishing slavery. States doing so added anti-Negro provisions that enraged Congress, which restored military control over the South. When Johnson removed Edwin M. Stanton, secretary of war, without notifying the Senate, thus repudiating the Tenure of Office Act, the House impeached him for this and other reasons. He was tried by the Senate, and acquitted by only one vote, May 26, 1868. He returned to the Senate in 1875. Johnson died July 31, 1875.

Ulysses Simpson Grant

Ulysses S. Grant, 18th president, Republican, was born at Point Pleasant, Oh., Apr. 27, 1822, son of Jesse R. Grant, a tanner, and Hannah Simpson. The next year the family moved to Georgetown, Oh. Grant was named Hiram Ulysses, but on entering West Point, 1839, his name was entered as Ulysses Simpson and he adopted it. he was graduated in 1843; served under Gens. Taylor and Scott in the Mexican War; resigned, 1854; worked in St. Louis until 1860, then went to Galena, Ill. With the start of the Civil War, he was

named colonel of the 21st Illinois Vols., 1861, then brigadier general; took Forts Henry and Donelson; fought at Shiloh, took Vicksburg. After his victory at Chattanooga, Lincoln placed him in command of the Union Armies. He accepted Lee's surrender at Appomattox, Apr., 1865. President Johnson appointed Grant secretary of war when he suspended Stanton, but Grant was not confirmed. He was nominated for president by the Republicans and elected over Horatio Seymour, Democrat. The 15th Amendment, amnesty bill, and civil service reform were events of his administration. The Liberal Republicans and Democrats opposed him with Horace Greeley, 1872, but he was reelected. An attempt by the Stalwarts (Old Guard) to nominate him in 1880 failed. In 1884 the collapse of Grant & Ward, investment house, left him penniless. He wrote his personal memoirs while ill with cancer and completed them 4 days before his death at Mt. McGregor, N.Y., July 23, 1885. The book realized over $450,000.

Rutherford Birchard Hayes

Rutherford B. Hayes, 19th president, Republican, was born in Delaware, Oh., Oct. 4, 1822, the posthumous son of Rutherford Hayes, a farmer, and Sophia Birchard. He was raised by his uncle Sardis Birchard. He graduated from Kenyon College, 1842, and Harvard Law School, 1845. He practiced law in Lower Sandusky, Oh., now Fremont; was city solicitor of Cincinnati, 1858-61. In the Civil War, he was major of the 23d Ohio Vols., was wounded several times, and rose to the rank of brevet major general, 1864. He served in Congress 1864-67, supporting Reconstruction and Johnson's impeachment. He was elected governor of Ohio, 1867 and 1869; beaten in the race for Congress, 1872; reelected governor, 1875. In 1876 he was nominated for president and believed he had lost the election to Samuel J. Tilden, Democrat. But a few Southern states submitted 2 different sets of electoral votes and the result was in dispute. An electoral commission, appointed by Congress, 8 Republicans and 7 Democrats, awarded all disputed votes to Hayes allowing him to become president by one electoral vote. Hayes, keeping a promise to southerners, withdrew troops from areas still occupied in the South, ending the era of Reconstruction. He proceeded to reform the civil service, alienating political spoilsmen. He advocated repeal of the Tenure of Office Act. He supported sound money and specie payments. Hayes died in Fremont, Oh., Jan. 17, 1893.

James Abram Garfield

James A. Garfield, 20th president, Republican, was born Nov. 19, 1831, in Orange, Cuyahoga Co., Oh., the son of Abram Garfield and Eliza Ballou. His father died in 1833. He worked as a canal bargeman, farmer, and carpenter; attended Western Reserve Eclectic, later Hiram College, and was graduated from Williams in 1856. He taught at Hiram, and later became principal. He was in the Ohio senate in 1859. Anti-slavery and anti-secession, he volunteered for the war, became colonel of the 42d Ohio Infantry and brigadier in 1862. He fought at Shiloh, was chief of staff for Rosecrans and was made major general for gallantry at Chickamauga. He entered Congress as a radical Republican in 1863; supported specie payment as against paper money (greenbacks). On the electoral commission in 1876 he voted for Hayes against Tilden on strict party lines. He was senator-elect in 1880 when he became the Republican nominee for president. He was chosen as a compromise over Gen. Grant, James G. Blaine, and John Sherman. This alienated the Grant following but Garfield was elected. On July 2, 1881, Garfield was shot by mentally disturbed office-seeker, Charles J. Guiteau, while entering a railroad station in Washington. He died Sept. 19, 1881, at Elberon, N.J.

Chester Alan Arthur

Chester A. Arthur, 21st president, Republican, was born at Fairfield, Vt., Oct. 5, 1829, the son of the Rev. William Arthur, from County Antrim, Ireland, and Malvina Stone. He graduated from Union College, 1848, taught school at Pownall, Vt., studied law in New York. In 1853 he argued in a fugitive slave case that slaves transported through N.Y. State were thereby freed; in 1885 he obtained a ruling that Negroes were to be treated the same as whites on street cars. He was made collector of the Port of New York, 1871. President Hayes, reforming the civil service, forced Arthur to resign, 1879. This made the New York machine stalwarts enemies of Hayes. Arthur and the stalwarts tried to nominate Grant for a 3d term in 1880. When Garfield was nominated, Arthur received 2d place in the interests of harmony. When Garfield died, Arthur became president. He supported civil service reform and the tariff of 1883. He was defeated for renomination by James G. Blaine. He died in New York City Nov. 18, 1886.

Grover Cleveland

(According to a ruling of the State Dept., Grover Cleveland is both the 22d and the 24th president, because his 2 terms were not consecutive. By individuals, he is only the 22d.)

Grover Cleveland, 22d and 24th president, Democrat, was born in Caldwell, N.J. Mar. 18, 1837, the son of Richard F. Cleveland, a Presbyterian minister, and Ann Neale. He was named Stephen Grover, but dropped the Stephen. He clerked in Clinton and Buffalo, N.Y.; taught at the N.Y. City Institution for the Blind; was admitted to the bar in Buffalo, 1859; became assistant district attorney, 1863; sheriff, 1871; mayor, 1881; governor of New York, 1882. He was an independent, honest administrator who hated corruption. He was nominated for president over Tammany Hall opposition, 1884, and defeated Republican James G. Blaine. He enlarged the civil service, vetoed many pension raids on the Treasury. In 1888 he was defeated by Benjamin Harrison, although his popular vote was larger. Reelected over Harrison in 1892, he faced a money crisis brought about by lowering of the gold reserve, circulation of paper and exorbitant silver purchases under the Sherman Act; obtained a repeal of the latter and a reduced tariff. A severe depression and labor troubles racked his administration but he refused to interfere in business matters and rejected Jacob Coxey's demand for unemployment relief. He broke the Pullman strike, 1894. In 1896, the Democrats repudiated his administration and chose silverite William Jennings Bryan as their candidate. Cleveland died in Princeton, N.J., June 24, 1908.

Benjamin Harrison

Benjamin Harrison, 23d president, Republican, was born at North Bend, Oh., Aug. 20, 1833. His great-grandfather, Benjamin Harrison, was a signer of the Declaration of Independence; his grandfather, William Henry Harrison, was 9th President; his father, John Scott Harrison, was a member of Congress. His mother was Elizabeth F. Irwin. He attended school on his father's farm; graduated from Miami Univ. at Oxford, Oh., 1852; admitted to the bar, 1853, and practiced in Indianapolis. In the Civil War, he rose to the rank of brevet brigadier general, fought at Kennesaw Mountain, Peachtree Creek, Nashville, and in the Atlanta campaign. He failed to be elected governor of Indiana, 1876; but became senator, 1881, and worked for the G. A. R. pensions vetoed by Cleveland. In 1888 he defeated Cleveland for president despite having fewer popular votes. He expanded the pension list; signed the McKinley high tariff bill and the Sherman Silver Purchase Act. During his administration, 6 states were admitted to the union. He was defeated for reelection, 1892. He represented Venezuela in a boundary arbitration with Great Britain in Paris, 1899. He died at Indianapolis, Mar. 13, 1901.

William McKinley

William McKinley, 25th president, Republican, was born in Niles, Oh., Jan. 29, 1843, the son of William McKinley, an ironmaker, and Nancy Allison. McKinley attended school in Poland, Oh., and Allegheny College, Meadville, Pa., and enlisted for the Civil War at 18 in the 23d Ohio, in which Rutherford B. Hayes was a major. He rose to captain and in 1865 was made brevet major. He studied law in the Albany, N.Y., law school; opened an office in Canton, Oh.,

in 1867, and campaigned for Grant and Hayes. He served in the House of Representatives, 1877-83, 1885-91, and led the fight for passage of the McKinley Tarriff, 1890. Defeated for reelection on the issue in 1890, he was governor of Ohio, 1892-96. He had support for president in the convention that nominated Benjamin Harrison in 1892. In 1896 he was elected president on a protective tariff, sound money (gold standard) platform over William Jennings Bryan, Democratic proponent of free silver. McKinley was reluctant to intervene in Cuba but the loss of the battleship Maine at Havana crystallized opinion. He demanded Spain's withdrawal from Cuba; Spain made some concessions but Congress announced state of war as of Apr. 21. He was reelected in the 1900 campaign, defeating Bryan's anti-imperialist arguments with the promise of a "full dinner pail." McKinley was respected for his conciliatory nature, but conservative on business issues. On Sept. 6, 1901, while welcoming citizens at the Pan-American Exposition, Buffalo, N.Y., he was shot by Leon Czolgosz, an anarchist. He died Sept. 14.

Theodore Roosevelt

Theodore Roosevelt, 26th president, Republican, was born in N.Y. City, Oct. 27, 1858, the son of Theodore Roosevelt, a glass importer, and Martha Bulloch. He was a 5th cousin of Franklin D. Roosevelt and an uncle of Mrs. Eleanor Roosevelt. Roosevelt graduated from Harvard, 1880; attended Columbia Law School briefly; sat in the N.Y. State Assembly, 1882-84; ranched in North Dakota, 1884-86; failed reelection as mayor of N.Y. City, 1886; member of U.S. Civil Service Commission, 1889; president, N.Y. Police Board, 1895, supporting the merit system; assistant secretary of the Navy under McKinley, 1897-98. In the war with Spain, he organized the 1st U.S. Volunteer Cavalry (Rough Riders) as lieutenant colonel; led the charge up Kettle Hill at San Juan. Elected New York governor, 1898-1900, he fought the spoils system and achieved taxation of corporation franchises. Nominated for vice president, 1900, he became nation's youngest president when McKinley died. As president he fought corruption of politics by big business; dissolved Northern Securities Co. and others for violating, anti-trust laws; intervened in coal strike on behalf of the public, 1902; obtained Elkins Law forbidding rebates to favored corporations, 1903; Hepburn Law regulating railroad rates, 1906; Pure Food and Drugs Act, 1906; Reclamation Act and employers' liability laws. He organized conservation, mediated the peace between Japan and Russia, 1905; won the Nobel Peace Prize. He was the first to use the Hague Court of International Arbitration. By recognizing the new Republic of Panama he made Panama Canal possible. He was reelected in 1904.

In 1908 he obtained the nomination of William H. Taft, who was elected. Feeling that Taft had abandoned his policies, Roosevelt unsuccessfully sought the nomination in 1912. He bolted the party and ran on the Progressive "Bull Moose", ticket against Taft and Woodrow Wilson, splitting the Republicans and insuring Wilson's election. He was shot during the campaign but recovered. In 1916 he supported Charles E. Hughes, Republican. A strong friend of Britain, he fought American isolation in World War I. He wrote some 40 books on many topics; his *Winning of the West* is best known. He died Jan. 6, 1919, at Sagamore Hill, Oyster Bay, N.Y.

William Howard Taft

William Howard Taft, 27th president, Republican, was born in Cincinnati, Oh., Sept. 15, 1857, the son of Alphonso Taft and Louisa Maria Torrey. His father was secretary of war and attorney general in Grant's cabinet; minister to Austria and Russia under Arthur. Taft was graduated from Yale, 1878; Cincinnati Law School, 1880; became law reporter for Cincinnati newspapers; was assistant prosecuting attorney, 1881-83; assistant county solicitor, 1885; judge, superior court, 1887; U.S. solicitor-general, 1890; federal circuit judge, 1892. In 1900 he became head of the U.S. Philippines Commission and was first civil governor of the Philippines, 1901-04; secretary of war, 1904; provisional governor of Cuba, 1906. He was groomed for president by Roosevelt and elected over Bryan, 1908. His administration dissolved Standard Oil and tobacco trusts; instituted Dept. of Labor; drafted direct election of senators and income tax amend-

ments. His tariff and conservation policies angered progressives; though renominated he was opposed by Roosevelt; the result was Democrat Woodrow Wilson's election. Taft, with some reservations, supported the League of Nations. He was professor of constitutional law, Yale, 1913-21; chief justice of the U.S., 1921-30; illness forced him to resign. He died in Washington, Mar. 8, 1930.

Woodrow Wilson

Woodrow Wilson, 28th president, Democrat, was born at Staunton, Va., Dec. 28, 1856, as Thomas Woodrow Wilson, son of a Presbyterian minister, the Rev. Joseph Ruggles Wilson and Janet (Jessie) Woodrow. In his youth Wilson lived in Augusta, Ga., Columbia, S.C., and Wilmington, N.C. He attended Davidson College, 1873-74; was graduated from Princeton, A.B., 1879; A.M., 1882; read law at the Univ. of Virginia, 1881; practiced law, Atlanta, 1882-83; Ph.D., Johns Hopkins, 1886. He taught at Bryn Mawr, 1885-88; at Wesleyan, 1888-90; was professor of jurisprudence and political economy at Princeton, 1890-1910; president of Princeton, 1902-1910; governor of New Jersey, 1911-13. In 1912 he was nominated for president with the aid of William Jennings Bryan, who sought to block James "Champ" Clark and Tammany Hall. Wilson won the election because the Republican vote for Taft was split by the Progressives under Roosevelt.

Wilson protected American interests in revolutionary Mexico and fought for American rights on the high seas. His sharp warnings to Germany led to the resignation of his secretary of state, Bryan, a pacifist. In 1916 he was reelected by a slim margin with the slogan, "He kept us out of war." Wilson's attempts to mediate in the war failed. After 4 American ships had been sunk by the Germans, he secured a declaration of war against Germany on Apr. 6, 1917.

Wilson proposed peace Jan. 8, 1918, on the basis of his "Fourteen Points," a state paper with worldwide influence. His doctrine of self-determination continues to play a major role in territorial disputes. The Germans accepted his terms and an armistice, Nov. 11.

Wilson went to Paris to help negotiate the peace treaty, the crux of which he considered the League of Nations. The Senate demanded reservations that would not make the U.S. subordinate to the votes of other nations in case of war. Wilson refused to consider any reservations and toured the country to get support. He suffered a stroke, Oct., 1919. An invalid for months, he clung to his executive powers while his wife and doctor sought to shield him from affairs which would tire him.

He was awarded the 1919 Nobel Peace Prize, but the treaty embodying the League of Nations was rejected by the Senate, 1920. He died Feb. 3, 1924.

Warren Gamaliel Harding

Warren Gamaliel Harding, 29th president, Republican, was born near Corsica, now Blooming Grove, Oh., Nov. 2, 1865, the son of Dr. George Tyron Harding, a physician, and Phoebe Elizabeth Dickerson. He attended Ohio Central College. He was state senator, 1900-04; lieutenant governor, 1904-06; defeated for governor, 1910; chosen U.S. senator, 1915. He supported Taft, opposed federal control of food and fuel; voted for anti-strike legislation, woman's suffrage, and the Volstead prohibition enforcement act over President Wilson's veto; and opposed the League of Nations. In 1920 he was nominated for president and defeated James M. Cox in the election. The Republicans capitalized on war weariness and fear that Wilson's League of Nations would curtail U.S. sovereignty. Harding stressed a return to "normalcy"; worked for tariff revision and repeal of excess profits law and high income taxes. Two Harding appointees, Albert B. Fall (interior) and Harry Daugherty (attorney general), became involved in the Teapot Dome scandal that embittered Harding's last days. He called the International Conference on Limitation of Armaments, 1921-22. Returning from a trip to Alaska he became ill and died in San Francisco, Aug. 2, 1923.

Calvin Coolidge

Calvin Coolidge, 30th president, Republican, was born in Plymouth, Vt., July 4, 1872, the son of John Calvin Coolidge, a storekeeper, and Victoria J. Moor, and named John

Calvin Coolidge. Coolidge graduated from Amherst in 1895. He entered Republican state politics and served as mayor of Northampton, Mass., state senator, lieutenant governor, and, in 1919, governor. In Sept., 1919, Coolidge attained national prominence by calling out the state guard in the Boston police strike. He declared: "There is no right to strike against the public safety by anybody, anywhere, anytime." This brought his name before the Republican convention of 1920, where he was nominated for vice president. He succeeded to the presidency on Harding's death. He opposed the League of Nations; approved the World Court; vetoed the soldiers' bonus bill, which was passed over his veto. In 1924 he was elected by a huge majority. He reduced the national debt by $2 billion in 3 years. He twice vetoed the McNary-Haugen farm bill, which would have provided relief to financially hard-pressed farmers. With Republicans eager to renominate him he announced, Aug. 2, 1927: "I do not choose to run for president in 1928." He died in Northampton, Jan. 5, 1933.

Herbert Hoover

Herbert C. Hoover, 31st president, Republican, was born at West Branch, Ia., Aug. 10, 1874, son of Jesse Clark Hoover, a blacksmith, and Hulda Randall Minthorn. Hoover grew up in Indian Territory (now Oklahoma) and Oregon; won his A.B. in engineering at Stanford, 1891. He worked briefly with U.S. Geological Survey and western mines; then was a mining engineer in Australia, Asia, Europe, Africa, America. While chief engineer, imperial mines, China, he directed food relief for victims of Boxer Rebellion, 1900. He directed American Relief Committee, London, 1914-15; U.S. Comm. for Relief in Belgium, 1915-1919; was U.S. Food Administrator, 1917-1919; American Relief Administrator, 1918-1923, feeding children in defeated nations; Russian Relief, 1918-1923. He was secy. of commerce, 1921-28. He was elected president over Alfred E. Smith, 1928. In 1929 the stock market crashed and the economy collapsed. During the depression, Hoover opposed federal aid to the unemployed. He was defeated in the 1932 election by Franklin D. Roosevelt. President Truman made him co-ordinator of European Food Program, 1947, chairman of the Commission for Reorganization of the Executive Branch, 1947-49. He founded the Hoover Institution on War, Revolution, and Peace at Stanford Univ. He died in N.Y. City, Oct. 20, 1964.

Franklin Delano Roosevelt

Franklin D. Roosevelt, 32d president, Democrat, was born near Hyde Park, N.Y., Jan. 30, 1882, the son of James Roosevelt and Sara Delano. He graduated from Harvard, 1904; attended Columbia Law School; was admitted to the bar. He went to the N.Y. Senate, 1910 and 1913. In 1913 President Wilson made him assistant secretary of the navy.

Roosevelt ran for vice president, 1920, with James Cox and was defeated. From 1920 to 1928 he was a N.Y. lawyer and vice president of Fidelity & Deposit Co. In Aug., 1921, polio paralyzed his legs. He learned to walk with leg braces and a cane.

Roosevelt was elected governor of New York, 1928 and 1930. In 1932, W. G. McAdoo, pledged to John N. Garner, threw his votes to Roosevelt, who was nominated. The depression and the promise to repeal prohibition insured his election. He asked emergency powers, proclaimed the New Deal, and put into effect a vast number of administrative changes. Foremost was the use of public funds for relief and public works, resulting in deficit financing. He greatly expanded the controls of the central government over business, and by an excess profits tax and progressive income taxes produced a redistribution of earnings on an unprecedented scale. The Wagner Act gave labor many advantages in organizing and collective bargaining. He was the last president inaugurated on Mar. 4 (1933) and the first inaugurated on Jan. 20 (1937).

Roosevelt was the first president to use radio for "fireside chats." When the Supreme Court nullified some New Deal laws, he sought power to "pack" the court with additional justices, but Congress refused to give him the authority. He was the first president to break the "no 3d term" tradition (1940) and was elected to a 4th term, 1944, despite failing health. He was openly hostile to fascist governments before

World War II and launched a lend-lease program on behalf of the Allies. He wrote the principles of fair dealing into the Atlantic Charter, Aug. 14, 1941 (with Winston Churchill), and urged the Four Freedoms (freedom of speech, of worship, from want, from fear) Jan. 6, 1941. When Japan attacked Pearl Harbor, Dec. 7, 1941, the U.S. entered the war. He conferred with allied heads of state at Casablanca, Jan., 1943; Quebec, Aug., 1943; Teheran, Nov.-Dec., 1943; Cairo, Dec., 1943; Yalta, Feb., 1945. He died at Warm Springs, Ga., Apr. 12, 1945.

Harry S Truman

Harry S. Truman, 33d president, Democrat, was born at Lamar, Mo., May 8, 1884, the son of John Anderson Truman and Martha Ellen Young. A family disagreement on whether his middle name was Shippe or Solomon, after names of 2 grandfathers, resulted in his using only the middle initial S. He attended public schools in Independence, Mo., worked for the Kansas City Star, 1901, and as railroad timekeeper, and helper in Kansas City banks up to 1905. He ran his family's farm, 1906-17. He was commissioned a first lieutenant and took part in the Vosges, Meuse-Argonne, and St. Mihiel actions in World War I. After the war he ran a haberdashery, became judge of Jackson Co. Court, 1922-24; attended Kansas City School of Law, 1923-25.

Truman was elected U.S. senator in 1934; reelected 1940. In 1944 with Roosevelt's backing he was nominated for vice president and elected. On Roosevelt's death Truman became president. In 1948 he was elected president.

Truman authorized the first uses of the atomic bomb (Hiroshima and Nagasaki, Aug. 6 and 9, 1945), bringing World War II to a rapid end. He was responsible for creating NATO, the Marshall Plan, and what came to be called the Truman Doctrine (to aid nations such as Greece and Turkey, threatened by Russian or other communist takeover). He broke a Russian blockade of West Berlin with a massive airlift, 1948-49. When communist North Korea invaded South Korea, June, 1950, he won UN approval for a "police action" and sent in forces under Gen. Douglas MacArthur. When MacArthur sought to pursue North Koreans into China, Truman removed him from command.

Truman was responsible for higher minimum-wage, increased social-security, and aid-for-housing laws. Truman died Dec. 26, 1972, in Kansas City, Mo.

Dwight David Eisenhower

Dwight D. Eisenhower, 34th president, Republican, was born Oct. 14, 1890, at Denison, Tex., the son of David Jacob Eisenhower and Ida Elizabeth Stover. The next year, the family moved to Abilene, Kan. He graduated from West Point, 1915. He was on the American military mission to the Philippines, 1935-39 and during 4 of those years on the staff of Gen. Douglas MacArthur. He was made commander of Allied forces landing in North Africa, 1942, full general, 1943. He became supreme Allied commander in Europe, 1943, and as such led the Normandy invasion June 6, 1944. He was given the rank of general of the army Dec. 20, 1944, made permanent in 1946. On May 7, 1945, he received the surrender of the Germans at Rheims. He returned to the U.S. to serve as chief of staff, 1945-1948. In 1948, Eisenhower published Crusade in Europe, his war memoirs, which quickly became a best seller. From 1948 to 1953, he was president of Columbia Univ., but took leave of absence in 1950, to command NATO forces.

Eisenhower resigned from the army and was nominated for president by the Republicans, 1952. He defeated Adlai E. Stevenson in the election. He again defeated Stevenson, 1956. He called himself a moderate, favored "free market system" vs. government price and wage controls; kept government out of labor disputes; reorganized defense establishment; promoted missile programs. He continued foreign aid; sped end of Korean fighting; endorsed Taiwan and SE Asia defense treaties; backed UN in condemning Anglo-French raid on Egypt; advocated "open skies" policy of mutual inspection to USSR. He sent U.S. troops into Little Rock, Ark., Sept., 1957, during the segregation crisis and ordered Marines into Lebanon July-Aug., 1958.

During his retirement at his farm near Gettysburg, Pa., Eisenhower took up the role of elder statesman, counseling

his 3 successors in the White House. He died Mar. 28, 1969, in Washington.

John Fitzgerald Kennedy

John F. Kennedy, 35th president, Democrat, was born May 29, 1917, in Brookline, Mass., the son of Joseph P. Kennedy, financier, who later became ambassador to Great Britain, and Rose Fitzgerald. He entered Harvard, attended the London School of Economics briefly in 1935, received a B.S., from Harvard, 1940. He served in the Navy, 1941-1945, commanded a PT boat in the Solomons and won the Navy and Marine Corps Medal. He wrote *Profiles in Courage,* which won a Pulitzer prize. He served as representative in Congress, 1947-1953; was elected to the Senate in 1952, reelected 1958. He nearly won the vice presidential nomination in 1956.

In 1960, Kennedy won the Democratic nomination for president and defeated Richard M. Nixon, Republican. He was the first Roman Catholic president.

Kennedy's most important act was his successful demand Oct. 22, 1962, that the Soviet Union dismantle its missile bases in Cuba. He established a quarantine of arms shipments to Cuba and continued surveillance by air. He defied Soviet attempts to force the Allies out of Berlin. He made the steel industry rescind a price rise. He backed civil rights, a mental health program, arbitration of railroad disputes, and expanded medical care for the aged. Astronaut flights and satellite orbiting were greatly developed during his administration.

On Nov. 22, 1963, Kennedy was assassinated in Dallas, Tex.

Lyndon Baines Johnson

Lyndon B. Johnson, 36th president, Democrat, was born near Stonewall, Tex., Aug. 27, 1908, son of Sam Ealy Johnson and Rebekah Baines. He received a B.S. degree at Southwest Texas State Teachers College, 1930, attended Georgetown Univ. Law School, Washington, 1935. He taught public speaking in Houston, 1930-32; served as secretary to Rep. R. M. Kleberg, 1932-35. In 1937 Johnson won a contest to fill the vacancy caused by the death of a representative and in 1938 was elected to the full term, after which he returned for 4 terms. He was elected U.S. senator in 1948 and reelected in 1954. He became Democratic leader, 1953. Johnson was Texas' favorite son for the Democratic presidential nomination in 1956 and had strong support in the 1960 convention, where the nominee, John F. Kennedy, asked him to run for vice president. His campaigning helped overcome religious bias against Kennedy in the South.

Johnson became president on the death of Kennedy. Johnson worked hard for welfare legislation, signed civil rights, anti-proverty, and tax reduction laws, and averted strikes on railroads. He was elected to a full term, 1964. The war in Vietnam overshadowed other developments, 1965-68.

In face of increasing division in the nation and his own party over his handling of the war, Johnson announced that he would not seek another term, Mar. 31, 1968.

Retiring to his ranch near Johnson City, Tex., Johnson wrote his memoirs and oversaw the construction of the Lyndon Baines Johnson Library on the campus of the Univ. of Texas in Austin. He died Jan. 22, 1973.

Richard Milhous Nixon

Richard M. Nixon, 37th president, Republican, was the only president to resign without completing an elected term. He was born in Yorba Linda, Cal., Jan. 9, 1913, the son of Francis Anthony Nixon and Hannah Milhous. Nixon graduated from Whittier College, 1934; Duke Univ. Law School, 1937. After practicing law in Whittier and serving briefly in the Office of Price Administration in 1942, he entered the navy, serving in the South Pacific, and was discharged as a lieutenant commander.

Nixon was elected to the House of Representatives in 1946 and 1948. He achieved prominence as the House Un-American Activities Committee member who forced the showdown that resulted in the Alger Hiss perjury conviction. In 1950 Nixon moved to the Senate.

He was elected vice president in the Eisenhower landslides of 1952 and 1956. With Eisenhower's endorsement, Nixon won the Republican nomination in 1960. He was defeated by Democrat John F. Kennedy, returned to Cal. and was defeated in his race for governor, 1962.

In 1968, he won the presidential nomination and went on to defeat Democrat Hubert H. Humphrey.

Nixon became the first U.S. president to visit China and Russia (1972). He and his foreign affairs advisor, Henry A. Kissinger, achieved a detente with China. Nixon appointed 4 new Supreme Court justices, including the chief justice, thus altering the court's balance in favor of a more conservative view.

Reelected 1972, Nixon secured a cease-fire agreement in Vietnam and completed the withdrawal of U.S. troops.

Nixon's 2d term was cut short by a series of scandals beginning with the burglary of Democratic party national headquarters in the Watergate office complex on June 17, 1972. Nixon denied any White House involvement in the Watergate break-in. On July 16, 1973, a White House aide, under questioning by a Senate committee, revealed that most of Nixon's office conversations and phone calls had been recorded. Nixon claimed executive privilege to keep the tapes secret and the courts and Congress sought the tapes for criminal proceedings against former White House aides and for a House inquiry into possible impeachment.

On Oct. 10, 1973, Nixon fired the Watergate special prosecutor and the attorney general resigned in protest. The public outcry which followed caused Nixon to appoint a new special prosecutor and to turn over to the courts a number of subpoenaed tape recordings. Public reaction also brought the initiation of a formal inquiry into impeachment.

On July 24, 1974, the Supreme Court ruled that Nixon's claim of executive privilege must fall before the special prosecutor's subpoenas of tapes relevant to criminal trial proceedings. That same day, the House Judiciary Committee opened debate on impeachment. On July 30, the committee recommended House adoption of 3 articles of impeachment charging Nixon with obstruction of justice, abuse of power, and contempt of Congress.

On Aug. 5, Nixon released transcripts of conversations held 6 days after the Watergate break-in showing that Nixon had known of, approved, and directed Watergate cover-up activities. Nixon resigned from office Aug. 9.

Gerald Rudolph Ford

Gerald R. Ford, 38th president, Republican, was born July 14, 1913, in Omaha, Neb., son of Leslie King and Dorothy Gardner, and was named Leslie Jr. When he was 2, his parents were divorced and his mother moved with the boy to Grand Rapids, Mich. There she met and married Gerald R. Ford, who formally adopted the boy and gave him his own name.

He graduated from the Univ. of Michigan, 1935 and Yale Law School, 1941.

He began practicing law in Grand Rapids, but in 1942 joined the navy and served in the Pacific, leaving the service in 1946 as a lieutenant commander.

He entered congress in 1948 and continued to win elections, spending 25 years in the House, 8 of them as Republican leader.

On Oct. 12, 1973, after Vice President Spiro T. Agnew resigned, Ford was nominated by President Nixon to replace him. It was the first use of the procedures set out in the 25th Amendment.

When Nixon resigned Aug. 9, 1974, Ford became president, the first to serve without being chosen in a national election. On Sept. 8 he pardoned Nixon for any federal crimes he might have committed as president. Ford veoted 48 bills in his first 21 months in office, saying most would prove too costly. He visited China. In 1976, he was defeated in the election by Democrat Jimmy Carter.

Jimmy (James Earl) Carter

Jimmy (James Earl) Carter, 39th president, Democrat, was the first president from the Deep South since before the Civil War. He was born Oct. 1, 1924, at Plains, Ga., where his parents, James and Lillian Gordy Carter, had a farm and several businesses.

He attended Georgia Tech, and graduated from the U.S. Naval Academy. He entered the Navy's nuclear submarine program as an aide to Adm. Hyman Rickover, and studied nuclear physics at Union College.

His father died in 1953 and Carter left the Navy to take over the family businesses — peanut-raising, warehousing, and cotton-ginning. He was elected to the Georgia state senate, was defeated for governor, 1966, but elected in 1970.

Carter won the Democratic nomination and defeated President Gerald R. Ford in the election of 1976.

In 1979, Carter played a major role in the peace negotiations between Israel and Egypt. In Nov., Iranian student militants attacked the U.S. embassy in Teheran and held members of the embassy staff hostage.

During 1980, Carter was widely criticized for the poor state of the economy and high inflation. He was also viewed as weak in his handling of foreign policy. He reacted to the Soviet invasion of Afghanistan by imposing a grain embargo and boycotting the Moscow Olympic games. His failure to obtain the release of the remaining 52 hostages held in Iran, whose first anniversary of capture fell on Election Day, plagued Carter to the end of his term. He was defeated by Ronald Reagan in the election. Carter finally succeeded in obtaining the release of the hostages on Inauguration Day, as the new president was taking the oath of office.

Ronald Wilson Reagan

Ronald Wilson Reagan, 40th president, Republican, was born Feb. 6, 1911, in Tampico, Ill., the son of John Edward Reagan and Nellie Wilson. Reagan graduated from Eureka (Ill.) College in 1932. Following his graduation, he worked for 5 years as a sports announcer in Des Moines, Ia.

Reagan began a successful career as a film actor in 1937, and starred in numerous movies, and later television, until the 1960s. He was a captain in the Army Air Force during World War II.

He served as president of the Screen Actors Guild from 1947 to 1952, and in 1959.

Once a liberal Democrat, Reagan became active in Republican politics during the 1964 presidential campaign of Barry Goldwater. He was elected governor of California in 1966, and reelected in 1970.

Following his retirement as governor, Reagan became the leading spokesman for the conservative wing of the Republican Party, and made a strong bid for the party's 1976 presidential nomination.

In 1980, he gained the Republican nomination and won a landslide victory over Jimmy Carter.

As president, he successfully forged a bipartisan coalition in Congress which led to enactment of an economic program which included the largest budget and tax cuts in U.S. history, and a Social Security reform bill designed to insure the long-term solvency of the system.

Reagan was plagued by a severe recession which caused a 9.7% unemployment rate in 1982, the highest since 1941.

In 1983, Reagan sent a task force to lead the invasion of Grenada, and joined 3 European nations in maintaining a peacekeeping force in Beirut, Lebanon. He has strongly supported the El Salvador and other anti-communist governments in Central America while aiding anti-government forces in Nicaragua.

In 1984, interest rates and inflation had declined and the economy had made a strong recovery. Reagan easily won reelection to a second term. Reagan's fiscal 1986 budget, with a projected deficit of $180 billion, called for deep cuts in domestic spending and an increase in military spending.

Wives and Children of the Presidents
Listed in order of presidential administrations,

Name	State	Born	Married	Died	Sons	Daughters
Martha Dandridge Custis Washington	Va.	1732	1759	1802	...	...
Abigail Smith Adams	Mass.	1744	1764	1818	3	2
Martha Wayles Skelton Jefferson	Va.	1748	1772	1782	1	5
Dorothea "Dolley" Payne Todd Madison	N.C.	1768	1794	1849	...	...
Elizabeth Kortright Monroe	N.Y.	1768	1786	1830	...(1)	2
Louise Catherine Johnson Adams	Md. (2)	1775	1797	1852	3	1
Rachel Donelson Robards Jackson	Va.	1767	1791	1828	...	...
Hannah Hoes Van Buren	N.Y.	1783	1807	1819	4	...
Anna Symmes Harrison	N.J.	1775	1795	1864	6	4
Letitia Christian Tyler	Va.	1790	1813	1842	3	4
Julia Gardiner Tyler	N.Y.	1820	1844	1889	5	2
Sarah Childress Polk	Tenn.	1803	1824	1891	...	...
Margaret Smith Taylor	Md.	1788	1810	1852	1	5
Abigail Powers Fillmore	N.Y.	1798	1826	1853	1	1
Caroline Carmichael McIntosh Fillmore	N.J.	1813	1858	1881	...	...
Jane Means Appleton Pierce	N.H.	1806	1834	1863	3	...
Mary Todd Lincoln	Ky.	1818	1842	1882	4	...
Eliza McCardle Johnson	Tenn.	1810	1827	1876	3	2
Julia Dent Grant	Mo.	1826	1848	1902	3	1
Lucy Ware Webb Hayes	Oh.	1831	1852	1889	7	1
Lucretia Rudolph Garfield	Oh.	1832	1858	1918	4	1
Ellen Lewis Herndon Arthur	Va.	1837	1859	1880	2	1
Frances Folsom Cleveland	N.Y.	1864	1886	1947	2	3
Caroline Lavinia Scott Harrison	Oh.	1832	1853	1892	1	1
Mary Scott Lord Dimmick Harrison	Pa.	1858	1896	1948	...	1
Ida Saxton McKinley	Oh.	1847	1871	1907	...	2
Alice Hathaway Lee Roosevelt	Mass.	1861	1880	1884	...	1
Edith Kermit Carow Roosevelt	Conn.	1861	1886	1948	4	1
Helen Herron Taft	Oh.	1861	1886	1943	2	1
Ellen Louise Axson Wilson	Ga.	1860	1885	1914	...	3
Edith Bolling Galt Wilson	Va.	1872	1915	1961	...	...
Florence Kling De Wolfe Harding	Oh.	1860	1891	1924	...	...
Grace Anna Goodhue Coolidge	Vt.	1879	1905	1957	2	...
Lou Henry Hoover	Ia.	1875	1899	1944	2	...
Anna Eleanor Roosevelt Roosevelt	N.Y.	1884	1905	1962	4 (1)	1
Bess Wallace Truman	Mo.	1885	1919	1982	...	1
Mamie Geneva Doud Eisenhower	Ia.	1896	1916	1979	1 (1)	...
Jacqueline Lee Bouvier Kennedy	N.Y.	1929	1953	...	1 (1)	1
Claudia "Lady Bird" Alta Taylor Johnson	Tex.	1912	1934	...	...	2
Thelma Catherine Patricia Ryan Nixon	Nev.	1912	1940	...	...	2
Elizabeth Bloomer Warren Ford	Ill.	1918	1948	...	3	1
Rosalynn Smith Carter	Ga.	1927	1946	...	3	1
Anne Frances "Nancy" Robbins Davis Reagan	N.Y.	1923	1952	...	1 (3)	1(3)

James Buchanan, 15th president, was unmarried. (1) plus one infant, deceased. (2) Born London, father a Md. citizen. (3) President Reagan has a son and daughter from a former marriage.

UNITED STATES FACTS
Superlative U.S. Statistics
Source: National Geographic Society, Washington, D.C.

Area for 50 states	Total	3,623,420 sq. mi.
	Land 3,543,883 sq. mi.—Water 79,537 sq. mi.	
Largest state	Alaska	591,004 sq. mi.
Smallest state	Rhode Island	1,212 sq. mi.
Largest county	San Bernardino County, California	20,102 sq. mi.
Smallest county	New York, New York	22 sq. mi.
Northernmost city	Barrow, Alaska	71°17'N.
Northernmost point	Point Barrow, Alaska	71°23'N.
Southernmost city	Hilo, Island of Hawaii	19°43'N.
Southernmost town	Naalehu, Island of Hawaii	19°03'N.
Southernmost point	Ka Lae (South Cape), Island of Hawaii	18°56'N. (155°41'W.)
Easternmost city	Eastport, Maine	66°59'02"W.
Easternmost town	Lubec, Maine	66°58'49"W.
Easternmost point	West Quoddy Head, Maine	66°57'W.
Westernmost city	Lihue, Island of Kauai, Hawaii	159°22'W.
Westernmost town	Adak, Aleutians, Alaska	176°45'W.
Westernmost point	Cape Wrangell, Attu Island, Aleutians, Alaska	172°27'E.
Highest city	Leadville, Colorado	10,200 ft.
Lowest town	Calipatria, California	−184 ft.
Highest point on Atlantic coast	Cadillac Mountain, Mount Desert Is., Maine	1,530 ft.
Oldest national park	Yellowstone National Park (1872), Wyoming, Montana, Idaho	3,468 sq. mi.
Largest national park	Wrangell-St. Elias, Alaska	12,730 sq. mi.
Largest national monument	Death Valley, California, Nevada	3,231 sq. mi.
Highest waterfall	Yosemite Falls—Total in three sections	2,425 ft.
	Upper Yosemite Fall	1,430 ft.
	Cascades in middle section	675 ft.
	Lower Yosemite Fall	320 ft.
Longest river	Mississippi-Missouri	3,710 mi.
Highest mountain	Mount McKinley, Alaska	20,320 ft.
Lowest point	Death Valley, California	−282 ft.
Deepest lake	Crater Lake, Oregon	1,932 ft.
Rainiest spot	Mt. Waialeale, Hawaii	Annual aver. rainfall 460 inches
Largest gorge	Grand Canyon, Colorado River, Arizona	277 miles long, 600 ft. to 18 miles wide, 1 mile deep
Deepest gorge	Hell's Canyon, Snake River, Idaho-Oregon	7,900 ft.
Strongest surface wind	Mount Washington, New Hampshire recorded 1934	231 mph
Biggest dam	New Cornelia Tailings, Ten Mile Wash, Arizona	274,026,000 cu. yds. material used
Tallest building	Sears Tower, Chicago, Illinois	1,454 ft.
Largest building	Boeing 747 Manufacturing Plant, Everett, Washington	205,600,000 cu. ft.; covers 47 acres.
Tallest structure	TV tower, Blanchard, North Dakota	2,063 ft.
Longest bridge span	Verrazano-Narrows, New York	4,260 ft.
Highest bridge	Royal Gorge, Colorado	1,053 ft. above water
Deepest well	Gas well, Washita County, Oklahoma	31,441 ft.

The 49 States, Including Alaska

Area for 49 states	Total	3,616,949 sq. mi.
	Land 3,537,458 sq. mi.—Water 79,491 sq. mi.	

The 48 Contiguous States

Area for 48 states	Total	3,025,945 sq. mi.
	Land 2,966,625 sq. mi.—Water 59,320 sq. mi.	
Largest state	Texas	267,338 sq. mi
Northernmost town	Angle Inlet, Minnesota	49°22'N.
Northernmost point	Northwest Angle, Minnesota	49°23'N.
Southernmost city	Key West, Florida	24°33'N.
Southernmost mainland city	Florida City, Florida	25°27'N.
Southernmost point	Key West, Florida	24°33'N.
Westernmost town	La Push, Washington	124°38'W.
Westernmost point	Cape Alava, Washington	124°44'W.
Highest mountain	Mount Whitney, California	14,494 ft.

Note to users: The distinction between cities and towns varies from state to state. In this table the U.S. Bureau of the Census usage was followed.

Geodetic Datum Point of North America

The geodetic datum point of the U.S. is the National Ocean Service's triangulation station Meades Ranch in Osborne County, Kansas, at latitude 39° 13'26". 686 N and longitude 98° 32'30". 506 W. This geodetic datum point is a fundamental point from which all latitude and longitude computations originate for North America and Central America.

Statistical Information about the U.S.

In the *Statistical Abstract of the United States* the Bureau of the Census, U.S. Dept. of Commerce, annually publishes a summary of social, political, and economic information. A book of more than 1,000 pages, it presents in 33 sections comprehensive data on population, housing, health, education, employment, income, prices, business, banking, energy, science, defense, trade, government finance, foreign country comparison, and other subjects. Special features include a section on Recent Trends and appendixes on state rankings and Metropolitan Statistical Areas. The book is prepared under the direction of Glenn W. King, Chief, Statistical Compendia Staff, Bureau of the Census. Supplements to the *Statistical Abstract* are *Pocket Data Book USA, 1979; County and City Data Book, 1983; Historical Statistics of the United States, Colonial Times to 1970;* and *State and Metropolitan Area Data Book, 1982* (1985, in production). Information concerning these and other publications may be obtained from the Supt. of Documents, Government Printing Office, Wash., D.C. 20402, or from the U.S. Bureau of the Census, Data User Services Division, Wash., D.C. 20233.

Highest and Lowest Altitudes in the U.S. and Territories

Source: Geological Survey, U.S. Interior Department. (Minus sign means below sea level; elevations are in feet.)

State	Highest Point Name	County	Elev.	Lowest Point Name	County	Elev.
Alabama	Cheaha Mountain	Cleburne	2,407	Gulf of Mexico		Sea level
Alaska	Mount McKinley		20,320	Pacific Ocean		Sea level
Arizona	Humphreys Peak	Coconino	12,633	Colorado R.	Yuma	70
Arkansas	Magazine Mountain	Logan	2,753	Ouachita R.	Ashley Union	55
California	Mount Whitney	Inyo-Tulare	14,494	Death Valley	Inyo	−282
Colorado	Mount Elbert	Lake	14,433	Arkansas R.	Prowers	3,350
Connecticut	Mount Frissell	Litchfield	2,380	L.I. Sound		Sea level
Delaware	On Ebright Road	New Castle	442	Atlantic Ocean		Sea level
Dist. of Col.	Tenleytown	N. W. part	410	Potomac R.		1
Florida	Sec. 30, T 6N, R 20W	Walton	345	Atlantic Ocean		Sea level
Georgia	Brasstown Bald	Towns-Union	4,784	Atlantic Ocean		Sea level
Guam	Mount Lamlam	Agat District	1,329	Pacific Ocean		Sea level
Hawaii	Mauna Kea	Hawaii	13,796	Pacific Ocean		Sea level
Idaho	Borah Peak	Custer	12,662	Snake R.	Nez Perce	710
Illinois	Charles Mound	Jo Daviess	1,235	Mississippi R.	Alexander	279
Indiana	Franklin Township	Wayne	1,257	Ohio R.	Posey	320
Iowa	Sec. 29, T 100N, R 41W	Osceola	1,670	Mississippi R.	Lee	480
Kansas	Mount Sunflower	Wallace	4,039	Verdigris R.	Montgomery	680
Kentucky	Black Mountain	Harlan	4,145	Mississippi R.	Fulton	257
Louisiana	Driskill Mountain	Bienville	535	New Orleans	Orleans	−5
Maine	Mount Katahdin	Piscataquis	5,268	Atlantic Ocean		Sea level
Maryland	Backbone Mountain	Garrett	3,360	Atlantic Ocean		Sea level
Massachusetts	Mount Greylock	Berkshire	3,491	Atlantic Ocean		Sea level
Michigan	Mount Curwood	Baraga	1,980	Lake Erie		572
Minnesota	Eagle Mountain	Cook	2,301	Lake Superior		602
Mississippi	Woodall Mountain	Tishomingo	806	Gulf of Mexico		Sea level
Missouri	Taum Sauk Mt.	Iron	1,772	St. Francis R.	Dunklin	230
Montana	Granite Peak	Park	12,799	Kootenai R.	Lincoln	1,800
Nebraska	Johnson Township	Kimball	5,426	S.E. cor. State	Richardson	840
Nevada	Boundary Peak	Esmeralda	13,143	Colorado R.	Clark	470
New Hamp.	Mt. Washington	Coos	6,288	Atlantic Ocean		Sea level
New Jersey	High Point	Sussex	1,803	Atlantic Ocean		Sea level
New Mexico	Wheeler Peak	Taos	13,161	Red Bluff Res.	Eddy	2,817
New York	Mount Marcy	Essex	5,344	Atlantic Ocean		Sea level
North Carolina	Mount Mitchell	Yancey	6,684	Atlantic Ocean		Sea level
North Dakota	White Butte	Slope	3,506	Red R.	Pembina	750
Ohio	Campbell Hill	Logan	1,550	Ohio R.	Hamilton	433
Oklahoma	Black Mesa	Cimarron	4,973	Little R.	McCurtain	287
Oregon	Mount Hood	Clackamas-Hood R.	11,239	Pacific Ocean		Sea level
Pennsylvania	Mt. Davis	Somerset	3,213	Delaware R.	Delaware	Sea level
Puerto Rico	Cerro de Punta	Ponce District	4,389	Atlantic Ocean		Sea level
Rhode Island	Jerimoth Hill	Providence	812	Atlantic Ocean		Sea level
Samoa	Lata Mountain	Tau Island	3,160	Pacific Ocean		Sea level
South Carolina	Sassafras Mountain	Pickens	3,560	Atlantic Ocean		Sea level
South Dakota	Harney Peak	Pennington	7,242	Big Stone Lake	Roberts	962
Tennessee	Clingmans Dome	Sevier	6,643	Mississippi R.	Shelby	182
Texas	Guadalupe Peak	Culberson	8,749	Gulf of Mexico		Sea level
Utah	Kings Peak	Duchesne	13,528	Beaverdam Cr.	Washington	2,000
Vermont	Mount Mansfield	Lamoille	4,393	Lake Champlain	Franklin	95
Virginia	Mount Rogers	Grayson-Smyth	5,729	Atlantic Ocean		Sea level
Virgin Islands	Crown Mountain	St. Thomas Island	1,556	Atlantic Ocean		Sea level
Washington	Mount Rainier	Pierce	14,410	Pacific Ocean		Sea level
West Virginia	Spruce Knob	Pendleton	4,863	Potomac R.	Jefferson	240
Wisconsin	Timms Hill	Price	1,951	Lake Michigan		581
Wyoming	Gannett Peak	Fremont	13,804	B. Fourche R.	Crook	3,100

U.S. Coastline by States

Source: NOAA, U.S. Commerce Department
(statute miles)

State	Coastline[1]	Shoreline[2]	State	Coastline[1]	Shoreline[2]
Atlantic coast	**2,069**	**28,673**	**Gulf coast**	**1,631**	**17,141**
Connecticut	0	618	Alabama	53	607
Delaware	28	381	Florida	770	5,095
Florida	580	3,331	Louisiana	397	7,721
Georgia	100	2,344	Mississippi	44	359
Maine	228	3,478	Texas	367	3,359
Maryland	31	3,190			
Massachusetts	192	1,519	**Pacific coast**	**7,623**	**40,298**
New Hampshire	13	131	Alaska	5,580	31,383
New Jersey	130	1,792	California	840	3,427
New York	127	1,850	Hawaii	750	1,052
North Carolina	301	3,375	Oregon	296	1,410
Pennsylvania	0	89	Washington	157	3,026
Rhode Island	40	384			
South Carolina	187	2,876	**Arctic coast, Alaska**	**1,060**	**2,521**
Virginia	112	3,315	**United States**	**12,383**	**88,633**

(1) Figures are lengths of general outline of seacoast. Measurements were made with a unit measure of 30 minutes of latitude on charts as near the scale of 1:1,200,000 as possible. Coastline of sounds and bays is included to a point where they narrow to width of unit measure, and includes the distance across at such point. (2) Figures obtained in 1939-40 with a recording instrument on the largest-scale charts and maps then available. Shoreline of outer coast, offshore islands, sounds, bays, rivers, and creeks is included to the head of tidewater or to a point where tidal waters narrow to a width of 100 feet.

States: Settled, Capitals, Entry into Union, Area, Rank

The **original 13 states**—The 13 colonies that seceded from Great Britain and fought the War of Independence (American Revolution) became the 13 original states. They were: Delaware, Pennsylvania, New Jersey, Georgia, Connecticut, Massachusetts, Maryland, South Carolina, New Hampshire, Virginia, New York, North Carolina, and Rhode Island. The order for the original 13 states is the order in which they ratified the Constitution.

State	Set-tled*	Capital	Entered Union Date	Order	Extent in miles Long (approx. mean)	Wide	Area in square miles Land	Inland water	Total	Rank in area
Ala. . .	1702	Montgomery	Dec.	14, 1819	22	330	190	50,708	901	51,609	29
Alas. .	1784	Juneau	Jan.	3, 1959	49	(a)1,480	810	569,600	20,157	589,757	1
Ariz. .	1776	Phoenix	Feb.	14, 1912	48	400	310	113,417	492	113,909	6
Ark. . .	1686	Little Rock	June	15, 1836	25	260	240	51,945	1,159	53,104	27
Cal. . .	1769	Sacramento	Sept.	9, 1850	31	770	250	156,361	2,332	158,693	3
Col. . .	1858	Denver	Aug.	1, 1876	38	380	280	103,766	481	104,247	8
Conn. .	1634	Hartford	Jan.	9, 1788	5	110	70	4,862	147	5,009	48
Del. . .	1638	Dover	Dec.	7, 1787	1	100	30	1,982	75	2,057	49
D.C. . .		Washington.	. .			. . .	. . .	61	6	67	51
Fla. . .	1565	Tallahassee	Mar.	3, 1845	27	500	160	54,090	4,470	58,560	22
Ga. . .	1733	Atlanta	Jan.	2, 1788	4	300	230	58,073	803	58,876	21
Ha. . .	1820	Honolulu	Aug.	21, 1959	50	. . .	. . .	6,425	25	6,450	47
Ida. . .	1842	Boise	July	3, 1890	43	570	300	82,677	880	83,557	13
Ill. . . .	1720	Springfield	Dec.	3, 1818	21	390	210	55,748	652	56,400	24
Ind. . .	1733	Indianapolis.	Dec.	11, 1816	19	270	140	36,097	194	36,291	38
Ia. . . .	1788	Des Moines	Dec.	28, 1846	29	310	200	55,941	349	56,290	25
Kan. . .	1727	Topeka	Jan.	29, 1861	34	400	210	81,787	477	82,264	14
Ky. . .	1774	Frankfort	June	1, 1792	15	380	140	39,650	745	40,395	37
La. . . .	1699	Baton Rouge.	Apr.	30, 1812	18	380	130	44,930	3,593	48,523	31
Me. . .	1624	Augusta	Mar.	15, 1820	23	320	190	30,920	2,295	33,215	39
Md. . .	1634	Annapolis.	Apr.	28, 1788	7	250	90	9,891	686	10,577	42
Mass. .	1620	Boston	Feb.	6, 1788	6	190	50	7,826	431	8,257	45
Mich. .	1668	Lansing	Jan.	26, 1837	26	490	240	56,817	1,399	58,216	23
Minn. .	1805	St. Paul	May	11, 1858	32	400	250	79,289	4,779	84,068	12
Miss. .	1699	Jackson.	Dec.	10, 1817	20	340	170	47,296	420	47,716	32
Mo. . .	1735	Jefferson City	Aug.	10, 1821	24	300	240	68,995	691	69,686	19
Mon. .	1809	Helena	Nov.	8, 1889	41	630	280	145,587	1,551	147,138	4
Neb.. .	1823	Lincoln	Mar.	1, 1867	37	430	210	76,483	744	77,227	15
Nev.. .	1849	Carson City	Oct.	31, 1864	36	490	320	109,889	651	110,540	7
N.H.. .	1623	Concord	June	21, 1788	9	190	70	9,027	277	9,304	44
N.J. . .	1664	Trenton	Dec.	18, 1787	3	150	70	7,521	315	7,836	46
N.M.. .	1610	Santa Fe	Jan.	6, 1912	47	370	343	121,412	254	121,666	5
N.Y.. .	1614	Albany	July	26, 1788	11	330	283	47,831	1,745	49,576	30
N.C.. .	1660	Raleigh	Nov.	21, 1789	12	500	150	48,798	3,788	52,586	28
N.D.. .	1812	Bismarck	Nov.	2, 1889	39	340	211	69,273	1,392	70,665	17
Oh. . .	1788	Columbus	Mar.	1, 1803	17	220	220	40,975	247	41,222	35
Okla. .	1889	Oklahoma City.	Nov.	16, 1907	46	400	220	68,782	1,137	69,919	18
Ore. . .	1811	Salem.	Feb.	14, 1859	33	360	261	96,184	797	96,981	10
Pa. . .	1682	Harrisburg	Dec.	12, 1787	2	283	160	44,966	367	45,333	33
R.I. . .	1636	Providence	May	29, 1790	13	40	30	1,049	165	1,214	50
S.C. . .	1670	Columbia	May	23, 1788	8	260	200	30,225	830	31,055	40
S.D. . .	1859	Pierre	Nov.	2, 1889	40	380	210	75,955	1,092	77,047	16
Tenn. .	1769	Nashville	June	1, 1796	16	440	120	41,328	916	42,244	34
Tex.. .	1682	Austin.	Dec.	29, 1845	28	790	660	262,134	5,204	267,338	2
Ut.. . .	1847	Salt Lake City	Jan.	4, 1896	45	350	270	82,096	2,820	84,916	11
Vt.. . .	1724	Montpelier	Mar.	4, 1791	14	160	80	9,267	342	9,609	43
Va.. . .	1607	Richmond.	June	25, 1788	10	430	200	39,780	1,037	40,817	36
Wash..	1811	Olympia	Nov.	11, 1889	42	360	240	66,570	1,622	68,192	20
W.Va..	1727	Charleston	June	20, 1863	35	240	130	24,070	111	24,181	41
Wis. . .	1766	Madison	May	29, 1848	30	310	260	54,464	1,690	56,154	26
Wy. . .	1834	Cheyenne	July	10, 1890	44	360	280	97,203	711	97,914	9

*First European permanent settlement. (a) Aleutian Islands and Alexander Archipelago are not considered in these lengths.

The Continental Divide

Source: Geological Survey, U.S. Interior Department

The Continental Divide: watershed, created by mountain ranges or table-lands of the Rocky Mountains, from which the drainage is easterly or westerly; the easterly flowing waters reaching the Atlantic Ocean chiefly through the Gulf of Mexico, and the westerly flowing waters reaching the Pacific Ocean through the Columbia River, or through the Colorado River, which flows into the Gulf of California.

The location and route of the Continental Divide across the United States may briefly be described as follows:

Beginning at point of crossing the United States-Mexican boundary, near long. 108°45'W., the Divide, in a northerly direction, crosses New Mexico along the western edge of the Rio Grande drainage basin, entering Colorado near long. 106°41'W.

Thence by a very irregular route northerly across Colorado along the western summits of the Rio Grande and of the Arkansas, the South Platte, and the North Platte River basins, and across Rocky Mountain National Park, entering Wyoming near long. 106°52'W.

Thence in a northwesterly direction, forming the western rims of the North Platte, Big Horn, and Yellowstone River basins, crossing the southwestern portion of Yellowstone National Park.

Thence in a westerly and then a northerly direction forming the common boundary of Idaho and Montana, to a point on said boundary near long. 114°00'W.

Thence northeasterly and northwesterly through Montana and the Glacier National Park, entering Canada near long. 114°04'W.

Chronological List of Territories

Source: National Archives and Records Service

Name of territory	Date of Organic Act	Organic Act effective	Admission as state	Yrs. terr.
Northwest Territory(a)	July 13, 1787	No fixed date.	Mar. 1, 1803(b)	16
Territory southwest of River Ohio	May 26, 1790	No fixed date.	June 1, 1796(c)	6
Mississippi	Apr. 7, 1798	When president acted.	Dec. 10, 1817	19
Indiana	May 7, 1800	July 4, 1800	Dec. 11, 1816	16
Orleans	Mar. 26, 1804	Oct. 1, 1804	Apr. 30, 1812(d)	7
Michigan	Jan. 11, 1805	June 30, 1805	Jan. 26, 1837	31
Louisiana-Missouri(e)	Mar. 3, 1805	July 4, 1805	Aug. 10, 1821	16
Illinois	Feb. 3, 1809	Mar. 1, 1809	Dec. 3, 1818	9
Alabama	Mar. 3, 1817	When Miss. became a state	Dec. 14, 1819	2
Arkansas	Mar. 2, 1819	July 4, 1819	June 15, 1836	17
Florida	Mar. 30, 1822	No fixed date.	Mar. 3, 1845	23
Wisconsin	Apr. 20, 1836	July 3, 1836	May 29, 1848	12
Iowa	June 12, 1838	July 3, 1838	Dec. 28, 1846	7
Oregon	Aug. 14, 1848	Date of act	Feb. 14, 1859	10
Minnesota	Mar. 3, 1849	Date of act	May 11, 1858	9
New Mexico	Sept. 9, 1850	On president's proclamation	Jan. 6, 1912	61
Utah	Sept. 9, 1850	Date of act	Jan. 4, 1896	44
Washington	Mar. 2, 1853	Date of act	Nov. 11, 1889	36
Nebraska	May 30, 1854	Date of act	Mar. 1, 1867	12
Kansas	May 30, 1854	Date of act	Jan. 29, 1861	6
Colorado	Feb. 28, 1861	Date of act	Aug. 1, 1876	15
Nevada	Mar. 2, 1861	Date of act	Oct. 31, 1864	3
Dakota	Mar. 2, 1861	Date of act	Nov. 2, 1889	28
Arizona	Feb. 24, 1863	Date of act	Feb. 14, 1912	49
Idaho	Mar. 3, 1863	Date of act	July 3, 1890	27
Montana	May 26, 1864	Date of act	Nov. 8, 1889	25
Wyoming	July 25, 1868	When officers were qualified	July 10, 1890	22
Alaska(f)	May 17, 1884	No fixed date.	Jan. 3, 1959	75
Oklahoma	May 2, 1890	Date of act	Nov. 16, 1907	17
Hawaii	Apr. 30, 1900	June 14, 1900	Aug. 21, 1959	59

(a) Included Ohio, Indiana, Illinois, Michigan, Wisconsin, eastern Minnesota; (b) as the state of Ohio; (c) as the state of Tennessee; (d) as the state of Louisiana; (e) organic act for Missouri Territory of June 4, 1812, became effective Dec. 7, 1812; (f) Although the May 17, 1884 act actually constituted Alaska as a district, it was often referred to as a territory, and unofficially administered as such. The Territory of Alaska was legally and formally organized by an act of Aug. 24, 1912.

Geographic Centers, U.S. and Each State

Source: Geological Survey, U.S. Interior Department

United States, including Alaska and Hawaii — South Dakota; Butte County, W of Castle Rock, Approx. lat. 44°58'N. long. 103°46'W.

Contiguous U. S. (48 states) — Near Lebanon, Smith Co., Kansas, lat. 39°50'N. long. 98°35'W.

North American continent — The geographic center is in Pierce County, North Dakota, 6 miles W of Balta, latitude 48°10', longitude 100°10'W.

State—county, locality

Alabama—Chilton, 12 miles SW of Clanton.
Alaska—lat. 63°50'N. long. 152°W. Approx. 60 mi. NW of Mt. McKinley.
Arizona—Yavapai, 55 miles ESE of Prescott.
Arkansas—Pulaski, 12 miles NW of Little Rock.
California—Madera, 38 miles E of Madera.
Colorado—Park, 30 miles NW of Pikes Peak.
Connecticut—Hartford, at East Berlin.
Delaware—Kent, 11 miles S of Dover.
District of Columbia—Near 4th and L Sts., NW.
Florida—Hernando, 12 miles NNW of Brooksville.
Georgia—Twiggs, 18 miles SE of Macon.
Hawaii—Hawaii, 20°15'N, 156°20'W, off Maui Island.
Idaho—Custer, at Custer, SW of Challis.
Illinois—Logan, 28 miles NE of Springfield.
Indiana—Boone, 14 miles NNW of Indianapolis.
Iowa—Story, 5 miles NE of Ames.
Kansas—Barton, 15 miles NE of Great Bend.
Kentucky—Marion, 3 miles NNW of Lebanon.
Louisiana—Avoyelles, 3 miles SE of Marksville.
Maine—Piscataquis, 18 miles north of Dover.

Maryland—Prince Georges, 4.5 miles NW of Davidsonville.
Massachusetts—Worcester, north part of city.
Michigan—Wexford, 5 miles NNW of Cadillac.
Minnesota—Crow Wing, 10 miles SW of Brainerd.
Mississippi—Leake, 9 miles WNW of Carthage.
Missouri—Miller, 20 miles SW of Jefferson City.
Montana—Fergus, 12 miles west of Lewistown.
Nebraska—Custer, 10 miles NW of Broken Bow.
Nevada—Lander, 26 miles SE of Austin.
New Hampshire—Belknap, 3 miles E of Ashland.
New Jersey—Mercer, 5 miles SE of Trenton.
New Mexico—Torrance, 12 miles SSW of Willard.
New York—Madison, 12 miles S of Oneida and 26 miles SW of Utica.
North Carolina—Chatham, 10 miles NW of Sanford.
North Dakota—Sheridan, 5 miles SW of McClusky.
Ohio—Delaware, 25 miles NNE of Columbus.
Oklahoma—Oklahoma, 8 miles N of Oklahoma City.
Oregon—Crook, 25 miles SSE of Prineville.
Pennsylvania—Centre, 2.5 miles SW of Bellefonte.
Rhode Island—Kent, 1 mile SSW of Crompton.
South Carolina—Richland, 13 miles SE of Columbia.
South Dakota—Hughes, 8 miles NE of Pierre.
Tennessee—Rutherford, 5 mi. NE of Murfreesboro.
Texas—McCulloch, 15 miles NE of Brady.
Utah—Sanpete, 3 miles N of Manti.
Vermont—Washington, 3 miles E of Roxbury.
Virginia—Buckingham, 5 miles SW of Buckingham.
Washington—Chelan, 10 mi. WSW of Wenatchee.
West Virginia—Braxton, 4 miles E of Sutton.
Wisconsin—Wood, 9 miles SE of Marshfield.
Wyoming—Fremont, 58 miles ENE of Lander.

There is no generally accepted definition of geographic center, and no satisfactory method for determining it. The geographic center of an area may be defined as the center of gravity of the surface, or that point on which the surface of the area would balance if it were a plane of uniform thickness.

No marked or monumented point has been established by any government agency as the geographic center of either the 50 states, the contiguous United States, or the North American continent. A monument was erected in Lebanon, Kan., contiguous U.S. center, by a group of citizens.

International Boundary Lines of the U.S.

The length of the northern boundary of the contiguous U.S. — the U.S.-Canadian border, excluding Alaska — is 3,987 miles according to the U.S. Geological Survey, Dept. of the Interior. The length of the Alaskan-Canadian border is 1,538 miles. The length of the U.S.-Mexican border, from the Gulf of Mexico to the Pacific Ocean, is approximately 1,933 miles (1963 boundary agreement).

Origin of the Names of U.S. States

Source: State officials, the Smithsonian Institution, and the Topographic Division, U.S. Geological Survey.

Alabama—Indian for tribal town, later a tribe (Alabamas or Alibamons) of the Creek confederacy.

Alaska—Russian version of Aleutian (Eskimo) word, alakshak, for "peninsula," "great lands," or "land that is not an island."

Arizona—Spanish version of Pima Indian word for "little spring place," or Aztec arizuma, meaning "silver-bearing."

Arkansas—French variant of Kansas, a Sioux Indian name for "south wind people."

California—Bestowed by the Spanish conquistadors (possibly by Cortez). It was the name of an imaginary island, an earthly paradise, in "Las Serges de Esplandian," a Spanish romance written by Montalvo in 1510. Baja California (Lower California, in Mexico) was first visited by Spanish in 1533. The present U.S. state was called Alta (Upper) California.

Colorado—Spanish, red, first applied to Colorado River.

Connecticut—From Mohican and other Algonquin words meaning "long river place."

Delaware—Named for Lord De La Warr, early governor of Virginia; first applied to river, then to Indian tribe (Lenni-Lenape), and the state.

District of Columbia—For Columbus, 1791.

Florida—Named by Ponce de Leon on Pascua Florida, "Flowery Easter," on Easter Sunday, 1513.

Georgia—For King George II of England by James Oglethorpe, colonial administrator, 1732.

Hawaii—Possibly derived from native world for homeland, Hawaiki or Owhyhee.

Idaho—A coined name with an invented Indian meaning: "gem of the mountains;" originally suggested for the Pike's Peak mining territory (Colorado), then applied to the new mining territory of the Pacific Northwest. Another theory suggests Idaho may be a Kiowa Apache term for the Comanche.

Illinois—French for Illini or land of Illini, Algonquin word meaning men or warriors.

Indiana—Means "land of the Indians."

Iowa—Indian word variously translated as "one who puts to sleep" or "beautiful land."

Kansas—Sioux word for "south wind people."

Kentucky—Indian word variously translated as "dark and bloody ground," "meadow land" and "land of tomorrow."

Louisiana—Part of territory called Louisiana by Sieur de La Salle for French King Louis XIV.

Maine—From Maine, ancient French province. Also: descriptive, referring to the mainland as distinct from the many coastal islands.

Maryland—For Queen Henrietta Maria, wife of Charles I of England.

Massachusetts—From Indian tribe named after "large hill place" identified by Capt. John Smith as being near Milton, Mass.

Michigan—From Chippewa words mici gama meaning "great water," after the lake of the same name.

Minnesota—From Dakota Sioux word meaning "cloudy water" or "sky-tinted water" of the Minnesota River.

Mississippi—Probably Chippewa; mici zibi, "great river" or "gathering-in of all the waters." Also: Algonquin word, "Messipi."

Missouri—Algonquin Indian tribe named after Missouri River, meaning "muddy water."

Montana—Latin or Spanish for "mountainous."

Nebraska—From Omaha or Otos Indian word meaning "broad water" or "flat river," describing the Platte River.

Nevada—Spanish, meaning snow-clad.

New Hampshire—Named 1629 by Capt. John Mason of Plymouth Council for his home county in England.

New Jersey—The Duke of York, 1664, gave a patent to John Berkeley and Sir George Carteret to be called Nova Caesaria, or New Jersey, after England's Isle of Jersey.

New Mexico—Spaniards in Mexico applied term to land north and west of Rio Grande in the 16th century.

New York—For Duke of York and Albany who received patent to New Netherland from his brother Charles II and sent an expedition to capture it, 1664.

North Carolina—In 1619 Charles I gave a large patent to Sir Robert Heath to be called Province of Carolana, from Carolus, Latin name for Charles. A new patent was granted by Charles II to Earl of Clarendon and others. Divided into North and South Carolina, 1710.

North Dakota—Dakota is Sioux for friend or ally.

Ohio—Iroquois word for "fine or good river."

Oklahoma—Choctaw coined word meaning red man, proposed by Rev. Allen Wright, Choctaw-speaking Indian.

Oregon—Origin unknown. One theory holds that the name may have been derived from that of the Wisconsin River shown on a 1715 French map as "Ouaricon-sint."

Pennsylvania—William Penn, the Quaker, who was made full proprietor by King Charles II in 1681, suggested Sylvania, or woodland, for his tract. The king's government owed Penn's father, Admiral William Penn, £16,000, and the land was granted as partial settlement. Charles II added the Penn to Sylvania, against the desires of the modest proprietor, in honor of the admiral.

Puerto Rico—Spanish for Rich Port.

Rhode Island—Exact origin is unknown. One theory notes that Giovanni de Verrazano recorded an island about the size of Rhodes in the Mediterranean in 1524, but others believe the state was named Roode Eylandt by Adriaen Block, Dutch explorer, because of its red clay.

South Carolina—See North Carolina.

South Dakota—See North Dakota.

Tennessee—Tanasi was the name of Cherokee villages on the Little Tennessee River. From 1784 to 1788 this was the State of Franklin, or Frankland.

Texas—Variant of word used by Caddo and other Indians meaning friends or allies, and applied to them by the Spanish in eastern Texas. Also written texias, tejas, teysas.

Utah—From a Navajo word meaning upper, or higher up, as applied to a Shoshone tribe called Ute. Spanish form is Yutta, English Uta or Utah. Proposed name Deseret, "land of honeybees," from Book of Mormon, was rejected by Congress.

Vermont—From French words vert (green) and mont (mountain). The Green Mountains were said to have been named by Samuel de Champlain. The Green Mountain Boys were Gen. Stark's men in the Revolution. When the state was formed, 1777, Dr. Thomas Young suggested combining vert and mont into Vermont.

Virginia—Named by Sir Walter Raleigh, who fitted out the expedition of 1584, in honor of Queen Elizabeth, the Virgin Queen of England.

Washington—Named after George Washington. When the bill creating the Territory of Columbia was introduced in the 32d Congress, the name was changed to Washington because of the existence of the District of Columbia.

West Virginia—So named when western counties of Virginia refused to secede from the United States, 1863.

Wisconsin—An Indian name, spelled Ouisconsin and Mesconsing by early chroniclers. Believed to mean "grassy place" in Chippewa. Congress made it Wisconsin.

Wyoming—The word was taken from Wyoming Valley, Pa., which was the site of an Indian massacre and became widely known by Campbell's poem, "Gertrude of Wyoming." In Algonquin it means "large prairie place."

Accession of Territory by the U.S.

Source: Statistical Abstract of the United States

Division	Year	Sq. mi.[1]	Division	Year	Sq. mi.[1]	Division	Year	Sq. mi.[1]
Total U.S.	1970	3,630,854	Oregon	1846	285,580	American Samoa . .	1900	76
50 states & D.C. . . .		3,618,467	Mexican Cession. . .	1848	529,017	Corn Islands[4]	1914	4
Territory in 1790[2]. . .		888,685	Gadsden Purchase . .	1853	29,640	Virgin Islands, U.S.. .	1917	133
Louisiana Purchase .	1803	827,192	Alaska.	1867	589,757	Trust Territory of		
By treaty with Spain:			Hawaii.	1898	6,450	the Pacific Is.. . . .	1947	8,489
Florida	1819	58,560	The Philippines[3] . . .	1898	115,600	All other[5]		42
Other areas	1819	13,443	Puerto Rico.	1899	3,435			
Texas	1845	390,143	Guam	1899	212			

(1) Gross area (land and water). (2) Includes drainage basin of Red River on the north, south of 49th parallel, sometimes considered a part of the Louisiana Purchase. (3) Area not included in total; became Republic of the Philippines July 4, 1946. (4) Leased from Nicaragua for 99 years but returned Apr. 25, 1971; area not included in total. (5) See index for Outlying Areas, U.S.

Public Lands of the U. S.

Source: Bureau of Land Management, U.S. Interior Department

Acquisition of the Public Domain 1781-1867

Acquisition	Area* (acres)	Land	Water	Total	Cost[1]
State Cessions (1781-1802)		233,415,680	3,409,920	236,825,600	[2]$6,200,000
Louisiana Purchase (1803)[3]		523,446,400	6,465,280	529,911,680	[5]$23,213,568
Red River Basin[4]		29,066,880	535,040	29,601,920	
Cession from Spain (1819)		43,342,720	2,801,920	46,144,640	6,674,057
Oregon Compromise (1846)		180,644,480	2,741,760	183,386,240	
Mexican Cession (1848)		334,479,360	4,201,600	338,680,960	16,295,149
Purchase from Texas (1850)		78,842,880	83,840	78,926,720	15,496,448
Gadsden Purchase (1853)		18,961,920	26,880	18,988,800	10,000,000
Alaska Purchase (1867)		362,516,480	12,787,200	375,303,680	7,200,000
Total		**1,804,716,800**	**33,053,440**	**1,837,770,240**	**$85,079,222**

*All areas except Alaska were computed in 1912, and have not been adjusted for the recomputation of the area of the United States which was made for the 1950 Decennial Census. (1) Cost data for all except "State Cessions" obtained from U.S. Geological Survey. (2) Paid by federal government for Georgia cession, 1802 (56,689,920 acres). (3) Excludes areas eliminated by Treaty of 1819 with Spain. (4) Basin of the Red River of the North, south of the 49th parallel. (5) Includes $8,221,321 in interest paid on bonds floated by U.S to France.

Disposition of Public Lands 1781 to 1982

Disposition by methods not elsewhere classified[1]	Acres	Granted to states for:	Acres
Granted or sold to homesteaders	303,500,000	Support of common schools	77,630,000
Granted to railroad corporations	287,500,000	Reclamation of swampland	64,920,000
Granted to veterans as military bounties. .	94,400,000	Construction of railroads	37,130,000
Confirmed as private land claims[2]	61,000,000	Support of misc. institutions[6]	21,700,000
Sold under timber and stone law[3].	34,000,000	Purposes not elsewhere classified[7] . . .	117,600,000
Granted or sold under timber culture law[4] .	13,900,000	Canals and rivers	6,100,000
Sold under desert land law[5]	10,900,000	Construction of wagon roads	3,400,000
	10,700,000	**Total granted to states . . . . . .**	**328,480,000**

(1) Chiefly public, private, and preemption sales, but includes mineral entries, script locations, sales of townsites and townlots. (2) The Government has confirmed title to lands claimed under valid grants made by foreign governments prior to the acquisition of the public domain by the United States. (3) The law provided for the sale of lands valuable for timber or stone and unfit for cultivation. (4) The law provided for the granting of public lands to settlers on condition that they plant and cultivate trees on the lands granted. (5) The law provided for the sale of arid agricultural public lands to settlers who irrigate them and bring them under cultivation. (6) Universities, hospitals, asylums, etc. (7) For construction of various public improvements (individual items not specified in the granting act) reclamation of desert lands, construction of water reservoirs, etc.

Public Lands Administered by Federal Agencies

Agency (Acres, March, 1, 1985)	Public domain	Acquired	Total
Forest Service	163,520,649.8	28,554,101.5	192,074,751.3
Bureau of Land Management.	338,751,552.0	2,307,693.5	341,059,245.5
Bureau of Reclamation	3,049,320.1	1,164,924.6	4,214,244.7
Fish and Wildlife Service	80,316,552.7	4,590,665.9	84,907,218.6
National Park Service	70,144,075.6	7,141,739.4	77,285,815.0
Tennessee Valley Authority.	—	1,010,270.0	1,010,270.0
Corps of Engineers	723,182.7	7,821,313.2	8,544,495.9
U.S. Army.	6,501,006.0	4,067,408.0	10,568,414.0
U.S. Navy.	2,170,475.4	958,166.3	3,128,641.7
Energy Research and Development Admin. . . .	1,435,273.4	665,687.7	2,100,961.1
Bureau of Indian Affairs	2,620,689.3	396,517.6	3,017,206.9
Other	775,032.1	1,154,564.6	1,929,596.7
Total	**670,007,809.1**	**59,833,052.3**	**729,840,861.4**

National Parks, Other Areas Administered by Nat'l Park Service

Figures given are date area initially protected by Congress or presidential proclamation, date given current designation, and gross area in acres 12/31/83.

National Parks

Acadia, Me. (1916/1929) 39,707. Includes Mount Desert Island, half of Isle au Haut, Schoodic Point on mainland. Highest elevation on Eastern seaboard.

Arches, Ut. (1929/1978) 73,379. Contains giant red sandstone arches and other products of erosion.

Badlands, S.D. (1929/1978) 243,302; eroded prairie, bison, bighorn and antelope. Contains animal fossils of 40 million years ago.

Big Bend, Tex. (1935/1944) 741,118. Rio Grande, Chisos Mts.

Biscayne, Fla. (1968/1980) 172,953. Aquatic park encompasses chain of islands south of Miami.

Bryce Canyon, Ut. (1923/1928) 35,835. Spectacularly colorful and unusual display of erosion effects.

Canyonlands, Ut. (1964) 337,570. At junction of Colorado and Green rivers, extensive evidence of prehistoric Indians.

Capitol Reef, Ut. (1937/1971) 241,904. A 60-mile uplift of sandstone cliffs dissected by high-walled gorges.

Carlsbad Caverns, N.M. (1923/1930) 46,755. Largest known caverns; not yet fully explored.

Channel Islands, Cal. (1938/1980) 249,354. Seal lion breeding place, nesting sea birds, unique plants.

Crater Lake, Ore. (1902) 183,227. Extraordinary blue lake in crater of extinct volcano encircled by lava walls 500 to 2,000 feet high.

Denali, Alas. (1917/1980) 4,700,000. Name changed from Mt. McKinley NP. Contains highest mountain in U.S.; wildlife.

Everglades, Fla. (1934) 1,398,937. Largest remaining subtropical wilderness in continental U.S.

Gates of the Arctic, Alas. (1978/1980) 7,500,000. Vast wilderness in north central region.

Glacier, Mon. (1910) 1,013,595. Superb Rocky Mt. scenery, numerous glaciers and glacial lakes. Part of Waterton-Glacier Intl. Peace Park established by U.S. and Canada in 1932.

Glacier Bay, Alas. (1925/1980) 3,225,198. Great tidewater glaciers that move down mountain sides and break up into the sea; much wildlife.

Grand Canyon, Ariz. (1908/1919) 1,218,375. Most spectacular part of Colorado River's greatest canyon.

Grand Teton, Wy. (1929) 310,528. Most impressive part of the Teton Mountains, winter feeding ground of largest American elk herd.

Great Smoky Mountains, N.C.-Tenn. (1926) 520,269. Largest eastern mountain range, magnificent forests.

Guadalupe Mountains, Tex. (1966/1972) 76,293. Extensive Permian limestone fossil reef; tremendous earth fault.

Haleakala, Ha. (1916/1960) 28,655. Dormant volcano on Maui with large colorful craters.

Hawaii Volcanoes, Ha. (1916/1961) 229,177. Contains Kilauea and Mauna Loa, active volcanoes.

Hot Springs, Ark. (1832/1921) 5,824. Government supervised bath houses use waters of 45 of the 47 natural hot springs.

Isle Royale, Mich. (1931) 571,790. Largest island in Lake Superior, noted for its wilderness area and wildlife.

Katmai, Alas. (1918/1980) 3,716,000. Valley of Ten Thousand Smokes, scene of 1917 volcanic eruption.

Kenai Fjords, Alas. (1978/1980) 670,000. Abundant mountain goats, marine mammals, birdlife; the Harding Icefield, one of the major icecaps in U.S.

Kings Canyon, Cal. (1890/1940) 461,636. Mountain wilderness, dominated by Kings River Canyons and High Sierra; contains giant sequoias.

Kobuk Valley, Alas. (1978/1980) 1,750,000. Broad river is core of native culture.

Lake Clark, Alas. (1978/1980) 2,874,000. Across Cook Inlet from Anchorage. A scenic wilderness rich in fish and wildlife.

Lassen Volcanic, Cal. (1907/1916) 106,372. Contains Lassen Peak, recently active volcano, and other volcanic phenomena.

Mammoth Cave, Ky. (1926) 52,369. 144 miles of surveyed underground passages, beautiful natural formations, river 300 feet below surface.

Mesa Verde, Col. (1906) 52,085. Most notable and best preserved prehistoric cliff dwellings in the United States.

Mount Rainier, Wash. (1899) 235,404. Greatest single-peak glacial system in the lower 48 states.

North Cascades, Wash. (1968) 504,781. Spectacular mountainous region with many glaciers, lakes.

Olympic, Wash. (1909/1938) 914,576. Mountain wilderness containing finest remnant of Pacific Northwest rain forest, active glaciers, Pacific shoreline, rare elk.

Petrified Forest, Ariz. (1906/1962) 93,493. Extensive petrified wood and Indian artifacts. Contains part of Painted Desert.

Redwood, Cal. (1968) 110,123. Forty miles of Pacific coastline, groves of ancient redwoods and world's tallest trees.

Rocky Mountain, Col. (1915) 265,193. On the continental divide, includes 107 named peaks over 11,000 feet.

Sequoia, Cal. (1890) 402,488. Groves of giant sequoias, highest mountain in contiguous United States — Mount Whitney (14,494 feet). World's largest tree.

Shenandoah, Va. (1926/1935) 195,072. Portion of the Blue Ridge Mountains; overlooks Shenandoah Valley; Skyline Drive.

Theodore Roosevelt, N.D. (1947/1978) 70,416. Contains part of T.R.'s ranch and scenic badlands.

Virgin Islands, V.I. (1956) 14,695. Covers 75% of St. John Island, lush growth, lovely beaches, Indian relics, evidence of colonial Danes.

Voyageurs, Minn. (1971/1975) 217,892. Abundant lakes, forests, wildlife, canoeing, boating.

Wind Cave, S.D. (1903) 28,292. Limestone caverns in Black Hills. Extensive wildlife includes a herd of bison.

Wrangell-St. Elias, Alas. (1978/1980) 8,945,000. Largest area in park system, most peaks over 16,000 feet, abundant wildlife; day's drive east of Anchorage.

Yellowstone, Ida., Mon., Wy., (1872) 2,219,823. Oldest national park. World's greatest geyser area has about 3,000 geysers and hot springs; spectacular falls and impressive canyons of the Yellowstone River; grizzly bear, moose, and bison.

Yosemite, Cal. (1890) 761,110. Yosemite Valley, the nation's highest waterfall, 3 groves of sequoias, and mountainous.

Zion, Ut. (1909/1919) 146,551. Unusual shapes and landscapes have resulted from erosion and faulting; Zion Canyon, with sheer walls ranging up to 2,500 feet, is readily accessible.

National Historical Parks

Appomattox Court House, Va. (1930/1954) 1,325. Where Lee surrendered to Grant.

Boston, Mass. (1974) 41. Includes Faneuil Hall, Old North Church, Bunker Hill, Paul Revere House.

Chaco Culture, N.M. (1907/1980) 33,978. Ruins of pueblos built by prehistoric Indians.

Chesapeake and Ohio Canal, Md.-W.Va.-D.C. (1961/1971) 20,781. 185 mile historic canal; D.C. to Cumberland, Md.

Colonial, Va. (1930/1936) 9,316. Includes most of Jamestown Island, site of first successful English colony; Yorktown, site of Cornwallis' surrender to George Washington; and the Colonial Parkway.

Cumberland Gap, Ky.-Tenn.-Va. (1940) 20,274. Mountain pass of the Wilderness Road which carried the first great migration of pioneers into America's interior.

George Rogers Clark, Vincennes, Ind. (1966) 24. Commemorates American defeat of British in west during Revolution.

Harpers Ferry, Md., W. Va. (1944/1963) 2,238. At the confluence of the Shenandoah and Potomac rivers, the site of John Brown's 1859 raid on the Army arsenal.

Independence, Pa. (1948/1956) 45. Contains several properties in Philadelphia associated with the Revolutionary War and the founding of the U.S.

Jean Laffite (and preserve), La. (1939/1978) 20,000. Includes Chalmette, site of 1814 Battle of New Orleans; French Quarter.

Kalaupapa, Ha. (1980) 10,902. Molokai's former leper colony site and other historic areas.

Kaloko-Honokohau, Ha. (1978) 1,161. Culture center has 234 historic features and grave of first king, Kamehameha.

Klondike Gold Rush, Alas.-Wash. (1976) 13,191. Alaskan Trails in 1898 Gold Rush. Museum in Seattle.

Lowell, Mass. (1978) 137. Seven mills, canal, 19th C. structures, park to show planned city of Industrial Revolution.

Lyndon B. Johnson, Tex. (1969/1980) 1,478. President's birthplace, boyhood home, ranch.

Minute Man, Mass. (1959) 748. Where the colonial Minute Men battled the British, April 19, 1775. Also contains Nathaniel Hawthorne's home.

Morristown, N.J. (1933) 1,676. Sites of important military encampments during the Revolutionary War; Washington's headquarters 1777, 1779-80.

Nez Perce, Ida. (1965) 2,109. Illustrates the history and culture of the Nez Perce Indian country. 22 separate sites.

Pu'uhonua o Honaunau, Ha. (1955/1978) 182. Until 1819, a sanctuary for Hawaiians vanquished in battle, and those guilty of crimes or breaking taboos.

San Antonio Missions, Tex. (1978) 477. Four of finest Spanish missions in U.S., 18th C. irrigation system.

San Juan Island, Wash. (1966) 1,752. Commemorates peaceful relations of the U.S., Canada and Great Britain since the 1872 boundary disputes.

Saratoga, N.Y. (1938) 3,415. Scene of a major battle which became a turning point in the War of Independence.

Sitka, Alas. (1910/1972) 106. Scene of last major resistance of the Tlingit Indians to the Russians, 1804.

Valley Forge, Pa. (1976) 3,465. Continental Army campsite in 1777-78 winter.

War in the Pacific, Guam (1978) 1,958. Scenic park memorial for WWII combatants in Pacific.

Women's Rights, N.Y. (1980) 4.99. Seneca Falls site where Susan B. Anthony, Elizabeth Cady Stanton began rights movement in 1848.

National Battlefields

Antietam, Md. (1890) 3,246. Battle ended first Confederate invasion of North, Sept. 17, 1862.

Big Hole, Mon. (1910/1963) 656. Site of major battle with Nez Perce Indians.

Cowpens, S.C. (1929/1972) 841. Revolutionary War battlefield.

Fort Necessity, Pa. (1931/1961) 903. First battle of French and Indian War.

Monocacy, Md. (1934/1976) 1,659. Civil War battle in defense of Wash., D.C., July 9, 1864.

Moores Creek, N.C. (1926) 87. Pre-Revolutionary War battle.

Petersburg, Va. (1926/1962) 2,735. Scene of 10-month Union campaign 1864-65.

Stones River, Tenn. (1927/1960) 331. Civil War battle leading to Sherman's "March to the Sea."

Tupelo, Miss. (1929/1961) 1. Crucial battle over Sherman's supply line.

Wilson's Creek, Mo. (1960/1970) 1,750. Civil War battle for control of Missouri.

National Battlefield Parks

Kennesaw Mountain, Ga. (1917/1935) 2,884. Two major battles of Atlanta campaign in Civil War.

Manassas, Va. (1940) 4,513. Two battles of Bull Run in Civil War, 1861 and 1862.

Richmond, Va. (1936) 771. Site of battles defending Confederate capital.

National Battlefield Site

Brices Cross Roads, Miss. (1929) 1. Civil War battlefield.

National Military Parks

Chickamauga and Chattanooga, Ga.-Tenn. (1890) 8,103. Four Civil War battlefields.

Fort Donelson, Tenn. (1928) 537. Site of first major Union victory.

Fredericksburg and Spotsylvania County, Va. (1927) 5,909. Sites of several major Civil War battles and campaigns.

Gettysburg, Pa. (1895) 3,865. Site of decisive Confederate defeat in North. Gettysburg Address.

Guilford Courthouse, N.C. (1917) 220. Revolutionary War battle site.

Horseshoe Bend, Ala. (1956) 2,040. On Tallapoosa River, where Gen. Andrew Jackson broke the power of the Creek Indian Confederacy.

Kings Mountain, S.C. (1931) 3,945. Revolutionary War battle.

Pea Ridge, Ark. (1956) 4,300. Civil War battle.

Shiloh, Tenn. (1894) 3,838. Major Civil War battle; site includes some well-preserved Indian burial mounds.

Vicksburg, Miss. (1899) 1,620. Union victory gave North control of the Mississippi and split the Confederacy in two.

National Memorials

Arkansas Post, Ark. (1960) 389. First permanent French settlement in the lower Mississippi River valley.

Arlington House, the Robert E. Lee Memorial, Va. (1925/1972) 28. Lee's home overlooking the Potomac.

Chamizal, El Paso, Tex. (1964/1966) 55. Commemorates 1963 settlement of 99-year border dispute with Mexico.

Coronado, Ariz. (1941/1952) 4,750. Commemorates first European exploration of the Southwest.

DeSoto, Fla. (1948) 27. Commemorates 16th-century Spanish explorations.

Federal Hall, N.Y. (1939/1955) 0.45. First seat of U.S. government under the Constitution.

Fort Caroline, Fla. (1950) 138. On St. Johns River, overlooks site of second attempt by French Huguenots to colonize North America.

Fort Clatsop, Ore. (1958) 125. Lewis and Clark encampment 1805-06.

General Grant, N.Y. (1958) 0.76. Tombs of Pres. and wife.

Hamilton Grange, N.Y. (1962) 0.71. Home of Alexander Hamilton.

John F. Kennedy Center for the Performing Arts, D.C. (1958/1964) 18.

Johnstown Flood, Pa. (1964) 163. Commemorates tragic flood of 1889.

Lincoln Boyhood, Ind. (1962) 192. Lincoln grew up here.

Lincoln Memorial, D.C. (1911) 164.

Lyndon B. Johnson Grove on the Potomac, D.C. (1973) 17.

Mount Rushmore, S.D. (1925) 1,278. World famous sculpture of 4 presidents.

Roger Williams, R.I. (1965) 5. Memorial to founder of Rhode Island.

Thaddeus Kosciuszko, Pa. (1972) 0.02. Memorial to Polish hero of American Revolution.

Theodore Roosevelt Island, D.C. (1932) 89.

Thomas Jefferson Memorial, D.C. (1934) 18.

USS Arizona, Ha. (1980). 00. Memorializes American losses at Pearl Harbor.

Washington Monument, D.C. (1848) 106.

Wright Brothers, N.C. (1927/1953) 431. Site of first powered flight.

Vietnam Veterans National Memorial, D.C. (1980) 2. Honors and recognizes the men and women of the armed forces who served in the Vietnam war.

National Historic Sites

Abraham Lincoln Birthplace, Hodgenville, Ky. (1916/1959) 117.

Adams, Quincy, Mass. (1946/1952) 10. Home of Presidents John Adams, John Quincy Adams, and celebrated descendants.

Allegheny Portage Railroad, Pa. (1964) 1,135. Part of the Pennsylvania Canal system.

Andersonville, Andersonville, Ga. (1970) 476. Noted Civil War prison.

Andrew Johnson, Greeneville, Tenn. (1935/1963) 17. Home of the President.

Bent's Old Fort, Col. (1960) 800. Old West fur-trading post.

Carl Sandburg Home, N.C. (1968/1972) 264. Poet's home.

Christiansted, St. Croix; V.I. (1952/1961) 27. Commemorates Danish colony.

Clara Barton, Md. (1974) 9. Home of founder of American Red Cross.

Edgar Allan Poe, Pa. (1978/1980) 1. Poet's home.

Edison, West Orange, N.J. (1955/1962) 21. Home and laboratory.

Eisenhower, Gettysburg, Pa. (1967/1969) 690. Home of 34th president.

Eleanor Roosevelt, Hyde Park, N.Y. (1977) 181.

Eugene O'Neill, Danville, Cal. (1976) 13. Playwright's home.

Ford's Theatre, Washington, D.C. (1866/1970) 0.29. Includes theater, now restored, where Lincoln was assassinated, house where he died, and Lincoln Museum.

Fort Bowie, Ariz. (1964/1972) 1,000. Focal point of operations against Geronimo and the Apaches.

Fort Davis, Tex. (1961) 460. Frontier outpost battled Comanches and Apaches.

Fort Laramie, Wy. (1938/1960) 832. Military post on Oregon Trail.

Fort Larned, Kan. (1964) 718. Military post on Santa Fe Trail.

Fort Point, San Francisco, Cal. (1970) 29. Largest West Coast fortification.

Fort Raleigh, N.C. (1941) 157. First English settlement.

Fort Scott, Kan. (1978) 17. Commemorates events of Civil War period.

Fort Smith, Ark. (1961) 73. Active post from 1817 to 1890.

Fort Union Trading Post, Mon., N.D. (1966) 434. Principal fur-trading post on upper Missouri, 1828-1867.

Fort Vancouver, Wash. (1948/1961) 209. Hdqts. for Hudson's Bay Company in 1825. Early military and political seat.

Frederick Law Olmsted, Mass. (1979) 2. Home of famous park planner (1822-1903).

Friendship Hill, Pa. (1978) 675. Home of Albert Gallatin, Jefferson's Sec'y of Treasury. Not open to public.

Golden Spike, Utah (1957) 2,735. Commemorates completion of first transcontinental railroad in 1869.

Grant-Kohrs Ranch, Mon. (1972) 1,499. Ranch house and part of 19th century ranch.

Hampton, Md. (1948) 59. 18th-century Georgian mansion.

Harry S Truman, Mo. (1980/1982). 0.78. Home of Pres. Truman after 1919.

Herbert Hoover, West Branch, Ia. (1965) 187. Birthplace and boyhood home of 31st president.

Home of Franklin D. Roosevelt, Hyde Park, N.Y. (1944) 290. Birthplace, home and "Summer White House".

Hopewell Village, Pa. (1938) 848. 19th-century iron making village.

Hubbell Trading Post, Ariz. (1965) 160. Indian trading post.

James A. Garfield, Mentor, Oh. (1980) 8. President's home.

Jefferson National Expansion Memorial, St. Louis, Mo. (1935/1954) 91. Commemorates westward expansion.

John Fitzgerald Kennedy, Brookline, Mass. (1967) 0.09. Birthplace and childhood home of the President.

John Muir, Martinez, Cal. (1964) 9. Home of early conservationist and writer.

Knife River Indian Villages, N.D. (1974) 1,293. Remnants of 5 Hidatsa villages.

Lincoln Home, Springfield, Ill. (1971) 12. Lincoln's residence when he was elected President, 1860.

Longfellow, Cambridge, Mass. (1972) 2. Longfellow's home, 1837-82, and Washington's hq. during Boston Siege, 1775-76. No federal facilities.

Maggie L. Walker, Va. (1978) 1. Richmond home of black leader and 1903 founder of bank.

Martin Luther King, Jr., Atlanta, Ga. (1980) 23. Birthplace, grave.

Martin Van Buren, N.Y. (1974) 40. Lindenwald, home of 8th president, near Kinderhook.

Ninety Six, S.C. (1976) 989. Colonial trading village.

Palo Alto Battlefield, Tex. (1978) 50. One of 2 Mexican War battles fought in U.S.

Puukohola Heiau, Ha. (1972) 78. Ruins of temple built by King Kamehameha.

Sagamore Hill, Oyster Bay, N.Y. (1962) 78. Home of President Theodore Roosevelt from 1885 until his death in 1919.

Saint-Gaudens, Cornish, N.H. (1964/1977) 148. Home, studio and gardens of American sculptor Augustus Saint-Gaudens.

Salem Maritime, Mass. (1938) 9. Only port never seized from the patriots by the British. Major fishing and whaling port.

San Juan, P.R. (1949) 75. 16th-century Spanish fortifications.

Saugus Iron Works, Mass. (1968) 9. Reconstructed 17th-century colonial ironworks.

Sewall-Belmont House, D.C. (1974) 0.35. National Women's Party headquarters 1929-74.

Springfield Armory, Mass. (1974) 55. Small arms manufacturing center for nearly 200 years.

Theodore Roosevelt Birthplace, N.Y., N.Y. (1962) 0.11.

Theodore Roosevelt Inaugural, Buffalo, N.Y. (1966) 1. Wilcox House where he took oath of office, 1901.

Thomas Stone, Md. (1978) 328. Home of signer of Declaration, built in 1771. Not open to public.

Tuskegee Institute, Ala. (1974) 74. College founded by Booker T. Washington in 1881 for blacks, includes student-made brick buildings.

Vanderbilt Mansion, Hyde Park, N.Y. (1940) 212. Mansion of 19th-century financier.

Whitman Mission, Wash. (1936/1963) 98. Site where Dr. and Mrs. Marcus Whitman ministered to the Indians until slain by them in 1847.

William Howard Taft, Cincinnati, Oh. (1969) 3. Birthplace and early home of the 27th president.

National Monuments

Name	State	Year	Acreage
Agate Fossil Beds	Neb.	1965	3,055
Alibates Flint Quarries	N.M.-Tex.	1965	1,371
Anakchak	Alas.	1978	139,500
Aztec Ruins	N.M.	1923	27
Bandelier	N.M.	1916	36,917
Black Canyon of the Gunnison	Col.	1933	20,763
Booker T. Washington	Va.	1956	224
Buck Island Reef	V.I.	1961	880
Cabrillo	Cal.	1913	144
Canyon de Chelly	Ariz.	1931	83,840
Cape Krusenstern	Alas.	1978	660,000

Name	State	Year	Acreage
Capulin Mountain	N.M.	1916	775
Casa Grande Ruins	Ariz.	1892	473
Castillo de San Marcos	Fla.	1924	20
Castle Clinton	N.Y.	1946	1
Cedar Breaks	Ut.	1933	6,155
Chiricahua	Ariz.	1924	11,135
Colorado	Col.	1911	20,454
Congaree Swamp	S.C.	1976	15,138
Craters of the Moon	Ida.	1924	53,545
Custer Battlefield	Mon.	1879	765
Death Valley	Cal.-Nev.	1933	2,067,628
Devils Postpile	Cal.	1911	798
Devils Tower	Wy.	1906	1,347
Dinosaur	Col.-Ut.	1915	211,272
Effigy Mounds	Ia.	1949	1,475
El Morro	N.M.	1906	1,279
Florissant Fossil Beds**	Col.	1969	5,998
Fort Frederica	Ga.	1936	214
Fort Jefferson	Fla.	1935	64,700
Fort Matanzas	Fla.	1924	299
Fort McHenry National Monument and Historic Shrine	Md.	1925	43
Fort Pulaski	Ga.	1924	5,623
Fort Stanwix	N.Y.	1935	16
Fort Sumter	S.C.	1948	67
Fort Union	N.M.	1954	721
Fossil Butte	Wy.	1972	8,198
G. Washington Birthplace	Va.	1930	538
George Washington Carver	Mo.	1943	210
Gila Cliff Dwellings	N.M.	1907	533
Grand Portage	Minn.	1951	710
Great Sand Dunes	Col.	1932	38,662
Hohokam Pima*	Ariz.	1972	1,690
Homestead Nat'l. Monument of America	Neb.	1936	195
Hovenweep	Col.-Ut.	1923	785
Jewel Cave	S.D.	1908	1,274
John Day Fossil Beds	Ore.	1974	14,012
Joshua Tree	Cal.	1936	559,960
Lava Beds	Cal.	1925	46,560
Lehman Caves	Nev.	1922	640
Montezuma Castle	Ariz.	1906	858
Mound City Group	Oh.	1923	218
Muir Woods	Cal.	1908	554
Natural Bridges	Ut.	1908	7,791
Navajo	Ariz.	1909	360
Ocmulgee	Ga.	1934	683
Oregon Caves	Ore.	1909	488
Organ Pipe Cactus	Ariz.	1937	330,689
Pecos	N.M.	1965	365
Pinnacles	Cal.	1908	16,222
Pipe Spring	Ariz.	1923	40
Pipestone	Minn.	1937	282
Rainbow Bridge	Ut.	1910	160
Russell Cave	Ala.	1961	310
Saguaro	Ariz.	1933	83,574
Saint Croix Island**	Me.	1949	35
Salinas	N.M.	1909	1,080
Scotts Bluff	Neb.	1919	2,997
Statue of Liberty	N.J.-N.Y.	1924	58
Sunset Crater	Ariz.	1930	3,040
Timpanogos Cave	Ut.	1922	250
Tonto	Ariz.	1907	1,120
Tumacacori	Ariz.	1908	17
Tuzigoot	Ariz.	1939	809
Walnut Canyon	Ariz.	1915	2,249
White Sands	N.M.	1933	144,458
Wupatki	Ariz.	1924	35,253
Yucca House*	Col.	1919	10

National Preserves

Name	State	Year	Acreage
Aniakchak	Alas.	1978	475,500
Bering Land Bridge	Alas.	1978	2,700,000
Big Cypress	Fla.	1974	570,000
Big Thicket	Tex.	1974	85,850
Denali	Alas.	1917	1,330,000
Gates of the Arctic	Alas.	1978	940,000

Name	State	Year	Acreage
Glacier Bay	Alas.	1925	55,000
Katmai	Alas.	1918	374,000
Lake Clark	Alas.	1978	1,171,000
Noatak	Alas.	1978	6,560,000
Wrangell-St. Elias	Alas.	1978	4,255,000
Yukon-Charley Rivers	Alas.	1978	2,520,000

National Seashores

Name	State	Year	Acreage
Assateague Island	Md.-Va.	1965	39,631
Canaveral	Fla.	1975	57,627
Cape Cod	Mass.	1961	43,526
Cape Hatteras	N.C.	1937	30,319
Cape Lookout**	N.C.	1966	28,415
Cumberland Island	Ga.	1972	36,410
Fire Island	N.Y.	1964	19,579
Gulf Islands	Fla.-Miss.	1971	139,775
Padre Island	Tex.	1962	130,697
Point Reyes	Cal.	1962	71,046

National Parkways

Name	State	Year	Acreage
Blue Ridge	Va.-N.C.	1936	82,117
George Washington Memorial	Va.-Md.	1930	7,142
John D. Rockefeller Jr. Mem.	Wy.	1972	23,777
Natchez Trace	Ala.-Miss.-Tenn.	1938	50,189

National Lakeshores

Name	State	Year	Acreage
Apostle Islands	Wis.	1970	67,885
Indiana Dunes	Ind.	1966	12,870
Pictured Rocks	Mich.	1966	72,899
Sleeping Bear Dunes	Mich.	1970	71,021

National Rivers

Name	State	Year	Acreage
Alagnak Wild River	Alas.	1980	24,038
Big South Fork	Ky.-Tenn.	1976	122,960
Buffalo	Ark.	1972	94,221
New River Gorge	W.Va.	1978	62,024

National Scenic Rivers and Riverways

Name	State	Year	Acreage
Delaware	N.Y.-N.J.-Pa.	1978	1,973
Lower Saint Croix	Minn.-Wis.	1972	9,365
Obed Wild	Tenn.	1976	5,101
Ozark	Mo.	1964	80,698
Rio Grande	Tex.	1978	9,600
Saint Croix	Minn.-Wis.	1968	68,793
Upper Delaware	N.Y.-N.J.	1978	75,000

Parks (no other classification)

Name	State	Year	Acreage
Catoctin Mountain	Md.	1954	5,770
Fort Benton	Mon.	1976	...
Fort Washington	Md.	1930	341
Frederick Douglass Home	D.C.	1962	8
Greenbelt	Md.	1950	1,176
Perry's Victory	Oh.	1936	25
Piscataway	Md.	1961	4,251
Prince William Forest	Va.	1948	18,572
Rock Creek	D.C.	1890	1,754
Wolf Trap Farm Park for the Performing Arts	Va.	1966	130

National Recreation Areas

Name	State	Year	Acreage
Amistad	Tex.	1965	57,272
Bighorn Canyon	Mon.-Wy.	1966	120,278
Chattahoochee R.	Ga.	1978	8,699
Chickasaw	Okla.	1902	9,522
Coulee Dam	Wash.	1946	100,059
Curecanti	Col.	1965	42,114
Cuyahoga Valley	Oh.	1974	32,460
Delaware Water Gap	N.J.-Pa.	1965	66,697
Gateway	N.Y.-N.J.	1972	26,311
Glen Canyon	Ariz.-Ut.	1958	1,236,880
Golden Gate	Cal.	1972	72,815
Lake Chelan	Wash.	1968	61,890
Lake Mead	Ariz.-Nev.	1936	1,496,601
Lake Meredith	Tex.	1965	44,978
Ross Lake	Wash.	1968	117,574
Santa Monica Mts.	Cal.	1978	150,000
Whiskeytown	Cal.	1965	42,503

National Mall

Name	State	Year	Acreage
	D.C.	1933	146

National Scenic Trail

Name	State	Year	Acreage
Appalachian	Me. to Ga.	1968	115,863

*Not open to the public **No federal facilities

National Recreation Areas Administered by Forest Service

Name	State	Year	Acreage	Name	State	Year	Acreage
Arapaho	Col.	1978	35,697	Rattlesnake	Mon.	1980	61,000
Flaming Gorge	Ut.-Wyo.	1968	20,114	Sawtooth	Ida.	1972	756,019
Hell's Canyon	Ida.-Ore.	1975	525,608	Whiskeytown Shasta-Trinity	Cal.	1965	203,587
Mount Rogers	Va.	1966	154,770	Spruce Knob-Seneca Rocks	W. Va.	1965	100,000
Oregon Dunes	Ore.	1972	31,566				

The Homestead Act; Sale of Public Land

On October 21, 1976 Congress repealed the Homestead Act of 1862 for all states except Alaska. The Homestead Act is scheduled to expire in Alaska in 1986.

The Homestead Act was repealed because there was no longer any land in the public domain suitable for cultivation. The law had been in effect for 114 years. During that

time it had exerted a profound influence on the settlement of the west. Under the authority of the Homestead Act more than 1.6 million settlers claimed more than 270 million acres of public lands. The influx of settlers into the west made such states as Oklahoma, Kansas, Nebraska, and North and South Dakota a reality and brought substantial numbers of settlers into many other western states.

Federal Indian Reservations[1]

Source: Bureau of Indian Affairs, U.S. Interior Department (data for persons and unemployment as of 1985, other data as of 1983)

State	No. of reser.	Tribally-owned acreage[2]	Allotted acreage[2]	No. of tribes[3]	No. of persons[4]	Avg. (%) unemp. rate[5]	Major tribes and/or natives
Alaska	1[6]	86,759	361,523	6	69,410	51	Aleut, Eskimo, Athapascan[7], Haida, Tlingit, Tsimpshian
Arizona	20	19,555,035	252,474	13	166,330	43	Navajo, Apache, Papago, Hopi, Yavapai, Pima
California	78	500,285	68,556	—[8]	25,263	55	Hoopa, Paiute, Yurok, Karok, Mission Bands
Colorado	2	752,461	3,623	1	2,427	47	Ute
Florida	3	79,014	—	1	1,873	26	Seminole, Miccosukee[9]
Idaho	4	461,543	332,240		7,218	46	Shoshone, Bannock, Nez Perce
Iowa	1	4,164	—		745	66	Sac and Fox[10]
Kansas	4	5,768	22,522		2,254	28	Potawatomi, Kickapoo, Iowa
Louisiana	2	416	—		781	18	Chitimacha, Coushatta
Maine	3	245,424	—		2,421	22	Passamaquoddy, Penobscot, Maliseet
Michigan	5	12,085	9,186		6,498	58	Chippewa, Potawatomi, Ottawa
Minnesota	14	713,076	50,914		17,886	59	Chippewa, Sioux
Mississippi	1	17,635	19		4,599	26	Choctaw
Montana	7	2,220,383	3,016,409		28,963	39	Blackfeet, Crow, Sioux, Assiniboine, Cheyenne
Nebraska	3	22,656	42,339		4,415	60	Omaha, Winnebago, Santee Sioux
Nevada	23	1,138,462	79,567		8,410	44	Paiute, Shoshone, Washoe
New Mexico	24	6,483,483	675,986		110,172	32	Zuni, Apache, Navajo
New York	6	—	—		11,079	56	Seneca, Mohawk, Onondaga, Oneida[11]
North Carolina	1	56,461	—		6,110	39	Cherokee
North Dakota	5	207,820	643,959		21,835	50	Sioux, Chippewa, Mandan, Arikara, Hidatsa
Oklahoma	—[12]	86,684	1,127,751		159,587	18	Cherokee, Creek, Choctaw, Chickasaw, Osage, Cheyenne, Arapahoe, Kiowa, Comanche
Oregon	5	617,797	139,045		4,856	37	Warm Springs, Wasco, Paiute, Umatilla, Siletz
S. Dakota	9	2,621,228	2,473,118		49,832	64	Sioux
Utah	6	2,251,749	33,647		7,480	25	Ute, Goshute, Southern Paiute
Washington	26	2,014,238	481,545		40,524	52	Yakima, Lummi, Quinault
Wisconsin	15	328,886	80,795		19,334	49	Chippewa, Oneida, Winnebago
Wyoming	1	1,792,166	94,536		5,254	65	Shoshone, Arapahoe

(1) As of 1985 the federal government recognized and acknowledged that it had a special relationship with, and a trust responsibility for, 506 Federally recognized Indian entities in the U.S., including Alaska. The term "Indian entities" encompasses Indian tribes, bands, villages, groups, pueblos, Eskimos, and Aleuts, eligible for federal services and classified in the following 3 categories: (a) Officially approved Indian organizations pursuant to federal statutory authority (Indian Reorganization Act; Oklahoma Indian Welfare Act and Alaska Native Act.) (b) Officially approved Indian organizations outside of specified federal statutory authority. (c) Traditional Indian organizations recognized without formal federal approval of organizational structure.
(2) The acreages refer only to Indian lands which are either owned by the tribes or individual Indians, and held in trust by the U.S. government.
(3) "Tribe" among the North American Indians originally meant a body of persons bound together by blood ties who were socially, politically, and religiously organized, and who lived together, occupying a definite territory and having a common language or dialect. With the relegation of Indians to reservations, the word "tribe" developed a number of different meanings. Today, it can be a distinct group within an Indian village or community, the entire community, a large number of communities, several different groups or villages speaking different languages but sharing a common government, or a widely scattered number of villages with a common language but no common government.
(4) Number of Indians living on or adjacent to federally recognized reservations comprising the BIA service population.
(5) Unemployment rate of Indian work force consisting of all those 16 years old and over who are able and actively seeking work.
(6) Alaskan Indian Affairs are carried out under the Alaska Native Claims Settlement Act (Dec. 18, 1971). The Act provided for the establishment of regional and village corporations to conduct business for profit and non-profit purposes. There are 13 such regional corporations, each one with organized village corporations. The Metlakatla Reservation remains the only federally recognized reservation in Alaska in the sense of specific reservation boundaries, trust lands, etc.
(7) Aleuts and Eskimos are racially and linguistically related. Athapascans are related to the Navaho and Apache Indians.
(8) Some 62 distinct tribes are known to have lived in or wandered through what is now California at some time in the past. Many of these were village groups and are historically associated with bands which settled near Spanish missions where much of the traditional culture was destroyed. Many of these bands, however, still retain some of their Indian language and customs. Excluding the 30 mission bands, who are primarily of the Cahuilla, Diegueno, or Luiseno, there are some 22 tribes represented on the California reservations.
(9) "Seminole" means "runaways" and these Indians from various tribes were originally refugees from whites in the Carolinas and Georgia. Later joined by runaway slaves, the Seminole were united by their hostility to the United States. Formal peace with the Seminoles in Florida was not achieved until 1934. The Miccosukee are a branch of the Seminole; they retain their Indian religion and have not made formal peace with the United States.
(10) Once two tribes, the Sac and Fox formed a political alliance in 1734.
(11) These 4 tribes along with the Cayuga and Tuscarora made up the Iroquois League, which ruled large portions of New York, New England and Pennsylvania and ranged into the Midwest and South. The Onondaga, who traditionally provide the president of the league, maintain that they are a foreign nation within New York and the United States.
(12) Indian land status in Oklahoma is unique and there are no reservations in the sense that the term is used elsewhere in the U.S. Likewise, many of the Oklahoma tribes are unique in their high degree of assimilation to the white culture.

Declaration of Independence

The Declaration of Independence was adopted by the Continental Congress in Philadelphia, on July 4, 1776. John Hancock was president of the Congress and Charles Thomson was secretary. A copy of the Declaration, engrossed on parchment, was signed by members of Congress on and after Aug. 2, 1776. On Jan. 18, 1777, Congress ordered that "an authenticated copy, with the names of the members of Congress subscribing the same, be sent to each of the United States, and that they be desired to have the same put upon record." Authenticated copies were printed in broadside form in Baltimore, where the Continental Congress was then in session. The following text is that of the original printed by John Dunlap at Philadelphia for the Continental Congress.

IN CONGRESS, July 4, 1776.

A DECLARATION

By the REPRESENTATIVES of the

UNITED STATES OF AMERICA,

In GENERAL CONGRESS assembled

When in the Course of human Events, it becomes necessary for one People to dissolve the Political Bands which have connected them with another, and to assume among the Powers of the Earth, the separate and equal Station to which the Laws of Nature and of Nature's God entitle them, a decent Respect to the Opinions of Mankind requires that they should declare the causes which impel them to the Separation.

We hold these Truths to be self-evident, that all Men are created equal, that they are endowed by their Creator with certain unalienable Rights, that among these are Life, Liberty, and the Pursuit of Happiness—That to secure these Rights, Governments are instituted among Men, deriving their just Powers from the Consent of the Governed, that whenever any Form of Government becomes destructive of these Ends, it is the Right of the People to alter or to abolish it, and to institute new Government, laying its Foundation on such Principles, and organizing its Powers in such Form, as to them shall seem most likely to effect their Safety and Happiness. Prudence, indeed, will dictate that Governments long established should not be changed for light and transient Causes; and accordingly all Experience hath shewn, that Mankind are more disposed to suffer, while Evils are sufferable, than to right themselves by abolishing the Forms to which they are accustomed. But when a long Train of Abuses and Usurpations, pursuing invariably the same Object, evinces a Design to reduce them under absolute Despotism, it is their Right, it is their Duty, to throw off such Government, and to provide new Guards for their future Security. Such has been the patient Sufferance of these Colonies; and such is now the Necessity which constrains them to alter their former Systems of Government. The History of the present King of Great-Britain is a History of repeated Injuries and Usurpations, all having in direct Object the Establishment of an absolute Tyranny over these States. To prove this, let Facts be submitted to a candid World.

He has refused his Assent to Laws, the most wholesome and necessary for the public Good.

He has forbidden his Governors to pass Laws of immediate and pressing Importance, unless suspended in their Operation till his Assent should be obtained; and when so suspended, he has utterly neglected to attend to them.

He has refused to pass other Laws for the Accommodation of large Districts of People, unless those People would relinquish the Right of Representation in the Legislature, a Right inestimable to them, and formidable to Tyrants only.

He has called together Legislative Bodies at Places unusual, uncomfortable, and distant from the Depository of their Public Records, for the sole Purpose of fatiguing them into Compliance with his Measures.

He has dissolved Representative Houses repeatedly, for opposing with manly Firmness his Invasions on the Rights of the People.

He has refused for a long Time, after such Dissolutions, to cause others to be elected; whereby the Legislative Powers, incapable of Annihilation, have returned to the People at large for their exercise; the State remaining in the mean time exposed to all the Dangers of Invasion from without, and Convulsions within.

He has endeavoured to prevent the Population of these States; for that Purpose obstructing the Laws for Naturalization of Foreigners; refusing to pass others to encourage their Migrations hither, and raising the Conditions of new Appropriations of Lands.

He has obstructed the Administration of Justice, by refusing his Assent to Laws for establishing Judiciary Powers.

He has made Judges dependent on his Will alone, for the Tenure of their Offices, and the Amount and payment of their Salaries.

He has erected a Multitude of new Offices, and sent hither Swarms of Officers to harrass our People, and eat out their Substance.

He has kept among us, in Times of Peace, Standing Armies, without the consent of our Legislatures.

He has affected to render the Military independent of, and superior to the Civil Power.

He has combined with others to subject us to a Jurisdiction foreign to our Constitution, and unacknowledged by our Laws; giving his Assent to their Acts of pretended Legislation:

For quartering large Bodies of Armed Troops among us:

For protecting them, by a mock Trial, from Punishment for any Murders which they should commit on the Inhabitants of these States:

For cutting off our Trade with all Parts of the World:

For imposing Taxes on us without our Consent:

For depriving us, in many Cases, of the Benefits of Trial by Jury:

For transporting us beyond Seas to be tried for pretended Offences:

For abolishing the free System of English Laws in a neighbouring Province, establishing therein an arbitrary Government, and enlarging its Boundaries, so as to render it at once an Example and fit Instrument for introducing the same absolute Rule into these Colonies:

For taking away our Charters, abolishing our most valuable Laws, and altering fundamentally the Forms of our Governments:

For suspending our own Legislatures, and declaring themselves invested with Power to legislate for us in all Cases whatsoever.

He has abdicated Government here, by declaring us out of his Protection and waging War against us.

He has plundered our Seas, ravaged our Coasts, burnt our towns, and destroyed the Lives of our People.

He is, at this Time, transporting large Armies of foreign Mercenaries to compleat the works of Death, Desolation, and Tyranny, already begun with circumstances of Cruelty and Perfidy, scarcely parallelled in the most barbarous Ages, and totally unworthy the Head of a civilized Nation.

He has constrained our fellow Citizens taken Captive on the high Seas to bear Arms against their Country, to become the Executioners of their Friends and Brethren, or to fall themselves by their Hands.

He has excited domestic Insurrections amongst us, and has endeavoured to bring on the Inhabitants of our Frontiers, the merciless Indian Savages, whose known Rule of Warfare, is an undistinguished Destruction, of all Ages, Sexes and Conditions.

In every stage of these Oppressions we have Petitioned for Redress in the most humble Terms: Our repeated Petitions have been answered only by repeated Injury. A Prince, whose Character is thus marked by every act which may de-

fine a Tyrant, is unfit to be the Ruler of a free People.

Nor have we been wanting in Attentions to our British Brethren. We have warned them from Time to Time of Attempts by their Legislature to extend an unwarrantable Jurisdiction over us. We have reminded them of the Circumstances of our Emigration and Settlement here. We have appealed to their native Justice and Magnanimity, and we have conjured them by the Ties of our common Kindred to disavow these Usurpations, which, would inevitably interrupt our Connections and Correspondence. They too have been deaf to the Voice of Justice and of Consanguinity. We must, therefore, acquiesce in the Necessity, which denounces our Separation, and hold them, as we hold the rest of Mankind, Enemies in War, in Peace, Friends.

We, therefore, the Representatives of the UNITED STATES OF AMERICA, in General Congress, Assembled, appealing to the Supreme Judge of the World for the Rectitude of our Intentions, do, in the Name, and by Authority of the good People of these Colonies, solemnly Publish and Declare, That these United Colonies are, and of Right ought to be, Free and Independent States; that they are absolved from all Allegiance to the British Crown, and that all political Connection between them and the State of Great-Britain, is and ought to be totally dissolved; and that as Free and Independent States, they have full Power to levy War, conclude Peace, contract Alliances, establish Commerce, and to do all other Acts and Things which Independent States may of right do. And for the support of this declaration, with a firm Reliance on the Protection of divine Providence, we mutually pledge to each other our lives, our Fortunes, and our sacred Honor.

JOHN HANCOCK, President

Attest.
CHARLES THOMSON, Secretary.

Signers of the Declaration of Independence

Delegate and state	Vocation	Birthplace	Born	Died
Adams, John (Mass.)	Lawyer	Braintree (Quincy), Mass.	Oct. 30, 1735	July 4, 1826
Adams, Samuel (Mass.)	Political leader	Boston, Mass.	Sept. 27, 1722	Oct. 2, 1803
Bartlett, Josiah (N.H.)	Physician, judge	Amesbury, Mass.	Nov. 21, 1729	May 19, 1795
Braxton, Carter (Va.)	Farmer	Newington Plantation, Va.	Sept. 10, 1736	Oct. 10, 1797
Carroll, Chas. of Carrollton (Md.)	Lawyer	Annapolis, Md.	Sept. 19, 1737	Nov. 14, 1832
Chase, Samuel (Md.)	Judge	Princess Anne, Md.	Apr. 17, 1741	June 19, 1811
Clark, Abraham (N.J.)	Surveyor	Roselle, N.J.	Feb. 15, 1726	Sept. 15, 1794
Clymer, George (Pa.)	Merchant	Philadelphia, Pa.	Mar. 16, 1739	Jan. 23, 1813
Ellery, William (R.I.)	Lawyer	Newport, R.I.	Dec. 22, 1727	Feb. 15, 1820
Floyd, William (N.Y.)	Soldier	Brookhaven, N.Y.	Dec. 17, 1734	Aug. 4, 1821
Franklin, Benjamin (Pa.)	Printer, publisher.	Boston, Mass.	Jan. 17, 1706	Apr. 17, 1790
Gerry, Elbridge (Mass.)	Merchant	Marblehead, Mass.	July 17, 1744	Nov. 23, 1814
Gwinnett, Button (Ga.)	Merchant	Down Hatherly, England.	c. 1735	May 19, 1777
Hall, Lyman (Ga.)	Physician	Wallingford, Conn.	Apr. 12, 1724	Oct. 19, 1790
Hancock, John (Mass.)	Merchant	Braintree (Quincy), Mass.	Jan. 12, 1737	Oct. 8, 1793
Harrison, Benjamin (Va.)	Farmer	Berkeley, Va.	Apr. 5, 1726	Apr. 24, 1791
Hart, John (N.J.)	Farmer	Stonington, Conn.	c. 1711	May 11, 1779
Hewes, Joseph (N.C.)	Merchant	Princeton, N.J.	Jan. 23, 1730	Nov. 10, 1779
Heyward, Thos. Jr. (S.C.)	Lawyer, farmer.	St. Luke's Parish, S.C.	July 28, 1746	Mar. 6, 1809
Hooper, William (N.C.)	Lawyer	Boston, Mass.	June 28, 1742	Oct. 14, 1790
Hopkins, Stephen (R.I.)	Judge, educator	Providence, R.I.	Mar. 7, 1707	July 13, 1785
Hopkinson, Francis (N.J.)	Judge, author.	Philadelphia, Pa.	Sept. 21, 1737	May 9, 1791
Huntington, Samuel (Conn.)	Judge	Windham County, Conn.	July 3, 1731	Jan. 5, 1796
Jefferson, Thomas (Va.)	Lawyer	Shadwell, Va.	Apr. 13, 1743	July 4, 1826
Lee, Francis Lightfoot (Va.)	Farmer	Westmoreland County, Va.	Oct. 14, 1734	Jan. 11, 1797
Lee, Richard Henry (Va.)	Farmer	Westmoreland County, Va.	Jan. 20, 1732	June 19, 1794
Lewis, Francis (N.Y.)	Merchant	Llandaff, Wales	Mar., 1713	Dec. 31, 1802
Livingston, Philip (N.Y.)	Merchant	Albany, N.Y.	Jan. 15, 1716	June 12, 1778
Lynch, Thomas Jr. (S.C.)	Farmer	Winyah, S.C.	Aug. 5, 1749	(at sea) 1779
McKean, Thomas (Del.)	Lawyer	New London, Pa.	Mar. 19, 1734	June 24, 1817
Middleton, Arthur (S.C.)	Farmer	Charleston, S.C.	June 26, 1742	Jan. 1, 1787
Morris, Lewis (N.Y.)	Farmer	Morrisania (Bronx County), N.Y.	Apr. 8, 1726	Jan. 22, 1798
Morris, Robert (Pa.)	Merchant	Liverpool, England	Jan. 20, 1734	May 9, 1806
Morton, John (Pa.)	Judge	Ridley, Pa.	1724	Apr., 1777
Nelson, Thos. Jr. (Va.)	Farmer	Yorktown, Va.	Dec. 26, 1738	Jan. 4, 1789
Paca, William (Md.)	Judge	Abingdon, Md.	Oct. 31, 1740	Oct. 23, 1799
Paine, Robert Treat (Mass.)	Judge	Boston, Mass.	Mar. 11, 1731	May 12, 1814
Penn, John (N.C.)	Lawyer	Near Port Royal, Va.	May 17, 1741	Sept. 14, 1788
Read, George (Del.)	Judge	Near North East, Md.	Sept. 18, 1733	Sept. 21, 1798
Rodney, Caesar (Del.)	Judge	Dover, Del.	Oct. 7, 1728	June 29, 1784
Ross, George (Pa.)	Judge	New Castle, Del.	May 10, 1730	July 14, 1779
Rush, Benjamin (Pa.)	Physician	Byberry, Pa. (Philadelphia).	Dec. 24, 1745	Apr. 19, 1813
Rutledge, Edward (S.C.)	Lawyer	Charleston, S.C.	Nov. 23, 1749	Jan. 23, 1800
Sherman, Roger (Conn.)	Lawyer	Newton, Mass.	Apr. 19, 1721	July 23, 1793
Smith, James (Pa.)	Lawyer	Dublin, Ireland	c. 1719	July 11, 1806
Stockton, Richard (N.J.)	Lawyer	Near Princeton, N.J.	Oct. 1, 1730	Feb. 28, 1781
Stone, Thomas (Md.)	Lawyer	Charles County, Md.	1743	Oct. 5, 1787
Taylor, George (Pa.)	Ironmaster	Ireland	1716	Feb. 23, 1781
Thornton, Matthew (N.H.)	Physician	Ireland	1714	June 24, 1803
Walton, George (Ga.)	Judge	Prince Edward County, Va.	1741	Feb. 2, 1804
Whipple, William (N.H.)	Merchant, judge	Kittery, Me.	Jan. 14, 1730	Nov. 28, 1785
Williams, William (Conn.)	Merchant	Lebanon, Conn.	Apr. 23, 1731	Aug. 2, 1811
Wilson, James (Pa.)	Judge	Carskerdo, Scotland	Sept. 14, 1742	Aug. 28, 1798
Witherspoon, John (N.J.)	Educator	Gifford, Scotland	Feb. 5, 1723	Nov. 15, 1794
Wolcott, Oliver (Conn.)	Judge	Windsor, Conn.	Dec. 1, 1726	Dec. 1, 1797
Wythe, George (Va.)	Lawyer	Elizabeth City Co. (Hampton), Va.	1726	June 8, 1806

Constitution of the United States
The Original 7 Articles

PREAMBLE

We, the people of the United States, in order to form a more perfect Union, establish justice, insure domestic tranquility, provide for the common defense, promote the general welfare, and secure the blessings of liberty to ourselves and our posterity do ordain and establish this Constitution for the United States of America.

ARTICLE I.

Section 1—Legislative powers; in whom vested:

All legislative powers herein granted shall be vested in a Congress of the United States, which shall consist of a Senate and House of Representatives.

Section 2—House of Representatives, how and by whom chosen. Qualifications of a Representative. Representatives and direct taxes, how apportioned. Enumeration. Vacancies to be filled. Power of choosing officers, and of impeachment.

1. The House of Representatives shall be composed of members chosen every second year by the people of the several States, and the electors in each State shall have the qualifications requisite for electors of the most numerous branch of the State Legislature.

2. No person shall be a Representative who shall not have attained to the age of twenty-five years, and been seven years a citizen of the United States, and who shall not, when elected, be an inhabitant of that State in which he shall be chosen.

3. *(Representatives and direct taxes shall be apportioned among the several States which may be included within this Union, according to their respective numbers, which shall be determined by adding to the whole number of free persons, including those bound to service for a term of years, and excluding Indians not taxed, three-fifths of all other persons.) (The previous sentence was superseded by Amendment XIV, section 2.)* The actual enumeration shall be made within three years after the first meeting of the Congress of the United States, and within every subsequent term of ten years, in such manner as they shall by law direct. The number of Representatives shall not exceed one for every thirty thousand; but each State shall have at least one Representative; and until such enumeration shall be made, the State of New Hampshire shall be entitled to choose three, Massachusetts eight, Rhode Island and Providence Plantations one, Connecticut five, New York six, New Jersey four, Pennsylvania eight, Delaware one, Maryland six, Virginia ten, North Carolina five, South Carolina five, and Georgia three.

4. When vacancies happen in the representation from any State, the Executive Authority thereof shall issue writs of election to fill such vacancies.

5. The House of Representatives shall choose their Speaker and other officers; and shall have the sole power of impeachment.

Section 3—Senators, how and by whom chosen. How classified. Qualifications of a Senator. President of the Senate, his right to vote. President pro tem., and other officers of the Senate, how chosen. Power to try impeachments. When President is tried, Chief Justice to preside. Sentence.

1. The Senate of the United States shall be composed of two Senators from each State, *(chosen by the Legislature thereof), (The preceding five words were superseded by Amendment XVII, section 1.)* for six years; and each Senator shall have one vote.

2. Immediately after they shall be assembled in consequence of the first election, they shall be divided as equally as may be into three classes. The seats of the Senators of the first class shall be vacated at the expiration of the second year, of the second class at the expiration of the fourth year, and of the third class at the expiration of the sixth year, so that one-third may be chosen every second year; *(and if vacancies happen by resignation, or otherwise, during the recess of the Legislature of any State, the Executive thereof may make temporary appointments until the next meeting of the Legislature, which shall then fill such vacancies.) (The words*

in parentheses were superseded by Amendment XVII, section 2.)

3. No person shall be a Senator who shall not have attained to the age of thirty years, and been nine years a citizen of the United States, and who shall not, when elected, be an inhabitant of that State for which he shall be chosen.

4. The Vice President of the United States shall be President of the Senate, but shall have no vote, unless they be equally divided.

5. The Senate shall choose their other officers, and also a President pro tempore, in the absence of the Vice President, or when he shall exercise the office of President of the United States.

6. The Senate shall have the sole power to try all impeachments. When sitting for that purpose, they shall be on oath or affirmation. When the President of the United States is tried, the Chief Justice shall preside: and no person shall be convicted without the concurrence of two-thirds of the members present.

7. Judgment in cases of impeachment shall not extend further than to removal from office, and disqualification to hold and enjoy any office of honor, trust or profit under the United States: but the party convicted shall nevertheless be liable and subject to indictment, trial, judgment and punishment, according to law.

Section 4—Times, etc., of holding elections, how prescribed. One session each year.

1. The times, places and manner of holding elections for Senators and Representatives, shall be prescribed in each State by the Legislature thereof; but the Congress may at any time by law make or alter such regulations, except as to the places of choosing Senators.

2. The Congress shall assemble at least once in every year, and such meeting shall *(be on the first Monday in December,) (The words in parentheses were superseded by Amendment XX, section 2).* unless they shall by law appoint a different day.

Section 5—Membership, quorum, adjournments, rules. Power to punish or expel. Journal. Time of adjournments, how limited, etc.

1. Each House shall be the judge of the elections, returns and qualifications of its own members, and a majority of each shall constitute a quorum to do business; but a smaller number may adjourn from day to day, and may be authorized to compel the attendance of absent members, in such manner, and under such penalties as each House may provide.

2. Each House may determine the rules of its proceedings, punish its members for disorderly behavior, and, with the concurrence of two-thirds, expel a member.

3. Each House shall keep a journal of its proceedings, and from time to time publish the same, excepting such parts as may in their judgment require secrecy; and the yeas and nays of the members of either House on any question shall, at the desire of one-fifth of those present, be entered on the journal.

4. Neither House, during the session of Congress, shall, without the consent of the other, adjourn for more than three days, nor to any other place than that in which the two Houses shall be sitting.

Section 6—Compensation, privileges, disqualifications in certain cases.

1. The Senators and Representatives shall receive a compensation for their services, to be ascertained by law, and paid out of the Treasury of the United States. They shall in all cases, except treason, felony and breach of the peace, be privileged from arrest during their attendance at the session of their respective Houses, and in going to and returning from the same; and for any speech or debate in either House, they shall not be questioned in any other place.

2. No Senator or Representative shall, during the time for which he was elected, be appointed to any civil office under the authority of the United States, which shall have been created, or the emoluments whereof shall have been increased during such time; and no person holding any office under the United States, shall be a member of either House

during his continuance in office.

Section 7—House to originate all revenue bills. Veto. Bill may be passed by two-thirds of each House, notwithstanding, etc. Bill, not returned in ten days, to become a law. Provisions as to orders, concurrent resolutions, etc.

1. All bills for raising revenue shall originate in the House of Representatives; but the Senate may propose or concur with amendments as on other bills.

2. Every bill which shall have passed the House of Representatives and the Senate, shall, before it becomes a law, be presented to the President of the United States; if he approves he shall sign it, but if not he shall return it, with his objections to that House in which it shall have originated, who shall enter the objections at large on their journal, and proceed to reconsider it. If after such reconsideration two-thirds of that House shall agree to pass the bill, it shall be sent, together with the objections, to the other House, by which it shall likewise be reconsidered, and if approved by two-thirds of that House, it shall become a law. But in all such cases the votes of both Houses shall be determined by yeas and nays, and the names of the persons voting for and against the bill shall be entered on the journal of each House respectively. If any bill shall not be returned by the President within ten days (Sundays excepted) after it shall have been presented to him, the same shall be a law, in like manner as if he had signed it, unless the Congress by their adjournment prevent its return, in which case it shall not be a law.

3. Every order, resolution, or vote to which the concurrence of the Senate and House of Representatives may be necessary (except on a question of adjournment) shall be presented to the President of the United States; and before the same shall take effect, shall be approved by him, or being disapproved by him, shall be repassed by two-thirds of the Senate and House of Representatives, according to the rules and limitations prescribed in the case of a bill.

Section 8—Powers of Congress.

The Congress shall have power

1. To lay and collect taxes, duties, imposts and excises, to pay the debts and provide for the common defense and general welfare of the United States; but all duties, imposts and excises shall be uniform throughout the United States;

2. To borrow money on the credit of the United States;

3. To regulate commerce with foreign nations, and among the several States, and with the Indian tribes;

4. To establish a uniform rule of naturalization, and uniform laws on the subject of bankruptcies throughout the United States;

5. To coin money, regulate the value thereof, and of foreign coin, and fix the standard of weights and measures;

6. To provide for the punishment of counterfeiting the securities and current coin of the United States;

7. To establish post-offices and post-roads;

8. To promote the progress of science and useful arts, by securing for limited times to authors and inventors the exclusive right to their respective writings and discoveries;

9. To constitute tribunals inferior to the Supreme Court;

10. To define and punish piracies and felonies committed on the high seas, and offenses against the law of nations;

11. To declare war, grant letters of marque and reprisal, and make rules concerning captures on land and water;

12. To raise and support armies, but no appropriation of money to that use shall be for a longer term than two years;

13. To provide and maintain a navy;

14. To make rules for the government and regulation of the land and naval forces;

15. To provide for calling forth the militia to execute the laws of the Union, suppress insurrections and repel invasions;

16. To provide for organizing, arming, and disciplining the militia, and for governing such part of them as may be employed in the service of the United States, reserving to the States respectively, the appointment of the officers, and the authority of training and militia according to the discipline prescribed by Congress;

17. To exercise exclusive legislation in all cases whatsoever, over such district (not exceeding ten miles square) as may, by cession of particular States, and the acceptance of Congress, become the seat of the Government of the United States, and to exercise like authority over all places purchased by the consent of the Legislature of the State in which the same shall be, for the erection of forts, magazines, arsenals, dockyards, and other needful buildings;—And

18. To make all laws which shall be necessary and proper for carrying into execution the foregoing powers, and all other powers vested by this Constitution in the Government of the United States, or in any department or officer thereof.

Section 9—Provision as to migration or importation of certain persons. Habeas corpus, bills of attainder, etc. Taxes, how apportioned. No export duty. No commercial preference. Money, how drawn from Treasury, etc. No titular nobility. Officers not to receive presents, etc.

1. The migration or importation of such persons as any of the States now existing shall think proper to admit, shall not be prohibited by the Congress prior to the year one thousand eight hundred and eight, but a tax or duty may be imposed on such importation, not exceeding ten dollars for each person.

2. The privilege of the writ of habeas corpus shall not be suspended, unless when in cases of rebellion or invasion the public safety may require it.

3. No bill of attainder or ex post facto law shall be passed.

4. No capitation, or other direct, tax shall be laid, unless in proportion to the census or enumeration herein before directed to be taken. (Modified by Amendment XVI.)

5. No tax or duty shall be laid on articles exported from any State.

6. No preference shall be given by any regulation of commerce or revenue to the ports of one State over those of another: nor shall vessels bound to, or from, one State, be obliged to enter, clear, or pay duties in another.

7. No money shall be drawn from the Treasury, but in consequence of appropriations made by law; and a regular statement and account of the receipts and expenditures of all public money shall be published from time to time.

8. No title of nobility shall be granted by the United States: and no person holding any office of profit or trust under them, shall, without the consent of the Congress, accept of any present, emolument, office, or title, of any kind whatever, from any king, prince, or foreign state.

Section 10—States prohibited from the exercise of certain powers.

1. No State shall enter into any treaty, alliance, or confederation; grant letters of marque and reprisal; coin money; emit bills of credit; make anything but gold and silver coin a tender in payment of debts; pass any bill of attainder, ex post facto law, or law impairing the obligation of contracts, or grant any title of nobility.

2. No State shall, without the consent of the Congress, lay any imposts or duties on imports or exports, except what may be absolutely necessary for executing its inspection laws: and the net produce of all duties and imposts, laid by any State on imports or exports, shall be for the use of the Treasury of the United States; and all such laws shall be subject to the revision and control of the Congress.

3. No State shall, without the consent of Congress, lay any duty of tonnage, keep troops, or ships of war in time of peace, enter into any agreement or compact with another State, or with a foreign power, or engage in war, unless actually invaded, or in such imminent danger as will not admit of delay.

ARTICLE II.

Section 1—President: his term of office. Electors of President; number and how appointed. Electors to vote on same day. Qualification of President. On whom his duties devolve in case of his removal, death, etc. President's compensation. His oath of office.

1. The Executive power shall be vested in a President of the United States of America. He shall hold his office during the term of four years, and together with the Vice President, chosen for the same term, be elected as follows

2. Each State shall appoint, in such manner as the Legis-

lature thereof may direct, a number of electors, equal to the whole number of Senators and Representatives to which the State may be entitled in the Congress: but no Senator or Representative, or person holding an office of trust or profit under the United States, shall be appointed an elector.

(The electors shall meet in their respective States, and vote by ballot for two persons, of whom one at least shall not be an inhabitant of the same State with themselves. And they shall make a list of all the persons voted for, and of the number of votes for each; which list they shall sign and certify, and transmit sealed to the seat of the Government of the United States, directed to the President of the Senate. The President of the Senate shall, in the presence of the Senate and House of Representatives, open all the certificates, and the votes shall then be counted. The person having the greatest number of votes shall be the President, if such number be a majority of the whole number of electors appointed; and if there be more than one who have such majority, and have an equal number of votes, then the House of Representatives shall immediately choose by ballot one of them for President; and if no person have a majority, then from the five highest on the list the said House shall in like manner choose the President. But in choosing the President, the votes shall be taken by States, the representation from each State having one vote; a quorum for this purpose shall consist of a member or members from two-thirds of the States, and a majority of all the States shall be necessary to a choice. In every case, after the choice of the President, the person having the greatest number of votes of the electors shall be the Vice President. But if there should remain two or more who have equal votes, the Senate shall choose from them by ballot the Vice President.)

(This clause was superseded by Amendment XII.)

3. The Congress may determine the time of choosing the electors, and the day on which they shall give their votes; which day shall be the same throughout the United States.

4. No person except a natural born citizen, or a citizen of the United States, at the time of the adoption of this Constitution, shall be eligible to the office of President; neither shall any person be eligible to that office who shall not have attained to the age of thirty-five years, and been fourteen years a resident within the United States.

(For qualification of the Vice President, see Amendment XII.)

5. In case of the removal of the President from office, or of his death, resignation, or inability to discharge the powers and duties of the said office, the same shall devolve on the Vice President, and the Congress may by law provide for the case of removal, death, resignation or inability, both of the President and Vice President, declaring what officer shall then act as President, and such officer shall act accordingly, until the disability be removed, or a President shall be elected.

(This clause has been modified by Amendments XX and XXV.)

6. The President shall, at stated times, receive for his services, a compensation, which shall neither be increased nor diminished during the period for which he shall have been elected, and he shall not receive within that period any other emolument from the United States, or any of them.

7. Before he enter on the execution of his office, he shall take the following oath or affirmation:

"I do solemnly swear (or affirm) that I will faithfully execute the office of President of the United States, and will to the best of my ability, preserve, protect and defend the Constitution of the United States."

Section 2—President to be Commander-in-Chief. He may require opinions of cabinet officers, etc., may pardon. Treaty-making power. Nomination of certain officers. When President may fill vacancies.

1. The President shall be Commander-in-Chief of the Army and Navy of the United States, and of the militia of the several States, when called into the actual service of the United States; he may require the opinion, in writing, of the principal officer in each of the executive departments, upon any subject relating to the duties of their respective offices, and he shall have power to grant reprieves and pardons for offenses against the United States, except in cases of impeachment.

2. He shall have power, by and with the advice and con-

sent of the Senate, to make treaties, provided two-thirds of the Senators present concur; and he shall nominate, and by and with the advice and consent of the Senate, shall appoint ambassadors, other public ministers and consuls, judges of the Supreme Court, and all other officers of the United States, whose appointments are not herein otherwise provided for, and which shall be established by law: but the Congress may by law vest the appointment of such inferior officers, as they think proper, in the President alone, in the courts of law, or in the heads of departments.

3. The President shall have power to fill up all vacancies that may happen during the recess of the Senate, by granting commissions, which shall expire at the end of their next session.

Section 3—President shall communicate to Congress. He may convene and adjourn Congress, in case of disagreement, etc. Shall receive ambassadors, execute laws, and commission officers.

He shall from time to time give to the Congress information of the state of the Union, and recommend to their consideration such measures as he shall judge necessary and expedient; he may, on extraordinary occasions, convene both Houses, or either of them, and in case of disagreement between them, with respect to the time of adjournment, he may adjourn them to such time as he shall think proper; he shall receive ambassadors and other public ministers; he shall take care that the laws be faithfully executed, and shall commission all the officers of the United States.

Section 4—All civil offices forfeited for certain crimes.

The President, Vice President, and all civil officers of the United States, shall be removed from office on impeachment for, and conviction of, treason, bribery, or other high crimes and misdemeanors.

ARTICLE III.

Section 1—Judicial powers, Tenure. Compensation.

The judicial power of the United States, shall be vested in one Supreme Court, and in such inferior courts as the Congress may from time to time ordain and establish. The judges, both of the Supreme and inferior courts, shall hold their offices during good behavior, and shall at stated times, receive for their services, a compensation, which shall not be diminished during their continuance in office.

Section 2—Judicial power; to what cases it extends. Original jurisdiction of Supreme Court; appellate jurisdiction. Trial by jury, etc. Trial, where.

1. The judicial power shall extend to all cases, in law and equity, arising under this Constitution, the laws of the United States, and treaties made, or which shall be made, under their authority; to all cases affecting ambassadors, other public ministers and consuls; to all cases of admiralty and maritime jurisdiction; to controversies to which the United States shall be a party; to controversies between two or more States; between a State and citizens of another State; between citizens of different States, between citizens of the same State claiming lands under grants of different States, and between a State, or the citizens thereof, and foreign states, citizens or subjects.

(This section is modified by Amendment XI.)

2. In all cases affecting ambassadors, other public ministers and consuls, and those in which a State shall be party, the Supreme Court shall have original jurisdiction. In all the other cases before mentioned, the Supreme Court shall have appellate jurisdiction, both as to law and fact, with such exceptions, and under such regulations as the Congress shall make.

3. The trial of all crimes, except in cases of impeachment, shall be by jury; and such trial shall be held in the State where the said crimes shall have been committed; but when not committed within any State, the trial shall be at such place or places as the Congress may by law have directed.

Section 3—Treason Defined, Proof of, Punishment of.

1. Treason against the United States, shall consist only in levying war against them, or in adhering to their enemies,

giving them aid and comfort. No person shall be convicted of treason unless on the testimony of two witnesses to the same overt act, or on confession in open court.

2. The Congress shall have power to declare the punishment of treason, but no attainder of treason shall work corruption of blood, or forfeiture except during the life of the person attainted.

ARTICLE IV.

Section 1—Each State to give credit to the public acts, etc., of every other State.

Full faith and credit shall be given in each State to the public acts, records, and judicial proceedings of every other State. And the Congress may by general laws prescribe the manner in which such acts, records and proceedings shall be proved, and the effect thereof.

Section 2—Privileges of citizens of each State. Fugitives from justice to be delivered up. Persons held to service having escaped, to be delivered up.

1. The citizens of each State shall be entitled to all privileges and immunities of citizens in the several States.

2. A person charged in any State with treason, felony, or other crime, who shall flee from justice, and be found in another State, shall on demand of the Executive authority of the State from which he fled, be delivered up, to be removed to the State having jurisdiction of the crime.

(3. No person held to service or labor in one State, under the laws thereof, escaping into another, shall in consequence of any law or regulation therein, be discharged from such service or labor, but shall be delivered up on claim of the party to whom such service or labor may be due.) (This clause was superseded by Amendment XIII.)

Section 3—Admission of new States. Power of Congress over territory and other property.

1. New States may be admitted by the Congress into this Union; but no new State shall be formed or erected within the jurisdiction of any other State; nor any State be formed by the junction of two or more States, or parts of States, without the consent of the Legislatures of the States concerned as well as of the Congress.

2. The Congress shall have power to dispose of and make all needful rules and regulations respecting the territory or other property belonging to the United States; and nothing in this Constitution shall be so construed as to prejudice any claims of the United States, or of any particular State.

Section 4—Republican form of government guaranteed. Each state to be protected.

The United States shall guarantee to every State in this Union a Republican form of government, and shall protect each of them against invasion; and on application of the Legislature, or of the Executive (when the Legislature cannot be convened) against domestic violence.

ARTICLE V.

Constitution: how amended; proviso.

The Congress, whenever two-thirds of both Houses shall deem it necessary, shall propose amendments to this Constitution, or, on the application of the Legislatures of two-thirds of the several States, shall call a convention for proposing amendments, which, in either case, shall be valid to all intents and purposes, as part of this Constitution, when ratified by the Legislatures of three-fourths of the several States, or by conventions in three-fourths thereof, as the one or the other mode of ratification may be proposed by the Congress; provided that no amendment which may be made prior to the year one thousand eight hundred and eight shall in any manner affect the first and fourth clauses in the Ninth Section of the First Article; and that no State, without its consent, shall be deprived of its equal suffrage in the Senate.

ARTICLE VI.

Certain debts, etc., declared valid. Supremacy of Constitution, treaties, and laws of the United States. Oath to support Constitution, by whom taken. No religious test.

1. All debts contracted and engagements entered into, before the adoption of this Constitution, shall be as valid against the United States under this Constitution, as under the Confederation.

2. This Constitution, and the laws of the United States which shall be made in pursuance thereof; and all treaties made, or which shall be made, under the authority of the United States, shall be the supreme law of the land; and the judges in every State shall be bound thereby, any thing in the Constitution or laws of any State to the contrary notwithstanding.

3. The Senators and Representatives before mentioned, and the members of the several State Legislatures, and all executive and judicial officers, both of the United States and of the several States, shall be bound by oath or affirmation, to support this Constitution; but no religious test shall ever be required as a qualification to any office or public trust under the United States.

ARTICLE VII.

What ratification shall establish Constitution.

The ratification of the Conventions of nine States, shall be sufficient for the establishment of this Constitution between the States so ratifying the same.

Done in convention by the unanimous consent of the States present the Seventeenth day of September in the year of our Lord one thousand seven hundred and eighty seven, and of the independence of the United States of America the Twelfth. In witness whereof we have hereunto subscribed our names.

George Washington, President and deputy from Virginia.

New Hampshire—John Langdon, Nicholas Gilman.

Massachusetts—Nathaniel Gorham, Rufus King.

Connecticut—Wm. Saml. Johnson, Roger Sherman.

New York—Alexander Hamilton.

New Jersey—Wil: Livingston, David Brearley, Wm. Paterson, Jona: Dayton.

Pennsylvania—B. Franklin, Thomas Mifflin, Robt. Morris, Geo. Clymer, Thos. FitzSimons, Jared Ingersoll, James Wilson, Gouv. Morris.

Delaware—Geo: Read, Gunning Bedford Jun., John Dickinson, Richard Bassett, Jaco: Broom.

Maryland—James McHenry, Daniel of Saint Thomas' Jenifer, Danl. Carroll.

Virginia—John Blair, James Madison Jr.

North Carolina—Wm. Blount, Rich'd. Dobbs Spaight, Hugh Williamson.

South Carolina—J. Rutledge, Charles Cotesworth Pinckney, Charles Pinckney, Pierce Butler.

Georgia—William Few, Abr. Baldwin.

Attest: William Jackson, Secretary.

Ten Original Amendments: The Bill of Rights
In force Dec. 15, 1791

(The First Congress, at its first session in the City of New York, Sept. 25, 1789, submitted to the states 12 amendments to clarify certain individual and state rights not named in the Constitution. They are generally called the Bill of Rights.

(Influential in framing these amendments was the Declaration of Rights of Virginia, written by George Mason (1725-1792) in 1776. Mason, a Virginia delegate to the Constitutional Convention, did not sign the Constitution and opposed its ratification on the ground that it did not sufficiently oppose slavery or safeguard individual rights.

(In the preamble to the resolution offering the proposed amendments, Congress said: "The conventions of a number of the States having at the time of their adopting the Constitution, expressed a desire, in order to prevent misconstruction or abuse of its powers, that further declaratory and restrictive clauses should be added, and as extending the ground of public confidence in the government will best insure the beneficent ends of its institution, be it resolved," etc.

(Ten of these amendments now commonly known as one to 10 inclusive, but originally 3 to 12 inclusive, were ratified by the states as follows: New Jersey, Nov. 20, 1789; Maryland, Dec. 19, 1789; North Carolina, Dec. 22, 1789; South Carolina, Jan. 19, 1790; New Hampshire, Jan 25, 1790; Delaware, Jan 28, 1790; New York, Feb. 24, 1790; Pennsylvania, Mar. 10, 1790; Rhode

Island, June 7, 1790; Vermont, Nov 3, 1791; Virginia, Dec. 15, 1791; Massachusetts, Mar. 2, 1939; Georgia, Mar. 18, 1939; Connecticut, Apr. 19, 1939. These original 10 ratified amendments follow as Amendments I to X inclusive.

(Of the two original proposed amendments which were not ratified by the necessary number of states, the first related to apportionment of Representatives; the second, to compensation of members.)

AMENDMENT I.
Religious establishment prohibited. Freedom of speech, of the press, and right to petition.

Congress shall make no law respecting an establishment of religion, or prohibiting the free exercise thereof; or abridging the freedom of speech, or of the press; or the right of the people peaceably to assemble, and to petition the Government for a redress of grievances.

AMENDMENT II.
Right to keep and bear arms.

A well-regulated militia, being necessary to the security of a free State, the right of the people to keep and bear arms, shall not be infringed.

AMENDMENT III.
Conditions for quarters for soldiers.

No soldier shall, in time of peace be quartered in any house, without the consent of the owner, nor in time of war, but in a manner to be prescribed by law.

AMENDMENT IV.
Right of search and seizure regulated.

The right of the people to be secure in their persons, houses, papers, and effects, against unreasonable searches and seizures, shall not be violated, and no warrants shall issue, but upon probable cause, supported by oath or affirmation, and particularly describing the place to be searched, and the persons or things to be seized.

AMENDMENT V.
Provisions concerning prosecution. Trial and punishment—private property not to be taken for public use without compensation.

No person shall be held to answer for a capital, or otherwise infamous crime, unless on a presentment or indictment of a Grand Jury, except in cases arising in the land or naval forces, or in the militia, when in actual service in time of war or public danger; nor shall any person be subject for the same offense to be twice put in jeopardy of life or limb; nor shall be compelled in any criminal case to be a witness against himself, nor be deprived of life, liberty, or property, without due process of law; nor shall private property be taken for public use without just compensation.

AMENDMENT VI.
Right to speedy trial, witnesses, etc.

In all criminal prosecutions, the accused shall enjoy the right to a speedy and public trial, by an impartial jury of the State and district wherein the crime shall have been committed, which district shall have been previously ascertained by law, and to be informed of the nature and cause of the accusation; to be confronted with the witnesses against him; to have compulsory process for obtaining witnesses in his favor, and to have the assistance of counsel for his defense.

AMENDMENT VII.
Right of trial by jury.

In suits at common law, where the value in controversy shall exceed twenty dollars, the right of trial by jury shall be preserved, and no fact tried by a jury shall be otherwise reexamined in any court of the United States, than according to the rules of the common law.

AMENDMENT VIII.
Excessive bail or fines and cruel punishment prohibited.

Excessive bail shall not be required, nor excessive fines imposed, nor cruel and unusual punishments inflicted.

AMENDMENT IX.
Rule of construction of Constitution.

The enumeration in the Constitution, of certain rights, shall not be construed to deny or disparage others retained by the people.

AMENDMENT X.
Rights of States under Constitution.

The powers not delegated to the United States by the Constitution, nor prohibited by it to the States, are reserved to the States respectively, or to the people.

Amendments Since the Bill of Rights

AMENDMENT XI.
Judicial powers construed.

The judicial power of the United States shall not be construed to extend to any suit in law or equity, commenced or prosecuted against one of the United States by citizens of another State, or by citizens or subjects of any foreign state.

(This amendment was proposed to the Legislatures of the several States by the Third Congress on March 4, 1794, and was declared to have been ratified in a message from the President to Congress, dated Jan. 8, 1798.

(It was on Jan 5, 1798, that Secretary of State Pickering received from 12 of the States authenticated ratifications, and informed President John Adams of that fact.

(As a result of later research in the Department of State, it is now established that Amendment XI became part of the Constitution on Feb. 7, 1795, for on that date it had been ratified by 12 States as follows:

(1. New York, Mar. 27, 1794. 2. Rhode Island, Mar. 31, 1794. 3. Connecticut, May 8, 1794. 4. New Hampshire, June 16, 1794. 5. Massachusetts, June 26, 1794. 6. Vermont, between Oct 9, 1794, and Nov. 9, 1794. 7. Virginia, Nov. 18, 1794. 8. Georgia, Nov. 29, 1794. 9. Kentucky, Dec. 7, 1794. 10. Maryland, Dec. 26, 1794. 11. Delaware, Jan 23, 1795. 12. North Carolina, Feb. 7, 1795.

(On June 1, 1796, more than a year after Amendment XI had become a part of the Constitution (but before anyone was officially aware of this), Tennessee had been admitted as a State; but not until Oct. 16, 1797, was a certified copy of the resolution of Congress proposing the amendment sent to the Governor of Tennessee (John Sevier) by Secretary of State Pickering, whose office was then at Trenton, New Jersey, because of the epidemic of yellow fever at Philadelphia; it seems, however, that the Legislature of Tennessee took no action on Amendment XI, owing doubtless to the fact that public announcement of its adoption was made soon thereafter.

(Besides the necessary 12 States, one other, South Carolina, ratified Amendment XI, but this action was not taken until Dec. 4, 1797; the two remaining States, New Jersey and Pennsylvania, failed to ratify.)

AMENDMENT XII.
Manner of choosing President and Vice-President.

(Proposed by Congress Dec. 9, 1803; ratification completed June 15, 1804.)

The Electors shall meet in their respective States and vote by ballot for President and Vice-President, one of whom, at least, shall not be an inhabitant of the same State with themselves; they shall name in their ballots the person voted for as President, and in distinct ballots the person voted for as Vice-President, and they shall make distinct lists of all persons voted for as President, and of all persons voted for as Vice-President, and of the number of votes for each, which lists they shall sign and certify, and transmit sealed to the seat of the Government of the United States, directed to the President of the Senate; the President of the Senate shall, in the presence of the Senate and House of Representatives, open all the certificates and the votes shall then be counted;—The person having the greatest number of votes for President, shall be the President, if such number be a majority of the whole number of Electors appointed; and if no person have such majority, then from the persons having the highest numbers not exceeding three on the list of those voted for as President, the House of Representatives shall

choose immediately, by ballot, the President. But in choosing the President, the votes shall be taken by States, the representation from each State having one vote; a quorum for this purpose shall consist of a member or members from two-thirds of the States, and a majority of all the States shall be necessary to a choice. *(And if the House of Representatives shall not choose a President whenever the right of choice shall devolve upon them, before the fourth day of March next following, then the Vice-President shall act as President, as in the case of the death or other constitutional disability of the President.) (The words in parentheses were superseded by Amendment XX, section 3.)* The person having the greatest number of votes as Vice-President, shall be the Vice-President, if such number be a majority of the whole number of Electors appointed, and if no person have a majority, then from the two highest numbers on the list, the Senate shall choose the Vice-President; a quorum for the purpose shall consist of two-thirds of the whole number of Senators, and a majority of the whole number shall be necessary to a choice. But no person constitutionally ineligible to the office of President shall be eligible to that of Vice-President of the United States.

THE RECONSTRUCTION AMENDMENTS

(Amendments XIII, XIV, and XV are commonly known as the Reconstruction Amendments, inasmuch as they followed the Civil War, and were drafted by Republicans who were bent on imposing their own policy of reconstruction on the South. Post-bellum legislatures there—Mississippi, South Carolina, Georgia, for example—had set up laws which, it was charged, were contrived to perpetuate Negro slavery under other names.)

AMENDMENT XIII.

Slavery abolished.

(Proposed by Congress Jan. 31, 1865; ratification completed Dec. 18, 1865. The amendment, when first proposed by a resolution in Congress, was passed by the Senate, 38 to 6, on Apr. 8, 1864, but was defeated in the House, 95 to 66 on June 15, 1864. On reconsideration by the House, on Jan. 31, 1865, the resolution passed, 119 to 56. It was approved by President Lincoln on Feb. 1, 1865, although the Supreme Court had decided in 1798 that the President has nothing to do with the proposing of amendments to the Constitution, or their adoption.)

1. Neither slavery nor involuntary servitude, except as a punishment for crime whereof the party shall have been duly convicted, shall exist within the United States or any place subject to their jurisdiction.

2. Congress shall have power to enforce this article by appropriate legislation.

AMENDMENT XIV.

Citizenship rights not to be abridged.

(The following amendment was proposed to the Legislatures of the several states by the 39th Congress, June 13, 1866, and was declared to have been ratified in a proclamation by the Secretary of State, July 28, 1868.

(The 14th amendment was adopted only by virtue of ratification subsequent to earlier rejections. Newly constituted legislatures in both North Carolina and South Carolina (respectively July 4 and 9, 1868), ratified the proposed amendment, although earlier legislatures had rejected the proposal. The Secretary of State issued a proclamation, which, though doubtful as to the effect of attempted withdrawals by Ohio and New Jersey, entertained no doubt as to the validity of the ratification by North and South Carolina. The following day (July 21, 1868), Congress passed a resolution which declared the 14th Amendment to be a part of the Constitution and directed the Secretary of State so to promulgate it. The Secretary waited, however, until the newly constituted Legislature of Georgia had ratified the amendment, subsequent to an earlier rejection, before the promulgation of the ratification of the new amendment.)

1. All persons born or naturalized in the United States, and subject to the jurisdiction thereof, are citizens of the United States and of the State wherein they reside. No State shall make or enforce any law which shall abridge the privileges or immunities of citizens of the United States; nor shall any State deprive any person of life, liberty, or property, without due process of law; nor deny to any person within its jurisdiction the equal protection of the laws.

2. Representatives shall be apportioned among the several States according to their respective numbers, counting the whole number of persons in each State, excluding Indians not taxed. But when the right to vote at any election for the choice of Electors for President and Vice-President of the United States, Representatives in Congress, the executive and judicial officers of a State, or the members of the Legislature thereof, is denied to any of the male inhabitants of such State, being twenty-one years of age, and citizens of the United States, or in any way abridged, except for participation in rebellion, or other crime, the basis of representation therein shall be reduced in the proportion which the number of such male citizens shall bear to the whole number of male citizens twenty-one years of age in such State.

3. No person shall be a Senator or Representative in Congress, or Elector of President and Vice-President, or hold any office, civil or military, under the United States, or under any State, who, having previously taken an oath, as a member of Congress, or as an officer of the United States, or as a member of any State Legislature, or as an executive or judicial officer of any State, to support the Constitution of the United States, shall have engaged in insurrection or rebellion against the same, or given aid or comfort to the enemies thereof. But Congress may by a vote of two-thirds of each House, remove such disability.

4. The validity of the public debt of the United States, authorized by law, including debts incurred for payment of pensions and bounties for services in suppressing insurrection or rebellion, shall not be questioned. But neither the United States nor any State shall assume or pay any debt or obligation incurred in aid of insurrection or rebellion against the United States, or any claim for the loss or emancipation of any slave; but all such debts, obligations and claims, shall be held illegal and void.

5. The Congress shall have power to enforce, by appropriate legislation, the provisions of this article.

AMENDMENT XV.

Race no bar to voting rights.

(The following amendment was proposed to the legislatures of the several States by the 40th Congress, Feb. 26, 1869, and was declared to have been ratified in a proclamation by the Secretary of State, Mar. 30, 1870.)

1. The right of citizens of the United States to vote shall not be denied or abridged by the United States or by any State on account of race, color, or previous condition of servitude.

2. The Congress shall have power to enforce this article by appropriate legislation.

AMENDMENT XVI.

Income taxes authorized.

(Proposed by Congress July 12, 1909; ratification declared by the Secretary of State Feb. 25, 1913.)

The Congress shall have power to lay and collect taxes on incomes, from whatever source derived, without apportionment among the several States, and without regard to any census or enumeration.

AMENDMENT XVII.

United States Senators to be elected by direct popular vote.

(Proposed by Congress May 13, 1912; ratification declared by the Secretary of State May 31, 1913.)

1. The Senate of the United States shall be composed of two Senators from each State, elected by the people thereof, for six years; and each Senator shall have one vote. The electors in each State shall have the qualifications requisite for electors of the most numerous branch of the State Legislatures.

2. When vacancies happen in the representation of any State in the Senate, the executive authority of such State shall issue writs of election to fill such vacancies: Provided, That the Legislature of any State may empower the Executive thereof to make temporary appointments until the peo-

ple fill the vacancies by election as the Legislature may direct.

3. This amendment shall not be so construed as to affect the election or term of any Senator chosen before it becomes valid as part of the Constitution.

AMENDMENT XVIII.

Liquor prohibition amendment.

(Proposed by Congress Dec. 18, 1917; ratification completed Jan. 16, 1919. Repealed by Amendment XXI, effective Dec. 5, 1933.)

(1. After one year from the ratification of this article the manufacture, sale, or transportation of intoxicating liquors within, the importation thereof into, or the exportation thereof from the United States and all territory subject to the jurisdiction thereof for beverage purposes is hereby prohibited.

(2. The Congress and the several States shall have concurrent power to enforce this article by appropriate legislation.

(3. This article shall be inoperative unless it shall have been ratified as an amendment to the Constitution by the Legislatures of the several States, as provided in the Constitution, within seven years from the date of the submission hereof to the States by the Congress.)

(The total vote in the Senates of the various States was 1,310 for, 237 against—84.6% dry. In the lower houses of the States the vote was 3,782 for, 1,035 against—78.5% dry.

(The amendment ultimately was adopted by all the States except Connecticut and Rhode Island.)

AMENDMENT XIX.

Giving nationwide suffrage to women.

(Proposed by Congress June 4, 1919; ratification certified by Secretary of State Aug. 26, 1920.)

1. The right of citizens of the United States to vote shall not be denied or abridged by the United States or by any State on account of sex.

2. Congress shall have power to enforce this Article by appropriate legislation.

AMENDMENT XX.

Terms of President and Vice President to begin on Jan. 20; those of Senators, Representatives, Jan. 3.

(Proposed by Congress Mar. 2, 1932; ratification completed Jan. 23, 1933.)

1. The terms of the President and Vice President shall end at noon on the 20th day of January, and the terms of Senators and Representatives at noon on the 3rd day of January, of the years in which such terms would have ended if this article had not been ratified; and the terms of their successors shall then begin.

2. The Congress shall assemble at least once in every year, and such meeting shall begin at noon on the 3rd day of January, unless they shall by law appoint a different day.

3. If, at the time fixed for the beginning of the term of the President, the President elect shall have died, the Vice President elect shall become President. If a President shall not have been chosen before the time fixed for the beginning of his term, or if the President elect shall have failed to qualify, then the Vice President elect shall act as President until a President shall have qualified; and the Congress may by law provide for the case wherein neither a President elect nor a Vice President elect shall have qualified, declaring who shall then act as President, or the manner in which one who is to act shall be selected, and such person shall act accordingly until a President or Vice President shall have qualified.

4. The Congress may by law provide for the case of the death of any of the persons from whom the House of Representatives may choose a President whenever the right of choice shall have devolved upon them, and for the case of the death of any of the persons from whom the Senate may choose a Vice President whenever the right of choice shall have devolved upon them.

5. Sections 1 and 2 shall take effect on the 15th day of October following the ratification of this article (Oct., 1933).

6. This article shall be inoperative unless it shall have been ratified as an amendment to the Constitution by the Legislatures of three-fourths of the several States within seven years from the date of its submission.

AMENDMENT XXI.

Repeal of Amendment XVIII.

(Proposed by Congress Feb. 20, 1933; ratification completed Dec. 5, 1933.)

1. The eighteenth article of amendment to the Constitution of the United States is hereby repealed.

2. The transportation or importation into any State, Territory, or Possession of the United States for delivery or use therein of intoxicating liquors, in violation of the laws thereof, is hereby prohibited.

3. This article shall be inoperative unless it shall have been ratified as an amendment to the Constitution by conventions in the several States, as provided in the Constitution, within seven years from the date of the submission hereof to the States by the Congress.

AMENDMENT XXII.

Limiting Presidential terms of office.

(Proposed by Congress Mar. 24, 1947; ratification completed Feb. 27, 1951.)

1. No person shall be elected to the office of the President more than twice, and no person who has held the office of President, or acted as President, for more than two years of a term to which some other person was elected President shall be elected to the office of the President more than once. But this Article shall not apply to any person holding the office of President when this Article was proposed by the Congress, and shall not prevent any person who may be holding the office of President, or acting as President, during the term within which this Article becomes operative from holding the office of President or acting as President during the remainder of such term.

2. This article shall be inoperative unless it shall have been ratified as an amendment to the Constitution by the Legislatures of three-fourths of the several States within seven years from the date of its submission to the States by the Congress.

AMENDMENT XXIII.

Presidential vote for District of Columbia.

(Proposed by Congress June 16, 1960; ratification completed Mar. 29, 1961.)

1. The District constituting the seat of Government of the United States shall appoint in such manner as the Congress may direct:

A number of electors of President and Vice President equal to the whole number of Senators and Representatives in Congress to which the District would be entitled if it were a State, but in no event more than the least populous State; they shall be in addition to those appointed by the States, but they shall be considered, for the purposes of the election of President and Vice President, to be electors appointed by a State; and they shall meet in the District and perform such duties as provided by the twelfth article of amendment.

2. The Congress shall have power to enforce this article by appropriate legislation.

AMENDMENT XXIV.

Barring poll tax in federal elections.

(Proposed by Congress Aug. 27, 1962; ratification completed Jan. 23, 1964.)

1. The right of citizens of the United States to vote in any primary or other election for President or Vice President, for electors for President or Vice President, or for Senator or Representative in Congress, shall not be denied or abridged by the United States or any State by reason of failure to pay any poll tax or other tax.

2. The Congress shall have power to enforce this article by appropriate legislation.

AMENDMENT XXV.

Presidential disability and succession.

(Proposed by Congress July 6, 1965; ratification completed Feb. 10, 1967.)

1. In case of the removal of the President from office or of

his death or resignation, the Vice President shall become President.

2. Whenever there is a vacancy in the office of the Vice President, the President shall nominate a Vice President who shall take office upon confirmation by a majority vote of both houses of Congress.

3. Whenever the President transmits to the President pro tempore of the Senate and the Speaker of the House of Representatives his written declaration that he is unable to discharge the powers and duties of his office, and until he transmits to them a written declaration to the contrary, such powers and duties shall be discharged by the Vice President as Acting President.

4. Whenever the Vice President and a majority of either the principal officers of the executive departments or of such other body as Congress may by law provide, transmit to the President pro tempore of the Senate and the Speaker of the House of Representatives their written declaration that the President is unable to discharge the powers and duties of his office, the Vice President shall immediately assume the powers and duties of the office as Acting President.

Thereafter, when the President transmits to the President pro tempore of the Senate and the Speaker of the House of Representatives his written declaration that no inability exists, he shall resume the powers and duties of his office unless the Vice President and a majority of either the principal officers of the executive department or of such other body as Congress may by law provide, transmit within four days to the President pro tempore of the Senate and the Speaker of the House of Representatives their written declaration that the President is unable to discharge the powers and duties of his office. Thereupon Congress shall decide the issue, assembling within forty-eight hours for that purpose if not in session. If the Congress, within twenty-one days after receipt of the latter written declaration, or, if Congress is not in session, within twenty-one days after Congress is required to

assemble, determines by two-thirds vote of both houses that the President is unable to discharge the powers and duties of his office, the Vice President shall continue to discharge the same as Acting President; otherwise, the President shall resume the powers and duties of his office.

AMENDMENT XXVI.

Lowering voting age to 18 years.

(Proposed by Congress Mar. 8, 1971; ratification completed July 1, 1971.)

1. The right of citizens of the United States, who are 18 years of age or older, to vote shall not be denied or abridged by the United States or any state on account of age.

2. The Congress shall have the power to enforce this article by appropriate legislation.

PROPOSED D.C. REPRESENTATION AMENDMENT

(Proposed by Congress Aug. 22, 1978; ratified, as of March, 1985, by 16 states.) Will become inoperative unless ratified by 22 more states before August 22, 1985.

1. For purposes of representation in the Congress, election of the President and Vice President, and article V of this Constitution, the District constituting the seat of government of the United States shall be treated as though it were a State.

2. The exercise of the rights and powers conferred under this article shall be by the people of the District constituting the seat of government, and as shall be provided by the Congress.

3. The twenty-third article of amendment to the Constitution of the United States is hereby repealed.

4. This article shall be inoperative, unless it shall have been ratified as an amendment to the Constitution by the legislatures of three-fourths of the several States within seven years from the date of its submission.

Origin of the Constitution

The War of Independence was conducted by delegates from the original 13 states, called the Congress of the United States of America and generally known as the Continental Congress. In 1777 the Congress submitted to the legislatures of the states the Articles of Confederation and Perpetual Union, which were ratified by New Hampshire, Massachusetts, Rhode Island, Connecticut, New York, New Jersey, Pennsylvania, Delaware, Virginia, North Carolina, South Carolina, and Georgia, and finally, in 1781, by Maryland.

The first article of the instrument read: "The stile of this confederacy shall be the United States of America." This did not signify a sovereign nation, because the states delegated only those powers they could not handle individually, such as power to wage war, establish a uniform currency, make treaties with foreign nations and contract debts for general expenses (such as paying the army). Taxes for the payment of such debts were levied by the individual states. The president under the Articles signed himself "President of the United States in Congress assembled," but here the United States were considered in the plural, a cooperating group. Canada was invited to join the union on equal terms but did not act.

When the war was won it became evident that a stronger federal union was needed to protect the mutual interests of the states. The Congress left the initiative to the legislatures. Virginia in Jan. 1786 appointed commissioners to meet with representatives of other states, with the result that delegates from Virginia, Delaware, New York, New Jersey, and Pennsylvania met at Annapolis. Alexander Hamilton prepared for their call by asking delegates from all states to meet in Philadelphia in May 1787 "to render the Constitution of the Federal government adequate to the exigencies of the union." Congress endorsed the plan Feb. 21, 1787. Delegates

were appointed by all states except Rhode Island.

The convention met May 14, 1787. George Washington was chosen president (presiding officer). The states certified 65 delegates, but 10 did not attend. The work was done by 55, not all of whom were present at all sessions. Of the 55 attending delegates, 16 failed to sign, and 39 actually signed Sept. 17, 1787, some with reservations. Some historians have said 74 delegates (9 more than the 65 actually certified) were named and 19 failed to attend. These 9 additional persons refused the appointment, were never delegates and never counted as absentees. Washington sent the Constitution to Congress with a covering letter and that body, Sept. 28, 1787, ordered it sent to the legislatures, "in order to be submitted to a convention of delegates chosen in each state by the people thereof."

The Constitution was ratified by votes of state conventions as follows: Delaware, Dec. 7, 1787, unanimous; Pennsylvania, Dec. 12, 1787, 43 to 23; New Jersey, Dec. 18, 1787, unanimous; Georgia, Jan 2, 1788, unanimous; Connecticut, Jan. 9, 1788, 128 to 40; Massachusetts, Feb. 6, 1788, 187 to 168; Maryland, Apr. 28, 1788, 63 to 11; South Carolina, May 23, 1788, 149 to 73; New Hampshire, June 21, 1788, 57 to 46; Virginia, June 26, 1788, 89 to 79; New York, July 26, 1788, 30 to 27. Nine states were needed to establish the operation of the Constitution "between the states so ratifying the same" and New Hampshire was the 9th state. The government did not declare the Constitution in effect until the first Wednesday in Mar. 1789 which was Mar. 4. After that North Carolina ratified it Nov. 21, 1789, 194 to 77; and Rhode Island, May 29, 1790, 34 to 32. Vermont in convention ratified it Jan. 10, 1791, and by act of Congress approved Feb. 18, 1791, was admitted into the Union as the 14th state, Mar. 4, 1791.

How the Declaration of Independence Was Adopted

On June 7, 1776, Richard Henry Lee, who had issued the first call for a congress of the colonies, introduced in the Continental Congress at Philadelphia a resolution declaring "that these United Colonies are, and of right ought to be, free and independent states, that they are absolved from all allegiance to the British Crown, and that all political connection between them and the state of Great Britain is, and ought to be, totally dissolved."

The resolution, seconded by John Adams on behalf of the Massachusetts delegation, came up again June 10 when a committee of 5, headed by Thomas Jefferson, was appointed to express the purpose of the resolution in a declaration of independence. The others on the committee were John Adams, Benjamin Franklin, Robert R. Livingston, and Roger Sherman.

Drafting the Declaration was assigned to Jefferson, who worked on a portable desk of his own construction in a room at Market and 7th Sts. The committee reported the result June 28, 1776. The members of the Congress suggested a number of changes, which Jefferson called "deplorable." They didn't approve Jefferson's arraignment of the British people and King George III for encouraging and fostering the slave trade, which Jefferson called "an execrable commerce." They made 86 changes, eliminating 480 words and leaving 1,337. In the final form capitalization was erratic. Jefferson had written that men were endowed with "inalienable" rights; in the final copy it came out as "unalienable" and has been thus ever since.

The Lee-Adams resolution of independence was adopted by 12 yeas July 2 — the actual date of the act of independence. The Declaration, which explains the act, was adopted July 4, in the evening.

After the Declaration was adopted, July 4, 1776, it was turned over to John Dunlap, printer, to be printed on broadsides. The original copy was lost and one of his broadsides

was attached to a page in the journal of the Congress. It was read aloud July 8 in Philadelphia, Easton, Pa., and Trenton, N.J. On July 9 at 6 p.m. it was read by order of Gen. George Washington to the troops assembled on the Common in New York City (City Hall Park).

The Continental Congress of July 19, 1776, adopted the following resolution:

"Resolved, That the Declaration passed on the 4th, be fairly engrossed on parchment with the title and stile of 'The Unanimous Declaration of the thirteen United States of America' and that the same, when engrossed, be signed by every member of Congress."

Not all delegates who signed the engrossed Declaration were present on July 4. Robert Morris (Pa.), William Williams (Conn.) and Samuel Chase (Md.) signed on Aug. 2, Oliver Wolcott (Conn.), George Wythe (Va.), Richard Henry Lee (Va.) and Elbridge Gerry (Mass.) signed in August and September, Matthew Thornton (N. H.) joined the Congress Nov. 4 and signed later. Thomas McKean (Del.) rejoined Washington's Army before signing and said later that he signed in 1781.

Charles Carroll of Carrollton was appointed a delegate by Maryland on July 4, 1776, presented his credentials July 18, and signed the engrossed Declaration Aug. 2. Born Sept. 19, 1737, he was 95 years old and the last surviving signer when he died Nov. 14, 1832.

Two Pennsylvania delegates who did not support the Declaration on July 4 were replaced.

The 4 New York delegates did not have authority from their state to vote on July 4. On July 9 the New York state convention authorized its delegates to approve the Declaration and the Congress was so notified on July 15, 1776. The 4 signed the Declaration on Aug. 2.

The original engrossed Declaration is preserved in the National Archives Building in Washington.

The Liberty Bell: Its History and Significance

The Liberty Bell, in Independence Hall, Philadelphia, is an object of great reverence to Americans because of its association with the historic events of the War of Independence.

The original Province bell, ordered to commemorate the 50th anniversary of the Commonwealth of Pennsylvania, was cast by Thomas Lister, Whitechapel, London, and reached Philadelphia in Aug. 1752. It bore an inscription from Leviticus XXV, 10: "Proclaim liberty throughout all the land unto all the inhabitants thereof."

The bell was cracked by a stroke of its clapper in Sept. 1752 while it hung on a truss in the State House yard for testing. Pass & Stow, Philadelphia founders, recast the bell, adding 1 1/2 ounces of copper to a pound of the original metal to reduce brittleness. It was found that the bell contained too much copper, injuring its tone, so Pass & Stow recast it again, this time successfully.

In June 1753 the bell was hung in the wooden steeple of the State House, erected on top of the brick tower. In use while the Continental Congress was in session in the State House, it rang out in defiance of British tax and trade restrictions, and proclaimed the Boston Tea Party and the first public reading of the Declaration of Independence.

On Sept. 18, 1777, when the British Army was about to occupy Philadelphia, the bell was moved in a baggage train of the American Army to Allentown, Pa. where it was hidden in the Zion Reformed Church until June 27, 1778. It was moved back to Philadelphia after the British left.

In July 1781 the wooden steeple became insecure and had to be taken down. The bell was lowered into the brick section of the tower. Here it was hanging in July, 1835, when it cracked while tolling for the funeral of John Marshall, chief justice of the United States. Because of its association with the War of Independence it was not recast but remained mute in this location until 1846, the year of the Mexican War, when it was placed on exhibition in the Declaration Chamber of Independence Hall.

In 1876, when many thousands of Americans visited Philadelphia for the Centennial Exposition, it was placed in its old walnut frame in the tower hallway. In 1877 it was hung from the ceiling of the tower by a chain of 13 links. It was returned again to the Declaration Chamber and in 1896 taken back to the tower hall, where it occupied a glass case. In 1915 the case was removed so that the public might touch it. On Jan. 1, 1976, just after midnight to mark the opening of the Bicentennial Year, the bell was moved to a new glass and steel pavilion behind Independence Hall for easier viewing by the larger number of visitors expected during the year.

The measurements of the bell follow: circumference around the lip, 12 ft.; circumference around the crown, 7 ft. 6 in.; lip to the crown, 3 ft.; height over the crown, 2 ft. 3 in.; thickness at lip, 3 in.; thickness at crown, 1 1/4 in.; weight, 2080 lbs.; length of clapper, 3 ft. 2 in.; cost, £60 14s 5d.

Confederate States and Secession

The American Civil War, 1861-65, grew out of sectional disputes over the continued existence of slavery in the South and the contention of Southern legislators that the states retained many sovereign rights, including the right to secede from the Union.

The war was not fought by state against state but by one

federal regime against another, the Confederate government in Richmond assuming control over the economic, political, and military life of the South, under protest from Georgia and South Carolina.

South Carolina voted an ordinance of secession from the Union, repealing its 1788 ratification of the U.S. Constitu-

tion on Dec. 20, 1860, to take effect Dec. 24. Other states seceded in 1861. Their votes in conventions were:

Mississippi, Jan. 9, 84-15; Florida, Jan. 10, 62-7; Alabama, Jan. 11, 61-39; Georgia, Jan. 19, 208-89; Louisiana, Jan. 26, 113-17; Texas, Feb. 1, 166-7, ratified by popular vote Feb. 23 (for 34,794, against 11,325); Virginia, Apr. 17, 88-55, ratified by popular vote May 23 (for 128,884; against 32,134); Arkansas, May 6, 69-1; Tennessee, May 7, ratified by popular vote June 8 (for 104,019, against 47,238); North Carolina, May 21.

Missouri Unionists stopped secession in conventions Feb. 28 and Mar. 9. The legislature condemned secession Mar. 7. Under the protection of Confederate troops, secessionist members of the legislature adopted a resolution of secession at Neosho, Oct. 31. The Confederate Congress seated the secessionists' representatives.

Kentucky did not secede and its government remained Unionist. In a part occupied by Confederate troops, Kentuckians approved secession and the Confederate Congress admitted their representatives.

The Maryland legislature voted against secession Apr. 27, 53-13. Delaware did not secede. Western Virginia held conventions at Wheeling, named a pro-Union governor June 11, 1861; admitted to Union as West Virginia June 30, 1863; its constitution provided for gradual abolition of slavery.

Confederate Government

Forty-two delegates from South Carolina, Georgia, Alabama, Mississippi, Louisiana, and Florida met in convention at Montgomery, Ala., Feb. 4, 1861. They adopted a provisional constitution of the Confederate States of America, and elected Jefferson Davis (Miss.) provisional president, and Alexander H. Stephens (Ga.) provisional vice president.

A permanent constitution was adopted Mar. 11; it abolished the African slave trade. The Congress moved to Richmond, Va. July 20. Davis was elected president in October, and was inaugurated Feb. 22, 1862.

The Congress adopted a flag, consisting of a red field with a white stripe, and a blue jack with a circle of white stars. Later the more popular flag was the red field with blue diagonal cross bars that held 13 white stars. The stars represented the 11 states actually in the Confederacy plus Kentucky and Missouri.

(See also Civil War, U.S., in Index)

Lincoln's Address at Gettysburg, 1863

Fourscore and seven years ago our fathers brought forth on this continent a new nation, conceived in liberty and dedicated to the proposition that all men are created equal.

Now we are engaged in a great civil war, testing whether that nation or any nation so conceived and so dedicated can long endure. We are met on a great battle field of that war. We have come to dedicate a portion of that field, as a final resting-place for those who here gave their lives that that nation might live. It is altogether fitting and proper that we should do this.

But, in a larger sense, we can not dedicate — we can not consecrate — we can not hallow — this ground. The brave men, living and dead, who struggled here, have consecrated it, far above our poor power to add or detract. The world will little note, nor long remember, what we say here, but it can never forget what they did here. It is for us the living, rather, to be dedicated here to the unfinished work which they who fought here have thus far so nobly advanced. It is rather for us to be here dedicated to the great task remaining before us — that from these honored dead we take increased devotion to that cause for which they gave the last full measure of devotion — that we here highly resolve that these dead shall not have died in vain — that this nation, under God, shall have a new birth of freedom — and that government of the people, by the people, for the people, shall not perish from the earth.

Origin of the United States National Motto

In God We Trust, designated as the U. S. National Motto by Congress in 1956, originated during the Civil War as an inscription for U. S. coins, although it was used by Francis Scott Key in a slightly different form when he wrote The Star Spangled Banner in 1814. On Nov. 13, 1861, when Union morale had been shaken by battlefield defeats, the Rev. M. R. Watkinson, of Ridleyville, Pa. wrote to Secy. of the Treasury Salmon P. Chase, "From my heart I have felt our national shame in disowning God as not the least of our present national disasters," the minister wrote, suggesting "recognition of the Almighty God in some form on our coins." Secy. Chase ordered designs prepared with the inscription In God We Trust and backed coinage legislation which authorized use of this slogan. It first appeared on some U. S. coins in 1864, disappeared and reappeared on various coins until 1955, when Congress ordered it placed on all paper money and all coins.

The National Anthem — The Star-Spangled Banner

The Star-Spangled Banner was ordered played by the military and naval services by President Woodrow Wilson in 1916. It was designated the National Anthem by Act of Congress, Mar. 3, 1931. It was written by Francis Scott Key, of Georgetown, D. C., during the bombardment of Fort McHenry, Baltimore, Md., Sept. 13-14, 1814. Key was a lawyer, a graduate of St. John's College, Annapolis, and a volunteer in a light artillery company. When a friend, Dr. Beanes, a physician of Upper Marlborough, Md., was taken aboard Admiral Cockburn's British squadron for interfering with ground troops, Key and J. S. Skinner, carrying a note from President Madison, went to the fleet under a flag of truce on a cartel ship to ask Beanes' release. Admiral Cockburn consented, but as the fleet was about to sail up the Patapsco to bombard Fort McHenry he detained them, first on H. M. S. Surprise, and then on a supply ship.

Key witnessed the bombardment from his own vessel. It began at 7 a.m., Sept. 13, 1814, and lasted, with intermissions, for 25 hours. The British fired over 1,500 shells, each weighing as much as 220 lbs. They were unable to approach closely because the Americans had sunk 22 vessels in the channel. Only four Americans were killed and 24 wounded. A British bomb-ship was disabled.

During the bombardment Key wrote a stanza on the back of an envelope. Next day at Indian Queen Inn, Baltimore, he wrote out the poem and gave it to his brother-in-law, Judge J. H. Nicholson. Nicholson suggested the tune, Anacreon in Heaven, and had the poem printed on broadsides, of which two survive. On Sept. 20 it appeared in the "Baltimore American." Later Key made 3 copies; one is in the Library of Congress and one in the Pennsylvania Historical Society.

The copy that Key wrote in his hotel Sept. 14, 1814, remained in the Nicholson family for 93 years. In 1907 it was sold to Henry Walters of Baltimore. In 1934 it was bought at auction in New York from the Walters estate by the Walters Art Gallery, Baltimore, for $26,400. The Walters Gallery in 1953 sold the manuscript to the Maryland Historical Society for the same price.

The flag that Key saw during the bombardment is preserved in the Smithsonian Institution, Washington. It is 30 by 42 ft., and has 15 alternate red and white stripes and 15 stars, for the original 13 states plus Kentucky and Vermont.

It was made by Mary Young Pickersgill. The Baltimore Flag House, a museum, occupies her premises, which were restored in 1953.

The Star-Spangled Banner

I

Oh, say can you see by the dawn's early light
   What so proudly we hailed at the twilight's last gleaming?
Whose broad stripes and bright stars thru the perilous fight,
   O'er the ramparts we watched were so gallantly streaming?
And the rocket's red glare, the bombs bursting in air,
   Gave proof through the night that our flag was still there.
Oh, say does that star-spangled banner yet wave
   O'er the land of the free and the home of the brave?

II

On the shore, dimly seen through the mists of the deep,
   Where the foe's haughty host in dread silence reposes,
What is that which the breeze, o'er the towering steep,
   As it fitfully blows, half conceals, half discloses?
Now it catches the gleam of the morning's first beam,
   In full glory reflected now shines in the stream:

'Tis the star-spangled banner! Oh long may it wave
   O'er the land of the free and the home of the brave!

III

And where is that band who so vauntingly swore
   That the havoc of war and the battle's confusion,
A home and a country should leave us no more!
   Their blood has washed out their foul footsteps' pollution.
No refuge could save the hireling and slave
   From the terror of flight, or the gloom of the grave:
And the star-spangled banner in triumph doth wave
   O'er the land of the free and the home of the brave!

IV

Oh! thus be it ever, when freemen shall stand
   Between their loved home and the war's desolation!
Blest with victory and peace, may the heav'n rescued land
   Praise the Power that hath made and preserved us a nation.
Then conquer we must, when our cause it is just,
   And this be our motto: "In God is our trust."
And the star-spangled banner in triumph shall wave
   O'er the land of the free and the home of the brave!

Statue of Liberty National Monument

Since 1886, the Statue of Liberty Enlightening the World has stood as a symbol of freedom in New York harbor. It also commemorates French-American friendship for it was given by the people of France, designed by Frederic Auguste Bartholdi (1834-1904). A $2.5 million building housing the American Museum of Immigration was opened by Pres. Nixon Sept. 26, 1972, at the base of the statue. It houses a permanent exhibition of photos, posters, and artifacts tracing the history of American immigration. The Monument is administered by the National Park Service.

Nearby Ellis Island, gateway to America for more than 12 million immigrants between 1892 and 1954, was proclaimed part of the National Monument in 1965 by Pres. Johnson.

Edouard de Laboulaye, French historian and admirer of American political institutions, suggested that the French present a monument to the United States, the latter to provide pedestal and site. Bartholdi visualized a colossal statue at the entrance of New York harbor, welcoming the peoples of the world with the torch of liberty.

On Washington's birthday, Feb. 22, 1877, Congress approved the use of a site on Bedloe's Island suggested by Bartholdi. This island of 12 acres had been owned in the 17th century by a Walloon named Isaac Bedloe. It was called Bedloe's until Aug. 3, 1956, when Pres. Eisenhower approved a resolution of Congress changing the name to Liberty Island.

The statue was finished May 21, 1884, and formally presented to U.S. Minister Morton July 4, 1884, by Ferdinand de Lesseps, head of the Franco-American Union, promoter of the Panama Canal, and builder of the Suez Canal.

On Aug. 5, 1884, the Americans laid the cornerstone for the pedestal. This was to be built on the foundations of Fort Wood, which had been erected by the Government in 1811. The American committee had raised $125,000, but this was found to be inadequate. Joseph Pulitzer, owner of the New York World, appealed on Mar. 16, 1885, for general donations. By Aug. 11, 1885, he had raised $100,000.

The statue arrived dismantled, in 214 packing cases, from Rouen, France, in June, 1885. The last rivet of the statue was driven Oct. 28, 1886, when Pres. Grover Cleveland dedicated the monument.

The statue weighs 450,000 lbs. or 225 tons. The copper sheeting weighs 200,000 lbs. There are 167 steps from the land level to the top of the pedestal, 168 steps inside the

statue to the head, and 54 rungs on the ladder leading to the arm that holds the torch.

Two years of restoration work, to be completed by the statue's centennial celebration on July 4, 1986, were begun in 1984. Among other repairs, the $39 million project will include replacing the 1,600 wrought iron bands that hold its copper skin to its frame, replacing its torch, and installing an elevator.

Dimensions of the Statue	Ft.	In.
Height from base to torch (45.3 meters)	151	1
Foundation of pedestal to torch (91.5 meters)	305	1
Heel to top of head	111	1
Length of hand	16	5
Index finger	8	0
Circumference at second joint	3	6
Size of finger nail . . . . 13x10 in.		
Head from chin to cranium	17	3
Head thickness from ear to ear	10	0
Distance across the eye	2	6
Length of nose	4	6
Right arm, length	42	0
Right arm, greatest thickness	12	0
Thickness of waist	35	0
Width of mouth	3	0
Tablet, length	23	7
Tablet, width	13	7
Tablet, thickness	2	0

Emma Lazarus' Famous Poem

A poem by Emma Lazarus is graven on a tablet within the pedestal on which the statue stands.

The New Colossus

Not like the brazen giant of Greek fame,
  With conquering limbs astride from land to land;
Here at our sea-washed, sunset gates shall stand
A mighty woman with a torch, whose flame
Is the imprisoned lightning, and her name
Mother of Exiles. From her beacon-hand
Glows world-wide welcome; her mild eyes command
The air-bridged harbor that twin cities frame.
"Keep ancient lands, your storied pomp!" cries she
With silent lips. "Give me your tired, your poor,
Your huddled masses yearning to breathe free,
The wretched refuse of your teeming shore.
Send these, the homeless, tempest-tost to me,
I lift my lamp beside the golden door!"

Forms of Address for Persons of Rank and Public Office

In these examples John Smith is used as a representative American name. The salutation Dear Sir or Dear Madam is always permissible when addressing a person not known to the writer.

President of the United States

Address: The President, The White House, Washington, DC 20500. Also, The President and Mrs. ___.

Salutation: Dear Sir or Mr. President or Dear Mr. President. More intimately: My dear Mr. President. Also: Dear Mr. President and Mrs. ___

The vice president takes the same forms.

Cabinet Officers

Address: Mr. John Smith, Secretary of State, Washington, D.C. or The Hon. John Smith. Similar addresses for other members of the cabinet. Also: Secretary and Mrs. John Smith.

Salutation: Dear Sir, or Dear Mr. Secretary. Also: Dear Mr. and Mrs. Smith.

The Bench
Address: The Hon. John Smith, Chief Justice of the United States. The Hon. John Smith, Associate Justice of the Supreme Court of the United States. The Hon. John Smith, Associate Judge, U.S. District Court.
Salutation: Dear Sir, or Dear Mr. Chief Justice. Dear Mr. Justice. Dear Judge Smith.

Members of Congress
Address: The Hon. John Smith, United States Senate, Washington, DC 20510, or Sen. John Smith, etc. Also The Hon. John Smith, House of Representatives, Washington, DC 20515, or Rep. John Smith, etc.
Salutation: Dear Mr. Senator or Dear Mr. Smith; for Representative, Dear Mr. Smith.

Officers of Armed Forces
Address: Careful attention should be given to the precise rank, thus: General of the Army John Smith, Fleet Admiral John Smith. Ranks in the Air Force are same as Army.
Salutation: Dear Sir, or Dear General. All general officers, whatever rank, are entitled to be addressed as generals. Likewise a lieutenant colonel is addressed as colonel and first and second lieutenants are addressed as lieutenant. Warrant officers and flight officers are addressed as Mister. Chaplains are addressed as Chaplain. A Catholic chaplain may be addressed as Father. Cadets of the United States Military Academy and Air Force Academy are addressed as Cadet. Noncommissioned officers are addressed by their titles. In the U. S. Navy all men from midshipman at Annapolis up to and including lieutenant commander are addressed as Mister.

Ambassador, Governor, Mayor
Address: The Hon. John Smith, followed by his or her title. They can be addressed either at their embassy, or at the Department of State, Washington, D.C. An ambassador from a foreign nation may be addressed as His or Her Excellency. An American is not to be so addressed.

Salutation: Dear Mr. or Madam Ambassador. An ambassador from a foreign nation may be called Your Excellency.

Governors and mayors are often addressed as The Hon. Jane Smith, Governor of _____, or The Hon. John Smith, Mayor of _____; also Governor John Smith, State House, Albany, N.Y., or Mayor Jane Smith, City Hall, Erie, Pa.

The Clergy
Address: His Holiness, the Pope, or His Holiness Pope (name), State of Vatican City, Italy.
Salutation: Your Holiness or Most Holy Father.

Also: His Eminence, John, Cardinal Smith; salutation: Your Eminence. An archbishop or a bishop is addressed The Most Reverend, and the salutation is Your Excellency. A monsignor who is a papal chamberlain is The Very Reverend Monsignor and the salutation is Dear Sir or Very Reverend Monsignor; a monsignor who is a domestic prelate is The Right Reverend Monsignor and salutation is Right Reverend Monsignor. A priest is addressed Reverend John Smith. A brother of an order is addressed Brother —. A sister takes the same form.

A bishop of the Protestant Episcopal Church is The Right Reverend John Smith; salutation is Right Reverend Sir, or Dear Bishop Smith. If a clergyman is a doctor of divinity, he is addressed: The Reverend John Smith, D.D., and the salutation is Reverend Sir, or Dear Dr. Smith. When a clergyman does not have the degree the salutation is Dear Mr. Smith.

A bishop of the Methodist Church is addressed Bishop John Smith with titles following.

Royalty and Nobility
An emperor is to be addressed in a letter as Sir, or Your Imperial Majesty.

A king or queen is addressed as His Majesty (Name), King of (Name), or Her Majesty (Name), Queen of (Name), Salutation: Sir, or Madam, or May it please Your Majesty.

Princes and princesses and other persons of royal blood are addressed as His (or Her) Royal Highness, and saluted with May it please Your Royal Highness.

A duke or marquis is My Lord Duke (or Marquis), a duke is His (or Your) Grace.

Code of Etiquette for Display and Use of the U.S. Flag

Although the Stars and Stripes originated in 1777, it was not until 146 years later that there was a serious attempt to establish a uniform code of etiquette for the U.S. flag. The War Department issued Feb. 15, 1923, a circular on the rules of flag usage. These were adopted almost in their entirety June 14, 1923, by a conference of 68 patriotic organizations in Washington. Finally, on June 22, 1942, a joint resolution of Congress, amended by Public Law 94-344 July 7, 1976, codified "existing rules and customs pertaining to the display and use of the flag. . ."

When to Display the Flag—The flag should be displayed on all days, especially on legal holidays and other special occasions, on official buildings when in use, in or near polling places on election days, and in or near schools when in session. A citizen may fly the flag at any time he wishes. It is customary to display the flag only from sunrise to sunset on buildings and on stationary flagstaffs in the open. However, it may be displayed at night on special occasions, preferably lighted. In Washington, the flag now flies over the White House both day and night. It flies over the Senate wing of the Capitol when the Senate is in session and over the House wing when that body is in session. It flies day and night over the east and west fronts of the Capitol, without floodlights at night but receiving light from the illuminated Capitol Dome. It flies 24 hours a day at several other places, including the Fort McHenry Nat'l Monument in Baltimore, where it inspired Francis Scott Key to write The Star Spangled Banner.

How to Fly the Flag—The flag should be hoisted briskly and lowered ceremoniously, and should never be allowed to touch the ground or the floor. When hung over a sidewalk from a rope extending from a building to a pole, the union should be away from the building. When hung over the center of a street it should have the union to the north in an east-west street and to the east in a north-south street. No other flag may be flown above or, if on the same level, to the right of the U.S. flag, except that at the United Nations Headquarters the UN flag may be placed above flags of all member nations and other national flags may be flown with equal prominence or honor with the flag of the U.S. At services by Navy chaplains at sea, the church pennant may be flown above the flag.

When two flags are placed against a wall with crossed staffs, the U.S. flag should be at right—its own right, and its staff should be in front of the staff of the other flag; when a number of flags are grouped and displayed from staffs, it should be at the center and highest point of the group.

Church and Platform Use—In an auditorium, the flag may be displayed flat, above and behind the speaker. When displayed from a staff in a church or public auditorium, the flag should hold the position of superior prominence, in advance of the audience, and in the position of honor at the clergyman's or speaker's right as he faces the audience. Any other flag so displayed should be placed on the left of the clergyman or speaker or to the right of the audience.

When the flag is displayed horizontally or vertically against a wall, the stars should be uppermost and at the observer's left.

When to Salute the Flag—All persons present should face the flag, stand at attention and salute on the following occasions: (1) When the flag is passing in a parade or in a review, (2) During the ceremony of hoisting or lowering, (3) When the National Anthem is played, and (4) During the Pledge of Allegiance. Those present in uniform should render the military salute. When not in uniform, men should remove the hat with the right hand holding it at the left shoulder, the hand being over the heart. Men without hats should salute in the same manner. Aliens should stand at attention. Women should salute by placing the right hand over the heart.

On Memorial Day, the flag should fly at half-staff until noon, then be raised to the peak.

As provided by Presidential proclamation the flag should fly at half-staff for 30 days from the day of death of a president or former president; for 10 days from the day of death of a vice president, chief justice or retired chief justice of the U.S., or speaker of the House of Representatives; from day of death until burial of an associate justice of the Supreme Court, cabinet member, former vice president, or Senate president pro tempore, majority or minority Senate leader, or majority or minority House leader; for a U.S. senator, representative, territorial delegate, or the resident commissioner of Puerto Rico, on day of death and the following day within the metropolitan area of the District of Columbia and from day of death until burial within the decedent's state, congressional district, territory or commonwealth; and for the death of the governor of a state, territory, or possession of the U.S., from day of

death until burial within that state, territory, or possession.

When used to cover a casket, the flag should be placed so that the union is at the head and over the left shoulder. It should not be lowered into the grave nor touch the ground.

Prohibited Uses of the Flag—The flag should not be dipped to any person or thing. (An exception—customarily, ships salute by dipping their colors.) It should never be displayed with the union down save as a distress signal. It should never be carried flat or horizontally, but always aloft and free.

It should not be displayed on a float, motor car or boat except from a staff.

It should never be used as a covering for a ceiling, nor have placed upon it any word, design, or drawing. It should never be used as a receptacle for carrying anything. It should not be used to cover a statue or a monument.

The flag should never be used for advertising purposes, nor be embroidered on such articles as cushions or hankerchiefs, printed or otherwise impressed on boxes or used as a costume or athletic uniform. Advertising signs should not be fastened to its staff or halyard.

The flag should never be used as drapery of any sort, never festooned, drawn back, nor up, in folds, but always allowed to fall free. Bunting of blue, white and red always arranged with the blue above and the white in the middle, should be used for covering a speaker's desk, draping the front of a platform, and for decoration in general.

An Act of Congress approved Feb. 8, 1917, provided certain penalties for the desecration, mutilation or improper use of the flag within the District of Columbia. A 1968 federal law provided penalties of up to a year's imprisonment or a $1,000 fine or both, for publicly burning or otherwise desecrating any flag of the United States. In addition, many states have laws against flag desecration.

How to Dispose of Worn Flags—The flag, when it is in such condition that it is no longer a fitting emblem for display, should be destroyed in a dignified way, preferably by burning in private.

Pledge of Allegiance to the Flag

I pledge allegiance to the flag of the United States of America and to the republic for which it stands, one nation under God, indivisible, with liberty and justice for all.

This, the current official version of the Pledge of Allegiance, has developed from the original pledge, which was first published in the Sept. 8, 1892, issue of the Youth's Companion, a weekly magazine then published in Boston. The original pledge contained the phrase "my flag," which was changed more than 30 years later to "flag of the United States of America." An act of Congress in 1954 added the words "under God."

The authorship of the pledge had been in dispute for many years. The Youth's Companion stated in 1917 that the original draft was written by James B. Upham, an executive of the magazine who died in 1910. A leaflet circulated by the magazine later named Upham as the originator of the draft "afterwards condensed and perfected by him and his associates of the Companion force."

Francis Bellamy, a former member of the Youth's Companion editorial staff, publicly claimed authorship of the pledge in 1923. The United States Flag Assn., acting on the advice of a committee named to study the controversy, upheld in 1939 the claim of Bellamy, who had died 8 years earlier. The Library of Congress issued in 1957 a report attributing the authorship to Bellamy.

The Flag of the U.S.—The Stars and Stripes

The 50-star flag of the United States was raised for the first time officially at 12:01 a.m. on July 4, 1960, at Fort McHenry National Monument in Baltimore, Md. The 50th star had been added for Hawaii; a year earlier the 49th, for Alaska. Before that, no star had been added since 1912, when N.M. and Ariz. were admitted to the Union.

History of the Flag

The true history of the Stars and Stripes has become so cluttered by a volume of myth and tradition that the facts are difficult, and in some cases impossible, to establish. For example, it is not certain who designed the Stars and Stripes, who made the first such flag, or even whether it ever flew in any sea fight or land battle of the American Revolution.

One thing all agree on is that the Stars and Stripes originated as the result of a resolution offered by the Marine Committee of the Second Continental Congress at Philadelphia and adopted June 14, 1777. It read:

Resolved: that the flag of the United States be thirteen stripes, alternate red and white; that the union be thirteen stars, white in a blue field, representing a new constellation.

Congress gave no hint as to the designer of the flag, no instructions as to the arrangement of the stars, and no information on its appropriate uses. Historians have been unable to find the original flag law.

The resolution establishing the flag was not even published until Sept. 2, 1777. Despite repeated requests, Washington did not get the flags until 1783, after the Revolutionary War was over. And there is no certainty that they were the Stars and Stripes.

Early Flags

Although it was never officially adopted by the Continental Congress, many historians consider the first flag of the United States to have been the Grand Union (sometimes called Great Union) flag. This was a modification of the British Meteor flag, which had the red cross of St. George and the white cross of St. Andrew combined in the blue canton. For the Grand Union flag, 6 horizontal stripes were imposed on the red field, dividing it into 13 alternate red and white stripes. On Jan. 1, 1776, when the Continental Army came into formal existence, this flag was unfurled on Prospect Hill, Somerville, Mass. Washington wrote that "we hoisted the Union Flag in compliment to the United Colonies."

One of several flags about which controversy has raged for years is at Easton, Pa. Containing the devices of the national flag in reversed order, this has been in the public library at Easton for over 150 years. Some contend that this flag was actually the first Stars and Stripes, first displayed on July 8, 1776. This flag has 13 red and white stripes in the canton, 13 white stars centered in a blue field.

A flag was hastily improvised from garments by the defenders of Fort Schuyler at Rome, N.Y., Aug. 3-22, 1777. Historians believe it was the Grand Union flag.

The Sons of Liberty had a flag of 9 red and white stripes, to signify 9 colonies, when they met in New York in 1765 to oppose the Stamp Tax. By 1775, the flag had grown to 13 red and white stripes, with a rattlesnake on it.

At Concord, Apr. 19, 1775, the minute men from Bedford, Mass., are said to have carried a flag having a silver arm with sword on a red field.

At Cambridge, Mass., the Sons of Liberty used a plain red flag with a green pine tree on it.

In June 1775, Washington went from Philadelphia to Boston to take command of the army, escorted to New York by the Philadelphia Light Horse Troop. It carried a yellow flag which had an elaborate coat of arms — the shield charged with 13 knots, the motto "For These We Strive" — and a canton of 13 blue and silver stripes.

In Feb., 1776, Col. Christopher Gadsden, member of the Continental Congress, gave the South Carolina Provincial Congress a flag "such as is to be used by the commander-in-chief of the American Navy." It had a yellow field, with a rattlesnake about to strike and the words "Don't Tread on Me."

At the battle of Bennington, Aug. 16, 1777, patriots used a flag of 7 white and 6 red stripes with a blue canton extending down 9 stripes and showing an arch of 11 white stars over the figure 76 and a star in each of the upper corners. The stars are seven-pointed. This flag is preserved in the Historical Museum at Bennington, Vt.

At the Battle of Cowpens, Jan. 17, 1781, the 3d Maryland Regt. is said to have carried a flag of 13 red and white stripes, with a blue canton containing 12 stars in a circle around one star.

Legends about the Flag

Who Designed the Flag? No one knows for a certainty. Francis Hopkinson, designer of a naval flag, declared he also had designed the flag and in 1781 asked Congress to reimburse him for his services. Congress did not do so. Dumas Malone of Columbia Univ. wrote: "This talented man . . . designed the American flag."

Who Called the Flag Old Glory? — The flag is said to have been named Old Glory by William Driver, a sea captain of Salem, Mass. One legend has it that when he raised the flag on his brig, the Charles Doggett, in 1824, he said: "I name thee Old Glory." But his daughter, who presented the flag to the Smithsonian Institution, said he named it at his 21st birthday celebration Mar. 17, 1824, when his mother presented the homemade flag to him.

The Betsy Ross Legend — The widely publicized legend that Mrs. Betsy Ross made the first Stars and Stripes in June 1776, at the request of a committee composed of George Washington, Robert Morris, and George Ross, an uncle, was first made public in 1870, by a grandson of Mrs. Ross. Historians have been unable to find a historical record of such a meeting or committee.

Adding New Stars

The flag of 1777 was used until 1795. Then, on the admission of Vermont and Kentucky to the Union, Congress passed and Pres. Washington signed an act that after May 1, 1795, the flag should have 15 stripes, alternate red and white, and 15 white stars on a blue field in the union.

When new states were admitted it became evident that the flag would become burdened with stripes. Congress thereupon ordered that after July 4, 1818, the flag should have 13 stripes, symbolizing the 13 original states; that the union have 20 stars, and that whenever a new state was admitted a new star should be added on the July 4 following admission. No law designates the permanent arrangement of the stars. However, since 1912 when a new state has been admitted, the new design has been announced by executive order. No star is specifically identified with any state.

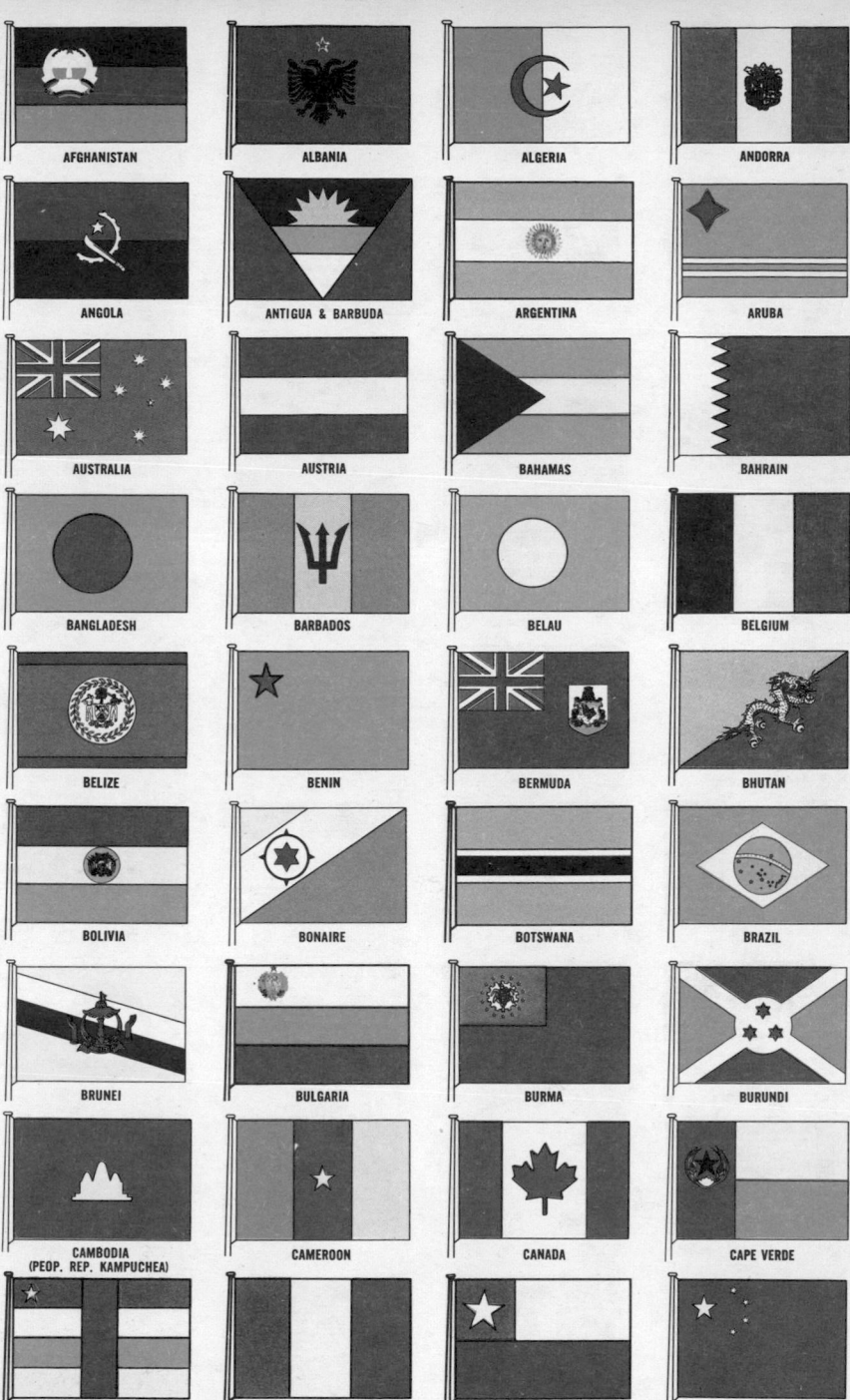

AFGHANISTAN

ALBANIA

ALGERIA

ANDORRA

ANGOLA

ANTIGUA & BARBUDA

ARGENTINA

ARUBA

AUSTRALIA

AUSTRIA

BAHAMAS

BAHRAIN

BANGLADESH

BARBADOS

BELAU

BELGIUM

BELIZE

BENIN

BERMUDA

BHUTAN

BOLIVIA

BONAIRE

BOTSWANA

BRAZIL

BRUNEI

BULGARIA

BURMA

BURUNDI

CAMBODIA
(PEOP. REP. KAMPUCHEA)

CAMEROON

CANADA

CAPE VERDE

CENTRAL AFRICAN REP.

CHAD

CHILE

CHINA (MAINLAND)

458

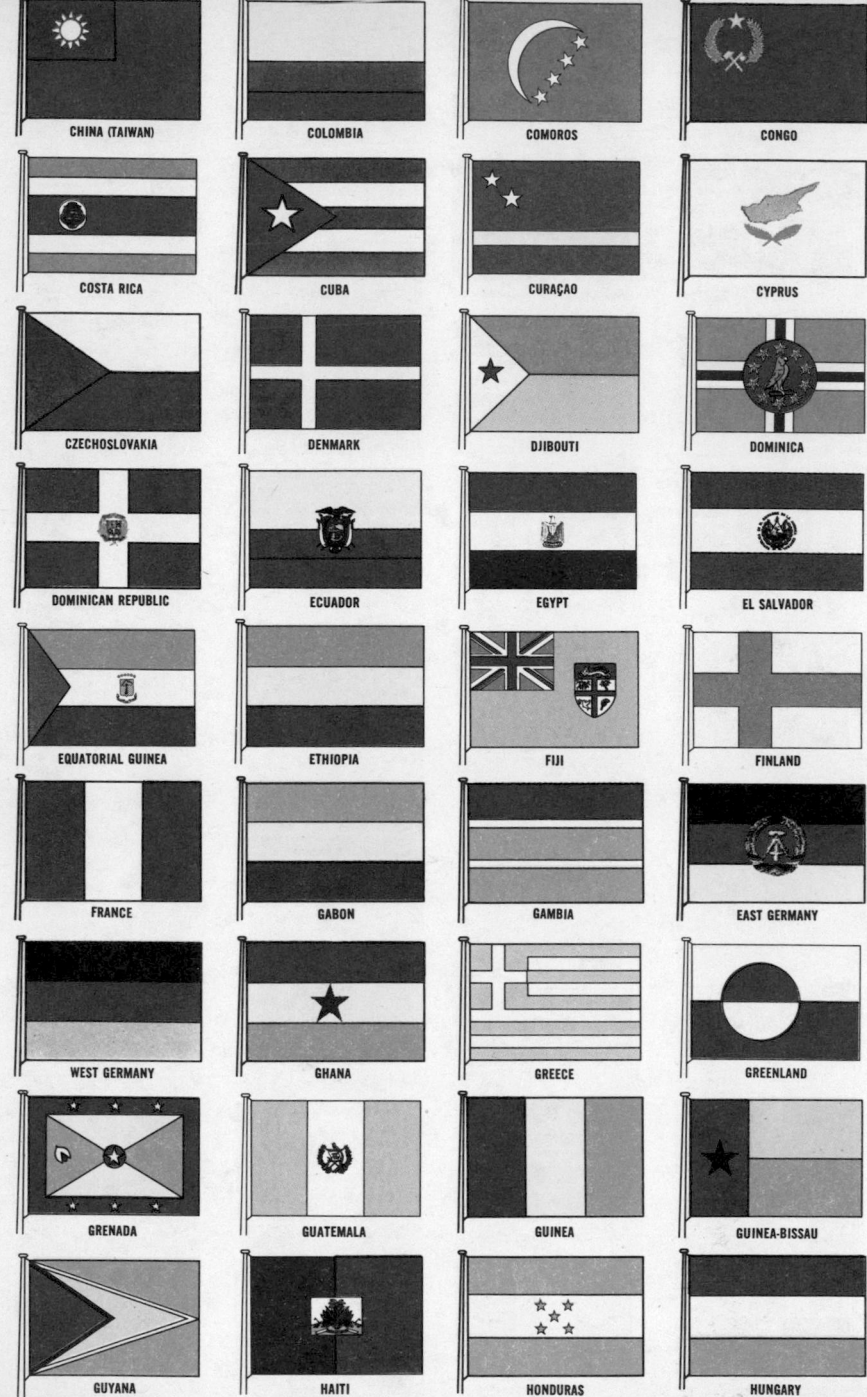

CHINA (TAIWAN)	COLOMBIA	COMOROS	CONGO
COSTA RICA	CUBA	CURAÇAO	CYPRUS
CZECHOSLOVAKIA	DENMARK	DJIBOUTI	DOMINICA
DOMINICAN REPUBLIC	ECUADOR	EGYPT	EL SALVADOR
EQUATORIAL GUINEA	ETHIOPIA	FIJI	FINLAND
FRANCE	GABON	GAMBIA	EAST GERMANY
WEST GERMANY	GHANA	GREECE	GREENLAND
GRENADA	GUATEMALA	GUINEA	GUINEA-BISSAU
GUYANA	HAITI	HONDURAS	HUNGARY

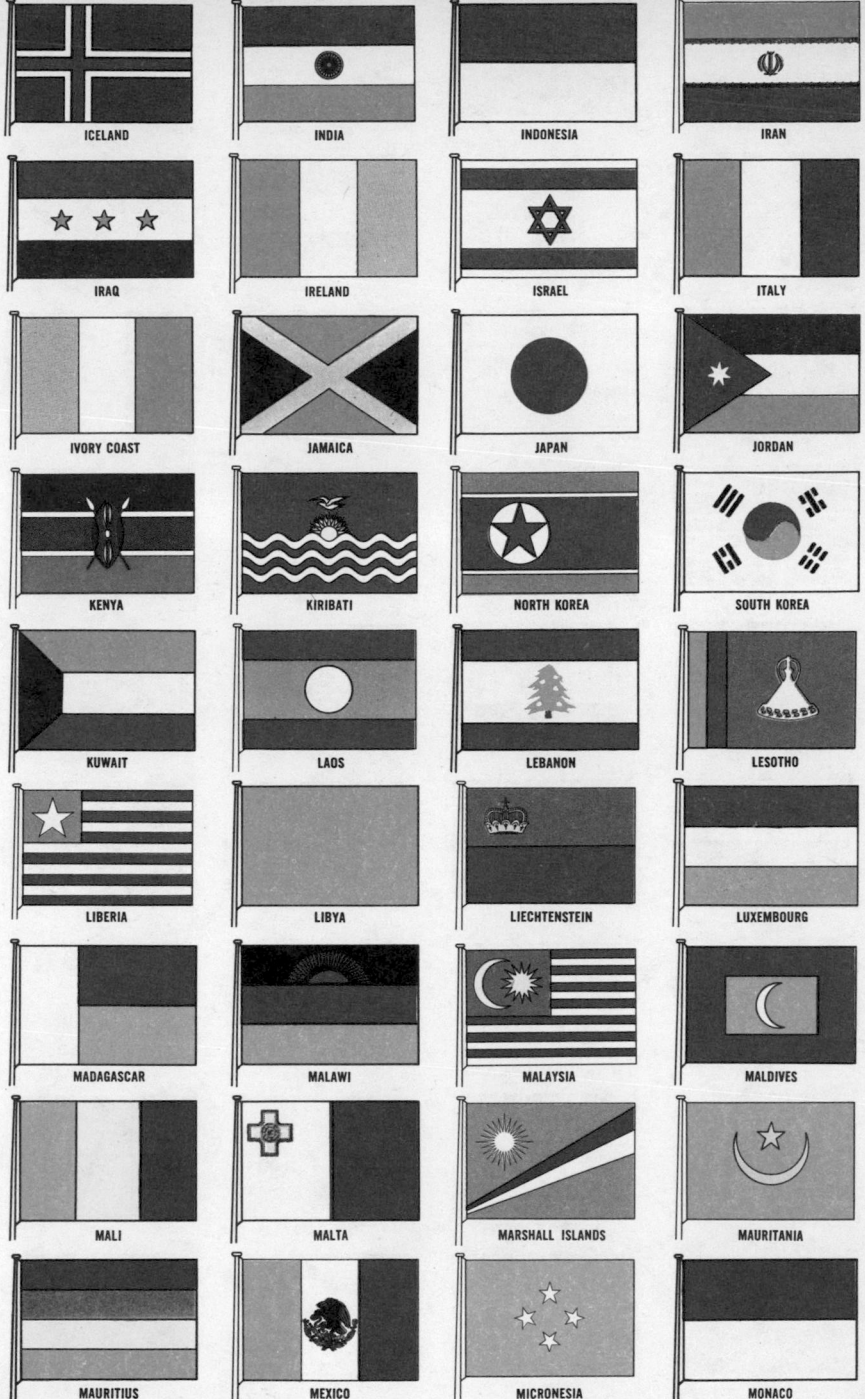

ICELAND

INDIA

INDONESIA

IRAN

IRAQ

IRELAND

ISRAEL

ITALY

IVORY COAST

JAMAICA

JAPAN

JORDAN

KENYA

KIRIBATI

NORTH KOREA

SOUTH KOREA

KUWAIT

LAOS

LEBANON

LESOTHO

LIBERIA

LIBYA

LIECHTENSTEIN

LUXEMBOURG

MADAGASCAR

MALAWI

MALAYSIA

MALDIVES

MALI

MALTA

MARSHALL ISLANDS

MAURITANIA

MAURITIUS

MEXICO

MICRONESIA

MONACO

MONGOLIA

MOROCCO

MOZAMBIQUE

NAMIBIA
(FLAG OF S. AFRICA)

NAURU

NEPAL

NETHERLANDS

NETHERLANDS ANTILLES

NEW ZEALAND

NICARAGUA

NIGER

NIGERIA

NORWAY

OMAN

PAKISTAN

PANAMA

PAPUA NEW GUINEA

PARAGUAY

PERU

PHILIPPINES

POLAND

PORTUGAL

QATAR

ROMANIA

RWANDA

ST. CHRISTOPHER AND NEVIS

ST. LUCIA

ST. VINCENT & GRENS.

SAN MARINO

SÃO TOMÉ E PRINCIPE

SAUDI ARABIA

SENEGAL

SEYCHELLES

SIERRA LEONE

SINGAPORE

SOLOMON ISLANDS

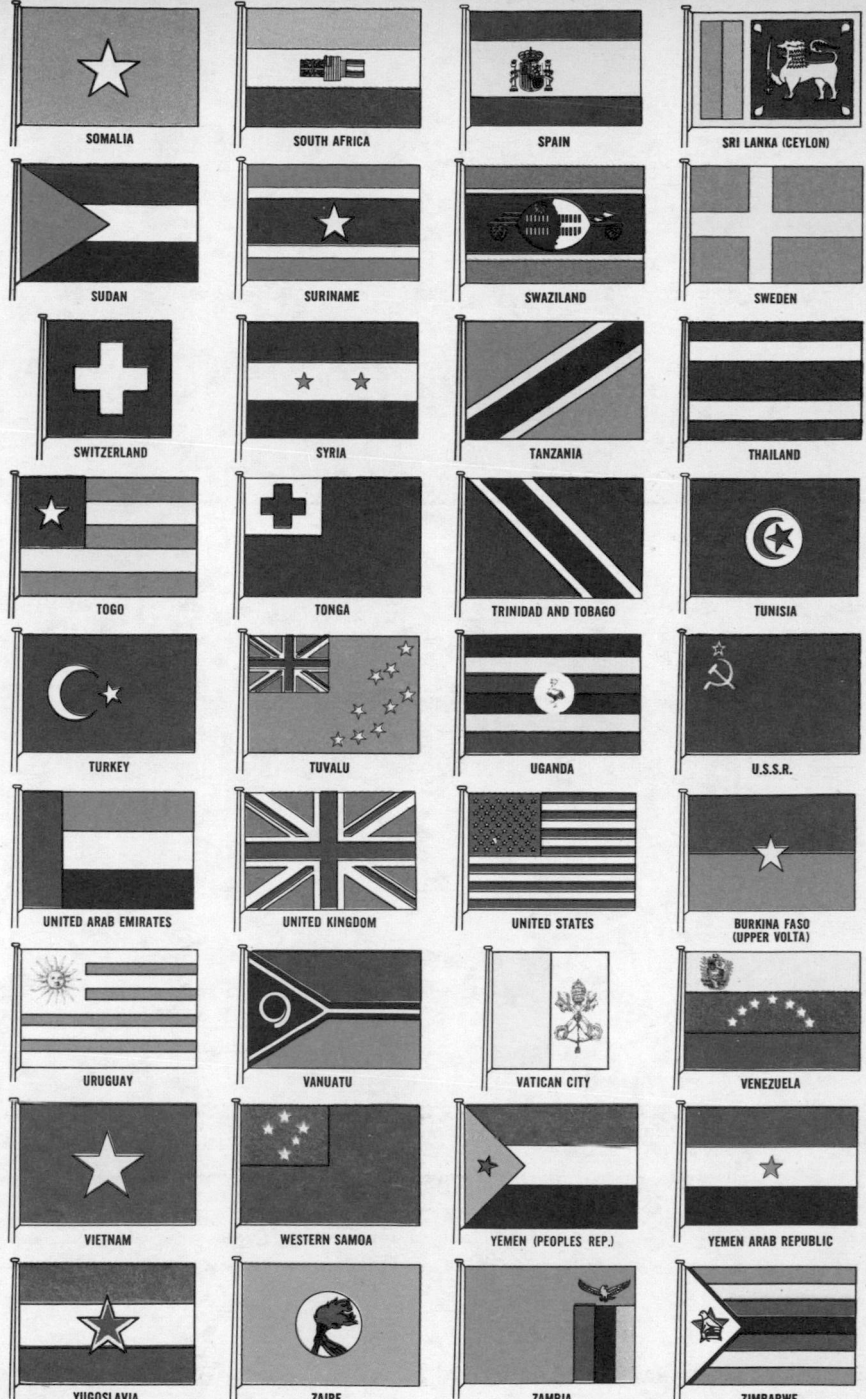

461

SOMALIA SOUTH AFRICA SPAIN SRI LANKA (CEYLON)

SUDAN SURINAME SWAZILAND SWEDEN

SWITZERLAND SYRIA TANZANIA THAILAND

TOGO TONGA TRINIDAD AND TOBAGO TUNISIA

TURKEY TUVALU UGANDA U.S.S.R.

UNITED ARAB EMIRATES UNITED KINGDOM UNITED STATES BURKINA FASO (UPPER VOLTA)

URUGUAY VANUATU VATICAN CITY VENEZUELA

VIETNAM WESTERN SAMOA YEMEN (PEOPLES REP.) YEMEN ARAB REPUBLIC

YUGOSLAVIA ZAIRE ZAMBIA ZIMBABWE

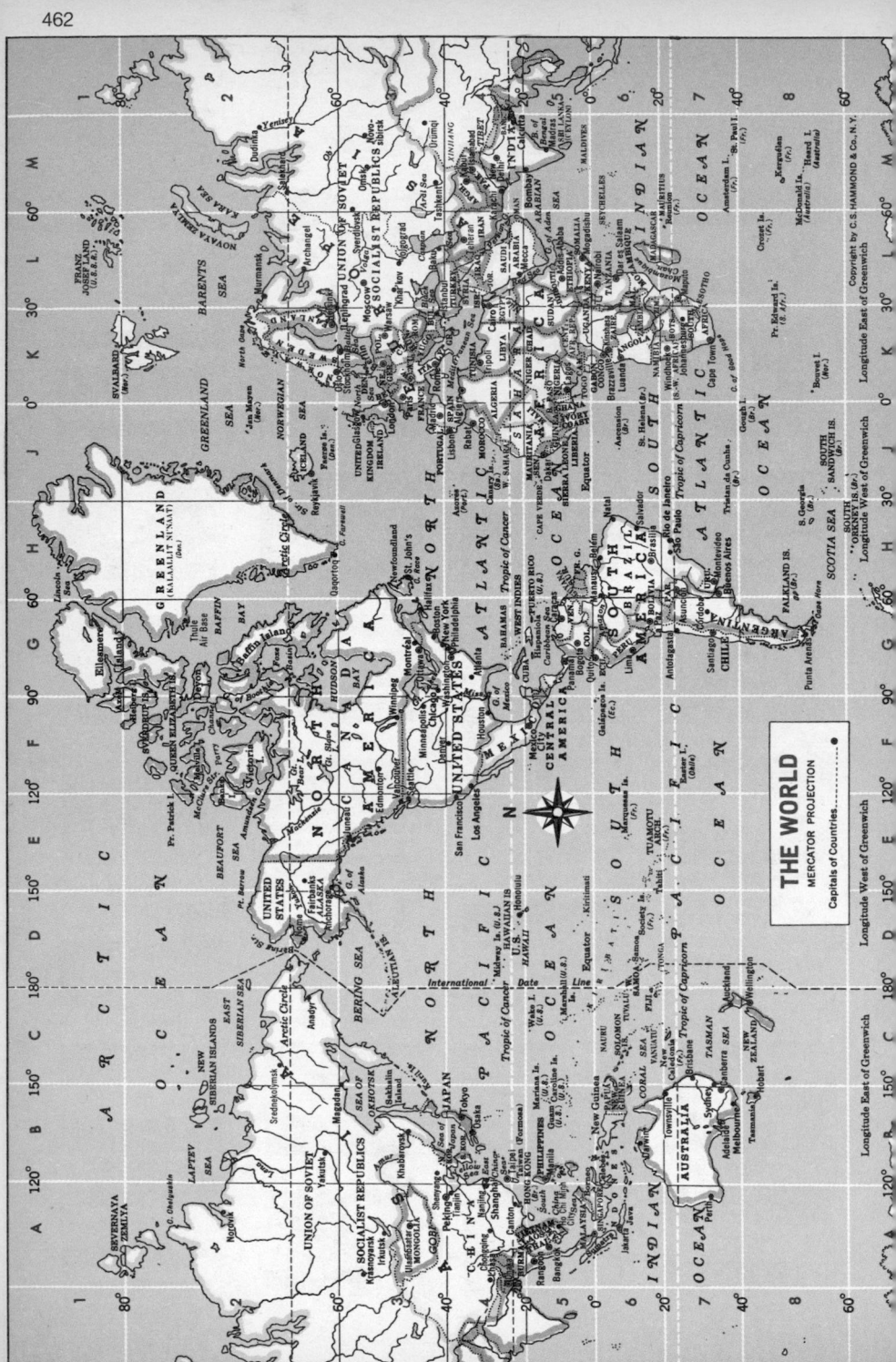

THE WORLD

MERCATOR PROJECTION

Capitals of Countries........ ●

Copyright by C.S. HAMMOND & Co., N.Y.

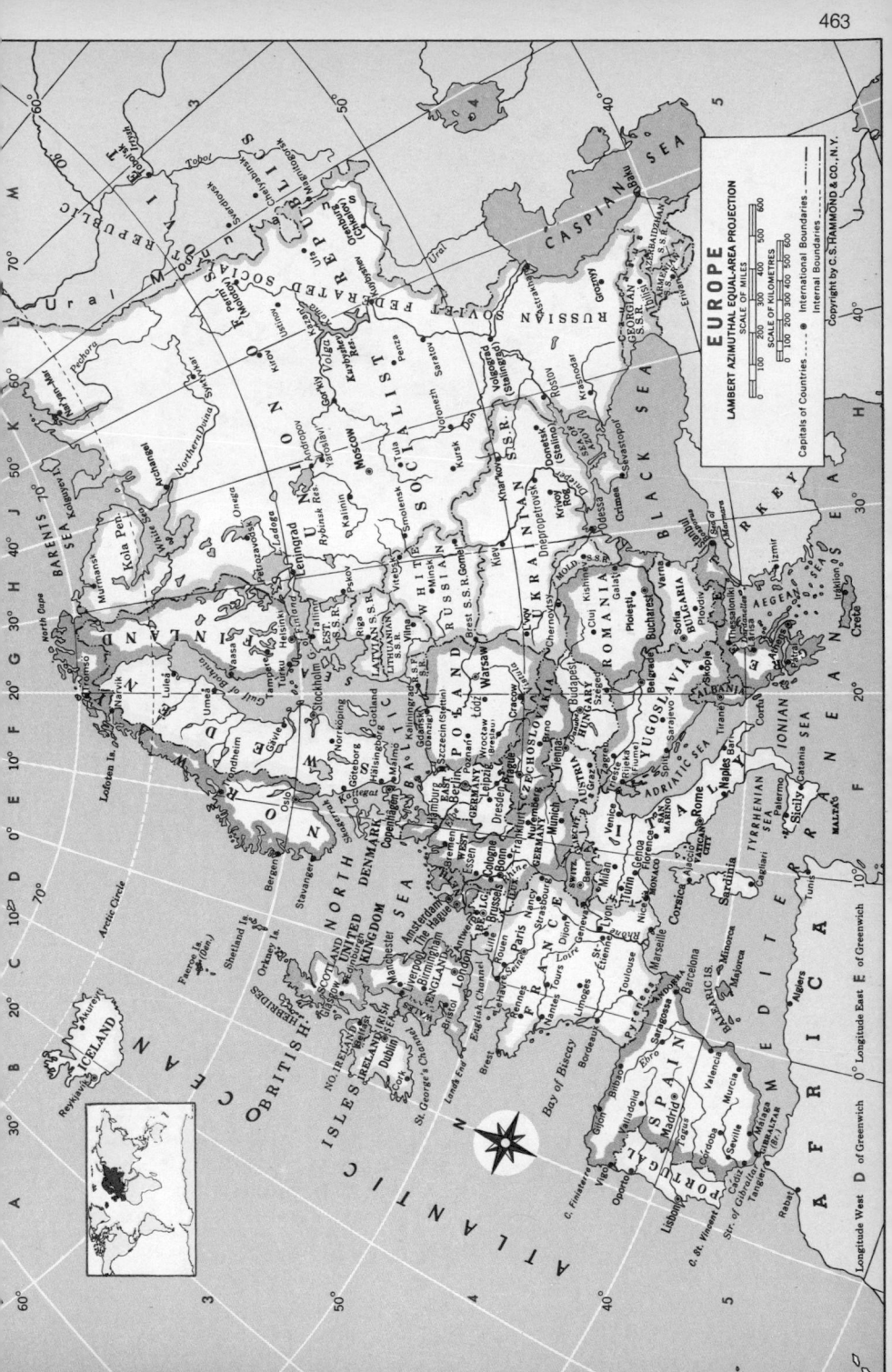

EUROPE

LAMBERT AZIMUTHAL EQUAL-AREA PROJECTION

SCALE OF MILES

100   200   300   400   500   600

SCALE OF KILOMETRES

100 200 300 400 500 600

Capitals of Countries........ ⊛   International Boundaries......
                                   Internal Boundaries........

Copyright by C. S. HAMMOND & CO., N.Y.

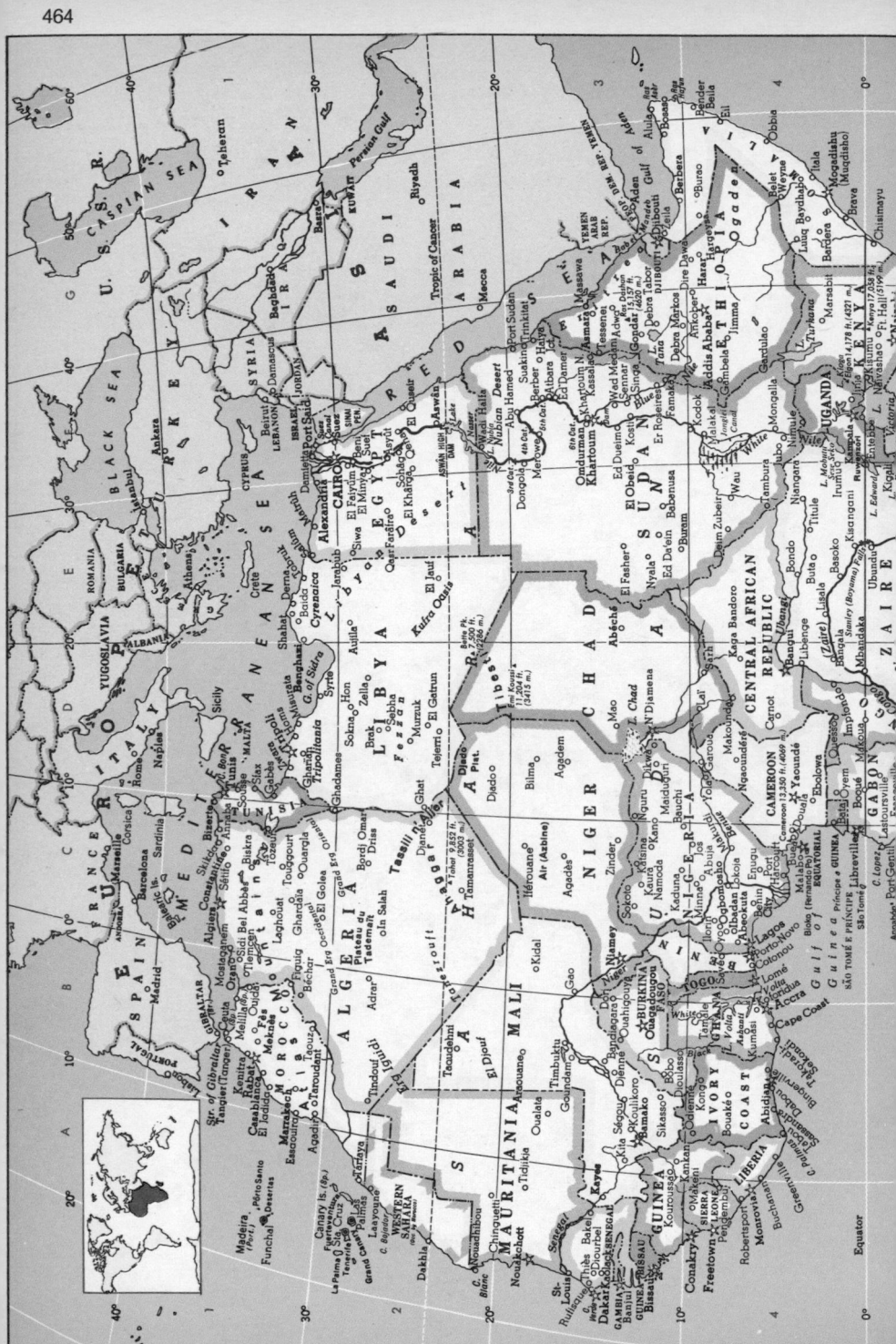

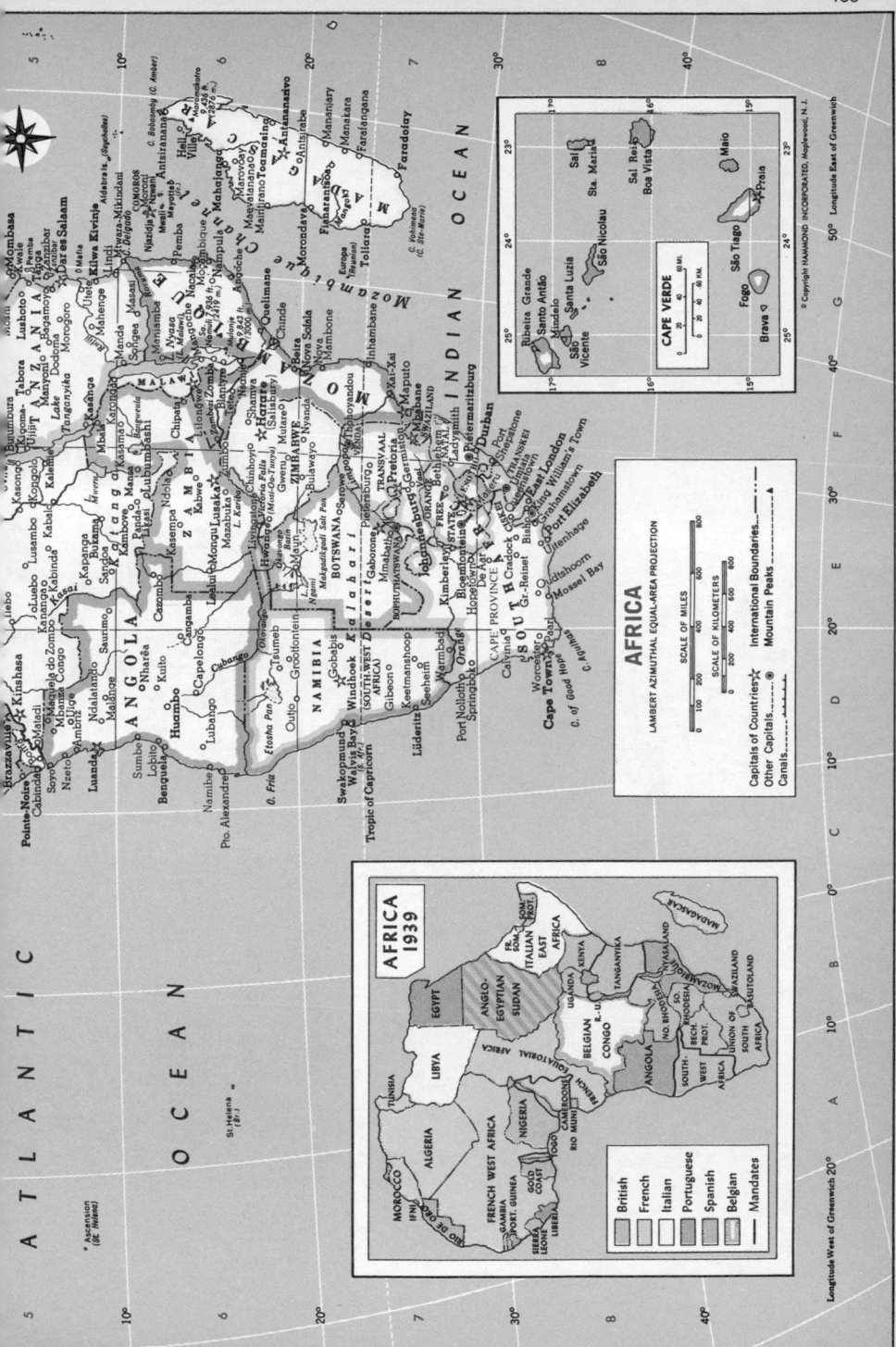

466

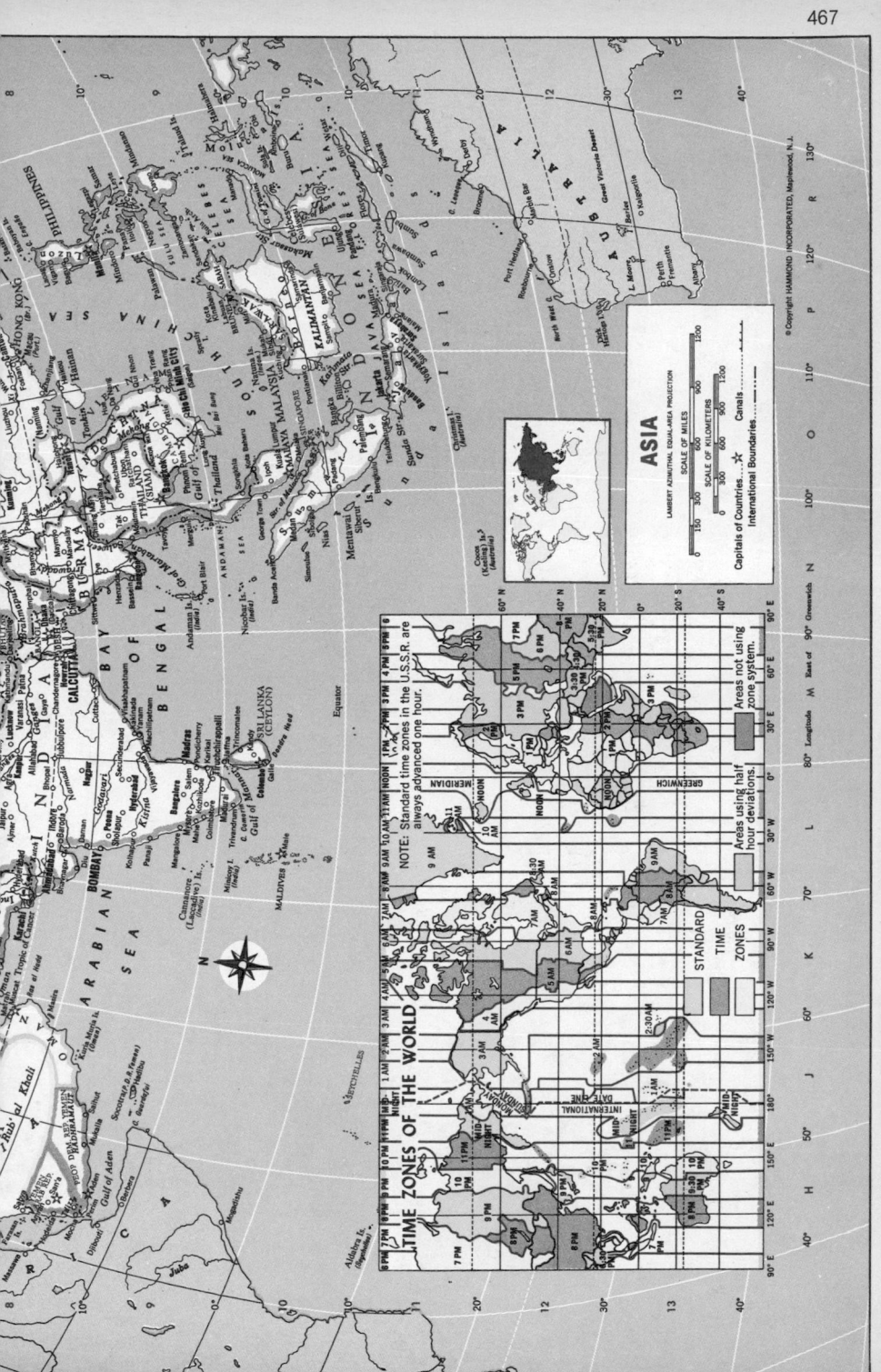

ASIA

LAMBERT AZIMUTHAL EQUAL-AREA PROJECTION

SCALE OF MILES

SCALE OF KILOMETERS

Capitals of Countries........☆   Canals ....
International Boundaries.......

TIME ZONES OF THE WORLD

STANDARD TIME ZONES

NOTE: Standard time zones in the U.S.S.R. are always advanced one hour.

Areas not using zone system.

Areas using half hour deviations.

INTERNATIONAL DATE LINE

THE NEAR and MIDDLE EAST
CONIC PROJECTION

SCALE OF MILES

| 0 | 100 | 200 | 300 | 400 |

KILOMETERS

| 0 | 100 | 200 | 300 | 400 |

Capitals of Countries ⊛
International Boundaries ▬▬▬
Other Boundaries ▪▪▪▪

© Copyright HAMMOND INC., Maplewood, N. J.

ARCTIC OCEAN

ATLANTIC OCEAN

GREENLAND SEA

GREENLAND
(KALAALLIT NUNAAT)
(Dan.)

UNITED KINGDOM

ICELAND

Denmark Strait

KING CHRISTIAN IX LAND

KING FREDERIK VI COAST

C. Farewell

KNUD RASMUSSEN LAND

KING FREDERIK VIII LAND

CHRISTIAN X LAND

Baffin Bay

Davis Strait

Baffin Island

LABRADOR

NEWFOUNDLAND

North Pole

QUEEN ELIZABETH ISLANDS

SVERDRUP IS.

Devon I.

Melville I.

Victoria I.

BEAUFORT SEA

BANKS I.

McClure Str.

ARCTIC OCEAN

NORTHWEST TERRITORY

Great Bear Lake

Great Slave Lake

Mackenzie

HUDSON Bay

QUEBEC

ONTARIO

MANITOBA

SASKATCHEWAN

ALBERTA

BRITISH COLUMBIA

YUKON TER.

UNITED STATES (ALASKA)

Brooks Range

Yukon

SEWARD PEN.

Kodiak I.

BERING SEA

ASIA
U.S.S.R.

Bering Strait

St. Lawrence I.

St. Matthew I.

Nunivak I.

Bristol Bay

Coast Mountains

Vancouver I.

QUEEN CHARLOTTE IS.

ALEXANDER ARCH.

Fraser

PACIFIC OCEAN

MONT.

IDAHO

WYO.

N. DAK.

S. DAK.

NEBR.

MINN.

WIS.

MICH.

IOWA

ILL.

IND.

OHIO

N.Y.

PA.

Winnipeg

Regina

Chicago

Rock Is.

Cedar Rapids

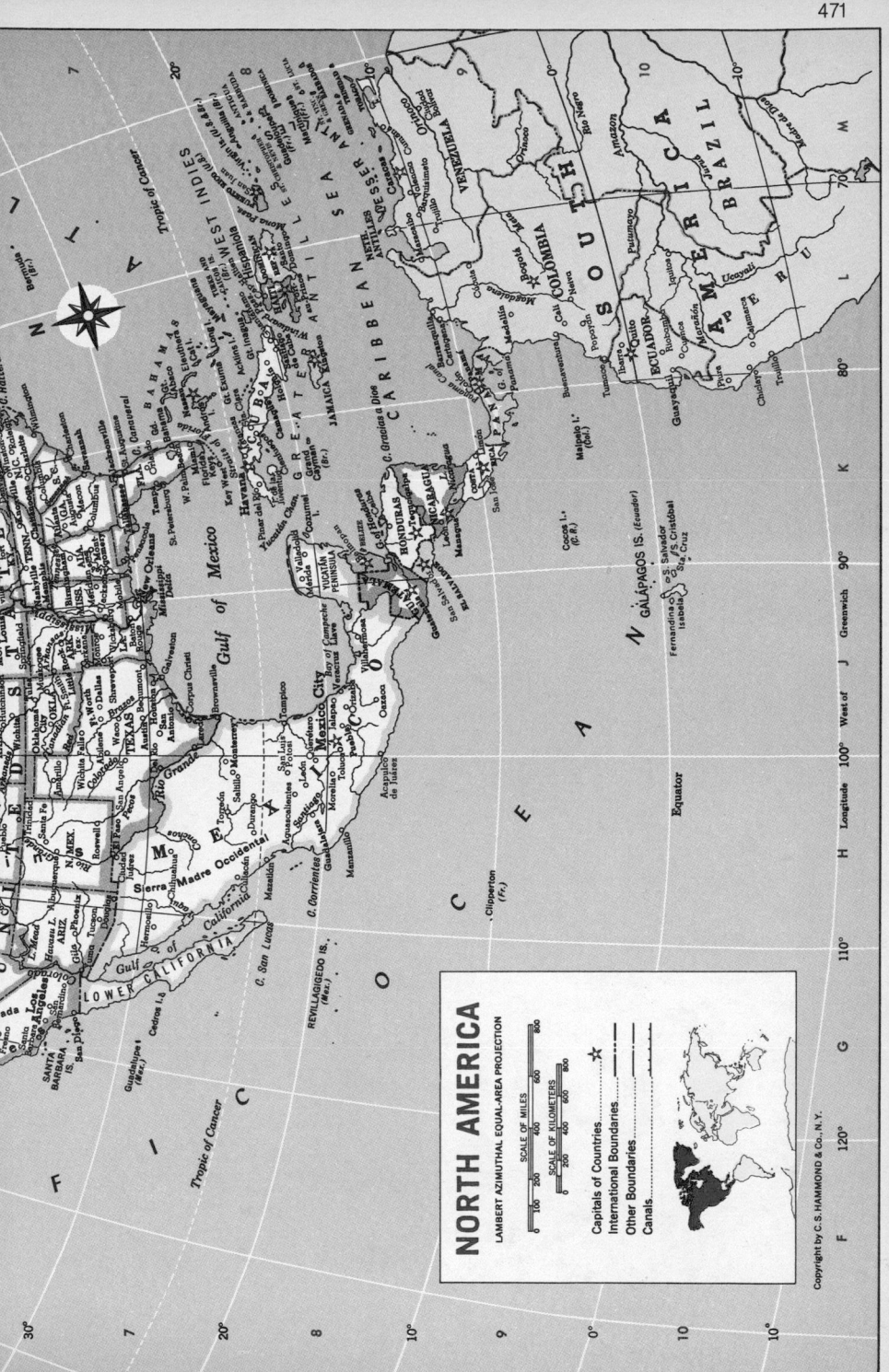

NORTH AMERICA

LAMBERT AZIMUTHAL EQUAL-AREA PROJECTION

SCALE OF MILES

0 200 400 600 800

SCALE OF KILOMETERS

0 200 400 600 800

Capitals of Countries .... ☆
International Boundaries ....
Other Boundaries ....
Canals ....

Copyright by C.S. HAMMOND & Co., N.Y.

472

HISTORY

Memorable Dates in U.S. History

1492
Christopher Columbus and crew sighted land Oct. 12 in the present-day Bahamas.

1497
John Cabot explored northeast coast to Delaware.

1513
Juan Ponce de Leon explored Florida coast.

1524
Giovanni da Verrazano led French expedition along coast from Carolina north to Nova Scotia; entered New York harbor.

1539
Hernando de Soto landed in Florida May 28; crossed Mississippi River, 1541.

1540
Francisco Vazquez de Coronado explored Southwest north of Rio Grande. Hernando de Alarcon reached Colorado River, Don Garcia Lopez de Cardenas reached Grand Canyon. Others explored California coast.

1565
St. Augustine, Fla. founded by Pedro Menendez. Razed by Francis Drake 1586.

1579
Francis Drake claimed California for Britain. Metal plate, found 1936, thought to be left by Drake, termed probable hoax 1979.

1607
Capt. John Smith and 105 cavaliers in 3 ships landed on Virginia coast, started first permanent English settlement in New World at Jamestown, May 13.

1609
Henry Hudson, English explorer of Northwest Passage, employed by Dutch, sailed into New York harbor in Sept., and up Hudson to Albany. The same year, Samuel de Champlain explored Lake Champlain just to the north. Spaniards settled Santa Fe., N.M.

1619
House of Burgesses, first representative assembly in New World, elected July 30 at Jamestown, Va.

First black laborers — indentured servants — in English N. American colonies, landed by Dutch at Jamestown in Aug. Chattel slavery legally recognized, 1650.

1620
Plymouth Pilgrims, Puritan separatists from Church of England, some living in Holland, left Plymouth, England Sept. 15 on Mayflower. Original destination Virginia, they reached Cape Cod Nov. 19, explored coast; 103 passengers landed Dec. 21 (Dec. 11 Old Style) at Plymouth. Mayflower Compact was agreement to form a government and abide by its laws. Half of colony died during harsh winter.

1624
Dutch left 8 men from ship New Netherland on Manhattan Island in May. Rest sailed to Albany.

1626
Peter Minuit bought Manhattan for Dutch from Man-a-hat-a Indians May 6 for trinkets valued at $24.

1634
Maryland founded as Catholic colony with religious tolerance.

1636
Harvard College founded Oct. 28, now oldest in U.S., Grammar school, compulsory education established at Boston.

Roger Williams founded Providence, R.I., June, as a democratically ruled colony with separation of church and state. Charter was granted, 1644.

1654
First Jews arrived in New Amsterdam.

1660
British Parliament passed **Navigation Act**, regulating colonial commerce to suit English needs.

1664
Three hundred British troops Sept. 8 seized New Netherland from Dutch, who yield peacefully. Charles II granted province of New Netherland and city of New Amsterdam to brother, Duke of York; both renamed New York. The Dutch recaptured the colony Aug. 9, 1673, but ceded it to Britain Nov. 10, 1674.

1676
Nathaniel Bacon led planters against autocratic British Gov. Berkeley, burned Jamestown, Va. Bacon died, 23 followers executed.

Bloody Indian war in New England ended Aug. 12. King Philip, Wampanoag chief, and many Narragansett Indians killed.

1682
Robert Cavelier, Sieur de La Salle, claimed lower Mississippi River country for France, called it Louisiana Apr. 9. Had French outposts built in Illinois and Texas, 1684. Killed during mutiny Mar. 19, 1687.

1683
William Penn signed treaty with Delaware Indians and made payment for Pennsylvania lands.

1692
Witchcraft delusion at Salem (now Danvers) Mass. inspired by preaching; 19 persons executed.

1696
Capt. William Kidd, American hired by British to fight pirates and take booty, becomes pirate. Arrested and sent to England, where he was hanged 1701.

1699
French settlements made in Mississippi, Louisiana.

1704
Indians attacked Deerfield, Mass. Feb. 28-29, killed 40, carried off 100.

Boston News Letter, first regular newspaper, started by John Campbell, postmaster. (*Publick Occurences* was suppressed after one issue 1690.)

1709
British-Colonial troops captured French fort, Port Royal, Nova Scotia, in Queen Anne's War 1701-13. France yielded Nova Scotia by treaty 1713.

1712
Slaves revolted in New York Apr. 6. Six committed suicide, 21 were executed. Second rising, 1741; 13 slaves hanged, 13 burned, 71 deported.

1716
First theater in colonies opened in Williamsburg, Va.

1728
Pennsylvania Gazette founded by Samuel Keimer in Philadelphia. Benjamin Franklin bought interest 1729.

1732
Benjamin Franklin published first *Poor Richard's Almanac;* published annually to 1757.

1735
Freedom of the press recognized in New York by acquittal of John Peter Zenger, editor of *Weekly Journal,* on charge of libeling British Gov. Cosby by criticizing his conduct in office.

1740-41
Capt. Vitus Bering, Dane employed by Russians, reached Alaska.

1744
King George's War pitted British and colonials vs. French. Colonials captured Louisburg, Cape Breton Is. June 17, 1745. Returned to France 1748 by Treaty of Aix-la-Chapelle.

1752
Benjamin Franklin, flying kite in thunderstorm, proved

lightning is electricity June 15; invented lightning rod.

1754

French and Indian War (in Europe called 7 Years War, started 1756) began when French occupied Ft. Duquesne (Pittsburgh). British moved Acadian French from Nova Scotia to Louisiana Oct. 1755. British captured Quebec Sept. 18, 1759 in battles in which French Gen. Montcalm and British Gen. Wolfe were killed. Peace signed Feb. 10 1763. French lost Canada and American Midwest. British tightened colonial administration in North America.

1764

Sugar Act placed duties on lumber, foodstuffs, molasses and rum in colonies.

1765

Stamp Act required revenue stamps to help defray cost of royal troops. Nine colonies, led by New York and Massachusetts at Stamp Act Congress in New York Oct. 7-25, 1765, adopted Declaration of Rights opposing taxation without representation in Parliament and trial without jury by admiralty courts. Stamp Act repealed Mar. 17, 1766.

1767

Townshend Acts levied taxes on glass, painter's lead, paper, and tea. In 1770 all duties except on tea were repealed.

1770

British troops fired Mar. 5 into Boston mob, killed 5 including Crispus Attucks, a black man, reportedly leader of group; later called Boston Massacre.

1773

East India Co. tea ships turned back at Boston, New York, Philadelphia in May. Cargo ship burned at Annapolis Oct. 14, cargo thrown overboard at Boston Tea Party Dec. 16.

1774

"Intolerable Acts" of Parliament curtailed Massachusetts self-rule; barred use of Boston harbor till tea was paid for.

First Continental Congress held in Philadelphia Sept. 5-Oct. 26; protested British measures, called for civil disobedience.

Rhode Island abolished slavery.

1775

Patrick Henry addressed Virginia convention, Mar. 23 said "Give me liberty or give me death."

Paul Revere and William Dawes on night of Apr. 18 rode to alert patriots that British were on way to Concord to destroy arms. At Lexington, Mass. Apr. 19 Minutemen lost 8 killed. On return from Concord British took 273 casualties.

Col. Ethan Allen (joined by Col. Benedict Arnold) captured Ft. Ticonderoga, N.Y. May 10; also Crown Point. Colonials headed for Bunker Hill, fortified Breed's Hill, Charlestown, Mass., repulsed British under Gen. William Howe twice before retreating June 17; British casualties 1,000; called Battle of Bunker Hill. Continental Congress June 15 named George Washington commander-in-chief.

1776

France and Spain each agreed May 2 to provide one million livres in arms to Americans.

In Continental Congress June 7, Richard Henry Lee (Va.) moved "that these united colonies are and of right ought to be free and independent states." Resolution adopted July 2. Declaration of Independence approved July 4.

Col. Moultrie's batteries at Charleston, S.C. repulsed British sea attack June 28.

Washington, with 10,000 men, lost Battle of Long Island Aug. 27, evacuated New York.

Nathan Hale executed as spy by British Sept. 22.

Brig. Gen. Arnold's Lake Champlain fleet was defeated at Valcour Oct. 11, but British returned to Canada. Howe failed to destroy Washington's army at White Plains Oct. 28. Hessians captured Ft. Washington, Manhattan, and 3,000 men Nov. 16; Ft. Lee, N.J. Nov. 18.

Washington in Pennsylvania, recrossed Delaware River Dec. 25-26, defeated 1,400 Hessians at Trenton, N.J. Dec. 26.

1777

Washington defeated Lord Cornwallis at Princeton Jan.

3. Continental Congress adopted Stars and Stripes. See Flag article.

Maj. Gen. John Burgoyne with 8,000 from Canada captured Ft. Ticonderoga July 6. Americans beat back Burgoyne at Bemis Heights Oct. 7 and cut off British escape route. Burgoyne surrendered 5,000 men at Saratoga N.Y. Oct. 17.

Marquis de Lafayette, aged 20, made major general.

Articles of Confederation and Perpetual Union adopted by Continental Congress Nov. 15

France recognized independence of 13 colonies Dec. 17.

1778

France signed treaty of aid with U.S. Feb. 6. Sent fleet; British evacuated Philadelphia in consequence June 18.

1779

John Paul Jones on the Bonhomme Richard defeated Serapis in British North Sea waters Sept. 23.

1780

Charleston, S.C. fell to the British May 12, but a British force was defeated near Kings Mountain, N.C. Oct. 7 by militiamen.

Benedict Arnold found to be a traitor Sept. 23. Arnold escaped, made brigadier general in British army.

1781

Bank of North America incorporated in Philadelphia May 26.

Cornwallis, harrassed by U.S. troops, retired to Yorktown, Va. Adm. De Grasse landed 3,000 French and stopped British fleet in Hampton Roads. Washington and Rochambeau joined forces, arrived near Williamsburg Sept. 26. When siege of Cornwallis began Oct. 6, British had 6,000, Americans 8,846, French 7,800. Cornwallis surrendered Oct. 19.

1782

New British cabinet agreed in March to recognize U.S. independence. Preliminary agreement signed in Paris Nov. 30.

1783

Massachusetts Supreme Court outlawed slavery in that state, noting the words in the state Bill of Rights "all men are born free and equal."

Britain, U.S. signed peace treaty Sept. 3 (Congress ratified it Jan. 14, 1784).

Washington ordered army disbanded Nov. 3, bade farewell to his officers at Fraunces Tavern, N.Y. City Dec. 4.

Noah Webster published American Spelling Book, great bestseller.

1784

First successful daily newspaper, Pennsylvania Packet & General Advertiser, published Sept. 21.

1786

Delegates from 5 states at Annapolis, Md. Sept. 11-14 asked Congress to call convention in Philadelphia to write practical constitution for the 13 states.

1787

Shays's Rebellion, of debt-ridden farmers in Massachusetts, failed Jan. 25.

Northwest Ordinance adopted July 13 by Continental Congress. Determined government of Northwest Territory north of Ohio River, west of New York; 60,000 inhabitants could get statehood. Guaranteed freedom of religion, support for schools, no slavery.

Constitutional convention opened at Philadelphia May 25 with George Washington presiding. Constitution adopted by delegates Sept. 17; ratification by 9th state, New Hampshire, June 21, 1788, meant adoption; declared in effect Mar. 4, 1789.

1789

George Washington chosen president by all electors voting (73 eligible, 69 voting, 4 absent); John Adams, vice president, 34 votes. Feb. 4. First Congress met at Federal Hall, N.Y. City; regular sessions began Apr. 6. Washington inaugurated there Apr. 30. Supreme Court created by Federal Judiciary Act Sept. 24.

1790

Congress met in Philadelphia Dec. 6, new temporary Cap-

ital.

1791
Bill of Rights went into effect **Dec. 15.**

1792
Gen. "Mad" **Anthony Wayne** made commander in Ohio-Indiana area, trained "American Legion"; established string of forts. Routed Indians at Fallen Timbers on Maumee River **Aug. 20, 1794,** checked British at Fort Miami, Ohio.

1793
Eli Whitney invented **cotton gin,** reviving southern slavery.

1794
Whiskey Rebellion, west Pennsylvania farmers protesting liquor tax of 1791, was suppressed by 15,000 militiamen **Sept. 1794.** Alexander Hamilton used incident to establish authority of the new federal government in enforcing its laws.

1795
U.S. bought peace from **Algiers and Tunis** by paying $800,000, supplying a frigate and annual tribute of $25,000 **Nov. 28.**
Gen. **Wayne** signed peace with Indians at Fort Greenville.
Univ. of North Carolina became first operating state university.

1796
Washington's Farewell Address as president delivered **Sept. 19.** Gave strong warnings against permanent alliances with foreign powers, big public debt, large military establishment and devices of "small, artful, enterprising minority" to control or change government.

1797
U.S. frigate **United States** launched at Philadelphia **July 10;** Constellation at **Baltimore Sept. 7;** Constitution (Old Ironsides) at Boston **Sept. 20.**

1798
War with France threatened over French raids on U.S. shipping and rejection of U.S. diplomats. Congress voided all treaties with France, ordered Navy to capture French armed ships. Navy (45 ships) and 365 privateers captured 84 French ships. USS Constellation took French warship Insurgente 1799. Napoleon stopped French raids after becoming First Consul.

1801
Tripoli declared war **June 10** against U.S., which refused added tribute to commerce-raiding Arab corsairs. Land and naval campaigns forced Tripoli to conclude peace **June 4, 1805.**

1803
Supreme Court, in **Marbury v. Madison** case, for the first time overturned a U.S. law **Feb. 24.**
Napoleon, who had recovered **Louisiana** from Spain by secret treaty, sold all of Louisiana, stretching to Canadian border, to U.S., for $11,250,000 in bonds, plus $3,750,000 indemnities to American citizens with claims against France. U.S. took title **Dec. 20.** Purchases doubled U.S. area.

1804
Lewis and Clark expedition ordered by Pres. Jefferson to explore what is now northwest U.S. Started from St. Louis **May 14;** ended **Sept. 23, 1806.** Sacajawea, an Indian woman, served as guide.
Vice Pres. **Aaron Burr,** after long political rivalry, **shot** Alexander Hamilton in a duel **July 11** in Weehawken, N.J.; Hamilton died the next day.

1807
Robert Fulton made first practical steamboat trip; left N.Y. City **Aug. 17,** reached Albany, 150 mi., in 32 hrs.

1808
Slave importation outlawed. Some 250,000 slaves were illegally imported **1808-1860.**

1811
William Henry Harrison, governor of Indiana, defeated Indians under the Prophet, in battle of Tippecanoe **Nov. 7.**
Cumberland Road begun at Cumberland, Md.; became important route to West.

1812
War of 1812 had 3 main causes: Britain seized U.S. ships trading with France; Britain seized 4,000 naturalized U.S. sailors by 1810; Britain armed Indians who raided western border. U.S. stopped trade with Europe 1807 and 1809. Trade with Britain only was stopped, 1810.
Unaware that Britain had raised the blockade 2 days before, **Congress declared war June 18** by a small majority. The West favored war, New England opposed it. The British were handicapped by war with France.
U.S. naval victories in 1812 included: USS Essex captured Alert **Aug. 13;** USS Constitution destroyed Guerriere **Aug. 19;** USS Wasp took Frolic **Oct. 18;** USS United States defeated Macedonian off Azores **Oct. 25;** Constitution beat Java **Dec. 29.** British captured Detroit **Aug. 16.**

1813
Oliver H. Perry defeated British fleet at Battle of Lake Erie, **Sept. 10.** U.S. victory at Battle of the Thames, Ont., **Oct. 5,** broke Indian allies of Britain, and made Detroit frontier safe for U.S. But Americans failed in Canadian invasion attempts. York (Toronto) and Buffalo were burned.

1814
British landed in Maryland in August, defeated U.S. force **Aug. 24,** burned Capitol and White House. Maryland militia stopped British advance **Sept. 12.** Bombardment of Ft. McHenry, Baltimore, for 25 hours, **Sept. 13-14,** by British fleet failed; Francis Scott Key wrote words to **Star Spangled Banner.**
U.S. won naval Battle of Lake Champlain **Sept. 11.** Peace treaty signed at Ghent **Dec. 24.**

1815
Some 5,300 British, unaware of peace treaty, attacked U.S. entrenchments near **New Orleans, Jan. 8.** British had over 2,000 casualties, Americans lost 71.
U.S. flotilla finally ended piracy by **Algiers, Tunis, Tripoli** by **Aug. 6.**

1816
Second Bank of the U.S. chartered.

1817
Rush-Bagot treaty signed **Apr. 28-29;** limited U.S., British armaments on the Great Lakes.

1819
Spain cedes **Florida** to U.S. **Feb. 22.**
American steamship Savannah made first part steam-powered, part sail-powered crossing of Atlantic, Savannah, Ga. to Liverpool, Eng., 29 days.

1820
Henry Clay's **Missouri Compromise** bill passed by Congress **May 3.** Slavery was allowed in Missouri, but not elsewhere west of the Mississippi River north of 36° 30' latitude (the southern line of Missouri). Repealed **1854.**

1821
Emma Willard founded Troy Female Seminary, first U.S. women's college.

1823
Monroe Doctrine enunciated **Dec. 2,** opposing European intervention in the Americas.

1824
Pawtucket, R.I. weavers strike in first such action by women.

1825
Erie Canal opened; first boat left Buffalo **Oct. 26,** reached N.Y. City **Nov. 4.** Canal cost $7 million but cut travel time one-third, shipping costs nine-tenths; opened Great Lakes area, made N.Y. City chief Atlantic port.
John Stevens of Hoboken, N.J., built and operated first experimental steam locomotive in U.S.

1828
South Carolina **Dec. 19** declared the right of state **nullification** of federal laws, opposing the "Tariff of Abominations."
Noah Webster published his *American Dictionary of the English Language.*
Baltimore & Ohio first U.S. passenger railroad, was be-

gun July 4.

1830
Mormon church organized by Joseph Smith in Fayette, N.Y. Apr. 6.

1831
Nat Turner, black slave in Virginia, led local slave rebellion, killed 57 whites in Aug. Troops called in, Turner captured, tried, and hanged.

1832
Black Hawk War (Ill.-Wis.) Apr.-Sept. pushed Sauk and Fox Indians west across Mississippi.

South Carolina convention passed Ordinance of Nullification in Nov. against permanent tariff, threatening to withdraw from the Union. Congress Feb. 1833 passed a compromise tariff act, whereupon South Carolina repealed its act.

1833
Oberlin College, first in U.S. to adopt coeducation; refused to bar students on account of race, 1835.

1835
Texas proclaimed right to secede from Mexico; Sam Houston put in command of Texas army, Nov. 2-4.

Gold discovered on Cherokee land in Georgia. Indians forced to cede lands Dec. 20 and to cross Mississippi.

1836
Texans besieged in Alamo in San Antonio by Mexicans under Santa Anna Feb. 23-Mar. 6; entire garrison killed. Texas independence declared, Mar. 2. At San Jacinto Apr. 21 Sam Houston and Texans defeated Mexicans.

Marcus Whitman, H.H. Spaulding and wives reached Fort Walla Walla on Columbia River, Oregon. First white women to cross plains.

Seminole Indians in Florida under Osceola began attacks Nov. 1, protesting forced removal. The unpopular 8-year war ended Aug. 14, 1842; Indians were sent to Oklahoma. War cost the U.S. 1,500 soldiers.

1841
First emigrant wagon train for California, 47 persons, left Independence, Mo. May 1, reached Cal. Nov. 4.

Brook Farm commune set up by New England transcendentalist intellectuals. Lasts to 1846.

1842
Webster-Ashburton Treaty signed Aug. 9, fixing the U.S.-Canada border in Maine and Minnesota.

First use of anesthetic (sulphuric ether gas).

Settlement of Oregon begins via Oregon Trail.

1844
First message over first telegraph line sent May 24 by inventor Samuel F.B. Morse from Washington to Baltimore: "What hath God wrought!"

1845
Texas Congress voted for annexation to U.S. July 4. U.S. Congress admits Texas to Union Dec. 29.

1846
Mexican War. Pres. James K. Polk ordered Gen. Zachary Taylor to seize disputed Texan land settled by Mexicans. After border clash, U.S. declared war May 13; Mexico May 23. Northern Whigs opposed war, southerners backed it.

Bear flag of Republic of California raised by American settlers at Sonoma June 14.

About 12,000 U.S. troops took Vera Cruz Mar. 27, 1847, Mexico City Sept. 14, 1847. By treaty, Feb. 1848, Mexico ceded claims to Texas, California, Arizona, New Mexico, Nevada, Utah, part of Colorado. U.S. assumed $3 million American claims and paid Mexico $15 million.

Treaty with Great Britain June 15 set boundary in Oregon territory at 49th parallel (extension of existing line). Expansionists had used slogan "54° 40' or fight."

Mormons, after violent clashes with settlers over polygamy, left Nauvoo, Ill. for West under Brigham Young, settled July 1847 at Salt Lake City, Utah.

Elias Howe invented sewing machine.

1847
First adhesive U.S. postage stamps on sale July 1; Benjamin Franklin 5¢, Washington 10¢.

Ralph Waldo Emerson published first book of poems; Henry Wadsworth Longfellow published *Evangeline*.

1848
Gold discovered Jan. 24 in California; 80,000 prospectors emigrate in 1849.

Lucretia Mott and Elizabeth Cady Stanton lead Seneca Falls, N.Y. Women's Rights Convention July 19-20.

1850
Sen. Henry Clay's Compromise of 1850 admitted California as 31st state Sept. 9, slavery forbidden; made Utah and New Mexico territories without decision on slavery; made Fugitive Slave Law more harsh; ended District of Columbia slave trade.

1851
Herman Melville's *Moby Dick*, Nathaniel Hawthorne's *House of the Seven Gables* published.

1852
Uncle Tom's Cabin, by Harriet Beecher Stowe, published.

1853
Commodore Matthew C. Perry, U.S.N., received by Lord of Toda, Japan July 14; negotiated treaty to open Japan to U.S. ships.

1854
Republican party formed at Ripon, Wis. Feb. 28. Opposed Kansas-Nebraska Act (became law May 30) which left issue of slavery to vote of settlers.

Henry David Thoreau published *Walden*.

1855
Walt Whitman published *Leaves of Grass*.

First railroad train crossed Mississippi on the river's first bridge, Rock Island, Ill.-Davenport, Ia. Apr. 21.

1856
Republican party's first nominee for president, John C. Fremont, defeated. Abraham Lincoln made 50 speeches for him.

Lawrence, Kan. sacked May 21 by slavery party; abolitionist John Brown led anti-slavery men against Missourians at Osawatomie, Kan. Aug. 30

1857
Dred Scott decision by U.S. Supreme Court Mar. 6 held, 6-3, that a slave did not become free when taken into a free state, Congress could not bar slavery from a territory, and blacks could not be citizens.

1858
First Atlantic cable completed by Cyrus W. Field Aug. 5; cable failed Sept. 1.

Lincoln-Douglas debates in Illinois Aug. 21-Oct. 15.

1859
First commercially productive oil well, drilled near Titusville, Pa., by Edwin L. Drake Aug. 27.

Abolitionist John Brown with 21 men seized U.S. Armory at Harpers Ferry (then Va.) Oct. 16. U.S. Marines captured raiders, killing several. Brown was hanged for treason by Virginia Dec. 2.

1860
New England shoe-workers, 20,000, strike, win higher wages.

Abraham Lincoln, Republican, elected president in 4-way race.

First Pony Express between Sacramento, Cal. and St. Joseph, Mo. started Apr. 3; service ended Oct. 24, 1861 when first transcontinental telegraph line was completed.

1861
Seven southern states set up Confederate States of America Feb. 8, with Jefferson Davis as president. Confederates fired on Ft. Sumter in Charleston, S.C. Apr. 12, captured it Apr. 14.

President Lincoln called for 75,000 volunteers Apr. 15. By May, 11 states had seceded. Lincoln blockaded southern ports Apr. 19, cutting off vital exports, aid.

Confederates repelled Union forces at first Battle of Bull Run July 21.

First transcontinental telegraph was put in operation.

1862
Homestead Act was approved May 20; it granted free

family farms to settlers.

Land Grant Act approved July 7, providing for public land sale to benefit agricultural education; eventually led to establishment of state university systems.

Union forces were victorious in western campaigns, took New Orleans. Battles in East were inconclusive.

1863

Lincoln issued Emancipation Proclamation Jan. 1, freeing "all slaves in areas still in rebellion."

The entire Mississippi River was in Union hands by July 4. Union forces won a major victory at Gettysburg, Pa. July 1-July 4. Lincoln read his Gettysburg Address Nov. 19.

Draft riots in N.Y. City killed about 1,000, including blacks who were hung by mobs July 13-16. Rioters protested provision allowing money payment in place of service. Such payments were ended 1864.

1864

Gen. Sherman marched through Georgia, taking Atlanta Sept. 1, Savannah Dec. 22.

Sand Creek massacre of Cheyenne and Arapaho Indians Nov. 29 in a raid by 900 cavalrymen who killed 150-500 men, women, and children; 9 soldiers died. The tribes were awaiting surrender terms when attacked.

1865

Robert E. Lee surrendered 27,800 Confederate troops to Grant at Appomattox Court House, Va. Apr. 9. J.E. Johnston surrendered 31,200 to Sherman at Durham Station, N.C. Apr. 18. Last rebel troops surrendered May 26.

President Lincoln was shot Apr. 14 by John Wilkes Booth in Ford's Theater, Washington; died the following morning. Booth was reported dead Apr. 26. Four co-conspirators were hung July 7.

Thirteenth Amendment, abolishing slavery, took effect Dec. 18.

1866

First post of the Grand Army of the Republic formed Apr. 6; was a major national political force for years. Last encampment, Aug. 31, 1949, attended by 6 of the 16 surviving veterans.

Ku Klux Klan formed secretly in South to terrorize blacks who voted. Disbanded 1869-71. A second Klan was organized 1915.

Congress took control of southern Reconstruction, backed freedmen's rights.

1867

Alaska sold to U.S. by Russia for $7.2 million Mar. 30 through efforts of Sec. of State William H. Seward.

Horatio Alger published first book, Ragged Dick.

The Grange was organized Dec 4, to protect farmer interests.

1868

The World Almanac, a publication of the New York World, appeared for the first time.

Pres. Andrew Johnson tried to remove Edwin M. Stanton, secretary of war; was impeached by House Feb. 24 for violation of Tenure of Office Act; acquitted by Senate March-May. Stanton resigned.

1869

Financial "Black Friday" in New York Sept. 24; caused by attempt to "corner" gold.

Transcontinental railroad completed; golden spike driven at Promontory, Utah May 10 marking the junction of Central Pacific and Union Pacific.

Knights of Labor formed in Philadelphia. By 1886, it had 700,000 members nationally.

Woman suffrage law passed in Territory of Wyoming Dec. 10.

1871

Great fire destroyed Chicago Oct. 8-11; loss est. at $196 million.

1872

Amnesty Act restored civil rights to citizens of the South May 22 except for 500 Confederate leaders.

Congress founded first national park — Yellowstone in Wyoming.

1873

First U.S. postal card issued May 1.

Banks failed, panic began in Sept. Depression lasted 5 years.

"Boss" William Tweed of N.Y. City convicted of stealing public funds. He died in jail in 1878.

Bellevue Hospital in N.Y. City started the first school of nursing.

1875

Congress passed Civil Rights Act Mar. 1 giving equal rights to blacks in public accommodations and jury duty. Act invalidated in 1883 by Supreme Court.

First Kentucky Derby held May 17 at Churchill Downs, Louisville, Ky.

1876

Samuel J. Tilden, Democrat, received majority of popular votes for president over Rutherford B. Hayes, Republican, but 22 electoral votes were in dispute; issue left to Congress. Hayes given presidency in Feb., 1877 after Republicans agree to end Reconstruction of South.

Col. George A. Custer and 264 soldiers of the 7th Cavalry killed June 25 in "last stand," Battle of the Little Big Horn, Mont., in Sioux Indian War.

Mark Twain published Tom Sawyer.

1877

Molly Maguires, Irish terrorist society in Scranton, Pa. mining areas, broken up by hanging of 11 leaders for murders of mine officials and police.

Pres. Hayes sent troops in violent national railroad strike.

1878

First commercial telephone exchange opened, New Haven, Conn. Jan. 28.

1879

F.W. Woolworth opened his first five-and-ten store in Utica, N.Y. Feb. 22.

Henry George published Progress & Poverty, advocating single tax on land.

1881

Pres. James A. Garfield shot in Washington, D.C. July 2; died Sept. 19.

Booker T. Washington founded Tuskegee Institute for blacks.

Helen Hunt Jackson published A Century of Dishonor about mistreatment of Indians.

1883

Pendleton Act, passed Jan. 16, reformed federal civil service.

Brooklyn Bridge opened May 24.

1886

Haymarket riot and bombing, evening of May 4, followed bitter labor battles for 8-hour day in Chicago; 7 police and 4 workers died, 66 wounded. Eight anarchists found guilty. Gov. John P. Altgeld denounced trial as unfair.

Geronimo, Apache Indian, finally surrendered Sept. 4.

American Federation of Labor (AFL) formed Dec. 8 by 25 craft unions.

1888

Great blizzard in eastern U.S. Mar. 11-14; 400 deaths.

1889

Johnstown, Pa. flood May 31; 2,200 lives lost.

1890

First execution by electrocution: William Kemmler Aug. 6 at Auburn Prison, Auburn, N.Y., for murder.

Battle of Wounded Knee, S.D. Dec. 29, the last major conflict between Indians and U.S. troops. About 200 Indian men, women, and children, and 29 soldiers were killed.

Castle Garden closed as N.Y. immigration depot; Ellis Island opened Dec. 31, closed 1954.

Sherman Antitrust Act begins federal effort to curb monopolies.

Jacob Riis published How the Other Half Lives, about city slums.

1892

Homestead, Pa., strike at Carnegie steel mills; 7 guards and 11 strikers and spectators shot to death July 6; setback for unions.

1893

Financial panic began, led to 4-year depression.

1894

Thomas A. Edison's kinetoscope (motion pictures) (invented **1887**) given first public showing **Apr. 14** in N.Y. City.

Jacob S. Coxey led 500 unemployed from the Midwest into Washington, D.C. **Apr. 29.** Coxey was arrested for trespassing on Capitol grounds.

1896

William Jennings Bryan delivered "Cross of Gold" speech at Democratic National Convention in Chicago **July 8.**

Supreme Court, in **Plessy v. Ferguson,** approved racial segregation under the "separate but equal" doctrine.

1898

U.S. battleship Maine blown up **Feb. 15** at Havana, 260 killed.

U.S. blockaded Cuba **Apr. 22** in aid of independence forces. Spain declared war **Apr. 24.** U.S. destroyed Spanish fleet in Philippines **May 1,** took Guam **June 20.**

Puerto Rico taken by U.S. **July 25-Aug. 12.** Spain agreed **Dec. 10** to cede Philippines, Puerto Rico, and Guam, and approved independence for Cuba.

U.S. annexed independent republic of **Hawaii.**

1899

Filipino insurgents, unable to get recognition of independence from U.S., started guerrilla war **Feb. 4.** Crushed with capture **May 23, 1901** of leader, Emilio Aguinaldo.

U.S. declared **Open Door Policy** to make China an open international market and to preserve its integrity as a nation.

John Dewey published *School and Society,* backing progressive education.

1900

Carry Nation, Kansas anti-saloon agitator, began raiding with hatchet.

U.S. helped suppress **"Boxers"** in Peking.

1901

Pres. William McKinley was shot **Sept. 6** by an anarchist, Leon Czolgosz; died **Sept. 14.**

1903

Treaty between U.S. and Colombia to have U.S. dig **Panama Canal** signed **Jan. 22,** rejected by Colombia. Panama declared independence with U.S. support **Nov. 3;** recognized by Pres. Theodore Roosevelt **Nov. 6.** U.S., Panama signed canal treaty **Nov. 18.**

Wisconsin set first **direct primary** voting system **May 23.**

First **automobile trip** across U.S. from San Francisco to New York **May 23-Aug. 1.**

First successful flight in heavier-than-air mechanically propelled airplane by **Orville Wright Dec. 17** near Kitty Hawk, N.C., 120 ft. in 12 seconds. Fourth flight same day by **Wilbur Wright,** 852 ft. in 59 seconds. Improved plane patented **May 22, 1906.**

Jack London published *Call of the Wild.*

Great Train Robbery, pioneering film, produced.

1904

Ida Tarbell published muckraking *History of Standard Oil.*

1905

First **Rotary Club** of local businessmen founded in Chicago.

1906

San Francisco earthquake and fire **Apr. 18-19** left 452 dead, $350 million damages.

Pure Food and Drug Act and Meat Inspection Act both passed **June 30.**

1907

Financial panic and depression started **Mar. 13.**

First round-world cruise of U.S. **"Great White Fleet";** 16 battleships, 12,000 men.

1909

Adm. Robert E. Peary reached **North Pole Apr. 6** on 6th attempt, accompanied by Matthew Henson, a black man, and 4 Eskimos.

National Conference on the Negro convened **May 30,** leading to founding of the National Association for the Advancement of Colored People.

1910

Boy Scouts of America founded **Feb. 8.**

1911

Supreme Court dissolved **Standard Oil Co.**

First **transcontinental airplane flight** (with numerous stops) by C.P. Rodgers, New York to Pasadena, **Sept. 17-Nov. 5;** time in air 82 hrs., 4 min.

1912

U.S. sent marines **Aug. 14** to **Nicaragua,** which was in default of loans to U.S. and Europe.

1913

N.Y. **Armory Show** introduced modern art to U.S. public **Feb. 17.**

U.S. blockaded Mexico in support of revolutionaries.

Charles Beard published his *Economic Interpretation of the Constitution.*

Federal Reserve System was authorized **Dec. 23,** in a major reform of U.S. banking and finance.

1914

Ford Motor Co. raised basic wage rates from $2.40 for 9-hr. day to $5 for 8-hr. day **Jan. 5.**

When U.S. sailors were arrested at Tampico **Apr. 9,** Atlantic fleet was sent to **Veracruz,** occupied city.

Pres. Wilson proclaimed **U.S. neutrality** in the European war **Aug. 4.**

The **Clayton Antitrust Act** was passed **Oct. 15,** strengthening federal anti-monopoly powers.

1915

First **telephone talk,** New York to San Francisco, **Jan. 25** by Alexander Graham Bell and Thomas A. Watson.

British ship **Lusitania** sunk **May 7** by German submarine; 128 American passengers lost (Germany had warned passengers in advance). As a result of U.S. campaign, Germany issued apology and promise of payments **Oct. 5.** Pres. Wilson asked for a military fund increase **Dec. 7.**

U.S. troops landed in **Haiti July 28.** Haiti became a virtual U.S. protectorate under **Sept. 16** treaty.

1916

Gen. John J. **Pershing entered Mexico** to pursue Francisco (Pancho) Villa, who had raided U.S. border areas. Forces withdrawn **Feb. 5, 1917.**

Rural Credits Act passed **July 17,** followed by Warehouse Act. **Aug. 11;** both provided financial aid to farmers.

Bomb exploded during **San Francisco** Preparedness Day parade **July 22,** killed 10. Thomas J. Mooney, labor organizer, and Warren K. Billings, shoe worker, were convicted; both pardoned in **1939.**

U.S. bought **Virgin Islands** from Denmark **Aug. 4.**

U.S. established military government in the **Dominican Republic Nov. 29.**

Trade and loans to European Allies soared during the year.

John Dewey published *Democracy in Education.*

Carl Sandburg published *Chicago Poems.*

1917

Germany, suffering from British blockade, declared almost unrestricted submarine warfare **Jan. 31.** U.S. cut diplomatic ties with Germany **Feb. 3,** and formally declared war **Apr. 6.**

Conscription law was passed **May 18.** First U.S. troops arrived in Europe **June 26.**

The 18th (**Prohibition**) Amendment to the Constitution was submitted to the states by Congress **Dec. 18.** On **Jan. 16, 1919,** the 36th state (Nebraska) ratified it. Franklin D. Roosevelt, as 1932 presidential candidate, endorsed repeal; 21st Amendment repealed 18th; ratification completed **Dec. 5, 1933.**

1918

Over one million **American troops** were in Europe by July. War ended Nov. 11.

Influenza epidemic killed an estimated 20 million worldwide, 548,000 in U.S.

1919

First **transatlantic flight**, by U.S. Navy seaplane, left Rockaway, N.Y. May 8, stopped at Newfoundland, Azores, Lisbon May 27.

Boston police strike Sept. 9; National Guard breaks strike.

Sherwood Anderson published *Winesburg, Ohio.*

About 250 alien radicals were deported Dec. 22.

1920

In national **Red Scare**, some 2,700 Communists, anarchists, and other radicals were arrested Jan.-May.

Senate refused Mar. 19 to ratify the League of Nations Covenant.

Nicola Sacco, 29, shoe factory employee and radical agitator, and **Bartolomeo Vanzetti**, 32, fish peddler and anarchist, accused of killing 2 men in Mass. payroll holdup **Apr. 15**. Found guilty **1921**. A 6-year worldwide campaign for release on grounds of want of conclusive evidence and prejudice failed. Both were executed **Aug. 23, 1927.** Vindicated July 19, 1977 by proclamation of Mass. Gov. Dukakis.

First regular licensed **radio** broadcasting begun **Aug. 20.**

Wall St., N.Y. City, bomb explosion killed 30, injured 100, did $2 million damage **Sept. 16.**

Sinclair Lewis' *Main Street,* F. Scott Fitzgerald's *This Side of Paradise* published.

1921

Congress sharply curbed **immigration,** set national quota system **May 19.**

Joint Congressional resolution declaring **peace with Germany, Austria, and Hungary** signed **July 2** by Pres. Harding; treaties were signed in Aug.

Limitation of Armaments Conference met in Washington **Nov. 12 to Feb. 6, 1922.** Major powers agreed to curtail naval construction, outlaw poison gas, restrict submarine attack on merchantmen, respect integrity of China. Ratified **Aug. 5, 1925.**

Ku Klux Klan began revival with violence against blacks in North, South, and Midwest.

1922

Violence during **coal-mine** strike at Herrin, Ill., **June 22-23** cost 36 lives, 21 of them non-union miners.

Reader's Digest founded.

1923

First **sound-on-film motion picture,** "Phonofilm" was shown by Lee de Forest at Rivoli Theater, N.Y. City, beginning in **April.**

1924

Law approved by Congress **June 15** making all **Indians** citizens.

Nellie Tayloe Ross elected governor of Wyoming **Nov. 9** after death of her husband **Oct. 2**; installed **Jan. 5, 1925,** first woman governor. Miriam (Ma) Ferguson was elected governor of Texas **Nov. 9**; installed **Jan. 20, 1925.**

George Gershwin wrote *Rhapsody in Blue.*

1925

John T. Scopes found guilty of having taught evolution in Dayton, Tenn. high school, fined $100 and costs **July 24.**

1926

Dr. **Robert H. Goddard** demonstrated practicality of rockets **Mar. 16** at Auburn, Mass. with first liquid fuel rocket; rocket traveled 184 ft. in 2.5 secs.

Air Commerce Act passed, providing federal aid for airlines and airports.

1927

About 1,000 **marines** landed in **China Mar. 5** to protect property in civil war. U.S. and British consulates looted by nationalists **Mar. 24.**

Capt. **Charles A. Lindbergh** left Roosevelt Field, N.Y. **May 20** alone in plane Spirit of St. Louis on first New York-

Paris nonstop flight. Reached Le Bourget airfield **May 21,** 3,610 miles in 33 ½ hours.

The Jazz Singer, with Al Jolson, demonstrated part-talking pictures in N.Y. City **Oct. 6.**

Show Boat opened in New York **Dec. 27.**

O. E. Rolvaag published *Giants in the Earth.*

1929

"St. Valentine's Day massacre" in Chicago **Feb. 14;** gangsters killed 7 rivals.

Farm price stability aided by **Agricultural Marketing Act,** passed **June 15.**

Albert B. Fall, former sec. of the interior, was convicted of accepting a bribe of $100,000 in the leasing of the **Elk Hills (Teapot Dome)** naval oil reserve; sentenced Nov. 1 to $100,000 fine and year in prison.

Stock Market crash Oct. 29 marked end of postwar prosperity as stock prices plummeted. Stock losses for 1929-31 estimated at $50 billion; worst American depression began.

Thomas Wolfe published *Look Homeward, Angel.* William Faulkner published *The Sound and the Fury.*

1930

London Naval Reduction Treaty signed by U.S., Britain, Italy, France, and Japan **Apr. 22;** in effect **Jan. 1, 1931;** expired **Dec. 31, 1936.**

Hawley-Smoot Tariff signed; rate hikes slash world trade.

1931

Empire State Building opened in N.Y. City **May 1.**

Pearl Buck published *The Good Earth.*

1932

Reconstruction Finance Corp. established **Jan. 22** to stimulate banking and business. Unemployment stood at 12 million.

Charles Lindbergh Jr. kidnaped Mar. 1, found dead **May 12.**

Bonus March on Washington **May 29** by World War I veterans demanding Congress pay their bonus in full. Army, under Gen. Douglas MacArthur, disbanded the marchers on Pres. Hoover's orders.

1933

All banks in the U.S. were ordered closed by Pres. Roosevelt **Mar. 6.**

In the "100 days" special session, **Mar. 9—June 16,** Congress passed New Deal social and economic measures.

Gold standard dropped by U.S.; announced by Pres. Roosevelt **Apr. 19,** ratified by Congress **June 5.**

Prohibition ended in the U.S. as 36th state ratified 21st Amendment **Dec. 5.**

U.S. foreswore armed intervention in **Western Hemisphere** nations **Dec. 26.**

1934

U.S. troops pull out of **Haiti Aug. 6.**

1935

Comedian **Will Rogers** and aviator Wiley Post killed **Aug. 15** in Alaska plane crash.

Social Security Act passed by Congress **Aug. 14.**

Huey Long, Senator from Louisiana and national political leader, was assassinated **Sept. 8.**

Porgy and Bess, George Gershwin opera on American theme, opened **Oct. 10** in N.Y. City.

Committee for Industrial Organization (CIO) formed to expand industrial unionism **Nov. 9.**

1936

Boulder Dam completed.

Margaret Mitchell published *Gone With the Wind.*

1937

Amelia Earhart Putnam, aviator, and co-pilot Fred Noonan lost **July 2** near Howland Is. in the Pacific.

Pres. Roosevelt asked for 6 additional Supreme Court justices; "packing" plan defeated.

Auto, steel labor unions won first big contracts.

1938

Naval Expansion Act passed **May 17.**

National minimum wage enacted **June 28.**

Orson Welles radio dramatization of *War of the Worlds* caused nationwide scare **Oct. 30.**

1939

Pres. Roosevelt asked defense budget hike Jan. 5, 12.

N.Y. World's Fair opened Apr. 30, closed Oct. 31; reopened May 11, 1940, and finally closed Oct. 21.

Einstein alerts FDR to A-bomb opportunity in Aug. 2 letter.

U.S. declares its neutrality in European war Sept. 5.

Roosevelt proclaimed a limited national emergency Sept. 8, an unlimited emergency May 27, 1941. Both ended by Pres. Truman Apr. 28, 1952.

John Steinbeck published Grapes of Wrath.

1940

U.S. authorized sale of surplus war material to Britain June 3; announced transfer of 50 overaged destroyers Sept. 3.

First peacetime draft approved Sept. 14.

Richard Wright published Native Son.

1941

The Four Freedoms termed essential by Pres. Roosevelt in speech to Congress Jan. 6; freedom of speech and religion, freedom from want and fear.

Lend-Lease Act signed Mar. 11, providing $7 billion in military credits for Britain. Lend-Lease for USSR approved in Nov.

U.S. occupied Iceland July 7.

The Atlantic Charter, 8-point declaration of principles, issued by Roosevelt and Winston Churchill Aug. 14.

Japan attacked Pearl Harbor, Hawaii, 7:55 a.m. Dec. 7, 19 ships sunk or damaged, 2,300 dead. U.S. declared war on Japan Dec. 8, on Germany and Italy Dec. 11 after those countries declared war.

1942

Federal government forcibly moved 110,000 Japanese-Americans (including 75,000 U.S. citizens) from West Coast to detention camps. Exclusion lasted 3 years.

Battle of Midway June 3-6 was Japan's first major defeat.

Marines landed on Guadalcanal Aug. 7; last Japanese not expelled until Feb. 9, 1943.

U.S., Britain invaded North Africa Nov. 8.

First nuclear chain reaction (fission of uranium isotope U-235) produced at Univ. of Chicago, under physicists Arthur Compton, Enrico Fermi, others Dec. 2.

1943

All war contractors barred from racial discrimination May 27.

Pres. Roosevelt signed June 10 the pay-as-you-go income tax bill. Starting July 1 wage and salary earners were subject to a paycheck withholding tax.

Race riot in Detroit June 21; 34 dead, 700 injured. Riot in Harlem section of N.Y. City; 6 killed.

U.S. troops invaded Italy Sept. 9.

Marines advanced in Gilbert Is. in Nov.

1944

U.S., Allied forces invaded Europe at Normandy June 6.

G.I. Bill of Rights signed June 22, providing veterans benefits.

U.S. forces landed on Leyte, Philippines Oct. 20.

1945

Yalta Conference met in the Crimea, USSR, Feb. 3-11. Roosevelt, Churchill, and Stalin agreed Russia would enter war against Japan.

Marines landed on Iwo Jima Feb. 19; U.S. forces invaded Okinawa Apr. 1.

Pres. Roosevelt, 63, died of cerebral hemorrhage in Warm Springs, Ga. Apr. 12.

Germany surrendered May 7.

First atomic bomb, produced at Los Alamos, N.M., exploded at Alamogordo, N.M. July 16. Bomb dropped on Hiroshima Aug. 6, on Nagasaki Aug. 9. Japan surrendered Aug. 15.

U.S. forces entered Korea south of 38th parallel to displace Japanese Sept. 8.

Gen. Douglas MacArthur took over supervision of Japan Sept. 9.

1946

Strike by 400,000 mine workers began Apr. 1; other industries followed.

Philippines given independence by U.S. July 4.

1947

Truman Doctrine: Pres. Truman asked Congress to aid Greece and Turkey to combat Communist terrorism Mar. 12. Approved May 15.

United Nations Security Council voted unanimously Apr. 2 to place under U.S. trusteeship the Pacific islands formerly mandated to Japan.

Jackie Robinson on Brooklyn Dodgers Apr. 11, broke the color barrier in major league baseball.

Taft-Hartley Labor Act curbing strikes was vetoed by Truman June 20; Congress overrode the veto.

Proposals later known as the Marshall Plan, under which the U.S. would extend aid to European countries, were made by Sec. of State George C. Marshall June 5. Congress authorized some $12 billion in next 4 years.

1948

USSR began a land blockade of Berlin's Allied sectors Apr. 1. This blockade and Western counter-blockade were lifted Sept. 30, 1949, after British and U.S. planes had lifted 2,343,315 tons of food and coal into the city.

Organization of American States founded Apr. 30.

Alger Hiss, former State Dept. official, indicted Dec. 15 for perjury, after denying he had passed secret documents to Whittaker Chambers for transmission to a communist spy ring. His second trial ended in conviction Jan. 21, 1950, and a sentence of 5 years in prison.

Kinsey Report on Sexuality in the Human Male published.

1949

U.S. troops withdrawn from Korea June 29.

North Atlantic Treaty Organization (NATO) established Aug. 24 by U.S., Canada, and 10 West European nations, agreeing that "an armed attack against one or more of them in Europe and North America shall be considered an attack against all."

Mrs. I. Toguri D'Aquino (Tokyo Rose of Japanese wartime broadcasts) was sentenced Oct. 7 to 10 years in prison for treason. Paroled 1956, pardoned 1977.

Eleven leaders of U.S. Communist party convicted Oct. 14, after 9-month trial in N.Y. City, of advocating violent overthrow of U.S. government. Ten defendants sentenced to 5 years in prison each and the 11th, to 3 years. Supreme Court upheld the convictions June 4, 1951.

1950

U.S. Jan 14 recalled all consular officials from China after the latter seized the American consulate general in Peking.

Masked bandits robbed Brink's Inc., Boston express office, Jan. 17 of $2.8 million, of which $1.2 million was in cash. Case solved 1956, 8 sentenced to life.

Pres. Truman authorized production of H-bomb Jan. 31.

United Nations asked for troops to restore Korea peace June 25.

Truman ordered Air Force and Navy to Korea June 27 after North Korea invaded South. Truman approved ground forces, air strikes against North June 30.

U.S. sent 35 military advisers to South Vietnam June 27, and agreed to provide military and economic aid to anti-Communist government.

Army seized all railroads Aug. 27 on Truman's order to prevent a general strike; roads returned to owners in 1952.

U.S. forces landed at Inchon Sept. 15; UN force took Pyongyang Oct. 20, reached China border Nov. 20, China sent troops across border Nov. 26.

Two members of a **Puerto Rican nationalist** movement tried to kill Pres. Truman **Nov. 1.** (see Assassinations)

U.S. Dec. 8 banned shipments to **Communist China** and to Asiatic ports trading with it.

1951

Sen. **Estes Kefauver** led Senate investigation into organized crime. Preliminary report **Feb. 28** said gambling take was over $20 billion a year.

Julius Rosenberg, his wife, Ethel, and Morton Sobell, all U.S. citizens, were found guilty **Mar. 29** of conspiracy to commit wartime espionage. Rosenbergs sentenced to death, Sobell to 30 years. Rosenbergs **executed June 19, 1953.** Sobell released Jan. 14, 1969.

Gen. **Douglas MacArthur** was removed from his Korea command **Apr. 11** for making unauthorized policy statements.

Korea cease-fire talks began in July; lasted 2 years. Fighting ended **July 27, 1953.**

Tariff concessions by the U.S. to the Soviet Union, Communist China, and all communist-dominated lands were suspended **Aug. 1.**

The U.S., **Australia,** and **New Zealand** signed a mutual security pact **Sept. 1.**

Transcontinental television inaugurated **Sept. 4** with Pres. Truman's address at the Japanese Peace Treaty Conference in San Francisco.

Japanese Peace Treaty signed in San Francisco **Sept. 8** by U.S., Japan, and 47 other nations.

J.D. Salinger published *Catcher in the Rye.*

1952

U.S. seizure of nation's steel mills was ordered by Pres. Truman **Apr. 8** to avert a strike. Ruled illegal by Supreme Court **June 2.**

Peace contract between West Germany, U.S., Great Britain, and France was signed **May 26.**

The last racial and ethnic barriers to naturalization were removed, **June 26-27,** with the passage of the **Immigration and Naturalization Act of 1952.**

First hydrogen device explosion **Nov. 1** at Eniwetok Atoll in Pacific.

1953

Pres. Eisenhower announced **May 8** that U.S. had given France $60 million for **Indochina War.** More aid was announced in **Sept.** In **1954** it was reported that three fourths of the war's costs were met by U.S.

1954

Nautilus, first atomic-powered submarine, was launched at Groton, Conn. **Jan. 21.**

Five members of Congress were wounded in the House **Mar. 1** by 4 **Puerto Rican independence supporters** who fired at random from a spectators' gallery.

Sen. **Joseph McCarthy** led televised hearings **Apr. 22-June 17** into alleged Communist influence in the Army.

Racial segregation in public schools was unanimously ruled unconstitutional by the Supreme Court **May 17,** as a violation of the 14th Amendment clause guaranteeing equal protection of the laws.

Southeast Asia Treaty Organization **(SEATO)** formed by collective defense pact signed in Manila **Sept. 8** by the U.S., Britain, France, Australia, New Zealand, Philippines, Pakistan, and Thailand.

Condemnation of Sen. **Joseph R. McCarthy** (R., Wis.) voted by Senate, 67-22 **Dec. 2** for contempt of a Senate elections subcommittee, for abuse of its members, and for insults to the Senate during his Army investigation hearings.

1955

U.S. agreed Feb. 12 to help train **South Vietnamese** army.

Supreme Court ordered **"all deliberate speed"** in integration of public schools **May 31.**

A summit meeting of leaders of U.S., Britain, France, and USSR took place **July 18-23** in Geneva, Switzerland.

Rosa Parks refused **Dec. 1** to give her seat to a white man on a bus in Montgomery, Ala. Bus segregation ordinance

declared unconstitutional by a federal court following boycott and NAACP protest.

Merger of America's 2 largest labor organizations was effected **Dec. 5** under the name American Federation of Labor and Congress of Industrial Organizations. The merged **AFL-CIO** had a membership estimated at 15 million.

1956

Massive resistance to Supreme Court desegregation rulings was called for **Mar. 12** by 101 Southern congressmen.

Federal-Aid Highway Act signed **June 29,** inaugurating interstate highway system.

First transatlantic telephone cable went into operation **Sept. 25.**

1957

Congress approved first **civil rights bill** for blacks since Reconstruction **Apr. 29,** to protect voting rights.

National Guardsmen, called out by Arkansas Gov. Orval Faubus **Sept. 4,** barred 9 black students from entering previously all-white Central High School in **Little Rock.** Faubus complied **Sept. 21** with a federal court order to remove the National Guardsmen. The blacks entered school **Sept. 23** but were ordered to withdraw by local authorities because of fear of mob violence. Pres. Eisenhower sent federal troops **Sept. 24** to enforce the court's order.

Jack Kerouac published *On the Road,* beatnik journal.

1958

First U.S. earth satellite to go into orbit, **Explorer I,** launched by Army **Jan. 31** at Cape Canaveral, Fla.; discovered Van Allen radiation belt.

Five thousand U.S. Marines sent to **Lebanon** to protect elected government from threatened overthrow **July-Oct.**

First domestic **jet airline** passenger service in U.S. opened by National Airlines **Dec. 10** between New York and Miami.

1959

Alaska admitted as 49th state **Jan. 3; Hawaii** admitted **Aug. 21.**

St. Lawrence Seaway opened **Apr. 25.**

The George Washington, first U.S. ballistic-missile submarine, launched at Groton, Conn. **June 9.**

N.S. Savannah, world's first atomic-powered merchant ship, launched **July 21** at Camden, N.J.

Soviet Premier **Khrushchev** paid unprecedented visit to U.S. **Sept. 15-27,** made transcontinental tour.

1960

A wave of **sit-ins** began **Feb. 1** when 4 black college students in Greensboro, N.C. refused to move from a Woolworth lunch counter when they were denied service. By **Sept. 1961** more than 70,000 students, whites and blacks, had participated in sit-ins.

U.S. launched first **weather satellite,** Tiros I, **Apr. 1.**

Congress approved a strong **voting rights act Apr. 21.**

A **U-2 reconnaisance plane** of the U.S. was shot down in the Soviet Union **May 1.** The incident led to cancellation of an imminent Paris summit conference.

Mobs attacked U.S. embassy in **Panama Sept. 17** in dispute over flying of U.S. and Panamanian flags.

U.S. announced **Dec. 15** it backed rightist group in Laos, which took power the next day.

1961

The U.S. severed diplomatic and consular relations with **Cuba Jan. 3,** after disputes over nationalizations of U.S. firms, U.S. military presence at Guantanamo base, etc.

Invasion of Cuba's **"Bay of Pigs" Apr. 17** by Cuban exiles trained, armed, and directed by the U.S., attempting to overthrow the regime of Premier Fidel Castro, was repulsed.

Commander Alan B. Shepard Jr. was rocketed from Cape Canaveral, Fla., 116.5 mi. above the earth in a Mercury capsule **May 5** in the first U.S. manned sub-orbital space flight.

1962

Lt. Col. John H. Glenn Jr. became the first American in orbit **Feb. 20** when he circled the earth 3 times in the Mercury capsule **Friendship 7.**

Pres. Kennedy said Feb. 14 U.S. military advisers in Vietnam would fire if fired upon.

Supreme Court Mar. 26 backed one-man one-vote apportionment of seats in state legislatures.

First U.S. communications satellite launched in July.

James Meredith became first black student at Univ. of Mississippi Oct. 1 after 3,000 troops put down riots.

A Soviet offensive missile buildup in Cuba was revealed Oct. 22 by Pres. Kennedy, who ordered a naval and air quarantine on shipment of offensive military equipment to the island. Kennedy and Soviet Premier Khrushchev reached agreement Oct. 28 on a formula to end the crisis. Kennedy announced Nov. 2 that Soviet missile bases in Cuba were being dismantled.

Rachel Carson's *Silent Spring* launched environmentalist movement.

1963

Supreme Court ruled Mar. 18 that all criminal defendants must have counsel and that illegally acquired evidence was not admissible in state as well as federal courts.

Supreme Court ruled, 8-1, June 17 that laws requiring recitation of the Lord's Prayer or Bible verses in public schools were unconstitutional.

A limited nuclear test-ban treaty was agreed upon July 25 by the U.S., Soviet Union and Britain, barring all nuclear tests except underground.

Washington demonstration by 200,000 persons Aug. 28 in support of black demands for equal rights. Highlight was speech in which Dr. Martin Luther King said: "I have a dream that this nation will rise up and live out the true meaning of its creed, 'We hold these truths to be self-evident: that all men are created equal.' "

South Vietnam Pres. Ngo Dinh Diem assassinated Nov. 2; U.S. had earlier withdrawn support.

Pres. John F. Kennedy was shot and fatally wounded by an assassin Nov. 22 as he rode in a motorcade through downtown Dallas, Tex. Vice Pres. Lyndon B. Johnson was inaugurated president shortly after in Dallas. Lee Harvey Oswald was arrested and charged with the murder. Oswald was shot and fatally wounded Nov. 24 by Jack Ruby, 52, a Dallas nightclub owner, who was convicted of murder Mar. 14, 1964 and sentenced to death. Ruby died of natural causes Jan. 3, 1967 while awaiting retrial.

U.S. troops in Vietnam totalled over 15,000 by year-end; aid to South Vietnam was over $500 million in 1963.

1964

Panama suspended relations with U.S. Jan. 9 after riots. U.S. offered Dec. 18 to negotiate a new canal treaty.

Supreme Court ordered Feb. 17 that congressional districts have equal populations.

U.S. reported May 27 it was sending military planes to Laos.

Omnibus civil rights bill passed June 29 banning discrimination in voting, jobs, public accommodations, etc.

Three civil rights workers were reported missing in Mississippi June 22; found buried Aug. 4. Twenty-one white men were arrested. On Oct. 20, 1967, an all-white federal jury convicted 7 of conspiracy in the slayings.

U.S. Congress Aug. 7 passed Tonkin Resolution, authorizing presidential action in Vietnam, after North Vietnam boats reportedly attacked 2 U.S. destroyers Aug. 2.

Congress approved War on Poverty bill Aug. 11.

The Warren Commission released Sept. 27 a report concluding that Lee Harvey Oswald was solely responsible for the Kennedy assassination.

1965

Pres. Johnson in Feb. ordered continuous bombing of North Vietnam below 20th parallel.

Some 14,000 U.S. troops sent to Dominican Republic during civil war Apr. 28. All troops withdrawn by following year.

New Voting Rights Act signed Aug. 6.

Los Angeles riot by blacks living in Watts area resulted in death of 35 persons and property damage est. at $200 million Aug. 11-16.

Water Quality Act passed Sept. 21 to meet pollution, shortage problems.

National origins quota system of immigration abolished Oct. 3.

Massive electric power failure blacked out most of northeastern U.S, parts of 2 Canadian provinces the night of Nov. 9-10.

U.S. forces in South Vietnam reached 184,300 by year-end.

1966

U.S. forces began firing into Cambodia May 1.

Bombing of Hanoi area of North Vietnam by U.S. planes began June 29. By Dec. 31, 385,300 U.S. troops were stationed in South Vietnam, plus 60,000 offshore and 33,000 in Thailand.

Medicare, government program to pay part of the medical expenses of citizens over 65, began July 1.

Edward Brooke (R, Mass.) elected Nov. 8 as first black U.S. senator in 85 years.

1967

Black representative Adam Clayton Powell (D, N.Y.) was denied Mar. 1 his seat in Congress because of charges he misused government funds. Reelected in 1968, he was seated, but fined $25,000 and stripped of his 22 years' seniority.

Pres. Johnson and Soviet Premier Aleksei Kosygin met June 23 and 25 at Glassboro State College in N.J.; agreed not to let any crisis push them into war.

Black riots in Newark, N.J. July 12-17 killed some 26, injured 1,500; over 1,000 arrested. In Detroit, Mich., July 23-30 at least 40 died; 2,000 injured, and 5,000 left homeless by rioting, looting, burning in city's black ghetto. Quelled by 4,700 federal paratroopers and 8,000 National Guardsmen.

Thurgood Marshall sworn in Oct. 2 as first black U.S. Supreme Court Justice. Carl B. Stokes (D, Cleveland) and Richard G. Hatcher (D, Gary, Ind.) were elected first black mayors of major U.S. cities Nov. 7.

By December 475,000 U.S. troops were in South Vietnam, all North Vietnam was subject to bombing. Protests against the war mounted in U.S. during year.

1968

USS Pueblo and 83-man crew seized in Sea of Japan Jan. 23 by North Koreans; 82 men released Dec. 22.

"Tet offensive": Communist troops attacked Saigon, 30 province capitals Jan. 30, suffer heavy casualties.

Pres. Johnson curbed bombing of North Vietnam Mar. 31. Peace talks began in Paris May 10. All bombing of North is halted Oct. 31.

Martin Luther King Jr., 39, assassinated Apr. 4 in Memphis, Tenn. James Earl Ray, an escaped convict, pleaded guilty to the slaying, was sentenced to 99 years.

Sen. Robert F. Kennedy (D, N.Y.) 42, shot June 5 in Hotel Ambassador, Los Angeles, after celebrating presidential primary victories. Died June 6. Sirhan Bishara Sirhan, Jordanian, convicted of murder.

1969

Expanded four-party Vietnam peace talks began Jan. 18. U.S. force peaked at 543,400 in April. Withdrawal started July 8. Pres. Nixon set Vietnamization policy Nov. 3.

A car driven by Sen. Edward M. Kennedy (D, Mass.) plunged off a bridge into a tidal pool on Chappaquiddick Is., Martha's Vineyard, Mass. July 18. The body of Mary Jo Kopechne, a 28-year-old secretary, was found drowned in the car.

U.S. astronaut Neil A. Armstrong, 38, commander of the Apollo 11 mission, became the first man to set foot on the moon July 20. Air Force Col. Edwin E. Aldrin Jr. accompanied Armstrong.

Anti-Vietnam War demonstrations reached peak in U.S.; some 250,000 marched in Washington, D.C. Nov. 15.

Massacre of hundreds of civilians at Mylai, South Vietnam in 1968 incident was reported Nov. 16.

1970

United Mine Workers official **Joseph A. Yablonski**, his wife, and their daughter were found shot **Jan. 5** in their Clarksville, Pa. home. UMW chief W. A. (Tony) Boyle was later convicted of the killing.

A federal jury **Feb. 18** found the defendants in the "Chicago 7" trial innocent of conspiring to incite riots during the 1968 Democratic National Convention. However, 5 were convicted of crossing state lines with intent to incite riots.

Millions of Americans participated in anti-pollution demonstrations **Apr. 22** to mark the first **Earth Day.**

U.S. and South Vietnamese forces crossed **Cambodian** borders **Apr. 30** to get at enemy bases. Four students were killed **May 4** at Kent St. Univ. in Ohio by National Guardsmen during a protest against the war.

Two **women** generals, the first in U.S. history, were named by Pres. Nixon **May 15.**

A **postal reform** measure was signed **Aug. 12,** creating an independent U.S. Postal Service, thus relinquishing governmental control of the U.S. mails after almost 2 centuries.

1971

Charles Manson, 36, and 3 of his followers were found guilty **Jan. 26** of first-degree murder in the 1969 slaying of actress Sharon Tate and 6 others.

U.S. air and artillery forces aided a 44-day incursion by South Vietnam forces into **Laos** starting **Feb. 8.**

A Constitutional Amendment lowering the **voting age to 18** in all elections was approved in the Senate by a vote of 94-0 **Mar. 10.** The proposed 26th Amendment got House approval by a 400-19 vote **Mar. 23.** Thirty-eighth state ratified **June 30.**

A court-martial jury **Mar. 29,** convicted **Lt. William L. Calley Jr.** of premeditated murder of 22 South Vietnamese at Mylai on **Mar. 16, 1968.** He was sentenced to life imprisonment **Mar. 31.** Sentence was reduced to 20 years **Aug. 20.**

Publication of classified **Pentagon papers** on the U.S. involvement in Vietnam was begun **June 13** by the New York Times. In a 6-3 vote, the U.S. Supreme Court **June 30** upheld the right of the Times and the Washington Post to publish the documents under the protection of the First Amendment.

U.S. bombers struck massively in North Vietnam for 5 days starting **Dec. 26,** in retaliation for alleged violations of agreements reached prior to the 1968 bombing halt. U.S. forces at year-end were down to 140,000.

1972

Pres. Nixon arrived in **Peking Feb. 21** for an 8-day visit to China, which he called a "journey for peace." The unprecedented visit ended with a joint communique pledging that both powers would work for "a normalization of relations."

By a vote of 84 to 8, the Senate approved **Mar. 22** a Constitutional Amendment banning **discrimination against women** because of their sex and sent the measure to the states for ratification.

North Vietnamese forces launched the biggest attacks in 4 years across the demilitarized zone **Mar. 30.** The U.S. responded **Apr. 15** by resumption of bombing of Hanoi and Haiphong after a 4-year lull.

Nixon announced **May 8** the mining of **North Vietnam** ports. Last U.S. combat troops left **Aug. 11.**

Alabama Gov. **George C. Wallace**, campaigning at a Laurel, Md. shopping center **May 15, was shot** and seriously wounded as he greeted a large crowd. Arthur H. Bremer, 21, was sentenced Aug. 4 to 63 years for shooting Wallace and 3 bystanders.

In the first visit of a U.S. president to Moscow, Nixon arrived **May 22** for a week of summit talks with Kremlin leaders which culminated in a landmark **strategic arms pact.**

Five men were arrested **June 17** for breaking into the offices of the Democratic National Committee in the Watergate office complex in Washington, D.C.

The White House announced **July 8** that the U.S. would sell to the USSR at least $750 million of **American wheat,** corn, and other grains over a period of 3 years.

1973

Five of seven defendants in the **Watergate** break-in trial pleaded guilty **Jan. 11 and 15,** and the other 2 were convicted **Jan. 30.**

The Supreme Court ruled 7-2, **Jan. 22,** that a state may not prevent a woman from having an **abortion** during the **first 6 months of pregnancy,** invalidating abortion laws in Texas and Georgia, and, by implication, overturning restrictive abortion laws in 44 other states.

Four-party **Vietnam peace pacts** were signed in Paris **Jan. 27,** and North Vietnam released some 590 U.S. prisoners by **Apr. 1.** Last U.S. troops left **Mar. 29.**

The end of the military draft was announced **Jan. 27.**

China and the U.S. agreed **Feb. 22** to set up permanent liaison offices in each other's country.

Top **Nixon** aides H.R. Haldeman, John D. Ehrlichman, and John W. Dean, and Attorney General Richard Kleindienst resigned **Apr. 30** amid charges of White House efforts to obstruct justice in the Watergate case.

The Senate Armed Services Committee **July 16** began a probe into allegations that the U.S. Air Force had made 3,500 secret **B-52 raids into Cambodia** in 1969 and 1970.

John Dean, former Nixon counsel, told Senate hearings **June 25** that Nixon, his staff and campaign aides, and the Justice Department all had conspired to cover up Watergate facts. Nixon refused July 23 to release tapes of relevant White House conversations. Some tapes were turned over to the court **Nov. 26.**

The U.S. officially ceased bombing in **Cambodia** at midnight **Aug. 14** in accord with a June Congressional action.

Vice Pres. Spiro T. Agnew Oct. 10 resigned and pleaded "nolo contendere" (no contest) to charges of tax evasion on payments made to him by Maryland contractors when he was governor of that state. Gerald Rudolph Ford **Oct. 12** became first appointed vice president under the 25th Amendment; sworn in **Dec. 6.**

A total ban on **oil exports** to the U.S. was imposed by Arab oil-producing nations **Oct. 19-21** after the outbreak of an Arab-Israeli war. The ban was lifted **Mar. 18, 1974.**

Atty. Gen. Elliot Richardson resigned, and his deputy William D. Ruckelshaus and Watergate Special Prosecutor Archibald Cox were fired by Pres. Nixon **Oct. 20** when Cox threatened to secure a judicial ruling that Nixon was violating a court order to turn tapes over to Watergate case Judge John Sirica.

Leon Jaworski, conservative Texas Democrat, was named **Nov. 1** by the Nixon administration to be special prosecutor to succeed Archibald Cox.

Congress overrode **Nov. 7** Nixon's veto of the war powers bill which curbed the president's power to commit armed forces to hostilities abroad without Congressional approval.

1974

Impeachment hearings were opened **May 9** against Nixon by the House Judiciary Committee.

John D. Ehrlichman and 3 White House "plumbers" were found guilty **July 12** of conspiring to violate the civil rights of Dr. Lewis Fielding, formerly psychiatrist to Pentagon Papers leaker Daniel Ellsberg, by breaking into his Beverly Hills, Cal. office.

The U.S. Supreme Court ruled, 8-0, **July 24** that Nixon had to turn over 64 tapes of White House conversations sought by Watergate Special Prosecutor Leon Jaworski.

The House Judiciary Committee, in televised hearings **July 24-30,** recommended 3 articles of impeachment against Nixon. The first, voted 27-11 **July 27,** charged Nixon with taking part in a criminal conspiracy to obstruct justice in the Watergate cover-up. The second, voted 28-10 **July 29,** charged he "repeatedly" failed to carry out his constitutional oath in a series of alleged abuses of power. The third, voted 27-17 **July 30,** accused him of unconstitutional defiance of committee subpoenas. The House of Representatives voted without debate Aug. 20, by 412-3, to accept the committee report, which included the recommended impeachment articles.

Nixon resigned Aug. 9. His support began eroding Aug. 5 when he released 3 tapes, admitting he originated plans to have the FBI stop its probe of the Watergate break-in for political as well as national security reasons. Vice President Gerald R. Ford was sworn in as the 38th U.S. president on Aug. 9.

An unconditional pardon to ex-Pres. Nixon for all federal crimes that he "committed or may have committed" while president was issued by Pres. Gerald Ford Sept. 8.

1975

Found guilty of Watergate cover-up charges Jan. 1 were ex-Atty. Gen. John N. Mitchell, ex-presidential advisers H.R. Haldeman and John D. Ehrlichman.

U.S. civilians were evacuated from Saigon Apr. 29 as communist forces completed takeover of South Vietnam.

U.S. merchant ship Mayaguez and crew of 39 seized by Cambodian forces in Gulf of Siam May 12. In rescue operation, U.S. Marines attacked Tang Is., planes bombed air base; Cambodia surrendered ship and crew; U.S. losses were 15 killed in battle and 23 dead in a helicopter crash.

Congress voted $405 million for South Vietnam refugees May 16; 140,000 were flown to the U.S.

Illegal CIA operations, including records on 300,000 persons and groups, and infiltration of agents into black, antiwar and political movements, were described by a "blueribbon" panel headed by Vice Pres. Rockefeller June 10.

FBI agents captured Patricia (Patty) Hearst, kidnaped Feb. 4, 1974, in San Francisco Sept. 18 with others. She was indicted for bank robbery; a San Francisco jury convicted her Mar. 20, 1976.

1976

Payments abroad of $22 million in bribes by Lockheed Aircraft Corp. to sell its planes were revealed Feb. 4 by a Senate subcommittee. Lockheed admitted payments in Japan, Turkey, Italy, and Holland.

The U.S. celebrated its Bicentennial July 4, marking the 200th anniversary of its independence with festivals, parades, and N.Y. City's Operation Sail, a gathering of tall ships from around the world viewed by 6 million persons.

A mystery ailment legionnaire's disease killed 29 persons who attended an American Legion convention July 21-24 in Philadelphia. The cause was found to be a bacterium, it was reported June 18, 1977.

The Viking II lander set down on Mars' Utopia Plains Sept. 3, following the successful landing by Viking I July 20.

1977

Pres. Jimmy Carter Jan. 27 pardoned most Vietnam War draft evaders, who numbered some 10,000.

Convicted murderer Gary Gilmore was executed by a Utah firing squad Jan. 17, in the first exercise of capital punishment anywhere in the U.S. since 1967. Gilmore had opposed all attempts to delay the execution.

Carter signed an act Aug. 4 creating a new Cabinet-level Energy Department.

1978

Sen. Hubert H. Humphrey (D., Minn.), 66, lost a battle with cancer Jan. 13, after 32 years of public service, including 4 years as vice-president of the United States.

U.S. Senate voted Apr. 18 to turn over the Panama Canal to Panama on Dec. 31, 1999, by a vote of 68-32, ending several months of heated debate; an earlier vote (Mar. 16) had given approval to a treaty guaranteeing the area's neutrality after the year 2000.

California voters June 6 approved (by a 65% majority) the Proposition 13 initiative to cut property taxes in the state by 57%, thus severely limiting government spending.

The U.S. Supreme Court June 28 voted 5-4 not to allow a firm quota system in affirmative action plans; the Court did uphold programs that were more "flexible" in nature.

The House Select Committee on Assassinations opened hearings Sept. 6 into assassinations of Pres. Kennedy and Martin Luther King Jr.; the committee recessed Dec. 30 after concluding conspiracies likely in both cases, but with no further hard evidence for further prosecutions.

Congress passed the Humphrey-Hawkins "full employment" Bill Oct. 15, which set national goal of reducing unemployment to 4% by 1983, while reducing inflation to 3% in same period; Pres. Carter signed bill, Oct. 27.

1979

A major accident occurred, Mar. 28, at a nuclear reactor on Three Mile Island near Middletown, Pa. Radioactive gases escaped through the plant's venting system and a large hydrogen gas bubble formed in the top of the reactor containment vessel.

In the worst disaster in U.S. aviation history, an American Airlines DC-10 jetliner lost its left engine and crashed shortly after takeoff in Chicago, May 25, killing 275 people.

Pope John Paul II, Oct. 1-6, visited the U.S. and reaffirmed traditional Roman Catholic teachings.

The federal government announced, Nov. 1, a $1.5 billion loan-guarantee plan to aid the nation's 3d largest automaker, Chrysler Corp., which had reported a loss of $460.6 million for the 3d quarter of 1979.

Some 90 people, including 63 Americans, were taken hostage, Nov. 3, at the American embassy in Teheran, Iran, by militant student followers of Ayatollah Khomeini who demanded the return of former Shah Mohammad Reza Pahlavi, who was undergoing medical treatment in New York City.

1980

Citing "an extremely serious threat to peace," Pres. Carter announced, Jan. 4, a series of punitive measures against the USSR, most notably an embargo on the sale of grain and high technology, in retaliation for the Soviet invasion of Afghanistan. At Carter's request, the U.S. Olympic Committee voted, Apr. 12, not to attend the Moscow Summer Olympics.

Eight Americans were killed and 5 wounded, Apr. 24, in an ill-fated attempt to rescue the hostages held by Iranian militants at the U.S. Embassy in Teheran.

In Washington, Mt. St. Helens erupted, May 18, in a violent blast estimated to be 500 times as powerful as the Hiroshima atomic bomb. The blast, followed by others on May 25 and June 12, left 25 confirmed dead, at least 40 missing, and economic losses estimated at nearly $3 billion.

In a sweeping victory, Nov. 4, Ronald Wilson Reagan was elected 40th President of the United States, defeating incumbent Jimmy Carter. The stunning GOP victory extended to the U.S. Congress where Republicans gained control of the Senate and wrested 33 House seats from the Democrats.

Former Beatle John Lennon was shot and killed, Dec. 8, outside his apartment building in New York City, by Mark David Chapman, a former psychiatric patient.

1981

Minutes after the inauguration of Pres. Ronald Reagan, Jan. 20, the 52 Americans who had been held hostage in Iran for 444 days were flown to freedom following an agreement in which the U.S. agreed to return to Iran $8 billion in frozen assets.

President Reagan was shot in the chest by John W. Hinckley, Jr., a would-be assassin, Mar. 30, in Washington, D.C., as he walked to his limousine following an address at the Washington Hilton.

The world's first reusable spacecraft, the Space Shuttle Columbia, was sent into space, Apr. 12, and completed its successful mission 2 days later.

Both houses of Congress passed, July 29, President Reagan's tax-cut legislation. The bill, the largest tax cut in the nation's history, was expected to reduce taxes by $37.6 billion in fiscal year 1982, and would save taxpayers $750 billion over the next 5 years.

Federal air traffic controllers, Aug. 3, began an illegal nationwide strike after their union rejected the government's final offer for a new contract. Most of the 13,000 striking controllers defied the back-to-work order, and were dismissed by President Reagan on Aug. 5.

In a 99-0 vote, the Senate confirmed, Sept. 21, the appointment of Sandra Day O'Connor as an associate justice of the U.S. Supreme Court. She was the first woman appointed to that body.

President Reagan ordered a series of sanctions against the new Polish military government, Dec. 23, in response to the imposition of martial law that had occurred in that country. This was followed, Dec. 29, by reprisals against the Soviet Union for its alleged role in the crackdown.

1982

The 13-year-old lawsuit brought against AT&T by the Justice Department was settled on Jan. 8. AT&T agreed to give up the 22 Bell System companies but, in return, was allowed to expand its operations into previously prohibited areas such as data processing, telephone and computer equipment sales, and computer communication devices.

On Mar. 2, the Senate voted 57-37 in favor of a bill that virtually eliminated busing for the purposes of racial integration.

On June 12, in New York's Central Park, hundreds of thousands of demonstrators gathered to protest nuclear arms.

The Senate adopted a bill on June 18 extending for an additional 25 years the section of the Voting Rights Act dealing with changes in election procedures.

The Equal Rights Amendment was defeated after a 10-year struggle for ratification.

Secretary of State Alexander M. Haig resigned on June 25. George P. Shultz, a former Secretary of the Treasury, was nominated and approved as Haig's replacement.

The elections on Nov. 2 resulted in gains for the Democrats—the margin in the new House was 269-166. In the Senate elections, Democrats won 20 out of 33 seats, but were still the minority, 54-46.

The highest unemployment rate since 1940, 10.4%, was reported on Nov. 5. The rate for Nov. reached 10.8%, with over 11 million unemployed.

Leonid Brezhnev, 75, general secretary of the central committee of the Communist Party and the Soviet Union, died of a heart attack on Nov. 10. On Nov. 12, the central committee unanimously elected Yuri V. Andropov, 68, to succeed him. Andropov was a member of the ruling Politburo and a former head of the state security police.

Lech Walesa, former leader of Solidarity, the Polish labor union, was freed Nov. 13, after 11 months of internment following the imposition of martial law and the outlawing of Solidarity in Dec. 1981. The Polish government declared Walesa "no longer a threat to internal security." In response, Pres. Reagan lifted the U.S. embargo on sales of oil and gas equipment to the Soviet Union.

The Space Shuttle Columbia completed its first operational flight on Nov. 16.

The 8-week-old National Football League players' strike ended Nov. 16. It was estimated that the strike had cost players, owners, media, cities, and businesses nearly $450 million.

Sen Edward M. Kennedy (D., Mass.) announced on Dec. 1 that he would not seek his party's 1984 nomination for the presidency. Kennedy had been regarded as the leading contender.

A retired dentist, Dr. Barney B. Clark, 61, became the first recipient of a permanent artificial heart during a 7½ hour operation in Salt Lake City on Dec. 2. The heart was designed by Dr. Robert Jarvik, who also served on the surgical team.

On Dec. 16, Anne M. Gorsuch, administrator of the Environmental Protection Agency, became the first Cabinet level official to be cited for contempt by the House when she declined to submit certain documents requested by a House subcommittee.

1983

Four aspirants for the 1984 Democratic presidential nomination declared their candidacy in Feb.: Sen. Alan Cranston (Cal.), the Senate Democratic whip; Sen. Gary Hart (Col.); former vice president Walter Mondale; and former two-term governor of Florida, Reuben Askew. Mondale was considered the front-runner.

Anne McGill (Gorsuch) Burford stepped down on Mar. 9 as administrator of the federal Environmental Protection Agency, as criticism of the agency continued to build.

On Mar. 14, for the first time in its 23-year-history, the Organization of Petroleum Exporting Countries (OPEC) agreed to cut the prices of its crude oil. The decision in London reflected falling worldwide demand for OPEC products.

In Apr., Sen. Ernest Hollings (S.C.), and Sen. John Glenn (Ohio) announced their candidacies for the 1984 Democratic presidential nomination.

On Apr. 20, Pres. Reagan signed into law a compromise and bipartisan bill designed to rescue the Social Security System from bankruptcy.

The National Commission on Excellence in Education issued its report on Apr. 26. The report labelled U.S. elementary and secondary education "mediocre," and recommended that: schools put more emphasis on English, math, social studies, and computer science; the school day be lengthened; teachers be rewarded for merit rather than seniority; and college admissions standards be raised.

In an 8-1 decision, the U.S. Supreme Court held, May 24, that the Internal Revenue Service could deny tax exemptions to private schools that practiced racial discrimination.

The House, May 24, and the Senate, May 25, voted to free $625 million for the MX missile, after Congress received assurances from Pres. Reagan that he would be more flexible in arms talks with the Soviet Union.

Sally Ride became the first American woman to travel in space, June 18, when the space shuttle Challenger was launched from Cape Canaveral, Fla.

The Soviet Union shot a South Korean airliner out of the sky on Sept. 1, killing all 269 people aboard. The attack occurred in Soviet air space, and the plane crashed into the Sea of Japan. The USSR charged that the plane, which carried 240 passengers and a crew of 29, had been on a spying mission. Most of the noncommunist world, led by Pres. Reagan, responded with condemnation.

The Big 3 auto companies reported, Oct. 4, that sales had increased 16.7 percent during the 1983 model year. It was the biggest gain from the previous year since 1978.

Lech Walesa, the founder of Solidarity, the Polish labor union, was named winner of the 1983 Nobel Peace Prize on Oct. 5.

On Oct. 23, 241 U.S. Marines and sailors, members of the multinational peacekeeping force in Lebanon, were killed when a TNT-laden suicide terrorist blew up Marine headquarters at Beirut Intl. Airport. Almost simultaneously, a second truck bomb blew up a French paratroop barracks two miles away, killing more than 40.

U.S. Marines and Rangers and a small force from 6 Caribbean nations invaded the island of Grenada on Oct. 25. Pres. Reagan said the action was in response to an Oct. 23 request from the Organization of Eastern Caribbean States to help restore order to Grenada, whose government had been overthrown the previous week, and also to protect the lives of the 1,000 U.S. citizens on the island. After a few days of intense fighting, Grenadian militia and Cuban "construction workers" were overcome, hundreds of U.S. citizens evacuated safely, and the hard-line Marxist regime deposed. Caches of Soviet-made arms were said to have been found, and 600 Cubans captured. A majority of members of the OAS, U.N. Security Council, and U.N. General Assembly voted for resolutions condemning the invasion. The U.S. Senate and the House approved resolutions applying the War Powers Resolution to the conflict, requiring U.S. troops to leave Grenada by Dec. 24. The Defense Dept. said, Nov. 2, that the hostilities had ended. Casualties were put at 45 Grenadians, 24 Cubans, and 18 Americans killed, with 115 Americans wounded in action. The last 190 U.S. combat troops left Grenada, Dec. 15, but some 300 noncombat troops remained.

1984

On Jan. 3, after the personal intervention of Rev. Jesse Jackson, a candidate for the Democratic presidential nomination, **Syria freed a captured Navy flier**, Lt. Robert Goodman, Jr., whose plane had been shot down, **Dec. 4**, over Syrian-controlled territory in Lebanon.

Pres. Ronald Reagan's **National Bipartisan Commission on Central America**, headed by Henry Kissinger, called, **Jan. 11**, for a sharp increase in economic and military aid and endorsed most of the Reagan administration policy.

In his **State of the Union address, Jan. 25**, Pres. Reagan called for budget cuts of $100 billion over 3 years, but opposed increased taxes.

Pres. Reagan announced, Jan. 29, that he would seek re-election in 1984.

Sen. Gary Hart (Col.) emerged as a surprisingly strong contender for the Democratic presidential nomination, **Feb. 28**, when he upset the overwhelming favorite for the nomination, former vice president **Walter Mondale** (Minn.) in the New Hampshire primary.

Soviet leader **Yuri V. Andropov**, 69, died in Moscow, Feb. 9, after a long illness. Chosen by the Politburo to replace him as general secretary of the party was **Konstantin U. Chernenko**, who had served as chief of staff for the Supreme Soviet and as head of administration and security for the Central Committee. At 72, Chernenko was the oldest man to assume power in the USSR.

On **Feb. 26**, as the position of Pres. Amin Gemayel of Lebanon deteriorated and his army crumbled, Pres. Reagan **removed U.S. Marines from Beirut** and placed them on U.S. ships offshore.

The space shuttle *Challenger* was launched on its 4th trip into space, Feb. 3. On Feb. 7, Navy Capt. Bruce McCandless, followed by Army Lt. Colonel Robert Stewart, flew free of the spacecraft, the first humans to do so without a tether.

During March, the U.S. Senate rejected 2 Constitutional amendments that would have permitted **prayer in the public schools.**

The U.S. Central Intelligence Agency **(CIA)** acknowledged in April that it had participated in the **mining of Nicaraguan harbors.** This touched off a controversy in Congress, and the Senate, **Apr. 10**, adopted a nonbinding resolution condemning U.S. participation in the mining. The Reagan administration, **Apr. 11**, said that the mining had been halted.

In a unanimous vote by the Supreme Soviet on **Apr. 11**, Konstantin Chernenko, general secretary of the Communist Party, was also named head of state.

From **Apr. 26 to May 1**, Pres. Reagan **visited China** for the first time, holding a series of discussions with Chinese leaders.

On **May 7**, American veterans of the Vietnam war reached an **out-of-court settlement with 7 chemical companies** in their class-action suit relating to the herbicide **Agent Orange.** The suit involved some 15,000 veterans and family members, but many more people could ultimately get a share of the $180 billion made available for compensation. In the settlement, the companies made no acknowledgement of culpability. Left open was the question of culpability by the federal government.

A federal judge in Salt Lake City held, **May 10**, that the **U.S. government had been negligent** in its above-ground testing of nuclear weapons in Nevada from 1951 to 1962.

Jose Napoleon Duarte, the candidate of the Christian Democratic Party and a political moderate, was **elected president of strife-torn El Salvador, May 7.**

An **undamaged Mayan tomb** was discovered by archaeologists, **May 15.** It was expected to add much new knowledge about the great civilization that flourished in Middle America 1,500 years ago.

On **June 6**, former vice president **Walter Mondale** claimed victory in his struggle with Sen. Gary Hart for the **Democratic presidental nomination.** In a historic move, July 12, Mondale chose a woman, **Rep. Geraldine Ferraro** (N.Y.) to run with him as candidate for **vice president.**

A report written by Italian State Prosecutor Antonio Albano and made public in June, linked the **Bulgarian secret service to the plot to assassinate Pope John Paul II** in 1981.

Vanessa Williams, the first black Miss America, resigned July 23, after several days of controversy related to nude photographs of her that were about to be published. The first runnerup, Suzette Charles, who was also black, succeeded Williams.

Pres. Reagan, **Aug. 11**, signed into law an act that would prohibit public high schools from barring students who wished to **assemble for religious or political activities** outside of school hours.

Pres. **Ronald Reagan and Vice Pres. George Bush** were **renominated, Aug. 23**, at the Republican National convention.

The XXIII Olympics, opening July 28, brought a record total of **174 medals to American athletes**—83 gold, 61 silver, and 30 bronze. Carl Lewis led the American domination with 4 gold medals in track and field, Mary Lou Retton won 4 medals in gymnastics, including a gold in the all-around competition, and Joan Benoit won the first Olympic marathon for women. The Olympics were boycotted by the USSR and other Soviet bloc nations.

Indira Gandhi, the prime minister of India, was **slain by 2 of her own bodyguards** in New Delhi, **Oct. 31.** Her assassins were reportedly members of the Sikh religious minority, who had been in violent confrontation with the Gandhi government for months. Gandhi was succeeded by her 40-year-old son, Rajiv, the ranking general secretary of his mother's party.

As **starvation threatened to engulf millions of people** in Ethiopia, the Reagan administration announced, **Oct. 24**, that it was sending $45 million in wheat and other foodstuffs. Ethiopia and other countries had suffered from a protracted drought throughout much of Africa.

Five men and two women, **the largest crew in the history of space flight**, rode the shuttle *Challenger* into space, Oct. 5.

The heart of a baboon was implanted in a 15-day-old girl, Oct. 26, in a 5-hour operation performed at Loma Linda University Medical Center in California. Identified only as Baby Fae, the baby lived for almost 3 weeks, dying Nov. 15, after her body appeared to rejected the new heart.

Pres. **Ronald Reagan and Vice Pres. George Bush** were **reelected, Nov. 6**, defeating Democrats former Vice Pres. Walter Mondale and Rep. Geraldine Ferraro, the first woman to run for vice president on a major-party ticket. Reagan and Bush **carried 49 states**, and Republicans won an all-time high of 525 electoral votes. Reagan, at 73 the oldest man ever elected president, drew majority support from almost all demographic groups.

For the second time, a human patient underwent an operation that **replaced a diseased heart with a mechanical one made of aluminum and plastic.** The operation, in Louisville, Ky., on **Nov. 25**, was performed on William Schroeder, 52, of Jasper, Ind., a retired federal worker. It took place at the Humana Heart Institute under the leadership of Dr. William DeVries, who had also headed the surgical team performing the first artificial-heart transplant in 1983 on Dr. Barney Clark.

Toxic fumes drifted through two densely-populated slum neighborhoods in the Indian city of Bhopal, Dec. 3, killing more than 2,000 people. The lethal gas, methyl isocyanate, leaked from a chemical plant where it was used in the manufacture of an insecticide. The plant was owned by Union Carbide India Ltd., a subsidiary of the U.S. Union Carbide Corp. The toll of injured, some of whom suffered serious damage to lungs, eyes, and other organs, was put at 50,000. The Madhya Pradesh state government said, **Dec. 30**, that it would file suit in the U.S. against Union Carbide.

WORLD HISTORY

Prehistory: Our Ancestors Take Over

Homo sapiens. The precise origins of *homo sapiens*, the species to which all humans belong, are subject to broad speculation based on a small number of fossils, genetic and anatomical studies, and the geological record. But most scientists agree that we evolved from ape-like primate ancestors in a process that began millions of years ago.

Current theories say the first hominid (human-like primate) was *Ramapithecus*, who emerged 12 million years ago. Its remains have been found in Asia, Europe, and Africa. Further development was apparently limited to Africa, where 2 lines of hominids appeared some 5 or 6 million years ago. One was *Australopithecus*, a tool-maker and social animal, who lived from perhaps 4 to 3 million years ago, and then apparently became extinct.

The 2nd was a human line, *Homo habillus*, a large-brained specimen that walked upright and had a dextrous hand. *Homo habillus* lived in semi-permanent camps and had a food-gathering and sharing economy.

Homo erectus, our nearest ancestor, appeared in Africa perhaps 1.75 million years ago, and began spreading into Asia and Europe soon after. It had a fairly large brain and a skeletal structure similar to ours. *Homo erectus* learned to control fire, and probably had primitive language skills. The final brain development to *Homo sapiens* and then to our sub-species *Homo sapiens sapiens* occurred between 500,000 and 50,000 years ago, over a wide geographic area and in many different steps and recombinations. All humans of all races belong to this sub-species.

The spread of mankind into the remaining habitable continents probably took place during the last ice age up to 100,000 years ago: to the Americas across a land bridge from Asia, and to Australia across the Timor Straits.

Earliest cultures. A variety of cultural modes — in tool-making, diet, shelter, and possibly social arrangements and spiritual expression, arose as early mankind adapted to different geographic and climatic zones.

Three basic tool-making traditions are recognized by archeologists as arising and often coexisting from one million years ago to the near past: the *chopper tradition*, found largely in E. Asia, with crude chopping tools and simple flake tools; the *flake tradition*, found in Africa and W. Europe, with a variety of small cutting and flaking tools, and

the *biface tradition*, found in all of Africa, W. and S. Europe, and S. Asia, producing pointed hand axes chipped on both faces. Later biface sites yield more refined axes and a variety of other tools, weapons, and ornaments using bone, antler, and wood as well as stone.

Only sketchy evidence remains for the different stages in man's increasing control over the environment. Traces of 400,000-year-old covered wood shelters have been found at Nice, France. Scraping tools at Neanderthal sites (200,000-30,000 BC in Europe, N. Africa, the Middle East and Central Asia) suggest the treatment of skins for clothing. Sites from all parts of the world show seasonal migration patterns and exploitation of a wide range of plant and animal food sources.

Painting and decoration, for which there is evidence at the Nice site, flourished along with stone and ivory sculpture after 30,000 years ago; 60 caves in France and 30 in Spain show remarkable examples of wall painting. Other examples have been found in Africa. Proto-religious rites are suggested by these works, and by evidence of ritual cannibalism by Peking Man, 500,000 BC, and of ritual burial with medicinal plants and flowers by Neanderthals at Shanidar in Iraq.

The Neolithic Revolution. Sometime after 10,000 BC, among widely separated human communities, a series of dramatic technological and social changes occurred that are summed up as the Neolithic Revolution. The cultivation of previously wild plants encouraged the growth of permanent settlements. Animals were domesticated as a work force and food source. The manufacture of pottery and cloth began. These techniques permitted a huge increase in world population and in human control over the earth.

No region can safely claim priority as the "inventor" of these techniques. Dispersed sites in Cen. and S. America, S.E. Europe, and the Middle East show roughly contemporaneous (10-8,000 BC) evidence of one or another "neolithic" trait. Dates near 6-3,000 BC have been given for E. and S. Asian, W. European, and sub-Saharan African neolithic remains. The variety of crops — field grains, rice, maize, and roots, and the varying mix of other traits suggest that the revolution occurred independently in all these regions.

History Begins: 4000 - 1000 BC

Near Eastern cradle. If history began with writing, the first chapter opened in Mesopotamia, the Tigris-Euphrates river valley. Clay tablets with pictographs were used by the Sumerians to keep records after 4000 BC. A cuneiform (wedge shaped) script evolved by 3000 BC as a full syllabic alphabet. Neighboring peoples adapted the script to their own language.

Sumerian life centered, from 4000 BC, on large cities (Eridu, Ur, Uruk, Nippur, Kish, Lagash) organized around temples and priestly bureaucracies, with the surrounding plains watered by vast irrigation works and worked with traction plows. Sailboats, wheeled vehicles, potters wheels, and kilns were used. Copper was smelted and tempered in Sumeria from c4000 BC and bronze was produced not long after. Ores, as well as precious stones and metals were obtained through long-distance ship and caravan trade. Iron was used from c2000 BC. Improved ironworking, developed partly by the Hittites, became widespread by 1200 BC.

Sumerian political primacy passed among cities and their kingly dynasties. Semitic-speaking peoples, with cultures derived from the Sumerian, founded a succession of dynasties that ruled in Mesopotamia and neighboring areas for most of 1800 years; among them the Akkadians (first under Sargon c2350 BC), the Amorites (whose laws, codified by Hammurabi, c1792-1750 BC, have Biblical parallels), and the Assyrians, with interludes of rule by the Hittites, Kassites, and Mitanni, all possibly Indo-Europeans. The political and cultural center of gravity shifted northwest with each successive empire.

Mesopotamian learning, maintained by scribes and preserved by successive rulers in vast libraries, was not abstract or theoretical. Algebraic and geometric problems could be solved on a practical basis in construction, commerce, or administration. Systematic lists of astronomical phenomena, plants, animals and stones were kept; medical texts listed ailments and their herbal cures.

The Sumerians worshipped anthropomorphic gods representing natural forces — Anu, god of heaven; Enlil (Ea), god of water. Epic poetry related these and other gods in a hierarchy. Sacrifices were made at ziggurats — huge stepped temples. Gods were thought to control all events, which could be foretold using oracular materials. This religious pattern persisted into the first millenium BC.

The Syria-Palestine area, site of some of the earliest urban remains (Jericho, 7000 BC), and of the recently uncovered Ebla civilization (fl. 2500 BC), experienced Egyptian cultural and political influence along with Mesopotamia. The Phoenician coast was an active commercial center. A phonetic alphabet was invented here before 1600 BC. It became the ancestor of all European, Middle Eastern, Indian, S.E.

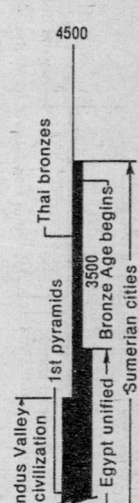

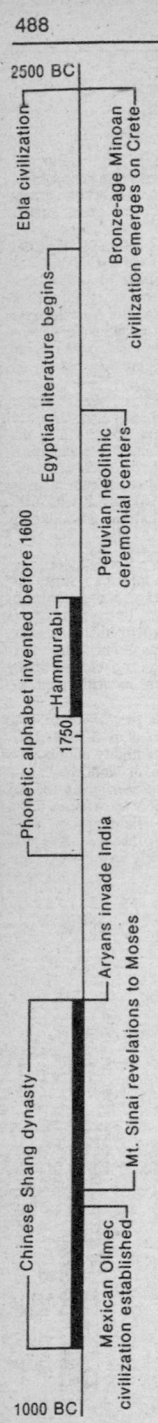

Asian, Ethiopian, and Korean alphabets.

Regional commerce and diplomacy were aided by the use of Akkadian as a *lingua franca*, later replaced by Aramaic.

Egypt. Agricultural villages along the Nile were united by 3300 BC into two kingdoms, Upper and Lower Egypt, unified under the Pharaoh Menes c3100 BC; Nubia to the south was added 2600 BC. A national bureaucracy supervised construction of canals and monuments (**pyramids** starting 2700 BC). Brilliant First Dynasty achievements in architecture, sculpture and painting, set the standards and forms for all subsequent Egyptian civilization and are still admired. **Hieroglyphic writing** appeared by 3400 BC, recording a sophisticated literature including romantic and philosophical modes after 2300 BC.

An ordered hierarchy of gods, including totemistic animal elements, was served by a powerful priesthood in Memphis. The pharaoh was identified with the falcon god Horus. Later trends were the belief in an afterlife, and the quasi-monotheistic reforms of **Akhenaton** (c1379-1362 BC).

After a period of conquest by Semitic Hyksos from Asia (c1700-1500 BC), the New Kingdom established an empire in Syria. Egypt became increasingly embroiled in Asiatic wars and diplomacy. Eventually it was conquered by Persia in 525 BC, and it faded away as an independent culture.

India. An urban civilization with a so-far-undeciphered writing system stretched across the Indus Valley and along the Arabian Sea c3000-1500 BC. Major sites are Harappa and **Mohenjo-Daro** in Pakistan, well-planned geometric cities with underground sewers and vast granaries. The entire region (600,000 sq. mi.) may have been ruled as a single state. Bronze was used, and arts and crafts were highly developed. Religious life apparently took the form of fertility cults.

Indus civilization was probably in decline when it was destroyed by **Aryan invaders** from the northwest, speaking an Indo-European language from which all the languages of Pakistan, north India and Bangladesh descend. Led by a warrior aristocracy whose legendary deeds are recorded in the **Rig Veda**, the Aryans spread east and south, bringing their pantheon of sky gods, elaborate priestly (Brahmin) ritual, and the beginnings of the caste system; local customs and beliefs were assimilated by the conquerors.

Europe. On Crete, the bronze-age **Minoan civilization** emerged c2500 BC. A prosperous economy and richly decorative art (e.g. at Knossos palace) was supported by seaborne commerce. Mycenae and other cities in Greece and Asia Minor (e.g. **Troy**) preserved elements of the culture to c1100 BC. Cretan Linear A script, c2000-1700 BC, is undeciphered; Linear B, c1300-1200 BC, records a Greek dialect.

Possible connection between Minoan-Mycenaean monumental stonework, and the great megalithic monuments and tombs of W. Europe, Iberia, and Malta (c4000-1500 BC) is unclear.

China. Proto-Chinese neolithic cultures had long covered northern and southeastern China when the first large political state was organized in the north by the **Shang dynasty** c1500 BC. Shang kings called themselves Sons of Heaven, and presided over a cult of human and animal sacrifice to ancestors and nature gods. The Chou dynasty, starting c1100 BC, expanded the area of the Son of Heaven's dominion, but feudal states exercised most temporal power.

A writing system with 2,000 different characters was already in use under the Shang, with **pictographs** later supplemented by phonetic characters. The system, with modifications, is still in use, despite changes in spoken Chinese.

Technical advances allowed urban specialists to create fine ceramic and jade products, and bronze casting after 1500 BC was the most advanced in the world.

Bronze artifacts have recently been discovered in northern Thailand dating to 3600 BC, hundreds of years before similar Middle Eastern finds.

Americas. Olmecs settled on the Gulf coast of Mexico, 1500 BC, and soon developed the first civilization in the Western Hemisphere. Temple cities and huge stone sculpture date to 1200 BC. A rudimentary calendar and writing system existed. Olmec religion, centering on a jaguar god, and art forms influenced all later Meso-American cultures.

Neolithic ceremonial centers were built on the Peruvian desert coast, c2000 BC.

Classical Era of Old World Civilizations

Greece. After a period of decline during the Dorian Greek invasions (1200-1000 BC), Greece and the Aegean area developed a unique civilization. Drawing upon Mycenaean traditions, Mesopotamian learning (weights and measures, lunisolar calendar, astronomy, musical scales), the Phoenician alphabet (modified for Greek), and Egyptian art, the revived **Greek city-states** saw a rich elaboration of intellectual life. Long-range commerce was aided by metal coinage (introduced by the Lydians in Asia Minor before 700 BC); colonies were founded around the Mediterranean and Black Sea shores (Cumae in Italy 760 BC, Massalia in France c600 BC).

Philosophy, starting with Ionian speculation on the nature of matter and the universe (Thales c634-546), and including mathematical speculation (Pythagoras c580-c500), culminated in Athens in the rationalist idealism of **Plato** (c428-347) and **Socrates** (c470-399); the latter was executed for alleged impiety. Aristotle (384-322) united all fields of study in his system. The arts were highly valued. Architecture culminated in the **Parthenon** in Athens (438, sculpture by Phidias); poetry and drama (Aeschylus 525-456) thrived. Male beauty and strength, a chief artistic theme, were enhanced at the gymnasium and the national games at Olympia.

Ruled by local tyrants or oligarchies, the Greeks were never politically united, but managed to resist inclusion in the Persian Empire (Darius defeated at Marathon 490 BC, Xerxes at Salamis, Plataea 479 BC). Local warfare was common; the **Peloponnesian Wars,** 431-404 BC, ended in Sparta's victory over Athens. Greek political power waned, but classical Greek cultural forms spread thoughout the ancient world from the Atlantic to India.

Hebrews. Nomadic Hebrew tribes entered Canaan before 1200 BC, settling among other Semitic peoples speaking the same language. They brought from the desert a **monotheistic faith** said to have been revealed to Abraham in Canaan c1800 BC and to Moses at Mt. Sinai c1250 BC, after the Hebrews' escape from bondage in Egypt. David (ruled 1000-961 BC) and Solomon (ruled 961-922 BC) united the Hebrews in a kingdom that briefly dominated the area. Phoenicians to the north established colonies

Paleontology: The History of Life

All dates are approximate, and are subject to change based on new fossil finds or new dating techniques; but the sequence of events is generally accepted. Dates are in years before the present.

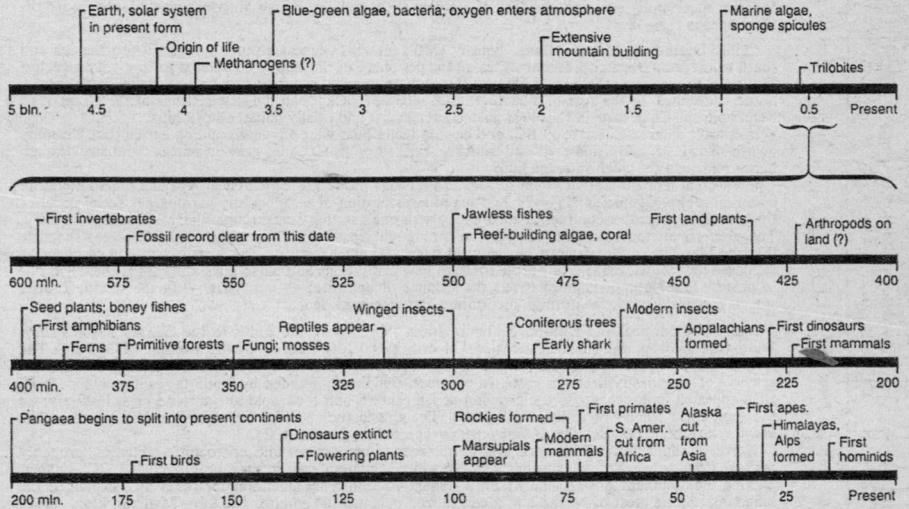

Ancient Near Eastern Civilizations 4000 B.C.-500 B.C.

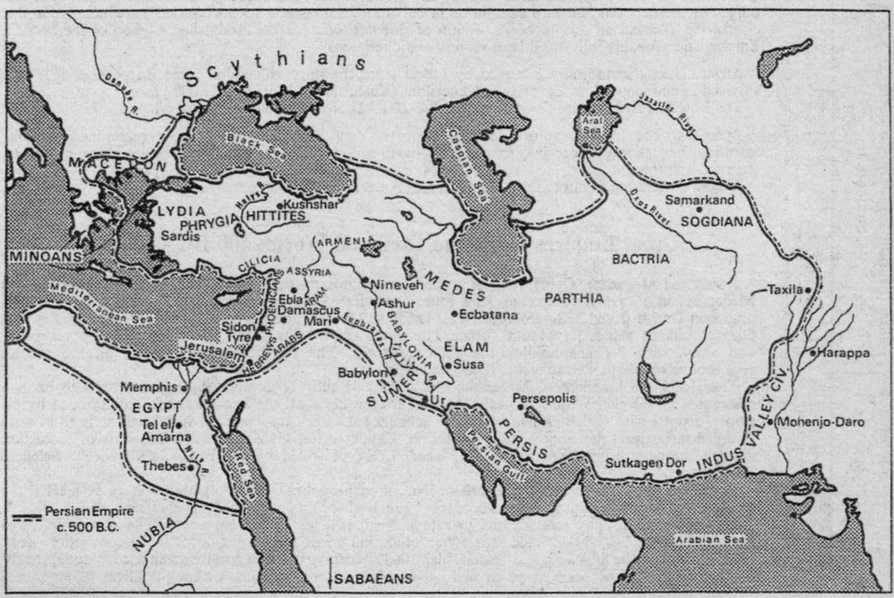

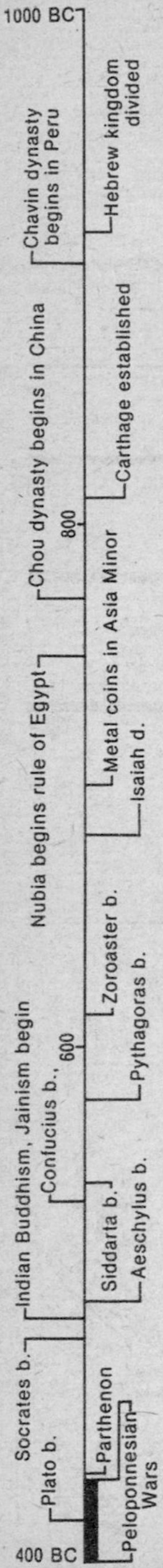

1000 BC

Timeline labels (left margin):
- Chavin dynasty begins in Peru
- Hebrew kingdom divided
- Chou dynasty begins in China
- Carthage established
- 800
- Nubia begins rule of Egypt
- Metal coins in Asia Minor
- Isaiah d.
- Zoroaster b.
- Pythagoras b.
- 600
- Indian Buddhism, Jainism begin
- Confucius b.
- Siddarta b.
- Aeschylus b.
- Socrates b.
- Plato b.
- Parthenon
- Peloponnesian Wars
- 400 BC

around the E. and W. Mediterranean (**Carthage** c814 BC) and sailed into the Atlantic.

A temple in Jerusalem became the national religious center, with sacrifices performed by a hereditary priesthood. Polytheistic influences, especially of the fertility cult of Baal, were opposed by **prophets** (Elijah, Amos, Isaiah).

Divided into **two kingdoms** after Solomon, the Hebrews were unable to resist the revived Assyrian empire, which conquered Israel, the northern kingdom in 722 BC. Judah, the southern kingdom, was conquered in 586 BC by the Babylonians under Nebuchadnezzar II. But with the fixing of most of the Biblical canon by the mid-fourth century BC, and the emergence of rabbis, arbiters of law and custom, Judaism successfully survived the loss of Hebrew autonomy. A Jewish kingdom was revived under the Hasmoneans (168-42 BC).

China. During the **Eastern Chou** dynasty (770-256 BC), Chinese culture spread east to the sea and south to the Yangtze. Large feudal states on the periphery of the empire contended for pre-eminence, but continued to recognize the Son of Heaven (king), who retained a purely ritual role enriched with courtly music and dance. In the Age of Warring States (403-221 BC), when the first sections of the **Great Wall** were built, the Ch'in state in the West gained supremacy, and finally united all of China.

Iron tools entered China c500 BC, and casting techniques were advanced, aiding agriculture. Peasants owned their land, and owed civil and military service to nobles. Cities grew in number and size, though barter remained the chief trade medium.

Intellectual ferment among noble scribes and officials produced the Classical Age of Chinese literature and philosophy. **Confucius** (551-479 BC) urged a restoration of a supposedly harmonious social order of the past through proper conduct in accordance with one's station and through filial and ceremonial piety. The *Analects*, attributed to him, are revered throughout East Asia. **Mencius** (d. 289 BC) added the view that the Mandate of Heaven can be removed from an unjust dynasty. The Legalists sought to curb the supposed natural wickedness of people through new institutions and harsh laws; they aided the Ch'in rise to power. The Naturalists emphasized the balance of opposites — yin, yang — in the world. Taoists sought mystical knowledge through meditation and disengagement.

India. The political and cultural center of India shifted from the Indus to the Ganges River Valley. Buddhism, Jainism, and mystical revisions of orthodox Vedism all developed around 500-300 BC. The *Upanishads*, last part of the *Veda*, urged escape from the illusory physical world. Vedism remained the preserve of the priestly Brahmin caste. In contrast, **Buddhism**, founded by Siddarta Gautama (c563-c483 BC), appealed to merchants in the growing urban centers, and took hold at first (and most lastingly) on the geographic fringes of Indian civilization. The classic Indian epics were composed in this era: The *Ramayana* around 300 BC, the *Mahabharata* over a period starting 400 BC.

Northern India was divided into a large number of monarchies and aristocratic republics, probably derived from tribal groupings, when the Magadha kingdom was formed in Bihar c542 BC. It soon became the dominant power. The **Maurya dynasty**, founded by Chandragupta c321 BC, expanded the kingdom, uniting most of N. India in a centralized bureaucratic empire. The third Mauryan king, **Asoka** (ruled c274-236) conquered most of the subcontinent: he converted to Buddhism, and inscribed its tenets on pillars throughout India. He downplayed the caste system and tried to end expensive sacrificial rites.

Before its final decline in India, Buddhism developed the popular worship of heavenly Bodhisatvas (enlightened beings), and produced a refined architecture (stupa—shrine—at Sanchi 100 AD) and sculpture (Gandhara reliefs 1-400 AD).

Persia. Aryan peoples (Persians, Medes) dominated the area of present Iran by the beginning of the first millenium BC. The prophet **Zoroaster** (born c628 BC) introduced a dualistic religion in which the forces of good (Ahura Mazda, Lord of Wisdom) and evil (Ahiram) battle for dominance; individuals are judged by their actions and earn damnation or salvation. Zoroaster's hymns (*Gathas*) are included in the *Avesta*, the Zoroastrian scriptures. A version of this faith became the established religion of the Persian Empire, and probably influenced later monotheistic religions.

Africa. Nubia, periodically occupied by Egypt since the third millenium, ruled Egypt c750-661, and survived as an independent Egyptianized kingdom (**Kush**; capital Meroe) for 1,000 years.
The Iron Age Nok culture flourished c500 BC-200 AD on the Benue Plateau of Nigeria.

Americas. The Chavin culture controlled north Peru from 900-200 BC. Its ceremonial centers, featuring the jaguar god, survived long after. Chavin architecture, ceramics, and textiles influenced other Peruvian cultures.
Mayan civilization began to develop in Central America in the 5th century BC.

Great Empires Unite the Civilized World: 400 BC - 400 AD

Persia and Alexander. Cyrus, ruler of a small kingdom in Persia from 559 BC, united the Persians and Medes within 10 years, conquered Asia Minor and Babylonia in another 10. His son Cambyses and grandson **Darius** (ruled 522-486) added vast lands to the east and north as far as the Indus Valley and Central Asia, as well as Egypt and Thrace. The whole empire was ruled by an international bureaucracy and army, with· Persians holding the chief positions. The resources and styles of all the subject civilizations were exploited to create a rich syncretic art.

The Hellenized kingdom of Macedon, which under Phillip II dominated Greece, passed to his son **Alexander** in 336 BC. Within 13 years, Alexander conquered all the Persian dominions. Imbued by his tutor Aristotle with Greek ideals, Alexander encouraged Greek colonization, and Greek-style cities were founded throughout the empire (e.g. Alexandria, Egypt). After his death in 323 BC, wars of succession divided the empire into three parts — Macedon, Egypt (ruled by the **Ptolemies**), and the **Seleucid** Empire.

In the ensuing 300 years (the **Hellenistic Era**), a cosmopolitan Greek-oriented culture permeated the ancient world from W. Europe to the borders of India, absorbing native elites everywhere.

Hellenistic philosophy stressed the private individual's search for happiness. The Cynics followed Diogenes (c372-287), who stressed satisfaction of animal needs and contempt for social convention. Zeno (c335-c263) and the Stoics exalted reason, identified it with virtue, and counseled an ascetic disregard for misfortune. The Epicureans tried to build lives of moderate pleasure without political or emotional

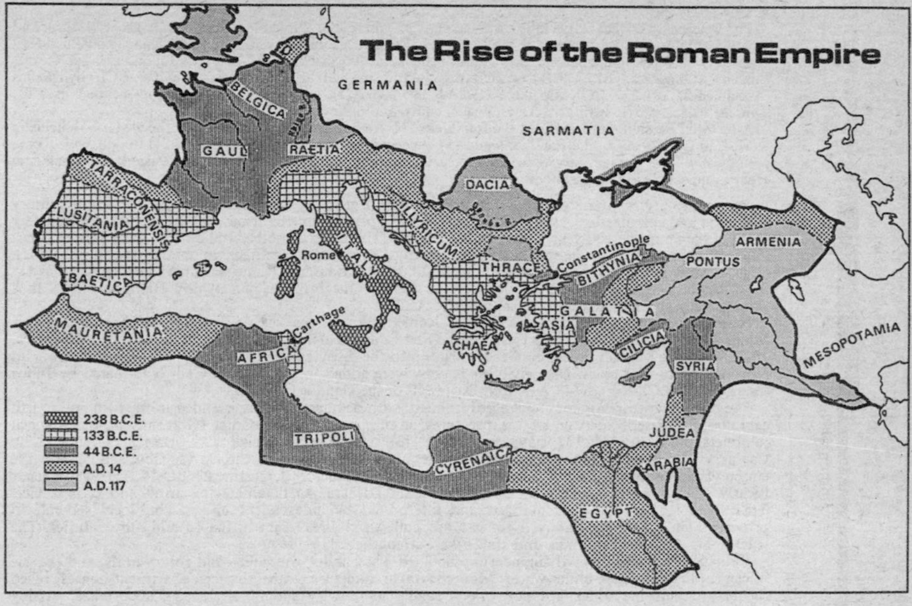

The Rise of the Roman Empire

GERMANIA

BELGICA

GAUL

RAETIA

SARMATIA

DACIA

TARRACONENSIS

LUSITANIA

ILLYRICUM

ARMENIA

BAETICA

Rome ITALY

THRACE

Constantinople

BITHYNIA

PONTUS

MAURETANIA

Carthage

ASIA

GALATIA

ACHAEA

CILICIA

MESOPOTAMIA

AFRICA

SYRIA

TRIPOLI

JUDEA

CYRENAICA

ARABIA

EGYPT

- 238 B.C.E.
- 133 B.C.E.
- 44 B.C.E.
- A.D. 14
- A.D. 117

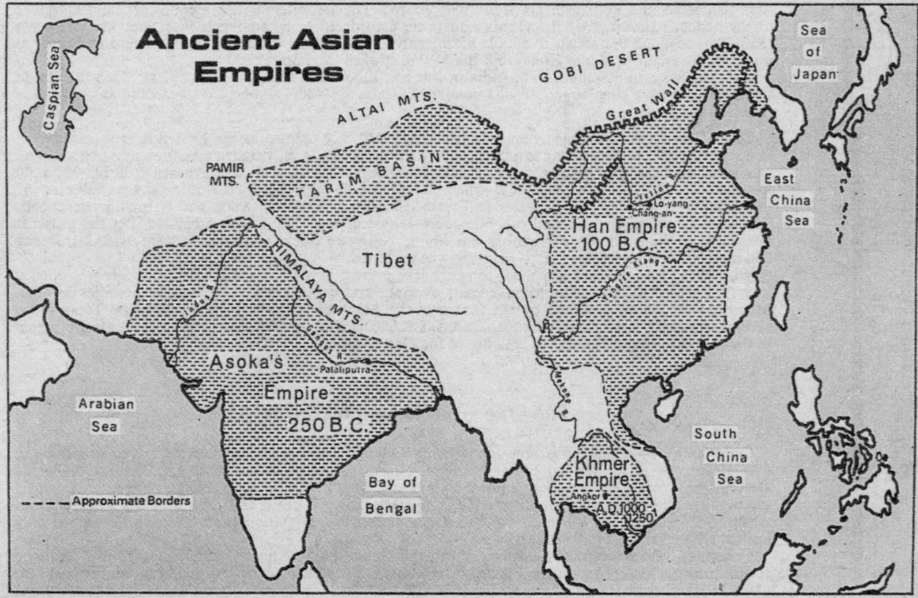

Ancient Asian Empires

Caspian Sea

GOBI DESERT

Sea of Japan

ALTAI MTS.

Great Wall

PAMIR MTS.

TARIM BASIN

East China Sea

HIMALAYA MTS.

Tibet

Han Empire 100 B.C.

Lo-yang

Chang-an

Arabian Sea

Asoka's Empire 250 B.C.

Pataliputra

Bay of Bengal

Khmer Empire

Angkor

A.D. 1000

South China Sea

- - - Approximate Borders

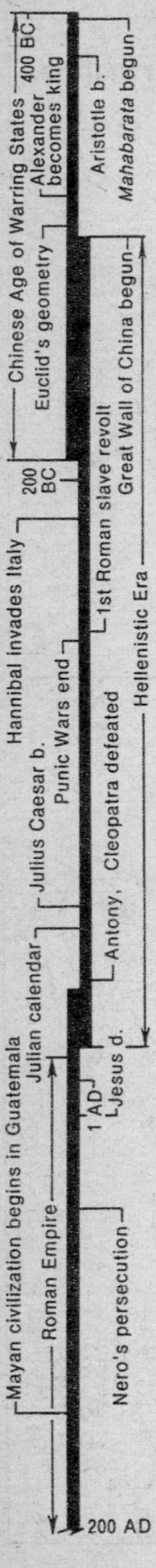

The timeline markers along the left margin read:

- 400 BC
- Alexander becomes king
- Chinese Age of Warring States
- Euclid's geometry
- Aristotle b.
- Mahabarata begun
- Hannibal invades Italy
- 200 BC
- Punic Wars end
- 1st Roman slave revolt
- Great Wall of China begun
- Julius Caesar b.
- Antony, Cleopatra defeated
- Hellenistic Era
- Julian calendar
- Jesus d.
- Mayan civilization begins in Guatemala
- Roman Empire
- 1 AD
- Nero's persecution
- 200 AD

involvement. Hellenistic arts imitated life realistically, especially in sculpture and literature (comedies of Menander, 342-292).

The sciences thrived, especially at Alexandria, where the Ptolemies financed a great library and museum. Fields of study included mathematics (**Euclid's** geometry, c300 BC; Menelaus' non-Euclidean geometry, c100 AD); astronomy (heliocentric theory of Aristarchus, 310-230 BC; Julian calendar 45 BC; Ptolemy's *Almagest*, c150 AD); geography (world map of Eratosthenes, 276-194 BC); hydraulics (**Archimedes**, 287-212 BC); medicine (Galen, 130-200 AD), and chemistry. Inventors refined uses for siphons, valves, gears, springs, screws, levers, cams, and pulleys.

A restored Persian empire under the **Parthians** (N. Iranian tribesmen) controlled the eastern Hellenistic world 250 BC-229 AD. The Parthians and the succeeding Sassanian dynasty (229-651) fought with Rome periodically. The **Sassanians** revived Zoroastrianism as a state religion, and patronized a nationalistic artistic and scholarly renaissance.

Rome. The city of Rome was founded, according to legend, by Romulus in 753 BC. Through military expansion and colonization, and by granting citizenship to conquered tribes, the city annexed all of Italy south of the Po in the 100-year period before 268 BC. The Latin and other Italic tribes were annexed first, followed by the Etruscans (a civilized people north of Rome) and the Greek colonies in the south. With a large standing army and reserve forces of several hundred thousand, Rome was able to defeat Carthage in the 3 **Punic Wars**, 264-241, 218-201, 149-146 (despite the invasion of Italy by Hannibal, 218), thus gaining Sicily and territory in Spain and North Africa.

New provinces were added in the East, as Rome exploited local disputes to conquer Greece and Asia Minor in the 2d century BC, and Egypt in the first (after the defeat and suicide of **Antony and Cleopatra**, 30 BC). All the Mediterranean civilized world up to the disputed Parthian border was now Roman, and remained so for 500 years. Less civilized regions were added to the Empire: Gaul (conquered by Julius Caesar, 56-49 BC), Britain (43 AD) and Dacia NE of the Danube (117 AD).

The original aristocratic republican government, with democratic features added in the fifth and fourth centuries BC, deteriorated under the pressures of empire and class conflict (**Gracchus** brothers, social reformers, murdered 133, 121; slave revolts 135, 73). After a series of civil wars (Marius vs. Sulla 88-82, Caesar vs. Pompey 49-45, triumvirate vs. Caesar's assassins 44-43, Antony vs. Octavian 32-30), the empire came under the rule of a deified monarch (first emperor, **Augustus**, 27 BC-14 AD). Provincials (nearly all granted citizenship by Caracalla, 212 AD) came to dominate the army and civil service. Traditional Roman law, systematized and interpreted by independent jurists, and local self-rule in provincial cities were supplanted by a vast tax-collecting bureaucracy in the 3d and 4th centuries. The legal rights of women, children, and slaves were strengthened.

Roman innovations in civil engineering included water mills, windmills, and rotary mills, and the use of cement that hardened under water. Monumental architecture (baths, theaters, apartment houses) relied on the arch and the dome. The network of roads (some still standing) stretched 53,000 miles, passing through mountain tunnels as long as 3.5 miles. Aqueducts brought water to cities, underground sewers removed waste.

Roman art and literature were derivative of Greek models. Innovations were made in sculpture (naturalistic busts and equestrian statues), decorative wall painting (as at Pompeii), satire (Juvenal, 60-127), history (Tacitus 56-120), prose romance (Petronius, d. 66 AD). Violence and torture dominated mass public amusements, which were supported by the state.

India. The **Gupta** monarchs reunited N. India c320 AD. Their peaceful and prosperous reign saw a revival of Hindu religious thought and Brahmin power. The old Vedic traditions were combined with devotion to a plethora of indigenous deities (who were seen as manifestations of Vedic gods). Caste lines were reinforced, and Buddhism gradually disappeared. The art (often erotic), architecture, and literature of the period, patronized by the Gupta court, are considered to be among India's finest achievements (Kalidasa, poet and dramatist, fl. c400). Mathematical innovations included the use of zero and decimal numbers. Invasions by White Huns from the NW destroyed the empire c550.

Rich cultures also developed in S. India in this era. Emotional Tamil religious poetry aided the Hindu revival. The Pallava kingdom controlled much of S. India c350-880, and helped spread Indian civilization to S.E. Asia.

China. The Ch'in ruler Shih Huang Ti (ruled 221-210 BC), known as the First Emperor, centralized political authority in China, standardized the written language, laws, weights, measures, and coinage, and conducted a census, but tried to destroy most philosophical texts. The Han dynasty (206 BC-220 AD) instituted the Mandarin bureaucracy, which lasted for 2,000 years. Local officials were selected by examination in the Confucian classics and trained at the imperial university and at provincial schools. The invention of paper facilitated this bureaucratic system. Agriculture was promoted, but the peasants bore most of the tax burden. Irrigation was improved; water clocks and sundials were used; astronomy and mathematics thrived; landscape painting was perfected.

With the expansion south and west (to nearly the present borders of today's China), trade was opened with India, S.E. Asia, and the Middle East, over sea and caravan routes. Indian missionaries brought Mahayana Buddhism to China by the first century AD, and spawned a variety of sects. Taoism was revived, and merged with popular superstitions. Taoist and Buddhist monasteries and convents multiplied in the turbulent centuries after the collapse of the Han dynasty.

The One God Triumphs: 1-750 AD

Christianity. Religions indigenous to particular Middle Eastern nations became international in the first 3 centuries of the Roman Empire. Roman citizens worshipped **Isis** of Egypt, **Mithras** of Persia, **Demeter** of Greece, and the great mother **Cybele** of Phrygia. Their cults centered on mysteries (secret ceremonies) and the promise of an afterlife, symbolized by the death and rebirth of the god. Judaism, which had begun as the national cult of Judea, also spread by emigration and conversion. It was the only ancient religion west of India to survive.

Christians, who emerged as a distinct sect in the second half of the 1st century AD, revered **Jesus**, a Jewish preacher said to have been killed by the Romans at the request of Jewish authorities in Jerusalem c30 AD. They considered him the Savior (Messiah, or Christ) who rose from the dead and could grant

eternal life to the faithful, despite their sinfulness. They believed he was an incarnation of the one god worshipped by the Jews, and that he would return soon to pass final judgment on the world. The missionary activities of such early leaders as Paul of Tarsus spread the faith, at first mostly among Jews or among quasi-Jews attracted by the Pauline rejection of such difficult Jewish laws as circumcision. Intermittent persecution, as in Rome under Nero in 64 AD, on grounds of suspected disloyalty, failed to disrupt the Christian communities. Each congregation, generally urban and of plebeian character, was tightly organized under a leader (bishop) elders (presbyters or priests), and assistants (deacons). Stories about Jesus (the Gospels) and the early church (Acts) were written down in the late first and early 2d centuries, and circulated along with letters of Paul. An authoritative canon of these writings was not fixed until the 4th century.

A school for priests was established at Alexandria in the second century. Its teachers (Origen c182-251) helped define Christian doctrine and promote the faith in Greek-style philosophical works. Pagan Neoplatonism was given Christian coloration in the works of Church Fathers such as Augustine (354-430). Christian hermits, often drawn from the lower classes, began to associate in monasteries, first in Egypt (St. Pachomius c290-345), then in other eastern lands, then in the West (St. Benedict's rule, 529). Popular devotion to saints, especially Mary, mother of Jesus, spread.

Under Constantine (ruled 306-337), Christianity became in effect the established religion of the Empire. Pagan temples were expropriated, state funds were used to build huge churches and support the hierarchy, and laws were adjusted in accordance with Christian notions. Pagan worship was banned by the end of the fourth century, and severe restrictions were placed on Judaism.

The newly established church was rocked by doctrinal disputes, often exacerbated by regional rivalries both within and outside the Empire. Chief heresies (as defined by church councils backed by imperial authority) were Arianism, which denied the divinity of Jesus; Donatism, which rejected the convergence of church and state and denied the validity of sacraments performed by sinful clergy; and the Monophysite position denying the dual nature of Christ.

Judaism. First century Judaism embraced several sects, including: the Sadducees, mostly drawn from the Temple priesthood, who were culturally Hellenized; the Pharisees, who upheld the full range of traditional customs and practices as of equal weight to literal scriptural law, and elaborated synagogue worship; and the Essenes, an ascetic, millenarian sect. Messianic fervor led to repeated, unsuccessful rebellions against Rome (66-70, 135). As a result, the Temple was destroyed, and the population decimated.

To avoid the dissolution of the faith, a program of codification of law was begun at the academy of Yavneh. The work continued for some 500 years in Palestine and Babylonia, ending in the final redaction of the Talmud (c600), a huge collection of legal and moral debates, rulings, liturgy, Biblical exegesis, and legendary materials.

Islam. The earliest Arab civilization emerged by the end of the 2d millenium BC in the watered highlands of Yemen. Seaborne and caravan trade in frankincense and myrrh connected the area with the Nile and Fertile Crescent. The Minaean, Sabean (Sheba), and Himyarite states successively held sway. By Mohammed's time (7th century AD), the region was a province of Sassanian Persia. In the North, the Nabataean kingdom at Petra and the kingdom of Palmyra were first Aramaicized and then Romanized, and finally absorbed like neighboring Judea into the Roman Empire. Nomads shared the central region with a few trading towns and oases. Wars between tribes and raids on settled communities were common, and were celebrated in a poetic tradition that by the 6th century helped establish a classic literary Arabic.

In 611 Mohammed, a wealthy 40-year-old Arab of Mecca, had a revelation from Allah, the one true god, calling on him to repudiate pagan idolatry. Drawing on elements of Judaism and Christianity, and eventually incorporating some Arab pagan traditions (such as reverence for the black stone at the kaaba shrine in Mecca), Mohammed's teachings, recorded in the Koran, forged a new religion, Islam (submission to Allah). Opposed by the leaders of Mecca, Mohammed made a hejira (migration) to Medina to the north in 622, the beginning of the Moslem lunar calendar. He and his followers defeated the Meccans in 624 in the first jihad (holy war); and by his death (632), nearly all the Arabian peninsula accepted his religious and secular leadership.

Under the first two caliphs (successors) Abu Bakr (632-34) and Oman (634-44), Moslem rule was confirmed over Arabia. Raiding parties into Byzantine and Persian border areas developed into campaigns of conquest against the two empires, which had been weakened by wars and by disaffection among subject peoples (including Coptic and Syriac Christians opposed to the Byzantine orthodox church). Syria, Palestine, Egypt, Iraq, and Persia all fell to the inspired Arab armies. The Arabs at first remained a distinct minority, using non-Moslems in the new administrative system, and tolerating Christians, Jews, and Zoroastrians as self-governing "Peoples of the Book," whose taxes supported the empire.

Disputes over the succession, and puritan reaction to the wealth and refinement that empire brought to the ruling strata, led to the growth of schismatic movements. The followers of Mohammed's son-in-law Ali (assassinated 661) and his descendants became the founders of the more mystical Shi'ite sect, still the largest non-orthodox Moslem sect. The Karijites, puritanical, militant, and egalitarian, persist as a minor sect to the present.

Under the Ummayad caliphs (661-750), the boundaries of Islam were extended across N. Africa and into Spain. Arab armies in the West were stopped at Tours in 732 by the Frank Charles Martel. Asia Minor, the Indus Valley, and Transoxiana were conquered in the East. The vast majority of the subject population gradually converted to Islam, encouraged by tax and career privileges. The Arab language supplanted the local tongues in the central and western areas, but Arab soldiers and rulers in the East eventually became assimilated to the indigenous languages.

New Peoples Enter History: 400-900

Barbarian invasions. Germanic tribes infiltrated S and E from their Baltic homeland during the 1st millenium BC, reaching S. Germany by 100 BC and the Black Sea by 214 AD. Organized into large federated tribes under elected kings, most resisted Roman domination and raided the empire in time of civil war (Goths took Dacia 214, raided Thrace 251-269). German troops and commanders came to dominate the Roman armies by the end of the 4th century. Huns, invaders from Asia, entered Europe 372, driving more Germans into the western empire. Emperor Valens allowed Visigoths to cross

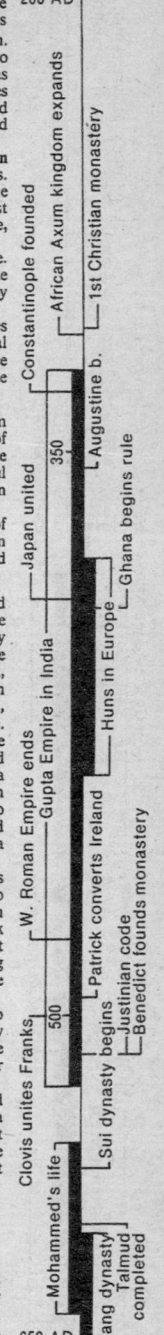

200 AD

African Axum kingdom expands — 1st Christian monastery

Constantinople founded — Augustine b.

Japan united — 350 — Ghana begins rule

Gupta Empire in India — Huns in Europe

W. Roman Empire ends — Patrick converts Ireland

Justinian code — Benedict founds monastery

Clovis unites Franks — 500 — Sui dynasty begins

Mohammed's life — Tang dynasty / Talmud completed

650 AD

Greek replaces Latin in Byzantium

Slav-Turk Bulgarian Empire begins

650

Chinese poet Li Po b.

Nara period begins, Japan

750

Baghdad founded

Charlemagne rules

Viking explorations, raids

850

Arab-Moslem golden age

Vietnam independent

950

the Danube 376. Huns under Attila (d. 453) raided Gaul, Italy, Balkans. The western empire, weakened by overtaxation and social stagnation, was overrun in the 5th century. Gaul was effectively lost 406-7, Spain 409, Britain 410, Africa 429-39. Rome itself was sacked 410 by Visigoths under Alaric, 455 by Vandals. The last western emperor, Romulus Augustulus, was deposed 476 by the Germanic chief Odoacer.

Celts. Celtic cultures, which in pre-Roman times covered most of W. Europe, were confined almost entirely to the British Isles after the Germanic invasions. St. Patrick completed the conversion of Ireland (c457-92). A strong monastic tradition took hold. Irish monastic missionaries in Scotland, England, and the continent (Columba c521-597; Columban c543-615) helped restore Christianity after the Germanic invasions. The monasteries became renowned centers of classic and Christian learning, and presided over the recording of a Christianized Celtic mythology, elaborated by secular writers and bards. An intricate decorative art style developed, especially in book illumination (Lindisfarne Gospels, c700, Book of Kells, 8th century).

Successor states. The Visigoth kingdom in Spain (from 419) and much of France (to 507) saw a continuation of much Roman administration, language, and law (Breviary of Alaric 506), until its destruction by the Moslems, 711. The Vandal kingdom in Africa, from 429, was conquered by the Byzantines, 533. Italy was ruled in succession by an Ostrogothic kingdom under Byzantine suzerainty 489-554, direct Byzantine government, and the German Lombards (568-774). The latter divided the peninsula with the Byzantines and the papacy under the dynamic reformer Pope Gregory the Great (590-604) and his successors.

King Clovis (ruled 481-511) united the Franks on both sides of the Rhine, and after his conversion to orthodox Christianity, defeated the Arian Burgundians (after 500) and Visigoths (507) with the support of the native clergy and the papacy. Under the Merovingian kings a feudal system emerged: power was fragmented among hierarchies of military landowners. Social stratification, which in late Roman times had acquired legal, hereditary sanction, was reinforced. The Carolingians (747-987) expanded the kingdom and restored central power. **Charlemagne** (ruled 768-814) conquered nearly all the Germanic lands, including Lombard Italy, and was crowned Emperor by Pope Leo III in Rome in 800. A centuries-long decline in commerce and the arts was reversed under Charlemagne's patronage. He welcomed Jews to his kingdom, which became a center of Jewish learning (Rashi 1040-1105). He sponsored the "Carolingian Renaissance" of learning under the Anglo-Latin scholar Alcuin (c732-804), who reformed church liturgy.

Byzantine Empire. Under Diocletian (ruled 284-305) the empire had been divided into 2 parts to facilitate administration and defense. Constantine founded **Constantinople,** 330, (at old Byzantium) as a fully Christian city. Commerce and taxation financed a sumptuous, orientalized court, a class of hereditary bureaucratic families, and magnificent urban construction (Hagia Sophia, 532-37). The city's fortifications and naval innovations (Greek fire) repelled assaults by Goths, Huns, Slavs, Bulgars, Avars, Arabs, and Scandinavians. Greek replaced Latin as the official language by c700. Byzantine art, a solemn, sacral, and stylized variation of late classical styles (mosaics at S. Vitale, Ravenna, 526-48) was a starting point for medieval art in E. and W. Europe.

Justinian (ruled 527-65) reconquered parts of Spain, N. Africa, and Italy, codified Roman law (*codex Justinianus,* 529, was medieval Europe's chief legal text), closed the Platonic Academy at Athens and ordered all pagans to convert. Lombards in Italy, Arabs in Africa retook most of his conquests. The Isaurian dynasty from Anatolia (from 717) and the Macedonian dynasty (867-1054) restored military and commercial power. The Iconoclast controversy (726-843) over the permissibility of images, helped alienate the Eastern Church from the papacy.

Arab Empire. Baghdad, founded 762, became the seat of the **Abbasid** Caliphate (founded 750), while Ummayads continued to rule in Spain. A brilliant cosmopolitan civilization emerged, inaugurating an Arab-Moslem golden age. Arab lyric poetry revived; Greek, Syriac, Persian, and Sanskrit books were translated into Arabic, often by Syriac Christians and Jews, whose theology and Talmudic law, respectively, influenced Islam. The arts and music flourished at the court of **Harun al-Rashid** (786-809), celebrated in *The Arabian Nights.* The sciences, medicine, and mathematics were pursued at Baghdad, Cordova, and Cairo (founded 969). Science and Aristotelian philosophy culminated in the systems of Avicenna (980-1037), Averroes (1126-98), and Maimonides (1135-1204), a Jew; all influenced later Christian scholarship and theology. The Islamic ban on images encouraged a sinuous, geometric decorative tradition, applied to architecture and illumination. A gradual loss of Arab control in Persia (from 874) led to the capture of Baghdad by Persians, 945. By the next century, Spain and N. Africa were ruled by Berbers, while Turks prevailed in Asia Minor and the Levant. The loss of political power by the caliphs allowed for the growth of non-orthodox trends, especially the mystical Sufi tradition (theologian Ghazali, 1058-1111).

Africa. Immigrants from Saba in S. Arabia helped set up the **Axum** kingdom in Ethiopia in the 2d century (their language, Ge'ez, is preserved by the Ethiopian Church). In the 4th century, when the kingdom became Christianized, it defeated Kushite Meroe and expanded into Yemen. Axum was the center of a vast ivory trade; it controlled the Red Sea coast until c1100. Arab conquest in Egypt cut Axum's political and economic ties with Byzantium.

The Iron Age entered W. Africa by the end of the 1st millenium BC. **Ghana,** the first known sub-Saharan state, ruled in the upper Senegal-Niger region c400-1240, controlling the trade of gold from mines in the S to trans-Sahara caravan routes to the N. The **Bantu** peoples, probably of W. African origin, began to spread E and S perhaps 2000 years ago, displacing the Pygmies and Bushmen of central

Japan. The advanced Neolithic Yayoi period, when irrigation, rice farming, and iron and bronze casting techniques were introduced from China or Korea, persisted to c400 AD. The myriad Japanese states were then united by the **Yamato** clan, under an emperor who acted as the chief priest of the animistic **Shinto** cult. Japanese political and military intervention in Korea by the 6th century quickened a Chinese cultural invasion, bringing Buddhism, the Chinese language (which long remained a literary and governmental medium), Chinese ideographs and Buddhist styles in painting, sculpture, literature, and architecture (7th c. Horyu-ji temple at Nara). The Taika Reforms, 646, tried to centralize Japan according to Chinese bureaucratic and Buddhist philosophical values, but failed to curb traditional Japanese decentralization. A nativist reaction against the Buddhist **Nara period** (710-94) ushered in the

Heian period (794-1185) centered at the new capital, Kyoto. Japanese elegance and simplicity modified Chinese styles in architecture, scroll painting, and literature; the writing system was also simplified. The courtly novel *Tale of Genji* (1010-20) testifies to the enhanced role of women.

Southeast Asia. The historic peoples of southeast Asia began arriving some 2500 years ago from China and Tibet, displacing scattered aborigines. Their agriculture relied on rice and tubers (yams), which they may have introduced to Africa. Indian cultural influences were strongest; literacy and Hindu and Buddhist ideas followed the southern India-China trade route. From the southern tip of Indochina, the kingdom of **Funan** (1st-7th centuries) traded as far west as Persia. It was absorbed by Chenla, itself conquered by the **Khmer Empire** (600-1300). The Khmers, under Hindu god-kings (Suryavarman II, 1113-c1150), built the monumental Angkor Wat temple center for the royal phallic cult. The **Nam-Viet** kingdom in Annam, dominated by China and Chinese culture for 1,000 years, emerged in the 10th century, growing at the expense of the Khmers, who also lost ground in the NW to the new, highly-organized **Thai** kingdom. On Sumatra, the **Srivijaya** Empire at Palembang controlled vital sea lanes (7th to 10th centuries). A Buddhist dynasty, the Sailendras, ruled central **Java** (8th-9th centuries), building at Borobudur one of the largest stupas in the world.

China. The short-lived Sui dynasty (581-618) ushered in a period of commercial, artistic, and scientific achievement in China, continuing under the T'ang dynasty (618-906). Such inventions as the magnetic compass, gunpowder, the abacus, and printing were introduced or perfected. Medical innovations included cataract surgery. The state, from the cosmopolitan capital, Ch'ang-an, supervised foreign trade which exchanged Chinese silks, porcelains, and art works for spices, ivory, etc., over Central Asian caravan routes and sea routes reaching Africa. A golden age of poetry bequeathed tens of thousands of works to later generations (Tu Fu 712-70, Li Po 701-62). Landscape painting flourished. Commercial and industrial expansion continued under the **Northern Sung** dynasty (960-1126), facilitated by paper money and credit notes. But commerce never achieved respectability; government monopolies expropriated successful merchants. The population, long stable at 50 million, doubled in 200 years with the introduction of early-ripening rice and the double harvest. In art, native Chinese styles were revived.

Americas. An Indian empire stretched from the Valley of Mexico to Guatemala, 300-600, centering on the huge city **Teotihuacan** (founded 100 BC). To the S, in Guatemala, a high **Mayan** civilization developed, 150-900, around hundreds of rural ceremonial centers. The Mayans improved on Olmec writing and the calendar, and pursued astronomy and mathematics (using the idea of zero). In S. America, a widespread pre-Inca culture grew from **Tiahuanaco** near Lake Titicaca (Gateway of the Sun, c700).

Christian Europe Regroups and Expands: 900-1300

Scandinavians. Pagan Danish and Norse (**Viking**) adventurers, traders, and pirates raided the coasts of the British Isles (Dublin founded c831), France, and even the Mediterranean for over 200 years beginning in the late 8th century. Inland settlement in the W was limited to Great Britain (King Canute, 994-1035) and Normandy, settled under Rollo, 911, as a fief of France. Other Vikings reached Iceland (874), Greenland (c986), and probably N. America (Leif Eriksson c1000). Norse traders (**Varangians**) developed Russian river commerce from the 8th-11th centuries, and helped set up a state at Kiev in the late 9th century. Conversion to Christianity occurred during the 10th century, reaching Sweden 100 years later. Eleventh century Norman bands conquered S. Italy and Sicily. Duke **William of Normandy** conquered England, 1066, bringing continental feudalism and the French language, essential elements in later English civilization.

East Europe. Slavs inhabited areas of E. Central Europe in prehistoric times, and reached most of their present limits by c850. The first Slavic states were in the Balkans (Slav-Turk **Bulgarian Empire**, 680-1018) and Moravia (628). Missions of St. Cyril (whose Greek-based Cyrillic alphabet is still used by S. and E. Slavs) converted Moravia, 863. The Eastern Slavs, part-civilized under the overlordship of the Turkish-Jewish **Khazar** trading empire (7th-10th centuries), gravitated toward Constantinople by the 9th century. The **Kievan state** adopted Eastern Christianity under Prince Vladimir, 989. King Boleslav I (992-1025) began **Poland's** long history of eastern conquest. The Magyars (**Hungarians**) in Europe since 896, accepted Latin Christianity, 1001.

Germany. The German kingdom that emerged after the breakup of Charlemagne's Empire remained a confederation of largely autonomous states. The Saxon Otto I, king from 936, established the **Holy Roman Empire** of Germany and Italy in alliance with Pope John XII, who crowned him emperor, 962; he defeated the Magyars, 955. Imperial power was greatest under the Hohenstaufens (1138-1254), despite the growing opposition of the papacy, which ruled central Italy, and the Lombard League cities. Frederick II (1194-1250) improved administration, patronized the arts; after his death German influence was removed from Italy.

Christian Spain. From its northern mountain redoubts, Christian rule slowly migrated south through the 11th century, when Moslem unity collapsed. After the capture of **Toledo** (1085), the kingdoms of Portugal, Castile, and Aragon undertook repeated crusades of reconquest, finally completed in 1492. Elements of Islamic civilization persisted in recaptured areas, influencing all W. Europe.

Crusades. Pope Urban II called, 1095, for a crusade to restore Asia Minor to Byzantium and conquer the Holy Land from the Turks. Some 10 crusades (to 1291) succeeded only in founding 4 temporary Frankish states in the Levant. The 4th crusade sacked Constantinople, 1204. In Rhineland (1096), England (1290), France (1306), Jews were massacred or expelled, and wars were launched against Christian heretics (**Albigensian** crusade in France, 1229). Trade in eastern luxuries expanded, led by the Venetian naval empire.

Economy. The agricultural base of European life benefitted from improvements in **plow design** c1000, and by draining of lowlands and clearing of forests, leading to a rural population increase. Towns grew in N. Italy, Flanders, and N. Germany (Hanseatic League). Improvements in **loom design** permitted factory textile production. **Guilds** dominated urban trades from the 12th century. Banking (centered in Italy, 12th-15th century) facilitated long-distance trade.

The Church. The split between the Eastern and Western churches was formalized in 1054. W. and

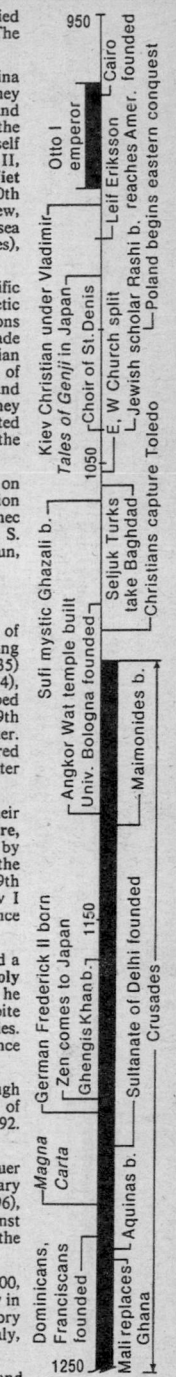

950 — Cairo
    Otto I emperor
    Leif Eriksson reaches Amer.
    Rashi b.
    Poland begins eastern conquest
    Kiev Christian under Vladimir
    Tales of Genji in Japan
    Choir of St. Denis
    E. W Church split
    Jewish scholar
1050 — Christians capture Toledo
    Seljuk Turks take Baghdad
    Sufi mystic Ghazali b.
    Angkor Wat temple built
    Univ. Bologna founded
    Maimonides b.
    German Frederick II born
1150 — Zen comes to Japan
    Ghengis Khan b.
    Sultanate of Delhi founded
    Crusades
    Magna Carta
    Aquinas b.
    Dominicans, Franciscans founded
    Mali replaces Ghana
1250

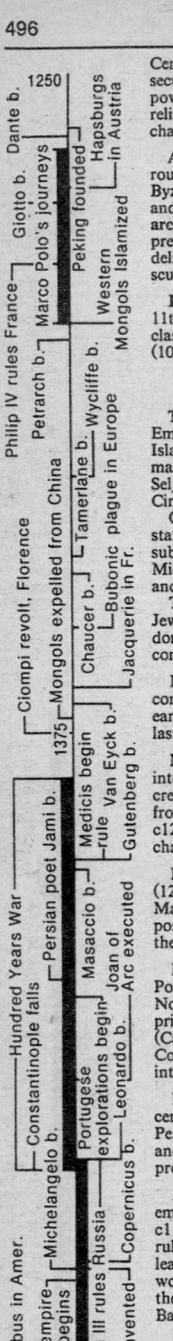

Central Europe was divided into 500 bishoprics under one united hierarchy, but conflicts between secular and church authorities were frequent (German **Investiture Controversy**, 1075-1122). Clerical power was first strengthened through the international monastic reform begun at Cluny, 910. Popular religious enthusiasm often expressed itself in heretical movements (Waldensians from 1173), but was channelled by the **Dominican** (1215) and **Franciscan** (1223) friars into the religious mainstream.

Arts. **Romanesque** architecture (11th-12th centuries) expanded on late Roman models, using the rounded arch and massed stone to support enlarged basilicas. Painting and sculpture followed Byzantine models. The literature of chivalry was exemplified by the epic (Chanson de Roland, c1100) and by courtly love poems of the troubadours of Provence and minnesingers of Germany. **Gothic** architecture emerged in France (choir of St. Denis, c1040) and spread as French cultural influence predominated in Europe. Rib vaulting and pointed arches were used to combine soaring heights with delicacy, and freed walls for display of stained glass. Exteriors were covered with painted relief sculpture and elaborate architectural detail.

Learning. Law, medicine, and philosophy were advanced at independent **universities** (Bologna, late 11th century), originally corporations of students and masters. Twelfth century translations of Greek classics, especially Aristotle, encouraged an analytic approach. Scholastic philosophy, from Anselm (1033-1109) to Aquinas (1225-74) attempted to reconcile reason and revelation.

Apogee of Central Asian Power; Islam Grows: 1250-1500

Turks. Turkic peoples, of Central Asian ancestry, were a military threat to the Byzantine and Persian Empires from the 6th century. After several waves of invasions, during which most of the Turks adopted Islam, the **Seljuk Turks** took Baghdad, 1055. They ruled Persia, Iraq, and, after 1071, Asia Minor, where massive numbers of Turks settled. The empire was divided in the 12th century into smaller states ruled by Seljuks, Kurds (**Saladin** c1137-93), and Mamelukes (a military caste of former Turk, Kurd, and Circassian slaves), which governed Egypt and the Middle East until the Ottoman era (c1290-1922).

Osman I (ruled c1290-1326) and succeeding sultans united Anatolian Turkish warriors in a militaristic state that waged holy war against Byzantium and Balkan Christians. Most of the Balkans had been subdued, and Anatolia united, when **Constantinople fell**, 1453. By the mid-16th century, Hungary, the Middle East, and North Africa had been conquered. The Turkish advance was stopped at Vienna, 1529, and at the naval battle of Lepanto, 1571, by Spain, Venice, and the papacy.

The Ottoman state was governed in accordance with orthodox Moslem law. Greek, Armenian, and Jewish communities were segregated, and ruled by religious leaders responsible for taxation; they dominated trade. State offices and most army ranks were filled by slaves through a system of child conscription among Christians.

India. Mahmud of Ghazni (971-1030) led repeated Turkish raids into N. India. Turkish power was consolidated in 1206 with the start of the **Sultanate at Delhi**. Centralization of state power under the early Delhi sultans went far beyond traditional Indian practice. Moslem rule of most of the subcontinent lasted until the British conquest some 600 years later.

Mongols. Genghis Khan (c1162-1227) first united the feuding Mongol tribes, and built their armies into an effective offensive force around a core of highly mobile cavalry. He and his immediate successors created the largest land empire in history; by 1279 it stretched from the east coast of Asia to the Danube, from the Siberian steppes to the Arabian Sea. East-West trade and contacts were facilitated (Marco Polo c1254-1324). The western Mongols were Islamized by 1295; successor states soon lost their Mongol character by assimilation. They were briefly reunited under the Turk Tamerlane (1336-1405).

Kublai Khan ruled China from his new capital Peking (founded 1264). Naval campaigns against Japan (1274, 1281) and Java (1293) were defeated, the latter by the Hindu-Buddhist maritime kingdom of Majapahit. The **Yuan** dynasty made use of Mongols and other foreigners (including Europeans) in official posts, and tolerated the return of Nestorian Christianity (suppressed 841-45) and the spread of Islam in the South and West. A native reaction expelled the Mongols, 1367-68.

Russia. The Kievan state in Russia, weakened by the decline of Byzantium and the rise of the Catholic Polish-Lithuanian state, was overrun by the Mongols, 1238-40. Only the northern trading republic of Novgorod remained independent. The grand dukes of Moscow emerged as leaders of a coalition of princes that eventually defeated the Mongols, by 1481. With the fall of Constantinople, the **Tsars** (Caesars) at Moscow (from Ivan III, ruled 1462-1505) set up an independent Russian Orthodox Church. Commerce failed to revive. The isolated Russian state remained agrarian, with the peasant class falling into serfdom.

Persia. A revival of Persian literature, using the Arab alphabet and literary forms, began in the 10th century (epic of Firdausi, 935-1020). An art revival, influenced by Chinese styles, began in the 12th. Persian cultural and political forms, and often the Persian language, were used for centuries by Turkish and Mongol elites from the Balkans to India. Persian mystics from Rumi (1207-73) to Jami (1414-92) promoted Sufism in their poetry.

Africa. Two Berber dynasties, imbued with Islamic militance, emerged from the Sahara to carve out empires from the Sahel to central Spain — the **Almoravids**, c1050-1140, and the fanatical **Almohads**, c1125-1269. The Ghanaian empire was replaced in the upper Niger by Mali, c1230-c1340, whose Moslem rulers imported Egyptians to help make **Timbuktu** a center of commerce (in gold, leather, slaves) and learning. The Songhay empire (to 1590) replaced Mali. To the S, forest kingdoms produced refined art works (Ife terra cotta, Benin bronzes). Other Moslem states in Nigeria (Hausas) and Chad originated in the 11th century, and continued in some form until the 19th century European conquest. Less developed Bantu kingdoms existed across central Africa.

Some 40 Moslem Arab-Persian trading colonies and city-states were established all along the E. African coast from the 10th century (Kilwa, Mogadishu). The interchange with Bantu peoples produced the **Swahili** language and culture. Gold, palm oil, and slaves were brought from the interior, stimulating the growth of the Monamatapa kingdom of the Zambezi (15th century). The Christian Ethiopian empire (from 13th century) continued the traditions of Axum.

Southeast Asia. Islam was introduced into Malaya and the Indonesian islands by Arab, Persian, and

ndian traders. Coastal Moslem cities and states (starting before 1300), enriched by trade, soon dominated the interior. Chief among these was the **Malacca** state, on the Malay peninsula, c1400-1511.

Arts and Statecraft Thrive in Europe: 1350-1600

Italian Renaissance & humanism. Distinctive Italian achievements in the arts in the late Middle Ages (Dante, 1265-1321, Giotto, 1276-1337) led to the vigorous new styles of the Renaissance (14th-16th centuries). Patronized by the rulers of the quarreling petty states of Italy (Medicis in Florence and the papacy, c1400-1737), the plastic arts perfected realistic techniques, including **perspective** (Masaccio, 1401-28, Leonardo 1452-1519). Classical motifs were used in architecture and increased talent and expense were put into secular buildings. The Florentine dialect was refined as a national literary language (Petrarch, 1304-74). Greek refugees from the E strengthened the respect of humanist scholars for the classic sources (Bruni 1370-1444). Soon an international movement aided by the spread of printing (Gutenberg c1400-1468), **humanism** was optimistic about the power of human reason (Erasmus of Rotterdam, 1466-1536, Thomas More's *Utopia*, 1516) and valued individual effort in the arts and in politics (Machiavelli, 1469-1527).

France. The French monarchy, strengthened in its repeated struggles with powerful nobles (Burgundy, Flanders, Aquitaine) by alliances with the growing commercial towns, consolidated bureaucratic control under Philip IV (ruled 1285-1314) and extended French influence into Germany and Italy (popes at Avignon, France, 1309-1417). The **Hundred Years War**, 1338-1453, ended English dynastic claims in France (battles of Crécy, 1346, Poitiers, 1356; Joan of Arc executed, 1431). A French Renaissance, dating from royal invasions of Italy, 1494, 1499, was encouraged at the court of Francis I (ruled 1515-47), who centralized taxation and law. French vernacular literature consciously asserted its independence (La Pleiade, 1549).

England. The evolution of England's unique political institutions began with the Magna Carta, 1215, by which King John guaranteed the privileges of nobles and church against the monarchy and assured jury trial. After the Wars of the Roses (1455-85), the **Tudor dynasty** reasserted royal prerogatives (Henry VIII, ruled 1509-47), but the trend toward independent departments and ministerial government also continued. English trade (wool exports from c1340) was protected by the nation's growing maritime power (**Spanish Armada** destroyed, 1588).
English replaced French and Latin in the late 14th century in law and literature (Chaucer, 1340-1400) and English translation of the Bible began (Wycliffe, 1380s). Elizabeth I (ruled 1558-1603) presided over a confident flowering of poetry (Spenser, 1552-99), drama (Shakespeare, 1564-1616), and music.

German Empire. From among a welter of minor feudal states, church lands, and independent cities, the Hapsburgs assembled a far-flung territorial domain, based in Austria from 1276. The family held the title Holy Roman Emperor from 1452 to the Empire's dissolution in 1806, but failed to centralize its domains, leaving Germany disunited for centuries. Resistance to Turkish expansion brought Hungary under Austrian control from the 16th century. The Netherlands, Luxembourg, and Burgundy were added in 1477, curbing French expansion.
The Flemish painting tradition of naturalism, technical proficiency, and bourgeois subject matter began in the 15th century (Jan Van Eyck, 1366-1440), the earliest northern manifestation of the Renaissance. Durer (1471-1528) typified the merging of late Gothic and Italian trends in 16th century German art. Imposing civic architecture flourished in the prosperous commercial cities.

Spain. Despite the unification of Castile and Aragon in 1479, the 2 countries retained separate governments, and the nobility, especially in Aragon and Catalonia, retained many privileges. Spanish lands in Italy (Naples, Sicily) and the Netherlands entangled the country in European wars through the mid-17th century, while explorers, traders, and conquerors built up a Spanish empire in the Americas and the Philippines.
From the late 15th century, a **golden age** of literature and art produced works of social satire (plays of Lope de Vega, 1562-1635; Cervantes, 1547-1616), as well as spiritual intensity (El Greco, 1541-1614; Velazquez, 1599-1660).

Black Death. The bubonic plague reached Europe from the E in 1348, killing as much as half the population by 1350. Labor scarcity forced a rise in wages and brought greater freedom to the peasantry, making possible **peasant uprisings** (Jacquerie in France, 1358, Wat Tyler's rebellion in England, 1381). In the *ciompi* revolt, 1378, Florentine wage earners demanded a say in economic and political power.

Explorations. Organized European maritime exploration began, seeking to evade the Venice-Ottoman monopoly of eastern trade and to promote Christianity. Expeditions from Portugal beginning 1418 explored the west coast of Africa, until **Vasco da Gama** rounded the Cape of Good Hope in 1497 and reached India. A Portuguese trading empire was consolidated by the seizure of Goa, 1510, and Malacca, 1551. Japan was reached in 1542. Spanish voyages (**Columbus**, 1492-1504) uncovered a new world, which Spain hastened to subdue. Navigation schools in Spain and Portugal, the development of large sailing ships (carracks), and the invention of the rifle, c1475, aided European penetration.

Mughals and Safavids. East of the Ottoman empire, two Moslem dynasties ruled unchallenged in the 16th and 17th centuries. The Mughal empire in India, founded by Persianized Turkish invaders from the NW under Babur, dates from their 1526 conquest of Delhi. The dynasty ruled most of India for over 200 years, surviving nominally until 1857. Akbar (ruled 1556-1605) consolidated administration at his glorious court, where Urdu (Persian-influenced Hindi) developed. Trade relations with Europe increased. Under Shah Jahan (1629-58), a secularized art fusing Hindu and Moslem elements flourished in miniature painting and architecture (**Taj Mahal**). Sikhism, founded c1519, combined elements of both faiths. Suppression of Hindus and Shi'ite Moslems in S India in the late 17th century weakened the empire.
Fanatical devotion to the Shi'ite sect characterized the Safavids of Persia, 1502-1736, and led to hostilities with the Sunni Ottomans for over a century. The prosperity and strength of the empire are evidenced by the mosques at its capital, **Isfahan**. The dynasty enhanced Iranian national consciousness.

China. The Ming emperors, 1368-1644, the last native dynasty in China, wielded unprecedented personal power, while the Confucian bureaucracy began to suffer from inertia. European trade (Portugese

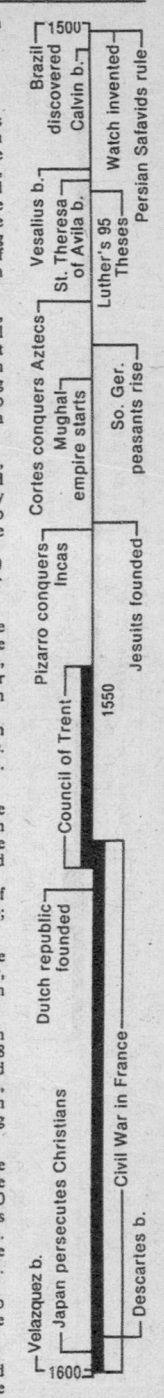

1500
Brazil discovered
Calvin b.
Watch invented
Persian Safavids rule
Vesalius b.
St. Theresa of Avila b.
Luther's 95 Theses
Cortes conquers Aztecs
Mughal empire starts
So. Ger. peasants rise
Pizarro conquers Incas
Jesuits founded
1550
Council of Trent
Dutch republic founded
Velazquez b.
Japan persecutes Christians
Civil War in France
Descartes b.
1600

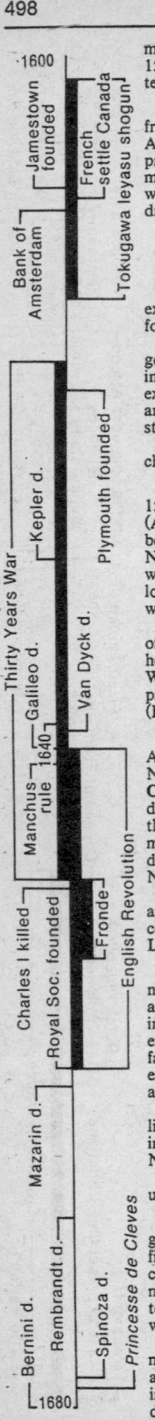

monopoly through **Macao** from 1557) was strictly controlled. Jesuit scholars and scientists (Matteo Ricci 1552-1610) introduced some Western science; their writings familiarized the West with China. Chinese technological inventiveness declined from this era, but the arts thrived, especially painting and ceramics.

Japan. After the decline of the first hereditary shogunate (chief generalship) at **Kamakura** (1185-1333), fragmentation of power accelerated, as did the consequent social mobility. Under Kamakura and the Ashikaga shogunate, 1338-1573, the daimyos (lords) and samurai (warriors) grew more powerful and promoted a martial ideology. Japanese pirates and traders plied the China coast. Popular Buddhist movements included the nationalist Nichiren sect (from c1250) and **Zen** (brought from China, 1191), which stressed meditation and a disciplined esthetic (tea ceremony, landscape gardening, judo, Noh drama).

Reformed Europe Expands Overseas: 1500-1700

Reformation begun. Theological debate and protests against real and perceived clerical corruption existed in the medieval Christian world, expressed by such dissenters as Wycliffe (c1320-84) and his followers, the Lollards, in England, and Huss (burned as a heretic, 1415) in Bohemia.

Luther (1483-1546) preached that only faith could lead to salvation, without the mediation of clergy or good works. He attacked the authority of the Pope, rejected priestly celibacy, and recommended individual study of the Bible (which he translated, c1525). His 95 Theses (1517) led to his excommunication (1520). **Calvin** (1509-64) said God's elect were predestined for salvation; good conduct and success were signs of election. Calvin in Geneva and Knox (1505-72) in Scotland erected theocratic states.

Henry VIII asserted English national authority and secular power by breaking away from the Catholic church, 1534. Monastic property was confiscated, and some Protestant doctrines given official sanction.

Religious wars. A century and a half of religious wars began with a South German peasant uprising, 1524, repressed with Luther's support. Radical sects—democratic, pacifist, millennarian—arose (Anabaptists ruled Muenster, 1534-35), and were suppressed violently. Civil war in France from 1562 between **Huguenots** (Protestant nobles and merchants) and Catholics ended with the 1598 Edict of Nantes tolerating Protestants (revoked 1685). Hapsburg attempts to restore Catholicism in Germany were resisted in 25 years of fighting; the 1555 Peace of Augsburg guarantee of religious independence to local princes and cities was confirmed only after the **Thirty Years War**, 1618-48, when much of Germany was devastated by local and foreign armies (Sweden, France).

A Catholic Reformation, or **counter-reformation**, met the Protestant challenge, clearly defining an official theology at the Council of Trent, 1545-63. The **Jesuit** order, founded 1534 by Loyola (1491-1556), helped reconvert large areas of Poland, Hungary, and S. Germany and sent missionaries to the New World, India, and China, while the Inquisition helped suppress heresy in Catholic countries. A revival of piety appeared in the devotional literature (Theresa of Avila, 1515-82) and the grandiose Baroque art (Bernini, 1598-1680) of Roman Catholic countries.

Scientific Revolution. The late nominalist thinkers (Ockham, c1300-49) of Paris and Oxford challenged Aristotelian orthodoxy, allowing for a freer scientific approach. But metaphysical values, such as the Neoplatonic faith in an orderly, mathematical cosmos, still motivated and directed subsequent inquiry. **Copernicus** (1473-1543) promoted the heliocentric theory, which was confirmed when Kepler (1571-1630) discovered the mathematical laws describing the orbits of the planets. The Christian-Aristotelian belief that heavens and earth were fundamentally different collapsed when **Galileo** (1564-1642) discovered moving sunspots, irregular moon topography, and moons around Jupiter. He and Newton (1642-1727) developed a mechanics that unified cosmic and earthly phenomena. To meet the needs of the new physics, Newton and Leibnitz (1646-1716) invented calculus, Descartes (1596-1650) invented analytic geometry.

An explosion of observational science included the discovery of blood circulation (Harvey, 1578-1657) and microscopic life (Leeuwenhoek, 1632-1723), and advances in anatomy (Vesalius, 1514-64, dissected corpses) and chemistry (Boyle, 1627-91). Scientific research institutes were founded: Florence, 1657, London (**Royal Society**), 1660, Paris, 1666. Inventions proliferated (Savery's steam engine, 1696).

Arts. Mannerist trends of the high Renaissance (**Michelangelo**, 1475-1564) exploited virtuosity, grace, novelty, and exotic subjects and poses. The notion of artistic genius was promoted, in contrast to the anonymous medieval artisan. Private commissions entered the art market. These trends were elaborated in the 17th century **Baroque** era, on a grander scale. Dynamic movement in painting and sculpture was emphasized by sharp lighting effects, use of rich materials (colored marble, gilt), realistic details. Curved facades, broken lines, rich, deep-cut detail, and ceiling decoration characterized Baroque architecture, especially in Germany. Monarchs, princes, and prelates, usually Catholic, used Baroque art to enhance and embellish their authority, as in royal portraits by Velazquez (1599-1660) and Van Dyck (1599-1641).

National styles emerged. In France, a taste for rectilinear order and serenity (Poussin, 1594-1665), linked to the new rational philosophy, was expressed in classical forms. The influence of **classical values** in French literature (tragedies of Racine, 1639-99) gave rise to the "battle of the Ancients and Moderns." New forms included the essay (Montaigne, 1533-92) and novel (*Princesse de Cleves*, La Fayette, 1678).

Dutch painting of the 17th century was unique in its wide social distribution. The Flemish tradition of undemonstrative realism reached its peak in Rembrandt (1606-69) and Vermeer (1632-75).

Economy. European economic expansion was stimulated by the new trade with the East, New World gold and silver, and a doubling of population (50 mln. in 1450, 100 mln. in 1600). New business and financial techniques were developed and refined, such as joint-stock companies, insurance, and letters of credit and exchange. The Bank of Amsterdam, 1609, and the Bank of England, 1694, broke the old monopoly of private banking families. The rise of a business mentality was typified by the spread of clock towers in cities in the 14th century. By the mid-15th century, portable clocks were available; the first watch was invented in 1502.

By 1650, most governments had adopted the **mercantile system**, in which they sought to amass metallic wealth by protecting their merchants' foreign and colonial trade monopolies. The rise in prices and the new coin-based economy undermined the craft guild and feudal manorial systems. Expanding industries, such as clothweaving and mining, benefitted from technical advances. Coal replaced disappearing wood as the chief fuel; it was used to fuel new 16th century blast furnaces making cast iron.

New World. The Aztecs united much of the Mesoamerican culture area in a militarist empire by 1519, om their capital, Tenochtitlan (pop. 300,000), which was the center of a cult requiring enormous levels f ritual human sacrifice. Most of the civilized areas of S. America were ruled by the centralized **Inca Empire** (1476-1534), stretching 2,000 miles from Ecuador to N.W. Argentina. Lavish and sophisticated traditions in pottery, weaving, sculpture, and architecture were maintained in both regions.

These empires, beset by revolts, fell in 2 short campaigns to gold-seeking Spanish forces based in the Antilles and Panama. **Cortes** took Mexico, 1519-21; **Pizarro** Peru, 1531-35. From these centers, land and sea expeditions claimed most of N. and S. America for Spain. The Indian high cultures did not survive the impact of Christian missionaries and the new upper class of whites and mestizos. In turn, New World silver, and such Indian products as potatoes, tobacco, corn, peanuts, chocolate, and rubber exercised a major economic influence on Europe. While the Spanish administration intermittently concerned itself with the welfare of Indians, the population remained impoverished at most levels, despite the growth of a distinct South American civilization. European diseases reduced the native population.

Brazil, which the Portuguese discovered in 1500 and settled after 1530, and the Caribbean colonies of several European nations developed a plantation economy where sugar cane, tobacco, cotton, coffee, rice, indigo, and lumber were grown commercially by slaves. From the early 16th to the late 19th centuries, some 10 million Africans were transported to **slavery** in the New World.

Netherlands. The urban, Calvinist northern provinces of the Netherlands rebelled against Hapsburg Spain, 1568, and founded an oligarchic mercantile republic. Their strategic control of the Baltic grain market enabled them to exploit Mediterranean food shortages. Religious refugees — French and Belgian Protestants, Iberian Jews — added to the cosmopolitan commercial talent pool. After Spain absorbed Portugal in 1580, the Dutch seized Portuguese possessions and created a vast, though generally short-lived commercial empire in Brazil, the Antilles, Africa, India, Ceylon, Malacca, Indonesia, and Taiwan, and challenged or supplanted Portuguese traders in China and Japan.

England. Anglicanism became firmly established under Elizabeth I after a brief Catholic interlude under "Bloody Mary," 1553-58. But religious and political conflicts led to a rebellion by Parliament, 1642. Roundheads (Puritans) defeated Cavaliers (Royalists); Charles I was beheaded, 1649. The new **Commonwealth** was ruled as a military dictatorship by Cromwell, who also brutally crushed an Irish rebellion, 1649-51. Conflicts within the Puritan camp (democratic Levelers defeated 1649) aided the Stuart restoration, 1660, but Parliament was permanently strengthened and the peaceful **"Glorious Revolution"**, 1688, advanced political and religious liberties (writings of Locke, 1632-1704). British privateers (Drake, 1540-96) challenged Spanish control of the New World, and penetrated Asian trade routes (Madras taken, 1639). N. American colonies (Jamestown, 1607, Plymouth, 1620) provided an outlet for religious dissenters.

France. Emerging from the religious civil wars in 1628, France regained military and commercial great power status under the ministries of **Richelieu** (1624-42), Mazarin (1643-61), and Colbert (1662-83). Under Louis XIV (ruled 1643-1715) royal absolutism triumphed over nobles and local *parlements* (defeat of Fronde, 1648-53). Permanent colonies were founded in Canada (1608), the Caribbean (1626), and India (1674).

Sweden. Sweden seceded from the Scandinavian Union in 1523. The thinly-populated agrarian state (with copper, iron, and timber exports) was united by the Vasa kings, whose conquests by the mid-17th century made Sweden the dominant Baltic power. The empire collapsed in the Great Northern War (1700-21).

Poland. After the union with Lithuania in 1447, Poland ruled vast territories from the Baltic to the Black Sea, resisting German and Turkish incursions. Catholic nobles failed to gain the loyalty of the Orthodox Christian peasantry in the East; commerce and trades were practiced by German and Jewish immigrants. The bloody 1648-49 cossack uprising began the kingdom's dismemberment.

China. A new dynasty, the **Manchus**, invaded from the NE and seized power in 1644, and expanded Chinese control to its greatest extent in Central and Southeast Asia. Trade and diplomatic contact with Europe grew, carefully controlled by China. New crops (sweet potato, maize, peanut) allowed an economic and population growth (300 million pop. in 1800). Traditional arts and literature were pursued with increased sophistication (*Dream of the Red Chamber*, novel, mid-18th century).

Japan. Tokugawa Ieyasu, shogun from 1603, finally unified and pacified feudal Japan. Hereditary daimyos and samurai monopolized government office and the professions. An urban merchant class grew, literacy spread, and a cultural renaissance occurred (haiku of Basho, 1644-94). Fear of European domination led to persecution of Christian converts from 1597, and stringent isolation from outside contact from 1640.

Philosophy, Industry, and Revolution: 1700-1800

Science and Reason. Faith in human reason and science as the source of truth and a means to improve the physical and social environment, espoused since the Renaissance (Francis Bacon, 1561-1626), was bolstered by scientific discoveries in spite of theological opposition (**Galileo's** forced retraction, 1633). Descartes applied the logical method of mathematics to discover "self-evident" scientific and philosophical truths, while Newton emphasized induction from experimental observation.

The challenge of reason to traditional religious and political values and institutions began with **Spinoza** (1632-77), who interpreted the Bible historically and called for political and intellectual freedom.

French philosophes assumed leadership of the "**Enlightenment**" in the 18th century. Montesquieu (1689-1755) used British history to support his notions of limited government. Voltaire's (1694-1778) diaries and novels of exotic travel illustrated the intellectual trends toward secular ethics and relativism. Rousseau's (1712-1778) radical concepts of the **social contract** and of the inherent goodness of the common man gave impetus to anti-monarchical republicanism. The *Encyclopedia*, 1751-72, edited by Diderot and d'Alembert, designed as a monument to reason, was largely devoted to practical technology.

In England, ideals of political and religious liberty were connected with empiricist philosophy and science in the followers of Locke. But the extreme **empiricism** of Hume (1711-76) and Berkeley

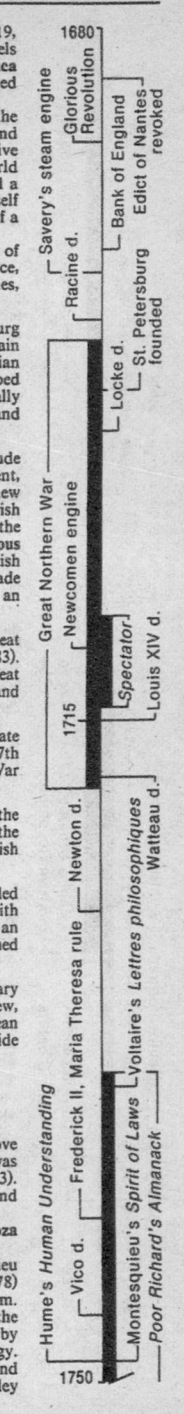

1680 — Glorious Revolution
Savery's steam engine
Cornelius
Racine d.
Bank of England
Edict of Nantes revoked
St. Petersburg founded
Locke d.
Great Northern War
Newcomen engine
1715
Spectator
Louis XIV d.
Newton d.
Frederick II, Maria Theresa rule
Voltaire's *Lettres philosophiques*
Watteau d.
Hume's *Human Understanding*
Vico d.
Montesquieu's *Spirit of Laws*
Poor Richard's Almanack
1750

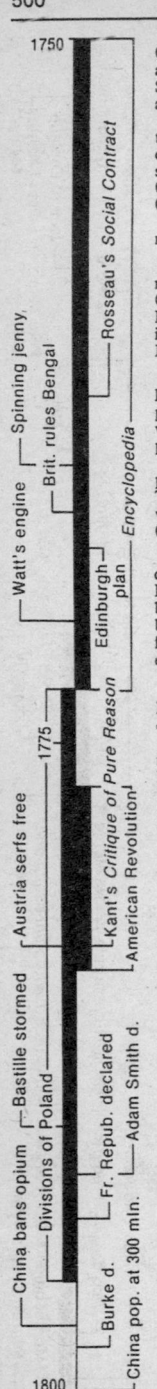

1750

Rosseau's Social Contract

Spinning jenny

Brit. rules Bengal

Watt's engine

Encyclopedia

Edinburgh plan

1775

Kant's Critique of Pure Reason

American Revolution

Austria serfs free

Bastille stormed

Fr. Repub. declared

Adam Smith d.

Divisions of Poland

Burke d.

China bans opium

China pop. at 300 mln.

1800

(1685-1753) posed limits to the identification of reason with absolute truth, as did the evolutionary approach to law and politics of Burke (1729-97) and the utilitarianism of Bentham (1748-1832). Adam Smith (1723-90) and other **physiocrats** called for a rationalization of economic activity by removing artificial barriers to a supposedly natural free exchange of goods.

Despite the political disunity and backwardness of most of Germany, German writers participated in the new philosophical trends popularized by Wolff (1679-1754). **Kant's** (1724-1804) **idealism**, unifying an empirical epistemology with *a priori* moral and logical concepts, directed German thought away from skepticism. Italian contributions included work on electricity by Galvani (1737-98) and Volta (1745-1827), the pioneer **historiography** of Vico (1668-1744), and writings on penal reform by Beccaria (1738-94). The American Franklin (1706-90) was celebrated in Europe for his varied achievements.

The growth of the **press** (*Spectator*, 1711-14) and the wide distribution of realistic but sentimental novels attested to the increase of a large bourgeois public.

Arts. Rococo art, characterized by extravagant decorative effects, asymmetries copied from organic models, and artificial pastoral subjects, was favored by the continental aristocracy for most of the century (Watteau, 1684-1721), and had musical analogies in the ornamentalized polyphony of late Baroque. The **Neoclassical** art after 1750, associated with the new scientific archeology, was more streamlined, and infused with the supposed moral and geometric rectitude of the Roman Republic (David, 1748-1825). In England, **town planning** on a grand scale began (Edinburgh, 1767).

Industrial Revolution in England. Agricultural improvements, such as the sowing drill (1701) and livestock breeding, were implemented on the large fields provided by enclosure of common lands by private owners. Profits from agriculture and from colonial and foreign trade (1800 volume, £ 54 million) were channelled through hundreds of banks and the **Stock Exchange** (founded 1773) into new industrial processes.

The Newcomen steam pump (1712) aided coal mining. Coal fueled the new efficient steam engines patented by Watt in 1769, and coke-smelting produced cheap, sturdy iron for machinery by the 1730s. The **flying shuttle** (1733) and **spinning jenny** (1764) were used in the large new cotton textile factories, where women and children were much of the work force. Goods were transported cheaply over **canals** (2,000 miles built 1760-1800).

American Revolution. The British colonies in N. America attracted a mass immigration of religious dissenters and poor people throughout the 17th and 18th centuries, coming from all parts of the British Isles, Germany, the Netherlands, and other countries. The population reached 3 million whites and blacks by the 1770s. The small native population was decimated by European diseases and wars with and between the various colonies. British attempts to control colonial trade, and to tax the colonists to pay for the costs of colonial administration and defense clashed with traditions of local self government, and eventually provoked the colonies to rebellion. (*See American Revolution in Index.*)

Central and East Europe. The monarchs of the three states that dominated eastern Europe — Austria, Prussia, and Russia — accepted the advice and legitimation of philosophes in creating more modern, centralized institutions in their kingdoms, enlarged by the division of Poland (1772-95).

Under **Frederick II** (ruled 1740-86) Prussia, with its efficient modern army, doubled in size. State monopolies and tariff protection fostered industry, and some legal reforms were introduced. Austria's heterogeneous realms were legally unified under **Maria Theresa** (ruled 1740-80) and **Joseph II** (1780-90). Reforms in education, law, and religion were enacted, and the Austrian serfs were freed (1781). With its defeat in the Seven Years' War in 1763, Austria lost Silesia and ceased its active role in Germany, but was compensated by expansion to the E and S (Hungary, Slavonia, 1699, Galicia, 1772).

Russia, whose borders continued to expand in all directions, adopted some Western bureaucratic and economic policies under Peter I (ruled 1682-1725) and Catherine II (ruled 1762-96). Trade and cultural contacts with the West multiplied from the new Baltic Sea capital, **St. Petersburg** (founded 1703).

French Revolution. The growing French middle class lacked political power, and resented aristocratic tax privileges, especially in light of liberal political ideals popularized by the American Revolution. Peasants lacked adequate land and were burdened with feudal obligations to nobles. Wars with Britain drained the treasury, finally forcing the king to call the **Estates-General** in 1789 (first time since 1614), in an atmosphere of food riots (poor crop in 1788).

Aristocratic resistance to absolutism was soon overshadowed by the reformist Third Estate (middle class), which proclaimed itself the **National Constituent Assembly** June 17 and took the "Tennis Court oath" on June 20 to secure a constitution. The storming of the **Bastille** July 14 by Parisian artisans was followed by looting and seizure of aristocratic property throughout France. Assembly reforms included abolition of class and regional privileges, a Declaration of Rights, suffrage by taxpayers (75% of males), and the **Civil Constitution of the Clergy** providing for election and loyalty oaths for priests. A republic was declared Sept. 22, 1792, in spite of royalist pressure from Austria and Prussia, which had declared war in April (joined by Britain the next year). Louis XVI was beheaded Jan. 21, 1793, Queen Marie Antoinette was beheaded Oct. 16, 1793.

Royalist uprisings in La Vendee and the S and military reverses led to a **reign of terror** in which tens of thousands of opponents of the Revolution and criminals were executed. Radical reforms in the **Convention** period (Sept. 1793-Oct. 1795) included the abolition of colonial slavery, economic measures to aid the poor, support of public education, and a short-lived de-Christianization.

Division among radicals (execution of Hebert, March 1794, Danton, April, and Robespierre, July) aided the ascendance of a moderate **Directory**, which consolidated military victories. Napoleon Bonaparte (1769-1821), a popular young general, exploited political divisions and participated in a coup Nov. 9, 1799, making himself first consul (dictator).

India. Sikh and Hindu rebels (Rajputs, Marathas) and Afghans destroyed the power of the Mughals during the 18th century. After France's defeat in the Seven Years War, 1763, Britain was the chief European trade power in India. Its control of inland Bengal and Bihar was recognized by the Mughal shah in 1765, who granted the **British East India Co.** (under Clive, 1727-74) the right to collect land revenue there. Despite objections from Parliament (1784 India Act) the company's involvement in local wars and politics led to repeated acquisitions of new territory. The company exported Indian textiles, sugar, and indigo.

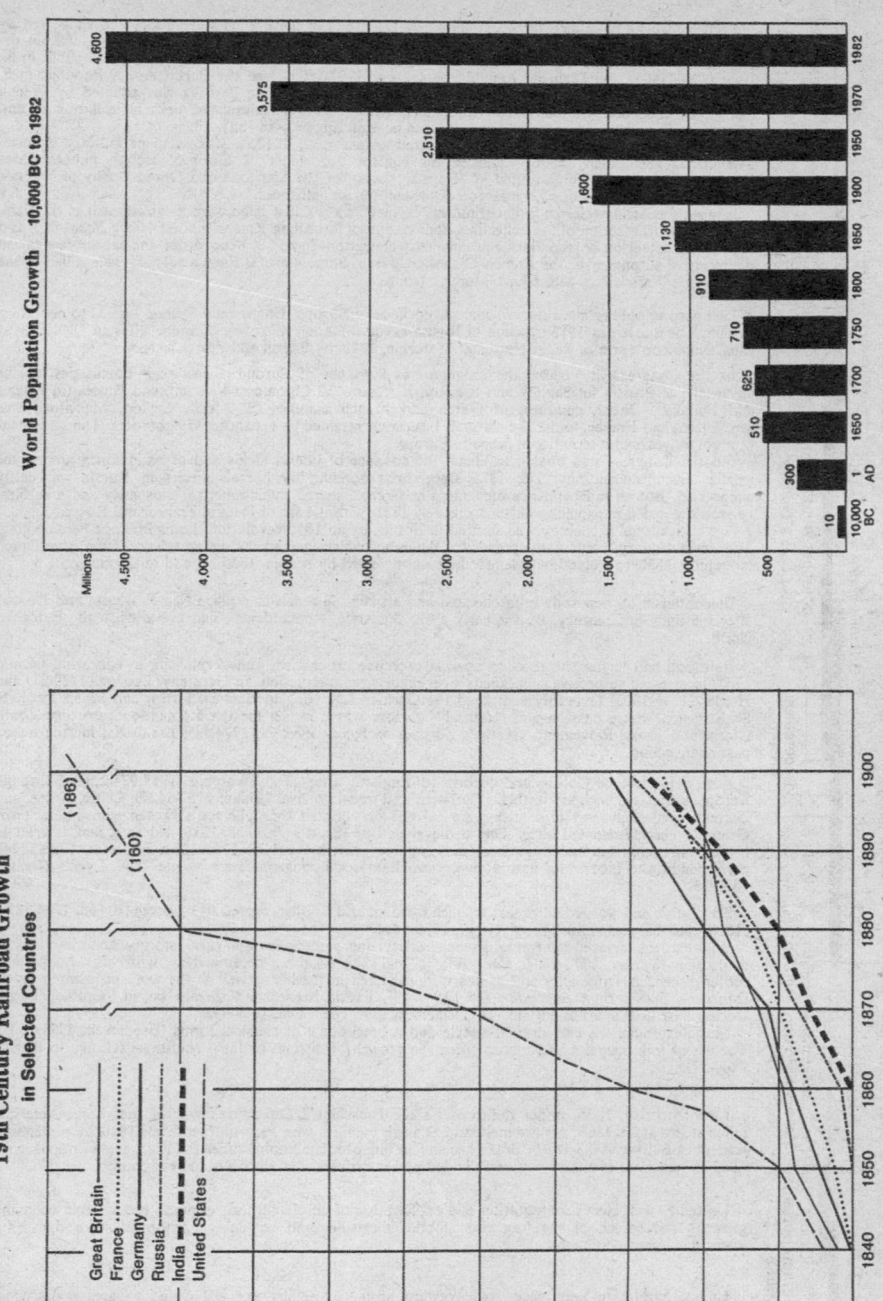

19th Century Railroad Growth
In Selected Countries

Miles (1,000)

Great Britain
France
Germany
Russia
India
United States

World Population Growth   10,000 BC to 1982

Millions

Change Gathers Steam: 1800-1840

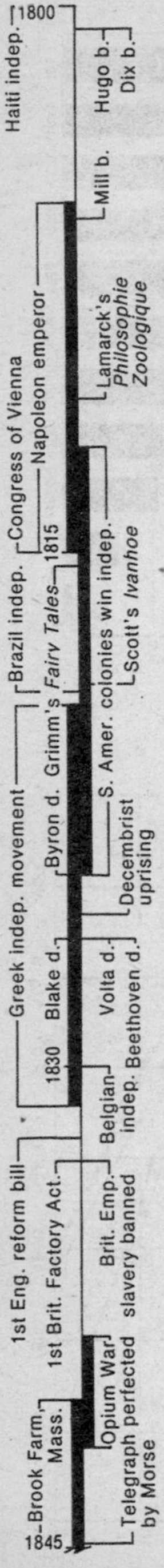
1800
1815
1830
1845
Haiti indep.
Hugo b.
Dix b.
Mill b.
Napoleon emperor
Lamarck's *Philosophie Zoologique*
Congress of Vienna
Brazil indep.
Grimm's *Fairy Tales*
S. Amer. colonies win indep.
Scott's *Ivanhoe*
Greek indep. movement
Byron d.
Decembrist uprising
Blake d.
Volta d.
Beethoven d.
Belgian indep.
1st Eng. reform bill
1st Brit. Factory Act.
Brit. Emp. slavery banned
Opium War
Brook Farm, Mass.
Telegraph perfected by Morse

French ideals and empire spread. Inspired by the ideals of the French Revolution, and supported by the expanding French armies, new republican regimes arose near France: the **Batavian** Republic in the Netherlands (1795-1806), the **Helvetic** Republic in Switzerland (1798-1803), the **Cisalpine** Republic in N. Italy (1797-1805), the **Ligurian** Republic in Genoa (1797-1805), and the **Parthenopean** Republic in S. Italy (1799). A Roman Republic existed briefly in 1798 after Pope Pius VI was arrested by French troops. In Italy and Germany, new nationalist sentiments were stimulated both in imitation of and reaction to France (anti-French and anti-Jacobin peasant uprisings in Italy, 1796-9).

From 1804, when Napoleon declared himself emperor, to 1812, a succession of military victories (Austerlitz, 1805, Jena, 1806) extended his control over most of Europe, through puppet states (**Confederation of the Rhine** united W. German states for the first time and **Grand Duchy of Warsaw** revived Polish national hopes), expansion of the empire, and alliances.

Among the lasting reforms initiated under Napoleon's absolutist reign were: establishment of the Bank of France, centralization of tax collection, codification of law along Roman models (*Code Napoleon*), and reform and extension of secondary and university education. In an 1801 concordat, the papacy recognized the effective autonomy of the French Catholic Church. Some 400,000 French soldiers were killed in the Napoleonic Wars, along with 600,000 foreign troops.

Last gasp of old regime. France's coastal blockade of Europe (**Continental System**) failed to neutralize Britain. The disastrous 1812 invasion of Russia exposed Napoleon's overextension. After an 1814 exile at Elba, Napoleon's armies were defeated at **Waterloo**, 1815, by British and Prussian troops.

At the **Congress of Vienna**, the monarchs and princes of Europe redrew their boundaries, to the advantage of Prussia (in Saxony and the Ruhr), Austria (in Illyria and Venetia), and Russia (in Poland and Finland). British conquest of Dutch and French colonies (S. Africa, Ceylon, Mauritius) was recognized, and France, under the restored Bourbons, retained its expanded 1792 borders. The settlement brought 50 years of international peace to Europe.

But the Congress was unable to check the advance of liberal ideals and of nationalism among the smaller European nations. The 1825 **Decembrist uprising** by liberal officers in Russia was easily suppressed. But an independence movement in **Greece**, stirred by commercial prosperity and a cultural revival, succeeded in expelling Ottoman rule by 1831, with the aid of Britain, France, and Russia.

A constitutional monarchy was secured in France by an **1830 revolution**; Louis Philippe became king. The revolutionary contagion spread to **Belgium**, which gained its independence from the Dutch monarchy, 1830; to **Poland**, whose rebellion was defeated by Russia, 1830-31; and to Germany.

Romanticism. A new style in intellectual and artistic life began to replace Neo-classicism and Rococo after the mid-18th century. By the early 19th, this style, Romanticism, had prevailed in the European world.

Rousseau had begun the reaction against excessive rationalism and skepticism; in education (*Emile*, 1762) he stressed subjective spontaneity over regularized instruction. In Germany, Lessing (1729-81) and Herder (1744-1803) favorably compared the German folk song to classical forms, and began a cult of Shakespeare, whose passion and "natural" wisdom was a model for the Romantic *Sturm und Drang* (storm and stress) movement. **Goethe's** *Sorrows of Young Werther* (1774) set the model for the tragic, passionate genius.

A new interest in **Gothic architecture** in England after 1760 (Walpole, 1717-97) spread through Europe, associated with an aesthetic Christian and mystic revival (Blake, 1757-1827). Celtic, Norse, and German mythology and folk tales were revived or imitated (Macpherson's Ossian translation, 1762, Grimm's *Fairy Tales*, 1812-22). The medieval revival (Scott's *Ivanhoe*, 1819) led to a new interest in history, stressing national differences and organic growth (Carlyle, 1795-1881; Michelet, 1798-1874), corresponding to theories of natural evolution (Lamarck's *Philosophie zoologique*, 1809, Lyell's *Geology*, 1830-33).

Revolution and war fed an obsession with freedom and conflict, expressed by poets (**Byron**, 1788-1824, **Hugo**, 1802-85) and philosophers (**Hegel**, 1770-1831).

Wild gardens replaced the formal French variety, and painters favored rural, stormy, and mountainous landscapes (**Turner**, 1775-1851; **Constable**, 1776-1837). Clothing became freer, with wigs, hoops, and ruffles discarded. Originality and genius were expected in the life as well as the work of inspired artists (Murger's *Scenes from Bohemian Life*, 1847-49). Exotic locales and themes (as in "Gothic" horror stories) were used in art and literature (Delacroix, 1798-1863, **Poe**, 1809-49).

Music exhibited the new dramatic style and a breakdown of classical forms (Beethoven, 1770-1827). The use of folk melodies and modes aided the growth of distinct national traditions (Glinka in Russia, 1804-57).

Latin America. Haiti, under the former slave **Toussaint L'Ouverture**, was the first Latin American independent state, 1800. All the mainland Spanish colonies won their independence 1810-24, under such leaders as **Bolivar** (1783-1830). Brazil became an independent empire under the Portuguese prince regent, 1822. A new class of military officers divided power with large landholders and the church.

United States. Heavy immigration and exploitation of ample natural resources fueled rapid economic growth. The spread of the franchise, public education, and antislavery sentiment were signs of a widespread democratic ethic.

China. Failure to keep pace with Western arms technology exposed China to greater European influence, and hampered efforts to bar imports of opium, which had damaged Chinese society and drained wealth overseas. In the **Opium War**, 1839-42, Britain forced China to expand trade opportunities and to cede Hong Kong.

Triumph of Progress: 1840-80

...idea of Progress. As a result of the cumulative scientific, economic, and political changes of the ...eceding eras, the idea took hold among literate people in the West that continuing growth and ...mprovement was the usual state of human and natural life.

Darwin's statement of the theory of evolution and survival of the fittest (*Origin of Species*, 1859), ...efended by intellectuals and scientists against theological objections, was taken as confirmation that progress was the natural direction of life. The controversy helped define popular ideas of the dedicated scientist and ever-expanding human knowledge of and control over the world (Foucault's demonstration of earth's rotation, 1851, Pasteur's germ theory, 1861).

Liberals following Ricardo (1772-1823) in their faith that unrestrained competition would bring continuous economic expansion sought to adjust political life to the new social realities, and believed that unregulated competition of ideas would yield truth (Mill, 1806-73). In England, successive reform bills (1832, 1867, 1884) gave representation to the new industrial towns, and extended the franchise to the middle and lower classes and to Catholics, Dissenters, and Jews. On both sides of the Atlantic, reformists tried to improve conditions for the mentally ill (Dix, 1802-87), women (Anthony, 1820-1906), and prisoners. Slavery was barred in the British Empire, 1833; the United States, 1865; and Brazil, 1888.

Socialist theories based on ideas of human perfectibility or historical progress were widely disseminated. Utopian socialists like Saint-Simon (1760-1825) envisaged an orderly, just society directed by a technocratic elite. A model factory town, New Lanark, Scotland, was set up by utopian Robert Owen (1771-1858), and utopian communal experiments were tried in the U.S. (Brook Farm, Mass., 1841-7). Bakunin's (1814-76) anarchism represented the opposite utopian extreme of total freedom. Marx (1818-83) posited the inevitable triumph of socialism in the industrial countries through a historical process of class conflict.

Spread of industry. The technical processes and managerial innovations of the English industrial revolution spread to Europe (especially Germany) and the U.S., causing an explosion of industrial production, demand for raw materials, and competition for markets. Inventors, both trained and self-educated, provided the means for larger-scale production (Bessemer steel, 1856, sewing machine, 1846). Many inventions were shown at the 1851 London Great Exhibition at the Crystal Palace, whose theme was universal prosperity.

Local specialization and long-distance trade were aided by a revolution in transportation and communication. Railroads were first introduced in the 1820s in England and the U.S. Over 150,000 miles of track had been laid worldwide by 1880, with another 100,000 miles laid in the next decade. Steamships were improved (*Savannah* crossed Atlantic, 1819). The telegraph, perfected by 1844 (Morse), connected the Old and New Worlds by cable in 1866, and quickened the pace of international commerce and politics. The first commercial telephone exchange went into operation in the U.S. in 1878.

The new class of industrial workers, uprooted from their rural homes, lacked job security, and suffered from dangerous overcrowded conditions at work and at home. Many responded by organizing trade unions (legalized in England, 1824; France, 1884). The U.S. Knights of Labor had 700,000 members by 1886. The First International, 1864-76, tried to unite workers internationally around a Marxist program. The quasi-Socialist Paris Commune uprising, 1871, was violently suppressed. Factory Acts to reduce child labor and regulate conditions were passed (1833-50 in England). Social security measures were introduced by the Bismarck regime in Germany, 1883-89.

Revolutions of 1848. Among the causes of the continent-wide revolutions were an international collapse of credit and resulting unemployment, bad harvests in 1845-7, and a cholera epidemic. The new urban proletariat and expanding bourgeoisie demanded a greater political role. Republics were proclaimed in France, Rome, and Venice. Nationalist feelings reached fever pitch in the Hapsburg empire, as Hungary declared independence under Kossuth, a Slav Congress demanded equality, and Piedmont tried to drive Austria from Lombardy. A national liberal assembly at Frankfurt called for German unification.

But riots fueled bourgeois fears of socialism (Marx and Engels' 1848 *Communist Manifesto*) and peasants remained conservative. The old establishment — The Papacy, the Hapsburgs (using Croats and Romanians against Hungary), the Prussian army — was able to rout the revolutionaries by 1849. The French Republic succumbed to a renewed monarchy by 1852 (Emperor Napoleon III).

Great nations unified. Using the "blood and iron" tactics of Bismarck from 1862, Prussia controlled N. Germany by 1867 (war with Denmark, 1864, Austria, 1866). After defeating France in 1870 (loss of Alsace-Lorraine), it won the allegiance of S. German states. A new German Empire was proclaimed, 1871. Italy, inspired by Mazzini (1805-72) and Garibaldi (1807-82), was unified by the reformed Piedmont kingdom through uprisings, plebiscites, and war.

The U.S., its area expanded after the 1846-47 Mexican War, defeated a secession attempt by slave states, 1861-65. The Canadian provinces were united in an autonomous Dominion of Canada, 1867. Control in India was removed from the East India Co. and centralized under British administration after the 1857-58 Sepoy rebellion, laying the groundwork for the modern Indian State. Queen Victoria was named Empress of India, 1876.

Europe dominates Asia. The Ottoman Empire began to collapse in the face of Balkan nationalisms and European imperial incursions in N. Africa (Suez Canal, 1869). The Turks had lost control of most of both regions by 1882. Russia completed its expansion south by 1884 (despite the temporary setback of the Crimean War with Turkey, Britain, and France, 1853-56) taking Turkestan, all the Caucasus, and Chinese areas in the East and sponsoring Balkan Slavs against the Turks. A succession of reformist and reactionary regimes presided over a slow modernization (serfs freed, 1861). Persian independence suffered as Russia and British India competed for influence.

China was forced to sign a series of unequal treaties with European powers and Japan. Overpopulation and an inefficient dynasty brought misery and caused rebellions (Taiping, Moslems) leaving tens of millions dead. Japan was forced by the U.S. (Commodore Perry's visits, 1853-54) and Europe to end its isolation. The Meiji restoration, 1868, gave power to a Westernizing oligarchy. Intensified empire-building gave Burma to Britain, 1824-86, and Indo-China to France, 1862-95. Christian missionary activity followed imperial and trade expansion in Asia.

Respectability. The fine arts were expected to reflect and encourage the progress of morals and

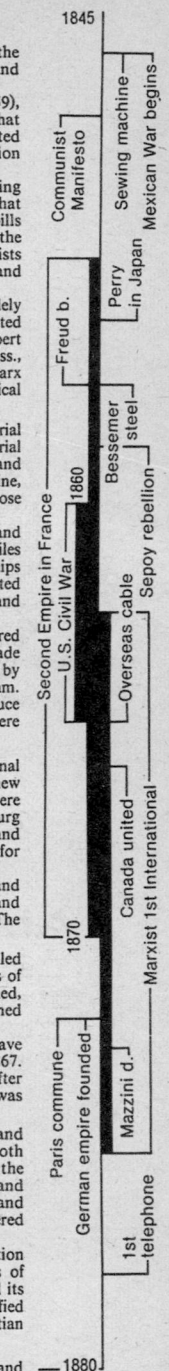

1845

Communist Manifesto

Sewing machine

Mexican War begins

Freud b.

Perry in Japan

Bessemer steel

1860

Second Empire in France

U.S. Civil War

Overseas cable

Sepoy rebellion

Canada united

1870

Marxist 1st International

Paris commune

Mazzini d.

German empire founded

1st telephone

1880

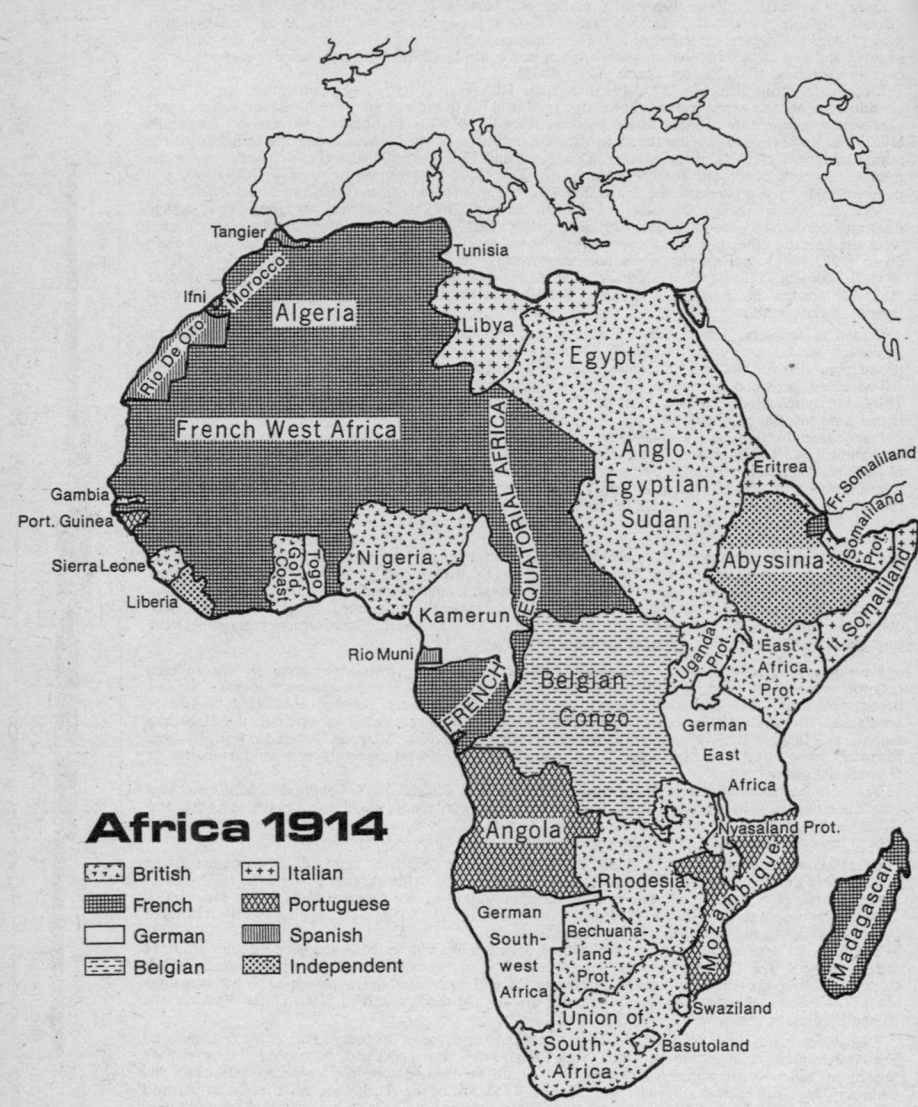

Tangier

Tunisia

Ifni

Morocco

Algeria

Libya

Rio De Oro

Egypt

French West Africa

EQUATORIAL AFRICA

Anglo
Egyptian
Sudan

Eritrea

Fr. Somaliland

Gambia

Port. Guinea

Gold Coast

Togo

Nigeria

Abyssinia

It. Somaliland

Sierra Leone

Liberia

Kamerun

FRENCH

Rio Muni

Belgian
Congo

Uganda Prot.

East
Africa
Prot.

German

East

Africa

Nyasaland Prot.

Africa 1914

	British		Italian
	French		Portuguese
	German		Spanish
	Belgian		Independent

Angola

Rhodesia

Mozambique

Madagascar

German
South-
west

Africa

Bechuana-
land
Prot.

Union of
South

Africa

Swaziland

Basutoland

...nners among the different classes. "Victorian" prudery, exaggerated delicacy, and familial piety were ...ralded by **Bowdler's** expurgated edition of Shakespeare (1818). Government-supported mass education ...culcated a work ethic as a means to escape poverty (Horatio Alger, 1832-99).

The official **Beaux Arts** school in Paris set an international style of imposing public buildings (Paris Opera, 1861-74, Vienna Opera, 1861-69) and uplifting statues (Bartholdi's *Statue of Liberty*, 1885). Realist painting, influenced by photography (Daguerre, 1837), appealed to a new mass audience with social or historical narrative (Wilkie, 1785-1841, Poynter, 1836-1919) or with serious religious, moral, or social messages (pre-Raphaelites, Millet's *Angelus*, 1858) often drawn from ordinary life. The **Impressionists** (Pissarro, 1830-1903, Renoir, 1841-1919) rejected the central role of serious subject matter in favor of a colorful and sensual depiction of a moment, but their sunny, placid depictions of bourgeois scenes kept them within the respectable consensus.

Realistic **novelists** presented the full panorama of social classes and personalities, but retained sentimentality and moral judgment (Dickens, 1812-70, Eliot, 1819-80, Tolstoy, 1828-1910, Balzac, 1799-1850).

Veneer of Stability: 1880-1900

Imperialism triumphant. The vast **African** interior, visited by European explorers (Barth, 1821-65, Livingstone, 1813-73) was conquered by the European powers in rapid, competitive thrusts from their coastal bases after 1880, mostly for domestic political and international strategic reasons. W. African Moslem kingdoms (Fulani), Arab slave traders (Zanzibar), and Bantu military confederations (Zulu) were alike subdued. Only Christian Ethiopia (defeat of Italy, 1896) and Liberia resisted successfully. France (W. Africa) and Britain ("Cape to Cairo," Boer War, 1899-1902) were the major beneficiaries. The ideology of "the white man's burden" (Kipling, *Barrack Room Ballads*, 1892) or of a "civilizing mission" (France) justified the conquests.

West European foreign capital investments soared to nearly $40 billion by 1914, but most was in E. Europe (France, Germany) the Americas (Britain) and the white colonies. The foundation of the modern interdependent world economy was laid, with cartels dominating raw material trade.

An industrious world. Industrial and technological proficiency characterized the 2 new great powers — Germany and the U.S. Coal and iron deposits enabled Germany to reach second or third place status in iron, steel, and shipbuilding by the 1900s. German electrical and chemical industries were world leaders. The U.S. post-civil war boom (interrupted by "panics," 1884, 1893, 1896) was shaped by massive immigration from S. and E. Europe from 1880, government subsidy of railroads, and huge private monopolies (Standard Oil, 1870, U.S. Steel, 1901). The **Spanish-American War**, 1898 (Phillipine rebellion, 1899-1901) and the Open Door policy in China (1899) made the U.S. a world power.

England led in **urbanization** (72% by 1890), with **London** the world capital of finance, insurance, and shipping. Electric subways (London, 1890), sewer systems (Paris, 1850s), parks, and bargain department stores helped improve living standards for most of the urban population of the industrial world.

Asians assimilate. Asian reaction to European economic, military, and religious incursions took the form of imitation of Western techniques and adoption of Western ideas of progress and freedom. The Chinese "self-strengthening" movement of the 1860s and 70s included rail, port, and arsenal improvements and metal and textile mills. Reformers like **K'ang Yu-wei** (1858-1927) won liberalizing reforms in 1898, right after the European and Japanese "scramble for concessions."

A universal education system in Japan and importation of foreign industrial, scientific, and military experts aided Japan's unprecedented rapid modernization after 1868, under the authoritarian Meiji regime. Japan's victory in the **Sino-Japanese War**, 1894-95, put Formosa and Korea in its power.

In India, the British alliance with the remaining princely states masked reform sentiment among the Westernized urban elite; higher education had been conducted largely in English for 50 years. The **Indian National Congress**, founded in 1885, demanded a larger government role for Indians.

"Fin-de-siecle" sophistication. Naturalist writers pushed realism to its extreme limits, adopting a quasi-scientific attitude and writing about formerly taboo subjects like sex, crime, extreme poverty, and corruption (Flaubert, 1821-80, Zola, 1840-1902, Hardy, 1840-1928). Unseen or repressed psychological motivations were explored in the clinical and theoretical works of **Freud** (1856-1939) and in the fiction of Dostoevsky (1821-81), James (1843-1916), Schnitzler (1862-1931) and others.

A contempt for bourgeois life or a desire to shock a complacent audience was shared by the French **symbolist** poets (Verlaine, 1844-96, Rimbaud, 1854-91), neo-pagan English writers (Swinburne, 1837-1909), continental dramatists (Ibsen, 1828-1906) and satirists (Wilde, 1854-1900). **Nietzsche** (1844-1900) was influential in his elitism and pessimism.

Post-impressionist art neglected long-cherished conventions of representation (Cezanne, 1839-1906) and showed a willingness to learn from primitive and non-European art (Gauguin, 1848-1903, Japanese prints).

Racism. Gobineau (1816-82) gave a pseudo-biological foundation to modern racist theories, which spread in the latter 19th century along with **Social Darwinism**, the belief that societies are and should be organized as a struggle for survival of the fittest. The Medieval period was interpreted as an era of natural Germanic rule (Chamberlain, 1855-1927) and notions of superiority were associated with German national aspirations (Treitschke, 1834-96). **Anti-Semitism**, with a new racist rationale, became a significant political force in Germany (Anti-Semitic Petition, 1880), Austria (Lueger, 1844-1910), and France (Dreyfus case, 1894-1906).

Last Respite: 1900-1909

Alliances. While the peace of Europe (and its dependencies) continued to hold (1907 **Hague Conference** extended the rules of war and international arbitration procedures), imperial rivalries, protectionist trade practices (in Germany and France), and the escalating arms race (British *Dreadnought* battleship launched, Germany widens Kiel canal, 1906) exacerbated minor disputes (German-French Moroccan "crises", 1905, 1911).

Security was sought through alliances: **Triple Alliance** (Germany, Austria-Hungary, Italy) renewed

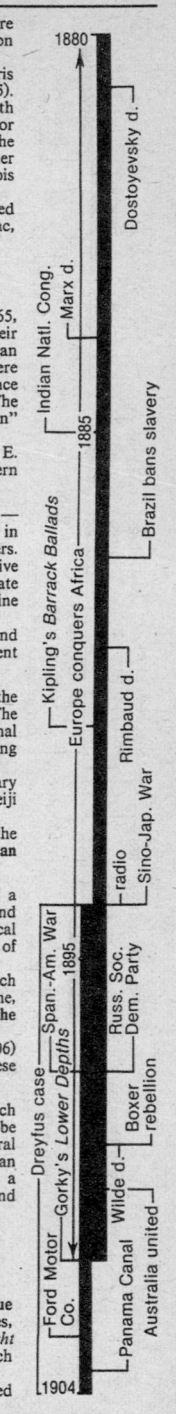

1880

Dostoyevsky d.

Indian Natl. Cong.

Marx d.

1885

Brazil bans slavery

Kipling's *Barrack Room Ballads*

Europe conquers Africa

Rimbaud d.

radio

Sino-Jap. War

Span.-Am. War

1895

Russ. Soc. Dem. Party

Boxer rebellion

Dreyfus case

Gorky's *Lower Depths*

Wilde d.

Ford Motor Co.

Panama Canal

Australia united

1904

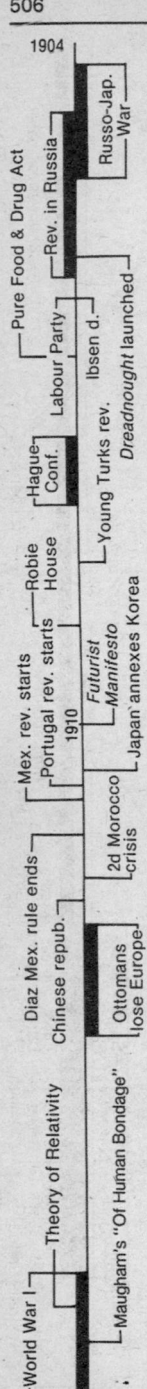

1904

Pure Food & Drug Act

Rev. in Russia

Russo-Jap. War

Labour Party

Ibsen d.

Dreadnought launched

Hague Conf.

Young Turks rev.

Robie House

Futurist Manifesto

Japan annexes Korea

Mex. rev. starts

Portugal rev. starts

1910

2d Morocco Crisis

Diaz Mex. rule ends

Chinese repub.

Ottomans lose Europe

Theory of Relativity

World War I

Maugham's "Of Human Bondage"

1916

1902, 1907; Anglo-Japanese Alliance, 1902; Franco-Russian Alliance, 1899; **Entente Cordiale** (Brit., France) 1904; Anglo-Russian Treaty, 1907; German-Ottoman friendship.

Ottomans decline. The inefficient, corrupt Ottoman government was unable to resist further loss of territory. Nearly all European lands were lost in 1912 to Serbia, Greece, Montenegro, and Bulgaria. Italy took Libya and the Dodecanese islands the same year, and Britain took Kuwait, 1899, and the Sinai, 1906. The **Young Turk** revolution in 1908 forced the sultan to restore a constitution, introduced some social reform, industrialization, and secularization.

British Empire. British trade and cultural influence remained dominant in the empire, but constitutional reforms presaged its eventual dissolution: the colonies of **Australia** were united in 1901 under a self-governing commonwealth. **New Zealand** acquired dominion status in 1907. The old Boer republics joined Cape Colony and Natal in the self-governing **Union of South Africa** in 1910.

The 1909 Indian Councils Act enhanced the role of elected province legislatures in **India.** The Moslem League, founded 1906, sought separate communal representation.

East Asia. Japan exploited its growing industrial power to expand its empire. Victory in the 1904-05 war against Russia (naval battle of Tsushima, 1905) assured Japan's domination of **Korea** (annexed 1910) and Manchuria (took Port Arthur 1905).

In China, central authority began to crumble (empress died, 1908). Reforms (Confucian exam system ended 1905, modernization of the army, building of railroads) were inadequate and secret societies of reformers and nationalists, inspired by the Westernized **Sun Yat-sen** (1866-1925) fomented periodic uprisings in the south.

Siam, whose independence had been guaranteed by Britain and France in 1896, was split into spheres of influence by those countries in 1907.

Russia. The population of the Russian Empire approached 150 million in 1900. Reforms in education, law, and local institutions (*zemstvos*), and an industrial boom starting in the 1880s (oil, railroads) created the beginnings of a modern state, despite the autocratic tsarist regime. Liberals (1903 Union of Liberation), Socialists (Social Democrats founded 1898, Bolsheviks split off 1903), and populists (Social Revolutionaries founded 1901) were periodically repressed, and national minorities persecuted (anti-Jewish pogroms, 1903, 1905-6).

An industrial crisis after 1900 and harvest failures aggravated poverty in the urban proletariat, and the 1904-05 defeat by Japan (which checked Russia's Asian expansion) sparked the revolution of 1905-06. A **Duma** (parliament) was created, and an agricultural reform (under Stolypin, prime minister 1906-11) created a large class of landowning peasants (kulaks).

The world shrinks. Developments in transportation and communication and mass population movements helped create an awareness of an interdependent world. Early **automobiles** (Daimler, Benz, 1885) were experimental, or designed as luxuries. Assembly-line mass production (Ford Motor Co., 1903) made the invention practicable, and by 1910 nearly 500,000 motor vehicles were registered in the U.S. alone. **Heavier-than-air flights** began in 1903 in the U.S. (Wright brothers), preceded by glider, balloon, and model plane advances in several countries. Trade was advanced by improvements in **ship design** (gyrocompass, 1907), speed (Lusitania crossed Atlantic in 5 days, 1907), and reach (Panama Canal begun, 1904).

The first transatlantic **radio** telegraphic transmission occurred in 1901, 6 years after Marconi discovered radio. Radio transmission of human speech had been made in 1900. Telegraphic transmission of photos was achieved in 1904, lending immediacy to news reports. **Phonographs,** popularized by Caruso's recordings (starting 1902) made for quick international spread of musical styles (ragtime). **Motion pictures,** perfected in the 1890s (Dickson, Lumiere brothers), became a popular and artistic medium after 1900; newsreels appeared in 1909.

Emigration from crowded European centers soared in the decade: 9 million migrated to the U.S., and millions more went to Siberia, Canada, Argentina, Australia, South Africa, and Algeria. Some 70 million Europeans emigrated in the century before 1914. Several million Chinese, Indians, and Japanese migrated to Southeast Asia, where their urban skills often enabled them to take a predominant economic role.

Social reform. The social and economic problems of the poor were kept in the public eye by realist fiction writers (Dreiser's *Sister Carrie*, 1900; Gorky's *Lower Depths*, 1902; Sinclair's *Jungle*, 1906), journalists (U.S. **muckrakers** — Steffens, Tarbell) and artists (Ashcan school). Frequent labor strikes and occasional assassinations by anarchists or radicals (Austrian Empress, 1898; King Umberto I of Italy, 1900; U.S. Pres. McKinley, 1901; Russian Interior Minister Plehve, 1904; Portugal's King Carlos, 1908) added to social tension and fear of revolution.

But democratic reformism prevailed. In Germany, Bernstein's (1850-1932) **revisionist Marxism,** downgrading revolution, was accepted by the powerful Social Democrats and trade unions. The British Fabian Society (the Webbs, Shaw) and the Labour Party (founded 1906) worked for reforms such as social security and union rights (1906), while women's suffragists grew more militant. U.S. **progressives** fought big business (Pure Food and Drug Act, 1906). In France, the 10-hour work day (1904) and separation of church and state (1905) were reform victories, as was universal suffrage in Austria (1907).

Arts. An unprecedented period of experimentation, centered in France, produced several new **painting** styles: fauvism exploited bold color areas (Matisse, *Woman with Hat*, 1905); expressionism reflected powerful inner emotions (the Brücke group, 1905); cubism combined several views of an object on one flat surface (Picasso's *Demoiselles*, 1906-07); futurism tried to depict speed and motion (Italian Futurist Manifesto, 1910). **Architects** explored new uses of steel structures, with facades either neo-classical (Adler and Sullivan in U.S.); curvilinear Art Nouveau (Gaudi's Casa Mila, 1905-10); or functionally streamlined (Wright's Robie House, 1909).

Music and Dance shared the experimental spirit. Ruth St. Denis (1877-1968) and Isadora Duncan (1878-1927) pioneered modern dance, while Diaghilev in Paris revitalized classic ballet from 1909. Composers explored atonal music (Debussy, 1862-1918) and dissonance (Schönberg, 1874-1951), or revolutionized classical forms (Stravinsky, 1882-71), often showing jazz or folk music influences.

War and Revolution: 1910-1919

War threatens. Germany under Wilhelm II sought a political and imperial role consonant with its industrial strength, challenging Britain's world supremacy and threatening France, still resenting the loss of Alsace-Lorraine. Austria wanted to curb an expanded Serbia (after 1912) and the threat it posed to its own Slav lands. Russia feared Austrian and German political and economic aims in the Balkans and Turkey. An accelerated arms race resulted: the German standing army rose to over 2 million men by 1914. Russia and France had over a million each, Austria and the British Empire nearly a million each. Dozens of enormous battleships were built by the powers after 1906.

The **assassination of Austrian Archduke Ferdinand** by a Serbian, June 28, 1914, was the pretext for war. The system of alliances made the conflict Europe-wide; Germany's invasion of Belgium to outflank France forced Britain to enter the war. Patriotic fervor was nearly unanimous among all classes in most countries.

World War I. German forces were stopped in France in one month. The rival armies dug **trench networks.** Artillery and improved machine guns prevented either side from any lasting advance despite repeated assaults (600,000 dead at **Verdun**, Feb.-July 1916). Poison gas, used by Germany in 1915, proved ineffective. Over one million U.S. troops tipped the balance after mid-1917, forcing Germany to sue for peace.

In the East, the Russian armies were thrown back (battle of **Tannenberg,** Aug. 20, 1914) and the war grew unpopular. An allied attempt to relieve Russia through Turkey failed (**Gallipoli** 1916). The new Bolshevik regime signed the capitulatory Brest-Litovsk peace in March, 1918. Italy entered the war on the allied side, Apr. 1915, but was pushed back by Oct. 1917. A renewed offensive with Allied aid in Oct.-Nov. 1918 forced Austria to surrender.

The British Navy successfully blockaded Germany, which responded with submarine U-boat attacks; **unrestricted submarine warfare** against neutrals after Jan. 1917 helped bring the U.S. into the war. Other battlefields included Palestine and Mesopotamia, both of which Britain wrested from the Turks in 1917, and the African and Pacific colonies of Germany, most of which fell to Britain, France, Australia, Japan, and South Africa.

From 1916, the civilian population and economy of both sides were mobilized to an unprecedented degree. Over 10 million soldiers died (May 1917 French mutiny crushed). *For further details, see 1978 and earlier editions of The World Almanac.*

Settlement. At the Versailles conference (Jan.-June 1919) and in subsequent negotiations and local wars (Russian-Polish War 1920), the map of Europe was redrawn with a nod to U.S. Pres. Wilson's principle of self-determination. Austria and Hungary were separated and much of their land was given to Yugoslavia (formerly Serbia), Romania, Italy, and the newly independent Poland and Czechoslovakia. Germany lost territory in the West, North, and East, while Finland and the Baltic states were detached from Russia. Turkey lost nearly all its Arab lands to British-sponsored Arab states or to direct French and British rule.

A huge reparations burden and partial demilitarization were imposed on Germany. Wilson obtained approval for a League of Nations, but the U.S. Senate refused to allow the U.S. to join.

Russian revolution. Military defeats and high casualties caused a contagious lack of confidence in Tsar Nicholas, who was forced to abdicate, Mar. 1917. A liberal provisional government failed to end the war, and massive desertions, riots, and fighting between factions followed. A moderate socialist government under Kerensky was overthrown in a violent **coup by the Bolsheviks** in Petrograd under Lenin, who disbanded the elected Constituent Assembly, Nov. 1917.

The Bolsheviks brutally suppressed all opposition and ended the war with Germany, Mar. 1918. **Civil war broke out** in the summer between the Red Army, including the Bolsheviks and their supporters, and monarchists, anarchists, nationalities (Ukrainians, Georgians, Poles) and others. Small U.S., British, French and Japanese units also opposed the Bolsheviks, 1918-19 (Japan in Vladivostok to 1922). The civil war, anarchy, and pogroms devastated the country until the 1920 Red Army victory. The wartime total monopoly of political, economic, and police power by the Communist Party leadership was retained.

Other European revolutions. An unpopular monarchy in **Portugal** was overthrown in 1910. The new republic took severe anti-clerical measures, 1911.

After a century of Home Rule agitation, during which **Ireland** was devastated by famine (one million dead, 1846-47) and emigration, republican militants staged an unsuccessful uprising in Dublin, Easter 1916. The execution of the leaders and mass arrests by the British won popular support for the rebels. The Irish Free State, comprising all but the 6 northern counties, achieved dominion status in 1922.

In the aftermath of the world war, radical revolutions were attempted in Germany (**Spartacist** uprising Jan. 1919), **Hungary** (Kun regime 1919), and elsewhere. All were suppressed or failed for lack of support.

Chinese revolution. The Manchu Dynasty was overthrown and a republic proclaimed, Oct. 1911. First president Sun Yat-sen resigned in favor of strongman Yuan Shih-k'ai. Sun organized the parliamentarian **Kuomintang** party.

Students launched protests May 4, 1919 against League of Nations concessions in China to Japan. Nationalist, liberal, and socialist ideas and political groups spread. The **Communist Party** was founded 1921. A communist regime took power in Mongolia with Soviet support in 1921.

India restive. Indian objections to British rule erupted in nationalist riots as well as in the non-violent tactics of Gandhi (1869-1948). Nearly 400 unarmed demonstrators were shot at **Amritsar,** Apr. 1919. Britain approved limited self-rule that year.

Mexican revolution. Under the long Diaz dictatorship (1876-1911) the economy advanced, but Indian and mestizo lands were confiscated, and concessions to foreigners (mostly U.S.) damaged the middle class. **A revolution in 1910** led to civil wars and U.S. intervention (1914, 1916-17). Land reform and a more democratic constitution (1917) were achieved.

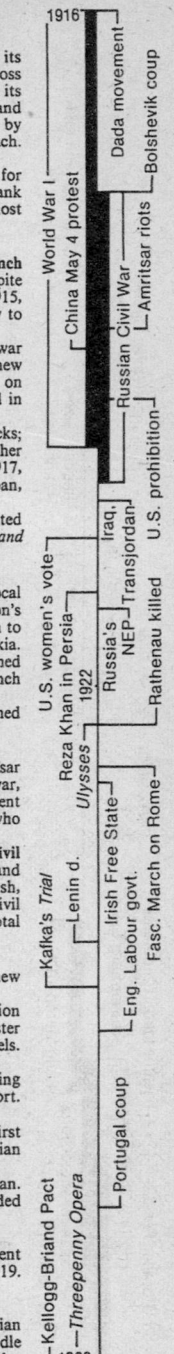

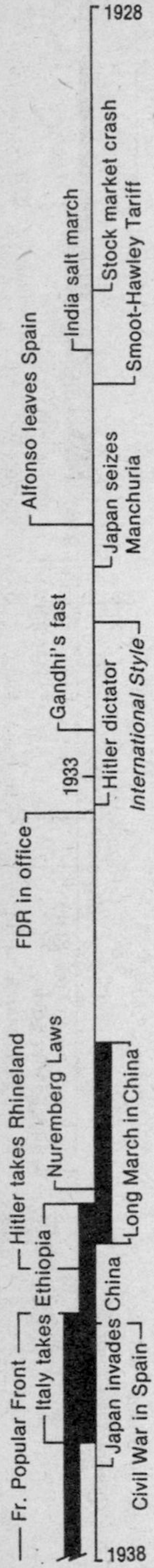

The Aftermath of War: 1920-29

U.S. Easy credit, technological ingenuity, and war-related industrial decline in Europe caused a long economic boom, in which ownership of the new products — autos, phones, radios — became democratized. Prosperity, an increase in women workers, women's suffrage (1920) and drastic change in fashion (flappers, mannish bob for women, clean-shaven men), created a wide perception of social change, despite prohibition of alcoholic beverages (1919-33). Union membership and strikes increased. Fear of radicals led to Palmer raids (1919-20) and Sacco/Vanzetti case (1921-27).

Europe sorts itself out. Germany's liberal **Weimar constitution** (1919) could not guarantee a stable government in the face of rightist violence (Rathenau assassinated 1922) and Communist refusal to cooperate with Socialists. Reparations and allied occupation of the Rhineland caused staggering inflation which destroyed middle class savings, but economic expansion resumed after mid-decade, aided by U.S. loans. A sophisticated, innovative culture developed in architecture and design (Bauhaus, 1919-28), film (Lang, *M*, 1931), painting (Grosz), music (Weill, *Threepenny Opera*, 1928), theater (Brecht, *A Man's a Man*, 1926), criticism (Benjamin), philosophy (Jung), and fashion. This culture was considered decadent and socially disruptive by rightists.
England elected its first labor governments (Jan. 1924, June 1929). A 10-day general strike in support of coal miners failed, May 1926. In **Italy**, strikes, political chaos and violence by small Fascist bands culminated in the Oct. 1922 Fascist March on Rome, which established Mussolini's dictatorship. Strikes were outlawed (1926), and Italian influence was pressed in the Balkans (Albania a protectorate 1926). A conservative dictatorship was also established in **Portugal** in a 1926 military coup.
Czechoslovakia, the only stable democracy to emerge from the war in Central or East Europe, faced opposition from Germans (in the Sudetenland), Ruthenians, and some Slovaks. As the industrial heartland of the old Hapsburg empire, it remained fairly prosperous. With French backing, it formed the Little Entente with Yugoslavia (1920) and **Romania** (1921) to block Austrian or Hungarian irredentism. **Hungary** remained dominated by the landholding classes and expansionist feeling. Croats and Slovenes in **Yugoslavia** demanded a federal state until King Alexander proclaimed a dictatorship (1929). Poland faced nationality problems as well (Germans, Ukrainians, Jews); Pilsudski ruled as dictator from 1926. The Baltic states were threatened by traditionally dominant ethnic Germans and by Soviet-supported communists.
An economic collapse and famine in **Russia**, 1921-22, claimed 5 million lives. The New Economic Policy (1921) allowed land ownership by peasants and some private commerce and industry. Stalin was absolute ruler within 4 years of Lenin's 1924 death. He inaugurated a brutal collectivization program 1929-32, and used foreign communist parties for Soviet state advantage.

Internationalism. Revulsion against World War I led to pacifist agitation, the Kellogg-Briand Pact renouncing aggressive war (1928), and **naval disarmament** pacts (Washington, 1922, London, 1930). But the League of Nations was able to arbitrate only minor disputes (Greece-Bulgaria, 1925).

Middle East. Mustafa Kemal (Ataturk) led **Turkish** nationalists in resisting Italian, French, and Greek military advances, 1919-23. The sultanate was abolished 1922, and elaborate reforms passed, including secularization of law and adoption of the Latin alphabet. Ethnic conflict led to persecution of **Armenians** (over 1 million dead in 1915, 1 million expelled), Greeks (forced Greek-Turk population exchange, 1923), and Kurds (1925 uprising).
With evacuation of the Turks from **Arab** lands, the puritanical Wahabi dynasty of eastern Arabia conquered present Saudi Arabia, 1919-25. British, French, and Arab dynastic and nationalist maneuvering resulted in the creation of two more Arab monarchies in 1921: Iraq and Transjordan (both under British control), and two French mandates: Syria and Lebanon. Jewish immigration into British-mandated **Palestine**, inspired by the Zionist movement, was resisted by Arabs, at times violently (1921, 1929 massacres).
Reza Khan ruled **Persia** after his 1921 coup (shah from 1925), centralized control, and created the trappings of a modern state.

China. The Kuomintang under **Chiang Kai-shek** (1887-1975) subdued the warlords by 1928. The Communists were brutally suppressed after their alliance with the Kuomintang was broken in 1927. Relative peace thereafter allowed for industrial and financial improvements, with some Russian, British, and U.S. cooperation.

Arts. Nearly all bounds of subject matter, style, and attitude were broken in the arts of the period. **Abstract** art first took inspiration from natural forms or narrative themes (Kandinsky from 1911), then worked free of any representational aims (Malevich's suprematism, 1915-19, Mondrian's geometric style from 1917). The **Dada** movement from 1916 mocked artistic pretension with absurd collages and constructions (Arp, Tzara, from 1916). Paradox, illusion, and psychological taboos were exploited by **surrealists** by the latter 1920s (Dali, Magritte). Architectural schools celebrated industrial values, whether vigorous abstract constructivism (Tatlin, *Monument to 3rd International*, 1919) or the machined, streamlined **Bauhaus** style, which was extended to many design fields (Helvetica type face).
Prose writers explored revolutionary narrative modes related to dreams (Kafka's *Trial*, 1925), internal monologue (Joyce's *Ulysses*, 1922), and word play (Stein's *Making of Americans*, 1925). Poets and novelists wrote of modern alienation (Eliot's *Waste Land*, 1922) and aimlessness (Lost Generation).

Sciences. Scientific specialization prevailed by the 20th century. Advances in knowledge and technological aptitude increased with the geometric increase in the number of practitioners. Physicists challenged common-sense views of causality, observation, and a mechanistic universe, putting science further beyond popular grasp (Einstein's general theory of relativity, 1915; Bohr's quantum mechanics, 1913; Heisinger's uncertainty principle, 1927).

Timeline markers (left margin):

1928

India salt march

Stock market crash

Smoot-Hawley Tariff

Alfonso leaves Spain

Japan seizes Manchuria

Gandhi's fast

Hitler dictator

International Style

1933

FDR in office

Hitler takes Rhineland

Nuremberg Laws

Long March in China

Fr. Popular Front

Italy takes Ethiopia

Japan invades China

Civil War in Spain

1938

Rise of the Totalitarians: 1930-39

Depression. A worldwide financial panic and economic depression began with the Oct. 1929 U.S. stock market crash and the May 1931 failure of the Austrian Credit-Anstalt. A credit crunch caused international bankruptcies and **unemployment:** 12 million jobless by 1932 in the U.S., 5.6 million in Germany, 2.7 million in England. Governments responded with **tariff restrictions** (Smoot-Hawley Act 1930; Ottawa Imperial Conference, 1932) which dried up world trade. Government public works programs were vitiated by deflationary budget balancing.

Germany. Years of agitation by violent extremists was brought to a head by the Depression. Nazi leader **Hitler** was named chancellor by Pres. Hindenburg Jan. 1933, and given dictatorial power by the Reichstag in Mar. Opposition parties were disbanded, strikes banned, and all aspects of economic, cultural, and religious life brought under central government and Nazi party control and manipulated by sophisticated propaganda. Severe persecution of Jews began (**Nuremberg Laws** Sept. 1935). Many Jews, political opponents and others were sent to concentration camps (Dachau, 1933) where thousands died or were killed. Public works, renewed conscription (1935), arms production, and a 4-year plan (1936) ended unemployment.

Hitler's expansionism started with reincorporation of the Saar (1935), occupation of the **Rhineland** (Mar. 1936), and annexation of Austria (Mar. 1938). At **Munich**, Sept. 1938, an indecisive Britain and France sanctioned German dismemberment of Czechoslovakia.

Russia. Urbanization and education advanced. Rapid industrialization was achieved through successive **5-year-plans** starting 1928, using severe labor discipline and mass forced labor. Industry was financed by a decline in living standards and exploitation of agriculture, which was almost totally collectivized by the early 1930s (*kolkhoz*, collective farm; *sovkhoz*, state farm, often in newly-worked lands). Successive **purges** increased the role of professionals and management at the expense of workers. Millions perished in a series of man-made disasters: elimination of kulaks (peasant land-owners), 1929-34; severe famine, 1932-33; party purges (Great Purge, 1936-38); suppression of nationalities; and poor conditions in labor camps.

Spain. An industrial revolution during World War I created an urban proletariat, which was attracted to socialism and anarchism; Catalan nationalists challenged central authority. The 5 years after King Alfonso left Spain, Apr. 1931, were dominated by tension between intermittent leftist and anti-clerical governments and clericals, monarchists and other rightists. Anarchist and communist rebellions were crushed, but a July, 1936, extreme right rebellion led by Gen. Francisco Franco and aided by Nazi Germany and Fascist Italy succeeded, after a 3-year **civil war** (over 1 million dead in battles and atrocities). The war polarized international public opinion.

Italy. Despite propaganda for the ideal of the Corporate State, few domestic reforms were attempted. An entente with Hungary and Austria, Mar. 1934, a pact with Germany and Japan, Nov. 1937, and intervention by 50-75,000 troops in Spain, 1936-39, sealed Italy's identification with the fascist bloc (anti-Semitic laws after Mar. 1938). Ethiopia was conquered, 1935-37, and **Albania** annexed, Jan. 1939, in conscious imitation of ancient Rome.

East Europe. Repressive regimes fought for power against an active opposition (liberals, socialists, communists, peasants, Nazis). Minority groups and Jews were restricted within national boundaries that did not coincide with ethnic population patterns. In the destruction of **Czechoslovakia,** Hungary occupied southern Slovakia (Mar. 1938) and Ruthenia (Mar. 1939), and a pro-Nazi regime took power in the rest of Slovakia. Other boundary disputes (e.g. Poland-Lithuania, Yugoslavia-Bulgaria, Romania-Hungary) doomed attempts to build joint fronts against Germany or Russia. Economic depression was severe.

East Asia. After a period of liberalism in **Japan**, nativist militarists dominated the government with peasant support. Manchuria was seized, Sept. 1931-Feb. 1932, and a puppet state set up (Manchukuo). Adjacent Jehol (inner Mongolia) was occupied in 1933. China proper was invaded July 1937; large areas were conquered by Oct. 1938.

In **China** Communist forces left Kuomintang-besieged strongholds in the South in a Long March (1934-35) to the North. The Kuomintang-Communist civil war was suspended Jan. 1937 in the face of threatening Japan.

The democracies. The Roosevelt Administration, in office Mar. 1933, embarked on an extensive program of social reform and economic stimulation, including protection for labor unions (heavy industries organized), social security, public works, wages and hours laws, assistance to farmers. Isolationist sentiment (1937 Neutrality Act) prevented U.S. intervention in Europe, but military expenditures were increased in 1939.

French political instability and polarization prevented resolution of economic and international security questions. The **Popular Front** government under Blum (June 1936-Apr. 1938) passed social reforms (40-hour week) and raised arms spending. National coalition governments ruled Britain from Aug. 1931, brought some economic recovery, but failed to define a consistent foreign policy until Chamberlain's government (from May 1937), which practiced deliberate **appeasement** of Germany and Italy.

India. Twenty years of agitation for autonomy and then for independence (Gandhi's **salt march,** 1930) achieved some constitutional reform (extended provincial powers, 1935) despite Moslem-Hindu strife. Social issues assumed prominence with peasant uprisings (1921), strikes (1928), Gandhi's efforts for untouchables (1932 "fast unto death"), and social and agrarian reform by the provinces after 1937.

Arts. The streamlined, geometric design motifs of Art Deco (from 1925) prevailed through the 1930s. Abstract art flourished (Moore sculptures from 1931) alongside a new realism related to social and political concerns (**Socialist Realism** the official Soviet style from 1934; Mexican muralists Rivera, 1886-1957, and Orozco, 1883-1949), which was also expressed in fiction and poetry (Steinbeck's *Grapes of Wrath,* 1939; Sandburg's *The People, Yes,* 1936). Modern architecture (*International Style,* 1932) was unchallenged in its use of man-made materials (concrete, glass), lack of decoration, and monumentality (Rockefeller Center, 1929-40). U.S.-made films captured a world-wide audience with their larger-than-life fantasies (*Gone with the Wind,* 1939).

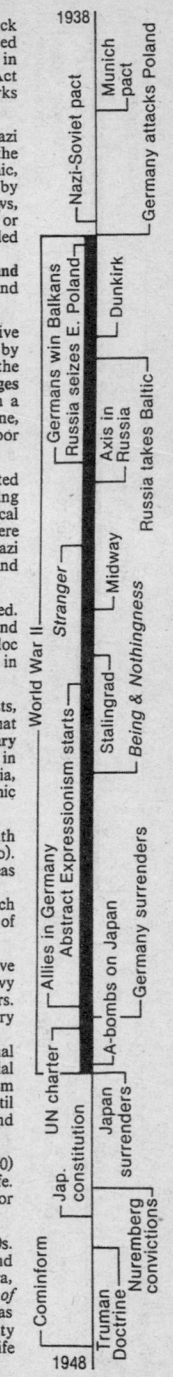

1938

Munich pact

Nazi-Soviet pact

Germany attacks Poland

Germans win Balkans

Russia seizes E. Poland

Dunkirk

Axis in Russia

Russia takes Baltic

Stranger

Midway

Being & Nothingness

Stalingrad

World War II

Abstract Expressionism starts

Allies in Germany

Germany surrenders

A-bombs on Japan

UN charter

Japan surrenders

Jap. constitution

Nuremberg convictions

Cominform

Truman Doctrine

1948

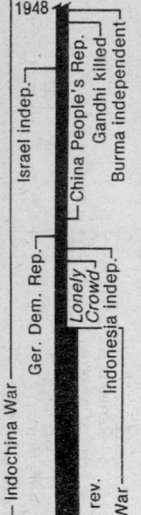

1948

- Israel indep.
- China People's Rep.
- Gandhi killed
- Burma independent
- Ger. Dem. Rep.
- *Lonely Crowd*
- Indonesia indep.
- Indochina War
- H-bomb
- Egypt rev.
- Korean War
- Stalin d.
- Ghana indep.
- Sputnik
- McCarthy censured
- Peron ousted
- Suez War
- Hungary rev.
- Bandung conf.
- *On the Road*
- SEATO founded
- EEC Treaty

1958

War, Hot and Cold: 1940-49

War in Europe. The Nazi-Soviet non-agression pact (Aug. '39) freed Germany to attack Poland (Sept.) Britain and France, who had guaranteed Polish independence, declared war on Germany. Russia seize East Poland (Sept.), attacked Finland (Nov.) and took the Baltic states (July '40). Mobile German force staged "blitzkrieg" attacks Apr.-June, '40, conquering neutral Denmark, Norway, and the low countrie and defeating France; 350,000 British and French troops were evacuated at Dunkirk (May). The Battle of Britain, June-Dec. '40, denied Germany air superiority, German-Italian campaigns won the Balkans by Apr. '41. Three million Axis troops **invaded Russia** June '41, marching through the Ukraine to the Caucasus, and through White Russia and the Baltic republics to Moscow and Leningrad.

Russian winter counterthrusts, '41-'42 and '42-'43 stopped the German advance (Stalingrad Sept. '42-Feb. '43). With British and U.S. Lend-Lease aid and sustaining great casualties, the Russians drove the Axis from all E. Europe and the Balkans in the next 2 years. Invasions of N. Africa (Nov. '42), Italy (Sept. '43), and Normandy (June '44) brought U.S., British, Free French and allied troops to Germany by spring '45. Germany surrendered May 7, 1945.

War in Asia-Pacific. Japan occupied Indochina Sept. '40, dominated Thailand Déc. '41, attacked Hawaii, the Philippines, Hong Kong, Malaya Dec. 7, 1941. Indonesia was attacked Jan. '42, Burma conquered Mar. 42. Battle of Midway (June '42) turned back the Japanese advance. "Island-hopping" battles (Guadalcanal Aug. '42-Jan. '43, **Leyte Gulf** Oct. '44, Iwo Jima Feb.-Mar. '45, Okinawa Apr. '45) and massive bombing raids on Japan from June '44 wore out Japanese defenses. Two U.S. atom bombs, dropped Aug. 6 and 9, forced Japan to surrender Aug. 14, 1945. *For further details, see 1978 and earlier editions of The World Almanac.*

Atrocities. The war brought 20th-century cruelty to its peak. Nazi murder camps (Auschwitz) systematically killed 6 million Jews. Gypsies, political opponents, sick and retarded people, and others deemed undesirable were murdered by the Nazis, as were vast numbers of Slavs, especially leaders.

Civilian deaths. German bombs killed 70,000 English civilians. Some 100,000 Chinese civilians were killed by Japanese forces in the capture of Nanking. Severe retaliation by the Soviet army, E. European partisans, Free French and others took a heavy toll. U.S. and British bombing of Germany killed hundreds of thousands, as did U.S. bombing of Japan (80-200,000 at Hiroshima alone). Some 45 million people lost their lives in the war.

Settlement. The United Nations charter was signed in San Francisco June 26, 1945 by 50 nations. The International Tribunal at Nuremberg convicted 22 German leaders for war crimes Sept. '46, 23 Japanese leaders were convicted Nov. '48. Postwar border changes included large gains in territory for the USSR, losses for Germany, a shift westward in Polish borders, and minor losses for Italy. Communist regimes, supported by Soviet troops, took power in most of E. Europe, including Soviet-occupied Germany (GDR proclaimed Oct. '49). Japan lost all overseas lands.

Recovery. Basic political and social changes were imposed on Japan and W. Germany by the western allies (Japan constitution Nov. '46, W. German basic law May '49). U.S. Marshall Plan aid ($12 billion '47-'51) spurred W. European economic recovery after a period of severe inflation and strikes in Europe and the U.S. The British Labour Party introduced a national health service and nationalized basic industries in 1946.

Cold War. Western fears of further Soviet advances (Cominform formed Oct. '47, Czechoslovakia coup, Feb. '48, Berlin blockade Apr.'48-Sept. '49) led to formation of NATO. Civil War in Greece and Soviet pressure on Turkey led to U.S. aid under the Truman Doctrine (Mar. '47). Other anti-communist security pacts were the Org. of American States (Apr. '48) and Southeast Asia Treaty Org. (Sept. '54). A new wave of Soviet purges and repression intensified in the last years of Stalin's rule, extending to E. Europe (Slansky trial in Czechoslovakia, 1951). Only Yugoslavia resisted Soviet control (expelled by Cominform, June '48; U.S. aid, June '49).

China, Korea. Communist forces emerged from World War II strengthened by the Soviet takeover of industrial Manchuria. In 4 years of fighting, the Kuomintang was driven from the mainland; the People's Republic was proclaimed Oct. 1, 1949. Korea was divided by Russian and U.S. occupation forces. Separate republics were proclaimed in the 2 zones Aug.-Sept. '48.

India. India and Pakistan became independent dominions Aug. 15, 1947. Millions of Hindu and Moslem refugees were created by the partition; riots, 1946-47, took hundreds of thousands of lives; Gandhi himself was assassinated Jan. '48. Burma became completely independent Jan. '48; Ceylon took dominion status in Feb.

Middle East. The UN approved partition of Palestine into Jewish and Arab states. Israel was proclaimed May 14, 1948. Arabs rejected partition, but failed to defeat Israel in war, May '48-July '49. Immigration from Europe and the Middle East swelled Israel's Jewish population. British and French forces left Lebanon and Syria, 1946. Transjordan occupied most of Arab Palestine.

Southeast Asia. Communists and others fought against restoration of French rule in Indochina from 1946; a non-communist government was recognized by France Mar. '49, but fighting continued. Both Indonesia and the Philippines became independent, the former in 1949 after 4 years of war with Netherlands, the latter in 1946. Philippine economic and military ties with the U.S. remained strong; a communist-led peasant rising was checked in '48.

Arts. New York became the center of the world art market; abstract expressionism was the chief mode (Pollock from '43, de Kooning from '47). Literature and philosophy explored existentialism (Camus' *Stranger*, 1942, Sartre's *Being and Nothingness*, 1943). Non-western attempts to revive or create regional styles (Senghor's Negritude, Mishima's novels) only confirmed the emergence of a universal culture. Radio and phonograph records spread American popular music (swing, bebop) around the world.

The American Decade: 1950-59

olite decolonization. The peaceful decline of European political and military power in Asia and Africa
elerated in the 1950s. Nearly all of **N. Africa** was freed by 1956, but France fought a bitter war to
ain Algeria, with its large European minority, until 1962. **Ghana**, independent 1957, led a parade of
ew black African nations (over 2 dozen by 1962) which altered the political character of the UN. Ethnic
sputes often exploded in the new nations after decolonization (UN troops in Cyprus 1964; **Nigeria** civil
var 1967-70). Leaders of the new states, mostly sharing socialist ideologies, tried to create an Afro-Asian
oloc (Bandung Conf. 1955), but Western economic influence and U.S. political ties remained strong
(Baghdad Pact, 1955).

Trade. World trade volume soared, in an atmosphere of monetary stability assured by international
accords (**Bretton Woods** 1944). In Europe, economic integration advanced (**European Economic
Community** 1957, European Free Trade Association 1960). Comecon (1949) coordinated the economies
of Soviet-bloc countries.

U.S. Economic growth produced an abundance of consumer goods (9.3 million motor vehicles sold,
1955). Suburban housing tracts changed life patterns for middle and working classes (Levittown
1946-51). **Eisenhower's** landside election victories (1952, 1956) reflected consensus politics. Censure of
McCarthy (Dec. '54) curbed the political abuse of anti-communism. A system of alliances and military
bases bolstered U.S. influence on all continents. Trade and payments surpluses were balanced by overseas
investments and foreign aid ($50 billion, 1950-59).

USSR. In the "thaw" after Stalin's death in 1953, relations with the West improved (evacuation of
Vienna, Geneva summit conf., both 1955). Repression of scientific and cultural life eased, and many
prisoners were freed or rehabilitated culminating in **de-Stalinization** (1956). Khrushchev's leadership
aimed at consumer sector growth, but farm production lagged, despite the virgin lands program (from
1954). The 1956 Hungarian revolution, the 1960 U-2 spy plane episode, and other incidents renewed
East-West tension and domestic curbs.

East Europe. Resentment of Russian domination and Stalinist repression combined with nationalist,
economic and religious factors to produce periodic violence. East Berlin workers rioted in 1953, Polish
workers rioted in Poznan, June 1956, and a broad-based revolution broke out in Hungary, Oct. 1956. All
were suppressed by Soviet force or threats (at least 7,000 dead in Hungary). But Poland was allowed to
restore private ownership of farms, and a degree of personal and economic freedom returned to Hungary.
Yugoslavia experimented with worker self-management and a market economy. ·

Korea. The 1945 division of Korea left industry in the North, which was organized into a militant
regime and armed by Russia. The South was politically disunited. Over 60,000 North Korean troops
invaded the South June 25, 1950. The U.S., backed by the UN Security Council, sent troops. UN troops
reached the Chinese border in Nov. Some 200,000 Chinese troops crossed the Yalu River and drove back
UN forces. Cease-fire in July 1951 found the opposing forces near the original 38th parallel border. After
2 years of sporadic fighting, an armistice was signed July 27, 1953. U.S. troops remained in the South,
and U.S. economic and military aid continued. The war stimulated rapid economic recovery in Japan. *For
details, see 1978 and earlier editions of The World Almanac.*

China. Starting in 1952, industry, agriculture, and social institutions were forcibly collectivized. As
many as several million people were executed as Kuomintang supporters or as class and political enemies.
The Great Leap Forward, 1958-60, unsuccessfully tried to force the pace of development by substituting
labor for investment.

Indochina. Ho's forces, aided by Russia and the new Chinese Communist government, fought French
and pro-French Vietnamese forces to a standstill, and captured the strategic Dienbienphu camp in May,
1954. The Geneva Agreements divided Vietnam in half pending elections (never held), and recognized
Laos and Cambodia as independent. The U.S. aided the anti-Communist Republic of Vietnam in the
South.

Middle East. Arab revolutions placed leftist, militantly nationalist regimes in power in Egypt (1952)
and Iraq (1958). But Arab unity attempts failed (United Arab Republic joined Egypt, Syria, Yemen
1958-61). Arab refusal to recognize Israel (Arab League economic blockade began Sept. 1951) led to a
permanent state of war, with repeated incidents (Gaza, 1955). Israel occupied Sinai, Britain and France
took the Suez Canal, Oct. 1956, but were replaced by the UN Emergency Force. The Mossadegh
government in Iran nationalized the British-owned oil industry May 1951, but was overthrown in a
U.S.-aided coup Aug. 1953.

Latin America. Dictator Juan Peron, in office 1946, enforced land reform, some nationalization,
welfare state measures, and curbs on the Roman Catholic Church, but crushed opposition. A Sept. 1955
coup deposed Pèron. The 1952 revolution in Bolivia brought land reform, nationalization of tin mines,
and improvement in the status of Indians, who nevertheless remained poor. The Batista regime in Cuba
was overthrown, Jan. 1959, by Fidel Castro, who imposed a communist dictatorship, aligned Cuba with
Russia, improved education and health care. A U.S.-backed anti-Castro invasion (Bay of Pigs, Apr. 1961)
was crushed. Self-government advanced in the British Caribbean.

Technology. Large outlays on research and development in the U.S. and USSR focussed on military
applications (H-bomb in U.S. 1952, USSR 1953, Britain 1957, intercontinental missiles late 1950s). Soviet
launching of the Sputnik satellite, Oct. 1957, spurred increases in U.S. science education funds (National
Defense Education Act).

Literature and letters. Alienation from social and literary conventions reached an extreme in the
theater of the absurd (Beckett's *Waiting for Godot* 1952), the "new novel" (Robbe-Grillet's *Voyeur* 1955),
and avant-garde film (Antonioni's *L'Avventura* 1960). U.S. Beatniks (Kerouac's *On the Road* 1957) and
others rejected the supposed conformism of Americans (Riesman's *Lonely Crowd* 1950).

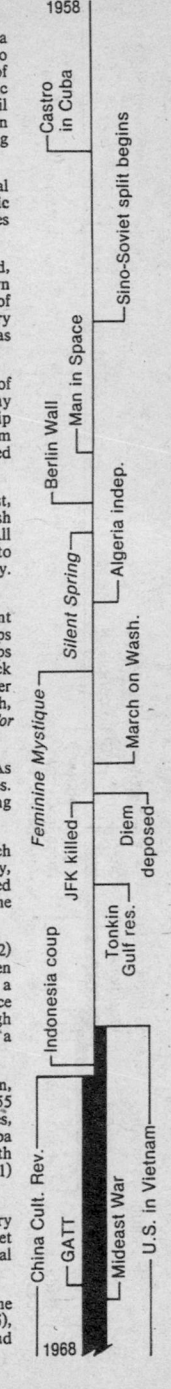

1958

Castro in Cuba

Sino-Soviet split begins

Berlin Wall

Man in Space

Algeria indep.

Silent Spring

March on Wash.

Feminine Mystique

JFK killed

Diem deposed

Indonesia coup

Tonkin Gulf res.

China Cult. Rev.

GATT

Mideast War

U.S. in Vietnam

1968

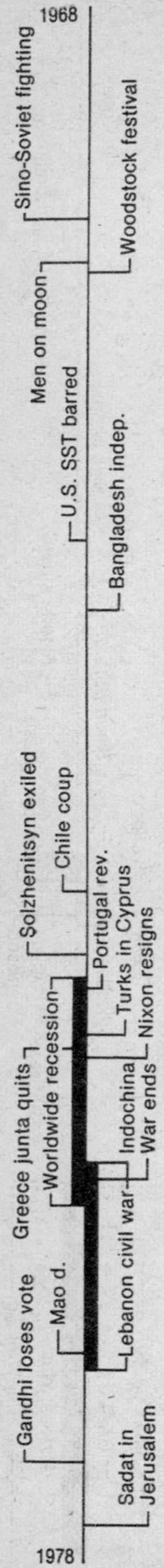
1968
Sino-Soviet fighting
Woodstock festival
Men on moon
U.S. SST barred
Bangladesh indep.
Solzhenitsyn exiled
Chile coup
Portugal rev.
Turks in Cyprus
Nixon resigns
Worldwide recession
Greece junta quits
Indochina
War ends
Lebanon civil war
Mao d.
Gandhi loses vote
Sadat in
Jerusalem
1978

Rising Expectations: 1960-69

Economic boom. The longest sustained economic boom on record spanned almost the entire decad the capitalist world; the closely-watched GNP figure doubled in the U.S. 1960-70, fueled by Vietn War-related budget deficits. The **General Agreement on Tariffs and Trade,** 1967, stimulated W European prosperity, which spread to peripheral areas (Spain, Italy, E. Germany). Japan became a t economic power ($20 billion exports 1970). Foreign investment aided the industrialization of Braz Soviet 1965 economic reform attempts (decentralization, material incentives) were limited; but growt continued.

Reform and radicalization. A series of political and social reform movements took root in the U.S. later spreading to other countries with the help of ubiquitous U.S. film and television programs and heavy overseas travel (2.2 million U.S. passports issued 1970). Blacks agitated peaceably and with partial success against segregation and poverty (1963 March on Washington, 1964 **Civil Rights Act**); but some urban ghettos erupted in extensive riots (Watts, 1965; Detroit, 1967; King assassination, Apr. 4, 1968). New concern for the poor (Harrington's *Other America,* 1963) led to Pres. Johnson's **"Great Society"** programs (Medicare, Water Quality Act, Higher Education Act, all 1965). Concern with the **environment** surged (Carson's *Silent Spring,* 1962). **Feminism** revived as a cultural and political movement (Friedan's *Feminine Mystique,* 1963, National Organization for Women founded 1966) and a movement for homosexual rights emerged (Stonewall riot, in NYC, 1969).

Opposition to U.S. involvement in Vietnam, especially among university students (**Moratorium** protest Nov. '69) turned violent (Weatherman Chicago riots Oct. '69). New Left and Marxist theories became popular, and membership in radical groups swelled (Students for a Democratic Society, Black Panthers). Maoist groups, especially in Europe, called for total transformation of society. In France, students sparked a nationwide strike affecting 10 million workers May-June '68, but an electoral reaction barred revolutionary change.

Arts and styles. The boundary between fine and popular arts were blurred by Pop Art (Warhol) and rock musicals (Hair, 1968). Informality and exaggeration prevailed in fashion (beards, miniskirts). A non-political "counterculture" developed, rejecting traditional bourgeois life goals and personal habits, and use of marijuana and hallucinogens spread (Woodstock festival Aug. '68). Indian influence was felt in music (Beatles), religion (Ram Dass), and fashion.

Science. Achievements in space (men on moon July '69) and electronics (lasers, integrated circuits) encouraged a faith in scientific solutions to problems in agriculture ("green revolution"), medicine (heart transplants 1967) and other areas. The harmful effects of science, it was believed, could be controlled (1963 nuclear weapon test ban treaty, 1968 non-proliferation treaty).

China. Mao's revolutionary militance caused disputes with Russia under "revisionist" Khrushchev, starting 1960. The two powers exchanged fire in 1969 border disputes. China used force to capture areas disputed with India, 1962. The "Great Proletarian Cultural Revolution" tried to impose a utopian egalitarian program in China and spread revolution abroad; political struggle, often violent, convulsed China 1965-68.

Indochina. Communist-led guerrillas aided by N. Vietnam fought from 1960 against the S. Vietnam government of Ngo Dinh Diem (killed 1963). The U.S. military role increased after the 1964 Tonkin Gulf incident. U.S. forces peaked at 543,400, Apr. '69. Massive numbers of N. Viet troops also fought. Laotian and Cambodian neutrality were threatened by communist insurgencies, with N. Vietnamese aid, and U.S. intrigues. *For details, see 1978 and earlier editions of The World Almanac.*

Third World. A bloc of authoritarian leftist regimes among the newly independent nations emerged in political opposition to the U.S.-led Western alliance, and came to dominate the conference of nonaligned nations (Belgrade 1961, Cairo 1964, Lusaka 1970). Soviet political ties and military bases were established in Cuba, Egypt, Algeria, Guinea, and other countries, whose leaders were regarded as revolutionary heros by opposition groups in pro-Western or colonial countries. Some leaders were ousted in coups by pro-Western groups—Zaire's Lumumba (killed 1961), Ghana's Nkrumah (exiled 1966), and Indonesia's Sukarno (effectively ousted 1965 after a Communist coup failed).

Middle East. Arab-Israeli tension erupted into a brief war June 1967. Israel emerged as a major regional power. Military shipments before and after the war brought much of the Arab world into the Soviet political sphere. Most Arab states broke U.S. diplomatic ties, while Communist countries cut their ties to Israel. Intra-Arab disputes continued: Egypt and Saudi Arabia supported rival factions in a bloody Yemen civil war 1962-70; Lebanese troops fought Palestinian commandos in 1969.

East Europe. To stop the large-scale exodus of citizens, E. German authorities built a fortified wall across Berlin Aug. '61. Soviet sway in the Balkans was weakened by Albania's support of China (USSR broke ties Dec. '61) and Romania's assertion of industrial and foreign policy autonomy in 1964. Liberalization in Czechoslovakia, spring 1968, was crushed by troops of 5 Warsaw Pact countries. West German treaties with Russia and Poland, 1970, facilitated the transfer of German technology and confirmed post-war boundaries.

Disillusionment: 1970-79

U.S.: Caution and neoconservatism. A relatively sluggish economy, energy and resource shortages (natural gas crunch 1975, gasoline shortage 1979), and environmental problems contributed to a **"limits of growth"** philosophy that affected politics (Cal. Gov. Brown). Suspicion of science and technology killed or delayed major projects (supersonic transport dropped 1971, DNA recombination curbed 1976, Seabrook A-plant protests 1977-78) and was fed by the Three Mile Island nuclear reactor accident in Mar. '79.

Mistrust of big government weakened support for government reform plans among liberals. School busing and racial quotas were opposed (**Bakke decision** June '78); the Equal Rights Amendment for women languished; civil rights for homosexuals were opposed (Dade County referendum June '77).

U.S. defeat in **Indochina** (evacuation Apr. '75), revelations of Central Intelligence Agency misdeeds (Rockefeller Commission report June '75), and the **Watergate** scandals (Nixon quit Aug. '74) reduced

in U.S. moral and material capacity to influence world affairs. Revelations of Soviet crimes (Solzhenitsyn's *Gulag Archipelago* from 1974) and Russian intervention in Africa aided a revival of anti-Communist sentiment.

Economy sluggish. The 1960s boom faltered in the 1970s; a severe recession in the U.S. and Europe 1974-75 followed a huge oil price hike Dec. '73. Monetary instability (U.S. cut ties to gold Aug. '71), the decline of the dollar, and protectionist moves by industrial countries (1977-78) threatened trade. Business investment and spending for research declined. Severe inflation plagued many countries (25% in Britain, 1975; 18% in U.S., 1979).

China picks up pieces. After the 1976 deaths of Mao and Chou, a power struggle for the leadership succession was won by pragmatists. A nationwide purge of orthodox Maoists was carried out, and the "Gang of Four", led by Mao's widow Chiang Ching, was arrested.

The new leaders freed over 100,000 political prisoners, and reduced public adulation of Mao. Political and trade ties were expanded with Japan, Europe, and the U.S. in the late 1970's, as relations worsened with Russia, Cuba, and Vietnam (4-week invasion by China in 1979). Ideological guidelines in industry, science, education, and the armed forces, which the ruling faction said had caused chaos and decline, were reversed (bonuses to workers, Dec. '77; exams for college entrance, Oct. '77). Severe restrictions on cultural expression were eased (Beethoven ban lifted Mar. '77).

Europe. European unity moves (EEC-EFTA trade accord 1972) faltered as economic problems appeared (Britain floated pound 1972; France floated franc 1974). Germany and Switzerland curbed guest workers from S. Europe. Greece and Turkey quarreled over Cyprus (Turks intervened 1974) and Aegean oil rights.

All of non-Communist Europe was under democratic rule after free elections were held in Spain June '76, 7 months after the death of Franco. The conservative, colonialist regime in Portugal was overthrown Apr. '74. In Greece, the 7-year-old military dictatorship yielded power in 1974. Northern Europe, though ruled mostly by Socialists (Swedish Socialists unseated 1976, after 44 years in power), turned conservative. The British Labour government imposed wage curbs 1975, and suspended nationalization schemes. Terrorism in Germany (1972 Munich Olympics killings) led to laws curbing some civil liberties. French "new philosophers" rejected leftist ideologies, and the shaky Socialist-Communist coalition lost a 1978 election bid.

Religion back in politics. The improvement in Moslem countries' political fortunes by the 1950s (with the exception of Central Asia under Soviet and Chinese rule), and the growth of Arab oil wealth, was followed by a resurgence of traditional piety. Libyan dictator Qaddafi mixed strict Islamic laws with socialism in his militant ideology and called for an eventual Moslem return to Spain and Sicily. The illegal Moslem Brotherhood in Egypt was accused of violence, while extreme Moslem groups bombed theaters, 1977, to protest secular values.

In Turkey, the National Salvation Party was the first Islamic group to share power (1974) since secularization in the 1920s. Religious authorities, such as Ayatollah Ruholla Khomeini, led the Iranian revolution and religiously motivated Moslems took part in the insurrection in Saudi Arabia that briefly seized the Grand Mosque in Mecca in 1979. Moslem puritan opposition to Pakistan Pres. Bhutto helped lead to his overthrow July '77. However, Moslem solidarity could not prevent Pakistan's eastern province (Bangladesh) from declaring independence, Dec. '71, after a bloody civil war.

Moslem and Hindu resentment against coerced sterilization in India helped defeat the Gandhi government, which was replaced Mar. '77 by a coalition including religious Hindu parties and led by devout Hindu Desai. Moslems in the southern Philippines, aided by Libya, conducted a long rebellion against central rule from 1973.

Evangelical Protestant groups grew in numbers and prosperity in the U.S. ("born again" Pres. Carter elected 1976), and the Catholic charismatic movement obtained respectability. A revival of interest in Orthodox Christianity occurred among Russian intellectuals (Solzhenitsyn). The secularist Israeli Labor party, after decades of rule, was ousted in 1977 by conservatives led by Begin, an observant Jew; religious militants founded settlements on the disputed West Bank, part of Biblically-promised Israel. U.S. Reform Judaism revived many previously discarded traditional practices.

The Buddhist Soka Gakkai movement launched the Komeito party in Japan, 1964, which became a major opposition party in 1972 and 1976 elections.

Old-fashioned religious wars raged intermittently in N. Ireland (Catholic vs. Protestant, 1969-) and Lebanon (Christian vs. Moslem, 1975-), while religious militancy complicated the Israel-Arab dispute (1973 Israel-Arab war. In spite of a 1979 peace treaty between Egypt and Israel which looked forward to a resolution of the Palestinian issue, increased religious militancy on the West Bank made such a resolution seem unlikely.

Latin America. Repressive conservative regimes strengthened their hold on most of the continent, with the violent coup against the elected Allende government in Chile, Sept. '73, the 1976 military coup in Argentina, and coups against reformist regimes in Bolivia, 1971 and 1979, and Peru, 1976. In Central America, increasing liberal and leftist militancy led to the ouster of the Somoza regime of Nicaragua in 1979 and civil conflict in El Salvador.

Indochina. Communist victory in Vietnam, Cambodia, and Laos by May '75 did not bring peace. Attempts at radical social reorganization left over one million dead in Cambodia during 1975-78 and caused hundreds of thousands of ethnic Chinese and others to flee Vietnam ("boat people," 1979). The Vietnamese invasion of Cambodia swelled the refugee population and contributed to widespread starvation in that devastated country.

Russian expansion. Soviet influence, checked in some countries (troops ousted by Egypt 1972) was projected further afield, often with the use of Cuban troops (Angola 1975- , Ethiopia 1977-), and aided by a growing navy, merchant fleet, and international banking ability. Detente with the West — 1972 Berlin pact, 1970 strategic arms pact (SALT) — gave way to a more antagonistic relationship in the late 1970s, exacerbated by the Soviet invasion of Afghanistan in 1979.

Africa. The last remaining European colonies were granted independence (Spanish Sahara 1976, Djibouti 1977) and, after 10 years of civil war and many negotiation sessions, a black government took over Zimbabwe (Rhodesia) in 1979; white domination remained in S. Africa. Great power involvement in local wars (Russia in Angola, Ethiopia; France in Chad, Zaire, Mauritania) and the use of tens of thousands of Cuban troops was denounced by some African leaders as neocolonialism. Ethnic or tribal clashes made Africa the chief world locus of sustained warfare in the late 1970s.

Arts. Traditional modes in painting, architecture, and music, pursued in relative obscurity for much of the 20th century, returned to popular and critical attention in the 1970s. The pictorial emphasis in neorealist and photorealist painting, the return of many architects to detail, decoration, and traditional natural materials, and the concern with ordered structure in musical composition were, ironically, novel experiences for artistic consumers after the exhaustion of experimental possibilities. However, these more conservative styles coexisted with modernist works in an atmosphere of variety and tolerance.

100 Years Ago

On October 28, 1886, President Grover Cleveland dedicated the Statue of Liberty on Bedloe's Island in New York Harbor. Originally called Liberty Enlightening the World, the statue was proposed by journalist and politician Edouard Laboulaye, and given by the people of France to the people of the U.S. in commemoration of the French and American revolutions. The statue was designed by sculptor Frederic Auguste Bartholdi and was constructed of hammered coppered sheets. Standing 302 feet high, including its pedestal, it represented a woman holding a torch in her raised right hand, and in her left hand a tablet showing the date July 4, 1776. "The New Colossus," a sonnet on the statue by American poet Emma Lazarus, would be engraved on the pedestal in 1903. The statue would be declared a national monument in 1924.

The American Federation of Labor (AF of L) was founded in 1886 by Samuel Gompers. Organizing skilled workers into national unions composed of members of the same craft, the AF of L hoped to achieve shorter hours, higher pay, and better working conditions. Gompers, an English-American cigarmaker, would become president of the AF of L and would continue in that position with only one year's interruption until his death thirty-eight years later.

There were more labor strikes in 1886 than in any other year in 19th-century America. Demands for an 8-hour day and improved working conditions caused 610,000 workers to strike, with monetary losses of more than $33.5 million. On May 4, the Haymarket Square riot took place in Chicago after police attempted to disperse a peaceful demonstration, and a bomb felled 60 policemen, killing one. In the melee, six other policemen were killed. More than 200 suspected radicals were arrested, and eight anarchist labor leaders were tried for murder. Although no evidence was produced that the leaders had made or had thrown the bomb, they were convicted of incitement to murder, on the grounds that they had aided or conspired with the unknown bomber. Four would be hanged in 1887, one would commit suicide, and three would serve seven years in prison until pardoned in 1893 by Illinois governor John Peter Altgeld, on the grounds that the trial had been unjust.

The last major Indian war ended September 4, when U.S. troops captured Geronimo, leader of the Chiricahua band of Apaches. As a prisoner of war, Geronimo was deported to Florida. After further imprisonment in Alabama, he would be permitted to settle in Fort Sill, Oklahoma, where he would become a prosperous farmer and a Christian. Later, appearances at the St. Louis World's Fair and in Teddy Roosevelt's inaugural procession would make him a national celebrity. Three years before his death, he would dictate his autobiography.

Anti-Chinese riots in Seattle drove 400 Chinese from their homes. The Supreme Court declared a municipal order discriminating against Chinese laundries a violation of the 14th Amendment.

Stanton Coit, an assistant to Felix Adler in the Society for Ethical Culture, returned from visiting the first settlement house, London's Toybee Hall, and began to establish neighborhood clubs. Coit would organize the poor to work for social improvement.

International

W.E. Gladstone became British Prime Minister for the third time. Gladstone introduced the first bill for Irish Home Rule, which split the Liberal party and was defeated. In 1892, Gladstone would again become Prime Minister, bringing with him a new Home Rule Bill, which would pass the House of Commons, but meet defeat in the House of Lords, leading to Gladstone's resignation.

Gold was discovered in the Watwatersrand of Transvaal, a province in South Africa, bringing a huge influx of British and European miners and financiers. The mines would supply much of the world's gold.

General Georges Boulanger became the French War Minister, made himself a national hero, and led a nationalist movement, Boulangism, resembling fascism. He would retain great popularity despite being forced from his ministry in 1887 and then deprived of his army command. Boulanger would be remembered as a would-be Napoleon.

Inventions and Practicalities

The New York Tribune became the first newspaper to use linotype machines. Invented by Otto Mergenthaler, the linotype could cast a full line of type from matrices assembled by a keyboard like that of a typewriter.

German inventor Paul Gottlieb Nipkov created a rotating scanning device that would become important in the development of television.

Commercial aluminum production was begun by Charles Martin Hall, a graduate student at Oberlin College. His manufacturing company would become the Aluminum Company of America.

The first ready-to-use surgical dressings were introduced by Johnson & Johnson in New Brunswick, New Jersey.

Samuel C. Johnson introduced Johnson's Wax in Racine, Wisconsin.

David J. McConnell, a Brooklyn-born door-to-door book salesman working in California, was so successful using free vials of perfume to gain entrance to homes that he abandoned books and started selling perfume. His firm, eventually called Avon Products, would become the world's largest cosmetic company.

Brothers Lyman, Joseph, and Gustave Bloomingdale opened a department store on Third Avenue at 59th Street in New York City. With the assistance of the Third Avenue El, Bloomingdale's would attract the city's middle class.

Coca-Cola, made by pharmacist John S. Pemberton from the dried leaves of the South American cocoa shrub, an extract of Kola nuts from Africa, and fruit syrup, went on sale at a drugstore in Atlanta. The drink was advertised as an "esteemed Brain Tonic and Intellectual Beverage" that would cure headaches and hangovers. The same year, Dr. Pepper was introduced in Waco, Texas as "The King of Beverages, Free from Caffeine," and Hires' Rootbeer came out in bottles as well as in an extract for home brewing.

Arts and Entertainment

The eighth and last show of French Impressionism opened in Paris. The show included the painting "Sunday afternoon on the Island of Grand Jatte" by Georges Seurat.

French sculptor Auguste Rodin created "The Kiss."

Moussorgsky's "A Night on Bald Mountain" had its first performance at St. Petersburg.

The English translation of Karl Marx's *Das Kapital* was published, as was Krafft-Ebbing's *Psychopathia Sexualis*, Thomas Hardy's *The Mayor of Casterbridge*, Henry James's *The Bostonians* and *The Princess Cassamassima*. Robert Louis Stevenson wrote *The Strange Case of Dr. Jekyll and Mr. Hyde* in three days and rewrote it in another three. Also published were Stevenson's *Kidnapped*, Frances Hodgson Burnett's *Little Lord Fauntleroy*, and poet Arthur Rimbaud's *Les Illuminations*.

Theater managers B.F. Keith and Edward F. Albee founded the Keith-Albee Vaudeville Circuit.

The tuxedo was introduced when tobacco heir Griswold Lorillard wore a short black coat with satin lapels, instead of a tailcoat, to the Autumn Ball of the Tuxedo Park County Club in Tuxedo, New York.

Milestones

David Green was born in Plonsk, Belorussia. As David Ben-Gurion, he would become the first prime minister of Israel. Considered by many the father of his country, the flamboyant and indefatigable Ben-Gurion would hold the premiership, with only a two-year voluntary interruption, for a dozen years.

Also born in 1886 was Ty Cobb, who would become one of the most brilliant baseball players in history. The fiery-tempered Cobb was nicknamed the "Georgia Peach." In 1936, Cobb, who had set 90 records, would be voted the first member of the Baseball Hall of Fame.

HISTORICAL FIGURES

Ancient Greeks and Latins

Greeks

Aeschines, orator, 389-314BC.
Aeschylus, dramatist, 525-456BC.
Aesop, fableist, c620-c560BC.
Alcibiades, politician, 450-404BC.
Anacreon, poet, c582-c485BC.
Anaxagoras, philosopher, c500-428BC.
Anaximander, philosopher, 611-546BC.
Antiphon, speechwriter, c480-411BC.
Apollonius, mathematician, c265-170BC.
Archimedes, math. c287-212BC.
Aristophanes, dramatist, c448-380BC.
Aristotle, philosopher, 384-322BC.
Athenaeus, scholar, fl.c200.
Callicrates, architect, fl.5th cent.BC.
Callimachus, poet, c305-240BC.
Cratinus, comic dramatist, 520-421BC.
Democritus, philosopher, c460-370BC.
Demosthenes, orator, 384-322BC.
Diodorus, historian, fl.20BC.
Diogenes, philosopher, c372-c287BC.

Dionysius, historian, d.c7BC.
Empedocles, philosopher, c490-430BC.
Epicharmus, dramatist, c530-440BC.
Epictetus, philosopher, c55-c135.
Epicurus, philosopher, 341-270BC.
Eratosthenes, scientist, c276-194BC.
Euclid, mathematician, fl.c300BC.
Euripides, dramatist, c484-406BC.
Galen, physician, c129-199.
Heraclitus, philosopher, c535-c475BC.
Herodotus, historian, c484-420BC.
Hesiod, poet, 8th cent. BC.
Hippocrates, physician, c460-377BC.
Homer, poet, believed lived c850BC.
Isocrates, orator, 436-338BC.
Menander, dramatist, 342-292BC.
Phidias, sculptor, c500-435BC.
Pindar, poet, c518-c438BC.
Plato, philosopher, c428-c347BC.
Plutarch, biographer, c46-120.

Polybius, historian, c200-c118BC.
Praxiteles, sculptor, 400-330BC.
Pythagoras, phil., math., c580-c500BC.
Sappho, poet, c610-c580BC.
Simonides, poet, 556-c468BC.
Socrates, philosopher, c470-399BC.
Solon, statesman, 640-560BC.
Sophocles, dramatist, C496-406BC.
Strabo, geographer, c63BC-AD24.
Thales, philosopher, c634-c546BC.
Themistocles, politician, c524-c460BC.
Theocritus, poet, c310-250BC.
Theophrastus, phil. c372-c287BC.
Thucydides, historian, fl.5th cent.BC.
Timon, philosopher, c320-c230BC.
Xenophon, historian, c434-c355BC.
Zeno, philosopher, c495-c430BC.

Latins

Ammianus, historian, c330-395.
Apuleius, satirist, c124-c170.
Boethius, scholar, c480-524
Caesar, Julius, general, 100-44BC.
Catilina, politician, c108-62BC.
Carus, poet, c98-55BC.
Cato(Elder), statesman, 234-149BC.
Catullus, poet, c84-54BC.
Cicero, orator, 106-43BC.
Claudian, poet, c370-c404.
Ennius, poet, 239-170BC.
Gellius, author, c130-c165.

Horace, poet, 65-8BC.
Juvenal, satirist, c60-c127.
Livy, historian, 59BC-AD17.
Lucan, poet, 39-65.
Lucilius, poet, c180-c102BC.
Lucretius, poet, c99-c55BC.
Martial, epigrammatist, c38-c103.
Nepos, historian, c100-c25BC.
Ovid,poet, 43BC-AD17.
Persius, satirist, 34-62.
Plautus, dramatist, c254-c184BC.
Pliny, scholar, 23-79.

Pliny(Younger), author, 62-113.
Quintilian, rhetorician, c35-c97.
Sallust, historian, 86-34BC.
Seneca, philosopher, 4BC-AD65.
Silius, poet, c25-101.
Statius, poet, c45-c96.
Suetonius, biographer, c69-c122.
Tacitus, historian, c56-c120.
Terence, dramatist, 185-c159BC.
Tibullus, poet, c55-c19BC.
Virgil, poet, 70-19BC.
Vitruvius, architect, fl.1st cent.BC.

Rulers of England and Great Britain

Name	England	Began	Died	Age	Rgd
Saxons and Danes					
Egbert	King of Wessex, won allegiance of all English	829	839	—	10
Ethelwulf	Son, King of Wessex, Sussex, Kent, Essex	839	858	—	19
Ethelbald	Son of Ethelwulf, displaced father in Wessex	858	860	—	2
Ethelbert	2d son of Ethelwulf, united Kent and Wessex	860	866	—	6
Ethelred I	3d son, King of Wessex, fought Danes	866	871	—	5
Alfred	The Great, 4th son, defeated Danes, fortified London	871	899	52	28
Edward	The Elder, Alfred's son, united English, claimed Scotland	899	924	55	25
Athelstan	The Glorious, Edward's son, King of Mercia, Wessex	924	940	45	16
Edmund I	3d son of Edward, King of Wessex, Mercia	940	946	25	6
Edred	4th son of Edward	946	955	32	9
Edwy	The Fair, eldest son of Edmund, King of Wessex	955	959	18	3
Edgar	The Peaceful, 2d son of Edmund, ruled all English	959	975	32	17
Edward	The Martyr, eldest son of Edgar, murdered by stepmother	975	978	17	4
Ethelred II	The Unready, 2d son of Edgar, married Emma of Normandy	978	1016	48	37
Edmund II	Ironside, son of Ethelred II, King of London	1016	1016	27	0
Canute	The Dane, gave Wessex to Edmund, married Emma	1016	1035	40	19
Harold I	Harefoot, natural son of Canute	1035	1040	—	5
Hardecanute	Son of Canute by Emma, Danish King	1040	1042	24	2
Edward	The Confessor, son of Ethelred II (Canonized 1161)	1042	1066	62	24
Harold II	Edward's brother-in-law, last Saxon King	1066	1066	44	0
House of Normandy					
William I	The Conqueror, defeated Harold at Hastings	1066	1087	60	21
William II	Rufus, 3d son of William I, killed by arrow	1087	1100	43	13
Henry I	Beauclerc, youngest son of William I	1100	1135	67	35
House of Blois					
Stephen	Son of Adela, daughter of William I, and Count of Blois	1135	1154	50	19
House of Plantagenet					
Henry II	Son of Geoffrey Plantagenet (Angevin) by Matilda, dau. of Henry I	1154	1189	56	35
Richard I	Coeur de Lion, son of Henry II, crusader	1189	1199	42	10
John	Lackland, son of Henry II, signed Magna Carta, 1215	1199	1216	50	17
Henry III	Son of John, acceded at 9, under regency until 1227	1216	1272	65	56
Edward I	Longshanks, son of Henry III	1272	1307	68	35
Edward II	Son of Edward I, deposed by Parliament, 1327	1307	1327	43	20
Edward III	Of Windsor, son of Edward II	1327	1377	65	50
Richard II	Grandson of Edw. III, minor until 1389, deposed 1399	1377	1400	34	22
House of Lancaster					
Henry IV	Son of John of Gaunt, Duke of Lancaster, son of Edw. III	1399	1413	47	13
Henry V	Son of Henry IV, victor of Agincourt	1413	1422	34	9
Henry VI	Son of Henry V, deposed 1461, died in Tower	1422	1471	49	39

House of York

Edward IV	Great-great-grandson of Edward III, son of Duke of York	1461	1483	41	22
Edward V	Son of Edward IV, murdered in Tower of London	1483	1483	13	0
Richard III	Crookback, bro. of Edward IV, fell at Bosworth Field	1483	1485	35	2

House of Tudor

Henry VII	Son of Edmund Tudor, Earl of Richmond, whose father had married the widow of Henry V; descended from Edward III through his mother, Margaret Beaufort via John of Gaunt. By marriage with dau. of Edward IV he united Lancaster and York	1485	1509	53	24
Henry VIII	Son of Henry VII by Elizabeth, dau. of Edward IV.	1509	1547	56	38
Edward VI	Son of Henry VIII, by Jane Seymour, his 3d queen. Ruled under regents. Was forced to name Lady Jane Grey his successor. Council of State proclaimed her queen July 10, 1553. Mary Tudor won Council, was proclaimed queen July 19, 1553. Mary had Lady Jane Grey beheaded for treason, Feb., 1554	1547	1553	16	6
Mary I	Daughter of Henry VIII, by Catherine of Aragon	1553	1558	43	5
Elizabeth I	Daughter of Henry VIII, by Anne Boleyn	1558	1603	69	44

Great Britain

House of Stuart

James I	James VI of Scotland, son of Mary, Queen of Scots. *First to call himself King of Great Britain. This became official with the Act of Union, 1707*	1603	1625	59	22
Charles I	Only surviving son of James I; beheaded Jan. 30, 1649	1625	1649	48	24

Commonwealth, 1649-1660
Council of State, 1649; Protectorate, 1653

The Cromwells	Oliver Cromwell, Lord Protector	1653	1658	59	—
	Richard Cromwell, son, Lord Protector, resigned May 25, 1659	1658	1712	86	—

House of Stuart (Restored)

Charles II	Eldest son of Charles I, died without issue	1660	1685	55	25
James II	2d son of Charles I. Deposed 1688. Interregnum Dec. 11, 1688, to Feb. 13, 1689	1685	1701	68	3
William III	Son of William, Prince of Orange, by Mary, dau. of Charles I	1689	1702	51	13
and Mary II	Eldest daughter of James II and wife of William III		1694	33	6
Anne	2d daughter of James II	1702	1714	49	12

House of Hanover

George I	Son of Elector of Hanover, by Sophia, grand-dau. of James I	1714	1727	67	13
George II	Only son of George I, married Caroline of Brandenburg	1727	1760	77	33
George III	Grandson of George II, married Charlotte of Mecklenburg	1760	1820	81	59
George IV	Eldest son of George III, Prince Regent, from Feb., 1811	1820	1830	67	10
William IV	3d son of George III, married Adelaide of Saxe-Meiningen	1830	1837	71	7
Victoria	Dau. of Edward, 4th son of George III; married (1840) Prince Albert of Saxe-Coburg and Gotha, who became Prince Consort	1837	1901	81	63

House of Saxe-Coburg and Gotha

Edward VII	Eldest son of Victoria, married Alexandra, Princess of Denmark	1901	1910	68	9

House of Windsor
Name Adopted July 17, 1917

George V	2d son of Edward VII, married Princess Mary of Teck	1910	1936	70	25
Edward VIII	Eldest son of George V; acceded Jan. 20, 1936, abdicated Dec. 11	1936	1972	77	1
George VI	2d son of George V; married Lady Elizabeth Bowes-Lyon	1936	1952	56	15
Elizabeth II	Elder daughter of George VI, acceded Feb. 6, 1952	1952	—	—	—

Rulers of Scotland

Kenneth I MacAlpin was the first Scot to rule both Scots and Picts, 846 AD.

Duncan I was the first general ruler, 1034. Macbeth seized the kingdom 1040, was slain by Duncan's son, Malcolm III MacDuncan (Canmore), 1057.

Malcolm married Margaret, Saxon princess who had fled from the Normans. Queen Margaret introduced English language and English monastic customs. She was canonized, 1250. Her son Edgar, 1097, moved the court to Edinburgh. His brothers Alexander I and David I succeeded. Malcolm IV, the Maiden, 1153, grandson of David I, was followed by his brother, William the Lion, 1165, whose son was Alexander II, 1214. The latter's son, Alexander III, 1249, defeated the Norse and regained the Hebrides. When he died, 1286, his granddaughter, Margaret, child of Eric of Norway and grandniece of Edward I of England, known as the Maid of Norway, was chosen ruler, but died 1290, aged 8.

John Baliol, 1292-1296. (Interregnum, 10 years.)

Robert Bruce (The Bruce), 1306-1329, victor at Bannockburn, 1314.

David II, only son of Robert Bruce, ruled 1329-1371.

Robert II, 1371-1390, grandson of Robert Bruce, son of Walter, the Steward of Scotland, was called The Steward, first of the so-called Stuart line.

Robert III, son of Robert II, 1390-1406.

James I, son of Robert III, 1406-1437.

James II, son of James I, 1437-1460.

James III, eldest son of James II, 1460-1488.

James IV, eldest son of James III, 1488-1513.

James V, eldest son of James IV, 1513-1542.

Mary, daughter of James V, born 1542, became queen when one week old; was crowned 1543. Married, 1558, Francis, son of Henry II of France, who became king 1559, died 1560. Mary ruled Scots 1561 until abdication, 1567. She also married (2) Henry Stewart, Lord Darnley, and (3) James, Earl of Bothwell. Imprisoned by Elizabeth I, Mary was beheaded 1587.

James VI, 1566-1625, son of Mary and Lord Darnley, became King of England on death of Elizabeth in 1603. Although the thrones were thus united, the legislative union of Scotland and England was not effected until the Act of Union, May 1, 1707.

Rulers of France: Kings, Queens, Presidents

Caesar to Charlemagne

Julius Caesar subdued the Gauls, native tribes of Gaul (France) 57 to 52 BC. The Romans ruled 500 years. The Franks, a Teutonic tribe, reached the Somme from the East ca. 250 AD. By the 5th century the Merovingian Franks ousted the Romans. In 451 AD, with the help of Visigoths, Burgundians and others,

they defeated Attila and the Huns at Chalons-sur-Marne.

Childeric I became leader of the Merovingians 458 AD. His son Clovis I (Chlodwig, Ludwig, Louis), crowned 481, founded the dynasty. After defeating the Alemanni (Germans) 496, he was baptized a Christian and made Paris his capital. His line ruled until Childeric III was deposed, 751.

The West Merovingians were called Neustrians, the eastern

...strasians. Pepin of Herstal (687-714) major domus, or head of ... palace, of Austrasia, took over Neustria as dux (leader) of ...e Franks. Pepin's son, Charles, called Martel (the Hammer) ...efeated the Saracens at Tours-Poitiers, 732; was succeeded ...y his son, Pepin the Short, 741, who deposed Childeric III and ruled as king until 768.

His son, Charlemagne, or Charles the Great (742-814) became king of the Franks, 768, with his brother Carloman, who died 771. He ruled France, Germany, parts of Italy, Spain, Austria, and enforced Christianity. Crowned Emperor of the Romans by Pope Leo III in St. Peter's, Rome, Dec. 25, 800 AD. Succeeded by son, Louis I the Pious, 814. At death, 840, Louis left empire to sons, Lothair (Roman emperor); Pepin I (king of Aquitaine); Louis II (of Germany); Charles the Bald (France). They quarreled and by the peace of Verdun, 843, divided the empire.

AD Name, year of accession

The Carolingians

843 Charles I (the Bald), Roman Emperor, 875
877 Louis II (the Stammerer), son
879 Louis III (died 882) and Carloman, brothers
885 Charles II (the Fat), Roman Emperor, 881
888 Eudes (Odo) elected by nobles
898 Charles III (the Simple), son of Louis II, defeated by
922 Robert, brother of Eudes, killed in war
923 Rudolph (Raoul) Duke of Burgundy
936 Louis IV, son of Charles III
954 Lothair, son, aged 13, defeated by Capet
986 Louis V (the Sluggard), left no heirs

The Capets

987 Hugh Capet, son of Hugh the Great
996 Robert II (the Wise), his son
1031 Henry I, his son, last Norman
1060 Philip I (the Fair), son
1108 Louis VI (the Fat), son
1137 Louis VII (the Younger), son
1180 Philip II (Augustus), son, crowned at Reims
1223 Louis VIII (the Lion), son
1226 Louis IX, son, crusader; Louis IX (1214-1270) reigned 44 years, arbitrated disputes with English King Henry III; led crusades, 1248 (captured in Egypt 1250) and 1270, when he died of plague in Tunis. Canonized 1297 as St. Louis.
1270 Philip III (the Hardy), son
1285 Philip IV (the Fair), son, king at 17
1314 Louis X (the Headstrong), son. His posthumous son, John I, lived only 7 days
1316 Philip V (the Tall), brother of Louis X
1322 Charles IV (the Fair), brother of Louis X

House of Valois

1328 Philip VI (of Valois), grandson of Philip III
1350 John II (the Good), his son, retired to England
1364 Charles V (the Wise), son
1380 Charles VI (the Beloved), son
1422 Charles VII (the Victorious), son. In 1429 Joan of Arc (Jeanne d'Arc) promised Charles to oust the English, who occupied northern France. Joan won at Orleans and Patay and had Charles crowned at Reims July 17, 1429. Joan was captured May 24, 1430, and executed May 30, 1431, at Rouen for heresy. Charles ordered her rehabilitation, effected 1455.
1461 Louis XI (the Cruel), son, civil reformer
1483 Charles VIII (the Affable), son
1498 Louis XII, great-grandson of Charles V
1515 Francis I, of Angouleme, nephew, son-in-law. Francis I (1494-1547) reigned 32 years, fought 4 big wars, was patron of the arts, aided Cellini, del Sarto, Leonardo da Vinci, Rabelais, embellished Fontainebleau.
1547 Henry II, son, killed at a joust in a tournament. He was the husband of Catherine de Medicis (1519-1589) and the lover of Diane de Poitiers (1499-1566). Catherine was born in Florence, daughter of Lorenzo de Medicis. By her marriage to Henry II she became the mother of Francis II, Charles IX, Henry III and Queen Margaret (Reine Margot) wife of Henry IV. She persuaded Charles IX to order the massacre of Huguenots on the Feast of St. Bartholomew, Aug. 24, 1572, the day her daughter was married to Henry of Navarre.
1559 Francis II, son. In 1548, Mary, Queen of Scots since infancy, was betrothed when 6 to Francis, aged 4. They were married 1558. Francis died 1560, aged 16; Mary ruled Scotland, abdicated 1567.
1560 Charles IX, brother

1574 Henry III, brother, assassinated

House of Bourbon

1589 Henry IV, of Navarre, assassinated. Henry IV made enemies when he gave tolerance to Protestants by Edict of Nantes, 1598. He was grandson of Queen Margaret of Navarre, literary patron. He married Margaret of Valois, daughter of Henry II and Catherine de Medicis; was divorced; in 1600 married Marie de Medicis, who became Regent of France, 1610-17 for her son, Louis XIII, but was exiled by Richelieu, 1631.
1610 Louis XIII (the Just), son. Louis XIII (1601-1643) married Anne of Austria. His ministers were Cardinals Richelieu and Mazarin.
1643 Louis XIV (The Grand Monarch), son. Louis XIV was king 72 years. He exhausted a prosperous country in wars for thrones and territory. By revoking the Edict of Nantes (1685) he caused the emigration of the Huguenots. He said: "I am the state."
1715 Louis XV, great-grandson. Louis XV married a Polish princess; lost Canada to the English. His favorites, Mme. Pompadour and Mme. Du Barry, influenced policies. Noted for saying "After me, the deluge."
1774 Louis XVI, grandson; married Marie Antoinette, daughter of Empress Maria Therese of Austria. King and queen beheaded by Revolution, 1793. Their son, called Louis XVII, died in prison, never ruled.

First Republic

1792 National Convention of the French Revolution
1795 Directory, under Barras and others
1799 Consulate, Napoleon Bonaparte, first consul. Elected consul for life, 1802.

First Empire

1804 Napoleon I, emperor. Josephine (de Beauharnais) empress, 1804-09; Marie Louise, empress, 1810-1814. Her son, Francois (1811-1832), titular King of Rome, later Duke de Reichstadt and "Napoleon II," never ruled. Napoleon abdicated 1814, died 1821.

Bourbons Restored

1814 Louis XVIII king; brother of Louis XVI.
1824 Charles X, brother; reactionary; deposed by the July Revolution, 1830.

House of Orleans

1830 Louis-Philippe, the "citizen king."

Second Republic

1848 Louis Napoleon Bonaparte, president, nephew of Napoleon I. He became:

Second Empire

1852 Napoleon III, emperor; Eugenie (de Montijo) empress. Lost Franco-Prussian war, deposed 1870. Son, Prince Imperial (1856-79), died in Zulu War. Eugenie died 1920.

Third Republic—Presidents

1871 Thiers, Louis Adolphe (1797-1877)
1873 MacMahon, Marshal Patrice M. de (1808-1893)
1879 Grevy, Paul J. (1807-1891)
1887 Sadi-Carnot, M. (1837-1894), assassinated
1894 Casimir-Perier, Jean P. P. (1847-1907)
1895 Faure, Francois Felix (1841-1899)
1899 Loubet, Emile (1838-1929)
1906 Fallieres, C. Armand (1841-1931)
1913 Poincare, Raymond (1860-1934)
1920 Deschanel, Paul (1856-1922)
1920 Millerand, Alexandre (1859-1943)
1924 Doumergue, Gaston (1863-1937)
1931 Doumer, Paul (1857-1932), assassinated
1932 Lebrun, Albert (1871-1950), resigned 1940
1940 **Vichy govt.** under German armistice: Henri Philippe Petain (1856-1951) Chief of State, 1940-1944.
Provisional govt. after liberation: Charles de Gaulle (1890-1970) Oct. 1944-Jan. 21, 1946; Felix Gouin (1884-1977) Jan. 23, 1946; Georges Bidault (1899-) June 24, 1946.

Fourth Republic—Presidents

1947 Auriol, Vincent (1884-1966)
1954 Coty, Rene (1882-1962)

Fifth Republic—Presidents

1959 de Gaulle, Charles Andre J. M. (1890-1970)
1969 Pompidou, Georges (1911-1974)
1974 Giscard d'Estaing, Valery (1926-   )
1981 Mitterrand, Francois (1916-   )

Rulers of Middle Europe; Rise and Fall of Dynasties

Carolingian Dynasty

Charles the Great, or Charlemagne, ruled France, Italy, and

Middle Europe; established Ostmark (later Austria); crowned Roman emperor by pope in Rome, 800 AD; died 814.
Louis I (Ludwig) the Pious, son; crowned by Charlemagne 814,

d. 840.

Louis II, the German, son; succeeded to East Francia (Germany) 843-876.

Charles the Fat, son; inherited East Francia and West Francia (France) 876, reunited empire, crowned emperor by pope, 881, deposed 887.

Arnulf, nephew, 887-899. Partition of empire.

Louis the Child, 899-911, last direct descendant of Charlemagne.

Conrad I, duke of Franconia, first elected German king, 911-918, founded House of Franconia.

Saxon Dynasty; First Reich

Henry I, the Fowler, duke of Saxony, 919-936.

Otto I, the Great, 936-973, son; crowned Holy Roman Emperor by pope, 962.

Otto II, 973-983, son; failed to oust Greeks and Arabs from Sicily.

Otto III, 983-1002, son; crowned emperor at 16.

Henry II, the Saint, duke of Bavaria, 1002-1024, great-grandson of Otto the Great.

House of Franconia

Conrad II, 1024-1039, elected king of Germany.

Henry III, the Black, 1039-1056, son; deposed 3 popes; annexed Burgundy.

Henry IV, 1056-1106, son; regency by his mother, Agnes of Poitou. Banned by Pope Gregory VII, he did penance at Canossa.

Henry V, 1106-1125, son; last of Salic House.

Lothair, duke of Saxony, 1125-1137. Crowned emperor in Rome, 1134.

House of Hohenstaufen

Conrad III, duke of Swabia, 1138-1152. In 2d Crusade.

Frederick I, Barbarossa, 1152-1190; Conrad's nephew.

Henry VI, 1190-1196, took lower Italy from Normans. Son became king of Sicily.

Philip of Swabia, 1197-1208, brother.

Otto IV, of House of Welf, 1198-1215; deposed.

Frederick II, 1215-1250, son of Henry VI; king of Sicily; crowned king of Jerusalem; in 5th Crusade.

Conrad IV, 1250-1254, son; lost lower Italy to Charles of Anjou.

Conradin (1252-1268) son, king of Jerusalem and Sicily, beheaded. Last Hohenstaufen.

Interregnum, 1254-1273, Rise of the Electors.

Transition

Rudolph I of Hapsburg, 1273-1291, defeated King Ottocar II of Bohemia. Bequeathed duchy of Austria to eldest son, Albert.

Adolph of Nassau, 1292-1298, killed in war with Albert of Austria.

Albert I, king of Germany, 1298-1308, son of Rudolph.

Henry VII, of Luxemburg, 1308-1313, crowned emperor in Rome. Seized Bohemia, 1310.

Louis IV of Bavaria (Wittelsbach), 1314-1347. Also elected was Frederick of Austria, 1314-1330 (Hapsburg). Abolition of papal sanction for election of Holy Roman Emperor.

Charles IV, of Luxemburg, 1347-1378, grandson of Henry VII, German emperor and king of Bohemia, Lombardy, Burgundy; took Mark of Brandenburg.

Wenceslaus, 1378-1400, deposed.

Rupert, Duke of Palatine, 1400-1410.

Hungary

Stephen I, house of Arpad, 997-1038. Crowned king 1000; converted Magyars; canonized 1083. After several centuries of feuds Charles Robert of Anjou became Charles I, 1308-1342.

Louis I, the Great, son, 1342-1382; joint ruler of Poland with Casimir III, 1370. Defeated Turks.

Mary, daughter, 1382-1395, ruled with husband. Sigismund of Luxemburg, 1387-1437, also king of Bohemia. As bro. of Wenceslaus he succeeded Rupert as Holy Roman Emperor, 1410.

Albert II, 1438-1439, son-in-law of Sigismund; also Roman emperor. (see under Hapsburg.)

Ulaszlo I of Poland, 1440-1444.

Ladislaus V, posthumous son of Albert II, 1444-1457. John Hunyadi (Hunyadi Janos) governor (1446-1452), fought Turks, Czechs; died 1456.

Matthias I (Corvinus) son of Hunyadi, 1458-1490. Shared rule of Bohemia, captured Vienna, 1485, annexed Austria, Styria, Carinthia.

Ladislas II (king of Bohemia), 1490-1516.

Louis II, son, aged 10, 1516-1526. Wars with Suleiman, Turk. In 1527 Hungary was split between Ferdinand I, Archduke o Austria, bro.-in-law of Louis II, and John Zapolya of Transylvania. After Turkish invasion, 1547, Hungary was split between Ferdinand, Prince John Sigismund (Transylvania) and the Turks.

House of Hapsburg'

Albert V of Austria, Hapsburg, crowned king of Hungary, Jan. 1438, Roman emperor, March, 1438, as Albert II; died 1439.

Frederick III, cousin, 1440-1493. Fought Turks.

Maximilian I, son, 1493-1519. Assumed title of Holy Roman Emperor (German), 1493.

Charles V, grandson, 1519-1556. King of Spain with mother co-regent; crowned Roman emperor at Aix, 1520. Confronted Luther at Worms; attempted church reform and religious conciliation; abdicated 1556.

Ferdinand I, king of Bohemia, 1526, of Hungary, 1527; disputed German king, 1531. Crowned Roman emperor on abdication of brother Charles V, 1556.

Maximilian II, son, 1564-1576.

Rudolph II, son, 1576-1612.

Matthias, brother, 1612-1619, king of Bohemia and Hungary.

Ferdinand II of Styria, king of Bohemia, 1617, of Hungary, 1618, Roman emperor, 1619. Bohemian Protestants deposed him, elected Frederick V of Palatine, starting Thirty Years War.

Ferdinand III, son, king of Hungary, 1625, Bohemia, 1627, Roman emperor, 1637. Peace of Westphalia, 1648, ended war. Leopold I, 1658-1705; Joseph I, 1705-1711; Charles VI, 1711-1740.

Maria Theresa, daughter, 1740-1780, Archduchess of Austria, queen of Hungary; ousted pretender, Charles VII, crowned 1742; in 1745 obtained election of her husband Francis I as Roman emperor and co-regent (d. 1765). Fought Seven Years' War with Frederick II (the Great) of Prussia. Mother of Marie Antoinette, Queen of France.

Joseph II, son 1765-1790, Roman emperor, reformer; powers restricted by Empress Maria Theresa until her death, 1780. First partition of Poland. Leopold II, 1790-1792.

Francis II, son, 1792-1835. Fought Napoleon. Proclaimed first hereditary emperor of Austria, 1804. Forced to abdicate as Roman emperor, 1806; last use of title. Ferdinand I, son, 1835-1848, abdicated during revolution.

Austro-Hungarian Monarchy

Francis Joseph I, nephew, 1848-1916, emperor of Austria, king of Hungary. Dual monarchy of Austria-Hungary formed, 1867. After assassination of heir, Archduke Francis Ferdinand, June 28, 1914, Austrian diplomacy precipitated World War I.

Charles I, grand-nephew, 1916-1918, last emperor of Austria and king of Hungary. Abdicated Nov. 11-13, 1918, died 1922.

Rulers of Prussia

Nucleus of Prussia was the Mark of Brandenburg. First margrave was Albert the Bear (Albrecht), 1134-1170. First Hohenzollern margrave was Frederick, burgrave of Nuremberg, 1417-1440.

Frederick William, 1640-1688, the Great Elector. Son, Frederick III, 1688-1713, was crowned King Frederick of Prussia, 1701.

Frederick William I, son, 1713-1740.

Frederick II, the Great, son, 1740-1786, annexed Silesia part of Austria.

Frederick William II, nephew, 1786-1797.

Frederick William III, son, 1797-1840. Napoleonic wars.

Frederick William IV, son, 1840-1861. Uprising of 1848 and first parliament and constitution.

Second and Third Reich

William I, 1861-1888, brother. Annexation of Schleswig and Hanover; Franco-Prussian war, 1870-71, proclamation of German Reich, Jan. 18, 1871, at Versailles; William, German emperor (Deutscher Kaiser); Bismarck, chancellor.

Frederick III, son, 1888.

William II, son, 1888-1918. Led Germany in World War I, abdicated as German emperor and king of Prussia, Nov. 9, 1918. Died in exile in Netherlands June 4, 1941. Minor rulers of Bavaria, Saxony, Wurttemberg also abdicated.

Germany proclaimed a republic at Weimar, July 1, 1919. Presidents: Frederick Ebert, 1919-1925, Paul von Hindenburg-Beneckendorff, 1925, reelected 1932, d. Aug. 2, 1934. Adolf Hitler, chancellor, chosen successor as Leader-Chancellor (Fuehrer & Reichskanzler) of Third Reich. Annexed Austria, March, 1938. Precipitated World War II, 1939-1945. Committed suicide April 30, 1945.

Rulers of Poland

House of Piasts

Miesko I, 962?-992; Poland Christianized 966. Expansion under 3 Boleslavs: I, 992-1025, son, crowned king 1024; II, 1058-1079, great-grandson, exiled after killing bishop Stanislav who became chief patron saint of Poland: III, 1106-1138, nephew, divided Poland among 4 sons eldest suzerain.

1138-1306, feudal division. 1226 founding in Prussia of military order Teutonic Knights. 1226 invasion by Tartars/Mongols.

Vladislav I, 1306-1333, reunited most Polish territories, crowned king 1320. Casimir III the Great, 1333-1370, son, developed economic, cultural life, foreign policy.

House of Anjou

Louis I, 1370-1382, nephew/identical with Louis I of Hungary.

Jadwiga, 1384-1399, daughter, married 1386 Jagiello, Grand Duke of Lituania.

House of Jagelloneans

Vladislav II, 1386-1434, Christianized Lituania, founded personal union between Poland & Lituania. Defeated 1410 Teutonic Knights at Grunwald.

Vladislav III, 1434-1444, son, simultaneously king of Hungary. Fought Turks, killed 1444 in battle of Varna.

Casimir IV, 1446-1492, brother, competed with Hapsburgs, put son Vladislav on throne of Bohemia, later also of Hungary.

Sigismund I, 1506-1548, brother, patronized science & arts, his & son's reign "Golden Age."

Sigismund II, 1548-1572, son, established 1569 real union of Poland and Lituania (lasted until 1795).

Elective kings

Polish nobles proclaimed 1572 Poland a Republic headed by king to be elected by whole nobility.

Stephen Batory, 1576-1586, duke of Transylvania, married Ann, sister of Sigismund II August. Fought Russians.

Sigismund III Vasa, 1587-1632, nephew of Sigismund II. 1592-1598 also king of Sweden. His generals fought Russians, Turks.

Vladislav IV Vasa, 1632-1648, son. Fought Russians.

John II Casimir Vasa, 1648-1668, brother. Fought Cossacks, Swedes, Russians, Turks, Tartars (the "Deluge"). Abdicated 1668.

John III Sobieski, 1674-1696. Won Vienna from Turks, 1683.

Stanislav II, 1764-1795, last king. Encouraged reforms; 1791 1st modern Constitution in Europe. 1772, 1793, 1795 Poland partitioned among Russia, Prussia, Austria. Unsuccessful insurrection against foreign invasion 1794 under Kosciuszko, Amer-Polish gen.

1795-1918 Poland under foreign rule

1807-1815 Grand Duchy of Warsaw created by Napoleon I, Frederick August of Saxony grand duke.

1815 Congress of Vienna proclaimed part of Poland "Kingdom" in personal union with Russia.

Polish uprisings: 1830 against Russia, 1846, 1848 against Austria, 1863 against Russia—all repressed.

1918-1939 Second Republic

1918-1922 Head of State Jozef Pilsudski. Presidents: Gabriel Narutowicz 1933, assassinated. Stanislav Wojsiechowski 1922-1926, had to abdicate after Pilsudski's coup d'état. Ignacy Mosciecki, 1926-1939, ruled with Pilsudski as (until 1935) virtual dictator.

1939-1945 Poland under foreign occupation

Nazi aggression Sept. 1939. Polish govt.-in-exile, first in France, then in England. Vladislav Raczkiewicz pres., Gen. Vladislav Sikorski, then Stanislav Mikolajczyk, prime ministers. Polish Committee of Natl. Liberation proclaimed at Lublin July 1944, transformed into govt. Jan. 1, 1945.

Rulers of Denmark, Sweden, Norway

Denmark

Earliest rulers invaded Britain; King Canute, who ruled in London 1016-1035, was most famous. The Valdemars furnished kings until the 15th century. In 1282 the Danes won the first national assembly, Danehof, from King Erik V.

Most redoubtable medieval character was Margaret, daughter of Valdemar IV, born 1353, married at 10 to King Haakon VI of Norway. In 1376 she had her first infant son Olaf made king of Denmark. After his death, 1387, she was regent of Denmark and Norway. In 1388 Sweden accepted her as sovereign. In 1389 she made her grand-nephew, Duke Erik of Pomerania, titular king of Denmark, Sweden, and Norway, with herself as regent. In 1397 she effected the Union of Kalmar of the three kingdoms and had Erik VII crowned. In 1439 the three kingdoms deposed him and elected, 1440, Christopher of Bavaria king (Christopher III). On his death, 1448, the union broke up.

Succeeding rulers were unable to enforce their claims as rulers of Sweden until 1520, when Christian II conquered Sweden. He was thrown out 1522, and in 1523 Gustavus Vasa united Sweden. Denmark continued to dominate Norway until the Napoleonic wars, when Frederick VI, 1808-1839, joined the Napoleonic cause after Britain had destroyed the Danish fleet, 1807. In 1814 he was forced to cede Norway to Sweden and Helgoland to Britain, receiving Lauenburg. Successors Christian VIII, 1839; Frederick VII, 1848; Christian IX, 1863; Frederick VIII, 1906; Christian X, 1912; Frederick IX, 1947; Margrethe II, 1972.

Sweden

Early kings ruled at Uppsala, but did not dominate the country. Sverker, c1130-c1156, united the Swedes and Goths. In 1435 Sweden obtained the Riksdag, or parliament. After the Union of Kalmar, 1397, the Danes either ruled or harried the country until Christian II of Denmark conquered it anew, 1520. This led to a rising under Gustavus Vasa, who ruled Sweden 1523-1560, and established an independent kingdom. Charles IX, 1599-1611, crowned 1604, conquered Moscow. Gustavus II Adolphus, 1611-1632, was called the Lion of the North. Later rulers: Christina, 1632; Charles X, Gustavus 1654; Charles XI, 1660; Charles XII (invader of Russia and Poland, defeated at Poltava, June 28, 1709), 1697; Ulrika Eleanora, sister, elected queen 1718; Frederick I (of Hesse), her husband, 1720; Adolphus Frederick, 1751; Gustavus III, 1771; Gustavus IV Adolphus, 1792; Charles XIII, 1809. (Union with Norway began 1814.) Charles XIV John, 1818. He was Jean Bernadotte, Napoleon's Prince of Ponte Corvo, elected 1810 to succeed Charles XIII. He founded the present dynasty: Oscar I, 1844, Charles XV, 1859; Oscar II, 1872; Gustavus V, 1907; Gustav VI Adolf, 1950; Carl XVI Gustaf, 1973.

Norway

Overcoming many rivals, Harald Haarfager, 872-930, conquered Norway, Orkneys, and Shetlands; Olaf I, great-grandson, 995-1000, brought Christianity into Norway, Iceland, and Greenland. In 1035 Magnus the Good also became king of Denmark. Haakon V, 1299-1319, had married his daughter to Erik of Sweden. Their son, Magnus, became ruler of Norway and Sweden at 6. His son, Haakon VI, married Margaret of Denmark; their son Olaf IV became king of Norway and Denmark, followed by Margaret's regency and the Union of Kalmar, 1397.

In 1450 Norway became subservient to Denmark. Christian IV, 1588-1648, founded Christiania, now Oslo. After Napoleonic wars, when Denmark ceded Norway to Sweden, a strong nationalist movement forced recognition of Norway as an independent kingdom united with Sweden under the Swedish kings, 1814-1905. In 1905 the union was dissolved and Prince Carl of Denmark became Haakon VII. He died Sept. 21, 1957, aged 85; succeeded by son, Olav V, b. July 2, 1903.

Rulers of the Netherlands and Belgium

The Netherlands (Holland)

William Frederick, Prince of Orange, led a revolt against French rule, 1813, and was crowned King of the Netherlands, 1815. Belgium seceded Oct. 4, 1830, after a revolt, and formed a separate government. The change was ratified by the two kingdoms by treaty Apr. 19, 1839.

Succession: William II, son, 1840; William III, son, 1849; Wilhelmina, daughter of William III and his 2d wife Princess Emma of Waldeck, 1890; Wilhelmina abdicated, Sept. 4, 1948, in favor of daughter, Juliana. Juliana abdicated Apr. 30, 1980, in favor of daughter, Beatrix.

Belgium

A national congress elected Prince Leopold of Saxe-Coburg King; he took the throne July 21, 1831, as Leopold I. Succession: Leopold II, son 1865; Albert I, nephew of Leopold II, 1909; Leopold III, son of Albert, 1934; Prince Charles, Regent 1944; Leopold returned 1950, yielded powers to son Baudouin, Prince Royal, Aug. 6, 1950, abdicated July 16, 1951. Baudouin I took throne July 17, 1951.

For political history prior to 1830 see articles on the Netherlands and Belgium.

Roman Rulers

From Romulus to the end of the Empire in the West. Rulers of the Roman Empire in the East sat in Constantinople and for a brief period in Nicaea, until the capture of Constantinople by the Turks in 1453, when Byzantium was succeeded by the Ottoman Empire.

BC	Name	BC	Name	AD	Name
	The Kingdom	534	L. Tarquinius Superbus	435	Censorship instituted
			The Republic	366	Praetorship established
753	Romulus (Quirinus)	509	Consulate established	366	Curule Aedileship created
716	Numa Pompilius	509	Quaestorship instituted	362	Military Tribunate elected
673	Tullus Hostilius	498	Dictatorship introduced	326	Proconsulate introduced
640	Ancus Marcius	494	Plebeian Tribunate created	311	Naval Duumvirate elected
616	L. Tarquinius Priscus	494	Plebeian Aedileship created	217	Dictatorship of Fabius Maximus
578	Servius Tullius	444	Consular Tribunate organized	133	Tribunate of Tiberius Gracchus

123 Tribunate of Gaius Gracchus	238 Gordianus I and Gordianus II;	**West (Rome) and East**
82 Dictatorship of Sulla	Pupienus and Balbinus	**(Constantinople)**
60 First Triumvirate formed	238 Gordianus III	364 Valentinianus I (West) and Valens
(Caesar, Pompeius, Crassus)	244 Philippus (the Arabian)	(East)
46 Dictatorship of Caesar	249 Decius	367 Valentinianus I with
43 Second Triumvirate formed	251 Gallus and Volusianus	Gratianus (West) and Valens (East)
(Octavianus, Antonius, Lepidus)	253 Aemilianus	375 Gratianus with Valentinianus
The Empire	253 Valerianus and Gallienus	II (West) and Valens (East)
27 Augustus (Gaius Julius	258 Gallienus (alone)	378 Gratianus with Valentinianus II
Caesar Octavianus)	268 Claudius II (the Goth)	(West) Theodosius I (East)
AD	270 Quintillus	383 Valentinianus II (West) and
	270 Aurelianus	Theodosius I (East)
14 Tiberius I	275 Tacitus	394 Theodosius I (the Great)
37 Gaius Caesar (Caligula)	276 Florianus	395 Honorius (West) and Arcadius
41 Claudius I	276 Probus	(East)
54 Nero	282 Carus	408 Honorius (West) and Theodosius II
68 Galba	283 Carinus and Numerianus	(East)
69 Galba; Otho, Vitellius	284 Diocletianus	423 Valentinianus III (West) and
69 Vespasianus	286 Diocletianus and Maximianus	Theodosius II (East)
79 Titus	305 Galerius and Constantius I	450 Valentinianus III (West)
81 Domitianus	306 Galerius, Maximinus II, Severus I	and Marcianus (East)
96 Nerva	307 Galerius, Maximinus	455 Maximus (West), Avitus
98 Trajanus	II, Constantinus I, Licinius,	(West); Marcianus (East)
117 Hadrianus	Maxentius	456 Avitus (West), Marcianus (East)
138 Antoninus Pius	311 Maximinus II, Constantinus I,	457 Majorianus (West), Leo I (East)
161 Marcus Aurelius and Lucius Verus	Licinius, Maxentius	461 Severus II (West), Leo I (East)
169 Marcus Aurelius (alone)	314 Maximinus II, Constantinus I,	467 Anthemius (West), Leo I (East)
180 Commodus	Licinius	472 Olybrius (West), Leo I (East)
193 Pertinax; Julianus I	314 Constantinus I and Licinius	473 Glycerius (West), Leo I (East)
193 Septimius Severus	324 Constantinus I (the Great)	474 Julius Nepos (West), Leo II (East)
211 Caracalla and Geta	337 Constantinus II, Constans I,	475 Romulus Augustulus (West) and
212 Caracalla (alone)	Constantius II	Zeno (East)
217 Macrinus	340 Constantius II and Constans I	476 End of Empire in West; Odovacar,
218 Elagabalus (Heliogabalus)	350 Constantius II	King, drops title of Emperor;
222 Alexander Severus	361 Julianus II (the Apostate)	murdered by King Theodoric of
235 Maximinus I (the Thracian)	363 Jovianus	Ostrogoths 493 AD

Rulers of Modern Italy

After the fall of Napoleon in 1814, the Congress of Vienna, 1815, restored Italy as a political patchwork, comprising the Kingdom of Naples and Sicily, the Papal States, and smaller units. Piedmont and Genoa were awarded to Sardinia, ruled by King Victor Emmanuel I of Savoy.

United Italy emerged under the leadership of Camillo, Count di Cavour (1810-1861), Sardinian prime minister. Agitation was led by Giuseppe Mazzini (1805-1872) and Giuseppe Garibaldi (1807-1882), soldier, Victor Emmanuel I abdicated 1821. After a brief regency for a brother, Charles Albert was King 1831-1849, abdicating when defeated by the Austrians at Novara. Succeeded by Victor Emmanuel II, 1849-1861.

In 1859 France forced Austria to cede Lombardy to Sardinia, which gave rights to Savoy and Nice to France. In 1860 Garibaldi led 1,000 volunteers in a spectacular campaign, took Sicily and expelled the King of Naples. In 1860 the House of Savoy annexed Tuscany, Parma, Modena, Romagna, the Two Sicilies, the Marches, and Umbria. Victor Emmanuel assumed the title of King

of Italy at Turin Mar. 17, 1861. In 1866 he allied with Prussia in the Austro-Prussian War, with Prussia's victory received Venetia. On Sept. 20, 1870, his troops under Gen. Raffaele Cadorna entered Rome and took over the Papal States, ending the temporal power of the Roman Catholic Church.

Succession: Umberto I; 1878, assassinated 1900; Victor Emmanuel III, 1900, abdicated 1946, died 1947; Umberto II, 1946, ruled a month. In 1921 Benito Mussolini (1883-1945) formed the Fascist party and became prime minister Oct. 31, 1922. He made the King Emperor of Ethiopia, 1937; entered World War II as ally of Hitler. He was deposed July 25, 1943.

At a plebiscite June 2, 1946, Italy voted for a republic; Premier Alcide de Gasperi became chief of state June 13, 1946. On June 28, 1946, the Constituent Assembly elected Enrico de Nicola, Liberal, provisional president. Successive presidents: Luigi Einaudi, elected May 11, 1948, Giovanni Gronchi, Apr. 29, 1955; Antonio Segni, May 6, 1962; Giuseppe Saragat, Dec. 28, 1964; Giovanni Leone, Dec. 29, 1971; Alessandro Pertini, July 9, 1978.

Rulers of Spain

From 8th to 11th centuries Spain was dominated by the Moors (Arabs and Berbers). The Christian reconquest established small competing kingdoms of the Asturias, Aragon, Castile, Catalonia, Leon, Navarre, and Valencia. In 1474 Isabella (Isabel), b. 1451, became Queen of Castile & Leon. Her husband, Ferdinand, b. 1452, inherited Aragon 1479, with Catalonia, Valencia, and the Balearic Islands, became Ferdinand V of Castile. By Isabella's request Pope Sixtus IV established the Inquisition, 1478. Last Moorish kingdom, Granada, fell 1492. Columbus opened New World of colonies, 1492. Isabella died 1504, succeeded by her daughter, Juana "the Mad," but Ferdinand ruled until his death 1516.

Charles I, b. 1500, son of Juana and grandson of Ferdinand and Isabella, and of Maximilian I of Hapsburg; succeeded later as Holy Roman Emperor, Charles V, 1520; abdicated 1556. Philip II, son, 1556-1598, inherited only Spanish throne; conquered Portugal, fought Turks, persecuted non-Catholics, sent Armada against England. Was briefly married to Mary I of England, 1554-1558. Succession: Philip III, 1598-1621; Philip IV, 1621-1665; Charles II, 1665-1700, left Spain to Philip of Anjou, grandson of Louis XIV, who as Philip V, 1700-1746, founded Bourbon dynasty. Ferdinand VI, 1746-1759; Charles III, 1759-1788; Charles IV, 1788-1808, abdicated.

Napoleon now dominated politics and made his brother Joseph King of Spain 1808, but the Spanish ousted him finally in 1813. Ferdinand VII, 1808, 1814-1833, lost American colonies; succeeded by daughter Isabella II, aged 3, with wife Maria Christina of Na-

ples regent until 1843. Isabella deposed by revolution 1868. Elected king by the Cortes, Amadeo of Savoy, 1870; abdicated 1873. First republic, 1873-1874. Alphonso XII, son of Isabella, 1875-1885. His posthumous son was Alphonso XIII, with his mother, Queen Maria Christina regent; Spanish-American war, Spain lost Cuba, gave up Puerto Rico, Philippines, Sulu Is., Marianas. Alphonso took throne 1902, aged 16, married British Princess Victoria Eugenia of Battenberg. The dictatorship of Primo de Rivera, 1923-30, precipitated the revolution of 1931. Alphonso agreed to leave without formal abdication. The monarchy was abolished and the second republic established, with strong socialist backing. Presidents were Niceto Alcala Zamora, to 1936, when Manuel Azaña was chosen.

In July, 1936, the army in Morocco revolted against the government and General Francisco Franco led the troops into Spain. The revolution succeeded by Feb., 1939, when Azaña resigned. Franco became chief of state, with provisions that if he was incapacitated the Regency Council by two-thirds vote may propose a king to the Cortes, which must have a two-thirds majority to elect him.

Alphonso XIII died in Rome Feb. 28, 1941, aged 54. His property and citizenship had been restored.

A succession law restoring the monarchy was approved in a 1947 referendum. Prince Juan Carlos, son of the pretender to the throne, was designated by Franco and the Cortes in 1969 as the future king and chief of state. Upon Franco's death, Nov. 20, 1975, Juan Carlos was proclaimed king, Nov. 22, 1975.

Leaders in the South American Wars of Liberation

Simon Bolivar (1783-1830), Jose Francisco de San Martin (1778-1850), and Francisco Antonio Gabriel Miranda (1750-1816),

are among the heroes of the early 19th century struggles of South American nations to free themselves from Spain. All three, and

their contemporaries, operated in periods of intense factional strife, during which soldiers and civilians suffered.

Miranda, a Venezuelan, who had served with the French in the American Revolution and commanded parts of the French Revolutionary armies in the Netherlands, attempted to start a revolt in Venezuela in 1806 and failed. In 1810, with British and American backing, he returned and was briefly a dictator, until the British withdrew their support. In 1812 he was overcome by the royalists in Venezuela and taken prisoner, dying in a Spanish prison in 1816.

San Martin was born in Argentina and during 1789-1811 served in campaigns of the Spanish armies in Europe and Africa. He first joined the independence movement in Argentina in 1812 and then in 1817 invaded Chile with 4,000 men over the high mountain passes. Here he and General Bernardo O'Higgins (1778-1842) defeated the Spaniards at Chacabuco, 1817, and O'Higgins was named Liberator and became first director of Chile, 1817-1823. In 1821 San Martin occupied Lima and Callao, Peru, and became protector of Peru.

Bolivar, the greatest leader of South American liberation from Spain, was born in Venezuela, the son of an aristocratic family. His organizing and administrative abilities were superior and he foresaw many of the political difficulties of the future. He first served under Miranda in 1812 and in 1813 captured Caracas, where he was named Liberator. Forced out next year by civil strife, he led a campaign that captured Bogota in 1814. In 1817 he was again in control of Venezuela and was named dictator. He organized Nueva Granada with the help of General Francisco de Paula Santander (1792-1840). By joining Nueva Granada, Venezuela, and the present terrain of Panama and Ecuador, the republic of Colombia was formed with Bolivar president. After numerous setbacks he decisively defeated the Spaniards in the second battle of Carabobo, Venezuela, June 24, 1821.

In May, 1822, Gen. Antonio Jose de Sucre, Bolivar's trusted lieutenant, took Quito. Bolivar went to Guayaquil to confer with San Martin, who resigned as protector of Peru and withdrew from politics. With a new army of Colombians and Peruvians Bolivar defeated the Spaniards in a saber battle at Junín in 1824 and cleared Peru.

De Sucre organized Charcas (Upper Peru) as Republica Bolivar (now Bolivia) and acted as president in place of Bolivar, who wrote its constitution. De Sucre defeated the Spanish faction of Peru at Ayacucho, Dec. 19, 1824.

Continued civil strife finally caused the Colombian federation to break apart. Santander turned against Bolivar, but the latter defeated him and banished him. In 1828 Bolivar gave up the presidency he had held precariously for 14 years. He became ill from tuberculosis and died Dec. 17, 1830. He was honored as the great liberator and is buried in the national pantheon in Caracas.

Rulers of Russia; Premiers of the USSR

First ruler to consolidate Slavic tribes was Rurik, leader of the Russians who established himself at Novgorod, 862 A.D. He and his immediate successors had Scandinavian affiliations. They moved to Kiev after 972 AD and ruled as Dukes of Kiev. In 988 Vladimir was converted and adopted the Byzantine Greek Orthodox service, later modified by Slav influences. Important as organizer and lawgiver was Yaroslav, 1019-1054, whose daughters married kings of Norway, Hungary, and France. His grandson, Vladimir II (Monomakh), 1113-1125, was progenitor of several rulers, but in 1169 Andrew Bogolubski overthrew Kiev and began the line known as Grand Dukes of Vladimir.

Of the Grand Dukes of Vladimir, Alexander Nevsky, 1246-1263, had a son, Daniel, first to be called Duke of Muscovy (Moscow) who ruled 1294-1303. His successors became Grand Dukes of Muscovy. After Dmitri III Donskoi defeated the Tartars in 1380, they also became Grand Dukes of all Russia. Independence of the Tartars and considerable territorial expansion were achieved under Ivan III, 1462-1505.

Tsars of Muscovy—Ivan III was referred to in church ritual as Tsar. He married Sofia, niece of the last Byzantine emperor. His successor, Basil III, died in 1533 when Basil's son Ivan was only 3. He became Ivan IV, "the Terrible"; crowned 1547 as Tsar of all the Russias, ruled till 1584. Under the weak rule of his son, Feodor I, 1584-1598, Boris Godunov had control. The dynasty died, and after years of tribal strife and intervention by Polish and Swedish armies, the Russians united under 17-year-old Michael Romanov, distantly related to the first wife of Ivan IV. He ruled 1613-1645 and established the Romanov line. Fourth ruler after Michael was Peter I.

Tsars, or Emperors of Russia (Romanovs)—Peter I, 1682-1725, known as Peter the Great, took title of Emperor in 1721. His successors and dates of accession were: Catherine, his widow, 1725; Peter II, his grandson, 1727-1730; Anne, Duchess of Courland, 1730, daughter of Peter the Great's brother, Tsar Ivan V; Ivan VI, 1740-1741, great-grandson of Ivan V, child, kept in prison and murdered 1764; Elizabeth, daughter of Peter I, 1741; Peter III, grandson of Peter I, 1761, deposed 1762 for his consort, Catherine II, former princess of Anhalt Zerbst (Germany) who is known as Catherine the Great, 1762-1796; Paul I, her son, 1796, killed 1801; Alexander I, son of Paul, 1801-1825, defeated Napoleon; Nicholas I, his brother, 1825; Alexander II, son of Nicholas, 1855, assassinated 1881 by terrorists; Alexander III, son, 1881-1894.

Nicholas II, son, 1894-1917, last Tsar of Russia, was forced to abdicate by the Revolution that followed losses to Germany in WWI. The Tsar, the Empress, the Tsesarevich (Crown Prince) and the Tsar's 4 daughters were murdered by the Bolsheviks in Ekaterinburg, July 16, 1918.

Provisional Government—Prince Georgi Lvov and Alexander Kerensky, premiers, 1917.

Union of Soviet Socialist Republics

Bolshevik Revolution, Nov. 7, 1917, displaced Kerensky; council of People's Commissars formed, Lenin (Vladimir Ilyich Ulyanov), premier. Lenin died Jan. 21, 1924. Aleksei Rykov (executed 1938) and V. M. Molotov held the office, but actual ruler was Joseph Stalin (Joseph Vissarionovich Djugashvili), general secretary of the Central Committee of the Communist Party. Stalin became president of the Council of Ministers (premier) May 7, 1941, died Mar. 5, 1953. Succeeded by Georgi M. Malenkov, as head of the Council and premier and Nikita S. Khrushchev, first secretary of the Central Committee. Malenkov resigned Feb. 8, 1955, became deputy premier, was dropped July 3, 1957. Marshal Nikolai A. Bulganin became premier Feb. 8, 1955; was demoted and Khrushchev became premier Mar. 27 1958. Khrushchev was ousted Oct. 14-15, 1964, replaced by Leonid I. Brezhnev as first secretary of the party and by Aleksei N. Kosygin as premier. On June 16, 1977, Brezhnev took office as president. Brezhnev died Nov. 10, 1982; 2 days later the Central Committee unanimously elected former KGB head Yuri V. Andropov president. Andropov died Feb. 9, 1984; on Feb. 13, Konstantin U. Chernenko was chosen by Central Committee to succeed Andropov as its general secretary. Chernenko died Mar. 10, 1985. On Mar. 22, he was succeeded as general secretary by Mikhail Gorbachev.

Governments of China

(Until 221 BC and frequently thereafter, China was not a unified state. Where dynastic dates overlap, the rulers or events referred to appeared in different areas of China.)

Hsia	c1994BC	-	c1523BC	ture; capital: Sian)	618	-	906
Shang	c1523	-	c1028	Five Dynasties (Yellow River basin)	902	-	960
Western Chou	c1027	-	770	Ten Kingdoms (southern China)	907	-	979
Eastern Chou	770	-	256	Liao (Khitan Mongols; capital: Peking)	947	-	1125
Warring States	403	-	222			
Ch'in (first unified empire)	221	-	206	Sung	960	-	1279
Han	202BC	-	220AD	Northern Sung (reunified central and southern China)	960	-	1126
Western Han (expanded Chinese state beyond the Yellow and Yangtze River valleys)	202BC	-	9AD	Western Hsai (non-Chinese rulers in northwest)	990	-	1227
Hsin (Wang Mang, usurper)	9AD	-	23AD	Chin (Tartars; drove Sung out of central China)	1115	-	1234
Eastern Han (expanded Chinese state into Indo-China and Turkestan)	25	-	220	Yuan (Mongols; Kublai Khan made Peking his capital in 1267)	1271	-	1368
Three Kingdoms (Wei, Shu, Wu)	220	-	265	Ming (China reunified under Chinese rule; capital: Nanking, then Peking in 1420)	1368	-	1644
Chin (western)	265	-	317			
(eastern)	317	-	420	Ch'ing (Manchus, descendents of Tartars)	1644	-	1911
Northern Dynasties (followed several short-lived governments by Turks, Mongols, etc.)	386	-	581	Republic (disunity; provincial rulers, warlords)	1912	-	1949
Southern Dynasties (capital: Nanking)	420	-	589	People's Republic of China (Nationalist China established on Taiwan)		
Sui (reunified China)	581	-	618		1949	-	—
Tang (a golden age of Chinese cul-						

Chronological List of Popes

Source: Annuario Pontificio. Table lists year of accession of each Pope.

The Roman Catholic Church names the Apostle Peter as founder of the Church in Rome. He arrived there c. 42, was martyred there c. 67, and raised to sainthood.

The Pope's temporal title is: Sovereign of the State of Vatican City.

The Pope's spiritual titles are: Bishop of Rome, Vicar of Jesus Christ, Successor of St. Peter, Prince of the Apostles, Supreme Pontiff of the Universal Church, Patriarch of the West, Primate of Italy, Archbishop and Metropolitan of the Roman Province.

Anti-Popes are in *Italics*. Anti-Popes were illegitimate claimants of or pretenders to the papal throne.

Year	Name of Pope	Year	Name of Pope	Year	Name of Pope	Year	Name of Pope
See above.	St. Peter	615	St. Deusdedit	974	Benedict VII	1305	Clement V
67	St. Linus		or Adeodatus	983	John XIV	1316	John XXII
76	St. Anacletus	619	Boniface V	985	John XV	*1328*	*Nicholas V*
	or Cletus	625	Honorius I	996	Gregory V	1334	Benedict XII
88	St. Clement I	640	Severinus	*997*	*John XVI*	1342	Clement VI
97	St. Evaristus	640	John IV	999	Sylvester II	1352	Innocent VI
105	St. Alexander I	642	Theodore I	1003	John XVII	1362	Bl. Urban V
115	St. Sixtus I	649	St. Martin I, Martyr	1004	John XVIII	1370	Gregory XI
125	St. Telesphorus	654	St. Eugene I	1009	Sergius IV	1378	Urban VI
136	St. Hyginus	657	St. Vitalian	1012	Benedict VIII	*1378*	*Clement VII*
140	St. Pius I	672	Adeodatus II	*1012*	*Gregory*	1389	Boniface IX
155	St. Anicetus	676	Donus	1024	John XIX	*1394*	*Benedict XIII*
166	St. Soter	678	St. Agatho	1032	Benedict IX	1404	Innocent VII
175	St. Eleutherius	682	St. Leo II	1045	Sylvester III	1406	Gregory XII
189	St. Victor I	684	St. Benedict II	1045	Benedict IX	*1409*	*Alexander V*
199	St. Zephyrinus	685	John V	1045	Gregory VI	*1410*	*John XXIII*
217	St. Callistus I	686	Conon	1046	Clement II	1417	Martin V
217	*St. Hippolytus*	*687*	*Theodore*	1047	Benedict IX	1431	Eugene IV
222	St. Urban I	*687*	*Paschal*	1048	Damasus II	*1439*	*Felix V*
230	St. Pontian	687	St. Sergius I	1049	St. Leo IX	1447	Nicholas V
235	St. Anterus	701	John VI	1055	Victor II	1455	Callistus III
236	St. Fabian	705	John VII	1057	Stephen IX (X)	1458	Pius II
251	St. Cornelius	708	Sisinnius	*1058*	*Benedict X*	1464	Paul II
251	*Novatian*	708	Constantine	1059	Nicholas II	1471	Sixtus IV
253	St. Lucius I	715	St. Gregory II	1061	Alexander II	1484	Innocent VIII
254	St. Stephen I	731	St. Gregory III	*1061*	*Honorius II*	1492	Alexander VI
257	St. Sixtus II	741	St. Zachary	1073	St. Gregory VII	1503	Pius III
259	St. Dionysius	752	Stephen II (III)	*1080*	*Clement III*	1503	Julius II
269	St. Felix I	757	St. Paul I	1086	Bl. Victor III	1513	Leo X
275	St. Eutychian	*767*	*Constantine*	1088	Bl. Urban II	1522	Adrian VI
283	St. Caius	*768*	*Philip*	1099	Paschal II	1523	Clement VII
296	St. Marcellinus	768	Stephen III (IV)	*1100*	*Theodoric*	1534	Paul III
308	St. Marcellus I	772	Adrian I	*1102*	*Albert*	1550	Julius III
309	St. Eusebius	795	St. Leo III	*1105*	*Sylvester IV*	1555	Marcellus II
311	St. Melchiades	816	Stephen IV (V)	1118	Gelasius II	1555	Paul IV
314	St. Sylvester I	817	St. Paschal I	*1118*	*Gregory VIII*	1559	Pius IV
336	St. Marcus	824	Eugene II	1119	Callistus II	1566	St. Pius V
337	St. Julius I	827	Valentine	1124	Honorius II	1572	Gregory XIII
352	Liberius	827	Gregory IV	*1124*	*Celestine II*	1585	Sixtus V
355	*Felix II*	*844*	*John*	1130	Innocent II	1590	Urban VII
366	St. Damasus I	844	Sergius II	*1130*	*Anacletus II*	1590	Gregory XIV
366	*Ursinus*	847	St. Leo IV	*1138*	*Victor IV*	1591	Innocent IX
384	St. Siricius	855	Benedict III	1143	Celestine II	1592	Clement VIII
399	St. Anastasius I	*855*	*Anastasius*	1144	Lucius II	1605	Leo XI
401	St. Innocent I	858	St. Nicholas I	1145	Bl. Eugene III	1605	Paul V
417	St. Zosimus	867	Adrian II	1153	Anastasius IV	1621	Gregory XV
418	St. Boniface I	872	John VIII	1154	Adrian IV	1623	Urban VIII
418	*Eulalius*	882	Marinus I	1159	Alexander III	1644	Innocent X
422	St. Celestine I	884	St. Adrian III	*1159*	*Victor IV*	1655	Alexander VII
432	St. Sixtus III	885	Stephen V (VI)	*1164*	*Paschal III*	1667	Clement IX
440	St. Leo I	891	Formosus	*1168*	*Callistus III*	1670	Clement X
461	St. Hilary	896	Boniface VI	*1179*	*Innocent III*	1676	Bl. Innocent XI
468	St. Simplicius	896	Stephen VI (VII)	1181	Lucius III	1689	Alexander VIII
483	St. Felix III (II)	897	Romanus	1185	Urban III	1691	Innocent XII
492	St. Gelasius I	897	Theodore II	1187	Gregory VIII	1700	Clement XI
496	Anastasius II	898	John IX	1187	Clement III	1721	Innocent XIII
498	St. Symmachus	900	Benedict IV	1191	Celestine III	1724	Benedict XIII
498	*Lawrence*	903	Leo V	1198	Innocent III	1730	Clement XII
	(501-505)	*903*	*Christopher*	1216	Honorius III	1740	Benedict XIV
514	St. Hormisdas	904	Sergius III	1227	Gregory IX	1758	Clement XIII
523	St. John I, Martyr	911	Anastasius III	1241	Celestine IV	1769	Clement XIV
526	St. Felix IV (III)	913	Landus	1243	Innocent IV	1775	Pius VI
530	Boniface II	914	John X	1254	Alexander IV	1800	Pius VII
530	*Dioscorus*	928	Leo VI	1261	Urban IV	1823	Leo XII
533	John II	928	Stephen VII (VIII)	1265	Clement IV	1829	Pius VIII
535	St. Agapitus I	931	John XI	1271	Bl. Gregory X	1831	Gregory XVI
536	St. Silverius, Martyr	936	Leo VII	1276	Bl. Innocent V	1846	Pius IX
537	Vigilius	939	Stephen VIII (IX)	1276	Adrian V	1878	Leo XIII
556	Pelagius I	942	Marinus II	1276	John XXI	1903	St. Pius X
561	John III	946	Agapitus II	1277	Nicholas III	1914	Benedict XV
575	Benedict I	955	John XII	1281	Martin IV	1922	Pius XI
579	Pelagius II	963	Leo VIII	1285	Honorius IV	1939	Pius XII
590	St. Gregory I	964	Benedict V	1288	Nicholas IV	1958	John XXIII
604	Sabinian	965	John XIII	1294	St. Celestine V	1963	Paul VI
607	Boniface III	973	Benedict VI	1294	Boniface VIII	1978	John Paul I
608	St. Boniface IV	*974*	*Boniface VII*	1303	Bl. Benedict XI	1978	John Paul II

WORLD FACTS
Early Explorers of the Western Hemisphere

The first men to discover the New World or Western Hemisphere are believed to have walked across a "land bridge" from Siberia to Alaska, an isthmus since broken by the Bering Strait. From Alaska, these ancestors of the Indians spread through North, Central, and South America. Anthropologists have placed these crossings at between 18,000 and 14,000 B.C.; but evidence found in 1967 near Puebla, Mex., indicates mankind reached there as early as 35,000-40,000 years ago.

At first, these people were hunters using flint weapons and tools. In Mexico, about 7000-6000 B.C., they founded farming cultures, developing corn, squash, etc. Eventually, they created complex civilizations — Olmec, Toltec, Aztec, and Maya and, in South America, Inca. Carbon-14 tests show men lived about 8000 B.C. near what are now Front Royal, Va., Kanawha, W. Va., and Dutchess Quarry, N.Y. The Hopewell Culture, based on farming, flourished about 1000 B.C.; remains of it are seen today in large mounds in Ohio and other states.

Norsemen (Norwegian Vikings sailing out of Iceland and Greenland) are credited by most scholars with being the first Europeans to discover America, with at least 5 voyages around 1000 A.D. to areas they called Helluland, Markland, Vinland—possibly Labrador, Nova Scotia or Newfoundland, and New England.

Christopher Columbus, most famous of the explorers, was born at Genoa, Italy, but made his discoveries sailing for the Spanish rulers Ferdinand and Isabella. Dates of his voyages, places he discovered, and other information follow:

1492—First voyage. Left Palos, Spain, Aug. 3 with 88 men (est.). Discovered San Salvador (Guanahani or Watling Is., Bahamas) Oct. 12. Also Cuba, Hispaniola (Haiti-Dominican Republic); built Fort La Navidad on latter.

1493—Second voyage, first part, Sept. 25, with 17 ships, 1,500 men. Dominica (Lesser Antilles) Nov. 3; Guadeloupe, Montserrat, Antigua, San Martin, Santa Cruz, Puerto Rico, Virgin Islands. Settled Isabela on Hispaniola. Second part (Columbus having remained in Western Hemisphere), Jamaica, Isle of Pines, La Mona Is.

1498—Third voyage. Left Spain May 30, 1498, 6 ships. Discovered Trinidad. Saw South American continent Aug. 1, 1498, but called it Isla Sancta (Holy Island). Entered Gulf of Paria and landed, first time on continental soil. At mouth of Orinoco Aug. 14 he decided this was the mainland.

1502—Fourth voyage, 4 caravels, 150 men. St. Lucia, Guanaja off Honduras; Cape Gracias a Dios, Honduras; San Juan River, Costa Rica; Almirante, Portobelo, and Laguna de Chiriqui, Panama.

Year	Explorer	Nationality and employer	Discovery or exploration
1497	John Cabot	Italian-English	Newfoundland or Nova Scotia
1498	John and Sebastian Cabot	Italian-English	Labrador to Hatteras
1499	Alonso de Ojeda	Spanish	South American coast, Venezuela
1500, Feb.	Vicente y Pinzon	Spanish	South American coast, Amazon River
1500, Apr.	Pedro Alvarez Cabral	Portuguese	Brazil (for Portugal)
1500-02	Gaspar Corte-Real	Portuguese	Labrador
1501	Rodrigo de Bastidas	Spanish	Central America
1513	Vasco Nunez de Balboa	Spanish	Pacific Ocean
1513	Juan Ponce de Leon	Spanish	Florida
1515	Juan de Solis	Spanish	Rio de la Plata
1519	Alonso de Pineda	Spanish	Mouth of Mississippi River
1519	Hernando Cortes	Spanish	Mexico
1520	Ferdinand Magellan	Portuguese-Spanish	Straits of Magellan, Tierra del Fuego
1524	Giovanni da Verrazano	Italian-French	Atlantic coast-New York harbor
1532	Francisco Pizarro	Spanish	Peru
1534	Jacques Cartier	French	Canada, Gulf of St. Lawrence
1536	Pedro de Mendoza	Spanish	Buenos Aires
1536	A.N. Cabeza de Vaca	Spanish	Texas coast and interior
1539	Francisco de Ulloa	Spanish	California coast
1539-41	Hernando de Soto	Spanish	Mississippi River near Memphis
1539	Marcos de Niza	Italian-Spanish	Southwest (now U.S.)
1540	Francisco V. de Coronado	Spanish	Southwest (now U.S.)
1540	Hernando Alarcon	Spanish	Colorado River
1540	Garcia de L. Cardenas	Spanish	Grand Canyon of the Colorado
1541	Francisco de Orellana	Spanish	Amazon River
1542	Juan Rodriguez Cabrillo	Portuguese-Spanish	San Diego harbor
1565	Pedro Menendez de Aviles	Spanish	St. Augustine
1576	Martin Frobisher	Engish	Frobisher's Bay, Canada
1577-80	Francis Drake	English	California coast
1582	Antonio de Espejo	Spanish	Southwest (named New Mexico)
1584	Amadas & Barlow (for Raleigh)	English	Virginia
1585-87	Sir Walter Raleigh's men	English	Roanoke Is., N.C.
1595	Sir Walter Raleigh	English	Orinoco River
1603-09	Samuel de Champlain	French	Canadian interior, Lake Champlain
1607	Capt. John Smith	English	Atlantic coast
1609-10	Henry Hudson	English-Dutch	Hudson River, Hudson Bay
1634	Jean Nicolet	French	Lake Michigan; Wisconsin
1673	Jacques Marquette, Louis Jolliet	French	Mississippi S to Arkansas
1682	Sieur de La Salle	French	Mississippi S to Gulf of Mexico
1789	Alexander Mackenzie	Canadian	Canadian Northwest

Arctic Exploration

Early Explorers

1587 — John Davis (England). Davis Strait to Sanderson's Hope, 72° 12' N.

1596 — Willem Barents and Jacob van Heemskerck (Holland). Discovered Bear Island, touched northwest tip of Spitsbergen, 79° 49' N, rounded Novaya Zemlya, wintered at Ice Haven.

1607 — Henry Hudson (England). North along Greenland's east coast to Cape Hold-with-Hope, 73° 30', then north of Spitsbergen to 80° 23'. Returning he discovered Hudson's Touches (Jan Mayen).

1616 — William Baffin and Robert Bylot (England). Baffin Bay to Smith Sound.

1728 — Vitus Bering (Russia). Proved Asia and America were separated by sailing through strait.

1733-40 — Great Northern Expedition (Russia). Surveyed Siberian Arctic coast.

1741 — Vitus Bering (Russia). Sighted Alaska from sea, named Mount St. Elias. His lieutenant, Chirikof, discovered coast.

1771 — Samuel Hearne (Hudson's Bay Co.). Overland from Prince of Wales Fort (Churchill) on Hudson Bay to mouth of Coppermine River.

1778 — James Cook (Britain). Through Bering Strait to Icy Cape, Alaska, and North Cape, Siberia.
1789 — Alexander Mackenzie (North West Co., Britain). Montreal to mouth of Mackenzie River.
1806 — William Scoresby (Britain). N. of Spitsbergen to 81° 30'.
1820-3 — Ferdinand von Wrangel (Russia). Completed a survey of Siberian Arctic coast. His exploration joined that of James Cook at North Cape, confirming separation of the continents.
1845 — Sir John Franklin (Britain) was one of many to seek the Northwest Passage—an ocean route connecting the Atlantic and Pacific via the Arctic. His 2 ships (the Erebus and Terror) were last seen entering Lancaster Sound July 26.
1888 — Fridtjof Nansen (Norway) crossed Greenland's icecap, 1893-96 — Nansen in Fram drifted from New Siberian Is. to Spitsbergen; tried polar dash in 1895, reached Franz Josef Land.
1896 — Salomon A. Andree (Sweden). In June, made first attempt to reach North Pole by balloon; failed and returned in August. On July 11, 1897, Andree and 2 others started in balloon from Danes, Is., Spitsbergen, to drift across pole to America, and disappeared. Over 33 years later, Aug. 6, 1930, their frozen bodies were found on White Is., 82° 57' N 29° 52' E.
1903-06 — Roald Amundsen (Norway) first sailed Northwest Passage.

Discovery of North Pole

Robert E. Peary explored Greenland's coast 1891-92, tried for North Pole 1893. In 1900 he reached northern limit of Greenland and 83° 50' N; in 1902 he reached 84° 06' N; in 1906 he went from Ellesmere Is. to 87° 06' N. He sailed in the *Roosevelt*, July, 1908, to winter off Cape Sheridan, Grant Land. The dash for the North Pole began Mar. 1 from Cape Columbia, Ellesmere Land. Peary reached the pole, 90° N, Apr. 6, 1909.
Peary had several supporting groups carrying supplies until the last group turned back at 87° 47' N. Peary, Matthew Henson, and 4 eskimos proceeded with dog teams and sleds. They crossed the pole several times, finally built an igloo at 90°, remained 36 hours. Started south Apr. 7 at 4 p.m. for Cape Columbia. Eskimos were Coqueeh, Ootah, Eginwah, and Seegloo.
1914 — Donald Macmillan (U.S.). Northwest, 200 miles, from Axel Heiberg Island to seek Peary's Crocker Land.

1915-17 — Vihjalmur Stefansson (Canada) discovered Borden, Brock, Meighen, and Lougheed Islands.
1918-20 — Roald Amundsen sailed Northeast Passage.
1925 — Amundsen and Lincoln Ellsworth (U.S.) reached 87° 44' N in attempt to fly to North Pole from Spitsbergen.
1926 — Richard E. Byrd and Floyd Bennett (U.S.) first over North Pole by air, May 9.
1926 — Amundsen, Ellsworth, and Umberto Nobile (Italy) flew from Spitsbergen over North Pole May 12, to Teller, Alaska, in dirigible *Norge*.
1928 — Nobile crossed North Pole in airship May 24, crashed May 25. Amundsen lost while trying to effect rescue by plane.

North Pole Exploration Records

On Aug. 3, 1958, the *Nautilus*, under Comdr. William R. Anderson, became the first ship to cross the North Pole beneath the Arctic ice.
The nuclear-powered U.S. submarine *Seadragon*, Comdr. George P. Steele 2d, made the first east-west underwater transit through the Northwest Passage during August, 1960. It sailed from Portsmouth N.H., headed between Greenland and Labrador through Baffin Bay, then west through Lancaster Sound and McClure Strait to the Beaufort Sea. Traveling submerged for the most part, the submarine made 850 miles from Baffin Bay to the Beaufort Sea in 6 days.
On Aug. 16, 1977, the Soviet nuclear icebreaker *Arktika* reached the North Pole and became the first surface ship to break through the Arctic ice pack to the top of the world.
On April 30, 1978, Naomi Uemura, a Japanese explorer, became the first man to reach the North Pole alone by dog sled. During the 54-day, 600-mile trek over the frozen Arctic, Uemura survived attacks by a marauding polar bear.
In April, 1982, Sir Ranulph Fiennes and Charles Burton, British explorers, reached the North Pole and became the first to circle the earth from pole to pole. They had reached the South Pole 16 months earlier. The 52,000-mile trek took 3 years, involved 23 people, and cost an estimated $18 million. The expedition was also the first to travel down the Scott Glacier and the first to journey up the Yukon and through the Northwest Passage in a single season.

Antarctic Exploration

Early History

Antarctica has been approached since 1773-75, when Capt. James Cook (Britain) reached 71° 10' S. Many sea and landmarks bear names of early explorers. Bellingshausen (Russia) discovered Peter I and Alexander I Islands, 1819-21. Nathaniel Palmer (U.S.) discovered Palmer Peninsula, 60° W, 1820, without realizing that this was a continent. James Weddell (Britain) found Weddell Sea, 74° 15' S, 1823.
First to announce existence of the continent of Antarctica was Charles Wilkes (U.S.), who followed the coast for 1,500 mi., 1840. Adelie Coast, 140° E, was found by Dumont d'Urville (France), 1840. Ross Ice Shelf was found by James Clark Ross (Britain), 1841-42.
1895 — Leonard Kristensen (Norway) landed a party on the coast of Victoria Land. They were the first ashore on the main continental mass. C.E. Borchgrevink, a member of that party, returned in 1899 with a British expedition, first to winter on Antarctica.
1902-04 — Robert F. Scott (Britain) discovered Edward VII Peninsula. He reached 82° 17' S, 146° 33' E from McMurdo Sound.
1908-09 — Ernest Shackleton (Britain) introduced the use of Manchurian ponies in Antarctic sledging. He reached 88° 23' S, discovering a route on to the plateau by way of the Beardmore Glacier and pioneering the way to the pole.

Discovery of South Pole

1911 — Roald Amundsen (Norway) with 4 men and dog teams reached the pole Dec. 14.
1912 — Capt. Scott reached the pole from Ross Island Jan. 18, with 4 companions. They found Amundsen's tent. None of Scott's party survived. They were found Nov. 12.
1928 — First man to use an airplane over Antarctica was Hubert Wilkins (Britain).
1929 — Richard E. Byrd (U.S.) established Little America on Bay of Whales. On 1,600-mi. airplane flight begun Nov. 28 he crossed South Pole Nov. 29 with 3 others.
1934-35 — Byrd led 2d expedition to Little America, explored 450,000 sq. mi., wintered alone at weather station, 80° 08' S.

1934-37 — John Rymill led British Graham Land expedition; discovered that Palmer Peninsula is part of Antarctic mainland.
1935 — Lincoln Ellsworth (U.S.) flew south along Palmer Peninsula's east coast, then crossed continent to Little America, making 4 landings on unprepared terrain in bad weather.
1939-41 — U.S. Antarctic Service built West Base on Ross Ice Shelf under Paul Siple, and East Base on Palmer Peninsula under Richard Black. U.S. Navy plane flights discovered about 150,000 sq. miles of new land.
1940 — Byrd charted most of coast between Ross Sea and Palmer Peninsula.
1946-47 — U.S. Navy undertook Operation High-jump under Byrd. Expedition included 13 ships and 4,000 men. Airplanes photomapped coastline and penetrated beyond pole.
1946-48 — Ronne Antarctic Research Expedition, Comdr. Finn Ronne, USNR, determined the Antarctic to be only one continent with no strait between Weddell Sea and Ross Sea; discovered 250,000 sq. miles of land by flights to 79° S Lat., and made 14,000 aerial photographs over 450,000 sq. miles of land. Mrs. Ronne and Mrs. H. Darlington were the first women to winter on Antarctica.
1955-57 — U.S. Navy's Operation Deep Freeze led by Adm. Byrd. Supporting U.S. scientific efforts for the International Geophysical Year, the operation was commanded by Rear Adm. George Dufek. It established 5 coastal stations fronting the Indian, Pacific, and Atlantic oceans and also 3 interior stations; explored more than 1,000,000 sq. miles in Wilkes Land.
1957-58 — During the International Geophysical year, July, 1957, through Dec. 1958, scientists from 12 countries conducted ambitious programs of Antarctic research. A network of some 60 stations on the continent and sub-Arctic islands studied oceanography, glaciology, meteorology, seismology, geomagnetism, the ionosphere, cosmic rays, aurora, and airglow.
Dr. V.E. Fuchs led a 12-man Trans-Antarctic Expedition on the first land crossing of Antarctica. Starting from the Weddell Sea, they reached Scott Station Mar. 2, 1958, after traveling 2,158 miles in 98 days.
1958 — A group of 5 U.S. scientists led by Edward C. Thiel, seismologist, moving by tractor from Ellsworth Station on Weddell Sea, identified a huge mountain range, 5,000 ft. above the ice sheet and 9,000 ft. above sea level. The range, originally seen by a Navy plane, was named the Dufek Massif, for Rear Adm. George Dufek.

1959 — Twelve nations — Argentina, Australia, Belgium, Chile, France, Japan, New Zealand, Norway, South Africa, the Soviet Union, the United Kingdom, and the U.S. — signed a treaty suspending any territorial claims for 30 years and reserving the continent for research.

1961-62 — Scientists discovered a trough, the Bentley Trench, running from Ross Ice Shelf, Pacific, into Marie Byrd Land, around the end of the Ellsworth Mtns., toward the Weddell Sea.

1962 — First nuclear power plant began operation at McMurdo Sound.

1963 — On Feb. 22 a U.S. plane made the longest nonstop flight ever made in the S. Pole area, covering 3,600 miles in 10 hours. The flight was from McMurdo Station south past the geographical S. Pole to Shackleton Mtns., southeast to the "Area of Inaccessibility" and back to McMurdo Station.

1964 — A British survey team was landed by helicopter on Cook Island, the first recorded visit since its discovery in 1775.

1964 — New Zealanders completed one of the last and most important surveys when they mapped the mountain area from Cape Adare west some 400 miles to Pennell Glacier.

Notable Active Volcanoes of the World

More than 75 per cent of the world's 850 active volcanoes lie within the "Ring of Fire," a zone running along the west coast of the Americas from Chile to Alaska and down the east coast of Asia from Siberia to New Zealand. Twenty per cent of these volcanoes are located in Indonesia. Other prominent groupings are located in Japan, the Aleutian Islands, and Central America. Almost all active regions are found at the boundaries of the large moving plates which comprise the earth's surface. The "Ring of Fire" marks the boundary between the plates underlying the Pacific Ocean and those underlying the surrounding continents. Other active regions, such as the Mediterranean Sea and Iceland, are located on plate boundaries.

Major Historical Eruptions

Approximately 7,000 years ago, Mazama, a 9,900-feet-high volcano in southern Oregon, erupted violently, ejecting ash and lava. The ash spread over the entire northwestern United States and as far away as Saskatchewan, Canada. During the eruption, the top of the mountain collapsed, leaving a caldera 6 miles across and about a half mile deep, which filled with rain water to form what is now called Crater Lake.

In 79 A.D., Vesuvio, or Vesuvius, a 4,190 feet volcano overlooking Naples Bay became active after several centuries of quiescence. On Aug. 24 of that year, a heated mud and ash flow swept down the mountain engulfing the cities of Pompeii, Herculaneum, and Stabiae with debris over 60 feet deep. About 10 percent of the population of the 3 towns was killed.

The largest eruptions in recent centuries have been in Indonesia. In 1883, an eruption similar to the Mazama eruption occurred on the island of Krakatau. On August 27, the 2,640-feet-high peak of the volcano collapsed to 1,000 feet below sea level, leaving only a small portion of the island standing above the sea. Ash from the eruption colored sunsets around the world for 2 years. A tsunami ("tidal wave") generated by the collapse killed 36,000 people in nearby Java and Sumatra and eventually reached England. A similar, but even more powerful, eruption had taken place 68 years earlier at Tambora volcano on the Indonesian island of Sumbawa.

Name, latest activity	Location	Feet	Name, latest activity	Location	Feet
Africa			Alaid (1972)	Kuril Is.	7,662
			Ulawun (1984)	New Britain	7,532
Cameroon (1982)	Cameroon	13,354	Ngauruhoe (1975)	New Zealand	7,515
Nyirangongo (1977)	Zaire	11,400	Chokai (1974)	Japan	7,300
Nyamuragira (1984)	Zaire	10,028	Galunggung (1982)	Java	7,113
Karthala (1977)	Comoro Is.	8,000	Amburombu (1969)	Indonesia	7,051
Piton de la Fournaise (1983)	Reunion Is.	5,981	Azuma (1978)	Japan	6,700
Erta-Ale (1973)	Ethiopia	1,650	Tangkuban Prahu (1967)	Java	6,637
			Sangeang Api (1966)	Indonesia	6,351
			Nasu (1977)	Japan	6,210
Antarctica			Tiatia (1973)	Kuril Islands	6,013
			Manam (1984)	Papua New	
Erebus (1984)	Ross Island	12,450		Guinea	6,000
Big Ben (1960)	Heard Island	9,007	Soputan (1984)	Indonesia	5,994
Deception Island (1970)	South Shetland		Siau (1976)	Indonesia	5,853
	Islands	1,890	Kelud (1967)	Java	5,679
			Batur (1968)	Bali	5,636
			Ternate (1963)	Indonesia	5,627
			Kirisima (1982)	Japan	5,577
Asia-Oceania			Keli Mutu (1968)	Indonesia	5,460
Klyuchevskaya (1974)	USSR	15,584	Akita Komaga take (1970)	Japan	5,449
Kerintji (1968)	Sumatra	12,467	Gamkonora (1981)	Indonesia	5,364
Rindjani (1966)	Indonesia	12,224	Aso (1984)	Japan	5,223
Semeru (1981)	Java	12,060	Lewotobi Laki-Laki (1968)	Indonesia	5,217
Slamet (1967)	Java	11,247	Lokon-Empung (1970)	Celebes	5,187
Raung (1982)	Java	10,932	Bulusan (1983)	Philippines	5,115
Shiveluch (1964)	USSR	10,771	Sarycheva (1976)	Kuril Islands	4,960
Agung (1964)	Bali	10,308	Me-akan (1966)	Japan	4,931
On-Take (1980)	Japan	10,049	Karkar (1981)	Papua New	
Mayon (1978)	Philippines	9,991		Guinea	4,920
Merapi (1984)	Java	9,551	Karymskaya (1976)	USSR	4,869
Bezymianny (1984)	USSR	9,514	Lopevi (1982)	New Hebrides	4,755
Marapi (1982)	Sumatra	9,485	Ambrym (1979)	New Hebrides	4,376
Ruapehu (1982)	New Zealand	9,175	Awu (1968)	Indonesia	4,350
Asama (1983)	Japan	8,300	Sakurazima (1985)	Japan	3,668
Niigata Yakeyama (1983)	Japan	8,111	Langila (1985)	New Britain	3,586
Yake Dake (1963)	Japan	8,064	Dukono (1971)	Indonesia	3,566

Name, latest activity	Location	Feet
Suwanosezima (1982)	Japan	2,640
O-Sima (1977)	Japan	2,550
Usu (1978)	Japan	2,400
White Island (1984)	New Zealand	1,075
Taal (1977)	Philippines	984

Central America—Caribbean

Name, latest activity	Location	Feet
Acatenango (1972)	Guatemala	12,992
Fuego (1980)	Guatemala	12,582
Santiaguito (Santa Maria) (1983)	Guatemala	12,362
Irazu (1967)	Costa Rica	11,260
Poas (1982)	Costa Rica	8,930
Pacaya (1984)	Guatemala	8,346
Izalco (1966)	El Salvador	7,749
San Miguel (1976)	El Salvador	6,994
Rincon de la Vieja (1968)	Costa Rica	6,234
El Viejo (San Cristobal) (1981)	Nicaragua	5,840
Ometepe (Concepcion) (1982)	Nicaragua	5,106
Arenal (1985)	Costa Rica	5,092
Momotombo (1982)	Nicaragua	4,199
Soufriere (1979)	St. Vincent	4,048
Telica (1982)	Nicaragua	3,409

South America

Name, latest activity	Location	Feet
Lascar (1968)	Chile	19,652
Cotopaxi (1975)	Ecuador	19,347
Tupungatito (1980)	Chile	18,504
Sangay (1976)	Ecuador	17,159
Guagua Pichincha (1982)	Ecuador	15,696
Purace (1977)	Colombia	15,604
Llaima (1984)	Chile	10,239
Villarica (1984)	Chile	9,318
Hudson (1973)	Chile	8,580
Alcedo (1970)	Galapagos Is.	3,599

Mid-Pacific

Name, latest activity	Location	Feet
Mauna Loa (1984)	Hawaii	13,680
Kilauea (1985)	Hawaii	4,077

Mid-Atlantic Ridge

Name, latest activity	Location	Feet
Beerenberg (1970)	Jan Mayen Is.	7,470
Hekla (1981)	Iceland	4,892
Leirhnukur (1975)	Iceland	2,145
Krafla (1984)	Iceland	2,145
Surtsey (1967)	Iceland	568

Europe

Name, latest activity	Location	Feet
Etna (1985)	Italy	11,053
Stromboli (1975)	Italy	3,038

North America

Name, latest activity	Location	Feet
Colima (1983)	Mexico	14,003
Redoubt (1966)	Alaska	10,197
Iliamna (1978)	Alaska	10,092
Mt. St. Helens (1985)	Washington	9,677
Shishaldin (1981)	Aleutian Is.	9,387
Pavlof (1984)	Aleutian Is.	8,215
El Chichon (1983)	Mexico	7,300
Makushin (1980)	Aleutian Is.	6,680
Pogromni (1964)	Alaska	6,568
Trident 1963)	Alaska	6,010
Great Sitkin (1974)	Aleutian Is.	5,710
Gareloi (1982)	Aleutian Is.	5,334
Akutan (1980)	Aleutian Is.	4,275
Kiska (1969)	Aleutian Is.	4,275
Augustine (1976)	Alaska	3,927
Seguam (1977)	Alaska	3,458

Record Oil Spills

Name, place	Date	Cause	Tons
Ixtoc I oil well, southern Gulf of Mexico	June 3, 1979	Blowout	600,000
Nowruz oil field, Persian Gulf	Feb., 1983	Blowout	600,000(est.)
Atlantic Empress & Aegean Captain, off Trinidad & Tobago	July 19, 1979	Collision	300,000
Castillo de Bellver, off Cape Town, South Africa	Aug. 6, 1983	Fire	250,000
Amoco Cadiz, near Portsall, France	March 16, 1978	Grounding	223,000
Torrey Canyon, off Land's End, England	March 18, 1967	Grounding	119,000
Sea Star, Gulf of Oman	Dec. 19, 1972	Collision	115,000
Urquiola, La Coruna, Spain	May 12, 1976	Grounding	100,000
Hawaiian Patriot, northern Pacific	Feb. 25, 1977	Fire	99,000
Othello, Tralhavet Bay, Sweden	March 20, 1970	Collision	60,000-100,000
Jacob Maersk, Porto do Leixoes, Portugal	Jan. 29, 1975	Grounding	84,000
Wafra, Cape Agulhas, South Africa	Feb. 27, 1971	Grounding	63,000
Epic Colacotroni, Caribbean	May, 1975	Grounding	57,000

Other Notable Oil Spills

Name, place	Date	Cause	Gallons
World Glory, off South Africa	June 13, 1968	Hull failure	13,524,000
Keo, off Massachusetts	Nov. 5, 1969	Hull failure	8,820,000
Storage tank, Sewaren, N.J.	Nov. 4, 1969	Tank rupture	8,400,000
Ekofisk oil field, North Sea	Apr. 22, 1977	Well blowout	8,200,000
Argo Merchant, Nantucket, Mass.	Dec. 15, 1976	Grounding	7,700,000
Pipeline, West Delta, La.	Oct. 15, 1967	Dragging anchor	6,720,000
Tanker off Japan	Nov. 30, 1971	Ship broke in half	6,258,000

Highest and Lowest Continental Altitudes

Source: National Geographic Society, Washington, D.C.

Continent	Highest point	Feet elevation	Lowest point	Feet below sea level
Asia	Mount Everest, Nepal-Tibet	29,028	Dead Sea, Israel-Jordan	1,312
South America	Mount Aconcagua, Argentina	22,834	Valdes Peninsula, Argentina	131
North America	Mount McKinley, Alaska	20,320	Death Valley, California	282
Africa	Kilimanjaro, Tanzania	19,340	Lake Assal, Djibouti	512
Europe	Mount El'brus, USSR	18,510	Caspian Sea, USSR	92
Antarctica	Vinson Massif	16,864	Unknown	...
Australia	Mount Kosciusko, New South Wales	7,310	Lake Eyre, South Australia	52

Height of Mount Everest

Mt. Everest was considered to be 29,002 ft. tall when Edmund Hillary and Tenzing Norgay scaled it in 1953. This triangulation figure had been accepted since 1850. In 1954 the Surveyor General of the Republic of India set the height at 29,028 ft., plus or minus 10 ft. because of snow. The National Geographic Society accepts the new figure, but many mountaineering groups still use 29,002 ft.

High Peaks in United States, Canada, Mexico

Name	Place	Feet	Name	Place	Feet	Name	Place	Feet
McKinley	Alas	20,320	Crestone	Col	14,294	Columbia	Col	14,073
Logan	Can	19,850	Lincoln	Col	14,286	Augusta	Alas-Can	14,070
Citlaltepec (Orizaba)	Mexico	18,700	Grays	Col	14,270	Missouri	Col	14,067
St. Elias	Alas-Can	18,008	Antero	Col	14,269	Humboldt	Col	14,064
Popocatepeti	Mexico	17,887	Torreys	Col	14,267	Bierstadt	Col	14,060
Foraker	Alas	17,400	Castle	Col	14,265	Sunlight	Col	14,059
Iztaccihuatl	Mexico	17,343	Quandary	Col	14,265	Split	Cal	14,058
Lucania	Can	17,147	Evans	Col	14,264	Nauhcampatepeti		
King	Can	16,971	Longs	Col	14,256	(Cofre de Perote)	Mexico	14,049
Steele	Can	16,644	McArthur	Can	14,253	Handies	Col	14,048
Bona	Alas	16,550	Wilson	Col	14,246	Culebra	Col	14,047
Blackburn	Alas	16,390	White	Cal	14,246	Langley	Cal	14,042
Kennedy	Alas	16,286	North Palisade	Cal	14,242	Lindsey	Col	14,042
Sanford	Alas	16,237	Shavano	Col	14,229	Middle Palisade	Cal	14,040
South Buttress	Alas	15,885	Belford	Col	14,197	Little Bear	Col	14,037
Wood	Can	15,885	Princeton	Col	14,197	Sherman	Col	14,036
Vancouver	Alas-Can	15,700	Crestone Needle	Col	14,197	Redcloud	Col	14,034
Churchill	Alas	15,638	Yale	Col	14,196	Tyndall	Cal	14,018
Fairweather	Alas-Can	15,300	Bross	Col	14,172	Pyramid	Col	14,018
Zinantecatl (Toluca)	Mexico	15,016	Kit Carson	Col	14,165	Wilson Peak	Col	14,017
Hubbard	Alas-Can	15,015	Wrangell	Alas	14,163	Muir	Cal	14,015
Bear	Alas	14,831	Shasta	Cal	14,162	Wetterhorn	Col	14,015
Walsh	Can	14,780	Sill	Cal	14,162	North Maroon	Col	14,014
East Buttress	Alas	14,730	El Diente	Col	14,159	San Luis	Col	14,014
Matlalcueyeti	Mexico	14,636	Maroon	Col	14,156	Huron	Col	14,005
Hunter	Alas	14,573	Tabeguache	Col	14,155	Holy Cross	Col	14,005
Alverstone	Alas-Can	14,565	Oxford	Col	14,153	Colima	Mexico	14,003
Browne Tower	Alas	14,530	Sneffels	Col	14,150	Sunshine	Col	14,001
Whitney	Cal	14,494	Point Success	Wash	14,150	Grizzly	Col	14,000
Elbert	Col	14,433	Democrat	Col	14,148	Barnard	Cal	13,990
Massive	Col	14,421	Capitol	Col	14,130	Stewart	Cal	13,980
Harvard	Col	14,420	Liberty Cap	Wash	14,112	Keith	Cal	13,977
Rainier	Wash	14,410	Pikes Peak	Col	14,110	Ouray	Col	13,971
Williamson	Cal	14,375	Snowmass	Col	14,092	Le Conte	Cal	13,960
Blanca	Col	14,345	Windom	Col	14,087	Meeker	Col	13,911
La Plata	Col	14,336	Russell	Cal	14,086	Kennedy	Can	13,905
Uncompahgre	Col	14,309	Eolus	Col	14,084			

South America

Peak, Country	Feet	Peak, Country	Feet	Peak, Country	Feet
Aconcagua, Argentina	22,834	Laudo, Argentina	20,997	Polleras, Argentina	20,456
Ojos del Salado, Arg.-Chile	22,572	Ancohuma, Bolivia	20,958	Pular, Chile	20,423
Bonete, Argentina	22,546	Ausangate, Peru	20,945	Chani, Argentina	20,341
Tupungato, Argentina-Chile	22,310	Toro, Argentina-Chile	20,932	Aucanquilcha, Chile	20,295
Pissis, Argentina	22,241	Illampu, Bolivia	20,873	Juncal, Argentina-Chile	20,276
Mercedario, Argentina	22,211	Tres Cruces, Argentina-Chile	20,853	Negro, Argentina	20,184
Huascaran, Peru	22,205	Huandoy, Peru	20,852	Quela, Argentina	20,128
Llullaillaco, Argentina-Chile	22,057	Parinacota, Bolivia-Chile	20,768	Condoriri, Bolivia	20,095
El Libertador, Argentina	22,047	Tortolas, Argentina-Chile	20,745	Palermo, Argentina	20,079
Cachi, Argentina	22,047	Ampato, Peru	20,702	Solimana, Peru	20,068
Yerupaja, Peru	21,709	Condor, Argentina	20,669	San Juan, Argentina-Chile	20,049
Galan, Argentina	21,654	Salcantay, Peru	20,574	Sierra Nevada, Arg.-Chile	20,023
El Muerto, Argentina-Chile	21,457	Chimborazo, Ecuador	20,561	Antofalla, Argentina	20,013
Sajama, Bolivia	21,391	Huancarhuas, Peru	20,531	Marmolejo, Argentina-Chile	20,013
Nacimiento, Argentina	21,302	Famatina, Argentina	20,505	Chachani, Peru	19,931
Illimani, Bolivia	21,201	Pumasillo, Peru	20,492	Licancabur, Argentina-Chile	19,425
Coropuna, Peru	21,083	Solo, Argentina	20,492		

The highest point in the West Indies is in the Dominican Republic, Pico Duarte (10,417 ft.)

Africa, Australia, and Oceania

Peak, country	Feet	Peak, country	Feet	Peak, country	Feet
Kilimanjaro, Tanzania	19,340	Meru, Tanzania	14,979	Toubkal, Morocco	13,665
Kenya, Kenya	17,058	Wilhelm, New Guinea	14,793	Kinabalu, Malaysia	13,455
Margherita Pk., Uganda-Zaire	16,763	Karisimbi, Zaire-Rwanda	14,787	Kerinci, Sumatra	12,467
Jaja, New Guinea	16,500	Elgon, Kenya-Uganda	14,178	Cook, New Zealand	12,349
Trikora, New Guinea	15,585	Batu, Ethiopia	14,131	Teide, Canary Islands	12,198
Mandala, New Guinea	15,420	Guna, Ethiopia	13,881	Semeru, Java	12,060
Ras Dashan, Ethiopia	15,158	Gughe, Ethiopia	13,780	Kosciusko, Australia	7,310

Europe

Peak, country	Feet	Peak, county	Feet	Peak, country	Feet
Alps		Breithorn, It., Switz.	13,665	Eiger, Switz.	13,025
		Bishorn, Switz.	13,645	Jagerhorn, Switz.	13,024
Mont Blanc, Fr. It.	15,771	Jungfrau, Switz.	13,642	Rottalhorn, Switz.	13,022
Monte Rosa (highest peak of group), Switz.	15,203	Ecrins, Fr.	13,461		
Dom, Switz.	14,911	Monch, Switz.	13,448	**Pyrenees**	
Liskamm, It., Switz.	14,852	Pollux, Switz.	13,422		
Weisshom, Switz.	14,780	Schreckhorn, Switz.	13,379	Aneto, Sp.	11,168
Taschhorn, Switz.	14,733	Ober Gabelhorn, Switz.	13,330	Posets, Sp.	11,073
Matterhorn, It., Switz.	14,690	Gran Paradiso, It.	13,323	Perdido, Sp.	11,007
Dent Blanche, Switz.	14,293	Bernina, It., Switz.	13,284	Vignemale, Fr., Sp.	10,820
Nadelhorn, Switz.	14,196	Fiescherhorn, Switz.	13,283	Long, Sp.	10,479
Grand Combin, Switz.	14,154	Grunhorn, Switz.	13,266	Estats, Sp.	10,304
Lenzpitze, Switz.	14,088	Lauteraarhorn, Switz.	13,261	Montcalm, Sp.	10,105
Finsteraarhorn, Switz.	14,022	Durrenhorn, Switz.	13,238		
Castor, Switz.	13,865	Allalinhorn, Switz.	13,213		
Zinalrothorn, Switz.	13,849	Weissmies, Switz.	13,199	**Caucasus (Europe-Asia)**	
Hohberghorn, Switz.	13,842	Lagginhorn, Switz.	13,156		
Alphubel, Switz.	13,799	Zupo, Switz.	13,120	El'brus, USSR	18,510
Rimpfischhom, Switz.	13,776	Fletschhorn, Switz.	13,110	Shkara, USSR	17,064
Aletschorn, Switz.	13,763	Adlerhorn, Switz.	13,081	Dykh Tau, USSR	17,054
Strahlhorn, Switz.	13,747	Gletscherhorn, Switz.	13,068	Kashtan Tau, USSR	16,877
Dent D'Herens, Switz.	13,686	Schalihorn, Switz.	13,040	Dzhangi Tau, USSR	16,565
		Scerscen, Switz.	13,028	Kazbek, USSR	16,558

Asia

Peak	Country	Feet	Peak	Country	Feet	Peak	Country	Feet
Everest	Nepal-Tibet.	29,028	Kungur.	Sinkiang.	25,325	Badrinath	India.	23,420
K2 (Godwin Austen)	Kashmir.	28,250	Tirich Mir	Pakistan.	25,230	Nunkun	Kashmir.	23,410
Kanchenjunga	India-Nepal.	28,208	Makalu II.	Nepal-Tibet.	25,120	Lenina Peak.	USSR.	23,405
Lhotse I (Everest)	Nepal-Tibet.	27,923	Minya Konka	China.	24,900	Pyramid	India-Nepal.	23,400
Makalu I	Nepal-Tibet.	27,824	Kula Gangri	Bhutan-Tibet	24,784	Api	Nepal.	23,399
Lhotse II (Everest)	Nepal-Tibet.	27,560	Changtzu (Everest)	Nepal-Tibet.	24,780	Pauhunri.	India-Tibet.	23,385
Dhaulagiri	Nepal.	26,810	Muz Tagh Ata.	Sinkiang.	24,757	Trisul.	India.	23,360
Manaslu I	Nepal.	26,760	Skyang Kangri	Kashmir.	24,750	Kangto.	India-Tibet.	23,260
Cho Oyu.	Nepal-Tibet.	26,750	Communism Peak	USSR	24,590	Nyenchhen Thanglha	Tibet.	23,255
Nanga Parbat.	Kashmir.	26,660	Jongsang Peak.	India-Nepal.	24,472	Trisuli	India.	23,210
Annapurna I.	Nepal.	26,504	Pobedy Peak	Sinkiang-USSR.	24,406	Pumori.	Nepal-Tibet.	23,190
Gasherbrum	Kashmir.	26,470	Sia Kangri	Kashmir.	24,350	Dunagiri	India.	23,184
Broad	Kashmir.	26,400	Haramosh Peak	Pakistan.	24,270	Lombo Kangra	Tibet.	23,165
Gosainthan	Tibet.	26,287	Istoro Nal	Pakistan.	24,240	Saipal.	Nepal.	23,100
Annapurna II	Nepal.	26,041	Tent Peak.	India-Nepal.	24,165	Macha Pucchare.	Nepal.	22,958
Gyachung Kang	Nepal-Tibet.	25,910	Chomo Lhari.	Bhutan-Tibet	24,040	Numbar.	Nepal.	22,817
Disteghil Sar	Kashmir.	25,868	Chamlang.	Nepal.	24,012	Kanjiroba.	Nepal.	22,580
Himalchuli	Nepal.	25,801	Kabru.	India-Nepal.	24,002	Ama Dablam.	Nepal.	22,350
Nuptse (Everest)	Nepal-Tibet.	25,726	Alung Gangri.	Tibet.	24,000	Cho Polu.	Nepal.	22,093
Masherbrum	Kashmir.	25,660	Baltoro Kangri.	Kashmir.	23,990	Lingtren.	Nepal-Tibet.	21,972
Nanda Devi	India.	25,645	Mussu Shan.	Sinkiang.	23,890	Khumbutse.	Nepal-Tibet.	21,785
Rakaposhi.	Kashmir.	25,550	Mana.	India.	23,860	Hlako Gangri.	Tibet.	21,266
Kamet.	India-Tibet.	25,447	Baruntse.	Nepal.	23,688	Mt. Grosvenor.	China.	21,190
Namcha Barwa.	Tibet.	25,445	Nepal Peak.	India-Nepal.	23,500	Thagchhab Gangri	Tibet.	20,970
Gurla Mandhata.	Tibet.	25,355	Amne Machin.	China.	23,490	Damavand.	Iran.	18,606
Ulugh Muz Tagh	Sinkiang-Tibet.	25,340	Gauri Sankar.	Nepal-Tibet.	23,440	Ararat.	Turkey.	16,804

Antarctica

Peak	Feet	Peak	Feet	Peak	Feet	Peak	Feet
Vinson Massif	16,864	Andrew Jackson	13,750	Shear	13,100	Campbell	12,434
Tyree.	16,290	Sidley	13,720	Odishaw	13,008	Don Pedro Christophersen	12,355
Shinn.	15,750	Ostenso	13,710	Donaldson	12,894		
Gardner	15,375	Minto.	13,668	Ray	12,808	Lysaght	12,326
Epperly	15,100	Miller.	13,650	Sellery	12,779	Huggins	12,247
Kirkpatrick	14,855	Long Gables	13,620	Waterman	12,730	Sabine	12,200
Elizabeth.	14,698	Dickerson	13,517	Anne	12,703	Astor	12,175
Markham	14,290	Giovinetto	13,412	Press	12,566	Mohl	12,172
Bell	14,117	Wade	13,400	Falla.	12,549	Frankes	12,064
Mackellar	14,098	Fisher	13,386	Rucker	12,520	Jones.	12,040
Anderson	13,957	Fridtjof Nansen	13,350	Goldthwait	12,510	Gjelsvik	12,008
Bentley.	13,934	Wexler.	13,202	Morris.	12,500	Coman.	12,000
Kaplan	13,878	Lister.	13,200	Erebus	12,450		

How Deep Is the Ocean?

Principal ocean depths. Source: Defense Mapping Agency Hydrographic/Topographic Center

Name of area	Location	Meters	Depth Fathoms	Feet
Pacific Ocean				
Mariana Trench . . . . 11°20'N	142°12'E	10,915	5,968	35,810
Tonga Trench . . . . 23°16'S	174°44'W	10,800	5,906	35,433
Philippine Trench . . . . 10°38'N	126°36'E	10,057	5,499	32,995
Kermadec Trench . . . . 31°53'S	177°21'W	10,047	5,494	32,963
Bonin Trench. . . . . 24°30'N	143°24'E	9,994	5,464	32,788
Kuril Trench . . . . 44°15'N	150°34'E	9,750	5,331	31,988
Izu Trench . . . . 31°05'N	142°10'E	9,695	5,301	31,808
New Britain Trench . . . . 06°19'S	153°45'E	8,940	4,888	29,331
Yap Trench. . . . . 08°33'N	138°02'E	8,527	4,663	27,976
Japan Trench . . . . 36°08'N	142°43'E	8,412	4,600	27,599
Peru-Chile Trench . . . . 23°18'S	71°14'W	8,064	4,409	26,457
Palau Trench. . . . . 07°52'N	134°56'E	8,054	4,404	26,424
Aleutian Trench . . . . 50°51'N	177°11'E	7,679	4,199	25,194
New Hebrides Trench. . . . . 20°36'S	168°37'E	7,570	4,139	24,836
North Ryukyu Trench . . . . 24°00'N	126°48'E	7,181	3,927	23,560
Mid. America Trench . . . . 14°02'N	93°39'W	6,662	3,643	21,857
Atlantic Ocean				
Puerto Rico Trench . . . . 19°55'N	65°27'W	8,605	4,705	28,232
So. Sandwich Trench . . . . 55°42'S	25°56'E	8,325	4,552	27,313
Romanche Gap . . . . 0°13'S	18°26'W	7,728	4,226	25,354
Cayman Trench . . . . 19°12'N	80°00'W	7,535	4,120	24,721
Brazil Basin. . . . . 09°10'S	23°02'W	6,119	3,346	20,076
Indian Ocean				
Java Trench . . . . 10°19'S	109°58'E	7,125	3,896	23,376
Ob' Trench. . . . . 09°45'S	67°18'E	6,874	3,759	22,553
Diamantina Trench . . . . 35°50'S	105°14'E	6,602	3,610	21,660
Vema Trench . . . . 09°08'S	67°15'E	6,402	3,501	21,004
Agulhas Basin . . . . 45°20'S	26°50'E	6,195	3,387	20,325
Arctic Ocean				
Eurasia Basin . . . . 82°23'N	19°31'E	5,450	2,980	17,881
Mediterranean Sea				
Ionian Basin . . . . 36°32'N	21°06'E	5,150	2,816	16,896

Ocean Areas and Average Depths

Four major bodies of water are recognized by geographers and mapmakers. They are: the Pacific, Atlantic, Indian, and Arctic oceans. The Atlantic and Pacific oceans are considered divided at the equator into the No. and So. Atlantic; the No. and So. Pacific. The Arctic Ocean is the name for waters north of the continental land masses in the region of the Arctic Circle.

	Sq. miles	Avg. depth in feet		Sq. miles	Avg. depth in feet
Pacific Ocean	64,186,300	12,925	Hudson Bay	281,900	305
Atlantic Ocean.	33,420,000	11,730	East China Sea	256,600	620
Indian Ocean.	28,350,500	12,598	Andaman Sea	218,100	3,667
Arctic Ocean.	5,105,700	3,407	Black Sea	196,100	3,906
South China Sea	1,148,500	4,802	Red Sea	174,900	1,764
Caribbean Sea	971,400	8,448	North Sea	164,900	308
Mediterranean Sea	969,100	4,926	Baltic Sea	147,500	180
Bering Sea.	873,000	4,893	Yellow Sea.	113,500	121
Gulf of Mexico	582,100	5,297	Persian Gulf	88,800	328
Sea of Okhotsk	537,500	3,192	Gulf of California	59,100	2,375
Sea of Japan	391,100	5,468			

Continental Statistics

Source: National Geographic Society, Washington, D.C.

Continents	Area (sq. mi.)	% of Earth	Population (est.)	% World total	Highest point (in feet)	Lowest point
Asia	16,999,000	29.7	2,896,700,000	59.8	Everest, 29,028	Dead Sea, −1,312
Africa	11,688,000	20.4	551,000,000	11.4	Kilimanjaro, 19,340	Lake Assal, −512
North America . .	9,366,000	16.3	400,000,000	8.3	McKinley, 20,320	Death Valley, −282
South America . .	6,881,000	12.0	271,000,000	5.6	Aconcagua, 22,834	Valdes Penin., −131
Europe.	4,017,000	7.0	702,300,000	14.5	El'brus, 18,510	Caspian Sea, −92
Australia.	2,966,000	5.2	15,800,000	0.3	Kosciusko, 7,310	Lake Eyre, −52
Antarctica	5,100,000	8.9			Vinson Massif, 16,864	Not Known
Est. World Population			4,845,000,000			

Important Islands and Their Areas

Source: National Geographic Society, Washington, D.C.

Figure in parentheses shows rank among the world's 10 largest islands; some islands have not been surveyed accurately; in such cases estimated areas are shown.

Location-Ownership
Area in square miles

Arctic Ocean

Canadian

Axel Heiberg	16,671
Baffin (5)	195,928
Banks	27,038
Bathurst	6,194
Devon	21,331
Ellesmere (10)	75,767
Melville	16,274
Prince of Wales	12,872
Somerset	9,570
Southampton	15,913
Victoria (9)	83,896

USSR

Franz Josef Land	8,000
Novaya Zemlya (two is.)	35,000
Wrangel	2,800

Norwegian

Svalbard	23,940
Nordaustlandet	5,410
Spitsbergen	15,060

Atlantic Ocean

Anticosti, Canada	3,066
Ascension, UK	34
Azores, Portugal	902
Faial	67
Sao Miguel	291
Bahamas	5,353
Bermuda Is., UK	20
Block, Rhode Island	10
Canary Is., Spain	2,808
Fuerteventura	668
Gran Canaria	592
Tenerife	795
Cape Breton, Canada	3,981
Cape Verde Is.	1,750
Faeroe Is., Denmark	540
Falkland Is., UK	4,700
Fernando de Noronha Archipelago, Brazil	7
Greenland, Denmark (1)	840,000
Iceland	39,769
Long Island, N. Y.	1,396
Bioko Is. Equatorial Guinea	785
Madeira Is., Portugal	307
Marajo, Brazil	15,528
Martha's Vineyard, Mass.	91
Mount Desert, Me.	108
Nantucket, Mass.	46
Newfoundland, Canada	42,030
Prince Edward, Canada	2,184
St. Helena, UK	47
South Georgia, UK	1,450
Tierra del Fuego, Chile and Argentina	18,800
Tristan da Cunha, UK	40

British Isles

Great Britain, mainland (8)	84,200
Channel Islands	75
Guernsey	24
Jersey	45
Sark	2
Hebrides	2,744
Ireland	32,599
Irish Republic	27,136
Northern Ireland	5,463
Man	227

Orkney Is.	390
Scilly Is.	6
Shetland Is.	567
Skye	670
Wight	147

Baltic Sea

Aland Is., Finland	581
Bornholm, Denmark	227
Gotland, Sweden	1,164

Caribbean Sea

Antigua	108
Aruba, Netherlands	75
Barbados	166
Cuba	44,218
Isle of Youth	1,182
Curacao, Netherlands	171
Dominica	290
Guadeloupe, France	687
Hispaniola, Haiti and Dominican Republic	29,530
Jamaica	4,244
Martinique, France	425
Puerto Rico, U.S.	3,515
Tobago	116
Trinidad	1,864
Virgin Is., UK	59
Virgin Is., U.S.	132

Indian Ocean

Andaman Is., India	2,500
Madagascar (4)	226,658
Mauritius	720
Pemba, Tanzania	380
Reunion, France	969
Seychelles	171
Sri Lanka	25,332
Zanzibar, Tanzania	640

Persian Gulf

Bahrain	258

Mediterranean Sea

Balearic Is., Spain	1,936
Corfu, Greece	229
Corsica, France	3,365
Crete, Greece	3,186
Cyprus	3,572
Elba, Italy	86
Euboea, Greece	1,409
Malta	122
Rhodes, Greece	542
Sardinia, Italy	9,262
Sicily, Italy	9,822

Pacific Ocean

Aleutian Is., U.S.	6,821
Adak	289
Amchitka	121
Attu	388
Kanaga	135
Kiska	110
Tanaga	209
Umnak	675
Unalaska	1,064
Unimak	1,600
Canton, Kiribati*	4
Caroline Is., U.S. trust terr.	472
Christmas, Kiribati*	94

Diomede, Big, USSR	11
Diomede, Little, U.S.	2
Easter, Chile	69
Fiji	7,056
Vanua Levu	2,242
Viti Levu	4,109
Funafuti, Tuvalu*	2
Galapagos Is., Ecuador	3,043
Guadalcanal, UK	2,500
Guam	209
Hainan, China	13,000
Hawaiian Is., U.S.	6,450
Hawaii	4,037
Oahu	593
Hong Kong, UK	29
Japan	145,809
Hokkaido	30,144
Honshu (7)	87,805
Iwo Jima	8
Kyushu	14,114
Okinawa	459
Shikoku	7,049
Kodiak, U.S.	3,670
Marquesas Is., France	492
Marshall Is., U.S. trust terr.	70
Bikini*	2
Nauru	8
New Caledonia, France	6,530
New Guinea (2)	306,000
New Zealand	103,883
Chatham	372
North	44,035
South	58,305
Stewart	674
Northern Mariana Is.	184
Philippines	115,831
Leyte	2,787
Luzon	40,880
Mindanao	36,775
Mindoro	3,790
Negros	4,907
Palawan	4,554
Panay	4,446
Samar	5,050
Quemoy	56
Sakhalin, USSR	29,500
Samoa Is.	1,177
American Samoa	77
Tutuila	52
Samoa (Western)	1,101
Savaii	670
Upolu	429
Santa Catalina, U.S.	72
Tahiti, France	402
Taiwan	13,823
Tasmania, Australia	26,178
Tonga Is.	270
Vancouver, Canada	12,079
Vanuatu	5,700

East Indies

Bali, Indonesia	2,147
Borneo, Indonesia-Malaysia, UK (3)	280,100
Celebes, Indonesia	69,000
Java, Indonesia	48,900
Madura, Indonesia	2,113
Moluccas, Indonesia	28,766
New Britain, Papua New Guinea	14,093
New Ireland, Papua New Guinea	3,707
Sumatra, Indonesia (6)	165,000
Timor	11,570

*Atolls: Bikini (lagoon area, 230 sq. mi., land area 2 sq. mi.), U.S. Trust Territory of the Pacific Islands; Canton (lagoon 20 sq. mi., land 4 sq. mi.), Kiribati; Christmas (lagoon 140 sq. mi., land 94 sq. mi.), Kiribati; Funafuti (lagoon 84 sq. mi., land 2 sq. mi.), Tuvalu.

Australia, often called an island, is a continent. Its mainland area is 2,939,975 sq. mi.

Islands in minor waters; Manhattan (22 sq mi.) Staten (59 sq. mi.) and Governors (173 acres), all in New York Harbor, U.S.; Isle Royale (209 sq. mi.), Lake Superior, U.S.; Manitoulin (1,068 sq. mi.), Lake Huron, Canada; Pinang (110 sq. mi.), Strait of Malacca, Malaysia; Singapore (239 sq. mi.), Singapore Strait, Singapore.

Major Rivers in North America
Source: U.S. Geological Survey

River	Source or Upper Limit of Length	Outflow	Miles
Alabama	Gilmer County, Ga.	Mobile River	735
Albany	Lake St. Joseph, Ont., Can.	James Bay	610
Allegheny	Potter County, Pa.	Ohio River	325
Altamaha-Ocmulgee	Junction of Yellow and South Rivers, Newton County, Ga.	Atlantic Ocean	392
Apalachicola-Chattahoochee	Towns County, Ga.	Gulf of Mexico, Fla.	524
Arkansas	Lake County, Col.	Mississippi River, Ark.	1,459
Assiniboine	Eastern Saskatchewan	Red River	450
Attawapiskat	Attawapiskat, Ont., Can.	James Bay	465
Big Black (Miss.)	Webster County, Miss.	Mississippi River	330
Black (N.W.T.)	Contwoyto Lake	Chantrey Inlet	600
Brazos	Junction of Salt and Double Mountain Forks, Stonewall County, Tex.	Gulf of Mexico	870
Canadian	Las Animas County, Col.	Arkansas River, Okla.	906
Cedar (Iowa)	Dodge County, Minn.	Iowa River, Ia.	329
Cheyenne	Junction of Antelope Creek and Dry Fork, Converse County, Wyo.	Missouri River	290
Churchill	Methy Lake	Hudson Bay	1,000
Cimarron	Colfax County, N.M.	Arkansas River, Okla.	600
Clark Fork-Pend Oreille	Silver Bow County, Mon.	Columbia River, B.C.	505
Colorado (Ariz.)	Rocky Mountain National Park, Col. (90 miles in Mexico)	Gulf of Cal., Mexico	1,450
Colorado (Texas)	West Texas	Matagorda Bay	840
Columbia	Columbia Lake, British Columbia	Pacific Ocean, bet. Ore. and Wash.	1,243
Columbia, Upper	Columbia Lake, British Columbia	To mouth of Snake River	890
Connecticut	Third Connecticut Lake, N.H.	L.I. Sound, Conn.	407
Coppermine (N.W.T.)	Lac de Gras	Coronation Gulf (Atlantic Ocean)	525
Cumberland	Letcher County, Ky.	Ohio River	720
Delaware	Schoharie County, N.Y.	Liston Point, Delaware Bay	390
Fraser	Near Mount Robson (on Continental Divide)	Strait of Georgia	850
Gila	Catron County, N.M.	Colorado River, Ariz.	630
Green (Ut.-Wyo.)	Junction of Wells and Trail Creeks, Sublette County, Wyo.	Colorado River, Ut.	730
Hamilton (Lab.)	Lake Ashuanipi	Atlantic Ocean	600
Hudson	Henderson Lake, Essex County, N.Y.	Upper N.Y. Bay, N.Y.,-N.J.	306
Illinois	St. Joseph County, Ind.	Mississippi River	420
James (N.D.-S.D.)	Wells County, N.D.	Missouri River, S.D.	710
James (Va.)	Junction of Jackson and Cowpasture Rivers, Botetourt County, Va.	Hampton Roads	340
Kanawha-New	Junction of North and South Forks of New River, N.C.	Ohio River	352
Kentucky	Junction of North and Middle Forks, Lee County, Ky.	Ohio River	259
Klamath	Lake Ewauna, Klamath Falls, Ore.	Pacific Ocean	250
Koyukuk	Endicott Mountains, Alaska	Yukon River	470
Kuskokwim	Alaska Range	Kuskokwim Bay	680
Liard	Southern Yukon, Alaska	Mackenzie River	693
Little Missouri	Crook County, Wyo.	Missouri River	560
Mackenzie	Great Slave Lake	Arctic Ocean	900
Milk	Junction of North and South Forks, Alberta Province	Missouri River, Mon.	625
Minnesota	Big Stone Lake, Minn.	Mississippi River, St. Paul, Minn.	332
Mississippi	Lake Itasca, Minn.	Mouth of Southwest Pass	2,348
Mississippi, Upper	Lake Itasca, Minn.	To mouth of Missouri R.	1,171
Mississippi-Missouri-Red Rock	Source of Red Rock, Beaverhead Co., Mon.	Mouth of Southwest Pass	3,710
Missouri	Junction of Jefferson, Madison, and Gallatin Rivers, Madison County, Mon.	Mississippi River	2,315
Missouri-Red Rock	Source of Red Rock, Beaverhead Co., Mon.	Mississippi River	2,533
Mobile-Alabama-Coosa	Gilmer County, Ga.	Mobile Bay	780
Nelson (Manitoba)	Lake Winnipeg	Hudson Bay	410
Neosho	Morris County, Kan.	Arkansas River, Okla.	460
Niobrara	Niobrara County, Wyo.	Missouri River, Neb.	431
North Canadian	Union County, N.M.	Canadian River, Okla.	760
North Platte	Junction of Grizzly and Little Grizzly Creeks, Jackson County, Col.	Platte River, Neb.	618
Ohio	Junction of Allegheny and Monongahela Rivers, Pittsburgh, Pa.	Mississippi River, Ill.-Ky.	981
Ohio-Allegheny	Potter County, Pa.	Mississippi River	1,306
Osage	East-central Kansas	Missouri River, Mo.	500
Ottawa	Lake Capimitchigama	St. Lawrence	790
Ouachita	Polk County, Ark.	Red River, La.	605
Peace	Stikine Mountains, B.C.	Slave River	1,195
Pearl	Neshoba County, Miss.	Gulf of Mexico, Miss.-La.	411
Pecos	Mora County, N.M.	Rio Grande, Tex.	735
Pee Dee-Yadkin	Watauga County, N.C.	Winyah Bay, S.C.	435
Pend Oreille	Near Butte, Mon.	Columbia River	490
Platte	Junction of North and South Platte Rivers, Neb.	Missouri River, Neb.	310
Porcupine	Ogilvie Mountains, Alaska	Yukon River, Alaska	460
Potomac	Garrett County, Md.	Chesapeake Bay	383
Powder	Junction of South and Middle Forks, Wyo.	Yellowstone River, Mon.	375
Red (Okla.-Tex.-La.)	Curry County, N.M.	Mississippi River	1,270
Red River of the North	Junction of Otter Tail and Bois de Sioux Rivers, Wilkin County, Minn.	Lake Winnipeg, Manitoba	545

River	Source or Upper Limit of Length	Outflow	Miles
Republican	Junction of North Fork and Arikaree River, Neb.	Kansas River, Kan.	445
Rio Grande	San Juan County, Col.	Gulf of Mexico	1,885
Roanoke	Junction of North and South Forks, Montgomery County, Va.	Albemarle Sound, N.C.	380
Rock (Ill.-Wis.)	Dodge County, Wis.	Mississippi River, Ill.	300
Sabine	Junction of South and Caddo Forks, Hunt County, Tex.	Sabine Lake, Tex.-La.	380
Sacramento	Siskiyou County, Cal.	Suisun Bay	377
St. Francis	Iron County, Mo.	Mississippi River, Ark.	425
St. Lawrence	Lake Ontario	Gulf of St. Lawrence (Atlantic Ocean)	800
Salmon (Idaho)	Custer County, Ida.	Snake River, Ida.	420
San Joaquin	Junction of South and Middle Forks, Madera County, Cal.	Suisun Bay	350
San Juan	Silver Lake, Archuleta County, Col.	Colorado River, Ut.	360
Santee-Wateree-Catawba	McDowell County, N.C.	Atlantic Ocean, S.C.	538
Saskatchewan, North	Rocky Mountains	Lake Winnipeg	1,100
Saskatchewan, South	Rocky Mountains	Lake Winnipeg	1,205
Savannah	Junction of Seneca and Tugaloo Rivers, Anderson County, S.C.	Atlantic Ocean, Ga.-S.C.	314
Severn (Ontario)	Sandy Lake	Hudson Bay	610
Smoky Hill	Cheyenne County, Col.	Kansas River, Kan.	540
Snake	Teton County, Wyo.	Columbia River, Wash.	1,038
South Platte	Junction of South and Middle Forks, Park County, Col.	Platte River, Neb.	424
Susitna	Alaska Range	Cook Inlet	300
Susquehanna	Otsego Lake, Otsego County, N.Y.	Chesapeake Bay, Md.	444
Tallahatchie	Tippah County, Miss.	Yazoo River, Miss.	301
Tanana	Wrangell Mountains	Yukon River, Alaska	620
Tennessee	Junction of French Broad and Holston Rivers	Ohio River, Ky.	652
Tennessee-French Broad	Bland County, Va.	Ohio River	900
Tombigbee	Prentiss County, Miss.	Mobile River, Ala.	525
Trinity	North of Dallas, Tex.	Galveston Bay, Tex.	360
Wabash	Darke County, Oh.	Ohio River, Ill.-Ind.	529
Washita	Hemphill County, Tex.	Red River, Okla.	500
White (Ark.-Mo.)	Madison County, Ark.	Mississippi River	720
Willamette	Douglas County, Ore.	Columbia River	270
Wind-Bighorn	Junction of Wind and Little Wind Rivers, Fremont Co., Wyo. (Source of Wind R. is Togwotee Pass, Teton Co., Wyo.)	Yellowstone R., Mon.	336
Wisconsin	LeVieux Desert, Vilas County, Wis.	Mississippi River	430
Yellowstone	Park County, Wyo.	Missouri River, N.D.	671
Yukon	Coast Mountains of British Columbia	Bering Sea, Alaska	1,979

Principal World Rivers

Source: National Geographic Society, Washington, D.C. (length in miles)

River	Outflow	Lgth	River	Outflow	Lgth	River	Outflow	Lgth
Albany	James Bay	610	Indus	Arabian Sea	1,800	Red River of N.	Lake Winnipeg	545
Amazon	Atlantic Ocean	4,000	Irrawaddy	Bay of Bengal	1,337	Rhine	North Sea	820
Amu	Aral Sea	1,578	Japura	Amazon River	1,750	Rhone	Gulf of Lions	505
Amur	Tatar Strait	2,744	Jordan	Dead Sea	200	Rio de la Plata	Atlantic Ocean	150
Angara	Yenisey River	1,151	Kootenay	Columbia River	485	Rio Grande	Gulf of Mexico	1,885
Arkansas	Mississippi	1,459	Lena	Laptev Sea	2,734	Rio Roosevelt	Aripuana	400
Back	Arctic Ocean	605	Loire	Bay of Biscay	634	Saguenay	St. Lawrence R.	434
Brahmaputra	Bay of Bengal	1,800	Mackenzie	Arctic Ocean	2,635	St. John	Bay of Fundy	418
Bug, Southern	Dnieper River	532	Madeira	Amazon River	2,013	St. Lawrence	Gulf of St. Law.	800
Bug, Western	Wisla River	481	Magdalena	Caribbean Sea	956	Salween	Andaman Sea	1,500
Canadian	Arkansas River	906	Marne	Seine River	326	Sao Francisco	Atlantic Ocean	1,988
Chang Jiang	E. China Sea	3,964	Mekong	S. China Sea	2,600	Saskatchewan	Lake Winnipeg	1,205
Churchill, Man.	Hudson Bay	1,000	Meuse	North Sea	580	Seine	English Chan.	496
Churchill, Que.	Atlantic Ocean	532	Mississippi	Gulf of Mexico	2,348	Shannon	Atlantic Ocean	230
Colorado	Gulf of Calif.	1,450	Missouri	Mississippi	2,533	Snake	Columbia River	1,038
Columbia	Pacific Ocean	1,243	Murray-Darling	Indian Ocean	2,310	Sungari	Amur River	1,150
Congo	Atlantic Ocean	2,900	Negro	Amazon	1,400	Syr	Aral Sea	1,370
Danube	Black Sea	1,776	Nelson	Hudson Bay	1,600	Tajo, Tagus	Atlantic Ocean	626
Dnieper	Black Sea	1,420	Niger	Gulf of Guinea	2,590	Tennessee	Ohio River	652
Dniester	Black Sea	877	Nile	Mediterranean	4,160	Thames	North Sea	236
Don	Sea of Azov	1,224	Ob-Irtysh	Gulf of Ob	3,362	Tiber	Tyrrhenian Sea	252
Drava	Danube River	447	Oder	Baltic Sea	567	Tigris	Shatt al-Arab	1,180
Dvina, North	White Sea	824	Ohio	Mississippi	975	Tisza	Danube River	600
Dvina, West	Gulf of Riga	634	Orange	Atlantic Ocean	1,300	Tocantins	Para River	1,677
Ebro	Mediterranean	565	Orinoco	Atantic Ocean	1,600	Ural	Caspian Sea	1,575
Elbe	North Sea	724	Ottawa	St. Lawrence R.	790	Uruguay	Rio de la Plata	1,000
Euphrates	Shatt al-Arab	1,700	Paraguay	Parana River	1,584	Volga	Caspian Sea	2,194
Fraser	Str. of Georgia	850	Parana	Rio de la Plata	2,485	Weser	North Sea	454
Gambia	Atlantic Ocean	700	Peace	Slave River	1,195	Wisla	Bay of Danzig	675
Ganges	Bay of Bengal	1,560	Pilcomayo	Paraguay River	1,000	Yellow (See Huang)		
Garonne	Bay of Biscay	357	Po	Adriatic Sea	405	Yenisey	Kara Sea	2,543
Hsi	S. China Sea	1,200	Purus	Amazon River	2,100	Yukon	Bering Sea	1,979
Huang	Yellow Sea	2,903	Red	Mississippi	1,270	Zambezi	Indian Ocean	1,700

Famous Waterfalls

Source: National Geographic Society, Washington, D.C.

The earth has thousands of waterfalls, some of considerable magnitude. Their importance is determined not only by height but volume of flow, steadiness of flow, crest width, whether the water drops sheerly or over a sloping surface, and in one leap or a succession of leaps. A

series of low falls flowing over a considerable distance is known as a cascade.

Sete Quedas or Guaira is the world's greatest waterfall when its mean annual flow (estimated at 470,000 cusecs, cubic feet per second) is combined with height. A greater volume of water passes over Boyoma Falls (Stanley Falls), though not one of its seven cataracts, spread over nearly 60 miles of the Congo River, exceeds 10 feet.

Estimated mean annual flow, in cusecs, of other major waterfalls are: Niagara, 212,200; Paulo Afonso, 100,000; Urubupunga, 97,000; Iguazu, 61,000; Patos-Maribondo, 53,000; Victoria, 35,400; and Kaieteur, 23,400.

Height = total drop in feet in one or more leaps. † = falls of more than one leap; * = falls that diminish greatly seasonally; ** = falls that reduce to a trickle or are dry for part of each year. If river names not shown, they are same as the falls. R. = river; L. = lake; (C) = cascade type.

Name and location	Ht.	Name and location	Ht.	Name and location	Ht.
Africa		Glomach.	370	Idaho	
Angola		Wales		**Shoshone, Snake R.	212
Duque de Braganca,		Cain	150	Twin, Snake R.	120
Lucala R.	344	Rhaiadr	240	Kentucky	
Ruacana, Cuene R.	406	Iceland—Detti	144	Cumberland.	68
Ethiopia		† Gull, Hvita R.	105	Maryland	
Dal Verme,		Italy—Frua, Toce R. (C).	470	*Great, Potomac R. (C)	71
Dorya R.	98	**Norway**		Minnesota	
Fincha	508	Mardalsfossen (Northern)	1,535	**Minnehaha	53
Tesissat, Blue Nile R.	140	† Mardalsfossen (Southern).	2,149	New Jersey	
Lesotho		† **Skjeggedal, Nybuai R.	1,378	Passaic	70
*Maletsunyane	630	**Skykje.	984	New York	
Zimbabwe-Zambia		Vetti, Morka-Koldedola R.	900	*Taughannock	215
*Victoria, Zambezi R.	343	Voring, Bjoreio R.	597	Oregon	
South Africa		**Sweden**		† Multnomah	620
*Augrabies, Orange R.	480	† Handol.	427	Highest fall.	542
Howick, Umgeni R.	364	† Tannforsen, Are R.	120	Tennessee	
† Tugela.	2,014	**Switzerland**		Fall Creek.	256
Highest fall	597	† Diesbach	394	Washington	
Tanzania-Zambia		Giessbach (C)	984	Mt. Rainier Natl. Park	
*Kalambo	726	Handegg, Aare R.	150	Narada, Paradise R.	168
Uganda		Iffigen	120	Sluiskin, Paradise R.	300
Kabalega (Murchison) Victoria		Pissevache, Salanfe R.	213	Palouse	197
Nile R.	130	† Reichenbach	656	**Snoqualmie.	268
		Rhine	79	Wisconsin	
Asia		† Simmen	459	*Big Manitou, Black R. (C).	165
India—*Cauvery	330	Staubbach.	984	Wyoming	
*Gokak, Ghataprabha R.	170	† Trummelbach.	1,312	Yellowstone Natl. Pk. Tower	132
*Jog (Gersoppa), Sharavathi R.	830			*Yellowstone (upper).	109
Japan		**North America**		*Yellowstone (lower).	308
*Kegon, Daiya R.	330	**Canada**		**Mexico**	
Laos		Alberta		El Salto	218
Khon Cataracts,		Panther, Nigel Cr.	600	**Juanacatlan, Santiago R.	72
Mekong R. (C)	70	British Columbia			
		† Della.	1,443	**South America**	
Australasia		† Takakkaw, Daly Glacier.	1,200	Argentina-Brazil	
Australia		Northwest Territories		Iguazu	230
New South Wales		Virginia, S. Nahanni R.	294	**Brazil**	
Wentworth.	614	Quebec		Glass	1,325
Highest fall.	360	Montmorency	274	Patos-Maribondo, Grande R.	115
Wollomombi.	1,100	**Canada—United States**		Paulo Afonso, Sao Francisco R.	275
Queensland		Niagara: American	182	Urubupunga, Parana R.	40
Coomera	210	Horseshoe	173	**Brazil-Paraguay**	
Tully	885	**United States**		Sete Quedas	
† Wallaman, Stony Cr.	1,137	California		Parana R.	130
Highest fall.	937	*Feather, Fall R.	640	**Colombia**	
New Zealand		Yosemite National Park		Catarata de Candelas,	
Bowen	540	*Bridalveil	620	Cusiana R.	984
Helena.	890	*Illilouette	370	*Tequendama, Bogota R.	427
Stirling	505	*Nevada, Merced R.	594	**Ecuador**	
† Sutherland, Arthur R.	1,904	**Ribbon.	1,612	*Agoyan, Pastaza R.	200
Highest fall	815	**Silver Strand, Meadow Br.	1,170	**Guyana**	
		*Vernal, Merced R.	317	Kaieteur, Potaro R.	741
Europe		† **Yosemite	2,425	Great, Kamarang R.	1,600
Austria—† Gastein	492	Yosemite (upper).	1,430	† Marina, Ipobe R.	500
Highest fall	280	Yosemite (lower).	320	Highest fall	300
† *Golling, Schwarzbach R.	250	Yosemite (middle) (C)	675	**Venezuela—**	
† Krimml.	1,312	Colorado		† *Angel.	3,212
France—*Gavarnie	1,385	† Seven, South Cheyenne Cr.	300	Highest fall	2,648
Great Britain—Scotland		Hawaii		Cuquenan	2,000
		Akaka, Kolekole Str.	442		

The Great Lakes

Source: National Ocean Service, U.S. Commerce Department

The Great Lakes form the largest body of fresh water in the world and with their connecting waterways are the largest inland water transportation unit. Draining the great North Central basin of the U.S., they enable shipping to reach the Atlantic via their outlet, the St. Lawrence R., and also the Gulf of Mexico via the Illinois Waterway, from Lake Michigan to the Mississippi R. A third outlet connects with the Hudson R. and thence the Atlantic via the N. Y. State Barge Canal System. Traffic on the Illinois Waterway and the N.Y. State Barge Canal System is limited to recreational boating and small shipping vessels.

Only one of the lakes, Lake Michigan, is wholly in the United States; the others are shared with Canada. Ships carrying grain, lumber and iron ore move from the shores of Lake Superior to Whitefish Bay at the east end of the lake, thence through the Soo (Sault Ste. Marie) locks, through the St. Mary's River and into Lake Huron. To reach the steel mills at Gary, and Port of Indiana and South Chicago, Ill., ore ships move west from Lake Huron to Lake Michigan through the Straits of Mackinac.

Lake Huron discharges its waters into Lake Erie through a narrow waterway, the St. Clair R., Lake St. Clair (both

included in the drainage basin figures) and the Detroit R. Lake St. Clair, a marshy basin, is 26 miles long and 24 miles wide at its maximum. A ship channel has been dredged through the lake.

Lake Superior is 600 feet above mean water level at Point-au-Pere, Quebec, on the International Great Lakes Datum (1955). From Duluth, Minn., to the eastern end of Lake Ontario is 1,156 mi.

	Superior	Michigan	Huron	Erie	Ontario
Length in miles	350	307	206	241	193
Breadth in miles	160	118	183	57	53
Deepest soundings in feet	1,330	923	750	210	802
Volume of water in cubic miles	2,900	1,180	850	116	393
Area (sq. miles) water surface—U.S.	20,600	22,300	9,100	4,980	3,560
Canada	11,100	.....	13,900	4,930	3,990
Area (sq. miles) entire drainage basin—U.S.	16,900	45,600	16,200	18,000	15,200
Canada	32,400	.....	35,500	4,720	12,100
Total Area (sq. miles) U.S. and Canada	**81,000**	**67,900**	**74,700**	**32,630**	**34,850**
Mean surface above mean water level at Point-au-Pere, Quebec, aver. level in feet (1900-1983)	600.59	578.25	578.25	570.42	244.71
Latitude, North	46° 25'	41° 37'	43° 00'	41° 23'	43° 11'
	49° 00'	46° 06'	46° 17'	42° 52'	44° 15'
Longitude, West	84° 22'	84° 45'	79° 43'	78° 51'	76° 03'
	92° 06'	88° 02'	84° 45'	83° 29'	79° 53'
National boundary line in miles	282.8	None	260.8	251.5	174.6
United States shore line (mainland only) miles	863	1,400	580	431	300

Lakes of the World

Source: National Geographic Society, Washington, D.C.

A lake is a body of water surrounded by land. Although some lakes are called seas, they are lakes by definition. The Caspian Sea is bounded by the Soviet Union and Iran and is fed by eight rivers.

Name	Continent	Area sq. mi.	Length mi.	Depth feet	Elev. feet
Caspian Sea	Asia-Europe	143,244	760	3,363	−92
Superior	North America	31,700	350	1,333	600
Victoria	Africa	26,828	250	270	3,720
Aral Sea	Asia	24,904	280	220	174
Huron	North America	23,000	206	750	579
Michigan	North America	22,300	307	923	579
Tanganyika	Africa	12,700	420	4,823	2,534
Baykal	Asia	12,162	395	5,315	1,493
Great Bear	North America	12,096	192	1,463	512
Malawi	Africa	11,150	360	2,280	1,550
Great Slave	North America	11,031	298	2,015	513
Erie	North America	9,910	241	210	570
Winnipeg	North America	9,417	266	60	713
Ontario	North America	7,550	193	802	245
Balkhash	Asia	7,115	376	85	1,115
Ladoga	Europe	6,835	124	738	13
Chad	Africa	6,300	175	24	787
Maracaibo	South America	5,217	133	115	Sea level
Onega	Europe	3,710	145	328	108
Eyre	Australia	3,600	90	4	−52
Volta	Africa	3,276	250	.....	.....
Titicaca	South America	3,200	122	922	12,500
Nicaragua	North America	3,100	102	230	102
Athabasca	North America	3,064	208	407	700
Reindeer	North America	2,568	143	720	1,106
Turkana	Africa	2,473	154	240	1,230
Issyk Kul	Asia	2,355	115	2,303	5,279
Torrens	Australia	2,230	130	.....	92
Vanern	Europe	2,156	91	328	144
Nettilling	North America	2,140	67	.....	95
Winnipegosis	North America	2,075	141	38	830
Albert	Africa	2,075	100	168	2,030
Kariba	Africa	2,050	175	390	1,590
Nipigon	North America	1,872	72	540	1,050
Gairdner	Australia	1,840	90	.....	112
Urmia	Asia	1,815	90	49	4,180
Manitoba	North America	1,799	140	12	813

Notable Deserts of the World

Arabian (Eastern), 70,000 sq. mi. in Egypt between the Nile river and Red Sea, extending southward into Sudan.

Atacama, 600 mi. long area rich in nitrate and copper deposits in N. Chile.

Chihuahuan, 140,000 sq. mi. in Tex., N.M., Ariz., and Mexico.

Death Valley, 3,300 sq. mi. in E. Cal. and SW Nev. Contains lowest point below sea level (282 ft.) in Western Hemisphere.

Gibson, 120,000 sq. mi. in the interior of W. Australia.

Gobi, 500,000 sq. mi. in Mongolia and China.

Great Sandy, 150,000 sq. mi. in W. Australia.

Great Victoria, 150,000 sq. mi. in W. and S. Australia.

Kalahari, 225,000 sq. mi. in southern Africa.

Kara-Kum, 120,000 sq. mi. in Turkmen SSR.

Kavir (Dasht-e Kavir), great salt waste in central Iran some 400 mi. long.

Kyzyl Kum, 100,000 sq. mi. in Kazakh and Uzbek SSRs.

Libyan, 450,000 sq. mi. in the Sahara extending from Lybia through SW Egypt into Sudan.

Lut (Dasht-e Lut), 20,000 sq. mi. in E. Iran.

Mojave, 15,000 sq. mi. in S. Cal.

Nafud (An Nafud), 40,000 sq. mi. near Jawf in Saudi Arabia.

Namib, long narrow area extending 800 miles along SW coast of Africa.

Nubian, 100,000 sq. mi. in the Sahara in NE Sudan.

Painted Desert, section of high plateau in N. Ariz. extending 150 mi.

Rub al Khali (Empty Quarter), 250,000 sq. mi. in the south Arabian Peninsula.

Sahara, 3,500,000 sq. mi. in N. Africa extending westward to the Atlantic. Largest desert in the world.

Simpson, 40,000 sq. mi. in central Australia.

Sonoran, 70,000 sq. mi. in SW Ariz. and SE Cal. extending into Mexico.

Syrian, 100,000 sq. mi. arid wasteland extending over much of N. Saudi Arabia, E. Jordan, S. Syria, and W. Iraq.

Taklimakan, 140,000 sq. mi. in Sinkiang Province, China.

Thar (Great Indian), 100,000 sq. mi. arid area extending 400 mi. along India-Pakistan border.

NATIONS OF THE WORLD

The nations of the world are listed in alphabetical order. Initials in the following articles include UN (United Nations), OAS (Org. of American States), NATO (North Atlantic Treaty Org.), EC (European Communities or Common Market), OAU (Org. of African Unity). Sources: U.S. Dept. of State; U.S. Census Bureau; International Monetary Fund; UN Statistical Yearbook; UN Demographic Yearbook; The Environmental Fund; International Iron and Steel Institute; The Statesman's Year-Book; Encyclopaedia Britannica. All embassy addresses are Wash., DC; area codes (202), unless otherwise noted. Literacy rates are usually based on the ability to read and write on a lower elementary school level. The concept of literacy is changing in the industrialized countries, where literacy is defined as the ability to read instructions necessary for a job or a license. By these standards, illiteracy may be more common than present rates suggest.

See special color section for maps and flags of all nations.

Afghanistan
Democratic Republic of Afghanistan

People: Population (1984 est.): 14,448,000. **Pop. density:** 70.1 per sq. mi. **Ethnic groups:** Pashtoon 50%; Tajiks 25%; Uzbek 9%; Hazara 9%. **Languages:** Pashta (Iranian), Dari Persian (spoken by Tajiks, Hazaras), Uzbek (Turkic). **Religions:** Sunni Muslim (80%), Shi'a Muslim (20%).
Geography: Area: 251,773 sq. mi., about the size of Texas. **Location:** Between Soviet Central Asia and the Indian subcontinent. **Neighbors:** Pakistan on E, S, Iran on W, USSR on N; the NE tip touches China. **Topography:** The country is landlocked and mountainous, much of it over 4,000 ft. above sea level. The Hindu Kush Mts. tower 16,000 ft. above Kabul and reach a height of 25,000 ft. to the E. Trade with Pakistan flows through the 35-mile long Khyber Pass. The climate is dry, with extreme temperatures, and large desert regions, though mountain rivers produce intermittent fertile valleys. **Capital:** Kabul. **Cities** (1984 est.): Kabul 1.4 mln.
Government: Type: People's Republic. **Head of state, and President of the Revolutionary Council:** Pres. Babrak Karmal; b. 1929; in office: Dec. 27, 1979. **Head of Government:** Prime Min. Sultan Ali Keshtmand; in office: 1981. **Local divisions:** 24 provinces, each under a governor. **Defense:** 3.0% of GNP (1981).
Economy: Industries: Textiles, carpets, cement. **Chief crops:** Cotton, wheat, fruits. **Minerals:** Copper, lead, gas, coal, zinc, iron. **Crude oil reserves** (1978): 284 mln. bbls. **Other resources:** Wool, hides, karacul pelts. **Per capita arable land:** 1.3 acres. **Meat prod.** (1980): beef: 67,000 metric tons; lamb: 125,000 metric tons. **Electricity prod.** (1981): 1 bln. kwh. **Labor force:** cannot be estimated due to war.
Finance: Currency: Afghani (Mar. 1985: 50.60 = $1 US). **Gross domestic product** (1982): $3.5 bln. **Per capita income** (1978): $168. **Imports** (1981): $562 mln.; partners: USSR 53%, Jap. 21%, Iran 13%. **Exports** (1982): $707 mln.; partners: USSR 60%, Pak. 12%, UK 12%. **International reserves less gold** (Jan. 1985): $232.7 mln. **Gold:** 965,000 oz t. **Consumer prices** (change in 1981): 4.9%
Transport: Motor vehicles: in use (1982): 30,000 passenger cars, 35,000 comm. vehicles. **Civil aviation** (1982): 291 mln. passenger-km; 18.6 mln. net ton-km.
Communications: Television sets: 12,000 in use (1982); **Radios:** 1.2 mln. in use (1982). **Telephones in use** (1980): 32,000. **Daily newspaper circ.** (1983): 3 per 1,000 pop.
Health: Life expectancy at birth (1975): 39.9 male; 40.7 female. **Births** (per 1,000 pop. 1979): 52. **Deaths** (per 1,000 pop. 1979): 30. **Natural increase** (1979): 2.2%. **Hospital beds:** 6,875. **Physicians:** 1,215 (1982).
Education (1982): **Literacy:** 10%.
Embassy: 2341 Wyoming Ave. NW, 20008; 234-3770.

Afghanistan, occupying a favored invasion route since antiquity, has been variously known as Ariana or Bactria (in ancient times) and Khorasan (in the Middle Ages). Foreign empires alternated rule with local emirs and kings until the 18th century, when a unified kingdom was established. In 1973, a military coup ushered in a republic.

Pro-Soviet leftists took power in a bloody 1978 coup, and concluded an economic and military treaty with the USSR.

Late in Dec. 1979, the USSR began a massive military airlift into Kabul. The three-month old regime of Hafizullah Amin ended with a Soviet backed coup, Dec. 27th. He was replaced by Babrak Karmal, considered a more pro-Soviet leader. Soviet troops, estimated at between 60,000-100,000, fanned out over Afghanistan, fighting rebels. Fighting continued during 1985 as the Soviets found themselves engaged in a long, protracted guerrilla war.

Albania
Socialist Republic of Albania

People: Population (1983 est.): 2,906,000. **Pop. density:** 246 per sq. mi. **Urban** (1983): 33%. **Ethnic groups:** Albanians (Gegs in N, Tosks in S) 95%, Greeks 2.5%. **Languages:** Albanian (Tosk is official dialect), Greek. **Religions:** officially atheist; (historically) mostly Moslems. All public worship and religious institutions were outlawed in 1967.
Geography: Area: 11,100 sq. mi., slightly larger than Maryland. **Location:** On SE coast of Adriatic Sea. **Neighbors:** Greece on S, Yugoslavia on N, E. **Topography:** Apart from a narrow coastal plain, Albania consists of hills and mountains covered with scrub forest, cut by small E-W rivers. **Capital:** Tirana. **Cities** (1983 est.): Tirana 272,000; Durres 127,000; Vlore 90,000.
Government: Type: Communist. **Head of state:** Pres. Ramiz Alia, in office: Nov. 22, 1982. **Head of government:** Premier Adil Carcani; in office: Jan. 18, 1982. **Head of Communist Party:** Ramiz Alia; b. Oct. 18, 1925; in office: Apr. 13, 1985. **Local divisions:** 27 districts. **Defense:** 13% of budget (1980).
Economy: Industries: Chem. fertilizers, textiles, electric cables. **Chief crops:** Grain, sugar beets, cotton, potatoes, tobacco, fruits. **Minerals:** Chromium, coal, oil. **Other resources:** Forests. **Arable land:** 43%. **Meat prod.** (1980): beef: 20,000 metric tons; pork: 12,000 metric tons; lamb; 24,000 metric tons. **Electricity prod.** (1980): 2.6 bln. kwh. **Labor force:** 60% agric; 40% industry and commerce.
Finance: Currency: Lek (Nov. 1984: 8.33 = $1 US). **Gross domestic product** (1981 est.) $2.3 bln. **Per capita income** (1979): $830. **Imports** (1976): $250 mln.; partners: Czech., Yugoslavia, China. **Exports** (1976): $200 mln.; partners: Czech., Yugoslavia, China, Italy.
Transport: Motor vehicles: in use (1971): 3,500 passenger cars, 11,200 comm. vehicles. **Chief ports:** Durres, Vlone.
Communications: Television sets: 20,500 in use (1983). **Radios:** 210,000 in use (1983). **Daily newspaper circ.** (1982): 52 per 1,000 pop.
Health: Life expectancy at birth (1983): 69 yrs. **Births** (per 1,000 pop. 1984): 26.0. **Deaths** (per 1,000 pop. 1984): 6.0. **Natural increase** 2.0%. **Hospital beds** (per 1,000 pop. 1982): 70. **Physicians** (1982): 4,476 doctors & dentists. **Infant mortality** (per 1,000 live births 1971): 86.8.
Major International Organizations: UN and its specialized agencies.
Education (1983): **Literacy:** 75%.

Ancient Illyria was conquered by Romans, Slavs, and Turks (15th century); the latter Islamized the population. Independent Albania was proclaimed in 1912, republic was formed in 1920. Self-styled King Zog I ruled 1925-39, until Italy invaded.

Communist partisans took over in 1944, allied Albania with USSR, then broke with USSR in 1960 over de-Stalinization. Strong political alliance with China followed, leading to several billion dollars in aid, which was curtailed after 1974. China cut off aid in 1978 when Albania attacked its policies after the death of Chinese ruler Mao Tse-tung.

Industrialization, pressed in 1960s, slowed in 1970s. Large-scale purges of officials occurred 1973-76. Enver Hoxha, the nation's ruler for 4 decades, died Apr. 11, 1985.

Algeria
Democratic and Popular Republic of Algeria

People: Population (1984 est.); 21,351,000. **Age distrib. (%):** 0–14: 47.9; 15–59: 46.3; 60+: 5.7. **Pop. density:** 22.7 per sq. mi. **Urban** (1983): 45%. **Ethnic groups:** Arabs 75%, Berbers 25%. **Languages:** Arabic (official), Berber (indigenous language), French. **Religions:** Sunni Moslem (state religion).

Geography: Area: 918,497 sq. mi., more than 3 times the size of Texas. **Location:** In NW Africa, from Mediterranean Sea into Sahara Desert. **Neighbors:** Morocco on W, Mauritania, Mali, Niger on S, Libya, Tunisia on E. **Topography:** The Tell, located on the coast, comprises fertile plains 50-100 miles wide, with a moderate climate and adequate rain. Two major chains of the Atlas Mts., running roughly E-W, and reaching 7,000 ft., enclose a dry plateau region. Below lies the Sahara, mostly desert with major mineral resources. **Capital:** Algiers (El Djazair). **Cities** (1982 est.): El Djazair 2,200,000; Wahran 633,000; Qacentina 384,000.

Government: Type: Republic. **Head of state:** Pres. Chadli Bendjedid; b. Apr. 14, 1929; in office: Feb. 9, 1979. **Head of government:** Premier Abdel Hamid Brahimi; in office: Jan. 22, 1984. **Local divisions:** 31 wilayaat (states). **Defense:** 1.9% of GDP (1982).

Economy: Industries: Oil, iron, steel, textiles, fertilizer, plastics. **Chief crops:** Grains, wine-grapes, potatoes, dates, tomatoes, oranges. **Minerals:** Mercury, oil, iron, zinc, lead, coal, copper, natural gas, phosphates. **Crude oil reserves** (1984): 8.3 bln. bbls. **Other resources:** Cork trees. **Arable land:** 13%. **Meat prod.** (1980): beef: 33,000 metric tons; lamb: 67,000 metric tons. **Electricity prod.** (1983): 8.9 bln. kwh. **Crude steel prod.** (1981): 550,000 metric tons. **Labor force:** 30% agric.; 40% ind. and commerce; 17% government; 10% services.

Finance: Currency: Dinar (Mar. 1985: 5.05 = $1 US). **Gross domestic product** (1982): $40 bln. **Per capita income** (1982): $1,951. **Imports** (1983): $10.3 bln.; partners: France 18%, W. Ger. 18%, It. 11%, Japan 9%. **Exports** (1982): $12.9 bln.; partners: U.S. 51%, W. Ger. 14%, France 11%, It. 7%. **National budget** (1983): $21.9 bln. **International reserves less gold** (Mar. 1985): $1.9 bln. **Gold:** 5.58 mln. oz t. **Consumer prices** (change in 1982): 6.7%

Transport: Railway traffic (1979): 1.8 bln. passenger-km; 2.5 bln. net ton-km. **Motor vehicles:** in use (1981): 573,000 passenger cars, 265,000 comm. vehicles; assembled (1977): 6,360 comm. vehicles. **Chief ports:** El Djazair.

Communications: Television sets: 1.2 mln. in use (1982). **Radios:** 3.2 mln. in use (1982). **Telephones in use** (1982): 606,000. **Daily newspaper circ.** (1982): 29 per 1,000 pop.

Health: Life expectancy at birth (1984): 56.7 male; 58.9 female. **Births** (per 1,000 pop. 1979): 46. **Deaths** (per 1,000 pop. 1979): 14. **Natural increase** (1979); 3.2%. **Hospital beds** (1980): 45,160. **Physicians** (1980): 6,081. **Infant mortality** (per 1,000 live births 1982): 110

Education (1978): **Literacy:** 46%. **School:** Free and compulsory to age 13; Attendance: 86% primary, 31% secondary.

Major international Organizations: UN and its specialized agencies, OAU, Arab League, OPEC.

Embassy: 2118 Kalorama Rd. NW; 328-5300.

Earliest known inhabitants were ancestors of Berbers, followed by Phoenicians, Romans, Vandals, and, finally, Arabs; but 25% still speak Berber dialects. Turkey ruled 1518 to 1830, when France took control.

Large-scale European immigration and French cultural inroads did not prevent an Arab nationalist movement from launching guerilla war. Peace, and French withdrawal, was negotiated with French Pres. Charles de Gaulle. One million Europeans left.

Ahmed Ben Bella was the victor of infighting, and ruled 1962-65, when an army coup installed Col. Houari Boumedienne as leader. Ben Bella remained under house arrest until 1979.

In 1967, Algeria declared war with Israel, broke with U.S., and moved toward eventual military and political ties with the USSR. French oil interests were partly seized in 1971, but relations with the West have since improved.

Algeria, strongly backing Saharan guerillas' demands for a cease fire and self-determination, encouraged Mauritania to come to terms with the Polisario Front, 1979.

The one-party Socialist regime faces endemic mass unemployment and poverty, despite land reform and industrialization attempts.

Andorra
Principality of Andorra

People: Population (1984 est.): 45,000. **Age distrib. (%):** 0–14: 29.2; 14–59: 61.7; 60+: 9.1. **Pop. density:** 223.5 per sq. mi. **Ethnic groups:** Spanish over 60%, Andorran 30%, French 6%. **Languages:** Catalan (official), Spanish, French. **Religion:** Roman Catholic.

Geography: Area: 188 sq. mi., half the size of New York City. **Location:** In Pyrenees Mtns. **Neighbors:** Spain on S, France on N. **Topography:** High mountains and narrow valleys over the country. **Capital:** Andorra la Vella.

Government: Type: Co-principality. **Head of state:** Co-princes are the president of France and the Roman Catholic bishop of Urgel in Spain. **Local divisions:** 7 parishes.

Economy: Industries: Tourism, (6 mln. visitors in 1982), tobacco products. **Labor force:** 20% agric.; 80% ind. and commerce; services; government.

Finance: Currency: French franc, Spanish peseta.

Communications: Television sets: 4,000 in use (1980). **Radios:** 7,000 in use (1980). **Telephones in use** (1982): 17,719.

Health: Births (per 1,000 pop. 1981): 14.8. **Deaths** (per 1,000 pop. 1981): 4.1. **Natural increase** (1981): 1.0%.

Education (1984): **Literacy:** 100%. School compulsory to age 16.

The present political status, with joint sovereignty by France and the bishop of Urgel, dates from 1278.

Tourism, especially skiing, is the economic mainstay. A free port, allowing for an active trading center, draws some 7 million tourists annually. The ensuing economic prosperity accompanied by Andorra's virtual law-free status, has given rise to calls for reform.

Angola
People's Republic of Angola

People: Population (1984 est.): 7,770,000. **Pop. density:** 15.2 per sq. mi. **Ethnic groups:** Ovimbundu 38%, Kimbundu 23%; Bakongo 13%, European 1%; Mesticos 2%. **Languages:** Portuguese (official), various Bantu languages. **Religions:** Roman Catholic 46%, Protestant 12%, animist 42%.

Geography: Area: 481,353 sq. mi., larger than Texas and California combined. **Location:** In SW Africa on Atlantic coast. **Neighbors:** Namibia (SW Africa) on S, Zambia on E, Zaire on N; Cabinda, an enclave separated from rest of country by short Atlantic coast of Zaire, borders Congo Republic. **Topography:** Most of Angola consists of a plateau elevated 3,000 to 5,000 feet above sea level, rising from a narrow coastal strip. There is also a temperate highland area in the west-central region, a desert in the S, and a tropical rain forest covering Cabinda. **Capital:** Luanda (1981 est.): 1.1 mln.

Government: Type: People's Republic, one-party rule. **Head of state:** Pres. Jose Eduardo dos Santos b. Aug. 28, 1942; in office: Sept. 20, 1979. **Local divisions:** 18 provinces. **Defense:** 20% of govt budget (1981).

Economy: Industries: Alcohol, cotton goods, fishmeal, paper, palm oil, footwear. **Chief crops:** Coffee, bananas. **Minerals:** Iron, diamonds (over 2 mln. carats a year), copper, manganese, sulphur, phosphates, oil. **Crude oil reserves** (1980): 1.2 bln. bbls. **Arable land:** 2%. **Meat prod.** (1980): beef: 51,000 metric tons; pork: 13,000 metric tons. **Fish catch** (1981): 121,000 metric tons. **Electricity prod.** (1982): 1.6 bln.kwh. **Labor force:** 60% agric., 15% industry.

Finance: Currency: Kwanza (Nov. 1984: 30.82 = $1 US). **Gross domestic product** (1982): $7.6 bln. **Per capita income** (1976): $500. **Imports** (1982): $1.1 bln.; partners: U.S. 16%, Fra. 12%; USSR 8%. **Exports** (1982): $1.7 bln.; partners: Bahamas 18%, U.S. 38%.

Transport: Motor vehicles: in use (1982): 75,000 passenger cars, 25,000 comm. vehicles. **Chief ports:** Cabinda, Lobito, Luanda.

Communications: Radios: 130,000 in use (1983). **Telephones in use** (1982): 40,000. **Daily newspaper circ.** (1982): 16 per 1,000 pop.

Health: Life expectancy at birth (1981): 40.6 male; 42.9 female. **Births** (per 1,000 pop. 1981): 48.8. **Deaths** (per 1,000 pop. 1981): 22.7. **Natural increase** (1981): 2.6%. **Hospital beds** (per 100,000 pop. 1977): 306. **Physicians** (per 100,000 pop 1977): 6. **Infant mortality** (per 1,000 live births 1981): 152.

Education (1980): **Literacy:** 20%. **Pop. 5-19:** in school: 28%, teachers per 1,000: 9.

From the early centuries AD to 1500, Bantu tribes penetrated most of the region. Portuguese came in 1583, allied with the Bakongo kingdom in the north, and developed the slave trade. Large-scale colonization did not begin until the 20th century, when 400,000 Portuguese immigrated.

A guerrilla war begun in 1961 lasted until 1974, when Portugal offered independence. Violence between the National Front, based in Zaire, the Soviet-backed Popular Movement, and the National Union, aided by the U.S. and S. Africa, killed thousands of blacks, drove most whites to emigrate, and completed economic ruin. Some 15,000 Cuban troops and massive Soviet aid helped the Popular Movement win most of the country after independence Nov. 11, 1975.

S. African troops crossed the southern Angolan border June 7, 1981, killing more than 300 civilians and occupying several towns. The S. Africans withdrew in Sept.

Russian influence, backed by 25,000 Cubans, East Germans, and Portuguese Communists, is strong in the Marxist regime.

Antigua and Barbuda

People: Population (1984 est.) 80,000. **Urban:** 34%. **Language:** English. **Religion:** Predominantly Church of England.

Geography: Area: 171 sq. mi. **Location:** Eastern Caribbean. **Neighbors:** approx. 30 mi. north of Guadeloupe. **Capital:** St. John's, (1983 est.) 27,000.

Government: Head of State: Queen Elizabeth II; represented by Sir Wilfred E. Jacobs. **Head of Government:** Prime Min. Vere Cornwall Bird; b. Dec. 7, 1910; in office Nov. 1, 1981.

Economy: Industries: manufacturing, tourists (visitors spent $43 mln. in 1983). **Arable Land:** 55%.

Finance: Currency: East Caribbean dollar (Apr. 1985): 2.67 = $1 U.S. **Consumer prices** (change in 1982): 4.4%.

Embassy: 2000 N St. NW; 296-6310.

Antigua was discovered by Columbus in 1493. The British colonized it in 1632.

The British associated state of Antigua achieved independence as Antigua and Barbuda on Nov. 1, 1981. The government maintains close relations with the U.S., United Kingdom, and Venezuela.

Argentina

Argentine Republic

People: Population (1984 est.) 30,097,000. **Age distrib. (%):** 0–14: 28.5; 15–59: 59.6; 60+: 11.9. **Pop. density:** 28 per sq. mi. **Urban** (1983): 80%. **Ethnic groups:** Europeans 97% (Spanish, Italian), Indians, Mestizos, Arabs. **Languages:** Spanish (official), English, Italian, German, French. **Religions:** Roman Catholic 92%.

Geography: Area: 1,065,189 sq. mi., 4 times the size of Texas, second largest in S. America. **Location:** Occupies most of southern S. America. **Neighbors:** Chile on W, Bolivia, Paraguay on N, Brazil, Uruguay on NE. **Topography:** The mountains in W: the Andean, Central, Misiones, and Southern. Aconcagua is the highest peak in the Western hemisphere, alt. 22,834 ft. E of the Andes are heavily wooded plains, called the Gran Chaco in the N, and the fertile, treeless Pampas in the central region. Patagonia, in the S, is bleak and arid. Rio de la Plata, 170 by 140 mi., is mostly fresh water, from 2,485-mi. Parana and 1,000-mi. Uruguay rivers. **Capital:** Buenos Aires. **Cities** (1982 cen.): Buenos Aires 2,908,000; Cordoba 969,000; Rosario 750,455; Mendoza 597,000; San Miguel de Tucuman 497,000.

Government: Type: Republic. **Head of state:** Pres. Raul Alfonsin; b. Mar. 3, 1926; in office: Dec. 10, 1983. **Local divisions:**

22 provinces, 1 natl. terr. and 1 federal dist., under military governors. **Defense:** 2.6% of GNP (1981).

Economy: Industries: Meat processing, flour milling, chemicals, textiles, machinery, autos. **Chief crops:** Grains, corn, grapes, linseed, sugar, tobacco, rice, soybeans, citrus fruits. **Minerals:** Oil, lead, zinc, iron, sulphur, silver, copper, gold. **Crude oil reserves** (1980): 2.40 bln. bbls. **Arable land:** 12%. **Meat prod.** (1980): beef: 2.92 mln. metric tons; pork: 246,000 metric tons; lamb: 117,000 metric tons. **Fish catch** (1983): 475,000 metric tons. **Electricity prod.** (1982): 36.2 bln. kwh. **Crude steel prod.** (1982): 2.9 mln. metric tons. **Labor force:** 19% agric.; 36% ind. and comm.; 20% services.

Finance: Currency: Austral (June 1985: 1.25 = $1 US). **Gross domestic product** (1983 est.): $53 bln. **Per capita income** (1978 est.): $2,331. **Imports** (1983): $4.5 bln.; partners: U.S. 22%, W. Ger. 10%, Braz. 12%, Jap. 10%. **Exports** (1983): $7.8 bln.; partners: USSR 21%, Braz. 7%, Neth. 8%, U.S. 13%.

Tourists (1980): receipts: $344 mln. **National budget** (1980): $4.9 bln. revenues; $5.7 bln. expenditures. **International reserves less gold** (Jan. 1985): $1.7 bln. **Gold:** 4.37 mln. oz t. **Consumer prices** (change in 1984): 626.7%.

Transport: Railway traffic (1983): 6.9 bln. passenger-km; 9.2 bln. net ton-km. **Motor vehicles:** in use (1983): 5.0 mln. passenger cars, 1.2 mln. comm. vehicles. **Civil aviation:** (1983) 3.7 mln. passenger-km; 131 mln. net ton-km. **Chief ports:** Buenos Aires, Bahia Blanca, La Plata.

Communications: Television sets: 5.9 mln. in use (1983). **Radios:** 10 mln. in use (1983). **Telephones in use** (1982): 3.0 mln. **Daily newspaper circ.** (1982): 85 per 1,000 pop.

Health: Life expectancy at birth (1983): 66.8 male; 73.2 female. **Births** (per 1,000 pop. 1983): 24.6. **Deaths** (per 1,000 pop. 1983): 8.7 **Natural increase** (1983): 1.5%. **Hospital beds** (per 100,000 pop. 1977): 524. **Physicians** (per 100,000 pop. 1977): 192. **Infant mortality** (per 1,000 live births 1984): 52.

Education (1984): Literacy: 94%. School attendence 21.5% through secondary school.

Major International Organizations: UN and its specialized agencies, OAS.

Embassy: 1600 New Hampshire Ave. NW 20009; 933-6400.

Nomadic Indians roamed the Pampas when Spaniards arrived, 1515-1516, led by Juan Diaz de Solis. Nearly all the Indians were killed by the late 19th century. The colonists won independence, 1810-1819, and a long period of disorders ended in a strong centralized government.

Large-scale Italian, German, and Spanish immigration in the decades after 1880 spurred modernization, making Argentina the most prosperous, educated, and industrialized of the major Latin American nations. Social reforms were enacted in the 1920s, but military coups prevailed 1930-46, until the election of Gen. Juan Peron as president.

Peron, with his wife Eva Duarte effected labor reforms, but also suppressed speech and press freedoms, closed religious schools, and ran the country into debt. A 1955 coup exiled Peron, who was followed by a series of military and civilian regimes. Peron returned in 1973, and was once more elected president. He died 10 months later, succeeded by his wife, Isabel, who had been elected vice president, and who became the first woman head of state in the Western hemisphere.

A military junta ousted Mrs. Peron in 1976 amid charges of corruption. Under a continuing state of siege, the army battled guerrillas and leftists, killed 5,000 people, and jailed and tortured others. The government rejected a report of the Inter-American Human Rights Commission, 1980, which charged widespread killing, torture, and arbitrary detention.

A severe worsening in economic conditions placed extreme pressure on the military government. In 1983, inflation was over 300% and payments on foreign debt were suspended.

Argentine troops seized control of the British-held Falkland Islands on Apr. 2, 1982. Both countries had claimed sovereignty over the islands, located 250 miles off the Argentine coast, since 1833. The British dispatched a task force and declared a total air and sea blockade around the Falklands. Fighting began May 1; several hundred lost their lives as the result of the destruction of a British destroyer and the sinking of an Argentine cruiser.

British troops landed in force on East Falkland Island May 21. By June 2, the British had surrounded Stanley, the capital city and Argentine stronghold. The Argentine troops surrendered,

June 14; Argentine President Leopoldo Galtieri resigned June 17.

Democratic rule returned to Argentina in 1983 as Raul Alfonsin's Radical Civic Union gained an absolute majority in the presidential electoral college and Congress. The nation was plagued by severe financial problems as inflation soared to an annual rate of 850% in Mar. 1985.

Australia

Commonwealth of Australia

People: Population (1984 est.): 15,462,000. **Age distrib. (%):** 0–14: 25; 15–44: 46.1; 45+: 28.9. **Pop. density:** 5.2 per sq. mi. **Urban** (1984): 85%. **Ethnic groups:** British 95%, other European 3%, aborigines (including mixed) 1.5%. **Languages:** English, aboriginal languages. **Religions:** Anglican 36%, other Protestant 25%, Roman Catholic 33%.

Geography: Area: 2,966,200 sq. mi., almost as large as the continental U.S. **Location:** SE of Asia, Indian O. is W and S, Pacific O. (Coral, Tasman seas) is E; they meet N of Australia in Timor and Arafura seas: Tasmania lies 150 mi. S of Victoria state, across Bass Strait. **Neighbors:** Nearest are Indonesia, Papua New Guinea on N, Solomons, Fiji, and New Zealand on E. **Topography:** An island continent. The Great Dividing Range along the E coast has Mt. Kosciusko, 7,310 ft. The W plateau rises to 2,000 ft., with arid areas in the Great Sandy and Great Victoria deserts. The NW part of Western Australia and Northern Terr. are arid and hot. The NE has heavy rainfall and Cape York Peninsula has jungles. The Murray R. rises in New South Wales and flows 1,600 mi. to the Indian O. **Capital:** Canberra. **Cities** (1982 est.): Sydney 3,310,500; Melbourne 2,836,800; Brisbane 1,124,200; Adelaide 960,000; Perth 948,900.

Government: Type: Democratic, federal state system. **Head of state:** Queen Elizabeth II, represented by Gov.-Gen. Ninian Martin Stephen; in office: July 29, 1982. **Head of government:** Prime Min. Robert James Lee Hawke; b. Dec. 9, 1929; in office: Mar. 11, 1983. **Local divisions:** 6 states, 2 territories. **Defense:** 2.9% of GNP (1983).

Economy: Industries: Iron, steel, textiles, electrical equip., chemicals, autos, aircraft, ships, machinery. **Chief crops:** Wheat (a leading export), barley, oats, corn, hay, sugar, wine, fruit, vegetables. **Minerals:** Bauxite, coal, copper, iron, lead, nickel, silver, tin, tungsten, uranium, zinc. **Crude oil reserves** (1980): 2.13 bln. bbls. **Other resources:** Wool (30% of world output). **Arable land:** 9%. **Meat prod.** (1983): beef: 1.55 mln. metric tons; pork: 237,000 metric tons; lamb: 517,000 metric tons. **Fish catch** (1978): 122,900 metric tons. **Electricity prod.** (1982): 106.1 bln. kwh. **Crude steel prod.** (1983): 5.3 mln. metric tons. **Labor force:** 7% agric.; 30% ind. and comm.; 32.6% service.

Finance: Currency: Dollar (Mar. 1985: .70 = $1 US). **Gross domestic product** (1983): $150.2 bln. **Per capita income** (1983): $9,960. **Imports** (1984): $26.4 bln; partners: U.S. 23%, Jap. 20%, UK 7%, W. Ger. 6%. **Exports** (1983): $23.7 bln.; partners: Jap. 27%, U.S. 11%, NZ 5%. **Tourists** (1982): 954,674. **National budget** (1981): $40.9 bln. **International reserves less gold** (Mar. 1985): $6.8 bln. **Gold:** 7.93 mln. oz t. **Consumer prices** (change in 1984): 3.9%.

Transport: Railway traffic (1983): 37.3 bln. net ton-km. **Motor vehicles:** in use (1983): 6.2 mln. passenger cars, 789,000 comm. vehicles; manuf. (1982): 379,000 passenger cars; 37,000 comm. vehicles. **Civil aviation** (1982): 25.2 mln. passenger-km.; 634 mln. freight ton-km. **Chief ports:** Sydney, Melbourne, Newcastle, Port Kembla, Fremantle, Geelong.

Communications: Television sets: 6.5 mln. (1983). **Radios:** 20 mln. (1983), 68,000 manuf. (1977). **Telephones in use** (1983): 8.2 mln. **Daily newspaper circ.** (1982): 426 per 1,000 pop.

Health: Life expectancy at birth (1980): 70.0 male; 76.0 female. **Births** (per 1,000 pop. 1983): 15.8. **Deaths** (per 1,000 pop. 1983): 7.3. **Natural increase** (1981): .8%. **Hospital beds** (per 100,000 pop. 1977): 1,244. **Physicians** (per 100,000 pop. 1977): 154. **Infant mortality** (per 1,000 live births 1984): 9.9.

Education (1984): **Literacy:** 100%. **School:** compulsory to age 15; attendance 94%.

Major International Organizations: UN and its specialized agencies, OECD, ANZUS, Commonwealth of Nations.

Embassy: 1601 Massachusetts Ave NW 20036; 797-3000.

Capt. James Cook explored the E coast in 1770, when the continent was inhabited by a variety of different tribes. Within decades, Britain had claimed the entire continent, which became a penal colony until immigration increased in the 1850s. The commonwealth was proclaimed Jan. 1, 1901. Northern Terr. was granted limited self-rule July 1, 1978. Their capitals and 1982 pop.:

	Area (sq. mi.)	Population
New South Wales, Sydney	309,418	5,307,900
Victoria, Melbourne	87,854	3,948,555
Queensland, Brisbane	666,699	2,295,123
South Aust., Adelaide	379,824	1,285,033
Western Aust., Perth	974,843	1,299,100
Tasmania, Hobart	26,178	427,300
Aust. Capital Terr., Canberra	926	232,000
Northern Terr., Darwin	519,633	130,000

Australia's racially discriminatory immigration policies were abandoned in 1973, after 3 million Europeans (half British) had entered since 1945. The 50,000 aborigines and 150,000 part-aborigines are mostly detribalized, but there are several preserves in the Northern Territory. They remain economically disadvantaged.

Australia's agricultural success makes it among the top exporters of beef, lamb, wool, and wheat. Major mineral deposits have been developed as well, largely for exports. Industrialization has been completed.

Australia harbors many plant and animal species not found elsewhere, including the kangaroo, koala bear, platypus, dingo (wild dog), Tasmanian devil (racoon-like marsupial), wombat (bear-like marsupial), and barking and frilled lizards.

Australian External Territories

Norfolk Is., area 13½ sq. mi., pop. (1981) 1,800, was taken over, 1914. The soil is very fertile, suitable for citrus fruits, bananas, and coffee. Many of the inhabitants are descendants of the Bounty mutineers, moved to Norfolk 1856 from Pitcairn Is. Australia offered the island limited home rule, 1978.

Coral Sea Is. Territory, 1 sq. mi., is administered from Norfolk Is.

Territory of Ashmore and Cartier Is., area 2 sq. mi., in the Indian O. came under Australian authority 1934 and are administered as part of Northern Territory. **Heard and McDonald Is.** are administered by the Dept. of Science.

Cocos (Keeling) Is., 27 small coral islands in the Indian O. 1,750 mi. NW of Australia. Pop. (1981) 569, area: 5½ sq. mi. The residents voted to become part of Australia, Apr. 1984.

Christmas Is., 52 sq. mi., pop. 3,018 (1982), 230 mi. S of Java, was transferred by Britain in 1958. It has phosphate deposits.

Australian Antarctic Territory was claimed by Australia in 1933, including 2,472,000 sq. mi. of territory S of 60th parallel S Lat. and between 160th-45th meridians E Long.

Austria

Republic of Austria

People: Population (1984 est.): 7,579,000. **Age distrib. (%):** 0–14: 22.8; 15–59: 57.0; 60+: 20.2. **Pop. density:** 233 per sq. mi. **Urban** (1981): 55.1%. **Ethnic groups:** German 98%, Slovene, Croatian. **Languages:** German 95%, Slovene. **Religions:** Roman Catholic 85%.

Geography: Area: 32,374 sq. mi., slightly smaller than Maine. **Location:** In S Central Europe. **Neighbors:** Switzerland, Liechtenstein on W, W. Germany, Czechoslovakia on N, Hungary on E, Yugoslavia, Italy on S. **Topography:** Austria is primarily mountainous, with the Alps and foothills covering the western and southern provinces. The eastern provinces and Vienna are located in the Danube River Basin. **Capital:** Vienna. **Cities** (1981 cen.): Vienna 1,504,200.

Government: Type: Parliamentary democracy. **Head of state:** Pres. Rudolf Kirchschlaeger; b. Mar. 20, 1915; in office: July 8, 1974. **Head of government:** Chancellor Fred Sinowatz; b. Feb. 5, 1929; in office: May 24, 1983. **Local divisions:** 9 lander (states), each with a legislature. **Defense:** 0.6% of GNP (1983).

Economy: Industries: Steel, machinery, autos, electrical and optical equip., glassware, sport goods, paper, textiles, chemi-

cals, cement. **Chief crops:** Grains, potatoes, beets, grapes. **Minerals:** Iron ore, oil, magnesite, aluminum, coal, lignite, copper. **Crude oil reserves** (1980): 140 mln. bbls. **Other resources:** Forests, hydro power. **Arable land:** 19.9%. **Meat prod.** (1983): beef: 212,000 metric tons; pork: 470,000 metric tons. **Electricity prod.** (1982): 44.4 bln. kwh. **Crude steel prod.** (1982): 4.2 mln. metric tons. **Labor force:** 13.8% agric.; 60% ind. & comm.; 25.5% service.

Finance: Currency: Schilling (Mar. 1985: 21.67 = $1 US). **Gross domestic product** (1983): $66.7 bln. **Per capita income** (1980): $8,280. **Imports** (1984): $19.6 bln.; partners: W. Ger. 41%, It. 9%, Switz. 5%. **Exports** (1984): $15.7 bln.; partners: W. Ger. 29%, It. 9%, Switz. 7%. **Tourists** (1982): 14.2 mln.; receipts: $5.6 bln. **National budget** (1979): $14.19 bln. revenues; $16.55 bln. expenditures. **International reserves less gold** (Mar. 1985): $3.67 bln. **Gold:** 21.14 mln. oz t. **Consumer prices** (change in 1984): 5.7%.

Transport: Railway traffic (1982): 7.3 bln. passenger-km; 10.1 bln. net ton-km. **Motor vehicles:** in use (1982): 2.3 mln. passenger cars, 220,000 comm. **Civil aviation** (1983): 1.2 bln. passenger-km; 21.3 mln. freight ton-km.

Communications: Television sets: 3.1 mln. licensed (1983). **Radios:** 5.5 mln. licensed (1983). **Telephones in use** (1983): 3.1 mln. **Daily newspaper circ.** (1983): 312 per 1,000 pop.

Health: Life expectancy at birth (1981): 69.3 male; 76.4 female. **Births** (per 1,000 pop. 1982): 12.5. **Deaths** (per 1,000 pop. 1982): 12.0. **Natural increase** (1982): −.5%. **Hospital beds** (1982): 83,830. **Physicians** (1982): 19,513. **Infant mortality** (per 1,000 live births 1983): 16.

Education (1983): Literacy: 98%. School years compulsory 9; attendance 95%.

Major International Organizations: UN and its specialized agencies, EFTA, OECD.

Embassy: 2343 Massachusetts Ave. NW 20008; 483-4474.

Rome conquered Austrian lands from Celtic tribes around 15 BC. In 788 the territory was incorporated into Charlemagne's empire. By 1300, the House of Hapsburg had gained control; they added vast territories in all parts of Europe to their realm in the next few hundred years.

Austrian dominance of Germany was undermined in the 18th century and ended by Prussia by 1866. But the Congress of Vienna, 1815, confirmed Austrian control of a large empire in southeast Europe consisting of Germans, Hungarians, Slavs, Italians, and others.

The dual Austro-Hungarian monarchy was established in 1867, giving autonomy to Hungary and almost 50 years of peace.

World War I, started after the June 28, 1914 assassination of Archduke Franz Ferdinand, the Hapsburg heir, by a Serbian nationalist, destroyed the empire. By 1918 Austria was reduced to a small republic, with the borders it has today.

Nazi Germany invaded Austria Mar. 13, 1938. The republic was reestablished in 1945, under Allied occupation. Full independence and neutrality were restored in 1955.

Austria produces most of its food, as well as an array of industrial products. A large part of Austria's economy is controlled by state enterprises. Socialists have shared or alternated power with the conservative People's Party.

Economic agreements with the Common Market give Austria access to a free-trade area encompassing most of West Europe.

The Bahamas
The Commonwealth of the Bahamas

People: Population (1984 est.): 228,000. **Age distrib. (%):** 0–14: 43.6; 15–59: 50.9; 60+: 5.5. **Pop. density:** 42.2 per sq. mi. **Urban** (1985): 75%. **Ethnic groups:** Black 85%, White (British, Canadian, U.S.) 15%. **Languages:** English. **Religions:** Baptist 29%, Anglican 23%, Roman Catholic 22%.

Geography: Area: 5,380 sq. mi., about the size of Connecticut. **Location:** In Atlantic O., E of Florida. **Neighbors:** Nearest are U.S. on W, Cuba on S. **Topography:** Nearly 700 islands (30 inhabited) and over 2,000 islets in the western Atlantic extend 760 mi. NW to SE. **Capital:** Nassau. **Cities:** (1985 est.) New Providence 135,437; Freeport 16,000.

Government: Type: Independent commonwealth. **Head of state:** Queen Elizabeth II, represented by Gov.-Gen. Gerald C. Cash; b. May 28, 1917, in office: Sept. 29, 1979. **Head of government:** Prime Min. Lynden Oscar Pindling; b. Mar. 22, 1930; in office: Jan. 16, 1967. **Local divisions:** 18 districts.

Economy: Industries: Tourism (70% of GNP), rum, drugs. **Chief crops:** Fruits, vegetables. **Minerals:** Salt. **Other resources:** Lobsters. **Arable land:** 2%. **Electricity prod.** (1982): 900 mln. kwh. **Labor force:** 6% agric.; 25% tourism, 30% government.

Finance: Currency: Dollar (Mar. 1985: 1 = $1 US). **Gross domestic product** (1981): $780 mln. **Per capita income** (1982): $5,756. **Imports** (1983): $801 mln.; partners: U.S. 74%, EC 30%. **Exports** (1983): $244 mln. (not incl. oil); partners: U.S. 41%, U.K. 7%. **Tourists** (1982): 1.9 mln.; receipts: $650 mln. **National budget** (1981): $278 mln. revenues; $278 mln. expenditures. **International reserves less gold** (Mar. 1985): $201.4 mln. **Consumer prices** (change in 1984): 3.9%.

Transport: Motor vehicles in use (1982): 63,000 passenger cars, 10,000 comm. vehicles. **Chief ports:** Nassau, Freeport.

Communications: Radios: 115,000 in use (1983). **Television sets** (1983): 50,000. **Telephones in use** (1982): 75,000. **Daily newspaper circ.** (1983): 163 per 1,000 pop.

Health: Life expectancy at birth (1985): 64.0 male; 70 female. **Births** (per 1,000 pop. 1979): 25. **Deaths** (per 1,000 pop. 1978): 5. **Natural increase** (1979): 2.0%. **Infant mortality** (per 1,000 live births 1985): 20.2.

Education (1985): Literacy: 93%; School compulsory through age 14.

Major International Organizations: UN and its specialized agencies, OAS.

Embassy: 600 New Hampshire Ave. NW 20037; 338-3940.

Christopher Columbus first set foot in the New World on San Salvador (Watling I.) in 1492, when Arawak Indians inhabited the islands. British settlement began in 1647; the islands became a British colony in 1783. Internal self-government was granted in 1964; full independence within the Commonwealth was attained July 10, 1973.

International banking and investment management has become a major industry alongside tourism, despite controversy over financial irregularities.

Bahrain
State of Bahrain

People: Population (1984 est.): 409,000. **Age distrib. (%):** 0–14: 32.9; 15–59: 63.4; 60+: 3.7. **Pop. density:** 1,517 per sq. mi. **Urban** (1981): 80.7%. **Ethnic groups:** Arabs 73%, Iranians 9%, Indians, Pakistanis 5%. **Languages:** Arabic (official), Persian. **Religions:** Sunni Moslem 40%, Shi'ah Moslem 60%.

Geography: Area: 258 sq. mi., smaller than New York City. **Location:** In Persian Gulf. **Neighbors:** Nearest are Saudi Arabia on W, Qatar on E. **Topography:** Bahrain Island, and several adjacent, smaller islands, are flat, hot and humid, with little rain. **Capital:** Manama. **Cities** (1981 cen.): Manama 121,986.

Government: Type: Traditional emirate. **Head of state:** Amir Isa bin Sulman al-Khalifa; b. July 3, 1933; in office: Nov. 2, 1961. **Head of government:** Prime Min. Kahlifa ibn Sulman al–Khalifa; b. 1935; in office: Jan. 19, 1970. **Local divisions:** 6 towns and cities. **Defense:** 8.1% of GNP (1982).

Economy: Industries: Oil products, aluminum smelting, shipping. **Chief crops:** Fruits, vegetables. **Minerals:** Oil, gas. **Crude oil reserves** (1980): 240 mln. bbls. **Arable land:** 5%. **Electricity prod.** (1982): 1.8 bln. kwh. **Labor force:** 5% agric.; 85% ind. and commerce; 5% services; 3% gov.

Finance: Currency: Dinar (Mar. 1985: 0.38 = $1 US). **Gross domestic product** (1981): $3.2 bln. **Per capita income** (1980 est.): $6,315. **Imports** (1983): $3.3 bln.; partners: Sau. Ar. 60%, UK 9%, U.S. 9%. **Exports** (1983): $3.2 bln.; partners: UAE 18%, Jap. 12%, Sing. 10%, U.S. 6%. **National Budget** (1980): $622 mln. revenues; $407 mln. expenditures. **International reserves less gold** (Mar. 1984): $1.3 bln. **Gold:** 150,000 oz t. **Consumer prices** (change in 1982): 8.9%.

Transport: Motor vehicles: in use (1981): 70,000 passenger cars, 13,200 comm. vehicles. **Chief ports:** Sitra.

Communications: Television sets: 121,000 in use (1983). **Radios:** 140,000 in use (1983). **Telephones in use** (1982): 84,593.

Health: Births (per 1,000 pop. 1981): 32.9. **Deaths** (per 1,000 pop. 1981): 5.5. **Natural Increase** (1981): 2.7. **Hospital beds** (per 100,000 pop. 1977): 303. **Physicians** (per 100,000 pop. 1977): 62.

Education (1982): **Literacy:** 40%. **Pop. 5–19:** in school: 58%, teachers per 1,000: 36.

Major International Organizations: UN and its specialized agencies, Arab League.

Embassy: 3502 International Dr. NW 20008; 342-0741.

Long ruled by the Khalifa family, Bahrain was a British protectorate from 1861 to 1971, when it regained independence.

Pearls, shrimp, fruits, and vegetables were the mainstays of the economy until oil was discovered in 1932. By the 1970s, oil reserves were depleted; international banking thrived.

Bahrain took part in the 1973-74 Arab oil embargo against the U.S. and other nations. The government bought controlling interest in the oil industry in 1975.

Saudi Arabia is building a 15-mile causeway linking Bahrain with the Arab mainland.

Bangladesh
People's Republic of Bangladesh

People: Population (1984 est.): 99,585,000. **Age distrib.** (%): 0–14: 43.2; 15–59: 52.4; 60+: 4.4. **Pop. density:** 1,740 per sq. mi. **Urban** (1981): 15%. **Ethnic groups:** Bengali 98%, Bihari, tribesmen. **Languages:** Bengali (official), English. **Religions:** Moslems 83%, Hindu 16%.

Geography: Area: 55,813 sq. mi. slightly smaller than Wisconsin. **Location:** In S Asia, on N bend of Bay of Bengal. **Neighbors:** India nearly surrounds country on W, N, E; Burma on SE. **Topography:** The country is mostly a low plain cut by the Ganges and Brahmaputra rivers and their delta. The land is alluvial and marshy along the coast, with hills only in the extreme SE and NE. A tropical monsoon climate prevails, among the rainiest in the world. **Capital:** Dacca. **Cities** (1984 est.): Dkaka (met.) 3.5 mln.; Chittagong (met.) 1.4 mln.; Khulna (met.) 623,000.

Government: Type: Martial law. **Head of state:** Pres. Hossain Mohammad Ershad, b. Feb. 1, 1930, in office: Dec. 11, 1983. **Local divisions:** 20 districts. **Defense:** 1.6% of GNP (1982).

Economy: Industries: Cement, jute, textiles, fertilizers, petroleum products. **Chief crops:** Jute (most of world output), rice. **Minerals:** Natural gas, offshore oil. **Fish catch** (1982): 736,000 metric tons. **Electricity prod.** (1982): 3.3 bln. kwh. **Labor force:** 74% agric.

Finance: Currency: Taka (Mar. 1985: 26.5 = $1 US). **Gross domestic product** (1983): $11.2 bln. **Per capita income** (1983) $119. **Imports** (1983): $2.4 bln.; partners: Jap. 13%, U.S. 8%. **Exports** (1983): $782 mln.; partners: U.S. 10%, Sing. 11%; Pak 5%. **International reserves less gold** (Mar. 1985): $357 mln. **Gold:** 54,000 oz t. **Consumer prices** (change in 1984): 12.1%.

Transport: Railway traffic (1982): 5.3 bln. passenger-km; 844 mln. net ton-km. **Motor vehicles:** in use (1981): 35,000 passenger cars, 21,000 comm. vehicles. **Chief ports:** Chittagong, Khulna.

Communications: Telephones in use (1982): 122,000. **Daily newspaper circ.** (1983) 6 per 1,000 pop.

Health: Life expectancy at birth (1978): 45 yrs. **Births** (per 1,000 pop. 1984): 45.2. **Deaths** (per 1,000 pop. 1978): 17.3. **Natural increase** (1982): 2.7%. **Hospital beds** (1979): 17,494. **Physicians** (per 100,000 pop. 1977): 8.

Education (1984): **Literacy:** 25%. **Attendance:** 65% primary school; 25% secondary school.

Major International Organizations: UN and its specialized agencies.

Embassy: 2201 Wisconsin Ave. NW 20007; 342-8372.

Moslem invaders conquered the formerly Hindu area in the 12th century. British rule lasted from the 18th century to 1947, when East Bengal became part of Pakistan.

Charging West Pakistani domination, the Awami League, based in the East, won National Assembly control in 1971. Assembly sessions were postponed; riots broke out. Pakistani troops attacked Mar. 25; Bangladesh independence was proclaimed the next day. In the ensuing civil war, one million died amid charges of Pakistani atrocities. Ten million fled to India.

War between India and Pakistan broke out Dec. 3, 1971. Pakistan surrendered in the East Dec. 15. Sheik Mujibur Rahman became prime minister. The country moved into the Indian and Soviet orbits, in response to U.S. support of Pakistan, and much of the economy was nationalized.

In 1974, the government took emergency powers to curb widespread violence; Mujibur was assassinated and a series of coups followed.

Chronic destitution among the densely crowded population has been worsened by the decline of jute as a major world commodity.

A Ganges waterpact with India, signed 1977, was recommitted by the 2 nations, 1979. Martial law, in force since 1975, was lifted on Apr. 6, 1979, prior to the opening of the new parliament.

On May 30, 1981, Pres. Ziaur Rahman was shot and killed in an unsuccessful coup attempt by army rivals. Vice President Abdus Sattar assumed the presidency but was ousted in a coup led by army chief of staff Gen. H.M. Ershad, Mar. 1982. Ershad promised a return to democracy but by 1985 was still ruling by martial law.

Barbados

People: Population (1984 est.): 252,000 **Age distrib.** (%): 0–14: 28.9%; 15–59: 57.7; 60+: 13.3. **Pop. density:** 1,526 per sq. mi. **Urban** (1980): 40%. **Ethnic groups:** African 80%, mixed 16%, Caucasian 4%. **Languages:** English. **Religions:** Anglican 70%, Methodist 9%, Roman Catholic 4%.

Geography: Area: 166 sq. mi. **Location:** In Atlantic, farthest E of W. Indies. **Neighbors:** Nearest are Trinidad, Grenada on SW. **Topography:** The island lies alone in the Atlantic almost completely surrounded by coral reefs. Highest point is Mt. Hillaby, 1,115 ft. **Capital:** Bridgetown. **Cities** (1982 est.): Bridgetown 7,600.

Government: Type: Independent sovereign state within the Commonwealth. **Head of state:** Queen Elizabeth II, represented by Gov.-Gen. Hugh Springer. **Head of government:** Prime Min. Bernard St. John; in office: Mar. 11, 1985. **Local divisions:** 11 parishes and Bridgetown.

Economy: Industries: Rum, molasses, tourism. **Chief crops:** Sugar, corn. **Minerals:** Lime. **Crude oil reserves** (1980): 1.5 mln. bbls. **Other resources:** Fish. **Arable land:** 76%. **Electricity prod.** (1982): 336.00 mln. kwh. **Labor force:** 6.9% agric.; 12.7% ind. and comm.; 80.9% services and government.

Finance: Currency: Dollar (Apr. 1985: 2.01 = $1 US). **Gross domestic product** (1982): $1 bln. **Per capita income** (1982): $3,040. **Imports** (1982): $650 mln.; partners: U.S. 36%, UK 9%, Trin./Tob. 12%, Can. 9%. **Exports** (1982): $543 mln.; partners: U.S. 30%, UK 9%, Trin./Tob. 15%. **Tourists** (1982): 352,555; receipts: $240 million. **National budget** (1984): $318 mln. **International reserves less gold** (Mar. 1985): $158.1 mln. **Consumer prices** (change in 1984): 4.6%.

Transport: Motor vehicles: in use (1980): 24,600 passenger cars; 5,100 comm. vehicles. **Chief ports:** Bridgetown.

Communications: Television sets: 52,000 in use (1983). **Radios:** 190,000 in use (1983). **Telephones in use** (1982): 72,850. **Daily newspaper circ.** (1983): 154 per 1,000 pop.

Health: Life expectancy at birth (1984): 70.8. **Births** (per 1,000 pop. 1983): 17.8. **Deaths** (per 1,000 pop. 1983): 6.9. **Natural increase** (1983): 1.0%. **Hospital beds** (per 100,000 pop. 1977): 833. **Physicians** (per 100,000 pop. 1977): 76. **Infant mortality** (per 1,000 live births 1984): 26.3.

Education (1984): **Literacy:** 99%. **Years compulsory:** 9.

Major International Organizations: UN and its specialized agencies, OAS.

Embassy: 2144 Wyoming Ave. NW 20008; 387-7374.

Barbados was probably named by Portuguese sailors in reference to bearded fig trees. An English ship visited in 1605, and British settlers arrived on the uninhabited island in 1627. Slaves worked the sugar plantations, but were freed in 1834.

Self-rule came gradually, with full independence proclaimed Nov. 30, 1966. British traditions have remained.

Belgium

Kingdom of Belgium

People: Population (1984 est.): 9,872,000. **Age distrib. (%):** 0–14: 20.0; 15–59: 61.4; 60+: 18.6 **Pop. density:** 836 per sq. mi. **Urban** (1980): 73%. **Ethnic groups:** Flemings 58%, Walloons 41%. **Languages:** Flemish (Dutch) 57%, French 33%, legally bilingual 10%, German 1%. **Religions:** Roman Catholic 75%, Protestant.

Geography: Area: 11,779 sq. mi., slightly larger than Maryland. **Location:** In NW Europe, on N. Sea. **Neighbors:** France on W, S, Luxembourg on SE, W. Germany on E, Netherlands on N. **Topography:** Mostly flat, the country is trisected by the Scheldt and Meuse, major commercial rivers. The land becomes hilly and forested in the SE (Ardennes) region. **Capital:** Brussels. **Cities** (1983 est.): Brussels (Met.) 989,877; Antwerp (met.) 490,524; Ghent 236,540; Charleroi 216,144; Liege 207,496.

Government: Type: Parliamentary democracy under a constitutional monarch. **Head of state:** King Baudouin; b. Sept. 7, 1930; in office: July 17, 1951. **Head of government:** Premier Wilfried Martens; b. Apr. 19, 1936; in office: Dec. 17, 1981. **Local divisions:** 9 provinces; 589 communes. **Defense:** 5.8% of govt. budget (1983).

Economy: Industries: Steel, glassware, diamond cutting, textiles, chemicals. **Chief crops:** Grains, barley, potatoes, sugar beets. **Minerals:** Coal, coke. **Other resources:** Forests. **Arable land** (incl. Lux.): 26.5%. **Meat prod.** (1983): beef: 290,000 metric tons; pork: 650,000 metric tons. **Fish catch** (1981): 49,000 metric tons. **Electricity prod.** (1982): 50.6 bln. kwh. **Crude steel prod.** (1982): 9.9 mln. metric tons. **Labor force:** 3% agric.; 33% ind. & comm.; 36% services; 21% public service.

Finance: Currency: Franc (Mar. 1985: 62.07 = $1 US). **Gross national product** (1983): $81 bln. **Per capita income** (1981): $9,827. *Note:* the following trade and tourist data includes Luxembourg. **Imports** (1983): $55.3 bln.; partners: W. Ger. 20%, Neth. 18%, France 14%, UK 7%, U.S. 7%. **Exports** (1983): $51.9 bln.; partners: W. Ger. 20%, France 19%, Neth. 14%, UK 10%. **Tourists** (1981): receipts: $1.5 bln. **National budget** (1983): $31.20 bln. **International reserves less gold** (Mar. 1985): $4.66 bln. **Gold:** 34.18 mln. oz t. **Consumer prices** (change in 1984): 6.3%.

Transport: Railway traffic (1982): 6.9 bln. passenger-km; 6.7 bln. net ton-km. **Motor vehicles:** in use (1983): 3.2 mln. passenger cars, 288,000 comm. vehicles; assembled (1978): 1.01 mln. passenger cars; 18,744 comm. vehicles. **Civil aviation** (1982): 5.2 bln. passenger-km; 492 mln. freight ton-km. **Chief ports:** Antwerp, Zeebrugge, Ghent.

Communications: Television sets: 2.9 mln. licensed (1983). **Radios:** 4.6 mln. licensed (1983); **Telephones in use** (1982): 3.8 mln. **Daily newspaper circ.** (1982): 314 per 1,000 pop.

Health: Life expectancy at birth (1980): 68.6 male; 75.1 female. **Births** (per 1,000 pop. 1982): 12.2. **Deaths** (per 1,000 pop. 1982): 11.1. **Natural increase** (1982) .01%. **Hospital beds** (1981): 92,436. **Physicians:** 25,629. **Infant mortality** (per 1,000 live births 1982): 11.7.

Education (1983): Literacy: 98%. School compulsory to age 16.

Major International Organizations: UN and its specialized agencies, NATO, EC, OECD.

Embassy: 3330 Garfield St. NW 20008; 333-6900

Belgium derives its name from the Belgae, the first recorded inhabitants, probably Celts. The land was conquered by Julius Caesar, and was ruled for 1800 years by conquerors, including Rome, the Franks, Burgundy, Spain, Austria, and France. After 1815, Belgium was made a part of the Netherlands, but it became an independent constitutional monarchy in 1830.

Belgian neutrality was violated by Germany in both world wars. King Leopold III surrendered to Germany, May 28, 1940. After the war, he was forced by political pressure to abdicate in favor of his son, King Baudouin.

The Flemings of northern Belgium speak Dutch while French is the language of the Walloons in the south. The language difference has been a perennial source of controversy. Antagonism between the 2 groups has continued.

Belgium lives by its foreign trade; about 50% of its entire production is sold abroad.

Belize

People: Population (1984 est.): 158,000. **Age distrib. (%):** 0–14: 46.1; 15–64: 49.2; 65+: 4.7. **Pop. density:** 17.8 per sq. mi. **Ethnic groups:** African, Mestizo, Amerindian, Creole. **Languages:** English (official), Spanish, native Creole dialects. **Religions:** Roman Catholic 66%, Methodist 13%, Anglican 13%.

Geography: Area: 8,867 sq. mi. **Location:** eastern coast of Central America. **Neighbors:** Mexico on N., Guatemala on W. and S. **Capital:** Belmopan. **Cities:** (1984 est.): Belize City 40,000.

Government: Type: Parliamentary. **Head of State:** Gov. Gen. Minita Gordon. **Head of government:** Prime Min. Manual Esquivel; b. 1940; in office: Dec. 17, 1984. **Local divisions:** 6 districts.

Economy: Sugar is the main export.

Finance: Currency: Belize dollar (Mar. 1985) 2 = $1 U.S. **Gross domestic product** (1983): 176 mln. **Per capita income** (1984): $1,000. **Imports** (1983) $113 mln.; partners: U.S. 42%, UK 15%. **Exports:** (1983): 77 mln.; partners: U.S. 47%, UK 44%. **National Budget** (1984): $67.3 mln.

Health: life expectancy (1981) 60 yrs. **Births** (per 1,000 pop. 1981): 40.7. **Deaths** (per 1,000 pop. 1981): 4.8. **Hospital beds:** 578; **Physicians:** 75 (1983). **Infant mortality** (per 1,000 live births, 1984): 56.

Education: (1985) **Literacy:** 80%.; **Years compulsory:** 9; attendance 55%.

Major International Organizations: UN and its specialized agencies, Commonwealth of Nations.

Embassy: 1575 I St. NW 20005; 289-1416.

Belize (formerly called British Honduras), Great Britain's last colony on the American mainland, achieved independence on Sept. 21, 1981. Guatemala claims territorial sovereignty over the country and has refused to recognize Belize's independence. There are 1,600 British troops in Belize to guarantee security.

Benin

People's Republic of Benin

People: Population (1984 est.): 3,910,000. **Age distrib. (%):** 0–14: 46.1; 15–59: 48.3; 60+: 5.6. **Pop. density:** 83.3 per sq. mi. **Urban** (1984): 20%. **Ethnic groups:** Fons, Adjas, Baribas, Yorubas. **Languages:** French (official), local dialects. **Religions:** Mainly animist with Christian, Muslim minorities.

Geography: Area: 43,483 sq. mi., slightly smaller than Pennsylvania. **Location:** In W Africa on Gulf of Guinea. **Neighbors:** Togo on W, Upper Volta, Niger on N, Nigeria on E. **Topography:** most of Benin is flat and covered with dense vegetation. The coast is hot, humid, and rainy. **Capital:** Porto–Novo. **Cities** (1984 est.): Cotonou 330,000.

Government: Type: Marxist-Leninist. **Head of state:** Pres. Ahmed Kerekou; b. Sept. 2, 1933; in office: Oct. 27, 1972. **Local divisions:** 6 provinces, 84 districts. **Defense:** 17% of govt. budget (1983).

Economy: Chief crops: Palm products, peanuts, cotton, kapok, coffee, tobacco. **Minerals:** Oil. **Arable land:** 16%. **Fish catch** (1980): 25,500 metric tons. **Electricity prod.** (1982): 5 mln. kwh. **Labor force:** 60% agric; 30% serv. & comm.

Finance: Currency: CFA franc (Mar. 1985: 471.35 = $1 US). **Gross domestic product** (1980): $1.0 bln. **Per capita income** (1982): $310. **Imports** (1982): $590 mln.; partners: Fr. 27%, UK 13%, W. Ger. 6%, Neth. 6%. **Exports** (1982): $304 mln.; partners: Neth. 28%, Jap. 27%, Fr. 24%. **International reserves less gold** (Jan. 1985): $2.5 mln.

Transport: Railway traffic (1981): 187.6 mln. passenger-km; 176 mln. net ton-km. **Motor vehicles:** in use (1981): 10,000 passenger cars, 7,500 comm. vehicles. **Chief ports:** Cotonou.

Communications: Radios: 68,000 in use (1983). **Daily newspaper circ.** (1983): 3 per 1,000 pop.

Health: Life expectancy at birth (1984): 46.9 yrs. **Births** (per 1,000 pop. 1981): 49. **Deaths** (per 1,000 pop. 1981): 17.1. **Natural increase** (1981): 3.1%. **Hospital beds** (per 100,000 pop. 1977): 137. **Physicians** (per 100,000 pop. 1977): 3. **Infant mortality** (per 1,000 live births 1982): 150.

Education (1984): **Literacy:** 11%. **Years compulsory** 6; attendance 43%.

Major International Organizations: UN and its specialized agencies, OAU.

Embassy: 2737 Cathedral Ave. NW 20008; 232-6656.

The Kingdom of Abomey, rising to power in wars with neighboring kingdoms in the 17th century, came under French domination in the late 19th century, and was incorporated into French West Africa by 1904.

Under the name Dahomey, the country became independent Aug. 1, 1960. The name was changed to Benin in 1975. In the fifth coup since independence Col. Ahmed Kerekou took power in 1972; two years later he declared a socialist state with a "Marxist-Leninist" philosophy. The economy relies on the development of agriculturally-based industries.

Bhutan
Kingdom of Bhutan

People: Population (1984 est.): 1,417,000. **Pop. density:** 91.8 per sq. mi. **Ethnic groups:** Bhotia (Tibetan) 60%. Nepalese 25%, Lepcha (indigenous), Indians. **Languages:** Dzongkha (official), Nepali. **Religions:** Buddhist 70%, Hindu 25%.

Geography: Area: 17,800 sq. mi., the size of Vermont and New Hampshire combined. **Location:** In eastern Himalayan Mts. **Neighbors:** India on W (Sikkim) and S, China on N. **Topography:** Bhutan is comprised of very high mountains in the N, fertile valleys in the center, and thick forests in the Duar Plain in the S. **Capital:** Thimphu. **City** (1982 est.): Thimphu 15,000.

Government: Type: Monarchy. **Head of state:** King Jigme Singye Wangchuk; b. Nov. 11, 1955; in office: July 21, 1972. **Local divisions:** 4 regions comprised of 17 districts.

Economy: Industries: Handicrafts. **Chief crops:** Rice, corn, wheat. **Other resources:** Timber. **Arable land:** 2%. **Labor force:** 95% agric.

Finance: Currency: Ngultrum (Oct. 1983: 10.21 = 1 US) (Indian Rupee also used). **Gross national product** (1981): $113 mln. **Per capita income** (1981): $100. **Imports** (1981): $19 mln.; partners India 99%. **Exports** (1982): $12 mln.; partners India 99%.

Communications: Radios: 12,000 licensed (1982). **Telephones in use** (1982): 14,000.

Health: Life expectancy at birth (1983): 46 male; 44.5 female. **Births** (per 1,000 pop. 1983): 39.3. **Deaths** (per 1,000 pop. 1983): 18. **Natural Increase** (1983): 2.1%. **Hospital beds** (1979): 536. **Physicians** (1979): 52.

Education (1983): **Literacy:** 5%.

Major International Organizations: UN and its specialized agencies.

The region came under Tibetan rule in the 16th century. British influence grew in the 19th century. A monarchy, set up in 1907, became a British protectorate by a 1910 treaty. The country became independent in 1949, with India guiding foreign relations and supplying aid.

Links to India have been strengthened by airline service and a road network. Most of the population engages in subsistence agriculture.

Bolivia
Republic of Bolivia

People: Population (1984 est.): 6,037,000. **Age distrib. (%):** 0–14: 41.9; 15–59: 52.0; 60+: 6.4. **Pop. density:** 14.7 per sq. mi. **Ethnic groups:** Quechua 30%, Aymara 25%, Mestizo (cholo) 25-30%, European 5-15%. **Languages:** Spanish (official), Quechua, Aymara. **Religions:** Roman Catholic 95%.

Geography: Area: 424,165 sq. mi., the size of Texas and California combined. **Location:** In central Andes Mts. **Neighbors:** Peru, Chile on W, Argentina, Paraguay on S, Brazil on E and N. **Topography:** The great central plateau, at an altitude of 12,000 ft., over 500 mi. long, lies between two great cordilleras having 3 of the highest peaks in S. America. Lake Titicaca, on Peruvian border, is highest lake in world on which steamboats ply (12,506 ft.). The E central region has semitropical forests; the llanos, or Amazon-Chaco lowlands are in E. **Capitals:** Sucre, (legal), La Paz (de facto). **Cities** (1984 est.): La Paz 953,400; Santa Cruz 419,000; Cochabamba 304,000.

Government: Type: Republic. **Head of state:** Pres. Hernan Siles Zuazo; in office: Oct. 10, 1982. **Local divisions:** 9 departments, 94 provinces.

Economy: Industry: Textiles, food processing, chemicals, plastics. **Chief crops:** Potatoes, sugar, coffee, barley, cocoa, rice, corn, bananas, citrus. **Minerals:** Antimony, tin, tungsten, silver, zinc, oil, gas, iron. **Crude oil reserves** (1980): 150 mln. bbls. **Other resources:** rubber, cinchona bark. **Arable land:** 3%. **Electricity prod.** (1982): 1.7 bln. kwh. **Labor force:** 47% agric., 19% ind. & comm, 34% serv. & govt.

Finance: Currency: Peso (Mar. 1985: 9,000 = $1 US). **Gross domestic product** (1982): $5.4 bln. **Per capita income** (1982): $570. **Imports** (1982): $522 mln.; partners: U.S. 29%, Jap. 5.4%, Arg. 14%, Braz. 10%. **Exports** (1982): $832 mln.; partners: U.S. 27%, Arg. 51%. **National budget** (1980): $3.8 bln. revenues; $4.7 bln. expenditures. **International reserves less gold** (Mar. 1985): $196 mln. **Gold:** 894,000 oz t. **Consumer prices** (change in 1984): 1,500+.

Transport: Railway traffic (1982): 482 mln. passenger-km; 620 mln. net ton-miles. **Motor vehicles** in use (1982): 40,000 passenger cars, 36,000 comm. vehicles. **Civil aviation** (1983): 786 mln. passenger-km.; 17.8 mln. freight ton-km.

Communications: Television sets: 386,000 (1983). **Radios:** 480,000 in use (1983). **Telephones in use** (1982): 144,000. **Daily newspaper circ.** (1983): 32 per 1,000 pop.

Health: Life expectancy at birth (1983): 49 yrs. **Births** (per 1,000 pop. 1980): 24.9. **Deaths** (per 1,000 pop. 1980): 4.8. **Natural increase** (1980): 2.0%. **Hospital beds** (per 100,000 pop. 1977): 228. **Physicians** (per 100,000 pop. 1977): 38. **Infant mortality** (per 1,000 live births 1983): 142.

Education (1983): **Literacy:** 75%. **Years compulsory:** ages 7-14; attendance 60%.

Major International Organizations: UN and its specialized agencies, OAS.

Embassy: 3014 Massachusetts Ave. NW 20008; 483-4410.

The Incas conquered the region from earlier Indian inhabitants in the 13th century. Spanish rule began in the 1530s, and lasted until Aug. 6, 1825. The country is named after Simon Bolivar, independence fighter.

In a series of wars, Bolivia lost its Pacific coast to Chile, the oilbearing Chaco to Paraguay, and rubber-growing areas to Brazil, 1879-1935.

Economic unrest, especially among the militant mine workers, has contributed to continuing political instability. A reformist government under Victor Paz Estenssoro, 1951-64, nationalized tin mines and attempted to improve conditions for the Indian majority, but was overthrown by a military junta. A series of coups and countercoups continued through 1981, until the military junta elected Gen. Villa as president.

In July 1982, the military junta assumed power amid a growing economic crisis and foreign debt difficulties. The junta resigned in October and allowed the Congress, elected democratically in 1980, to take power. The Congress elected Hernan Siles Zuazo to a 4-year term as president.

In 1985, Bolivia had the highest inflation rate in the world and $4.1 billion in outstanding debt. There were 2 unsuccessful coups in Jan. and a general strike in Mar.

Botswana
Republic of Botswana

People: Population (1984 est.): 1,038,000. **Age distrib. (%):** 0–14: 46.1; 15–59: 43.1; 60+: 7.4. **Pop. density:** 4.9 per sq. mi. **Urban** (1984): 17%. **Ethnic groups:** Batswana, others. **Languages:** English (official), Setswana (national). **Religions:** indigenous beliefs (majority), Christian 15%.

Geography: Area: 231,804 sq. mi., slightly smaller than Texas. **Location:** In southern Africa. **Neighbors:** Namibia (S.W. Africa) on N and W, S. Africa on S, Zimbabwe on NE; Botswana claims border with Zambia on N. **Topography:** The Kalahari Desert, supporting nomadic Bushmen and wildlife, spreads over SW; there are swamplands and farming areas in N, and rolling plains in E where livestock are grazed. **Capital:** Gaborone. **Cities** (1984): Gaborone 79,000.

Government: Type: Republic, parliamentary democracy. **Head of state:** Pres. Quett Masire; b. 1925; in office: July 13,

1980. Local divisions: 9 districts and 4 independent towns, all with local councils. **Defense:** 2.7% of GNP (1982).
Economy: Industries: Tourism. **Chief crops:** Corn, sorghum, peanuts. **Minerals:** Copper, coal, nickel, diamonds. **Other resources:** Big game. **Arable land:** 2%. **Electricity prod.** (1982): 604 mln. kwh. **Labor force:** 70% agric.
Finance: Currency: Pula (Mar. 1985: 0.42 = $1 US). **Gross domestic product** (1982): $620 mln. **Per capita income** (1978): $544. **Imports** (1981): $610 mln.; partners: S. Africa 88%. **Exports** (1981): $504 mln.; partners: Europe 67%, U.S. 17%, S. Africa 7%. **National budget** (1980): $221 mln. **International reserves less gold** (Mar. 1985): $505 mln. **Consumer prices** (change in 1984): 7.4%
Transport: Railway traffic (1982): 1.2 bln. net ton km. **Motor vehicles:** in use (1983): 11,000 passenger cars, 20,500 comm. vehicles.
Communications: Radios: 75,000 in use (1983). **Daily newspaper circ.** (1983): 19 per 1,000 pop.
Health: Life expectancy at birth (1980): 56.0 male; 62.0 female. **Births** (annual per 1,000 pop. 1984): 50.5. **Deaths** (per 1,000 pop. 1984): 15.6. **Natural increase** (1984): 3.4%. **Hospital beds** (per 100,000 pop. 1980): 970. **Physicians** (per 100,000 pop. 1977): 14.
Education (1983): **Literacy:** 30%.
Major International Organizations: UN and its specialized agencies, OAU, Commonwealth of Nations.
Embassy: 4301 Connecticut Ave. NW 20008; 244-4990.

First inhabited by bushmen, then by Bantus, the region became the British protectorate of Bechuanaland in 1886, halting encroachment by Boers and Germans from the south and southwest. The country became fully independent Sept. 30, 1966, changing its name to Botswana.
Cattle-raising and mining (diamonds, copper, nickel) have contributed to the country's economic growth.

Brazil
Federative Republic of Brazil

People: Population (1984 est.): 134,380,000. **Age distrib.** (%): 0–14: 39.1; 15–59: 55.0; 60+: 5.9. **Pop. density:** 40.6 per sq. mi. **Urban** (1981): 56%. **Ethnic groups:** Portuguese, Africans, and mulattoes make up the vast majority; Italians, Germans, Japanese, Indians, Jews, Arabs. **Languages:** Portuguese (official), English. **Religions:** Roman Catholic 89%.
Geography: Area: 3,286,470 sq. mi., larger than contiguous 48 U.S. states; largest country in S. America. **Location:** Occupies eastern half of S. America. **Neighbors:** French Guiana, Suriname, Guyana, Venezuela on N, Colombia, Peru, Bolivia, Paraguay, Argentina on W, Uruguay on S. **Topography:** Brazil's Atlantic coastline stretches 4,603 miles. In N is the heavily-wooded Amazon basin covering half the country. Its network of rivers navigable for 15,814 mi. The Amazon itself flows 2,093 miles in Brazil, all navigable. The NE region is semiarid scrubland, heavily settled and poor. The S central region, favored by climate and resources, has 45% of the population, produces 75% of farm goods and 80% of industrial output. The narrow coastal belt includes most of the major cities. Almost the entire country has a tropical or semitropical climate. **Capital:** Brasília. **Cities** (1980 cen.): Sao Paulo 7 mln.; Rio de Janeiro 5 mln.; Belo Horizonte 1.4 mln.; Recife 1.1 mln.; Salvador 1.4 mln.; Porto Alegre 1.1 mln.
Government: Type: Federal Republic. **Head of state:** Pres. Jose Sarney; b. Apr. 30, 1930; in office: Apr. 22, 1985. **Local divisions:** 23 states, with individual constitutions and elected governments; 3 territories, federal district. **Defense:** 7% of govt. budget (1981).
Economy: Industries: Steel, autos, chemicals, ships, appliances, shoes, paper, petrochemicals, machinery. **Chief crops:** Coffee (largest grower), cotton, soybeans, sugar, cocoa, rice, corn, fruits. **Minerals:** Chromium, iron, manganese, tin, quartz crystals, beryl, sheet mica, columbium, titanium, diamonds, thorium, gold, nickel, gem stones, coal, tin, tungsten, bauxite, oil. **Crude oil reserves** (1980): 1.22 bln. bbls. **Arable land:** 9%. **Meat prod.** (1983): beef: 2.5 mln. metric tons; pork: 970 metric tons; lamb: 52,000 metric tons. **Fish catch** (1983): 900,000 metric tons. **Electricity prod.** (1982): 152.0 bln. kwh. **Crude steel prod.** (1982): 12.8 mln. metric tons. **Labor force:** 41% service, 36% agric.; 23% ind.

Finance: Currency: Cruzeiro (Mar. 1985: 4,450 = $1 US). **Gross domestic product** (1982): $190 bln. **Per capita income** (1978): $1,523. **Imports** (1983): $15.4 bln.; partners: U.S. 15%, Iraq 19%, Sau. Ar. 15%, Jap. 5%. **Exports** (1984): $26.9 bln.; partners: U.S. 20%, W. Ger. 6%, Neth. 6%, Japan 7%. **Tourists** (1980): 1.2 mln.; receipts: $182 mln. **National budget** (1979): $18.91 mln. revenues; $18.83 bln. expenditures. **International reserves less gold** (Jan. 1985): $9.8 bln. **Gold:** 2.5 mln. oz t. **Consumer prices** (change in 1984): 196.7%.
Transport: Railway traffic (1982): 8.2 bln. passenger-km; 77 bln. net ton-km. **Motor vehicles:** in use (1982): 9.9 mln. passenger cars, 1.4 mln. comm. vehicles; manuf. (1982): 659,000 passenger cars; 143,000 comm. vehicles. **Civil aviation** (1982): 16.3 bln. passenger-km: 670 mln. freight ton-km: **Chief ports:** Santos, Rio de Janeiro, Vitoria, Salvador, Rio Grande, Recife.
Communications: Television sets: 25 mln. in use (1983). **Radios:** 85 mln. in use (1983). **Telephones in use** (1982): 8.5 mln. **Daily newspaper circ.** (1982): 44 per 1,000 pop.
Health: Life expectancy at birth (1981): 61.6 male; 65.7 female. **Births** (per 1,000 pop. 1981): 30.5. **Deaths** (per 1,000 pop. 1981): 8.2. **Natural increase** (1981): 2.2%. **Hospital beds** (1980): 488,323. **Physicians** (per 100,000 pop. 1980): 68.1. **Infant mortality** (per 1,000 live births 1981): 92.
Education (1983): **Literacy:** 75%.
Major International Organizations: UN and its specialized agencies, OAS.
Embassy: 3006 Massachusetts Ave. NW 20008; 797-0100.

Pedro Alvares Cabral, a Portuguese navigator, is generally credited as the first European to reach Brazil, in 1500. The country was thinly settled by various Indian tribes. Only a few have survived to the present, mostly in the Amazon basin.
In the next centuries, Portuguese colonists gradually pushed inland, bringing along large numbers of African slaves. Slavery was not abolished until 1888.
The King of Portugal, fleeing before Napoleon's army, moved the seat of government to Brazil in 1808. Brazil thereupon became a kingdom under Dom Joao VI. After his return to Portugal, his son Pedro proclaimed the independence of Brazil, Sept. 7, 1822, and was acclaimed emperor. The second emperor, Dom Pedro II, was deposed in 1889, and a republic proclaimed, called the United States of Brazil. In 1967 the country was renamed the Federative Republic of Brazil.
A military junta took control in 1930; dictatorial power was assumed by Getulio Vargas, who alternated with military coups until finally forced out by the military in 1954. A democratic regime prevailed 1956-64, during which time the capital was moved from Rio de Janeiro to Brasilia in the interior.
The next 5 presidents were all military leaders. Censorship was imposed, and much of the opposition was suppressed amid charges of torture. In 1974 elections, the official opposition party made gains in the chamber of deputies; some relaxation of censorship occurred, though church liberals, labor leaders, and intellectuals continued to report cases of arrest and torture.
Since 1930, successive governments have pursued industrial and agricultural growth and the development of interior areas. Exploiting vast mineral resources, fertile soil in several regions, and a huge labor force, Brazil became the leading industrial power of Latin America by the 1970s, while agricultural output soared. The 1979 government declared an amnesty and enacted democratic reforms.
However, income maldistribution, inflation and government land policies have all led to severe economic recession. Foreign debt was $100 bln. in 1985, the largest in the world.

Brunei

People: Population (1984 est.): 218,000. **Ethnic groups:** Malay 62%, Chinese 20%, Indian 3%. **Language:** Malay (official), English. **Religion:** Muslim 64%, Buddhist 14%, Christian 10%.
Geography: Area: 2,226 sq. mi. **Location:** on the north coast of the island of Borneo; it is surrounded on its landward side by the Malaysian state of Sarawak. **Capital:** Bandar Seri Begawan. **Cities** (1982 est.): Bandar Seri Begawan 51,000.
Government: Type: Independent sultanate. **Head of Government:** Sultan Sir Muda Hassanal Bolkiah Mu'izzadin Waddaulah; in office: Jan. 1, 1984.
Economy: Industries: petroleum (about 90% of revenue is derived from oil exports). **Chief crops:** rice, bananas, cassava

Finance: Currency: Brunei dollar (Oct 1984: 2.15 = $1).
Communications: Television sets: 32,000 (1982). Radios:
38,000 (1982). Telephones: 21,928 (1982).

The Sultanate of Brunei was a powerful state in the early 16th
century with authority over all of the island of Borneo as well as
parts of the Sulu Islands and the Philippines. In 1888, a treaty
was signed which placed the state under the protection of Great
Britain.

Brunei became a fully sovereign and independent state at the
end of 1983.

Bulgaria
People's Republic of Bulgaria

People: Population (1984 est.): 8,969,000. Age distrib. (%):
0–14: 22.3; 15–59: 61.7; 60+: 16.0. Pop. density: 209 per sq.
mi. Urban (1983): 64%. Ethnic groups: Bulgarians 85%, Turks
8.5%. Languages: Bulgarian, Turkish, Greek. Religions: Orthodox 85%, Moslem 13%.

Geography: Area: 44,365 sq. mi., about the size of Ohio. Location: In eastern Balkan Peninsula on Black Sea. Neighbors:
Romania on N, Yugoslavia on W, Greece, Turkey on S. Topography: The Stara Planina (Balkan) Mts. stretch E-W across the
center of the country, with the Danubian plain on N, the Rhodope
Mts. on SW, and Thracian Plain on SE. Capital: Sofia. Cities
(1981 est.): Sofia 1,070,000; Plovdiv 307,414; Varna 257,731.

Government: Type: Communist. Head of state: Pres. Todor
Zhivkov; b. Sept. 7, 1911; in office: July 7, 1971. Head of government: Premier Grisha Filipov; in office: June 16, 1981. Head
of Communist Party: First Sec. Todor Zhivkov; b. 1911; in office: Jan. 1954. Local divisions: 27 provinces, one city. Defense: 10% of GNP (1982).

Economy: Industries: Chemicals, machinery, metals, textiles,
fur, leather goods, vehicles, wine, processed food. Chief crops:
Grains, fruit, corn, potatoes, tobacco. Minerals: Lead, bauxite,
coal, oil, zinc. Arable land: 38%. Meat prod. (1983): beef:
130,000 metric tons; pork: 359,000 metric tons; lamb: 101,000
metric tons. Fish catch (1980): 140,000 metric tons. Electricity
prod. (1982): 40.4 bln. kwh. Crude steel prod. (1982): 2.5 mln.
metric tons. Labor force: 23% agric.; 42% Ind. & comm.

Finance: Currency: Lev (Oct. 1984: 1.08 = $1 US). Gross
National Product (1982): $26 bln. Per capita income (1980):
$2,625. Imports (1982): $11.3 bln.; partners: USSR 54%, E.
Ger. 6%, W. Ger. 5%. Exports (1982): $11.2 bln.; partners:
USSR 48%, E. Ger. 6%. Tourists (1982): 5.6 mln: revenues
$260 min.

Transport: Railway traffic (1982): 8.0 bln. passenger-km; 1
bln. net ton-km. Motor vehicles: in use (1980) 815,549 passenger cars, 130,000 commercial; manuf. (1977): 15,000 passenger
cars, 6,900 comm. vehicles. Chief ports: Burgas, Varna.

Communications: Television sets: 1.6 mln. licensed (1983).
Radios: 2.1 mln. licensed (1983). Telephones in use (1983):
1.5 mln. Daily newspaper circ. (1982): 245 per 1,000 pop.

Health: Life expectancy at birth (1983): 69 male; 74 female.
Births (per 1,000 pop. 1981): 14.0. Deaths (per 1,000 pop.
1981): 10.7. Hospital beds (1983): 81,000. Physicians: 23,100.
Infant mortality (per 1,000 live births 1983): 20.2

Education (1983): Literacy: 95%. Years compulsory: 8.

Major International Organizations: UN and its specialized
agencies, Warsaw Pact.

Embassy: 1621-22d St. NW 20008; 387-7969.

Bulgaria was settled by Slavs in the 6th century. Turkic Bulgars arrived in the 7th century, merged with the Slavs, became
Christians by the 9th century, and set up powerful empires in the
10th and 12th centuries. The Ottomans prevailed in 1396 and
remained for 500 years.

A revolt in 1876 led to an independent kingdom in 1908. Bulgaria expanded after the first Balkan War but lost its Aegean
coastline in World War I, when it sided with Germany. Bulgaria
joined the Axis in World War II, but withdrew in 1944. Communists took power with Soviet aid; the monarchy was abolished
Sept. 8, 1946.

The U.S. and Italy have asserted that Bulgaria was involved in
the May 1981 shooting of Pope John Paul II.

Burkina Faso
Republic of Burkina Faso

People: Population (1984 est.): 6,733,000. Pop. density: 64
per sq. mi. Ethnic groups: Voltaic groups (Mossi, Bobo),
Mande. Languages: French (official), More, Sudanic tribal languages. Religions: animist 50%, Moslems 16%, Roman Catholics 8%, others.

Geography: Area: 105,869 sq. mi., the size of Colorado. Location: In W. Africa, S of the Sahara. Neighbors: Mali on NW,
Niger on NE, Benin, Togo, Ghana, Ivory Coast on S. Topography: Landlocked Burkina Faso is in the savannah region of W.
Africa. The N is arid, hot, and thinly populated. Capital: Ouagadougou. Cities (1984): Ouagadougou 236,000; Bobo-Dioulasso
140,000.

Government: Type: Republic. Head of state: Pres. Thomas
Sankara; b. 1948; in office: Aug. 4, 1983. Local divisions: 10
departments. Defense: 17.8% of govt. budget. (1982).

Economy: Chief crops: Millet, sorghum, rice, peanuts, grain.
Minerals: Manganese, gold, diamonds. Arable land: 10%. Meat
prod. (1980): beef: 29,000 metric tons; lamb: 8,000 metric tons.
Electricity prod. (1980): 140 mln. kwh. Labor force: 83%
agric.; 12% industry.

Finance: Currency: CFA franc (Mar. 1985: 471.00 = $1 US).
Gross domestic product (1981 est.): $1.2 bln. Per capita in-
come (1981): $180. Imports (1981): $325 mln.; partners: EC,
Ivory Coast. Exports (1981): $73 mln.; partners: Ivory Coast,
EC, China. International reserves less gold (Jan. 1985):
$106.3 mln. Gold: 11,000 oz t. Consumer prices (change in
1984): 4.8%.

Transport: Motor vehicles: in use (1982): 16,000 passenger
cars, 15,000 comm. vehicles.

Communications: Television sets: 15,000 in use (1983).
Radios: 116,000 in use (1983). Telephones in use (1981):
10,000. Daily newspaper circ. (1982): 2 per 1,000 pop.

Health: Life expectancy at birth (1984): 42 yrs. Births (per
1,000 pop. 1981): 47.8. Deaths (per 1,000 pop. 1981): 21.5.
Natural increase (1981): 2.3%. Hospital beds (1980): 4,587.
Physicians (1980): 131. Infant mortality (per 1,000 live births
1984): 182.

Education (1984): Literacy: 7%. Only 8% attend school.

Major International Organizations: UN and its specialized
agencies, OAU.

Embassy: 2340 Massachusetts Ave. NW 20008; 332-5577.

The Mossi tribe entered the area in the 11th to 13th centuries.
Their kingdoms ruled until defeated by the Mali and Songhai empires.

French control came by 1896, but Upper Volta (name
changed to Burkina Faso on Aug. 4, 1984), was not finally established as a separate territory until 1947. Full independence
came Aug. 5, 1960, and a pro-French government was elected.
A 1982 coup established the current regime.

Several hundred thousand farm workers migrate each year to
Ivory Coast and Ghana. Droughts brought famine in the 1970s.
Burkina Faso is heavily dependent on foreign aid.

Burma
Socialist Republic of the Union of Burma

People: Population (1984 est.): 36,196,000. Age distrib.
(%): 0–14: 40.5; 15–59: 53.5; 60+: 6.0. Pop. density: 139.2 per
sq. mi. Ethnic groups: Burmans (related to Tibetans) 72%; Karen 7%, Shan 6%, Indians 6%, others. Languages: Burmese
(official). Religions: Buddhist 85%; Animists, Christians.

Geography: Area: 261,288 sq. mi., nearly as large as Texas.
Location: Between S. and S.E. Asia, on Bay of Bengal. Neighbors: Bangladesh, India on W, China, Laos, Thailand on E. Topography: Mountains surround Burma on W, N, and E, and
dense forests cover much of the nation. N-S rivers provide habitable valleys and communications, especially the Irrawaddy, navigable for 900 miles. The country has a tropical monsoon climate.
Capital: Rangoon. Cities (1983 est.): Rangoon 2,458,712;

Mandalay 458,000; Karbe ('73 cen.): 253,600; Moulmein 188,000.

Government: Type: Socialist Republic. **Head of state:** Pres. U San Yu in office: Nov. 9, 1981. **Head of government:** Prime Min. U. Maung Maung Kha; b. Nov. 2, 1917; in office: Mar. 29, 1977. **Local divisions:** 7 states and 7 divisions. **Defense:** 3.4% of GDP (1982).

Economy: Chief crops: Rice, sugarcane, peanuts, beans. **Minerals:** Oil, lead, silver, tin, tungsten, precious stones. **Crude oil reserves** (1980): 25 mln. bbls. **Other resources:** Rubber, teakwood. **Arable land:** 15%. **Meat prod.** (1980): beef: 94,000 metric tons; pork: 81,000 metric tons; lamb: 4,000 metric tons. **Fish catch** (1982): 585,000 metric tons. **Electricity prod.** (1982): 1.7 bln. kwh. **Labor force:** 67% agric; 9% ind.

Finance: Currency: Kyat (Mar. 1985: 8.70 = $1 US). **Gross domestic product** (1982): $5.9 bln. **Per capita income** (1981): $174. **Imports** (1982): $863 mln.; partners: Jap. 34%, U.S. 12%, UK 9%, W. Ger. 9%. **Exports** (1982): $390 mln.; partners: Switz. 12%, Sing. 10%. **National budget** (1983): $4.4 bln. **International reserves less gold** (Mar. 1985): $45.8 mln. **Gold:** 251,000 oz t. **Consumer prices** (change in 1984): 4.8%.

Transport: Railway traffic (1982): 3.1 bln. passenger-km; 698 mln. net ton-km. **Motor vehicles:** in use (1980): 43,000 passenger cars, 44,000 comm. vehicles. **Civil aviation** (1982): 199 mln. passenger-km.; 1.2 mln. net ton-km. **Chief ports:** Rangoon, Sittwe, Bassein, Moulmein, Tavoy.

Communications: Radios: 1.6 mln. in use (1982). **Telephones in use** (1983): 49,000. **Daily newspaper circ.** (1983): 15 per 1,000 pop.

Health: Life expectancy at birth (1982): 51.4 male; 54.5 female. **Births** (per 1,000 pop. 1982): 34. **Deaths** (per 1,000 pop. 1982): 14. **Natural increase** (1982): 2.0%. **Hospital beds** (per 100,000 pop. 1977): 89. **Physicians** (per 100,000 pop. 1977): 19. **Infant mortality** (per 1,000 live births 1982): 100.

Education (1984): **Literacy:** 78%. **Years compulsory:** 4; **Attendance:** 90%.

Major International Organizations: UN and its specialized agencies.

Embassy: 2300 S St. NW 20008; 332-9044.

The Burmese arrived from Tibet before the 9th century, displacing earlier cultures, and a Buddhist monarchy was established by the 11th. Burma was conquered by the Mongol dynasty of China in 1272, then ruled by Shans as a Chinese tributary, until the 16th century.

Britain subjugated Burma in 3 wars, 1824-84, and ruled the country as part of India until 1937, when it became self-governing. Independence outside the Commonwealth was achieved Jan. 4, 1948.

Gen. Ne Win dominated politics during the 1960s and 1970s. He led a Revolutionary Council set up in 1962, which drove Indians from the civil service and Chinese from commerce. Socialization of the economy was advanced, isolation from foreign countries enforced. Lagging production and export have begun to turn around, due to government incentives in the agriculture and petroleum sectors and receptivity to foreign investment in the economy.

Burundi
Republic of Burundi

People: Population (1984 est.): 4,691,000. **Age distrib.** (%): 0–14: 44.1; 15–59: 51.9; 60+: 4.1. **Pop. density:** 465 per sq. mi. **Urban** (1981): 2.3%. **Ethnic groups:** Hutu 85%, Tutsi 14%, Twa (pygmy) 1%. **Languages:** French, Kirundi (both official). **Religions:** Roman Catholic 62%, traditional African 32%.

Geography: Area: 10,759 sq. mi., the size of Maryland. **Location:** In central Africa. **Neighbors:** Rwanda on N, Zaire on W, Tanzania on E. **Topography:** Much of the country is grassy highland, with mountains reaching 8,900 ft. The southernmost source of the White Nile is located in Burundi. Lake Tanganyika is the second deepest lake in the world. **Capital:** Bujumbura. **Cities** (1983 est.): Bujumbura 141,000.

Government: Type: Republic. **Head of state and head of government:** Pres. Jean Baptiste Bagaza; b. Aug. 29, 1946; in office: Nov. 9, 1976 (govt: Oct. 1978). **Local divisions:** 15 provinces, 114 communes. **Defense** (1982): 19.3% of govt. budget.

Economy: Chief crops: Coffee (90% of exports), cotton, tea. **Minerals:** Nickel. **Arable land:** 61%. **Fish catch** (1982): 11,000

metric tons. **Electricity prod.** (1982): 20 mln. kwh. **Labor force:** 93% agric.

Finance: Currency: Franc (Apr. 1985: 1.24 = $1 US). **Gross domestic product** (1982): $1.2 bln. **Per capita income** (1982) $235. **Imports** (1980): $168 mln.; partners: Iran 14%, Belg.-Lux. 16%, Jap. 8%. **Exports** (1980): $65.1 mln.; partners: U.S. 32%, Belg. 10%. **National budget** (1982): $238 mln. **International reserves less gold** (Mar. 1985): $26.0 mln. **Gold:** 17,000 oz t. **Consumer prices** (change in 1984): 14%

Transport: Motor vehicles: in use (1981): 6,000 passenger cars, 2,400 comm. vehicles.

Communications: Radios: 152,000 in use (1982). **Telephones in use** (1982): 5,601.

Health: Life expectancy at birth (1983): 45.3 male; 48.6 female. **Births** (per 1,000 pop. 1981): 46.3. **Deaths** (per 1,000 pop. 1981): 20.3. **Natural increase** (1981): 2.6%. **Hospital beds** (per 100,000 pop. 1977): 118. **Physicians** (per 100,000 pop. 1977): 3. **Infant mortality** (per 1,000 live births 1983): 121.

Education (1983): **Literacy:** 25%.

Major International Organizations: UN and its specialized agences, OAU.

Embassy: 2233 Wisconsin Ave. NW 20007; 342-2574.

The pygmy Twa were the first inhabitants, followed by Bantu Hutus, who were conquered in the 16th century by the tall Tutsi (Watusi), probably from Ethiopia. Under German control in 1899, the area fell to Belgium in 1916, which exercised successively a League of Nations mandate and UN trusteeship over Ruanda-Urundi (now 2 countries).

Independence came in 1962, and the monarchy was overthrown in 1966. An unsuccessful Hutu rebellion in 1972-73 left 10,000 Tutsi and 150,000 Hutu dead. Over 100,000 Hutu fled to Tanzania and Zaire. The present regime is pledged to ethnic reconciliation, but Burundi remains one of the poorest and most densely populated countries in Africa.

Cambodia (Kampuchea)
Cambodian People's Republic

People: Population (1984 est.): 6,300,000. **Pop. density:** 90 per sq. mi. **Ethnic groups:** Khmers 90%, Vietnamese, Chinese. **Languages:** Khmer (official), French. **Religions:** Theravada Buddhism, animism.

Geography: Area: 69,900 sq. mi., the size of Missouri. **Location:** In Indochina Peninsula. **Neighbors:** Thailand on W, N, Laos on NE, Vietnam on E. **Topography:** The central area, formed by the Mekong R. basin and Tonle Sap lake, is level. Hills and mountains are in SE, a long escarpment separates the country from Thailand on NW. 75% of the area is forested. **Capital:** Phnom Penh. **Cities** (1984 est.): Phnom Penh 200,000.

Government: Type: No single authority controls the whole country. Vietnamese-installed government controls Phnom Penh. **Head of government:** Pres., People's Revolutionary Council Heng Samrin; in office: Jan. 7, 1979. **Head of State:** Premier Hun Sen; in office: Jan. 14, 1985. **Local divisions:** 18 provinces.

Economy: Industries: Textiles, cement. **Chief crops:** Rice, sugar. **Minerals:** Iron, copper, manganese, gold. **Other resources:** Forests, rubber, kapok. **Meat prod.** (1980): beef: 17,000 metric tons; pork: 26,000 metric tons. **Fish catch** (1978): 84,700 metric tons. **Electricity prod.** (1982): 136.00 mln. kwh.

Finance: Currency: Riel (Jan. 1984: 4 = $1 US). **Per capita income** (1984): $100. **Imports** (1981): $103 mln. **Exports** (1981): $43 mln.

Transport: Railway traffic (1981): 54 mln. passenger-miles; 6.8 mln. net ton-miles. **Motor vehicles:** in use (1972): 27,200 passenger cars, (1973) 10,100 comm. vehicles. **Chief ports:** Kompong Som.

Communications: Television sets: 35,000 in use (1977). **Radios:** 171,000 in use (1978). **Telephones in use** (1977): 71,000.

Health: Life expectancy at birth (1982): 42.0 male; 44.9 female. **Births** (per 1,000 pop. 1975): 45.9. **Deaths** (per 1,000 pop. 1975): 16.9. **Health:** Conditions are poor.

Education (1978): **Literacy:** 48%.

Major International Organizations: UN.

Early kingdoms dating from that of Funan in the 1st century AD culminated in the great Khmer empire which flourished from the 9th century to the 13th, encompassing present-day Thailand,

Cambodia, Laos, and southern Vietnam. The peripheral areas were lost to invading Siamese and Vietnamese, and France established a protectorate in 1863. Independence came in 1953.

Prince Norodom Sihanouk, king 1941-1955 and head of state from 1960, tried to maintain neutrality. Relations with the U.S. were broken in 1965, after South Vietnam planes attacked Vietcong forces within Cambodia. Relations were restored in 1969, after Sihanouk charged Viet communists with arming Cambodian insurgents.

In 1970, pro-U.S. premier Lon Nol seized power, demanding removal of 40,000 North Viet troops; the monarchy was abolished. Sihanouk formed a government-in-exile in Peking, and open war began between the government and Khmer Rouge. The U.S. provided heavy military and economic aid. U.S. troops fought Vietcong forces within Cambodia for 2 months in 1970.

Khmer Rouge forces captured Phnom Penh April 17, 1975. Over 100,000 people had died in 5 years of fighting. The new government evacuated all cities and towns, and shuffled the rural population, sending virtually the entire population to clear jungle, forest, and scrub, which covered half the country. Over one million people were killed in executions and enforced hardships.

Severe border fighting broke out with Vietnam in 1978; developed into a full-fledged Vietnamese invasion. The Vietnamese-backed Kampuchean National United Front for National Salvation, a Cambodian rebel movement, announced, Jan. 8, 1979, the formation of a government one day after the Vietnamese capture of Phnom Pehn. Thousands of refugees flowed into Thailand. Widespread starvation was reported; by Sept., when the UN confirmed diplomatic recognition to the ousted Pol Pot government, international food assistance was allowed to aid the famine-stricken country. In July 1981, renewed efforts to bring about a Vietnamese troop withdrawal and institute supervised elections were pursued in a UN conference on Cambodia, but Vietnam and the Soviet Union boycotted the proceedings.

On Jan. 10, 1983, Vietnam launched an offensive against rebel forces in the west. They overran a refugee camp, Jan. 31, driving 30,000 residents into Thailand. In March, Vietnam launched a major offensive against camps on the Cambodian-Thailand border, engaged Khmer Rouge guerrillas, and crossed the border instigating clashes with Thai troops. By Feb. 1985, Vietnamese forces had overrun all major Khmer Rouge bases. Thailand, Feb. 9, accused Vietnam of using poison gas against the Cambodian rebels.

Cameroon

United Republic of Cameroon

People: Population (1984 est.): 9,506,000. **Age distrib. (%):** 0–14: 43.4; 15–59: 50.8; 60+: 5.8. **Pop. density:** 51.5 per sq. mi. **Urban** (1981): 33.8%. **Ethnic groups:** Some 200 tribes; largest are Bamileke 30%, Fulani 7%. **Languages:** English, French (both official), Bantu, Sudanic. **Religions:** Roman Catholic 35%, animist 25%, Moslim 22%, Protestant 18%.

Geography: Area: 179,558 sq. mi., somewhat larger than California. **Location:** Between W and central Africa. **Neighbors:** Nigeria on NW, Chad, Central African Republic on E, Congo, Gabon, Equatorial Guinea on S. **Topography:** A low coastal plain with rain forests is in S; plateaus in center lead to forested mountains in W, including Mt. Cameroon, 13,000 ft.; grasslands in N lead to marshes around Lake Chad. **Capital:** Yaounde. **Cities** (1984 est.): Douala 850,000; Yaounde 650,000.

Government: Type: Independent Republic. **Head of state:** Pres. Paul Biya; b. Feb. 13, 1933; in office: Nov. 6, 1982. **Local divisions:** 7 provinces with appointed governors.

Economy: Industries: Aluminum processing, palm products. **Chief crops:** Cocoa, coffee, peanuts, tea, bananas, cotton, tobacco. **Crude oil reserves** (1980): 140 mln. bbls. **Other resources:** Timber, rubber. **Arable land:** 14%. **Fish catch** (1984): 75,000 metric tons. **Electricity prod.** (1982): 1.9 bln. kwh. **Labor force:** 83% agric., 7% ind. and commerce.

Finance: Currency: CFA franc (Mar. 1985: 471 = $1 US). **Gross domestic product** (1981): $5.2 bln. **Per capita income** (1979): $628. **Imports** (1983): 7 bln.; partners: Fr. 41%, W. Ger. 5%, Jap. 6%. **Exports** (1983): $976 mln.; partners: Fr. 19%, Neth. 15%, U.S. 38%, It. 5%. **National budget** (1980): $928 mln. revenues; $928 mln. expenditures. **International reserves**

less gold (Oct. 1984): $64.4 mln. **Gold:** 30,000 oz t. **Consumer prices** (change in 1983): 16.6%.

Transport: Railway traffic (1981): 280 mln. passenger-km; 710 mln. net ton-km. **Motor vehicles:** in use (1980): 66,800 passenger cars, 47,100 comm. vehicles. **Chief ports:** Douala.

Communications: Radios: 240,000 in use (1980). **Telephones in use** (1979): 26,000. **Daily newspaper circ.** (1982): 6 per 1,000 pop.

Health: Life expectancy at birth (1980): 46.9 male; 50.1 female. **Births** (per 1,000 pop. 1978): 46. **Deaths** (per 1,000 pop. 1978): 20. **Natural increase** (1978): 2.6%. **Hospital beds** (per 100,000 pop. 1977): 269. **Physicians** (per 100,000 pop. 1977): 6.

Education (1976): **Literacy:** 34%. **Pop. 5-19:** in school: 52%, teachers per 1,000: 10.

Major International Organizations: UN, OAU.

Embassy: 2349 Massachusetts Ave. NW 20008; 265-8790.

Portuguese sailors were the first Europeans to reach Cameroon, in the 15th century. The European and American slave trade was very active in the area. German control lasted from 1884 to 1916, when France and Britain divided the territory, later receiving League of Nations mandates and UN trusteeships. French Cameroon became independent Jan. 1, 1960; one part of British Cameroon joined Nigeria in 1961, the other part joined Cameroon. Stability has allowed for development of roads, railways, agriculture, and petroleum production.

An attempted coup by the Republican Guards was crushed, Apr. 9, 1985.

Canada

See also Canada in Index.

People: Population (1984 est.): 25,142,000. **Age distrib. (%):** 0–14: 22.5; 15–44: 48.6; 44+: 28.8. **Pop. density:** 7 per sq. mi. **Urban** (1981): 75.7%. **Cities** (met. 1982 est.): Montreal 2,850,000; Toronto 3,029,000; Vancouver 1,100,000; Ottawa 695,000; Winnipeg 570,000; Edmonton 529,000.

Government: Type: Confederation with parliamentary democracy. **Head of state:** Queen Elizabeth II, represented by Gov.-Gen. Jeanne Suave; in office: May 14, 1985. **Head of government:** Brian Mulroney; born: Mar. 20, 1939; in office: Sept. 4, 1984. **Local divisions:** 10 provinces, 2 territories. **Defense:** 2.2% of GNP (1983).

Economy: Minerals: Nickel, zinc, copper, gold, lead, molybdenum, potash, silver. **Crude oil reserves** (1980): 6.8 bln. bbls. **Meat prod.** (1983): beef: 1.2 mln. metric tons; pork 850,000 metric tons. **Fish catch** (1982): 1.3 mln. metric tons. **Electricity prod.** (1983): 395 bln. kwh. **Crude steel prod.** (1982): 11.9 mln. metric tons. **Labor force:** 5% agric.; 43.5% ind. & comm., 38% service.

Finance: Currency: Dollar (June 1985: 1.36 = $1 US). **Gross domestic product** (1984): $317 bln. **Per capita income** (1982 est.) $10,193. **Imports** (1984): $78 bln.; partners: U.S. 71%, Jap. 5%. **Exports** (1984): $90 bln.; partners: U.S. 68%, Jap. 5%. **Tourists** (1982): 34.4 mln.; receipts: $2.5 bln. **National budget** (1983-84): 71.1 bln. **International reserves less gold** (Mar. 1985): $3.0 bln. **Gold:** 20.14 mln. oz t. **Consumer prices** (change in 1984): 4.3%.

Transport: Railway traffic (1983): 2.1 bln. passenger-km; 220 bln. net ton-km. **Motor vehicles:** in use (1982): 10.1 mln. passenger cars, 3.1 mln. comm. vehicles; manuf. (1982): 814,000 passenger cars; 470,000 comm. vehicles. **Civil aviation** (1983): 28.7 bln. passenger-km: 916 mln. net ton-km.

Communications: Television sets: 12.4 mln. in use (1983). **Radios:** 28 mln. in use (1983). **Telephones in use** (1983): 16.2 mln. **Daily newspaper circ.** (1983): 215 per 1,000 pop.

Health: Life expectancy at birth (1983): 69 male; 76 female. **Births** (per 1,000 pop. 1983): 14.8. **Deaths** (per 1,000 pop. 1983): 7.0. **Natural increase** (1983): .7%. **Hospital beds** (per 100,000 pop. 1977): 875. **Physicians** (per 100,000 pop. 1977): 178. **Infant mortality** (per 1,000 live births 1982): 15.

Education (1982): **Literacy:** 99%. **Pop. 5-19:** in school: 75%, teachers per 1,000: 40.

Major International Organizations: UN and its specialized agencies, NATO, OECD, Commonwealth of Nations.

Embassy: 1746 Massachusetts Ave. NW 20036; 785-1400.

Cape Verde
Republic of Cape Verde

People: Population (1984 est.): 300,000. **Age distrib. (%):** 0–14: 46.9; 15–59: 44.9; 60+: 7.9. **Pop. density:** 192 per sq. mi. **Urban** (1980): 26.2%. **Ethnic groups:** Creole (mulatto) 71%, African 28%, European 1%. **Languages:** Portuguese (official), Crioulo. **Religions:** 80% Roman Catholic.

Geography: Area: 1,557 sq. mi., a bit larger than Rhode Island. **Location:** In Atlantic O., off western tip of Africa. **Neighbors:** Nearest are Mauritania, Senegal. **Topography:** Cape Verde Islands are 15 in number, volcanic in origin (active crater on Fogo). The landscape is eroded and stark, with vegetation mostly in interior valleys. **Capital:** Praia. **Cities** (1984 est.): Mindelo 40,000; Praia 50,000.

Government: Type: Republic. **Head of state:** Pres. Aristide Pereira; b. Nov. 17, 1923; in office: July 5, 1975. **Head of government:** Prime Min. Pedro Pires, b. Apr. 29, 1934; in office: July 5, 1975. **Local divisions:** 14 administrative districts.

Economy: Chief crops: Bananas, coffee, sugarcane, corn, beans. **Minerals:** Salt. **Other resources:** Fish. **Arable land:** 10%. **Electricity prod.** (1982): 12 mln. kwh.

Finance: Currency: Escudo (Sept. 1983: 72.67 = $1 US). **Gross domestic product** (1980 est.): $96 mln. **Per capita income** (1980): $300. **Imports** (1981): $104 mln.; partners: Port. 58%, Neth. 5%. **Exports** (1981): $6 mln.; partners: Port. 63%, Ang. 14%, UK 5%, Zaire 5%.

Transport: Motor vehicles: in use (1981): 4,000 passenger cars, 1,343 comm. vehicles. **Chief ports:** Mindelo, Praia.

Communications: Radios: 42,000 licensed (1982). **Telephones in use** (1981): 1,739.

Health: Life expectancy at birth (1980): 60 yrs. **Births** (per 1,000 pop. 1978): 29. **Deaths** (per 1,000 pop. 1978): 8. **Natural increase** (1978): 2.1%. **Pop. per hospital bed** (1977): 516. **Pop. per physician** (1977): 7,750. **Infant mortality** (per 1,000 live births 1983): 60.

Education (1984): **Literacy:** 37%.

Major International Organizations: UN and its specialized agencies, OAU.

Embassy: 3415 Massachusetts Ave. NW 20007; 965-6820.

The uninhabited Cape Verdes were discovered by the Portuguese in 1456 or 1460. The first Portuguese colonists landed in 1462; African slaves were brought soon after, and most Cape Verdeans descend from both groups. Cape Verde independence came July 5, 1975. The islands have suffered from repeated extreme droughts and famines, especially 1978. Emphasis is placed on the development of agriculture and on fishing.

Central African Republic

People: Population (1984 est.): 2,585,000. **Pop. density:** 10.82 per sq. mi. **Ethnic groups:** Banda 27%, Baya 34%, Mandja 21%, Sara 10%. **Languages:** French (official), local dialects. **Religions:** Protestant 25%, Roman Catholic 25%, traditional 24%.

Geography: Area: 240,324 sq. mi., slightly smaller than Texas. **Location:** In central Africa. **Neighbors:** Chad on N, Cameroon on W, Congo, Zaire on S, Sudan on E. **Topography:** Mostly rolling plateau, average altitude 2,000 ft., with rivers draining S to the Congo and N to Lake Chad. Open, well-watered savanna covers most of the area, with an arid area in NE, and tropical rainforest in SW. **Capital:** Bangui. **Cities** (1983 est.): Bangui (met.) 375,000.

Government: Type: Republic. **Head of state:** Gen. Andre Kolingba; in office: Sept. 1, 1981. **Local divisions:** 16 prefectures. **Defense:** 14.2% of govt. budget.

Economy: Industries: Textiles, light manuf. **Chief crops:** Cotton, coffee, peanuts, corn, sorghum. **Minerals:** Diamonds (chief export), uranium, iron, copper. **Other resources:** Timber. **Arable land:** 15%. **Electricity prod.** (1983): 68 mln. kwh. **Labor force:** 88% agric.

Finance: Currency: CFA franc (Mar. 1985: 471 = $1 US). **Gross domestic product** (1982): $627 mln. **Per capita income** (1982): $310. **Imports** (1981): $145 mln.; partners (1981): Fr. 58%. **Exports** (1981): $118 mln.; partners (1980): Fr. 52%,

Bel.-Lux. 14%. **International reserves less gold** (Oct. 1984): $59.8 mln. **Gold:** 11,000 oz t. **Consumer prices** (change in 1983): 13.3%.

Transport: Motor vehicles: in use (1979): 10,000 passenger cars, 6,000 comm. vehicles.

Communications: Radios: 120,000 in use (1980).

Health: Life expectancy at birth (1983): 44 years. **Births** (per 1,000 pop. 1980): 35.5. **Deaths** (per 1,000 pop. 1980): 8.5%. **Natural increase** (1980): 2.7%. **Hospital beds** (per 100,000 pop. 1977): 138. **Physicians** (per 100,000 pop. 1977): 5. **Infant mortality** (per 1,000 live births 1983): 148.

Education (1983): **Literacy:** 20%. **Attendance:** primary school 64%; secondary school 11%.

Embassy: 1618 22d St. NW 20008; 483-7800.

Various Bantu tribes migrated through the region for centuries before French control was asserted in the late 19th century, when the region was named Ubangi-Shari. Complete independence was attained Aug. 13, 1960.

All political parties were dissolved in 1960, and the country became a center for Chinese political influence in Africa. Relations with China were severed after 1965. Elizabeth Domitien, premier 1975-76, was the first woman to hold that post in an African country. Pres. Jean-Bedel Bokassa, who seized power in a 1965 military coup, proclaimed himself constitutional emperor of the renamed Central African Empire Dec. 1976.

Emp. Bokassa's rule was characterized by virtually unchecked ruthless and cruel authority, and human rights violations. Bokassa was ousted in a bloodless coup aided by the French government, Sept. 20, 1979, and replaced by his cousin David Dacko, former president from 1960 to 1965. In 1981, the political situation deteriorated amid strikes and economic crisis. Gen. Kolingba replaced Dacko as head of state in a bloodless coup.

Chad
Republic of Chad

People: Population (1984 est.): 5,116,000. **Age distrib. (%):** 0–14: 40.7; 15–59: 54.9; 60+: 4.4. **Pop. density:** 9.8 per sq. mi. **Urban** (1980): 17.8%. **Ethnic groups:** Sudanese Arab 30%, Sudanic tribes 25%, Nilotic, Saharan tribes. **Languages:** French (official), Arabic, others. **Religions:** Moslems 44%, animist 23%, Christian 33%.

Geography: Area: 495,755 sq. mi., four-fifths the size of Alaska. **Location:** In central N. Africa. **Neighbors:** Libya on N, Niger, Nigeria, Cameroon on W, Central African Republic on S, Sudan on E. **Topography:** Southern wooded savanna, steppe, and desert, part of the Sahara, in the N. Southern rivers flow N to Lake Chad, surrounded by marshland. **Capital:** N'Djamena. **Cities** (1983 est.): N'Djamena 225,000.

Government: Head of state: Hissen Habre; b. 1942; in office: June 19, 1982. **Local divisions:** 14 prefectures with appointed governors. **Armed forces:** regulars 20,000.

Economy: Chief crops: Cotton. **Minerals:** Uranium. **Arable land:** 7%. **Fish catch** (1982): 115,000 metric tons. **Electricity prod.** (1982): 65 mln. kwh. **Labor force:** 85% agric.

Finance: Currency: CFA franc (Mar. 1985: 471 = $1 US). **Gross domestic product** (1981): $550 mln. **Per capita income** (1976): $73. **Imports** (1979): $140 mln.; partners (1976): Fr. 47%, Nigeria 22%. **Exports** (1979): $58 mln.; partners (1976): Nigeria 19%, Fr. 13%, Jap. 13%. **Tourist receipts** (1981): $2 mln. **National budget** (1978): $64 mln. revenues; $64 mln. expenditures. **International reserves less gold** (Oct. 1984): $40.1 mln. **Gold:** 11,000 oz t.

Transport: Motor vehicles: in use (1982): 7,000 passenger cars, 5,000 comm. vehicles.

Communications: Radios: 75,000 in use (1983). **Telephones in use** (1981): 1,000.

Health: Life expectancy at birth (1981): 41.5 male; 43.9 female. **Births** (per 1,000 pop. 1981): 42.9. **Deaths** (per 1,000 pop. 1981): 21.9. **Natural increase** (1981): 2.1%. **Hospital beds** (per 100,000 pop. 1977): 82. **Physicians** (per 100,000 pop. 1977): 2. **Infant mortality** (per 1,000 live births 1981): 146.

Education (1978): **Literacy:** 15%. **Pop. 5-19:** in school: 18%, teachers per 1,000: 2.

Embassy: 2002 R St. NW 20009; 462-4009.

Chad was the site of paleolithic and neolithic cultures before the Sahara Desert formed. A succession of kingdoms and Arab slave traders dominated Chad until France took control around 1900. Independence came Aug. 11, 1960.

Northern Moslem rebels, have fought animist and Christian southern government and French troops from 1966, despite numerous cease-fires and peace pacts.

Libyan troops entered the country at the request of the Chad government, December 1980. On Jan. 6, 1981 Libya and Chad announced their intention to unite. France together with several African nations condemned the agreement as a menace to African security. The Libyan troops were withdrawn from Chad in November 1981.

Rebel forces, led by Hissen Habre, captured the capital and forced Pres. Oueddei to flee the country in June 1982.

In 1983, France sent some 3,000 troops to Chad to assist Habre in opposing Libyan-backed rebels. France and Libya agreed to a simultaneous withdrawal of troops from Chad in September 1984.

Chile
Republic of Chile

People: Population (1984 est.): 11,655,000. **Age distrib.** (%): 0–14: 32.2; 15–59: 59.7; 60+: 8.1. **Pop. density:** 38.76 per sq. mi. **Urban** (1983): 82%. **Ethnic groups:** Mestizo 66%, Spanish 25%, Indian 5%. **Languages:** Spanish. **Religions:** Predominantly Roman Catholic.

Geography: Area: 292,135 sq. mi., larger than Texas. **Location:** Occupies western coast of southern S. America. **Neighbors:** Peru on N, Bolivia on NE, Argentina on E. **Topography:** Andes Mtns. are on E border including some of the world's highest peaks; on W is 2,650-mile Pacific Coast. Width varies between 100 and 250 miles. In N is Atacama Desert, in center are agricultural regions, in S are forests and grazing lands. **Capital:** Santiago. **Cities** (1983 metro est.) Santiago 4,085,000.

Government: Head of state: Pres. Augusto Pinochet Ugarte; b. Nov. 25, 1915; in office: Sept. 11, 1973. **Local divisions:** 12 regions and Santiago region. **Defense:** 6.5% of GNP (1982).

Economy: Industries: Steel, textiles, wood products. **Chief crops:** Grain, onions, beans, potatoes, peas, fruits, grapes. **Minerals:** Copper (27% world resources), molybdenum, nitrates, iodine (half world output), iron, coal, oil, gas, gold, cobalt, zinc, manganese, borate, mica, mercury, salt, sulphur, marble, onyx. **Crude oil reserves** (1983): 440 mln. bbls. **Other resources:** Water, forests. **Arable land:** 6%. **Meat prod.** (1983): beef: 205,000 metric tons; pork: 61,000 metric tons; lamb: 21,000 metric tons. **Fish catch** (1982): 3.8 mln. metric tons. **Electricity prod.** (1982): 11.8 bln. kwh. **Crude steel prod.** (1982): 481,000 metric tons. **Labor force:** 9% agric.; 33% ind & comm., 31% serv.

Finance: Currency: Peso (Apr. 1985: 146 = $1 US). **Gross domestic product** (1982): $23.6 bln. **Per capita income** (1979): $1,950. **Imports** (1984): $3.1 bln.; partners: U.S. 26%, Braz. 7%. **Exports** (1984): $3.6 bln.; partners: W. Ger. 11%, Jap. 11%, U.S. 21%. **Tourists** (1982): 307,495. **National budget** (1982): $9.4 bln. **International reserves less gold** (Feb. 1985): $1.9 bln. **Gold:** 1.53 mln. oz. t. **Consumer prices** (change in 1984): 19.9%.

Transport: Railway traffic (1982): 1.5 bln. passenger-km; 1.7 bln. net ton-km. **Motor vehicles:** in use (1981): 505,000 passenger cars, 210,000 comm. vehicles. **Civil aviation** (1982): 1.7 bln. passenger-km; 137 mln. net ton-km. **Chief ports:** Valparaiso, Arica, Antofagasta.

Communications: Television sets: 1.2 mln. in use (1980). **Radios:** 3.2 mln. in use (1980). **Telephones in use** (1982): 595,000.

Health: Life expectancy at birth (1983): 63.8 male; 70.4 female. **Births** (per 1,000 pop. 1980): 22. **Deaths** (per 1,000 pop. 1978): 7. **Natural increase** (1980): 1.5%. **Hospital beds** 39,000. **Infant mortality** (per 1,000 live births 1981): 27.2.

Education (1983): Literacy: 90%. Compulsory ages 6-14.

Major International Organizations: UN and its specialized agencies, OAS.

Embassy: 1732 Massachusetts Ave. NW 20036; 785-1746.

Northern Chile was under Inca rule before the Spanish conquest, 1536-40. The southern Araucanian Indians resisted until the late 19th century. Independence was gained 1810-18, under Jose de San Martin and Bernardo O'Higgins; the latter, as supreme director 1817-23, sought social and economic reforms until deposed. Chile defeated Peru and Bolivia in 1836-39 and 1879-84, gaining mineral-rich northern land.

Eduardo Frei Montalva came into office in 1964, instituting social programs and gradual nationalization of foreign-owned mining companies. In 1970, Salvador Allende Gossens, a Marxist, became president with a third of the national vote.

The Allende government furthered nationalizations, and improved conditions for the poor. But illegal and violent actions by extremist supporters of the government, the regime's failure to attain majority support, and poorly planned socialist economic programs led to political and financial chaos.

A military junta seized power Sept. 11, 1973, and said Allende killed himself. The junta named a mostly military cabinet, and announced plans to "exterminate Marxism."

Repression continued during 1984 with no sign of any political liberalization. There were waves of violent protests in Oct. The government imposed a state of siege, implemented curbs on the media, and arrested thousands.

Tierra del Fuego is the largest (18,800 sq. mi.) island in the archipelago of the same name at the southern tip of South America, an area of majestic mountains, tortuous channels, and high winds. It was discovered 1520 by Magellan and named the Land of Fire because of its many Indian bonfires. Part of the island is in Chile, part in Argentina. Punta Arenas, on a mainland peninsula, is a center of sheep-raising and the world's southernmost city (pop. 67,600); Puerto Williams, pop. 949, is the southernmost settlement.

China
People's Republic of China

People: Population (1984 est.): 1,034,907,000. **Pop. density:** 290 per sq. mi. **Ethnic groups:** Han Chinese 94%, Mongol, Korean, Manchu, others. **Languages:** Mandarin Chinese (official), Shanghai, Canton, Fukien, Hakka dialects; Tibetan, Vigus (Turkic). **Religions:** officially atheist; Confucianism, Buddhism, Taoism, are traditional.

Geography: Area: 3,691,521 sq. mi., slightly larger than the U.S. **Location:** Occupies most of the habitable mainland of E. Asia. **Neighbors:** Mongolia on N, USSR on NE and NW, Afghanistan, Pakistan on W, India, Nepal, Bhutan, Burma, Laos, Vietnam on S, N. Korea on NW. **Topography:** Two-thirds of the vast territory is mountainous or desert, and only one-tenth is cultivated. Rolling topography rises to high elevations in the N in the Daxinganlingshanmai separating Manchuria and Mongolia; the Tienshan in Xinjiang; the Himalayan and Kunlunshanmai in the SW and in Tibet. Length is 1,860 mi. from N to S, width E to W is more than 2,000 mi. The eastern half of China is one of the best-watered lands in the world. Three great river systems, the Changjiang, the Huanghe, and the Xijiang provide water for vast farmlands. **Capital:** Peking. **Cities** (1981 est.): Shanghai 12,000,000; Peking 8,500,000; Tianjin 7,200,000; Canton 5,200,000; Shenyang 4,800,000; Wuhan 4,400,000; Chendu 4,000,000.

Government: Type: People's Republic. **Head of state:** Pres. Li Xiannian; in office: June 18, 1983. **Head of government:** Party Chairman Hu Yaobang, b. 1915; in office: June 29, 1981. **Effective head of government:** Premier Zhao Ziyang; b. 1919; in office: Sept. 1980. **Local divisions:** 21 provinces, 5 autonomous regions, and 3 cities. **Defense:** 8.5% of GNP (1982).

Economy: Industries: Iron and steel, plastics, agriculture implements, trucks. **Chief crops:** Grain, rice, cotton, tea. **Minerals:** Tungsten, antimony, coal, iron, lead, manganese, mercury, molybdenum, phosphates, potash, tin. **Crude oil reserves** (1980): 20 bln. bbls. **Other resources:** Silk. **Arable land:** 11%. **Meat prod.** (1983): beef: 2.5 mln. metric tons; pork: 17 mln. metric tons; lamb: 793,000 metric tons. **Fish catch** (1983): 4.9 mln. metric tons. **Electricity prod.** (1982): 327 bln. kwh. **Crude steel prod.** (1982): 37.1 mln. metric tons. **Labor force:** 74% agric.; 15% ind. & comm.

Finance: Currency: Yuan (Mar. 1985): 2.81 = $1 US). **Gross national product** (1983): $313 bln. **Per capita income** (1980): $566. **Imports** (1983): $21.3 bln.; partners: Jap. 22%, U.S. 18%, Hong Kong 12%. **Exports** (1983): $22.1 bln.; partners: Hong Kong 24%, Jap. 23%, U.S. 10%. **Tourism** (1982): $7.9 bln. receipts. **National budget** (1982): $56.8 bln. revenues,

$58.3 bln. expenditures. **International reserves less gold** (Feb. 1985): 13.0 bln. **Gold:** 12.7 mln. oz t. **Consumer prices** (change in 1983): 2.1%.

Transport: Railway traffic (1983): 177 bln. net ton-km. **Motor vehicles:** in use (1982): 70,000 passenger cars, 900,000 comm. vehicles. **Civil aviation** (1982): 6 bln. passenger km, 200 mln. net ton-km. **Chief ports:** Shanghai, Tianjin, Luda.

Communications: Television sets: over 15 mln. in use (1983). **Radios:** 190 mln. in use (1983). **Telephones** (1983): 2.4 mln.; **Daily newspaper circ.** (1982): 74 per 1,000 pop.

Health: Life expectancy at birth (1984): 68 years. **Births** (per 1,000 pop. 1983): 18.6. **Deaths** (per 1,000 pop. 1983): 7.1. **Natural increase** (1983): 1.1%. **Hospital beds** (1982): 2.2 mln. **Physicians** (1982): 1.3 mln.

Education (1984): **Literacy:** 75%. Years compulsory 5; first grade enrollment 93%.

Major International Organizations: UN and its specialized agencies.

Embassy: 2300 Conn. Ave. NW 20008; 328-2520.

History. Remains of various man-like creatures who lived as early as several hundred thousand years ago have been found in many parts of China. Neolithic agricultural settlements dotted the Huanghe basin from about 5,000 BC. Their language, religion, and art were the sources of later Chinese civilization.

Bronze metallurgy reached a peak and Chinese pictographic writing, similar to today's, was in use in the more developed culture of the Shang Dynasty (c. 1500 BC–c. 1000 BC) which ruled much of North China.

A succession of dynasties and interdynastic warring kingdoms ruled China for the next 3,000 years. They expanded Chinese political and cultural domination to the south and west, and developed a brilliant technologically and culturally advanced society. Rule by foreigners (Mongols in the Yuan Dynasty, 1271-1368, and Manchus in the Ch'ing Dynasty, 1644-1911) did not alter the underlying culture.

A period of relative stagnation left China vulnerable to internal and external pressures in the 19th century. Rebellions left tens of millions dead, and Russia, Japan, Britain, and other powers exercised political and economic control in large parts of the country. China became a republic Jan. 1, 1912, following the Wuchang Uprising inspired by Dr. Sun Yat-sen.

For a period of 50 years, 1894-1945, China was involved in conflicts with Japan. In 1895, China ceded Korea, Taiwan, and other areas. On Sept. 18, 1931, Japan seized the Northeastern Provinces (Manchuria) and set up a puppet state called Manchukuo. The border province of Jehol was cut off as a buffer state in 1933. Japan invaded China proper July 7, 1937. After its defeat in World War II, Japan gave up all seized land.

Following World War II, internal disturbances arose involving the Kuomintang, communists, and other factions. China came under domination of communist armies, 1949-1950. The Kuomintang government moved to Taiwan, 90 mi. off the mainland, Dec. 8, 1949.

The People's Republic of China was proclaimed in Peking Sept. 21, 1949, by the Chinese People's Political Consultative Conference under Mao Tse-tung.

China and the USSR signed a 30-year treaty of "friendship, alliance and mutual assistance," Feb. 15, 1950.

The U.S. refused recognition of the new regime. On Nov. 26, 1950, the People's Republic sent armies into Korea against U.S. troops and forced a stalemate.

By the 1960s, relations with the USSR deteriorated, with disagreements on borders, ideology and leadership of world communism. The USSR cancelled aid accords, and China, with Albania, launched anti-Soviet propaganda drives. High level talks have been held with the USSR to seek improved trade and cultural contracts; little progress was reported.

On Oct. 25, 1971, the UN General Assembly ousted the Taiwan government from the UN and seated the People's Republic in its place. The U.S. had supported the mainland's admission but opposed Taiwan's expulsion.

U.S. Pres. Nixon visited China Feb. 21-28, 1972, on invitation from Premier Chou En-lai, ending years of antipathy between the 2 nations. China and the U.S. opened liaison offices in each other's capitals, May-June 1973. The U.S., Dec. 15, 1978, formally recognized the People's Republic of China as the sole legal government of China; diplomatic relations between the 2 nations were established, Jan. 1, 1979.

In a continuing "reassessment" of the policies of Mao Zedong, Mao's widow, Jiang Quing, and other Gang of Four members were convicted of "committing crimes during the 'Cultural Revolution,'" Jan. 25, 1981.

Internal developments. After an initial period of consolidation, 1949-52, industry, agriculture, and social and economic institutions were forcibly molded according to Maoist ideals. However, frequent drastic changes in policy and violent factionalism interfered with economic development.

In 1957, Mao Tse-tung admitted an estimated 800,000 people had been executed 1949-54; opponents claimed much higher figures.

The Great Leap Forward, 1958-60, tried to force the pace of economic development through intensive labor on huge new rural communes, and through emphasis on ideological purity and enthusiasm. The program caused resistance and was largely abandoned. Serious food shortages developed, and the government was forced to buy grain from the West.

The Great Proletarian Cultural Revolution, 1965, was an attempt to oppose pragmatism and bureaucratic power and instruct a new generation in revolutionary principles. Massive purges took place. A program of forcibly relocating millions of urban teenagers into the countryside was launched.

By 1968 the movement had run its course; many purged officials returned to office in subsequent years, and reforms in education and industry that had placed ideology above expertise were gradually weakened.

In the mid-1970s, factional and ideological fighting increased, and emerged into the open after the 1976 deaths of Mao and Premier Chou En-lai. Mao's widow and 3 other leading leftists were purged and placed under arrest, after reportedly trying to seize power. Their opponents said the "gang of four" had used severe repression and mass torture, had sparked local fighting and had disrupted production. The new ruling group modified Maoist policies in education, culture, and industry, and sought better ties with non-communist countries.

Relations with Vietnam deteriorated in 1978 as China charged persecution of ethnic Chinese. In retaliation for Vietnam's invasion of Cambodia, China attacked 4 Vietnamese border provinces Feb. 17, 1979; heavy border fighting ensued.

Sweeping reforms of the central bureaucracy were announced March 1982.

Manchuria. Home of the Manchus, rulers of China 1644-1911, Manchuria has accommodated millions of Chinese settlers in the 20th century. Under Japanese rule 1931-45, the area became industrialized. China no longer uses the name Manchuria for the region, which is divided into the 3 NE provinces of Heilongjiang, Jilin, and Liaoning.

Guandong is the southernmost part of Manchuria. Russia in 1898 forced China to lease it Guandong, and built Port Arthur (Lushun) and the port of Dairen (Luda). Japan seized Port Arthur in 1905. It was turned over to the USSR by the 1945 Yalta agreement, but finally returned to China in 1950.

Inner Mongolia was organized by the People's Republic in 1947. Its boundaries have undergone frequent changes, reaching its greatest extent (and restored in 1979) in 1956, with an area of 460,000 sq. mi., allegedly in order to dilute the minority Mongol population. Chinese settlers outnumber the Mongols more than 10 to 1. Total pop., 8.5 million. Capital: Hohhot.

Xinjiang Uygur Autonomous Region, in Central Asia, is 633,802 sq. mi., pop. 11 million (75% Uygurs, a Turkic Moslem group, with a heavy Chinese increase in recent years). Capital: Urumqi. It is China's richest region in strategic minerals. Some Uygurs have fled to the USSR, claiming national oppression.

Tibet, 470,000 sq. mi., is a thinly populated region of high plateaus and massive mountains, the Himalayas on the S, the Kunluns on the N. High passes connect with India and Nepal; roads lead into China proper. Capital: Lhasa. Average altitude is 15,000 ft. Jiachan, 15,870 ft., is believed to be the highest inhabited town on earth. Agriculture is primitive. Pop. 1.7 million (of whom 500,000 are Chinese). Another 4 million Tibetans form the majority of the population of vast adjacent areas that have long been incorporated into China.

China ruled all of Tibet from the 18th century, but independence came in 1911. China reasserted control in 1951, and a communist government was installed in 1953, revising the theocratic Lamaist Buddhist rule. Serfdom was abolished, but all land remained collectivized.

A Tibetan uprising within China in 1956 spread to Tibet in 1959. The rebellion was crushed with Chinese troops, and Buddhism was almost totally suppressed. The Dalai Lama and 100,000 Tibetans fled to India.

Colombia

Republic of Colombia

People: Population (1984 est.): 28,248,000. **Age distrib. (%):** 0–14: 44.6; 15–59: 50.7; 60+: 4.7. **Pop. density:** 64 per sq. mi. **Urban** (1983): 65.4%. **Ethnic groups:** Mestizo 58%, Caucasian 20%, Mulatto 14%, Negro 4%, Indian 1%. **Languages:** Spanish. **Religions:** Roman Catholic 97%.

Geography: Area: 440,831 sq. mi., about the size of Texas and New Mexico combined. **Location:** At the NW corner of S. America. **Neighbors:** Panama on NW, Ecuador, Peru on S, Brazil, Venezuela on E. **Topography:** Three ranges of Andes, the Western, Central, and Eastern Cordilleras, run through the country from N to S. The eastern range consists mostly of high table lands, densely populated. The Magdalena R. rises in Andes, flows N to Carribean, through a rich alluvial plain. Sparsely-settled plains in E are drained by Orinoco and Amazon systems. **Capital:** Bogota. **Cities** (1981 est.): Bogota 4,486,200; (1973 cen.); Medellin 1,112,390; Cali 967,908; Barranquilla 690,471.

Government: Type: Republic. **Head of state:** Pres. Belisario Betancur Cuartas; in office: Aug. 7, 1982. **Local divisions:** 23 departments, 8 national territories, and special district of Bogota. **Defense:** 0.8% of GNP (1983).

Economy: Industries: Textiles, processed goods, hides, steel, cement, chemicals. **Chief crops:** Coffee (50% of exports), rice, tobacco, cotton, sugar, bananas. **Minerals:** Oil, gas, emeralds (90% world output), gold, copper, lead, coal, iron, nickel, salt. **Crude oil reserves** (1981): 3.2 bln. bbls. **Other resources:** Rubber, balsam, dye-woods, copaiba, hydro power. **Arable land:** 5%. **Meat prod.** (1983): beef: 542,000 metric tons; pork: 61,000 metric tons; lamb 13,000 metric tons. **Fish catch** (1983): 49,000 metric tons. **Electricity prod.** (1982): 25.6 bln. kwh. **Crude steel prod.** (1982): 215,000 metric tons. **Labor force:** 27% agric.; 21% man.; 18% services.

Finance: Currency: Peso (Mar. 1985: 126 = $1 US). **Gross national product** (1983): $42.5 bln. **Per capita income** (1981): $1,112. **Imports** (1983): $4.9 bln.; partners: U.S. 34%, Jap. 10%. **Exports** (1983): $3.0 bln.; partners: U.S. 23%, W. Ger. 20%, Venez. 12%. **Tourists** (1982): 1.2 mln.; receipts: $624 mln. **National budget** (1981): $4.8 bln. **International reserves less gold** (Mar. 1985): $1.1 bln. **Gold** 1.89 mln. oz t. **Consumer prices** (change in 1984): 16.1.

Transport: Railway traffic (1982): 157 mln. passenger-km; 553 mln. net ton-km. **Motor vehicles:** in use (1981): 672,385 passenger cars, 110,943 comm. vehicles; assembled (1976): 26,900 passenger cars; 9,500 comm. vehicles. **Civil aviation** (1982): 4.1 bln. passenger-km; 240 mln. net ton-km. **Chief ports:** Buena Ventura, Santa Marta, Barranquilla, Cartagena.

Communications: Television sets: 1.8 mln. in use (1983). **Radios:** 3.2 mln. in use (1984). **Telephones in use** (1981): 1.1 mln. **Daily newspaper circ.** (1983): 44 per 1,000 pop.

Health: Life expectancy at birth (1985): 61.4 male; 66 female. **Births** (per 1,000 pop. 1985): 31. **Deaths** (per 1,000 pop. 1985): 7.7. **Natural increase** (1985): 2.3%. **Hospital beds** (per 100,000 pop. 1977): 161. **Physicians** (per 100,000 pop. 1977): 51. **Infant mortality** (per 1,000 live births 1982): 65%.

Education (1981): **Literacy:** 82%. Only 28% finish primary school.

Major International Organizations: UN and its specialized agencies, OAS.

Embassy: 2118 Leroy Pl. NW, 20008; 387-8338.

Spain subdued the local Indian kingdoms (Funza, Tunja) by the 1530s, and ruled Colombia and neighboring areas as New Granada for 300 years. Independence was won by 1819. Venezuela and Ecuador broke away in 1829-30, and Panama withdrew in 1903.

One of the few functioning Latin American democracies, Colombia is nevertheless plagued by rural and urban violence, though scaled down from "La Violencia" of 1948-58, which claimed 200,000 lives. Attempts at land and social reform, and progress in industrialization have not yet succeeded in reducing massive social problems aggravated by a very high birth rate.

Comoros

Federal Islamic Republic of the Comoros

People: Population (1984 est.): 445,000. **Age distrib. (%):** 0–14: 43.0; 15–59: 47.0; 60+: 8.0. **Pop. density:** 540 per sq. mi. **Ethnic groups:** Arabs, Africans, East Indians. **Languages:** Arabic, French (official), Comoran. **Religions:** Islam (official).

Geography: Area: 838 sq. mi., half the size of Delaware. **Location:** 3 islands (Grande Comore, Anjouan, and Moheli) in the Mozambique Channel between NW Madagascar and SE Africa. **Neighbors:** Nearest are Mozambique on W, Madagascar on E. **Topography:** The islands are of volcanic origin, with an active volcano on Grand Comoro. **Capital:** Moroni. **Cities** (1982 est.): Moroni (met.) 22,000.

Government: Type: Republic. **Head of state:** Pres. Ahmed Abdallah Abderemane; b. 1919; in office: May 23, 1978. **Head of govt.:** Prime Min. Ali Mroudjae; in office: Feb. 8, 1982. **Local divisions:** each of the 3 main islands is a prefecture.

Economy: Industries: Perfume. **Chief crops:** Vanilla, copra, perfume plants, fruits. **Arable land:** 3%. **Electricity prod.** (1982): 10 mln. kwh. **Labor force:** 87% agric.

Finance: Currency: CFA franc (Sept. 1984: 470 = $1 US). **Gross national product** (1982): $92.3 mln. **Per capita income** (1982): $240. **Imports** (1979): $24 mln.; partners: Fr. 41%, Madag. 20%, Pak. 8%, Ken. 5%. **Exports** (1979): $15 mln.; partners: Fr. 65%, U.S. 21%, Mad. 5%.

Transport: Chief ports: Dzaoudzi.

Communications: Radios: 37,000 in use (1982). **Telephones in use** (1981): 3,000.

Health: Life expectancy at birth (1984): 46.4 male; 49.7 female. **Births** (per 1,000 pop. 1984): 46.2. **Deaths** (per 1,000 pop. 1984): 18.1. **Natural increase** (1982): 2.8%. **Infant mortality** (per 1,000 live births 1980): 97.

Education (1982): **Literacy:** 15%; less than 20% attend secondary school.

Major International Organizations: UN and its specialized agencies, OAF.

The islands were controlled by Moslem sultans until the French acquired them 1841-1909. A 1974 referendum favored independence, with only the Christian island of Mayotte preferring association with France. The French National Assembly decided to allow each of the islands to decide its own fate. The Comoro Chamber of Deputies declared independence July 6, 1975. In a referendum in 1976, Mayotte voted to remain French. A leftist regime that seized power in 1975 was deposed in a pro-French 1978 coup.

Congo

People's Republic of the Congo

People: Population (1984 est.): 1,745,000. **Pop. density:** 13.2 per sq. mi. **Ethnic groups:** Bakongo 45%, Bateke 20%, others. **Languages:** French (official), Bantu dialects. **Religions:** Christians 50% (two-thirds Roman Catholic), animists 47%, Muslim 2%.

Geography: Area: 132,046 sq. mi., slightly smaller than Montana. **Location:** In western central Africa. **Neighbors:** Gabon, Cameroon on W, Central African Republic on N, Zaire on E, Angola (Cabinda) on SW. **Topography:** Much of the Congo is covered by thick forests. A coastal plain leads to the fertile Niari Valley. The center is a plateau; the Congo R. basin consists of flood plains in the lower and savanna in the upper portion. **Capital:** Brazzaville. **Cities** (1980 est.): Brazzaville (met.) 200,000; Pointe-Noire 135,000; Loubomo 34,000.

Government: Type: People's Republic. **Head of state:** Pres. Denis Sassou-Nguesso; b. 1943; in office: Feb. 8, 1979. **Head of government:** Prime Min. Ange Edouard Poungui; in office: Aug. 12, 1984. **Local divisions:** 9 regions and capital district. **Defense:** 17% of govt. budget (1978).

Economy: Chief crops: Palm oil and kernels, cocoa, coffee, tobacco. **Minerals:** Oil, potash, natural gas, lead, copper, zinc.

Crude oil reserves (1980): 400 mln. bbls. **Arable land:** 2%. **Fish catch** (1983): 20,000 metric tons. **Electricity prod.** (1981): 165 mln. kwh. **Labor force:** 90% agric.

Finance: Currency: CFA franc (Mar. 1985: 471 = $1 US). **Gross domestic product** (1982 est.): $2 bln. **Per capita income** (1978): $500. **Imports** (1978): $261 mln.; partners (1978): Fr. 50%, W. Ger. 5%. **Exports** (1977): $185 mln.; partners (1978): Ital. 31%, Fr. 24%, Sp. 8%. **Tourist receipts** (1982): $13 mln. **International reserves less gold** (Oct. 1984): $5.5 mln. **Gold:** 11,000 oz t. **Consumer prices** (change in 1983): 7.8%.

Transport: Railway traffic (1981): 358 mln. passenger-km; 546 mln. net ton-km. **Motor vehicles:** in use (1982): 41,000 passenger cars, 79,000 comm. vehicles. **Chief ports:** Pointe-Noire, Brazzaville.

Communications: Television sets: 3,500 in use (1981). **Radios:** 92,000 in use (1981). **Telephones in use** (1982): 9,000.

Health: Life expectancy at birth (1980): 46.9 male; 50.2 female. **Births** (per 1,000 pop. 1984): 44.2. **Deaths** (per 1,000 pop. 1984): 17.2. **Natural increase** (1984): 2.7%. **Hospital beds** (per 100,000 pop. 1977): 499. **Physicians** (per 100,000 pop. 1977): 14. **Infant mortality** (per 1,000 live births 1984): 134.

Education (1980): **Literacy:** 80%. Years compulsory 10; attendance 80%.

Major International Organizations: UN, OAU.
Embassy: 4891 Colorado Ave. NW 20011; 726-5500.

The Loango Kingdom flourished in the 15th century, as did the Anzico Kingdom of the Batekes; by the late 17th century they had become weakened. France established control by 1885. Independence came Aug. 15, 1960.

After a 1963 coup sparked by trade unions, the country adopted a Marxist-Leninist stance, with the USSR and China vying for influence. Tribal divisions remain strong. France remains a dominant trade partner and source of technical assistance, and French-owned private enterprise retained a major economic role. However, the government of Pres. Sassou-Nguesso favored a strengthening of relations with the USSR, a socialist constitution was adopted, 1979, and on May 13, 1981 a treaty of friendship and cooperation was signed with the Soviets.

Costa Rica
Republic of Costa Rica

People: Population (1984 est.): 2,693,000. **Age distrib.** (%): 0–14: 44.0; 15–59: 50.4; 60+: 5.6. **Pop. density:** 124 per sq. mi. **Urban** (1982): 43%. **Ethnic groups:** Spanish (with Mestizo minority). **Language:** Spanish (official). **Religions:** Roman Catholicism prevails.

Geography: Area: 19,653 sq. mi., smaller than W. Virginia. **Location:** in central America. **Neighbors:** Nicaragua on N, Panama on S. **Topography:** Lowlands by the Caribbean are tropical. The interior plateau, with an altitude of about 4,000 ft., is temperate. **Capital:** San Jose. **Cities** (1982 est.): San Jose 867,800; Alajuela (1979 est.) 40,000; Cartago (1979 est.) 40,000.

Government: Type: Democratic Republic. **Head of state:** Pres. Luis Alberto Monge Alvarez; b. Dec. 29, 1925; in office May 8, 1982. **Local divisions:** 7 provinces and 80 cantons. **Armed forces:** para-military 5,000.

Economy: Industries: Fiberglass, aluminum, textiles, fertilizers, roofing, cement. **Chief crops:** Coffee (chief export), bananas, sugar, cocoa, cotton, hemp. **Minerals:** Gold, salt, sulphur, iron. **Other resources:** Fish, forests. **Arable land:** 10%. **Meat prod.** (1980): beef: 81,000 metric tons; pork: 10,000 metric tons. **Fish catch** (1983): 15,000 metric tons. **Electricity prod.** (1982): 2.5 bln. kwh. **Labor force:** 33% agric.; 40% ind. & comm.; 25% service and government.

Finance: Currency: Colone (Mar. 1985: 48.6 = $1 US). **Gross domestic product** (1982): $2.0 bln. **Per capita income** (1981): $2,238. **Imports** (1980): $1.46 bln.; partners: U.S. 33%, Jap. 10%, Guat. 5%, W. Ger. 5%. **Exports** (1980): $1.0 bln.; partners: U.S. 33%, W. Ger. 11%. **Tourists** (1982): 345,000; receipts $131 mln. **National budget** (1979): $217 mln. revenues; $332 mln. expenditures. **International reserves less gold** (Mar. 1985): $395.1 mln. **Gold:** 26,000 oz t. **Consumer prices** (change in 1984): 12.0%.

Transport: Railway traffic (1983): 81 mln. passenger-km; 14 mln. net ton-km. **Motor vehicles:** in use (1982): 90,000 passenger cars, 85,000 comm. vehicles. **Civil aviation** (1982): 624 mln. passenger-km; 21 mln. net ton-km. **Chief ports:** Limon, Puntarenas, Golfito.

Communications: Television sets: 255,000 in use (1982). **Radios:** 190,000 in use (1982). **Telephones in use** (1982): 256,000. **Daily newspaper circ.** (1982): 121 per 1,000 pop.

Health: Life expectancy at birth (1981): 67.5 male; 71.9 female. **Births** (per 1,000 pop. 1981): 29.7. **Deaths** (per 1,000 pop. 1981): 4.3. **Natural increase** (1981): 2.5%. **Hospital beds** (per 100,000 pop 1977): 345. **Physicians** (per 100,000 pop. 1977): 72. **Infant mortality** (per 1,000 live births 1982): 37.6.

Education (1982): **Literacy:** 90%. Years compulsory 6; attendance 99%.

Major International Organizations: UN and its specialized agencies, OAS.

Embassy: 2112 S St. NW, 20008; 234-2945.

Guaymi Indians inhabited the area when Spaniards arrived, 1502. Independence came in 1821. Costa Rica seceded from the Central American Federation in 1838. Since the civil war of 1948-49, there has been little violent social conflict, and free political institutions have been preserved.

Costa Rica, though still a largely agricultural country, has achieved a relatively high standard of living and social services, and land ownership is widespread.

Cuba
Republic of Cuba

People: Population (1984 est.): 9,995,000. **Age distrib. (%):** 0–29: 57.8; 30–59: 31.3; 60+: 10.9. **Pop. density:** 232 per sq. mi. **Urban** (1982): 69%. **Ethnic groups:** Spanish, African. **Languages:** Spanish. **Religions:** Roman Catholic 42%, none 49%.

Geography: Area: 44,218 sq. mi., nearly as large as Pennsylvania. **Location:** Westernmost of West Indies. **Neighbors:** Bahamas, U.S., on N, Mexico on W, Jamaica on S, Haiti on E. **Topography:** The coastline is about 2,500 miles. The N coast is steep and rocky, the S coast low and marshy. Low hills and fertile valleys cover more than half the country. Sierra Maestra, in the E is the highest of 3 mountain ranges. **Capital:** Havana. **Cities** (1981 cen.): Havana 1,924,886; Santiago de Cuba 563,455; Camaguey 480,620.

Government: Type: Communist state. **Head of state:** Pres. Fidel Castro Ruz; b. Aug. 13, 1926; in office: Dec. 3, 1976 (formerly Prime Min. since Feb. 16, 1959). **Local divisions:** 14 provinces, 169 municipal assemblies. **Defense:** 5% of GNP (1982).

Economy: Industries: Texiles, wood products, cement, chemicals, cigars. **Chief crops:** Sugar (83% of exports), tobacco, coffee, pineapples, bananas, citrus fruit, coconuts. **Minerals:** Cobalt, nickel, iron, copper, manganese, salt. **Other resources:** Forests. **Arable land:** 28%. **Meat prod.** (1983): beef: 162,000 metric tons; pork: 73,000 metric tons. **Fish catch** (1981): 98,200 metric tons. **Electricity prod.** (1982): 10.7 bln. kwh. **Crude steel prod.** (1981): 300,000 metric tons. **Labor force:** 30% agric.; 45% ind. & comm.; 20% services.

Finance: Currency: Peso (Oct. 1984: 1.14 = $1 US). **Gross national product** (1979): $13.9 bln. **Per capita income** (1981): $840. **Imports** (1979): $5.1 bln.; partners (1980): USSR 62%, Jap. 8%, Canada 6%. **Exports** (1979): $5.3 bln.; partners (1980): USSR 64%.

Transport: Railway traffic (1981): 1.8 bln. passenger-km; 2.6 bln. net ton-km. **Motor vehicles:** in use (1979): 152,600 passenger cars, 40,000 comm. vehicles. **Civil aviation** (1981): 1.2 bln. passenger-km; 14.5 mln. net ton-km. **Chief ports:** Havana, Matanzas, Cienfuegos, Santiago de Cuba.

Communications: Television sets: 750,000 in use (1984). **Radios:** 2.1 mln. in use (1984). **Telephones in use** (1982): 406,355. **Daily newspaper circ.** (1983): 195 per 1,000 pop.

Health: Life expectancy at birth: (1980): 71.0 male; 74.0 female. **Births** (per 1,000 pop. 1982): 16.3. **Deaths** (per 1,000 pop. 1982): 5.8. **Natural increase** (1982): 1.05%. **Physicians** 16,193 serve 266 hospitals (1981). **Infant mortality** (per 1,000 live births 1983): 25.

Education (1983): **Literacy:** 96%. School is free & compulsory between ages 6–14.

Major International Organizations: UN and its specialized agencies.

Some 50,000 Indians lived in Cuba when it was discovered by Columbus in 1492. Its name derives from the Indian Cubanacan. Except for British occupation of Havana, 1762-63, Cuba remained Spanish until 1898. A slave-based sugar plantation economy developed from the 18th century, aided by early mechanization of milling. Sugar remains the chief product and chief export despite government attempts to diversify.

A ten-year uprising ended in 1878 with guarantees of rights by Spain, which Spain failed to carry out. A full-scale movement under Jose Marti began Feb. 24, 1895.

The U.S. declared war on Spain in April, 1898, after the sinking of the U.S.S. Maine in Havana harbor, and defeated it in the short Spanish-American War. Spain gave up all claims to Cuba. U.S. troops withdrew in 1902, but under 1903 and 1934 agreements, the U.S. leases a site at Guantanamo Bay in the SE as a naval base. U.S. and other foreign investments acquired a dominant role in the economy. In 1952, former president Fulgencio Batista seized control and established a dictatorship, which grew increasingly harsh and corrupt. Former student leader Fidel Castro assembled a rebel band in 1956; guerrilla fighting intensified in 1958. Batista fled Jan. 1, 1959, and in the resulting political vacuum Castro took power, becoming premier Feb. 16.

The government, quickly dominated by extreme leftists, began a program of sweeping economic and social changes, without restoring promised liberties. Opponents were imprisoned and some were executed. Some 700,000 Cubans emigrated in the years after the Castro takeover, mostly to the U.S.

Cattle and tobacco lands were nationalized, while a system of cooperatives was instituted. By the end of 1960 all banks and industrial companies had been nationalized, including over $1 billion worth of U.S.-owned properties, mostly without compensation.

Poor sugar crops resulted in collectivization of farms, stringent labor controls, and rationing, despite continued aid from the USSR and other Communist countries.

The U.S. cut back Cuba's sugar quota in 1960, and imposed a partial export embargo, which became total in 1962, severely damaging the economy. In 1961, some 1,400 Cubans, trained and backed by the U.S. Central Intelligence Agency, unsuccessfully tried to invade and overthrow the regime.

In the fall of 1962, the U.S. learned that the USSR had brought nuclear missiles to Cuba. After an Oct. 22 warning from Pres. Kennedy, the missiles were removed.

In 1977, Cuba and the U.S. signed agreements to exchange diplomats, without restoring full ties, and to regulate offshore fishing. In 1978, and again in 1980, the U.S. agreed to accept political prisoners released by Cuba some of whom, it was later discovered, were criminals and mental patients .

But relations are strained by ongoing Cuban military involvement abroad. In 1975-78, Cuba sent over 20,000 troops to aid one faction in the Angola Civil War. Cuban troops or advisers are stationed in several African countries. This presence, along with Cuba's growing involvement in Central America and the Caribbean has contributed to worsening relations with the U.S.

In 1983, 24 Cubans died and over 700 were captured, later repatriated, as a result of the U.S. led invasion of Grenada.

Cyprus
Republic of Cyprus

People: Population (1984 est.): 662,000. **Age distrib. (%):** 0–14: 25.0; 15–59: 61.0; 60+: 14.0. **Pop. density:** 183 per sq. mi. **Urban** (1982): 53%. **Ethnic groups:** Greeks 80%, Turks 18.7%, Armenians, Maronites. **Languages:** Greek, Turkish (both official), English. **Religions:** Orthodox 77%, Moslems 18%.

Geography: Area: 3,572 sq. mi., smaller than Connecticut. **Location:** In eastern Mediterranean Sea, off Turkish coast. **Neighbors:** Nearest are Turkey on N, Syria, Lebanon on E. **Topography:** Two mountain ranges run E-W, separated by a wide, fertile plain. **Capital:** Nicosia. **Cities** (1984 est.): Nicosia 124,300.

Government: Type: Republic. **Head of state:** Pres. Spyros Kyprianou; b. Oct. 28, 1932; in office: Aug. 3, 1977. **Local divisions:** 6 districts. **Defense:** 6.3% of govt. budget (1981). Greek: regulars 9,000; Turkish: 4,500 (1980).

Economy: Industries: Wine, clothing, construction, chemicals. **Chief crops:** Grains, grapes, carobs, citrus fruits, potatoes,

olives. **Minerals:** Copper, pyrites, asbetos, gypsum, umber. **Per capita arable land:** 1.5 acres. **Meat prod.** (1980): pork: 15,000 metric tons; lamb: 10,000 metric tons. **Electricity prod.** (1982): 1.1 mln. kwh. **Labor force:** 21% agric.; 20% ind., 18% comm., 19% serv.

Finance: Currency: Pound (Mar. 1985: 0.66 = $1 US). **GNP** (1983): $2.11 bln. **Per capita income** (1983): $3,986. **Imports** (1983): $1.21 bln.; partners: UK 13%, Gre. 7%. **Exports** (1983): $495 mln.; partners (1982): UK 20%, Leb. 12%, Sau. Ar. 9%. **Tourists** (1983): 621,000; receipts: $244 mln. **National budget** (1983): $540 mln. revenues; $737 mln. expenditures. **International reserves less gold** (Mar. 1985): $508.6 mln. **Gold:** 459,000 oz. t. **Consumer prices** (change in 1984): 6%.

Transport: Motor vehicles: in use (1983): 110,000 passenger cars, 38,000 comm. vehicles. **Civil aviation** (1982): 854 mln. passenger-km; 19.9 mln. net ton-km. **Chief ports:** Famagusta, Limassol.

Communications: Television sets: 110,000 (1983). **Radios:** 400,000 (1983). **Telephones in use** (1981): 113,400. **Daily newspaper circ.** (1983): 106 per 1,000 pop.

Health: Life expectancy at birth (1984): 72.3 male; 76.0 female. **Births** (per 1,000 pop. 1982): 22.1. **Deaths** (per 1,000 pop. 1982): 8.3. **Natural increase** (1978): .7%. **Hospital beds** (per 100,000 pop. 1981): 600. **Physicians** (per 100,000 pop. 1981): 100. **Infant mortality** (per 1,000 live births 1984): 17.

Education (1984): **Literacy:** 99%. **Years compulsory:** 9; attendance 99%.

Major International Organizations: UN and its specialized agencies, Commonwealth of Nations, EC (Assoc.).

Embassy: 2211 R St. NW, 20008; 462-5772.

Agitation for enosis (union) with Greece increased after World War II, with the Turkish minority opposed, and broke into violence in 1955-56. In 1959, Britain, Greece, Turkey, and Cypriot leaders approved a plan for an independent republic, with constitutional guarantees for the Turkish minority and permanent division of offices on an ethnic basis. Greek and Turkish Communal Chambers dealt with religion, education, and other matters.

Archbishop Makarios, formerly the leader of the enosis movement, was elected president, and full independence became final Aug. 16, 1960. Makarios was re-elected in 1968 and 1973.

Further communal strife led the United Nations to send a peace-keeping force in 1964; its mandate has been repeatedly renewed.

The Cypriot National Guard, led by officers from the army of Greece, seized the government July 15, 1974, and named Nikos Sampson, an advocate of union with Greece, president. Makarios fled the country. On July 20, Turkey invaded the island; Greece mobilized its forces but did not intervene. A cease-fire was arranged July 22. On the 23d, Sampson turned over the presidency to Glafkos Clerides (on the same day, Greece's military junta resigned). A peace conference collapsed Aug. 14; fighting resumed. By Aug. 16 Turkish forces had occupied the NE 40% of the island, despite the presence of UN peace forces. Makarios resumed the presidency in Dec., until his death, 1977.

Turkish Cypriots voted overwhelmingly, June 8, 1975, to form a separate Turkish Cypriot federated state. A president and assembly were elected in 1976. Some 200,000 Greeks have been expelled from the Turkish-controlled area, replaced by thousands of Turks, some from the mainland.

A unilateral declaration of independence was announced by Turkish-Cypriot leader Rauf Denktash, Nov. 15, 1983. The new state, which was not recognized by other nations, was named the Turkish Rep. of Northern Cyprus.

Czechoslovakia
Czechoslovak Socialist Republic

People: Population (1984 est.): 15,466,000. **Age distrib. (%):** 0–14: 24.3; 15–59: 59.9; 60+: 15.7. **Pop. density:** 309 per sq. mi. **Urban** (1983): 73%. **Ethnic groups:** Czechs 65%, Slovaks 30%, Hungarians 4%, Germans, Poles, Ukrainians. **Languages:** Czech, Slovak (both official). **Religions:** Roman Catholics were majority, Lutherans, Orthodox.

Geography: Area: 49,365 sq. mi., the size of New York. **Location:** In E central Europe. **Neighbors:** Poland, E. Germany on N, W. Germany on W. Austria, Hungary on S, USSR on E. **Topography:** Bohemia, in W, is a plateau surrounded by moun-

...ains; Moravia is hilly, Slovakia, in E, has mountains (Carpathi-ans) in N, fertile Danube plain in S. Vltava (Moldau) and Labe (Elbe) rivers flow N from Bohemia to G. **Capital:** Prague. **Cities** (1984 est.): Prague 1.1 mln.; Brno 382,000; Bratislava 404,000; Ostrava 324,000.

Government: Type: Communist. **Head of state:** Pres. Gustav Husak; b. Jan 10, 1913; in office: May 29, 1975; **Head of government:** Prime Min. Lubomir Strougal; b. Oct. 19, 1924; in office: Jan. 28, 1970. **Head of Communist Party:** First Sec. Gustav Husak; in office: Apr. 17, 1969. **Local divisions:** Czech and Slovak republics each have an assembly. **Defense:** 5.2% of GNP (1983).

Economy: Industries: Machinery, oil products, iron and steel, glass, chemicals, motor vehicles, cement. **Chief crops:** Wheat, sugar beets, potatoes, rye, corn, barley. **Minerals:** Mercury, coal, iron. Jachymor has Europe's greatest pitchblende (for uranium and radium) deposits. **Per capita arable land:** 0.8 acres. **Meat prod.** (1983): beef: 375,000 metric tons; pork: 770,000 metric tons; lamb 7,000 metric tons. **Electricity prod.** (1983): 76 bln. kwh. **Crude steel prod.** (1982): 14.9 mln. metric tons. **Labor force:** 12% agric.; 66% ind., comm.; 18% service, govt.

Finance: Currency: Koruna (Nov. 1984: 6.67 = $1 US). **Gross national product** (1982): $85.8 bln. **Per capita income** (1980): $5,800. **Imports** (1982): $15.6 bln.; partners (1982): USSR 43%, E. Ger. 9%, Pol. 6%, W. Ger. 5%. **Exports** (1982): $15.7 bln.; partners (1981): USSR 38%, E. Ger. 10%, Pol. 7%, Hung. 5%. **Tourists** (1978): 14.4 mln. **Consumer prices** (change in 1982): 8%.

Transport: Railway traffic (1983): 19.0 bln. passenger-km; 66.1 bln. net ton-km. **Motor vehicles:** in use (1982): 2.4 mln. passenger cars, 385,000 comm. vehicles; manuf. (1982): 173,000 passenger cars; 90,000 comm. vehicles. **Civil aviation** (1982): 1.5 bln. passenger-km; 17.1 mln. net ton-km.

Communications: Television sets: 4.3 mln. (1983). **Radios:** 4.3 mln. (1983), 241,000 manuf. (1978). **Telephones in use** (1981): 3.2 mln. **Daily newspaper circ.** (1983): 284 per 1,000 pop.

Health: Life expectancy at birth (1982): 67 male; 74 female. **Births** (per 1,000 pop. 1982): 15.2 **Deaths** (per 1,000 pop. 1982): 11.7. **Natural increase** (1982): .3%. **Hospital beds** 120,000; **Physicians and Dentists:** 50,992 (1981). **Infant mortality** (per 1,000 live births 1981): 16.8.

Education (1981): **Literacy:** 99%. **Pop. 5–19:** in school: 60%, teachers per 1,000: 30.

Major International Organizations: UN and its specialized agencies, Warsaw Pact.

Embassy: 3900 Linnean Ave. NW 20008; 263-6315.

Bohemia, Moravia and Slovakia were part of the Great Moravian Empire in the 9th century. Later, Slovakia was overrun by Magyars, while Bohemia and Moravia became part of the Holy Roman Empire. Under the kings of Bohemia, Prague in the 14th century was the cultural center of Central Europe. Bohemia and Hungary became part of Austria-Hungary.

In 1914-1918 Thomas G. Masaryk and Eduard Benes formed a provisional government with the support of Slovak leaders including Milan Stefanik. They proclaimed the Republic of Czechoslovakia Oct. 30, 1918.

By 1938 Nazi Germany had worked up disaffection among German-speaking citizens in Sudetenland and demanded its cession. Prime Min. Neville Chamberlain of Britain, with the acquiescence of France, signed with Hitler at Munich, Sept. 30, 1938, an agreement to the cession, with a guarantee of peace by Hitler and Mussolini. Germany occupied Sudetenland Oct. 1-2.

Hitler on Mar. 15, 1939, dissolved Czechoslovakia, made protectorates of Bohemia and Moravia, and supported the autonomy of Slovakia, which was proclaimed independent Mar. 14, 1939, with Josef Tiso president.

Soviet troops with some Czechoslovak contingents entered eastern Czechoslovakia in 1944 and reached Prague in May 1945; Benes returned as president. In May 1946 elections, the Communist Party won 38% of the votes, and Benes accepted Klement Gottwald, a Communist, as prime minister. Tiso was executed in 1947.

In February, 1948, the Communists seized power in advance of scheduled elections. In May 1948 a new constitution was approved. Benes refused to sign it. On May 30 the voters were offered a one-slate ballot and the Communists won full control. Benes resigned June 7. Gottwald became president and Benes

died Sept. 3. A harsh Stalinist period followed, with complete and violent suppression of all opposition.

In Jan. 1968 a liberalization movement spread explosively through Czechoslovakia. Antonin Novotny, long the Stalinist boss of the nation, was deposed as party leader and succeeded by Alexander Dubcek, a Slovak, who declared he intended to make communism democratic. On Mar. 22 Novotny resigned as president and was succeeded by Gen. Ludvik Svoboda. On Apr. 6, Premier Joseph Lenart resigned and was succeeded by Oldrich Cernik, whose new cabinet was pledged to carry out democratization and economic reforms.

In July 1968 the USSR and 4 Warsaw Pact nations demanded an end to liberalization. On Aug. 20, the Russian, Polish, East German, Hungarian, and Bulgarian armies invaded Czechoslovakia.

Despite demonstrations and riots by students and workers, press censorship was imposed, liberal leaders were ousted from office and promises of loyalty to Soviet policies were made by some old-line Communist Party leaders.

On Apr. 17, 1969, Dubcek resigned as leader of the Communist Party and was succeeded by Gustav Husak. In Jan. 1970, Premier Cernik was ousted. Censorship was tightened and the Communist Party expelled a third of its members. In 1972, more than 40 liberals were jailed on subversion charges. In 1973, amnesty was offered to some of the 40,000 who fled the country after the 1968 invasion, but repressive policies continue to remain in force.

More than 700 leading Czechoslovak intellectuals and former party leaders signed a human rights manifesto in 1977, called Charter 77, prompting a renewed crackdown by the regime.

Czechoslovakia has long been an industrial and technological leader of the eastern European countries, though its relative standing has declined in recent years because of the government's rejection of economic reforms.

Denmark
Kingdom of Denmark

People: Population (1984 est.): 5,112,000. **Age distrib. (%):** 0–14: 19.5 15–44: 44.2; 45+: 35.8. **Pop. density:** 307 per sq. mi. **Urban** (1982): 84%. **Ethnic groups:** Almost all Scandinavian. **Languages:** Danish. **Religions:** Predominantly Lutherans.

Geography: Area: 16,633 sq. mi., the size of Massachusetts and New Hampshire combined. **Location:** In northern Europe, separating the North and Baltic seas. **Neighbors:** W. Germany on S., Norway on NW, Sweden on NE. **Topography:** Denmark consists of the Jutland Peninsula and about 500 islands, 100 inhabited. The land is flat or gently rolling, and is almost all in productive use. **Capital:** Copenhagen. **Cities** (1983): Copenhagen 641,904; Arhus 246,679.

Government: Type: Constitutional Monarchy. **Head of state:** Queen Margrethe II; b. Apr. 16, 1940; in office: Jan. 14, 1972. **Head of government:** Prime Min. Poul Schluter; b. 1929; in office: Sept. 10, 1982. **Local divisions:** 14 counties and one city (Copenhagen). **Defense:** 2.6% of GNP (1982).

Economy: Industries: Machinery, textiles, furniture, electronics. **Chief crops:** Dairy products. **Crude oil reserves** (1980): 375 mln. bbls. **Arable land:** 62%. **Meat prod.** (1983): beef: 375,000 metric tons; pork: 1 mln. metric tons. **Fish catch** (1981): 1.8 mln. metric tons. **Electricity prod.** (1982): 22.0 bln. kwh. **Crude steel prod.** (1982): 560,000 metric tons. **Labor force:** 8.2% agric.; 45% manuf.

Finance: Currency: Krone (Mar. 1985: 11.0 = $1 US). **Gross domestic product** (1983): $50.4 bln. **Per capita income** (1980): $12,956. **Imports** (1984): $16.6 bln.; partners: W. Ger. 20%, Swed. 12%, UK 11%, Neth. 7%. **Exports** (1984): $15.9 bln.; partners (1982): W. Ger. 17%, UK 14%, Swed. 11%, Nor. 6%. **Tourists** (1980): 3.5 mln. visitors; receipts: 1.2 bln. **National budget** (1980): $15.4 bln. revenues; $16.9 bln. expenditures. **International reserves less gold** (Mar. 1985): $3.9 bln. **Gold:** 1.62 mln. oz t. **Consumer prices** (change in 1984): 6.3%.

Transport: Railway traffic (1982): 4.2 bln. passenger-km; 1.6 bln. net ton-km. **Motor vehicles:** in use (1982): 1.3 mln. passenger cars, 388,000 comm. vehicles. **Civil aviation** (1982): 2.9 bln. passenger-km; 128.6 mln. net ton-km. **Chief ports:** Copenhagen, Alborg, Arhus, Odense.

Communications: Television sets: 1.8 mln. licensed (1983). **Radios:** 2 mln. licensed (1983). **Telephones in use** (1983): 3.4 mln. **Daily newspaper circ.** (1983): 353 per 1,000 pop.

Health: Life expectancy at birth (1981): 71.3 male; 77.4 female. **Births** (per 1,000 pop. 1982): 10.3. **Deaths** (per 1,000 pop. 1982): 10.8. **Hospital beds** (per 100,000 pop. 1977): 853. **Physicians** (per 100,000 pop. 1977): 204. **Infant mortality** (per 1,000 live births 1982): 7.9.

Education (1981): **Literacy:** 99%. Years compulsory 9; attendance 100%.

Major International Organizations: UN and its specialized agencies, OECD, EC.

Embassy: 3200 Whitehaven St. NW 20008; 234-4300.

The origin of Copenhagen dates back to ancient times, when the fishing and trading place named Havn (port) grew up on a cluster of islets, but Bishop Absalon (1128-1201) is regarded as the actual founder of the city.

Danes formed a large component of the Viking raiders in the early Middle Ages. The Danish kingdom was a major north European power until the 17th century, when it lost its land in southern Sweden. Norway was separated in 1815, and Schleswig-Holstein in 1864. Northern Schleswig was returned in 1920.

There was severe labor strife in 1985.

The **Faeroe Islands** in the N. Atlantic, about 300 mi. NE of the Shetlands, and 850 mi. from Denmark proper, 18 inhabited, have an area of 540 sq. mi. and pop. (1982) of 45,000. They are self-governing in most matters.

Greenland

(Kalaallit Nunaat)

Greenland, a huge island between the N. Atlantic and the Polar Sea, is separated from the North American continent by Davis Strait and Baffin Bay. Its total area is 840,000 sq. mi., 84% of which is ice-capped. Most of the island is a lofty plateau 9,000 to 10,000 ft. in altitude. The average thickness of the cap is 1,000 ft. The population (1982 est.) is 51,000. Under the 1953 Danish constitution the colony became an integral part of the realm with representatives in the Folketing. The Danish parliament, 1978, approved home rule for Greenland, effective May 1, 1979. Accepting home rule the islanders elected a socialist-dominated legislature, Apr. 4th. With home rule, Greenlandic place names came into official use. The technically-correct name for Greenland is now Kalaallit Nunaat; its capital is Nuuk, rather than Gothab. Fish is the principal export.

Djibouti

Republic of Djibouti

People: Population (1984 est.): 289,000. **Pop. density:** 37 per sq. mi. **Ethnic groups:** Issa (Somali) 60%; Afar 35%; European, Arab. **Languages:** French (official); Somali, Saho-Afar, Arabic. **Religions:** Most are Moslems.

Geography: Area: 8,996 sq. mi., about the size of New Hampshire. **Location:** On E coast of Africa, separated from Arabian Peninsula by the strategically vital strait of Bab el-Mandeb. **Neighbors:** Ethiopia on N (Eritrea) and W, Somalia on S. **Topography:** The territory, divided into a low coastal plain, mountains behind, and an interior plateau, is arid, sandy, and desolate. The climate is generally hot and dry. **Capital:** Djibouti. **Cities** (1980): Djibouti (met.) 200,000.

Government: Type: Republic. **Head of state:** Pres. Hassan Gouled Aptidon b. 1916; in office: June 24, 1977; **Head of government:** Prem. Barkat Gourat Hamadou; in office: Sept. 30, 1978. **Local divisions:** 5 cercles (districts).

Economy: Minerals: Salt. **Electricity prod.** (1982): 130 mln. kwh.

Finance: Currency Franc (Nov. 1984: 177 = $1 US). **Gross domestic product:** (1981): $180 mln. **Per capita income** (1982): $400. **Imports** (1979): $140 mln.; partners (1979): Fr. 47%, Jap. 8%, UK 8%. **Exports** (1979): $20 mln.; partners (1979): Fr. 87%.

Transport: Motor vehicles: in use (1982): 9,000 passenger cars, 1,500 commercial vehicles. **Chief ports:** Djibouti.

Communications: Television sets: 10,000 in use (1982). **Radios:** 17,200 in use (1982). **Telephones in use** (1982): 3,000.

Health: Life expectancy at birth (1982): 50 years. **Births** (per 1,000 pop. 1978): 49. **Deaths** (per 1,000 pop. 1978): 23. **Natural increase** (1978): 2.6%.

Education (1981): **Literacy:** 20%.

Major International Organizations: UN, OAU, Arab League.

Embassy: 866 United Nations Plaza, New York, NY 10017; (212) 753-3163.

France gained control of the territory in stages between 1862 and 1900.

Ethiopia and Somalia have renounced their claims to the area, but each has accused the other of trying to gain control. There were clashes between Afars (ethnically related to Ethiopians) and Issas (related to Somalis) in 1976. Immigrants from both countries continued to enter the country up to independence, which came June 27, 1977.

Unemployment is very high. There are few natural resources; trade is the main contributor to domestic product. French aid is the mainstay of the economy and some 5,000 French troops are present.

Dominica

Commonwealth of Dominica

People: Population (1984 est.): 74,000. **Pop. density:** 258 per sq. mi. **Ethnic groups:** nearly all African or mulatto, Caribs. **Languages:** English (official), French patois. **Religions:** mainly Roman Catholic.

Geography: Area: 290 sq. mi., about one-fourth the size of Rhode Island. **Location:** In Eastern Caribbean, most northerly Windward Is. **Neighbors:** Guadeloupe to N, Martinique to S. **Topography:** Mountainous, a central ridge running from N to S, terminating in cliffs; volcanic in origin, with numerous thermal springs; rich deep topsoil on leeward side, red tropical clay on windward coast. **Capital** (1983 est.) Roseau 18,000.

Government: Head of state: Pres. Clarence Augustus Seignoret; in office: 1984. **Head of government:** Prime Min. Mary Eugenia Charles; b. 1919; in office: July 21, 1980. **Local divisions:** 25 village councils and 2 town councils.

Economy: Industries: Agriculture, tourism. **Chief crops:** Bananas, citrus fruits, coconuts. **Minerals:** Pumice. **Other resources:** Forests. **Arable land:** 23%. **Electricity prod.** (1982): 17 mln. kwh.

Finance: Currency: East Caribbean dollar (Mar. 1985: 2.70 = $1 US). **Gross domestic product** (1982): $60 mln. **Per capita income** (1976): $460. **Imports** (1978): $28.4 mln.; partners (1978): UK 27%, U.S. 15%, Can. 5%. **Exports** (1978): $15.8 mln.; partners (1978): UK 67%. **Tourists** (1983): 19,638. **National budget** (1976): $6.29 mln. revenues; $7.51 mln. expenditures. **Consumer prices** (change in 1984): 2.2%.

Transport: Chief ports: Roseau.

Communications: Telephones in use (1982): 2,972.

Health: Life expectancy at birth (1962): 56.97 male; 59.18 female. **Births** (per 1,000 pop. 1978): 21.4. **Deaths** (per 1,000 pop. 1978): 5.3. **Natural increase** (1978): 1.6%. **Hospital beds** (1983): 237. **Physicians** (1983): 26. **Infant mortality** (per 1,000 live births 1978): 19.6.

Education: Literacy: 80%.

A British colony since 1805, Dominica was granted self government in 1967. Independence was achieved Nov. 3, 1978.

Hurricane David struck, Aug. 30, 1979, devastating the island and destroying the banana plantations, Dominica's economic mainstay. Coups were attempted in 1980 and 1981.

Dominica took a leading role in the instigation of the October 1983 invasion of Grenada.

Dominican Republic

People: Population (1984 est.): 6,416,000. **Age distrib. (%):** 0–14: 47.5; 15–59: 47.5; 60+: 4.9. **Pop. density:** 316 per sq. mi. **Urban** (1983): 52.0%. **Ethnic groups:** Caucasian 16%, mulatto

73%, Negro 11%. **Languages:** Spanish. **Religions:** Roman Catholic 98%.

Geography: Area: 18,704 sq. mi., the size of Vermont and New Hampshire combined. **Location:** In West Indies, sharing I. of Hispaniola with Haiti. **Neighbors:** Haiti on W. **Topography:** The Cordillera Central range crosses the center of the country, rising to over 10,000 ft., highest in the Caribbean. The Cibao valley to the N is major agricultural area. **Capital:** Santo Domingo. **Cities** (1982 est.): Santo Domingo 1,600,000; Santiago de Los Caballeros 326,000.

Government: Type: Representative democracy. **Head of state:** Pres. Salvador Jorge Blanco; b. July 5, 1926; in office: Aug. 16, 1982. **Local divisions:** 26 provinces and Santo Domingo. **Defense:** 1.4% of GDP. (1982).

Economy: Industries: Sugar refining, cement, textiles, pharmaceuticals. **Chief crops:** sugar, cocoa, coffee, tobacco, rice. **Minerals:** Nickel, gold, silver, bauxite. **Other resources:** Timber. **Arable land:** 25%. **Meat prod.** (1980): beef: 43,000 metric tons; pork: 12,000 metric tons. **Electricity prod.** (1982): 2.9 bln. kwh. **Labor force:** 47% agric.; 23% manuf.

Finance: Currency: Peso (Mar. 1985: 3.32 = $1 US). **Gross domestic product** (1981): $7.0 bln. **Per capita income** (1980): $1,221. **Imports** (1983): $1.4 bln.; partners (1982): U.S. 39%, Venez. 18%, Mex. 14%. **Exports** (1983): $780 mln.; partners (1982): U.S. 54%, Swit. 12%, USSR 8%, Neth. 5%. **Tourists** (1980): 173 mln. receipts. **National budget** (1979): $745.6 mln. revenues; $973.9 mln. expenditures. **International reserves less gold** (Mar. 1985): $263 mln. **Gold:** 18,000 oz t. **Consumer prices** (change in 1983): 4.8%

Transport: Motor vehicles: in use (1982): 102,100 passenger cars, 66,000 comm. vehicles. **Chief ports:** Santo Domingo, San Pedro de Macoris, Puerto Plata.

Communications: Television sets: 388,000 in use (1983). **Radios:** 225,000 in use (1983). **Telephones in use** (1982): 175,054. **Daily newspaper circ.** (1982): 52 per 1,000 pop.

Health: Life expectancy at birth (1983): 60.7 male; 64.6 female. **Births** (per 1,000 pop. 1983): 38.6. **Deaths** (per 1,000 pop. 1983): 8.5. **Natural increase** (1983): 3.0%. **Hospital beds** (per 100,000 pop. 1977): 233. **Physicians** (per 100,000 pop. 1977): 53. **Infant mortality** (per 1,000 live births 1983): 28.3.

Education (1981): **Literacy:** 62%. Years compulsory 8; attendance 60%.

Major International Organizations: UN and its specialized agencies, OAS.

Embassy: 1715-22d St. NW 20008; 332-6280.

Carib and Arawak Indians inhabited the island of Hispaniola when Columbus landed in 1492. The city of Santo Domingo, founded 1496, is the oldest settlement by Europeans in the hemisphere and has the supposed ashes of Columbus in an elaborate tomb in its ancient cathedral.

The western third of the island was ceded to France in 1697. Santo Domingo itself was ceded to France in 1795. Haitian leader Toussaint L'Ouverture seized it, 1801. Spain returned intermittently 1803-21, as several native republics came and went. Haiti ruled again, 1822-44, and Spanish occupation occurred 1861-63.

The country was occupied by U.S. Marines from 1916 to 1924, when a constitutionally elected government was installed.

In 1930, Gen. Rafael Leonidas Trujillo Molina was elected president. Trujillo ruled brutally until his assassination in 1961. Pres. Joaquin Balaguer, appointed by Trujillo in 1960, resigned under pressure in 1962. Juan Bosch, elected president in the first free elections in 38 years, was overthrown in 1963.

On April 24, 1965, a revolt was launched by followers of Bosch and others, including a few communists. Four days later U.S. Marines intervened against the pro-Bosch forces. Token units were later sent by 5 So. American countries as a peacekeeping force.

A provisional government supervised a June 1966 election, in which Balaguer defeated Bosch by a 3-2 margin; there were some charges of election fraud. The Inter-American Peace Force completed its departure Sept. 20, 1966.

Continued depressed world prices have affected the main export commodity, sugar.

Ecuador
Republic of Ecuador

People: Population (1984 est.): 9,091,000. **Age distrib. (%):** 0–14: 44.5; 15–59: 49.6; 60+: 6.0. **Pop. density:** 81 per sq. mi. **Urban** (1984): 55% **Ethnic groups:** Indians 25%, Mestizo 55%, Spanish 10%, African 10%. **Languages:** Spanish (official), Quechuan, Jivaroan. **Religions:** Predominantly Roman Catholic.

Geography: Area: 104,506 sq. mi., the size of Colorado. **Location:** In NW S. America, on Pacific coast, astride Equator. **Neighbors:** Colombia to N, Peru to E and S. **Topography:** Two ranges of Andes run N and S, splitting the country into 3 zones: hot, humid lowlands on the coast; temperate highlands between the ranges, and rainy, tropical lowlands to the E. **Capital:** Quito. **Cities** (1984 est.): Guayaquil 1,278,900; Quito 890,000.

Government: Type: Republic. **Head of state:** Pres. Leon Febres-Cordero; b. Mar. 9, 1931; in office: Aug. 10, 1984. **Local divisions:** 20 provinces. **Defense:** 8.2% of govt. budget (1983).

Economy: Industries: Food processing, wood prods., textiles. **Chief crops:** Bananas (largest exporter), coffee, rice, sugar, corn. **Minerals:** Oil, copper, iron, lead, coal, sulphur. **Crude oil reserves** (1980): 1.1 bln. bbls. **Other resources:** Rubber, bark. **Arable land:** 18%. **Meat prod.** (1980): beef: 92,000 metric tons; pork: 63,000 metric tons; lamb: 10,000 metric tons. **Fish catch** (1982): 636,000 metric tons. **Electricity prod.** (1982): 3.3 bln. kwh. **Labor force:** 49% agric., 11% ind., 17% services.

Finance: Currency: Sucre (Mar. 1985: 67.1 = $1 US). **Gross domestic product** (1983): $12.9 bln. **Per capita income** (1983): $1,428. **Imports** (1984): $1.7 bln.; partners: U.S. 37%, EC 19%, Jap. 12%. **Exports** (1984): $2.5 bln.; partners: U.S. 48%. **National budget** (1983): $1.7 bln. **International reserves less gold** (Mar. 1985): $550 mln. **Gold:** 414,000 oz t. **Consumer prices** (change in 1984): 31.2%.

Transport: Railway traffic (1983) 69 mln. passenger-km; 29 mln. net ton-km. **Motor vehicles:** in use (1981): 232,600 passenger cars, 23,900 comm. vehicles. **Civil aviation** (1982): 862 mln. passenger-km; 39.4 mln. net ton-km. **Chief ports:** Guayaquil, Manta, Esmeraldas, Puerto Bolivar.

Communications: Television sets: 135,000 in use (1983). **Radios:** 1.8 mln. in use (1983). **Telephones in use** (1982): 290,000. **Daily newspaper circ.** (1983): 60 per 1,000 pop.

Health: Life expectancy at birth (1979): 62 yrs. **Births** (per 1,000 pop. 1981): 39.6. **Deaths** (per 1,000 pop. 1981): 9.2. **Natural increase** (1981): 3.0%. **Hospital beds** (per 100,000 pop.1977): 204. **Physicians** (per 100,000 pop. 1977): 64. **Infant mortality** (per 1,000 live births 1981): 79.

Education (1984): **Literacy:** 90%. Attendance through 6th grade—76% urban, 33% rural.

Major International Organizations: UN and its specialized agencies, OAS, OPEC.

Embassy: 2535 15th St. NW 20009; 234-7200.

Spain conquered the region, which was the northern Inca empire, in 1633. Liberation forces defeated the Spanish May 24, 1822, near Quito. Ecuador became part of the Great Colombia Republic but seceded, May 13, 1830.

Ecuador had been ruled by civilian and military dictatorships since 1968. A peaceful transfer of power from the military junta to the democratic civilian government took place, 1979.

Since 1972, the economy has revolved around its petroleum exports, which have declined since 1982 causing severe economic problems.

Ecuador and Peru have long disputed their Amazon Valley boundary.

The **Galapagos Islands,** 600 mi. to the W, are the home of hugh tortoises and other unusual animals.

Egypt
Arab Republic of Egypt

People: Population (1984 est.): 47,000,000. **Pop. density:** 122 per sq. mi. **Urban** (1980): 45.1%. **Ethnic groups:** Egyptian, Bedouin, Nubian. **Languages:** Arabic, English. **Religions:** 90% Sunni Moslem.

Geography: Area: 386,650 sq. mi, the size of Texas, Oklahoma, and Arkansas combined. **Location:** NE corner of Africa. **Neighbors:** Libya on W, Sudan on S, Israel on E. **Topography:** Almost entirely desolate and barren, with hills and mountains in E and along Nile. The Nile Valley, where most of the people live, stretches 550 miles. **Capital:** Cairo. **Cities** (1976 cen.): Cairo 5,084,463; Alexandria 2,318,655; Giza 1,246,713; Subra-El Khema 393,700; El-Mahalla El-Kubra 292,853.

Government: Type: Republic. **Head of state:** Pres. Hosni Mubarak; b. 1929; in office: Oct. 14, 1981. **Head of Government:** Kamal Hassan Ali; in office: June, 1984. **Local divisions:** 26 governorates. **Defense:** 8.2% of GNP (1982).

Economy: Industries: Textiles, chemicals, petrochemicals, cement. **Chief crops:** Cotton (one of largest producers), rice, beans, fruits, grains, vegetables, sugar, corn. **Minerals:** Oil, phosphates, gypsum, iron, manganese, limestone. **Crude oil reserves** (1983): 6 bln. bbls. **Arable land:** 4%. **Meat prod.** (1983): beef: 278,000 metric tons; lamb: 48,000 metric tons. **Fish catch** (1983): 100,000 metric tons. **Electricity prod.** (1982): 17.7 bln. kwh. **Crude steel prod.** (1981 est.): 900,000 metric tons. **Labor force:** 50% agric.; 26% services.

Finance: Currency: Pound (Mar. 1985: .72 = $1 US). **Gross domestic product** (1983): $32 bln. **Per capita income** (1983): $686. **Imports** (1983): $10.2 bln.; partners: U.S. 19%, W. Ger. 10%, lt. 8%, France 8%. **Exports** (1983): $3.2 bln.; partners: lt. 22%, lsr. 14%. **Tourists** (1983): 1.5 mln. visitors. **International reserves less gold** (Jan. 1985): $736 mln. **Gold:** 2.43 mln. oz t. **Consumer prices** (change in 1984): 17.1%.

Transport: Railway traffic (1982): 18.7 bln. passenger-km; 2.3 bln. net ton-km. **Motor vehicles:** in use (1983): 597,000 passenger cars, 227,000 comm. vehicles. **Civil aviation** (1982): 3.6 bln. passenger-km, 56 mln. freight ton-km. **Chief ports:** Alexandria, Port Said, Suez.

Communications: Television sets: 6 mln. in use (1982). **Radios:** 12 mln. in use (1982). **Telephones in use** (1982): 522,000. **Daily newspaper circ.** (1983): 54 per 1,000 pop.

Health: Life expectancy at birth (1983): 55.9 male; 58.4 female. **Births** (per 1,000 pop. 1982): 36.9. **Deaths** (per 1,000 pop. 1982): 10.3. **Natural increase** (1982): 2.6%. **Hospital beds** (1983): 85,350. **Physicians** (1983): 73,300. **Infant mortality** (per 1,000 live births 1983): 69.

Education (1985): Literacy: 44%. Compulsory ages 6-12.

Major International Organizations: UN and its specialized agencies, OAU, Islamic Conference Org.

Embassy: 2310 Decatur Pl. NW 20008; 232-5400.

Archeological records of ancient Egyptian civilization date back to 4000 BC. A unified kingdom arose around 3200 BC, and extended its way south into Nubia and north as far as Syria. A high culture of rulers and priests was built on an economic base of serfdom, fertile soil, and annual flooding of the Nile banks.

Imperial decline facilitated conquest by Asian invaders (Hyksos, Assyrians). The last native dynasty fell in 341 BC to the Persians, who were in turn replaced by Greeks (Alexander and the Ptolemies), Romans, Byzantines, and Arabs, who introduced Islam and the Arabic language. The ancient Egyptian language is preserved only in the liturgy of the Coptic Christians.

Egypt was ruled as part of larger Islamic empires for several centuries. The Mamluks, a military caste of Caucasian origin, ruled Egypt from 1250 until defeat by the Ottoman Turks in 1517. Under Turkish sultans the khedive as hereditary viceroy had wide authority. Britain intervened in 1882 and took control of administration, though nominal allegiance to the Ottoman Empire continued until 1914.

The country was a British protectorate from 1914 to 1922. A 1936 treaty strengthened Egyptian autonomy, but Britain retained bases in Egypt and a condominium over the Sudan. Britain fought German and Italian armies from Egypt, 1940-42, but Egypt did not declare war against Germany until 1945. In 1951 Egypt abrogated the 1936 treaty. The Sudan became independent in 1956.

The uprising of July 23, 1952, led by the Society of Free Officers, named Maj. Gen. Mohammed Naguib commander in chief and forced King Farouk to abdicate. When the republic was proclaimed June 18, 1953, Naguib became its first president and premier. Lt. Col. Gamal Abdel Nasser removed Naguib and became premier in 1954. In 1956, he was voted president. Nasser died in 1970 and was replaced by Vice Pres. Anwar Sadat.

A series of decrees in July, 1961, nationalized about 90% of industry. Economic liberalization was begun, 1974, with more emphasis on private domestic and foreign investment.

In July, 1956, the U. S. and UK withdrew support for loans to start the Aswan High Dam. Nasser obtained credits and technicians from the USSR to build the dam. The billion-dollar Aswan High Dam project, begun 1960, completed 1971, provided irrigation for more than a million acres of land and a potential of 10 billion kwh of electricity per year. Artesian wells, drilled in the Western Desert, reclaimed 43,000 acres, 1960-66.

When the state of Israel was proclaimed in 1948, Egypt joined other Arab nations invading Israel and was defeated.

After terrorist raids across its border, Israel invaded Egypt's Sinai Peninsula, Oct. 29, 1956. Egypt rejected a cease-fire demand by Britain and France; on Oct. 31 the 2 nations dropped bombs and on Nov. 5-6 landed forces. Egypt and Israel accepted a UN cease-fire; fighting ended Nov. 7.

A UN Emergency Force guarded the 117-mile long border between Egypt and Israel until May 19, 1967, when it was withdrawn at Nasser's demand. Egyptian troops entered the Gaza Strip and the heights of Sharm el Sheikh and 3 days later closed the Strait of Tiran to all Israeli shipping. Full-scale war broke out June 5 and before it ended under a UN cease-fire June 10, Israel had captured Gaza and the Sinai Peninsula, controlled the east bank of the Suez Canal and reopened the gulf.

Sporadic fighting with Israel broke out late in 1968 and continued almost daily, 1969-70. Military and economic aid was received from the USSR. Israel and Egypt agreed, Aug. 7, 1970, to a cease-fire and peace negotiations proposed by the U.S. Negotiations failed to achieve results, but the cease-fire continued into 1973.

In July 1972 Sadat ordered most of the 20,000 Soviet military advisers and personnel to leave Egypt.

In a surprise attack Oct. 6, 1973, Egyptian forces crossed the Suez Canal into the Sinai. (At the same time, Syrian forces attacked Israelis on the Golan Heights.) Egypt was supplied by a USSR military airlift; the U.S. responded with an airlift to Israel. Israel counter-attacked, crossed the canal, surrounded Suez City. A UN cease-fire took effect Oct. 24.

A disengagement agreement was signed Jan. 18, 1974. Under it, Israeli forces withdrew from the canal's W bank; limited numbers of Egyptian forces occupied a strip along the E bank. A second accord was signed in 1975, with Israel yielding Sinai oil fields. Pres. Sadat's surprise visit to Jerusalem, Nov. 1977, opened the prospect of peace with Israel, but worsened relations with Libya (border clashes, July 1977). On Mar. 26, 1979, Egypt and Israel signed a formal peace treaty, ending 30 years of war, and establishing diplomatic relations. Israel returned control of the Sinai to Egypt in April 1982.

Tension between Muslim fundamentalists and Christians in 1981 caused street riots and culminated in a nationwide security crackdown in September. Pres Sadat was assassinated on Oct. 6.

The **Suez Canal,** 103 mi. long, links the Mediterranean and Red seas. It was built by a French corporation 1859-69, but Britain obtained controlling interest in 1875. The last British troops were removed June 13, 1956. On July 26, Egypt nationalized the canal. French and British stockholders eventually received some compensation.

Egypt had barred Israeli ships and cargoes destined for Israel since 1948, and closed the canal to all shipping after the 1967 Arab-Israeli War. The canal was reopened in 1975; Egypt agreed to allow passage to Israeli cargo in third party ships. A $1.3 billion expansion project will enable the canal to accommodate larger tankers.

El Salvador
Republic of El Salvador

People: Population (1984 est.): 5,100,000. **Age distrib. (%):** 0–14; 46.2; 15–59: 48.4; 60+: 5.4. **Pop. density:** 661 per sq. mi. **Urban** (1978): 40.1%. **Ethnic groups:** Mestizos 89%, Indians 10%, Caucasians 1%. **Languages:** Spanish, Nahuatl (among some Indians). **Religions:** Roman Catholicism prevails. **Geography: Area:** 8,260 sq. mi., the size of Massachusetts. **Location:** In Central America. **Neighbors:** Guatemala on W, Honduras on N. **Topography:** A hot Pacific coastal plain in the south rises to a cooler plateau and valley region, densely populated. The N is mountainous, including many volcanoes. **Capital:** San Salvador. **Cities** (1982 est.): San Salvador 440,000.
Government: Type: Republic. **Head of state:** Pres., Jose Napoleon Duarte; b. Nov. 23, 1926; in office: June 1, 1984. **Local divisions:** 14 departments. **Defense:** 23% of expenditures (1984).
Economy: Industries: Food and beverages, textiles, petroleum products. **Chief crops:** Coffee, cotton, corn, sugar. **Other resources:** Rubber, forests. **Arable land:** 67%. **Meat prod.** (1980): beef: 28,000 metric tons; pork: 16,000 metric tons. **Electricity prod.** (1981): 1.5 bln. kwh. **Labor force:** 50% agric.; 22% ind.; 27% services.
Finance: Currency: Colon (Mar. 1985: 2.50 = $1 US). **Gross domestic product** (1984): $4.3 bln. **Per capita income** (1984): $854. **Imports** (1983): $870 mln.; partners: U.S. 35%, CACM 22%. **Exports** (1983): $732 mln.; partners: U.S. 35%, CACM 23%. **National budget** (1984): $944 mln. expenditures. **International reserves less gold** (Mar. 1985): $149 mln. **Gold:** 469,000 oz t. **Consumer prices** (change in 1984): 11.5%.
Transport: Railway traffic (1981): 14 mln. passenger-km; 31 mln. net ton-km. **Motor vehicles:** in use (1981): 77,300 passenger cars, 63,000 comm. vehicles. **Chief ports:** La Union, Acajutla.
Communications: Television sets: 300,000 in use (1981). **Radios:** 1.5 mln. in use (1981). **Telephones in use** (1982): 86,000. **Daily newspaper circ.** (1982): 71 per 1,000 pop.
Health: Life expectancy at birth (1985): 62.6 male; 66.3 female. **Births** (per 1,000 pop. 1982): 31.4. **Deaths** (per 1,000 pop. 1982): 6.7. **Natural increase** (1982): 2.4%. **Hospital beds** (per 100,000 pop. 1977): 161. **Physicians** (per 100,000 pop. 1977): 27. **Infant mortality** (per 1,000 live births 1985): 71.
Education (1985): **Literacy:** 62% (urban areas); 40% (rural areas). Years compulsory 6; attendance 82%.
Major International Organizations: UN and its specialized agencies, OAS, CACM.
Embassy: 2308 California St. NW 20008; 265-3480.

El Salvador became independent of Spain in 1821, and of the Central American Federation in 1839.

A fight with Honduras in 1969 over the presence of 300,000 Salvadorean workers left 2,000 dead. Clashes were renewed 1970 and 1974.

A military coup overthrew the Romero government, 1979, but the ruling military-civilian junta failed to quell the civil war which has resulted in some 50,000 deaths. Some 10,000 leftists insurgents, armed by Cuba and Nicaragua, control about 25% of the country, mostly in the east. Extreme right-wing death squads organized to eliminate suspected leftists were blamed for over 1,000 deaths in 1983. The Reagan administration has staunchly supported the government with military aid.

Voters turned out in large numbers in the May 1984 presidential election. Christian Democrat Jose Napoleon Duarte, a moderate, was victorious with 54% of the vote.

Leftist guerrillas continued their offensive in 1985 including attacks on U.S. servicemen stationed in the country (See Chronology).

Equatorial Guinea
Republic of Equatorial Guinea

People: Population (1984 est.): 275,000. **Age distrib. (%):** 0–14: 35.2; 15–59: 57.1; 60+: 7.7. **Pop. density:** 28 per sq. mi. **Ethnic groups:** Fangs 80%, several other groups. **Languages:** Spanish (official), Fang, English. **Religions:** Roman Catholics 83%, Protestants, others.

Geography: Area: 10,832 sq. mi., the size of Maryland. **Location:** Bioko Is. off W. Africa coast in Gulf of Guinea, and Rio Muni, mainland enclave. **Neighbors:** Gabon on S, Cameroon on E, N. **Topography:** Bioko Is. consists of 2 volcanic mountains and a connecting valley. Rio Muni, with over 90% of the area, has a coastal plain and low hills beyond. **Capital:** Malabo. **Cities** (1984 est.): Malabo 34,980.
Government: Type: Unitary Republic. **Head of state:** Pres., Supreme Military Council Teodoro Obiang Nguema Mbasogo; b. June 5, 1942; in office: Oct. 10, 1979. **Local divisions:** 2 provinces.
Economy: Chief crops: Cocoa, coffee, bananas, sweet potatoes. **Other resources:** Timber. **Per capita arable land:** 0.9 acres. **Electricity prod.** (1982): 26 mln. kwh. **Labor force:** 76% agric.
Finance: Currency: Ekuele (Nov. 1984: 344 = $1 US). **Gross domestic product** (1983 est.): $75 mln. **Per capita income** (1983): $250. **Imports** (1982): $41 mln.; partners (1981): Spain 54%, China 17%. **Exports** (1982): $16 mln.; partners (1981): Sp. 40%, Neth. 28%, W. Ger. 23%.
Transport: Chief ports: Malabo, Bata.
Communications: Radios: 90,000 in use (1982).
Health: Life expectancy at birth (1984): 44.4 male; 47.6 female. **Births** (per 1,000 pop. 1978): 42. **Deaths** (per 1,000 pop. 1978): 19. **Natural increase** (1978): 2.3% **Hospital beds** (per 100,000 pop. 1977): 704. **Physicians** (per 100,000 pop. 1977): 2. **Infant mortality** (per 1,000 live births 1975): 53.2.
Education (1984): **Literacy:** 55%. About 65% attend primary school.
Major International Organizations: UN, OAU.
Embassy: 801 2d Ave., New York, NY 10017; (212) 599-1523.

Fernando Po (now Bioko) Island was discovered by Portugal in the late 15th century and ceded to Spain in 1778. Independence came Oct. 12, 1968. Riots occurred in 1969 over disputes between the island and the more backward Rio Muni province on the mainland. Masie Nguema Biyogo, himself from the mainland, became president for life in 1972.

Masie's 11-year reign was one of the most brutal in Africa, resulting in a bankrupted nation. Most of the nation's 7,000 Europeans emigrated. In 1976, 45,000 Nigerian workers were evacuated amid charges of a reign of terror. Masie was ousted in a military coup, Aug., 1979.

Ethiopia
Socialist Ethiopia

People: Population (1984 est.): 31,998,000. **Age distrib. (%):** 0–14: 43.1; 15–59: 52.5; 60+: 4.4. **Pop. density:** 88 per sq. mi. **Urban** (1984): 11%. **Ethnic groups:** Oromo 40%, Amhara 25%, Tigre 12%, Somali, Afar, Sidama. **Languages:** Amharic, Tigre (Semitic languages); Galla (Hamitic), Arabic, others. **Religions:** Orthodox Christian 40%, Moslem 40%.
Geography: Area: 472,400 sq. mi., four-fifths the size of Alaska. **Location:** In E. Africa. **Neighbors:** Sudan on W, Kenya on S. Somalia, Djibouti on E. **Topography:** A high central plateau, between 6,000 and 10,000 ft. high, rises to higher mountains near the Great Rift Valley, cutting in from the SW. The Blue Nile and other rivers cross the plateau, which descends to plains on both W and SE. **Capital:** Addis Ababa. **Cities** (1984 est.): Addis Ababa 1,412,000.
Government: Type: Provisional military govt. **Head of state and head of gov't.:** Chmn. of Provisional Military Administrative Council Mengistu Haile Mariam; b. 1937; in office: Feb. 11, 1977. **Local divisions:** 14 administrative regions. **Defense:** 9.8% of GDP (1982).
Economy: Industries: Food processing, cement, textiles. **Chief crops:** Coffee (61% export earnings), grains. **Minerals:** Coal, platinum, gold, copper, asbestos, potash. **Other resources:** Hydro power potential. **Arable land:** 12%. **Meat prod.** (1980): beef: 214,000 metric tons; lamb: 132,000 metric tons. **Fish catch** (1978): 26,800 metric tons. **Electricity prod.** (1982): 679 mln. kwh. **Labor force:** 80% agric.
Finance: Currency: Birr (Mar. 1985: 2.07 = $1 US). **Gross domestic product** (1982): $7 bln. **Per capita income** (1980): $117. **Imports** (1983): $875 mln.; partners: USSR 20%, U.S. 8%, Jap. 7%, W.Ger. 9%. **Exports** (1983): $403 mln.; partners: U.S. 21%, Italy 7%, Saud. Ar. 9%. **National budget** (1980):

$985 mln. revenues; $1.8 bln. expenditures. International reserves less gold (Mar. 1985): $50.6 mln. Gold: 209,000 oz t. Consumer prices (change in 1982): 5.9%.

Transport: Railway traffic (1983): 247 mln. passenger-km; 148 mln. net ton-km. Motor vehicles: in use (1984): 41,300 passenger cars, 11,800 comm. vehicles. Civil aviation (1982): 762 mln. passenger-km; 26.2 mln. net ton-km. Chief ports: Masewa, Aseb.

Communications: Television sets: 45,000 in use (1982), Radios: 250,000 in use (1981). Telephones in use (1981): 87,800. Daily newspaper circ. (1982): 1 per 1,000 pop.

Health: Life expectancy at birth (1981): 40 yrs. Births (per 1,000 pop. 1978): 48. Deaths (per 1,000 pop. 1978): 23. Natural increase (1978): 2.5%. Hospital beds (per 100,000 pop. 1977): 29. Physicians (per 100,000 pop. 1977): 1. Infant mortality (per 1,000 live births 1981): 155.

Education (1984): Literacy: 15%.

Major International Organizations: UN and its specialized agencies, OAU.

Embassy: 2134 Kalorama Rd. NW 20008; 234-2281.

Ethiopian culture was influenced by Egypt and Greece. The ancient monarchy was invaded by Italy in 1880, but maintained its independence until another Italian invasion in 1936. British forces freed the country in 1941.

The last emperor, Haile Selassie I, established a parliament and judiciary system in 1931, but barred all political parties.

A series of droughts since 1972 have killed hundreds of thousands. An army mutiny, strikes, and student demonstrations led to the dethronement of Selassie in 1974. The ruling junta pledged to form a one-party socialist state, and instituted a successful land reform; opposition was violently suppressed. The influence of the Coptic Church, embraced in 330 AD, was curbed, and the monarchy was abolished in 1975.

The regime, torn by bloody coups, faced uprisings by tribal and political groups in part aided by Sudan and Somalia. Ties with the U.S., once a major arms and aid source, deteriorated, while cooperation accords were signed with the USSR in 1977. In 1978, Soviet advisors and 20,000 Cuban troops helped defeat Somali rebels & Somalia forces.

A world-wide relief effort began in 1984, as an extended drought caused millions to face starvation and death.

Fiji
Dominion of Fiji

People: Population (1984 est.): 686,000. Age distrib. (%): 0–14: 41.1; 15–59: 54.7; 60+: 4.0. Pop. density: 97 per sq. mi. Urban (1983): 45%. Ethnic groups: Indian 50%, Fijian (Melanesian-Polynesian) 45%, Europeans 2%. Languages: English (official), Fijian, Hindustani. Religions: Christian 49%, Hindu 40%.

Geography: Area: 7,056 sq. mi., the size of Massachusetts. Location: In western S. Pacific O. Neighbors: Nearest are Solomons on NW, Tonga on E. Topography: 322 islands (106 inhabited), many mountainous, with tropical forests and large fertile areas. Viti Levu, the largest island, has over half the total land area. Capital: Suva. Cities (1983 est.): Suva 65,000.

Government: Type: Parliamentary democracy. Head of state: Queen Elizabeth II, represented by Gov. Gen. Penaia Ganilau; in office: 1984. Head of government: Prime Min. Kamisese Mara; b. May 13, 1920; in office: Oct. 10, 1970. Local divisions: 4 divisions.

Economy: Industries: Sugar refining, light industry, tourism. Chief crops: Sugar, bananas, ginger. Minerals: Gold. Other resources: Timber. Arable land: 12%. Electricity prod. (1982): 327 mln. kwh. Labor force: 44% agric.

Finance: Currency: Dollar (Mar. 1985: 1.09 = $1 US). Gross domestic product (1983): $1.0 bln. Per capita income (1982): $1,852. Imports (1983): $500 mln.; partners: Austral. 39%, Jap. 16%, N.Z. 16%. Exports (1983): $280 mln.; partners: UK 30%, Aust. 14%. Tourists (1982): 200,000; receipts $143 mln. National budget (1982): $258 mln. revenues; $273 mln. expenditures. International reserves less gold (Mar. 1985): $119 mln. Gold: 11,000 oz t. Consumer prices (change in 1983): 6.7%.

Transport: Motor vehicles: in use (1983): 27,000 passenger cars, 19,700 comm. vehicles. Civil aviation (1983): 409 mln. passenger-km; 3.2 mln. net ton-km. Chief ports: Suva, Lautoka.

Communications: Radios: 400,000 in use (1983). Telephones in use (1983): 46,252. Daily newspaper circ. (1983): 106 per 1,000 pop.

Health: Life expectancy at birth (1975): 68.5 male; 71.7 female. Births (per 1,000 pop. 1982): 30.9. Deaths (per 1,000 pop. 1982): 58. Natural increase (1982): 2.5%. Hospital beds (1981): 1,716. Physicians (1981): 318. Infant mortality (per 1,000 live births 1983): 29.

Education (1978): Literacy: 75%. Pop. 5-19: in school: 73%, teachers per 1,000 27.

Major International Organizations: UN and its specialized agencies, Commonwealth of Nations.

Embassy: 1140 19th St. NW 20036; 296-3928.

A British colony since 1874, Fiji became an independent parliamentary democracy Oct. 10, 1970.

Cultural differences between the majority Indian community, descendants of contract laborers brought to the islands in the 19th century, and the less modernized native Fijians, who by law own 83% of the land in communal villages, have led to political polarization.

The discovery of copper on Viti Levu along with increased sugar production bode well for the economy.

Finland
Republic of Finland

People: Population (1984 est.): 4,873,000. Age distrib. (%): 0–14: 20.2; 15–59: 63.4; 60+: 16.5. Pop. density: 41 per sq. mi. Urban (1982): 59.9%. Ethnic groups: Finns, Swedes. Languages: Finnish 93.5%, Swedish 6.5% (both official). Religions: Lutheran 97%.

Geography: Area: 130,119 sq. mi., slightly smaller than Montana. Location: In northern Baltic region of Europe. Neighbors: Norway on N, Sweden on W, USSR on E. Topography: South and central Finland are mostly flat areas with low hills and many lakes. The N has mountainous areas, 3,000-4,000 ft. Capital: Helsinki. Cities (1984 est.). Helsinki 483,051; Tampere 167,028; Turku 163,526.

Government: Type: Constitutional Republic. Head of state: Pres. Mauno Koivisto; b. Nov. 25, 1923; in office: Jan. 27, 1982. Head of government: Prime Min. Kaleva Sorsa; b. 1930; in office: Feb. 25, 1982. Local divisions: 12 laanit (provinces). Defense: 1.8% of GNP (1982).

Economy: Industries: Machinery, metal, shipbuilding, textiles, clothing. Chief crops: Grains, potatoes, dairy prods. Minerals: Copper, iron, zinc. Other resources: Forests (40% of exports). Arable land: 7%. Meat prod. (1980): beef: 115,000 metric tons; pork: 176,000 metric tons. Fish catch (1983): 145,000 metric tons. Electricity prod. (1982): 39.3 bln. kwh. Crude steel prod. (1982): 2.4 mln. metric tons. Labor force: 11% agric.; 46% ind. & comm.; 24% services.

Finance: Currency: Markkaa (Mar. 1985: 6.42 = $1 US). Gross domestic product (1983): $46.3 bln. Per capita income (1980): $10,477. Imports (1984): $12.4 bln.; partners: USSR 25%, Swed. 12%, W. Ger. 13%, UK 7%. Exports (1984): $13.4 bln.; partners: USSR 27%, Swed. 12%, UK 11%, W. Ger. 9%. Tourists (1982): $579 mln. receipts. National budget (1980): $11.67 bln. revenues; $12.03 bln. expenditures. International reserves less gold (Mar. 1985): $3.1 bln. Gold 1.5 mln. oz t. Consumer prices (change in 1984): 7.1%.

Transport: Railway traffic (1982): 3.3 bln. passenger-km; 8.0 bln. net ton-km. Motor vehicles: in use (1982): 1.3 mln. passenger cars, 161,700 comm. vehicles; Civil aviation (1982): 2.5 bln. passenger-km; 66.8 mln. freight ton-km. Chief ports: Helsinki, Turku.

Communications: Television sets: 2.2 mln. licensed (1983). Radios: 2.5 mln. licensed (1983). Telephones in use (1983): 2.5 mln. Daily newspaper circ. (1982): 506 per 1,000 pop.

Health: Life expectancy at birth (1981): 69.5 male; 77.8 female. Births (per 1,000 pop. 1982): 13.7. Deaths (per 1,000 pop. 1982): 9.0. Hospital beds (1981): 74,381. Physicians (1981): 9,538. Infant mortality (per 1,000 live births 1982): 6.0.

Education (1982): Literacy: 99%. Years compulsory 9; attendance 99%.

Major International Organizations: UN and its specialized agencies, EC, OECD.

Embassy: 3216 New Mexico Ave. NW 20016; 363-2430.

The early Finns probably migrated from the Ural area at about the beginning of the Christian era. Swedish settlers brought the country into Sweden, 1154 to 1809, when Finland became an autonomous grand duchy of the Russian Empire. Russian exactions created a strong national spirit; on Dec. 6, 1917, Finland declared its independence and in 1919 became a republic. On Nov. 30, 1939, the Soviet Union invaded, and the Finns were forced to cede 16,173 sq. mi., including the Karelian Isthmus, Viipuri, and an area on Lake Ladoga. After World War II, in which Finland tried to recover its lost territory, further cessions were exacted. In 1948, Finland signed a treaty of mutual assistance with the USSR. In 1956 Russia returned Porkkala, which had been ceded as a military base.

Finland is an integral member of the Nordic group of five countries and maintains good relations with the Soviet Union. The governing coalition usually includes the Communist Party.

Aland, constituting an autonomous department, is a group of small islands, 572 sq. mi., in the Gulf of Bothnia, 25 mi. from Sweden, 15 mi. from Finland. Mariehamn is the principal port.

France
French Republic

People: Population (1984 est.): 54,872,000. **Age distrib. (%):** 0–14: 22.0; 15–59: 60; 60+: 17.6. **Pop. density:** 259.6 per sq. mi. **Urban** (1975): 73.0%. **Ethnic groups:** A mixture of various European and Mediterranean groups. **Languages:** French; minorities speak Breton, Alsatian German, Flemish, Italian, Basque, Catalan. **Religions:** Mostly Roman Catholic.

Geography: Area: 210,040 sq. mi., four-fifths the size of Texas. **Location:** In western Europe, between Atlantic O. and Mediterranean Sea. **Neighbors:** Spain on S, Italy, Switzerland, W. Germany on E, Luxembourg, Belgium on N. **Topography:** A wide plain covers more than half of the country, in N and W, drained to W by Seine, Loire, Garonne rivers. The Massif Central is a mountainous plateau in center. In E are Alps (Mt. Blanc is tallest in W. Europe, 15,771 ft.), the lower Jura range, and the forested Vosges. The Rhone flows from Lake Geneva to Mediterranean. Pyrenees are in SW, on border with Spain. **Capital:** Paris. **Cities** (1975 cen.): Paris 2,296,945; Marseille 912,130; Lyon 457,410; Toulouse 371,835; Nice 344,040; Nantes 255,700; Strasbourg 253,355; Bordeaux 223,845.

Government: Type: Republic. **Head of state:** Pres. François Mitterrand; b. Oct. 26, 1916; in office: May 21, 1981. **Head of government:** Prime Min. Laurent Fabius; b. Aug. 20, 1946; in office: July 17, 1984. **Local divisions:** 95 departments. **Defense:** 18% of govt. budget. (1984).

Economy: Industries: Steel, chemicals, autos, textiles, wine, perfume, aircraft, ships, electronic equipment. **Chief crops:** Grains, corn, rice, fruits, vegetables. France is largest food producer, exporter, in W. Eur. **Minerals:** Bauxite, iron, coal. **Crude oil reserves** (1980): 50 mln. bbls. **Other resources:** Forests. **Arable land:** 32%. **Meat prod.** (1984): beef: 2 mln. metric tons; pork: 1.86 mln. metric tons; lamb: 171,000 metric tons. **Fish catch** (1982): 640,000 metric tons. **Electricity prod.** (1983): 277.1 bln. kwh. **Crude steel prod.** (1982): 18.4 mln. metric tons. **Labor force:** 9% agric.; 45% ind. & comm.; 46% services.

Finance: Currency: Franc (June 1985: 9.26 = $1 US). **Gross domestic product** (1983). $920 bln. **Per capita income** (1983): $7,179. **Imports** (1984): $103.7 bln.; partners: W. Ger. 17%, It. 10%, Belg. 8%, U.S. 8%. **Exports** (1984): $97.5 bln.; partners: W. Ger. 14%, It. 11%, Belg. 8%, UK 7%. **Tourists** (1982) receipts: $6.9 bln. **National budget** (1980): $113.5 bln. revenues; $113.6 bln. expenditures. **International reserves less gold** (Feb. 1985): $21.3 bln. **Gold:** 81.85 mln. oz t. **Consumer prices** (change in 1984): 7.3%.

Transport: Railway traffic (1982): 56.8 bln. passenger-km; 61.1 bln. net ton-km. **Motor vehicles:** in use (1983): 20.6 mln. passenger cars, 3.2 mln. comm. vehicles; manuf. (1982): 3 mln. passenger cars; 466,000 comm. vehicles. **Civil aviation** (1982): 37.8 bln. passenger-km; 2.2 bln net ton-km. **Chief ports:** Marseille, LeHavre, Nantes, Bordeaux, Rouen.

Communications: Television sets: 19 mln. in use (1983). **Radios:** 20 mln. in use (1983). **Telephones in use** (1982): 18 mln. **Daily newspaper circ.** (1983): 209 per 1,000 pop.

Health: Life expectancy at birth (1982): 70.2 male; 78.5 female. **Births** (per 1,000 pop. 1982): 12.8. **Deaths** (per 1,000 pop. 1982): 7.1. **Natural increase** (1982): .5%. **Hospital beds**

(1982): 446,901. **Physicians** (1981): 104,073. **Infant mortality** (per 1,000 live births 1983): 8.9.

Education (1984): **Literacy:** 99%. Years compulsory 10; 17.7% of natl. budget.

Major International Organizations: UN and its specialized agencies, OECD, EC, NATO.

Embassy: 2535 Belmont Rd. NW 20008; 328-2600.

Celtic Gaul was conquered by Julius Caesar 58-51 BC; Romans ruled for 500 years. Under Charlemagne, Frankish rule extended over much of Europe. After his death France emerged as one of the successor kingdoms.

The monarchy was overthrown by the French Revolution (1789-93) and succeeded by the First Republic; followed by the First Empire under Napoleon (1804-15), a monarchy (1814-48), the Second Republic (1848-52), the Second Empire (1852-70), the Third Republic (1871-1946), the Fourth Republic (1946-58), and the Fifth Republic (1958 to present).

France suffered severe losses in manpower and wealth in the first World War, 1914-18, when it was invaded by Germany. By the Treaty of Versailles, France exacted return of Alsace and Lorraine, French provinces seized by Germany in 1871. Germany invaded France again in May, 1940, and signed an armistice with a government based in Vichy. After France was liberated by the Allies Sept. 1944, Gen. Charles de Gaulle became head of the provisional government, serving until 1946.

De Gaulle again became premier in 1958, during a crisis over Algeria, and obtained voter approval for a new constitution, ushering in the Fifth Republic. Using strong executive powers, he promoted French economic and technological advances in the context of the European Economic Community, and guarded French foreign policy independence.

France had withdrawn from Indochina in 1954, and from Morocco and Tunisia in 1956. Most of its remaining African territories were freed 1958-62, but France retained strong economic and political ties.

France tested atomic bombs in the Sahara beginning in 1960. Land-based and submarine launched strategic missiles were also developed. In 1966, France withdrew all its troops from the integrated military command of NATO, though 60,000 remained stationed in Germany. France continued to attend political meetings of NATO.

In May 1968 rebellious students in Paris and other centers rioted, battled police, and were joined by workers who launched nationwide strikes. The government awarded pay increases to the strikers May 26. In elections to the Assembly in June, de Gaulle's backers won a landslide victory. Nevertheless, he resigned from office in April, 1969, after losing a nationwide referendum on constitutional reform. De Gaulle's policies were largely continued after his death in 1970.

On May 10, 1981, France elected François Mitterrand, a Socialist candidate, president in a stunning victory over Valéry Giscard d'Estaing. In September, the government nationalized 5 major industries and most private banks.

France committed troops and military aid to the government of Chad, June 1983. On Oct. 23, 58 members of the French peacekeeping force in Lebanon were killed in a suicide terrorist attack.

The island of **Corsica**, in the Mediterranean W of Italy and N of Sardinia, is an official region of France comprising 2 departments. Area: 3,369 sq. mi.; pop. (1975 cen.): 289,842. The capital is Ajaccio, birthplace of Napoleon.

Overseas Departments

French Guiana is on the NE coast of South America with Suriname on the W and Brazil on the E and S. Its area is 32,252 sq. mi.; pop. (1982 cen.): 73,022. Guiana sends one senator and one deputy to the French Parliament. Guiana is administered by a prefect and has a Council General of 16 elected members; capital is Cayenne.

The famous penal colony, Devil's Island, was phased out between 1938 and 1951.

Immense forests of rich timber cover 90% of the land. Placer gold mining is the most important industry. Exports are shrimp, timber, and machinery.

Guadeloupe, in the West Indies' Leeward Islands, consists of 2 large islands, Basse-Terre and Grande-Terre, separated by the Salt River, plus Marie Galante and the Saintes group to the S and, to the N, Desirade, St. Barthelemy, and over half of St. Martin (the Netherlands portion is St. Maarten). A French pos-

session since 1635, the department is represented in the French Parliament by 2 senators and 3 deputies; administration consists of a prefect (governor) and an elected General Council.

Area of the islands is 687 sq. mi.; pop. (1982 est.) 314,800, mainly descendants of slaves; capital is Basse-Terre on Basse-Terre Is. The land is fertile; sugar, rum, and bananas are exported; tourism is an important industry.

Martinique, one of the Windward Islands, in the West Indies, has been a possession since 1635, and a department since March, 1946. It is represented in the French Parliament by 2 senators and 3 deputies. The island was the birthplace of Napoleon's Empress Josephine.

It has an area of 425 sq. mi.; pop. (1982 cen.) 328,566, mostly descendants of slaves. The capital is Fort-de-France. It is a popular tourist stop. The chief exports are rum, bananas, and petroleum products.

Mayotte, formerly part of Comoros, voted in 1976 to become an overseas department of France. An island NW of Madagascar, area is 144 sq. mi.; pop. (1982 est.) 53,000.

Reunion is a volcanic island in the Indian O. about 420 mi. E of Madagascar, and has belonged to France since 1665. Area, 969 sq. mi.; pop. (1982 cen.) 515,814, 30% of French extraction. Capital: Saint-Denis. The chief export is sugar. It elects 3 deputies, 2 senators to the French Parliament.

St. Pierre and Miquelon, formerly an Overseas Territory, made the transition to department status in 1976. It consists of 2 groups of rocky islands near the SW coast of Newfoundland, inhabited by fishermen. The exports are chiefly fish products. The St. Pierre group has an area of 10 sq. mi.; Miquelon, 83 sq. mi. Total pop. (1982 cen.), 6,041. The capital is St. Pierre. A deputy and a senator are elected to the French Parliament.

Overseas Territories

French Polynesia Overseas Territory, comprises 130 islands widely scattered among 5 archipelagos in the South Pacific; administered by a governor. Territorial Assembly and a Council with headquarters at Papeete, Tahiti, one of the Society Islands (which include the Windward and Leeward islands). A deputy and a senator are elected to the French Parliament.

Other groups are the **Marquesas Islands**, the Tuamotu Archipelago, including the Gambier Islands, and the Austral Islands.

Total area of the islands administered from Tahiti is 1,544 sq. mi.; pop. (1983 est.), 148,000, more than half on Tahiti. Tahiti is picturesque and mountainous with a productive coastline bearing coconut, banana and orange trees, sugar cane and vanilla.

Tahiti was visited by Capt. James Cook in 1769 and by Capt. Bligh in the Bounty, 1788-89. Its beauty impressed Herman Melville, Paul Gauguin, and Charles Darwin.

French Southern and Antarctic Lands Overseas Territory, comprises Adelie Land, on Antarctica, and 4 island groups in the Indian O. Adelie, discovered 1840, has a research station, a coastline of 185 mi. and tapers 1,240 mi. inland to the South Pole. The U.S. does not recognize national claims in Antarctica. There are 2 huge glaciers, Ninnis, 22 mi. wide, 99 mi. long, and Mentz, 11 mi. wide, 140 mi. long. The Indian O. groups are:

Kerguelen Archipelago, discovered 1772, one large and 300 small islands. The chief is 87 mi. long, 74 mi. wide, and has Mt. Ross, 6,429 ft. tall. Principal research station is Port-aux-Francais. Seals often weigh 2 tons; there are blue whales, coal, peat, semi-precious stones. **Crozet Archipelago**, discovered 1772, covers 195 sq. mi. Eastern Island rises to 6,560 ft. **Saint Paul**, in southern Indian O., has warm springs with earth at places heating to 120° to 390° F. **Amsterdam** is nearby; both produce cod and rock lobster.

New Caledonia and its dependencies, an overseas territory, are a group of islands in the Pacific O. about 1,115 mi. E of Australia and approx. the same distance NW of New Zealand. Dependencies are the **Loyalty Islands**, the **Isle of Pines**, **Huon Islands** and the **Chesterfield Islands**.

New Caledonia, the largest, has 6,530 sq. mi. Total area of the territory is 8,548 sq. mi.; population (1981 est.) 142,500. The group was acquired by France in 1853.

The territory is administered by a governor and government council. There is a popularly elected Territorial Assembly. A deputy and a senator are elected to the French Parliament. Capital: Noumea.

Mining is the chief industry. New Caledonia is one of the world's largest nickel producers. Other minerals found are chrome, iron, cobalt, manganese, silver, gold, lead, and copper.

Agricultural products include coffee, copra, cotton, manioc (cassava), corn, tobacco, bananas and pineapples.

A referendum on New Caledonian independence is scheduled for 1987.

Wallis and Futuna Islands, 2 archipelagos raised to status of overseas territory July 29, 1961, are in the SW Pacific S of the Equator between Fiji and Samoa. The islands have a total area of 106 sq. mi. and population (1982 cen.) of 11,943. **Alofi**, attached to Futuna, is uninhabited. Capital: Mata-Utu. Chief products are copra, yams, taro roots, bananas. A senator and a deputy are elected to the French Parliament.

Gabon
Gabonese Republic

People: Population (1984 est.): 958,000. **Pop. density:** 12.6 per sq. mi. **Urban** (1980): 35%. **Ethnic groups:** Fangs 25%, Bapounon 10%, others. **Languages:** French (official), Bantu dialects. **Religions:** Tribal beliefs, Christian minority.

Geography: Area: 102,317 sq. mi., the size of Colorado. **Location:** On Atlantic coast of central Africa. **Neighbors:** Equatorial Guinea, Cameroon on N, Congo on E, S. **Topography:** Heavily forested, the country consists of coastal lowlands plateaus in N, E, and S, mountains in N, SE, and center. The Ogooue R. system covers most of Gabon. **Capital:** Libreville. **Cities** (1983 est.): Libreville 180,000.

Government: Type: Republic. **Head of state:** Pres. Omar Bongo; b. Dec. 30, 1935; in office: Dec. 2, 1967. **Head of government:** Prime Min. Leon Mebiame, b. Sept. 1, 1934; in office: Apr. 16, 1975. **Local divisions:** 9 provinces, 37 prefectures. **Defense:** 2.7% of GNP (1982).

Economy: Industries: Oil products. **Chief crops:** Cocoa, coffee, rice, peanuts, palm products, cassava, bananas. **Minerals:** Manganese, uranium, oil, iron, gas. **Crude oil reserves** (1980): 500 mln. bbls. **Other resources:** Timber. **Arable land:** 1%. **Electricity prod.** (1983): 734 mln. kwh. **Labor force:** 65% agric.; 30% ind. & comm.; 2.5% services.

Finance: Currency: CFA franc (Mar. 1985: 471 = $1 US). **Gross domestic product** (1981) $3.7 bln. **Per capita income** (1981): $2,974. **Imports** (1983): $853 mln.; partners: Fr. 51%, U.S. 14%. **Exports** (1983): $1.9 bln.; partners: Fr. 26%, U.S. 25%. **Tourists receipts** (1980): $13 mln. **National budget** (1982): $545 mln. **International reserves less gold** (Oct. 1984): $265 mln. **Gold:** 13,000 oz t. **Consumer prices** (change in 1983): 10.7%.

Transport: Motor vehicles: in use (1982): 16,000 passenger cars, 10,000 comm. vehicles. **Civil aviation** (1982): 430 mln. passenger-km. **Chief ports** Port-Gentil, Owendo, Mayumba.

Communications: Television sets: 10,000 licensed (1982). **Radios:** 98,000 licensed (1982). **Telephones in use** (1982): 11,113.

Health: Life expectancy at birth (1961): 25 male; 45 female. **Births** (per 1,000 pop. 1978): 34. **Deaths** (per 1,000 pop. 1978): 22. **Natural increase** (1978): 1.2%. **Hospital beds** (per 100,000 pop. 1977): 736. **Physicians** (per 100,000 pop. 1977): 32. **Infant mortality** (per 1,000 live births 1983): 117.

Education (1983): **Literacy:** 65%. Compulsory to age 16; attendance: 84% primary, 14% secondary.

Major International Organizations: UN and its specialized agencies, OAU, OPEC.

Embassy: 2034 20th St NW 20009; 797-1000.

France established control over the region in the second half of the 19th century. Gabon became independent Aug. 17, 1960. It is one of the most prosperous black African countries, thanks to abundant natural resources, foreign private investment, and government development programs.

The Gambia
Republic of The Gambia

People: Population (1983 cen.): 695,886. **Age distrib. (%):** 0–14: 45.9; 15–59: 54.4; 60+: 3.8. **Pop. density:** 206 per sq. mi. **Urban** (1983): 21%. **Ethnic groups:** Mandinka 37.7%, Fula 16.2%, Wolof 14%, others. **Languages:** English (official), Mandinka, Wolof. **Religions:** Moslems 85%, Christian 14%.

Geography: Area: 4,361 sq. mi., smaller than Connecticut. **Location:** On Atlantic coast near western tip of Africa. **Neighbors:** Surrounded on 3 sides by Senegal. **Topography:** A narrow strip of land on each side of the lower Gambia. **Capital:** Banjul. **Cities** (1983 cen.): Banjul 44,536.

Government: Type: Republic. **Head of state:** Pres. Dawda Kairaba Jawara; b. May 16, 1924; in office: Apr. 24, 1970 (prime min. from June 12, 1962). **Local divisions:** 5 divisions and Banjul.

Economy: Industries: Tourism. **Chief crops:** Peanuts (main export), rice. **Arable land:** 28%. **Fish catch** (1982): 35,000 metric tons. **Electricity prod.** (1982): 40 mln. kwh. **Labor force:** 75% agric.; 18% ind. & comm.

Finance: Currency: Dalasi (Mar. 1985: 2.78 = $1 US). **Gross domestic product** (1981): $198 mln. **Per capita income** (1981): $330. **Imports** (1983): $53 mln.; partners: UK 21%, China 11%. **Exports** (1983): $40 mln.; partners: EEC 40%. **Tourists** (1983): 24,800. **National budget** (1980): $35.1 mln. revenues; $33.3 mln. expenditures. **International reserves less gold** (Mar. 1985): $1.4 mln. **Consumer prices** (change in 1984): 22.1%.

Transport: Motor vehicles: in use (1983): 6,500 passenger cars, 1,500 comm. vehicles. **Chief ports:** Banjul.

Communications: Radios: 100,000 in use (1983). **Telephones in use** (1980): 3,500.

Health: Life expectancy at birth (1982): 32 male; 34 female. **Births** (per 1,000 pop. 1980): 47.5. **Deaths** (per 1,000 pop. 1980): 21.7. **Natural increase** (1980): 2.5%. **Hospital beds** (1980): 635. **Physicians** (1980): 65. **Infant mortality** (per 100,000 live births 1979): 217.

Education (1982): **Literacy:** 12%. **Pop. 5-19:** in school: 14.2%.

Major International Organizations: UN and its specialized agencies, OAU.

Embassy: 1785 Massachusetts Ave. NW 20036; 265-3252.

The tribes of Gambia were at one time associated with the West African empires of Ghana, Mali, and Songhay. The area became Britain's first African possession in 1588.

Independence came Feb. 18, 1965; republic status within the Commonwealth was achieved in 1970. Gambia is one of the only functioning democracies in Africa. The country suffered from severe famine in 1977-78.

An unsuccessful coup was launched July 30, 1981, while Pres. Jawara was in the UK for the royal wedding. Gambia has a treaty with Senegal to form a confederation of the 2 countries under the name of Senegambia. However, each country will retain its sovereignty.

Germany

Now comprises 2 nations: **Federal Republic of Germany (West Germany), German Democratic Republic (East Germany).**

Germany, prior to World War II, was a central European nation composed of numerous states which had a common language and traditions and which had been united in one country since 1871; since World War II it has been split in 2 parts.

History and government. Germanic tribes were defeated by Julius Caesar, 55 and 53 BC, but Roman expansion N of the Rhine was stopped in 9 AD. Charlemagne, ruler of the Franks, consolidated Saxon, Bavarian, Rhenish, Frankish, and other lands; after him the eastern part became the German Empire. The Thirty Years' War, 1618-1648, split Germany into small principalities and kingdoms. After Napoleon, Austria contended with Prussia for dominance, but lost the Seven Weeks' War to Prussia, 1866. Otto von Bismarck, Prussian chancellor, formed the North German Confederation, 1867.

In 1870 Bismarck maneuvered Napoleon III into declaring war. After the quick defeat of France, Bismarck formed the German Empire and on Jan. 18, 1871, in Versailles, proclaimed King Wilhelm I of Prussia German emperor (Deutscher kaiser).

The German Empire reached its peak before World War I in 1914, with 208,780 sq. mi., plus a colonial empire. After that war Germany ceded Alsace-Lorraine to France; West Prussia and Posen (Poznan) province to Poland; part of Schleswig to Denmark; lost all of its colonies and the ports of Memel and Danzig.

Republic of Germany, 1919-1933, adopted the Weimar constitution; met reparation payments and elected Friedrich Ebert and Gen. Paul von Hindenburg presidents.

Third Reich, 1933-1945, Adolf Hitler led the National Socialist German Workers' (Nazi) party after World War I. In 1923 he attempted to unseat the Bavarian government and was imprisoned. Pres. von Hindenburg named Hitler chancellor Jan. 30, 1933; on Aug. 3, 1934, the day after Hindenburg's death, the cabinet joined the offices of president and chancellor and made Hitler fuehrer (leader). Hitler abolished freedom of speech and assembly, and began a long series of persecutions climaxed by the murder of millions of Jews and opponents.

Hitler repudiated the Versailles treaty and reparations agreements. He remilitarized the Rhineland 1936 and annexed Austria (Anschluss, 1938). At Munich he made an agreement with Neville Chamberlain, British prime minister, which permitted Hitler to annex part of Czechoslovakia. He signed a non-aggression treaty with the USSR, 1939. He declared war on Poland Sept. 1, 1939, precipitating World War II.

With total defeat near, Hitler committed suicide in Berlin Apr. 1945. The victorious Allies voided all acts and annexations of Hitler's Reich.

Postwar changes. The zones of occupation administered by the Allied Powers and later relinquished gave the USSR Saxony, Saxony-Anhalt, Thuringia, and Mecklenburg, and the former Prussian provinces of Saxony and Brandenburg.

The territory E of the Oder-Neisse line within 1937 boundaries comprising the provinces of Silesia, Pomerania, and the southern part of East Prussia, totaling about 41,220 sq. mi., was taken by Poland. Northern East Prussia was taken by the USSR.

The Western Allies ended the state of war with Germany in 1951. The USSR did so in 1955.

There was also created the area of Greater Berlin, within but not part of the Soviet zone, administered by the 4 occupying powers under the Allied Command. In 1948 the USSR withdrew, established its single command in East Berlin, and cut off supplies. The Allies utilized a gigantic airlift to bring food to West Berlin, 1948-1949. In Aug. 1961 the East Germans built a wall dividing Berlin, after over 3 million E. Germans had emigrated.

East Germany
German Democratic Republic

People: Population (1984 est.): 16,718,000. **Age distrib. (%):** 0–14: 20.6; 15–59: 58.7; 60+: 20.7. **Pop. density:** 399 per sq. mi. **Urban** (1983): 76.4%. **Ethnic groups:** German 99%. **Languages:** German. **Religions:** traditionally 80% Protestant.

Geography: Area: 41,825 sq. mi., the size of Virginia. **Location:** In E. Central Europe. **Neighbors:** W. Germany on W, Czechoslovakia on S, Poland on E. **Topography:** E. Germany lies mostly on the North German plains, with lakes in N, Harz Mtns., Elbe Valley, and sandy soil of Bradenburg in center, and highlands in S. **Capital:** East Berlin. **Cities** (1982 est.): East Berlin 1,166,641; Leipzig 558,414; Dresden 521,011.

Government: Type: Communist. **Head of state:** Chmn. Erich Honecker; b. Aug. 25, 1912; in office: Oct. 29, 1976. **Head of government:** Prime Min. Willi Stoph; b. July 9, 1914; in office: Oct. 29, 1976. **Head of Communist Party:** Sec.-Gen. Erich Honecker; in office: May 3, 1971. **Local divisions:** 14 districts. **Defense:** 8% of GNP (1982).

Economy: Industries: Steel, chemicals, electrical prods., textiles, machinery. **Chief crops:** Grains, potatoes, sugarbeets. **Minerals:** Potash, lignite, uranium, coal. **Arable land:** 47%. **Meat prod.** (1983): beef: 370,000 metric tons; pork: 1.2 mln. metric tons; lamb: 17,000 metric tons. **Fish catch** (1982): 269,867 metric tons. **Electricity prod.** (1983): 104 bln. kwh. **Crude steel prod.** (1982): 7.1 mln metric tons. **Labor force:** 10% agric.; 42.5% ind. & construction.

Finance: Currency: Mark (Nov. 1984: 3.06 = $1 US). **Produced national income** (1982): $152 bln. **Per capita income** (1984): $8,000. **Imports** (1983): $22.4 bln.; partners: USSR, E. Europe. **Exports** (1983): $24 bln.; partners: USSR, E. Europe. **Tourists** (1977): 1,100,000. **National budget** (1984): $78 bln.

Transport: Railway traffic (1983): 22.6 bln. passenger-km; 54.8 bln. net ton-km. **Motor vehicles:** in use (1982): 2.9 mln. passenger cars, 228,368 comm. vehicles; manuf. (1982): 183,000 passenger cars; 39,000 comm. vehicles. **Civil aviation** (1980): 2 bln. passenger-km; 67 mln. freight ton-km. **Chief ports:** Rostack, Wismar, Stralsund.

Communications: Television sets: 5.8 mln. licensed (1982). **Radios:** 6.4 mln. licensed (1982). **Telephones in use** (1982): 3.2 mln. **Daily newspaper circ.** (1982): 515 per 1,000 pop.
Health: Life expectancy at birth (1984): 68.8 male; 74.7 female. **Births** (per 1,000 pop. 1983): 14.4. **Deaths** (per 1,000 pop. 1983): 13.7. **Natural increase** (1983): 0.0%. **Hospital beds** (1980): 171,895. **Physicians** (1982): 35,377. **Infant mortality** (per 1,000 live births 1985): 13.1.
Education (1985): **Literacy:** 99%. **Years compulsory:** through 10th grade.
Major International Organizations: UN and affiliated organizations, Warsaw Pact.
Embassy: 1717 Massachusetts Ave. NW 20036; 232-3134.

The German Democratic Republic was proclaimed in the Soviet sector of Berlin Oct. 7, 1949. It was proclaimed fully sovereign in 1954, but 400,000 Soviet troops remain on grounds of security and the 4-power Potsdam agreement.
Coincident with the entrance of W. Germany into the European Defense community in 1952, the East German government decreed a prohibited zone 3 miles deep along its 600-mile border with W. Germany and cut Berlin's telephone system in two. Berlin was further divided by erection of a fortified wall in 1961, but the exodus of refugees to the West continued, though on a smaller scale.
E. Germany suffered severe economic problems until the mid-1960s. A "new economic system" was introduced, easing the former central planning controls and allowing factories to make profits provided they were reinvested in operations or redistributed to workers as bonuses. By the early 1970s, the economy was highly industrialized. In May 1972 the few remaining private firms were ordered sold to the government. The nation was credited with the highest standard of living among communist countries. But growth slowed in the late 1970s, due to shortages of natural resources and labor, and a huge debt to lenders in the West.

West Germany
Federal Republic of Germany

People: Population (1984 est.): 61,387,000. **Age distrib.** (%): 0–14: 16.8; 15–59: 61.5; 60+: 21.7. **Pop. density:** 638 per sq. mi. **Ethnic groups:** Primarily German. **Languages:** German. **Religions:** Protestant 44%, Roman Catholic 45%.
Geography: Area: 95,975 sq. mi. (incl. W. Berlin), the size of Wyoming. **Location:** In central Europe. **Neighbors:** Denmark on N, Netherlands, Belgium, Luxembourg, France on W, Switzerland, Austria on S, Czechoslovakia, E. Germany on E. **Topography:** West Germany is flat in N, hilly in center and W, and mountainous in Bavaria. Chief rivers are Elbe, Weser, Ems, Rhine, and Main, all flowing toward North Sea, and Danube, flowing toward Black Sea. **Capital:** Bonn. **Cities** (1984 est.): Berlin 1.8 mln.; Hamburg 1.6 mln.; Munich 1.2 mln.; Cologne 940,000; Essen 635,000; Frankfurt 614,000; Dortmund 595,000; Dusseldorf 579,000; Stuttgart 571,000.
Government: Type: Federal republic. **Head of state:** Pres. Richard von Weizsacker; b. Apr. 15, 1920; in office: May 23, 1984. **Head of government:** Chan. Helmut Kohl; b. Apr. 3, 1930; in office: Oct. 1, 1982. **Local divisions:** West Berlin and 10 laender (states) with substantial powers: Schleswig-Holstein, Hamburg, Lower Saxony, Bremen, North Rhine-Westphalia, Hessen, Rhineland-Palatinate, Baden-Wurttemberg, Bavaria, Saarland. **Defense:** 5% of GNP (1985).
Economy: Industries: Steel, ships, autos, machinery, coal, cement, chemicals. **Chief crops:** Grains, potatoes, sugar beets. **Minerals:** Coal, mercury, potash, lignite, iron, zinc, lead, copper, salt, oil. **Crude oil reserves** (1980): 480 mln. bbls. **Arable land:** 30%. **Meat prod.** (1983): beef: 1.4 mln. metric tons; pork: 3.2 mln. metric tons; lamb: 27,000 metric tons. **Fish catch** (1982): 313,000 metric tons. **Electricity prod.** (1983): 371 bln. kwh. **Crude steel prod.** (1982): 36.3 mln. metric tons. **Labor force:** 6% agric.; 42% ind. & comm.; 42% service.
Finance: Currency: Mark (Mar. 1985: 3.09 = $1 US). **Gross domestic product** (1984): $583 bln. **Per capita income** (1985): $9,450. **Imports** (1984): $153.0 bln.; partners: Neth. 12%, Fr. 11%, It. 8%, Belg. 7%. **Exports** (1984): $171.7 bln.; partners: Fr. 14%, Neth. 8%, Belg. 7%, It. 8%. **Tourists** (1982): receipts $5.6 bln. **National budget** (1985): $81.3 bln. **Interna-**

tional reserves less gold (Mar. 1985): $37.1 bln. **Gold:** 95.18 mln. oz t. **Consumer prices** (change in 1984): 2.4%.
Transport: Railway traffic (1983): 39 bln. passenger-km; 55 bln. net ton-km. **Motor vehicles:** in use (1983): 24 mln. passenger cars, 1.5 mln. comm. vehicles; manuf. (1982): 3.7 mln. passenger cars; 286,000 comm. vehicles. **Civil aviation** (1983): 22.8 bln. passenger-km; 4.2 bln. freight ton-km. **Chief ports:** Hamburg, Bremen, Lubeck.
Communications: Television sets: 21.8 mln. in use (1983), 4.2 mln. manuf. (1978). **Radios:** 24.3 mln. in use (1983), 4.6 mln. manuf. (1978). **Telephones in use** (1983): 30.1 mln. **Daily newspaper circ.** (1983): 141 per 1,000 pop.
Health: Life expectancy at birth (1985): 67.2 male; 73.4 female. **Births** (per 1,000 pop. 1983): 9.7. **Deaths** (per 1,000 pop. 1983): 11.7. **Natural increase** (1983): −.2%. **Hospital beds** (1983): 707,000. **Physicians** (1983): 146,000. **Infant mortality** (per 1,000 live births 1985): 13.5.
Education (1985): **Literacy:** 99%. **Years compulsory:** 10; attendance 100%.
Major International Organizations: UN and its specialized agencies, EC, OECD, NATO.
Embassy: 4645 Reservoir Rd. NW 20007; 298-4000.

The Federal Republic of Germany was proclaimed May 23, 1949, in Bonn, after a constitution had been drawn up by a consultative assembly formed by representatives of the 11 laender (states) in the French, British, and American zones. Later reorganized into 9 units, the laender numbered 10 with the addition of the Saar, 1957. Berlin also was granted land (state) status, but the 1945 occupation agreements placed restrictions on it.
The occupying powers, the U.S., Britain, and France, restored the civil status, Sept. 21, 1949. The U. S. resumed diplomatic relations July 2, 1951. The powers lifted controls and the republic became fully independent May 5, 1955.
Dr. Konrad Adenauer, Christian Democrat, was made chancellor Sept. 15, 1949, re-elected 1953, 1957, 1961. Willy Brandt, heading a coalition of Social Democrats and Free Democrats, became chancellor Oct. 21, 1969.
In 1970 Brandt signed friendship treaties with the USSR and Poland. In 1971, the U.S., Britain, France, and the USSR signed an agreement on Western access to West Berlin. In 1972 the Bundestag approved the USSR and Polish treaties and East and West Germany signed their first formal treaty, implementing the agreement easing access to West Berlin. In 1973 a West Germany-Czechoslovakia pact normalized relations and nullified the 1938 "Munich Agreement."
In May 1974 Brandt resigned, saying he took full responsibility for "negligence" for allowing an East German spy to become a member of his staff. Helmut Schmidt, Brandt's finance minister, succeeded him.
West Germany has experienced tremendous economic growth since the 1950s. The country leads Europe in provisions for worker participation in the management of industry.
The NATO decision to deploy medium-range nuclear missiles in Western Europe sparked a demonstration by some 400,000 protesters in April 1983. Chancellor Kohl has supported the U.S. "Star Wars" antimissile program.
Helgoland, an island of 130 acres in the North Sea, was taken from Denmark by a British Naval Force in 1807 and later ceded to Germany to become a part of Schleswig-Holstein province in return for rights in East Africa. The heavily fortified island was surrendered to UK, May 23, 1945, demilitarized in 1947, and returned to W. Germany, Mar 1, 1952. It is a free port.

Ghana
Republic of Ghana

People: Population (1984 est.): 13,804,000. **Age distrib.** (%): 0–14: 46.9; 15–59: 47.7; 60+: 5.3. **Pop. density:** 132 per sq. mi. **Urban** (1981): 36.6%. **Ethnic groups:** Akan 44%, Moshi-Dagomba 16%, Ewe 13%, Ga 8%, others. **Languages:** English (official), 50 tribal languages. **Religions:** Christian 43%, traditional beliefs 45%.
Geography: Area: 92,098 sq. mi., slightly smaller than Oregon. **Location:** On southern coast of W. Africa. **Neighbors:** Ivory Coast on W, Upper Volta on N, Togo on E. **Topography:** Most of Ghana consists of low fertile plains and scrubland, cut

...y rivers and by the artificial Lake Volta. **Capital:** Accra. **Cities** (1982 est.): Accra 1,045,000.

Government: Type: Authoritarian. **Head of government: Pres.** Jerry Rawlings; b. 1947; in office: Dec. 31, 1981. **Local divisions:** 10 regions.

Economy: Industries: Aluminum, light industry. **Chief crops:** Cocoa (70% of exports), coffee. **Minerals:** Gold, manganese, industrial diamonds, bauxite. **Crude oil reserves** (1980): 7 mln. bbls. **Other resources:** Timber, rubber. **Arable land:** 12%. **Fish catch** (1981): 240,000 metric tons. **Electricity prod.** (1982): 4.9 bln. kwh. **Labor force:** 60% agric.; 10% ind.

Finance: Currency: Cedi (Mar. 1985: 5.00 = $1 US). **Gross domestic product** (1981): $4.8 bln. **Per capita income** (1980): $420. **Imports** (1983): $2.0 bln.; partners: UK 18%, W. Ger. 12%, Nigeria 12%. **Exports** (1983): $2.2 bln.; partners: UK 16%, U.S. 16%, Neth. 9%, W. Ger. 9%. **National budget** (1979): $1.2 bln. revenues; $1.0 bln. expenditures. **International reserves less gold** (Mar. 1985): 300 mln. **Gold:** 307,000 oz t. **Consumer prices** (change in 1983): 122.9%.

Transport: Railway traffic (1980): 521 mln. passenger-km; 312 mln. net ton-km. **Motor vehicles:** in use (1983): 52,000 passenger cars, 24,000 comm. vehicles. **Civil aviation** (1982): 291 mln. passenger-km; 4.8 mln. freight ton-km. **Chief ports:** Tema, Takoradi.

Communications: Television sets: 71,000 in use (1983). **Radios:** 2 mln. in use (1983). **Telephones in use** (1982): 70,653.

Health: Life expectancy at birth (1975): 41.9 male; 45.1 female. **Births** (per 1,000 pop. 1978): 46. **Deaths** (per 1,000 pop. 1978): 14. **Natural increase** (1978): 3.2%. **Physicians** (1980): 1,244. **Infant mortality** (per 1,000 live births 1975): 156.

Education (1983): Literacy: 30%.

Major International Organizations: UN and its specialized agencies, OAU.

Embassy: 2460 16th St. NW 20009; 462-0761.

Named for an African empire along the Niger River, 400-1240 AD, Ghana was ruled by Britain for 113 years as the Gold Coast. The UN in 1956 approved merger with the British Togoland trust territory. Independence came March 6, 1957. Republic status within the Commonwealth was attained in 1960.

Pres. Kwame Nkrumah built hospitals and schools, promoted development projects like the Volta R. hydroelectric and aluminum plants, but ran the country into debt, jailed opponents, and was accused of corruption. A 1964 referendum gave Nkrumah dictatorial powers and set up a one-party socialist state.

Nkrumah was overthrown in 1966 by a police-army coup, which expelled Chinese and East German teachers and technicians. Elections were held in 1969, but 4 further coups occurred in 1972, 1978, 1979, and 1981. The 1979 and 1981 coups were led by Flight Lieut. Jerry Rawlings. The stagnant economy has continued to deteriorate.

Greece
Hellenic Republic

People: Population (1984 est.): 9,884,000. **Age distrib. (%):** 0–14: 23.7; 15–59: 58.9; 60+: 17.5. **Pop. density:** 194 per sq. mi. **Urban** (1981): 58.1%. **Ethnic groups:** Greeks 98.5%. **Languages:** Greek, others. **Religions:** Greek Orthodox 97%.

Geography: Area: 50,962 sq. mi., the size of New York State. **Location:** Occupies southern end of Balkan Peninsula in SE Europe. **Neighbors:** Albania, Yugoslavia, Bulgaria on N, Turkey on E. **Topography:** About 75% of Greece is non-arable, with mountains in all areas. Pindus Mts. run through the country N to S. The heavily indented coastline is 9,385 mi. long. Of over 2,000 islands, only 169 are inhabited, among them Crete, Rhodes, Milos, Kerkira (Corfu), Chios, Lesbos, Samos, Euboea, Delos, Mykonos. **Capital:** Athens. **Cities** (1981 est.): Athens (met.) 3,016,457; Thessaloniki (met.) 800,000; Patras 120,000.

Government: Type: Presidential Parliamentary Republic. **Head of state:** Pres. Christos Sartzetakis; in office: Mar. 30, 1985. **Head of government:** Prime Min. Andreas Papandreou; b. Feb. 5, 1919, in office: Oct. 21, 1981. **Local divisions:** 51 prefectures. **Defense:** 6.9% of GNP (1982).

Economy: Industries: Textiles, chemicals, metals, wine, food processng, cement. **Chief crops:** Grains, corn, rice, cotton, tobacco, olives, citrus fruits, raisins, figs. **Minerals:** Bauxite, lignite, oil, manganese. **Crude oil reserves** (1980): 150 mln. bbls. **Ara-

ble land:** 30%. **Meat prod.** (1983): beef: 90,000 metric tons; pork: 155,000 metric tons; lamb: 120,000 metric tons. **Fish catch** (1982): 106,000 metric tons. **Electricity prod.** (1982): 21.0 bln. kwh. **Crude steel prod.** (1982): 910,000 metric tons. **Labor force:** 29% agric.; 30% manuf. 41% service.

Finance: Currency: Drachma (Mar. 1985: 133.85 = $1 US). **Gross domestic product** (1983): $34.8 bln. **Per capita income** (1980): $4,590. **Imports** (1983): $9.5 bln.; partners: W. Ger. 18%, It. 9%, Fr. 7%. **Exports** (1983): $4.4 bln.; partners: W. Ger. 19%, It. 14%, Fr. 7%, Saudi Ar. 6%. **Tourists** (1982): receipts $1.5 bln. **National budget** (1982): $6.7 bln. revenues; $6.9 bln. expenditures. **International reserves less gold** (Mar. 1985): $904.9 mln. **Gold:** 4.1 mln. oz t. **Consumer prices** (change in 1984): 18.4%.

Transport: Railway traffic (1982): 1.5 bln. passenger-km; 585 mln. net ton-km. **Motor vehicles:** in use (1983): 1 mln. passenger cars, 574,000 comm. vehicles. **Civil aviation** (1983): 5.5 bln. passenger-km; 67.7 mln. freight ton-km. **Chief ports:** Piraeus, Thessaloniki, Patrai.

Communications: Television sets: 1.5 mln. in use (1983). **Radios:** 3.3 mln. in use (1983). **Telephones in use** (1982): 2.9 mln. **Daily newspaper circ.** (1982): 88 per 1,000 pop.

Health: Life expectancy at birth (1982): 72 male; 76 female. **Births** (per 1,000 pop. 1983): 13.4. **Deaths** (per 1,000 pop. 1983): 9.2. **Natural increase** (1983): .4%. **Hospital beds** (1982): 59,914. **Physicians** (1982): 24,724. **Infant mortality** (per 1,000 live births 1982): 14.3.

Education (1978): Literacy: 95%. **Pop. 5–19:** in school: 70%, teachers per 1,000: 25.

Major International Organizations: UN, EC, NATO, OECD.

Embassy: 2221 Massachusetts Ave. NW 20008; 667-3168.

The achievements of ancient Greece in art, architecture, science, mathematics, philosophy, drama, literature, and democracy became legacies for succeeding ages. Greece reached the height of its glory and power, particularly in the Athenian city-state, in the 5th century BC.

Greece fell under Roman rule in the 2d and 1st centuries BC. In the 4th century AD it became part of the Byzantine Empire and, after the fall of Constantinople to the Turks in 1453, part of the Ottoman Empire.

Greece won its war of independence from Turkey 1821-1829, and became a kingdom. A republic was established 1924; the monarchy was restored, 1935, and George II, King of the Hellenes, resumed the throne. In Oct., 1940, Greece rejected an ultimatum from Italy. Nazi support resulted in its defeat and occupation by Germans, Italians, and Bulgarians. By the end of 1944 the invaders withdrew. Communist resistance forces were defeated by Royalist and British troops. A plebiscite recalled King George II. He died Apr. 1, 1947, was succeeded by his brother, Paul I.

Communists waged guerrilla war 1947-49 against the government but were defeated with the aid of the U.S.

A period of reconstruction and rapid development followed, mainly with conservative governments under Premier Constantine Karamanlis. The Center Union led by George Papandreou won elections in 1963 and 1964. King Constantine, who acceded in 1964, forced Papandreou to resign. A period of political maneuvers ended in the military takeover of April 21, 1967, by Col. George Papadopoulos. King Constantine tried to reverse the consolidation of the harsh dictatorship Dec. 13, 1967, but failed and fled to Italy. Papadopoulos was ousted Nov. 25, 1973, in a coup led by rightist Brig. Demetrius Ioannides.

Greek army officers serving in the National Guard of Cyprus staged a coup on the island July 15, 1974. Turkey invaded Cyprus a week later, precipitating the collapse of the Greek junta, which was implicated in the Cyprus coup.

The military turned the government over to Karamanlis, who named a civilian cabinet, freed political prisoners, and sought to solve the Cyprus crisis. In Nov. 1974 elections his party won a large parliamentary majority, reduced by socialist gains in 1977. A Dec. 1974 referendum resulted in the proclamation of a republic.

Greece was reintegrated into the military wing of NATO in October 1980, and it became the 10th full member of the European Community on Jan. 1, 1981.

The 1981 victory of the Panhellenic Socialist Movement (Pasok) of Andreas Papandreou has brought about substantial changes in the internal and external policies that Greece has pursued for the past 5 decades. Relations with the U.S. were

strained during 1985 due to disputes over NATO and Cyprus policies.

Grenada

State of Grenada

People: Population (1984 est.): 113,000. **Pop. density:** 842 per sq. mi. **Ethnic groups:** Mostly African descent. **Languages:** English (official), French-African patois. **Religions:** Catholic 64%, Anglican 22%.

Geography: Area: 133 sq. mi., twice the size of Washington, D.C. **Location:** 90 mi. N. of Venezuela. **Topography:** Main island is mountainous; country includes Carriacon and Petit Martinique islands. **Capital:** St. George's. **Cities** (1980 est.): St. George's 7,500.

Government: Head of state: Queen Elizabeth II, represented by Gov.-Gen. Paul Scoon, b. July 4, 1935; in office: Sept. 30, 1978. **Head of government:** Prime Minister: Herbert Blaize; in office: Dec. 4, 1984. **Local divisions:** 6 parishes and one dependency.

Economy: Industries: Rum. **Chief crops:** Nutmegs, bananas, cocoa, mace. **Arable land:** 45%. **Electricity prod.** (1977): 28.00 mln. kwh. **Labor force:** 23% agric.; 24% ind.

Finance: Currency: East Caribbean dollar (Apr. 1985: 2.70 = $1 US). **Gross domestic product** (1982): $56 mln. **Per capita income** (1977): $500. **Imports** (1982): $56 mln.; partners: UK 16%, Trin./Tob. 19%. **Exports** (1982): $17 mln.; partners: UK 35%, W. Ger. 9%, Neth. 15%. **Tourists** (1981): 102,668. **National budget** (1980): $38.1 mln. revenues; $38.1 mln. expenditures. **International reserves less gold** (Jan. 1985): $23 mln.

Transport: Motor vehicles: in use (1981): 4,700 passenger cars, 1,000 comm. vehicles. **Chief ports:** Saint George's.

Communications: Radios: 65,000 in use (1982). **Telephones in use** (1983): 5,000.

Health: Life expectancy at birth (1984): 69 yrs. **Births** (per 1,000 pop. 1980): 23.6. **Deaths** (per 1,000 pop. 1980): 6.6. **Natural increase** (1980): 1.7%. **Infant mortality** (per 1,000 live births 1984): 16.7.

Education (1984): **Literacy:** 85%; **Years compulsory:** 6. **Major International Organizations:** UN and its specialized agencies, OAS.

Embassy: 1701 New Hampshire Ave. NW 20009; 265-2561.

Columbus sighted the island 1498. First European settlers were French, 1650. The island was held alternately by France and England until final British occupation, 1784. Grenada became fully independent Feb. 7, 1974 during a general strike. It is the smallest independent nation in the Western Hemisphere. The U.S. has criticized the government for following Soviet and Cuban policies.

On Oct. 14, 1983, a military coup ousted Prime Minister Maurice Bishop, who was put under house arrest, later freed by supporters, rearrested, and, finally, on Oct. 19, executed. U.S. forces, with a token force from 6 area nations, invaded Grenada, Oct. 25. Resistance from the Grenadian army and Cuban advisors was quickly overcome as most of the population welcomed the invading forces as liberators. U.S. troops were due to leave Grenada by Sept. 1985.

Guatemala

Republic of Guatemala

People: Population (1984 est.): 7,956,000. **Age distrib.** (%): 0–14: 45.1; 15–59: 50.6; 60+: 4.4. **Pop. density:** 180 per sq. mi. **Urban** (1981): 34.3%. **Ethnic groups:** Indians 54%, Mestizos 42%, whites 4%. **Languages:** Spanish, Indian dialects. **Religions:** Roman Catholics over 88%; Mayan religion practiced.

Geography: Area: 42,042 sq. mi., the size of Tennessee. **Location:** In Central America. **Neighbors:** Mexico N, W; El Salvador on S, Honduras, Belize on E. **Topography:** The central highland and mountain areas are bordered by the narrow Pacific coast and the lowlands and fertile river valleys on the Caribbean. There are numerous volcanoes in S, more than half a dozen over 11,000 ft. **Capital:** Guatemala City. **Cities** (1983 est.): Guatemala City 1,307,300.

Government: Type: Military. **Head of state:** Pres. Oscar Humberto Mejía Victores; b. 1930; in office: Aug. 8, 1983. **Local**

divisions: Guatemala City and 22 departments. **Defense:** 1.6% of GNP (1983).

Economy: Industries: Prepared foods, tires, textiles. **Chief crops:** Coffee (one third of exports), sugar, bananas, cotton, corn. **Minerals:** Oil, nickel. **Crude oil reserves** (1981): 120 mln. bbls. **Other resources:** Rare woods, fish, chicle. **Arable land:** 15%. **Electricity prod.** (1982): 1.6 bln. kwh. **Labor force:** 50% agric.; 27% ind. & comm., 12% services.

Finance: Currency: Quetzal (Apr. 1985: 1.00 = $1 US). **Gross domestic product** (1984): $9.9 bln. **Per capita income** (1984): $1,085. **Imports** (1983): $1.1 bln.; partners: U.S. 31%, Jap. 8%, Venez. 7%. **Exports** (1983): $1.1 bln.; partners: U.S. 27%, W. Ger. 8%. **National budget** (1984): $1.3 bln. **International reserves less gold** (Mar. 1985): $237.1 mln. **Gold:** 522,000 oz t. **Consumer prices** (change in 1983): 0.5%.

Transport: Railway traffic. Motor vehicles: in use (1983): 166,900 passenger cars, 81,500 comm. vehicles. **Civil aviation** (1982) 160 mln. passenger-km; 5.5 mln. freight ton-km. **Chief ports:** Puerto Barrios, San Jose.

Communications: Television sets: 192,000 in use (1982). **Radios:** 500,000 in use (1983). **Telephones in use** (1982): 97,670. **Daily newspaper circ.** (1982): 47 per 1,000 pop.

Health: Life expectancy at birth (1984): 55 yrs. **Births** (per 1,000 pop. 1978): 42. **Deaths** (per 1,000 pop. 1978): 11. **Natural increase** (1984): 3.1% **Health:** There are about 1,250 doctors, 60 hospitals, and 100 dispensaries. **Infant mortality** (per 1,000 live births 1984): 79.

Education (1984): **Literacy:** 48%. **Years compulsory:** 6; **Attendance:** 35%.

Major International Organizations: UN and its specialized agencies, OAS.

Embassy: 2220 R St. NW 20008; 745-4952.

The old Mayan Indian empire flourished in what is today Guatemala for over 1,000 years before the Spanish.

Guatemala was a Spanish colony 1524-1821; briefly a part of Mexico and then of the U.S. of Central America, the republic was established in 1839.

Since 1945 when a liberal government was elected to replace the long-term dictatorship of Jorge Ubico, the country has seen a swing toward socialism, an armed revolt, renewed attempts at social reform and a military coup. Assassinations and political violence from left and right plagued the country. The Guerrilla Army of the Poor, an insurgent group founded 1975, has stepped up their military offensive by attacking army posts and has succeeded in incorporating segments of the large Indian population in its struggle against the government.

Dissident army officers seized power, Mar. 23, 1982, denouncing the Mar. 7 Presidential election as fraudulent and pledging to restore "authentic democracy" to the nation. Political violence has caused some 200,000 Guatemalans to seek refuge in Mexico. A second military coup occurred Oct. 8, 1983; elections were scheduled for October 1985.

Guinea

Republic of Guinea

People: Population (1984 est.): 5,579,000. **Pop. density:** 58 per sq. mi. **Ethnic groups:** Foulah 40%, Malinké 25%, Soussous 10%, 15 other tribes. **Languages:** French (official), tribal languages. **Religions:** Muslims 75%, tribal 24%, Christian 1%.

Geography: Area: 94,925 sq. mi., slightly smaller than Oregon. **Location:** On Atlantic coast of W. Africa. **Neighbors:** Guinea-Bissau, Senegal, Mali on N, Ivory Coast on E, Liberia on S. **Topography:** A narrow coastal belt leads to the mountainous middle region, the source of the Gambia, Senegal, and Niger rivers. Upper Guinea, farther inland, is a cooler upland. The SE is forested. **Capital:** Conakry. **Cities** (1983 est.): Conakry 656,000; Labe 273,000; N'Zerekore 250,000; Kankan 278,000.

Government: Type: Republic. **Head of state:** Pres. Col. Lansana Conte; b. 1944; in office: Apr. 5, 1984. **Local divisions:** 33 districts. **Defense:** 5.1% of GNP (1981).

Economy: Chief crops: Bananas, pineapples, rice, corn, palm nuts, coffee, honey. **Minerals:** Bauxite, iron, diamonds. **Arable land:** 7%. **Meat prod.** (1980): beef 18,000 metric tons. **Electricity prod.** (1982) 498 mln. kwh. **Labor force:** 82% agric.; 11% ind. & comm.

Finance: Currency: Syli (Nov. 1984: 24.80 = $1 US). **Gross domestic product** (1981): $1.6 bln. **Per capita income** (1980):

93. **Imports** (1981): $375 mln.; partners (1979): Fr. 36%, SSR 11%, U.S. 6% It. 6%. **Exports** (1981): $385 mln.; partners (1979): U.S. 18%, Fr. 13%, W. Ger. 12%, USSR 12%. **National budget** (1982): 140 mln. **Consumer prices** (change in 1981): 5.6%.

Transport: Motor vehicles: in use (1982): 10,000 passenger cars, 10,000 comm. vehicles. **Chief ports:** Conakry.

Communications: Radios: 144,000 in use (1981). **Daily newspaper circ.** (1982): 2 per 1,000 pop.

Health: Life expectancy at birth (1980): 44 male; 47 female. **Births** (per 1,000 pop. 1978): 47. **Deaths** (per 1,000 pop. 1978): 26. **Natural increase** (1978): 2.1%. **Hospital beds** (per 100,000 pop. 1977): 158. **Physicians** (per 100,000 pop. 1977): 6. **Infant mortality** (per 1,000 live births 1980): 172.

Education (1983): **Literacy:** 48%. **Years compulsory:** 12; attendance: 34% primary, 15% secondary.

Major International Organizations: UN and its specialized agencies, OAU.

Embassy: 2112 Leroy Pl. NW 20008; 438-9420.

Part of the ancient West African empires, Guinea fell under French control 1849-98. Under Sekou Toure, it opted for full independence in 1958, and France withdrew all aid.

Toure turned to communist nations for support, and set up a militant one-party state. Western firms, as well as the Soviet government, have invested in Guinea's vast bauxite mines.

Thousands of opponents were jailed in the 1970s, in the aftermath of an unsuccessful Portuguese invasion. Many were tortured and killed.

The military took control of the government in a bloodless coup after the March 1984 death of Toure.

Guinea-Bissau
Republic of Guinea-Bissau

People: Population (1984 est.): 842,000. **Pop. density:** 63.2 per sq. mi. **Ethnic groups:** Balanta 30%, Fula 20%, Mandyako 14%, Mandinga 13%. **Languages:** Portuguese (official), Criolo, tribal languages. **Religion:** Traditional 66%, Moslems 30%, Christians 5%.

Geography: Area: 13,948 sq. mi. **Location:** On Atlantic coast of W. Africa. **Neighbors:** Senegal on N, Guinea on E, S. **Topography:** A swampy coastal plain covers most of the country; to the east is a low savanna region. **Capital:** Bissau. **Cities** (1979): Bissau 109,500.

Government: Type: Republic. **Head of government:** Gen. Joao Bernardo Vieira; b. 1939; in office: Nov. 14,1980. **Local divisions:** 8 regions. **Defense:** 7% of GNP (1982).

Economy: Chief crops: Peanuts, cotton, rice. **Minerals:** Bauxite. **Arable land:** 8%. **Electricity prod.** (1982): 13 mln. kwh. **Labor force:** 90% agric.

Finance: Currency: Peso (Nov. 1984: 84.44 = $1 US). **Gross domestic product** (1981): $150 mln. **Per capita income** (1979): $170. **Imports** (1980): $60 mln.; partners: Port. 32%, It. 11%, Fr. 7%. **Exports** (1980): $10 mln.; partners: Port. 65%.

Communications: Radios: 7,000 licensed (1981). **Daily newspaper circ.** (1984): 7 per 1,000 pop.

Health: Life expectancy at birth (1982): 35 years. **Births** (per 1,000 pop. 1981): 40.9. **Deaths** (per 1,000 pop. 1981): 21.9. **Natural increase** (1981): 1.9%. **Infant mortality** (per 1,000 live births 1982): 250.

Education (1982): Literacy 9%. **Years compulsory:** 4.

Major International Organizations: UN and its specialized agencies, OAU.

Embassy: 211 E 43d St., New York, NY 10017; (212) 661-3977.

Portuguese mariners explored the area in the mid-15th century; the slave trade flourished in the 17th and 18th centuries, and colonization began in the 19th.

Beginning in the 1960s, an independence movement waged a guerrilla war and formed a government in the interior that achieved international support. Full independence came Sept. 10, 1974, after the Portuguese regime was overthrown.

The November 1980 coup gave Joao Bernardo Vieira absolute power.

Guyana
Cooperative Republic of Guyana

People: Population (1984 est.): 775,000. **Age distrib.** (%): 0–14: 43.7; 5–59: 50.7; 60+: 5.6. **Pop. density:** 12.3 per sq. mi. **Urban** (1983): 28%. **Ethnic groups:** East Indians 51%, African and mixed 43%. **Languages:** English (official), Amerindian dialects. **Religions:** Christians 57%, Hindus 34%, Moslems 9%.

Geography: Area: 83,000 sq. mi., the size of Idaho. **Location:** On N coast of S. America. **Neighbors:** Venezuela on W, Brazil on S, Suriname on E. **Topography:** Dense tropical forests cover much of the land, although a flat coastal area up to 40 mi. wide, where 90% of the population lives, provides rich alluvial soil for agriculture. A grassy savanna divides the 2 zones. **Capital:** Georgetown. **Cities** (1985 est.): Georgetown 170,000.

Government: Type: Republic within the Commonwealth of Nations. **Head of state:** President Linden Forbes Burnham; b. Feb. 20, 1923; in office: Dec. 14, 1964. **Head of Government:** Prime Min. Desmond Hoyte; in office: Aug. 16, 1984. **Local divisions:** 10 regions. **Defense:** 9% of GDP (1985).

Economy: Industries: Cigarettes, rum, clothing, furniture, drugs. **Chief crops:** Sugar, rice, citrus and other fruits. **Minerals:** Bauxite, diamonds. **Other resources:** Timber, shrimp. **Arable land:** 2%. **Electricity prod.** (1982): 359 bln. kwh. **Labor force:** 33% agric.; 45% ind. & comm.; 22% services.

Finance: Currency: Dollar (Mar. 1985: 4.15 = $1 US). **Gross national product** (1983): $419 mln. **Per capita income** (1983): $457. **Imports** (1983): $243 mln.; partners: U.S. 28%, Trin-Tob. 24%, UK 20%. **Exports** (1983): $193 mln.; partners: UK 28%, U.S. 18%, Trin-Tob. 7%. **National budget** (1984): $441 mln. **International reserves less gold** (Oct. 1984): $3.8 mln. **Consumer prices** (change in 1983): 14.9%.

Transport: Railway traffic (1974): 6 mln. passenger-km. **Motor vehicles:** in use (1982): 20,000 passenger cars, 4,000 comm. vehicles. **Chief ports:** Georgetown.

Communications: Radios: 300,000 in use (1983). **Telephones in use** (1982): 28,000. **Daily newspaper circ.** (1983): 63 per 1,000 pop.

Health: Life expectancy at birth (1985): 70 years. **Births** (per 1,000 pop. 1983): 29.0. **Deaths** (per 1,000 pop. 1983): 7.0. **Natural increase** (1983): 2.2% **Health** (1982): 270 doctors, 29 hospitals, 149 health centers. **Infant mortality** (per 1,000 live births 1985): 41.

Education (1985): **Literacy:** 86%. **Years compulsory:** ages 5-14.

Major International Organizations: UN and its specialized agencies, CARICOM, Commonwealth of Nations.

Embassy: 2490 Tracy Pl. NW 20008; 265-6900.

Guyana became a Dutch possession in the 17th century, but sovereignty passed to Britain in 1815. Indentured servants from India soon outnumbered African slaves. Ethnic tension has affected political life.

Guyana became independent May 26, 1966. A Venezuelan claim to the western half of Guyana was suspended in 1970 but renewed in 1982. The Suriname border is also disputed. The government has nationalized most of the economy which has remained severely depressed.

The Port Kaituma ambush of U.S. Rep. Leo J. Ryan and others investigating mistreatment of American followers of the Rev. Jim Jones' People's Temple cult, triggered a mass suicide-execution of 911 cultists in the Guyana jungle, Nov. 18, 1978.

Haiti
Republic of Haiti

People: Population (1984 est.): 5,803,000. **Age distrib.** (%): 4–14: 41.5; 15–59: 51.8; 60+: 6.7. **Pop. density:** 501 per sq. mi. **Urban** (1984): 20.7%. **Ethnic groups:** African descent 95%. **Languages:** French (official), Creole (majority). **Religions:** Roman Catholics 80%, Protestants 10%; Voodoo widely practiced.

Geography: Area: 10,714 sq. mi., the size of Maryland. **Location:** In West Indies, occupies western third of I. of Hispaniola. **Neighbors:** Dominican Republic on E, Cuba on W. **Topography:** About two-thirds of Haiti is mountainous. Much of the rest is

semiarid. Coastal areas are warm and moist. **Capital:** Port-au-Prince. **Cities** (1984 est.): Port-au-Prince 550,000.

Government: Type: Republic. **Head of state:** Pres. Jean-Claude Duvalier; b. July 3, 1951; in office: Apr. 22, 1971. **Local divisions:** 9 departments. **Defense** (1982): About 4.5% of govt. budget.

Economy: Industries: Rum, molasses, tourism. **Chief crops:** Coffee, sisal, cotton, sugar, bananas, cocoa, tobacco, rice. **Minerals:** Bauxite, copper, gold, silver, metric tons. **Other resources:** Timber. **Arable land:** 32%. **Meat prod.** (1980): beef: 24,000 metric tons; pork: 33,000 metric tons; lamb: 6,000 metric tons. **Electricity prod.** (1981): 325 mln. kwh. **Labor force:** 79% agric.; 7% ind. & comm.; 14% services.

Finance: Currency: Gourde (Apr. 1985: 5.00 = $1 US). **Gross national product** (1983): $1.6 bln. **Per capita income** (1983): $300. **Imports** (1982): $330 mln.; partners: U.S. 45%, Neth. Ant. 10%, Jap. 9%. Can. 8%. **Exports** (1982): $150 mln.; partners: U.S. 59%, Fr. 13%, It. 7%, Belg. 6%. **Tourists** (1981): receipts $26 mln. **National budget** (1979): $94 mln. revenues; $94 mln. expenditures. **International reserves less gold** (Mar. 1985): $11 mln. **Gold:** 18,000 oz t. **Consumer prices** (change in 1984): 10.7%.

Transport: Motor vehicles: in use (1981): 17,400 passenger cars, 3,100 comm. vehicles. **Chief ports:** Port-au-Prince, Les Cayes.

Communications: Television sets: 65,000 in use (1982). **Radios:** 105,000 in use (1982). **Telephones in use** (1982): 80,000 **Daily newspaper circ.** (1982): 4 per 1,000 pop.

Health: Life expectancy at birth (1984): 45 yrs. **Births** (per 1,000 pop. 1978): 42. **Deaths** (per 1,000 pop. 1978): 16. **Natural increase** (1978): 2.6%. **Hospital beds** (per 100,000 pop. 1977): 72. **Physicians** (per 100,000 pop. 1977): 7. **Infant mortality rate** (per 1,000 live births, 1984): 130.

Education (1984): **Literacy:** 20%. **Years compulsory:** 6; attendance 20%.

Major International Organizations: UN and its specialized agencies, OAS.

Embassy: 2311 Massachusetts Ave. NW 20008; 332-4090.

Haiti, visited by Columbus, 1492, and a French colony from 1677, attained its independence, 1804, following the rebellion led by former slave Toussaint L'Ouverture. Following a period of political violence, the U.S. occupied the country 1915-34.

Dr. Francois Duvalier was voted president in 1957; in 1964 he was named president for life. Upon his death in 1971, he was succeeded by his son, Jean-Claude. Drought in 1975-77 brought famine, and Hurricane Allen in 1980 destroyed most of the rice, bean, and coffee crops.

Haiti is the poorest nation in the Western hemisphere. Amnesty International has charged Haitian authorities with arbitrarily arresting, torturing, and killing opponents of Duvalier.

Honduras
Republic of Honduras

People: Population (1984 est.): 4,424,000. **Age distrib.** (%): 0–14: 48.1; 15–59: 47.5; 60+: 4.5. **Pop. density:** 97.8 per sq. mi. **Urban** (1982): 36.4%. **Ethnic groups:** Mestizo 90%, Europeans, Negroes, Indians. **Languages:** Spanish, Indian dialects. **Religions:** Roman Catholics, small Protestant minority.

Geography: Area: 43,277 sq. mi., slightly larger than Tennessee. **Location:** In Central America. **Neighbors:** Guatemala on W, El Salvador, Nicaragua on S. **Topography:** The Caribbean coast is 500 mi. long. Pacific coast, on Gulf of Fonseca, is 40 mi. long. Honduras is mountainous, with wide fertile valleys and rich forests. **Capital:** Tegucigalpa. **Cities** (1984 est.) Tegucigalpa 450,000; San Pedro Sula 342,800.

Government: Type: Democratic constitutional republic. **Head of State:** Pres. Roberto Suazo Cordova; in office: Jan. 27, 1982. **Local divisions:** 18 departments. **Defense:** 7% of govt. budget (1983).

Economy: Industries: Clothing, textiles, cement, wood prods. **Chief crops:** Bananas (chief export), coffee, corn, beans. **Minerals:** Gold, silver, copper, lead, zinc, iron, antimony, coal. **Other resources:** Timber. **Arable land:** 16%. **Meat prod.** (1980): beef: 56,000 metric tons; pork: 9,000 metric tons. **Electricity prod.** (1982): 1 bln. kwh. **Labor force:** 59% agric.; 20% ind. & comm.; 12% service.

Finance: Currency: Lempira (Apr. 1985): 2.00 = $1 US. **Gross national product** (1983): $2.8 bln. **Per capita income** (1982): $590. **Imports** (1982): $1 bln.; partners: U.S. 41%, Jap 7%, Guat. 6%. **Exports** (1982): $791 mln.; partners: U.S. 52%, W. Ger. 8%, Jap. 5%. **Tourists** (1981): 188,177. **National budget** (1984): $805 mln. revenues; $1.3 bln. expenditures. **International reserves less gold** (Feb. 1985): $136.4 mln. **Gold:** 16,000 oz t. **Consumer prices** (change in 1983): 9.4%.

Transport: Motor vehicles: in use (1983) 58,900 passenger cars, 24,000 comm. vehicles. **Civil aviation** (1982): 331 mln. passenger-km; 3.1 mln. freight ton-km. **Chief ports:** Puerto Cortes, La Ceiba.

Communications: Television sets: 135,000 in use (1983). **Radios:** 1.5 mln. in use (1983). **Telephones in use** (1982): 33,000. **Daily newspaper circ.** (1983): 60 per 1,000 pop.

Health: Life expectancy at birth (1984): 58.7 yrs. **Births** (per 1,000 pop. 1980): 49.3. **Deaths** (per 1,000 pop. 1980): 12.4. **Natural increase** (1980): 3.6%. **Hospital beds** (1981): 5,230. **Physicians** (1981): 1,370. **Infant mortality** (per 1,000 live births 1984): 78.

Education (1984): **Literacy:** 55%. **Years compulsory:** 6; attendance 70%.

Major International Organizations: UN, OAS.

Embassy: 4301 Connecticut Ave. NW 20008; 966-7700.

Mayan civilization flourished in Honduras in the 1st millenium AD. Columbus arrived in 1502. Honduras became independent after freeing itself from Spain, 1821 and from the Fed. of Central America, 1838.

Gen. Oswaldo Lopez Arellano, president for most of the period 1963-75 by virtue of one election and 2 coups, was ousted by the Army in 1975 over charges of pervasive bribery by United Brands Co. of the U.S.

The government has resumed land distribution, raised minimum wages, and started a literacy campaign. An elected civilian government took power in 1982, the country's first in 10 years.

The U.S. has provided military aid and advisors to help withstand pressures from Nicaragua and help block arms shipments from Nicaragua to rebel forces in El Salvador. The U.S. contributed $84 mln. in economic aid, and $41 mln. in military aid in 1984. Joint military exercises were held in 1985.

Hungary
Hungarian People's Republic

People: Population (1984 est.): 10,681,000. **Age distrib.** (%): 0–14: 21.7; 15–59: 61.4; 60+: 16.9. **Pop. density:** 297 per sq. mi. **Urban** (1983): 54%. **Ethnic groups:** Magyar 92%, German 2.5%, Gypsy 3%. **Languages:** Hungarian (Magyar). **Religions:** Roman Catholics 67%, Protestant 25%.

Geography: Area: 35,919 sq. mi., slightly smaller than Indiana. **Location:** In East Central Europe. **Neighbors:** Czechoslovakia on N, Austria on W, Yugoslavia on S, Romania, USSR on E. **Topography:** The Danube R. forms the Czech border in the NW, then swings S to bisect the country. The eastern half of Hungary is mainly a great fertile plain, the Alfold; the W and N are hilly. **Capital:** Budapest. **Cities** (1984 est.): Budapest 2,064,000; Miskolc 212,000; Debrecen 205,000.

Government: Type: Communist unitary state. **Head of state:** Pres. Pal Losonczi; b. Sept. 18, 1919; in office: Apr. 14, 1967. **Head of government:** Prem. Gyorgy Lazar; b. Sept. 15, 1924; in office: May 15, 1975. **Head of Communist Party:** Janos Kadar; b. May 26, 1912; in office: Oct. 25, 1956. **Local divisions:** 19 counties, 5 cities with county status. **Defense:** 3.9% of govt. budget (1983).

Economy: Industries: Iron and steel, machinery, pharmaceuticals, vehicles, communications equip., milling, distilling. **Chief crops:** Grains, vegetables, fruits, grapes. **Minerals:** Bauxite, natural gas. **Arable land:** 57%. **Meat prod.** (1983): beef: 133,000 metric tons; pork: 1.1 mln. metric tons. **Electricity prod.** (1983): 25.6 bln. kwh. **Crude steel prod.** (1982): 3.7 mln. metric tons. **Labor force:** 20% agric.; 42% ind. & comm.; 32% services.

Finance: Currency: Forint (Mar. 1985: 50.88 = $1 US). **Gross domestic product** (1983): $18.6 bln. **Per capita income** (1982): $4,180. **Imports** (1984): $8.0 bln.; partners: USSR 29%, W. Ger. 11%, E. Ger. 7%, Czech. 5%. **Exports** (1984): $8.5 bln.; partners: USSR 34%, E. Ger. 6%, W. Ger.

%, Czech. 6%. **National budget** (1983): $13.4 bln. **Tourists** 982): 9.8 mln. **Consumer prices** (change in 1984): 7.2%.

Transport: Railway traffic (1983): 11.1 bln. passenger-km; 23.2 bln. net ton-km. **Motor vehicles:** in use (1983): 1.2 mln. passenger cars, 153,000 comm. vehicles; manuf. (1982): 11,000 comm. vehicles. **Civil aviation** (1983): 1.1 bln. Passenger-km; 29.4 mln. net freight-km.

Communications: Television sets: 2.8 mln. licensed (1982). **Radios:** 2.7 mln. licensed (1981). **Telephones in use** (1982): 1.2 mln. **Daily newspaper circ.** (1983): 265 per 1,000 pop.

Health: Life expectancy at birth (1981): 66.0 male; 73.4 female. **Births** (per 1,000 pop. 1982): 12.5 **Deaths** (per 1,000 pop. 1982): 12.5. **Natural increase** (1982): 0%. **Hospital beds** (1982): 98,535. **Physicians** (1982): 32,476. **Infant mortality** (per 1,000 live births 1983): 20.6

Education (1983): **Literacy:** 98%. **Years compulsory:** to age 16; attendance 99%.

Major International Organizations: UN and its specialized agencies, Warsaw Pact.

Embassy: 3910 Shoemaker St. NW 20008; 362-6730.

Earliest settlers, chiefly Slav and Germanic, were overrun by Magyars from the east. Stephen I (997-1038) was made king by Pope Sylvester II in 1000 AD. The country suffered repeated Turkish invasions in the 15th-17th centuries. After the defeats of the Turks, 1686-1697, Austria dominated, but Hungary obtained concessions until it regained internal independence in 1867, with the emperor of Austria as king of Hungary in a dual monarchy with a single diplomatic service. Defeated with the Central Powers in 1918, Hungary lost Transylvania to Romania, Croatia and Bacska to Yugoslavia, Slovakia and Carpatho-Ruthenia to Czechoslovakia, all of which had large Hungarian minorities. A republic under Michael Karolyi and a bolshevist revolt under Bela Kun were followed by a vote for a monarchy in 1920 with Admiral Nicholas Horthy as regent.

Hungary joined Germany in World War II, and was allowed to annex most of its lost territories. Russian troops captured the country, 1944-1945. By terms of an armistice with the Allied powers Hungary agreed to give up territory acquired by the 1938 dismemberment of Czechoslovakia and to return to its borders of 1937.

A republic was declared Feb. 1, 1946; Zoltan Tildy was elected president. In 1947 the communists forced Tildy out. Premier Imre Nagy, in office since mid-1953, was ousted for his moderate policy of favoring agriculture and consumer production, April 18, 1955.

In 1956, popular demands for the ousting of Erno Gero, Communist party secretary, and for formation of a government by Nagy, resulted in the latter's appointment Oct. 23; demonstrations against communist rule developed into open revolt. Gero called in Soviet forces. On Nov. 4 Soviet forces launched a massive attack against Budapest with 200,000 troops, 2,500 tanks and armored cars.

Estimates varied from 6,500 to 32,000 dead, and thousands deported. About 200,000 persons fled the country. In the spring of 1963 the regime freed many anti-communists and captives from the revolution in a sweeping amnesty. Nagy was executed by the Russians.

Some 60,000 Soviet troops are stationed in Hungary. Hungarian troops participated in the 1968 Warsaw Pact invasion of Czechoslovakia.

Major economic reforms were launched early in 1968, switching from a central planning system to one in which market forces and profit control much of production. Productivity and living standards have improved. Hungary leads the communist states in comparative tolerance for cultural freedoms and small private enterprise.

Iceland
Republic of Iceland

People: Population (1984 est.): 239,000. **Age distrib.** (%): 0-14: 26.7; 15-59: 59.5; 60+: 13.8. **Pop. density:** 6 per sq. mi. **Urban** (1983): 88.9% **Ethnic groups:** Homogeneous, descendants of Norwegians, Celts. **Language:** Icelandic. **Religion:** Evangelical Lutheran 97%.

Geography: Area: 39,769 sq. mi., the size of Virginia. **Location:** At N end of Atlantic O. **Neighbors:** Nearest is Greenland. **Topography:** Iceland is of recent volcanic origin. Three-quarters

of the surface is wasteland: glaciers, lakes, a lava desert. There are geysers and hot springs, and the climate is moderated by the Gulf Stream. **Capital:** Reykjavik. **Cities** (1983 est.): Reykjavik 85,782.

Government: Type: Constitutional Republic. **Head of state:** Pres. Vigdis Finnbogadottir; b. Apr. 15, 1930; in office: Aug. 1, 1980. **Head of government:** Prime Min. Steingrimur Hermannsson; b. June 22, 1928; in office: May 26, 1983. **Local divisions:** 7 districts.

Economy: Industries: Fish products (some 80% of exports), aluminum. **Chief crops:** Potatoes, turnips, hay. **Arable land:** 0.5%. **Meat prod.** (1983): lamb: 14,000 metric tons. **Fish catch** (1982): 776,000 metric tons. **Electricity prod.** (1982): 3.2 bln. kwh. **Labor force:** 19% agric.; 43% ind. & comm.; 34% services & govt.

Finance: Currency: Kronur (Mar. 1985: 40.5 = $1 US). **Gross domestic product** (1983): $2.1 bln. **Per capita income** (1979): $9,000. **Imports** (1980): $1.00 bln.; partners: USSR 10%, W. Ger. 12%, UK 9%, Den. 10%. **Exports** (1980): $929 mln.; partners: U.S. 28%, UK 13%, Port. 12%. **Tourists** (1983): receipts: $58 mln. **National budget** (1980): $455 mln. revenues; $451 mln. expenditures. **International reserves less gold** (Mar. 1985): $116.3 mln. **Gold:** 49,000 oz t. **Consumer prices** (change in 1984): 30.8%.

Transport: Motor vehicles: in use (1982): 91,457 passenger cars, 9,479 comm. vehicles. **Civil aviation** (1982): 1.4 bln. passenger-km ; 23.7 mln. freight ton-km . **Chief ports:** Reykjavik.

Communications: Television sets: 62,500 in use (1982). **Radios:** 69,700 licensed (1982). **Telephones in use** (1982): 111,358. **Daily newspaper circ.** (1982): 557 per 1,000 pop.

Health: Life expectancy at birth (1983): 73.5 male; 79.5 female. **Births** (per 1,000 pop. 1982): 18.5. **Deaths** (per 1,000 pop. 1982): 6.8. **Natural increase** (1982): 1.1%. **Hospital beds** (per 100,000 pop. 1977): 1,700. **Physicians** (per 100,000 pop. 1977): 180. **Infant mortality** per (1,000 live births 1982): 7.1.

Education (1984): **Literacy:** 99.9%.

Major International Organizations: UN and its specialized agencies, NATO, OECD.

Embassy: 2022 Connecticut Ave. NW 20008; 265-6653.

Iceland was an independent republic from 930 to 1262, when it joined with Norway. Its language has maintained its purity for 1,000 years. Danish rule lasted from 1380-1918; the last ties with the Danish crown were severed in 1941. The Althing, or assembly, is the world's oldest surviving parliament.

A four-year dispute with Britain ended in 1976 when the latter accepted Iceland's 200-mile territorial waters claim.

India
Republic of India

People: Population (1984 est.): 746,388,000. **Age distrib.** (%): 0-14: 40.8; 15-59: 53.9; 60+: 5.3. **Pop. density:** 582 per sq. mi. **Urban** (1981): 21.5%. **Ethnic groups:** Indo-Aryan groups 72%, Dravidians 25%, Mongoloids 3%. **Languages:** 16 languages, including Hindi (official) and English (associate official). **Religions:** Hindu 83%, Moslem 11%, Christian 3%, Sikh 2%.

Geography: Area: 1,269,420 sq. mi., one third the size of the U.S. **Location:** Occupies most of the Indian subcontinent in S. Asia. **Neighbors:** Pakistan on W, China, Nepal, Bhutan on N, Burma, Bangladesh on E. **Topography:** The Himalaya Mts., highest in world, stretch across India's northern borders. Below, the Ganges Plain is wide, fertile, and among the most densely populated regions of the world. The area below includes the Deccan Peninsula. Close to one quarter the area is forested. The climate varies from tropical heat in S to near-Arctic cold in N. Rajasthan Desert is in NW; NE Assam Hills get 400 in. of rain a year. **Capital:** New Delhi. **Cities** (1980 cen.): Calcutta 9.1 mln.; Bombay (met.) 8.2 mln.; Delhi 5.2 mln.; Madras 4.3 mln.; Bangalore 2.9 mln.; Hyderabad 1.5 mln.; Ahmedabad 2.5 mln.; Kanpur 1.7 mln.; Pune 1.7 mln.; Nagpur 1.3 mln.

Government: Type: Federal Republic. **Head of state:** Pres. Zail Singh; b. May 5, 1916; in office: July 12, 1982. **Head of government:** Prime Min. Rajiv Gandhi, b. Aug. 20, 1944; in office: Oct. 31, 1984. **Local divisions:** 22 states, 9 union territories. **Defense:** 3.5% of GNP (1982).

Economy: Industries: Textiles, steel, processed foods, cement, machinery, chemicals, fertilizers, consumer appliances,

autos. **Chief crops:** Rice, grains, coffee, sugar cane, spices, tea, cashews, cotton, copra, coir, juta, linseed. **Minerals:** Chromium, coal, iron, manganese, mica salt, bauxite, gypsum, oil. **Crude oil reserves** (1980): 2.60 bln. bbls. **Other resources:** Rubber, timber. **Arable land:** 57%. **Meat prod.** (1984): beef: 220,000 metric tons; pork: 84,000 metric tons; lamb: 438,000 metric tons. **Fish catch** (1982): 2.4 mln. metric tons. **Electricity prod.** (1982): 138 bln. kwh. **Crude steel prod.** (1982): 10.8 mln. metric tons. **Labor force:** 70% agric.; 19% ind. & comm.

Finance: Currency: Rupee (Mar. 1985: 12.4 = $1 US). **Gross domestic product** (1982): $173 bln. **Per capita income** (1977): $150. **Imports** (1983): $13.6 bln.; partners: U.S. 12%, USSR 8%, W. Ger. 6%, Iran 11%. **Exports** (1983): $8.6 bln.; partners: U.S. 11%, USSR 18%, UK 6%, Jap. 9%. **Tourists** (1982): receipts: $800 mln. **National budget** (1980): $13.4 bln. revenues; $14.7 bln. expenditures. **International reserves less gold** (Jan. 1985): $5.8 bln. **Gold:** 8.7 mln. oz. t. **Consumer prices** (change in 1984): 8.3%.

Transport: Railway traffic (1982): 221 bln. passenger-km; 173 bln. net ton-km. **Motor vehicles:** in use (1982): 900,000 passenger cars, 791,000 comm. vehicles; manuf. (1982): 63,000 passenger cars, 87,000 comm. vehicles. **Civil aviation:** (1982): 13.2 bln. passenger-km; 446 mln. freight ton-km. **Chief ports:** Calcutta, Bombay, Madras, Cochin, Vishakhapatnam.

Communications: Television sets: 2 mln. licensed (1983). **Radios:** 22 mln. licensed (1983).**Telephones in use** (1982): 2.9 mln. **Daily newspaper circ.** (1981): 21 per. 1,000 pop.

Health: Life expectancy at birth (1981): 52 male; 50 female. **Births** (per 1,000 pop. 1980): 33.5. **Deaths** (per 1,000 pop. 1980): 12.5. **Natural increase** (1980): 2.1%. **Hospital beds** (per 100,000 pop. 1977): 75. **Physicians** (per 100,000 pop. 1977): 26. **Infant mortality** (per 1,000 live births 1981): 117.

Education (1981): Literacy: 36%. **Pop. 5-19:** in school: 42%, teachers per 1,000: 13.

Major International Organizations: UN and its specialized agencies.

Embassy: 2107 Massachusetts Ave. NW 20008; 265-5050.

India has one of the oldest civilizations in the world. Excavations trace the Indus Valley civilization back for at least 5,000 years. Paintings in the mountain caves of Ajanta, richly carved temples, the Taj Mahal in Agra, and the Kutab Minar in Delhi are among relics of the past.

Aryan tribes, speaking Sanskrit, invaded from the NW around 1500 BC, and merged with the earlier inhabitants to create classical Indian civilization.

Asoka ruled most of the Indian subcontinent in the 3d century BC, and established Buddhism. But Hinduism revived and eventually predominated. During the Gupta kingdom, 4th-6th century AD, science, literature, and the arts enjoyed a "golden age."

Arab invaders established a Moslem foothold in the W in the 8th century, and Turkish Moslems gained control of North India by 1200. The Mogul emperors ruled 1526-1857.

Vasco da Gama established Portuguese trading posts 1498-1503. The Dutch followed. The British East India Co. sent Capt. William Hawkins, 1609, to get concessions from the Mogul emperor for spices and textiles. Operating as the East India Co. the British gained control of most of India. The British parliament assumed political direction; under Lord Bentinck, 1828-35, rule by rajahs was curbed. After the Sepoy troops mutinied, 1857-58, the British supported the native rulers.

Nationalism grew rapidly after World War I. The Indian National Congress and the Moslem League demanded constitutional reform. A leader emerged in Mohandas K. Gandhi (called Mahatma, or Great Soul), born Oct. 2, 1869, assassinated Jan. 30, 1948. He began advocating self-rule, non-violence, removal of untouchability in 1919. In 1930 he launched "civil disobedience," including boycott of British goods and rejection of taxes without representation.

In 1935 Britain gave India a constitution providing a bicameral federal congress. Mohammed Ali Jinnah, head of the Moslem League, sought creation of a Moslem nation, Pakistan.

The British government partitioned British India into the dominions of India and Pakistan. Aug. 15, 1947, was designated Indian Independence Day. India became a self-governing member of the Commonwealth and a member of the UN. It became a democratic republic, Jan. 26, 1950.

More than 12 million Hindu & Moslem refugees crossed the India-Pakistan borders in a mass transferral of some of the peoples during 1947; about 200,000 were killed in communal fighting.

After Pakistan troops began attacks on Bengali separatists in East Pakistan, Mar. 25, 1971, some 10 million refugees fled into India. On Aug. 9, India and the USSR signed a 20-year friendship pact while U.S.-India relations soured. India and Pakistan went to war Dec. 3, 1971, on both the East and West fronts. Pakistan troops in the East surrendered Dec. 16; Pakistan agreed to a cease-fire in the West Dec. 17.

India and Pakistan signed a pact agreeing to withdraw troops from their borders and seek peaceful solutions, July 3, 1972. In Aug. 1973 India agreed to release 93,000 Pakistanis held prisoner since 1971; the return was completed in Apr. 1974. The 2 countries resumed full relations in 1976.

In 2 days of carnage, the Bengali population of the village of Mandai, Tripura State, 700 people, were massacred in a raid by indigenous tribal residents of the area, June 8-9, 1980. A similar year-long campaign against Bengali immigrants had been going on in Assam State.

Prime Min. Mrs. Indira Gandhi, named Jan. 19, 1966, was the 2d successor to Jawaharlal Nehru, India's prime minister from 1947 to his death, May 27, 1964.

Long the dominant power in India's politics, the Congress party lost some of its near monopoly by 1967. The party split into New and Old Congress parties in 1969. Mrs. Gandhi's New Congress party won control of the House.

Threatened with adverse court rulings in a voting law case, an opposition protest campaign and strikes, Gandhi invoked emergency provisions of the constitution June, 1975. Thousands of opponents were arrested and press censorship imposed. Measures to control prices, protect small farmers, and improve productivity were adopted.

The emergency, especially enforcement of coercive birth control measures in some areas, and the prominent extra-constitutional role of Indira Gandhi's son Sanjay, was widely resented. Opposition parties, united in the Janata coalition, scored massive victories in federal and state parliamentary elections in 1977, turning the New Congress Party from power.

Amid growing political tensions within the majority Janata party, and facing a censure vote in Parliament, Prime Min. Morarji R. Desai resigned, July 15, 1979. He was succeeded by a coalition government which only lasted 24 days.

With 350 candidates of her party winning seats to Parliament, Indira Gandhi became prime minister for the second time, Jan. 14, 1980. Gandhi was assassinated by Sikh extremists Oct. 31, 1984. Widespread rioting followed causing over 1,000 deaths. Rajiv, her son, replaced her as prime minister.

On Dec. 3, 1984, methyl isocyanate, a deadly gas, escaped from a tank owned by the Union Carbide Corp. at Bhopal and killed over 2,500, in history's worst industrial accident.

Sikkim, bordered by Tibet, Bhutan and Nepal, formerly British protected, became a protectorate of India in 1950. Area, 2,818 sq. mi.; pop. 1981 cen. 315,000; capital, Gangtok. In Sept. 1974 India's parliament voted to make Sikkim an associate Indian state, absorbing it into India. The monarchy was abolished in an April, 1975, referendum.

Kashmir, a predominantly Moslem region in the northwest, has been in dispute between India and Pakistan since 1947. A cease-fire was negotiated by the UN Jan. 1, 1949; it gave Pakistan control of one-third of the area, in the west and northwest, and India the remaining two-thirds, the Indian state of Jammu and Kashmir, which enjoys internal autonomy. Repeated clashes broke out along the line.

There were also clashes in April 1965 along the Assam-East Pakistan border and in the **Rann** (swamp) **of Kutch** area along the West Pakistan-Gujarat border near the Arabian Sea. An international arbitration commission on Feb. 19, 1968, awarded 90% of the Rann to India, 10% to Pakistan.

France, 1952-54, peacefully yielded to India its 5 colonies, former French India, comprising Pondicherry, Karikal, Mahe, Yanaon (which became Pondicherry Union Territory, area 185 sq. mi., pop. 1981, 604,136) and Chandernagor (which was incorporated into the state of West Bengal).

ɔa, 1,429 sq. mi., pop., 1981, 1 mln., which had been ruled ɔortugal since 1505 AD, was taken by India by military action c. 18, 1961, together with 2 other Portuguese enclaves, Da- an and Diu, located near Bombay.

Indonesia

Republic of Indonesia

People: Population (1984 est.): 169,442,000. **Age distrib. (%):** 0–14: 44.8; 15–59: 50.0; 60+: 5.1. **Pop. density:** 221 per sq. mi. **Urban** (1980): 22.3%. **Ethnic groups:** Malay, Chinese, Irianese. **Languages:** Bahasa Indonesian (Malay) (official), Java- nese, other Austronesian languages. **Religions:** Muslims 90%. **Geography: Area:** 741,101 sq. mi. **Location:** Archipelago SE of Asia along the Equator. **Neighbors:** Malaysia on N, Papua New Guinea on E. **Topography:** Indonesia comprises 13,500 islands, including Java (one of the most densely populated areas in the world with 1,500 persons to the sq. mi.), Sumatra, Kali- mantan (most of Borneo), Sulawesi (Celebes), and West Irian (Irian Jaya, the W. half of New Guinea). Also: Bangka, Billiton, Madura, Bali, Timor. The mountains and plateaus on the major islands have a cooler climate than the tropical lowlands. **Capital:** Jakarta. **Cities** (1981 est.): Jakarta 5,500,000; Surabaja 2,000,000; Bandung 1,400,000; Medan 1,000,000.

Government: Type: Independent Republic. **Head of state:** Pres. Suharto; b. June 8, 1921; in office: Mar. 6, 1967. **Local divisions:** 27 provinces, 281 regencies. **Defense:** 3% of govt. budget (1982).

Economy: Industries: Food processing, textiles, light indus- try. **Chief crops:** Rice, coffee, sugar. **Minerals:** Nickel, tin, oil, bauxite, copper, natural gas. **Crude oil reserves** (1980): 9.6 bln. bbls. **Other resources:** Rubber. **Arable land:** 11%. **Meat prod.** (1983): beef: 164,000 metric tons; pork: 94,000 metric tons, lamb: 61,000 metric tons. **Fish catch** (1982): 2 mln. metric tons. **Electricity prod.** (1982): 7.3 bln. kwh. **Crude steel prod.** (1981): 375,000 metric tons. **Labor force:** 66% agric.; 23% ind. & comm.; 10% services.

Finance: Currency: Rupiah (Mar. 1985: 1,102 = $1 US). **Gross domestic product** (1982): $87 bln. **Per capita income** (1982): $560. **Imports** (1983): $16.7 bln.; partners: Jap. 30%, U.S. 14%, Sing. 9%. **Exports** (1983): $20.9 bln.; partners: Jap. 47%, U.S. 18%, Sing. 10%. **Tourists** (1981): $288 mln. re- ceipts. **National budget** (1984): $20.7 bln. **International re- serves less gold** (Feb. 1985): $5.04 bln. **Gold:** 3.10 mln. oz t. **Consumer prices** (change in 1984): 10.5%.

Transport: Railway traffic (1982): 6.2 bln. passenger-km; 890 mln. net ton-km. **Motor vehicles:** in use (1982): 791,500 passenger cars, 791,000 comm. **Civil aviation** (1982): 8.4 bln. passenger-km; 190 mln. freight ton-km. **Chief ports:** Jakarta, Surabaja, Medan, Palembang, Semarang.

Communications: Television sets: 3 mln. in use (1983). **Ra- dios:** 6.5 mln. in use (1983). **Telephones in use** (1982): 600,000.

Health: Life expectancy at birth (1983): male: 51.4; female 54.2 years. **Births** (per 1,000 pop. 1983): 30.3. **Deaths** (per 1,000 pop. 1983): 12.9. **Natural increase** (1983) 1.7%. **Hospi- tal beds** (per 100,000 pop. 1977): 60. **Physicians** (per 100,000 pop. 1977): 7. **Infant mortality** (per 1,000 live births 1983): 100.

Education (1981): **Literacy:** 64%. 86% attend primary school; 15% secondary school.

Major International Organizations: UN and its specialized agencies, ASEAN, OPEC.

Embassy: 2020 Massachusetts Ave. NW 20036; 393-1745.

Hindu and Buddhist civilization from India reached the peoples of Indonesia nearly 2,000 years ago, taking root especially in Java. Islam spread along the maritime trade routes in the 15th century, and became predominant by the 16th century. The Dutch replaced the Portuguese as the most important European trade power in the area in the 17th century. They secured territo- rial control over Java by 1750. The outer islands were not finally subdued until the early 20th century, when the full area of pres- ent-day Indonesia was united under one rule for the first time in history.

Following Japanese occupation, 1942-45, nationalists led by Sukarno and Hatta proclaimed a republic. The Netherlands ceded sovereignty Dec. 27, 1949, after 4 years of fighting. West Irian, on New Guinea, remained under Dutch control.

After the Dutch in 1957 rejected proposals for new negotia- tions over West Irian, Indonesia stepped up the seizure of Dutch property. A U.S. mediator's plan was adopted in 1962. In 1963 the UN turned the area over to Indonesia, which promised a plebiscite. In 1969, voting by tribal chiefs favored staying with Indonesia, despite an uprising and widespread opposition.

Sukarno suspended Parliament in 1960, and was named pres- ident for life in 1963. Russian-armed Indonesian troops staged raids in 1964 and 1965 into Malaysia, whose formation Sukarno had opposed.

Indonesia's popular, pro-Peking Communist party tried to seize control in 1965; the army smashed the coup, later inti- mated that Sukarno had played a role in it. In parts of Java, Communists seized several districts before being defeated; over 300,000 Communists were executed.

Gen. Suharto, head of the army, was named president for 5 years in 1968, reelected 1973 and 1978. A coalition of his sup- porters won a strong majority in House elections in 1971, the first national vote in 16 years. Moslem opposition parties made gains in 1977 elections but lost ground in the 1982 elections. The military retains a predominant political role.

In 1966 Indonesia and Malaysia signed an agreement ending hostility. After ties with Peking were cut in 1967, there were riots against the economically important ethnic Chinese minority. Ri- ots against Chinese and Japanese also occurred in 1974.

The former Portuguese Timor became Indonesia's 27th prov- ince in 1976 during a local civil war.

Oil export earnings, and political stability have made Indone- sia's economy one of the most stable in the world.

Iran

Islamic Republic of Iran

People: Population (1984 est.): 43,280,000. **Age distrib. (%):** 0–14: 44.4; 15–59: 50.3; 60+: 5.2. **Pop. density:** 65.4 per sq. mi. **Urban** (1980): 50%. **Ethnic groups:** Persian 63%, Tur- komans & Baluchis 19%, Kurds 3%, Arabs 4%. **Languages:** Farsi, Turk, Kurdish, Arabic, English, French. **Religions:** Shi'a Moslems 93%.

Geography: Area: 636,363 sq. mi. **Location:** Between the Middle East and S. Asia. **Neighbors:** Turkey, Iraq on W, USSR of N (Armenia, Azerbaijan, Turkmenistan), Afghanistan, Pakistan on E. **Topography:** Interior highlands and plains are surrounded by high mountains, up to 18,000 ft. Large salt deserts cover much of the area, but there are many oases and forest areas. Most of the population inhabits the N and NW. **Capital:** Teheran. **Cities** (1976 cen.): Teheran 4,496,159; Isfahan 671,825; Mashhad 670,180; Tabriz 598,576.

Government: Type: Islamic republic. **Religious head (Faghi):** Ayatollah Ruhollah Khomeini, b. 1901. **Head of gov- ernment:** Pres. Sayyed Ali Khamenei. **Head of state:** Prime Minister Mir Hussein Moussavi; b. 1937; in office: Oct. 29, 1981. **Local divisions:** 23 provinces, 9 governates. **Defense:** 15% of govt. budget (1982).

Economy: Industries: Steel, petrochemicals, cement, auto assembly, sugar refining, carpets. **Chief crops:** Grains, rice, fruits, sugar beets, cotton, grapes. **Minerals:** Chromium, oil, gas, copper, iron, lead, manganese, zinc, barite, sulphur, coal, emer- alds, turquoise. **Crude oil reserves** (1980): 58.00 bln. bbls. **Other resources:** Gums, wool, silk, caviar. **Arable land:** 10%. **Meat prod.** (1984): beef: 175,000 metric tons; lamb: 278,000 metric tons. **Electricity prod.** (1981): 16.9 bln. kwh. **Crude steel prod.** (1982) 1.2 mln. metric tons. **Labor force:** 40% agric.; 33% ind. & comm; 27% services.

Finance: Currency: Rial (Mar. 1985: 93.11 = $1 US). **Gross domestic product** (1977): $76.37 bln. **Per capita income** (1977): $2,160. **Imports** (1983): $18.1 bln.; partners: W. Ger. 14%, Jap. 9%, UK 6%. **Exports** (1984): $12.4 bln.; partners: Jap. 13%, Bah. 7%, It. 14%. **National budget** (1983): $33.3 bln. expenditures. **International reserves less gold** (Jun. 1980): $15.48 bln. **Gold:** 4.34 mln. oz t. **Consumer prices** (change in 1983) 20%.

Transport: Motor vehicles: in use (1981): 1.5 mln. passen- ger cars, 313,000 comm. vehicles. **Chief ports:** Bandar Abbas.

Communications: Television sets: 2.1 mln. in use (1983). **Radios:** 7.5 mln. in use (1983). **Telephones in use** (1981): 1.2 mln. **Daily newspaper circ.** (1982): 25 per 1,000 pop.

Health: Life expectancy at birth (1981): 57.1 male; 59.0 female. **Births** (per 1,000 pop. 1978): 41. **Deaths** (per 1,000 pop. 1978): 11. **Natural increase** (1978): 3.0%. **Hospital beds** (1981): 62,056. **Physicians** (1981): 10,054. **Infant mortality** (per 1,000 live births 1982): 14.

Education (1980): **Literacy:** 48%. **Pop. 5-19:** in school: 52%, teachers per 100,000: 20.

Major International Organizations: UN, OPEC.

Iran is the official name of the country long known as Persia. The Iranians, who supplanted an earlier agricultural civilization, came from the E during the 2d millenium BC; they were an Indo-European group related to the Aryans of India.

In 549 BC Cyrus the Great united the Medes and Persians in the Persian Empire, conquered Babylonia in 538 BC, restored Jerusalem to the Jews. Alexander the Great conquered Persia in 333 BC, but Persians regained their independence in the next century under the Parthians, themselves succeeded by Sassanian Persians in 226 AD. Arabs brought Islam to Persia in the 7th century, replacing the indigenous Zoroastrian faith. After Persian political and cultural autonomy was reasserted in the 9th century, the arts and sciences flourished for several centuries.

Turks and Mongols ruled Persia in turn from the 11th century to 1502, when a native dynasty reasserted full independence. The British and Russian empires vied for influence in the 19th century, and Afghanistan was severed from Iran by Britain in 1857.

The previous dynasty was founded by Reza Khan, a military leader, in 1925. He abdicated as shah in 1941, and was succeeded by his son, Mohammad Reza Pahlavi.

British and Russian forces entered Iran Aug. 25, 1941, withdrawing later. Britain and the USSR signed an agreement Jan. 29, 1942, to respect Iranian integrity and give economic aid. In 1946 a Soviet attempt to take over the Azerbaijan region in the NW was defeated when a puppet regime was ousted by force.

Parliament, under Premier Mohammed Mossadegh, nationalized the oil industry in 1951, leading to a British blockade. Mossadegh was overthrown in 1953; the shah assumed control. Under his rule, Iran underwent economic and social change. However, political opposition was not tolerated. Thousands were arrested in the 1970s, while hundreds of purported terrorists were executed.

Conservative Moslem protests led to 1978 violence. Martial law in 12 cities was declared Sept. 8. A military government was appointed Nov. 6 to deal with striking oil workers. Continued clashes with demonstrators led to greater violence; oil production fell to a 27-year low, Dec. 27. In a 3d change of government in 5 months, Prime Min. Shahpur Bakhtiar was designated by the shah to head a regency council in his absence. The shah left Iran Jan. 16, 1979.

Violence continued throughout January. Exiled religious leader Ayatollah Ruhollah Khomeini named a provisional government council in preparation for his return to Iran, Jan. 31. Clashes between Khomeini's supporters and government troops culminated in a rout of Iran's elite Imperial Guard Feb. 11, leading to the fall of Bakhtiar's government. Ayatollah Khomeini's choice for prime minister, Mehdi Bazargan, headed an interim government pledged to establish an Islamic republic, but resigned Nov. 6, 1979, conceding power to the Islamic authority of Ayatollah Khomeini.

The Iranian revolution was marked by revolts among the ethnic minorities and by a continuing struggle between the clerical forces and westernized intellectuals and liberals. The Islamic Constitution, drafted under the domination of the clergy, established final authority to be vested in a Faghi, the Ayatollah Khomeini.

Iranian militants seized the U.S. embassy, Nov. 4, 1979, and took hostages including 62 Americans. The militants vowed to stay in the embassy until the deposed shah was returned to Iran. Despite international condemnations and U.S. efforts, including an abortive Apr., 1980, rescue attempt, the crisis continued. The U.S. broke diplomatic relations with Iran, Apr. 7th. The shah died in Egypt, July 27th. The hostage drama finally ended Jan. 21, 1981 when an accord, involving the release of frozen Iranian assets, was reached.

On June 28, 1981, a bomb destroyed the Teheran headquarters of Iran's ruling Islamic Party, killing the party's leader, and 71 other persons.

Turmoil continued in Teheran however. The ruling Islamic Party, increasingly dissatisfied with President Abolhassan Bani-Sadr, declared him unfit for office. In the weeks following Bani-

Sadr's dismissal, June 22, 1981, a new wave of executions began. Over 2,000 people, reportedly members of the Mujaheddin-i-Khalq and smaller Marxist-Leninist/Maoist factions, died before revolutionary firing squads by the end of 1981.

The political upheavals have brought Iran to virtual civil war and almost total isolation from other countries. In May, 1983 Iran's Communist Party was dissolved and 18 Soviet diplomats ordered to leave the country amid charges of treason and espionage.

A dispute over the Shatt al-Arab waterway that divides the two countries brought Iran and Iraq, Sept. 22, 1980, into open warfare. Iraqi planes attacked Iranian air fields including Teheran airport. Iranian planes bombed Iraqi bases. Iraqi troops occupied Iranian territory including the port city of Khorramshahr in October. Iranian troops recaptured the city and drove Iraqi troops back across the border, May 1982. Iran launched several offenses in 1983, but they were unable to break through Iraqi lines. At least 50,000 Iranians were killed in action. Iran's threat to close the Strait of Hormuz to maritime traffic brought a strong response from Western nations. Iraq, and later Iran, attacked several oil tankers in the Persian Gulf during 1984. Saudi Arabian war planes shot down 2 Iranian jets, June 5, which they felt were threatening Saudi shipping.

Iraq
Republic of Iraq

People: Population (1984 est.): 15,000,000. **Age distrib.** (%): 0–14: 48.3; 15–59: 46.5; 60+: 5.3. **Pop. density:** 88.6 per sq. mi. **Urban** (1980): 71.6%. **Ethnic groups:** Arabs, 75% Kurds, 15% Turks. **Languages:** Arabic (official), Kurdish, others. **Religions:** Moslems 95% (Shiites 55%, Sunnis 40%), Christians 5%.

Geography: Area: 167,924 sq. mi., larger than California. **Location:** In the Middle East, occupying most of historic Mesopotamia. **Neighbors:** Jordan, Syria on W, Turkey on N, Iran on E, Kuwait, Saudi Arabia on S. **Topography:** Mostly an alluvial plain, including the Tigris and Euphrates rivers, descending from mountains in N to desert in SW. Persian Gulf region is marshland. **Capital:** Baghdad. **Cities** (1984 est.): Baghdad (met.) 3,800,000.

Government: Type: Ruling council. **Head of state:** Pres. Saddam Hussein At-Takriti, b. 1935 in office: July 16, 1979. **Local divisions:** 18 provinces. **Defense:** 46% of GNP (1981).

Economy: Industries: Textiles, petrochemicals, oil refining, cement. **Chief crops:** Grains, rice, dates, cotton. **Minerals:** Oil, gas. **Crude oil reserves** (1983): 59 bln. bbls. **Other resources:** Wool, hides. **Arable land:** 13%. **Meat prod.** (1983): lamb: 60,000 metric tons. **Electricity prod.** (1982): 6.3 bln. kwh. **Labor force:** 50% agric.

Finance: Currency: Dinar (Mar. 1985: 0.30 = $1 US). **Gross domestic product** (1981): $22 bln. **Per capita income** (1981): $2,410. **Imports** (1983): $12.2 bln.; partners: W. Ger. 16%, Jap. 14%, Fr. 7%. **Exports** (1983): $9.7 bln.; partners: It. 13%, Tur. 11%, Braz. 22%, Jap. 6%. **Consumer prices** (change in 1984): 25%

Transport: Railway traffic (1982): 874 mln. passenger-km; 2.8 bln. net ton-km. **Motor vehicles:** in use (1982): 229,000 passenger cars, 118,700 comm. vehicles. **Civil aviation** (1982): 1.7 bln. passenger-km; 54.7 mln. freight ton-km. **Chief ports:** Basra.

Communications: Television sets: 650,000 in use (1981). **Radios:** 2 mln. in use (1981). **Telephones in use** (1978): 319,600. **Daily newspaper circ.** (1982): 19 per 1,000 pop.

Health: Life expectancy at birth (1982): 56.1 yrs. **Births** (per 1,000 pop. 1978): 47. **Deaths** (per 1,000 pop. 1978): 13. **Natural increase** (1978): 3.4%. **Hospital beds** (per 100,000 pop. 1977): 199. **Physicians** (per 100,000 pop. 1977): 44. **Infant mortality** (per 1,000 live births 1984): 25.

Major International Organizations: UN and its specialized agencies, Arab League, OPEC.

Education (1984): **Literacy:** 70%. Compulsory to age 10.

The Tigris-Euphrates valley, formerly called Mesopotamia, was the site of one of the earliest civilizations in the world. The Sumerian city-states of 3,000 BC originated the culture later developed by the Semitic Akkadians, Babylonians, and Assyrians.

Mesopotamia ceased to be a separate entity after the conquests of the Persians, Greeks, and Arabs. The latter founded

..ghdad, from where the caliph ruled a vast empire in the 8th ..d 9th centuries. Mongol and Turkish conquests led to a de-..ine in population, the economy, cultural life, and the irrigation system.

Britain secured a League of Nations mandate over Iraq after World War I. Independence under a king came in 1932. A leftist, pan-Arab revolution established a republic in 1958, which oriented foreign policy toward the USSR. Most industry has been nationalized, and large land holdings broken up.

A local faction of the international Baath Arab Socialist party has ruled by decree since 1968. Russia and Iraq signed an aid pact in 1972, and arms were sent along with several thousand advisers. The 1978 execution of 21 Communists and a shift of trade to the West signalled a more neutral policy, straining relations with the USSR. In the 1973 Arab-Israeli war Iraq sent forces to aid Syria. Relations with Syria were improving steadily to negotiations of uniting the 2 nations as a single political entity, but were halted by the Hussein government, July, 1979. Within a month of assuming power, Saddam Hussein instituted a bloody purge in the wake of a reported coup attempt against the new regime.

Years of battling with the Kurdish minority resulted in total defeat for the Kurds in 1975, when Iran withdrew support. Kurdish rebels continued their war, 1979; fighting led to Iraqi bombing of Kurdish villages in Iran, causing relations with Iran to deteriorate.

After skirmishing intermittently for 10 months over the sovereignty of the disputed Shatt al-Arab waterway that divides the two countries, Iraq and Iran, Sept. 22, 1980, entered into open warfare when Iraqi fighter-bombers attacked 10 Iranian airfields, including Teheran airport, and Iranian planes retaliated with strikes on 2 Iraqi bases. In the following days, there was heavy ground fighting around Abadan and the adjacent port of Khorramshahr as Iraq pressed its attack on Iran's oil-rich province of Khuzistan. In May 1982, Iraqi troops were driven back across the border. A fierce border war continued through 1985 with both sides suffering heavy casualties.

Israeli airplanes destroyed a nuclear reactor near Baghdad on June 7, 1981, claiming that it could be used to produce nuclear weapons.

Iraq and Iran expanded their war to the Persian Gulf in Apr. 1984. Several attacks on oil tankers were reported, prompting Lloyd's of London to increase insurance rates in the area.

Ireland

People: Population (1984 est.): 3,575,000. **Age distrib. (%):** 0–14: 31.2; 15–59: 53.5; 60+:15.3. **Pop. density:** 129 per sq. mi. **Urban** (1981): 55.6%. **Ethnic groups:** Irish, Anglo-Irish minority. **Languages:** English predominates, Irish (Gaelic) spoken by minority. **Religions:** Roman Catholics 94%, Anglican 4%.

Geography: Area: 27,137 sq. mi. **Location:** In the Atlantic O. just W of Great Britain. **Neighbors:** United Kingdom (Northern Ireland). **Topography:** Ireland consists of a central plateau surrounded by isolated groups of hills and mountains. The coastline is heavily indented by the Atlantic O. **Capital:** Dublin. **Cities** (1984 est.): Dublin 525,360; Cork (met.) 136,269.

Government: Type: Parliamentary Republic. **Head of State:** Pres. Patrick J. Hillery; b. May 2, 1923; in office: Dec. 3, 1976. **Head of government:** Prime Min. Garret FitzGerald; in office: Dec. 14, 1982. **Local divisions:** 26 counties. **Defense:** 2% of GNP (1984).

Economy: Industries: Food processing, auto assembly, metals, textiles, chemicals, brewing, electrical and non-electrical machinery, tourism. **Chief crops:** Potatoes, grain, sugar beets, fruits, vegetables. **Minerals:** Zinc, lead, silver, gas. **Arable land:** 15%. **Meat prod.** (1983): beef: 360,000 metric tons; pork: 154,000 metric tons; lamb: 42,000 metric tons. **Fish catch** (1982): 195,000 metric tons. **Electricity prod.** (1982): 10.9 bln. kwh. **Crude steel prod.** (1981): 32,000 metric tons. **Labor force:** 26% agric.; 19% manuf.; 15% comm.

Finance: Currency: Pound (Mar. 1985: 0.98 = $1 US). **Gross national product** (1983): $16.5 bln. **Per capita income** (1984): $4,750. **Imports** (1984): $9.6 bln.; partners: UK 48%, U.S. 13%, W. Ger. 8%, Fr. 5%. **Exports** (1984): $9.6 bln.; partners: UK 39%, Fr. 9%, W. Ger. 9%, U.S. 7%. **Tourists** (1982): 2.3 mln; receipts: $710 mln. **National budget** (1983): $5.70 bln. revenues; $6.6 bln. expenditures. **International reserves less gold** (Feb. 1985): $2.72 bln. **Gold:** 360,000 oz. t. **Consumer prices** (change in 1984): 8.6%.

Transport: Railway traffic (1982): 832 mln. passenger-km; 629 mln. net ton-km. **Motor vehicles:** in use (1982): 709,000

passenger cars, 74,000 comm. vehicles. **Civil aviation:** (1982): 2.3 bln. passenger-km; 79.4 mln. freight ton-km. **Chief ports:** Dublin, Cork.

Communications: Television sets: 695,500 licensed (1983). **Radios:** 1.5 mln. licensed (1981). **Telephones in use** (1983): 580,000. **Daily newspaper circ.** (1982): 224 per 1,000 pop.

Health: Life expectancy at birth (1984): 72 years. **Births** (per 1,000 pop. 1983): 19.0. **Deaths** (per 1,000 pop. 1983): 9.3. **Natural increase** (1983): .09%. **Hospital beds** (per 100,000 pop. 1977): 1,051. **Physicians** (per 100,000 pop. 1977): 116. **Infant mortality** (per 1,000 live births 1984): 12.4

Education (1984): **Literacy:** 99%. **Years compulsory:** 10; attendance 91%.

Major International Organizations: UN and its specialized agencies, EC.

Embassy: 2234 Massachusetts Ave. NW 20008; 462-3939.

Celtic tribes invaded the islands about the 4th century BC; their Gaelic culture and literature flourished and spread to Scotland and elsewhere in the 5th century AD, the same century in which St. Patrick converted the Irish to Christianity. Invasions by Norsemen began in the 8th century, ended with defeat of the Danes by the Irish King Brian Boru in 1014. English invasions started in the 12th century; for over 700 years the Anglo-Irish struggle continued with bitter rebellions and savage repressions.

The Easter Monday Rebellion (1916) failed but was followed by guerrilla warfare and harsh reprisals by British troops, the "Black and Tans." The Dail Eireann, or Irish parliament, reaffirmed independence in Jan. 1919. The British offered dominion status to Ulster (6 counties) and southern Ireland (26 counties) Dec. 1921. The constitution of the Irish Free State, a British dominion, was adopted Dec. 11, 1922. Northern Ireland remained part of the United Kingdom.

A new constitution adopted by plebiscite came into operation Dec. 29, 1937. It declared the name of the state Eire in the Irish language (Ireland in the English) and declared it a sovereign democratic state.

On Dec. 21, 1948, an Irish law declared the country a republic rather than a dominion and withdrew it from the Commonwealth. The British Parliament recognized both actions, 1949, but reasserted its claim to incorporate the 6 northeastern counties in the United Kingdom. This claim has not been recognized by Ireland. *(See United Kingdom — Northern Ireland.)*

Irish governments have favored peaceful unification of all Ireland. Ireland cooperated with England against terrorist groups.

Israel
State of Israel

People: Population (1984 est.): 4,024,000. **Age distrib. (%):** 0–14: 33.2; 15–59: 63.0; 60+: 11.7. **Pop. density:** 539 per sq. mi. **Urban** (1984): 86%. **Ethnic groups:** Jewish 83%, Arab, Christian. **Languages:** Hebrew and Arabic (official), Yiddish, various European and West Asian languages. **Religions:** Jewish 83%, Moslems, Christians, others.

Geography: Area: 7,850 sq. mi. about the size of New Jersey. **Location:** On eastern end of Mediterranean Sea. **Neighbors:** Lebanon on N, Syria, Jordan on E, Egypt on W. **Topography:** The Mediterranean coastal plain is fertile and well-watered. In the center is the Judean Plateau. A triangular-shaped semidesert region, the Negev, extends from south of Beersheba to an apex at the head of the Gulf of Aqaba. The eastern border drops sharply into the Jordan Rift Valley, including Lake Tiberias (Sea of Galilee) and the Dead Sea, which is 1,296 ft. below sea level, lowest point on the earth's surface. **Capital:** Jerusalem. Most countries maintain their embassy in Tel Aviv. **Cities** (1982 est.): Jerusalem 415,000; Tel Aviv-Yafo 329,000; Haifa 227,000.

Government: Type: Parliamentary democracy. **Head of state:** Pres. Chaim Herzog; b. Sept. 17, 1918; in office: May 5, 1983. **Head of government:** Prime Min. Shimon Peres; b. Aug. 1, 1923; in office: Sept. 14, 1984. **Local divisions:** 6 administrative districts. **Defense:** 25.5% of GNP (1982).

Economy: Industries: Diamond cutting, textiles, electronics, machinery, plastics, tires, drugs, aircraft, munitions, wine. **Chief crops:** Citrus fruit, grains, olives, cotton, vegetables. **Minerals:** Potash, limestone, copper, phosphates, magnesium, manganese, salt, sulphur. **Crude oil reserves** (1980): 1.0 mln. bbls. **Arable land:** 20%. **Meat prod.** (1980): beef: 21,000 metric tons; pork: 13,000 metric tons. **Fish catch** (1978): 25,900 metric tons.

Electricity prod. (1983): 14.5 bln. kwh. **Crude steel prod.** (1981 est.): 114,000 metric tons. **Labor force:** 6% agric.; 23% ind., 30% public services.

Finance: Currency: Shekel (Mar. 1985: 858 = $1 US). **GNP** (1983): $23 bln. **Per capita income** (1983): $5,609. **Imports** (1983): $8.3 bln.; partners: U.S. 19%, Switz. 6%. W. Ger. 11%, UK 8%. **Exports** (1983): $4.8 bln.; partners: U.S. 26%, W. Ger. 7%, UK 8%. **Tourists** (1982): 1.0 mln.; receipts $866 mln. **National budget** (1980): $20.8 bln. revenues; $959 bln. expenditures. **International reserves less gold** (Jan. 1985): $2.6 bln. **Gold:** 1.01 mln. oz t. **Consumer prices** (change in 1984): 378.8%.

Transport: Railway traffic (1982): 242 mln. passenger-km; 805 mln. net ton-km. **Motor vehicles:** in use (1982): 459,000 passenger cars, 103,000 comm. vehicles. **Civil aviation** (1982): 4.6 bln. passenger-km; 301 mln. freight ton-km. **Chief ports:** Haifa, Ashdod, Eilat.

Communications: Television sets: 600,000 in use (1983). **Radios:** 1 mln. in use (1983). **Telephones in use** (1982): 1.4 mln. **Daily newspaper circ.** (1982): 205 per 1,000 pop.

Health: Life expectancy at birth (1984) Jewish pop. only 72:1 male; 75.7 female. **Births** (per 1,000 pop. 1981): 23.6. **Deaths** (per 1,000 pop. 1981): 6.6%. **Natural increase** (1981): 1.7%. **Hospital beds** (1982): 27,000. **Physicians** (per 100,000 pop. 1977): 277. **Infant mortality** (per 1,000 live births 1984): 14.1.

Education (1984): **Literacy:** 88% (Jewish), 48% (Arab).

Major International Organizations: UN and its specialized agencies.

Embassy: 3541 International Dr. NW 20008; 364-5500.

Occupying the SW corner of the ancient Fertile Crescent, Israel contains some of the oldest known evidence of agriculture and of primitive town life. A more advanced civilization emerged in the 3d millenium BC. The Hebrews probably arrived early in the 2d millenium BC. Under King David and his successors (c.1000 BC-597 BC), Judaism was developed and secured. After conquest by Babylonians, Persians, and Greeks, an independent Jewish kingdom was revived, 168 BC, but Rome took effective control in the next century, suppressed Jewish revolts in 70 AD and 135 AD, and renamed Judea Palestine, after the earlier coastal inhabitants, the Philistines.

Arab invaders conquered Palestine in 636. The Arabic language and Islam prevailed within a few centuries, but a Jewish minority remained. The land was ruled from the 11th century as a part of non-Arab empires by Seljuks, Mamluks, and Ottomans (with a crusader interval, 1098-1291).

After 4 centuries of Ottoman rule, during which the population declined to a low of 350,000 (1785), the land was taken in 1917 by Britain, which in the Balfour Declaration that year pledged to support a Jewish national homeland there, as foreseen by the Zionists. In 1920 a British Palestine Mandate was recognized; in 1922 the land east of the Jordan was detached.

Jewish immigration, begun in the late 19th century, swelled in the 1930s with refugees from the Nazis; heavy Arab immigration from Syria and Lebanon also occurred. Arab opposition to Jewish immigration turned violent in 1920, 1921, 1929, and 1936. The UN General Assembly voted in 1947 to partition Palestine into an Arab and a Jewish state. Britain withdrew in May 1948.

Israel was declared an independent state May 14, 1948; the Arabs rejected partition. Egypt, Jordan, Syria, Lebanon, Iraq, and Saudi Arabia invaded, but failed to destroy the Jewish state, which gained territory. Separate armistices with the Arab nations were signed in 1949; Jordan occupied the West Bank, Egypt occupied Gaza, but neither granted Palestinian autonomy. No peace settlement was obtained, and the Arab nations continued policies of economic boycott, blockade in the Suez Canal, and support of guerrillas. Several hundred thousand Arabs left the area of Jewish control; an equal number of Jews left the Arab countries for Israel 1949-53.

After persistent terrorist raids, Israel invaded Egypt's Sinai, Oct. 29, 1956, aided briefly by British and French forces. A UN cease-fire was arranged Nov. 6.

An uneasy truce between Israel and the Arab countries, supervised by a UN Emergency Force, prevailed until May 19, 1967, when the UN force withdrew at the demand of Egypt's Pres. Nasser. Egyptian forces reoccupied the Gaza Strip and closed the Gulf of Aqaba to Israeli shipping. In a 6-day war that started June 5, the Israelis took the Gaza Strip, occupied the Sinai Peninsula to the Suez Canal, and captured Old Jerusalem,

Syria's Golan Heights, and Jordan's West Bank. The fightin was halted June 10 by UN-arranged cease-fire agreements.

Egypt and Syria attacked Israel, Oct. 6, 1973 (Yom Kippur, most solemn day on the Jewish calendar). Egypt and Syria were supplied by massive USSR military airlifts; the U.S. responded with an airlift to Israel. Israel counter-attacked, driving the Syrians back, and crossed the Suez Canal.

A cease fire took effect Oct. 24; a UN peace-keeping force went to the area. A disengagement agreement was signed Jan. 18, 1974, following negotiations by U.S. Secretary of State Henry Kissinger. Israel withdrew from the canal's W bank. A second withdrawal was completed in 1976; Israel returned the Sinai to Egypt in 1982.

Israel and Syria agreed to disengage June 1; Israel completed withdrawing from its salient (and a small part of the land taken in the 1967 war) June 25.

In the wake of the war, Golda Meir, long Israel's premier, resigned; severe inflation gripped the nation. Palestinian guerrillas staged massacres, killing scores of civilians 1974-75. Israel conducted preventive attacks in Lebanon through 1975. Israel aided Christian forces in the 1975-76 Lebanese civil war.

Israeli forces raided Entebbe, Uganda, July 3, 1976, and rescued 103 hostages seized by Arab and German terrorists.

In 1977, the conservative opposition, led by Menachem Begin, was voted into office for the first time. Egypt's Pres. Sadat visited Jerusalem Nov. 1977 and on Mar. 26, 1979. Egypt and Israel signed a formal peace treaty, ending 30 years of war, and establishing diplomatic relations.

Israel invaded S. Lebanon, March 1978, following a Lebanon-based terrorist attack in Israel. Israel withdrew in favor of a 6,000-man UN force, but continued to aid Christian militiamen.

A 5-day occupation of Israeli forces in southern Lebanon took place April 1980, in retaliation to the Palestinian raid on a kibbutz earlier that month. Violence on the Israeli-occupied West Bank rose in 1982 when Israel announced plans to build new Jewish settlements.

Israel affirmed the entire city of Jerusalem as its capital, July, 1980, encompassing the annexed Arab East Jerusalem.

Israel shot down, Apr. 28, 1981, two Syrian helicopters Israel claimed were attacking Lebanese Christian militia forces in the Beirut-Zahle area of Lebanon. Syria responded by installing Soviet-built surface-to-air missiles in Lebanon. Both the U.S. and Israel were unable to persuade Syria to withdraw the missiles, and Israel threatened to destroy them.

On June 7, 1981, Israeli jets destroyed an Iraqi atomic reactor near Baghdad that, Israel claimed, would have enabled Iraq to manufacture nuclear weapons.

In a close election, June 30, 1981, Prime Min. Menachem Begin was able to assemble a narrow coalition, he survived a no confidence motion in the Knesset by one vote, May 1982. He retired Oct. 1983.

Israeli jets bombed Palestine Liberation Organization (PLO) strongholds in Lebanon April, May 1982. In reaction to the wounding of the Israeli ambassador to Great Britain, Israeli forces in a coordinated land, sea, and air attack invaded Lebanon, June 6, to destroy PLO strongholds in that country. Israeli and Syrian forces engaged in the Bekka Valley, June 9, but quickly agreed to a truce. Israeli forces encircled Beirut June 14. Following massive Israeli bombing of West Beirut, the PLO agreed to evacuate the city.

Israeli troops entered West Beirut after newly-elected Lebanese president Bashir Gemayel was assassinated on Sept. 14. Israel received widespread condemnation when Lebanese Christian forces, Sept. 16, entered 2 West Beirut refugee camps and slaughtered hundreds of Palestinian refugees. Israeli Defense Minister Ariel Sharon resigned Feb. 11, 1983, after Israel's State Board of Inquiry cited him for neglect of duty during the massacre.

Shiite terrorists hijacked a TWA jet, June 14, 1985, and demanded that Israel release Shiite prisoners being held in Israel. (*See Chronology*).

Italy

Italian Republic

People: Population (1984 est.): 56,998,000. **Age distrib.** (%): 0–14: 23.7; 15–59: 58.8; 60+: 17.5. **Pop. density:** 488 per

mi. **Ethnic groups:** Italians, small minorities of Germans, ovenes, Albanians, French, Ladins, Greeks. **Languages:** Ital-n. **Religions:** Predominantly Roman Catholic.

Geography: Area: 116,303 sq. mi., slightly larger than Ari-zona. **Location:** In S Europe, jutting into Mediterranean S. **Neighbors:** France on W, Switzerland, Austria on N, Yugoslavia on E. **Topography:** Occupies a long boot-shaped peninsula, extending SE from the Alps into the Mediterranean, with the islands of Sicily and Sardinia offshore. The alluvial Po Valley drains most of N. The rest of the country is rugged and mountainous, except for intermittent coastal plains, like the Campajna, S of Rome. Appenine Mts. run down through center of peninsula. **Capital:** Rome. **Cities** (1981 cen.): Rome 2.8 mln.; Milan 1.6 mln.; Naples 1.2 mln.; Turin 1.1 mln.

Government: Type: Republic. **Head of state:** Pres. Francesco Cossiga; b. 1929; in office: July 8, 1985; **Head of government:** Prime Min. Bettino Craxi; b. Feb. 24, 1934; in office: Aug. 4, 1983. **Local divisions:** 20 regions with some autonomy, 94 provinces. **Defense:** 2.6% of GNP (1982).

Economy: Industries: Steel, machinery, autos, textiles, shoes, machine tools, chemicals. **Chief crops:** Grapes, olives, citrus fruits, vegetables, wheat, rice. **Minerals:** Mercury, potash, gas, marble, sulphur, coal. **Crude oil reserves** (1980): 645 mln. bbls. **Arable land:** 41%. **Meat prod.** (1984): beef: 1.16 mln. metric tons; pork: 1.1 mln. metric tons; lamb: 70,000 metric tons. **Fish catch** (1983): 468,000 metric tons. **Electricity prod.** (1982): 180.6 bln. kwh. **Crude steel prod.** (1982): 23.9 mln. metric tons. **Labor force:** 10% agric.; 30% ind. and comm.; 60% services and govt.

Finance: Currency: Lira (June 1985: 1,944 = $1 US). **Gross domestic product** (1983): $350 bln. **Per capita income** (1980): $6,914. **Imports** (1984): $84.2 bln.; partners: W. Ger. 16%, Fr. 12%, U.S. 7%. **Exports** (1983): $73.3 bln.; partners: W. Ger. 16%, Fr. 15%, U.S. 7%, UK 6%. **Tourists** (1982): receipts $8.2 bln. **National budget** (1980): $108.12 bln. revenues; $141.90 bln. expenditures. **International reserves less gold** (Apr. 1985): $18.5 bln. **Gold:** 66.67 mln. oz t. **Consumer prices** (change in 1984): 10.8%.

Transport: Railway traffic (1983): 37.3 bln. passenger-km; 15.8 bln. net ton-km. **Motor vehicles:** in use (1982): 19.6 mln. passenger cars, 1.6 mln. comm. vehicles; manuf. (1981): 1.2 mln. passenger cars, 175,000 comm. vehicles. **Civil aviation** (1983): 12.6 bln. passenger-km; 633 mln. freight ton-km. **Chief ports:** Genoa, Venice, Trieste, Taranto, Naples, La Spezia.

Communications: Television sets: 13.4 mln. licensed (1982). **Radios:** 13.4 mln. licensed (1982). **Telephones in use** (1982): 20.4 mln. **Daily newspaper circ.** (1983): 124 per 1,000 pop.

Health: Life expectancy at birth (1980): 70.0 male; 76.1 female. **Births** (per 1,000 pop. 1982): 11.7. **Deaths** (per 1,000 pop. 1982): 9.5. **Natural increase** (1982): .2%. **Hospital beds** (per 100,000 pop. 1977): 1,036. **Physicians** (per 100,000 pop. 1977): 208. **Infant mortality** (per 1,000 live births 1983): 12.3.

Education (1984): **Literacy:** 98%. **Years compulsory:** 6–14.

Major International Organizations: UN and its specialized agencies, NATO, OECD, EC.

Embassy: 1601 Fuller St. NW 20009; 328-5500.

Rome emerged as the major power in Italy after 500 BC, dominating the more civilized Etruscans to the N and Greeks to the S. Under the Empire, which lasted until the 5th century AD, Rome ruled most of Western Europe, the Balkans, the Near East, and North Africa.

After the Germanic invasions, lasting several centuries, a high civilization arose in the city-states of the N, culminating in the Renaissance. But German, French, Spanish, and Austrian intervention prevented the unification of the country. In 1859 Lombardy came under the crown of King Victor Emmanuel II of Sardinia. By plebiscite in 1860, Parma, Modena, Romagna, and Tuscany joined, followed by Sicily and Naples, and by the Marches and Umbria. The first Italian parliament declared Victor Emmanuel king of Italy Mar. 17, 1861. Mantua and Venetia were added in 1866 as an outcome of the Austro-Prussian war. The Papal States were taken by Italian troops Sept. 20, 1870, on the withdrawal of the French garrison. The states were annexed to the kingdom by plebiscite. Italy recognized the State of Vatican City as independent Feb. 11, 1929.

Fascism appeared in Italy Mar. 23, 1919, led by Benito Mussolini, who took over the government at the invitation of the king Oct. 28, 1922. Mussolini acquired dictatorial powers. He made war on Ethiopia and proclaimed Victor Emmanuel III emperor,

defied the sanctions of the League of Nations, joined the Berlin-Tokyo axis, sent troops to fight for Franco against the Republic of Spain and joined Germany in World War II.

After Fascism was overthrown in 1943, Italy declared war on Germany and Japan and contributed to the Allied victory. It surrendered conquered lands and lost its colonies. Mussolini was killed by partisans Apr. 28, 1945.

Victor Emmanuel III abdicated May 9, 1946; his son Humbert II was king until June 10, when Italy became a republic after a referendum, June 2-3.

Reorganization of the Fascist party is forbidden. The cabinet normally represents a coalition of the Christian Democrats, largest of Italy's many parties, and one or 2 other parties.

The Vatican agreed in 1976 to revise its 1929 concordat with the state, depriving Roman Catholicism of its status as state religion. In 1974 Italians voted by a 3-to-2 margin to retain a 3-year-old law permitting divorce, which was opposed by the church.

Italy has enjoyed an extraordinary growth in industry and living standards since World War II, in part due to membership in the Common Market. Italy joined the European Monetary System, 1980. But in 1973-74, a fourfold increase in international oil prices helped disrupt the economy. Taxes were boosted and Western aid helped ease the crisis. A wave of left-wing political violence worsened in the late 1970s with kidnappings and assassinations and continued through the 1980s. Christian Dem. leader and former Prime Min. Moro was murdered May 1978 by Red Brigade terrorists.

U.S. Brig. Gen. James Dozier, a senior NATO officer, was kidnapped by terrorists in 1981, but was later rescued by Italian police.

The Cabinet of Prime Min. Arnaldo Forlani resigned, May 26, 1981, in the wake of revelations that numerous high-ranking officials were members of an illegally secret Masonic lodge. The June 1983 elections saw Bettino Craxi chosen the nation's first Socialist premier. Italy has accepted U.S. cruise missiles. Some 2,000 troops were contributed to the Lebanese peace-keeping force.

Sicily, 9,822 sq. mi., pop. (1980) 5,000,000, is an island 180 by 120 mi., seat of a region that embraces the island of **Pantelleria,** 32 sq. mi., and the **Lipari** group, 44 sq. mi., 63 14,000, including 2 active volcanoes: **Vulcano,** 1,637 ft. and **Stromboli,** 3,038 ft. From prehistoric times Sicily has been settled by various peoples; a Greek state had its capital at Syracuse. Rome took Sicily from Carthage 215 BC. **Mt. Etna,** 10,705 ft. active volcano, is tallest peak.

Sardinia, 9,262 sq. mi., pop. (1980) 1,610,000, lies in the Mediterranean, 115 mi. W of Italy and 7-½ mi. S of Corsica. It is 160 mi. long, 68 mi. wide, and mountainous, with mining of coal, zinc, lead, copper. In 1720 Sardinia was added to the possessions of the Dukes of Savoy in Piedmont and Savoy to form the Kingdom of Sardinia. Giuseppe Garibaldi is buried on the nearby isle of Caprera. **Elba,** 86 sq. mi., lies 6 mi. W of Tuscany. Napoleon I lived in exile on Elba 1814-1815.

Trieste. An agreement, signed Oct. 5, 1954, by Italy and Yugoslavia, confirmed, Nov. 10, 1975, gave Italy provisional administration over the northern section and the seaport of Trieste, and Yugoslavia the part of Istrian peninsula it has occupied.

Ivory Coast
Republic of Ivory Coast

People: Population (1984 est.): 9,178,000. **Age distrib. (%):** 0–14: 44.6; 15–59: 52.0; 60+: 3.4. **Pop. density:** 77.2 per sq. mi. **Urban** (1980): 32%. **Ethnic groups:** Baule 23%, Bete 18%, Senufo 15%, Malinke 11%, over 60 tribes. **Languages:** French (official), tribal languages. **Religions:** Moslems 15%, Christians 12%, indigenous 63%.

Geography: Area: 124,503 sq. mi., slightly larger than New Mexico. **Location:** On S. coast of W. Africa. **Neighbors:** Liberia, Guinea on W, Mali, Burkina Faso on N, Ghana on E. **Topography:** Forests cover the W half of the country, and range from a coastal strip to halfway to the N on the E. A sparse inland plain leads to low mountains in NW. **Capital:** Abidjan. **Cities** (1981 est.): Abidjan 1,686,100 (met.)

Government: Type: Republic. **Head of state:** Pres. Felix Houphouet-Boigny; b. Oct. 18, 1905; in office: Aug. 7, 1960. **Local divisions:** 25 departments.

Economy: Chief crops: Coffee, cocoa. **Minerals:** Diamonds, manganese. **Other resources:** Timber, rubber. **Arable land:** 12%. **Meat prod.** (1980): beef: 41,000 metric tons; pork: 13,000 metric tons; lamb: 13,000 metric tons. **Fish catch** (1981): 80,000 metric tons. **Electricity prod.** (1982): 1.9 bln. kwh. **Labor force:** 75% agric.; 25% ind. and commerce.

Finance: Currency: CFA franc (Mar. 1985: 471 = $1 US). **Gross domestic product** (1981 est.): $9.8 bln. **Per capita income** (1984): $1,100. **Imports** (1983): $1.8 bln.; partners: Fr. 31%, Venez. 8%, Jap. 5%, U.S. 5%. **Exports** (1983): $2.0 bln.; partners: Fr. 19%, Neth. 13%, U.S. 11%, It. 8%. **Tourists** (1980): 137,000; **International reserves less gold** (Jan. 1985): $5.4 mln. **Gold:** 45,000 oz t. **Consumer prices** (changed in 1984): 4.3%.

Transport: Railway traffic (1983): 998 mln. passenger-km; 526 mln. net ton-km. **Motor vehicles:** in use (1982): 166,000 passenger cars, 69,500 comm. vehicles. **Chief ports:** Abidjan, Sassandra.

Communications: Television sets: 562,000 in use (1983). **Radios:** 800,000 in use (1983). **Telephones in use** (1981): 88,000. **Daily newspaper circ.** (1983): 8 per 1,000 pop.

Health: Life expectancy at birth (1983): 46.9 male; 50.2 female. **Births** (per 1,000 pop. 1978): 47. **Deaths** (per 1,000 pop. 1978): 18. **Natural increase** (1978): 2.9%. **Hospital beds** (1978): 9,962. **Physicians** (1978): 429. **Infant mortality** (per 1,000 live births 1982): 127.

Education (1983): **Literacy:** 24%. **Years compulsory:** none; attendance 75%.

Major International Organizations: UN and its specialized agencies, OAU.

Embassy: 2424 Massachusetts Ave. NW 20008; 483-2400.

A French protectorate from 1842, Ivory Coast became independent in 1960. It is the most prosperous of tropical African nations, due to diversification of agriculture for export, close ties to France, and encouragement of foreign investment. About 20% of the population are workers from neighboring countries. Ivory Coast is a leader of the pro-Western bloc in Africa.

Jamaica

People: Population (1984 est.): 2,388,000. **Age distrib. (%):** 0–14: 36.7; 15–59: 52.8; 60+: 8.5. **Pop. density:** 493 per sq. mi. **Urban** (1981): 41.9%. **Ethnic groups:** African 76%, mixed 15%, Chinese, Caucasians, East Indians. **Languages:** English, Jamaican Creole. **Religions:** Protestant 70%.

Geography: Area: 4,244 sq. mi., slightly smaller than Connecticut. **Location:** In West Indies. **Neighbors:** Nearest are Cuba on N, Haiti on E. **Topography:** The country is four-fifths covered by mountains. **Capital:** Kingston. **Cities** (1984 est.): St. Andrews 393,100, Kingston 100,000.

Government: Type: Constitutional monarchy. **Head of state:** Queen Elizabeth II, represented by Gov.-Gen. Florizel A. Glasspole; b. Sept. 25, 1909; in office: Mar. 2, 1973. **Head of government:** Prime Min. Edward Seaga; b. May 28, 1930; in office: Oct., 1980. **Local divisions:** 12 parishes; Kingston and St. Andrew corporate area. **Defense:** 1.3% of GDP (1984).

Economy: Industries: Rum, molasses, cement, paper, tourism. **Chief crops:** Sugar cane, coffee, bananas, coconuts, citrus fruits. **Minerals:** Bauxite, limestone, gypsum. **Arable land:** 24%. **Meat prod.** (1980): beef: 13,000 metric tons; pork: 9,000 metric tons. **Electricity prod.** (1982): 1.3 bln. kwh. **Labor force:** 35% agric.; 25% services; 11.5% manuf.

Finance: Currency: Dollar (Apr. 1985: 5.48 = $1 US). **Gross domestic product** (1982): $3.0 bln. **Per capita income** (1981): $1,340. **Imports** (1984): $1.1 bln.; partners: U.S. 35%, Venez. 14%, Neth. Ant. 13%, UK 8%. **Exports** (1984): $714 mln.; partners: U.S. 33%, UK 18%, Nor. 8%, Can. 12%. **Tourists** (1983): 800,000; receipts: $399 mln. **National budget** (1982): $825 mln. revenues. **International reserves less gold** (Feb. 1985): $120.7 mln. **Consumer prices** (change in 1984): 27.8%.

Transport: Railway traffic (1983): 49 mln. passenger-km; 129 mln. net ton-km. **Chief ports:** Kingston, Montego Bay.

Communications: Television sets: 180,000 in use (1982). **Radios:** 850,000 in use (1982). **Telephones in use** (1982): 124,000. **Daily newspaper circ.** (1982): 137 per 1,000 pop.

Health: Life expectancy at birth (1984): 65 years. **Births** (per 1,000 pop. 1982): 27.6. **Deaths** (per 1,000 pop. 1982): 5.7. **Natural increase** (1982): 2.1%. **Hospital beds** (1980): 6,229.

Physicians (1980): 700. **Infant mortality** (per 1,000 live birth 1984): 16.8.

Education (1984): **Literacy:** 76%. Compulsory to age 14.

Major International Organizations: UN and its specialized agencies, OAS.

Embassy: 1850 K St. NW 20008; 452-0660.

Jamaica was visited by Columbus, 1494, and ruled by Spain (under whom Arawak Indians died out) until seized by Britain, 1655. Jamaica won independence Aug. 6, 1962.

In 1974 Jamaica sought an increase in taxes paid by U.S. and Canadian companies which mine bauxite on the island. The socialist government acquired 50% ownership of the companies' Jamaican interests in 1976, and was reelected that year. Rudimentary welfare state measures were passed, but unemployment increased. Relations with the U.S. improved greatly in 1981; Prime Minister Seaga was the first official visitor to Washington after Pres. Ronald Reagan's inauguration. Jamaica broke diplomatic relations with Cuba in December.

In 1982, Reagan became the first U.S. President to visit Jamaica and voiced strong support for the free-enterprise policies of the Seaga government. Jamaica took part in the October 1983 invasion of Grenada.

Japan

People: Population (1984 est.): 119,896,000. **Age distrib. (%):** 0–14: 23.5; 15–59: 63.6; 60+: 12.9. **Pop. density:** 822 per sq. mi. **Urban** (1980): 76.2%. **Language:** Japanese. **Ethnic groups:** Japanese 99.4%, Korean 0.5%. **Religions:** Buddhism, Shintoism shared by large majority.

Geography: Area: 147,470 sq. mi., slightly smaller than California. **Location:** Archipelago off E. coast of Asia. **Neighbors:** USSR on N, S. Korea on W. **Topography:** Japan consists of 4 main islands: Honshu ("mainland"), 87,805 sq. mi.; Hokkaido, 30,144 sq. mi.; Kyushu, 14,114 sq. mi.; and Shikoku, 7,049 sq. mi. The coast, deeply indented, measures 16,654 mi. The northern islands are a continuation of the Sakhalin Mts. The Kunlun range of China continues into southern islands, the ranges meeting in the Japanese Alps. In a vast transverse fissure crossing Honshu E-W rises a group of volcanoes, mostly extinct or inactive, including 12,388 ft. Fuji-San (Fujiyama) near Tokyo. **Capital:** Tokyo. **Cities** (1982 est.): Tokyo 8.3 mln.; Osaka 2.5 mln.; Yokohama 2.8 mln.; Nagoya 2 mln.; Kyoto 1.4 mln.; Kobe 1.3 mln.; Sapporo 1.4 mln.; Kitakyushu 1 mln.; Kawasaki 1 mln.

Government: Type: Parliamentary democracy. **Head of state:** Emp. Hirohito; b. Apr. 29, 1901; in office: Dec. 25, 1926. **Head of government:** Prime Min. Yasuhiro Nakasone; in office: Nov. 26, 1982. **Local divisions:** 47 prefectures. **Defense:** Less than 1% of GNP (1984).

Economy: Industries: Electrical & electronic equip., autos, machinery, chemicals. **Chief crops:** Rice, grains, vegetables, fruits. **Minerals:** negligible. **Crude oil reserves** (1980): 55 mln. bbls. **Arable land:** 19%. **Meat prod.** (1984): beef: 534,000 metric tons; pork: 1.43 mln. metric tons. **Fish catch** (1983): 11.8 mln. metric tons. **Electricity prod.** (1983): 555.5 bln. kwh. **Crude steel prod.** (1983): 97.2 mln. metric tons. **Labor force:** 11% agric.; 34% manuf; 48% services.

Finance: Currency: Yen (June 1985: 250.55 = $1 US). **Gross national product** (1984): $1.2 trl. **Per capita income** (1980): $8,460. **Imports** (1984): $136 bln.; partners: U.S. 18%, Saudi Ar. 16%, Austral. 5%, Indon. 9%. **Exports** (1984): $149 bln.; partners: U.S. 26%. **Tourists** (1981): 1.5 mln. **National budget** (1980): $190.1 bln. revenues; $190.1 bln. expenditures. **International reserves less gold** (Mar. 1985): $26.6 bln. **Gold:** 24.23 mln. **Consumer prices** (change in 1984): 4.1%.

Transport: Railway traffic (1982): 314.9 bln. passenger-km; 31.3 bln. net ton-km. **Motor vehicles:** in use (1983): 24.2 mln. passenger cars, 8.9 mln. comm. vehicles; manuf. (1982): 6.8 mln. passenger cars; 3.8 mln. comm. vehicles. **Civil aviation** (1983): 58.4 bln. passenger-km; 2.5 bln. freight ton-km. **Chief ports:** Yokohama, Tokyo, Kobe, Osaka, Nagoya, Chiba, Kawasaki, Hakodate.

Communications: Television sets: 30 mln. in use (1983), 16.3 mln. manuf. (1980). **Radios:** 93 mln. in use (1983), 15.1 mln. manuf. (1981). **Telephones in use** (1982): 58.6 mln. **Daily newspaper circ.** (1982): 569 per 1,000 pop.

Health: Life expectancy at birth (1983): 73 male; 78 female. **Births** (per 1,000 pop. 1983): 12.7. **Deaths** (per 1,000 pop. 1983): 6.1. **Natural increase** (1983): .06%. **Hospital beds** (1981): 1.3 mln. **Physicians** (1981): 162,882. **Infant mortality** (per 1,000 live births 1983): 6.2.

Education (1983): **Literacy:** 99%. Most attend school for 12 years.

Major International Organizations: UN and its specialized agencies, OECD.

Embassy: 2520 Massachusetts Ave. NW 20008; 234-2266.

According to Japanese legend, the empire was founded by Emperor Jimmu, 660 BC, but earliest records of a unified Japan date from 1,000 years later. Chinese influence was strong in the formation of Japanese civilization. Buddhism was introduced before the 6th century.

A feudal system, with locally powerful noble families and their samurai warrior retainers, dominated from 1192. Central power was held by successive families of shoguns (military dictators), 1192-1867, until recovered by the Emperor Meiji, 1868. The Portuguese and Dutch had minor trade with Japan in the 16th and 17th centuries; U.S. Commodore Matthew C. Perry opened it to U.S. trade in a treaty ratified 1854. Japan fought China, 1894-95, gaining Taiwan. After war with Russia, 1904-05, Russia ceded S half of Sakhalin and gave concessions in China. Japan annexed Korea 1910. In World War I Japan ousted Germany from Shantung, took over German Pacific islands. Japan took Manchuria 1931, started war with China 1932. Japan launched war against the U.S. by attack on Pearl Harbor Dec. 7, 1941. Japan surrendered Aug. 14, 1945.

In a new constitution adopted May 3, 1947, Japan renounced the right to wage war; the emperor gave up claims to divinity; the Diet became the sole law-making authority.

The U.S. and 48 other non-communist nations signed a peace treaty and the U.S. a bilateral defense agreement with Japan, in San Francisco Sept. 8, 1951, restoring Japan's sovereignty as of April 28, 1952. Japan signed separate treaties with Nationalist China, 1952; India, 1952; a declaration with USSR ending a technical state of war, 1956. In Dec. 1965 Japan and South Korea agreed to resume diplomatic relations.

On June 26, 1968, the U.S. returned to Japanese control the Bonin Is., the Volcano Is. (including Iwo Jima) and Marcus Is. On May 15, 1972, Okinawa, the other Ryukyu Is. and the Daito Is. were returned to Japan by the U.S.; it was agreed the U.S. would continue to maintain military bases on Okinawa. Japan and the USSR have failed to resolve disputed claims of sovereignty over 4 of the Kurile Is. and over offshore fishing rights.

In 1972, Japan and China resumed diplomatic relations; Japan and Taiwan severed diplomatic relations.

Industrialization was begun in the late 19th century. After World War II, Japan emerged as one of the most powerful economies in the world, and as a leader in technology.

The U.S. and EC member nations have criticized Japan for its restrictive policy on imports which has given Japan a substantial trade surplus. In 1984, Japan, under the threat of sanctions, agreed to increase the import quotas on U.S. beef and citrus products.

Jordan

Hashemite Kingdom of Jordan

Population (1984 est.): 2,689,000. **Age distrib.** (%): 0–14: 51.8; 15–59: 44.0; 60+: 4.2. **Pop. density:** 70.1 per sq. mi. **Urban** (1979): 59.5%. **Ethnic groups:** Arabs, small minorities of Circassians, Armenians, Kurds. **Languages:** Arabic (official), English. **Religions:** Sunni Moslems 93.6%, Christians 5%.

Geography: Area: 37,297 sq. mi., slightly larger than Indiana. **Location:** In W Asia. **Neighbors:** Israel on W, Saudi Arabia on S, Iraq on E, Syria on N. **Topography:** About 88% of Jordan is arid. Fertile areas are in W. Only port is on short Aqaba Gulf coast. Country shares Dead Sea (1,296 ft. below sea level) with Israel. **Capital:** Amman. **Cities** (1980 est.): Amman 1,232,600; Irbid 634,200.

Government: Type: Constitutional monarchy. **Head of state:** King Hussein I; b. Nov. 14, 1935; in office: Aug. 11, 1952. **Head of government:** Prime Min. Zaid Rifai; b. 1937; in office: Apr. 4, 1985. **Local divisions:** 8 governorates. **Defense:** 21% of GNP (1982).

Economy: Industries: Textiles, cement, food processing. **Chief crops:** Grains, olives, vegetables, fruits. **Minerals:** Phosphate, potash. **Arable land:** 14%. **Electricity prod.** (1981): 1.2 bln. kwh. **Labor force:** 30% agric.

Finance: Currency: Dinar (Mar. 1985: 0.34 = $1 US). **Gross domestic product** (1983): $3.8 bln. **Per capita income** (1976): $552. **Imports** (1982): $3.2 bln.; partners: Saudi Ar. 17%, W. Ger. 11%, Jap. 8%. **Exports** (1982): $752 mln.; partners: Saudi Ar. 12%, Syria 6%, Iraq. 38%. **Tourists** (1982): 1.5 mln.; receipts: $510 mln. **National budget** (1980): $751.59 mln. revenues; $1.68 bln. expenditures. **International reserves less gold** (Mar. 1985): $355.5 mln. **Gold:** 1.06 mln. oz t. **Consumer prices** (change in 1984): 3.8%.

Transport: Motor vehicles: in use (1982): 118,900 passenger cars, 43,600 comm. vehicles. **Civil aviation** (1982): 3.2 bln. passenger-km; 131 mln. freight ton-km. **Chief ports:** Aqaba.

Communications: Television sets: 171,000 licensed (1981). **Radios:** 536,000 in use (1981). **Telephones in use** (1983): 86,000. **Daily newspaper circ.** (1982): 73 per 1,000 pop.

Health: Life expectancy at birth (1980): 60.3 male; 64.2 female. **Births** (per 1,000 pop. 1978): 49. **Deaths** (per 1,000 pop. 1978): 11. **Natural increase** (1978): 3.8%. **Hospital beds** (1980): 2,743. **Physicians** (1980): 1,715. **Infant mortality** (per 1,000 live births 1981): 67.

Education (1978): **Literacy:** 58%. **Pop. 5-19:** in school: 56%, teachers per 1,000: 20.

Major International Organizations: UN and its specialized agencies.

Embassy: 2319 Wyoming Ave NW 20008; 265-1606.

From ancient times to 1922 the lands to the E of the Jordan were culturally and politically united with the lands to the W. Arabs conquered the area in the 7th century; the Ottomans took control in the 16th. Britain's 1920 Palestine Mandate covered both sides of the Jordan. In 1921, Abdullah, son of the ruler of Hejaz in Arabia, was installed by Britain as emir of an autonomous Transjordan, covering two-thirds of Palestine. An independent kingdom was proclaimed, 1946.

During the 1948 Arab-Israeli war the West Bank and old city of Jerusalem were added to the kingdom, which changed its name to Jordan. All these territories were lost to Israel in the 1967 war, which swelled the number of Arab refugees on the East Bank. A 1974 Arab summit conference designated the Palestine Liberation Organization as the sole representative of Arabs on the West Bank. Jordan accepted the move, and was granted an annual subsidy by Arab oil states. The U.S. has also provided substantial economic and military support.

King Hussein actively promoted rejection of the Egyptian-Israeli peace treaty; Jordan was the first Arab country to sever diplomatic relations with Egypt, Mar. 1979; relations were restored, Sept., 1984.

Kenya

Republic of Kenya

People: Population (1984 est.): 19,362,000. **Age distrib.** (%): 0–14: 48.4; 15–59: 46.3; 60+: 5.4. **Pop. density:** 89.7 per sq. mi. **Urban** (1981): 10%. **Ethnic groups:** Kikuyu 21%, Luo 13%, Luhya 14%, Kelenjin 11%, Kamba 11%, others, including 280,000 Asians, Arabs, Europeans. **Languages:** Swahili (official), English. **Religions:** Protestants 38%, Roman Catholics 28%, Moslems 6%, others.

Geography: Area: 224,081 sq. mi., slightly smaller than Texas. **Location:** On Indian O. coast of E. Africa. **Neighbors:** Uganda on W, Tanzania on S, Somalia on E, Ethopia, Sudan on N. **Topography:** The northern three-fifths of Kenya is arid. To the S, a low coastal area and a plateau varying from 3,000 to 10,000 ft. The Great Rift Valley enters the country N-S, flanked by high mountains. **Capital:** Nairobi. **Cities** (1978): Nairobi (met.) 959,000; Mombasa (met.) 401,000.

Government: Type: Republic. **Head of state:** Pres. Daniel arap Moi, b. Sept., 1924; in office: Aug. 22, 1978. **Local divisions:** Nairobi and 7 provinces. **Defense:** 5.4% of GDP (1982).

Economy: Industries: Tourism, light industry. **Chief crops:** Coffee, corn, tea, cereals, cotton, sisal. **Minerals:** Gold, limestone, diatomite, salt, barytes, magnesite, felspar, sapphires, fluospar, garnets. **Other resources:** Timber, hides. **Arable land:** 4%. **Meat prod.** (1984): beef: 203,000 metric tons; lamb: 56,000

metric tons. **Fish catch** (1982): 70,000 metric tons. **Electricity prod.** (1981): 1.7 bln. kwh. **Labor force:** 17% agric.; 18% ind. and commerce; 13% services; 47% public sector.

Finance: Currency: Shilling (Mar. 1985: 16.10 = $1 US). **Gross domestic product** (1982): $6.0 bln. **Per capita income** (1981): $196. **Imports** (1983): $1.2 bln.; partners: UK 17%, W. Ger. 8%, Jap. 8, Saudi Ar. 19%. **Exports** (1983): $876 mln.; partners: W. Ger. 11%, UK 11%, Ugan. 9%. **Tourists** (1981): 373,500; receipts: $240 mln. **National budget** (1981): $1.4 bln. **International reserves less gold** (Mar. 1985): $438.3 mln. **Gold:** 80,000 oz t. **Consumer prices** (change in 1984): 10.2%.

Transport: Motor vehicles: in use (1982): 114,000 passenger cars, 88,000 comm. vehicles. **Chief ports:** Mombasa.

Communications: Television sets: 100,000 in use (1982). **Radios:** 1.5 mln. in use (1982). **Telephones in use** (1982): 216,000. **Daily newspaper circ.** (1982): 13 per 1,000 pop.

Health: Life expectancy at birth (1983): 56.3 male; 60.0 female. **Births** (per 1,000 pop. 1978): 54. **Deaths** (per 1,000 pop. 1978): 14. **Natural increase** (1978): 4.0%. **Hospital beds** (per 100,000 pop. 1977): 128. **Physicians** (per 100,000 pop. 1977): 8. **Infant mortality** (per 1,000 live births 1982): 83.

Education (1978): **Literacy:** 40%. **Pop. 5-19:** in school: 62%, teachers per 1,000: 18.

Major international Organizations: UN and its specialized agencies, OAU, Commonwealth of Nations.

Embassy: 2249 R St. NW 20008; 387-6101.

Arab colonies exported spices and slaves from the Kenya coast as early as the 8th century. Britain obtained control in the 19th century. Kenya won independence Dec. 12, 1963, 4 years after the end of the violent Mau Mau uprising.

Kenya has shown steady growth in industry and agriculture under a modified private enterprise system, and has had a relatively free political life. But stability was shaken in 1974-5, with opposition charges of corruption and oppression.

In 1968 ties with Somalia were restored after 4 years of skirmishes. Tanzania closed its Kenya border in 1977 in a dispute over the collapse of the East African Community.

Kenya has close ties to the West.

Kiribati
Republic of Kiribati

People: Population (1984 est.): 61,000. **Pop. density:** 223 per sq. mi. **Ethnic groups:** nearly all Micronesian, some Polynesians. **Languages:** Gilbertese and English (official). **Religions:** evenly divided between Protestant and Roman Catholic.

Geography: Area: 266 sq. mi., slightly smaller than New York City. **Location:** 33 Micronesian islands (the Gilbert, Line, and Phoenix groups) in the mid-Pacific scattered in a 2-mln. sq. mi. chain around the point where the International Date Line cuts the Equator. **Neighbors:** Nearest are Nauru to SW, Tuvalu and Tokelau Is. to S. **Topography:** except Banaba (Ocean) I., all are low-lying, with soil of coral sand and rock fragments, subject to erratic rainfall. **Capital** (1980): Tarawa 22,148.

Government: Head of state and of government: Pres. Ieremia Tabai, b. Dec. 16, 1950; in office: July 12, 1979.

Economy: Industries: Copra. **Chief crops:** Coconuts, breadfruit, pandanus, bananas, paw paw. **Other resources:** Fish. **Electricity prod.** (1982): 6 mln. kwh.

Finance: Currency: Australian dollar. **Imports** (1979): $15.0 mln.; partners: Austral. 57%, NZ 5%, UK 6%, Jap. 13%. **Exports** (1979): $20 mln.; partners: UK 89%. **National budget** (1978): $16.3 mln. revenues; $14 mln. expenditures.

Transport: Chief port: Tarawa.

Communications: Radios: 58,000 in use (1983). **Telephones in use** (1982): 1,821.

Health: Hospital beds (1981): 307; **Physicians:** 16.

Education: Literacy (1982): 90%.

A British protectorate since 1892, the Gilbert and Ellice Islands colony was completed with the inclusion of the Phoenix islands, 1937. Self-rule was granted 1971; the Ellice Islands separated from the colony 1975 and became independent Tuvalu, 1978. Kiribati (pronounced *Kiribass)* independence was attained July 12, 1979. Under a Treaty of Friendship, pending ratification by the U.S. Senate, the U.S. relinquishes its claims to several of the Line and Phoenix islands, including Christmas, Canton, and Enderbury.

Tarawa Atoll was the scene of some of the bloodiest fighting in the Pacific during WW II.

North Korea
Democratic People's Republic of Korea

People: Population (Jan. 1984 est.): 19,630,000. **Pop. density:** 417 per sq. mi. **Ethnic groups:** Korean. **Languages:** Korean. **Religions:** activities discouraged; traditionally Buddhism, Confucianism, Chondokyo.

Geography: Area: 47,077 sq. mi., slightly smaller than Mississippi. **Location:** In northern E. Asia. **Neighbors:** China, USSR on N, S. Korea on S. **Topography:** Mountains and hills cover nearly all the country, with narrow valleys and small plains in between. The N and the E coast are the most rugged areas. **Capital:** Pyongyang. **Cities** (1981 est.): Pyongyang 1,283,000.

Government: Type: Communist state. **Head of state:** Pres. Kim Il-Sung; b. Apr. 15, 1912; in office: Dec. 28, 1972. **Head of government:** Premier Kang Song-san; in office: 1984. **Head of Communist Party:** Gen. Sec. Kim Il-Sung; in office: 1945. **Local divisions:** 9 provinces, 4 municipalities. **Defense** (1983 est.): 25% of GNP.

Economy: Industries: Textiles, petrochemicals, cement. **Chief crops:** Corn, potatoes, fruits, vegetables, rice. **Minerals:** Coal, lead tungsten, zinc, graphite, magnesite, iron, copper, gold, phosphate, salt, fluorspar. **Arable land:** 19%. **Meat prod.** (1984): pork: 136,000 metric tons. **Fish catch** (1983): 1.5 mln. metric tons. **Crude steel prod.** (1982) 3.5 mln. metric tons. **Labor force:** 48% agric.

Finance: Currency: Won (Nov. 1984): 1.30 = $1 US). **Gross national product** (1982 est.): $18.1 bln. **Per capita income** (1978, in 1975 U.S. dollars): $570. **Imports** (1980): $2.1 bln.; partners: China 17%, USSR 22%, Jap. 18%. **Exports** (1980): $1.9 bln.; partners: USSR 26% China 17%, Saudi Ar. 9%, Jap. 9%.

Transport: Chief ports: Chonglin, Hamhung, Nampo.

Health: Life expectancy at birth (1980): 70 male; 76 female. **Births** (per 1,000 pop. 1983): 31. **Deaths** (per 1,000 pop. 1983): 7.5. **Natural increase** (1983): 2.3%. **Hospital beds** (per 10,000 pop. 1982): 130. **Physicians** (per 10,000 pop. 1982): 24. **Education** (1984): **Literacy:** 99%. **Years compulsory:** 11.

The Democratic People's Republic of Korea was founded May 1, 1948, in the zone occupied by Russian troops after World War II. Its armies tried to conquer the south, 1950. After 3 years of fighting with Chinese and U.S. intervention, a cease-fire was proclaimed.

Industry, begun by the Japanese during their 1910-45 occupation, and nationalized in the 1940s, had grown substantially, using N. Korea's abundant mineral and hydroelectric resources.

Two N. Korean Army officers were sentenced to death by Burmese authorities after they confessed to the October 9, 1983 bombing which killed 17, including 4 S. Korean cabinet ministers, in Rangoon.

South Korea
Republic of Korea

People: Population (1984 est.): 41,999,000. **Age distrib. (%):** 0–14: 34; 15–59: 56.3; 60+: 6.1. **Pop. density:** 1,061 per sq. mi. **Urban** (1983): 62.9%. **Ethnic groups:** Korean. **Languages:** Korean. **Religions:** Buddhism, Confucianism, Christian.

Geography: Area: 38,211 sq. mi., slightly larger than Indiana. **Location:** In Northern E. Asia. **Neighbors:** N. Korea on N. **Topography:** The country is mountainous, with a rugged east coast. The western and southern coasts are deeply indented, with many islands and harbors. **Capital:** Seoul. **Cities** (1980 cen.): Seoul 9,204,344; Pusan 3,395,171; Taegu 1,958,112.

Government: Type: Republic, with power centralized in a strong executive. **Head of state:** Pres. Chun Doo Hwan; b. Jan. 18, 1931; in office: Dec. 1979. **Head of government:** Prime Min. Chin Lee Chong; in office: Oct. 14, 1983. **Local divisions:** 9 provinces and Seoul, Pusan, Inchon, and Taegu. **Defense:** 6% of GNP (1983).

Economy: Industries: Electronics, ships, textiles, clothing, motor vehicles. **Chief crops:** Rice, barley, vegetables. **Minerals:**

Tungsten, coal, graphite. **Arable land:** 22%. **Meat prod.** (1984): pork: 375,000 metric tons. **Fish catch:** (1983): 2.7 mln. metric tons. **Electricity prod.** (1983): 42.6 bln. kwh. **Crude steel prod.** (1981): 3.5 mln. metric tons. **Labor force:** 30% agric.; 22% manuf. & mining; 47% services.

Finance: Currency: Won (Mar. 1985: 850 = $1 US). **Gross national product** (1983): $73.3 bln. **Per capita income** (1978): $1,187. **Imports** (1984): $30.6 bln.; partners: Jap. 24%, U.S. 23%, Saudi Ar. 14%, Kuw. 6%. **Exports** (1984): $29.2 bln.; partners: U.S. 27%, Jap. 16%. **Tourists** (1982): 1.1 mln.; receipts: $502 mln. **National budget** (1983): 13.9 bln. expenditures. **International reserves less gold** (Mar. 1985): $2.1 bln. **Gold:** 310,000 oz t. **Consumer prices** (change in 1984): 2.3%.

Transport: Railway traffic (1984): 21.0 bln. passenger-km; 10.8 bln. net ton-km. **Motor vehicles:** in use (1983): 380,000 passenger cars, 390,000 comm. vehicles; assembled (1978): 92,328 passenger cars; 65,616 comm. vehicles. **Civil aviation** (1982): 12.1 bln. passenger-km; 1 bln. freight ton-km. **Chief ports:** Pusan, Inchon.

Communications: Television sets: 7.2 mln. in use (1984), 5.8 mln. manuf. (1979). **Radios:** 15 mln. in use (1981), 4.7 mln. manuf. (1979). **Telephones in use** (1983): 5.3 mln. **Daily newspaper circ.** (1982): 190 per 1,000 pop.

Health: Life expectancy at birth (1979): 68 years. **Births** (per 1,000 pop. 1981): 23.4. **Deaths** (per 1,000 pop. 1981): 6.6. **Natural increase** (1981): 1.6%. **Hospital beds** (1980): 11,181. **Physicians** (1982): 28,365. **Infant mortality** (per 1,000 live births 1982): 32.

Education (1983): **Literacy:** 92%. **Attendance:** High school 57%, college 14%.

Embassy: 2320 Massachusetts Ave. NW 20008; 483-6892.

Korea, once called the Hermit Kingdom, has a recorded history since the 1st century BC. It was united in a kingdom under the Silla Dynasty, 668 AD. It was at times associated with the Chinese empire; the treaty that concluded the Sino-Japanese war of 1894-95 recognized Korea's complete independence. In 1910 Japan forcibly annexed Korea as Chosun.

At the Potsdam conference, July, 1945, the 38th parallel was designated as the line dividing the Soviet and the American occupation. Russian troops entered Korea Aug. 10, 1945, U.S. troops entered Sept. 8, 1945. The Soviet military organized socialists and communists and blocked efforts to let the Koreans unite their country. *(See Index for Korean War.)*

The South Koreans formed the Republic of Korea in May 1948 with Seoul as the capital. Dr. Syngman Rhee was chosen president but a movement spearheaded by college students forced his resignation Apr. 26, 1960.

In an army coup May 16, 1961, Gen. Park Chung Hee became chairman of the ruling junta. He was elected president, 1963; a 1972 referendum allowed him to be reelected for 6 year terms unlimited times. Park was assassinated by the chief of the Korean CIA, Oct. 26, 1979. The calm of the new government was halted by the rise of Gen. Chon Too Hwan, head of the military intelligence, who reinstated martial law, and reverted South Korea to the police state it was under Park.

North Korean raids across the border tapered off in 1971, but incidents occurred in 1973 and 1974. In July 1972 South and North Korea agreed on a common goal of reunifying the 2 nations by peaceful means. But there had been no sign of a thaw in relations between the two regimes until 1985 when they agreed to discuss economic issues.

A Korean Air Lines passenger airliner was shot down by a Soviet jet fighter, Sept. 1, 1983, after it strayed into Soviet airspace; all 269 people aboard died.

During a 6-nation tour by Pres. Chun Doo Hwan, Oct. 9, a bomb exploded in Rangoon, Burma killing 17 S. Koreans, including 4 cabinet ministers. Two N. Korean Army officers confessed to the bombing.

Kuwait
State of Kuwait

People: Population (1984 est.): 1,758,000. **Age distrib. (%):** 0–14: 40.2; 15–59: 57.6; 60+: 2.3. **Pop. density:** 273 per sq. mi. **Ethnic groups:** Arabs 83%, Iranians, Indians, Pakistanis 13%. **Languages:** Arabic, others. **Religions:** Islam 95%.

Geography: Area: 6,532 sq. mi., slightly smaller than New Jersey. **Location:** In Middle East, at N end of Persian Gulf.

Neighbors: Iraq on N, Saudi Arabia on S. **Topography:** The country is flat, very dry, and extremely hot. **Capital:** Kuwait. **Cities** (1980 cen.): Hawalli 152,300; Kuwait City 60,400.

Government: Type: Constitutional monarchy. **Head of state:** Emir Shaikh Jabir al-Ahmad al-Jabir as-Sabah; b. 1928; in office: Jan. 1, 1978. **Head of government:** Prime Min. Shaikh Saad Abdulla as-Salim as-Sabah; in office: Feb. 8, 1978. **Local divisions:** 4 governorates.

Economy: Industries: Oil products. **Minerals:** Oil, gas. **Crude oil reserves** (1981): 70 bln. bbls. **Cultivated land:** 1%. **Electricity prod.** (1982): 10.3 bln. kwh. **Labor force:** 2% agric.; 8%. manuf.; 53% services.

Finance: Currency: Dinar (Mar. 1985: 0.29 = $1 US). **Gross domestic product** (1981): $24.3 bln. **Per capita income** (1975): $11,431. **Imports** (1983): $7.4 bln.; partners: Jap. 21%, U.S. 14%, UK 9%, W. Ger. 9%. **Exports** (1983): $9.7 bln.; partners: Jap. 20%, U.S. 14%, UK 9%, It. 6%. **National budget** (1982): $11.1 bln. revenues; $10 bln. expenditures. **International reserves less gold** (Feb. 1985): $4.5 bln. **Gold:** 2.53 mln. oz t. **Consumer prices** (change in 1983): 4.7%.

Transport: Motor vehicles: in use (1982): 480,000 passenger cars, 171,000 comm. vehicles. **Civil aviation** (1982): 3.5 bln. passenger-km; 115.6 mln. freight ton-km. **Chief ports:** Mina al-Ahmadi.

Communications: Television sets: 575,000 in use (1984). **Radios:** 710 in use (1984). **Telephones in use** (1982): 231,000. **Daily newspaper circ.** (1983): 208 per 1,000 pop.

Health: Life expectancy at birth (1980): 67.3 male; 71.6 female. **Births** (per 1,000 pop. 1981): 37.2. **Deaths** (per 1,000 pop. 1981): 3.6. **Natural increase** (1978): 5.9%. **Hospital beds** (1981): 5,563 plus 232 clinics and health centers. **Physicians** (1981): 2,348. **Infant mortality** (per 1,000 live births 1983): 33.9.

Education (1983): **Literacy:** 71%. **Years compulsory:** 8.

Major International Organizations: UN and its specialized agencies, Arab League, OPEC.

Embassy: 2940 Tilden St. NW 20008; 966-0702.

Kuwait is ruled by the Al-Sabah dynasty, founded 1759. Britain ran foreign relations and defense from 1899 until independence in 1961. The majority of the population is non-Kuwaiti, with many Palestinians, and cannot vote.

Iraqi troops crossed the Kuwait border in 1973 but soon withdrew. Kuwait has ordered weapons from France and the U.S.

Oil, first exported in 1946, is the fiscal mainstay, providing most of Kuwait's income. Oil pays for free medical care, education, and social security. There are no taxes, except customs duties.

Two Kuwaiti oil tankers were attacked in the Persian Gulf by Iranian planes, May 1984.

Laos
Lao People's Democratic Republic

People: Population (1984 est.): 3,732,000. **Pop. density:** 47.2 per sq. mi. **Urban** (1980): 13.4%. **Ethnic groups:** Lao 50%, Thai 20%, Meo and Yao 15%, others. **Languages:** Lao (official), French, English. **Religions:** Buddhists 58%, tribal 34%.

Geography: Area: 91,428 sq. mi., slightly larger than Utah. **Location:** In Indochina Peninsula in SE Asia. **Neighbors:** Burma, China on N, Vietnam on E, Cambodia on S, Thailand on W. **Topography:** Landlocked, dominated by jungle. High mountains along the eastern border are the source of the E-W rivers slicing across the country to the Mekong R., which defines most of the western border. **Capital:** Vientiane. **Cities** (1978 est.): Vientiane 200,000.

Government: Type: Communist. **Head of state:** Pres. Souphanouvong; b. July 13, 1909; in office: Dec. 2, 1975. **Head of government:** Prime Min. Kaysone Phomvihan; b. Dec. 13, 1920; in office: Dec. 2, 1975. **Local divisions:** 13 provinces. **Armed forces: Defense:** 14% of GNP (1980).

Economy: Industries: Wood products. **Chief crops:** Rice, corn, tobacco, cotton, opium, citrus fruits, coffee. **Minerals:** Tin. **Other resources:** Forests. **Arable land:** 4%. **Meat prod.** (1980): beef: 12,000 metric tons; pork: 30,000 metric tons. **Fish catch** (1982): 20,000 metric tons. **Electricity prod.** (1982): 1.1 bln. kwh. **Labor force:** 76% agric.

Finance: Currency: New kip (Nov. 1984): 35.07 = $1 US). **Gross domestic product** (1981): $290 mln. **Per capita income** (1976 est.): $85. **Imports** (1982): $150.1 mln.; partners

(1974): Thai. 49%, Jap. 19%, Fr. 7%, W. Ger. 7%. **Exports** (1982): $14 mln.; partners (1974): Thai. 73%, Malaysia 11%, HK 10%.

Transport: Motor vehicles: in use (1982): 15,100 passenger cars, 3,000 comm. vehicles. **Civil Aviation** (1982): 8 mln. passenger km; 100,000 net ton-km.

Communications: Radios: 225,000 licensed (1983).

Health: Life expectancy at birth (1975): 39.1 male; 41.8 female. **Births** (per 1,000 pop. 1976): 44. **Deaths** (per 1,000 pop. 1978): 21. **Natural increase** (1978): 2.3%. **Hospital beds** (1981): 8,729. **Physicians** (1981): 30.

Education: (1981): **Literacy:** 85%.

Major International Organizations: UN and its specialized agencies.

Embassy: 2222 S St. NW 20008; 332-6416.

Laos became a French protectorate in 1893, but regained independence as a constitutional monarchy July 19, 1949.

Conflicts among neutralist, communist and conservative factions created a chaotic political situation. Armed conflict increased after 1960.

The 3 factions formed a coalition government in June 1962, with neutralist Prince Souvanna Phouma as premier. A 14-nation conference in Geneva signed agreements, 1962, guaranteeing neutrality and independence. By 1964 the Pathet Lao had withdrawn from the coalition, and, with aid from N. Vietnamese troops, renewed sporadic attacks. U.S. planes bombed the Ho Chi Minh trail, supply line from N. Vietnam to communist forces in Laos and S. Vietnam. An estimated 2.75 million tons of bombs were dropped on Laos during the fighting.

In 1970 the U.S. stepped up air support and military aid. There were an est. 67,000 N. Vietnamese troops in Laos, and some 15,000 Thais financed by the U.S.

After Pathet Lao military gains, Souvanna Phouma in May 1975 ordered government troops to cease fighting; the Pathet Lao took control. A Lao People's Democratic Republic was proclaimed Dec. 3, 1975; it is strongly influenced by Vietnam.

Lebanon

Republic of Lebanon

People: Population (1984 est.): 2,601,000. **Age distrib. (%):** 0–14: 42.6; 15–59: 49.6; 60+: 7.7. **Pop. density:** 784 per sq. mi. **Urban** (1984): 64%. **Ethnic groups:** Arabs 93%, Armenians 6%. **Languages:** Arabic (official), French, Armenian. **Religions:** Predominately Moslems and Christians; Druze minority.

Geography: Area: 3,950 sq. mi., smaller than Connecticut. **Location:** On Eastern end of Mediterranean Sea. **Neighbors:** Syria on E. Israel on S. **Topography:** There is a narrow coastal strip, and 2 mountain ranges running N-S enclosing the fertile Beqaa Valley. The Litani R. runs S through the valley, turning W to empty into the Mediterranean. **Capital:** Beirut. **Cities** (1984 est.): Beirut 1,100,000; Tripoli 240,000.

Government: Type: Parliamentary republic. **Head of state:** Pres. Amin Gemayel; in office: Sept. 23, 1982; **Head of government:** Prime Min. Rashid Abdul Hamid Karami; b. Dec. 30, 1921; in office: Apr. 30, 1984. **Local divisions:** 6 provinces. **Defense:** 18% of govt. budget (1984).

Economy: Industries: Trade, food products, textiles, cement, oil products. **Chief crops:** Fruits, olives, tobacco, grapes, vegetables, grains. **Minerals:** Iron. **Arable land:** 35%. **Meat prod.** (1980): beef: 13,000 metric tons; lamb: 13,000 metric tons. **Electricity prod.** (1981): 1.8 bln. kwh. **Labor force:** 17% agric.; 75% ind., comm., services.

Finance: Currency: Pound (Mar. 1985: 17.65 = $1 US). **Gross domestic product** (1983): $3.0 bln. **Per capita income** (1983): $1,150. **Imports** (1983): $3.6 bln.; partners: It. 15%, Fr. 10%, U.S. 9%, Saudi Ar. 6%. **Exports** (1983): $691 mln.; partners: Saudi Ar. 33%, Syria 8%, Jor. 6%, Kuw. 8%. **National budget** (1983): $1.8 bln. **International reserves less gold** (Mar. 1985): $673 mln. **Gold:** 9.22 mln. oz t.

Transport: Railway traffic (1982): 5.3 mln. passenger-km; 42 mln. net ton-km. **Motor vehicles:** in use (1982): 460,000 passenger cars, 21,000 comm. vehicles. **Civil aviation** (1982): 968 mln. passenger-km; 465 mln. freight ton-km. **Chief ports:** Beirut, Tripoli, Sidon.

Communications: Television sets: 450,000 in use (1983). **Radios:** 1.5 mln. in use (1983). **Telephones:** in use (1978): 231,000. **Daily newspaper circ.** (1983): 89 per 1,000 pop.

Health: Life expectancy at birth (1975): 61.4 male; 65.1 female. **Births** (per 1,000 pop. 1982): 29.9. **Deaths** (per 1,000 pop. 1982): 8.3. **Natural increase** (1982): 2.1%. **Hospital beds** (per 100,000 pop. 1977): 384. **Physicians** (per 100,000 pop. 1977): 75. **Infant mortality** (per 1,000 live births 1982): 45.

Education: (1984): **Literacy:** 75%. **Years compulsory:** 5; attendance 93%.

Major International Organizations: UN and its specialized agencies.

Embassy: 2560 28th St. NW 20008; 939-6300.

Formed from 5 former Turkish Empire districts, Lebanon became an independent state Sept. 1, 1920, administered under French mandate 1920-41. French troops withdrew in 1946.

Under the 1943 National Covenant, all public positions were divided among the various religious communities, with Christians in the majority. By the 1970s, Moslems became the majority, and demanded a larger political and economic role.

U.S. Marines intervened, May-Oct. 1958, during a Syrian-aided revolt. Lebanon's efforts to restrain Palestinian commandos caused armed clashes in 1969. Continued raids against Israeli civilians, 1970-75, brought Israeli attacks against guerrilla camps and villages. Israeli troops occupied S. Lebanon, March 1978, but were replaced by a UN force, and again in Apr. 1980.

An estimated 60,000 were killed and billions of dollars in damage inflicted in a 1975-76 civil war. Palestinian units and leftist Moslems fought against the Maronite militia, the Phalange, and other Christians. Several Arab countries provided political and arms support to the various factions, while Israel aided Christian forces. Up to 15,000 Syrian troops intervened in 1976, and fought Palestinian groups. Arab League troops from several nations tried to impose a cease-fire.

Clashes between Syrian troops and Christian forces erupted, Apr. 1, 1981, near Zahle, Lebanon, bringing to an end the cease-fire that had been in place. By Apr. 22, fighting had broken out not only between Syrians and Christians, but also between two Moslem factions. Israeli commandos attacked Palestinian positions at Tyre and Tulin. In July, Israeli air raids on Beirut killed or wounded some 800 persons. A cease-fire between Israel and the Palestinians was concluded July 24, but hostilities continued.

Israeli forces invaded Lebanon June 6, 1982, in a coordinated land, sea, and air attack aimed at crushing strongholds of the Palestine Liberation Organization (PLO). Israeli and Syrian forces engaged in the Bekka Valley. By June 14, Israeli troops had encircled Beirut. On Aug. 21, the PLO evacuated West Beirut following massive Israeli bombings of the city. The withdrawal was supervised by U.S., French, and Italian troops.

Israeli troops entered West Beirut following the Sept. 14 assassination of newly-elected Lebanese Pres. Bashir Gemayel. On Sept. 16, Lebanese Christian troops entered 2 refugee camps and massacred hundreds of Palestinian refugees.

In 1983, terrorist bombings became a way of life in Beirut as some 50 people were killed in an explosion at the U.S. Embassy, Apr. 18; 241 U.S. servicemen and 58 French soldiers died in separate Muslim suicide attacks, Oct. 23.

PLO leader Yasir Arafat and PLO dissidents backed by Syria fought a 6-week battle in Tripoli until negotiations allowed Arafat and some 4,000 followers to evacuate the city.

On Apr. 26, 1984, pro-Syrian Rashid Karami was appointed premier. The appointment failed to end virtual civil war in Beirut between Christian forces, and Druse and Shiite Moslem militias. There was heavy fighting between Shiite militiamen and Palestinian guerrillas in May 1985. Beirut Airport was the scene of a hostage crisis where Shiite terrorists held U.S. citizens for 17 days. (*See Chronology*)

Lesotho

Kingdom of Lesotho

People: Population (1984 est.): 1,474,000. **Age distrib. (%):** 0–14: 39.5; 15–59: 53.9; 60+: 6.6. **Pop. density:** 125 per sq. mi. **Ethnic groups:** Sotho 99%. **Languages:** English, Sesotho (official). **Religions:** Roman Catholic 43%, Protestant 49%.

Geography: Area: 11,716 sq. mi., slightly larger than Maryland. **Location:** In Southern Africa. **Neighbors:** Completely surrounded by Republic of South Africa. **Topography:** Landlocked and mountainous, with altitudes ranging from 5,000 to 11,000 ft. **Capital:** Maseru. **Cities** (1984 est.): Maseru 80,250.

Government: Type: Constitutional monarchy. **Head of state:** King Moshoeshoe II, b. May 2, 1938; in office: Mar. 12, 1960. **Head of government:** Prime Min. Leabua Jonathan; b. Oct. 31, 1914; in office: Oct. 4, 1966. **Local divisions:** 10 districts. **Defense:** 4.5% of govt. budget (1982).

Economy: Industries: Diamond polishing, food processing. **Chief crops:** Corn, grains, peas, beans. **Other resources:** Wool, mohair. **Arable land:** 13%. **Electricity prod.** (1967): 5.00 mln. kwh. **Labor force:** 36% agric.; 5% ind. and comm., 53% services.

Finance: Currency: Maloti (Mar. 1985: 1.96 = $1 US). **Gross national product** (1981): $678.2 mln. **Per capita income** (1979): $355. **Imports** (1982): $396 mln.; partners: Mostly So. Afr. **Exports** (1982): $50 mln.; partners: Mostly So. Afr. **National budget** (1983): $153.5 mln.

Transport: Motor vehicles: in use (1979): 4,000 passenger cars, 8,000 comm. vehicles.

Communications: Radios: 37,000 licensed (1983). **Daily newspaper circ.** (1983): 30 per 1,000 pop.

Health: Life expectancy at birth (1983): 51.5 yrs. **Births** (per 1,000 pop. 1978): 37. **Deaths** (per 1,000 pop. 1978): 14. **Natural increase** (1978): 2.3%. **Hospital beds** (per 100,000 pop. 1977): 205. **Physicians** (per 100,000 pop. 1977): 8. **Infant mortality** (per 1,000 live births 1983): 104.

Education (1984): **Literacy:** 65%.

Major International Organizations: UN and its specialized organizations, OAU.

Embassy: 1601 Connecticut Ave. NW 20009; 462-4190.

Lesotho (once called Basutoland) became a British protectorate in 1868 when Chief Moshesh sought protection against the Boers. Independence came Oct. 4, 1966. Elections were suspended in 1970. Over 50% of males work abroad in So. Africa. Livestock raising is the chief industry; diamonds are the chief export.

Liberia
Republic of Liberia

People: Population (1984 est.): 2,180,000. **Age distrib. (%):** 0–14: 40.9; 15–59: 53.1; 60+: 5.9. **Pop. density:** 59.4 per sq. mi. **Urban** (1981): 37.1%. **Ethnic groups:** Americo-Liberians 5%, 16 tribes 95% **Languages:** English (official), tribal dialects. **Religions:** Moslems 20%, Christians 15%, traditional 65%.

Geography: Area: 38,250 sq. mi., slightly smaller than Pennsylvania. **Location:** On SW coast of W. Africa. **Neighbors:** Sierra Leone on W, Guinea on N, Ivory Coast on E. **Topography:** Marshy Atlantic coastline rises to low mountains and plateaus in the forested interior; 6 major rivers flow in parallel courses to the ocean. **Capital:** Monrovia. **Cities** (1984 est.): Monrovia 306,000.

Government: Type: Military. **Head of state:** Pres. Samuel K. Doe; in office: Apr. 12, 1980. **Local divisions:** 10 counties and 5 territories. **Defense:** 5.1% of GDP (1982).

Economy: Industries: Food processing and other light industry. **Chief crops:** Rice, cassava, coffee, cocoa, sugar. **Minerals:** Iron, diamonds, gold. **Other resources:** Rubber, timber. **Arable land:** 4%. **Fish catch** (1982): 13,500 metric tons. **Electricity prod.** (1982): 1.1 bln. kwh. **Labor force:** 70.5% agric.

Finance: Currency: Dollar (Apr. 1985: 1.00 = $1 US). **Gross domestic product** (1981): $372 mln. **Per capita income** (1982): $400. **Imports** (1981): $477 mln.; partners: U.S. 29%, W. Ger. 10%, Saudi Ar. 19%, Jap. 5%, Neth. 8%. **Exports** (1981): $601 mln.; partners: W. Ger. 25%, U.S. 23%, It. 13%, Fr. 10%. **National budget** (1984): $387 mln. **International reserves less gold** (Feb. 1985): $2.2 mln. **Consumer prices** (change in 1983): 1.6%.

Transport: Motor vehicles: in use (1980): 22,000 passenger cars, 20,000 comm. vehicles. **Chief ports:** Monrovia, Buchanan.

Communications: Television sets: 21,000 in use (1982). **Radios:** 320,000 in use (1982). **Telephones** in use (1980): 7,740. **Daily newspaper circ.** (1982): 6 per 1,000 pop.

Health: Life expectancy at birth (1984): 54 yrs.; **Births** (per 1,000 pop. 1978): 50. **Deaths** (per 1,000 pop. 1978): 20. **Natural increase** (1978): 3.0%. **Hospital beds** (1981): 3,000. **Physicians** (1981): 236. **Infant mortality** (per 1,000 live births 1984): 152.

Education (1984): **Literacy:** 24%. **School attendance:** primary 50%, secondary 20%.

Major International Organizations: UN and its specialized agencies, OAU.

Embassy: 5201 16th St. NW 20011; 723-9437.

Liberia was founded in 1822 by U.S. black freedmen who settled at Monrovia with the aid of colonization societies. It became a republic July 26, 1847, with a constitution modeled on that of the U.S. Descendants of freedmen dominated politics.

Charging rampant corruption, an Army Redemption Council of enlisted men staged a bloody predawn coup, April 12, 1980, in which Pres. Tolbert was killed and replaced as head of state by Sgt. Samuel Doe. Doe promised a return to civilian rule in 1985.

Libya
Socialist People's Libyan Arab Jamahiriya

People: Population: (1984 est.): 3,684,000. **Age distrib. (%):** 0–14: 51.4; 15–59: 42.6; 60+: 5.9. **Pop. density:** 5 per sq. mi. **Urban** (1983): 53%. **Ethnic groups:** Arab-Berber 82%, foreign nationals 17%. **Languages:** Arabic. **Religions:** Sunni Moslem 97%.

Geography: Area: 679,536 sq. mi., larger than Alaska. **Location:** On Mediterranean coast of N. Africa. **Neighbors:** Tunisia, Algeria on W, Niger, Chad on S, Sudan, Egypt on E. **Topography:** Desert and semidesert regions cover 92% of the land, with low mountains in N, higher mountains in S, and a narrow coastal zone. **Capital:** Tripoli. **Cities** (1982 est.): Tripoli 820,000.

Government: Type: Centralized republic, under military control. **Head of state:** Col. Muammar al-Qaddafi; b. Sept. 1942; in office: Sept. 1969. **Head of government:** Premier Muhammad az-Zaruq Rajab; in office: Feb. 16, 1984. **Local divisions:** 10 regions. **Defense:** 2.8% of GNP (1982).

Economy: Industries: Carpets, textiles, shoes. **Chief crops:** Dates, olives, citrus and other fruits, grapes, tobacco. **Minerals:** Gypsum, oil, gas. **Crude oil reserves** (1980): 23.5 bln. bbls. **Arable land:** 2%. **Meat prod.** (1980): beef: 33,000 metric tons; lamb: 53,000 metric tons. **Electricity prod.** (1982): 6 bln. kwh. **Labor force:** 20% agric.; 20% manuf.; 10% oil ind.

Finance: Currency: Dinar (Feb. 1985: 0.33 = $1 US). **Gross domestic product** (1982): $25 bln. **Per capita income** (1978): $6,335. **Imports** (1983): $7.3 bln.; partners: It. 30%, W. Ger. 11%, Fr. 6%, Jap. 8%. **Exports** (1984): $11.1 bln.; partners: U.S. 27%, It. 24%, W. Ger. 10%, Sp. 7%. **International reserves less gold** (Mar. 1985): $3.3 bln. **Gold:** 3.6 mln. oz t.

Transport: Motor vehicles: in use (1982): 415,000 passenger cars, 334,000 comm. vehicles. **Chief ports:** Tripoli, Benghazi.

Communications: Television sets: 170,000 licensed (1982). **Radios:** 165,000 (1982). **Daily newspaper circ.** (1983): 11 per 1,000 pop.

Health: Life expectancy at birth (1980): 56.1 male; 59.4 female. **Births** (per 1,000 pop. 1978): 48. **Deaths** (per 1,000 pop. 1978): 13. **Natural increase** (1978): 3.5%. **Hospital beds** (1980): 14,472. **Physicians** (1980): 4,300.

Education (1983): **Literacy:** 40%.

Major International Organizations: UN, Arab League, OAU, OPEC.

First settled by Berbers, Libya was ruled by Carthage, Rome, and Vandals, the Ottomans, Italy from 1912, and Britain and France after WW II. It became an independent constitutional monarchy Jan. 2, 1952. In 1969 a junta lead by Col. Muammar al-Qaddafi seized power.

In the mid-1970s, Libya helped arm violent revolutionary groups in Egypt and Sudan, and had aided terrorists of various nationalities. The USSR sold Libya advanced arms, and established close political ties.

Libya and Egypt fought several air and land battles along their border in July, 1977. Chad charged Libya with military occupation of its uranium-rich northern region in 1977. Libya's 1979 offensive into the Aouzou Strip was repulsed by Chadian forces. Libyan forces withdrew from Chad, Nov. 1981 but have since returned.

Widespread nationalization, arrests, imposition of currency regulations, wholesale conscription of civil servants into the army, and the fall in crude oil prices have hurt the economy.

On May 6, 1981, the U.S., citing "a wide range of Libyan provocations and misconduct," closed the Libyan mission in Wash. In

August, 2 Libyan jets were shot down by U.S. Navy planes taking part in naval exercises in the Gulf of Sidra. Great Britain severed diplomatic relations with Libya April 22, 1984, following the death of a British policewoman and the wounding of 10 Libyan-exile demonstrators by machine-gun fire from within the Libyan embassy in London.

There were signs of internal opposition to Qaddafi in 1985.

Liechtenstein

Principality of Liechtenstein

People: Population (1984 est.): 27,000. **Age distrib. (%):** 0–14: 27.9; 15–59: 60.2; 60+: 11.9. **Pop. density:** 427 per sq. mi. **Ethnic groups:** Alemannic. **Languages:** German (official), Alemannic dialect. **Religions:** Roman Catholic 85%, Protestants 8%.

Geography: Area: 62 sq. mi., the size of Washington, D.C. **Location:** In the Alps. **Neighbors:** Switzerland on W, Austria on E. **Topography:** The Rhine Valley occupies one-third of the country, the Alps cover the rest. **Capital:** Vaduz. **Cities** (1984 cen.): Vaduz 4,980.

Government: Type: Hereditary constitutional monarchy. **Head of state:** Prince Franz Josef II; b. Aug. 16, 1906; in office: Mar. 30, 1938. **Head of government:** Hans Brunhart; b. Mar. 28, 1945; in office: Apr. 26, 1978. **Local divisions:** 2 districts, 11 communities.

Economy: Industries: Machines, instruments, chemicals, furniture, ceramics. **Arable land:** 25%. **Labor force:** 54.6% industry, trade and building; 41.5% services; 3.9% agric., fishing, forestry.

Finance: Currency: Swiss Franc (Mar. 1985): 2.61 = $1. **Tourists** (1982): 79,757.

Communications: Radios: 7,608 in use (1982). **Telephones in use** (1982): 10,980. **Daily newspaper circ.** (1982): 558 per 1,000 pop.

Health: Births (per 1,000 pop. 1983): 13.2. **Deaths** (per 1,000 pop. 1983): 5.7. **Natural increase** (1983): .7%. **Infant mortality** (per 1,000 live births 1983): 5.8.

Education: Literacy: 100%. **Years compulsory** 9; attendance 100%.

Liechtenstein became sovereign in 1866. Austria administered Liechtenstein's ports up to 1920; Switzerland has administered its postal services since 1921. Liechtenstein is united with Switzerland by a customs and monetary union. Taxes are low; many international corporations have headquarters there. Foreign workers comprise a third of the population.

Luxembourg

Grand Duchy of Luxembourg

People: Population (1984 est.): 366,000. **Age distrib. (%):** 0–14: 19.0; 15–59: 63.5; 60+: 17.6. **Pop. density:** 374 per sq. mi. **Urban** (1980): 78.4%. **Ethnic groups:** Mixture of French and Germans predominate. **Languages:** French, German, Luxembourgian. **Religions:** Roman Catholic 94%.

Geography: Area: 1,034 sq. mi., smaller than Rhode Island. **Location:** In W. Europe. **Neighbors:** Belgium on W, France on S, W. Germany on E. **Topography:** Heavy forests (Ardennes) cover N, S is a low, open plateau. **Capital:** Luxembourg. **Cities** (1982 est.): Luxembourg 80,000.

Government: Type: Constitutional monarchy. **Head of state:** Grand Duke Jean; b. Jan. 5, 1921; in office: Nov. 12, 1964. **Head of government:** Prime Min. Jacques Santer; in office: July 21, 1984. **Local divisions:** 3 districts, 12 cantons. **Defense:** 2.8% of govt. budget (1982).

Economy: Industries: Steel, chemicals, beer, tires, tobacco, metal products, cement. **Chief crops:** Corn, wine. **Minerals:** Iron. **Arable land:** 27%. **Electricity prod.** (1982): 972 mln. kwh. **Crude steel prod.** (1982): 3.5 mln. metric tons. **Labor force:** 1% agric.; 42% ind. & comm.; 45% services.

Finance: Currency: Franc (Mar. 1985: 62.07 = $1 US). **Gross domestic product** (1981): $3.8 bln. **Per capita income** (1981): $10,444. **Note:** trade and tourist data included in Belgian statistics. **Consumer prices** (change in 1984): 5.6%.

Transport: Railway traffic (1982): 310 mln. passenger-km; 551 mln. net ton-km. **Motor vehicles:** in use (1982): 137,900

passenger cars, 10,800 comm. vehicles. **Civil aviation:** (1980): 55 mln. passenger-miles; 200,000 freight ton-miles.

Communications: Television sets: 91,000 in use (1983). **Radios:** 205,000 in use (1983). **Telephones in use** (1982): 228,000. **Daily newspaper circ.** (1982): 352 per 1,000 pop.

Health: Life expectancy at birth (1978): 68.0 male; 75 female. **Births** (per 1,000 pop. 1980): 11.4. **Deaths** (per 1,000 pop. 1980): 11.3. **Hospital beds** (1982): 4,816. **Physicians** (1982): 580. **Infant mortality** (per 1,000 live births 1982): 12.

Education (1982): **Literacy:** 100%. **Years compulsory** 9; attendance 100%.

Major International Organizations: UN and its specialized agencies, OECD, EC, NATO.

Embassy: 2200 Massachusetts Ave. NW 20008; 265-4171.

Luxembourg, founded about 963, was ruled by Burgundy, Spain, Austria, and France from 1448 to 1815. It left the Germanic Confederation in 1866. Overrun by Germany in 2 world wars, Luxembourg ended its neutrality in 1948, when a customs union with Belgium and Netherlands was adopted.

Madagascar

Democratic Republic of Madagascar

People: Population (1984 est.): 9,645,000. **Pop. density:** 42 per sq. mi. **Urban** (1980): 18%. **Ethnic groups:** 18 Malayan-Indonesian tribes (Merina 26%), with Arab and African presence. **Languages:** Malagasy (national), French. **Religions:** animists 47%, Christian 51%, Muslim 2%.

Geography: Area: 228,880 sq. mi., slightly smaller than Texas. **Location:** In the Indian O., off the SE coast of Africa. **Neighbors:** Comoro Is., Mozambique (across Mozambique Channel). **Topography:** Humid coastal strip in the E, fertile valleys in the mountainous center plateau region, and a wider coastal strip on the W. **Capital:** Antananarivo. **Cities** (1984 est.): Antananarivo 650,000.

Government: Type: Republic. **Head of state:** Pres. Didier Ratsiraka; b. Nov. 4, 1936; in office: June 15, 1975. **Head of government:** Prime Min. Desire Rakotoarijaona, b. June 19, 1934; in office: Aug. 4, 1977. **Local divisions:** 6 provinces. **Defense:** 10.2% of govt. budget (1984).

Economy: Industries: Light industry. **Chief crops:** Coffee (over 50% of exports), cloves, vanilla, rice, sugar, sisal, tobacco, peanuts. **Minerals:** Chromium, graphite. **Arable land:** 5%. **Meat prod.** (1984): beef: 138,000 metric tons; pork: 34,000 metric tons. **Fish catch** (1983): 48,000 metric tons. **Electricity prod.** (1982): 425 mln. kwh. **Labor force:** 88% agric.

Finance: Currency: Franc (Mar. 1985: 686 = $1 US). **Gross domestic product** (1982): $2.7 bln. **Per capita income** (1982): $279. **Imports** (1982): $487 mln.; partners: Fr. 41%, W. Ger. 10%. **Exports** (1982): $325 mln.; partners: Fr. 20%, U.S. 19%. **National budget** (1984): $660 mln. **International reserves less gold** (Mar. 1985): $40.7 mln. **Consumer prices** (change in 1983): 19.7%.

Transport: Railway traffic (1983): 279 mln. passenger-km; 222 mln. net ton-km. **Motor vehicles:** in use (1982): 55,000 passenger cars, 50,000 comm. vehicles. **Civil aviation:** (1983): 384 mln. passenger-km; 20 mln. freight ton-km. **Chief ports:** Tamatave, Diego-Suarez, Majunga, Tulear.

Communications: Television sets: 71,000 in use (1983). **Radios:** 910 mln. in use (1983). **Telephones in use** (1983): 37,000.

Health: Life expectancy at birth (1984): 46 years. **Births** (per 1,000 pop. 1981): 45. **Deaths** (per 1,000 pop. 1981): 18. **Natural increase** (1981): 2.7%. **Hospital beds** (per 100,000 pop. 1977): 245. **Physicians** (per 100,000 pop. 1977): 10. **Infant mortality** (per 1,000 live births 1984): 177.

Education (1984): **Literacy:** 53%. **Years compulsory:** 5; attendance 83%.

Major International Organizations: UN and its specialized agencies, OAU.

Embassy: 2374 Massachusetts Ave. NW 20008; 265-5525.

Madagascar was settled 2,000 years ago by Malayan-Indonesian people, whose descendants still predominate. A unified kingdom ruled the 18th and 19th centuries. The island became a French protectorate, 1885, and a colony 1896. Independence came June 26, 1960.

Discontent with inflation and French domination led to a coup in 1972. The new regime nationalized French-owned financial interests, closed French bases and a U.S. space tracking station, and obtained Chinese aid. The government conducted a program of arrests, expulsion of foreigners, and repression of strikes, 1979.

Malawi
Republic of Malawi

People: Population (1984 est.): 6,829,000. **Age distrib. (%):** 0–14: 43.9; 15–59: 50.4; 60+: 5.6. **Pop. density:** 187 per sq. mi. **Urban** (1980): 9.6%. **Ethnic groups:** Chewa, 90%, Nyanja, Lomwe, other Bantu tribes. **Languages:** English, Chichewa (both official). **Religions:** Christian 75%, Muslim 20%.

Geography: Area: 45,747 sq. mi., the size of Pennsylvania. **Location:** In SE Africa. **Neighbors:** Zambia on W, Mozambique on SE, Tanzania on N. **Topography:** Malawi stretches 560 mi. N-S along Lake Malawi (Lake Nyasa), most of which belongs to Malawi. High plateaus and mountains line the Rift Valley the length of the nation. **Capital:** Lilongwe. **Cities** (1983 est.): Blantyre 250,000; Lilongwe 130,000.

Government: Type: Republic. **Head of state:** Pres. Hastings Kamuzu Banda, b. May 14, 1906; in office: July 6, 1966. **Local divisions:** 24 administrative districts. **Defense:** 8% of gov't. budget (1983).

Economy: Industries: Textiles, sugar, farm implements. **Chief crops:** Tea, tobacco, sugar, coffee. **Other resources:** Rubber. **Arable land:** 25%. **Fish catch** (1983): 70.0 metric tons. **Electricity prod.** (1983): 445 mln. kwh. **Labor force:** 45% agric.; 17% ind. and comm.; 20% govt.; 18% services.

Finance: Currency: Kwacha (Mar. 1985: 1.53 = $1 US). **Gross national product** (1981): $1.23 bln. **Per capita income** (1979): $220. **Imports** (1981): $263 mln.; partners: So. Afr. 32%, UK 10%, Jap. 6%. **Exports** (1981): $230 mln.; partners: UK 17%, U.S. 28%, Neth. 5%. W. Ger. 7%. **National budget** (1983): $386.4 mln. **International reserves less gold** (Mar. 1985): $25.0 mln. **Gold:** 13,000 oz t. **Consumer prices** (change in 1983): 13.5%.

Transport: Railway traffic (1982): 95 mln. passenger-km; 187 mln. net ton-km. **Motor vehicles:** in use (1981): 14,100 passenger cars, 13,600 comm. vehicles. **Civil aviation** (1982) 96 mln. passenger-km; 1.5 freight ton-km.

Communications: Radios: 500,000 in use (1983). **Telephones in use** (1981): 15,130. **Daily newspaper circ.** (1983): 2 per 1,000 pop.

Health: Life expectancy at birth (1981): 42.7 male; 45.4 female. **Births** (per 1,000 pop. 1981): 56.2. **Deaths** (per 1,000 pop. 1981): 22.8. **Natural increase** (1981): 3.3%. **Hospital beds** (1979): 8,991. **Infant mortality** (per 1,000 live births 1983): 14.

Education (1983): **Literacy:** 25%. About 45% attend school. **Major International Organizations:** UN and its specialized agencies, OAU, Commonwealth of Nations. **Embassy:** 1400 20th St. NW 20036; 296-5530.

Bantus came in the 16th century, Arab slavers in the 19th. The area became the British protectorate Nyasaland, in 1891. It became independent July 6, 1964, and a republic in 1966. It has a pro-West foreign policy and cooperates economically with Zimbabwe and S. Africa.

Malaysia

People: Population (1984 est.): 15,330,000. **Age distrib. (%):** 0–14: 41.5; 15–59: 53.0; 60+: 5.4. **Pop. density:** 119 per sq. mi. **Urban** (1980): 34.2%. **Ethnic groups:** Malays 50%, Chinese 36%, Indians 10%, others. **Languages:** Malay (official), English, Chinese, Indian languages. **Religions:** Moslem, Hindu, Buddhist, Confucian, Taoist, local religions.

Geography: Area: 127,316 sq. mi., slightly larger than New Mexico. **Location:** On the SE tip of Asia, plus the N. coast of the island of Borneo. **Neighbors:** Thailand on N, Indonesia on S. **Topography:** Most of W. Malaysia is covered by tropical jungle, including the central mountain range that runs N-S through the peninsula. The western coast is marshy, the eastern, sandy. E. Malaysia has a wide, swampy coastal plain, with interior jungles

and mountains. **Capital:** Kuala Lumpur. **Cities** (1980 est.): Kuala Lumpur 1,081,000 (met.).

Government: Type: Federal parliamentary democracy with a constitutional monarch. **Head of state:** Paramount Ruler Mahmood Iskander; b. 1932; in office: Apr. 26, 1984. **Head of government:** Prime Min. Datuk Seri Mahathir bin Mohamad; b. Dec. 20, 1925; in office: July 16, 1981. **Local divisions:** 13 states and capital. **Defense:** 8.2% of GNP (1982).

Economy: Industries: Rubber goods, steel, electronics. **Chief crops:** Palm oil, copra, rice, pepper. **Minerals:** Tin (35% world output), iron. **Crude oil reserves** (1980): 2.80 bln. bbls. **Other resources:** Rubber (35% world output). **Arable land:** 13%. **Meat prod.** (1980): beef: 17,000 metric tons; pork: 71,000 metric tons. **Fish catch** (1983): 713,000 metric tons. **Electricity prod.** (1983): 12.2 bln. kwh. **Crude steel prod.** (1981 est.): 210,000 metric tons. **Labor force:** 41% agric.; 24% ind. and comm.; 21% service & trade.

Finance: Currency: Ringgit (Mar. 1985: 2.52 = $1 US). **Gross national product** (1983): $29.7 bln. **Per capita income** (1975): $714. **Imports** (1982): $13.2 bln.; partners: Jap. 25%, U.S. 18%, Sing. 14%. **Exports** (1982): $12 bln.; partners: Jap. 20%, U.S. 12% Sing. 25%, Neth. 6%. **National budget** (1982): $14.2 bln. **International reserves less gold** (Mar. 1985): $3.2 bln. **Gold:** 2.33 mln. oz t. **Consumer prices** (change in 1984): 3.9%.

Transport: Railway traffic (incl. Singapore) (1982): 2 bln. passenger-km; 1.1 bln. net ton-km. **Motor vehicles:** in use (1983): 1.1 mln. passenger cars, 266,000 comm. vehicles. **Civil aviation:** (1982): 5.4 bln. passenger-km; 148 mln. freight ton-km. **Chief ports:** George Town, Kelang, Melaka, Kuching.

Communications: Television sets: 1.3 mln. in use (1982). **Radios:** 2 mln. in use (1982). **Telephones in use** (1983): 976,000. **Daily newspaper circ.** (1983): 133 per 1,000 pop.

Health: Life expectancy at birth (1983): 64 years. **Births** (per 1,000 pop. 1983): 28.6. **Deaths** (per 1,000 pop. 1983): 6.4. **Natural increase** (1983): 2.2%. **Hospital beds** (per 100,000 pop. 1977): 308. **Physicians** (per 100,000 pop. 1977): 12. **Infant mortality** (per 1,000 live births 1983): 31.8.

Education (1983): **Literacy:** 75%; 94% attend primary school, 48% attend secondary.

Major International Organizations: UN and its specialized agencies, ASEAN.

Embassy: 2401 Massachusetts Ave. NW 20008; 328-2700.

European traders appeared in the 16th century; Britain established control in 1867. Malaysia was created Sept. 16, 1963. It included Malaya (which had become independent in 1957 after the suppression of Communist rebels), plus the formerly-British Singapore, Sabah (N Borneo), and Sarawak (NW Borneo). Singapore was separated in 1965, in order to end tensions between Chinese, the majority in Singapore, and Malays in control of the Malaysian government. Chinese have charged economical and political discrimination.

A monarch is elected by a council of hereditary rulers of the Malayan states every 5 years.

Abundant natural resources have assured prosperity, and foreign investment has aided industrialization.

Maldives
Republic of Maldives

People: Population (1984 est.): 173,000. **Age distrib. (%):** 0–14: 44.9; 15–59: 51.3; 60+: 3.8. **Pop. density:** 1,400 per sq. mi. **Urban** (1978): 20.7%. **Ethnic groups:** Sinhalese, Dravidian, Arab mixture. **Languages:** Divehi (Sinhalese dialect). **Religions:** Sunni Moslem.

Geography: Area: 115 sq. mi., twice the size of Washington, D.C. **Location:** In the Indian O. SW of India. **Neighbors:** Nearest is India on N. **Topography:** 19 atolls with 1,087 islands, about 200 inhabited. None of the islands are over 5 sq. mi. in area, and all are nearly flat. **Capital:** Male. **Cities** (1984 est.): Male 37,700.

Government: Type: Republic. **Head of state:** Pres. Maumoon Abdul Gayoom; b. Dec. 29, 1939; in office: Nov. 11, 1978. **Local divisions:** 19 atolls, each with an elected committee and a government-appointed chief.

Economy: Industries: Fish processing, tourism. **Chief crops:** Coconuts, fruit, millet. **Other resources:** Shells. **Fish catch**

1978): 25,800 metric tons. **Electricity prod.** (1982): 8 mln. kwh. **Labor force:** 80% fishing, agriculture, & manufacturing.

Finance: Currency: Rufiyaa (Nov. 1984: 7.57 = $1 US). **Gross national product** (1982): $59 mln. **Per capita income** (1982): $373. **Imports** (1981): $42.6 min.; partners: Sing., Jap., Sri Lan. **Exports** (1982): $14.3 mln.; partners: Jap., Europe. **Tourists** (1983): 74,000.

Transport: Chief ports: Male Atoll.

Communications: Radios: 11,000 licensed (1983). **Telephones in use** (1982): 1,500.

Health: Life expectancy at birth (1984): 46.5 yrs. **Births** (per 1,000 pop. 1977): 40.5. **Deaths** (per 1,000 pop. 1977): 11.8. **Pop. per hospital bed** (1977): 3,500. **Pop. per physician** (1977): 15,555. **Infant morality** (per 1,000 live births 1984): 88.

Education (1984): **Literacy:** 85%. (claimed by govt.). Only 6% of those aged 11-15 attend school.

Major International Organizations: UN and its specialized agencies.

The islands had been a British protectorate since 1887. The country became independent July 26, 1965. Long a sultanate, the Maldives became a republic in 1968. Natural resources and tourism are being developed; however, it remains one of the world's poorest countries.

Mali
Republic of Mali

People: Population (1984 est.): 7,562,000. **Age distrib. (%):** 0–14: 47.9; 15–59: 49.1; 60+: 3.0. **Pop. density:** 16.1 per sq. mi. **Urban** (1983): 16.6%. **Ethnic groups:** Mande (Bambara, Malinke, Sarakolle) 50%, Peul 17%, Voltaic 12%, Songhai, Tuareg, Moors. **Languages:** French (official), Bambara. **Religions:** Moslem 90%.

Geography: Area: 478,841 sq. mi., larger than Texas and California combined. **Location:** In the interior of W. Africa. **Neighbors:** Mauritania, Senegal on W, Guinea, Ivory Coast, Burkina Faso on S, Niger on E, Algeria on N. **Topography:** A landlocked grassy plain in the upper basins of the Senegal and Niger rivers, extending N into the Sahara. **Capital:** Bamako. **Cities** (1984 est.): Bamako (met.) 620,000.

Government: Type: Republic. **Head of state and head of govt.:** Pres. Moussa Traore; b. Sept. 25, 1936; in office: Dec. 6, 1968 (state); Sept. 19, 1969 (govt.) **Local divisions:** 7 regions and a capital district. **Defense:** 2.4% of GDP (1982).

Economy: Chief crops: Millet, rice, peanuts, cotton. **Other resources:** Bauxite, iron, gold. **Arable land:** 2%. **Meat prod.** (1984): lamb: 43,000 metric tons. **Fish catch** (1982): 90,000 metric tons. **Electricity prod.** (1982): 110 mln. kwh. **Labor force:** 73% agric.; 12% ind. & comm.; 16% services.

Finance: Currency: Franc (Mar. 1985: 471.35 = $1 US). **Gross domestic product** (1981): $1.1 bln. **Per capita income** (1981): $140. **Imports** (1980): $417 mln.; partners: Fr. 38% Ivory Coast 19%, Sen. 19%. **Exports** (1980): $176 mln.; partners: Fr. 29%, Ivory Coast 14%, China 12%. **Tourists** (1977): 19,500; receipts: $8 mln. **International reserves less gold** (Feb. 1985): $26 mln. **Gold:** 19,000 oz t.

Transport: Railway traffic (1982): 314 mln. passenger-km; 136 mln. net ton-km. **Motor vehicles:** in use (1982): 20,000 passenger cars, 5,000 comm. vehicles.

Communications: Radios: 95,000 in use (1982). **Telephones in use** (1982): 8,485.

Health: Life expectancy at birth (1975): 39.4 male; 42.5 female. **Births** (per 1,000 pop. 1978): 52. **Deaths** (per 1,000 pop. 1978): 24. **Natural increase** (1978): 2.8%. **Hospital beds** (1980): 3,200. **Physicians** (1980): 337. **Infant mortality** (per 1,000 live births 1984): 152.

Education (1984): **Literacy:** 10%. **Attendance:** 28% under 15 attend school.

Major International Organizations: UN and its specialized agencies, OAU, EC.

Embassy: 2130 R St. NW 20008; 332-2250.

Until the 15th century the area was part of the great Mali Empire. Timbuktu was a center of Islamic study. French rule was secured, 1898. The Sudanese Rep. and Senegal became independent as the Mali Federation June 20, 1960, but Senegal withdrew, and the Sudanese Rep. was renamed Mali.

Mali signed economic agreements with France and, in 1963, with Senegal. In 1968, a coup ended the socialist regime. Famine struck in 1973-74, killing as many as 100,000 people. Drought conditions returned in the 1980s.

Malta

People: Population (1984 est.): 356,000. **Age distrib. (%):** 0–14: 24.6; 15–59: 63.2; 60+: 12.2. **Pop. density:** 2,673 per sq. mi. **Ethnic groups:** Italian, Arab, French. **Languages:** Maltese, English both official. **Religions:** Mainly Roman Catholics.

Geography: Area: 122 sq. mi., twice the size of Washington, D.C. **Location:** In center of Mediterranean Sea. **Neighbors:** Nearest is Italy on N. **Topography:** Island of Malta is 95 sq. mi.; other islands in the group: Gozo, 26 sq. mi., Comino, 1 sq. mi. The coastline is heavily indented. Low hills cover the interior. **Capital:** Valletta. **Cities** (1983 est.): Valletta 14,000; Sliema 20,000.

Government: Type: Republic. **Head of state:** Pres. Agatha Barbara; in office: Feb. 16, 1982. **Head of government:** Prime Min. Carmelo Mifsud Bonnici; in office: Dec. 17, 1984.

Economy: Industries: Textiles, tourism. **Chief crops:** Potatoes, onions, beans. **Arable land:** 44%. **Electricity prod.** (1982): 561.00 mln. kwh. **Labor force:** 27.8% manuf.; 31.4% market services; 21.5% gov.

Finance: Currency: Pound (Mar. 1985: 0.53 = $1 US). **Gross domestic product** (1982): $1.2 bln. **Per capita income** (1978): $2,036. **Imports** (1983): $316 mln.; partners: UK 18%, It. 27%, W. Ger. 14%, U.S. 7%. **Exports** (1983): $156 mln.; partners: W. Ger. 31%, UK 20%, Libya 8%. **Tourists** (1982): receipts: $184 mln. **National budget** (1981): $561 mln. revenues; $562 mln. expenditures. **International reserves less gold** (Mar. 1985): 990 mln. **Gold:** 466,000 oz t. **Consumer prices** (change in 1984): −0.4% .

Transport: Motor vehicles: in use (1982): 69,973 passenger cars, 17,288 comm. vehicles. **Civil aviation** (1982): 644 mln. passenger-km; 3.8 mln. freight ton-km. **Chief ports:** Valletta.

Communications: Television sets: 76,000 licensed (1981). **Radios:** 137,000 in use (1981). **Telephones in use** (1982): 90,997.

Health: Life expectancy at birth (1976): 68.27 male; 73.10 female. **Births** (per 1,000 pop. 1983): 15.0. **Deaths** (per 1,000 pop. 1983): 8.3. **Natural increase** (1983): .6%. **Hospital beds** (per 100,000 pop. 1977): 1,040. **Physicians** (per 100,000 pop. 1977): 127. **Infant mortality** (per 1,000 live births 1980): 15.

Education (1981): **Literacy:** 83%. **Compulsory:** until age 16.

Major International Organizations: UN and its specialized agencies, Commonwealth of Nations.

Embassy: 2017 Connecticut Ave. NW 20008; 462-3611.

Malta was ruled by Phoenicians, Romans, Arabs, Normans, the Knights of Malta, France, and Britain (since 1814). It became independent Sept. 21, 1964. Malta became a republic in 1974. The withdrawal of the last of its sailors, Apr. 1, 1979, ended 179 years of British military presence on the island.

Malta is democratic but nonaligned.

Mauritania
Islamic Republic of Mauritania

People: Population (1984 est.): 1,632,000. **Age distrib. (%):** 0–14: 42.2; 15–59: 49.8; 60+: 13.4. **Pop. density:** 4.2 per sq. mi. **Urban** (1981): 24.4%. **Ethnic groups:** Arab-Berber 80%, Negroes 20%. **Languages:** French (official), Hassanya Arabic (national), Toucouleur, Fula, Sarakole, Wolof. **Religion:** Predominately Moslems.

Geography: Area: 419,229 sq. mi., the size of Texas and California combined. **Location:** In W. Africa. **Neighbors:** Morocco on N, Algeria, Mali on E, Senegal on S. **Topography:** The fertile Senegal R. valley in the S gives way to a wide central region of sandy plains and scrub trees. The N is arid and extends into the Sahara. **Capital:** Nouakchott. **Cities** (1981 est.): Nouakchott 250,000; Nouadhibou 22,000; Kaedi 21,000.

Government: Type: Military republic. **Head of Government:** President & Premier Maaouya Ould Sidi Ahmed Taya; in office:

Apr. 25, 1981. **Local divisions:** 8 regions, one district. **Defense:** 17% of GDP (1983).

Economy: Chief crops: Dates, grain. **Minerals:** Iron, ore, gypsum. **Meat prod.** (1980): beef: 17,000 metric tons; lamb: 12,000 metric tons. **Fish catch** (1983): 312,118 metric tons. **Electricity prod.** (1982): 103 mln. kwh. **Labor force:** 47% agric., 14% ind. & comm., 29% services.

Finance: Currency: Ouguiya (Mar. 1985: 77.51 = $1 US). **Gross domestic product** (1984): $614 mln. **Per capita income** (1984): $466. **Imports** (1984): $382 mln.; partners: Fr. 29%, Sp. 9%. **Exports** (1984): $286 mln.; partners: Fr. 21%, It. 26%, Jap. 20%. **International reserves less gold** (Feb. 1985): $64.9 mln. **Gold:** 12,000 oz t. **Consumer prices** (change in 1984): 7%.

Transport: Motor vehicles: in use (1980): 11,000 passenger cars, 8,000 comm. vehicles. **Chief ports:** Nouakchott, Nouadhibou.

Communications: Radios: 95,000 in use (1983).

Health: Life expectancy at birth (1985): 45 years. **Births** (per 1,000 pop. 1980): 50.2. **Deaths** (per 1,000 pop. 1980): 22.3. **Natural increase** (1980): 2.7%. **Hospital beds** (per 100,000 pop. 1977): 38. **Physicians** (per 100,000 pop. 1977): 7. **Infant mortality** (per 1,000 live births 1985): 138.

Education (1985): **Literacy:** 17%. **Attendance:** 36% in primary school, 4% in secondary school.

Major International Organizations: UN, OAU, Arab League. **Embassy:** 2129 Leroy Pl. NW 20008; 232-5700.

Mauritania became independent Nov. 28, 1960. It annexed the south of former Spanish Sahara in 1976. Saharan guerrillas stepped up attacks in 1977; 8,000 Moroccan troops and French bomber raids aided the government. Mauritania signed a peace treaty with the Polsario Front, 1980, resumed diplomatic relations with Algeria while breaking a defense treaty with Morocco, and renounced sovereignty over its share of former Spanish Sahara. Morocco annexed the territory.

Famine has struck repeatedly during the last decade.

Mauritius

People: Population (1984 est.): 1,018,000. **Age distrib.** (%): 0–14: 36.3; 15–59: 57.2; 60+: 6.4. **Pop. density:** 1,280 per sq. mi. **Urban** (1982): 42.5%. **Ethnic groups:** Indo-Mauritians 68%, Creoles 27%, others. **Languages:** English (official), French, Creole. **Religions:** Hindu 51%, Christian 30%, Moslem 16%.

Geography: Area: 787 sq. mi., smaller than Rhode Island. **Location:** In the Indian O., 500 mi. E of Madagascar. **Neighbors:** Nearest is Madagascar on W. **Topography:** A volcanic island nearly surrounded by coral reefs. A central plateau is encircled by mountain peaks. **Capital:** Port Louis. **Cities** (1982 est.): Port Louis 146,884.

Government: Type: Parliamentary democracy under a constitutional monarch. **Head of state:** Queen Elizabeth II, represented by Gov.-Gen. Sir Seewoosagur Ramgoolam; in office: 1983. **Head of government:** Prime Min. Aneerood Jugnauth; in office: June 12, 1982. **Local divisions:** 9 administrative divisions.

Economy: Industries: Tourism. **Chief crops:** Sugar cane, tea. **Arable land:** 55%. **Electricity prod.** (1982): 362 mln. kwh. **Labor force:** 29% agric. & fishing; 23% ind. and commerce; 28% govt. services.

Finance: Currency: Rupee (Mar. 1985: 15.93 = $1 US). **Gross national product** (1981): $988 mln. **Per capita income** (1981): $1,052. **Imports** (1983): $441 mln.; partners: UK 9%, Fr. 10%, So. Afr. 9%. **Exports** (1983): $367 mln.; partners: UK 53%, Fr. 22%, U.S. 8%. **Tourists** (1982): 118,000; receipts: $47 mln. **National budget** (1981): $450 mln. **International reserves less gold** (Feb. 1985): $24.2 mln. **Gold:** 38,000 oz t. **Consumer prices** (change in 1984): 7.4%.

Transport: Motor vehicles: in use (1982): 25,006 passenger cars, 17,000 comm. vehicles. **Chief ports:** Port Louis.

Communications: Television sets: 92,000 in use (1983). **Radios:** 120,000 in use (1983). **Telephones in use** (1982): 37,812. **Daily newspaper circ.** (1982): 69 per 1,000 pop.

Health: Life expectancy at birth (1982): 69 years. **Births** (per 1,000 pop. 1982): 22.8. **Deaths** (per 1,000 pop. 1982): 6.7. **Natural increase** (1982): 1.6%. **Hospital beds** (1982): 2,862. **Physicians** (1982): 634. **Infant mortality** (per 1,000 live births 1982): 33.

Education (1982): **Literacy:** 61%. **Attendance:** primary school 78%.

Major International Organizations: UN and its specialized agencies, OAU, Commonwealth of Nations.

Embassy: 4301 Connecticut Ave. NW 20008; 244-1491.

Mauritius was uninhabited when settled in 1638 by the Dutch, who introduced sugar cane. France took over in 1721, bringing African slaves. Britain ruled from 1810 to Mar. 12, 1968, bringing Indian workers for the sugar plantations.

The economy has suffered in the 1980s because of low world sugar prices.

Mexico
United Mexican States

People: Population (1984 est.): 77,659,000. **Age distrib.** (%): 0–14: 42.9; 15–59: 52.3; 60+: 5.9. **Pop. density:** 101 per sq. mi. **Urban** (1980): 66%. **Ethnic groups:** Mestizo 55%, American Indian 29%, Caucasian 10%. **Languages:** Spanish. **Religions:** Roman Catholics 97%.

Geography: Area: 761,604 sq. mi., three times the size of Texas. **Location:** In southern N. America. **Neighbors:** U.S. on N, Guatemala, Belize on S. **Topography:** The Sierra Madre Occidental Mts. run NW-SE near the west coast; the Sierra Madre Oriental Mts., run near the Gulf of Mexico. They join S of Mexico City. Between the 2 ranges lies the dry central plateau, 5,000 to 8,000 ft. alt., rising toward the S, with temperate vegetation. Coastal lowlands are tropical. About 45% of land is arid. **Capital:** Mexico City. **Cities** (1980 est.): Mexico City (metro) 15 mln.; Guadalajara (metro) 2.4 mln.; Monterrey (metro) 2 mln.

Government: Type: Federal republic. **Head of state:** Pres. Miguel de la Madrid Hurtado; b. Dec. 12, 1934; in office: Dec. 1, 1982. **Local divisions:** Federal district and 31 states. **Defense:** 0.5% of GNP (1984).

Economy: Industries: Steel, chemicals, electric goods, textiles, rubber, petroleum handicrafts, tourism. **Chief crops:** Cotton, coffee, sugar cane, vegetables, corn. **Minerals:** Silver, lead, zinc, gold, oil, natural gas. **Crude oil reserves** (1982): 72 bln. bbls. **Arable land:** 19%. **Meat prod.** (1983): beef: 780,000 metric tons; pork: 500,000 metric tons; lamb: 38,000 metric tons. **Fish catch** (1982): 1.9 mln. metric tons. **Electricity prod.** (1982): 80.5 bln. kwh. **Crude steel prod.** (1982): 6.9 mln. metric tons. **Labor force:** 41% agric.; 18% manuf.

Finance: Currency: Peso (Mar. 1985: 208.48 = $1 US). **Gross domestic product** (1982): $162 bln. **Per capita income** (1980): $1,800. **Imports** (1984): $11.2 bln.; partners: U.S. 64%, Jap. 5%, W. Ger. 5%. **Exports** (1984): $24.3 bln.; partners: U.S. 55% Spa. 10%. **Tourists** (1981): 4.0 mln.; receipts: $1.7 bln. **National budget** (1981): $93.3 bln. revenues; $93.3 bln. expenditures. **International reserves less gold** (Jan. 1985): $6.9 bln. **Gold:** 2.4 mln. oz t. **Consumer prices** (change in 1984): 65.4%.

Transport: Railway traffic (1982): 5.3 bln. passenger-km; 38.8 bln. net ton-km. **Motor vehicles:** in use (1982): 5.2 mln. passenger cars, 1.8 mln. comm. vehicles; manuf. (1981): 357,000 passenger cars, 171,000 comm. vehicles. **Civil aviation** (1982): 13.4 bln. passenger-km; 118 mln. freight ton-km. **Chief ports:** Veracruz, Tampico, Mazatlan, Coatzacoalcos.

Communications: Television sets: 7.5 mln. in use (1983), 964,000 manuf. (1981). **Radios:** 21 mln. in use (1983), 1.2 mln. manuf. (1980). **Telephones in use** (1982): 5.4 mln. **Daily newspaper circ.** (1982): 130 per 1,000 pop.

Health: Life expectancy at birth (1980): 62.0 male; 67.0 female. **Births** (per 1,000 pop. 1983): 32.7. **Deaths** (per 1,000 pop. 1983): 7.0. **Natural increase** (1983): 2.5%. **Hospital beds** (per 100,000 pop. 1977): 115. **Physicians** (per 100,000 pop. 1977): 57. **Infant mortality** (per 1,000 live births 1983): 53.

Education (1983): **Literacy:** 74%. **Years compulsory:** 10. **Major International Organizations:** UN, OAS. **Embassy:** 2829 16th St. NW 20009; 234-6000.

Mexico was the site of advanced Indian civilizations. The Mayas, an agricultural people, moved up from Yucatan, built immense stone pyramids, invented a calendar. The Toltecs were overcome by the Aztecs, who founded Tenochtitlan 1325 AD, now Mexico City. Hernando Cortes, Spanish conquistador, destroyed the Aztec empire, 1519-1521.

After 3 centuries of Spanish rule the people rose, under Fr. Miguel Hidalgo y Costilla, 1810, Fr. Morelos y Payon, 1812, and Gen. Agustin Iturbide, who made independence effective Sept. 27, 1821, but made himself emperor as Agustin I. A republic was declared in 1823.

Mexican territory extended into the present American Southwest and California until Texas revolted and established a republic in 1836; the Mexican legislature refused recognition but was unable to enforce its authority there. After numerous clashes, the U.S.-Mexican War, 1846-48, resulted in the loss by Mexico of the lands north of the Rio Grande.

French arms supported an Austrian archduke on the throne of Mexico as Maximilian I, 1864-67, but pressure from the U.S. forced France to withdraw. A dictatorial rule by Porfirio Diaz, president 1877-80, 1884-1911, led to fighting by rival forces until the new constitution of Feb. 5, 1917 provided social reform. Since then Mexico has developed large-scale programs of social security, labor protection, and school improvement. A constitutional provision requires management to share profits with labor.

The Institutional Revolutionary Party has been dominant in politics since 1929. Radical opposition, including some guerrilla activity, has been contained by strong measures.

The presidency of Luis Echeverria, 1970-76, was marked by a more leftist foreign policy and domestic rhetoric. Some land redistribution begun in 1976 was reversed under the succeeding administration.

Some gains in agriculture, industry, and social services have been achieved. The land is rich, but the rugged topography and lack of sufficient rainfall are major obstacles. Crops and farm prices are controlled, as are export and import. Economic prospects brightened with the discovery of vast oil reserves, perhaps the world's greatest. But much of the work force is jobless or underemployed.

Inflation and the drop in world oil prices has caused economic problems in the 1980s. The peso was devalued and private banks were nationalized to restore financial stability.

President de la Madrid has urged the U.S. to avoid the use of force to solve differences in Central America. Mexico has friendly relations with Cuba and Nicaragua.

Monaco
Principality of Monaco

People: Population (1984 est.): 28,000. **Age distrib. (%):** 0–14: 12.7; 15–59: 56.3 60+: 30.7. **Ethnic groups:** French 58%, Italian 17%, Monegasque 15%. **Languages:** French (official). **Religions:** Predominantly Roman Catholic.

Geography: Area: 0.73 sq. mi. **Location:** On the NW Mediterranean coast. **Neighbors:** France to W, N, E. **Topography:** Monaco-Ville sits atop a high promontory, the rest of the principality rises from the port up the hillside. **Capital:** Monaco-Ville (1979 est.): 1,700.

Government: Type: Constitutional monarchy. **Head of state:** Prince Rainier III; b. May 31, 1923; in office: May 9, 1949. **Head of government:** Min. of State Jean Herly; in office: July, 1981.

Economy: Industries: Tourism, gambling, chemicals, precision instruments, plastics.

Finance: Currency: French franc or Monégasque franc. **Tourists** (1981): 209,000.

Transport: Chief ports: La Condamine.

Communications: Television sets: 16,000 in use (1976). **Radios:** 7,500 in use (1976). **Telephones in use** (1978): 32,000. **Daily newspaper circ.** (1977): 11,000; 420 per 1,000 pop.

Health: Births (per 1,000 pop. 1980): 20.6. **Deaths** (per 1,000 pop. 1980): 21.1. **Natural increase** (1980): −.5%. **Infant mortality** (per 1,000 live births 1970): 9.3.

Education: (1983): **Literacy:** 80%. **Years compulsory:** 10; attendance 99%.

An independent principality for over 300 years, Monaco has belonged to the House of Grimaldi since 1297 except during the French Revolution. It was placed under the protectorate of Sardinia in 1815, and under that of France, 1861. The Prince of Monaco was an absolute ruler until a 1911 constitution.

Monaco's fame as a tourist resort is widespread. It is noted for its mild climate and magnificent scenery. The area has been extended by land reclamation.

Mongolia
Mongolian People's Republic

People: Population (1984 est.): 1,860,000. **Pop. density:** 2.9 per sq. mi. **Urban** (1982): 45%. **Ethnic groups:** Khalkha Mongols 75%, other Mongols 8%, Kazakhs 5%. **Languages:** Khalkha Mongolian (official, written in Cyrillic letters since 1941), Russian, Chinese. **Religions:** Lama Buddhism prevailed, has been curbed.

Geography: Area: 604,247 sq. mi., more than twice the size of Texas. **Location:** In E Central Asia. **Neighbors:** USSR on N, China on S. **Topography:** Mostly a high plateau with mountains, salt lakes, and vast grasslands. Arid lands in the S are part of the Gobi Desert. **Capital:** Ulaanbaatar. **Cities** (1983 est.): Ulaanbaatar 435,400, Darhan 56,000.

Government: Type: Communist state. **Head of state:** Chmn. Zhambyn Batmunkh; b. May 10, 1926; in office: Aug. 23, 1984. **Head of government:** Premier Dumaagiyn Sodnom; in office: Aug. 23, 1984. **Local divisions:** 18 provinces, 3 autonomous municipalities. **Defense:** 12% of GNP.

Economy: Industries: Food processing, textiles, chemicals, cement. **Chief crops:** Grain. **Minerals:** Coal, tungsten, copper, molybdenum, gold, tin. **Arable land:** 1%. **Meat prod.** (1983): beef: 70,000 metric tons; lamb: 129,000 metric tons. **Electricity prod.** (1982): 1.6 bln. kwh. **Labor force:** 52% agric.; 10% manuf.

Finance: Currency: Tugrik (Nov. 1984: 3.78 = $1 US). **Gross domestic product** (1976 est.): $1.20 bln. **Per capita income** (1976 est.): $750. **Imports** (1982): $1.4 bln.; partners: USSR 91%. **Exports** (1982): $550 mln.; partners: USSR 80%.

Transport: Railway traffic (1982): 297 mln. passenger-km; 3.4 bln. net ton-km.

Communications: Television sets: 65,000 in use (1982). **Radios:** 180,000 in use (1982). **Telephones in use** (1983): 43,000. **Daily newspaper circ.** (1983): 99 per 1,000 pop.

Health: Life expectancy at birth (1979): 63 years. **Births** (per 1,000 pop. 1982): 36.6. **Deaths** (per 1,000 pop. 1982): 9.4. **Natural increase** (1982): 2.7%. **Hospital beds** (per 10,000 pop. 1983): 107. **Physicians** (per 10,000 pop. 1983): 22.

Major International Organizations: UN and its specialized agencies.

Education (1983): **Literacy:** 80%. **Years compulsory:** 7 in major population centers.

One of the world's oldest countries, Mongolia reached the zenith of its power in the 13th century when Genghis Khan and his successors conquered all of China and extended their influence as far W as Hungary and Poland. In later centuries, the empire dissolved and Mongolia came under the suzerainty of China.

With the advent of the 1911 Chinese revolution, Mongolia, with Russian backing, declared its independence. A Mongolian Communist regime was established July 11, 1921.

Mongolia has been changed from a nomadic culture to one of settled agriculture and growing industries with aid from the USSR and East European nations.

Mongolia has sided with the Russians in the Sino-Soviet dispute. A Mongolian-Soviet mutual assistance pact was signed Jan. 15, 1966, and thousands of Soviet troops are based in the country.

Morocco
Kingdom of Morocco

People: Population (1984 est.): 23,565,000. **Age distrib. (%):** 0–14: 46.4; 15–59: 49.2; 60+: 4.2. **Pop. density:** 130.5 per sq. mi. **Urban** (1984): 42%. **Ethnic groups:** Arab-Berber 99%. **Languages:** Arabic (official), with Berber, French, Spanish minorities. **Religions:** Sunni Moslems 99%.

Geography: Area: 171,117 sq. mi., larger than California. **Location:** on NW coast of Africa. **Neighbors:** W. Sahara on S, Algeria on E. **Topography:** Consists of 5 natural regions: mountain ranges (Riff in the N, Middle Atlas, Upper Atlas, and Anti-Atlas); rich plains in the W; alluvial plains in SW; well-cultivated plateaus in the center; a pre-Sahara arid zone extending from SE. **Capital:** Rabat. **Cities** (1982): Casablanca 2,136,000; Rabat 518,000, Fes 448,000.

Government: Type: Constitutional monarchy. **Head of state:** King Hassan II; b. July 9, 1929; in office: Mar. 3, 1961. **Head of government:** Prime Min. Mohammad Karim Lamrani; in office: Nov. 30, 1983. **Local divisions:** 6 prefectures, 35 provinces. **Defense:** 8.8% of GNP (1982).

Economy: Industries: Carpets, clothing, leather goods, tourism. **Chief crops:** Grain, fruits, dates, grapes. **Minerals:** Antimony, cobalt, manganese, phosphates, lead, oil, coal. **Crude oil reserves** (1980): 100 mln. bbls. **Arable land:** 18%. **Meat prod.** (1980): beef: 77,000 metric tons; lamb: 58,000 metric tons. **Fish catch** (1983): 439,000 metric tons. **Electricity prod.** (1982): 5.4 bln. kwh. **Labor force:** 50% agric., 26% services.

Finance: Currency: Dirham (Mar. 1985: 9.70 = $1 US). **Gross domestic product** (1981): $16 bln. **Per capita income** (1981): $800. **Imports** (1983): $3.5 bln.; partners: Fr. 25%, Sp. 7%, Saudi Ar. 15%. **Exports** (1983): $2.0 bln.; partners: Fr. 22%, W. Ger. 7%, Sp. 7%, It. 5%. **Tourists** (1983): 1.2 mln. **National budget** (1981): $6 bln. revenues; $6.6 bln. expenditures. **International reserves less gold** (Jan. 1985): $109 mln. **Gold:** 704,000 oz t. **Consumer prices** (change in 1984): 12.4%.

Transport: Railway traffic (1982): 1.3 bln. passenger-km; 3.8 bln. net ton-km. **Motor vehicles:** in use (1983): 470,000 passenger cars, 232,000 comm. vehicles. **Civil aviation** (1982): 1.8 bln. passenger-km; 38.9 mln. freight ton-km. **Chief ports:** Tangier, Casablanca, Kenitra.

Communications: Television sets: 800,000 licensed (1983). **Radios:** 2.5 mln. licensed (1983). **Telephones in use** (1982): 241,000. **Daily newspaper circ.** (1982): 12 per 1,000 pop.

Health: Life expectancy at birth (1980): 56.1 male; 59.4 female. **Births** (per 1,000 pop. 1978): 43. **Deaths** (per 1,000 pop. 1978): 14. **Natural increase** (1978): 2.9%. **Hospital beds** (1981): 24,453. **Physicians** (1981): 1,153. **Infant mortality** (per 1,000 live births 1980): 114.

Education (1978): **Literacy:** 24%. **Major International Organizations:** UN, OAU, Arab League. **Embassy:** 1601 21st St. NW 20009; 462-7979.

Berbers were the original inhabitants, followed by Carthaginians and Romans. Arabs conquered in 683. In the 11th and 12th centuries, a Berber empire ruled all NW Africa and most of Spain from Morocco.

Part of Morocco came under Spanish rule in the 19th century; France controlled the rest in the early 20th. Tribal uprisings lasted from 1911 to 1933. The country became independent Mar. 2, 1956. Tangier, an internationalized seaport, was turned over to Morocco, 1956. Ifni, a Spanish enclave, was ceded in 1969.

Morocco annexed over 70,000 sq. mi. of phosphate-rich land Apr. 14, 1976, two-thirds of former Spanish Sahara, with the remainder annexed by Mauritania. Spain had withdrawn in February. Polisario, a guerrilla movement, proclaimed the region independent Feb. 27, and launched attacks with Algerian support. Morocco accepted U.S. military and economic aid. When Mauritania signed a treaty with the Polisario Front, and gave up its portion of the former Spanish Sahara, Morocco occupied the area, 1980. Morocco accused Algeria of instigating Polisario attacks.

After years of bitter fighting, Morocco controls the main urban areas, but the Polisario Front's guerrillas move freely in the vast, sparsely populated deserts.

Mozambique
People's Republic of Mozambique

People: Population (1984 est.): 13,413,000. **Age distrib.** (%): 0–14: 45.3; 15–59: 50.6; 60+: 4.1. **Pop. density:** 42.8 per sq. mi. **Ethnic groups:** Bantu tribes. **Languages:** Portuguese (official), Bantu languages predominate. **Religions:** Traditional beliefs 60%, Christians 30%, Moslems 10%.

Geography: Area: 308,650 sq. mi., larger than California. **Location:** On SE coast of Africa. **Neighbors:** Tanzania on N, Malawi, Zambia, Zimbabwe on W, South Africa, Swaziland on S. **Topography:** Coastal lowlands comprise nearly half the country with plateaus rising in steps to the mountains along the western border. **Capital:** Maputo. **Cities:** (1982 est.): Maputo 785,000.

Government: Type: Marxist one-party state. **Head of state:** Pres. Samora Machel; b. Sept. 29, 1933; in office: June 25, 1975. **Local divisions:** 10 provinces. **Defense:** 29% of govt. budget (1982).

Economy: Industries: Cement, alcohol, textiles. **Chief crops:** Cashews, cotton, sugar, copra, tea. **Minerals:** Coal, bauxite. **Arable land:** 4%. **Meat prod.** (1980): beef: 36,000 metric tons; pork: 8,000 metric tons. **Fish catch** (1981): 30,000 metric tons. **Electricity prod.** (1982): 3.4 bln. kwh. **Labor force:** 85% agric., 9% ind. & comm., 2% services.

Finance: Currency: Metical (Nov. 1984: 43.73 = $1 US). **Gross domestic product** (1981): $2.7 bln. **Per capita income** (1980): $220. **Imports** (1981): $737 mln.; partners: So. Afr. 20%, W. Ger. 15%, Port. 10%. **Exports** (1981): $385 mln.; partners: U.S. 27%, Port. 16%, UK 7%, So. Afr. 7%. **National budget** (1982): $611 mln.

Transport: Railway traffic (1983): 570 mln. passenger-km; 1.5 bln. net ton-km. **Motor vehicles:** in use (1981): 49,000 passenger cars, 24,700 comm. vehicles. **Chief ports:** Maputo, Beira, Nacala, Quelimane.

Communications: Television sets: 1,000 in use (1983). **Radios:** 275,000 licensed (1983). **Telephones in use** (1982): 56,000. **Daily newspaper circ.** (1982): 6 per 1,000 pop.

Health: Life expectancy at birth (1982): 47 years. **Births** (per 1,000 pop. 1978): 44. **Deaths** (per 1,000 pop. 1978): 19. **Natural increase** (1978): 3.1%. **Hospital beds** (1980): 13,180. **Physicians** (1980): 823. **Infant mortality** (per 1,000 live births 1982): 115.

Education (1982): **Literacy:** 14%.

The first Portuguese post on the Mozambique coast was established in 1505, on the trade route to the East. Mozambique became independent June 25, 1975, after a ten-year war against Portuguese colonial domination. The 1974 revolution in Portugal paved the way for the orderly transfer of power to Frelimo (Front for the Liberation of Mozambique). Frelimo took over local administration Sept. 20, 1974, over the opposition, in part violent, of some blacks and whites. The new government, led by Maoist Pres. Samora Machel, promised a gradual transition to a communist system. Private schools were closed, rural collective farms organized, and private homes nationalized. Economic problems included the emigration of most of the country's 160,000 whites, a politically untenable economic dependence on white-ruled South Africa, and a large external debt.

In 1984, severe drought caused famine and heavy loss of life.

Nauru
Republic of Nauru

People: Population (1984): 8,000. **Pop density:** 975 per sq. mi. **Ethnic groups:** Nauruans 57%, Pacific Islanders 26%, Chinese 8%, European 8%. **Languages:** Nauruan (official), English. **Religions:** Predominately Christian.

Geography: Area: 8 sq. mi. **Location:** In Western Pacific O. just S of Equator. **Neighbors:** Nearest are Solomon Is. **Topography:** Mostly a plateau bearing high grade phosphate deposits, surrounded by a coral cliff and a sandy shore in concentric rings. **Capital:** Yaren.

Government: Type: Republic. **Head of state:** Pres. Hammer DeRoburt, b. Sept. 25, 1922; in office: May 11, 1978. **Local divisions:** 14 districts.

Economy: Phosphate mining. **Electricity prod.** (1982): 26.00 mln. kwh.

Finance: Currency: Australian dollar. **Gross domestic product** (1981): $155 mln. **Per capita income** (1981): $21,400. **Imports** (1979): $11 mln. **Exports** (1979): $75 mln. **National budget** (1979): $46 mln. revenues; $38 mln. expenditures.

Communications: Radios: 5,000 in use (1983). **Telephones in use** (1980): 1,500.

Health: Births (per 1,000 pop. 1981): 24.0. **Deaths** (per 1,000 pop. 1981): 10.5. **Natural increase** (1981): 1.3%. **Infant mortality** (per 1,000 live births 1981): 31.2.

Education: Literacy 99%; Compulsory ages 6-16.

The island was discovered in 1798 by the British but was formally annexed to the German Empire in 1886. After World War I, Nauru became a League of Nations mandate administered by Australia. During World War II the Japanese occupied the island and shipped 1,200 Nauruans to the fortress island of Truk as slave laborers.

In 1947 Nauru was made a UN trust territory, administered by Australia. Nauru became an independent republic Jan. 31, 1968.

Phosphate exports provide one of the world's highest per capita revenues for the Nauru people. The deposits are expected to be nearly exhausted by 1990.

Nepal
Kingdom of Nepal

People: Population (1984 est.): 16,578,000. **Age distrib.** (%): 0–14: 40.5; 15–59: 53.9; 60+: 5.6. **Pop. density:** 283 per sq. mi. **Urban** (1981): 6.4%. **Ethnic groups:** The many tribes are descendants of Indian, Tibetan, and Central Asian migrants. **Languages:** Nepali (official) (an Indic language), 12 others. **Religions:** Hindus 90%, Buddhists 7%.

Geography: Area: 56,136 sq. mi., the size of North Carolina. **Location:** Astride the Himalaya Mts. **Neighbors:** China on N, India on S. **Topography:** The Himalayas stretch across the N, the hill country with its fertile valleys extends across the center, while the southern border region is part of the flat, subtropical Ganges Plain. **Capital:** Kathmandu. **Cities** (1982 est.): Kathmandu 125,000, Pokhara, Biratnagar, Birganj.

Government: Type: Constitutional monarchy. **Head of state:** King Birendra Bir Bikram Shah Dev; b. Dec. 28, 1945; in office: Jan. 31, 1972. **Head of government:** Prime Min. Lokendra Bahadur Chand; in office: July 12, 1983. **Local divisions:** 14 zones; 75 districts. **Defense:** 4% of govt. budget (1982).

Economy: Industries: Hides, drugs, tourism. **Chief crops:** Jute, rice, grain. **Minerals:** Quartz. **Other resources:** Forests. **Arable land:** 17%. **Meat prod.** (1980): beef: 23,000 metric tons; pork: 5,000 metric tons; lamb: 18,000 metric tons. **Electricity prod.** (1982): 232 mln. kwh. **Labor force:** 93% agric.

Finance: Currency: Rupee (Mar. 1985: 18.10 = $1 US). **Gross domestic product** (1980): $1.99 bln. **Per capita income** (1982): $140. **Imports** (1981): $369 mln.; partners: India 20%, Jap. 15%. **Exports** (1981): $134 mln.; partners: India 14%, W. Ger. 12%. **Tourists** (1981): 162,000; receipts: $52 mln. **National budget** (1982): $539 mln. **International reserves less gold** (Mar. 1985): $84.1 mln. **Gold:** 151,000 oz t. **Consumer prices** (change in 1983): 12.4%.

Communications: Radios: 300,000 in use (1983). **Telephones in use** (1980): 9,000. **Daily newspaper circ.** (1983): 5 per 1,000 pop.

Health: Life expectancy at birth (1980): 44.0 male; 42.5 female. **Births** (per 1,000 pop. 1983): 41.5. **Deaths** (per 1,000 pop. 1983): 18.2. **Natural increase** (1983): 2.3%. **Hospital beds** (1979): 2,586. **Physicians** (1979): 420.

Education (1981): **Literacy:** 20%. **Years compulsory:** 3; Attendance: 71% primary, 14% secondary.

Major International Organizations: UN and its specialized agencies.

Embassy: 2131 Leroy Pl. NW 20008; 667-4550.

Nepal was originally a group of petty principalities, the inhabitants of one of which, the Gurkhas, became dominant about 1769. In 1951 King Tribhubana Bir Bikram, member of the Shah family, ended the system of rule by hereditary premiers of the Ranas family, who had kept the kings virtual prisoners, and established a cabinet system of government.

Virtually closed to the outside world for centuries, Nepal is now linked to India and Pakistan by roads and air service and to Tibet by road. Polygamy, child marriage, and the caste system were officially abolished in 1963.

A wave of protests, 1979, led to a change in premiers.

Netherlands
Kingdom of the Netherlands

People: Population (1984 est.) 14,437,000. **Age distrib.** (%): 0–14: 21.5; 15–44: 46.9; 45+: 31.6. **Pop. density:** 1,094.62 per sq. mi. **Urban** (1983): 88.3%. **Ethnic groups:** Dutch. **Languages:** Dutch. **Religions:** Roman Catholics 36%, Dutch Reformed 27%.

Geography: Area: 16,464 sq. mi., the size of Mass., Conn., and R.I. combined. **Location:** In NW Europe on North Sea. **Topography:** The land is flat, an average alt. of 37 ft. above sea level, with much land below sea level reclaimed and protected by 1,500 miles of dikes. Since 1927 the government has been

draining the IJsselmeer, formerly the Zuider Zee. By 1972, 410,000 of a planned 550,000 acres had been drained and reclaimed. **Capital:** Amsterdam. **Cities** (1983): Amsterdam 687,397; Rotterdam 558,832; Hague 456,886.

Government: Type: Parliamentary democracy under a constitutional monarch. **Head of state:** Queen Beatrix; b. Jan. 31, 1938; in office: Apr. 30, 1980. **Head of government:** Prime Min. Ruud Lubbers; in office: Nov. 4, 1982. **Seat of govt.:** The Hague. **Local divisions:** 11 provinces. **Defense:** 3.2% of GNP (1983).

Economy: Industries: Metals, machinery, chemicals, oil refinery, diamond cutting, electronics, tourism. **Chief crops:** Grains, potatoes, sugar beets, vegetables, fruits, flowers. **Minerals:** Natural gas, oil. **Crude oil reserves** (1980): 60 mln. bbls. **Arable land:** 26%. **Meat prod.** (1984): beef: 510,000 metric tons; pork: 1.3 mln. metric tons; lamb: 10,000 metric tons. **Fish catch** (1981): 399,438 metric tons. **Electricity prod.** (1982): 60.3 bln. kwh. **Crude steel prod.** (1982): 4.3 mln. metric tons. **Labor force:** 6% agric.; 36% ind. and commerce, 34% services, 15% govt.

Finance: Currency: Guilder (June 1985: 3.43 = $1 US). **Gross national product** (1983): $131.2 bln. **Per capita income** (1983): $9,175. **Imports** (1984): $62.3 bln.; partners: W. Ger. 22%, Belg. 11%, U.S. 9%, U.K. 9%. **Exports** (1984): $65.7 bln.; partners: W. Ger. 30%, Belg. 14%, Fr. 10%, UK 9%. **Tourists** (1982): 2.8 mln.; receipts: $1.5 bln. **National budget** (1980): $58.02 bln. revenues; $63.33 bln. expenditures. **International reserves less gold** (Mar. 1985): $8.8 bln. **Gold:** 43.94 mln. oz t. **Consumer prices** (change in 1984): 3.3%.

Transport: Railway traffic (1982): 9.3 bln. passenger-km; 2.8 bln. net ton-km. **Motor vehicles:** in use (1982): 4.6 mln. passenger cars, 317,000 comm. vehicles; manuf. (1978): 62,400 passenger cars; 11,520 comm. vehicles. **Civil aviation** (1982): 16.2 bln. passenger-km; 1 bln. freight ton-km. **Chief ports:** Rotterdam, Amsterdam, IJmuiden.

Communications: Television sets: 4.4 mln. licensed (1983). **Radios:** 4.3 mln. licensed (1981). **Telephones in use** (1982): 5.1 mln. **Daily newspaper circ.** (1982): 325 per 1,000 pop.

Health: Life expectancy at birth (1984): 72 male; 78 female. **Births** (per 1,000 pop. 1982): 12.0. **Deaths** (per 1,000 pop. 1982): 8.2. **Natural increase** (1982): .3%. **Hospital beds** (1983): 69,600. **Physicians** (1983): 28,807. **Infant mortality** (per 1,000 live births 1984): 6.

Education (1984): **Literacy:** 98%. **Years compulsory:** 10; attendance: 100%.

Major International Organizations: UN, NATO.

Embassy: 4200 Linnean Ave. NW 20008; 244-5300.

Julius Caesar conquered the region in 55 BC, when it was inhabited by Celtic and Germanic tribes.

After the empire of Charlemagne fell apart, the Netherlands (Holland, Belgium, Flanders) split among counts, dukes and bishops, passed to Burgundy and thence to Charles V of Spain. His son, Philip II, tried to check the Dutch drive toward political freedom and Protestantism (1568-1573). William the Silent, prince of Orange, led a confederation of the northern provinces, called Estates, in the Union of Utrecht, 1579. The Estates retained individual sovereignty, but were represented jointly in the States-General, a body that had control of foreign affairs and defense. In 1581 they repudiated allegiance to Spain. The rise of the Dutch republic to naval, economic, and artistic eminence came in the 17th century.

The United Dutch Republic ended 1795 when the French formed the Batavian Republic. Napoleon made his brother Louis king of Holland, 1806; Louis abdicated 1810 when Napoleon annexed Holland. In 1813 the French were expelled. In 1815 the Congress of Vienna formed a kingdom of the Netherlands, including Belgium, under William I. In 1830, the Belgians seceded and formed a separate kingdom.

The constitution, promulgated 1814, and subsequently revised, assures a hereditary constitutional monarchy.

The Netherlands maintained its neutrality in World War I, but was invaded and brutally occupied by Germany from 1940 to 1945. After the war, neutrality was abandoned, and the country joined NATO, the Western European Union, the Benelux Union, and, in 1957, became a charter member of the Common Market.

In 1949, after several years of fighting, the Netherlands granted independence to Indonesia, where it had ruled since the 17th century. In 1963, West New Guinea was turned over to In-

donesia, after five years of controversy and seizure of Dutch property in Indonesia.

The independence of former Dutch colonies has instigated mass emigrations to the Netherlands, adding to problems of unemployment.

Though the Netherlands has been heavily industrialized, its productive small farms export large quantities of pork and dairy foods.

Rotterdam, located along the principal mouth of the Rhine, handles the most cargo of any ocean port in the world. Canals, of which there are 3,478 miles, are important in transportation.

Netherlands Antilles

The **Netherlands Antilles**, constitutionally on a level of equality with the Netherlands homeland within the kingdom, consist of 2 groups of islands in the West Indies. **Curacao, Aruba,** and **Bonaire** are near the South American coast; **St. Eustatius, Saba,** and the southern part of **St. Maarten** are SE of Puerto Rico. Northern two-thirds of St. Maarten belong to French Guadeloupe; the French call the island St. Martin. Total area of the 2 groups is 385 sq. mi., including: Aruba 75, Bonaire 111, Curacao 171, St. Eustatius 11, Saba 5, St. Maarten (Dutch part) 13.

Total pop. (est. 1981) was 253,300. Willemstad, on Curacao, is the capital. Chief products are corn, pulse, salt and phosphate; principal industry is the refining of crude oil from Venezuela. Tourism is an important industry, as are electronics and shipbuilding.

New Zealand

People: Population: (1984 est.): 3,238,000. **Age distrib. (%):** 0–14: 26.8; 15–59: 59.1; 60+: 14.1 **Pop. density:** 31.5 per sq. mi. **Urban** (1984): 83.0%. **Ethnic groups:** European (mostly British) 85%, Polynesian (mostly Maori) 8.9%. **Languages:** English (official), Maori. **Religions:** Anglican 29%, Presbyterian 18%, Roman Catholics 15%, others.

Geography: Area: 103,883 sq. mi., the size of Colorado. **Location:** In SW Pacific O. **Neighbors:** Nearest are Australia on W, Fiji, Tonga on N. **Topography:** Each of the 2 main islands (North and South Is.) is mainly hilly and mountainous. The east coasts consist of fertile plains, especially the broad Canterbury Plains on South Is. A volcanic plateau is in center of North Is. South Is. has glaciers and 15 peaks over 10,000 ft. **Capital:** Wellington. **Cities** (1982 cen.): Christchurch 322,000; Auckland 839,000; Wellington 343,000.

Government: Type: Parliamentary. **Head of state:** Queen Elizabeth II, represented by Gov.-Gen. David Stuart Beattie; in office: Nov. 6, 1980. **Head of government:** Prime Min. David Lange; b. Aug. 4, 1942; elected: July 14, 1984. **Local divisions:** 96 counties, 132 boroughs, 3 towns, 4 districts. **Defense:** 1.9% of GNP (1984).

Economy: Industries: Food processing, textiles, machinery, fish, forest prods. **Chief crops:** Grain. **Minerals:** Oil, gas, iron, coal. **Crude oil reserves** (1980): 110 mln. bbls. **Other resources:** Wool, timber. **Arable land:** 78%. **Meat prod.** (1984): beef: 442,000 metric tons; pork: 44,000 metric tons; lamb: 693,000 metric tons. **Fish catch** (1983): 86,000 metric tons. **Electricity prod.** (1982): 23.9 bln. kwh. **Crude steel prod.** (1981): 221,000 metric tons. **Labor force:** 10.3% agric.; 34% ind. and commerce, 55% services and gov.

Finance: Currency: Dollar (Mar. 1985: 1.54 = $1 US). **Gross national product** (1984): $21.4 bln. **Per capita income** (1982): $7,916. **Imports** (1984): $5.7 bln.; partners: Austral. 20%, U.S. 16%, Jap. 17%. **Exports** (1984): $5.5 bln.; partners: UK 14%, U.S. 13%, Jap. 13%, Austral. 15%. **Tourists** (1981): 478,000; receipts $252 mln. **National budget** (1984): $7.5 bln. **International reserves less gold** (Feb. 1985): $1.4 bln. **Gold:** 22,000 oz t. **Consumer prices** (change in 1983): 3.6%.

Transport: Railway traffic (1982): 429 mln. passenger-km; 3.2 bln. net ton-km. **Motor vehicles:** in use (1983): 1.4 mln. passenger cars; 303,000 comm. vehicles; assembled (1978): 51,828 passenger cars; 11,088 comm. vehicles. **Civil aviation:** (1982): 5.8 bln. passenger-km, 229 mln. freight ton-km. **Chief ports:** Auckland, Wellington, Lyttleton, Tauranga.

Communications: Television sets: 921,724 mln. licensed (1983): 90,000 manuf. (1978). **Radios:** 2.7 mln. in use (1983): 143,000 manuf. (1978). **Telephones in use** (1983): 1.9 mln. **Daily newspaper circ.** (1982): 326 per 1,000 pop.

Health: Life expectancy at birth (1982): 70.6 male; 76.6 female. **Births** (per 1,000 pop. 1982): 15.6. **Deaths** (per 1,000 pop. 1982): 8.0 **Natural increase** (1982): .7%. **Hospital beds** (1982): 25,524. **Physicians** (1982): 8,565. **Infant mortality** (per 1,000 live births 1984): 11.3

Education (1984): **Literacy:** 99%. Compulsory ages 6-15; attendance: 100%.

Major International Organizations: UN and its specialized agencies, Commonwealth of Nations, OECD.

Embassy: 37 Observatory Cir. NW 20008; 328-4800.

The Maoris, a Polynesian group from the eastern Pacific, reached New Zealand before and during the 14th century. The first European to sight New Zealand was Dutch navigator Abel Janszoon Tasman, but Maoris refused to allow him to land. British Capt. James Cook explored the coasts, 1769-1770.

British sovereignty was proclaimed in 1840, with organized settlement beginning in the same year. Representative institutions were granted in 1853. Maori Wars ended in 1870 with British victory. The colony became a dominion in 1907, and is an independent member of the Commonwealth.

New Zealand fought on the side of the Allies in both world wars, and signed the ANZUS Treaty of Mutual Security with the U.S. and Australia in 1951. New Zealand's refusal to allow U.S. ships with nuclear weapons to use their port facilities caused a strain on the ANZUS alliance in 1985. New Zealand joined with Australia and Britain in a pact to defend Singapore and Malaysia; New Zealand units are stationed in those 2 countries.

A labor tradition in politics dates back to the 19th century. Private ownership is basic to the economy, but state ownership or regulation affects many industries. Transportation, broadcasting, mining, and forestry are largely state-owned.

The native Maoris number about 250,000. Four of 92 members of the House of Representatives are elected directly by the Maori people.

New Zealand comprises **North Island,** 44,035 sq. mi.; **South Island,** 58,304 sq. mi.; **Stewart Island,** 674 sq. mi.; **Chatham Islands,** 372 sq. mi.

In 1965, the **Cook Islands** (pop. 1983 est., 16,900; area 93 sq. mi.) became self-governing although New Zealand retains responsibility for defense and foreign affairs. **Niue** attained the same status in 1974; it lies 400 mi. to W (pop. 1981 est., 3,400; area 100 sq. mi.). **Tokelau Is.,** (pop. 1981 est., 1,600; area 4 sq. mi.) are 300 mi. N of Samoa.

Ross Dependency, administered by New Zealand since 1923, comprises 160,000 sq. mi. of Antarctic territory.

Nicaragua

Republic of Nicaragua

People: Population (1984 est.): 2,914,000. **Age distrib. (%):** 0–14: 48.1; 15–59: 47.2; 60+: 4.7. **Pop. density:** 63.7 per sq. mi. **Urban** (1983): 55.3%. **Ethnic groups:** Mestizo 69%, Caucasian 17%, Negro 9%, Indian 5%. **Languages:** Spanish, English (on Caribbean coast). **Religions:** Predominantly Roman Catholics.

Geography: Area: 49,291 sq. mi., about the size of Iowa. **Location:** In Central America. **Neighbors:** Honduras on N, Costa Rica on S. **Topography:** Both Atlantic and Pacific coasts are over 200 mi. long. The Cordillera Mtns., with many volcanic peaks, runs NW-SE through the middle of the country. Between this and a volcanic range to the E lie Lakes Managua and Nicaragua. **Capital:** Managua. **Cities** (1981): Managua 819,679.

Government: Head of Government: Daniel Ortega Saavedra; in office Jan. 10, 1985. **Local divisions:** 16 departments; one national district. **Defense:** 13.3% of govt. budget (1980).

Economy: Industries: Oil refining, food processing, chemicals, textiles. **Chief crops:** Bananas, cotton, fruit, yucca, coffee, sugar, corn, beans, cocoa, rice, sesame, tobacco, wheat. **Minerals:** Gold, silver, copper, tungsten. **Other resources:** Forests, shrimp. **Arable land:** 11%. **Meat prod.** (1980): beef: 69,000 metric tons; pork: 11,000 metric tons. **Fish catch:** (1983): 5,900 metric tons. **Electricity prod.** (1982): 1.1 bln. kwh. **Labor force:** 65% agric.

Finance: Currency: Cordoba (Apr. 1985: 10.05 = $1 US). **Gross domestic product** (1983): $3.4 bln. **Per capita income** (1980): $804. **Imports** (1981): $877 mln.; partners (1980): U.S. 27%, Venez. 18%, Costa Rica 13%, Guat. 12%. **Exports**

(1981): $526 mln.; partners (1980): U.S. 39%, W. Ger. 14%, Costa Rica 8%. National budget (1980): $622 mln. expenditures. International reserves less gold (June 1983): $233 mln. Gold: 18,000 oz t. Consumer prices (change in 1984): 35.7%.

Transport: Railway traffic (1983): 16 mln. passenger-miles; 10 mln. net ton-miles. Motor vehicles: in use (1982): 25,000 passenger cars, 7,900 comm. vehicles. Civil aviation (1982): 20 mln. passenger-km; 14 mln. freight ton-km. Chief ports: Corinto, Puerto Somoza, San Juan del Sur.

Communications: Television sets: 127,000 in use (1983). Radios: 700,000 in use (1981). Telephones in use (1982): 51,000 Daily newspaper circ. (1983): 50 per 1,000 pop.

Health: Life expectancy at birth (1982): 56 male; 60 female. Births (per 1,000 pop. 1980): 44.6. Deaths (per 1,000 pop. 1980): 10.6. Natural increase (1980): 3.4%. Hospital beds (1980): 4,573. Physicians (1980): 1,600. Infant mortality (per 1,000 live births 1982): 37.0.

Education (1982): Literacy: 87%. Pop. 5-19: in school: 48%, teachers per 1,000: 13.

Major International Organizations: UN and its specialized agencies, OAS.

Embassy: 1627 New Hampshire Ave. NW 20009; 387-4371.

Nicaragua, inhabited by various Indian tribes, was conquered by Spain in 1552. After gaining independence from Spain, 1821, Nicaragua was united for a short period with Mexico, then with the United Provinces of Central America, finally becoming an independent republic, 1838.

U.S. Marines occupied the country at times in the early 20th century, the last time from 1926 to 1933.

Gen. Anastasio Somoza-Debayle was elected president 1967. He resigned 1972, but was elected president again in 1974. Martial law was imposed in Dec. 1974, after officials were kidnapped by the Marxist Sandinista guerrillas. The country's Roman Catholic bishops charged in 1977 that the government had mistreated civilians in its anti-guerrilla campaign. Violent opposition spread to nearly all classes, 1978; a nationwide strike called against the government Aug. 25 touched off a state of civil war at Matagalpa.

Months of simmering civil war erupted when Sandinist guerrillas invaded Nicaragua May 29, 1979, touching off a 7-week-offensive that culminated in the resignation and exile of Somoza, July 17.

Relations with the U.S. have been strained due to Nicaragua's military aid to leftist guerrillas in El Salvador and the U.S. backing contra rebels.

In 1983, Nicaragua accused the U.S. of aiding anti-Sandinista rebels who were invading from Honduras. The charge sparked a debate in the U.S. Congress over funds for covert aid to the rebels. In 1985, the U.S. House rejected Pres. Reagan's request for military aid to the contras; but in June voted to provide $27 mln. in humanitarian aid.

Nicaragua accused the U.S. CIA of directing the mining of its ports, Apr. 6, 1984. It asked the International Court of Justice in The Hague to order the U.S. to halt the mining and cease aiding attacks on its territory. The Court ruled, May 10, that the U.S. should immediately halt any actions to blockade or mine Nicaragua's ports.

Pres. Ortega visited the USSR and other eastern bloc nations in 1985.

Niger
Republic of Niger

People: Population (1984 est.): 6,284,000. Age distrib. (%): 0–14: 43.0; 15–59: 52.2; 60+: 4.8. Pop. density: 13.1 per sq. mi. Ethnic groups: Hausa 56%, Djerma 22%, Fulani 8%, Tuareg 8%. Languages: French (official), Hausa, Djerma. Religions: Moslems 85%, animists 14%.

Geography: Area: 459,100 sq. mi., almost 3 times the size of California. Location: In the interior of N. Africa. Neighbors: Libya, Algeria on N, Mali, Burkina Faso on W, Benin, Nigeria on S, Chad on E. Topography: Mostly arid desert and mountains. A narrow savanna in the S and the Niger R. basin in the SW contain most of the population. Capital: Niamey. Cities (1984 est.): Niamey 300,000.

Government: Type: Republic. Head of state: Pres. Seyni Kountche; b. 1931; in office: Apr. 15, 1974. Head of government: Premier Hamid Algabid; in office: Nov. 11, 1983. Local

divisions: 7 departments. Defense: 4.3% of govt. budget (1983).

Economy: Chief crops: Peanuts, cotton. Minerals: Uranium. Arable land: 3%. Meat prod. (1980): beef: 37,000 metric tons; lamb: 33,000 metric tons. Electricity prod. (1982): 62 mln. kwh. Labor force: 90% agric.

Finance: Currency: CFA franc (Mar. 1985: 471 = $1 US). Gross domestic product (1982): $2.3 bln. Per capita income (1981) : $475. Imports (1982): $270 mln.; partners: Fr. 36%, Nig. 13%. Exports (1982): $178 mln.; partners: Fr. 36%, Nig. 17%. National budget (1983): $232 mln. International reserves less gold (Jan. 1985): $88.7 mln. Gold: 11,000 oz t. Consumer prices (change in 1984): 8.4%.

Transport: Motor vehicles: in use (1983): 33,000 passenger cars, 5,500 comm. vehicles.

Communications: Radios: 160,000 in use (1982). Telephones in use (1981): 10,000. Daily newspaper cir. (1984): 1 per 1,000 pop.

Health: Life expectancy at birth (1984): 43 years. Births (per 1,000 pop. 1978): 51. Deaths (per 1,000 pop. 1978): 23. Natural increase (1978): 2.8%. Health (1982): 2 hospitals, 36 medical centers. Infant mortality (per 1,000 live births 1984): 139.

Education (1984): Literacy: 8%. Years compulsory: 6; attendance: 15%.

Major International Organizations: UN and specialized agencies, OAU.

Embassy: 2204 R St. NW 20008; 483-4224.

Niger was part of ancient and medieval African empires. European explorers reached the area in the late 18th century. The French colony of Niger was established 1900-22, after the defeat of Tuareg fighters, who had invaded the area from the N a century before. The country became independent Aug. 3, 1960. The next year it signed a bilateral agreement with France retaining close economic and cultural ties, which have continued. Hamani Diori, Niger's first president, was ousted in a 1974 coup. Drought and famine struck in 1973-74, and again in 1975.

Nigeria
Federal Republic of Nigeria

People: Population (1984 est.): 88,148,000. Pop. density: 265 per sq. mi. Ethnic groups: Hausa 21%, Yoruba 20%, Ibo 17%, Fulani 9%, others. Languages: English (official), Hausa, Yoruba, Ibo. Religions: Moslems 47% (in N), Christians 34% (in S), others.

Geography: Area: 356,700 sq. mi., more than twice the size of California. Location: On the S coast of W. Africa. Neighbors: Benin on W, Niger on N, Chad, Cameroon on E. Topography: 4 E-W regions divide Nigeria: a coastal mangrove swamp 10-60 mi. wide, a tropical rain forest 50-100 mi. wide, a plateau of savanna and open woodland, and semidesert in the N. Capital: Lagos. Cities: (1983 est.): Lagos 1,097,000; Ibadan 1,060,000.

Government: Type: Military. Head of state: Gen. Mohammed Buhari; b. Dec. 17, 1942; in office: Dec. 31, 1983. Local divisions: 19 states plus federal capital territory. Defense: 9.3% of govt. budget (1984).

Economy: Industries: Crude oil (95% of export), food processing, assembly of vehicles and other equipment. Chief crops: Cocoa (main export crop), tobacco, palm products, peanuts, cotton, soybeans. Minerals: Oil, gas, coal, iron, limestone, columbium, tin. Crude oil reserves (1980): 17.4 bln. bbls. Other resources: Timber, rubber, hides. Arable land: 34%. Meat prod. (1984): beef: 225,000 metric tons; pork: 48,000 metric tons; lamb: 178,000 metric tons. Fish catch (1983): 511,000 metric tons. Electricity prod. (1982): 7.5 bln. kwh. Labor force: 60% agric., 19% ind., comm. and serv.

Finance: Currency: Naira (Feb. 1985: .53 = $1 US). Gross domestic product (1983): $65 bln. Per capita income (1980): $750. Imports (1983): $13 bln.; partners: U.S., EC. Exports (1983): $11.7 bln.; partners: U.S., EC. Tourist receipts (1981): $55 mln. National budget (1984): $13.4 bln. International reserves less gold (Jan. 1985): $1.2 bln. Gold: 687,000 oz t. Consumer prices (change in 1983): 20%.

Transport: Motor vehicles: in use (1980): 215,000 passenger cars, 33,100 comm. vehicles. Civil aviation (1982): 2.3 bln.

passenger-km; 26.9 mln. freight ton-km. **Chief ports:** Port Harcourt, Lagos, Warri, Calabar.

Communications: Television sets: 450,000 licensed (1982). **Radios:** 5.6 mln. licensed (1982). **Telephones in use** (1980): 154,200. **Daily newspaper circ.** (1982): 15 per 1,000 pop.

Health: Life expectancy at birth (1983): 48.3 male; 51.7 female. **Births** (per 1,000 pop. 1980): 49.5. **Deaths** (per 1,000 pop. 1980): 16. **Natural increase** (1980): 3.3%. **Hospital beds** (per 100,000 pop. 1977): 80. **Physicians** (per 100,000 pop. 1977): 7.

Education (1984): **Literacy:** 25-35%. **Primary school attendance:** 42%.

Major International Organizations: UN and its specialized agencies, OPEC, OAU, Commonwealth of Nations.

Embassy: 2201 M St. NW 20037; 822-1500.

Early cultures in Nigeria date back to at least 700 BC. From the 12th to the 14th centuries, more advanced cultures developed in the Yoruba area, at Ife, and in the north, where Moslem influence prevailed.

Portuguese and British slavers appeared from the 15th-16th centuries. Britain seized Lagos, 1861, during an anti-slave trade campaign, and gradually extended control inland until 1900. Nigeria became independent Oct. 1, 1960, and a republic Oct. 1, 1963.

On May 30, 1967, the Eastern Region seceded, proclaiming itself the Republic of Biafra, plunging the country into civil war. Casualties in the war were est. at over 1 million, including many "Biafrans" (mostly Ibos) who died of starvation despite international efforts to provide relief. The secessionists, after steadily losing ground, capitulated Jan. 12, 1970. Within a few years, the Ibos were reintegrated into national life, but mistrust among the regions persists.

Oil revenues have made possible a massive economic development program, largely using private enterprise, but agriculture has lagged. Oil revenues have declined in the 1980s.

After 13 years of military rule, the nation experienced a peaceful return to civilian government, Oct., 1979.

Nigeria announced that it would expel 2 million illegal immigrants from Ghana, Niger, and other neighboring countries, Feb. 1983. Another 700,000 illegals were ordered to leave in 1985. Military rule returned to Nigeria, Dec. 31, 1983 as a coup ousted the democratically-elected government.

Norway

Kingdom of Norway

People: Population (1984 est.): 4,145,000. **Age distrib. (%):** 0–14: 23.5; 15–59: 57.2; 60+: 19.6. **Pop. density:** 33 per sq. mi. **Urban** (1981): 70%. **Ethnic groups:** Germanic (Nordic, Alpine, Baltic), minority Lapps. **Languages:** Norwegian (official), Lapp. **Religions:** Lutherans 97%.

Geography: Area: 125,057 sq. mi., slightly larger than New Mexico. **Location:** Occupies the W part of Scandinavian peninsula in NW Europe (extends farther north than any European land). **Neighbors:** Sweden, Finland, USSR on E. **Topography:** A highly indented coast is lined with tens of thousands of islands. Mountains and plateaus cover most of the country, which is only 25% forested. **Capital:** Oslo. **Cities** (1983): Oslo 448,775; Bergen 207,292.

Government: Type: Hereditary constitutional monarchy. **Head of state:** King Olav V, b. July 2, 1903; in office: Sept. 21, 1957. **Head of government:** Prime Min. Kåre Isaachsen Willoch, b. Oct. 3, 1928; in office: Oct. 14, 1981. **Local divisions:** Oslo, Svalbard and 18 fylker (counties). **Defense:** 3.1% of GNP (1984).

Economy: Industries: Paper, shipbuilding, engineering, metals, chemicals, food processing oil, gas. **Chief crops:** Grains, potatoes, fruits. **Minerals:** Oil, copper, pyrites, nickel, iron, zinc, lead. **Crude oil reserves** (1980): 5.75 bln. bbls. **Other resources:** Timber. **Cultivated land:** 3%. **Meat prod.** (1984): beef: 74,000 metric tons; pork: 83,000 metric tons; lamb: 25,000 metric tons. **Fish catch** (1982): 2.4 mln. metric tons. **Electricity prod.** (1983): 106.2 bln. kwh. **Crude steel prod.** (1982): 767,000 metric tons. **Labor force:** 8% agric.; 20% ind., 32% services, 29% govt.

Finance: Currency: Kroner (Mar. 1985: 8.88 = $1 US). **Gross national product** (1982): $56 bln. **Per capita income** (1980): $12,432. **Imports** (1984): $13.8 bln.; partners: Swed.

17%, W. Ger. 16%, UK 12%, U.S. 9%. **Exports** (1984): $18.9 bln.; partners: UK 37%, W. Ger. 20%, Swed. 9%. **Tourists** (1982): receipts: $815 mln. **National budget** (1984): $24 bln. expenditures. **International reserves less gold** (Mar. 1985): $10.3 bln. **Gold:** 1.18 mln. oz t. **Consumer prices** (change in 1984): 6.3%.

Transport: Railway traffic (1983): 2.2 bln. passenger-km; 2.5 bln. net ton-km. **Motor vehicles:** in use (1983): 1.3 mln. passenger cars, 180,000 comm. vehicles. **Civil aviation:** (1982): 4.1 bln. passenger-km; 139 mln. net ton-km. **Chief ports:** Bergen, Stavanger, Oslo, Tonsberg.

Communications: Television sets: 1.2 mln. licensed (1983). **Radios:** 1.5 mln. in use (1983) **Telephones in use** (1983): 2.2 mln. **Daily newspaper circ.** (1982): 479 per 1,000 pop.

Health: Life expectancy at birth (1984): 72.5 male; 79.7 female. **Births** (per 1,000 pop. 1983): 12.0. **Deaths** (per 1,000 pop. 1983): 10.2. **Natural increase** (1983): .1%. **Hospital beds** (1981): 67,384. **Physicians** (1981): 9,329. **Infant mortality** (per 1,000 live births 1984): 7.5.

Education (1984): **Literacy:** 100%. **Years Compulsory:** 9.

Major International Organizations: UN and its specialized agencies, NATO, OECD.

Embassy: 2720 34th St. NW 20008; 333-6000.

The first supreme ruler of Norway was Harald the Fairhaired who came to power in 872 AD. Between 800 and 1000, Norway's Vikings raided and occupied widely dispersed parts of Europe.

The country was united with Denmark 1381-1814, and with Sweden, 1814-1905. In 1905, the country became independent with Prince Charles of Denmark as king.

Norway remained neutral during World War I. Germany attacked Norway Apr. 9, 1940, and held it until liberation May 8, 1945. The country abandoned its neutrality after the war, and joined the NATO alliance. Norway rejected membership in the Common Market in a 1972 referendum.

Abundant hydroelectric resources provided the base for Norway's industrialization, producing one of the highest living standards in the world.

Norway's merchant marine is one of the world's largest.

Norway and the Soviet Union have disputed their territorial waters boundary in the Barents Sea, north of the 2 countries' common border.

Petroleum output from oil and mineral deposits under the continental shelf has raised state revenues.

Svalbard is a group of mountainous islands in the Arctic O., c. 23,957 sq. mi., pop. varying seasonally from 1,500 to 3,600. The largest, Spitsbergen (formerly called West Spitsbergen), 15,060 sq. mi., seat of governor, is about 370 mi. N of Norway. By a treaty signed in Paris, 1920, major European powers recognized the sovereignty of Norway, which incorporated it in 1925. Both Norway and the USSR mine rich coal deposits. Mt. Newton (Spitsbergen) is 5,633 ft. tall.

Oman

Sultanate of Oman

People: Population (1984 est.): 1,009,000. **Pop. density:** 8.7 per sq. mi. **Ethnic groups:** Arab 88%, Baluchi 4%, Persian 3%, Indian 2%, African 2%. **Languages:** Arabic (official), English, Urdu, others. **Religions:** Ibadhi Moslems 75%, Sunni Moslems.

Geography: Area: 120,000 sq. mi., about the size of New Mexico. **Location:** On SE coast of Arabian peninsula. **Neighbors:** United Arab Emirates, Saudi Arabia, South Yemen on W. **Topography:** Oman has a narrow coastal plain up to 10 mi. wide, a range of barren mountains reaching 9,900 ft., and a wide, stony, mostly waterless plateau, avg. alt. 1,000 ft. Also the tip of the Ruus-al-Jebal peninsula controls access to the Persian Gulf. **Capital:** Muscat. **Cities** (1982 est.): Muscat 85,000.

Government: Type: Absolute monarchy. **Head of state:** Sultan Qabus bin Said; b. Nov. 18, 1942; in office: July 23, 1970. **Local divisions:** 1 province, numerous districts. **Defense:** 28% of GNP (1982).

Economy: Chief crops: Dates, fruits vegetables, wheat, bananas. **Minerals:** Oil (95% of exports). **Crude oil reserves** (1984): 2.9 bln. bbls. **Fish catch** (1982): 89,000 metric tons. **Electricity prod.** (1983): 1.3 bln. kwh. **Labor force:** 66% agric.

Finance: Currency: Rial Omani (Mar. 1985: .34 = $1 US). **Gross national product** (1982): $6.4 bln. **Per capita income**

(1978): $2,400. **Imports** (1982): $2.7 bln.; partners: Jap. 21%, UAE 14%, UK 14%. **Exports** (1982): $4.4 bln.; partners: Jap. 52%, Europe 30%. **National budget** (1983): $4.8 bln. revenues; $4.8 bln. expenditures. **International reserves less gold** (Mar. 1985): $743 mln. **Gold:** 288,000 oz t.
Transport: Chief ports: Matrah, Muscat.
Communications: Telephones in use (1982): 20,000.
Health: (1982): 14 hospitals, 12 health centers, 60 clinics.
Education (1983): **Literacy:** 20%. **Attendance:** 60% primary, 10% secondary.
Major International Organizations: UN and its specialized agencies, Arab League, OPEC.
Embassy: 2342 Massachusetts Ave. NW 20008; 387-1980.

A long history of rule by other lands, including Portugal in the 16th century, ended with the ouster of the Persians in 1744. By the early 19th century, Muscat and Oman was one of the most important countries in the region, controlling much of the Persian and Pakistan coasts, and ruling far-away Zanzibar, which was separated in 1861 under British mediation.

British influence was confirmed in a 1951 treaty, and Britain helped suppress an uprising by traditionally rebellious interior tribes against control by Muscat in the 1950s. Enclaves on the Pakistan coast were sold to that country in 1958.

On July 23, 1970, Sultan Said bin Taimur was overthrown by his son. The new sultan changed the nation's name to Sultanate of Oman. He launched a domestic development program, and battled leftist rebels in the southern Dhofar area to their defeat, Dec. 1975.

Oil has been the major source of income. Oman has close political ties to the U.S.

Pakistan

Islamic Republic of Pakistan

People: Population (1984 est.): 96,628,000. **Pop. density:** 298 per sq. mi. **Urban** (1981): 28.2%. **Ethnic groups:** Punjabi 66%, Sindhi 13%, Pushtun (Iranian) 8.5%, Urdu 7.6%, Baluchi 2.5%, others. **Languages:** Urdu, English are both official. **Religions:** Muslim 97%.
Geography: Area: 310,524 sq. mi., larger than Texas. **Location:** In W part of South Asia. **Neighbors:** Iran on W, Afghanistan, China on N, India on E. **Topography:** The Indus R. rises in the Hindu Kush and Himalaya mtns. in the N (highest is K2, or Godwin Austen, 28,250 ft., 2d highest in world), then flows over 1,000 mi. through fertile valley and empties into Arabian Sea. Thar Desert, Eastern Plains flank Indus Valley. **Capital:** Islamabad. **Cities** (1981 cen.): Karachi 5.1 mln.; Lahore 2.9 mln.; Faisalabad 1 mln.; Hyderabad 795,000; Rawalpindi 928,000.
Government: Type: Martial law regime. **Head of government:** Pres. Mohammad Zia ul-Haq; b. 1924; in office: July 5, 1977. **Head of state:** Muhammad Khan Junejo; in office: Mar. 24, 1985. **Local divisions:** Federal capital, 4 provinces, tribal areas. **Defense:** 6.1% of GNP (1982).
Economy: Industries: Textiles, food processing, chemicals, tobacco, **Chief crops:** Rice, wheat. **Minerals:** Natural gas, iron ore. **Crude oil reserves** (1980): 200 mln. bbls. **Other resources:** Wool. **Arable land:** 26%. **Meat prod.** (1984): beef: 470,000 metric tons; lamb: 420,000 metric tons. **Fish catch** (1982): 337,000 metric tons. **Electricity prod.** (1982): 18.0 bln. kwh. **Labor force:** 55% agric.; 20% ind.
Finance: Currency: Rupee (Mar. 1985: 15.90 = $1 US). **Gross domestic product** (1980): $31.6 bln. **Per capita income** (1980): $280. **Imports** (1984): $5.8 bln.; partners: Sau. Ar. 15%, Jap. 12%, U.S. 9%, Kuwait 10%. **Exports** (1984): $2.5 bln.; partners: China 6%, Jap. 8%, U.S. 7%. **National budget** (1984): $7.2 bln. **International reserves less gold** (Mar. 1985): $934 mln. **Gold:** 1.86 mln. oz t. **Consumer prices** (change in 1984): 7.1%.
Transport: Railway traffic (1982): 17.0 bln. passenger-km; 7.2 bln. net ton-km. **Motor vehicles:** in use (1983): 197,000 passenger cars, 82,000 comm. vehicles. **Civil aviation** (1982): 6.2 bln. passenger-km; 230.4 mln. freight ton-km. **Chief ports:** Karachi.
Communications: Television sets: 800,000 in use (1981). **Radios:** 5.5 mln. in use (1981). **Telephones in use** (1982): 393,000. **Daily newspaper circ.** (1982): 24 per 1,000 pop.
Health: Life expectancy at birth (1983): 54.4 male; 54.2 female. **Births** (per 1,000 pop. 1983): 42.5. **Deaths** (per 1,000 pop. 1983): 15. **Natural increase** 1983): 2.7%. **Hospital beds**

(1983): 52,161. **Physicians** (1983): 33,584. **Infant mortality** (per 1,000 live births 1983): 119.
Education (1984): **Literacy:** 24%.
Major International Organizations: UN and its specialized agencies.
Embassy: 2315 Massachusetts Ave. NW 20008; 939-6200.

Present-day Pakistan shares the 5,000-year history of the India-Pakistan sub-continent. At present day Harappa and Mohenjo Daro, the Indus Valley Civilization, with large cities and elaborate irrigation systems, flourished c. 4,000-2,500 BC.

Aryan invaders from the NW conquered the region around 1,500 BC, forging a Hindu civilization that dominated Pakistan as well as India for 2,000 years.

Beginning with the Persians in the 6th century BC, and continuing with Alexander the Great and with the Sassanians, successive nations to the west ruled or influenced Pakistan, eventually separating the area from the Indian cultural sphere.

The first Arab invasion, 712 AD, introduced Islam. Under the Mogul empire (1526-1857), Moslems ruled most of India, yielding to British encroachment and resurgent Hindus.

After World War I the Moslems of British India began agitation for minority rights in elections. Mohammad Ali Jinnah (1876-1948) was the principal architect of Pakistan. A leader of the Moslem League from 1916, he worked for dominion status for India; from 1940 he advocated a separate Moslem state.

When the British withdrew Aug. 14, 1947, the Islamic majority areas of India acquired self-government as Pakistan, with dominion status in the Commonwealth. Pakistan was divided into 2 sections, West Pakistan and East Pakistan. The 2 areas were nearly 1,000 mi. apart on opposite sides of India.

Pakistan became a republic in 1956. Pakistan had a National Assembly (legislature) with equal membership from East and West Pakistan, and 2 Provincial Assemblies. In Oct. 1958, Gen. Mohammad Ayub Khan took power in a coup. He was elected president in 1960, reelected in 1965.

As a member of the Central Treaty Organization, Pakistan had been aligned with the West. Following clashes between India and China in 1962, Pakistan made commercial and aid agreements with China.

Ayub resigned Mar. 25, 1969, after several months of violent rioting and unrest, most of it in East Pakistan, which demanded autonomy. The government was turned over to Gen. Agha Mohammad Yahya Khan and martial law was declared.

The Awami League, which sought regional autonomy for East Pakistan, won a majority in Dec. 1970 elections to a National Assembly which was to write a new constitution. In March, 1971 Yahya postponed the Assembly. Rioting and strikes broke out in the East.

On Mar. 25, 1971, government troops launched attacks in the East. The Easterners, aided by India, proclaimed the independent nation of Bangladesh. In months of widespread fighting, countless thousands were killed. Some 10 million Easterners fled into India.

Full scale war between India and Pakistan had spread to both the East and West fronts by December 3. Pakistan troops in the East surrendered Dec. 16; Pakistan agreed to a cease-fire in the West Dec. 17. On July 3, 1972, Pakistan and India signed a pact agreeing to withdraw troops from their borders and seek peaceful solutions to all problems. Diplomatic relations were resumed in 1976.

Zulfikar Ali Bhutto, leader of the Pakistan People's party, which had won the most West Pakistan votes in the Dec. 1970 elections, became president Dec. 20.

Bhutto was overthrown in a military coup July, 1977. Convicted of complicity in a 1974 political murder, Bhutto was executed Apr.4, 1979.

In June 1981, the U.S., pressured by the Soviet threat in Afghanistan, agreed to a six-year economic and military aid program with Pakistan. There are some 2 million Afghan refugees now in Pakistan.

Panama

Republic of Panama

People: Population (1984 est.): 2,101,000. **Age distrib. (%):** 0–14: 31.6; 15–59: 57.2; 60+: 11.1. **Pop. density:** 70.2 per sq. mi. **Urban** (1980): 49.3%. **Ethnic groups:** Mestizo 70%, West Indian 14%, Caucasian 10%, Indian 6%. **Languages:** Spanish (official), English. **Religions:** Roman Catholics 93%, Protestants.

Geography: Area: 29,762 sq. mi., slightly larger than West Virginia. **Location:** In Central America. **Neighbors:** Costa Rica on W., Colombia on E. **Topography:** 2 mountain ranges run the length of the isthmus. Tropical rain forests cover the Caribbean coast and eastern Panama. **Capital:** Panama. **Cities** (1981 est.): Panama 655,000; Colon 117,000.

Government: Type: Centralized republic. **Head of state and head of government:** Pres. Nicholas Ardito-Barletta; b. Aug. 21, 1938; in office: Oct. 11, 1984. **Local divisions:** 9 provinces, 1 territory. **Defense:** 0.8% of GNP (1982).

Economy: Industries: Oil refining, international banking. **Chief crops:** Bananas, pineapples, cocoa, corn, coconuts, sugar. **Minerals:** Copper. **Other resources:** Forests (mahogany), shrimp. **Arable land:** 24%. **Meat prod.** (1980): beef: 52,000 metric tons; pork: 7,000 metric tons. **Fish catch** (1982): 91,144 metric tons. **Electricity prod.** (1982): 2.7 bln. kwh. **Labor force:** 29% agric., 29.4% ind. and commerce.

Finance: Currency: Balboa (Apr. 1985: 1.00 = $1 US). **Gross domestic product** (1983): $4.1 bln. **Per capita income** (1978): $1,116. **Imports** (1981): $1.5 bln.; partners: U.S. 35%, Saudi Ar. 8%. **Exports** (1981): $315 mln.; partners: U.S. 51%, W. Ger. 5%. **Tourists** (1982): $169 mln. receipts. **National budget** (1982): $2.8 bln. **International reserves less gold** (Jan. 1985): $147 mln. **Consumer prices** (change in 1984): 1.6%.

Transport: Motor vehicles: in use (1982): 104,000 passenger cars, 35,000 comm. vehicles. **Civil aviation** (1982): 400 mln. passenger-km; 15 mln. net ton-km. **Chief ports:** Balboa, Cristobal.

Communications: Television sets: 226,000 in use (1983). **Radios:** 290,000 in use (1983). **Telephones in use** (1982): 212,000. **Daily newspaper circ.** (1982): 95 per 1,000 pop.

Health: Life expectancy at birth (1980): 68.0 male; 72.0 female. **Births** (per 1,000 pop. 1982): 25.5. **Deaths** (per 1,000 pop. 1982): 3.8. **Natural increase** (1982): 2.1%. **Hospital beds** (per 100,000 pop. 1977): 386. **Physicians** (per 100,000 pop. 1977): 78. **Infant mortality** (per 1,000 live births 1981): 29.

Education (1982): **Literacy:** 85%. **Primary school attendance:** 93%.

Major International Organizations: UN and its specialized agencies.

Embassy: 2862 McGill Terrace NW 20008; 483-1407.

The coast of Panama was sighted by Rodrigo de Bastidas, sailing with Columbus for Spain in 1501, and was visited by Columbus in 1502. Vasco Nunez de Balboa crossed the isthmus and "discovered" the Pacific O. Sept. 13, 1513. Spanish colonies were ravaged by Francis Drake, 1572-95, and Henry Morgan, 1668-71. Morgan destroyed the old city of Panama which had been founded in 1519. Freed from Spain, Panama joined Colombia in 1821.

Panama declared its independence from Colombia Nov. 3, 1903, with U.S. recognition. U.S. naval forces deterred action by Colombia. On Nov. 18, 1903, Panama granted use, occupation and control of the Canal Zone to the U.S. by treaty, ratified Feb. 26, 1904. *(See also Panama Canal.)*

Rioting began Jan. 9, 1964, in a dispute over the flying of the U.S. and Panamanian flags and terms of the 1903 treaty.

New treaties were proposed in 1967 and 1974. In 1977, the U.S. and Panama initialed two treaties that would provide for a gradual takeover by Panama of the canal, and withdrawal of U.S. troops, to be completed by 1999. U.S. payments would be substantially increased in the interim. The permanent neutrality of the canal would also be guaranteed. The treaties were ratified by the U.S. Senate in 1978.

Due to easy Panama ship regulations and strictures in the U.S., merchant tonnage registered in Panama since World War II ranks high in size. Similarly easy financial regulations have made Panama a center for international banking.

Papua New Guinea

People: Population (1984 est.): 3,353,000. **Age distrib.** (%): 0–14: 43.8; 15–59: 50.3; 60+: 11.4. **Pop. density:** 18.2 per sq. mi. **Urban** (1980): 13.1%. **Ethnic groups:** Papuans (in S and interior), Melanesian (N,E), pygmies, minorities of Chinese, Australians, Polynesians. **Languages:** Melanesian Pidgin, Police Motu, English, numerous local languages. **Religions:** Protestant 63%, Roman Catholic 31%, local religions.

Geography: Area: 178,704 sq. mi., slightly larger than California. **Location:** Occupies eastern half of island of New Guinea.

Neighbors: Indonesia (West Irian) on W, Australia on S. **Topography:** Thickly forested mtns. cover much of the center of the country, with lowlands along the coasts. Included are some of the nearby islands of Bismarck and Solomon groups, including Admiralty Is., New Ireland, New Britain, and Bougainville. **Capital:** Port Moresby. **Cities** (1984 est.): Port Moresby 144,000.

Government: Type: Parliamentary democracy. **Head of state:** Queen Elizabeth II, represented by Gov. Gen. Sir Kingsford Dibela; in office: Mar. 1, 1983. **Head of government:** Prime Min. Michael Somare; b. 1936; in office: Aug. 2, 1982. **Local divisions:** National capital and 19 provinces with elected legislatures. **Defense:** approx. 1% of GDP (1982).

Economy: Chief crops: Coffee, coconuts, cocoa. **Minerals:** Gold, copper, silver, gas. **Arable land:** 1%. **Meat prod.** (1980): pork: 22,000 metric tons. **Fish catch** (1982): 26,000 metric tons. **Electricity prod.** (1982): 1.2 bln. kwh. **Labor force:** 75% agric., 8% ind. and commerce, 2% services.

Finance: Currency: Kina (Mar. 1985: 1.02 = $1 US). **Gross domestic product** (1981): $1.9 bln. **Per capita income** (1976): $480. **Imports** (1982): $1.08 bln.; partners: Austral. 41%, Jap. 14%, Sing. 15%. **Exports** (1982): $816 mln.; partners: Jap. 33%, W. Ger. 25%, Austral. 8%. **National budget** (1983): 853 mln. **International reserves less gold** (Mar. 1985): $417 mln. **Gold:** 63,000 oz t. **Consumer prices** (change in 1983): 7.9%.

Transport: Motor vehicles: in use (1981): 17,700 passenger cars, 24,400 comm. vehicles. **Chief ports:** Port Moresby, Lae.

Communications: Telephones in use (1982): 50,000. **Daily newspaper circ.** (1983) 8 per 1,000 pop.

Health: Life expectancy at birth (1984): 49 yrs. **Births** (per 1,000 pop. 1983): 39. **Deaths** (per 1,000 pop. 1983): 17. **Natural increase** (1980): 2.2%. **Hospital beds** (per 100,000 pop. 1977): 469. **Physicians** (per 100,000 pop. 1977): 7.

Education (1984): **Literacy:** 25%. **Attendance:** 63% primary school; 13% secondary school.

Major International Organizations: UN and its specialized agencies, Commonwealth of Nations.

Embassy: 1800 K St. NW 20006.

Human remains have been found in the interior of New Guinea dating back at least 10,000 years and possibly much earlier. Successive waves of peoples probably entered the country from Asia through Indonesia. Europeans visited in the 15th century, but land claims did not begin until the 19th century, when the Dutch took control of the western half of the island.

The southern half of eastern New Guinea was first claimed by Britain in 1884, and transferred to Australia in 1905. The northern half was claimed by Germany in 1884, but captured in World War I by Australia, which was granted a League of Nations mandate and then a UN trusteeship over the area. The 2 territories were administered jointly after 1949, given self-government Dec. 1, 1973, and became independent Sept. 16, 1975.

The indigenous population consists of a huge number of tribes, many living in almost complete isolation with mutually unintelligible languages.

Paraguay
Republic of Paraguay

People: Population (1984 est.): 3,623,000. **Age distrib.** (%): 0–14: 41.0; 15–59: 52.0; 60+: 7.0. **Pop. density:** 19.8 per sq. mi. **Urban** (1982): 42.2%. **Ethnic groups:** Mestizos 95%, small Caucasian, Indian, Negro minorities. **Languages:** Spanish (official), Guarani (used by 90%). **Religions:** Roman Catholic (official) 97%.

Geography: Area: 157,047 sq. mi., the size of California. **Location:** One of the 2 landlocked countries of S. America. **Neighbors:** Bolivia on N, Argentina on S, Brazil on E. **Topography:** Paraguay R. bisects the country. To E are fertile plains, wooded slopes, grasslands. To W is the Chaco plain, with marshes and scrub trees. Extreme W is arid. **Capital:** Asunción. **Cities** (1984 cen.): Asunción 570,000.

Government: Type: Constitutional republic with powerful executive branch. **Head of state:** Pres. Alfredo Stroessner; b. Nov. 3, 1912; in office: Aug. 15, 1954. **Local divisions:** 19 departments. **Defense:** 14.4% of govt. budget (1984).

Economy: Industries: Food processing, wood products, textiles, cement. **Chief crops:** Corn, wheat, cotton, beans, peanuts, tobacco, citrus fruits, yerba mate. **Minerals:** Iron, manganese, limestone. **Other resources:** Forests. **Arable land:** 2%. **Meat**

prod. (1980): beef: 110,000 metric tons; pork: 79,000 metric tons. **Electricity prod.** (1981): 1 bln. kwh. **Labor force:** 44% agric., 34% ind. and commerce, 18% services.

Finance: Currency: Guarani (Mar. 1985 240.00 = $1 US). **Gross domestic product** (1983): $5.6 bln. **Per capita income** (1983): $1,614. **Imports** (1983): $570 mln.; partners: Braz. 20%, Arg. 19%, U.S. 8%. **Exports** (1983): $251 mln.; partners: Arg. 18%, W. Ger. 13%, Braz. 25%. **Tourists** (1982): 178,454. **National budget** (1984): $300 mln. **International reserves less gold** (Mar. 1985): $497 mln. **Gold:** 35,000 oz t. **Consumer prices** (change in 1984): 20.3%.

Transport: Railway traffic (1978): 23 mln. passenger-km; 17 mln. net ton-km. **Motor vehicles:** in use (1982): 35,000 passenger cars, 26,000 comm. vehicles. **Civil aviation** (1982): 479 mln. passenger-km; 2.9 mln. net ton-km. **Chief ports:** Asuncion.

Communications: Television sets: 81,000 in use (1983). **Radios:** 198,000 in use (1983). **Telephones in use** (1981): 58,713. **Daily newspaper circ.** (1982): 78 per 100,000 pop.

Health: Life expectancy at birth (1984): 63 yrs. **Births** (per 1,000 pop. 1978): 34. **Deaths** (per 1,000 pop. 1978): 7. **Natural increase** (1978): 2.5%. **Hospital beds** (per 100,000 pop. 1977): 135. **Physicians** (per 100,000 pop. 1977): 77. **Infant mortality** (per 1,000 live births 1982): 64.

Education (1984): **Literacy:** 83%. **Years compulsory:** 7; **Attendance:** 83%.

Major International Organizations: UN and its specialized agencies, OAS.

Embassy: 2400 Massachusetts Ave. NW 20008; 483-6960.

The Guarani Indians were settled farmers speaking a common language before the arrival of Europeans.

Visited by Sebastian Cabot in 1527 and settled as a Spanish possession in 1535, Paraguay gained its independence from Spain in 1811. It lost much of its territory to Brazil, Uruguay, and Argentina in the War of the Triple Alliance, 1865-1870. Large areas were won from Bolivia in the Chaco War, 1932-35.

Gen. Alfredo Stroessner has ruled since 1954. Suppression of the opposition and decimation of small Indian groups has been charged by international rights groups.

Peru
Republic of Peru

People: Population (1984 est.): 19,157,000. **Age distrib. (%):** 0–14: 41.4; 15–59: 54.4; 60+: 4.2. **Pop. density:** 38.7 per sq. mi. **Urban** (1981): 72.6%. **Ethnic groups:** Indians 45%, Mestizos 37%, Caucasians 15%, blacks, Asians. **Languages:** Spanish, Quechua both official; Aymara; 30% speak no Spanish. **Religions:** Roman Catholics over 90%.

Geography: Area: 496,222 sq. mi., five-sixths the size of Alaska. **Location:** On the Pacific coast of S. America. **Neighbors:** Ecuador, Colombia on N, Brazil, Bolivia on E, Chile on S. **Topography:** An arid coastal strip, 10 to 100 mi. wide, supports much of the population thanks to widespread irrigation. The Andes cover 27% of land area. The uplands are well-watered, as are the eastern slopes reaching the Amazon basin, which covers half the country with its forests and jungles. **Capital:** Lima. **Cities** (1981 cen.): Lima 4,164,597.

Government: Type: Constitutional republic. **Head of state:** Pres. Alan Garcia Perez; in office: July 28, 1985. **Head of government:** Prime Min. Luis Roca Percovich; in office: Oct. 10, 1984. **Local divisions:** 24 departments, 1 province. **Defense:** 5% of GDP (1983).

Economy: Industries: Fish meal, steel, cement. **Chief crops:** Cotton, sugar, coffee, corn. **Minerals:** Copper, lead, molybdenum, silver, zinc, iron, oil. **Crude oil reserves** (1983): 696 mln. bbls. **Other resources:** Wool, sardines. **Arable land:** 3%. **Meat prod.** (1984): beef: 90,000 metric tons; pork: 75,000 metric tons; lamb: 27,000 metric tons. **Fish catch** (1981): 2.7 mln. metric tons. **Electricity prod.** (1982): 10.4 bln. kwh. **Crude steel prod.** (1981): 359,000 metric tons. **Labor force:** 40% agric.; 19% ind. and mining; 41% govt. and other services.

Finance: Currency: Sol (Mar. 1985: 8,245 = $1 US). **Gross domestic product** (1983): $15.9 bln. **Per capita income** (1979): $655. **Imports** (1984): $2.2 bln.; partners: U.S. 33%, W. Ger. 7%. **Exports** (1984): $3.1 bln.; partners: U.S. 33%, Jap. 15%. **Tourists** (1981): 336,000. **National budget** (1984): $4.3 bln. **International reserves less gold** (Jan. 1985): $1.5 bln.

Gold: 1.39 mln. oz t. **Consumer prices** (change in 1984): 110%.

Transport: Railway traffic (1982): 424 mln. passenger-km; 518 mln. net ton-km. **Motor vehicles:** in use (1982): 359,000 passenger cars, 196,000 comm. vehicles. **Civil aviation** (1982): 1.6 bln. passenger-km; 94.3 mln. net ton-km. **Chief ports:** Callao, Chimbate, Mollendo.

Communications: Television sets: 1.2 mln. in use (1982). **Radios:** 2.2 mln. in use (1982). **Telephones in use** (1982): 130,000. **Daily newspaper circ.** (1982): 118 per 1,000 pop.

Health: Life expectancy at birth (1983): 56.7 male; 59.7 female. **Births** (per 1,000 pop. 1982): 35.4. **Deaths** (per 1,000 pop. 1982): 10.8. **Natural increase** (1982): 2.5%. **Hospital beds** (per 100,000 pop. 1977): 184. **Physicians** (per 100,000 pop. 1977): 64. **Infant mortality** (per 1,000 live births 1985): 80.

Education (1978): **Literacy:** 72%. **Years compulsory:** 10.

Major International Organizations: UN and its specialized agencies, OAS.

Embassy: 1700 Massachusetts Ave. NW 20036; 833-9860.

The powerful Inca empire had its seat at Cuzco in the Andes covering most of Peru, Bolivia, and Ecuador, as well as parts of Colombia, Chile, and Argentina. Building on the achievements of 800 years of Andean civilization, the Incas had a high level of skill in architecture, engineering, textiles, and social organization.

A civil war had weakened the empire when Francisco Pizarro, Spanish conquistador, began raiding Peru for its wealth, 1532. In 1533 he had the seized ruling Inca, Atahualpa, fill a room with gold as a ransom, then executed him and enslaved the natives.

Lima was the seat of Spanish viceroys until the Argentine liberator, Jose de San Martin, captured it in 1821; Spain was defeated by Simon Bolivar and Antonio J. de Sucre; recognized Peruvian independence, 1824. Chile defeated Peru and Bolivia, 1879-84, and took Tarapaca, Tacna, and Arica; returned Tacna, 1929.

On Oct. 3, 1968, a military coup ousted Pres. Fernando Belaunde Terry. In 1968-74, the military government put through sweeping agrarian changes, and nationalized oil, mining, fishmeal, and banking industries.

Food shortages, escalating foreign debt, and strikes led to another coup, Aug. 29, 1976, and to a slowdown of socialist programs.

After 12 years of military rule, Peru returned to democratic leadership under former Pres. Fernando Belaunde Terry, July 1980. The new government encouraged the return of private enterprise to stimulate the inflation-ridden economy.

Fighting again erupted, Jan. 28, 1981, in the ongoing border dispute between Peru and Ecuador. The border was reopened in April. There was a wave of terrorist bombings during 1981, including the U.S. embassy in August. Terrorist activity, mostly by Maoist groups, continued in 1983 and 1984.

In 1984, there were strikes by farmers, Mar. 1–3, and by the 4 major labor unions, Mar. 22, to protest the government's economic policies.

Philippines
Republic of the Philippines

People: Population (1984 est.): 55,528,000. **Age distrib. (%):** 0–14: 42.9; 15–59: 52.5; 60+: 4.6. **Pop. density:** 459 per sq. mi. **Urban** (1970): 31.8%. **Ethnic groups:** Malays the large majority, Chinese, Americans, Spanish are minorities. **Languages:** Pilipino (based on Tagalog), English both official; numerous others spoken. **Religions:** Roman Catholics 83%, Protestants 9%, Moslems 5%.

Geography: Area: 115,831 sq. mi., slightly larger than Nevada. **Location:** An archipelago off the SE coast of Asia. **Neighbors:** Nearest are Malaysia, Indonesia on S, Taiwan on N. **Topography:** The country consists of some 7,100 islands stretching 1,100 mi. N-S. About 95% of area and population are on 11 largest islands, which are mountainous, except for the heavily indented coastlines and for the central plain on Luzon. **Capital:** Quezon City (Manila is de facto capital). **Cities** (1981 est.): Manila 1.6 mln.; Quezon City 1.1 mln.; Davao 611,311.

Government: Type: Republic. **Head of state:** Pres. Ferdinand E. Marcos; b. Sept. 11, 1917; in office: Dec. 30, 1965 (pres.), Jan. 17, 1973 (premier). **Head of govt:** Prime Min. Cesar Virata; b. Dec. 12, 1930; in office: Apr. 8, 1981. **Local divi-**

sions: 13 regions, 73 provinces, 60 cities. Defense: 2.1% of GNP (1983).

Economy: Industries: Food processing, textiles, clothing, drugs, wood prods., appliances. Chief crops: Sugar, rice, corn, pineapple, coconut. Minerals: Cobalt, copper, gold, nickel, silver, iron, petroleum. Crude oil reserves (1980): 25 mln. bbls. Other resources: Forests (42% of area). Arable land: 34%. Meat prod. (1984): beef: 118,000 metric tons; pork: 483,000 metric tons. Fish catch (1981): 1.7 mln. metric tons. Electricity prod. (1982): 17.6 bln. kwh. Crude steel prod. (1981 est.): 350,000 metric tons. Labor force: 47% agric., 20% ind. and comm., 13% services.

Finance: Currency: Peso (Mar. 1985: 18.46 = $1 US). Gross national product (1982): $39.2 bln. Per capita income (1982): $772. Imports (1984): $6.3 bln.; partners: U.S. 22%, Jap. 23%, Saudi Ar. 12%. Exports (1984): $5.2 bln.; partners: U.S. 31%, Jap. 23%. Tourists (1981): 939,000; receipts: $344 mln. National budget (1982): $72 bln. International reserves less gold (Mar. 1985): $278 mln. Gold: 947,000 oz t. Consumer prices (change in 1984): 50.3%.

Transport: Railway traffic (1982): 209 mln. passenger-km; 22 mln. net ton-km. Motor vehicles: in use (1980): 465,000 passenger cars, 294,800 comm. vehicles. Civil aviation (1982): 7.3 bln. passenger-km; 187 mln. freight ton-km. Chief ports: Cebu, Manila, Iloilo, Davao.

Communications: Television sets: 955,000 in use (1983). Radios: 2.1 mln. in use (1983). Telephones in use (1982): 732,000. Daily newspaper circ. (1982): 52 per 1,000 pop.

Health: Life expectancy at birth (1983): 63.0 male; 66.5 female. Births (per 1,000 pop. 1983): 32. Deaths (per 1,000 pop. 1983): 6.8. Natural increase (1983): 2.5%. Hospital beds (1982): 80,465. Physicians (1981): 43,736. Infant mortality (per 1,000 live births 1983): 50.

Education (1983): Literacy: 88%. Attendance: 95% in elementary, 57% secondary.

Major International Organizations: UN and its specialized agencies, ASEAN.

Embassy: 1617 Massachusetts Ave. NW 20036; 483-1414

The Malay peoples of the Philippine islands, whose ancestors probably migrated from Southeast Asia, were mostly hunters, fishers, and unsettled cultivators when first visited by Europeans.

The archipelago was visited by Magellan, 1521. The Spanish founded Manila, 1571. The islands, named for King Philip II of Spain, were ceded by Spain to the U.S. for $20 million, 1898, following the Spanish-American War. U.S. troops suppressed a guerrilla uprising in a brutal 6-year war, 1899-1905.

Japan attacked the Philippines Dec. 8, 1941 (Far Eastern time). Japan occupied the islands during WW II.

On July 4, 1946, independence was proclaimed in accordance with an act passed by the U.S. Congress in 1934. A republic was established.

A rebellion by Communist-led Huk guerrillas was put down by 1954. But urban and rural political violence periodically reappears.

The Philippines and the U.S. have treaties for U.S. military and naval bases and a mutual defense treaty. Riots by radical youth groups and terrorism by leftist guerrillas and outlaws, increased from 1970. On Sept. 21, 1972, Marcos declared martial law. Ruling by decree, he ordered some land reform and stabilized prices. But opposition was suppressed, and a high population growth rate aggravated poverty and unemployment. Political corruption was believed to be widespread. On Jan. 17, 1973, Marcos proclaimed a new constitution with himself as president. His wife received wide powers in 1978 to supervise planning and development.

Martial law was lifted Jan. 17, 1981. Marcos turned over legislative power to the National Assembly, released political prisoners, and said he would no longer rule by decree. He was elected to a new 6-year term as president, June, with 88% of the vote.

The assassination of prominent opposition leader Benigno S. Aquino Jr, Aug. 21, 1983, sparked demonstrations calling for the resignation of Marcos. An independent commission appointed by Marcos concluded that a military conspiracy was responsible for Aquino's death. The May 1984 elections saw Marcos retain his majority in the National Assembly although opponents made a strong showing in key areas like Manila.

Government troops battled Moslem (Moro) secessionists, 1973-76, in southern Mindanao. Fighting resumed, 1977, after a Libyan-mediated agreement on autonomy was rejected by the region's mainly Christian voters.

The archipelago has a coastline of 10,850 mi. Manila Bay, with an area of 770 sq. mi., and a circumference of 120 mi., is the finest harbor in the Far East.

All natural resources of the Philippines belong to the state; their exploitation is limited to citizens of the Philippines or corporations of which 60% of the capital is owned by citizens.

Poland
Polish People's Republic

People: Population (1984 est.): 36,887,000. Age distrib. (%): 0–14: 23.9; 15–59: 62.7; 60+: 13.5. Pop. density: 308 per sq. mi. Urban (1983): 59.5%. Ethnic groups: Polish 98%, Germans, Ukrainians, Byelorussians. Language: Polish. Religions: Roman Catholic 95%.

Geography: Area: 120,727 sq. mi. Location: On the Baltic Sea in E Central Europe. Neighbors: E. Germany on W, Czechoslovakia on S, USSR (Lithuania, Byelorussia, Ukraine) on E. Topography: Mostly lowlands forming part of the Northern European Plain. The Carpathian Mts. along the southern border rise to 8,200 ft. Capital: Warsaw. Cities (1982): Warsaw 1.6 mln., Lodz 845,000, Cracow 723,000, Wroclaw 627,000, Poznan 563,000.

Government: Type: Communist. Head of state: Chairman, council of state: Henryk Jablonski, b. Dec. 27, 1909; in office: Mar. 28, 1972. Head of government: Premier Wojciech Jaruzelski; in office: Oct. 18, 1981. Local divisions: 49 provinces. Defense: 4.9% of govt. budget (1982).

Economy: Industries: Shipbuilding, chemicals, metals, autos, food processing. Chief crops: Grains, potatoes, sugar beets, tobacco, flax. Minerals: Coal, copper, zinc, silver, zinc, sulphur, natural gas. Arable land: 49%. Meat prod. (1984): beef: 700,000 metric tons; pork: 1.2 mln. metric tons; lamb: 17,000 metric tons. Fish catch (1982): 582,000 metric tons. Electricity prod. (1982): 117 bln. kwh. Crude steel prod. (1982): 14.4 mln. metric tons. Labor force: 27% agric.; 41% manuf.

Finance: Currency: Zloty (Nov. 1984: 125 = $1 US). Gross national product (1982): $170 bln. Per capita income (1982): $4,670. Imports (1982): $4.6 bln.; partners: USSR 38%, E. Ger. 7% W. Ger. 7% Czech. 5%. Exports (1982): $4.9 bln.; partners: USSR 30%, E. Ger. 6%, Czech. 6%, W. Ger. 10%. National budget (1982): 19.1 mln. Tourists (1982): 1.4 mln. Consumer prices (change in 1982): 100%.

Transport: Railway traffic (1982): 48.9 bln. passenger-km; 112.6 bln. net ton-km. Motor vehicles: in use (1982): 2.8 mln. passenger cars, 615,000 comm. vehicles; manuf. (1982): 229,000 passenger cars; 47,000 comm. vehicles. Civil aviation (1982): 778 mln. passenger-km; 6.4 mln. freight ton-km. Chief ports: Gdansk, Gdynia, Szczecin.

Communications: Television sets: 8.3 mln. licensed (1983), 972,000 manuf. (1978). Radios: 8.8 mln. licensed (1983), 2.5 mln. manuf. (1978). Telephones in use (1982): 3.6 mln. Daily newspaper circ. (1982): 287 per 1,000 pop.

Health: Life expectancy at birth (1980): 66 male; 74.4 female. Births (per 1,000 pop. 1982): 19.4. Deaths (per 1,000 pop. 1982): 9.2. Natural increase (1982): 1.0%. Hospital beds (1982): 240,000. Physicians (1982): 66,848. Infant mortality (per 1,000 live births 1982): 20.2.

Education (1983): Literacy: 98%. Years compulsory: 8; attendance 98%.

Major International Organizations: UN and its specialized agencies, Warsaw Pact.

Embassy: 2640 16th St. NW 20009; 234-3800.

Slavic tribes in the area were converted to Latin Christianity in the 10th century. Poland was a great power from the 14th to the 17th centuries. In 3 partitions (1772, 1793, 1795) it was apportioned among Prussia, Russia, and Austria. Overrun by the Austro-German armies in World War I, its independence, self-declared on Nov.11, 1918, was recognized by the Treaty of Versailles, June 28, 1919. Large territories to the east were taken in a war with Russia, 1921.

Nazi Germany and the USSR invaded Poland Sept. 1-27, 1939, and divided the country. During the war, some 6 million Polish citizens were killed by the Nazis, half of them Jews. With Germany's defeat, a Polish government-in-exile in London was recognized by the U.S., but the USSR pressed the claims of a

rival group. The election of 1947 was completely dominated by the Communists.

In compensation for 69,860 sq. mi. ceded to the USSR, 1945, Poland received approx. 40,000 sq. mi. of German territory E of the Oder-Neisse line comprising Silesia, Pomerania, West Prussia, and part of East Prussia.

In 12 years of rule by Stalinists, large estates were abolished, industries nationalized, schools secularized, and Roman Catholic prelates jailed. Farm production fell off. Harsh working conditions caused a riot in Poznan June 28-29, 1956.

A new Politburo, committed to development of a more independent Polish Communism, was named Oct. 1956, with Wladyslaw Gomulka as first secretary of the Communist Party. Collectivization of farms was ended and many collectives were abolished.

In Dec. 1970 workers in port cities rioted because of price rises and new incentive wage rules. On Dec. 20 Gomulka resigned as party leader; he was succeeded by Edward Gierek; the incentive rules were dropped, price rises were revoked.

Poland was the first Communist state to get most-favored nation trade terms from the U.S.

A law promulgated Feb. 13, 1953, required government consent to high Roman Catholic church appointments. In 1956 Gomulka agreed to permit religious liberty and religious publications, provided the church kept out of politics. In 1961 religious studies in public schools were halted. Government relations with the Church improved in the 1970s. The number of priests and churches was greater in 1971 than in 1939.

After 2 months of labor turmoil had crippled the country, the Polish government, Aug. 30, 1980, met the demands of striking workers at the Lenin Shipyard, Gdansk. Among the 21 concessions granted were the right to form independent trade unions and the right to strike — unprecedented political developments in the Soviet bloc. By 1981, 9.5 mln. workers had joined the independent trade union (Solidarity). Farmers won official recognition for their independent trade union in May. Solidarity leaders proposed, Dec. 12, a nationwide referendum on establishing a non-Communist government if the government failed to agree to a series of demands which included access to the mass media and free and democratic elections to local councils in the provinces.

Spurred by the fear of Soviet intervention, the government, Dec. 13, imposed martial law. Public gatherings, demonstrations, and strikes were banned and an internal and external blackout was imposed. Solidarity leaders called for a nationwide strike, but there were only scattered work stoppages. Lech Walesa and other Solidarity leaders were arrested. The U.S. imposed economic sanctions which were lifted when martial law was suspended December 1982.

In 1983 there were demonstrations outside the Lenin Shipyards in March, and antigovernment protests in some 20 cities in May. Pope John Paul II visited his homeland in June.

A government directive ordering the removal of crucifixes from public schools and hospitals sparked student demonstrations in the Mietno region, March 1984.

Portugal
Republic of Portugal

People: Population (1984 est.): 10,045,000. **Age distrib. (%):** 0–14: 27.9; 15–59: 57.9; 60+: 14.3. **Pop. density:** 277 per sq. mi. **Ethnic groups:** Homogeneous Mediterranean stock with small African minority. **Languages:** Portuguese. **Religions:** Roman Catholics 97%.

Geography: Area: 36,390 sq. mi., slightly smaller than Indiana. **Location:** At SW extreme of Europe. **Neighbors:** Spain on N, E. **Topography:** Portugal N of Tajus R, which bisects the country NE-SW, is mountainous, cool and rainy. To the S there are drier, rolling plains, and a warm climate. **Capital:** Lisbon. **Cities** (1981 est.): Lisbon 812,400.

Government: Type: Parliamentary democracy. **Head of state:** Pres. Antonio das Santos Ramalho Eanes; b. Jan. 25, 1935; in office: July 14, 1976. **Head of government:** Prime Min. Mario Soares; b. Dec. 7, 1924; in office: June 9, 1983. **Local divisions:** 18 districts, 2 autonomous regions, one dependency. **Defense:** 3% of GNP (1983).

Economy: Industries: Textiles, footwear, cork, chemicals, fish canning, wine, paper. **Chief crops:** Grains, potatoes, rice, grapes, olives, fruits. **Minerals:** Tungsten, uranium, iron. **Other**

resources: Forests (world leader in cork production). **Arable land:** 39%. **Meat prod.** (1984): beef: 102,000 metric tons; pork: 180,000 metric tons; lamb: 25,000 metric tons. **Fish catch** (1982): 253,000 metric tons. **Electricity prod.** (1982): 14.6 bln. kwh. **Crude steel prod.** (1982): 362,000 metric tons. **Labor force:** 24% agric.; 31% ind. and comm.; 44% services and govt.

Finance: Currency: Escudo (Mar. 1985: 171.32 = $1 US). **Gross domestic product** (1984): $19.4 bln. **Per capita income** (1984): $1,930. **Imports** (1984): $7.3 bln.; partners: W. Ger. 12%, U.S. 11%, UK 8%, Fr. 9%. **Exports** (1984): $5.2 bln.; partners: UK 15%, W. Ger. 13%, Fr. 13%, U.S. 6%. **Tourists** (1982): 3.0 mln. **National budget** (1985): $6.2 bln. expenditures. **International reserves less gold** (Jan. 1985): $568 mln. **Gold:** 20.28 mln. oz t. **Consumer prices** (change in 1984): 28.9%.

Transport: Railway traffic (1982): 5.4 bln. passenger-km; 1.0 bln. net ton-km. **Motor vehicles:** in use (1980): 1.2 mln. passenger cars, 186,100 comm. vehicles. **Civil aviation** (1982): 4.1 bln. passenger-km; 106.7 mln. freight ton-km. **Chief ports:** Lisbon, Setubal, Leixoes.

Communications: Television sets: 1.4 mln. licensed (1983). **Radios:** 2.1 licensed (1983). **Telephones in use** (1982): 1.4 mln. **Daily newspaper circ.** (1982): 74 per 1,000 pop.

Health: Life expectancy at birth (1980): 66 male; 74 female. **Births** (per 1,000 pop. 1981): 15.7. **Deaths** (per 1,000 pop. 1981): 9.9. **Natural increase** (1981): .5%. **Hospital beds** (per 100,000 pop. 1977): 528. **Physicians** (per 100,000 pop. 1977): 142. **Infant mortality** (per 1,000 live births 1985): 39.

Education (1985): **Literacy:** 80%, **Years compulsory:** 6; attendance 60%.

Major International Organizations: UN and its specialized agencies, NATO, EFTA, OECD.

Embassy: 2125 Kalorama Rd. NW 20008; 265-1643.

Portugal, an independent state since the 12th century, was a kingdom until a revolution in 1910 drove out King Manoel II and a republic was proclaimed.

From 1932 a strong, repressive government was headed by Premier Antonio de Oliveira Salazar. Illness forced his retirement in Sept. 1968; he was succeeded by Marcello Caetano.

On Apr. 25, 1974, the government was seized by a military junta led by Gen. Antonio de Spinola, who was named president.

The new government reached agreements providing independence for Guinea-Bissau, Mozambique, Cape Verde Islands, Angola, and Sao Tome and Principe. Spinola resigned Sept. 30, 1974, in face of increasing pressure from leftist officers. Despite a 64% victory for democratic parties in April 1975, the Soviet-supported Communist party increased its influence. Banks, insurance companies, and other industries were nationalized. A countercoup in November halted this trend. After years of turmoil the economy and political life were in disarray, despite aid from the U.S. and West European countries.

Azores Islands, in the Atlantic, 740 mi. W. of Portugal, have an area of 888 sq. mi. and a pop. (1975) of 292,000. A 1951 agreement gave the U.S. the rights to use defense facilities in the Azores. The **Madeira Islands,** 350 mi. off the NW coast of Africa, have an area of 307 sq. mi. and a pop. (1976) of 270,000. Both groups were offered partial autonomy in 1976.

Macao, area of 6 sq. mi., is an enclave, a peninsula and 2 small islands, at the mouth of the Canton R. in China. Portugal granted broad autonomy in 1976. Pop. (1984 est.): 400,000.

Qatar
State of Qatar

People: Population (1984 est.): 276,000. **Pop. density:** 62.7 per sq. mi. **Ethnic groups:** Arabs 40%, Pakistani 18%, Indian 18%, Iranian 10%, others. **Languages:** Arabic (official), English. **Religions:** Moslems 95%.

Geography: Area: 4,247 sq. mi., smaller than Connecticut. **Location:** Occupies peninsula on W coast of Persian Gulf. **Neighbors:** Saudi Arabia on W, United Arab Emirates on S. **Topography:** Mostly a flat desert, with some limestone ridges, vegetation of any kind is scarce. **Capital:** Doha. **Cities** (1985 est.): Doha 190,000.

Government: Type: Traditional emirate. **Head of state and head of government:** Khalifah ibn Hamad ath-Thani; b. 1932; in office: Feb. 22, 1972 (amir), 1970 (prime min.) **Defense:** 25% of govt. budget (1983).

Economy: Crude oil reserves (1984): 3.3 mln. bbls. **Arable land:** 2.9%. **Electricity prod.** (1982): 2.7 bln. kwh. **Crude steel prod.** (1981 est.): 469,000 metric tons. **Labor force:** 10% agric., 70% ind., services and commerce.

Finance: Currency: Riyal (Mar. 1985: 3.64 = $1 US). **Gross domestic product** (1982 est.): $7.8 bln. **Per capita income** (1982): $35,000. **Imports** (1982): $1.9 bln.; partners: Jap. 20%, UK 16%, U.S. 11%. **Exports** (1982): $4.5 bln.; partners: Neth. 11%, Jap. 35%, Fr. 13%. **National budget** (1983): $3.7 bln. expenditures.

Transport: Chief ports: Doha, Musayid.

Communications: Radios: 75,000 in use (1983). **Telephones in use** (1982): 67,500.

Health: Life expectancy at birth (1985): 57.5 years. **Hospital beds** (per 100,000 pop. 1977): 389. **Physicians** (per 100,000 pop. 1977): 105.

Education (1985): **Literacy:** 60%. **Compulsory:** ages 6-16; attendance: 98%.

Major International Organizations: UN and its specialized agencies, Arab League, OPEC.

Embassy: 600 New Hampshire Ave. NW 20037; 338-0111.

Qatar was under Bahrain's control until the Ottoman Turks took power, 1872 to 1915. In a treaty signed 1916, Qatar gave Great Britain responsibility for its defense and foreign relations. After Britain announced it would remove its military forces from the Persian Gulf area by the end of 1971, Qatar sought a federation with other British protected States in the area; this failed and Qatar declared itself independent, Sept. 1 1971.

Oil revenues give Qatar a per capita income among the highest in the world, but lack of skilled labor hampers development plans.

Romania
Socialist Republic of Romania

People: Population (1984 est.): 22,683,000. **Age distrib.** (%): 0–14: 25.4; 15–59; 60.5; 60+: 14.2. **Pop. density:** 246 per sq. mi. **Urban** (1982): 49.6%. **Ethnic groups:** Romanians 88.1%, Hungarians 7.9%, Germans 1.6%. **Languages:** Romanian, Hungarian, German. **Religions:** Orthodox 80%, Roman Catholics 6%.

Geography: Area: 91,699 sq. mi., slightly smaller than New York and Pennsylvania combined. **Location:** In SE Europe on the Black Sea. **Neighbors:** USSR on E (Moldavia) and N (Ukraine), Hungary, Yugoslavia on W, Bulgaria on S. **Topography:** The Carpathian Mts. encase the north-central Transylvanian plateau. There are wide plains S and E of the mountains, through which flow the lower reaches of the rivers of the Danube system. **Capital:** Bucharest. **Cities** (1982): Bucharest 1,979,076, Brasov 334,136, Timisoara 301,612, Constanta 306,879.

Government: Type: Communist. **Head of state:** Pres. Nicolae Ceausescu; b. Jan. 26, 1918; in office; Dec. 9, 1967. **Head of government:** Prime Min. Constantin Dascalescu; in office; May 21, 1982. **Head of Communist Party:** Pres. Nicolae Ceausescu; in office: Mar. 23, 1965. **Local divisions:** Bucharest and 40 counties. **Defense:** 4.6% of GNP (1982).

Economy: Industries: Steel, metals, machinery, oil products, chemicals, textiles, shoes, tourism. **Chief crops:** Corn, wheat, oilseeds, potatoes. **Minerals:** Oil, gas, coal. **Other resources:** Timber. **Arable land:** 45%. **Meat prod.** (1984): beef: 198,000 metric tons; pork: 840,000 metric tons; lamb: 70,000 metric tons. **Fish catch** (1978): 137,700 metric tons. **Electricity prod.** (1982): 68.9 bln. kwh. **Crude steel prod.** (1983): 13.6 mln. metric tons. **Labor force:** 28% agric.; 44% ind. and commerce.

Finance: Currency: Leu (Mar. 1985: 17.99 = $1 US). **Gross domestic product** (1980): $116 bln. **Per capita income** (1980): $5,250. **Imports** (1982): $10.5 bln.; partners: USSR 18%, W. Ger. 6%, U.S. 8%, Iran 7%. **Exports** (1982): $11.5 bln.; partners: USSR 18%, W. Ger. 7%. **Tourists** (1983): 6 mln. **National budget** (1979): $76 mln. revenues; $75 mln. expenditures. **International reserves less gold** (Dec. 1984): $605 mln. **Gold:** 3.72 mln. oz t.

Transport: Railway traffic (1983): 25.7 bln. passenger-km; 73.3 bln. net ton-km. **Motor vehicles:** in use (1980): 250,000 passenger cars; 130,000 comm. vehicles. **Civil aviation** (1983): 2.3 bln. passenger-km; 39 mln. freight ton-km. **Chief ports:** Constanta, Galati, Braila.

Communications: Television sets: 3.8 mln. licensed (1983). **Radios:** 3.2 mln. licensed (1983). **Telephones in use** (1981): 1.6 mln. **Daily newspaper circ.** (1982): 181 per 1,000 pop.

Health: Life expectancy at birth (1982): 67.4 male; 72.4 female. **Births** (per 1,000 pop. 1982): 15.3. **Deaths** (per 1,000 pop. 1982): 10. **Natural increase** (1982): 5.3%. **Hospital beds** (1982): 210,088. **Physicians** (1982): 44,030. **Infant mortality** (per 1,000 live births 1983): 31.

Education (1983): **Literacy:** 98%. **Years compulsory:** 10; attendance 98%.

Major International Organizations: UN and its specialized agencies, Warsaw Pact.

Embassy: 1607 23d St. NW 20008; 232-4747.

Romania's earliest known people merged with invading Proto-Thracians, preceding by centuries the Dacians. The Dacian kingdom was occupied by Rome, 106 AD-271 AD; people and language were Romanized. The principalities of Wallachia and Moldavia, dominated by Turkey, were united in 1859, became Romania in 1861. In 1877 Romania proclaimed independence from Turkey, became an independent state by the Treaty of Berlin, 1878, a kingdom, 1881, under Carol I. In 1886 Romania became a constitutional monarchy with a bicameral legislature.

Romania helped Russia in its war with Turkey, 1877-78. After World War I it acquired Bessarabia, Bukovina, Transylvania, and Banat. In 1940 it ceded Bessarabia and Northern Bukovina to the USSR and part of Southern Dobrudja to Bulgaria.

Marshal Ion Antonescu, leader of a militarist movement, forced Romania to join Germany against the USSR in World War II in 1941. In 1944 Antonescu was overthrown by King Michael with Soviet help and Romania joined the Allies.

With occupation by Soviet troops the Communist-headed National Democratic Front displaced the National Peasant party. A People's Republic was proclaimed, Dec. 30, 1947; Michael was forced to abdicate. Land owners were dispossessed; most banks, factories and transportation units were nationalized.

On Aug. 22, 1965, a new constitution proclaimed Romania a Socialist, rather than a People's Republic. Since 1959, USSR troops have not been permitted to enter Romania.

Internal policies remain oppressive. Ethnic Hungarians have protested cultural and job discrimination.

Romania has become industrialized, but lags in consumer goods and in personal freedoms. All industry is state owned, and state farms and cooperatives own over 90% of arable land.

A major earthquake struck Bucharest in March, 1977, killing over 1,300 people and causing extensive damage to housing and industry.

In 1982, Romania asked Western creditors for a rescheduling of debt repayments which totaled some $3 billion.

Rwanda
Republic of Rwanda

People: Population (1984 est.): 5,836,000. **Age distrib.** (%): 0–14: 50.8; 15–59: 46.2; 60+: 3.0. **Pop. density:** 573 per sq. mi. **Urban** (1985): 5.1%. **Ethnic groups:** Hutu 90%, Tutsi 9%, Twa (pygmies) 1%. **Languages:** French, Kinyarwandu (both official), Swahili. **Religions:** Christian 68%, traditional 23%.

Geography: Area: 10,169 sq. mi., the size of Maryland. **Location:** In E central Africa. **Neighbors:** Uganda on N, Zaire on W, Burundi on S, Tanzania on E. **Topography:** Grassy uplands and hills cover most of the country, with a chain of volcanoes in the NW. The source of the Nile R. has been located in the headwaters of the Kagera (Akagera) R., SW of Kigali. **Capital:** Kigali. **Cities** (1983 est.): Kigali 150,000.

Government: Type: Republic. **Head of state:** Pres. Juvenal Habyarimana; b. Mar. 8, 1937; in office: July 5, 1973. **Local divisions:** 10 prefectures, 143 communes. **Defense:** 1.7% of GNP (1982).

Economy: Chief crops: Coffee, tea. **Minerals:** Tin, gold, wolframite. **Arable land:** 40%. **Electricity prod.** (1982): 163 mln. kwh. **Labor force:** 93% agric.

Finance: Currency: Franc (Apr. 1985: 104.03 = $1 US). **Gross domestic product** (1982): $1.4 bln. **Per capita income** (1982): $250. **Imports** (1982): $219 mln.; partners: Belg. 16%, Jap. 12%, W. Ger. 9%. **Exports** (1982): $116 mln.; partners: Tanz. 63%, Kenya 13%. **National budget** (1983): $174 mln. revenues; $193 mln. expenditures. **International reserves less**

gold (Mar. 1985): $112 mln. **Consumer prices** (change in 1984): 5.4%.

Transport: Motor vehicles: in use (1982): 6,100 passenger cars, 7,000 comm. vehicles.

Communications: Radios: 47,000 in use (1983). **Telephones in use** (1980): 5,000.

Health: Life expectancy at birth (1983): 45.2 years. **Births** (per 1,000 pop. 1980): 19.5. **Deaths** (per 1,000 pop. 1980): 5.2. **Natural increase** (1980): 1.4%. **Hospital beds** (per 100,000 pop. 1977): 154. **Physicians** (per 100,000 pop. 1977): 13. **Infant mortality** (per 1,000 live births 1983): 137.

Education (1983): **Literacy:** 37%. **Years compulsory:** ro 8; attendance: 70%.

Major International Organizations: UN, OAU.

Embassy: 1714 New Hampshire Ave. NW 20009; 232-2882.

For centuries, the Tutsi (an extremely tall people) dominated the Hutus (90% of the population). A civil war broke out in 1959 and Tutsi power was ended. A referendum in 1961 abolished the monarchic system.

Rwanda, which had been part of the Belgian UN trusteeship of Rwanda-Urundi, became independent July 1, 1962. The government was overthrown in a 1973 military coup. Rwanda is one of the most densely populated countries in Africa. All available arable land is being used, and is being subject to erosion. The government has carried out economic and social improvement programs, using foreign aid and volunteer labor on public works projects.

St. Christopher (St. Kitts) and Nevis
St. Christopher Nevis

People: Population (1984 est.): 44,500. **Ethnic groups:** black 95%. **Language:** English. **Religion:** Protestant 76%.

Geography: Area: 101 sq. mi. in the northern part of the Leeward group of the Lesser Antilles in the eastern Caribbean Sea. **Capitol:** Basseterre. **Cities** (1982 est.): 18,500.

Government: Head of State: Queen Elizabeth represented by Sir Clement Arrindell. **Head of Government:** Prime Minister Kennedy A. Simmonds; b. Apr. 12, 1936; in office: Sept. 19, 1983.

Economy: Sugar is the principal industry.

Finance: Currency: E. Caribbean Dollar (Mar. 1985): 2.70 = $1 U.S. **Tourists** (1982): 34,575.

Communications: 3,259 telephones (1983).

Education: Literacy (1984): 90%; school compulsory ages 5–14.

St. Christopher (known by the natives as Liamuiga) and Nevis were discovered and named by Columbus in 1493. They were settled by Britain in 1623, but ownership was disputed with France until 1713. They were part of the Leeward Islands Federation, 1871-1956, and the Federation of the W. Indies, 1958-62. The colony achieved self-government as an Associated State of the UK in 1967, and became fully independent Sept. 19, 1983. Nevis, the smaller of the islands, has the right of secession.

Saint Lucia

People: Population (1984 est.): 120,000. **Age distrib.** (%): 0–20: 49.6; 21–64: 42.7; 65+: 7.7. **Pop. density:** 521 per sq. mi. **Ethnic groups:** Predominantly African descent. **Languages:** English (official), French patois. **Religions:** Roman Catholic 90%.

Geography: Area: 238 sq. mi., about one-fifth the size of Rhode Island. **Location:** In Eastern Caribbean, 2d largest of the Windward Is. **Neighbors:** Martinique to N, St. Vincent to SW. **Topography:** Mountainous, volcanic in origin; Soufriere, a volcanic crater, in the S. Wooded mountains run N-S to Mt. Gimie, 3,145 ft., with streams through fertile valleys. **Capital:** Castries. **City:** Castries (1984 est.): 45,000.

Government: Type: Parliamentary democracy. **Head of state:** Queen Elizabeth II, represented by Gov.-Gen. Sir Allen Lewis; **Head of government:** Prime Min. John Compton; in office: May 3, 1982. **Local divisions:** 16 parishes and Castries.

Economy: Industries: Agriculture, tourism, manufacturing. **Chief crops:** Bananas, coconuts, cocoa, citrus fruits. **Other resources:** Forests. **Arable land:** 50%. **Electricity prod.** (1982):

60 mln. kwh. **Labor force:** 36% agric., 20% ind. & commerce, 18% servioos.

Finance: Currency: East Caribbean dollar (Mar. 1985: 2.70 = $1 US). **Gross national product** (1982): $133 mln. **Per capita income** (1978): $698. **Imports** (1982): $118 mln.; partners: U.S. 36%, UK 12%, Trin./Tob. 11%. **Exports** (1982): $41 mln.; partners: U.S. 28%, UK 25%. **Tourists** (1982): 98,181; receipts: $34 mln.

Transport: Motor vehicles: in use (1983): 4,500 passenger cars, 1,200 comm. vehicles. **Chief ports:** Castries, Vieux Fort.

Communications: Television sets: 90 in use (1983). **Radios:** 121,000 in use (1983). **Telephones in use** (1982): 9,500. **Daily newspaper circ.** (1976): 4,000; 36 per 1,000 pop.

Health: Life expectancy at birth (1983): 65 male; 71 female. **Births** (per 1,000 pop. 1983): 31.0. **Deaths** (per 1,000 pop. 1983): 6.2. **Natural increase** (1983): 2.4%. **Hospital beds** (1983): 213. **Infant mortality** (per 1,000 live births 1983): 27.4.

Education: Literacy (1984) 78%; **Years compulsory:** ages 5-15; **Attendance:** 80%.

Major International Organizations: UN and its specialized agencies, CARICOM, OAS.

St. Lucia was ceded to Britain by France at the Treaty of Paris, 1814. Self government was granted with the West Indies Act, 1967. Independence was attained Feb. 22, 1979.

Saint Vincent and the Grenadines

People: Population (1984 est.): 138,000. **Pop. density:** 876 per sq. mi. **Ethnic groups:** Mainly of African descent. **Languages:** English. **Religions:** Methodists, Anglicans, Roman Catholics.

Geography: Area: 150 sq. mi., about twice the size of Washington, D.C. **Location:** In the eastern Caribbean, St. Vincent (133 sq. mi.) and the northern islets of the Grenadines form a part of the Windward chain. **Neighbors:** St. Lucia to N, Barbados to E, Grenada to S. **Topography:** St. Vincent is volcanic, with a ridge of thickly-wooded mountains running its length; Soufriere, rising in the N, erupted in Apr. 1979. **Capital:** Kingstown. **Cities** (1982 est.): Kingstown 23,500.

Government: Head of state: Queen Elizabeth II, represented by Gov.-Gen. Sir Sydney Douglas Gun-Munro; b. Nov. 29, 1916; in office: Jan. 1, 1977. **Head of government:** James Mitchell; in office: July 30, 1984.

Economy: Industries: Agriculture, tourism. **Chief crops:** Bananas (62% of exports), arrowroot, coconuts. **Arable land:** 50%. **Electricity prod.** (1982): 29 mln. kwh. **Labor force:** 30% agric.

Finance: Currency: East Caribbean dollar (Mar. 1985: 2.70 = $1 US). **Per capita income** (1979): $250. **Imports** (1981): $60 mln.; partners: UK 17%, Trin./Tob. 14%, U.S. 32%. **Exports** (1981): $12 mln.; partners: UK 45%, Trin./Tob. 23%. **Tourists** (1981): 82,196. **National budget** (1981): $17 mln. revenues; $20.3 mln. expenditures.

Transport: Motor vehicles: in use (1983): 4,500 passenger cars, 1,700 comm. vehicles. **Chief port:** Kingstown.

Communications: Telephones in use (1982): 6,000.

Health: Life expectancy at birth (1970): 62.4 male; 63.2 female. **Births** (per 1,000 pop. 1981): 25.7. **Deaths** (per 1,000 pop. 1981): 6.1. **Natural increase** (1981): 1.9%. **Infant mortality** (per 1,000 pop. under 1 yr. 1981): 46.

Education (1981): **Literacy:** 85%.

Columbus landed on St. Vincent on Jan. 22, 1498 (St. Vincent's Day). Britain and France both laid claim to the island in the 17th and 18th centuries; the Treaty of Versailles, 1783, finally ceded it to Britain. Associated State status was granted 1969; independence was attained Oct. 27, 1979.

The entire economic life of St. Vincent is dependent upon agriculture and tourism.

San Marino
Most Serene Republic of San Marino

People: Population (1984 est.): 23,000. **Age distrib.** (%): 0–14: 24.4; 15–59: 60.3; 60+: 15.3. **Pop. density:** 965 per sq.

mi. **Urban** (1981): 92.4%. **Ethnic groups:** Sanmarinese, Italian. **Languages:** Italian. **Religions:** Roman Catholics predominate.

Geography: Area: 24 sq. mi. **Location:** In N central Italy near Adriatic coast. **Neighbors:** Completely surrounded by Italy. **Topography:** The country lies on the slopes of Mt. Titano. **Capital:** San Marino. **City** (1982 est.): San Marino 4,000.

Government: Type: Independent republic. **Head of state:** Two co-regents appt. every 6 months. **Local divisions:** 11 districts, 9 sectors.

Economy: Industries: Postage stamps, tourism, woolen goods, paper, cement, ceramics. **Arable land:** 17%.

Finance: Currency: Italian lira. **Tourists** (1983): 2.7 mln.

Communications: Television sets: 5,000 licensed (1981). **Radios:** 6,000 licensed (1976). **Telephones in use** (1982): 8,712. **Daily newspaper circ.** (1983): 60 per 1,000 pop.

Births (per 1,000 pop. 1983): 11.1. **Deaths** (per 1,000 pop. 1983): 7.4. **Natural increase** (1983): 3.7%. **Infant mortality** (per 1,000 live births 1985): 9.6.

San Marino claims to be the oldest state in Europe and to have been founded in the 4th century. A communist-led coalition ruled 1947-57; a similar coalition took power in 1978. It has had a treaty of friendship with Italy since 1862.

Sao Tome and Principe

Democratic Republic of Sao Tome and Principe

People: Population (1984 est.): 89,000. **Pop. density:** 268 per sq. mi. **Ethnic groups:** Portuguese-African mixture, African minority (Angola, Mozambique immigrants). **Languages:** Portuguese. **Religions:** Roman Catholic 99%.

Geography: Area: 372 sq. mi., slightly larger than New York City. **Location:** In the Gulf of Guinea about 125 miles off W Central Africa. **Neighbors:** Gabon, Equatorial Guinea on E. **Topography:** Sao Tome and Principe Islands, part of an extinct volcano chain, are both covered by lush forests and croplands. **Capital:** Sao Tome. **Cities** (1981 est.): Sao Tome 20,000.

Government: Type: Republic. **Head of state and head of government:** Pres. Manuel Pinto da Costa, b. 1910; in office: July 12, 1975. **Local divisions:** 2 provinces, 12 counties.

Economy: Chief crops: Cocoa (82% of exports), coconut products, cinchona. **Arable land:** 38%. **Electricity prod.** (1982): 14 mln. kwh.

Finance: Currency: Dobra (Nov. 1984): 45.46 = $1 US). **Gross domestic product** (1982 est.): $53 mln. **Per capita income** (1981): $300. **Imports** (1981): $20 mln.; partners: Port. 61%, Angola 13%. **Exports** (1981): $8 mln.; partners: Neth. 52%, Port. 33%, W. Ger. 8%.

Transport: Motor vehicles: in use (1979): 1,300 passenger cars, 1,900 comm. vehicles. **Chief ports:** Sao Tome, Santo Antonio.

Communications: Radios: 25,000 in use (1983).

Health: Births (per 1,000 pop. 1982): 38.7. **Deaths** (per 1,000 pop. 1982): 10.2. **Natural increase** (1982): 2.8%. **Pop. per hospital bed** (1976): 160. **Pop. per physician** (1973): 6,666. **Infant mortality** (per 1,000 live births 1982): 69.5.

Education (1983): Literacy: 50%.

Major International Organizations: UN, OAU.

The islands were uninhabited when discovered in 1471 by the Portuguese, who brought the first settlers — convicts and exiled Jews. Sugar planting was replaced by the slave trade as the chief economic activity until coffee and cocoa were introduced in the 19th century.

Portugal agreed, 1974, to turn the colony over to the Gabon-based Movement for the Liberation of Sao Tome and Principe, which proclaimed as first president its East German-trained leader Manuel Pinto da Costa. Independence came July 12, 1975.

Agriculture and fishing are the mainstays of the economy. There was severe draught in 1984.

Saudi Arabia

Kingdom of Saudi Arabia

People: Population (1984 est.): 10,794,000. **Pop. density:** 12.5 per sq. mi. **Ethnic groups:** Arab tribes, immigrants from other Arab and Moslem countries. **Languages:** Arabic. **Religions:** Moslems 99%.

Geography: Area: 830,000 sq. mi., one-third the size of the U.S. **Location:** Occupies most of Arabian Peninsula in Middle East. **Neighbors:** Kuwait, Iraq, Jordan on N, Yemen, South Yemen, Oman on S, United Arab Emirates, Qatar on E. **Topography:** The highlands on W, up to 9,000 ft., slope as an arid, barren desert to the Persian Gulf. **Capital:** Riyadh. **Cities** (1983 est.): Riyadh 1,793,000; Jidda 983,000; Mecca 463,000.

Government: Type: Monarchy with council of ministers. **Head of state and head of government:** King Fahd; b. 1922; in office: June 13, 1982. **Local divisions:** 14 provinces. **Defense:** 29.6% of govt. budget (1983).

Economy: Industries: Oil products. **Chief crops:** Dates, wheat, barley, fruit. **Minerals:** Oil, gas, gold, silver, iron. **Crude oil reserves** (1981): 178 bln. bbls. **Arable land:** 2%. **Meat prod.** (1980): beef: 19,000 metric tons, lamb: 29,000 metric tons. **Electricity prod.** (1982): 25 bln. kwh. **Labor force:** 28% agric.; 4% ind; 44% serv., comm., & govt.; 21% construction.

Finance: Currency: Riyal (Mar. 1985: 3.60 = $1 US). **Gross domestic product** (1983): $110.5 bln. **Per capita income** (1979): $11,500. **Imports** (1983): $39.1 bln.; partners: US 21%, Jap. 18%, W. Ger. 10%. **Exports** (1984): $46.8 bln.; partners: US 13%, Jap., 17%, Fr. 10%. **Tourist receipts** (1981): $1.5 bln. **International reserves less gold** (Mar. 1985): $23.7 bln. **Gold:** 4.59 mln. oz t. **Consumer prices** (change in 1984): 0.9%.

Transport: Railway traffic (1983): 95 mln. passenger-km; 272 mln. net ton-km. **Motor vehicles:** in use (1983): 1.8 mln. passenger cars, 1.7 mln. comm. vehicles. **Civil aviation** (1983): 14.9 bln. passenger-km. 1.8 bln. net ton-km. **Chief ports:** Jidda, Ad-Dammam, Ras Tannurah.

Communications: Television sets: 3.5 mln. in use (1983). **Radios:** 2.7 mln. in use (1983). **Telephones in use** (1982): 788,000. **Daily newspaper circ.** (1983): 23 per 1,000 pop.

Health: Life expectancy at birth (1982): 54 years. **Births** (per 1,000 pop. 1978): 49. **Deaths** (per 1,000 pop. 1978): 18. **Natural increase** (1978): 3.1%. **Hospital beds** (1979): 10,978. **Physicians** (1979): 2,883.

Education (1978): Literacy: 15%. **Pop. 5-19:** in school: 36%, teachers per 1,000: 22.

Major International Organizations: UN and its specialized agencies, Arab League, OPEC.

Embassy: 1520 18th Street NW 20036; 483-2100.

Arabia was united for the first time by Mohammed, in the early 7th century. His successors conquered the entire Near East and North Africa, bringing Islam and the Arabic language. But Arabia itself soon returned to its former status as political and cultural backwater.

Nejd, long an independent state and center of the Wahhabi sect, fell under Turkish rule in the 18th century, but in 1913 Ibn Saud, founder of the Saudi dynasty, overthrew the Turks and captured the Turkish province of Hasa; took the Hejaz in 1925 and by 1926, most of Asir. The discovery of oil by a U.S. oil company in the 1930s transformed the new country.

Crown Prince Khalid was proclaimed king on Mar. 25, 1975, after the assassination of King Faisal. Fahd became king on June 13, 1982 following Khalid's death. There is no constitution and no parliament. The king exercises authority together with a Council of Ministers. The Islamic religious code is the law of the land. Alcohol and public entertainments are restricted, and women have an inferior legal status.

Saudi units fought against Israel in the 1948 and 1973 Arab-Israeli wars. Many billions of dollars of advanced arms have been purchased from Britain, France, and the U.S., including jet fighters, missiles, and, in 1981, 5 airborne warning and control system (AWACS) aircraft from the U.S., despite strong opposition from Israel. Beginning with the 1967 Arab-Israeli war, Saudi Arabia provided large annual financial gifts to Egypt; aid was later extended to Syria, Jordan, and Palestinian guerrilla groups, as well as to other Moslem countries. The country has aided anti-radical forces in Yemen and Oman.

Faisal played a leading role in the 1973-74 Arab oil embargo against the U.S. and other nations in an attempt to force them to adopt an anti-Israel policy. Saudi Arabia joined most other Arab states, 1979, in condemning Egypt's peace treaty with Israel.

Between 1973 and 1976, Saudi Arabia acquired full ownership of Aramco (Arabian American Oil Co.). In the 1980s, Saudi Arabia's moderate position on crude oil prices has often prevailed at OPEC meetings. Saudi Arabia announced, 1979, it will build a $1

billion causeway linking the island state Bahrain to the Arab mainland.

The Hejaz contains the holy cities of Islam — Medina where the Mosque of the Prophet enshrines the tomb of Mohammed, who died in the city June 7, 632, and Mecca, his birthplace. More than 600,000 Moslems from 60 nations pilgrimage to Mecca annually. The regime faced its first serious opposition when Moslem fundamentalists seized the Grand Mosque in Mecca, Nov. 20, 1979.

Two Saudi oil tankers were attacked May 1984, as Iran and Iraq began air attacks against shipping in the Persian Gulf. On May 29, the U.S., citing grave concern over the growing escalation of the Iran-Iraq war in the Persian Gulf, authorized the sale of 400 Stinger antiaircraft missiles to the Saudis. Saudi warplanes shot down 2 Iranian jets, June 5.

Senegal
Republic of Senegal

People: Population (1984 est.): 6,541,000. **Age distrib. (%):** 0–14: 44.2; 15–59: 50.5; 60+: 5.3. **Pop. density:** 83.6 per sq. mi. **Urban** (1986): 30%. **Ethnic groups:** Wolof 36%, Serer 17%, Peulh 17%, Diola 9%, Mandingo 9%. **Languages:** French (official), tribal languages. **Religions:** Moslems 75%, Christians 5%.

Geography: Area: 75,995 sq. mi., the size of South Dakota. **Location:** At western extreme of Africa. **Neighbors:** Mauritania on N, Mali on E, Guinea, Guinea-Bissau on S, Gambia surrounded on three sides. **Topography:** Low rolling plains cover most of Senegal, rising somewhat in the SE. Swamp and jungles are in SW. **Capital:** Dakar. **Cities** (1982): Dakar 1.3 mln.; Thies 126,889; Kaolack 115,679.

Government: Type: Republic. **Head of state:** Pres. Abdou Diouf; b. Sept. 7, 1935; in office: Jan. 1, 1981. **Local divisions:** 10 regions. **Defense:** 3% of GNP (1982).

Economy: Industries: Food processing, fishing. **Chief crops:** Peanuts are chief export; millet, rice. **Minerals:** Phosphates. **Arable land:** 27%. **Meat prod.** (1980): beef: 40,000 metric tons; pork: 8,000 metric tons; lamb: 11,000 metric tons. **Fish catch** (1981): 359,200 metric tons. **Electricity prod.** (1982): 631 mln. kwh. **Labor force:** 70% agric.

Finance: Currency: CFA franc (Mar. 1985: 471 = $1 US). **Gross national product** (1982): $2.3 bln. **Per capita income** (1975): $342. **Imports** (1982): $713 mln.; partners Fr. 37%, U.S. 6%. **Exports** (1982): $476 mln.; partners Fr. 25%, UK 6%. **Tourists** (1982): $62 mln. receipts. **International reserves less gold** (Jan. 1985): $3.7 mln. **Gold:** 29,000 oz t. **Consumer prices** (change in 1984): 11.8%.

Transport: Railway traffic (1979): 133 mln. passenger-km; 309 mln. net ton-km. **Motor vehicles:** in use (1979): 65,000 passenger cars, 10,000 comm. vehicles. **Chief ports:** Dakar, Saint-Louis.

Communications: Television sets: 50,000 in use (1982). **Radios:** 450,000 in use (1982). **Telephones in use** (1982): 56,000. **Daily newspaper circ.** (1983): 7 per 1,000 pop.

Health: Life expectancy at birth (1984): 44 yrs. **Births** (per 1,000 pop. 1978): 47. **Deaths** (per 1,000 pop. 1978): 20. **Natural increase** (1978): 2.7%. **Hospital beds** (per 100,000 pop. 1977): 111. **Physicians** (per 100,000 pop. 1977): 2. **Infant mortality** (per 1,000 live births 1984): 158.

Education (1984): **Literacy:** 10%. **Attendance:** 53% primary, 11% secondary.

Major International Organizations: UN and its specialized agencies, OAU.

Embassy: 2112 Wyoming Ave. NW 20008; 234-0540.

Portuguese settlers arrived in the 15th century, but French control grew from the 17th century. The last independent Moslem state was subdued in 1893. Dakar became the capital of French West Africa.

Independence as part, along with the Sudanese Rep., of the Mali Federation, came June 20, 1960. Senegal withdrew Aug. 20 that year. French political and economic influence is strong.

A long drought brought famine, 1972-73, and again in 1978.

Senegal is recognized as the most democratic of the French-speaking West African nations.

Senegal, Dec. 17, 1981, signed an agreement with The Gambia for confederation of the 2 countries under the name of Senegambia. The confederation began Feb. 1, 1982. The 2 nations

retained their individual sovereignty but adopted joint defense and monetary policies.

Seychelles
Republic of Seychelles

People: Population (1984 est.): 66,000. **Age distrib. (%):** 0–14: 39.7; 15–59: 51.1; 60+: 9.1. **Pop. density:** 369 per sq. mi. **Urban** (1977): 37.1% **Ethnic groups:** Creoles (mixture of Asians, Africans, and French) predominate. **Languages:** English and French (both official), Creole. **Religions:** Roman Catholics 96%.

Geography: Area: 171 sq. mi. **Location:** In the Indian O. 700 miles NE of Madagascar. **Neighbors:** Nearest are Madagascar on SW, Somalia on NW. **Topography:** A group of 86 islands, about half of them composed of coral, the other half granite, the latter predominantly mountainous. **Capital:** Victoria. **Cities** (1980): Port Victoria 23,000.

Government: Type: Single party republic. **Head of state:** Pres. France-Albert Rene, b. Nov. 16, 1935; in office: June 5, 1977. **Defense:** 11.7% of govt. budget (1983).

Economy: Industries: Food processing. **Chief crops:** Coconut products, cinnamon, vanilla, patchouli. **Other resources:** Guano, shark fins, tortoise shells, fish. **Electricity prod.** (1983): 56.7 mln. kwh. **Labor force:** 18.5% agric.; 19.4% ind. & comm.; 13.5% serv.; 49% govt.

Finance: Currency: Rupee (Mar. 1985: 7.32 = $1 US). **Gross domestic product** (1982): $143 mln. **Per capita income** (1980): $1,030. **Imports** (1981): $88.5 mln.; partners: UK 25%, So. Afr. 10%, Bah. 24%. **Exports** (1981): $13 mln.; partners: Pak. 45%. **National Budget** (1983): $65 mln. **Tourists** (1982): 47,280; receipts: $41 mln. **International reserves less gold** (Mar. 1985): $9.2 mln. **Consumer prices** (change in 1984): 4.0%.

Transport: Motor vehicles: in use (1983): 3,500 passenger cars, 1,000 comm. vehicles. **Port:** Victoria.

Communications: Radios: 18,000 in use (1979). **Telephones in use** (1981): 7,105. **Daily newspaper circ.** (1982): 63 per 1,000 pop.

Health: Life expectancy at birth (1983): 66 years. **Births** (per 1,000 pop. 1982): 24.0. **Deaths** (per 1,000 pop. 1982): 7.5. **Natural increase** (1982): 1.6%. **Hospital beds** (1983): 32.6. **Physicians** (1983): 41. **Infant mortality** (per 1,000 live births 1982): 19.4.

Education (1983): **Literacy:** 60%. **Years compulsory** 9; attendance 95%.

Major International Organizations: UN, OAU, Commonwealth of Nations.

Embassy: 820 2d Ave., New York, NY 10017; (212) 687-9766.

The islands were occupied by France in 1768, and seized by Britain in 1794. Ruled as part of Mauritius from 1814, the Seychelles became a separate colony in 1903. The ruling party had opposed independence as impractical, but pressure from the OAU and the UN became irresistible, and independence was declared June 29, 1976. The first president was ousted in a coup a year later by a socialist leader.

A new Constitution, announced Mar. 1979, turned the country into a one-party state.

Sierra Leone
Republic of Sierra Leone

People: Population (1984 est.): 3,805,000. **Age distrib. (%):** 0–14: 40.6; 15–59: 51.5; 60+: 7.8. **Pop. density:** 139 per sq. mi. **Ethnic groups:** Temne 30%, Mende 30%, others. **Languages:** English (official), tribal languages. **Religions:** animist 30%, Moslems 60%.

Geography: Area: 27,699 sq. mi., slightly smaller than South Carolina. **Location:** On W coast of W. Africa. **Neighbors:** Guinea on N, E, Liberia on S. **Topography:** The heavily-indented, 210-mi. coastline has mangrove swamps. Behind are wooded hills, rising to a plateau and mountains in the E. **Capital:** Freetown. **Cities** (1982 est.): Freetown 375,000; Bo, Kenema, Makeni.

Government: Type: Republic. **Head of state and head of government:** Pres. Siaka P. Stevens; b. Aug. 24, 1905; in office: Apr. 21, 1971 (state), June 14, 1978 (gov't.). **Local divisions:** 3 provinces and one region including Freetown.
Economy: Industries: Mining, tourism. **Chief crops:** Cocoa, coffee, palm kernels, rice, ginger. **Minerals:** Diamonds, bauxite. **Arable land:** 25%. **Fish catch** (1982): 121,000 metric tons. **Electricity prod.** (1982): 236 mln. kwh. **Labor force:** 75% agric.; 15% ind. & serv.
Finance: Currency: Leone (Mar. 1985: 6.00 = $1 US). **Gross national product** (1982): $1.2 bln. **Per capita income** (1980): $176. **Imports** (1982): $323 mln.; partners: UK 22%, Fr. 11%. **Exports** (1982): $80 mln.; partners: UK 40%, U.S. 27%. **National budget** (1981): $185 mln. revenues; $161 mln. expenditures. **International reserves less gold** (Mar. 1985): $2.8 mln. **Consumer prices** (change in 1984): 72.9%.
Transport: Motor Vehicles: in use (1982): 47,000 passenger cars, 30,000 comm. vehicles. **Chief ports:** Freetown, Bonthe.
Communications: Television sets: 20,000 in use (1981). **Radios:** 500,000 in use (1981). **Telephones in use** (1981): 220,000. **Daily newspaper circ.** (1982): 3 per 1,000 pop.
Health: Life expectancy at birth (1984): 46 yrs. **Births** (per 1,000 pop. 1978): 45. **Deaths** (per 1,000 pop. 1978): 27. **Natural increase** (1978): 1.9%. **Hospital beds** (per 100,000 pop. 1977): 99. **Physicians** (per 100,000 pop. 1979): 7.
Education (1984): **Literacy:** 15%.
Major International Organizations: UN and its specialized agencies, Commonwealth of Nations, OAU.
Embassy: 1701 19th St. NW 20009; 939-9261.

Freetown was founded in 1787 by the British government as a haven for freed slaves. Their descendants, known as Creoles, number more than 60,000.
Successive steps toward independence followed the 1951 constitution. Full independence arrived Apr. 27, 1961. Sierra Leone became a republic Apr. 19, 1971. A one-party state approved by referendum 1978, brought political stability, but the economy has been plagued by inflation, corruption, and dependence upon the International Monetary Fund and creditors.

Singapore
Republic of Singapore

People: Population (1984 est.): 2,531,000. **Age distrib.** (%): 0–14: 27; 15–59: 65.8; 60+: 7.2. **Pop. density:** 10,582 per sq. mi. **Ethnic groups:** Chinese 77%, Malays 15%, Indians 6%. **Languages:** Chinese, Malay, Tamil, English all official. **Religions:** Buddhism, Taoism, Islam, Hinduism, Christianity.
Geography: Area: 239 sq. mi., smaller than New York City. **Location:** Off tip of Malayan Peninsula in S.E. Asia. **Neighbors:** Nearest are Malaysia on N, Indonesia on S. **Topography:** Singapore is a flat, formerly swampy island. The nation includes 40 nearby islets. **Capital:** Singapore. **Cities** (1978 est.): Singapore 2,334,400.
Government: Type: Parliamentary democracy. **Head of state:** Pres. Chengara Veetil Devan Nair; in office: Oct. 21, 1981. **Head of government:** Prime Min. Lee Kuan Yew; b. Sept. 16, 1923; in office: June 5, 1959. **Defense:** 5.6% of GNP (1982).
Economy: Industries: Shipbuilding, oil refining, electronics, banking, textiles, food, rubber, lumber processing, tourism. **Meat prod.** (1980): pork: 43,000 metric tons. **Fish catch** (1982): 19,000 metric tons. **Electricity prod.** (1983): 8.6 bln. kwh. **Crude steel prod.** (1981): 350,000 metric tons. **Labor force:** 1% agric.; 59% ind. & comm.; 34% services.
Finance: Currency: Dollar (Mar. 1985: 2.20 = $1 US). **Gross national product** (1983): $16.3 bln. **Per capita income** (1983): $6,526. **Imports** (1984): $28.6 bln.; partners: Jap. 18%, Malay. 13%, U.S. 13%, Sau. Ar. 16%. **Exports** (1984): $24.0 bln., partners: U.S. 13%, Malay. 18%, Jap. 11%, HK 8%. **Tourists** (1982): 2.9 mln.; receipts $1 bln. **National budget** (1984): $5.1 bln. revenues; $8.1 bln. expenditures. **Consumer prices** (change in 1984): 2.6%.
Transport: Motor vehicles: in use (1983): 216,400 passenger cars, 113,000 comm. vehicles. **Civil aviation:** (1982) 18.1 bln. passenger-km; 758 mln. freight ton-km.
Communications: Television sets: 424,100 licensed (1983). **Radios:** 608,000 licensed (1983). **Telephones in use** (1983): 852,000. **Daily newspaper circ.** (1983): 335 per 1,000 pop.

Health: Life expectancy at birth (1984): 69 male; 74 female. **Births** (per 1,000 pop. 1983): 16.2. **Deaths** (per 1,000 pop. 1983): 5.3. **Natural increase** (1983): 1%. **Hospital beds** (1982): 8,246. **Physicians** (1982): 2,225. **Infant mortality** (per 1,000 live births 1984): 10.7.
Education (1984): **Literacy:** 85%. **Years compulsory:** none; attendance 84%.
Major International Organizations: UN and its specialized agencies, ASEAN.
Embassy: 1824 R St. NW 20009; 667-7555.

Founded in 1819 by Sir Thomas Stamford Raffles, Singapore was a British colony until 1959 when it became autonomous within the Commonwealth. On Sept. 16, 1963, it joined with Malaya, Sarawak and Sabah to form the Federation of Malaysia.
Tensions between Malayans, dominant in the federation, and ethnic Chinese, dominant in Singapore, led to an agreement under which Singapore became a separate nation, Aug. 9, 1965.
Singapore is one of the world's largest ports. Standards in health, education, and housing are high. International banking has grown.

Solomon Islands

People: Population (1984 est.): 263,000. **Age distrib.** (%): 0–14: 49; 15–59: 47.5; 60+: 3.5. **Pop. density:** 24.3 per sq. mi. **Urban** (1980): 25.2%. **Ethnic groups:** A variety of Melanesian groups and mixtures, some Polynesians. **Languages:** English (official), Pidgin, local languages. **Religions:** Anglican 34%, Roman Catholic 19%, Evangelical 24%, traditional religions.
Geography: Area: 10,640 sq. mi., slightly larger than Maryland. **Location:** Melanesian archipelago in the western Pacific O. **Neighbors:** Nearest is Papua New Guinea on W. **Topography:** 10 large volcanic and rugged islands and 4 groups of smaller ones. **Capital:** Honiara. **Cities:** (1981): Honiara 19,200.
Government: Type: Parliamentary democracy within the Commonwealth of Nations. **Head of state:** Queen Elizabeth II, represented by Gov.-Gen. Baddeley Devesi; b. Oct. 16, 1941; in office: July 7, 1978. **Head of government:** Prime Min. Peter Kenilorea; in office: 1984. **Local divisions:** 7 provinces and Honiara.
Economy: Industries: Fish canning. **Chief crops:** Coconuts, rice, bananas, yams. **Other resources:** Forests, marine shell. **Arable land:** 2%. **Fish catch** (1982): 33,000 metric tons. **Electricity prod.** (1982): 21.00 mln. kwh. **Labor force:** 32% agric., 32% services, 18% ind. & comm.
Finance: Currency: Dollar (Nov. 1984: 1.31 = $1 US). **Gross domestic product** (1978): $93.9 mln. **Per capita income** (1978): $440. **Imports** (1979): $57 mln.; partners: Austral. 29%, Jap. 14%, UK 7%, Sing. 23%. **Exports** (1979): $67 mln.; partners: Jap. 37%, U.S. 22%, UK 12%, Neth. 12%.
Communications: Radios: 25,000 in use (1982). **Telephones in use** (1981): 2,474.
Health: Births (per 1,000 pop. 1982): 44.6. **Deaths** (per 1,000 pop. 1982): 11.7. **Natural increase** (1982): 3.2%. **Infant mortality** (per 1,000 live births 1982): 46.
Major International Organizations: UN, Commonwealth of Nations.

The Solomon Islands were sighted in 1568 by an expedition from Peru. Britain established a protectorate in the 1890s over most of the group, inhabited by Melanesians. The islands saw major World War II battles. Self-government came Jan. 2, 1976, and independence was formally attained July 7, 1978.

Somalia
Somali Democratic Republic

People: Population (1984 est.): 6,393,000. **Pop. density:** 22.4 per sq. mi. **Ethnic groups:** mainly Hamitic, others. **Languages:** Somali, Arabic (both official). **Religions:** Sunni Muslims 99%.
Geography: Area: 246,300 sq. mi., slightly smaller than Texas. **Location:** Occupies the eastern horn of Africa. **Neighbors:** Djibouti, Ethiopia, Kenya on W. **Topography:** The coastline extends for 1,700 mi. Hills cover the N; the center and S are flat. **Capital:** Mogadishu. **Cities** (1984 est.): Mogadishu 600,000.

Government: Type: Independent republic. **Head of state:** Pres. Mohammed Siad Barrah; b. 1919; in office: Oct. 21, 1969. **Local divisions:** 15 regions. **Defense:** 29% of govt. expenditures (1983).

Economy: Chief crops: Incense, sugar, bananas, sorghum, corn, gum. **Minerals:** Iron, tin, gypsum, bauxite, uranium. **Arable land:** 2%. **Meat prod.** (1980): beef: 45,000 metric tons; lamb: 66,000 metric tons. **Fish catch** (1982): 6,500 metric tons. **Electricity prod.** (1982): 75 mln. kwh. **Labor force:** 82% agric.

Finance: Currency: Shilling (Mar. 1985: 37.00 = $1 US). **Gross national product** (1981): $1.8 bln. **Per capita income** (1983): less than $500. **Imports** (1982): $510 mln.; partners: It. 35%, UK 8%, U.S. 9%. **Exports** (1982): $167 mln.; partners: Saudi Ar. 66%, It. 12%. **International reserves less gold** (Sept. 1984): $1.5 mln. **Gold:** 19,000 oz t. **Consumer prices** (change in 1984): 92.2%.

Transport: Motor vehicles: in use (1980): 17,200 passenger cars, 8,050 comm. vehicles. **Chief ports:** Mogadishu, Berbera.

Communications: Radios: 95,000 in use (1983).

Health: Life expectancy at birth (1984): 43.9 yrs. **Births** (per 1,000 pop. 1978): 48. **Deaths** (per 1,000 pop. 1978): 22. **Natural increase** (1978): 2.6%. **Hospital beds** (per 100,000 pop. 1977): 179. **Physicians** (per 100,000 pop. 1977): 3.

Education (1984): Literacy: 5%. 50% attend primary school, 7% attend secondary school.

Major International Organizations: UN, OAS, Arab League.
Embassy: 600 New Hampshire Ave. NW 20037; 342-1575.

Arab trading posts developed into sultanates. The Italian Protectorate of Somalia, acquired from 1885 to 1927, extended along the Indian O. from the Gulf of Aden to the Juba R. The UN in 1949 approved eventual creation of Somalia as a sovereign state and in 1950 Italy took over the trusteeship held by Great Britain since World War II.

British Somaliland was formed in the 19th century in the NW. Britain gave it independence June 26, 1960; on July 1 it joined with the former Italian part to create the independent Somali Republic.

On Oct. 21, 1969, a Supreme Revolutionary Council seized power in a bloodless coup, named a Council of Secretaries of State, and abolished the Assembly. In May, 1970, several foreign companies were nationalized.

A severe drought in 1975 killed tens of thousands, and spurred efforts to resettle nomads on collective farms.

Somalia has laid claim to Ogaden, the huge eastern region of Ethiopia, peopled mostly by Somalis. Ethiopia battled Somali rebels and accused Somalia of sending troops and heavy arms in 1977. Russian forces were expelled in 1977 in retaliation for Soviet support of Ethiopia. Some 11,000 Cuban troops with Soviet arms defeated Somali army troops and ethnic Somali rebels in Ethiopia, 1978. As many as 1.5 mln. refugees entered Somalia. Guerrilla fighting in Ogaden has continued, although the Somali government no longer officially supports the Ogaden secessionists.

There was severe drought in 1984.

South Africa
Republic of South Africa

People: Population (1984 est.): 31,698,000. **Age distrib.** (%):** 0–14: 41.5; 15–59: 54.5; 60+: 3.8. **Pop. density:** 70.1 per sq. mi. **Urban** (1980): 52%. **Ethnic groups:** black 68%, white 18%, coloured 10%, Asian 3%. **Religions:** Mainly Christian. **Languages:** Afrikaans, English (both official), Bantu languages predominate.

Geography: Area: 435,868 sq. mi., four-fifths the size of Alaska. **Location:** At the southern extreme of Africa. **Neighbors:** Namibia (SW Africa), Botswana, Zimbabwe on N, Mozambique, Swaziland on E; surrounds Lesotho. **Topography:** The large interior plateau reaches close to the country's 2,700-mi. coastline. There are few major rivers or lakes; rainfall is sparse in W, more plentiful in E. **Capitals:** Cape Town (legislative). Pretoria (administrative), and Bloemfontein (judicial). **Cities** (1980): Durban 505,963; Cape Town 213,830; Johannesburg 1,536,457; Pretoria 528,407.

Government: Type: Parliamentary (limited to white adults). **Head of State:** Pres. and Prime Min. Pieter Willem Botha; b. Jan. 12, 1916; in office: Sept. 28, 1978. **Local divisions:** 4 provinces. **Defense:** 15% of govt. budget (1984).

Economy: Industries: Steel, tires, motors, textiles, plastics. **Chief crops:** Corn, wool, dairy products, grain, tobacco, sugar, fruit, peanuts, grapes. **Minerals:** Gold (largest producer), chromium, antimony, coal, iron, manganese, nickel, phosphates, tin, uranium, gem diamonds, platinum, copper, vanadium. **Other resources:** Wool. **Arable land:** 10%. **Meat prod.** (1984): beef: 620,000 metric tons; pork: 107,000 metric tons; lamb: 164,000 metric tons. **Fish catch** (1982): 624,000 metric tons. **Electricity prod.** (1982): 119.8 bln. kwh. **Crude steel prod.** (1982): 8.2 mln. metric tons. **Labor force:** 30% agric.; 29% ind. and commerce; 34% serv.; 7% mining.

Finance: Currency: Rand (Mar. 1985: 1.90 = $1 US). **Gross domestic product** (1983): $75.6 bln. **Per capita income** (1978): $1,296. **Imports** (1983): $15.7 bln.; partners (1981): W. Ger. 15%, U.S. 15%, UK 12%, Jap. 10%. **Exports** (1983): $18.6 bln.; partners: U.S. 8%, UK 7%, Jap. 8%. **Tourist receipts** (1977): $321 mln. **National budget** (1984): $20.7 bln. **International reserves less gold** (Mar. 1985): $326 mln. **Gold:** 6.23 mln. oz t. **Consumer prices** (change in 1984): 11.7%.

Transport: Railway traffic (1982): 103 bln. net ton-km. **Motor vehicles:** in use (1983): 2.7 mln. passenger cars, 1.1 mln. comm. vehicles. **Civil aviation** (1983): 8.6 bln. passenger-km: 338.8 mln. freight ton-km. **Chief ports:** Durban, Cape Town, East London, Port Elizabeth.

Communications: Television sets (1983): 2 mln.; **Radios:** 8 mln. in use (1983). **Telephones in use** (1983): 2.4 mln. **Daily newspaper circ.** (1982): 70 per 1,000 pop.

Health: Life expectancy at birth (1982): White: 70 years; Asians: 65 years; Africans: 59 years. **Births** (per 1,000 pop. 1978): 36. **Deaths** (per 1,000 pop. 1978): 13. **Natural increase** (1978): 2.3%. **Health** (1982): 16,787 medical practitioners, 3,904 specialists, 2,286 interns. **Infant mortality** (per 1,000 live births 1982): Africans 94, Asians 25.3, whites 14.9.

Education (1982): Literacy: 98% (whites), 85% (Asians), 75% (coloureds), 50% (Africans).

Major International Organizations: UN.
Embassy: 3051 Massachusetts Ave. NW 20008; 232-4400.

Bushmen and Hottentots were the original inhabitants. Bantus, including Zulu, Xhosa, Swazi, and Sotho, had occupied the area from Transvaal to south of Transkei before the 17th century.

The Cape of Good Hope area was settled by Dutch, beginning in the 17th century. Britain seized the Cape in 1806. Many Dutch trekked north and founded 2 republics, the Transvaal and the Orange Free State. Diamonds were discovered, 1867, and gold, 1886. The Dutch (Boers) resented encroachments by the British and others; the Anglo-Boer War followed, 1899-1902. Britain won and, effective May 31, 1910, created the Union of South Africa, incorporating the British colonies of the Cape and Natal, the Transvaal and the Orange Free State. After a referendum, the Union became the Republic of South Africa, May 31, 1961, and withdrew from the Commonwealth.

With the election victory of Daniel Malan's National party in 1948, the policy of separate development of the races, or apartheid, already existing unofficially, became official. This called for separate development, separate residential areas, and ultimate political independence for the whites, Bantus, Asians, and Coloreds. In 1959 the government passed acts providing the eventual creation of several Bantu nations or Bantustans on 13% of the country's land area, though most black leaders have opposed the plan.

Under apartheid, blacks are severely restricted to certain occupations, and are paid far lower wages than are whites for similar work. Only whites may vote or run for public office, and militant white opposition has been curbed. There is an advisory Indian Council, partly elected, partly appointed. In 1969, a Colored People's Representative Council was created. Some liberalization measures were allowed in the 1980s.

At least 600 persons, mostly Bantus, were killed in 1976 riots protesting apartheid. Black protests continued through 1985 as violence broke out in several black townships. Police reaction to the protests caused several hundred deaths. A new constitution was approved by referendum, Nov. 1983, which extended the parliamentary franchise to the Coloured and Asian minorities. Laws banning interracial sex and marriage were repealed in 1985.

In 1963, the Transkei, an area in the SE, became the first of these partially self-governing territories or "Homelands." Transkei became independent on Oct. 26, 1976, Bophuthatswana on Dec. 6, 1977, and Venda on Sept. 13, 1979; none received international recognition.

In 1981, So. Africa launched military operations in Angola and Mozambique to combat terrorists groups; So. African troops attacked the South West African People's Organization (SWAPO) guerrillas in Angola, March, 1982. South Africa and Mozambique signed a non-agression pact in 1984.

A car bomb exploded outside air force headquarters in Pretoria, May 20, 1983, killing or injuring hundreds of people. The African National Congress (ANC), a black nationalist group, claimed responsibility. In the U.S., there were nationwide antiapartheid protests in 1985; some 20 bills were pending in Congress proposing various economic sanctions against So. Africa unless racial reforms were enacted. (*See Chronology*).

Bophuthatswana: Population (1984 est.): 1,417,000. **Area:** 15,571 sq. mi., 6 discontinuous geographic units. **Capital:** Mmabatho. **Cities:** (1980 est.): Ga-Rankawa 48,300. **Head of state:** Pres. Kgosi Lucas Manyane Mangope, b. Dec. 27, 1923; in office: Dec. 6, 1977.

Ciskei: Population (1984 est.): 706,000. **Area:** 3,080 sq. mi. **Capitol:** Bisho. **Head of State:** Pres. Lennox Sebe.

Transkei: Population (1984 est.): 2,517,000. **Area:** 16,816 sq. mi., 3 discontinuous geographic units. **Capital:** Umtata (1978 est.): 30,000. **Head of state:** Pres. Kaiser Matanzima; in office: Feb. 20, 1979. **Head of government:** Prime Min. George Matanzima; in office: Feb. 20, 1979.

Venda: Population (1984 est.): 396,000. **Area:** 2,390 sq. mi., 2 discontinuous geographic units. **Capital:** Thohoyandou. **City:** Makearela (1976 est.): 1,972. **Head of state:** Patrick Mphephu; in office: Sept. 13, 1979.

Namibia (South-West Africa)

South-West Africa is a sparsely populated land twice the size of California. Made a German protectorate in 1884, it was surrendered to South Africa in 1915 and was administered by that country under a League of Nations mandate. S. Africa refused to accept UN authority under the trusteeship system.

Other African nations charged S. Africa imposed apartheid, built military bases, and exploited S-W Africa. The UN General Assembly, May 1968, created an 11-nation council to take over administration of S-W Africa and lead it to independence. The council charged that S. Africa had blocked its efforts to visit S-W Africa.

In 1968 the UN General Assembly gave the area the name Namibia. In Jan. 1970 the UN Security Council condemned S. Africa for "illegal" control of the area. In an advisory opinion, June 1971, the International Court of Justice declared S. Africa was occupying the area illegally.

In a 1977 referendum, white voters backed a plan for a multiracial interim government to lead to independence. The Marxist South-West Africa People's Organization (SWAPO) rejected the plan, and launched a guerrilla war. Both S. Africa and Namibian rebels agreed to a UN plan for independence by the end of 1978. S. Africa rejected the plan, Sept. 20, 1978, and held elections, without UN supervision, for Namibia's constituent assembly, Dec., that were ignored by the major black opposition parties.

The UN peace plan, proposed 1980, called for a cease-fire and a demilitarized zone 31 miles deep on each side of S-W Africa's borders with Angola and Zambia that would be patrolled by UN peacekeeping forces against guerrilla actions. Impartial elections would follow. In 1982, So. African and SWAPO agreed in principal on a cease-fire and the holding of UN-supervised elections. So. Africa, however, insisted on the withdrawal of Cuban forces from Angola as a precondition to Namibian independence. On Jan. 18, 1983, South Africa dissolved the Namibian National Assembly and resumed direct control of the territory.

Most of Namibia is a plateau, 3,600 ft. high, with plains in the N, Kalahari Desert to the E, Orange R. on the S, Atlantic O. on the W. Area is 318,827 sq. mi.; pop. (1982 est.) 1,038,000; capital, Windhoek.

Products include cattle, sheep, diamonds, copper, lead, zinc, fish. People include Namas (Hottentots), Ovambos (Bantus), Bushmen, and others.

Walvis Bay, the only deepwater port in the country, was turned over to South African administration in 1922. S. Africa said in 1978 it would discuss sovereignty only after Namibian independence.

Spain
Spanish State

People: Population (1984 est.): 38,435,000 **Age distrib. (%):** 0–14: 27.6; 15–59: 58.0; 60+: 14.4. **Pop. density:** 196 per sq. mi. **Ethnic groups:** Spanish (Castilian, Valencian, Andalusian, Asturian) 72.8%, Catalan 16.4%, Galician 8.2%, Basque 2.3%. **Languages:** Spanish (official), Catalan, Galician, Basque. **Religions:** Roman Catholic.

Geography: Area: 195,988 sq. mi., the size of Arizona and Utah combined. **Location:** In SW Europe. **Neighbors:** Portugal on W. France on N. **Topography:** The interior is a high, arid plateau broken by mountain ranges and river valleys. The NW is heavily watered, the south has lowlands and a Mediterranean climate. **Capital:** Madrid. **Cities** (1981 cen.): Madrid 3,188,297; Barcelona 1,754,900; Valencia 751,734; Seville 653,833; Zaragoza 590,750.

Government: Type: Constitutional monarchy. **Head of state:** King Juan Carlos I de Borbon y Borbon, b. Jan. 5, 1938; in office: Nov. 22, 1975. **Head of government:** Prime Min. Felipe Gonzalez Marquez; in office: Dec. 2, 1982. **Local divisions:** 50 provinces, 2 territories, 3 islands. **Defense:** 2.1% of GNP (1982).

Economy: Industries: Machinery, steel, textiles, shoes, autos, ships. **Chief crops:** Grains, olives, grapes, citrus fruits, vegetables, olives. **Minerals:** Mercury, potash, uranium, lead, iron, copper, zinc, coal. **Crude oil reserves** (1980): 150 mln. bbls. **Other resources:** Forests (cork). **Arable land:** 40%. **Meat prod.** (1984): beef: 410,000 metric tons; pork: 1.1 mln. metric tons; lamb: 140,000 metric tons. **Fish catch** (1981): 1.2 mln. tons. **Electricity prod.** (1982): 113.7 bln. kwh. **Crude steel prod.** (1982): 12.7 mln. metric tons. **Labor force:** 17% agric.; 34% ind. and comm.; 49% serv.

Finance: Currency: Peseta (Mar. 1985: 173 = $1 US). **Gross domestic product** (1984): $160.4 bln. **Per capita income** (1979): $5,500. **Imports** (1984): $28.8 bln.; partners: U.S. 11%, EC 33%. **Exports** (1984): $23.5 bln.; partners: EC 49%, U.S. 10%. **Tourists** (1982): receipts: $7.1 bln. **National budget** (1985): $25.8 bln. revenues; $35.5 bln. expenditures. **International reserves less gold** (Jan. 1985): $12.1 bln. **Gold:** 14.63 min. oz t. **Consumer prices** (change in 1984): 11.3%.

Transport: Railway traffic (1983): 15 bln. passenger-km; 10.5 bln. net ton-km. **Motor vehicles:** in use (1983): 8.7 mln. passenger cars, 1.6 mln. comm. vehicles; manuf. (1982): 915,000 passenger cars; 111,000 comm. vehicles. **Civil aviation:** (1983): 15.5 bln. passenger-km; 440 mln. freight ton-km. **Chief ports:** Barcelona, Bilbao, Valencia, Cartagena, Gijon.

Communications: Television sets: 11.6 mln. in use (1983). **Radios:** 10.4 mln. in use (1983). **Telephones in use** (1982): 12.8 mln. **Daily newspaper circ.** (1980): 116 per 1,000 pop.

Health: Life expectancy at birth (1980): 70.0 male; 76.0 female. **Births** (per 1,000 pop. 1981): 14.1. **Deaths** (per 1,000 pop. 1981): 7.6. **Natural increase** (1981): .6%. **Hospital beds** (per 100,000 pop. 1977): 543. **Physicians** (per 100,000 pop. 1977): 176. **Infant mortality** (per 1,000 live births 1981): 10.3.

Education (1985): Literacy: 97%. **School compulsory:** to age 14.

Major International Organizations: UN and its specialized agencies, NATO, OECD.

Embassy: 2700 15th St. NW 2009; 265-0190.

Spain was settled by Iberians, Basques, and Celts, partly overrun by Carthaginians, conquered by Rome c.200 BC. The Visigoths, in power by the 5th century AD, adopted Christianity but by 711 AD lost to the Islamic invasion from Africa. Christian reconquest from the N led to a Spanish nationalism. In 1469 the kingdoms of Aragon and Castile were united by the marriage of Ferdinand II and Isabella I, and the last Moorish power was broken by the fall of the kingdom of Granada, 1492. Spain became a bulwark of Roman Catholicism.

Spain obtained a colonial empire with the discovery of America by Columbus, 1492, the conquest of Mexico by Cortes, and Peru by Pizarro. It also controlled the Netherlands and parts of Italy and Germany. Spain lost its American colonies in the early 19th century. It lost Cuba, the Philippines, and Puerto Rico during the Spanish-American War, 1898.

Primo de Rivera became dictator in 1923. King Alfonso XIII revoked the dictatorship, 1930, but was forced to leave the country 1931. A republic was proclaimed which disestablished the church, curtailed its privileges, and secularized education. A conservative reaction occurred 1933 but was followed by a Popular Front (1936-1939) composed of socialists, communists, republicans, and anarchists.

Army officers under Francisco Franco revolted against the government, 1936. In a destructive 3-year war, in which some one million died, Franco received massive help and troops from Italy and Germany, while the USSR, France, and Mexico supported the republic. War ended Mar. 28, 1939. Franco was named caudillo, leader of the nation. Spain was neutral in World War II but its relations with fascist countries caused its exclusion from the UN until 1955.

In July 1969, Franco and the Cortes designated Prince Juan Carlos as the future king and chief of state. After Franco's death, Nov. 20, 1975, Juan Carlos was sworn in as king. He presided over the formal dissolution of the institutions of the Franco regime. In free elections June 1977, moderates and democratic socialists emerged as the largest parties.

In an unsuccessful attempt at a military coup, Feb. 23, 1981, rightist Civil Guards seized the lower house of Parliament and took most of the country's leaders hostage. The plot collapsed the next day when the army remained loyal to King Juan Carlos.

Catalonia and the Basque country were granted autonomy, Jan. 1980, following overwhelming approval in home-rule referendums. Basque extremists, however, have continued their campaign for independence.

Spain's unemployment reached 18.6% in 1985, the highest in Europe.

The **Balearic Islands** in the western Mediterranean, 1,935 sq. mi., are a province of Spain; they include **Majorca** (Mallorca), with the capital, Palma; **Minorca, Cabrera, Ibiza** and **Formentera.** The **Canary Islands,** 2,807 sq. mi., in the Atlantic W of Morocco, form 2 provinces, including the islands of **Tenerife, Palma, Gomera, Hierro, Grand Canary, Fuerteventura,** and **Lanzarote** with Las Palmas and Santa Cruz thriving ports. **Ceuta** and **Melilla,** small enclaves on Morocco's Mediterranean coast, are part of Metropolitan Spain.

Spain has sought the return of Gibraltar, in British hands since 1704.

Sri Lanka

Democratic Socialist Republic of Sri Lanka

People: Population (1984 est.): 15,925,000. **Age distrib. (%):** 0–14: 35.3; 15–59: 58.1; 60+: 6.6. **Pop. density:** 622 per sq. mi. **Urban** (1981): 21.5%. **Ethnic groups:** Sinhalese 75%, Tamils 18%, Moors 7%. **Languages:** Sinhala (official), Tamil, English. **Religions:** Buddhists 69%, Hindus 15%, Christians 7%, Muslims 7%.

Geography: Area: 25,332 sq. mi. **Location:** In Indian O. off SE coast of India. **Neighbors:** India on NW. **Topography:** The coastal area and the northern half are flat; the S-central area is hilly and mountainous. **Capital:** Colombo. **Cities** (1983): Colombo 1,262,000.

Government: Type: Republic. **Head of state:** Pres. Junius Richard Jayawardene; b. Sept. 17, 1906; in office: Feb. 4, 1978. **Head of government:** Prime Minister Ranasinghe Premadasa, b. June 23, 1924, in office: Feb. 6, 1978. **Local divisions:** 24 districts. **Defense:** 0.5% of GNP (1982).

Economy: Industries: Plywood, paper, milling, chemicals, textiles. **Chief crops:** Tea, coconuts, rice. **Minerals:** Graphite, limestone, gems, phosphate. **Other resources:** Forests, rubber. **Arable land:** 34%. **Meat prod.** (1980): beef: 18,000 metric tons. **Fish catch** (1982): 207,000 metric tons. **Electricity prod.** (1982): 2 bln. kwh. **Labor force:** 46% agric.; 29% ind. and comm.; 19% serv.

Finance: Currency: Rupee (Mar. 1985: 26.95 = $1 US). **Gross domestic product** (1981): $4 bln. **Per capita income** (1981): $266. **Imports** (1983): $1.8 bln.; partners: Jap. 15%, Saudi Ar. 12%, UK 7%. **Exports** (1983): $1.06 bln.; partners: U.S. 14%, UK 7%. **Tourists** (1982): 407,230. **National budget** (1982): $873 mln. revenues; $1.8 bln. expenditures. **International reserves less gold** (Mar. 1985): $544 mln. **Gold:** 63,000 oz t. **Consumer prices** (change in 1984): 16.6%

Transport: Railway traffic (1982): 3.1 bln. passenger-km; 218 mln. net ton-km. **Motor vehicles:** in use (1981): 126,000 passenger cars, 67,200 comm. vehicles. **Civil aviation** (1982): 1.9 bln. passenger-km; 43 mln. freight ton-km. **Chief ports:** Colombo, Trincomalee, Galle.

Communications: Radios: 4.9 mln. in use (1982). **Telephones in use** (1982): 109,900.

Health: Life expectancy at birth (1983): 68 years. **Births** (per 1,000 pop. 1981): 28.0. **Deaths** (per 1,000 pop. 1981): 6.0. **Natural increase** (1981): 2.2%. **Hospital beds** (1982): 43,389. **Physicians** (1981): 2,889. **Infant mortality** (per 1,000 live births 1983): 37.

Education (1983): **Literacy:** 84%. **Years compulsory:** To age 12; attendance 84%.

Major International Organizations: UN and its specialized agencies, Commonwealth of Nations.

Embassy: 2148 Wyoming Ave. NW 20008; 483-4025.

The island was known to the ancient world as Taprobane (Greek for copper-colored) and later as Serendip (from Arabic). Colonists from northern India subdued the indigenous Veddahs about 543 BC; their descendants, the Buddhist Sinhalese, still form most of the population. Hindu descendants of Tamil immigrants from southern India account for one-fifth of the population; separatism has grown. Parts were occupied by the Portuguese in 1505 and by the Dutch in 1658. The British seized the island in 1796. As Ceylon it became an independent member of the Commonwealth in 1948. On May 22, 1972, Ceylon became the Republic of Sri Lanka.

Prime Min. W. R. D. Bandaranaike was assassinated Sept. 25, 1959. In new elections, the Freedom Party was victorious under Mrs. Sirimavo Bandaranaike, widow of the former prime minister. In Apr., 1962, the government expropriated British and U.S. oil companies. In Mar. 1965 elections, the conservative United National Party won; the new government agreed to pay compensation for the seized oil companies.

After May 1970 elections, Mrs. Bandaranaike became prime minister again. In 1971 the nation suffered economic problems and terrorist activities by ultra-leftists, thousands of whom were executed. Massive land reform and nationalization of foreign-owned plantations was undertaken in the mid-1970s. Mrs. Bandaranaike was ousted in 1977 elections by the United Nationals. A presidential form of government was installed in 1978 to restore stability.

Tension between the Sinhalese and Tamil separatists erupted into violence in 1985.

Sudan

Democratic Republic of the Sudan

People: Population (1984 est.): 21,103,000. **Pop. density:** 21.3 per sq. mi. **Urban** (1983): 35%. **Ethnic groups:** North: Arabs, Nubians; South: Nilotic; Sudanic, Negro tribes. **Languages:** Arabic (official), various tribal languages. **Religions:** Muslims 73%, animist 18%, Christians 9%.

Geography: Area: 966,757 sq. mi., the largest country in Africa, over one-fourth the size of the U.S. **Location:** At the E end of Sahara desert zone. **Neighbors:** Egypt on N, Libya, Chad, Central African Republic on W, Zaire, Uganda, Kenya on S, Ethiopia on E. **Topography:** The N consists of the Libyan Desert in the W, and the mountainous Nubia desert in E, with narrow Nile valley between. The center contains large, fertile, rainy areas with fields, pasture, and forest. The S has rich soil, heavy rain. **Capital:** Khartoum. **Cities** (1983 est.): Khartoum 476,000; Omdurman 526,000; North Khartoum 341,000; Port Sudan 206,000.

Government: Type: Republic, single party. **Head of state and head of government:** Pres., Prime Min. Abdel Rahman Siwar el-Dahab; b 1934; in office: Apr. 6, 1985. **Local divisions:** 15 provinces; the southern 3 have a regional government. **Defense:** 24% of GNP (1982).

Economy: Industries: Textiles, food processing. **Chief crops:** Gum arabic (principal world source), durra (sorghum), cotton (main export), sesame, peanuts, rice, coffee, sugar cane, tobacco, wheat, dates. **Minerals:** Chrome, gold, copper, white mica, vermiculite, asbestos. **Other resources:** Mahogany. **Arable land:** 12%. **Meat prod.** (1983): beef: 239,000 metric tons; lamb: 137,000 metric tons. **Electricity prod.** (1982): 1 bln. kwh. **Labor force:** 78% agric.; 9% ind., commerce, serv.

Finance: Currency: Pound (Mar. 1985: 2.30 = $1 US). **Gross domestic product** (1981 est.): $8.8 bln. **Per capita income** (1982 est.): $370. **Imports** (1983): $1.3 bln.; partners: UK

13%, W. Ger. 8%, Saudi Ar. 11%. **Exports** (1983): $624 mln.; partners: China 6%, It. 9%, Saudi Ar. 21%. **National Budget** (1983): $1.5 bln. expenditures. **International reserves less gold** (Mar. 1985): $10.4 mln. **Consumer prices** (change in 1983): 30.6%.

Transport: Railway traffic (1982): 1.1 bln. net ton-km. **Motor vehicles:** in use (1982): 150,000 passenger cars, 22,000 comm. vehicles. **Civil aviation:** (1982): 657 mln. passenger-km; 6.3 mln. freight ton-km. **Chief ports:** Port Sudan.

Communications: Television sets: 107,000 in use (1982). **Radios:** 1.4 mln. licensed (1982). **Telephones in use** (1982): 68,503. **Daily newspaper circ.** (1983): 6 per 1,000 pop.

Health: Life expectancy at birth (1975): 43 male; 45 female. **Births** (per 1,000 pop. 1978): 49. **Deaths** (per 1,000 pop. 1978): 18 **Natural increase** (1978): 3.1%. **Hospital beds** (per 100,000 pop. 1977): 100. **Physicians** (per 100,000 pop. 1977): 50. **Infant mortality** (per 1,000 live births 1979): 141.

Education (1982): **Literacy:** 20%. **Years compulsory:** 9; attendance 50%.

Major International Organizations: UN and its specialized agencies, Arab League, OAU.

Embassy: 2210 Massachusetts Ave. NW 20008; 338-8565.

Northern Sudan, ancient Nubia, was settled by Egyptians in antiquity, and was converted to Coptic Christianity in the 6th century. Arab conquests brought Islam in the 15th century.

In the 1820s Egypt took over the Sudan, defeating the last of earlier empires, including the Fung. In the 1880s a revolution was led by Mohammed Ahmed who called himself the Mahdi (leader of the faithful) and his followers, the dervishes.

In 1898 an Anglo-Egyptian force crushed the Mahdi's successors. In 1951 the Egyptian Parliament abrogated its 1899 and 1936 treaties with Great Britain, and amended its constitution, to provide for a separate Sudanese constitution.

Sudan voted for complete independence as a parliamentary government effective Jan. 1, 1956. Gen. Ibrahim Abboud took power 1958, but resigned under pressure, 1964.

In 1969, in a second military coup, a Revolutionary Council took power, but a civilian premier and cabinet were appointed; the government announced it would create a socialist state. The northern 12 provinces are predominantly Arab-Moslem and have been dominant in the central government. The 3 southern provinces are Negro and predominantly pagan. A 1972 peace agreement gave the South regional autonomy.

The government nationalized a number of businesses in May 1970.

Sudan charged Libya with aiding an unsuccessful coup in Sudan in 1976. Sudan claimed that Libyan planes bombed several border towns, Sept. 1981, and the city of Omdurman, 1984.

Economic problems plagued the nation in the 1980s, aggravated by a hugh influx of refugees from neighboring countries. After 16 years in power, Pres. Nimeiry was overthrown in a bloodless military coup, Apr. 6, 1985.

Suriname

People: Population (1984 est.): 370,000. **Pop. density:** 5.6 per sq. mi. **Ethnic groups** Hindustanis 37%, Creole 31%, Javanese 15%. **Languages:** Dutch (official), Sranan (Creole), English, others. **Religions:** Muslim, Hindu, Christian.

Geography: Area: 63,037 sq. mi., slightly larger than Georgia. **Location:** On N shore of S. America. **Neighbors:** Guyana on W, Brazil on S, French Guiana on E. **Topography:** A flat Atlantic coast, where dikes permit agriculture. Inland is a forest belt; to the S, largely unexplored hills cover 75% of the country. **Capital:** Paramaribo. **Cities** (1984): Paramaribo 180,000.

Government: Type: Military-civilian executive. **Head of Military Council:** Col. Desire Bouterse; in office: Feb. 5, 1982. **Local divisions:** 9 districts.

Economy: Industries: Aluminum. **Chief crops:** Rice, sugar, fruits. **Minerals:** Bauxite. **Other resources:** Forests, shrimp. **Arable land:** 1%. **Electricity prod.** (1982): 1.7 bln. kwh. **Labor force:** 29% agric.; 15% ind. and commerce; 42% govt.

Finance: Currency: Guilder (Mar. 1985: 1.78 = $1 US). **Gross domestic product** (1983): $1.0 bln. **Per capita income** (1981): $2,600. **Imports** (1982): $449 mln.; partners: U.S. 31%, Neth. 19%, Trin./Tob. 15%, Jap. 7%. **Exports** (1982): $366 mln.; partners: U.S. 36%, Neth. 17%, Nor. 13%. **Tourists** (1981): receipts: $17 mln. **National budget** (1983): $454. **Inter-**

national reserves less gold (Mar. 1985): $25.2 mln. **Gold:** 54,000 oz t. **Consumer prices** (change in 1983): 4.4%.

Transport: Motor vehicles: in use (1983): 31,000 passenger cars, 12,000 comm. vehicles. **Chief ports:** Paramaribo, Nieuw-Nickerie.

Communications: Television sets: 42,000 in use (1983). **Radios:** 185,000 in use (1983). **Telephones in use** (1982): 27,495. **Daily newspaper circ.** (1983): 22 per 1,000 pop.

Health: Life expectancy at birth (1980): 64.8 male; 69.8 female. **Births** (per 1,000 pop. 1978): 29. **Deaths** (per 1,000 pop. 1978): 7. **Natural increase** (1978): 2.1%. **Infant mortality** (per 1,000 live births 1984): 23.

Education (1984): Literacy: 65%; compulsory ages 6–12.

Major International Organizations: UN and its affiliated agencies, OAS.

Embassy: 2600 Virginia Ave. NW 20037; 338-6980.

The Netherlands acquired Suriname in 1667 from Britain, in exchange for New Netherlands (New York). The 1954 Dutch constitution raised the colony to a level of equality with the Netherlands and the Netherlands Antilles. In the 1970s the Dutch government pressured for Suriname independence, which came Nov. 25, 1975, despite objections from East Indians and some Bush Negroes. Some 40% of the population (mostly East Indians) emigrated to the Netherlands in the months before independence. The Netherlands promised $1.5 billion in aid for the first decade of independence.

The National Military Council took over control of the government, Feb. 1982. The Netherlands has suspended aid.

Swaziland
Kingdom of Swaziland

People: Population (1984 est.): 651,000. **Age distrib. (%):** 0–14: 47.7; 15–59: 46.8; 60+: 5.4. **Pop. density:** 92.9 per sq. mi. **Urban** (1980): 8.9%. **Ethnic groups:** Swazi 90%, Zulu 2.3%, European 2.1%, other African, non-African groups. **Languages:** siSwati, English, (both official). **Religions:** Christians 77%, animist 23%.

Geography: Area: 6,704 sq. mi., slightly smaller than New Jersey. **Location:** In southern Africa, near Indian O. coast. **Neighbors:** South Africa on N, W, S, Mozambique on E. **Topography:** The country descends from W-E in broad belts, becoming more arid in the lowveld region, then rising to a plateau in the E. **Capital:** Mbabane. **Cities** (1983 est.): Mbabane 39,000.

Government: Type: Monarchy. **Head of state:** Queen Ntombi; as of: Aug. 10, 1983. **Head of government:** Prime Min. Prince Bhekimpi Dlamini; in office: Mar. 25, 1983. **Local divisions:** 4 districts, 2 municipalities, 40 regions.

Economy: Type: Industries: Wood pulp. **Chief crops:** Sugar, corn, cotton, rice, pineapples, sugar, citrus fruits. **Minerals:** Asbestos, iron, coal. **Other resources:** Forests. **Arable land:** 19%. **Meat prod.** (1980): beef: 14,000 metric tons. **Electricity prod.** (1981): 310 mln. kwh. **Labor force:** 53% agric.; 9% ind. and commerce; 9% serv.

Finance: Currency: Lilangeni (Mar. 1985: 1.90 = $1 US). **Gross domestic product** (1981): $425 mln. **Per capita income** (1981 est.): $840. **Imports** (1981): $635 mln.; partners: So. Afr., 96%. **Exports** (1981): $353 mln.; partners: UK 33%, So. Afr. 20%. **National budget** (1982): $182 mln. **International reserves less gold** (Feb. 1985): $66.8 mln. **Consumer prices** (change in 1983): 11.6%.

Transport: Motor vehicles: in use (1982): 21,000 passenger cars, 8,000 comm. vehicles.

Communications: Radios: 70,000 in use (1982). **Telephones in use** (1982): 15,357. **Daily newspaper circ.** (1982): 17 per 1,000 pop.

Health: Life expectancy at birth (1983): 46.8 male; 50.0 female. **Births** (per 1,000 pop. 1978): 47. **Deaths** (per 1,000 pop. 1978): 19. **Natural increase** (1978): 2.7%. **Hospital beds** (1980): 1,560. **Physicians** (1981): 80. **Infant mortality rate** (per 1,000 live births 1982): 156.

Education (1983): **Literacy:** 65%. Almost all attend primary school.

Major International Organizations: UN and its specialized agencies, OAU, Commonwealth of Nations.

Embassy: 4301 Connecticut Ave. NW 20008; 362-6683.

The royal house of Swaziland traces back 400 years, and is one of Africa's last ruling dynasties. The Swazis, a Bantu people, were driven to Swaziland from lands to the N by the Zulus in 1820. Their autonomy was later guaranteed by Britain and Transvaal, with Britain assuming control after 1903. Independence came Sept. 6, 1968. In 1973 the king repealed the constitution and assumed full powers.

A new Parliament was opened, 1979. Under the new constitution political parties were forbidden; Parliament's role in government was limited to debate and advice.

Sweden
Kingdom of Sweden

People: Population (1984 est.): 8,335,000. **Age distrib. (%):** 0–14: 19.4; 15–59: 57.5; 60+: 22.1. **Pop. density:** 52.4 per sq. mi. **Urban** (1980): 87.2%. **Ethnic groups:** Swedish 93%, Finnish 3%, Lapps, European immigrants. **Languages:** Swedish, Finnish. **Religions:** Lutherans (official) 95%, other Protestants 5%.

Geography: Area: 179,896 sq. mi., larger than California. **Location:** On Scandinavian Peninsula in N. Europe. **Neighbors:** Norway on W, Denmark on S (across Kattegat), Finland on E. **Topography:** Mountains along NW border cover 25% of Sweden, flat or rolling terrain covers the central and southern areas, which includes several large lakes. **Capital:** Stockholm. **Cities** (1983 est.): Stockholm 649,686; Goteborg 425,875; Malmo 230,381.

Government: Type: Constitutional monarchy. **Head of state:** King Carl XVI Gustaf; b. Apr. 30, 1946; in office: Sept. 19, 1973. **Head of government:** Prime Min. Olof Palme; b. Jan. 27, 1927; in office: Oct. 7, 1982. **Local divisions:** 24 lan (counties). **Defense:** 3.3% of GNP (1982).

Economy: Industries: Steel, machinery, instruments, autos, shipbuilding, shipping, paper. **Chief crops:** Grains, potatoes, sugar beets. **Minerals:** Zinc, iron, lead, copper, gold, silver. **Other resources:** Forests (half the country); yield one fourth exports. **Arable land:** 7%. **Meat prod.** (1984): beef: 155,000 metric tons; pork: 322,000 metric tons. **Fish catch** (1983): 180,000 metric tons. **Electricity prod.** (1983): 105.8 bln. kwh. **Crude steel prod.** (1983): 8.2 mln. metric tons. **Labor force:** 5% agric.; 39% ind. and commerce, 20% serv, 35% govt.

Finance: Currency: Krona (June 1985: 8.79 = $1 US). **Gross national product** (1983): $88 bln. **Per capita income** (1980): $14,821. **Imports** (1984): $26.3 bln.; partners: W. Ger. 17%, UK 13%, U.S. 9%, Fin. 7%. **Exports** (1984): $29.3 bln.; partners: UK 10%, W. Ger. 10%, Nor. 11%, Den. 8%. **National budget** (1982): $28.9 bln. revenues; $42.9 bln. expenditures. **International reserves less gold** (Mar. 1985): $3.6 bln. **Gold:** 6.06 mln. oz t. **Consumer prices** (change in 1984): 8.0%.

Transport: Railway traffic (1983): 6.4 bln. passenger-km; 14.9 bln. net ton-km. **Motor vehicles:** in use (1983): 2.9 mln. passenger cars, 206,738 comm. vehicles; manuf. (1982): 269,000 passenger cars. **Civil aviation** (1982): 5.5 bln. passenger-km: 189 mln. freight ton-km. **Chief ports:** Goteborg, Stockholm, Malmo.

Communications: Television sets: 3.2 mln. licensed (1983). **Radios:** 8.3 mln. (1977). **Telephones in use** (1982): 6.8 mln. **Daily newspaper circ.** (1982): 578 per 1,000 pop.

Health: Life expectancy at birth (1982): 73.4 male; 79.4 female. **Births** (per 1,000 pop. 1982): 11.1. **Deaths** (per 1,000 pop. 1982): 10.9. **Natural increase** (1982): 0.2%. **Hospital beds** (per 100,000 pop. 1977): 1,496. **Physicians** (per 100,000 pop. 1977): 178. **Infant mortality** (per 1,000 live births 1982): 6.8.

Education (1982): **Literacy:** 99%. **Years compulsory:** 9; attendance 100%.

Major International Organizations: UN and its specialized agencies, EFTA, OECD.

Embassy: 600 New Hampshire Ave. NW 20037; 298-3500.

The Swedes have lived in present-day Sweden for at least 5,000 years, longer than nearly any other European people. Gothic tribes from Sweden played a major role in the disintegration of the Roman Empire. Other Swedes helped create the first Russian state in the 9th century.

The Swedes were Christianized from the 11th century, and a strong centralized monarchy developed. A parliament, the Riksdag, was first called in 1435, the earliest parliament on the European continent, with all classes of society represented.

Swedish independence from rule by Danish kings (dating from 1397) was secured by Gustavus I in a revolt, 1521-23; he built up the government and military and established the Lutheran Church. In the 17th century Sweden was a major European power, gaining most of the Baltic seacoast, but its international position subsequently declined.

The Napoleonic wars, in which Sweden acquired Norway (it became independent 1905), were the last in which Sweden participated. Armed neutrality was maintained in both world wars.

Over 4 decades of Social Democratic rule was ended in 1976 parliamentary elections but the party was returned to power in the 1982 elections. Although 90% of the economy is in private hands, the government holds a large interest in water power production and the railroads are operated by a public agency.

Consumer cooperatives are in extensive operation and also are important in agriculture and housing. Per capita GNP is among the highest in the world.

A labor crisis of strikes locking out more than 800,000 workers, May 1980, brought the country to an industrial standstill.

A Soviet submarine went aground inside Swedish territorial waters near the Karlskrona Naval Base, Oct. 27, 1981. Sweden claimed the submarine was armed with nuclear weapons and the incident a "flagrant violation" of Swedish neutrality. The submarine was towed back to international waters Nov. 6. Sweden charged that the USSR has repeatedly violated its territorial waters and airspace.

Switzerland
Swiss Confederation

People: Population (1984 est.): 6,500,000. **Age distrib. (%):** 0–14: 19.8; 15–59: 62.1; 60+: 17.2. **Pop. density:** 403 per sq. mi. **Urban** (1980): 50.9%. **Ethnic groups:** Mixed European stock. **Languages:** German 65%, French 18%, Italian 12%, Romansh 1%. (all official). **Religions:** Roman Catholic 49%, Protestant 48%.

Geography: Area: 15,941 sq. mi., as large as Mass., Conn., and R.I. combined. **Location:** In the Alps Mts. in Central Europe. **Neighbors:** France on W, Italy on S, Austria on E, W. Germany on N. **Topography:** The Alps cover 60% of the land area, the Jura, near France, 10%. Running between, from NE to SW, are midlands, 30%. **Capital:** Bern. **Cities** (1985 est.): Zurich 375,000; Basel 183,200; Geneva 157,000.

Government: Type: Federal state. **Head of government:** Pres. Kurt Furgler; in office: Jan. 1, 1985. **Local divisions:** 20 full cantons, 6 half cantons. **Defense:** 2.1% of GNP (1984).

Economy: Industries: Machinery, machine tools, steel, instruments, watches, textiles, foodstuffs (cheese, chocolate), chemicals, drugs, banking, tourism. **Chief crops:** Grains, potatoes, sugar beets, vegetables, tobacco. **Minerals:** Salt. **Other resources:** Hydro power potential. **Arable land:** 10%. **Meat prod.** (1984): beef: 172,000 metric tons; pork: 272,000 metric tons. **Electricity prod.** (1982): 50.7 bln. kwh. **Crude steel Prod.** (1982): 950,000 metric tons. **Labor force:** 39% ind. and commerce, 7% agric., 50% serv.

Finance: Currency: Franc (June 1985: 2.56 = $1 US). **Gross domestic product** (1984): $93.7 bln. **Per capita income** (1984): $14,408. **Imports** (1984): $29.6 bln.; partners: W. Ger. 30%, Fr. 11%, It. 10%, U.K. 5%. **Exports** (1984): $25.5 bln.; partners: W. Ger. 18%, Fr. 9%, It. 8%, U.S. 8%. **Tourists** (1983): receipts: $3.0 bln. **National budget** (1984): $10.1 bln. **International reserves less gold** (Mar. 1985): $13.1 bln. **Gold:** 83.28 mln. oz t. **Consumer prices** (change in 1984): 3.0%.

Transport: Railway traffic (1983): 9.0 bln. passenger-km; 6.4 bln. net ton-km. **Motor vehicles:** in use (1983): 2.5 mln. passenger cars, 201,000 comm. vehicles. **Civil aviation** (1983): 12.2 bln. passenger-km; 539 mln. freight ton-km.

Communications: Television sets: 2 mln. licensed (1983). **Radios:** 2.3 mln. licensed (1983). **Telephones in use** (1982): 4.7 mln. **Daily newspaper circ.** (1983): 605 per 1,000 pop.

Health: Life expectancy at birth (1985): 70.3 male; 76.2 female. **Births** (per 1,000 pop. 1983): 11.4. **Deaths** (per 1,000 pop. 1983): 9.3. **Natural increase** (1983): .2%. **Hospital beds** (per 100,000 pop. 1977): 1,141. **Physicians** (per 100,000 pop. 1977): 201. **Infant mortality** (per 1,000 live births 1985): 9.

Education (1984): **Literacy:** 100%. **Years compulsory:** 9; attendance 100%.

Major International Organizations: Many UN specialized agencies (though not a member).
Embassy: 2900 Cathedral Ave. NW 20008; 745-7900.

Switzerland, the Roman province of Helvetia, is a federation of 23 cantons (20 full cantons and 6 half cantons), 3 of which in 1291 created a defensive league and later were joined by other districts. Voters in the French-speaking part of Canton Bern voted for self-government, 1978; Canton Jura was created Jan. 1, 1979.

In 1648 the Swiss Confederation obtained its independence from the Holy Roman Empire. The cantons were joined under a federal constitution in 1848, with large powers of local control retained by each canton.

Switzerland has maintained an armed neutrality since 1815, and has not been involved in a foreign war since 1515. It is not a member of NATO or the UN. However, the Cabinet took steps, Mar. 28, 1979, to recommend Swiss membership in the UN. Switzerland is a member of several UN agencies and of the European Free Trade Assoc. and has ties with the EC. It is also the seat of many UN and other international agencies.

Switzerland is a leading world banking center; stability of the currency brings funds from many quarters. In 1984, voters rejected a proposal that would have opened bank records to authorities investigating domestic and foreign tax evasion. Some 20% of all workers are foreign residents.

Syria
Syrian Arab Republic

People: Population (1984 est.): 10,075,000. **Age distrib. (%):** 0–14: 47.9; 15–59: 47.6; 60+: 4.5. **Pop. density:** 138 per sq. mi. **Urban** (1981): 47.9%. **Ethnic groups:** Arabs 90%, Kurds, Armenians, Turks, Circassians, Assyrians. **Languages:** Arabic (official), Kurdish, Armenian, French, English. **Religions:** Sunni Muslim 70%, Christian 13%.
Geography: Area: 71,498 sq. mi., the size of North Dakota. **Location:** At eastern end of Mediterranean Sea. **Neighbors:** Lebanon, Israel on W, Jordan on S, Iraq on E, Turkey on N. **Topography:** Syria has a short Mediterranean coastline, then stretches E and S with fertile lowlands and plains, alternating with mountains and large desert areas. **Capital:** Damascus. **Cities** (1984 est.): Damascus 1,178,000; Aleppo 1,109,000; Homs 406,000.
Government: Type: Socialist. **Head of state:** Pres. Hafez al-Assad; b. Mar. 1930; in office: Feb. 22, 1971. **Head of government:** Prime Min. Abdul Rauf al-Kassem; in office: Jan. 16, 1980. **Local divisions:** Damascus and 13 provinces. **Defense:** 14.4% of GNP (1982).
Economy: Industries: Oil products, textiles, cement, tobacco, glassware, sugar, brassware. **Chief crops:** Cotton, grain, olives, fruits, vegetables. **Minerals:** Oil, phosphate, gypsum. **Crude oil reserves** (1980): 2.00 bln. bbls. **Other resources:** Wool. **Arable land:** 31%. **Meat prod.** (1983): beef: 26,000 metric tons; lamb: 99,000 metric tons. **Electricity prod.** (1982): 5.4 bln. kwh. **Labor force:** 32% agric.; 29% ind. & comm.; 39% services.
Finance: Currency: Pound (Mar. 1985: 3.92 = $1 US). **Gross domestic product** (1981): $15.3 bln. **Per capita income** (1975): $702. **Imports** (1982): $4.0 bln.; partners: Iraq 19%, It. 10%, W. Ger. 7%, Fr. 5%. **Exports** (1983): $2.0 bln.; partners: It. 42%, Rom. 10%. **Tourists** (1982): receipts: $150 mln. **Consumer prices** (change in 1983): 6.0%.
Transport: Railway traffic (1982): 412 mln. passenger-km; 708 mln. net ton-km. **Motor vehicles** in use (1982): 79,000 passenger cars, 113,000 comm. vehicles **Civil aviation** (1983): 1.1 bln. passenger-km; 9.2 mln. net ton-km. **Chief ports:** Latakia, Tartus.
Communications: Television sets: 387,000 in use (1982). **Radios:** 1.8 mln. in use (1982). **Telephones in use** (1982): 355,000. **Daily newspaper circ.** (1982): 7 per 1,000 pop.
Health: Life expectancy at birth (1980): 64.9 male; 67.6 female. **Births** (per 1,000 pop. 1983): 43.6. **Deaths** (per 1,000 1983): 5.3. **Natural increase** (1983): 8%. **Hospital beds** (1977): 7,479. **Infant mortality** (per 1,000 live births 1976): 15.3.
Education (1981): **Literacy:** 65%. **Years compulsory:** 6; attendance: 90%.
Major International Organizations: UN and its specialized agencies.
Embassy: 2215 Wyoming Ave. NW 20008; 232-6313.

Syria contains some of the most ancient remains of civilization. It was the center of the Seleucid empire, but later became absorbed in the Roman and Arab empires. Ottoman rule prevailed for 4 centuries, until the end of World War I.

The state of Syria was formed from former Turkish districts, made a separate entity by the Treaty of Sevres 1920 and divided into the states of Syria and Greater Lebanon. Both were administered under a French League of Nations mandate 1920-1941.

Syria was proclaimed a republic by the occupying French Sept. 16, 1941, and exercised full independence effective Jan. 1, 1944. French troops left in 1946. Syria joined in the Arab invasion of Israel in 1948.

Syria joined with Egypt in Feb. 1958 in the United Arab Republic but seceded Sept. 30, 1961. The Socialist Baath party and military leaders seized power in Mar. 1963. The Baath, a pan-Arab organization, became the only legal party. The government has been dominated by members of the minority Alawite sect.

In the Arab-Israeli war of June 1967, Israel seized and occupied the Golan Heights area inside Syria, from which Israeli settlements had for years been shelled by Syria.

Syria aided Palestinian guerrillas fighting Jordanian forces in Sept. 1970 and, after a renewal of that fighting in July 1971, broke off relations with Jordan. But by 1975 the 2 countries had entered a military coordination pact.

On Oct. 6, 1973, Syria joined Egypt in an attack on Israel. Arab oil states agreed in 1974 to give Syria $1 billion a year to aid anti-Israel moves. Military supplies used or lost in the 1973 war were replaced by the USSR in 1974. Some 30,000 Syrian troops entered Lebanon in 1976 to mediate in a civil war, and fought Palestinian guerrillas and, later, fought Christian militiamen. Syrian troops again battled Christian forces in Lebanon, Apr. 1981, ending a ceasefire that had been in place.

Following the June 6, 1982 Israeli invasion of Lebanon, Israeli planes destroyed 17 Syrian antiaircraft missile batteries in the Bekka Valley, June 9. Some 25 Syrian planes were downed during the engagement. Syrian and Israeli troops exchanged fire in central Lebanon. Israel and Syria agreed to a cease fire June 11. Syria has rejected a peace settlement in Lebanon until Israel withdraws its forces from Lebanon and the Golan Heights. In 1983, Syria backed the PLO rebels who ousted Yasir Arafat's forces from Tripoli.

In Feb. 1982, an uprising by antigovernment Muslim brotherhood militants brought heavy fighting and caused some 5,000 deaths.

Taiwan
Republic of China

People: Population (1984 est.): 19,117,000. **Pop. density:** 1,347 per sq. mi. **Ethnic groups:** Han Chinese 98% (18% from mainland), aborigines (of Indonesian origin) 2%. **Languages:** Mandarin Chinese (official), Taiwan, Hakka dialects. **Religions:** Buddhism, Taoism, Confucianism prevail.
Geography: Area: 13,814 sq. mi., the size of Maryland and Delaware combined. **Location:** Off SE coast of China, between E. and S. China Seas. **Neighbors:** Nearest is China. **Topography:** A mountain range forms the backbone of the island; the eastern half is very steep and craggy, the western slope is flat, fertile, and well-cultivated. **Capital:** Taipei. **Cities** (1984 est.): Taipei (met.) 2,388,000; Kaohsiung 1,262,000; Taichung 636,734; Tainan 622,000.
Government: Type: One-party system. **Head of state:** Chiang Ching-kuo; b. Mar. 18, 1910; in office: May 20, 1978. **Head of government:** Prime Min. Yu Kuo-hwa; in office: May 20, 1984. **Local divisions:** Taiwan province, Taipei and Kaohsiung municipalities. **Defense:** 7.2% of GNP (1982).
Economy: Industries: Textiles, clothing, electronics, processed foods, chemicals, plastics. **Chief crops:** Rice, bananas, pineapples, sugarcane, sweet potatoes, peanuts. **Minerals:** Coal, limestone, marble. **Crude oil reserves** (1980): 10.2 mln. bbls. **Cultivated land:** 25%. **Meat prod.** (1977): beef: 15,798 metric tons; pork: 574,656 metric tons. **Fish catch** (1982): 922,520 metric tons. **Electricity prod.** (1982): 40.8 bln. kwh. **Crude steel prod.** (1982): 4.1 mln. metric tons. **Labor force:** 20% agric.; 41% ind. & comm.; 32% services.
Finance: Currency: New Taiwan dollar (Nov. 1984: 39.13 = $1 US). **Gross national product** (1983): $49.7 bln. **Per capita**

income (1984): $3,000. **Imports** (1981): $21.1 bln.; partners: U.S. 21%, Jap. 27%, Kuw. 6%, Saudi Ar. 10%. **Exports** (1981): $22.6 bln.; partners: U.S. 45%, Jap. 10%, Hong Kong 6%. **Tourists** (1982): 1.1 bln.; receipts: $953 mln. **National budget** (1981): $23.2 bln. **International reserves less gold** (Mar. 1980): $1.51 bln. **Gold:** 2.49 mln. oz t. **Consumer prices** (change in 1979): 9.7%.

Transport: Motor vehicles: in use (1984): 712,000 passenger cars, 95,000 comm. vehicles. **Civil Aviation** (1983): 9.1 bln. passenger-km; 1.5 mln. net ton-km. **Chief ports:** Kaohsiung, Keelung, Hualien, Taichung.

Communications: Television sets: 5 mln. in use (1983). **Radios:** 5 mln. in use (1983). **Telephones in use** (1982): 4.3 mln. **Daily newspaper circ.** (1983): 215 per 1,000 pop.

Health: Life expectancy at birth (1983): 69.6 male; 74.5 female. **Births** (per 1,000 pop. 1983): 20.6. **Deaths** (per 1,000 pop. 1983): 4.9. **Natural increase** (1983): 1.5%. **Physicians** (1982): 21,526 serve some 11,000 medical care facilities. **Infant mortality** (per 1,000 live births 1983): 11.1.

Education (1983): **Literacy:** 89%. Years compulsory 9; attendance 99%.

Large-scale Chinese immigration began in the 17th century. The island came under mainland control after an interval of Dutch rule, 1620-62. Taiwan (also called Formosa) was ruled by Japan 1895-1945. Two million Kuomintang supporters fled to Taiwan in 1949. Both the Taipei and Peking governments consider Taiwan an integral part of China. Taiwan has rejected Peking's efforts at reunification.

The U.S. upon its recognition of the People's Republic of China, Dec. 15, 1978, severed diplomatic ties with Taiwan. It maintains the unofficial American Institute in Taiwan, while Taiwan has established the Coordination Council for North American Affairs in Washington, D.C.

Land reform, government planning, U.S. aid and investment, and free universal education have brought huge advances in industry, agriculture, and mass living standards.

The **Penghu** (Pescadores), 50 sq. mi., pop. 120,000, lie between Taiwan and the mainland. **Quemoy** and **Matsu,** pop. (1980) 61,000 lie just off the mainland.

Tanzania
United Republic of Tanzania

People: Population (1984 est.) 21,202,000. **Pop. density:** 55.9 per sq. mi. **Urban** (1984): 20%. **Ethnic groups:** African. **Languages:** Swahili, English are official. **Religions:** Moslems 35%, Christians 35%, traditional beliefs 30%.

Geography: Area: 364,886 sq. mi., more than twice the size of California. **Location:** On coast of E. Africa. **Neighbors:** Kenya, Uganda on N, Rwanda, Burundi, Zaire on W, Zambia, Malawi, Mozambique on S. **Topography:** Hot, arid central plateau, surrounded by the lake region in the W, temperate highlands in N and S, the coastal plains. Mt. Kilimanjaro, 19,340 ft., is highest in Africa. **Capital:** Dar-es-Salaam. **Cities** (1984): Dar-es-Salaam 1.4 mln.

Government: Type: Republic. **Head of state:** Pres. Julius Kambarage Nyerere; b. Mar. 1922; in office: Apr. 26, 1964. **Head of government:** Salim Ahmed Salim; b. 1942; in office: Apr. 24, 1984. **Local divisions:** 25 regions (20 on mainland). **Defense:** 5.5% of GDP (1982).

Economy: Industries: Food processing, clothing. **Chief crops:** Sisal, cotton, coffee, tea, tobacco. **Minerals:** Diamonds, gold, nickel. **Other resources:** Hides. **Arable land:** 15%. **Meat prod.** (1980): beef: 139,000 metric tons; lamb: 34,000 metric tons. **Fish catch** (1982): 226,000 metric tons. **Electricity prod.** (1982): 720 mln. kwh. **Labor force:** 83% agric., 17% ind. & comm.

Finance: Currency: Shilling (Mar. 1985: 17.89 = $1 US). **Gross domestic product** (1982): $4.56 bln. **Per capita income** (1982): $240. **Imports** (1983): $773 mln.; partners: UK 14%, Jap. 12%, W. Ger. 10%. **Exports** (1983): $364 mln.; partners: W. Ger. 15%, UK 13%. **Tourists** (1981): 91,600; receipts: $15 mln. **National budget** (1980): $973 mln. revenues; $933 mln. expenditures. **International reserves less gold** (Jan. 1984): $20.7 mln. **Consumer prices** (change in 1984): 35.8%.

Transport: Motor vehicles: in use (1982): 48,000 passenger cars, 31,000 comm. vehicles. **Chief ports:** Dar-es-Salaam, Mtwara, Tanga.

Communications: Radios: 2 mln. in use (1983). **Telephones in use** (1982): 99,000. **Daily newspaper circ.** (1982): 7 per 1,000 pop.

Health: Life expectancy at birth (1984): 52 yrs. **Births** (per 1,000 pop. 1978): 47. **Deaths** (per 1,000 pop. 1978): 17. **Natural increase** (1978): 3.0%. **Hospital beds** (1981): 21,352. **Physicians** (1981): 599. **Infant mortality** (per 1,000 live births 1984): 103.

Education (1984): **Literacy:** 66%. **Attendance:** 87%.

Major International Organizations: UN and its specialized agencies, OAU, Commonwealth of Nations.

Embassy: 2139 R. St. NW 20008; 939-6125.

The Republic of Tanganyika in E. Africa and the island Republic of Zanzibar, off the coast of Tanganyika, joined into a single nation, the United Republic of Tanzania, Apr. 26, 1964. Zanzibar retains internal self-government.

Tanganyika. Arab colonization and slaving began in the 8th century AD; Portuguese sailors explored the coast by about 1500. Other Europeans followed.

In 1885 Germany established German East Africa of which Tanganyika formed the bulk. It became a League of Nations mandate and, after 1946, a UN trust territory, both under Britain. It became independent Dec. 9, 1961, and a republic within the Commonwealth a year later.

In 1967 the government set on a socialist course; it nationalized all banks and many industries. The government also ordered that Swahili, not English, be used in all official business. Nine million people have been moved into cooperative villages.

Tanzania exchanged invasion attacks with Uganda, 1978-79. Tanzanian forces drove Idi Amin from Uganda, Mar., 1979.

Zanzibar, the Isle of Cloves, lies 23 mi. off the coast of Tanganyika; its area is 640 sq. mi. The island of **Pemba,** 25 mi. to the NE, area 380 sq. mi., is included in the administration. The total population (1978 cen.) is 475,655.

Chief industry is the production of cloves and clove oil of which Zanzibar and Pemba produce the bulk of the world's supply.

Zanzibar was for centuries the center for Arab slave-traders. Portugal ruled for 2 centuries until ousted by Arabs around 1700. Zanzibar became a British Protectorate in 1890; independence came Dec. 10, 1963. Revolutionary forces overthrew the Sultan Jan. 12, 1964. The new government ousted Western diplomats and newsmen, slaughtered thousands of Arabs, and nationalized farms. Union with Tanganyika followed, 1964. The ruling parties of Tanganyika and Zanzibar were united in 1977, as political tension eased.

Thailand
Kingdom of Thailand

People: Population (1984 est.): 51,725,000. **Age distrib.** (%): 0–14: 38.5; 15–59: 54.9; 60+: 6.6. **Pop. density:** 254 per sq. mi. **Urban** (1984): 17%. **Ethnic groups:** Thais 75%, Chinese 14%, others 11%. **Languages:** Thai, Chinese. **Religions:** Buddhists 95%, Moslems 4%.

Geography: Area: 198,500 sq. mi., about the size of Texas. **Location:** On Indochinese and Malayan Peninsulas in S.E. Asia. **Neighbors:** Burma on W. Laos on N, Cambodia on E, Malaysia on S. **Topography:** A plateau dominates the NE third of Thailand, dropping to the fertile alluvial valley of the Chao Phraya R. in the center. Forested mountains are in N, with narrow fertile valleys. The southern peninsula region is covered by rain forests. **Capital:** Bangkok. **Cities** (1980 est.): Bangkok (met.): 4.7 mln.

Government: Type: Constitutional monarchy. **Head of state:** King Bhumibol Adulyadej; b. Dec. 5, 1927; in office: June 9, 1946. **Head of government:** Prime Min. Prem Tinsulanond; b. 1920; in office: Mar. 3, 1980. **Local divisions:** 73 provinces. **Defense:** 4.2% of GNP (1982).

Economy: Industries: Auto assembly, drugs, textiles, electrical goods. **Chief crops:** Rice (a major export), corn tapioca, jute, sugar, coconuts, tobacco, pepper, peanuts, beans, cotton.

Minerals: Antimony, tin (5th largest producer), tungsten, iron, manganese, gas. **Crude oil reserves** (1979): 200 bbls. **Other resources:** Forests (teak is exported), rubber. **Arable land:** 36%. **Meat prod.** (1984): beef: 220,000 metric tons; pork: 255,000 metric tons. **Fish catch** (1982): 1.9 mln. metric tons. **Electricity prod.** (1982): 17.2 bln. kwh. **Crude steel prod.** (1981): 450,000 metric tons. **Labor force:** 76% agric.; 9% ind. & comm.; 9% serv.; 6% govt.

Finance: Currency: Baht (Mar. 1985: 27.55 = $1 US). **Gross domestic product** (1983): $39.2 bln. **Per capita income** (1981): $758. **Imports** (1984): $10.4 bln.; partners: Jap. 24%, U.S. 13%, Saudi Ar. 13%. **Exports** (1984): $7.4 bln.; partners: Jap. 14%, U.S. 13%, Sing. 14%. **Tourists** (1981): 2 mln. receipts: $983 mln. **National budget** (1982): $7 bln. **International reserves less gold** (Mar. 1985): $1.7 bln. **Gold:** 2.48 mln. oz t. **Consumer prices** (change in 1984): 0.9%.

Transport: Railway traffic (1982): 9.4 bln. passenger-km; 2.3 bln. net ton-km. **Motor vehicles:** in use (1982): 451,000 passenger cars, 64,000 comm. vehicles. **Civil aviation** (1982): 8.6 bln. passenger-km; 320 mln. freight ton-km. **Chief ports:** Bangkok, Sattahip.

Communication: Television sets: 3 mln. in use (1983). **Radios:** 7 mln. in use (1983). **Telephones in use** (1982): 529,106. **Daily newspaper circ.** (1983): 48 per 1,000 pop.

Health: Life expectancy at birth (1983): 59.5 male; 65.1 female. **Births** (per 1,000 pop. 1982): 22.5. **Deaths** (per 1,000 pop. 1982): 5.1. **Natural increase** (1982): 1.7%. **Health** (1982): 434 hospitals, 6,496 health centers. **Physicians** (1982): 6,550. **Infant mortality** (per 1,000 live births 1982): 68.

Education (1983): **Literacy:** 84%. **Years compulsory:** 7; attendance 83%.

Major International Organizations: UN and its specialized agencies.

Embassy: 2300 Kalorama Rd. NW 20008; 667-1446.

Thais began migrating from southern China in the 11th century. Thailand is the only country in SE Asia never taken over by a European power, thanks to King Mongkut and his son King Chulalongkorn who ruled from 1851 to 1910, modernized the country, and signed trade treaties with both Britain and France. A bloodless revolution in 1932 limited the monarchy.

Japan occupied the country in 1941. After the war, Thailand followed a pro-West foreign policy. Some 11,000 Thai troops fought in S. Vietnam, but were withdrawn by 1972.

The military took over the government in a bloody 1976 coup. Kriangsak Chomanan, prime minister since a 1977 military coup, resigned, Feb. 1980, under opposition over soaring inflation, oil price increases, labor unrest and growing crime.

Vietnamese troops have crossed the border and been repulsed by Thai forces in the 1980s.

Togo
Republic of Togo

People: Population (1984 est.): 2,926,000. **Age distrib. (%):** 0-14: 49.8; 15-59: 44.6; 60+:5.6.**Pop. density:** 134 per sq. mi. **Urban** (1981): 15.2%. **Ethnic groups:** Ewe 35%, Mina 6%, Kabye 22%. **Languages:** French (official), others. **Religions:** Traditional 60%, Christian 20%, Moslem 20%.

Geography: Area: 21,853 sq. mi., slightly smaller than West Virginia. **Location:** On S coast of W. Africa. **Neighbors:** Ghana on W, Upper Volta on N, Benin on E. **Topography:** A range of hills running SW-NE splits Togo into 2 savanna plains regions. **Capital:** Lomé. **Cities** (1984 est.): Lomé 250,000.

Government: Type: Republic. **Head of state:** Pres. Gnassingbe Eyadema; b. Dec. 26, 1937; in office: Apr. 14, 1967. **Local divisions:** 21 prefectures.

Economy: Industries: Textiles, shoes. **Chief crops:** Coffee, cocoa, yams, manioc, millet, rice. **Minerals:** Phosphates. **Arable land:** 26%. **Electricity prod.** (1982): 85 mln. kwh. **Labor force:** 67% agric.; 15% industry.

Finance: Currency: CFA franc (Mar. 1985: 471 = $1 US). **Gross domestic product** (1982): $812.5 mln. **Per capita income** (1981): $348. **Imports** (1982): $390 mln.; partners: Fr., U.K., W. Ger. **Exports** (1982): $177 mln.; partners: Neth., Fr., W. Ger. **International reserves less gold** (Jan. 1985): $203.3 mln. **Gold:** 13,000 oz t. **Consumer prices** (change in 1984): −3.8%.

Transport: Railway traffic (1981): 84.5 mln. passenger-km; 37.7 mln. net ton-km. **Motor vehicles:** in use (1981): 26,000 passenger cars, 13,000 comm. vehicles. **Chief ports:** Lome.

Communications: Radios: 190,000 in use (1983). **Telephones in use** (1981): 7,870. **Daily newspaper circ.** (1982): 5 per 1,000 pop.

Health: Life expectancy at birth (1984): 47 yrs. **Births** (per 1,000 pop. 1980): 47.8. **Deaths** (per 1,000 pop. 1980): 17. **Natural increase** (1980): 3.0%. **Hospital beds** (per 100,000 pop. 1977): 143. **Physicians** (per 100,000 pop. 1977): 6. **Infant mortality** (per 1,000 live births 1980): 114.

Education (1984): **Literacy:** 18%.

Major International Organizations: UN, OAU.

Embassy: 2208 Massachusetts Ave. NW 20008; 234-4212.

The Ewe arrived in southern Togo several centuries ago. The country later became a major source of slaves. Germany took control from 1884 on. France and Britain administered Togoland as UN trusteeships. The French sector became the republic of Togo Apr. 27, 1960.

The population is divided between Bantus in the S and Hamitic tribes in the N. Togo has actively promoted regional integration, as a means of stimulating the economy.

Tonga
Kingdom of Tonga

People: Population (1984 est.): 106,000. **Age distrib. (%):** 0-14: 44.4; 15-59; 50.5; 60+:5.1. **Pop. density:** 245 per sq. mi. **Ethnic groups:** Tongans 98%, other Polynesian, European. **Languages:** Tongan, English. **Religions:** Free Wesleyan 47%, Roman Catholics 14%, Free Church of Tonga 14%, Mormons 9%, Church of Tonga 9%.

Geography: Area: 270 sq. mi., smaller than New York City. **Location:** In western S. Pacific O. **Neighbors:** Nearest is Fiji, on W, New Zealand, on S. **Topography:** Tonga comprises 169 volcanic and coral islands, 45 inhabited. **Capital:** Nuku'alofa. **Cities** (1983 est.): Nuku'alofa (met.) 20,000.

Government: Type: Monarchy. **Head of state:** King Taufa'ahau Tupou IV; b. July 4, 1918; in office: Dec. 16, 1965. **Head of government:** Prime Min. Fatafehi Tu'ipelehake; b. Jan. 7, 1922; in office: Dec. 16, 1965. **Local divisions:** 3 island districts.

Economy: Industries: Tourism. **Chief crops:** Coconut products, bananas are exported. **Other resources:** Fish. **Per capita arable land:** 0.4 acres. **Electricity prod.** (1982): 12 mln. kwh. **Labor force:** 75% agric.

Finance: Currency: Pa'anga (Nov. 1984: 1.19 = $1 US). **Gross domestic product** (1981): $50 mln. **Per capita income** (1976): $430. **Imports** (1982): $39 mln.; partners: N Z 37%, Austral. 23%, Jap. 6%, Fiji 7%. **Exports** (1982): $4 mln.; partners: Aust. 45%, N Z 38%.

Transport: Motor vehicles: in use (1981): 622 passenger cars, 1,000 comm. vehicles. **Chief ports:** Nuku'alofa.

Communications: Radios: 65,000 in use (1983). **Telephones in use** (1982): 2,608.

Health: Births (per 1,000 pop. 1983): 27.1. **Deaths** (per 1,000 pop. 1983): 3.3. **Natural increase** (1983): 2.3%. **Pop. per hospital bed** (1976): 300. **Pop. per physician** (1976): 3,000. **Infant mortality** (per 1,000 live births 1983): 6.4.

The islands were first visited by the Dutch in the early 17th century. A series of civil wars ended in 1845 with establishment of the Tupou dynasty. In 1900 Tonga became a British protectorate. On June 4, 1970, Tonga became completely independent and a member of the Commonwealth.

Trinidad and Tobago
Republic of Trinidad and Tobago

People: Population (1984 est.): 1,168,000. **Age distrib. (%):** 0-14: 38.0; 15-59: 55.4; 60+: 6.6. **Pop. density:** 632 per sq. mi. **Urban** (1970): 49.4%. **Ethnic groups:** Africans 40%, East Indians 49%, mixed 14%. **Languages:** English (official), Hindi, French, Spanish. **Religions:** Roman Catholics 33%, Protestants 14%, Hindus 24%, Muslims 6%.

Geography: Area: 1,970 sq. mi., the size of Delaware. **Location:** Off eastern coast of Venezuela. **Neighbors:** Nearest is Venezuela on SW. **Topography:** Three low mountain ranges cross Trinidad E-W, with a well-watered plain between N and Central Ranges. Parts of E and W coasts are swamps. Tobago, 116 sq. mi., lies 20 mi. NE. **Capital:** Port-of-Spain. **Cities** (1984 est.): Port-of-Spain (met.) 300,000; San Fernando 50,000.

Government: Type: Parliamentary democracy. **Head of state:** Pres. Ellis E. I. Clarke; b. Dec. 28, 1917; in office: July 31, 1976. **Head of government:** Prime Min. George Chambers; b. Oct. 4, 1928; in office: Mar. 30, 1981. **Local divisions:** 7 counties, Tobago, 4 cities.

Economy: Industries: Oil products, rum, cement, tourism. **Chief crops:** Sugar, cocoa, coffee, citrus fruits, bananas. **Minerals:** Asphalt, oil, **Crude oil reserves** (1983): 750 mln. bbls. **Arable land:** 30%. **Electricity prod.** (1982): 2 bln. kwh. **Labor force:** 7% agric., 60% construction, mining, commerce, 22% services.

Finance: Currency: Dollar (Mar. 1985: 2.40 = $1 US). **Gross domestic product** (1983): $8.4 bln. **Per capita income** (1982): $6,800. **Imports** (1983): $2.5 bln.; partners: Saudi Ar. 26%, U.S. 26%, UK 9%. **Exports** (1983): $2.3 bln.; partners: U.S. 59%, Neth. 5%. **National budget** (1980): $2.5 bln. revenues; $2.6 bln. expenditures. **International reserves less gold** (Mar. 1985): $1.0 bln. **Gold:** 54,000 oz t. **Consumer prices** (change in 1984): 13.3%.

Transport: Motor vehicles: in use (1983): 180,000 passenger cars, 35,000 comm. vehicles. **Civil aviation:** (1982): 1.5 bln. passenger-km; 5.5 mln. freight ton-km. **Chief ports:** Port-of-Spain.

Communications: Television sets: 300,000 in use (1983). **Radios:** 355,000 licensed (1983). **Telephones in use** (1980): 77,800. **Daily newspaper circ.** (1982): 143 per 1,000 pop.

Health: Life expectancy at birth (1980): 66 male; 72 female. **Births** (per 1,000 pop. 1979): 23.8. **Deaths** (per 1,000 pop. 1979): 6.6. **Natural increase** (1978): 1.9%. **Hospital beds** (per 100,000 pop. 1977): 445. **Physicians** (per 100,000 pop 1977): 54. **Infant mortality** (per 1,000 pop. 1980): 197.

Education (1984): **Literacy:** 96%. **Years compulsory:** 8.

Major International Organizations: UN and its specialized agencies, Commonwealth of Nations, OAS.

Embassy: 1708 Massachusetts Ave. NW 20036; 467-6490.

Columbus sighted Trinidad in 1498. A British possession since 1802, Trinidad and Tobago won independence Aug. 31, 1962. It became a republic in 1976. The People's National Movement party has held control of the government since 1956.

The nation is one of the most prosperous in the Caribbean. Oil production has increased with offshore finds. Middle Eastern oil is refined and exported, mostly to the U.S.

Tunisia
Republic of Tunisia

People: Population (1984 est.): 7,202,000. **Age distrib.** (%) 0–14: 43.3 15–59: 50.9; 60+: 5.8. **Pop. density:** 117 per sq. mi. **Ethnic groups:** Arab 98%. **Languages:** Arabic (official), French. **Religions:** Mainly Moslem, Christian and Jewish minorities.

Geography: Area: 63,378 sq. mi., about the size of Missouri. **Location:** On N coast of Africa. **Neighbors:** Algeria on W, Libya on E. **Topography:** The N is wooded and fertile. The central coastal plains are given to grazing and orchards. The S is arid, approaching Sahara Desert. **Capital:** Tunis. **Cities** (1984 est.) Tunis 1,000,000, Sfax 475,000.

Government: Type: Republic. **Head of state:** Pres. Habib Bourguiba; b. Aug. 3, 1903; in office: July 25, 1957. **Head of government:** Prime Min. Mohammed Mzali; b. Dec. 23, 1925; in office: Apr. 23, 1980. **Local divisions:** 21 governorates. **Defense:** less than 3% of GDP (1982).

Economy: Industries: Food processing, textiles, oil products, construction materials, tourism. **Chief crops:** Grains, dates, olives, citrus fruits, figs, vegetables, grapes. **Minerals:** Phosphates, iron, oil, lead, zinc. **Crude oil reserves** (1980): 2.25 bln. bbls. **Arable land:** 30%. **Meat prod.** (1980): beef: 26,000 metric tons; lamb: 27,000 metric tons. **Fish catch** (1981): 57,500 metric tons. **Electricity prod.** (1982): 3.0 bln. kwh. **Crude steel prod.** (1982): 106,000 metric tons. **Labor force:** 35% agric.; 22% industry; 11% serv.

Finance: Currency: Dinar (Mar. 1985: .85 = $1 US). **Gross domestic product** (1983): $5.8 bln. **Per capita income** (1983) $844. **Imports** (1984): $3.1 bln.; partners: Fr. 20%, W. Ger. 11%, It. 15%. **Exports** (1984): $1.7 bln.; partners: It. 17%, Fr. 19%, W. Ger. 10%, U.S. 23%. **Tourists** (1982): 2.2 mln.; receipts: $581 mln. **National budget** (1982): $2.6 bln. expenditures. **International reserves less gold** (Mar. 1985): $225.6 mln. **Gold:** 187,000 oz t. **Consumer prices** (change in 1984): 8.4%.

Transport: Railway traffic (1982): 930 mln. passenger-km; 1.5 bln. net ton-km. **Motor vehicles:** in use (1982): 141,000 passenger cars, 141,000 comm. vehicles; **Civil aviation:** (1982): 1.5 bln. passenger-km; 17.3 mln. freight ton-km. **Chief ports:** Tunis, Sfax, Bizerte.

Communications: Television sets: 300,000 in use (1983). **Radios:** 1.1 mln. in use (1983). **Telephones in use** (1981): 188,000. **Daily newspaper circ.** (1982): 49 per 1,000 pop.

Health: Life expectancy at birth (1980): 56.3 male; 58.4 female. **Births** (per 1,000 pop. 1982): 32.9. **Deaths** (per 1,000 pop. 1982): 7.3. **Natural increase** (1982): 2.5%. **Hospital beds** (per 100,000 pop. 1977): 229. **Physicians** (per 100,000 pop. 1977): 4. **Infant mortality** (per 1,000 pop. under 1 yr. 1984): 90.

Education (1984): **Literacy:** 62%. **Years compulsory:** 8; attendance 85%.

Major International Organizations: UN, Arab League.

Embassy: 2408 Massachusetts Ave. NW 20008; 234-6644.

Site of ancient Carthage, and a former Barbary state under the suzerainty of Turkey, Tunisia became a protectorate of France under a treaty signed May 12, 1881. The nation became independent Mar. 20, 1956, and ended the monarchy the following year. Habib Bourguiba has headed the country since independence.

Although Tunisia is a member of the Arab League, Bourguiba in the 1960s urged negotiations to end Arab-Israeli disputes and was denounced by other members. In 1966 he broke relations with Egypt but resumed them after the 1967 Arab-Israeli war.

Tunisia survived a Libyan-engineered raid against the southern mining center of Gafsa, Jan. 1980. A liberal-minded government undertook steps to ease the blocked political situation. Some 1,000 rioters were arrested in 1984 following an announced 125% increase in the price of bread.

Turkey
Republic of Turkey

People: Population (1984 est.): 50,207,000. **Age distrib.** (%): 0–14: 38.5; 15–59: 54.9; 60+: 6.6. **Pop. density:** 161 per sq. mi. **Urban** (1977): 44.6%. **Ethnic groups:** Turks 85%, Kurds 12%. **Languages:** Turkish (official), Kurdish, Arabic. **Religions:** Muslims 98%, Christians, Jews.

Geography: Area: 300,948 sq. mi., twice the size of California. **Location:** Occupies Asia Minor, between Mediterranean and Black Seas. **Neighbors:** Bulgaria, Greece on W, USSR (Georgia, Armenia) on N, Iran on E, Iraq, Syria on S. **Topography:** Central Turkey has wide plateaus, with hot, dry summers and cold winters. High mountains ring the interior on all but W, with more than 20 peaks over 10,000 ft. Rolling plains are in W; mild, fertile coastal plains are in S, W. **Capital:** Ankara. **Cities** (1980 cen.): Istanbul 2,772,708; Ankara 1,877,755; Izmir 757,854; Adana 574,515.

Government: Type: Republic. **Head of state:** Pres. Kenan Evren; b. 1918; in office: Oct. 27, 1980. **Head of government:** Prime Min. Turgut Ozal; b. 1927; in office: Dec. 13, 1983. **Local divisions:** 67 provinces, with appointed governors. **Defense:** 3.7% of GNP (1982).

Economy: Industries: Silk, textiles, steel, shoes, furniture, cement, paper, glassware, appliances. **Chief crops:** Tobacco (6th largest producer), cereals, cotton, olives, figs, nuts, sugar, opium gums. **Minerals:** Antimony, chromium, mercury, borate, copper, coal. **Crude oil reserves** (1980): 125 mln. bbls. **Other resources:** Wool, silk, forests. **Arable land:** 37%. **Meat prod.** (1984): beef: 245,000 metric tons; lamb: 383,000 metric tons. **Fish catch** (1982): 466,000 metric tons. **Electricity prod.** (1982): 26.4 bln. kwh. **Crude steel prod.** (1982): 2.1 mln. metric tons. **Labor force:** 61% agric.; 12% ind. and comm.; 27% serv.

Finance: Currency: Lira (Mar. 1985: 491 = $1 US). **Gross domestic product** (1983): $51 bln. **Per capita income** (1984):

$1,000 **Imports** (1983): $9.2 bln.; partners: Iraq 16%, W. Ger. 11%, Libya 10%, U.S. 9%. **Exports** (1983): $5.7 bln.; partners: W. Ger. 12%, Iraq 10%, Iran 14%. **Tourists** (1982): 1.4 mln.; receipts: $370 mln. **National budget** (1984): $8.7 bln. expenditures. **International reserves less gold** (Feb. 1985): $1.04 bln. **Gold:** 3.8 mln. oz t. **Consumer prices** (change in 1983): 28.9%.

Transport: Railway traffic (1982): 5.6 bln. passenger-km; 6.3 bln. net ton-km. **Motor vehicles:** in use (1982): 746,000 passenger cars, 341,000 comm. vehicles. **Civil aviation** (1982): 1.1 bln. passenger-km; 20 mln. freight ton-km. **Chief ports:** Istanbul, Izmir, Mersin, Samsun.

Communications: Television sets: 4.5 mln. in use (1982). **Radios:** 4.2 mln. licensed (1982). **Telephones in use** (1982): 1.2 mln.

Health: Life expectancy at birth (1985): 57 years. **Births** (per 1,000 pop. 1978): 35. **Deaths** (per 1,000 pop. 1978): 12. **Natural increase** (1978): 2.3%. **Hospital beds** (1982): 96,138. **Physicians** (1982): 30,956. **Infant mortality** (per 1,000 live births 1985): 15.3.

Education (1985): **Literacy:** 70%. **Years compulsory:** 6; attendance 95%.

Major International Organizations: UN, NATO, OECD. **Embassy:** 1606 23d St. NW 20008; 667-6400.

Ancient inhabitants of Turkey were among the worlds first agriculturalists. Such civilizations as the Hittite, Phrygian, and Lydian flourished in Asiatic Turkey (Asia Minor), as did much of Greek civilization. After the fall of Rome in the 5th century, Constantinople was the capital of the Byzantine Empire for 1,000 years. It fell in 1453 to Ottoman Turks, who ruled a vast empire for over 400 years.

Just before World War I, Turkey, or the Ottoman Empire, ruled what is now Syria, Lebanon, Iraq, Jordan, Israel, Saudi Arabia, Yemen, and islands in the Aegean Sea.

Turkey joined Germany and Austria in World War I and its defeat resulted in loss of much territory and fall of the sultanate. A republic was declared Oct. 29, 1923. The Caliphate (spiritual leadership of Islam) was renounced 1924.

Long embroiled with Greece over Cyprus, off Turkey's south coast, Turkey invaded the island July 20, 1974, after Greek officers seized the Cypriot government as a step toward unification with Greece. Turkey sought a new government for Cyprus, with Greek Cypriot and Turkish Cypriot zones. In reaction to Turkey's moves, the U.S. cut off military aid in 1975. Turkey, in turn, suspended the use of most U.S. bases. Aid was restored in 1978. There was a military takeover, Sept. 12, 1980.

Religious and ethnic tensions and active left and right extremists have caused endemic violence. Martial law, imposed since 1978, was lifted in 1984. The military formally transferred power to an elected parliament in 1983.

Tuvalu

People: Population (1984 est.): 8,000. **Pop. density:** 937 per sq. mi. **Ethnic group:** Polynesian. **Languages:** Tuvaluan, English. **Religions:** mainly Protestant.

Geography: Area: 10 sq. mi., less than one-half the size of Manhattan. **Location:** 9 islands forming a NW-SE chain 360 mi. long in the SW Pacific O. **Neighbors:** Nearest are Samoa on SE, Fiji on S. **Topography:** The islands are all low-lying atolls, nowhere rising more than 15 ft. above sea level, composed of coral reefs. **Capital:** Funafuti (pop. 1983): 2,620.

Government: Head of state: Queen Elizabeth II, represented by Gov.-Gen. Penitala Fiatau Teo, b. July 23, 1911; in office: Oct. 1, 1978. **Head of government:** Prime Min. Tomasi Puapua; in office: Sept. 8, 1981. **Local divisions:** 8 island councils on the permanently inhabited islands.

Economy: Industries: Copra. **Chief crops:** Coconuts. **Labor force:** Approx. 1,500 Tuvaluans work overseas in the Gilberts' phosphate industry, or as overseas seamen.

Finance: Currency: Australian dollar.

Transport: Chief port: Funafuti.

Health: (including former Gilbert Is.) **Life expectancy at birth** (1979): 57 male; 60 female. **Births** (per 1,000 pop. 1982): 34.8. **Deaths** (per 1,000 pop. 1982): 7.6. **Natural increase** (1982): 2.7%. **Infant mortality** (per 1,000 pop. under 1 yr. 1979) : 42. **Education:** Literacy (1979): 96%.

The Ellice Islands separated from the British Gilbert and Ellice Islands colony, 1975, and became independent Tuvalu Oct. 1, 1978.

Britain is committed to providing extensive economic aid. Australian funding has provided for a marine training school and a deep-sea wharf.

Uganda
Republic of Uganda

People: Population (1984 est.): 14,268,000. **Age distrib. (%):** 0–14: 46.1; 15–59: 47.9; 60+: 5.8. **Pop. density:** 175 per sq. mi. **Urban** (1980): 8.1%. **Ethnic groups:** Bantu, Nilotic, Nilo-Hamitic, Sudanic tribes. **Languages:** English (official), Luganda, Swahili. **Religions:** Christians 63%, Moslems 6%, traditional beliefs.

Geography: Area: 93,104 sq. mi., slightly smaller than Oregon. **Location:** In E. Central Africa. **Neighbors:** Sudan on N, Zaire on W, Rwanda, Tanzania on S, Kenya on E. **Topography:** Most of Uganda is a high plateau 3,000-6,000 ft. high, with high Ruwenzori range in W (Mt. Margherita 16,750 ft.), volcanoes in SW, NE is arid, W and SW rainy. Lakes Victoria, Edward, Albert form much of borders. **Capital:** Kampala. **Cities** (1980): Kampala 458,000.

Government: Type: Republic. **Head of state:** Pres. Milton Obote; b. 1925; assumed full control Sept. 17, 1980; elections held Dec. 1980. **Head of government:** Prime Min. Erifasi Otema Allimadi; in office: Dec. 1980. **Local divisions:** 10 provinces, 34 districts. **Defense:** 0.9% of GNP (1982).

Economy: Chief Crops: Coffee, cotton, tea, corn, peanuts, bananas, sugar. **Minerals:** Copper, cobalt. **Arable land:** 29%. **Meat prod.** (1980): beef: 92,000 metric tons; lamb: 13,000 metric tons. **Fish catch** (1981): 167,000 metric tons. **Electricity prod.** (1982): 668 mln. kwh. **Labor force:** 90% agric.

Finance: Currency: Shilling (Mar. 1985: 575 = $1 US). **Gross domestic product** (1981): $2.8 bln. **Per capita income** (1976): $240. **Imports** (1981): $400 mln.; partners: (1979): Kenya 28%, UK 17%, W. Ger. 13%, Jap. 8%, It. 7%. **Exports** (1981): $220 mln.; partners (1978): U.S. 21%, UK 16%, Fr. 10%, Jap. 9%. **National budget** (1981): $641 mln. revenues; $871 mln. expenditures. **International reserves less gold** (Apr. 1981): $45.3 mln.

Transport: Motor vehicles: in use (1982): 10,000 passenger cars, 11,000 comm. vehicles.

Communications: Television sets: 75,000 in use (1983). **Radios:** 275,000 in use (1982). **Telephones in use** (1981): 47,000. **Daily newspaper circ.** (1982): 2 per 1,000 pop.

Health: Life expectancy at birth (1975): 48.3 male; 51.7 female. **Births** (per 1,000 pop. 1978): 48. **Deaths** (per 1,000 pop. 1978): 17. **Natural increase** (1978): 3.2%. **Hospital beds** (per 100,000 pop. 1977): 157. **Physicians** (per 100,000 pop. 1977): 20. **Infant mortality** (per 1,000 live births (1981): 120.

Education (1978): **Literacy:** 25%. **Pop. 5-19:** in school: 27%, teachers per 1,000: 8.

Major International Organizations: UN, OAU, Commonwealth of Nations. **Embassy:** 5909 16th St. NW 20011; 726-7100.

Britain obtained a protectorate over Uganda in 1894. The country became independent Oct. 9, 1962, and a republic within the Commonwealth a year later. In 1967, the traditional kingdoms, including the powerful Buganda state, were abolished and the central government strengthened.

Gen. Idi Amin seized power from Prime Min. Milton Obote in 1971. As many as 300,000 of his opponents were reported killed in subsequent years. Amin was named president for life in 1976.

In 1972 Amin expelled nearly all of Uganda's 45,000 Asians. In 1973 the U.S., Canada, and Norway ended economic aid programs; the U.S. withdrew all diplomatic personnel.

A June 1977 Commonwealth conference condemned the Amin government for its "disregard for the sanctity of human life."

Amid worsening economic and domestic crises, Uganda's troops exchanged invasion attacks with long-standing foe Tanzania, 1978 to 1979. Tanzanian forces, coupled with Ugandan exiles and rebels, ended the dictatorial rule of Amin, Apr. 11, 1979.

The U.S. reopened its embassy, reinstated economic aid, and ended its trade embargo in 1979.

Four governments have been in power since Amin fled. The country remains in economic and social chaos. (*See Chronology.*)

Union of Soviet Socialist Republics

People: Population (1983 est.): 272,500,000. **Age distrib.** (%): 0–19: 36.7; 20-59: 50.5; 60+: 12.7. **Pop. density:** 31 per sq. mi. **Urban** (1984): 64%. **Ethnic groups:** Russians 52% Ukrainians 16%, Uzbeks 5%, Byelorussians 4%, many others. **Languages:** Slavic (Russian, Ukrainian, Byelorussian, Polish), Altaic (Turkish, etc.), other Indo-European, Uralian, Caucasian. **Religions:** Russian Orthodox 18%, Moslems 9%, other Orthodox, Protestants, Jews, Buddhists.

Geography: Area: 8,649,490 sq. mi., the largest country in the world, nearly 2½ times the size of the U.S. **Location:** Stretches from E. Europe across N Asia to the Pacific O. **Neighbors:** Finland, Poland, Czechoslovakia, Hungary, Norway, Romania on W, Turkey, Iran, Afghanistan, China, Mongolia, N. Korea on S. **Topography:** Covering one-sixth of the earth's land area, the USSR contains every type of climate except the distinctly tropical, and has a varied topography.

The European portion is a low plain, grassy in S, wooded in N with Ural Mtns. on the E. Caucasus Mts. on the S. Urals stretch N-S for 2,500 mi. The Asiatic portion is also a vast plain, with mountains on the S and in the E; tundra covers extreme N, with forest belt below; plains, marshes are in W, desert in SW. **Capital:** Moscow. **Cities** (1983 est.): Moscow 8.3 mln.; Leningrad 4.7 mln.; Kiev 2.3 mln.; Tashkent 1.9 mln.; Kharkov 1.5 mln.; Gorky 1.3 mln.; Novosibirsk 1.4 mln.; Minsk 1.4 mln.; Kuibyshev 1.2 mln.; Sverdlovsk 1.2 mln.

Government: Type: Federal Union. **Head of state:** Pres. Andrei Gromyko; b. July 18, 1909; in office: July 2, 1985. **Head of government:** Premier Nikolai A. Tikhonov; b. May 1, 1905; in office: Oct. 23, 1980. **Head of Communist Party:** Mikhail Sergeyvich Gorbachev; b. Mar. 2, 1931; in office: Mar. 11, 1985. **Local divisions:** 15 union republics, within which are 20 autonomous republics, 6 krays (territories), 120 oblasts (regions), 8 autonomous oblasts, 10 national areas. **Defense:** 15% of GNP (1982).

Economy: Industries: Steel, machinery, machine tools, vehicles, chemicals, cement, textiles, appliances, paper. **Chief crops:** Grain, cotton, sugar beets, potatoes, vegetables, sunflowers. **Minerals:** Iron, manganese, mercury, potash, antimony, bauxite, cobalt, chromium, copper, coal, gold, lead, molybdenum, nickel, phosphates, silver, tin, tungsten, zinc, oil (59%), potassium salts. **Crude oil reserves** (1980): 67.00 bln. bbls. **Other resources:** Forests (25% of world reserves). **Arable land:** 11%. **Meat prod.** (1980): beef: 6.7 mln. metric tons; pork; 5.0 mln. metric tons; lamb: 853,000 metric tons. **Fish catch** (1982): 9.5 mln. metric tons. **Electricity prod.** (1983): 1.4 bln. kwh. **Crude steel prod.** (1982): 147 mln. metric tons. **Labor force:** 20% agric.; 29% industry, 21% services.

Finance: Currency: Ruble (Nov. 1984: 1.15 = $1 US). **Gross national product** (1983): $706 bln. **Per capita income** (1976): $2,600. **Imports** (1982): $55 bln.; partners: E. Ger. 10%, Pol. 7%, Czech. 8%, Bulg. 8%. **Exports** (1982): $62 bln.; partners: E. Ger. 10%, Pol. 8%, Bulg. 8%, Czech. 8%. **National budget** (1982): $350 bln. **Tourists** (1981): 23.9 mln.

Transport: Railway traffic (1983): 348 bln. passenger-km; 3.4 bln. net ton-km. **Motor vehicles:** in use (1980): 9.2 mln. passenger cars, 7.9 mln. comm. vehicles; manuf. (1982): 1.3 mln. passenger cars; 874,000 comm. vehicles. **Civil aviation** (1982): 172 bln. passenger-km; 3 bln. freight ton-km. **Chief ports:** Leningrad, Odessa, Murmansk, Kaliningrad, Archangelsk, Riga, Vladivostok.

Communications: Television sets: 75 mln. in use (1983). **Radios:** 164 mln. in use (1983). **Telephones in use** (1983): 26.4 mln. **Daily newspaper circ.** (1983): 314 per 1,000 pop.

Health: Life expectancy at birth (1972): 64 male; 74 female. **Births** (per 1,000 pop. 1982): 18.9. **Deaths** (per 1,000 pop. 1982): 10.1. **Natural increase** (1982): .8%. **Hospital beds** (1982): 3.4 mln. **Physicians** (1982): 1 mln. **Infant mortality** (per 1,000 live births 1982): 27.9.

Education (1981): Literacy: 99%. Most receive 10 years of schooling.

Major International Organizations: UN and its specialized agencies, Warsaw Pact.

Embassy: 1125 16th St. NW 20036, 628-7551.

The USSR is nominally a federation consisting of 15 union republics, the largest being the Russian Soviet Federated Socialist Republic. Important positions in the republics are filled by centrally chosen appointees, often ethnic Russians.

Beginning in 1939 the USSR by means of military action and negotiation overran contiguous territory and independent republics, including all or part of Lithuania, Latvia, Estonia, Poland, Czechoslovakia, Romania, Germany, Finland, Tannu Tuva, and Japan. The union republics are:

Republic	Area sq. mi.	Pop. (cen. 1979)
Russian SFSR	6,593,391	137,552,000
Ukrainian SSR	232,046	49,757,000
Uzbek SSR	158,069	15,391,000
Kazakh SSR	1,064,092	14,685,000

Republic	Area sq. mi.	Pop. (cen. 1979)
Byelorussian SSR	80,154	9,559,000
Azerbaijan SSR	33,436	6,028,000
Georgian SSR	26,911	5,016,000
Moldavian SSR	13,012	3,948,000
Tadzhik SSR	54,019	3,801,000
Kirghiz SSR	76,642	3,529,000
Lithuanian SSR	26,173	3,399,000
Armenian SSR	11,306	3,031,000
Turkmen SSR	188,417	2,759,000
Latvian SSR	24,695	2,521,000
Estonian SSR	17,413	1,466,000

The **Russian Soviet Federated Socialist Republic** contains over 50% of the population of the USSR and includes 76% of its territory. It extends from the old Estonian, Latvian, and Finnish borders and the Byelorussian and Ukrainian lines on the W, to the shores of the Pacific, and from the Arctic on the N to the Black and Caspian seas and the borders of Kazakh SSR, Mongolia, and Manchuria on the S. Siberia encompasses a large part of the RSFSR area. Capital: Moscow.

Parts of eastern and western Siberia have been transformed by steel mills, huge dams, oil and gas industries, electric railroads, and highways.

The **Ukraine**, the most densely populated of the republics, borders on the Black Sea, with Poland, Czechoslovakia, Hungary, and Romania on the W and SW. Capital: Kiev.

The Ukraine contains the arable black soil belt, the chief wheat-producing section of the Soviet Union. Sugar beets, potatoes, and livestock are important.

The Donets Basin has large deposits of coal, iron and other metals. There are chemical and machine industries and salt mines.

Byelorussia (White Russia). Capital: Minsk. Chief industries include machinery, tools, appliances, tractors, clocks, cameras, steel, cement, textiles, paper, leather, glass. Main crops are grain, flax, potatoes, sugar beets.

Azerbaijan boasts near Baku, the capital, important oil fields. Its natural wealth includes deposits of iron ore, cobalt, etc. A high-yield winter wheat is grown, as are fruits. It produces iron, steel, cement, fertilizers, synthetic rubber, electrical and chemical equipment. It borders on Iran and Turkey.

Georgia, in the western part of Transcaucasia, contains the largest manganese mines in the world. There are rich timber resources and coal mines. Basic industries are food, textiles, iron, steel. Grain, tea, tobacco, fruits, grapes are grown. Capital: Tbilisi (Tiflis). Despite massive party and government purges since 1972, illegal private enterprise and Georgian nationalist feelings persist; attempts to repress them have led to violence.

Armenia is mountainous, sub-tropical, extensively irrigated. Copper, zinc, aluminum, molybdenum, and marble are mined. Instrument making is important. Capital: Erevan.

Uzbekistan, most important economically of the Central Asia republics, produces 67% of USSR cotton, 50% of rice, 33% of silk, 34% of astrakhan, 85% of hemp. Industries include iron, steel, cars, tractors, TV and radio sets, textiles, food. Mineral wealth includes coal, sulphur, copper, and oil. Capital: Tashkent.

Turkmenistan in Central Asia, produces cotton, maize, carpets, chemicals. Minerals: oil, coal, sulphur, barite, lime, salt, gypsum. The Kara Kum desert occupies 80% of the area. Capital: Ashkhabad.

Tadzhikistan borders on China and Afghanistan. Over half the population are Tadzhiks, mostly Moslems, speaking an Iranian dialect. Chief occupations are farming and cattle breeding.

Cotton, grain, rice, and a variety of fruits are grown. Heavy industry, based on rich mineral deposits, coal and hydroelectric power, has replaced handicrafts. Capital: Dushanbe.

Kazakhstan extends from the lower reaches of the Volga in Europe to the Altai Mtns. on the Chinese border. It has vast deposits of coal, oil, iron, tin, copper, lead, zinc, etc. Fish for its canning industry are caught in Lake Balkhash and the Caspian and Aral seas. The capital is Alma-Ata. About 50% of the population is Russian or Ukrainian, working in the virgin-grain lands opened up after 1954, and in the growing industries. Capital: Alma-Ata.

Kirghizia is the eastern part of Soviet Central Asia, on the frontier of Xinjiang, China. The people breed cattle and horses and grow tobacco, cotton, rice, sugar beets. Industries include machine and instrument making, chemicals. Capital: Frunze.

Moldavia, in the SW part of the USSR, is a fertile black earth plain bordering Romania and includes Bessarabia. It is an agricultural region that grows grains, fruits, vegetables, and tobacco. Textiles, wine, food and electrical equipment industries have been developed. Capital: Kishinev. The region was taken from Romania in 1940; the people speak Romanian.

Lithuania, on the Baltic, produces cattle, hogs, electric motors, and appliances. The capital is Vilnius (Vilna). **Latvia** on the Baltic and the Gulf of Riga, has timber and peat resources est. at 3 bln. tons. In addition to agricultural products it produces rubber goods, dyes, fertilizers, glassware, telephone apparatus, TV and radio sets, railroad cars. Capital: Riga.

Estonia, also on the Baltic, has textiles, shipbuilding, timber, roadmaking and mining equipment industries and a shale oil refining industry. Capital: Tallinn. The 3 Baltic states were provinces of imperial Russia before World War I, were independent nations between World Wars I and II, but were conquered by Russia in 1940. The U.S. has never formally recognized the takeover.

Economy. Almost all legal economic enterprises are state-owned. There were 29,600 collective farms in 1976, along with 18,064 larger state farms. A huge illegal black market plays an important role in distribution; illegal private production and service firms are periodically exposed.

The USSR is incalculably rich in natural resources; distant Siberian reserves are being exploited with Japanese assistance. Its heavy industry is 2d only to the U.S. It leads the world in oil and steel production. Consumer industries have lagged comparatively. Agricultural output has expanded, but in poor crop years the USSR has been forced to make huge grain purchases from the West. Shortages and rationing of basic food products periodically occur.

Exports include petroleum and its products, iron and steel, rolled non-ferrous metals, industrial plant equipment, arms, lumber, cotton, asbestos, gold, manganese, and others.

Industrial growth has dropped, due to short falls in oil, coal, and steel industries, as well as poor grain harvests since 1979.

History. Slavic tribes began migrating into Russia from the W in the 5th century AD. The first Russian state, founded by Scandinavian chieftains, was established in the 9th century, centering in Novgorod and Kiev.

In the 13th century the Mongols overran the country. It recovered under the grand dukes and princes of Muscovy, or Moscow, and by 1480 freed itself from the Mongols. Ivan the Terrible was the first to be formally proclaimed Tsar (1547). Peter the Great (1682-1725), extended the domain and in 1721, founded the Russian Empire.

Western ideas and the beginnings of modernization spread through the huge Russian empire in the 19th and early 20th centuries. But political evolution failed to keep pace.

Military reverses in the 1905 war with Japan and in World War I led to the breakdown of the Tsarist regime. The 1917 Revolution began in March with a series of sporadic strikes for higher wages by factory workers. A provisional democratic government under Prince Georgi Lvov was established but was quickly followed in May by the second provisional government, led by Alexander Kerensky. The Kerensky government and the freely-elected Constituent Assembly were overthrown in a Communist coup led by Vladimir Ilyich Lenin Nov. 7.

Lenin's death Jan. 21, 1924, resulted in an internal power struggle from which Joseph Stalin eventually emerged the absolute ruler of Russia. Stalin secured his position at first by exiling opponents, but from the 1930s to 1953, he resorted to a series of "purge" trials, mass executions, and mass exiles to work camps. These measures resulted in millions of deaths, according to most estimates.

Germany and the USSR signed a non-aggression pact Aug. 1939; Nazi forces launched a massive invasion of the Soviet Union, June 1941. Notable heroic episode was the "900 days" siege of Leningrad, lasting to Jan. 1944, and causing 1,000,000 deaths; the city was never taken. Russian winter counterthrusts, 1941 to '42 and 1942 to '43, stopped the German advance. Turning point was the failure of German troops to take and hold Stalingrad, Sept. 1942 to Feb. 1943. With British and U.S. Lend-Lease aid and sustaining great casualties, the Russians drove the Axis from eastern Europe and the Balkans in the next 2 years.

After Stalin died, Mar. 5, 1953, Nikita Khrushchev was elected first secretary of the Central Committee. In 1956 he condemned Stalin. "De-Stalinization" of the country on all levels was effected after Stalin's body was removed from the Lenin-Stalin tomb in Moscow.

Under Khrushchev the open antagonism of Poles and Hungarians toward domination by Moscow was brutally suppressed in 1956. He advocated peaceful co-existence with the capitalist countries, but continued arming the USSR with nuclear weapons. He aided the Cuban revolution under Fidel Castro but withdrew Soviet missiles from Cuba during confrontation by U.S. Pres. Kennedy, Sept.-Oct. 1962.

The USSR, the U.S., and Great Britain initialed a joint treaty July 25, 1963, banning above-ground nuclear tests.

Khrushchev was suddenly deposed, Oct. 1964, and replaced as party first secretary by Leonid I. Brezhnev, and as premier by Aleksei N. Kosygin.

In Aug. 1968 Russian, Polish, East German, Hungarian, and Bulgarian military forces invaded Czechoslovakia to put a curb on liberalization policies of the Czech government.

The USSR in 1971 continued heavy arms shipments to Egypt. In July 1972 Egypt ordered most of the 20,000 Soviet military personnel in that country to leave. When Egypt and Syria attacked Israel in Oct. 1973, the USSR launched huge arms airlifts to the 2 Arab nations. In 1974, the Soviet replenished the arms used or lost by the Syrians in the 1973 war, and continued some shipments to Egypt.

Massive Soviet military aid to North Vietnam in the late 1960s and early 1970s helped assure Communist victories throughout Indo-China. Soviet arms aid and advisers were sent to several African countries in the 1970s, including Algeria, Angola, Somalia, and Ethiopia.

In 1972, the U.S. and USSR reached temporary agreements to freeze intercontinental missiles at their current levels, to limit defensive missiles to 200 each and to cooperate on health, environment, space, trade, and science.

More than 130,000 Jews and over 40,000 ethnic Germans were allowed to emigrate from the USSR in the 1970s, following pressure from the West. Many leading figures in the arts also left the country.

A limitation on grain sales, imposed by Pres. Carter, Jan. 4, 1980, in response to the Soviet invasion of Afghanistan, was lifted, Apr. 24, 1981, by the Reagan administration. Nevertheless, there were serious food shortages reported, and a new agricultural program, covering 1982-90, was announced in May amid Soviet fears of becoming dependent on foreign, especially U.S., grain imports. The Afghan invasion continued to go badly in 1985 with no end in sight.

The USSR drew international condemnation on Sept. 1, 1983 when it shot down a Korean 747 commercial airliner, killing 269. The airliner had strayed off course. The Soviets have been unable to prevent U.S. Pershing II and cruise missiles from being deployed in Western Europe. The Soviets led the Eastern bloc boycott of the 1984 Los Angeles Olympics.

Government. The Communist Party leadership dominates all areas of national life. A Politburo of 14 full members and 8 candidate members makes all major political, economic, and foreign policy decisions. Party membership in 1978 was reported to be over 16,000,000.

United Arab Emirates

People: Population (1984 est.): 1,523,000. **Pop. density:** 41.8 per sq. mi. **Ethnic groups:** Arab, Iranian, Pakistani and Indian. **Languages:** Arabic (official), Farsi, English, Hindi, Urdu. **Religions:** Moslems 90%, Christian, Hindu.

Geography: Area: 32,000 sq. mi., the size of Maine. **Location:** On the S shore of the Persian Gulf. **Neighbors:** Qatar on

N, Saudi Ar. on W, S, Oman on E. **Topography:** A barren, flat coastal plain gives way to uninhabited sand dunes on the S. Hajar Mtns. are on E. **Capital:** Abu Dhabi. **Cities** (1982 est.): Abu Dhabi 516,000; Dubai 296,000.

Government: Type: Federation of emirates. **Head of state:** Pres. Zaid ibn Sultan an-Nahayan b. 1923; in office: Dec. 2, 1971. **Head of government:** Prime Min. Rashid ibn Said al-Maktum; in office: June 25, 1979. **Local divisions:** 7 autonomous emirates: Abu Dhabi, Ajman, Dubai, Fujaira, Ras al-Khaimah, Sharjah, Umm al-Qaiwain. **Defense:** 8% of GNP (1982).

Economy: Chief crops: Vegetables, dates, limes. **Minerals:** Oil. **Crude oil reserves** (1981): 26.9 bln. bbls. **Arable land:** 1%. **Electricity prod.** (1982): 6 bln. kwh. **Labor force:** 5% agric. 85% ind. and commerce; 5% serv.; 5% gvt.

Finance: Currency: Dirham (Apr. 1985: 3.67 = $1 US). **Gross domestic product** (1981): $27 bln. **Per capita income** (1981 est.) $24,000. **Imports** (1981): $9.6 bln.; partners: Jap. 18%, UK 11%, W. Ger. 6%. **Exports** (1982): $16.9 bln.; partners: Jap. 36%, U.S. 7%, Fr. 10%. **International reserves less gold** (Nov. 1984): $2.1 bln. **Gold:** 817,000 oz t.

Transport: Chief ports: Dubai, Abu Dhabi.

Communications: Radios: 260,000 in use (1981). **Telephones in use** (1982): 240,167.

Health: Life Expectancy at Birth (1982):62.4 years. **Hospital beds** (1980): 2,972. **Physicians** (1980): 1,202.

Education (1982): **Literacy:** 53%. **Years Compulsory:** ages 6-12.

Major International Organizations: UN and its specialized agencies, Arab League, OPEC.

Embassy: 600 New Hampshire Ave. NW 20037; 338-6500.

The 7 "Trucial Sheikdoms" gave Britain control of defense and foreign relations in the 19th century. They merged to become an independent state Dec. 2, 1971.

The Abu Dhabi Petroleum Co. was fully nationalized in 1975. Oil revenues have given the UAE one of the highest per capita GNPs in the world. International banking has grown in recent years.

United Kingdom of Great Britain and Northern Ireland

People: Population (1984 est.): 56,023,000. **Age distrib.** (%): 0–4: 21.1; 15–59: 59.0; 60+: 19.9. **Pop. density:** 596 per sq. mi. **Urban** (1981): Eng. & Wales: 76.9%, N. Ire.: 54.7%, Scot. (1974): 70.0%. **Ethnic groups:** English 81.5%, Scottish 9.6%, Irish 2.4, Welsh 1.9%, Ulster 1.8%; West Indian, Indian, Pakistani over 2%; others. **Languages:** English, Welsh spoken in western Wales; Gaelic. **Religions:** Church of England 19%, Roman Catholic, 8%.

Geography: Area: 94,222 sq. mi., slightly smaller than Oregon. **Location:** Off the NW coast of Europe, across English Channel, Strait of Dover, and North Sea. **Neighbors:** Ireland to W, France to SE. **Topography:** England is mostly rolling land, rising to Uplands of southern Scotland; Lowlands are in center of Scotland, granite Highlands are in N. Coast is heavily indented, especially on W. British Isles have milder climate than N Europe, due to the Gulf Stream, and ample rainfall. Severn, 220 mi., and Thames, 215 mi., are longest rivers. **Capital:** London. **Cities** (1981 cen.): London 6,696,008; Birmingham 1,058,800; Glasgow 832,097; Leeds 744,500; Sheffield 588,000; Liverpool 539,700; Manchester 490,000; Edinburgh 463,923; Bradford 458,900; Bristol 416,300; Belfast 357,600.

Government: Type: Constitutional monarchy. **Head of state:** Queen Elizabeth II; b. Apr. 21, 1926; in office: Feb. 6, 1952. **Head of government:** Prime Min. Margaret Thatcher; b. Oct. 13, 1925; in office: May 4, 1979. **Local divisions:** England and Wales: 47 non-metro counties, 6 metro counties, Greater London; Scotland: 9 regions, 3 island areas; N. Ireland: 26 districts. **Defense:** 6.2% of GDP (1982).

Economy: Industries: Steel, metals, vehicles, shipbuilding, shipping, banking, insurance, textiles, chemicals, electronics, aircraft, machinery, distilling. **Chief crops:** Grains, sugar beets, fruits, vegetables. **Minerals:** Coal, tin, oil, gas, limestone, iron, salt, clay, chalk, gypsum, lead, silica. **Crude oil reserves** (1980): 15.4 bln. bbls. **Arable land:** 30%. **Meat prod.** (1984): beef: 1.1 mln. metric tons; pork: 940,000 metric tons; lamb: 284,000 metric tons. **Fish catch** (1982): 911,000 metric tons. **Electricity prod.** (1983): 276 bln. kwh. **Crude steel prod.**

(1982): 13.6 mln. metric tons. **Labor force:** 1.5% agric.; 30% manuf. & eng., 59% services.

Finance: Currency: Pound (June 1985: .77 = $1 US). **Gross domestic product** (1983): $458 bln. **Per capita income** (1979): $7,216. **Imports** (1984): $104.8 bln.; partners: W. Ger. 13%, U.S. 12%, Fr. 7%, Neth. 8%. **Exports** (1984): $93.7 bln.; partners: U.S. 13%, W. Ger. 10%, Fr. 8%, Neth. 8%. **Tourists** (1982): receipts: $5.1 bln.; **National budget** (1982): $182 bln. **International reserves less gold** (Mar. 1985): $9.8 bln. **Gold:** 19.03 mln. oz t. **Consumer prices** (change in 1984): 5.0%.

Transport: Railway traffic (1983): 30.1 bln. passenger-km; 17.1 bln. net ton-km. **Motor vehicles:** in use (1982): 16 mln. passenger cars, 1.8 mln. comm. vehicles; manuf. (1982): 888,000 passenger cars; 269,000 comm. vehicles. **Civil aviation** (1982): 43.9 bln. passenger-km: 1.2 mln. freight ton-km. **Chief ports:** London, Liverpool, Glasgow, Southampton, Cardiff, Belfast.

Communications: Television sets: 18.7 mln. licensed (1984). **Radios:** 18 mln. licensed (1983). **Telephones in use** (1983): 28 mln. **Daily newspaper circ.** (1983): 407 per 1,000 pop.

Health: Life expectancy at birth: (1983): 70.2 male; 76.2 female. **Births:** (per 1,000 pop. 1984): 12.6. **Deaths:** (per 1,000 pop. 1984): 12. **Natural increase:** (1984): .02%. **Hospital beds** (per 100,000 pop. 1977): 894. **Physicians** (per 100,000 pop. 1977): 153. **Infant mortality:** (per 1,000 live births 1984): 13.3.

Education (1984): **Literacy:** 99%. **Years compulsory:** 12; attendance 99%.

Major International Organizations: UN and its specialized agencies, NATO, EC, OECD.

Embassy: 3100 Massachusetts Ave. NW 20008; 462-1340.

The United Kingdom of Great Britain and Northern Ireland comprises England, Wales, Scotland, and Northern Ireland.

Queen and Royal Family. The ruling sovereign is Elizabeth II of the House of Windsor, born Apr. 21, 1926, elder daughter of King George VI. She succeeded to the throne Feb. 6, 1952, and was crowned June 2, 1953. She was married Nov. 20, 1947, to Lt. Philip Mountbatten, born June 10, 1921, former Prince of Greece. He was created Duke of Edinburgh, Earl of Merioneth, and Baron Greenwich, and given the style H.R.H., Nov. 19, 1947; he was given the title Prince of the United Kingdom and Northern Ireland Feb. 22, 1957. Prince Charles Philip Arthur George, born Nov. 14, 1948, is the Prince of Wales and heir apparent. His son, William Philip Arthur Louis, born June 21, 1982, is second in line to the throne.

Parliament is the legislative governing body for the United Kingdom, with certain powers over dependent units. It consists of 2 houses: The **House of Lords** includes 763 hereditary and 314 life peers and peeresses, certain judges, 2 archbishops and 24 bishops of the Church of England. Total membership is over 1,000. The **House of Commons** has 635 members, who are elected by direct ballot and divided as follows: England 516; Wales 36; Scotland 71; Northern Ireland 12.

Resources and Industries. Great Britain's major occupations are manufacturing and trade. Metals and metal-using industries contribute more than 50% of the exports. Of about 60 million acres of land in England, Wales and Scotland, 46 million are farmed, of which 17 million are arable, the rest pastures.

Large oil and gas fields have been found in the North Sea. Commercial oil production began in 1975. There are large deposits of coal.

The railroads, nationalized since 1948, have been reduced in total length, with a basic network, Dec. 1978, of 11,123 mi. The merchant marine totaled 126,000 gross registered tons in 1982.

A year-long coal strike costing some $3 bln. ended March 1985. The issue of the closing of uneconomic mines was unresolved.

Britain imports all of its cotton, rubber, sulphur, 80% of its wool, half of its food and iron ore, also certain amounts of paper, tobacco, chemicals. Manufactured goods from these basic materials have been exported since the industrial age began. Main exports are machinery, chemicals, woolen and synthetic textiles, clothing, autos and trucks, iron and steel, locomotives, ships, jet aircraft, farm machinery, drugs, radio, TV, radar and navigation equipment, scientific instruments, arms, whisky.

Religion and Education. The Church of England is Protestant Episcopal. The queen is its temporal head, with rights of appointments to archbishoprics, bishoprics, and other offices. There are 2 provinces, Canterbury and York, each headed by an archbishop. About 48% of the population is baptized into the Church,

ess than 10% is confirmed. Most famous church is Westminster Abbey (1050-1760), site of coronations, tombs of Elizabeth I, Mary of Scots, kings, poets, and of the Unknown Warrior.

The most celebrated British universities are Oxford and Cambridge, each dating to the 13th century. There are about 40 other universities.

History. Britain was part of the continent of Europe until about 6,000 BC, but migration of peoples across the English Channel continued long afterward. Celts arrived 2,500 to 3,000 years ago. Their language survives in Welsh, Cornish, and Gaelic enclaves.

England was added to the Roman Empire in 43 AD. After the withdrawal of Roman legions in 410, waves of Jutes, Angles, and Saxons arrived from German lands. They contended with Danish raiders for control from the 8th through 11th centuries.

The last successful invasion was by French speaking Normans in 1066, who united the country with their dominions in France.

Opposition by nobles to royal authority forced King John to sign the Magna Carta in 1215, a guarantee of rights and the rule of law. In the ensuing decades, the foundations of the parliamentary system were laid.

English dynastic claims to large parts of France led to the Hundred Years War, 1338-1453, and the defeat of England. A long civil war, the War of the Roses, lasted 1455-85, and ended with the establishment of the powerful Tudor monarchy. A distinct English civilization flourished. The economy prospered over long periods of domestic peace unmatched in continental Europe. Religious independence was secured when the Church of England was separated from the authority of the Pope in 1534.

Under Queen Elizabeth I, England became a major naval power, leading to the founding of colonies in the new world and the expansion of trade with Europe and the Orient. Scotland was united with England when James VI of Scotland was crowned James I of England in 1603.

A struggle between Parliament and the Stuart kings led to a bloody civil war, 1642-49, and the establishment of a republic under the Puritan Oliver Cromwell. The monarchy was restored in 1660, but the "Glorious Revolution" of 1688 confirmed the sovereignty of Parliament: a Bill of Rights was granted 1689.

In the 18th century, parliamentary rule was strengthened. Technological and entrepreneurial innovations led to the Industrial Revolution. The 13 North American colonies were lost, but replaced by growing empires in Canada and India. Britain's role in the defeat of Napoleon, 1815, strengthened its position as the leading world power.

The extension of the franchise in 1832 and 1867, the formation of trade unions, and the development of universal public education were among the drastic social changes which accompanied the spread of industrialization and urbanization in the 19th century. Large parts of Africa and Asia were added to the empire during the reign of Queen Victoria, 1837-1901.

Though victorious in World War I, Britain suffered huge casualties and economic dislocation. Ireland became independent in 1921, and independence movements became active in India and other colonies.

The country suffered major bombing damage in World War II, but held out against Germany singlehandedly for a year after the fall of France in 1940.

Industrial growth continued in the postwar period, but Britain lost its leadership position to other powers. Labor governments passed socialist programs nationalizing some basic industries and expanding social security. The 1983 re-election of Thatcher's Conservative Party, however, indicated an increased role for private enterprise.

Britain broke diplomatic relations with Libya, Apr. 22, 1984, 5 days after a policewoman was killed and 10 Libyan exile demonstrators wounded by machine-gun fire from within the Libyan embassy in London. The embassy occupants, including the killer, left Britain, Apr. 27.

Britain joined the NATO alliance and, in 1973, the European Communities (Common Market).

Wales

The Principality of Wales in western Britain has an area of 8,016 sq. mi. and a population (1981 cen.) of 2,790,000. Cardiff is the capital, pop. (1981 est.) 273,856.

England and Wales are administered as a unit. Less than 20% of the population of Wales speak both English and Welsh; about 32,000 speak Welsh solely. Welsh nationalism is advocated by a segment. A 1979 referendum rejected, 4-1, the creation of an elected Welsh Assembly.

Early Anglo-Saxon invaders drove Celtic peoples into the mountains of Wales, terming them Waelise (Welsh, or foreign). There they developed a distinct nationality. Members of the ruling house of Gwynedd in the 13th century fought England but were crushed, 1283. Edward of Caernarvon, son of Edward I of England, was created Prince of Wales, 1301.

Scotland

Scotland, a kingdom now united with England and Wales in Great Britain, occupies the northern 37% of the main British island, and the Hebrides, Orkney, Shetland and smaller islands. Length, 275 mi., breadth approx. 150 mi., area, 30,405 sq. mi., population (1981 cen.) 5,117,146.

The Lowlands, a belt of land approximately 60 mi. wide from the Firth of Clyde to the Firth of Forth, divide the farming region of the Southern Uplands from the granite Highlands of the North, contain 75% of the population and most of the industry. The Highlands, famous for hunting and fishing, have been opened to industry by many hydroelectric power stations.

Edinburgh, pop. (1981 cen.) 419,187, is the capital. Glasgow, pop. (1981 cen.) 762,288, is Britain's greatest industrial center. It is a shipbuilding complex on the Clyde and an ocean port. Aberdeen, pop. (1981 cen.) 190,200, NE of Edinburgh, is a major port, center of granite industry, fish processing, and North Sea oil exploitation. Dundee, pop. (1981 cen.) 174,746, NE of Edinburgh, is an industrial and fish processing center. About 90,000 persons speak Gaelic as well as English.

History. Scotland was called Caledonia by the Romans who battled early Pict and Celtic tribes and occupied southern areas from the 1st to the 4th centuries. Missionaries from Britain introduced Christianity in the 4th century; St. Columba, an Irish monk, converted most of Scotland in the 6th century.

The Kingdom of Scotland was founded in 1018. William Wallace and Robert Bruce both defeated English armies 1297 and 1314, respectively.

In 1603 James VI of Scotland, son of Mary, Queen of Scots, succeeded to the throne of England as James I, and effected the Union of the Crowns. In 1707 Scotland received representation in the British Parliament, resulting from the union of former separate Parliaments. Its executive in the British cabinet is the Secretary of State for Scotland. The growing Scottish National Party urges independence. A 1979 referendum on the creation of an elected Scotland Assembly was defeated.

There are 8 universities. Memorials of Robert Burns, Sir Walter Scott, John Knox, Mary, Queen of Scots draw many tourists, as do the beauties of the Trossachs, Loch Katrine, Loch Lomond and abbey ruins.

Industries. Engineering products are the most important industry, with growing emphasis on office machinery, autos, electronics and other consumer goods. Oil has been discovered offshore in the North Sea, stimulating on-shore support industries.

Scotland produces fine woolens, worsteds, tweeds, silks, fine linens and jute. It is known for its special breeds of cattle and sheep. Fisheries have large hauls of herring, cod, whiting. Whisky is the biggest export.

The Hebrides are a group of c. 500 islands, 100 inhabited, off the W coast. The inner Hebrides include **Skye, Mull,** and **Iona,** the last famous for the arrival of St. Columba, 563 AD. The Outer Hebrides include **Lewis** and **Harris.** Industries include sheep raising and weaving. The **Orkney Islands,** c. 90, are to the NE. The capital is Kirkwall, on Pomona Is. Fish curing, sheep raising and weaving are occupations. NE of the Orkneys are the 200 **Shetland Islands,** 24 inhabited, home of Shetland pony. The Orkneys and Shetlands have become centers for the North Sea oil industry.

Northern Ireland

Six of the 9 counties of Ulster, the NE corner of Ireland, constitute Northern Ireland, with the parliamentary boroughs of Belfast and Londonderry. Area 5,463 sq. mi., 1981 cen. pop. 1,490,228, capital and chief industrial center, Belfast, (1981 cen.) 297,862.

Industries. Shipbuilding, including large tankers, has long been an important industry, centered in Belfast, the largest port. Linen manufacture is also important, along with apparel, rope, and twine. Growing diversification has added engineering products, synthetic fibers, and electronics. They are large numbers of

cattle, hogs, and sheep, potatoes, poultry, and dairy foods are also produced.

Government. An act of the British Parliament, 1920, divided Northern from Southern Ireland, each with a parliament and government. When Ireland became a dominion, 1921, and later a republic, Northern Ireland chose to remain a part of the United Kingdom. It elects 12 members to the British House of Commons.

During 1968-69, large demonstrations were conducted by Roman Catholics who charged they were discriminated against in voting rights, housing, and employment. The Catholics, a minority comprising about a third of the population, demanded abolition of property qualifications for voting in local elections. Violence and terrorism intensified, involving branches of the Irish Republican Army (outlawed in the Irish Republic), Protestant groups, police, and up to 15,000 British troops.

A succession of Northern Ireland prime ministers pressed reform programs but failed to satisfy extremists on both sides. Over 2,000 were killed in over 13 years of bombings and shootings through 1984, many in England itself. Britain suspended the Northern Ireland parliament Mar. 30, 1972, and imposed direct British rule. A coalition government was formed in 1973 when moderates won election to a new one-house Assembly. But a Protestant general strike overthrew the government in 1974 and direct rule was resumed.

The turmoil and agony of Northern Ireland was dramatized in 1981 by the deaths of 10 imprisoned Irish nationalist hunger strikers in Maze Prison near Belfast. The inmates had starved themselves to death in an attempt to achieve status as political prisoners, but the British government refused to yield to their demands.

Education and Religion. Northern Ireland is 2/3 Protestant, 1/3 Roman Catholic. Education is compulsory through age 15. There are 2 universities and 24 technical colleges.

Channel Islands

The Channel Islands, area 75 sq. mi., cen. pop. 1980 130,000, off the NW coast of France, the only parts of the one-time Dukedom of Normandy belonging to England, are **Jersey, Guernsey** and the dependencies of Guernsey — **Alderney, Brechou, Great Sark, Little Sark, Herm, Jethou and Lihou.** Jersey and Guernsey have separate legal existences and lieutenant governors named by the Crown. The islands were the only British soil occupied by German troops in World War II.

Isle of Man

The Isle of Man, area 227 sq. mi., 1982 est. pop. 61,000, is in the Irish Sea, 20 mi. from Scotland, 30 mi. from Cumberland. It is rich in lead and iron. The island has its own laws and a lieutenant governor appointed by the Crown. The Tynwald (legislature) consists of the Legislative Council, partly elected, and House of Keys, elected. Capital: Douglas. Farming, tourism (413,000 visitors in 1982), fishing (kippers, scallops) are chief occupations. Man is famous for the Manx tailless cat.

Gibraltar

Gibraltar, a dependency on the southern coast of Spain, guards the entrance to the Mediterranean. The Rock has been in British possession since 1704. The Rock is 2.75 mi. long, 3/4 of a mi. wide and 1,396 ft. in height; a narrow isthmus connects it with the mainland. Est. pop. 1982, 30,000.

In 1966 Spain called on Britain to give "substantial sovereignty" of Gibraltar to Spain and imposed a partial blockade. In 1967, residents voted 12,138 for remaining under Britain, 44 for returning to Spain. A new constitution, May 30, 1969, gave an elected House of Assembly more control in domestic affairs. A UN General Assembly resolution requested Britain to end Gibraltar's colonial status by Oct. 1, 1969. No settlement has been reached.

British West Indies

Swinging in a vast arc from the coast of Venezuela NE, then N and NW toward Puerto Rico are the Leeward Islands, forming a coral and volcanic barrier sheltering the Caribbean from the open Atlantic. Many of the islands are self-governing British possessions. Universal suffrage was instituted 1951-54; ministerial systems were set up 1956-1960.

The **Leeward Islands**, are **Montserrat** (1980 pop. 11,600, area 32 sq. mi., capital Plymouth), and **St. Kitts (St. Christopher)-Nevis**, 2 islands (1980 pop. 44,400, area 104 sq. mi., cap-

ital Basseterre on St. Kitts). Nearby are the small **British Virgin Islands.**

Britain granted self-government to 5 of these islands (exception, Montserrat) and island groups in 1967-1969; each became an Associated State, with Britain controlling foreign affairs and defense.

Anguilla gained its independence from St. Kitts Dec. 19, 1980. A 1976 constitution provides for an autonomous elected government. Area 35 sq. mi., pop. (1982 est.) 7,000.

The three **Cayman Islands**, a dependency, lie S of Cuba, NW of Jamaica. Pop. 18,000 (1981), most of it on Grand Cayman. It is a free port; in the 1970s Grand Cayman became a tax-free refuge for foreign funds and branches of many Western banks were opened there. Total area 102 sq. mi., capital Georgetown.

The **Turks and Caicos Islands**, at the SE end of the Bahama Islands, are a separate possession. There are about 30 islands, only 6 inhabited, 1980 pop. est. 7,000, area 193 sq. mi., capital Grand Turk. Salt, crayfish and conch shells are the main exports.

Bermuda

Bermuda is a British dependency governed by a royal governor and an Assembly, dating from 1620, the oldest legislative body among British dependencies. Capital is Hamilton.

It is a group of 360 small islands of coral formation, 20 inhabited, comprising 21 sq. mi. in the western Atlantic, 580 mi. E of North Carolina. Pop., 1980 cen., was 54,893 (about 61% of African descent). Density is high.

The U.S. has air and naval bases under long-term lease, and a NASA tracking station.

Bermuda boasts many resort hotels, serving 429,000 visitors in 1981. The government raises most revenue from import duties. Exports: petroleum products, drugs.

South Atlantic

Falkland Islands and Dependencies, a British dependency, lies 300 mi. E of the Strait of Magellan at the southern end of South America.

The Falklands or Islas Malvinas include about 200 islands, area 4,700 sq. mi., pop. (1980 est.) 1,800. Sheep-grazing is the main industry; wool is the principal export. There are indications of large oil and gas deposits. The islands are also claimed by Argentina though 97% of inhabitants are of British origin. Argentina invaded the islands Apr. 2, 1982. The British responded by sending a task force to the area, landing their main force on the Falklands, May 21, and forcing an Argentine surrender at Port Stanley, June 14. **South Georgia**, area 1,450 sq. mi., and the uninhabited **South Sandwich Is.** are dependencies of the Falklands.

British Antarctic Territory, south of 60° S lat., was made a separate colony in 1962 and comprises mainly the **South Shetland Islands,** the **South Orkneys** and **Graham's Land.** A chain of meteorological stations is maintained.

St. Helena, an island 1,200 mi. off the W coast of Africa and 1,800 E of South America, has 47 sq. mi. and est. pop., 1981 of 5,300. Flax, lace and rope making are the chief industries. After Napoleon Bonaparte was defeated at Waterloo the Allies exiled him to St. Helena, where he lived from Oct. 16, 1815, to his death, May 5, 1821. Capital is Jamestown.

Tristan da Cunha is the principal of a group of islands of volcanic origin, total area 40 sq. mi., half way between the Cape of Good Hope and South America. A volcanic peak 6,760 ft. high erupted in 1961. The 262 inhabitants were removed to England, but most returned in 1963. The islands are dependencies of St. Helena.

Ascension is an island of volcanic origin, 34 sq. mi. in area, 700 mi. NW of St. Helena, through which it is administered. It is a communications relay center for Britain, and has a U.S. satellite tracking center. Est. pop., 1976, was 1,179, half of them communications workers. The island is noted for sea turtles.

Asia and Indian Ocean

Hong Kong is a Crown Colony at the mouth of the Canton R. in China, 90 mi. S of Canton. Its nucleus is Hong Kong Is., 35½ sq. mi., acquired from China 1841, on which is located Victoria, the capital. Opposite is Kowloon Peninsula, 3 sq. mi. and Stonecutters Is., ¼ sq. mi., added, 1860. An additional 355 sq. mi. known as the New Territories, a mainland area and islands, were leased from China, 1898, for 99 years. China has indicated its intention to reclaim sovereignty over Hong Kong when the

lease expires in 1997. Total area of the colony is 409 sq. mi., with a population, 1983 est., of 5,287,000 including fewer than 20,000 British. From 1949 to 1962 Hong Kong absorbed more than a million refugees from the mainland.

Hong Kong harbor was long an important British naval station and one of the world's great trans-shipment ports.

Principal industries are textiles and apparel (25% of exports); also tourism, 2.5 mln. visitors, $1.5 bln. expenditures (1981), shipbuilding, iron and steel, fishing, cement, and small manufactures.

Spinning mills, among the best in the world, and low wages compete with textiles elsewhere and have resulted in the protective measures in some countries. Hong Kong also has a booming electronics industry.

British Indian Ocean Territory was formed Nov. 1965, embracing islands formerly dependencies of Mauritius or Seychelles: the Chagos Archipelago (including Diego Garcia), Aldabra, Farquhar and Des Roches. The latter 3 were transferred to Seychelles, which became independent in 1976. Area 22 sq mi. No civilian population remains.

Pacific Ocean

Pitcairn Island is in the Pacific, halfway between South America and Australia. The island was discovered in 1767 by Carteret but was not inhabited until 23 years later when the mutineers of the Bounty landed there. The area is 18 sq. mi. and pop. 1983, was 61. It is a British colony and is administered by a British Representative in New Zealand and a local Council. The uninhabited islands of **Henderson, Ducie** and **Oeno** are in the Pitcairn group.

United States of America

People: Population (1984 est.): 236,413,000. **Age distrib.(%):** 0–14: 22.0; 15–59: 61.7; 60+: 16.3. **Pop. density:** 65.3 per sq. mi. **Urban** (1980): 79.2%.
Defense: 6.4% of GNP (1982).
Economy: Minerals: Coal, copper, lead, molybdenum, phosphates, uranium, bauxite, gold, iron, mercury, nickel, potash, silver, tungsten, zinc. **Crude oil reserves** (1980): 26.50 bln. bbls. **Arable land:** 21%. **Meat prod.** (1984): beef: 10 mln. metric tons; pork: 6.6 mln. metric tons; lamb: 171,000 metric tons. **Fish catch** (1983): 2.9 mln. metric tons. **Electricity prod.** (1983): 2,310 bln. kwh. **Crude steel prod.** (1983): 75 mln. metric tons.
Finance: Gross domestic product (1984): $3,701 bln. **Per capita income** (1983): $11,675. **Imports** (1984): $341.1 bln.; partners: Can. 18%, Jap. 16%, Mex. 6%. **Exports** (1984): $217.8 bln.; partners: Can. 16%, Jap. 10%, Mex. 6%, UK 5%. **Tourists** (1982): 23.1 mln.; receipts $11 bln. **National budget** (1984): $668 bln. revenues; $848 bln. expenditures and lending. **International reserves less gold** (Mar. 1985): $24.4 bln. **Gold:** 262.7 mln. oz t. **Consumer prices** (change in 1984): 4.3%.
Transport: Railway traffic (1981): .17.6 bln. passenger-km; 1.3 bln. net ton-km. **Motor vehicles:** in use (1983): 124 mln. passenger cars, 35 mln. comm. vehicles; manuf. (1982): 5.0 mln. passenger cars; 1.9 mln. comm. vehicles. **Civil aviation** (1983): 406 bln. passenger-km; 10.6 bln. freight ton-km.
Communications: Television sets: 143 mln. in use (1983). **Radios:** 485 mln. in use (1983). **Telephones in use** (1984): 134 mln. **Daily newspaper circ.** (1983): 370 per 1,000 pop.
Health: Life expectancy at birth (1983): 71.6 male; 76.3 female. **Births** (per 1,000 pop. 1984): 15.5. **Deaths** (per 1,000 pop. 1984): 8.6. **Natural increase** (1984): .6%. **Hospital beds** (1982): 1.3 mln. **Physicians** (1982): 455,000. **Infant mortality** (per 1,000 live births 1984): 10.6.
Education (1984): **Literacy:** 99%.

Uruguay
Oriental Republic of Uruguay

People: Population (1984 est.): 2,926,000. **Age distrib. (%):** 0–14: 27.0; 15–59: 58.7; 60+: 14.3. **Pop. density:** 44.3 per sq. mi. **Urban** (1983): 83.0%. **Ethnic groups:** Caucasians (Iberians, Italians) 89%, mestizos 10%, mulatto and Negro. **Languages:** Spanish. **Religions:** 60% Roman Catholic.
Geography: Area: 68,037 sq. mi., the size of Washington State. **Location:** In southern S. America, on the Atlantic O. **Neighbors:** Argentina on W, Brazil on N. **Topography:** Uruguay

is composed of rolling, grassy plains and hills, well-watered by rivers flowing W to Uruguay R. **Capital:** Montevideo. **Cities** (1983 est.): Montevideo 1,255,600.
Government: Type: Republic. **Head of state:** Pres. Julio Maria Sanguinetti; in office: Mar. 1, 1985. **Local divisions:** 19 departments. **Defense:** 3.7% of GDP (1982).
Economy: Industries: Meat-packing, metals, textiles, wine, cement, oil products. **Chief crops:** Corn, wheat, citrus fruits, rice, oats, linseed. **Arable land:** 12%. **Meat prod.** (1984): beef: 355,000 metric tons; pork: 18,000 metric tons; lamb: 41,000 metric tons. **Fish catch** (1982): 123,000 metric tons. **Electricity prod.** (1982): 6.1 bln. kwh. **Labor force** 16% agric.; 31% ind. and commerce; 12% serv.; 19% govt.
Finance: Currency: New Peso (Mar. 1985: 91.50 = $1 US). **Gross domestic product** (1983): $5 bln. **Per capita income** (1980): $2,780. **Imports** (1983): $706 mln.; partners: Braz. 12%, Arg. 8%, U.S. 12%. **Exports** (1983): $1.0 bln.; partners: Braz. 14%, U.S. 7%, W. Ger. 9%, Arg. 11%. **Tourists** (1981): 480,000 mln.; receipts: $283 mln. **National budget** (1979): $1.30 bln. revenues; $1.24 bln. expeditures. **International reserves less gold** (Jan. 1985): $156 mln. **Gold:** 2.61 mln. oz t. **Consumer prices** (change in 1984): 55.3%.
Transport: Railway traffic (1982): 270 mln. passenger-km; 180 mln. net ton-km. **Motor vehicles:** in use (1981): 281,000 passenger cars, 43,000 comm. vehicles. **Civil aviation** (1982): 293 mln. passenger-km; 1.1 mln. freight ton-km. **Chief ports:** Montevideo.
Communications: Television sets: 368,000 in use (1982). **Radios:** 1.6 mln. in use (1982). **Telephones in use** (1982): 294,000. **Daily newspaper circ.** (1982): 337 per 1,000 pop.
Health: Life expectancy at birth (1983): 67.1 male; 73.7 female. **Births** (per 1,000 pop. 1981): 18.3. **Deaths** (per 1,000 pop. 1981): 9.0. **Natural increase** (1981): 0.9%. **Hospital beds** (1981): 23,000. **Physicians:** (1981): 5,600. **Infant mortality** (per 1,000 live births 1983): 32.
Education (1978): **Literacy:** 94%.
Major International Organizations: UN and its specialized agencies, OAS.
Embassy: 1918 F St. NW 20006; 331-1313.

Spanish settlers did not begin replacing the indigenous Charrua Indians until 1624. Portuguese from Brazil arrived later, but Uruguay was attached to the Spanish Viceroyalty of Rio de la Plata in the 18th century. Rebels fought against Spain beginning in 1810. An independent republic was declared Aug. 25, 1825.

Liberal governments adopted socialist measures as far back as 1911. More than a third of the workers are employed by the state, which owns the power, telephone, railroad, cement, oil-refining and other industries. Social welfare programs are among the most advanced in the world.

Uruguay's standard of living was one of the highest in South America, and political and labor conditions among the freest. Economic stagnation, inflation, plus floods, drought in 1967 and a general strike in 1968 brought attempts by the government to strengthen the economy through a series of devaluations of the peso and wage and price controls. But inflation continued in the 1980s and the country was forced to ask international creditors to restructure $2.7 billion in debt in 1983.

Tupamaros, leftist guerrillas drawn from the upper classes, increased terrorist actions in 1970. Violence continued and in Feb. 1973 Pres. Juan Maria Bordaberry agreed to military control of his administration. In June he abolished Congress and set up a Council of State in its place. By 1974 the military had apparently defeated the Tupamaros, using severe repressive measures. Bordaberry was removed by the military in a 1976 coup. Civilian government was restored to the country in 1985.

Vanuatu
Republic of Vanuatu

People: Population (1984 est.): 130,000. **Population density:** 28.4 per sq. mi. **Ethnic groups:** Mainly Melanesian, some European, Polynesian, Micronesian. **Languages:** Bislama (national), French and English both official. **Religions:** Presbyterian 40%, Anglican 14%, Roman Catholic 16%, animist 15%.
Geography: Area: 4,707 sq. mi. **Location:** SW Pacific, 1,200 mi NE of Brisbane, Australia. **Topography:** dense forest with narrow coastal strips of cultivated land. **Capital:** Vila. **Cities** (1979): 15,100.

Government: Type: Republic. **Head of state:** Pres. George Sokomanu; in office: July 30, 1980. **Head of gov't:** Prime Min. Rev. Walter Lini; in office: July 30, 1980.

Economy: Industries: Fish-freezing, meat canneries, tourism. **Chief crops:** Copra (38% of export), cocoa, coffee. **Minerals:** Manganese. **Other resources:** Forests, cattle. **Fish catch** (1981): 2.7 metric tons.

Finance: Currency: Australian dollar and Vanuatu franc (Nov. 1984: 98 vatu = $1 US). **Imports** (1982): $66 mln.; partners: Aus. 39%, Fr. 10%, Japan 13%. **Exports** (1982): $22 mln.; partners: Fr. 27%, Belg.-Lux. 34%.

Education: Education not compulsory, but 85-90% of children of primary school age attend primary schools.

The Anglo-French condominium of the New Hebrides, administered jointly by France and Great Britain since 1906, became the independent Republic of Vanuatu on July 30, 1980.

Vatican City

State of the Vatican City

People: Population (1984 est.): 1,000. **Ethnic groups:** Italians, Swiss. **Languages:** Italian, Latin. **Religion:** Roman Catholicism.

Geography: Area: 108.7 acres. **Location:** In Rome, Italy. **Neighbors:** Completely surrounded by Italy.

Currency: Lira.

Apostolic Nunciature in U.S.: 3339 Massachusetts Ave. NW 20008; 222-7121.

The popes for many centuries, with brief interruptions, held temporal sovereignty over mid-Italy (the so-called Papal States), comprising an area of some 16,000 sq. mi., with a population in the 19th century of more than 3 million. This territory was incorporated in the new Kingdom of Italy, the sovereignty of the pope being confined to the palaces of the Vatican and the Lateran in Rome and the villa of Castel Gandolfo, by an Italian law, May 13, 1871. This law also guaranteed to the pope and his successors a yearly indemnity of over $620,000. The allowance, however, remained unclaimed.

A Treaty of Conciliation, a concordat and a financial convention were signed Feb. 11, 1929, by Cardinal Gaspari and Premier Mussolini. The documents established the independent state of Vatican City, and gave the Catholic religion special status in Italy. The treaty (Lateran Agreement) was made part of the Constitution of Italy (Article 7) in 1947. Italy and the Vatican reached preliminary agreement in 1976 on revisions of the concordat, that would eliminate Roman Catholicism as the state religion and end required religious education in Italian schools.

Vatican City includes St. Peter's, the Vatican Palace and Museum covering over 13 acres, the Vatican gardens, and neighboring buildings between Viale Vaticano and the Church. Thirteen buildings in Rome, outside the boundaries, enjoy extraterritorial rights; these buildings house congregations or officers necessary for the administration of the Holy See.

The legal system is based on the code of canon law, the apostolic constitutions and the laws especially promulgated for the Vatican City by the pope. The Secretariat of State represents the Holy See in its diplomatic relations. By the Treaty of Conciliation the pope is pledged to a perpetual neutrality unless his mediation is specifically requested. This, however, does not prevent the defense of the Church whenever it is persecuted.

The present sovereign of the State of Vatican City is the Supreme Pontiff John Paul II, Karol Wojtyla, born in Wadowice, Poland, May 18, 1920, elected Oct. 16, 1978 (the first non-Italian to be elected Pope in 456 years).

The U.S. restored formal relations in 1984 after the U.S. Congress repealed an 1867 ban on diplomatic relations with the Vatican.

Venezuela

Republic of Venezuela

People: Population (1984 est.): 18,552,000. **Age distrib. (%):** 0–14: 42.8; 15–59: 52.4; 60+: 4.8. **Pop. density:** 47.3 per sq. mi. **Urban** (1984): 80%. **Ethnic groups:** Mestizo 69%, white (Spanish, Portuguese, Italian) 20%, Negro 9%, Indian 2%. **Languages:** Spanish (official), Indian languages 2%. **Religions:** Predominantly Roman Catholic.

Geography: Area: 352,143 sq. mi., more than twice the size of California. **Location:** On the Caribbean coast of S. America. **Neighbors:** Colombia on W, Brazil on S, Guyana on E. **Topography:** Flat coastal plain and Orinoco Delta are bordered by Andes Mtns. and hills. Plains, called llanos, extend between mountains and Orinoco. Guyana Highlands and plains are S of Orinoco, which stretches 1,600 mi. and drains 80% of Venezuela. **Capital:** Caracas. **Cities** (1981 est.): Caracas 2,700,000; Maracaibo 845,000; Barquisimeto 459,000; Valencia 471,000.

Government: Type: Federal republic. **Head of state:** Pres. Jaime Lusinchi; b. 1924; in office: Feb. 2, 1984. **Local divisions:** 20 states, 2 federal territories, federal district, federal dependency. **Defense:** 1.4% of GNP (1982).

Economy: Industries: Steel, oil products, textiles, containers, paper, shoes. **Chief crops:** Coffee, rice, fruits, sugar. **Minerals:** Oil (5th largest producer), iron (extensive reserves and production), gold. **Crude oil reserves** (1980): 17.87 bln. bbls. **Arable land:** 4%. **Meat prod.** (1984): beef: 365,000 metric tons; pork: 118,000 metric tons; lamb: 12,000 metric tons. **Fish catch** (1981): 181,000 metric tons. **Electricity prod.** (1981): 37.5 bln. kwh. **Crude steel prod.** (1982): 2.0 mln. metric tons. **Labor force:** 18% agric.; 42% ind. and commerce; 41% services.

Finance: Currency: Bolivar (Apr. 1985: 7.50 = $1 US). **Gross national product** (1982): $69.4 bln. **Per capita income** (1982): $4,716. **Imports** (1983): $10.2 bln.; partners: U.S. 48%, W. Ger. 6%, Jap. 8%. **Exports** (1982): $16.4 bln.; partners: U.S. 25%, Neth Ant. 21%, Can. 9%. **Tourists** (1983): 201,560. **National budget** (1982): $19.3 bln. expenditures. **International reserves less gold** (Mar. 1985): $9.4 bln. **Gold:** 11.46 mln. oz t. **Consumer prices** (change in 1984): 12.2%.

Transport: Railway traffic (1979): 25 mln. passenger-km; 18 mln. net ton-km. **Motor vehicles:** in use (1981): 1.5 mln. passenger cars, 763,000 comm. vehicles. **Civil aviation** (1982): 5.0 bln. passenger-km; 144.6 mln. freight ton-km. **Chief ports:** Maracaibo, La Guaira, Puerto Cabello.

Communications: Television sets: 1.7 mln. in use (1981). **Radios:** 5.3 mln. in use (1981). **Telephones in use** (1982): 1.3 mln. **Daily newspaper circ.** (1982): 120 per 1,000 pop.

Health: Life expectancy at birth (1980): 64.0 male; 69.0 female. **Births** (per 1,000 pop. 1980): 35.6 **Deaths** (per 1,000 pop. 1980): 5.5. **Natural increase** (1980): 3.0%. **Hospital beds** (per 100,000 pop. 1977): 292. **Physicians** (per 100,000 pop. 1977): 107. **Infant mortality** (per 1,000 live births 1984): 36.2.

Education (1984): **Literacy:** 85.6%. **Years compulsory:** 9; attendance 82%.

Major International Organizations: UN and its specialized agencies, OAS, OPEC.

Embassy: 2445 Massachusetts Ave. NW 20008; 797-3800.

Columbus first set foot on the South American continent on the peninsula of Paria, Aug. 1498. Alonso de Ojeda, 1499, found Lake Maracaibo, called the land Venezuela, or Little Venice, because natives had houses on stilts. Venezuela was under Spanish domination until 1821. The republic was formed after secession from the Colombian Federation in 1830.

Military strongmen ruled Venezuela for most of the 20th century. They promoted the oil industry; some social reforms were implemented. Since 1959, the country has enjoyed progressive, democratically-elected governments.

Venezuela helped found the Organization of Petroleum Exporting States (OPEC). The government, Jan. 1, 1976, nationalized the oil industry with compensation. Development has begun of the Orinoco tar belt, believed to contain the world's largest oil reserves. Oil accounts for much of total export earnings and the economy suffered a severe cash crisis in 1983 and 1984 as the result of falling oil revenues.

Oil profits help finance a $150 billion national development plan for 1981-85. The funds were spent for housing, education, and industrial expansion.

A dispute with Guyana over the Essequibo border region was renewed in 1982.

Vietnam

Socialist Republic of Vietnam

People: Population (1984 est.): 59,030,000. **Pop. density:** 455 per sq. mi. **Ethnic groups:** Vietnamese 84%, Chinese 2%, remainder Muong, Thai, Meo, Khmer, Man, Cham. **Languages:** Vietnamese (official), French, English. **Religions:** Buddhists,

...cians, and Taoists most numerous, Roman Catholics, ani-
..., Muslims, Protestants.
...eography: Area: 127,207 sq. mi., the size of New Mexico.
...ation: On the E coast of the Indochinese Peninsula in SE
...a. Neighbors: China on N, Laos, Cambodia on W. Topogra-
...y: Vietnam is long and narrow, with a 1,400-mi. coast. About
..4% of country is readily arable, including the densely settled
..ed R. valley in the N, narrow coastal plains in center, and the
wide, often marshy Mekong R. Delta in the S. The rest consists
of semi-arid plateaus and barren mountains, with some stretches
of tropical rain forest. Capital: Hanoi. Cities (1981): Ho Chi Minh
City 3.5 mln.; Hanoi 2 mln.

Government: Type: Communist people's republic. **Head of
state:** Chairman State Council Truong Chinh; in office: July 4,
1981. **Head of government:** Prime Min. Pham Van Dong; b.
1906; in office: Sept. 20, 1955. **Head of Communist Party:** First
Sec. Le Duan; b. 1907; in office: Sept. 10, 1960. **Local divisions:** 39 provinces. **Defense:** 50% of govt. budget (1982 est.)

Economy: Industries: Food processing, textiles, cement,
chemical fertilizers, steel. **Chief crops:** Rice, rubber, fruits and
vegetables, corn, manioc, sugarcane. **Minerals:** Phosphates,
coal, iron, manganese, bauxite, apatite, chromate. **Other resources:** Forests. **Arable land:** 18%. **Meat prod.** (1984): beef:
129,000 metric tons; pork: 570,000 metric tons. **Fish catch**
(1982): 800,000 metric tons. **Electricity prod.** (1983): 4.3 bln.
kwh, **Labor force:** 70% agric.; 8% ind. and commerce.

Finance: Currency: Dong (Nov. 1984: 10.42 = $1 US).
Gross national product (1982): $9 bln. **Per capita income**
(1982): $189. **Imports** (1982): $1.9 bln.; partners: USSR 58%,
Jap. 6%. **Exports** (1982): $550 mln.; partners: USSR 52%, Jap.
6%.

Transport: Motor vehicles: in use (1976): 100,000 passenger cars, 200,000 comm. vehicles. **Chief ports:** Ho Chi Minh
City, Haiphong, Da Nang.

Communications: Television sets (1983) 2 mln. **Radios:** 3
mln. in use (1983). **Daily newspaper circ.** (1983): 10 per 1,000
pop.

Health: Life expectancy at birth (1981): 52 years. **Births**
(per 1,000 pop. 1983): 31.7. **Deaths** (per 1,000 pop. 1983): 10.9.
Natural increase (1983): 2.0%. **Hospital beds** (1980): 197,000.
Physicians (1980): 13,300.

Education (1978): **Literacy:** 78%.

Vietnam's recorded history began in Tonkin before the Christian era. Settled by Viets from central China, Vietnam was held
by China, 111 BC-939 AD, and was a vassal state during subsequent periods. Vietnam defeated the armies of Kublai Khan,
1288. Conquest by France began in 1858 and ended in 1884
with the protectorates of Tonkin and Annam in the N. and the
colony of Cochin-China in the S.

In 1940 Vietnam was occupied by Japan; nationalist aims
gathered force. A number of groups formed the Vietminh (Independence) League, headed by Ho Chi Minh, communist guerrilla
leader. In Aug. 1945 the Vietminh forced out Bao Dai, former
emperor of Annam, head of a Japan-sponsored regime. France,
seeking to reestablish colonial control, battled communist and
nationalist forces, 1946-1954, and was finally defeated at Dienbienphu, May 8, 1954. Meanwhile, on July 1, 1949, Bao Dai had
formed a State of Vietnam, with himself as chief of state, with
French approval. Communist China backed Ho Chi Minh.

A cease-fire accord signed in Geneva July 21, 1954, divided
Vietnam along the Ben Hai R. It provided for a buffer zone, withdrawal of French troops from the North and elections to determine the country's future. Under the agreement the communists
gained control of territory north of the 17th parallel, 22 provinces
with area of 62,000 sq. mi. and 13 million pop., with its capital at
Hanoi and Ho Chi Minh as president. South Vietnam came to
comprise the 39 southern provinces with approx. area of 65,000
sq. mi. and pop. of 12 million. Some 900,000 North Vietnamese
fled to South Vietnam. Neither South Vietnam nor the U.S.
signed the agreement.

On Oct. 26, 1955, Ngo Dinh Diem, premier of the interim government of South Vietnam, proclaimed the Republic of Vietnam
and became its first president.

The Democratic Republic of Vietnam, established in the North,
adopted a constitution Dec. 31, 1959, based on communist principles and calling for reunification of all Vietnam. North Vietnam
sought to take over South Vietnam beginning in 1954. Fighting
persisted from 1956, with the communist Vietcong, aided by
North Vietnam, pressing war in the South and South Vietnam
receiving U.S. aid. Northern aid to Vietcong guerrillas was intensified in 1959, and large-scale troop infiltration began in 1964,

with Soviet and Chinese arms assistance. Large Northern forces
were stationed in border areas of Laos and Cambodia.

A serious political conflict arose in the South in 1963 when
Buddhists denounced authoritarianism and brutality. This paved
the way for a military coup Nov. 1-2, 1963, which overthrew
Diem. Several military coups followed. In elections Sept. 3,
1967, Chief of State Nguyen Van Thieu was chosen president.

In 1964, the U.S. began air strikes against North Vietnam. Beginning in 1965, the raids were stepped up and U.S. troops became combatants. U.S. troop strength in Vietnam, which
reached a high of 543,400 in Apr. 1969, was ordered reduced by
President Nixon in a series of withdrawals, beginning in June
1969. U.S. bombings were resumed in 1972-73.

A ceasefire agreement was signed in Paris Jan. 27, 1973 by
the U.S., North and South Vietnam, and the Vietcong. It was
never implemented. U.S. aid was curbed in 1974 by the U.S.
Congress. Heavy fighting continued for two years throughout
Indochina.

North Vietnamese forces launched attacks against remaining
government outposts in the Central Highlands in the first months
of 1975. Government retreats turned into a rout, and the Saigon
regime surrendered April 30. A Provisional Revolutionary Government assumed control, aided by officials and technicians
from Hanoi, and first steps were taken to transform society
along communist lines. All businesses and farms were collectivized.

The U.S. accepted over 165,000 Vietnamese refugees, while
scores of thousands more sought refuge in other countries.

The war's toll included — Combat deaths: U.S. 47,752; South
Vietnam over 200,000; other allied forces 5,225. Civilian casualties were over a million. Displaced war refugees in South Vietnam totaled over 6.5 million.

After the fighting ended, 8 Northern divisions remained stationed in the South. Over 1 million urban residents and 260,000
Montagnards were resettled in the countryside by 1978, the first
of 10 million scheduled for forced resettlement. Many were sent
to long-term re-education camps, including thousands of adherents of the Hoa Hao sect.

The first National Assembly of both parts of the country met
and the country was officially reunited July 2, 1976. The Northern capital, flag, anthem, emblem, and currency were applied to
the new state. Nearly all major government posts went to officials of the former Northern government.

Heavy fighting with Cambodia took place, 1977-80, amid mutual charges of aggression and atrocities against civilians. Increasing numbers of Vietnamese civilians, ethnic Chinese, escaped the country, via the sea, or the overland route across
Cambodia. Vietnam launched an offensive against Cambodian
refugee strongholds along the Thai-Cambodian border in 1985;
they also engaged Thai troops.

Relations with China soured as 140,000 ethnic Chinese left
Vietnam charging discrimination; China cut off economic aid. Re-
acting to Vietnam's invasion of Cambodia, China attacked 4 Vietnamese border provinces, Feb., 1979, instigating heavy fighting.
Several border clashes were reported with China in 1984.

Western Samoa

Independent State of Western Samoa

People: Population (1984 est.): 162,000. **Age distrib.** (%):
0-14: 50.4; 15-59: 45.4; 60+: 4.3. **Pop. density:** 146 per sq. mi.
Urban (1981): 21.2%. **Ethnic groups:** Samoan (Polynesian)
88%, Euronesian (mixed) 10%, European, other Pacific Islanders. **Languages:** Samoan, English both official. **Religions:** Protestants 70%, Roman Catholics 20%.

Geography: Area: 1,133 sq. mi., the size of Rhode Island.
Location: In the S. Pacific O. **Neighbors:** Nearest are Fiji on W,
Tonga on S. **Topography:** Main islands, Savai'i (670 sq. mi.)
and Upolu (429 sq. mi.), both ruggedly mountainous, and small
islands Manono and Apolima. **Capital:** Apia. **Cities** (1983 est.):
Apia 35,000.

Government: Type: Parliamentary democracy. **Head of
state:** King Malietoa Tanumafili II; b. Jan. 4, 1913; in office: Jan.
1, 1962. **Head of government:** Prime Min. Tupuola Efi; b. Mar.
1, 1938; in office: Sept. 18, 1982. **Local divisions:** 24 districts.

Economy: Chief crops: Cocoa, copra, bananas. **Other resources:** Hardwoods, fish. **Arable land:** 43%. **Electricity prod.**
(1982): 39 mln. kwh. **Labor force:** 67% agric.

Finance: Currency: Tala (Mar. 1985: 2.24 = $1 US). **Gross domestic product** (1978): $65 mln. **Per capita income** (1978): $400. **Imports** (1982): $38 mln.; partners: NZ 24% Austral. 16%, Jap. 9%, U.S. 23%. **Exports** (1982): $9 mln.; partners: NZ 33%, W. Ger. 13%, Neth. 13%. **Tourists** (1977): 22,000; receipts (1976): $3 mln. **International reserves less gold** (Mar. 1985): $11.6 mln. **Consumer prices** (change in 1981): 20.5%.

Transport: Motor vehicles: in use (1983): 3,000 passenger cars, 2,503 comm. vehicles. **Chief ports:** Apia, Asau.

Communications: Radios: 70,000 in use (1983). **Telephones in use** (1982): 5,857.

Health: Life expectancy at birth (1983): 63 years. **Births** (per 1,000 pop. 1978): 20.0. **Deaths** (per 1,000 pop. 1978): 2.8. **Natural increase** (1978): 1.7%. **Hospital beds** (1980): 674. **Physicians** (1980): 34. **Infant mortality** (per 1,000 live births 1983): 36.

Education (1983): **Literacy:** 90%. 95% attend elementary school.

Major International Organizations: UN and its specialized agencies, Commonwealth of Nations.

Western Samoa was a German colony, 1899 to 1914, when New Zealand landed troops and took over. It became a New Zealand mandate under the League of Nations and, in 1945, a New Zealand UN Trusteeship.

An elected local government took office in Oct. 1959 and the country became fully independent Jan. 1, 1962.

North Yemen

Yemen Arab Republic

People: Population (1984 est.): 4,890,000. **Pop. density:** 122 per sq. mi. **Ethnic groups:** Arabs, some Negroids. **Languages:** Arabic. **Religions:** Sunni Moslems 50%, Shiite Moslems 50%.

Geography: Area: 77,200 sq. mi., slightly smaller than South Dakota. **Location:** On the southern Red Sea coast of the Arabian Peninsula. **Neighbors:** Saudi Arabia on NE, South Yemen on S. **Topography:** A sandy coastal strip leads to well-watered fertile mountains in interior. **Capital:** Sanaa. **Cities** (1985 est.): Sanaa 275,000.

Government: Type: Republic. **Head of state:** Pres. Ali Abdullah Saleh, b. 1942; in office: July 17, 1978. **Head of government:** Prime Min. Abdul Aziz Abdel Ghani; in office: Nov. 13, 1983. **Local divisions:** 10 governorates. **Defense:** 35% of govt. budget.

Economy: Industries: Textiles, cement. **Chief crops:** Wheat, sorghum, qat, fruits, coffee, cotton. **Minerals:** Salt. **Crude oil reserves** (1978): 370 mln. bbls. **Arable land:** 14%. **Meat prod.** (1984): beef: 14,000 metric tons; lamb: 47,000 metric tons. **Fish catch** (1980): 17,000 metric tons. **Electricity prod.** (1982): 230 mln. kwh. **Labor force:** 74% agric.; 17% ind. and commerce; 9% serv.

Finance: Currency: Rial (Apr. 1985: 6.48 = $1 US). **Gross domestic product** (1982): $3.2 bln. **Per capita income** (1977-78): $475. **Imports** (1982): $1.5 bln.; partners: Saudi Ar. 20%, Fr. 8%, Jap. 16%. **Exports** (1982): $39 mln.; partners: S. Yemen 23%, Saudi Ar. 8%, Pak. 19%. **National budget** (1984): 1.5 bln. **International reserves less gold** (Mar. 1985): $290.9 mln. **Gold:** 9,000 oz t. **Consumer prices** (change in 1982): 2.7%.

Transport: Chief ports: Al-Hudaydah, Al-Mukha.

Communications: Television sets: (1983): 25,000. **Radios:** 110,000 in use (1983). **Telephones in use** (1981): 90,350.

Health: Life expectancy at birth (1975): 37.3 male; 38.7 female. **Births** (per 1,000 pop. 1978): 48. **Deaths** (per 1,000 pop. 1978): 25. **Natural increase** (1978): 2.3%. **Hospital beds** (1983): 4,000.

Education (1985): **Literacy:** 20%. **Primary school attendance:** 29%.

Major International Organizations: UN and its specialized agencies, Arab League.

Embassy: 600 New Hampshire Ave. NW 20037; 965-4760.

Yemen's territory once was part of the ancient kindgom of Sheba, or Saba, a prosperous link in trade between Africa and India. A Biblical reference speaks of its gold, spices and precious stones as gifts borne by the Queen of Sheba to King Solomon.

Yemen became independent in 1918, after years of Ottoman Turkish rule, but remained politically and economically backward. Imam Ahmed ruled 1948-1962. The king was reported

assassinated Sept. 26, 1962, and a revolutionary group he by Brig. Gen. Abdullah al-Salal declared the country to be Yemen Arab Republic.

The Imam Ahmed's heir, the Imam Mohamad al-Badr, fled the mountains where tribesmen joined royalist forces; inter warfare between them and the republican forces continue Egypt sent troops and Saudi Arabia military aid to the royalists. About 150,000 people died in the fighting.

After its defeat in the June 1967 Arab-Israeli war, Egypt announced it would withdraw its troops from Yemen.

There was a bloodless coup Nov. 5, 1967.

In April 1970 hostilities ended with an agreement between Yemen and Saudi Arabia and appointment of several royalists to the Yemen government. There were border skirmishes with forces of the People's Democratic Republic of Yemen in 1972-73.

On June 13, 1974, an Army group, led by Col. Ibrahim al-Hamidi, seized the government. Hamidi pursued close Saudi and U.S. ties; he was assassinated in 1977.

The People's Democratic Republic of Yemen went to war with Yemen on Feb. 24, 1979. Swift Arab mediation led to a ceasefire and a mutual withdrawal of forces, Mar. 19. An Arab League-sponsored agreement between North and South Yemen on unification of the 2 countries was signed Mar. 29th.

The remittances from 400,000 Yemenis living in Arab oil countries provide most of foreign earnings.

South Yemen

People's Democratic Republic of Yemen

People: Population (1984 est.): 2,147,000. **Age distrib. (%):** 0–14: 49.4; 15–59: 45.5; 60+: 5.5. **Pop. density:** 15.9 per sq. mi. **Urban** (1973): 33.3%. **Ethnic groups:** Arabs, 75%, Indians 11%, Somalis 8%, others. **Languages:** Arabic. **Religions:** Muslims (Sunni) 91%, Christians 4%, Hindus 3.5%.

Geography: Area: 130,541 sq. mi., the size of Nevada. **Location:** On the southern coast of the Arabian Peninsula. **Neighbors:** Yemen on W, Saudi Arabia on N, Oman on E. **Topography:** The entire country is very hot and very dry. A sandy coast rises to mountains which give way to desert sands. **Capital:** Aden. **Cities** (1981 est.): Aden 365,000.

Government: Type: Republic. **Head of state:** Chairman, Council of Ministers Ali Nasir Muhammad Husani; b. 1938; in office: Apr. 21, 1980. **Head of Communist Party:** Sec. Gen. Ali Nasir Muhammad Husani; in office: April 21, 1980. **Local divisions:** 6 governorates. **Defense:** 15.5% of GNP (1982).

Economy: Industries: Transshipment. **Chief crops:** Cotton (main export), grains. **Meat prod.** (1980) lamb: 11,000 metric tons. **Fish catch** (1982): 69,000 metric tons. **Electricity prod.** (1982) 257 mln. kwh. **Labor force:** 43.8% agric.; 28% ind. and commerce; 28% serv.

Finance: Currency: Dinar (Mar. 1985: .35 = $1 US). **Gross domestic product** (1981 est.): $910 mln. **Per capita income** (1977): $310. **Imports** (1983) $756 mln.; partners: UAE 28%, Kuw. 9%, Jap. 6%. **Exports** (1983): $30 mln.; partners: It. 11%, UAE 22%. **National budget** (1977): $101 mln. revenues; $137 mln. expenditures. **International reserves less gold** (Jan. 1985): $236.9 mln. **Gold:** 42,000 oz t. **Consumer prices** (change in 1981): 3.8%.

Transport: Motor vehicles: in use (1980): 12,200 passenger cars, 15,300 comm. vehicles. **Chief ports:** Aden.

Communications: Television sets: 26,000 in use (1983). **Radios:** 150,000 in use (1983). **Daily newspaper circ.** (1982): 6 per 1,000 pop.

Health: Life expectancy at birth (1975): 40.6 male; 42.4 female. **Births** (per 1,000 pop. 1978): 47. **Deaths** (per 1,000 pop. 1978): 21. **Natural increase** (1978): 1.8%. **Hospital beds** (1980): 2,700. **Physicians** (1980): 250. **Infant mortality rate** (per 1,000 live births in 1980): 114.

Major International Organizations: UN, Arab League.

Education (1980): **Literacy:** 39%. About 90% attend primary school.

Aden, mentioned in the Bible, has been a port for trade in incense, spice and silk between the East and West for 2,000 years. British rule began in 1839. Aden provided Britain with a controlling position at the southern entrance to the Red Sea.

A war for independence began in 1963. The National Liberation Front (NLF) and the Egypt-supported Front for the Libera-

Occupied South Yemen, waged a guerrilla war against ...sh and local dynastic rulers. The 2 groups vied with each ...or control. The NLF won out. Independence came Nov. ...67. In 1969, the left wing of the NLF seized power and in-...rated a thorough nationalization of the economy and regi-...tation of daily life.

...he new government broke off relations with the U.S. and na-...nalized some foreign firms. Aid has been furnished by the ...SSR and China.

In 1972-73 there were border skirmishes with forces of the Yemen Arab Republic. South Yemen aided leftist guerrillas in neighboring Oman. Relations with Saudi Arabia later improved. S. Yemen troops fought in Ethiopia against Eritrean rebels in 1978.

Pres. Salem Robaye Ali, who had tried to improve relations with Yemen, Saudi Arabia, Oman, and the U.S., was executed after a bloody coup June 1978. The new ruling faction was accused by N. Yemen of the murder of N. Yemen's president 2 days earlier. N. Yemen, Egypt, and Saudi Arabia froze ties with S. Yemen in July.

The People's Democratic Republic of Yemen went to war with Yemen on Feb. 24, 1979. Swift Arab mediation led to a ceasefire and a mutual withdrawal of forces, Mar. 19th. An Arab League-sponsored agreement between North and South Yemen on unification of the 2 countries was signed Mar. 29th.

The Port of Aden is the country's most valuable resource.

Socotra, the largest island in the Arabian Sea, Kamaran, an island in the Red Sea near the coast of North Yemen, and Perim, an island in the strait between the Gulf of Aden and the Red Sea, are controlled by South Yemen.

Yugoslavia
Socialist Federal Republic of Yugoslavia

People: Population (1984 est.): 22,997,000. **Age distrib. (%):** 0–14: 24.7; 15-59: 63.7; 60+: 12.6. **Pop. density:** 233 per sq. mi. **Urban** (1971): 38.6%. **Ethnic groups:** Serbs 36%, Croats 20%, Bosnian Muslims 9%, Slovenes 8%, Macedonians 6%, Albanians 8%. **Languages:** Serbo-Croatian, Macedonian, Slovenian (all official), Albanian. **Religions:** Orthodox 50%, Roman Catholics 30%, Moslems 10%, Protestants 1%.

Geography: Area: 98,766 sq. mi., the size of Wyoming. **Location:** On the Adriatic coast of the Balkan Peninsula in SE Europe. **Neighbors:** Italy on W, Austria, Hungary on N, Romania, Bulgaria on E, Greece, Albania on S. **Topography:** The Dinaric Alps run parallel to the Adriatic coast, which is lined by offshore islands. Plains stretch across N and E river basins. S and NW are mountainous. **Capital:** Belgrade. **Cities** (1980 est.): Belgrade 1,300,000; Zagreb 700,000; Skopje 440,000; Sarajevo 400,000; Ljubljana 300,000.

Government: Type: Federal republic. **Head of state:** Pres. Veselin Djuranovic; in office: May 15, 1984. **Head of government:** Prime Min. Milka Planinc; b. 1924; in office: May 16, 1982; **Head of Communist Party:** Mitja Ribicic; in office: June 29, 1982. **Local divisions:** 6 republics, 2 autonomous provinces. **Defense:** 5.2% of GNP (1983).

Economy: Industries: Steel, wood products, cement, textiles, tourism. **Chief crops:** Corn, grains, tobacco, sugar beets. **Minerals:** Antimony, bauxite, lead, mercury, coal, iron, copper, chrome, zinc, salt. **Crude oil reserves** (1980): 275 mln. bbls. **Arable land:** 31%. **Meat prod.** (1984): beef: 350,000 metric tons; pork: 870,000 metric tons; lamb: 60,000 metric tons. **Fish catch:** (1981): 71,000 metric tons. **Electricity prod.** (1982): 60.3 bln. kwh. **Crude steel prod.** (1982): 2.8 mln. metric tons. **Labor force:** 30% agric.; 70% ind.

Finance: Currency: Dinar (Mar. 1985: 249 = $1 US). **Gross national product** (1982): $46.4 bln. **Per capita income:** $3,109. **Imports** (1984): $11.9 bln.; partners: W. Ger. 15%, USSR 19%, It. 8%, U.S. 6%. **Exports** (1984): $10.2 bln.; partners: USSR 33%, It. 9%, W. Ger. 8%, Czech. 5%. **Tourists** (1981): 6.6 mln.; receipts: 1.1 bln. **National budget** (1980): $3.5 bln. revenues; $3.5 bln. expenditures. **International reserves less gold** (Mar. 1985): $1.0 bln. **Gold:** 2.02 mln. oz t. **Consumer prices** change in 1984): 55.4%.

Transport: Railway traffic (1982): 10.8 bln. passenger-km; 25.8 bln. net ton-km. **Motor vehicles:** in use (1982): 2.7 mln. passenger cars, 237,000 comm. vehicles; manuf. (1981): 175,000 passenger cars; 73,000 comm. vehicles. **Civil aviation** (1982): 2.8 bln. passenger-km; 59.7 mln. freight ton-km. **Chief ports:** Rijeka, Split, Dubrovnik.

Communications: Television sets: 4.6 mln. licensed (1982), 599,000 manuf. (1979). **Radios:** 4.9 mln. licensed (1982), 172,000 manuf. (1978). **Telephones in use** (1982): 2.5 mln. **Daily newspaper circ.** (1982): 97 per 1,000 pop.

Health: Life expectancy at birth (1983): 68 male; 73 female. **Births** (per 1,000 pop. 1982): 16.5. **Deaths** (per 1,000 pop. 1982): 8.9. **Natural increase** (1982): .7%. **Hospital beds** (1981): 136,280. **Physicians** (1981): 33,517. **Infant mortality** (per 1,000 live births 1981): 32.8.

Education (1983): **Literacy:** 90%. Almost all attend primary school.

Major International Organizations: UN and its specialized agencies.

Embassy: 2410 California St. NW 20008; 462-6566.

Serbia, which had since 1389 been a vassal principality of Turkey, was established as an independent kingdom by the Treaty of Berlin, 1878. Montenegro, independent since 1389, also obtained international recognition in 1878. After the Balkan wars Serbia's boundaries were enlarged by the annexation of Old Serbia and Macedonia, 1913.

When the Austro-Hungarian empire collapsed after World War I, the Kingdom of the Serbs, Croats, and Slovenes was formed from the former provinces of Croatia, Dalmatia, Bosnia, Herzegovina, Slovenia, Voyvodina and the independent state of Montenegro. The name was later changed to Yugoslavia.

Nazi Germany invaded in 1941. Many Yugoslav partisan troops continued to operate. Among these were the Chetniks led by Draja Mikhailovich, who fought other partisans led by Josip Broz, known as Marshal Tito. Tito, backed by the USSR and Britain from 1943, was in control by the time the Germans had been driven from Yugoslavia in 1945. Mikhailovich was executed July 17, 1946, by the Tito regime.

A constituent assembly proclaimed Yugoslavia a republic Nov. 29, 1945. It became a federated republic Jan. 31, 1946, and Marshal Tito, a communist, became head of the government.

The Stalin policy of dictating to all communist nations was rejected by Tito. He accepted economic aid and military equipment from the U.S. and received aid in foreign trade also from France and Great Britain. Tito also supported the liberal government of Czechoslovakia in 1968 before the Russian invasion.

A separatist movement among Croatians, 2d to the Serbs in numbers, brought arrests and a change of leaders in the Croatian Republic in Jan. 1972. Violence by extreme Croatian nationalists and fears of Soviet political intervention have led to restrictions on political and intellectual dissent, which had previously been freer than in other East European countries. Serbians, Montenegrins, and Macedonians use Cyrillic, Croatians and Slovenians use Latin letters. Croatia and Slovenia have been the most prosperous republics.

Most industry is socialized and private enterprise is restricted to small-scale production. Since 1952 workers are guaranteed a basic wage and a share in cooperative profits. Management of industrial enterprises is handled by workers' councils. Farmland is 85% privately owned but farms are restricted to 25 acres.

Beginning in 1965, reforms designed to decentralize the administration of economic development and to force industries to produce more efficiently in competition with foreign producers were introduced.

Yugoslavia has developed considerable trade with Western Europe as well as with Eastern Europe. Money earned by Yugoslavs working temporarily in Western Europe helps pay for imports.

Pres. Tito died May 4, 1980; with his death, the post as head of the Collective Presidency and also that as head of the League of Communists became a rotating system of succession among the members representing each republic and autonomous province.

Zaire
Republic of Zaire

People: Population (1983 est.): 32,158,000. **Pop. density:** 35.4 per sq. mi. **Urban** (1981): 30.3%. **Ethnic groups:** Bantu tribes 80%, over 200 other tribes. **Languages:** French (official), Bantu dialects. **Religions:** Christian 70%, Muslim 10%.

Geography: Area: 905,365 sq. mi., one-fourth the size of the U.S. **Location:** In central Africa. **Neighbors:** Congo on W, Central African Republic, Sudan on N, Uganda, Rwanda, Burundi,

Tanzania on E, Zambia, Angola on S. **Topography:** Zaire includes the bulk of the Zaire (Congo) R. Basin. The vast central region is a low-lying plateau covered by rain forest. Mountainous terraces in the W, savannas in the S and SE, grasslands toward the N, and the high Ruwenzori Mtns. on the E surround the central region. A short strip of territory borders the Atlantic O. The Zaire R. is 2,718 mi. long. **Capital:** Kinshasa. **Cities** (1983 est.): Kinshasa 3,000,000; Kananga 601,239.

Government: Type: Republic with strong presidential authority. **Head of state:** Pres. Mobutu Sese Seko; b. Oct. 14, 1930; in office: Nov. 25, 1965. **Local divisions:** 9 regions, Kinshasa. **Defense:** 1.4% of GNP (1981).

Economy: Chief crops: Coffee, cotton, rice, sugar cane, bananas, plantains, coconuts, manioc, mangoes, tea, cacao, palm oil. **Minerals:** Cobalt (60% of world reserves), copper, cadmium, gold, silver, tin, germanium, zinc, iron, manganese, uranium, radium. **Crude oil reserves** (1980): 135 mln. bbls. **Other resources:** Forests, rubber, ivory. **Arable land:** 3%. **Meat prod.** (1984): pork: 28,000 metric tons; lamb: 9,000 metric tons. **Fish catch** (1982): 100,000 metric tons. **Electricity prod.** (1981): 4.5 bln. kwh. **Labor force:** 75% agric..

Finance: Currency: Zaire (Mar. 1985: 47.20 = $1 US). **Gross domestic product** (1982): $9.9 bln. **Per capita income** (1975): $127. **Imports** (1983): $529 mln.; partners: Belg. 22%, U.S. 10%, W. Ger. 10%, Fra. 13%. **Exports** (1983): $1.0 bln.; partners: Belg.-Lux. 31%, U.S. 36%. **National budget** (1978): $886 mln. revenues; $1.8 bln. expenditures. **International reserves less gold** (Jan. 1985): $71.6 mln. **Gold:** 470,000 oz t. **Consumer prices** (change in 1984): 52.2%.

Transport: Railway traffic (1981): 389 mln. passenger-km; 1.7 bln. net ton-km. **Motor vehicles:** in use (1982): 89,000 passenger cars, 16,000 comm. vehicles. **Civil aviation** (1982): 683 mln. passenger-km. 31.5 mln. freight ton-km. **Chief ports:** Matadi, Boma.

Communications: Television sets: 8,000 in use (1981). **Radios:** 150,000 mln. in use (1981). **Telephones in use** (1980): 30,300. **Daily newspaper circ.** (1982): 1 per 1,000 pop.

Health: Life expectancy at birth (1983): 46 male; 49 female. **Births** (per 1,000 pop. 1978): 46. **Deaths** (per 1,000 pop. 1978): 18. **Natural increase** (1978): 2.8%. **Hospital beds** (1979): 79,244. **Physicians** (1979): 1,900. **Infant mortality** (per 1,000 live births 1983): 117.

Education (1980): Literacy: males 40%, females 15%.

Major International Organizations: UN and its specialized agencies, OAU.

Embassy: 1800 New Hampshire Ave. NW 20009; 234-7690.

The earliest inhabitants of Zaire may have been the pygmies, followed by Bantus from the E and Nilotic tribes from the N. The large Bantu Bakongo kingdom ruled much of Zaire and Angola when Portuguese explorers visited in the 15th century.

Leopold II, king of the Belgians, formed an international group to exploit the Congo in 1876. In 1877 Henry M. Stanley explored the Congo and in 1878 the king's group sent him back to organize the region and win over the native chiefs. The Conference of Berlin, 1884-85, organized the Congo Free State with Leopold as king and chief owner. Exploitation of native laborers on the rubber plantations caused international criticism and led to granting of a colonial charter, 1908.

Belgian and Congolese leaders agreed Jan. 27, 1960, that the Congo would become independent June 30. In the first general elections, May 31, the National Congolese movement of Patrice Lumumba won 35 of 137 seats in the National Assembly. He was appointed premier June 21, and formed a coalition cabinet.

Widespread violence caused Europeans and others to flee. The UN Security Council Aug. 9, 1960, called on Belgium to withdraw its troops and sent a UN contingent. President Kasavubu removed Lumumba as premier. Lumumba fought for control backed by Ghana, Guinea and India; he was murdered in 1961.

The last UN troops left the Congo June 30, 1964, and Moise Tshombe became president.

On Sept. 7, 1964, leftist rebels set up a "People's Republic" in Stanleyville. Tshombe hired foreign mercenaries and sought to rebuild the Congolese Army. In Nov. and Dec. 1964 rebels slew scores of white hostages and thousands of Congolese; Belgian paratroops, dropped from U.S. transport planes, rescued hundreds. By July 1965 the rebels had lost their effectiveness.

In 1965 Gen. Joseph D. Mobutu was named president. He later changed his name to Mobutu Sese Seko. The country changed its name to Republic of Zaire on Oct. 27, 1971; in 1972 Zairians with Christian names were ordered to change them to African names.

In 1969-74, political stability under Mobutu was refle... improved economic conditions. In 1974 most foreign-owne... nesses were ordered sold to Zaire citizens, but in 1977 the... ernment asked the original owners to return.

In 1977, a force of Zairians invaded Shaba province (Katar... from Angola. Zaire repelled the attack, with the aid of Egypt... pilots and Moroccan troops flown in by France. But many Eur... pean mining experts failed to return after a 2d unsuccessful inva... sion from Angola in May 1978.

Serious economic difficulties, amid charges of corruption by... government officials, have plagued Zaire in the 1980s.

Zambia
Republic of Zambia

People: Population (1984 est.): 6,554,000. **Age distrib. (%):** 0-14: 46.5; 15-59: 49.3; 60+: 4.1. **Pop. density:** 22.1 per sq. mi. **Urban** (1984): 40%. **Ethnic groups:** Mostly Bantu tribes. **Languages:** English (official), Bantu dialects. **Religions:** Predominantly animists, Roman Catholics 21%, Protestant, Hindu, Muslim minorities.

Geography: Area: 290,586 sq. mi., larger than Texas. **Location:** In southern central Africa. **Neighbors:** Zaire on N, Tanzania, Malawi, Mozambique on E, Zimbabwe, Namibia on S, Angola on W. **Topography:** Zambia is mostly high plateau country covered with thick forests, and drained by several important rivers, including the Zambezi. **Capital:** Lusaka. **Cities** (1984 est.): Lusaka 538,000; Kitwe 314,794; Ndola 282,439.

Government: Type: Republic. **Head of state:** Pres. Kenneth David Kaunda; b. Apr. 28, 1924; in office: Oct. 24, 1964. **Head of government:** Prime Min. Nalumino Mundia; in office: Feb. 18, 1981. **Local divisions:** 9 provinces. **Defense:** 20% of GDP (1984 est).

Economy: Chief crops: Corn, tobacco, peanuts, cotton, sugar. **Minerals:** Cobalt, copper, zinc, gold, lead, vanadium, manganese, coal. **Other resources:** Rubber, ivory. **Arable land:** 7%. **Meat prod.** (1980): beef: 24,000 metric tons; pork: 7,000 metric tons. **Fish catch** (1982): 55,600 metric tons. **Electricity prod.** (1982): 10.5 bln. kwh. **Labor force:** 60% agric.; 40% ind. and commerce.

Finance: Currency: Kwacha (Mar. 1985: 2.16 = $1 US). **Gross domestic product** (1982): $3.8 bln. **Per capita income** (1982): $570. **Imports** (1983): $816 mln.; partners: UK 26%, Saudi Ar. 18%, W. Ger. 18%, U.S. 9%. **Exports** (1983): $836 mln.; partners: Jap. 19%, Fr. 15%, UK 13%, U.S. 10%, W. Ger. 9%. **National budget** (1982): $510 mln. revenues; $750 mln. expenditures. **International reserves less gold** (Jan. 1985): $57.3 mln. **Gold:** 2,000 oz t. **Consumer prices** (change in 1984): 19.6%.

Transport: Motor vehicles: in use (1980): 103,500 passenger cars, 66,300 comm. vehicles. **Civil aviation** (1982): 55.7 mln. passenger-km; 23.5 mln. freight ton-km.

Communications: Television sets: 80,000 in use (1982). **Radios:** 200,000 in use (1982). **Telephones in use** (1982): 32,000. **Daily newspaper circ.** (1982): 20 per 1,000 pop.

Health: Life expectancy at birth (1984): 47 yrs. **Births** (per 1,000 pop. 1978): 49. **Deaths** (per 1,000 pop. 1978): 17. **Natural increase** (1978): 3.2%. **Hospital beds** (per 100,000 pop. 1977): 366. **Physicians** (per 100,000 pop. 1977): 5. **Infant mortality** (per 1,000 live births 1984): 140.

Education (1984): Literacy: 54%. **Attendance:** less than 50% in grades 1-7.

Major International Organizations: UN, OAU, Commonwealth of Nations.

Embassy: 2419 Massachusetts Ave. NW 20008; 265-9717.

As Northern Rhodesia, the country was under the administration of the South Africa Company, 1889 until 1924, when the office of governor was established, and, subsequently, a legislature. The country became an independent republic within the Commonwealth Oct. 24, 1964.

After the white government of Rhodesia declared its independence from Britain Nov. 11, 1965, relations between Zambia and Rhodesia became strained and use of their jointly owned railroad was disputed.

Britain gave Zambia an extra $12 million aid in 1966 after imposing an oil embargo on Rhodesia, and Zambia set up a temporary airlift to carry copper out from its mines and gasoline in. In Aug. 1968 a 1,058-mi. pipeline was completed, bringing oil

anzania. In 1973 a truck road to carry copper to Tanza-
ort of Dar es Salaam was completed with U.S. aid. A rail-
built with Chinese aid across Tanzania, reached the Zam-
border in 1974.

s part of a program of government participation in major in-
stries, a government corporation in 1970 took over 51% of the
wnership of 2 foreign-owned copper mining companies. Private-
-held land and other enterprises were nationalized in 1975, as
were all newspapers. In the 1980s, decline in copper prices has
hurt the economy and severe drought has caused famine.

Zimbabwe

People: Population (1984 est.): 8,325,000. **Age distrib. (%):**
0–14: 49.2; 15–59: 47.8; 60+: 3.0. **Pop. density:** 52.7 per sq.
mi. **Urban** (1982): 23%. **Ethnic groups:** Shona 77%, Ndebele
19%, white 3%. **Languages:** English (official), Shona, Sin-
debele. **Religions:** Predominantly traditional tribal beliefs, Christian minority.

Geography: Area: 150,873 sq. mi., nearly as large as California. **Location:** In southern Africa. **Neighbors:** Zambia on N, Botswana on W, S. Africa on S, Mozambique on E. **Topography:**
Rhodesia is high plateau country, rising to mountains on eastern
border, sloping down on the other borders. **Capital:** Harare. **Cities** (1982 cen.): Harare (met.) 656,000; Bulawayo (met.)
414,000.

Government: Type: Parliamentary democracy. **Head of
state:** Pres. Rev. Cannan Banana, b. Mar. 5, 1936; in office: Apr.
18, 1980. **Head of government:** Prime Min. Robert G. Mugabe;
b. Apr. 14, 1928; in office: Apr. 18, 1980. **Local divisions:** 8
provinces. **Defense:** 7% of GNP (1982).

Economy: Industries: Clothing, chemicals, light industries.
Chief crops: Tobacco, sugar, cotton, corn, wheat. **Minerals:**
Chromium, gold, nickel, asbestos, copper, iron, coal. **Arable
land:** 7%. **Meat prod.** (1980): beef: 125,000 metric tons; pork:
9,000 metric tons; lamb: 7,000 metric tons. **Electricity prod.**
(1982): 4.1 bln. kwh. **Crude steel prod.** (1981): 691,000 metric
tons. **Labor force:** 35% agric.; 30% ind. and commerce; 20%
serv.; 15% gvt.

Finance: Currency: Dollar (Mar. 1985: 1.46 = $1 US).
Gross domestic product (1982): $4.4 bln. **Per capita income**
(1981): White $13,480, African $314-655. **Imports** (1981): $1.3
bln.; partners: UK 10%, So. Afr. 27%, U.S. 7%, W. Ger. 7%.
Exports (1981): $937 mln.; partners: UK 7%, So. Afr. 22%, W.
Ger. 8%. **Consumer prices** (change in 1984): 23.1%.

Transport: Railway traffic (1982): 6.2 bln. net ton-km. **Motor
vehicles:** in use (1982): 224,000 passenger cars, 17,000 comm.
vehicles.

Communications: Television sets: 82,000 in use (1982).

Radios: 170,000 in use (1982). **Telephones in use** (1983):
242,252. **Daily newspaper circ.** (1982): 20 per 1,000 pop.

Health: Life expectancy at birth (1981): 53.3 male; 56.8 female. **Births** (per 1,000 pop. 1978): 49. **Deaths** (per 1,000 pop.
1978): 16. **Natural increase** (1978): 3.3%. **Health** (1983): 161
hospitals, 438 rural clinics. **Infant mortality** (per 1,000 live births
1975): 122.

Education (1982): **Literacy:** 45%. **Attendance:** 90% primary, 15% secondary for Africans; higher for whites, Asians.

Major International Organizations: UN and its specialized
agencies, OAU, Commonwealth of Nations.

Embassy: 2852 McGill Terrace NW 20008; 332-7100.

Britain took over the area as Southern Rhodesia in 1923 from
the British South Africa Co. (which, under Cecil Rhodes, had
conquered the area by 1897) and granted internal self-
government. Under a 1961 constitution, voting was restricted to
maintain whites in power. On Nov. 11, 1965, Prime Min. Ian D.
Smith announced his country's unilateral declaration of independence. Britain termed the act illegal, and demanded Rhodesia
broaden voting rights to provide for eventual rule by the majority
Africans.

Urged by Britain, the UN imposed sanctions, including embar-
goes on oil shipments to Rhodesia. Some oil and gasoline
reached Rhodesia, however, from South Africa and Mozambique, before the latter became independent in 1975. In May
1968, the UN Security Council ordered a trade embargo.

A new constitution came into effect, Mar. 2, 1970, providing for
a republic with a president and prime minister. The election law
effectively prevented full black representation through income
tax requirements.

A proposed British-Rhodesian settlement was dropped in May
1972 when a British commission reported most Rhodesian
blacks opposed it. Intermittent negotiations between the government and various black nationalist groups failed to prevent increasing skirmishes. By mid-1978, over 6,000 soldiers and civilians had been killed. Rhodesian troops battled guerrillas within
Mozambique and Zambia. An "internal settlement" signed Mar.
1978 in which Smith and 3 popular black leaders share control
until transfer of power to the black majority was rejected by
guerrilla leaders.

In the country's first universal-franchise election, Apr. 21,
1979, Bishop Abel Muzorewa's United African National Council
gained a bare majority control of the black-dominated parliament. Britain's Thatcher government, 1979, began efforts to nor-
malize its relationship with Zimbabwe. A British cease-fire was
accepted by all parties, Dec. 5th. Independence was finally
achieved Apr. 18, 1980.

Population of the World's Largest Cities

The table below represents one attempt at comparing the world's largest cities. The figures are for the city proper unless
otherwise indicated. City proper is defined as a large locality with legally fixed boundaries and an administratively recognized
urban status which is usually characterized by some form of local government.

City	Population	City	Population
Ahmedabad, India, metro (1981 census)	2,515,195	Los Angeles, Cal. (1980 census)	2,966,850
Baghdad, Iraq (1984 est.)	3,800,000	Madras, India, metro (1981 census)	4,276,635
Bangalore, India, metro (1981 census)	2,913,537	Madrid, Spain (1981 estimate)	3,267,500
Bangkok, Thailand, metro (1979 census)	4,870,509	Manchester, England, greater (1981 census)	2,594,000
Berlin (1980 estimate)	3,039,200	Melbourne, Australia (1980 census)	2,836,800
East	1,140,300	Mexico City, Mexico (1978 estimate)	8,988,230
West	1,898,900	Moscow, USSR (1983 estimate)	8,300,000
Bogota, Colombia (1978 estimate)	3,800,000	Nanjing, China (1977 estimate)	3,000,000
Bombay, India, metro (1981 census)	8,202,759	New York City (1980 census)	7,071,039
Buenos Aires, Argentina (1980 estimate)	2,908,000	Osaka, Japan (1980 census)	2,648,000
Cairo, Egypt (1979 estimate)	5,399,000	Paris, France (1975 census)	2,317,227
Calcutta, India (1981 estimate)	9,165,650	Peking, China, metro (1980 estimate)	9,029,000
Canton, China (1977 estimate)	5,000,000	Pusan, South Korea (1980 census)	3,395,171
Chicago, Ill. (1980 census)	3,005,072	Rio de Janeiro, Brazil (1980 census)	5,093,232
Chongquig, China (1977 estimate)	6,000,000	Rome, Italy (1980 census)	2,916,414
Delhi, India, metro (1981 census)	5,277,730	Santiago, Chile, metro (1983 estimate)	4,085,300
Dhaka, Bangladesh (1984 estimate)	3,400,000	Sao Paulo, Brazil (1980 census)	7,033,529
Ho Chi Minh City, Vietnam (1981 estimate)	3,500,000	Seoul, South Korea (1983 census)	9,204,344
Hong Kong (1981 census)	5,021,066	Shanghai, metro (1979 estimate)	11,000,000
Hyderabad, India, metro (1981 census)	2,565,536	Shenyang, China (1977 estimate)	4,400,000
Istambul, Turkey (1980 census)	2,772,708	Sydney, Australia (1980 estimate)	3,310,500
Jakarta, Indonesia (1980 estimate)	6,503,400	Teheran, Iran (1976 census)	4,496,159
Karachi, Pakistan, metro (1980 estimate)	5,005,000	Tianjin, China, metro (1980 estimate)	7,390,000
Leningrad, USSR (1983 estimate)	4,700,000	Tokyo, Japan (1980 census)	8,349,000
Lima, Peru (1981 census)	4,164,597	Wuhan, China (1977 census)	3,500,000
London, England, greater (1981 census)	6,696,000	Yokohama, Japan (1980 census)	2,774,000

Selected World Statistics

For sources and further information see pages 535-621.

Country	Yearly Per Cap. Income	Literacy	Life Expectancy M/F	Defense % of GNP
Afghanistan	$168	10%	39.9/40.7	3.0%
Albania	830	75	69	*13
Algeria	1,951	46	56.7/58.9	1.9
Angola	500	20	40.6/42.9	*20
Argentina	2,331	94	66.8/73.2	2.6
Australia	9,960	100	70/76	2.9
Austria	8,280	98	69.3/76.4	0.6
Bahamas	5,756	93	64/70	...
Bahrain	6,315	40	...	8.1
Bangladesh	119	25	45	1.6
Barbados	3,040	99	70.8	...
Belgium	9,827	98	68.6/75.1	*5.8
Belize	1,000	80	60	...
Benin	310	11	46.9	*7
Bhutan	100	5	46/44.5	...
Bolivia	570	75	49	...
Botswana	544	30	56/62	2.7
Brazil	1,523	75	61.6/65.7	*7
Bulgaria	2,625	95	69/74	10
Burkina Faso	180	7	42	*17.8
Burma	174	78	51.4/54.5	3.4
Burundi	235	25	45.3/48.6	*19.3
Cambodia	100	48	42/44.9	...
Cameroon	628	34	46.9/50.1	...
Canada	10,193	99	69/76	2.2
Cape Verde	300	37	60	...
Ctr. African Rep.	310	20	44	*14.2
Chad	73	15	41.5/43.9	...
Chile	1,950	90	63.8/70.4	6.5
China	566	75	68	8.5
Colombia	1,112	82	61.4/66.0	0.8
Comoros	240	15	46.4/49.7	...
Congo	500	80	46.9/50.2	*17
Costa Rica	2,238	90	67.5/71.9	...
Cuba	840	96	71/74	5
Cyprus	3,986	99	72.3/76.0	*6.3
Czechoslovakia	5,800	99	67/74	5.2
Denmark	12,956	99	71.3/77.4	2.6
Djibouti	400	20	50	...
Dominica	460	80	56.9/59.1	...
Dom. Republic	1,221	62	60.7/64.6	1.4
Ecuador	1,428	90	62	*8.2
Egypt	686	44	55.9/58.4	8.2
El Salvador	854	62	62.6/66.3	*23
Equatorial Guinea	250	55	44.4/47.6	...
Ethiopia	117	15	40	9.8
Finland	10,477	99	69.5/77.8	1.8
France	7,179	99	70.2/78.5	*18
Gabon	2,974	65	25/45	2.7
Gambia, The	330	12	32/34	...
Germany, East	8,000	99	68.8/74.7	8.0
Germany, West	11,142	99	67.2/73.4	5.8
Ghana	420	30	41.9/45.1	...
Greece	4,590	95	72/76	6.9
Grenada	500	85	69	...
Guatemala	1,085	48	55	1.6
Guinea	293	48	44/47	5.1
Guinea-Bissau	170	9	35	7
Guyana	457	86	70	9
Haiti	300	20	45	*4.5
Honduras	590	55	58.7	*7
Hungary	4,180	98	66/73.4	*3.9
Iceland	9,000	99.9	73.5/79.5	...
India	150	36	52/50	3.5
Indonesia	560	64	51.4/54.2	*3.0
Iran	2,160	48	57.1/59.0	*15
Iraq	2,410	70	56.1	46
Ireland	4,750	99	72	2.0
Israel	5,609	88	72.1/75.7	25.5
Italy	6,914	98	70.0/76.1	2.6
Ivory Coast	1,100	24	46.9/50.2	...
Jamaica	1,340	76	65	1.3
Japan	8,460	99	73/78	1.0
Jordan	552	58	60.3/64.2	21
Kenya	196	40	56.3/60.0	5.4
Korea, South	1,187	92	68	6.0
Korea, North	570	99	70/76	25
Kuwait	11,431	71	67.3/71.6	...
Laos	85	85	39.1/41.8	14
Lebanon	1,150	75	61.4/65.1	*18
Lesotho	355	65	51.5	*4.5
Liberia	400	24	54	5.1
Libya	6,335	40	56.1/59.4	2.8
Luxembourg	10,444	100	68/75	*2.8
Madagascar	279	53	46	*10.2
Malawi	220	25	42.7/45.4	*8.0
Malaysia	714	75	64	8.2
Maldives	373	85	...	...
Mali	140	10	39.4/42.5	2.4
Malta	2,036	83	68.2/73.1	...
Mauritania	466	17	45	17
Mauritius	1,052	61	69	...
Mexico	1,800	74	62/67	0.5
Mongolia	750	80	63	12
Morocco	800	24	56.1/59.4	8.8
Mozambique	220	14	47	*29
Nauru	21,400	99	...	...
Nepal	140	20	44.0/42.5	*4.0
Netherlands	9,175	98	72/78	3.2
New Zealand	7,363	99	70.6/76.6	1.9
Nicaragua	804	87	56/60	*13.3
Niger	475	8	43	*4.3
Nigeria	750	25	48.3/51.7	*9.3
Norway	12,432	100	72.5/79.7	3.1
Oman	2,400	20	...	25
Pakistan	280	24	54.4/54.2	6.1
Panama	1,116	85	68/72	0.8
Papua New Guinea	480	25	49	1.0
Paraguay	1,614	83	63	*14.4
Peru	655	72	56.7/59.7	5.0
Philippines	772	88	63.0/66.5	2.1
Poland	4,670	98	66.0/74.4	*4.9
Portugal	1,930	80	66/74	3.0
Qatar	35,000	46	57.5	*25
Romania	5,250	98	67.4/72.4	4.6
Rwanda	250	37	45.2	1.7
St. Lucia	698	78	65/71	...
St. Vincent	250	85	62.4/63.2	...
Sao Tome and Principe	300	50	...	...
Saudi Arabia	11,500	15	54	*29.6
Senegal	342	10	44	3.0
Seychelles	1,030	60	66	*11.7
Sierra Leone	176	15	46	...
Singapore	6,526	85	69/74	5.6
Somalia	500	5	43.9	*29
South Africa	1,296	98[1]	70[1]	*15
Spain	5,500	97	70/76	2.1
Sri Lanka	266	84	68	0.5
Sudan	370	20	43/45	24
Suriname	2,600	65	64.8/69.8	...
Swaziland	840	65	46.8/50.0	...
Sweden	14,821	99	73.4/79.4	3.3
Switzerland	14,408	100	70.3/76.2	2.1
Syria	702	65	64.9/67.6	14.4
Taiwan	3,000	89	69.6/74.5	7.2
Tanzania	240	66	52	5.5
Thailand	758	84	59.5/65.1	4.2
Togo	348	18	47	...
Trinidad & Tobago	6,800	96	66/72	...
Tunisia	844	62	56.3/58.4	3.0
Turkey	1,000	70	57	3.7
Uganda	240	25	48.3/51.7	0.9
USSR	2,600	99	64/74	15
United Arab Emirates	24,000	53	62.4	8.0
U.K.	7,216	99	70.2/76.2	6.2
United States	11,675	99	71.6/76.3	6.4
Uruguay	2,780	94	67.1/73.7	3.7
Venezuela	4,716	85	64/69	1.4
Vietnam	189	78	52	*50
W. Samoa	400	90	63	...
Yemen, North	475	20	37.3/38.7	*35
Yemen, South	310	39	40.6/42.4	15.5
Yugoslavia	3,109	80	68/73	5.2
Zaire	127	40[2]	46/49	1.4
Zambia	570	54	47	20
Zimbabwe	655[3]	45	53.3/56.8	7.0

* of govt. budget. (1) whites. (2) males. (3) African.

U.S. Aid to Foreign Nations

Source: Bureau of Economic Analysis, U.S. Commerce Department

...gures are in millions of dollars. (*Less than $500,000.) Data include military supplies and services furnished under the ...eign Assistance Act and direct Defense Department appropriations, and include credits extended to private entities.

...Net grants and credits take into account all known returns to the U.S., including reverse grants, returns of grants, and pay-...ents of principal. A minus sign (—) indicates that the total of these returns is greater than the total of grants or credits.

Other assistance represents the transfer of U.S. farm products in exchange for foreign currencies, less the government's dis-ursements of the currencies as grants, credits, or for purchases.

Amounts do not include investments in the following: Asian Development Bank, $80 mln.; Inter-American Development Bank, $353 mln.; International Development Assn., $892 mln. International Bank for Reconstruction and Development, $27 mln.; African Development Bank, $18 mln.; African Development Fund, $57 mln.

	Total	Net grants	Net credits	Net other		Total	Net grants	Net credits	Net other
Calendar Year 1984					Burkina Faso	39	39	(*)	(*)
Total	12,611	8,857	3,745	9	Burundi	12	12		
					Cameroon	20	12	8	
Military grants	1,295	1,295	—	—	Cape Verde	6	6		
Western Europe	269	385	—116	1	Cen. African Rep.	2	2	(*)	
Austria	3	—	3		Chad	21	21	—	
Belgium-Luxembourg	—17	—	—17		Congo	1	2	(*)	(*)
Denmark	—12	—	—12		Djibouti	7	7		
Finland	—11	—	—11	(*)	Equatorial Guinea	2	2		
France	—17	(*)	—17		Ethiopia	19	24	—4	(*)
Germany, West	—5	(*)	—5		Gabon	—1	2	—2	
Ireland	—4	—	—4		Gambia	10	10		
Italy	—12	20	—32		Ghana	19	26	—7	(*)
Liechtenstein	—2	—	—2		Guinea	4	4	—1	1
Netherlands	—14	—	—14		Guinea-Bissau	5	5		
Norway	—4	—	—4		Ivory Coast	2	(*)	1	(*)
Portugal	83	134	—50		Kenya	61	50	12	
Spain	225	23	201	1	Lesotho	36	36	—	
Sweden	—3	—	—3		Liberia	106	85	21	
Switzerland	—14	—	—14		Madagascar	19	8	11	(*)
United Kingdom	—134	(*)	—134		Malawi	10	7	2	
Yugoslavia	16	(*)	16	1	Mali	31	32	(*)	(*)
Atomic EC	—4	—	—4		Mauritania	24	24		
Other & unspecified	195	209	—14		Mauritius	3	4	—1	(*)
Eastern Europe	—20	54	—72	—2	Morocco	312	60	253	(*)
Czechoslovakia	—3	—	—3		Mozambique	20	18	2	
Hungary	—2	—	—2		Niger	23	22	1	
Poland	42	54	—10	—2	Nigeria	49	1	49	
Romania	—18	—	—18		Rwanda	18	18	—1	(*)
Soviet Union	—39	—	—39		Sao Tome-Principe	2	2		
Near East & South Asia	6,459	4,331	128	—1	Senegal	73	74	(*)	(*)
Afghanistan	—4	(*)	—4		Seychelles	3	3		
Bangladesh	259	164	94	(*)	Sierra Leone	9	6	3	
Bhutan	1	1			Somalia	113	92	21	(*)
Cyprus	1	1	—		Sudan	220	141	79	(*)
Egypt	1,922	1,185	734	4	Swaziland	7	7	1	
Greece	—15	1	—17	1	Tanzania	22	20	2	(*)
India	81	140	—52	—7	Togo	7	8	(*)	
Iraq	—8	—	—8		Tunisia	111	39	72	(*)
Israel	3,094	2,277	817	(*)	Uganda	3	3	(*)	
Jordan	—23	10	—33	(*)	Zaire	207	26	180	(*)
Lebanon	31	29	2		Zambia	53	11	42	
Nepal	24	24	(*)	(*)	Zimbabwe	74	71	3	
Oman	14	2	12		Other & unspecified	70	71	(*)	
Pakistan	414	98	314	2	**Western Hemisphere**	2,102	1,174	926	2
Saudi Arabia	—2	—	—2		Argentina	16	(*)	16	
Sri Lanka (Ceylon)	83	12	71	(*)	Barbados	1	1	(*)	
Syria	1	(*)	1	(*)	Belize	6	6	(*)	
Turkey	439	240	199	(*)	Bolivia	38	30	8	(*)
Yemen (Sanaa)	32	31	1		Brazil	79	14	65	
Other & unspecified	116	116	—		Canada	98	—	98	
East Asia & Pacific	694	431	255	8	Cayman Islands	—1	—	—1	
Australia	—5	—	—5		Chile	—28	10	—40	2
Burma	7	7	—1		Colombia	103	2	101	(*)
China-mainland	20	—	20		Costa Rica	182	112	70	(*)
Hong Kong	—14	(*)	—14		Dominican Republic	140	67	73	(*)
Indonesia	222	38	182	1	Ecuador	45	24	21	
Japan	—99	—1	—98	(*)	El Salvador	441	365	75	
Kampuchea (Cambodia)	4	4	(*)		Grenada	26	25	1	
Korea (So.)	206	—2	208	(*)	Guatemala	24	20	4	
Laos	2	2	—		Guyana	—1	1	—2	
Malaysia	—7	(*)	—7		Haiti	43	32	10	
New Zealand	—13	—	—13		Honduras	207	175	33	(*)
Philippines	135	121	10	4	Jamaica	151	17	134	
Singapore	56	(*)	56		Mexico	—137	20	117	
Taiwan	—144	(*)	—147	3	Nicaragua	3	3	(*)	
Thailand	107	42	65		Panama	53	47	6	
Trust Terr. Pacific	178	178	—		Paraguay	(*)	3	—2	(*)
Other & unspecified	41	42	—1		Peru	211	57	153	(*)
Africa	1,776	1,147	628	1	Trinidad-Tobago	19	(*)	19	
Algeria	—108	—	—108		Uruguay	—4	(*)	—4	
Angola	—5	7	—13		Venezuela	37	(*)	4	
Benin	4	4	(*)		Other & unspecified	147	141	6	
Botswana	27	23	4		**Intl. orgs. & unspecified**	1,332	1,335	—3	

Ambassadors and Envoys
As of mid-1985.
The address of U.S. embassies abroad is the appropriate foreign capital. The U.S. does not have diplomatic relations
the following countries: Albania,[1] Angola,[2] Cambodia,[3] Taiwan,[4] Cuba,[5] Iran,[6] Libya,[8] Vietnam,[3] S. Yemen.[3]

Countries	Envoys from United States	Envoys to United States
Afghanistan	*Vacant*	M. Haider Refq, Chargé
Algeria	L. Craig Johnstone, Amb.	Mohamed Sahnoun, Amb.
Antigua & Barbuda	Thomas H. Anderson, Amb.	Edmund H. Lake, Amb.
Argentina	Frank V. Ortiz Jr., Amb.	Lucio Garcia Del Solar, Amb.
Australia	Robert D. Nesen, Amb.	Robert Cotton, Amb.
Austria	Helene A. von Damm, Amb.	Thomas Klestil, Amb.
Bahamas	Lev Dobriansky, Amb.	Reginald L. Wood, Amb.
Bahrain	Donald C. Leidel, Amb.	Ghazi M. Algosaibi, Amb.
Bangladesh	Howard B. Schaffer, Amb.	A.Z.M. Obaidullah Khan, Amb.
Barbados	Thomas H. Anderson, Amb.	Peter D. Laurie, Amb.
Belgium	Geoffrey Swaebe, Amb.	J. Raoul Schoumaker, Amb.
Belize	Malcolm R. Barnebey, Amb.	F. R. Galvez Jr., Chargé
Benin	George E. Moose, Amb.	Guy L. Hazoume, Amb.
Bolivia	*Vacant*	Mariano Baptista Gumucio, Amb.
Botswana	Theodore C. Maino, Amb.	Serara T. Ketlogetswe, Amb.
Brazil	Diego C. Asencio, Amb.	Sergeo C. da Costa, Amb.
Brunei	Barrington King, Amb.	Pengiran Haji Idriss, Amb.
Bulgaria	Melvin Levitsky, Amb.	Stoyan I. Zhulev, Amb.
Burkina Faso	Leonardo Neher, Amb.	Melegue Traore, Chargé
Burma	Daniel A. O'Donohue, Amb.	U Maung Maung Gyi, Amb.
Burundi	James R. Bullington, Amb.	Simon Sabimbona, Amb.
Cameroon	Myles R. Frechette, Amb.	Paul Pondi, Amb.
Canada	Paul H. Robinson Jr., Amb.	Allan Gotlieb, Amb.
Cape Verde	John M. Yates, Amb.	Jose Luis Fernandes Lopes, Amb.
Central African Rep.	Ernest T. Dejarnette, Amb.	Christian Lingama-Toleque, Amb.
Chad	Jay P. Moffat	Mahamat Ali Adoum, Amb.
Chile	James D. Theberge	Hernan F. Errazuriz, Amb.
China	Arthur W. Hummel Jr., Amb.	Han Xu, Amb.
Colombia	Lewis A. Tambs, Amb.	Rodrigo Lloreda, Amb.
Comoros	Fernando E. Rondon, Amb.	Ali Mlahaili, Amb.
Congo	Alan W. Lukens, Amb.	Nicolas Mondjo, Amb.
Costa Rica	Curtin Winsor Jr., Amb.	Luis Guardia, Chargé
Cyprus	Richard W. Boehm, Amb.	Andrew J. Jacovides, Amb.
Czechoslovakia	William H. Luers, Amb.	Stanislav Suja, Amb.
Denmark	Terence A. Todman, Amb	Eigil Jorgensen, Amb.
Djibouti	Alvin P. Adams Jr.	Salah Hadji Farah Dirir, Amb.
Dominica	Thomas H. Anderson, Amb.	Franklin Baron, Amb.
Dominican Republic	Robert Anderson, Amb.	Carlos Despradel, Amb.
Ecuador	Samuel F. Hart, Amb.	Mario Ribadeniera, Amb.
Egypt	Nicholas A. Veliotes, Amb.	El Sayed A. R. El Reedy, Amb.
El Salvador	Edwin G. Corr, Amb.	Pablo M. Alvergue, Amb.
Equatorial Guinea	*Vacant*	Florencio Maye Ela, Amb.
Estonia[7]		Ernst Jaakson, Consul General
Ethiopia	David A. Korn, Chargé	Tamene Eshete, Chargé
Fiji	*Vacant*	Ratu Radrodro, Amb.
Finland	Keith F. Nyborg, Amb.	Richard Muller, Amb.
France	Evan G. Galbraith, Amb.	Emmanuel de Margerie, Amb.
Gabon	Larry C. Williamson, Amb.	Mocktar Abdoulaye-Mbingt, Amb.
Gambia, The	Robert T. Hennemeyer, Amb.	Lamin A. Mbye, Amb.
Germany, East	*Vacant*	Gerhard Herder, Amb.
Germany, West	Richard Burt, Amb.	Guenther van Well, Amb.
Ghana	Robert E. Fritts, Amb.	Eric K. Otoo, Amb.
Greece	Monteagle Stearns, Amb.	George D. Papaulias, Amb.
Grenada	Loren E. Lawrence, Chargé	*Vacant*
Guatemala	Alberto M. Piedra, Amb.	Eduardo Palomo, Amb.
Guinea	James D. Rosenthal, Amb.	Tolo Beavogui, Amb.
Guinea-Bissau	*Vacant*	Inacio Semedo Jr., Amb.
Guyana	Clint A. Lauderdale, Amb.	Cedric H. Grant, Amb.
Haiti	Clayton E. McManaway Jr., Amb.	Adrien L. Raymond, Amb.
Honduras	John D. Negroponte, Amb.	Juan Agurcia Ewing, Amb.
Hungary	Nicholas M. Salgo, Amb.	Vencel Hazi, Amb.
Iceland	Nicholas Ruwe, Amb.	Hans G. Andersen, Amb.
India	Harry G. Barnes, Amb.	K. S. Bajpai, Amb.
Indonesia	John H. Holdridge, Amb.	A. Hasnan Habib, Amb.
Iraq	David G. Newton, Chargé	Nizar Hamdoon, Amb.
Ireland	Robert E. Kane, Amb.	Tadhg F. O'Sullivan, Amb.
Israel	Thomas P. Pickering, Amb.	Meir Rosenne, Amb.
Italy	Maxwell M. Rabb, Amb.	Rinaldo Petrignani, Amb.
Ivory Coast	Robert H. Miller, Amb.	Rene Amany, Amb.
Jamaica	William A. Hewitt, Amb.	Keith Johnson, Amb.
Japan	Michael J. Mansfield, Amb.	Yoshio Okawara, Amb.
Jordan	Paul H. Boeker, Amb.	Ibrahim Izziddin, Amb.
Kenya	Gerald E. Thomas, Amb.	Wafula Wabuge, Amb.
Kiribati	William Bodde Jr., Min.	Atanradi Baiteke, Amb.
Korea, South	Richard L. Walker, Amb.	Byong H. Lew, Amb.
Kuwait	Anthony C. Quainton, Amb.	Shaikh S. N. Al-Sabah, Amb.
Laos	*Vacant*	Bounkeut Sangsomsak, Chargé
Latvia[7]		Anatol Dinbergs, Chargé
Lebanon	Reginald Bartholomew, Amb.	Adballah Bouhabib, Amb.
Lesotho	S. L. Abbott, Amb.	'M'alineo N. Tau, Amb.
Liberia	William Swing, Amb.	G. Toe Washington, Amb.
Lithuania[7]		Stasys A. Backis, Chargé
Luxembourg	John E. Dolibois, Amb.	Paul Peters, Amb.
Madagascar	Robert B. Keating, Amb.	Leon M. Rajaobelina, Amb.

Countries	Envoys from United States	Envoys to United States
...awi	Weston Adams, Amb.	Nelson T. Mizere, Amb.
...alaysia	Thomas P. Shoesmith, Amb.	Dato Lew Sip Hon, Amb.
...aldives	John H. Reed, Amb.	*Vacant*
...ali	Robert J. Ryan, Amb.	Lassana Keita, Amb.
Malta	James M. Rentschler, Amb.	Lawrence Farrugia, Chargé
Mauritania	Edward L. Peck, Amb.	Abdellah Ould Daddah, Amb.
Mauritius	George R. Andrews, Amb.	Chitmansing Jesseramsing, Amb.
Mexico	John A. Gavin, Amb.	J. Espinosa de los Reyes, Amb.
Morocco	Joseph V. Reed, Amb.	Maati Jorio, Amb.
Mozambique	Peter Jon de Vos, Amb.	Valeriano Ferrao, Amb.
Nauru	Robert D. Nesen, Amb.	T.W. Star, Amb.
Nepal	Leon J. Weil, Amb.	Bhekh B. Thapa, Amb.
Netherlands	L. Paul Bremer 3d, Amb.	Richard H. Fein, Amb.
New Zealand	H. Monroe Browne, Amb.	Wallace E. Rowling, Amb.
Nicaragua	Harry E. Bergold Jr., Amb.	Carlos Tunnermann, Amb.
Niger	William R. Casey Jr., Amb.	Joseph Diatta, Amb.
Nigeria	Thomas W. M. Smith, Amb.	Ignatius C. Olisemeka, Amb.
Norway	Robert D. Stuart Jr., Amb.	Kjell Eliassen, Amb.
Oman	John R. Countryman, Amb.	Ali Salim Bader Al-Hanai, Amb.
Pakistan	Deane R. Hinton, Amb.	Ejaz Azim, Amb.
Panama	Everett E. Briggs, Amb.	Lawrence E. Ghewning Fabrega, Chargé
Papua New Guinea	Paul F. Gardner, Amb.	Renagi Lohia Obe, Amb.
Paraguay	Arthur H. Davis, Amb.	Marcos Martinez Mendieta, Amb.
Peru	David C. Jordan, Amb.	Luis Marchand, Amb.
Philippines	Stephen W. Bosworth, Amb.	Benjamin T. Romualdez, Amb.
Poland	*Vacant*	Zdzislaw Ludwiczak, Chargé
Portugal	H. Allen Holmes, Amb.	Leonardo Mathias, Amb.
Qatar	Charles F. Dunbar, Amb.	Abdelkader B. Al-Ameri, Amb.
Romania	David B. Funderburk, Amb.	Alexander Gheorghiu, Chargé
Rwanda	John Blane, Amb.	Simon Insonere, Amb.
St. Christopher & Nevis	*Vacant*	William Herbert
St. Lucia	Thomas H. Anderson	Joseph E. Edmunds, Amb.
St. Vincent and The Grenadines	Thomas H. Anderson	*Vacant*
Samoa, Western	Anne C. Martindell, Amb.	Maiava I. Toma, Amb.
Sao Tome and Principe	Francis T. McNamera, Amb.	*Vacant*
Saudi Arabia	Walter L. Cutler, Amb.	Bandar Bin Sultan, Amb.
Senegal	Charles W. Bray, Amb.	Falilou Kane, Amb.
Seychelles	David J. Fischer, Amb.	Giovinella Gonthier, Amb.
Sierra Leone	Arthur W. Lewis, Amb.	Dauda S. Kamara, Amb.
Singapore	J. Stapleton Roy, Amb.	Tommy T. B. Koh, Amb.
Solomon Islands	Paul F. Gardner, Amb.	Francis Saemala, Amb.
Somalia	Peter S. Bridges, Amb.	Mohamud Haji Nur, Amb.
South Africa	Herman W. Nickel, Amb.	Bernardus G. Fourie, Amb.
Spain	Thomas O. Enders, Amb.	Gabriel Manueco, Amb.
Sri Lanka	John H. Reed, Amb.	Ernest Corea, Amb.
Sudan	Hume A. Horan, Amb.	Omer Salih Eissa, Amb.
Suriname	*Vacant*	Donald McLeod, Amb.
Swaziland	*Vacant*	Peter H. Mtetwa, Amb.
Sweden	Franklin S. Forsberg, Amb.	Wilhelm Wachtmeister, Amb.
Switzerland	John D. Lodge, Amb.	Klaus Jacobi, Amb.
Syria	*Vacant*	Rafic Jouejati, Amb.
Tanzania	John W. Shirley, Amb.	Asterius M. Hyera, Amb.
Thailand	John G. Dean, Amb.	Kasem S. Kasemsri, Amb.
Togo	Owen W. Roberts, Amb.	Ellom-Kodjo Schuppius, Amb.
Tonga	*Vacant*	S. T. Taumoepeau, Amb.
Trinidad and Tobago	*Vacant*	James O'Neil-Lewis, Amb.
Tunisia	Peter Sebastian, Amb.	Habib B. Yahia, Amb.
Turkey	Robert Strausz-Hupe, Amb.	Sukru Elekdag, Amb.
Tuvalu	*Vacant*	Ionatana Ionatana, Amb.
Uganda	Allen C. Davis, Amb.	John Wycliffe Lwamafa, Amb.
USSR	Arthur A. Hartman, Amb.	Anatoliy F. Dobrynin, Amb.
United Arab Emirates	G. Quincy Lumsden Jr., Amb.	A.S. Al-Mokarrab, Amb.
United Kingdom	Charles S. Price 2d, Amb.	Oliver Wright, Amb.
Uruguay	Thomas Aranda Jr., Amb.	Walter Ravenna, Amb.
Vatican	William Wilson, Amb.	Pio Laghi, Amb.
Venezuela	George W. Landau, Amb.	Valentin Hernandez, Amb.
Yemen Arab Rep.	William A. Rugh, Amb.	Mohsin A. Alaini, Amb.
Yugoslavia	David Anderson, Amb.	Mico Rakic, Amb.
Zaire	Brandon H. Grove Jr., Amb.	Kasongo Mutuale, Amb.
Zambia	Nicholas Platt, Amb.	Putteho M. Ngonda, Amb.
Zimbabwe	David C. Miller Jr., Amb.	Edmund R. M. Garwe, Amb.

Ambassadors at Large: Daniel J. Terra, Richard T. Kennedy, Howard E. Douglas, Harry W. Shlaudeman, Richard Fairbanks.

Special Missions

U.S. Mission to North Atlantic Treaty Organization, Brussels—David M. Abshire
U.S. Mission to the European Communities, Brussels—George S. Vest
U.S. Mission to the United Nations, New York—Vernon Walters
U.S. Mission to the European Office of the UN, Geneva—Gerald P. Carmen
U.S. Mission to the Organization for Economic Cooperation and Development, Paris—Edward J. Streator
U.S. Mission to the Organization of American States, Washington—J. William Middendorf, Amb.
U.S. Mission to International Civic Aviation Organization, Montreal—Edmond P. Stohr

(1) Relations severed in 1939. (2) Post closed in 1975. (3) U.S. embassy closed in 1975. (4) U.S. severed relations in 1978; unofficial relations are maintained. (5) Relations severed in 1961; limited ties restored in 1977. (6) U.S. severed relations on Apr. 7, 1980. (7) U.S. does not officially recognize 1940 annexation by USSR. (8) Embassy closed, May 2, 1980. U.S. closed the Libyan mission in Wash., DC, May 6, 1981.

Major International Organizations

Association of Southeast Asian Nations (ASEAN),was formed in 1967 to promote political and economic cooperation among the non-communist states of the region. Members in 1985 are Brunei, Indonesia, Malaysia, Philippines, Singapore, Thailand. Annual ministerial meetings set policy; a central Secretariat in Jakarta and 9 permanent committees work in trade, transportation, communications, agriculture, science, finance, and culture.

Commonwealth of Nations originally called the British Commonwealth of Nations, is an association of nations and dependencies loosely joined by a common interest based on having been parts of the old British Empire. The British monarch is the symbolic head of the Commonwealth.

There are 48 self-governing independent nations in the Commonwealth, plus various colonies and protectorates. As of Jan. 1984, the members were the United Kingdom of Great Britain and Northern Ireland and 17 other nations recognizing the British monarch, represented by a governor-general, as their head of state: Antigua and Barbuda, Australia, Bahamas, Barbados, Belize, Canada, Fiji, Grenada, Jamaica, Mauritius, New Zealand, Papua New Guinea, St. Kitts-Nevis, St. Lucia, St. Vincent and the Grenadines (a special member), Solomon Islands, and Tuvalu (a special member); and 28 countries with their own heads of state: Bangladesh, Botswana, Cyprus, Dominica, The Gambia, Ghana, Guyana, India, Kenya, Kiribati, Lesotho, Malawi, Malaysia, The Maldives (a special member), Malta, Nauru (a special member), Nigeria, Samoa, Seychelles, Sierra Leone, Singapore, Sri Lanka, Swaziland, Tanzania, Tonga, Trinidad and Tobago, Uganda, Vanuatu, Zambia, and Zimbabwe. In addition various Caribbean dependencies take part in certain Commonwealth activities.

The Commonwealth facilitates consultation among member states through meetings of prime ministers and finance ministers, and through a permanent Secretariat. Members consult on economic, scientific, educational, financial, legal, and military matters, and try to coordinate policies.

European Communities (EC, the Common Market) is the collective designation of three organizations with common membership: the European Economic Community (Common Market), the European Coal and Steel Community, and the European Atomic Energy Community. The 10 full members are: Belgium, Denmark, France, West Germany, Greece, Ireland, Italy, Luxembourg, Netherlands, United Kingdom. Spain and Portugal will join the EC in 1986. Some 60 nations in Africa, the Caribbean, and the Pacific are affiliated under the Lomé Convention.

A merger of the 3 communities executives went into effect July 1, 1967, though the component organizations date back to 1951 and 1958. A Council of Ministers, a Commission, a European Parliament, and a Court of Justice comprise the permanent structure. The communities aim to integrate their economies, coordinate social developments, and bring about political union of the democratic states of Europe.

European Free Trade Association (EFTA), consisting of Austria, Iceland, Norway, Portugal, Sweden, Switzerland and associated member Finland, was created Jan. 4, 1960, to gradually reduce customs duties and quantitative restrictions between members on industrial products. By Dec. 31, 1966, all tariffs and quotas had been eliminated. The association entered into free trade agreements with the EC, Jan. 1, 1973. Trade barriers were removed July 1, 1976.

League of Arab States (The Arab League) was created Mar. 22, 1945, by Egypt, Iraq, Jordan, Lebanon, Saudi Arabia, Syria, and Yemen. Joining later were Algeria, Bahrain, Djibouti, Kuwait, Libya, Mauritania, Morocco, Oman, Qatar, Somalia, Sudan, Tunisia, United Arab Emirates and South Yemen. The Palestine Liberation Org. has been admitted as a full member. The League fosters cultural, economic, and communication ties and mediates disputes among the Arab states; it represents Arab states in certain international negotiations, and coordinates a military, economic, and diplomatic offensive against Israel. As a result of Egypt signing a peace treaty with Israel, the League, Mar.

1979, suspended Egypt's membership and transferred League's headquarters from Cairo to Tunis.

North Atlantic Treaty Org. (NATO) was created by treaty (signed Apr. 4, 1949; in effect Aug. 24, 1949) among Belgium, Canada, Denmark, France, Iceland, Italy, Luxembourg, Netherlands, Norway, Portugal, United Kingdom, and the U.S. Greece, Turkey, West Germany, and Spain have joined since. The members agreed to settle disputes by peaceful means; to develop their individual and collective capacity to resist armed attack; to regard an attack on one as an attack on all, and to take necessary action to repel an attack under Article 51 of the United Nations Charter.

The NATO structure consists of a Council and a Military Committee of 3 commands (Allied Command Europe, Allied Command Atlantic, Allied Command Channel) and the Canada-U.S. Regional Planning Group.

Following announcement in 1966 of nearly total French withdrawal from the military affairs of NATO, organization hq. moved, 1967, from Paris to Brussels. In August, 1974, Greece announced a total withdrawal of armed forces from NATO, in response to Turkish intervention in Cyprus. Greece rejoined NATO's military wing, Oct. 20, 1980.

Organization of African Unity (OAU), formed May 25, 1963, by 32 African countries (51 in 1985) to coordinate cultural, political, scientific and economic policies; to end colonialism in Africa; and to promote a common defense of members' independence. It holds annual conferences of heads of state. Hq. is in Addis Ababa, Ethiopia.

Organization of American States (OAS) was formed in Bogota, Colombia, in 1948. Hq. is in Washington, D.C. It has a Permanent Council, Inter-American Economic and Social Council, and Inter-American Council for Education, Science and Culture, a Juridical Committee and a Commission on Human Rights. The Permanent Council can call meetings of foreign ministers to deal with urgent security matters. A General Assembly meets annually. A secretary general and assistant are elected for 5-year terms. There are 32 members, each with one vote in the various organizations: Antigua, Argentina, Bahamas, Barbados, Bolivia, Brazil, Chile, Colombia, Costa Rica, Cuba, Dominica, Dominican Republic, Ecuador, El Salvador, Grenada, Guatemala, Haiti, Honduras, Jamaica, Mexico, Nicaragua, Panama, Paraguay, Peru, St. Kitts-Nevis, St. Lucia, St. Vincent, Suriname, Trinidad & Tobago, U.S., Uruguay, Venezuela. In 1962, the OAS excluded Cuba from OAS activities but not from membership.

Organization for Economic Cooperation and Development (OECD) was established Sept. 30, 1961 to promote economic and social welfare in member countries, and to stimulate and harmonize efforts on behalf of developing nations. Nearly all the industrialized "free market" countries belong, with Yugoslavia as an associate member. OECD collects and disseminates economic and environmental information. Members in 1985 were: Australia, Austria, Belgium, Canada, Denmark, Finland, France, West Germany, Greece, Iceland, Ireland, Italy, Japan, Luxembourg, Netherlands, New Zealand, Norway, Portugal, Spain, Sweden, Switzerland, Turkey, United Kingdom, United States, Yugoslavia (special member). Hq. is in Paris.

Organization of Petroleum Exporting Countries (OPEC) was created Nov. 14, 1960 at Venezuelan initiative. The group has often been successful in determining world oil prices, and in advancing members' interests in trade and development dealings with industrialized oil-consuming nations. Members in 1985 were Algeria, Ecuador, Gabon, Indonesia, Iran, Iraq, Kuwait, Libya, Nigeria, Qatar, Saudi Arabia, United Arab Emirates, Venezuela.

Warsaw Pact was created May 14, 1955, as a mutual defense alliance. Members in 1985 were Bulgaria, Czechoslovakia, East Germany, Hungary, Poland, Romania, and the USSR. Hq. is in Moscow. It provides for a unified military command; if one member is attacked, the others will aid it with all necessary steps including armed force.

United Nations

The 39th regular session of the United Nations General Assembly was scheduled to open in September, 1985. *See chronology for developments at UN sessions during 1985.*

UN headquarters are in New York, N.Y., between First Ave. and Roosevelt Drive and E. 42d St. and E. 48th St. The General Assembly Bldg., Secretariat, Conference and Library bldgs. are interconnected. A new UN office building-hotel was opened in New York in 1976.

A European office at Geneva includes Secretariat and agency staff members. Other offices of UN bodies and related organizations are scattered throughout the world.

The UN has a post office originating its own stamps.

Proposals to establish an organization of nations for maintenance of world peace led to the United Nations Conference on International Organization at San Francisco, Apr. 25-June 26, 1945, where the charter of the United Nations was drawn up. It was signed June 26 by 50 nations, and by Poland, one of the original 51, on Oct. 15, 1945. The charter came into effect Oct. 24, 1945, upon ratification by the permanent members of the Security Council and a majority of other signatories.

Roster of the United Nations

(As of mid-1985)

The 159 members of the United Nations, with the years in which they became members.

Member	Year	Member	Year	Member	Year	Member	Year
Afghanistan	1946	Ecuador	1945	Lesotho	1966	Samoa (Western)	1976
Albania	1955	Egypt²	1945	Liberia	1945	Sao Tome e Principe	1975
Algeria	1962	El Salvador	1945	Libya	1955	Saudi Arabia	1945
Angola	1976	Equatorial Guinea	1968	Luxembourg	1945	Senegal	1960
Antigua and Barbuda	1981	Ethiopia	1945			Seychelles	1976
Argentina	1945					Sierra Leone	1961
Australia	1945	Fiji	1970	Madagascar (Malagasy)	1960	Singapore¹	1965
Austria	1955	Finland	1955	Malawi	1964	Solomon Islands	1978
		France	1945	Malaysia¹	1957	Somalia	1960
Bahamas	1973			Maldives	1965	South Africa⁵	1945
Bahrain	1971	Gabon	1960	Mali	1960	Spain	1955
Bangladesh	1974	Gambia	1965	Malta	1964	Sri Lanka	1955
Barbados	1966	Germany, East	1973	Mauritania	1961	Sudan	1956
Belgium	1945	Germany, West	1973	Mauritius	1968	Suriname	1975
Belize	1981	Ghana	1957	Mexico	1945	Swaziland	1968
Benin	1960	Greece	1945	Mongolia	1961	Sweden	1946
Bhutan	1971	Grenada	1974	Morocco	1956	Syria²	1945
Bolivia	1945	Guatemala	1945	Mozambique	1975		
Botswana	1966	Guinea	1958				
Brazil	1945	Guinea-Bissau	1974	Nepal	1955	Tanzania³	1961
Brunei	1984	Guyana	1966	Netherlands	1945	Thailand	1946
Bulgaria	1955			New Zealand	1945	Togo	1960
Burkina Faso	1960	Haiti	1945	Nicaragua	1945	Trinidad & Tobago	1962
Burma	1948	Honduras	1945	Niger	1960	Tunisia	1956
Burundi	1962	Hungary	1955	Nigeria	1960	Turkey	1945
Byelorussia	1945			Norway	1945		
		Iceland	1946			Uganda	1962
Cambodia (Kampuchea)	1955	India	1945	Oman	1971	Ukraine	1945
Cameroon	1960	Indonesia⁶	1950			USSR	1945
Canada	1945	Iran	1945	Pakistan	1947	United Arab Emirates	1971
Cape Verde	1975	Iraq	1945	Panama	1945	United Kingdom	1945
Central Afr. Rep.	1960	Ireland	1955	Papua New Guinea	1975	United States	1945
Chad	1960	Israel	1949	Paraguay	1945	Uruguay	1945
Chile	1945	Italy	1955	Peru	1945		
China⁴	1945	Ivory Coast	1960	Philippines	1945		
Colombia	1945			Poland	1945	Vanuatu	1981
Comoros	1975			Portugal	1955	Venezuela	1945
Congo	1960	Jamaica	1962			Vietnam	1977
Costa Rica	1945	Japan	1956	Qatar	1971		
Cuba	1945	Jordan	1955				
Cyprus	1960			Romania	1955	Yemen	1947
Czechoslovakia	1945			Rwanda	1962	Yemen, South	1967
		Kenya	1963			Yugoslavia	1945
		Kuwait	1963	Saint Christopher & Nevis	1983		
Denmark	1945			Saint Lucia	1979	Zaire	1960
Djibouti	1977			Saint Vincent and the		Zambia	1964
Dominica	1978	Laos	1955	Grenadines	1980	Zimbabwe	1980
Dominican Rep.	1945	Lebanon	1945				

(1) Malaya joined the UN in 1957. In 1963, its name was changed to Malaysia following the accession of Singapore, Sabah, and Sarawak. Singapore became an independent UN member in 1965. (2) Egypt and Syria were original members of the UN. In 1958, the United Arab Republic was established by a union of Egypt and Syria and continued as a single member of the UN. In 1961, Syria resumed its separate membership. (3) Tanganyika was a member of the United Nations from 1961 and Zanzibar was a member from 1963. Following the ratification in 1964 of Articles of Union between Tanganyika and Zanzibar, the United Republic of Tanganyika and Zanzibar continued as a single member of the United Nations, later changing its name to United Republic of Tanzania. (4) The General Assembly voted in 1971 to expel the Chinese government on Taiwan and admit the Peking government in its place. (5) The General Assembly rejected the credentials of the South African delegates in 1974, and suspended the country from the Assembly. (6) Indonesia withdrew from the UN in 1965 and rejoined in 1966.

Organization

The text of the UN Charter, and further information, may be obtained from the Office of Public Information, United Natio N.Y.

General Assembly. The General Assembly is composed of representatives of all the member nations. Each nation is entitled to one vote.

The General Assembly meets in regular annual sessions and in special session when necessary. Special sessions are convoked by the Secretary General at the request of the Security Council or of a majority of the members of the UN.

On important questions a two-thirds majority of members present and voting is required; on other questions a simple majority is sufficient.

The General Assembly must approve the budget and apportion expenses among members. A member in arrears will have no vote if the amount of arrears equals or exceeds the amount of the contributions due for the preceeding two full years.

Security Council. The Security Council consists of 15 members, 5 with permanent seats. The remaining 10 are elected for 2-year terms by the General Assembly; they are not eligible for immediate reelection.

Permanent members of the Council: China, France, USSR, United Kingdom, United States.

Non-permanent members are Burkina Faso, Egypt, India, Peru, and Ukraine, (until Dec. 31, 1985); Australia, Denmark, Madagascar, Thailand, and Trinidad & Tobago (until Dec. 31, 1986).

The Security Council has the primary responsiblity within the UN for maintaining international peace and security. The Council may investigate any dispute that threatens international peace and security.

Any member of the UN at UN headquarters may participate in its discussions and a nation not a member of UN may appear if it is a party to a dispute.

Decisions on procedural questions are made by an affirmative vote of 9 members. On all other matters the affirmative vote of 9 members must include the concurring votes of all permanent members; it is this clause which gives rise to the so-called "veto." A party to a dispute must refrain from voting.

The Security Council directs the various truce supervisory forces deployed in the Middle East, India-Pakistan, and Cyprus.

Economic and Social Council. The Economic and Social Council consists of 54 members elected by the General Assembly for 3-year terms of office. The council is responsible under the General Assembly for carrying out the functions of the United Nations with regard to international eco-

nomic, social, cultural, educational, health and related mat ters. The council meets usually twice a year.

Trusteeship Council. The administration of trust territories is under UN supervision. The only remaining trust territory is the Pacific Islands, administered by the U.S.

Secretariat. The Secretary General is the chief administrative officer of the UN. He may bring to the attention of the Security Council any matter that threatens international peace. He reports to the General Assembly.

Javier Perez de Cuellar (Peru), secretary general, was elected to a 5-year term beginning Jan. 1, 1982.

The 1984-85 budget is $1.5 billion, exclusive of trust funds, special contributions, and expenses for the Specialized or the Related Organizations.

The U.S. contributes 25% of the regular budget, the Soviet Union 11.33%, Japan 8.66%, W. Germany 7.74%, and France, China, and Britain about 5% each.

International Court of Justice. The International Court of Justice is the principal judicial organ of the United Nations. All members are *ipso facto* parties to the statute of the Court, as are three nonmembers — Liechtenstein, San Marino, and Switzerland. Other states may become parties to the Court's statute.

The jurisdiction of the Court comprises cases which the parties submit to it and matters especially provided for in the charter or in treaties. The Court gives advisory opinions and renders judgments. Its decisions are only binding between the parties concerned and in respect to a particular dispute. If any party to a case fails to heed a judgment, the other party may have recourse to the Security Council.

The 15 judges are elected for 9-year terms by the General Assembly and the Security Council. Retiring judges are eligible for re-election. The Court remains permanently in session, except during vacations. All questions are decided by majority. The Court sits in The Hague, Netherlands.

Judges: 9-year term in office ending 1991: Nagendra Singh, India. Jose Maria Ruda, Argentina. Robert Y. Jennings, United Kingdom. Guy Ladreit de Lacharriere, France. Keba Mbaye, Senegal. **9-year term in office ending 1988:** Robert Ago, Italy. Stephen M. Schwebel, U.S. Mohammed Bedjaoui, Algeria. Platon D. Morozov, USSR. Jose Sette Camara, Brazil. **9-year term in office ending 1985:** Taslim Olawala Elias, Nigeria. Hermann Mosier, W. Germany. Shigeru Oda, Japan. Abdullah Fikri Al-Khani, Syria. Manfred Lachs, Poland.

United Nations Secretaries General

Year	Secretary, Nation	Year	Secretary, Nation	Year	Secretary, Nation
1946	Trygve Lie, Norway	1961	U Thant, Burma	1982	Javier Perez de Cuellar, Peru
1953	Dag Hammarskjold, Sweden	1972	Kurt Waldheim, Austria		

U.S. Representatives to the United Nations

The U.S. Representative to the United Nations is the Chief of the U.S. Mission to the United Nations in New York and holds the rank and status of Ambassador Extraordinary and Plenipotentiary.

Year	Representative	Year	Representative	Year	Representative
1946	Edward R. Stettinius Jr.	1965	Arthur J. Goldberg	1975	Daniel P. Moynihan
1946	Hershel V. Johnson (act.)	1968	George W. Ball	1976	William W. Scranton
1947	Warren R. Austin	1968	James Russell Wiggins	1977	Andrew Young
1953	Henry Cabot Lodge Jr.	1969	Charles W. Yost	1979	Donald McHenry
1960	James J. Wadsworth	1971	George Bush	1981	Jeane J. Kirkpatrick
1961	Adlai E. Stevenson	1973	John A. Scali	1985	Vernon A. Walters

Specialized and Related Agencies

These agencies are autonomous, with their own memberships and organs which have a functional relationship or working agreement with the UN (headquarters.)

International Labor Org. (ILO) aims to promote employment; improve labor conditions and living standards. (4 route de Morillons, CH-1211, Geneva 22, Switzerland.)

Food & Agriculture Org. (FAO) aims to increase production from farms, forests, and fisheries; improve distribution,

marketing, and nutrition; better conditions for rural people. (Viale delle Terme di Caracalla, 00100 Rome, Italy.)

United Nations Educational, Scientific, & Cultural Org. (UNESCO) aims to promote collaboration among nations through education, science, and culture. The U.S. withdrew

this organization in 1985 because of UNESCO's anti-_ern bias. (9 Place de Fontenoy, 75700 Paris, France.)

World Health Org. (WHO) aims to aid the attainment of highest possible level of health. (20 Ave. Appia, 1211 _eneva, Switzerland.)

International Monetary Fund (IMF) aims to promote in-_ernational monetary co-operation and currency stabiliza-_ion; expansion of international trade. (700 19th St., NW, Washington, DC, 20431.)

International Civil Aviation Org. (ICAO) promotes inter-national civil aviation standards and regulations. (1000 Sher-brooke St. W., Montreal, Quebec, Canada H3A 2R2.)

Universal Postal Union (UPU) aims to perfect postal ser-vices and promote international collaboration. (Weltpost-strasse 4, 3000 Berne, 15 Switzerland.)

International Telecommunication Union (ITU) sets up international regulations of radio, telegraph, telephone and space radio-communications. Allocates radio frequencies. (Place des Nations, 1211 Geneva 20, Switzerland.)

World Meteorological Org. (WMO) aims to co-ordinate and improve world meteorological work. (Case Postale 5, CH-1211, Geneva, Switzerland.)

International Fund for Agricultural Development (IFAD) aims to mobilize funds for agricultural and rural projects in developing countries. (107 Via del Serafico, 00142 Rome, Italy.)

International Maritime Org. (IMO) aims to promote co-operation on technical matters affecting international ship-ping. (4 Albert Embankment, London, SE1 7SR, England.)

World Intellectual Property Organization (WIPO) seeks to protect, through international cooperation, literary, in-dustrial, scientific, and artistic works. (34, Chemin des Co-lom Bettes, 1211 Geneva, Switzerland.)

International Atomic Energy Agency (IAEA) aims to pro-mote the safe, peaceful uses of atomic energy. (Vienna Inter-national Centre, PO Box 100, A-1400, Vienna, Austria.)

General Agreement on Tariffs and Trade (GATT) is the only treaty setting rules for world trade. Provides a forum for settling trade disputes and negotiating trade liberaliza-tion. (Centre William Rappard, 154 rue de Lausanne, 1211 Geneva 21, Switzerland.)

International Bank for Reconstruction and Development (IBRD) (World Bank) provides loans and technical assist-ance for economic development projects in developing mem-ber countries; encourages cofinancing for projects from other public and private sources. International Development Association (IDA), an affiliate of the Bank, provides funds for development projects on concessionary terms to the poorer developing member countries. (both 1818 H St., NW, Washington, DC 20433.) International Finance Corporation (IFC) an affiliate of the Bank, promotes the growth of the private sector in developing member countries; encourages the development of local capital markets; stimulates the in-ternational flow of private capital. (1818 H St., NW, Wash-ington, DC 20433.)

United Nations Children's Fund (UNICEF) provides aid and development assistance to children and mothers in de-veloping countries. (1 UN Plaza, New York, NY 10017).

The World's Refugees in 1984
Source: U. S. Committee for Refugees

Country of Asylum	From	Number[1]
Total Africa		**2,734,000**
Algeria	Mostly Western Sahara	168,000[2]
Angola	Namibia, Zaire, S. Africa	96,000
Botswana	Zimbabwe	5,000
Burundi	Rwanda, Zaire	57,000[2]
Cameroon	Chad	4,000
Central African Rep.	Chad	7,000
Djibouti	Ethiopia	23,000[2]
Egypt	Ethiopia, Afghanistan	7,000
Ethiopia	Sudan	46,000
Kenya	Ethiopia, Rwanda, Uganda	24,000
Lesotho	South Africa	1,000[2]
Mozambique	Zimbabwe	1,000
Nigeria	Chad, others	5,000
Rwanda	Uganda, Burundi	50,000[2]
Senegal	Guinea Bissau	5,000
Somalia	Ethiopia	761,000[2]
Sudan	Ethiopia, Uganda, Chad, Zaire	690,000
Swaziland	South Africa	13,000
Tanzania	Burundi, Zaire, Uganda	180,000
Uganda	Rwanda, Zaire	132,000[2]
Zaire	Angola, Uganda, Zambia	304,000
Zambia	Angola, Namibia, Zaire	113,000
Zimbabwe	Mozambique	44,000
Total East Asia/Pacific		**742,000**
Australia	various	103,000
Burma	China, Malaysia	1,000
China	Vietnam	293,000[2]
Hong Kong	Vietnam	17,000
Indonesia	Vietnam	10,000
Japan	Vietnam	5,000
Korea, S.	N. Korea, Vietnam	1,000
Malaysia	Philippines, Vietnam	114,000[2]
New Zealand	various	6,000
Papua New Guinea	Indonesia	12,000
Philippines	Vietnam, Cambodia, Laos	20,000
Taiwan	SE Asia	13,000
Thailand*	Vietnam, Laos, Cambodia	126,000
Vietnam	Cambodia	21,000
*Not including border camps		
Total Europe		**308,000**
Austria	Eastern Europe, Vietnam	23,000
Belgium	various	2,000
Denmark	Eastern Europe, Vietnam	4,000
France	Africa, E. Europe, SE Asia	119,000
W. Germany	E. Europe, SE Asia	45,000
Greece	Near East	4,000
Italy	E. Europe	14,000
Netherlands	various	19,000
Norway	various	6,000[3]
Portugal	various	3,000[3]
Spain	various	26,000
Switzerland	Poland, SE Asia	17,000
Sweden	various	23,000
Turkey	Afghanistan	5,000
United Kingdom	various	6,000[3]
Yugoslavia	Eastern Europe	2,000
Total Latin America/Caribbean		**404,000**
Argentina	Europe, Latin America, SE Asia	14,000[2]
Belize	El Salvador	7,000
Brazil	Europe, other	5,000[2]
Chile	Europe	3,000
Costa Rica	El Salvador, Latin America	19,000
Cuba	Latin America	2,000
Dominican Rep.	Haiti	5,000
Guatemala	El Salvador	70,000[2]
Honduras	El Salvador, Nicaragua, oth-ers	22,000
Mexico	El Salvador, Guatemala	170,000[2]
Nicaragua	El Salvador, Guatemala	45,000
Panama	El Salvador	2,000
Venezuela	Latin America	1,000
Other		2,000
Total North America		**1,037,000**
Canada	various	142,000
United States	various	895,000
Total Middle East/South Asia		**5,760,600**
India	Afghanistan, Iran	6,000
Iran	Afghanistan, Iraq	810,000[2]
Pakistan	Afghanistan	2,925,000[2]
Palestinians		
Gaza Strip		402,000
Jordan		775,000
Lebanon		258,000
Syria		232,000
West Bank		350,000
Total Refugees		**9,091,000**

(1) Includes refugees in need of protection and assistance, and refugees who have entered and resettled, 1975-83; (2) Significant variance among sources in number reported; (3) Reflects 1982 and 1983 entries.

Sources of Largest Refugee Groups

Afghanistan	3,656,000	Angola	301,000
Palestinians	2,017,000	El Salvador	244,000
Ethiopia	1,209,000	Western Sahara	165,000
Uganda	310,000	Poland	120,000

Customs Exemptions and Advice to Travelers

U.S. residents returning after a stay abroad of at least 48 hours are usually granted customs exemptions of $400 each. The duty-free articles must accompany the traveler at the time of his return, be for personal or household use, have been acquired as an incident of his trip, and be properly declared to Customs. Not more than one liter of alcoholic beverages may be included in the $400 exemption.

If a U.S. resident arrives directly or indirectly from American Samoa, Guam, or the U.S. Virgin Islands, the purchase may be valued up to $800 fair retail value, but not more than $400 of the exemption may be applied to the value of articles acquired elsewhere than in such insular possessions, and 5 liters of alcoholic beverages may be included in the exemption, but not more than 1 liter of such beverages may have been acquired elsewhere than in the designated islands.

The exemption for alcoholic beverages is accorded only when the returning resident has attained 21 years of age at the time of his arrival. One hundred cigars and 200 cigarettes may be included in either exemption. Cuban cigars may be included if obtained in Cuba and all articles acquired there do not exceed $100 in retail value.

The $400 or $800 exemption may be granted only if the exemption, or any part of it, has not been used within preceding 30-day period and the stay abroad was for at le 48 hours. The 48-hour absence requirement does not apply you return from Mexico or the U.S. Virgin Islands.

Gifts costing no more than $50 fair retail value or $10(from American Samoa, Guam, or the Virgin Islands, may be mailed duty-free.

Most items—including alcoholic beverages, cigars, cigarettes and perfume—made in designated Caribbean and Central American countries may enter the U.S. duty-free under the Caribbean Basin Economic Recovery Act. Countries currently designated for such duty-free treatment are: Antigua and Barbuda, Barbados, Belize, British Virgin Islands, Costa Rica, Dominica, Dominican Republic, El Salvador, Grenada, Guatemala, Haiti, Honduras, Jamaica, Montserrat, Netherlands Antilles, Panama, Saint Christopher-Nevis, Saint Lucia, Saint Vincent and the Grenadines, and Trinidad and Tobago. Exceptions are: most textiles (incl. clothing), footwear, handbags, luggage, flat goods, work gloves and leather wearing apparel, and certain watches and watch parts. Alcoholic beverages and perfumes, remain subject to IRS tax.

U.S. Passport, Visa, and Health Requirements

Source: Passport Services, U.S. State Department as of May, 1984

Passports are issued by the United States Department of State to citizens and nationals of the United States for the purpose of documenting them for foreign travel and identifying them as Americans.

How to Obtain a Passport

An applicant for a passport who has never been previously issued a passport in his own name, must execute an application in person before (1) a passport agent; (2) a clerk of any federal court or state court of record or a judge or clerk of any probate court, accepting applications; (3) a postal employee designated by the postmaster at a Post Office which has been selected to accept passport applications; or (4) a diplomatic or consular officer of the U.S. abroad. It is no longer possible to include family members of any age in a U.S. passport. All persons are required to obtain individual passports in their own name.

A passport previously issued to the applicant, or one in which he was included, will be accepted as proof of citizenship in lieu of the following documents. A person born in the United States shall present his birth certificate. To be acceptable, the certificate must show the given name and surname, the date and place of birth and that the birth record was filed shortly after birth. A delayed birth certificate (a record filed more than one year after the date of birth) is acceptable provided that it shows that the report of birth was supported by acceptable secondary evidence of birth.

If such primary evidence is not obtainable, a notice from the registrar shall be submitted stating that no birth record exists. The notice shall be accompanied by the best obtainable secondary evidence such as a baptismal certificate, a certificate of circumcision, or a hospital birth record.

A person who has been issued a passport in his own name within the last eight years may obtain a new passport by filling out, signing and mailing a passport by mail application together with his previous passport, two recent identical signed photographs and $35.00 to the nearest Passport Agency or to the Passport Services in Wash., D.C. Those persons applying for a passport for the first time, or whose prior passport was issued before their 18th birthday, must execute a passport application in person.

A naturalized citizen should present his naturalization certificate. A person born abroad claiming citizenship through either a native-born or naturalized citizen must submit a certificate of citizenship issued by the Immigration and Naturalization Service; or a Consular Report of Birth or Certification of Birth issued by the Dept. of State. If one of the above documents has not been obtained, he must submit evidence of citizenship of the parent(s) through whom citizenship is claimed and evidence which would establish the parent/child relationship. Additionally, if through birth to citizen parent(s), parents' marriage certificate plus an affidavit from parent(s) showing periods and places of residence or physical presence in the U.S. and abroad, specifying periods spent abroad in the employment of the U.S. government, including the armed forces, or with certain international organizations; if through naturalization of parents, evidence of admission to the U.S. for permanent residence.

Under certain conditions, married women must present evidence of marriage. Special laws govern women married prior to Mar. 3, 1931.

Aliens — An alien leaving the U.S. must request passport facilities from his home government. He must have a permit from his local Collector of Internal Revenue, and if he wishes to return he should request a re-entry permit from the Immigration and Naturalization Service if it is required.

Contract Employees — Persons traveling because of a contract with the Government must submit with their applications letters from their employer stating position, destination and purpose of travel, armed forces contract number, and expiration date of contract when pertinent.

Photographs and Fees

Photographs — Two identical photographs which are sufficiently recent (normally not more than 6 months old) to be a good likeness of and satisfactorily identify the applicant. Photographs should be 2 × 2 inches in size. The image size measured from the bottom of the chin to the top of the head (including hair) should be not less than one inch nor more than 1 3/8 inches. Photographs must be signed in the center on the reverse. Photographs should be portrait-type prints. They must be clear, front view, full face, with a plain light (white or off-white) background. Photographs which depict the applicant as relaxed and smiling are encouraged.

Fees — As of Jan. 1, 1985, the passport fee is $20.00 for passports issued to persons under 18 years of age and the passports are valid for 5 years from the date of issue. The passport fee is $35.00 for passports issued to persons 18 years old and older and the passports are valid for 10 years from the date of issuance except where limited by the Secretary of State to a shorter period. A fee of $7.00 shall be charged for the execution of the application. No execution fee is payable when using DSP-82, "Application For Passport By Mail." Applicants eligible to use this procedure will pay only the $35.00 passport fee.

The loss or theft of a valid passport is a serious matter and should be reported in writing immediately to Passport Services, Dept. of State, Wash., D.C. 20524, or to the nearest passport agency, or to the nearest consular office of the U.S. when abroad.

Foreign Regulations

A visa, usually rubber stamped in a passport by a representative of the country to be visited, certifies that the bearer of the passport is permitted to enter that country for a certain purpose and length of time. Visa information can be obtained by writing directly to foreign consular officials.

U.S. Immigration Law

Source: Immigration and Naturalization Service, U.S. Justice Department

The Immigration and Nationality Act, as amended, provides for the numerical limitation of most immigration. Not subject to any numerical limitations are immigrants classified as immediate relatives who are spouses or children of U.S. citizens, or parents of citizens who are 21 years of age or older; returning residents; certain former U.S. citizens; ministers of religion; and certain long-term U.S. government employees.

The Refugee Act of 1980 (P.L. 96-212) became effective on April 1, 1980. Congress stated that the objectives of the Refugee Act are to provide a permanent and systematic procedure for the admission of refugees who are of special humanitarian concern to the United States, and to provide uniform provisions for the effective settlement and absorption of those refugees. The number of refugees who may be admitted is determined by the President, after consultation with the Committees on the Judiciary of the Senate and of the House of Representatives. For fiscal year 1984, the ceiling was set at 72,000 authorized refugee admissions.

Numerical Limitation of Immigrants

Immigration to the U.S. is numerically limited to 270,000 per year. Within this quota there is an annual limitation of 20,000 for each country. The colonies and dependencies of foreign states are limited to 600 per year, chargeable to the country limitation of the mother country.

Visa Categories

Of those immigrants subject to numerical limitations, applicants for immigration are classified as either preference or nonpreference. The preference visa categories are based on certain relationships to persons in the U.S., i.e., unmarried sons and daughters over 21 of U.S. citizens, spouses and unmarried sons and daughters of resident aliens, married sons and daughters of U.S. citizens, brothers and sisters of U.S. citizens 21 or over (first, 2d, 4th, and 5th preference, respectively); members of the professions or persons of exceptional ability in the sciences and arts whose services are sought by U.S. employers (3d preference); and skilled and unskilled workers in short supply (6th preference). Spouses and children of preference applicants are entitled to the same preference if accompanying or following to join such persons.

Preference status is based upon approved petitions, filed with the Immigration and Naturalization Service, by the appropriate relative or employer (or in the 3d preference by the alien himself).

Other immigrants not within one of the above-mentioned preference groups may qualify as nonpreference applicants and receive only those visa numbers not needed by preference applicants. The nonpreference category has not been available since 1978 due to 6 preferences using the allocation.

Labor Certification

The Act of October 3, 1965, established new controls to protect the American labor market from an influx of skilled and unskilled foreign labor. Prior to the issuance of a visa, the potential 3d, 6th, and nonpreference immigrant must obtain the Secretary of Labor's certification, establishing that there are not sufficient workers in the U.S. at the alien's destination who are able, willing, and qualified to perform the job; and that the employment of the alien will not adversely affect the wages and working conditions of workers in the U.S. similarly employed; or that there is satisfactory evidence that the provisions of that section do not apply to the alien's case.

Immigrants Admitted from All Countries

Fiscal Year Ends June 30 through 1976, Sept. 30 thereafter

Year	Number	Year	Number	Year	Number	Year	Number
1820	8,385	1871-1880. . .	2,812,191	1931-1940. . .	528,431	1979	460,348
1821-1830. . .	143,439	1881-1890. . .	5,246,613	1941-1950. . .	1,035,039	1980	530,639
1831-1840. . .	599,125	1891-1900. . .	3,687,564	1951-1960. . .	2,515,479	1981	596,600
1841-1850. . .	1,713,251	1901-1910. . .	8,795,386	1961-1970. . .	3,321,677	1982	594,131
1851-1860. . .	2,598,214	1911-1920. . .	5,735,811	1971-1975. . .	1,936,281	1983	559,763
1861-1870. . .	2,314,824	1921-1930. . .	4,107,209	1976	398,613	1984	543,903
				1976 July-Sept.	103,676	1820-1984. . .	51,950,349

Naturalization: How to Become an American Citizen

Source: The Federal Statutes

A person who desires to be naturalized as a citizen of the United States may obtain the necessary application form as well as detailed information from the nearest office of the Immigration and Naturalization Service or from the clerk of a court handling naturalization cases.

An applicant must be at least 18 years old. He must have been a lawful resident of the United States continuously for 5 years. For husbands and wives of U.S. citizens the period is 3 years in most instances. Special provisions apply to certain veterans of the Armed Forces.

An applicant must have been physically present in this country for at least half of the required 5 years' residence.

Every applicant for naturalization must:

(1) demonstrate an understanding of the English language, including an ability to read, write, and speak words in ordinary usage in the English language (persons physically unable to do so, and persons who, on the date of their examinations, are over 50 years of age and have been lawful permanent residents of the United States for 20 years or more are exempt).

(2) have been a person of good moral character, attached to the principles of the Constitution, and well disposed to the good order and happiness of the United States for five years just before filing the petition or for whatever other period of residence is required in his case and continue to be such a person until admitted to citizenship; and

(3) demonstrate a knowledge and understanding of the fundamentals of the history, and the principles and form of government, of the U.S.

The petitioner also is obliged to have two credible citizen witnesses. These witnesses must have personal knowledge of the applicant.

When the applicant files his petition he pays the court clerk $25. At the preliminary hearing he may be represented by a lawyer or social service agency. There is a 30-day wait. If action is favorable, there is a final hearing before a judge, who administers the following oath of allegiance:

I hereby declare, on oath, that I absolutely and entirely renounce and abjure all allegiance and fidelity to any foreign prince, potentate, state or sovereignty, to whom or which I have heretofore been a subject or citizen; that I will support and defend the Constitution and laws of the United States of America against all enemies, foreign and domestic; that I will bear true faith and allegiance to the same; that I will bear arms on behalf of the United States when required by the law; that I will perform noncombatant service in the armed forces of the United States when required by the law; that I will perform work of national importance under civilian direction when required by the law; and that I take this obligation freely without any mental reservation or purpose of evasion; so help me God.

STATES AND OTHER AREAS OF THE U.S.

Sources: Population: Commerce Dept., Bureau of the Census (July, 1984 provisional estimates, inc. armed forces person in each state but excluding such personnel stationed overseas); area: Bureau of the Census, Geography Division; fores land: Agriculture Dept., Forest Service; lumber production: Bureau of the Census, Industry Division; mineral production: I terior Dept., Bureau of Mines; commercial fishing: Commerce Dept., Natl. Marine Fisheries Service; value of construction McGraw-Hill Information Systems Co., F.W. Dodge Division; per capita income (estimate): Commerce Dept., Bureau o Economic Analysis; unemployment: Labor Dept., Bureau of Labor Statistics; finance: Federal Deposit Insurance Corp., Federal Home Loan Bank Bd.; federal employees: Labor Dept., Office of Personnel Management; energy: Energy Dept., Energy Information Administration; education: Education Dept., Natl. Center for Education Statistics, National Education Assn. Other information from sources in individual states, usually Commerce Dept.

Alabama

Heart of Dixie, Camellia State

People. Population (1984): 3,990,000; **rank:** 22. **Pop. density:** 78.6 per sq. mi. **Urban** (1980): 60%. **Racial distrib.** (1980): 73.7% White; 26.3% Black; Hispanic 33,100. **Net migration** (1970-80): +151,880.

Geography. Total area: 51,609 sq. mi.; **rank:** 29. **Land area:** 50,708 sq. mi. **Acres forested land:** 21,361,100. **Location:** in the east south central U.S., extending N-S from Tenn. to the Gulf of Mexico; east of the Mississippi River. **Climate:** long, hot summers; mild winters; generally abundant rainfall. **Topography:** coastal plains inc. Prairie Black Belt give way to hills, broken terrain; highest elevation, 2,407 ft. **Capital:** Montgomery.

Economy. Principal industries: pulp and paper, chemicals, electronics, apparel, textiles, primary metals, lumber and wood, food processing, fabricated metals, automotive tires. **Principal manufactured goods:** electronics, cast iron and plastic pipe, fabricated steel prods., ships, paper products, chemicals, steel, mobile homes, fabrics, poultry processing. **Agriculture:** Chief crops: soybeans, peanuts, corn, hay, wheat, cotton, pecans, peaches, potatoes, tomatoes. **Livestock** (1982): 1.9 mln. cattle; 480,000 hogs/pigs; 17.4 mln. poultry. **Timber/lumber** (1983): pine, hardwoods; 1.5 bln. bd. ft. **Minerals** (1984): $411.1 mostly cement, clays, lime, sand & gravel, stone. **Commercial fishing** (1983): $43.6 mln. **Chief ports:** Mobile. **Value of construction** (1984): $3.0 bln. **Employment distribution:** 25.4% manuf.; 20.4% trade; 16.4% serv. **Per capita income** (1984): $9,981. **Unemployment** (1984): 11.1%. **Tourism** (1984): tourists spent $3.3 bln.

Finance. No. banks (1983): 273; **No. savings assns.** (1983): 35.

Federal government. No. federal civilian employees (Mar. 1984): 49,617. **Avg. salary:** $24,974. **Notable federal facilities:** George C. Marshall NASA Space Center, Huntsville; Maxwell AFB, Montgomery; Ft. Rucker, Ozark; Ft. McClellan, Anniston; Natl. Fertilizer Development Center, Muscle Shoals; U.S. Corps of Engineers, Mobile.

Energy. Electricity production (1984, mwh, by source): Hydroelectric: 10.8 mln. Mineral: 72.0 mln. Nuclear: 24.2 mln.

Education. No. schools (1982): 1,347 public elem. and second.; 60 higher ed. **Avg. salary, public school teachers** (1984): $20,209.

State data. Motto: We dare defend our rights. **Flower:** Camellia. **Bird:** Yellowhammer. **Tree:** Southern pine. **Song:** Alabama. **Entered union** Dec. 14, 1819; rank, 22d. **State fair** at: Birmingham; Oct. 5-14.

History. First Europeans were Spanish explorers in the early 1500s. The French made the first permanent settlement, on Mobile Bay, 1701-02; later, English settled in the northern areas. France ceded the entire region to England at the end of the French and Indian War, 1763, but Spanish Florida claimed the Mobile Bay area until U. S. troops took it, 1813. Gen. Andrew Jackson broke the power of the Creek Indians, 1814, and they were removed to Oklahoma. The Confederate States were organized Feb. 4, 1861, at Montgomery, the first capital.

Tourist attractions. Jefferson Davis' "first White House" of the Confederacy; Ivy Green, Helen Keller's birthplace at Tuscumbia; statue of Vulcan in Birmingham; George Washington Carver Museum at Tuskegee Institute; Alabama Space and Rocket Center at Huntsville.

At Russell Cave National Monument, near Bridgeport, may be seen a detailed record of occupancy by humans from about 10,000 BC to 1650 AD.

Famous Alabamians include Hank Aaron, Tallulah Bankhead, Hugo L. Black, Paul "Bear" Bryant, George Washington Carver, Nat King Cole, William C. Handy, Helen Keller, Harper Lee, Joe Louis, John Hunt Morgan, Jesse Owens, Booker T. Washington, Hank Williams.

Chamber of Commerce: 468 S. Perry St., P.O. Box 76, Montgomery, AL 36195.

Alaska

No official nickname

People. Population (1984): 500,000; **rank:** 50. **Pop. density:** 0.88 per sq. mi., **Urban** (1980): 64.3%. **Net migration** (1970-82): +60,130.

Geography. Total area: 586,412 sq. mi.; **rank:** 1. **Land area:** 569,600 sq. mi. **Acres forested land:** 119,114,900. **Location:** NW corner of North America, bordered on east by Canada. **Climate:** SE, SW, and central regions, moist and mild; far north extremely dry. Extended summer days, winter nights, throughout. **Topography:** includes Pacific and Arctic mountain systems, central plateau, and Arctic slope. Mt. McKinley, 20,320 ft., is the highest point in North America. **Capital:** Juneau.

Economy. Principal industries: oil, gas, tourism, commercial fishing. **Principal manufactured goods:** fish products, lumber and pulp, furs. **Agriculture:** Chief crops: barley, hay, silage, potatoes, lettuce, milk, eggs. **Livestock:** 9,600 cattle; 3,200 hogs/pigs; 3,100 sheep; 78,000 poultry; 25,000 reindeer. **Timber/lumber:** spruce, yellow cedar, hemlock. **Minerals** (1984): $98.7 mln.; sand & gravel, crushed stone, gold. **Commercial fishing** (1983): $543.9 mln. **Chief ports:** Anchorage, Dutch Harbor, Seward, Skagway, Juneau, Sitka, Valdez, Wrangell. **International airports at:** Anchorage, Fairbanks, Ketchikan, Juneau. **Value of construction** (1984): $1.8 bln. **Employment distribution:** 29.3% gvt.; 19.7% trade; 18.3% serv.; 8.7% transp. **Per capita income** (1984): $17,155. **Unemployment** (1984): 10.0%. **Tourism** (1983): out-of-state visitors spent $535 mln.

Finance. No. banks: (1983): 15; **No. savings assns.:** (1983): 5.

Federal government. No. federal civilian employees (Mar. 1984): 10,463. **Avg. salary:** $29,173.

Energy. Electricity production (1983, mwh, by source): Hydroelectric: 693,000. Mineral: 3.3 mln.

Education. No. schools (1982): 407 public elem. and second.; 15 higher ed. **Avg. salary, public school teachers** (1984): $39,751.

State data. Motto: North to the future. **Flower:** Forget-me-not. **Bird:** Willow ptarmigan. **Tree:** Sitka spruce. **Song:** Alaska's Flag. **Entered union:** Jan. 3, 1959; rank, 49th. **State fair at:** Palmer; late Aug.—early Sept.

...ory. Vitus Bering, a Danish explorer working for ...a, was the first European to land in Alaska, 1741. ...ander Baranov, first governor of Russian America, set ...headquarters at Archangel, near present Sitka, in ...9. Secretary of State William H. Seward in 1867 ...ught Alaska from Russia for $7.2 million, a bargain ...me called "Seward's Folly." In 1896 gold was discov-...red and the famed Gold Rush was on.

Tourist attractions: Glacier Bay National Park, Katmai National Park & Preserve, Denali National Park, one of North America's great wildlife sanctuaries, Pribilof Islands fur seal rookeries, restored St. Michael's Russian Ortho-dox Cathedral, Sitka.

Famous Alaskans include Carl Eielson, Ernest Gruen-ing, Joe Juneau, Sydney Laurence, James Wickersham.

Chamber of Commerce: 310 Second St., Juneau, AK 99801.

Arizona

Grand Canyon State

People. Population (1984): 3,053,000; **rank: 28. Pop. density:** 26.9 per sq. mi. **Urban** (1980): 83.8% **Racial distrib.** (1980): 82.4% White; 2.7% Black; 14.8% Other (includes American Indians); Hispanic 440,915. **Net mi-gration** (1970-79): +464,000.

Geography. Total area: 113,909 sq. mi.; **rank: 6. Land area:** 113,417 sq. mi. **Acres forested land:** 18,493,900. **Location:** in the southwestern U.S. **Climate:** clear and dry in the southern regions and northern plateau; high central areas have heavy winter snows. **Topography:** Colorado plateau in the N, containing the Grand Canyon; Mexican Highlands running diagonally NW to SE; Sonoran Desert in the SW. **Capital:** Phoenix.

Economy. Principal industries: manufacturing, tour-ism, mining, agriculture. **Principal manufactured goods:** electronics, printing and publishing, foods, primary and fabricated metals, aircraft and missiles, apparel. **Agricul-ture: Chief crops:** cotton, sorghum, barley, corn, wheat, sugar beets, citrus fruits. **Livestock:** 980,000 cattle; 150,000 hogs/pigs; 306,000 sheep; 400,000 poultry. **Tim-ber/lumber** (1984): pine, fir, spruce; 326 mln. bd. ft. **Min-erals** (1984): $1.2 bln.; copper, molybdenum, gold, silver. **International airports at:** Phoenix, Tucson, Yuma. **Value of construction** (1984): $5.9 bln. **Employment distribu-tion** (1984): 24% trade, 17% gvt., 23% serv., 15% manuf. **Per capita income** (1984): $11,629. **Unemploy-ment** (1984): 5.0%. **Tourism** (1983): tourists spent $4.8 bln.

Finance. No. banks: (1983): 48; **No. savings assns.** (1983): 8.

Federal government. No. federal civilian employees (Mar. 1984): 26,302. **Avg. salary:** $23,065. **Notable fed-eral facilities:** Williams, Luke, Davis-Monthan AF bases; Ft. Huachuca Army Base; Yuma Proving Grounds.

Energy. Electricity production (1984, mwh, by source): Hydroelectric: 15.7 mln.; Mineral: 30.1.

Education. No. schools (1982): 867 public elem. and second.; 29 higher ed. **Avg. salary, public school teach-ers** (1984): $23,380.

State data. Motto: Ditat Deus (God enriches). **Flower:** Blossom of the Seguaro cactus. **Bird:** Cactus wren. **Tree:** Paloverde. **Song:** Arizona. **Entered union** Feb. 14, 1912; rank, 48th. **State fair at:** Phoenix; late Oct.–early Nov.

History. Marcos de Niza, a Franciscan, and Estevan, a black slave, explored the area, 1539. Eusebio Francisco Kino, Jesuit missionary, taught Indians Christianity and farming, 1690-1711, left a chain of missions. Spain ceded Arizona to Mexico, 1821. The U. S. took over at the end of the Mexican War, 1848. The area below the Gila River was obtained from Mexico in the Gadsden Purchase, 1854. Long Apache wars did not end until 1886, with Ge-ronimo's surrender.

Tourist attractions. The Grand Canyon of the Colo-rado, an immense, vari-colored fissure 217 mi. long, 4 to 13 mi. wide at the brim, 4,000 to 5,500 ft. deep; the Painted Desert, extending for 30 mi. along U.S. 66; the Petrified Forest; Canyon Diablo, 225 ft. deep and 500 ft. wide; Meteor Crater, 4,150 ft. across, 570 ft. deep, made by a prehistoric meteor. Also, London Bridge at Lake Havasu City.

Famous Arizonans include Cochise, Geronimo, Barry Goldwater, Zane Grey, George W. P. Hunt, Helen Jacobs, Percival Lowell, William H. Pickering, Morris Udall, Stewart Udall, Frank Lloyd Wright.

Chamber of Commerce: 1366 E. Thomas, Suite 202, Phoenix, AZ 85014.

Arkansas

Land of Opportunity

People. Population (1984): 2,349,000; **rank: 33. Pop. density:** 45.2 per sq. mi. **Urban** (1980): 51.5%. **Racial distrib.** (1980): 66.1% White; 16.3% Black; Hispanic 17,873. **Net migration** (1970-80): +14,616.

Geography. Total area: 53,104 sq. mi.; **rank: 27. Land area:** 51,945 sq. mi. **Acres forested land:** 18,281,500. **Location:** in the west south-central U.S. **Climate:** long, hot summers, mild winters; generally abundant rainfall. **Topography:** eastern delta and prairie, southern lowland forests, and the northwestern highlands, which include the Ozark Plateaus. **Capital:** Little Rock.

Economy. Principal industries: manufacturing, agri-culture, tourism. **Principal manufactured goods:** poultry products, forestry products, aluminum, electric motors, transformers, garments, bricks, fertilizer, petroleum prod-ucts. **Agriculture: Chief crops:** soybeans, rice, cotton, hay, wheat, sorghum, tomatoes, strawberries, peaches. **Livestock:** 2 mln. cattle; 395,000 hogs/pigs; 6.73 mln. poultry. **Timber/lumber** (1984): oak, hickory, gum, cy-press, pine; 1.4 bln. bd. ft. **Minerals** (1984): $279.0; abra-sives, bauxite, bromine, stone, sand & gravel. **Commer-cial fishing** (1983): $14.3 mln. **Chief ports:** Little Rock, Pine Bluff, Osceola, Helena, Fort Smith, Van Buren, Cam-den. **Value of construction** (1984): $1.7 bln. **Employ-ment distribution:** 20.2% manuf.; 7.4% trade; 5.8% agric. **Per capita income** (1984): $9,724. **Unemploy-ment** (1984): 8.9% **Tourism** (1984): travelers spent $1.7 bln.

Finance. No. banks (1983): 262; **No. savings assns.** (1983): 37.

Federal government. No. federal civilian employees (Mar. 1984): 12,230. **Avg. salary:** $22,413. **Notable fed-eral facilities:** Nat'l. Center for Toxicological Research, Jefferson; Pine Bluff Arsenal.

Energy. Electricity production (1984, mwh, by source): Hydroelectric: 2.7 mln.; Mineral: 16.5 mln.; Nu-clear: 10.8 mln.

Education. No. schools (1982): 1,179 public elem. and second.; 35 higher ed. **Avg. salary, public school teach-ers** (1984): $18,933.

State data. Motto: Regnat Populus (The people rule). **Flower:** Apple Blossom. **Bird:** Mockingbird. **Tree:** Pine. **Song:** Arkansas. **Entered union:** June 15, 1836; rank, 25th. **State fair at:** Little Rock; late Sept.- early Oct.

History. First European explorers were de Soto, 1541, Jolliet, 1673; La Salle, 1682. First settlement was by the French under Henri de Tonty, 1686, at Arkansas Post. In 1762 the area was ceded by France to Spain, then back again in 1800, and was part of the Louisiana Purchase by the U.S. in 1803. Arkansas seceded from the Union in 1861, only after the Civil War began, and more than 10,000 Arkansans fought on the Union side.

Tourist attractions. Hot Springs National Park, water ranging from 95° to 147°F; Eureka Springs, resort since 1880s; Blanchard Caverns, near Mountain View, are among the nation's largest; Crater of Diamonds, near Murfreesboro, only U.S. diamond mine; Buffalo Natl. River; Mid-America Museum, Dogpatch, U.S.A.

Famous Arkansans include Hattie Caraway, "Dizzy" Dean, Orval Faubus, James W. Fulbright, Douglas MacArthur, John L. McClellan, James S. McDonnel, Win-throp Rockefeller, Edward Durell Stone, Archibald Yell.

Chamber of Commerce: One Spring Bldg., Little Rock, AR 72201.

Famous Californians include Luther Burbank, Joh Fremont, Bret Harte, Wm. R. Hearst, Jack London, Ai Semple McPherson, John Muir, William Saroyan, Junip Serra, Leland Stanford, John Steinbeck, Earl Warren.
Chamber of Commerce: 1027 10th, Sacramento, C 95814.

California
Golden State

People. Population (1984): 25,622,000; **rank:** 1. **Pop. density:** 163.9 per sq. mi. **Urban** (1980): 91.3%. **Racial distrib.** (1980): 76.1% White; 7.6% Black; 16.1% Other (includes American Indians, Asian Americans, and Pacific Islanders); Hispanic 4,543,770. **Net migration** (1984): +189,020.

Geography. Total area 158,693 sq. mi.; **rank:** 3. **Land area:** 156,361 sq. mi. **Acres forested land:** 40,152,100. **Location:** on western coast of the U.S. **Climate:** moderate temperatures and rainfall along the coast; extremes in the interior. **Topography:** long mountainous coastline; central valley; Sierra Nevada on the east; desert basins of the southern interior; rugged mountains of the north. **Capital:** Sacramento.

Economy. Principal industries: agriculture, manufacturing, aerospace, construction, recreation. **Principal manufactured goods:** foods, primary and fabricated metals, machinery, electric and electronic equipment, chemicals and allied products. **Agriculture: Chief crops:** grapes, cotton, flowers, oranges, nursery products, hay, tomatoes, lettuce, strawberries, almonds. **Livestock** (1982): 1.9 mln. cattle; 1.8 mln. hogs/pigs; 1.5 mln. sheep; 209.8 mln. poultry. **Timber/ lumber** (1983): fir, pine, redwood, oak; 3.8 bln. bd. ft. **Minerals:** (1984): leading state in U.S. in nonfuel minerals, with value of $1.9 bln.; mostly cement, boron minerals, sand & gravel, crushed stone. **Commercial fishing** (1983): $202.1 mln. **Chief ports:** Long Beach, San Diego, Oakland, San Francisco, Sacramento, Stockton. **International airports at:** Los Angeles, San Francisco. **Value of construction** (1984): $26.8 bln. **Employment distribution** (1984): 24.0% serv.; 23.8% trade; 19.4% mfg; 16.4% gvt. **Per capita income** (1984): $14,344. **Unemployment** (1984): 7.8% **Tourism** (1983): out-of-state visitors spent $28.5 bln.

Finance. No. banks (1983): 441; **No. savings assns.** (1983): 172.

Federal government. No. federal civilian employees (Mar. 1984): 205,188. **Avg. salary:** $24,723. **Notable federal facilities:** Vandenberg, Beale, Travis, McClellan AF bases, San Francisco Mint.

Energy. Electricity production (1984, mwh, by source): Hydroelectric: 43.2 mln.; Mineral: 99.8 mln.; Nuclear: 13.6 mln.

Education. No. schools (1982): 6,818 public elem. and second.; 268 higher ed. **Avg. salary, public school teachers** (1984): $26,300.

State Data. Motto: Eureka (I have found it). **Flower:** Golden poppy. **Bird:** California valley quail. **Tree:** California redwood. **Song:** I Love You, California. **Entered Union** Sept. 9, 1850; rank, 31st. **State fair at:** Sacramento; late Aug.—early Sept.

History. First European explorers were Cabrillo, 1542, and Drake, 1579. First settlement was the Spanish Alta California mission at San Diego, 1769, first in a string founded by Franciscan Father Junipero Serra. U. S. traders and settlers arrived in the 19th century and staged the abortive Bear Flag Revolt, 1846; the Mexican War began later in 1846 and U.S. forces occupied California; Mexico ceded the province to the U.S., 1848, the same year the Gold Rush began.

Tourist attractions. Scenic regions are Yosemite Valley; Lassen and Sequoia-Kings Canyon national parks; Lake Tahoe; the Mojave and Colorado deserts; San Francisco Bay; and Monterey Peninsula. Oldest living things on earth are believed to be a stand of Bristlecone pines in the Inyo National Forest, est. to be 4,600 years old. The world's tallest tree, the Howard Libbey redwood, 362 ft. with a girth of 44 ft., stands on Redwood Creek, Humboldt County.

Also, Palomar Observatory; Disneyland; J. Paul Getty Museum, Malibu; Tournament of Roses and Rose Bowl.

Colorado
Centennial State

People. Population (1984): 3,178,000; **rank:** 26. **Pop. density:** 30.6 per sq. mi. **Urban** (1980): 80.6%. **Racial distrib.** (1980): 88.9% White; 3.5% Black; Hispanic 339,300. **Net migration** (1970-80): +668,811.

Geography. Total area: 104,247 sq. mi.; **rank:** 8. **Land area:** 103,766 sq. mi. **Acres forested land:** 22,271,000. **Location:** in west central U.S. **Climate:** low relative humidity, abundant sunshine, wide daily, seasonal temperatures ranges; alpine conditions in the high mountains. **Topography:** eastern dry high plains; hilly to mountainous central plateau; western Rocky Mountains of high ranges alternating with broad valleys and deep, narrow canyons. **Capital:** Denver.

Economy. Principal industries: manufacturing, government, mining, tourism, agriculture, aerospace, electronics equipment. **Principal manufactured goods:** computer equipment, instruments, foods, machinery, aerospace products, rubber, steel. **Agriculture: Chief crops:** corn, wheat, hay, sugar beets, barley, potatoes, apples, peaches, pears, soy beans. **Livestock** (1982): 3.0 mln. cattle; 330,000 hogs/pigs; 710,000 sheep; (1981) 7.4 mln. poultry. **Timber/lumber** (1983): oak, ponderosa pine, Douglas fir; 151 mln. bd. ft. **Minerals** (1984): $422.1; cement, sand & gravel, molybdenum. **International airports at:** Denver. **Value of construction** (1984): $4.7 bln. **Employment distribution** (1983): 21.8% trade; 19.1% serv.; 15.9% gvt.; 12.0% manuf. **Per capita income** (1984): $13,742. **Unemployment** (1984): 5.6%. **Tourism** (1983): $4.0 bln.

Finance. No. banks (1983): 551; **No. savings assns.** (1983): 37.

Federal government. No. federal civilian employees (Mar. 1984): 35,365. **Avg. salary:** $25,474. **Notable federal facilities:** U.S. Air Force Academy; U.S. Mint; Ft. Carson, Lowry AFB; Solar Energy Research Institute; U.S. Rail Transport. Test Center; N. Amer. Aerospace Defense Command; Consolidated Space Operations Center; U.S. Documents Center.

Energy. Electricity production (1984, mwh, by source): Hydroelectric: 2.2 mln.; Mineral: 25.4 mln.; Nuclear: 55,000.

Education. No. schools (1982): 1,271 public elem. and second.; 47 higher ed. **Avg. salary, public school teachers** (1984): $24,456.

State data. Motto: Nil Sine Numine (Nothing without Providence). **Flower:** Rocky Mountain columbine. **Bird:** Lark bunting. **Tree:** Colorado blue spruce. **Song:** Where the Columbines Grow. Entered union Aug. 1, 1876; rank 38th. **State fair** at: Pueblo; last week in Aug.

History. Early civilization centered around Mesa Verde 2,000 years ago. The U.S. acquired eastern Colorado in the Louisiana Purchase, 1803; Lt. Zebulon M. Pike explored the area, 1806, discovering the peak that bears his name. After the Mexican War, 1846-48, U.S. immigrants settled in the east, former Mexicans in the south.

Tourist attractions. Rocky Mountain National Park; Garden of the Gods; Great Sand Dunes, Dinosaur, Black Canyon of the Gannison, and Colorado national monuments; Pikes Peak and Mt. Evans highways; Mesa Verde National Park (pre-historic cliff dwellings); 35 major ski areas. The Grand Mesa tableland comprises Grand Mesa Forest, 659,584 acres, with 200 lakes stocked with trout.

Famous Coloradans include Frederick Bonfils, William N. Byers, M. Scott Carpenter, Jack Dempsey, Mamie Eisenhower, Douglas Fairbanks, Scott Hamilton, Lowell Thomas, Byron R. White, Paul Whiteman.

ist information: Dept. of Local Affairs, 1313 Sher-
.t., Denver, CO 80203.

Connecticut

Constitution State, Nutmeg State

People. Population (1984): 3,154,000; **rank:** 27. **Pop. density:** 648.7 per sq. mi. **Urban** (1980): 78.8% **Racial distrib.** (1980): 90.0% White; 6.9% Black; Hispanic 124,499. **Net migration** (1970-80): +75,576.

Geography. Total area: 5,009 sq. mi.; **rank:** 48. **Land area:** 4,862 sq. mi. **Acres forested land:** 1,860,800. **Location:** New England state in the northeastern corner of the U.S. **Climate:** moderate; winters avg. slightly below freezing, warm, humid summers. **Topography:** western upland, the Berkshires, in the NW, highest elevations; narrow central lowland N-S; hilly eastern upland drained by rivers. **Capital:** Hartford.

Economy. Principal industries: manufacturing, retail trade, government, services. **Principal manufactured goods:** aircraft engines and parts, submarines, copper wire and tubing, helicopters, bearings, instruments, electrical equipment, machine tools. **Agriculture: Chief crops:** tobacco, hay, apples, potatoes, nursery stock. **Livestock:** 107,000 cattle; 8,000 hogs/pigs; 4,800 sheep; 5.9 mln. poultry. **Timber/lumber:** oak, birch, beech, maple. **Minerals** (1984): $75.3 mln; sand & gravel; crushed stone. **Commercial fishing** (1983): $11.9 mln. **Chief ports:** New Haven, Bridgeport, New London. **International airports at:** Windsor Locks. **Value of construction** (1984): $2.7 bln. **Employment distribution:** 28% manuf.; 22% serv. **Per capita income** (1984): $16,369. **Unemployment** (1984): 4.6%. **Tourism** (1984): out-of-state visitors spent $2.25 bln.

Finance. No. banks (1983): 108; **No. savings assns.** (1983): 32.

Federal Government. No. federal civilian employees (Mar. 1984): 9,289. **Avg. salary:** $25,504. **Notable federal facilities:** U.S. Coast Guard Academy; U.S. Navy Submarine Base.

Energy. Electricity production (1984, mwh, by source): Hydroelectric: 372,000; Mineral: 12.6 mln.; Nuclear: 14.3 mln.

Education. No. schools (1982): 962 public elem. and second.; 47 higher ed. **Avg. salary, public school teachers** (1984): $24,520.

State data. Motto: Qui Transtulit Sustinet (He who transplanted still sustains). **Flower:** Mountain laurel. **Bird:** American robin. **Tree:** White oak. **Song:** Yankee Doodle Dandy. **Fifth** of the 13 original states to ratify the Constitution, Jan. 9, 1788.

History. Adriaen Block, Dutch explorer, was the first European visitor, 1614. By 1634, settlers from Plymouth Bay started colonies along the Connecticut River and in 1637 defeated the Pequot Indians. In the Revolution, Connecticut men fought in most major campaigns and turned back British raids on Danbury and other towns, while Connecticut privateers captured British merchant ships.

Tourist attractions. Mark Twain House, Hartford; Yale University's Art Gallery, Peabody Museum, all in New Haven; Mystic Seaport; Mystic Marine Life Aquarium; P.T. Barnum Museum, Bridgeport; Gillette Castle, Hadlyme.

Famous "Nutmeggers" include Ethan Allen, Phineas T. Barnum, Samuel Colt, Jonathan Edwards, Nathan Hale, Katharine Hepburn, Isaac Hull, J. Pierpont Morgan, Israel Putnam, Harriet Beecher Stowe, Mark Twain, Noah Webster, Eli Whitney.

Tourist Information: State Dept. of Economic Development, 210 Washington St., Hartford, CT 06106.

Delaware

First State, Diamond State

People. Population (1984): 613,000; **rank:** 47. **Pop. density:** 309.3 per sq. mi. **Urban** (1980): 70.6%. **Racial distrib.** (1980): 82.0% White; 16.1% Black; Hispanic 9,671. **Net migration** (1970-80): +8,000.

Geography. Total area: 2,057 sq. mi.; **rank:** 49. **Land area:** 1,982 sq. mi. **Acres forested land:** 391,800. **Location:** occupies the Delmarva Peninsula on the Atlantic coastal plain. **Climate:** moderate. **Topography:** Piedmont plateau to the N, sloping to a near sea-level plain. **Capital:** Dover.

Economy. Principal industries: chemistry, agriculture, poultry, shellfish, tourism, auto assembly, food processing, transportation equipment. **Principal manufactured goods:** nylon, apparel, luggage, foods, autos, processed meats and vegetables, railroad and aircraft equipment. **Agriculture: Chief crops:** soybeans, potatoes, corn, mushrooms, lima beans, green peas, barley, cucumbers, snap beans, watermelons, apples. **Livestock:** 30,000 cattle; 1.82 mln. poultry. **Timber/Lumber:** (1982) forest products $1.8 mln. **Minerals** (1984): $3.0 mln; sand & gravel, magnesium compounds. **Commercial fishing** (1983): $2.0 mln. **Chief ports:** Wilmington. **International airports at:** Philadelphia/Wilmington. **Value of construction** (1984): $488.3 mln. **Employment distribution:** 74.9% non-manufacturing; 25.1% manuf. **Per capita income** (1984): $13,545. **Unemployment** (1984): 6.2%. **Tourism** (1983): out-of-state visitors spent $461 mln.

Finance. No. banks (1983): 34; **No. savings assns.** (1983): 4.

Federal government. No. federal civilian employees (Mar. 1984): 3,043. **Avg. salary:** $23,480. **Notable federal facilities:** Dover Air Force Base, Federal Wildlife Refuge, Bombay Hook.

Energy. Electricity production (1984, mwh, by source): Mineral: 9.4 mln.

Education. No. schools (1982): 146 public elem. and second.; 8 higher ed. **Avg. salary, public school teachers** (1984): $23,300.

State data. Motto: Liberty and independence. **Flower:** Peach blossom. **Bird:** Blue hen chicken. **Tree:** American holly. **Song:** Our Delaware. **First** of original 13 states to ratify the Constitution, Dec. 7, 1787. **State fair** at: Harrington; end of July.

History. The Dutch first settled in Delaware near present Lewes, 1631, but were wiped out by Indians. Swedes settled at present Wilmington, 1638; Dutch settled anew, 1651, near New Castle and seized the Swedish settlement, 1655, only to lose all Delaware and New Netherland to the British, 1664.

Tourist attractions. Ft. Christina Monument, the site of founding of New Sweden; John Dickinson "Penman of the Revolution" home, Dover; Henry Francis du Pont Winterthur Museum; Hagley Museum, Wilmington; Rehobeth Beach, "nation's summer capital," Rehobeth; Dover Downs Intl. Speedway, Dover; Old Swedes (Trinity Parish) Church, erected 1698, is the oldest Protestant church in the U.S. still in use.

Famous Delawareans include Thomas F. Bayard, Henry Seidel Canby, E. I. du Pont, John P. Marquand, Howard Pyle, Caesar Rodney.

Chamber of Commerce: One Commerce Center, Wilmington, DE 19801.

Florida

Sunshine State

People. Population (1984): 10,976,000; **rank:** 6. **Pop. density:** 202.7 per sq. mi. **Urban** (1980): 84.3%. **Racial distrib.** (1980): 83.9% White; 13.7% Black; Hispanic 858,158. **Net migration** (1970-84): +3,763,546.

Geography. Total area: 58,560 sq. mi.; **rank:** 22. **Land area:** 54,136 sq. mi. **Acres forested land:** 17,932,900. **Location:** peninsula jutting southward 500 mi. bet. the Atlantic and the Gulf of Mexico. **Climate:** subtropical N of Bradenton-Lake Okeechobee-Vero Beach line; tropical S of line. **Topography:** land is flat or rolling; highest point is 345 ft. in the NW. **Capital:** Tallahassee.

Economy. Principal industries: services, trade, gvt., manufacturing, tourism. **Principal manufactured goods:** electric & electronic equip., transp. equipment; food; printing & publishing; apparel & textile. **Agriculture: Chief crops:** citrus fruits, vegetables, corn sourbean, avocados, sugarcane, peanuts, hay crops, tobacco, strawberries, watermelon. **Livestock** (1984): 2.2 mln. cattle; 160,000 hogs/pigs; 4,500 sheep; 11.5 mln. poultry. **Timber/lumber** (1983): pine, cypress, cedar; 557 mln. bd. ft. **Minerals** (1984): $1.5 bln.; mostly crushed stone, cement, and phosphate rock. **Commercial fishing** (1983): $177.4 mln. **Chief ports:** Tampa, Jacksonville, Miami, Pensacola. **International airports at:** Miami, Tampa, Jacksonville, Orlando, Ft. Lauderdale, W. Palm Beach. **Value of construction** (1984): $16.9 bln. **Per capita income** (1984): $12,553. **Unemployment** (1984): 6.3% **Tourism** (1983): out-of-state visitors spent $20 bln.

Finance. No. banks (1983): 472; **No. savings assns.** (1983): 109.

Federal government. No. federal civilian employees (Mar. 1984): 53,948. **Avg. salary:** $24,699. **Notable federal facilities:** John F. Kennedy Space Center, Cape Canaveral; Eglin Air Force Base.

Energy. Electricity production (1984, mwh, by source): Hydroelectric: 213,000; Mineral: 70.1 mln.; Nuclear: 24.1 mln.

Education. No. schools (1982): 1,994 public elem. and second.; 79 higher ed. **Avg. salary, public school teachers** (1984): $21,057.

State data. Motto: In God we trust. **Flower:** Orange blossom. **Bird:** Mockingbird. **Tree:** Sabal palmetto palm. **Song:** Swanee River. **Entered union** Mar. 3, 1845; rank, 27th. **State fair at:** Tampa; Feb. 5-16.

History. First European to see Florida was Ponce de Leon, 1513. France established a colony, Fort Caroline, on the St. Johns River, 1564; Spain settled St. Augustine, 1565, and Spanish troops massacred most of the French. Britain's Francis Drake burned St. Augustine, 1586. Britain held the area briefly, 1763-83, returning it to Spain. After Andrew Jackson led a U.S. invasion, 1818, Spain ceded Florida to the U.S., 1819. The Seminole War, 1835-42, resulted in removal of most Indians to Oklahoma. Florida seceded from the Union, 1861, was readmitted, 1868.

Tourist attractions. Miami, with the nation's greatest concentration of luxury hotels at Miami Beach; St. Augustine, oldest city in U.S.; Walt Disney World and EPCOT; Kennedy Space Center, Cape Canaveral.

Everglades National Park, 3d largest of U.S. national parks, preserves the beauty of the vast Everglades swamp. Castillo de San Marcos, St. Augustine, is a national monument. Also, the Ringling Museum of Art, and the Ringling Museum of the Circus, both in Sarasota; Sea World, and Circus World, Orlando; Busch Gardens, Tampa.

Famous Floridians include Henry M. Flagler, James Weldon Johnson, MacKinlay Kantor, Henry B. Plant, Marjorie Kinnan Rawlings, Joseph W. Stilwell, Charles P. Summerall.

Chamber of Commerce: P.O. Box 1639, Tallahassee, FL 32302.

Georgia

Empire State of the South, Peach State

People. Population (1984): 5,837,000; **rank:** 11. **Pop. density:** 100.5 per sq. mi. **Urban** (1980): 62.4%. **Racial distrib.** (1980): 72.2% White; 26.8% Black; Hispanic 61,261. **Net migration** (1970-80): +441,658.

Geography. Total area: 58,876 sq. mi.; **rank:** 21. **Land area:** 58,073 sq. mi. **Acres forested land:** 25,256,100. **Location:** South Atlantic state. **Climate:** maritime tropical air masses dominate in summer; continental polar air masses in winter; east central area drier. **Topography:** most southerly of the Blue Ridge Mtns. cover NE and N central; central Piedmont extends to the fall line of rivers; coastal plain levels to the coast flatlands. **Capital:** Atlanta.

Economy. Principal industries: manufacturing, forestry, agriculture, chemicals. **Principal manufactured goods:** textiles, transportation equipment, foods, clothing, paper and wood products, chemical products. **Agriculture: Chief crops:** peanuts, corn, soybeans, tobacco, oats and wheat, cotton and cottonseed. **Livestock** (1983): 1.87 mln. cattle; 1.57 mln. hogs/pigs; 5,000 sheep; 68 mln. poultry. **Timber/lumber** (1983): pine, hardwood; 2.0 bln. bd. ft. **Minerals** (1984): $952.6 mln.; clays, crushed stone. **Commercial fishing** (1983): $25.4 mln. **Chief ports:** Savannah, Brunswick. **International airports at:** Atlanta. **Value of construction** (1984): $6.6 bln. **Employment distribution:** 32% trade; 25% mfg.; 20% gvt.; 23% serv. **Per capita income** (1984): $11,441. **Unemployment** (1984): 6.0% **Tourism** (1983): tourists spent $7.6 bln.

Finance. No. banks (1983): 394. **No. savings assns.** (1983): 62.

Federal government. No. federal civilian employees (Mar. 1984): 61,661. **Avg. salary:** $24,120. **Notable federal facilities:** Dobbins AFB; Fts. Benning, Gordon, McPherson; Nat'l. Law Enforcement Training Ctr., Glynco.

Energy. Electricity production (1984, mwh, by source): Hydroelectric: 4.1 mln.; Mineral: 64.0 mln.; Nuclear: 5.5 mln.

Education. No. schools (1982): 1,768 elem. and second.; 80 higher ed. **Avg. salary, public school teachers** (1984): $20,494.

State data. Motto: Wisdom, justice and moderation. **Flower:** Cherokee rose. **Bird:** Brown thrasher. **Tree:** Live oak. **Song:** Georgia On My Mind. **Fourth** of the 13 original states to ratify the Constitution, Jan. 2, 1788.

History. Gen. James Oglethorpe established the first settlements, 1733, for poor and religiously-persecuted Englishmen. Oglethorpe defeated a Spanish army from Florida at Bloody Marsh, 1742. In the Revolution, Georgians seized the Savannah armory, 1775, and sent the munitions to the Continental Army; they fought seesaw campaigns with Cornwallis' British troops, twice liberating Augusta and forcing final evacuation by the British from Savannah, 1782.

Tourist attractions. The Little White House in Warm Springs where Pres. Franklin D. Roosevelt died Apr. 12, 1945, 2,500-acre Callaway Gardens, Jekyll Island State Park, the restored 1850s farming community of Westville; Alpine Helen, tiny mountain town converted to Alpine Village. Dahlonega, site of America's first gold rush; Stone Mountain, and Six Flags Over Georgia.

Okefenokee in the SE is one of the largest swamps in the U.S., a wetland wilderness and peat bog covering 660 sq. mi. A large part of it is a National Wildlife Refuge, a home for wild birds, alligators, bear, deer.

Famous Georgians include Hank Aaron, James Bowie, Erskine Caldwell, Jimmy Carter, Lucius D. Clay, Ty Cobb, John C. Fremont, Joel Chandler Harris, Martin Luther King Jr., Sidney Lanier, Margaret Mitchell, Jackie Robinson, Joseph Wheeler.

Chamber of Commerce: 1200 Commerce Bldg., Atlanta, GA 30303.

Hawaii

The Aloha State

eople. Population (1984): 1,039,000; **rank:** 39. **Pop. nsity:** 161.7 per sq. mi. **Urban** (1980): 86.5%. **Racial strib.** (1980): 33.0% White; 1.7% Black; 65.1% Other ncludes Asian Americans and Pacific Islanders); Hispanic 1,479. **Net migration.** (1970-83): +15,000.

Geography. Total area: 6,450 sq. mi.; **rank:** 47. **Land area:** 6,425 sq. mi. **Acres forested land:** 1,986,000. **Location:** Hawaiian Islands lie in the North Pacific, 2,397 mi. SW from San Francisco. **Climate:** temperate, mountain regions cooler; Waialeale, on Kauai, wettest spot in the U.S. annual rainfall 451 in. **Topography:** islands are tops of a chain of submerged volcanic mountains; active volcanoes: Mauna Loa, Kilauea. **Capital:** Honolulu.

Economy. Principal industries: tourism, defense and other government, sugar refining, pineapple and diversified agriculture, aquaculture, fishing, motion pictures, manufacturing. **Principal manufactured goods:** sugar, canned pineapple, clothing, foods, printing and publishing. **Agriculture: Chief crops:** sugar, pineapples, macadamia nuts, fruits, coffee, vegetables, melons, and floriculture. **Livestock:** 230,000 cattle; 49,000 hogs/pigs; 1.15 mln. poultry. **Minerals** (1984): $54 mln.; cement, crushed stone. **Commercial fishing** (1983): $17.9 mln. **Chief ports:** Honolulu, Nawiliwili, Barber's Point, Kahului, Hilo. **International airports at:** Honolulu. **Value of construction** (1984): $880.7 mln. **Employment distribution:** 22.8% serv.; 20.4% gvt.; 23.9% trade. **Per capita income** (1984): $12,761. **Unemployment** (1984): 5.6%. **Tourism** (1982): visitors spent $3.7 bln.

Finance. No. banks (1983): 18; **No. savings assns.** (1983): 5.

Federal government. No. federal civilian employees (Mar. 1984): 22,868. **Avg. salary:** $25,774. **Notable federal facilities:** Pearl Harbor Naval Shipyard; Hickam AFB; Schofield Barracks.

Energy. Electricity production (1984, mwh, by source): Hydroelectric: 15,000; Mineral: 6.6 mln.

Education. No. schools (1982): 232 public elem. and second.; 12 higher ed. **Avg. salary, public school teachers** (1984): $24,628.

State data. Motto: The life of the land is perpetuated in righteousness. **Flower:** Hibiscus. **Bird:** Hawaiian goose. **Tree:** Candlenut. **Song:** Hawaii Ponoi. **Entered union** Aug. 21, 1959; rank, 50th. **State fair** at: Honolulu; late May through mid-June.

History. Polynesians from islands 2,000 mi. to the south settled the Hawaiian Islands, probably about 700 A.D. First European visitor was British Capt. James Cook, 1778. Missionaries arrived, 1820, taught religion, reading and writing. King Kamehameha III and his chiefs created the first Constitution and a Legislature which set up a public school system. Sugar production began in 1835 and it became the dominant industry. In 1893, Queen Liliuokalani was deposed, followed, 1894, by a republic headed by Sanford B. Dole. Annexation by the U.S. came in 1898.

Tourist attractions. Natl. Memorial Cemetery of the Pacific, USS Arizona Memorial, Pearl Harbor; Hawaii Volcanoes, Haleakala National Parks; Polynesian Cultural Center, Diamond Head, Waikiki Beach, Nuuanu Pali, Oahu.

Famous Islanders include Bernice Pauahi Bishop, John A. Burns, Father Joseph Damien, Sanford B. Dole, Wallace R. Farrington, Hiram L. Fong, Daniel K. Inouye, Duke Kahanamoku, King Kameheha the Great, Queen Kaahumanu, Queen Liliuokalani.

Chamber of Commerce: Dillingham Bldg., 735 Bishop St., Honolulu, HI 96813.

Idaho

Gem State

People. Population (1984): 1,001,000; **rank:** 40. **Pop. density:** 12.1 per sq. mi. **Urban** (1980): 54.0%. **Racial distrib.** (1980): 95.5% White; 0.3% Black; Hispanic 36,615. **Net migration** (1970-83): +130,000.

Geography. Total area: 83,557 sq. mi.; **rank:** 13. **Land area:** 82,677 sq. mi. **Acres forested land:** 21,726,600. **Location:** Pacific Northwest-Mountain state bordering on British Columbia. **Climate:** tempered by Pacific westerly winds; drier, colder, continental clime in SE; altitude an important factor. **Topography:** Snake R. plains in the S; central region of mountains, canyons, gorges (Hells Canyon, 7,000 ft., deepest in N.A.); subalpine northern region. **Capital:** Boise.

Economy. Principal industries: agriculture, manufacturing, tourism, lumber, mining, electronics. **Principal manufactured goods:** processed foods, lumber and wood products, chemical products, primary metals, fabricated metal products, machinery, electronic components. **Agriculture: Chief crops:** potatoes, peas, sugar beets, alfalfa seed, wheat, hops, barley, plums and prunes, mint, onions, corn, cherries, apples, hay. **Livestock:** 1.89 mln. cattle; 120,000 hogs/pigs; 383,000 sheep; 1.27 mln. poultry. **Timber/lumber** (1983): yellow, white pine; Douglas fir; white spruce; 2.0 bln. bd. ft. **Minerals** (1984): $424 mln.; silver, copper, crushed stone. **Commercial fishing** (1983): $69,000. **Chief ports:** Lewiston. **Value of construction** (1984) $633.7 mln. **Employment distribution:** 21% trade; 15% serv., 14% manuf.; 10% agric. **Per capita income** (1984): $10,174. **Unemployment** (1984): 7.2%. **Tourism** (1982): travellers spent $1.2 bln.

Finance. No. banks (1983): 26; **No. savings assns.** (1983): 9.

Federal government. No. federal civilian employees (Mar. 1984): 7,093. **Avg. salary:** $24,767. **Notable federal facilities:** Ida. Nat'l. Engineering Lab, Idaho Falls; Nat'l. Reactor Testing Sta., Upper Snake River Plains.

Energy. Electricity production (1984, mwh, by source): Hydroelectric: 13.2 mln.

Education. No. schools (1982): 569 public elem. and second.; 9 higher ed. **Avg. salary, public school teachers** (1984): $19,700.

State data. Motto: Esto Perpetua (It is perpetual). **Flower:** Syringa. **Bird:** Mountain bluebird. **Tree:** White pine. **Song:** Here We Have Idaho. **Entered union** July 3, 1890; rank, 43d. **State fair** at: Boise, late Aug.; and Blackfoot, early Sept.

History. Exploration of the Idaho area began with Lewis and Clark, 1805-06. Next came fur traders, setting up posts, 1809-34, and missionaries, establishing missions, 1830s-1850s. Mormons made their first permanent settlement at Franklin, 1860. Idaho's Gold Rush began that same year, and brought thousands of permanent settlers. Strangest of the Indian Wars was the 1,300-mi. trek in 1877 of Chief Joseph and the Nez Perce tribe, pursued by troops that caught them a few miles short of the Canadian border. In 1890, Idaho adopted a progressive Constitution and became a state.

Tourist attractions. Hells Canyon, deepest gorge in N.A.; Craters of the Moon; Sun Valley, year-round resort in the Sawtooth Mtns.; Crystal Falls Cave; Shoshone Falls; Lava Hot Springs; Lake Pend Oreille; Lake Coeur d'Alene; Sawtooth Natl. Recreation Area; River of No Return Wilderness Area.

Famous Idahoans include William E. Borah, Frank Church, Fred T. Dubois, Chief Joseph, Sacagawea.

Tourist Information: Department of Commerce, Room 108, State House, Boise, ID 83720.

Illinois

The Prairie State

People. Population (1984): 11,511,000; **rank:** 5. **Pop. density:** 206.5 per sq. mi. **Urban** (1980): 83.3%. **Racial distrib.** (1980): 80.7% White; 14.6% Black; Hispanic 635,525. **Net migration** (1970-80): −686,300.

Geography. Total area: 56,400 sq. mi.; **rank:** 24. **Land area:** 55,748 sq. mi. **Acres forested land:** 3,810,400. **Location:** east-north central state; western, southern, and eastern boundaries formed by Mississippi, Ohio, and Wabash Rivers, respectively. **Climate:** temperate; typically cold, snowy winters, hot summers. **Topography:** prairie and fertile plains throughout; open hills in the southern region. **Capital:** Springfield.

Economy. Principal industries: manufacturing, wholesale and retail trade, finance, insurance, real estate, agriculture, services. **Principal manufactured goods:** machinery, electric and electronic equipment, foods, primary and fabricated metals, chemical products, printing and publishing. **Agriculture: Chief crops:** corn, soybeans, wheat, oats, hay. **Livestock** (1984): 2.6 mln. cattle; 5.4 mln. hogs/pigs; 145,000 sheep; 2.86 mln. poultry. **Timber/lumber** (1983): oak, hickory, maple, cottonwood; 63 mln. bd. ft. **Minerals** (1984): $446.5 mln.; mostly crushed stone, cement, sand & gravel. **Commercial fishing** (1983): $1.9 mln. **Chief ports:** Chicago. **International airports at:** Chicago. **Value of construction** (1984): $7.1 bln. **Employment distribution:** 21.3% manuf.; 24.7% trade; 22.6% serv.; 1% agric. **Per capita income** (1984): $13,728. **Unemployment** (1984) 9.1%. **Tourism** (1984): out-of-state visitors spent $6.1 bln.

Finance. No. banks (1983): 1,297; **No. savings assns.** (1983): 274.

Federal government. No. federal civilian employees (Mar. 1984): 53,564. **Avg. salary:** $24,991. **Notable federal facilities:** Fermi Nat'l. Accelerator Lab; Argonne Nat'l. Lab; Ft. Sheridan; Rock Island; Great Lakes, Rantoul, Scott Field.

Energy. Electricity production (1984, mwh, by source): Hydroelectric: 124,000; Mineral: 65.9 mln.; Nuclear: 34.0 mln.

Education. No. schools (1982): 4,188 public elem. and second.; 157 higher ed. **Avg. salary, public school teachers** (1984): $25,829.

State data. Motto: State sovereignty—national union. **Flower:** Native violet. **Bird:** Cardinal. **Tree:** White oak. **Song:** Illinois. **Entered union** Dec. 3, 1818; **rank,** 21st. **State fair at:** Springfield; early Aug.

History. Fur traders were the first Europeans in Illinois, followed shortly, 1673, by Jolliet and Marquette, and, 1680, La Salle, who built a fort near present Peoria. First settlements were French, at Fort St. Louis on the Illinois River, 1692, and Kaskaskia, 1700. France ceded the area to Britain, 1763; Amer. Gen. George Rogers Clark, 1778, took Kaskaskia from the British without a shot. Defeat of Indian tribes in Black Hawk War, 1832, and railroads in 1850s, inspired immigration.

Tourist attractions: Lincoln shrines at Springfield, New Salem, Sangamon; Cahokia Mounds, E. St. Louis; Starved Rock State Park; Crab Orchard Wildlife Refuge; Mormon settlement at Nauvoo; Fts. Kaskaskia, Chartres, Massac (parks).

Famous Illinoisans include Jane Addams, Saul Bellow, Jack Benny, Ray Bradbury, Gwendolyn Brooks, William Jennings Bryan, St. Francis Xavier Cabrini, Clarence Darrow, Stephen A. Douglas, James T. Farrell, Ulysses S. Grant, Ernest Hemingway, Abraham Lincoln, Edgar Lee Masters, Ronald Reagan, Carl Sandburg, Adlai Stevenson, Frank Lloyd Wright.

Tourist Information: Illinois Dept. of Commerce and Community Affairs, 620 E. Adams St., Springfield, IL 62701.

Indiana

Hoosier State

People. Population (1984): 5,498,000; **rank:** 14. **Pop. density:** 152.3 per sq. mi. **Urban** (1980): 64.2%. **Racial distrib.** (1980): 91.1% White; 7.5% Black; Hispanic 87,020. **Net migration** (1980-83): −134,000.

Geography. Total area: 36,291 sq. mi.; **rank:** 38. **Land area:** 36,097 sq. mi. **Acres forested land:** 3,942,900. **Location:** east north-central state; Lake Michigan on northern border. **Climate:** 4 distinct seasons with a temperate climate. **Topography:** hilly southern region; fertile rolling plains of central region; flat, heavily glaciated north; dunes along Lake Michigan shore. **Capital:** Indianapolis.

Economy. Principal industries: manufacturing, wholesale and retail trade, agriculture, government, services. **Principal manufactured goods:** primary and fabricated metals, transportation equipment, electrical and electronic equipment, non-electrical machinery, chemical products, foods. **Agriculture: Chief crops** (1983): corn, soybeans, wheat, hay. **Livestock** (1983): 1.7 mln. cattle; 4.4 mln. hogs/pigs; 118,000 sheep; 23.5 mln. poultry. **Timber/lumber:** oak, tulip, beech, sycamore; 252 mln. bd. ft. **Minerals** (1984): $293.0 mln.; mostly crushed stone, abrasives, cement, gypsum, lime, sand & gravel. **Commercial fishing** (1983): $60,000. **Chief ports:** Lake Michigan facility, east of Gary, Southwind Maritime Centre at Mt. Vernon. **International airports at:** Indianapolis. **Value of construction** (1984): $3.6 bln. **Employment distribution** (1983): 28.7% manuf.; 22.9% trade; 18.0% serv. **Per capita income** (1984): $11,799. **Unemployment** (1984): 8.6%. **Tourism** (1983): tourists spent $2.3 bln.

Finance. No. banks (1983): 396; **No. savings assns.** (1983): 117.

Federal government. No. federal civilian employees (Mar. 1984): 23,569. **Avg. salary:** $23,404. **Notable federal facilities:** Naval Avionics Ctr.; Ft. Benjamin Harrison; Grissom AFB; Navy Weapons Support Ctr., Crane.

Energy. Electricity production (1984 mwh, by source): Hydroelectric: 436,000; Mineral: 79.3 mln.

Education. No. schools (1982): 2,006 public elem. and second.; 74 higher ed. **Avg. salary, public school teachers** (1984): $23,089.

State data. Motto: Crossroads of America. **Flower:** Peony. **Bird:** Cardinal. **Tree:** Tulip poplar. **Song:** On the Banks of the Wabash, Far Away. **Entered union** Dec. 11, 1816; **rank,** 19th. **State fair at:** Indianapolis; mid-Aug.

History: Pre-historic Indian Mound Builders of 1,000 years ago were the earliest known inhabitants. A French trading post was built, 1731-32, at Vincennes and La Salle visited the present South Bend area, 1679 and 1681. France ceded the area to Britain, 1763. During the Revolution, American Gen. George Rogers Clark captured Vincennes, 1778, and defeated British forces 1779; at war's end Britain ceded the area to the U.S. Miami Indians defeated U.S. troops twice, 1790, but were beaten, 1794, at Fallen Timbers by Gen. Anthony Wayne. At Tippecanoe, 1811, Gen. William H. Harrison defeated Tecumseh's Indian confederation.

Tourist attractions. Lincoln, George Rogers Clark memorials; Wyandotte Cave; Vincennes, Tippecanoe sites; Indiana Dunes; Hoosier Nat'l. Forest; Benjamin Harrison Home.

Famous "Hoosiers" include Ambrose Burnside, Hoagy Carmichael, Eugene V. Debs, Theodore Dreiser, Paul Dresser, Cole Porter, Gene Stratton Porter, Ernie Pyle, James Whitcomb Riley, Booth Tarkington, Lew Wallace, Wendell L. Willkie, Wilbur Wright.

Chamber of Commerce: One North Capital, Indianapolis, IN 46204.

Iowa

Hawkeye State

People. Population (1984): 2,910,000; **rank:** 29. **Pop. density:** 52.0 per sq. mi. **Urban** (1980): 58.6%. **Racial distrib.** (1980): 97.4% White; 1.4% Black; Hispanic 15,852. **Net migration** (1970-80): −60,491.

Geography. Total area: 56,290 sq. mi.; **rank:** 25. **Land area:** 55,941 sq. mi. **Acres forested land:** 1,561,300. **Location:** Midwest state bordered by Mississippi R. on the E and Missouri R. on the W. **Climate:** humid, continental. **Topography:** Watershed from NW to SE; soil especially rich and land level in the N central counties. **Capital:** Des Moines.

Economy. Principal industries: manufacturing, agriculture. **Principal manufactured goods:** tires, farm machinery, electronic products, appliances, office furniture, chemicals, fertilizers, auto accessories. **Agriculture: Chief crops:** silage and grain corn, soybeans, oats, hay. **Livestock** (1983): 2.5 mln. cattle; 22.6 mln. hogs/pigs; 336,000 sheep; 7.6 mln. poultry. **Timber/lumber:** red cedar. **Minerals** (1984): $259.7 mln.; mostly crushed stone, cement, sand & gravel. **Commercial fishing** (1983): 1.5 mln. **Value of construction** (1984): 1.7 bln. **Employment distribution** (1984): 25.2% trade; 20.1% serv; 20.1% manuf.; 19.9% gvt. **Per capita income** (1984): $12,090. **Unemployment** (1984): 7.0%. **Tourism** (1982): tourists spent $1.6 bln.

Finance. No. banks (1983): 642; **No. savings assns.** (1983): 51.

Federal government. No. federal civilian employees (Mar. 1984): 7,787. **Avg. salary:** $23,748.

Energy. Electricity production (1984, mwh, by source): Hydroelectric: 917,000; Mineral: 11.1 mln.; Nuclear: 2.7 mln.

Education. No. schools (1982): 1,718 public elem. and second.; 60 higher ed. **Avg. salary, public school teachers** (1984): $20,934.

State data. Motto: Our liberties we prize and our rights we will maintain. **Flower:** Wild rose. **Bird:** Eastern goldfinch. **Tree:** Oak. **Rock:** Geode. **Entered union** Dec. 28, 1846; **rank,** 29th. **State fair** at: Des Moines; mid-to-late Aug.

History. A thousand years ago several groups of prehistoric Indian Mound Builders dwelt on Iowa's fertile plains. Marquette and Jolliet gave France its claim to the area, 1673. It became U.S. territory through the 1803 Louisiana Purchase. Indian tribes were moved into the area from states further east, but by mid-19th century were forced to move on to Kansas. Before and during the Civil War, Iowans strongly supported Abraham Lincoln and became traditional Republicans.

Tourist attractions. Herbert Hoover birthplace and library, West Branch; Effigy Mounds Nat'l. Monument, Marquette, a pre-historic Indian burial site; Amana colonies; Davenport Municipal Art Gallery's collection of Grant Wood's paintings and memorabilia.

Famous Iowans include James A. Van Allen, Marquis Childs, Buffalo Bill Cody, Susan Glaspell, James Norman Hall, Harry Hansen, Billy Sunday, Carl Van Vechten, Henry Wallace, Meredith Willson, Grant Wood.

Tourist information: Visitors and Tourism, Iowa Development Commission, 600 E. Court, Suite A, Des Moines, IA 50309.

Kansas

Sunflower State

People. Population (1984): 2,438,000; **rank:** 32. **Pop. density:** 29.8 per sq. mi. **Urban** (1980): 66.7%. **Racial distrib.** (1980): 91.7% White; 5.3% Black; Hispanic 63,333. **Net migration** (1970-80): −20,334.

Geography. Total area: 82,264 sq. mi.; **rank:** 14. **Land area:** 81,787 sq. mi. **Acres forested land:** 1,344,400. **Location:** West North Central state, with Missouri R. on E. **Climate:** temperate but continental, with great extremes bet. summer and winter. **Topography:** hilly Osage Plains

in the E; central region level prairie and hills; high plains in the W. **Capital:** Topeka.

Economy. Principal industries: agriculture, machinery, mining, aerospace. **Principal manufactured goods:** processed foods, aircraft, petroleum products, farm machinery. **Agriculture: Chief crops:** wheat, sorghum, corn, hay. **Livestock:** 6.0 mln. cattle; 1.53 mln. hogs/pigs; 225,000 sheep; 1.89 mln. poultry. **Timber/lumber:** oak, walnut. **Minerals** (1984): $297.4 mln.; cement, salt, crushed stone. **Commercial fishing** (1983): $165,000 **Chief ports:** Kansas City. **International airports at:** Wichita. **Value of construction** (1984): $2.3 bln. **Employment distribution** (1984): 20.1% trade; 15.7% manuf.; 16.6% gvt.; 15.5% serv. **Per capita income** (1984): $13,319. **Unemployment** (1984): 5.2%. **Tourism** (1981): out-of-state visitors spent $1.5 bln.

Finance. No. banks (1983): 624; **No. savings assns.** (1983): 63.

Federal government. No. federal civilian employees (Mar. 1984): 14,035. **Avg. salary:** $22,964. **Notable federal facilities:** McConnell AFB; Fts. Riley, Leavenworth.

Energy. Electricity production (1984, mwh, by source): Hydroelectric: 7,000; Mineral: 26.2 mln.

Education. No. schools (1982): 1,518 public elem. and second.; 53 higher ed. **Avg. salary, public school teachers** (1984): $21,208.

State data. Motto: Ad Astra per Aspera (To the stars through difficulties). **Flower:** Native sunflower. **Bird:** Western meadowlark. **Tree:** Cottonwood. **Song:** Home on the Range. **Entered union** Jan. 29, 1861; **rank,** 34th. **State fair** at: Hutchinson; 2d week of Sept.

History. Coronado marched through the Kansas area, 1541; French explorers came next. The U.S. took over in the Louisiana Purchase, 1803. In the pre-war North-South struggle over slavery, so much violence swept the area it was called Bleeding Kansas. Railroad construction after the war made Abilene and Dodge City terminals of large cattle drives from Texas.

Tourist attractions. Eisenhower Center and "Place of Meditation," Abilene; Agricultural Hall of Fame and National Ctr., Bonner Springs, displays farm equipment; Dodge City; Ft. Scott; Kansas Cosmosphere and Space Discovery Center, Hutchinson.

Famous Kansans include Thomas Hart Benton, John Brown, Walter P. Chrysler, Amelia Earhart, Cyrus Holliday, William Inge, Walter Johnson, Alf Landon, Carry Nation, Gordon Parks, William Allen White.

Chamber of Commerce: 500 First National Tower, One Townsite Plaza, Topeka, KS 66603.

Kentucky

Bluegrass State

People. Population (1984): 3,723,000 **rank:** 23. **Pop. density:** 93.9 per sq. mi. **Urban** (1980): 50.9% **Racial Distrib.** (1980): 92.3% White; 7.1% Black; Hispanic (1980): 27,406. **Net migration** (1970-80): +206,237.

Geography. Total area: 40,409 sq. mi.; **rank:** 37. **Land area:** 39,650 sq. mi. **Acres forested land:** 12,160,800. **Location:** east south central state, bordered on N by Illinois, Indiana, Ohio; on E by West Virginia and Virginia; in S by Tennessee; on W by Missouri. **Climate:** moderate, with plentiful rainfall. **Topography:** mountainous in E; rounded hills of the Knobs in the N; Bluegrass, heart of state; wooded rocky hillsides of the Pennyroyal; Western Coal Field; the fertile Purchase the SW. **Capital:** Frankfort.

Economy. Principal industries: manufacturing, coal mining, construction, agriculture. **Principal manufactured goods:** nonelectrical machinery, food products, electrical & electronic products, chemical & allied products, primary metals. **Agriculture: Chief crops:** tobacco, soybeans, corn, wheat, hay, fruit. **Livestock:** 2.7 mln. cattle; 920,000 hogs/pigs; 23,000 sheep; 2.1 mln. chickens. **Timber/lumber** (1983): hardwoods, pines; 296 mln. bd. ft. **Minerals** (1984): $259.7 mln.; crushed stone, ball clay, lime, primary aluminum. **Commercial fishing** (1978): $923,000. **Chief ports:** Paducah, Louisville, Covington, Owensboro,

Ashland, Henderson County, Lyon County, Hickman-Fulton County. **International airports at:** Covington. **Value of construction** (1984): $2.5 bln. **Employment distribution:** mfg. 20.9%; trade 23.0%; gvt. 15.5%; serv. 19.4%. **Per capita income** (1984): $10,374. **Unemployment** (1984): 9.3%. **Tourism** (1982): tourists spent $2.1 bln.

Finance. No. banks (1983): 338; **No. savings assns.** (1983): 71.

Federal government. No. federal civilian employees (Mar. 1984): 25,817. **Avg. salary:** $22,145. **Notable federal facilities:** U.S. Gold Bullion Depository; Ft. Knox; Addiction Research Center and Federal Correction Institution, Lexington.

Energy. Electricity production (1984, mwh, by source): Hydroelectric: 3.5 mln.; Mineral: 56.4 mln.

Education. No. schools (1982): 1,341 public elem. and second.; 57 higher ed. **Avg. salary, public school teachers** (1984): $20,100.

State data. Motto: United we stand, divided we fall. **Flower:** Goldenrod. **Bird:** Cardinal. **Tree:** Kentucky coffee tree. **Song:** My Old Kentucky Home. **Entered union** June 1, 1792; rank, 23rd. **State fair** at: Louisville.

History. Kentucky was the first area west of the Alleghenies settled by American pioneers; first permanent settlement, Harrodsburg, 1774. Daniel Boone blazed the Wilderness Trail through the Cumberland Gap and founded Fort Boonesborough, 1775. Indian attacks, spurred by the British, were unceasing until, during the Revolution, Gen. George Rogers Clark captured British forts in Indiana and Illinois, 1778. In 1792, after Virginia dropped its claims to the region, Kentucky became the 15th state.

Tourist attractions. Kentucky Derby and accompanying festivities, Louisville; Land Between the Lakes Nat'l. Recreation Area encompassing Kentucky Lake and Lake Barkley; Mammoth Cave with 300 mi. of explored passageways, 200-ft. high rooms, blind fish, and Echo River, 360 ft. below ground; Old Ft. Harrod State Park; Lincoln birthplace, Hodgenville; My Old Kentucky Home, Bardstown.

Famous Kentuckians include Muhammad Ali, John James Audubon, Alben Barkley, Daniel Boone, Louis D. Brandeis, John C. Breckinridge, Kit Carson, Albert B. "Happy" Chandler, Henry Clay, Jefferson Davis, John Fox Jr., John Marshall Harlan, Abraham Lincoln, Thomas Hunt Morgan, Elizabeth Madox Roberts, Col. Harland Sanders, Jesse Stuart, Adlai Stevenson, Zachary Taylor, Robert Penn Warren.

Chamber of Commerce: 452 Versailles Rd., P.O. Box 817, Frankfort, KY 40602.

Louisiana

Pelican State

People. Population (1984): 4,462,000; **rank:** 18. **Pop. density:** 99.3 per sq. mi. **Urban** (1980): 68.7%. **Racial distrib.** (1980): 69.2% White; 29.4% Black; Hispanic 99,105. **Net migration** (1980-83): +79,000.

Geography. Total area: 48,523 sq. mi.; **rank:** 31. **Land area:** 44,930 sq. mi. **Acres forested land:** 14,558,100. **Location:** south central Gulf Coast state. **Climate:** subtropical, affected by continental weather patterns. **Topography:** lowlands of marshes and Mississippi R. flood plain; Red R. Valley lowlands; upland hills in the Florida Parishes; average elevation, 100 ft. **Capital:** Baton Rouge.

Economy. Principal industries: wholesale and retail trade, government, manufacturing, construction, transportation, mining. **Principal manufactured goods:** chemical products, foods, transportation equipment, electronic equipment, apparel, petroleum products. **Agriculture: Chief crops:** soybean, sugarcane, rice, corn, cotton, sweet potatoes, melons, pecans. **Livestock:** 1.3 mln. cattle; 240,000 hogs/pigs; 21,000 sheep; 3.2 mln. poultry. **Timber/lumber** (1983): pines, hardwoods, oak; 633 mln. bd. ft. **Minerals** (1984): Led U.S. in salt, second in Frasch sulfur. Total nonfuel minerals $568.3 mln., mostly salt, sulfur, cement, sand & gravel, stone. **Commercial fishing**

(1983): $230.3 mln. **Chief ports:** New Orleans, Baton Rouge, Lake Charles, S. Louisiana Port Commission at Place. **International airports at:** New Orleans. **Value of construction** (1984): $4.3 bln. **Employment distribution:** 29% trade; 25% gvt.; 24% serv.; 14% manuf.; 9% constr. **Per capita income** (1984): $10,850. **Unemployment** (1984): 10.0%. **Tourism** (1981): out-of-state visitors spent $3.3 bln.

Finance. No. banks (1983): 286; **No. savings assn.** (1983): 103.

Federal government. No. federal civilian employees (Mar. 1984): 20,043. **Avg. salary:** $23,073. **Notable federal facilities:** Barksdale, England, Ft. Polk military bases; Strategic Petroleum Reserve, New Orleans; Michoud Assembly Plant, New Orleans; U.S. Public Service Hospital, Carville.

Energy. Electricity production (1984, mwh, by source): Mineral: 39.3 mln.

Education. No. schools (1982): 1,462 public elem. and second.; 32 higher ed. **Avg. salary, public school teachers** (1984): $19,690.

State data. Motto: Union, justice and confidence. **Flower:** Magnolia. **Bird:** Eastern brown pelican. **Tree:** Cypress. **Song:** Give Me Louisiana. **Entered union** Apr. 30, 1812; rank, 18th. **State fair** at: Shreveport; Oct.

History. The area was first visited, 1530, by Cabeza de Vaca and Panfilo de Narvaez. The region was claimed for France by LaSalle, 1682. First permanent settlement was by French at Biloxi, now in Mississippi, 1699. France ceded the region to Spain, 1762, took it back, 1800, and sold it to the U.S., 1803, in the Louisiana Purchase. During the Revolution, Spanish Louisiana aided the Americans. Admitted to statehood, 1812, Louisiana was the scene of the Battle of New Orleans, 1815.

Louisiana Creoles are descendants of early French and/or Spanish settlers. About 4,000 Acadians, French settlers in Nova Scotia, Canada, were forcibly transported by the British to Louisiana in 1755 (an event commemorated in Longfellow's *Evangeline*) and settled near Bayou Teche; their descendants became known as Cajuns. Another group, the Islenos, were descendants of Canary Islanders brought to Louisiana by a Spanish governor in 1770. Traces of Spanish and French survive in local dialects.

Tourist attractions. Mardi Gras, French Quarter, Superdome, Dixieland jazz, all New Orleans; Battle of New Orleans site; Longfellow-Evangeline Memorial Park; Kent House Museum, Alexandria; Hodges Gardens, Natchiloches.

Famous Louisianians include Louis Armstrong, Pierre Beauregard, Judah P. Benjamin, Braxton Bragg, Grace King, Huey Long, Leonidas K. Polk, Henry Miller Shreve, Edward D. White Jr.

Tourist Information: State Dept. of Commerce, P.O. Box 94185, Baton Rouge, LA 70804-9185.

Maine

Pine Tree State

People. Population (1984): 1,156,000; **rank:** 38. **Pop. density:** 37.4 per sq. mi. **Urban** (1980): 47.5% **Racial distrib.** (1980): 98.3% White; 0.3% Black; Hispanic: 5,005. **Net migration** (1970-83): +76,131.

Geography. Total area: 33,215 sq. mi.; **rank:** 39. **Land area:** 30,920 sq. mi. **Acres forested land:** 17,718,300. **Location:** New England state at northeastern tip of U.S. **Climate:** Southern interior and coastal, influenced by air masses from the S and W; northern clime harsher, avg. +100 in. snow in winter. **Topography:** Appalachian Mtns. extend through state; western borders have rugged terrain; long sand beaches on southern coast; northern coast mainly rocky promontories, peninsulas, fjords. **Capital:** Augusta.

Economy. Principal industries: manufacturing, services, trade, government, agriculture, fisheries, forestry. **Principal manufactured goods:** paper and wood products, textiles, leather, processed foods. **Agriculture: Chief crops:** potatoes, apples, blueberries, sweet corn,

peas, beans. **Livestock:** 141,000 cattle; 9,000 hogs/pigs; 17,000 sheep; 17.2 mln. poultry. **Timber/lumber** (1983): pine, spruce, fir; more 1.3 bln. bd ft. **Minerals** (1984): $34.1 mln.; sand & gravel, crushed stone. **Commercial fishing** (1983): $107.9 mln. **Chief ports:** Searsport, Portland, Eastport. **International airports at:** Portland, Bangor. **Value of construction** (1984): $681.7 mln. **Employment distribution** (1983): 25.8% manuf.; 22.2% trade; 19.6% gvt.; 19.9% serv. **Per capita income** (1984): $10,678. **Unemployment** (1984): 6.1% **Tourism** (1984): $700 mln.

Finance. No. banks (1983): 52; **No. savings assns.** (1983): 14.

Federal government. No. federal civilian employees (Mar. 1984): 4,696. **Avg. salary:** $23,043. **Notable federal facilities:** Kittery Naval Shipyard; Brunswick Naval Air Station; Loring Air Force Base.

Energy. Electricity production (1984, mwh, by source): Hydroelectric: 2.0 mln.; Mineral: 2.1 mln.; Nuclear: 5.1 mln.

Education. No. schools (1982): 745 public elem. and second.; 29 higher ed. **Avg. salary, public school teachers** (1984): $18,329.

State data. Motto: Dirigo (I direct). **Flower:** White pine cone and tassel. **Bird:** Chickadee. **Tree:** Eastern white pine. **Song:** State of Maine Song. **Entered union:** Mar. 15, 1820; rank, 23d.

History. Maine's rocky coast was explored by the Cabots, 1498-99. French settlers arrived, 1604, at the St. Croix River; English, 1607, on the Kennebec. In 1691, Maine was made part of Massachusetts. In the Revolution, a Maine regiment fought at Bunker Hill; a British fleet destroyed Falmouth (now Portland), 1775, but the British ship Margaretta was captured near Machiasport. In 1820, Maine broke off from Massachusetts, became a separate state.

Tourist attractions. Acadia Nat'l. Park, Bar Harbor, on Mt. Desert Is.; Bath Iron Works and Marine Museum; Boothbay (Harbor) Railway Museum; Portland Art Museum; Sugarloaf/USA Ski Area; Ogunquit, Portland, York.

Famous "Down Easters" include James G. Blaine, Cyrus H.K. Curtis, Hannibal Hamlin, Longfellow, Sir Hiram and Hudson Maxim, Edna St. Vincent Millay, Kate Douglas Wiggin, Ben Ames Williams.

Chamber of Commerce and Industry: 126 Sewall St., Augusta, ME 04330.

Maryland

Old Line State, Free State

People. Population (1984): 4,349,000; rank: 19. **Pop. density:** 439.7 per sq. mi. **Urban** (1980): 80.3% **Racial distrib.** (1980): 74.9% White; 22.7% Black; Hispanic 64,740. **Net migration** (1970-80): +48,000.

Geography. Total area: 10,577 sq. mi.; rank: 42. **Land area:** 9,891 sq. mi. **Acres forested land:** 2,653,200. **Location:** Middle Atlantic state stretching from the Ocean to the Allegheny Mtns. **Climate:** continental in the west; humid subtropical in the east. **Topography:** Eastern Shore of coastal plain and Maryland Main of coastal plain, piedmont plateau, and the Blue Ridge, separated by the Chesapeake Bay. **Capital:** Annapolis.

Economy. Principal industries: food, manufacturing, tourism. **Principal manufactured goods:** food and kindred products, primary metals, electric and electronic equipment. **Agriculture: Chief crops:** tobacco, corn, soybeans. **Livestock:** 405,000 cattle; 200,000 hogs/pigs; 19,000 sheep; 4.4 mln. poultry. **Timber/lumber:** hardwoods. **Minerals** (1984): $232.9 mln.; crushed stone, sand & gravel, clay, shale. **Commercial fishing** (1983): $45.5 mln. **Chief ports:** Baltimore. **International airports at:** Baltimore. **Value of construction** (1984): 4.7 bln. **Employment distribution:** 24% government; 23.8% wholesale and retail trade; 19.9% services and mining. **Per capita income** (1984): $14,111. **Unemployment** (1984): 5.4%. **Tourism** (1980): tourists spent $3 bln.

Finance. No. banks (1983): 92; **No. savings assns.** (1983): 56.

Federal government. No. federal civilian employees (Mar. 1983): 105,601. **Avg. salary:** $27,843. **Notable federal facilities:** U.S. Naval Academy, Annapolis; Natl. Agric. Research Cen.; Ft. George C. Meade, Aberdeen Proving Ground.

Energy. Electricity production (1984, mwh, by source): Hydroelectric: 2.0 mln.; Mineral: 22.0 mln.; Nuclear: 11.7 mln.

Education. No. schools (1982): 1,217 public elem. and second.; 57 higher ed. **Avg. salary, public school teachers** (1984): $25,861.

State data. Motto. Fatti Maschii, Parole Femine (Manly deeds, womanly words). **Flower:** Black-eyed susan. **Bird:** Baltimore oriole. **Tree:** White oak. **Song:** Maryland, My Maryland. **Seventh** of the original 13 states to ratify Constitution, Apr. 28, 1788. **State fair** at: Timonium; end-Aug. to Sept. 7.

History. Capt. John Smith first explored Maryland, 1608. William Claiborne set up a trading post on Kent Is. in Chesapeake Bay, 1631. Britain granted land to Cecilius Calvert, Lord Baltimore, 1632; his brother led 200 settlers to St. Marys River, 1634. The bravery of Maryland troops in the Revolution, as at the Battle of Long Island, won the state its nickname, The Old Line State. In the War of 1812, when a British fleet tried to take Fort McHenry, Marylander Francis Scott Key, 1814, wrote *The Star-Spangled Banner.*

Tourist Attractions. Racing events include the Preakness, at Pimlico track, Baltimore; the International at Laurel Race Course; the John B. Campbell Handicap at Bowie. Also Annapolis yacht races; Ocean City summer resort; restored Ft. McHenry, Baltimore, near which Francis Scott Key wrote *The Star-Spangled Banner;* Antietam Battlefield, 1862, near Hagerstown; South Mountain Battlefield, 1862; Edgar Allan Poe house, Baltimore; The State House, Annapolis, 1772, the oldest still in use in the U.S.

Famous Marylanders include Benjamin Banneker, Francis Scott Key, H.L. Mencken, William Pinkney, Upton Sinclair, Roger B. Taney, Charles Willson Peale.

Chamber of Commerce: 60 West St., Suite 405, Annapolis, MD 21401.

Massachusetts

Bay State, Old Colony

People. Population (1984): 5,798,000; rank: 12. **Pop. density:** 740.9 per sq. mi. **Urban** (1980): 83.8% **Racial distrib.** (1980): 93.4% White; 3.8% Black; Hispanic 141,043. **Net migration** (1970-79): —145,225.

Geography. Total area: 8,257 sq. mi.; rank: 45. **Land area:** 7,826 sq. mi. **Acres forested land:** 2,952,300. **Location:** New England state along Atlantic seaboard. **Climate:** temperate, with colder and drier clime in western region. **Topography:** jagged indented coast from Rhode Island around Cape Cod; flat land yields to stony upland pastures near central region and gentle hilly country in west; except in west, land is rocky, sandy, and not fertile. **Capital:** Boston.

Economy. Principal industries: manufacturing, services, trade, construction. **Principal manufactured goods** (1983): electronics, machinery, instruments, fabricated metals, printing and publishing. **Agriculture: Chief crops:** cranberries, greenhouse, nursery, vegetables. **Livestock** (1983): 120,000 cattle; 50,000 hogs/pigs; 8,000 sheep; 125,000 horses, ponies; 3.6 mln. poultry. **Timber/lumber** (1983): white pine, oak, other hard woods; 84 mln. bd. ft. **Minerals** (1984): $101.1 mln.; mostly sand & gravel, crushed stone, lime. **Commercial fishing** (1983): $244.9 mln. **Chief ports:** Boston, Fall River, New Bedford, Salem, Gloucester. **International airport at:** Boston. **Value of construction** (1984): $4.7 bln. **Employment distribution** (1983): 25.6% manuf.; 23.7% serv.; 22.3% trade. **Per capita income** (1984): $14,574. **Unemployment** (1984): 4.8%. **Tourism** (1983): out-of-state visitors spent $3.0 bln.

Finance. No. banks (1983): 286; **No. savings assns.** (1983): 17.

Federal government. No. federal civilian employees (Mar. 1984): 30,490. **Avg. salary:** $24,846. **Notable federal facilities:** Ft. Devens; U.S. Customs House, John Fitzgerald Kennedy Federal Bldg., Boston; Q.M. Laboratory, Natick.

Energy. Electricity production (1984, mwh, by source): Hydroelectric: 234,000; Mineral: 31.6 mln.; Nuclear: 1.0 mln.

Education. No. schools (1982): 1,837 public elem. and second.; 117 higher ed. **Avg. salary, public school teachers** (1984): $24,110.

State data. Motto: Ense Petit Placidam Sub Libertate Quietem (By the sword we seek peace, but peace only under liberty). **Flower:** Mayflower. **Bird:** Chickadee. **Tree:** American elm. **Song:** All Hail to Massachusetts. **Sixth** of the original 13 states to ratify Constitution, Feb. 6, 1788.

History. The Pilgrims, seeking religious freedom, made their first settlement at Plymouth, 1620; the following year they gave thanks for their survival with the first Thanksgiving Day. Indian opposition reached a high point in King Philip's War, 1675-76, won by the colonists. Demonstrations against British restrictions set off the "Boston Massacre," 1770, and Boston "tea party," 1773. First bloodshed of the Revolution was at Lexington, 1775.

Tourist attractions. Cape Cod with Provincetown artists' colony; Freedom Trail; Berkshire Music Festival, Tanglewood; Boston "Pops" concerts; Museum of Fine Arts, Arnold Arboretum, all Boston; Jacob's Pillow Dance Festival, West Becket; historical Shaker Village, Old Sturbridge, Lexington, Concord, Salem, Plymouth Rock.

Famous "Bay Staters" include Samuel Adams, Louisa May Alcott, Horatio Alger, Clara Barton, Emily Dickinson, Emerson, Hancock, Hawthorne, Oliver W. Holmes, Winslow Homer, Elias Howe, Samuel F.B. Morse, Poe, Revere, Sargent, Thoreau, Whistler, Whittier.

Tourist information: Massachusetts Dept. of Commerce, 100 Cambridge St., Boston, MA 02202.

eral facilities: Isle Royal, Sleeping Bear Dunes national parks.

Energy. Electricity production (1984, mwh, by source): Hydroelectric: 954,000 mln; Mineral: 56.9 mln.; Nuclear: 14.1 mln.

Education. No. schools (1982): 3,688 public elem. and second.; 92 higher ed. **Avg. salary, public school teachers** (1984): $28,401.

State data. Motto: Si Quaeris Peninsulam Amoenam Circumspice (If you seek a pleasant peninsula, look about you). **Flower:** Apple blossom. **Bird:** Robin. **Tree:** White pine. **Song:** Michigan, My Michigan. **Entered union** Jan. 26, 1837; rank, 26th. **State fair** at: Detroit, Aug. 23–Sept. 2; Upper Peninsula (Escanaba) Aug. 13–Aug. 18.

History. French fur traders and missionaries visited the region, 1616, set up a mission at Sault Ste. Marie, 1641, and a settlement there, 1668. The whole region went to Britain, 1763. During the Revolution, the British led attacks from the area on American settlements to the south until Anthony Wayne defeated their Indian allies at Fallen Timbers, Ohio, 1794. The British returned, 1812, seized Ft. Mackinac and Detroit. Oliver H. Perry's Lake Erie victory and William H. Harrison's troops, who carried the war to the Thames River in Canada, 1813, freed Michigan once more.

Tourist attractions. Henry Ford Museum, Greenfield Village, reconstruction of a typical 19th cent. American village, both in Dearborn; Michigan Space Ctr., Jackson; Tahquamenon *(Hiawatha)* Falls; DeZwaan windmill and Tulip Festival, Holland; "Soo Locks," St. Marys Falls Ship Canal, Sault Ste. Marie.

Famous Michiganders include George Custer, Paul de Kruif, Thomas Dewey, Edna Ferber, Henry Ford, Edgar Guest, Betty Hutton, Robert Ingersoll, Will Kellogg, Danny Thomas, Stewart Edward White.

Chamber of Commerce: 200 N. Washington Sq., Suite 400, Lansing, MI 48933.

Michigan

Great Lake State, Wolverine State

People. Population (1984): 9,075,000; **rank:** 8. **Pop. density:** 159.7 per sq. mi. **Urban** (1980): 70.7%. **Racial distrib.** (1980): 84.9% White; 12.9% Black; Hispanic 162,388. **Net migration** (1975-80): −169,123.

Geography. Total area: 58,216 sq. mi.; **rank:** 23. **Land area:** 56,817 sq. mi. **Acres forested land:** 19,270,400. **Location:** east north central state bordering on 4 of the 5 Great Lakes, divided into an Upper and Lower Peninsula by the Straits of Mackinac, which link lakes Michigan and Huron. **Climate:** well-defined seasons tempered by the Great Lakes. **Topography:** low rolling hills give way to northern tableland of hilly belts in Lower Peninsula; Upper Peninsula is level in the east, with swampy areas; western region is higher and more rugged. **Capital:** Lansing.

Economy. Principal industries: manufacturing, mining, agriculture, food processing, tourism, fishing. **Principal manufactured goods:** automobiles, machine tools, chemicals, foods, primary metals and metal products, plastics. **Agriculture: Chief crops:** corn, winter wheat, soybeans, dry beans, oats, hay, sugar beets, honey, asparagus, sweet corn, apples, cherries, grapes, peaches, blueberries, flowers. **Livestock** (1983): 1.5 mln. cattle; 690,000 mln. hogs/pigs; 100,000 sheep; 8.7 mln. poultry. **Timber/lumber:** maple, oak, aspen; 266 mln. bd. ft. **Minerals** (1984): $1.3 bln.; mostly cement, salt, crushed stone, sand & gravel. **Commercial fishing** (1983): $6.4 mln. **Chief ports:** Detroit, Saginaw River, Escanaba. **International airports at:** Detroit, Grand Rapids. **Value of construction** (1984): $4.9 bln. **Employment distribution** (1983): 28% manuf.; 20% serv.; **Per capita income** (1984): $12,518. **Unemployment** (1984): 11.2%. **Tourism** (1983): out-of-state visitors spent $3.4 bln.

Finance. No. banks (1983): 374; **No. savings assns.** (1983): 50.

Federal government. No. federal civilian employees (Mar. 1984): 26,640. **Avg. salary:** $24,863. **Notable fed-**

Minnesota

North Star State, Gopher State

People. Population (1984): 4,162,000; **rank:** 21. **Pop. density:** 52.5 per sq. mi. **Urban** (1980): 66.9%. **Racial distrib.** (1980): 96.5% White; 1.3% Black; Hispanic 32,124. **Net migration** (1980-82): −12,800 est.

Geography. Total area: 84,068 sq. mi.; **rank:** 12. **Land area:** 79,289 sq. mi. **Acres forested land:** 16,709,200. **Location:** north central state bounded on the E by Wisconsin and Lake Superior, on the N by Canada, on the W by the Dakotas, and on the S by Iowa. **Climate:** northern part of state lies in the moist Great Lakes storm belt; the western border lies at the edge of the semi-arid Great Plains. **Topography:** central hill and lake region covering approx. half the state; to the NE, rocky ridges and deep lakes; to the NW, flat plain; to the S, rolling plains and deep river valleys. **Capital:** St. Paul.

Economy. Principal industries: agri business, forest products, mining, manufacturing, tourism. **Principal manufactured goods:** food processing, non-electrical machinery, chemicals, paper, electric and electronic equipment, printing and publishing, instruments, fabricated metal products. **Value added by manufacture** (1978): $10.9 bln. **Agriculture: Chief crops:** corn, soybeans, wheat, sugar beets, sunflowers, barley. **Livestock** (1984): 3.6 mln. cattle; 4.3 mln. hogs/pigs; 255,000 sheep; 40.9 mln. poultry. **Timber/lumber** (1983): needle-leaves and hardwoods; 170 mln. bd. ft. **Minerals** (1984): 1.7 bln.; mostly iron ore, manganiferous ore, sand and gravel, peat. **Commercial fishing** (1983): $3.3 mln. **Chief ports:** Duluth, St. Paul, Minneapolis. **International airports at:** Minneapolis-St. Paul. **Value of construction** (1984): $3.8 bln. **Employment distribution** (1984): 25.2% trade; 20.5% manuf.; 22.9% serv.; 16.0% gvt. **Per capita income** (1984): $13,219. **Unemployment** (1983): 6.3%. **Tourism** (1982): out-of-state visitors spent $1.4 bln.

Finance. No. banks (1983): 754; **No. savings assns.** (1983): 39.

Federal government. No. federal civilian employees (Mar. 1984): 13,020. **Avg. salary:** $25,145.

Energy. Electricity production (1984, mwh, by source): Hydroelectric: 826,000; Mineral: 19.3 mln.; Nuclear: 8.3 mln.

Education. No. schools (1982): 1,588 public elem. and second.; 67 higher ed. **Avg. salary, public school teachers** (1984): $25,920.

State data. Motto: L'Etoile du Nord (The star of the north). **Flower:** Pink and white lady's-slipper. **Bird:** Common loon. **Tree:** Red pine. **Song:** Hail! Minnesota. **Entered union** May 11, 1858; rank, 32d. **State fair** at: Saint Paul; end-Aug. to early Sept.

History. Fur traders and missionaries from French Canada opened the region in the 17th century. Britain took the area east of the Mississippi, 1763. The U.S. took over that portion after the Revolution and in 1803 bought the western area as part of the Louisiana Purchase. The U.S. built present Ft. Snelling, 1820, bought lands from the Indians, 1837. Sioux Indians staged a bloody uprising, 1862, and were driven from the state.

Tourist attractions. Minnehaha Falls, Minneapolis, inspiration for Longfellow's *Hiawatha;* over 10,000 lakes; 64 state parks; 20 historical sites; Minneapolis Aquatennial; Ordway Theater, St. Paul; Guthrie Theater, Minneapolis; professional baseball, football, hockey. Voyageurs Nat'l. Park, a water wilderness along the Canadian border; Mayo Clinic, Rochester; St. Paul Winter Carnival.

Famous Minnesotans include F. Scott Fitzgerald, Cass Gilbert, Hubert Humphrey, Sister Elizabeth Kenny, Sinclair Lewis, Paul Manship, E. G. Marshall, William and Charles Mayo, Walter F. Mondale, Charles Schulz, Harold Stassen, Thorstein Veblen.

Tourist Information: Minnesota Tourism Division, 419 N. Robert St., 240 Bremer Bldg., St. Paul, MN 55101.

Mississippi
Magnolia State

People. Population (1984): 2,598,000; **rank:** 31. **Pop. density:** 54.9 per sq. mi. **Urban** (1980): 47.3%. **Racial distrib.** (1980): 64.1% White; 35.2% Black; Hispanic (1970): 8,182. **Net migration** (1970-80): +84,879.

Geography. Total area: 47,716 sq. mi.; **rank:** 32. **Land area:** 47,296 sq. mi. **Acres forested land:** 16,715,600. **Location:** south central state bordered on the W by the Mississippi R. and on the S by the Gulf of Mexico. **Climate:** semi-tropical, with abundant rainfall, long growing season, and extreme temperatures unusual. **Topography:** low, fertile delta bet. the Yazoo and Mississippi rivers; loess bluffs stretching around delta border; sandy Gulf coastal terraces followed by piney woods and prairie; rugged, high sandy hills in extreme NE followed by black prairie belt. Pontotoc Ridge, and flatwoods into the north central highlands. **Capital:** Jackson.

Economy. Principal industries: manufacturing, food processing, seafood, government, wholesale and retail trade, agriculture. **Principal manufactured goods:** apparel, transportation equipment, lumber and wood products, foods, electrical machinery and equipment. **Agriculture: Chief crops:** soybeans, cotton, rice, catfish. **Livestock:** 1.80 mln. cattle; 410,000 hogs/pigs; 4,500 sheep; 10.18 mln. poultry. **Timber/lumber** (1983): pine, oak, hardwoods; 1.6 bln. bd. ft. **Minerals** (1984): $95.4 mln., mostly cement, clays, sand & gravel, crushed stone. **Commercial fishing** (1983): $50.2 mln. **Chief ports:** Pascagoula, Vicksburg, Gulfport, Natchez, Greenville. **Value of construction** (1984): $1.7 bln. **Employment distribution** (1983): 21.8% manuf.; 19.3% gvt.; 17.6% trade; 13.4% serv. **Per capita income** (1983): $8,857. **Unemployment** (1984): 10.8%. **Tourism** (1982): out-of-state visitors spent $1.2 bln.

Finance. No. banks (1983): 162; **No. savings assns.** (1983): 47.

Federal government. No. federal civilian employees (Mar. 1984): 17,957. **Avg. salary:** $23,588. **Notable federal facilities:** Columbus, Keesler AF bases; Meridian Naval Air Station, NASA/NOAA International Earth Sciences Center.

Energy. Electricity production (1984, mwh, by source): Mineral 15.2 mln; Nuclear 165,000.

Education. No. schools (1982): 816 public elem. and second.; 42 higher ed. **Avg. salary, public school teachers** (1984): $15,971.

State data. Motto: Virtute et Armis (By valor and arms). **Flower:** Magnolia. **Bird:** Mockingbird. **Tree:** Magnolia. **Song:** Go, Mississippi! **Entered union** Dec. 10, 1817; rank, 20th. **State fair** at: Jackson; Fall.

History. De Soto explored the area, 1540, discovered the Mississippi River, 1541. La Salle traced the river from Illinois to its mouth and claimed the entire valley for France, 1682. First settlement was the French Ft. Maurepas, near Ocean Springs, 1699. The area was ceded to Britain, 1763; American settlers followed. During the Revolution, Spain seized part of the area and refused to leave even after the U.S. acquired title at the end of the Revolution, finally moving out, 1798. Mississippi seceded 1861. Union forces captured Corinth and Vicksburg and destroyed Jackson and much of Meridian.

Tourist attractions. Vicksburg National Military Park and Cemetery, other Civil War sites; Natchez Trace; Indian mounds; estate pilgrimage at Natchez; Mardi Gras and blessing of the shrimp fleet, Aug., both in Biloxi.

Famous Mississippians include Dana Andrews, William Faulkner, L.Q.C. Lamar, Elvis Presley, Leontyne Price, Charlie Pride, Eudora Welty.

Chamber of Commerce: P.O. Box 1849, Jackson, MS 39205.

Missouri
Show Me State

People. Population (1984): 5,008,000; **rank:** 15. **Pop. density:** 72.6 per sq. mi. **Urban** (1980): 68.1%. **Racial distrib.** (1980): 88.3% White; 10.4% Black; Hispanic 51,667. **Net migration** (1970-80): +10,726.

Geography. Total area: 69,686 sq. mi.; **rank:** 19. **Land area:** 68,995 sq. mi. **Acres forested land:** 12,876,000. **Location:** West North central state near the geographic center of the conterminous U.S.; bordered on the E by the Mississippi R., on the NW by the Missouri R. **Climate:** continental, susceptible to cold Canadian air, moist, warm Gulf air, and drier SW air. **Topography:** Rolling hills, open, fertile plains, and well-watered prairie N of the Missouri R.; south of the river land is rough and hilly with deep, narrow valleys; alluvial plain in the SE; low elevation in the west. **Capital:** Jefferson City.

Economy. Principal industries: agriculture, manufacturing, aerospace, tourism. **Principal manufactured goods:** transportation equipment, food and related products, electrical and electronic equipment, chemicals. **Agriculture: Chief crops:** soybeans, corn, wheat, cotton. **Livestock** (1983): 5.2 mln. cattle; 3.6 mln. hogs/pigs; 128,000 sheep; 20 mln. poultry. **Timber/lumber** (1983): oak, hickory; 169 mln. bd. ft. **Minerals** (1984): $749.7 mln., mostly cement, lead, zinc. **Commercial fishing** (1983) $376,000. **Chief ports:** St. Louis, Kansas City. **International airports at:** St. Louis, Kansas City. **Value of construction** (1984): $3.8 bln. **Employment distribution** (1983): 24% trade; 21.4% serv.; 21% manuf.; 17% gvt.; 7% transp. **Per capita income** (1984): $12,129. **Unemployment** (1984): 7.2%. **Tourism** (1983): total travelers spent $4.5 bln.

Finance. No. banks (1983): 739; **No. savings assns.** (1983): 85.

Federal government. No. federal civilian employees (Mar. 1984): 43,928. **Avg. salary:** $24,007. **Notable federal facilities:** Federal Reserve banks, St. Louis, Kansas City; Ft. Leonard Wood, Rolla; Jefferson Barracks, St. Louis; Whiteman AFB, Knob Noster.

Energy. Electricity production (1984 mwh, by source): Hydroelectric: 1.6 mln.; Mineral: 53.5 mln; Nuclear 920,000.

Education. No. schools (1982): 2,015 public elem. and second.; 92 higher ed. **Avg. salary, public school teachers** (1984): $20,452.

State data. Motto: Salus Populi Suprema Lex Esto (The welfare of the people shall be the supreme law). **Flower:** Hawthorn. **Bird:** Bluebird. **Tree:** Dogwood. **Song:** Missouri Waltz. **Entered union** Aug. 10, 1821; rank, 24th. **State fair** at: Sedalia; 3d week in Aug.

History. DeSoto visited the area, 1541. French hunters and lead miners made the first settlement, c. 1735, at Ste. Genevieve. The U.S. acquired Missouri as part of the Louisiana Purchase, 1803. The fur trade and the Santa Fe Trail provided prosperity; St. Louis became the "jump-off" point for pioneers on their way West. Pro- and anti-slavery forces battled each other there during the Civil War.

Tourist attractions. Mark Twain Area, Hannibal; Pony Express Museum, St. Joseph; Harry S. Truman Library, Independence; Gateway Arch, St. Louis; Silver Dollar City, Branson Worlds of Fun, Kansas City; Lake of the Ozarks, Churchill Memorial, Fulton.

Famous Missourians include Thomas Hart Benton, George Caleb Bingham, Gen. Omar Bradley, George Washington Carver, Walter Cronkite, Dale Carnegie, Walt Disney, T.S. Eliot, Jesse James, J. C. Penney, John J. Pershing, Joseph Pulitzer, Ginger Rogers, Bess Truman, Harry Truman, Mark Twain, Tennessee Williams.

Chamber of Commerce: 400 E. High St., P.O. Box 149, Jefferson City, MO 65101.

Montana

Treasure State

People. Population (1984): 824,000; **rank:** 44. **Pop. density:** 5.66 per sq. mi. **Urban** (1980): 52.9%. **Racial distrib.** (1980): 94.0% White; 0.2% Black; 5.6% Other (includes American Indians); Hispanic 9,974. **Net migration** (1970-82): +34,000.

Geography. Total area: 147,138 sq. mi.; **rank:** 4. **Land area:** 145,587 sq. mi. **Acres forested land:** 22,559,300. **Location:** Mountain state bounded on the E by the Dakotas, on the S by Wyoming, on the S/SW by Idaho, and on the N by Canada. **Climate:** colder, continental climate with low humidity. **Topography:** Rocky Mtns. in western third of the state; eastern two-thirds gently rolling northern Great Plains. **Capital:** Helena.

Economy. Principal industries: manufacturing, agriculture, mining, tourism. **Principal manufactured goods:** lumber and wood products, petroleum products, primary metals and minerals, farm machinery, processed foods. **Agriculture: Chief crops:** wheat, barley, sugar beets, hay, flax, oats. **Livestock** (1983): 3.15 mln. cattle; 180,000 hogs/pigs; 509,000 sheep; 940,200 poultry. **Timber/lumber** (1983): Douglas fir, pines, larch; 1.3 bln. bd. ft. **Minerals** (1984): $248 mln. mostly metallics. **International airports** at: Great Falls, Billings. **Value of construction** (1984): 723.8 mln. **Employment distribution** (1983): 23% trade; 19% gvt.; 22% serv.; 11% agric; 7% manuf. **Per capita income** (1984): $10,216. **Unemployment** (1984): 7.4%. **Tourism** (1983): out-of-state visitors spent $423 mln.

Finance. No. banks (1983): 169; **No. savings assns.** (1983): 9.

Federal government. No. federal civilian employees (Mar. 1984): 8,404. **Avg. salary:** $24,308. **Notable federal facilities:** Malmstrom AFB; Ft. Peck, Hungry Horse, Libby, Yellowtail dams.

Energy. Electricity production (1984, mwh, by source): Hydroelectric: 11.1 mln; Mineral: 7.7 mln.

Education. No. schools (1982): 782 public elem. and second.; 16 higher ed. **Avg. salary, public school teachers** (1984): $21,705.

State data. Motto: Oro y Plata (Gold and silver). **Flower:** Bitterroot. **Bird:** Western meadowlark. **Tree:** Ponderosa pine. **Song:** None. **Entered union** Nov. 8, 1889; rank, 41st. **State fair** at: Great Falls; end July to early Aug.

History. French explorers visited the region, 1742. The U.S. acquired the area partly through the Louisiana Pur-

chase, 1803, and partly through the explorations of Lewis and Clark, 1805-06. Fur traders and missionaries established posts in the early 19th century. Indian uprisings reached their peak with the Battle of the Little Big Horn, 1876. The coming of the Northern Pacific Railway, 1883, brought population growth.

Tourist attractions. Glacier National Park, on the Continental Divide, is a scenic and recreational wonderland, with 60 glaciers, 200 lakes, and many trout streams.

Also, Museum of the Plains Indian, Blackfeet Reservation near Browning; Custer Battlefield National Cemetery; Flathead Lake, in the NW, Lewis and Clark Cavern, Morrison Cave State Park, near Whitehall.

There are 7 Indian reservations, covering over 5 million acres; tribes are Blackfeet, Crow, Confederated Salish & Kootenai, Assiniboine, Gros Ventre, Sioux, Northern Cheyenne, Chippewa, Cree. Population of the reservations is approximately 25,500.

Famous Montanans include Gary Cooper, Marcus Daly, Chet Huntley, Will James, Myrna Loy, Mike Mansfield, Jeannette Rankin, Charles M. Russell, Brent Musberger.

Chamber of Commerce: 110 Neil Ave., P.O. Box 1730, Helena, MT 59624.

Nebraska

Cornhusker State

People. Population (1984): 1,606,000; **rank:** 36. **Pop. density:** 21.0 per sq. mi. **Urban** (1980): 62.9%. **Racial distrib.** (1980): 94.9% White; 3.1% Black; Hispanic 28,020. **Net migration** (1980-83): −13,000.

Geography. Total area: 77,227 sq. mi.; **rank:** 15. **Land area:** 76,483 sq. mi. **Acres forested land:** 1,029,100. **Location:** West North Central state with the Missouri R. for a N/NE border. **Climate:** continental semi-arid. **Topography:** till plains of the central lowland in the eastern third rising to the Great Plains and hill country of the north central and NW. **Capital:** Lincoln.

Economy. Principal industries: agriculture, food processing, manufacturing. **Principal manufactured goods:** foods, machinery, electric and electronic equipment, primary and fabricated metal products, chemicals. **Agriculture: Chief crops:** corn, sorghum, wheat, soy beans, hay, beans, popcorn, oats, potatoes, sugar beets. **Livestock:** 6.1 mln. cattle; 3.7 mln. hogs/pigs; 165,000 sheep; 4.0 mln. poultry. **Minerals** (1984): $102.4 mln.; mostly cement, crushed stone, sand & gravel. **Commercial fishing** (1983): $47,000. **Chief ports:** Omaha, Sioux City, Brownville, Blair, Plattsmouth, Nebraska City. **Value of construction** (1984): $1.1 bln. **Employment distribution:** 25.6% trade; 21.0% gvt.; 21.5% serv.; 14.2% manuf. **Per capita income** (1984): $12,280. **Unemployment** (1984): 4.4%. **Tourism** (1984): traveler expenditures $1.2 bln.

Finance. No. banks (1982): 482; **No. savings assns.** (1983): 23.

Federal government. No. federal civilian employees (Mar. 1984): 8,627. **Avg. salary:** $24,308. **Notable federal facilities:** Strategic Air Command Base, Omaha.

Energy. Electricity production (1984, mwh, by source): Hydroelectric: 1.3 mln.; Mineral: 10.9 mln.; Nuclear: 5.8 mln.

Education. No. schools (1982): 1,699 public elem. and second.; 28 higher ed. **Avg. salary, public school teachers** (1984): $20,153.

State data. Motto: Equality before the law. **Flower:** Goldenrod. **Bird:** Western meadowlark. **Tree:** Cottonwood. **Song:** Beautiful Nebraska. **Entered union** Mar. 1, 1867; rank, 37th. **State fair** at: Lincoln; Aug. 29-Sept. 7.

History. Spanish and French explorers and fur traders visited the area prior to the Louisiana Purchase, 1803. Lewis and Clark passed through, 1804-06. First permanent settlement was Bellevue, near Omaha, 1823. Many Civil War veterans settled under free land terms of the 1862 Homestead Act; struggles followed between homesteaders and ranchers.

Tourist attractions. Boys Town, founded by Fr. Flanagan, west of Omaha, is a self-contained community of un-

der-privileged and homeless boys. Arbor Lodge State Park, Nebraska City, is a memorial to J. Sterling Morton, founder of Arbor Day. Buffalo Bill Ranch State Historical Park, North Platte, contains Cody's home and memorabilia of his Wild West Show.

Also, Pioneer Village, Minden; Oregon Trail, landmarks, Scotts Bluff National Monument and Chimney Rock Historic Site.

Famous Nebraskans include Fred Astaire, Charles W. and William Jennings Bryan, Johnny Carson, Willa Cather, William F. "Buffalo Bill" Cody, Michael and Edward A. Cudahy, Loren Eiseley, Rev. Edward J. Flanagan, Henry Fonda, Rollin Kirby, Harold Lloyd, Wright Morris, Gen. John J. Pershing, Mari Sandoz, Malcolm X, Roscoe Pound.

Chamber of Commerce: Suite 200, 1320 Lincoln Mall, Box 95128, Lincoln, NE 68509.

Nevada

Sagebrush State, Battle Born State, Silver State

People. Population (1984): 911,000; **rank:** 43. **Pop. density:** 8.3 per sq. mi. **Urban** (1980): 85.3%. **Racial distrib.** (1980): 87.5% White; 6.3% Black; Hispanic 53,786. **Net migration** (1980-83): +765,000.

Geography. Total area: 110,540 sq. mi.; **rank:** 7. **Land area:** 109,889 sq. mi. **Acres forested land:** 7,683,300. **Location:** Mountain state bordered on N by Oregon and Idaho, on E by Utah and Arizona, on SE by Arizona, and on SW/W by California. **Climate:** semi-arid. **Topography:** rugged N-S mountain ranges; southern area is within the Mojave Desert; lowest elevation, Colorado R. Canyon, 470 ft. **Capital:** Carson City.

Economy. Principal industries: gaming, tourism, mining, manufacturing, government, agriculture, warehousing, trucking. **Principal manufactured goods:** gaming devices, electronics, chemicals, stone-clay-glass products. **Agriculture: Chief crops:** alfalfa, potatoes, hay, barley, wheat, cotton. **Livestock** (1984): 660,000 cattle; 14,000 hogs/pigs; 94,000 sheep; 13,000 poultry. **Timber/lumber:** pine, fir, juniper, spruce. **Minerals** (1984): $622 mln.; mostly barite, gold, mercury. **International airports** at Las Vegas, Reno. **Value of construction** (1984): $1.3 bln. **Employment distribution** (1985): 45% serv.; 20% trade; 14% gvt. **Per capita income** (1984): $13,216. **Unemployment** (1984): 7.8% **Tourism** (1981): out-of-state visitors spent $2.6 bln.

Finance. No. banks (1983): 15; **No. savings assns.** (1983): 7.

Federal government. No. federal civilian employees (Mar. 1984): 6,174. **Avg. salary:** $25,716. **Notable federal facilities:** Nevada Test Site; Hawthorne Munitions Plant.

Energy. Electricity production (1984, mwh, by source): Hydroelectric: 5.6 mln.; Mineral: 14.9 mln.

Education. No. schools (1982): 292 public elem. and second.; 8 higher ed. **Avg. salary, public school teachers** (1984): $22,520.

State data. Motto: All for our country. **Flower:** Sagebrush. **Bird:** Mountain bluebird. **Tree:** Single-leaf pinon. **Song:** Home Means Nevada. **Entered union** Oct. 31, 1864; **rank,** 36th. **State fair** at Reno; early Sept.

History. Nevada was first explored by Spaniards in 1776. Hudson's Bay Co. trappers explored the north and central region, 1825; trader Jedediah Smith crossed the state, 1826 and 1827. The area was acquired by the U.S., in 1848, at the end of the Mexican War. First settlement, Mormon Station, now Genoa, was est. 1849. In the early 20th century, Nevada adopted progressive measures such as the initiative, referendum, recall, and woman suffrage.

Tourist attractions. Legalized gambling provided the impetus for the development of resort areas Lake Tahoe, Reno, and Las Vegas. Ghost towns, rodeos, trout fishing, water sports and hunting important.

Notable are Helldorado Week in May, Las Vegas; Basque Festival, Elko; Reno Rodeo, 4th of July; Valley of Fire State Park, Overton; Death Valley, on the California border; Lehman Caves National Monument.

Famous Nevadans include Walter Van Tilburg Clark, Sarah Winnemucca Hopkins, Paul Laxalt, John William MacKay, Pat McCarran, Dat So La Lee, William Morris Stewart.

Tourist Information: Department of Economic Development, 1100 E. William St., Carson City, NV 89710.

New Hampshire

Granite State

People. Population (1984): 977,000; **rank:** 41. **Pop. density:** 108.2 per sq. mi. **Urban** (1980): 52.2%. **Racial distrib.** (1980): 98.8% White; 0.4% Black; Hispanic 5,587. **Net migration** (1980-82): +15,000.

Geography. Total area: 9,304 sq. mi.; **rank:** 44. **Land area:** 9,027 sq. mi. **Acres forested land:** 5,013,500. **Location:** New England state bounded on S by Massachusetts, on W by Vermont, on N/NW by Canada, on E by Maine and the Atlantic O. **Climate:** highly varied, due to its nearness to high mountains and ocean. **Topography:** low, rolling coast followed by countless hills and mountains rising out of a central plateau. **Capital:** Concord.

Economy. Principal industries: manufacturing, tourism, agriculture, trade, mining. **Principal manufactured goods:** machinery, computers, electrical & electronic equipment, pulp & paper, lumber & furniture, leather prod. **Agriculture: Chief crops:** dairy products, nursery and greenhouse products, hay, vegetables, apples, maple syrup & sugar prods. **Livestock** (1982): 69,207 cattle; 6,343 hogs/pigs; 9,000 sheep; 693,765 poultry. **Timber/lumber** (1983): white pine, hemlock, oak, birch; 903 mln. bd. ft. **Minerals** (1984): $21.1 mln.; mostly sand & gravel. **Commercial fishing** (1983): $4.3 mln. **Chief ports:** Portsmouth, Hampton, Rye. **Value of construction** (1984): $1.0 bln. **Employment distribution** (1983): 32.5% manuf.; 27% trade; 23% serv; 17 gvt. **Per capita income** (1984): $13,148. **Unemployment** (1984): 4.3%. **Tourism** (1984): out-of-state visitors spent $4.2 bln.

Finance. No. banks (1983): 88; **No. savings assns.** (1983): 8.

Federal government. No. federal civilian employees (Mar. 1984): 11,680. **Avg. salary:** $23,348. **Notable federal facilities:** Pease Air Base, Newington.

Energy. Electricity production (1984, mwh, by source): Hydroelectric: 1.1 mln.; Mineral: 5.2 mln.

Education. No. schools (1982): 431 elem. and second.; 27 higher ed. **Avg. salary, public school teachers** (1984): $18,577.

State data. Motto: Live free or die. **Flower:** Purple lilac. **Bird:** Purple finch. **Tree:** White birch. **Song:** Old New Hampshire. **Ninth** of the original 13 states to ratify the Constitution, June 21, 1788.

History. First explorers to visit the New Hampshire area were England's Martin Pring, 1603, and Champlain, 1605. First settlement was Little Harbor, near Rye, 1623. Indian raids were halted, 1759, by Robert Rogers' Rangers. Before the Revolution, New Hampshire men seized a British fort at Portsmouth, 1774, and drove the royal governor out, 1775. Three regiments served in the Continental Army and scores of privateers raided British shipping.

Tourist attractions. Mt. Washington, highest peak in Northeast, hub of network of trails; Lake Winnipesaukee; White Mt. Natl. Forest; Crawford, Franconia, Pinkham notches in White Mt. region—Franconia famous for the Old Man of the Mountains, described by Hawthorne as the Great Stone Face; the Flume, a spectacular gorge; the aerial tramway on Cannon Mt; Strawbery Banke, Portsmouth; Shaker Village, Canterbury.

Famous New Hampshirites include Salmon P. Chase, Ralph Adams Cram, Mary Baker Eddy, Daniel Chester French, Robert Frost, Horace Greeley, Sarah Buell Hale, Franklin Pierce, Augustus Saint-Gaudens, Daniel Webster.

Tourist Information: Department of Resources and Economic Development, Office of Vacation Travel, P.O. Box 856, Concord, NH 03301.

New Jersey
Garden State

People. Population (1984): 7,515,000; **rank:** 9. **Pop. density:** 999.2 per sq. mi. **Urban** (1980): 89.0%. **Racial distrib.** (1980): 83.2% White; 12.5% Black; Hispanic 491,867. **Net migration** (1980-83): +7,000.

Geography. Total area: 7,836 sq. mi.; **rank:** 46. **Land area:** 7,521 sq. mi. **Acres forested land:** 1,928,400. **Location:** Middle Atlantic state bounded on the N and E by New York and the Atlantic O., on the S and W by Delaware and Pennsylvania. **Climate:** moderate, with marked difference bet. NW and SE extremities. **Topography:** Appalachian Valley in the NW also has highest elevation, High Pt., 1,801 ft.; Appalachian Highlands, flat-topped NE-SW mountain ranges; Piedmont Plateau, low plains broken by high ridges (Palisades) rising 400-500 ft.; Coastal Plain, covering three-fifths of state in SE, gradually rises from sea level to gentle slopes. **Capital:** Trenton.

Economy. Principal industries: trade, services, manufacturing. **Principal manufactured goods:** chemicals, electronic and electrical equipment, non-electrical machinery, fabricated metals. **Agriculture: Chief crops:** hay, corn, soybeans, tomatoes, blueberries, peaches, cranberries. **Livestock:** 95,000 cattle; 53,800 hogs/pigs; 11,900 sheep; 966,800 poultry. **Timber/lumber** (1983): pine, cedar, mixed hardwoods; 16 mln. bd. ft. **Minerals** (1984): $155.6 mln.; mostly crushed stone, sand & gravel. **Commercial fishing** (1983): $53.9 mln. **Chief ports:** Newark, Elizabeth, Hoboken, Ameri-Port (Delaware R.). **International airports at:** Newark. **Value of construction** (1984): $6.4 bln. **Employment distribution** (1984): 23.8% trade, 22.6% serv., 21.8% manuf., 15.7% govt. **Per capita income** (1984): $15,282. **Unemployment** (1984): 6.2%. **Tourism** (1984): tourists spent $9 bln.

Finance. No. banks (1983): 152; **No. savings assns.** (1983): 136.

Federal government. No. federal civilian employees (Mar. 1984): 39,044. **Avg. salary:** $25,438. **Notable federal facilities:** McGuire AFB Fort Dix; Fort Monmouth; Picatinny Arsenal; Lakewood Naval Air Station, Lakehurst Naval Air Engineering Center.

Energy. Electricity production (1984, mwh, by source): Mineral: 21.0 mln.; Nuclear: 5.6 mln.

Education. No. schools (1982): 2,207 public elem. and second.; 60 higher ed. **Avg. salary, public school teachers** (1984): $25,125.

State Data. Motto: Liberty and prosperity. **Flower:** Purple violet. **Bird:** Eastern goldfinch. **Tree:** Red oak. **Third** of the original 13 states to ratify the Constitution, Dec. 18, 1787. **State fair:** usually Sept.

History. The Lenni Lenape (Delaware) Indians had mostly peaceful relations with European colonists who arrived after the explorers Verrazano, 1524, and Hudson, 1609. The Dutch were first; when the British took New Netherland, 1664, the area between the Delaware and Hudson Rivers was given to Lord John Berkeley and Sir George Carteret. New Jersey was the scene of nearly 100 battles, large and small, during the Revolution, including Trenton, 1776, Princeton, 1777, Monmouth, 1778.

Tourist attractions. 127 miles of beaches; Miss America Pageant and hotel-casinos, Atlantic City; Grover Cleveland birthplace, Caldwell. Cape May Historic District; Edison Labs, W. Orange; Great Adventure amusement park; Liberty State Park; Meadowlands Sports Complex; Pine Barrens wilderness area; Princeton University; numerous Revolutionary War historical sites.

Famous New Jerseyites include Count Basie, Aaron Burr, James Fenimore Cooper, Stephen Crane, Thomas Edison, Albert Einstein, Alexander Hamilton, Joyce Kilmer, Gen. George McClellan, Thomas Paine, Molly Pitcher, Paul Robeson, Walter Schirra, Walt Whitman, Woodrow Wilson.

Chamber of Commerce: 5 Commerce St., Newark, NJ 07102.

New Mexico
Land of Enchantment

People. Population (1984): 1,424,000; **rank:** 37. **Pop. density:** 11.7 per sq. mi. **Urban** (1980): 72.1%. **Racial distrib.** (1980): 75.1% White; 1.8% Black; 15.3% Other (includes American Indians); Hispanic 476,089. **Major ethnic groups:** Spanish, Indian, English. **Net migration** (1970-82): +284,000.

Geography. Total area: 121,666 sq. mi.; **rank:** 5. **Land area:** 121,412 sq. mi. **Acres forested land:** 18,059,800. **Location:** southwestern state bounded by Colorado on the N, Oklahoma, Texas, and Mexico on the E and S, and Arizona on the W. **Climate:** dry, with temperatures rising or falling 5°F with every 1,000 ft. elevation. **Topography:** eastern third, Great Plains; central third Rocky Mtns. (85% of the state is over 4,000 ft. elevation); western third high plateau. **Capital:** Santa Fe.

Economy. Principal industries: extractive industries, tourism, agriculture. **Principal manufactured goods:** foods, electrical machinery, apparel, lumber, printing, transportation equipment. **Agriculture: Chief crops:** wheat, hay, sorghum, grain, onions, cotton, corn. **Livestock:** 1.72 mln. cattle; 72,000 hogs/pigs; 578,000 sheep; 1.21 mln. poultry. **Timber/lumber** (1983): Ponderosa pine, Douglas fir; 218 mln. bd. ft. **Minerals** (1984): $645.6 mln.; mostly potassium salts, sand & gravel. **International airports at:** Albuquerque. **Value of construction** (1984): $1.8 bln. **Employment distribution:** 23.0% serv.; 18.0% agric.; 10% manuf.; 8.9% gvt. **Per capita income** (1984): $10,330. **Unemployment** (1984): 7.5%. **Tourism** (1983): out-of-state visitors spent $1.47 bln.

Finance. No. banks (1983): 94; **No. savings assns.** (1983): 23.

Federal government. No. federal civilian employees (Mar. 1984): 22,023. **Avg. salary:** $23,935. **Notable federal facilities:** Kirtland, Cannon, Holloman AF bases; Los Alamos Scientific Laboratory; White Sands Missile Range.

Energy. Electricity production (1984, mwh, by source): Hydroelectric: 94,000; Mineral: 27.0 mln.

Education. No. schools (1982): 625 public elem. and second.; 20 higher ed. **Avg. salary, public school teachers** (1984): $22,064.

State data. Motto: Crescit Eundo (It grows as it goes). **Flower:** Yucca. **Bird:** Roadrunner. **Tree:** Pinon. **Song:** O, Fair New Mexico, Asi Es Nuevo Mexico. **Entered union** Jan. 6, 1912; rank, 47th. **State fair at:** Albuquerque; mid-Sept.

History. Franciscan Marcos de Niza and a black slave Estevan explored the area, 1539, seeking gold. First settlements were at San Juan Pueblo, 1598, and Santa Fe, 1610. Settlers alternately traded and fought with the Apaches, Comanches, and Navajos. Trade on the Santa Fe Trail to Missouri started 1821. The Mexican War was declared May, 1846, Gen. Stephen Kearny took Santa Fe, August. In the 1870s, cattlemen staged the famed Lincoln County War in which Billy (the Kid) Bonney played a leading role. Pancho Villa raided Columbus, 1916.

Tourist Attractions. Carlsbad Caverns, a national park, has caverns on 3 levels and the largest natural cave "room" in the world, 1,500 by 300 ft., 300 ft. high; White Sands Natl. Monument, the largest gypsum deposit in the world.

Pueblo ruins from 100 AD, Chaco Canyon; Acoma, the "sky city," built atop a 357-ft. mesa; 19 Pueblo, 4 Navajo, and 2 Apache reservations. Also, ghost towns, dude ranches, skiing, hunting, and fishing.

Famous New Mexicans include Billy (the Kid) Bonney, Kit Carson, Peter Hurd, Archbishop Jean Baptiste Lamy, Bill Mauldin, Georgia O'Keeffe, Kim Stanley, Lew Wallace.

Tourist information: New Mexico Travel Division, Bataan Bldg., Santa Fe, N.M. 87503.

New York

Empire State

People. Population (1984): 17,735,000; **rank:** 2. **Pop. density:** 370.8 per sq. mi. **Urban** (1980): 84.6%. **Racial distrib.** (1980): 79.5% White; 13.68% Black; Hispanic (1980): 1,659,245. **Net migration** (1980-83): −136,000.

Geography. Total area: 49,576 sq. mi.; **rank:** 30. **Land area:** 47,831 sq. mi. **Acres forested land:** 17,218,400. **Location:** Middle Atlantic state, bordered by the New England states, Atlantic Ocean, New Jersey and Pennsylvania, Lakes Ontario and Erie, and Canada. **Climate:** variable; the SE region moderated by the ocean. **Topography:** highest and most rugged mountains in the NE Adirondack upland; St. Lawrence-Champlain lowlands extend from Lake Ontario NE along the Canadian border; Hudson-Mohawk lowland follows the flows of the rivers N and W, 10-30 mi. wide; Atlantic coastal plain in the SE; Appalachian Highlands, covering half the state westward from the Hudson Valley, include the Catskill Mtns., Finger Lakes; plateau of Erie-Ontario lowlands. **Capital:** Albany.

Economy. Principal industries: manufacturing, finance, communications, tourism, transportation, services. **Principal manufactured goods:** books and periodicals, clothing and apparel, pharmaceuticals, machinery, instruments, toys and sporting goods, electronic equipment, automotive and aircraft components. **Agriculture: Chief crops:** apples, cabbage, cauliflower, celery, cherries, grapes, corn, peas, snap beans, sweet corn. **Products:** milk, cheese, maple syrup, wine. **Livestock:** 2.05 mln. cattle; 110,000 hogs/pigs; 61,000 sheep; 14.0 mln. poultry. **Timber/lumber** (1983): saw log production; 355 mln. bd. ft. **Minerals** (1984): $541.4 mln.; mostly stone, cement, salt. **Commercial fishing** (1983): $38.5 mln. **Chief ports:** New York, Buffalo, Albany. **International airports at:** New York, Buffalo, Syracuse, Massena, Ogdensburg, Watertown, Monroe and Sullivan counties. **Value of construction** (1984): $9.3 bln. **Employment distribution:** 1.3% agric.; 21% manuf.; 33% serv.; 19% trade. **Per capita income** (1984): $14,121. **Unemployment** (1984): 7.2%. **Tourism** (1983): tourists spent $12.4 bln.

Finance. No. banks (1983): 451; **No. savings assns.** (1983): 75.

Federal government. No. federal civilian employees (Mar. 1984): 69,546. **Avg. salary:** $24,165. **Notable federal facilities:** West Point Military Academy; Merchant Marine Academy; Ft. Drum; Griffiss, Plattsburgh AF bases; Watervliet Arsenal.

Energy. Electricity production (1984, mwh, by source): Hydroelectric: 26.6 mln.; Mineral: 61.4 mln.; Nuclear: 20.9 mln.

Education. No. schools (1982): 3,890 public elem. and second.; 296 higher ed. **Avg. salary, public school teachers** (1984): $29,000.

State data. Motto: Excelsior (Ever upward). **Flower:** Rose. **Bird:** Bluebird. **Tree:** Sugar maple. **Song:** I Love New York. **Eleventh** of the original 13 states to ratify the Constitution, July 26, 1788. **State fair** at: Syracuse, Aug. 23-Sept. 3.

History. In 1609 Henry Hudson discovered the river that bears his name and Champlain explored the lake, far upstate, which was named for him. Dutch built posts near Albany 1614 and 1624; in 1626 they settled Manhattan. A British fleet seized New Netherland, 1664. Ninety-two of the 300 or more engagements of the Revolution were fought in New York, including the Battle of Bemis Heights-Saratoga, a turning point of the war.

Tourist attractions. New York City; Adirondack and Catskill mtns.; Finger Lakes, Great Lakes; Long Island beaches; Thousand Islands; Niagara Falls; Saratoga Springs racing and spas; Philipsburg Manor, Sunnyside, the restored home of Washington Irving, The Dutch Church of Sleepy Hollow, all in North Tarrytown; Corning Glass Center and Steuben factory, Corning; Fenimore House, National Baseball Hall of Fame and Museum, both in Cooperstown; Ft. Ticonderoga overlooking lakes George and Champlain; Albany's Empire State Plaza, Lake Placid Olympic Village.

The Franklin D. Roosevelt National Historic Site, Hyde Park, includes the graves of Pres. and Mrs. Roosevelt, the family home since 1867, the Roosevelt Library. Sagamore Hill, Oyster Bay, the Theodore Roosevelt estate, includes his home.

Famous New Yorkers include Susan B. Anthony, Peter Cooper, George Eastman, Julia Ward Howe, Charles Evans Hughes, Henry and William James, Herman Melville, Alfred E. Smith, Elizabeth Cady Stanton, Walt Whitman.

Tourist information: N.Y. State Dept. of Commerce, 1 Commerce Plaza, Albany, NY 12245.

North Carolina

Tar Heel State, Old North State

People. Population (1984): 6,165,000; **rank:** 10. **Pop. density:** 126.3 per sq. mi. **Urban** (1980): 42.9%. **Racial distrib.** (1980): 75.8% White; 22.4% Black; Hispanic (1980): 56,607. **Net migration** (1970-80): +393,369.

Geography. Total area: 52,586 sq. mi.; **rank:** 28. **Land area:** 48,798 sq. mi. **Acres forested land:** 20,043,300. **Location:** South Atlantic state bounded by Virginia, South Carolina, Georgia, Tennessee, and the Atlantic O. **Climate:** sub-tropical in SE, medium-continental in mountain region; tempered by the Gulf Stream and the mountains in W. **Topography:** coastal plain and tidewater, two-fifths of state, extending to the fall line of the rivers; piedmont plateau, another two-fifths, 200 mi. wide of gentle to rugged hills; southern Appalachian Mtns. contains the Blue Ridge and Great Smoky mtns. **Capital:** Raleigh.

Economy. Principal industries: manufacturing, agriculture, tobacco, tourism. **Principal manufactured goods:** textiles, tobacco products, electrical/electronic equip., chemicals, furniture, food products, non-electrical machinery. **Agriculture: Chief crops:** tobacco, soybeans, corn, peanuts, small sweet potatoes, grains, vegetables, fruits. **Livestock:** 1.10 mln. cattle; 2.15 mln. hogs/pigs; 7,000 sheep; 19.2 mln. chickens. **Timber/lumber** (1983): yellow pine, oak, hickory, poplar, maple. 1.4 bln. bd. ft. **Minerals** (1984): Total $429.1 mln., mostly crushed stone, sand & gravel, feldspar. **Commercial fishing** (1983): $57.4 mln. **Chief ports:** Morehead City, Wilmington. **Value of construction** (1984): $5.6 bln. **Employment distribution:** 34.5% manuf.; 19.8% trade; 17.2% gvt.; 14.3% serv. **Per capita income** (1984): $10,758. **Unemployment** (1984): 6.7%. **Tourism** (1983): out-of-state visitors spent $3.4 bln.

Finance. No. banks (1983): 71; **No. savings assns.** (1983): 115.

Federal government. No. federal civilian employees (Mar. 1984): 27,715. **Avg. salary:** $22,629. **Notable federal facilities:** Ft. Bragg; Camp LeJeune Marine Base; U.S. EPA Research and Development Labs, Cherry Point Marine Corps Air Station.

Energy. Electricity production (1984, mwh, by source): Hydroelectric: 6.4 mln.; Mineral: 52.5 mln.; Nuclear: 20.2 mln.

Education. No. schools (1982): 1,986 public elem. and second.; 128 higher ed. **Avg. salary, public school teachers** (1984): $20,691.

State data. Motto: Esse Quam Videri (To be rather than to seem). **Flower:** Dogwood. **Bird:** Cardinal. **Tree:** Pine. **Song:** The Old North State. **Twelfth** of the original 13 states to ratify the Constitution, Nov. 21, 1789. **State fair** at: Raleigh; mid-Oct.

History. The first English colony in America was the first of 2 established by Sir Walter Raleigh on Roanoke Is., 1585 and 1587. The first group returned to England; the second, the "Lost Colony," disappeared without trace. Permanent settlers came from Virginia, c. 1660. Roused by British repressions, the colonists drove out the royal governor, 1775; the province's congress was the first to vote for independence; ten regiments were furnished to the Continental Army. Cornwallis' forces were defeated at Kings Mountain, 1780, and forced out after Guilford Courthouse, 1781.

Tourist attractions. Cape Hatteras and Cape Lookout national seashores; Great Smoky Mtns. (half in Tennessee); Guilford Courthouse and Moore's Creek parks, Rev-

olutionary battle sites; Bennett Place, NW of Durham, where Gen. Joseph Johnston surrendered the last Confederate army to Gen. Wm. Sherman; Ft. Raleigh, Roanoke Is., where Virginia Dare, first child of English parents in the New World, was born Aug. 18, 1587; Wright Brothers National Memorial, Kitty Hawk.

Famous North Carolinians include Richard J. Gatling, Billy Graham, Wm. Rufus King, Dolley Madison, Edward R. Murrow, Enos Slaughter, Moses Waddel.

Tourist information: Division of Travel & Tourism Development, P.O. Box 25249, Raleigh, NC 27611.

North Dakota

Peace Garden State

People. Population (1984): 686,000; **rank:** 46. **Pop. density:** 9.9 per sq. mi. **Urban** (1980): 48.8%. **Racial distrib.** (1980): 95.8% White; 0.39% Black; Hispanic (1980): 3,903. **Net migration** (1980-84): —6,800.

Geography. Total area: 70,665 sq. mi.; **rank:** 17. **Land area:** 69,273 sq. mi. **Acres forested land:** 421,800. **Location:** West North Central state, situated exactly in the middle of North America, bounded on the N by Canada, on the E by Minnesota, on the S by South Dakota, on the W by Montana. **Climate:** continental, with a wide range of temperature and moderate rainfall. **Topography:** Central Lowland in the E comprises the flat Red River Valley and the Rolling Drift Prairie; Missouri Plateau of the Great Plains on the W. **Capital:** Bismarck.

Economy. Principal industries: agriculture, mining, tourism, manufacturing. **Principal manufactured goods:** farm equipment, processed foods. **Agriculture: Chief crops:** spring wheat, durum, barley, rye, flaxseed, oats, potatoes, dried edible beans, honey, soybeans, sugarbeets, sunflowers, hay. **Livestock:** 2.1 mln. cattle; 260,000 hogs/pigs; 224,000 sheep; 1.5 mln. poultry. **Minerals** (1984): $12.7 mln. mostly sand & gravel, salt, lime. **Commercial fishing** (1983): $190,000. **International airports at:** Fargo, Grand Forks, Bismarck, Minot. **Value of construction** (1984): $596.8 mln. **Employment distribution:** 21.9% trade; 20.4% gvt.; 18.6% serv.; 17.2% agric. **Per capita income** (1984): $12,461. **Unemployment** (1984): 5.1%. **Tourism** (1983): out-of-state visitors spent $11.6 mln.

Finance No. banks (1983): 181; **No. savings assns.** (1983): 6.

Federal government. No. federal civilian employees (Mar. 1984): 5,093. **Avg. salary:** $22,900. **Notable federal facilities:** Strategic Air Command bases at Minot, Grand Forks; Northern Prairie Wildlife Research Center; Garrison Dam; Theodore Roosevelt Natl. Park; Grand Forks Energy Research Center; Ft. Union Natl. Historic Site.

Energy. Electricity production (1984, mwh, by source): Hydroelectric: 2.4 mln.; Mineral: 17.3 mln.

Education. No. schools (1982): 655 public elem. and second.; 18 higher ed. **Avg. salary, public school teachers** (1984): $19,900.

State data. Motto: Liberty and union, now and forever, one and inseparable. **Flower:** Wild prairie rose. **Bird:** Western Meadowlark. **Tree:** American elm. **Song:** North Dakota Hymn. **Entered union** Nov. 2, 1889; rank, 39th. **State fair** at: Minot; 3d week in July.

History. Pierre La Verendrye was the first French fur trader in the area, 1738, followed later by the English. The U.S. acquired half the territory in the Louisiana Purchase, 1803. Lewis and Clark built Ft. Mandan, spent the winter of 1804-05 there. In 1818, American ownership of the other half was confirmed by agreement with Britain. First permanent settlement was at Pembina, 1812. Missouri River steamboats reached the area, 1832; the first railroad, 1873, bringing many homesteaders. The state was first to hold a presidential primary, 1912.

Tourist attractions. International Peace Garden, a 2,200-acre tract extending across the border into Manitoba, commemorates the friendly relations between the U.S. and Canada; 65,000-acre Theodore Roosevelt Na-

tional Park, Badlands, contains the president's Elkhorn Ranch; Ft. Abraham Lincoln State Park and Museum, S of Mandan.

Famous North Dakotans include Maxwell Anderson, Angie Dickinson, John Bernard Flannagan; Louis L'Amour, Peggy Lee, Eric Sevareid, Vilhjalmur Stefansson, Lawrence Welk.

Chamber of Commerce: P.O. Box 2467, Fargo, ND 58108.

Ohio

Buckeye State

People. Population (1984): 10,752,000; **rank:** 7. **Pop. density:** 262.4 per sq. mi. **Urban** (1980): 73.3%. **Racial distrib.** (1980): 88.8% White; 9.9% Black; Hispanic (1980): 119,880. **Net migration** (1970-80): —635,662.

Geography. Total area: 41,222 sq. mi.; **rank:** 35. **Land area:** 40,975 sq. mi. **Acres forested land:** 6,146,600. **Location:** East North Central state bounded on the N by Michigan and Lake Erie; on the E and S by Pennsylvania, West Virginia, and Kentucky; on the W by Indiana. **Climate:** temperate but variable; weather subject to much precipitation. **Topography:** generally rolling plain; Allegheny plateau in E; Lake [Erie] plains extend southward; central plains in the W. **Capital:** Columbus.

Economy. Principal industries: manufacturing, tourism, government, trade. **Principal manufactured goods:** transportation equipment, machinery, primary and fabricated metal products. **Agriculture: Chief crops:** corn, hay, winter wheat, oats, soybeans. **Livestock** (1983): 1.9 mln. cattle; 2.1 mln. hogs/pigs; 265,000 sheep; 16.3 mln. poultry. **Timber/lumber** (1984): oak, ash, maple, walnut, beech; 269 mln. bd. ft. **Minerals** (1984): $554.9 mln.; mostly crushed stone, sand & gravel, salt, lime, clays, cement. **Commercial fishing** (1983): $1.5 mln. **Chief ports:** Toledo, Conneaut, Cleveland, Ashtabula. **International airports at:** Cleveland, Cincinnati, Columbus, Dayton. **Value of construction** (1984): $6.2 bln. **Employment distribution:** 23.8% manuf.; 20.6% trade; 19.5% serv.; 14.7% gvt. **Per capita income** (1984): $12,314. **Unemployment** (1984): 9.4%. **Tourism** (1982): travelers spent nearly $5.4 bln.

Finance. No. banks (1983): 344; **No. savings assns.** (1983): 229.

Federal government. No. federal civilian employees (Mar. 1984): 53,878. **Avg. salary:** $26,141. **Notable federal facilities:** Wright Patterson, Rickenbacker AF bases; Defense Construction Supply Center; Lewis Research Ctr.; Portsmouth Gaseous Diffusion Plant; Mound Laboratory.

Energy. Electricity production (1984, mwh, by source): Hydroelectric: 164,000; Mineral: 103.6 mln.; Nuclear: 4.3 mln.

Education. No. schools (1982): 3,824 public elem. and second.; 139 higher ed. **Avg. salary, public school teachers** (1984): $22,737.

State data. Motto: With God, all things are possible. **Flower:** Scarlet carnation. **Bird:** Cardinal. **Tree:** Buckeye. **Song:** Beautiful Ohio. **Entered union** Mar. 1, 1803; rank, 17th. **State fair** at: Columbus; mid-Aug.

History. LaSalle visited the Ohio area, 1669. American fur-traders arrived, beginning 1685; the French and Indians sought to drive them out. During the Revolution, Virginians defeated the Indians, 1774, but hostilities were renewed, 1777. The region became U.S. territory after the Revolution. First organized settlement was at Marietta, 1788. Indian warfare ended with Anthony Wayne's victory at Fallen Timbers, 1794. In the War of 1812, Oliver H. Perry's victory on Lake Erie and William H. Harrison's invasion of Canada, 1813, ended British incursions.

Tourist attractions. Mound City Group National Monuments, a group of 24 prehistoric Indian burial mounds; Neil Armstrong Air and Space Museum, Wapakoneta; Air Force Museum, Dayton; Pro Football Hall of Fame, Canton; King's Island amusement park, King's Island; Cedar Point amusement park, Sandusky. birthplaces, homes,

and memorials to Ohio's 8 U.S. presidents: Wm. Henry Harrison, U.S. Grant, Garfield, Hayes, McKinley, Harding, Taft, Benjamin Harrison.

Famous Ohioans include Sherwood Anderson, Neil Armstrong, George Bellows, Ambrose Bierce, Clarence Darrow, Paul Laurence Dunbar, Thomas Edison, Clark Gable, John Glenn, Bob Hope, Jack Nicklaus, Eddie Rickenbacker, John D. Rockefeller Sr. and Jr., Pete Rose, Gen. Wm. Sherman, Harriet Beecher Stowe, Charles Taft, Robert A. Taft, William H. Taft, James Thurber, Orville Wright.

Chamber of Commerce: 17 S. High St., 8th Fl., Columbus, OH 43215.

Oklahoma
Sooner State

People. Population (1984): 3,298,000; **rank:** 25. **Pop. density:** 47.9 per sq. mi. **Urban** (1980): 67.3%. **Racial distrib.** (1980): 85.8% White; 6.76% Black; 5.6% Amer. Ind. **Net migration** (1980-84): +165,000.

Geography. Total area: 69,919 sq. mi.; **rank:** 18. **Land area:** 68,782 sq. mi. **Acres forested land:** 8,513,300. **Location:** West South Central state bounded on the N by Colorado and Kansas; on the E by Missouri and Arkansas; on the S and W by Texas and New Mexico. **Climate:** temperate; southern humid belt merging with colder northern continental; humid eastern and dry western zones. **Topography:** high plains predominate the W, hills and small mountains in the E; the east central region is dominated by the Arkansas R. Basin, and the Red R. Plains, in the S. **Capital:** Oklahoma City.

Economy. Principal industries: manufacturing, mineral and energy exploration and production, agriculture. **Principal manufactured goods:** non-electrical machinery, oil field machinery and equipment, fabricated metal products, petroleum. **Agriculture: Chief crops:** wheat, cotton, sorghum grain, peanuts, hay, soybeans, corn, barley, oats, pecans. **Livestock:** 5.5 mln. cattle; 290,000 hogs/pigs; 115,000 sheep; 55 mln. poultry. **Timber/lumber** (1983): pine, oaks, hickory; 211 mln. bd. ft. **Minerals** (1984): $253.2 mln.; mostly crushed stone, cement, sand & gravel, gypsum, lime. **Commercial fishing** (1979): $2.8 mln. **Chief ports:** Catoosa, Muskogee. **International airports at:** Oklahoma City, Tulsa. **Value of construction** (1984): $3.3 bln. **Employment distribution** (1983): 16% trade; 17.4% gvt.; 16.6% serv.; 12.4% manuf. **Per capita income** (1984): $11,745. **Unemployment** (1984): 7.0%. **Tourism** (1983): tourists spent $2.6 bln.

Finance. No. banks (1983): 533; **No. savings assns.** (1983): 49.

Federal government. No. federal civilian employees (Mar. 1984): 36,646. **Avg. salary:** $23,216. **Notable federal facilities:** Federal Aviation Agency and Tinker AFB, both Oklahoma City; Ft. Sill, Lawton; Altus AFB, Altus; Vance AFB, Enid.

Energy. Electricity production (1984, mwh, by source): Hydroelectric: 2.3 mln.; Mineral: 42.7 mln.

Education. No. schools (1982): 1,850 public elem. and second.; 45 higher ed. **Avg. salary, public school teachers** (1984): $18,930.

State data. Motto: Labor Omnia Vincit (Labor conquers all things). **Flower:** Mistletoe. **Bird:** Scissortailed flycatcher. **Tree:** Redbud. **Song:** Oklahoma! **Entered union** Nov. 16, 1907; **rank,** 46th. **State fair** at: Oklahoma City; last week of Sept.

History. Part of the Louisiana Purchase, 1803, Oklahoma was known as Indian Territory (but was not given territorial government) after it became the home of the "Five Civilized Tribes"—Cherokee, Choctaw, Chickasaw, Creek, and Seminole—1828-1846. The land was also used by Comanche, Osage, and other Plains Indians. As white settlers pressed west, land was opened for homesteading by runs and lottery, the first run taking place Apr. 22, 1889. The most famous run was to the Cherokee Outlet, 1893.

Tourist attraction. Will Rogers Memorial, Claremore; National Cowboy Hall of Fame, Oklahoma City; restored Ft. Gibson Stockade, near Muskogee, the Army's largest outpost in Indian lands; Indian pow-wows; rodeos; fishing; hunting; Ouachita National Forest; Enterprise Square, museum devoted to American economic system.

Famous Oklahomans include Carl Albert, Woody Guthrie, Gen. Patrick J. Hurley, Karl Jansky, Mickey Mantle, Wiley Post, Oral Roberts, Will Rogers, Maria Tallchief, Jim Thorpe.

Chamber of Commerce: 4020 N. Lincoln Blvd., Oklahoma City, OK 73105.

Oregon
Beaver State

People. Population (1984): 2,674,000; **rank:** 30. **Pop. density:** 27.8 per sq. mi. **Urban** (1980): 67.9%. **Racial distrib.** (1980): 94.5% White; 1.4% Black; Hispanic (1980): 65,883. **Net migration** (1970-83): +568,467.

Geography. Total area: 96,981 sq. mi.; **rank:** 10. **Land area:** 96,184 sq. mi. **Acres forested land:** 29,810,000. **Location:** Pacific state, bounded on N by Washington; on E by Idaho; on S by Nevada and California; on W by the Pacific. **Climate:** coastal mild and humid climate; continental dryness and extreme temperatures in the interior. **Topography:** Coast Range of rugged mountains; fertile Willamette R. Valley to E and S; Cascade Mtn. Range of volcanic peaks E of the valley; plateau E of Cascades, remaining two-thirds of state. **Capital:** Salem.

Economy. Principal industries: manufacturing, agriculture, forestry, tourism. **Principal manufactured goods:** lumber & wood products, foods, machinery, fabricated metals, paper, printing & publishing, primary metals. **Agriculture: Chief crops:** wheat, hay, potatoes, pears, barley, onions, strawberries, sweet corn, cherries, hops. **Livestock:** 1,710,000 cattle; 85,000 hogs/pigs; 495,000 sheep; 20 mln. poultry. **Timber/lumber** (1983): Douglas fir, hemlock, ponderosa pine; 7.1 bln. bd. ft. **Minerals** (1984): $129 mln.; mostly sand & gravel, stone, cement. **Commercial fishing** (1983): $38.5 mln. **Chief ports:** Portland, Astoria, Newport, Coos Bay. **International airports at:** Portland. **Value of construction** (1984): $1.8 bln. **Employment distribution:** 25% trade; 20% serv.; 20% govt.; 19% manuf. **Per capita income** (1984): $11,582. **Unemployment** (1984): 9.4%. **Tourism** (1983): out-of-state visitors spent $964.3 mln.

Finance. No. banks (1983): 91; **No. savings assns.** (1983): 19.

Federal government. No. federal civilian employees (Mar. 1984): 18,856. **Avg. salary:** $25,161. **Notable federal facilities:** Bonneville Power Administration.

Energy: Electricity production (1984, mwh, by source): Hydroelectric: 46.6 mln.; Mineral: 721,000; Nuclear: 4.7 mln.

Education. No. schools (1982): 1,269 public elem. and second.; 45 higher ed. **Avg. salary, public school teachers** (1984): $24,889.

State data. Motto: The union. **Flower:** Oregon grape. **Bird:** Western meadowlark. **Tree:** Douglas fir. **Song:** Oregon, My Oregon. **Entered union** Feb. 14, 1859; **rank,** 33d. **State fair** at: Salem; end-Aug. to early Sept.

History. American Capt. Robert Gray discovered and sailed into the Columbia River, 1792; Lewis and Clark, traveling overland, wintered at its mouth 1805-06; fur traders followed. Settlers arrived in the Willamette Valley, 1834. In 1843 the first large wave of settlers arrived via the Oregon Trail. Early in the 20th century, the "Oregon System," reforms which included the initiative, referendum, recall, direct primary, and woman suffrage, were adopted.

Tourist attractions. John Day Fossil Beds National Monument; Columbia River Gorge; Mt. Hood & Timberline Lodge; Crater Lake National Park; Oregon Dunes National Recreation Area; Ft. Clatsop National Memorial; Oregon Caves National Monument; Shakespearean Festival,

Ashland; High Desert Museum, Bend. Also, skiing, fishing; Annual Albany Timber Carnival, Pendelton Round-Up, Portland Rose Festival.

Famous Oregonians include Ernest Bloch, Ernest Haycox, Chief Joseph, Edwin Markham, Tom McCall, Dr. John McLoughlin, Joaquin Miller, Linus Pauling, John Reed, Alberto Salazar, Mary Decker, William Simon U'Ren.

Tourist Information: Economic Development Department, 595 Cottage St. NE, Salem, OR 97310.

Pennsylvania

Keystone State

People. Population (1984): 11,901,000; **rank:** 4. **Pop. density:** 264.7 per sq. mi. **Urban** (1980): 69.3%. **Racial distrib.** (1980): 89.7% White; 8.8% Black; Hispanic (1980): 154,004. **Net migration** (1970-79): −478,000.

Geography. Total area: 45,333 sq. mi.; **rank:** 33. **Land area:** 44,966 sq. mi. **Acres forested land:** 16,825,900. **Location:** Middle Atlantic state, bordered on the E by the Delaware R., on the S by the Mason-Dixon Line; on the W by West Virginia and Ohio; on the N/NE by Lake Erie and New York. **Climate:** continental with wide fluctuations in seasonal temperatures. **Topography:** Allegheny Mtns. run SW to NE, with Piedmont and Coast Plain in the SE triangle; Allegheny Front a diagonal spine across the state's center; N and W rugged plateau falls to Lake Erie Lowland. **Capital:** Harrisburg.

Economy. Principal industries: steel, travel, health, apparel, machinery, food & agriculture. **Principal manufactured goods:** primary metals, foods, fabricated metal products, non-electrical machinery, electrical machinery. **Agriculture: Chief crops:** corn, hay, mushrooms, apples, potatoes, winter wheat, oats, vegetables, tobacco, grapes. **Livestock:** 2.0 mln. cattle; 950,000 hogs/pigs; 104,000 sheep; 23.8 mln. poultry. **Timber/lumber** (1983): pine, oak, maple; 444 mln. bd. ft. **Minerals** (1984): $657.6 mln.; mostly cement, lime, crushed stone. **Commercial fishing** (1983): $281,000. **Chief ports:** Philadelphia, Pittsburgh, Erie. **International airports at:** Philadelphia, Pittsburgh, Erie, Harrisburg. **Value of construction** (1984): $6.7 bln. **Employment distribution:** 23.6% manuf.; 22.4% trades; 23.8% serv.; 14.6% gvt. **Per capita income** (1984): $12,343. **Unemployment** (1984): 9.1%. **Tourism** (1983): out-of-state visitors spent $7.4 bln.

Finance. No. banks (1983): 355; **No. savings and loan assns.** (1983): 186.

Federal government. No. federal civilian employees (Mar. 1984): 83,585. **Avg. salary:** $23,113. **Notable federal facilities:** Army War College, Carlisle; Ships Control Ctr., Mechanicsburg; New Cumberland Army Depot; Philadelphia Navy Yard, Philadelphia.

Energy. Electricity production (1984, mwh, by source): Hydroelectric: 1.5 mln.; Mineral: 108.9 mln. Nuclear: 21.6 mln.

Education. No. schools (1982): 3,362 public elem. and second.; 201 higher ed. **Avg. salary, public school teachers** (1984): $24,435.

State data. Motto: Virtue, liberty and independence. **Flower:** Mountain laurel. **Bird:** Ruffed grouse. **Tree:** Hemlock. **Second** of the original 13 states to ratify the Constitution, Dec. 12, 1787. **State fair** at: Harrisburg; 2d week in Jan.

History. First settlers were Swedish, 1643, on Tinicum Is. In 1655 the Dutch seized the settlement but lost it to the British, 1664. The region was given by Charles II to William Penn, 1681, Philadelphia (brotherly love) was the capital of the colonies during most of the Revolution, and of the U.S., 1790-1800. Philadelphia was taken by the British, 1777; Washington's troops encamped at Valley Forge in the bitter winter of 1777-78. The Declaration of Independence, 1776, and the Constitution, 1787, were signed in Philadelphia.

Tourist attractions. Independence Hall, Liberty Bell, Carpenters Hall, all in Philadelphia; Valley Forge; Gettysburg battlefield; Amish festivals, Lancaster Cty., Hershey Chocolate World; Pocono Mtns.; Delaware Water Gap;

Longwood Gardens, near Kennett Square; Pine Creek Gorge; hunting, fishing, winter sports.

Famous Pennsylvanians include Marian Anderson, Maxwell Anderson, Andrew Carnegie, Stephen Foster, Benjamin Franklin, George C. Marshall, Andrew W. Mellon, Robert E. Peary, Mary Roberts Rinehart, Betsy Ross.

Chamber of Commerce: 222 N. 3d St., Harrisburg, PA 17101.

Rhode Island

Little Rhody, Ocean State

People. Population (1984): 962,000; **rank:** 42. **Pop. density:** 917.1 per sq. mi. **Urban** (1980): 87.0% **Racial distrib.** (1980): 94.6% White; 2.9% Black; Hispanic (1980): 19,707. **Net migration** (1970-80): −33,000.

Geography. Total area: 1,214 sq. mi.; **rank:** 50. **Land area:** 1,049 sq. mi. **Acres forested land:** 404,200. **Location:** New England state. **Climate:** invigorating and changeable. **Topography:** eastern lowlands of Narragansett Basin; western uplands of flat and rolling hills. **Capital:** Providence.

Economy. Principal industries: manufacturing, services. **Principal manufactured goods:** costume jewelry, machinery, textiles, electronics, silverware. **Agriculture: Chief crops:** potatoes, apples, corn. **Livestock:** 10,000 cattle; 8,700 hogs/pigs; 2,100 sheep; 260,000 poultry. **Timber/lumber:** oak, chestnut. **Minerals** (1984): $9.1 mln.; sand & gravel, stone. **Commercial fishing** (1983): $66.2 mln. **Chief ports:** Providence, Newport, Tiverton. **Value of construction** (1984): $544.6 mln. **Employment distribution** (1984): 29.3% manuf.; 23.6% serv.; 21.3% trade. **Per capita income** (1984): $12,730. **Unemployment** (1984): 5.3%. **Tourism** (1983): out-of-state visitors spent $500 mln.

Finance. No. banks (1983): 24; **No. savings assns.** (1983): 4.

Federal government. No. federal civilian employees (Mar. 1984): 5,707. **Avg. salary:** $24,738. **Notable federal facilities:** Naval War College; Naval Underwater Systems Center.

Energy. Electricity production (1984, mwh, by source): Hydroelectric: 2,000; Mineral: 601,000.

Education. No. schools (1982): 283 public elem. and second.; 13 higher ed. **Avg. salary, public school teachers** (1984): $27,384.

State data. Motto: Hope. **Flower:** Violet. **Bird:** Rhode Island red. **Tree:** Red maple. **Song:** Rhode Island. **Thirteenth** of original 13 states to ratify the Constitution, May 29, 1790. **State fair** at: E. Greenwich; mid-Aug.

History. Rhode Island is distinguished for its battle for freedom of conscience and action, begun by Roger Williams, founder of Providence, who was exiled from Massachusetts Bay Colony in 1636, and Anne Hutchinson, exiled in 1638. Rhode Island gave protection to Quakers in 1657 and to Jews from Holland in 1658.

The colonists broke the power of the Narragansett Indians in the Great Swamp Fight, 1675, the decisive battle in King Philip's War. British trade restrictions angered the colonists and they burned the British revenue cutter Gaspee, 1772. The colony declared its independence May 4, 1776. Gen. John Sullivan and Lafayette won a partial victory, 1778, but failed to oust the British.

Tourist attractions. Newport mansions; summer resorts and water sports; various yachting races inc. Newport to Bermuda. Touro Synagogue, Newport, 1763; first Baptist Church in America, Providence, 1638; Gilbert Stuart birthplace, Saunderstown; Narragansett Indian Fall Festival.

Famous Rhode Islanders include Ambrose Burnside, George M. Cohan, Nelson Eddy, Jabez Gorham, Nathanael Greene, Christopher and Oliver La Farge, Matthew C. and Oliver Perry, Gilbert Stuart.

Chamber of Commerce: 91 Park St., Providence, RI 02908.

South Carolina

Palmetto State

People. Population (1984): 3,300,000; **rank:** 24. **Pop. density:** 109.3 per sq. mi. **Urban** (1980): 54.1%. **Racial distrib.** (1980): 68.8% White; 30.4% Black; Hispanic (1980): 33,414. **Net migration** (1980-84): +70,000.

Geography. Total area: 31,055 sq. mi.; **rank:** 40. **Land area:** 30,203.37 sq. mi. **Acres forested land:** 12,249,400. **Location:** south Atlantic coast state, bordering North Carolina on the N; Georgia on the SW and W; the Atlantic O. on the E, SE and S. **Climate:** humid sub-tropical. **Topography:** Blue Ridge province in NW has highest peaks; piedmont lies between the mountains and the fall line; coastal plain covers two-thirds of the state. **Capital:** Columbia.

Economy: Principal industries: tourism, textiles, apparel, chemical, agriculture, manufacturing. **Principal manufactured goods:** textiles, chemicals and allied products, machinery & fabricated metal products, apparel and related products. **Agriculture: Chief crops:** tobacco, soybeans, corn, cotton, peaches, hay. **Livestock** (1982): 700,000 cattle; 440,000 hogs/pigs; 8.55 mln. poultry. **Timber/lumber** (1983): pine, oak; 1.0 bln. **Minerals** (1984): $255.9 mln.; mostly cement, clay, sand & gravel, stone. **Commercial fishing** (1983): $25.2 mln. **Chief ports:** Charleston, Georgetown, Port Royal. **International airports at:** Charleston. **Value of construction** (1984): $2.9 bln. **Employment distribution** (1983): 30.6% manuf.; 19.4% gvt.; 15.0% serv. **Per capita income** (1984): $10,075. **Unemployment** (1984): 7.1%. **Tourism** (1982): out-of-state visitors spent $2.5 bln.

Finance. No. banks (1983): 72; **No. savings assns.** (1983): 42.

Federal government: No. federal civilian employees (Mar. 1984): 25,263. **Avg. Salary:** $22,708. **Notable federal facilities:** Polaris Submarine Base; Barnwell Nuclear Power Plant; Ft. Jackson.

Energy. Electricity production (1984, mwh, by source): Hydroelectric: 3.1 mln.; Mineral: 18.6 mln.; Nuclear: 23.2 mln.

Education. No. schools (1982): 1,112 public elem. and second.; 62 higher ed. **Avg. salary, public school teachers** (1984): $19,800.

State data. Motto: Dum Spiro Spero (While I breathe, I hope). **Flower:** Carolina jessamine. **Bird:** Carolina wren. **Tree:** Palmetto. **Song:** Carolina. **Eighth** of the original 13 states to ratify the Constitution, May 23, 1788. **State fair** at: Columbia; Oct.

History. The first English colonists settled, 1670, on the Ashley River, moved to the site of Charleston, 1680. The colonists seized the government, 1775, and the royal governor fled. The British took Charleston, 1780, but were defeated at Kings Mountain that year, and at Cowpens and Eutaw Springs, 1781. In the 1830s, South Carolinians, angered by federal protective tariffs, adopted the Nullification Doctrine, holding a state can void an act of Congress. The state was the first to secede and, in 1861, Confederate troops fired on and forced the surrender of U. S. troops at Ft. Sumter, in Charleston Harbor, launching the Civil War.

Tourist attractions. Restored historic Charleston harbor area and Charleston gardens: Middleton Place, Magnolia, Cypress; other gardens at Brookgreen, Edisto, Glencairn; state parks; coastal islands; shore resorts such as Myrtle Beach and Hilton Head Island; fishing and quail hunting; Ft. Sumter National Monument, in Charleston Harbor; Charleston Museum, est. 1773, is the oldest museum in the U.S.

Famous South Carolinians include James F. Byrnes, John C. Calhoun, DuBose Heyward, Ernest F. Hollings, James Longstreet, Francis Marion, Charles Pinckney, John Rutledge, Thomas Sumter, Strom Thurmond.

Chamber of Commerce: 1301 Gervais St., Suite 520, Bankers Trust Tower, Columbia, SC 29201.

South Dakota

Coyote State, Sunshine State

People. Population (1984): 706,000; **rank:** 45. **Pop. density:** 9.3 per sq. mi. **Urban** (1980): 46.4%. **Racial distrib.** (1980): 92.6% White; 0.31% Black; 7.1% Other (includes American Indians); Hispanic (1980): 4,028. **Net migration** (1970-83): −29,000.

Geography. Total area: 77,047 sq. mi.; **rank:** 16. **Land area:** 75,955 sq. mi. **Acres forested land:** 1,702,000. **Location:** West North Central state bounded on the N by North Dakota; on the E by Minnesota and Iowa; on the S by Nebraska; on the W by Wyoming and Montana. **Climate:** characterized by extremes of temperature, persistent winds, low precipitation and humidity. **Topography:** Prairie Plains in the E; rolling hills of the Great Plains in the W; the Black Hills, rising 3,500 ft. in the SW corner. **Capital:** Pierre.

Economy: Principal industries: agriculture, tourism, manufacturing. **Principal manufactured goods:** apparel, machinery, fabricated metals and stone, clay and glass products. **Agriculture: Chief crops:** wheat, corn, oats, hay, rye, sorghum, barley, soybeans, flaxseed, sunflowers. **Livestock** (1984): 4.16 mln. cattle; 1.6 mln. hogs/pigs; 730,000 sheep; 3.65 mln. poultry. **Timber/lumber** (1983): ponderosa pine; 172 mln. bd. ft. **Minerals** (1984): $227.5 mln.; mostly gold, cement, stone. **Commercial fishing** (1983): $579,000. **Value of construction** (1984): $515.7 mln. **Employment distribution:** 18.5% agric.; 17.5% serv.; 9.5% manuf. **Per capita income** (1984): $11,049. **Unemployment** (1984): 4.3%. **Tourism** (1982): out-of-state visitors spent $450 mln.

Finance. No. banks (1983): 146; **No. savings assns.** (1983): 14.

Federal government. No. federal civilian employees (Mar. 1984): 6,648. **Avg. salary:** $22,390. **Notable federal facilities:** Bureau of Indian Affairs, Ellsworth AFB, Corp of Engineers, Nat'l Park Service.

Energy. Electricity production (1984, mwh, by source): Hydroelectric: 5.7 mln.; Mineral: 2.5 mln.

Education. No. schools (1982): 699 public elem. and second.; 20 higher ed. **Avg. salary, public school teachers** (1984): $17,356.

State data. Motto: Under God, the people rule. **Flower:** Pasque flower. **Bird:** Ringnecked pheasant. **Tree:** Black Hills spruce. **Song:** Hail, South Dakota. **Entered union** Nov. 2, 1889; **rank,** 40th. **State fair** at: Huron; late Aug.-early Sept.

History. Les Verendryes explored the region, 1742-43. Lewis and Clark passed through the area, 1804 and 1806. First white American settlement was at Fort Pierre, 1817. Gold was discovered, 1874, on the Sioux Reservation; miners rushed in. The U.S. first tried to stop them, then relaxed its opposition. Custer's defeat by the Sioux followed; the Sioux relinquished the land, 1877 and the "great Dakota Boom" began, 1879. A new Indian uprising came in 1890, climaxed by the massacre of Indian families at Wounded Knee.

Tourist attractions. Needles Highway through the Black Hills; Badlands National Park "moonscape"; Custer State Park's bison and burro herds; Ft. Sisseton, a restored army frontier post of 1864; the "Great Lakes of South Dakota," reservoirs created behind Oahe, Big Bend, Ft. Randall, and Gavins Point dams on the Missouri R.

Mount Rushmore, in the Black Hills, has an altitude of 6,200 ft. Sculptured on its granite face are the heads of Washington, Jefferson, Lincoln, and Theodore Roosevelt. These busts by Gutzon Borglum are proportionate to men 465 ft. tall. Rushmore is visited by about 2 million persons annually.

Famous South Dakotans include Tom Brokaw, "Calamity Jane," Crazy Horse, Alvin H. Hansen, Dr. Ernest O. Lawrence, George McGovern, Sacagawea, Sitting Bull, Laura Ingalls Wilder.

Chamber of Commerce: P.O. Box 190, Pierre, SD 57501.

Tennessee
Volunteer State

People. Population (1984): 4,717,000; **rank:** 17. **Pop. density:** 114.1 per sq. mi. **Urban** (1980): 60.4%. **Racial distrib.** (1980): 83.5% White; 15.8% Black; Hispanic (1980): 34,081. **Major ethnic groups:** German, English, Italian. **Net migration** (1970-80): +231,925.

Geography. Total area: 42,244 sq. mi.; **rank:** 34. **Land area:** 41,328 sq. mi. **Acres forested land:** 13,160,500. **Location:** East South Central state bounded on the N by Kentucky and Virginia; on the E by North Carolina; on the S by Georgia, Alabama, and Mississippi; on the W by Arkansas and Missouri. **Climate:** humid continental to the N; humid sub-tropical to the S. **Topography:** rugged country in the E; the Great Smoky Mtns. of the Unakas; low ridges of the Appalachian Valley; the flat Cumberland Plateau; slightly rolling terrain and knobs of the Interior Low Plateau, the largest region; Eastern Gulf Coastal Plain to the W, is laced with meandering streams; Mississippi Alluvial Plain, a narrow strip of swamp and flood plain in the extreme W. **Capital:** Nashville.

Economy. Principal industries: trade, services, construction; transp., commun., public utilities; finance, ins., real estate. **Principal manufactured goods:** chemicals & allied prods.; food & kindred prods.; nonelectrical machinery; electric/electronic equip.; apparel; fabr. metal prods.; transp. equip.; rubber/misc. plastic prods.; paper & allied prods. **Agriculture: Chief crops:** soybeans, tobacco, wheat, cotton, corn. **Livestock:** 2.4 mln. cattle; 1.1 mln. hogs/pigs; 11,000 sheep; 5.7 mln. poultry. **Timber/lumber** (1983): red oak, white oak, yellow poplar, hickory; 364 mln. bd. ft. **Minerals** (1984): $461.2 mln.; mostly crushed stone, zinc. **Chief ports:** Memphis, Nashville, Chattanooga, Knoxville. **International airports at:** Memphis. **Value of construction** (1984): $4.2 bln. **Employment distribution** (1983): 27.3% manuf.; 22.7% trade; 18.7% serv.; 13.7% gvt. **Per capita income** (1984): $10,400. **Unemployment** (1984): 8.6%. **Tourism** (1982): out-of-state visitors spent $2.1 bln.

Finance. No. banks (1983): 336; **No. savings assns.** (1983): 70.

Federal government. No. federal civilian employees (Mar. 1984): 45,503. **Avg. salary:** $24,811. **Notable federal facilities:** Tennessee Valley Authority; Oak Ridge Nat'l. Laboratories.

Energy. Electricity production (1984, mwh, by source): Hydroelectric: 10.2 mln.; Mineral: 46.2 mln.; Nuclear: 12.5 mln.

Education. No. schools (1982): 1,682 public elem. and second.; 80 higher ed. **Avg. salary, public school teachers** (1984): $20,080.

State data. Motto: Agriculture and commerce. **Flower:** Iris. **Bird:** Mockingbird. **Tree:** Tulip poplar. **Song:** The Tennessee Waltz. **Entered union** June 1, 1796; **rank,** 16th. **State fair** at: Nashville; 3d week of Sept.

History. Spanish explorers first visited the area, 1541. English traders crossed the Great Smokies from the east while France's Marquette and Jolliet sailed down the Mississippi on the west, 1673. First permanent settlement was by Virginians on the Watauga River, 1769. During the Revolution, the colonists helped win the Battle of Kings Mountain, N.C., 1780, and joined other eastern campaigns. The state seceded from the Union 1861, and saw many engagements of the Civil War, but 30,000 soldiers fought for the Union.

Tourist attractions. Natural wonders include Reelfoot Lake, the reservoir basin of the Mississippi R. formed by the 1811 earthquake; Lookout Mountain, Chattanooga; Fall Creek Falls, 256 ft. high; Great Smoky Mountains National Park.

Also, the Hermitage, 13 mi. E of Nashville, home of Andrew Jackson; the homes of presidents Polk and Andrew Johnson; the Parthenon, Nashville, a replica of the Parthenon of Athens; the Grand Old Opry, Nashville.

Famous Tennesseans include Davy Crockett, David Farragut, William C. Handy, Sam Houston, Cordell Hull, Grace Moore, Dinah Shore, Alvin York.

Tourist Information: Tourist Development Office, 601 Broadway, Nashville, TN 37202.

Texas
Lone Star State

People. Population (1984): 15,989,000; **rank:** 3. **Pop. density:** 61.0 per sq. mi. **Urban** (1980): 79.6%. **Racial distrib.** (1980): 78.6% White; 12.0% Black; Hispanic (1980): 2,985,643. **Net migration** (1970-80): +1,760,000.

Geography. Total area: 267,338 sq. mi.; **rank:** 2. **Land area:** 262,134 sq. mi.; **Acres forested land:** 23,279,300. **Location:** Southwestern state, bounded on the SE by the Gulf of Mexico; on the SW by Mexico, separated by the Rio Grande; surrounding states are Louisiana, Arkansas, Oklahoma, New Mexico. **Climate:** extremely varied; driest region is the Trans-Pecos; wettest is the NE. **Topography:** Gulf Coast Plain in the S and SE; North Central Plains slope upward with some hills; the Great Plains extend over the Panhandle, are broken by low mountains; the Trans-Pecos is the southern extension of the Rockies. **Capital:** Austin.

Economy. Principal industries: petroleum, manufacturing, construction. **Principal manufactured goods:** machinery, transportation equipment, foods, refined petroleum, apparel. **Agriculture: Chief crops:** cotton, grain sorghum, grains, vegetables, citrus and other fruits, pecans, peanuts. **Livestock:** 14.4 mln. cattle; 590,000 hogs/pigs; 1.97 mln. sheep; 17.4 mln. poultry. **Timber/lumber** (1983): pine, cypress; 940 mln. bd. ft. **Minerals** (1984): $1.7 bln.; mostly cement, stone, sand & gravel. **Commercial fishing** (1983): $188.2 mln. **Chief ports:** Houston, Galveston, Brownsville, Beaumont, Port Arthur, Corpus Christi. **Major international airports at:** Houston, Dallas/Ft. Worth, San Antonio. **Value of construction** (1984) $20.4 bln. **Employment distribution** (1984): 15.5% manuf.; 19.5% serv.; 5.3% transp. **Per capita income** (1984): $12,636. **Unemployment** (1984): 5.9%. **Tourism** (1982): out-of-state visitors spent $12.5 mln.

Finance. No. banks (1983) 1,733; **No. savings assns.** (1983): 270.

Federal government. No. federal civilian employees (Mar. 1984): 110,048. **Avg. salary:** $23,211. **Notable federal facilities:** Fort Hood (Killeen); Kelly AFB, and Ft. Sam Houston, both San Antonio.

Energy. Electricity production (1984, mwh, by source): Hydroelectric: 1.0 mln.; Mineral: 216.9 mln.

Education. No. schools (1982): 5,507 public elem. and second.; 157 higher ed. **Avg. salary, public school teachers** (1984): $22,600.

State data. Motto: Friendship. **Flower:** Bluebonnet. **Bird:** Mockingbird. **Tree:** Pecan. **Song:** Texas, Our Texas. **Entered union** Dec. 29, 1845; **rank,** 28th. **State fair** at: Dallas; mid-Oct.

History. Pineda sailed along the Texas coast, 1519; Cabeza de Vaca and Coronado visited the interior, 1541. Spaniards made the first settlement at Ysleta, near El Paso, 1682. Americans moved into the land early in the 19th century. Mexico, of which Texas was a part, won independence from Spain, 1821; Santa Anna became dictator, 1835. Texans rebelled; Santa Anna wiped out defenders of the Alamo, 1836. Sam Houston's Texans defeated Santa Anna at San Jacinto and independence was proclaimed the same year. In 1845, Texas was admitted to the Union.

Tourist attractions. Padre Island National Seashore; Big Bend, Guadalupe Mtns. national parks; The Alamo; Ft. Davis; Six Flags Amusement Park. Named for Pres. Lyndon B. Johnson are a state park, a natl. historic site marking his birthplace, boyhood home, and ranch, all near Johnson City, and a library in Austin.

Famous Texans include Stephen Austin, James Bowie, Carol Burnett, J. Frank Dobie, Sam Houston, Howard Hughes, Lyndon B. Johnson, Mary Martin, Chester Nimitz, Katharine Ann Porter, Sam Rayburn.

Chamber of Commerce: 1012 Perry-Brooks Bldg., Austin, TX 78701.

Utah

Beehive State

People. Population (1984): 1,652,000; **rank:** 35. **Pop. density:** 20.1 per sq. mi. **Urban** (1980): 84.4%. **Racial distrib.** (1980): 92.6% White; 4.1% Hispanic. **Net migration** (1970-80): +149,000.

Geography. Total area: 84,916 sq. mi.; **rank:** 11. **Land area:** 82,096 sq. mi. **Acres forested land:** 15,557,400. **Location:** Middle Rocky Mountain state; its southeastern corner touches Colorado, New Mexico, and Arizona, and is the only spot in the U.S. where 4 states join. **Climate:** arid; ranging from warm desert in SW to alpine in NE. **Topography:** high Colorado plateau is cut by brilliantly-colored canyons of the SE; broad, flat, desert-like Great Basin of the W; the Great Salt Lake and Bonneville Salt Flats to the NW; Middle Rockies in the NE run E-W; valleys and plateaus of the Wasatch Front. **Capital:** Salt Lake City.

Economy. Principal industries: manufacturing, tourism, trade, services, mining, transportation. **Principal manufactured goods:** guided missiles and parts, electronic components, food products, primary metals, electrical and transportation equipment. **Agriculture: Chief crops:** wheat, hay, apples, barley, alfalfa seed, corn, potatoes, cherries, onions. **Livestock:** 850,000 cattle; 40,000 hogs/pigs; 650,000 sheep; 3.8 mln. poultry. **Timber/lumber:** aspen, spruce, pine. **Minerals** (1984): $525.3 mln.; salt, sand & gravel, lime, stone. **International airports at:** Salt Lake City. **Value of construction** (1984): $1.6 bln. **Employment distribution:** (1984) 23.4% trade; 21.8% govt., 20.2% serv.; 15.7% manuf. **Per capita income** (1984): $9,719. **Unemployment** (1984): 6.5%. **Tourism** (1984): out-of-state visitors spent $754 mln.

Finance. No. banks (1983): 63; **No. savings assns.** (1983): 15.

Federal government. No. federal civilian employees (Mar. 1984): 31,510. **Avg. salary:** $23,129. **Notable federal facilities:** Hill AFB; Tooele Army Depot, IRS Western Service Center.

Energy. Electricity production (1984, mwh, by source): Hydroelectric: 1.4 mln.; Mineral: 12.4 mln.

Education. No. schools (1982): 652 public elem. and second.; 14 higher ed. **Avg. salary, public school teachers** (1984): $21,307.

State data. Motto: Industry. **Flower:** Sego lily. **Bird:** Seagull. **Tree:** Blue spruce. **Song:** Utah, We Love Thee. **Entered union** Jan. 4, 1896; rank, 45th. **State fair at:** Salt Lake City; Sept.

History. Spanish Franciscans visited the area, 1776, the first white men to do so. American fur traders followed. Permanent settlement began with the arrival of the Mormons, 1847. They made the arid land bloom and created a prosperous economy, organized the State of Deseret, 1849, and asked admission to the Union. This was not achieved until 1896, after a long period of controversy over the Mormon Church's doctrine of polygamy, which it discontinued in 1890.

Tourist attractions. Temple Square, Mormon Church hdqtrs., Salt Lake City; Great Salt Lake; fishing streams; lakes and reservoirs, numerous winter sports; campgrounds. Natural wonders may be seen at Zion, Canyonlands, Bryce Canyon, Arches, and Capitol Reef national parks; Dinosaur, Rainbow Bridge, Timpanogas Cave, and Natural Bridges national monuments. Also Lake Powell and Flaming Gorge Dam.

Famous Utahans include Maude Adams, Ezra Taft Benson, John Moses Browning, Philo Farnsworth, Osmond Family, Merlin Olsen, Ivy Baker Priest, George Romney, Brigham Young, Loretta Young.

Tourist information: Utah Travel Council, Council Hall, Salt Lake City, UT 84114.

Vermont

Green Mountain State

People. Population (1984): 530,000; **rank:** 48. **Pop. density:** 57.2 per sq. mi. **Urban** (1980): 33.8%. **Racial distrib.** (1980): 99.0% White; 0.22% Black; Hispanic (1980): 3,304. **Net migration** (1970-82): +38,000.

Geography. Total area: 9,609 sq. mi.; **rank:** 43. **Land area:** 9,267 sq. mi. **Acres forested land:** 4,511,700. **Location:** northern New England state. **Climate:** temperate, with considerable temperature extremes; heavy snowfall in mountains. **Topography:** Green Mtns. N-S backbone 20-36 mi. wide; avg. altitude 1,000 ft. **Capital:** Montpelier.

Economy. Principal industries: manufacturing, tourism, agriculture, mining, government. **Principal manufactured goods:** machine tools, furniture, scales, books, computer components, skis, fishing rods. **Agriculture: Chief crops:** apples, maple syrup, silage corn, hay; also, dairy products. **Livestock:** 339,000 cattle; 8,000 hogs/pigs; 9,200 sheep; 435,000 poultry. **Timber/lumber** (1983): pine, spruce, fir, hemlock; 102 mln. bd. ft. **Minerals** (1984): $42.9 mln.; mostly asbestos, dimension stone, talc. **International airports at:** Burlington. **Value of construction** (1984): $429.7 mln. **Employment distribution:** 22% manuf.; 19% serv.; 15% retail trade. **Per capita income** (1984): $10,692. **Unemployment** (1984): 5.2%. **Tourism** (1983): out-of-state visitors spent $1.2 bln.

Finance. No. banks (1983): 33; **No. savings assns.** (1983): 3.

Federal government. No. federal civilian employees (Mar. 1984): 2,238. **Avg. salary:** $23,528.

Energy. Electricity production (1984, mwh, by source): Hydroelectric: 879,000; Mineral: 76,000; Nuclear: 3.3 mln.

Education. No. schools (1982): 374 public elem. and second.; 22 higher ed. **Avg. salary, public school teachers** (1984): $19,014.

State data. Motto: Freedom and unity. **Flower:** Red clover. **Bird:** Hermit thrush. **Tree:** Sugar maple. **Song:** Hail, Vermont. **Entered union** Mar. 4, 1791; rank, 14th. **State fair at:** Rutland; early Sept.

History. Champlain explored the lake that bears his name, 1609. First American settlement was Ft. Dummer, 1724, near Brattleboro. Ethan Allen and the Green Mountain Boys captured Ft. Ticonderoga, 1775; John Stark defeated part of Burgoyne's forces near Bennington, 1777. In the War of 1812, Thomas MacDonough defeated a British fleet on Champlain off Plattsburgh, 1814.

Tourist attractions. Year-round outdoor sports, esp. hiking, camping and skiing; there are over 56 ski areas in the state. Popular are the Shelburne Museum; Rock of Ages Tourist Center, Graniteville; Vermont Marble Exhibit, Proctor; Bennington Battleground; Pres. Coolidge homestead, Plymouth; Maple Grove Maple Museum, St. Johnsbury.

Famous Vermonters include Ethan Allen, Adm. George Dewey, John Dewey, Stephen A. Douglas, Dorothy Canfield Fisher, James Fisk.

Tourist information: Vermont Travel Division, 134 State St., Montpelier, VT 05602.

Virginia

Old Dominion

People. Population (1984): 5,636,000; **rank:** 13. **Pop. density:** 141.7 per sq. mi. **Urban** (1980): 66.0% **Racial distrib.** (1980): 79.1% White; 18.9% Black; Hispanic (1980): 79,873. **Net migration** (1980-83): +81,100.

Geography. Total area: 40,817 sq. mi.; **rank:** 36. **Land area:** 39,780 sq. mi. **Acres forested land:** 16,417,400. **Location:** South Atlantic state bounded by the Atlantic O. on the E and surrounded by North Carolina, Tennessee, Kentucky, West Virginia, and Maryland. **Climate:** mild and

equable. **Topography:** mountain and valley region in the W, including the Blue Ridge Mtns.; rolling piedmont plateau; tidewater, or coastal plain, including the eastern shore. **Capital:** Richmond.

Economy. Principal industries: government, trade, manufacturing, tourism, agriculture. **Principal manufactured goods:** textiles, transportation equipment, electric & electronic equipment, food processing, chemicals. **Agriculture: Chief crops:** tobacco, soybeans, peanuts, corn. **Livestock:** 2.02 mln. cattle; 550,000 hogs/pigs; 130,000 sheep; 4.78 mln. poultry. **Timber/lumber** (1983): pine and hardwoods; 864 mln. bd. ft. **Minerals** (1984): $317.7 mln.; mostly crushed stone, sand & gravel, lime. **Commercial fishing** (1983): $84.7 mln. **Chief ports:** Hampton Roads. **International airports at:** Norfolk, Dulles, Richmond, Newport News. **Value of construction** (1984): $6.6 bln. **Employment distribution:** 18% manuf.; 22% trade; 21% serv.; 22% gvt. **Per capita income** (1984): $13,067. **Unemployment** (1984): 5.0%. **Tourism** (1984): out-of-state visitors spent $4.1 bln.

Finance. No. banks (1983): 191; **No. savings assns.** (1983): 66.

Federal government. No. federal civilian employees (Mar. 1984): 131,575. **Avg. salary:** $26,404. **Notable federal facilities:** Pentagon; Naval Sta., Norfolk; Naval Air Sta., Norfolk, Virginia Beach; Naval Shipyard, Portsmouth; Marine Corps Base, Quantico; Langley AFB; NASA at Langley.

Energy. Electricity production (1984, mwh, by source): Hydroelectric: 1.2 mln.; Mineral: 20.0 mln.; Nuclear: 16.4 mln.

Education. No. schools (1982): 1,763 public elem. and second.; 69 higher ed. **Avg. salary, public school teachers** (1984): $21,536.

State data. Motto: Sic Semper Tyrannis (Thus always to tyrants). **Flower:** Dogwood. **Bird:** Cardinal. **Tree:** Dogwood. **Song:** Carry Me Back to Old Virginia. **Tenth** of the original 13 states to ratify the Constitution, June 26, 1788. **State fair** at: Richmond; late Sept.-early Oct.

History. English settlers founded Jamestown, 1607. Virginians took over much of the government from royal Gov. Dunmore in 1775, forcing him to flee. Virginians under George Rogers Clark freed the Ohio-Indiana-Illinois area of British forces. Benedict Arnold burned Richmond and Petersburg for the British, 1781. That same year, Britain's Cornwallis was trapped at Yorktown and surrendered.

Tourist attractions. Colonial Williamsburg; Busch Gardens; Wolf Trap Farm, near Falls Church; Arlington National Cemetery; Mt. Vernon, home of George Washington; Jamestown Festival Park; Yorktown; Jefferson's Monticello, Charlottesville; Robert E. Lee's birthplace, Stratford Hall, and grave, at Lexington; Appomattox; Shenandoah National Park; Blue Ridge Parkway; Virginia Beach.

Famous Virginians include Richard E. Byrd, James B. Cabell, Patrick Henry, Joseph E. Johnston, Robert E. Lee, Meriwether Lewis and William Clark, John Marshall, Edgar Allan Poe, Walter Reed, Booker T. Washington.

Chamber of Commerce: 611 E. Franklin St., Richmond, VA 23219.

Washington

Evergreen State

People. Population (1984): 4,302,000; **rank:** 20. **Pop. density:** 64.6 per sq. mi. **Urban** (1980): 73.5%. **Racial distrib.** (1980): 91.4% White; 2.5% Black; Hispanic (1980): 119,986. **Net migration** (1970-83): +514,600.

Geography. Total area: 68,192 sq. mi.; **rank:** 20. **Land area:** 66,570 sq. mi. **Acres forested land:** 23,181,000. **Location:** northwestern coastal state bordered by Canada on the N; Idaho on the E; Oregon on the S; and the Pacific O. on the W. **Climate:** mild, dominated by the Pacific O. and protected by the Rockies. **Topography:** Olympic Mtns. on NW peninsula; open land along coast to Columbia R.; flat terrain of Puget Sound Lowland; Cascade Mtns. region's high peaks to the E; Columbia Basin

in central portion; highlands to the NE; mountains to the SE. **Capital:** Olympia.

Economy. Principal industries: aerospace, forest products, food products, petroleum refining, primary metals, agriculture. **Principal manufactured goods:** aircraft, pulp and paper, lumber and plywood, aluminum, processed fruits and vegetables. **Agriculture: Chief crops:** wheat, apples, hay, potatoes, barley, nursery/greenhouse products, hops, corn, pears. **Livestock** (1983): 1.65 mln. cattle; 53,000 hogs/pigs; 62,000 sheep; 6.13 mln. poultry. **Timber/lumber** (1983): Douglas fir, hemlock, cedar, pine; 4.6 bln. bd. ft. **Minerals** (1984): $195 mln.; mostly sand & gravel, stone, cement. **Commercial fishing** (1983): $61.3 mln. **Chief ports:** Seattle, Tacoma, Vancouver, Kelso-Longview. **International airports at:** Seattle/Tacoma, Spokane, Boeing Field. **Value of construction** (1984): $3.8 bln. **Employment distribution:** 25% trade; 21% serv.; 18% mfg.; 14% gvt. **Per capita income** (1984): $12,728. **Unemployment** (1984): 9.5%. **Tourism** (1983): $3.6 bln.

Finance. No. banks (1983): 123; **No. savings assns.** (1983): 41.

Federal government. No. federal civilian employees (Mar. 1984): 47,683. **Avg. salary:** $25,103. **Notable federal facilities:** Bonneville Power Admin.; Ft. Lewis; McChord AFB; Hanford Nuclear Reservation; Bremerton Naval Shipyards.

Energy. Electricity production (1984, mwh, by source): Hydroelectric: 83.3 mln.; Mineral: 6.5 mln.; Nuclear: 5.3 mln.

Education. No. schools (1982): 1,723 public elem. and second.; 50 higher ed. **Avg. salary, public school teachers** (1984): $25,610.

State data. Motto: Alki (By and by). **Flower:** Western rhododendron. **Bird:** Willow goldfinch. **Tree:** Western hemlock. **Song:** Washington, My Home. **Entered union** Nov. 11, 1889; rank, 42d.

History. Spain's Bruno Hezeta sailed the coast, 1775. American Capt. Robert Gray sailed up the Columbia River, 1792. Canadian fur traders set up Spokane House, 1810; Americans under John Jacob Astor established a post at Fort Okanogan, 1811. Missionary Marcus Whitman settled near Walla Walla, 1836. Final agreement on the border of Washington and Canada was made with Britain, 1846, and gold was discovered in the state's northeast, 1855, bringing new settlers.

Tourist attractions. Mt. Rainier, Olympic and North Cascades National Parks; Mt. St. Helens; Pacific beaches; Puget Sound; wineries; Indian cultures; year-round outdoor sports.

Famous Washingtonians include Bing Crosby, William O. Douglas, Henry M. Jackson, Mary McCarthy, Edward R. Murrow, Theodore Roethke, Marcus Whitman, Minoru Yamasaki.

Local Chambers of Commerce: P.O. Box 658, Olympia, WA 98507.

West Virginia

Mountain State

People. Population (1984): 1,952,000. **rank:** 34. **Pop. density:** 81.1 per sq. mi. **Urban** (1980): 36.2. **Racial distrib.** (1980): 96.1% White; 3.3% Black; Hispanic (1980): 12,707. **Net migration** (1980-83): −13,000.

Geography. Total area: 24,181 sq. mi.; **rank:** 41. **Land area:** 24,070 sq. mi. **Acres forested land:** 11,668,600. **Location:** South Atlantic state bounded on the N by Ohio, Pennsylvania, Maryland; on the S and W by Virginia, Kentucky, Ohio; on the E by Maryland and Virginia. **Climate:** humid continental climate except for marine modification in the lower panhandle. **Topography:** ranging from hilly to mountainous; Allegheny Plateau in the W, covers two-thirds of the state; mountains here are the highest in the state, over 4,000 ft. **Capital:** Charleston.

Economy. Principal industries: mining, mineral and chemical production, primary metals and stone, clay, and glass prods., timber, tourism. **Principal manufactured**

goods: machinery, plastic and hardwood prods., fabricated metals, basic organic and inorganic chemicals, aluminum, steel. **Agriculture: Chief crops:** apples, peaches, hay, tobacco, corn, wheat, oats, barley. **Chief products:** milk, eggs, honey. **Livestock** (1983): 590,000 cattle; 38,000 hogs/pigs; 91,000 sheep; 870,000 chickens. **Timber/ lumber** (1983): oak, yellow poplar, hickory, walnut, cherry; 260 mln. bd. ft. **Minerals** (1984): $102.6 mln.; mostly crushed stone, sand & gravel, salt, cement, dimension stone. **Commercial fishing** (1983): $25,000. **Chief port:** Huntington. **Value of construction** (1984): $831.9 mln. **Employment distribution:** 15% manuf., 22% trade, 22% govt., 18% serv. **Per capita income** (1984): $9,846. **Unemployment** (1984): 15.0%. **Tourism** (1982): travel-related expenditures were $1.4 bln.

Finance. No. banks (1983): 231; **No. savings assns.** (1983): 18.

Federal government. No. federal civilian employees (Mar. 1984): 9,482. **Avg. salary:** $23,836. **Notable federal facilities:** National Radio Astronomy Observatory, Green Bank; Bureau of Public Debt. Bldg., Parkersburg; Natl. Park, Harper's Ferry; Correctional Institution for Women, Alderson.

Energy. Electricity production (1984, mwh, by source): Hydroelectric: 448,000; Mineral: 77.4 mln.

Education. No. schools (1982): 1,095 public elem. and second.; 30 higher ed. **Avg. salary, public school teachers** (1984): $19,563.

State Data. Motto: Montani Semper Liberi (Mountaineers are always free) **Flower:** Big rhododendron. **Bird:** Cardinal. **Tree:** Sugar maple. **Songs:** The West Virginia Hills; This Is My West Virginia; West Virginia, My Home, Sweet Home. **Entered union** June 20, 1863; rank, 35th. **State fair** at: Lewisburg (Fairlea), Aug. 17-25.

History. Early explorers included George Washington, 1753, and Daniel Boone. The area became part of Virginia and often objected to rule by the eastern part of the state. When Virginia seceded, 1861, the Wheeling Conventions repudiated the act and created a new state, Kanawha, subsequently changed to West Virginia. It was admitted to the Union as such, 1863.

Tourist attractions. Harpers Ferry National Historic Park has been restored to its condition in 1859, when John Brown seized the U.S. Armory.

Also Science and Cultural Center, Charleston; White Sulphur and Berkeley Springs mineral water spas; Monongahela Natl. Forest; state parks and forests; trout fishing; turkey, deer, and bear hunting.

Famous West Virginians include Newton D. Baker, Pearl Buck, John W. Davis, Thomas "Stonewall" Jackson, Don Knotts, Dwight Whitney Morrow, Michael Owens, Cyrus Vance, Col. Charles "Chuck" Yeager.

Tourist information: Governor's Office of Economic Development, State Capitol, Charleston WV 25305.

Wisconsin

Badger State

People. Population (1984): 4,766,000; **rank:** 16. **Pop. density:** 87.5 per sq. mi. **Urban** (1980): 64.2%. **Racial distrib.** (1980): 94.4% White; 3.8% Black; Hispanic (1980): 62,981. **Net migration** (1970-80): +9,000.

Geography. Total area: 56,154 sq. mi.; **rank:** 26. **Land area:** 54,464 sq. mi. **Acres forested land:** 14,907,700. **Location:** North central state, bounded on the N by Lake Superior and Upper Michigan; on the E by Lake Michigan; on the S by Illinois; on the W by the St. Croix and Mississippi rivers. **Climate:** long, cold winters and short, warm summers tempered by the Great Lakes. **Topography:** narrow Lake Superior Lowland plain met by Northern Highland which slopes gently to the sandy crescent Central Plain; Western Upland in the SW; 3 broad parallel limestone ridges running N-S are separated by wide and shallow lowlands in the SE. **Capital:** Madison.

Economy. Principal industries: manufacturing, trade, services, government, transportation, communications, agriculture, tourism. **Principal manufactured goods:** machinery, foods, fabricated metals, transportation equipment, paper and wood products. **Agriculture: Chief crops:** corn, beans, beets, peas, hay, oats, cabbage, cranberries. **Chief products:** milk, butter, cheese. **Livestock:** 4.4 mln. cattle, 1.3 mln. hogs/pigs; 84,000 sheep; 11.6 mln. poultry. **Timber/lumber** (1983): maple, birch, oak, evergreens; 315 mln. bd. ft. **Minerals** (1984): $121.6 mln.; mostly crushed stone, sand & gravel. (mainly nonmetallic minerals). **Commercial fishing** (1983): $6.3 mln. **Chief ports:** Superior, Ashland, Milwaukee, Green Bay, Kewaunee, Pt. Washington, Manitowoc, Sheboygan, Marinette, Kenosha. **International airports at:** Milwaukee. **Value of construction** (1984): $2.8 bln. **Employment distribution** (1984): 25.8% manuf.; 23.6% trade; 20.7% serv.; 16.9% gvt. **Per capita income** (1984): $12,309. **Unemployment** (1984): 7.3%. **Tourism** (1982): out-of-state visitors spent $6.4 bln.

Finance. No. banks (1983): 611; **No. savings assns.** (1983): 84.

Federal government. No. federal civilian employees (Mar. 1984): 11,963. **Avg. salary:** $23,701. **Notable federal facilities:** Ft. McCoy.

Energy. Electricity production (1984, mwh, by source): Hydroelectric: 2.1 mln.; Mineral: 29.0 mln.; Nuclear: 10.7 mln.

Education. No. schools (1982): 2,033 elem and second.; 63 higher ed. **Avg. salary, public school teachers** (1984): $24,780.

State data. Motto: Forward. **Flower:** Wood violet. **Bird:** Robin. **Tree:** Sugar maple. **Song:** On, Wisconsin! **Entered union** May 29, 1848; rank, 30th. **State fair** at: West Allis; mid-Aug.

History. Jean Nicolet was the first European to see the Wisconsin area, arriving in Green Bay, 1634; French missionaries and fur traders followed. The British took over, 1763. The U.S. won the land after the Revolution but the British were not ousted until after the War of 1812. Lead miners came next, then farmers. Railroads were started in 1851, serving growing wheat harvests and iron mines.

Tourist attractions. Old Wade House and Carriage Museum, Greenbush; Villa Louis, Prairie du Chien; Circus World Museum, Baraboo; Wisconsin Dells; Old World Wisconsin, Eagle; Door County peninsula; Chequamegon and Nicolet national forests; Lake Winnebago; numerous lakes for water sports, ice boating and fishing; skiing and hunting.

Famous Wisconsinites include Edna Ferber, King Camp Gillette, Harry Houdini, Robert LaFollette, Alfred Lunt, Spencer Tracy, Thorstein Veblen, Orson Welles, Thornton Wilder, Frank Lloyd Wright.

Tourist information: Wisconsin Dept. of Development, Division of Tourism, 123 W. Washington Ave., Madison, WI 53702.

Wyoming

Equality State

People. Population (1984) 511,000; **rank:** 49. **Pop. density:** 5.3 per sq. mi. **Urban** (1980): 62.7%. **Racial distrib.** (1980): 95.0% White; 0.71% Black; Hispanic (1980): 24,499. **Major ethnic groups:** German, English, Russian. **Net migration** (1970-82): +103,000.

Geography. Total area: 97,914 sq. mi.; **rank:** 9. **Land area:** 97,203 sq. mi. **Acres forested land:** 9.8 mln. **Location:** Mountain state lying in the high western plateaus of the Great Plains. **Climate:** semi-desert conditions throughout; true desert in the Big Horn and Great Divide basins. **Topography:** the eastern Great Plains rise to the foothills of the Rocky Mtns.; the Continental Divide crossed the state from the NW to the SE. **Capital:** Cheyenne.

Economy. Principal industries: mineral extraction, tourism and recreation, agriculture. **Principal manufactured goods:** refined petroleum products, foods, wood products, stone, clay and glass products. **Agriculture: Chief crops:** wheat, beans, barley, oats, sugar beets, hay. **Livestock:** 1.39 mln. cattle; 65,000 hogs/pigs; 1.09 mln. sheep. **Timber/lumber** (1983): aspen, yellow pine; 215 mln. bd. ft. **Minerals** (1984): $525 mln.; mostly clays, stone, sand & gravel. **International airports at:** Casper.

Value of construction (1984): $570.0 mln. **Employment distribution** (1983): 31% serv.; 15% mining; 24% trade. **Per capita income** (1984): $12,586. **Unemployment** (1984): 6.3%. **Tourism** (1982): out-of-state visitors spent $750 mln.

Finance. No. banks (1983): 112; **No. savings and loan assns.** (1983): 10.

Federal government. No. federal civilian employees (Mar. 1984): 4,554. **Avg. salary:** $24,241. **Notable federal facilities:** Warren AFB.

Energy. Electricity production (1984, mwh, by source): Hydroelectric: 1.3 mln. Mineral: 30.3 mln.

Education. No. schools (1982): 371 public elem. and second.; 8 higher ed. **Avg. salary, public school teachers** (1984): $26,709.

State data. Motto: Equal Rights. **Flower:** Indian paintbrush. **Bird:** Meadowlark. **Tree:** Cottonwood. **Song:** Wyoming. **Entered union** July 10, 1890; rank, 44th. **State fair** at: Douglas; end of Aug.

History. Francés Francois and Louis Verendrye were the first Europeans, 1743. John Colter, American, was first to traverse Yellowstone Park, 1807-08. Trappers and fur traders followed in the 1820s. Forts Laramie and Bridger became important stops on the pioneer trail to the West Coast. Indian wars followed massacres of army detachments in 1854 and 1866. Population grew after the Union Pacific crossed the state, 1869. Women won the vote, for the first time in the U.S., from the Territorial Legislature, 1869.

Tourist attractions. Yellowstone National Park, 3,472 sq. mi. in the NW corner of Wyoming and the adjoining edges of Montana and Idaho, the oldest U.S. national park, est. 1872, has some 10,000 geysers, hot springs, mud volcanoes, fossil forests, a volcanic glass (obsidian) mountain, the 1,000-ft.-deep canyon and 308-ft.-high waterfall of the Yellowstone River, and a wide variety of animals living free in their natural habitat.

Also, Grand Teton National Park, with mountains 13,000 ft. high; National Elk Refuge, covering 25,000 acres; Devils Tower, a columnar rock of igneous origin 865 ft. high; Fort Laramie and surrounding areas of pioneer trails; Buffalo Bill Museum, Cody; Cheyenne Frontier Days Celebration, last full week in July, the state's largest rodeo, and world's largest purse.

Famous Wyomingites include James Bridger, Buffalo Bill Cody, Nellie Tayloe Ross.

Tourist information: Travel Commission, Etchepare Circle, Cheyenne, WY 82002.

District of Columbia

Area: 67 sq. mi. **Population:** (1984): 623,000. **Motto:** Justitia omnibus, Justice for all. **Flower:** American beauty rose. **Tree:** Scarlet oak. **Bird:** Wood thrush. The city of Washington is coextensive with the District of Columbia.

The District of Columbia is the seat of the federal government of the United States. It lies on the west central edge of Maryland on the Potomac River, opposite Virginia. Its area was originally 100 sq. mi. taken from the sovereignty of Maryland and Virginia. Virginia's portion south of the Potomac was given back to that state in 1846.

The 23d Amendment, ratified in 1961, granted residents the right to vote for president and vice president for the first time and gave them 3 members in the Electoral College. The first such votes were cast in Nov. 1964.

Congress, which has legislative authority over the District under the Constitution, established in 1878 a government of 3 commissioners appointed by the president. The Reorganization Plan of 1967 substituted a single commissioner (also called mayor), assistant, and 9-member City Council. Funds were still appropriated by Congress; residents had no vote in local government, except to elect school board members.

In Sept. 1970, Congress approved legislation giving the District one delegate to the House of Representatives. The delegate could vote in committee but not on the House floor. The first was elected 1971.

In May 1974 voters approved a charter giving them the right to elect their own mayor and a 13-member city council; the first took office Jan. 2, 1975. The district won the right to levy its own taxes but Congress retained power to veto council actions, and approve the city's annual budget.

Proposals for a "federal town" for the deliberations of the Continental Congress were made in 1783, 4 years before the adoption of the Constitution that gave the Confederation a national government. Rivalry between northern and southern delegates over the site appeared in the First Congress, 1789. John Adams, presiding officer of the Senate, cast the deciding vote of that body for Germantown, Pa. In 1790 Congress compromised by making Philadelphia the temporary capital for 10 years. The Virginia members of the House wanted a capital on the eastern bank of the Potomac; they were defeated by the Northerners, while the Southerners defeated the Northern attempt to have the nation assume the war debts of the 13 original states, the Assumption Bill fathered by Alexander Hamilton. Hamilton and Jefferson arranged a compromise: the Virginia men voted for the Assumption Bill, and the Northerners conceded the capital to the Potomac. President Washington chose the site in Oct. 1790 and persuaded landowners to sell their holdings to the government at £25, then about $66, an acre. The capital was named Washington.

Washington appointed Pierre Charles L'Enfant, a French engineer who had come over with Lafayette, to plan the capital on an area not over 10 mi. square. The L'Enfant plan, for streets 100 to 110 feet wide and one avenue 400 feet wide and a mile long, seemed grandiose and foolhardy. But Washington endorsed it. When L'Enfant ordered a wealthy landowner to remove his new manor house because it obstructed a vista, and demolished it when the owner refused, Washington stepped in and dismissed the architect. The official map and design of the city was completed by Benjamin Banneker, a distinguished black architect and astronomer, and Andrew Ellicott.

On Sept. 18, 1793, Pres. Washington laid the cornerstone of the north wing of the Capitol. On June 3, 1800, Pres. John Adams moved to Washington and on June 10, Philadelphia ceased to be the temporary capital. The City of Washington was incorporated in 1802; the District of Columbia was created as a municipal corporation in 1871, embracing Washington, Georgetown, and Washington County.

Outlying U.S. Areas

Commonwealth of Puerto Rico

(Estado Libre Asociado de Puerto Rico)

People. Population (1985): 3,389,686. **Pop. density:** 987 per sq. mi. **Urban** (1980): 66.8%. **Racial distribution** (1980): 99.9% Hispanic. **Net migration** (1983): −44,601.

Geography. Total area: 3,435 sq. mi. **Land area:** 3,421 sq. mi. **Location:** island lying between the Atlantic to the N and the Caribbean to the S; it is easternmost of the West Indies group called the Greater Antilles, of which Cuba, Hispaniola, and Jamaica are the larger units. **Climate:** mild, with a mean temperature of 76°. **Topography:** mountainous throughout three-fourths of its rectangular area, surrounded by a broken coastal plain; highest peak is Cerro de Punta, 4,389 ft. **Capital:** San Juan.

Economy. Principal industries: manufacturing. **Principal manufactured goods:** pharmaceuticals; chemicals, machinery and metals, electric machinery and equipment, petroleum refining, food products, apparel. **Agriculture: Chief crops:** coffee; plantains; bananas; yams; taniers; pineapples; pidgeon peas; peppers; pumpkins; coriander; lettuce; tobacco. **Livestock** (1984): 591,972 cattle; 205,764 pigs; 6.4 mln. poultry. **Minerals** (1984): crushed stone, sand and gravel, lime; $120.3 mln., mostly marble. **Commercial fishing** (1984): $8.9 mln. **Chief ports/river shipping:** San Juan, Ponce, Mayaguez, Guayanillá,

Guánica, Yabucoa, Aguirre. **Major airports at:** San Juan, Ponce, Mayaguez, Aguadilla. **Value of construction** (1983): $1.0 bln. **Employment distribution:** 24% gvt.; 19% manuf.; 19% trade; 19% serv. **Per capita income** (1983): $3,900. **Unemployment** (1984): 22%. **Tourism** (1984): Out-of-area visitors spent $660 mln.

Finance. No. banks (1983): 20; No. savings and loan assns. (1984): 8; Other: 4 retirement fund systems; over 100 credit unions; 268 credit and saving co-operatives.

Federal government. No. federal civilian employees (1984): 9,989. **Notable federal facilities:** U.S. Naval Station at Roosevelt Roads; U.S. Army Salinas Training Area and Ft. Allen; Sabana SECA Communications Center (U.S. Navy); Ft. Buchanan.

Energy Production (1984): Steam and gas: 12,147 mln. kwh; Other: 134 mln. kwh.

Education. No. schools (1984): 1,766 public, 818 private elem. and second.; 69 higher ed. **Avg. salary, public school teachers** (1984): $8,163.

Misc. Data. Motto. Joannes Est Nomen Eius (John is his name). **Flower:** Maga. **Bird:** Reinita. **Tree:** Ceiba. **Song:** La Borinqueña.

History: Puerto Rico (or Borinquen, after the original Arawak Indian name Boriquen), was discovered by Columbus, Nov. 19, 1493. Ponce de Leon conquered it for Spain, 1509, and established the first settlement at Caparra, across the bay from San Juan.

Sugar cane was introduced, 1515, and slaves were imported 3 years later. Gold mining petered out, 1570. Spaniards fought off a series of British and Dutch attacks; slavery was abolished, 1873. Under the treaty of Paris, Puerto Rico was ceded to the U.S. after the Spanish-American War, 1898.

General tourist attractions: Ponce Museum of Art; forts El Morro and San Cristobal; Old Walled City of San Juan; Arecibo Observatory; Cordillera Central and state parks; El Yunque Rain Forest; San Juan Cathedral; Porta Coeli Chapel and Museum of Religious Art, San Germán; Condado Convention Center; Casa Blanca, Ponce de León family home, Puerto Rican Family Museum of 16th and 17 centuries and the Fine Arts Center in San Juan.

Cultural facilities, festivals, etc.: Festival Casals classical music concerts, mid-June; Puerto Rico Symphony Orchestra at Music Conservatory; Botanical Garden and Museum of Anthropology, Art, and History at the University of Puerto Rico; Institute of Puerto Rican Culture, at the Dominican Convent.

The Commonwealth of Puerto Rico is a self-governing part of the U.S. with a primary Hispanic culture. Puerto Ricans are U.S. citizens and about 2.0 million now live on the mainland, although since 1974 there has also been a reverse migration flow.

The current commonwealth political status of Puerto Rico gives the island's citizens virtually the same control over their internal affairs as the fifty states of the U.S. However, they do not vote in national elections, although they do vote in national primary elections.

Puerto Rico is represented in Congress solely by a resident commissioner who has a voice but no vote, except in committees.

No federal income tax is collected from residents on income earned from local sources in Puerto Rico.

Puerto Rico's famous "Operation Bootstrap," begun in the late 1940s, succeeded in changing the island from "The Poorhouse of the Caribbean" to an area with the highest per capita income in Latin America. This pioneering program encouraged manufacturing and the development of the tourist trade by selective tax exemption, low-interest loans, and other incentives. Despite the marked success of Puerto Rico's development efforts over an extended period of time, per capita income in Puerto Rico is low in comparison to that of the U.S. In calendar year 1984, the transfer payments from the U.S. government to individuals and governments in Puerto Rico totalled $3.4 bln., or 24% of the Gross Domestic Product of $14.0 bln.

Famous Puerto Ricans include: José Celso Barbosa, Julia de Burgos, Pablo Casals, Orlando Cepeda, Roberto Clemente, José de Diego, José Feliciano, Luis A. Ferré, José Ferrer, Doña Felisa Rincón de Gautier, Commodore Diégo E. Hernández, Rafael Hernández (El Jibarito), Raúl Julia, Luis Muñoz Marín, René Marqués, Luis Palés Matos, Concha Meléndez, Rita Moreno, Adm. Horacio Rivero.

Chamber of Commerce: 100 Tetuán P.O.Box. S-3789, San Juan, PR 00904; Ponce & South: El Señorial Bldg., Ponce, PR 00731.

Guam

Where America's Day Begins

People. Population (1984): 110,800. **Pop. density:** 531.5 per sq. mi. **Urban** (1970): 25.5%. Native Guamanians, ethnically called chamorros, are basically of Indonesian stock, with a mixture of Spanish and Filipino. In addition to the offical language, they speak the native Chamorro.

Geography. Total area: 209 sq. mi. land, 30 mi. long and 4 to 8.5 mi. wide. **Location:** largest and southernmost of the Mariana Islands in the West Pacific, 3,700 mi. W of Hawaii. **Climate:** tropical, with temperatures from 70° to 90°F; avg. annual rainfall, about 70 in. **Topography:** coralline limestone plateau in the N; southern chain of low volcanic mountains sloping gently to the W, more steeply to coastal cliffs on the E; general elevation, 500 ft.; highest pt., Mt. Lamlam, 1,334 ft. **Capital:** Agana.

Economy. Principal industries: construction, light manufacturing, tourism, petroleum refining, banking. **Principal manufactured goods:** textiles, foods, petroleum products. **Value added by manufacture:** $187.5 million/yr. **Agriculture: Chief crops:** cabbages, eggplants, cucumber, long beans, tomatoes, bananas, coconuts, watermelon, yams, canteloupe, papayas, maize, sweet potatoes. **Livestock:** 1,011 cattle; 9,842 hogs/pigs; 108,862 poultry. **Commercial fishing:** $187,000. **Chief ports:** Apra Harbor. **International airports at:** Tamuning. **Value of construction** (1980): $80.61 mln. **Employment distribution:** 45% gvt.; 13% construct.; 3% manufacturing; 12% services; 18% trade. **Per capita income** (1979): $4,769. **Unemployment** (1980): 10%. **Tourism** (1980): No. out-of-area visitors: 300,000.

Finance. Notable industries: insurance, real estate, finance. **No. banks:** 13; **No. savings and loan assns.:** 2.

Federal government. No. federal employees (1980): 6,600. **Notable federal facilities:** Andersen AFB; other naval and air bases.

Education. No. public schools: 27 elementary; 9 secondary; 1 higher education. **Avg. salary, public school teachers** (1979): $12,684.

Misc. Data. Flower: Puti Tai Nobio (Bougainvillea). **Bird:** Toto (Fruit dove). **Tree:** Ifit (Intsiabijuga). **Song:** Stand Ye Guamanians.

History. Magellan arrived in the Marianas Mar. 6, 1521, and called them the Ladrones (thieves). They were colonized in 1668 by Spanish missionaries who renamed them the Mariana Islands in honor of Maria Anna, queen of Spain. When Spain ceded Guam to the U.S., it sold the other Marianas to Germany. Japan obtained a League of Nations mandate over the German islands in 1919; in Dec. 1941 it seized Guam; the island was retaken by the U.S. in July 1944.

Guam is under the jurisdiction of the Interior Department. It is administered under the Organic Act of 1950, which provides for a governor and a 21-member unicameral legislature, elected biennially by the residents who are American citizens but do not vote for president.

Beginning in Nov., 1970, Guamanians elected their own governor, previously appointed by the U.S. president. He took office in Jan. 1971. In 1972 a U.S. law gave Guam one delegate to the U.S. House of Representatives; the delegate may vote in committee but not on the House floor.

General tourist attractions. annual mid-Aug. Merizo Water Festival; Tarzan Falls; beaches; water sports, duty-free port shopping.

Virgin Islands

St. John, St. Croix, St. Thomas

People. Population (1984): 101,500. **Pop. density:** 765.2 per sq. mi. **Urban** (1970): 25%. **Racial distribution:** 15% White; 85% Black. **Major ethnic groups:** West Indian, Chachas.

Geography. Total area: 133 sq. mi.; **Land area:** 132 sq. mi. **Location:** 3 larger and 50 smaller islands and cays in the S and W of the V.I. group (British V.I. colony to the N and E) which is situated 70 mi. E of Puerto Rico, located W of the Anegada Passage, a major channel connecting the Atlantic O. and the Caribbean Sea. **Climate:** subtropical; the sun tempered by gentle trade winds; humidity is low; average temperature, 78° F. **Topography:** St. Thomas is mainly a ridge of hills running E and W, and has little tillable land; St. Croix rises abruptly in the N but slopes to the S to flatlands and lagoons; St. John has steep, lofty hills and valleys with little level tillable land. **Capital:** Charlotte Amalie, St. Thomas.

Economy. Principal industries: tourism, rum, petroleum refining, bauxite processing, watch assembly, textiles. **Principal manufactured goods:** rum, textiles, pharmaceuticals, perfumes. **Gross Domestic Product** (1977): $500 million. **Agriculture: Chief crops:** truck garden produce. **Minerals:** sand, gravel. **Chief ports:** Cruz Bay, St. John; Frederiksted and Christiansted, St. Croix; Charlotte Amalie, St. Thomas. **International airports on:** St. Thomas, St. Croix. **Value of construction** (1976): $42,303,000. **Per capita income** (1980 est.): $5,500. **Unemployment** (Dec. 1981): 7.0%. **Tourism** (1980): No. out-of-area visitors: 1,172,113; $355 mln. spent. **No. banks** (1979): 6.

Education: No. public schools: 33 elem. and second.; 1 higher education. **Avg. salary, public school teachers** (1980): $13,575.

Misc. data. Flower: Yellow elder or yellow cedar. **Bird:** Yellow breast. **Song:** Virgin Islands March.

History. The islands were discovered by Columbus in 1493, who named them for the virgins of St. Ursula, the sailor's patron saint. Spanish forces, 1555, defeated the Caribes and claimed the territory; by 1596 the native population was annihilated. First permanent settlement in the U.S. territory, 1672, by the Danes; U.S. purchased the islands, 1917, for defense purposes.

The inhabitants have been citizens of the U.S. since 1927. Legislation originates in a unicameral house of 15 senators, elected for 2 years. The governor, formerly appointed by the U.S. president, was popularly elected for the first time in Nov. 1970. In 1972 a U.S. law gave the Virgin Islands one delegate to the U.S. House of Representatives; the delegate may vote in committee but not in the House.

General tourist attractions. Megen Bay, St. Thomas; duty-free shopping; Virgin Islands National Park, 14,488 acres on St. John of lush growth, beaches, Indian relics, and evidence of colonial Danes.

Chamber of Commerce: for St. Thomas and St. John: P.O. Box 324, St. Thomas, VI 00802; for St. Croix: 17 Church St., Christiansted, St. Croix, VI 00820.

American Samoa

Capital: Pago Pago, Island of Tutuila. **Area:** 77 sq. mi. **Population:** (1984) 33,800. **Motto:** Samoa Muamua le Atua (In Samoa, God Is First). **Song:** Amerika Samoa. **Flower:** Paogo (Ula-fala). **Plant:** Ava.

Blessed with spectacular scenery and delightful South Seas climate, American Samoa is the most southerly of all lands under U. S. ownership. It is an unincorporated territory consisting of 6 small islands of the Samoan group: **Tutuila, Aunu'u, Manu'a Group (Ta'u, Olosega and Ofu),** and **Rose.** Also administered as part of American Samoa is **Swain's Island,** 210 mi. to the NW, acquired by the U.S. in 1925. The islands are 2,600 mi. SW of Honolulu.

American Samoa became U. S. territory by a treaty with the United Kingdom and Germany in 1899. The islands were ceded by local chiefs in 1900 and 1904.

Samoa (Western), comprising the larger islands of the Samoan group, was a New Zealand mandate and UN Trusteeship until it became an independent nation Jan. 1, 1962 *(see Index.)*

Tutuila and Annu'u have an area of 53 sq. mi. Ta'u has an area of 17 sq. mi., and the islets of Ofu and Olosega, 5 sq. mi. with a population of a few thousand. Swain's Island has nearly 2 sq. mi. and a population of about 100.

About 70% of the land is bush. Chief products and exports are fish products, copra, and handicrafts. Taro, bread-fruit, yams, coconuts, pineapples, oranges, and bananas are also produced.

Formerly under jurisdiction of the Navy, since July 1, 1951, it has been under the Interior Dept. On Jan. 3, 1978, the first popularly elected Samoan governor and lieutenant governor were inaugurated. Previously, the governor was appointed by the Secretary of the Interior. American Samoa has a bicameral legislature and an elected delegate to appear before U.S. agencies in Washington.

The American Samoans are of Polynesian origin. They are nationals of the U.S.; there are more than 15,000 in Hawaii and 90,000 on the U.S. west coast.

Minor Caribbean Islands

Quita Sueño Bank, Roncador and Serrana, lie in the Caribbean between Nicaragua and Jamaica. They are uninhabited. U.S. claim to the islands was relinquished in a treaty with Colombia, which entered into force on Sept. 17, 1981.

Navassa lies between Jamaica and Haiti, covers about 2 sq. mi., is reserved by the U.S. for a lighthouse and is uninhabited.

Wake, Midway, Other Islands

Wake Island, and its sister islands, **Wilkes and Peale,** lie in the Pacific Ocean on the direct route from Hawaii to Hong Kong, about 2,300 mi. W of Hawaii and 1,290 mi. E of Guam. The group is 4.5 mi. long, 1.5 mi. wide, and totals less than 3 sq. mi.

The U.S. flag was hoisted over Wake Island, July 4, 1898, formal possession taken Jan. 17, 1899; Wake has been administered by the U.S. Air Force since 1972. Population (1983) was 1,600.

The **Midway Islands,** acquired in 1867, consist of 2, **Sand** and **Eastern,** in the North Pacific 1,150 mi. NW of Hawaii, with area of about 2 sq. mi., administered by the Navy Dept. Population (1983) was 2,220.

Johnston Atoll, SW of Hawaii, area 1 sq. mi., pop. 300 (1978), is operated by Nuclear Defense Agency, and **Kingman Reef,** S of Hawaii, is under Navy control.

Howland, Jarvis, and **Baker Islands,** 1500-1650 miles southwest of the Hawaiian group, uninhabited since World War II, are under the Interior Dept.

Palmyra is an atoll about 1,000 miles south of Hawaii, 4 sq. mi. Privately owned, it is under the Interior Dept.

Islands Under Trusteeship

The U. S. Trust Territory of the Pacific Islands, also called Micronesia, includes 3 major archipelagoes: the **Caroline Islands, Marshall Islands,** and **Mariana Islands** (except Guam: see above). There are 2,141 islands, 98 of them inhabited. Total land area is 715.8 sq. mi., but the islands are scattered over 3 million sq. mi. in the western Pacific N of the equator and E of the Philippines. Population (1984): 120,400.

The Marianas

In process of becoming a U.S. commonwealth are the Northern Mariana Islands, which since 1947 have been part of the Trust Territory of the Pacific Islands, assigned to U.S. administration by the United Nations. The Northern Marianas comprise all the Marianas except Guam, stretching N-S in a 500-mi. arc of tropical islands east of the Philippines and southeast of Japan.

Residents of the islands on June 17, 1975, voted 78% in favor of becoming a commonwealth of the U.S. rather than continuing with the Carolines and Marshalls in the U.S.-UN Trusteeship. On Mar. 24, 1976, U.S. Pres. Ford signed a congressionally-approved commonwealth covenant giving the Marianas control of domestic affairs and giving the U.S. control of foreign relations and defense, and the right to maintain military bases on the islands. The full force of commonwealth status will come into effect at the termination of the trusteeship.

Pres. Carter, on Oct. 24, 1977, approved the Constitution of the Northern Mariana Islands with the effective date of Jan. 9, 1978. In December 1977, the voters of the Northern Marianas elected a governor, lieutenant governor, and members of a bicameral legislature for the new government.

Ferdinand Magellan was the first European to visit the Marianas, 1521. Spain, Germany, and Japan held the islands in turn until World War II when the U.S. seized them in bitter battles on 2 of the main islands, Saipan and Tinian.

Population in 1984 was estimated at 17,700, mostly on Saipan. English is the official language, Roman Catholicism the major religion. The people are descendants of the early Chamorros, Spanish, Japanese, Filipinos, and Mexicans. Land area is 181.9 sq. mi.

Tourism is an important industry; visitors are mostly from Japan. Crops include coconuts, breadfruit, melons and tomatoes.

The Carolines and Marshalls

In 1885, many of the Carolines, Marshalls, and Marianas were claimed by Germany. Others, held by Spain, were sold to Germany at the time of the Spanish-American War, 1898. After the outbreak of World War I, Japan took over the 3 archipelagoes; following that war, League of Nations mandates over them were awarded to Japan.

After World War II, the United Nations assigned them, 1947, as a Trust Territory to be administered by the U.S. They were placed, 1951, under administration of the U.S. Interior Dept.

There is a high commissioner, appointed by the U.S. president. Saipan is the headquarters of the administration. The Congress of Micronesia, an elected legislature with limited powers, held its first meeting, 1965.

In 1969, a commission of the Congress of Micronesia recommended that Micronesia be given internal self-government in free association with the U.S. All the Micronesian entities now have their own locally-elected governments, including legislatures, which have preempted the Congress of Micronesia.

A U.S. offer of commonwealth status was rejected by Micronesian leaders in 1970.

The U.S. and three Trust Territory negotiating commissions representing, respectively, the Marshall Islands, Palau, and the Federated States of Micronesia, comprised of Truk, Yap, Ponape and Kosrae, are negotiating a free association arrangement: the three Micronesian areas would enjoy full self-government; the U.S. would retain responsibility for defense. The Compacts of Free Association, initialled in late 1980, must be approved by the people locally and by the U.S. Congress. If the new status is approved, the U.N. will take action to terminate the trusteeship agreement.

Among the noted islands are the former Japanese strongholds of **Belau, Peleliu, Truk,** and **Yap** in the Carolines; **Bikini** and **Enewetak,** where U.S. nuclear tests were staged, and **Kwajalein,** another World War II battle scene, all in the Marshalls.

Many of the islands are volcanic with luxuriant vegetation; others are of coral formation. Only a few are self-sustaining. Principal exports are copra, trochus shells, fish products, handicrafts, and vegetables.

Disputed Pacific Islands

In the central Pacific, S and SW of Hawaii lie 25 islands that were claimed by the U.S.; 18 of them were also claimed by the United Kingdom and 7 by New Zealand. **Kiribati** achieved its independence from the U.K. in July, 1979.

The **Tuvalu (Ellice) Islands,** including Funafuti, Nukufetau, Nukulailai, and Nurakita, became independent of UK, Oct. 1, 1978.

The **Cook Islands,** including Danger, Manahiki, Rakahanga, and Penrhyn (Tongareva), are self-governing in free association with New Zealand. **Tokelau** is a New Zealand territory.

The U.S. signed a treaty with Kiribati on Sept. 20, 1979; with Tuvalu on Feb. 7, 1979; and with the Cook Islands and New Zealand for Tokelau on Dec. 2, 1980. These treaties, which relinquished U.S. claim to the disputed islands, were ratified in August, 1983.

Estimated Changes in State Population 1980-84

Source: Census Bureau, Dept. of Commerce

Region, division, and state	July 1, 1984 (provisional, in thousands)	Change, 1980-84 Percent	Region, division and state	July 1, 1984 (provisional in thousands)	Change, 1980-84 Percent	Region, division and state	July 1, 1984 (provisional, in thousands)	Change, 1980-84 Percent
New England			Mo.	5,000	1.9	Ark.	2,349	2.7
Me.	1,156	2.8	N.D.	686	5.2	La.	4,462	6.1
N.H.	977	6.1	S.D.	706	2.2	Okla. . . .	3,298	9.0
Vt.	530	3.6	Neb.	1,606	2.3	Tex.	15,989	12.4
Mass.	5,798	1.1	Kan.	2,438	3.1	Mountain		
R.I.	962	1.6	South Atlantic			Mont.	824	4.7
Conn.	3,154	1.5	Del.	613	3.1	Ida.	1,001	6.0
Middle Atlantic			Md.	4,349	3.1	Wyo. . . .	511	8.9
N.Y.	17,735	1.0	Va.	5,636	5.4	Col.	3,178	10.0
N.J.	7,515	2.0	W.Va.	1,952	0.1	N.M. . . .	1,424	9.3
Pa.	11,901	0.3	N.C.	6,165	4.8	Ariz. . . .	3,053	12.3
East North Central			S.C.	3,300	5.7	Ut.	1,652	13.0
Oh.	10,752	-0.4	Ga.	5,837	6.8	Nev.	911	13.8
Ind.	5,498	0.1	Fla.	10,976	12.6	Pacific		
Ill.	11,511	0.7	East South Central			Wash.	4,349	5.2
Mich.	9,075	-2.0	Ky.	3,723	1.7	Ore.	2,674	1.6
Wis.	4,766	1.3	Tenn.	4,717	2.7	Cal.	25,622	8.3
West North Central			Ala.	3,990	2.5	Alas.	500	24.4
Minn.	4,162	2.1	Miss.	2,598	3.1	Ha.	1,039	7.7
ia.	2,910	-0.1	West South Central					

NORTH AMERICAN CITIES[1]

Sources: Bureau of the Census: population (1982 estimates); population growth (1970-1980); population over 65 and under 35 (1980). Geography Division, Bureau of the Census: population density (1980); area (1980). Bureau of Labor Statistics: employment (Jan. 1985). Bureau of Economic Analysis: per capita personal income (MSA, 1983). For Canadian cities: Statistics Canada. All other information was gathered from sources in the individual cities.

Akron, Ohio

Population: 231,659; **Pop. density:** 4,312 per sq. mi.; **Pop. growth:** −13.9%; **Pop. over 65:** 13.5%; **Pop. under 35:** 57.1%. **Area:** 55 sq. mi. **Employment:** 89,453 employed, 11.4% unemployed; **Per capita income:** $11,584.
Transportation: Akron-Canton airport; major trucking industry; Conrail; metro transit system. **Communications:** 1 TV, and 7 radio stations; 2 public broadcast outlets. **Medical facilities:** 11 hospitals; specialized children's treatment center. **Educational facilities:** Univ. of Arkon and 12 others; 68 public schools. **Further information:** Akron Regional Development Board or Akron-Summit Convention and Visitors Bureau, both One Cascade Plaza, Akron, OH 44308.

Albuquerque, New Mexico

Population: 341,978; **Pop. density:** 3,492 per sq. mi.; **Pop. growth:** 35.7%; **Pop. over 65:** 8.4%; **Pop. under 35:** 61.6%. **Area:** 95 sq. mi. **Employment:** 185,920 employed, 5.5% unemployed; **Per capita income:** $11,520.
Transportation: 1 international airport; 2 railroads; 2 bus lines. **Communications:** 5 TV, 21 radio stations; 3 cable TV systems. **Medical facilities:** 9 major hospitals. **Educational facilities:** 2 universities. **Further information:** Chamber of Commerce, 401 2d NW, Albuquerque, NM 87102.

Anaheim, California

Population: 226,467; **Pop. density:** 5,349 per sq. mi.; **Pop. growth:** 31.6%; **Pop. over 65:** 7.7%; **Pop. under 35:** 60.7%. **Area:** 41 sq. mi. **Employment:** 147,578 employed. 4.8% unemployed; **Per capita income:** $15,250.
Transportation: John Wayne, Fullerton, and Long Beach Municipal airports; 4 railroads; Greyhound buses. **Communications:** 12 TV channels, one CATV; 4 radio stations. **Medical facilities:** 6 general hospitals. **Educational facilities:** 3 colleges, 5 junior colleges; 62 elementary, 8 junior high, 8 high schools. **Further information:** Chamber of Commerce, 100 South Anaheim Blvd., Suite 300, Anaheim, CA 92805.

Anchorage, Alaska

Population: 194,675; **Pop. density:** 100 per sq. mi.; **Pop. growth:** 259.5%; **Pop. over 65:** 2.0%; **Pop. under 35:** 70.2%. **Area:** 1,732 sq. mi. **Employment:** 108,300 employed, 8.2% unemployed; **Per capita income:** $19,020.
Transportation: Anchorage International Airport, 5 other airports. **Communications:** 4 TV, 11 radio stations. **Medical facilities:** 3 hospitals. **Educational facilities:** Univ. of Alaska, Alaska Pacific Univ. **Further information:** Chamber of Commerce, 415 F St., Anchorage, AK 99501.

Arlington, Texas

Population: 182,975; **Pop. density:** 2,024 per sq. mi.; **Pop. growth:** 77.5%; **Pop. over 65:** 4.5%; **Pop. under 35:** 67.3%. **Area:** 79 sq. mi.; **Employment:** 102,354 employed, 4.0% unemployed; **Per capita income:** $13,103.
Transportation: Dallas/Ft. Worth airport is 20 minutes away; 12 railway lines; intracity transport system in planning stage. **Communications:** 9 TV stations; 39 radio stations. **Medical facilities:** almost 1,000 beds in hospital network. **Educational facilities:** 43 public schools; Univ. of Texas at Arlington. **Further information:** Chamber of Commerce, 316 W. Main St., Arlington, TX 76010.

Atlanta, Georgia

Population: 428,153; **Pop. density:** 3,244 per sq. mi.; **Pop. growth:** −14.1%; **Pop. over 65:** 11.5%; **Pop. under 35:** 60.7%. **Area:** 131 sq. mi.. **Employment:** 210,277 employed, 6.7% unemployed; **Per capita income:** $12,492.
Transportation: 1 international airport; 7 railroad lines, 2 systems; bus terminal; rapid rail under construction; 6 legs of 3 interstate highways intersecting downtown interchange. **Communications:** 8 TV, 41 radio stations; 8 cable TV companies. **Medical facilities:** 56 hospitals; VA hospital; Natl. Centers for Disease Control; Natl. Cancer Center. **Educational facilities:** 28 colleges, universities, seminaries, junior colleges. **Further information:** Chamber of Commerce, 1300 N. Omni Intl., Atlanta, GA 30302.

Aurora, Colorado

Population: 184,372; **Pop. density:** 2,652 per sq. mi.; **Pop. growth:** 111.5%; **Pop. over 65:** 4.3%; **Pop. under 35:** 67.3%. **Area:** 60 sq. mi. **Employment:** 98,586 employed, 5.5% unemployed; **Per capita income:** $14,504.
Transportation: 1 international airport; 4 railroads; 2 bus lines; city bus system. **Further information:** Chamber of Commerce, Suite 303, 14001 E. Lliff Ave., Aurora, CO 80014.

Austin, Texas

Population: 368,135; **Pop. density:** 2,978 per sq. mi.; **Pop. growth:** 36.3%; **Pop. over 65:** 7.5%; **Pop. under 35:** 69%. **Area:** 116 sq. mi. **Employment:** 237,387 employed, 4.1% unemployed; **Per capita income:** $11,937.
Transportation: 1 international airport; 4 railroads. **Communications:** 4 TV, 18 radio stations. **Medical facilities:** 9 hospitals. **Educational facilities:** 10 universities and colleges. **Further information:** Chamber of Commerce, 901 W. Riverside Dr., Austin, TX 78701.

Baltimore, Maryland

Population: 774,113; **Pop. density:** 9,835 per sq. mi.; **Pop. growth:** −13.1%; **Pop. over 65:** 12.8%; **Pop. under 35:** 56.9%. **Area:** 80 sq. mi. **Employment:** 356,538 employed, 8.5% unemployed; **Per capita income:** $12,254.
Transportation: 1 major airport; 3 railroads, bus system; subway system: 1 underwater tunnel. **Communications:** 6 TV stations; 33 radio stations. **Medical facilities:** 29 hospitals; 2 major medical centers. **Educational facilities:** 189 public schools; over 30 universities and colleges; major public library system. **Further information:** Greater Baltimore Committee, Suite 900, Two Hopkins Plaza, Baltimore, MD 21202.

Baton Rouge, Louisiana

Population: 361,572; **Pop. density:** 5,673 per sq. mi.; **Pop. growth:** 32.2%; **Pop. over 65:** 8.7%; **Pop. under 35:** 64.0%. **Area:** 61 sq. mi. **Employment:** 168,084 employed, 7.5% unemployed; **Per capita income:** $11,254.
Transportation: 1 airport with 5 airlines; 3 bus lines; 4 railroad trunk lines; Port of Baton Rouge is one of largest in U.S. **Communications:** 4 TV, 13 radio stations. **Medical facilities:** 7 hospitals. **Educational facilities:** 97 public schools; Louisiana St. Univ., center of 8-campus system; Southern Univ. **Further information:** Chamber of Commerce, P.O. Box 3217, Baton Rouge, LA 70821.

[1] The 100 most populated cities, excluding Mexico.

660

Birmingham, Alabama

Population: 283,239; **Pop. density:** 2,872 per sq. mi.; **Pop. growth:** −5.5%; **Pop. over 65%:** 13.9%; **Pop. under 35:** 57.5%. **Area:** 99 sq. mi.. **Employment:** 115,557 employed, 11.2% unemployed; **Per capita income:** $10,621.

Transportation: 1 airport; 5 major rail freight lines, Amtrak; 2 bus lines; 75 truck line terminals; 3 interstate highways. **Communications:** 3 TV, 16 radio stations; 1 educational TV, 1 educational radio station. **Medical facilities:** Univ. of Alabama in Birmingham Medical Center; VA hospital with organ transplant program; 15 other hospitals. **Educational facilities:** 1 university, 3 colleges, 2 junior colleges. **Further information:** Chamber of Commerce, 2027 First Ave. N., Birmingham, AL 35202.

Boston, Massachusetts

Population: 560,847; **Pop. density:** 11,979 per sq. mi.; **Pop. growth:** −12.2%; **Pop. over 65:** 12.7%; **Pop. under 35:** 60.4%. **Area:** 47 sq. mi. **Employment:** 274,388 employed, 5.0% unemployed; **Per capita income:** $14,297.

Transportation: 1 major airport; 2 railroads; city rail and subway system; 2 underwater tunnels. **Communications:** 8 TV stations; 33 radio stations. **Medical facilities:** numerous hospitals; 3 major medical research centers. **Educational facilities:** 25 universities and colleges; major public library system. **Further information:** Chamber of Commerce, 125 High Street, Boston, MA 02110.

Buffalo, New York

Population: 358,035; **Pop. density:** 8,520 per sq. mi.; **Pop. growth:** −22.7%; **Pop. over 65:** 15.0%; **Pop. under 35:** 55.3%. **Area:** 42 sq. mi. **Employment:** 125,098 employed, 11.5% unemployed; **Per capita income:** $11,398.

Transportation: 1 international airport; 6 major railroads, metro rail system; direct highway & rail to all of Canada; water service to Great Lakes-St. Lawrence seaways system, overseas, and Atlantic seaboard. **Communications:** 5 TV, 23 AM & FM radio stations, 3 cable systems. **Medical facilities:** 21 hospitals. **Educational facilities:** 2 universities; 9 colleges. **Further information:** Chamber of Commerce, 107 Delaware Ave., Buffalo, NY 14202.

Calgary, Alberta

Population: 625,143 (1985); **Pop. density:** 3,071 per sq. mi.; **Pop. growth:** 37.8% (1975-85); **Pop. over 65:** 6.1%; **Pop. under 35:** 66.2%. **Area:** 203.5 sq. mi. **Employment:** 302,000 employed, 11.6% unemployed (Apr. 1985).

Transportation: International Airport served by 10 airlines; railway passenger service on VIA Rail, freight service on CN and CP Rail. **Communications:** 15 radio and 3 TV stations plus cable. **Medical facilities:** 7 major hospitals with 2,900 beds, 5 auxiliary hospitals with 1,276 beds for extended care. **Educational facilities:** 296 public and separate schools, 5 private schools, Univ. of Calgary, Mount Royal College, Southern Alberta Institute of Technology, Alberta Vocational Centre. **Further information:** Economic Development Authority, P.O. Box 2100, Postal Station "M", Calgary, AB, T2P, 2M5.

Charlotte, North Carolina

Population: 323,972; **Pop. density:** 2,278 per sq. mi.; **Pop. growth:** 30.2%; **Pop. over 65:** 8.6%; **Pop. under 35:** 60.4%. **Area:** 138 sq. mi. **Employment:** 170,840 employed, 4.7% unemployed; **Per capita income:** $11,152.

Transportation: Charlotte/Douglas Airport; 2 major railway lines; 3 bus lines; 150 trucking firms. **Communications:** 6 TV, 12 radio stations. **Medical facilities:** 7 hospitals, 1 medical center. **Educational facilities:** 2 universities, 5 colleges. **Further information:** Chamber of Commerce, P.O. Box 32785, Charlotte, NC 28232.

Chicago, Illinois

Population: 2,997,155; **Pop. density:** 13,180 per sq. mi.; **Pop. growth:** −10.8%; **Pop. over 65:** 11.4%; **Pop. under 35:** 58.5%. **Area:** 228 sq. mi. **Employment:** 1,396,179 employed, 9.3% unemployed; **Per capita income:** $13,456.

Transportation: 3 airports; major railroad system; major trucking industry. **Communications:** 9 TV stations; 31 radio stations. **Medical facilities:** over 123 hospitals. **Educational facilities:** 95 institutions of higher learning; major public library system. **Further information:** Association of Commerce and Industry, 200 N. Lasalle St., Chicago, IL 60601.

Cincinnati, Ohio

Population: 380,118; **Pop. density:** 4,941 per sq. mi.; **Pop. growth:** −15.0%; **Pop. over 65:** 14.5%; **Pop. under 35:** 58.5%. **Area:** 78 sq. mi.. **Employment:** 164,081 employed, 9.1% unemployed; **Per capita income:** $11,777.

Transportation: 1 international airport; 3 railroads; 1 bus system. **Communications:** 8 TV, 9 AM & 16 FM radio stations. **Medical facilities:** 30 hospitals; Children's Hospital Medical Center; VA hospital. **Educational facilities:** 3 universities; 6 4-year colleges, 8 technical & 2-year colleges. **Further information:** Chamber of Commerce, 120 W. 5th St., Cincinnati, OH 45202.

Cleveland, Ohio

Population: 558,869; **Pop. density:** 7,264 per sq. mi.; **Pop. growth:** −23.6%; **Pop. over 65:** 13.0%; **Pop. under 35:** 56.7%. **Area:** 79 sq. mi.. **Employment:** 209,544 employed, 12.2% unemployed; **Per capita income:** $13,103.

Transportation: 2 airports; rail service; major port; rapid transit system. **Communications:** 7 TV stations; 53 radio stations. **Medical facilities:** numerous hospitals; major medical research center. **Educational facilities:** 8 universities and colleges; major public library system. **Further information:** Convention Visitor's Bureau, 1301 E. 6th Street, Cleveland, OH 44114.

Colorado Springs, Colorado

Population: 231,699; **Pop. density:** 2,088 per sq. mi.; **Pop. growth:** 58.8%; **Pop. over 65:** 8.3%; **Pop. under 35:** 62.3%. **Area:** 103 sq. mi.. **Employment:** 116,131 employed, 6.7% unemployed; **Per capita income:** $11,218.

Transportation: Municipal airport served by 6 air lines; Denver & Rio Grande, Santa Fe, Burlington railroads; Greyhound, Continental Trailways buses. **Communications:** 13 TV, 15 radio stations. **Medical facilities:** 9 hospitals, 1,418 beds. **Educational facilities:** Univ. of Colorado at Colo. Springs, U.S. Air Force Acad., Pikes Peak Comm. College. **Further information:** Chamber of Commerce, P.O. Drawer B, Colorado Springs, CO 80901.

Columbus, Georgia

Population: 174,348; **Pop. density:** 779 per sq. mi.; **Pop. growth:** 9.3%; **Pop. over 65:** 8.9%; **Pop. under 35:** 61.5%. **Area:** 218 sq. mi. **Employment:** 64,586 employed, 6.0% unemployed; **Per capita income:** $9,328.

Transportation: Metropolitan airport; metro bus system; 2 bus lines; 2 railroads. **Communications:** 5 TV stations, 11 radio stations. **Medical facilities:** 5 hospitals. **Educational facilities:** 53 public schools; 1 college. **Further information:** Chamber of Commerce, P.O. Box 1200, Columbus, GA 31902.

Columbus, Ohio

Population: 570,588; **Pop. density:** 3,121 per sq. mi.; **Pop. growth:** 4.6%; **Pop. over 65:** 8.9%; **Pop. under 35:** 64.4%. **Area:** 181 sq. mi.. **Employment:** 272,950 employed, 7.0% unemployed; **Per capita income:** $11,445. **Transportation:** 2 airports; 3 railroads; 4 intercity bus lines; major highway system. **Communications:** 5 TV stations; 19 radio stations. **Medical facilities:** 22 hospitals. **Educational facilities:** 12 universities and colleges; major public library system. **Further information:** Chamber of Commerce, P.O. Box 1527, Columbus, OH 43216.

Corpus Christi, Texas

Population: 246,081; **Pop. density:** 2,230 per sq. mi.; **Pop. growth:** 13.4%; **Pop. over 65:** 8.2%; **Pop. under 35:** 63.2%. **Area:** 104 sq. mi.. **Employment:** 110,497 employed, 8.9% unemployed; **Per capita income:** $10,503. **Transportation:** 5 airlines; 2 bus lines, metro bus system; 3 freight railroads. **Communications:** 6 TV stations; 17 radio stations. **Medical facilities:** 10 hospitals including a children's center. **Educational facilities:** 54 public schools; Del Mar Coll., Corpus Christi State Univ. **Further information:** Chamber of Commerce, PO Box 640, Corpus Christi, TX 78403.

Dallas, Texas

Population: 943,848; **Pop. density:** 2,715 per sq. mi.; **Pop. growth:** 7%; **Pop. over 65:** 9.5%; **Pop. under 35:** 61.1%. **Area:** 333 sq. mi.. **Employment:** 557,807 employed, 5.0% unemployed; **Per capita income:** $14,222. **Transportation:** 1 international airport; 6 railroads; major transit system. **Communications:** 9 TV stations; 38 radio stations. **Medical facilities:** 42 hospitals; major medical center. **Educational facilities:** 37 universities and colleges; major public library system; 186 public schools. **Further information:** Chamber of Commerce, 1507 Pacific Ave., Dallas, TX 75201.

Dayton, Ohio

Population: 188,499; **Pop. density:** 4,236 per sq, mi.; **Pop, growth:** −16.3%; **Pop. over 65:** 11.8%; **Pop. under 35:** 59.8%. **Area:** 48 sq. mi. **Employment:** 75,175 employed, 10.3% unemployed; **Per capita income:** $11,395. **Transportation:** 1 international airport; 9 airlines, 3 railroads; 4 bus lines; countywide Dayton Regional Transit Authority. **Communications:** 5 TV, 8 radio stations. **Medical facilities:** 14 hospitals including VA facility. **Educational facilities:** Univ. of Dayton, Wright St. Univ.. **Further information:** Chamber of Commerce, Suite 1980, Kettering Tower, Dayton Oh 45423.

Denver, Colorado

Population: 505,563; **Pop. density:** 4,435 per sq. mi.; **Pop. growth:** −4.3%; **Pop. over 65:** 12.6%; **Pop. under 35:** 58.9%. **Area:** 111 sq. mi.. **Employment:** 279,442 employed, 6.1% unemployed; **Per capita income:** $14,504. **Transportation:** 1 international airport; 5 major rail freight lines, Amtrak; 2 bus lines; 3 interstate highways intersect city. **Communications:** 7 TV, 35 radio stations. **Medical facilities:** 34 hospitals. **Educational facilities:** 2 universities; 3 colleges. **Further information:** Chamber of Commerce, 1301 Welton St., Denver, CO 80204.

Des Moines, Iowa

Population: 191,506; **Pop. density:** 2,890 per sq. mi.; **Pop. growth:** −5.2%; **Pop. over 65:** 12.5; **Pop. under 35:** 58.4%. **Area:** 66 sq. mi.. **Employment:** 93,321 employed, 8.5% unemployed; **Per capita income:** $12,880. **Transportation:** 1 international airport; 3 bus lines; 4 railroads; metro bus system. **Communications:** 5 TV, 18 radio stations; CATV. **Medical facilities:** 8 hospitals with 2,700 beds. **Educational facilities:** Drake Univ.; 2 Bible colleges. **Further information:** Chamber of Commerce, 8th & High Sts., Des Moines, IA 50309.

Detroit, Michigan

Population: 1,138,717; **Pop. density:** 8,848 per sq. mi.; **Pop. growth:** −20.5%; **Pop. over 65:** 11.7%; **Pop. under 35:** 59.5%. **Area:** 136 sq. mi.. **Employment:** 424,934 employed, 12.8% unemployed (Dec. 1984); **Per capita income:** $12,537. **Transportation:** 1 international airport; 10 railroads; major international port; public transit system. **Communications:** 9 TV stations, 37 radio stations. **Medical facilities:** 28 hospitals, major medical center. **Educational facilities:** 13 universities and colleges; major public library system. **Further information:** Chamber of Commerce, 150 Michigan Avenue, Detroit, MI 48226.

Edmonton, Alberta

Population: 564,000 (1984). **Pop. density:** 2,150 per sq. mi.; **Pop. growth:** 26.5% (1974-84); **Pop. over 65:** 7.0%; **Pop. under 35:** 64%. **Area:** 263 sq. mi.. **Employment:** 328,000 (metro) employed, 14.1% unemployed (1984). **Transportation:** Canadian National (VIA), Canadian Pacific; 2 airports with 9 airlines; Light Rail Transit System. **Communications:** 18 (including 1 French) radio stations, 4 (including 1 French) TV stations. **Medical facilities:** 6 major hospitals. **Educational facilities:** 2 universities and 4 colleges. **Further information:** Chamber of Commerce, 600 Sun Life Place, 10123–99 St., Edmonton, T5J 3G9.

El Paso, Texas

Population: 445,071; **Pop. density:** 1,779 per sq. mi.. **Pop. growth:** 32.0%; **Pop. over 65:** 6.9%; **Pop. under 35:** 65%. **Area:** 239 sq. mi. **Employment:** 163,363 employed, 11.4% unemployed; **Per capita income:** $8,290. **Transportation:** International airport; 5 major rail lines; 8 bus lines; 9 major highways; gateway to Mexico. **Communications:** 6 TV, 23 radio stations. **Medical facilities:** 16 hospitals; 1 medical school; 1 nursing school; 1 cancer treatment center. **Educational facilities:** 2 colleges and universities. **Further information:** Convention and Visitors Bureau, 5 Civic Center Plaza, El Paso, TX 79901.

Fort Worth, Texas

Population: 401,402; **Pop. density:** 1,604 per sq. mi.; **Pop. growth:** −21.1%; **Pop. over 65:** 11.8%; **Pop. under 35:** 58.5%. **Area:** 240 sq. mi. **Employment:** 211,358 employed, 6.0% unemployed; **Per capita income:** $13,103. **Transportation:** Dallas/Fort Worth airport; 8 major railroads, Amtrak; 41 motor carriers; local bus service; 2 transcontinental, 2 intrastate bus lines. **Communications:** 9 TV, 37 radio stations. **Medical facilities:** 35 hospitals; 2 children's hospitals; 4 government hospitals. **Educational facilities:** 8 colleges & universities. **Further information:** Chamber of Commerce, 700 Throckmorton, Fort Worth, TX 76102.

Fresno, California

Population: 244,623; **Pop. density:** 3,356 per sq. mi.; **Pop. growth:** 31.7%; **Pop. over 65:** 10.9%; **Pop. under 35:** 62.5%. **Area:** 65 sq. mi. **Employment:** 108,668 employed, 12.9% unemployed; **Per capita income:** $10,922. **Transportation:** 7 airlines; Amtrak; freeways connect to all major areas in state; U.S. port of entry. **Communications:** one public, 6 commercial TV stations, 5 CATV services; 18 commercial, 2 public radio stations. **Medical facilities:** 6 general hospitals including a VA facility. **Educational facilities:** Cal. State-Fresno, Pacific Coll., Fresno City Coll. (oldest jr. coll. in Cal.). **Further information:** Chamber of Commerce, P.O. Box 1469, Fresno, CA 93721.

Grand Rapids, Michigan

Population: 182,774; **Pop. density:** 4,190 per sq. mi.; **Pop. growth:** −8.0%; **Pop. over 65:** 13.4%; **Pop. under 35:** 60.5%. **Area:** 43.4 sq. mi. **Employment:** 88,565 employed, 12.2% unemployed (Dec. 1984); **Per capita income:** $11,334.

Transportation: 4 railroads; 1 international airport; 3 bus lines. **Communications:** 6 TV stations; 20 radio stations. **Medical facilities:** 12 hospitals. **Educational facilities:** 60 public schools; 7 colleges. **Further information:** Chamber of Commerce, 17 Fountain St., NW, Grand Rapids, MI 49503.

Hamilton, Ontario

Population: 306,434 (1981); **Pop. density:** 6,456 per sq. mi.; **Pop. growth:** −1.0% (1971-81); **Pop. over 65:** 11.9%; **Pop. under 35:** 55.0%. **Area:** 47.4 sq. mi. **Employment:** 144,320 employed, 6.5% unemployed (1981, city).

Transportation: airport served by Nordair flights to Ottawa and Montreal; VIA passenger rail service, GO Transit links to nearby municipalities. **Communications:** 1 local TV station plus cable; 4 radio stations. **Medical facilities:** 7 general hospitals including McMaster Hospital and Hamilton Psychiatric Hospital. **Educational facilities:** 75 public schools; McMaster University, Mohawk College, 2 private business colleges. **Further information:** Hamilton & District Chamber of Commerce, 100 King St. West, Suite 830, Hamilton, Ont. L8P 1A2.

Honolulu Co., Hawaii

Population: 781,899; **Pop. density:** 1,280 per sq. mi.; **Pop. growth:** 20.9%; **Pop. over 65:** 7.4%; **Pop. under 35:** 62.4%. **Area:** 596 sq. mi.. **Employment:** 339,582 employed, 4.7% unemployed; **Per capita income:** $12,697.

Transportation: 1 major airport; large, active port for passengers and cargo. **Communications:** 5 TV stations; 23 radio stations. **Medical facilities:** 43 hospitals. **Educational facilities:** 230 public schools (state); 146 private schools (state); 1 university (9 campus centers); major public library system. **Further information:** Visitors Bureau, 2270 Kalakaua Avenue, Honolulu, HI 96815.

Houston, Texas

Population: 1,725,617; **Pop. density:** 2,869 per sq. mi.; **Pop. growth:** 29.3%; **Pop. over 65:** 6.9%; **Pop. under 35:** 64.4%. **Area:** 556 sq. mi.. **Employment:** 901,403 employed; 7.9% unemployed; **Per capita income:** $13,655.

Transportation: 2 airports; 5 railroads; major bus transit system; major international port. **Communications:** 8 TV stations; 40 radio stations. **Medical facilities:** 59 hospitals; major medical center. **Educational facilities:** 29 universities and colleges; 7th largest U.S. public school system; major public library system. **Further information:** Chamber of Commerce, 1100 Milam, Houston, TX 77002.

Huntington Beach, California

Population: 176,314; **Pop. density:** 6,315 per sq. mi.; **Pop. growth:** 47%. **Area:** 27 sq. mi.. **Employment:** 116,826 employed, 4.2% unemployed; **Per capita income:** $11,089.

Transportation: 1 airport; 4 railroads; 2 bus lines. **Communications:** TV, radio stations. **Medical facilities:** 2 hospitals. **Educational facilities:** 38 public schools; 2 colleges. **Further information:** Chamber of Commerce, Seacliff Village, 2213 Main #32, Huntington Beach, CA 92648.

Indianapolis, Indiana

Population: 707,655; **Pop. density:** 1,991 per sq. mi.; **Pop. growth:** −4.9%; **Pop. over 65:** 10.3%; **Pop. under 35:** 59.4%. **Area:** 352 sq. mi.. **Employment:** 368,685 employed, 8.2% unemployed; **Per capita income:** $11,858.

Transportation: 1 international airport; 6 railroads; 3 interstate bus lines. **Communications:** 7 TV stations; 27 radio stations. **Medical facilities:** 17 hospitals; major medical center. **Educational facilities:** 6 universities and colleges; major public library system. **Further information:** Chamber of Commerce, 320 N. Meridian Street, Indianapolis, IN 46204.

Jackson, Mississippi

Population: 204,195; **Pop. density:** 1,914 per sq. mi.; **Pop. growth:** 31.8%; **Pop. over 65:** 9.9%; **Pop. under 35:** 59.3%. **Area:** 106.2 sq. mi.. **Employment:** 90,446 employed, 7.2% unemployed; **Per capita income:** $10,449.

Transportation: American, Delta, Royale, and Sunbelt airlines; Greyhound, Trailways buses; Ill. Central Gulf railroad. **Communications:** 4 TV, 18 radio stations. **Medical facilities:** 11 hospitals including a VA facility. **Educational facilities:** Jackson St. Univ.; Belhaven, Millsaps, Mississippi, Tougaloo, and Wesley colleges. **Further information:** Chamber of Commerce, P.O. Box 22548, Jackson, MS 39205.

Jacksonville, Florida

Population: 556,370; **Pop. density:** 712 per sq. mi.; **Pop. growth:** 7.3%; **Pop. over 65:** 9.6%; **Pop. under 35:** 60.0%. **Area:** 760 sq. mi.. **Employment:** 265,928 employed, 5.8% unemployed; **Per capita income:** $11,149.

Transportation: 1 international airport; 3 railroads; 2 interstate bus lines. **Communications:** 6 TV stations; 21 radio stations. **Medical facilities:** 14 hospitals. **Educational facilities:** 5 universities and colleges; major public library system. **Further information:** Chamber of Commerce, 3 Independent Drive, P.O. Box 329, Jacksonville, FL 32201.

Jersey City, New Jersey

Population: 222,881; **Pop. density:** 16,934 per sq. mi.; **Pop. growth:** −14.1%; **Pop. over 65:** 11.8%; **Pop. under 35:** 57.6%. **Area:** 13.2 sq. mi. **Employment:** 77,978 employed, 13.6% unemployed; **Per capita income:** $11,194.

Transportation: bus and subway system. **Medical facilities:** 10 hospitals. **Educational facilities:** 3 colleges. **Further information:** Chamber of Commerce & Industry of Hudson County, 911 Bergen Ave., Jersey City, NJ 07303.

Kansas City, Missouri

Population: 445,221; **Pop. density:** 1,418 per sq. mi.; **Pop. growth:** −11.7%; **Pop. over 65:** 12.3%; **Pop. under 35:** 57.1%. **Area:** 316 sq. mi. **Employment:** 211,358 employed, 7.3% unemployed; **Per capita income:** $12,654.

Transportation: 1 international airport; a major rail center; 191 trunk lines; several barge companies. **Communications:** 6 TV, 14 AM, 18 FM radio stations. **Medical facilities:** 41 hospitals; 18 clinics. **Educational facilities:** 13 colleges & universities. **Further information:** Chamber of Commerce, 600 Charterbank Center, 920 Main St., Kansas City, MO 64105.

Knoxville, Tennessee

Population: 175,298; **Pop. density:** 2,273 per sq. mi.; **Pop. growth:** 2.5%; **Pop. over 65:** 13.8%; **Pop. under 35:** 57.8%. **Area:** 77 sq. mi.. **Employment:** 70,929 employed, 7.8% unemployed; **Per capita income:** $9,831.

Transportation: 8 airlines, 2 bus lines, 34 motor freight carriers; 2 railroads. **Communications:** 5 TV, 24 radio stations. **Medical facilities:** 9 hospitals. **Educational facilities:** 91 public schools; Univ. of Tennessee, Knoxville College. **Further information:** Chamber of Commerce, P.O. Box 2688, Knoxville, TN 37901.

Las Vegas, Nevada

Population: 179,587; **Pop. density:** 2,994 per sq. mi.; **Pop. growth:** 30.9%; **Pop. over 65:** 8.3%; **Pop. under 35:** 58.4%. **Area:** 55 sq. mi. **Employment:** 91,592 employed, 9.5% unemployed; **Per capita income:** $12,052.
Transportation: 1 international airport; 2 railroads; bus system. **Communcations:** 5 TV and 18 radio stations. **Medical facilities:** 8 hospitals. **Educational facilities:** 113 public schools; Clark Comm. College; Univ. of Nevada. **Further information:** Chamber of Commerce, 2301 E. Sahara Ave., Las Vegas, NV, 89104.

Laval, Quebec

Population: 273,000 (1983); **Pop. density:** 2,916 per sq. mi.; **Pop. growth:** 18.0% (1971-1981); **Pop. over 65:** 5.7%; **Pop. under 35:** 59.4%. **Area:** 94.7 sq. mi.. **Employment:** 126,040 employed, 7.6% unemployed (1981, city).
Transportation: (see City of Montreal). **Communications:** 2 radio stations; see also City of Montreal. **Medical facilities:** 4 hospitals; see also City of Montreal. **Educational facilities:** 116 public schools. **Further information:** La Chambre de Commerce, 1435 St-Martin Ouest, Suite 600, Laval, Que. H7S 2C6.

Lexington–Fayette, Kentucky

Population: 207,668; **Pop. density:** 719 per sq. mi.; **Pop. growth:** 88.8%; **Pop. over 65:** 8.6%; **Pop. under 35:** 63.3%. **Area:** 284 sq. mi. **Employment:** 116,388 employed, 4.4% unemployed; **Per capita income:** $12,582.
Transportation: 5 airlines, 4 railroads; city buses. **Communications:** 4 TV stations, CATV; 7 radio stations. **Medical facilities:** 4 general, 5 specialized hospitals. **Educational facilities:** Univ. of Kentucky, Transylvania Univ., Lexington Baptist College. **Further information:** Chamber of Commerce, 421 North Broadway, Lexington, KY 40508.

Lincoln, Nebraska

Population: 177,340; **Pop. density:** 2,866 per sq. mi.; **Pop. growth:** 15.0%; **Pop. over 65:** 10.3%; **Pop. under 35:** 63.9%. **Area:** 60 sq. mi. **Employment:** 97,644 employed, 4.1% unemployed; **Per capita income:** $11,698.
Transportation: 5 airlines serve Lincoln Municipal Airport; Greyhound, Trailways buses; Amtrak. **Communications:** 5 TV, 13 radio stations; CATV. **Medical facilities:** 4 hospitals including a VA facility. **Educational facilities:** 4 4-year colleges with 26,946 enrollment; 8 business, professional, or technical schools. **Further information:** Chamber.of Commerce, 1221 N St., Lincoln, NE 68508.

London, Ontario

Population: 268,051 (1983); **Pop. density:** 4,254 per sq. mi.; **Pop. growth:** 14% (1971-81); **Pop. over 65:** 10.2%; **Pop. under 35:** 58.5%. **Area:** 62.2 sq. mi.. **Employment:** 141,000 employed, 11.0% unemployed (1985, city).
Transportation: London International Airport served by Air Canada and Air Ontario; passenger train service on VIA Rail and Amtrak; 3 inter-city bus lines. **Communications:** 1 television station; 7 radio stations. **Medical facilities:** 3 general hospitals, London Psychiatric Hospital, and Shute Institute for Clinical and Laboratory Medicine. **Educational facilities:** Univ. of Western Ontario, Fanshawe College. **Further information:** Visitors & Convention Services, 300 Dufferin Ave., P.O. Box 5035, London, Ont. N6A 4L9.

Long Beach, California

Population: 371,426; **Pop. density:** 7,226 per sq. mi.; **Pop. growth:** 0.7%; **Pop. over 65:** 14.0%; **Pop. under 35:** 56.6%. **Area:** 49.8 sq. mi.. **Employment:** 171,832 employed, 7.7% unemployed; **Per capita income:** $13,417.
Transportation: 1 airport; 3 railroads. **Communications:** 1 cable TV station; 2 AM, 6 FM radio stations. **Medical facilities:** 10 hospitals. **Educational facilities:** 1 university; 1 college. **Further information:** Chamber of Commerce, 50 Oceangate Plaza, Long Beach, CA 90802.

Los Angeles, California

Population: 3,022,247; **Pop. density:** 6,380 per sq. mi.; **Pop. growth:** +0.5%; **Pop. over 65:** 10.6%; **Pop. under 35:** 58.1%. **Area:** 465 sq. mi.. **Employment:** 1,472,090 employed, 8.9% unemployed; **Per capita income:** $13,417.
Transportation: 1 major airport; 4 railroads; major bus carrier service; major freeway system. **Communications:** 19 TV stations; 71 radio stations. **Medical facilities:** 822 hospitals and clinics; 409 nursing homes. **Educational facilities:** 11 universities and colleges; 1,642 public schools; 800 private schools; 61 public libraries. **Further information:** Chamber of Commerce, P.O. Box 3696, Terminal Annex, Los Angeles, CA 90051.

Louisville, Kentucky

Population: 293,531; **Pop. density:** 4,974 per sq. mi.; **Pop. growth:** −17.5%; **Pop. over 65:** 15.3%; **Pop. under 35:** 54.1%. **Area:** 60 sq. mi. **Employment:** 126,421 employed, 6.8% unemployed. **Per capita income:** $11,507.
Transportation: 2 municipal airports; 1 terminal, 6 trunk-line railroads; 3 bus lines; 125 inter-city truck lines; 5 barge lines. **Communications:** 4 TV, 20 radio stations, 2 educational, 3 cable. **Medical facilities:** 21 hospitals. **Educational facilities:** 10 colleges & universities, 3 business colleges & technical schools. **Further information:** Chamber of Commerce, 300 W. Liberty, Louisville, KY 40202.

Lubbock, Texas

Population: 176,588; **Pop. density:** 1,933 per sq. mi.; **Pop. growth:** 16.7%; **Pop. over 65:** 7.8%; **Pop. under 35:** 66.9%. **Area:** 90 sq. mi. **Employment:** 88,798 employed, 5.3% unemployed; **Per capita income:** $11,123.
Transportation: Lubbock International Airport; 2 railroads, bus line. **Communications:** 5 TV, 18 radio stations. **Medical facilities:** 7 hospitals. **Educational facilities:** 51 public schools; Texas Tech Univ., Lubbock Christian College. **Further information:** Chamber of Commerce, P.O. Box 561, Lubbock, TX 79408.

Madison, Wisconsin

Population: 172,640; **Pop. density:** 3,219 per sq. mi.; **Pop. growth:** −0.7%; **Pop. over 65:** 8.7%; **Pop. under 35:** 66.5%. **Area:** 53 sq. mi. **Employment:** 95,305 employed, 4.8% unemployed; **Per capita income:** $13,021.
Transportation: Dane County Regional Airport with 5 airlines; 4 bus lines; highways I-90, I-94. **Communications:** 3 commercial, 1 public, 2 cable TV stations; 17 radio stations. **Medical facilities:** 5 hospitals including Univ. of Wis. and a VA facility; 21 clinics. **Educational facilities:** Univ. of Wisconsin; Madison Area Technical colleges. **Further information:** Chamber of Commerce, 625 W. Washington Ave., Madison, WI 53701.

Memphis, Tennessee

Population: 645,760; **Pop. density:** 2,448 per sq. mi.; **Pop. growth:** 3.6%; **Pop. over 65:** 10.4%; **Pop. under 35:** 60.5%. **Area:** 264 sq. mi.. **Employment:** 300,800 employed, 7.5% unemployed; **Per capita income:** $10,590.
Transportation: 1 major airport; 6 railroads; bus system. **Communications:** 6 TV stations; 24 radio stations. **Medical facilities:** 19 hospitals. **Educational facilities:**

10 universities and colleges; 149 public schools; 76 private schools. **Further information:** Chamber of Commerce, Box 224, Memphis TN 38101.

Miami, Florida

Population: 382,726; **Pop. density:** 8,671 per sq. mi.; **Pop. growth:** 3.6%; **Pop. over 65:** 17.0%; **Pop. under 35:** 46.5%. **Area:** 34 sq. mi.. **Employment:** 171,800 employed; 9.9% unemployed; **Per capita income:** $12,131.
Transportation: 1 international airport; 2 passenger railroads, 1 all-freight; 2 bus lines; 65 truck lines. **Communications:** 6 commercial, 5 educational TV stations; 31 radio stations. **Medical facilities:** 41 hospitals, 39 nursing homes; VA Hospital. **Educational facilities:** 6 colleges & universities. **Further information:** Metro-Dade Department of Tourism, 234 W. Flagler St., Miami, FL 33130.

Milwaukee, Wisconsin

Population: 631,509; **Pop. density:** 6,627 per sq. mi.; **Pop. growth:** −11.3%; **Pop. over 65:** 12.5%; **Pop. under 35:** 59.8%. **Area:** 96 sq. mi.. **Employment:** 300,071 employed, 7.4% unemployed; **Per capita income:** $13,001.
Transportation: 1 major airport; 4 railroads; major port; 4 bus lines. **Communications:** 7 TV stations; 31 radio stations. **Medical facilities:** 27 hospitals; major medical center. **Educational facilities:** 11 universities and colleges; major public school and library system. **Further information:** Association of Commerce, 756 N. Milwaukee Street, Milwaukee, WI 53202.

Minneapolis, Minnesota

Population: 369,161; **Pop. density:** 6,744 per sq. mi.; **Pop. growth:** −14.6%; **Pop. over 65:** 15.4%; **Pop. under 35:** 59.4%. **Area:** 55 sq. mi.. **Employment:** 201,780 employed; 4.4% unemployed; **Per capita income:** $13,781.
Transportation: 1 international airport; 5 trunk railroads; 150 trucking firms; 5 major barge lines. **Communications:** 6 TV, 39 radio stations. **Medical facilities:** 14 hospitals, including leading heart hospital at Univ. of Minnesota. **Educational facilities:** 13 colleges and universities. **Further information:** Chamber of Commerce, 15 S. 5th St., Minneapolis, MN 55402.

Mississauga, Ontario

Population: 355,900 (1984); **Pop. density:** 3,367 per sq. mi.; **Pop. growth:** 60.0% (1974-84); **Pop. over 65:** 6.1%; **Pop. under 35:** 59.3%. **Area:** 111 sq. mi.. **Employment:** 174,933 employed, 5.1% unemployed (1982, city).
Transportation: Pearson International Airport is within Mississauga; GO Transit connects with Toronto and other municipalities; bus connections to Metro Toronto subway system. **Communications:** 1 TV, 2 local radio station; see also City of Toronto. **Medical facilities:** Mississauga General Hospital; Credit Valley Hospital. **Educational facilities:** Erindale Campus of the University of Toronto, Sheridan College; 132 public and separate schools, 2 schools for trainable mentally retarded. **Further information:** Public Relations Office, Mississauga City Hall, One City Centre Drive, Mississauga, Ont. L5B 1M2.

Mobile, Alabama

Population: 204,586; **Pop. density:** 1,630 per sq. mi.; **Pop. growth:** 5.5%; **Pop. over 65:** 11.1%; **Pop. under 35:** 59.3%. **Area:** 123 sq. mi.. **Employment:** 79,378 employed, 12.0% unemployed; **Per capita income:** $9,171.
Transportation: 4 railroads, 4 major airlines, 55 truck lines; leading river system. **Communications:** 5 TV, 12 radio stations; CATV. **Medical facilities:** 6 hospitals. **Educational facilities:** Univ. of South Alabama; Spring Hill,

Mobile colleges. **Further information:** Chamber of Commerce, P.O. Box 2187, Mobile, AL 36652.

Montgomery, Alabama

Population: 182,406; **Pop. density:** 1,389 per sq. mi.; **Pop. growth:** 33.3%; **Pop. over 65:** 10.1%; **Pop. under 35:** 60.7%. **Area:** 128 sq. mi.. **Employment:** 80,336 employed, 8.6% unemployed; **Per capita income:** $10,432.
Transportation: 3 airlines, 5 railroads, 2 bus lines, city bus line; Interstate 65 and 85 intersect in city; Alabama River is navigable to Gulf of Mexico. **Communications:** 4 TV, 14 radio stations; CATV. **Medical facilities:** 5 general hospitals; VA and mental health facilities. **Educational facilities:** 5 colleges and universities. **Further information:** Chamber of Commerce, P.O. Box 79, Montgomery, AL 36192.

Montreal, Quebec

Population: 1,018,609 (1984); **Pop. density:** 15,046 per sq. mi.; **Pop. growth:** −19% (1971-81); **Pop. over 65:** 13.1%; **Pop. under 35:** 51.6%. **Area:** 67.7 sq. mi.. **Employment:** 1,051,500 (metro) employed, 12.3% unemployed (May 1985).
Transportation: served by 2 major airports at Dorval and Mirabel; headquarters of Canadian National (VIA) and Canadian Pacific railways; major port on St. Lawrence Seaway; subway system (Metro). **Communications:** 5 TV stations, 20 radio stations. **Medical facilities:** over 70 hospitals, including the renowned Montreal Neurological Institute and the Montreal Children's Hospital. **Educational facilities:** Concordia University, McGill University, Universite du Montreal, Universite de Quebec. **Further information:** Convention and Tourism Bureau of Greater Montreal, Mart F-1 Frontenac, Box 889, Place Bonaventure, Montreal, Quebec H5A 1E6.

Nashville-Davidson, Tennessee

Population: 455,252; **Pop. density:** 949 per sq. mi.; **Pop. growth:** 7.0%; **Pop. over 65:** 11.0%; **Pop. under 35:** 58.7%. **Area:** 480 sq. mi.. **Employment:** 254,038 employed, 4.4% unemployed; **Per capita income:** $11,058.
Transportation: 1 airport; 2 railroads; more than 100 motor freight lines; 9 U.S. highways, 6 branches of interstate system. **Communications:** 5 TV, 30 radio stations. **Medical facilities:** 17 hospitals; 2 medical schools; VA Hospital, speech-hearing center. **Educational facilities:** 16 colleges & universities. **Further information:** Chamber of Commerce, 161 4th Ave., Nashville, TN 37219.

Newark, New Jersey

Population: 320,512; **Pop. density:** 13,718 per sq. mi.; **Pop. growth:** −13.8%; **Pop. over 65:** 8.8%; **Pop. under 35:** 61.6%. **Area:** 24 sq. mi.. **Employment:** 119,430 employed, 13.3% unemployed; **Per capita income:** $14,847.
Transportation: 1 international airport; 2 railroads; bus system; 2 subways. **Communications:** 3 TV, 5 radio stations. **Medical facilities:** 6 hospitals. **Educational facilities:** 5 universities and colleges; 71 public schools. **Further information:** Chamber of Commerce, 50 Park Pl., Newark, NJ 07102.

New Orleans, Louisiana

Population: 564,561; **Pop. density:** 2,802 per sq. mi.; **Pop. growth:** −6%; **Pop. over 65:** 11.7%; **Pop. under 35:** 60.1%. **Area:** 199 sq. mi.. **Employment:** 220,071 employed, 11.0% unemployed; **Per capita income:** $11,706.
Transportation: 2 airports; major railroad center; major international port. **Communications:** 5 TV stations; 20 radio stations. **Medical facilities:** numerous hospitals; major medical research center. **Educational facilities:** 13 universities and colleges; major public library system. **Further information:** Chamber of Commerce, 301 Camp Street, New Orleans, LA 70130.

New York City, New York

Population: 7,086,096; **Pop. density:** 23,494 per sq. mi.; **Pop. growth:** −10.4%; **Pop. over 65:** 13.5%; **Pop. under 35:** 53.7%. **Area:** 301 sq. mi.. **Employment:** 2,855,000 employed, 8.2% unemployed; **Per capita income:** $13,808.

Transportation: 2 airports; 4 heliports; 2 rail terminals; 34 bus carriers; major subway network; ferry system; 4 underwater tunnels. **Communications:** 15 TV stations, 39 radio stations. **Medical facilities:** over 100 hospitals; 5 medical research centers. **Educational facilities:** 29 universities and colleges; 1,000 public schools, 879 private schools; 201 public libraries. **Further information:** Convention and Visitors Bureau, 2 Columbus Circle, New York, NY 10019.

Norfolk, Virginia

Population: 266,874; **Pop. density:** 5,037 per sq. mi.; **Pop. growth:** −13.3%; **Pop. over 65:** 9.2%; **Pop. under 35:** 68.6%. **Area:** 53 sq. mi.. **Employment:** 107,952 employed, 4.8% unemployed; **Per capita income:** $11,314.

Transportation: 1 international airport; 4 major railroad systems in area. **Communications:** 7 TV, 38 radio stations. **Medical facilities:** 10 hospitals, 1 medical school. **Educational facilities:** 53 public schools; 2 universities, 1 college. **Further information:** Chamber of Commerce, 480 Bank St., Norfolk, VA 23510.

North York, Ontario

Population (1983): 555,276; **Pop. density:** 8,129 per sq. mi.; **Pop. growth:** 2.0% (1974-84); **Pop. over 65:** 14.0%; **Pop. under 35:** 49.0%. **Area:** 68.3 sq. mi.. **Employment:** 243,049 employed, 7.3% unemployed (1985).

Transportation: (see City of Toronto). **Communications:** (see City of Toronto). **Medical facilities:** 10 hospitals; see also City of Toronto. **Educational facilities:** York University, Seneca College; 270 public and private elementary, intermediate and secondary schools. **Further information:** Public Information Office, 5100 Yonge St., North York, Ont. M2N 5V7.

Oakland, California

Population: 344,652; **Pop. density:** 6,284 per sq. mi.; **Pop. growth:** −6.2%; **Pop. over 65:** 13.2%; **Pop. under 35:** 57%. **Area:** 54 sq. mi.. **Employment:** 149,961 employed, 10.0% unemployed; **Per capita income:** $14,653.

Transportation: 1 international airport; western terminus for 3 railroads; underground, underwater 75-mile subway. **Communications:** 1 TV, 3 radio stations. **Medical facilities:** 9 hospitals, including Children's Hospital Medical Center, VA hospital. **Educational facilities:** 1 university; 6 colleges. **Further information:** Chamber of Commerce, 1320 Webster St., Oakland, CA 94612.

Oklahoma City, Oklahoma

Population: 427,714; **Pop. density:** 667 per sq. mi.; **Pop. growth:** 9.5%; **Pop. over 65:** 11.3%; **Pop. under 35:** 58.2%. **Area:** 604 sq. mi.. **Employment:** 212,378 employed, 7.2% unemployed; **Per capita income:** $12,427.

Transportation: 1 international airport; 2 railroads; 5 major bus lines. **Communications:** 8 TV, 24 radio stations; cable TV. **Medical facilities:** 19 hospitals. **Educational facilities:** 90 public schools; 5 colleges and universities. **Further information:** Chamber of Commerce, One Santa Fe Plaza, Oklahoma City, OK 73102.

Omaha, Nebraska

Population: 328,557; **Pop. density:** 3,453 per sq. mi.; **Pop. growth:** −9.5%; **Pop. over 65:** 12.2%; **Pop. under 35:** 41.9%. **Area:** 91 sq. mi.. **Employment:** 151,020 employed, 6.6% unemployed; **Per capita income:** $12,105.

Transportation: 8 major airlines; major rail center, with 6 major railroads; 98 truck lines; 2 interstate highways; 2 intercity bus lines; 5 barge lines. **Communications:** 6 TV, 16 radio stations. **Medical facilities:** 16 hospitals; 2 medical, 1 dental, 7 nursing schools; institute for cancer research. **Educational facilities:** 83 public schools; 3 universities, 6 colleges. **Further information:** Chamber of Commerce, 1301 Harney St., Omaha, NE 68102.

Ottawa, Ontario

Population: 304,776 (1984); **Pop. density:** 7,171 per sq. mi.; **Pop. growth:** 1.0% (1976-81); **Pop. over 65:** 9.0% (1981); **Pop. under 35:** 58.0% (1981). **Area:** 42.5 sq. mi.. **Employment:** 154,690 employed, 6.3% unemployed (1981, city).

Transportation: Ottawa International Airport, served by 8 airlines, more than 100 flights daily; surface transport by VIA Rail and intercity bus service. **Communications:** 6 TV and 14 radio stations. **Medical facilities:** 10 hospitals with more than 2,000 beds. **Educational facilities:** Carleton Univ., the bi-lingual Univ. of Ottawa, Algonquin Community College. **Further information:** Canada's Capital Visitors Bureau, 7th Floor, 222 Queen St., Ottawa, Ont. K1P 5V9.

Philadelphia, Pennsylvania

Population: 1,665,382; **Pop. density:** 12,413 per sq. mi.; **Pop. growth:** −13.4%; **Pop. over 65:** 14.1%; **Pop. under 35:** 54.4%. **Area:** 136 sq. mi.. **Employment:** 741,093 employed, 6.8% unemployed; **Per capita income:** $12,700.

Transportation: 1 major airport; 3 railroads; biggest freshwater port in world; subway, el, rail commuter, bus, and streetcar system. **Communications:** 6 TV stations; 53 radio stations. **Medical facilities:** 124 hospitals. **Educational facilities:** 88 degree-granting institutions; major public library system. **Further information:** Office of City Representative, 1660 Municipal Services Bldg., Philadelphia, PA 19107.

Phoenix, Arizona

Population: 824,230; **Pop. density:** 2,438 per sq. mi.; **Pop. growth:** 35.1%; **Pop. over 65:** 9.3%; **Pop. under 35:** 60.4%. **Area:** 324 sq. mi.. **Employment:** 495,680 employed, 4.4% unemployed; **Per capita income:** $11,779.

Transportation: 1 major airport; 2 railroads; 2 transcontinental bus lines; public transit system. **Communications:** 8 TV stations; 38 radio stations. **Medical facilities:** 33 hospitals, 1 medical research center. **Educational facilities:** 8 universities and colleges; 6 community colleges; major public library system. **Further information:** Chamber of Commerce, 34 W. Monroe, Suite 900, Phoenix, AZ 85003.

Pittsburgh, Pennsylvania

Population: 414,936; **Pop. density:** 7,707 per sq. mi.; **Pop. growth:** −18%; **Pop. over 65:** 16.0%; **Pop. under 35:** 52.9%. **Area:** 55 sq. mi.. **Employment:** 159,203 employed, 8.7% unemployed; **Per capita income:** $11,920.

Transportation: 1 international airport; 20 railroads; 2 bus lines; trolley/subway system. **Communications:** 6 TV, 25 radio stations. **Medical facilities:** 32 hospitals; VA installation. **Educational facilities:** 86 public schools; 3 universities; 6 colleges. **Further information:** Chamber of Commerce, 3 Gateway Ctr., Pittsburgh, PA 15222.

Portland, Oregon

Population: 367,530; **Pop. density:** 3,557 per sq. mi.; **Pop. growth:** −3.6%; **Pop. over 65:** 10.9%; **Pop. under 35:** 58.9%. **Area:** 103 sq. mi.. **Employment:** 184,144 employed, 9.1% unemployed; **Per capita income:** $12,268.

Transportation: 1 international airport; 3 major rail freight lines, Amtrak; 2 bus lines; 27-mi. frontage freshwater port; mass transit system. **Communications:** 5 TV, 27

radio stations. **Medical facilities:** 32 hospitals; Oregon Health Sciences University Hospital; VA hospital. **Educational facilities:** 9 universities; 4 community colleges. **Further information:** Chamber of Commerce, 824 SW 5th, Portland, OR 97204.

Richmond, Virginia

Population: 218,237; **Pop. density:** 3,650 per sq. mi.; **Pop. growth:** −12.1%; **Pop. over 65:** 14.1%; **Pop. under 35:** 56.9%. **Area:** 60 sq. mi.. **Employment:** 108,493 employed, 5.8% unemployed; **Per capita income:** $13,039.

Transportation: 4 commercial, 3 commuter air lines; 4 railroads, 5 intercity bus lines; deepwater terminal accessible to ocean-going ships. **Communications:** 6 TV, 24 radio stations. **Medical facilities:** Medical Coll. of Virginia renowned for heart and kidney transplants; 17 other hospitals including VA facility. **Educational facilities:** 54 public schools; Va. Commonwealth, Univ. of Richmond, Va. Union, Randolph-Macon College. **Further information:** Chamber of Commerce, 201 E. Franklin St., Richmond, VA 23219.

Riverside, California

Population: 174,023; **Pop. density:** 2,406 per sq. mi.; **Pop. growth:** 22.0%; **Pop. over 65:** 8.8%; **Pop. under 35:** 62.8%. **Area:** 71 sq. mi. **Employment:** 79,536 employed, 8.2% unemployed; **Per capita income:** $11,188.

Communications: 11 TV, 13 radio stations. **Educational facilities:** Univ. of Cal.- Riverside, Cal. Baptist. **Further information:** Chamber of Commerce, 4261 Main St., Riverside, CA 92501.

Rochester, New York

Population: 244,094; **Pop. density:** 7,068 per sq. mi.; **Pop. growth:** −18.1%; **Pop. over 65:** 14.0%; **Pop. under 35:** 60.0%. **Area:** 34 sq. mi.. **Employment:** 101,361 employed, 7.4% unemployed; **Per capita income:** $12,649.

Transportation: Amtrak; Greyhound, Trailways, Blue Bird bus lines; Monroe Co. airport with 8 major airlines; Rochester Transit Service; Port of Rochester; some 75 motor freight firms. **Communications:** 5 TV, 18 radio stations. **Medical facilities:** 8 general hospitals including Strong Memorial. **Educational facilities:** 8 private and 2 public 4-year colleges; 3 community colleges. **Further information:** Chamber of Commerce, 55 St. Paul St., Rochester, NY 14604.

Sacramento, California

Population: 288,597; **Pop. density:** 2,872 per sq. mi.; **Pop. growth:** 10.7%; **Pop. over 65:** 9.6%; **Pop. under 35:** 59%. **Area:** 96 sq. mi.. **Employment:** 126,102 employed, 9.3% unemployed; **Per capita income:** $11,676.

Transportation: metropolitan airport; 2 mainline transcontinental rail carriers; bus and light rail system. **Communications:** 7 TV, 22 radio stations. **Medical facilities:** 15 hospitals. **Educational facilities:** 3 universities, 4 community colleges. **Further information:** Chamber of Commerce, 917 7th St., P.O. Box 1017, Sacramento, CA 95805.

St. Louis, Missouri

Population: 437,354; **Pop. density:** 7,427 per sq. mi.; **Pop. growth:** −27.2%; **Pop. over 65:** 17.6%; **Pop. under 35:** 54%. **Area:** 61 sq. mi.. **Employment:** 193,085 employed, 9.4% unemployed; **Per capita income:** $12,710.

Transportation: 1 airport; 2d largest rail center in U.S.; 17 trunk line railroads; largest inland port in U.S.; 9 major highways; 14 bus lines; 350 motor freight lines, 14 barge lines. **Communications:** 6 TV, 35 radio stations. **Medical facilities:** 65 hospitals. **Educational facilities:** 4 universities, 26 colleges and seminaries. **Further information:** Convention and Visitors Bureau, 500 N. Broadway, St. Louis, MO 63101.

St. Paul, Minnesota

Population: 270,443; **Pop. density:** 5,196 per sq. mi.; **Pop. growth:** −12.8%; **Pop. over 65:** 15.0%; **Pop. under 35:** 41.5%. **Area:** 52 sq. mi.. **Employment:** 147,821 employed, 5.5% unemployed; **Per capita income:** $13,781.

Transportation: 1 international airport; 5 major rail lines; 3 interstate bus lines; 60 barge firms. **Communications:** 5 TV, 36 radio stations. **Medical facilities:** 12 private hospitals; community hospital and research center. **Educational facilities:** 1 university; 5 colleges; 51 public schools. **Further information:** Chamber of Commerce, 701 N. Central Tower, 445 Minnesota St., St. Paul, MN 55101.

St. Petersburg, Florida

Population: 241,214; **Pop. density:** 4,186 per sq. mi.; **Pop. growth:** 10.4%; **Pop. over 65:** 25.8%; **Pop. under 35:** 43.7%. **Area:** 57 sq. mi.. **Employment:** 111,951 employed, 5.9% unemployed; **Per capita income:** $11,362.

Transportation: 1 international airport; bus system; 2 full-service ports. **Communications:** 9 TV, 49 radio stations. **Medical facilities:** 9 hospitals. **Educational facilities:** 106 public schools; 7 colleges. **Further information:** Chamber of Commerce, P.O. Box 1371, St. Petersburg, FL 33731.

San Antonio, Texas

Population: 819,021; **Pop. density:** 2,988 per sq. mi.; **Pop. growth:** 20%; **Pop. over 65:** 9.5%; **Pop. under 35:** 62.1%. **Area:** 263 sq. mi.. **Employment:** 363,960 employed, 6.0% unemployed; **Per capita income:** $10,569.

Transportation: 1 major airport; 4 railroads; 6 bus lines; major freeway system. **Communications:** 5 TV, 20 radio stations. **Medical facilities:** 16 hospitals; major medical center. **Educational facilities:** 7 universities and colleges; major public library system. **Further information:** Chamber of Commerce, 602 E. Commerce, P.O. Box 1628, San Antonio, TX 78296.

San Diego, California

Population: 915,956; **Pop. density:** 2,736 per sq. mi.; **Pop. growth:** 25.5%; **Pop. over 65:** 9.7%; **Pop. under 35:** 62.1%. **Area:** 320 sq. mi.. **Employment:** 395,985 employed, 6.1% unemployed; **Per capita income:** $12,272.

Transportation: 1 major airport; 1 railroad; major freeway system; bus system. **Communications:** 8 TV, 33 radio stations. **Medical facilities:** 18 hospitals; 2 major medical research centers. **Educational facilities:** 8 universities and colleges; major public library system. **Further information:** Chamber of Commerce, 110 West "C," Suite 1600, San Diego, CA 92101.

San Francisco, California

Population: 691,637; **Pop. density:** 14,760 per sq. mi.; **Pop. growth:** −5.1%; **Pop. over 65:** 15.4%; **Pop. under 35:** 51.7%. **Area:** 46 sq. mi.. **Employment:** 370,775 employed, 6.4% unemployed; **Per capita income:** $17,875.

Transportation: 1 major airport; intra-city railway system; 2 railway transit systems; bus and railroad service; ferry system; 1 underwater tunnel. **Communications:** 7 TV stations; 45 radio stations. **Medical facilities:** 29 hospitals; 1 major medical center. **Educational facilities:** 4 universities and colleges; major public library system. **Further information:** Chamber of Commerce, 465 California Street, San Francisco, CA 94104.

San Jose, California

Population: 659,181; **Pop. density:** 3,984 per sq. mi.; **Pop. growth:** 36.9%; **Pop. over 65:** 6.2%; **Pop. under 35:** 64.7%. **Area:** 158 sq. mi.. **Employment:** 394,379 employed, 6.0% unemployed; **Per capita income:** $15,583.
Transportation: 1 international airport; 2 railroads; bus system. **Communications:** 4 TV stations; 14 radio stations. **Medical facilities:** 6 hospitals. **Educational facilities:** 3 universities and colleges; major public library system. **Further information:** Chamber of Commerce, One Paseo de San Antonio, San Jose, CA 95113.

Santa Ana, California

Population: 217,219; **Pop. density:** 7,544 per sq. mi.; **Pop. growth:** 30.8%; **Pop. over 65:** 7.4%; **Pop. under 35:** 66.9%. **Area:** 27 sq. mi.. **Employment:** 124,188 employed, 5.6% unemployed (county); **Per capita income:** $15,250.
Transportation: John Wayne airport; 8 major freeways including main Los Angeles-San Diego artery; Amtrak. **Communications:** $27 mln. installation of CATV system. **Medical facilities:** 4 hospitals with 561 beds. **Educational facilities:** 1 university, 1 community college, 1 law school. **Further information:** Chamber of Commerce, 1616 E. 4th St., P.O. Box 205, Santa Ana, CA 92702.

Seattle, Washington

Population: 490,077; **Pop. density:** 5,879 per sq. mi.; **Pop. growth:** −7.0%; **Pop. over 65:** 15.4%; **Pop. under 35:** 54.9%. **Area:** 84 sq. mi.. **Employment:** 264,723 employed, 8.8% unemployed; **Per capita income:** $13,955.
Transportation: 1 international airport; 3 railroads; ferries serve Puget Sound, Alaska, Canada. **Communications:** 7 TV, 23 AM & 19 FM radio stations. **Medical facilities:** 27 hospitals. **Educational facilities:** 4 colleges; 11 community colleges. **Further information:** Chamber of Commerce, 215 Columbia St., Seattle, WA 98104.

Shreveport, Louisiana

Population: 210,881; **Pop. density:** 2,572 per sq. mi.; **Pop. growth:** 13%; **Pop. over 65:** 11.7%; **Pop. under 35:** 59.4%. **Area:** 80 sq. mi.. **Employment:** 89,964 employed, 8.3% unemployed; **Per capita income:** $10,942.
Transportation: 6 air lines service Shreveport Regional airport; Continental Trailways buses. **Communications:** 4 TV, 17 radio stations; CATV. **Medical facilities:** 11 hospitals with over 3,000 beds. **Educational facilities:** La. Tech., Northwestern St., and Grambling univs.; Centenary Coll., Bossier Parish Comm. College. **Further information:** Chamber of Commerce, P.O. Box 20074, Shreveport, LA 71120.

Tampa, Florida

Population: 276,413; **Pop. density:** 3,232 per sq. mi.; **Pop. growth:** −2.2%; **Pop. over 65:** 14.8%; **Pop. under 35:** 54%. **Area:** 84 sq. mi.. **Employment:** 147,661 employed, 6.5% unemployed; **Per capita income:** $11,362.
Transportation: 1 international airport; Port of Tampa, 140 steamship lines; 2 bus lines. **Communications:** 7 TV, 27 radio stations. **Medical facilities:** 19 hospitals. **Educational facilities:** 130 public schools; 4 colleges and universities. **Further information:** Chamber of Commerce, 801 E. Kennedy Blvd., Tampa, FL 33601.

Toledo, Ohio

Population: 350,565; **Pop. density:** 4,221 per sq. mi.; **Pop. growth:** −7.4%; **Pop. over 65:** 12.5%; **Pop. under 35:** 58.5%. **Area:** 84 sq. mi.. **Employment:** 148,065 employed, 9.3% unemployed; **Per capita income:** $11,613.
Transportation: 9 major airlines; 7 railroads; 100 motor freight lines; 2 interstate bus lines; 13 major highways.

Communications: 4 TV, 13 radio stations; 1 cablevision company. **Medical facilities:** 10 major hospital complexes. **Educational facilities:** 2 universities; 3 colleges. **Further information:** Convention and Visitors Bureau, 218 Huron, Toledo, OH 43604.

Toronto, Ontario

Population: 599,217 (1981); **Pop. density:** 15,979 per sq. mi.; **Pop. growth:** −16.0% (1971-81); **Pop. over 65:** 12.4% **Pop. under 35:** 54.5%. **Area:** 37.5 sq. mi.. **Employment:** 327,610 employed, 4.7% unemployed (1981, city).
Transportation: bus system, subway system; Pearson International Airport; passenger and freight train service. **Communications:** 7 TV stations including educational and French-language channels; 18 radio stations. **Medical facilities:** 40 active treatment hospitals (metro) including Hospital for Sick Children. **Educational facilities:** Univ. of Toronto, Ryerson Polytechnical Institute, George Brown College (plus York Univ. and 3 more community colleges within metro), Ontario College of Art, Royal Conservatory of Music, Osgoode Hall Law School (at York Univ.). **Further information:** Convention and Visitors Association, 220 Yonge St., Suite 110, Box 510, Toronto, Ontario M5B 2H1.

Tucson, Arizona

Population: 352,455; **Pop. density:** 3,338 per sq. mi.; **Pop. growth:** 25.7%; **Pop. over 65:** 11.7%; **Pop. under 35:** 60.7%. **Area:** 99 sq. mi.. **Employment:** 165,542 employed, 5.2% unemployed; **Per capita income:** $10,694.
Transportation: 1 international airport; 3 railroads; bus system. **Communications:** 7 TV, 19 radio stations. **Medical facilities:** 12 hospitals. **Educational facilities:** 1 university, 1 college; 157 public schools. **Further information:** Chamber of Commerce, P.O. Box 991, Tucson, AZ 85702.

Tulsa, Oklahoma

Population: 375,300; **Pop. density:** 1,940 per sq. mi.; **Pop. growth:** 9.3%; **Pop. over 65:** 10.8%; **Pop. under 35:** 58.1%. **Area:** 185.6 sq. mi.. **Employment:** 185,521 employed, 7.8% unemployed; **Per capita income:** $12,381.
Transportation: 1 international airport; 4 rail lines; 2 regional bus lines, 2 national bus lines. **Communications:** 6 TV, 21 radio stations. **Medical facilities:** 6 hospitals. **Educational facilities:** 89 public schools; 6 colleges and universities. **Further information:** Chamber of Commerce, 616 S. Boston Ave., Tulsa, OK 74119.

Vancouver, British Columbia

Population: 414,281 (1981). **Pop. density:** 9,480 per sq. mi.; **Pop. growth:** −2.8%; **Pop. over 65:** 15.3%; **Pop. under 35:** 51.3%. **Area:** 43.7 sq. mi.. **Employment:** 217,000 employed, 6.0% unemployed (1981, city).
Transportation: International Airport served by 8 major airlines; western terminus of Canada's 2 national railways, Canadian National (VIA passenger service) and Canadian Pacific; provincially operated British Columbia linked to U.S. by Amtrak; 3 long-distance bus carriers (Trailways, Greyhound, Pacific Coach Lines); Canada's busiest port. **Communications:** 19 radio stations, 4 local TV stations. **Medical facilities:** General and St. Paul's are largest hospitals; also Shaughnessy and New Children's in Vancouver, Royal Columbian in New Westminster, Burnaby General, Lion's Gate in North Vancouver, and Riverview Psychiatric Hospital. **Educational facilities:** Univ. of British Columbia and Simon Fraser Univ.; 5 institutes of technology, 4 community colleges, Trinity Western (private) Univ., Open Learning Institute. **Further information:** Convention & Visitors Bureau, P.O. Box 11142-1055 West Georgia Street, Vancouver B.C., V6E 4C8.

Virginia Beach, Virginia

Population: 282,588; **Pop. density:** 1,028 per sq. mi.; **Pop. growth:** 52.3%; **Pop. over 65:** 4.5%; **Pop. under 35:** 66.0%. **Area:** 255 sq. mi.. **Employment:** 125,022 employed, 3.7% unemployed; **Per capita income:** $11,314.
Transportation: 10 airlines serve Norfolk/Virginia Beach Airport; Greyhound, Trailways buses. **Communications:** 6 TV, 39 radio stations. **Medical facilities:** 2 hospitals. **Educational facilities:** 59 public schools; 1 university. **Further information:** Chamber of Commerce, 4512 Virginia Beach Blvd., Virginia Beach, VA 23462.

Washington, District of Columbia

Population: 633,425; **Pop. density:** 10,121 per sq. mi.; **Pop. growth:** −15.7%; **Pop. over 65:** 11.6%; **Pop. under 35:** 56.9%. **Area:** 63 sq. mi.. **Employment:** 300,078 employed, 8.6% unemployed; **Per capita income:** $16,173.
Transportation: 2 airports; rail transit system; extensive local bus service; long distance rail and bus service. **Communications:** 8 TV stations; 40 radio stations. **Medical facilities:** 43 hospitals; major medical research center. **Educational facilities:** 6 universities and colleges; 24 public libraries. **Further information:** Convention and Visitors Association, 1575 I Street NW, Suite 250, Washington, DC 20005.

Wichita, Kansas

Population: 288,723; **Pop. density:** 2,765 per sq. mi.; **Pop. growth:** 1.0%; **Pop. over 65:** 10.6%; **Pop. under 35:** 59.9%. **Area:** 101.4 sq. mi.. **Employment:** 144,858 employed, 6.4% unemployed; **Per capita income:** $12,981.
Transportation: 2 airports; 4 major rail freight lines; 1 bus line; 72 truck lines; 9 major highways. **Communications:** 4 TV, 7 AM, 6 FM radio stations; cable TV. **Medical facilities:** 6 hospital complexes, including a VA; world's largest speech & hearing rehabilitation center. **Educational facilities:** 3 universities, 1 college. **Further information:** Chamber of Commerce, 350 W. Douglas, Wichita, KS 67202.

Windsor, Ontario

Population: 194,338 (1984); **Pop. density:** 4,158 per sq. mi.; **Pop. growth:** −5.5% (1971-81); **Pop. over 65:** 12.1%; **Pop. under 35:** 55.6%. **Area:** 46.2 sq. mi.. **Employment:** 80,170 employed, 12.2% unemployed (1981, city).
Transportation: VIA Rail passenger service; Windsor International Airport served by Air Canada; linked to Detroit by vehicular tunnel and suspension bridge. **Communications:** 8 radio stations; 1 TV station. **Medical facilities:** 4 major hospitals, regional children's center; handicapped children's rehabilitation center. **Educational facilities:** Univ. of Windsor, St. Clair College of Applied Arts & Technology. **Further information:** Chamber of Commerce, 500 Riverside Drive West, Windsor, Ont. N9A 5K6; Tourist Information, 80 Chatham St. East.

Winnipeg, Manitoba

Population: 564,473; **Pop. density:** 2,559 per sq. mi.; **Pop. growth:** 129.0% (1971-81); **Pop. over 65:** 11.6%; **Pop. under 35:** 57.2%. **Area:** 220.6 sq. mi.. **Employment:** 283,780 employed, 5.2% unemployed (1981, city).
Transportation: International Airport served by 10 airlines; 2 national railways, VIA Rail passenger service; one rail line to U.S.; 5 national and regional bus lines; trucking hub. **Communications:** 4 TV and 11 radio stations. **Medical facilities:** 13 active treatment hospitals, including 2 major teaching centres plus the Univ. of Manitoba Rh Institute. **Educational facilities:** Univ. of Manitoba with 4 affiliated colleges; Univ. of Winnipeg, Red River Community College. **Further information:** Chamber of Commerce, 500-167 Lombard Ave., Winnipeg, Man. R3B 3E5; Winnipeg Visitor and Convention Bureau, 226 - 375 York Ave.

Yonkers, New York

Population: 192,342; **Pop. density:** 10,852 per sq. mi.; **Pop. growth:** −4%. **Area:** 18 sq. mi.. **Employment:** 98,808 employed, 5.8% unemployed; **Per capita income:** $13,808.
Transportation: intracity bus system; rail service. **Medical facilities:** St. Joseph's Medical Center, St. John's Riverside Hospital, Yonkers General Hospital. **Educational facilities:** Elizabeth Seton, Mercy, Sarah Lawrence colleges. **Further information:** Chamber of Commerce, 101 N. Broadway, Yonkers, NY 10701.

Consumer Price Index—Selected Cities

Source: U.S. Bureau of Labor Statistics

1967 = 100, except as noted.	1982, all items	All Items	Food and beverages	Housing	Fuel and other utilities	Apparel and upkeep	Transportation	Medical care	Entertainment
City average[1]	289.1	298.4	284.4	323.1	370.3	196.5	298.4	357.3	246.0
Anchorage, AK[2]	260.1	264.8	291.2	261.4	247.2	201.8	269.2	359.2	259.7
Atlanta, GA	289.5	301.3	290.5	333.8	330.0	194.6	282.1	356.5	201.8
Baltimore, MD	285.8	298.8	282.4	329.9	346.4	211.7	291.2	337.6	243.7
Boston, MA	277.7	290.0	265.2	307.9	378.3	214.7	323.7	328.4	250.3
Buffalo, NY	267.2	284.5	278.5	303.6	496.1	221.7	278.2	293.4	250.4
Chicago, IL-Northwestern IN . .	287.4	298.8	273.6	332.5	339.3	165.5	295.2	361.4	259.3
Cincinnati, OH-KY-IN	293.5	312.0	298.8	341.9	414.1	223.8	278.0	375.3	232.6
Cleveland, OH	301.2	324.3	289.0	363.2	405.6	193.5	293.5	402.0	241.5
Dallas-Fort Worth, TX	301.3	312.6	295.1	347.4	350.4	204.8	298.3	357.9	248.2
Denver-Boulder, CO	317.0	335.1	267.9	411.6	344.9	184.4	301.4	340.1	279.4
Detroit, MI	288.3	296.5	270.0	327.7	402.6	166.6	293.7	365.5	221.4
Honolulu, HI.	267.6	273.5	296.0	257.5	339.9	207.7	253.7	357.6	257.6
Houston, TX.	312.2	320.6	314.3	355.9	455.2	236.3	274.9	406.5	266.8
Kansas City, MO-KS.	282.0	298.4	280.6	322.4	383.1	215.1	287.0	372.4	230.6
Los Angeles-Long Beach-Anaheim, CA.	287.6	292.7	280.9	314.9	322.4	171.7	305.7	381.8	213.5
Miami, FL[3].	155.8	161.0	152.9	164.6	153.7	133.9	172.9	174.5	129.0
Milwaukee, WI	296.3	309.5	275.4	347.4	413.3	222.3	301.1	349.6	256.8
Minneapolis-St. Paul, MN-WI . .	306.2	312.6	288.9	362.1	387.0	191.4	279.0	329.4	271.3
New York, NY-Northeast NJ . .	275.6	288.6	285.4	300.5	390.8	184.7	317.8	352.4	254.3
Northeast PA	273.8	283.6	269.2	301.7	450.5	196.5	285.2	363.1	231.6
Philadelphia, PA-NJ	279.0	287.1	291.2	294.3	369.3	181.4	304.7	376.3	233.7
Pittsburgh, PA	288.0	308.4	289.8	343.9	355.8	197.6	315.7	375.7	245.8
Portland, OR-WA.	287.0	290.1	284.0	300.1	372.5	195.4	288.7	363.0	233.6
St. Louis, MO-IL	286.9	297.2	284.0	326.8	330.9	192.3	281.3	339.6	241.7
San Diego, CA	325.3	334.6	295.6	404.1	344.6	201.5	296.4	335.6	241.1
San Francisco-Oakland, CA . .	300.0	302.5	283.2	334.9	359.5	201.9	301.5	348.2	236.5
Seattle-Everett, WA	297.8	302.8	279.3	335.6	359.7	193.8	280.1	346.8	248.5
Washington, DC-MD-VA.	281.9	294.7	295.4	306.9	349.0	206.7	291.0	375.8	226.6

(1) Based on 56 urban areas and 85 areas beginning 1978. (2) Oct. 1967 = 100. (3) Nov. 1977 = 100.

Washington, Capital of the U.S.

Arlington National Cemetery

Arlington National Cemetery, on the former Custis estate in Virginia, is the site of the Tomb of the Unknown Soldier and the final resting place of John Fitzgerald Kennedy, president of the United States, who was buried there Nov. 25, 1963. A torch burns day and night over his grave. The remains of his brother Sen. Robert F. Kennedy (N.Y.) were interred on June 8, 1968, in an area adjacent. Many other famous Americans are also buried at Arlington, as well as American soldiers from every major war.

Arlington House, The Robert E. Lee Memorial

On a hilltop above the cemetery, stands Arlington House, the Robert E. Lee Memorial, which from 1955 to 1972 was officially called the Custis-Lee Mansion.

U.S. Marine Corps War Memorial

North of the National Cemetery, approximately 350 yards, stands the bronze statue of the raising of the United States flag on Iwo Jima, executed by Felix de Weldon from the photograph by Joe Rosenthal, and presented to the nation by members and friends of the U.S. Marine Corps.

Vietnam War Memorial

On November 13, 1982, a memorial was dedicated to the American soldiers killed or missing during the Vietnam War. It is located near the Lincoln Memorial and the Washingtom Monument.

The Capitol

The United States Capitol was originally designed by Dr. William Thornton, an amateur architect, who submitted a plan in the spring of 1793 that won him $500 and a city lot.

The south, or House wing, was completed in 1807 under the direction of Benjamin H. Latrobe.

The present Senate and House wings and the iron dome were designed and constructed by Thomas U. Walter, the 4th architect of the Capitol, between 1851-1863.

The present cast iron dome at its greatest exterior measures 135 ft. 5 in., and it is topped by the bronze Statue of Freedom that stands 19½ ft. and weighs 14,985 pounds. On its base are the words "E Pluribus Unum (Out of Many One).

The Capitol is normally open from 9 a.m. to 4:30 p.m. daily, closed Christmas, New Year's Day, and Thanksgiving Day.

Tours through the Capitol, including the House and Senate Galleries, are conducted from 9 a.m. to 4 p.m. without charge.

Folger Shakespeare Library

The Folger Shakespeare Library on Capitol Hill, Washington, D. C., is a research institution devoted to the advancement of learning in the background of Anglo-American civilization in the 16th and 17th centuries and in most aspects of the continental Renaissance. It has the largest collection of Shakespeareana in the world with 79 copies of the First Folio.

Library of Congress

Established by and for Congress in 1800, the Library of Congress has extended its services over the years to other Government agencies and other libraries, to scholars, and to the general public, and it now serves as the national library.

The library's exhibit halls are open to the public. Guided tours are given every hour from 9 a.m. through 4 p.m. Monday through Friday. Arrangements for groups should be made in advance with the Tour Coordinator.

Thomas Jefferson Memorial

The Thomas Jefferson Memorial stands on the south shore of the Tidal Basin in West Potomac park. It is a circular stone structure, with Vermont marble on the exterior and Georgia white marble inside and combines architectural elements of the dome of the Pantheon in Rome and the rotunda designed by Jefferson for the University of Virginia.

The memorial is open daily from 8 a.m. to midnight, except Christmas Day. An elevator and curb ramps for the handicapped are in service.

Lincoln Memorial

The Lincoln Memorial in West Potomac Park, on the axis of the Capitol and the Washington Monument, consists of a large marble hall enclosing a heroic statue of Abraham Lincoln in meditation sitting on a large armchair. It was dedicated on Memorial Day, May 30, 1922. The Memorial was designed by Henry Bacon. The statue was made by Daniel Chester French. Murals and ornamentation on the bronze ceiling beams are by Jules Guerin.

The memorial is open daily from 8 a.m. to midnight, except Christmas Day. A new elevator for the handicapped is in service.

John F. Kennedy Center

John F. Kennedy Center for the Performing Arts, designated by Congress as the National Cultural Center and the official memorial in Washington to President Kennedy, opened September 8, 1971. Tours are available daily, free of charge, between 10:00 a.m. and 1:15 p.m.

Mount Vernon

Mount Vernon on the south bank of the Potomac, 16 miles below Washington, D. C., is part of a large tract of land in northern Virginia which was originally included in a royal grant made to Lord Culpepper, who in 1674 granted 5,000 acres to Nicholas Spencer and John Washington.

The present house is an enlargement of one apparently built on the site of an earlier one by John's grandson, Augustine Washington, who lived there 1735-1738. His son Lawrence came there in 1743, when he renamed the plantation Mount Vernon in honor of Admiral Vernon under whom he had served in the West Indies. Lawrence Washington died in 1752 and was succeeded as proprietor of Mount Vernon by his half-brother, George Washington.

National Arboretum

The National Arboretum, one of Washington's great showplaces, occupies 444 acres in the northeastern section of the city. The National Herb Garden and National Bonsai Collection are special attractions in the nation's only federally-supported gardens.

The Arboretum is open every day of the year except Christmas.

National Archives

The Declaration of Independence, the Constitution of the United States, and the Bill of Rights are on permanent display in the National Archives Exhibition Hall. They are sealed in glass-and-bronze cases. The National Archives also holds the permanently valuable federal records of the United States government.

National Gallery of Art

The National Gallery of Art, situated in an area bounded by Constitution Avenue and the Mall, between Third and Seventh Streets, was established by Joint Resolution of Congress Mar. 24, 1937, and opened Mar. 17, 1941.

Open daily except Christmas and New Year's, from 10 a.m. to 5 p.m. Monday through Saturday and noon to 9 p.m. Sunday. Summer, 10 a.m. to 9 p.m., noon to 9 p.m. on Sunday.

The Pentagon

The Pentagon, headquarters of the Department of Defense, is the world's largest office building, with 3 times the floor space of the Empire State Building in New York. Situated in Arlington, Va., it houses more than 23,000 employees in offices that occupy 3,707,745 square feet.

Tours are available Monday through Friday (excluding federal holidays), from 9 a.m. to 3:30 p.m.

Smithsonian Institution

The Smithsonian Institution is one of the world's great historical, scientific, educational, and cultural establishments. It comprises numerous facilities, mostly in Wash., D.C.

Washington Monument

The Washington Monument is a tapering shaft or obelisk of white marble, 555 ft., 5-⅛ inches in height and 55 ft., 1-½ inches square at base. Eight small windows, 2 on each side, are located at the 500-ft. level, where Washington points of interest are indicated.

The Monument is open 7 days a week, 9 a.m. to 5 p.m., 8 a.m. to 12 midnight in the summer. It is closed Christmas Day.

The White House

The White House, the president's residence, stands on 18 acres on the south side of Pennsylvania Avenue, between the Treasury and the Executive Office Building.

The walls are of sandstone, quarried at Aquia Creek, Va. The exterior walls were painted, causing the building to be termed the "White House." On Aug. 24, 1814, during Madison's administration, the house was burned by the British. James Hoban rebuilt it by Oct. 1817, for President Monroe to move in. .

The White House is open from 10 a.m. to 12 noon, Tuesday through Friday, except on Thanksgiving, Christmas, and New Year. Also Saturdays, 10 a.m. to 2 p.m. Jun. 1 through Labor Day, and 10 a.m. to noon Labor Day through May 31. Only the public rooms on the ground floor and state floor may be visited.

Notable Tall Buildings in North American Cities

Height from sidewalk to roof, including penthouse and tower if enclosed as integral part of structure; actual number of stories beginning at street level. Asterisks (*) denote buildings still under construction Jan. 1986.

City	Hgt. ft.	Stories
Akron, Oh.		
First National Tower	330	28
National City Center.	301	23
Albany, N.Y.		
Erastus Corning II Tower	589	44
State Office Building	388	34
Agency (4 bldgs.), So. Mall. . .	310	23
Atlanta, Ga.		
Westin Peachtree Plaza	723	71
Georgia Pacific Tower	697	51
Southern Bell Telephone. . .	677	47
First National Bank, 2 Peachtree	556	44
Marriott Marquis	554	52
Equitable Building, 100 Peachtree . .	453	34
101 Marietta Tower, 101 Marietta St. . . .	446	36
Atlanta Center	443	35
National Bank of Georgia. . .	409	32
Peachtree Summit No. 1 . . .	406	31
North Avenue Tower, 310 North Ave. . . .	403	26
Tower Place, 3361 Piedmont Road	401	29
Richard B. Russell, Federal Bldg. . . .	383	26
Atlanta Hilton Hotel	383	32
Peachtree Center, Harris Bldg. . .	382	31
Park Place, 2660 Peachtree	380	38
AT&T Long Line Bldg..	380	...
Marquis One.	378	30
Trust Company Bank	377	28
Coastal States Insurance.	377	27
Peachtree Center Cain Building	376	30
Peachtree Center Building	374	31
Life of Georgia Tower.	371	29
Georgia Power Tower, 333 Piedmont .	349	24
Peachtree Center South	332	27
Gas Light Tower, 235 Peachtree .	331	27
Hyatt Regency Hotel, 265 Peachtree . . .	330	23
100 Colony Square, 1175 Peachtree .	328	25
Austin, Tex.		
Austin National Bank	328	26
American Bank	313	21
State Capitol.	309	...
Univ. of Texas Admin. Bldg.	307	29
Baltimore, Md.		
*Merritt Tower	625	29
U.S. Fidelity & Guaranty Co.. . . .	529	40
Maryland National Bank Bldg. . .	509	34
World Trade Center Bldg. . .	405	32
Saint-Paul Apartments Bldg.. .	385	37
Arlington Federal S & L Bldg. . .	370	28
Blaustein Bldg..	370	30
Charles Plaza Apts. So.	350	31
Charles Center South.	330	26
Tower Bldg.	330	16
Baltimore Arts Tower	319	15
First National Bank of Maryland . .	315	22
Lord Baltimore Hotel	315	24
Mercantile-Safe Deposit and Trust Co. . . .	315	21
Charles Plaza Apts. No.	315	28
Baton Rouge, La.		
State Capitol.	460	34
American Bank Bldg.	315	24
Birmingham, Ala.		
First Natl. Southern Natural Bldg. . .	390	30
South Central Bell Hdqts. Bldg. . .	390	30
City Federal Bldg.	325	27
Boston, Mass.		
John Hancock Tower	790	60
Prudential Tower	750	52
Boston Co. Bldg., Court St.. . .	605	41
Federal Reserve Bldg.	604	32
First National Bank of Boston . .	591	37
One Financial Center	590	46
Shawmut Bank Bldg.	520	38
Exchange Place, 53 State St. . .	510	39
Sixty State St.	509	38
One Post Office Sq..	507	40
One Beacon St.	507	40
New England Merch. Bank Bldg..	500	40

City	Hgt. ft.	Stories
U.S. Custom House	496	32
John Hancock Bldg..	495	26
State St. Bank Bldg.	477	34
One Hundred Summer St. . . .	450	33
McCormack Bldg.	401	22
Keystone Custodian Funds. . . .	400	32
Saltonstall Office Bldg.	396	22
Devonshire, 250 Wash. St. . .	396	40
Harbor Towers (2 bldgs.). . . .	396	40
Westin Hotel, Copley Place	395	36
John F. Kennedy Bldg.	387	24
Marriott Hotel, Copley Place	383	39
Longfellow Towers (2 bldgs.)	380	38
Federal Bldg. & Post Office	345	22
Suffolk County Courthouse. .	330	19
Jamaicaway Towers	320	30
Sheraton-Boston Hotel	310	29
Buffalo, N.Y.		
Marine Midland Center	529	40
City Hall	378	32
Rand Bldg., not incl. 40-ft. beacon.	351	29
Main Place Tower	350	26
One M&T Plaza	317	21
Liberty Bank	305	23
Calgary, Alta.		
Petro-Canada Tower #2. . . .	689	52
Calgary Tower.	626	...
First Canadian Centre.	547	44
Scotia Centre	504	38
Nova Bldg., 801 7th Ave. SW	500	37
Petro-Canada Tower #1. . . .	469	33
Two Bow Valley Square . . .	468	39
Fifth & Fifth Bldg.	460	35
Oxford Square North	463	34
Shell Tower	460	34
Oxford Square South	449	33
Four Bow Valley Square . . .	441	37
Esso Plaza (twin towers) . . .	435	34
Cascade 300.	432	31
T.D. Square	421	33
Family Life Bldg..	410	33
Pan Canadian Bldg., 150 9th Ave. SW	410	28
Norcen Tower	408	33
Sun Oil Bldg..	397	34
Western Centre	385	40
Three Bow Valley Square . .	382	33
Sun Life Bldg. (twin towers)	374	28
Mobil Tower	369	29
A.G.T. Tower, 411 1st St. SE.	366	28
Amgoy Bldg..	358	31
One Palliser Square.	350	28
Charlotte, N.C.		
NCNB Plaza	503	40
First Union Plaza	433	32
Wachovia Center	420	32
Charlotte Plaza	388	27
Southern National Center, ...	300	22
Chicago, Ill.		
Sears Tower (world's tallest).	1,454	110
Standard Oil (Indiana).	1,136	80
John Hancock Center.	1,127	100
Water Tower Place (a)	859	74
First Natl. Bank	850	60
Three First National Plaza . . .	775	57
One Magnificent Mile	770	58
Olympia Centre	727	63
Huron Apts.	723	56
IBM Bldg.	695	52
Neiman-Marcus Tower	690	65
Daley Center.	662	31
Lake Point Tower	645	70
Board of Trade, incl. 81 ft. statue	605	44
Prudential Bldg., 130 E. Randolph . .	601	41
Antenna tower, 311 ft., makes total. . .	912	...
1000 Lake Shore Plaza Apts.	590	55
Marina City Apts., 2 buildings	588	61
Mid Continental Plaza, 55 E. Monroe	580	50
Pittsfield, 55 E. Washington St.. . .	557	38
Kemper Insurance Bldg. . . .	555	45
Newberry Plaza, State & Oak	553	56
One South Wacker Dr.	550	40

City	Hgt. ft.	Stories
Harbor Point	550	54
LaSalle Natl. Bank, 135 S. LaSalle St.	535	44
One LaSalle Street	530	49
111 E. Chestnut St.	529	56
River Plaza, Rush & Hubbard	524	56
Pure Oil, 35 E. Wacker Drive	523	40
United Ins. Bldg., 1 E. Wacker Dr.	522	41
Lincoln Tower, 75 E. Wacker Dr.	519	42
Carbide & Carbon, 230 N. Mich.	503	37
Walton Colonnade	500	44
LaSalle-Wacker, 221 N. LaSalle St.	491	41
Amer. Nat'l. Bank, 33 N. LaSalle St.	479	40
Bankers, 105 W. Adams St.	476	41
Brunswick Bldg.	475	37
Continental Companies	475	45
American Furniture Mart	474	24
333 Wacker Dr.	472	36
Sheraton Hotel, 505 N. Mich. Ave.	471	42
Playboy Bldg., 919 N. Mich. Ave.	468	37
188 Randolph Tower	465	45
Tribune Tower, 435 N. Mich. Ave.	462	36
Chicago Marriott, Mich. & Ohio Sts.	460	45
(a) World's tallest reinforced concrete bldg.		

Cincinnati, Oh.

City	Hgt. ft.	Stories
Carew Tower	568	49
Central Trust Tower	504	33
Dubois Tower, 5th & Walnut	423	32
Netherland Plaza	372	31
Central Trust Center	355	27
Atrium Two	350	30
First Natl. Bank Center	351	26
Clarion North Tower	350	33
Cinn. Commerce Center	346	29
Kroger Bldg.	320	25
Federated Bldg.	317	21

Cleveland, Oh.

City	Hgt. ft.	Stories
Terminal Tower	708	52
Sohio Tower	650	46
Erieview Plaza Tower	529	40
One Cleveland Center	450	31
Justice Center, 1250 Ontario	420	26
Federal Bldg.	419	32
National City Complex	410	35
Cleveland Trust Tower No. 1	383	29
Eaton Center	360	28
Ohio-Bell Hqs.	360	22

Columbus, Oh.

City	Hgt. ft.	Stories
James A. Rhodes (State Office Tower)	624	41
LeVeque Tower, 50 W. Broad	555	47
Huntington Center, 41 S. High St.	512	37
One Nationwide Plaza	485	40
One Riverside Plaza	456	31
Borden Bldg., 180 E. Broad	438	34
Columbus Center, 100 E. Broad	357	24
Capitol Square	348	26
Ohio Bell Bldg., 150 E. Gay St.	346	26

Dallas, Tex.

City	Hgt. ft.	Stories
Main Centre, 901 Main St.	939	73
First International Bldg.	710	56
LTV Center	686	50
Arco Tower, 1601 Bryan St.	660	49
Thanksgiving Tower, 1600 Pacific Ave.	645	50
Two Dallas Centre	635	50
First National Bank	625	52
Republic Bank Tower	598	50
First City Center, 1700 Pacific Ave.	595	49
SW Bell Admin. Tower	580	37
One Lincoln Plaza	579	45
Olympia York, 1999 Bryan St.	562	37
Reunion Tower	560	50
Southland Life Tower	550	42
Diamond Shamrock, 717 N. Harwood St.	550	34
2001 Bryan St.	512	40
San Jacinto Tower	456	33
Republic Bank Bldg., not incl. 150-ft. ornamental tower	452	36
Wyndham Hotel	451	29
One Main Place	445	34
LTV Tower	434	31

City	Hgt. ft.	Stories
Mercantile Natl. Bank Bldg., not incl. 115-ft. weather beacon	430	31
Mobil Bldg.	430	31
Mart Hotel	400	29
Fidelity Union Tower	400	33
One Dallas Centre	386	30
Southwestern Bell Toll Bldg.	372	22
Court House & Fedl. Office Bldg.	362	16
Mercantile Dallas Bldg.	360	22
Sheraton Hotel	352	38

Dayton, Oh.

City	Hgt. ft.	Stories
Kettering Tower	405	30
Mead Tower, 10 W. 2d St.	365	28
Centre City Office Bldg.	297	21
Hulman Bldg.	295	23
Miami Valley Tower	290	22

Denver, Col.

City	Hgt. ft.	Stories
Republic Plaza	714	56
City Center Four	706	54
United Bank of Denver	697	52
1999 Broadway	544	43
Arco Tower	527	41
Anaconda Tower	507	40
One Denver Place	467	35
Amoco Bldg., 17th Ave. & Broadway	450	36
17th Street Plaza	438	34
Brooks Towers, 1020 15th St.	420	42
First of Denver Plaza	415	32
Stellar Plaza	410	32
Tabor Center, #1	405	32
Energy Center 1	404	29
Colorado Nat'l. Bank, 17th & Curtis	389	26
First National Bank	385	28
Security Life Bldg.	384	33
Centennial Plaza	374	31
Dominion Plaza	368	30
Lincoln Center	366	30
Denver Natl. Bank Plaza	363	29
Western Fed. Savings	357	27
Colorado State Bank	352	26
Executive Tower	350	30
Larimer Place	335	32
410 Building	335	24
Mountain Bell, 17th & Curtis	330	21
D&F Tower	330	20

Des Moines, Ia.

City	Hgt. ft.	Stories
Ruan Center	457	36
Financial Center, 7th & Walnut	345	25
Marriott Hotel, 700 Grand Ave.	340	33
Equitable Bldg.	318	19

Detroit, Mich.

City	Hgt. ft.	Stories
Detroit Plaza Hotel	720	71
Penobscot Bldg.	557	47
15000 Town Center Dr.	554	40
Guardian	485	40
Renaissance Center (4 bldgs.)	479	39
Book Tower	472	35
Prudential Town Center	448	32
13000 Town Center Dr.	443	32
Cadillac Tower	437	40
David Stott	436	38
Mich. Cons. Gas Co. Bldg.	430	32
Fisher	420	28
J. L. Hudson Bldg.	397	28
McNamara Federal Office Bldg.	393	27
American Center	374	27
Top of Troy Bldg.	374	27
Comerica Bldg., 211 N. Fort	370	28
Edison Plaza	365	25
Woodward Tower at the Park	358	34
Amer. Center Bldg. #2	350	25
Buhl, 535 Griswold	350	26
Ford Bldg.	346	25
Michigan Bell Telephone	340	19
1st Federal of Michigan	338	23
Pontchartrain Motor Hotel	336	23
Troy Center Tower	332	24
1st Natl. Bldg.	330	25

City	Hgt. ft.	Stories

Edmonton, Alta.

City	Hgt. ft.	Stories
Manulife Place, 10170-101 St.	479	39
Royal Trust Tower.	476	30
AGT Tower, 10020-100 St.	441	34
CCB Tower, 10124-103 Ave.. . . .	410	34
Principal Plaza, 10303 Jasper Ave.	370	30
Scotia Place, 10060 Jasper Ave. . . .	366	30
CN Tower, 1004-104 Ave.	365	26
Phipps McKinnon	359	21
Toronto Dominion Tower	325	27
Oxford Tower	325	29
Sun Life Bldg.	320	25

Fort Wayne, Ind.

	Hgt. ft.	Stories
One Summit Square, 911 S. Calhoun. . .	442	27
Ft. Wayne Natl. Bank	339	26
Lincoln Bank Tower.	312	23

Fort Worth, Tex.

	Hgt. ft.	Stories
Center Tower II	546	38
1st United Tower	536	40
Continental Plaza	525	40
1st City Bank Tower.	475	33
Texas American Bank.	454	37
Continental Natl. Bank Bldg.	380	30
Continental Life	307	24
First National Bank, 500 W. 7th	300	21
One Tandy Center	300	20
Two Tandy Center.	300	20

Hamilton, Ont.

	Hgt. ft.	Stories
Century Twenty One	418	43
Stelco Tower.	339	25
The Olympia	321	33

Harrisburg, Pa.

	Hgt. ft.	Stories
State Office Tower #2	334	21
333 Market St. (incl. tower).	327	19

Hartford, Conn.

	Hgt. ft.	Stories
City Place	535	38
Travelers Ins. Co. Bldg.	527	34
Hartford Plaza	420	22
Hartford Natl. Bank & Trust	360	26
One Commercial Plaza	349	27
One Financial Plaza, 755 Main.	335	26

Honolulu, Ha.

	Hgt. ft.	Stories
Ala Moana Americana Hotel	396	36
Pacific Tower.	350	30
Franklin Towers	350	41
Honolulu Tower	350	40
Discovery Bay	350	42
Hyatt Regency Waikiki	350	39
Mehelani Waikiki Lodge.	350	43
Regency Tower, 2525 Date St.	350	42
Pearlridge Square.	350	43
Yacht Harbor Towers	350	40
Canterbury Place	350	40
Royal Iolani.	350	38
Island Colony	350	44
Century Center	350	41
Pacific Beach Hotel	350	43
Hawaiian Monarch Hotel	350	43
Waikiki Hobron.	350	43

Houston, Tex.

	Hgt. ft.	Stories
Texas Commerce Tower	1,002	75
Allied Bank Plaza, 1000 Louisiana.	985	71
Transco Tower.	899	64
RepublicBank Center	780	56
Interfirst Plaza	744	55
1600 Smith St..	729	54
Gulf Tower, 1301 McKinney	725	52
One Shell Plaza		
(not incl. 285 ft. TV tower)	714	50
Four Allen Center	692	50
Capital Natl. Bank Plaza	685	50
One Houston Center	678	47
First City Tower	662	47
1100 Milam Bldg.	651	47
*San Felipe Plaza	620	45

City	Hgt. ft.	Stories
Exxon Bldg.	606	44
The America Tower	577	42
Marathon Oil Tower	572	41
Two Houston Center	570	40
Dresser Tower.	550	40
1415 Louisiana Tower.	550	44
Pennzoil, 700 Milam (2 bldgs.)	523	36
Two Allen Center	521	36
Entex Bldg.	518	35
Huntington	506	34
Tenneco Bldg.	502	33
Conoco Tower	465	32
One Allen Center	452	34
Summit Tower West	441	31
Coastal Tower.	441	31
Four Leafs Towers (2 bldgs.).	439	40
*Phoenix Tower	434	34
Gulf Bldg..	428	37
The Spires	426	41
Central Tower (4 Oaks Place)	420	30
First City Natl. Bank.	410	32
Houston Lighting & Power	410	27
Neils Esperson Bldg.	409	31
Hyatt Regency Houston	401	34

Hull, Que.

	Hgt. ft.	Stories
Les Terrasses De La Chaudiere	383	30
Place Du Portage, Phase 1.	333	24

Indianapolis, Ind.

	Hgt. ft.	Stories
American United Life Ins. Co.	533	38
Indiana Natl. Bank Tower.	504	37
City-County Bldg.	377	26
Merchants Plaza/Hyatt Regency Hotel. .	328	26
Indiana Bell Telephone	320	20

Jacksonville, Fla.

	Hgt. ft.	Stories
Independent Life & Accident Ins. Co.. . .	535	37
Gulf Life Ins. Co. Bldg.	432	28

Kansas City, Mo.

	Hgt. ft.	Stories
Kansas City Power and Light Bldg.	476	32
City Hall	443	29
Federal Office Bldg..	413	35
Commerce Tower.	402	32
Southwest Bell Telephone Bldg.	394	27
Pershing Road Associates	352	28
A. T. & T. Long Line Bldg.	331	20

Las Vegas, Nev.

	Hgt. ft.	Stories
Sundance Hotel	400	33
Landmark Hotel	356	31
Las Vegas Hilton	345	30

Little Rock, Ark.

	Hgt. ft.	Stories
First National Bank	454	30
Worthen Bank & Trust	375	23
Tower Bldg.	350	18
Union National Bank.	331	21

Los Angeles, Cal.

	Hgt. ft.	Stories
First Interstate Bank.	858	62
Crocker Center, North	750	53
Security Pacific Natl. Bank	735	55
Atlantic Richfield Plaza (2 bldgs.)	699	52
Wells Fargo Bank	625	48
Crocker-Citizen Plaza.	620	42
California Plaza	578	42
Century Plaza Towers (2 bldgs.).	571	44
*Citycorp Plaza	534	42
Union Bank Square	516	41
*Wilshire/Bixel.	496	36
City Hall	454	28
Equitable Life Bldg.	454	34
Transamerica Center	452	32
Mutual Benefit Life Ins. Bldg..	435	31
Broadway Plaza	414	33
1900 Ave. of Stars	398	27
1 Wilshire Bldg.	395	28
The Evian, 10490 Wilshire Blvd.	390	31
Bonaventure Hotel, 404 S. Figueroa . . .	367	35
Beaudry Center	365	26
400 S. Hope St.	375	26
Cal. Fed. Savings & Loan Bldg.	363	28
Century City Office Bldg.	363	26
Bunker Hill Towers	349	32
International Industries Plaza	347	24
Century City Hotel.	340	27

City	Hgt. ft.	Stories

Louisville, Ky.

City	Hgt. ft.	Stories
First Natl. Bank	512	40
Citizen's Plaza	420	30
Humana Bldg.	350	27
Meindinger Tower	338	26
Brown & Williamson Tower	338	26
Galt House	325	25
United Kentucky Bldg.	312	24

Memphis, Tenn.

City	Hgt. ft.	Stories
100 N. Main Bldg.	430	37
Commerce Square	396	31
Sterick Bldg.	365	31
Clark, 5100 Poplar	365	32
First Natl. Bank Bldg.	332	25
Hyatt Regency	329	28

Miami, Fla.

City	Hgt. ft.	Stories
Southeast Financial Center	764	55
*Centrust Tower	562	35
Metro-Dade Administration Bldg.	510	30
Edward Ball Bldg.	484	35
One Biscayne Corp.	456	40
First Federal Savings & Loan	375	32
Pavillon Hotel	366	35
Dade County Court House	357	28
New World Center	340	30
Plaza Venetia	332	33
Flagler Center Bldg.	318	25

Milwaukee, Wis.

City	Hgt. ft.	Stories
First Wis. Center & Office Tower	625	42
411 Bldg.	385	30
City Hall	350	9
Hyatt Regency	320	22
Wisconsin Telephone Co.	317	19
Marine Plaza	309	20

Minneapolis, Minn.

City	Hgt. ft.	Stories
* Northwest Center	950	66
IDS Center	775	57
Multifoods Tower	668	52
Piper Tower	579	44
Pillsbury Bldg., 200 S. 6th St.	561	40
Foshay Tower, not including 163-ft. antenna tower	447	32
Amfac Hotel	440	32
Northwestern Bell	416	26
Hennepin County Government Center	403	24
First Natl. Bank Bldg.	366	28
100 South Fifth	356	25
Municipal Building	355	14
100 Washington Square	340	22
Cedar-Riverside	337	39

Montreal, Que.

City	Hgt. ft.	Stories
Place Victoria	624	47
Place Ville Marie	616	42
Canadian Imperial Bank of Commerce	604	43
Le Complexe Desjardins		
La Tour du Sud	498	40
La Tour du L'Est	428	32
La Tour du Nord	355	27
La Tour Laurier	425	36
C.I.L. House	429	32
Chateau Champlain Hotel	420	38
Port Royal Apts.	400	33
Royal Bank Tower	397	22
Sun Life Bldg.	390	26
Banque Canadienne National	390	32
Place du Canada	372	33
Hydro Quebec	360	27
Alexis Nihon Plaza	331	33

Nashville, Tenn.

City	Hgt. ft.	Stories
American General Center	452	31
Landmark Center	409	30
James K. Polk State Office Bldg.	392	32
First American N.A. Bank	354	28
One Nashville Plaza	340	23
Hyatt Regency	300	28

Newark, N.J.

City	Hgt. ft.	Stories
Midlantic Natl. Bank	465	36
Raymond-Commerce	448	36
Park Plaza Bldg.	400	26
Prudential Plaza	370	24
Public Service Elec. & Gas	360	26
Prudential Ins. Co., 753 Broad St.	360	26
Western Electric Bldg.	359	31
Gateway 1	355	30
American Insurance Company	326	21

New Orleans, La.

City	Hgt. ft.	Stories
One Shell Square	697	51
Place St. Charles	645	53
Plaza Tower	531	45
Energy Centre	530	39
Sheraton Hotel	478	47
Marriott Hotel	450	42
Texaco Bldg.	442	33
Canal Place One	439	32
1010 Common	438	31
Int'l. Trade Mart Bldg.	407	33
225 Baronne St.	362	28
One Poydras Plaza	360	28
Hyatt-Regency Hotel, Poydras Plaza	360	25
Hibernia Bank Bldg.	355	23
1250 Poydras Plaza	341	24
1515 Poydras	340	27
New Orleans Hilton	340	27
American Bank Bldg.	330	23
Pan American Life Bldg.	323	27

New York, N.Y.

City	Hgt. ft.	Stories
World Trade Center (2 towers)	1,350	110
Empire State, 34th St. & 5th Ave.	1,250	102
TV tower, 164 ft., makes total	1,414	...
Chrysler, Lexington Ave. & 43d St.	1,046	77
American International Bldg., 70 Pine St.	950	67
40 Wall Tower	927	71
Citicorp Center	914	46
RCA Bldg., Rockefeller Center	850	70
1 Chase Manhattan Plaza	813	60
Pan Am Bldg., 200 Park Ave.	808	59
*Eichner Bldg.	799	70
Woolworth, 233 Broadway	792	60
1 Penn Plaza	764	57
Exxon, 1251 Ave. of Americas	750	54
1 Liberty Plaza	743	50
Citibank	741	57
One Astor Plaza	730	54
*Metropolitan Tower, 146 W. 57th St.	716	78
Union Carbide Bldg., 270 Park Ave.	707	52
General Motors Bldg.	705	50
Metropolitan Life, 1 Madison Ave.	700	50
500 5th Ave.	697	60
9 W. 57th St.	688	50
Chem. Bank, N.Y. Trust Bldg.	687	50
55 Water St.	687	53
Chanin, Lexington Ave. & 42d St.	680	56
Gulf & Western Bldg.	679	44
Marine Midland Bldg., 140 Bway.	677	52
McGraw Hill, 1221 Ave. of Am.	674	51
Lincoln, 60 E. 42d Street	673	53
1633 Broadway	670	48
Trump Tower, 725 5th Ave.	664	68
Museum Tower Apts.	650	58
American Brands, 245 Park Ave.	648	47
A. T. & T. Tower, 570 Madison Ave.	648	37
General Electric, 570 Lexington	640	50
Irving Trust, 1 Wall St.	640	50
345 Park Ave.	634	44
Grace Plaza, 1114 Ave. of Am.	630	50
1 New York Plaza	630	50
Home Insurance Co. Bldg.	630	44
N.Y. Telephone, 1095 Ave. of Am.	630	40
888 7th Ave.	628	42
1 Hammarskjold Plaza	628	50
Waldorf-Astoria, 301 Park Ave.	625	47
Burlington House, 1345 Ave. of Am.	625	50
Olympic Tower, 645 5th Ave.	620	51
10 E. 40th St.	620	48
101 Park Ave.	618	50
New York Life, 51 Madison Ave.	615	40
Penney Bldg., 1301 Ave. of Am.	609	46
IBM, 590 Madison Ave.	603	41
780 3rd Ave.	600	50
560 Lexington Ave.	600	22
Celanese Bldg., 1211 Ave. of Am.	592	45
U.S. Court House, 505 Pearl St.	590	37
Federal Bldg., Foley Square	587	41
Time & Life, 1271 Ave. of Am.	587	47
Cooper Bregstein Bldg., 1250 Bway.	580	40
1185 Ave. of Americas	580	42
Municipal, Park Row & Centre St.	580	34
1 Madison Square Plaza	576	42
Westvaco Bldg. 299 Park Ave.	574	42
Socony Mobil Bldg., East 42d St.	572	45
Sperry Rand Bldg., 1290 Ave. of Am.	570	43
600 3d Ave.	570	42
Helmsley Bldg., 230 Park Ave.	565	35

City	Hgt. ft.	Stories
1 Bankers Trust Plaza	565	40
Palace Hotel, Madison & 51st St.	563	51
30 Broad St.	562	48
Sherry-Netherland, 5th Ave. & 59th St.	560	40
Continental Can, 633 3d Ave.	557	39
Sperry & Hutchinson, 330 Madison	555	39
Galleria, 117 E. 57th St.	552	57
Interchem Bldg., 1133 Ave. of Am.	552	45
151 E. 44th St.	550	44
N.Y. Telephone, 323 Bway.	550	45
919 3d Ave.	550	47
Burroughs Bldg., 605 3d Ave.	550	44
Bankers Trust, 33 E. 48 St.	547	41
Transportation Bldg., 225 Bway.	546	45
Equitable, 120 Broadway	545	42
1 Brooklyn Bridge Plaza	540	42
Equitable Life, 1285 Ave. of Am.	540	42
Ritz Tower, Park Ave. & 57th St.	540	41
Sterling Drug Bldg., 90 Park Ave.	515	41
First National City Bank.	515	41
Bank of New York, 48 Wall St.	513	32
Navarre, 512 7th Ave.	513	43
Williamsburgh Savings Bank, Bklyn.	512	42
ITT—American, 437 Madison Ave.	512	40
International, Rockefeller Center	512	41
1407 Broadway Realty Corp.	512	44
United Nations, 405 E. 42 St.	505	39
Bankers Trust, 6 Wall St.	540	39
1166 Ave. of Americas	540	44
1700 Broadway	533	41
Downtown Athletic Club, 19 West St.	530	45
Nelson Towers, 7th Ave. & 34th St.	525	45
767 3d Ave.	525	39
Hotel Pierre, 5th Ave. & 61st St.	525	44
House of Seagram, 375 Park Ave.	525	38
7 World Trade Center.	525	44
Random House, 825 3d Ave.	522	40
3 Park Ave.	522	42
North American Plywood, 800 3d Ave.	520	41
Du Mont Bldg., 515 Madison Ave.	520	42
26 Broadway.	520	31
Newsweek Bldg., 444 Madison Ave.	518	43
Sterling Drug Bldg., 90 Park Ave.	515	41
First National City Bank.	515	41
Bank of New York, 48 Wall St.	513	32
Navarre, 512 7th Ave.	513	43
Williamsburgh Savings Bank, Bklyn.	512	42
ITT—American, 437 Madison Ave.	512	40
International, Rockefeller Center	512	41
1407 Broadway Realty Corp.	512	44
United Nations, 405 E. 42 St.	505	39

Oakland, Cal.

City	Hgt. ft.	Stories
Ordway Bldg., 2150 Valdez St.	404	28
Kaiser Bldg.	390	28
Lake Merritt Plaza	371	27
Raymond Kaiser Engineer Bldg.	336	25
Clorox Bldg.	330	24
Tribune Tower	305	21

Oklahoma City, Okla.

City	Hgt. ft.	Stories
Liberty Tower	500	36
First National Bank	493	33
City National Bank Tower.	440	32
First Oklahoma Tower	425	31
Kerr-McGee Center	393	30
Mid America Plaza	362	19
Penn Bank Tower	321	21

Omaha, Neb.

City	Hgt. ft.	Stories
Woodmen Tower	469	30
Northwestern Bell Telephone Hdqrs.	334	16
Masonic Manor	320	22

Ottawa, Ont.

City	Hgt. ft.	Stories
Place de Ville, Tower C	368	29
R.H. Coats Bldg.	326	27
Place Bell Canada.	318	26

Philadelphia, Pa.

City	Hgt. ft.	Stories
City Hall Tower, incl. 37-ft. statue of Wm. Penn.	548	7
1818 Market St.	500	40
Provident Mutual Life	491	40
Fidelity Mutual Life Ins. Bldg.	490	38
Phila. Saving Fund Society	490	40
Central Penn Natl. Bank	490	36
Centre Square (2 towers)	490/416	38/32
Industrial Valley Bank Bldg.	482	32
Philadelphia National Bank	475	25
Two Girard Plaza	450	30
2000 Market St. Bldg.	435	29
One Reading Center	417	32
Fidelity Bank Bldg.	405	30

City	Hgt. ft.	Stories
Lewis Tower, 15th & Locust	400	33
1500 Locust St.	390	44
Academy House, 1420 Locust St.	390	37
Philadelphia Electric Co.	384	27
INA Annex, 1600 Arch St.	383	27
Penn Mutual Life.	375	20
The Drake, 15th & Spruce	375	33
Medical Tower, 255 So. 17th.	364	33
State Bldg., 1400 Spring Garden	351	18
One Logan Square	350	30
United Engineers, 17th & Ludlow	344	20
Land Title, Broad & Chestnut	344	22
Packard, 15th & Chestnut	340	25
Inquirer Building	340	18

Phoenix, Ariz.

City	Hgt. ft.	Stories
Valley National Bank	483	40
Arizona Bank Downtown	407	31
First Interstate Bank Plaza	372	27
United Bank Plaza.	356	28
First Federal Savings Bldg.	341	26
Hyatt Regency.	317	20

Pittsburgh, Pa.

City	Hgt. ft.	Stories
U.S. Steel Bldg.	841	64
One Mellon Bank Center	725	54
One PPG Place	635	40
One Oxford Centre	615	46
Gulf, 7th Ave. and Grant St.	582	44
University of Pittsburgh	535	42
Mellon Bank Bldg.	520	41
1 Oliver Plaza	511	39
Grant, Grant St. at 3rd Ave.	485	40
Koppers, 7th Ave. and Grant.	475	34
Equibank Bldg.	445	34
Pittsburgh National Bldg.	424	30
Alcoa Bldg., 425 Sixth Ave.	410	30
Liberty Tower	358	29
Westinghouse Bldg.	355	23
Oliver, 535 Smithfield St.	347	25
Gateway Bldg. No. 3	344	24
Centre City Tower.	341	26
Federal Bldg., 1000 Liberty Ave.	340	23
Bell Telephone, 416 7th Ave.	339	21
Hilton Hotel.	333	22
Frick, 437 Grant St.	330	20

Portland, Ore.

City	Hgt. ft.	Stories
First Interstate Tower	546	41
U.S. Bancorp Tower.	536	39
Georgia Pacific Bldg.	367	27

Providence, R.I.

City	Hgt. ft.	Stories
Fleet National Bank	420	26
Rhode Island Hospital Trust Tower	410	30
40 Westminster Bldg.	301	24

Richmond, Va.

City	Hgt. ft.	Stories
James Monroe Bldg.	450	29
City Hall (incl. penthouse)	425	17
United Virginia Bank Bldg.	400	24
Federal Reserve Bank	393	26
First & Merchants Natl. Bank.	333	25

Rochester, N.Y.

City	Hgt. ft.	Stories
Xerox Tower.	443	30
Lincoln First Tower	390	26
Eastman Kodak Bldg.	360	19

St. Louis, Mo.

City	Hgt. ft.	Stories
Gateway Arch.	630	...
S.W. Bell Telephone Bldg.	560	44
Mercantile Trust Bldg.	550	37
Centerre Bldg.	433	31
Laclede Gas. Bldg., 8th & Olive	400	30
S.W. Bell Telephone Bldg.	398	31
Civil Courts.	387	13
Queeny Tower.	321	24
Counsel House Plaza	320	30

St. Paul, Minn.

City	Hgt. ft.	Stories
First Natl. Bank Bldg., incl. 100-ft. sign.	517	32
*Minn. World Trade Center.	500	40
Osborn Bldg., 320 Wabasha	368	20
Kellogg Square Apts.	366	32
Northwestern Bell Telephone (2 bldgs.).	340	16
American National Bank Bldg.	335	25
North Central Tower, 445 Minn.	328	27
Amhoist/Park Tower	324	26
Minn. Mutual Life Center	315	21
St. Paul Cathedral.	307	...

Salt Lake City, Ut.

City	Hgt. ft.	Stories
L.D.S. Church Office Bldg.	420	30
Beneficial Life Tower	351	21
Amer. Towers (2 bldgs.)	324	27

San Antonio, Tex.

Tower of the Americas	622	...
Tower Life	404	30
Interfirst Plaza	387	28
Nix Professional Bldg.	375	23
Natl. Bank of Commerce	310	24
First Natl. Bank Tower	302	20
Frost Bank Tower	300	21
Marriot Hotel	300	25

San Diego, Cal.

California First Bank	388	27
Columbia Centre	379	27
Imperial Bank	355	24
Wells Fargo Bldg.	348	20
Wickes Bldg.	340	25
Financial Square	339	24
Central Federal	320	22
Union Bank	320	22

San Francisco, Cal.

Transamerica Pyramid	853	48
Bank of America	778	52
101 California St.	600	48
5 Fremont Center	600	43
Embarcadero Center, No. 4	570	45
Security Pacific Bank	569	45
One Market Plaza, Spear St.	565	43
Wells Fargo Bldg.	561	43
Standard Oil, 575 Market St.	551	39
One Sansome-Citicorp	550	39
Shaklee Bldg., 444 Market	537	38
Aetna Life	529	38
First & Market Bldg.	529	38
Metropolitan Life	524	38
Crocker National Bank	500	38
Hilton Hotel	493	46
Pacific Gas & Electric	492	34
Union Bank	487	37
Pacific Insurance	476	34
Bechtel Bldg., Fremont St.	475	33
333 Market Bldg.	474	33
Hartford Bldg.	465	33
Mutual Benefit Life	438	32
Russ Bldg.	435	31
Pacific Telephone Bldg.	435	26
Pacific Gateway	416	30
Embarcadero Center, No. 3	412	31
Embarcadero Center, No. 2	412	31
595 Market Bldg.	410	31
101 Montgomery St.	405	28
Cal. State Automobile Assn.	399	29
Alcoa Bldg.	398	27
St. Francis Hotel	395	32
Shell Bldg.	386	29
Del Monte	378	28
Pacific 3-Apparel Mart	376	30
Meridien Hotel	374	34
Union Square Hyatt House Hotel	355	35

Seattle, Wash.

Columbia Center	954	76
Seattle-1st Natl. Bank Bldg.	609	50
Space Needle	605	...
First Interstate Center	574	48
Seafirst 5th Ave. Plaza	543	42
Bank of Cal., 900 4th Ave.	536	42
Rainer Bank Tower, 4th & Univ.	514	42
Smith Tower	500	42
Federal Office Bldg.	487	37
Pacific Northwest Bell	466	33
One Union Square	456	38
1111 3d Ave. Bldg.	454	35
Washington Plaza Second Tower	448	44
Westin Bldg., 2001 6th Ave.	409	34
Washington Plaza	397	40
Financial Center	389	30
Daon Bldg., 840 Olive Way	381	19
Sheraton Seattle Hotel	371	34
Sixth & Pike Bldg.	365	29
Fourth & Blanchard Bldg.	360	24
Park Hilton Hotel	352	33

Tampa, Fla.

Barnett Plaza	577	42
Tampa City Center	537	39
First Financial Tower	458	36

Toledo, Oh.

Owens-Illinois Corp. Headquarters	411	32
Owens-Corning Fiberglas Tower	400	30
Ohio Citizens Bank Bldg.	368	27
Toledo Govt. Center	327	22
City-County State Office Bldg.	300	22

Toronto, Ont.

CN Tower, World's tallest self-supporting structure	1,821	...
First Canadian Place	952	72
*Scotia Plaza	886	68
Commerce Court West	784	57
Toronto-Dominion Tower (TD Centre)	758	56
Royal Trust Tower (TD Centre)	600	46
Royal Bank Plaza—South Tower	589	41
Manulife Centre	545	53
IBM Tower TD Centre	493	36
Two Bloor West	486	34
Exchange Tower	480	36
Commerce Court North	476	34
Simpson Tower	473	33
Cadillac-Fairview Bldg., 10 Queen St.	465	36
Palace Pier	452	46
Continental Bank Bldg.	450	35
Sheraton Centre	443	43
Hudson's Bay Centre	442	35
Leaside Towers (2 bldgs.)	423	44
Commercial Union Tower (TD Centre)	420	32
Maple Leaf Mills Tower	419	30
Plaza 2 Hotel	415	41
Sun Life Bldg., 150 King St.	410	28
Royal York Hotel	399	27
390 Bay St.	394	31
Royal Bank Plaza—North Tower	387	26
Eaton Tower	385	29
Maclean-Hunter Bldg.	380	30
Harborside Apts.	380	39
Harbour Castle Hilton, East	374	35
Travellers Tower	369	27
360 Sun Life, 200 King St.	360	34
York Centre	360	27
*Standard Life Bldg.	360	26
3 Massey Square	354	38
Harbour Castle Hilton, West	353	35
Mowat Block	349	24
Toronto Professional Tower	346	26
L'Apartel at Harbour Square	344	36
Sutton Place Hotel	340	32
Richmond-Adelaide Centre	340	27
50 Cordova Ave.	340	36

Tulsa, Okla.

Bank of Oklahoma Tower	667	52
City of Faith Clinic Tower	648	60
Mid-Continent Tower	530	36
1st National Tower	516	41
4th Natl. Bank of Tulsa	412	33
320 South Boston Bldg.	400	24
Cities Service Bldg.	388	28
Univ. Club Tower	377	32
City of Faith Hospital	348	30
Philtower	343	24

Vancouver, B.C.

Royal Bank Tower	460	37
Canada Trust Tower, 1055 Melville	454	35
Scotiabank Tower	451	36
Vancouver Centre	450	36
Park Place	450	35
Bentall IV	443	34
T-D Bank Tower	432	30
Harbour Centre	428	32
200 Granville Square	403	30
Bentall III, 595 Burrand	399	31
Sheraton-Landmark Hotel	380	45
Hyatt Regency Vancouver	357	36
Hotel Vancouver	353	22
Board of Trade Tower	323	26

Winnipeg, Man.

Richardson Bldg., 375 Main	406	32
Commodity Exchange Tower	393	32

Winston-Salem, N.C.

Wachovia Bldg.	410	30
Reynolds Bldg.	315	21

Other Notable Tall Buildings

Cape Canaveral, Fla., Vehicle Assembly Bldg., 40 (552); Allentown, Pa., Power & Light Bldg., 23 (320); Amarillo, Tex., American Natl. Bank, 33 (374); Bethlehem, Pa., Martin Tower, 21 (332); Charleston, W. Va., Kanawha Valley Bldg., 20 (384); Frankfort, Ky., Capital Plaza Office Tower, 28 (338); Galveston, Tex., American National Ins., 20 (358); Knoxville, Tenn., United American Bank, 30 (400); Lansing, Mich., Michigan Natl. Tower, 25 (300, not including antenna tower); Lexington, Ky., Kinkaid Tower, 22 (333); Lincoln, Neb., State Capitol (432); Mobile, Ala., First Natl. Bank, 33 (420); New Haven, Conn., Knights of Columbus Hqs. (319); Niagara Falls, Ont., Skylon, (520); Springfield, Mass., Valley Bank Tower, 29 (370); Tallahassee, Fla., State Capitol Tower, 22 (345).

Notable Bridges in North America

Source: State Highway Engineers; Canadian Civil Engineering — ASCE

Asterisk (*) designates railroad bridge. Span of a bridge is distance (in feet) between its supports.

Suspension

Year	Bridge	Location	Longest span
1964	Verrazano-Narrows	New York, N.Y.	4,260
1937	Golden Gate	San Fran. Bay, Cal.	4,200
1957	Mackinac	Sts. of Mackinac	3,800
1931	Geo. Washington	Hudson River	3,500
1950	Tacoma Narrows	Washington	2,800
1936	*Transbay	San Fran. Bay, Cal.	2,310
1939	Bronx-Whitestone	East R., N.Y.C.	2,300
1970	Pierre Laporte	Quebec	2,190
1951	Del. Memorial	Wilmington, Del.	2,150
1968	Del. Mem. (new)	Wilmington, Del.	2,150
1957	Walt Whitman	Phila., Pa.	2,000
1929	Ambassador	Detroit-Canada	1,850
1961	Throgs Neck	Long Is. Sound	1,800
1926	Benjamin Franklin	Philadelphia	1,750
1924	Bear Mt., N.Y.	Hudson River	1,632
1952	²Wm. Preston Lane Mem.	Sandy Point, Md.	1,600
1903	Williamsburg	East R., N.Y.C.	1,600
1969	Newport	Narragansett Bay, R.I.	1,600
1883	Brooklyn	East R., N.Y.C.	1,595
1939	Lion's Gate	Burrard Inlet, B.C.	1,550
1930	Mid-Hudson, N.Y.	Poughkeepsie	1,500
1964	Vincent Thomas	Los Angeles Harbor	1,500
1909	Manhattan	East R., N.Y.C.	1,470
1936	Triboro	East R., N.Y.C.	1,380
1931	St. Johns	Portland, Ore.	1,207
1929	Mount Hope	Rhode Island	1,200
1960	Ogdensburg, N.Y.	St. Lawrence R.	1,150
1939	Deer Isle	Maine	1,080
1931	Maysville (Ky.)	Ohio River	1,060
1867	Cincinnati	Ohio River	1,057
1971	Dent	Clearwater Co., Ida.	1,050
1900	Miampimi	Mexico	1,030
1849	Wheeling, W. Va.	Ohio River	1,010

Cantilever

Year	Bridge	Location	Longest span
1917	Quebec	Quebec	1,800
1974	Commodore Barry	Chester, Pa.	1,644
1958	New Orleans, La.	Mississippi R.	1,575
1936	Transbay	San Fran. Bay	1,400
1968	Baton Rouge, La.	Mississippi R.	1,235
1955	Tappan Zee	Hudson River	1,212
1930	Longview, Wash.	Columbia River	1,200
1909	Queensboro	East R., N.Y.C.	1,182
1927	Carquinez Strait	California	1,100
1958	Parallel Span	"	1,100
1930	Jacques Cartier	Montreal, P.Q.	1,097
1968	Isaiah D. Hart	Jacksonville, Fla.	1,088
1957	³Richmond	San Fran. Bay, Cal.	1,070
1929	Grace Memorial	Charleston, S.C.	1,050
1963	Newburgh-Beacon	Hudson, R., N.Y.	1,000
1975	Caruthersville, Mo.	Mississippi R.	920
1977	Saint Marys	Saint Marys, W. Va.	900
1969	Silver Memorial	Pt. Pleasant, W. Va.	900
1940	Natchez	Mississippi R.	875
1938	Blue Water	Pt. Huron, Mich.	871
1972	Vicksburg	Mississippi River	870
1954	Sunshine Skyway	St. Petersburg, Fla.	864
1972	N. Fork American R.	Auburn, Cal.	862
1940	*Baton Rouge	Mississippi R.	848
1899	*Cornwall	St. Lawrence R.	843
1940	Greenville	Mississippi R.	840
1961	Helena, Ark.	Mississippi R.	840
1963	Brent Spence	Covington, Ky.	831
1963	Cincinnati, Oh.	Ohio River	830
1963	Sunshine, Don'ville	Mississippi, La.	825
1930	*Vicksburg	Mississippi R.	825
1929	Louisville	Ohio River	820
1961	Campbellton-Cross Point	New Brunswick-Quebec	815
1950	Maurice J. Tobin	Boston, Mass.	800
1935	Rip Van Winkle	Catskill, N.Y.	800
1938	Cairo	Ohio River, Ill.-Ky.	800
1940	Ludlow Ferry	Potomac R.	800
1932	Washington Mem.	Seattle, Wash.	800
1936	McCullough	Coos Bay, Ore.	793
1935	⁴Huey P Long	New Orleans	790
1916	*Memphis (Harahan)	Mississippi R.	790
1892	*Memphis	Mississippi R.	790
1949	Memphis-Arkansas	Mississippi R.	790

(Suspension continued)

Year	Bridge	Location	Longest span
1904	*Mingo Jct., W. Va.	Ohio River	769
1910	*Beaver, Pa.	Ohio River	767
1966	⁵S.N. Pearman	Charleston, S.C.	760
1940	Owensboro	Ohio River	750
1911	Sewickley, Pa.	Ohio River	750
1928	Outerbridge, N.Y.-N.J.	Arthur Kill	750

Simple Truss

Year	Bridge	Location	Longest span
1977	Chester	Chester, W. Va.	746
1917	*Metropolis	Ohio River	720
1929	Irvin S. Cobb	Ohio River-Ill.-Ky.	716
1922	*Tanana River	Nenana, Alaska	700
1933	*Henderson	Ohio River-Ind.-Ky.	665
1967	I-77, Ohio River	Marietta, Oh.	650
1917	*MacArthur, Ill.-Mo.	St. Louis	647
1919	Louisville	Ohio River	644
1933	Atchafalaya	Morgan City, La.	608
1924	*Castleton	Hudson River	598
1889	*Cincinnati	Ohio River	542
1951	Allegheny River	Allegheny Co., Pa.	533
1914	Pittsburgh	Allegheny R.	531
1930	*Martinez	California	528
1967	Tanana River	Alaska	500

Steel Truss

Year	Bridge	Location	Longest span
1940	Gov. Nice Mem.	Potomac River, Md.	800
1973	Atchafalaya R.	Krotz Springs, La.	780
1975	I-24	Tenn R., Ky.	720
1938	US-62, Ky.	Green River	700
1952	US-62, Ky.	Cumberland River.	700
1940	Jamestown	Jamestown, R.I.	640
1940	Greenville	Mississippi R., Ark.	640
1949	Memphis	Mississippi R., Ark.	621
1938	US-22	Delaware River, N.J.	540
1910	*McKinley, St. Louis	Mississippi River.	517
1972	Mississippi River	Muscatine, Ia.	512
1942	Wax Lake Outlet	Louisiana	511
1896	Newport	Ohio River, Ky.	511
1931	US-60	Cumberland R., Ky.	500
1958	Lake Oahe	Mobridge, S.D.	500
1958	Lake Oahe	Gettysburg, S.D.	500
1963	Millard E. Tydings	Susquehanna R., Md.	490
1955	Four Bears	Missouri R., N.D.	475
1930	Lake Champlain	Lake Champlain, N.Y.	434

Continuous Truss

Year	Bridge	Location	Longest span
1966	Astoria, Ore.	Columbia R.	1,232
1977	Francis Scott Key	Baltimore, Md.	1,200
1966	*Marquam	Willamette R., Ore.	1,044
1943	Dubuque, Ia.	Mississippi R.	845
1956	*Earl C. Clements	Ohio R., Ill-Ky.	825
1953	John E. Mathews	Jacksonville, Fla.	810
1957	Kingston-Rhinecliff	Hudson R., N.Y.	800
1918	*Sciotoville	Ohio River	775
1974	Betsy Ross	Philadelphia, Pa.	729
1929	Madison-Milton	Ohio River	727
1966	⁶Matthew E. Welsh	Mauckport	707
1962	Champlain	Montreal, P.Q.	707
1975	Girard Point	Philadelphia, Pa.	700
1938	Port Arthur-Orange	Texas	680
1929	*Cincinnati	Ohio River	675
1928	Cape Girardeau, Mo.	Mississippi R.	672
1946	Chester, Ill.	Mississippi R.	670
1930	Quincy, Ill.	Mississippi R.	628
1959	US 181, over harbor	Corpus Christi, Tex.	620
1934	Bourne	Cape Cod Canal	616
1935	Sagamore	Cape Cod Canal	616
1965	Clarion River	Clarion Co., Pa.	612
1957	Blatnik	Duluth, Minn.	600
1965	Rio Grande Gorge	Taos, N.M.	600
1941	Columbia River	Kettle Falls, Wash.	600
1954	Columbia River	Umatilla, Ore.	600
1954	Columbia River	The Dalles, Ore.	576
1962	W. Br. Feather River	Oroville, Cal.	576
1936	Meredosia	Illinois River	567
1936	Mark Twain Mem.	Hannibal, Mo.	562
1957	Mackinac	Mackinac Straits, Mich.	560
1937	Homestead	Pittsburgh	553
1961	Ship Canal	Seattle, Wash.	552
1932	Pulaski Skyway	Passaic R., N.J.	550
1973	I-95, Thames River	New London, Conn.	540
1927	Ross Island	Portland, Ore.	535

Continuous Box and Plate Girder

Year	Bridge	Location	Longest span
1983	Lüling-Destrehan	Luling, La.	1,222
1982	Houston Ship Chan	Texas.	750
1967	San Mateo-Hayward No. 2.	San Fran. Bay, Cal..	750
1963	Gunnison River	Gunnison, Col..	720
1969	⁷San Diego-Coronado.	San Diego Bay, Cal..	660
1973	Ship Channel	Houston, Tex..	630
1981	Douglas.	Juneau, Alaska	620
1967	Poplar St..	St. Louis, Mo..	600
1982	Illinois R..	Perkin, Ill..	550
1982	I-440	Arkansas R..	540
1977	US-64, Tennessee R..	Savannah, Tenn..	525
1965	McDonald-Cartier	Ottawa, Ont..	520
1971	Lake Koocanusa.	Lincoln Co., Mon..	500
1972	Sitka Harbor.	Sitka, Alaska	450
1970	I-205	Willamette R., Ore..	430
1974	I-430	Arkansas R..	430
1985	I-435	Missouri R., Ks.-Mo.	425
1984	US-36.	Missouri R., Ks.-Mo.	425
1972	I-635, Kansas City	Missouri R., Kan.-Mo..	425
1967	I-24, Tennessee R..	Marion Co., Tenn..	420
1978	Snake River	Clarkston, Wash..	420
1979	Arkansas R.	Clarksville, Ark..	410
1975	Yukon River	Alaska	410
1972	I-75, Tennessee River.	Loudon Co., Tenn..	400
1941	Susquehanna	Susquehanna R., Md..	400
1963	Lake Charles B'Pass.	Louisiana.	399
1957	Conn. Turnpike	Quinnipiac R..	387
1960	Route 34	New Haven, Conn..	379
1971	US-165	Pendleton, Ark..	377
1960	I-24, Tennessee R..	Chattanooga, Tenn..	375
1966	I-80, LeClaire, Ia..	Mississippi	370
1971	Sacramento R..	Bryte, Cal..	370
1963	I-40, Tennessee River.	Benton Co., Tenn..	365
1950	US-62, Kentucky Dam.	Tennessee R., Ky..	350
1972	Franklin Falls.	Snoq'lmie Pass, Wash..	350
1971	Don Pedro Reserv	Tuolumne Co., Cal..	350

Continuous Plate

Year	Bridge	Location	Longest span
1971	W. Atchafalaya	Henderson, La..	573
1981	Illinois 23	Illinois R., Ill..	510
1968	Trinity R..	Dallas, Tex..	480
1975	I-129	Missouri R., Ia..	450
1967	Mississippi River.	LaCrescent, Minn..	450
1966	I-480	Missouri R., Ia.-Neb..	425
1970	I-435	Missouri R., Mo..	425
1972	I-80	Missouri R., Ia.-Neb..	425
1971	St. Croix River	Hudson, Wisc..	390
1968	Lafayette St..	St. Paul, Minn..	362
1967	San Mateo Creek	Hillsborough, Cal..	360
1969	Fort Smith	Arkansas River	353
1961	Whiskey Creek	Shasta Co., Cal..	350
1964	Lexington Ave..	St. Paul, Minn..	340

I-Beam Girder

Year	Bridge	Location	Longest span
1980	Shreveport Int..	Louisiana.	438
1941	US-31E.	Rolling Fork R., Ky..	340
1948	US-27.	Licking River, Ky..	316
1947	US-31E.	Green River, Ky..	316
1941	US-62.	Rolling Fork, Ky..	240
1942	Licking River.	Owingsville, Ky..	240
1954	Fuller Warren	Jacksonville, Fla..	224

Steel Arch

Year	Bridge	Location	Longest span
1977	New River Gorge	Fayetteville, W. Va..	1,700
1931	Bayonne, N.J.	Kill Van Kull	1,652
1973	Fremont	Portland, Ore..	1,255
1964	Port Mann	British Columbia.	1,200
1916	*Hell Gate	East R., N.Y.C..	1,038
1959	Glen Canyon	Colorado River	1,028
1967	Trois-Rivieres	St. Lawrence R., P.Q..	1,100
1962	Lewiston-Queenston	Niagara River, Ont..	1,000
1976	Perrine	Twin Falls, Ida..	993
1941	Rainbow	Niagara Falls	984
1984	I-255	Mississippi R., Mo..	909
1972	¹⁰I-40, Mississippi R..	Memphis, Tenn..	900
1970	Lake Quinsigamond.	Worcester, Mass..	849
1966	Charles Braga	Somerset, Mass..	840
1936	Henry Hudson	Harlem River, N.Y.C..	840
1967	Lincoln Trail	Ohio R., Ind.-Ky..	625
1978	I-57, Cairo, Ill..	Mississippi R..	821
1961	Sherman Minton	Louisville, Ky..	800
1936	French King	Conn. R. (Rt. 2, Mass.)	782

Year	Bridge	Location	Longest span
1931	West End.	Pittsburgh	778
1972	Piscataqua R..	I-95, N.H.-Me..	756
1979	SR 156, Tennessee R.	So. Pittsburgh, Tenn..	750
1973	I-24, Paducah, Ky..	Ohio River.	730

Concrete Arch

Year	Bridge	Location	Longest span
1971	Selah Creek (twin)	Selah, Wash..	549
1968	Cowlitz River.	Mossyrock, Wash..	520
1931	Westinghouse	Pittsburgh	425
1923	Cappelen.	Minneapolis	400
1930	Jack's Run	Pittsburgh	400
1973	Elwha River	Port Angeles, Wash..	380
1931	Bixby Creek	Monterey Coast, Cal..	330
1953	Arroyo Seco	Pasadena, Cal..	320

Twin Concrete Trestle

Year	Bridge	Location	Longest span
1963	⁹Slidell, La..	L. Pontchartrain	28,547

Concrete Slab Dam

Year	Bridge	Location	Longest span
1927	Conowingo Dam.	Maryland.	4,611
1952	John H. Kerr Dam.	Roanoke River, Va..	2,785
1936	Hoover Dam.	Boulder City, Nev..	1,324

Drawbridges

Vertical Lift

Year	Bridge	Location	Longest span
1937	Marine Parkway	Jamaica Bay, N.Y.C..	590
1959	*Arthur Kill	N.Y.-N.J..	558
1935	*Cape Cod Canal	Massachusetts	544
1960	*Delair, N.J.	Delaware River	542
1931	Burlington, N.J..	Delaware R..	534
1968	Second Narrows	Vancouver, B.C..	493
1912	*A-S-B Fratt	Kansas City	428
1945	*Harry S. Truman	Kansas City	427
1955	Roosevelt Island.	East River, N.Y.C..	418
1979	James River	Newport News, Va..	415
1932	*M-K-T R.R.	Missouri R..	414
1969	Wilm'gtn Mem.	Wilmington, N.C..	408
1930	Aerial	Duluth, Minn..	386
1941	Main St..	Jacksonville, Fla..	386
1962	Burlington	Ontario	370
1941	Acosta	St. Johns R., Fla..	365
1922	*Cincinnati	Ohio River	365
1967	Benj. Harrison Mem..	James River, Va..	363
1936	Tribo	Harlem River, N.Y.C..	344
1961	*Corpus Christi Harbor.	Corpus Christi, Tex..	344
1941	U.S. 1&9, Passaic R.	Newark, N.J..	332
1929	Carlton	Bath-Woolwich, Me..	328
1930	*Martinez	California.	328
1960	St. Andrews Bay.	Panama City, Fla..	327
1929	*Penn-Lehigh	Newark Bay	322
1920	*Chattanooga	Tennessee R..	310
1936	Hardin	Illinois River	309
1960	Sacramento River.	Rio Vista, Cal..	306
1957	Claiborne Ave.	New Orleans	305
1927	Cochrane	Mobile, Ala..	300
1929	Dumbarton	California.	300
1926	*Missouri Pacific.	Kragen, Ark..	300

Bascule

Year	Bridge	Location	Longest span
1969	Pearl River	Slidell, La..	482
1917	SR-8, Tennessee River.	Chattanooga, Tenn..	306
1940	Lorain, Ohio	Black River	300
1958	Morrison	Portland, Ore..	285
1969	Elizabeth River.	Chesapeake, Va..	281
1954	Fuller Warren	St. Johns R., Fla..	267
1977	Curtis Creek	Baltimore, Md..	251
1957	Craig Memorial	I-280, Toledo, Oh..	245

Swing Bridges

Year	Bridge	Location	Longest span
1926	*Fort Madison	Mississippi R..	525
1930	Rigolets Pass	New Orleans, La..	400
1950	Douglass Memorial	Wash. D.C..	386
1916	Keokuk Municipal	Mississippi R., Ia..	377
1945	Lord Delaware	Mattaponi River, Va..	252
1957	Eltham	Pamunkey River, Va..	237
1939	Chickahominy River.	Route 5, Va..	222
1930	Nansemond River	Route 125, Va..	200

Swing Span

Year	Bridge	Location	Longest span
1908	*Willamette R..	Portland, Ore..	521
1903	*East Omaha	Missouri R..	519
1952	Yorktown	York River, Va..	500
1897	*Duluth, Minn.	St. Louis Bay	486
1899	*C.M.&N.R.R.	Chicago	474
1914	*Coos Bay.	Oregon	458

Floating Pontoon

Year	Bridge	Location	Longest span
1963	Evergreen Pt.	Seattle, Wash..	7,518
1940	Lacey V. Murrow	Seattle	6,561
1961	Hood Canal	Pt. Gamble, Wash..	6,471

(1) The Transbay Bridge has 2 spans of 2,310 ft. each. (2) A second bridge in parallel was completed in 1973. (3) The Richmond Bridge has twin spans 1,070 ft. each. (4) Railroad and vehicular bridge. (5) Two spans each 760 ft. (6) Two spans each 707 ft. (7) Two spans each 660 ft. (8) Two spans each 825 ft. (9) Total length of bridge. (10) Two spans each 900 ft.

Notable International Bridges

Angostura, suspension type, span 2,336 feet, 1967 at Ciudad Bolivar, Venezuela. Total length, 5,507.

Bendorf Bridge on the Rhine River, 5 mi. n. of Coblenz, completed 1965, is a 3-span cement girder bridge, 3,378 ft. overall length, 101 ft. wide, with the main span 682 ft.

Gladesville Bridge at Sydney, Australia, has the longest concrete arch in the world (1,000 ft. span).

Humber Bridge, with a suspension span of 4,626 ft., the longest in the world, crosses the Humber estuary 5 miles west of the city of Kingston upon Hull, England. Unique in a large suspension bridge are the towers of reinforced concrete instead of steel.

Second Narrow's Bridge, Canada's longest railway lift span connecting Vancouver and North Vancouver over Burrard Inlet.

Oland Island Bridge in Sweden was completed in 1972. It is 19,882 feet long, Europe's longest.

Oosterscheldebrug, opened Dec. 15, 1965, is a 3.125-mile causeway for automobiles over a sea arm in Zeeland, the Netherlands. It completes a direct connection between Flushing and Rotterdam.

Rio-Niteroi, Guanabara Bay, Brazil, completed in 1972, is world's longest continuous box and plate girder bridge. 8 miles, 3,363 feet long, with a center span of 984 feet and a span on each side of 656 feet.

Tagus River Bridge near Lisbon, Portugal, has a 3,323-ft. main span. Opened Aug. 6, 1966, it was named Salazar Bridge for the former premier.

Zoo Bridge across the Rhine at Cologne, with steel box girders, has a main span of 850 ft.

Underwater Vehicular Tunnels in North America
(3,000 feet in length or more)

Name	Location	Waterway	Lgth. Ft.
Bart Trans-Bay Tubes (Rapid Transit). .	San Francisco, Cal..	S.F. Bay	3.6 miles
Brooklyn-Battery	New York, N.Y..	East River	9,117
Holland Tunnel.	New York, N.Y..	Hudson River	8,557
Lincoln Tunnel.	New York, N.Y..	Hudson River	8,216
Baltimore Harbor Tunnel.	Baltimore, Md.	Patapsco River	7,650
Hampton Roads	Norfolk, Va..	Hampton Roads.	7,479
Queens Midtown	New York, N.Y..	East River	6,414
Thimble Shoal Channel	Cape Henry, Va..	Chesapeake Bay	5,738
Sumner Tunnel	Boston, Mass.	Boston Harbor	5,650
Chesapeake Channel	Cape Charles, Va.. . . .	Chesapeake Bay	5,450
Louis-Hippolyte Lafontaine Tunnel	Montreal, Que.	St. Lawrence River . . .	5,280
Detroit-Windsor	Detroit, Mich.	Detroit River	5,135
Callahan Tunnel	Boston, Mass.	Boston Harbor.	5,046
Midtown Tunnel	Norfolk, Va..	Elizabeth River	4,194
Baytown Tunnel.	Baytown, Tex.	Houston Ship Channel .	4,111
Posey Tube	Oakland, Cal..	Oakland Estuary . . .	3,500
Downtown Tunnel.	Norfolk, Va..	Elizabeth River	3,350
Webster St..	Alameda, Cal.	Oakland Estuary . . .	3,350
Bankhead Tunnel.	Mobile, Ala..	Mobile River	3,109
I-10 Twin Tunnel	Mobile, Ala..	Mobile River	3,000

Land Vehicular Tunnels in U.S.
(over 2,000 feet in length.)

Name	Location	Lgth. Ft.	Name	Location	Lgth. Ft.
E. Johnson Memorial . .	I-70, Col.	8,959	Fort Pitt	Pittsburgh, Pa.	3,560
Eisenhower Memorial . .	I-70, Col.	8,941	Mall Tunnel	Dist. of Columbia. . . .	3,400
Allegheny (twin)	Penna. Turnpike . . .	6,070	Caldecott	Oakland, Cal.	3,371
Liberty Tubes.	Pittsburgh, Pa.. . . .	5,920	Cody No. 1	U.S. 14, 16, 20, Wyo. . . .	3,224
Zion Natl. Park	Rte. 9, Utah.	5,766	Kalihi.	Honolulu, Ha..	2,780
East River Mt. (twin) . . .	Interstate 77, W. Va.-Va.	5,661	Memorial	W. Va. Tpke. (I-77). . .	2,669
Tuscarora (twin)	Penna. Turnpike . . .	5,326	Ft. Cronkhite	Sausalito, Cal.	2,690
Kittatinny (twin).	Penna. Turnpike . . .	4,727	Cross-Town.	178 St. N.Y.C.	2,414
Lehigh	Penna. Turnpike . . .	4,379	F.D. Roosevelt Dr.	81-89 Sts. N.Y.C. . . .	2,400
Blue Mountain (twin). . .	Penna. Turnpike . . .	4,339	Dewey Sq.	Boston, Mass.	2,400
Wawona.	Yosemite Natl. Park . .	4,233	Battery Park	N.Y.C..	2,300
Squirrel Hill	Pittsburgh, Pa.. . . .	4,225	Battery St..	Seattle, Wash..	2,140
Big Walker Mt.	Route I-77, Va.. . . .	4,200	Big Oak Flat	Yosemite Natl. Park	2,083

World's Longest Railway Tunnels
Source: Railway Directory & Year Book 1980. Tunnels over 5 miles in length.

Tunnel	Date	Miles	Operating railway	Country
Seikan.	1985	33.5	Japanese National.	Japan
Dai-shimizu	1979	13	Japanese National.	Japan
Simplon No. 1 and 2	1906, 1922	12	Swiss Fed. & Italian St..	Switz.-Italy
Kanmon	1975	11	Japanese National.	Japan
Apennine.	1934	11	Italian State.	Italy
Rokko	1972	10	Japanese National.	Japan
Gotthard	1882	9	Swiss Federal	Switzerland
Lotschberg	1913	9	Bern-Lotschberg-Simplon.	Switzerland
Hokuriku	1962	8	Japanese National.	Japan
Mont Cenis (Frejus)	1871	8	Italian State.	France-Italy
Shin-Shimizu	1961	8	Japanese National.	Japan
Aki	1975	8	Japanese National.	Japan
Cascade	1929	7	Burlington Northern	U.S.
Flathead	1970	7	Great Northern	U.S.
Keijo	1970	7	Japanese National.	Japan
Lierasen	1973	6	Norwegian State.	Norway
Santa Lucia	1977	6	Italian State.	Italy
Arlberg	1884	6	Austrian Federal	Austria
Moffat	1928	6	Denver & Rio Grande Western.	U.S.
Shimizu	1931	6	Japanese National.	Japan

Scientific Achievements and Discoveries: 1984-1985

As of mid-1985

Origins of Life

Scientists at NASA's Ames Research Center in Mountainview, Calif. reported a major discovery that supports the emerging theory that life on earth began in clay rather than the sea. The findings showed that ordinary clay contains two basic properties essential to life: the capacities to store and transfer energy. With such energy, coming from radioactive decay and other sources, the early clays could have acted as "chemical factories" for processing inorganic raw materials into the more complex molecules from which the first life arose some four billion years ago.

Recent analysis of fossils from Olduvai Gorge in Tanzania raised doubts about the popular theory that early humans lived the hunter-gatherer way of life with its attendant family structure, division of labor between sexes, and interfamily sharing of food. According to Richard Potts of Yale Univ., the Olduvai assemblages could be the remains of "stone caches" where hominids stored stone tools to provide convenient butchering sites, rather than home bases or campsites, as they foraged for meat. This suggests that the hunter-gatherer life style might have developed later in human history than previously thought, and that the associated social patterns might be less central to "humanness" than is often asserted.

Human genetic material, largely undamaged after 2,400 years, was extracted from an Egyptian mummy and was cloned in a laboratory. The achievement, by Svante Paabo of Univ. of Uppsala in Sweden, was believed to be the first in which DNA, the genetic material in all forms of life, was resurrected and duplicated from an ancient human. Previously, scientists at Univ. of Calif. at Berkeley extracted and reproduced DNA from an African mammal called a quagga, a relative of the zebra and the horse, which became extinct a century ago. Reproduction of fragments of its genetic material represented the first time such a biochemical resurrection was achieved with the DNA of any extinct animal.

The skeleton of what was believed to be the earliest known dinosaur, a creature the size of a small ostrich, was discovered in Arizona's Painted Desert by scientists from the Univ. of Calif. at Berkeley. The skeleton was estimated to be 3-4 million years older than any dinosaur ever found in North America.

Space Exploration

The search for intelligent life elsewhere in the universe yielded no clear evidence that life exists beyond Earth, but new discoveries and new methods of searching are attracting the interest of scientists and the financial backing of NASA ($1.5 million yearly). One suggestion states that the civilizations might be trying to establish contact on a radio wavelength, based on the radiation given off by free atoms of hydrogen, the most common element in the universe.

American astronomers, led by Donald W. McCarthy Jr. of Univ. of Ariz. at Tucson, have discovered what they believe is the first planet to be detected outside the solar system. If the object is actually a planet, the discovery would be the first direct evidence to support a premise underlying theories of possible extraterrestrial life, which is that planetary systems are not unique to the Sun and might even be common in the universe. Other astronomers, however, believed the object might be too hot and massive to be called a planet in the usual sense. Rather, it could be the first evidence of a new class of objects, "brown dwarfs," believed to be too small to get their nuclear fires ignited and become true stars. The object was said to be about 21 light years from earth, with a mass estimated to be 30-80 times greater than Jupiter, and a surface temperature of 2,000°F.

Astronomers from the Univ. of Maryland, Calif. Inst. of Technology, and the Univ. of Washington confirmed that quasars, the mysterious, starlike objects that are the most powerful energy sources known, are near the edge of the universe and are not simply illusions reflecting some unknown law of physics. Detailed observations led to the conclusion that quasars were born when the universe began, and that, in turn, could mean that we are seeing light that originated billions of years ago, at the beginning of time, from material that was part of the original expansion of matter that created the universe.

Medicine

A new genetically engineered drug that could effectively open closed arteries by dissolving blood clots was produced by Genetech Inc., a biotechnology company in San Francisco. The experimental drug, actually a human blood substance that can now be produced in large quantities by genetic splicing methods, was said to be twice as effective as medications now used in halting heart attacks.

Tests began, in humans, of a new anticancer drug. Instead of killing cancer cells with toxic chemicals, the standard approach, the new drug seeks to change the cancer cells so that they stop their uncontrolled proliferation and resume more normal behavior. The new drug and others like it, known as differentiation modifiers or differentiation inducers, appear to operate primarily against tumor cells while leaving normal cells relatively untouched. Dr. Charlotte Friend of Mt. Sinai School of Medicine in N.Y. City described the first observed effects of a differentiating agent in 1971.

A critical defect in the immune system of patients suffering from acquired immune deficiency syndrome (AIDS) was identified by U.S. government scientists led by Anthony S. Fauci of the National Inst. of Allergy and Infectious Diseases. The AIDS virus selectively destroys a key set of blood cells, the T4 helper cells, that are supposed to detect invading viruses and set the immune system into motion to destroy them. The practical importance of the finding is that in order to treat the AIDS virus itself, the patient's immune system will have to be reconstituted, and scientists will need to know precisely which immune cells are defective. As of Jan. 14, 1985, a total of 7,857 cases of AIDS have been reported in the U.S. Of these, 3,737 patients have already died.

A transplant of fetal brain cells into the brains of monkeys suffering from Parkinson's disease was performed at Emory University's Yerkes Primate Center. The transplant alleviated the symptoms of the disease. Parkinson's disease afflicts an estimated 500,000 Americans.

French doctors Bernard Jaquetin and Jean-Luc Meyer successfully exchanged the blood of a fetus whose life was at risk because its blood was incompatible with that of its mother. Although a virtually total replacement of blood has been carried out for newborn babies, this was the first time such a procedure had been performed with a fetus.

Patents

Among the many inventions to receive patents in 1985 were: a magazine page containing dehydrated foods in plastic bags (Penny Stone Cooper, the inventor, said that the idea came to her in a dream); a clinically tested method of reducing the duration of the common cold by administration of zinc glutonate in lozenge form; a device to detect the presence of the human body for such purposes as finding lost children in the woods, although military applications are likely as well; an alarm to alert car drivers that they are excessively fatigued; a sensor to let golfers know when they are guilty of excessive head movement during their swing; a radio antenna that would survive a nuclear blast; a method of identifying individuals by inscribing personal data on a tiny disk beneath the face of a person's tooth; a voice control system for home appliances such as automatic clothes dryers; a vacuum cane for picking up light articles from the floor; and a flag-waving machine that waves the staff in a figure-8 pattern and maintains the flag in an outstretched condition similar to that afforded by a good breeze.

The 1984 report of the Patent and Trademark Office showed the issuance of 72,149 patents during its fiscal year ending Sept. 30, 1984, compared with 59,715 in the previous fiscal year. The number of foreign inventors getting patents increased to 30,087 in the 1984 fiscal year from 24,593 and U.S. residents received 42,062 patents compared with 35,122 the year before.

INVENTIONS AND DISCOVERIES

Invention	Date	Inventor	Nation.
Adding machine	1642	Pascal	French
Adding machine	1885	Burroughs	U.S.
Addressograph	1892	Rotheim	Norwegian
Aerosol spray	1926	Goodhue	U.S.
Air brake	1868	Westinghouse	U.S.
Air conditioning	1911	Carrier	U.S.
Air pump	1654	Guericke	German
Airplane, automatic pilot	1912	Sperry	U.S.
Airplane, experimental	1896	Langley	U.S.
Airplane jet engine	1939	Ohain	German
Airplane with motor	1903	Wright bros.	U.S.
Airplane, hydro	1911	Curtiss	U.S.
Airship	1852	Giffard	French
Airship, rigid dirigible	1900	Zeppelin	German
Arc welder	1919	Thomson	U.S.
Autogyro	1920	de la Cierva	Spanish
Automobile, differential gear	1885	Benz	German
Automobile, electric	1892	Morrison	U.S.
Automobile, exp'mtl	1864	Marcus	Austrian
Automobile, gasoline	1889	Daimler	German
Automobile, gasoline	1892	Duryea	U.S.
Automobile magneto	1897	Bosch	German
Automobile muffler	...	Maxim, H.P.	U.S.
Automobile self-starter	1911	Kettering	U.S.
Babbitt metal	1839	Babbitt	U.S.
Bakelite	1907	Baekeland	Belg., U.S.
Balloon	1783	Montgolfier	French
Barometer	1643	Torricelli	Italian
Bicycle, modern	1885	Starley	English
Bifocal lens	1780	Franklin	U.S.
Block signals, railway	1867	Hall	U.S.
Bomb, depth	1916	Tait	U.S.
Bottle machine	1895	Owens	U.S.
Braille printing	1829	Braille	French
Burner, gas	1855	Bunsen	German
Calculating machine	1833	Babbage	English
Camera—see also Photography			
Camera, Kodak	1888	Eastman, Walker	U.S.
Camera, Polaroid Land	1948	Land	U.S.
Car coupler	1873	Janney	U.S.
Carburetor, gasoline	1893	Maybach	German
Card time recorder	1894	Cooper	U.S.
Carding machine	1797	Whittemore	U.S.
Carpet sweeper	1876	Bissell	U.S.
Cash register	1879	Ritty	U.S.
Cathode ray tube	1878	Crookes	English
Cellophane	1908	Brandenberger	Swiss
Celluloid	1870	Hyatt	U.S.
Cement, Portland	1824	Aspdin	English
Chronometer	1761	Harrison	English
Circuit breaker	1925	Hilliard	U.S.
Clock, pendulum	1657	Huygens	Dutch
Coaxial cable system	1929	Affel, Espensched	U.S.
Coke oven	1893	Hoffman	Austrian
Compressed air rock drill	1871	Ingersoll	U.S.
Comptometer	1887	Felt	U.S.
Computer, automatic sequence	1944	Aiken et al.	U.S.
Condenser microphone (telephone)	1916	Wente	U.S.
Corn, hybrid	1917	Jones	U.S.
Cotton gin	1793	Whitney	U.S.
Cream separator	1878	DeLaval	Swedish
Cultivator, disc	1878	Mallon	U.S.
Cystoscope	1878	Nitze	German
Diesel engine	1895	Diesel	German
Dynamite	1866	Nobel	Swedish
Dynamo, continuous current	1871	Gramme	Belgian
Dynamo, hydrogen cooled	1915	Schuler	U.S.
Electric battery	1800	Volta	Italian
Electric fan	1882	Wheeler	U.S.
Electrocardiograph	1903	Einthoven	Dutch
Electroencephalograph	1929	Berger	German
Electromagnet	1824	Sturgeon	English
Electron spectrometer	1944	Deutsch, Elliott, Evans	U.S.
Electron tube multigrid	1913	Langmuir	U.S.
Electroplating	1805	Brugnatelli	Italian
Electrostatic generator	1929	Van de Graaff	U.S.
Elevator brake	1852	Otis	U.S.
Elevator, push button	1922	Larson	U.S.
Engine, coal-gas 4-cycle	1876	Otto	German
Engine, compression ignition	1883	Daimler	German
Engine, electric ignition	1883	Benz	German
Engine, gas, compound	1926	Eickemeyer	U.S.
Engine, gasoline	1872	Brayton, Geo.	U.S.
Engine, gasoline	1889	Daimler	German
Engine, steam, piston	1705	Newcomen	English
Engine, steam, piston	1769	Watt	Scottish
Engraving, half-tone	1852	Talbot	U.S.
Filament, tungsten	1913	Coolidge	U.S.
Flanged rail	1831	Stevens	U.S.
Flatiron, electric	1882	Seely	U.S.
Furnace (for steel)	1858	Siemens	German
Galvanometer	1820	Sweigger	German
Gas discharge tube	1922	Hull	U.S.
Gas lighting	1792	Murdoch	Scottish
Gas mantle	1885	Welsbach	Austrian
Gasoline (lead ethyl)	1922	Midgley	U.S.
Gasoline, cracked	1913	Burton	U.S.
Gasoline, high octane	1930	Ipatieff	Russian
Geiger counter	1913	Geiger	German
Glass, laminated safety	1909	Benedictus	French
Glider	1853	Cayley	English
Gun, breechloader	1811	Thornton	U.S.
Gun, Browning	1897	Browning	U.S.
Gun, magazine	1875	Hotchkiss	U.S.
Gun, silencer	1908	Maxim, H.P.	U.S.
Guncotton	1847	Schoenbein	German
Gyrocompass	1911	Sperry	U.S.
Gyroscope	1852	Foucault	French
Harvester-thresher	1818	Lane	U.S.
Helicopter	1939	Sikorsky	U.S.
Hydrometer	1768	Baume	French
Ice-making machine	1851	Gorrie	U.S.
Iron lung	1928	Drinker, Slaw.	U.S.
Kaleidoscope	1817	Brewster	Scottish
Kinetoscope	1889	Edison	U.S.
Lacquer, nitrocellulose	1921	Flaherty	U.S.
Lamp, arc	1847	Staite	English
Lamp, incandescent	1879	Edison	U.S.
Lamp, incand., frosted	1924	Pipkin	U.S.
Lamp, incand., gas	1913	Langmuir	U.S.
Lamp, Klieg	1911	Kliegl, A.&J.	U.S.
Lamp, mercury vapor	1912	Hewitt	U.S.
Lamp, miner's safety	1816	Davy	English
Lamp, neon	1909	Claude	French
Lathe, turret	1845	Fitch	U.S.
Launderette	1934	Cantrell	U.S.
Lens, achromatic	1758	Dollond	English
Lens, fused bifocal	1908	Borsch	U.S.
Leydenjar (condenser)	1745	von Kleist	German
Lightning rod	1752	Franklin	U.S.
Linoleum	1860	Walton	English
Linotype	1884	Mergenthaler	U.S.
Lock, cylinder	1851	Yale	U.S.
Locomotive, electric	1851	Vail	U.S.
Locomotive, exp'mtl	1802	Trevithick	English
Locomotive, exp'mtl	1812	Fenton et al.	English
Locomotive, exp'mtl	1813	Hedley	English
Locomotive, exp'mtl	1814	Stephenson	English
Locomotive practical	1829	Stephenson	English
Locomotive, 1st U.S.	1830	Cooper, P.	U.S.
Loom, power	1785	Cartwright	English
Loudspeaker, dynamic	1924	Rice, Kellogg	U.S.
Machine gun	1861	Gatling	U.S.
Machine gun, improved	1872	Hotchkiss	U.S.
Machine gun (Maxim)	1883	Maxim, H.S.	U.S., Eng.
Magnet, electro	1828	Henry	U.S.
Mantle, gas	1885	Welsbach	Austrian
Mason jar	1858	Mason, J.	U.S.
Match, friction	1827	John Walker	English
Mercerized textiles	1843	Mercer, J.	English

Invention	Date	Inventor	Nation.	Invention	Date	Inventor	Nation.
Meter, induction	1888	Shallenberg	U.S.	Refrigerator car	1868	David	U.S.
Metronome	1816	Maelzel	German	Resin, synthetic	1931	Hill	English
Micrometer	1636	Gascoigne	English	Rifle, repeating	1860	Spencer	U.S.
Microphone	1877	Berliner	U.S.	Rocket engine	1926	Goddard	U.S.
Microscope, compound	1590	Janssen	Dutch	Rubber, vulcanized	1839	Goodyear	U.S.
Microscope, electronic	1931	Knoll, Ruska	German				
Microscope, field ion.	1951	Mueller	Germany	Saw, band	1808	Newberry	English
Monitor, warship	1861	Ericsson	U.S.	Saw, circular	1777	Miller	English
Monotype	1887	Lanston	U.S.	Searchlight, arc	1915	Sperry	U.S.
Motor, AC	1892	Tesla	U.S.	Sewing machine	1846	Howe	U.S.
Motor, DC	1837	Davenport	U.S.	Shoe-sewing machine	1860	McKay	U.S.
Motor, induction	1887	Tesla	U.S.	Shrapnel shell	1784	Shrapnel	English
Motorcycle	1885	Daimler	German	Shuttle, flying	1733	Kay	English
Movie machine	1894	Jenkins	U.S.	Sleeping-car	1865	Pullman	U.S.
Movie, panoramic	1952	Waller	U.S.	Slide rule	1620	Oughtred	English
Movie, talking	1927	Warner Bros.	U.S.	Soap, hardwater	1928	Bertsch	German
Mower, lawn	1831	Budding,		Spectroscope	1859	Kirchoff,	
		Ferrabee	English			Bunsen	German
Mowing machine	1822	Bailey	U.S.	Spectroscope (mass)	1918	Dempster	U.S.
				Spinning jenny	1767	Hargreaves	English
Neoprene	1930	Carothers	U.S.	Spinning mule	1779	Crompton	English
Nylon synthetic	1930	Carothers	U.S.	Steamboat, exp'mtl	1778	Jouffroy	French
Nylon	1937	Du Pont lab.	U.S.	Steamboat, exp'mtl	1785	Fitch	U.S.
				Steamboat, exp'mtl	1787	Rumsey	U.S.
Oil cracking furnace	1891	Gavrilov	Russian	Steamboat, exp'mtl	1788	Miller	Scottish
Oil filled power cable	1921	Emanueli	Italian	Steamboat, exp'mtl	1803	Fulton	U.S.
Oleomargarine	1869	Mege-Mouries	French	Steamboat, exp'mtl	1804	Stevens	U.S.
Ophthalmoscope	1851	Helmholtz	German	Steamboat, practical	1802	Symington	Scottish
				Steamboat, practical	1807	Fulton	U.S.
Paper machine	1809	Dickinson	U.S.	Steam car	1770	Cugnot	French
Parachute	1785	Blanchard	French	Steam turbine	1884	Parsons	English
Pen, ballpoint	1888	Loud	U.S.	Steel	1856	Bessemer	English
Pen, fountain	1884	Waterman	U.S.	Steel alloy	1891	Harvey	U.S.
Pen, steel	1780	Harrison	English	Steel alloy, high-speed	1901	Taylor, White	U.S.
Pendulum	1583	Galileo	Italian	Steel, electric	1900	Heroult	French
Percussion cap	1807	Forsythe	Scottish	Steel, manganese	1884	Hadfield	English
Phonograph	1877	Edison	U.S.	Steel, stainless	1916	Brearley	English
Photo, color	1892	Ives	U.S.	Stereoscope	1838	Wheatstone	English
Photo film, celluloid	1893	Reichenbach	U.S.	Stethoscope	1819	Laennec	French
Photo film, transparent	1884	Eastman,		Stethoscope, binaural	1840	Cammann	U.S.
		Goodwin	U.S.	Stock ticker	1870	Edison	U.S.
Photoelectric cell	1895	Elster	German	Storage battery, recharge-			
Photographic paper	1835	Talbot	U.S.	able	1859	Plante	French
Photography	1835	Talbot	English	Stove, electric	1896	Hadaway	U.S.
Photography	1835	Daguerre	French	Submarine	1891	Holland	U.S.
Photography	1816	Niepce	French	Submarine, even keel	1894	Lake	U.S.
Photophone	1880	Bell	U.S.-Scot.	Submarine, torpedo	1776	Bushnell	U.S.
Phototelegraphy	1925	Bell Labs	U.S.				
Piano	1709	Cristofori	Italian	Tank, military	1914	Swinton	English
Piano, player	1863	Fourneaux	French	Tape recorder, magnetic	1899	Poulsen	Danish
Pin, safety	1849	Hunt	U.S.	Telegraph, magnetic	1837	Morse	U.S.
Pistol (revolver)	1836	Colt	U.S.	Telegraph, quadruplex	1864	Edison	U.S.
Plow, cast iron	1785	Ransome	English	Telegraph, railroad	1887	Woods	U.S.
Plow, disc	1896	Hardy	U.S.	Telegraph, wireless			
Pneumatic hammer	1890	King	U.S.	high frequency	1895	Marconi	Italian
Powder, smokeless	1884	Vieille	French	Telephone	1876	Bell	U.S.-Scot.
Printing press, rotary	1845	Hoe	U.S.	Telephone amplifier	1912	De Forest	U.S.
Printing press, web	1865	Bullock	U.S.	Telephone, automatic	1891	Stowger	U.S.
Propeller, screw	1804	Stevens	U.S.	Telephone, radio	1900	Poulsen,	
Propeller, screw	1837	Ericsson	Swedish			Fessenden	Danish
Punch card accounting	1889	Hollerith	U.S.	Telephone, radio	1906	De Forest	U.S.
				Telephone, radio, l. d	1915	AT&T	U.S.
Radar	1940	Watson-Watt	Scottish	Telephone, recording	1898	Poulsen	Danish
Radio amplifier	1906	De Forest	U.S.	Telephone, wireless	1899	Collins	U.S.
Radio beacon	1928	Donovan	U.S.	Telescope	1608	Lippershey	Neth.
Radio crystal oscillator	1918	Nicolson	U.S.	Telescope	1609	Galileo	Italian
Radio receiver, cascade				Telescope, astronomical	1611	Kepler	German
tuning	1913	Alexanderson	U.S.	Teletype	1928	Morkrum,	
Radio receiver,						Kleinschmidt	U.S.
heterodyne	1913	Fessenden	U.S.	Television, iconoscope	1923	Zworykin	U.S.
Radio transmitter triode				Television, electronic	1927	Farnsworth	U.S.
modulation	1914	Alexanderson	U.S.	Television, (mech.			
Radio tube-diode	1905	Fleming	English	scanner)	1923	Baird	Scottish
Radio tube oscillator	1915	De Forest	U.S.	Thermometer	1593	Galileo	Italian
Radio tube triode	1906	De Forest	U.S.	Thermometer	1730	Reaumur	French
Radio, signals	1895	Marconi	Italian	Thermometer, mercury	1714	Fahrenheit	German
Radio, magnetic				Time recorder	1890	Bundy	U.S.
detector	1902	Marconi	Italian	Time, self-regulator	1918	Bryce	U.S.
Radio FM 2-path	1933	Armstrong	U.S.	Tire, double-tube	1845	Thomson	Scottish
Rayon	1883	Swan	English	Tire, pneumatic	1888	Dunlop	Scottish
Razor, electric	1928	Schick	U.S.	Toaster, automatic	1918	Strite	U.S.
Razor, safety	1895	Gillette	U.S.	Tool, pneumatic	1865	Law	English
Reaper	1834	McCormick	U.S.	Torpedo, marine	1804	Fulton	U.S.
Record, cylinder	1887	Bell, Tainter	U.S.	Tractor, crawler	1904	Holt	U.S.
Record, disc	1887	Berliner	U.S.	Transformer A.C.	1885	Stanley	U.S.
Record, long playing	1947	Goldenmark	U.S.	Transistor	1947	Shockley,	
Record, wax cylinder	1888	Edison	U.S.			Brattain,	
Refrigerants, low-boiling	Midgely and					Bardeen	U.S.
fluorine compound	1930	co-workers	U.S.				

Invention	Date	Inventor	Nation.	Invention	Date	Inventor	Nation.
Trolley car, electric	1884	Van DePoele,		Washer, electric	1901	Fisher	U.S.
	-87	Sprague	U.S.	Welding, atomic		Langmuir,	
Tungsten, ductile	1912	Coolidge	U.S.	hydrogen	1924	Palmer	U.S.
Turbine, gas	1849	Bourdin	French	Welding, electric	1877	Thomson	U.S.
Turbine, hydraulic	1849	Francis	U.S.	Wind tunnel	1912	Eiffel	French
Turbine, steam	1884	Parsons	English	Wire, barbed	1874	Glidden	U.S.
Type, movable	1447	Gutenberg	German	Wire, barbed	1875	Haisn	U.S.
Typewriter	1867	Sholes, Soule,		Wrench, double-acting	1913	Owen	U.S.
		Glidden	U.S.	X-ray tube	1913	Coolidge	U.S.
Vacuum cleaner, electric	1907	Spangler	U.S.	Zipper	1891	Judson	U.S.

Discoveries and Innovations: Chemistry, Physics, Biology, Medicine

	Date	Discoverer	Nation.		Date	Discoverer	Nation.
Acetylene gas	1892	Wilson	U.S.	Erythromycin	1952	McGuire	U.S.
ACTH	1949	Armour & Co.	U.S.	Evolution, natural			
Adrenalin	1901	Takamine	Japanese	selection	1858	Darwin	English
Aluminum, electro-				Falling bodies, law	1590	Galileo	Italian
lytic process	1886	Hall	U.S.				
Aluminum, isolated	1825	Oersted	Danish	Gases, law of			
Analine dye	1856	Perkin	English	combining volumes	1808	Gay-Lussac	French
Anesthesia, ether	1842	Long	U.S.	Geometry, analytic	1619	Descartes	French
Anesthesia, local	1885	Koller	Austrian	Gold (cyanide process		MacArthur,	
Anesthesia, spinal	1898	Bier	German	for extraction)	1887	Forest	British
Anti-rabies	1885	Pasteur	French	Gravitation, law	1687	Newton	English
Antiseptic surgery	1867	Lister	English				
Antitoxin, diphtheria	1891	Von Behring	German	Holograph	1948	Gabor	British
Argyrol	1901	Barnes	U.S.	Human heart			
Arsphenamine	1910	Ehrlich	German	transplant	1967	Barnard	S. African
Aspirin	1889	Dresser	German	Indigo, synthesis of	1880	Baeyer	German
Atabrine	...	Mietzsch, et al.	German	Induction, electric	1830	Henry	U.S.
Atomic numbers	1913	Moseley	English	Insulin	1922	Banting, Best,	Canadian,
Atomic theory	1803	Dalton	English			Macleod	Scottish
Atomic time clock	1947	Libby	U.S.	Intelligence testing	1905	Binet, Simon	French
Atom-smashing				Isinazid	1952	Hoffman-	
theory	1919	Rutherford	English			La-Roche	U.S.
Aureomycin	1948	Duggar	U.S.			Domagk	German
				Isotopes, theory	1912	Soddy	English
Bacitracin	1945	Johnson, et al.	U.S.				
Bacteria (described)	1676	Leeuwenhoek	Dutch	Laser (light amplification by stimulated emission			
Barbital	1903	Fischer	German	of radiation)	1958	Townes, Schaw-	
Bleaching powder	1798	Tennant	English			low	U.S.
Blood, circulation	1628	Harvey	English	Light, velocity	1675	Roemer	Danish
Bordeaux mixture	1885	Millardet	French	Light, wave theory	1690	Huygens	Dutch
Bromine from sea	1924	Edgar Kramer	U.S.	Lithography	1796	Senefelder	Bohemian
Calcium carbide	1888	Wilson	U.S.	Lobotomy	1935	Egas Moniz	Portuguese
Calculus	1670	Newton	English	LSD-25	1943	Hoffman	Swiss
Camphor synthetic	1896	Haller	French				
Canning (food)	1804	Appert	French	Mendelian laws	1866	Mendel	Austrian
Carbomycin	1952	Tanner	U.S.	Mercator projection			
Carbon oxides	1925	Fisher	German	(map)	1568	Mercator (Kremer)	Flemish
Chlorine	1810	Davy	English	Methanol	1925	Patard	French
Chloroform	1831	Guthrie, S.	U.S.	Milk condensation	1853	Borden	U.S.
Chloromycetin	1947	Burkholder	U.S.	Molecular hypothesis	1811	Avogadro	Italian
Classification of				Motion, laws of	1687	Newton	English
plants and animals	1735	Linnaeus	Swedish				
Cocaine	1860	Niermann	German	Neomycin	1949	Waksman,	
Combustion explained	1777	Lavoisier	French			Lechevalier	U.S.
Conditioned reflex	1914	Pavlov	Russian	Neutron	1932	Chadwick	English
Conteben	1950	Belmisch,		Nitric acid	1648	Glauber	German
		Mietzsch,		Nitric oxide	1772	Priestley	English
		Domagk	German	Nitroglycerin	1846	Sobrero	Italian
Cortisone	1936	Kendall	U.S.				
Cortisone, synthesis	1946	Sarett	U.S.	Oil cracking process	1891	Dewar	U.S.
Cosmic rays	1910	Gockel	Swiss	Oxygen	1774	Priestley	English
Cyanimide	1905	Frank, Caro	German	Ozone	1840	Schonbein	German
Cyclotron	1930	Lawrence	U.S.				
				Paper, sulfite process	1867	Tilghman	U.S.
DDT	1874	Zeidler	German	Paper, wood pulp,			
(not applied as insecticide until 1939)				sulfate process	1884	Dahl	German
Deuterium	1932	Urey, Brickwedde,		Penicillin	1929	Fleming	Scottish
		Murphy	U.S.	practical use	1941	Florey, Chain	English
DNA (structure)	1951	Crick	English	Periodic law and			
		Watson	U.S.	table of elements	1869	Mendeleyev	Russian
		Wilkins	English	Planetary motion, laws	1609	Kepler	German
Electric resistance				Plutonium fission	1940	Kennedy, Wahl,	
(law)	1827	Ohm	German			Seaborg, Segre	U.S.
Electric waves	1888	Hertz	German	Polymixin	1947	Ainsworth	English
Electrolysis	1852	Faraday	English	Positron	1932	Anderson	U.S.
Electromagnetism	1819	Oersted	Danish	Proton	1919	Rutherford	N. Zealand
Electron	1897	Thomson, J.	English	Psychoanalysis	1900	Freud	Austrian
Electron diffraction	1936	Thomson, G.	English				
		Davisson	U.S.	Quantum theory	1900	Planck	German
				Quasars	1963	Matthews,	
Electroshock treat-						Sandage	U.S.
ment	1938	Cerletti, Bini	Italian				

	Date	Discoverer	Nation.		Date	Discoverer	Nation.
Quinine synthetic	1918	Rabe	German	Uranium fission		Hahn, Meitner,	
				(theory)	1939	Strassmann	German
Radioactivity	1896	Becquerel	French			Bohr	Danish
Radium	1898	Curie, Pierre	French			Fermi	Italian
		Curie, Marie	Pol.-Fr.			Einstein, Pegram,	
Relativity theory	1905	Einstein	German			Wheeler	U.S.
Reserpine	1949	Jal Vaikl	Indian	Uranium fission,		Fermi,	
				atomic reactor	1942	Szilard	U.S.
Salvarsan (606)	1910	Ehrlich	German	Vaccine, measles	1954	Enders, Peebles	U.S.
Schick test	1913	Schick	U.S.	Vaccine, polio	1953	Salk	U.S.
Silicon	1823	Berzelius	Swedish	Vaccine, polio, oral	1955	Sabin	U.S.
Streptomycin	1945	Waksman	U.S.	Vaccine, rabies	1885	Pasteur	French
Sulfadiazine	1940	Roblin	U.S.	Vaccine, smallpox	1796	Jenner	English
Sulfanilamide	1934	Domagk	German	Vaccine, typhus	1909	Nicolle	French
Sulfanilamide theory	1908	Gelmo	German	Van Allen belts,			
Sulfapyridine	1938	Ewins, Phelps	English	radiation	1958	Van Allen	U.S.
Sulfathiazole	...	Fosbinder, Walter	U.S.	Vitamin A	1913	McCollum, Davis	U.S.
Sulfuric acid	1831	Phillips	English	Vitamin B	1916	McCollum	U.S.
Sulfuric acid, lead	1746	Roebuck	English	Vitamin C	1912	Holst, Froelich	Norwegian
				Vitamin D	1922	McCollum	U.S.
				Wassermann test	1906	Wassermann	German
Terramycin	1950	Finlay, et al.	U.S.	Xerography	1938	Carlson	U.S.
Tuberculin	1890	Koch	German	X-ray	1895	Roentgen	German

Chemical Elements, Discoverers, Atomic Weights

Atomic weights, based on the exact number 12 as the assigned atomic mass of the principal isotope of carbon, carbon 12, are provided through the courtesy of the International Union of Pure and Applied Chemistry and Butterworth Scientific Publications.

For the radioactive elements, with the exception of uranium and thorium, the mass number of either the isotope of longest half-life (*) or the better known isotope (**) is given.

Chemical element	Symbol	Atomic number	Atomic weight	Year discov.	Discoverer
Actinium	Ac	89	227*	1899	Debierne
Aluminum	Al	13	26.9815	1825	Oersted
Americium	Am	95	243*	1944	Seaborg, et al.
Antimony	Sb	51	121.75	1450	Valentine
Argon	Ar	18	39.948	1894	Rayleigh, Ramsay
Arsenic	As	33	74.9216	13th c.	Albertus Magnus
Astatine	At	85	210*	1940	Corson, et al.
Barium	Ba	56	137.34	1808	Davy
Berkelium	Bk	97	249**	1949	Thompson, Ghiorso, Seaborg
Beryllium	Be	4	9.0122	1798	Vauquelin
Bismuth	Bi	83	208.980	15th c.	Valentine
Boron	B	5	10.811a	1808	Gay-Lussac, Thenard
Bromine	Br	35	79.904b	1826	Balard
Cadmium	Cd	48	112.40	1817	Stromeyer
Calcium	Ca	20	40.08	1808	Davy
Californium	Cf	98	251*	1950	Thompson, et al.
Carbon	C	6	12.01115a	B.C.	
Cerium	Ce	58	140.12	1803	Klaproth
Cesium	Cs	55	132.905	1860	Bunsen, Kirchhoff
Chlorine	Cl	17	35.453b	1774	Scheele
Chromium	Cr	24	51.996b	1797	Vauquelin
Cobalt	Co	27	58.9332	1735	Brandt
Copper	Cu	29	63.546b	B.C.	
Curium	Cm	96	247*	1944	Seaborg, James, Ghiorso
Dysprosium	Dy	66	162.50	1886	Boisbaudran
Einsteinium	Es	99	254*	1952	Ghiorso, et al.
Erbium	Er	68	167.26	1843	Mosander
Europium	Eu	63	151.96	1901	Demarcay
Fermium	Fm	100	257*	1953	Ghiorso, et al.
Fluorine	F	9	18.9984	1771	Scheele
Francium	Fr	87	223*	1939	Perey
Gadolinium	Gd	64	157.25	1886	Marignac
Gallium	Ga	31	69.72	1875	Boisbaudran
Germanium	Ge	32	72.59	1886	Winkler
Gold	Au	79	196.967	B.C.	
Hafnium	Hf	72	178.49	1923	Coster, Hevesy
Hahnium	Ha	105	262*	1970	Ghiorso, et al.
Helium	He	2	4.0026	1868	Janssen, Lockyer
Holmium	Ho	67	164.930	1878	Soret, Delafontaine
Hydrogen	H	1	1.00797a	1766	Cavendish
Indium	In	49	114.82	1863	Reich, Richter
Iodine	I	53	126.9044	1811	Courtois
Iridium	Ir	77	192.2	1804	Tennant
Iron	Fe	26	55.847b	B.C.	
Krypton	Kr	36	83.80	1898	Ramsay, Travers
Lanthanum	La	57	138.91	1839	Mosander
Lawrencium	Lr	103	260*	1961	Ghiorso, T. Sikkeland, A.E. Larsh, and R.M. Latimer
Lead	Pb	82	207.19	B.C.	
Lithium	Li	3	6.939	1817	Arfvedson
Lutetium	Lu	71	174.97	1907	Welsbach, Urbain
Magnesium	Mg	12	24.312	1829	Bussy

Chemical element	Symbol	Atomic number	Atomic weight	Year discov.	Discoverer
Manganese	Mn	25	54.9380	1774	Gahn
Mendelevium	Md	101	258*	1955	Ghiorso, et al.
Mercury	Hg	80	200.59	B.C.	
Molybdenum	Mo	42	95.94	1782	Hjelm
Neodymium	Nd	60	144.24	1885	Welsbach
Neon	Ne	10	20.183	1898	Ramsay, Travers
Neptunium	Np	93	237*	1940	McMillan, Abelson
Nickel	Ni	28	58.71	1751	Cronstedt
Niobium[1]	Nb	41	92.906	1801	Hatchett
Nitrogen	N	7	14.0067	1772	Rutherford
Nobelium	No	102	258*	1958	Ghiorso, et al.
Osmium	Os	76	190.2	1804	Tennant
Oxygen	O	8	15.9994a	1774	Priestley, Scheele
Palladium	Pd	46	106.4	1803	Wollaston
Phosphorus	P	15	30.9738	1669	Brand
Platinum	Pt	78	195.09	1735	Ulloa
Plutonium	Pu	94	242**	1940	Seaborg, et al.
Polonium	Po	84	210**	1898	P. and M. Curie
Potassium	K	19	39.102	1807	Davy
Praseodymium	Pr	59	140.907	1885	Welsbach
Promethium	Pm	61	147**	1945	Glendenin, Marinsky, Coryell
Protactinium	Pa	91	231*	1917	Hahn, Meitner
Radium	Ra	88	226*	1898	P. & M. Curie, Bemont
Radon	Rn	86	222*	1900	Dorn
Rhenium	Re	75	186.2	1925	Noddack, Tacke, Berg
Rhodium	Rh	45	102.905	1803	Wollaston
Rubidium	Rb	37	85.47	1861	Bunsen, Kirchhoff
Ruthenium	Ru	44	101.07	1845	Klaus
Rutherfordium	Rf	104	261*	1969	Ghiorso, et al.
Samarium	Sm	62	150.35	1879	Boisbaudran
Scandium	Sc	21	44.956	1879	Nilson
Selenium	Se	34	78.96	1817	Berzelius
Silicon	Si	14	28.086a	1823	Berzelius
Silver	Ag	47	107.868b	B.C.	
Sodium	Na	11	22.9898	1807	Davy
Strontium	Sr	38	87.62	1790	Crawford
Sulfur	S	16	32.064a	B.C.	
Tantalum	Ta	73	180.948	1802	Ekeberg
Technetium	Tc	43	99**	1937	Perrier and Segre
Tellurium	Te	52	127.60	1782	Von Reichenstein
Terbium	Tb	65	158.924	1843	Mosander
Thallium	Tl	81	204.37	1861	Crookes
Thorium	Th	90	232.038	1828	Berzelius
Thulium	Tm	69	168.934	1879	Cleve
Tin	Sn	50	118.69	B.C.	
Titanium	Ti	22	47.90	1791	Gregor
Tungsten (Wolfram)	W	74	183.85	1783	d'Elhujar
Uranium	U	92	238.03	1789	Klaproth
Vanadium	V	23	50.942	1830	Sefstrom
Xenon	Xe	54	131.30	1898	Ramsay, Travers
Ytterbium	Yb	70	173.04	1878	Marignac
Yttrium	Y	39	88.905	1794	Gadolin
Zinc	Zn	30	65.37	B.C.	
Zirconium	Zr	40	91.22	1789	Klaproth

(1) Formerly Columbium. (a) Atomic weights so designated are known to be variable because of natural variations in isotopic composition. The observed ranges are: hydrogen±0.0001; boron±0.003; carbon±0.005; oxygen±0.0001; silicon±0.001; sulfur±0.003. (b) Atomic weights so designated are believed to have the following experimental uncertainties: chlorine±0.001; chromium±0.001; iron±0.003; bromine±0.001; silver±0.001; copper±0.001.

Copyright Law of The United States

Source: Copyright Office, Library of Congress

Original works of authorship in any tangible medium of expression are entitled to protection under the copyright law (Title 17 of the United States Code). The law came into effect on January 1, 1978 (Public Law 94-553, 90 Stat. 2541); it superseded the Copyright Act of 1909, as amended. Before the 1976 Act, there had been only three general revisions of the original copyright law of 1790, namely those of 1831, 1870, and 1909.

Categories of Works

Copyright protection under the new law extends to original works of authorship fixed in any tangible medium of expression, now known or later developed, from which they can be perceived, reproduced, or otherwise communicated, either directly or with the aid of a machine or device. Works of authorship include books, periodicals, computer programs and other literary works, musical compositions with accompanying lyrics, dramas and dramatico-musical compositions, pantomimes and choreographic works, motion pictures and other audiovisual works, and sound recordings.

The owner of a copyright is given the exclusive right to reproduce the copyrighted work in copies or phonorecords and distribute them to the public by sale, rental, lease, or lending. The owner of a copyright also enjoys the exclusive right to make derivative works based upon the copyrighted work, to perform the work publicly if it be a literary, musical, dramatic, or choreographic work, a pantomime, motion picture, or other audiovisual work, and in the case of literary, musical, dramatic, and choreographic works, pantomimes, and pictorial, graphic, or sculptural works, including the individual images of a motion picture or other audiovisual work, to display the copyrighted work publicly. All of these rights are subject to certain specified exceptions, including the so-called judicial doctrine of "fair use," which is included in the law for the first time.

The act also provides special provisions permitting compulsory licensing for the recording and distribution of phonorecords of nondramatic musical compositions, noncommercial transmissions by public broadcasters of published musical, pictorial, sculptural, and graphic works, performances of copyrighted nondramatic music by means of jukeboxes, and the secondary transmission of copyrighted works on cable television systems.

Single National System

The law establishes a single national system of statutory protection for all copyrightable works fixed in tangible form, whether published or unpublished. Before Jan. 1, 1978 unpublished works were entitled to protection under the common law of the various states while published works came under the Federal statute.

Registration of a claim to copyright in any work, whether published or unpublished, may be made voluntarily at any time during the copyright term by the owner of the copyright or of any exclusive right in the work. Registration is not a condition of copyright protection, but is a prerequisite to an infringement suit. Subject to certain exceptions, the remedies of statutory damages and attorney's fees are not available for those infringements occurring before registration. Even if registration is not made, copies or phonorecords of works published in the U.S. with notice of copyright are required to be deposited for the collections of the Library of Congress. This deposit requirement is not a condition of protection, but does render the copyright owner subject to penalties for failure to deposit after a demand by the Register of Copyrights.

Duration of Copyright

For works created on or after Jan. 1, 1978, copyright subsists from their creation for a term consisting of the life of the author and 50 years after the author's death. For works made for hire, and for anonymous and pseudonymous works (unless the author's identity is revealed in Copyright Office records), the term is 100 years from creation or 75 years from first publication, whichever is shorter.

The law retains for works that were under statutory protection on January 1, 1978, the 28 year term of copyright from first publication (or from registration in some cases), renewable by certain persons for a second term of protection of 47 years. Copyrights in their first 28-year term on Jan. 1, 1978, have to be renewed in order to be protected for the full maximum term of 75 years. Copyrights in their second term on Jan. 1, 1978 were automatically extended to last for a total term of 75 years.

For works that had been created before the law came into effect but had neither been published nor registered for copyright before Jan. 1, 1978, the term of copyright is generally computed in the same way as for new works: the life-plus-50 or 75/100-year terms will apply. However, all works in this category are guaranteed at least 25 years of statutory protection. The law specifies that copyright in a work of this kind will not expire before Dec. 31, 2002, and if the work is published before that date the term is extended by another 25 years, through the end of the year 2027.

Notice of Copyright

Under the 1909 copyright law the copyright notice was the most important requirement for obtaining copyright protection for a published work. For published works, all copies had to bear the prescribed notice from the time of first publication. If a work was published before Jan. 1, 1978 without the required notice, copyright protection was lost permanently and cannot be regained.

The present copyright law requires a notice on copies or phonorecords of sound recordings that are distributed to the public. Errors and omissions, however, do not immediately result in forfeiture of the copyright and can be corrected within prescribed time limits. Innocent infringers misled by an omission or error in the notice generally are shielded from liability.

The notice of copyright required on all visually perceptible copies published in the U.S. or elsewhere under the 1976 Act consists of the symbol © (the letter C in a circle), the word "Copyright," or the abbreviation "Copr.," and the year of first publication, and the name of the owner of copyright in the work. Example: © 1985 JOHN DOE

The notice must be affixed in such manner and location as to give reasonable notice of the claim of copyright.

The notice of copyright prescribed for all published phonorecords of sound recordings consists of the symbol ℗ (the letter P in a circle), the year of first publication of the sound recording, and the name of the owner of copyright in the sound recording, placed on the surface of the phonorecord, or on the phonorecord label or container in such manner and location as to give reasonable notice of the claim of copyright. Example: ℗ 1985 DOE RECORDS, INC.

Manufacturing Requirements

The requirement in the copyright law, known as the manufacturing clause, mandating that certain textual literary works be manufactured in the U.S. was preserved in the copyright law until July 1, 1986, after Congress elected to override a veto of the extension by President Ronald Reagan. The manufacturing clause, section 601 of the 1976 Copyright Act, requires that works consisting preponderantly of nondramatic literary material (textual material) be manufactured in the United States or Canada to receive full copyright protection. The clause, which was due to expire in July 1982, was extended by Congress for another 4 years.

The manufacturing clause applies only to published works in the English language; as an exception to its provisions, the statute prescribes that, when manufacture has taken place outside the United States or Canada, a maximum of 2,000 copies of the foreign edition may be imported into the United States without affecting the copyright owners' rights. For this purpose, the copyright Office will issue an Import Statement (Form IS) upon request and payment of a fee of $3 at the time of registration or at any later time.

International Protection

The U.S. has copyright relations with more than 70 countries, under which works of American authors are protected in those countries, and the works of their authors are protected in the U.S. The basic feature of this protection is "national treatment," under which the alien author is treated by a country in the same manner that it treats its own authors. Relations exist by virtue of bilateral agreements or through the Buenos Aires Convention or the Universal Copyright Convention. U.S. legislation implementing the latter convention, which became effective Sept. 16, 1955, gives the works of foreign authors the benefit of exemptions from the manufacturing requirements of the U.S. copyright law, provided the works are first published abroad with a copyright notice including the symbol © , the name of the copyright owner and the year date of first publication, and that the work either is by an "author" who is a citizen or subject of a foreign country which belongs to the Convention or is first published in a foreign member country. Conversely, works of U.S. authors are exempt from certain burdensome requirements in particular foreign member countries.

Works published on or after Jan. 1, 1978, are subject to protection under the copyright statute if, on the date of first publication, one or more of the authors is a national or domiciliary of the U.S., or is a national, domiciliary, or sovereign authority of a foreign nation that is a party to a copyright treaty to which the United States is also a party, or is a stateless person, regardless of domicile, or if the work is first published either in the U.S. or in a foreign nation that, on the date of first publication is a party to the Universal Copyright Convention. All unpublished works are protected here regardless of the citizenship or domicile of the author.

A U.S. author may obtain copyright protection in all countries that are members of the Universal Copyright Convention (UCC). In member countries, where no formalities are required, the works of U.S. authors are protected automatically. Member countries whose laws impose formalities protect U.S. works if all published copies bear a convention notice which consists of the symbol ©, together with the name of the copyright owner and the year date of publication. Example: © JOHN DOE 1985.

Further information and application forms may be obtained free of charge by writing to the Information Section LM-455, Copyright Office, The Library of Congress, Washington, D.C. 20559.

Copyright registration application forms may be ordered on a 24-hour basis by calling (202) 287-9100.

DISASTERS

Some Notable Marine Disasters Since 1850

(Figures indicate estimated lives lost)

1854, Mar.—City of Glasgow; British steamer missing in North Atlantic; 480.

1854, Sept. 27—Arctic; U.S. (Collins Line) steamer sunk in collision with French steamer Vesta near Cape Race; 285-351.

1856, Jan. 23—Pacific; U.S. (Collins Line) steamer missing in North Atlantic; 186-286.

1858, Sept. 23—Austria; German steamer destroyed by fire in North Atlantic; 471.

1863, Apr. 27—Anglo-Saxon; British steamer wrecked at Cape Race; 238.

1865, Apr. 27—Sultana; a Mississippi River steamer blew up near Memphis, Tenn; 1,400.

1869, Oct. 27—Stonewall; steamer burned on Mississippi River below Cairo, Ill.; 200.

1870, Jan. 25—City of Boston; British (Inman Line) steamer vanished between New York and Liverpool; 177.

1870, Oct 19—Cambria; British steamer wrecked off northern Ireland; 196.

1872, Nov. 7—Mary Celeste; U.S. half-brig sailed from New York for Genoa; found abandoned in Atlantic 4 weeks later in mystery of sea; crew never heard from; loss of life unknown.

1873, Jan. 22—Northfleet; British steamer foundered off Dungeness, England; 300.

1873, Apr. 1—Atlantic; British (White Star) steamer wrecked off Nova Scotia; 585.

1873, Nov. 23—Ville du Havre; French steamer, sunk after collision with British sailing ship Loch Earn; 226.

1875, May 7—Schiller; German steamer wrecked off Scilly Isles; 312.

1875, Nov. 4—Pacific; U.S. steamer sunk after collision off Cape Flattery; 236.

1878, Sept. 3—Princess Alice; British steamer sank after collision in Thames; 700.

1878, Dec. 18—Byzantin; French steamer sank after Dardanelles collision; 210.

1881, May 24—Victoria; steamer capsized in Thames River, Canada; 200.

1883, Jan. 19—Cimbria; German steamer sunk in collision with British steamer Sultan in North Sea; 389.

1887, Nov. 15—Wah Yeung; British steamer burned at sea; 400.

1890, Feb. 17—Duburg; British steamer wrecked, China Sea; 400.

1890, Sept. 19—Ertogrul; Turkish frigate foundered off Japan; 540.

1891, Mar. 17—Utopia; British steamer sank in collision with British ironclad Anson off Gibraltar; 562.

1895, Jan. 30—Elbe; German steamer sank in collision with British steamer Craithie in North Sea; 332.

1895, Mar. 11—Reina Regenta; Spanish cruiser foundered near Gibraltar; 400.

1898, Feb. 15—Maine; U.S. battleship blown up in Havana Harbor; 266.

1898, July 4—La Bourgogne; French steamer sunk in collision with British sailing ship Cromartyshire off Nova Scotia; 549.

1904, June 15—General Slocum; excursion steamer burned in East River, New York City; 1,030.

1904, June 28—Norge; Danish steamer wrecked on Rockall Island, Scotland; 620.

1906, Aug. 4—Sirio; Italian steamer wrecked off Cape Palos, Spain; 350.

1908, Mar. 23—Matsu Maru; Japanese steamer sank in collision near Hakodate, Japan; 300.

1909, Aug. 1—Waratah; British steamer, Sydney to London, vanished; 300.

1910, Feb. 9—General Chanzy; French steamer wrecked off Minorca, Spain; 200.

1911, Sept. 25—Liberté; French battleship exploded at Toulon; 285.

1912, Apr. 14-15—Titanic; British (White Star) steamer hit iceberg in North Atlantic; 1,503.

1912, Sept. 28—Kichemaru; Japanese steamer sank off Japanese coast; 1,000.

1914, May 29—Empress of Ireland; British (Canadian Pacific) steamer sunk in collision with Norwegian collier in St. Lawrence River; 1,014.

1915, May 7—Lusitania; British (Cunard Line) steamer torpedoed and sunk by German submarine U. 20 off Ireland; 1,198.

1915, July 24—Eastland; excursion steamer capsized in Chicago River; 812.

1916, Feb. 26—Provence; French cruiser sank in Mediterranean; 3,100.

1916, Mar. 3—Principe de Asturias; Spanish steamer wrecked near Santos, Brazil; 558.

1916, Aug. 29—Hsin Yu; Chinese steamer sank off Chinese coast; 1,000.

1917, Dec. 6—Mont Blanc, Imo; French ammunition ship and Belgian steamer collided in Halifax Harbor; 1,600.

1918, Apr. 25—Kiang-Kwan; Chinese steamer sank in collision off Hankow; 500.

1918, July 12—Kawachi; Japanese battleship blew up in Tokayama Bay; 500.

1918, Oct. 25—Princess Sophia; Canadian steamer sank off Alaskan coast; 398.

1919, Jan. 17—Chaonia; French steamer lost in Straits of Messina, Italy; 460.

1919, Sept. 9—Valbanera; Spanish steamer lost off Florida coast; 500.

1921, Mar. 18—Hong Kong; steamer wrecked in South China Sea; 1,000.

1922, Aug. 26—Niitaka; Japanese cruiser sank in storm off Kamchatka, USSR; 300.

1927, Oct. 25—Principessa Mafalda; Italian steamer blew up, sank off Porto Seguro, Brazil; 314.

1934, Sept. 8—Morro Castle; U.S. steamer, Havana to New York, burned off Asbury Park, N.J.; 125.

1939, May 23—Squalus; U.S. submarine sank off Portsmouth, N.H.; 26.

1939, June 1—Thetis; British submarine, sank in Liverpool Bay; 99.

1942, Feb. 18—Truxtun and Pollux; U.S. destroyer and cargo ship ran aground, sank off Newfoundland; 204.

1942, Oct. 2—Curacao; British cruiser sank after collision with liner Queen Mary; 335.

1947, Jan. 8—Himera; Greek steamer hit a mine off Athens; 392.

1947, Apr. 16—Grandcamp; French freighter exploded in Texas City, Tex., Harbor, starting fires; 510.

1952, Apr. 26—Hobson and Wasp; U.S. destroyer and aircraft carrier collided in Atlantic; 176.

1953, Jan. 31—Princess Victoria; British ferry foundered off northern Irish coast; 134.

1954, Sept. 26—Toya Maru; Japanese ferry sank in Tsugaru Strait, Japan; 1,172.

1956, July 26—Andrea Doria and Stockholm; Italian liner and Swedish liner collided off Nantucket; 51.

1957, July 14—Eshghabad; Soviet ship ran aground in Caspian Sea; 270.

1961, Apr. 8—Dara; British liner burned in Persian Gulf; 212.

1961, July 8—Save; Portuguese ship ran aground off Mozambique; 259.

1963, Apr. 10—Thresher; U.S. Navy atomic submarine sank in North Atlantic; 129.

1964, Feb. 10—Voyager, Melbourne; Australian destroyer sank after collision with Australian aircraft carrier Melbourne off New South Wales; 82.

1968, Jan. 5—Dakar; Israeli submarine vanished in Mediterranean; 69.

1968, Jan. 27—Minerve; French submarine vanished in Mediterranean; 52.

1968, May 21—Scorpion; U.S. nuclear submarine sank in Atlantic near Azores; 99.

1969, June 2—Evans; U.S. destroyer cut in half by Australian carrier Melbourne, S. China Sea; 74.

1970, Mar. 4—Eurydice; French submarine sank in Mediterranean near Toulon; 57.

1970, Dec. 15—Namyong-Ho; South Korean ferry sank in Korea Strait; 308.

1974, May 1— Motor launch capsized off Bangladesh; 250.

1974, Sept. 26— Soviet destroyer burned and sank in Black Sea; est. 200.

1976, Oct. 20—George Prince and Frosta; ferryboat and Norwegian tanker collided on Mississippi R. at Luling, La.; 77.

1976, Dec. 25—Patria; Egyptian liner caught fire and sank in the Red Sea; c. 100.

1977, Jan. 11—Grand Zenith; Panamanian-registered tanker sank off Cape Cod, Mass.; 38.

1977, Jan. 17— Spanish freighter collided with launch in Barcelona, Spain harbor; 46.

1979, Aug. 14—23 yachts competing in Fastnet yacht race sunk or abandoned during storm in S. Irish Sea; 18.

1981, Jan. 27—Tamponas II; Indonesian passenger ship caught fire and sank in Java Sea; 580.

1981, May 26—Nimitz; U.S. Marine combat jet crashed on deck of U.S. aircraft carrier; 14.

1983, Feb. 12—Marine Electric; coal freighter sank during storm off Chincoteague, Va.; 33.

Major Earthquakes

Magnitude of earthquakes (Mag.), distinct from deaths or damage caused, is measured on the Richter scale, on which each higher number represents a tenfold increase in energy measured in ground motion. Adopted in 1935, the scale has been applied in the following table to earthquakes as far back as reliable seismograms are available.

Date	Place	Deaths	Mag.	Date	Place	Deaths	Mag.
526 May 20	Syria, Antioch.	250,000	N.A.	1956 June 10-17	N. Afghanistan	2,000	7.7
856	Greece, Corinth	45,000	"	1957 July 2	Northern Iran	2,500	7.4
1057	China, Chihli	25,000	"	1957 Dec. 13	Western Iran	2,000	7.1
1268	Asia Minor, Cilicia	60,000	"	1960 Feb. 29	Morocco, Agadir	12,000	5.8
1290 Sept. 27	China, Chihli	100,000	"	1960 May 21-30	Southern Chile	5,000	8.3
1293 May 20	Japan, Kamakura	30,000	"	1962 Sept. 1	Northwestern Iran	12,230	7.1
1531 Jan. 26	Portugal, Lisbon	30,000	"	1963 July 26	Yugoslavia, Skopje	1,100	6.0
1556 Jan. 24	China, Shaanxi	830,000	"	1964 Mar. 27	Alaska.	114	8.5
1667 Nov.	Caucasia, Shemaka	80,000	"	1966 Aug. 19	Eastern Turkey.	2,520	6.9
1693 Jan. 11	Italy, Catania	60,000	"	1968 Aug. 31	Northeastern Iran	12,000	7.4
1730 Dec. 30	Japan, Hokkaido	137,000	"	1970 Mar. 28	Western Turkey	1,086	7.4
1737 Oct. 11	India, Calcutta	300,000	"	1970 May 31	Northern Peru	66,794	7.7
1755 June 7	Northern Persia	40,000	"	1971 Feb. 9	Cal., San Fernando Val-		
1755 Nov. 1	Portugal, Lisbon	60,000	8.75*		ley.	65	6.5
1783 Feb. 4	Italy, Calabria.	30,000	N.A.	1972 Apr. 10	Southern Iran	5,057	6.9
1797 Feb. 4	Ecuador, Quito	41,000	N.A.	1972 Dec. 23	Nicaragua.	5,000	6.2
1822 Sept. 5	Asia Minor, Aleppo.	22,000	N.A.	1974 Dec. 28	Pakistan (9 towns)	5,200	6.3
1828 Dec. 28	Japan, Echigo	30,000	"	1975 Sept. 6	Turkey (Lice, etc.)	2,312	6.8
1868 Aug. 13-15	Peru and Ecuador	40,000	"	1976 Feb. 4	Guatemala	22,778	7.5
1875 May 16	Venezuela, Colombia	16,000	"	1976 May 6	Northeast Italy	946	6.5
1896 June 15	Japan, sea wave.	27,120	"	1976 June 26	New Guinea, Irian Jaya	443	7.1
1906 Apr. 18-19	Cal., San Francisco	503	8.3	1976 July 28	China, Tangshan	800,000	8.2
1906 Aug. 16	Chile, Valparaiso.	20,000	8.6	1976 Aug. 17	Philippines, Mindanao	8,000	7.8
1908 Dec. 28	Italy, Messina.	83,000	7.5	1976 Nov. 24	Eastern Turkey.	4,000	7.9
1915 Jan. 13	Italy, Avezzano.	29,980	7.5	1977 Mar. 4	Romania, Bucharest, etc.	1,541	7.5
1920 Dec. 16	China, Gansu.	100,000	8.6	1977 Aug. 19	Indonesia	200	8.0
1923 Sept. 1	Japan, Tokyo.	99,330	8.3	1977 Nov. 23	Northwestern Argentina	100	8.2
1927 May 22	China, Nan-Shan.	200,000	8.3	1978 June 12	Japan, Sendai	21	7.5
1932 Dec. 26	China, Gansu.	70,000	7.6	1978 Sept. 16	Northeast Iran	25,000	7.7
1933 Mar. 2	Japan	2,990	8.9	1979 Sept. 12	Indonesia	100	8.1
1934 Jan. 15	India, Bihar-Nepal	10,700	8.4	1979 Dec. 12	Colombia, Ecuador	800	7.9
1935 May 31	India, Quetta	30,000	7.5	1980 Oct. 10	Northwestern Algeria	4,500	7.3
1939 Jan. 24	Chile, Chillan	28,000	8.3	1980 Nov. 23	Southern Italy	4,800	7.2
1939 Dec. 26	Turkey, Erzincan	30,000	7.9	1982 Dec. 13	North Yemen	2,800	6.0
1946 Dec. 21	Japan, Honshu	2,000	8.4	1983 Mar. 31	Southern Colombia	250	5.5
1948 June 28	Japan, Fukui	5,131	7.3	1983 May 26	N. Honshu, Japan	81	7.7
1949 Aug. 5	Ecuador, Pelileo	6,000	6.8	1983 Oct. 30	Eastern Turkey.	1,300	7.1
1950 Aug. 15	India, Assam	1,530	8.7	1985 Mar. 3	Chile.	146	7.8
1953 Mar. 18	NW Turkey	1,200	7.2				

(*) estimated from earthquake intensity. (N.A.) not available.

Some Recent Earthquakes

Source: Scientific Event Alert Network, Smithsonian Institution

Attached is a list of recent earthquakes. Magnitude of earthquakes is measured on the Richter scale, on which each higher number represents a tenfold increase in energy measured in ground motion.

Date	Place	Magnitude	Date	Place	Magnitude
Apr. 24, 1985	Luzon Is. Philippines	6.0	Dec. 28	E. of Kamchatka, USSR	6.7
Apr. 13	Molucca Sea, Indonesia	6.8	Nov. 23	NE of Vanuatu	6.7
Apr. 13	Bali, Indonesia	6.3	Nov. 20	S. of Mindanao, Philippines	7.1
Apr. 3	Chile	7.2	Nov. 17	Off W. Sumatra, Indonesia	7.2
Mar. 19	Chile	6.7	Nov. 1	Central Atlantic Ocean	7.2
Mar. 18	Mindanao, Philippines	6.5	Oct. 18	Central Wyoming	5.3
Mar. 17	Chile	6.6	Sept. 18	Off E. Honshu, Japan	6.8
Mar. 4	Chile	6.5	Sept. 13	Central Honshu, Japan	6.2
Mar. 3	Chile	7.8	Sept. 10	Off N. California	6.7
Mar. 2	Sulawesi, Indonesia	6.6	Aug. 6	Kyushu, Japan	6.8
Feb. 2	S. Iran	5.2	July 5	Solomon Sea	6.5
Dec. 30, 1984	NE India	5.8	June 24	S. of Hispaniola, Dom. Rep.	6.5
Dec. 30	New Zealand	6.7			

Some Major Tornadoes In U.S. Since 1925

Source: National Climatic Center, NOAA, U.S. Commerce Department

Date			Place	Deaths	Date			Place	Deaths
1925	Mar.	18	Mo., Ill. Ind.	689	1949	Jan.	3	La. & Ark.	58
1927	Apr.	12	Rock Springs, Tex.	74	1952	Mar.	21	Ark., Mo., Tenn. (series)	208
1927	May	9	Arkansas, Poplar Bluff, Mo.	92	1953	May	11	Waco, Tex.	114
1930	May	6	Hill & Ellis Co., Tex.	41	1953	June	8	Flint to Lakeport, Mich.	116
1932	Mar.	21	Ala. (series of tornadoes)	268	1953	June	9	Worcester and vicinity, Mass.	90
1936	Apr.	5	Tupelo, Miss.	216	1953	Dec.	5	Vicksburg, Miss.	38
1936	Apr.	6	Gainesville, Ga.	203	1955	May	25	Udall, Kan.	80
1938	Sept.	29	Charleston, S.C.	32	1957	May	20	Kan., Mo.	48
1942	Mar.	16	Central to NE Miss.	75	1958	June	4	Northwestern Wisconsin	30
1942	Apr.	27	Rogers & Mayes Co., Okla.	52	1959	Feb.	10	St. Louis, Mo.	21
1944	June	23	Oh., Pa., W. Va., Md.	150	1960	May	5, 6	SE Oklahoma, Arkansas	30
1945	Apr.	12	Okla.-Ark.	102	1965	Apr.	11	Ind., Ill., Oh., Mich., Wis.	271
1947	Apr.	9	Tex., Okla. & Kan.	169	1966	Mar.	3	Jackson, Miss.	57
1948	Mar.	19	Bunker Hill & Gillespie, Ill.	33	1966	Mar.	3	Mississippi, Alabama.	61

Date			Place	Deaths	Date			Place	Deaths
1967	Apr.	21	Illinois	33	1982	Mar.	2-4	South, Midwest (series)	17
1968	May	15	Arkansas	34	1982	May	29	So. Ill.	10
1969	Jan.	23	Mississippi.	32	1983	May	18-22	Tex.	12
1971	Feb.	21	Mississippi delta	110	1984	Mar.	28	N. Carolina; S. Carolina	67
1973	May	26-7	South, Midwest (series)	47	1984	Apr.	21-22	Mississippi.	15
1974	Apr.	3-4	Ala., Ga., Tenn., Ky., Oh.	350	1984	Apr.	26	Series Okla to Minn.	17
1977	Apr.	4	Ala., Miss., Ga.	22	1984	June	9	W. USSR	400
1979	Apr.	10	Tex., Okla.	60	1985	May	31	N.Y., Pa., Oh., Ont. (series)	90
1980	June	3	Grand Island, Neb. (series)	4					

Hurricanes, Typhoons, Blizzards, Other Storms

Names of hurricanes and typhoons in italics—H.—hurricane; T.—typhoon

Date	Location	Deaths	Date	Location	Deaths
1888 Mar. 11-14	Blizzard, Eastern U.S.	400	1965 Dec. 15	Windstorm, Bangladesh	10,000
1900 Sept. 8	H., Galveston, Tex.	6,000	1966 June 4-10	H. Alma, Honduras, SE U.S.	51
1926 Sept. 16-22	H., Fla., Ala.	372	1966 Sept. 24-30	H. Inez, Carib., Fla., Mex.	293
1926 Oct. 20	H., Cuba.	600	1967 July 9	T. Billie, Japan	347
1928 Sept. 12-17	H., W. Indies, Fla.	4,000	1967 Sept. 5-23	H. Beulah, Carib., Mex., Tex.	54
1930 Sept. 3	H., San Domingo	2,000	1967 Dec. 12-20	Blizzard, Southwest, U.S.	51
1938 Sept. 21	H., New England	600	1968 Nov. 18-28	T. Nina, Philippines	63
1942 Oct. 15-16	H., Bengal, India	11,000	1969 Aug. 17-18	H. Camille, Miss., La.	256
1944 Sept. 12-16	H., N.C. to New Eng.	389	1970 July 30-		
1953 Sept. 25-27	T., Vietnam, Japan	1,300	Aug. 5	H. Celia, Cuba, Fla., Tex.	31
1954 Aug. 30	H. Carol, Northeast U.S.	68	1970 Aug. 20-21	H. Dorothy, Martinique	42
1954 Oct. 12-13	H. Hazel, Eastern, U.S., Haiti	347	1970 Sept. 15	T. Georgia, Philippines	300
1955 Aug. 12-13	H. Connie, Carolinas, Va., Md.	43	1970 Oct. 14	T. Sening, Philippines.	583
1955 Aug. 18-19	H. Diane, Eastern U.S.	400	1970 Oct. 15	T. Titang, Philippines	526
1955 Sept. 19	H. Hilda, Mexico	200	1970 Nov. 13	Cyclone, Bangladesh	300,000
1955 Sept. 22-28	H. Janet, Caribbean	500	1971 Aug. 1	T. Rose, Hong Kong	130
1956 Feb. 1-29	Blizzard, Western Europe	1,000	1972 June 19-29	H. Agnes, Fla. to N.Y.	118
1957 June 27-30	H. Audrey, La., Tex.	430	1972 Dec. 3	T. Theresa, Philippines.	169
1958 Feb. 15-16	Blizzard, NE U.S.	171	1973 June-Aug.	Monsoon rains in India	1,217
1959 Sept. 17-19	T. Sarah, Far East	2,000	1974 June 11	Storm Dinah, Luzon Is., Philip..	71
1959 Sept. 26-27	T. Vera, Honshu, Japan	4,466	1974 July 11	T. Gilda, Japan, S. Korea	108
1960 Sept. 4-12	H. Donna, Caribbean, E. U.S.	148	1974 Sept. 19-20	H. Fifi, Honduras	2,000
1961 Oct. 31	H. Hattie, Br. Honduras	400	1974 Dec. 25	Cyclone leveled Darwin, Aus.	50
1962 Feb. 17	Flooding, German Coast.	343	1975 Sept. 13-27	H. Eloise, Caribbean, NE U.S.	71
1962 Sept. 27	Flooding, Barcelona, Spain	445	1976 May 20	T. Olga, floods, Philippines	215
1963 May 28-29	Windstorm, Bangladesh	22,000	1977 July 25, 31	T. Thelma, T. Vera, Taiwan	39
1963 Oct. 4-8	H. Flora, Cuba, Haiti	6,000	1978 Oct. 27	T. Rita, Philippines	c. 400
1964 Oct. 4-7	H. Hilda, La., Miss., Ga.	38	1979 Aug. 30-		
1964 June 30	T. Winnie, N. Philippines	107	Sept. 7	H. David, Caribbean, E U.S.	1,100
1964 Sept. 5	T. Ruby, Hong Kong and China	735	1980 Aug. 4-11	H. Allen, Caribbean, Texas	272
1964 Sept. 14	Flooding, central S. Korea	563	1981 Nov. 25	T. Irma, Luzon Is., Philip.	176
1964 Nov. 12	Flooding, S. Vietnam	7,000	1983 June	Monsoon rains in India	900
1965 May 11-12	Windstorm, Bangladesh	17,000	1983 Aug. 18	H. Alicia, Southern Texas	17
1965 June 1-2	Windstorm, Bangladesh	30,000	1984 Sept. 2	T. Ike, Southern Philippines	1,363
1965 Sept. 7-10	H. Betsy, Fla., Miss., La.	74	1985 May 25	Cyclone, Bangladesh.	10,000

Floods, Tidal Waves

Date	Location	Deaths	Date	Location	Deaths
1887	....	Huang He River, China	900,000	1969	Sept. 15	South Korea	250
1889	May 31	Johnstown, Pa.	2,200	1969	Oct. 1-8	Tunisia	500
1900	Sept. 8	Galveston, Tex.	5,000	1970	May 20	Central Romania	160
1903	June 15	Heppner, Ore.	325	1970	July 22	Himalayas, India.	500
1911	....	Chang Jiang River, China.	100,000	1971	Feb. 26	Rio de Janeiro, Brazil	130
1913	Mar. 25-27	Ohio, Indiana.	732	1972	Feb. 26	Buffalo Creek, W. Va.	118
1915	Aug. 17	Galveston, Tex.	275	1972	June 9	Rapid City, S.D.	236
1928	Mar. 13	Collapse of St. Francis		1972	Aug. 7	Luzon Is., Philippines	454
		Dam, Santa Paula, Cal.	450	1974	Mar. 29	Tubaro, Brazil	1,000
1928	Sept. 13	Lake Okeechobee, Fla.	2,000	1974	Aug. 12	Monty-Long, Bangladesh	2,500
1931	Aug.	Huang He River, China	3,700,000	1975	Jan. 11	Southern Thailand.	131
1937	Jan. 22	Ohio, Miss. Valleys	250	1976	June 5	Teton Dam collapse, Ida.	11
1939	....	Northern China	200,000	1976	July 31	Big Thompson Canyon, Col.	130
1947	....	Honshu Island, Japan.	1,900	1976	Nov. 17	East Java, Indonesia	136
1951	Aug.	Manchuria	1,800	1977	July 19-20	Johnstown, Pa.	68
1953	Jan. 31	Western Europe	2,000	1978	June-Sept.	Northern India	1,200
1954	Aug. 17	Farahzad, Iran	2,000	1979	Jan.-Feb.	Brazil	204
1955	Oct. 7-12	India, Pakistan	1,700	1979	July	Lomblem Is., Indonesia	539
1959	Nov. 1	Western Mexico	2,000	1979	Aug. 11	Morvi, India	5,000-15,000
1959	Dec. 2	Frejus, France	412	1980	Feb. 13-22	So. Cal., Ariz.	26
1960	Oct. 10	Bangladesh	6,000	1981	Apr.	Northern China	550
1960	Oct. 31	Bangladesh	4,000	1981	July	Sichuan, Hubei Prov., China	1,300
1962	Feb. 17	German North Sea coast	343	1982	Jan. 23	Nr. Lima, Peru	600
1962	Sept. 27	Barcelona, Spain	445	1982	May 12	Guangdong, China	430
1963	Oct. 9	Dam collapse, Vaiont, Italy	1,800	1982	June 6	So. Conn.	12
1966	Nov. 4-6	Florence, Venice, Italy	113	1982	Sept. 17-21	El Salvador, Guatemala	1,300+
1967	Jan. 18-24	Eastern Brazil	894	1982	Dec. 2-9	Ill., Mo., Ark.	22
1967	Mar. 19	Rio de Janeiro, Brazil	436	1983	Feb.-Mar.	Cal. coast	13
1968	Aug. 7-14	Gujarat State, India	1,000	1983	Apr. 6-12	Ala., La., Miss., Tenn.	15
1968	Oct. 7	Northeastern India.	780	1984	May 27	Tulsa, Okla.	13
1969	Mar. 17	Mundau Valley, Alagoas, Brazil	218	1984	Aug-Sept.	S. Korea	200+
1969	Aug. 25	Western Virginia	189				

Explosions

Date			Location	Deaths
1910	Oct.	1	Los Angeles Times Bldg.,	21
1913	Mar.	7	Dynamite, Baltimore harbor	55
1915	Sept.	27	Gasoline tank car, Ardmore, Okla.	47
1917	Apr.	10	Munitions plant, Eddystone, Pa.	133
1917	Dec.	6	Halifax Harbor, Canada	1,654
1918	May	18	Chemical plant, Oakdale, Pa.	193
1918	July	2	Explosives, Split Rock, N.Y.	50
1918	Oct.	4	Shell plant, Morgan Station, N.J.	64
1919	May	22	Food plant, Cedar Rapids, Ia.	44
1920	Sept.	16	Wall Street, New York, bomb	30
1924	Jan.	3	Food plant, Pekin, Ill.	42
1928	April	13	Dance hall, West Plains, Mo.	40
1937	Mar.	18	New London, Tex., school	294
1940	Sept.	11	Hercules Powder, Kenvil, N.J.	51
1942	June	5	Ordnance plant, Elwood, Ill.	49
1944	Apr.	14	Bombay, India, harbor	700
1944	July	17	Port Chicago, Cal., pier	322
1944	Oct.	21	Liquid gas tank, Cleveland	135
1947	Apr.	16	Texas City, Tex., pier	561
1948	July	28	Farben works, Ludwigshafen, Ger.	184
1950	May	19	Munitions barges, S. Amboy, N. J.	30
1956	Aug.	7	Dynamite trucks, Cali, Colombia	1,100
1958	Apr.	18	Sunken munitions ship, Okinawa	40
1958	May	22	Nike missiles, Leonardo, N.J.	10
1959	Apr.	10	World War II bomb, Philippines	38
1959	June	28	Rail tank cars, Meldrin, Ga.	25
1959	Aug.	7	Dynamite truck, Roseburg, Ore.	13
1959	Nov.	2	Jamuri Bazar, India, explosives	46
1959	Dec.	13	Dortmund, Ger., 2 apt. bldgs.	26
1960	Mar.	4	Belgian munitions ship, Havana	100
1960	Oct.	25	Gas, Windsor, Ont., store	11
1962	Jan.	16	Gas pipeline, Edson, Alberta, Canada.	8
1962	Oct.	3	Telephone Co. office, N. Y. City	23
1963	Jan.	2	Packing plant, Terre Haute, Ind.	16
1963	Mar.	9	Dynamite plant, S. Africa	45
1963	Aug.	13	Explosives dump, Gauhiti, India	32
1963	Oct.	31	State Fair Coliseum, Indianapolis	73
1964	July	23	Bone, Algeria, harbor munitions	100
1965	Mar.	4	Gas pipeline, Natchitoches, La.	17
1965	Aug.	9	Missile silo, Searcy, Ark.	53
1965	Oct.	21	Bridge, Tila Bund, Pakistan	80
1965	Oct.	30	Cartagena, Colombia	48
1965	Nov.	24	Armory, Keokuk, Ia.	20
1966	Oct.	13	Chemical plant, La Salle, Que.	11
1967	Feb.	17	Chemical plant, Hawthorne, N.J.	11
1967	Dec.	25	Apartment bldg., Moscow	20
1968	Apr.	6	Sports store, Richmond, Ind.	43
1970	Apr.	8	Subway construction, Osaka, Japan	73
1971	June	24	Tunnel, Sylmar, Cal.	17
1971	June	28	School, fireworks, Pueblo, Mex.	13
1971	Oct.	21	Shopping center, Glasgow, Scot.	20
1973	Feb.	10	Liquified gas tank, Staten Is., N.Y.	40
1975	Dec.	27	Chasnala, India, mine	431
1976	Apr.	13	Lapua, Finland, munitions works	45
1977	Nov.	11	Freight train, Iri, S. Korea	57
1977	Dec.	22	Grain elevator, Westwego, La.	35
1978	Feb.	24	Derailed tank car, Waverly, Tenn.	12
1978	July	11	Propylene tank truck, Spanish coastal campsite.	150
1980	Oct.	23	School, Ortuella, Spain	64
1981	Feb.	13	Sewer system, Louisville, Ky.	0
1982	Apr.	7	Tanker truck, tunnel, Oakland, Cal.	7
1982	Apr.	25	Antiques exhibition, Todi, Italy.	33
1982	Nov.	2	Salang Tunnel, Afghanistan.	1,000-3,000
1984	Feb.	25	Oil pipeline, Cubatao, Brazil.	508
1984	June	21	Naval supply depot, Severomorsk, USSR.	200+
1984	Nov.	19	Gas storage area, NE Mexico City.	334
1984	Dec.	5	Coal mine, Taipei, Taiwan.	94

Fires

Date			Location	Deaths
1845	May		Theater, Canton, China	1,670
1871	Oct.	8	Chicago, $196 million loss.	250
1871	Oct.	8	Peshtigo, Wis., forest fire	1,182
1876	Dec.	5	Brooklyn (N.Y.), theater	295
1877	June	20	St. John, N. B., Canada	100
1881	Dec.	8	Ring Theater, Vienna.	850
1887	May	25	Opera Comique, Paris	200
1887	Sept.	4	Exeter, England, theater.	200
1894	Sept.	1	Hinckley, Minn., forest fire	413
1897	May	4	Charity bazaar, Paris.	150
1900	June	30	Hoboken, N. J., docks	326
1902	Sept.	20	Church, Birmingham, Ala.	115
1903	Dec.	30	Iroquois Theater, Chicago	602
1908	Jan.	13	Rhoads Theater, Boyertown, Pa.	170
1908	Mar.	4	School, Collinwood, Oh.	176
1911	Mar.	25	Triangle factory, N. Y. City	145
1913	Oct.	14	Colliery, Mid Glamorgan, Wales	439
1918	Apr.	13	Norman Okla., state hospital	38
1918	Oct.	12	Cloquet, Minn., forest fire	400
1919	June	20	Mayaguez Theater, San Juan.	150
1923	May	17	School, Camden, S. C.	76
1924	Dec.	24	School, Hobart, Okla.	35
1929	May	15	Clinic, Cleveland, Oh.	125
1930	Apr.	21	Penitentiary, Columbus, Oh.	320
1931	July	24	Pittsburgh, Pa., home for aged	48
1934	Dec.	11	Hotel Kerns, Lansing, Mich.	34
1938	May	16	Atlanta, Ga., Terminal Hotel.	35
1940	Apr.	23	Dance hall, Natchez, Miss.	198
1942	Nov.	28	Cocoanut Grove, Boston	491
1942			Hostel, St. John's, Newfoundland	100
1943	Sept.	7	Gulf Hotel, Houston	55
1944	July	6	Ringling Circus, Hartford.	168
1946	June	5	LaSalle Hotel, Chicago	61
1946	Dec.	7	Winecoff Hotel, Atlanta	119
1946	Dec.	12	New York, ice plant, tenement	37
1949	Apr.	5	Hospital, Effingham, Ill.	77
1950	Jan.	7	Davenport, Ia., Mercy Hospital	41
1953	Mar.	29	Largo, Fla., nursing home	35
1953	Apr.	16	Chicago, metalworking plant	35
1957	Feb.	17	Home for aged, Warrenton, Mo.	72
1958	Mar.	19	New York City loft building	24
1958	Dec.	1	Parochial school, Chicago	95
1958	Dec.	16	Store, Bogota, Colombia	83
1959	June	23	Resort hotel, Stalheim, Norway.	34
1960	Mar.	12	Pusan, Korea, chemical plant	68
1960	July	14	Mental hospital, Guatemala City	225
1960	Nov.	13	Movie theater, Amude, Syria	152
1961	Jan.	6	Thomas Hotel, San Francisco.	20
1961	Dec.	8	Hospital, Hartford, Conn.	16
1961	Dec.	17	Circus, Niteroi, Brazil.	323
1963	May	4	Theater, Diourbel, Senegal	64
1963	Nov.	18	Surfside Hotel, Atlantic City, N.J.	25
1963	Nov.	23	Rest home, Fitchville, Oh.	63
1963	Dec.	29	Roosevelt Hotel, Jacksonville, Fla.	22
1964	May	8	Apartment building, Manila	30
1964	Dec.	18	Nursing home, Fountaintown, Ind.	20
1965	Mar.	1	Apartment, LaSalle, Canada	28
1966	Mar.	11	Numata, Japan, 2 ski resorts	31
1966	Aug.	13	Melbourne, Australia, hotel	29
1966	Sept.	12	Anchorage, Alaska, hotel	14
1966	Oct.	17	N. Y. City bldg. (firemen)	12
1966	Dec.	1	Erzurum, Turkey, barracks	68
1967	Feb.	7	Restaurant, Montgomery, Ala.	25
1967	May	22	Store, Brussels, Belgium	322
1967	July	16	State prison, Jay, Fla.	37
1968	Feb.	26	Shrewsbury, England, hospital	22
1968	May	11	Vijayawada, India, wedding hall.	58
1968	Nov.	18	Glasgow, Scotland, factory	24
1969	Jan.	26	Victoria Hotel, Dunnville, Ont.	13
1969	Dec.	2	Nursing home, Notre Dame, Can.	54
1970	Jan.	9	Nursing home, Marietta, Oh.	27
1970	Mar.	20	Hotel, Seattle, Wash.	19
1970	Nov.	1	Dance hall, Grenoble, France	145
1970	Dec.	20	Hotel, Tucson, Arizona.	28
1971	Mar.	6	Psychiatric clinic, Burghoezli, Switzerland.	28
1971	Apr.	20	Hotel, Bangkok, Thailand	24
1971	Oct.	19	Nursing home, Honesdale, Pa.	15
1971	Dec.	25	Hotel, Seoul, So. Korea	162
1972	May	13	Osaka, Japan, nightclub	116
1972	July	5	Sherborne, England, hospital	30
1973	Feb.	6	Paris, France, school.	21
1973	Nov.	6	Fukui, Japan, train	28
1973	Nov.	29	Kumamoto, Japan, department store.	107
1973	Dec.	2	Seoul, Korea, theater	50
1974	Feb.	1	Sao Paulo, Brazil, bank building	189
1974	June	30	Port Chester, N. Y., discotheque	24
1974	Nov.	3	Seoul, So. Korea, hotel discotheque	88
1975	Dec.	12	Mina, Saudi Arabia, tent city.	138
1976	Oct.	24	Bronx, N.Y., social club	25
1977	Feb.	25	Rossiya Hotel, Moscow	45

Date			Location	Deaths	Date			Location	Deaths
1977	May	28	Southgate, Ky., nightclub	164	1981	Feb.	10	Las Vegas Hilton	8
1977	June	9	Abidjan, Ivory Coast nightclub	41	1981	Feb.	14	Dublin, Ireland, discotheque	44
1977	June	26	Columbia, Tenn., jail	42	1982	Sept.	4	Los Angeles, apartment house	24
1977	Nov.	14	Manila, PI, hotel	47	1982	Nov.	8	Biloxi, Miss., county jail	29
1978	Jan.	28	Kansas City, Coates House Hotel	16	1983	Feb.	13	Turin, Italy, movie theater	64
1979	Dec.	31	Chapais, Quebec, social club	42	1983	Dec.	17	Madrid, Spain, discotheque	83
1980	May	20	Kingston, Jamaica, nursing home	157	1985	Apr.	21	Tabaco, Philippines movie theater	44
1980	Nov.	21	MGM Grand Hotel, Las Vegas	84	1985	Apr.	26	Buenos Aires, Argentina hospital	79
1980	Dec.	4	Stouffer Inn, Harrison, N.Y.	26	1985	May	11	Bradford, England soccer stadium	53
1981	Jan.	9	Keansburg, N.J., boarding home	30					

Major U.S. Railroad Wrecks

Date			Location	Deaths	Date			Location	Deaths
1876	Dec.	29	Ashtabula, Oh.	92	1925	June	16	Hackettstown, N. J.	50
1880	Aug.	11	Mays Landing, N. J.	40	1925	Oct.	27	Victoria, Miss.	21
1887	Aug.	10	Chatsworth, Ill.	81	1926	Sept.	5	Waco, Col.	30
1888	Oct.	10	Mud Run, Pa.	55	1928	Aug.	24	I.R.T. subway, Times Sq., N. Y.	18
1896	July	30	Atlantic City, N. J.	60	1938	June	19	Saugus, Mont.	47
1903	Dec.	23	Laurel Run, Pa.	53	1939	Aug.	12	Harney, Nev.	24
1904	Aug.	7	Eden, Col.	96	1940	Apr.	19	Little Falls, N. Y.	31
1904	Sept.	24	New Market Tenn.	56	1940	July	31	Cuyahoga Falls, Oh.	43
1906	Mar.	16	Florence, Col.	35	1943	Aug.	29	Wayland, N. Y.	27
1906	Oct.	28	Atlantic City, N. J.	40	1943	Sept.	6	Frankford Junction, Philadelphia, Pa.	79
1906	Dec.	30	Washington, D. C.	53	1943	Dec.	16	Between Rennert and Buie, N. C.	72
1907	Jan.	2	Volland, Kan.	33	1944	July	6	High Bluff, Tenn.	35
1907	Jan.	19	Fowler, Ind.	29	1944	Aug.	4	Near Stockton, Ga.	47
1907	Feb.	16	New York, N.Y.	22	1944	Sept.	14	Dewey, Ind.	29
1907	Feb.	23	Colton, Cal.	26	1944	Dec.	31	Bagley, Utah	50
1907	July	20	Salem, Mich.	33	1945	Aug.	9	Michigan, N. D.	34
1910	Mar.	1	Wellington, Wash.	96	1946	Apr.	25	Naperville, Ill.	45
1910	Mar.	21	Green Mountain, Ia.	55	1947	Feb.	18	Gallitzin, Pa.	24
1911	Aug.	25	Manchester, N. Y.	29	1950	Feb.	17	Rockville Centre, N. Y.	31
1912	July	4	East Corning, N. Y.	39	1950	Sept.	11	Coshocton, Oh.	33
1912	July	5	Ligonier, Pa.	23	1950	Nov.	22	Richmond Hill, N. Y.	79
1914	Aug.	5	Tipton Ford, Mo.	43	1951	Feb.	6	Woodbridge, N. J.	84
1914	Sept.	15	Lebanon, Mo.	28	1951	Nov.	12	Wyuta, Wyo.	17
1916	Mar.	29	Amherst, Oh.	27	1951	Nov.	25	Woodstock, Ala.	17
1917	Sept.	28	Kellyville, Okla.	23	1953	Mar.	27	Conneaut, Oh.	21
1917	Dec.	20	Shepherdsville, Ky.	46	1956	Jan.	22	Los Angeles, Cal.	30
1918	June	22	Ivanhoe, Ind.	68	1956	Feb.	28	Swampscott, Mass.	13
1918	July	9	Nashville, Tenn.	101	1956	Sept.	5	Springer, N. M.	20
1918	Nov.	2	Brooklyn, N. Y., Malbone St. Tunnel	97	1957	June	11	Vroman, Col.	12
1919	Jan.	12	South Byron, N. Y.	22	1958	Sept.	15	Elizabethport, N. J.	48
1919	July	1	Dunkirk, N. Y.	12	1960	Mar.	14	Bakersfield, Cal.	14
1919	Dec.	20	Onawa, Maine	23	1962	July	28	Steelton, Pa.	19
1921	Feb.	27	Porter, Ind.	37	1966	Dec.	28	Everett, Mass.	13
1921	Dec.	5	Woodmont, Pa.	27	1971	June	10	Salem, Ill.	11
1922	Aug.	5	Sulphur Spring, Mo.	34	1972	Oct.	30	Chicago, Ill.	45
1922	Dec.	13	Humble, Tex.	22	1977	Feb.	4	Chicago, Ill., elevated train	11
1923	Sept.	27	Lockett, Wy.	31					

World's worst train wreck occurred Dec. 12, 1917, Modane, France, passenger train derailed, 543 killed.

Some Notable Aircraft Disasters Since 1937

Date			Aircraft	Site of accident	Deaths
1937	May	6	German zeppelin Hindenburg	Burned at mooring, Lakehurst, N.J.	36
1944	Aug.	23	U.S. Air Force B-24	Hit school, Freckelton, England	76[1]
1945	July	28	U.S. Army B-25	Hit Empire State bldg., N.Y.C.	14[1]
1947	May	30	Eastern Air Lines DC-4	Crashed near Port Deposit, Md.	53
1952	Dec.	20	U.S. Air Force C-124	Fell, burned, Moses Lake, Wash.	87
1953	Mar.	3	Canadian Pacific Comet Jet	Karachi, Pakistan	11[2]
1953	June	18	U.S. Air Force C-124	Crashed, burned near Tokyo	129
1955	Nov.	1	United Air Lines DC-6B	Exploded, crashed near Longmont, Col.	44[3]
1956	June	20	Venezuelan Super-Constellation	Crashed in Atlantic off Asbury Park, N.J.	74[1]
1956	June	30	TWA Super-Const., United DC-7	Collided over Grand Canyon, Arizona	128
1960	Dec.	16	United DC-8 jet, TWA Super-Const.	Collided over N.Y. City	134[4]
1962	Mar.	4	Br. Caledonian Airlines DC-7C	Crashed near Douala, Cameroon	111
1962	Mar.	16	Flying Tiger Super-Const.	Vanished in Western Pacific	107
1962	June	3	Air France Boeing 707 jet	Crashed on takeoff from Paris	130
1962	June	22	Air France Boeing 707 jet	Crashed in storm, Guadeloupe, W.I.	113
1963	June	3	Chartered Northw. Airlines DC-7	Crashed in Pacific off British Columbia	101
1963	Nov.	29	Trans-Canada Airlines DC-8F	Crashed after takeoff from Montreal	118
1965	May	20	Pakistani Boeing 720-B	Crashed at Cairo, Egypt, airport	121
1966	Jan.	24	Air India Boeing 707 jetliner	Crashed on Mont Blanc, France-Italy	117
1966	Feb.	4	All-Nippon Boeing 727	Plunged into Tokyo Bay	133
1966	Mar.	5	BOAC Boeing 707 jetliner	Crashed on Mount Fuji, Japan	124
1966	Dec.	24	U.S. military-chartered CL-44	Crashed into village in So. Vietnam	129[1]
1967	Apr.	20	Swiss Britannia turboprop	Crashed at Nicosia, Cyprus	126
1967	July	19	Piedmont Boeing 727, Cessna 310	Collided in air, Hendersonville, N.C.	82
1968	Apr.	20	S. African Airways Boeing 707	Crashed on takeoff, Windhoek, SW Africa	122
1968	May	3	Braniff International Electra	Crashed in storm near Dawson, Tex.	85
1969	Mar.	16	Venezuelan DC-9	Crashed after takeoff from Maracaibo, Venezuela	155[5]
1969	Mar.	20	United Arab Ilyushin-18	Crashed at Aswan airport, Egypt	87
1969	June	4	Mexican Boeing 727	Rammed into mountain near Monterrey, Mexico	79
1969	Dec.	8	Olympia Airways DC-6B	Crashed near Athens in storm	93
1970	Feb.	15	Dominican DC-9	Crashed into sea on takeoff from Santo Domingo	102

Date		Aircraft	Site of accident	Deaths
1970	July	3	British chartered jetliner	Crashed near Barcelona, Spain.	112
1970	July	5	Air Canada DC-8.	Crashed near Toronto International Airport	108
1970	Aug.	9	Peruvian turbojet.	Crashed after takeoff from Cuzco, Peru	101[1]
1970	Nov.	14	Southern Airways DC-9	Crashed in mountains near Huntington, W. Va.	75[6]
1971	July	30	All-Nippon Boeing 727 and Japanese Air Force F-86.	Collided over Morioka, Japan	162[7]
1971	Aug.	11	Soviet Aeroflot Tupolev-104	Crashed at Irkutsk airport, USSR.	97
1971	Sept.	4	Alaska Airlines Boeing 727	Crashed into mountain near Juneau, Alaska	111
1972	Aug.	14	E. German Ilyushin-62.	Crashed on take-off East Berlin.	156
1972	Oct.	13	Aeroflot Ilyushin-62	E. German airline crashed near Moscow	176
1972	Dec.	3	Chartered Spanish airliner	Crashed on take-off, Canary Islands	155
1972	Dec.	29	Eastern Airlines Lockheed Tristar	Crashed on approach to Miami Int'l. Airport	101
1973	Jan.	22	Chartered Boeing 707.	Burst into flames during landing, Kano Airport, Nigeria.	176
1973	Apr.	10	British Vanguard turboprop	Crashed during snowstorm at Basel, Switzerland	104
1973	June	3	Soviet Supersonic TU-144	Exploded in air near Goussainville, France	14[8]
1973	July	11	Brazilian Boeing 707.	Crashed on approach to Orly Airport, Paris	122
1973	July	31	Delta Airlines jetliner.	Crashed, landing in fog at Logan Airport, Boston	89
1973	Dec.	23	French Caravelle jet.	Crashed in Morocco	106
1974	Jan.	31	Pan American Boeing 707 jet.	Crashed in Pago Pago, American Samoa	96
1974	Mar.	3	Turkish DC-10 jet	Crashed at Ermenonville near Paris	346
1974	Apr.	23	Pan American 707 jet	Crashed in Bali, Indonesia	107
1974	Sept.	8	TWA 707 jet	Crashed in Ionian Sea off Greece, after bomb explosion.	80
1974	Dec.	1	TWA-727	Crashed in storm, Upperville, Va.	92
1974	Dec.	4	Dutch-chartered DC-8.	Crashed in storm near Colombo, Sri Lanka.	191
1975	Apr.	4	Air Force Galaxy C-58.	Crashed near Saigon, So. Vietnam, after takeoff with load of orphans	172
1975	June	24	Eastern Airlines 727 jet	Crashed in storm, JFK Airport, N.Y. City.	113
1975	Aug.	3	Chartered 707	Hit mountainside, Agadir, Morocco	188
1976	Sept.	10	British Airways Trident, Yugoslav DC-9	Collided near Zagreb, Yugoslavia	176
1976	Sept.	19	Turkish 727	Hit mountain, southern Turkey	155
1976	Oct.	6	Cuban DC-8	Crashed near Barbados after bomb explosion	73
1976	Oct.	12	Indian Caravelle jet	Crashed after takeoff, Bombay airport.	95
1976	Oct.	13	Bolivian 707 cargo jet	Crashed in Santa Cruz, Bolivia	100[9]
1976	Dec.	28	Aeroflot TU-104	Crashed at Moscow's Sheremetyevo airport	72
1977	Jan.	13	Aeroflot TU-104	Exploded and crashed at Alma-Ata, Central Asia.	90
1977	Mar.	27	KLM 747, Pan American 747	Collided on runway, Tenerife, Canary Islands.	581
1977	Nov.	19	TAP Boeing 727	Crashed on Madeira	130
1977	Dec.	4	Malaysian Boeing 737.	Hijacked, then exploded in mid-air over Straits of Johore	100
1977	Dec.	13	U.S. DC-3.	Crashed after takeoff at Evansville, Ind.	29[10]
1978	Jan.	1	Air India 747	Exploded, crashed into sea off Bombay	213
1978	Mar.	16	Bulgarian TU-134	Crashed at Vratsa, Bulgaria.	73
1978	Sept.	25	Boeing 727, Cessna 172	Collided in air, San Diego, Cal.	150
1978	Nov.	15	Chartered DC-8	Crashed near Colombo, Sri Lanka	183
1979	May	25	American Airlines DC-10	Crashed after takeoff at O'Hare Intl. Airport, Chicago	275[11]
1979	Aug.	17	Two Soviet Aeroflot jetliners	Collided over Ukraine	173
1979	Oct.	31	Western Airlines DC-10	Mexico City Airport	74
1979	Nov.	26	Pakistani Boeing 707	Crashed near Jidda, Saudi Arabia	156
1979	Nov.	28	New Zealand DC-10.	Crashed into mountain in Antarctica	257
1980	Mar.	14	Polish Ilyushin 62.	Crashed making emergency landing, Warsaw	87[12]
1980	Aug.	19	Saudi Arabian Tristar	Burned after emergency landing, Riyadh	301
1981	Dec.	1	Yugoslavian DC-9	Crashed into mountain in Corsica.	174
1982	Jan.	13	Air Florida Boeing 737.	Crashed into Potomac River after takeoff	78
1982	July	9	Pan-Am Boeing 727	Crashed after takeoff in Kenner, La.	153[13]
1982	Sept.	11	U.S. Army CH-47 Chinook helicopter	Crashed during air show in Mannheim, W. Germany	46
1983	Sept.	1	S. Korean Boeing 747.	Shot down after violating Soviet airspace	269
1983	Nov.	27	Colombian Boeing 747	Crashed near Barajas Airport, Madrid	183
1985	Feb.	19	Spanish Boeing 727	Crashed into Mt. Oiz, Spain	148
1985	June	23	Air-India Boeing 747	Crashed into Atlantic Ocean S. of Ireland	329
1985	Aug.	2	Delta Air Lines jumbo jet	Crashed at Dallas-Ft. Worth Intl. Airport.	132

(1) Including those on the ground and in buildings. (2) First fatal crash of commercial jet plane. (3) Caused by bomb planted by John G. Graham in insurance plot to kill his mother, a passenger. (4) Including all 128 aboard the planes and 6 on ground. (5) Killed 84 on plane and 71 on ground. (6) Including 43 Marshall U. football players and coaches. (7) Airliner-fighter crash, pilot of fighter parachuted to safety, was arrested for negligence. (8) First supersonic plane crash killed 6 crewmen and 8 on the ground; there were no passengers. (9) Crew of 3 killed; 97, mostly children, killed on ground. (10) Including U. of Evansville basketball team. (11) Highest death toll in U.S. aviation history. (12) Including 22 members of U.S. boxing team. (13) Including 8 on ground.

Principal U.S. Mine Disasters

Source: Bureau of Mines, U.S. Interior Department

Note: Prior to 1968, only disasters with losses of 60 or more lives are listed; since 1968, all disasters in which 5 or more people were killed are listed. Only fatalities to mining company employees are included. All Bituminous-coal mines unless otherwise noted.

Date	Location	Deaths	Date	Location	Deaths
1867 Apr. 3	Winterpock, Va.	69	1907 Dec. 19	Jacobs Creek, Pa.	239
1869[1] Sept. 6	Plymouth, Pa.	110	1908 Nov. 28	Marianna, Pa.	154
1883 Feb. 16	Braidwood, Ill.	69	1909 Jan. 12	Switchback, W. Va.	67
1884 Mar. 13	Pocahontas, Va.	112	1909 Nov. 13	Cherry, Ill.	259
1891 Jan. 27	Mount Pleasant, Pa.	109	1910 Jan. 31	Primero, Col.	75
1892 Jan. 7	Krebs, Okla.	100	1910 May 5	Palos, Ala.	90
1895 Mar. 20	Red Canyon, Wy.	60	1910 Nov. 8	Delagua, Col.	79
1900 Jan. 1	Scofield, Ut.	200	1911 Apr. 7	Throop, Pa.	72
1902 May 19	Coal Creek, Tenn.	184	1911 Apr. 8	Littleton, Ala.	128
1902 July 10	Johnstown, Pa.	112	1911 Dec. 9	Briceville, Tenn.	84
1903 June 30	Hanna, Wy.	169	1912 Mar. 20	McCurtain, Okla.	73
1904 Jan. 25	Cheswick, Pa.	179	1912 Mar. 26	Jed, W. Va.	83
1905 Feb. 20	Virginia City, Ala.	112	1913 Apr. 23	Finleyville, Pa.	96
1907 Jan. 29	Stuart W. Va.	84	1913 Oct. 22	Dawson, N.M.	263
1907 Dec. 6	Monongah, W. Va.	361	1914 Apr. 28	Eccles, W. Va.	181

Date	Location	Deaths	Date	Location	Deaths
1915 Mar. 2	Layland, W. Va.	112	1940 Mar. 16	St. Clairsville, Oh.	72
1917 Apr. 27	Hastings, Col.	121	1940 July 15	Portage, Pa.	63
1917[2]June 8	Butte, Mon.	163	1943 Feb. 27	Washoe, Mon.	74
1917 Aug. 4	Clay, Ky.	62	1944 July 5	Belmont, Oh.	66
1919[1]June 5	Wilkes-Barre, Pa.	92	1947 Mar. 25	Centralia, Ill.	111
1922 Nov. 6	Spangler, Pa.	77	1951 Dec. 21	West Frankfort, Ill.	119
1922 Nov. 22	Dolomite, Ala.	90	1968[3]Mar. 6	Calumet, La.	21
1923 Feb. 8	Dawson, N.M.	120	1968 Nov. 20	Farmington, W. Va.	78
1923 Aug. 14	Kemmerer, Wy.	99	1970 Dec. 30	Hyden, Ky.	38
1924 Mar. 8	Castle Gate, Ut.	171	1972[2]May 2	Kellogg, Ida.	91
1924 Apr. 28	Benwood, W. Va.	119	1976 Mar. 9, 11	Oven Fork, Ky.	26
1926 Jan. 13	Wilburton, Okla.	91	1977 Mar. 1	Tower City, Pa.	9
1926[2]Nov. 3	Ishpeming, Mich.	51	1981 Apr. 15	Redstone, Col.	15
1927 Apr. 30	Everettville, W. Va.	97	1981 Dec. 7	Topmost, Ky.	8
1928 May 19	Mather, Pa.	195	1981 Dec. 8	nr. Chattanooga, Tenn.	13
1929 Dec. 17	McAlester, Okla.	61	1982 Jan. 20	Floyd County, Ky.	7
1930 Nov. 5	Millfield, Oh.	79	1983 June 21	McClure, Va	7
1940 Jan. 10	Bartley, W. Va.	91	1984 Dec. 19	Huntington, Ut.	27

(1) Anthracite mine. (2) Metal mine. (3) Nonmetal mine.
World's worst mine disaster killed 1,549 workers in Honkeiko Colliery in Manchuria Apr. 25, 1942.

Historic Assassinations Since 1865

1865—Apr. 14. U. S. Pres. Abraham Lincoln, shot in Washington, D. C.; died Apr. 15.

1881—Mar. 13. Alexander II, of Russia—July 2. U. S. Pres. James A. Garfield, Washington; died Sept. 19.

1900—July 29. Umberto I, king of Italy.

1901—Sept. 6. U. S. Pres. William McKinley in Buffalo, N. Y., died Sept. 14. Leon Czolgosz executed for the crime Oct. 29.

1913—Feb. 23. Mexican Pres. Francisco, I, Madero and Vice Pres. Jose Pino Suarez.—Mar. 18. George, king of Greece.

1914—June 28. Archduke Francis Ferdinand of Austria-Hungary and his wife in Sarajevo, Bosnia (later part of Yugoslavia), by Gavrilo Princip.

1916—Dec. 30. Grigori Rasputin, politically powerful Russian monk.

1918—July 12. Grand Duke Michael of Russia, at Perm.—July 16. Nicholas II, abdicated as czar of Russia; his wife, the Czarina Alexandra, their son, Czarevitch Alexis, and their daughters, Grand Duchesses Olga, Tatiana, Marie, Anastasia, and 4 members of their household were executed by Bolsheviks at Ekaterinburg.

1920—May 20. Mexican Pres. Gen. Venustiano Carranza in Tlaxcalantongo.

1922—Aug. 22. Michael Collins, Irish revolutionary.

1923—July 20. Gen. Francisco "Pancho" Villa, ex-rebel leader, in Parral, Mexico.

1928—July 17. Gen. Alvaro Obregon, president-elect of Mexico, in San Angel, Mexico.

1933—Feb. 15. In Miami, Fla. Joseph Zangara, anarchist, shot at Pres.-elect Franklin D. Roosevelt, but a woman seized his arm, and the bullet fatally wounded Mayor Anton J. Cermak, of Chicago, who died Mar. 6. Zangara was electrocuted on Mar. 20, 1933.

1934—July 25. In Vienna, Austrian Chancellor Engelbert Dollfuss by Nazis.

1935—Sept. 8. U. S. Sen. Huey P. Long, shot in Baton Rouge, La., by Dr. Carl Austin Weiss, who was slain by Long's bodyguards.

1940—Aug. 20. Leon Trotsky (Lev Bronstein), 63, exiled Russian war minister, near Mexico City. Killer identified as Ramon Mercador del Rio, a Spaniard, served 20 years in Mexican prison.

1948—Jan. 30. Mohandas K. Gandhi, 78, shot in New Delhi, India, by Nathuran Vinayak Godse.—Sept. 17. Count Folke Bernadotte, UN mediator for Palestine, ambushed in Jerusalem.

1951—July 20. King Abdullah ibn Hussein of Jordan.

1956—Sept. 21. Pres. Anastasio Somoza of Nicaragua, in Leon; died Sept. 29.

1957—July 26. Pres. Carlos Castillo Armas of Guatemala, in Guatemala City by one of his own guards.

1958—July 14. King Faisal of Iraq; his uncle, Crown Prince Abdul Illah, and July 15, Premier Nuri as-Said, by rebels in Baghdad.

1959—Sept. 25. Prime Minister Solomon Bandaranaike of Ceylon, by Buddhist monk in Colombo.

1961—Jan. 17. Ex-Premier Patrice Lumumba of the Congo, in Katanga Province—May 30. Dominican dictator Rafael Leonidas Trujillo Molina shot to death by assassins near Ciudad Trujillo.

1963—June 12. Medgar W. Evers, NAACP's Mississippi field secretary, in Jackson, Miss.—Nov. 2. Pres. Ngo Dinh Diem of the Republic of Vietnam and his brother, Ngo Dinh Nhu, in a military coup.—Nov. 22. U. S. Pres. John F. Kennedy fatally shot in Dallas, Tex.; accused Lee Harvey Oswald murdered while awaiting trial.

1965—Jan. 21. Iranian premier Hassan Ali Mansour fatally wounded by assassin in Teheran; 4 executed.—Feb. 21. Malcolm X, black nationalist, fatally shot in N. Y. City; 3 sentenced to life.

1966—Sept. 6. Prime Minister Hendrik F. Verwoerd of South Africa stabbed to death in parliament at Capetown.

1968—Apr. 4. Rev. Dr. Martin Luther King Jr. fatally shot in Memphis, Tenn.; James Earl Ray sentenced to 99 years.—June 5. Sen. Robert F. Kennedy (D-N. Y.) fatally shot in Los Angeles; Sirhan Sirhan, resident alien, convicted of murder.

1971—Nov. 28. Jordan Prime Minister Wasfi Tal, in Cairo, by Palestinian guerrillas.

1973—Mar. 2. U. S. Ambassador Cleo A. Noel Jr., U. S. Charge d'Affaires George C. Moore and Belgian Charge d'Affaires Guy Eid killed by Palestinian guerrillas in Khartoum, Sudan.

1974—Aug. 15. Mrs. Park Chung Hee, wife of president of So. Korea, hit by bullet meant for her husband.—Aug. 19. U. S. Ambassador to Cyprus, Rodger P. Davies, killed by sniper's bullet in Nicosia.

1975—Feb. 11. Pres. Richard Ratsimandrava, of Madagascar, shot in Tananarive.—Mar. 25. King Faisal of Saudi Arabia shot by nephew Prince Musad Abdel Aziz, in royal palace, Riyadh.—Aug. 15. Bangladesh Pres. Sheik Mujibur Rahman killed in coup.

1976—Feb. 13. Nigerian head of state, Gen. Murtala Ramat Mohammed, slain by self-styled "young revolutionaries."

1977—Mar. 16. Kamal Jumblat, Lebanese Druse chieftain, was shot near Beirut.—Mar. 18. Congo Pres. Marien Ngouabi shot in Brazzaville.

1978—July 9. Former Iraqi Premier Abdul Razak Al-Naif shot in London.

1979—Feb. 14. U.S. Ambassador Adolph Dubs shot and killed by Afghan Moslem extremists in Kabul.—Mar. 30. British Tory MP Airey Neave killed when bomb in his car exploded. IRA claimed responsibility.—Aug. 27. Lord Mountbatten, WW2 hero, and 2 others were killed when a bomb exploded on his fishing boat off the coast of Co. Sligo, Ire. The IRA claimed responsibility.—Oct. 26. So. Korean President Park Chung Hee and 6 bodyguards fatally shot by Kim Jae Kyu, head of Korean CIA, and 5 aides in Seoul.

1980—Apr. 12. Liberian President William R. Tolbert slain in military coup.—Sept. 17. Former Nicaraguan President Anastasio Somoza Debayle and 2 others shot in Paraguay.

1981—Aug. 30. Iranian President Mohammed Ali Raji and Premier Mohammed Jad Bahonar killed by bomb in Teheran.—Oct. 6. Egyptian President Anwar El-Sadat fatally shot by a band of commandos while reviewing a military parade in Cairo.

1982—Sept. 14. Lebanese President-elect Bishir Gemayel killed by bomb in east Beirut.

1983—Apr. 10. PLO representative Dr. Issam Sartawi was fatally shot by an unknown gunman in Albufeira, Portugal. A PLO splinter group claimed responsibility.—Aug. 21. Philippine opposition political leader Benigno Aquino Jr. fatally shot by a gunman at Manila International Airport.—Oct. 9. Four S. Korea cabinet ministers and 17 others killed by bomb blast in Rangoon, Burma.

1984—Oct. 31. Indian Prime Minister Indira Gandhi shot and killed by 2 of her bodyguards, who were members of the minority Sikh sect, in New Delhi.

Assassination Attempts

1910—Aug. 6. N. Y. City Mayor William J. Gaynor shot and seriously wounded by discharged city employee.

1912—Oct. 14. Former U. S. President Theodore Roosevelt shot and seriously wounded by demented man in Milwaukee.

1950—Nov. 1. In an attempt to assassinate President Truman, 2 members of a Puerto Rican nationalist movement—Griselio Torresola and Oscar Collazo—tried to shoot their way into Blair House. Torresola was killed, and a guard, Pvt. Leslie Coffelt was fatally shot. Collazo was convicted Mar. 7, 1951 for the murder of Coffelt.

1970—Nov. 27. Pope Paul VI unharmed by knife-wielding assailant who attempted to attack him in Manila airport.

1972—May 15. Alabama Gov. George Wallace shot in Laurel, Md. by Arthur Bremer; seriously crippled.

1972—Dec. 7. Mrs. Ferdinand E. Marcos, wife of the Philippine president, was stabbed and seriously injured in Pasay City, Philippines.

1975—Sept. 5. Pres. Gerald R. Ford was unharmed when a Secret Service agent grabbed a pistol aimed at him by Lynette (Squeaky) Fromme, a Charles Manson follower, in Sacramento.

1975—Sept. 22. Pres. Gerald R. Ford escaped unharmed when Sara Jane Moore, a political activist, fired a revolver at him.

1980—Apr. 14. Indian Prime Minister Indira Gandhi was unharmed when a man threw a knife at her in New Delhi.

1981—Jan. 16. Irish political activist Bernadette Devlin McAlis-

key and her husband were shot and seriously wounded by 3 members of a protestant paramilitary group in Co. Tyrone, Ire.

1981—Mar. 30. Pres. Ronald Reagan, Press Secy. James Brady, Secret Service agent Timothy J. McCarthy, and Washington, D.C. policeman Thomas Delahanty were shot and seriously wounded by John W. Hinckley Jr. in Washington, D.C.

1981—May 13. Pope John Paul II and 2 bystanders were shot and wounded by Mehmet Ali Agca, an escaped Turkish murderer, in St. Peter's Square, Rome.

1982—May 12. Pope John Paul II was unharmed when a man with a knife was overpowered by security guards, in Fatima, Portugal.

1982—June 3. Israel's ambassador to Britain Shlomo Argov was shot and seriously wounded by Arab terrorists in London.

Major Kidnapings

Edward A. Cudahy Jr., 16, in Omaha, Neb., Dec. 18, 1900. Returned Dec. 20 after $25,000 paid. Pat Crowe confessed.

Robert Franks, 13, in Chicago, May 22, 1924, by 2 youths, Richard Loeb and Nathan Leopold, who killed boy. Demand for $10,000 ignored. Loeb died in prison, Leopold paroled 1958.

Charles A. Lindbergh Jr., 20 mos. old, in Hopewell, N.J., Mar. 1, 1932; found dead May 12. Ransom of $50,000 was paid to man identified as Bruno Richard Hauptmann, 35, paroled German convict who entered U.S. illegally. Hauptmann was convicted after spectacular trial at Flemington, and electrocuted at Trenton, N.J., prison, Apr. 3. 1936.

William A. Hamm Jr., 39, in St. Paul, June 15, 1933. $100,000 paid. Alvin Karpis given life, paroled in 1969.

Charles F. Urschel, in Oklahoma City, July 22, 1933. Released July 31 after $200,000 paid. George (Machine Gun) Kelly and 5 others given life.

Brooke L. Hart, 22, in San Jose, Cal. Thomas Thurmond and John Holmes arrested after demanding $40,000 ransom. When Hart's body was found in San Francisco Bay, Nov. 26, 1933, a mob attacked the jail at San Jose and lynched the 2 kidnappers.

George Weyerhaeuser, 9, in Tacoma, Wash., May 24, 1935. Returned home June 1 after $200,000 paid. Kidnappers given 20 to 60 years.

Charles Mattson, 10, in Tacoma, Wash., Dec. 27, 1936. Found dead Jan. 11, 1937. Kidnaper asked $28,000, failed to contact.

Arthur Fried, in White Plains, N.Y., Dec. 4, 1937. Body not found. Two kidnapers executed.

Robert C. Greenlease, 6, taken from school Sept. 28, 1953, and held for $600,000. Body found Oct. 7. Mrs. Bonnie Brown Heady and Carl A. Hall pleaded guilty and were executed.

Peter Weinberger, 32 days old, Westbury, N.Y., July 4, 1956, for $2,000 ransom, not paid. Child found dead. Angelo John LaMarca, 31, convicted, executed.

Cynthia Ruotolo, 6 wks old, taken from carriage in front of Hamden, Conn. store Sept. 1, 1956. Body found in lake.

Lee Crary, 8 in Everett, Wash., Sept. 22, 1957, $10,000 ransom, not paid. He escaped after 3 days, led police to George E. Collins, who was convicted.

Eric Peugeot, 4, taken from playground at St. Cloud golf course, Paris, Apr. 12, 1960. Released unharmed 3 days later after payment of undisclosed sum. Two sentenced to prison.

Frank Sinatra Jr., 19, from hotel room in Lake Tahoe, Cal., Dec. 8, 1963. Released Dec. 11 after his father paid $240,000 ransom. Three men sentenced to prison; most of ransom recovered.

Barbara Jane Mackle, 20, abducted Dec. 17, 1968, from Atlanta, Ga., motel, was found unharmed 3 days later, buried in a coffin-like wooden box 18 inches underground, after her father had paid $500,000 ransom; Gary Steven Krist sentenced to life, Ruth Eisenmann-Schier to 7 years; most of ransom recovered.

Anne Katherine Jenkins, 22, abducted May 10, 1969, from her Baltimore apartment, freed 3 days later after her father paid $10,000 ransom.

Mrs. Roy Fuchs, 35, and 3 children held hostage 2 hours, May 14, 1969, in Long Island, N. Y., released after her husband, a bank manager, paid kidnapers $129,000 in bank funds; 4 men arrested, ransom recovered.

C. Burke Elbrick, U.S. ambassador to Brazil, kidnaped by revolutionaries in Rio de Janeiro Sept. 4, 1969; released 3 days later after Brazil yielded to kidnaper's demands to publish manifesto and release 15 political prisoners.

Patrick Dolan, 18, found shot to death near Sao Paulo, Brazil, Nov. 5, 1969, after he was kidnaped and $12,500 paid.

Sean M. Holly, U.S. diplomat, in Guatemala Mar. 6, 1970; freed 2 days later upon release of 3 terrorists from prison.

Lt. Col. Donald J. Crowley, U.S. air attache, in Dominican Republic Mar. 24, 1970; released after government allowed 20 prisoners to leave the country.

Count Karl von Spreti, W. German ambassador to Guatemala, Mar. 31, 1970; slain after Guatemala refused demands for $700,000 and release of 22 prisoners.

Pedro Eugenio Aramburu, former Argentine president, by terrorists May 29, 1970; body found July 17.

Ehrenfried von Holleben, W. German ambassador to Brazil, by terrorists June 11, 1970; freed after release of 40 prisoners.

Daniel A. Mitrione, U.S. diplomat, July 31, 1970, by terrorists in Montevideo, Uruguay; body found Aug. 10 after government rejected demands for release of all political prisoners.

James R. Cross, British trade commissioner, Oct. 5, 1970, by French Canadian separatists in Quebec; freed Dec. 3 after 3 kidnapers and relatives flown to Cuba by government.

Pierre Laporte, Quebec Labor Minister, by separatists Oct. 10, 1970; body found Oct. 18.

Giovanni E. Bucher, Swiss ambassador Dec. 7, 1970, by revolutionaries in Rio de Janeiro; freed Jan. 16, 1971, after Brazil released 70 political prisoners.

Geoffrey Jackson, British ambassador, in Montevideo, Jan. 8, 1971, by Tupamaro terrorists. Held as ransom for release of imprisoned terrorists; released Sept. 9; prisoners escaped.

Ephraim Elrom, Israel consul general in Istanbul, May 17, 1971. Held as ransom for imprisoned terrorists; found dead May 23.

Mrs. Virginia Piper, 49 abducted July 27, 1972, from her home in suburban Minneapolis; found unharmed near Duluth 2 days later after her husband paid $1 million ransom to the kidnapers.

Victor E. Samuelson, Exxon executive, Dec. 6, 1973, in Campana, Argentina, by Marxist guerrillas, freed Apr. 29, 1974, after payment of record $14.2 million ransom.

J. Paul Getty 3d, 17, grandson of the U.S. oil mogul, released Dec. 15, 1973, in southern Italy after $2.8 million ransom paid.

Patricia (Patty) Hearst, 19, taken from her Berkeley, Cal., apartment Feb. 4, 1974. Symbionese Liberation Army demanded her father, Randolph A. Hearst, publisher, give millions to poor. Hearst offered $2 million in food; the Hearst Corp. offered $4 million worth. Patricia said she had joined SLA; she was identified by FBI as taking part in a San Francisco bank holdup, Apr. 15; she claimed she had been coerced. Again identified by FBI in a store holdup, May 16, she was classified by FBI as "an armed, dangerous fugitive." FBI, Sept. 18, 1975, captured Patricia and others in San Francisco; they were indicted on various charges. Patricia for bank robbery. Convicted, Mar. 20, 1976. She was released from prison under executive clemency, Feb. 1, 1979. In 1978, William and Emily Harris were sentenced to 10 years to life for the Hearst kidnaping. Both were paroled in 1983.

J. Reginald Murphy, 40, an editor of Atlanta (Ga.) Constitution, kidnaped Feb. 20, 1974, freed Feb. 22 after payment of $700,000 ransom by the newspaper. Police arrested William A. H. Williams, a contractor; most of the money was recovered.

J. Guadalupe Zuno Hernandez, 83, father-in-law of Mexican President Luis Echeverria Alvarez, seized by 4 terrorists Aug. 28, 1974; government refused to negotiate; he was released Sept. 8.

E. B. Reville, Hepzibah, Ga., banker, and wife Jean, kidnaped Sept. 30, 1974. Ransom of $30,000 paid. He was found alive; Mrs. Reville was found dead in car trunk Oct. 2.

Jack Teich, Kings Point, N.Y., steel executive, seized Nov. 12, 1974; released Nov. 19 after payment of $750,000.

Hanns-Martin Schleyer, a West German industrialist, was kidnaped in Cologne, Sept. 5, 1977 by armed terrorists. Schleyer was found dead, Oct. 19, in an abandoned car shortly after 3 jailed terrorist leaders of the Baader-Meinhof gang were found dead in their prison cells near Stuttgart, West Germany.

Aldo Moro, former Italian premier, kidnaped in Rome, Mar. 16, 1978, by left-wing terrorists. Five of his bodyguards killed during abduction. Moro's bullet-ridden body was found in a parked car, May 9, in Rome. Six members of the Red Brigades arrested, charged, June 5, with complicity in the kidnaping.

James L. Dozier, a U.S. Army general, kidnapped from his apartment in Verona, Italy, Dec. 17, 1981, by members of the Red Brigades terrorist organization. He was rescued, Jan. 28, 1982.

Enrique Camarena Salazar, and Alfredo Zavala Avelar, U.S. Drug Enforcement Agency employees were kidnapped in Guadalajara, Mexico, Feb. 7, 1985. Their bodies were found Mar. 6.

CANADA

See Index for Calgary, Edmonton, Hamilton, Laval, London, Mississauga, Montreal, North York, Ottawa, Quebec, Regina, Toronto, Vancouver, Windsor, Winnipeg.

Capital: Ottawa. Area: 3,849,670 sq. mi. Population (est., Jan. 1985): 25,262,500. Monetary unit: Canadian dollar.

The Land

The world's second largest country in land size, Canada stretches 3,223 miles from east to west and extends southward from the North Pole to the U.S. border. Its seacoast includes 36,356 miles of mainland and 115,133 miles of islands, including the Arctic islands almost from Greenland to near the Alaskan border.

Canada's continental climate, while generally temperate, varies from freezing winter cold to blistering summer heat - a range beyond 100 degrees Fahrenheit.

Major cities, industrial centres, agricultural regions, and the vast majority of the population are situated along a thin, southern fringe bordering the United States. To the north lie vast expanses of varied, virgin land. The remote north, due to extreme cold, is virtually uninhabitable.

Fragmented by history, geography, and economic factors, the country is as diverse as it is large. Regionally, Canada's 10 provinces can be put into 5 groups: the industrially-poor Atlantic Provinces of New Brunswick, Newfoundland, Nova Scotia, and Prince Edward Island; predominantly French-speaking Quebec; Ontario, financial and governmental heartland of the nation; the Prairies, including Manitoba, Saskatchewan, and oil-rich Alberta; and British Columbia, separated from the rest of the country by the Rocky Mountains.

Despite continuing problems of regional disparity in political, economic, and cultural outlook, Canada has survived as a nation by accepting the need to recognize and tolerate differences. Unlike the U.S., Canada has never been a melting pot, nor has it strived to become one.

History

French explorer Jacques Cartier, who discovered the Gulf of St. Lawrence in 1534, is generally regarded as the founder of Canada. But English seaman John Cabot sighted Newfoundland 37 years earlier, in 1497, and Vikings are believed to have reached the Atlantic coast centuries before either explorer.

Canadian settlement was pioneered by the French who established Quebec City (1608) and Montreal (1642) and declared New France a colony in 1663.

Britain, as part of its American expansion, acquired Acadia (later Nova Scotia) in 1717 and, through military victory over French forces in Canada (an extension of a European conflict between the 2 powers), captured Quebec (1759) and obtained control of the rest of New France in 1763. The French, through the Quebec Act of 1774, retained the rights to their own language, religion, and civil law.

The British presence in Canada increased during the American Revolution when many colonials, proudly calling themselves United Empire Loyalists, moved north to Canada.

Fur traders and explorers led Canadians westward across the continent. Sir Alexander Mackenzie reached the Pacific in 1793 and scrawled on a rock by the ocean, "from Canada by land."

In Upper and Lower Canada (later called Ontario and Quebec) and in the Maritimes, legislative assemblies appeared in the 18th century and reformers called for responsible government. But the War of 1812 intervened. The war, a conflict between Great Britain and the United States fought mainly in Upper Canada, ended in a stalemate in 1814.

In 1837 political agitation for more democratic government culminated in rebellions in Upper and Lower Canada. Britain sent Lord Durham to investigate and, in a famous report (1839), he recommended union of the 2 parts into one colony called Canada. The union lasted until Confederation, July 1, 1867, when proclamation of the British North America (BNA) Act launched the Dominion of Canada, consisting of Ontario, Quebec, and the former colonies of Nova Scotia and New Brunswick.

Since 1840 the Canadian colonies had held the right to internal self-government. The BNA act, which became the country's written constitution, established a federal system of government on the model of a British parliament and cabinet structure under the crown. Canada was proclaimed a self-governing Dominion within the British Empire in 1931. Empire has given way to Commonwealth, of which Canada is an independent member.

In 1982 Canada severed its last formal legislative link with Britain by obtaining the right to amend its constitution (the British North America Act of 1867). The new Constitution Act, 1982 includes a formula allowing the federal Parliament to make constitutional changes with the support of 7 provinces representing at least 50% of the Canadian population.

The Government

Canada is a constitutional monarchy with a parliamentary system of government. It is also a federal state. Official head of state remains England's Queen Elizabeth, represented by a resident governor-general. But in practice the nation is governed by the Prime Minister, leader of the party able to command the support of a majority of members of the House of Commons, dominant chamber of Canada's bicameral Parliament.

The Commons' 282 members are elected at least every 5 years - sooner if the Prime Minister so chooses or if the government is defeated in Parliament. This can occur either through passage of a motion of nonconfidence in the government or by defeat of a major piece of government legislation.

The upper house of Canada's Parliament is the Senate, comprised of 104 members traditionally appointed by party patronage and serving to age 75.

Legislation becomes law by receiving 3 "readings" in the Commons, passing in the Senate and obtaining assent from the governor-general. The latter 2 steps are, in practice, mere formality.

The Prime Minister heads the executive branch of government composed of the cabinet and governor-general. The cabinet is chosen by the Prime Minister, almost always from among members of his party holding seats in the House of Commons.

Provincial governments follow a modified version of the Ottawa pattern, with a unicameral legislature and an executive head usually referred to as the Premier.

Politics

Major changes occurred at the provincial political level in 1985 with the retirement of 3 prominent leaders. Premiers Bill Davis of Ontario, Peter Lougheed of Alberta and Rene Levesque of Quebec had shaped Canadian politics, both provincially and nationally, for more than a decade.

Following Davis' retirement, his Progressive Conservatives were ousted from power in Ontario after 42 years of rule. A Liberal minority govt., under David Peterson, was formed after a May 1985, election in which the Liberals obtained slightly fewer seats than the Conservatives but were able to form the govt. with support from the Ontario New Democratic Party. In Alberta, Lougheed, who had cham-

pioned the rights of the powerful western province, stepped down after 14 years as premier during which he led his provincial Progressive Conservatives to several landslide victories; a successor was to be chosen late in 1985.

Levesque's departure after 9 years as Quebec premier followed the fragmentation of his Parti Quebecois (PQ) over the issue of whether the PQ should make Quebec's separation from Canada a major issue in the upcoming provincial election. Levesque, who led the PQ to power in 1976 and 1981 but failed to gain support to negotiate a form of separation from Canada in a 1980 provisional referendum, did not want to make separation an election issue. He was supported by a majority of his party but opposed by PQ hardliners, some of whom left the party. Levesque's successor was to be chosen in the fall of 1985; a provincial election must be held by early 1986.

Nationally, the Progressive Conservative govt. of Prime Minister Brian Mulroney began a cautious shift to the right, announcing plans to lower the federal deficit and reduce govt. intervention in the economy. This followed Mulroney's landslide victory in the Sept. 1984 federal election in which his Conservatives won over 50% of the vote and 211 of 282 seats in the House of Commons. The Liberals, who had governed for more than 19 of the previous 20 years, obtained only 28% of the vote and 40 seats.

Underscoring the Conservative victory was the party's ability to obtain strong support in all areas of the country. Federal elections in 1979 and 1980 had been marked by regional political fragmentation, with voting split along geographic and linguistic lines. Mulroney, the first Conservative leader from Quebec in 90 years, captured 58 of 75 seats in the predominantly french-speaking province, traditionally a Liberal stronghold. In 1980 the Conservatives had held only one seat in Quebec while the Liberals won 74 seats there but only 2 in western Canada.

Federal-provincial conflicts have been less pronounced in recent years following the Nov. 1981 constitutional agreement reached between Ottawa and 9 (all except Quebec) of the 10 provinces. But the constitutional accord further isolated Quebec's separatist Parti Quebecois (PQ) government which viewed it as a challenge to the province's legislative autonomy, particularly regarding minority language rights—an area in which the new constitution's Charter of Rights is in conflict with Quebec's own language legislation. The PQ was re-elected by a wide margin in April 1981, when it chose not to make separation from Canada a major issue. But the party, which has until early 1986 to call the next provincial election, has said it will base its next campaign on separation.

The Economy

The Canadian economy continued its recovery throughout 1984 and early 1985. Real (after inflation) growth in the Gross Domestic Product (the value of all goods and services produced in the country and considered the best measure of economic performance) was 5% in 1984, the highest in 8 years. Only 2 years earlier, real GNP had fallen by 4.4%, the worst decline since the Depression.

The rate of inflation as measured by the Consumer Price Index fell in 1984 to 4.4%, lowest in more than a decade; during the first half of 1985 inflation was running slightly below 4%. Interest rates also declined despite upward pressure caused by the declining value of Canadian currency relative to the American dollar. The Canadian dollar hit an all-time low of approximately .71 U.S. in Feb. 1985, but had risen to the .74 level by mid summer. Normally, a fallen Canadian dollar fuels inflation by increasing Canadian costs for imported American products; more than 2/3 of all Canadian imports are from the U.S. The devalued dollar also puts pressure on the federal govt. to try to protect the value of Canadian currency by allowing interest rates to rise.

Unemployment remained high, despite a slight improvement, during 1984 and the first half of 1985. The annual 1984 rate was 11.3%, down from 11.9% in 1983 and a post-Depression high of 12.8% in Dec. 1982.

Principal Canadian industries are motor vehicle manufacturing, petroleum refining, pulp and paper production, slaughtering and meat processing, iron and steel production, the manufacture of miscellaneous machinery and equipment, saw and planing mill industries, and smelting and refining.

In Canada, an historical tradition of state aid necessitated by a harsh climate and sparse population has fostered development of a mixed economic system in which publicly-owned corporations exist alongside—and sometimes compete with—private enterprise. Most hydroelectric and many transportation and communication enterprises are government-owned. Air Canada and the Canadian National Railways, both large federal Crown corporations, compete with the privately-owned Canadian Pacific Ltd., whose 1984 operating revenue was the 2d largest of any company in Canada.

Foreign Policy

Canada's chief foreign ally and trading partner remains the United States with whom she shares a broad range of mutually beneficial ties. More than two thirds of all 1984 Canadian exports went to the U.S.; the U.S., in turn, sells almost twice as much to Canada as to its next largest trading partner, Japan.

Plans for even closer ties between the 2 nations, especially in the area of trade, were announced by Canadian Prime Minister Brian Mulroney soon after the Sept. 1984 election of his Progressive Conservative govt. Mulroney warned against "protectionist" trade barrier policies by either govt. and urged greater "trade liberalization." Mulroney also announced that Canada would encourage foreign investment by dismantling the National Energy Program and the Foreign Investment Review Agency. Both of these, established under the previous Liberal govt. of Pierre Trudeau, had sought to reduce foreign dominance of Canada's economy, especially in the energy industry; U.S. politicians had claimed these policies discriminated against American firms in Canada.

Efforts to strengthen U.S.-Canada relations were highlighted during a March 1985 visit to Canada by President Ronald Reagan during which Mulroney announced Canada's support for Reagan's Strategic Defence Initiative ("Star Wars") proposal. The 2 nations also agreed to a new northern air defence radar system; most (88%) of the $7 billion cost is to be paid by the U.S.

Canada and the U.S. have, since 1958, provided for joint air defence of the continent through the North American Aerospace Defence Command (NORAD) and are founding members of the North Atlantic Treaty Organization (NATO). Canada's NATO committment is based on the premise that by contributing to the direct defence of Europe, Canada is also contributing to its own defence. While continuing to advocate joint East-West nuclear arms reduction, Canada has supported NATO's policy of matching the Soviet arms buildup in Europe if reductions can't be negotiated. Canada has given the U.S. permission to test unarmed cruise missiles over northern Alberta, British Columbia and the Northwest Territories.

In 1985, the Canadian govt. announced a public review of foreign policy, to be completed in 1986. A preliminary discussion paper advocated increased defence spending, reduced foreign aid, renewed international trading competition, and closer ties with the U.S.

In July 1985, Canada announced trade sanctions against South Africa in a bid to force that govt. to abandon its apartheid racial segregation policy. External Affairs Minister Joe Clark said the move, which includes an embargo on imports of South African arms to Canada and a public monitoring of the employment practices of Canadian firms operating in South Africa, was a "first step" towards pressuring for change in South African policy.

Canada's Native Peoples

Canada's native population consists of 3 groups, the Indian, Inuit (Eskimo), and Métis. The Indian and Inuit are thought to have crossed from Asia via the Bering Sea several thousand years before the arrival of Europeans in North America. Metis are of mixed native Indian and non-Indian ancestry.

There are approximately 348,800 "status" Indians - those registered under the federal Indian Act - most of whom belong to one of the 592 Indian bands. About 70% live on one of the 2,256 federal reserves or on other government lands set aside for their use. The majority (82%) live in Ontario and the 4 western provinces. In addition, there are an estimated one million non-registered Indians and Metis.

The number of Inuit (meaning "the people" in their language, Inuktitut; Eskimo is an Indian word adopted by European settlers) in Canada is approximately 28,000. More than 60% live in the Northwest Territories, the remainder in Arctic Quebec and northern Labrador.

Due to the remoteness of their settlements close to the northern coasts where sea mammals provided the chief source of food, fuel and clothing, the Inuit lifestyle was affected later and less directly than that of the Indian by the encroachment of western civilization. Many Inuit still live by their traditional skills of hunting, trapping and fishing as well as through the production and sale of artwork. But increasing numbers now find work outside their communities, particularly since the search for oil, gas and minerals has brought more jobs to the north.

Both Inuit and status Indians are entitled to a broad range of government benefits administered through the federal Dept. of Indian Affairs and Northern Development as well as through provincial and territorial governments. Indian people living on reserves are eligible for direct federal assistance in such areas as education, housing, social services, and community development.

In addition, approximately half the registered Indians in Canada (mainly those living in Ontario and the 3 Prairie provinces) are in areas covered by treaties that granted reserves of land to their ancestors during the late 19th and early 20th centuries. In remote and less-settled areas, however, no such claims were made, and now Indian and Inuit groups are negotiating land claims in British Columbia, the Yukon and Northwest Territories, Quebec and Labrador.

In 1982 the federal government re-affirmed a 1973 commitment to settle both comprehensive (based on aboriginal rights) and specific (based on treaties or the Indian Act) claims. A 1975 agreement settled the claims of the Inuit and Cree of northern Quebec; in 1978 this settlement was extended to include the Naskapis of Schefferville. In June 1984, the government signed a final agreement with the Committee for Original Peoples' Entitlement, representing the Inuit of the western Arctic (the Inuvialiut). In 1984 an agreement in principle was also reached with the Council for Yukon Indians.

Inuit cultural and legal interests are represented by district Inuit associations and nationally by the Inuit Tapirisat, founded in 1971. The interests of status Indians are represented by provincial Indian associations and, at the national level, by the Assembly of First Nations. The Métis and non-status Indians are represented by the Native Council of Canada.

Provinces of Canada

Alberta

People. Population (Jan. 1985): 2,337,500; **rank:** 4. **Pop. density:** 9.4 per sq. mi. **Urban** (1981) 77%. **Ethnic distrib.** (1981): English 81%; German 4.1%; Ukrainian 3%; French 2.8%. **Net interprovincial migration** (1983-84): −42,784.

Geography: Total area: 255,290 sq. mi.; **rank:** 4. **Land area:** 248,800 sq. mi. **Forested land:** 134,714 sq. mi. **Location:** Canada's 2d most westerly province, bounded to the W by British Columbia, to the E by Saskatchewan, to the N by the Northwest Territories, and to the S by Montana. **Climate:** great variance in temperatures between regions and seasons; summer highs can range between 16°C and 32°C; winter temperatures can drop as low as −45°C; mean Jan. temperature in Edmonton is −14°C. **Topography:** ranges from the Rocky Mountains in the SW to flat prairie in the SE; the far north is a wilderness of forest and muskeg.

Economy. Principal industries: mining, oil production, agriculture, manufacturing, construction. **Principal manufactured goods:** foods and beverages, wood products, fabricated metal, transportation equipment, refined petroleum. **GDP, manufacturing** (1982): $3.1 billion. **Gross Domestic Product** (1983): $56.5 billion. **Agriculture: Chief crops:** wheat, barley, rapeseed, sugar beets, flaxseed. **Livestock** (1983): 3,485,000 cattle; 1,185,000 pigs; 134,000 sheep. **GDP, forestry** (1982): $48.2 million. **Mineral production** (1983): total value, $24.1 billion; fuels, $23.8 billion (85% of national production of petroleum, 93% of natural gas); structural materials, $279 million. **GDP, fishing** (1982): $.6 million. **GDP, construction** (1982): $4.4 billion. **Employment distribution** (1983): 31% services; 18% trade; 8% construction; 8% manufacturing; 7% agriculture; 7% public administration. **Per capita income** (1983): $14,652. **Unemployment** (1984): 11.2%.

Finance. No. banks: 813; **No. credit unions, caisses populaires:** 285.

International airports: Edmonton, Calgary.

Federal government: No. federal employees (Dec. 1984): 31,521; **Federal payroll** (1984): $814.1 million.

Energy. Electricity production, by mwh, (1984): mineral, 28,059,999; hydroelectric, 1,427,137.

Education. No schools: 1,449 elementary; 177 secondary; 23 higher education. **Avg. salary, public school teachers** (1983-84): N.A.

Provincial data. Motto: none. **Flower:** The Wild Rose. **Bird:** Great horned owl. **Date entered Confederation:** 1905. **Capital:** Edmonton.

Politics. Premier: Peter Lougheed (Progressive Conservative). **Leaders, opposition parties:** Ray Martin (New Democratic). **Composition of legislature** (June, 1985): PC 75; NDP 2; 2 independent. **Date of last general election:** Nov. 2, 1982.

Tourist attractions: Banff, Jasper, and Waterton Lakes, Elk Island and Wood Buffalo national parks; resorts at Banff, Jasper and Lake Louise; spectacular skiing, hiking, trail riding and camping in the Canadian Rockies; Dinosaur Park in Drumheller.

British Columbia

People. Population (Jan. 1985): 2,883,000; **rank:** 3. **Pop. density:** 8 per sq. mi. **Urban** (1981) 78%. **Ethnic distrib.** (1981): English 82%; German 3.4%; Chinese 2.8%; French 1.7%. **Net interprovincial migration** (1983-84): +13,125.

Geography. Total area: 365,950 sq. mi.; **rank:** 3. **Land area:** 358,970 sq. mi. **Forested land:** 244,338 sq. mi. **Location:** bounded to the N by the Yukon and Northwest Territories, to the NW by the Alaskan panhandle, to the W by the Pacific Ocean, to the E by Alberta, and to the S by Washington, Idaho and Montana. **Climate:** maritime with mild termperatures and abundant rainfall in the coastal areas; continental climate with temperature extremes in the interior and northeast. **Topography:** mostly mountainous except for the NE corner which is an extension of the Great Plains.

Economy. Principal industries: forestry, mining, tourism, agriculture, fishing, manufacturing. **Principal manufactured goods:** wood products, paper and allied products, food and beverages, petroleum and coal products, primary metals, transportation equipment. **GDP, manufacturing** (1982): $5 billion. **Gross Domestic Product** (1983): $47,238 billion. **Agriculture: Chief crops:** fruits and vegetables, barley, oats. **Livestock** (1983): 658,000 cattle; 250,000 pigs; 40,000 sheep. **GDP, forestry** (1982): $915 million. **Mineral production** (1983): $2.9 billion; fuels, $1.4 billion; metals, $1.2 billion; structural materials, $221 million. **GDP, fishing** (1982): $166.7 million. **GDP, construction** (1982): $2.6 billion. **Employment distribution** (1983): 33% services; 18% trade; 13% manufacturing; 7% public administration; 6% construction; 2.8% agriculture. **Per capita income** (1984): $14,339. **Unemployment** (1984): 14.7%.

Finance: No. banks: 846; **No. credit unions, caisses populaires:** 314.

International airports: Vancouver, Victoria.

Federal government: No. federal employees (Dec. 1984): 44,500. **Federal payroll** (1984): $814.1 million.

Energy. Electricity production, by mwh, (1984): hydroelectric, 50,243,139; mineral 1,938,847.

Education. No. schools: 1,567 elementary; 335 secondary; 27 higher education. **Avg. salary, public school teachers** (1983-84): $34,214.

Provincial data. Motto: Splendor Sine Occasu (Spendor Without Diminishment). **Flower:** Dogwood. **Bird:** None. **Date entered Confederation:** 1871. **Capital:** Victoria.

Politics. Premier: William R. Bennett (Social Credit). **Leaders, opposition parties:** Bob Skelly (New Democratic), Arthur Lee (Liberal), Peter Pollen (Progressive Conservative), Graham Lea (United). **Composition of legislature** (June, 1985): SC 34; NDP 22; 1 United. **Date of last general election:** May 5, 1983.

Tourist attractions. Victoria: Butchart Gardens, Crystal Garden, Provincial Museum; Vancouver: Stanley Park Zoo, Capilano Canyon, Gastown, Public Aquarium, Grouse Mountain, Planetarium; also National Parks, the Gulf Islands, Okanagan Valley, Totem Triangle Tour, fishing, skiing.

Manitoba

People. Population (Jan. 1985): 1,065,000; **rank:** 5. **Pop. density:** 5 per sq. mi. **Urban** (1981) 71.2%. **Ethnic distrib.** (1981): English 71.7%; German 7.3%; Ukrainian 5.7%; French 5.1%; Native Indians 2.5%. **Net interprovincial migration** (1983-84): −708.

Geography. Total area: 250,950 sq. mi.; **rank:** 6. **Land area:** 211,720 sq. mi. **Forested land:** 134,714 sq. mi. **Location:** bounded to the N by the Northwest Territories, to the S by Minnesota and North Dakota, to the E by Ontario and Hudson Bay, to the W by Saskatchewan. **Climate:** continental, with seasonal extremes: Winnipeg avg. Jan. low −23°C, avg. July high 26°C. **Topography:** the land rises gradually S and W from Hudson Bay; most of the province is between 500 and 1,000 feet above sea level.

Economy. Principal industries: manufacturing, agriculture, slaughtering and meat processing, mining. **Principal manufactured goods:** agricultural implements, processed food, machinery, transportation equipment, clothing. **GDP, manufacturing** (1982): $1.6 billion. **Gross Domestic Product** (1983): $15 billion. **Agriculture: Chief crops:** cereal grains, mustard seed, sunflower seeds, rape, flax. **Livestock** (1983): 955,000 cattle; 900,000 pigs; 24,500 sheep; **GDP, forestry** (1982): $15.8 million. **Mineral production** (1983): total value, $733 million; metals, $487 million; structural materials, $72 million; petroleum, $153 million. **GDP, fishing:** (1982): $11 million. **GDP, construction** (1982): $428.7 million. **Employment distribution** (1983): 31% services; 18% trade; 13% manufacturing; 9% agriculture; 8% public administration; 4% construction. **Per capita income** (1983): $12,603. **Unemployment** (1984): 8.3%.

Finance: No. banks: 345; **No. credit unions, caisses populaires:** 192.

International airports: Winnipeg.

Federal Government: No. federal employees (Dec. 1984): 20,343. **Federal payroll** (1984): $542.8 million.

Energy. Electricity production, by mwh, (1984): mineral, 200,238; hydroelectric, 21,226,145.

Education. No. schools: 723 elementary; 113 secondary; 12 higher education. **Avg. salary, public school teachers** (1983-84): $33,148.

Provincial data. Motto: None. **Flower:** Prairie crocus. **Bird:** none. **Date entered Confederation:** July 15, 1870. **Capital:** Winnipeg.

Politics. Premier: Howard Pawley (New Democratic). **Leaders, opposition parties:** Gary Filmon (Progressive Conservative). **Composition of legislature:** (June, 1985): NDP 31; PC 23; 2 independent; 1 vacant. **Date of last general election:** Nov. 17, 1981.

Tourist attractions. Museum of Man and Nature (Winnipeg), Lower Fort Garry (near Lockport), Red River cruises, Riding Mountain National Park, canoeing, fishing and camping on northern lakes.

New Brunswick

People. Population (Jan. 1985): 717,200; **rank:** 8. **Pop. density:** 25.8 per sq. mi. **Urban** (1981) 51.1%. **Ethnic distrib.** (1981): English 65%; French 33.6%. **Net interprovincial migration** (1983-84): +1,387.

Geography. Total area: 28,360 sq. mi.; **rank:** 8. **Land area:** 27,840 sq. mi. **Forested land:** 25,090 sq. mi. **Location:** bounded by Quebec to the N, Nova Scotia and the Bay of Fundy to the S, the Gulf of St. Lawrence and Northumberland Strait to the E, and Maine to the W. **Climate:** humid continental climate except along the shores where there is a marked maritime effect; avg. Jan. low in Fredericton is −14°C, avg. July high 22°C. **Topography:** upland, lowland and plateau regions throughout the province.

Economy. Principal industries: manufacturing, fishing, mining, forestry, pulp and paper. **Principal manufactured goods:** paper and allied products, wood products, fish products, semi-processed mineral products. **GDP, manufacturing** (1982): $850.9 million. **Gross Domestic Product** (1983): $7.3 billion. **Agriculture: Chief crops:** potatoes, apples, blueberries, oats. **Livestock** (1983): 102,000 cattle; 125,000 pigs; 8,300 sheep. **GDP, forestry** (1982): $94.3 million. **Mineral production** (1983): total value, $506 million; metals, $421 million; structural materials, $38 million; coal, $30 million. **GDP, fishing** (1982): $46.7 million. **GDP, construction** (1982): $348.5 million. **Employment distribution** (1983): 32% services; 19% trade; 13% manufacturing; 9% public administration; 6% construction; 2.8% agriculture. **Per capita income** (1983): $10,040. **Unemployment** (1984): 14.9%.

Finance: No. banks: 179; **No. credit unions, caisses populaires:** 130.

International airports: none.

Federal Government: No. federal employees (Dec. 1984): 14,617. **Federal payroll** (1984): $382.1 million.

Energy. Electricity production, by mwh, (1984): mineral, 4,126,983; hydroelectric, 3,093,106; nuclear, 5,011,393.

Education. No. schools: 409 elementary; 66 secondary; 13 higher education. **Avg. salary, public school teachers** (1983-84): $30,132.

Provincial Data. Motto: Spem Reduxit (Hope Restored). **Flower:** Purple violet. **Bird:** none. **Date entered Confederation:** 1867. **Capital:** Fredericton.

Politics. Premier: Richard Hatfield (Progressive Conservative). **Leaders, opposition parties:** Frank McKenna (Liberal). **Composition of legislature** (June, 1985): P.C. 38; Lib. 18; NDP 2. **Date of last general election:** Oct. 12, 1982.

Tourist attractions: Roosevelt-Campobello International Memorial Park; the tidal bore (Moncton); Magnetic Hill (Moncton); sport salmon fishing in the Miramichi River; world's longest covered bridge at Hartland; Fundy and Kouchibouguac national parks.

Newfoundland

People. Population (Jan. 1985): 578,900; **rank:** 9. **Pop. density:** 4 per sq. mi. **Urban** (1981) 58.6%. **Ethnic distrib.** (1981): English 98.7%. **Net interprovincial migration** (1983-84): −2,444.

Geography. Total area: 156,650 sq. mi.; **rank:** 7. **Land area:** 143,510 sq. mi. **Forested land:** 54,812 sq. mi. **Location:** 2 parts: a 43,010 sq. mi. Atlantic island and 100,500 sq. mi. mainland Labrador, bordered to the W by northern Quebec and to the E by the Atlantic Ocean. **Climate:** ranges from subarctic in Labrador and northern tip of island to humid continental with cool summers and heavy precipitation. **Topography:** highlands of the Long Range (max. elev. 2,673 ft.) along the western coast; central plateau contains uplands descending to lowlands towards the northeast; interior barren and rocky with many lakes and bogs; Labrador is part of the Canadian Shield.

Economy. Principal industries: mining, manufacturing, fishing, pulp and paper, electricity production. **Principal manufactured goods:** fish products, paper products. **GDP, manufacturing** (1982): $483.5 million. **Gross Domestic Product** (1983): $5.4 billion. **Agriculture: GDP, forestry** (1982): $55.4 million. **Livestock** (1983) 6,400 cattle; 23,000 pigs; 4,000 sheep. **Mineral production** (1983): total value, $752 million; metals, $807 million; asbestos, $7 million; structural materials, $31 million. **GDP, fishing:** (1982) $332 million. **GDP, construction** (1982): $122.1 million. **Employment distribution** (1983): 30% services; 18% trade; 13% manufacturing; 10% public administration; 6% construction. **Per capita income** (1983): $9,179. **Unemployment** (1984): 20.5%.

Finance: No. banks: 139; **no. credit unions, caisses populaires:** 20.

International airports: Gander.

Federal Government: No. federal employees (Dec. 1984): 9,738. **Federal payroll** (1984): $246.5 million.

Energy. Electricity production, by mwh, (1984): mineral, 783,230; hydroelectric, 44,753,460.

Education. No. schools: 509 elementary; 135 secondary; 7 higher education. **Avg. salary, public school teachers** (1983-84): $29,367.

Provincial data. Motto: Quaerite prime regnum Dei (Seek ye first the kingdom of God). **Flower:** Pitcher plant. **Bird:** none. **Date entered Confederation:** 1949. **Capital:** St. John's.

Politics. Premier: Brian Peckford (Progressive Conservative). **Leaders, opposition parties:** Leo Barry, (Liberal) Peter Fenwick, (New Democratic). **Composition of legislature** (June, 1985): PC 36; Lib. 15; NDP 1. **Date of last general election:** April 2, 1985.

Tourist attractions: numerous picturesque "outport" fishing villages; Signal Hill National Historical Park (St. John's); the Aviation Museum at Gander International Airport; Witless Bay Island Seabird Sanctuary.

Nova Scotia

People. Population (Jan. 1985): 878,300; **rank:** 7. **Pop. density:** 43.1 per sq. mi. **Urban** (1981) 55.19. **Ethnic distrib.** (1981): English 93.6%; French 4.3%. **Net interprovincial migration** (1983-84): +4,668.

Geography. Total area: 21,420 sq. mi.; **rank:** 9. **Land area:** 20,400 sq. mi. **Forested land:** 15,826 sq. mi. **Location:** connected to New Brunswick by a 17-mi. isthmus, otherwise surrounded by water - the Gulf of St. Lawrence, Atlantic Ocean and Bay of Fundy. **Climate:** humid continental, with some moderating effects due to the province's maritime location; avg. July temperature high in Halifax is 23°C, avg. Jan. low −10°C. **Topography:** the Atlantic Uplands in the southern half of the province descend to lowlands in the northern portion; 6,479 mi. of coastline, 3,000 lakes, hundreds of rivers.

Economy. Principal industries: manufacturing, fishing, mining, tourism, agriculture, forestry. **Principal manufactured goods:** paper and allied products, petroleum and coal products, fish products, automobiles and parts. **GDP, manufacturing** (1982): $1.0 billion. **Gross Domestic Product** (1983): $9.4 billion. **Agriculture: Chief crops:**

apples, blueberrries, strawberries, oats, potatoes. **Livestock** (1983): 133,000 cattle; 140,000 pigs; 29,000 sheep. **GDP, Forestry** (1982): $29.5 million. **Mineral production** (1983): total value, $260 million; coal, $146 million; structural materials, $47 million; gypsum, $37 million. **GDP, fishing** (1982): $180.3 million. **GDP, construction** (1982): $438.1 million. **Employment distribution** (1983): 33% services; 18% trade; 13% manufacturing; 10% public administration; 6% construction; 1.9% agriculture. **Per capita income** (1983): $10,889. **Unemployment** (1984): 13.1%.

Finance: No. banks: 243; **No. credit unions, caisses populaires:** 120.

International airports: Halifax.

Federal Government: No. federal employees (Dec. 1984): 35,068. **Federal payroll** (1984): $920 million.

Energy. Electricity production, by mwh, (1984): mineral, 6,190,962; hydroelectric, 1,031,021.

Education. No. schools: 524 elementary; 78 secondary; 23 higher education. **Avg. salary, public school teachers** (1983-84): $32,913.

Provincial Data. Motto: Munit Haec et Altera Vincit (One Defends and the Other Conquers). **Flower:** Trailing arbutus. **Bird:** None. **Date entered Confederation:** 1867. **Capital:** Halifax.

Politics. Premier: John M. Buchanan (Progressive conservative). **Leaders, opposition parties:** Vincent J. MacLean (Liberal); Alexa McDonough (New Democratic Party); Paul MacEwan (Cape Breton Labour Party). **Composition of legislature** (June, 1985): P.C. 42; Lib. 6; NDP 1; C.B. Labour Party 1. **Date of last general election:** Nov. 6, 1984.

Tourist attractions: Cabot Trail around Cape Breton Island; Fortress Louisbourg; Peggy's Cove; Alexander Graham Bell Museum (Baddeck); the Miners' Museum (Glace Bay); Nova Scotia Museum (Halifax); Citadel Hill (Halifax).

Ontario

People. Population (Jan. 1985); 9,023,900; **rank:** 1. **Pop. density:** 26.2 per sq. mi. **Urban** (1981) 81.7% **Ethnic distrib.** (1981): English 77.4%; French 5.5%; Italian 3.9%; German 2%; Portuguese 1.3%. **Net interprovincial migration** (1983-84): +42,078.

Geography. Total area: 412,580 sq. mi.; **rank:** 2. **Land area:** 344,090 sq. mi. **Forested land:** 311,502 sq. mi. **Location:** Canada's most centrally-situated province, with Quebec on the E and Manitoba to the W; extends N to shores of James and Hudson Bays; southern boundary with New York, Michigan, Minnesota, and 4 Great Lakes. **Climate:** ranges from humid continental in southern regions to subarctic in the far north, westerly winds bring winter storms; the Great Lakes moderate winter temperatures. **Topography:** 2/3 of province is Precambrian rock of the Canadian Shield; lowland areas lie along the shores of Hudson Bay, the St. Lawrence River and the southern Great Lakes region.

Economy. Principal industries: manufacturing, construction, tourism, agriculture, mining, forestry, fisheries and wildlife. **Principal manufactured goods:** motor vehicles, iron and steel, motor vehicle parts and accessories, foods and beverages, paper and allied products. **GDP, manufacturing** (1982): $30.4 billion. **Gross Domestic Product** (1983): $151.6 billion. **Agriculture: Chief crops:** corn, wheat, oats, barley, soybeans, tobacco, tree fruits. **Livestock** (1983): 2,730,000 cattle; 3,400,000 pigs; 175,000 sheep. **GDP, forestry** (1982): $319.6 million. **Mineral production** (1983): total value, $3.7 billion; metals, $2.7 billion; structural materials, $682 million. **GDP, fishing** (1982): $25.6 million. **GDP, construction** (1982): $4.6 billion. **Employment distribution** (1983): 31% services; 23% manufacturing; 17% trade; 7% public administration; 5% construction; 3.3% agriculture. **Per capita income:** (1983): $14,784. **Unemployment** (1984): 9.1%.

Finance: No. banks: 2,777; **No. credit unions, caisses populaires:** 980

International airports: Pearson (at Toronto), Ottawa.

Federal Government: No. federal employees (Dec. 1984): 173,623 **Federal payroll** (1984): $5 billion.

Energy. Electricity production, by mwh, (1984): mineral, 38,115,625; hydroelectric, 40,835,902; nuclear, 40,821,228.

Education. No. schools: 4,684 elementary; 847 secondary; 52 higher education. **Avg. salary, public school teachers** (1983-84): $34,521.

Provincial data. Motto: Ut Incepit Fidelis Sic Permanet (Loyal she began, loyal she remains). **Flower:** White trillium. **Bird:** none. **Date entered Confederation:** 1867. **Capital:** Toronto.

Politics. Premier: David Peterson (Liberal). **Leaders, opposition parties:** Frank Miller (Progressive Conservative); Bob Rae (New Democratic). **Composition of legislature** (June, 1985): PC 52; Lib. 48; NDP 25. **Date of last general election:** May 2, 1985.

Tourist attractions. Toronto C.N. Tower, Ontario Science Centre, Ontario Place, Metro Toronto Zoo, McLaughlin Planetarium, Black Creek Pioneer Village, Canadian Nation Exhibition (mid Aug. to Labor Day); Ottawa's Parliament buildings; Niagara Falls; Polar Bear Express and Agawa Canyon train rides into northern Ontario.

Prince Edward Island

People. Population (Jan. 1985): 126,800; **rank:** 10. **Pop. density:** 58.2 per sq. mi. **Urban** (1981) 36.3% **Ethnic distrib.** (1981): English 93.9%; French 5%. **Net interprovincial migration** (1983-84): +484.

Geography. Total area: 2,180 sq. mi.; **rank:** 10. **Land area:** 2,180 sq. mi. **Forested land:** 1,158 sq. mi. **Location:** an island 140 mi. long, between 40 and 140 mi. wide, situated in the Gulf of St. Lawrence approx. 10 mi. from the coasts of Nova Scotia and New Brunswick. **Climate:** humid continental with temperatures moderated by maritime location; avg. Jan. low in Charlottetown is −11°C, avg. July high 23°C. **Topography:** gently rolling hills; sharply indented coastline; many streams but only small rivers and lakes.

Economy. Principal industries: agriculture, tourism, fisheries, light manufacturing. **Principal manufactured goods:** paint, farm vehicles, metal products, electronic equipment. **GDP, manufacturing** (1982): $63 million. **Gross Domestic Product** (1983): $1.2 billion. **Agriculture: Chief crops:** potatoes, mixed grains, oats, barley. **Livestock** (1983): 99,000 cattle; 109,000 pigs; 5,000 sheep. **Mineral production** (1983): total value, $726,000, all from sand and gravel. **GDP, fishing:** (1982): $25 million. **GDP, construction** (1982): $47.4 million. **Employment distribution** (1983): 33% services; 17% trade; 10% agriculture; 8% manufacturing; 10% public administration. **Per capita income** (1983): $10,056. **Unemployment** (1984): 12.8%.

Finance: No. banks: 30; **No. credit unions, caisses populaires:** 11.

International airports: none.

Federal Government: No. federal employees (Dec. 1984): 3,593. **Federal payroll:** (1984): $93.7 million.

Energy. Electricity production, by mwh, (1984): mineral, 1,428.

Education. No. schools: 59 elementary; 13 secondary; 3 higher education. **Avg. salary, public school teachers** (1983-84): $28,570.

Provincial Data. Motto: Parva Sub Ingenti (The small under the protection of the large). **Flower:** Lady's slipper. **Bird:** Blue jay. **Date entered Confederation:** 1873. **Capital:** Charlottetown.

Politics. Premier: James M. Lee (Progressive Conservative). **Leaders, opposition parties:** Joe Ghiz (Liberal), Jim Mayne (New Democratic). **Composition of legislature** (June, 1985): P.C. 20; Lib. 12. **Date of last general election:** Sept. 27, 1982.

Tourist attractions. P.E.I. National Park; beaches all along the coastline; 9 golf courses; 70 campgrounds; Summerside Lobster Carnival, 3d wk. in July; Charlottetown Old Home Week, 3d wk. in Aug.; Charlottetown Confederation Centre; Woodleigh Replicas (Burlington).

Quebec

People. Population (Jan. 1985): 6,562,200; **rank:** 2. **Pop. density:** 12.5 per sq. mi. **Urban** (1981) 77.6%. **Ethnic distrib.** (1981): French 82.4%; English 11%; Italian 2%. **Net interprovincial migration** (1983-84): −19,077. **Geography. Total area:** 594,860 sq. mi.; **rank:** 1. **Land area:** 523,860 sq. mi. **Forested land:** 362,840 sq. mi. **Location:** borders Ontario on the W and Labrador and New Brunswick on the E; extends N to Hudson Strait and NW to James and Hudson Bays; the southern border touches New York, Vermont, New Hampshire and Maine. **Climate:** varies from subarctic in the northern half of the province to continental in the southern populated regions; avg. Jan. low in Montreal is −14°C, avg. Jan. High 26°C. **Topography:** half a million sq. mi. of Quebec consists of the Laurentian Uplands, part of the Canadian Shield; Appalachian Highlands are in southeastern Quebec; lowlands form a small area along the shore of the St. Lawrence River.

Economy. Principal industries: manufacturing, agriculture, electrical production, mining, meat processing, petroleum refining. **Principal manufactured goods:** foods and beverages, clothing, textiles, paper and paper products, furniture. **GDP, manufacturing** (1982): $15.6 billion. **Gross Domestic Product** (1983): $90.4 billion. **Agriculture: Chief crops:** oats, corn grains, potatoes, mixed grains, tame hay, apples. **Livestock** (1983): 1,500,000 cattle; 3,260,000 pigs; 88,000 sheep. **GDP, forestry** (1982): $324 million. **Mineral production** (1983): total value, $2 billion; metals, $1.2 billion; asbestos, $321 million; structural materials, $364 million. **GDP, fishing** (1982): $35.6 million. **GDP, construction** (1982): $3.3 billion. **Employment distribution** (1983): 32% services; 20% manufacturing; 17% trade; 7% public administration; 4% construction; 3% agriculture. **Per capita income** (1983): $12,531. **Unemployment** (1984): 12.8%.

Finance: No. banks: 1,276; **no. credit unions, caisses populaires:** 1,666.

International airports: Dorval, Mirabel (both near Montreal).

Federal Government: No. federal employees (Dec. 1984): 83,838. **Federal payroll** (1984): $2.3 billion.

Energy. Electricity production, by mwh, (1984): hydroelectric, 118,505,837; nuclear 3,422,087.

Education. No. schools: 1,921 elementary; 700 secondary; 91 higher education. **Avg. salary, public school teachers** (1983-84): N.A.

Provincial Data. Motto Je me souviens (I remember). **Flower:** Fleur de Lys. **Birds:** Alouette (lark). **Date entered Confederation:** 1867. **Capital:** Quebec City.

Politics. Premier: Rene Levesque (Parti Quebecois). **Leaders, opposition parties:** Robert Bourassa (Liberal); **Composition of legislature** (June, 1985): PQ 61; Lib. 53; 8 independent. **Date of last general election:** April 13, 1981.

Tourist attractions: Quebec City, often described as North America's "most European city", and sophisticated Montreal each offer numerous attractions; the north shore of the St. Lawrence River and the Gaspé Peninsula are picturesque.

Saskatchewan

People. Population (Jan. 1985): 1,016,400; **rank:** 6. **Pop. density:** 4.6 per sq. mi. **Urban** (1981) 58.2% **Ethnic distrib.** (1981): English 79.6%; German 5.2%; Ukrainian 4.6%; French 2.6%; Native Indian 2.4%. **Net interprovincial migration** (1983-84): 4,202.

Geography. Total area: 251,870 sq. mi.; **rank:** 5. **Land area:** 220,350 sq. mi. **Forested land:** 66,708 sq. mi. **Location:** borders on the Northwest Territories to the N, Manitoba to the E, Alberta to the W, and Montana and North Dakota to the S. **Climate:** continental, with cold winters (Jan. avg. low in Regina is −23°C) and hot summers (July avg. high in Regina is 26°C). **Topography:** southern 2/3ds of province is plains and grassland; northern 3d is Canadian Shield.

Economy. Principal industries: agriculture, mining of

potash and uranium, meat processing, electricity production, petroleum refining. **Principal manufactured goods:** foods, printing and publishing, metal fabrication, machines, non-metallic mineral products, chemicals and chemical products. **GDP, manufacturing** (1982): $644.3 million. **Gross domestic product** (1983): $16.3 billion. **Agriculture: Chief crops:** wheat (57% of national total), barley, oats, mustard seed, rapeseed, flax. **Livestock** (1983): 1,930,000 cattle; 530,000 pigs; 46,000 sheep. **GDP, forestry** (1982): $30 million. **Mineral production** (1983): total value, $2.8 billion; petroleum, $1.8 billion; metals, $146 million. **GDP, fishing** (1982): $1.8 million. **GDP, construction** (1982): $734.1 million. **Employment distribution** (1983): 29% services; 20% agriculture; 17% trade; 8% public administration; 6% construction; 6% manufacturing. **Per capita income** (1983): $12,686. **Unemployment** (1984): 8%.
Finance: No. banks: 398; **No. credit unions, caisses populaires:** 358.
International airports: none.

Federal Government: No. Federal employees (Dec. 1984): 12,906. **Federal payroll** (1984): $338.9 million.
Energy. Electricity production, by mwh, (1984): mineral, 9,773,872; hydroelectric, 1,704,615.
Education. No. schools: 927 elementary; 143 secondary; 7 higher education. **Avg. salary, public school teachers** (1983-84): $31,332.
Provincial Data. Motto: none. **Flower:** Western red lily. **Bird:** Prairie sharp-tailed grouse. **Date entered Confederation:** 1905. **Capital:** Regina.
Politics. Premier: Grant Devine (Progressive Conservative). **Leader, opposition party:** Allan Blakeney (New Democratic). **Composition of legislature** (June, 1985): PC 54; NDP 8; 1 independent; 1 vacant. **Date of last general election:** Apr. 26, 1982.

Tourist attractions. Regina: RCMP Museum, Museum of Natural History, Wascana Centre; Western Development Museums located at Saskatoon, Yorkton, North Battleford, Moose Jaw.

Territories of Canada

In addition to its 10 provinces, Canada contains the Yukon and Northwest Territories making up more than a third of the nation's land area but less than .3% of its population. A resident commissioner in each territory is appointed by the federal government which retains control over natural resources excluding wildlife. An elected legislative assembly in each territory exercises jurisdiction over such matters as education, housing, social services and renewable resources. The Commissioner of the Northwest Territories serves as chairman of and acts on the advice of a 9-member executive

council, 8 of them appointed from a 24-member elected assembly. The Yukon commissioner acts on the advice of a 6-member executive council, all of whom are appointed on the recommendation of the leader of the majority party in the legislature.

The NWT elects 2 members to the federal parliament, Yukon one member. Each territory has one Senate representative. There is strong support in both territories for increased autonomy or provincial status.

Yukon

*Data apply to both territories.

People. Population (Jan. 1985): 22,800; **Pop. density:** 0.1 per sq. mi. **Urban** (1981) 64%. **Ethnic distrib. by mother tongue** (1981): English 87.4%; Native Indian 3.6%; French 2.5%; German 2.1%. (Using other criteria Native Indians make up 19% of the population). **Net migration** (1983-84): −732.
Geography. Total area: 186,660 sq. mi. **Land area:** 184,930 sq. mi. **Forested land:** 93,412 sq. mi. **Location:** extreme northwestern area of mainland Canada; bounded on the N by the Beaufort Sea, on the S by British Columbia, on the E by the Mackenzie District of the Northwest Territories, and on the W by Alaska. **Climate:** great variance in temperatures; warm summers, very cold winters; low precipitation. **Topography:** main feature is the Yukon plateau with 21 peaks exceeding 10,000 ft.; open tundra in the far north.
Economy. Principal industries: mining, tourism. **Principal manufactured goods:** small amounts of cement, explosives, forest products, canoes, native Indian products. **GDP, manufacturing** (1982): $9.1 million.* **Gross domestic product** (1983): $1.4 billion.* **Agriculture:** hay, oats, vegetable gardens for local use. **Mineral production** (1983): total value, $63 million—almost all from metals. **GDP, fishing** (1982): $1.3 million.* **GDP, construction** (1982): $357.1 million.* **Per capita income** (1983): $14,282.* **No. of banks:** 11.
Federal Government: No. federal employees (Dec. 1984): 1,289. **Federal payroll** (1984): $37.6 million.
Energy. Electricity production, by mwh, (1984): hydroelectric, 232,659.
Education. No. schools: 23 elementary; 2 secondary; 0 higher education. **Avg. salary, public school teachers** (1983-84): $39,774.
Territorial Data. Flower: Fireweed. **Date established:** June 13, 1898. **Capital:** Whitehorse. **Commissioner:** Doug Bell. **Government leader:** Tony Penikett (New Democrat). **Other party leaders:** Willard Phelps (Progressive Conservative); Roger Coles (Liberal). **Composition of assembly** (June, 1985): NDP 8; PC 6; Lib. 2. **Date of last general election:** May 13, 1985.
Tourist attractions: Historic sites from the Gold Rush period in Whitehorse and Dawson City; Miles Canyon; Kluane National Park; Takhini Hot Springs.

The Northwest Territories

People. Population (Jan. 1985): 50,500; **Pop. density:** 0.04 per sq. mi. **Urban** (1981) 48% **Ethnic distrib. by mother tongue** (1981): English 54.1%; Inuit 28.9%; Native Indian 10.7%; French 2.7%. (Using other criteria the Inuit make up 34% of the population, Native Indians 18%.) **Net migration** (1983-84): −199.
Geography. Total area: 1,322,900 sq. mi. **Land area:** 1,271,440 sq. mi. **Forested land:** 237,390 sq. mi. **Location:** all land north of the 60th parallel between the Yukon Territory and Hudson Bay and all northern islands east to Greenland; land area bounded by the Yukon Territory to the W, Hudson Bay to the E, the Beaufort Sea to the N and B.C, Alta., Sask. and Man. to S. **Climate:** extreme temperatures and low precipitation; Arctic and sub-Arctic. **Topography:** mostly tundra plains formed on the rocks of the Canadian Shield; the Mackenzie Lowland is a continuation of the Great Plains; the Mackenzie River Valley is forested.
Economy. Principal industries: mining, mineral and hydrocarbon exploration; oil refining. **GDP, manufacturing** (1982): see Yukon. **Gross domestic product** (1983): see Yukon. **Agriculture:** scattered market gardening in the southern Mackenzie area only. **Mineral production** (1983): total value, $595 million; metals, $497 million; fuels, $38 million. **GDP, fishing:** (1982): see Yukon. **GDP, construction** (1982): see Yukon. **Per capita income** (1983): see Yukon. **No. of banks** 17.
Federal Government: No. federal employees (Dec. 1984): 13,453. **Federal payroll** (1984): $73.1 million.
Energy. Electricity production, by mwh, (1984): hydroelectric, 317,120.
Education. No. schools: 67 elementary; 5 secondary; 1 higher education. **Avg. salary, public school teachers** (1983-84): $39,389.
Territorial Data. Flower: Mountain avens. **Date Established:** June 22, 1869. **Capital:** Yellowknife. **Commissioner:** John H. Parker. **Council:** 24 independent elected representatives.

Tourist attractions: Wood Buffalo, Auyuittuq, and Nahanni National Parks; Mackenzie River and Delta; annual Midnight Golf Tournament in Yellowknife June 21.

Head of State and Cabinet

Canada's official head of state, Queen Elizabeth of England, who succeeded to the throne in 1952, is represented by Governor-General Jeanne Sauvé, appointed in 1984. Titles: Minister unless otherwise stated or *Minister of State.

(Aug. 20, 1985)

Prime Minister — Brian Mulroney
Veterans Affairs — George Hees
Senate Government Leader — Duff Roblin
External Affairs — Joe Clark
Employment and Immigration — Flora MacDonald
Deputy Prime Minister, Defense, and President of Privy Council — Erik Nielsen
Justice, Attorney-General — John Crosbie
Public Works — Roch LaSalle
Transport — Donald Mazankowski
Solicitor-General — Perrin Beatty
Health and Welfare — Jake Epp
Fisheries and Oceans — John Fraser
Regional Industrial Expansion — Sinclair Stevens
Agriculture — John Wise
Government House Leader — Raymon Hnatyshyn
Indian Affairs and Northern Development — David Crombie
President of the Treasury Board — Robert René de Contret
National Revenue — Elmer MacKay
Finance — Michael Wilson
*Immigration, Min. responsible for the Status of Women —

Walter McLean
Assoc. Min. of Defense — Harvie Andre
Supply and Services — Stewart McInnes
*Fitness and Amateur Sport and Multiculturalism — Otto Jelinek
*Science and Technology — Thomas Siddon
*Wheat Board — Charles Mayer
*Labor — William McKnight
*Secretary of State — Benoit Bouchard
*Tourism — Jack Murta
Energy, Mines and Resources — Pat Carney
*Small Business — André Bissonnette
Environment — Thomas McMillan
*Transport — Suzanne Blais-Grenier
*Youth — Andrée Champagne
Consumer and Corporate Affairs — Michael Coté
*International Trade — James Kelleher
Mines —Robert Layton
*Finance — Barbara McDougall
*Forestry — Gerald Merrithew
External Relations — Monique Vézina

Governors-General of Canada Since Confederation, 1867

Name	Term	Name	Term
The Viscount Monck of Ballytrammon	1867-1868	General The Baron Byng of Vimy	1921-1926
The Baron Lisgar of Lisgar and Bailieborough	1869-1872	The Viscount Willingdon of Ratton	1926-1931
The Earl of Dufferin	1872-1878	The Earl of Bessborough	1931-1935
The Marquis of Lorne	1878-1883	The Baron Tweedsmuir of Elsfield	1935-1940
The Marquis of Lansdowne	1883-1888	Major General The Earl of Athlone	1940-1946
The Baron Stanley of Preston	1888-1893	Field Marshal The Viscount Alexander of Tunis	1946-1952
The Earl of Aberdeen	1893-1898	The Right Hon. Vincent Massey	1952-1959
The Earl of Minto	1898-1904	General The Right Hon. Georges P. Vanier	1959-1967
The Earl Grey	1904-1911	The Right Hon. Roland Michener	1967-1974
Field Marshal H.R.H. The Duke of Connaught	1911-1916	The Right Hon. Jules Leger	1974-1979
The Duke of Devonshire	1916-1921	The Right Hon. Edward Schreyer	1979-1984
		The Right Hon. Jeanne Sauvé	1984-

Fathers of Confederation

Union of the British North American colonies into the Dominion of Canada was discussed and its terms negotiated at 3 confederation conferences held at Charlottetown (C), Sept. 1, 1864; Quebec (Q), Oct. 10, 1864; and London (L), Dec. 4, 1866. The names of delegates are followed by the provinces they represented. Canada refers to what are now the provinces of Ontario and Quebec.

Adams G. Archibald, N.S.	(C,Q,L)	Hector L. Langevin, Canada	(C,Q,L)
George Brown, Canada	(C,Q)	Jonathan McCully, N.S.	(C,Q,L)
Alexander Campbell, Canada	(C,Q)	A.A. Macdonald, P.E.I.	(C,Q)
Frederick B.T. Carter, Nfld.	(Q)	John A. Macdonald, Canada	(C,Q,L)
George-Etienne Cartier, Canada	(C,Q,L)	William McDougall, Canada	(C,Q,L)
Edward B. Chandler, N.B.	(C,Q)	Thomas D'Arcy McGee, Canada	(C,Q)
Jean-Charles Chapais, Canada	(Q)	Peter Mitchell, N.B.	(Q,L)
James Cockburn, Canada	(Q)	Oliver Mowat, Canada	(Q)
George H. Coles, P.E.I.	(C,Q)	Edward Palmer, P.E.I.	(C,Q)
Robert B. Dickey, N.S.	(Q)	William H. Pope, P.E.I.	(C,Q)
Charles Fisher, N.B.	(Q,L)	John W. Ritchie, N.S.	(L)
Alexander T. Galt, Canada	(C,Q,L)	J. Ambrose Shea, Nfld.	(L)
John Hamilton Gray, N.B.	(C,Q)	William H. Steeves, N.B.	(C,Q)
John Hamilton Gray, P.E.I.	(C,Q)	Sir Etienne-Paschal Tache, Canada	(Q)
Thomas Heath Haviland, P.E.I.	(Q)	Samuel Leonard Tilley, N.B.	(C,Q,L)
William A. Henry, N.S.	(C,Q,L)	Charles Tupper, N.S.	(C,Q,L)
William P. Howland, Canada	(L)	Edward Whelan, P.E.I.	(Q)
John M. Johnson, N.B.	(C,Q,L)	R.D. Wilmot, N.B.	(L)

The Political Parties

Canadian parties, from whatever point in the political spectrum they begin, gravitate towards the middle of the road where most of the votes lie. Despite variations in outlook and policy, all 3 official parties tend to adopt a practical rather than dogmatic line on most issues.

Progressive Conservatives — Canada's oldest party and

theoretically the furthest to the right, the Conservatives have nevertheless endorsed an extension of social welfare. Though their support is based in western Canada, the Conservatives received strong support in all provinces in 1984. Until the '84 victory the party had held office only 9 months during the preceeding 21 years, mainly due to a failure to gain support in Quebec. Leader: Brian Mulroney.

Liberals — Though politically situated between the Conservatives to the right and the New Democrats on the left, the Liberals are flexible enough to lean in either direction depending on specific issues and political situations. In 1975 they belatedly adopted a Conservative proposal for wage and price controls; in 1979 they sided with the NDP to oppose Conservative plans to return some government-owned corporations to the private sector. Most of their traditional electoral support comes from middle and upper class urban residents, from ethnic voters, and among French-speaking Canadians. **Leader:** John Turner.

New Democratic Party — Successor to the Cooperative Commonwealth Federation, which combined the agrarian protest movement in western Canada with a democratic socialism of the British Labor Party variety, the NDP was founded in 1961. It now attempts to attract the vote of middle-class Canadians and fuse it with the party's labor support. **Leader:** Ed Broadbent.

Political power in Canada has been dominated by the Conservative and Liberal parties. Of 33 federal elections since Confederation, the Conservatives have won 14, holding power for 48 years; the Liberals have gained office 19 times, governing for 70 years.

Despite the dominance of the Liberals and Conservatives, third parties have played an important role under Canada's parliamentary system in which a governing party holding less than half the seats in the House of Commons can remain in office and pass legislation only with the support of a minor party. A minority Conservative Government lost power in 1979 when none of the opposition parties supported its proposed budget.

The NDP has been the most influential of the third parties, consistently winning between 15% and 20% of the popular vote—though its proportion of elected members is always less. NDP pressure from the left has influenced policy decisions by both major parties. The Social Credit Party, once a strong political force with federal support in Quebec and the western provinces, has declined in stature over the past 2 decades and has failed to elect any members to Parliament in the past two elections.

Prime Ministers of Canada

Name	Party	Term	Name	Party	Term
Sir John A. MacDonald	Conservative	1867-1873			1926-1930
		1878-1891			1935-1948
Alexander Mackenzie	Liberal	1873-1878	R. B. Bennett.	Conservative	1930-1935
Sir John J. C. Abbott	Conservative	1891-1892	Louis St. Laurent	Liberal	1948-1957
Sir John S. D. Thompson . . .	Conservative	1892-1894	John G. Diefenbaker.	Prog. Cons.	1957-1963
Sir Mackenzie Bowell	Conservative	1894-1896	Lester B. Pearson	Liberal	1963-1968
Sir Charles Tupper.	Conservative	1896	Pierre Elliott Trudeau	Liberal	1968-1979
Sir Wilfrid Laurier	Liberal	1896-1911	Joe Clark	Prog. Cons.	1979-1980
Sir Robert L. Borden	Conservative	1911-1920	Pierre Elliott Trudeau	Liberal	1980-1984
	Unionist		John Turner	Liberal	1984-1984
Arthur Meighen	Cons. Union.	1920-1921	Brian Mulroney	Prog. Cons.	1984-
W.L. Mackenzie King	Liberal	1921-1926[1]			

(1) King's term was interrupted from June 26-Sept. 25, 1926, when Arthur Meighen again served as prime minister.

Canadian Political Party Leaders

Progressive Conservative Party[1]

Leader	Term				
John A.		Robert Borden	2/6/1901-7/10/1920	George Drew	10/2/1948-12/14/1956
MacDonald	1854-6/6/1891	Arthur Meighen	7/10/1920-10/11/1926	John G.	
J.C. Abbott	6/16/1891-12/5/1892	Hugh Guthrie	10/11/1926-10/12/1927	Diefenbaker	12/14/1956-9/9/1967
John Thompson	12/5/1892-12/12/1894	R.B. Bennett	11/12/1927-7/7/1938	Robert	
Mackenzie		R.J. Manion	7/7/1938-5/13/1940	Stanfield	9/9/1967-2/22/1976
Bowell	12/21/1894-4/27/1896	R.B. Hanson	5/13/1940-1/27/1943	Joe Clark	2/22/1976-6/13/1983
Charles Tupper	5/1/1896-2/5/1901	Arthur Meighen	11/12/1941-12/11/1942	Brian Mulroney	6/13/1983-
		John Bracken	12/11/1942-10/2/1948		

Liberal Party

Leader	Term				
Alexander		W.L. Mackenzie		Lester B.	
Mackenzie	3/6/1873-4/27/1880	King	8/7/1919-8/7/1948	Pearson	1/16/1958-4/2/1968
Edward Blake	5/4/1880-6/2/1887	Louis St.		Pierre Elliott	
Wilfrid Laurier	June/1887-2/17/1919	Laurent	8/7/1948-1/16/1958	Trudeau	4/6/1968-6/16/1984
				John Turner	6/16/1984-

New Democratic Party[2]

Leader	Term				
James S.		Hazen Argue	Aug./1960-Aug./1961	Ed Broadbent	Jul./1975-present
Woodsworth	Aug./1932-Jul./1942	Tommy			
M.J. Coldwell	Jul./1942-Aug./1960	Douglas	Aug./1961-Apr./1971		
		David Lewis	Apr./1971-Jul./1975		

(1) Changed name from Conservative to Progressive Conservative Dec., 1942. (2) Prior to August 1961 was called the Co-operative Commonwealth Federation.

Election Results by Province and Party, September 4, 1984

Province	Total Valid Votes	Liberal	Conservative	New Dem.	Other
Alberta	1,017,394	129,945	701,344	143,588	42,517
British Columbia.	1,432,795	235,394	668,432	502,331	26,638
Manitoba.	513,834	112,123	221,947	139,999	39,765
New Brunswick.	377,350	120,326	202,144	53,332	1,548
Newfoundland.	241,159	87,778	138,867	13,993	521
Nova Scotia	460,418	154,954	233,713	70,190	1,561
Ontario	4,399,974	1,323,835	2,113,187	921,504	41,448
Prince Edward Island	73,091	30,075	38,160	4,737	119
Quebec	3,439,267	1,219,124	1,728,196	301,928	190,019
Saskatchewan	522,800	95,143	218,000	200,918	8,739
N.W. Territories	19,510	5,254	8,059	5,511	686
Yukon	11,704	2,535	6,648	1,884	637
TOTAL.	12,509,296	3,516,486	6,278,697	2,359,915	354,198
Percent.	100	28.02	50.03	18.81	3.14
Seats.	282	40	211	30	1

Party Representation by Regions, 1953-1984

	1953	1957	1958	1962	1963	1965	1968	1972	1974	1979	1980	1984
Canada												
Liberal.	171	105	48	100	129	131	155	109	141	114	147	40
Conservative	51	112	208	116	95	97	72	107	95	136	103	211
New Democratic[1]	23	25	8	19	17	21	22	31	16	26	32	30
Social Credit	15	19	—	30	24	14	14	15	11	6	0	—
Other	5	4	1	—	—	2	1	2	1	0	0	1
Ontario												
Liberal.	51	21	14	44	52	51	64	36	55	32	52	14
Conservative	33	61	67	35	27	25	17	40	25	57	38	67
New Democratic[1]	1	3	3	6	6	9	6	11	8	6	5	13
Quebec												
Liberal.	66	62	25	35	47	56	56	56	60	67	74	17
Conservative	4	9	50	14	8	8	4	2	3	2	1	58
Social Credit	—	—	—	26	20	9	14	15	11	6	—	—
Atlantic												
Liberal.	27	12	8	14	20	15	7	10	13	12	19	7
Conservative	5	21	25	18	13	18	25	22	17	18	13	25
New Democratic[1]	1	—	—	1	—	—	—	—	1	2	—	—
Western[2]												
Liberal.	27	10	1	7	10	9	28	7	13	3	2	2
Conservative	9	21	66	49	47	46	26	43	50	59	51	61
New Democratic[1]	21	22	5	12	11	12	16	20	7	18	27	17
Social Credit	15	19	—	4	4	5	—	—	—	—	—	—

(1) Prior to 1962 election was known as the Cooperative Commonwealth Federation.
(2) Includes the Yukon and Northwest Territories.

Canadian Armed Forces

Canada has an all-volunteer Armed Forces which, since 1968, has been a single body composed of what had been a separate army, navy, and air force. Canada's defense budget for 1984-85 (ending Mar. 31) was $8,752,743,000. The projected 1985-86 budget is $9,367,723,000.

Chief of the Defense Staff: Gen. Gerard C.E. Theriault
Vice Chief of the Defense Staff: Lieut. Gen. John E. Vance

Maritime Command — Vice Admiral J.C. Wood
Mobile Command — Lieut. Gen. C. H. Belzile
Air Command — Lieut. Gen. D.M. McNaughton

Communications Command — Brig. Gen. G. D. Simpson
Canadian Forces Europe — Maj. Gen. D.P. Wightman

Regular Forces Strength

(as of March 31)

Year	Navy	Army	Air Force	Total	Year	Total	Year	Total	Year	Total
1945	92,529	494,258	174,254	761,041	1970	91,433	1980	78,909	1983	82,905
1955	19,207	49,409	49,461	118,077	1975	78,448	1981	79,549	1984	81,675
1965	19,756	46,264	48,144	114,164	1979	78,974	1982	82,858	1985	83,740

Canadian Military Participation in Major Conflicts

Northwest Rebellion (1885)[1]
Participants—3,323
Killed—38
Last veteran died at the age of 104 in 1971.
South African War (1899-1902)
Participants—7,368[2]
Killed—89
Living Veterans—1
First World War (1914-1918)
Participants—626,636[3]

Killed—61,332[4]
Living Veterans—18,500[5]
Second World War (1939-1945)
Participants—1,086,343 (inc. 45,423 women)
Killed—32,714 (inc. 8 women)
Living Veterans—630,800[5]
Korean War (1950-1953)
Participants—25,583
Killed—314
Living Veterans—23,100[6]

(1) First battle in history to be fought entirely by Canadian troops. (2) Includes Canadians in the South African constabulary and 8 nursing sisters. (3) Includes 2,854 nursing sisters. (4) Includes 21 nursing sisters and 1,563 airmen serving with the British air forces. (5) 1985 est. based on mortality rates applied to 1971 census data. (6) Includes 3,300 who also served in WWII.

Canadian Peacekeeping Operations

Canada has played a major role in the United Nations' efforts to preserve peace and promote international security, participating in almost all UN peacekeeping operations to date - in Egypt, Israel, Syria, Lebanon, Cyprus, Korea, India, Pakistan, West New Guinea, the Congo, Yemen and Nigeria.

Nearly 900 Canadian soldiers served in the Gaza Strip following the Israeli-Egyptian crisis of 1956 until the peacekeeping force there was disbanded in 1967. Another 850 Canadians served with the United Nations Emergency Force in the Middle East from 1973 until it was disbanded in Nov., 1979.

In the Congo, a 300-man signals unit provided communications for the UN force from 1960 to 1964.

Canadian participation in the International Commission for Control and Supervision in Vietnam and Laos began in 1954, and, at its height following U.S. military withdrawal from Vietnam in 1973, involved 245 Canadian Forces personnel. The Canadian Vietnam supervisory contingent was withdrawn in July 1973, the Laos mission in 1974.

Canadian peacekeeping operations in 1985:
—some 515 Canadians in the UN Peacekeeping Force in Cyprus where Canadian participation began in 1964 and was augmented in 1974.
—224 Canadians, mostly logistics troops, with the UN Disengagement Observer Force in the Middle East.
—20 Canadian combat arms officers with the UN Truce Supervisory Organization, Israel.

Area of Canada by Provinces
Source: Energy, Mines, and Resources Canada

Province, territory	Capital	Area in square miles			Area in square kilometers		
		Land	Fresh water	Total	Land	Fresh water	Total
Newfoundland	St. John's	143,510	13,140	156,650	371,690	34,030	405,720
Prince Edward Island	Charlottetown	2,180	...	2,180	5,660	...	5,660
Nova Scotia	Halifax	20,400	1,020	21,420	52,840	2,650	55,490
New Brunswick	Fredericton	27,840	520	28,360	72,090	1,350	73,440
Quebec	Quebec	523,860	71,000	594,860	1,356,790	183,890	1,540,680
Ontario	Toronto	344,090	68,490	412,580	891,190	177,390	1,068,580
Manitoba	Winnipeg	211,720	39,230	250,950	548,360	101,590	649,950
Saskatchewan	Regina	220,350	31,520	251,870	570,700	81,630	652,330
Alberta	Edmonton	248,800	6,490	255,290	644,390	16,800	661,190
British Columbia	Victoria	358,970	6,980	365,950	929,730	18,070	947,800
Yukon Territory	Whitehorse	184,930	1,730	186,660	478,970	4,480	483,450
Northwest Territories	Yellowknife	1,271,440	51,460	1,322,900	3,293,020	133,300	3,426,320
Total		**3,558,090**	**291,580**	**3,849,670**	**9,215,430**	**755,180**	**9,970,610**

Population of Canada by Province, 1871 - 1981

Source: Statistics Canada

Province, territory	1871 census	1901 census	1941 census	1951 census	1961 census	1971 census	1976 census	1981 census
Newfoundland	—	—	—	361,416	457,853	522,104	557,725	567,681
Prince Edward Island	94,021	103,259	95,047	98,429	104,629	111,641	118,229	122,506
Nova Scotia	387,800	459,574	577,942	642,584	737,007	788,960	828,571	847,442
New Brunswick	285,594	331,120	457,401	515,697	597,936	634,557	677,250	691,403
Quebec	1,191,516	1,648,898	3,331,882	4,055,681	5,259,211	6,027,764	6,234,445	6,438,403
Ontario	1,620,851	2,182,947	3,787,655	4,597,542	6,236,092	7,703,106	8,264,465	8,625,107
Manitoba	25,228	255,211	729,744	776,541	921,686	988,247	1,021,506	1,026,241
Saskatchewan	—	91,279	895,992	831,728	925,181	926,242	921,323	968,313
Alberta	—	73,022	796,169	939,501	1,331,944	1,627,874	1,838,037	2,237,724
British Columbia	36,247	178,657	817,861	1,165,210	1,629,082	2,184,621	2,466,608	2,744,467
Yukon	—	27,219	4,914	9,096	14,628	18,388	21,836	23,153
Northwest Territories	48,000	20,129	12,028	16,004	22,998	34,807	42,609	45,741
Total	**3,689,257**	**5,371,315**	**11,506,655**	**14,009,429**	**18,238,247**	**21,568,311**	**22,992,604**	**24,343,181**

Population of Major Canadian Cities and Metropolitan Areas

Source: Statistics Canada, from 1981 Census.

	City	Metro Area[1]		City	Metro Area[1]
Montreal, Quebec	980,354	2,828,349	Regina, Saskatchewan	162,613	164,313
Toronto, Ontario	599,217	2,998,947[2]	Saskatoon, Saskatchewan	154,210	154,210
Calgary, Alberta	592,743	592,743	Brampton, Ontario	149,030	—
Winnipeg, Manitoba	564,473	584,842	Kitchener, Ontario	139,734	287,801
North York, Ontario	559,521	—	Longueuil, Quebec	124,320	—
Edmonton, Alberta	532,246	657,057	St. Catharines, Ontario	124,018	304,353
Vancouver, British Columbia	414,281	1,268,183	Oshawa, Ontario	117,519	154,217
Mississauga, Ontario	315,056	—	Burlington, Ontario	114,853	—
Hamilton, Ontario	306,434	542,095	Halifax, Nova Scotia	114,594	277,727
Ottawa, Ontario	295,163	717,578[3]	Thunder Bay, Ontario	112,486	121,379
Laval, Quebec	268,335	—	Sudbury, Ontario	91,829	149,923
London, Ontario	254,280	283,668	St. John's, Newfoundland	83,770	154,820
Windsor, Ontario	192,083	246,110	Saint John, New Brunswick	80,521	112,974
Quebec, Quebec	166,474	576,075	Victoria, British Columbia	64,379	233,481

(1) Figures are for Census Metro Areas which, in some cases, include municipalities outside of metro political boundaries. (2) Census area includes Mississauga; actual metro political area (pop. 2,137,395) is composed of the cities of North York, Scarborough, Etobicoke, York and the borough of East York. (3) Includes Hull, Que.

Superlative Canadian Statistics

Source: Statistics Canada; Energy, Mines and Resources Canada

Area	Total: Land 3,558,090 sq. mi.; Water 291,580 sq. mi.	3,849,670 sq. mi.
Largest city in area	Timmins, Ont.	1,160 sq. mi.
Smallest city in area (east)	Vanier, Ont.	1.1 sq. mi.
Smallest city in area (west)	Chilliwack, B.C.	1.6 sq. mi.
Northernmost point	Cape Columbia, Ellesmere Island, N.W.T.	83°07′30″N, 70°32′07″W.
Southernmost point	Middle Island (Lake Erie), Ont.	41°41′N, 82°40′47″W.
Easternmost point	Cape Spear, Nfld.	47°31′12″N, 52°37′28″W.
Westernmost point	Mount St. Elias, Yukon (at Alaskan border)	60°18′24″N, 141°W.
Highest city	Rossland, B.C. at R.R. Stn. (49°05′N,117°47′W)	3,465 ft.
Highest town	Lake Louise, Alta.	5,051 ft.
Highest waterfall	Takakkaw Falls (Daly Glacier), B.C. (51°30′N,116°29′W)	1,650 ft.
Longest river	Mackenzie (from head of Finlay R.)	2,635 mi.
Highest mountain	Mt. Logan (Yukon)	19,524 ft.
Rainiest spot	Henderson Lake, Vancouver Is. yrly. avg. rainfall	262 inches
Highest lake	Chilco Lake (51°20′N,124°05′W) 75.1 sq. mi.	3,842 ft.

Immigration to Canada by Country of Last Permanent Residence

Source: Canadian Statistical Review, April 1985

Year	Total	UK and Ireland	France	Germany	Nether- lands	Greece	Italy
1980	143,117	18,924	1,900	1,643	1,866	1,093	1,740
1981	128,618	21,964	2,089	2,188	1,797	958	2,043
1982	121,147	17,075	2,393	4,425	1,827	885	1,506
1983	89,157	6,036	1,651	2,518	672	601	826
1984	88,199	5,385	1,379	1,727	545	554	837

Year	Portugal	Other Europe	Asia	Austral- asia	United States	West Indies	All Other
1980	4,228	9,774	71,602	1,555	9,926	7,254	11,612
1981	1,866	13,374	48,831	1,318	10,559	8,566	13,045
1982	1,388	16,657	41,686	938	9,360	8,630	14,377
1983	820	11,188	36,906	478	7,381	7,179	12,901
1984	852	9,601	41,908	535	6,909	5,600	12,367

Canadian Population by Mother Tongue, 1981

Source: Statistics Canada: 1981 Census

Province	English	French	Italian	German	Ukrain- ian	Indian, Inuit	Chinese	Portu- guese	Other
Newfoundland	560,460	2,655	90	445	50	1,600	725	205	1,450
Prince Edward Island	115,045	6,080	20	175	35	90	115	20	925
Nova Scotia	793,165	36,030	1,055	1,865	640	3,055	1,305	235	1,440
New Brunswick	453,310	234,030	525	1,220	195	2,115	730	165	4,115
Quebec.	706,115	5,307,010	133,710	24,060	10,765	28,080	15,270	25,495	187,895
Ontario	6,678,770	475,605	338,980	174,545	81,595	22,255	89,355	114,275	649,725
Manitoba	735,920	52,560	6,170	75,180	58,855	27,185	6,075	6,840	57,455
Saskatchewan	770,815	25,535	1,280	59,625	44,660	24,265	5,000	335	36,795
Alberta	1,810,545	62,145	16,175	91,480	68,130	27,565	28,910	5,560	127,215
British Columbia	2,249,310	45,615	30,595	93,380	26,950	11,445	76,270	12,340	198,560
Yukon.	20,245	580	45	495	170	835	125	5	655
Northwest Territories	24,755	1,240	130	385	210	18,090	145	25	765
Total	14,918,445	6,249,095	528,775	522,855	292,265	166,575	224,030	165,510	1,275,630

Population by Religious Denomination

Source: Statistics Canada

Denomination	1971	1981	Denomination	1971	1981
Adventist	28,590	41,605	Jewish.	276,025	296,425
Anglican.	2,543,180	2,436,375	Latter Day Saints (Mormons)	66,635	89,865
Baptist.	667,245	696,850	Lutheran.	715,740	702,905
Buddhist.	16,175	51,955	Mennonite.	168,150	189,370
Chr. & Miss'nary Alliance	23,630	33,895	Pentecostal	220,390	338,790
Christian Reformed	83,390	77,370	Presbyterian	872,335	812,110
Ch. of Christ, Disciples	16,405	15,350	Roman Catholic	9,974,895	11,210,385
Doukhobors.	9,170	6,700	Salvation Army	119,665	125,085
Free Methodist	19,125	12,270	Sikh	(1)	67,710
Greek Orthodox	316,605	314,670	Ukrainian Catholic	227,730	190,585
Hindu	(1)	69,500	Unitarian.	20,995	14,500
Hutterite.	13,650	16,530	United Church	3,768,800	3,758,015
Islam.	(1)	98,165	Other	293,240	476,225
Jehovah's Witnesses	174,810	143,485	No religion	929,575	1,788,995

(1) Not included in census data prior to 1981.

Births and Deaths in Canada by Province

Source: Statistics Canada

Province	Births 1982	Births 1983	Deaths 1982	Deaths 1983	Province	Births 1982	Births 1983	Deaths 1982	Deaths 1983
Newfoundland	9,173	8,929	3,385	3,498	Saskatchewan	17,722	17,847	8,202	7,611
Prince Edward Island	1,924	1,907	980	1,050	Alberta	45,036	45,555	12,968	12,588
Nova Scotia	12,325	12,401	6,941	7,047	British Columbia . . .	42,747	42,919	20,707	19,827
New Brunswick. . . .	10,489	10,851	5,197	5,206	Yukon.	525	540	118	113
Quebec	90,600	88,154	43,497	44,275	Northwest Territories	1,362	1,491	232	241
Ontario	124,856	126,826	63,696	64,507					
Manitoba	16,123	16,602	8,490	8,521	Total	372,882	373,689	174,413	174,484

Marriages, Divorces in Canada

Source: Statistics Canada
(Rates per 1,000 population)

Year	Marriages No.	Marriages Rate	Divorces No.	Divorces Rate	Year	Marriages No.	Marriages Rate	Divorces No.	Divorces Rate
1940.	125,709	10.8	2,416	0.21	1975.	197,585	8.7	50,611	2.22
1950.	125,083	9.1	5,386	0.39	1980.	191,069	8.0	62,019	2.59
1960.	130,338	7.3	6,980	0.39	1982.	188,119	7.6	70,436	2.86
1970.	188,428	8.8	29,775	1.39	1983.	184,675	7.4	68,567	2.76

Canadian Legal or Public Holidays, 1986

Legal public holidays in all provinces are: New Year's Day, Good Friday, Easter Monday, Victoria Day, Canada Day, Labor Day, Remembrance Day and Christmas Day. Additional holidays may be proclaimed provincially by the Lieutenant-Governor or in the municipalities by an order of the local council. For some holidays, government and business closing practices vary. In most provinces the provincial Ministry or Department of Labor can provide details of holiday closings.

Chief Legal or Public Holidays

Jan. 1 (Wednesday) - New Year's Day. All provinces.

March 28 - Good Friday. All provinces.

March 31 - Easter Monday. Que. (businesses remain open in other provinces)

May 19 (the Monday preceding May 25) - Victoria Day. All provinces.

July 1 (Tuesday) - Canada Day. All provinces.

Aug. 4 (1st Monday in Aug.) - Civic Holiday. Alb., B.C., Man., N.B., N.S., NWT, Ont., Sask.

Sept. 1 (1st Monday in Sept.) - Labor Day. All provinces.

Oct. 13 (2d Monday in Oct.) - Thanksgiving. All provinces.

Nov. 11 (Tuesday) - Remembrance Day. Observed in all provinces but most businesses remain open except in N.B.

Dec. 25 (Thursday) - Christmas Day. All provinces.

Dec. 26 (Friday) - Boxing Day. All provinces except Que.

Other Legal or Public Holidays

Jan. 11 (Saturday) - Sir John A. MacDonald's Birthday. Schools closed in some provinces.

March 17 (Monday nearest March 17) - St. Patrick's Day. Nfld.

April 23 (Wednesday) - St. George's Day. Nfld.

June 24 (Tuesday) - St. John the Baptist's Day. Que.

June 23 (Monday nearest June 24) - Discovery Day. Nfld.

July 14 (Monday nearest July 12) - Orangemen's Day. Nfld.

Aug. 18 (3d Monday in Aug.) - Discovery Day. Yukon.

Widely Known Canadians of the Present

Statesmen, authors, performers, artists, industrialists, and other prominent persons. (Canadians widely known in the North American entertainment industry are found on pages 393-408; some sports personalities can be found in sports section).

Doris Anderson, b. Calgary, Alta., 11/20/25, women's rights activist, journalist and author.

Margaret Atwood, b. Ottawa, Ont., 11/18/39, poet and author; *Lady Oracle* (1976), *Bodily Harm* (1981).

Harold Ballard, b. Toronto, Ont., 7/30/03, majority owner of Toronto Maple Leafs, Hamilton Tiger-Cats, Maple Leaf Gardens.

Carling Bassett, b. Toronto, Ont., 10/9/67, Canadian women's tennis champion.

Alex Baumann, b. Prague, Czechoslovakia, 4/21/64, winner of 2 gold medals for swimming at the 1984 Summer Olympics.

William Bennett, b. Kelowna, B.C., 4/14/32, leader of British Columbia Social Credit Party since 1973, B.C. premier (1975-   ).

Pierre Berton, b. Whitehorse, Yukon, 7/12/20, author; *The National Dream* (1970), *The Last Spike* (1971).

Conrad Black, b. Montreal, Que., 8/25/44, businessman, including chairman of the board of Argus Corp. Ltd.

Gaetan Boucher, b. Charlesbourg, Que., 5/10/58, speed skater, winner of 2 gold and 1 bronze medal in the 1984 Olympics, a silver in 1980 Olympics.

Gerald Bouey, b. Axford, Sask., 4/2/20, governor of the Bank of Canada (1973-   ).

Robert Boûrassa, b. Montreal, Que., 7/14/33, Quebec Premier 1970-76, Quebec Liberal leader (1970-76) and (1983-   ).

Ed Broadbent, b. Oshawa, Ont., 3/21/36, national leader of New Democratic Party (1975-   ).

Charles Bronfman, b. Montreal, Que., 6/27/31, deputy chairman of the Seagram Co. Ltd.; Chairman of the Montreal Expos.

John M. Buchanan, b. Sydney, N.S., 4/22/31, leader of Nova Scotia Progressive Conservative Party since 1971; Nova Scotia premier (1978-   ).

Jean Chrétien, b. Shawinigan, Que., 1/11/34, minister of energy, mines and resources (1982-1984), justice minister (1980-1982); finished 2d in 1984 Liberal leadership contest.

Joe Clark, b. High River, Alta., 6/5/39, former prime minister (May 1979-Feb. 1980), former leader of Progressive Conservative Party (1976-1983); External Affairs Minister (1984-   ).

Leonard Cohen, b. Montreal, Que., 9/21/34, poet, novelist, songwriter.

Alex Colville, b. Toronto, Ont., 8/24/20, artist.

David Crombie, b. Toronto, Ont. 4/24/36, candidate for Progressive Conservative leadership 1983, mayor of Toronto 1972-78, minister of Indian Affairs and Northern Development (1984-   ).

John Crosbie, b. St. John's, Nfld., 1/30/31, former finance minister (1979), finished 3d in 1983 Progressive Conservative leadership contest, Justice Minister (1984-   ).

Ken Danby, b. Sault Ste. Marie, Ont., 3/16/40, artist.

Robertson Davies, b. Thamesville, Ont., 8/28/13, educator, author of *The Rebel Angels* (1981).

Bill Davis, b. Brampton, Ont., 7/30/29, Ontario premier (1971-84).

Paul Desmarais, b. Sudbury, Ont., 1/4/27, industrial executive, including chairman of Power Corp. of Canada.

Grant Devine, b. Regina, Sask., 7/5/44, leader Saskatchewan Progressive Conservative Party since 1979, Saskatchewan premier (1982-   ).

Brian Dickson, b. Yorkton, Sask., 5/25/16, chief justice, Supreme Court of Canada (1984-   ).

Jean Drapeau, b. Montreal, Que., 2/18/16, mayor of Montreal (1954-57 and 1960-   ).

Alan Eagleson, b. St. Catharines, Ont., 4/24/33, executive director of National Hockey League Players' Assn.; arranges international hockey competition.

Maureen Forrester, b. Montreal, Que., 7/25/30, contralto.

Barbara Frum, b. Niagara Falls, Ont., 9/8/38, broadcaster.

Northrop Frye, b. Sherbrooke, Que., 7/14/12, educator, literary critic and author *The Great Code* (1982).

Peter Gzowski, b. Toronto, Ont., 7/13/34, radio host and author of *The Game of Our Lives* (1981).

Don Harron, b. Toronto, Ont., 9/19/24, comedian and actor, best known for alter-ego Charlie Farquharson.

Richard Hatfield, b. Hartland, N.B., 4/9/31, New Brunswick premier (1970-   ).

Mel Hurtig, b. Edmonton, Alta., 6/24/32, book publisher, proponent of Canadian nationalism.

Donald Johnston, b. Ottawa, Ont., 6/26/36, finished 3d in 1984 Liberal leadership contest.

Karen Kain, b. Hamilton, Ont., 3/28/51, principal dancer of the National Ballet of Canada.

Yousuf Karsh, b. Armenia-in-Turkey, 12/23/08, portrait photographer.

Margaret (Trudeau) Kemper, b. Vancouver, B.C., 9/10/48, author of autobiographies *Beyond Reason* and *Consequences,* television host.

Margaret Laurence, b. Neapawa, Man., 7/18/26, novelist; *The Stone Angel* (1964), *The Diviners* (1974).

Irving Layton, b. Neamtz, Romania, 3/12/12, poet.

René Lévesque, b. New Carlisle, Que., 8/24/22,

leader of Quebec separatist Parti Quebecois 1968-85, Quebec premier (1976-85).

James Lee, b. Charlottetown, P.E.I., 3/26/37, leader P.E.I. Progressive Conservative Party and premier (1981-).

Stephen Lewis, b. Ottawa, Ont., 11/11/37, Canadian ambassador to the United Nations (1984-); leader Ont. New Democratic Party 1970-78.

Peter Lougheed, b. Calgary, Alta., 7/26/28, Alberta Progressive Conservative leader (1965-85), Alberta premier (1971-85).

Dennis McDermott, b. Portsmouth, Eng., 11/3/22, president of Canadian Labour Congress (1978-).

W.O. Mitchell, b. Weyburn, Sask., 3/13/14, author; *Who Has Seen the Wind* (1947), *How I Spent My Summer Holidays* (1981).

Farlay Mowat, b. Belleville, Ont., 5/12/21, author, known for books on the North.

Brian Mulroney, b. Baie Comeau, Que., 3/20/39, Canada's 18th prime minister, elected 9/4/84; leader of Progressive Conservative Party since June 1983, finished 3d for P.C. leadership 1976, former pres. of Iron Ore Co. of Canada, labor lawyer.

Mila Mulroney, b. Sarajevo, Yugoslavia, 7/13/53, wife of Prime Minister Brian Mulroney, campaigned actively in 1984 elections.

Knowlton Nash, b. Toronto, Ont., 11/18/27, broadcaster, announcer for CBC national news.

Peter C. Newman, b. Vienna, Austria, 5/10/29, author, editor of Maclean's magazine (1971-82); *The Canadian Establishment* (1975), *Bronfman Dynasty* (1978), *The Acquisitors* (1981).

Erik Nielsen, b. Regina, Sask., 2/24/24, interim fed. PC party leader Feb-Aug 1983, deputy prime minister (1984-) and defence minister (1985-).

Howard Pawley, b. Brampton, Ont., 11/21/34, leader of Manitoba New Democratic Party since 1979, Manitoba premier (1981-).

Brian Peckford, b. Whitehorse, Nfld., 8/27/42, leader of Newfoundland Progressive Conservative Party and premier since 1979.

Peter Pocklington, b. Regina, Sask., 11/18/41, entrepreneur, owner of Edmonton Oilers and other sports franchises.

Steve Podborski, b. Toronto, Ont., 7/25/57, 1982 men's downhill World Cup skiing champion.

Christopher Pratt, b. St. John's, Nfld., 12/9/35, artist, has developed style known as "conceptual realism."

Mordecai Richler, b. Montreal, Que., 1/27/31, author; *The Apprenticeship of Duddy Kravitz* (1959), *Joshua Then and Now* (1980).

Jeanne Sauvé, b. Howell, Sask., 4/26/22, governorgeneral of Canada (1984-), speaker of the House of Commons (1980-83).

Edward Schreyer, b. Beausejour, Man., 12/21/35, premier of Manitoba (1969-77); governor-general of Canada, (1979-1984).

Joey Smallwood, b. Gambo, Nfld., 12/24/00, led Newfoundland into Canada and served as province's first premier (1949-72).

David Suzuki, b. Vancouver, B.C., 3/24/36, scientist, educator, television personality.

E.P. (Edward Plunket) **Taylor,** b. Ottawa, Ont., 1/29/01, industrialist, financier; now lives in the Bahamas.

Ken Taylor, b. Calgary, Alta., 10/5/34, diplomat, engineered escape of 6 U.S. embassy staff members from Iran (1980); Canadian counsul general in New York (1981-1984).

Ken Thomson, b. Toronto, Ont., 9/1/23, chairman of the board of Thomson Newspapers Ltd.

Pierre Elliott Trudeau, b. Montreal, Que., 10/18/19, Canadian prime minister (1968-79) and (1980-1984); leader federal Liberal Party (1968-1984).

John Turner, b. Richmond, Eng., 6/7/29, leader of Liberal Party since June 1984; Canada's 17th prime minister (6/84-9/84); practiced corporate law (1975-84); cabinet minister (1965-75).

Galen Weston, b. England, 10/26/40, chairman and president of George Weston Ltd.

Michael Wilson, b. Toronto, Ont., 11/4/37, Finance Minister (1984-).

Noted Canadians of the Past

William Aberhart, 1878-1943, b. Hibbard twp., Ont., spellbinding orator, founded Social Credit Party in Canada, premier of Alberta (1935-43).

Frederick G. Banting, 1891-1941, b. Alliston, Ont., co-discoverer of insulin, demonstrated its beneficial effects on diabetes (1922), awarded Nobel prize (1923).

W. "Max" Aitken (Baron Beaverbrook), 1879-1964, b. Maple, Ont., best known in Canada as publisher and philanthropist, held several positions in British Cabinet up to 1945.

Charles H. Best, 1899-1978, b. West Pembroke, Me., co-discoverer of insulin.

Norman Bethune, 1890-1939, b. Gravenhurst, Ont., died in northern China as a surgeon with the Chinese revolutionary army.

Billy Bishop, 1894-1956, b. Owen Sound, Ont., WWI flying ace, shot down 72 enemy aircraft, including 25 in a 10-day period in 1918.

Samuel Bronfman, 1891-1971, b. Brandon, Man., industrialist, established Distiller's Corporation—Seagram's Limited.

Emily Carr, 1871-1945, b. Victoria, B.C., painter, best known for sketches of Indian life.

George Etienne Cartier, 1814-1873, b. St. Antoine, Upper Canada; leading French-Canadian Father of Confederation, joint premier of United Canada (1857-62).

John Diefenbaker, 1895-1979, b. Grey Co., Ont., leader of Progressive Conservative Party (1956-67) and prime minister of Canada (1957-63).

Terry Fox, 1958-1981, b. Winnipeg, Man., in 1980, with an artificial leg, began "Marathon of Hope" run across Canada to raise funds for cancer research; run halted by recurring cancer but succeeded in raising more than $20 million.

Glenn Gould, 1932-1982, b. Toronto, Ont., classical pianist and composer.

Joseph Howe, 1804-1873, b. Halifax, N.S., politician, orator and writer, at first fought Nova Scotia entry into Canadian union but later accepted post in federal cabinet.

A.Y. Jackson, 1882-1974, b. Montreal Que., best known of "Group of Seven" Canadian painters.

Pauline Johnson, 1862-1913, b. Six Nations Indian Reserve, Ont., poet.

Cornelius Krieghoff, 1815-1872, b. Amsterdam, Holland, painter, did finest work after moving to Canada in 1846.

W.L. Mackenzie King, 1874-1950, b. Kitchener, Ont., prime minister of Canada a record 22 years (1921-26, 1926-30, 1935-48).

Wilfrid Laurier, 1841-1919, b. Saint Lin, Lower Canada, leader of Canadian Liberal Party (1887-1919) and prime minister (1896-1911).

Stephen Leacock, 1869-1944, b. Swanmoor, Hants, Eng., humorist, author, *Sunshine Sketches of a Little Town.*

John A. Macdonald, 1815-1891, b. Glasgow, Scotland, chief architect of Confederation and Canada's first prime minister (1867-1873 and 1878-1891).

William Lyon Mackenzie, 1795-1861, b. Scotland; politician and rebel, chief organizer of 1837 rebellion for political reform in Upper Canada, first mayor of Toronto (1835).

Vincent Massey, 1887-1967, b. Toronto, Ont., first native-born governor-general of Canada (1952-1959).

Thomas D'Arcy McGee, 1825-1868, b. Carlingford, Ireland, eloquent advocate of confederation; assassinated Apr. 7, 1868.

Marshall McLuhan, 1911-1980, b. Edmonton, Alta., author and educator best known for theories on communication. *The Medium is the Massage* (1967).

Nellie McClung, 1873-1951, b. Chatsworth, Ont., author and feminist.

John McCrae, 1872-1918, b. Guelph, Ont., poet, best known for *In Flanders Fields.*

Lucy Maud Montgomery, 1874-1942, b. Clifton, P.E.I., author, *Anne of Green Gables* (1908).

Susanna Moodie, 1803-1885, b. Suffolk, Eng., author, best known for *Roughing It In the Bush* (1852).

William Osler, 1849-1919, b. Bond Head, Upper Canada, physician and author.

Louis Joseph Papineau, 1786-1871, b. Montreal, Lower Canada, led movement for political reform in Lower Canada.

Lester B. Pearson, 1897-1972, b. Toronto, Ont., Canadian prime minister (1963-68); awarded Nobel peace prize (1957) for organizing United Nations intervention in 1956 Suez Canal crisis.

Edwin J. Pratt, 1883-1964, b. Western Bay, Nfld., poet.

Louis Riel, 1844-1885, b. St. Boniface, Man., led Metis of Western Canada in North West rebellions of 1870 and 1885, hung for treason in Regina.

Hans Selye, 1907-1982, b. Vienna, Austria, discovered evidence (1936) that mental stress affects the body's physical state.

Robert W. Service, 1874-1958, b. Preston, Eng., poet, *Songs of a Sourdough* (1907).

Roy Thomson (Lord Thomson of Fleet), 1894-1976, b. Toronto, Ont., newspaper publisher.

Tom Thomson, 1877-1917, b. Claremont, Ont., painter, influenced "Group of Seven" Canadian artists.

W. Garfield Weston, 1898-1978, b. Toronto, Ont., industrialist.

James S. Woodsworth, 1874-1942, b. Etobicoke, Ont., a founder of the Co-operative Commonwealth Federation, forerunner of the New Democratic Party.

Canadian Government Budget
Source: Canadian Statistical Review
(millions of Canadian dollars)

Expenditures

Fiscal Year	National defense	Health and welfare	Agriculture	Public debt Charges	Public works	Transport	Veterans affairs	Payments to provinces	Total expenditures
1978-79..	4,108	13,204	768	7,058	1,657	1,725	890	3,028	46,923
1979-80..	4,389	14,038	782	8,465	1,615	1,726	933	3,522	52,297
1980-81..	5,078	15,792	881	10,686	1,883	2,640	1,006	3,788	58,813
1981-82..	6,028	17,818	1,125	15,168	2,188	2,279	1,140	4,535	67,440
1982-83..	6,993	19,588	1,009	16,970	2,669	2,906	1,282	5,390	79,466
1983-84..	7,970	22,554	1,254	18,147	3,172	3,258	1,389	5,647	88,614

Revenues[1]

Fiscal year	Personal income tax	Corporation income tax	Sales tax	Other excise tax	Excise duties	Customs duties	Estate taxes	Return on investments	Total budgetary revenues
1978-79..	14,048	6,262	5,245	827	878	2,747	77	3,158	35,216
1979-80..	16,327	7,537	5,119	1,252	895	3,000	96	3,344	40,159
1980-81..	19,837	8,133	5,882	1,602	1,042	3,188	99	4,130	46,731
1981-82..	24,046	9,136	6,621	2,079	1,175	3,439	595	5,095	54,068
1982-83..	26,329	9,099	6,302	2,341	1,274	2,831	132	5,020	53,446
1983-84..	26,902	9,392	7,046	1,494	1,356	3,380	126	4,746	56,261

(1) This statement includes only receipts relating to revenue. Excluded are non-budgetary revenues such as Old Age Security Fund taxes, Prairie Farm Assistance Act levies, employer and employee contributions to government-held funds.

Budget Surplus or Deficit by Province
Source: Statistics Canada
(millions of $ Canadian)

	1976	1977	1978	1979	1980	1981	1982	1983
Newfoundland	−820	−927	−1,128	−1,178	−1,364	−1,377	−1,829	−2,575
Prince Edward Island	−227	−273	−328	−332	−357	−375	−423	−490
Nova Scotia	−1,465	−1,659	−1,977	−2,181	−2,779	−3,009	−3,195	−3,434
New Brunswick	−1,040	−1,190	−1,233	−1,298	−2,072	−1,958	−2,264	−2,130
Quebec	−2,479	−3,146	−3,863	−4,193	−6,233	−6,958	−8,609	−9,434
Ontario	+1,161	+551	−130	+1,525	+799	+2,020	−2,658	−3,841
Manitoba	−459	−664	−915	−991	−1,177	−1,259	−1,908	−2,083
Saskatchewan	−204	−256	−362	−231	+121	+241	−782	−1,172
Alberta	+2,874	+3,295	+3,886	+4,673	+5,870	+7,809	+6,979	+4,826
British Columbia	+524	+549	+478	+1,136	+796	+1,304	−243	+1,164
Yukon & NWT	−264	−285	−343	−346	−328	−461	−1,172	−966

(1) The difference between provincial govt. revenues and expenditures on a national account (calendar year) basis.

Canada: Taxable Returns by Income, 1982
Source: Revenue Canada Taxation Statistics

Total income in dollars	Number of tax returns	Percent of tax returns	Total income (millions)	Percent of total income	Taxed income (millions)	Federal tax (millions)	Percent of Fed. tax	Fed. Tax rate on total income
$1-5,000	2,537,654	16.68	6,217.8	2.24	197.1	.6	—	—
5,000-10,000	2,684,737	17.63	20,016.7	7.82	6,180.7	379.9	1.38	1.9
10,000-15,000	2,325,041	15.28	28,926.7	11.29	14,586.4	1,722.5	6.22	6.0
15,000-20,000	1,948,993	12.80	33,913.9	13.25	20,356.5	2,907.1	10.51	8.6
20,000-25,000	1,535,855	10.09	34,414.9	13.44	22,514.3	3,550.3	12.83	10.3
25,000-30,000	1,187,831	7.81	32,488.8	12.68	22,258.7	3,773.2	13.64	11.6
30,000-35,000	789,621	5.19	25,516.6	9.97	18,135.8	3,275.1	11.84	12.8
35,000-40,000	479,213	3.14	17,882.8	6.98	13,033.1	2,436.6	8.81	13.6
40,000-50,000	465,553	3.06	20,568.2	8.03	15,410.1	3,013.3	10.89	14.7
50,000-70,000	270,918	1.78	15,628.7	6.10	12,227.9	2,470.2	8.93	15.8
70,000-100,000	98,608	.65	8,065.8	3.15	6,364.9	1,439.0	5.20	17.8
100,000-200,000	53,959	.36	7,090.1	2.77	5,462.3	1,421.6	5.14	20.1
200,000 and over	14,372	.09	5,832.4	2.28	4,003.9	1,275.1	4.61	21.9

Average Canadian Income and Taxes by Occupation, 1982

Source: Revenue Canada Taxation Statistics

Occupation	Number[1]	Average income[2]	Average federal tax	Occupation	Number[1]	Average income[2]	Average federal tax
Self-employed doctors and surgeons	30,577	$75,175	$15,556	Other self-employed professionals	48,415	20,632	2,569
Self-employed dentists	8,276	66,151	13,307	Investors	1,283,943	19,946	1,951
Self-employed lawyers and notaries	16,929	57,882	10,822	Business employees	6,903,677	18,812	2,151
Self-employed accountants	10,699	43,330	7,040	Institutional employees	866,581	17,627	1,787
Self-employed engineers and architects	4,329	40,070	6,836	Property owners	114,366	16,697	1,924
Teachers and professors	307,206	31,178	4,123	Farmers	270,264	15,535	1,112
Federal government employees	342,032	25,053	3,059	Self-employed salesmen	28,632	15,432	1,578
Provincial government employees	514,907	23,589	2,821	Fishermen	38,105	13,004	956
Armed forces employees	82,725	23,487	2,752	Business proprietors	488,406	12,463	1,125
Municipal government employees	551,326	21,304	2,434	Unclassified employees	478,423	10,947	908
				Self-employed entertainers and artists	18,736	10,638	924
				Unclassified	1,823,691	3,679	176
				Total	10,046,877	19,346	2,206

(1) Based on number of tax returns. (2) Average total income after business expense deductions but before personal deductions.

Average Income in Selected Canadian Cities, 1982

Source: Revenue Canada Taxation Statistics

City	Average income[1]	Rank	No. of tax returns	City	Average income[1]	Rank	No. of tax returns
West Vancouver, B.C.	$29,532	1	24,066	Burnaby, B.C.	$18,973	21	89,789
Markham, Ont.	23,814	2	65,689	Brossard, Que.	18,947	22	30,765
Calgary, Alta.	22,297	3	413,969	Whitby, Ont.	18,750	23	24,015
Oakville, Ont.	22,196	4	49,476	Regina, Sask.	18,722	24	107,438
North Vancouver, B.C.	20,820	5	67,244	Red Deer, Alta.	18,640	25	34,257
Burlington, Ont.	20,485	6	71,308	Victoria, B.C.	18,440	28	145,386
Delta, B.C.	20,434	7	44,437	Toronto, Ont.	18,253	31	751,474
Ottawa, Ont.	20,309	8	248,292	Saskatoon, Sask.	17,816	36	103,673
Etobicoke, Ont.	20,179	9	111,882	Scarborough, Ont.	17,662	38	282,046
North York, Ont.	20,174	10	276,276	Halifax, N.S.	16,876	45	79,389
Nepean, Ont.	20,164	11	39,662	London, Ont.	16,839	46	168,447
Edmonton, Alta.	19,941	12	369,980	Hamilton, Ont.	15,908	62	198,643
Gloucester, Ont.	19,902	13	34,840	Kitchener, Ont.	15,836	64	94,386
Richmond, B.C.	19,710	14	63,644	Quebec, Que.	15,771	65	109,011
Vancouver, B.C.	19,654	15	300,544	St. John's, Nfld.	15,754	66	58,123
Mississauga, Ont.	19,561	16	206,986	Fredericton, N.B.	15,662	70	37,525
Richmond Hill, Ont.	19,509	17	24,772	Montreal, Que.	15,564	71	643,668
Coquitlam, B.C.	19,400	18	33,910	Winnipeg, Man.	15,479	72	415,714
Pickering, Ont.	19,270	19	26,542	Drummondville, Que.	13,283	100	26,532
Sarnia, Ont.	19,043	20	44,712				

(1) Average total income after business deductions but before personal deductions.

Canadian Labor Force

Source: Statistics Canada; 1984 annual averages (thousands of persons)

	Can.	Nfld.	P.E.I.	N.S.	N.B.	Que.	Ont.	Man.	Sask.	Alta.	B.C.
Labor force	12,399	211	56	387	291	3,123	4,666	515	477	1,254	1,410
Employed	11,000	176	49	337	248	2,722	4,243	472	439	1,114	1,202
Unemployed	1,399	45	7	51	44	400	423	43	38	140	208
Percent unemployed	11.3	20.5	12.8	13.1	14.9	12.8	9.1	8.3	8.0	11.2	14.7

Canadian Labor Force Characteristics

Source: Statistics Canada (thousands of workers 15 yrs. and over)

Year	Labor force	Employed	Unemployed	Agriculture	Manufacturing	Participation Rate[1] Male	Participation Rate[1] Female	Participation Rate[1] Both Sexes
1975	9,974	9,284	690	497	2,020	78.4	44.4	61.1
1979	11,231	10,395	836	505	2,222	78.5	49.0	63.4
1980	11,573	10,708	865	500	2,292	78.4	50.4	64.1
1981	11,904	11,006	898	508	2,303	78.4	51.7	64.8
1982	11,958	10,644	1,314	493	2,228	77.0	51.7	64.1
1983	12,183	10,734	1,448	513	2,167	76.7	52.6	64.4
1984	12,399	11,000	4,399	511	2,211	76.6	53.5	64.8

(1) Percent in labor force.

Average Weekly Canadian Wages and Salaries, by Province

Source: Statistics Canada (Canadian dollars)

Year & month	Canada[1]	Nfld.	P.E.I.	N.S.	N.B.	Que.	Ont.	Man.	Sask.	Alta.	B.C.
1970	126.82	117.70	83.82	104.21	104.01	122.38	131.52	115.88	114.87	128.15	137.97
1975	203.34	196.50	149.84	172.40	182.40	199.22	204.86	186.01	188.31	207.39	229.97
1981	355.28	328.08	250.13	296.35	313.37	351.57	347.92	314.26	336.78	390.40	407.03
1982	390.79	361.82	278.53	329.06	342.14	386.11	381.88	346.49	373.80	435.47	445.43
1983 (Jan.) . . .	405.61	376.92	297.52	343.01	369.57	397.74	396.26	358.20	384.98	455.89	465.29
1984 (Jan.) . . .	435.42	399.36	296.92	370.13	391.75	431.17	427.71	394.18	412.39	487.18	478.80
1985 (Jan.) . . .	451.13	429.82	299.75	380.53	404.39	444.77	446.44	404.10	430.16	493.58	496.88

(1) Includes Yukon and Northwest Territories.

Canadian Minimum Wages

(hourly rate for experienced adult workers)

Source: Labour Canada

	Fed.[1]	Newf.	P.E.I.	N.S.	N.B.	Que.	Ont.	Man.	Sask.	Alb.	B.C.	Yukon	N.W.T.
1985*	$3.50	$4.00	$4.00	$4.00	$3.80	$4.00	$4.00	$4.30	$4.50	$3.80	$3.65	$4.25	$4.25
1984	3.50	3.75	3.75	3.75	3.80	4.00	4.00	4.00	4.25	3.80	3.65	3.60	4.25
1983	3.50	3.75	3.75	3.75	3.80	4.00	3.50	4.00	4.25	3.80	3.65	3.60	4.25
1982	3.50	3.75	3.75	3.75	3.80	4.00	3.50	4.00	4.25	3.80	3.65	3.60	4.25
1980	3.25	3.15	3.00	3.00	3.05	3.65	3.00	3.15	3.65	3.50	3.65	3.35	3.50
1975	2.60	2.20	2.30	2.25	2.30	2.80	2.40	2.60	2.50	2.50	2.75	2.70	2.50
1970	1.65	1.25(M) 1.00(F)	1.25(M) .95(F)	1.25(M) 1.00(F)	1.15	1.40	1.50	1.50	1.25	1.55	1.50	1.50	1.50
1965	1.25	.70(M) .50(F)	1.00	1.05(M) .80(F)	.80	.85	1.00	.85	$38/wk	1.00	1.00	. . .	. . .

*Announced as of July 1, 1985   M = male; F = female

(1) Applies to work under federal govt. jurisdiction as defined by the Constitution Act, 1867, Sections 91 and 92. (2) Minimum wage rates (1984) for other categories of workers are as follows: **Federal:** under 17, $3.25; **Newf.:** domestics, $2.25; **P.E.I.:** under 18, $3.00; **N.S.:** 14-18 yrs., $3.40; **Que.:** under 18, $3.54; receiving gratuities, $3.28 (18 and over) or $2.95 (under 18); live-in domestics, $134/wk.; other domestics and agricultural workers, $4.00 (18 and over) or $3.54 (under 18); **Ont.:** students under 18 (working up to 28 hrs./wk.), $3.15; serving alcohol, $3.50; construction workers, $4.25; domestics (working more than 24 hrs./wk.), $3.50; **Man.:** under 18, $3.55; serving alcohol, $4.00; **Alb.:** under 18 not attending school, $3.65; under 18 attending school, $3.30; salespersons, $125/wk.; **B.C.:** under 18 $3.00; domestics, farm workers, $29.20 per day or part day; **N.W.T.:** under 17, $3.75.

Canadian Unemployment Insurance Commission

Source: Canadian Statistical Review, April, 1985
(Canadian dollars)

	Claims data				Benefits paid				
Year	Benefi- ciaries[1][2] (000)	Claims received (000)	Weeks paid	Total paid (thousands of dollars)	Regular	Sickness	Maternity	Retirement	Fishing
1979 . .	713	2,602	36,896	4,008,002	3,341,216	145,183	207,649	15,055	70,897
1980 . .	703	2,762	36,333	4,393,307	3,748,551	154,671	234,746	15,950	82,570
1981 . .	720	2,895	37,013	4,828,273	4,115,888	164,262	273,054	17,582	92,444
1982 . .	1,138	3,921	60,440	8,575,445	7,646,023	174,415	315,973	18,166	111,856
1983 . .	1,248	3,434	66,584	10,169,064	9,069,503	179,476	344,170	18,515	141,836
1984 . .	1,193	3,493	61,862	9,985,625	8,825,128	204,560	395,918	19,159	163,373

(1) Refer to the number of persons receiving $1.00 or more in unemployment insurance benefits during a specific week each month. (2) Annual figures are average of 12 months.

Canadian Provincial Unemployment Rates

Source: Statistics Canada

Year	Can.	Nfld.	P.E.I.	N.S.	N.B.	Que.	Ont.	Man.	Sask.	Alta.	B.C.
1979 . .	7.5	15.4	11.3	10.2	11.1	9.6	6.5	5.4	4.2	3.9	7.7
1980 . .	7.5	13.5	10.8	9.8	11.1	9.9	6.9	5.5	4.4	3.7	6.8
1981 . .	7.6	14.1	11.4	10.2	11.7	10.4	6.6	6.0	4.6	3.8	6.7
1982 . .	11.0	16.8	12.9	13.2	14.0	13.8	9.8	8.5	6.2	7.7	12.1
1983 . .	11.9	18.8	12.2	13.2	14.8	13.9	10.4	9.4	7.4	10.8	13.8
1984 . .	13.3	20.5	12.8	13.1	14.9	12.8	9.1	8.3	8.0	11.2	14.7

Canadian Consumer Price Index

Source: Statistics Canada
(All items: 1971 = 100)

Year	Avg.	Year	Avg.	Year	Avg.	Year	Avg.
1965	80.5	1973	112.7	1977	160.8	1981	236.9
1969	94.1	1974	125.0	1978	175.2	1982	262.5
1970	97.2	1975	138.5	1979	191.2	1983	277.6
1971	100.0	1976	148.9	1980	210.6	1984	289.7

Price Indexes By Item

Source: Canadian Statistical Review, April, 1984 (1971 = 100)

Year and month	All items	Food	Shelter	Clothing	Trans- portation	Health, personal	Recreation, education	Tobacco, alcohol	Total services
1980	210.6	260.6	192.4	178.7	200.7	199.3	173.5	185.3	201.8
1981	236.9	290.4	213.2	191.4	237.6	221.0	191.0	209.2	225.0
1982	262.5	311.3	239.2	202.1	271.1	244.4	207.6	241.6	254.0
1983	277.6	322.9	255.4	210.2	284.6	261.2	221.2	272.0	270.5
1984	289.7	340.9	270.1	215.3	296.5	271.4	228.6	294.1	280.8
1985 (Jan.). .	295.2	345.9	276.3	215.5	305.1	275.6	231.9	302.7	285.5

Personal Expenditure on Consumer Goods and Services in Current Dollars

Source: Statistics Canada   (millions of dollars)

	1970	1975	1978	1979	1980	1981	1982	1983
Food and non-alcoholic beverages	7,923	15,206	20,014	22,475	24,883	28,226	30,607	32,194
Alcoholic beverages	1,898	3,501	4,464	4,867	5,514	6,330	7,215	7,777
Tobacco products.	1,396	2,050	2,689	2,973	3,313	3,872	4,439	5,108
Clothing and footwear.	4,034	7,155	9,507	10,632	11,614	12,988	13,475	14,329
Gross rent, fuel and power.	9,861	16,445	25,613	28,824	32,964	38,014	44,368	48,715
Furniture, appliances, and other household furnishing & services	4,785	9,884	13,006	14,333	15,494	16,995	17,356	19,294
Medical care and health services	1,758	2,896	4,346	4,791	5,502	6,335	7,070	7,884
New and used cars	2,337	5,132	6,546	7,527	7,721	8,379	7,438	9,394
Car repairs and parts.	1,038	1,980	2,755	3,139	3,406	3,744	3,891	4,072
Gasoline, oil and grease	1,383	2,948	4,100	4,640	5,639	7,465	8,377	8,639
Recreation and reading.	3,065	7,249	7,245	8,148	9,057	10,088	10,584	11,499
Educational and cultural services	1,402	2,723	3,838	4,171	4,627	5,266	5,935	6,358
Personal goods and services	7,133	15,062	21,679	24,285	27,698	31,338	33,171	35,587
Total, consumer goods and services . . .	**50,327**	**96,995**	**136,532**	**152,088**	**170,179**	**193,280**	**209,974**	**229,184**

Canada's Largest Corporations

Source: The Financial Post 500; Toronto, Canada; June, 1985

Company (Home office)	Sales or operating revenue C$000	Assets C$000	Foreign owner- ship %	Major Shareholders
General Motors of Canada Ltd. (Oshawa, Ont.)	16,297,747	3,862,831	100	General Motors Corp., Detroit
Canadian Pacific Ltd. (Montreal, Que.)	14,635,095	18,796,122		Power Corp. of Canada 11%
Ford Motor Co. of Canada (Oakville, Ont.)	12,122,000	2,762,500	90	Ford Motor Co., Dearborn, Mich.
Bell Canada Enterprises Inc. (Montreal, Que.)	10,578,700	17,486,000		Wide distribution
Imperial Oil Ltd. (Toronto, Ont.)	8,448,000	8,781,000	70	Exxon Corp., New York
George Weston Ltd. (Toronto, Ont.)	8,254,700	2,279,000		Wittington Investments Ltd. 57%
Alcan Aluminium Ltd. (Montreal, Que.)	7,078,672[1]	8,842,173	44	Wide distribution
Chrysler Canada Ltd. (Windsor, Ont.)	6,292,000	1,119,600	100	Chrysler Corp., Detroit
Texaco Canada Inc. (Toronto, Ont.)	6,156,000	3,409,000	90	Texaco Inc. 68%, Texaco International 22%
Shell Canada Ltd. (Calgary, Alta.)	5,734,000	5,776,000	72	Shell Investments Ltd., Neth./Brit.
Gulf Canada Ltd. (Toronto, Ont.)	5,316,000	5,635,000	70	Chevron Corp., San Francisco, 60%
Canadian Wheat Board (Winnipeg, Man.)	5,191,000[2]	5,029,850		Federal govt. 100%
Canadian National Railway (Montreal, Que.)	5,002,500	7,466,611		Federal govt. 100%
PetroCanada (Calgary, Alta.)	4,881,293	9,055,282		Federal govt. 100%
Hudson's Bay Co. (Winnipeg, Man.)	4,829,325	3,950,812		Woodbridge Co. 73%
Provigo Inc. (Montreal, Que.)	4,367,372	728,966		Caisse de depot 26%, Sobeys Stores 17%
TransCanada Pipelines Ltd. (Calgary, Alta.)	4,231,500	5,799,200		Bell Canada Enterprises Inc. 47%
Ontario Hydro (Toronto, Ont.)	4,212,000	27,301,000		Ontario govt. 100%
Brascan Ltd. (Toronto, Ont.)	4,209,000[3]	3,640,500	16	Brascan Holdings Corp. 44%
Canada Development Corp. (Vancouver, B.C.)	4,180,900	7,648,900		Federal govt. 47%

(1) All figures converted from U.S.$. (2) Sales include grain purchases for the account and delivered to CWB; assets include grain held for the account of CWB. (3) Includes beneficial interest in gross revenues of consumer products, natural resources and other operations; excludes financial services.

Work Stoppages (Strikes and Lockouts) in Canada

Source: Labour Canada

Year	Number of stoppages	Workers involved	Person days idle	% of working time	Year	Number of stoppages	Workers involved	Person days idle	% of working time
1965	501	171,870	2,349,870	.17	1975	1,171	506,443	10,908,810	.53
1966	617	411,459	5,178,170	.34	1976	1,039	1,570,940	11,609,890	.55
1967	522	252,018	3,974,760	.25	1977	803	217,557	3,307,880	.15
1968	582	223,562	5,082,732	.32	1978	1,058	401,688	7,392,820	.34
1969	595	306,799	7,751,880	.46	1979	1,050	462,504	7,834,230	.34
1970	542	261,706	6,539,560	.39	1980	1,028	441,025	8,975,390	.38
1971	569	239,631	2,866,590	.16	1981	1,048	338,548	8,878,490	.37
1972	598	706,474	7,753,530	.43	1982	677	444,302	5,795,420	.25
1973	724	348,470	5,776,080	.30	1983	645	329,309	4,443,960	.19
1974	1,218	580,912	9,221,890	.46	1984	717	184,924	3,890,480	.18

Canadian Economic Indicators

Source: Statistics Canada; Dept. of Finance

Year	Per capita personal income	Unemploy -ment rate	Inflation rate(1)	Federal budget surplus or deficit(2) (millions of $)	Per capita national debt(3)(4)	Gross national product(5) (millions of $)	GNP real growth(6)
1950	$ 1,040	3.6%	2.9%	+650	$ 837	33,762	7.6%
1955	1,355	4.4%	.1%	+202	783	43,891	9.4%
1960	1,656	7.0%	1.4%	−229	801	53,231	2.9%
1965	2,091	3.9%	2.4%	+544	870	69,981	6.7%
1970	3,129	5.7%	3.3%	+266	878	88,390	2.5%
1975	6,001	6.9%	10.8%	−3,805	1,317	113,005	1.2%
1979	9,069	7.4%	9.2%	−9,131	2,966	130,362	3.2%
1980	10,178	7.5%	10.2%	−10,393	3,465	131,675	1.1%
1982	12,887	11.0%	10.8%	−18,904	4,942	130,065	−4.4%
1983	13,542	11.9%	5.8%	−24,100	6,162	134,361	3.3%
1984	14,412	11.3%	4.4%	−29,659	7,518	141,097	5.0%

(1) As measured by % change in the Consumer Price Index from previous year. (2) Difference between federal govt. revenues and expenditures. (3) For fiscal year ending March 31 of the following calendar year. (4) Federal govt. debt measured by accumulated budgetary deficits since 1867, divided by Canadian population. (5) Gross National Product is a measure of all goods and services produced in the country; in constant dollars. (6) Real (after inflation) change in Gross National Product over the previous year.

Canadian Direct Investment Abroad[1]

Source: Statistics Canada
(millions of Canadian dollars)

Location	1979	%	1980	%	1981	%	1982	%	1983	%
North America and Caribbean	13,633	68.1	18,254	70.7	23,868	73.4	25,081	74.1	27,130	75.7
United States	12,104	60.4	16,395	63.5	21,832	67.1	22,990	67.9	25,027	69.8
Europe	3,729	18.7	4,353	16.9	4,745	14.6	4,572	13.5	3,870	10.8
United Kingdom	2,082	10.4	2,439	9.4	2,451	7.5	2,174	6.4	1,852	5.2
South and Central America	979	4.9	1,037	4.0	1,170	3.6	1,324	3.9	1,402	3.9
Asia	783	3.9	1,129	4.4	1,320	4.1	1,460	4.3	2,057	5.7
Australasia	643	3.2	752	2.9	1,057	3.2	1,096	3.2	1,044	2.9
Africa	260	1.3	278	1.1	377	1.2	332	0.9	330	0.9
Total	20,027		25,803		32,537		33,865		35,833	

(1) Long-term Canadian capital invested in companies outside Canada in which the Canadian investor has a voice in the management of the operation.

Canadian Foreign Trade with Leading Countries

Source: Statistics Canada

(millions of dollars)

Exports from Canada to the following areas and countries and imports into Canada from those areas and countries:	Imports			Exports		
	1982	1983	1984	1982	1983	1984
Total	67,856	75,587	95,754	81,825	88,506	109,543
United States	47,866	54,103	68,450	55,847	64,528	82,796
Western Europe	7,026	7,527	10,028	8,516	7,560	7,932
United Kingdom	1,904	1,810	2,317	2,670	2,449	2,443
West Germany	1,384	1,577	2,173	1,234	1,156	1,221
France	877	841	1,219	707	626	701
Italy	725	798	1,116	695	549	578
Netherlands	267	349	545	1,044	958	1,063
Belgium and Luxembourg	264	296	448	773	700	677
Asia	6,182	7,828	10,331	8,066	8,629	9,743
Japan	3,527	4,409	5,711	4,568	4,728	5,629
Taiwan	661	925	1,224	290	342	401
Hong Kong	669	820	966	243	221	215
South Korea	586	791	1,152	484	556	713
China, People's Republic of	204	246	334	1,228	1,607	1,272
India	91	101	147	288	262	468
South America	2,694	2,047	2,440	1,501	1,316	1,531
Venezuela	1,805	1,004	1,207	424	232	248
Brazil	482	500	669	537	596	775
Middle East	967	865	452	1,822	1,412	1,664
Saudi Arabia	731	94	1	443	365	362
Central America and Antilles	1,627	1,765	2,280	1,470	1,412	1,427
Mexico	998	1,079	1,438	446	375	351
Cuba	95	56	63	324	361	336
Jamaica	125	110	139	68	64	74
Africa	659	678	952	1,154	937	1,125
Oceania	592	521	513	836	576	816
Australia	444	357	381	649	438	617
New Zealand	140	157	122	156	122	189
Eastern Europe	240	250	306	2,579	2,110	2,480
USSR	42	33	29	2,069	1,762	2,122

Canadian Imports and Exports of Leading Commodities

Source: Statistics Canada

(millions of dollars)

Commodity	Imports 1982	Imports 1983	Imports 1984	Exports 1982	Exports 1983	Exports 1984
Total	67,856	75,587	95,754	81,825	88,506	109,543
Live animals	136	132	94	325	340	520
Food, beverages, tobacco	4,802	4,870	5,810	9,896	10,074	10,298
Meat.	326	356	437	780	701	755
Fish	352	418	487	1,582	1,546	1,572
Fruits and vegetables	1,873	1,880	2,169	400	394	412
Wheat	. . .	. . .	. . .	4,289	4,648	4,710
Crude petroleum	4,979	3,274	3,376	2,729	3,457	4,390
Natural gas.	. . .	. . .	. . .	4,755	3,958	3,886
Coal.	932	840	1,094	1,269	1,313	1,847
Sulphur	. . .	. . .	. . .	720	572	831
Wood and paper.	873	1,198	1,423	11,717	12,840	15,156
Textiles	1,193	1,479	1,734	242	227	276
Chemicals	3,586	4,392	5,210	4,035	4,337	5,299
Iron and steel	1,238	1,175	1,642	1,965	1,643	2,227
Aluminum, including alloys	367	438	715	1,428	1,744	1,900
General and industrial machinery	5,657	5,292	6,617	2,485	2,368	2,844
Agricultural machinery	277	264	361	651	551	655
Transportation equipment	17,481	22,519	30,248	19,471	23,781	32,345
Cars and chassis.	4,043	6,209	7,889	7,358	9,573	13,890
Trucks, tractors, chassis	935	1,167	2,036	3,938	4,215	5,383
Motor vehicle parts, except engines	7,944	9,333	13,011	3,926	5,753	7,639
Motor vehicle engines	1,276	1,403	1,868	926	1,549	2,119
Other equipment and tools	9,695	11,320	15,126	2,466	2,761	3,436

Canadian Sea Fish Catch and Exports

Source: Fisheries and Oceans Canada

Year	Total Value	Landings of Sea Fish Total	Nfld.	P.E.I.	N.S.	N.B.	Que.	B.C.	Exports to[1] Total	U.S.	Other
		(in metric tons)							(in metric tons)		
1977 . . .	456,130,000	1,211,408	394,148	19,801	407,368	131,937	54,292	203,862	376,758	204,436	172,322
1978 . . .	668,191,000	1,352,027	463,959	25,660	444,869	151,393	67,350	198,796	422,390	224,077	198,177
1979 . . .	840,267,000	1,393,295	569,107	31,059	421,154	137,217	79,165	155,593	425,746	233,421	192,325
1980 . . .	692,356,000	1,286,014	499,199	33,463	436,822	105,356	81,248	129,926	430,917	220,494	210,106
1981 . . .	804,323,000	1,377,694	498,721	38,515	467,473	102,257	87,591	183,137	531,866	276,308	255,558
1982 . . .	829,184,000	1,355,475	504,458	36,788	460,792	109,001	86,593	157,843	550,078	294,106	255,972
1983 . . .	831,971,000	1,299,982	455,839	40,424	425,854	107,919	78,403	191,543	497,435	298,521	198,914

Marketed Value of Canadian Fish Catches

Source: Fisheries and Oceans Canada (thousands of Canadian dollars)

Province	1983[1]	1982[1]	Province	1983[1]	1982[1]
Newfoundland	461,529	504,453	Manitoba.	26,965	31,941
Prince Edward Island	84,782	58,153	Saskatchewan	5,037	6,988
Nova Scotia	497,664	523,191	Alberta	1,874	1,748
New Brunswick	316,435	289,167	British Columbia.	471,654	466,899
Quebec	120,334	104,543	Yukon & NWT.	2,022	2,948
Ontario	55,676	73,576	Total[2]	1,980,713	2,022,051

(1) Value after processing, both sea and freshwater fisheries; includes marine plants, aquatic mammals etc. (2) The sum of the provincial totals differs from the Canada total due to removal of inter-provincial shipments.

Canadian Balance of International Payments

Source: Statistics Canada (millions of Canadian dollars)

Year	Total current receipts	Total current payments	Current account balance	Goods and Services Receipts	Goods and Services Payments	Goods and Services Balance	Merchandise trade Exports	Merchandise trade Imports	Merchandise trade Balance	Service transactions Receipts	Service transactions Payments	Service transactions Balance
1930	1,297	1,634	−337	1,272	1,579	−307	880	973	−93	392	606	−214
1935	1,152	1,027	+125	1,129	1,000	+129	732	526	+206	397	474	−77
1940	1,799	1,648	+151	1,749	1,606	+143	1,202	1006	+196	547	600	−53
1945	4,486	3,797	+689	4,402	2,889	1,513	3,474	1,442	2,032	928	1,447	−519
1950	4,284	4,603	−319	4,158	4,492	−334	3,139	3,132	+7	1,019	1,360	−341
1955	5,926	6,613	−687	5,737	6,390	−653	4,332	4,543	−211	1,405	1,847	−442
1960	7,215	8,448	−1,233	6,982	8,089	−1,107	5,392	5,540	−148	1,590	2,549	−959
1965	11,648	12,778	−1,130	11,182	12,341	−1,159	8,745	8,627	+118	2,437	3,714	−1,277
1970	21,932	20,826	+1,106	21,167	20,214	+953	16,921	13,869	+3,052	4,246	6,345	−2,099
1975	41,940	46,597	−4,757	40,452	45,589	−5,137	33,511	33,962	−451	6,941	11,627	−4,686
1980	92,921	94,825	−1,904	90,258	93,443	−3,185	76,170	68,360	+7,810	14,088	25,083	−10,995
1981	102,543	107,889	−5,346	99,468	106,375	−6,907	84,221	76,870	7,351	15,247	29,505	−14,258
1982	104,617	101,600	+3,017	101,438	99,863	+1,575	84,577	66,239	+18,338	16,861	33,624	−16,763
1983	110,905	109,219	+1,686	108,167	107,263	+904	90,825	73,120	+17,705	17,342	34,143	−16,801
1984	134,980	133,025	+1,955	131,867	130,707	+1,160	112,511	91,679	+20,831	19,357	39,028	−19,671

Canadian Farm Cash Receipts by Province

Source: Statistics Canada
(millions of Canadian dollars)

Province	1977	1978	1979	1980	1981	1982	1983	1984
Newfoundland	21.9	23.4	26.4	28.1	32.1	35.1	35.7	40.7
Prince Edward Island	89.7	100.4	123.1	138.8	189.2	162.3	175.7	193.2
Nova Scotia	134.6	157.7	180.6	197.1	226.3	235.5	235.4	263.8
New Brunswick	110.7	122.7	141.7	151.0	201.5	199.7	197.3	225.2
Quebec	1,449.0	1,694.2	1,982.9	2,279.8	2,708.5	2,795.1	2,718.4	3,033.7
Ontario	2,859.1	3,422.7	4,021.9	4,393.5	4,972.6	4,935.0	5,067.7	5,330.0
Manitoba	893.6	1,141.0	1,326.9	1,480.6	1,658.9	1,672.0	1,720.9	1,946.5
Saskatchewan	2,160.9	2,507.9	3,021.8	3,302.5	4,008.3	4,008.9	3,937.3	4,315.8
Alberta	1,961.9	2,283.9	2,829.9	3,143.0	3,867.6	3,796.8	3,683.5	3,910.4
British Columbia	508.7	579.6	669.5	768.6	888.9	942.1	887.3	971.3
Total	**10,190.2**	**12,033.5**	**14,324.7**	**15,883.0**	**18,753.9**	**18,782.5**	**18,659.2**	**20,230.6**

Harvested Acreage of Principal Canadian Crops

Source: Statistics Canada (thousands of acres)

Province	1981	1982	1983	1984	Province	1981	1982	1983	1984
Prince Edward Island	373	376	371	374	Saskatchewan	28,390	28,631	29,193	30,307
Nova Scotia	231	237	239	242	Alberta	20,097	20,430	20,786	20,990
New Brunswick	290	294	295	298	British Columbia	1,235	1,351	1,402	1,424
Quebec	3,940	4,053	4,158	4,271					
Ontario	8,456	8,396	8,416	8,559					
Manitoba	10,629	10,630	10,857	11,353	Total	73,641[1]	74,398[1]	75,726[1]	77,827[1]

Crops included are winter wheat, spring wheat, oats, barley, fall rye, flaxseed, mixed grains, corn for grain, buckwheat, peas, dry beans, soybeans, rapeseed, potatoes, mustard seed, sunflower seed, tame hay, fodder corn, and sugar beets. (1) Totals include Newfoundland potatoes; (1981) 840 acres; (1982) 800 acres; (1983) 700 acres; (1984) 700 acres.

Production of Principal Field Crops in Canada

Source: Statistics Canada

1984	Wheats 1,000 bushels	Oats 1,000 bushels	Barley 1,000 bushels	Ryes 1,000 bushels	Flaxseed 1,000 bushels
Canada[1]	778,920	173,197	470,891	26,131	26,600
Prince Edward Island	392	1,740	2,544	—	—
Nova Scotia	287	1,167	648	224	—
New Brunswick	420	1,758	680	—	—
Quebec	4,409	23,343	18,372	197	—
Ontario	30,412	17,989	28,247	3,180	—
Manitoba	137,500	29,000	89,000	7,710	16,500
Saskatchewan	422,000	31,000	113,000	9,050	8,800
Alberta	178,500	64,000	211,000	5,400	1,300
British Columbia	5,000	3,200	7,400	370	—

	Mixed grains 1,000 bushels	Corn grains 1,000 bushels	Soybeans 1,000 bushels	Rapeseed 1,000 bushels	Potatoes 1,000 c.w.t.
Canada[1]	70,826	276,500	34,302	143,120	60,049
Prince Edward Island	4,756	—	—	—	19,080
Nova Scotia	309	480	—	—	861
New Brunswick	115	—	—	—	10,530
Quebec	7,349	53,147	—	—	4,039
Ontario	42,897	212,223	34,302	920	7,486
Manitoba	5,800	9,300	—	24,000	5,829
Saskatchewan	2,400	—	—	58,000	456
Alberta	6,500	1,350	—	57,000	4,675
British Columbia	700	—	—	3,200	2,093

	Mustard seed 1,000 pounds	Sunflower seed 1,000 pounds	Tame hay 1,000 tons	Fodder corn 1,000 tons	Sugar beets 1,000 tons
Canada[1]	222,000	180,000	28,284	11,705	1,027
Prince Edward Island	—	—	281	50	—
Nova Scotia	—	—	425	89	—
New Brunswick	—	—	378	53	—
Quebec	—	—	5,842	3,307	143
Ontario	—	—	7,843	7,206	—
Manitoba	34,000	168,000	2,300	270	374
Saskatchewan	150,000	12,000	2,300	—	—
Alberta	38,000	—	7,000	380	510
British Columbia	—	—	1,900	350	—

(1) Excluding Newfoundland.

Off-Beat News Stories of 1985

Calling Rambo — *Soldier of Fortune* magazine offerred $1 million to anyone who defected from Nicaragua and flew a Soviet Mi-24 helicopter back. The magazine called the craft "the world's most lethal attack helicopter"—with 32 rockets, 4 laser-guided anti-tank missiles, and a 4-barrel machine gun. Only Nicaraguan, Soviet, E. German, or Cuban pilots, crew members or trainers were eligible for the reward. Mercenaries, hijackers, and U.S. citizens need not apply.

Talk about slow negotiations — The mayors of Carthage and Rome officially made peace when they put their names on a symbolic friendship and collaboration pact at a ceremony at the ruins of ancient Carthage in Tunisia. Over 2,000 years earlier, Carthage sent Hannibal and his elephants across the Alps against the Romans, who retaliated by razing Carthage.

Sports legends — Marc Magnan, of the Indianapolis Checkers hockey team had the tip of his nose bitten off during a fight with Chris McSorley. He was sueing for $100,000.

Angelo Spagnolo was recognized as the Worst Avid Golfer by Golf Magazine when he shot a 257—185 over par on the Tournament Players Club Course at Ponte Vedra, Fla. On the 17th Hole, Spagnolo lost 27 balls in the lake and took a 66.

The 8th Congressional District in Indiana was without a representative because of a dispute over the 1984 election. The district's most famous citizen, Larry Bird of the Boston Celtics, didn't seem overly concerned. Bird claimed that the district didn't need a congressman, and suggested that the representative should be "the guy who can drink the most beer."

The oldest profession — The 350-member Moapa band of Paiute Indians decided that the answer to poverty and an unemployment rate of 83 percent was to open a brothel on their reservation. The brothel, which was to become the closest legal brothel to Las Vegas, would be used as a springboard to other enterprises such as a gas station, truck stop, and RV park. Currently, the main industry on the reservation is bagging manure from a nearby dairy plant for fertilizer. The U.S. Interior Department rejected the idea as "not the kind of economic development envisioned by federal policy." The tribe took the Interior Department to court to settle the issue.

You think your train is late — The Soviet Union has been having trouble keeping track of things lately. A train consisting of 28 freight cars with crushed rock left a Ukrainian factory on June 24, 1983 and hasn't been seen since. When the situation came up at the central national office of the Soviet rail ministry in Moscow 2 years later on June 2, 1985, it was decided that it was impossible to do anything, since all the documents concerning shipments were kept for one year and destroyed.

A tankless job — The Soviets, however, did find out what happened to the tank that was lost in Czechoslovakia during Warsaw Pact maneuvers. Authorities discovered that 4 Soviet soldiers traded their tank to a tavern owner for 24 bottles of vodka, 7 pounds of herring, and some pickles. The owner dismantled the tank and sold the pieces to a metal-recycling center.

You're all wet ... sir — The U.S. Army announced that men in uniform would not be permitted to carry umbrellas. Although the Army would not discuss the reasoning behind their decision, a source indicated that the Army leadership considered the image of male Army officers walking around with umbrellas "somehow intrinsically unmilitary" and "an artificial affectation." The Air Force allows its men to use umbrellas and women in all the services are permitted to use them.

Did Tarzan have insurance?— The British Medical Journal issued a report citing trees as the most common cause of injuries in several sections of Melanesia. Their 4-year study of admissions to the Provincial Hospital in Milne Bay Province, Papua New Guinea found that tree-associated accidents accounted for 41 percent of admissions for wounds and injuries. The types of accidents included falling off a tree while climbing, being struck by a falling tree limb or by a falling coconut, tripping over fallen tree limbs, and being struck by a crashing tree while trying to cut it down.

A pocketfull of miracles — Margaret Burke had visited St. Jude's Catholic Church every day for 9 days to pray to St. Jude, the patron saint of hopeless causes, to help her to keep her home. On the ninth day, she found an envelope at the saint's statue containing one hundred $100 bills. The Rev. John Steger, the pastor of the suburban Rochester N.Y. church, reported the missing money as a theft after learning from another parishioner about Burke's good fortune. The money, it was later discovered, was left by a parishioner as an anonymous donation for prayers answered by St. Jude. Burke took the money thinking that it was the answer to her prayers. Larceny charges against her were dropped.

Looking out for number one — Jay Shaheri sued the estate of Mildred Walker for $20 million after Walker leaped to her death from a window of her 19th-floor New York City apartment and hit Shaheri, who was walking on the street below. His suit claimed that he suffered "neurological and psychological" injuries when he was struck by Walker. Punitive damages were sought against Walker's estate because of her alleged "willful, reckless, and wanton" disregard for the safety of others.

There's no place like home — A guard at the Litchfield Correctional Center in Connecticut was surprised when he discovered William Tilley trying to break into the institution, especially since Tilley was supposed to be inside the prison. An investigation revealed that prisoners had been using sheets hanging from a second-story window to come and go as they pleased. Tilley, after taking a prison break was apprehended when he broke a first-floor window while trying to get back into jail.

"You dirty rat ..."— A Regensburg, West Germany policeman, struggling with a suspected shoplifter, was attacked by the suspect's pet rat. The rat came to its master's defense by springing onto the head of the arresting officer. The policeman was able to subdue and arrest the suspect, who was described as a punk rocker.

No soaps, but lots of suds — Hundreds of British pubs banned American prime-time soap operas such as *Dallas* and *Dynasty* from their bar television sets because customers became so engrossed that they forgot to drink. A spokesman for a pub chain said that the soaps were "killing the art of good conversation" over the traditional pint.

What do you expectorate?— Spitting is now recognized as a major social ill in China. A major campaign has begun in Peking, where as many as 150,000 health inspectors roam the streets of the city handing out pamphlets and fines of 18 cents. Stalls are set up at busy intersections, where offenders are required to peer through microscopes at bacteria. Citizens are often confronted by flag-waving school children chanting: "To spit on the streets is unhealthy. On no account spit on the ground."

Chinese ratatouille — In some rural areas of China, it was reported that the popularity of rat steaks and rat-skin shoes have helped to control the pests that are said to consume 15 million tons of grain a year. It was reported that in areas of southern China, live rats were sold for 50 cents a pound, about the same as chicken. In Fujian Province, people hail rat steak as the best steak in the world.

Thai-ing the tubes — In Thailand, over 1,000 men, lured by prizes and a holiday atmosphere, celebrated the king's birthday by receiving free vasectomies. T-shirts were handed out that said, "I am safe now," and prizes such as hotel lunches and airline tickets to Singapore and Hong Kong were raffled off. Sterilization clinics for women are set up on the queen's birthday. In the past 10 years, the birthrate in Thailand has dropped from 3.3 to 1.6 children per family.

Poetic justice — The Brookfield, Conn. police arrested a man they believed could be the world's dumbest robber. The suspect was hitchhiking and was picked up by a passing motorist. He punched the driver in the nose and stole his wallet. When he got home he not only found that the stolen wallet was empty, but also found that he had left his own wallet, which contained $70, in the victim's car. The hitchhiker then called the victim and offered to exchange wallets. The victim agreed to a meeting and called the police.

ASTRONOMY AND CALENDAR

Edited by Dr. Kenneth L. Franklin, Astronomer Emeritus
American Museum-Hayden Planetarium

Celestial Events Highlights, 1986

The year 1986 gets off to a rather slow start with respect to an evening planet show. January is saved somewhat by Jupiter, visible low in the western sky after sunset, and by the presence of Halley's Comet in the same neighborhood. The comet will be 9° north of the bright planet on the 20th, and it sets about an hour later. At the present writing, in mid-1985, the brightness of Halley's Comet in January is not predictable. Its being in our sky this month is about the best viewers in the northern hemisphere can expect, for when it is lost in the western twilight's glow by the end of the month, it will emerge in the dawn's light by late February. It will then begin a steady march to the south, reaching its "low" just when it is closest to the earth in the second week of April. At that time Halley's Comet, although at opposition and due south about midnight, will be invisible for any one staying north of a line running roughly from New York City to San Francisco. As it comes back to the north, it is also leaving the neighborhood of the earth, heading for the cold of distant space. Thus it will fade more quickly each day.

Saturn will begin to take prominence in our evening sky as the comet declines. The ringed planet rises about 9 pm by the end of April, followed by Mars an hour and a half later. Saturn spends much time north of Antares in the scorpion, passing the star three times. Mars is to the east, mostly in Sagittarius, and Jupiter is 2 constellations away, in Aquarius. But Mars puts on a spectacular show in the southern skies when it comes to opposition in July, following Saturn's opposition in May. Then it's Jupiter's turn in September. Check the following listings for some close approaches among the planets, and for monthly conjunctions of Venus and the crescent moon beginning surely in May.

There are several occultations (hiding) of planets by the moon this year, but you must be in the right place on the earth at the right time. View these remarks as indications of the moon's being quite near the object a night before or after the date. And the moon begins a long series of occultations of Antares, some of which may be visible from parts of North America. Keep your eye on the moon at these times, remembering that it moves eastward about one diameter every hour, and make your own prediction of when the event may take place. It is a dramatic experience when viewed with a telescope.

January, 1986

Mercury is a morning object all month, but effectively lost in the dawn twilight.

Venus is on the far side of the sun, passing through superior conjunction on the 19th, thus invisible to us.

Mars rises before 3 am, appearing as a reddish star fainter than first magnitude, but becoming brighter through the month, as it moves east through Virgo.

Jupiter may be visible low in the west just after sunset, but it will set earlier each evening, and be virtually lost to view by the end of the month.

Saturn rises about an hour after Mars, looking like a first magnitude star north of Antares; it passes into Ophiuchus in the middle of the month.

Moon passes Mars on the 6th, Saturn on the 7th, is at perigee and passes Uranus on the 8th, Jupiter on the 12th, and is at apogee on the 20th.

Jan. 2—Earth at perihelion, 91.4 million miles from the sun.

Jan. 3—Quadrantid meteor shower harmed slightly by the 3rd quarter moon.

Jan. 8—Mercury close to Neptune.

Jan. 19—Venus in superior conjunction; Sun enters Capricornus.

Jan. 20—Jupiter 9° south at Halley's Comet.

February

Mercury passes beyond the sun on the first and will not be visible this month.

Venus is still lost in the glare of the sun, although technically an evening object.

Mars continues to brighten as it moves rapidly eastward from Libra, through Scorpius, into Ophiuchus, passing 1°.3 south of Saturn the evening of the 17th, an event visible for watchers from North America.

Jupiter is lost all month as it passes beyond the sun in conjunction on the 18th.

Saturn continues its stately march through Ophiuchus, and is passed by speedy Mars on the 17th .

Moon passes Mars on the 3rd, Saturn and Uranus and is at perigee on the 4th, passes Neptune on the 5th, and is at apogee on the 16th.

Feb. 1—Mercury in superior conjunction.
Feb. 4—Halley's Comet in conjunction.
Feb. 9—Halley's Comet at perihelion.
Feb. 10—Saturn passes Antares.
Feb. 16—Sun enters Aquarius.
Feb. 17—Mars passes Antares.
Feb. 18—Mars passes Saturn; Jupiter in conjunction.
Feb. 28—Mercury at greatest elongation, 18° east of the sun.

March

Mercury is a difficult object to find low in the western sky after sunset early in the month, becoming impossible later, when it is in inferior conjunction on the 16th.

Venus is still lost in the evening twilight, setting before 8 pm by the end of the month.

Mars rises before 2 am in Ophiuchus, passing into Sagittarius by the third week, brightening as it goes.

Jupiter becomes a prominent object in the eastern dawn twilight by the end of the month.

Saturn in Ophiuchus, north of Antares, is stationary on the 19th, beginning its retrograde (western) motion for this year.

Moon is at perigee on the first, passes Saturn and Mars on the 3rd, Uranus on the 4th, Neptune on the 5th, Venus on the 11th, is at apogee on the 16th, at perigee again on the 28th, passes Saturn again on the 30th, and Uranus the second time on the 31st. On the 30th, the moon occults Antares, but a telescope will be needed to observe this daylight event from North America.

Mar. 6—Mercury stationary, begins retrograde motion.
Mar. 8—Mercury close to Venus.
Mar. 11—Sun enters Pisces.
Mar. 16—Mercury at inferior conjunction.
Mar. 19—Saturn stationary, begins retrograde motion.
Mar. 20—Equinox, Spring begins in the northern hemisphere at 10:03 pm GMT (5:03 pm EST).
Mar. 27—Uranus stationary, begins retrograde motion.
Mar. 29—Mercury stationary, resumes direct (eastward) motion.
Mar. 30—Occultation of Antares.

April

Mercury looks brighter than a first magnitude star in the eastern twilight at dawn, being at greatest elongation, 28° west of the sun on the 13th.

Venus is getting more prominent in the western sky after sunset, standing 1°.3 south of the 2-day crescent moon. Watch for this delightful scene each month until October.

Mars rises just after midnight in Sagittarius, looking brighter than a zero magnitude ruddy star.

Jupiter rises before 3 am by the end of the month, appearing nearly as bright as a -2 magnitude star in Aquarius.

Saturn is brightening all month, rising in the early evening, due north of Antares on the 26th.

Moon passes Mars and Neptune on the 1st, Jupiter and Mercury on the 6th, eclipses the sun on the 9th, passes Venus on the 11th, is at apogee on the 13th, in eclipse on the 24th, at perigee on the 25th, passes Saturn on the 26th, Uranus on the 27th, Neptune again on the 28th, and Mars the second time on the 29th.

Apr. 7—Neptune stationary, begins retrograde motion.

Apr. 9—Partial solar eclipse.

Apr. 11—Halley's Comet closest to earth, 39 million miles away.

Apr. 13—Mercury at greatest elongation, 28° west of the sun.

Apr. 18—Sun enters Aries.

Apr. 24—Total lunar eclipse.

Apr. 26—Pluto at opposition; Saturn due north of Antares.

May

Mercury is invisible this month, passing through superior conjunction on the 23rd.

Venus, bright in our evening western sky, passes 6° north of Aldebaran on the 5th, and is 3° south of the crescent moon on 11th.

Mars rises before midnight, looking brighter than a -1 magnitude star in Sagittarius.

Jupiter rises about 1 am by month's end, still in Aquarius.

Saturn is in opposition to the sun on the 28th, having moved back into Scorpius.

Moon passes Jupiter on the 3rd, occults the asteroid Vesta on the 4th, passes Mercury on the 7th, is at apogee on the 10th, passes Venus on the 11th, is at perigee, passes Saturn, and occults Antares on the 24th, passes Uranus on the 25th, Neptune on the 26th, Mars on the 27th, and Jupiter again on the 31st.

May 4—Vesta occulted; the fading moon will help with the observation of the Eta Aquarid meteor shower. It this shower is indeed related to Halley's Comet, there may be quite a show, because the comet passed this way only a few weeks ago.

May 5—Venus 6° north of Aldebaran.

May 11—Venus 3° south of the crescent moon.

May 13—Sun enters Taurus.

May 23—Mercury in superior conjunction.

May 28—Saturn at opposition.

June

Mercury may give us a rare chance at an easy sighting in the western evening twilight when early this month it is quite bright (and the crescent moon will be just 3° north of it on the 9th) and, on the 25th, it is at greatest elongation, 25° east of the sun.

Venus again gives us a good show with the crescent moon on the 10th, in the western evening twilight, on which date it is also near Pollux in Gemini.

Mars is stationary on the 10th, beginning its retrograde loop in anticipation of its opposition next month. Bright now, it gets even brighter in the next few weeks as it outshines Jupiter for awhile.

Jupiter rises before midnight in Aquarius and brightens somewhat, as we get closer together in our particular journeys around the sun.

Saturn, fading a little, is in the narrow northern part of Scorpius, still in retrograde after its opposition last month.

Moon is at apogee on the 7th, passes Mercury on the 9th, Venus on the 10th, Saturn on the 20th, passes Uranus and is at perigee on the 21st, passes Neptune on the 22nd, occults Mars on the 23rd, and passes Jupiter on the 27th.

June 10—Mars stationary, begins retrograde motion.

June 11—Uranus at opposition.

June 20—Sun enters Gemini.

June 21—Solstice, 4:30 pm GMT (11:30 am EST); summer begins in the northern hemisphere.

June 25—Mercury at greatest elongation, 25° east of the sun.

June 26—Neptune at opposition.

July

Mercury rapidly drops from sight in the western twilight as it heads for inferior conjunction on the 23rd.

Venus, 3° south of the crescent moon on the 10th, is getting slowly brighter in the western evening twilight.

Mars, at opposition on the 10th, and only 37.5 million miles from us on the 16th, clearly dominates the southern sky this month as it penetrates "the Milk Maid's Dipper," the handle of the "teapot", all asterisms of Sagittarius.

Jupiter temporarily allows Mars to outshine it as it begins retrograde motion in Aquarius on the 13th.

Saturn continues in retrograde motion in northern Scorpius, as it begins to fade toward its magnitude.

Moon is at apogee on the 4th, passes Mercury on the 8th, Venus on the 10th, Saturn on the 17th, occults Antares and passes Uranus on the 18th, passes Neptune and is at perigee on the 19th, occults Mars on the 20th, passes Jupiter on the 25th, and is again at apogee on the 31st.

July 5—Earth at aphelion, 94.4 million miles from the sun.

July 9—Mercury stationary, beginning retrograde motion.

July 10—Mars at opposition.

July 11—Venus 1°.1 north of Regulus in Leo.

July 13—Jupiter stationary, beginning retrograde motion.

July 16—Mars closest approach to the earth, 37.5 million miles away.

July 17—Antares is occulted by the moon just before midnight EST.

July 20—Mars occulted by the moon; sun enters Cancer.

July 21—Pluto stationary, resuming its direct motion.

July 23—Mercury in inferior conjunction.

August

Mercury is stationary in the eastern dawn sky on the 2nd, but its greatest elongation on the 11th is only 19° west of the sun.

Venus, which has dominated our western evening twilights, plays its little tableau with the moon on the 9th, reaches its greatest elongation on the 27th, 46° east of the sun, and is only 0°.5 from Spica on the 31st.

Mars is stationary on the 12th, resuming its direct motion in Sagittarius, and is occulted on the 16th.

Jupiter is at its brightest this year for 7 weeks beginning this month as it approaches opposition in September, still in Aquarius.

Saturn is stationary on the 7th, when it resumes its direct motion, still in Scorpius.

Moon passes Mercury on the 4th, Venus on the 9th, Saturn on the 14th, Uranus on the 15th, passes Neptune, occults Mars, and is at perigee on the 16th, passes Jupiter on the 21st, and is at apogee on the 28th.

Aug. 2—Mercury is stationary, resuming its direct motion.

Aug. 7—Saturn is stationary, resuming direct motion.

Aug. 10—Sun enters Leo.

Aug. 11—Mercury at greatest elongation, 19° west of the sun.

Aug. 12—Mars stationary, resuming its direct motion; Perseid meteor shower should not be bothered by the first quarter moon which sets about midnight.

Aug. 16—Mars is occulted.

Aug. 27—Venus at greatest elongation, 46° east of the sun

September

Mercury is beyond the sun this month, in superior conjunction on the 5th, so is unavailable for any attempt at viewing.

Venus plays with the moon on the 7th, still looking beautiful in the western evening sky.

Mars is again occulted by the moon, on the 13th this month, still in Sagittarius.

Jupiter clearly dominates the night sky as it takes its turn at brilliance in the faint constellation of Aquarius where it is in opposition on the 10th.

Saturn begins to pick up eastern speed in Scorpius where it is still prominent north of Antares.

Moon passes Venus on the 7th, Saturn on the 10th, Uranus on the 11th, is at perigee and passes Neptune on the 12th, occults Mars on the 13th, passes Jupiter on the 17th, and is at apogee on the 25th.

Sept. 5—Mercury in superior conjunction.

Sept. 10—Jupiter at opposition.

Sept. 13—Mars occulted.

Sept. 14—Neptune stationary, resuming its direct motion.

Sept. 16—Sun enters Virgo.

Sept. 23—Equinox; Autumn begins at 7:59 am GMT (2:59 EST) in the northern hemisphere.

Sept. 29—Mercury 1°.5 north of Spica.

October

Mercury is teasing us again this month, for it is 26° east of the sun in our western evening sky on the 21st (its greatest elongation this time), but it will be rather far to the south (left) of the sunset point, perhaps lost in the twilight.

Venus is at greatest brilliancy, magnitude -4.3, on the 1st, but it will leave out evening view by the end of the month; if you have a small telescope, watch Venus at this time. You will be amazed at how thin its crescent appears.

Mars will make it over half way through Capricornus by the end of the month.

Jupiter is still in retrograde motion in Aquarius, and still quite bright.

Saturn manages to get back into Ophiuchus by mid-month.

Moon eclipses the sun in an annular-total mode on the 3rd, occults Mercury on the 5th, passes Venus on the 6th, is at perigee and passes Saturn on the 7th, Uranus on the 8th, Neptune on the 9th, Mars on the 11th, Jupiter on the 14th, is totally eclipsed on the 17th, and is at apogee on the 23rd.

Oct. 1—Venus at greatest brilliancy.

Oct. 3—Annular-total solar eclipse.

Oct. 5—Mercury occulted by the moon.

Oct. 15—Venus stationary, begins retrograde motion.

Oct. 17—Total lunar eclipse.

Oct. 18—Mercury 4° north of Venus.

Oct. 21—Mercury at greatest elongation, 24° east of the sun; the Orionid meteor shower may be hurt by the fat gibbous moon, but if this shower is related to Halley's Comet, it may put on quite a show.

Oct. 30—Sun enters Libra.

Oct. 31—Pluto in conjunction.

November

Mercury passes over to the west side of the sun this month, in inferior conjunction on the 13th, thus lost to view, except for those observers in the Australian area who may witness a transit of Mercury across the face of the sun.

Venus is in inferior conjunction on the 5th, becoming visible in the dawn's early light only by the end of the month.

Mars enters Aquarius about the 21st, still as bright as a zero magnitude star.

Jupiter, in Aquarius, perhaps alarmed by the rush of Mars, resumes its direct motion on the 8th.

Saturn, for the third time this year, lies due north of Antares which it will not encounter in this manner again for about 30 years.

Moon occults Mercury on the 3rd, is at perigee and passes Saturn on the 4th, Uranus and Neptune on the 5th, Mars on the 9th, Jupiter on the 10th, is at apogee on the 19th, passes Venus on the 29th, and Mercury again on the 30th.

Nov. 2—Mercury stationary, begins retrograde motion.

Nov. 3—Saturn 6° north of Antares; Mercury occulted.

Nov. 5—Venus in inferior conjunction.

Nov. 8—Jupiter stationary, resumes its direct motion.

Nov. 13—Mercury in inferior conjunction, and transit over the sun.

Nov. 22—Mercury stationary, resuming direct motion; Sun enters Scorpius.

Nov. 24—Venus stationary, resuming direct motion.

Nov. 29—Sun enters Ophiuchus.

Nov. 30—Mercury at greatest elongation, 20° west of the sun.

December

Mercury is totally unexciting this month passing near some planets and Antares, but they, too, are invisible near the sun.

Venus attains greatest brilliancy in the dawn sky on the 11th.

Mars, still a respectably bright object, threatening Jupiter last month, overtakes it this month, passing just 0°.5 north of the giant planet on the 19th.

Jupiter, a very bright -2 magnitude most of the month is passed by Mars on the 19th; but on the 8th, it will be just 1°.8 north of the first quarter moon.

Saturn is in conjunction on the 4th, and will be hard to see in the dawn sky by the end of the month.

Moon is at perigee on the 2nd, passes Neptune on the 3rd, Mars on the 7th, Jupiter on the 8th, is at apogee on the 17th, passes Venus on the 28th, Saturn on the 29th, and is at perigee again on the 30th.

Dec. 4—Saturn in conjunction.

Dec. 11—Venus in greatest brilliancy.

Dec. 13—Geminid meteor shower tonight; watch for fireballs.

Dec. 14—Uranus in conjunction.

Dec. 16—Sun enters Sagittarius.

Dec. 19—Mars close to Jupiter.

Dec. 22—Solstice; 4:02 am GMT (Dec 21, 11:02 pm EST) winter begins in the northern hemisphere.

Dec. 27—Neptune in conjunction.

Planets and the Sun

The planets of the solar system, in order of their mean distance from the sun, are Mercury, Venus, Earth, Mars, Jupiter, Saturn, Uranus, Neptune and Pluto. Both Uranus and Neptune are visible through good field glasses, but Pluto is so distant and so small that only large telescopes or long exposure photographs can make it visible.

Since Mercury and Venus are nearer to the sun than is the earth, their motions about the sun are seen from the earth as wide swings first to one side of the sun and then to the other, although they are both passing continuously around the sun in orbits that are almost circular. When their passage takes them either between the earth and the sun, or beyond the sun as seen from the earth, they are invisible to us. Because of the laws which govern the motions of planets about the sun, both Mercury and Venus require much less time to pass between the earth and the sun than around the far side of the sun, so their periods of visibility and invisibility are unequal.

The planets that lie farther from the sun than does the earth may be seen for longer periods of time and are invisible only when they are so located in our sky that they rise and set about the same time as the sun when, of course, they are overwhelmed by the sun's great brilliance. None of the planets has any light of its own but each

shines only by reflecting sunlight from its surface. Mercury and Venus, because they are between the earth and the sun, show phases very much as the moon does. The planets farther from the sun are always seen as full, although Mars does occasionally present a slightly gibbous phase — like the moon when not quite full.

The planets move rapidly among the stars because they are very much nearer to us. The stars are also in motion, some of them at tremendous speeds, but they are so far away that their motion does not change their apparent positions in the heavens sufficiently for anyone to perceive that change in a single lifetime. The very nearest star is about 7,000 times as far away as the most distant planet.

Planets of the Solar System
Mercury, Venus, Mars, Jupiter and Saturn

Mercury

Mercury, nearest planet to the sun, is the second smallest of the nine planets known to be orbiting the sun. Its diameter is 3,100 miles and its mean distance from the sun is 36,000,000 miles.

Mercury moves with great speed in its journey about the sun, averaging about 30 miles a second to complete its circuit in 88 of our days. Mercury rotates upon its axis over a period of nearly 59 days, thus exposing all of its surface periodically to the sun. It is believed that the surface passing before the sun may have a temperature of about 800° F., while the temperature on the side turned temporarily away from the sun does not fall as low as might be expected. This night temperature has been described by Russian astronomers as "room temperature" — possibly about 70°. This would contradict the former belief that Mercury did not possess an atmosphere, for some sort of atmosphere would be needed to retain the fierce solar radiation that strikes Mercury. A shallow but dense layer of carbon dioxide would produce the "greenhouse" effect, in which heat accumulated during exposure to the sun would not completely escape at night. The actual presence of a carbon dioxide atmosphere is in dispute. Other research, however, has indicated a nighttime temperature approaching −300°.

This uncertainty about conditions upon Mercury and its motion arise from its shorter angular distance from the sun as seen from the earth, for Mercury is always too much in line with the sun to be observed against a dark sky, but is always seen during either morning or evening twilight.

Mariner 10 made 3 passes by Mercury in 1974 and 1975. A large fraction of the surface was photographed from varying distances, revealing a degree of cratering similar to that of the moon. An atmosphere of hydrogen and helium may be made up of gases of the solar wind temporarily concentrated by the presence of Mercury. The discovery of a weak but permanent magnetic field was a surprise. It has been held that both a fluid core and rapid rotation were necessary for the generation of a planetary magnetic field. Mercury may demonstrate these conditions to be unnecessary, or the field may reveal something about the history of Mercury.

Venus

Venus, slightly smaller than the earth, moves about the sun at a mean distance of 67,000,000 miles in 225 of our days. Its synodical revolution — its return to the same relationship with the earth and the sun, which is a result of the combination of its own motion and that of the earth — is 584 days. Every 19 months, then, Venus will be nearer to the earth than any other planet of the solar system. The planet is covered with a dense, white, cloudy atmosphere that conceals whatever is below it. This same cloud reflects sunlight efficiently so that when Venus is favorably situated, it is the third brightest object in the sky, exceeded only by the sun and the moon.

Spectral analysis of sunlight reflected from Venus' cloud tops has shown features that can best be explained by identifying the material of the clouds as sulphuric acid (oil of vitriol). Infrared spectroscopy from a balloon-borne telescope nearly 20 miles above the earth's surface gave indications of a small amount of water vapor present in the same region of the atmosphere of Venus. In 1956, radio astronomers at the Naval Research Laboratories in Washington, D. C., found a temperature for Venus of about 600° F., in marked contrast to minus 125° F., previously found at the cloud tops. Subsequent radio work confirmed a high temperature and produced evidence for this temperature to be associated with the solid body of Venus. With this peculiarity in mind, space scientists devised experiments for the U.S. space probe Mariner 2 to perform when it flew by in 1962. Mariner 2 con-

firmed the high temperature and the fact that it pertained to the ground rather than to some special activity of the atmosphere. In addition, Mariner 2 was unable to detect any radiation belts similar to the earth's so-called Van Allen belts. Nor was it able to detect the existence of a magnetic field even as weak as 1/100,000 of that of the earth.

In 1967, a Russian space probe, Venera 4, and the American Mariner 5 arrived at Venus within a few hours of each other. Venera 4 was designed to allow an instrument package to land gently on the planet's surface via parachute. It ceased transmission of information in about 75 minutes when the temperature it read went above 500° F. After considerable controversy, it was agreed that it still had 20 miles to go to reach the surface. The U.S. probe, Mariner 5, went around the dark side of Venus at a distance of about 6,000 miles. Again, it detected no significant magnetic field but its radio signals passed to earth through Venus' atmosphere twice — once on the night side and once on the day side. The results are startling. Venus' atmosphere is nearly all carbon dioxide and must exert a pressure at the planet's surface of up to 100 times the earth's normal sea-level pressure of one atmosphere. Since the earth and Venus are about the same size, and were presumably formed at the same time by the same general process from the same mixture of chemical elements, one is faced with the question: which is the planet with the unusual history — earth or Venus?

Radar astronomers using powerful transmitters as well as sensitive receivers and computers have succeeded in determining the rotation period of Venus. It turns out to be 243 days clockwise — in other words, contrary to the spin of most of the other planets and to its own motion around the sun. If it were exactly 243.16 days, Venus would always present the same face toward the earth at every inferior conjunction. This rate and sense of rotation allows a "day" on Venus of 117.4 earth days. Any part of Venus will receive sunlight on its clouds for over 58 days and will be in darkness for 58 days. Recent radar observations have shown surface features below the clouds. Large craters, continent-sized highlands, and extensive, dry "ocean" basins have been identified.

Mariner 10 passed Venus before traveling on to Mercury in 1974. The carbon dioxide molecule found in such abundance in the atmosphere is rather opaque to certain ultraviolet wavelengths, enabling sensitive television cameras to take pictures of the Venusian cloud cover. Photos radioed to earth show a spiral pattern in the clouds from equator to the poles.

In December, 1978, two U. S. Pioneer probes arrived at Venus. One went into orbit about Venus, the other split into 5 separate probes targeted for widely-spaced entry points to sample different conditions. The instrumentation ensemble was selected on the basis of previous missions that had shown the range of conditions to be studied. The probes confirmed expected high surface temperatures and high winds aloft. Winds of about 200 miles per hour, there, may account for the transfer of heat into the night side in spite of the low rotation speed of the planet. Surface winds were light at the time, however. Atmosphere and cloud chemistries were examined in detail, providing much data for continued analysis. The probes detected 4 layers of clouds and more light on the surface than expected solely from sunlight. This light allowed Russian scientists to obtain at least two photos showing rocks on the surface. Sulphur seems to play a large role in the chemistry of Venus, and reactions involving sulphur may be responsible for the glow. To learn more about the weather and atmospheric circulation on Venus, the orbiter takes daily photos of the daylight side cloud cover. It confirms the cloud pattern and its circulation

shown by Mariner 10. The ionosphere shows large variability. The orbiter's radar operates in 2 modes: one, for ground elevation variability, and the second for ground reflectivity in 2 dimensions, thus "imaging" the surface. Radar maps of the entire planet that show the features mentioned above have been produced.

Mars

Mars is the first planet beyond the earth, away from the sun. Mars' diameter is about 4,200 miles, although a determination of the radius and mass of Mars by the space-probe, Mariner 4, which flew by Mars on July 14, 1965 at a distance of less than 6,000 miles, indicated that these dimensions were slightly larger than had been previously estimated. While Mars' orbit is also nearly circular, it is somewhat more eccentric than the orbits of many of the other planets, and Mars is more than 30 million miles farther from the sun in some parts of its year than it is at others. Mars takes 687 of our days to make one circuit of the sun, traveling at about 15 miles a second. Mars rotates upon its axis in almost the same period of time that the earth does — 24 hours and 37 minutes. Mars' mean distance from the sun is 141 million miles, so that the temperature on Mars would be lower than that on the earth even if Mars' atmosphere were about the same as ours. The atmosphere is not, however, for Mariner 4 reported that atmospheric pressure on Mars is between 1% and 2% of the earth's atmospheric pressure. This thin atmosphere appears to be largely carbon dioxide. No evidence of free water was found.

There appears to be no magnetic field about Mars. This would eliminate the previous conception of a dangerous radiation belt around Mars. The same lack of a magnetic field would expose the surface of Mars to an influx of cosmic radiation about 100 times as intense as that on earth.

Deductions from years of telescopic observation indicate that 5/8ths of the surface of Mars is a desert of reddish rock, sand, and soil. The rest of Mars is covered by irregular patches that appear generally green in hues that change through the Martian year. These were formerly held to be some sort of primitive vegetation, but with the findings of Mariner 4 of a complete lack of water and oxygen, such growth does not appear possible. The nature of the green areas is now unknown. They may be regions covered with volcanic salts whose color changes with changing temperatures and atmospheric conditions, or they may be gray, rather than green. When large gray areas are placed beside large red areas, the gray areas will appear green to the eye.

Mars' axis of rotation is inclined from a vertical to the plane of its orbit about the sun by about 25° and therefore Mars has seasons as does the earth, except that the Martian seasons are longer because Mars' year is longer. White caps form about the winter pole of Mars, growing through the winter and shrinking in summer. These polar caps are now believed to be both water ice and carbon dioxide ice. It is the carbon dioxide that is seen to come and go with the seasons. The water ice is apparently in many layers with dust between them, indicating climatic cycles.

The canals of Mars have become more of a mystery than they were before the voyage of Mariner 4. Markings forming a network of fine lines crossing much of the surface of Mars have been seen there by men who have devoted much time to the study of the planet, but no canals have shown clearly enough in previous photographs to be universally accepted. A few of the 21 photographs sent back to earth by Mariner 4 covered areas crossed by canals. The pictures show faint, ill-defined, broad, dark markings, but no positive identification of the nature of the markings.

Mariners 6 & 7 in 1969 sent back many more photographs of higher quality than those of the pioneering Mariner 4. These pictures showed cratering similar to the earlier views, but in addition showed 2 other types of terrain. Some regions seemed featureless for many square miles, but others were chaotic, showing high relief without apparent organization into mountain chains or craters.

Mariner 9, the first artificial body to be placed in an orbit about Mars, has transmitted over 10,000 photographs covering 100% of the planet's surface. Preliminary study of these photos and other data shows that Mars resembles no other planet we know. Using terrestrial terms, however, scientists describe features that seem to be clearly of volcanic origin.

One of these features is Nix Olympica, (now called Olympus Mons), apparently a shield volcano whose caldera is over 50 miles wide, and whose outer slopes are over 300 miles in diameter, and which stands about 90,000 feet above the surrounding plain. Some features may have been produced by cracking (faulting) of the surface and the sliding of one region over or past another. Many craters seem to have been produced by impacting bodies such as may have come from the nearby asteroid belt. Features near the south pole may have been produced by glaciers that are no longer present. Flowing water, non-existent on Mars at the present time, probably carved canyons, one 10 times longer and 3 times deeper than the Grand Canyon.

Although the Russians landed a probe on the Martian surface, it transmitted for only 20 seconds. In 1976, the U.S. landed 2 Viking spacecraft on the Martian surface. The landers had devices aboard to perform chemical analyses of the soil in search of evidence of life. The results have been inconclusive. The 2 Viking orbiters have returned the best pictures yet of Martian topographic features. Many features can be explained only if Mars once had large quantities of flowing water.

Mars' position in its orbit and its speed around that orbit in relation to the earth's position and speed bring Mars fairly close to the earth on occasions about two years apart and then move Mars and the earth too far apart for accurate observation and photography. Every 15-17 years, the close approaches are especially favorable to close observation.

Mars has 2 satellites, discovered in 1877 by Asaph Hall. The outer satellite, Deimos, revolves around Mars in about 31 hours. The inner satellite, Phobos, whips around Mars in a little more than 7 hours, making 3 trips around the planet each Martian day. Mariner and Viking photos show these bodies to be irregularly shaped and pitted with numerous craters. Phobos also shows a system of linear grooves, each about 1/3-mile across and roughly parallel. Phobos measures about 8 by 12 miles and Deimos about 5 by 7.5 miles in size.

Jupiter

Jupiter is the largest of the planets. Its equatorial diameter is 88,000 miles, 11 times the diameter of the earth. Its polar diameter is about 6,000 miles shorter. This is an equilibrium condition resulting from the liquidity of the planet and its extremely rapid rate of rotation: a Jupiter day is only 10 earth hours long. For a planet this size, this rotational speed is amazing, and it moves a point on Jupiter's equator at a speed of 22,000 miles an hour, as compared with 1,000 miles an hour for a point on the earth's equator. Jupiter is at an average distance of 480 million miles from the sun and takes almost 12 of our years to make one complete circuit of the sun.

The only directly observable chemical constituents of Jupiter's atmosphere are methane (CH_4) and ammonia (NH_3), but it is reasonable to assume the same mixture of elements available to make Jupiter as to make the sun. This would mean a large fraction of hydrogen and helium must be present also, as well as water (H_2O). The temperature at the tops of the clouds may be about minus 260° F. The clouds are probably ammonia ice crystals, becoming ammonia droplets lower down. There may be a space before water ice crystals show up as clouds: in turn, these become water droplets near the bottom of the entire cloud layer. The total atmosphere may be only a few hundred miles in depth, pulled down by the surface gravity (= 2.64 times earth's) to a relatively thin layer. Of course, the gases become denser with depth until they may turn into a slush or a slurry. Perhaps there is no surface — no real interface between the gaseous atmosphere and the body of Jupiter. Pioneers 10 and 11 provided evidence for considering Jupiter to be almost entirely liquid hydrogen. Long before a rocky core about the size of the earth is reached, hydrogen mixed with helium becomes a liquid metal at very high temperature. Jupiter's cloudy atmosphere is a fairly good reflector of sunlight and makes it appear far brighter than any of the stars.

Fourteen of Jupiter's 17 or more satellites have been found through earth-based observations. Four of the moons are large and bright, rivaling our own moon and the planet Mercury in diameter, and may be seen through a field glass. They move rapidly around Jupiter and their change of position from night to night is extremely interesting to watch.

The other satellites are much smaller and in all but one instance much farther from Jupiter and cannot be seen except through powerful telescopes. The 4 outermost satellites are revolving around Jupiter clockwise as seen from the north, contrary to the motions of the great majority of the satellites in the solar system and to the direction of revolution of the planets around the sun. The reason for this retrograde motion is not known, but one theory is that Jupiter's tremendous gravitational power may have captured 4 of the minor planets or asteroids that move about the sun between Mars and Jupiter, and that these would necessarily revolve backward. At the great distance of these bodies from Jupiter — some 14 million miles — direct motion would result in decay of the orbits, while retrograde orbits would be stable. Jupiter's mass is more than twice the mass of all the other planets put together, and accounts for Jupiter's tremendous gravitational field and so, probably, for its numerous satellites and its dense atmosphere.

In December, 1973, Pioneer 10 passed about 80,000 miles from the equator of Jupiter and was whipped into a path taking it out of our solar system in about 50 years, and beyond the system of planets, on June 13, 1983. In December, 1974, Pioneer 11 passed within 30,000 miles of Jupiter, moving roughly from south to north, over the poles.

Photographs from both encounters were useful at the time but were far surpassed by those of Voyagers I and II. Thousands of high resolution multi-color pictures show rapid variations of features both large and small. The Great Red Spot exhibits internal counterclockwise rotation. Much turbulence is seen in adjacent material passing north or south of it. The satellites Amalthea, Io, Europa, Ganymede, and Callisto were photographed, some in great detail. Each is individual and unique, with no similarities to other known planets or satellites. Io has active volcanoes that probably have ejected material into a doughnut-shaped ring enveloping its orbit about Jupiter. This is not to be confused with the thin flat disk-like ring closer to Jupiter's surface. Now that such a ring has been seen by the Voyagers, older uncertain observations from Earth can be reinterpreted as early sightings of this structure.

Saturn

Saturn, last of the planets visible to the unaided eye, is almost twice as far from the sun as Jupiter, almost 900 million miles. It is second in size to Jupiter but its mass is much smaller. Saturn's specific gravity is less than that of water. Its diameter is about 71,000 miles at the equator; its rotational speed spins it completely around in a little more than 10 hours, and its atmosphere is much like that of Jupiter, except that its temperature at the top of its cloud layer is at least 100° lower. At about 300° F. below zero, the ammonia would be frozen out of Saturn's clouds. The theoretical construction of Saturn resembles that of Jupiter; it is either all gas, or it has a small dense center surrounded by a layer of liquid and a deep atmosphere.

Until Pioneer 11 passed Saturn in September 1979 only 10 satellites of Saturn were known. Since that time, the situation is quite confused. Added to data interpretations from the fly-by are earth-based observations using new techniques while the rings were edge-on and virtually invisible. It was hoped that the Voyager I and II fly-bys would help sort out the system. It is now believed that Saturn has at least 22 satellites, some sharing orbits. The Saturn satellite system is still confused.

Saturn's ring system begins about 7,000 miles above the visible disk of Saturn, lying above its equator and extending about 35,000 miles into space. The diameter of the ring system visible from Earth is about 170,000 miles; the rings are estimated to be no thicker than 10 miles. In 1973, radar observation showed the ring particles to be large chunks of material averaging a meter on a side.

Voyager I and II observations showed the rings to be considerably more complex than had been believed, so much so that interpretation will take much time. To the untrained eye, the Voyager photographs could be mistaken for pictures of a colorful phonograph record.

Uranus

Voyager II, after passing Saturn in August 1981, heads for a rendezvous with Uranus in 1986. Uranus, discovered by Sir William Herschel on Mar. 13, 1781, lies at a distance of 1.8 billion miles from the sun, taking 84 years to make its circuit around our star. Uranus has a diameter of about 32,000 miles and spins once in some 15.5 hours. One of the most fascinating features of Uranus is how far it is tipped over. Its north pole lies 98° from being directly up and down to its orbit plane. Thus, its seasons are extreme. If the sun rises at the north pole, it will stay up for 42 years; then it will set and the north pole will be in darkness (and winter) for 42 years.

Uranus has 5 satellites (known to date) whose orbits lie in the plane of the planet's equator. In that plane there are also 9 rings, discovered in 1978. Virtually invisible from Earth, the rings were found by observers watching Uranus pass before a star. As they waited, they saw their photoelectric equipment register a short eclipse of the star, then another, and another. Then the planet occulted the star as expected. After the star came out from behind Uranus, the star winked out several more times. Subsequent observations and analyses indicate 9 narrow, nearly opaque, rings circling Uranus.

The structure of Uranus is subject to some debate. Basically, however, it may have a rocky core surrounded by a thick icy mantle on top of which is a crust of hydrogen and helium that gradually becomes an atmosphere. Perhaps Voyager II will shed some light on this problem.

Neptune

Neptune, currently the most distant planet from the sun (until 1999), lies at an average distance of 2.8 billion miles. Having a diameter of about 31,000 miles and a rotation period of 18.2 hours, it is a virtual twin of Uranus. It is significantly more dense than Uranus, however, and this increases the debate over its internal structure. Neptune circles the sun in 164 years in a nearly circular orbit.

Neptune has 3 satellites, the third being found in 1981. The largest, Triton, is in a retrograde orbit suggesting that it was captured rather than being co-eval with Neptune. Triton is sufficiently large to raise significant tides on Neptune which will one day, say 100 million years from now, cause Triton to come close enough to Neptune for it to be torn apart. Nereid was found in 1949, and is in a long looping orbit suggesting it, too, was captured. The orbit of the third body is under analysis at this writing. Observations made in 1968 but not interpreted until 1982 suggest that Neptune, too, has a ring system.

As with the other giant planets, Neptune is emitting more energy than it receives from the sun. These excesses are thought to be cooling from internal heat sources and from the heat of the formation of the planets.

Little is known of Neptune beyond its distance, but Voyager II, if all continues to operate, will send us pictures and observations in 1989.

Pluto

Although Pluto on the average stays about 3.6 billion miles from the sun, its orbit is so eccentric that it is now approaching its minimum distance of 2.7 billion miles, less than the current distance of Neptune. Thus Pluto, until 1999, is temporarily planet number 8 from the sun. At its mean distance, Pluto takes 247.7 years to circumnavigate the sun. Until recently that was about all that was known of Pluto.

About a century ago, a hypothetical planet was believed to lie beyond Neptune and Uranus. Little more than a guess, a mass of one Earth was assigned to the mysterious body and mathematical searches were begun. Amid some controversy about the validity of the predictive process, Pluto was found nearly where it was predicted to be. It was found by Clyde Tombaugh at the Lowell Observatory in Flagstaff, Ariz., in 1930.

At the U.S. Naval Observatory, also in Flagstaff, on July 2, 1978, James Christy obtained a photograph of Pluto that was distinctly elongated. Repeated observations of this shape and its variation were convincing evidence of the discovery of a satellite of Pluto. Now named Charon, it may be 500 miles across, at a distance of over 10,000 miles, and taking 6.4 days to move around Pluto, the same length of time Pluto takes to rotate once. Gravitational laws allow these interactions to give us the mass of Pluto as 0.0017 of the Earth and a diameter of 1,500 miles. This makes the density about the same as that of water.

It is now clear that Pluto, the body found by Tombaugh, could not have influenced Neptune and Uranus to go astray. Theorists are again at work looking for a new planet X.

Greenwich Sidereal Time for 0h GMT, 1986

(Add 12 hours to obtain Right Ascension of Mean Sun)

Date		h	m	Date		h	m	Date		h	m	Date		h	m
Jan.	1	06	41.4	Apr.	1	12	36.2	July	10	19	10.5	Oct.	8	01	05.3
	11	07	20.8		11	13	15.7		20	19	49.9		18	01	44.8
	21	08	00.3		21	13	55.1		30	20	29.4		28	02	24.2
	31	08	39.7	May	1	14	34.5	Aug.	9	21	08.8	Nov.	7	03	03.6
Feb.	10	09	19.1		11	15	14.0		19	21	48.2		17	03	43.0
	20	09	58.5		21	15	53.4		29	22	27.6		27	04	22.5
Mar.	2	10	38.0		31	16	32.8	Sept.	8	23	07.0	Dec.	7	05	01.9
	12	11	17.4	June	10	17	12.2		18	23	46.5		17	05	41.3
	22	11	56.8		20	17	51.6		28	00	25.9		27	06	20.7
					30	18	31.1								

Astronomical Signs and Symbols

☉	The Sun	⊕	The Earth	♅	Uranus	□	Quadrature
☾	The Moon	♂	Mars	♆	Neptune	☍	Opposition
☿	Mercury	♃	Jupiter	♇	Pluto	☊	Ascending Node
♀	Venus	♄	Saturn	☌	Conjunction	☋	Descending Node

Two heavenly bodies are in "conjunction" (☌) when they are due north and south of each other, either in Right Ascension (with respect to the north celestial pole) or in Celestial Longitude (with respect to the north ecliptic pole). If the bodies are seen near each other, they will rise and set at nearly the same time. They are in "opposition" (☍) when their Right Ascensions differ by exactly 12 hours, or their Celestial Longitudes differ by 180°. One of the two objects in opposition will rise while the other is setting. "Quadrature" (□) refers to the arrangement when the coordinates of two bodies differ by exactly 90°. These terms may refer to the relative positions of any two bodies as seen from the earth, but one of the bodies is so frequently the sun that mention of the sun is omitted; otherwise both bodies are named. The geocentric angular separation between sun and object is termed "elongation." Elongation is limited only for Mercury and Venus; the "greatest elongation" for each of these bodies is noted in the appropriate tables and is approximately the time for longest observation. When a planet is in its "ascending" (☊) or "descending" (☋) node, it is passing northward or southward, respectively, through the plane of the earth's orbit, across the celestial circle called the ecliptic. The term "perihelion" means nearest to the sun, and "aphelion," farthest from the sun. An "occultation" of a planet or star is an eclipse of it by some other body, usually the moon.

Planetary Configurations, 1986

Greenwich Mean Time (0 designates midnight; 12 designates noon)

Mo.	D. h. m.		
Jan.	2 05	-	⊕ at perihelion.
	6 01	- ☌ ♂ ☽	♂ 1°.7 N
	7 14	- ☌ ♄ ☽	♄ 4° N
	8 10	- ☌ ☿ ♆	☿ 1°.7 S
	8 12	- ☌ ♅ ☽	♅ 3° N
	12 14	- ☌ ♃ ☽	♃ 4° N
	19 16	- ☌ ♀ ☉	Superior
Feb.	1 01	- ☌ ☿ ☉	Superior
	3 12	- ☌ ♂ ☽	♂ 3° N
	4 01	- ☌ ♄ ☽	♄ 5° N
	4 22	- ☌ ♅ ☽	♅ 4° N
	5 20	- ☌ ♆ ☽	♆ 5°N
	10 03	- ☌ ♄ *	♄ 7° N of Antares
	13 21	-	♇ stationary
	17 06	- ☌ ♂ *	♂ 5° N of Antares
	18 00	- ☌ ♂ ♄	♂ 1°.3 S
	18 10	- ☌ ♃ ☉	
	28 16	-	☿ Gr Elong 18° East of ☉
Mar.	3 08	- ☌ ♄ ☽	♄ 5° N
	3 20	- ☌ ♂ ☽	♂ 4° N
	4 05	- ☌ ♅ ☽	♅ 4°N
	5 03	- ☌ ♆ ☽	♆ 6° N
	6 23	-	☿ stationary
	8 13	- ☌ ☿ ♀	☿ 5° N
	11 15	- ☌ ♀ ☽	♀ 1°.3 N
	13 09	- ☌ ♂ ♅	♂ 0°.3 N
	16 20	- ☌ ☿ ☉	Inferior
	19 14	-	♄ stationary
	20 22 03		Vernal Equinox; Spring Begins; N hemisphere
	27 14	-	♅ stationary
	29 06	-	☿ stationary
	30 15	- ☌ ♄ ☽	♄ 5° N
	31 11	- ☌ ♅ ☽	♅ 4° N
Apr.	1 03	- ☌ ♂ ☽	♂ 5° N
	1 09	- ☌ ♆ ☽	♆ 6° N
	6 02	- ☌ ♃ ☽	♃ 3° N
	6 21	- ☌ ☿ ☽	☿ 2° N
	7 12	-	♆ stationary
	8 22	- ☌ ♂ ♆	♂ 1°.4 S
	9 06	-	Partial Solar Eclipse
	11 02	- ☌ ♀ ☽	♀ 1°.3 S
	13 15	-	☿ Gr Elong 28° West of ☉
	24 13	-	Total Lunar Eclipse
	26 13	- ☍ ♇ ☉	
	26 21	- ☌ ♄ ☽	♄ 5° N
	26 22	- ☌ ♄ *	♄ 7° N of Antares
	27 18	- ☌ ♅ ☽	♅ 4° N
	28 16	- ☌ ♆ ☽	♆ 6° N
	29 06	- ☌ ♂ ☽	♂ 4° N
May	3 18	- ☌ ♃ ☽	♃ 3° N
	5 11	- ☌ ♀ *	♀ 6° N of Aldebaran
	7 11	- ☌ ☿ ☽	☿ 2° S
	11 11	- ☌ ♀ ☽	♀ 3° S
	23 01	- ☌ ☿ ☉	Superior
	24 05	- ☌ ♄ ☽	♄ 5° N
	25 03	- ☌ ♅ ☽	♅ 4° N
	26 00	- ☌ ♆ ☽	♆ 6° N
	27 03	- ☌ ♂ ☽	♂ 3° N
	28 01	- ☍ ♄ ☉	
	31 08	- ☌ ♃ ☽	♃ 2° S
June	9 06	- ☌ ☿ ☽	☿ 3° S
	10 00	-	♂ stationary
	10 14	- ☌ ♀ *	♀ 5° S of Pollux
	10 16	- ☌ ♀ ☽	♀ 3° S
	11 15	- ☍ ♅ ☉	
	20 13	- ☌ ♄ ☽	♄ 5° N
	20 23	- ☌ ☿ *	☿ 6° S of Pollux
	21 12	- ☌ ♅ ☽	♅ 4° N
	21 16 30		Summer Solstice; Summer begins in Northern hemisphere
	22 10	- ☌ ♆ ☽	♆ 6° N
	23 13	- ☌ ♂ ☽	♂ 0°.5 N; Occultation
	25 20	-	☿ Gr Elong 25° East of ☉
	26 08	- ☍ ♆ ☉	
	27 20	- ☌ ♃ ☽	♃ 1°.9 N
July	5 10	-	⊕ at aphelion
	8 20	- ☌ ☿ ☽	☿ 8° S

Mo.	D. h. m.			
	9 01	-		☿ stationary
	10 05	-	☍ ♂ ☉	
	10 17	-	☌ ♀ ☽	♀ 3° S
	11 01	-	☌ ♀ *	♀ 1°.1 N of Regulus
	13 09	-		♃ stationary
	16 11	-		♂ closest to ⊕
	17 20	-	☌ ♄ ☽	♄ 5° N
	18 20	-	☌ ♅ ☽	♅ 4° N
	19 19	-	☌ ♆ ☽	♆ 6° N
	20 13	-	☌ ♂ ☽	♂ 0°.9 S; Occultation
	21 10	-		♇ stationary
	23 11	-	☌ ☿ ☉	Inferior
	25 06	-	☌ ♃ ☽	♃ 1°.5 N
Aug.	2 15	-		☿ stationary
	4 06	-	☌ ☿ ☽	☿ 8° S
	7 16	-		♄ stationary
	9 11	-	☌ ♀ ☽	♀ 2° S
	11 16	-		☿ Gr Elong 19° West of ☉
	12 12	-		♂ stationary
	14 02	-	☌ ♄ ☽	♄ 5° N
	15 03	-	☌ ♅ ☽	♅ 4° N
	16 03	-	☌ ♆ ☽	♆ 6° N
	16 16	-	☌ ♂ ☽	♂ 0°.5 S; Occultation
	21 11	-	☌ ♃ ☽	♃ 1°.4 N
	27 09	-		♀ Gr Elong 46° E of ☉
	27 21	-		♅ stationary
	31 15	-	☌ ♀ *	♀ 0°.5 S of Spica
Sept	5 18	-	☌ ☿ ☉	Superior
	7 20	-	☌ ♀ ☽	♀ 3° S
	10 09	-	☌ ♄ ☽	♄ 5° N
	10 21	-	☍ ♃ ☉	
	11 09	-	☌ ♅ ☽	♅ 4° N
	12 08	-	☌ ♆ ☽	♆ 6° N
	13 10	-	☌ ♂ ☽	♂ 0°.9 N; Occultation
	14 19	-		♆ stationary
	17 14	-	☌ ♃ ☽	♃ 1°.6 N
	23 07 59			Autumnal Equinox; Autumn Begins; N Hemisphere
	29 08	-	☌ ☿ *	☿ 1°.5 N of Spica
Oct.	1 10	-		♀ Gr Brilliancy
	3 19	-		Annular—Total Solar Eclipse
	5 07	-	☌ ☿ ☽	☿ 0°.4 S; Occultation

Mo.	D. h. m.			
	6 10	-	☌ ♀ ☽	♀ 4° S
	7 18	-	☌ ♄ ☽	♄ 5° N
	8 15	-	☌ ♅ ☽	♅ 4° N
	9 14	-	☌ ♆ ☽	♆ 6° N
	11 13	-	☌ ♂ ☽	♂ 2° N
	14 16	-	♂ ♃ ☽	♃ 1°.9 N
	15 12	-		♀ stationary
	17 19	-		Total Lunar Eclipse
	18 14	-	☌ ☿ ♀	☿ 4° N
	21 22	-		☿ Gr Elong 24° E of ☉
	31 01	-	☌ ♇ ☉	
Nov.	2 12	-		☿ stationary
	3 14	-	☌ ♄ *	♄ 6° N of Antares
	3 14	-	☌ ☿ ☽	☿ 0°.8 N; Occultation
	4 07	-	☌ ♄ ☽	♄ 6° N
	5 01	-	☌ ♅ ☽	♅ 4° N
	5 10	-	☌ ♀ ☉	Inferior
	5 22	-	☌ ♆ ☽	♆ 6° N
	8 20	-		♃ stationary
	9 00	-	☌ ♂ ☽	♂ 3° N
	10 19	-	☌ ♃ ☽	♃ 2° N
	13 04	-	☌ ☿ ☉	Inferior; transit over ☉
	22 05	-		☿ stationary
	24 04	-		♀ stationary
	29 11	-	☌ ♀ ☽	♀ 2° N
	30 03	-		☿ Gr Elong 20°W of ☉
	30 09	-	☌ ☿ ☽	☿ 5° N
Dec.	3 08	-	☌ ♆ ☽	♆ 6° N
	4 16	-	☌ ♄ ☉	
	7 16	-	☌ ♂ ☽	♂ 3° N
	8 04	-	☌ ♃ ☽	♃ 1°.8 N
	11 20	-		♀ Gr Brilliancy
	14 21	-	☌ ♅ ☉	
	16 01	-	☌ ☿ *	☿ 5° N of Antares
	19 07	-	☌ ♂ ♃	♂ 0°.5 N
	19 15	-	☌ ☿ ♄	☿ 1°.3 S
	22 04 02			Winter Solstice; Winter begins N Hemisphere
	25 14	-	☌ ☿ ♅	☿ 0°.4 S
	27 14	-	☌ ♆ ☉	
	28 01	-	☌ ♀ ☽	♀ 7° N
	29 15	-	☌ ♄ ☽	♄ 6° N

Rising and Setting of Halley's Comet, 1986

		20° N. Latitude		30° N. Latitude		40° N. Latitude		50° N. Latitude		60° N. Latitude	
		Rise	Set	Rise	Set	Rise	Set	Rise	Set	Rise	Set
Jan.	10	8:48	20:35	8:51	20:32	8:56	20:27	9:02	20:21	9:11	20:12
	20	7:53	19:59	7:58	19:30	8:05	19:24	8:13	19:15	8:27	19:02
	30	6:59	18:36	7:06	18:29	7:14	18:20	7:26	18:09	7:43	17:51
Feb.	9	6:05	17:35	6:13	17:26	6:24	17:15	6:39	17:00	7:02	16:37
	19	5:11	16:33	5:22	16:22	5:36	16:08	5:55	15:49	6:25	15:19
Mar.	1	4:20	15:31	4:34	15:17	4:51	14:59	5:16	14:35	5:55	13:56
	11	3:28	14:26	3:46	14:08	4:09	13:45	4:41	13:13	5:36	12:19
	21	2:31	13:07	2:56	12:42	3:28	12:10	4:15	11:24	5:47	9:51
	31	1:09	11:01	1:49	10:21	2:43	9:27	4:24	7:46	...	...
Apr.	10	21:05	6:42	22:53	5:39	0:43	3:49	...	...	...	...
	20	17:10	3:20	17:44	2:47	18:28	2:02	19:40	0:51	...	...
	30	14:59	2:00	15:17	1:42	15:39	1:20	16:09	0:50	17:01	23:58
May	10	13:46	1:08	13:56	0:57	14:10	0:44	14:29	0:25	14:58	23:56
	20	12:52	0:25	13:00	0:18	13:09	0:08	13:22	23:55	13:42	23:35
	30	12:07	23:47	12:13	23:41	12:21	23:33	12:31	23:23	12:46	23:08
June	9	11:27	23:10	11:32	23:05	11:38	22:59	11:47	22:50	12:00	22:37
	19	10:50	22:34	10:55	22:30	11:00	22:24	11:08	22:16	11:20	22:05
	29	10:14	21:59	10:19	21:55	10:24	21:49	10:32	21:42	10:43	21:31

Rising and Setting of Planets, 1986

Greenwich Mean Time (0 designates midnight)

		20° N. Latitude		30° N. Latitude		40° N. Latitude		50° N. Latitude		60° N. Latitude	
		Rise	Set	Rise	Set	Rise	Set	Rise	Set	Rise	Set
						Venus, 1986					
Jan.	10	6:33	17:22	6:55	17:01	7:21	16:34	7:59	15:56	9:07	14:48
	20	6:45	17:40	7:04	17:20	7:28	16:56	8:02	16:22	9:01	15:23
	30	6:52	17:57	7:09	17:41	7:29	17:20	7:58	16:52	8:45	16:05
Feb.	9	6:57	18:13	7:10	18:01	7:26	17:45	7:47	17:23	8:22	16:48
	19	6:59	18:29	7:08	18:20	7:18	18:09	7:33	17:54	7:56	17:31
Mar.	1	6:59	18:43	7:03	18:39	7:09	18:33	7:16	18:25	7:28	18:14
	11	6:57	18:57	6:58	18:56	6:58	18:56	6:58	18:56	6:59	18:55
	21	6:56	19:10	6:52	19:14	6:46	19:19	6:39	19:26	6:29	19:37

		20° N. Latitude		30° N. Latitude		40° N. Latitude		50° N. Latitude		60° N. Latitude	
		Rise	Set	Rise	Set	Rise	Set	Rise	Set	Rise	Set
	31	6:54	19:23	6:45	19:31	6:35	19:42	6:21	19:56	5:58	20:18
Apr.	10	6:55	19:38	6:43	19:51	6:27	20:06	6:05	20:28	5:31	21:02
	20	6:58	19:54	6:42	20:10	6:21	20:30	5:52	20:59	5:05	21:46
	30	7:03	20:10	6:44	20:29	6:19	20:54	5:44	21:29	4:44	22:29
May	10	7:12	20:26	6:50	20:48	6:22	21:16	5:42	21:55	4:30	23:08
	20	7:23	20:41	7:00	21:04	6:31	21:34	5:48	22:16	4:29	23:36
	30	7:37	20:54	7:14	21:17	6:44	21:47	6:02	22:29	4:43	23:48
June	9	7:52	21:05	7:30	21:26	7:02	21:54	6:23	22:33	5:12	23:44
	19	8:06	21:11	7:47	21:30	7:23	21:55	6:48	22:29	5:50	23:28
	29	8:19	21:14	8:04	21:30	7:44	21:50	7:16	22:18	6:30	23:04
July	9	8:31	21:13	8:19	21:25	8:04	21:41	7:43	22:02	7:10	22:35
	19	8:41	21:09	8:33	21:18	8:23	21:28	8:09	21:42	7:48	22:03
	29	8:49	21:03	8:45	21:07	8:40	21:12	8:34	21:19	8:23	21:29
Aug.	8	8:56	20:55	8:56	20:55	8:56	20:54	8:57	20:54	8:57	20:54
	18	9:00	20:45	9:05	20:41	9:10	20:35	9:18	20:28	9:29	20:16
	28	9:03	20:34	9:12	20:25	9:22	20:15	9:37	20:00	9:59	19:38
Sept.	7	9:04	20:21	9:16	20:08	9:32	19:53	9:54	19:31	10:28	18:57
	17	9:01	20:06	9:17	19:49	9:38	19:29	10:06	19:01	10:53	18:14
	27	8:52	19:46	9:12	19:27	9:36	19:02	10:11	18:26	11:10	17:28
Oct.	7	8:34	19:20	8:56	18:59	9:23	18:31	10:03	17:52	11:14	16:40
	17	8:01	18:45	8:24	18:22	8:53	17:53	9:34	17:11	10:51	15:55
	27	7:10	17:57	7:31	17:36	7:59	17:08	8:38	16:29	9:48	15:19
Nov.	6	6:04	17:03	6:23	16:44	6:46	16:21	7:18	15:49	8:13	14:55
	16	5:00	16:12	5:15	15:57	5:33	15:40	5:57	15:15	6:37	14:35
	26	4:11	15:32	4:23	15:21	4:37	15:06	4:57	14:47	5:28	14:15
Dec.	6	3:40	15:04	3:51	14:53	4:04	14:40	4:22	14:23	4:50	13:54
	16	3:22	14:45	3:33	14:34	3:47	14:22	4:06	14:02	4:35	13:32
	26	3:14	14:32	3:27	14:20	3:42	14:05	4:03	13:44	4:36	13:10

Mars, 1986

		20° N. Latitude		30° N. Latitude		40° N. Latitude		50° N. Latitude		60° N. Latitude	
		Rise	Set	Rise	Set	Rise	Set	Rise	Set	Rise	Set
Jan.	10	2:02	13:15	2:16	13:01	2:33	12:44	2:57	12:20	3:35	11:42
	20	1:50	12:57	2:05	12:42	2:24	12:22	2:51	11:56	3:35	11:12
	30	1:37	12:40	1:54	12:23	2:15	12:01	2:45	11:32	3:34	10:43
Feb.	9	1:24	12:22	1:42	12:04	2:05	11:41	2:39	11:09	3:32	10:15
	19	1:11	12:06	1:30	11:46	1:55	11:22	2:29	10:47	3:28	9:48
Mar.	1	0:57	11:49	1:17	11:29	1:43	11:03	2:19	10:27	3:23	9:23
	11	0:43	11:32	1:04	11:11	1:30	10:45	2:08	10:07	3:14	9:00
	21	0:27	11:15	0:49	10:54	1:16	10:26	1:54	9:48	3:04	8:38
	31	0:10	10:57	0:32	10:36	1:00	10:08	1:39	9:29	2:50	8:18
Apr.	10	23:52	10:39	0:14	10:17	0:42	9:49	1:22	9:10	2:33	7:58
	20	23:33	10:19	23:55	9:57	0:22	9:29	1:02	8:49	2:14	7:38
	30	23:11	9:57	23:33	9:35	0:00	9:07	0:40	8:28	1:52	7:16
May	10	22:46	9:33	23:08	9:11	23:36	8:43	0:16	8:03	1:28	6:51
	20	22:19	9:05	22:41	8:42	23:09	8:14	23:49	7:34	1:03	6:21
	30	21:48	8:33	22:11	8:10	22:39	7:41	23:20	7:00	0:36	5:45
June	9	21:13	7:55	21:36	7:32	22:05	7:03	22:48	6:20	0:07	5:01
	19	20:33	7:12	20:57	6:48	21:28	6:17	22:12	5:33	23:38	4:07
	29	19:48	6:24	20:13	5:58	20:45	5:26	21:33	4:39	23:07	3:04
July	9	18:59	5:31	19:25	5:05	19:59	4:31	20:49	3:40	22:35	1:55
	19	18:04	4:34	18:31	4:06	19:07	3:31	19:59	2:39	21:55	0:42
	29	17:15	3:43	17:43	3:15	18:18	2:40	19:12	1:46	21:14	23:43
Aug.	8	16:30	2:58	16:57	2:30	17:33	1:55	18:26	1:01	20:29	22:59
	18	15:50	2:19	16:17	1:52	16:52	1:17	17:45	0:25	19:41	22:28
	28	15:16	1:47	15:42	1:21	16:16	0:46	17:07	23:56	19:55	22:08
Sept.	7	14:46	1:21	15:12	0:55	15:45	0:22	16:34	23:34	18:12	21:55
	17	14:21	0:59	14:46	0:34	15:17	0:03	16:03	23:17	17:32	21:47
	27	13:59	0:41	14:22	0:17	14:52	23:48	15:34	23:05	16:54	21:45
Oct.	7	13:38	0:25	14:00	0:03	14:27	23:36	15:07	22:57	16:18	21:46
	17	13:19	0:12	13:39	23:52	14:04	23:27	14:40	22:51	15:42	21:49
	27	13:01	24:00	13:19	23:42	13:41	23:19	14:13	22:48	15:06	21:54
Nov.	6	12:43	23:49	12:58	23:33	13:18	23:13	13:46	22:46	14:31	22:01
	16	12:25	23:39	12:38	23:25	12:55	23:08	13:18	22:45	13:56	22:08
	26	12:07	23:29	12:18	23:17	12:32	23:04	12:51	22:45	13:20	22:15
Dec.	6	11:48	23:19	11:57	23:10	12:08	22:59	12:23	22:45	12:45	22:22
	16	11:30	23:09	11:36	23:03	11:44	22:55	11:54	22:45	12:10	22:29
	26	11:12	22:59	11:15	22:56	11:20	22:51	11:26	22:45	11:35	22:36

Jupiter, 1986

		20° N. Latitude		30° N. Latitude		40° N. Latitude		50° N. Latitude		60° N. Latitude	
		Rise	Set	Rise	Set	Rise	Set	Rise	Set	Rise	Set
Jan.	10	8:38	19:51	8:52	19:38	9:09	19:21	9:32	18:57	10:10	18:20
	20	8:06	19:22	8:19	19:09	8:35	18:53	8:57	18:31	9:33	17:55
	30	7:35	18:53	7:46	18:41	8:02	18:25	8:23	18:05	8:56	17:31
Feb.	9	7:03	18:24	7:15	18:12	7:29	17:58	7:49	17:39	8:20	17:08
	19	6:32	17:55	6:42	17:44	6:56	17:31	7:14	17:13	7:43	16:44
Mar.	1	6:00	17:26	6:10	17:16	6:23	17:04	6:40	16:47	7:06	16:20
	11	5:29	16:57	5:38	16:48	5:49	16:36	6:05	16:21	6:29	15:56
	21	4:57	16:28	5:05	16:19	5:16	16:09	5:30	15:54	5:52	15:32
	31	4:25	15:58	4:32	15:50	4:42	15:41	4:55	15:28	5:15	15:07
Apr.	10	3:52	15:28	3:59	15:21	4:08	15:12	4:20	15:00	4:38	14:42
	20	3:19	14:58	3:26	14:51	3:34	14:43	3:44	14:33	4:01	14:16
	30	2:46	14:26	2:52	14:21	2:59	14:14	3:09	14:04	3:24	13:49
May	10	2:12	13:55	2:18	13:49	2:24	13:43	2:33	13:34	2:46	13:21
	20	1:38	13:22	1:43	13:17	1:49	13:12	1:56	13:04	2:08	12:52
	30	1:03	12:49	1:07	12:44	1:13	12:39	1:20	12:32	1:31	12:21
June	9	0:27	12:14	0:31	12:10	0:36	12:05	0:43	11:59	0:53	11:49
	19	23:51	11:38	23:54	11:35	23:59	11:30	0:05	11:24	0:14	11:15
	29	23:13	11:02	23:17	10:58	23:21	10:54	23:27	10:48	23:36	10:39
July	9	22:35	10:23	22:38	10:20	22:43	10:16	22:48	10:10	22:57	10:01

	20° N. Latitude		30° N. Latitude		40° N. Latitude		50° N. Latitude		60° N. Latitude	
	Rise	Set	Rise	Set	Rise	Set	Rise	Set	Rise	Set
19	21:56	9:44	21:59	9:40	22:03	9:36	22:09	9:30	22:18	9:21
29	21:15	9:03	21:19	8:59	21:23	8:55	21:29	8:49	21:39	8:39
Aug. 8	20:34	8:20	20:38	8:17	20:43	8:12	20:49	8:05	20:59	7:55
18	19:52	7:37	19:56	7:33	20:01	7:28	20:08	7:20	20:19	7:10
28	19:09	6:53	19:13	6:48	19:19	6:42	19:27	6:34	19:39	6:23
Sept. 7	18:25	6:08	18:30	6:03	18:37	5:56	18:45	5:48	18:58	5:35
17	17:38	5:19	17:43	5:13	17:50	5:06	18:00	4:57	18:14	4:43
27	16:54	4:34	17:00	4:28	17:08	4:20	17:18	4:10	17:33	3:55
Oct. 7	16:11	3:50	16:18	3:43	16:26	3:36	16:36	3:25	16:53	3:08
17	15:29	3:07	15:36	3:00	15:44	2:52	15:55	2:41	16:12	2:24
27	14:48	2:25	14:55	2:18	15:03	2:09	15:14	1:58	15:32	1:40
Nov. 6	14:08	1:44	14:14	1:37	14:23	1:29	14:34	1:17	14:52	1:00
16	13:28	1:05	13:35	0:58	13:43	0:50	13:55	0:38	14:12	0:21
26	12:50	0:27	12:57	0:21	13:05	0:13	13:16	0:02	13:33	23:44
Dec. 6	12:13	23:51	12:19	23:45	12:27	23:37	12:38	23:26	12:54	23:10
16	*11:37	23:16	11:43	23:10	11:50	23:03	12:00	22:53	12:15	22:38
26	11:01	22:42	11:07	22:37	11:14	22:30	11:23	22:21	11:37	22:07

Saturn, 1986

	20° N. Latitude		30° N. Latitude		40° N. Latitude		50° N. Latitude		60° N. Latitude	
	Rise	Set	Rise	Set	Rise	Set	Rise	Set	Rise	Set
Jan. 10	3:31	14:32	3:48	14:14	4:10	13:52	4:41	13:21	5:33	12:30
20	2:56	13:56	3:13	13:38	3:35	13:16	4:07	12:45	4:59	11:53
30	2:20	13:20	2:38	13:02	3:00	12:39	3:31	12:08	4:24	11:15
Feb. 9	1:43	12:43	2:01	12:25	2:24	12:02	2:55	11:31	3:48	10:38
19	1:06	12:06	1:24	11:48	1:47	11:25	2:18	10:53	3:12	10:00
Mar. 1	0:29	11:28	0:47	11:10	1:09	10:47	1:41	10:15	2:34	9:22
11	23:50	10:49	0:08	10:31	0:31	10:09	1:02	9:37	1:56	8:44
21	23:11	10:10	23:29	9:52	23:52	9:30	0:23	8:58	1:17	8:04
31	22:31	9:30	22:49	9:12	23:12	8:50	23:43	8:18	0:36	7:25
Apr. 10	21:50	8:50	22:08	8:32	22:31	8:09	23:02	7:38	23:55	6:45
20	21:09	8:09	21:27	7:51	21:49	7:29	22:21	6:57	23:13	6:05
30	20:27	7:27	20:45	7:10	21:07	6:47	21:38	6:16	22:31	5:24
May 10	19:45	6:45	20:03	6:28	20:25	6:06	20:56	5:35	21:47	4:43
20	19:02	6:03	19:20	5:46	19:42	5:24	20:12	4:53	21:04	4:02
30	18:16	5:17	18:33	4:59	18:55	4:38	19:25	4:07	20:16	3:16
June 9	17:33	4:35	17:50	4:17	18:12	3:56	18:42	3:25	19:33	2:35
19	16:50	3:52	17:08	3:35	17:29	3:14	17:59	2:44	18:49	1:54
29	16:08	3:11	16:26	2:53	16:47	2:32	17:17	2:02	18:07	1:12
July 9	15:27	2:29	15:44	2:12	16:05	1:51	16:35	1:21	17:24	0:31
19	14:46	1:48	15:03	1:31	15:24	1:10	15:54	0:40	16:43	23:51
29	14:05	1:08	14:22	0:51	14:44	0:30	15:13	24:00	16:03	23:10
Aug. 8	13:26	0:28	13:43	0:11	14:04	23:50	14:34	23:20	15:23	22:30
18	12:47	23:49	13:04	23:32	13:25	23:10	13:55	22:41	14:45	21:51
28	12:08	23:10	12:26	22:53	12:47	22:32	13:17	22:02	14:07	21:12
Sept. 7	11:31	22:32	11:48	22:15	12:10	21:53	12:40	21:23	13:30	20:33
17	10:54	21:55	11:11	21:38	11:33	21:16	12:04	20:45	12:55	19:54
27	10:18	21:18	10:35	21:01	10:57	20:39	11:28	20:08	12:20	19:16
Oct. 7	9:42	20:42	10:00	20:24	10:22	20:02	10:53	19:31	11:45	18:38
17	9:06	20:06	9:24	19:48	9:47	19:26	10:18	18:54	11:11	18:01
27	8:32	19:30	8:50	19:12	9:12	18:50	9:44	18:18	10:38	17:24
Nov. 6	7:57	18:55	8:15	18:37	8:38	18:14	9:11	17:42	10:05	16:47
16	7:23	18:20	7:41	18:02	8:04	17:38	8:37	17:06	9:32	16:10
26	6:48	17:45	7:07	17:27	7:31	17:03	8:04	16:30	9:00	15:34
Dec. 6	6:14	17:11	6:33	16:52	6:57	16:28	7:30	15:55	8:27	14:58
16	5:40	16:36	5:59	16:17	6:23	15:53	6:57	15:19	7:54	14:22
26	5:06	16:01	5:25	15:42	5:49	15:18	6:23	14:44	7:21	13:46

Moonrise Tonight

The idea of estimating the time of moonrise tonight may have scared you off in the past because you assumed that it involved a difficult and mysterious series of calculations. The actual process is quite easy to do, however, especially with the little pocket calculators that seem ubiquitous today. The first major step involves finding three numbers for your city obtained from the latitude and longitude figures listed on pages 734 to 735. If your city is not here, find the information from a map, atlas or other source. These answers are permanent and never need to be determined for that city again. You can write these numbers down and use them every year you stay in that city. The second step involves taking the correct four figures from the tables of moonrise and moonset for the date you want. The third major step involves adjusting this answer to standard time.

Let us determine the time of moonrise on April 23, 1986 at Charleston, South Carolina.

First we must find the 3 numbers for Charleston:

I. Latitude: 32°46'35"; Longitude: 79°55'53".
A. Convert the Lat. and Long. to decimal numbers:
　　35" ÷ 60 = 0.'58
　　46' + 0.'58 = 46.'58
　　46.'58 ÷ 60 = 0.°776
　　32° + 0.°776 = 32.°776 for the Lat.
　　53" ÷ 60 = 0.'88
　　55' + 0.'88 = 55.'88
　　55.'88 ÷ 60 = 0.°931
　　79° + 0.°931 = 79.°931 for the Long.
B. Fraction between 30° and 40° that Charleston's latitude lies:
　　40° − 30° = 10°
　　32.°776 − 30° = 2.°776
　　2.°776 ÷ 10 = 0.2776

C. Fraction of earth that Charleston lies west of Greenwich:
　　79.°931 ÷ 360 = 0.2220
D. Correction from Local to Standard time:
　　(Standard time meridian for Charleston: 75°)
　　79.°931 − 75° = 4.°931 west (it happens *later* in Charleston by 4 minutes for each degree away from the Standard Time Meridian)
　　4.931 × 4 = 19.72 minutes later (round to 20 min.).
E. These numbers are permanent for Charleston, SC.
II. Find time of moonrise at GMT meridian for Charleston's latitude:
A. From the calendar page 739 for April:

(continued)

	30°	40°
Apr 23	17:37	17:46
24	18:47	19:04

B. What we want lies 0.2776 (Ans. IB) times the difference in time between 30 and 40 added to the time for 30 for each date. We are taking a proportion of the time difference.

For the 23rd:
17:46 − 17:37 = :09 (9 minutes)
9 × 0.2776 = 2.5 minutes (call it 2 minutes)
17:37 + 2 = 17:39 on the 23rd.

For the 24th:
19:04 − 18:47 = :17
17 × 0.2776 = 4.7 minutes (call it 5 minutes)
18.47 + 5 = 18:52 on the 24th.

Thus for Charleston's latitude at Greenwich:

Apr 23	17:39
24	18:52

C. How much later is the 24th time than the 23rd time?
18:52 − 17:39 = 73 minutes

D. How much of it passed before the moon rose at the longitude of Charleston? The fraction of the world from Greenwich (Ans. IC). (Another proportion.)
73 × 0.2220 = 16.2 minutes (call it 16 minutes)
17:39 + :16 = 17:55, local time at Charleston.

III. What did the clock read? (Since it happened later in Charleston than at the 75th meridian, we must add the time correction (Ans. II).
17:55 + :20 = 18:15, or 6:15 pm, EST.

Star Tables

These tables include stars of visual magnitude 2.5 and brighter. Co-ordinates are for mid-1986. Where no parallax figures are given, the trigonometric parallax figure is smaller than the margin for error and the distance given is obtained by indirect methods. Stars of variable magnitude designated by v.

To find the time when the star is on meridian, subtract R.A.M.S. of the sun table on page 723 from the star's right ascension, first adding 24h to the latter, if necessary. Mark this result P.M., if less than 12h; but if greater than 12, subtract 12h and mark the remainder A.M.

Star	Magnitude	Parallax "	Light yrs.	Right ascen. h. m.	Declination ° '	Star	Magnitude	Parallax "	Light yrs.	Right ascen. h. m.	Declination ° '
α Andromedae (Alpheratz)	2.06	0.02	90	0 07.6	+29 01	(Merak)	2.37	0.04	78	11 01.0	+56 28
β Cassiopeiae	2.26v	0.07	-45	0 08.4	+59 04	α Ursae Majoris (Dubhe)	1.81	0.03	105	11 02.8	+61 50
α Phoenicis	2.39	0.04	93	0 25.6	−42 23	β Leonis (Denebola)	2.14	0.08	43	11 48.3	+14 40
α Cassiopeiae (Schedir)	2.22	0.01	150	0 39.7	+56 27	γ Ursae Majoris (Phecda)	2.44	0.02	90	11 53.1	+53 47
β Ceti	2.02	0.06	57	0 42.9	−18 04	α Crucis	1.39		370	12 25.6	−63 01
γ Cassiopeiae	2.13v	0.03	96	0 55.8	+60 38	γ Crucis	1.69		220	12 30.4	−57 02
β Andromedae	2.02	0.04	76	1 08.9	+35 33	γ Centauri	2.17		160	12 40.7	−48 53
α Eridani (Achernar)	0.51	0.02	118	1 37.2	−57 19	β Crucis	1.28v		490	12 46.8	−59 37
γ Andromedae	2.14		260	2 03.0	+42 16	ε Ursae Majoris (Alioth)	1.79v	0.01	68	12 53.4	+56 02
α Arietis	2.00	0.04	76	2 06.4	+23 24	ζ Ursae Majoris (Mizar)	2.26	0.04	88	13 23.3	+55 00
α Ursae Min. (Pole Star)	1.99v		680	2 16.9	+89 12	α Virginis (Spica)	0.91v	0.02	220	13 24.4	−11 05
ο Ceti	2.00v	0.01	103	2 18.6	−3 03	α Centauri	2.33v		570	13 39.0	−53 24
β Persei (Algol)	2.06v	0.03	105	3 07.2	+40 54	η Ursae Majoris (Alkaid)	1.87		210	13 47.0	+49 23
α Persei	1.80	0.03	570	3 23.3	+49 49	β Centauri	0.63v	0.02	490	14 02.8	−60 18
α Tauri (Aldebaran)	0.86v	0.05	68	4 35.1	+16 29	θ Centauri	2.04	0.06	55	14 05.8	−36 18
β Orionis (Rigel)	0.14v		900	5 13.8	−8 13	α Bootis (Arcturus)	−0.06	0.09	36	14 15.0	+19 15
α Aurigae (Capella)	0.05	0.07	45	5 15.6	+45 59	η Centauri	2.39v		390	14 34.6	−42 06
γ Orionis (Bellatrix)	1.64	0.03	470	5 24.4	+6 20	α Centauri	0.01	0.75	4.3	14 38.6	−60 47
β Tauri (El Nath)	1.65	0.02	300	5 25.4	+28 36	α Lupi	2.32v		430	14 41.0	−47 20
δ Orionis	2.20v		1500	5 31.3	−0 18	ε Bootis	2.37	0.01	103	14 44.4	+27 08
ε Orionis	1.70		1600	5 35.5	−1 13	β Ursae Minoris	2.07	0.03	105	14 50.7	+74 13
ζ Orionis	1.79	0.02	1600	5 40.0	−1 57	α Coronae Borealis	2.23v	0.04	76	15 34.1	+26 46
κ Orionis	2.06	0.01	2100	5 47.1	−9 40	δ Scorpii	2.34		590	15 59.5	−22 35
α Orionis (Betelgeuse)	0.41v		520	5 54.4	+7 24	α Scorpii (Antares)	0.92v	0.02	520	16 28.5	−26 25
β Aurigae	1.86	0.04	88	5 58.5	+44 57	α Trianguli Australis	1.93	0.02	82	16 47.1	−69 00
β Canis Majoris	1.96	0.01	750	6 22.1	−17 57	ε Scorpii	2.28	0.05	66	16 49.2	−34 16
α Carinae (Canopus)	−0.72	0.02	98	6 23.6	−52 41	η Ophiuchi	2.43	0.05	69	17 09.5	−15 42
γ Geminorum	1.93	0.03	105	6 36.9	+16 25	λ Scorpii	1.60v		310	17 32.6	−37 06
α Canis Majoris (Sirius)	−1.47	0.38	8.7	6 44.5	−16 42	α Ophiuchi	2.09	0.06	58	17 34.3	+12 34
ε Canis Majoris	1.48		680	6 58.1	−28 57	θ Scorpii	1.86	0.02	650	17 36.3	−42 59
δ Canis Majoris	1.85		2100	7 07.8	−26 22	κ Scorpii	2.39v		470	17 41.5	−39 01
η Canis Majoris	2.46		2700	7 23.5	−29 16	γ Draconis	2.21	0.02	108	17 56.3	+51 29
α Geminorum (Castor)	1.97	0.07	45	7 33.7	+31 55	ε Sagittarii	1.81	0.02	124	18 23.2	−34 24
α Canis Minoris (Procyon)	0.37	0.29	11.3	7 38.5	+5 16	α Lyrae (Vega)	0.04	0.12	26.5	18 36.4	+38 46
β Geminorum (Pollux)	1.16	0.09	35	7 44.4	+28 04	σ Sagittarii	2.12		300	18 54.4	−26 19
ζ Puppis	2.23		2400	8 03.1	−39 58	α Aquilae (Altair)	0.77	0.20	16.5	19 50.1	+8 50
γ Velorum	1.88		520	8 09.1	−47 18	α Cygni	2.22		750	20 21.7	+40 13
ε Carinae	1.90		340	8 22.2	−59 28	α Pavonis	1.95		310	20 24.5	−56 47
δ Velorum	1.95	0.04	76	8 44.3	−54 39	α Cygni (Deneb)	1.26		1600	20 40.9	+45 14
λ Velorum	2.24	0.02	750	9 07.5	−43 22	ε Cygni	2.46	0.04	74	20 45.6	+33 55
β Carinae	1.67	0.04	86	9 13.0	−69 39	α Cephei	2.44	0.06	52	21 18.2	+62 31
ι Carinae	2.25		750	9 16.7	−59 13	ε Pegasi	2.38		780	21 43.5	+9 48
κ Velorum	2.49	0.01	470	9 21.7	−54 57	α Gruis	1.76	0.05	64	22 07.3	−47 02
α Hydrae	1.98	0.02	94	9 26.9	−8 36	β Gruis	2.17v		280	22 41.8	−46 58
α Leonis (Regulus)	1.36	0.04	84	10 07.6	+12 02	α Piscis Austrinis (Fomalhaut)	1.15	0.14	22.6	22 56.9	−29 42
γ Leonis	1.99	0.02	90	10 19.2	+19 55	β Pegasi	2.50v	0.02	210	23 03.1	+28 00
β Ursae Majoris						α Pegasi	2.50	0.03	109	23 04.0	+15 08

Astronomical Constants; Speed of Light

The following were adopted in 1968, in accordance with the resolutions and recommendations of the International Astronomical Union (Hamburg 1964): Velocity of light, 299,792.5 kilometers per second, or about 186,282.3976 statute miles per second; solar parallax, 8″.794; constant of nutation, 9″.210; and constant of aberration, 20″.496.

Aurora Borealis and Aurora Australis

The Aurora Borealis, also called the Northern Lights, is a broad display of rather faint light in the northern skies at night. The Aurora Australis, a similar phenomenon, appears at the same time in southern skies. The aurora appears in a wide variety of forms. Sometimes it is seen as a quiet glow, almost foglike in character; sometimes as vertical streamers in which there may be considerable motion; sometimes as a series of luminous expanding arcs. There are many colors, with white, yellow, and red predominating.

The auroras are most vivid and most frequently seen at about 20 degrees from the magnetic poles, along the northern coast of the North American continent and the eastern part of the northern coast of Europe. They have been seen as far south as Key West, and as far north as Australia and New Zealand, but rarely.

While the cause of the auroras is not known beyond question, there does seem to be a definite correlation between auroral displays and sun-spot activity. It is thought that atomic particles expelled from the sun by the forces that cause solar flares speed through space at velocities of 400 to 600 miles per second. These particles are entrapped by the earth's magnetic field, forming what are termed the Van Allen belts. The encounter of these clouds of the solar wind with the earth's magnetic field weakens the field so that previously trapped particles are allowed to impact the upper atmosphere. The collisions between solar and terrestrial atoms result in the glow in the upper atmosphere called the aurora. The glow may be vivid where the lines of magnetic force converge near the magnetic poles.

The auroral displays appear at heights ranging from 50 to about 600 miles and have given us a means of estimating the extent of the earth's atmosphere.

The auroras are often accompanied by magnetic storms whose forces, also guided by the lines of force of the earth's magnetic field, disrupt electrical communication.

Transit of Mercury, November 1986

An uncommon event occurs in November, 1986, although invisible in North and South America: a transit of the planet Mercury across the face of the sun. The entire event may be seen from India and eastern Asia, southeast Asia, the east Indies, Australia, and southern New Zealand; the beginning will be visible from most of the Pacific Ocean except the eastern part; the end will be visible from western Asia, the U.S.S.R., eastern Europe, Africa except the extreme western part. There are only 14 transits of Mercury in the 20th cen-tury, the last on November 10, 1973, the next on November 6, 1993.

NOTE: Any one observing a transit of Mercury will necessarily be using a telescope aimed directly at the sun for about 6 hours. The very powerful energy from the sun trapped in the telescope may cause severe damage to the instrument. Under no circumstances should the instrument be used for direct viewing by eye.

Geocentric Circumstances of the Transit
Greenwich Mean Time

	d	h	m		d	h	m
Ingress, exterior contact	13	1	14.0	Egress, exterior contact	13	6	31.1
Ingress, interior contact	13	1	44.9	Egress, interior contact	13	6	29.1
Least angular distance	13	4	07.0	Least angular distance, center-to-center 7'50.6"			

Eclipses, 1986

(E.S.T.)

There are four eclipses, two of the sun and two of the moon.

1. *Partial eclipse of the sun*, April 9: visible only in Australia, parts of southern New Guinea, Tasmania, parts of New Zealand, and parts of Antarctica.

		EST		
		d	h	m
Eclipse begins	Apr.	8	23	09.7
Greatest eclipse		9	01	20.4
Eclipse ends		9	03	31.7

2. *Total eclipse of the moon*, Apr. 24: the beginning of the umbral phase visible in the western half of North America, the Pacific Ocean, eastern U.S.S.R. and Asia, southeast Asia, Australia, New Zealand, eastern Indian Ocean, and Antarctica except the Atlantic coast; the end visible in western Alaska, the Pacific Ocean, the Indian Ocean, except the eastern edge, Antarctica except Palmer Peninsula and Princess Margaret Coast, Australia, New Zealand, and central, eastern, and southeast Asia.

		d	h	m
Moon enters penumbra	Apr.	24	5	04.7
Moon enters umbra		24	6	02.8
Moon enters totality		24	7	10.3
Middle of eclipse		24	7	42.6
Moon leaves totality		24	8	14.9
Moon leaves umbra		24	9	22.3
Moon leaves penumbra		24	10	20.4

Magnitude of the eclipse 1.208

3. *Annular—Total eclipse of the sun*, Oct. 3: the partial phases of this eclipse will be generally visible in North America, except in California, parts of Oregon, and parts of western Mexico. The path in which the eclipse is central (i.e., where the center of the moon nearly coincides with the center of the sun) is a short arc in the Atlantic Ocean southeast of Greenland. Globally, the duration of central eclipse is 20.2 minutes, totality taking 17.9 minutes; but in any one place in the path, the total duration of centrality will last less than 3.5 seconds.

		d	h	m
Eclipse begins	Oct.	3	11	57.4
Annular eclipse begins		3	13	55.5
Total eclipse begins		3	13	56.9
Total eclipse ends		3	14	14.8
Annular eclipse ends		3	14	15.7
Eclipse ends		3	16	13.5

4. *Total eclipse of the moon*, Oct. 17: the beginning of the umbral phase visible in New Zealand, Australia, western Pacific Ocean, eastern Antarctica, Asia, Europe except extreme west, Africa except the western extremity; the end visible in extreme western Australia, eastern Antarctica, Indian Ocean, Asia except the extreme eastern parts, Europe, Africa, Greenland, extreme northeastern North America, eastern South America, and the Atlantic Ocean.

		d	h	m
Moon enters penumbra	Oct.	17	11	19.7
Moon enters umbra		17	12	29.2
Moon enters totality		17	13	40.7
Middle of the eclipse		17	14	18.0
Moon leaves totality		17	14	55.2
Moon leaves umbra		17	16	06.7
Moon leaves penumbra		17	17	16.3

Magnitude of the eclipse 1.250

The Planets and the Solar System

Planet	Mean daily motion "	Orbital velocity miles per sec.	Sidereal revolution days	Synodical revolution days	Dist. from sun in millions of mi. Max.	Dist. from sun in millions of mi. Min.	Dist. from Earth in millions of mi. Max.	Dist. from Earth in millions of mi. Min.	Light at[1] peri- helion	Light at[1] aphe- lion
Mercury . .	14732	29.75	88.0	115.9	43.4	28.6	136	50	10.58	4.59
Venus . . .	5768	21.76	224.7	583.9	67.7	66.8	161	25	1.94	1.89
Earth. . . .	3548	18.51	365.3	—	94.6	91.4	—	—	1.03	0.97
Mars	1887	14.99	687.0	779.9	155.0	128.5	248	35	0.524	0.360
Jupiter . . .	299	8.12	4332.1	398.9	507.0	460.6	600	368	0.0408	0.0336
Saturn . . .	120	5.99	10825.9	378.1	937.5	838.4	1031	745	0.01230	0.00984
Uranus . . .	42	4.23	30676.1	369.7	1859.7	1669.3	1953	1606	0.00300	0.00250
Neptune . .	21	3.38	59911.1	367.5	2821.7	2760.4	2915	2667	0.00114	0.00109
Pluto . . .	14	2.95	90824.2	366.7	4551.4	2756.4	4644	2663	0.00114	0.00042

1. Light at perihelion and aphelion is solar illumination in units of mean illumination at Earth.

Planet	Mean longitude of:* ascending node ° ' "			Mean longitude of:* perihelion ° ' "			Inclination* of orbit to ecliptic ° ' "			Mean* distance**	Eccentricity* of orbit	Mean longitude at the epoch* ° ' "		
Mercury. . . .	48	09	04	77	13	19	7	00	17	0.387098	0.205636	242	06	54
Venus.	76	32	42	131	29	24	3	23	40	0.723330	0.006759	298	45	24
Earth	—	—	—	102	42	22	—	—	—	0.999994	0.016755	35	32	32
Mars	49	26	35	335	43	16	1	50	59	1.523712	0.093348	329	44	05
Jupiter	100	20	20	15	23	56	1	18	19	5.20270	0.048061	293	28	58
Saturn.	113	32	20	93	29	13	2	29	08	9.57542	0.050822	224	21	44
Uranus	73	59	17	177	07	23	0	46	27	19.2998	0.047552	248	05	03
Neptune . . .	131	37	34	354	40	12	1	46	15	30.2813	0.006608	271	32	56
Pluto	110	12	58	224	15	00	17	07	56	39.7138	0.253364	216	55	28

*Consistent for the standard Epoch: 1984 Oct. 27.0 Ephemeris Time   **Astronomical units

Sun and planets	Semi-diameter at unit dis- tance ' "	Semi-diameter at mean least dist. "	Semi-diameter in miles mean s.d.	Volume ⊕=1.	Mass. ⊕=1.	Den- sity ⊕=1.	Sidereal period of rotation d.	Sidereal period of rotation h.	Sidereal period of rotation m.	Sidereal period of rotation s.	Gravi- ty at sur- face ⊕=1.	Re- flect- ing power Pct.	Prob- able tem- per- ature °F.
Sun	959.62	—	432560	1303730	332830	0.26	24	16	48	27.9	—		+ 10,000
Mercury . . .	3.37	5.5	1515	0.0559	0.0553	0.99	58	21	58		0.37	0.06	+ 620
Venus	8.34	30.1	3760	0.8541	0.8150	0.95	243	R			0.88	0.72	+ 900
Earth	—	—	3963	1.000	1.000	1.00		23	56	4.1	1.00	0.39	+ 72
Moon	2.40	932.4	1080	0.020	0.0123	0.62	27	7	43		0.17	0.07	— 10
Mars	4.69	8.95	2108.4	0.1506	0.1074	0.71		24	37	23	0.38	0.16	— 10
Jupiter	98.35	23.4	44362	1403	317.83	0.23		9	3	30	2.64	0.70	— 240
Saturn	82.83	9.7	37280	832	95.16	0.11		10	30		1.15	0.75	— 300
Uranus . . .	35.4	1.9	15800	63	14.50	0.23		15	36	R	1.15	0.90	— 340
Neptune . . .	33.4	1.2	15100	55	17.20	0.31		18	26		1.12	0.82	— 370
Pluto*.	1.9	0.05	930	0.01	0.0025	0.25	6	9	17		0.04	0.14	?	?

*Much of this information is too new to be verified, but observers at the U.S. Naval Observatory have derived values similar to these after having discovered that Pluto has a satellite. It apparently revolves about Pluto in a period equal to Pluto's rotation period. (R) retrograde of Venus and Uranus.

Largest Telescopes Are in Northern Hemisphere

Most of the world's major astronomical installations are in the northern hemisphere, while many of astronomy's major problems are found in the southern sky. This imbalance has long been recognized and is being remedied.

In the northern hemisphere the largest reflector is the 236-inch mirror at the Special Astrophysical Observatory in the Caucasus in the Soviet Union. The largest reflectors in the U.S. include 3 in California: at Palomar Mtn., 200 inches; at Lick Observatory, Mt. Hamilton, 120 inches; and at Mt. Wilson Observatory, 100 inches. Also in the U.S. are a 158 inch reflector at Kitt Peak, Arizona, dedicated in June 1973, and a 107-inch telescope at the McDonald Observatory on Mt. Locke in Texas. A telescope at the Crimean Astrophysical Observatory in the Soviet Union has a 104-inch mirror.

Placed in service in 1975 were three large reflectors for the southern hemisphere. Associated Universities for Research in Astronomy (AURA), the operating organization of Kitt Peak National Observatory, dedicated the 158-inch reflector (twin of the telescope on Kitt Peak) at Cerro Tololo International Observatory, Chile; the European Southern Observatory has a 141-inch reflector at La Silla, Chile; and the Anglo-Australian telescope, 152 inches in diameter, is at Siding Spring Observatory in Australia.

Optical Telescopes

Optical astronomical telescopes are of two kinds, refracting and reflecting. In the first, light passes through a lens which brings the light rays into focus, where the image may be examined after being magnified by a second lens, the eyepiece, or directly photographed.

The reflector consists of a concave parabolic mirror, gen-

erally of Pyrex or now of a relatively heat insensitive material, cervit, coated with silver or aluminum, which reflects the light rays back toward the upper end of the telescope, where they are either magnified and observed by the eyepiece or, as in the case of the refractors, photographed. In most reflecting telescopes, the light is reflected again by a secondary mirror and comes to a focus after passing through a hole in the side of the telescope, where the eye-piece or camera is located, or after passing through a hole in the center of the primary mirror.

World's Largest Refractors

Location and diameter in inches

Yerkes Obs., Williams Bay, Wis.	40
Lick Obs., Mt. Hamilton, Cal.	36
Astrophys. Obs., Potsdam, E. Germany	32
Paris Observatory, Meudon, France	32
Allegheny Obs., Pittsburgh, Pa.	30
Univ. of Paris, Nice, France	30
Royal Greenwich Obs., Herstmonceux, England . .	28
Union Obs., Johannesburg, South Africa	26.5
Universitats-Sternwarte, Vienna, Austria	26.5
Leander McCormick Obs., Univ. of Virginia, Charlottesville, Va.	26
Obs., Academy of Sciences, Pulkova, USSR	26
Astronomical Obs., Belgrade, Yugoslavia	26
Obs. Mitaka, Tokyo-to, Japan	26
US Naval Obs., Washington, D.C.	26
Mt. Stromlo Obs., Canberra, Australia	26

The Sun

The sun, the controlling body of our solar system, is a star whose dimensions cause it to be classified among stars as average in size, temperature, and brightness. Its proximity to the earth makes it appear to us as tremendously large and bright. A series of thermo-nuclear reactions involving the atoms of the elements of which it is composed produces the heat and light that make life possible on earth.

The sun has a diameter of 864,000 miles and is distant, on the average, 92,900,000 miles from the earth. It is 1.41 times as dense as water. The light of the sun reaches the earth in 499.012 seconds or slightly more than 8 minutes. The average solar surface temperature has been measured by several indirect methods which agree closely on a value of 6,000° Kelvin or about 10,000° F. The interior temperature of the sun is about 35,000,000 F.°.

When sunlight is analyzed with a spectroscope, it is found to consist of a continuous spectrum composed of all the colors of the rainbow in order, crossed by many dark lines. The "absorption lines" are produced by gaseous materials in the atmosphere of the sun. More than 60 of the natural terrestrial elements have been identified in the sun, all in gaseous form because of the intense heat of the sun.

Spheres and Corona

The radiating surface of the sun is called the photosphere, and just above it is the chromosphere. The chromosphere is visible to the naked eye only at times of total solar eclipses, appearing then to be a pinkish-violet layer with occasional great prominences projecting above its general level. With proper instruments the chromosphere can be seen or photographed whenever the sun is visible without waiting for a total eclipse. Above the chromosphere is the corona, also visible to the naked eye only at times of total eclipse. Instruments also permit the brighter portions of the corona to be studied whenever conditions are favorable. The pearly light of the corona surges millions of miles from the sun. Iron, nickel, and calcium are believed to be principal contributors to the composition of the corona, all in a state of extreme attenuation and high ionization that indicates temperatures on the order of a million degrees Fahrenheit.

Sunspots

There is an intimate connection between sunspots and the corona. At times of low sunspot activity, the fine streamers of the corona will be much longer above the sun's equator than over the polar regions of the sun, while during high sunspot activity, the corona extends fairly evenly outward from all regions of the sun, but to a much greater distance in space. Sunspots are dark, irregularly-shaped regions whose diameters may reach tens of thousands of miles. The average life of a sunspot group is from two to three weeks, but there have been groups that have lasted for more than a year, being carried repeatedly around as the sun rotated upon its axis. The record for the duration of a sunspot is 18 months. Sunspots reach a low point every 11.3 years, with a peak of activity occurring irregularly between two successive minima.

The sun is 400,000 times as bright as the full moon and gives the earth 6 million times as much light as do all the other stars put together. Actually, most of the stars that can be easily seen on any clear night are brighter than the sun.

The Zodiac

The sun's apparent yearly path among the stars is known as the ecliptic. The zone 16° wide, 8° on each side of the ecliptic, is known as the zodiac. Inside of this zone are the apparent paths of the sun, moon, earth, and major planets. Beginning at the point on the ecliptic which marks the position of the sun at the vernal equinox, and thence proceeding eastward, the zodiac is divided into twelve signs of 30° each, as shown herewith.

These signs are named from the twelve constellations of the zodiac with which the signs coincided in the time of the astronomer Hipparchus, about 2,000 years ago. Owing to the precession of the equinoxes, that is to say, to the retrograde motion of the equinoxes along the ecliptic, each sign in the zodiac has, in the course of 2,000 years, moved backward 30° into the constellation west of it; so that the sign Aries is now in the constellation Pisces, and so on. The vernal equinox will move from Pisces into Aquarius about the middle of the 26th century. The signs of the zodiac with their Latin and English names are as follows:

Spring	1.	♈	Aries.	The Ram.
	2.	♉	Taurus.	The Bull.
	3.	♊	Gemini.	The Twins.
Summer	4.	♋	Cancer.	The Crab.
	5.	♌	Leo.	The Lion.
	6.	♍	Virgo.	The Virgin.
Autumn	7.	♎	Libra.	The Balance.
	8.	♏	Scorpio.	The Scorpion.
	9.	♐	Sagittarius.	The Archer.
Winter	10.	♑	Capricorn.	The Goat.
	11.	♒	Aquarius.	The Water Bearer.
	12.	♓	Pisces.	The Fishes.

Moon's Perigee and Apogee, 1986

		Perigee							Apogee			
Day		GMT	EST	Day		GMT	EST	Day		GMT	EST	
Jan	8	07	02	July	19 ...	20	15	Jan	20 ...	01	20*	July 31 ... 21 16
Feb	4	16	11	Aug	16 ...	17	12	Feb	16 ...	22	17	Aug 28 ... 15 10
Mar	1	10	05	Sep	12 ...	00	19*	Mar	16 ...	19	14	Sep 25 ... 10 05
Mar	28 ...	14	09	Oct	7	10	05	Apr	13 ...	12	07	Oct 23 ... 06 01
Apr	25 ...	18	13	Nov	4	02	21*	May	10 ...	23	18	Nov 19 ... 22 17
May	24 ...	03	22*	Dec	2	11	06	June	7 ...	02	21*	Dec 17 ... 05 00
June	21 ...	13	08	Dec	30 ...	23	18	July	4	08	03	
*Previous day												

Major U.S. Planetariums

Academy Planetarium, U.S. Air Force Academy
Adler Planetarium, Chicago, Ill.
American Museum-Hayden Planetarium, N.Y.C.
Buhl Planetarium, Pittsburgh, Pa.
Charles Hayden Planetarium, Boston, Mass.
Einstein Spacearium, Washington, D.C.
Fels Planetarium, Philadelphia, Pa.
Fernbank Science Center Planetarium, Altanta, Ga.

Griffith Planetarium, Los Angeles, Cal.
La. Arts and Science Planetarium, Baton Rouge, La.
McDonnell Planetarium, St. Louis, Mo.
Morehead Planetarium, Chapel Hill, N.C.
Morrison Planetarium, San Francisco, Cal.
Robert T. Longway Planetarium, Flint, Mich.
Strassenburgh Planetarium, Rochester, N.Y.

The Moon

The moon completes a circuit around the earth in a period whose mean or average duration is 27 days 7 hours 43.2 minutes. This is the moon's sidereal period. Because of the motion of the moon in common with the earth around the sun, the mean duration of the lunar month — the period from one new moon to the next new moon — is 29 days 12 hours 44.05 minutes. This is the moon's synodical period.

The mean distance of the moon from the earth according to the American Ephemeris is 238,857 miles. Because the orbit of the moon about the earth is not circular but elliptical, however, the maximum distance from the earth that the moon may reach is 252,710 miles and the least distance is 221,463 miles. All distances are from the center of one object to the center of the other.

The moon's diameter is 2,160 miles. If we deduct the radius of the moon, 1,080 miles, and the radius of the earth, 3,963 miles from the minimum distance or perigee, given above, we shall have for the nearest approach of the bodies' surfaces 216,420 miles.

The moon rotates on its axis in a period of time exactly equal to its sidereal revolution about the earth — 27.321666 days. The moon's revolution about the earth is irregular because of its elliptical orbit. The moon's rotation, however, is regular and this, together with the irregular revolution, produces what is called "libration in longitude" which permits us to see first farther around the east side and then farther around the west side of the moon. The moon's variation north or south of the ecliptic permits us to see farther over first one pole and then the other of the moon and this is "libration in latitude." These two libration effects permit us to see a total of about 60% of the moon's surface over a period of time. The hidden side of the moon was photographed in 1959 by the Soviet space vehicle Lunik III. Since then many excellent pictures of nearly all of the moon's surface have been transmitted to earth by Lunar Orbiters launched by the U.S.

The tides are caused mainly by the moon, because of its proximity to the earth. The ratio of the tide-raising power of the moon to that of the sun is 11 to 5.

Harvest Moon and Hunter's Moon

The Harvest Moon, the full moon nearest the Autumnal Equinox, ushers in a period of several successive days when the moon rises soon after sunset. This phenomenon gives farmers in temperate latitudes extra hours of light in which to harvest their crops before frost and winter come. The 1986 Harvest Moon falls on Sept. 18 GMT. Harvest moon in the south temperate latitudes falls on March 26.

The next full moon after Harvest Moon is called the Hunter's Moon, accompanied by a similar phenomenon but less marked; — Oct. 17, northern hemisphere; April 24, southern hemisphere.

The Earth: Size, Computation of Time, Seasons

Size and Dimensions

The earth is the fifth largest planet and the third from the sun. Its mass is 6 sextillion, 588 quintillion short tons. Using the parameters of an ellipsoid adopted by the International Astronomical Union in 1964 and recognized by the International Union of Geodesy and Geophysics in 1967, the length of the equator is 24,901.55 miles, the length of a meridian is 24,859.82 miles, the equatorial diameter is 7,926.41 miles, and the area of this reference ellipsoid is approximately 196,938,800 square miles.

The earth is considered a solid, rigid mass with a dense core of magnetic, probably metallic material. The outer part of the core is probably liquid. Around the core is a thick shell or mantle of heavy crystalline rock which in turn is covered by a thin crust forming the solid granite and basalt base of the continents and ocean basins. Over broad areas of the earth's surface the crust has a thin cover of sedimentary rock such as sandstone, shale, and limestone formed by weathering of the earth's surface and deposition of sands, clays, and plant and animal remains.

The temperature in the earth increases about 1°F. with every 100 to 200 feet in depth, in the upper 100 kilometers of the earth, and the temperature near the core is believed to be near the melting point of the core materials under the conditions at that depth. The heat of the earth is believed to be derived from radioactivity in the rocks, pressures developed within the earth, and original heat (if the earth in fact was formed at high temperatures).

Atmosphere of the Earth

The earth's atmosphere is a blanket composed of nitrogen, oxygen, and argon, in amounts of about 78, 21, and 1% by volume. Also present in minute quantities are carbon dioxide, hydrogen, neon, helium, krypton, and xenon.

Water vapor displaces other gases and varies from nearly zero to about 4% by volume. The height of the ozone layer varies from approximately 12 to 21 miles above the earth. Traces exist as low as 6 miles and as high as 35 miles. Traces of methane have been found.

The atmosphere rests on the earth's surface with the weight equivalent to a layer of water 34 ft. deep. For about 300,000 ft. upward the gases remain in the proportions stated. Gravity holds the gases to the earth. The weight of the air compresses it at the bottom, so that the greatest density is at the earth's surface. Pressure, as well as density, decreases as height increases because the weight pressing upon any layer is always less than that pressing upon the layers below.

The temperature of the air drops with increased height until the tropopause is reached. This may vary from 25,000 to 60,000 ft. The atmosphere below the tropopause is the troposphere; the atmosphere for about twenty miles above the tropopause is the stratosphere, where the temperature generally increases with height except at high latitudes in winter. A temperature maximum near the 30-mile level is called the stratopause. Above this boundary is the mesosphere where the temperature decreases with height to a minimum, the mesopause, at a height of 50 miles. Extending above the mesosphere to the outer fringes of the atmosphere is the thermosphere, a region where temperature increases with height to a value measured in thousands of degrees Fahrenheit. The lower portion of this region, extending from 50 to about 400 miles in altitude, is characterized by a high ion density, and is thus called the ionosphere. The outer region is called exosphere; this is the region where gas molecules traveling at high speed may escape into outer space, above 600 miles.

Latitude, Longitude

Position on the globe is measured by means of meridians and parallels. Meridians, which are imaginary lines drawn around the earth through the poles, determine longitude. The meridian running through Greenwich, England, is the prime meridian of longitude, and all others are either east or west. Parallels, which are imaginary circles parallel with the equator, determine latitude. The length of a degree of longitude varies as the cosine of the latitude. At the equator a degree is 69.171 statute miles; this is gradually reduced toward the poles. Value of a longitude degree at the poles is zero.

Latitude is reckoned by the number of degrees north or south of the equator, an imaginary circle on the earth's surface everywhere equidistant between the two poles. According to the IAU Ellipsoid of 1964, the length of a degree of latitude is 68.708 statute miles at the equator and varies slightly north and south because of the oblate form of the globe; at the poles it is 69.403 statute miles.

Computation of Time

The earth rotates on its axis and follows an elliptical orbit around the sun. The rotation makes the sun appear to move across the sky from East to West. It determines day and

night and the complete rotation, in relation to the sun, is called the **apparent** or **true solar day**. This varies but an average determines the **mean solar day** of 24 hours.

The mean solar day is in universal use for civil purposes. It may be obtained from apparent solar time by correcting observations of the sun for the equation of time, but when high precision is required, the mean solar time is calculated from its relation to sidereal time. These relations are extremely complicated, but for most practical uses, they may be considered as follows:

Sidereal time is the measure of time defined by the diurnal motion of the vernal equinox, and is determined from observation of the meridian transits of stars. One complete rotation of the earth relative to the equinox is called the **sidereal day**. The mean sidereal day is 23 hours, 56 minutes, 4.091 seconds of mean solar time.

The **Calendar Year** begins at 12 o'clock midnight precisely local clock time, on the night of Dec. 31-Jan. 1. The day and the calendar month also begin at midnight by the clock. The interval required for the earth to make one absolute revolution around the sun is a **sidereal year**; it consisted of 365 days, 6 hours, 9 minutes, and 9.5 seconds of mean solar time (approximately 24 hours per day) in 1900, and is increasing at the rate of 0.0001-second annually.

The **Tropical Year**, on which the return of the seasons depends, is the interval between two consecutive returns of the sun to the vernal equinox. The tropical year consists of 365 days, 5 hours, 48 minutes, and 46 seconds in 1900. It is decreasing at the rate of 0.530 seconds per century.

In 1956 the unit of time interval was defined to be identical with the second of **Ephemeris Time**, 1/31,556,925.9747 of the tropical year for 1900 January 0d 12th hour E.T. A physical definition of the second based on a quantum transition of cesium (atomic second) was adopted in 1964. The atomic second is equal to 9,192,631,770 cycles of the emitted radiation. In 1967 this atomic second was adopted as the unit of time interval for the Intern'l System of Units.

The Zones and Seasons

The five zones of the earth's surface are Torrid, lying between the Tropics of Cancer and Capricorn; North Temperate, between Cancer and the Arctic Circle; South Temperate, between Capricorn and the Antarctic Circle; The Frigid Zones, between the polar Circles and the Poles.

The inclination or tilt of the earth's axis with respect to the sun determines the seasons. These are commonly marked in the North Temperate Zone, where spring begins at the vernal equinox, summer at the summer solstice, autumn at the autumnal equinox and winter at the winter solstice.

In the South Temperate Zone, the seasons are reversed. Spring begins at the autumnal equinox, summer at the winter solstice, etc.

If the earth's axis were perpendicular to the plane of the earth's orbit around the sun there would be no change of seasons. Day and night would be of nearly constant length and there would be equable conditions of temperature. But the axis is tilted 23° 27′ away from a perpendicular to the orbit and only in March and September is the axis at right angles to the sun:

The points at which the sun crosses the equator are the equinoxes, when day and night are most nearly equal. The points at which the sun is at a maximum distance from the equator are the solstices. Days and nights are then most unequal.

In June the North Pole is tilted 23° 27′ toward the sun and the days in the northern hemisphere are longer than the nights, while the days in the southern hemisphere are shorter than the nights. In December the North Pole is tilted 23° 27′ away from the sun and the situation is reversed.

The Seasons in 1986

In 1986 the 4 seasons will begin as follows: add one hour to EST for Atlantic Time; subtract one hour for Central, two hours for Mountain, 3 hours for Pacific, 4 hours for Yukon, 5 hours for Alaska-Hawaii and six hours for Bering Time. Also shown in Greenwich Mean Time.

		Date	GMT	EST
Vernal Equinox	Spring	Mar. 20	22:03	17.03
Summer Solstice	Summer	June 21	16:30	11:30
Autumnal Equinox	Autumn	Sept. 23	07:59	02:59
Winter Solstice	Winter	Dec. 21	04:02	23:02*
*Previous Day				

Poles of The Earth

The geographic (rotation) poles, or points where the earth's axis of rotation cuts the surface, are not absolutely fixed in the body of the earth. The pole of rotation describes an irregular curve about its mean position.

Two periods have been detected in this motion: (1) an annual period due to seasonal changes in barometric pressure, load of ice and snow on the surface and to other phenomena of seasonal character; (2) a period of about 14 months due to the shape and constitution of the earth.

In addition there are small but as yet unpredictable irregularities. The whole motion is so small that the actual pole at any time remains within a circle of 30 or 40 feet in radius centered at the mean position of the pole.

The pole of rotation for the time being is of course the pole having a latitude of 90° and an indeterminate longitude.

Magnetic Poles

The **north magnetic pole** of the earth is that region where the magnetic force is vertically downward and the **south magnetic pole** that region where the magnetic force is vertically upward. A compass placed at the magnetic poles experiences no directive force.

There are slow changes in the distribution of the earth's magnetic field. These changes were at one time attributed in part to a periodic movement of the magnetic poles around the geographical poles, but later evidence refutes this theory and points, rather, to a slow migration of "disturbance" foci over the earth.

There appear shifts in position of the magnetic poles due to the changes in the earth's magnetic field. The center of the area designated as the north magnetic pole was estimated to be in about latitude 70.5° N and longitude 96° W in 1905; from recent nearby measurements and studies of the secular changes, the position in 1970 is estimated as latitude 76.2° N and longitude 101° W. Improved data rather than actual motion account for at least part of the change.

The position of the south magnetic pole in 1912 was near 71° S and longitude 150° E; the position in 1970 is estimated at latitude 66° S and longitude 139.1° E.

The direction of the horizontal components of the magnetic field at any point is known as magnetic north at that point, and the angle by which it deviates east or west of true north is known as the magnetic declination, or in the mariner's terminology, the **variation of the compass**.

A compass without error points in the direction of magnetic north. (In general this is *not* the direction of the magnetic north pole.) If one follows the direction indicated by the north end of the compass, he will travel along a rather irregular curve which eventually reaches the north magnetic pole (though not usually by a great-circle route). However, the action of the compass should not be thought of as due to any influence of the distant pole, but simply as an indication of the distribution of the earth's magnetism at the place of observation.

Rotation of The Earth

The speed of rotation of the earth about its axis has been found to be slightly variable. The variations may be classified as:

(A) **Secular.** Tidal friction acts as a brake on the rotation and causes a slow secular increase in the length of the day, about 1 millisecond per century.

(B) **Irregular.** The speed of rotation may increase for a number of years, about 5 to 10, and then start decreasing. The maximum difference from the mean in the length of the day during a century is about 5 milliseconds. The accumulated difference in time has amounted to approximately 44 seconds since 1900. The cause is probably motion in the interior of the earth.

(C) **Periodic.** Seasonal variations exist with periods of one year and six months. The cumulative effect is such that each year the earth is late about 30 milliseconds near June 1 and is ahead about 30 milliseconds near Oct. 1. The maximum seasonal variation in the length of the day is about 0.5 millisecond. It is believed that the principal cause of the annual variation is the seasonal change in the wind patterns of the Northern and Southern Hemispheres. The semiannual variation is due chiefly to tidal action of the sun, which distorts the shape of the earth slightly.

The secular and irregular variations were discovered by comparing time based on the rotation of the earth with time based on the orbital motion of the moon about the earth and of the planets about the sun. The periodic variation was determined largely with the aid of quartz-crystal clocks. The introduction of the cesium-beam atomic clock in 1955 made it possible to determine in greater detail than before the nature of the irregular and periodic variations.

Morning and Evening Stars 1986

(GMT)

	Morning	Evening		Morning	Evening
Jan.	Mercury Venus (to 19) Mars Saturn	Venus (from 19) Jupiter		Jupiter	Mars (from 10) Saturn
			Aug.	Mercury Jupiter	Venus Mars
Feb.	Mars Jupiter (from 18) Saturn	Mercury Venus Jupiter (to 18)	**Sept.**	Mercury (to 5) Jupiter (to 10)	Saturn Mercury (from 5) Venus
Mar.	Mercury (from 16) Mars Jupiter Saturn	Mercury (to 16) Venus	**Oct.**	(None)	Mars Jupiter (from 10) Saturn Mercury
Apr.	Mercury Mars Jupiter Saturn	Venus			Venus Mars Jupiter Saturn
May	Mercury (to 23) Mars Jupiter Saturn (to 28)	Mercury (from 23) Venus Saturn (from 28)	**Nov.**	Mercury (from 13) Venus (from 5)	Mercury (to 13) Venus (to 5) Mars Jupiter
June	Mars Jupiter	Mercury Venus Saturn	**Dec.**	Mercury Venus Saturn (from 4)	Saturn Mars Jupiter Saturn (to 4)
July	Mercury (from 23) Mars (to 10)	Mercury (to 23) Venus			

Astronomical Twilight—Meridian of Greenwich

Date 1986	20° Begin	20° End	30° Begin	30° End	40° Begin	40° End	50° Begin	50° End	60° Begin	60° End
	h m	h m	h m	h m	h m	h m	h m	h m	h m	h m
Jan. 1	5 16	6 50	5 30	6 35	5 45	6 21	6 00	6 07	6 18	5 49
11	5 19	6 56	5 33	6 43	5 46	6 30	6 00	6 17	6 15	6 01
21	5 21	7 01	5 32	6 51	5 43	6 40	5 55	6 30	6 06	6 18
Feb. 1	5 21	7 07	5 29	6 58	5 38	6 51	5 45	6 44	5 51	6 38
11	5 18	7 11	5 24	7 05	5 29	7 01	5 32	6 59	5 32	7 01
21	5 13	7 15	5 17	7 12	5 17	7 12	5 16	7 14	5 09	7 23
Mar. 1	5 08	7 18	5 08	7 19	5 06	7 21	4 59	7 29	4 44	7 45
11	5 00	7 21	4 58	7 24	4 50	7 32	4 38	7 46	4 12	8 12
21	4 52	7 24	4 45	7 32	4 33	7 44	4 14	8 04	3 37	8 43
Apr. 1	4 42	7 28	4 31	7 39	4 14	7 57	3 47	8 25	2 53	9 21
11	4 32	7 32	4 18	7 47	3 56	8 09	3 20	8 47	2 03	10 10
21	4 23	7 36	4 04	7 54	3 37	8 23	2 52	9 11	0 37	11 47
May 1	4 14	7 41	3 52	8 04	3 19	8 37	2 22	9 39		
11	4 08	7 46	3 41	8 13	3 03	8 53	1 49	10 09		
21	4 02	7 52	3 32	8 22	2 48	9 07	1 13	10 46		
June 1	3 58	7 58	3 26	8 30	2 36	9 20	0 21	11 52		
11	3 56	8 03	3 22	8 36	2 29	9 30				
21	3 57	8 06	3 22	8 40	2 28	9 35				
July 1	3 59	8 07	3 25	8 41	2 30	9 35				
11	4 03	8 06	3 30	8 39	2 40	9 30				
21	4 08	8 03	3 39	8 33	2 52	9 18	1 12	11 23		
Aug. 1	4 15	7 56	3 48	8 23	3 09	9 01	1 49	10 20		
11	4 20	7 50	3 56	8 13	3 22	8 46	2 21	9 46		
21	4 24	7 41	4 05	8 01	3 34	8 27	2 47	9 15		
Sept. 1	4 29	7 31	4 14	7 46	3 51	8 08	3 13	8 43	1 40	10 02
11	4 32	7 20	4 20	7 33	4 02	7 50	3 33	8 16	2 36	9 12
21	4 35	7 11	4 26	7 19	4 14	7 31	3 52	7 52	3 11	8 31
Oct. 1	4 38	7 02	4 33	7 05	4 25	7 13	4 10	7 28	3 41	7 54
11	4 40	6 53	4 40	6 53	4 35	6 58	4 26	7 05	4 07	7 23
21	4 43	6 47	4 45	6 44	4 45	6 43	4 41	6 46	4 32	6 55
Nov. 1	4 46	6 41	4 52	6 34	4 56	6 30	4 58	6 27	4 56	6 27
11	4 50	6 38	4 59	6 28	5 06	6 21	5 13	6 14	5 17	6 08
21	4 55	6 36	5 06	6 25	5 16	6 15	5 26	6 04	5 37	5 52
Dec. 1	5 00	6 37	5 13	6 24	5 25	6 11	5 38	5 58	5 53	5 42
11	5 06	6 40	5 20	6 26	5 34	6 12	5 48	5 57	6 06	5 38
21	5 11	6 45	5 25	6 30	5 39	6 16	5 55	6 00	6 15	5 40
31	5 15	6 50	5 30	6 35	5 44	6 21	6 00	6 06	6 18	5 48

Latitude, Longitude, and Altitude of North American Cities

Source: National Oceanic and Atmospheric Administration, U.S. Commerce Department for geographic positions.
Source for Canadian cities: Geodetic Survey of Canada, Dept. of Energy, Mines, and Resources.
Altitudes U.S. Geological Survey and various sources. *Approx. altitude at downtown business area U.S.; in Canada at city hall except where (a) is at tower of major airport.

City	Lat. N °	'	"	Long. W °	'	"	Alt.* feet
Abilene, Tex.	32	27	05	99	43	51	1710
Akron, Oh.	41	05	00	81	30	44	874
Albany, N.Y.	42	39	01	73	45	01	20
Albuquerque, N.M.	35	05	01	106	39	05	4,945
Allentown, Pa.	40	36	11	75	28	06	255
Alert, N.W.T.	82	29	50	62	21	15	95
Altoona, Pa.	40	30	55	78	24	03	1,180
Amarillo, Tex.	35	12	27	101	50	04	3,685
Anchorage, Alas.	61	10	00	149	59	00	118
Ann Arbor, Mich.	42	16	59	83	44	52	880
Asheville, N.C.	35	35	42	82	33	26	1,985
Ashland, Ky.	38	28	36	82	38	23	536
Atlanta, Ga.	33	45	10	84	23	37	1,050
Atlantic City, N.J.	39	21	32	74	25	53	10
Augusta, Ga.	33	28	20	81	58	00	143
Augusta, Me.	44	18	53	69	46	29	45
Austin, Tex.	30	16	09	97	44	37	505
Bakersfield, Cal.	35	22	31	119	01	18	400
Baltimore, Md.	39	17	26	76	36	45	20
Bangor, Me.	44	48	13	68	46	18	20
Baton Rouge, La.	30	26	58	91	11	00	57
Battle Creek, Mich.	42	18	58	85	10	48	820
Bay City, Mich.	43	36	04	83	53	15	595
Beaumont, Tex.	30	05	20	94	06	09	20
Belleville, Ont.	44	09	42	77	23	11	257
Bellingham, Wash.	48	45	34	122	28	36	60
Berkeley, Cal.	37	52	10	122	16	17	40
Bethlehem, Pa.	40	37	16	75	22	34	235
Billings, Mon.	45	47	00	108	30	04	3,120
Biloxi, Miss.	30	23	48	88	53	00	20
Binghamton, N.Y.	42	06	03	75	54	47	865
Birmingham, Ala.	33	31	01	86	48	36	600
Bismarck, N.D.	46	48	23	100	47	17	1,674
Bloomington, Ill.	40	28	58	88	59	36	800
Boise, Ida.	43	37	07	116	11	58	2,704
Boston, Mass.	42	21	24	71	03	25	21
Bowling Green, Ky.	36	59	41	86	26	33	510
Brandon, Man.	49	51	00	99	57	00	1,265(a)
Brantford, Ont.	43	08	34	80	15	39	705(a)
Brattleboro, Vt.	42	51	06	72	33	48	300
Bridgeport, Conn.	41	10	49	73	11	22	10
Brockton, Mass.	42	05	02	71	01	25	130
Brownsville, Tex.	25	54	07	97	29	58	35
Buffalo, N.Y.	42	52	52	78	52	21	585
Burlington, Ont.	43	19	33	79	47	57	284
Burlington, Vt.	44	28	34	73	12	46	110
Butte, Mon.	46	01	06	112	32	11	5,765
Calgary, Alta.	51	02	46	114	03	24	3,427
Cambridge, Mass.	42	22	01	71	06	22	20
Camden, N.J.	39	56	41	75	07	14	30
Canton, Oh.	40	47	50	81	22	37	1,030
Carson City, Nev.	39	10	00	119	46	00	4,680
Cedar Rapids, Ia.	41	58	01	91	39	53	730
Central Islip, N.Y.	40	47	24	73	12	00	80
Champaign, Ill.	40	07	05	88	14	48	740
Charleston, S.C.	32	46	35	79	55	53	9
Charleston, W.Va.	38	21	01	81	37	52	601
Charlotte, N.C.	35	13	44	80	50	45	720
Charlottetown, P.E.I.	46	14	07	63	07	49	31
Chattanooga, Tenn.	35	02	41	85	18	32	675
Cheyenne, Wy.	41	08	09	104	49	07	6,100
Chicago, Ill.	41	52	28	87	38	22	595
Churchill, Man.	58	45	15	94	10	00	94(a)
Cincinnati, Oh.	39	06	07	84	30	35	550
Cleveland, Oh.	41	29	51	81	41	50	660
Colorado Springs	38	50	07	104	49	16	5,980
Columbia, Mo.	38	57	03	92	19	46	730
Columbia, S.C.	34	00	02	81	02	00	190
Columbus, Ga.	32	28	07	84	59	24	265
Columbus, Oh.	39	57	47	83	00	17	780
Concord, N.H.	43	12	22	71	32	25	290
Corpus Christi, Tex.	27	47	51	97	23	45	35
Dallas, Tex.	32	47	09	96	47	37	435
Dartmouth, N.S.	44	39	50	63	34	08	24
Davenport, Ia.	41	31	19	90	34	33	590
Dawson, Yukon	64	03	30	139	26	00	1,211(a)
Dayton, Oh.	39	45	32	84	11	43	574
Daytona Beach, Fla.	29	12	44	81	01	10	7
Decatur, Ill.	39	50	42	88	56	47	682
Denver, Col.	39	44	58	104	59	22	5,280
Des Moines, Ia.	41	35	14	93	37	00	805
Detroit, Mich.	42	19	48	83	02	57	585
Dodge City, Kan.	37	45	17	100	01	09	2,480
Dubuque, Ia.	42	29	55	90	40	08	620
Duluth, Minn.	46	46	56	92	06	24	610
Durham, N.C.	36	00	00	78	54	45	405
Eau Claire, Wis.	44	48	31	91	29	49	790
Edmonton, Alta.	53	32	43	113	29	21	2,186
El Paso, Tex.	31	45	36	106	29	11	3,695
Elizabeth, N.J.	40	39	43	74	12	59	21
Enid, Okla.	36	23	40	97	52	35	1,240
Erie, Pa.	42	07	15	80	04	57	685
Eugene, Ore.	44	03	16	123	05	30	422
Eureka, Cal.	40	48	08	124	09	46	45
Evansville, Ind.	37	58	20	87	34	21	385
Fairbanks, Alas.	64	48	00	147	51	00	448
Fall River, Mass.	41	42	06	71	09	18	40
Fargo, N.D.	46	52	30	96	47	18	900
Flagstaff, Ariz.	35	11	36	111	39	06	6,900
Flint, Mich.	43	00	50	83	41	33	750
Ft. Smith, Ark.	35	23	10	94	25	36	440
Ft. Wayne, Ind.	41	04	21	85	08	26	790
Fort Worth, Tex.	32	44	55	97	19	44	670
Fredericton, N.B.	45	57	47	66	38	38	29
Fresno, Cal.	36	44	12	119	47	11	285
Gadsden, Ala.	34	00	57	86	00	41	555
Gainesville, Fla.	29	38	56	82	19	19	175
Gallup, N.M.	35	31	30	108	44	30	6,540
Galveston, Tex.	29	18	10	94	47	43	5
Gary, Ind.	41	36	12	87	20	19	590
Grand Junction, Col.	39	04	06	108	33	54	4,590
Grand Rapids, Mich.	42	58	03	85	40	13	610
Great Falls, Mon.	47	29	33	111	18	23	3,340
Green Bay, Wis.	44	30	48	88	00	50	590
Greensboro, N.C.	36	04	17	79	47	25	839
Greenville, S.C.	34	50	50	82	24	01	966
Guelph, Ont.	43	32	35	80	-14	54	1,065
Gulfport, Miss.	30	22	04	89	05	36	20
Halifax, N.S.	44	38	54	63	34	30	60
Hamilton, Ont.	43	15	20	79	52	30	329
Hamilton, Oh.	39	23	59	84	33	47	600
Harrisburg, Pa.	40	15	43	76	52	59	365
Hartford, Conn.	41	46	12	72	40	49	40
Helena, Mon.	46	35	33	112	02	24	4,155
Hilo, Hawaii	19	43	30	155	05	24	40
Holyoke, Mass.	42	12	29	72	36	36	115
Honolulu, Ha.	21	18	22	157	51	35	21
Houston, Tex.	29	45	26	95	21	37	40
Hull, Que.	45	25	42	75	42	41	185
Huntington, W.Va.	38	25	12	82	26	33	565
Huntsville, Ala.	34	44	18	86	35	19	640
Indianapolis, Ind.	39	46	07	86	09	46	710
Iowa City, Ia.	41	39	37	91	31	53	685
Jackson, Mich.	42	14	43	84	24	22	940
Jackson, Miss.	32	17	56	90	11	06	298
Jacksonville, Fla.	30	19	44	81	39	42	20
Jersey City, N.J.	40	43	50	74	03	56	20
Johnstown, Pa.	40	19	35	78	55	03	1,185
Joplin, Mo.	37	05	26	94	30	00	990
Juneau, Alas.	58	18	12	134	24	30	50
Kalamazoo, Mich.	42	17	29	85	35	14	755
Kansas City, Kan.	39	07	04	94	38	24	750
Kansas City, Mo.	39	04	56	94	35	20	750
Kenosha, Wis.	42	35	43	87	50	11	610
Key West, Fla.	24	33	30	81	48	12	5
Kingston, Ont.	44	13	53	76	28	48	264
Kitchener, Ont.	43	26	58	80	29	12	1,100
Knoxville, Tenn.	35	57	39	83	55	07	890
Lafayette, Ind.	40	25	11	86	53	39	550
Lancaster, Pa.	40	02	25	76	18	29	355
Lansing, Mich.	42	44	01	84	33	15	830
Laredo, Tex.	27	30	22	99	30	30	440
La Salle, Que.	45	25	30	73	39	30	110
Las Vegas, Nev.	36	10	20	115	08	37	2,030
Laval, Que.	45	33	05	73	44	42	142
Lawrence, Mass.	42	42	16	71	10	08	40
Lethbridge, Alta.	49	41	38	112	49	58	2,985
Lexington, Ky.	38	02	50	84	29	46	955
Lihue, Ha.	21	58	48	159	22	30	210
Lima, Oh.	40	44	35	84	06	20	865
Lincoln, Neb.	40	48	59	96	42	15	1,150
Little Rock, Ark.	34	44	42	92	16	37	286
London, Ont.	42	59	17	81	14	03	822
Long Beach, Cal.	33	46	14	118	11	18	35
Lorain, Oh.	41	28	05	82	10	49	610
Los Angeles, Cal.	34	03	15	118	14	28	340
Louisville, Ky.	38	14	47	85	45	49	450
Lowell, Mass.	42	38	25	71	19	14	100
Lubbock, Tex.	33	35	05	101	50	33	3,195

City	Lat. N °	′	″	Long. W °	′	″	Alt.* Feet
Macon, Ga.	32	50	12	83	37	36	335
Madison, Wis.	43	04	23	89	22	55	860
Manchester, N.H.	42	59	28	71	27	41	175
Marshall, Tex.	32	33	00	94	23	00	410
Memphis, Tenn.	35	08	46	90	03	13	275
Meriden, Conn.	41	32	06	72	47	30	190
Mexico City, Mexico	19	25	45	99	07	00	7,347
Miami, Fla.	25	46	37	80	11	32	10
Milwaukee, Wis.	43	02	19	87	54	15	635
Minneapolis, Minn.	44	58	57	93	15	43	815
Minot, N.D.	48	14	09	101	17	38	1,550
Mississauga, Ont.	43	33	00	79	35	00	260(a)
Mobile, Ala.	30	41	36	88	02	33	5
Moline, Ill.	41	30	31	90	30	49	585
Moncton, N.B.	46	05	18	64	46	41	38
Montgomery, Ala.	32	22	33	86	18	31	160
Montpelier, Vt.	44	15	36	72	34	41	485
Montreal, Que.	45	30	33	73	33	14	90
Moose Jaw, Sask.	50	23	34	105	32	04	1,784
Muncie, Ind.	40	11	28	85	23	16	950
Nashville, Tenn.	36	09	33	86	46	55	450
Natchez, Miss.	31	33	48	91	23	30	210
Newark, N.J.	40	44	14	74	10	19	55
New Bedford, Mass.	41	38	13	70	55	41	15
New Britain, Conn.	41	40	08	72	46	59	200
New Haven, Conn.	41	18	25	72	55	30	40
New Orleans, La.	29	56	53	90	04	10	5
New York, N.Y.	40	45	06	73	59	39	55
Niagara Falls, N.Y.	43	05	34	79	03	26	570
Niagara Falls, Ont.	43	06	22	79	03	51	590
Nome, Alas.	64	30	00	165	25	00	25
Norfolk, Va.	36	51	10	76	17	21	10
North Bay, Ont.	46	18	35	79	27	45	670
Oakland, Cal.	37	48	03	122	15	54	25
Ogden, Ut.	41	13	31	111	58	21	4,295
Oklahoma City	35	28	26	97	31	04	1,195
Omaha, Neb.	41	15	42	95	56	14	1,040
Orlando, Fla.	28	32	42	81	22	38	70
Oshawa, Ont.	43	53	46	78	51	57	350
Ottawa, Ont.	45	26	24	75	41	42	185
Paducah, Ky.	37	05	13	88	35	56	345
Pasadena, Cal.	34	08	44	118	08	41	830
Paterson, N.J.	40	55	01	74	10	21	100
Pensacola, Fla.	30	24	51	87	12	56	15
Peoria, Ill.	40	41	42	89	35	33	470
Peterborough, Ont.	44	18	32	78	19	13	673
Philadelphia, Pa.	39	56	58	75	09	21	100
Phoenix, Ariz.	33	27	12	112	04	28	1,090
Pierre, S.D.	44	22	18	100	20	54	1,480
Pittsburgh, Pa.	40	26	19	80	00	00	745
Pittsfield, Mass.	42	26	53	73	15	14	1,015
Pocatello, Ida.	42	51	38	112	27	01	4,460
Port Arthur, Tex.	29	52	30	93	56	15	10
Portland, Me.	43	39	33	70	15	19	25
Portland, Ore.	45	31	06	122	40	35	77
Portsmouth, N.H.	43	04	30	70	45	24	20
Portsmouth, Va.	36	50	07	76	18	14	10
Prince Rupert, B.C.	54	19	00	130	19	00	125(a)
Providence, R.I.	41	49	32	71	24	41	80
Provo, Ut.	40	14	06	111	39	24	4,550
Pueblo, Col.	38	16	17	104	36	33	4,690
Quebec City, Que.	46	48	51	71	12	30	163
Racine, Wis.	42	43	49	87	47	12	630
Rapid City, S.D.	44	04	52	103	13	11	3,230
Raleigh, N.C.	35	46	38	78	38	21	365
Reading, Pa.	40	20	09	75	55	40	265
Regina, Sask.	50	26	55	104	36	50	1,894(a)
Reno, Nev.	39	31	27	119	48	40	4,490
Richmond, Va.	37	32	15	77	26	09	160
Roanoke, Va.	37	16	13	79	56	44	905
Rochester, Minn.	44	01	21	92	28	03	990
Rochester, N.Y.	43	09	41	77	36	21	515
Rockford, Ill.	42	16	07	89	05	48	715
Sacramento, Cal.	38	34	57	121	29	41	30
Saginaw, Mich.	43	25	52	83	56	05	595
St. Catharines, Ont.	43	09	33	79	14	50	362(a)
St. Cloud, Minn.	45	34	00	94	10	24	1,040
Saint John, N.B.	45	16	22	66	03	48	27
St. John's, Nfld.	47	33	42	52	42	48	200(a)
St. Joseph, Mo.	39	45	57	94	51	02	850
St. Louis, Mo.	38	37	45	90	12	22	455
St. Paul, Minn.	44	57	19	93	06	07	780
St. Petersburg, Fla.	27	46	18	82	38	19	20
Salem, Ore.	44	56	24	123	01	59	155

City	Lat. N °	′	″	Long. W °	′	″	Alt.* Feet
Salina, Kan.	38	50	36	97	36	46	1,229
Salt Lake City, Ut.	40	45	23	111	53	26	4,390
San Angelo, Tex.	31	27	39	100	26	03	1,845
San Antonio, Tex.	29	25	37	98	29	06	650
San Bernardino, Cal.	34	06	30	117	17	28	1,080
San Diego, Cal.	32	42	53	117	09	21	20
San Francisco, Cal.	37	46	39	122	24	40	65
San Jose, Cal.	37	20	16	121	53	24	90
San Juan, P.R.	18	27	00	66	04	15	35
Santa Barbara, Cal.	34	25	18	119	41	55	100
Santa Cruz, Cal.	36	58	18	122	01	18	20
Santa Fe, N.M.	35	41	11	105	56	10	6,950
Sarasota, Fla.	27	20	05	82	32	30	20
Saskatoon, Sask.	52	07	49	106	39	35	1,587
Sault Ste. Marie, Ont.	46	30	24	84	20	04	589
Savannah, Ga.	32	04	42	81	05	37	20
Schenectady, N.Y.	42	48	42	73	55	42	245
Scranton, Pa.	41	24	32	75	39	46	725
Seattle, Wash.	47	36	32	122	20	12	10
Sheboygan, Wis.	43	45	03	87	42	55	630
Sherbrooke, Que.	45	24	27	71	51	07	535(a)
Sheridan, Wy.	44	47	55	106	57	10	3,740
Shreveport, La.	32	30	46	93	44	58	204
Sioux City, Ia.	42	29	46	96	24	30	1,110
Sioux Falls, S.D.	43	32	35	96	43	35	1,395
Somerville, Mass.	42	23	15	71	06	07	13
South Bend, Ind.	41	40	33	86	15	01	710
Spartanburg, S.C.	34	57	03	81	56	06	875
Spokane, Wash.	47	39	32	117	25	33	1,890
Springfield, Ill.	39	47	58	89	38	51	610
Springfield, Mass.	42	06	21	72	35	32	85
Springfield, Mo.	37	13	03	93	17	32	1,300
Springfield, Oh.	39	55	38	83	48	29	980
Stamford, Conn.	41	03	09	73	32	24	35
Steubenville, Oh.	40	21	42	80	36	53	660
Stockton, Cal.	37	57	30	121	17	16	20
Sudbury, Ont.	46	29	24	80	59	24	850(a)
Superior, Wis.	46	43	14	92	06	07	630
Sydney, N.S.	46	08	15	60	11	48	15
Syracuse, N.Y.	43	03	04	76	09	14	400
Tacoma, Wash.	47	14	59	122	26	15	110
Tallahassee, Fla.	30	26	30	84	16	56	150
Tampa, Fla.	27	56	58	82	27	25	15
Terre Haute, Ind.	39	28	03	87	24	26	496
Texarkana, Tex.	33	25	48	94	02	30	324
Thunder Bay, Ont.	48	22	54	89	14	42	616
Toledo, Oh.	41	39	14	83	32	39	585
Topeka, Kan.	39	03	16	95	40	23	930
Toronto, Ont.	43	39	10	79	23	00	300
Trenton, N.J.	40	13	14	74	46	13	35
Trois-Rivieres, Que.	46	20	36	72	32	37	115(a)
Troy, N.Y.	42	43	45	73	40	58	35
Tucson, Ariz.	32	13	15	110	58	08	2,390
Tulsa, Okla.	36	09	12	95	59	34	804
Urbana, Ill.	40	06	42	88	12	06	725
Utica, N.Y.	43	06	12	75	13	33	415
Vancouver, B.C.	49	18	56	123	04	44	141
Victoria, B.C.	48	25	43	123	21	49	57
Waco, Tex.	31	33	12	97	08	00	405
Walla Walla, Wash.	46	04	08	118	20	24	936
Washington, D.C.	38	53	51	77	00	33	25
Waterbury, Conn.	41	33	13	73	02	31	260
Waterloo, Ia.	42	29	40	92	20	20	850
West Palm Beach, Fla.	26	42	36	80	03	07	15
Wheeling, W. Va.	40	04	03	80	43	20	650
Whitehorse, Yukon	60	43	17	135	03	03	2,305(a)
White Plains, N.Y.	41	02	00	73	45	48	220
Wichita, Kan.	37	41	30	97	20	16	1,290
Wichita Falls, Tex.	33	54	34	98	29	28	945
Wilkes-Barre, Pa.	41	14	32	75	53	17	640
Wilmington, Del.	39	44	46	75	32	51	135
Wilmington, N.C.	34	14	14	77	56	58	35
Windsor, Ont.	42	18	56	83	02	10	603
Winnipeg, Man.	49	53	56	97	08	23	762
Winston-Salem, N.C.	36	05	52	80	14	42	860
Worcester, Mass.	42	15	37	71	48	17	475
Yakima, Wash.	46	36	09	120	30	39	1,060
Yellowknife, N.W.T.	62	27	16	114	22	33	674(a)
Yonkers, N.Y.	40	55	55	73	53	54	10
York, Pa.	39	57	35	76	43	36	370
Youngstown, Oh.	41	05	57	80	39	02	840
Yuma, Ariz.	32	42	54	114	37	24	160
Zanesville, Oh.	39	56	18	82	00	30	720

World Cities

City	Lat. N °	′	″	Long. W °	′	″	Alt.* Feet
London, UK (Greenwich)	51	30	00N	0	0	0	245
Paris, France	48	50	14N	2	20	14E	300
Berlin, Germany	52	32	00N	13	25	00E	110
Rome, Italy	41	53	00N	12	30	00E	95
Warsaw, Poland	52	15	00N	21	00	00E	360
Moscow, USSR	55	45	00N	37	42	00E	394
Athens, Greece	37	58	00N	23	44	00E	300
Jerusalem, Israel	31	47	00N	35	13	00E	2,500
Johannesburg, So. Afr.	26	10	00S	28	02	00E	5,740
New Delhi, India	28	38	00N	77	12	00E	770
Peking, China	39	54	00N	116	28	00E	600
Rio de Janeiro, Brazil	22	53	43S	43	13	22W	30
Tokyo, Japan	35	45	00N	139	45	00E	30
Sydney, Australia	33	52	00S	151	12	00E	25

1st Month   January, 1986   31 days

Greenwich Mean Time

NOTE: Light figures indicate Sun. **Dark** figures indicate **Moon.** *Degrees are North Latitude.*

CAUTION: Must be converted to local time. For instruction see page 726.

Day of month / week / year	Sun on Meridian / Moon phase (h m s)	Sun's Declination (° ')	20° Rise Sun/Moon (h m)	20° Set Sun/Moon (h m)	30° Rise (h m)	30° Set (h m)	40° Rise (h m)	40° Set (h m)	50° Rise (h m)	50° Set (h m)	60° Rise (h m)	60° Set (h m)
1 We	12 03 30	−23 03	6 35	17 32	6 56	17 11	7 22	16 45	7 59	16 09	9 02	14 44
1			22 23	10 29	22 15	10 39	22 06	10 51	21 53	11 08	21 33	11 33
2 Th	12 03 58	−22 58	6 35	17 33	6 56	17 12	7 22	16 46	7 59	16 10	9 02	14 46
2			23 18	11 05	23 16	11 10	23 14	11 16	23 11	11 23	23 07	11 34
3 Fr	12 04 26	−22 52	6 36	17 34	6 56	17 13	7 22	16 47	7 59	16 11	9 01	14 48
3	19 47 ☾		—	11 42	—	11 40	—	11 39	—	11 37	—	11 35
4 Sa	12 04 54	−22 47	6 36	17 34	6 56	17 13	7 22	16 48	7 58	16 12	9 00	14 50
4			0 15	12 19	0 19	12 12	0 24	12 04	0 31	11 52	0 42	11 35
5 Su	12 05 21	−22 40	6 36	17 34	6 57	17 14	7 22	16 49	7 58	16 13	9 00	14 51
5			1 13	12 59	1 23	12 46	1 36	12 31	1 53	12 09	2 21	11 37
6 Mo	12 05 48	−22 33	6 37	17 35	6 57	17 15	7 22	16 50	7 58	16 14	8 59	14 53
6			2 15	13 43	2 31	13 25	2 51	13 02	3 19	12 31	4 07	11 39
7 Tu	12 06 14	−22 26	6 37	17 36	6 57	17 16	7 22	16 51	7 58	16 15	8 58	14 55
7			3 20	14 34	3 42	14 11	4 09	13 42	4 48	13 00	5 59	11 46
8 We	12 06 39	−22 19	6 37	17 36	6 57	17 16	7 22	16 52	7 57	16 16	8 57	14 58
8			4 28	15 32	4 54	15 05	5 27	14 31	6 15	13 41	7 52	12 03
9 Th	12 07 05	−22 11	6 37	17 37	6 57	17 17	7 22	16 53	7 56	16 18	8 56	15 00
9			5 36	16 35	6 04	16 08	6 39	15 32	7 32	14 39	9 25	12 46
10 Fr	12 07 29	−22 02	6 37	17 38	6 57	17 18	7 22	16 54	7 56	16 19	8 55	15 02
10	12 22 ●		6 40	17 42	7 07	17 16	7 41	16 42	8 32	15 53	10 14	14 12
11 Sa	12 07 53	−21 53	6 37	17 38	6 57	17 19	7 22	16 55	7 55	16 20	8 54	15 04
11			7 37	18 48	8 01	18 25	8 31	17 57	9 14	17 16	10 33	16 00
12 Su	12 08 17	−21 44	6 38	17 39	6 57	17 19	7 22	16 56	7 55	16 22	8 52	15 07
12			8 27	19 50	8 46	19 33	9 10	19 11	9 44	18 40	10 40	17 48
13 Mo	12 08 40	−21 34	6 38	17 39	6 57	17 20	7 21	16 57	7 54	16 23	8 51	15 10
13			9 10	20 49	9 24	20 37	9 42	20 22	10 06	20 01	10 43	19 28
14 Tu	12 09 02	−21 24	6 38	17 40	6 57	17 21	7 21	16 58	7 54	16 25	8 50	15 12
14			9 48	21 43	9 57	21 37	10 08	21 29	10 22	21 18	10 45	21 00
15 We	12 09 24	−21 13	6 38	17 41	6 57	17 22	7 20	16 59	7 53	16 26	8 48	15 14
15			10 22	22 34	10 26	22 33	10 30	22 32	10 36	22 30	10 45	22 27
16 Th	12 09 45	−21 02	6 38	17 41	6 56	17 23	7 20	17 00	7 52	16 28	8 46	15 17
16			10 55	23 24	10 53	23 28	10 51	23 33	10 49	23 41	10 45	23 52
17 Fr	12 10 05	−20 51	6 38	17 42	6 56	17 24	7 19	17 01	7 52	16 30	8 45	15 20
17	22 13 ☽		11 27	—	11 20	—	11 12	—	11 01	—	10 45	—
18 Sa	12 10 24	−20 39	6 38	17 43	6 56	17 25	7 19	17 02	7 51	16 31	8 43	15 22
18			11 59	0 13	11 48	0 23	11 34	0 34	11 15	0 50	10 45	1 15
19 Su	12 10 43	−20 27	6 38	17 44	6 56	17 26	7 18	17 03	7 50	16 32	8 41	15 25
19			12 34	1 03	12 18	1 17	11 58	1 35	11 31	1 59	10 47	2 40
20 Mo	12 11 01	−20 14	6 38	17 44	6 55	17 26	7 18	17 04	7 49	16 34	8 40	15 28
20			13 12	1 54	12 51	2 13	12 26	2 36	11 50	3 10	10 50	4 07
21 Tu	12 11 18	−20 01	6 38	17 45	6 55	17 27	7 17	17 06	7 48	16 36	8 38	15 30
21			13 54	2 47	13 30	3 09	12 59	3 38	12 16	4 10	10 57	5 30
22 We	12 11 35	−19 48	6 38	17 46	6 55	17 28	7 17	17 07	7 47	16 37	8 36	15 33
22			14 40	3 41	14 14	4 07	13 40	4 39	12 51	5 28	11 13	7 04
23 Th	12 11 50	−19 34	6 38	17 46	6 55	17 29	7 16	17 08	7 46	16 39	8 34	15 36
23			15 04	4 35	15 04	5 03	14 29	5 37	13 57	6 29	11 48	8 18
24 Fr	12 12 05	−19 20	6 37	17 47	6 54	17 30	7 16	17 09	7 44	16 40	8 32	15 38
24			16 01	5 29	16 01	5 56	15 27	6 30	14 37	7 21	12 54	9 04
25 Sa	12 12 19	−19 06	6 37	17 47	6 54	17 31	7 15	17 11	7 43	16 42	8 30	15 41
25			17 25	6 19	17 25	6 44	16 31	7 16	15 47	8 01	14 23	9 27
26 Su	12 12 32	−18 51	6 37	17 48	6 54	17 32	7 14	17 12	7 42	16 44	8 28	15 44
26	00 31 ○		18 23	7 06	18 23	7 27	17 39	7 54	17 03	8 32	16 02	9 37
27 Mo	12 12 45	−18 35	6 37	17 49	6 54	17 33	7 13	17 13	7 41	16 46	8 26	15 47
27			19 21	7 49	19 21	8 06	18 48	8 27	18 23	8 55	17 40	9 42
28 Tu	12 12 56	−18 16	6 36	17 49	6 53	17 34	7 12	17 14	7 39	16 47	8 24	15 50
28			20 18	8 29	20 18	8 40	19 58	8 55	19 42	9 14	19 17	9 44
29 We	12 13 07	−18 04	6 36	17 50	6 52	17 35	7 12	17 16	7 38	16 48	8 21	15 53
29			21 14	9 06	21 14	9 12	21 07	9 20	21 01	9 30	20 52	9 45
30 Th	12 13 17	−17 48	6 36	17 51	6 52	17 35	7 11	17 16	7 37	16 50	8 19	15 56
30			22 10	9 43	22 10	9 43	22 16	9 44	22 20	9 44	22 27	9 45
31 Fr	12 13 27	−17 32	6 36	17 52	6 51	17 36	7 10	17 17	7 36	16 52	8 17	15 59
31			23 08	10 19	23 08	10 14	23 27	10 07	23 41	9 59	—	9 46

2nd Month   **February, 1986**   **28 Days**

Greenwich Mean Time

NOTE: Light figures indicate Sun. **Dark** figures indicate **Moon**. *Degrees are North Latitude.*

CAUTION: Must be converted to local time. For instruction see page 726.

Day of month week year	Sun on meridian Moon phase	Sun's Declination	20° Rise Sun/Moon	20° Set Sun/Moon	30° Rise Sun/Moon	30° Set Sun/Moon	40° Rise Sun/Moon	40° Set Sun/Moon	50° Rise Sun/Moon	50° Set Sun/Moon	60° Rise Sun/Moon	60° Set Sun/Moon
	h m s	° ′	h m	h m	h m	h m	h m	h m	h m	h m	h m	h m
1 Sa	12 13 35	−17 15	6 36	17 52	6 50	17 37	7 09	17 18	7 34	16 54	8 14	16 14
32				10 58		10 47		10 33		10 15	0 04	9 46
2 Su	12 13 43	−16 58	6 35	17 52	6 50	17 38	7 08	17 20	7 32	16 55	8 12	16 16
33	04 41 ☾		0 07	11 40	0 22	11 23	0 40	11 02	1 05	10 34	1 46	9 48
3 Mo	12 13 50	−16 40	6 35	17 53	6 49	17 39	7 07	17 21	7 31	16 57	8 10	16 19
34			1 10	12 27	1 30	12 05	1 55	11 38	2 31	10 59	3 34	9 53
4 Tu	12 13 56	−16 23	6 34	17 54	6 48	17 40	7 06	17 22	7 29	16 59	8 08	16 22
35			2 15	13 20	2 39	12 54	3 11	12 22	3 56	11 34	5 25	10 04
5 We	12 14 01	−16 05	6 34	17 54	6 48	17 40	7 05	17 24	7 28	17 00	8 05	16 24
36			3 21	14 20	3 48	13 52	4 23	13 16	5 15	12 24	7 06	10 32
6 Th	12 14 06	−15 46	6 33	17 55	6 47	17 41	7 04	17 25	7 26	17 02	8 02	16 26
37			4 25	15 24	4 52	14 56	5 28	14 21	6 20	13 29	8 11	11 39
7 Fr	12 14 09	−15 28	6 33	17 55	6 47	17 42	7 03	17 26	7 25	17 04	8 00	16 29
38			5 24	16 29	5 49	16 04	6 22	15 33	7 09	14 48	8 39	13 20
8 Sa	12 14 12	−15 09	6 33	17 56	6 46	17 43	7 02	17 27	7 23	17 06	7 58	16 32
39			6 16	17 32	6 37	17 13	7 05	16 48	7 43	16 12	8 49	15 09
9 Su	12 14 14	−14 50	6 32	17 56	6 45	17 44	7 00	17 28	7 22	17 08	7 55	16 34
40	00 55 ●		7 01	18 33	7 18	18 18	7 39	18 00	8 07	17 35	8 53	16 53
10 Mo	12 14 16	−14 31	6 32	17 57	6 45	17 44	6 59	17 30	7 20	17 09	7 52	16 37
41			7 42	19 29	7 53	19 20	8 07	19 09	8 26	18 54	8 55	18 30
11 Tu	12 14 16	−14 11	6 32	17 57	6 44	17 45	6 58	17 31	7 18	17 11	7 50	16 40
42			8 18	20 23	8 24	20 19	8 31	20 15	8 41	20 09	8 55	20 01
12 We	12 14 16	−13 52	6 31	17 58	6 43	17 46	6 57	17 32	7 16	17 13	7 47	16 42
43			8 51	21 14	8 52	21 16	8 53	21 19	8 54	21 22	8 55	21 27
13 Th	12 14 15	−13 32	6 30	17 58	6 42	17 46	6 56	17 33	7 14	17 14	7 44	16 45
44			9 24	22 04	9 19	22 11	9 14	22 20	9 06	22 33	8 55	22 52
14 Fr	12 14 13	−13 12	6 30	17 59	6 41	17 47	6 54	17 34	7 13	17 16	7 42	16 48
45			9 57	22 54	9 47	23 07	9 35	23 22	9 19	23 43	8 55	
15 Sa	12 14 11	−12 51	6 29	17 59	6 40	17 48	6 53	17 35	7 11	17 18	7 39	16 50
46			10 31	23 45	10 16		9 58		9 34		8 56	0 18
16 Su	12 14 07	−12 31	6 28	17 59	6 39	17 49	6 52	17 36	7 09	17 20	7 36	16 53
47	19 55 ☽		11 07		10 48	0 02	10 25	0 24	9 52	0 54	8 58	1 45
17 Mo	12 14 03	−12 10	6 28	18 00	6 38	17 50	6 50	17 38	7 08	17 21	7 34	16 56
48			11 47	0 37	11 24	0 59	10 56	1 26	10 15	2 05	9 03	3 15
18 Tu	12 13 59	−11 49	6 27	18 00	6 38	17 51	6 49	17 39	7 06	17 23	7 31	16 58
49			12 32	1 31	12 06	1 56	11 33	2 27	10 46	3 14	9 13	4 44
19 We	12 13 53	−11 28	6 27	18 01	6 37	17 52	6 48	17 40	7 04	17 25	7 28	17 01
50			13 21	2 25	12 54	2 52	12 19	3 27	11 27	4 18	9 38	6 06
20 Th	12 13 47	−11 06	6 26	18 01	6 36	17 53	6 47	17 41	7 02	17 26	7 25	17 04
51			14 15	3 18	13 47	3 46	13 12	4 21	12 20	5 14	10 31	7 04
21 Fr	12 13 40	−10 45	6 25	18 02	6 35	17 54	6 46	17 42	7 00	17 28	7 22	17 06
52			15 12	4 10	14 46	4 36	14 14	5 10	13 27	5 58	11 53	7 33
22 Sa	12 13 33	−10 23	6 25	18 02	6 34	17 54	6 44	17 44	6 58	17 30	7 20	17 08
53			16 10	4 59	15 49	5 22	15 21	5 51	14 42	6 32	13 30	7 46
23 Su	12 13 25	−10 01	6 24	18 03	6 33	17 55	6 43	17 45	6 56	17 31	7 17	17 11
54			17 09	5 43	16 52	6 02	16 31	6 26	16 01	6 58	15 11	7 52
24 Mo	12 13 16	−09 39	6 24	18 03	6 32	17 56	6 42	17 46	6 54	17 33	7 14	17 14
55	15 02 ○		18 08	6 25	17 56	6 39	17 42	6 56	17 22	7 19	16 51	7 55
25 Tu	12 13 07	−09 17	6 23	18 03	6 31	17 56	6 40	17 47	6 52	17 34	7 11	17 16
56			19 05	7 04	19 00	7 12	18 53	7 22	18 44	7 35	18 29	7 56
26 We	12 12 57	−08 55	6 22	18 04	6 30	17 57	6 38	17 48	6 50	17 36	7 08	17 18
57			20 03	7 41	20 03	7 44	20 04	7 47	20 05	7 50	20 07	7 56
27 Th	12 12 47	−08 32	6 22	18 04	6 29	17 57	6 37	17 49	6 48	17 38	7 05	17 21
58			21 01	8 19	21 08	8 15	21 16	8 11	21 28	8 05	21 46	7 56
28 Fr	12 12 36	−08 10	6 21	18 04	6 28	17 58	6 38	17 50	6 46	17 40	7 02	17 24
59			22 01	8 57	22 14	8 48	22 30	8 36	22 52	8 21	23 29	7 57

3rd Month   March, 1986   31 Days

Greenwich Mean Time

NOTE: Light figures indicate Sun. **Dark** figures indicate **Moon.** *Degrees are North Latitude.*

CAUTION: Must be converted to local time. For instruction see page 726.

Day of month week year	Sun on meridian Moon phase h m s	Sun's Decli-nation °	20° Rise Sun/Moon h m	20° Set Sun/Moon h m	30° Rise Sun/Moon h m	30° Set Sun/Moon h m	40° Rise Sun/Moon h m	40° Set Sun/Moon h m	50° Rise Sun/Moon h m	50° Set Sun/Moon h m	60° Rise Sun/Moon h m	60° Set Sun/Moon h m
1 Sa	12 12 25	− 07 47	6 20	18 05	6 26	17 58	6 34	17 52	6 44	17 42	7 00	17 26
60			23 04	9 39	23 22	9 23	23 46	9 05		8 39		7 58
2 Su	12 12 13	− 07 24	6 20	18 05	6 25	17 59	6 32	17 53	6 42	17 43	6 57	17 29
61				10 24		10 04		9 38	0 19	9 02	1 16	8 01
3 Mo	12 12 00	− 07 01	6 19	18 06	6 24	18 00	6 31	17 54	6 40	17 45	6 54	17 32
62	12 17 ☾		0 08	11 15	0 32	10 51	1 02	10 19	1 45	9 33	3 08	8 08
4 Tu	12 11 47	− 06 38	6 18	18 06	6 23	18 01	6 30	17 55	6 38	17 46	6 51	17 34
63			1 14	12 12	1 40	11 45	2 15	11 09	3 06	10 17	4 54	8 28
5 We	12 11 34	− 06 15	6 17	18 06	6 22	18 02	6 28	17 56	6 36	17 48	6 48	17 37
64			2 17	13 14	2 45	12 46	3 21	12 10	4 15	11 17	6 12	9 20
6 Th	12 11 20	− 05 52	6 16	18 07	6 21	18 02	6 26	17 57	6 34	17 50	6 45	17 40
65			3 16	14 17	3 43	13 52	4 17	13 19	5 07	12 30	6 47	10 52
7 Fr	12 11 06	− 05 29	6 15	18 07	6 20	18 03	6 25	17 58	6 32	17 51	6 42	17 42
66			4 09	15 20	4 33	14 58	5 02	14 31	5 44	13 51	7 00	12 38
8 Sa	12 10 52	− 05 05	6 14	18 07	6 19	18 04	6 24	17 59	6 30	17 53	6 39	17 44
67			4 56	16 21	5 15	16 04	5 38	15 43	6 11	15 13	7 05	14 23
9 Su	12 10 37	− 04 42	6 14	18 08	6 18	18 04	6 22	18 00	6 28	17 54	6 36	17 47
68			5 37	17 18	5 51	17 06	6 08	16 52	6 31	16 33	7 07	16 01
10 Mo	12 10 22	− 04 18	6 13	18 08	6 16	18 05	6 20	18 01	6 25	17 56	6 33	17 50
69	14 52 ●		6 14	18 12	6 23	18 06	6 33	17 59	6 46	17 49	7 07	17 34
11 Tu	12 10 06	− 03 55	6 12	18 08	6 15	18 06	6 19	18 02	6 23	17 58	6 30	17 52
70			6 49	19 04	6 52	19 04	6 55	19 03	7 00	19 03	7 07	19 02
12 We	12 09 50	− 03 31	6 11	18 08	6 14	18 06	6 17	18 03	6 21	17 59	6 27	17 54
71			7 22	19 54	7 19	20 00	7 16	20 06	7 12	20 15	7 06	20 29
13 Th	12 09 34	− 03 08	6 10	18 09	6 12	18 07	6 16	18 04	6 19	18 01	6 24	17 56
72			7 54	20 45	7 47	20 55	7 37	21 08	7 25	21 26	7 06	21 55
14 Fr	12 09 18	− 02 44	6 10	18 09	6 11	18 08	6 14	18 05	6 17	18 02	6 21	17 59
73			8 28	21 36	8 15	21 51	8 00	22 11	7 39	22 38	7 06	23 22
15 Sa	12 09 01	− 02 20	6 09	18 10	6 10	18 08	6 12	18 06	6 15	18 04	6 18	18 01
74			9 03	22 28	8 46	22 48	8 25	23 13	7 55	23 49	7 07	
16 Su	12 08 44	− 01 57	6 08	18 10	6 09	18 09	6 10	18 07	6 13	18 06	6 15	18 04
75			9 42	23 21	9 20	23 45	8 53		8 16		7 10	0 52
17 Mo	12 08 27	− 01 33	6 07	18 10	6 08	18 10	6 09	18 08	6 10	18 08	6 12	18 06
76			10 25		10 00		9 28	0 15	8 42	0 59	7 17	2 23
18 Tu	12 08 10	− 01 09	6 06	18 11	6 07	18 10	6 08	18 10	6 08	18 09	6 09	18 08
77	16 39 ☽		11 12	0 15	10 44	0 41	10 10	1 15	9 18	2 06	7 33	3 50
19 We	12 07 52	− 00 46	6 05	18 11	6 06	18 11	6 06	18 11	6 06	18 11	6 06	18 11
78			12 03	1 08	11 35	1 36	10 59	2 12	10 06	3 05	8 12	4 59
20 Th	12 07 34	− 00 22	6 04	18 11	6 05	18 12	6 04	18 12	6 04	18 12	6 03	18 14
79			12 58	2 00	12 31	2 27	11 57	3 02	11 06	3 53	9 22	5 39
21 Fr	12 07 17	+ 00 02	6 04	18 11	6 04	18 12	6 02	18 13	6 02	18 14	6 00	18 16
80			13 55	2 49	13 31	3 14	13 01	3 46	12 17	4 31	10 55	5 56
22 Sa	12 06 59	+ 00 26	6 03	18 12	6 02	18 13	6 01	18 14	5 59	18 16	5 57	18 18
81			14 53	3 35	14 34	3 56	14 09	4 23	13 35	5 00	12 34	6 03
23 Su	12 06 40	+ 00 49	6 02	18 12	6 01	18 13	5 59	18 15	5 57	18 17	5 54	18 21
82			15 52	4 18	15 38	4 34	15 20	4 54	14 55	5 22	14 15	6 07
24 Mo	12 06 22	+ 01 13	6 01	18 12	6 00	18 14	5 58	18 16	5 55	18 18	5 51	18 24
83			16 50	4 58	16 42	5 09	16 31	5 22	16 17	5 40	15 55	6 08
25 Tu	12 06 04	+ 01 37	6 00	18 13	5 58	18 14	5 56	18 17	5 52	18 20	5 48	18 26
84			17 48	5 36	17 46	5 41	17 43	5 47	17 40	5 56	17 34	6 08
26 We	12 05 46	+ 02 00	5 59	18 13	5 57	18 15	5 54	18 18	5 50	18 22	5 45	18 28
85	03 02 ○		18 48	6 14	18 52	6 13	18 57	6 12	19 04	6 10	19 15	6 08
27 Th	12 05 27	+ 02 24	5 58	18 13	5 56	18 15	5 53	18 19	5 48	18 23	5 42	18 31
86			19 49	6 52	19 59	6 45	20 12	6 37	20 30	6 25	20 59	6 08
28 Fr	12 05 09	+ 02 47	5 57	18 13	5 55	18 16	5 51	18 20	5 46	18 25	5 39	18 34
87			20 52	7 34	21 09	7 21	21 30	7 05	21 59	6 43	22 49	6 08
29 Sa	12 04 51	+ 03 11	5 56	18 14	5 54	18 16	5 50	18 21	5 44	18 26	5 36	18 36
88			21 58	8 19	22 21	8 00	22 49	7 37	23 30	7 04		6 10
30 Su	12 04 33	+ 03 34	5 56	18 14	5 52	18 17	5 48	18 22	5 42	18 28	5 32	18 38
89			23 06	9 10	23 32	8 46		8 16		7 33	0 44	6 15
31 Mo	12 04 15	+ 03 57	5 55	18 14	5 51	18 18	5 46	18 23	5 40	18 30	5 29	18 41
90				10 06		9 39	0 06	9 04	0 55	8 13	2 38	6 29

4th Month   April, 1986   30 Days

Greenwich Mean Time

NOTE: Light figures indicate Sun. **Dark** figures indicate **Moon.** *Degrees are North Latitude.*

CAUTION: Must be converted to local time. For instruction see page 726.

Day of month / week / year	Sun on meridian / Moon phase h m s	Sun's Declination ° '	Rise Sun/Moon 20° h m	Set Sun/Moon 20° h m	Rise Sun/Moon 30° h m	Set Sun/Moon 30° h m	Rise Sun/Moon 40° h m	Set Sun/Moon 40° h m	Rise Sun/Moon 50° h m	Set Sun/Moon 50° h m	Rise Sun/Moon 60° h m	Set Sun/Moon 60° h m
1 Tu	12 03 57	+04 20	5 54	18 14	5 50	18 18	5 44	18 24	5 38	18 32	5 26	18 43
91	19 30 ☾		0 11	11 08	0 39	10 39	1 16	10 03	2 10	9 09	4 10	7 09
2 We	12 03 39	+04 44	5 53	18 14	5 48	18 19	5 43	18 25	5 36	18 33	5 23	18 45
92			1 12	12 11	1 40	11 44	2 15	11 10	3 07	10 19	4 56	8 32
3 Th	12 03 21	+05 07	5 52	18 14	5 47	18 19	5 42	18 26	5 33	18 34	5 20	18 48
93			2 07	13 14	2 32	12 50	3 03	12 21	3 48	11 38	5 12	10 17
4 Fr	12 03 04	+05 30	5 51	18 15	5 46	18 20	5 40	18 27	5 31	18 36	5 17	18 50
94			2 55	14 14	3 15	13 56	3 41	13 32	4 17	12 59	5 17	12 02
5 Sa	12 02 46	+05 53	5 50	18 15	5 46	18 21	5 38	18 28	5 29	18 38	5 14	18 52
95			3 37	15 11	3 52	14 58	4 12	14 41	4 38	14 18	5 19	13 41
6 Su	12 02 29	+06 15	5 50	18 16	5 44	18 21	5 37	18 29	5 27	18 39	5 11	18 55
96			4 14	16 05	4 25	15 57	4 37	15 48	4 54	15 35	5 20	15 14
7 Mo	12 02 12	+06 38	5 49	18 16	5 43	18 22	5 35	18 30	5 25	18 40	5 08	18 58
97			4 49	16 57	4 54	16 55	5 00	16 52	5 07	16 48	5 19	16 42
8 Tu	12 01 55	+07 01	5 48	18 16	5 42	18 23	5 34	18 31	5 23	18 42	5 05	19 00
98			5 22	17 47	5 21	17 51	5 21	17 55	5 20	18 00	5 19	18 08
9 We	12 01 39	+07 23	5 47	18 16	5 41	18 24	5 32	18 32	5 21	18 44	5 02	19 02
99	06 08 ●		5 54	18 38	5 48	18 46	5 41	18 57	5 32	19 11	5 18	19 34
10 Th	12 01 23	+07 45	5 46	18 17	5 39	18 24	5 30	18 33	5 18	18 45	4 59	19 05
100			6 27	19 28	6 16	19 42	6 03	19 59	5 45	20 22	5 18	21 00
11 Fr	12 01 07	+08 08	5 46	18 17	5 38	18 25	5 29	18 34	5 16	18 47	4 56	19 08
101			7 01	20 20	6 46	20 38	6 27	21 01	6 00	21 34	5 18	22 30
12 Sa	12 00 51	+08 30	5 45	18 17	5 37	18 25	5 27	18 35	5 14	18 49	4 53	19 10
102			7 39	21 13	7 19	21 35	6 54	22 04	6 19	22 45	5 20	
13 Su	12 00 36	+08 52	5 44	18 17	5 36	18 26	5 26	18 36	5 12	18 50	4 50	19 12
103			8 20	22 06	7 56	22 32	7 26	23 05	6 43	23 54	5 25	0 01
14 Mo	12 00 21	+09 13	5 44	18 17	5 35	18 26	5 24	18 37	5 10	18 52	4 48	19 15
104			9 05	23 00	8 38	23 28	8 04		7 15		5 36	1 31
15 Tu	12 00 06	+09 35	5 43	18 18	5 34	18 27	5 22	18 38	5 08	18 54	4 45	19 18
105			9 54	23 52	9 26		8 51	0 03	7 57	0 56	6 03	2 50
16 We	11 59 51	+09 56	5 42	18 18	5 33	18 28	5 21	18 39	5 06	18 55	4 42	19 20
106			10 47		10 20	0 20	9 44	0 55	8 52	1 48	7 00	3 41
17 Th	11 59 37	+10 18	5 41	18 18	5 32	18 28	5 20	18 40	5 04	18 56	4 39	19 22
107	10 35 ☽		11 43	0 42	11 17	1 08	10 45	1 41	9 58	2 30	8 25	4 04
18 Fr	11 59 24	+10 39	5 40	18 19	5 30	18 29	5 18	18 41	5 02	18 58	4 36	19 25
108			12 39	1 28	12 18	1 51	11 50	2 20	11 11	3 01	10 01	4 14
19 Sa	11 59 10	+11 00	5 40	18 19	5 29	18 29	5 16	18 42	5 00	18 59	4 33	19 28
109			13 36	2 11	13 19	2 29	12 58	2 53	12 29	3 25	11 39	4 18
20 Su	11 58 57	+11 21	5 39	18 20	5 28	18 30	5 15	18 43	4 58	19 01	4 30	19 30
110			14 33	2 51	14 22	3 04	14 08	3 21	13 48	3 44	13 17	4 20
21 Mo	11 58 45	+11 41	5 38	18 20	5 27	18 31	5 14	18 44	4 56	19 02	4 27	19 32
111			15 31	3 29	15 25	3 37	15 18	3 47	15 09	4 00	14 55	4 20
22 Tu	11 58 33	+12 01	5 38	18 20	5 26	18 32	5 12	18 45	4 54	19 04	4 24	19 35
112			16 29	4 06	16 30	4 08	16 31	4 11	16 32	4 15	16 35	4 20
23 We	11 58 21	+12 22	5 37	18 21	5 25	18 32	5 11	18 46	4 52	19 06	4 21	19 37
113			17 29	4 44	17 37	4 40	17 46	4 36	17 58	4 29	18 18	4 20
24 Th	11 58 10	+12 42	5 36	18 21	5 24	18 33	5 10	18 47	4 50	19 07	4 18	19 40
114	12 46 ○		18 33	5 25	18 47	5 14	19 04	5 02	19 28	4 46	20 07	4 18
25 Fr	11 57 59	+13 01	5 35	18 21	5 23	18 33	5 08	18 48	4 48	19 09	4 15	19 42
115			19 40	6 09	20 00	5 53	20 25	5 33	21 00	5 05	22 03	4 21
26 Sa	11 57 49	+13 21	5 34	18 21	5 22	18 34	5 07	18 49	4 46	19 10	4 12	19 45
116			20 49	6 59	21 14	6 37	21 46	6 09	22 32	5 31		4 24
27 Su	11 57 39	+13 40	5 34	18 22	5 21	18 34	5 06	18 50	4 45	19 12	4 10	19 48
117			21 58	7 55	22 26	7 29	23 02	6 55	23 56	6 07	0 04	4 33
28 Mo	11 57 30	+13 59	5 33	18 22	5 20	18 35	5 04	18 51	4 43	19 14	4 07	19 50
118			23 04	8 56	23 32	8 28		7 52		6 58	1 52	5 00
29 Tu	11 57 21	+14 18	5 32	18 22	5 19	18 36	5 03	18 52	4 41	19 16	4 04	19 52
119				10 02		9 24	0 08	8 58	1 02	8 05	2 58	6 10
30 We	11 57 13	+14 37	5 32	18 23	5 18	18 37	5 02	18 53	4 39	19 17	4 02	19 54
120			0 03	11 06	0 28	10 42	1 01	10 10	1 49	9 24	3 21	7 54

5th Month   May, 1986   31 days

Greenwich Mean Time

NOTE: Light figures indicate Sun. **Dark** figures indicate **Moon.** *Degrees are North Latitude.*

CAUTION: Must be converted to local time. For instruction see page 726.

Day of month / week / year	Sun on meridian / Moon phase (h m s)	Sun's Decli-nation (° ')	20° Rise Sun/Moon (h m)	20° Set Sun/Moon (h m)	30° Rise (h m)	30° Set (h m)	40° Rise (h m)	40° Set (h m)	50° Rise (h m)	50° Set (h m)	60° Rise (h m)	60° Set (h m)
1 Th	11 57 05	+14 55	5 31	18 24	5 18	18 37	5 00	18 54	4 37	19 18	3 59	19 57
121	03 22 ☾		0 54	12 09	1 15	11 48	1 43	11 23	2 22	10 47	3 29	9 42
2 Fr	11 56 58	+15 13	5 31	18 24	5 17	18 38	4 59	18 55	4 35	19 20	3 56	19 59
122			1 38	13 07	1 55	12 52	2 16	12 33	2 45	12 07	3 32	11 24
3 Sa	11 56 52	+15 31	5 30	18 24	5 16	18 38	4 58	18 56	4 33	19 21	3 53	20 02
123			2 16	14 02	2 28	13 52	2 42	13 41	3 02	13 24	3 33	12 59
4 Su	11 56 46	+15 49	5 29	18 24	5 15	18 39	4 57	18 57	4 32	19 23	3 51	20 04
124			2 51	14 54	2 58	14 50	3 05	14 45	3 16	14 38	3 32	14 27
5 Mo	11 56 41	+16 06	5 29	18 25	5 14	18 39	4 56	18 58	4 30	19 24	3 48	20 06
125			3 24	15 44	3 25	15 54	3 27	15 47	3 29	15 49	3 32	15 53
6 Tu	11 56 36	+16 24	5 28	18 25	5 13	18 40	4 55	18 59	4 28	19 26	3 46	20 09
126			3 56	16 33	3 52	16 40	3 47	16 48	3 41	17 00	3 31	17 17
7 We	11 56 32	+16 40	5 28	18 26	5 12	18 41	4 54	19 00	4 26	19 27	3 43	20 12
127			4 28	17 23	4 19	17 35	4 08	17 50	3 53	18 10	3 30	18 43
8 Th	11 56 28	+16 57	5 27	18 26	5 12	18 41	4 52	19 01	4 25	19 29	3 40	20 14
128	22 10 ●		5 02	18 14	4 48	18 31	4 31	18 52	4 07	19 21	3 30	20 11
9 Fr	11 56 25	+17 13	5 26	18 27	5 11	18 42	4 51	19 02	4 24	19 30	3 38	20 16
129			5 38	19 07	5 19	19 28	4 56	19 55	4 07	20 33	3 32	21 41
10 Sa	11 56 22	+17 29	5 26	18 27	5 10	18 43	4 50	19 03	4 22	19 32	3 35	20 19
130			6 17	20 00	5 55	20 25	5 27	20 56	4 24	21 43	3 35	23 12
11 Su	11 56 20	+17 45	5 25	18 17	5 09	18 44	4 49	19 04	4 20	19 33	3 32	20 22
131			7 01	20 54	6 35	21 21	6 03	21 56	4 46	22 47	3 44	
12 Mo	11 56 19	+18 00	5 25	18 28	5 08	18 44	4 48	19 05	4 19	19 34	3 30	20 24
132			7 49	21 46	7 21	22 14	6 46	22 50	5 15	23 43	4 04	0 36
13 Tu	11 56 18	+18 15	5 24	18 28	5 08	18 45	4 47	19 06	4 18	19 36	3 28	20 26
133			8 41	22 37	8 13	23 03	7 37	23 38	5 54		4 50	1 38
14 We	11 56 18	+18 30	5 24	18 28	5 07	18 46	4 46	19 07	4 16	19 37	3 25	20 29
134			9 35	23 23	9 09	23 48	8 35		6 44	0 28	6 05	2 10
15 Th	11 56 18	+18 45	5 24	18 29	5 06	18 46	4 45	19 08	4 15	19 38	3 23	20 31
135			10 30		10 07		9 38	0 18	7 46	1 02	7 37	2 23
16 Fr	11 56 19	+18 59	5 23	18 29	5 06	18 47	4 44	19 09	4 14	19 40	3 20	20 34
136			11 26	0 07	11 07	0 27	10 43	0 53	8 56	1 28	9 13	2 29
17 Sa	11 56 20	+19 13	5 23	18 29	5 05	18 48	4 43	19 10	4 12	19 42	3 18	20 36
137	01 00 ☽		12 21	0 47	12 07	1 02	11 50	1 22	10 10	1 48	10 48	2 31
18 Su	11 56 22	+19 26	5 23	18 30	5 05	18 48	4 42	19 11	4 11	19 43	3 16	20 38
138			13 16	1 24	13 08	1 35	12 58	1 48	11 27	2 05	12 23	2 32
19 Mo	11 56 25	+19 40	5 23	18 30	5 04	18 49	4 41	19 12	4 10	19 44	3 14	20 40
139			14 12	2 00	14 10	2 05	14 07	2 11	12 44	2 20	13 58	2 32
20 Tu	11 56 28	+19 52	5 22	18 31	5 04	18 49	4 40	19 12	4 08	19 46	3 12	20 42
140			15 10	2 37	15 14	2 36	15 19	2 35	14 04	2 34	15 37	2 31
21 We	11 56 31	+20 05	5 22	18 31	5 03	18 50	4 40	19 13	4 07	19 47	3 10	20 45
141			16 11	3 15	16 21	3 08	16 34	3 00	15 26	2 48	17 21	2 31
22 Th	11 56 35	+20 17	5 22	18 32	5 03	18 51	4 39	19 14	4 06	19 48	3 08	20 47
142			17 16	3 57	17 33	3 44	17 53	3 28	16 52	3 06	19 13	2 32
23 Fr	11 56 40	+20 29	5 22	18 32	5 02	18 51	4 38	19 15	4 05	19 49	3 06	20 49
143	20 45 ○		18 25	4 43	18 47	4 24	19 16	4 01	18 23	3 28	21 13	2 34
24 Sa	11 56 45	+20 40	5 22	18 32	5 02	18 52	4 38	19 16	4 04	19 50	3 04	20 52
144			19 36	5 37	20 03	5 13	20 37	4 42	19 57	3 59	23 13	2 40
25 Su	11 56 51	+20 51	5 21	18 33	5 01	18 52	4 38	19 17	4 02	19 52	3 02	20 54
145			20 46	6 38	21 14	6 10	21 51	5 35	21 28	4 43		2 56
26 Mo	11 56 57	+21 02	5 21	18 33	5 01	18 53	4 37	19 18	4 01	19 53	3 00	20 56
146			21 50	7 44	22 17	7 16	22 52	6 40	22 45	5 45	0 45	3 46
27 Tu	11 57 03	+21 13	5 21	18 33	5 01	18 54	4 36	19 19	4 00	19 64	2 58	20 58
147			22 46	8 52	23 10	8 26	23 40	7 52	23 42	7 03	1 25	5 22
28 We	11 57 10	+21 23	5 20	18 34	5 00	18 54	4 36	19 19	3 59	19 55	2 56	20 59
148			23 34	9 58	23 53	9 36		9 08		8 28	1 38	7 15
29 Th	11 57 18	+21 32	5 20	18 34	5 00	18 54	4 35	19 20	3 59	19 57	2 55	21 01
149				10 59		10 43	0 17	10 22	0 22	9 52	1 43	9 02
30 Fr	11 57 26	+21 42	5 20	18 35	5 00	18 55	4 34	19 21	3 58	19 58	2 53	21 03
150	12 55 ☾		0 16	11 56	0 29	11 45	0 46	11 31	0 49	11 12	1 44	10 41
31 Sa	11 57 34	+21 51	5 20	18 35	5 00	18 55	4 34	19 22	3 57	19 59	2 52	21 05
151			0 52	12 50	1 01	12 44	1 10	12 37	1 08	12 28	1 44	12 13

6th Month   June, 1986   30 days

Greenwich Mean Time

NOTE: Light figures indicate Sun. **Dark** figures indicate **Moon.** *Degrees are North Latitude.*

CAUTION: Must be converted to local time. For instruction see page 726.

Day of month week year	Sun on meridian / Moon phase h m s	Sun's Decli-nation	20° Rise Sun/Moon h m	20° Set Sun/Moon h m	30° Rise Sun/Moon h m	30° Set Sun/Moon h m	40° Rise Sun/Moon h m	40° Set Sun/Moon h m	50° Rise Sun/Moon h m	50° Set Sun/Moon h m	60° Rise Sun/Moon h m	60° Set Sun/Moon h m
1 Su 152	11 57 43	+21 59	5 20	18 36	5 00	18 56	4 34	19 22	3 56	20 00	2 50	21 06
			2 26	13 41	1 29	13 41	1 32	13 40	1 37	13 40	1 44	13 40
2 Mo 153	11 57 53	+22 07	5 20	18 36	4 59	18 57	4 33	19 23	3 56	20 01	2 48	21 08
			1 58	14 31	1 56	14 36	1 53	14 42	1 49	14 51	1 43	15 04
3 Tu 154	11 58 02	+22 15	5 20	18 36	4 59	18 57	4 33	19 24	3 55	20 02	2 47	21 10
			2 30	15 20	2 23	15 30	2 13	15 43	2 01	16 01	1 43	16 29
4 We 155	11 58 13	+22 22	5 20	18 37	4 59	18 58	4 32	19 24	3 54	20 03	2 46	21 11
			3 03	16 11	2 51	16 26	2 35	16 45	2 15	17 11	4 45	17 55
5 Th 156	11 58 23	+22 29	5 20	18 37	4 58	18 58	4 32	19 25	3 54	20 04	2 44	21 13
			3 38	17 02	3 21	17 22	3 00	17 47	2 31	18 22	4 43	19 24
6 Fr 157	11 58 34	+22 36	5 20	18 38	4 58	18 59	4 31	19 25	3 53	20 05	2 43	21 14
			4 17	17 55	3 55	18 19	3 29	18 49	2 51	19 33	1 46	20 55
7 Sa 158	14 00 ●	+22 42	5 20	18 38	4 58	18 59	4 31	19 26	3 52	20 06	2 42	21 16
	11 58 45		4 59	18 49	4 34	19 15	4 03	19 49	3 18	20 39	1 53	22 22
8 Su 159	11 58 56	+22 48	5 20	18 39	4 58	19 00	4 31	19 27	3 52	20 06	2 41	21 17
			5 46	19 42	5 19	20 10	4 44	20 45	3 53	21 38	2 09	23 32
9 Mo 160	11 59 08	+22 53	5 20	18 39	4 58	19 00	4 31	19 28	3 52	20 07	2 40	21 18
			6 36	20 33	6 09	21 00	5 33	21 35	4 40	22 27	2 46	
10 Tu 161	11 59 20	+22 58	5 20	18 39	4 58	19 01	4 31	19 28	3 51	20 07	2 39	21 20
			7 30	21 21	7 03	21 46	6 29	22 18	5 38	23 04	3 53	0 13
11 We 162	11 59 32	+23 03	5 20	18 39	4 58	19 01	4 31	19 29	3 51	20 08	2 28	21 21
			8 25	22 05	8 01	22 27	7 30	22 54	6 46	23 32	5 21	0 30
12 Th 163	11 59 44	+23 07	5 20	18 40	4 58	19 01	4 31	19 29	3 51	20 09	2 38	21 22
			9 20	22 45	9 00	23 03	8 34	23 24	7 58	23 54	6 55	0 38
13 Fr 164	11 59 57	+23 11	5 20	18 40	4 58	19 02	4 30	19 30	3 50	20 09	2 37	21 23
			10 14	23 23	9 59	23 35	9 40	23 50	9 13		8 29	0 41
14 Sa 165	12 00 09	+23 14	5 20	18 40	4 58	19 02	4 30	19 30	3 50	20 10	2 37	21 24
			12 02	23 59	10 58		10 46		10 29	0 11	10 02	0 43
15 Su 166	12 00 22	+23 17	5 20	18 40	4 58	19 02	4 30	19 30	3 50	20 11	2 36	21 25
	12 00 ☽		12 57		11 58	0 06	11 53	0 14	11 45	0 25	11 34	0 43
16 Mo 167	12 00 35	+23 20	5 20	18 41	4 58	19 03	4 30	19 30	3 50	20 11	2 36	21 25
			13 55	0 34	12 59	0 35	13 01	0 37	13 03	0 39	13 07	0 43
17 Tu 168	12 00 48	+23 22	5 22	18 41	4 58	19 03	4 30	19 31	3 50	20 12	2 35	21 26
			14 56	1 10	14 02	1 05	14 12	1 00	14 24	0 53	14 45	0 42
18 We 169	12 01 01	+23 24	5 21	18 42	4 59	19 04	4 31	19 31	3 50	20 12	2 35	21 26
			16 01	1 48	15 09	1 38	15 26	1 25	15 50	1 08	16 29	0 42
19 Th 170	12 01 14	+23 25	5 21	18 42	4 59	19 04	4 31	19 32	3 50	20 12	2 35	21 27
			17 10	2 31	16 21	2 15	16 45	1 55	17 21	1 27	18 23	0 44
20 Fr 171	12 01 27	+23 26	5 21	18 42	4 59	19 04	4 31	19 32	3 50	20 12	2 35	21 27
			18 21	3 20	17 35	2 58	18 07	2 31	18 53	1 53	20 23	0 47
21 Sa 172	12 01 40	+23 26	5 21	18 42	4 59	19 04	4 31	19 32	3 50	20 12	2 36	21 27
			19 30	4 17	18 49	3 51	19 25	3 18	20 18	2 30	22 14	0 57
22 Su 173	12 01 53	+23 27	5 22	18 42	5 00	19 04	4 32	19 33	3 51	20 13	2 36	21 28
	03 42 ○		20 31	5 21	19 58	4 53	20 33	4 17	21 27	3 23	23 20	1 26
23 Mo 174	12 02 05	+23 26	5 22	18 42	5 00	19 04	4 32	19 33	3 51	20 13	2 36	21 28
			21 25	6 30	20 57	6 02	21 29	5 27	22 15	4 35	23 43	2 42
24 Tu 175	12 02 18	+23 25	5 22	18 42	5 00	19 04	4 32	19 33	3 51	20 13	2 36	21 28
			22 10	7 39	21 46	7 15	22 12	6 44	22 49	5 59	23 51	4 34
25 We 176	12 02 31	+23 24	5 22	18 42	5 00	19 05	4 32	19 33	3 51	20 13	2 37	21 28
			22 50	8 44	22 26	8 25	22 45	8 02	23 12	7 28	23 54	6 28
26 Th 177	12 02 44	+23 23	5 23	18 43	5 01	19 05	4 33	19 33	3 52	20 13	2 37	21 27
			23 26	9 45	23 00	9 32	23 12	9 16	23 29	8 52	23 55	8 15
27 Fr 178	12 02 56	+23 21	5 23	18 43	5 01	19 05	4 33	19 33	3 52	20 13	2 38	21 27
			23 59	10 42	23 30	10 34	23 36	10 25	23 43	10 12	23 55	9 52
28 Sa 179	12 03 08	+23 18	5 23	18 43	5 01	19 05	4 33	19 33	3 53	20 13	2 39	21 26
				11 35	23 58	11 33	23 55	11 31	23 56	11 27	23 54	11 22
29 Su 180	12 03 21	+23 16	5 25	18 43	5 01	19 05	4 34	19 33	3 54	20 13	2 40	21 26
	00 53 ☾		0 31	12 26		12 29		12 34		12 40	23 54	12 49
30 Mo 181	12 03 30	+23 12	5 24	18 43	5 02	19 05	4 34	19 33	3 54	20 13	2 41	21 25
			1 04	13 16	0 25	13 25	0 18	13 36	0 08	13 50	23 53	14 14

7th Month   July, 1986   31 Days

Greenwich Mean Time

NOTE: Light figures indicate Sun. **Dark** figures indicate **Moon**. *Degrees are North Latitude.*

CAUTION: Must be converted to local time. For instruction see page 726.

Day of month week year	Sun on meridian Moon phase h m s	Sun's Decli-nation °	20° Rise Sun Moon h m	20° Set Sun Moon h m	30° Rise Sun Moon h m	30° Set Sun Moon h m	40° Rise Sun Moon h m	40° Set Sun Moon h m	50° Rise Sun Moon h m	50° Set Sun Moon h m	60° Rise Sun Moon h m	60° Set Sun Moon h m
1 Tu 182	12 03 44	+23 09	5 24	18 43	5 02	19 05	4 35	19 33	3 55	20 13	2 42	21 25
			1 04	14 06	0 53	14 20	0 40	14 37	0 22	15 01	23 54	15 40
2 We 183	12 03 56	+23 05	5 24	18 43	5 02	19 05	4 35	19 33	3 55	20 12	2 43	21 24
			1 39	14 58	1 23	15 16	1 03	15 39	0 37	16 12	23 56	17 09
3 Th 184	12 04 07	+23 00	5 24	18 43	5 03	19 05	4 36	19 32	3 56	20 12	2 44	21 24
			2 16	15 50	1 56	16 13	1 31	16 42	0 56	17 23		18 39
4 Fr 185	12 04 18	+22 55	5 25	18 44	5 03	19 05	4 36	19 32	3 56	20 11	2 45	21 23
			2 57	16 44	2 33	17 10	2 03	17 43	1 20	18 31	0 02	20 08
5 Sa 186	12 04 29	+22 50	5 25	18 44	5 04	19 05	4 37	19 32	3 57	20 11	2 46	21 22
			3 42	17 37	3 16	18 05	2 42	18 40	1 53	19 33	0 14	21 25
6 Su 187	12 04 39	+22 45	5 25	18 44	5 04	19 05	4 37	19 32	3 58	20 10	2 47	21 21
			4 32	18 29	4 04	18 57	3 29	19 32	2 36	20 24	0 43	22 14
7 Mo 188	12 04 49 04 55 ●	+22 39	5 26	18 43	5 05	19 04	4 38	19 31	3 59	20 10	2 49	21 20
			5 25	19 19	4 58	19 44	4 23	20 17	3 31	21 05	1 42	22 37
8 Tu 189	12 04 59	+22 32	5 26	18 43	5 05	19 04	4 38	19 31	4 00	20 09	2 50	21 18
			6 20	20 04	5 55	20 27	5 23	20 55	4 37	21 36	3 06	22 47
9 We 190	12 05 08	+22 25	5 27	18 43	5 06	19 04	4 39	19 31	4 01	20 09	2 52	21 17
			7 16	20 46	6 54	21 04	6 27	21 27	5 49	21 59	4 40	22 52
10 Th 191	12 05 17	+22 18	5 27	18 43	5 06	19 04	4 40	19 30	4 02	20 08	2 54	21 16
			8 11	21 24	7 54	21 38	7 33	21 54	7 04	22 17	6 15	22 53
11 Fr 192	12 05 25	+22 11	5 27	18 43	5 07	19 03	4 40	19 30	4 03	20 08	2 55	21 14
			9 04	22 00	8 53	22 08	8 39	22 18	8 19	22 32	7 47	22 54
12 Sa 193	12 05 33	+22 03	5 28	18 43	5 07	19 03	4 41	19 29	4 04	20 07	2 57	21 12
			9 58	22 34	9 52	22 37	9 44	22 41	9 34	22 46	9 19	22 53
13 Su 194	12 05 41	+21 54	5 28	18 43	5 08	19 03	4 42	19 29	4 05	20 06	2 59	21 11
			10 51	23 09	10 51	23 06	10 51	23 03	10 50	22 59	10 50	22 53
14 Mo 195	12 05 47 20 10 ☾	+21 46	5 28	18 43	5 08	19 03	4 43	19 28	4 06	20 05	3 01	21 09
			11 46	23 45	11 52	23 37	11 59	23 27	12 08	23 13	12 23	22 53
15 Tu 196	12 05 54	+21 37	5 29	18 42	5 09	19 02	4 44	19 28	4 07	20 04	3 03	21 07
			12 44		12 55		13 10	23 54	13 30	23 30	14 02	22 53
16 We 197	12 06 00	+21 27	5 29	18 42	5 09	19 02	4 44	19 27	4 08	20 03	3 05	21 06
			13 45	0 25	14 03	0 11	14 24		14 55	23 52	15 48	22 55
17 Th 198	12 06 05	+21 17	5 30	18 42	5 10	19 02	4 45	19 27	4 09	20 02	3 07	21 04
			14 51	1 10	15 13	0 50	15 42	0 26	16 24		17 42	23 01
18 Fr 199	12 06 10	+21 07	5 30	18 42	5 10	19 02	4 46	19 26	4 10	20 01	3 09	21 02
			15 59	2 01	16 26	1 37	17 00	1 06	17 51	0 22	19 37	23 18
19 Sa 200	12 06 14	+20 57	5 30	18 41	5 11	19 01	4 46	19 26	4 11	20 00	3 11	21 00
			17 08	3 00	17 36	2 33	18 13	1 58	19 07	1 06	21 06	
20 Su 201	12 06 18	+20 46	5 31	18 41	5 11	19 01	4 47	19 25	4 12	19 59	3 13	20 58
			18 13	4 06	18 40	3 38	19 14	3 02	20 04	2 08	21 46	0 09
21 Mo 202	12 06 21 10 40 ○	+20 34	5 31	18 41	5 12	19 00	4 48	19 24	4 13	19 58	3 15	20 56
			19 10	5 15	19 33	4 49	20 03	4 16	20 44	3 27	21 59	1 48
22 Tu 203	12 06 24	+20 23	5 31	18 41	5 12	19 00	4 49	19 23	4 14	19 57	3 17	20 54
			20 00	6 24	20 18	6 02	20 41	5 35	21 12	4 55	22 03	3 44
23 We 204	12 06 26	+20 11	5 32	18 40	5 13	18 59	4 50	19 22	4 15	19 56	3 19	20 52
			20 43	7 28	20 56	7 12	21 11	6 52	21 32	6 24	22 05	5 37
24 Th 205	12 06 27	+19 59	5 32	18 40	5 13	18 59	4 51	19 22	4 16	19 55	3 22	20 50
			21 21	8 28	21 28	8 18	21 37	8 06	21 48	7 48	22 05	7 21
25 Fr 206	12 06 28	+19 46	5 33	18 40	5 14	18 58	4 52	19 21	4 17	19 53	3 24	20 48
			21 56	9 24	21 58	9 20	21 59	9 15	22 01	9 08	22 05	8 56
26 Sa 207	12 06 28	+19 33	5 33	18 40	5 15	18 58	4 53	19 20	4 18	19 52	3 26	20 46
			22 30	10 17	22 26	10 19	22 21	10 21	22 14	10 23	22 04	10 27
27 Su 208	12 06 28	+19 20	5 33	18 39	5 15	18 57	4 54	19 19	4 19	19 50	3 28	20 44
			23 03	11 09	22 54	11 16	22 42	11 24	22 27	11 36	22 04	11 54
28 Mo 209	12 06 27 15 34 ☽	+19 06	5 34	18 39	5 16	18 57	4 54	19 18	4 20	19 48	3 31	20 41
			23 37	12 00	23 23	12 12	23 06	12 27	22 42	12 48	22 04	13 22
29 Tu 210	12 06 25	+18 53	5 34	18 38	5 17	18 56	4 55	19 17	4 21	19 47	3 33	20 39
				12 51	23 55	13 08	23 32	13 30	22 59	14 00	22 05	14 51
30 We 211	12 06 23	+18 38	5 34	18 38	5 17	18 55	4 56	19 16	4 22	19 46	3 35	20 36
			0 14	13 44		14 05		14 32	23 21	15 11	22 09	16 21
31 Th 212	12 06 21	+18 24	5 35	18 37	5 18	18 55	4 57	19 15	4 23	19 44	3 38	20 34
			0 54	14 37	0 31	15 02	0 02	15 34	23 51	16 21	22 18	17 52

8th Month   August, 1986   31 Days

Greenwich Mean Time

NOTE: Light figures indicate Sun. **Dark** figures indicate **Moon.** *Degrees are North Latitude.*

CAUTION: Must be converted to local time. For instruction see page 726.

Day of month week year	Sun on meridian Moon phase h m s	Sun's Declination ° '	20° Rise Sun Moon h m	20° Set Sun Moon h m	30° Rise Sun Moon h m	30° Set Sun Moon h m	40° Rise Sun Moon h m	40° Set Sun Moon h m	50° Rise Sun Moon h m	50° Set Sun Moon h m	60° Rise Sun Moon h m	60° Set Sun Moon h m
1 Fr	12 06 18	+18 09	5 36	18 37	5 18	18 54	4 58	19 14	4 28	19 42	3 40	20 32
213			1 38	15 31	1 12	15 58	0 39	16 33		17 25	22 40	19 15
2 Sa	12 06 14	+17 54	5 36	18 37	5 19	18 53	4 59	19 13	4 30	19 41	3 42	20 29
214			2 26	16 24	1 59	16 52	1 23	17 27	0 31	18 21	23 28	20 15
3 Su	12 06 09	+17 39	5 36	18 36	5 19	18 52	5 00	19 12	4 32	19 40	3 44	20 26
215			3 18	17 14	2 51	17 41	2 15	18 15	1 22	19 05		20 45
4 Mo	12 06 04	+17 23	5 36	18 36	5 20	18 52	5 01	19 11	4 33	19 38	3 47	20 24
216			4 13	18 01	3 47	18 25	3 14	18 55	2 25	19 39	0 47	20 57
5 Tu	12 05 59	+17 07	5 37	18 36	5 21	18 51	5 02	19 10	4 34	19 36	3 50	20 22
217	18 36 ●		5 09	18 44	4 47	19 04	4 18	19 29	3 36	20 04	2 20	21 02
6 We	12 05 52	+16 51	5 37	18 35	5 22	18 50	5 03	19 09	4 36	19 35	3 52	20 19
218			6 05	19 24	5 47	19 39	5 24	19 58	4 52	20 24	3 57	21 04
7 Th	12 05 46	+16 34	5 37	18 34	5 22	18 49	5 04	19 08	4 38	19 33	3 54	20 16
219			7 00	20 01	6 47	20 11	6 31	20 23	6 08	20 39	5 31	21 05
8 Fr	12 05 38	+16 17	5 38	18 34	5 23	18 48	5 04	19 06	4 39	19 32	3 56	20 14
220			7 54	20 36	7 47	20 40	7 37	20 46	7 24	20 53	7 04	21 05
9 Sa	12 05 30	+16 00	5 38	18 33	5 24	18 47	5 05	19 05	4 40	19 30	3 59	20 11
221			8 48	21 10	8 46	21 09	8 44	21 08	8 41	21 07	8 36	21 04
10 Su	12 05 22	+15 43	5 38	18 32	5 24	18 46	5 06	19 04	4 42	19 28	4 02	20 08
222			9 42	21 46	9 46	21 39	9 51	21 31	9 58	21 20	10 09	21 04
11 Mo	12 05 12	+15 25	5 38	18 32	5 25	18 45	5 07	19 03	4 43	19 26	4 04	20 05
223			10 39	22 24	10 48	22 11	11 01	21 56	11 18	21 36	11 45	21 03
12 Tu	12 05 13	+15 08	5 38	18 31	5 25	18 44	5 08	19 02	4 44	19 24	4 06	20 02
224			11 38	23 06	11 53	22 48	12 13	22 26	12 41	21 55	13 27	21 04
13 We	12 04 52 02 21)	+14 50	5 39	18 30	5 26	18 43	5 09	19 00	4 46	19 23	4 08	20 00
225			12 40	23 54	13 01	23 31	13 28	23 02	14 07	22 21	15 16	21 08
14 Th	12 04 41	+14 31	5 39	18 30	5 26	18 42	5 10	18 59	4 47	19 21	4 11	19 57
226			13 46		14 11		14 44	23 47	15 33	22 58	17 10	21 18
15 Fr	12 04 30	+14 13	5 40	18 29	5 27	18 41	5 11	18 58	4 48	19 19	4 13	19 54
227			14 53	0 48	15 21	0 22	15 57		16 51	23 50	18 51	21 50
16 Sa	12 04 18	+13 54	5 40	18 28	5 28	18 40	5 12	18 56	4 50	19 17	4 16	19 52
228			15 57	1 50	16 25	1 21	17 01	0 45	17 54		19 48	23 09
17 Su	12 04 05	+13 35	5 40	18 28	5 28	18 39	5 13	18 54	4 52	19 15	4 18	19 49
229			16 57	2 56	17 22	2 29	17 54	1 54	18 40	1 01	20 07	
18 Mo	12 03 52	+13 16	5 41	18 27	5 29	18 38	5 14	18 53	4 53	19 13	4 20	19 46
230			17 49	4 04	18 10	3 40	18 36	3 10	19 12	2 25	20 14	1 01
19 Tu	12 03 38 18 54 ○	+12 57	5 41	18 26	5 29	18 37	5 15	18 52	4 54	19 11	4 22	19 43
231			18 35	5 09	18 50	4 51	19 09	4 27	19 35	3 54	20 16	2 56
20 We	12 03 24	+12 37	5 42	18 25	5 30	18 36	5 16	18 50	4 56	19 09	4 25	19 40
232			19 15	6 11	19 25	5 59	19 36	5 42	19 52	5 20	20 16	4 44
21 Th	12 03 10	+12 17	5 42	18 25	5 30	18 35	5 17	18 48	4 58	19 07	4 28	19 37
233			19 52	7 10	19 55	7 03	20 00	6 54	20 06	6 42	20 16	6 24
22 Fr	12 02 55	+11 57	5 42	18 24	5 31	18 34	5 18	18 47	4 59	19 05	4 30	19 34
234			20 26	8 05	20 24	8 04	20 22	8 02	20 19	8 01	20 15	7 58
23 Sa	12 02 39	+11 37	5 42	18 23	5 31	18 33	5 19	18 46	5 00	19 03	4 32	19 31
235			21 00	8 58	20 53	9 03	20 44	9 08	20 32	9 16	20 14	9 28
24 Su	12 02 23	+11 17	5 42	18 22	5 32	18 32	5 20	18 44	5 02	19 01	4 35	19 28
236			21 34	9 50	21 22	10 00	21 07	10 13	20 46	10 30	20 14	10 58
25 Mo	12 02 07	+10 56	5 43	18 22	5 32	18 31	5 21	18 43	5 04	18 59	4 38	19 25
237			22 10	10 42	21 53	10 58	21 32	11 17	21 02	11 44	20 14	12 28
26 Tu	12 01 50	+10 36	5 43	18 21	5 33	18 30	5 22	18 41	5 05	18 57	4 40	19 22
238			22 49	11 35	22 28	11 55	22 01	12 20	21 23	12 56	20 17	14 00
27 We	12 01 33	+10 15	5 43	18 20	5 34	18 29	5 23	18 40	5 06	18 55	4 42	19 19
239	08 38 (		23 32	11 35	23 07	12 53	22 35	13 23	21 49	14 08	20 22	15 32
28 Th	12 01 16	+09 54	5 43	18 19	5 34	18 28	5 24	18 38	5 08	18 53	4 44	19 16
240				13 23	23 51	13 50	23 16	14 24	22 25	15 15	20 37	17 01
29 Fr	12 00 58	+09 33	5 44	18 18	5 35	18 26	5 24	18 36	5 10	18 51	4 47	19 14
241			0 19	14 16		14 44		15 20	23 11	16 14	21 13	18 12
30 Sa	12 00 40	+09 11	5 44	18 17	5 36	18 25	5 25	18 35	5 11	18 49	4 49	19 11
242			1 09	15 07	0 41	15 35	0 05	16 10		17 02	22 23	18 51
31 Su	12 00 22	+08 50	5 44	18 16	5 36	18 24	5 26	18 34	5 12	18 47	4 52	19 08
243			2 03	15 56	1 36	16 21	1 02	16 53	0 11	17 39	23 53	19 07

9th Month   September, 1986   30 Days

Greenwich Mean Time

NOTE: Light figures indicate Sun. **Dark** figures indicate **Moon**. *Degrees are North Latitude.*

CAUTION: Must be converted to local time. For instruction see page 726.

Day of month week year	Sun on meridian Moon phase h m s	Sun's Decli- nation ° '	20° Rise Sun Moon h m	20° Set Sun Moon h m	30° Rise Sun Moon h m	30° Set Sun Moon h m	40° Rise Sun Moon h m	40° Set Sun Moon h m	50° Rise Sun Moon h m	50° Set Sun Moon h m	60° Rise Sun Moon h m	60° Set Sun Moon h m
1 Mo 244	12 00 03	+08 28	5 44	18 16	5 37	18 23	5 27	18 32	5 14	18 45	4 54	19 05
			2 59	16 40	2 35	17 02	2 04	17 29	1 19	18 08		19 14
2 Tu 245	11 59 44	+08 06	5 45	18 15	5 38	18 22	5 28	18 30	5 16	18 43	4 56	19 02
			3 55	17 21	3 35	17 38	3 10	18 00	2 34	18 29	1 31	19 16
3 We 246	11 59 25	+07 45	5 45	18 14	5 38	18 21	5 29	18 29	5 17	18 41	4 59	18 59
			4 51	17 59	4 36	18 11	4 17	18 26	3 51	18 46	3 08	19 17
4 Th 247	11 59 05 07 10 ●	+07 23	5 45	18 13	5 39	18 20	5 30	18 28	5 18	18 39	5 01	18 56
			5 47	18 36	5 37	18 42	5 25	18 50	5 09	19 01	4 43	19 17
5 Fr 248	11 58 45	+07 00	5 46	18 12	5 39	18 18	5 31	18 26	5 20	18 36	5 04	18 53
			6 41	19 11	6 38	19 12	6 35	19 13	6 29	19 14	6 16	19 16
6 Sa 249	11 58 25	+06 38	5 46	18 11	5 40	18 17	5 32	18 24	5 22	18 34	5 06	18 50
			7 37	19 46	7 39	19 41	7 41	19 35	7 45	19 27	7 51	19 15
7 Su 250	11 58 05	+06 16	5 46	18 10	5 40	18 16	5 33	18 23	5 23	18 32	5 08	18 47
			8 33	20 24	8 41	20 13	8 51	20 00	9 05	19 42	9 27	19 15
8 Mo 251	11 57 45	+05 53	5 46	18 09	5 41	18 15	5 34	18 21	5 24	18 30	5 10	18 44
			9 32	21 05	9 46	20 48	10 04	20 28	10 29	20 00	11 09	19 15
9 Tu 252	11 57 24	+05 31	5 46	18 08	5 41	18 14	5 35	18 20	5 26	18 28	5 12	18 40
			10 34	21 51	10 54	21 29	11 19	22 02	11 55	20 23	12 58	19 17
10 We 253	11 57 03	+05 08	5 46	18 08	5 42	18 12	5 36	18 18	5 28	18 25	5 15	18 37
			11 39	20 43	12 03	22 17	12 35	21 44	13 21	21 07	14 51	19 24
11 Th 254	11 56 42 07 41 ☽	+04 45	5 46	18 07	5 42	18 11	5 37	18 16	5 29	18 23	5 17	18 34
			12 44	23 41	13 12	23 13	13 48	22 37	14 42	21 56	16 39	19 44
12 Fr 255	11 56 21	+04 23	5 46	18 06	5 42	18 10	5 38	18 14	5 30	18 21	5 20	18 31
			13 49		14 17		14 54	23 40	15 49	22 59	17 50	20 45
13 Sa 256	11 56 00	+04 00	5 47	18 05	5 43	18 08	5 38	18 12	5 32	18 18	5 22	18 28
			14 48	0 45	15 15	0 17	15 49		16 39		18 17	22 28
14 Su 257	11 55 39	+03 37	5 47	18 04	5 43	18 07	5 39	18 11	5 34	18 16	5 24	18 25
			15 42	1 51	16 04	1 25	16 33	0 52	17 14	0 16	18 25	
15 Mo 258	11 55 17	+03 14	5 57	18 03	5 44	18 06	5 40	18 09	5 35	18 14	5 27	18 22
			16 29	2 55	16 46	2 34	17 08	2 08	17 38	1 39	18 28	0 21
16 Tu 259	11 54 56	+02 51	5 47	18 02	5 44	18 05	5 41	18 08	5 36	18 12	5 29	18 19
			17 10	3 58	17 22	3 42	17 37	3 23	17 57	3 02	18 28	2 10
17 We 260	11 54 34	+02 27	5 48	18 01	5 45	18 04	5 42	18 06	5 38	18 10	5 31	18 16
			17 47	4 56	17 54	4 47	18 02	4 35	18 12	4 22	18 28	3 52
18 Th 261	11 54 13 05 34 ○	+02 04	5 48	18 00	5 45	18 02	5 43	18 04	5 40	18 08	5 34	18 13
			18 22	5 52	18 23	5 49	18 24	5 44	18 25	5 39	18 27	5 28
19 Fr 262	11 53 51	+01 41	5 48	17 59	5 46	18 01	5 44	18 03	5 41	18 06	5 36	18 10
			18 56	6 46	18 52	6 48	18 46	6 51	18 38	6 54	18 26	7 00
20 Sa 263	11 53 30	+01 18	5 48	17 58	5 47	18 00	5 45	18 01	5 42	18 04	5 38	18 07
			19 31	7 39	19 20	7 47	19 08	7 56	18 51	8 06	18 25	8 30
21 Su 264	11 53 09	+00 54	5 49	17 58	5 47	17 58	5 46	18 00	5 44	18 02	5 41	18 04
			20 06	8 31	19 51	8 45	19 32	9 01	19 06	9 19	18 25	10 01
22 Mo 265	11 52 47	+00 31	5 49	17 57	5 47	17 57	5 47	17 58	5 46	17 59	5 44	18 01
			20 44	9 25	20 24	9 43	19 59	10 06	19 25	10 31	18 26	11 34
23 Tu 266	11 52 26	+00 08	5 49	17 56	5 49	17 56	5 48	17 56	5 47	17 57	5 46	17 58
			21 26	10 19	21 02	10 41	20 31	11 10	19 48	11 42	18 29	13 08
24 We 267	11 52 05	−00 16	5 49	17 55	5 49	17 55	5 49	17 54	5 48	17 55	5 48	17 55
			22 11	11 13	21 44	11 39	21 10	12 12	20 20	12 49	18 39	14 41
25 Th 268	11 51 45	−00 39	5 50	17 54	5 50	17 54	5 50	17 53	5 50	17 52	5 50	17 52
			23 00	12 07	22 32	12 35	21 56	13 11	21 02	13 51	19 04	16 02
26 Fr 269	11 51 24 03 17 ☾	−01 02	5 50	17 53	5 50	17 52	5 51	17 52	5 52	17 50	5 53	17 49
			23 53	12 59	23 25	13 27	22 49	14 03	21 56	14 44	19 59	16 54
27 Sa 270	11 51 04	−01 26	5 50	17 52	5 51	17 51	5 52	17 50	5 53	17 48	5 55	17 46
				13 48		14 15	23 49	14 49	23 00	15 26	21 24	17 17
28 Su 271	11 50 43	−01 49	5 50	17 51	5 51	17 50	5 53	17 48	5 54	17 46	5 58	17 43
			0 47	14 34	0 22	14 57		15 27		15 59	22 59	17 25
29 Mo 272	11 50 23	−02 12	5 50	17 50	5 52	17 48	5 54	17 46	5 56	17 44	6 00	17 40
			1 43	15 16	1 21	15 35	0 53	15 59	0 13	16 25		17 29
30 Tu 273	11 50 04	−02 36	5 51	17 49	5 52	17 47	5 55	17 45	5 57	17 41	6 02	17 37
			2 39	15 55	2 21	16 09	1 59	16 27	1 29	16 46	0 36	17 29

10th Month   October, 1986   31 Days

Greenwich Mean Time

NOTE: Light figures indicate Sun. **Dark** figures indicate **Moon**. *Degrees are North Latitude.*

CAUTION: Must be converted to local time. For instruction see page 726.

Day of month / week / year	Sun on meridian Moon phase h m s	Sun's Decli-nation ° '	20° Rise Sun/Moon h m	20° Set Sun/Moon h m	30° Rise h m	30° Set h m	40° Rise h m	40° Set h m	50° Rise h m	50° Set h m	60° Rise h m	60° Set h m
1 We	11 49 44	−02 59	5 51	17 48	5 53	17 46	5 56	17 43	5 59	17 39	6 05	17 34
274			3 34	16 32	3 22	16 41	3 07	16 52	2 46	17 07	2 17	17 29
2 Th	11 49 25	−03 22	5 51	17 47	5 54	17 45	5 57	17 42	6 01	17 37	6 07	17 31
275			4 29	17 08	4 23	17 11	4 15	17 15	4 04	17 20	3 47	17 28
3 Fr	11 49 06	−03 46	5 52	17 46	5 54	17 44	5 58	17 40	6 02	17 35	6 10	17 28
276	18 55 ●		5 25	17 44	5 25	17 41	5 24	17 38	5 24	17 34	5 23	17 27
4 Sa	11 48 48	−04 09	5 52	17 46	5 55	17 42	5 59	17 38	6 04	17 33	6 12	17 25
277			6 22	18 21	6 28	18 12	6 35	18 02	6 45	17 48	7 00	17 27
5 Su	11 48 30	−04 32	5 52	17 45	5 55	17 41	6 00	17 37	6 06	17 31	6 14	17 22
278			7 22	19 02	7 34	18 47	7 49	18 29	8 09	18 05	8 43	17 26
6 Mo	11 48 12	−04 55	5 53	17 44	5 56	17 40	6 01	17 35	6 08	17 29	6 16	17 19
279			8 24	19 47	8 32	19 27	9 05	19 02	9 37	18 26	10 32	17 2·
7 Tu	11 47 54	−05 18	5 53	17 44	5 56	17 38	6 02	17 34	6 09	17 26	6 19	17 16
280			9 30	20 38	9 53	20 13	10 23	19 41	11 06	18 56	12 28	17 32
8 We	11 47 37	−05 41	5 53	17 43	5 57	17 37	6 03	17 32	6 10	17 24	6 22	17 13
281			10 37	21 35	11 04	21 07	11 39	20 32	12 31	19 38	14 22	17 46
9 Th	11 47 21	−06 04	5 53	17 42	5 58	17 36	6 04	17 30	6 12	17 22	6 24	17 10
282			11 43	22 38	12 11	22 09	12 48	21 33	13 44	20 37	15 50	18 31
10 ·	11 47 05	−06 27	5 54	17 41	5 58	17 35	6 05	17 28	6 14	17 20	6 26	17 07
283	13 28 ☽		12 44	23 43	13 12	23 17	13 47	22 42	14 39	21 52	16 26	20 06
11 Sa	11 46 49	−06 50	5 54	17 40	5 59	17 34	6 06	17 27	6 15	17 18	6 29	17 04
284			13 39		14 03		14 33	23 56	15 17	23 15	16 37	21 58
12 Su	11 46 34	−07 12	5 54	17 39	6 00	17 33	6 07	17 26	6 16	17 16	6 32	17 01
285			14 27	0 48	14 46	0 25	15 10		15 44		16 41	23 47
13 Mo	11 46 19	−07 35	5 54	17 38	6 00	17 32	6 08	17 24	6 18	17 14	6 34	16 58
286			15 09	1 49	15 23	1 32	15 40	1 10	16 04	0 39	16 41	
14 Tu	11 46 04	−07 57	5 54	17 37	6 01	17 31	6 09	17 22	6 20	17 12	6 36	16 55
287			15 46	2 48	15 55	2 36	16 05	2 22	16 19	2 01	16 41	1 29
15 We	11 45 51	−08 20	5 55	17 36	6 02	17 30	6 10	17 21	6 21	17 10	6 38	16 52
288			16 21	3 44	16 24	3 38	16 28	3 30	16 33	3 20	16 40	3 05
16 Th	11 45 37	−08 42	5 55	17 36	6 02	17 29	6 11	17 20	6 22	17 08	6 41	16 49
289			16 55	4 37	16 52	4 37	16 49	4 37	16 45	4 36	16 39	4 36
17 Fr	11 45 25	−09 04	5 55	17 35	6 03	17 28	6 12	17 18	6 24	17 06	6 43	16 46
290	19 22 ○		17 29	5 29	17 21	5 35	17 11	5 42	16 58	5 51	16 38	6 06
18 Sa	11 45 13	−09 26	5 56	17 34	6 04	17 27	6 13	17 16	6 26	17 04	6 45	16 43
291			18 03	6 22	17 50	6 33	17 34	6 47	17 12	7 05	16 37	7 36
19 Su	11 45 01	−09 48	5 56	17 34	6 04	17 26	6 14	17 15	6 28	17 02	6 48	16 40
292			18 40	7 15	18 22	7 31	18 00	7 51	17 28	8 20	16 40	9 07
20 Mo	11 44 51	−10 09	5 56	17 33	6 05	17 24	6 15	17 14	6 29	17 00	6 50	16 38
293			19 20	8 09	18 58	8 30	18 30	8 56	17 50	9 34	16 46	10 41
21 Tu	11 44 40	−10 31	5 57	17 32	6 06	17 23	6 16	17 12	6 31	16 58	6 53	16 35
294			20 04	9 03	19 38	9 28	19 06	10 00	18 18	10 46	17 03	12 16
22 We	11 44 31	−10 52	5 57	17 32	6 06	17 22	6 17	17 11	6 32	16 56	6 56	16 32
295			20 52	9 58	20 24	10 25	19 48	11 00	18 55	11 52	17 44	13 44
23 Th	11 44 22	−11 13	5 57	17 31	6 07	17 21	6 18	17 10	6 34	16 54	6 58	16 30
296			21 43	10 50	21 15	11 19	20 39	11 55	19 44	12 49	18 58	14 50
24 Fr	11 44 14	−11 34	5 58	17 31	6 08	17 20	6 20	17 08	6 36	16 52	7 00	16 27
297			22 37	11 41	22 10	12 08	21 36	12 43	20 45	13 35	20 30	15 22
25 Sa	11 44 07	−11 55	5 58	17 30	6 08	17 19	6 19	17 07	6 37	16 50	7 03	16 24
298	22 26 ☾		23 31	12 27		12 52	22 37	13 24	21 53	14 10	22 05	15 35
26 Su	11 44 00	−12 16	5 58	17 29	6 09	17 18	6 22	17 06	6 39	16 48	7 06	16 21
299				13 10	0 06	13 32	23 42	13 58	23 07	14 36	23 40	15 40
27 Mo	11 43 54	−12 36	5 59	17 28	6 10	17 17	6 23	17 04	6 40	16 46	7 08	16 18
300			0 26	13 50	1 06	14 06		14 27		14 55		15 41
28 Tu	11 43 49	−12 57	5 59	17 28	6 10	17 17	6 24	17 03	6 42	16 45	7 11	16 16
301			1 21	14 27	2 06	14 38	0 48	14 53	0 22	15 12	1 14	15 41
29 We	11 43 45	−13 17	6 00	17 27	6 11	17 16	6 25	17 02	6 44	16 43	7 14	16 13
302			2 15	15 02	3 06	15 08	1 54	15 16	1 39	15 26	2 48	15 41
30 Th	11 43 41	−13 37	6 00	17 26	6 12	17 15	6 26	17 01	6 46	16 41	7 16	16 10
303			3 10	15 38	4 08	15 38	3 02	15 38	2 56	15 39	4 23	15 40
31 Fr	11 43 38	−13 56	6 01	17 26	6 12	17 14	6 27	17 00	6 48	16 40	7 19	16 08
304			4 06	16 14	5 13	16 09	4 12	16 02	4 16	15 53	6 04	15 39

11th Month   November, 1986   30 Days

Greenwich Mean Time

NOTE: Light figures indicate Sun. **Dark** figures indicate **Moon**. *Degrees are North Latitude.*

CAUTION: Must be converted to local time. For instruction see page 726.

Day of month / week / year	Sun on meridian / Moon phase (h m s)	Sun's Decli- nation (° ')	20° Rise Sun/Moon (h m)	20° Set Sun/Moon (h m)	30° Rise Sun/Moon (h m)	30° Set Sun/Moon (h m)	40° Rise Sun/Moon (h m)	40° Set Sun/Moon (h m)	50° Rise Sun/Moon (h m)	50° Set Sun/Moon (h m)	60° Rise Sun/Moon (h m)	60° Set Sun/Moon (h m)
1 Sa 305	11 43 36	−14 16	6 02	17 26	6 13	17 13	6 29	16 58	6 49	16 38	7 22	16 05
			5 04	16 54	5 13	16 42	5 24	16 28	5 40	16 08	6 04	15 38
2 Su 306	11 43 35 · 06 07 ●	−14 35	6 02	17 25	6 14	17 12	6 30	16 57	6 51	16 36	7 24	16 02
			6 07	17 37	6 22	17 20	6 41	16 58	7 08	16 28	7 52	15 39
3 Mo 307	11 43 35	−14 54	6 02	17 25	6 15	17 11	6 31	16 56	6 52	16 34	7 26	16 00
			7 13	18 28	7 34	18 04	8 01	17 36	8 39	16 54	9 49	15 42
4 Tu 308	11 43 35	−15 13	6 03	17 24	6 16	17 10	6 32	16 54	6 54	16 32	7 29	15 57
			8 22	19 25	8 48	18 57	9 21	18 23	10 10	17 32	11 49	15 51
5 We 309	11 43 36	−15 31	6 03	17 24	6 16	17 10	6 33	16 53	6 56	16 31	7 32	15 54
			9 31	20 28	9 59	19 59	10 36	19 22	11 31	18 27	13 35	16 22
6 Th 310	11 43 38	−15 50	6 04	17 23	6 17	17 09	6 34	16 52	6 57	16 29	7 34	15 52
			10 36	21 34	11 04	21 07	11 41	20 31	12 34	19 38	14 30	17 44
7 Fr 311	11 43 41	−16 08	6 04	17 23	6 18	17 08	6 35	16 51	6 59	16 28	7 36	15 50
			11 35	22 40	12 00	22 17	12 32	21 46	13 19	21 01	14 47	19 36
8 Sa 312	11 43 45 · 21 11 ☽	−16 25	6 05	17 22	6 19	17 08	6 36	16 50	7 00	16 26	7 39	15 48
			12 25	23 44	12 46	23 25	13 12	23 01	13 49	22 27	14 52	21 28
9 Su 313	11 43 50	−16 43	6 05	17 22	6 20	17 07	6 38	16 49	7 02	16 24	7 41	15 45
			13 09		13 25		13 44		14 11	23 50	14 53	23 12
10 Mo 314	11 43 55	−17 00	6 06	17 22	6 21	17 07	6 39	16 48	7 04	16 23	7 44	15 43
			13 48	0 43	13 58	0 30	14 10	0 13	14 27		14 53	
11 Tu 315	11 44 01	−17 17	6 06	17 22	6 22	17 06	6 40	16 47	7 06	16 22	7 47	15 40
			14 23	1 39	14 28	1 32	14 33	1 22	14 41	1 09	14 52	0 48
12 We 316	11 44 08	−17 33	6 07	17 21	6 22	17 06	6 42	16 46	7 08	16 20	7 50	15 38
			14 56	2 32	14 55	2 30	14 54	2 28	14 53	2 25	14 51	2 20
13 Th 317	11 44 16	−17 50	6 07	17 21	6 23	17 05	6 43	16 46	7 09	16 19	7 52	15 36
			15 29	3 24	15 23	3 28	15 16	3 32	15 05	3 38	14 50	3 48
14 Fr 318	11 44 25	−18 06	6 08	17 21	6 24	17 05	6 44	16 45	7 11	16 18	7 55	15 33
			16 03	4 16	15 52	4 25	15 38	4 36	15 19	4 52	14 49	5 16
15 Sa 319	11 44 34	−18 21	6 08	17 21	6 25	17 04	6 45	16 44	7 12	16 17	7 58	15 31
			16 39	5 08	16 22	5 33	16 02	5 40	15 34	6 05	14 50	6 46
16 Su 320	11 44 44 · 12 12 ○	−18 36	6 09	17 20	6 26	17 04	6 46	16 44	7 14	16 16	8 00	15 29
			17 17	6 01	16 57	6 20	16 30	6 44	15 54	7 19	14 51	8 18
17 Mo 321	11 44 56	−18 51	6 09	17 20	6 26	17 03	6 47	16 43	7 16	16 14	8 02	15 27
			18 00	6 55	17 35	7 18	17 04	7 48	16 19	8 31	14 56	9 53
18 Tu 322	11 45 08	−19 06	6 10	17 20	6 27	17 03	6 48	16 42	7 17	16 13	8 05	15 25
			18 46	7 50	18 19	8 16	17 44	8 50	16 53	9 40	15 08	11 24
19 We 323	11 45 21	−19 20	6 11	17 20	6 28	17 02	6 49	16 41	7 18	16 12	8 07	15 23
			19 36	8 43	19 08	9 11	18 32	9 47	17 38	10 41	15 39	12 40
20 Th 324	11 45 34	−19 34	6 11	17 20	6 29	17 02	6 50	16 40	7 20	16 10	8 10	15 21
			20 29	9 34	20 02	10 02	19 26	10 38	18 34	11 31	16 42	13 24
21 Fr 325	11 45 49	−19 48	6 12	17 19	6 30	17 01	6 52	16 40	7 22	16 09	8 12	15 19
			21 23	10 22	20 58	10 48	20 26	11 21	19 40	12 09	18 08	13 42
22 Sa 326	11 46 04	−20 01	6 13	17 19	6 31	17 01	6 53	16 39	7 23	16 08	8 14	15 17
			22 17	11 06	21 56	11 29	21 29	11 57	20 50	12 38	19 42	13 49
23 Su 327	11 46 20	−20 14	6 13	17 19	6 32	17 01	6 54	16 38	7 24	16 07	8 16	15 15
			23 10	11 46	22 54	12 05	22 33	12 28	22 04	12 59	21 15	13 52
24 Mo 328	11 46 37 · 16 50 ☾	−20 27	6 14	17 19	6 33	17 00	6 55	16 38	7 26	16 06	8 19	15 14
				12 23	23 52	12 37	23 37	12 54	23 18	13 16	22 46	13 52
25 Tu 329	11 46 55	−20 39	6 14	17 19	6 33	17 00	6 56	16 37	7 28	16 05	8 22	15 12
			0 03	12 58		13 07		13 17		13 31		13 52
26 We 330	11 47 14	−20 51	6 15	17 19	6 34	17 00	6 57	16 37	7 29	16 05	8 24	15 10
			0 56	13 32	0 50	13 35	0 42	13 39	0 32	13 44	0 16	13 51
27 Th 331	11 47 33	−21 02	6 16	17 19	6 35	17 00	6 58	16 36	7 30	16 04	8 26	15 08
			1 50	14 07	1 49	14 04	1 49	14 01	1 49	13 57	1 48	13 50
28 Fr 332	11 47 53	−21 13	6 16	17 19	6 36	17 00	6 59	16 36	7 32	16 03	8 28	15 07
			2 46	14 44	2 51	14 36	2 58	14 25	3 08	14 11	3 24	13 50
29 Sa 333	11 48 14	−21 23	6 17	17 19	6 36	17 00	7 00	16 36	7 34	16 03	8 30	15 06
			3 45	15 25	3 57	15 11	4 12	14 53	4 32	14 28	5 06	13 50
30 Su 334	11 48 35	−21 34	6 18	17 19	6 37	17 00	7 01	16 36	7 35	16 02	8 32	15 04
			4 49	16 12	5 07	15 52	5 30	15 26	6 02	14 51	6 58	13 51

12th Month   December, 1986   31 days

Greenwich Mean Time

NOTE: Light figures indicate Sun. **Dark** figures indicate **Moon.** *Degrees are North Latitude.*

CAUTION: Must be converted to local time. For instruction see page 726.

Day of month / week / year	Sun on meridian / Moon phase (h m s)	Sun's Declination (°)	20° Rise Sun/Moon (h m)	20° Set Sun/Moon (h m)	30° Rise Sun/Moon (h m)	30° Set Sun/Moon (h m)	40° Rise Sun/Moon (h m)	40° Set Sun/Moon (h m)	50° Rise Sun/Moon (h m)	50° Set Sun/Moon (h m)	60° Rise Sun/Moon (h m)	60° Set Sun/Moon (h m)
1 Mo 335	11 48 57	−21 43	6 18	17 19	6 38	17 00	7 02	16 36	7 36	16 01	8 84	15 03
	16 43 ●		5 57	17 06	6 21	16 41	6 51	16 09	7 35	15 23	8 58	13 57
2 Tu 336	11 49 20	−21 53	6 19	17 19	6 38	17 00	7 03	16 36	7 37	16 01	8 36	15 02
			7 08	18 08	7 36	17 40	8 11	17 04	9 04	16 10	10 57	14 15
3 We 337	11 49 43	−22 02	6 20	17 20	6 39	17 00	7 04	16 35	7 39	16 00	8 38	15 01
			8 18	19 16	8 47	18 48	9 24	18 11	10 19	17 17	12 21	15 15
4 Th 338	11 50 07	−22 10	6 20	17 20	6 40	17 00	7 05	16 35	7 40	16 00	8 40	15 00
			9 22	20 26	9 49	20 00	10 23	19 27	11 13	18 39	12 52	17 02
5 Fr 339	11 50 32	−22 18	6 21	17 20	6 41	17 00	7 06	16 35	7 41	15 59	8 42	14 59
			10 18	21 33	10 41	21 12	11 09	20 46	11 50	20 08	13 01	19 00
6 Sa 340	11 50 57	−22 26	6 21	17 21	6 42	17 00	7 07	16 35	7 42	15 59	8 44	14 58
			11 06	22 36	11 24	22 21	11 45	22 02	12 15	21 35	13 04	20 51
7 Su 341	11 51 23	−22 33	6 22	17 21	6 42	17 00	7 08	16 35	7 44	15 58	8 45	14 57
			11 47	23 34	11 59	23 25	12 14	23 13	12 34	22 57	13 04	22 32
8 Mo 342	11 51 49	−22 40	6 23	17 21	6 43	17 00	7 09	16 35	7 45	15 58	8 47	14 56
	08 01 ☽		12 24		12 30		12 38		12 48		13 04	
9 Tu 343	11 52 15	−22 46	6 24	17 21	6 44	17 00	7 10	16 35	7 46	15 58	8 48	14 56
			12 58	0 29	12 59	0 25	13 00	0 21	13 01	0 15	13 03	0 05
10 We 344	11 52 42	−22 46	6 24	17 22	6 44	17 00	7 10	16 35	7 47	15 58	8 50	14 55
			13 31	1 21	13 27	1 23	13 21	1 26	13 13	1 29	13 02	1 34
11 Th 345	11 53 09	−22 52	6 25	17 22	6 45	17 01	7 11	16 35	7 48	15 58	8 52	14 54
			14 05	2 13	13 55	2 20	13 43	2 29	13 26	2 42	13 01	3 02
12 Fr 346	11 53 37	−22 57	6 25	17 22	6 46	17 01	7 12	16 35	7 49	15 58	8 53	14 54
			14 39	3 04	14 24	3 17	14 06	3 32	13 41	3 55	13 01	4 30
13 Sa 347	11 54 05	−23 02	6 26	17 22	6 47	17 01	7 13	16 35	7 50	15 58	8 54	14 54
			15 17	3 56	14 57	4 14	14 33	4 36	13 59	5 07	13 02	6 01
14 Su 348	11 54 34	−23 07	6 26	17 23	6 47	17 01	7 14	16 36	7 51	15 58	8 56	14 53
			15 58	4 49	15 34	5 12	15 04	5 40	14 22	6 20	13 06	7 34
15 Mo 349	11 55 02	−23 15	6 27	17 23	6 48	17 02	7 14	16 36	7 52	15 58	8 57	14 53
			16 43	5 44	16 16	6 09	15 42	6 42	14 53	7 30	13 16	9 06
16 Tu 350	11 55 31	−23 15	6 28	17 23	6 49	17 04	7 15	16 36	7 53	15 58	8 58	14 53
	07 04 ○		17 32	6 38	17 04	7 05	16 28	7 41	15 34	8 34	13 40	10 28
17 We 351	11 56 00	−23 20	6 28	17 24	6 49	17 02	7 16	16 36	7 54	15 58	8 59	14 53
			18 24	7 30	17 56	7 58	17 20	8 34	16 27	9 27	14 32	11 22
18 Th 352	11 56 30	−23 22	6 29	17 24	6 50	17 03	7 16	16 36	7 54	15 59	9 00	14 53
			19 17	8 19	18 52	8 45	18 19	9 19	17 30	10 09	15 53	11 47
19 Fr 353	11 56 59	−23 24	6 30	17 24	6 50	17 03	7 17	16 37	7 55	15 59	9 00	14 54
			20 11	9 04	19 49	9 27	19 20	9 57	18 40	10 40	17 25	11 57
20 Sa 354	11 57 29	−23 25	6 30	17 25	6 51	17 04	7 18	16 37	7 55	16 00	9 01	14 54
			21 04	9 45	20 46	10 05	20 24	10 29	19 52	11 04	18 57	12 01
21 Su 355	11 57 59	−23 26	6 30	17 25	6 51	17 04	7 18	16 37	7 56	16 00	9 02	14 54
			21 57	10 22	21 44	10 37	21 27	10 56	21 04	11 22	20 28	12 03
22 Mo 356	11 58 28	−23 27	6 31	17 26	6 52	17 05	7 19	16 38	7 56	16 01	9 02	14 55
			22 48	10 57	22 40	11 07	22 31	11 20	22 17	11 37	21 56	12 03
23 Tu 357	11 58 58	−23 26	6 31	17 26	6 52	17 05	7 19	16 38	7 56	16 01	9 03	14 55
			23 40	11 30	23 37	11 35	23 34	11 42	23 30	11 50	23 24	12 02
24 We 358	11 59 28	−23 26	6 32	17 27	6 53	17 06	7 20	16 39	7 57	16 02	9 03	14 56
	09 17 ◑			12 04		12 03		12 03		12 02		12 01
25 Th 359	11 59 58	−23 25	6 32	17 27	6 53	17 06	7 20	16 40	7 57	16 03	9 03	14 57
			0 33	12 38	0 36	12 32	0 40	12 25	0 46	12 15	0 54	12 00
26 Fr 360	12 00 28	−23 23	6 33	17 28	6 54	17 07	7 20	16 40	7 57	16 04	9 03	14 58
			1 28	13 16	1 37	13 04	1 49	12 50	2 04	12 30	2 29	12 00
27 Sa 361	12 00 57	−23 21	6 33	17 28	6 54	17 07	7 21	16 41	7 58	16 04	9 04	14 58
			2 28	13 58	2 43	13 41	3 02	13 19	3 28	12 49	4 13	12 01
28 Su 362	12 01 27	−23 19	6 34	17 29	6 55	17 08	7 21	16 42	7 58	16 05	9 04	14 59
			3 32	14 47	3 53	14 24	4 19	13 56	4 57	13 15	6 06	12 04
29 Mo 363	12 01 56	−23 16	6 34	17 30	6 55	17 09	7 21	16 43	7 58	16 06	9 04	15 00
			4 41	15 45	5 07	15 18	5 39	14 43	6 28	13 53	8 06	12 14
30 Tu 364	12 02 26	−23 12	6 35	17 30	6 55	17 10	7 22	16 43	7 58	16 06	9 04	15 01
			5 52	16 50	6 20	16 21	6 57	15 45	7 51	14 50	9 53	12 47
31 We 365	12 02 55	−23 08	6 35	17 31	6 56	17 10	7 22	16 45	7 59	16 07	9 03	15 03
	03 10 ●		7 00	18 01	7 28	17 33	8 04	16 58	8 57	16 06	10 50	14 15

Perpetual Calendar

The number shown for each year indicates which Gregorian calendar to use. For 1583-1802, or for Julian calendar, see page 750. For years 1803-1820, use numbers for 1983-2000, respectively.

Year	No.		Year	No.		Year	No.		Year	No.
1821	2		1847	6		1873	4		1899	1
1822	3		1848	14		1874	5		1900	2
1823	4		1849	2		1875	6		1901	3
1824	12		1850	3		1876	14		1902	4
1825	7		1851	4		1877	2		1903	5
1826	1		1852	12		1878	3		1904	13
1827	2		1853	7		1879	4		1905	1
1828	10		1854	1		1880	12		1906	2
1829	5		1855	2		1881	7		1907	3
1830	6		1856	10		1882	1		1908	11
1831	7		1857	5		1883	2		1909	6
1832	8		1858	6		1884	10		1910	7
1833	3		1859	7		1885	5		1911	1
1834	4		1860	8		1886	6		1912	9
1835	5		1861	3		1887	7		1913	4
1836	13		1862	4		1888	8		1914	5
1837	1		1863	5		1889	3		1915	6
1838	2		1864	13		1890	4		1916	14
1839	3		1865	1		1891	5		1917	2
1840	11		1866	2		1892	13		1918	3
1841	6		1867	3		1893	1		1919	4
1842	7		1868	11		1894	2		1920	12
1843	1		1869	6		1895	3		1921	7
1844	9		1870	7		1896	11		1922	1
1845	4		1871	1		1897	6		1923	2
1846	5		1872	9		1898	7		1924	10

Year	No.		Year	No.		Year	No.		Year	No.
1925	5		1951	2		1977	7		2003	4
1926	6		1952	10		1978	1		2004	12
1927	7		1953	5		1979	2		2005	7
1928	8		1954	6		1980	10		2006	1
1929	3		1955	7		1981	5		2007	2
1930	4		1956	8		1982	6		2008	10
1931	5		1957	3		1983	7		2009	5
1932	13		1958	4		1984	8		2010	6
1933	1		1959	5		1985	3		2011	7
1934	2		1960	13		1986	4		2012	8
1935	3		1961	1		1987	5		2013	3
1936	11		1962	2		1988	13		2014	4
1937	6		1963	3		1989	1		2015	5
1938	7		1964	11		1990	2		2016	13
1939	1		1965	6		1991	3		2017	1
1940	9		1966	7		1992	11		2018	2
1941	4		1967	1		1993	6		2019	3
1942	5		1968	9		1994	7		2020	11
1943	6		1969	4		1995	1		2021	6
1944	14		1970	5		1996	9		2022	7
1945	2		1971	6		1997	4		2023	1
1946	3		1972	14		1998	5		2024	9
1947	4		1973	2		1999	6		2025	4
1948	12		1974	3		2000	14		2026	5
1949	7		1975	4		2001	2		2027	6
1950	1		1976	12		2002	3		2028	14

Year	No.		Year	No.
2029	4		2055	6
2030	5		2056	14
2031	6		2057	2
2032	14		2058	3
2033	7		2059	4
2034	1		2060	12
2035	2		2061	7
2036	10		2062	1
2037	5		2063	2
2038	6		2064	10
2039	7		2065	5
2040	8		2066	6
2041	3		2067	7
2042	4		2068	8
2043	5		2069	3
2044	13		2070	4
2045	1		2071	5
2046	2		2072	13
2047	3		2073	1
2048	11		2074	2
2049	6		2075	3
2050	7		2076	11
2051	1		2077	6
2052	9		2078	7
2053	4		2079	1
2054	5		2080	9

The remainder of the page consists of fourteen reference calendars (numbered **1** through **6**, and including the example years **1985**, **1986**, **1987**), each showing the twelve months — JANUARY, FEBRUARY, MARCH, APRIL, MAY, JUNE, JULY, AUGUST, SEPTEMBER, OCTOBER, NOVEMBER, DECEMBER — with weekday columns S M T W T F S.

7

January
S	M	T	W	T	F	S
						1
2	3	4	5	6	7	8
9	10	11	12	13	14	15
16	17	18	19	20	21	22
23	24	25	26	27	28	29
30	31					

February
S	M	T	W	T	F	S
		1	2	3	4	5
6	7	8	9	10	11	12
13	14	15	16	17	18	19
20	21	22	23	24	25	26
27	28					

March
S	M	T	W	T	F	S
		1	2	3	4	5
6	7	8	9	10	11	12
13	14	15	16	17	18	19
20	21	22	23	24	25	26
27	28	29	30	31		

April
S	M	T	W	T	F	S
					1	2
3	4	5	6	7	8	9
10	11	12	13	14	15	16
17	18	19	20	21	22	23
24	25	26	27	28	29	30

May
S	M	T	W	T	F	S
1	2	3	4	5	6	7
8	9	10	11	12	13	14
15	16	17	18	19	20	21
22	23	24	25	26	27	28
29	30	31				

June
S	M	T	W	T	F	S
			1	2	3	4
5	6	7	8	9	10	11
12	13	14	15	16	17	18
19	20	21	22	23	24	25
26	27	28	29	30		

July
S	M	T	W	T	F	S
					1	2
3	4	5	6	7	8	9
10	11	12	13	14	15	16
17	18	19	20	21	22	23
24	25	26	27	28	29	30
31						

August
S	M	T	W	T	F	S
	1	2	3	4	5	6
7	8	9	10	11	12	13
14	15	16	17	18	19	20
21	22	23	24	25	26	27
28	29	30	31			

September
S	M	T	W	T	F	S
				1	2	3
4	5	6	7	8	9	10
11	12	13	14	15	16	17
18	19	20	21	22	23	24
25	26	27	28	29	30	

October
S	M	T	W	T	F	S
						1
2	3	4	5	6	7	8
9	10	11	12	13	14	15
16	17	18	19	20	21	22
23	24	25	26	27	28	29
30	31					

November
S	M	T	W	T	F	S
		1	2	3	4	5
6	7	8	9	10	11	12
13	14	15	16	17	18	19
20	21	22	23	24	25	26
27	28	29	30			

December
S	M	T	W	T	F	S
				1	2	3
4	5	6	7	8	9	10
11	12	13	14	15	16	17
18	19	20	21	22	23	24
25	26	27	28	29	30	31

8

January
S	M	T	W	T	F	S
1	2	3	4	5	6	7
8	9	10	11	12	13	14
15	16	17	18	19	20	21
22	23	24	25	26	27	28
29	30	31				

February
S	M	T	W	T	F	S
			1	2	3	4
5	6	7	8	9	10	11
12	13	14	15	16	17	18
19	20	21	22	23	24	25
26	27	28	29			

March
S	M	T	W	T	F	S
				1	2	3
4	5	6	7	8	9	10
11	12	13	14	15	16	17
18	19	20	21	22	23	24
25	26	27	28	29	30	31

April
S	M	T	W	T	F	S
1	2	3	4	5	6	7
8	9	10	11	12	13	14
15	16	17	18	19	20	21
22	23	24	25	26	27	28
29	30					

May
S	M	T	W	T	F	S
		1	2	3	4	5
6	7	8	9	10	11	12
13	14	15	16	17	18	19
20	21	22	23	24	25	26
27	28	29	30	31		

June
S	M	T	W	T	F	S
					1	2
3	4	5	6	7	8	9
10	11	12	13	14	15	16
17	18	19	20	21	22	23
24	25	26	27	28	29	30

July
S	M	T	W	T	F	S
1	2	3	4	5	6	7
8	9	10	11	12	13	14
15	16	17	18	19	20	21
22	23	24	25	26	27	28
29	30	31				

August
S	M	T	W	T	F	S
			1	2	3	4
5	6	7	8	9	10	11
12	13	14	15	16	17	18
19	20	21	22	23	24	25
26	27	28	29	30	31	

September
S	M	T	W	T	F	S
						1
2	3	4	5	6	7	8
9	10	11	12	13	14	15
16	17	18	19	20	21	22
23	24	25	26	27	28	29
30						

October
S	M	T	W	T	F	S
	1	2	3	4	5	6
7	8	9	10	11	12	13
14	15	16	17	18	19	20
21	22	23	24	25	26	27
28	29	30	31			

November
S	M	T	W	T	F	S
				1	2	3
4	5	6	7	8	9	10
11	12	13	14	15	16	17
18	19	20	21	22	23	24
25	26	27	28	29	30	

December
S	M	T	W	T	F	S
						1
2	3	4	5	6	7	8
9	10	11	12	13	14	15
16	17	18	19	20	21	22
23	24	25	26	27	28	29
30	31					

9

January
S	M	T	W	T	F	S
	1	2	3	4	5	6
7	8	9	10	11	12	13
14	15	16	17	18	19	20
21	22	23	24	25	26	27
28	29	30	31			

February
S	M	T	W	T	F	S
				1	2	3
4	5	6	7	8	9	10
11	12	13	14	15	16	17
18	19	20	21	22	23	24
25	26	27	28	29		

March
S	M	T	W	T	F	S
					1	2
3	4	5	6	7	8	9
10	11	12	13	14	15	16
17	18	19	20	21	22	23
24	25	26	27	28	29	30
31						

April
S	M	T	W	T	F	S
	1	2	3	4	5	6
7	8	9	10	11	12	13
14	15	16	17	18	19	20
21	22	23	24	25	26	27
28	29	30				

May
S	M	T	W	T	F	S
			1	2	3	4
5	6	7	8	9	10	11
12	13	14	15	16	17	18
19	20	21	22	23	24	25
26	27	28	29	30	31	

June
S	M	T	W	T	F	S
						1
2	3	4	5	6	7	8
9	10	11	12	13	14	15
16	17	18	19	20	21	22
23	24	25	26	27	28	29
30						

July
S	M	T	W	T	F	S
	1	2	3	4	5	6
7	8	9	10	11	12	13
14	15	16	17	18	19	20
21	22	23	24	25	26	27
28	29	30	31			

August
S	M	T	W	T	F	S
				1	2	3
4	5	6	7	8	9	10
11	12	13	14	15	16	17
18	19	20	21	22	23	24
25	26	27	28	29	30	31

September
S	M	T	W	T	F	S
1	2	3	4	5	6	7
8	9	10	11	12	13	14
15	16	17	18	19	20	21
22	23	24	25	26	27	28
29	30					

October
S	M	T	W	T	F	S
		1	2	3	4	5
6	7	8	9	10	11	12
13	14	15	16	17	18	19
20	21	22	23	24	25	26
27	28	29	30	31		

November
S	M	T	W	T	F	S
					1	2
3	4	5	6	7	8	9
10	11	12	13	14	15	16
17	18	19	20	21	22	23
24	25	26	27	28	29	30

December
S	M	T	W	T	F	S
1	2	3	4	5	6	7
8	9	10	11	12	13	14
15	16	17	18	19	20	21
22	23	24	25	26	27	28
29	30	31				

10

January
S	M	T	W	T	F	S
		1	2	3	4	5
6	7	8	9	10	11	12
13	14	15	16	17	18	19
20	21	22	23	24	25	26
27	28	29	30	31		

February
S	M	T	W	T	F	S
					1	2
3	4	5	6	7	8	9
10	11	12	13	14	15	16
17	18	19	20	21	22	23
24	25	26	27	28	29	

March
S	M	T	W	T	F	S
						1
2	3	4	5	6	7	8
9	10	11	12	13	14	15
16	17	18	19	20	21	22
23	24	25	26	27	28	29
30	31					

April
S	M	T	W	T	F	S
		1	2	3	4	5
6	7	8	9	10	11	12
13	14	15	16	17	18	19
20	21	22	23	24	25	26
27	28	29	30			

May
S	M	T	W	T	F	S
				1	2	3
4	5	6	7	8	9	10
11	12	13	14	15	16	17
18	19	20	21	22	23	24
25	26	27	28	29	30	31

June
S	M	T	W	T	F	S
1	2	3	4	5	6	7
8	9	10	11	12	13	14
15	16	17	18	19	20	21
22	23	24	25	26	27	28
29	30					

July
S	M	T	W	T	F	S
		1	2	3	4	5
6	7	8	9	10	11	12
13	14	15	16	17	18	19
20	21	22	23	24	25	26
27	28	29	30	31		

August
S	M	T	W	T	F	S
					1	2
3	4	5	6	7	8	9
10	11	12	13	14	15	16
17	18	19	20	21	22	23
24	25	26	27	28	29	30
31						

September
S	M	T	W	T	F	S
	1	2	3	4	5	6
7	8	9	10	11	12	13
14	15	16	17	18	19	20
21	22	23	24	25	26	27
28	29	30				

October
S	M	T	W	T	F	S
			1	2	3	4
5	6	7	8	9	10	11
12	13	14	15	16	17	18
19	20	21	22	23	24	25
26	27	28	29	30	31	

November
S	M	T	W	T	F	S
						1
2	3	4	5	6	7	8
9	10	11	12	13	14	15
16	17	18	19	20	21	22
23	24	25	26	27	28	29
30						

December
S	M	T	W	T	F	S
	1	2	3	4	5	6
7	8	9	10	11	12	13
14	15	16	17	18	19	20
21	22	23	24	25	26	27
28	29	30	31			

11

January
S	M	T	W	T	F	S
			1	2	3	4
5	6	7	8	9	10	11
12	13	14	15	16	17	18
19	20	21	22	23	24	25
26	27	28	29	30	31	

February
S	M	T	W	T	F	S
						1
2	3	4	5	6	7	8
9	10	11	12	13	14	15
16	17	18	19	20	21	22
23	24	25	26	27	28	29

March
S	M	T	W	T	F	S
1	2	3	4	5	6	7
8	9	10	11	12	13	14
15	16	17	18	19	20	21
22	23	24	25	26	27	28
29	30	31				

April
S	M	T	W	T	F	S
			1	2	3	4
5	6	7	8	9	10	11
12	13	14	15	16	17	18
19	20	21	22	23	24	25
26	27	28	29	30		

May
S	M	T	W	T	F	S
					1	2
3	4	5	6	7	8	9
10	11	12	13	14	15	16
17	18	19	20	21	22	23
24	25	26	27	28	29	30
31						

June
S	M	T	W	T	F	S
	1	2	3	4	5	6
7	8	9	10	11	12	13
14	15	16	17	18	19	20
21	22	23	24	25	26	27
28	29	30				

July
S	M	T	W	T	F	S
			1	2	3	4
5	6	7	8	9	10	11
12	13	14	15	16	17	18
19	20	21	22	23	24	25
26	27	28	29	30	31	

August
S	M	T	W	T	F	S
						1
2	3	4	5	6	7	8
9	10	11	12	13	14	15
16	17	18	19	20	21	22
23	24	25	26	27	28	29
30	31					

September
S	M	T	W	T	F	S
		1	2	3	4	5
6	7	8	9	10	11	12
13	14	15	16	17	18	19
20	21	22	23	24	25	26
27	28	29	30			

October
S	M	T	W	T	F	S
				1	2	3
4	5	6	7	8	9	10
11	12	13	14	15	16	17
18	19	20	21	22	23	24
25	26	27	28	29	30	31

November
S	M	T	W	T	F	S
1	2	3	4	5	6	7
8	9	10	11	12	13	14
15	16	17	18	19	20	21
22	23	24	25	26	27	28
29	30					

December
S	M	T	W	T	F	S
		1	2	3	4	5
6	7	8	9	10	11	12
13	14	15	16	17	18	19
20	21	22	23	24	25	26
27	28	29	30	31		

12

January
S	M	T	W	T	F	S
				1	2	3
4	5	6	7	8	9	10
11	12	13	14	15	16	17
18	19	20	21	22	23	24
25	26	27	28	29	30	31

February
S	M	T	W	T	F	S
1	2	3	4	5	6	7
8	9	10	11	12	13	14
15	16	17	18	19	20	21
22	23	24	25	26	27	28
29						

March
S	M	T	W	T	F	S
	1	2	3	4	5	6
7	8	9	10	11	12	13
14	15	16	17	18	19	20
21	22	23	24	25	26	27
28	29	30	31			

April
S	M	T	W	T	F	S
				1	2	3
4	5	6	7	8	9	10
11	12	13	14	15	16	17
18	19	20	21	22	23	24
25	26	27	28	29	30	

May
S	M	T	W	T	F	S
						1
2	3	4	5	6	7	8
9	10	11	12	13	14	15
16	17	18	19	20	21	22
23	24	25	26	27	28	29
30	31					

June
S	M	T	W	T	F	S
		1	2	3	4	5
6	7	8	9	10	11	12
13	14	15	16	17	18	19
20	21	22	23	24	25	26
27	28	29	30			

July
S	M	T	W	T	F	S
				1	2	3
4	5	6	7	8	9	10
11	12	13	14	15	16	17
18	19	20	21	22	23	24
25	26	27	28	29	30	31

August
S	M	T	W	T	F	S
1	2	3	4	5	6	7
8	9	10	11	12	13	14
15	16	17	18	19	20	21
22	23	24	25	26	27	28
29	30	31				

September
S	M	T	W	T	F	S
			1	2	3	4
5	6	7	8	9	10	11
12	13	14	15	16	17	18
19	20	21	22	23	24	25
26	27	28	29	30		

October
S	M	T	W	T	F	S
					1	2
3	4	5	6	7	8	9
10	11	12	13	14	15	16
17	18	19	20	21	22	23
24	25	26	27	28	29	30
31						

November
S	M	T	W	T	F	S
	1	2	3	4	5	6
7	8	9	10	11	12	13
14	15	16	17	18	19	20
21	22	23	24	25	26	27
28	29	30				

December
S	M	T	W	T	F	S
			1	2	3	4
5	6	7	8	9	10	11
12	13	14	15	16	17	18
19	20	21	22	23	24	25
26	27	28	29	30	31	

13

January
S	M	T	W	T	F	S
					1	2
3	4	5	6	7	8	9
10	11	12	13	14	15	16
17	18	19	20	21	22	23
24	25	26	27	28	29	30
31						

February
S	M	T	W	T	F	S
	1	2	3	4	5	6
7	8	9	10	11	12	13
14	15	16	17	18	19	20
21	22	23	24	25	26	27
28	29					

March
S	M	T	W	T	F	S
		1	2	3	4	5
6	7	8	9	10	11	12
13	14	15	16	17	18	19
20	21	22	23	24	25	26
27	28	29	30	31		

April
S	M	T	W	T	F	S
					1	2
3	4	5	6	7	8	9
10	11	12	13	14	15	16
17	18	19	20	21	22	23
24	25	26	27	28	29	30

May
S	M	T	W	T	F	S
1	2	3	4	5	6	7
8	9	10	11	12	13	14
15	16	17	18	19	20	21
22	23	24	25	26	27	28
29	30	31				

June
S	M	T	W	T	F	S
			1	2	3	4
5	6	7	8	9	10	11
12	13	14	15	16	17	18
19	20	21	22	23	24	25
26	27	28	29	30		

July
S	M	T	W	T	F	S
					1	2
3	4	5	6	7	8	9
10	11	12	13	14	15	16
17	18	19	20	21	22	23
24	25	26	27	28	29	30
31						

August
S	M	T	W	T	F	S
	1	2	3	4	5	6
7	8	9	10	11	12	13
14	15	16	17	18	19	20
21	22	23	24	25	26	27
28	29	30	31			

September
S	M	T	W	T	F	S
				1	2	3
4	5	6	7	8	9	10
11	12	13	14	15	16	17
18	19	20	21	22	23	24
25	26	27	28	29	30	

October
S	M	T	W	T	F	S
						1
2	3	4	5	6	7	8
9	10	11	12	13	14	15
16	17	18	19	20	21	22
23	24	25	26	27	28	29
30	31					

November
S	M	T	W	T	F	S
		1	2	3	4	5
6	7	8	9	10	11	12
13	14	15	16	17	18	19
20	21	22	23	24	25	26
27	28	29	30			

December
S	M	T	W	T	F	S
				1	2	3
4	5	6	7	8	9	10
11	12	13	14	15	16	17
18	19	20	21	22	23	24
25	26	27	28	29	30	31

14

January
S	M	T	W	T	F	S
						1
2	3	4	5	6	7	8
9	10	11	12	13	14	15
16	17	18	19	20	21	22
23	24	25	26	27	28	29
30	31					

February
S	M	T	W	T	F	S
		1	2	3	4	5
6	7	8	9	10	11	12
13	14	15	16	17	18	19
20	21	22	23	24	25	26
27	28	29				

March
S	M	T	W	T	F	S
			1	2	3	4
5	6	7	8	9	10	11
12	13	14	15	16	17	18
19	20	21	22	23	24	25
26	27	28	29	30	31	

April
S	M	T	W	T	F	S
						1
2	3	4	5	6	7	8
9	10	11	12	13	14	15
16	17	18	19	20	21	22
23	24	25	26	27	28	29
30						

May
S	M	T	W	T	F	S
	1	2	3	4	5	6
7	8	9	10	11	12	13
14	15	16	17	18	19	20
21	22	23	24	25	26	27
28	29	30	31			

June
S	M	T	W	T	F	S
				1	2	3
4	5	6	7	8	9	10
11	12	13	14	15	16	17
18	19	20	21	22	23	24
25	26	27	28	29	30	

July
S	M	T	W	T	F	S
						1
2	3	4	5	6	7	8
9	10	11	12	13	14	15
16	17	18	19	20	21	22
23	24	25	26	27	28	29
30	31					

August
S	M	T	W	T	F	S
		1	2	3	4	5
6	7	8	9	10	11	12
13	14	15	16	17	18	19
20	21	22	23	24	25	26
27	28	29	30	31		

September
S	M	T	W	T	F	S
					1	2
3	4	5	6	7	8	9
10	11	12	13	14	15	16
17	18	19	20	21	22	23
24	25	26	27	28	29	30

October
S	M	T	W	T	F	S
1	2	3	4	5	6	7
8	9	10	11	12	13	14
15	16	17	18	19	20	21
22	23	24	25	26	27	28
29	30	31				

November
S	M	T	W	T	F	S
			1	2	3	4
5	6	7	8	9	10	11
12	13	14	15	16	17	18
19	20	21	22	23	24	25
26	27	28	29	30		

December
S	M	T	W	T	F	S
					1	2
3	4	5	6	7	8	9
10	11	12	13	14	15	16
17	18	19	20	21	22	23
24	25	26	27	28	29	30
31						

Julian and Gregorian Calendars; Leap Year

Calendars based on the movements of sun and moon have been used since ancient times, but none has been perfect. The Julian calendar, under which western nations measured time until 1582 A.D., was authorized by Julius Caesar in 46 B.C., the year 709 of Rome. His expert was a Greek, Sosigenes. The Julian calendar, on the assumption that the true year was 365 1/4 days long, gave every fourth year 366 days. The Venerable Bede, an Anglo-Saxon monk, announced in 730 A.D. that the 365 1/4-day Julian year was 11 min., 14 sec. too long, making a cumulative error of about a day every 128 years, but nothing was done about it for over 800 years.

By 1582 the accumulated error was estimated to have amounted to 10 days. In that year Pope Gregory XIII decreed that the day following Oct. 4, 1582, should be called Oct. 15, thus dropping 10 days.

However, with common years 365 days and a 366-day leap year every fourth year, the error in the length of the year would have recurred at the rate of a little more than 3 days every 400 years. So 3 of every 4 centesimal years (ending in 00) were made common years, not leap years. Thus 1600 was a leap year, 1700, 1800 and 1900 were not, but 2000 will be. Leap years are those divisible by 4 except centesimal years, which are common unless divisible by 400.

The Gregorian calendar was adopted at once by France, Italy, Spain, Portugal and Luxembourg. Within 2 years most German Catholic states, Belgium and parts of Switzerland and the Netherlands were brought under the new calendar, and Hungary followed in 1587. The rest of the Netherlands, along with Denmark and the German Protestant states made the change in 1699-1700 (German Protestants retained the old reckoning of Easter until 1776).

The British Government imposed the Gregorian calendar on all its possessions, including the American colonies, in 1752. The British decreed that the day following Sept. 2, 1752, should be called Sept. 14, a loss of 11 days. All dates preceding were marked O.S., for Old Style. In addition New Year's Day was moved to Jan. 1 from Mar. 25. (e.g., under the old reckoning, Mar. 24, 1700 had been followed by Mar. 25, 1701.) George Washington's birth date, which was Feb. 11, 1731, O.S., became Feb. 22, 1732, N.S. In 1753 Sweden too went Gregorian, retaining the old Easter rules until 1844.

In 1793 the French Revolutionary Government adopted a calendar of 12 months of 30 days each with 5 extra days in September of each common year and a 6th extra day every 4th year. Napoleon reinstated the Gregorian calendar in 1806.

The Gregorian system later spread to non-European regions, first in the European colonies, then in the independent countries, replacing various traditional calendars at least for official purposes. Japan in 1873, Egypt in 1875, China in 1912 and Turkey in 1917 made the change, usually in conjunction with political upheavals. In China, the republican government began reckoning years from its 1911 founding — e.g., 1948 was designated the year 37. After 1949, the Communists adopted the Common, or Christian Era year count, even for the traditional lunar calendar.

In 1918 the revolutionary government in Russia decreed that the day after Jan. 31, 1918, Old Style, would become Feb. 14, 1918, New Style. Greece followed in 1923. (In Russia the Orthodox Church has retained the Julian calendar, as have various Middle Eastern Christian sects.) For the first time in history, all major cultures have one calendar.

To change from the Julian to the Gregorian calendar, add 10 days to dates Oct. 5, 1582, through Feb. 28, 1700; after that date add 11 days through Feb. 28, 1800; 12 days through Feb. 28, 1900; and 13 days through Feb. 28, 2100.

A century consists of 100 consecutive calendar years. The 1st century consisted of the years 1 through 100. The 20th century consists of the years 1901 through 2000 and will end Dec. 31, 2000. The 21st century will begin Jan. 1, 2001.

Julian Calendar

To find which of the 14 calendars printed on pages 748-749 applies to any year, starting Jan. 1, under the Julian system, find the century for the desired year in the three left-hand columns below; read across. Then find the year in the four top rows; read down. The number in the intersection is the calendar designation for that year.

Year (last two figures of desired year)

		01 02 03 04	05 06 07 08	09 10 11 12	13 14 15 16	17 18 19 20	21 22 23 24	25 26 27 28
		29 30 31 32	33 34 35 36	37 38 39 40	41 42 43 44	45 46 47 48	49 50 51 52	53 54 55 56
		57 58 59 60	61 62 63 64	65 66 67 68	69 70 71 72	73 74 75 76	77 78 79 80	81 82 83 84
Century		00 85 86 87	88 89 90 91	92 93 94 95	96 97 98 99			
0	700 1400	12 7 1 2	10 5 6 7	8 3 4 5	13 1 2 3	11 6 7 1	9 4 5 6	14 2 3 4 12
100	800 1500	11 6 7 1	9 4 5 6	14 2 3 4	12 7 1 2	10 5 6 7	8 3 4 5	13 1 2 3 11
200	900 1600	10 5 6 7	8 3 4 5	13 1 2 3	11 6 7 1	9 4 5 6	14 2 3 4	12 7 1 2 10
300	1000 1700	9 4 5 6	14 2 3 4	12 7 1 2	10 5 6 7	8 3 4 5	13 1 2 3	11 6 7 1 9
400	1100 1800	8 3 4 5	13 1 2 3	11 6 7 1	9 4 5 6	14 2 3 4	12 7 1 2	10 5 6 7 8
500	1200 1900	14 2 3 4	12 7 1 2	10 5 6 7	8 3 4 5	13 1 2 3	11 6 7 1	9 4 5 6 14
600	1300 2000	13 1 2 3	11 6 7 1	9 4 5 6	14 2 3 4	12 7 1 2	10 5 6 7	8 3 4 5 13

Gregorian Calendar

Pick desired year from table below or on page 748 (for years 1800 to 2059). The number shown with each year shows which calendar to use for that year, as shown on pages 748-749 (The Gregorian calendar was inaugurated Oct. 15, 1582. From that date to Dec. 31, 1582, use calendar 6.)

1583-1802

1583 . . 7	1603 . . 4	1623 . . 1	1643 . . 5	1663 . . 2	1683 . . 6	1703 . . 2	1723 . . 6	1743 . . 3	1763 . . 7	1783 . . 4
1584 . . 8	1604 . 12	1624 . . 9	1644 . 13	1664 . 10	1684 . 14	1704 . 10	1724 . 14	1744 . 11	1764 . . 8	1784 . 12
1585 . . 3	1605 . . 7	1625 . . 4	1645 . . 1	1665 . . 5	1685 . . 2	1705 . . 5	1725 . . 2	1745 . . 6	1765 . . 3	1785 . . 7
1586 . . 4	1606 . . 1	1626 . . 5	1646 . . 2	1666 . . 6	1686 . . 3	1706 . . 6	1726 . . 3	1746 . . 7	1766 . . 4	1786 . . 1
1587 . . 5	1607 . . 2	1627 . . 6	1647 . . 3	1667 . . 7	1687 . . 4	1707 . . 7	1727 . . 4	1747 . . 1	1767 . . 5	1787 . . 2
1588 . 13	1608 . 10	1628 . 14	1648 . 11	1668 . . 8	1688 . 12	1708 . . 8	1728 . 12	1748 . . 9	1768 . 13	1788 . 10
1589 . . 1	1609 . . 5	1629 . . 2	1649 . . 6	1669 . . 3	1689 . . 7	1709 . . 3	1729 . . 7	1749 . . 4	1769 . . 1	1789 . . 5
1590 . . 2	1610 . . 6	1630 . . 3	1650 . . 7	1670 . . 4	1690 . . 1	1710 . . 4	1730 . . 1	1750 . . 5	1770 . . 2	1790 . . 6
1591 . . 3	1611 . . 7	1631 . . 4	1651 . . 1	1671 . . 5	1691 . . 2	1711 . . 5	1731 . . 2	1751 . . 6	1771 . . 3	1791 . . 7
1592 . 11	1612 . . 8	1632 . 12	1652 . . 9	1672 . 13	1692 . 10	1712 . 13	1732 . 10	1752 . 14	1772 . 11	1792 . . 8
1593 . . 6	1613 . . 3	1633 . . 7	1653 . . 4	1673 . . 1	1693 . . 5	1713 . . 1	1733 . . 5	1753 . . 2	1773 . . 6	1793 . . 3
1594 . . 7	1614 . . 4	1634 . . 1	1654 . . 5	1674 . . 2	1694 . . 6	1714 . . 2	1734 . . 6	1754 . . 3	1774 . . 7	1794 . . 4
1595 . . 1	1615 . . 5	1635 . . 2	1655 . . 6	1675 . . 3	1695 . . 7	1715 . . 3	1735 . . 7	1755 . . 4	1775 . . 1	1795 . . 5
1596 . . 9	1616 . 13	1636 . 10	1656 . 14	1676 . 11	1696 . . 8	1716 . 11	1736 . . 8	1756 . 12	1776 . . 9	1796 . 13
1597 . . 4	1617 . . 1	1637 . . 5	1657 . . 2	1677 . . 6	1697 . . 3	1717 . . 6	1737 . . 3	1757 . . 7	1777 . . 4	1797 . . 1
1598 . . 5	1618 . . 2	1638 . . 6	1658 . . 3	1678 . . 7	1698 . . 4	1718 . . 7	1738 . . 4	1758 . . 1	1778 . . 5	1798 . . 2
1599 . . 6	1619 . . 3	1639 . . 7	1659 . . 4	1679 . . 1	1699 . . 5	1719 . . 1	1739 . . 5	1759 . . 2	1779 . . 6	1799 . . 3
1600 . 14	1620 . 11	1640 . . 8	1660 . 12	1680 . . 9	1700 . . 6	1720 . . 9	1740 . 13	1760 . 10	1780 . 14	1800 . . 4
1601 . . 2	1621 . . 6	1641 . . 3	1661 . . 7	1681 . . 4	1701 . . 7	1721 . . 4	1741 . . 1	1761 . . 5	1781 . . 2	1801 . . 5
1602 . . 3	1622 . . 7	1642 . . 4	1662 . . 1	1682 . . 5	1702 . . 1	1722 . . 5	1742 . . 2	1762 . . 3	1782 . . 3	1802 . . 6

The Julian Period

How many days have you lived? To determine this, you must multiply your age by 365, add the number of days since your last birthday until today, and account for all leap years. Chances are your answer would be wrong. Astronomers, however, find it convenient to express dates and long time intervals in days rather than in years, months and days. This is done by placing events within the Julian period.

The Julian period was devised in 1582 by Joseph Scaliger and named after his father Julius (not after the Julian calendar). Scaliger had Julian Day (JD) #1 begin at noon, Jan. 1, 4713 B. C., the most recent time that three major chronological cycles began on the same day — 1) the 28-year solar cycle, after which dates in the Julian calendar (e.g., Feb. 11)

return to the same days of the week (e.g., Monday); 2) the 19-year lunar cycle, after which the phases of the moon return to the same dates of the year; and 3) the 15-year indiction cycle, used in ancient Rome to regulate taxes. It will take 7980 years to complete the period, the product of 28, 19, and 15.

Noon of Dec. 31, 1985, marks the beginning of JD 2,446,430; that many days will have passed since the start of the Julian period. The JD at noon of any date in 1984 may be found by adding to this figure the day of the year for that date, which is given in the left hand column in the chart below. Simple JD conversion tables are used by astronomers.

Days Between Two Dates

Table covers period of two ordinary years. Example—Days between Feb. 10, 1985 and Dec. 15, 1986; subtract 41 from 714; answer is 673 days. For leap year, such as 1984, one day must be added: final answer is 674.

Date	Jan.	Feb.	Mar.	April	May	June	July	Aug.	Sept.	Oct.	Nov.	Dec.	Date	Jan.	Feb.	Mar.	April	May	June	July	Aug.	Sept.	Oct.	Nov.	Dec.
1	1	32	60	91	121	152	182	213	244	274	305	335	1	366	397	425	456	486	517	547	578	609	639	670	700
2	2	33	61	92	122	153	183	214	245	275	306	336	2	367	398	426	457	487	518	548	579	610	640	671	701
3	3	34	62	93	123	154	184	215	246	276	307	337	3	368	399	427	458	488	519	549	580	611	641	672	702
4	4	35	63	94	124	155	185	216	247	277	308	338	4	369	400	428	459	489	520	550	581	612	642	673	703
5	5	36	64	95	125	156	186	217	248	278	309	339	5	370	401	429	460	490	521	551	582	613	643	674	704
6	6	37	65	96	126	157	187	218	249	279	310	340	6	371	402	430	461	491	522	552	583	614	644	675	705
7	7	38	66	97	127	158	188	219	250	280	311	341	7	372	403	431	462	492	523	553	584	615	645	676	706
8	8	39	67	98	128	159	189	220	251	281	312	342	8	373	404	432	463	493	524	554	585	616	646	677	707
9	9	40	68	99	129	160	190	221	252	282	313	343	9	374	405	433	464	494	525	555	586	617	647	678	708
10	10	41	69	100	130	161	191	222	253	283	314	344	10	375	406	434	465	495	526	556	587	618	648	679	709
11	11	42	70	101	131	162	192	223	254	284	315	345	11	376	407	435	466	496	527	557	588	619	649	680	710
12	12	43	71	102	132	163	193	224	255	285	316	346	12	377	408	436	467	497	528	558	589	620	650	681	711
13	13	44	72	103	133	164	194	225	256	286	317	347	13	378	409	437	468	498	529	559	590	621	651	682	712
14	14	45	73	104	134	165	195	226	257	287	318	348	14	379	410	438	469	499	530	560	591	622	652	683	713
15	15	46	74	105	135	166	196	227	258	288	319	349	15	380	411	439	470	500	531	561	592	623	653	684	714
16	16	47	75	106	136	167	197	228	259	289	320	350	16	381	412	440	471	501	532	562	593	624	654	685	715
17	17	48	76	107	137	168	198	229	260	290	321	351	17	382	413	441	472	502	533	563	594	625	655	686	716
18	18	49	77	108	138	169	199	230	261	291	322	352	18	383	414	442	473	503	534	564	595	626	656	687	717
19	19	50	78	109	139	170	200	231	262	292	323	353	19	384	415	443	474	504	535	565	596	627	657	688	718
20	20	51	79	110	140	171	201	232	263	293	324	354	20	385	416	444	475	505	536	566	597	628	658	689	719
21	21	52	80	111	141	172	202	233	264	294	325	355	21	386	417	445	476	506	537	567	598	629	659	690	720
22	22	53	81	112	142	173	203	234	265	295	326	356	22	387	418	446	477	507	538	568	599	630	660	691	721
23	23	54	82	113	143	174	204	235	266	296	327	357	23	388	419	447	478	508	539	569	600	631	661	692	722
24	24	55	83	114	144	175	205	236	267	297	328	358	24	389	420	448	479	509	540	570	601	632	662	693	723
25	25	56	84	115	145	176	206	237	268	298	329	359	25	390	421	449	480	510	541	571	602	633	663	694	724
26	26	57	85	116	146	177	207	238	269	299	330	360	26	391	422	450	481	511	542	572	603	634	664	695	725
27	27	58	86	117	147	178	208	239	270	300	331	361	27	392	423	451	482	512	543	573	604	635	665	696	726
28	28	59	87	118	148	179	209	240	271	301	332	362	28	393	424	452	483	513	544	574	605	636	666	697	727
29	29	—	88	119	149	180	210	241	272	302	333	363	29	394	—	453	484	514	545	575	606	637	667	698	728
30	30	—	89	120	150	181	211	242	273	303	334	364	30	395	—	454	485	515	546	576	607	638	668	699	729
31	31	—	90	—	151	—	212	243	—	304	—	365	31	396	—	455	—	516	—	577	608	—	669	—	730

Lunar Calendar, Chinese New Year, Vietnamese Tet

The ancient Chinese lunar calendar is divided into 12 months of either 29 or 30 days (compensating for the fact that the mean duration of the lunar month is 29 days, 12 hours, 44.05 minutes). The calendar is synchronized with the solar year by the addition of extra months at fixed intervals.

The Chinese calendar runs on a sexagenary cycle, i.e., 60 years. The cycles 1876-1935 and 1936-1995, with the years grouped under their twelve animal designations, are printed below. The Year 1986 is found in the third column, under Tiger, and is known as a "Year of the Tiger." Readers can find the animal name for the year of their birth, marriage, etc., in the same chart. (Note: the first 3-7 weeks of each of the western years belong to the previous Chinese year and animal designation.)

Both the western (Gregorian) and traditional lunar calendars are used publicly in China, and two New Year's celebrations are held. On Taiwan, in overseas Chinese communities, and in Vietnam, the lunar calendar has been used only to set the dates for traditional festivals, with the Gregorian system in general use.

The four-day Chinese New Year, Hsin Nien, and the three-day Vietnamese New Year festival, Tet, begin at the first new moon after the sun enters Aquarius. The day may fall, therefore, between Jan. 21 and Feb. 19 of the Gregorian calendar. Feb. 9, 1986 marks the start of the new Chinese year. The date is fixed according to the date of the new moon in the Far East. Since this is west of the International Date Line the date may be one day later than that of the new moon in the United States.

Rat	Ox	Tiger	Hare (Rabbit)	Dragon	Snake	Horse	Sheep (Goat)	Monkey	Rooster	Dog	Pig
1876	1877	1878	1879	1880	1881	1882	1883	1884	1885	1886	1887
1888	1889	1890	1891	1892	1893	1894	1895	1896	1897	1898	1899
1900	1901	1902	1903	1904	1905	1906	1907	1908	1909	1910	1911
1912	1913	1914	1915	1916	1917	1918	1919	1920	1921	1922	1923
1924	1925	1926	1927	1928	1929	1930	1931	1932	1933	1934	1935
1936	1937	1938	1939	1940	1941	1942	1943	1944	1945	1946	1947
1948	1949	1950	1951	1952	1953	1954	1955	1956	1957	1958	1959
1960	1961	1962	1963	1964	1965	1966	1967	1968	1969	1970	1971
1972	1973	1974	1975	1976	1977	1978	1979	1980	1981	1982	1983
1984	1985	1986	1987	1988	1989	1990	1991	1992	1993	1994	1995

Chronological Eras, 1986

The year 1986 of the Christian Era comprises the latter part of the 210th and the beginning of the 211th year of the independence of the United States of America.

Era	Year	Begins in 1986	Era	Year	Begins in 1986
Byzantine	7495	Sept. 14	Grecian	2298	Sept. 14
Jewish	5747	Oct. 3 (sunset)	(Seleucidae)		or Oct. 14
			Diocletian	1703	Sept. 11
Roman (Ab Urbe Condita)	2739	Jan. 14	Indian (Saka)	1908	Mar. 22
Nabonassar (Babylonian)	2735	Apr. 27	Mohammedan (Hegira)	1407	Sept. 5
Japanese	2646	Jan. 1			

Chronological Cycles, 1986

Dominical Letter .... E	Golden Number (Lunar Cycle) XI	Roman Indiction 9
Epact 19	Solar Cycle 7	Julian Period (year of) 6699

Standard Time Differences — North American Cities

At 12 o'clock noon, Eastern Standard Time, the standard time in N.A. cities is as follows:

Akron, Oh.	12.00	Noon	Frankfort, Ky.	12.00	Noon	Pierre, S.D.	11.00	A.M.
Albuquerque, N.M.	10.00	A.M.	Galveston, Tex.	11.00	A.M.	Pittsburgh, Pa.	12.00	Noon
Atlanta, Ga.	12.00	Noon	Grand Rapids, Mich.	12.00	Noon	Portland, Me.	12.00	Noon
Austin, Tex.	11.00	A.M.	Halifax, N.S.	1.00	P.M.	Portland, Ore.	9.00	A.M.
Baltimore, Md.	12.00	Noon	Hartford, Conn.	12.00	Noon	Providence, R.I.	12.00	Noon
Birmingham, Ala.	11.00	A.M.	Helena, Mon.	10.00	A.M.	*Regina, Sask.	11.00	A.M.
Bismarck, N.D.	11.00	A.M.	*Honolulu, Ha.	7.00	A.M.	Reno, Nev.	9.00	A.M.
Boise, Ida.	10.00	A.M.	Houston, Tex.	11.00	A.M.	Richmond, Va.	12.00	Noon
Boston, Mass.	12.00	Noon	*Indianapolis, Ind.	12.00	Noon	Rochester, N.Y.	12.00	Noon
Buffalo, N.Y.	12.00	Noon	Jacksonville, Fla.	12.00	Noon	Sacramento, Cal.	9.00	A.M.
Butte, Mon.	10.00	A.M.	Juneau, Alas.	8.00	A.M.	St. John's, Nfld.	1.30	P.M.
Calgary, Alta.	10.00	A.M.	Kansas City, Mo.	11.00	A.M.	St. Louis, Mo.	11.00	A.M.
Charleston, S.C.	12.00	Noon	Knoxville, Tenn.	12.00	Noon	St. Paul, Minn.	11.00	A.M.
Charleston, W.Va.	12.00	Noon	Lexington, Ky.	12.00	Noon	Salt Lake City, Ut.	10.00	A.M.
Charlotte, N.C.	12.00	Noon	Lincoln, Neb.	11.00	A.M.	San Antonio, Tex.	11.00	A.M.
Charlottetown, P.E.I.	1.00	P.M.	Little Rock, Ark.	11.00	A.M.	San Diego, Cal.	9.00	A.M.
Chattanooga, Tenn.	12.00	Noon	Los Angeles, Cal.	9.00	A.M.	San Francisco, Cal.	9.00	A.M.
Cheyenne, Wy.	10.00	A.M.	Louisville, Ky.	12.00	Noon	Santa Fe, N.M.	10.00	A.M.
Chicago, Ill.	11.00	A.M.	*Mexico City	11.00	A.M.	Savannah, Ga.	12.00	Noon
Cleveland, Oh.	12.00	Noon	Memphis, Tenn.	11.00	A.M.	Seattle, Wash.	9.00	A.M.
Colorado Spr., Col.	10.00	A.M.	Miami, Fla.	12.00	Noon	Shreveport, La.	11.00	A.M.
Columbus, Oh.	12.00	Noon	Milwaukee, Wis.	11.00	A.M.	Sioux Falls, S.D.	11.00	A.M.
Dallas, Tex.	11.00	A.M.	Minneapolis, Minn.	11.00	A.M.	Spokane, Wash.	9.00	A.M.
*Dawson, Yuk.	9.00	A.M.	Mobile, Ala.	11.00	A.M.	Tampa, Fla.	12.00	Noon
Dayton, Oh.	12.00	Noon	Montreal, Que.	12.00	Noon	Toledo, Oh.	12.00	Noon
Denver, Col.	10.00	A.M.	Nashville, Tenn.	11.00	A.M.	Topeka, Kan.	11.00	A.M.
Des Moines, Ia.	11.00	A.M.	New Haven, Conn.	12.00	Noon	Toronto, Ont.	12.00	Noon
Detroit, Mich.	12.00	Noon	New Orleans, La.	11.00	A.M.	*Tucson, Ariz.	10.00	A.M.
Duluth, Minn.	11.00	A.M.	New York, N.Y.	12.00	Noon	Tulsa, Okla.	11.00	A.M.
El Paso, Tex.	10.00	A.M.	Nome, Alas.	8.00	A.M.	Vancouver, B.C.	9.00	A.M.
Erie, Pa.	12.00	Noon	Norfolk, Va.	12.00	Noon	Washington, D.C.	12.00	Noon
Evansville, Ind.	11.00	A.M.	Okla. City, Okla.	11.00	A.M.	Wichita, Kan.	11.00	A.M.
Fairbanks, Alas.	8.00	A.M.	Omaha, Neb.	11.00	A.M.	Wilmington, Del.	12.00	Noon
Flint, Mich.	12.00	Noon	Peoria, Ill.	11.00	A.M.	Winnipeg, Man.	11.00	A.M.
*Fort Wayne, Ind.	12.00	Noon	Philadelphia, Pa.	12.00	Noon			
Fort Worth, Tex.	11.00	A.M.	*Phoenix, Ariz.	10.00	A.M.			

*Cities with an asterisk do not observe daylight savings time. During much of the year, it is necessary to add one hour to the cities which do observe daylight savings time to get the proper time relation.

Standard Time Differences—World Cities

The time indicated in the table is fixed by law and is called the legal time, or, more generally, Standard Time. Use of Daylight Saving Time varies widely. *Indicates morning of the following day. At 12:00 noon, Eastern Standard Time, the standard time (in 24-hour time) in foreign cities is as follows:

Addis Ababa	20 00	Caracas	13 00	Lima	12 00	Rome	18 00
Alexandria	19 00	Casablanca	17 00	Lisbon	18 00	Santiago (Chile)	13 00
Amsterdam	18 00	Copenhagen	18 00	Liverpool	17 00	Seoul	2 00*
Athens	19 00	Dacca	23 00	London	17 00	Shanghai	1 00*
Auckland	5 00*	Delhi	22 30	Madrid	18 00	Singapore	00 30*
Baghdad	20 00	Dublin	17 00	Manila	1 00*	Stockholm	18 00
Bangkok	0 00	Gdansk	18 00	Mecca	20 00	Sydney (Australia)	3 00*
Belfast	17 00	Geneva	18 00	Melbourne	3 00*	Tashkent	23 00
Berlin	18 00	Havana	12 00	Mexico City	11 00	Teheran	20 30
Bogota	12 00	Helsinki	19 00	Montevideo	14 00	Tel Aviv	19 00
Bombay	22 30	Ho Chi Minh City	1 00*	Moscow	20 00	Tokyo	2 00*
Bremen	18 00	Hong Kong	1 00*	Nagasaki	2 00*	Valparaiso	13 00
Brussels	18 00	Istanbul	19 00	Oslo	18 00	Vladivostok	3 00*
Bucharest	19 00	Jakarta	0 00	Paris	18 00	Vienna	18 00
Budapest	18 00	Jerusalem	19 00	Peking	1 00*	Warsaw	18 00
Buenos Aires	14 00	Johannesburg	19 00	Prague	18 00	Wellington (N.Z.)	5 00*
Cairo	19 00	Karachi	22 00	Rangoon	23 30	Yokohama	2 00*
Calcutta	22 30	Le Havre	18 00	Rio De Janeiro	14 00	Zurich	18 00
Cape Town	19 00	Leningrad	20 00				

Standard Time, Daylight Saving Time, and Others

Source: Defense Mapping Agency Hydrographic Center; Department of Transportation; National Bureau of Standards; U.S. Naval Observatory

Standard Time

Standard time is reckoned from Greenwich, England, recognized as the Prime Meridian of Longitude. The world is divided into 24 zones, each 15° of arc, or one hour in time apart. The Greenwich meridian (0°) extends through the center of the initial zone, and the zones to the east are numbered from 1 to 12 with the prefix "minus" indicating the number of hours to be subtracted to obtain Greenwich Time.

Westward zones are similarly numbered, but prefixed "plus" showing the number of hours that must be added to get Greenwich Time. While these zones apply generally to sea areas, it should be noted that the Standard Time maintained in many countries does not coincide with zone time. A graphical representation of the zones is shown on the Standard Time Zone Chart of the World published by the Defense Mapping Agency Hydrographic Center, Washington, DC 20390.

The United States and possessions are divided into eight Standard Time zones, as set forth by the Uniform Time Act of 1966, which also provides for the use of Daylight Saving Time therein. Each zone is approximately 15° of longitude in width. All places in each zone use, instead of their own local time, the time counted from the transit of the "mean sun" across the Standard Time meridian which passes near the middle of that zone.

These time zones are designated as Atlantic, Eastern, Central, Mountain, Pacific, Yukon, Alaska-Hawaii, and Bering, and the time in these zones is basically reckoned from the 60th, 75th, 90th, 105th, 120th, 135th, 150th, 165th meridians west of Greenwich. The line wanders to conform to local geographical regions. The time in the various zones is earlier than Greenwich Time by 4, 5, 6, 7, 8, 9, 10, and 11 hours respectively.

24-Hour Time

24-hour time is widely used in scientific work throughout the world. In the United States it is used also in operations of the Armed Forces. In Europe it is used in preference to the 12-hour a.m. and p.m. system. With the 24-hour system the day begins at midnight and hours are numbered 0 through 23.

International Date Line

The Date Line is a zig-zag line that approximately coincides with the 180th meridian, and it is where each calendar day begins. The date must be advanced one day when crossing in a westerly direction and set back one day when crossing in an easterly direction.

The line is deflected between north latitude 48° and 75°, so that all Asia lies to the west of it.

Daylight Saving Time

Daylight Saving Time is achieved by advancing the clock one hour. Under the Uniform Time Act, which became effective in 1967, all states, the District of Columbia, and U.S. possessions were to observe Daylight Saving Time beginning at 2 a.m. on the last Sunday in April and ending at 2 a.m. on the last Sunday in October. Any state could, by law, exempt itself; a 1972 amendment to the act authorized states split by time zones to take that into consideration in exempting themselves. Arizona, Hawaii, Puerto Rico, the Virgin Islands, American Samoa, and part of Indiana are now exempt. Some local zone boundaries in Kansas, Texas, Florida, Michigan, and Alaska have been modified in the last several years by the Dept. of Transportation, which oversees the act. To conserve energy Congress put most of the nation on year-round Daylight Saving Time for two years effective Jan. 6, 1974 through Oct. 26, 1975; but a further bill, signed in October, 1974, restored Standard Time from the last Sunday in that month to the last Sunday in February, 1975. At the end of 1975, Congress failed to renew this temporary legislation and the nation returned to the older end-of April to end-of October DST system.

Legal or Public Holidays, 1986

Technically there are no national holidays in the United States; each state has jurisdiction over its holidays, which are designated by legislative enactment or executive proclamation. In practice, however, most states observe the federal legal public holidays, even though the President and Congress can legally designate holidays only for the District of Columbia and for federal employees.

Federal legal public holidays are New Year's Day, Washington's Birthday, Memorial Day, Independence Day, Labor Day, Columbus Day, Veterans' Day, Thanksgiving, and Christmas.

Chief Legal or Public Holidays

When a holiday falls on a Sunday or a Saturday it is usually observed on the following Monday or preceding Friday. For some holidays, government and business closing practices vary. In most states, the office of the Secretary of State can provide details of holiday closings. In most states, the following will be legal or public holidays in 1986:

Jan. 1 (Wednesday) — New Year's Day.

Feb. 12 (Wednesday) — Lincoln's Birthday.

Feb. 17 (3d Mon. in Feb.) — Washington's Birthday, or Presidents' Day, or Washington-Lincoln Day.

May 26 (last Mon. in May) — Memorial Day, or Decoration Day.

July 4 (Friday) — Independence Day.

Sept. 1 (1st Mon. in Sept.) — Labor Day.

Oct. 13 (2d Mon. in Oct.) — Columbus Day, or Discoverers' Day, or Pioneers' Day.

Nov. 11 (Tuesday) — Veterans' Day.

Nov. 27 (4th Thurs. in Nov.) — Thanksgiving Day.

Dec. 25 (Thursday) — Christmas Day.

In some states, the following will be legal or public holidays in 1986:

Jan. 15 (Wednesday) — Martin Luther King Day. In some states, combined with Robert E. Lee Day and/or observed on the 3rd Mon. in Jan.

Mar. 28 (Friday) — Good Friday. In some states, observed for half or part of day.

Nov. 4 (1st Tues. after the 1st Mon. in Nov.) — Election Day.

Other Legal or Public Holidays

Dates are for 1986 observance, when known.

Jan. 12 — Volunteer Fireman Day (2d Sunday in Jan.). In New Jersey.

Jan. 19 — Confederate Heroes' Day. In various southern states.

Jan. 20 — Robert E. Lee's Birthday (3d Monday in Jan). In several southern states.

Jan. 30 — Franklin D. Roosevelt Day. In Kentucky.

Feb. 11 — Mardi Gras Day. In Alabama and Louisiana.

Feb. 14 — Admission Day. In Arizona.

Mar. 2 — Texas Independence Day. In that state.

Mar. 4 — Town Meeting Day (1st Tuesday in Mar.). In Vermont.

Mar. 26 — Prince Jonah Kuhio Kalanianaole Day. In Hawaii.

Mar. 31 — Seward's Day (last Sunday in Mar.). In Alaska.

Apr. 2 — Florida Day. In that state.

Apr. 14 — Thomas Jefferson's Birthday. In Alabama.

Apr. 21 — Patriot's Day. (3d Monday in Apr.). In Maine and Massachusetts.

Apr. 21 — San Jacinto Day. In Texas.

Apr. 28 — Fast Day (4th Monday in Apr.). In New Hampshire.

May 4 — Independence Day. In Rhode Island.

May 8 — Harry Truman's Birthday. In Missouri.

May 10 — Confederate Memorial Day. In North Carolina.

May 25 — Grandparents' Day (last Sunday in May). In New Jersey.

June 3 — Jefferson Davis' Birthday. In Florida, Georgia, and Louisiana. In Alabama and Mississippi, observed on the 1st Monday in June (June 2 in 1986).

June 11 — King Kamehameha I Day. In Hawaii.

June 14 — Flag Day. In New York, observed on the 2d Sunday in June (June 8 in 1986).

June 17 — Bunker Hill Day. In Boston and Suffolk County, Massachusetts.

June 19 — Emancipation Day. In Texas.

June 20 — West Virginia Day. In that state.

July 24 — Pioneer Day. In Utah.

Aug. 4 — Colorado Day (1st Monday in August). In that state.

Aug. 11 — Victory Day (2d Monday in August). In Arkansas.

Aug. 15 — Admission Day (3d Friday in August). In Hawaii.

Sept. 9 — California Admission Day. In that state.

Sept. 12 — Defenders' Day. In Maryland.

Oct 13 — Pioneer Day (2d Monday in October). In South Dakota.

Oct. 17 — Alaska Day (3d Monday in Oct.) In that state.

Oct. 31 — Nevada Day. In that state.

Nov. 6 — Return Day. In Sussex County, Delaware.

Days Usually Observed

American Family Day (Aug. 3 in 1986). Observed first Sunday in Aug. in Arizona.

Arbor Day. Tree-planting day. First observed April 10, 1872, in Nebraska. Now observed in most states, usually on the last Friday in Apr. (Apr. 25 in 1986).

Armed Forces Day (May 17 in 1986). Always third Saturday of May, by presidential proclamation. Replaced Army, Navy, and Air Force Days.

Bill of Rights Day, Dec. 15. By Act of Congress. Bill of Rights took effect Dec. 15, 1791.

Bird Day. Often observed with Arbor Day.

Child Health Day (Oct. 6 in 1986). Always first Monday in Oct., by presidential proclamation.

Citizenship Day, Sept. 17. President Truman, Feb. 29, 1952, signed bill designating Sept. 17 as annual Citizenship Day. It replaced I Am An American Day, formerly 3d Sunday in May, and Constitution Day, formerly Sept. 17.

Easter Sunday (Mar. 30 in 1986).

Easter Monday (Mar. 31 in 1986). A statutory day in Canada.

Elizabeth Cady Stanton Day, Nov. 12. Birthday of pioneer leader for equal rights for women.

Father's Day (June 15 in 1986). Always third Sunday in June.

Forefathers' Day, Dec. 21. Landing on Plymouth Rock, in 1620. Is celebrated with dinners by New England societies, especially "Down East."

Gen. Pulaski Memorial Day, Oct. 11. Native of Poland and Revolutionary War hero; died (Oct. 11, 1779) from wounds received at the siege of Savannah, Ga.

Georgia Day, Feb. 12. Observed in that state. Commemorates landing of first colonists in 1733.

Grandparents' Day (Sept. 7 in 1986). Always first Sunday after Labor Day. Legislated in 1979.

Groundhog Day, Feb. 2. A popular belief is that if the groundhog sees his shadow on this day, he returns to his burrow and winter continues 6 weeks longer.

Halloween, Oct. 31. The evening before All Saints or All-Hallows Day. Informally observed in the U.S. with masquerading and pumpkin decorating. Traditionally an occasion for children to play pranks.

Loyalty Day, May 1. By Act of Congress.

May Day. Name popularly given to May 1st. Celebrated as Labor Day in most of the world, and by some groups in the U.S. Observed in many schools as a Spring Festival.

Mother's Day (May 11 in 1986). Always second Sunday in that month. First celebrated in Philadelphia in 1908, Mother's Day has become an international holiday.

National Day of Prayer. By presidential proclamation each year on a day other than a Sunday.

National Freedom Day, Feb. 1. To commemorate the signing of the Thirteenth Amendment, abolishing slavery, Feb. 1, 1865. By presidential proclamation.

National Maritime Day, May 22. First proclaimed 1935 in commemoration of the departure of the SS Savannah, from Savannah, Georgia, on May 22, 1819, on the first successful transatlantic voyage under steam propulsion. By presidential proclamation.

Pan American Day, Apr. 14. In 1890 the First Intl. Conference of American States, meeting in Washington, was held on that date. A resolution was adopted which resulted in the creation of the organization known today as the Pan American Union. By presidential proclamation.

Primary Election Day. Observed usually only when presidential or general elections are held.

Reformation Day, Oct. 31. Observed by Protestant groups.

Sadie Hawkins Day (Nov. 15 in 1986). First Saturday after November 11.

St. Patrick's Day, Mar. 17. Observed by Irish societies, especially with parades.

St. Valentine's Day, Feb. 14. Festival of a martyr beheaded at Rome under Emperor Claudius. Association of this day with lovers has no connection with the saint and probably had its origin in an old belief that on this day birds begin to choose their mates.

Susan B. Anthony Day, Feb. 15. Birthday of a pioneer crusader for equal rights for women.

United Nations Day, Oct. 24. By presidential proclamation, to commemorate founding of United Nations.

Verrazano Day, Apr. 7. Observed by New York State, to commemorate the probable discovery of New York harbor by Giovanni da Verrazano in April, 1524.

Victoria Day (May 18 in 1986). Birthday of Queen Victoria, a statutory day in Canada, celebrated the first Monday before May 25.

World Poetry Day, Oct. 15.

Wright Brothers Day, Dec. 17. By presidential designation, to commemorate first successful flight by Orville and Wilbur Wright, Dec. 17, 1903.

Other Holidays, Anniversaries — 1986

Jan. 1, 1935	— Orange Bowl, Sugar Bowl held for first time.
Feb. 1, 1960	— U.S. blacks start to "sit-in" to desegregate Greensboro, N.C. lunch counters.
Feb. 11 (Tues.)	— National Inventors' Day; birthday of Thomas Edison.
Feb. 13, 1960	— France explodes her first atomic bomb, joining "atomic club" of U.S., USSR, Britain.
Feb. 12	— Ash Wednesday.
Mar. 11 (Tues.)	— Johnny Appleseed Day.
Mar. 12 (Wed.)	— Girl Scout Day.
Apr. 1 (Tues.)	— April Fool's Day.
Apr. 13 (Sun.)	— Birthday of Thomas Jefferson.
Apr. 24 (Thurs.)	— Passover begins.
May 6, 1935	— Works Progress Administration (WPA) created by FDR.
May 14, 1935	— First major league night baseball game played.
May 30, 1910	— First Indianapolis 500 car race.
June 24 (Tues.)	— San Juan Day in Puerto Rico; St. Jean Day in Quebec.
July 1 (Tues.)	— Canada Day.
July 5, 1935	— Congress passes Wagner-Connery Act, creating Natl. Labor Relations Bd., reasserting right of collective bargaining.
Aug. 1, 1960	— Echo I, world's first communications satellite, launched by U.S.
Aug. 12 (Tues.)	— Ponce De Leon Day in Puerto Rico.
Aug. 14, 1935	— Social Security Act passed by Congress.
Sept. 8, 1910	— N.Y.'s Penn Station opens to trains.
Sept. 14, 1960	— OPEC meets for first time, with 5 charter members—Saudi Arabia, Iran, Iraq, Kuwait, Qatar.
Oct. 4 (Sat.)	— Rosh Hashanah.
Oct. 13 (Mon.)	— Yom Kippur.
Nov. 8, 1960	— Mass. sen. John F. Kennedy, 43, defeats vice president Richard M. Nixon to become youngest man and first Roman Catholic elected U.S. president.
Dec. 27 (Sat.)	— Channukah.
Dec. 14, 1910	— 5 Norwegians and 17 huskies, headed by Roald Amundsen, are first to reach South Pole.

Wind Chill Table

Source: National Weather Service, NOAA, U.S. Commerce Department

Both temperature and wind cause heat loss from body surfaces. A combination of cold and wind makes a body feel colder than the actual temperature. The table shows, for example, that a temperature of 20 degrees Fahrenheit, plus a wind of 20 miles per hour, causes a body heat loss equal to that in minus 10 degrees with no wind. In other words, the wind makes 20 degrees feel like minus 10.

Top line of figures shows actual temperatures in degrees Fahrenheit. Column at left shows wind speeds.

MPH	35	30	25	20	15	10	5	0	−5	−10	−15	−20	−25	−30	−35	−40	−45
5	33	27	21	16	12	7	0	−5	−10	−15	−21	−26	−31	−36	−42	−47	−52
10	22	16	10	3	−3	−9	−15	−22	−27	−34	−40	−46	−52	−58	−64	−71	−77
15	16	9	2	−5	−11	−18	−25	−31	−38	−45	−51	−58	−65	−72	−78	−85	−92
20	12	4	−3	−10	−17	−24	−31	−39	−46	−53	−60	−67	−74	−81	−88	−95	−103
25	8	1	−7	−15	−22	−29	−36	−44	−51	−59	−66	−74	−81	−88	−96	−103	−110
30	6	−2	−10	−18	−25	−33	−41	−49	−56	−64	−71	−79	−86	−93	−101	−109	−116
35	4	−4	−12	−20	−27	−35	−43	−52	−58	−67	−74	−82	−89	−97	−105	−113	−120
40	3	−5	−13	−21	−29	−37	−45	−53	−60	−69	−76	−84	−92	−100	−107	−115	−123
45	2	−6	−14	−22	−30	−38	−46	−54	−62	−70	−78	−85	−93	−102	−109	−117	−125

(Wind speeds greater than 45 mph have little additional chilling effect.)

Heat Index

The index is a measure of the contribution that high humidity makes with abnormally high temperatures in reducing the body's ability to cool itself. For example, the index shows that for an actual air temperature of 100 degrees Fahrenheit and a relative humidity of 50 percent, the effect on the human body would be same as 120 degrees. Sunstroke and heat exhaustion are likely when the heat index reaches 105. This index is a measure of what hot weather "feels like" to the average person for various temperatures and relative humidities.

Relative Humidity	Air Temperature*										
	70	75	80	85	90	95	100	105	110	115	120
	Apparent Temperature*										
0%	64	69	73	78	83	87	91	95	99	103	107
10%	65	70	75	80	85	90	95	100	105	111	116
20%	66	72	77	82	87	93	99	105	112	120	130
30%	67	73	78	84	90	96	104	113	123	135	148
40%	68	74	79	86	93	101	110	123	137	151	
50%	69	75	81	88	96	107	120	135	150		
60%	70	76	82	90	100	114	132	149			
70%	70	77	85	93	106	124	144				
80%	71	78	86	97	113	136					
90%	71	79	88	102	122						
100%	72	80	91	108							

*Degrees Fahrenheit.

Tides and Their Causes

Source: NOAA, U.S. Department of Commerce

The tides are a natural phenomenon involving the alternating rise and fall in the large fluid bodies of the earth caused by the combined gravitational attraction of the sun and moon. The combination of these two variable force influences produce the complex recurrent cycle of the tides. Tides may occur in both oceans and seas, to a limited extent in large lakes, the atmosphere, and, to a very minute degree, in the earth itself. The period between succeeding tides varies as the result of many factors and force influences.

The tide-generating force represents the difference between (1) the centrifugal force produced by the revolution of the earth around the common center-of-gravity of the earth-moon system and (2) the gravitational attraction of the moon acting upon the earth's overlying waters. Since, on the average, the moon is only 238,852 miles from the earth compared with the sun's much greater distance of 92,956,000 miles, this closer distance outranks the much smaller mass of the moon compared with that of the sun, and the moon's tide-raising force is, accordingly, $2\frac{1}{5}$ times that of the sun.

The effect of the tide-generating forces of the moon and sun acting tangentially to the earth's surface (the so-called "tractive force") tends to cause a maximum accumulation of the waters of the oceans at two diametrically opposite positions on the surface of the earth and to withdraw compensating amounts of water from all points 90° removed from the positions of these tidal bulges. As the earth rotates beneath the maxima and minima of these tide-generating forces, a sequence of two high tides, separated by two low tides, ideally is produced each day.

Twice in each lunar month, when the sun, moon, and earth are directly aligned, with the moon between the earth and the sun (at new moon) or on the opposite side of the

earth from the sun (at full moon), the sun and the moon exert their gravitational force in a mutual or additive fashion. Higher high tides and lower low tides are produced. These are called *spring* tides. At two positions 90° in between, the gravitational forces of the moon and sun — imposed at right angles—tend to counteract each other to the greatest extent, and the range between high and low tides is reduced. These are called *neap* tides. This semi-monthly variation between the spring and neap tides is called the *phase inequality.*

The inclination of the moon's orbit to the equator also produces a difference in the height of succeeding high tides and in the extent of depression of succeeding low tides which is known as the *diurnal inequality.* In extreme cases, this phenomenon can result in only one high tide and one low tide each day.

The actual range of tide in the waters of the open ocean may amount to only one or two feet. However, as this tide approaches shoal waters and its effects are augmented the tidal range may be greatly increased. In Nova Scotia along the narrow channel of the Bay of Fundy, the range of tides or difference between high and low waters, may reach 43 1/2 feet or more (under spring tide conditions) due to resonant amplification.

At New Orleans, the periodic rise and fall of the tide varies with the state of the Mississippi, being about 10 inches at low stage and zero at high. The Canadian Tide Tables for 1972 gave a maximum range of nearly 50 feet at Leaf Basin, Ungava Bay, Quebec.

In every case, actual high or low tide can vary considerably from the average due to weather conditions such as strong winds, abrupt barometric pressure changes, or prolonged periods of extreme high or low pressure.

The Average Rise and Fall of Tides

Places	Ft.	In.	Places	Ft.	In.	Places	Ft.	In.
Baltimore, Md.	1	1	Mobile, Ala.	1	6[1]	San Diego, Cal.	5	9[1]
Boston, Mass.	9	6	New London, Conn.	2	7	Sandy Hook, N.J.	4	8
Charleston, S.C.	5	3	Newport, R.I.	3	6	San Francisco, Cal.	5	10[1]
Colon, Panama	1	1[1]	New York, N.Y.	4	7	Savannah, Ga.	7	5
Eastport, Me.	18	4	Old Pt. Comfort, Va.	2	6	Seattle, Wash.	11	4[1]
Galveston, Tex.	1	5[1]	Philadelphia, Pa.	6	2	Tampa, Fla.	2	10[1]
Halifax, N.S.	4	5	Portland, Me.	9	1	Vancouver, B.C.	10	6[1]
Key West, Fla.	1	10[1]	St. John's, Nfld.	2	7	Washington, D.C.	2	9

(1) Diurnal range.

Speed of Winds in the U.S.

Source: National Oceanic and Atmospheric Administration, U.S. Department of Commerce

Miles per hour — average through 1984. High through 1984. Wind velocities in true values.

Station	Avg.	High	Station	Avg.	High	Station	Avg.	High
Albuquerque, N.M.	9.1	90	Honolulu, Ha.	11.6	67	New York, N.Y.(c)	9.4	70
Anchorage, Alas.	6.8	61	Jacksonville, Fla.	8.2	82	Omaha, Neb.	10.6	109
Atlanta, Ga.	9.1	60	Key West, Fla.	11.2	58	Pensacola, Fla.	8.4	53
Bismarck, N.D.	10.3	72	Knoxville, Tenn.	7.1	36	Philadelphia, Pa.	9.5	73
Boston, Mass.	12.4	61	Lexington, Ky.	9.5	46	Pittsburgh, Pa.	9.2	58
Buffalo, N.Y.	12.1	91	Little Rock, Ark.	8.0	65	Portland, Ore.	7.9	88
Cape Hatteras, N.C.	11.4	(b)110	Louisville, Ky.	8.3	61	Rochester, N.Y.	9.8	73
Chattanooga, Tenn.	6.2	37	Memphis, Tenn.	9.0	46	St. Louis, Mo.	9.7	60
Chicago, Ill.	10.3	58	Miami, Fla.	9.2	(a)74	Salt Lake City, Ut.	8.8	71
Cleveland, Oh.	10.7	74	Minneapolis, Minn.	10.5	92	San Diego, Cal.	6.8	56
Denver, Col.	8.8	56	Mobile, Ala.	9.0	(b)63	San Francisco, Cal.	8.7	47
Detroit, Mich.	10.2	46	Montgomery, Ala.	6.7	72	Savannah, Ga.	7.9	66
Fort Smith, Ark.	7.6	60	Mt. Washington, N.H.	35.1	231	Spokane, Wash.	8.7	59
Galveston, Tex.	11.0	(d)100	Nashville, Tenn.	8.0	41	Toledo, Oh.	9.4	72
Helena, Mont.	7.8	73	New Orleans, La.	8.2	(b)98	Washington, D.C.	9.3	78

(a) Highest velocity ever recorded in Miami area was 132 mph, at former station in Miami Beach in September, 1926. (b) Previous location. (c) Data for Central Park, Battery Place data through 1960, avg. 14.5, high 113. (d) Recorded before anemometer blew away. Estimated high 120.

The Meaning of "One Inch of Rain"

An acre of ground contains 43,560 square feet. Consequently, a rainfall of 1 inch over 1 acre of ground would mean a total of 6,272,640 cubic inches of water. This is equivalent to 3,630 cubic feet.

As a cubic foot of pure water weighs about 62.4 pounds, the exact amount varying with the density, it follows that the weight of a uniform coating of 1 inch of rain over 1 acre of surface would be 226,512 pounds, or about 113 short tons. The weight of 1 U.S. gallon of pure water is about 8.345 pounds. Consequently a rainfall of 1 inch over 1 acre of ground would mean 27,143 gallons of water.

National Weather Service Watches and Warnings

Source: National Weather Service, NOAA, U.S. Commerce Department; Glossary of Meteorology, American Meteorological Society

National Weather Service forecasters issue a Tornado Watch for a specific area where tornadoes are most likely to occur during the valid time of the watch. A Watch is to alert people to watch for threatening weather, make plans for action, and listen for a Tornado Warning. A Tornado Warning means that a tornado has been sighted or indicated by radar, and that safety precautions should be taken at once. A Hurricane Watch means that an existing hurricane poses a threat to coastal and inland communities in the area specified by the Watch. A Hurricane Warning means hurricane force winds and/or dangerously high water and exceptionally high waves are expected in a specified coastal area within 24 hours.

Tornado—A violent rotating column of air in contact with the ground and pendant from a thundercloud, usually recognized as a funnel-shaped vortex accompanied by a loud roar. With rotating winds est. up to 300 mph., on a local scale, it is the most destructive storm. Tornado paths have varied in length from a few feet to nearly 300 miles (avg. 5 mi.); diameter from a few feet to over a mile (average 220 yards); average forward speed, 30 mph.

Cyclone—An atmospheric circulation of winds rotating counterclockwise in the northern hemisphere and clockwise in the southern hemisphere. Tornadoes, hurricanes, and the lows shown on weather maps are all examples of cyclones having various sizes and intensities. Cyclones are usually accompanied by precipitation or stormy weather.

Hurricane—A severe cyclone originating over tropical ocean waters and having winds 74 miles an hour or higher. (In the western Pacific, such storms are known as typhoons.) The area of strong winds takes the form of a circle or an oval, sometimes as much as 500 miles in diameter. In the lower latitudes hurricanes usually move toward the west or northwest at 10 to 15 mph. When the center approaches 25° to 30° North Latitude, direction of motion often changes to northeast, with increased forward speed.

Blizzard—A severe weather condition characterized by strong winds bearing a great amount of snow. The National Weather Service specifies, for blizzard, a wind of 35 miles an hour or higher, and sufficient falling and/or blowing snow to reduce visibility to less than $1/4$ of a mile for a duration of three hours or longer.

Monsoon—A name for seasonal winds (derived from Arabic "mausim," a season). It was first applied to the winds over the Arabian Sea, which blow for six months from northeast and six months from southwest, but it has been extended to similar winds in other parts of the world. The monsoons are strongest on the southern and eastern sides of Asia.

Flood—The condition that occurs when water overflows the natural or artificial confines of a stream or other body of water, or accumulates by drainage over low-lying areas.

National Weather Service Marine Warnings and Advisories

Small Craft Advisory: A Small Craft Advisory alerts mariners to sustained (exceeding two hours) weather and/or sea conditions either present or forecast, potentially hazardous to small boats. Hazardous conditions may include winds of 18 to 33 knots and/or dangerous wave or inlet conditions. It is the responsibility of the mariner, based on his experience and size or type of boat, to determine if the conditions are hazardous. When a mariner becomes aware of a Small Craft Advisory, he should immediately obtain the latest marine forecast to determine the reason for the Advisory.

Gale Warning indicates that winds within the range 34 to 47 knots are forecast for the area.

Storm Warning indicates that winds 48 knots and above, no matter how high the speed, are forecast for the area.

However, if the winds are associated with a tropical cyclone (hurricane), the storm warning indicates that winds within the range 48 to 63 knots are forecast.

Hurricane Warning indicates that winds 64 knots and above are forecast for the area.

Primary sources of dissemination are commercial radio, TV, U.S. Coast Guard Radio stations, and NOAA VHF-FM broadcasts. These broadcasts on 162.40 to 162.55 MHz can usually be received 20-40 miles from the transmitting antenna site, depending on terrain and quality of the receiver used. Where transmitting antennas are on high ground, the range is somewhat greater, reaching 60 miles or more.

Hurricane Names in 1986

U.S. government agencies responsible for weather and related communications have used girls' names to identify major tropical storms since 1953. A U.S. proposal that both male and female names be adopted for hurricanes, starting in 1979, was accepted by a committee of the World Meteorological Organization.

Names assigned to Atlantic hurricanes, 1986 — Andrew, Bonnie, Charley, Danielle, Earl, Frances, Georges, Hermine, Ivan, Jeanne, Karl, Lisa, Mitch, Nicole, Otto, Paula, Richard, Shary, Thomas, Virginie, Walter.

Names assigned to Eastern Pacific hurricanes, 1986 — Agatha, Blas, Celia, Darby, Estelle, Frank, Georgette, Howard, Isis, Javier, Kay, Lester, Madeline, Newton, Orlene, Paine, Roslyn, Seymour, Tina, Virgil, Winifred.

Explanation of Normal Temperatures

Normal temperatures listed in the tables on pages 758 and 760 are based on records of the National Weather Service for the 30-year period from 1951-1980 inclusive. To obtain the average maximum or minimum temperature for any month, the daily temperatures are added; the total is then divided by the number of days in that month.

The normal maximum temperature for January, for example, is obtained by adding the average maximums for Jan., 1951, Jan., 1952, etc., through Jan., 1980. The total is then divided by 30. The normal minimum temperature is obtained in a similar manner by adding the average minimums for each January in the 30-year period and dividing by 30. The normal temperature for January is one half of the sum for the normal maximum and minimum temperatures for that month. The mean temperature for any one day is one-half the total of the maximum and minimum temperatures for that day.

Monthly Normal Temperature and Precipitation

Source: NOAA, U.S. Department of Commerce

These normals are based on records for the 30-year period 1951 to 1980 inclusive. See explanation on page 757. For stations that did not have continuous records from the same instrument site for the entire 30 years, the means have been adjusted to the record at the present site.

Airport station; *city office stations. T, temperature in Fahrenheit; P, precipitation in inches; L, less than .05 inch.

	Jan.		Feb.		Mar.		Apr.		May		June		July		Aug.		Sept.		Oct.		Nov.		Dec.	
Station	T.	P.	T.	P.	T.	P.	T.	P.	T.	P.	T.	P.	T.	P.	T.	P.	T.	P.	T.	P.	T.	P.	T.	P.
Albany, N.Y.	21	2.4	23	2.3	34	3.0	47	2.9	58	3.3	67	3.3	71	3.0	69	3.3	61	3.2	51	2.9	39	3.0	26	3.0
Albuquerque, N.M.	35	0.4	39	0.4	46	0.5	55	0.4	64	0.5	75	0.5	79	1.3	76	1.5	69	0.9	57	0.9	44	0.4	36	0.5
Anchorage, Alas.	13	0.8	18	0.9	24	0.7	35	0.7	46	0.6	54	1.1	58	2.0	56	2.1	48	2.5	35	1.7	22	1.1	14	1.1
Asheville, N.C.	37	3.5	39	3.6	46	5.1	56	3.8	63	4.2	70	4.2	73	4.4	73	4.8	70	4.0	56	3.3	46	3.3	39	3.5
Atlanta, Ga.	42	4.9	45	4.4	53	5.9	62	4.4	69	4.0	76	3.4	79	4.7	78	3.4	73	3.2	62	2.5	52	3.4	45	4.2
Atlantic City, N.J.	34	3.3	35	3.2	42	3.7	51	3.1	60	2.9	68	2.9	74	3.9	74	4.5	68	2.7	58	2.8	48	3.5	38	3.5
Baltimore, Md.	33	3.0	35	3.0	43	3.7	54	3.4	63	3.4	72	3.8	77	3.9	76	4.6	69	3.5	57	3.1	46	3.1	37	3.4
Barrow, Alas.	-14	0.2	-20	0.2	-16	0.2	-2	0.2	19	0.2	33	0.4	39	0.9	38	1.0	31	0.6	14	0.6	-1	0.3	-13	0.2
Birmingham, Ala.	42	5.2	46	4.7	54	6.6	63	5.0	70	4.5	77	3.7	80	5.4	80	3.9	74	4.3	62	2.7	52	3.6	45	5.0
Bismarck, N.D.	7	0.5	15	0.5	26	0.7	43	1.5	55	2.2	64	3.0	70	2.0	69	1.7	57	1.4	46	0.8	29	0.5	15	0.5
Boise, Ida.	30	1.6	36	1.1	41	1.0	49	1.2	57	1.2	66	1.0	75	0.3	72	0.4	63	0.6	52	0.8	40	1.3	32	1.3
Boston, Mass.	30	4.0	31	3.7	38	4.1	49	3.7	59	3.5	68	2.9	74	2.7	72	3.7	65	3.4	55	3.4	45	4.2	34	4.9
Buffalo, N.Y.	24	3.0	25	2.4	33	3.0	45	3.0	56	2.9	66	2.7	71	3.0	69	4.2	62	3.4	52	2.9	40	3.6	29	3.4
Burlington, Vt.	17	1.9	18	1.7	29	2.2	43	2.8	55	3.0	65	3.6	70	3.4	67	3.9	59	3.2	48	2.8	37	2.8	23	2.4
Caribou, Me.	11	2.4	13	2.1	24	2.4	37	2.6	50	2.9	60	3.2	65	4.0	63	4.0	54	3.5	43	3.1	31	3.2	16	3.1
Charleston, S.C.	49	3.3	51	3.4	57	4.4	66	2.6	73	4.4	79	6.5	82	7.3	81	6.5	77	4.9	68	2.9	59	2.2	52	3.1
Chicago, Ill.	21	1.6	26	1.3	36	2.6	49	3.7	59	3.2	69	4.1	73	3.6	72	3.5	65	3.4	54	2.3	40	2.1	28	2.1
Cleveland, Oh.	26	2.5	27	2.2	37	3.0	48	3.3	58	3.3	68	3.5	72	3.4	70	3.4	64	2.9	53	2.5	42	2.8	31	2.8
Columbus, Oh.	27	2.8	30	2.2	40	3.2	51	3.4	61	3.8	70	4.0	74	4.0	72	3.7	66	2.8	54	1.9	42	2.6	32	2.6
Dallas-Ft. Worth, Tex.	44	1.7	49	1.9	56	2.4	66	3.6	74	4.3	82	2.6	86	2.0	86	1.8	79	3.3	68	2.5	56	1.8	48	1.7
Denver, Col.	30	0.5	34	0.7	38	1.2	47	1.8	57	2.5	67	1.6	73	1.9	71	1.5	63	1.2	52	1.0	39	0.8	33	0.6
Des Moines, Ia.	19	1.0	25	1.1	35	2.2	51	3.2	62	4.0	72	4.2	76	3.2	74	4.1	65	3.1	54	2.2	39	1.5	26	1.5
Detroit, Mich.	23	1.9	26	1.7	35	2.5	47	3.2	58	2.8	68	3.4	72	3.1	71	3.2	63	2.3	52	2.1	40	2.3	29	2.5
Dodge City, Kan.	30	0.5	35	0.5	42	1.5	54	1.8	64	3.3	75	3.0	80	3.1	78	2.5	69	1.9	58	1.3	43	0.8	34	0.5
Duluth, Minn.	6	1.2	12	0.9	23	1.8	38	2.2	50	3.2	59	4.0	65	4.0	63	4.1	54	3.3	44	2.2	28	1.7	14	1.3
Eureka, Cal.*	47	7.0	49	5.2	48	5.1	49	2.9	52	1.6	55	0.6	56	0.1	57	0.4	57	0.9	54	2.7	51	5.9	48	6.2
Fairbanks, Alas.	-13	0.5	-4	0.5	9	0.4	30	0.3	48	0.6	59	1.3	62	1.8	57	1.9	45	1.1	25	0.7	4	0.7	-10	0.7
Fresno, Cal.	46	2.0	51	1.9	54	1.6	60	1.2	68	0.3	75	0.1	81	L	79	L	74	0.2	65	0.4	53	1.2	45	1.6
Galveston, Tex.*	54	3.0	56	2.3	62	2.1	69	2.6	76	3.3	81	3.5	83	3.8	83	4.4	80	5.8	73	2.6	63	3.2	57	3.6
Grand Junction, Col.	26	0.6	34	0.5	42	0.8	52	0.7	62	0.8	72	0.4	79	0.5	76	0.9	67	0.7	55	0.9	40	0.6	28	0.6
Gr. Rapids, Mich.	22	1.9	24	1.5	33	2.5	46	3.6	58	3.0	67	3.9	71	3.0	70	3.5	62	3.1	51	2.9	39	2.9	27	2.6
Hartford, Conn.	25	3.5	28	3.2	37	4.2	49	4.0	59	3.4	69	3.4	73	3.1	71	4.0	63	3.9	52	3.5	42	4.1	29	4.2
Helena, Mon.	18	0.7	26	0.4	32	0.7	42	1.0	52	1.7	60	2.0	68	1.0	66	1.2	56	0.8	45	0.7	31	0.5	23	0.6
Honolulu, Ha.	73	3.8	73	2.7	74	3.5	76	1.5	78	1.2	79	0.5	80	0.5	81	0.6	81	0.6	80	1.9	77	3.2	74	3.4
Houston, Tex.	51	3.2	55	3.3	61	2.7	69	4.2	75	4.7	81	4.0	83	3.3	83	3.7	78	4.9	70	3.7	60	3.4	54	3.7
Huron, S.D.	11	0.4	18	0.8	29	1.2	46	2.0	57	2.7	68	3.3	74	2.3	72	2.0	61	1.4	49	1.4	32	0.7	19	0.5
Indianapolis, Ind.	26	2.7	30	2.5	40	3.6	52	3.7	63	3.7	72	4.0	75	4.3	73	3.5	67	2.7	55	2.5	42	3.0	32	3.0
Jackson, Miss.	46	5.0	49	4.9	56	5.9	65	5.9	73	4.8	79	2.9	82	4.4	81	3.7	76	3.6	65	2.6	55	4.2	49	5.4
Jacksonville, Fla.	53	3.1	55	3.5	61	3.7	68	3.3	74	4.9	79	5.4	81	6.5	81	7.2	78	7.3	70	3.4	61	1.9	55	2.6
Juneau, Alas.	22	3.7	28	3.7	31	3.3	39	2.9	46	3.4	53	3.0	56	4.1	55	5.0	49	6.4	42	7.7	33	5.2	27	4.7
Kansas City, Mo.	26	1.0	32	1.0	42	2.1	55	2.7	65	3.4	76	4.1	79	3.5	77	3.2	68	3.3	58	2.5	43	1.2	32	1.1
Knoxville, Tenn.	38	4.7	42	4.2	50	5.5	60	3.9	67	3.7	74	4.0	78	4.3	77	3.0	72	3.0	60	2.7	49	3.8	41	4.6
Lander, Wyo.	20	0.5	26	0.6	32	1.1	42	2.2	53	2.7	62	1.5	71	0.7	69	0.5	58	0.9	47	1.2	31	0.8	23	0.5
Lexington, Ky.	32	3.6	35	3.3	44	4.8	55	4.0	64	4.2	72	4.3	76	5.0	75	4.0	69	3.3	57	2.3	45	3.3	36	3.8
Little Rock, Ark.	40	3.9	44	3.8	52	4.7	62	5.4	71	5.3	79	3.7	82	3.6	81	3.1	74	4.3	63	2.8	51	4.4	43	4.2
Los Angeles, Cal.*	57	3.7	59	3.0	60	2.4	62	1.2	65	0.2	69	L	74	L	75	0.1	73	0.3	69	0.2	63	1.9	58	2.0
Louisville, Ky.	33	3.4	36	3.2	45	4.7	57	4.1	65	4.2	74	3.6	78	4.1	76	3.3	70	3.6	58	2.6	46	3.5	37	3.5
Marquette, Mich.*	12	2.0	14	1.9	23	2.8	37	3.6	50	4.0	60	3.9	65	3.2	63	3.3	54	3.9	44	3.3	30	2.9	18	2.4
Memphis, Tenn.	40	4.6	44	4.3	52	5.4	63	5.8	71	5.1	79	3.6	82	4.0	81	3.7	74	3.6	63	2.4	51	4.2	43	4.9
Miami, Fla.	67	2.1	68	2.1	72	1.9	75	3.1	79	6.5	81	9.2	83	6.0	83	7.0	82	8.1	78	7.1	73	2.7	69	1.9
Milwaukee, Wis.	19	1.6	23	1.3	32	2.6	45	3.4	55	2.6	65	3.6	71	3.5	69	3.1	62	2.9	51	2.3	37	2.0	25	2.0
Minneapolis, Minn.	11	0.8	18	0.9	29	1.7	46	2.1	59	3.2	68	4.1	73	3.5	71	3.6	61	2.5	50	1.9	33	1.3	19	0.9
Mobile, Ala.	51	4.6	54	4.9	60	6.5	68	5.4	75	5.5	81	5.1	82	7.7	82	6.8	78	6.6	69	2.6	59	3.7	53	5.4
Moline, Ill.	20	1.6	25	1.3	36	2.8	50	4.0	61	4.2	71	4.3	75	4.9	73	3.8	65	3.7	54	2.7	39	2.0	26	1.9
Nashville, Tenn.	37	4.5	40	4.0	49	5.6	60	4.8	68	4.6	76	3.7	79	3.8	78	3.4	72	3.7	60	2.6	49	3.5	41	4.6
Newark, N.J.	31	3.1	33	3.1	41	4.2	52	3.6	62	3.6	72	2.9	77	3.9	76	4.3	68	3.7	57	3.1	47	3.6	36	3.4
New Orleans, La.	52	5.0	55	5.2	61	4.7	69	4.5	75	5.1	80	4.6	82	6.7	82	6.0	79	5.9	69	2.7	60	4.1	55	5.3
New York, N.Y.*	32	3.2	33	3.1	41	4.2	53	3.8	62	3.8	71	3.2	77	3.8	75	4.0	68	3.7	58	3.4	47	4.1	36	3.8
Nome, Alas.	9	0.8	3	0.5	7	0.6	18	0.6	36	0.5	45	1.2	51	2.2	50	3.1	42	2.3	28	1.3	16	0.9	4	0.7
Norfolk, Va.	40	3.7	41	3.3	49	3.9	58	2.9	67	3.8	76	3.5	78	5.2	78	5.3	72	4.4	61	3.4	52	2.9	44	3.2
Okla. City, Okla.	36	1.0	41	1.3	49	2.1	60	2.9	68	5.5	77	3.9	82	3.0	81	2.4	73	3.4	62	2.7	49	1.5	40	1.2
Omaha, Neb.	19	0.8	25	0.9	35	1.9	50	2.9	62	4.3	71	4.1	76	3.6	74	4.1	64	2.5	54	2.1	38	1.3	26	0.8
Pago Pago, Amer. Samoa	81	13	81	13	81	11	81	11	80	11	80	8.6	79	6.5	79	7.1	79	6.7	80	11	80	11	81	14
Philadelphia, Pa.	31	3.2	33	2.8	42	3.9	53	3.5	63	3.2	72	3.9	77	3.9	75	4.1	68	3.4	57	2.8	46	3.3	36	3.5
Phoenix, Ariz.	52	0.7	56	0.6	61	0.8	68	0.3	77	0.1	87	0.2	92	0.7	90	1.0	85	0.6	73	0.6	61	0.5	53	0.8
Pittsburgh, Pa.	27	2.9	29	2.4	39	3.6	50	3.3	60	3.5	68	3.3	72	3.8	71	3.3	64	2.8	53	2.5	42	2.3	31	2.6
Portland, Me.	22	3.8	23	3.6	32	4.0	43	3.9	53	3.3	62	3.1	68	2.8	67	2.8	59	3.3	49	3.8	38	4.7	26	4.5
Portland, Ore.	39	6.2	43	3.9	46	3.6	50	2.3	57	2.1	63	1.5	68	0.5	67	1.1	63	1.6	54	3.1	46	5.2	41	6.4
Providence, R.I.	28	4.1	29	3.7	37	4.3	48	4.0	58	3.5	67	2.8	73	3.0	71	4.0	64	3.5	53	3.8	43	4.2	32	4.5
Raleigh, N.C.	40	3.6	42	3.4	49	3.7	59	2.9	67	3.7	74	3.7	78	4.4	77	4.4	71	3.3	60	2.7	50	2.9	42	3.1
Rapid City, S.D.	21	0.4	26	0.6	33	1.0	45	2.0	56	2.6	65	3.3	73	2.1	71	1.4	61	1.0	50	0.8	35	0.5	26	0.5
Reno, Nev.	32	1.2	37	1.0	41	0.7	46	0.5	55	0.7	62	0.3	70	0.3	67	0.3	60	0.3	50	0.3	40	0.6	33	1.2
Richmond, Va.	37	3.2	39	3.1	47	3.6	58	2.9	66	3.6	74	3.6	78	5.1	77	5.0	70	3.5	59	3.7	49	3.3	40	3.4
St. Louis, Mo.	29	1.7	34	2.1	43	3.3	56	3.6	66	3.5	75	3.7	79	3.6	77	2.6	70	2.7	58	2.3	45	2.5	34	2.2
Salt Lake City, Ut.	29	1.4	34	1.3	41	1.7	49	2.2	59	1.5	68	1.0	78	0.7	75	0.9	65	0.9	53	1.1	40	1.2	30	1.4
San Antonio, Tex.	50	1.6	54	1.9	62	1.3	70	2.7	76	3.7	82	3.0	85	1.9	84	2.7	79	3.8	70	2.9	60	2.3	53	1.4
San Diego, Cal.	57	2.1	58	1.4	59	1.6	61	0.8	63	0.2	66	0.1	70	L	72	0.1	71	0.2	68	0.3	62	1.1	57	1.4
San Francisco, Cal.	49	4.7	52	3.2	53	2.6	55	1.5	58	0.3	61	0.1	62	L	63	0.1	64	0.2	61	1.1	55	2.4	49	3.6
San Juan, P.R.	77	3.0	77	2.0	78	2.3	80	3.6	79	5.6	80	4.7	82	4.9	82	5.9	82	6.0	81	5.9	80	5.6	78	4.7
Sault Ste. Marie, Mich.*	13	2.2	14	1.7	24	2.0	38	2.4	50	2.9	58	3.3	64	3.0	63	3.5	55	3.9	45	2.9	33	3.2	20	2.6
Savannah, Ga.	49	3.1	52	3.2	58	3.8	66	3.2	73	4.6	79	5.7	81	7.4	81	6.7	77	5.2	67	2.3	58	1.9	51	2.8
Seattle, Wash.	39	6.0	43	4.2	44	3.6	49	2.4	55	1.6	60	1.4	65	0.7	64	1.3	60	2.0	52	3.4	45	5.6	41	6.3
Spokane, Wash.	26	2.5	32	1.6	38	1.4	46	1.1	54	1.4	62	1.2	70	0.5	68	0.7	60	0.7	48	1.1	35	2.1	29	2.5
Springfield, Mo.	32	1.6	36	2.1	45	3.4	56	4.0	65	4.3	73	4.7	78	3.6	77	2.8	70	4.2	58	3.2	45	2.9	36	2.6
Syracuse, N.Y.	23	2.6	24	2.7	33	3.1	46	3.3	57	3.2	66	3.6	71	3.8	69	3.8	62	3.3	51	3.1	41	3.5	28	3.2
Tampa, Fla.	60	2.2	61	3.0	66	3.5	72	1.8	77	3.4	81	5.3	82	7.4	82	7.6	81	6.2	74	2.3	67	1.9	61	2.1
Washington, D.C.	31	2.8	34	2.6	42	3.4	53	3.1	62	3.6	71	4.2	76	3.8	74	4.2	67	3.3	55	3.0	45	3.0	35	3.3
Wilmington, Del.	31	3.1	33	3.0	42	3.9	52	3.4	62	3.2	71	3.5	76	3.9	75	4.0	68	3.6	56	2.9	46	3.3	36	3.5

Annual Climatological Data

Source: NOAA, U.S. Department of Commerce

1984	Elev. ft	Temperature °F				Precipitation[1]			Sleet or snow			Fastest Wind		No. of days			
		Highest	Date	Lowest	Date	Total (in.)	Greatest in 24 hrs.	Date	Total (in.)	Greatest in 24 hours	Date	MPH	Date	Clear*	Cloudy*	Prec. .01 in. or more	Snow, sleet 1 in. or more
Albany, N.Y.	275	93	6/9	−20	1/22	37.13	2.14	5/28	65.8	17.0	3/13	38	3/11	63	201	138	13
Albuquerque, N.M.	5311	97	7/20	8	1/19	12.08	1.25	10/14	10.6	3.0	4/25	—	—	152	87	76	5
Anchorage, Alas.	114	76	8/15	−18	1/24	14.97	1.32	8/24	67.0	10.2	12/29	23	12/30	51	249	109	18
Asheville, N.C.	2140	90	7/11	5	1/22	45.71	3.13	2/13	3.1	2.6	2/5	31	12/6	100	143	118	1
Atlanta, Ga.	1010	97	6/21	15	2/6	55.39	2.99	8/25	1.3	1.0	2/5	60	7/27	126	138	109	1
Barrow, Alas.	31	71	7/2	−48	2/2	3.98	0.33	8/16	16.8	2.1	8/25	39	12/16	69	134	83	3
Birmingham, Ala.	678	96	6/20	12	1/22	45.79	2.82	11/27	1.3	0.7	2/28	—	—			115	0
Bismarck, N.D.	1647	99	8/12	−32	12/31	14.77	1.16	4/26	72.5	11.9	4/27	43	3/7	77	180	108	21
Boise, Ida.	2838	104	7/25	−13	1/18	13.24	0.90	4/8	16.9	3.1	12/15	45	11/2	104	178	88	7
Boston, Mass.	15	98	7/15	1	1/22	50.24	4.17	6/1	44.1	9.7	1/10	45	3/29	82	175	122	12
Buffalo, N.Y.	705	89	6/8	−10	1/16	37.42	2.44	6/23	75.4	19.4	2/27	55	4/30	44	208	160	16
Burlington, Vt.	332	92	6/9	−17	1/22	35.81	1.56	7/6	80.7	13.4	12/6	30	11/1	59	206	147	24
Charleston, S.C.	40	99	6/19	21	1/22	46.23	2.77	4/22	T	T	1/21	37	3/25	123	146	104	0
Charleston, W.Va.	939	96	6/12	−13	1/21	40.90	1.67	9/3	28.6	5.6	2/28	30	3/8	57	192	160	9
Chicago, Ill.	658	99	7/10	−22	1/21	34.00	1.68	7/20	38.1	5.9	1/29	43	4/30	85	185	132	14
Cincinnati, Oh.	869	94	9/2	−21	1/21	42.00	1.72	12/20	23.6	7.3	12/5	39	4/30	81	204	140	8
Cleveland, Oh.	777	90	7/10	−17	1/21	41.33	2.26	8/13	72.2	11.5	2/27	37	4/30	47	240	166	19
Columbus, Oh.	812	93	9/2	−16	1/21	33.42	1.83	3/20	38.1	8.0	2/27	38	8/4	63	208	144	10
Concord, N.H.	342	95	6/9	−33	1/22	42.24	3.00	10/1	74.6	14.4	3/13	35	12/25	88	182	131	19
Dallas, Tex.	551	106	8/19	10	1/19	33.89	2.15	10/20	0	0	—	37	3/28	144	120	76	0
Denver, Co.	5283	97	7/21	−19	1/18	16.49	1.22	10/4	65.7	12.3	4/20	40	5/12	126	113	96	20
Des Moines, Ia.	938	100	8/28	−16	1/20	41.78	2.73	7/14	37.9	4.5	1/1	42	9/7	116	149	116	11
Detroit, Mich.	633	96	7/23	−21	1/21	26.27	1.55	5/25	38.7	6.3	2/27	39	4/30	65	194	137	14
Dodge City, Kan.	2582	106	8/29	−13	1/1	18.97	2.00	12/14	21.8	7.0	3/22	39	11/1	137	131	82	7
Duluth, Minn.	1428	92	8/27	−30	1/20	26.83	2.18	9/23	51.6	9.2	1/11	46	10/19	77	185	130	20
Fairbanks, Alas.	436	84	7/1	−46	2/3	12.35	1.02	7/24	102.9	12.4	12/16	32	5/27	70	212	117	31
Fresno, Cal.	328	111	7/6	31	12/17	6.77	0.82	12/19	0	0	—	32	4/25	194	104	40	0
Galveston, Tex.	7	95	7/23	28	1/19	35.64	4.15	5/18	0	0	—	40	3/28	—	—	86	0
Grand Rapids, Mich.	784	92	8/7	−15	1/21	28.68	1.82	5/28	47.6	5.6	12/31	41	4/30	57	204	138	18
Hartford, Conn.	169	97	6/11	−21	1/22	42.85	2.93	5/29	39.2	8.9	3/13	30	3/29	72	176	130	13
Helena, Mont.	3828	89	8/10	−19	12/17	9.00	1.12	4/19	40.1	5.1	11/24	48	1/25	79	185	81	15
Honolulu, Ha.	7	94	10/6	57	2/4	17.08	4.33	12/24	0	0	—	28	12/9	107	67	81	0
Houston, Tex.	96	98	8/19	20	1/19	48.19			0	0	—	46	2/12	86	143	104	0
Huron, S.D.	1281	100	8/28	−22	1/20	29.73	2.17	6/20	38.5	10.8	3/3	42	9/21	98	187	101	12
Indianapolis, Ind.	792	93	7/10	−21	1/21	42.13	2.41	7/26	39.6	9.5	2/27	37	4/30	71	201	152	14
Jackson, Miss.	291	98	7/12	12	1/22	49.76	4.21	10/20	T	T	12/4	40	6/22	106	136	102	0
Jacksonville, Fla.	26	95	6/21	25	2/8	48.96	4.80	9/28	0	0	—	35	3/28	106	138	103	0
Kansas City, Mo.	1014	109	8/29	−7	1/20	38.77	3.63	7/4	17.9	6.7	12/31	52	4/29	118	152	112	5
Lander, Wyo.	5557	98	7/29	−21	1/18	13.19	1.13	4/26	123.1	13.1	4/25	56	12/23	117	112	81	30
Little Rock, Ark.	257	99	6/22	5	1/21	63.96	5.17	10/18	6.2	4.5	3/10	—	—			120	2
Los Angeles, Cal.	97	96	9/16	41	12/17	7.81	1.64	12/18	0	0	—	—	—	170	68	29	0
Louisville, Ky.	477	94	7/10	−9	1/21	49.38	4.88	7/4	17.7	4.8	12/5	47	9/14	81	189	137	4
Marquette, Mich.	1415	83	8/28	−24	1/21	32.48	2.35	3/21	159.9	24.9	3/21	38	10/31	—	—	151	36
Memphis, Tenn.	258	96	7/11	8	1/19	57.24	3.00	5/1	2.5	2.0	1/17	40	10/20	115	150	123	2
Miami, Fla.	7	96	8/11	44	3/1	60.02	4.15	5/28	0	0	—	35	8/11	109	77	137	0
Milford, Ut.	5028	101	7/6	−20	1/18	13.91	1.73	8/19	64.6	7.2	3/29	57	5/14	143	102	88	22
Milwaukee, Wis.	672	95	7/23	−19	1/21	39.60	2.05	7/9	38.5	8.4	12/26	54	7/10	80	194	146	11
Minneapolis, Minn.	834	94	7/22	−25	1/20	36.95	2.94	6/7	65.6	10.4	3/4	41	4/27	96	180	125	23
Mobile, Ala.	211	96	6/20	18	1/22	53.82	5.67	8/1	T	T	2/28	35	2/26	102	149	100	0
Moline, Ill.	582	99	7/9	−16	1/21	39.39	2.33	11/1	34.8	5.7	12/31	49	4/30	106	160	120	13
Nashville, Tenn.	590	95	6/19	−5	1/21	56.49	4.27	5/6	9.8	3.5	1/18	41	5/7	104	156	120	4
Newark, N.J.	7	97	6/8	−1	1/22	59.01	3.73	4/4	32.1	6.4	3/8	58	6/13	89	181	135	11
New Orleans, La.	4	96	8/21	21	1/1	52.07	3.33	8/3	0	0	—	32	2/26	79	174	111	0
New York, N.Y.	132	96	6/9	8	1/21	57.03	4.22	4/4	29.3	6.9	3/8	35	3/29	96	154	136	9
Nome, Alas.	13	80	6/26	−39	2/20	14.92	1.13	8/1	44.0	4.1	4/27	32	12/15	120	177	113	16
Norfolk, Va.	24	96	9/3	16	1/22	44.82	3.13	5/30	5.2	5.2	2/6	39	2/28	83	169	106	1
Oklahoma City, Okla.	1285	106	8/29	−3	1/19	33.59	3.57	10/26	13.7	5.7	12/4	35	11/10	135	122	87	7
Omaha, Neb.	997	100	7/8	−13	1/20	33.12	3.03	12/15	24.5	5.0	12/13	—	—	—		115	13
Philadelphia, Pa.	5	94	6/10	−7	1/22	43.66	3.18	5/29	21.0	7.3	3/8	52	5/8	86	171	131	6
Phoenix, Ariz.	1110	113	5/28	36	12/14	14.91	2.75	7/27	0	0	—	32	8/9	203	67	45	0
Pittsburgh, Pa.	1137	91	6/13	−15	1/21	35.32	1.25	5/28	38.9	7.5	2/28	37	5/11	49	205	168	12
Portland, Me.	43	95	6/9	−19	1/22	48.17	3.23	5/30	75.0	15.5	3/13	34	4/21	98	191	133	19
Portland, Ore.	21	100	7/24	18	12/20	37.50	2.55	11/1	2.9	2.4	12/20	35	11/27	65	223	168	1
Providence, R.I.	51	95	6/9	−9	1/22	48.74	5.17	5/30	33.6	6.5	1/10	37	4/5	83	182	121	8
Raleigh, N.C.	434	94	7/11	8	1/22	46.27	3.11	1/10	6.9	6.9	2/6	44	2/27	105	160	107	1
Rapid City, S.D.	3162	98	8/13	−15	12/24	15.23	1.72	4/25	41.7	9.1	4/25	61	7/8	118	123	90	10
Reno, Nev.	4404	101	7/4	1	1/17	4.28	0.68	11/27	16.0	5.5	1/15	54	3/13	144	110	44	6
Richmond, Va.	164	99	9/3	8	1/22	46.04	2.54	3/25	4.2	1.5	2/6	—	—	84	181	116	2
Rochester, N.Y.	547	90	6/10	−12	1/16	33.64	1.63	2/27	94.0	15.6	2/28	59	4/30	55	204	175	27
St. Louis, Mo.	535	107	8/29	−6	1/21	51.65	2.99	9/10	20.9	6.6	2/26	48	3/15	104	178	130	6
Salt Lake City, Ut.	4221	100	7/18	−6	1/18	21.55	1.76	10/17	97.8	18.4	10/17	49	5/14	103	164	119	25
San Antonio, Tex.	788	101	8/19	18	1/19	25.95	1.83	8/14	0	0	—	42	2/12	110	137	79	0
San Diego, Cal.	13	100	9/6	42	12/14	8.71	1.65	12/26	0	0	—	32	12/13	154	88	42	0
San Francisco, Cal.	8	100	9/8	34	12/23	14.13	1.91	11/12	0	0	—	41	11/27	183	91	57	0
Sault Ste Marie, Mich.	721	88	6/6	−33	1/21	34.91	2.40	9/12	98.4	12.5	12/2	40	7/14	61	221	177	33
Savannah, Ga.	46	101	6/20	20	1/1	50.66	3.58	1/26	T	T	1/21	44	5/3	119	142	98	0
Seattle, Wash.	400	91	7/23	20	12/18	36.99	1.61	6/20	2.4	1.6	12/20	44	3/16	47	221	165	1
Shreveport, La.	254	102	8/19	16	1/21	48.35	3.49	5/7	T	T	2/27	33	4/10	101	166	99	0
Sioux City, Ia.	1095	98	8/28	−16	1/20	34.02	1.77	6/7	43.3	9.9	2/18	52	7/16	97	159	127	12
Spokane, Wash.	2356	101	7/25	−12	12/18	18.01	0.91	12/9	55.1	8.9	12/29	43	11/3	79	202	120	19
Springfield, Mo.	1268	106	8/29	−13	1/19	45.78	2.05	9/8	22.8	9.0	2/26	41	2/18	109	162	119	7
Syracuse, N.Y.	410	89	7/23	−19	1/22	37.97	1.97	7/4	110.2	11.9	3/1	40	3/11	54	212	183	28
Tampa, Fla.	19	94	8/16	26	1/1	32.31	2.62	7/29	0	0	—	30	3/29	127	106	96	0
Washington, D.C.	10	97	6/11	3	1/22	37.73	2.28	3/28	8.6	3.9	1/18	52	5/8	65	189	119	3
Wilmington, Del.	74	98	7/11	−14	1/22	41.72	2.25	5/29	15.2	5.1	1/18	46	5/8	89	184	134	5

*To get partly cloudy days deduct the total of clear and cloudy days from 365 (1 yr.). T—trace. (1) Date shown is the starting date of the storm (in some cases it lasted more than one day).

Normal Temperatures, Highs, Lows, Precipitation

Source: National Oceanic and Atmospheric Administration, U.S. Commerce Department

These normals are based on records for the thirty-year period 1951-1980. (See explanation on page 757.) The extreme temperatures (through 1984) are listed for the stations shown and may not agree with the states records shown on page 761.

Airport stations; * designates city office stations. The minus (−) sign indicates temperatures below zero. Fahrenheit thermometer registration.

State	Station	Normal temperature January Max.	Min.	July Max.	Min.	Extreme temperature Highest	Lowest	Normal annual precipitation (inches)
Alabama	Mobile	61	41	91	73	104	7	64.64
Alabama	Montgomery	57	36	92	72	105	4	49.16
Alaska	Juneau	27	16	64	47	90	−22	53.15
Arizona	Phoenix	65	39	105	80	80	17	7.11
Arkansas	Little Rock	50	30	93	71	109	−5	49.20
California	Los Angeles*	67	48	84	64	110	28	14.85
California	San Francisco	55	42	71	53	106	20	19.71
Colorado	Denver	43	16	88	59	104	−30	15.31
Connecticut	Hartford	34	17	85	62	102	−26	44.39
Delaware	Wilmington	39	23	86	66	102	−14	41.38
Dist. of Col.	Washington	43	28	88	70	103	−5	39.00
Florida	Jacksonville	65	42	91	72	105	11	52.76
Florida	Key West	72	66	89	80	95	41	39.42
Florida	Miami	75	59	89	76	98	31	57.55
Georgia	Atlanta	51	33	88	69	105	−5	48.61
Hawaii	Honolulu	80	65	87	73	94	53	23.47
Idaho	Boise	37	23	91	59	111	−23	11.71
Illinois	Chicago-Midway	29	14	83	63	102	−26	33.34
Indiana	Indianapolis	34	18	85	65	104	−21	39.12
Iowa	Des Moines	27	10	86	66	108	−24	30.83
Iowa	Dubuque	24	7	82	62	99	−28	38.59
Kansas	Wichita	40	19	93	70	113	−21	28.61
Kentucky	Louisville	41	24	88	68	105	−20	43.56
Louisiana	New Orleans	62	43	91	74	102	14	59.74
Maine	Portland	31	12	79	57	103	−39	43.52
Maryland	Baltimore	41	24	87	67	105	−7	41.84
Massachusetts	Boston	36	23	82	65	102	−12	43.84
Michigan	Detroit	31	16	83	61	102	−21	30.97
Michigan	Sault Ste. Marie*	21	5	75	52	98	−36	33.48
Minnesota	Minn.-St. Paul	20	2	83	63	104	−34	26.36
Mississippi	Jackson	57	35	93	68	106	3	52.82
Missouri	St. Louis	38	20	89	69	107	−15	33.91
Montana	Helena	28	8	84	52	105	−42	11.37
Nebraska	Omaha	30	10	89	67	114	−23	30.34
Nevada	Winnemucca	42	17	93	51	108	−34	7.87
New Hampshire	Concord	31	9	83	56	102	−37	36.53
New Jersey	Atlantic City	41	23	84	65	106	−11	41.93
New Mexico	Albuquerque	47	22	93	65	105	−17	8.12
New Mexico	Roswell	55	27	94	69	109	−9	9.70
New York	Albany	30	12	83	60	100	−28	35.74
New York	New York-La Guardia	37	26	84	69	107	−2	42.82
No. Carolina	Charlotte	50	31	88	68	104	−3	43.16
No. Carolina	Raleigh	50	29	88	67	105	−1	41.76
No. Dakota	Bismarck	18	−4	84	56	109	−44	15.36
Ohio	Cincinnati-Greater.	37	20	86	65	102	−25	40.14
Ohio	Cleveland	33	19	82	61	103	−19	35.40
Oklahoma	Oklahoma City	47	25	94	71	110	−4	30.89
Oregon	Portland	44	34	80	56	107	−3	37.39
Pennsylvania	Harrisburg	37	22	86	65	107	−9	39.09
Pennsylvania	Philadelphia	39	24	86	67	104	−7	41.42
Rhode Island	Block Island	37	25	76	64	92	−4	41.91
So. Carolina	Charleston	59	37	89	72	103	8	51.59
So. Dakota	Huron	22	0	87	61	112	−39	18.66
So. Dakota	Rapid City	32	9	87	59	110	−27	16.27
Tennessee	Nashville	46	28	90	69	107	−15	48.49
Texas	Amarillo	49	22	91	66	108	−14	19.10
Texas	Galveston*	59	48	87	79	101	8	40.24
Texas	Houston	62	41	94	73	107	11	44.76
Utah	Salt Lake City	37	20	93	62	107	−30	15.31
Vermont	Burlington	25	8	81	59	101	−30	33.69
Virginia	Norfolk	48	32	90	70	104	5	45.22
Washington	Seattle-Tacoma	44	34	75	54	99	0	38.60
Washington	Spokane	31	20	84	55	108	−25	16.71
West Virginia	Huntington	41	25	86	65	100	−15	40.74
Wisconsin	Madison	25	7	83	58	104	−37	30.84
Wisconsin	Milwaukee	26	11	80	61	101	−26	30.94
Wyoming	Cheyenne	37	15	83	55	100	−34	13.31
Puerto Rico	San Juan	83	70	88	76	98	60	53.99

Mean Annual Snowfall (inches) based on record through 1980: Boston, Mass. 42; Sault Ste. Marie, Mich., 113; Albany, N.Y. 65.2; Rochester, N.Y. 89.2; Burlington, Vt., 78.6; Cheyenne, Wyo., 53.3; Juneau, Alas. 105.8.

Wettest Spot: Mount Waialeale, Ha., on the island of Kauai, is the rainiest place in the world, according to the National Geographic Society, with an average annual rainfall of 460 inches.

Highest Temperature: A temperature of 136° F. observed at Azizia, Tripolitania in Northern Africa on Sept. 13, 1922, is generally accepted as the world's highest temperature recorded under standard conditions.

The record high in the United States was 134° in Death Valley, Cal., July 10, 1913.

Lowest Temperature: A record low temperature of −128.6° F. was recorded at the Soviet Antarctica station Vostok on July 21, 1983.

The record low in the United States was −80° at Prospect Creek, Alas., Jan. 23, 1971.

The lowest official temperature on the North American continent was recorded at 81 degrees below zero in February, 1947, at a lonely airport in the Yukon called Snag.

These are the meteorological champions—the official temperature extremes—but there are plenty of other claimants to thermometer fame. However, sun readings are unofficial records, since meteorological data to qualify officially must be taken on instruments in a sheltered and ventilated location.

Record Temperatures by States Through 1984

Source: National Oceanic and Atmospheric Administration, U.S. Commerce Department

State	Lowest °F	Highest	Latest date	Station	Approximate elevation in feet
Alabama	−27		Jan. 30, 1966	New Market	725
		112	Sept. 5, 1925	Centerville	345
Alaska	−80		Jan. 23, 1971	Prospect Creek Camp	1,100
		100	June 27, 1915	Fort Yukon	419
Arizona	−40		Jan. 7, 1971	Hawley Lake	8,180
		127	July 7, 1905	Parker	345
Arkansas	−29		Feb. 13, 1905	Pond	1,250
		120	Aug. 10, 1936	Ozark	396
California	−45		Jan. 20, 1937	Boca	5,532
		134	July 10, 1913	Greenland Ranch	−178
Colorado	−61		Feb. 1, 1951	Taylor Park	9,206
		118	July 11, 1888	Bennett	5,484
Connecticut	−32		Feb. 16, 1943	Falls Village	585
		105	July 22, 1926	Waterbury	409
Delaware	−17		Jan. 17, 1893	Millsboro	20
		110	July 21, 1930	Millsboro	20
Dist. of Col.	−15		Feb. 11, 1899	Washington	112
		106	July 20, 1930	Washington	112
Florida	−2		Feb. 13, 1899	Tallahassee	193
		109	June 29, 1931	Monticello	207
Georgia	−17		Jan. 27, 1940	CCC Camp F-16	1,000
		112	Jul. 24, 1952	Louisville	132
Hawaii	14		Jan. 2, 1961	Haleakala, Maui	9,750
		100	Apr. 27, 1931	Pahala	850
Idaho	−60		Jan. 16, 1943	Island Park Dam	6,285
		118	July 28, 1934	Orofino	1,027
Illinois	−35		Jan. 22, 1930	Mount Carroll	817
		117	July 14, 1954	E. St. Louis	410
Indiana	−35		Feb. 2, 1951	Greensburg	954
		116	July 14, 1936	Collegeville	672
Iowa	−47		Jan. 12, 1912	Washta	1,157
		118	July 20, 1934	Keokuk	614
Kansas	−40		Feb. 13, 1905	Lebanon	1,812
		121	July 24, 1936	Alton (near)	1,651
Kentucky	−34		Jan. 28, 1963	Cynthiana	719
		114	July 28, 1930	Greensburg	581
Louisiana	−16		Feb. 13, 1899	Minden	194
		114	Aug. 10, 1936	Plain Dealing	268
Maine	−48		Jan. 19, 1925	Van Buren	510
		105	July 10, 1911	North Bridgton	450
Maryland	−40		Jan. 13, 1912	Oakland	2,461
		109	July 10, 1936	Cumberland and Frederick	623-325
Massachusetts	−34		Jan. 18, 1957	Birch Hill Dam	840
		107	Aug. 2, 1975	Chester and New Bedford	120-640
Michigan	−51		Feb. 9, 1934	Vanderbilt	785
		112	July 13, 1936	Mio	963
Minnesota	−59		Feb. 16, 1903	Pokegama Dam	1,280
		114	July 6, 1936	Moorhead	904
Mississippi	−19		Jan. 30, 1966	Corinth	420
		115	July 29, 1930	Holly Springs	600
Missouri	−40		Feb. 13, 1905	Warsaw	700
		118	July 14, 1954	Warsaw and Union	687-560
Montana	−70		Jan. 20, 1954	Rogers Pass	5,470
		117	July 5, 1937	Medicine Lake	1,950
Nebraska	−47		Feb. 12, 1899	Camp Clarke	3,700
		118	July 24, 1936	Minden	2,169
Nevada	−50		Jan. 8, 1937	San Jacinto	5,200
		122	June 23, 1954	Overton	1,240
New Hampshire	−46		Jan. 28, 1925	Pittsburg	1,575
		106	July 4, 1911	Nashua	125
New Jersey	−34		Jan. 5, 1904	River Vale	70
		110	July 10, 1936	Runyon	18
New Mexico	−50		Feb. 1, 1951	Gavilan	7,350
		116	July 14, 1934	Orogrande	4,171
New York	−52		Feb. 9, 1984	Stillwater Reservoir	1,670
		108	July 22, 1926	Troy	35
North Carolina	−34		Jan. 21, 1985	Mt. Mitchell	6,525
		110	Aug. 21, 1983	Fayetteville	213
North Dakota	−60		Feb. 15, 1936	Parshall	1,929
		121	July 6, 1936	Steele	1,857
Ohio	−39		Feb. 10, 1899	Milligan	800
		113	July 21, 1934	Gallipolis (near)	673
Oklahoma	−27		Jan. 18, 1930	Watts	958
		120	July 26, 1943	Tishmoningo	670
Oregon	−54		Feb. 10, 1933	Seneca	4,700
		119	Aug. 10, 1938	Pendleton	1,074
Pennsylvania	−42		Jan. 5, 1904	Smethport	1,469
		111	July 10, 1936	Phoenixville	100
Rhode Island	−23		Jan. 11, 1942	Kingston	100
		104	Aug. 2, 1975	Providence	51
South Carolina	−19		Jan. 21, 1985	Caesar's Head	3,100
		111	June 28, 1954	Camden	170
South Dakota	−58		Feb. 17, 1936	McIntosh	2,277
		120	July 5, 1936	Gannvalley	1,750

State	Lowest °F	Highest	Latest date	Station	Approximate elevation in feet
Tennessee	−32		Dec. 30, 1917	Mountain City	2,471
		113	Aug. 9, 1930	Perryville	377
Texas	−23		Feb. 8, 1933	Seminole	3,275
		120	Aug. 12, 1936	Seymour	1,291
Utah	−69		Feb. 1, 1985	Peter's Sink	8,092
		116	June 28, 1892	Saint George	2,880
Vermont	−50		Dec. 30, 1933	Bloomfield	915
		105	July 4, 1911	Vernon	310
Virginia	−30		Jan. 22, 1985	Mtn. Lake Bio. Stn.	3,870
		110	July 15, 1954	Balcony Falls	725
Washington	−48		Dec. 30, 1968	Mazama	2,120
	−48		Dec. 30, 1968	Winthrop	1,755
		118	Aug. 5, 1961	Ice Harbor Dam	475
West Virginia	−37		Dec. 30, 1917	Lewisburg	2,200
		112	July 10, 1936	Martinsburg	435
Wisconsin	−54		Jan. 24, 1922	Danbury	908
		114	July 13, 1936	Wisconsin Dells	900
Wyoming	−63		Feb. 9, 1933	Moran	6,770
		114	July 12, 1900	Basin	3,500

International Temperature and Precipitation

Source: Environmental Data Service, U.S. Commerce Department

A standard period of 30 years has been used to obtain the average daily maximum and minimum temperatures and precipitation. The length of record of extreme maximum and minimum temperatures includes all available years of data for a given location and is usually for a longer period.

Station	Elev. Ft.	Average Daily January Max.	Min.	July Max.	Min.	Extreme Max.	Min.	Average annual precipitation (inches)
Addis Ababa, Ethiopia	8,038	75	43	69	50	94	32	48.7
Algiers, Algeria	194	59	49	83	70	107	32	30.0
Amsterdam, Netherlands	5	40	34	69	59	95	3	25.6
Athens, Greece	351	54	42	90	72	109	20	15.8
Auckland, New Zealand	23	73	60	56	46	90	33	49.1
Bangkok, Thailand	53	89	67	90	76	104	50	57.8
Beirut, Lebanon	111	62	51	87	73	107	30	35.1
Belgrade, Yugoslavia	453	37	27	84	61	107	−14	24.6
Berlin, Germany	187	35	26	74	55	96	−15	23.1
Bogota, Colombia	8,355	67	48	64	50	75	30	41.8
Bombay, India	27	88	62	88	75	110	46	71.2
Bucharest, Romania	269	33	20	86	61	105	−18	22.8
Budapest, Hungary	394	35	26	82	61	103	−10	24.2
Buenos Aires, Argentina	89	85	63	57	42	104	22	37.4
Cairo, Egypt	381	65	47	96	70	117	34	1.1
Capetown, South Africa	56	78	60	63	45	103	28	20.0
Caracas, Venezuela	3,418	75	56	78	61	91	45	32.9
Casablanca, Morocco	164	63	45	79	65	110	31	15.9
Copenhagen, Denmark	43	36	29	72	55	91	−3	23.3
Damascus, Syria	2,362	53	36	96	64	113	21	8.6
Dublin, Ireland	155	47	35	67	51	86	8	29.7
Geneva, Switzerland	1,329	39	29	77	58	101	−1	33.9
Havana, Cuba	80	79	65	89	75	104	43	48.2
Hong Kong	109	64	56	87	78	97	32	85.1
Istanbul, Turkey	59	45	36	81	65	100	17	31.5
Jerusalem, Israel	2,654	55	41	87	63	107	26	19.7
Lagos, Nigeria	10	88	74	83	74	104	60	72.3
La Paz, Bolivia	12,001	63	43	62	33	80	26	22.6
Lima, Peru	394	82	66	67	57	93	49	1.6
London, England	149	44	35	73	55	99	9	22.9
Madrid, Spain	2,188	47	33	87	62	102	14	16.5
Manila, Philippines	49	86	69	88	75	101	58	82.0
Mexico City, Mexico	7,340	66	42	74	54	92	24	23.0
Moscow, U.S.S.R.	505	21	9	76	55	96	−27	24.8
Nairobi, Kenya	5,971	77	54	69	51	87	41	37.7
Oslo, Norway	308	30	20	73	56	93	−21	26.9
Paris, France	164	42	32	76	55	105	1	22.3
Prague, Czechoslovakia	662	34	25	74	58	98	−16	19.3
Reykjavik, Iceland	92	36	28	58	48	74	4	33.9
Rome, Italy	377	54	39	88	64	104	20	29.5
San Salvador, El Salvador	2,238	90	60	89	65	105	45	70.0
Santiago, Chile	1,706	85	53	59	37	99	24	14.2
Sao Paolo, Brazil	2,628	77	63	66	53	100	32	57.3
Shanghai, China	16	47	32	91	75	104	10	45.0
Singapore	33	86	73	88	75	97	66	95.0
Stockholm, Sweden	146	31	23	70	55	97	−26	22.4
Sydney, Australia	62	78	65	60	46	114	35	46.5
Teheran, Iran	3,937	45	27	99	72	109	−5	9.7
Tokyo, Japan	19	47	29	83	70	101	17	61.6
Tripoli, Libya	72	61	47	85	71	114	33	15.1
Vienna, Austria	664	34	26	75	59	98	−14	25.6
Warsaw, Poland	294	30	21	75	56	98	−22	22.0

Canadian Normal Temperature and Precipitation

Source: Atmospheric Environment Service, Environment Canada

Normal refers to the mean daily temperature and total monthly precipitation based on varying periods of record over the thirty-year period 1951 to 1980 inclusive. Airport station unless * designates city office station. T, temperature in Celsius; P, precipitation in millimeters.

Station	Jan. T.	Jan. P.	Feb. T.	Feb. P.	Mar. T.	Mar. P.	Apr. T.	Apr. P.	May T.	May P.	June T.	June P.	July T.	July P.	Aug. T.	Aug. P.	Sept. T.	Sept. P.	Oct. T.	Oct. P.	Nov. T.	Nov. P.	Dec. T.	Dec. P.
Calgary, Alta..	-12	16	-7	16	-4	16	3	33	9	49	14	89	16	65	15	55	11	38	6	18	-3	13	-8	16
Charlottetown, P.E.I..	-7	117	-8	97	-3	95	2	82	9	84	15	80	18	84	18	88	14	86	8	106	3	121	-4	129
Churchill, Man.	-28	15	-26	13	-20	18	-11	23	-2	32	6	44	12	46	11	58	5	51	-2	43	-12	39	-22	21
Dawson, Yukon*	-31	17	-24	16	-15	10	-2	10	8	21	14	39	16	47	13	44	7	28	-4	29	-17	22	-26	25
Edmonton, Alta.	-15	24	-10	18	-5	16	4	20	11	42	15	77	17	92	16	78	11	46	6	15	-4	17	-10	22
Fredericton, N.B..	-9	103	-8	90	-2	85	4	80	11	83	16	85	19	89	18	87	13	87	8	97	1	106	-7	118
Frobisher Bay, N.W.T..	-26	26	-26	23	-23	23	-14	26	-3	25	3	39	8	63	7	60	2	46	-5	44	-13	34	-22	22
Halifax, N.S.	-6	153	-6	134	-2	125	3	109	9	109	15	90	18	94	18	101	14	96	9	136	3	167	-3	163
Hamilton, Ont.	-6	63	-6	53	-1	71	6	79	13	66	18	65	21	71	20	75	16	74	9	61	3	68	-3	76
Kitchener, Ont.*	-7	60	-6	57	-1	72	6	75	13	77	18	86	21	84	20	89	16	72	10	69	3	80	-4	76
London, Ont.	-7	75	-6	61	-1	75	6	81	12	67	18	74	20	72	20	80	15	79	9	73	3	85	-4	88
Moncton, N.B.	-8	125	-8	99	-3	112	3	90	9	84	15	90	19	95	18	79	13	76	8	99	2	110	-5	121
Montreal, Que.	-10	72	-9	65	-3	74	6	74	13	66	18	82	21	90	20	92	15	88	9	76	2	81	-7	87
Ottawa, Ont.	-11	61	-10	60	-3	68	6	69	13	68	18	73	21	86	19	88	14	79	8	68	1	78	-8	80
Quebec City, Que.	-12	90	-11	78	-5	82	3	73	11	87	16	110	19	117	18	117	13	119	7	91	0	97	-9	114
Regina, Sask.	-18	17	-14	16	-8	18	3	24	11	64	16	80	19	53	18	45	12	37	5	19	-5	14	-13	17
Saint John, N.B.	-8	149	-8	116	-3	114	3	107	9	108	14	94	17	103	17	102	13	112	8	128	2	146	-5	166
St. John's, Nfld.	-4	156	-5	140	-2	132	1	116	5	102	11	86	16	75	15	122	12	117	7	146	3	163	-2	161
Saskatoon, Sask.	-19	18	-15	16	-9	18	3	21	11	40	16	59	19	54	17	38	11	31	5	17	-6	15	-14	20
Sault Ste. Marie, Ont.	-10	74	-10	68	-5	60	3	64	9	84	15	74	17	56	17	83	13	95	8	74	1	86	-7	80
Toronto, Ont.*	-5	61	-4	52	-1	70	8	73	14	66	19	64	22	74	21	73	17	66	11	61	5	68	-2	73
Vancouver, B.C.	3	154	5	115	6	101	9	60	12	52	15	45	17	32	17	41	14	67	10	114	6	150	4	182
Victoria, B.C.	3	154	5	99	6	72	8	39	12	29	14	29	16	16	16	27	14	40	10	78	6	131	4	157
Whitehorse, Yukon.	-21	18	-13	13	-8	14	0	10	7	13	12	31	14	34	13	38	8	30	1	22	-9	20	-17	20
Windsor, Ont.	-5	55	-4	50	1	72	8	83	14	70	20	89	22	83	21	84	17	67	11	57	4	65	-2	73
Winnipeg, Man.	-19	21	-16	18	-8	23	3	39	11	66	17	80	20	76	18	75	12	53	6	31	-5	25	-14	19
Yellowknife, N.W.T.	-29	13	-25	11	-19	12	-7	10	5	17	13	17	16	34	14	44	7	31	-2	35	-14	25	-24	18

Canadian Annual Climatological Data

Source: Atmospheric Environment Service, Environment Canada

Station 1984	Elev. meters	Temperature (Celsius) Highest	Date D/Mo.	Lowest	Date D/Mo.	Total (mm)	Precipitation Greatest in 24 hrs.	Date D/Mo.	Snowfall Total (cm)	Greatest in 24 hrs.	Date D/Mo.	Fastest wind Km/h	Date D/Mo.	No. of days Precip., measurable	Snow, measurable
Calgary, Alta..	1084	35.3	26/7	-36.2	29/12	366.8	40.8	6/9	104.2	7.6	21/9	111	6/9	119	68
Charlottetown, P.E.I..	55	29.9	6/8	-24.0	22/1	1298.8	52.4	14/8	250.9	18.5	9/4	65	10/4	185	71
Churchill, Man.	29	32.2	sev.	-39.6	7/1	412.8	34.4	28/4	292.7	34.4	28/4	98	30/10	145	94
Dawson, Yukon	369	28.3	21/6	-49.9	25/1	303.3	20.6	10/7	163.9	9.6	19/12	56	21/11	138	79
Edmonton, Alta.	671	33.4	26/7	-33.7	29/12	496.8	26.4	6/7	149.0	22.3	18/10	95	18/7	130	62
Fredericton, N.B.	20	34.9	9/6	-32.2	22/1	1288.4	45.9	26/6	332.9	53.8	14/3	82	sev.	167	62
Frobisher Bay, N.W.T.	34	24.4	14/7	-44.9	14/1	442.6	27.2	30/7	278.9	19.2	9/6	91	3/4	164	126
Halifax, N.S.	145	30.6	2/7	-21.1	10/2	1343.4	62.9	4/5	150.4	13.0	9/3	94	26/12	179	43
Hamilton, Ont.	237	30.5	sev.	-24.7	21/1	1008.2	66.6	17/6	179.4	27.4	28/2	78	30/4	154	61
Moncton, N.B.	71	32.5	9/6	-28.4	22/1	1294.7	38.6	sev.	419.6	35.6	sev.	100	9/4	185	75
Montreal, Que.	36	31.5	4/8	-28.3	16/1	860.7	53.8	18/6	174.3	18.7	28/2	80	sev.	150	55
Ottawa, Ont.	114	32.6	sev.	-29.4	16/1	923.3	41.6	12/8	201.4	34.7	28/2	78	30/4	150	57
Quebec, Que.	73	31.7	9/7	-30.9	21/1	1052.9	55.2	15/7	278.0	20.0	14/3	89	29/2	182	70
Regina, Sask.	577	36.1	23/8	-37.6	30/12	272.6	21.8	21/9	121.9	28.2	sev.	109	29/8	104	54
St. John, N.B.	109	29.8	5/8	-28.9	22/1	1490.1	81.8	19/6	273.4	22.6	31/1	98	29/2	176	59
St. John's, Nfld.	140	28.7	10/7	-19.7	27/12	1711.8	74.9	18/8	238.9	36.8	27/3	122	27/1	211	75
Saskatoon, Sask.	501	38.1	27/7	-38.5	29/12	310.2	24.4	20/6	119.5	28.2	16/10	87	19/8	98	51
Sault Ste. Marie, Ont.	192	29.8	6/6	-32.9	15/1	902.9	57.4	12/9	249.5	17.0	30/12	100	10/3	228	75
Thunder Bay, Ont.	199	31.5	22/7	-34.6	20/1	683.6	40.3	sev.	115.3	11.6	sev.	91	11/7	146	56
Toronto, Ont.	111	31.8	4/7	-20.6	15/1	756.3	35.6	13/2	138.6	24.4	28/2	100	30/4	137	46
Vancouver, B.C.	2	27.0	16/8	-11.3	31/12	1421.9	43.8	3/1	38.6	13.0	20/12	74	16/3	183	9
Victoria, B.C.	69	30.3	24/7	-7.1	18/12	953.0	44.0	2/11	55.5	19.6	29/12	70	12/10	176	11
Waterloo/Wellington, Ont.	314	29.9	23/7	-31.9	16/1	946.2	66.0	17/6	151.8	12.0	5/3	98	30/4	162	60
Whitehorse, Yukon	703	30.2	4/8	-44.4	29/12	252.7	26.8	7/8	144.4	17.2	sev.	87	29/1	205	80
Windsor, Ont.	190	33.5	23/7	-27.2	21/1	781.4	62.2	18/8	187.6	15.6	27/2	59	30/4	151	23
Winnipeg, Man.	239	36.5	26/8	-34.5	31/12	606.3	69.8	21/6	93.2	8.2	14/3	98	16/10	124	56
Yellowknife, N.W.T.	205	31.0	27/7	-44.2	11/12	328.5	22.6	30/6	159.3	9.2	sev.	72	17/10	123	74

Speed of Winds in Canada

Source: Atmospheric Environment Service, Environment Canada

Kilometers-per-hour average is for the period of record 1951 to 1980. High is for gust wind speed based on varying periods of record, depending on the origin of the station, through 1984.

Station	Avg.	High	Station	Avg.	High	Station	Avg.	High
Calgary, Alta..	16.2	127	London, Ont.	16.0	128	Sault Ste. Marie, Ont. .	15.1	119
Charlottetown, P.E.I..	19.3	177	Moncton, Que.	18.1	161	Thunder Bay, Ont. ..	13.4	122
Churchill, Man.	22.7	151	Montreal, Que.	15.6	161	Toronto, Ont.	18.0	124
Dawson, Yukon.	3.7	57	Ottawa, Ont.	14.6	135	Vancouver, B.C.	12.0	129
Edmonton, Alta.	14.1	117	Quebec City, Que.	16.0	177	Victoria, B.C.	17.7	145
Fredericton, N.B.	13.8	132	Regina, Sask.	20.8	153	Whitehorse, Yukon	14.1	106
Frobisher Bay, N.W.T.	16.7	156	Saint John, N.B.	18.5	146	Windsor, Ont.	17.0	148
Halifax, N.S.	18.2	132	Saint John's, Nfld.	24.3	193	Winnipeg, Man.	18.6	129
Hamilton, Ont.	17.7	133	Saskatoon, Sask.	17.5	151	Yellowknife, N.W.T.	15.5	105

WEIGHTS AND MEASURES

Source: National Bureau of Standards, U.S. Commerce Department

U.S. Moving, Inch by 25.4 mm, to Metric System

On July 2, 1971, following the report of a metric conversion study committee, Commerce Secy. Maurice H. Stans recommended a gradual U.S. changeover during a 10-year period at the end of which the U.S. would be predominantly, but not exclusively, on the metric system. The Metric Conversion Act of 1975, signed Dec. 23, 1975, declared a national policy of coordinating voluntary increasing use of the Metric System and established a U. S. Metric Board to coordinate the change over. That Board terminated its operations on Sept. 30, 1982 and transferred its functions to the Office of Metric Programs, U.S. Department of Commerce.

Currently conversion to metric for the most part is confined to the following industries: automotive, construction and farm equipment, computer, and bottling. In addition, with encouragement of the U.S. Office of Education, our school systems are emphasizing teaching of the metric system.

The International System of Units

Two systems of weights and measures exist side by side in the United States today, with roughly equal but separate legislative sanction: the U.S. Customary System and the International (Metric) System. Throughout U.S. history, the Customary System (inherited from, but now different from, the British Imperial System) has been, as its name implies, customarily used; a plethora of federal and state legislation has given it, through implication, standing as our primary voluntary weights and measures system. However, the Metric System (incorporated in the scientists' new SI or Systeme International d'Unites) is the only system that has ever received specific legislative sanction by Congress. The "Law of 1866" reads:

It shall be lawful throughout the United States of America to employ the weights and measures of the metric system; and no contract or dealing, or pleading in any court, shall be deemed invalid or liable to objection because the weights or measures expressed or referred to therein are weights or measures of the metric system.

Over the last 100 years, the Metric System has seen slow, steadily increasing use in the United States and, today, is of importance nearly equal to the Customary System.

On Feb. 10, 1964, the National Bureau of Standards issued the following bulletin:

Henceforth it shall be the policy of the National Bureau of Standards to use the units of the International System (SI), as adopted by the 11th General Conference on Weights and Measures (October 1960), except when the use of these units would obviously impair communication or reduce the usefulness of a report.

What had been the Metric System became the International System (SI), a more complete scientific system.

Seven units have been adopted to serve as the base for the International System as follows: length—meter; mass—kilogram; time—second; electric current—ampere; thermodynamic temperature—kelvin; amount of substance—mole; and luminous intensity—candela.

Prefixes

The following prefixes, in combination with the basic unit names, provide the multiples and submultiples in the International System. For example, the unit name "meter," with the prefix "kilo" added, produces "kilometer," meaning "1,000 meters."

Prefix	Symbol	Multiples	Equivalent	Prefix	Symbol	Submultiples	Equivalent
exa	E	10^{18}	quintillionfold	deci	d	10^{-1}	tenth part
peta	P	10^{15}	quadrillionfold	centi	c	10^{-2}	hundredth part
tera	T	10^{12}	trillionfold	milli	m	10^{-3}	thousandth part
giga	G	10^{9}	billionfold	micro	μ	10^{-6}	millionth part
mega	M	10^{6}	millionfold	nano	n	10^{-9}	billionth part
kilo	k	10^{3}	thousandfold	pico	p	10^{-12}	trillionth part
hecto	h	10^{2}	hundredfold	femto	f	10^{-15}	quadrillionth part
deka	da	10	tenfold	atto	a	10^{-18}	quintillionth part

Tables of Metric Weights and Measures

Linear Measure

10 millimeters (mm)	= 1 centimeter (cm)
10 centimeters	= 1 decimeter (dm) = 100 millimeters
10 decimeters	= 1 meter (m) = 1,000 millimeters
10 meters	= 1 dekameter (dam)
10 dekameters	= 1 hectometer (hm) = 100 meters
10 hectometers	= 1 kilometer (km) = 1,000 meters

Area Measure

100 square millimeters (mm²)	= 1 square centimeter (cm²)
10,000 square centimeters	= 1 square meter (m²) = 1,000,000 square millimeters
100 square meters	= 1 are (a)
100 ares	= 1 hectare (ha) = 10,000 square meters
100 hectares	= 1 square kilometer (km²) = 1,000,000 square meters

Fluid Volume Measure

10 milliliters (mL)	= 1 centiliter (cL)
10 centiliters	= 1 deciliter (dL) = 100 milliliters

10 deciliters	= 1 liter (L) = 1,000 milliliters
10 liters	= 1 dekaliter (daL)
10 dekaliters	= 1 hectoliter (hL) = 100 liters
10 hectoliters	= 1 kiloliter (kL) = 1,000 liters

Cubic Measure

1,000 cubic millimeters (mm³)	= 1 cubic centimeter (cm³)
1,000 cubic centimeters	= 1 cubic decimeter (dm³) = 1,000,000 cubic millimeters
1,000 cubic decimeters	= 1 cubic meter (m³) = 1 stere = 1,000,000 cubic centimeters = 1,000,000,000 cubic millimeters

Weight

10 milligrams (mg)	= 1 centigram (cg)
10 centigrams	= 1 decigram (dg) = 100 milligrams
10 decigrams	= 1 gram (g) = 1,000 milligrams
10 grams	= 1 dekagram (dag)
10 dekagrams	= 1 hectogram (hg) = 100 grams
10 hectograms	= 1 kilogram (kg) = 1,000 grams
1,000 kilograms	= 1 metric ton (t)

Table of U.S. Customary Weights and Measures

Linear Measure

12 inches (in)	= 1 foot (ft)
3 feet	= 1 yard (yd)
5 ½ yards	= 1 rod (rd), pole, or perch (16 ½ feet)

40 rods	= 1 furlong (fur) = 220 yards = 660 feet
8 furlongs	= 1 statute mile (mi) = 1,760 yards = 5,280 feet
3 miles	= 1 league = 5,280 yards = 15,840 feet
6076.11549 feet	= 1 International Nautical Mile

Liquid Measure

When necessary to distinguish the liquid pint or quart from the dry pint or quart, the word "liquid" or the abbreviation "liq" should be used in combination with the name or abbreviation of the liquid unit.

4 gills	= 1 pint (pt) = 28.875 cubic inches
2 pints	= 1 quart (qt) = 57.75 cubic inches
4 quarts	= 1 gallon (gal) = 231 cubic inches = 8 pints = 32 gills

Area Measure

Squares and cubes of units are sometimes abbreviated by using "superior" figures. For example. ft² means square foot, and ft³ means cubic foot.

144 square inches	= 1 square foot (ft²)
9 square feet	= 1 square yard (yd²) = 1,296 square inches
30 ¼ square yards	= 1 square rod (rd²) = 272 ¼ square feet
160 square rods	= 1 acre = 4,840 square yards = 43,560 square feet
640 acres	= 1 square mile (mi²)
1 mile square	= 1 section (of land)
6 miles square	= 1 township = 36 sections = 36 square miles

Cubic Measure

1 cubic foot (ft³)	= 1,728 cubic inches (in³)
27 cubic feet	= 1 cubic yard (yd³)

Gunter's or Surveyors' Chain Measure

7.92 inches (in)	= 1 link
100 links	= 1 chain (ch) = 4 rods = 66 feet
80 chains	= 1 survey mile (mi) = 320 rods = 5,280 feet

Troy Weight

24 grains	= 1 pennyweight (dwt)
20 pennyweights	= 1 ounce troy (oz t) = 480 grains
12 ounces troy	= 1 pound troy (lb t) = 240 pennyweights = 5,760 grains

Dry Measure

When necessary to distinguish the dry pint or quart from the liquid pint or quart, the word "dry" should be used in combination with the name or abbreviation of the dry unit.

2 pints (pt)	= 1 quart (qt) = 67.2006 cubic inches
8 quarts	= 1 peck (pk) = 537.605 cubic inches = 16 pints
4 pecks	= 1 bushel (bu) = 2,150.42 cubic inches = 32 quarts

Avoirdupois Weight

When necessary to distinguish the avoirdupois ounce or pound from the troy ounce or pound, the word "avoirdupois" or the abbreviation "avdp" should be used in combination with the name or abbreviation of the avoirdupois unit.

(The "grain" is the same in avoirdupois and troy weight.)

27 ¹¹/₃₂ grains	= 1 dram (dr)
16 drams	= 1 ounce (oz) = 437 ½ grains
16 ounces	= 1 pound (lb) = 256 drams = 7,000 grains
100 pounds	= 1 hundredweight (cwt)°
20 hundredweights	= 1 ton = 2,000 pounds°

In "gross" or "long" measure, the following values are recognized.

112 pounds	= 1 gross or long hundredweight°
20 gross or long hundredweights	= 1 gross or long ton = 2,240 pounds°

°When the terms "hundredweight" and "ton" are used unmodified, they are commonly understood to mean the 100-pound hundredweight and the 2,000-pound ton, respectively: these units may be designated "net" or "short" when necessary to distinguish them from the corresponding units in gross or long measure.

Tables of Equivalents

In this table it is necessary to distinguish between the "international" and the "survey" foot. The international foot, defined in 1959 as exactly equal to 0.3048 meter, is shorter than the old survey foot by exactly 2 parts in one million. The survey foot is still used in data expressed in feet in geodetic surveys within the U.S. In this table the survey foot is italicized.

When the name of a unit is enclosed in brackets thus, [1 hand], this indicates (1) that the unit is not in general current use in the United States, or (2) that the unit is believed to be based on "custom and usage" rather than on formal definition.

Equivalents involving decimals are, in most instances, rounded off to the third decimal place except where they are exact, in which cases these exact equivalents are so designated.

Lengths

1 angstrom (A)	0.1 nanometer (exactly) 0.000 1 micrometer (exactly) 0.000 000 1 millimeter (exactly) 0.000 000 004 inch
1 cable's length	120 fathoms (exactly) 720 *feet* (exactly) 219 meters
1 centimeter (cm)	0.3937 inch
1 chain (ch) (Gunter's or surveyors)	66 *feet* (exactly) 20.1168 meters
1 chain (engineers)	100 feet 30.48 meters (exactly)
1 decimeter (dm)	3.937 inches
1 degree (geographical)	364,566.929 feet 69.047 miles (avg.) 111.123 kilometers (avg.)
-of latitude	68.708 miles at equator 69.403 miles at poles
-of longitude	69.171 miles at equator
1 dekameter (dam)	32.808 feet
1 fathom	6 *feet* (exactly) 1.8288 meters (exactly)
1 foot (ft)	0.3048 meters (exactly)
1 furlong (fur)	10 chains (surveyors) (exactly) 660 *feet* (exactly) ⅛ statute mile (exactly) 201.168 meters
[1 hand] (height measure for horses from ground to top of shoulders)	4 inches
1 inch (in)	2.54 centimeters (exactly)
1 kilometer (km)	0.621 mile 3,281.5 feet

1 league (land)	3 survey miles (exactly) 4.828 kilometers
1 link (Gunter's or surveyors)	7.92 inches (exactly) 0.201 meter
1 link engineers	1 foot 0.305 meter
1 meter (m)	39.37 inches 1.094 yards
1 micrometer (μm) [the Greek letter mu]	0.001 millimeter (exactly) 0.000 039 37 inch
1 mil	0.001 inch (exactly) 0.025 4 millimeter (exactly)
1 mile (mi) (statute or land)	5,280 *feet* (exactly) 1.609 kilometers
1 international nautical mile (nmi)	1.852 kilometers (exactly) 1.150779 survey miles 6,076.11549 feet
1 millimeter (mm)	0.039 37 inch
1 nanometer (nm)	0.001 micrometer (exactly) 0.000 000 039 37 inch
1 pica (typography)	12 points
1 point (typography)	0.013 837 inch (exactly) 0.351 millimeter
1 rod (rd), pole, or perch	16 ½ *feet* (exactly) 5.029 meters
1 yard (yd)	0.9144 meter (exactly)

Areas or Surfaces

1 acre	43,560 square *feet* (exactly) 4,840 square yards 0.405 hectare
1 are (a)	119.599 square yards 0.025 acre

(continued)

1 bolt (cloth measure):

length . . . . 100 yards (on modern looms)

width . . . . { 42 inches (usually, for cotton)
{ 60 inches (usually, for wool)

1 hectare (ha) . . . . 2.471 acres

[1 square (building)] . . . . 100 square feet

1 square centimeter (cm²) . . . . 0.155 square inch

1 square decimeter (dm²) . . . . 15.500 square inches

1 square foot (ft²) . . . . 929.030 square centimeters

1 square inch (in²) . . . . . . 6.4516 square centimeters (exactly)

1 square kilometer (km²) . . . { 247.104 acres
{ 0.386 square mile

1 square meter (m²) . . . . . . { 1.196 square yards
{ 10.764 square feet

1 square mile (mi²) . . . . 258.999 hectares

1 square millimeter (mm²) . . . . 0.002 square inch

1 square rod (rd²) sq. pole, or
sq. perch . . . . 25.293 square meters

1 square yard (yd²) . . . . 0.836 square meter

Capacities or Volumes

1 barrel (bbl) liquid . . . . 31 to 42 gallons°

°There are a variety of "barrels," established by law or usage. For example: federal taxes on fermented liquors are based on a barrel of 31 gallons; many state laws fix the "barrel for liquids" as 31½ gallons; one state fixes a 36-gallon barrel for cistern measurement; federal law recognizes a 40-gallon barrel for "proof spirits"; by custom, 42 gallons comprise a barrel of crude oil or petroleum products for statistical purposes, and this equivalent is recognized "for liquids" by 4 states.

1 barrel (bbl), standard,
for fruits, vegetables,
and other dry com-
modities except dry
cranberries . . . . { 7,056 cubic inches
{ 105 dry quarts
{ 3.281 bushels, struck
{ measure

1 barrel (bbl), standard,
cranberry . . . . { 5,826 cubic inches
{ 86⁴⁵/₆₄ dry quarts
{ 2.709 bushels, struck
{ measure

1 board foot (lumber measure) . . a foot-square board 1 inch thick

1 bushel (bu) (U.S.)
(struck measure) . . . . . { 2,150.42 cubic inches
{ (exactly)
{ 35.239 liters

[1 bushel, heaped (U.S.)] . . . { 2,747.715 cubic inches
{ 1.278 bushels, struck
{ measure°

°Frequently recognized as 1¼ bushels, struck measure.

[1 bushel (bu) (British
Imperial) (struck
measure)] . . . . { 1.032 U.S. bushels
{ struck measure
{ 2,219.36 cubic inches

1 cord (cd) firewood . . . . . 128 cubic feet (exactly)

1 cubic centimeter (cm³) . . . . 0.061 cubic inch

1 cubic decimeter (dm³) . . . . 61.024 cubic inches

1 cubic inch (in³) . . . . . . { 0.554 fluid ounce
{ 4.433 fluid drams
{ 16.387 cubic centimeters

1 cubic foot (ft³) . . . . . . { 7.481 gallons
{ 28.317 cubic decimeters

1 cubic meter (m³) . . . . 1.308 cubic yards

1 cubic yard (yd³) . . . . 0.765 cubic meter

1 cup, measuring . . . . { 8 fluid ounces (exactly)
{ ½ liquid pint (exactly)

[1 dram, fluid (fl dr)
(British)] . . . . { 0.961 U.S. fluid dram
{ 0.217 cubic inch
{ 3.552 milliliters

1 dekaliter (daL) . . . . { 2.642 gallons
{ 1.135 pecks

1 gallon (gal) (U.S.) . . . . . { 231 cubic inches (exactly)
{ 3.785 liters
{ 0.833 British gallon
{ 128 U.S. fluid ounces (exactly)

[1 gallon (gal)
British Imperial] . . . . . { 277.42 cubic inches
{ 1.201 U.S. gallons
{ 4.546 liters
{ 160 British fluid ounces (exactly)

1 gill (gi) . . . . { 7.219 cubic inches
{ 4 fluid ounces (exactly)
{ 0.118 liter

1 hectoliter (hL) . . . . { 26.418 gallons
{ 2.838 bushels
{ 1.057 liquid quarts

1 liter (L) (1 cubic decimeter exactly) . . . . { 0.908 dry quart
{ 61.025 cubic inches

---

1 milliliter (mL) (1 cu cm exactly) . . . . . { 0.271 fluid dram
{ 16.231 minims
{ 0.061 cubic inch

1 ounce, liquid
(U.S.) . . . . { 1.805 cubic inches
{ 29.573 milliliters
{ 1.041 British fluid ounces
{ 0.961 U.S. fluid ounce

[1 ounce, fluid (fl oz) (British)] { 1.734 cubic inches
{ 28.412 milliliters

1 peck (pk) . . . . 8.810 liters

1 pint (pt), dry . . . . { 33.600 cubic inches
{ 0.551 liter

1 pint (pt), liquid . . . . . . { 28.875 cubic inches (exactly)
{ 0.473 liter

1 quart (qt) dry (U.S.) . . . . { 67.201 cubic inches
{ 1.101 liters
{ 0.969 British quart

1 quart (qt) liquid (U.S.) . . . { 57.75 cubic in (exactly)
{ 0.946 liter
{ 0.833 British quart

[1 quart (qt) (British)] . . . . { 69.354 cubic inches
{ 1.032 U.S. dry quarts
{ 1.201 U.S. liquid quarts

1 tablespoon . . . . { 3 teaspoons°(exactly)
{ 4 fluid drams
{ ½ fluid ounce (exactly)

1 teaspoon . . . . { ⅓ tablespoon°(exactly)
{ 1⅓ fluid drams°

°The equivalent "1 teaspoon—1⅓ fluid drams" has been found by the bureau to correspond more closely with the actual capacities of "measuring" and silver teaspoons than the equivalent "1 teaspoon—1 fluid dram" which is given by many dictionaries.

Weights or Masses

1 assay ton°° (AT) . . . . 29.167 grams

°°Used in assaying. The assay ton bears the same relation to the milligram that a ton of 2,000 pounds avoirdupois bears to the ounce troy; hence the weight in milligrams of precious metal obtained from one assay ton of ore gives directly the number of troy ounces to the net ton.

1 bale (cotton measure) . . . . { 500 pounds in U.S.
{ 750 pounds in Egypt

1 carat (c) . . . . { 200 milligrams (exactly)
{ 3.086 grains

1 dram avoirdupois (dr avdp) { 27¹¹/₁₂ (=27.344) grains
gamma, see microgram { 1.772 grams

1 grain . . . . 64.799 milligrams

1 gram . . . . { 15.432 grains
{ 0.035 ounce, avoirdupois

1 hundredweight, gross or
long°°° (gross cwt) . . . . { 112 pounds (exactly)
{ 50.802 kilograms

1 hundredweight, net or short
(cwt. or net cwt.) . . . . . { 100 pounds (exactly)
{ 45.359 kilograms

1 kilogram (kg) . . . . 2.205 pounds

1 microgram (μg [The Greek letter mu in
combination with the letter g]) . . . 0.000001 gram (exactly)

1 milligram (mg) . . . . 0.015 grain

1 ounce, avoirdupois
(oz avdp) . . . . { 437.5 grains (exactly)
{ 0.911 troy ounce
{ 28.350 grams

1 ounce, troy (oz t) . . . . . { 480 grains (exactly)
{ 1.097 avoirdupois ounces
{ 31.103 grams

1 pennyweight (dwt) . . . . . 1.555 grams

1 pound, avoirdupois
(lb avdp) . . . . { 7,000 grains (exactly)
{ 1.215 troy pounds
{ 453.592 37 grams (exactly)

1 pound, troy (lb t) . . . . . { 5,760 grains (exactly)
{ 0.823 avoirdupois pound
{ 373.242 grams

1 ton, gross or long°°°
(gross ton) . . . . { 2,240 pounds (exactly)
{ 1.12 net tons (exactly)
{ 1.016 metric tons

°°°The gross or long ton and hundredweight are used commercially in the United States to only a limited extent, usually in restricted industrial fields. These units are the same as British "ton" and "hundredweight."

1 ton, metric (t) . . . . { 2,204.623 pounds
{ 0.984 gross ton
{ 1.102 net tons

1 ton, net or short (sh ton) . . { 2,000 pounds (exactly)
{ 0.893 gross ton
{ 0.907 metric ton

Tables of Interrelation of Units of Measurement

Units of length and area of the international and survey measures are included in the following tables. Units unique to the survey measure are italicized. See pg 765, Tables of Equivalents, 1st para.

1 international foot	= 0.999 998 survey foot (exactly)
1 survey foot	= 1200/3937 meter (exactly)
1 international foot	= 12 × 0.0254 meter (exactly)

Bold face type indicates exact values

Units of Length

Units	Inches	Links	Feet	Yards	Rods	Chains	Miles	cm	Meters
1 inch=	1	0.126 263	0.083 333	0.027 778	0.005 051	0.001 263	0.000 016	2.54	0.025 4
1 link=	7.92	1	0.66	0.22	0.04	0.01	0.000 125	20.117	0.201 168
1 foot=	12	1.515 152	1	0.333 333	0.060 606	0.015 152	0.000 189	30.48	0.304 8
1 yard=	36	4.545 45	3	1	0.181 818	0.045 455	0.000 568	91.44	0.914 4
1 rod=	198	25	16.5	5.5	1	0.25	0.003 125	502.92	5.029 2
1 chain=	792	100	66	22	4	1	0.012 5	2011.68	20.116 8
1 mile=	63 360	8000	5280	1760	320	80	1	160 934.4	1609.344
1 cm=	0.3937	0.049 710	0.032 808	0.010 936	0.001 988	0.000 497	0.000 006	1	0.01
1 meter=	39.37	4.970 960	3.280 840	1.093 613	0.198 838	0.049 710	0.000 621	100	1

Units of Area

Units	Sq. inches	Sq. links	Sq. feet	Sq. yards	Sq. rods	Sq. chains
1 sq. inch=	1	.015 942 3	0.006 944	0.000 771 605	0.000 025 5	0.000 001 594
1 sq. link=	62.726 4	1	0.435 6	0.0484	0.0016	0.000 1
1 sq. foot=	144	2.295 684	1	0.111 111 1	0.003 673 09	0.000 229 568
1 sq. yard=	1296	20.661 16	9	1	0.033 057 85	0.002 066 12
1 sq. rod=	39 204	625	272.25	30.25	1	0.062 5
1 sq. chain=	627 264	10 000	4 356	484	16	1
1 acre=	6 272 640	100 000	43 560	4 840	160	10
1 sq. mile=	4 014 489 600	64 000 000	27 878 400	3 097 600	102 400	6400
1 sq. cm=	0.155 000 3	0.002 471 05	0.001 076	0.000 119 599	0.000 003 954	0.000 000 247
1 sq. meter=	1550.003	24.710 44	10.763 91	1.195 990	0.039 536 70	0.002 471 044
1 hectare=	15 500 031	247 104	107 639.1	11 959.90	395.367 0	24.710 44

Units	Acres	Sq. miles	Sq. cm	Sq. meters	Hectares
1 sq. inch=	0.000 000 159 423	0.000 000 000 249 10	6.451 6	0.000 645 16	0.000 000 065
1 sq. link=	0.000 01	0.000 000 015 625	404.685 642 24	0.040 468 56	0.000 004 047
1 sq. foot=	0.000 022 956 84	0.000 000 035 870 06	929.034 1	0.092 903 41	0.000 009 290
1 sq. yard=	0.000 206 611 6	0.000 000 322 830 6	8 361.273 6	0.836 127 36	0.000 083 613
1 sq. rod=	0.006 25	0.000 009 765 625	252 929.5	25.292 95	0.002 529 295
1 sq. chain=	0.1	0.000 156 25	4 046 873	404.687 3	0.040 468 73
1 acre=	1	0.001 562 5	40 468 73	4 046.873	0.404 687 3
1 sq. mile=	640	1	25 899 881 103	2 589 988.11	258.998 811 034
1 sq. cm=	0.000 000 024 711	0.000 000 000 038 610	1	0.000 1	0.000 000 01
1 sq. meter=	0.000 247 104 4	0.000 000 386 102 2	10 000	1	0.0001
1 hectare=	2.471 044	0.003 861 006	100 000 000	10 000	1

Units of Mass Not Greater than Pounds and Kilograms

Units	Grains	Pennyweights	Avdp drams	Avdp ounces
1 grain=	1	0.041 666 67	0.036 571 43	0.002 285 71
1 pennyweight=	24	1	0.877 714 3	0.054 857 14
1 dram avdp=	27.343 75	1.139 323	1	0.062 5
1 ounce avdp=	437.5	18.229 17	16	1
1 ounce troy=	480	20	17.554 29	1.097 143
1 pound troy=	5760	240	210.651 4	13.165 71
1 pound avdp=	7000	291.666 7	256	16
1 milligram=	0.015 432	0.000 643 015	0.000 564 383	0.000 035 274
1 gram=	15.432 36	0.643 014 9	0.564 383 4	0.035 273 96
1 kilogram=	15 432.36	643.014 9	564.383 4	35.273 96

Units	Troy ounces	Troy pounds	Avdp pounds	Milligrams	Grams	Kilograms
1 grain=	0.002 083 33	0.000 173 611	0.000 142 857	64.798 91	0.064 798 91	0.000 064 799
1 pennyw't.=	0.05	0.004 166 667	0.003 428 571	1555.173 84	1.555 173 84	0.001 555 174
1 dram avdp=	0.056 966 15	0.004 747 179	0.003 906 25	1771.845 195	1.771 845 195	0.001 771 845
1 oz avdp=	0.911 458 3	0.075 954 86	0.062 5	28 349.523 125	28.349 523 125	0.028 349 52
1 oz troy=	1	0.083 333 333	0.068 571 43	31 103.476 8	31.103 476 8	0.031 103 48
1 lb troy=	12	1	0.822 857 1	373 241.721 6	373.241 721 6	0.373 241 722
1 lb avdp=	14.583 33	1.215 278	1	453 592.37	453.592 37	0.453 592 37
1 milligram=	0.000 032 151	0.000 002 679	0.000 002 205	1	0.001	0.000 001
1 gram=	0.032 150 75	0.002 679 229	0.002 204 623	1000	1	0.001
1 kilogram=	32.150 75	2.679 229	2.204 623	1 000 000	1000	1

Units of Mass Not Less than Avoirdupois Ounces

Units	Avdp oz	Avdp lb	Short cwt	Short tons	Long tons	Kilograms	Metric tons
1 oz av=	1	0.0625	0.000 625	0.000 031 25	0.000 027 902	0.028 349 523	0.000 028 350
1 lb av=	16	1	0.01	0.000 5	0.000 446 429	0.453 592 37	0.000 453 592
1 sh cwt=	1 600	100	1	0.05	0.044 642 86	45.359 237	0.045 359 237
1 sh ton=	32 000	2000	20	1	0.892 857 1	907.184 74	0.907 184 74
1 long ton=	35 840	2240	22.4	1.12	1	1016.046 908 8	1.016 046 909
1 kg=	35.273 96	2.204 623	0.022 046 23	0.001 102 311	0.000 984 207	1	0.001
1 metric ton=	35 273.96	2 204.623	22.046 23	1.102 311	0.984 206 5	1000	1

(continued)

Units of Volume

Units	Cubic inches	Cubic feet	Cubic yards	Cubic cm	Cubic dm	Cubic meters
1 cubic inch=	1	0.000 578 704	0.000 021 433	16.387 064	0.016 387	0.000 016 387
1 cubic foot=	1728	1	0.037 037 04	28 316.846 592	28.316 847	0.028 316 847
1 cubic yard=	46 656	27	1	764 554.857 984	764.554 858	0.764 554 858
1 cubic cm=	0.061 023 74	0.000 035 315	0.000 001 308	1	0.001	0.000 000 1
1 cubic dm=	61.023 74	0.035 314 67	0.001 307 951	1 000	1	0.001
1 cubic meter	61 023.74	35.314 67	1.307 951	1 000 000	1000	1

Units of Capacity (Liquid Measure)

Units	Minims	Fluid drams	Fluid ounces	Gills	Liquid pt
1 minim=	1	0.016 666 7	0.002 083 33	0.000 520 833	0.000 130 208
1 fluid dram=	60	1	0.125	0.031 25	0.007 812 5
1 fluid ounce=	480	8	1	0.25	0.062 5
1 gill=	1920	32	4	1	0.25
1 liquid pint=	7680	128	16	4	1
1 liquid quart=	15 360	256	32	8	2
1 gallon=	61 440	1024	128	32	8
1 cubic inch=	265.974	4.432 900	0.554 112 6	0.138 528 1	0.034 632 03
1 cubic foot=	459 603.1	7 660.052	957.506 5	239.376 6	59.844 16
1 milliliter=	16.230 73	0.270 512 18	0.033 814 02	0.008 453 506	.002 113 376
1 liter=	16 230.73	270.512 18	33.814 02	8.453 506	2.113 376

Units	Liquid quarts	Gallons	Cubic inches	Cubic feet	Liters
1 minim=	0.000 065 104 17	0.000 016 276 04	0.003 759 766	0.000 002 175 790	0.000 061 611 52
1 flu. dram=	0.003 906 25	0.000 976 562 5	0.225 585 9	0.000 130 547 4	0.003 696 691
1 fluid oz=	0.031 25	0.007 812 5	1.804 687 5	0.001 044 379	0.029 573 53
1 gill=	0.125	0.031 25	7.218 75	0.004 177 517	0.118 294 118
1 liquid pt=	0.5	0.125	28.875	0.016 710 07	0.473 176 473
1 liquid qt=	1	0.25	57.75	0.033 420 14	0.946 352 946
1 gallon=	4	1	231	0.133 680 6	3.785 411 784
1 cubic in.=	0.017 316 02	0.004 329 004	1	0.000 578 703 7	0.016 387 064
1 cubic foot=	29.922 08	7.480 519	1728	1	28.316 846 592
1 liter=	1.056 688	0.264 172 05	61.023 74	0.035 314 67	1

Units of Capacity (Dry Measure)

Units	Dry pints	Dry quarts	Pecks	Bushels	Cubic in.	Liters
1 dry pint=	1	0.5	0.062 5	0.015 625	33.600 312 5	0.550 610 47
1 dry quart=	2	1	0.125	0.031 25	67.200 625	1.101 220 9
1 peck=	16	8	1	0.25	537.605	8.809 767 5
1 bushel=	64	32	4	1	2150.42	35.239 07
1 cubic inch=	0.029 761 6	0.014 880 8	0.001 860 10	0.000 465 025	1	0.016 387 06
1 liter=	1.816 166	0.908 083	0.113 510 37	0.028 377 59	61.023 74	1

Miscellaneous Measures

Caliber—the diameter of a gun bore. In the U.S., caliber is traditionally expressed in hundredths of inches, eg. .22 or .30. In Britain, caliber is often expressed in thousandths of inches, eg. .270 or .465. Now, it is commonly expressed in millimeters, eg. the 7.62 mm. M14 rifle and the 5.56 mm. M16 rifle. Heavier weapons' caliber has long been expressed in millimeters, eg. the 81 mm. mortar, the 105 mm. howitzer (light), the 155 mm. howitzer (medium or heavy).

Naval guns' caliber refers to the barrel length as a multiple of the bore diameter. A 5-inch, 50-caliber naval gun has a 5-inch bore and a barrel length of 250 inches.

Carat, karat—a measure of the amount of alloy per 24 parts in gold. Thus 24-carat gold is pure; 18-carat gold is one-fourth alloy.

Decibel (dB)—a measure of the relative loudness or intensity of sound. A 20-decibel sound is 10 times louder than a 10-decibel sound; 30 decibels is 100 times louder; 40 decibels is 1,000 times louder, etc. One decibel is the smallest difference between sounds detectable by the human ear. A 140-decibel sound is painful.

10 decibels	– a light whisper
20	– quiet conversation
30	– normal conversation
40	– light traffic
50	– typewriter, loud conversation
60	– noisy office
70	– normal traffic, quiet train
80	– rock music, subway
90	– heavy traffic, thunder
100	– jet plane at takeoff

Em—a printer's measure designating the square width of any given type size. Thus, an em of 10-point type is 10 points. An en is half an em.

Gauge—a measure of shotgun bore diameter. Gauge numbers originally referred to the number of lead balls of the gun barrel diameter in a pound. Thus, a 16 gauge shotgun's bore was smaller than a 12-gauge shotgun's. Today, an international agreement assigns millimeter measures to each gauge, eg:

Gauge	Bore diameter in mm
6	23.34
10	19.67
12	18.52
14	17.60
16	16.81
20	15.90

Horsepower—the power needed to lift 550 pounds one foot in one second, or to lift 33,000 pounds one foot in one minute. Equivalent to 746 watts or 2,546.0756 Btu/h.

Quire—25 sheets of paper

Ream—500 sheets of paper

Electrical Units

The **watt** is the unit of power (electrical, mechanical, thermal, etc.). Electrical power is given by the product of the voltage and the current.

Energy is sold by the **joule**, but in common practice the billing of electrical energy is expressed in terms of the kilowatt-hour, which is 3,600,000 joules or 3.6 megajoules.

The **horsepower** is a non-metric unit sometimes used in mechanics. It is equal to 746 watts.

The **ohm** is the unit of electrical resistance and represents the physical property of a conductor which offers a resistance to the flow of electricity, permitting just 1 ampere to flow at 1 volt of pressure.

Compound Interest

Compounded Annually

Principal	Period	4%	5%	6%	7%	8%	9%	10%	12%	14%	16%
$100	1 day	0.011	0.014	0.016	0.019	0.022	0.025	0.027	0.033	0.038	0.044
	1 week	0.077	0.096	0.115	0.134	0.153	0.173	0.192	0.230	0.268	0.307
	6 mos.	2.00	2.50	3.00	3.50	4.00	4.50	5.00	6.00	7.00	8.00
	1 year	4.00	5.00	6.00	7.00	8.00	9.00	10.00	12.00	14.00	16.00
	2 years	8.16	10.25	12.36	14.49	16.64	18.81	21.00	25.44	29.96	34.56
	3 years	12.49	15.76	19.10	22.50	25.97	29.50	33.10	40.49	48.15	56.09
	4 years	16.99	21.55	26.25	31.08	36.05	41.16	46.41	57.35	68.90	81.06
	5 years	21.67	27.63	33.82	40.26	46.93	53.86	61.05	76.23	92.54	110.03
	6 years	26.53	34.01	41.85	50.07	58.69	67.71	77.16	97.38	119.50	143.64
	7 years	31.59	40.71	50.36	60.58	71.38	82.80	94.87	121.07	150.23	182.62
	8 years	36.86	47.75	59.38	71.82	85.09	99.26	114.36	147.60	185.26	227.84
	9 years	42.33	55.13	68.95	83.85	99.90	117.19	135.79	177.31	225.19	280.30
	10 years	48.02	62.89	79.08	96.72	115.89	136.74	159.37	210.58	270.72	341.14
	12 years	60.10	79.59	101.22	125.22	151.82	181.27	213.84	289.60	381.79	493.60
	15 years	80.09	107.89	139.66	175.90	217.22	264.25	317.72	447.36	613.79	826.55
	20 years	119.11	165.33	220.71	286.97	366.10	460.44	572.75	864.63	1,274.35	1,846.08

Ancient Measures

Biblical		Greek		Roman	
Cubit	= 21.8 inches	Cubit	= 18.3 inches	Cubit	= 17.5 inches
Omer	= 0.45 peck	Stadion	= 607.2 or 622 feet	Stadium	= 202 yards
	3.964 liters	Obolos	= 715.38 milligrams	As, libra,	= 325.971 grams,
Ephah =	10 omers	Drachma	= 4.2923 grams	pondus	.71864 pounds
Shekel =	0.497 ounce	Mina	= 0.9463 pounds		
	14.1 grams	Talent	= 60 mina		

Weight of Water

1	cubic inch	.0360 pound	1	imperial gallon	10.0 pounds
12	cubic inches	.433 pound	11.2	imperial gallons	112.0 pounds
1	cubic foot	62.4 pounds	224	imperial gallons	2240.0 pounds
1	cubic foot	7.48052 U.S. gal	1	U.S. gallon	8.33 pounds
1.8	cubic feet	112.0 pounds	13.45	U.S. gallons	112.0 pounds
35.96	cubic feet	2240.0 pounds	269.0	U.S. gallons	2240.0 pounds

Density of Gases and Vapors

at 0°C and 760 mmHg
Source: National Bureau of Standards (kilograms per cubic meter)

Gas	Wgt.	Gas	Wgt.	Gas	Wgt.
Acetylene	1.171	Ethylene	1.260	Methyl fluoride	1.545
Air	1.293	Fluorine	1.696	Mono methylamine	1.38
Ammonia	.759	Helium	.178	Neon	.900
Argon	1.784	Hydrogen	.090	Nitric oxide	1.341
Arsene	3.48	Hydrogen bromide	3.50	Nitrogen	1.250
Butane-iso.	2.60	Hydrogen chloride	1.639	Nitrosyl chloride	2.99
Butane-n	2.519	Hydrogen iodide	5.724	Nitrous oxide	1.997
Carbon dioxide	1.977	Hydrogen selenide	3.66	Oxygen	1.429
Carbon monoxide	1.250	Hydrogen sulfide	1.539	Phosphine	1.48
Carbon oxysulfide	2.72	Krypton	3.745	Propane	2.020
Chlorine	3.214	Methane	.717	Silicon tetrafluoride	4.67
Chlorine monoxide	3.89	Methyl chloride	2.25	Sulfur dioxide	2.927
Ethane	1.356	Methyl ether	2.091	Xenon	5.897

Temperature Conversion Table

The numbers in **bold face type** refer to the temperature either in degrees Celsius or Fahrenheit which are to be converted. If converting from degrees Fahrenheit to Celsius, the equivalent will be found in the column on the left, while if converting from degrees Celsius to Fahrenheit the answer will be found in the column on the right.

For temperatures not shown. To convert Fahrenheit to Celsius subtract 32 degrees and multiply by 5, divide by 9; to convert Celsius to Fahrenheit, multiply by 9, divide by 5 and add 32 degrees.

Celsius		Fahrenheit	Celsius		Fahrenheit	Celsius		Fahrenheit
− 273.2	− 459.7	. . . .	− 17.8	0	32	35.0	95	203
− 184	− 300	. . . .	− 12.2	10	50	36.7	98	208.4
− 169	− 273	− 459.4	− 6.67	20	68	37.8	100	212
− 157	− 250	− 418	− 1.11	30	86	43	110	230
− 129	− 200	− 328	4.44	40	104	49	120	248
− 101	− 150	− 238	10.0	50	122	54	130	266
− 73.3	− 100	− 148	15.6	60	140	60	140	284
− 45.6	− 50	− 58	21.1	70	158	66	150	302
− 40.0	− 40	− 40	23.9	75	167	93	200	392
− 34.4	− 30	− 22	26.7	80	176	121	250	482
− 28.9	− 20	− 4	29.4	85	185	149	300	572
− 23.3	− 10	14	32.2	90	194			

Water boils at 212°F at sea level. For every 550 feet above sea level, boiling point of water is lower by about 1°F. Methyl alcohol boils at 148°F. Average human oral temperature, 98.6°F. Water freezes at 32°F. Although "Centigrade" is still frequently used, the International Committee on Weights and Measures and the National Bureau of Standards have recommended since 1948 that this scale be called "Celsius."

Breaking the Sound Barrier; Speed of Sound

The prefix Mach is used to describe supersonic speed. It derives from Ernst Mach, a Czech-born German physicist, who contributed to the study of sound. When a plane moves at the speed of sound it is Mach 1. When twice the speed of sound it is Mach 2. When it is near but below the speed of sound its speed can be designated at less than Mach 1, for example, Mach .90. Mach is defined as "in jet propulsion, the ratio of the velocity of a rocket or a jet to the velocity of sound in the medium being considered."

When a plane passes the sound barrier—flying faster than sound travels—listeners in the area hear thunderclaps, but pilots do not hear them.

Sound is produced by vibrations of an object and is transmitted by alternate increase and decrease in pressures that radiate outward through a material media of molecules —somewhat like waves spreading out on a pond after a rock has been tossed into it.

The frequency of sound is determined by the number of times the vibrating waves undulate per second, and is measured in cycles per second. The slower the cycle of waves, the lower the sound. As frequencies increase, the sound is higher.

Sound is audible to human beings only if the frequency falls within a certain range. The human ear is usually not sensitive to frequencies of less than 20 vibrations per second, or more than about 20,000 vibrations per second—although this range varies among individuals. Anything at a pitch higher than the human ear can hear is termed ultrasonic.

Intensity or loudness is the strength of the pressure of these radiating waves, and is measured in decibels. The human ear responds to intensity in a range from zero to 120 decibels. Any sound with pressure over 120 decibels is painful.

The speed of sound is generally placed at 1,088 ft. per second at sea level at 32°F. It varies in other temperatures and in different media. Sound travels faster in water than in air, and even faster in iron and steel. If in air it travels a mile in 5 seconds, it does a mile under water in 1 second, and through iron in ⅓ of a second. It travels through ice cold vapor at approximately 4,708 ft. per sec., ice-cold water, 4,938; granite, 12,960; hardwood, 12,620; brick, 11,960; glass, 16,410 to 19,690; silver, 8,658; gold, 5,717.

Colors of the Spectrum

Color, an electromagnetic wave phenomenon, is a sensation produced through the excitation of the retina of the eye by rays of light. The colors of the spectrum may be produced by viewing a light beam refracted by passage through a prism, which breaks the light into its wave lengths.

Customarily, the primary colors of the spectrum are thought of as those 6 monochromatic colors which occupy relatively large areas of the spectrum: red, orange, yellow, green, blue, and violet. However, Sir Isaac Newton named a 7th, indigo, situated between blue and violet on the spectrum. Aubert estimated (1865) the solar spectrum to contain approximately 1,000 distinguishable hues of which according to Rood (1881) 2 million tints and shades can be distinguished; Luckiesh stated (1915) that 55 distinctly different hues have been seen in a single spectrum.

By many physicists only 3 primary colors are recognized: red, yellow, and blue (Mayer, 1775); red, green, and violet (Thomas Young, 1801); red, green, and blue (Clerk Maxwell, 1860).

The color sensation of black is due to complete lack of stimulation of the retina, that of white to complete stimulation. The infra-red and ultra-violet rays, below the red (long) end of the spectrum and above the violet (short) end respectively, are invisible to the naked eye. Heat is the principal effect of the infra-red rays and chemical action that of the ultra-violet rays.

Common Fractions Reduced to Decimals

8ths	16ths	32ds	64ths		8ths	16ths	32ds	64ths		8ths	16ths	32ds	64ths	
			1	.015625				23	.359375				45	.703125
		1	2	.03125	3	6	12	24	.375			23	46	.71875
			3	.046875				25	.390625				47	.734375
	1	2	4	.0625				26	.40625	6	12	24	48	.75
			5	.078125			13	27	.421875				49	.765625
		3	6	.09375		7	14	28	.4375			25	50	.78125
			7	.109375				29	.453125				51	.796875
1	2	4	8	.125			15	30	.46875		13	26	52	.8125
			9	.140625				31	.484375				53	.828125
		5	10	.15625	4	8	16	32	.5			27	54	.84375
			11	.171875				33	.515625				55	.859375
	3	6	12	.1875			17	34	.53125	7	14	28	56	.875
			13	.203125				35	.546875				57	.890625
		7	14	.21875		9	18	36	.5625			29	58	.90625
			15	.234375				37	.578125				59	.921875
2	4	8	16	.25			19	38	.59375		15	30	60	.9375
			17	.265625				39	.609375				61	.953125
		9	18	.28125	5	10	20	40	.625			31	62	.96875
			19	.296875				41	.640625				63	.984375
	5	10	20	.3125			21	42	.65625	8	16	32	64	1.
			21	.328125				43	.671875					
		11	22	.34375		11	22	44	.6875					

Spirits Measures

Pony	0.5 jigger			For champagne only:
Shot	{ 0.666 jigger / 1.0 ounce	Quart	{ 32 shots / 1.25 fifth	Rehoboam . . . . 3 magnums
Jigger	1.5 shot	Magnum	{ 2 quarts / 2.49797 bottles (wine)	Methuselah . . . . 4 magnums
Pint	{ 16 shots / 0.625 fifth			Salmanazar . . . . 6 magnums
	{ 25.6 shots / 1.6 pints			Balthazar . . . . 8 magnums
		For champagne and brandy only:		Nebuchadnezzar . 10 magnums
Fifth	{ 0.8 quart / 0.75706 liter	Jeroboam	{ 6.4 pints / 1.6 magnum / 0.8 gallon	Wine bottle (standard): { 0.800633 quart / 0.7576778 liter

Mathematical Formulas

To find the CIRCUMFERENCE of a:

Circle — Multiply the diameter by 3.14159265 (usually 3.1416).

To find the AREA of a:

Circle — Multiply the square of the diameter by .785398 (usually .7854).
Rectangle — Multiply the length of the base by the height.
Sphere (surface) — Multiply the square of the radius by 3.1416 and multiply by 4.

Square — Square the length of one side.
Trapezoid — Add the two parallel sides, multiply by the height and divide by 2.
Triangle — Multiply the base by the height and divide by 2.

To find the VOLUME of a:

Cone — Multiply the square of the radius of the base by 3.1416, multiply by the height, and divide by 3.
Cube — Cube the length of one edge.
Cylinder — Multiply the square of the radius of the base by 3.1416 and multiply by the height.
Pyramid — Multiply the area of the base by the height and

divide by 3.
Rectangular Prism — Multiply the length by the width by the height.
Sphere — Multiply the cube of the radius by 3.1416, multiply by 4 and divide by 3.

Playing Cards and Dice Chances

Poker Hands

Hand	Number possible	Odds against
Royal flush	4	649,739 to 1
Other straight flush	36	72,192 to 1
Four of a kind	624	4,164 to 1
Full house	3,744	693 to 1
Flush	5,108	508 to 1
Straight	10,200	254 to 1
Three of a kind	54,912	46 to 1
Two pairs	123,552	20 to 1
One pair	1,098,240	4 to 3 (1.37 to 1)
Nothing	1,302,540	1 to 1
Total	**2,598,960**	

Dice
(probabilities on 2 dice)

Total	Odds against (Single toss)	Total	Odds against (Single toss)
2	35 to 1	8	31 to 5
3	17 to 1	9	8 to 1
4	11 to 1	10	11 to 1
5	8 to 1	11	17 to 1
6	31 to 5	12	35 to 1
7	5 to 1		

Dice
(Probabilities of consecutive winning plays)

No. consecutive wins	By 7, 11 or point	No. consecutive wins	By 7, 11 or point
1	244 in 495	6	1 in 70
2	6 in 25	7	1 in 141
3	3 in 25	8	1 in 287
4	1 in 17	9	1 in 582
5	1 in 34		

Pinochle Auction
(Odds against finding in "widow" of 3 cards)

Open places	Odds against	Open places	Odds against
1	5 to 1	4	3 to 2 for
2	2 to 1	5	2 to 1 for
3	Even		

Bridge
The odds—against suit distribution in a hand of 4-4-3-2 are about 4 to 1, against 5-4-2-2 about 8 to 1, against 6-4-2-1 about 20 to 1, against 7-4-1-1 about 254 to 1, against 8-4-1-0 about 2,211 to 1, and against 13-0-0-0 about 158,753,389,899 to 1.

Measures of Force and Pressure

Dyne = force necessary to accelerate a 1-gram mass 1 centimeter per second squared = 0.000072 poundal
Poundal = force necessary to accelerate a 1-pound mass 1 foot per second squared = 13,825.5 dynes = 0.138255 newtons
Newton = force needed to accelerate a 1-kilogram mass 1 meter per second squared

Pascal (pressure) = 1 newton per square meter = 0.020885 pound per square foot
Atmosphere (air pressure at sea level) = 2,116.102 pounds per square foot = 14.6952 pounds per square inch = 1.0332 kilograms per square centimeter = 101,323 newtons per square meter.

Large Numbers

U.S.	Number of zeros	French British, German	U.S.	Number of zeros	French British, German
million	6	million	sextillion	21	1,000 trillion
billion	9	milliard	septillion	24	quadrillion
trillion	12	billion	octillion	27	1,000 quadrillion
quadrillion	15	1,000 billion	nonillion	30	quintillion
quintillion	18	trillion	decillion	33	1,000 quintillion

Roman Numerals

I	–	1	VI	–	6	XI	–	11	L	–	50	CD	–	400	$\overline{X}$	–	10,000
II	–	2	VII	–	7	XIX	–	19	LX	–	60	D	–	500	$\overline{L}$	–	50,000
III	–	3	VIII	–	8	XX	–	20	XC	–	90	CM	–	900	$\overline{C}$	–	100,000
IV	–	4	IX	–	9	XXX	–	30	C	–	100	M	–	1,000	$\overline{D}$	–	500,000
V	–	5	X	–	10	XL	–	40	CC	–	200	$\overline{V}$	–	5,000	$\overline{M}$	–	1,000,000

POSTAL INFORMATION

U.S. Postal Service

The Postal Reorganization Act, creating a government-owned postal service under the executive branch and replacing the old Post Office Department, was signed into law by President Nixon on Aug. 12, 1970. The service officially came into being on July 1, 1971.

The new U.S. Postal Service is governed by an 11-man Board of Governors. Nine members are appointed to 9-year terms by the president with Senate approval. These 9, in turn, choose a postmaster general, who is no longer a member of the president's cabinet. The board and the new postmaster general choose the 11th member, who serves as deputy postmaster general. An independent Postal Rate Commission of 5 members, appointed by the president, recommends postal rates to the governors for their approval.

The first postmaster general under the new system was Winton M. Blount. He resigned Oct. 29, 1971, and was replaced by his deputy, E. T. Klassen, Dec. 7, 1971. Benjamin F. Bailar succeeded him Feb. 16, 1975, and was succeeded by William F. Bolger on March 15, 1978.

As of Oct. 1, 1984, there were 39,386 post offices throughout the U.S. and possessions.

U.S. Domestic Rates

(In effect Feb. 17, 1985.)

Domestic includes the U.S., territories and possessions, APO and FPO.

First Class

Letters written, and matter sealed against inspection, 22¢ for 1st oz. or fraction, 17¢ for each additional oz. or fraction.
U.S. Postal cards; single 14¢; double 28¢; private postcards, same.

First class includes written matter, namely letters, postal cards, postcards (private mailing cards) and all other matter wholly or partly in writing, whether sealed or unsealed, except manuscripts for books, periodical articles and music, manuscript copy accompanying proofsheets or corrected proofsheets of the same and the writing authorized by law on matter of other classes. Also matter sealed or closed against inspection, bills and statements of accounts.

Greeting Cards

May be sent first class or single piece third class.

Express Mail

Express Mail Service is available for any mailable article up to 70 pounds, and guarantees delivery between major U.S. cities or your money back. Articles received by the acceptance time authorized by the postmaster at a postal facility offering Express Mail will be delivered by 3 p.m. the next day or, if you prefer, your shipment can be picked up as early as 10 a.m. the next business day. Rates include insurance, Shipment Receipt, and Record of Delivery at the destination post office.

Consult Postmaster for other Express Mail Services and rates. (The Postal Service will refund, upon application to originating office, the postage for any Express Mail shipments not meeting the service standard except for those delayed by strike or work stoppage.)

Second Class

Single copy mailings by general public 22¢ for first ounce, 39¢ for over 1 to 2 ozs., 56¢ for over 2 to 3 ozs. 73¢ for over 3 to 4 ozs., 88¢ for 4–5 ozs. and 10¢ for each additional ounce up to 16 ozs.

Third Class

Third class (limit up to but not including 16 ounces): Mailable matter not in 1st and 2d classes.

Single mailing: Greeting cards (sealed or unsealed), small parcels, printed matter, booklets and catalogs, 22¢ the first ounce, 39¢ for over 1 to 2 ozs., 56¢ for over 2 to 3 ozs., 73¢ for over 3 to 4 ozs., 88¢ for over 4 to 6 ozs., 98¢ for over 6 to 8 ozs., $1.08 for over 8 to 10 ozs., $1.18 for over 10 to 12 ozs., $1.28 for over 12 to 14 ozs., $1.38 for over 14 but less than 16 ozs.

Bulk material: books, catalogs of 24 pages or more, seeds, cuttings, bulbs, roots, scions, and plants. 38¢ per pound, 12.5¢ minimum per piece.

Other matter: newsletters, shopper's guides, advertising circulars, 45¢ per pound, 10.9¢ minimum per piece. Separate rates for some nonprofit organizations. Bulk mailing fee, $40 per calendar year. Apply to postmaster for permit. One-time fee for permit imprint, $50.

Parcel Post—Fourth Class

Fourth class or parcel post (16 ounces and over): merchandise, printed matter, etc., may be sealed, subject to inspection.

On parcels weighing less than 15 lbs. and measuring more than 84 inches, but not more than 100 inches in length and girth combined, the minimum postal charge shall be the zone charge applicable to a 15-pound parcel.

Priority Mail

First class mail of more than 12 ounces can be sent "Priority Mail (Heavy Pieces)" service. The most expeditious handling and transportation available will be used for fastest delivery.

Forwarding Addresses

The mailer, in order to obtain a forwarding address, must endorse the envelope or cover "Address Correction Requested." The destination post office then will determine whether a forwarding address has been left on file and provide it for a fee of 30¢.

Priority Mail

Packages weighing up to 70 pounds and exceeding 100 inches in length and girth combined, including written and other material of the first class, whether sealed or unsealed, fractions of a pound being charged as a full pound, except in the 1 to 5 pound weight category where half-pound weight increments apply.

Rates according to zone apply between the U.S. and Puerto Rico and Virgin Islands.

Parcels weighing less than 15 pounds, measuring over 84 inches but not exceeding 100 inches in length and girth combined are chargeable with a minimum rate equal to that for a 15 pound parcel for the zone to which addressed.

Zones	To 1 lb.	1½	2	2½	3	3½	4	4½	5*
1, 2, 3, ...	$2.24	$2.30	$2.54	$2.78	$3.01	$3.25	$3.49	3.73	$3.97
4.	2.24	2.42	2.70	2.98	3.25	3.53	3.81	4.09	4.37
5.	2.24	2.56	2.88	3.21	3.53	3.85	4.18	4.50	4.83
6.	2.34	2.72	3.09	3.47	3.85	4.22	4.60	4.97	5.35
7.	2.45	2.87	3.30	3.73	4.16	4.59	5.02	5.45	5.88
8.	2.58	3.07	3.57	4.06	4.56	5.05	5.55	6.05	6.54

*Consult postmaster for parcels over 5 lbs.

Special Handling

Third and fourth class parcels will be handled and delivered as expeditiously as practicable (but not special delivery) upon payment, in addition to the regular postage: up to 10 lbs., $1.10; over 10 lbs., $1.30. Such parcels must be endorsed, Special Handling.

Special Delivery

First class mail up to 2 lbs. $2.95, over 2 lbs. and up to 10 lbs., $3.15; over 10 lbs. $4.00. All other classes up to 2 lbs. $3.10, over 2 and up to 10 lbs., $3.60, over 10 lbs. $4.50.

Bound Printed Matter Rates
(Fourth class single piece zone rate)

Weight lbs.	Local	1&2	3	4	5	6	7	8
1.5	$0.55	$0.77	$0.81	$0.89	$1.00	$1.11	$1.26	$1.38
2	0.58	0.81	0.87	0.97	1.12	1.27	1.46	1.62
2.5	0.60	0.85	0.92	1.05	1.23	1.42	1.67	1.86
3	0.63	0.89	0.98	1.12	1.35	1.58	1.87	2.10
3.5	0.65	0.93	1.03	1.20	1.47	1.73	2.07	2.34
4	0.68	0.97	1.09	1.28	1.58	1.89	2.28	2.59
4.5	0.70	1.01	1.14	1.36	1.70	2.04	2.48	2.83
5	0.73	1.06	1.20	1.44	1.82	2.20	2.69	3.07
6	0.77	1.14	1.30	1.60	2.05	2.50	3.09	3.55
7	0.82	1.22	1.41	1.76	2.28	2.81	3.50	4.04
8	0.87	1.30	1.52	1.91	2.51	3.12	3.91	4.52
9	0.92	1.38	1.63	2.07	2.75	3.43	4.31	5.01
10	0.97	1.46	1.74	2.23	2.98	3.74	4.72	5.49

Domestic Mail Special Services

Registry — Only matter prepaid with postage at First-class postage rates may be registered. Stamps or meter stamps must be attached. The face of the article must be at least 5" long, 3½" high. The mailer is required to declare the value of mail presented for registration.

Registered Mail

	Insured	Uninsured
$0.00 to $100.	$3.60	$3.55
$100.01 to $500	3.90	3.80
$500.01 to $1,000 . . .	4.25	4.15
$1,000.01 to $2,000 . .	4.60	4.40
$2,000.01 to $3,000 . .	4.95	4.65
$3,000.01 to $4,000 . .	5.30	4.90
$4,000.01 to $5,000 . .	5.65	5.15
$5,000.01 to $6,000 . .	6.00	5.40
$6,000.01 to $7,000 . .	6.35	5.65
$7,000.01 to $8,000 . .	6.70	5.90
$8,000.01 to $9,000 . .	7.05	6.15
$9,000.01 to $10,000 . .	7.40	6.40

Consult postmaster for registry rates above $10,000.

C.O.D.: Unregistered — is applicable to 3d and 4th class matter and sealed domestic mail of any class bearing postage at the 1st class rate. Such mail must be based on bona fide orders or be in conformity with agreements between senders and addressees. **Registered** — for details consult postmaster.

Insurance — is applicable to 3d and 4th class matter. Matter for sale addressed to prospective purchasers who have not ordered it or authorized its sending will not be insured.

Insured Mail

$0.01 to $25.	$1.50
25.01 to 50	1.80
50.01 to 100.	2.10
100.01 to 200.	2.40
200.01 to 300.	3.00
300.01 to 400.	3.70
400.01 to 500.	4.70

Liability for insured mail is limited to $400.

Certified mail — service is available for any matter having no intrinsic value on which 1st class or air mail postage is paid. Receipt is furnished at time of mailing and evidence of delivery obtained. The fee is 75¢ ($1.25 restricted delivery) in addition to postage. Return receipt, restricted delivery, and special delivery are available upon payment of additional fees. No indemnity.

Special Fourth Class Rate
(limit 70 lbs.)

First pound or fraction, 69¢ (47¢ if 500 pieces or more of special rate matter are presorted to 5 digit ZIP code or 60¢ if 500 pieces or more are presorted to Bulk Mail Cntrs.); each additional pound or fraction through 7 pounds, 25¢; each additional pound, 15¢. Only following specific articles: books 24 pages or more, at least 22 of which are printed consisting wholly of reading matter or scholarly bibliography containing no advertisement other than incidental announcements of books; 16 millimeter films in final form (except when mailed to or from commercial theaters); printed music in bound or sheet form; printed objective test materials; sound recordings, playscripts, and manuscripts for books, periodicals, and music; printed educational reference charts; loose-leaf pages and binders therefor consisting of medical information for distribution to doctors, hospitals, medical schools, and medical students. Package must be marked "Special 4th Class Rate" stating item contained.

Library Rate (limit 70 lbs.)

First pound 40¢, each additional pound through 7 pounds, 14¢; each additional pound, 8¢. Books when loaned or exchanged between schools, colleges, public libraries, and certain non-profit organizations; books, printed music, bound academic theses, periodicals, sound recordings, other library materials, museum materials (specimens, collections), scientific or mathematical kits, instruments or other devices; also catalogs, guides or scripts for some of these materials. Must be marked "Library Rate".

Postal Union Mail Special Services

Registration — available to practically all countries. Fee $3.60. The maximum indemnity payable — generally only in case of complete loss (of both contents and wrapper) — is $20.40. To Canada only the fee is $3.60 providing indemnity for loss up to $100, $3.90 for loss up to $200.

Parcel Post Rate Schedule
Zones

Single Piece Zone Rates Not Exceeding (pounds)	Local	1 and 2	Zone 3	Zone 4	Zone 5
2	1.19	1.25	1.35	1.50	1.73
3	1.25	1.33	1.49	1.71	2.05
4	1.31	1.41	1.62	1.92	2.38
5	1.36	1.49	1.76	2.13	2.70
6	1.42	1.58	1.89	2.34	3.02
7	1.47	1.66	2.03	2.55	3.35
8	1.53	1.74	2.16	2.76	3.67
9	1.59	1.83	2.30	2.97	3.99
10	1.64	1.91	2.43	3.18	4.32
11	1.69	1.97	2.54	3.33	4.55
12	1.74	2.04	2.63	3.49	4.78
13	1.78	2.10	2.73	3.63	4.99
14	1.82	2.16	2.82	3.76	5.19
15	1.86	2.21	2.90	3.88	5.38
16	1.90	2.26	2.98	4.00	5.55
17	1.94	2.32	3.06	4.11	5.72
18	1.98	2.36	3.13	4.22	5.87
19	2.02	2.41	3.20	4.32	6.02
20	2.05	2.46	3.27	4.42	6.17
21	2.09	2.51	3.33	4.51	6.31
22	2.12	2.55	3.40	4.60	6.44
23	2.16	2.59	3.46	4.69	6.57
24	2.19	2.64	3.52	4.78	6.69
25	2.23	2.68	3.58	4.86	6.81

Return receipt—showing to whom and date deliv'd, 70¢.

Special delivery — Available to most countries. Consult post office. Fees: for post cards, letter mail, and airmail "other articles," $2.95 up to 2 pounds; over 2 to 10 pounds, $3.15; over 10 pounds, $4.00. For surface "other articles," $3.10, $3.60, and $4.50, respectively.

Marking — an article intended for special delivery service must have affixed to the cover near the name of the country of destination "EXPRESS" (special delivery) label, obtainable at the post office, or it may be marked on the cover boldly in red "EXPRESS" (special delivery).

Special handling — entitles AO surface packages to prior-ity handling between mailing point and U.S. point of dispatch. Fees: $1.10 for packages to 10 pounds, and $1.60 for packages over 10 pounds.

Airmail — there is daily air service to practically all countries.

Prepayment of replies from other countries — a mailer who wishes to prepay a reply by letter from another country may do so by sending his correspondent one or more international reply coupons, which may be purchased at United States post offices. One coupon should be accepted in any country in exchange for stamps to prepay a surface letter of the first unit of weight to the U.S.

Post Office-Authorized 2-Letter State Abbreviations

The abbreviations below are approved by the U.S. Postal Service for use in addresses only. They do not replace the traditional abbreviations in other contexts. The official list follows, including the District of Columbia, Guam, Puerto Rico, the Canal Zone, and the Virgin Islands (all capital letters are used):

Alabama . . . . AL	Hawaii . . . . HI	Missouri . . . . MO	Puerto Rico . . . . PR
Alaska . . . . AK	Idaho . . . . ID	Montana . . . . MT	Rhode Island . . . . RI
American Samoa . . . . . AS	Illinois IL	Nebraska . . . . NE	South Carolina . . . . . . SC
Arizona . . . . AZ	Indiana . . . . IN	Nevada . . . . NV	South Dakota . . . . SD
Arkansas . . . . AR	Iowa . . . . IA	New Hampshire . . . . . NH	Tennessee . . . . TN
California . . . . CA	Kansas . . . . KS	New Jersey . . . . NJ	Texas . . . . TX
Canal Zone . . . . CZ	Kentucky . . . . KY	New Mexico . . . . NM	Trust Territories . . . . . TT
Colorado . . . . CO	Louisiana . . . . LA	New York . . . . NY	Utah . . . . UT
Connecticut . . . . CT	Maine . . . . ME	North Carolina . . . . . . NC	Vermont . . . . VT
Delaware . . . . DE	Maryland . . . . MD	North Dakota . . . . ND	Virginia . . . . VA
Dist. of Col. . . . . DC	Massachusetts . . . . . MA	Northern Mariana Is. . . . CM	Virgin Islands VI
Florida . . . . FL	Michigan . . . . MI	Ohio . . . . OH	Washington . . . . WA
Georgia . . . . GA	Minnesota . . . . MN	Oklahoma . . . . OK	West Virginia . . . . . . WV
Guam . . . . GU	Mississippi . . . . MS	Oregon . . . . OR	Wisconsin . . . . WI
		Pennsylvania . . . . PA	Wyoming . . . . WY

Also approved for use in addressing mail are the following abbreviations:

Alley . . . . Aly	Court . . . . Ct	Grove . . . . Grv	Rural . . . . R
Arcade . . . . Arc	Courts . . . . Cts	Heights . . . . Hts	Square . . . . Sq
Avenue . . . ., . . Ave	Crescent . . . . Cres	Highway . . . . Hwy	Street . . . . St
Boulevard . . . . Blvd	Drive. . . . . Dr	Lane . . . . Ln	Terrace . . . . Ter
Branch . . . . Br	Expressway . . . . . . Expy	Manor . . . . Mnr	Trail . . . . Trl
Bypass . . . . Byp	Extended . . . . Ext	Place . . . . Pl	Turnpike . . . . Tpke
Causeway . . . . Cswy	Extension . . . . Ext	Plaza . . . . Plz	Viaduct . . . . Via
Center . . . . Ctr	Freeway . . . . Fwy	Point . . . . Pt	Vista . . . . Vis
Circle. . . . . Cir	Gardens . . . . Gdns	Road . . . . Rd	

Size Standards for Domestic Mail

Minimum Size

Pieces which do not meet the following requirements are prohibited from the mails:

   a. All pieces must be at least .007 of an inch thick, and

   b. All pieces (except keys and identification devices) which are ¼ inch or less thick must be:

      (1) Rectangular in shape,

      (2) At least 3½ inches high, and

      (3) At least 5 inches long.

Note: Pieces greater than ¼ inch thick can be mailed even if they measure less than 3½ by 5 inches.

Nonstandard Mail

All First-Class Mail weighing one ounce or less and all single-piece rate Third-Class mail weighing one ounce or less is nonstandard (and subject to a 9¢ surcharge in addition to the applicable postage and fees) if:

   1. Any of the following dimensions are exceeded:
      Length—11½ inches,
      Height—6⅛ inches,
      Thickness—¼ inch, or

   2. The piece has a height to length (aspect) ratio which does not fall between 1 to 1.3 and 1 to 2.5 inclusive. (The aspect ratio is found by dividing the length by the height. If the answer is between 1.3 and 2.5 inclusive, the piece has a standard aspect ratio.)

Envelopes Available at Post Offices

Kind	Size	Denomination	Item No.	Less than 500 each	500	1,000
Regular	6¾	22 cents	631	$0.27	115.90	231.80
	10	22 cents	131	.27	117.40	234.80
Window	6¾	22 cents	632		116.50	233.00
	10	22 cents	132		118.00	236.00
Precanceled	6¾	6.0 cents	666		35.90	71.80
(Regular)	10	6.0 cents	166		37.40	74.80
Precanceled	6¾	6.0 cents	667		36.50	73.00
(Window)	10	6.0 cents	167		38.00	76.00

Postal Receipts at Large Cities

Fiscal year	Boston	Chicago	L.A.	New York	Phila.	St. Louis	Wash., D.C.
1975	$136,453,079	$365,376,795	$193,229,077	$453,905,277	$134,571,376	$85,591,774	$115,489,343
1979	211,082,724	506,395,438	273,563,824	627,445,984	211,571,818	126,031,314	175,467,893
1980	224,428,760	528,233,991	271,136,828	666,377,778	221,161,624	127,427,555	187,334,312
1981	256,524,082	551,988,015	301,159,594	741,286,845	235,116,018	142,548,957	201,191,995
1982	292,971,572	597,246,568	338,798,409	848,507,590	265,242,959	160,596,946	215,772,861
1983	294,932,399	589,476,264	330,734,928	856,569,717	273,210,529	165,000,437	212,117,368
1984	314,230,399	598,141,605	338,760,060	907,426,500	295,917,848	177,041,331	225,378,646

Other cities for fiscal year 1984: Dallas, $324,161,294; Atlanta, $307,400,593; Houston, $269,171,666; Minneapolis, $209,878,305; San Francisco, $207,732,787; Denver, $177,924,297; Hartford, $166,413,863; Cleveland, $163,865,745; Baltimore, $163,173,315; Pittsburgh, $158,431,804; Miami, $153,399,597.

Air Mail, Parcel Post International Rates

Aerogrammes — 36¢ each to all countries.
Air mail postcards (single) - 33¢ to all countries except Canada and Mexico (14¢)

Country	First 4 oz.	Air parcel post rates — Each add'l. 4 oz. or fraction up to first 5 lbs.	Each add'l. ½ lb. or fraction of ½ lb.
Afghanistan	$7.05	1.35	2.50
Albania	6.00	1.10	2.00
Algeria	7.05	1.35	2.50
Andorra	4.95	.90	1.50
Angola	8.10	1.60	3.00
Argentina	7.05	1.35	2.50
Ascension	No Air Service		
Australia	7.05	1.35	2.50
Austria	4.95	.90	1.50
Azores	6.00	1.10	2.00
Bahamas	3.90	.65	1.00
Bahrain	7.05	1.35	2.50
Bangladesh	8.10	1.60	3.00
Barbados	4.95	.90	1.50
Belgium	8.10	1.60	3.00
Belize	3.90	.65	1.00
Benin	7.05	1.35	2.50
Bermuda	3.90	.65	1.00
Bhutan	No Parcel Post Service		
Bolivia	4.95	.90	1.50
Botswana	8.10	1.60	3.00
Brazil	8.10	1.60	3.00
Brunei	7.05	1.35	2.50
Bulgaria	7.05	1.35	2.50
Burma	7.05	1.35	2.50
Burundi	8.10	1.60	3.00
Cameroon	6.00	1.10	2.00
Canada¹	No Air Service		
Cape Verde	7.05	1.35	2.50
Cayman Islands	3.90	.65	1.00
Central African Rep.	8.10	1.60	3.00
Chad	7.05	1.35	2.50
Chile	7.05	1.35	2.50
China (People's Republic of)	7.05	1.35	2.50
Colombia	4.95	.90	1.50
Comoros	8.10	1.60	3.00
Congo	7.05	1.35	2.50
Corsica	8.10	1.60	3.00
Costa Rica	3.90	.65	1.00
Cuba	No Parcel Post Service		
Cyprus	7.05	1.35	2.50
Czechoslovakia	6.00	1.10	2.00
Denmark	4.95	.90	1.50
Djibouti	8.10	1.60	3.00
Dominica	3.90	.65	1.00
Dominican Republic	3.90	.65	1.00
East Timor	No Parcel Post Service		
Ecuador	4.95	.90	1.50
Egypt	6.00	1.10	2.00
El Salvador	3.90	.65	1.00
Equatorial Guinea	7.05	1.35	2.50
Estonia	8.10	1.60	3.00
Ethiopia	7.05	1.35	2.50
Faeroe Islands	6.00	1.10	2.00
Falkland Islands	7.05	1.35	2.50
Fiji	4.95	.90	1.50
Finland	7.05	1.35	2.50
France (Including Monaco)	8.10	1.60	3.00
French Guiana	6.00	1.10	2.00
French Polynesia	7.05	1.35	2.50
Gabon	7.05	1.35	2.50
Gambia	4.95	.90	1.50
German Democratic Republic (East Germany)	6.00	1.10	2.00
Germany, Federal Rep. of (West Germany)	6.00	1.10	2.00
Ghana	7.05	1.35	2.50
Gibraltar	7.05	1.35	2.50
Great Britain	6.00	1.10	2.00
Greece	6.00	1.10	2.00
Greenland	7.05	1.35	2.50
Grenada	4.95	.90	1.50
Guadeloupe	3.90	.65	1.00
Guatemala	3.90	.65	1.00
Guinea	4.95	.90	1.50
Guinea-Bissau	4.95	.90	1.50

Country	First 4 oz.	Air parcel post rates — Each add'l. 4 oz. or fraction up to first 5 lbs.	Each add'l. ½ lb. or fraction of ½ lb.
Guyana	4.95	.90	1.50
Haiti	3.90	.65	1.00
Honduras	4.95	.90	1.50
Hong Kong	6.00	1.10	2.00
Hungary	6.00	1.10	2.00
Iceland	7.05	1.35	2.50
India	7.05	1.35	2.50
Indonesia	8.10	1.60	3.00
Iran	7.05	1.35	2.50
Iraq	7.05	1.35	2.50
Ireland (Eire)	6.00	1.10	2.00
Israel	6.00	1.10	2.00
Italy	6.00	1.10	2.00
Ivory Coast	7.05	1.35	2.50
Jamaica	3.90	.65	1.00
Japan	8.10	1.60	3.00
Jordan	6.00	1.10	2.00
Kampuchea	No Parcel Post Service		
Kenya	7.05	1.35	2.50
Kiribati	4.95	.90	1.50
Korea, Democratic People's Rep. (North)	No Parcel Post Service		
Korea, Rep. of (South)	7.05	1.35	2.50
Kuwait	6.00	1.10	2.00
Lao	8.10	1.60	3.00
Latvia	8.10	1.60	3.00
Lebanon	6.00	1.10	2.00
Leeward Islands	3.90	.65	1.00
Lesotho	8.10	1.60	3.00
Liberia	4.95	.90	1.50
Libya	6.00	1.10	2.00
Lithuania	8.10	1.60	3.00
Luxembourg	4.95	.90	1.50
Macao	6.00	1.10	2.00
Madagascar	6.00	1.10	2.00
Madeira Islands	4.95	.90	1.50
Malawi	7.05	1.35	2.50
Malaysia	7.05	1.35	2.50
Maldives	7.05	1.35	2.50
Mali	6.00	1.10	2.00
Malta	6.00	1.10	2.00
Martinique	3.90	.65	1.00
Mauritania	7.05	1.35	2.50
Mauritius	8.10	1.60	3.00
Mexico	3.90	.65	1.00
Mongolia	No Parcel Post Service		
Morocco	6.00	1.10	2.00
Mozambique	8.10	1.60	3.00
Nauru	6.00	1.10	2.00
Nepal	7.05	1.35	2.50
Netherlands	6.00	1.10	2.00
Nertherlands Antilles	3.90	.65	1.00
New Caledonia	7.05	1.35	2.50
New Zealand	7.05	1.35	2.50
Nicaragua	4.95	.90	1.50
Niger	7.05	1.35	2.50
Nigeria	6.00	1.10	2.00
Norway	7.05	1.35	2.50
Oman	7.05	1.35	2.50
Pakistan	7.05	1.35	2.50
Panama	3.90	.65	1.00
Papua New Guinea	7.05	1.35	2.50
Paraguay	6.00	1.10	2.00
Peru	4.95	.90	1.50
Philippines	7.05	1.35	2.50
Pitcairn Islands	4.95	.90	1.50
Poland	6.00	1.10	2.00
Portugal	4.95	.90	1.50
Qatar	6.00	1.10	2.00
Reunion	8.10	1.60	3.00
Romania	6.00	1.10	2.00
Rwanda	7.05	1.35	2.50
St. Helena	4.95	.90	1.50
St. Lucia	3.90	.65	1.00
St. Pierre & Miquelon	3.90	.65	1.00
St. Thomas & Principe	7.05	1.35	2.50
St. Vincent & The Grenadines	3.90	.65	1.00
Santa Cruz Islands	4.95	.90	1.50

Country	First 4 oz.	Air parcel post rates Each add'l. 4 oz. or fraction up to first 5 lbs.	post rates Each add'l. ½ lb. or fraction of ½ lb.
Qatar	6.00	1.10	2.00
Reunion	8.10	1.60	3.00
Romania	6.00	1.10	2.00
Rwanda	7.05	1.35	2.50
St. Helena	4.95	.90	1.50
St. Lucia	3.90	.65	1.00
St. Pierre & Miquelon	3.90	.65	1.00
St. Thomas & Principe	7.05	1.35	2.50
St. Vincent & The Grenadines	3.90	.65	1.00
Santa Cruz Islands	4.95	.90	1.50
Saudi Arabia	6.00	1.10	2.00
Senegal	7.05	1.35	2.50
Seychelles	7.05	1.35	2.50
Sierra Leone	6.00	1.10	2.00
Singapore	7.05	1.35	2.50
Solomon Islands	6.00	1.10	2.00
Somalia (Southern Region)	7.05	1.35	2.50
Somalia (Northern Region)	7.05	1.35	2.50
South Africa	8.10	1.60	3.00
Spain	6.00	1.10	2.00
Sri Lanka	7.05	1.35	2.50
Sudan	7.05	1.35	2.50
Suriname	4.95	.90	1.50
Swaziland	7.05	1.35	2.50
Sweden	7.05	1.35	2.50
Switzerland	4.95	.90	1.50

Country	First 4 oz.	Air parcel post rates Each add'l. 4 oz. or fraction up to first 5 lbs.	post rates Each add'l. ½ lb. or fraction of ½ lb.
Syria	6.00	1.10	2.00
Taiwan	6.00	1.10	2.00
Tanzania	8.10	1.60	3.00
Thailand	7.05	1.35	2.50
Togo	7.05	1.35	2.50
Tonga	4.95	.90	1.50
Trinidad & Tobago	4.95	.90	1.50
Tristan da Cunha	4.95	.90	1.50
Tunisia	6.00	1.10	2.00
Turkey	6.00	1.10	2.00
Turks & Caicos Islands	3.90	.65	1.00
Tuvalu (Ellice Islands)	4.95	.90	1.50
Uganda	7.05	1.35	2.50
USSR[2]	8.10	1.60	3.00
United Arab Emirates	7.05	1.35	2.50
Upper Volta	6.00	1.10	2.00
Uruguay	4.95	.90	1.50
Vanuatu	4.95	.90	1.50
Vatican City State	6.00	1.10	2.00
Venezuela	4.95	.90	1.50
Vietnam[1]	No Parcel Post Service		
Western Samoa	4.95	.90	1.50
Yemen Arab Republic	7.05	1.35	2.50
Yemen, Peoples Democratic Republic of	7.05	1.35	2.50
Yugoslavia	6.00	1.10	2.00
Zaire	7.05	1.35	2.50
Zambia	8.10	1.60	3.00
Zimbabwe	8.10	1.60	3.00

Weight limits: minimum 1 lb., maximum 66 lbs.; up to 1½ lbs., $3.38; each add'l 8 oz. or fraction, up to first 5 lbs., 54¢; each add'l 8 oz. or fraction, $1.08.

(1) Restrictions apply; consult post office. (2) To facilitate distribution and delivery, include "Union of Soviet Socialist Republics" or "USSR" as part of the address.

Miscellaneous International Rates

Letters and Letter Pkgs (Surface)

Over Lbs.	Over Ozs.	Through Lbs.	Through Ozs.	Canada and Mexico	All other countries
0	0	0	1	$.22	$.37
0	1	0	2	.40	.57
0	2	0	3	.58	.77
0	3	0	4	.76	.97
0	4	0	5	.94	1.17
0	5	0	6	1.12	1.37
0	6	0	7	1.30	1.59
0	7	0	8	1.48	1.79
0	8	0	9	1.66	1.77
0	9	0	10	1.84	1.77
0	10	0	11	2.02	1.77
0	11	0	12	2.20	1.77
0	12	1	0	2.84	1.77
1	0	1	8	3.38	3.40
1	8	2	0	3.92	4.66
2	0	2	8	4.46	5.92
2	8	3	0	5.00	6.84
3	0	3	8	5.54	7.76
3	8	4	0	6.08	8.68

Maximum limit: 66 pounds to Canada, 4 pounds to Mexico and all other countries.

Letters and Letter Pkgs (Air)

Canada and Mexico: Refer to rates listed under Letter and Letter Pkgs. (Surface). Mail paid at this rate receives First-Class service in the United States and air service in Canada and Mexico.

Colombia, Venezuela, Central America, the Caribbean Islands, Bahamas, Bermuda, St. Pierre & Miquelon; also from Amer. Samoa to Western Samoa and from Guam to Philippines: 39 cents per half ounce up to and including 2 ounces; 33 cents each additional half ounce up to and including 32 ounces; 33 cents per additional ounce over 32 ounces.

All Other Countries: 44 cents per half ounce up to and including 2 ounces; 39 cents each additional half ounce up to and including 32 ounces; 39 cents per additional ounce over 32 ounces.

Parcel Post (Surface)

Canada: $3.35 for over 1 lb. and up to 2 lbs.; $1.05 each add'l lb.

Mexico, Central America, The Caribbean Islands, Bahamas, Bermuda, St. Pierre and Miquelon: $3.70 for the first 2 pounds and $1.20 each additional pound or fraction.

All Other Countries: $3.90 for the first 2 pounds and $1.30 for each additional pound or fraction.

For Parcel Post air rates, see tables, pages 775-776.

Postcards

Surface rates to Canada and Mexico, 14¢; to all other countries, 25¢. By air, Canada and Mexico, 14¢; to all other countries, 33¢. Maximum size permitted, 6 x 4¼ in.; minimum, 5½ x 3½.

International Parcel Post

For rates see pages 775-776, and Addenda

General dimensional limits — greatest length, 3½ feet; greatest length and girth combined, 6 feet.

Prohibited articles. Before sending goods abroad the mailer should consult the post office that they will not be confiscated or returned because their importation is prohibited or restricted by the country of address.

Packing. Parcels for transmission overseas should be even more carefully packed than those intended for delivery within the continental U.S. Containers should be used which will be strong enough to protect the contents from the weight of other mail, from pressure and friction, climatic changes, and repeated handlings.

Sealing. Registered or insured parcels must be sealed. To some countries the sealing of ordinary (unregistered and uninsured) parcels is optional, and to others compulsory. Consult post office.

Customs declarations and other forms. At least one customs declaration is required for parcel post packages (surface or air) mailed to another country. In addition, to some countries, a dispatch note is required. The forms may be obtained at post offices.

Air-AO (Printed Matter, Matter for the Blind and Small Packets) Canada & Mexico

Weight Not Over	Rate	Weight Not Over	Rate	Weight Not Over	Rate
1 oz.	$0.22	2.5 lbs.	$4.46	15.0 lbs.	$17.96
2	0.40	3.0	5.00	16.0	19.04
3	0.58	3.5	5.54	17.0	20.12
4	0.76	4.0	6.08	18.0	21.20
5	0.94	4.5	6.62	19.0	22.28
6	1.12	5.0	7.16	20.0	23.36
7	1.30	6.0	8.24	21.0	24.44
8	1.48	7.0	9.32	22.0	25.52
9	1.66	8.0	10.40	23.0	26.60
10	1.84	9.0	11.48	24.0	27.68
11	2.02	10.0	12.56	25.0	28.76
12	2.20	11.0	13.64	26.0	29.84
16	2.84	12.0	14.72	27.0	30.92
24	3.38	13.0	15.80	28.0	32.00
32	3.92	14.0	16.88	29.0	33.08
				30.0	34.16

All Other Countries

Weight Not Over	Columbia, Venezuela, Central America, Caribbean Islands, Bahamas, Bermuda, St. Pierre & Miquelon (Also, from American Samoa to Western Samoa, & from Guam to the Philippines)	South America (except Colombia & Venezuela), Europe (except Estonia, Latvia, Lithuania, & U.S.S.R.), & North Africa (Morocco, Algeria, Tunisia, Libya & Egypt)	Estonia, Latvia, Lithuania, U.S.S.R., Asia, Australia & New Zealand, Pacific Ocean Islands, Africa (other than North Africa), the Indian Ocean Islands & the Middle East
1 ozs.	$0.58	$0.70	$0.82
2 ozs.	.89	1.12	1.35
3 ozs.	1.20	1.54	1.88
4 ozs.	1.51	1.96	2.41
6 ozs.	1.82	2.50	3.18
8 ozs.	2.13	3.04	3.95
10 ozs.	2.44	3.58	4.72
12 ozs.	2.75	4.12	5.49
14 ozs.	3.06	4.66	6.26
16 ozs.	3.37	5.20	7.03
18 ozs.	3.68	5.74	7.80
20 ozs.	3.99	6.28	8.57
22 ozs.	4.30	6.82	9.34
24 ozs.	4.61	7.36	10.11
26 ozs.	4.92	7.90	10.88
28 ozs.	5.23	8.44	11.65
30 ozs.	5.54	8.98	12.42
32 ozs.	5.85	9.52	13.19
2.5 lbs.	7.07	11.68	16.29
3.0 lbs.	8.29	13.84	19.39
3.5 lbs.	9.51	16.00	22.49
4.0 lbs.	10.73	18.16	25.59
Each additional 1/2 lb. over 4 lbs.	1.22	2.16	3.10

Small Packets (Surface)

Weight Not Over	Canada	Mexico	All Other Countries
1 oz.	$0.22	$0.22	$0.29
2	0.39	0.39	.47
3	0.56	0.56	.65
4	0.73	0.73	.83
6	0.91	0.91	1.02
8	1.09	1.09	1.21
10	1.27	1.27	1.40
12	1.45	1.45	1.59
14	1.63	1.63	1.78
16	1.81	1.81	1.97
18	...	1.99	2.16
20	...	2.17	2.35
22	...	2.35	2.54
24	...	2.53	2.73
26	...	2.71	2.92
28	...	2.89	3.11
30	...	3.07	3.30
32	...	3.25	3.49

Printed Matter (Surface)

Weight Not Over	Canada and Mexico	All Other Countries
1 oz.	$0.22	$0.29
2	0.39	0.47
3	0.56	0.65
4	0.73	0.83
6	0.91	1.02
8	1.09	1.21
10	1.27	1.40
12	1.45	1.59
14	1.63	1.78
16	1.81	1.97
18	1.99	2.16
20	2.17	2.35
22	2.35	2.54
24	2.53	2.73
26	2.71	2.92
28	2.89	3.11
30	3.07	3.30
32	3.25	3.49
3 lbs.	3.57	4.19
4 lbs.	3.89	4.89
Each additional 1 lb.	.97	1.22

Books and Sheet Music (Surface)

Weight Not Over	All Countries
1 lb.	$0.96
2	1.76
3	2.10
4	2.44
5	3.05
6	3.66
7	4.27
8	4.88
9	5.49
10	6.10
11	6.71
Each Additional 1 lb.	0.61

Publishers' Periodicals (Surface)

Weight Not Over	All Countries
1 oz.	$0.15
2	0.22
3	0.29
4	0.36
6	0.46
8	0.56
10	0.66
12	0.76
14	0.86
16	0.96
18	1.06
20	1.16
22	1.26
24	1.36
26	1.46
28	1.56
30	1.66
32	1.76
3 lbs.	2.10
4 lbs.	2.44
Each additional 1 lb.	0.61

INTELPOST-A USPS International Service Offering

The U.S. Postal Service, in conjunction with several foreign countries is making available to the public a new service offering called INTELPOST. INTELPOST is an acronym for International Electronic Post.

The INTELPOST system is a very high speed digital facsimile network between the United States and participating countries. INTELPOST utilizes existing international postal acceptance and delivery mechanisms for the acceptance and distribution of the INTELPOST original and facsimile documents. The INTELPOST original document and a transmittal form are scanned by a facsimile reader operated by USPS personnel at the INTELPOST transmitting facility and sent via international satellite communications to its destination.

A black and white image of the original document is printed by a facsimile printer operated by foreign postal personnel and is inserted into an INTELPOST envelope for delivery by participating postal administration personnel according to the service offerings available in the particular country.

The cost of an INTELPOST transmission is $5.00 per page including First Class (normal) delivery in the destinating foreign country. If an optional express type delivery service is available and is selected, the cost of such service will be added to the price of the message. Service is currently available to Canada, the United Kingdom and the Netherlands. Several additional countries are in the process of building INTELPOST Centers.

VITAL STATISTICS

Source: National Center for Health Statistics, U.S. Department of Health and Human Services

January-March 1985 (Provisional Data)

Births

During the first 3 months of 1985 there were 896,000 live births, slightly more than the number reported for the same period in 1984. The birth rate was 15.3, unchanged from the Jan.-March 1984 rate; the fertility rate was 64.4, slightly below the rate for Jan.-March 1984.

Marriages

For the first quarter of 1985 a total of 424,000 marriages was reported, yielding a marriage rate of 7.2 per 1,000 population. Both the number and rate of marriages in the first quarter of 1985 were 5% below comparable figures for 1984.

Divorces

In the 3 months from January through March, a cumulative total of 276,000 divorces was reported, and the divorce rate for the period was 4.7 per 1,000 population. This was an increase of 2% over the level recorded in the first 3 months of 1984.

Deaths

The provisional count of deaths for March 1985 totaled 185,000 resulting in a rate of 9.2 deaths per 1,000 population. This rate was the same as the rate for March 1984. Among the 185,000 deaths for March 1985 were 3,300 deaths at ages under 1 year, yielding an infant mortality rate of 10.7 deaths per 1,000 live births.

The provisional death rate for the 12 months ending with February 1985 was 8.8 deaths per 1,000 population. This was 2% higher than the rate for the 12 months ending with February 1984.

Provisional Statistics
12 months ending with March

	Number		Rate*	
	1985	1984	1985	1984
Live births	3,699,000	3,617,000	15.6	15.4
Deaths	2,073,000	2,019,000	8.8	8.6
Natural increase.	1,626,000	1,598,000	6.8	6.8
Marriages	2,458,000	2,452,000	10.4	10.5
Divorces	1,159,000	1,167,000	4.9	5.0
Infant deaths. . .	39,000	39,200	10.5	10.9
Population base (in millions)			236.7	234.4

*Per 1,000 population
Note: Rates are based on the 1980 Census of Population.

Annual Report for the Year 1984 (Provisional Statistics)

Births

During 1984 an estimated 3,697,000 babies were born in the United States, 2% more than in 1983. The birth rate was 15.7 per 1,000 population (15.5 in 1983) and the fertility rate was 66.0 per 1,000 women aged 15-44 years, 1% higher than the rate in 1983 (65.4).

The 2% increase in the number of births in 1984, along with the 1% increase in the fertility rate, seem to indicate that at least some age-specific birth rates increased between 1983 and 1984. A 2% decline in the number of women 15-24 yrs.—the age at which nearly half all U.S. births occur—indicates that the childbearing population is becoming older.

As a result of natural increase, the number of births over deaths, an estimated 1,650,000 persons were added to the population in 1984. The rate of increase was 7.0 per 1,000 population, 1% below that of 1983. This increase was due to the increase in birth rate.

Deaths

The provisional count of deaths in the United States during 1984 totaled 2,047,000, a rate of 8.7 deaths per 1,000 population. This rate was 1% higher than in 1983. Among these deaths were 39,200 at ages under 1 year, resulting in an infant mortality rate of 10.6 per 1,000 live births. This rate was 3% lower than the provisional infant mortality rate of 10.9 for 1983.

Marriages and Divorces

The number of marriages rose from 2,444,000 in 1983 to 2,487,000 in 1984, an increase of 2%.

The marriage rate was 10.5 per 1,000 population. This rate was the same as in 1983 but lower than in any other year since 1979. In December, 1984, 196,000 couples married, and the marriage rate was 9.8 per 1,000 population compared with 9.2 in December 1983.

Provisional data indicate that 1,155,000 couples were divorced during 1984, 24,000 (2%) fewer than in 1983 and 58,000 (5%) fewer than in 1981 when the national divorce total reached a historic high of 1,213,000.

The divorce rate declined from 5.0 per 1,000 population in 1983 to 4.9 in 1984. The divorce rate has not been as low since 1975.

Births and Deaths in the U.S.

Refers only to events occurring within the U.S., including Alaska and Hawaii beginning in 1960. Excludes fetal deaths. Rates per 1,000 population enumerated as of April 1 for 1960, and 1970; estimated as of July 1 for all other years. (p) provisional. (NA) not available. Beginning 1970 excludes births and deaths occurring to nonresidents of the U.S.

	Births		Deaths	
Year	Total number	Rate	Total number	Rate
1955.	4,097,000	25.0	1,528,717	9.3
1960.	4,257,850	23.7	1,711,982	9.5
1965.	3,760,358	19.4	1,828,136	9.4
1970.	3,731,386	18.4	1,921,031	9.5
1975.	3,144,198	14.6	1,892,879	8.8
1980.	3,612,258	15.9	1,986,000	8.7
1981.	3,646,000	15.9	1,987,000	8.7
1982.	3,614,000	16.0	1,975,550	8.6
1983.	3,614,000	15.5	2,010,000	8.6
1984.	3,697,000	15.7	2,047,000	8.7

Births and Deaths by States

Source: National Center for Health Statistics, U.S. Department of Health and Human Services

State	Births 1984ᴾ	Births 1983	Deaths 1984ᴾ	Deaths 1983	State	Births 1984ᴾ	Births 1983	Deaths 1984ᴾ	Deaths 1983
Alabama	58,604	57,685	37,551	34,885	Montana	13,846	13,794	6,644	6,697
Alaska	12,247	11,500	1,993	34,885	Nebraska	26,483	26,816	14,973	14,819
Arizona	54,821	52,659	24,384	23,183	Nevada	15,276	14,251	7,302	6,948
Arkansas	33,440	33,630	23,478	23,093	New Hampshire	12,656	13,973	7,749	7,771
California	455,075	413,915	195,430	187,938	New Jersey	94,044	90,627	66,511	65,620
Colorado	54,471	55,159	20,941	19,978	New Mexico	26,285	30,186	9,806	9,927
Connecticut	39,237	34,978	27,633	25,273	New York	251,062	249,618	168,852	170,464
Delaware	9,487	9,538	5,098	5,071	North Carolina	86,705	84,655	51,496	50,602
Dist. of Col.	19,123	18,592	8,302	8,349	North Dakota	12,738	13,200	5,897	5,880
Florida	155,236	148,695	116,515	114,443	Ohio	159,939	160,330	96,937	98,234
Georgia	91,761	91,090	47,303	45,988	Oklahoma	53,425	54,085	29,258	28,414
Hawaii	18,658	19,005	5,966	5,712	Oregon	39,536	41,045	23,229	21,579
Idaho	17,072	18,541	6,649	6,951	Pennsylvania	159,911	159,210	122,204	121,592
Illinois	175,907	175,679	98,151	99,964	Rhode Island	13,219	13,061	9,589	9,407
Indiana	79,134	82,169	47,195	48,268	South Carolina	48,215	48,513	25,340	25,300
Iowa	42,611	43,783	26,093	27,169	South Dakota	12,383	12,409	6,417	6,545
Kansas	38,570	39,498	21,742	21,365	Tennessee	70,407	67,739	45,570	42,148
Kentucky	51,964	55,252	33,449	33,590	Texas	306,192	287,044	119,531	115,128
Louisiana	83,195	80,610	36,549	35,755	Utah	39,677	40,752	9,295	8,834
Maine	16,513	16,323	10,796	11,242	Vermont	7,419	7,671	4,455	4,908
Maryland	58,790	57,436	34,875	33,981	Virginia	79,342	77,448	43,899	43,226
Massachusetts	79,386	78,670	59,104	54,275	Washington	73,605	63,729	35,212	31,039
Michigan	134,517	131,873	75,515	74,302	West Virginia	25,059	26,911	19,114	19,210
Minnesota	65,788	64,698	33,525	34,099	Wisconsin	73,088	72,611	41,274	41,124
Mississippi	42,695	44,025	22,464	23,122	Wyoming	9,026	9,515	3,000	2,990
Missouri	78,517	76,739	52,332	50,419	(p) provisional				

Marriages and Divorces by States

Source: National Center for Health Statistics, U.S. Department of Health and Human Services

1984 provisional figures; divorces include reported annulments.

State	Marriages	Divorces	State	Marriages	Divorces	State	Marriages	Divorces
Alabama	47,487	25,483	Louisiana	41,295	NA	Oklahoma	38,612	24,002
Alaska	6,519	3,904	Maine	884	5,864	Oregon	22,594	15,463
Arizona	31,506	19,796	Maryland	46,815	15,817	Pennsylvania	92,596	40,581
Arkansas	31,427	15,553	Massachusetts	53,198	16,957	Rhode Island	7,942	3,640
California	226,580	NA	Michigan	89,391	42,112	South Carolina	55,882	13,753
Colorado	34,630	18,413	Minnesota	36,893	14,696	South Dakota	8,035	2,506
Connecticut	25,080	11,226	Mississippi	26,158	12,524	Tennessee	55,205	30,684
Delaware	5,463	2,908	Missouri	54,148	25,038	Texas	207,631	98,074
Dist. of Col.	5,488	2,874	Montana	7,677	4,407	Utah	17,579	8,134
Florida	124,088	75,342	Nebraska	13,341	6,487	Vermont	5,375	2,173
Georgia	75,817	34,084	Nevada	107,422	12,487	Virginia	65,976	24,837
Hawaii	14,891	4,756	New Hampshire	11,363	4,808	Washington	44,730	27,313
Idaho	12,518	6,033	New Jersey	62,429	28,469	West Virginia	15,456	9,491
Illinois	102,504	48,914	New Mexico	15,171	9,205	Wisconsin	41,104	16,552
Indiana	52,705	NA	New York	176,654	61,075	Wyoming	5,723	3,700
Iowa	26,960	10,406	North Carolina	52,123	29,125			
Kansas	24,795	12,915	North Dakota	5,806	2,258	NA = Not Available		
Kentucky	44,006	17,369	Ohio	98,708	53,492			

Marriages, Divorces, and Rates in the U.S.

Source: National Center for Health Statistics, Public Health Service

Data refer only to events occurring within the United States, including Alaska and Hawaii beginning with 1960. Rates per 1,000 population.

Year	Marriages[1] No.	Marriages[1] Rate	Divorces[2] No.	Divorces[2] Rate	Year	Marriages[1] No.	Marriages[1] Rate	Divorces[2] No.	Divorces[2] Rate
1890	570,000	9.0	33,461	0.5	1945	1,612,992	12.2	485,000	[3]3.5
1895	620,000	8.9	40,387	0.6	1950	1,667,231	11.1	385,144	2.6
1900	709,000	9.3	55,751	0.7	1955	1,531,000	9.3	377,000	2.3
1905	842,000	10.0	67,976	0.8	1960	1,523,000	8.5	393,000	2.2
1910	948,166	10.3	83,045	0.9	1965	1,800,000	9.3	479,000	2.5
1915	1,007,595	10.0	104,298	1.0	1970	2,158,802	10.6	708,000	3.5
1920	1,274,476	12.0	170,505	1.6	1975	2,152,662	10.0	1,036,000	4.8
1925	1,188,334	10.3	175,449	1.5	1980	2,413,000	10.6	1,182,000	5.2
1930	1,126,856	9.2	195,961	1.6	1981	2,438,000	10.6	1,219,000	5.3
1935	1,327,000	10.4	218,000	1.7	1982	2,495,000	10.8	1,180,000	5.1
1940	1,595,879	12.1	264,000	2.0	1983	2,444,000	10.5	1,179,000	5.0
					1984	2,487,000	10.5	1,155,000	4.9

(1) Includes estimates and marriage licenses for some states for all years. (2) Includes reported annulments. (3) Divorce rates for 1945 based on population including armed forces overseas.

Deaths and Death Rates for Selected Causes

Source: National Center for Health Statistics, U.S. Department of Health and Human Services

1984 Cause of death (est.)	Number[1]	Rate[2]	1984 Cause of death (est.)	Number[1]	Rate[2]
All causes	185,587	863.4	Influenza and pneumonia	5,303	24.7
Viral hepatitis	76	0.4	Influenza	124	0.6
Tuberculosis, all forms	157	0.7	Pneumonia	5,179	24.1
Septicemia	1,352	6.3	Chronic obstructive pulmonary diseases . .	6,354	29.6
Syphilis and its sequelae	6	0.0	Chronic and unspecified bronchitis. . . .	307	1.4
All other infective and parasitic diseases . .	539	2.5	Emphysema	1,215	5.7
Malignant neoplasms, including			Asthma	344	1.6
neoplasms of lymphatic and			Ulcer of stomach and duodenum	607	2.8
hematopoietic tissues	41,130	791.3	Hernia and intestinal obstruction.	509	2.4
Diabetes mellitus	3,246	15.1	Cirrhosis of liver	2,435	11.3
Meningitis.	98	0.5	Cholelithiasis, cholecystitis, and cholangitis.	297	1.4
Major cardiovascular diseases.	87,967	409.2	Nephritis, nephrosis and nephrotic syn. . .	1,883	8.8
Diseases of heart	69,137	321.6	Infections of kidney	166	0.8
Rheumatic fever and			Hyperplasia of prostate	49	0.2
rheumatic heart disease	625	2.9	Congenital anomalies	1,188	5.5
Hypertensive heart disease	1,867	8.7	Certain causes of mortality in early infancy.	1,724	8.0
Ischemic heart disease	48,830	227.2	Symptoms and ill-defined conditions . . .	3,719	17.3
Acute myocardial infarction	25,331	117.8	All other diseases	12,267	57.1
All other forms of heart disease . . .	14,045	65.3	Accidents.	8,571	39.9
Hypertension	622	2.9	Motor vehicle accidents	4,136	19.2
Cerebrovascular diseases	14,045	65.3	Suicide	2,528	11.8
Artherosclerosis	2,196	10.2	Homicide	1,778	8.3
Other diseases of arteries,			All other external causes	249	1.2
arterioles, and capillaries	1,967	9.2			
Acute bronchitis and bronchiolitis	48	0.2			

Due to rounding estimates of death, figures may not add to total. (1) Data represent a 10% sampling of all death certificates for an 11-month (Jan.-Nov.) period. (2) Rates per 100,000 population.

Principal Types of Accidental Deaths

Source: National Safety Council

Year	Motor vehicle	Falls	Fires, Burns	Drown-ing	Fire-arms	Injestion of Food, Object	Poison by gas	Other poisons
1965 . .	49,163	19,984	7,347	5,485	2,344	1,973	1,526	2,110
1970 . .	54,633	16,926	6,718	6,391	2,406	2,877	1,620	3,679
1975 . .	45,853	14,896	6,071	6,640	2,380	3,106	1,577	4,694
1980 . .	52,600	12,300	5,500	7,000	1,800	3,249	1,500	2,800
1981 . .	50,800	11,700	4,900	6,000	1,900	3,200	1,700	2,600
1982 . .	46,000	11,600	5,000	6,200	1,900	3,200	1,400	3,000
1983 . .	44,600	11,700	4,600	6,600	1,900	3,200	1,300	3,000
			Death rates per 100,000 population					
1965 . .	25.4	10.3	3.8	2.8	1.2	1.1	0.8	1.1
1970 . .	26.9	8.3	3.3	3.1	1.2	1.4	0.8	1.8
1975 . .	21.5	7.0	2.8	3.1	1.1	1.1	0.7	2.2
1980 . .	23.2	5.4	2.4	3.1	0.8	1.4	0.7	1.2
1981 . .	22.2	5.1	2.1	2.6	0.8	1.4	0.8	1.1
1982 . .	19.9	5.0	2.2	2.7	0.8	1.4	0.6	1.3
1983 . .	19.1	5.0	2.0	2.8	0.8	1.4	0.6	1.3

U.S. Civil Aviation Accidents

Source: National Safety Council

1984	Accidents Total	Accidents Fatal	Deaths[1]	Per 100,000 Aircraft-Hours Total	Per 100,000 Aircraft-Hours Fatal	Per million Aircraft-Miles Total	Per million Aircraft-Miles Fatal
Large airlines	12	1	4	0.164	0.014	0.004	0.0003
Commuter airlines. . . .	21	7	45	1.20	0.40	0.07	0.02
On-demand air taxis .	140	22	51	4.21	0.66	—	—
General aviation	2,999	529	998	9.82	1.73	—	—

(1) Includes passengers, crew members and others.

Transportation Accident Passenger Death Rates, 1983

Source: National Safety Council

Kind of transportation	Passenger miles (billions)	Passenger deaths	Rate per 100,000,000 pass. miles	1981-1983 aver. death rate
Passenger automobiles and taxis[1]	2,321.5	22,739	0.98	1.08
Buses	90.0	49	0.05	0.05
Intercity buses[2].	26.5	8	0.03	—
Railroad passenger trains.	11.1	4	0.04	0.05
Scheduled air transport planes (domestic)	231.7	17	0.01	0.04

(1) Drivers of passenger automobiles are considered passengers. (2) Class 1 only, representing 65 per cent of total intercity bus passenger mileage.

Motor Vehicle Traffic Deaths by State

Source: National Safety Council

Place of accidents	Number 1984	Number 1983	Mileage Rate[b] 1984	Mileage Rate[b] 1983	Place of accidents	Number 1984	Number 1983	Mileage Rate[b] 1984	Mileage Rate[b] 1983
Total U.S.[a]	46,200	44,400	2.7	2.7					
Alabama	939	942	3.1	3.0	Montana	238	286	3.1	4.0
Alaska	131	150	2.4	4.5	Nebraska	285	255	2.3	2.2
Arizona	869	675	3.3	3.4	Nevada	249	253	3.6	3.7
Arkansas	524	554	2.8	3.3	New Hampshire	192	191	2.6	2.7
California	4,999	4,571	2.9	2.5	New Jersey	927	932	1.6	1.8
Colorado	610	646	2.5	2.7	New Mexico	497	531	4.3	4.5
Connecticut	471	445	2.2	2.2	New York	2,065	2,077	2.4	2.5
Delaware	130	112	2.6	2.3	North Carolina	1,446	1,242	3.0	2.8
Dist. of Col.	64	72	2.3	2.3	North Dakota	100	116	1.7	2.2
Florida	2,845	2,703	3.3	3.3	Ohio	1,645	1,556	2.2	2.1
Georgia	1,409	1,296	2.9	2.7	Oklahoma	816	854	2.8	2.9
Hawaii	136	139	1.9	2.4	Oregon	571	548	3.4	2.7
Idaho	242	263	2.8	3.2	Pennsylvania	1,752	1,752	2.4	2.4
Illinois	1,572	1,553	2.3	2.3	Rhode Island	82	100	1.3	1.7
Indiana	927	1,019	2.5	2.6	South Carolina	915	845	3.6	3.4
Iowa	420	509	2.1	2.6	South Dakota	143	175	2.3	2.8
Kansas	510	411	2.7	2.3	Tennessee	1,111	1,046	3.0	2.9
Kentucky	765	790	2.8	3.0	Texas	3,913	3,823	2.9	2.9
Louisiana	958	941	3.6	3.4	Utah	315	283	2.7	2.5
Maine	231	224	2.5	2.8	Vermont	115	94	2.7	2.3
Maryland	650	663	2.1	2.2	Virginia	1,014	900	2.4	2.1
Massachusetts	663	643	1.7	1.7	Washington	761	705	2.2	2.0
Michigan	1,549	1,331	2.4	2.2	West Virginia	440	428	4.0	3.7
Minnesota	584	558	1.8	1.8	Wisconsin	834	735	2.4	2.2
Mississippi	680	716	3.8	4.0	Wyoming	157	173	3.2	3.4
Missouri	991	921	2.6	2.5					

(a) Includes both traffic and nontraffic motor-vehicle deaths. (b) The mileage death rate is deaths per 100,000,000 vehicle miles. 1984 mileage death rates are National Safety Council estimates.

Accidental Deaths and Injuries by Severity of Injury

Source: National Safety Council

In 1984 accidental deaths were estimated to number 92,000, an increase of 500 or 1 percent above the 1983 total. This was the third year since 1962 that accidental deaths were estimated to number less than 100,000. The death rate per 100,000 population was 39.0.

1984 Severity of injury	Total*	Motor vehicle	Work	Home	Public[1]
Deaths*	92,000	46,200	11,500	20,000	18,500
Disabling injuries*	8,700,000	1,700,000	1,900,000	3,000,000	2,300,000
Permanent impairments	330,000	140,000	70,000	80,000	50,000
Temporary total disabilities	8,400,000	1,600,000	1,800,000	2,900,000	2,300,000

Certain Costs of Accidental Deaths or Injuries, 1984 ($ billions)					
Total*	$96.9	$47.6	$33.0	$10.8	$7.2
Wage loss	28.8	15.2	6.8	4.0	4.1
Medical expense	13.8	4.7	4.3	3.2	2.0
Insurance administration	13.4	8.9	4.3	0.1	0.1

*Duplication between motor vehicle, work, and home are eliminated in the total column. (1) Excludes motor vehicle and work accidents in public places.

Home Accident Deaths

Source: National Safety Council

Year	Total home	Falls	Fires, burns[2]	Suffo., ingesting object	Suffo., mech-anical	Poison (solid, liquid)	Poison by gas	Fire-arms	Other
1950	29,000	14,800	5,000	(1)	1,600	1,300	1,250	950	4,100
1955	28,500	14,100	5,400	(1)	1,250	1,150	900	1,100	4,600
1960	28,000	12,300	6,350	1,850	1,500	1,350	900	1,200	2,550
1965	28,500	11,700	6,100	1,300*	1,200	1,700	1,100	1,300	4,100
1970	27,000	9,700	5,600	1,800	1,100	3,000	1,100	1,400	3,300
1975	25,000	8,000	5,000	1,800	800	3,700	1,000	1,300	3,400
1980	23,000	6,600	4,400	1,700	500	2,300	700	1,000	5,800[3]
1983	20,000	6,300	3,900	2,000	600	2,400	800	1,100	2,900
1984	20,000	6,100	3,900	1,900	600	3,100	800	900	2,700

*Data for this year and subsequent years not comparable with previous years due to classification changes. (1) Included in Other. (2) Includes deaths resulting from conflagration, regardless of nature of injury. (3) Includes 1,000 excessive deaths due to summer heat wave.

Pedalcycle Accidents

Source: National Safety Council

Year	Pedalcycles (millions)	Deaths	Death Rate[a]	Percent of Deaths by Age 0-14	Percent of Deaths by Age 15-24	Percent of Deaths by Age 25 & over
1940	7.8	750	9.59	48	39	13
1950	13.8	440	3.18	82	9	9
1960	28.2	460	1.63	78	9	13
1970	56.5	780	1.38	66	15	19
1980	100.0	1,200	1.20	35	36	29
1983	105.5	1,100	1.04	42	31	27
1984	106.1	1,000	0.94	36	32	32

(a) Deaths per 100,000 pedalcycles.

U.S. Deaths and Death Rates, 1981
By Region, Division, State; Race and Sex

Source: National Center for Health Statistics

Race, Sex, Area	Total Deaths Number	Rate[1]	Infant Deaths (under 1 year) Number	Rate[2]	Race, Sex, Area	Total Deaths Number	Rate[1]	Infant Deaths (under 1 year) Number	Rate[2]
United States...	1,977,981	862.4	43,305	11.9	Nebraska.....	14,616	926.8	270	9.9
Male	1,063,772	954.5	24,452	13.1	Kansas.....	21,701	909.9	470	11.4
Female.....	914,209	775.4	18,853	10.7	**South**				
White	1,731,233	880.3	30,478	10.5	South Atlantic ...	335,949	891.3	7,501	13.6
Male	925,490	965.1	17,411	11.7	Delaware....	5,073	849.7	123	13.4
Female.....	805,743	799.6	13,067	9.2	Maryland....	33,949	797.1	771	12.6
All other.....	246,748	755.0	12,827	17.8	District of				
Male	138,282	889.4	7,041	19.2	Columbia..	6,954	1,098.6	231	25.1
Female.....	108,466	633.0	5,786	16.3	Virginia	42,237	778.6	991	12.5
Black	228,560	841.7	11,757	20.0	West Virginia..	19,053	979.1	363	13.0
Male	127,296	991.6	6,451	21.7	North Carolina..	49,236	827.2	1,101	13.1
Female.....	101,264	707.3	5,306	18.3	South Carolina..	25,428	802.1	837	16.1
Regions					Georgia.....	44,892	806.7	1,238	13.8
Northeast...	466,887	946.2	7,678	11.6	Florida	109,127	1,075.5	1,846	13.3
North Central...	518,871	880.1	11,407	12.2	East South Central	132,664	899.7	3,054	13.2
South	666,174	866.8	16,019	13.0	Kentucky....	33,283	908.1	697	12.2
West.......	326,049	737.8	8,201	10.4	Tennessee....	40,509	876.1	847	12.6
Northeast					Alabama....	35,412	903.4	799	13.0
New England...	111,334	894.4	1,721	10.5	Mississippi...	23,460	925.1	711	15.4
Maine......	10,387	918.4	180	10.9	West South Central	197,561	809.1	5,464	12.1
New Hampshire	7,701	821.9	131	9.7	Arkansas....	22,372	975.7	425	11.9
Vermont	4,322	839.2	61	7.7	Louisiana....	36,024	838.7	1,130	13.7
Massachusetts.	52,982	917.6	720	9.7	Oklahoma....	28,617	921.9	637	11.9
Rhode Island..	9,174	960.6	147	11.8	Texas.....	110,548	750.8	3,272	11.6
Connecticut ..	26,768	853.6	482	12.1	**West**				
Middle Atlantic..	355,553	963.7	5,957	11.9	Mountain	80,474	687.5	2,398	10.4
New York	168,184	955.7	3,006	12.4	Montana	6,729	846.4	153	10.7
New Jersey ...	67,280	906.6	1,038	10.7	Idaho	6,929	723.3	181	9.2
Pennsylvania..	120,089	1,011.3	1,913	11.9	Wyoming	3,165	645.9	115	10.6
North Central					Colorado....	19,388	651.5	519	10.0
East North Central	362,017	868.6	8,243	12.6	New Mexico ..	8,678	651.0	261	9.8
Ohio.......	96,487	894.0	2,059	12.3	Arizona....	21,358	765.2	606	11.8
Indiana.....	47,309	862.5	993	11.7	Utah.....	8,343	550.3	405	9.8
Illinois......	101,819	889.7	2,573	13.9	Nevada....	5,884	695.5	158	11.2
Michigan	75,842	823.0	1,845	13.1	Pacific.....	245,575	755.8	5,803	10.3
Wisconsin ...	40,560	855.7	773	10.4	Washington ..	32,031	759.0	733	10.5
West North Central	156,854	907.8	3,164	11.1	Oregon.....	21,843	820.2	467	10.9
Minnesota ...	32,837	798.4	706	10.3	California....	184,987	764.0	4,297	10.2
Iowa.......	26,949	924.8	459	10.0	Alaska....	1,723	414.2	128	12.7
Missouri	48,848	988.8	973	12.6	Hawaii	4,991	509.8	178	9.8
North Dakota .	5,452	826.1	139	11.2					
South Dakota .	6,451	934.9	147	11.5					

(1) Per 100,000 population in each race-sex group and area. (2) Per 1,000 live births in each race-sex group and area.

Leading Causes of Death, by Sex and Race

Source: National Center for Health Statistics

Rank (1981)	Cause of Death	Ratio of Male to Female	Ratio of Black to White	Rank (1981)	Cause of Death	Ratio of Male to Female	Ratio of Black to White
	All causes.............	1.79	1.47	6	Pneumonia and influenza	1.80	1.52
1	Diseases of heart	2.00	1.28	7	Diabetes mellitus.	1.04	2.21
2	Malignant neoplasms, including neo-			8	Chronic liver disease and cirrhosis..	2.16	1.82
	plasms of lymphatic and hemato-			9	Atherosclerosis..............	1.30	1.09
	poietic tissues	1.50	1.33	10	Suicide	3.15	0.52
3	Cerebrovascular diseases	1.17	1.80	11	Homicide and legal intervention ...	3.88	5.89
4	Accidents and adverse effects ...	2.95	1.16	12	Certain conditions originating in the		
	Motor vehicle accidents.	2.89	0.81		perinatal period	1.25	2.26
	All other accidents and adverse			13	Nephritis, nephrotic syndrome, and		
	effects	3.02	1.64		nephrosis.	1.55	2.92
5	Chronic obstructive pulmonary dis-			14	Congenital anomalies	1.09	0.98
	eases and allied conditions.	2.75	0.75	15	Septicemia	1.41	2.72

Leading Causes of Infant Deaths

Source: National Center for Health Statistics

Rank (1981)	Cause of Death	Number	Rate	Rank (1981)	Cause of Death	Number	Rate
	All causes................	43,305	1,193.2	6	Intrauterine hypoxia and birth asphyxia	1,405	38.7
1	Congenital anomalies..........	8,914	245.6	7	Accidents and adverse effects	981	27.0
2	Sudden infant death syndrome.	5,295	145.9	8	Newborn affected by complications of		
3	Respiratory distress syndrome.....	4,319	119.0		placenta, cord, and membranes...	977	26.9
4	Disorders relating to short gestation			9	Birth trauma	918	25.3
	and unspecified low birthweight ...	3,658	100.8	10	Neonatal hemorrhage	909	25.0
5	Newborn affected by maternal compli-				All other causes	14,471	398.7
	cations of pregnancy	1,458	40.2				

Accidental Deaths by Month and Type, 1982 and 1984

Source: National Safety Council

Month	1984 totals	1982 totals	Motor vehicle	Falls	Drown-ing†	Fires, burns*	Ingest. of food, object	Fire-arms	Poison (solid, liquid)	Poison by gas
All months.	92,000	94,082	45,779	12,077	6,351	5,210	3,254	1,756	3,474	1,259
January	6,900	7,737	3,081	1,116	180	866	296	133	269	237
February	6,400	6,498	2,906	951	200	567	253	110	278	168
March	7,200	7,221	3,450	1,000	320	475	259	106	315	111
April	7,050	7,455	3,668	962	411	506	281	120	244	92
May	7,600	3,294	4,022	1,040	820	389	284	147	297	52
June	8,500	8,132	4,005	989	980	265	246	124	284	63
July	9,000	9,318	4,488	963	1,410	240	243	130	310	51
August	8,650	8,592	4,391	1,040	870	222	252	118	323	53
September	8,100	7,780	4,089	956	460	284	278	137	274	57
October	7,550	7,947	4,247	1,020	300	355	297	193	267	95
November	7,250	7,333	3,642	999	190	445	257	217	289	129
December	7,800	7,775	3,790	1,041	210	596	308	221	324	151
Average	7,670	7,840	3,815	1,006	529	434	271	146	290	105

‡ Includes some deaths not shown separately. † Includes drowning in water transport accidents. Some totals partly estimated. * Includes deaths resulting from conflagration regardless of nature of injury.

Average Lifetime in the U.S.

Source: National Center for Health Statistics, U.S. Department of Health and Human Services

1981 Age interval	Number living[1]	Avg. life expect.[2]	1981p Age interval	Number living[1]	Avg. life expect.[2]
0-1	100,000	74.2	40-45	95,097	37.0
1-5	98,806	74.1	45-50	93,820	32.5
5-10	98,570	70.2	50-55	91,767	28.1
10-15	98,426	65.3	55-60	88,606	24.0
15-20	98,280	60.4	60-65	83,989	20.2
20-25	97,833	55.7	65-70	77,468	16.7
25-30	97,235	51.0	70-75	68,631	13.5
30-35	96,611	46.3	75-80	57,322	10.7
35-40	95,956	41.6	80-85	43,936	8.1
			85 and over	28,778	6.1

(1) Of 100,000 born alive, number living at beginning of age interval. (2) Average number of years of life remaining at beginning of age interval.

Years of Life Expected at Birth

Year	Total pop.	White, male	White, female	Black, male	Black, female
1983p	74.5	71.4	78.7	66.5	75.2
1982p	74.7	71.6	78.8	67.1	75.3
1981	74.2	71.1	78.5	64.4	73.0
1980	73.7	70.7	78.1	63.7	72.3
1969-1971	70.8	67.9	75.5	60.0	68.3
1959-61	69.9	67.6	74.2	—	—
1900-1902[1] . . .	49.2	48.2	51.1	32.5	35.0

[1] Based on data for death-registration states only. p = preliminary

Ownership of Life Insurance in the U.S. and Assets of U.S. Life Insurance Companies

Source: American Council of Life Insurance

Legal Reserve Life Insurance Companies (millions of dollars)

	Purchases of life insurance				Insurance in force					
Year	Ordi-nary	Group	Indus-trial	Total	Ordi-nary	Group	Indus-trial	Credit	Total	Assets
1940	7,022	747	3,318	11,087	79,346	14,938	20,866	380	115,530	30,802
1950	18,260	6,237	5,492	29,989	149,116	47,793	33,415	3,844	234,168	64,020
1960	56,183	15,328	6,906	78,417	341,881	175,903	39,563	29,101	586,448	119,576
1965	89,643	52,867*	7,302	149,812*	499,638	308,078	39,818	53,020	900,554	158,884
1970	134,802	65,381*	6,612	206,795*	734,730	551,357	38,644	77,392	1,402,123	207,254
1975	207,052	102,659*	6,741	316,452*	1,083,421	904,695	39,423	112,032	2,139,571	289,304
1979	329,571	157,906	5,335	492,812	1,585,878	1,419,418	37,794	179,250	3,222,340	432,282
1980	385,575	183,418	3,609	572,602	1,760,474	1,579,355	35,994	165,215	3,541,038	479,210
1981	463,843	346,351*	2,097	812,291*	1,978,080	1,888,612	34,547	162,356	4,063,595	525,803
1982	585,444	250,532	1,898	837,874	2,216,388	2,066,361	32,766	161,144	4,476,659	588,163
1983	753,444	271,609	1,388	1,026,441	2,544,275	2,219,573	31,354	170,659	4,965,861	654,948
1984	820,315	293,521	943	1,114,779	2,887,574	2,392,558	30,104	189,951	5,499,987	722,979

*Includes Servicemen's Group Life Insurance $27.4 billion in 1965, $16.8 billion in 1970, and $1.7 billion in 1975, and $45.6 billion in 1981, as well as $84.4 billion of Federal Employees' Group Life Insurance in 1981.

Families, 1960-1983

Source: U.S. Bureau of Census
(in thousands)

	All Families Number	Married Couple Number	Male Householder[1] Number	Female Householder[1] Number	Black Families Number
1960.	45,111	39,329	1,275	4,507	[2]4,242
1965.	47,956	41,749	1,181	5,026	[2]4,767
1970.	51,586	44,755	1,239	5,591	4,887
1975.	55,712	46,971	1,499	7,242	5,498
1979.	57,804	47,692	1,655	8,458	5,906
1980.	59,550	49,112	1,733	8,705	6,184
1981.	60,309	49,294	1,933	9,082	6,317
1982.	61,019	49,630	1,986	9,403	6,413

	Number	%	Number	%	Number	%	Number	%	Number	%
1983, total.	61,393	100.0	49,908	100.0	2,016	100.0	9,469	100.0	6,530	100.
White	53,407	87.0	42,252	90.7	1,648	81.7	6,507	68.7	(x)	(x)
Black	6,530	10.6	3,486	7.0	309	15.3	2,734	28.9	6,530	100.0
Spanish origin[3]	3,369	5.5	2,448	4.9	153	7.6	767	8.1	(x)	(x)
Size of family:										
2 persons	24,392	39.7	18,736	37.5	1,290	64.0	4,366	46.1	2,131	32.6
3 persons	14,189	23.1	11,063	22.2	448	22.2	2,677	28.3	1,554	23.8
4 persons	13,039	21.2	11,530	23.1	159	7.9	1,350	14.3	1,267	19.4
5 persons	5,970	9.7	5,289	10.6	72	3.6	609	6.4	792	12.1
6 persons	2,329	3.8	2,035	4.1	35	1.7	258	2.7	379	5.8
7 or more persons	1,475	2.4	1,255	2.5	11	.5	209	2.2	406	6.2
Median size[4]	3.26	(x)	3.33	(x)	2.66	(x)	3.04	(x)	3.66	(x)
Own children under age 18:										
None	30,575	49.8	25,544	51.2	1,279	63.4	3,751	39.6	2,639	40.4
1.	12,854	20.9	9,730	19.5	477	23.7	2,648	28.0	1,557	23.8
2.	11,470	18.7	9,406	18.8	204	10.1	1,859	19.6	1,221	18.7
3.	4,492	7.3	3,652	7.3	41	2.0	798	8.4	697	10.7
4 or more.	2,002	3.3	1,575	3.2	15	.7	413	4.4	416	6.4
Own children under age 6:										
None	47,593	77.5	38,448	77.0	1,814	90.0	7,330	77.4	4,757	72.8
1.	9,477	15.4	7,761	15.6	172	8.5	1,543	16.3	1,230	18.8
2.	3,690	6.0	3,174	6.4	29	1.4	487	5.1	434	6.6
3 or more.	634	1.0	525	1.1	—	—	108	1.1	109	1.7

x = Not applicable; (1) No spouse present; (2) Black and other races; (3) Persons of Spanish origin may be of any race.

Marital Status of the Population, By Sex and Age, 1983

Source: U.S. Bureau of the Census

	Number of Persons (1,000)					Percent Distribution				
Sex and Age	Total	Single	Married	Widowed	Divorced	Total	Single	Married	Widowed	Divorced
Male	79,346	19,903	52,884	1,940	4,623	100.0	25.1	66.6	2.4	5.8
18-19 years.	3,965	3,813	145	—	7	100.0	96.2	3.7	—	.2
20-24 years.	10,379	7,594	2,625	7	154	100.0	73.2	25.3	.1	1.5
25-29 years.	10,221	3,909	5,688	14	610	100.0	38.2	55.7	.1	6.0
30-34 years.	9,217	1,804	6,612	3	798	100.0	19.6	71.7	—	8.7
35-44 years.	14,075	1,214	11,518	45	1,298	100.0	8.6	81.8	.3	9.2
45-54 years.	10,721	638	9,054	148	881	100.0	6.0	84.5	1.4	8.2
55-64 years.	10,253	430	8,974	323	527	100.0	4.2	87.5	3.2	5.1
65-74 years.	6,939	390	5,674	622	254	100.0	5.6	81.8	9.0	3.7
75 years old and over	3,576	111	2,594	778	94	100.0	3.1	72.5	21.8	2.6
Female	87,719	16,026	53,831	10,896	6,966	100.0	18.3	61.4	12.4	7.9
18-19 years.	4,020	3,497	501	—	23	100.0	87.0	12.5	—	.6
20-24 years.	10,682	5,933	4,337	19	393	100.0	55.5	40.6	.2	3.7
25-29 years.	10,416	2,579	6,892	50	894	100.0	24.8	66.2	.5	8.6
30-34 years.	9,487	1,230	7,147	69	1,042	100.0	13.0	75.3	.7	11.0
35-44 years.	14,676	929	11,527	308	1,911	100.0	6.3	78.5	2.1	13.0
45-54 years.	11,484	517	9,028	718	1,221	100.0	4.5	78.6	6.3	10.6
55-64 years.	11,732	512	8,286	2,077	857	100.0	4.4	70.6	17.7	7.3
65-74 years.	9,042	458	4,576	3,542	467	100.0	5.1	50.6	39.2	5.2
75 years old and over	6,180	371	1,537	4,113	158	100.0	6.0	24.9	66.6	2.6

Never-Married Persons as Percent of Population, 1960-1983

	Male					Female				
Age	1960	1970	1975	1980	1983	1960	1970	1975	1980	1983
Total	17.3	18.9	20.8	23.8	25.1	11.9	13.7	14.6	17.1	18.3
18 years	94.6	95.1	96.8	97.4	98.0	75.6	82.0	83.7	88.0	90.6
19 years	87.1	89.9	89.3	90.9	94.2	59.7	68.8	71.4	77.6	83.4
20-24 years.	53.1	54.7	59.9	68.8	73.2	28.4	35.8	40.3	50.2	55.5
25-29 years.	20.8	19.1	22.3	33.1	38.2	10.5	10.5	13.8	20.9	24.8
30-34 years.	11.9	9.4	11.1	15.9	19.6	6.9	6.2	7.5	9.5	13.0
35-39 years.	8.8	7.2	8.6	7.8	10.1	6.1	5.4	5.0	6.2	7.2
40-44 years.	7.3	6.3	7.2	7.1	6.8	6.1	4.9	4.8	4.8	5.2
45-54 years.	7.4	7.5	6.3	6.1	6.0	7.0	4.9	4.6	4.7	4.5
55-64 years.	8.0	7.8	6.5	5.3	4.2	8.0	6.8	5.1	4.5	4.4
65 years old and over	7.7	7.5	4.7	4.9	4.8	8.5	7.7	5.8	5.9	5.4

Persons Living Alone, By Sex and Age, 1960-1983

Source: U.S. Bureau of Census

Sex and age	Number of Persons (1,000)							Percent Distribution				
	1960	1970	1975	1980	1981	1982	1983	1960	1970	1975	1980	1983
Both sexes ..	7,064	10,851	13,939	18,296	18,936	19,354	19,250	100.0	100.0	100.0	100.0	100.0
14–24 years....	234	556	1,111	1,726	1,651	1,511	1,303	3.3	5.1	8.0	9.4	6.8
25–44 years....	1,212	1,604	2,744	4,729	5,138	5,560	5,576	17.2	14.8	19.7	25.8	29.0
45–64 years....	2,720	3,622	4,076	4,514	4,663	4,611	4,515	38.5	33.4	29.2	24.7	23.5
65 years old and over	2,898	5,071	6,008	7,328	7,484	7,673	7,856	41.0	46.7	43.1	40.1	40.8
Male.......	2,628	3,532	4,918	6,966	7,253	7,482	7,451	37.2	32.5	35.3	38.1	38.7
14–24 years....	124	274	610	947	899	841	672	1.8	2.5	4.4	5.2	3.5
25–44 years....	686	933	1,689	2,920	3,189	3,365	3,441	9.7	8.6	12.1	16.0	17.9
45–64 years....	965	1,152	1,329	1,613	1,715	1,784	1,714	13.7	10.6	9.5	8.8	8.9
65 years old and over	853	1,174	1,290	1,486	1,450	1,492	1,624	12.1	10.8	9.3	8.1	8.4
Female	4,436	7,319	9,021	11,330	11,683	11,872	11,799	62.8	67.5	64.7	61.9	61.3
14–24 years....	110	282	501	779	752	670	631	1.6	2.6	3.6	4.3	3.3
25–44 years....	526	671	1,055	1,809	1,949	2,196	2,135	7.4	6.2	7.6	9.9	11.1
45–64 years....	1,755	2,470	2,747	2,901	2,948	2,826	2,801	24.8	22.8	19.7	15.9	14.6
65 years old and over	2,045	2,897	4,718	5,842	6,034	6,180	6,232	28.9	35.9	33.8	31.9	32.4

Unmarried Couples

Source: U.S. Bureau of the Census

Presence of Children and Age of householders	1970	1980	1983	1984	Presence of Children and Age of Householder	1970	1980	1983	1984
Unmarried couples...	523	1,589	1,891	1,988					
No children under 15 yr ..	327	1,159	1,366	1,373	25-44 yr. old..........	103	837	1,082	1,208
Some children under 15 yr.	196	431	525	614	45-64 yr. old..........	186	221	233	234
Under 25 yr. old.......	55	411	455	432	65 yr. old or over	178	119	121	114

Women, Age 18-44, Who Gave Birth in 1982

Source: U.S. Bureau of the Census

	Total 18-44 Years old			18-29 Years Old			30-44 Years Old		
	Number of women (1,000)	Women who have had a child in the last year		Number of women (1,000)	Women who have had a child in the last year		Number of women (1,000)	Women who have had a child in the last year	
		Total births per 1,000 women	First births per 1,000 women		Total births per 1,000 women	First births per 1,000 women		Total births per 1,000 women	First births per 1,000 women
Total[1]........	48,666	70.5	25.9	25,087	97.5	44.3	23,579	41.9	6.4
White	41,107	68.1	25.9	20,990	93.9	44.5	20,118	41.3	6.6
Black	6,118	83.6	25.4	3,394	114.3	41.9	2,724	45.3	4.8
Spanish origin[2]	3,215	97.9	29.2	1,675	126.1	49.8	1,540	67.3	6.8
Married, spouse present	28,336	96.8	34.7	11,159	167.6	75.8	17,177	50.8	8.0
Married, spouse absent[3]	2,085	71.5	15.6	868	131.0	35.4	1,216	29.0	1.5
Widowed or divorced	4,710	26.3	4.7	1,431	51.9	9.0	3,278	15.1	2.9
Single	13,536	30.9	16.6	11,629	33.3	19.1	1,907	16.4	1.2
Labor force status: In labor force	33,229	45.4	19.2	17,492	59.4	30.9	15,737	29.8	6.2
Employed	29,704	41.9	17.7	15,095	55.3	29.2	14,610	28.0	5.9
Unemployed....	3,525	74.9	31.5	2,398	85.3	41.5	1,127	52.7	10.3
Not in labor force ..	15,437	124.7	40.5	7,594	185.0	75.2	7,842	66.3	6.9
Family income: Under $5,000	3,662	98.5	31.1	2,375	135.0	47.9	1,288	31.2	.2
$5,000–$9,999....	5,570	75.0	27.2	3,198	100.0	44.3	2,372	41.2	4.1
$10,000–$14,999 ..	7,322	73.5	26.1	4,313	99.0	40.7	3,009	37.1	5.1
$15,000–$19,999 ..	6,123	83.4	30.8	3,311	121.0	53.7	2,812	39.3	4.0
$20,000–$24,999 ..	6,403	78.7	27.1	3,080	113.8	50.8	3,323	46.2	5.2
$25,000 and over ..	16,728	55.9	22.6	7,072	72.4	41.7	9,655	43.7	8.6
Years of school completed: Not a high school graduate	8,621	80.0	23.8	4,485	122.0	44.4	4,136	34.4	1.4
High school, 4 years ..	21,830	73.2	26.9	11,358	110.5	49.4	10,472	32.7	2.6
College, 1–3 years ..	10,438	60.3	25.6	6,012	67.5	35.1	4,426	50.5	12.7
College, 4 years ...	5,118	64.0	24.6	2,439	68.1	39.8	2,679	60.3	10.7
College, 5 or more years	2,659	71.4	29.0	792	89.9	55.4	1,867	63.6	17.9

(1) Includes women of other races and women with family income not reported, not shown separately. (2) Persons of Spanish origin may be of any race. (3) Includes separated women.

Prevalence of Mental Disorders in the U.S.

Source: Alcohol, Drug Abuse, and Mental Health Administration, National Institute of Mental Health; based on a survey of 9,000 people age 18 or older, relating to 6-month period; estimates based on 1980 census.

Overall, the study found that in the course of 6 months, almost 19 percent of adult Americans suffered from at least one psychiatric disorder. Only about one-fifth of those with a disorder sought treatment during the six-month period, most consulting a physician rather than a mental health specialist.

Disorder	Estimated # of Americans (millions)	Estimated % of Americans	Disorder	Estimated # of Americans (millions)	Estimated % of Americans
Any Disorder	29.4	18.7	Manic Episode	1.0	0.7
Substance Use Disorder	10.0	6.4	Major Depressive Episode	4.9	3.1
Alcohol Abuse/Dependence	7.9	5.0	Dysthemia	5.1	3.2
Alcohol Abuse	7.2	4.6	Anxiety/Somatoform Disorders	13.1	8.3
Alcohol Dependence	4.6	2.9	Phobia	11.1	7.0
Drug Abuse/Dependence	3.1	2.0	Panic	1.2	0.8
Drug Abuse	2.1	1.3	Obsessive Compulsive	2.4	1.5
Drug Dependence	1.7	1.1	Somatization	0.1	0.1
Schizophrenia	1.4	0.9	Antisocial Personality	1.4	0.9
Affective Disorder	9.4	6.0	Severe Cognitive Impairment	1.6	1.0

Patients' Expenditures in Mental Hospitals

Source: National Institute of Mental Health

Based on reports of 280 state and county hospitals on the Jan., 1981, Inventory of Mental Health Facilities.

State	No. patients	Tot. expend. ($000)	State	No. patients	Tot. expend. ($000)	State	No. patients	Tot. expend. ($000)	State	No. patients	Tot. expend. ($000)
U.S...	132,164	4,085,765	Ida...	208	6,040	Mo...	3,053	115,125	Pa...	10,308	344,821
Ala...	2,024	49,533	Ill...	4,090	171,387	Mon..	316	10,981	R.I...	723	28,345
Alas.	143	8,056	Ind...	2,766	71,441	Neb...	609	21,260	S.C...	3,233	65,615
Ariz..	328	17,733	Ia....	1,139	32,726	Nev...	116	6,921	S.D...	437	9,748
Ark..	258	12,836	Kan..	1,155	37,900	N.H...	456	22,894	Tenn..	2,614	69,247
Cal..	6,508	252,607	Ky...	554	33,544	N.J...	5,294	160,107	Tex...	5,709	152,891
Col..	1,138	40,092	La...	2,271	54,925	N.M...	227	9,701	Ut...	281	8,298
Conn..	2,360	71,062	Me...	654	18,104	N.Y...	24,713	740,061	Vt...	244	9,812
Del...	630	17,010	Md...	3,334	98,629	N.C...	3,303	100,045	Va...	4,982	88,092
D.C..	2,090	110,530	Mass..	2,648	79,180	N.D...	573	14,141	Wash..	1,225	33,730
Fla...	5,385	113,415	Mich..	4,464	218,469	Oh....	5,915	183,984	W.Va..	1,746	20,094
Ga...	4,241	138,997	Minn.	2,325	62,616	Okla..	1,240	42,202	Wis...	856	41,169
Ha...	239	7,746	Miss..	1,767	28,300	Ore...	1,011	25,882	Wy...	261	7,721

Selected Statistics on State and County Mental Hospitals

Source: National Institute of Mental Health

Year	Total admitted	Net releases	Deaths in hospital	Residents end of year	Expense per patient[1]
1955	178,033	NA	44,384	558,922	$1,116.59
1960	234,791	NA	49,748	535,540	1,702.41
1970	393,174	394,627	30,804	338,592	5,435.38
1975	376,156	391,345	13,401	193,436	13,634.53
1977	414,703	408,667*	9,716	159,523	NA
1978	406,407	NA	9,080	153,544	NA
1979	383,323	NA	7,830	140,423	NA
1980	370,344	NA	6,800	132,164	NA

*Includes estimates; NA-not available. (p)-provisional data. (1) Per average daily resident patient population.

Handicapped Persons in the United States

Chronic Conditions, by Sex and Age, 1981

Source: National Center for Health Statistics

(in millions)

Impairments	Total	Male	Female	Under 17 yrs.	17-44 yrs.	45-64 yrs.	65 yrs. and over
Visual Impairments	9.1	5.1	3.9	0.6	2.7	2.4	3.4
Hearing Impairments	18.7	9.9	8.8	10.4	4.3	6.3	7.1
Speech Impairments	2.2	1.5	0.7	0.9	0.7	0.4	0.2
Absence of Extremities	2.0	1.6	0.4	0.1	0.5	0.7	0.7
Absence of Entire Finger	1.3	1.0	0.2	0.1	0.4	0.5	0.3
Other Extremities Absent	0.8	0.6	0.2	0.0	0.2	0.1	0.4
Paralysis, Complete or Partial	1.3	0.8	0.6	1.5	0.4	0.3	0.5
Deformities	18.4	9.4	9.0	12.4	8.8	5.2	3.1
Of Back	11.7	5.5	6.2	6.4	5.7	3.5	1.1
Upper Extremities	3.0	1.7	1.3	1.7	1.3	0.9	0.7
Lower Extremities	5.2	3.0	2.2	5.3	2.3	12.6	1.1
Other	3.0	0.2	0.1	—	1.5	1.8	0.5

Surgery in Short-Stay Hospitals 1971-1982

Source: National Center For Health Statistics

Sex and Type of Operation	Number of Operations (mil.)						Rate Per 1,000 Population					
	1971	1975	1978	1980	1981	1982	1971	1975	1978	1980	1981	1982
Total	15.77	20.04	20.75	24.49	25.62	25.82	77.0	93.7	94.1	108.6	112.6	112.3
Male.	6.16	7.37	7.83	8.50	8.77	9.06	62.4	71.4	73.6	78.1	79.8	81.7
Operations on the musculoskeletal system	1.07	1.34	1.47	1.54	1.56	1.65	10.8	13.0	13.8	14.2	14.1	14.9
Operations on the cardiovascular system.	.30	.52	.71	.80	.89	1.02	3.0	5.1	6.7	7.4	8.1	9.2
Biopsy	.24	.35	.45	.55	.55	.60	2.4	3.4	4.2	5.0	5.0	5.4
Repair of inguinal hernia	.44	.48	.45	.48	.46	.57	4.9	4.7	4.2	4.4	4.2	4.4
Operations on the eye	.25	.33	.37	.45	.51	.49	2.6	3.2	3.5	4.1	4.6	5.1
Prostatectomy.	.21	.27	.30	.34	.35	.36	2.1	2.6	2.8	3.1	3.2	3.2
Tonsillectomy with or without adenoidectomy	.45	.30	.23	.20	.19	.31	4.5	2.9	2.2	1.8	1.7	1.6
Cardiac catheterization.	.06	.13	.21	.23	.27	.18	.6	1.2	2.0	2.1	2.5	2.6
Appendectomy	.16	.16	.15	.15	.17	.15	1.7	1.5	1.4	1.3	1.6	1.3
Female	9.59	12.66	12.92	15.99	16.85	16.76	90.4	114.6	113.3	137.1	143.1	141.0
Operations on the female genital organs	2.79	3.89	3.82	4.26	4.22	4.00	26.3	35.2	33.5	36.5	35.8	33.7
Diagnostic dilation and curettage of uterus	.77	.98	.97	.92	.83	.74	7.3	8.8	8.5	7.9	7.1	6.2
Hysterectomy.	.57	.73	.64	.65	.67	.65	5.4	6.6.	5.6	5.6	5.7	5.5
Bilateral destruction or occlusion of Fallopian tubes	.21	.37	.55	.64	.65	.60	2.0	3.3	4.9	5.5	5.5	5.1
Obstetrical procedures	.97	1.25	1.47	3.80	3.93	3.95	9.2	11.3	12.9	30.9	33.4	33.2
Cesarean section	.19	.33	.51	.62	.70	.73	1.8	3.0	4.5	5.3	6.0	6.1
Operations on the musculoskeletal system	.88	1.26	1.36	1.49	1.63	1.67	8.3	11.4	11.9	12.7	13.8	14.1
Biopsy	.52	.75	.73	.80	.86	.84	4.9	6.8	6.4	6.9	7.3	6.9
Operations on the eye	.31	.42	.51	.60	.73	.82	2.9	3.8	4.5	5.1	6.2	7.0
Cholecystectomy	.29	.34	.32	.34	.35	.36	2.7	3.1	2.8	2.9	3.0	3.0
Appendectomy	.15	.16	.15	.15	.14	.26	1.4	1.4	1.3	1.2	1.2	1.1
Tonsillectomy with or without adenoidectomy	.52	.39	.32	.27	.27	.13	4.9	3.5	2.8	2.3	2.3	2.2

Legal Abortions in the U.S.

Source: Centers for Disease Control, U.S. Department of Health and Human Services

Legal abortions, according to selected characteristics of the patient.

	1974	1975	1976	1978	1979	1980	1981
Number	763,476	854,853	988,267	1,157,776	1,251,921	1,297,606	1,300,760
Age Characteristic				Percent distribution			
Under 20 years.	32.7	33.1	32.1	30.0	30.0	29.2	28.0
20-24 years.	31.8	31.9	33.3	35.0	35.4	35.5	35.3
25 years and over	35.6	35.0	34.6	34.9	34.6	35.3	36.7
Marital status							
Married	27.4	26.1	24.6	26.4	24.7	23.1	22.1
Unmarried	72.6	73.9	75.4	73.6	75.3	76.9	77.9
Number of living children							
0	47.8	47.1	47.7	56.6	58.1	58.4	58.3
1	19.6	20.2	20.7	19.2	19.1	19.5	19.7
2	14.8	15.5	15.4	14.1	13.8	13.7	13.7
3	8.7	8.7	8.3	5.9	5.5	5.3	5.3
4	4.5	4.4	4.1	4.2*	3.5	3.2	3.0
5 or more	4.5	4.2	3.7	—	—	—	—
Location of abortion facility							
In state of residence	86.6	89.2	90.0	93.8	90.1	92.6	92.5
Out of state of residence	13.4	10.8	10.0	6.2	9.9	7.4	7.5
Period of gestation							
Under 8 weeks	42.6	44.6	47.0	53.2	52.1	51.7	51.2
9-10 weeks	28.7	28.4	28.0	26.9	27.0	26.2	26.8
11-12 weeks	15.4	14.9	14.4	12.3	12.5	12.2	12.1
13-15 weeks	5.5	5.0	4.5	4.0	4.2	5.2	5.2
16-20 weeks	6.5	6.1	5.1	3.7	3.4	3.9	3.7
21 weeks and over.	1.2	1.0	0.9	0.9	0.9	0.9	1.0

*Beginning with 1978, 4 or more.

Canadian Motor Vehicle Traffic Deaths

Source: Statistics Canada

Province	Number		Province	Number	
	1982	1983		1982	1983
Newfoundland.	70	94	Saskatchewan	239	226
Prince Edward Island.	15	27	Alberta	461	432
Nova Scotia.	173	171	British Columbia.	562	582
New Brunswick	187	117	Yukon	8	8
Quebec	1,006	1,158	Northwest Territories.	6	9
Ontario.	1,185	1,185	Total	4,073	4,156
Manitoba.	161	147			

Hospitals Facilities, 1982

Source: *Hospital Statistics,* 1984 © 1983 by American Hospital Association

	Number of Hospitals		Beds (1,000)		Patients admitted (mil.)		Average Daily census[2]		Occupancy rate[3]		Person-nel (1,000)	Total out-patient visits (mil.)
	Total	Short-term[1]	Total	Short-term[1]	Total	Short-term[1]	Total	Short-term[1]	Total	Short-term[1]		
Alabama	146	130	25.9	20.0	.8	.8	19.8	14.8	76.5	74.0	68	4.0
Alaska	25	16	1.7	1.0	.1	—	1.1	.7	63.3	65.4	5	1.2
Arizona	80	59	12.1	9.5	.4	.4	8.6	6.7	71.2	71.0	41	5.0
Arkansas	97	92	13.6	11.4	.5	.4	9.	7.8	71.3	68.4	35	1.9
California	593	502	111.5	83.2	3.4	3.2	80.3	56.8	72.0	68.3	358	31.2
Colorado	97	81	15.1	11.8	.5	.4	11.3	8.4	74.6	71.7	48	6.6
Connecticut. . . .	65	41	18.2	11.0	.5	.4	15.3	8.9	84.0	81.2	56	4.9
Delaware	14	8	4.0	2.1	.1	.1	3.5	1.8	88.6	85.0	11	.9
District of Columbia. . . .	17	12	8.8	4.7	.2	.2	7.1	3.9	81.7	82.8	33	2.3
Florida	253	217	59.6	48.4	1.9	1.8	45.4	35.8	76.1	74.0	170	10.8
Georgia	191	165	33.0	25.0	1.1	1.0	24.3	17.6	73.5	70.4	93	7.9
Hawaii.	27	19	4.1	2.8	.1	.1	3.3	2.3	81.1	80.8	14	1.4
Idaho	52	47	4.0	3.5	.1	.1	2.7	2.3	66.0	65.9	11	1.0
Illinois	281	245	71.2	57.8	2.0	1.9	53.7	42.4	75.4	73.4	215	15.3
Indiana	133	115	31.9	24.3	.9	.9	25.2	19.0	78.9	78.0	90	6.7
Iowa.	139	128	20.5	16.6	.6	.5	14.8	11.5	72.1	69.4	52	3.0
Kansas	166	149	18.5	14.0	.5	.4	13.0	9.1	70.3	65.2	48	3.4
Kentucky	118	106	18.8	15.5	.7	.7	14.7	12.2	78.4	78.3	53	4.4
Louisiana	157	138	26.0	19.1	.8	.8	19.1	13.4	73.4	70.1	72	6.2
Maine	47	43	6.6	5.0	.2	.2	5.0	3.6	76.4	71.9	20	2.6
Maryland	85	55	24.9	15.4	.6	.6	20.6	12.6	82.7	81.9	75	6.4
Massachusetts. .	178	118	41.4	25.9	.9	.9	34.6	21.4	83.6	82.6	144	12.4
Michigan	233	205	48.3	39.8	1.5	1.4	38.1	30.7	78.8	77.2	157	14.0
Minnesota	182	170	29.3	23.5	.7	.7	21.9	17.0	74.8	72.2	74	3.2
Mississippi	118	108	17.5	13.0	.5	.5	12.8	9.1	73.4	69.5	40	2.8
Missouri.	169	149	34.2	27.5	1.0	.9	25.8	20.1	75.3	73.3	102	7.5
Montana	67	60	5.2	4.5	.1	.1	3.6	3.0	68.5	67.0	11	.9
Nebraska.	110	100	11.8	10.1	.3	.3	8.3	7.0	69.9	68.7	30	1.8
Nevada	25	19	3.6	3.2	.1	.1	2.5	2.2	69.0	68.8	12	1.0
New Hampshire .	34	29	4.7	3.5	.1	.1	3.6	2.6	75.9	73.5	14	1.3
New Jersey. . . .	131	102	42.4	30.5	1.1	1.1	35.3	24.9	83.3	81.6	114	9.4
New Mexico . . .	57	42	6.3	4.4	.2	.2	4.6	3.1	73.2	71.0	19	2.9
New York.	344	273	125.9	79.9	2.8	2.6	110.6	69.8	87.9	87.3	357	29.1
North Carolina . .	159	133	32.5	24.1	1.0	.9	25.4	18.5	77.9	76.6	89	6.1
North Dakota. . .	59	52	6.0	4.8	.2	.1	4.1	3.2	67.7	67.3	14	.9
Ohio.	237	204	62.7	50.9	1.9	1.8	50.1	40.2	79.9	79.0	199	13.5
Oklahoma	142	122	17.7	13.7	.6	.5	12.3	10.0	69.7	69.9	52	3.6
Oregon	83	75	11.9	9.0	.4	.4	8.3	6.0	69.8	66.4	36	2.5
Pennsylvania . . .	310	248	82.9	57.3	2.1	2.0	68.2	46.1	82.3	80.4	241	21.7
Rhode Island . . .	21	14	5.9	3.5	.1	.1	5.0	3.0	85.2	84.9	20	1.5
South Carolina. .	91	75	17.1	12.1	.5	.4	13.3	9.1	77.4	75.4	44	4.5
South Dakota. . .	68	57	5.7	4.4	.1	.1	3.9	3.0	68.8	67.3	13	.9
Tennessee	164	147	31.8	25.6	1.0	1.0	24.0	19.1	75.6	74.7	85	4.5
Texas	561	497	84.6	64.7	2.8	2.6	62.5	46.5	73.9	71.9	237	16.6
Utah.	42	37	5.3	4.3	.2	.2	3.8	3.1	72.8	71.4	19	1.9
Vermont	19	16	2.9	2.2	.1	.1	2.2	1.7	75.9	75.1	9	.6
Virginia	137	103	31.6	21.8	.9	.8	24.9	17.0	78.8	77.7	85	6.8
Washington	121	106	15.7	12.5	.6	.6	11.6	8.8	73.7	71.0	53	5.3
West Virginia . . .	76	66	12.9	10.4	.4	.4	9.8	7.8	76.0	75.1	35	2.7
Wisconsin.	163	141	29.0	23.9	.8	.7	21.3	17.0	73.5	71.3	79	5.7
Wyoming	31	27	2.7	1.8	.1	.1	1.8	1.1	64.8	59.1	6	.6
Total	**6,915**	**5,863**	**1,359.8**	**1,015,2**	**39.1**	**36.4**	**1,052.7**	**763.3**	**77.4**	**75.2**	**3,959**	**313.7**

(1) Short term hospitals have an average stay of less than 30 days. (2) Excludes newborns. (3) Ratio of average daily census to every 100 beds.

U.S. Health Expenditures

Source: Health Care Financing Administration, U.S. Department of Health and Human Services

	1960	1965	1970	1975	1980	1981	1982	1983
Total (billions)	$26.9	$41.7	$74.7	$132.7	$249.0	$286.6	$322.3	$355.4
Type of expenditure								
Health services and supplies.	25.2	38.2	69.3	124.3	237.1	273.5	308.1	340.1
Hospital care.	9.1	13.9	27.8	52.1	100.4	118.0	134.9	147.2
Physician services.	5.7	8.5	14.3	24.9	46.8	54.8	61.8	69.0
Dentist services	2.0	2.8	4.7	8.2	15.4	17.3	19.5	21.8
Nursing home care	.5	2.1	4.7	10.1	20.6	24.2	26.5	28.8
Other professional services	.9	1.0	1.6	2.6	5.6	6.4	7.1	8.0
Drugs and drug sundries	3.7	5.2	8.0	11.9	19.3	21.3	21.8	23.7
Eyeglasses and appliances.	.8	1.2	1.9	3.2	5.1	5.7	5.5	6.2
Expenses for prepayment and administration	1.1	1.7	2.7	4.4	10.7	11.1	13.4	15.6
Gov't public health activities	.4	.8	1.4	3.2	7.0	7.7	10.0	11.2
Other health services	1.1	1.1	2.1	3.7	6.0	6.9	7.6	8.5
Research and medical facilities construction.	1.7	3.5	5.4	8.4	11.8	13.1	14.8	15.3
Research.	.7	1.5	2.0	3.3	5.3	5.7	5.9	6.2
Construction	1.0	2.0	3.4	5.1	6.5	7.5	8.3	9.1

Physicians, by State

(Source: AMA Physician Masterfile, 1982; Division of Survey and Data Resources, AMA, 1984)

Location	1970	1975	1980	1982	Percent Change 1970-1982	1980-1982
Total Physicians	334,028	393,742	467,679	501,958	50.2	7.3
Alabama	3,377	3,961	5,229	5,677	68.1	8.6
Alaska	324	468	627	721	122.5	15.0
Arizona	2,938	4,440	5,859	6,447	119.4	10.0
Arkansas	1,955	2,348	3,070	3,328	70.2	8.4
California	41,640	49,744	60,752	65,478	57.2	7.8
Colorado	4,386	5,163	6,391	6,803	55.1	6.4
Connecticut	6,072	7,170	8,322	8,866	46.0	6.5
Delaware	783	945	1,047	1,160	48.1	10.8
District of Columbia	4,073	4,209	4,164	4,083	0.2	-1.9
Florida	11,451	16,198	21,131	23,481	105.1	11.1
Georgia	5,546	6,810	8,549	9,368	68.9	9.6
Hawaii	1,235	1,587	2,265	2,453	98.6	8.3
Idaho	718	894	1,134	1,255	74.8	10.6
Illinois	16,323	19,276	22,228	23,893	46.4	7.5
Indiana	5,470	6,349	7,527	7,962	45.6	5.8
Iowa	3,061	3,373	3,917	4,191	36.9	7.0
Kansas	2,910	3,341	4,043	4,306	48.0	6.5
Kentucky	3,560	4,382	5,212	5,673	59.4	8.8
Louisiana	4,768	5,385	6,997	7,638	60.2	9.2
Maine	1,186	1,504	1,927	2,103	77.3	9.1
Maryland	9,518	11,236	13,282	14,481	52.1	9.0
Massachusetts	12,576	14,381	16,661	17,875	42.1	7.3
Michigan	11,364	13,537	15,571	16,440	44.7	5.6
Minnesota	6,145	7,129	8,297	8,854	44.1	6.7
Mississippi	2,077	2,475	3,015	3,273	57.6	8.6
Missouri	6,314	7,400	8,508	9,127	44.6	7.3
Montana	787	943	1,153	1,230	56.3	6.7
Nebraska	1,855	2,203	2,509	2,623	41.4	4.5
Nevada	595	808	1,233	1,442	142.4	17.0
New Hampshire	1,098	1,389	1,701	1,899	73.0	11.6
New Jersey	10,923	13,208	15,067	16,539	51.4	9.8
New Mexico	1,390	1,718	2,292	2,542	82.9	10.9
New York	44,800	48,088	49,978	53,380	19.2	6.8
North Carolina	6,069	7,558	9,742	10,541	73.7	8.2
North Dakota	660	728	956	1,049	58.9	9.7
Ohio	14,740	16,334	18,781	20,197	37.0	7.5
Oklahoma	2,899	3,328	4,194	4,634	59.8	10.5
Oregon	3,181	4,093	5,232	5,529	73.8	5.7
Pennsylvania	18,712	20,867	23,742	25,822	38.0	8.8
Rhode Island	1,638	1,913	2,163	2,246	37.1	3.8
South Carolina	2,670	3,485	4,607	5,007	87.2	8.7
South Dakota	629	693	884	960	52.6	8.6
Tennessee	5,022	6,146	7,686	8,246	64.2	7.3
Texas	14,952	18,307	24,058	26,628	78.1	10.7
Utah	1,569	1,993	2,570	2,832	80.5	10.2
Vermont	868	1,019	1,215	1,338	54.1	10.1
Virginia	6,552	8,236	10,476	11,353	73.3	8.4
Washington	5,562	6,585	8,450	9,123	64.0	8.0
West Virginia	1,946	2,366	2,857	3,111	59.9	8.9
Wisconsin	5,588	6,593	8,005	8,593	53.8	7.3
Wyoming	364	452	610	694	47.6	13.8

Physicians by Specialty, Age, and Sex

Source: American Medical Association; Dec. 31, 1982

Specialty	Male Under 35 yrs.	Female Under 35 yrs.	Male 35-44	Female 35-44	Male 45-54	Female 45-54	Male 55 and over	Female 55 and over
Total	107,876	27,999	114,837	18,075	84,474	7,654	70,524	10,519
Aerospace Med.	137	18	143	9	175	2	150	1
Allergy	67	16	328	46	410	17	595	46
Anesthesiology	3,920	996	4,717	1,112	3,672	567	3,408	412
Cardiovascular	2,043	125	3,899	161	2,407	64	2,189	46
Child Psychiatry	369	223	931	379	694	235	453	184
Dermatology	1,053	387	1,819	270	1,152	88	1,219	78
Diagnostic Radiol.	3,656	866	3,629	354	1,264	95	818	50
Emergency Med.	2,538	367	2,972	306	1,026	95	1,120	48
Family Practice	12,112	2,523	6,932	811	4,761	312	6,117	263
Gastroenterology	1,095	69	2,001	72	905	11	568	8
General Practice	1,065	313	2,924	593	5,931	465	16,430	787
General Surgery	10,139	1,061	8,081	254	6,872	73	9,220	75
Internal Med.	27,191	6,630	17,852	2,664	11,120	865	12,985	673
Neurology	1,754	369	2,222	249	1,216	106	705	54
Neurological Surg.	802	49	1,113	16	971	4	771	0
Nuclear Medicine	130	28	383	47	329	17	194	14
Obstet./Gynec.	5,379	2,259	6,731	1,129	5,989	421	6,077	398
Occupational Med.	127	35	281	40	530	43	1,476	55
Ophthalmology	2,752	436	4,032	228	3,034	104	3,154	101
Orthopedic Surgery	4,036	143	5,048	35	3,541	13	2,735	20
Otorhinolaryngology	1,464	129	2,207	46	1,617	16	1,381	13
Pathology	2,474	1,065	3,289	993	3,271	410	2,711	300
Pediatrics	6,690	4,891	6,319	3,053	4,233	1,099	4,197	933

(continued)

Specialty	Male Under 35 yrs.	Female Under 35 yrs.	Male 35-44	Female 35-44	Male 45-54	Female 45-54	Male 55 and over	Female 55 and over
Pediat. Cardiology	116	37	222	51	157	35	99	17
Physical Med./Rehab.	435	240	539	251	418	147	553	102
Plastic Surgery	477	56	1,459	69	865	13	524	19
Psychiatry	4,313	1,727	6,738	1,637	6,166	995	7,024	1,074
Public Health	107	44	345	89	368	90	857	229
Pulmonary Dis.	1,162	95	1,649	94	604	47	603	45
Radiology	578	134	2,399	271	2,794	134	2,642	82
Therapeutic Radiol.	313	90	665	127	371	29	282	18
Thoracic Surgery	233	10	657	6	633	2	598	1
Urological Surgery	1,528	41	2,748	13	2,052	5	1,847	2

Suicide Rates

Source: National Center for Health Statistics, U.S. Department of Health and Human Services

(Rates per 100,000 population)

Rates by Age Group, 1979-81

Age Group	1981	1980	1979
Total	12.0	11.9	12.1
5-14 years	0.5	0.4	0.4
12-24 years	12.3	12.3	12.4
25-34 years	16.3	16.0	16.3
35-44 years	15.9	15.4	15.4
45-54 years	16.1	15.9	16.5
55-64 years	16.4	15.9	16.6
65-74 years	16.2	16.9	17.8
75-84 years	18.6	19.1	20.8
85 years and over	17.7	19.2	17.9

By Sex and Race, 1981

	Number	Rate
Total	27,596	12.0
Male	20,809	18.7
Female	6,787	5.8
White	25,452	12.9
White male	19,166	20.0
White female	6,286	6.2
Black	1,658	6.1
Black male	1,315	10.2
Black female	343	2.4

Average Height and Weight for Children

Source: Physicians Handbook, 1983.

Boys Age Years	Height ft	Height in	Height cm	Weight lb	Weight kg	Girls Age Years	Height ft	Height in	Height cm	Weight lb	Weight kg
(Birth)	1	8	45.7	7½	3.4	(Birth)	1	8	50.8	7½	3.4
½	2	2	66.0	17	7.7	½	2	2	66.0	16	7.2
1	2	5	73.6	21	9.5	1	2	5	73.6	20	9.1
2	2	9	83.8	26	11.8	2	2	9	83.8	25	11.3
3	3	0	91.4	31	14.0	3	3	0	91.4	30	13.6
4	3	3	99.0	34	15.4	4	3	3	99.0	33	15.0
5	3	6	106.6	39	17.7	5	3	5	104.1	38	17.2
6	3	9	114.2	46	20.9	6	3	8	111.7	45	20.4
7	3	11	119.3	51	23.1	7	3	11	119.3	49	22.2
8	4	2	127.0	57	25.9	8	4	2	127.0	56	25.4
9	4	4	132.0	63	28.6	9	4	4	132.0	62	28.1
10	4	6	137.1	69	31.3	10	4	6	137.1	69	31.3
11	4	8	142.2	77	34.9	11	4	8	142.2	77	34.9
12	4	10	147.3	83	37.7	12	4	10	147.3	86	39.0
13	5	0	152.4	92	41.7	13	5	0	152.4	98	45.5
14	5	2	157.5	107	48.5	14	5	2	157.5	107	48.5

This table gives a general picture of American children at specific ages. When used as a standard, the individual variation in children's growth should not be overlooked. In most cases the height-weight relationship is probably a more valid index of weight status than a weight-for-age assessment.

Average Weight of Americans by Height and Age

Source: Society of Actuaries; from the *1979 Build and Blood Pressure Study*
The figures represent weights in ordinary indoor clothing and shoes, and heights with shoes.

Men Height	20-24	25-29	30-39	40-49	50-59	60-69	Women Height	20-24	25-29	30-39	40-49	50-59	60-69
5'2"	130	134	138	140	141	140	4'10"	105	110	113	118	121	123
5'3"	136	140	143	144	145	144	4'11"	110	112	115	121	125	127
5'4"	139	143	147	149	150	149	5'0"	112	114	118	123	127	130
5'5"	143	147	151	154	155	153	5'1"	116	119	121	127	131	133
5'6"	148	152	156	158	159	158	5'2"	120	121	124	129	133	136
5'7"	153	156	160	163	164	163	5'3"	124	125	128	133	137	140
5'8"	157	161	165	167	168	167	5'4"	127	128	131	136	141	143
5'9"	163	166	170	172	173	172	5'5"	130	132	134	139	144	147
5'10"	167	171	174	176	177	176	5'6"	133	134	137	143	147	150
5'11"	171	175	179	181	182	181	5'7"	137	138	141	147	152	155
6'0"	176	181	184	186	187	186	5'8"	141	142	145	150	156	158
6'1"	182	186	190	192	193	191	5'9"	146	148	150	155	159	161
6'2"	187	191	195	197	198	196	5'10"	149	150	153	158	162	163
6'3"	193	197	201	203	204	200	5'11"	155	156	159	162	166	167
6'4"	198	202	206	208	209	207	6'0"	157	159	164	168	171	172

U.S. Crime Rate Down Again in 1984

For the third consecutive year, the crime rate declined in 1984. According to the FBI's Uniform Crime Reporting figures, overall serious crime decreased 2 percent in 1984. The 1984 annual report, "Crime in the U.S.," showed an estimated 11,881,800 Crime Index Offenses reported to nearly 16,000 law enforcement agencies covering 96 percent of the nation's population. This marked the first time since 1978 that the Index total dropped below 12 million offenses. Violent crime rose 1 percent in 1984, while property crime was down 2 percent. The number of total arrests showed virtually no change from the previous year.

According to the Bureau of Justice Statistics, although almost 23 million households were touched by crime in 1984, this figure represented the smallest number of criminal victimizations in nine years. The 1984 figure continued a downward trend that characterized the measure since its introduction in 1975. In that year 32 percent of households were touched by crime. In 1984, as in previous years, larceny affected the highest percentage of households, almost one in five. Five percent of households had a member victimized by violent crime and 6 percent had an attempted or completed burglary.

Federal Bureau of Investigation

The Federal Bureau of Investigation (FBI) is the principal investigative arm of the U.S. Department of Justice, and is located at 10th Street and Pennsylvania Avenue, Northwest, Washington, D.C. 20535. It investigates all violations of Federal law except those specifically assigned to some other agency by legislative action. The FBI's jurisdiction includes a wide range of responsibilities in the criminal, civil, and security fields. Priority has been assigned to four areas—organized crime, including drug trafficking; foreign counterintelligence; terrorism; and white-collar crime. On Jan. 28, 1982, the Attorney General assigned concurrent jurisdiction for the enforcement of the Controlled Substances Act to the FBI and the Drug Enforcement Administration (DEA).

The FBI also offers cooperative services to duly authorized law enforcement agencies; these services include fingerprint identification, laboratory examination, police training, and the National Crime Information Center.

The FBI has 59 field offices in the principal cities of the country. (Consult telephone directories for locations and phone numbers.)

An applicant for the position of Special Agent of the FBI must be a citizen of the U.S., at least 23 and under 35 years old, and a graduate of an accredited law school or of an accredited college or university with a major in accounting. In addition, applicants with a four-year degree from an accredited college or university with a major in other academic areas may qualify with three additional years of full-time work experience. Specialized need areas include languages, science, and financial analysis. Those appointed to the Special Agent position must complete an initial training period of 15 weeks at the FBI Academy, Quantico, Virginia.

William H. Webster, a Federal Appeals Court judge from St. Louis, was sworn in as FBI Director for a ten-year term on February 23, 1978.

U.S. Crime Reports

Source: Federal Bureau of Investigation

Offense	Number 1984	% Change over 1983	1975
Murder	18,690	−3.2	−8.9
Forcible Rape	84,230	+6.7	+50.2
Robbery	485,010	−4.3	+3.1
Aggravated Assault. . . .	685,350	+4.9	+39.1
Burglary	2,984,400	−4.6	−8.6
Larceny-theft	6,591,900	−1.8	+10.3
Motor Vehicle theft	1,032,200	+2.4	+2.2

Percent of Households Touched by Crime, by Selected Characteristics, 1984

Source: Bureau of Justice Statistics

Crime	Race of Head		Annual Family Income				Residence		
	White	Black	Low Under $7,500	Medium $7,500–$14,999	$15,000–$24,999	High $25,000 or more	Urban	Suburban	Rural
Crime	25.5%	29.4%	23.8%	24.1%	26.3%	30.3%	31.2%	26.2%	20.9%
Violent crime	4.8	6.1	5.6	4.8	4.8	5.1	6.3	4.9	3.7
Rape	0.2	0.4	0.3	0.2	0.1	0.2	0.3	0.2	0.1
Robbery	0.9	2.0	1.4	1.0	0.8	1.0	1.9	0.9	0.5
Assault	4.0	4.4	4.5	3.9	4.1	4.3	4.7	4.1	3.4
Aggravated	1.4	2.1	1.8	1.5	1.4	1.4	1.7	1.5	1.3
Simple	2.9	2.6	3.0	2.8	3.1	3.1	3.4	3.0	2.3
Total larceny	18.5	19.1	15.1	16.8	19.4	23.0	21.0	19.6	15.1
Personal larceny	12.3	11.8	8.6	10.2	12.8	16.7	13.6	13.5	9.5
Household larceny	8.3	10.0	8.5	8.9	8.8	8.8	10.7	8.2	6.9
Burglary	5.2	7.5	7.3	5.5	4.9	5.2	7.3	4.8	4.5
Motor vehicle theft	1.2	2.3	1.0	1.2	1.4	1.7	2.1	1.4	0.7
Serious violent crime[1]	2.4	4.1	3.3	2.6	2.2	2.4	3.7	2.4	1.8
Crimes of high concern[2]	7.7	10.4	9.8	7.7	7.6	8.1	11.0	7.4	6.1

(1) Rape, robbery, aggravated assault. (2) Rape, robbery, assault by stranger, or burglary.

Percent of Households Touched by Crime, 1975-1984

Source: Bureau of Justice Statistics

	1975	1976	1977	1978	1979	1980	1981	1982	1983	1984
Any crime	32.0%	31.5%	31.3%	31.3%	31.3%	30.0%	30.0%	29.3%	27.4%	26.0%
Violent crime	5.8	5.6	5.7	5.7	5.9	5.5	5.9	5.6	5.1	4.9
Rape	0.2	0.2	0.2	0.2	0.2	0.2	0.2	0.2	0.1	0.2
Robbery	1.4	1.2	1.2	1.1	1.2	1.2	1.3	1.4	1.1	1.0
Assault	4.5	4.4	4.7	4.6	4.8	4.4	4.7	4.5	4.2	4.1
Personal larceny	16.4	16.2	16.3	16.2	15.4	14.2	13.9	13.9	13.0	12.3
Burglary	7.7	7.4	7.2	7.2	7.1	7.0	7.4	6.9	6.1	5.5
Household larceny	10.2	10.3	10.2	9.9	10.8	10.4	10.2	9.6	8.9	8.5
Motor vehicle theft	1.8	1.6	1.5	1.7	1.6	1.6	1.6	1.6	1.4	1.4
Households touched by crime (thousands)	23,377	23,504	23,741	24,277	24,730	24,222	24,863	24,989	23,621	22,786
Households in U.S. (thousands)	72,123	74,528	75,904	77,578	78,964	80,622	82,797	85,178	86,146	87,693

Note: Detail does not add to total because of overlap in thousands touched by various crimes.

Changes in Victimization, 1983–84

Source: Bureau of Justice Statistics

	Victimization levels (in thousands)			Victimization rate (per thousand)		
	1983	1984ᴾ	Percent change	1983	1984ᴾ	Percent change
All Crimes	37,001	35,321	−4.5			
Personal sector						
Crimes of violence	5,903	5,951	0.8	31.0	31.0	−0.1
Rape	154	186	21.0	0.8	1.0	19.9
Completed rape	50	52	5.4	0.3	0.3	4.6
Attempted rape	105	136	29.8	0.5	0.7	28.8
Robbery	1,149	1,129	−1.8	6.0	5.9	−2.7
Robbery with injury	377	408	8.1	2.0	2.1	6.7
From serious assault	187	208	11.2	1.0	1.1	10.4
From minor assault	190	198	4.1	1.0	1.0	3.0
Robbery without injury	772	720	−6.7	4.0	3.7	−7.5
Assault	4,600	4,636	0.8	24.1	24.1	−0.1
Aggravated assault	1,517	1,611	6.2	8.0	8.4	5.2
With injury	537	555	3.3	2.8	2.9	2.3
Attempted with weapon	980	1,057	7.8	5.1	5.5	6.8
Simple assault	3,083	3,022	−2.0	16.2	15.7	−2.9
With injury	824	832	1.0	4.3	4.3	0.1
Attempted without weapon	2,259	2,190	−3.0	11.9	11.4	−3.9
Crimes of theft	14,657	13,992	−4.5	76.9	72.8	−5.4
Personal larceny with contact	563	561	−0.3	3.0	2.9	−1.2
Purse snatching	177	155	−12.1	0.9	0.8	−12.8
Completed purse snatching	127	121	−4.9	0.7	0.6	−5.9
Attempted purse snatching	50	36	−27.6	0.3	0.2	−28.4
Pocket picking	386	403	4.3	2.0	2.1	3.4
Personal larceny without contact	14,095	13,432	−4.7	74.0	69.9	−5.6
Total population 12 and over	190,504	192,267	0.9			
Household sector						
Household burglary	6,063	5,473	−9.7	70.0	62.1	−11.3
Forcible entry	1,903	1,736	−8.8	22.0	19.7	−10.4
Unlawful entry without force	2,607	2,411	−7.5	30.1	27.3	−9.2
Attempted forcible entry	1,553	1,326	−14.6	17.9	15.0	−16.1
Household larceny	9,114	8,621	−5.4	105.2	97.8	−7.1
Less than $50	4,429	4,003	−9.6	51.1	45.4	−11.2
$50 or more	3,699	3,729	0.8	42.7	42.3	−1.0
Amount not available	410	391	−4.6	4.7	4.4	−6.3
Attempted larceny	576	501	−13.0	6.6	5.7	−14.6
Motor vehicle theft	1,264	1,283	1.6	14.6	14.6	−0.2
Completed theft	810	772	−4.6	9.3	8.8	−6.3
Attempted theft	454	514	13.2	5.2	5.8	11.2
Total number of households	86,635	88,187	1.8			

P = Preliminary. Note: Numbers and percents may not add to total shown because of rounding; percent change calculated based on unrounded numbers.

Family Violence

The National Crime Survey (NCS), sponsored by the Bureau of Justice Statistics, collects information on criminal victimization, whether or not the event was reported to the police. Therefore, the survey provides statistical information about various aspects of family violence—but only for those events that a victim is willing to report to a crime survey. Survey findings indicate that family violence may be significantly under-reported. The figures below are estimates of the amount of family violence that people considered to be criminal and that victims chose to and were able to relate to survey interviewers. A relative of the victim was identified as the offender in 7 percent of all violent victimizations measured by the NCS during 1973-81; this represented 4.1 million violent victimizations by relatives during the 9-year period.

Reported Family Violence

Relationship	1973-81 Total	Yearly Average
Total by all relatives	4,108,000	456,000
Spouses or ex-spouses	2,333,000	259,000
Parents	263,000	29,000
Children	173,000	19,000
Brothers or sisters	351,000	39,000
Other relatives	988,000	110,000

All estimates rounded to nearest thousand.

Weapons Used in Family Violence

Type of Weapon	All Family Violence	Spousal Violence
Weapon	31%	26%
Gun	11	9
Knife	9	8
Other	10	8
Not known	3	2
No weapon or don't know	69	74

Women in State and Federal Prisons, 1978-1983

Source: Bureau of Justice Statistics

According to the FBI's "Crime in the United States," females accounted for 17 percent of arrests in 1984. Females were arrested more often for larceny-theft than for any other offense; thirty percent of larceny-theft arrests were females, and twenty percent of all female arrests were for this crime.

According to the Bureau of Justice Statistics, there were 13 women on death row at the end of 1982, triple the number in 1972, but still representing only about 1 percent of all death row inmates.

Year	Number	Percent change	Percent of prison population	Year	Number	Percent change	Percent of prison population
1978	12,746	3.8	4.2	1981	15,537	15.8	4.2
1979	12,995	2.0	4.3	1982	17,923	15.4	4.3
1980	13,420	3.3	4.1	1983	19,019	6.1	4.3

State and Federal Prison Population; Death Penalty

Prison population as of Jan. 1985; death penalty as of July, 1984.

Source: Bureau of Justice Statistics, U.S. Justice Department

	Prisoners	Sentenced to more than a year	Sentenced per 100,000 population	Death penalty Under sentence of death	Executions	Death penalty
Total	463,866	445,381	188	1,202	5	37
Federal institutions	34,263	27,602	12	0	0	Yes
State institutions	429,603	417,779	176	1,202	0	...
Male	443,013	425,986	369	1,189	0	...
Female	20,853	19,395	16	13	0	...
Alabama	10,482	10,246	256	49	1	Yes
Alaska	1,995	1,290	252	0	0	No
Arizona	7,845	7,638	247	51	0	Yes
Arkansas	4,454	4,427	188	22	0	Yes
California	43,314	41,780	162	149	0	Yes
Colorado	3,364	3,347	104	1	0	Yes
Connecticut	5,718	3,748	119	0	0	Yes
Delaware	2,200	1,615	263	6	0	Yes
Dist. of Columbia	4,834	4,031	649	0	0	No
Florida	27,106	26,933	242	193	1	Yes
Georgia	15,731	14,944	252	102	1	Yes
Hawaii	1,934	1,299	124	0	0	No
Idaho	1,282	1,282	127	7	0	Yes
Illinois	17,187	17,187	149	64	0	Yes
Indiana	9,328	9,063	165	21	0	Yes
Iowa	2,836	2,836	97	0	0	No
Kansas	4,238	4,238	173	0	0	No
Kentucky	4,793	4,793	128	19	0	Yes
Louisiana	13,919	13,919	310	24	1	Yes
Maine	1,025	840	72	0	0	No
Maryland	13,124	12,442	285	11	0	Yes
Massachusetts	4,890	4,890	84	0	0	No
Michigan	14,604	14,604	161	0	0	No
Minnesota	2,167	2,167	52	0	0	No
Mississippi	6,115	5,974	229	37	1	Yes
Missouri	8,808	8,808	175	23	0	Yes
Montana	1,005	1,005	121	4	0	Yes
Nebraska	1,623	1,535	95	10	0	Yes
Nevada	3,510	3,510	380	23	0	Yes
New Hampshire	561	561	57	0	0	Yes
New Jersey	10,363	10,363	138	3	0	Yes
New Mexico	2,129	1,908	133	6	0	Yes
New York	33,155	33,155	187	1	0	Yes
North Carolina	16,371	15,219	246	33	0	Yes
North Dakota	434	374	54	0	0	No
Ohio	18,694	18,694	174	18	0	Yes
Oklahoma	7,872	7,872	236	39	0	Yes
Oregon	4,563	4,563	170	0	0	No
Pennsylvania	13,090	12,998	109	33	0	Yes
Rhode Island	1,220	888	92	0	0	No
South Carolina	10,035	9,434	284	28	0	Yes
South Dakota	917	900	127	0	0	Yes
Tennessee	7,302	7,302	154	31	0	Yes
Texas	36,682	36,682	226	163	0	Yes
Utah	1,419	1,407	84	4	0	Yes
Vermont	515	392	74	0	0	Yes
Virginia	10,667	10,493	185	20	0	Yes
Washington	6,821	6,821	156	0	0	Yes
West Virginia	1,599	1,599	82	0	0	No
Wisconsin	5,023	5,023	105	0	0	No
Wyoming	740	740	143	3	0	Yes

NA-figure not available

Greatest Prison Population Increases, by State

10 states with largest prison population, 1984	Number	Increase, 1983-84	10 states with greatest percent change, 1983-84	Percent change	10 states with greatest percent change, 1980-84	Percent change	10 states with highest incarceration rates, 1984	Prisoners per 100,000 residents
California	43,314	3,941	Alaska	22.1	Alaska	142.7	Nevada	380
Texas	36,682	1,423	New Hampshire	17.1	Hawaii	96.3	Louisiana	310
New York	33,155	2,614	Oregon	15.8	Nevada	90.9	Maryland	285
Florida	27,106	772	Kansas	14.4	Arizona	79.4	South Carolina	284
Ohio	18,694	687	Hawaii	13.8	California	76.3	Delaware	263
Illinois	17,187	1,592	New Jersey	12.7	New Jersey	76.1	Alabama	256
North Carolina	16,371	976	Utah	11.4	New Hampshire	72.1	Georgia	254
Georgia	15,731	373	Montana	11.3	North Dakota	71.5	Alaska	252
Michigan	14,604	222	Pennsylvania	11.2	Kansas	69.9	Arizona	247
Louisiana	13,919	1,107	South Dakota	11.0	Maryland	69.8	North Carolina	246

Police Roster

Source: Uniform Crime Reports

Police officers and civilian employees in large cities as of Oct. 31, 1984

City	Officer	Civilian	City	Officer	Civilian	City	Officer	Civilian
Anchorage, Alas...	290	104	Indianapolis, Ind. ...	939	301	Phoenix, Ariz.....	1,648	631
Atlanta, Ga......	1,276	287	Jacksonville, Fla. ..	915	699	Pittsburgh, Pa. ...	1,231	119
Baltimore, Md...	3,031	510	Kansas City, Mo...	1,105	531	Portland, Ore.....	714	176
Birmingham, Ala. ..	623	186	Little Rock, Ark....	305	85	Sacramento, Cal...	501	235
Boston, Mass....	1,762	326	Los Angeles, Cal...	6,966	2,398	St. Louis, Mo.	1,711	492
Bridgeport, Conn...	387	27	Louisville, Ky.....	663	188	St. Petersburg, Fla..	395	205
Buffalo, N.Y......	1,017	115	Memphis, Tenn....	1,159	363	San Antonio, Tex...	1,214	284
Chicago, Ill......	11,960	1,885	Miami, Fla.......	1,019	416	San Diego, Cal....	1,378	499
Cincinnati, Oh. ...	894	140	Milwaukee, Wis....	2,062	310	San Francisco, Cal.	1,926	831
Cleveland, Oh. ...	1,757	253	Minneapolis, Minn. .	673	87	San Jose, Cal. ...	919	220
Columbus, Oh. ...	1,160	327	Newark, N.J......	918	260	Santa Ana, Cal....	315	160
Dallas, Tex......	2,087	494	New Orleans, La...	1,323	505	Seattle, Wash. ...	991	394
Denver, Col......	1,368	304	New York, N.Y.....	25,044	7,970	Stockton, Cal.....	241	115
Detroit, Mich.....	3,825	640	Norfolk, Va......	622	75	Tampa, Fla......	662	202
Ft. Worth, Tex. ...	760	262	Oakland, Cal.....	617	306	Toledo, Oh.	747	54
Fresno, Cal.....	351	175	Oklahoma City, Ok.	763	207	Tucson, Ariz.....	557	188
Hartford, Conn...	497	123	Omaha, Neb.....	578	163	Washington, D.C...	3,879	497
Honolulu, Ha.....	1,645	353	Pasadena, Cal....	203	110	Wichita, Kan.....	452	118
Houston, Tex.....	3,957	1,306	Philadelphia, Pa. ...	7,075	819			

Law Enforcement Officers

Source: F.B.I. Uniform Crime Reports

As of Oct. 31, 1984, there was an average of 2 full-time law enforcement officers for every 1,000 inhabitants in the U.S. A total of 11,912 city, county, and state police agencies reported employing 467,117 officers; including full-time civilian employees, the total law enforcement employee force was 511,488—a rate of 2.7 per 1,000 inhabitants.

City law enforcement employee averages in 1984 ranged from 2 per 1,000 inhabitants in those cities with populations from 25,000 to 49,999 to 3.4 for those with populations of 250,000 or more. The suburban counties averaged 2.9 full-time law enforcement employees per 1,000 inhabitants; the average rate for rural counties was 3.2.

Geographically, the highest law enforcement employee rate per 1,000 inhabitants was in the South Atlantic Division, with 3.2. The fewest number of employees per 1,000 population was in the West North Central Division, with an average of 2.2.

Nationwide, 94 percent of law enforcement personnel, excluding civilians, were males. Civilians represented 20 percent of all city law enforcement personnel, 29 percent in suburban counties, 30 percent in rural counties. Nationally, the percentage was 24.

During 1984, 72 law enforcement officers were killed in the line of duty; assaults on officers numbered 60,153—16.2 per 100 officers; 5.4 of every 100 officers suffered personal injuries as a result.

U.S. Fires

Source: National Fire Protection Assn.

Fires attended by the public fire service (1983 estimates)

Civilian Fire Deaths and Injuries

	Deaths	Percent	Injuries	Percent
Residential (total)	4,820	81.4	21,450	68.6
One- and Two-Family Dwellings[1]	3,825	64.6	16,450	52.6
Apartment	845	14.2	4,300	13.8
Hotels and Motels	80	1.4	450	1.4
Other Residential. ...	70	1.2	250	.8
Non Residential Structures[2]	270	4.6	4,700	15.0
Highway Vehicles	670	11.3	3,400	10.9
Other Vehicles[3]	55	.9	400	1.3
All Other[4]	105	1.8	1,325	4.2
Total	**5,920**		**31,275**	

Structure Fires by Property Use

	No. of fires	Property loss
Public assembly	24,500	$354,000,000
Educational...........	11,500	103,000,000
Institutional............	23,000	14,000,000
Residential.............	641,500	3,306,000,000
One-/2-family dwellings[5]..	523,500	2,792,000,000
Apartments	102,000	413,000,000
Hotels, motels.......	9,000	64,000,000
Other residential	7,000	37,000,000
Stores and offices.......	50,500	686,000,000
Industry, utility, defense[6]	36,000	763,000,000
Storage in structures[6]......	48,000	473,000,000
Special structures.......	33,500	127,000,000
Total[6].............	**868,500**	**$5,826,000,000**

(1) Includes mobile homes. (2) Includes public assembly, educational, institutional, stores and offices, industry, utility, storage, and special structure properties. (3) Includes trains, boats, ships, aircraft, farm vehicles and construction vehicles. (4) Includes properties outside with value, brush, rubbish, and other. (5) Includes mobile homes. (6) The results represent only those fires reported to the NFPA.

Fire Fighters: Deaths and Injuries

Source: National Fire Protection Assn.

Year	Line of Duty Deaths	Line of Duty Injuries	% of Deaths by Cause		% of Deaths by Nature of Injury		% of Fire Ground Injuries by Cause		% of Fire Ground Injuries by Nature of Injury	
1977	149	112,540	Stress	51.9	Heart Attack	49.1	Exposure to smoke	28.1	Strain, sprain	32.9
1978	170	101,100	Falls, struck by object	27.4	Internal injury/ fracture	27.4	Fell, slipped	19.8	Wound, cut, bruise	25.7
1979	120	95,780			Burns & smoke inhalation	10.4	Stepped on, contact with object	14.2	Smoke or gas inhalation	12.2
1980	138	98,070	Caught or trapped	15.1	Drowning	6.6			Other	10.8
1981	132	103,340	Exposure to smoke	8.9	Stroke	1.9	Overexertion	12.8	Eye irritation	7.0
1982	122	98,150					Struck by object	10.1	Burns (fire or chemical)	7.0
1983	110	103,150	Structural collapse	4.7			Other	15.0	Dislocation, fracture	3.5

SPORTS IN 1985

Olympic Games Records

The modern Olympic Games, first held in Athens, Greece, in 1896, were the result of efforts by Baron Pierre de Coubertin, a French educator, to promote interest in education and culture, also to foster better international understanding through the universal medium of youth's love of athletics.

His source of inspiration for the Olympic Games was the ancient Greek Olympic Games, most notable of the four Panhellenic celebrations. The games were combined patriotic, religious, and athletic festivals held every four years. The first such recorded festival was that held in 776 B.C., the date from which the Greeks began to keep their calendar by "Olympiads," or four-year spans between the games.

The first Olympiad is said to have consisted merely of a 200-yard foot race near the small city of Olympia, but the games gained in scope and became demonstrations of national pride. Only Greek citizens — amateurs — were permitted to participate. Winners received laurel, wild olive, and palm wreaths and were accorded many special privileges. Under the Roman emperors, the games deteriorated into professional carnivals and circuses. Emperor Theodosius banned them in 394 A.D.

Baron de Coubertin enlisted 9 nations to send athletes to the first modern Olympics in 1896; now more than 100 nations compete. Winter Olympic Games were started in 1924.

Sites and Unofficial Winners of Games

1896 Athens (U.S.)	1920 Antwerp (U.S.)	1952 Helsinki (U.S.)	1972 Munich (USSR)
1900 Paris (U.S.)	1924 Paris (U.S.)	1956 Melbourne (USSR)	1976 Montreal (USSR)
1904 St. Louis (U.S.)	1928 Amsterdam (U.S.)	1960 Rome (USSR)	1980 Moscow (USSR)
1906 Athens (U.S.)*	1932 Los Angeles (U.S.)	1964 Tokyo (U.S.)	1984 Los Angeles (U.S.)
1908 London (U.S.)	1936 Berlin (Germany)	1968 Mexico City (U.S.)	1988 Seoul, S. Korea (scheduled)
1912 Stockholm (U.S.)	1948 London (U.S.)		

*Games not recognized by International Olympic Committee. Games 6 (1916), 12 (1940), and 13 (1944) were not celebrated. The 1980 games were boycotted by 62 nations, including the U.S. The 1984 games were boycotted by the USSR and most eastern bloc nations. East and West Germany began competing separately in 1968.

Olympic Games Champions, 1896—1984

(*Indicates Olympic Records)

Track and Field — Men

100-Meter Run

1896	Thomas Burke, United States	12s
1900	Francis W. Jarvis, United States	10.8s
1904	Archie Hahn, United States	11s
1908	Reginald Walker, South Africa	10.8s
1912	Ralph Craig, United States	10.8s
1920	Charles Paddock, United States	10.8s
1924	Harold Abrahams, Great Britain	10.6s
1928	Percy Williams, Canada	10.8s
1932	Eddie Tolan, United States	10.3s
1936	Jesse Owens, United States	10.3s
1948	Harrison Dillard, United States	10.3s
1952	Lindy Remigino, United States	10.4s
1956	Bobby Morrow, United States	10.5s
1960	Armin Hary, Germany	10.2s
1964	Bob Hayes, United States	10.0s
1968	Jim Hines, United States	9.9s*
1972	Valeri Borzov, USSR	10.14s
1976	Hasely Crawford, Trinidad	10.06s
1980	Allan Wells, Great Britain	10.25s
1984	Carl Lewis, United States	9.99s

200-Meter Run

1900	Walter Tewksbury, United States	22.2s
1904	Archie Hahn, United States	21.6s
1908	Robert Kerr, Canada	22.4s
1912	Ralph Craig, United States	21.7s
1920	Allan Woodring, United States	22s
1924	Jackson Scholz, United States	21.6s
1928	Percy Williams, Canada	21.8s
1932	Eddie Tolan, United States	21.2s
1936	Jesse Owens, United States	20.7s
1948	Mel Patton, United States	21.1s
1952	Andrew Stanfield, United States	20.7s
1956	Bobby Morrow, United States	20.6s
1960	Livio Berruti, Italy	20.5s
1964	Henry Carr, United States	20.3s
1968	Tommie Smith, United States	19.83s
1972	Valeri Borzov, USSR	20.00s
1976	Donald Quarrie, Jamaica	20.23s
1980	Pietro Mennea, Italy	20.19s
1984	Carl Lewis, United States	19.80s*

400-Meter Run

1896	Thomas Burke, United States	54.2s
1900	Maxey Long, United States	49.4s
1904	Harry Hillman, United States	49.2s
1908	Wyndham Halswelle, Great Britain, walkover	50s

1912	Charles Reidpath, United States	48.2s
1920	Bevil Rudd, South Africa	49.6s
1924	Eric Liddell, Great Britain	47.6s
1928	Ray Barbuti, United States	47.8s
1932	William Carr, United States	46.2s
1936	Archie Williams, United States	46.5s
1948	Arthur Wint, Jamaica, B W I	46.2s
1952	George Rhoden, Jamaica, B W I	45.9s
1956	Charles Jenkins, United States	46.7s
1960	Otis Davis, United States	44.9s
1964	Michael Larrabee, United States	45.1s
1968	Lee Evans, United States	43.8s*
1972	Vincent Matthews, United States	44.66s
1976	Alberto Juantorena, Cuba	44.26s
1980	Viktor Markin, USSR	44.60s
1984	Alonzo Babers, United States	44.27s

800-Meter Run

1896	Edwin Flack, Great Britain	2m. 11s
1900	Alfred Tysoe, Great Britain	2m. 1.4s
1904	James Lightbody, United States	1m. 56s
1908	Mel Sheppard, United States	1m. 52.8s
1912	James Meredith, United States	1m. 51.9s
1920	Albert Hill, Great Britain	1m. 53.4s
1924	Douglas Lowe, Great Britain	1m. 52.4s
1928	Douglas Lowe, Great Britain	1m. 51.8s
1932	Thomas Hampson, Great Britain	1m. 49.8s
1936	John Woodruff, United States	1m. 52.9s
1948	Mal Whitfield, United States	1m. 49.2s
1952	Mal Whitfield, United States	1m. 49.2s
1956	Thomas Courtney, United States	1m. 47.7s
1960	Peter Snell, New Zealand	1m. 46.3s
1964	Peter Snell, New Zealand	1m. 45.1s
1968	Ralph Doubell, Australia	1m. 44.3s
1972	Dave Wottle, United States	1m. 45.9s
1976	Alberto Juantorena, Cuba	1m. 43.50s
1980	Steve Ovett, Great Britain	1m. 45.40s
1984	Joaquim Cruz, Brazil	1m. 43.00*

1,500-Meter Run

1896	Edwin Flack, Great Britain	4m. 33.2s
1900	Charles Bennett, Great Britain	4m. 6s
1904	James Lightbody, United States	4m. 5.4s
1908	Mel Sheppard, United States	4m. 3.4s
1912	Arnold Jackson, Great Britain	3m. 56.8s
1920	Albert Hill, Great Britain	4m. 1.8s
1924	Paavo Nurmi, Finland	3m. 53.6s

795

1928	Harry Larva, Finland	3m. 53.2s
1932	Luigi Beccali, Italy	3m. 51.2s
1936	Jack Lovelock, New Zealand	3m. 47.8s
1948	Henri Eriksson, Sweden	3m. 49.8s
1952	Joseph Barthel, Luxemburg	3m. 45.2s
1956	Ron Delany, Ireland	3m. 41.2s
1960	Herb Elliott, Australia	3m. 35.6s
1964	Peter Snell, New Zealand	3m. 38.1s
1968	Kipchoge Keino, Kenya	3m. 34.9s
1972	Pekka Vasala, Finland	3m. 36.3s
1976	John Walker, New Zealand	3m. 39.17s
1980	Sebastian Coe, Great Britain	3m. 38.4s
1984	Sebastian Coe, Great Britain	3m. 32.53*

3,000-Meter Steeplechase

1920	Percy Hodge, Great Britain	10m. 0.4s
1924	Willie Ritola, Finland	9m. 33.6s
1928	Toivo Loukola, Finland	9m. 21.8s
1932	Volmari Iso-Hollo, Finland	10m. 33.4s
	(About 3,450 mtrs. extra lap by error)	
1936	Volmari Iso-Hollo, Finland	9m. 3.8s
1948	Thure Sjoestrand, Sweden	9m. 4.6s
1952	Horace Ashenfelter, United States	8m. 45.4s
1956	Chris Brasher, Great Britain	8m. 41.2s
1960	Zdzislaw Krzyszkowiak, Poland	8m. 34.2s
1964	Gaston Roelants, Belgium	8m. 30.8s
1968	Amos Biwott, Kenya	8m. 51s
1972	Kipchoge Keino, Kenya	8m. 23.6s
1976	Anders Garderud, Sweden	8m. 08.2s*
1980	Bronislaw Malinowski, Poland	8m. 09.7s
1984	Julius Korir, Kenya.	8m. 11.8s

5,000-Meter Run

1912	Hannes Kolehmainen, Finland	14m. 36.6s
1920	Joseph Guillemot, France	14m. 55.6s
1924	Paavo Nurmi, Finland	14m. 31.2s
1928	Willie Ritola, Finland	14m. 38s
1932	Lauri Lehtinen, Finland	14m. 30s
1936	Gunnar Hockert, Finland	14m. 22.2s
1948	Gaston Reiff, Belgium	14m. 17.6s
1952	Emil Zatopek, Czechoslovakia	14m. 6.6s
1956	Vladimir Kuts, USSR.	13m. 39.6s
1960	Murray Halberg, New Zealand	13m. 43.4s
1964	Bob Schul, United States	13m. 48.8s
1968	Mohamed Gammoudi, Tunisia	14m. 05.0s
1972	Lasse Viren, Finland	13m. 26.4s
1976	Lasse Viren, Finland	13m. 24.76s
1980	Miruts Yifter, Ethiopia	13m. 21.0s
1984	Said Aouita, Morocco	13m. 05.59s*

10,000-Meter Run

1912	Hannes Kolehmainen, Finland	31m. 20.8s
1920	Paavo Nurmi, Finland	31m. 45.8s
1924	Willie Ritola, Finland	30m. 23.2s
1928	Paavo Nurmi, Finland	30m. 18.8s
1932	Janusz Kusocinski, Poland	30m. 11.4s
1936	Ilmari Salminen, Finland	30m. 15.4s
1948	Emil Zatopek, Czechoslovakia	29m. 59.6s
1952	Emil Zatopek, Czechoslovakia	29m. 17.0s
1956	Vladimir Kuts, USSR.	28m. 45.6s
1960	Pytor Bolotnikov, USSR.	28m. 32.2s
1964	Billy Mills, United States.	28m. 24.4s
1968	Naftali Temu, Kenya	29m. 27.4s
1972	Lasse Viren, Finland	27m. 38.4s*
1976	Lasse Viren, Finland	27m. 40.38s
1980	Miruts Yifter, Ethiopia	27m. 42.7s
1984	Alberto Cova, Italy	27m. 47.54

Marathon

1896	Spiridon Loues, Greece	2h. 58m. 50s
1900	Michel Teato, France	2h. 59m. 45s
1904	Thomas Hicks, United States.	3h. 28m. 53s
1908	John J. Hayes, United States.	2h. 55m. 18.4s
1912	Kenneth McArthur, South Africa	2h. 36m. 54.8s
1920	Hannes Kolehmainen, Finland	2h. 32m. 35.8s
1924	Albin Stenroos, Finland	2h. 41m. 22.6s
1928	A.B. El Ouafi, France	2h. 32m. 57s
1932	Juan Zabala, Argentina	2h. 31m. 36s
1936	Kitei Son, Japan	2h. 29m. 19.2s
1948	Delfo Cabrera, Argentina	2h. 34m. 51.6s
1952	Emil Zatopek, Czechoslovakia	2h. 23m. 03.2s
1956	Alain Mimoun, France	2h. 25m.
1960	Abebe Bikila, Ethiopia	2h. 15m. 16.2s
1964	Abebe Bikila, Ethiopia	2h. 12m. 11.2s
1968	Mamo Wolde, Ethiopia	2h. 20m. 26.4s
1972	Frank Shorter, United States	2h. 12m. 19.8s
1976	Waldemar Cierpinski, E. Germany	2h. 09m. 55s
1980	Waldemar Cierpinski, E. Germany	2h. 11m. 03s
1984	Carlos Lopes, Portugal	2h. 09m. 21 s*

10,000-Meter Cross-Country

1920	Paavo Nurmi, Finland	27m. 15s*
1924	Paavo Nurmi, Finland	32m. 54.8s

20-Kilometer Walk

1956	Leonid Spirine, USSR	1h. 31m. 27.4s
1960	Vladimir Golubnichy, USSR	1h. 34m. 7.2s
1964	Kenneth Mathews, Great Britain	1h. 29m. 34.0s
1968	Vladimir Golubnichy, USSR.	1h. 35m. 58.4s
1972	Peter Frenkel, E. Germany	1h. 26m. 42.4s
1976	Daniel Bautista, Mexico	1h. 24m. 40.6s
1980	Maurizio Damilano, Italy.	1h. 23m. 35.5s
1984	Ernesto Canto, Mexico.	1h. 23m. 13.2s*

50-Kilometer Walk

1932	Thomas W. Green, Great Britain	4h. 50m. 10s
1936	Harold Whitlock, Great Britain	4h. 30m. 41.4s
1948	John Ljunggren, Sweden	4h. 41m. 52s
1952	Giuseppe Dordoni, Italy	4h. 28m. 07.8s
1956	Norman Read, New Zealand	4h. 30m. 42.8s
1960	Donald Thompson, Great Britain	4h. 25m. 30s
1964	Abdon Parnich, Italy	4h. 11m. 11.4s
1968	Christoph Hohne, E. Germany	4h. 20m. 13.6s
1972	Bern Kannenberg, W. Germany	3h. 56m. 11.6s
1980	Hartwig Gauter, E. Germany	3h. 49m. 24.0s
1984	Raul Gonzalez, Mexico	3h. 47m. 26.05*

110-Meter Hurdles

1896	Thomas Curtis, United States	17.6s
1900	Alvin Kraenzlein, United States	15.4s
1904	Frederick Schule, United States	16s
1908	Forrest Smithson, United States	15s
1912	Frederick Kelly, United States.	15.1s
1920	Earl Thomson, Canada.	14.8s
1924	Daniel Kinsey, United States	15s
1928	Sydney Atkinson, South Africa	14.8s
1932	George Saling, United States.	14.6s
1936	Forrest Towns, United States	14.2s
1948	William Porter, United States	13.9s
1952	Harrison Dillard, United States	13.7s
1956	Lee Calhoun, United States	13.5s
1960	Lee Calhoun, United States	13.8s
1964	Hayes Jones, United States	13.6s
1968	Willie Davenport, United States	13.3s
1972	Rod Milburn, United States.	13.24s
1976	Guy Drut, France	13.30s
1980	Thomas Munkelt, E. Germany	13. 39s
1984	Roger Kingdom, United States.	13.20s*

400-Meter Hurdles

1900	J.W.B. Tewksbury, United States.	57.6s
1904	Harry Hillman, United States	53s
1908	Charles Bacon, United States	55s
1920	Frank Loomis, United States	54s
1924	F. Morgan Taylor, United States	52.6s
1928	Lord Burghley, Great Britain.	53.4s
1932	Robert Tisdall, Ireland	51.8s
1936	Glenn Hardin, United States.	52.4s
1948	Roy Cochran, United States.	51.1s
1952	Charles Moore, United States	50.8s
1956	Glenn Davis, United States	50.1s
1960	Glenn Davis, United States	49.3s
1964	Rex Cawley, United States	49.6s
1968	Dave Hemery, Great Britain	48.1s
1972	John Akii-Bua, Uganda	47.82s
1976	Edwin Moses, United States	47.64s*
1980	Volker Beck, E. Germany	48.70s
1984	Edwin Moses, United States	47.75s

High Jump

1896	Ellery Clark, United States	5ft. 11 1-4 in.
1900	Irving Baxter, United States	6ft. 2 4-5 in.
1904	Samuel Jones, United States	5ft. 11 in.
1908	Harry Porter, United States	6ft. 3 in.
1912	Alma Richards, United States	6ft. 4 in.
1920	Richard Landon, United States	6ft. 4 1-4 in.
1924	Harold Osborn, United States	6ft. 6 in.
1928	Robert W. King, United States	6ft. 4 3-8 in.
1932	Duncan McNaughton, Canada.	6ft. 5 5-8 in.
1936	Cornelius Johnson, United States	6ft. 7 15-16 in.
1948	John L. Winter, Australia	6ft. 6 in.
1952	Walter Davis, United States.	6ft. 8.32 in.
1956	Charles Dumas, United States	6ft. 11 1-4 in.
1960	Robert Shavlakadze, USSR	7ft. 1 in.

1964	Valery Brumel, USSR . . . . 7ft. 1 3-4 in.
1968	Dick Fosbury, United States . . . . 7ft. 4 1-4 in.
1972	Yuri Tarmak, USSR . . . . 7ft. 3 3-4 in.
1976	Jacek Wszola, Poland . . . . 7ft. 4 1-2 in.
1980	Gerd Wessig, E. Germany . . . . 7ft. 8 3-4 in.*
1984	Dietmar Mogenburg, W. Germany . . . . . . 7 ft. 8 1-2 in.

Long Jump

1896	Ellery Clark, United States . . . . 20ft. 9 3-4 in.
1900	Alvin Kraenzlein, United States. . . . . . 23ft. 6 7-8 in.
1904	Myer Prinstein, United States . . . . 24ft. 1 in.
1908	Frank Irons, United States . . . . . . 24ft. 6 1-2 in.
1912	Albert Gutterson, United States. . . . . 24ft. 11 1-4 in.
1920	William Pettersson, Sweden . . . . . . 23ft. 5 1-2 in.
1924	DeHart Hubbard, United States . . . . . 24ft. 5 1-8 in.
1928	Edward B. Hamm, United States. . . . . . 25ft. 4 3-4 in.
1932	Edward Gordon, United States . . . . . . 25ft. 3-4 in.
1936	Jesse Owens, United States . . . . . . 26ft. 5 5-16 in.
1948	William Steele, United States . . . . 25ft. 8 in.
1952	Jerome Biffle, United States . . . . 24ft. 10 in.
1956	Gregory Bell, United States . . . . . . 25ft. 8 1-4 in.
1960	Ralph Boston, United States. . . . . . 26ft. 7 3-4 in.
1964	Lynn Davies, Great Britain . . . . . . 26ft. 5 3-4 in.
1968	Bob Beamon, United States. . . . . . . 29ft. 2 1-2 in.*
1972	Randy Williams, United States . . . . . . 27ft. 1-2 in.
1976	Arnie Robinson, United States . . . . . 27ft. 4 1-2 in.
1980	Lutz Dombrowski, E. Germany . . . . . . 28ft. 1-4 in.
1984	Carl Lewis, United States . . . . 28ft. 1-4 in.

400-Meter Relay

1912	Great Britain 42.4s
1920	United States 42.2s
1924	United States 41s
1928	United States 41s
1932	United States 40s
1936	United States 39.8s
1948	United States 40.6s
1952	United States 40.1s
1956	United States 39.5s
1960	Germany (U.S. disqualified) 39.5s
1964	United States 39.0s
1968	United States 38.2s
1972	United States 38.19s
1976	United States 38.33s
1980	USSR 38.26s
1984	United States 37.83s*

1,600-Meter Relay

1908	United States. 3m. 27.2s
1912	United States. 3m. 16.6s
1920	Great Britain 3m. 22.2s
1924	United States 3m. 16s
1928	United States 3m. 14.2s
1932	United States 3m. 8.2s
1936	Great Britain 3m. 9s
1948	United States 3m. 10.4s
1952	Jamaica, B.W.I. 3m. 03.9s
1956	United States 3m. 04.8s
1960	United States 3m. 02.2s
1964	United States 3m. 00.7s
1968	United States 2m. 56.1s*
1972	Kenya 2m. 59.8s
1976	United States 2m. 59.52s
1980	USSR 3m. 01.1s
1984	United States . . . . 2m.57.91 s

Pole Vault

1896	William Hoyt, United States. . . . . . . 10ft. 9 3-4 in.
1900	Irving Baxter, United States. . . . . . . 10ft. 9 7-8 in.
1904	Charles Dvorak, United States . . . . 11ft. 6 in.
1908	A. C. Gilbert, United States
	Edward Cook Jr., United States . . . . . 12ft. 2 in.
1912	Harry Babcock, United States . . . . 12ft. 11 1-2 in.
1920	Frank Foss, United States . . . . 13ft. 5 in.
1924	Lee Barnes, United States . . . . . . 12ft. 11 1-2 in.
1928	Sabin W. Carr, United States . . . . . . 13ft. 9 3-8 in.
1932	William Miller, United States . . . . . . 14ft. 1 7-8 in.
1936	Earle Meadows, United States . . . . . 14ft. 3 1-4 in.
1948	Guinn Smith, United States . . . . . . 14ft. 1 1-4 in.
1952	Robert Richards, United States . . . . 14ft. 11 1-8 in.
1956	Robert Richards, United States . . . . 14ft. 11 1-2 in.
1960	Don Bragg, United States . . . . 15ft. 5 1-8 in.
1964	Fred Hansen, United States . . . . . . 16ft. 8 3-4 in.
1968	Bob Seagren, United States . . . . . . 17ft. 8 1-2 in.
1972	Wolfgang Nordwig, E. Germany . . . . . 18ft. 1-2 in.
1976	Tadeusz Slusarski, Poland . . . . 18ft. 1-2 in.
1980	Wladyslaw Kozakiewicz, Poland . . . . 18ft. 11 1-2 in.*
1984	Pierre Quinon, France . . . . 18ft. 10 1-4 in.

Hammer Throw

1900	John Flanagan, United States . . . . 167ft. 4 in.
1904	John Flanagan, United States . . . . 168ft. 1 in.
1908	John Flanagan, United States . . . . 170ft. 4 1-4 in.
1912	Matt McGrath, United States . . . . 179ft. 7 1-8 in.
1920	Pat Ryan, United States . . . . 173ft. 5 5-8 in.
1924	Fred Tootell, United States . . . . 174ft. 10 1-8 in.
1928	Patrick O'Callaghan, Ireland . . . . 168ft. 7 1-2 in.
1932	Patrick O'Callaghan, Ireland. . . . . . 176ft. 11 1-8 in.
1936	Karl Hein, Germany. . . . . 185ft. 4 in.
1948	Imre Nemeth, Hungary . . . . 183ft. 11 1-2 in.
1952	Jozsef Csermak, Hungary . . . . 197ft. 11 9-16 in.
1956	Harold Connolly, United States . . . . . 207ft. 3 1-2 in.
1960	Vasily Rudenkov, USSR. . . . . 220ft. 1 5-8 in.
1964	Romuald Klim, USSR . . . . 228ft. 9 1-2 in.
1968	Gyula Zsivotsky, Hungary . . . . 240ft. 8 in.
1972	Anatoli Bondarchuk, USSR . . . . 248ft. 8 in.
1976	Yuri Syedykh, USSR . . . . 254ft. 4 in.
1980	Yuri Syedykh, USSR . . . . 268ft. 4 1-2 in.*
1984	Juha Tiainen, Finland . . . . 256ft. 2 in.

Discus Throw

1896	Robert Garrett, United States . . . . . . 95ft. 7 1-2 in.
1900	Rudolf Bauer, Hungary . . . . 118ft. 2.9-10 in.
1904	Martin Sheridan, United States . . . . 128ft. 10 1-2 in.
1908	Martin Sheridan, United States. . . . . . . 134ft. 2 in.
1912	Armas Taipale, Finland. . . . . 148ft. 4 in.
	Both hands—Armas Taipale, Finland. . . 271ft. 10 1-4 in.
1920	Elmer Niklander, Finland . . . . 146ft. 7 1-4 in.
1924	Clarence Houser, United States . . . . . 151ft. 5 1-8 in.
1928	Clarence Houser, United States . . . . . . 155ft. 3 in.
1932	John Anderson, United States . . . . . . 162ft. 4 7-8 in.
1936	Ken Carpenter, United States. . . . . . 165ft. 7 3-8 in.
1948	Adolfo Consolini, Italy . . . . 173ft. 2 in.
1952	Sim Iness, United States . . . . 180ft. 6.85 in.
1956	Al Oerter, United States . . . . 184ft. 10 1-2 in.
1960	Al Oerter, United States . . . . 194ft. 2 in.
1964	Al Oerter, United States . . . . 200ft. 1 1-2 in.
1968	Al Oerter, United States . . . . 212ft. 6 1-2 in.
1972	Ludvik Danek, Czechoslovakia . . . . . . 211ft. 3 in.
1976	Mac Wilkins, United States . . . . 221ft. 5.4 in.*
1980	Viktor Rashchupkin, USSR . . . . 218ft. 8 in.
1984	Rolf Dannenberg, W. Germany . . . . 218ft. 6 in.

Triple Jump

1896	James Connolly, United States. . . . . 45ft.
1900	Myer Prinstein, United States. . . . . . . 47ft. 4 1-4 in.
1904	Myer Prinstein, United States . . . . 47 ft.
1908	Timothy Aheame, Great Britain . . . . . 48ft. 11 1-4 in.
1912	Gustaf Lindblom, Sweden. . . . . 48ft. 5 1-8 in.
1920	Vilho Tuulos, Finland . . . . 47ft. 6 7-8 in.
1924	Archie Winter, Australia . . . . 50ft. 11 1-4 in.
1928	Mikio Oda, Japan . . . . 49ft. 11 in.
1932	Chuhei Nambu, Japan. . . . . 51ft. 7 in.
1936	Naoto Tajima, Japan . . . . 52ft. 5 7-8 in.
1948	Arne Ahman, Sweden. . . . . 50ft. 6 1-4 in.
1952	Adhemar de Silva, Brazil . . . . 53ft. 2 9-16 in.
1956	Adhemar de Silva, Brazil . . . . 53ft. 7 1-2 in.
1960	Jozef Schmidt, Poland . . . . 55ft. 1 3-4 in.
1964	Jozef Schmidt, Poland . . . . 55ft. 3 1-4 in.
1968	Viktor Saneev, USSR . . . . 57ft. 3-4 in.
1972	Viktor Saneev, USSR . . . . 56ft. 11 in.
1976	Viktor Saneev, USSR . . . . 56ft. 8 3-4 in.
1980	Jaak Uudmae, USSR . . . . 56ft. 11 1-8 in.
1984	Al Joyner, United States . . . . 56ft. 7 1-2 in.*

16-lb. Shot Put

1896	Robert Garrett, United States . . . . 36ft. 9 3-4 in.
1900	Robert Sheldon, United States . . . . 46ft. 3 1-8 in.
1904	Ralph Rose, United States . . . . 48ft. 7 in.
1908	Ralph Rose, United States . . . . 46ft. 7 1-2 in.
1912	Pat McDonald, United States . . . . 50ft. 4 in.
	Both hands—Ralph Rose,
	United States. . . . . 90ft. 5 1-2 in.
1920	Ville Porhola, Finland . . . . 48ft. 7 1-8 in.
1924	Clarence Houser, United States . . . . . 49ft. 2 1-2 in.
1928	John Kuck, United States . . . . 52ft. 3-4 in.
1932	Leo Sexton, United States . . . . 52ft. 6 3-16 in.
1936	Hans Woellke, Germany . . . . 53ft. 1 3-4 in.
1948	Wilbur Thompson, United States . . . . . . 56ft. 2 in.
1952	Parry O'Brien, United States . . . . . 57ft. 1 7-16 in.
1956	Parry O'Brien, United States . . . . 60ft. 11 in.
1960	William Nieder, United States . . . . . . 64ft. 6 3-4 in.
1964	Dallas Long, United States . . . . 66ft. 8 1-4 in.
1968	Randy Matson, United States . . . . . . 67ft. 4 3-4 in.
1972	Wladyslaw Komar, Poland . . . . 69ft. 6 in.
1976	Udo Beyer, E. Germany . . . . 69ft. 3-4 in.
1980	Vladimir Kiselyov, USSR . . . . 70ft. 1-2 in.*
1984	Alessandro Andrei, Italy. . . . . 69ft. 9 in.

Javelin

1908	Erik Lemming, Sweden	178ft. 7 1-2 in.
	Held in middle—Erik Lemming,	
	Sweden	179ft. 10 1-2 in.
1912	Erik Lemming, Sweden	198ft. 11 1-4 in.
	Both hands, Julius Saaristo,	
	Finland	358ft. 11 7-8 in.
1920	Jonni Myrra, Finland	215ft. 9 3-4 in.
1924	Jonni Myrra, Finland	206ft. 6 3-4 in.
1928	Eric Lundquist, Sweden	218ft. 6 1-8 in.
1932	Matti Jarvinen, Finland	238ft. 7 in.
1936	Gerhard Stoeck, Germany	235ft. 8 5-16 in.
1948	Kaj Rautavaara, Finland	228ft. 10 1-2 in.
1952	Cy Young, United States	242ft. 0.79 in.
1956	Egil Danielsen, Norway	281ft. 2 1-4 in.
1960	Viktor Tsibulenko, USSR	277ft. 8 3-8 in.
1964	Pauli Nevala, Finland	271ft. 2 1-2 in.
1968	Janis Lusis, USSR	295ft. 7 1-4 in.
1972	Klaus Wolfermann, W. Germany	296ft. 10 in.
1976	Miklos Nemeth, Hungary	310ft. 4 in.*
1980	Dainis Kula, USSR	299ft. 2 3-8 in.
1984	Arto Haerkoenen, Finland	284ft. 8 in.

Decathlon

1912	Hugo Wieslander, Sweden	7,724.49 pts.(a)
1920	Helge Lovland, Norway	6,804.35 pts.
1924	Harold Osborn, United States	7,710.77 pts.
1928	Paavo Yrjola, Finland	8,053.29 pts.
1932	James Bausch, United States	8,462.23 pts.
1936	Glenn Morris, United States	7,900 pts.
1948	Robert Mathias, United States	7,139 pts.
1952	Robert Mathias, United States	7,887 pts.
1956	Milton Campbell, United States	7,937 pts.
1960	Rafer Johnson, United States	8,392 pts.
1964	Willi Holdorf, Germany	7,887 pts.
1968	Bill Toomey, United States	8,193 pts.
1972	Nikola Avilov, USSR	8,454 pts.
1976	Bruce Jenner, United States	8,618 pts.
1980	Daley Thompson, Great Britain	8,495pts.
1984	Daley Thompson, Great Britain	8,797 pts.*
	Former point systems used prior to 1964.	

(a) Jim Thorpe of the U.S. won the 1912 Decathlon with 8,413 pts. but was disqualified and had to return his medals because he had played professional baseball prior to the Olympic games. The medals were restored posthumously in 1982.

Track and Field—Women

100-Meter Run

1928	Elizabeth Robinson, United States	12.2s
1932	Stella Walsh, Poland	11.9s
1936	Helen Stephens, United States	11.5s
1948	Francina Blankers-Koen, Netherlands	11.9s
1952	Marjorie Jackson, Australia	11.5s
1956	Betty Cuthbert, Australia	11.5s
1960	Wilma Rudolph, United States	11.0s
1964	Wyomia Tyus, United States	11.4s
1968	Wyomia Tyus, United States	11.0s
1972	Renate Stecher, E. Germany	11.07s
1976	Annegret Richter, W. Germany	11.08s
1980	Ludmila Kondratyeva, USSR	11.6s
1984	Evelyn Ashford, United States	10.97s*

200-Meter Run

1948	Francina Blankers-Koen, Netherlands	24.4s
1952	Marjorie Jackson, Australia	23.7s
1956	Betty Cuthbert, Australia	23.4s
1960	Wilma Rudolph, United States	24.0s
1964	Edith McGuire, United States	23.0s
1968	Irena Szewinska, Poland	22.5s
1972	Renate Stecher, E. Germany	22.40s
1976	Barbel Eckert, E. Germany	22.37s
1980	Barbel Wockel, E. Germany	22.03
1984	Valerie Brisco-Hooks, United States	21.81s*

400-Meter Run

1964	Betty Cuthbert, Australia	52s
1968	Colette Besson, France	52s
1972	Monika Zehrt, E. Germany	51.08s
1976	Irena Szewinska, Poland	49.29s
1980	Marita Koch, E. Germany	48.88s
1984	Valerie Brisco-Hooks, United States	48.83s*

800-Meter Run

1928	Lina Radke, Germany	2m. 16.8s
1960	Ludmila Shevcova, USSR	2m. 4.3s
1964	Ann Packer, Great Britain	2m. 1.1s
1968	Madeline Manning, United States	2m. 0.9s
1972	Hildegard Flack, W. Germany	1m. 58.6s
1976	Tatyana Kazankina, USSR	1m. 54.94s
1980	Nadezhda Olizayrenko, USSR	1m. 53.5s*
1984	Doina Melinte, Romania	1m. 57.6s

1,500-Meter Run

1972	Ludmila Bragina, USSR	4m. 01.4s
1976	Tatyana Kazankina, USSR	4m. 05.48s
1980	Tatyana Kazankina, USSR	3m. 56.6s*
1984	Gabriella Dorio, Italy	4m. 03.26s

3,000-Meter Run

| 1984 | Maricica Puica, Romania | 8:35.96* |

400-Meter Relay

1928	Canada	48.4s
1932	United States	47.0s
1936	United States	46.9s
1948	Netherlands	47.5s
1952	United States	45.9s
1956	Australia	44.5s
1960	United States	44.5s
1964	Poland	43.6s
1968	United States	42.8s
1972	West Germany	42.81s
1976	East Germany	42.55s
1980	East Germany	41.60s*
1984	United States	41.65s

1,600-Meter Relay

1972	East Germany	3m. 23s
1976	East Germany	3m. 19.23s
1980	USSR	3m. 20.02s
1984	United States	3m. 18.29s*

80-Meter Hurdles

1932	Mildred Didrikson, United States	11.7s
1936	Trebisonda Villa, Italy	11.7s
1948	Francina Blankers-Koen, Netherlands	11.2s
1952	Shirley Strickland de la Hunty, Australia	10.9s
1956	Shirley Strickland de la Hunty, Australia	10.7s
1960	Irina Press, USSR	10.8s
1964	Karen Balzer, Germany	10.5s
1968	Maureen Caird, Australia	10.3s*

100-Meter Hurdles

1972	Annelie Ehrhardt, E. Germany	12.59s
1976	Johanna Schaller, E. Germany	12.77s
1980	Vera Komisova, USSR	12.56s*
1984	Benita Brown-Fitzgerald, United States	12.84s

400-Meter Hurdles

| 1984 | Nawal el Moutawakii, Morocco | 54.61s* |

Heptathlon

| 1984 | Glynis Nunn, Australia | 6,390 pts.* |

High Jump

1928	Ethel Catherwood, Canada	5ft. 3 in.
1932	Jean Shiley, United States	5ft. 5 1-4 in.
1936	Ibolya Csak, Hungary	5ft. 3 in.
1948	Alice Coachman, United States	5ft. 6 1-8 in.
1952	Esther Brand, South Africa	5ft. 5 3-4 in.
1956	Mildred L. McDaniel, United States	5ft. 9 1-4 in.
1960	Iolanda Balas, Romania	6ft. 3-4 in.
1964	Iolanda Balas, Romania	6ft. 2 3-4 in.
1968	Miloslava Reskova, Czechoslovakia	5ft. 11 3-4 in.
1972	Ulrike Meyfarth, W. Germany	6ft. 3 1-4 in.
1976	Rosemarie Ackermann, E. Germany	6ft. 3 3-4 in.
1980	Sara Simeoni, Italy	6ft. 5 1-2 in.
1984	Ulrike Meyfarth, W. Germany	6ft. 7 1-2 in.*

Discus Throw

1928	Helena Konopacka, Poland	129ft. 11 7-8 in.
1932	Lillian Copeland, United States	133ft. 2 in.
1936	Gisela Mauermayer, Germany	156ft. 3 3-16 in.
1948	Micheline Ostermeyer, France	137ft. 6 1-2 in.
1952	Nina Romaschkova, USSR	168ft. 8 1-2 in.
1956	Olga Fikotova, Czechoslovakia	176ft. 1 1-2 in.
1960	Nina Ponomareva, USSR	180ft. 8 1-4 in.
1964	Tamara Press, USSR	187ft. 10 1-2 in.
1968	Lia Manoliu, Romania	191ft. 2 1-2 in.
1972	Faina Melnik, USSR	218ft. 7 in.
1976	Evelin Schlaak, E. Germany	226ft. 4 1-2 in.
1980	Evelin Jahl, E. Germany	229ft. 6 1-4 in.*
1984	Ria Stalman, Netherlands	214ft. 5 in.

Javelin Throw

| 1932 | Mildred Didrikson, United States | 143ft. 4 in. |

1936	Tilly Fleischer, Germany	148ft. 2 3-4 in.
1948	Herma Bauma, Austria	149ft. 6 in.
1952	Dana Zatopkova, Czechoslovakia	165ft. 7 in.
1956	Inessa Janzeme, USSR	176ft. 8 in.
1960	Elvira Ozolina, USSR	183ft. 8 in.
1964	Mihaela Penes, Romania	198ft. 7 1-2 in.
1968	Angela Nemeth, Hungary	198ft. 1-2 in.
1972	Ruth Fuchs, E. Germany	209ft. 7 in.
1976	Ruth Fuchs, E. Germany	216ft. 4 in.
1980	Maria Colon, Cuba	224ft. 5 in.
1984	Tessa Sanderson, Great Britain	228ft. 2 in.*

Shot Put (8lb., 13oz.)

1948	Micheline Ostermeyer, France	45ft. 1 1-2 in.
1952	Galina Zybina, USSR	50ft. 1 1-2 in.
1956	Tamara Tishkyevich, USSR	54ft. 5 in.
1960	Tamara Press, USSR	56ft. 9 7-8 in.
1964	Tamara Press, USSR	59ft. 6 1-4 in.
1968	Margitta Gummel, E. Germany	64ft. 4 in.
1972	Nadezhda Chizova, USSR	69ft.
1976	Ivanka Christova, Bulgaria	69ft. 5 in.
1980	Ilona Slupianek, E. Germany	73ft. 6 1-4 in. *
1984	Claudia Losch, W. Germany	67ft. 2 1-4 in.

Long Jump

1948	Olga Gyarmati, Hungary	18ft. 8 1-4 in.
1952	Yvette Williams, New Zealand	20ft. 5 3-4 in.
1956	Elzbieta Krzeskinska, Poland	20ft. 9 3-4 in.
1960	Vyera Krepkina, USSR	20ft. 10 3-4 in.
1964	Mary Rand, Great Britain	22ft. 2 1-4 in.
1968	Viorica Viscopoleanu, Romania	22ft. 4 1-2 in.
1972	Heidemarie Rosendahl, W. Germany	22ft. 3 in.
1976	Angela Voigt, E. Germany	22ft. 2 1-2 in.
1980	Tatyana Kolpakova, USSR	23ft. 2 in.*
1984	Anisoara Stanciu, Romania	22ft. 10 in.

Pentathlon

1964	Irina Press, USSR	5,246 pts.
1968	Ingrid Becker, W. Germany	5,098 pts.
1972	Mary Peters, England	4,801 pts.
1976	Sigrun Siegl, E. Germany	4,745 pts.
1980	Nadyezhda Tkachenko, USSR	5,083pts.*

Former point system, 1964–1968

Marathon

| 1984 | Joan Benoit, United States | 2h. 24m. 52s* |

Swimming—Men

100-Meter Freestyle

1896	Alfred Hajos, Hungary	1:22.2
1904	Zoltan de Halmay, Hungary (100 yards)	1:02.8
1908	Charles Daniels, U.S.	1:05.6
1912	Duke P. Kahanamoku, U.S.	1:03.4
1920	Duke P. Kahanamoku, U.S.	1:01.4
1924	John Weissmuller, U.S.	59.0
1928	John Weissmuller, U.S.	58.6
1932	Yasuji Miyazaki, Japan	58.2
1936	Ferenc Csik, Hungary	57.6
1948	Wally Ris, U.S.	57.3
1952	Clark Scholes, U.S.	57.4
1956	Jon Henricks, Australia	55.4
1960	John Devitt, Australia	55.2
1964	Don Schollander, U.S.	53.4
1968	Mike Wenden, Australia	52.2
1972	Mark Spitz, U.S.	51.22
1976	Jim Montgomery, U.S.	49.99
1980	Jorg Woithe, E. Germany	50.40
1984	Rowdy Gaines, U.S.	49.80*

200-Meter Freestyle

1968	Mike Wenden, Australia	1:55.2
1972	Mark Spitz, U.S.	1:52.78
1976	Bruce Furniss, U.S.	1:50.29
1980	Sergei Kopliakov, USSR	1:49.81
1984	Michael Gross, W. Germany	1:47.44*

400-Meter Freestyle

1904	C. M. Daniels, U.S. (440 yards)	6:16.2
1908	Henry Taylor, Great Britain	5:36.8
1912	George Hodgson, Canada	5:24.4
1920	Norman Ross, U.S.	5:26.8
1924	John Weissmuller, U.S.	5:04.2
1928	Albert Zorilla, Argentina	5:01.6
1932	Clarence Crabbe, U.S.	4:48.4
1936	Jack Medica, U.S.	4:44.5
1948	William Smith, U.S.	4:41.0
1952	Jean Boiteux, France	4:30.7
1956	Murray Rose, Australia	4:27.3
1960	Murray Rose, Australia	4:18.3
1964	Don Schollander, U.S.	4:12.2
1968	Mike Burton, U.S.	4:09.0
1972	Brad Cooper, Australia	4:00.27
1976	Brian Goodell, U.S.	3:51.93
1980	Vladimir Salnikov, USSR	3:51.31
1984	George DiCarlo, U.S.	3:51.23*

1,500-Meter Freestyle

1908	Henry Taylor, Great Britain	22:48.4
1912	George Hodgson, Canada	22:00.0
1920	Norman Ross, U.S.	22:23.2
1924	Andrew Charlton, Australia	20:06.6
1928	Arne Borg, Sweden	19:51.8
1932	Kusuo Kitamura, Japan	19:12.4
1936	Noboru Terada, Japan	19:13.7
1948	James McLane, U.S.	19:18.5
1952	Ford Konno, U.S.	18:30.0
1956	Murray Rose, Australia	17:58.9
1960	Jon Konrads, Australia	17:19.6
1964	Robert Windle, Australia	17:01.7
1968	Mike Burton, U.S.	16:38.9
1972	Mike Burton, U.S.	15:52.58
1976	Brian Goodell, U.S.	15:02.40
1980	Vladimir Salnikov, USSR	14:58.27*
1984	Michael O'Brien, U.S.	15:05.20

400-Meter Medley Relay

1960	United States	4:05.4
1964	United States	3:58.4
1968	United States	3:54.9
1972	United States	3:48.16
1976	United States	3:42.22
1980	Australia	3:45.70
1984	United States	3:39.30*

400-Meter Freestyle Relay

1964	United States	3:33.2
1968	United States	3:31.7
1972	United States	3:26.42
1984	United States	3:19.03*

800-Meter Freestyle Relay

1908	Great Britain	10:55.6
1912	Australia	10:11.6
1920	United States	10:04.4
1924	United States	9:53.4
1928	United States	9:36.2
1932	Japan	8:58.4
1936	Japan	8:51.5
1948	United States	8:46.0
1952	United States	8:31.1
1956	Australia	8:23.6
1960	United States	8:10.2
1964	United States	7:52.1
1968	United States	7:52.3
1972	United States	7:35.78
1976	United States	7:23.22
1980	USSR	7:23.50
1984	United States	7:15.69*

100-Meter Backstroke

1904	Walter Brack, Germany (100 yds.)	1:16.8
1908	Arno Bieberstein, Germany	1:24.6
1912	Harry Hebner, U.S.	1:21.2
1920	Warren Kealoha, U.S.	1:15.2
1924	Warren Kealoha, U.S.	1:13.2
1928	George Kojac, U.S.	1:08.2
1932	Masaji Kiyokawa, Japan	1:08.6
1936	Adolph Kiefer, U.S.	1:05.9
1948	Allen Stack, U.S.	1:06.4
1952	Yoshi Oyakawa, U.S.	1:05.4
1956	David Thiele, Australia	1:02.2
1960	David Thiele, Australia	1:01.9
1968	Roland Matthes, E. Germany	58.7
1972	Roland Matthes, E. Germany	56.58
1976	John Naber, U.S.	55.49*
1980	Bengt Baron, Sweden	56.53
1984	Rick Carey, U.S.	55.79

200-Meter Backstroke

1964	Jed Graef, U.S.	2:10.3
1968	Roland Matthes, E. Germany	2:09.6
1972	Roland Matthes, E. Germany	2:02.82
1976	John Naber, U.S.	1:59.19*
1980	Sandor Wladar, Hungary	2:01.93
1984	Rick Carey, U.S.	2:00.23

100-Meter Breaststroke

1968	Don McKenzie, U.S.	1:07.7
1972	Nobutaka Taguchi, Japan	1:04.94
1976	John Hencken, U.S.	1:03.11
1980	Duncan Goodhew, Great Britain	1:03.34
1984	Steve Lundquist, U.S.	1:01.65*

200-Meter Breaststroke

1908	Frederick Holman, Great Britain	3:09.2
1912	Walter Bathe, Germany	3:01.8
1920	Haken Malmroth, Sweden	3:04.4
1924	Robert Skelton, U.S.	2:56.6
1928	Yoshiyuki Tsuruta, Japan	2:48.8
1932	Yoshiyuki Tsuruta, Japan	2:45.4
1936	Tetsuo Hamuro, Japan	2:42.5
1948	Joseph Verdeur, U.S.	2:39.3
1952	John Davies, Australia	2:34.4
1956	Masura Furukawa, Japan	2:34.7
1960	William Mulliken, U.S.	2:37.4
1964	Ian O'Brien, Australia	2:27.8
1968	Felipe Munoz, Mexico	2:28.7
1972	John Hencken, U.S.	2:21.55
1976	David Wilkie, Great Britain	2:15.11
1980	Robertas Zulpa, USSR	2:15.85
1984	Victor Davis, Canada	2:13.34*

100-Meter Butterfly

1968	Doug Russell, U.S.	55.9
1972	Mark Spitz, U.S.	54.27
1976	Matt Vogel, U.S.	54.35
1980	Par Arvidsson, Sweden	54.92
1984	Michael Gross, W. Germany	53.08*

200-Meter Butterfly

1956	William Yorzyk, U.S.	2:19.3
1960	Michael Troy, U.S.	2:12.8
1964	Kevin J. Berry, Australia	2:06.6
1968	Carl Robie, U.S.	2:08.7
1972	Mark Spitz, U.S.	2:00.70
1976	Mike Bruner, U.S.	1:59.23
1980	Sergei Fesenko, USSR	1:59.76
1984	Jon Sieben, Australia	1:57.04*

200-Meter Individual Medley

1968	Charles Hickcox, U.S.	2:12.0
1972	Gunnar Larsson, Sweden	2:07.17
1984	Alex Baumann, Canada	2:10.42*

400-Meter Individual Medley

1964	Dick Roth, U.S.	4:45.4
1968	Charles Hickcox, U.S.	4:48.4
1972	Gunnar Larsson, Sweden	4:31.98
1976	Rod Strachan, U.S.	4:23.68
1980	Aleksandr Sidorenko, USSR	4:22.89
1984	Alex Baumann, Canada	4:17.41*

Springboard Diving

		Points
1908	Albert Zurner, Germany	85.5
1912	Paul Guenther, Germany	79.23
1920	Louis Kuehn, U.S.	675.00
1924	Albert White, U.S.	696.40
1928	Pete Desjardins, U.S.	185.04
1932	Michael Galitzen, U.S.	161.38
1936	Richard Degener, U.S.	161.57
1948	Bruce Harlan, U.S.	163.64
1952	David Browning, U.S.	205.29
1956	Robert Clotworthy, U.S.	159.56
1960	Gary Tobian, U.S.	170.00
1964	Kenneth Sitzberger, U.S.	159.90
1968	Bernie Wrightson, U.S.	170.15
1972	Vladimir Vasin, USSR	594.09
1976	Phil Boggs, U.S.	619.52
1980	Aleksandr Portnov, USSR	905.02
1984	Greg Louganis, U.S.	754.41

Platform Diving

		Points
1904	Dr. G.E. Sheldon, U.S.	12.75
1908	Hjalmar Johansson, Sweden	83.75
1912	Erik Adlerz, Sweden	73.94
1920	Clarence Pinkston, U.S.	100.67
1924	Albert White, U.S.	487.30
1928	Pete Desjardins, U.S.	98.74
1932	Harold Smith, U.S.	124.80
1936	Marshall Wayne, U.S.	113.58
1948	Sammy Lee, U.S.	130.05
1952	Sammy Lee, U.S.	156.28
1956	Joaquin Capilla, Mexico	152.44
1960	Robert Webster, U.S.	165.56
1964	Robert Webster, U.S.	148.58
1968	Klaus Dibiasi, Italy	164.18
1972	Klaus Dibiasi, Italy	504.12
1976	Klaus Dibiasi, Italy	600.51
1980	Falk Hoffmann, E. Germany	835.65
1984	Greg Louganis, U.S.	710.91

Swimming—Women

100-Meter Freestyle

1912	Fanny Durack, Australia	1:22.2
1920	Ethelda Bleibtrey, U.S.	1:13.6
1924	Ethel Lackie, U.S.	1:12.4
1928	Albina Osipowich, U.S.	1:11.0
1932	Helene Madison, U.S.	1:06.8
1936	Hendrika Mastenbroek, Holland	1:05.9
1948	Greta Anderson, Denmark	1:06.3
1952	Katalin Szoke, Hungary	1:06.3
1956	Dawn Fraser, Australia	1:02.0
1960	Dawn Fraser, Australia	1:01.2
1964	Dawn Fraser, Australia	59.5
1968	Jan Henne, U.S.	1:00.0
1972	Sandra Neilson, U.S.	58.59
1976	Kornelia Ender, E. Germany	55.65
1980	Barbara Krause, E. Germany	54.79*
1984	(tie) Carrie Steinseifer, U.S.	55.92
	Nancy Hogshead, U.S.	55.92

200-Meter Freestyle

1968	Debbie Meyer, U.S.	2:10.5
1972	Shane Gould, Australia	2:03.56
1976	Kornelia Ender, E. Germany	1:59.26
1980	Barbara Krause, E. Germany	1:58.33*
1984	Mary Wayte, U.S.	1:59.23

400-Meter Freestyle

1924	Martha Norelius, U.S.	6:02.2
1928	Martha Norelius, U.S.	5:42.8
1932	Helene Madison, U.S.	5:28.5
1936	Hendrika Mastenbroek, Netherlands	5:26.4
1948	Ann Curtis, U.S.	5:17.8
1952	Valerie Gyenge, Hungary	5:12.1
1956	Lorraine Crapp, Australia	4:54.6
1960	Susan Chris von Saltza, U.S.	4:50.6
1964	Virginia Duenkel, U.S.	4:43.3

1968	Debbie Meyer, U.S.	4:31.8
1972	Shane Gould, Australia	4:19.04
1976	Petra Thuemer E. Germany	4:09.89
1980	Ines Diers, E. Germany	4:08.76
1984	Tiffany Cohen, U.S.	4:07.10*

800-Meter Freestyle

1968	Debbie Meyer, U.S.	9:24.0
1972	Keena Rothhammer, U.S.	8:53.68
1976	Petra Thuemer, E. Germany	8:37.14
1980	Michelle Ford, Australia	8:28.90
1984	Tiffany Cohen, U.S.	8:24.95*

100-Meter Backstroke

1924	Sybil Bauer, U.S.	1:23.3
1928	Marie Braun, Netherlands	1:22.0
1932	Eleanor Holm, U.S.	1:19.4
1936	Dina Senff, Netherlands	1:18.9
1948	Karen Harup, Denmark	1:14.4
1952	Joan Harrison, South Africa	1:14.3
1956	Judy Grinham, Great Britain	1:12.9
1960	Lynn Burke, U.S.	1:09.3
1964	Cathy Ferguson, U.S.	1:07.7
1968	Kaye Hall, U.S.	1:06.2
1972	Melissa Belote, U.S.	1:05.78
1976	Ulrike Richter, E. Germany	1:01.83
1980	Rica Reinisch, E. Germany	1:00.86*
1984	Theresa Andrews, U.S.	1:02.55

200-Meter Backstroke

1968	Pokey Watson, U.S.	2:24.8
1972	Melissa Belote, U.S.	2:19.19
1976	Ulrike Richter, E. Germany	2:13.43
1980	Rica Reinisch, E. Germany	2:11.77*
1984	Jolanda De Rover, Netherlands	2:13.38

100-Meter Breaststroke
1968	Djurdjica Bjedov, Yugoslavia	1:15.8
1972	Cathy Carr, U.S.	1:13.58
1976	Hannelore Anke, E. Germany	1:11:16
1980	Ute Geweniger, E. Germany	1:10.22
1984	Petra Van Staveren, Netherlands	1:09.88*

200-Meter Breaststroke
1924	Lucy Morton, Great Britain	3:32.2
1928	Hilde Schrader, Germany	3:12.6
1932	Clare Dennis, Australia	3:06.3
1936	Hideko Maehata, Japan	3:03.6
1948	Nelly Van Vliet, Netherlands	2:57.2
1952	Eva Szekely, Hungary	2:51.7
1956	Ursula Happe, Germany	2:53.1
1960	Anita Lonsbrough, Great Britain	2:49.5
1964	Galina Prozumenschikova, USSR	2:46.4
1968	Sharon Wichman, U.S.	2:44.4
1972	Beverly Whitfield, Australia	2:41.71
1976	Marina Koshevaia, USSR	2:33.35
1980	Lina Kachushite, USSR	2:29.54*
1984	Anne Ottenbrite, Canada	2:30.38

200-Meter Individual Medley
1968	Claudia Kolb, U.S.	2:24.7
1972	Shane Gould, Australia	2:23.07
1984	Tracy Caulkins, U.S.	2:12.64*

400-Meter Individual Medley
1964	Donna de Varona, U.S.	5:18.7
1968	Claudia Kolb, U.S.	5:08.5
1972	Gail Neall, Australia	5:02.97
1976	Ulrike Tauber, E. Germany	4:42.77
1980	Petra Schneider, E. Germany	4:36.29*
1984	Tracy Caulkins, U.S.	4:39.24

100-Meter Butterfly
1956	Shelley Mann, U.S.	1:11.0
1960	Carolyn Schuler, U.S.	1:09.5
1964	Sharon Stouder, U.S.	1:04.7
1968	Lynn McClements, Australia	1:05.5
1972	Mayumi Aoki, Japan	1:03.34
1976	Kornelia Ender, E. Germany	1:00.13
1980	Caren Metschuck, E. Germany	1:00.42
1984	Mary T. Meagher, U.S.	59.26*

200-Meter Butterfly
1968	Ada Kok, Netherlands	2:24.7
1972	Karen Moe, U.S.	2:15.57
1976	Andrea Pollack, E. Germany	2:11.41
1980	Ines Geissler, E. Germany	2:10.44
1984	Mary T. Meagher, U.S.	2:06.90*

400-Meter Medley Relay
1960	United States	4:41.1
1960	United States	4:33.9
1968	United States	4:28.3

1972	United States	4:20.75
1976	East Germany	4:07.95
1980	East Germany	4:06.67*
1984	United States	4:08.34

400-Meter Freestyle Relay
1912	Great Britain	5:52.8
1920	United States	5:11.6
1924	United States	4:58.8
1928	United States	4:47.6
1932	United States	4:38.0
1936	Netherlands	4:36.0
1948	United States	4:29.2
1952	Hungary	4:24.4
1956	Australia	4:17.1
1960	United States	4:08.9
1964	United States	4:03.8
1968	United States	4:02.5
1972	United States	3:55.19
1976	United States	3:44.82
1980	East Germany	3:42.71*
1984	United States	3:43.43

Springboard Diving
		Points
1920	Aileen Riggin, U.S.	539.90
1924	Elizabeth Becker, U.S.	474.50
1928	Helen Meany, U.S.	78.62
1932	Georgia Coleman U.S.	87.52
1936	Marjorie Gestring, U.S.	89.27
1948	Victoria M. Draves, U.S.	108.74
1952	Patricia McCormick, U.S.	147.30
1956	Patricia McCormick, U.S.	142.36
1960	Ingrid Kramer, Germany	155.81
1964	Ingrid Engel-Kramer, Germany	145.00
1968	Sue Gossick, U.S.	150.77
1972	Micki King, U.S.	450.03
1976	Jenni Chandler, U.S.	506.19
1980	Irina Kalinina, USSR	725.91
1984	Sylvie Bernier, Canada	530.70

Platform Diving
		Points
1912	Greta Johansson, Sweden	39.90
1920	Stefani Fryland-Clausen, Denmark	34.60
1924	Caroline Smith, U.S.	166.00
1928	Elizabeth B. Pinkston, U.S.	31.60
1932	Dorothy Poynton, U.S.	40.26
1936	Dorothy Poynton Hill, U.S.	33.93
1948	Victoria M. Draves, U.S.	68.87
1952	Patricia McCormick, U.S.	79.37
1956	Patricia McCormick, U.S.	84.85
1960	Ingrid Kramer, Germany	91.28
1964	Lesley Bush, U.S.	99.80
1968	Milena Duchkova, Czech.	109.59
1972	Ulrika Knape, Sweden	390.00
1976	Elena Vaytsekhouskaya, USSR	406.59
1980	Martina Jaschke, E. Germany	596.25
1984	Zhou Jihong, China	435.51

Other Summer Olympics Gold Medalists in 1984

Archery
Men—Darrell Pace, U.S.
Women—Hyang-Soun Seo, S. Korea.

Basketball
Men—1. U.S.; 2. Spain; 3. Yugoslavia.
Women—1. U.S.; 2. S. Korea; 3. China.

Boxing
106 lbs.—Paul Gonzales, U.S.
112 lbs.—Steve McCrory, U.S.
119 lbs.—Maurizio Stecca, Italy.
126 lbs.—Meldrick Taylor, U.S.
132 lbs.—Pernell Whitaker, U.S.
139 lbs.—Jerry Page, U.S.
147 lbs.—Mark Breland, U.S.
157 lbs.—Frank Tate, U.S.
165 lbs.—Joun-Sup Shin, S. Korea.
178 lbs.—Anton Josipovic, Yugoslavia.
201 lbs.—Henry Tillman, U.S.
Over 201 lbs.—Tyrell Biggs, U.S.

Canoeing—Men
500m One-Man Canoe—Larry Cain, Canada.
500m Two-Man Canoe—Yugoslavia.
500m One-Man Kayak—Ian Ferguson, New Zealand.
500m Two-Man Kayak—New Zealand.
1,000m One-Man Kayak—Alan Thompson, New Zealand.
1,000m Two-Man Kayak—Canada.
1,000m Four-Man Kayak—New Zealand.
1,000m One-Man Canoe—Ulrich Eiche, W. Germany.
1,000m Two-Man Canoe—Romania.

Canoeing—Women
500m One-Woman Kayak—Agneta Andersson, Sweden.
500m Two-Woman Kayak—Sweden.
500m Four-Woman Kayak—Romania.

Cycling
4,000 Individual Pursuit—Steve Hegg, U.S.
Individual Road Race—Alexi Grewal, U.S.
1,000m Time Trials—Fredy Schmidtke, W. Germany.

4,000m Team Pursuit—Australia.
Sprint—Mark Gorski, U.S.
Points Race—Roger Ilegems, Belgium.
100km Road Team Trials—Italy.
Women's Individual Road Race—Connie Carpenter, U.S.

Diving

Men's Springboard—Greg Louganis, U.S.
Men's Platform—Greg Louganis, U.S.
Women's Springboard—Sylvie Bernier, Canada.
Women's Platform—Zhou Jihong, China.

Equestrian

Individual 3-Day Event—Mark Todd, New Zealand.
Team 3-Day Event—U.S.
Team Jumping—U.S.
Team Dressage—W. Germany.
Individual Dressage—Reiner Klimke, W. Germany.
Individual Jumping—Jose Fargis, U.S.

Fencing—Men

Individual Epee—Phillippe Boisse, France.
Individual Foil—Mauro Numa, Italy.
Individual Sabre—Jean Francois Lamour, France.
Team Foil—Italy.
Team Epee—W. Germany.
Team Sabre—Italy.

Fencing—Women

Individual Foil—Luan Jujie, China.
Team Foil—W. Germany.

Field Hockey

Men—1. Pakistan; 2. W. Germany; 3. Great Britain.
Women—1. Netherlands; 2. W. Germany; 3. U.S.

Gymnastics—Men

All Around—Koji Gushiken, Japan.
Team—U.S.
Floor Exercise—Li Ning, China.
Horizontal Bar—Shinji Morisue, Japan.
Parallel Bars—Bart Connor, U.S.
Pommel Horse—Li Ning, China & Peter Vidmar, U.S. (tie).
Rings—Koji Gushiken, Japan & Li Ning, China (tie).
Vault—Lou Yung, China.

Gymnastics—Women

Floor Exercise—Ecaterina Szabo, Romania.
Balance Beam—Simona Pauca & Ecaterina Szabo, both Romania (tie).
Vault—Ecaterina Szabo, Romania.
Uneven Parallel Bars—Ma Yanhonjg, China & Julianne McNamara, U.S. (tie).
All-Around—Mary Lou Retton, U.S.
Team—Romania.
Rhythmic—Lori Fung, Canada.

Team Handball

Men—1. Yugoslavia; 2. W. Germany; 3. Romania.
Women—1. Yugoslavia; 2. S. Korea; 3. China.

Judo

Lightweight—Byeong-Keun Ahn, S. Korea.
Extra Lightweight—Shinji Hosokawa, Japan.
Half Lightweight—Yoshiyuki Matsuoka, Japan.
Half Middleweight—Frank Wieneke, W. Germany.
Middleweight—Peter Seisenbacher, Austria.
Half Heavyweight—Hyong-Zoo Ha, S. Korea.
Heavyweight—Hitoshi Saito, Japan.
Open—Yasuhiro Yamashita, Japan.

Modern Pentathlon

Individual—Daniele Masala, Italy.
Team—1. Italy; 2. U.S.; 3. France.

Rowing

Single Sculls—Pertti Karppinen, Finland.
Double Sculls—U.S.

Quadruple Sculls—W. Germany.
Pair Oars With Coxswain—Italy.
Pair Oars Without Coxswain—Romania.
Four Oars With Coxswain—Great Britain.
Four Oars Without Coxswain—New Zealand.
Eight Oars With Coxswain—Canada.

Rowing—Women

Single Sculls—Valarie Racila, Romania.
Double Sculls—Romania.
Quadruple Sculls with Coxswain—Romania.
Pair Oars Without Coxswain—Romania.
Four Oars Without Coxswain—Romania.
Eight Oars—U.S.

Shooting—Men

Air Rifle—Philippe Heberle, France.
Clay Target Trap—Luciano Giovanetti, Italy.
English Small Bore Rifle—Ed Etzel, U.S.
Free Pistol—Xu Haifeng, China.
Rapid-Fire Pistol—Takeo Kamachi, Japan
Running Game Targets—Li Yuwei, China.
Small Bore Rifle, 3 Positions—Malcolm Cooper, Great Britain.
Clay Target Skeet—Matthew Dryke, U.S.

Shooting—Women

Air Rifle—Pat Spurgin, U.S.
Small Bore Rifle, 3 Positions—Wu Xiaoxuan, China.
Sport Pistol—Linda Thom, Canada.

Soccer

Championship—1. France; 2. Brazil; 3. Yugoslavia.

Synchronized Swimming

Solo—Tracie Ruiz, U.S.
Duet—1. U.S.; 2. Canada; 3. Japan.

Volleyball

Men—1. U.S.; 2. Brazil; 3. Italy.
Women—1. China; 2. U.S.; 3. Japan.

Water Polo

Championship—1. Yugoslavia; 2. U.S.; 3. W. Germany.

Weight Lifting

Bantamweight—Wu Shude, China.
Flyweight—Zeng Guoqiang, China.
Featherweights—Chen Weiquiang, China.
Lightweights—Yao Jingyuang, China.
Middleweights—Karl-Heinz Radschinsky, W. Germany.
Light Heavyweights—Petre Becheru, Romania.
Middle Heavyweights—Niku Vlad, Romania.
100 Kilograms—Rolf Milser, W. Germany.
110 Kilograms—Norberto Oberburger, Italy.
Super Heavyweights—Dinko Lukim, Australia.

Wrestling—Freestyle

106 Pounds—Robert Weaver, U.S.
115 Pounds—Saban Trstena, Yugoslavia.
126 Pounds—Hideaki Tomiyama, Japan.
137 Pounds—Randy Lewis, U.S.
150 Pounds—In Tak Yoo, S. Korea.
163 Pounds—Dave Schultz, U.S.
181 Pounds—Mark Schultz, U.S.
198 Pounds—Ed Banach, U.S.
220 Pounds—Lou Banach, U.S.
Over 220 Pounds—Bruce Baumgartner, U.S.

Wrestling—Greco-Roman

106 Pounds—Vicenzo Maenza, Italy.
115 Pounds—Atsuji Miyahara, Japan.
126 Pounds—Pasquale Passarelli, W. Germany.
137 Pounds—Weon Kee Kim, S. Korea.
150 Pounds—Vlado Lisjak, Yugoslavia.
163 Pounds—Jouko Salomaki, Finland.

181 Pounds—Ion Draica, Romania.
198 Pounds—Steven Fraser, U.S.
202 Pounds—Vasile Andrei, Romania.
Over 202 Pounds—Jeff Blatnick, U.S.

Yachting

Windglider Class—Stephen Van Den Berg, Netherlands.

Soling Class—1. U.S.; 2. Brazil; 3. Canada.
Flying Dutchman Class—1. U.S.; 2. Canada; 3. Great Britain.
Star Class—1. U.S.; 2. W. Germany; 3. Italy.
Finn Class—1. Russell Coutts, New Zealand.
Tornado Class—1. New Zealand; 2. U.S.; 3. Australia.
470 Class—1. Spain; 2. U.S.; 3. France.

23d Summer Olympics

Los Angeles, Cal., July 29-Aug. 12, 1984

Final Medal Standings

(nations in alphabetical order)

	Gold	Silver	Bronze	Total		Gold	Silver	Bronze	Total
Algeria	0	0	2	2	Mexico	2	3	1	6
Australia	4	8	12	24	Morocco	2	0	0	2
Austria	1	1	1	3	Netherlands	5	2	6	13
Belgium	1	1	2	4	New Zealand	8	1	2	11
Brazil	1	5	2	8	Nigeria	0	1	1	2
Cameroon	0	0	1	1	Norway	0	1	2	3
Canada	10	18	16	44	Pakistan	1	0	0	1
China	15	8	9	32	Peru	0	1	0	1
Columbia	0	1	0	1	Portugal	1	0	2	3
Denmark	0	3	3	6	Puerto Rico	0	1	1	2
Dom. Republic	0	0	1	1	Romania	20	16	17	53
Egypt	0	1	0	1	Spain	1	2	2	5
Finland	4	3	6	13	Sweden	2	11	6	19
France	5	7	15	27	Switzerland	0	4	4	8
Germany, West	17	19	23	59	Syria	0	1	0	1
Great Britain	5	10	22	37	Taipei	0	0	1	1
Greece	0	1	1	2	Thailand	0	1	0	1
Iceland	0	0	1	1	Turkey	0	0	3	3
Ireland	0	1	0	1	United States	83	61	30	174
Italy	14	6	12	32	Venezuela	0	0	3	3
Ivory Coast	0	1	0	1	Yugoslavia	7	4	7	18
Jamaica	0	1	2	3	Zambia	0	0	1	1
Japan	10	8	14	32	Duplicate medals awarded in some events				
Kenya	1	0	1	2					
Korea, South	6	6	7	19					

Olympic Information

Symbol: Five rings or circles, linked together to represent the sporting friendship of all peoples. The rings also symbolize the 5 continents—Europe, Asia, Africa, Australia, and America. Each ring is a different color—blue, yellow, black, green, and red.

Flag: The symbol of the 5 rings on a plain white background.

Motto: "Citius, Altius, Fortius." Latin meaning "faster, higher, braver," or the modern interpretation "swifter, higher, stronger". The motto was coined by Father Didon, a French educator, in 1895.

Creed: "The most important thing in the Olympic Games is not to win but to take part, just as the most important thing in life is not the triumph but the struggle. The essential thing is not to have conquered but to have fought well."

Oath: An athlete of the host country recites the following at the opening ceremony. "In the name of all competitors I promise that we will take part in these Olympic Games, respecting and abiding by the rules which govern them, in the true spirit of sportsmanship for the glory of sport and the honor of our teams." Both the oath and the creed were composed by Pierre de Coubertin, the founder of the modern Games.

Flame: Symbolizes the continuity between the ancient and modern Games. The modern version of the flame was adopted in 1936. The torch used to kindle the flame is first lit by the sun's rays at Olympia, Greece, and then carried to the site of the Games by relays of runners. Ships and planes are used when necessary.

Winter Olympic Games Champions, 1924-1984

Sites and Unofficial Winners of Games

1924 Chamonix, France (Norway)
1928 St. Moritz, Switzerland (Norway)
1932 Lake Placid, N.Y. (U.S.)
1936 Garmisch-Partenkirchen (Norway)
1948 St. Moritz (Sweden)
1952 Oslo, Norway (Norway)

1956 Cortina d'Ampezzo, Italy (USSR)
1960 Squaw Valley, Cal. (USSR)
1964 Innsbruck, Austria (USSR)
1968 Grenoble, France (Norway)
1972 Sapporo, Japan (USSR)
1976 Innsbruck, Austria (USSR)

1980 Lake Placid, N.Y. (E. Germany)
1984 Sarajevo, Yugoslavia (USSR)
1988 Calgary, Alberta (scheduled)

Biathlon

10 Kilometers	Time
1980 Frank Ulrich, E. Germany	32:10.69
1984 Eirik Kvalfoss, Norway	30:53.8

20 Kilometers	Time
1960 Klas Lestander, Sweden	1:33:21.6

	Time
1964 Vladimir Melanin, USSR	1:20:26.8
1968 Magnar Solberg, Norway	1:13:45.9
1972 Magnar Solberg, Norway	1:15:55.50
1976 Nikolai Kruglov, USSR	1:14:12.26
1980 Anatoly Alabyev, USSR	1:08:16.31
1984 Peter Angerer, W. Germany	1:11:52.7

40-Kilometer Relay

		Time
1968	USSR, Norway, Sweden	2:13:02
1972	USSR, Finland, E. Germany	1:51:44
1976	USSR, Finland, E. Germany	1:57:55.64
1980	USSR, E. Germany, W. Germany (30 km.)	1:34:03.27
1984	USSR, Norway, W. Germany	1:38:51.70

Bobsledding
4-Man Bob

	(Driver in parentheses)	Time
1924	Switzerland (Edward Scherrer)	5:45.54
1928	United States (William Fiske) (5-man)	3:20.50
1932	United States (William Fiske)	7:53.68
1936	Switzerland (Pierre Musy)	5:19.85
1948	United States (Edward Rimkus)	5:20.10
1952	Germany (Andreas Ostler)	5:07.84
1956	Switzerland (Franz Kapus)	5:10.44
1964	Canada (Victor Emery)	4:14.46
1968	Italy (Eugenio Monti) (2 races)	2:17.39
1972	Switzerland (Jean Wicki)	4:43.07
1976	E. Germany (Meinhard Nehmer)	3:40.43
1980	E. Germany (Mainhard Nehmer)	3:59.92
1984	E. Germany (Wolfgang Hoppe)	3:20.22

2-Man Bob

		Time
1932	United States (Hubert Stevens)	8:14.74
1936	United States (Ivan Brown)	5:29.29
1948	Switzerland (F. Endrich)	5:29.20
1952	Germany (Andreas Ostler)	5:24.54
1956	Italy (Dalla Costa)	5:30.14
1964	Great Britain (Antony Nash)	4:21.90
1968	Italy (Eugenio Monti)	4:41.54
1972	W. Germany (Wolfgang Zimmerer)	4:47.07
1976	E. Germany (Meinhard Nehmer)	3:40.43
1980	Switzerland (Erich Schaerer)	4:09.36
1984	E.Germany (Wolfgang Hoppe)	3:25.56

Figure Skating
Men's Singles

1908	Ulrich Sachow, Sweden
1920	Gillis Grafstrom, Sweden
1924	Gillis Grafstrom, Sweden
1928	Gillis Grafstrom, Sweden
1932	Karl Schaefer, Austria
1936	Karl Schaefer, Austria
1948	Richard Button, U.S.
1952	Richard Button, U.S.
1956	Hayes Alan Jenkins, U.S.
1960	David W. Jenkins, U.S.
1964	Manfred Schnelldorfer, Germany
1968	Wolfgang Schwartz, Austria
1972	Ondrej Nepela, Czechoslovakia
1976	John Curry, Great Britain
1980	Robin Cousins, Great Britain
1984	Scott Hamilton, U.S.

Women's Singles

1908	Madge Syers, Great Britain
1920	Magda Julin-Mauroy, Sweden
1924	Heima von Szabo-Planck, Austria
1928	Sonja Henie, Norway
1932	Sonja Henie, Norway
1936	Sonja Henie, Norway
1948	Barbara Ann Scott, Canada
1952	Jeanette Altwegg, Great Britain
1956	Tenley Albright, U.S.
1960	Carol Heiss, U.S.
1964	Sjoukje Dijkstra, Netherlands
1968	Peggy Fleming, U.S.
1972	Beatrix Schuba, Austria
1976	Dorothy Hamill, U.S.
1980	Anett Poetzsch, E. Germany
1984	Katarina Witt, E. Germany

Pairs

1908	Anna Hubler & Heinrich Burger, Germany
1920	Ludovika & Walter Jakobsson, Finland
1924	Helene Engelman & Alfred Berger, Austria
1928	Andree Joly & Pierre Brunet, France
1932	Andree Joly & Pierre Brunet, France
1936	Maxie Herber & Ernest Baier, Germany
1948	Micheline Lannoy & Pierre Baugniet, Belgium
1952	Ria and Paul Falk, Germany
1956	Elisabeth Schwarz & Kurt Oppelt, Austria
1960	Barbara Wagner & Robert Paul, Canada
1964	Ludmila Beloussova & Oleg Protopopov, USSR
1968	Ludmila Beloussova & Oleg Protopopov, USSR
1972	Irina Rodnina & Alexei Ulanov, USSR
1976	Irina Rodnina & Aleksandr Zaitzev, USSR
1980	Irina Rodnina & Aleksandr Zaitzev, USSR
1984	Elena Valova & Oleg Vassiliev, USSR

Ice Dancing

1976	Ludmila Pakhomova & Aleksandr Gorschkov, USSR
1980	Natalya Linichuk & Gennadi Karponosov, USSR
1984	Jayne Torvill & Christopher Dean, Great Britain

Ice Hockey

1920	Canada, U.S., Czechoslovakia
1924	Canada, U.S., Great Britain
1928	Canada, Sweden, Switzerland
1932	Canada, U.S., Germany
1936	Great Britain, Canada, U.S.
1948	Canada, Czechoslovakia, Switzerland
1952	Canada, U.S., Sweden
1956	USSR, U.S., Canada
1960	U.S., Canada, USSR
1964	USSR, Sweden, Czechoslovakia
1968	USSR, Czechoslovakia, Canada
1972	USSR, U.S., Czechoslovakia,
1976	USSR, Czechoslovakia, W. Germany
1980	U.S., USSR, Sweden
1984	USSR, Czechoslovakia, Sweden

Luge
Men's Singles

		Time
1964	Thomas Keohler, Germany	3:26.77
1968	Manfred Schmid, Austria	2:52.48
1972	Wolfgang Scheidel, E. Germany	3:27.58
1976	Detlef Guenther, E. Germany	3:27.688
1980	Bernhard Glass, E. Germany	2:54.796
1984	Paul Hildgartner, Italy	3:04.258

Men's Doubles

		Time
1964	Austria	1:41.62
1968	E. Germany	1:35.85
1972	Italy, E. Germany (tie)	1:28.35
1976	E. Germany	1:25.604
1980	E. Germany	1:19.331
1984	W. Germany	1:23.620

Women's Singles

		Time
1964	Ortun Enderlein, Germany	3:24.67
1968	Erica Lechner, Italy	2:28.66
1972	Anna M. Muller, E. Germany	2:59.18
1976	Margit Schumann, E. Germany	2:50.621
1980	Vera Zozulya, USSR	2:36.537
1984	Steffi Martin, E. Germany	2:46.570

Alpine Skiing
Men's Downhill

		Time
1948	Henri Oreiller, France	2:55.0
1952	Zeno Colo, Italy	2:30.8
1956	Anton Sailer, Austria	2:52.2
1960	Jean Vuarnet, France	2:06.0
1964	Egon Zimmermann, Austria	2:18.16
1968	Jean Claude Killy, France	1:59.85
1972	Bernhard Russi, Switzerland	1:51.43
1976	Franz Klammer, Austria	1:45.73
1980	Leonhard Stock, Austria	1:45.50
1984	Bill Johnson, U.S.	1:45:59

Men's Giant Slalom

		Time
1952	Stein Eriksen, Norway	2:25.0
1956	Anton Sailer, Austria	3:00.1
1960	Roger Staub, Switzerland	1:48.3
1964	Francois Bonlieu, France	1:46.71

1968	Jean Claude Killy, France	3:29.28
1972	Gustavo Thoeni, Italy	3:09.62
1976	Heini Hemmi, Switzerland	3:26.97
1980	Ingemar Stenmark, Sweden	2:40.74
1984	Max Julen, Switzerland	2:41.18

Men's Slalom — Time

1948	Edi Reinalter, Switzerland	2:10.3
1952	Othmar Schneider, Austria	2:00.0
1956	Anton Sailer, Austria	194.7 pts.
1960	Ernst Hinterseer, Austria	2:08.9
1964	Josef Stiegler, Austria	2:11.13
1968	Jean Claude Killy, France	1:39.73
1972	Francesco Fernandez Ochoa, Spain	1:49.27
1976	Piero Gros, Italy	2:03.29
1980	Ingemar Stenmark, Sweden	1:44.26
1984	Phil Mahre, U.S.	1:39.41

Women's Downhill — Time

1948	Heidi Schlunegger, Switzerland	2:28.3
1952	Trude Jochum-Beiser, Austria	1:47.1
1956	Madeline Berthod, Switzerland	1:40.7
1960	Heidi Biebl, Germany	1:37.6
1964	Christi Haas, Austria	1:55.39
1968	Olga Pall, Austria	1:40.87
1972	Marie Therese Nadig, Switzerland	1:36.68
1976	Rosi Mittermaier, W. Germany	1:46.16
1980	Annemarie Proell Moser, Austria	1:37.52
1984	Michela Figini, Switzerland	1:13.36

Women's Giant Slalom — Time

1952	Andrea Mead Lawrence, U.S.	2:06.8
1956	Ossi Reichert, Germany	1:56.5
1960	Yvonne Ruegg, Switzerland	1:39.9
1964	Marielle Goitschel, France	1:52.24
1968	Nancy Greene, Canada	1:51.97
1972	Marie Therese Nadig, Switzerland	1:29.90
1976	Kathy Kreiner, Canada	1:29.13
1980	Hanni Wenzel, Liechtenstein (2 runs)	2:41.66
1984	Debbie Armstrong, U.S.	2:20.98

Women's Slalom — Time

1948	Gretchen Fraser, U.S.	1:57.2
1952	Andrea Mead Lawrence, U.S.	2:10.6
1956	Renee Colliard, Switzerland	112.3 pts.
1960	Anne Heggtveigt, Canada	1:49.6
1964	Christine Goitschel, France	1:29.86
1968	Marielle Goitschel, France	1:25.86
1972	Barbara Cochran, U.S.	1:31.24
1976	Rosi Mittermaier, W. Germany	1:30.54
1980	Hanni Wenzel, Liechtenstein	1:25.09
1984	Paoletta Magoni, Italy	1:36.47

Nordic Skiing

Men's Cross-Country Events
15 kilometers (9.3 miles) — Time

1924	Thorleif Haug, Norway	1:14:31
1928	Johan Grottumsbraaten, Norway	1:37:01
1932	Sven Utterstrom, Sweden	1:23:07
1936	Erik-August Larsson, Sweden	1:14:38
1948	Martin Lundstrom, Sweden	1:13:50
1952	Hallgeir Brenden, Norway	1:01:34
1956	Hallgeir Brenden, Norway	49:39.0
1960	Haakon Brusveen, Norway	51:55.0
1964	Eero Maentyranta, Finland	50:54.1
1968	Harald Groenningen, Norway	47:54.2
1972	Sven-Ake Lundback, Sweden	45:28.24
1976	Nikolai Bajukov, USSR	43:58.47
1980	Thomas Wassberg, Sweden	41:57.63
1984	Gunde Svan, Sweden	41:25.6
	(Note: approx. 18-km. course 1924-1952)	

30 kilometers (18.6 miles) — Time

1956	Veikko Hakulinen, Finland	1:44:06.0
1960	Sixten Jernberg, Sweden	1:51:03.9
1964	Eero Maentyranta, Finland	1:30:50.7
1968	Franco Nones, Italy	1:35:39.2
1972	Vyacheslav Vedenin, USSR	1:36:31.15
1976	Sergei Saveliev, USSR	1:30:29.38
1980	Nikolai Zimyatov, USSR	1:27:02.80
1984	Nikolai Zimyatov, USSR	1:28:56.3

50 kilometers (31.2 miles) — Time

1924	Thorleif Haug, Norway	3:44:32.0
1928	Per Erik Hedlund, Sweden	4:52:03.0

1932	Veli Saarinen, Finland	4:28:00.0
1936	Elis Viklund, Sweden	3:30:11.0
1948	Nils Karlsson, Sweden	3:47:48.0
1952	Veikko Hakulinen, Finland	3:33:33.0
1956	Sixten Jernberg, Sweden	2:50:27.0
1960	Kalevi Hamalainen, Finland	2:59:06.3
1964	Sixten Jernberg, Sweden	2:43:52.6
1968	Ole Ellefsaeter, Norway	2:28:45.8
1972	Paal Tyldum, Norway	2:43:14.75
1976	Ivar Formo, Norway	2:37:30.05
1980	Nikolai Zimyatov, USSR	2:27:24.60
1984	Thomas Wassberg, Sweden	2:15:55.8

40-km. Cross-Country Relay — Time

1936	Finland, Norway, Sweden	2:41:33.0
1948	Sweden, Finland, Norway	2:32:08.0
1952	Finland, Norway, Sweden	2:20:16.0
1956	USSR, Finland, Sweden	2:15:30.0
1960	Finland, Norway, USSR	2:18:45.6
1964	Sweden, Finland, USSR	2:18:34.6
1968	Norway, Sweden, Finland	2:08:33.5
1972	USSR, Norway, Switzerland	2:04:47.94
1976	Finland, Norway, USSR	2:07:59.72
1980	USSR, Norway, Finland	1:57:03.46
1984	Sweden, USSR, Finland	1:55:06.30

Combined Cross-Country & Jumping — Points

1924	Thorleif Haug, Norway	453.800
1928	Johan Grottumsbraaten, Norway	427.800
1932	Johan Grottumsbraaten, Norway	446.200
1936	Oddbjorn Hagen, Norway	430.300
1948	Heikki Hasu, Finland	448.800
1952	Simon Slattvik, Norway	451.621
1956	Sverre Stenersen, Norway	455.000
1960	Georg Thoma, Germany	457.952
1964	Tormod Knutsen, Norway	469.280
1968	Franz Keller, W. Germany	449.040
1972	Ulrich Wehling, E. Germany	413.340
1976	Ulrich Wehling, E. Germany	423.390
1980	Ulrich Wehling, E. Germany	432.200
1984	Tom Sandberg, Norway	422.595

Ski Jumping (90 meters) — Points

1924	Jacob Thams, Norway	227.5
1928	Alfred Andersen, Norway	230.5
1932	Birger Ruud, Norway	228.0
1936	Birger Ruud, Norway	232.0
1948	Petter Hugsted, Norway	228.1
1952	Anders Bergmann, Norway	226.0
1956	Antti Hyvarinen, Finland	227.0
1960	Helmut Recknagel, Germany	227.2
1964	Toralf Engan, Norway	230.7
1968	Vladimir Beloussov, USSR	231.3
1972	Wojiech Fortuna, Poland	219.9
1976	Karl Schnabl, Austria	234.8
1980	Jouko Tormanen, Finland	231.5
1984	Matti Nykaenen, Finland	231.2

Ski Jumping (70 meters) — Points

1964	Veikko Kankkonen, Finland	229.9
1968	Jiri Raska, Czechoslovakia	216.5
1972	Yukio Kasaya, Japan	244.2
1976	Hans Aschenbach, E. Germany	252.0
1980	Anton Innauer, Austria	266.3
1984	Jens Weissflog, E. Germany	215.2

Women's Events
5 kilometers (approx. 3.1 miles) — Time

1964	Claudia Boyarskikh, USSR	17:50.5
1968	Toini Gustafsson, Sweden	16:45.2
1972	Galina Koulacova, USSR	17:00.50
1976	Helena Takalo, Finland	15:48.69
1980	Raisa Smetanina, USSR	15:06.92
1984	Marja-Liisa Haemaelainen, Finland	17:04.0

10 kilometers — Time

1952	Lydia Wideman, Finland	41:40.0
1956	Lyubov Kosyreva, USSR	38:11.0
1960	Maria Gusakova, USSR	39:46.6
1964	Claudia Boyarskikh, USSR	40:24.3
1968	Toini Gustafsson, Sweden	36:46.5
1972	Galina Koulacova, USSR	34:17.82
1976	Raisa Smetanina, USSR	30:13.41
1980	Barbara Petzold, E. Germany	30:31.54
1984	Marja-Liisa Haemaelainen, Finland	31:44.2

20 kilometers	Time
1984 Marja-Liisa Haemaelainen, Finland	1:01:45.0

20-km. Cross-Country Relay	Time
1956 Finland, USSR, Sweden (15 km.)	1:09:01.0
1960 Sweden, USSR, Finland (15 km.)	1:04:21.4
1964 USSR, Sweden, Finland (15 km.)	59:20.2
1968 Norway, Sweden, USSR (15 km.)	57:30.0
1972 USSR, Finland, Norway (15 km.)	48:46.1
1976 USSR, Finland, E. Germany	1:07:49.75
1980 E. Germany, USSR, Norway	1:02:11.10
1984 Norway, Czechoslovakia, Finland	1:06:49.70

Speed Skating

Men's 500 meters

	Time
1924 Charles Jewtraw, U.S.	0:44.0
1928 Thunberg, Finland & Evensen, Norway (tie)	0:43.4
1932 John A. Shea, U.S.	0:43.4
1936 Ivar Ballangrud, Norway.	0:43.4
1948 Finn Helgesen, Norway	0:43.1
1952 Kenneth Henry, U.S.	0:43.2
1956 Evgeniy Grishin, USSR	0:40.2
1960 Evgeniy Grishin, USSR	0:40.2
1964 Terry McDermott, U.S.	0:40.1
1968 Erhard Keller, W. Germany	0:40.3
1972 Erhard Keller, W. Germany	0:39.44
1976 Evgeny Kulikov, USSR	0:39.17
1980 Eric Heiden, U.S.	0:38.03
1984 Sergei Fokichev, USSR	0:38.19

Men's 1,000 meters

	Time
1976 Peter Mueller, U.S.	1:19.32
1980 Eric Heiden, U.S.	1:15.18
1984 Gaetan Boucher, Canada	1:15.80

Men's 1,500 meters

	Time
1924 Clas Thunberg, Finland	2:20.8
1928 Clas Thunberg, Finland	2:21.1
1932 John A. Shea, U.S.	2:57.2
1936 Charles Mathiesen, Norway	2:19.2
1948 Sverre Farstad, Norway.	2:17.6
1952 Hjalmar Andersen, Norway	2:20.4
1956 Grishin, & Mikhailov, both USSR (tie) . .	2:08.6
1960 Aas, Norway & Grishin, USSR (tie)	2:10.4
1964 Ants Anston, USSR	2:10.3
1968 Cornetis Verkerk, Netherlands	2:03.4
1972 Ard Schenk, Netherlands	2:02.96
1976 Jan Egil Storholt, Norway	1:59.38
1980 Eric Heiden, U.S.	1:55.44
1984 Gaetan Boucher, Canada	1:58.36

Men's 5,000 meters

	Time
1924 Clas Thunberg, Finland	8:39.0
1928 Ivar Ballangrud, Norway.	8:50.5
1932 Irving Jaffee, U.S.	9:40.8

1936 Ivar Ballangrud, Norway.	8:19.6
1948 Reidar Liaklev, Norway	8:29.4
1952 Hjalmar Andersen, Norway	8:10.6
1956 Boris Shilkov, USSR	7:48.7
1960 Viktor Kosichkin, USSR	7:51.3
1964 Knut Johannesen, Norway	7:38.4
1968 F. Anton Maier, Norway	7:22.4
1972 Ard Schenk, Netherlands	7:23.61
1976 Sten Stensen, Norway.	7:24.48
1980 Eric Heiden, U.S.	7:02.29
1984 Sven Tomas Gustafson, Sweden.	7:12:28

Men's 10,000 meters

	Time
1924 Julius Skutnabb, Finland.	18:04.8
1928 Event not held, thawing of ice	
1932 Irving Jaffee, U.S.	19:13.6
1936 Ivar Ballangrud, Norway.	17:24.3
1948 Ake Seyffarth, Sweden	17:26.3
1952 Hjalmar Andersen, Norway	16:45.8
1956 Sigvard Ericsson, Sweden	16:35.9
1960 Knut Johannesen, Norway	15:46.6
1964 Jonny Nilsson, Sweden	15:50.1
1968 Jonny Hoeglin, Sweden	15:23.6
1972 Ard Schenk, Netherlands	15:01.3
1976 Piet Kleine, Netherlands	14:50.59
1980 Eric Heiden, U.S.	14:28.13
1984 Igor Malkov, USSR	14:39.90

Women's 500 meters

	Time
1960 Helga Haase, Germany	0:45.9
1964 Lydia Skoblikova, USSR	0:45.0
1968 Ludmila Titova, USSR	0:46.1
1972 Anne Henning, U.S.	0:43.44
1976 Sheila Young, U.S.	0:42.76
1980 Karin Enke, E. Germany	0:41.78
1984 Christa Rothenburger, E. Germany	0:41.02

Women's 1,000 meters

	Time
1960 Klara Guseva, USSR	1:34.1
1964 Lydia Skoblikova, USSR	1:33.2
1968 Caroline Geijssen, Netherlands.	1:32.6
1972 Monika Pflug, W. Germany	1:31.40
1976 Tatiana Averina, USSR	1:28.43
1980 Natalya Petruseva, USSR.	1:24.10
1984 Karin Enke, E. Germany.	1:21.61

Women's 1,500 meters

	Time
1960 Lydia Skoblikova, USSR	2:52.2
1964 Lydia Skoblikova, USSR	2:22.6
1968 Kaija Mustonen, Finland	2:22.4
1972 Dianne Holum, U.S.	2:20.85
1976 Galina Stepanskaya, USSR.	2:16.58
1980 Anne Borckink, Netherlands	2:10.95
1984 Karin Enke, E. Germany.	2:03.42

Women's 3,000 meters

	Time
1960 Lydia Skoblikova, USSR	5:14.3
1964 Lydia Skoblikova, USSR	5:14.9
1968 Johanna Schut, Netherlands	4:56.2
1972 Stien Baas-Kaiser, Netherlands	4:52.14
1976 Tatiana Averina, USSR	4:45.19
1980 Bjoerg Eva Jensen, Norway	4:32.13
1984 Andrea Schoene, E. Germany	4:24.79

Winter Olympic Medal Winners in 1984

Sarajevo, Yugoslavia, Feb. 7-18, 1984

	Gold	Silver	Bronze	Total
Austria	0	0	1	1
Canada	2	1	1	4
Czechoslovakia	0	2	4	6
Finland	4	3	6	13
France	0	1	2	3
Germany, East	9	9	6	24
Germany, West	2	1	1	4
Great Britain	1	0	0	1
Italy	2	0	0	2

	Gold	Silver	Bronze	Total
Japan	0	1	0	1
Liechtenstein	0	0	2	2
Norway	3	2	4	9
Sweden	4	2	2	8
Switzerland	2	2	1	5
USSR	6	10	9	25
United States	4	4	0	8
Yugoslavia	0	1	0	1

National Hockey League, 1984-85

Final Standings

Wales Conference

Adams Division

	W	L	T	Pts	GA	GF
Montreal	41	27	12	94	309	262
Quebec	41	30	9	91	323	275
Buffalo	38	28	14	90	290	237
Boston	36	34	10	82	303	287
Hartford	30	41	9	69	268	318

Patrick Division

	W	L	T	Pts	GA	GF
Philadelphia	53	20	7	113	348	241
Washington	46	25	9	101	322	240
N.Y. Islanders	40	34	6	86	345	312
N.Y. Rangers	26	44	10	62	295	345
New Jersey	22	48	10	54	264	346
Pittsburgh	24	51	5	53	276	385

Campbell Conference

Norris Division

	W	L	T	Pts	GA	GF
St. Louis	37	31	12	86	299	288
Chicago	38	35	7	83	309	299
Detroit	27	41	12	66	313	357
Minnesota	25	43	12	62	268	321
Toronto	20	52	8	48	253	358

Smythe Division

	W	L	T	Pts	GA	GF
Edmonton	49	20	11	109	401	298
Winnipeg	43	27	10	96	358	332
Calgary	41	27	12	94	363	302
Los Angeles	34	32	14	82	339	326
Vancouver	25	46	9	59	284	401

Stanley Cup Playoff Results

Wales Conference

Philadelphia defeated N.Y. Rangers 3 games to 0.
N.Y. Islanders defeated Washington 3 games to 2.
Montreal defeated Boston 3 games to 2.
Quebec defeated Buffalo 3 games to 2.
Philadelphia defeated N.Y. Islanders 4 games to 1.
Quebec defeated Montreal 4 games to 3.
Philadelphia defeated Quebec 4 games to 2.

Campbell Conference

Minnesota defeated St. Louis 3 games to 0.
Chicago defeated Detroit 3 games to 0.
Winnipeg defeated Calgary 3 games to 1.
Edmonton defeated Los Angeles 3 games to 0.
Edmonton defeated Winnipeg 4 games to 0.
Chicago defeated Minnesota 4 games to 2.
Edmonton defeated Chicago 4 games to 2.

Finals

Edmonton defeated Philadelphia 4 games to 1.

Stanley Cup Champions Since 1928

Year	Champion	Coach	Final opponent	Year	Champion	Coach	Final opponent
1928	New York	Lester Patrick	Montreal	1957	Montreal	Toe Blake	Boston
1929	Boston	Cy Denneny	N.Y. Rangers	1958	Montreal	Toe Blake	Boston
1930	Montreal	Cecil Hart	Boston	1959	Montreal	Toe Blake	Toronto
1931	Montreal	Cecil Hart	Chicago	1960	Montreal	Toe Blake	Toronto
1932	Toronto	Dick Irvin	N.Y. Rangers	1961	Chicago	Rudy Pilous	Detroit
1933	New York	Lester Patrick	Toronto	1962	Toronto	Punch Imlach	Chicago
1934	Chicago	Tommy Gorman	Detroit	1963	Toronto	Punch Imlach	Detroit
1935	Montreal Maroons	Tommy Gorman	Toronto	1964	Toronto	Punch Imlach	Detroit
1936	Detroit	Jack Adams	Toronto	1965	Montreal	Toe Blake	Chicago
1937	Detroit	Jack Adams	N.Y. Rangers	1966	Montreal	Toe Blake	Detroit
1938	Chicago	Bill Stewart	Toronto	1967	Toronto	Punch Imlach	Montreal
1939	Boston	Art Ross	Toronto	1968	Montreal	Toe Blake	St. Louis
1940	N.Y. Rangers	Frank Boucher	Toronto	1969	Montreal	Claude Ruel	St. Louis
1941	Boston	Cooney Weiland	Detroit	1970	Boston	Harry Sinden	St. Louis
1942	Toronto	Hap Day	Detroit	1971	Montreal	Al MacNeil	Chicago
1943	Detroit	Jack Adams	Boston	1972	Boston	Tom Johnson	N.Y. Rangers
1944	Montreal	Dick Irvin	Chicago	1973	Montreal	Scotty Bowman	Chicago
1945	Toronto	Hap Day	Detroit	1974	Philadelphia	Fred Shero	Boston
1946	Montreal	Dick Irvin	Boston	1975	Philadelphia	Fred Shero	Buffalo
1947	Toronto	Hap Day	Montreal	1976	Montreal	Scotty Bowman	Philadelphia
1948	Toronto	Hap Day	Detroit	1977	Montreal	Scotty Bowman	Boston
1949	Toronto	Hap Day	Detroit	1978	Montreal	Scotty Bowman	Boston
1950	Detroit	Tommy Ivan	N.Y. Rangers	1979	Montreal	Scotty Bowman	N.Y. Rangers
1951	Toronto	Joe Primeau	Montreal	1980	N.Y. Islanders	Al Arbour	Philadelphia
1952	Detroit	Tommy Ivan	Montreal	1981	N.Y. Islanders	Al Arbour	Minnesota
1953	Montreal	Dick Irvin	Boston	1982	N.Y. Islanders	Al Arbour	Vancouver
1954	Detroit	Tommy Ivan	Montreal	1983	N.Y. Islanders	Al Arbour	Edmonton
1955	Detroit	Jimmy Skinner	Montreal	1984	Edmonton	Glen Sather	N.Y. Islanders
1956	Montreal	Toe Blake	Detroit	1985	Edmonton	Glen Sather	Philadelphia

Conn Smythe Trophy (MVP in Playoffs)

1965 Jean Beliveau, Montreal	1972 Bobby Orr, Boston	1979 Bob Gainey, Montreal
1966 Roger Crozier, Detroit	1973 Yvan Cournoyer, Montreal	1980 Bryan Trottier, N.Y. Islanders
1967 Dave Keon, Toronto	1974 Bernie Parent, Philadelphia	1981 Butch Goring, N.Y. Islanders
1968 Glenn Hall, St. Louis	1975 Bernie Parent, Philadelphia	1982 Mike Bossy, N.Y. Islanders
1969 Serge Savard, Montreal	1976 Reg Leach, Philadelphia	1983 Billy Smith, N.Y. Islanders
1970 Bobby Orr, Boston	1977 Guy Lafleur, Montreal	1984 Mark Messier, Edmonton
1971 Ken Dryden, Montreal	1978 Larry Robinson, Montreal	1985 Wayne Gretzky, Edmonton

Individual Leaders

Points

Gretzky, Edmonton, 208; Kurri, Edmonton, 135; Hawerchuk, Winnipeg, 130; Dionne, Los Angeles, 126; Coffey, Edmonton, 121.

Goals

Gretzky, Edmonton, 73; Kurri, Edmonton, 71; Bossy, N.Y. Islanders, 58; Goulet, Quebec, 55; Ogrodnick, Detroit, 55.

Assists

Gretzky, Edmonton, 135; Coffey, Edmonton, 84; Dionne, Los Angeles, 80; Hawerchuk, Winnipeg, 77; Federko, St. Louis, 73.

Power-play goals

Kerr, Philadelphia, 21; Gartner, Washington, 17; Goulet, Quebec, 17; Hawerchuk, Winnipeg, 17; Dionne, Los Angeles, 16; Stevens, Washington, 16.

Shorthanded goals

Gretzky, Edmonton, 11; Propp, Philadelphia 7; Derlago, Toronto, 5; Kasper, Boston, 5; Messier, Edmonton, 5; Trottier, N.Y. Islanders, 5.

Game-winning goals

Kurri, Edmonton, 13; Gartner, Washington, 11; Kerr, Philadelphia, 9; P. Stastny, Quebec, 9.

Shooting percentage
(minimum 80 shots)

Young, Pittsburgh, 30.8; Kurri, Edmonton, 27.2; Simmer, Boston, 25.4; Taylor, Los Angeles, 23.8; Naslund, Montreal, 23.5..

Goaltenders
Goals-against average
(minimum 25 games)

Barrasso, Buffalo, 2.66; Riggin, Washington, 2.98; Lindbergh, Philadelphia, 3.02; Penney, Montreal, 3.08; Sauve, Buffalo, 3.22; Skorodenski, Chicago, 3.22.

Wins

Lindbergh, Philadelphia, 40; Hayward, Winnipeg, 33; Lemelin, Calgary, 30; Riggin, Washington, 28; Bannerman, Chicago, 27.

Save percentage

Skorodenski, Chicago, .903; Lindbergh, Philadelphia, .899; Moog, Edmonton, .894; Lemelin, Calgary, .889; Liut, Hartford, .887.

Shutouts

Barrasso, Buffalo, 5; Skorodenski, Chicago, Weeks, Hartford, Liut, Hartford, Janecyk, Los Angeles, Hrudey, N.Y. Islanders, Lindbergh, Philadelphia, Riggin, Washington, 2.

Individual Scoring
(40 or more games played)

Boston Bruins

	GP	G	A	Pts	+/−	PIM
Ray Bourque	73	20	66	86	29	53
Rick Middleton	80	30	46	76	1	6
Ken Linseman	74	25	49	74	20	126
Tom Fergus	79	30	43	73	13	75
Keith Crowder	79	32	38	70	30	152
Charlie Simmer	68	34	30	64	8	39
Mike O'Connell	78	15	40	55	4	64
Butch Goring	68	15	26	41	20−	8
Steve Kasper	77	16	24	40	11−	33
Louis Sleigher	76	13	21	34	3−	45
Terry O'Reilly	63	13	17	30	16−	168
Geoff Courtnall	64	12	16	28	3−	82
Morris Lukowich	69	10	17	27	8−	52
Mats Thelin	73	5	13	18	8	78
John Blum	75	3	13	16	1−	263
Mike Milbury	78	3	13	16	7−	152
Frank Simonetti	43	1	5	6	1−	26
Brian Curran	56	0	1	1	7−	158

Buffalo Sabres

	GP	G	A	Pts	+/−	PIM
Gilbert Perreault	78	30	53	83	5	42
Phil Housley	73	16	53	69	13	28
Dave Andreychuk	64	31	30	61	2−	54
Mike Foligno	77	27	29	56	14	154
John Tucker	64	22	27	49	6	21
Gilles Hamel	80	18	30	48	1−	36
Paul Cyr	71	22	24	46	5−	63
Sean McKenna	65	20	16	36	6−	41
Brent Peterson	74	12	22	34	16	47
Craig Ramsay	79	12	21	33	17	16
Ric Seiling	73	16	15	31	28	86
Mike Ramsey	79	8	22	30	29	102
Mal Davis	47	17	9	26	2−	26
Dave Maloney	68	3	22	25	20	51
Hannu Virta	51	1	23	24	1−	16
Bill Hajt	57	5	13	18	30	14
Larry Playfair	72	3	14	17	2−	157
Dave Fenyves	60	1	8	9	1	27

Calgary Flames

	GP	G	A	Pts	+/−	PIM
Kent Nilsson	77	37	62	99	4−	14
Hakan Loob	78	37	35	72	14	14
Carey Wilson	74	24	48	72	20	27
Paul Reinhart	75	23	46	69	2	18
Eddy Beers	74	28	40	68	7	94
Al MacInnis	67	14	52	66	6	75
Dan Quinn	74	20	38	58	10	22
Richard Kromm	73	20	32	52	18	32
Jim Peplinski	80	16	29	45	12	111
Colin Patterson	57	22	21	43	17	5
Mike Eaves	56	14	29	43	14	10
Jamie Macoun	70	9	30	39	45	67
Lanny McDonald	43	19	18	37	4−	36
Steve Bozek	54	13	22	35	12	6
Steve Tambellini	47	19	10	29	8	4
Steve Konroyd	64	3	23	26	10	73
Tim Hunter	71	11	11	22	13	259
Paul Baxter	70	5	14	19	38	126
Kari Eloranta	65	2	11	13	0	39
Charles Bourgeois	47	2	10	12	13	134

Chicago Black Hawks

	GP	G	A	Pts	+/−	PIM
Denis Savard	79	38	67	105	16	56
Steve Larmer	80	46	40	86	17	16
Doug Wilson	78	22	54	76	24	44
Troy Murray	80	26	40	66	17	82
Bill Gardner	74	17	34	51	7	12
Curt Fraser	73	25	25	50	3	109
Ed Olczyk	70	20	30	50	12	67
Tom Lysiak	74	16	30	46	15−	13
Bob Murray	80	5	38	43	14	56
Darryl Sutter	49	20	18	38	8	12
Behn Wilson	76	10	23	33	5	185
Steve Ludzik	79	11	20	31	5	86
Al Secord	51	15	11	26	0	183
Ken Yaremchuk	63	10	16	26	8−	16
Keith Brown	56	1	22	23	2	55
Rick Paterson	79	7	12	19	6	25
Jack O'Callahan	66	6	8	14	4	105
Jerome Dupont	55	3	10	13	7	100
Marc Bergevin	60	0	6	6	9	54

Detroit Red Wings

	GP	G	A	Pts	+/-	PIM
John Ogrodnick	79	55	50	105	2	30
Ron Duguay	80	38	51	89	16-	51
Steve Yzerman	80	30	59	89	17-	58
Reed Larson	77	17	45	62	8	139
Kelly Kisio	75	20	41	61	4	56
Danny Gare	71	27	29	56	6	163
Ivan Boldirev	75	19	30	49	26-	16
Brad Park	67	13	30	43	14-	55
Dwight Foster	50	16	16	32	12	56
Bob Manno	74	10	22	32	0	32
Randy Ladouceur	80	3	27	30	2	108
Darryl Sittler	61	11	16	27	11-	37
Lane Lambert	69	14	11	25	3-	104
John Barrett	71	6	19	25	14-	117
Greg Smith	73	2	18	20	26-	117
Dave Silk	41	10	5	15	3-	32
Larry Trader	40	3	7	10	11	39
Frank Cernik	49	5	4	9	7-	13
Colin Campbell	57	1	5	6	14-	124

Edmonton Oilers

	GP	G	A	Pts	+/-	PIM
Wayne Gretzky	80	73	135	208	99	52
Jari Kurri	73	71	64	135	77	30
Paul Coffey	80	37	84	121	55	97
Mike Krushelnyski	80	43	45	88	56	60
Glenn Anderson	80	42	39	81	24	69
Mark Napier	72	19	44	63	6	21
Mark Messier	55	23	31	54	9	57
Charlie Huddy	80	7	44	51	50	46
Dave Hunter	80	17	19	36	0	122
Willy Lindstrom	80	12	20	32	5	18
Dave Lumley	60	9	23	32	18-	111
Kevin Lowe	80	4	22	26	11	104
Pat Hughes	73	12	13	25	7-	85
Kevin McClelland	62	8	15	23	11-	212
Randy Gregg	57	3	20	23	28	32
Don Jackson	78	3	17	20	28	141
Dave Semenko	69	6	12	18	5	167
Lee Fogolin	79	4	14	18	17	126
Bill Carroll	65	8	9	17	0	22

Hartford Whalers

	GP	G	A	Pts	+/-	PIM
Ron Francis	80	24	57	81	23-	66
Sylvain Turgeon	64	31	31	62	10-	67
Ray Neufeld	76	27	35	62	29-	129
Greg Malone	76	22	39	61	16-	67
Risto Siltanen	76	12	33	45	25-	30
Kevin Dineen	57	25	16	41	7-	120
Torrie Robertson	74	11	30	41	14-	337
Bobby Crawford	45	14	14	28	3-	8
Ray Ferraro	44	11	17	28	2-	40
Joel Quenneville	79	6	16	22	16-	96
Dave Tippett	80	7	12	19	23-	12
Pat Boutette	47	7	11	18	12-	75
Mike Zuke	67	4	12	16	4-	12
Sylvain Cote	67	3	9	12	31-	17
Mike Crombeen	46	4	7	11	0	16
Mark Fusco	63	3	8	11	14-	40
Ulf Samuelsson	41	2	6	8	8-	83

Los Angeles Kings

	GP	G	A	Pts	+/-	PIM
Marcel Dionne	80	46	80	126	11	46
Bernie Nicholls	80	46	54	100	4-	76
Dave Taylor	79	41	51	92	13	132
Brian MacLellan	80	31	54	85	2	53
Jim Fox	79	30	53	83	4	10
Mark Hardy	78	14	39	53	20-	97
Terry Ruskowski	78	16	33	49	2	144
Steve Shutt	69	18	25	43	13-	19
Doug Smith	62	21	20	41	14-	58
Craig Redmond	79	6	33	39	8-	57
Garry Galley	78	8	30	38	4	82
Phil Sykes	79	17	15	32	18-	38
Anders Hakansson	73	12	12	24	3-	28
Brian Engblom	79	4	19	23	2-	70
Bob Miller	63	4	16	20	17-	35
John Paul Kelly	73	8	10	18	9-	55
Tiger Williams	67	7	11	18	16-	201
Rick LaPointe	73	4	13	17	10-	46
Jay Wells	77	2	9	11	5	185

Minnesota North Stars

	GP	G	A	Pts	+/-	PIM
Brian Bellows	78	26	36	62	18-	72
Dennis Maruk	71	19	41	60	2-	56
Keith Acton	78	20	38	58	3-	90
Neal Broten	80	19	37	56	18-	39
Steve Payne	76	29	22	51	14-	61
Tony McKegney	57	23	22	45	11	16
Gordie Roberts	78	6	36	42	12-	112
Tom McCarthy	44	16	21	37	3	36
Dino Ciccarelli	51	15	17	32	10-	41
Gord Shevren	69	11	19	30	1	18
Curt Giles	77	5	25	30	3	49
Willi Plett	47	14	14	28	4	157
Bo Berglund	45	10	10	20	1-	14
Ken Solheim	55	8	10	18	15-	19
Scott Bjugstad	72	11	4	15	21-	32
Randy Velischek	52	4	9	13	7	26
Brian Lawton	40	5	6	11	2-	24
Bob Rouse	63	2	9	11	14-	113
Dave Richter	55	2	8	10	3	221
Harold Snepsts	71	0	7	7	19-	232

Montreal Canadiens

	GP	G	A	Pts	+/-	PIM
Mats Naslund	80	42	37	79	19	14
Mario Tremblay	75	31	35	66	22	120
Chris Chelios	74	9	55	64	11	87
Guy Carbonneau	79	23	34	57	28	43
Pierre Mondou	67	18	39	57	15	21
Bobby Smith	65	16	40	56	9-	59
Larry Robinson	76	14	33	47	32	44
Tom Kurvers	75	10	35	45	2-	30
Mike McPhee	70	17	22	39	1	120
Ryan Walter	72	19	19	38	18-	59
Chris Nilan	77	21	16	37	3-	358
Mark Hunter	72	21	12	33	13-	123
Bob Gainey	79	19	13	32	13	40
Petr Svoboda	73	4	27	31	16	65
Ron Flockhart	54	10	17	27	7	18
Alfie Turcotte	53	8	16	24	1-	35
Lucien Deblois	51	12	11	23	9	20
Craig Ludwig	72	5	14	19	5	90
Rick Green	77	1	18	19	11-	30

New Jersey Devils

	GP	G	A	Pts	+/-	PIM
Mel Bridgman	80	22	39	61	17-	105
Aaron Broten	80	22	35	57	17-	38
Dave Pichette	71	17	40	57	20-	41
Kirk Muller	80	17	37	54	31-	69
Tim Higgins	71	19	29	48	10-	30
Paul Gagne	79	24	19	43	12-	28
Doug Sulliman	57	22	16	38	11-	4
Pat Verbeek	78	15	18	33	24-	162
John MacLean	61	13	20	33	11-	44
Bruce Driver	67	9	23	32	22-	36
Jan Ludvig	74	12	19	31	19-	53
Rick Meagher	71	11	20	31	14-	22
Uli Hiemer	53	5	24	29	15-	70
Rich Preston	75	12	15	27	24-	26
Joe Cirella	66	6	18	24	46-	143
Phil Russell	66	4	16	20	15-	110
Don Lever	67	10	8	18	30-	31
Dave Lewis	74	3	9	12	29-	78
Bob Lorimer	46	2	6	8	6	35

N.Y. Islanders

	GP	G	A	Pts	+/-	PIM
Mike Bossy	76	58	59	117	37	38
Brent Sutter	72	42	60	102	42	51
John Tonelli	80	42	58	100	50	95
Denis Potvin	77	17	51	68	36	96
Bryan Trottier	68	28	31	59	5	47
Pat LaFontaine	67	19	35	54	9	32
Patrick Flatley	78	20	31	51	8-	104
Tomas Jonsson	69	16	34	50	1-	58
Duane Sutter	78	17	24	41	12-	172
Greg Gilbert	58	13	25	38	4-	36
Paul Boutilier	78	12	23	35	0	90
Clark Gillies	54	15	17	32	0	73
Stefan Persson	54	3	19	22	8	30
Bob Bourne	44	8	12	20	8-	51
Anders Kallur	51	10	8	18	9-	26
Gord Dineen	48	1	12	13	10	89

	GP	G	A	Pts	+/−	PIM
Dave Langevin	56	0	13	13	6−	35
Gerald Diduck	65	2	8	10	2	80
Gord Lane	57	1	8	9	10	83

N.Y. Rangers

	GP	G	A	Pts	+/−	PIM
Reijo Ruotsalainen	80	28	45	73	27−	32
Mike Rogers	78	26	38	64	27−	24
Pierre Larouche	65	24	36	60	17−	8
Tomas Sandstrom	74	29	29	58	1	51
Anders Hedberg	64	20	31	51	14−	10
Ron Greschner	48	16	29	45	19−	42
Mark Pavelich	48	14	31	45	2	29
Peter Sundstrom	76	18	25	43	26−	34
James Patrick	75	8	28	36	17−	71
Steve Patrick	57	13	20	33	7−	67
Jan Erixon	66	7	22	29	11−	33
George McPhee	49	12	15	27	8−	139
Barry Beck	56	7	19	26	11−	65
Grant Ledyard	42	8	12	20	6	53
Robbie Ftorek	48	9	10	19	7−	35
Bob Brooke	72	7	9	16	18−	79
Willie Huber	49	3	11	14	20−	55
Tom Laidlaw	61	1	11	12	11−	52
Nick Fotiu	46	4	7	11	7−	54

Philadelphia Flyers

	GP	G	A	Pts	+/−	PIM
Tim Kerr	74	54	44	98	24	57
Brian Propp	76	43	53	96	46	43
Dave Poulin	73	30	44	74	42	59
Ilkka Sinisalo	70	36	37	73	31	16
Murray Craven	80	26	35	61	45	30
Peter Zezel	65	15	46	61	22	26
Mark Howe	73	18	39	57	51	31
Ron Sutter	73	16	29	45	12	94
Brad McCrimmon	66	8	35	43	51	81
Lindsay Carson	77	20	19	39	1−	123
Derrick Smith	77	17	22	39	27	31
Rick Tocchet	75	14	25	39	6	181
Thomas Eriksson	72	10	29	39	24	36
Doug Crossman	80	4	33	37	30	65
Len Hachborn	40	5	17	22	15	23
Brad Marsh	77	2	18	20	42	91
Miroslav Dvorak	47	3	14	17	11	4
Rich Sutter	56	6	10	16	1−	89
Dave Brown	57	3	6	9	3−	163
Ed Hospodar	50	3	4	7	6	130

Pittsburgh Penguins

	GP	G	A	Pts	+/−	PIM
Mario Lemieux	73	43	57	100	35−	54
Warren Young	80	40	32	72	19−	176
Doug Shedden	80	35	32	67	50−	30
Mike Bullard	68	32	31	63	42−	75
John Chabot	77	9	51	60	34−	14
Wayne Babych	65	20	34	54	8−	35
Moe Mantha	71	11	40	51	31−	54
Doug Bodger	65	5	26	31	23−	67
Andy Brickley	45	7	15	22	14−	10
Randy Hillier	45	2	19	21	12−	56
Mitch Lamoureux	62	11	8	19	8−	53
Gary Rissling	56	10	9	19	6−	209
Kevin McCarthy	64	9	10	19	20−	30
Troy Loney	46	10	8	18	11−	59
Joe McDonnell	40	2	9	11	19−	20
Rod Buskas	69	2	7	9	21−	191
Todd Charlesworth	67	1	8	9	23−	31
Roger Belanger	44	3	5	8	13−	32
Wally Weir	48	2	6	8	6−	90
Bryan Maxwell	44	0	8	8	23−	57

Quebec Nordiques

	GP	G	A	Pts	+/−	PIM
Peter Stastny	75	32	68	100	23	95
Michel Goulet	69	55	40	95	10	55
Anton Stastny	79	38	42	80	18	30
Dale Hunter	80	20	52	72	24	209
Brent Ashton	78	31	31	62	19	53
Wilf Paiement	68	23	28	51	13	165
Mario Marois	76	6	37	43	2	91

	GP	G	A	Pts	+/−	PIM
Paul Gillis	77	14	28	42	13	168
J. F. Sauve	64	13	29	42	10	21
Brad Maxwell	68	10	31	41	14	172
Bruce Bell	75	6	31	37	32	44
Alain Cote	80	13	22	35	13	31
Randy Moller	79	7	22	29	30	120
Alain Lemieux	49	15	13	28	2	12
Pat Price	68	1	26	27	18	118
Normand Rochefort	73	3	21	24	14	74
Marian Stastny	50	7	14	21	1	4
Mark Kumpel	42	8	7	15	4	26

St. Louis Blues

	GP	G	A	Pts	+/−	PIM
Bernie Federko	76	30	73	103	11−	27
Joe Mullen	79	40	52	92	4	6
Brian Sutter	77	37	38	75	11	121
Mark Johnson	66	23	34	57	26−	25
Doug Gilmour	78	21	36	57	4	49
Jorgen Pettersson	75	23	32	55	7	20
Doug Wickenheiser	68	23	20	43	9	36
Greg Paslawski	72	22	20	42	7	23
Mark Reeds	80	9	30	39	8	25
Rob Ramage	80	7	31	38	7−	178
Dave Barr	75	16	18	34	4	32
Craig Levie	61	6	23	29	1	33
Tim Bothwell	79	4	22	26	27	62
Rik Wilson	51	8	16	24	14	39
Pat Hickey	57	10	13	23	3−	32
Perry Anderson	71	9	9	18	2	146
Gilbert Delorme	74	2	12	14	7	53
Luc Dufour	53	3	6	9	13−	45
Jim Pavese	51	2	5	7	4−	69
Terry Johnson	74	0	7	7	14	120
Dwight Schofield	43	1	4	5	4−	184

Toronto Maple Leafs

	GP	G	A	Pts	+/−	PIM
Rick Vaive	72	35	33	68	30−	112
John Anderson	75	32	31	63	24−	27
Bill Derlago	62	31	31	62	17−	21
Miroslav Frycer	65	25	30	55	7−	55
Dan Daoust	79	17	37	54	28−	98
Peter Ihnacak	70	22	22	44	28−	24
Jim Benning	80	9	35	44	42−	55
Borje Salming	73	6	33	39	30−	76
Greg Terrion	72	14	17	31	16−	20
Gary Leeman	53	5	26	31	12−	72
Stewart Gavin	73	12	13	25	22−	38
Russ Courtnall	69	12	10	22	23−	44
Al Iafrate	68	5	16	21	22−	51
Gary Nylund	76	3	17	20	41−	99
Jeff Brubaker	68	8	4	12	17−	209
Jim Korn	41	5	5	10	10−	171
Bob McGill	72	0	5	5	0	250

Vancouver Canucks

	GP	G	A	Pts	+/−	PIM
Patrik Sundstrom	71	25	43	68	17−	46
Stan Smyl	80	27	37	64	17−	100
Thomas Gradin	76	22	42	64	19−	43
Tony Tanti	68	39	20	59	18−	45
Moe Lemay	74	21	31	52	10−	68
Peter McNab	75	23	25	48	21−	10
Cam Neely	72	21	18	39	27−	137
Petri Skriko	72	21	14	35	25−	10
Al MacAdam	80	14	20	34	29−	27
Doug Halward	71	7	27	34	39−	82
Michel Petit	69	5	26	31	25−	127
Doug Lidster	78	6	24	30	11−	55
Gary Lupul	66	12	17	29	14−	82
J. J. Daigneault	67	4	23	27	13−	69
Mark Kirton	62	17	5	22	22−	21
Rick Lanz	57	2	17	19	22−	69
Jiri Bubla	56	2	15	17	15−	54
Garth Butcher	75	3	9	12	30−	152

Washington Capitals

	GP	G	A	Pts	+/−	PIM
Mike Gartner	80	50	52	102	17	71
Bob Carpenter	80	53	42	95	21	87

	GP	G	A	Pts	+/-	PIM
Dave Christian	80	26	43	69	21	14
Scott Stevens	80	21	44	65	20	221
Larry Murphy	79	13	42	55	21	51
Craig Laughlin	78	16	34	50	13	38
Alan Haworth	76	23	26	49	21	48
Bengt Gustafsson	51	14	29	43	14	8
Gaetan Duchesne	67	15	23	38	18	32
Mike McEwen	56	11	27	38	24	42
Doug Jarvis	80	9	28	37	21	32
Bob Gould	78	14	19	33	11	69
Bryan Erickson	57	15	13	28	11	23
Rod Langway	79	4	22	26	38	54
Gary Sampson	46	10	15	25	20	13
Darren Veitch	75	3	18	21	32	37
Mark Taylor	56	8	11	19	8—	21
Greg Adams	51	6	12	18	8	72
Peter Andersson	57	0	10	10	6	21
Glen Currie	44	1	5	6	2	19
Timo Blomqvist	53	1	4	5	11	51

Winnipeg Jets

	GP	G	A	Pts	+/-	PIM
Dale Hawerchuk	80	53	77	130	24	74
Paul MacLean	79	41	60	101	5	119
Thomas Steen	79	30	54	84	1—	80
Laurie Boschman	80	32	44	76	8—	180
Brian Mullen	69	32	39	71	16	32
Doug Smail	80	31	35	66	10	45
Dave Babych	78	13	49	62	16—	78
Randy Carlyle	71	13	38	51	23	98
Scott Arniel	79	22	22	44	7	81
Perry Turnbull	66	22	21	43	9	130
Dave Ellett	80	11	27	38	20	85
Robert Picard	78	12	22	34	31	107
Bengt Lundholm	77	12	18	30	8	20
Jim Nill	69	9	17	26	9—	100
Andrew McBain	77	7	15	22	2—	45
Tim Watters	63	2	20	22	20	74
Ron Wilson	75	10	9	19	8—	31
Wade Campbell	40	1	6	7	11	21
Jim Kyte	71	0	3	3	26—	111

NHL Trophy Winners

Ross Trophy
Leading scorer

1985	Wayne Gretzky, Edmonton
1984	Wayne Gretzky, Edmonton
1983	Wayne Gretzky, Edmonton
1982	Wayne Gretzky, Edmonton
1981	Wayne Gretzky, Edmonton
1980	Marcel Dionne, Los Angeles
1979	Bryan Trottier, N.Y. Islanders
1978	Guy Lafleur, Montreal
1977	Guy Lafleur, Montreal
1976	Guy Lafleur, Montreal
1975	Bobby Orr, Boston
1974	Phil Esposito, Boston
1973	Phil Esposito, Boston
1972	Phil Esposito, Boston
1971	Phil Esposito, Boston
1970	Bobby Orr, Boston
1969	Phil Esposito, Boston
1968	Stan Mikita, Chicago
1967	Stan Mikita, Chicago
1966	Bobby Hull, Chicago
1965	Stan Mikita, Chicago

Norris Trophy
Best defenseman

1985	Paul Coffey, Edmonton
1984	Rod Langway, Washington
1983	Rod Langway, Washington
1982	Doug Wilson, Chicago
1981	Randy Carlyle, Pittsburgh
1980	Larry Robinson, Montreal
1979	Denis Potvin, N.Y. Islanders
1978	Denis Potvin, N.Y. Islanders
1977	Larry Robinson, Montreal
1976	Denis Potvin, N.Y. Islanders
1975	Bobby Orr, Boston
1974	Bobby Orr, Boston
1973	Bobby Orr, Boston
1972	Bobby Orr, Boston
1971	Bobby Orr, Boston
1970	Bobby Orr, Boston
1969	Bobby Orr, Boston
1968	Bobby Orr, Boston
1967	Harry Howell, N.Y. Rangers
1966	Jacques Laperriere, Montreal
1965	Pierre Pilote, Chicago

Calder Trophy
Best rookie

1985	Mario Lemieux, Pittsburgh
1984	Tom Barrasso, Buffalo
1983	Steve Larmer, Chicago
1982	Dale Hawerchuk, Winnipeg
1981	Peter Stastny, Quebec
1980	Ray Bourque, Boston
1979	Bob Smith, Minnesota
1978	Mike Bossy, N.Y. Islanders
1977	Willi Plett, Atlanta
1976	Bryan Trottier, N.Y. Islanders
1975	Eric Vail, Atlanta
1974	Denis Potvin, N.Y. Islanders
1973	Steve Vickers, N.Y. Rangers
1972	Ken Dryden, Montreal
1971	Gil Perreault, Buffalo
1970	Tony Esposito, Chicago
1969	Danny Grant, Minnesota
1968	Derek Sanderson, Boston
1967	Bobby Orr, Boston
1966	Brit Selby, Toronto
1965	Roger Crozier, Detroit

Hart Trophy
MVP

1985	Wayne Gretzky, Edmonton
1984	Wayne Gretzky, Edmonton
1983	Wayne Gretzky, Edmonton
1982	Wayne Gretzky, Edmonton
1981	Wayne Gretzky, Edmonton
1980	Wayne Gretzky, Edmonton
1979	Bryan Trottier, N.Y. Islanders
1978	Guy Lafleur, Montreal
1977	Guy Lafleur, Montreal
1976	Bobby Clarke, Philadelphia
1975	Bobby Clarke, Philadelphia
1974	Phil Esposito, Boston
1973	Bobby Clarke, Philadelphia
1972	Bobby Orr, Boston
1971	Bobby Orr, Boston
1970	Bobby Orr, Boston
1969	Phil Esposito, Boston
1968	Stan Mikita, Chicago
1967	Stan Mikita, Chicago
1966	Bobby Hull, Chicago
1965	Bobby Hull, Chicago

Vezina Trophy
Leading goalie[1]

1985	Pelle Lindbergh, Philadelphia
1984	Tom Barrasso, Buffalo
1983	Pete Peeters, Boston
1982	Billy Smith, N.Y. Islanders
1981	Sevigny, Herron, Larocque, Montreal
1980	Edwards, Sauve, Buffalo
1979	Dryden, Larocque, Montreal
1978	Dryden, Larocque, Montreal
1977	Dryden, Larocque, Montreal
1976	Ken Dryden, Montreal
1975	Bernie Parent, Philadelphia
1974	Tony Esposito, Chicago
	Bernie Parent, Philadelphia
1973	Ken Dryden, Montreal
1972	Esposito, Smith, Chicago
1971	Giacomin, Villemure, N.Y. Rangers
1970	Tony Esposito, Chicago
1969	Hall, Plante, St. Louis
1968	Worsley, Vachon, Montreal
1967	Hall, De Jordy, Chicago
1966	Hodge, Worsley, Montreal
1965	Sawchuck, Bower, Toronto

Lady Byng Trophy
Sportsmanship

1985	Jari Kurri, Edmonton
1984	Mike Bossy, N.Y. Islanders
1983	Mike Bossy, N.Y. Islanders
1982	Rick Middleton, Boston
1981	Rick Kehoe, Pittsburgh
1980	Wayne Gretzky, Edmonton
1979	Bob MacMillan, Atlanta
1978	Butch Goring, Los Angeles
1977	Marcel Dionne, Los Angeles
1976	Jean Ratelle, Boston
1975	Marcel Dionne, Detroit
1974	John Bucyk, Boston
1973	Gilbert Perreault, Buffalo
1972	Jean Ratelle, N.Y. Rangers
1971	John Bucyk, Boston
1970	Phil Goyette, St. Louis
1969	Alex Devecchio, Detroit
1968	Stan Mikita, Chicago
1967	Stan Mikita, Chicago
1966	Alex Devecchio, Detroit
1965	Bobby Hull, Chicago

Frank Selke Trophy (best defensive forward)—1978-81, Bob Gainey, Montreal; 1982, Steve Kasper, Boston; 1983, Bobby Clarke, Philadelphia; 1984, Doug Jarvis, Washington; 1985, Craig Ramsey, Buffalo.
(1) Most valuable goalie beginning in 1982.

NHL All Star Team, 1985

First team	Position	Second team
Pelle Lindbergh, Philadelphia	Goalie	Tom Barrasso, Buffalo
Ray Bourque, Boston	Defense	Rod Langway, Washington
Paul Coffey, Edmonton	Defense	Doug Wilson, Chicago
Wayne Gretzky, Edmonton	Center	Dale Hawerchuk, Winnipeg
Jari Kurri, Edmonton	Right Wing	Mike Bossy, N.Y. Islanders
John Ogrodnick, Detroit	Left Wing	John Tonelli, N.Y. Islanders

NCAA Hockey Champions

1948	Michigan	1958	Denver	1968	Denver	1977	Wisconsin
1949	Boston College	1959	North Dakota	1969	Denver	1978	Boston Univ.
1950	Colorado College	1960	Denver	1970	Cornell	1979	Minnesota
1951	Michigan	1961	Denver	1971	Boston Univ.	1980	North Dakota
1952	Michigan	1962	Michigan Tech	1972	Boston Univ	1981	Wisconsin
1953	Michigan	1963	North Dakota	1973	Wisconsin	1982	North Dakota
1954	RPI	1964	Michigan	1974	Minnesota	1983	Wisconsin
1955	Michigan	1965	Michigan Tech	1975	Michigan Tech	1984	Bowling Green
1956	Michigan	1966	Michigan State	1976	Minnesota	1985	RPI
1957	Colorado College	1967	Cornell				

Thoroughbred Racing

Triple Crown Turf Winners, Jockeys, and Trainers

(Kentucky Derby, Preakness, and Belmont Stakes)

Year	Horse	Jockey	Trainer	Year	Horse	Jockey	Trainer
1919	Sir Barton	J. Loftus	H. G. Bedwell	1946	Assault	Mehrtens	M. Hirsch
1930	Gallant Fox	E. Sande	J. Fitzsimmons	1948	Citation	E. Arcaro	H.A. Jones
1935	Omaha	W. Sanders	J. Fitzsimmons	1973	Secretariat	R. Turcotte	L. Laurin
1937	War Admiral	C. Kurtsinger	G. Conway	1977	Seattle Slew	J. Cruguet	W.H. Turner Jr.
1941	Whirlaway	E. Arcaro	B.A. Jones	1978	Affirmed	S. Cauthen	L.S. Barrera
1943	Count Fleet	J. Longden	G.D. Cameron				

Annual Leading Money-Winning Horses

Year	Horse	Dollars	Year	Horse	Dollars	Year	Horse	Dollars
1944	Pavot	179,040	1958	Round Table	662,780	1972	Droll Roll	471,633
1945	Busher	273,735	1959	Sword Dancer	537,004	1973	Secretariat	860,404
1946	Assault	424,195	1960	Bally Ache	455,045	1974	Chris Evert	551,063
1947	Armed	376,325	1961	Carry Back	565,349	1975	Foolish Pleasure	716,278
1948	Citation	709,470	1962	Never Bend	402,969	1976	Forego	491,701
1949	Ponder	321,825	1963	Candy Spots	604,481	1977	Seattle Slew	641,370
1950	Noor	346,940	1964	Gun Bow	580,100	1978	Affirmed	901,541
1951	Counterpoint	250,525	1965	Buckpasser	568,096	1979	Spectacular Bid.	1,279,334
1952	Crafty Admiral	277,255	1966	Buckpasser	669,078	1980	Temperance Hill	1,130,452
1953	Native Dancer	513,425	1967	Damascus	817,941	1981	John Henry	1,148,800
1954	Determine	328,700	1968	Forward Pass	546,674	1982	Perrault	1,197,400
1955	Nashua	752,550	1969	Arts and Letters	555,604	1983	All Along	2,138,963
1956	Needles	440,850	1970	Personality	444,049	1984	Slew O'Gold	2,627,944
1957	Round Table	600,383	1971	Riva Ridge	503,263			

Annual Leading Jockey—Money Won

Year	Jockey	Dollars	Year	Jockey	Dollars	Year	Jockey	Dollars
1952	Eddie Arcaro	1,859,591	1963	Willie Shoemaker	2,526,925	1974	Laffit Pincay Jr.	4,251,060
1953	Willie Shoemaker	1,784,187	1964	Willie Shoemaker	2,649,553	1975	Braulio Baeza	3,695,198
1954	Willie Shoemaker	1,876,760	1965	Braulio Baeza	2,582,702	1976	Angel Cordero Jr.	4,709,500
1955	Eddie Arcaro	1,864,796	1966	Braulio Baeza	2,951,022	1977	Steve Cauthen	6,151,750
1956	Bill Hartack	2,343,955	1967	Braulio Baeza	3,088,888	1978	Darrel McHargue	6,029,885
1957	Bill Hartack	3,060,501	1968	Braulio Baeza	2,835,108	1979	Laffit Pincay Jr.	8,193,535
1958	Willie Shoemaker	2,961,693	1969	Jorge Velasquez	2,542,315	1980	Chris McCarron	7,663,300
1959	Willie Shoemaker	2,843,133	1970	Laffit Pincay Jr.	2,626,526	1981	Chris McCarron	8,397,604
1960	Willie Shoemaker	2,123,961	1971	Laffit Pincay Jr.	3,784,377	1982	Angel Cordero Jr.	9,483,590
1961	Willie Shoemaker	2,690,819	1972	Laffit Pincay Jr.	3,225,827	1983	Angel Cordero Jr.	10,116,697
1962	Willie Shoemaker	2,916,844	1973	Laffit Pincay Jr.	4,093,492	1984	Chris McCarron	12,045,813

Leading Money-Winning Horses

As of June, 1985

Horse	Sts.	1st	Dollars	Horse	Sts.	1st	Dollars	Horse	Sts.	1st	Dollars
John Henry	83	39	6,597,947	Spectacular Bid	30	26	2,781,607	Majesty's Price	43	12	2,075,299
Spend a Buck	13	9	3,998,509	Trinycarol	25	18	2,644,516	Kelso	63	39	1,977,896
Slew O'Gold	21	12	3,533,134	Affirmed	29	22	2,393,818	Forego	57	34	1,938,957
All Along	21	9	3,015,764	Wild Again	24	8	2,088,109	Round Table	66	43	1,749,869

Eclipse Awards in 1984

Sponsored by the Thoroughbred Racing Assn., Daily Racing Form, and the National Turf Writers Assn.

Horse of the Year—John Henry
Best 2-year-old colt—Chief's Crown
Best 2-year-old filly—Outstandingly
Best 3-year-old colt—Swale
Best 3-year-old filly—Life's Magic
Best colt, horse, or gelding (4-year-olds & up)—Slew O'Gold
Best filly or mare (4-year-olds & up)—Princess Rooney
Best male turf horse—John Henry

Best turf filly or mare—Royal Heroine
Best sprinter—Eillo
Best steeplechase horse—Flatterer
Best trainer—Jack Van Berg
Best jockey—Pat Day
Best apprentice jockey—Wesley Ward
Best owner—John Franks

Kentucky Derby

Churchill Downs, Louisville, Ky.; inaugurated 1875; distance 1-1/4 miles; 1-1/2 miles until 1896. 3-year olds.
Times—seconds in fifths.

Year	Winner	Jockey	Trainer	Wt.	Second	Winner's share	Time
1911	Meridian	G. Archibald	A. Ewing	117	Governor Gray	$4,850	2:05
1912	Worth	C. H. Shilling	F. M. Taylor	117	Duval	4,850	2:09.2
1913	Donerail	R. Goose	T. P. Hayes	117	Ten Point	5,475	2:04.4
1914	Old Rosebud	J. McCabe	F. D. Weir	114	Hodge	9,125	2:03.2
1915	Regret*	J. Notter	J. Rowe Sr.	112	Pebbles	11,450	2:05.2
1916	George Smith	J. Loftus	H. Hughes	117	Star Hawk	16,600	2:04.3
1917	Omar Khayyam	C. Borel	C. T. Patterson	117	Ticket	9,750	2:04.
1918	Exterminator	W. Knapp	H. McDaniel	114	Escoba	14,700	2:10.4
1919	Sir Barton	J. Loftus	H. G. Bedwell	112	Billy Kelly	20,825	2:09.4
1920	Paul Jones	T. Rice	W. Garth	126	Upset	30,375	2:09.
1921	Behave Yourself	C. Thompson	H. J. Thompson	126	Black Servant	38,450	2:04.1
1922	Morvich	A. Johnson	F. Burlew	126	Bet Mosie	46,775	2:04.3
1923	Zev	E. Sande	D. J. Leary	126	Martingale	53,600	2:05.2
1924	Black Gold	J. D. Mooney	H. Webb	126	Chilhowee	52,775	2:05.1
1925	Flying Ebony	E. Sande	W. B. Duke	126	Captain Hal	52,950	2:07.3
1926	Bubbling Over	A. Johnson	H. J. Thompson	126	Bagenbaggage	50,075	2:03.4
1927	Whiskery	L. McAtee	F. Hopkins	126	Osmand	51,000	2:06.
1928	Reigh Count	C. Lang	B. S. Michell	126	Misstep	55,375	2:10.2
1929	Clyde Van Dusen	L. McAtee	C. Van Dusen	126	Naishapur	53,950	2:10.4
1930	Gallant Fox	E. Sande	J. Fitzsimmons	126	Gallant Knight	50,725	2:07.3
1931	Twenty Grand	C. Kurtsinger	J. Rowe Jr.	126	Sweep All	48,725	2:01.4
1932	Burgoo King	E. James	H. J. Thompson	126	Economic	52,350	2:05.1
1933	Brokers Tip	D. Meade	H. J. Thompson	126	Head Play	48,925	2:06.4
1934	Cavalcade	M. Garner	R. A. Smith	126	Discovery	28,175	2:04.
1935	Omaha	W. Saunders	J. Fitzsimmons	126	Roman Soldier	39,525	2:05.
1936	Bold Venture	I. Hanford	M. Hirsch	126	Brevity	37,725	2:03.3
1937	War Admiral	C. Kurtsinger	G. Conway	126	Pompoon	52,050	2:03.1
1938	Lawrin	E. Arcaro	B. A. Jones	126	Dauber	47,050	2:04.4
1939	Johnstown	J. Stout	J. Fitzsimmons	126	Challedon	46,350	2:03.2
1940	Gallahadion	C. Bierman	R. Waldron	126	Bimelech	60,150	2:05.
1941	Whirlaway	E. Arcaro	B. A. Jones	126	Staretor	61,275	2:01.2
1942	Shut Out	W. D. Wright	J. M. Gaver	126	Alsab	64,225	2:04.2
1943	Count Fleet	J. Longden	G. D. Cameron	126	Blue Swords	60,275	2:04.
1944	Pensive	C. McCreary	B. A. Jones	126	Broadcloth	64,675	2:04.1
1945	Hoop, Jr.	E. Arcaro	I. H. Parke	126	Pot o'Luck	64,850	2:07.
1946	Assault	W. Mehrtens	M. Hirsch	126	Spy Song	96,400	2:06.3
1947	Jet Pilot	E. Guerin	T. Smith	126	Phalanx	92,160	2:06.3
1948	Citation	E. Arcaro	B. A. Jones	126	Coaltown	83,400	2:05.2
1949	Ponder	S. Brooks	B. A. Jones	126	Capot	91,600	2:04.1
1950	Middleground	W. Boland	M. Hirsch	126	Hill Prince	92,650	2:01.3
1951	Count Turf	C. McCreary	S. Rutchick	126	Royal Mustang	98,050	2:02.3
1952	Hill Gail	E. Arcaro	B. A. Jones	126	Sub Fleet	96,300	2:01.3
1953	Dark Star	H. Moreno	E. Hayward	126	Native Dancer	90,050	2:02.
1954	Determine	R. York	W. Molter	126	Hasty Road	102,050	2:03.
1955	Swaps	W. Shoemaker	M. A. Tenney	126	Nashua	108,400	2:01.4
1956	Needles	D. Erb	H. L. Fontaine	126	Fabius	123,450	2:03.2
1957	Iron Liege	W. Hartack	H. A. Jones	126	Gallant Man	107,950	2:02.1
1958	Tim Tam	I. Valenzuela	H. A. Jones	126	Lincoln Road	116,400	2:05.
1959	Tomy Lee	W. Shoemaker	F. Childs	126	Sword Dancer	119,650	2:02.1
1960	Venetian Way	W. Hartack	V. Sovinski	126	Bally Ache	114,850	2:02.2
1961	Carry Back	J. Sellers	J. A. Price	126	Crozier	120,500	2:04.
1962	Decidedly	W. Hartack	H. Luro	126	Roman Line	119,650	2:00.2
1963	Chateaugay	B. Baeza	J. Conway	126	Never Bend	108,900	2:01.4
1964	Northern Dancer	W. Hartack	H. Luro	126	Hill Rise	114,300	2:00.
1965	Lucky Debonair	W. Shoemaker	F. Catrone	126	Dapper Dan	112,000	2:01.1
1966	Kauai King	D. Brumfield	H. Forrest	126	Advocator	120,500	2:02.
1967	Proud Clarion	R. Ussery	L. Gentry	126	Barbs Delight	119,700	2:00.3
1968	Dancer's Image (a)	R. Ussery	H. Forrest	126	Forward Pass	122,600	2:02.1
1969	Majestic Prince	W. Hartack	J. Longden	126	Arts and Letters	113,200	2:01.4
1970	Dust Commander	M. Manganello	D. Combs	126	My Dad George	127,800	2:03.2
1971	Canonero II	G. Avila	J. Arias	126	Jim French	145,500	2:03.1
1972	Riva Ridge	R. Turcotte	L. Laurin	126	No Le Hace	140,300	2:01.4
1973	Secretariat	R. Turcotte	L. Laurin	126	Sham	155,050	1:59.2
1974	Cannonade	A. Cordero	W. Stephens	126	Hudson County	274,000	2:04.
1975	Foolish Pleasure	J. Vasquez	L. Jolley	126	Avatar	209,611	2:02.
1976	Bold Forbes	A. Cordero	L. Barrera	126	Honest Pleasure	165,200	2:01.3
1977	Seattle Slew	J. Cruguet	W. H. Turner Jr.	126	Run Dusty Run	214,700	2:02.1
1978	Affirmed	S. Cauthen	L. Barrera	126	Alydar	186,900	2:01.1
1979	Spectacular Bid	R. Franklin	G. Delp	126	General Assembly	228,650	2:02.2
1980	Genuine Risk*	J. Vasquez	L. Jolley	121	Rumbo	250,550	2:02
1981	Pleasant Colony	J. Velasquez	J. Campo	126	Woodchopper	317,200	2:02
1982	Gato del Sol	E. Delahoussaye	E. Gregson	126	Laser Light	428,850	2:02.2
1983	Sunny's Halo	E. Delahoussaye	D. Cross	126	Desert Wine	426,000	2:02.1
1984	Swale	L. Pincay	W. Stephens	126	Coax Me Chad	537,000	2:02.2
1985	Spend a Buck	A. Cordero	C. Gambolati	126	Stephen's Odyssey	406,800	2:00.1

(a) Dancer's Image was disqualified from purse money after tests disclosed that he had run with a pain-killing drug, phenylbutazone, in his system. All wagers were paid on Dancer's Image. Forward Pass was awarded first place money.

The Kentucky Derby has been won five times by two jockeys, Eddie Arcaro, 1938, 1941, 1945, 1948 and 1952; and Bill Hartack, 1957, 1960, 1962, 1964 and 1969; and three times by each of four jockeys, Isaac Murphy, 1884, 1890, and 1891; Earle Sande, 1923, 1925 and 1930, Willie Shoemaker, 1955, 1959, 1965, and Angel Cordero in 1974, 1976 and 1985. *Regret and Genuine Risk are the only fillies to win the Derby.

Preakness

Pimlico, Baltimore, Md.; inaugurated 1873; 1 3-16 miles, 3 yr. olds. Time—seconds in fifths.

Year	Winner	Jockey	Trainer	Wt.	Second	Winner's share	Time
1947	Faultless	D. Dodson	H.A. Jones	126	On Trust	$98,005	1:59
1948	Citation	E. Arcaro	H.A. Jones	126	Vulcan's Forge	91,870	2:02.2
1949	Capot	T. Atkinson	J.M. Gaver	126	Palestinian	79,985	1:56
1950	Hill Prince	E. Arcaro	J.H. Hayes	126	Middleground	56,115	1:59.1
1951	Bold	E. Arcaro	P.M. Burch	126	Counterpoint	83,110	1:56.2
1952	Blue Man	C. McCreary	W.C. Stephens	126	Jampol	86,135	1:57.2
1953	Native Dancer	E. Guerin	W.C. Winfrey	126	Jamie K	65,200	1:57.4
1954	Hasty Road	J. Adams	H. Trotsek	126	Correlation	91,600	1:57.2
1955	Nashua	E. Arcaro	J. Fitzsimmons	126	Saratoga	67,550	1:54.3
1956	Fabius	W. Hartack	H.A. Jones	126	Needles	84,250	1:58.2
1957	Bold Ruler	E. Arcaro	J. Fitzsimmons	126	Iron Liege	65,250	1:56.1
1958	Tim Tam	I. Valenzuela	H.A. Jones	126	Lincoln Road	97,900	1:57.1
1959	Royal Orbit	W. Harmatz	R. Cornell	126	Sword Dancer	136,200	1:57
1960	Bally Ache	R. Ussery	H.J. Pitt	126	Victoria Park	121,000	1:57.3
1961	Carry Back	J. Sellers	J.A. Price	126	Globemaster	126,200	1:57.3
1962	Greek Money	J.L. Rotz	V.W. Raines	126	Ridan	135,800	1:56.1
1963	Candy Spots	W. Shoemaker	M.A. Tenney	126	Chateaugay	127,500	1:56.1
1964	Northern Dancer	W. Hartack	H. Luro	126	The Scoundrel	124,200	1:56.4
1965	Tom Rolfe	R. Turcotte	F.Y Whiteley Jr.	126	Dapper Dan	128,100	1:56.1
1966	Kauai King	D. Brumfield	H. Forrest	126	Stupendous	129,000	1:55.2
1967	Damascus	W. Shoemaker	F.Y. Whiteley Jr.	126	In Reality	141,500	1:55.1
1968	Forward Pass	I. Valenzuela	H. Forrest	126	Out of the Way	142,700	1:56.4
1969	Majestic Prince	W. Hartack	J. Longden	126	Arts and Letters	129,500	1:55.3
1970	Personality	E. Belmonte	J.W. Jacobs	126	My Dad George	151,300	1:56.1
1971	Canonero II	G. Avila	J. Arias	126	Eastern Fleet	137,400	1:54
1972	Bee Bee Bee	E. Nelson	D.W. Carroll	126	No Le Hace	135,300	1:55.3
1973	Secretariat	R. Turcotte	L. Laurin	126	Sham	129,900	1:54.2
1974	Little Current	M. Rivera	L. Rondinello	126	Neopolitan Way	156,000	1:54.3
1975	Master Derby	D. McHargue	W.E. Adams	126	Foolish Pleasure	158,100	1:56.2
1976	Elocutionist	J. Lively	P.T. Adwell	126	Play The Red	129,700	1:55
1977	Seattle Slew	J. Cruguet	W.H. Turner Jr.	126	Iron Constitution	138,600	1:54.2
1978	Affirmed	S. Cauthen	L. Barrera	126	Alydar	136,200	1:54.2
1979	Spectacular Bid	R. Franklin	G. Delp	126	Golden Act	165,300	1:54.1
1980	Codex	A. Cordero	D.W. Lucas	126	Genuine Risk	180,600	1:54.1
1981	Pleasant Colony	J. Velasquez	J. Campo	126	Bold Ego	270,800	1:54.3
1982	Aloma's Ruler	J. Kaenel	J. Lenzini	126	Linkage	209,990	1:55.2
1983	Deputed Testamony	D. Miller	J.W. Boniface	126	Desert Wine	251,200	1:55.2
1984	Gate Dancer	A. Cordero	J. Van Berg	126	Play On	243,600	1:53.3
1985	Tank's Prospect	P. Day	D.W. Lucas	126	Chief's Crown	423,200	1:53.2

Belmont Stakes

Elmont, N.Y.; inaugurated 1867; 1 ½ miles, 3 year olds. Time—seconds in fifths.

Year	Winner	Jockey	Trainer	Wt.	Second	Winner's share	Time
1947	Phalanx	R. Donoso	S. Veitch	126	Tide Rips	$78,900	2:29.2
1948	Citation	E. Arcaro	H.A. Jones	126	Better Self	77,700	2:28.1
1949	Capot	T. Atkinson	J.M. Gaver	126	Ponder	60,900	2:30.1
1950	Middleground	W. Boland	M. Hirsch	126	Lights Up	61,350	2:28.3
1951	Counterpoint	D. Gorman	S. Veitch	125	Battlefield	82,000	2:29
1952	One Count	E. Arcaro	O. White	126	Blue Man	82,400	2:30.1
1953	Native Dancer	E. Guerin	W.C. Winfrey	126	Jamie K.	82,500	2:28.3
1954	High Gun	E. Guerin	M. Hirsch	126	Fisherman	89,000	2:30.4
1955	Nashua	E. Arcaro	J. Fitzsimmons	126	Blazing Count	83,700	2:29
1956	Needles	D. Erb	H. Fontaine	126	Career Boy	83,600	2:29.4
1957	Gallant Man	W. Shoemaker	J. Nerud	126	Inside Tract	77,300	2:26.3
1958	Cavan	P. Anderson	T.J. Barry	126	Tim Tam	73,440	2:30.1
1959	Sword Dancer	W. Shoemaker	J.E. Burch	126	Bagdad	93,525	2:28.2
1960	Celtic Ash	W. Hartack	T.J. Barry	126	Venetian Way	96,785	2:29.3
1961	Sherluck	B. Baeza	H. Young	126	Globemaster	104,900	2:29.1
1962	Jaipur	W. Shoemaker	W.F. Mulholland	126	Admiral's Voyage	109,550	2:28.4
1963	Chateaugay	B. Baeza	J.P. Conway	126	Candy Spots	101,700	2:30.1
1964	Quadrangle	M. Ycaza	J.E. Burch	126	Roman Brother	110,850	2:28.2
1965	Hail to All	J. Sellers	E. Yowell	126	Tom Rolfe	104,150	2:28.2
1966	Amberoid	W. Boland	L. Laurin	126	Buffle	117,700	2:29.3
1967	Damascus	W. Shoemaker	F.Y. Whiteley Jr.	126	Cool Reception	104,950	2:28.4
1968	Stage Door Johnny	H. Gustines	J.M. Gaver	126	Forward Pass	117,700	2:27.1
1969	Arts and Letters	B. Baeza	J.E. Burch	126	Majestic Prince	104,050	2:28.4
1970	High Echelon	J.L. Rotz	J.W. Jacobs	126	Needles N Pens	115,000	2:34
1971	Pass Catcher	W. Blum	E. Yowell	126	Jim French	97,710	2:30.2
1972	Riva Ridge	R. Turcotte	L. Laurin	126	Ruritania	93,950	2:28
1973	Secretariat	R. Turcotte	L. Laurin	126	Twice A Prince	90,120	2:24
1974	Little Current	M. Rivera	L. Rondinello	126	Jolly Johu	101,970	2:29.1
1975	Avatar	W. Shoemaker	A.T. Doyle	126	Foolish Pleasure	116,160	2:28.1
1976	Bold Forbes	A. Cordero	Laz Barrera	126	McKenzie Bridge	116,850	2:29
1977	Seattle Slew	J. Cruguet	W.H. Turner Jr.	126	Run Dusty Run	109,080	2:29.3
1978	Affirmed	S. Cauthen	Laz Barrera	126	Alydar	110,580	2:26.4
1979	Coastal	R. Hernandez	D.A. Whiteley	126	Golden Act	161,400	2:28.3
1980	Temperence Hill	E. Maple	J. Cantey	126	Genuine Risk	176,220	2:29.4
1981	Summing	G. Martens	Luis Barrera	126	Highland Blade	170,580	2:29
1982	Conquistador Cielo	L. Pincay	W. Stephens	126	Gato Del Sol	159,720	2:28.1
1983	Caveat	L. Pincay	W. Stephens	126	Slew o'Gold	215,100	2:27.4
1984	Swale	L. Pincay	W. Stephens	126	Pine Circle	310,020	2:27.1
1985	Creme Fraiche	E. Maple	W. Stephens	126	Stephan's Odyssey	307,740	2:27

College Basketball

Final Regular Season Conference Standings, 1984-85

Atlantic Coast

	Conference W	L	All Games W	L
North Carolina	9	5	22	7
Georgia Tech	9	5	21	7
North Carolina St.	9	5	19	8
Duke	8	6	21	6
Maryland	8	6	23	10
Clemson	5	9	16	11
Wake Forest	5	9	15	12
Virginia	3	11	14	14

Champion—Georgia Tech

Atlantic 10

	Conference W	L	All Games W	L
West Virginia	16	2	20	7
Temple	15	3	21	5
St. Joseph's	13	5	17	10
Rutgers	9	9	14	13
George Washington	9	9	14	13
Massachusetts	9	9	13	14
St. Bonaventure	7	11	13	14
Duquesne	6	12	10	17
Penn State	4	14	8	18
Rhode Island	2	16	8	19

Champion—Temple

Big East

	Conference W	L	All Games W	L
St. John's	15	1	25	2
Georgetown	14	2	27	2
Syracuse	9	7	20	7
Villanova	9	7	18	9
Pittsburgh	8	8	17	10
Boston College	7	9	18	9
Connecticut	6	10	13	14
Providence	3	13	10	19
Seton Hall	1	15	10	17

Champion—Georgetown

Big Eight

	Conference W	L	All Games W	L
Oklahoma	13	1	25	5
Kansas	11	3	24	6
Iowa State	7	7	19	11
Missouri	7	7	18	11
Kansas State	5	9	14	13
Colorado	5	9	11	16
Nebraska	5	9	15	12
Oklahoma State	3	11	12	15

Champion—Oklahoma

Big Sky

	Conference W	L	All Games W	L
Nevada-Reno	11	3	18	9
Montana	10	4	22	6
Weber State	9	5	20	8
Northern Arizona	8	6	16	11
Montana State	7	7	11	16
Boise State	5	9	15	12
Idaho State	5	9	13	17
Idaho	1	13	8	21

Champion—Nevada-Reno

Big Ten

	Conference W	L	All Games W	L
Michigan	14	2	23	3
Illinois	10	6	22	8
Iowa	10	6	21	8
Ohio State	10	6	18	8
Michigan State	9	7	18	8
Purdue	9	7	18	8
Indiana	7	9	15	11
Minnesota	6	10	13	13
Wisconsin	4	13	13	14
Northwestern	2	15	6	21

Champion—Michigan

East Coast

	Conference W	L	All Games W	L
Bucknell	10	4	19	9
Lafayette	8	6	15	13
Drexel	8	6	10	18
Rider	7	7	14	15
Delaware	7	7	12	16
Lehigh	6	8	11	18
Hofstra	5	9	14	15
Towson State	5	9	7	21

Champion—Lehigh

ECAC Metro

	Conference W	L	All Games W	L
Marist	11	3	17	12
FDU	10	4	20	9
LIU	9	5	15	13
Loyola, Md.	8	6	16	13
St. Francis, Pa.	6	8	9	19
Wagner	5	9	11	17
Robert Morris	4	10	9	19
St. Francis, N.Y.	3	11	7	21
Monmouth	—	—	12	15

Champion—FDU

ECAC North Atlantic

	Conference W	L	All Games W	L
Canisius	13	3	19	8
Northeastern	13	3	19	8
Siena	12	4	21	6
Niagara	11	5	16	11
Boston Univ.	9	7	13	14
Maine	5	11	11	16
Vermont	5	11	9	18
New Hampshire	4	12	6	21
Colgate	0	16	5	20
Hartford	—	—	7	21

Champion—Northeastern

ECAC South

	Conference W	L	All Games W	L
Navy	11	3	21	5
Richmond	11	3	18	9
George Mason	10	4	17	10
William & Mary	9	5	15	11
James Madison	7	7	14	13
N.C.-Wilmington	4	10	12	15
American	3	11	9	18
East Carolina	1	13	7	21

Champion—Navy

Ivy League

	Conference W	L	All Games W	L
Penn	9	3	13	12
Harvard	7	5	15	7
Cornell	7	5	13	11
Columbia	7	5	11	13
Princeton	7	5	11	13
Yale	6	7	13	12
Brown	4	9	8	18
Dartmouth	3	11	5	21

Champion—Penn

Metro

	Conference W	L	All Games W	L
Memphis State	13	1	24	3
Virginia Tech	10	4	20	7
Cincinnati	8	6	15	12
South Carolina	6	8	15	12
Louisville	6	8	15	15
Tulane	6	8	15	12
Florida State	4	10	12	15
S. Mississippi	3	11	7	20

Champion—Memphis State

Metro Atlantic Athletic

	Conference W	L	All Games W	L
Iona	11	3	25	4
Fordham	9	5	19	10
La Salle	8	6	15	13
Holy Cross	8	6	9	19
Army	7	7	15	13
St. Peter's	5	9	15	13
Fairfield	4	10	11	17
Manhattan	4	10	8	20

Champion—Iona

Mid-American

	Conference W	L	All Games W	L
Ohio Univ.	14	4	20	7
Miami, Ohio	13	5	18	9
Toledo	11	7	16	11
Kent State	11	7	16	11
E. Michigan	9	9	15	12
Ball State	8	10	13	14
Western Michigan	7	11	12	15
Northern Illinois	7	11	11	16
Bowling Green	6	12	9	18
Central Michigan	4	14	9	18

Champion—Ohio Univ.

Mid-Eastern Athletic

	Conference W	L	All Games W	L
North Carolina A&T	10	2	17	9
Howard	9	3	15	11
Delaware State	7	4	10	16
S.C. State	7	4	11	15
Bethune-Cookman	4	6	7	17
Md.-Eastern Shore	2	10	3	24
Morgan State	1	11	3	25

Champion—North Carolina A&T

Midwestern City

	Conference W	L	All Games W	L
Loyola, Ill.	13	1	22	5
Butler	9	5	18	8
Oral Roberts	8	6	13	14
Detroit	8	6	16	11
Xavier, Ohio	7	7	15	12
St. Louis	6	8	12	14
Evansville	4	10	14	13
Oklahoma City	1	13	6	19

Champion—Loyola, Ill.

Missouri Valley

	Conference W	L	All Games W	L
Tulsa	12	4	21	6
Illinois State	11	5	21	6
Wichita State	11	5	15	12
Bradley	9	7	16	11
Creighton	9	7	20	11
Southern Illinois	6	10	14	13
Indiana State	6	10	13	14
West Texas State	4	12	11	16
Drake	4	12	12	15

Champion—Wichita State

Ohio Valley

	Conference W	L	All Games W	L
Tennessee Tech	11	3	19	8
Youngstown State	10	5	20	11
Eastern Kentucky	9	5	16	13
Murray State	8	6	19	9
Middle Tenn. State	7	7	17	13
Akron	6	8	12	14
Austin Peay	4	10	8	19
Morehead State	2	13	7	21

Champion—Middle Tenn. State

Pacific Coast Athletic

	Conference W	L	All Games W	L
Nevada-Las Vegas	17	1	24	3
Fresno State	15	3	20	7
Fullerton State	11	7	15	12
San Jose State	10	8	15	12
Utah State	10	8	17	10
Cal-Irvine	8	10	13	16
Santa Barbara	8	10	12	15
Pacific	5	13	9	18
New Mexico State	4	14	7	20
Long Beach State	2	16	4	23

Champion—Nevada-Las Vegas

Pacific-10

	Conference W	L	All Games W	L
USC	12	4	18	8
Oregon State	11	5	21	7
Washington	11	5	20	9
Arizona	11	6	20	9
UCLA	10	6	14	12
Oregon	8	8	15	14
Arizona State	7	10	12	15
California	4	12	12	14
Washington State	4	12	12	14
Stanford	3	13	11	15

Champion—USC; Washington

Southeastern

	Conference W	L	All Games W	L
LSU	13	5	19	8
Georgia	12	6	20	7
Alabama	11	7	19	8
Kentucky	11	7	16	11
Florida	9	9	17	10
Mississippi State	9	9	13	14
Auburn	8	10	16	11
Tennessee	8	10	17	13
Mississippi	5	13	11	16
Vanderbilt	4	14	11	16

Champion—Auburn

	Confer-ence W L		All Games W L	
Southern				
UT-Chattanooga...	14	2	22	7
Marshall........	12	4	21	12
Citadel........	11	5	18	11
Western Carolina..	8	8	14	14
VMI........	7	9	16	14
Appalachian State..	7	9	14	14
Davidson........	6	10	10	20
Furman........	4	12	7	21
Eastern Tenn. State.	3	13	9	18
Champion—Marshall				
Southwest				
Texas Tech......	12	4	20	7
SMU........	10	6	21	8
Texas A&M.......	10	6	18	9
Arkansas........	10	6	19	11
Texas Christian...	8	8	16	11
Houston........	8	8	16	12
Texas........	7	9	15	12
Baylor........	4	12	11	16
Rice........	3	13	10	16
Champion—Texas Tech				
Southwestern Athletic				
Alcorn State.....	13	1	22	5
Southern Univ.....	9	5	17	9
Alabama State....	7	7	11	16
Miss. Valley State..	6	7	14	10
Texas Southern...	6	8	11	16
Jackson State....	6	8	10	16
Grambling......	4	9	8	18
Prairie View A&M...	4	10	5	22
Champion—Alcorn State				

	Confer-ence W L		All Games W L	
Southland				
Louisiana Tech....	11	1	25	2
McNeese State....	9	3	17	9
Lamar........	8	4	17	10
Arkansas State...	6	6	14	13
NE Louisiana.....	4	8	16	11
Texas-Arlington...	3	9	12	15
North Texas State..	1	11	5	22
Champion—Louisiana Tech				
Sun Belt				
Va. Commonwealth.	12	2	25	5
Ala.-Birmingham...	11	3	24	8
Old Dominion.....	9	5	19	11
South Florida.....	6	8	16	11
Jacksonville.....	6	8	15	14
South Alabama...	6	8	15	13
Western Kentucky..	5	9	14	14
UNC-Charlotte....	1	13	5	23
Champion—Va. Commonwealth				
Trans America				
Georgia Southern..	11	3	24	4
Houston Baptist...	10	4	21	7
Mercer........	10	4	20	6
Ark.-Little Rock...	9	5	16	12
Samford........	7	7	18	12
Hardin-Simmons...	7	7	11	17
Centenary......	2	12	7	21
Georgia State....	0	14	2	26
Champion—Mercer				
West Coast Athletic				
Pepperdine.....	11	1	23	8
Santa Clara.....	8	3	19	8
St. Mary's.....	7	4	15	11
San Diego.....	5	6	16	10
Gonzaga.....	4	7	15	12
Portland.....	2	9	13	14
Loyola, Cal.....	2	9	10	16
Champion—Pepperdine				

	Confer-ence W L		All Games W L	
Western Athletic				
Texas-El Paso....	12	4	20	8
San Diego State...	11	5	21	7
New Mexico.....	9	7	17	11
Brigham Young...	9	7	15	13
Colorado State...	9	7	17	11
Utah........	8	8	13	15
Wyoming......	7	9	15	13
Hawaii.......	5	11	10	17
Air Force......	2	14	7	19
Champion—San Diego State				

Major Independents	W	L
Dayton........	19	8
DePaul........	18	8
Notre Dame......	18	8
Marquette......	17	9
Texas-San Antonio..	17	11
Chicago State....	16	11
Radford........	16	11
Utica........	15	12
SW Louisiana.....	16	13
Brooklyn........	15	13
Baptist........	13	15
Pan American....	12	14
Stetson........	12	16
Eastern Washington.	12	15
Florida A&M.....	10	17
Central Florida...	10	18
New Orleans....	10	19
Tennessee State...	9	18
Augusta........	8	20
Campbell......	5	21
U.S. International...	1	27

NCAA Basketball Championships in 1985

East
First round—Georgetown 68, Lehigh 43; Temple 60, Virginia Tech 57; SMU 85, Old Dominion 68; Loyola (Ill.) 59, Iona 58; Georgia 67, Wichita St. 59; Illinois 76, Northeastern 57; Syracuse 70, DePaul 65; Georgia Tech 65, Mercer 58.

Second round—Georgetown 63, Temple 46; Loyola 70, SMU 57; Illinois 74, Georgia 58; Georgia Tech 70, Syracuse 53.

Regionals—Georgetown 65, Loyola 53; Georgia Tech 61, Illinois 53.

Championship—Georgetown 60, Georgia Tech 54.

Southeast
First round—Auburn 59, Purdue 58; Kansas 49, Ohio U. 38; Notre Dame 79, Oregon St. 70; North Carolina 76, Middle Tennessee 57; Michigan 59, FDU 55; Villanova 51, Dayton 49; Maryland 69, Miami (Ohio) 68; Navy 78, Louisiana St. 55.

Second round—Auburn 66, Kansas 64; North Carolina 60, Notre Dame 58; Villanova 59, Michigan 55; Maryland 64, Navy 59.

Regionals—North Carolina 62, Auburn 56; Villanova 46, Maryland 43.

Championship—Villanova 56, North Carolina 44.

Midwest
First round—Oklahoma 96, North Carolina A&T 83; Illinois St. 58, USC 55; Louisiana Tech 78, Pittsburgh 54; Ohio St. 75, Iowa St. 64; Boston College 55, Texas Tech 53; Duke 75, Pepperdine

62; Alabama-Birmingham 70, Michigan St. 68; Memphis St. 67, Pennsylvania 55.

Second round—Oklahoma 75, Illinois St. 69; Louisiana Tech 79, Ohio St. 67; Boston College 74, Duke 73; Memphis St. 67, Alabama-Birmingham 66.

Regionals—Oklahoma 86, Louisiana Tech 84; Memphis St. 59, Boston College 57.

Championship—Memphis St. 63, Oklahoma 61.

West
First round—St. John's 83, Southern Univ. 59; Arkansas 63, Iowa 54; Kentucky 66, Washington 58; UNLV 85, San Diego St. 80; UTEP 79, Tulsa 75; North Carolina St. 65, Nevada-Reno 56; Alabama 50, Arizona 41; Va. Commonwealth 81, Marshall 65.

Second round—St. John's 68, Arkansas 65; Kentucky 64, UNLV 61; North Carolina St. 86, UTEP 73; Alabama 63, Va. Commonwealth 52.

Regionals—St. John's 86, Kentucky 70; North Carolina St. 61, Alabama 55.

Championship—St. John's 69, North Carolina St. 60.

National Semifinals
Georgetown 77, St. John's 59; Villanova 52, Memphis St. 45.

Championship
Villanova 66, Georgetown 64.

National Invitation Tournament Champions

Year	Champion	Year	Champion	Year	Champion	Year	Champion
1938	Temple	1950	CCNY	1962	Dayton	1974	Purdue
1939	Long Island Univ.	1951	Brigham Young	1963	Providence	1975	Princeton
1940	Colorado	1952	LaSalle	1964	Bradley	1976	Kentucky
1941	Long Island Univ.	1953	Seton Hall	1965	St. John's	1977	St. Bonaventure
1942	West Virginia	1954	Holy Cross	1966	Brigham Young	1978	Texas
1943	St. John's	1955	Duquesne	1967	Southern Illinois	1979	Indiana
1944	St. John's	1956	Louisville	1968	Dayton	1980	Virginia
1945	De Paul	1957	Bradley	1969	Temple	1981	Tulsa
1946	Kentucky	1958	Xavier (Ohio)	1970	Marquette	1982	Bradley
1947	Utah	1959	St. John's	1971	North Carolina	1983	Fresno State
1948	St. Louis	1960	Bradley	1972	Maryland	1984	Michigan
1949	San Francisco	1961	Providence	1973	Virginia Tech	1985	UCLA

NCAA Division I Champions

Year	Champion	Coach	Final opponent	Score	MVP	Site
1939	Oregon	Howard Hobson	Ohio St.	46-33	None	Evanston, Ill.
1940	Indiana	Branch McCracken	Kansas	60-42	Marvin Huffman, Indiana	Kansas City, Mo.
1941	Wisconsin	Harold Foster	Washington St.	39-34	John Kotz, Wisconsin	Kansas City, Mo.
1942	Stanford	Everett Dean	Dartmouth	53-38	Howard Dallmar, Stanford	Kansas City, Mo.
1943	Wyoming	Everett Shelton	Georgetown	46-34	Ken Sailors, Wyoming	New York, N.Y.
1944	Utah	Vadal Peterson	Dartmouth	42-40(1)	Arnold Ferrin, Utah	New York, N.Y.
1945	Oklahoma St.	Henry Iba	NYU	49-45	Bob Kurland, Oklahoma St.	New York, N.Y.
1946	Oklahoma St.	Henry Iba	North Carolina	43-40	Bob Kurland, Oklahoma St.	New York, N.Y.
1947	Holy Cross	Alvin Julian	Oklahoma	58-47	George Kaftan, Holy Cross	New York, N.Y.
1948	Kentucky	Adolph Rupp	Baylor	58-42	Alex Groza, Kentucky	New York, N.Y.
1949	Kentucky	Adolph Rupp	Oklahoma St.	46-36	Alex Groza, Kentucky	Seattle, Wash.
1950	CCNY	Nat Holman	Bradley	71-68	Irwin Dambrot, CCNY	New York, N.Y.
1951	Kentucky	Adolph Rupp	Kansas St.	68-58	None	Minneapolis, Minn.
1952	Kansas	Forrest Allen	St. John's	80-63	Clyde Lovellette, Kansas	Seattle, Wash.
1953	Indiana	Branch McCracken	Kansas	69-68	B.H. Born, Kansas	Kansas City, Mo.
1954	La Salle	Kenneth Loeffler	Bradley	92-76	Tom Gola, La Salle	Kansas City, Mo.
1955	San Francisco	Phil Woolpert	LaSalle	77-63	Bill Russell, San Francisco	Kansas City, Mo.
1956	San Francisco	Phil Woolpert	Iowa	83-71	Hal Lear, Temple	Evanston, Ill.
1957	N. Carolina	Frank McGuire	Kansas	54-53(1)	Wilt Chamberlin, Kansas	Kansas City, Mo.
1958	Kentucky	Adolph Rupp	Seattle	84-72	Elgin Baylor, Seattle	Louisville, Ky.
1959	California	Pete Newell	W. Virginia	71-70	Jerry West, W. Virginia	Louisville, Ky.
1960	Ohio St.	Fred Taylor	California	75-55	Jerry Lucas, Ohio St.	San Francisco, Cal.
1961	Cincinnati	Edwin Jucker	Ohio St.	70-65(1)	Jerry Lucas, Ohio St.	Kansas City, Mo.
1962	Cincinnati	Edwin Jucker	Ohio St.	71-59	Paul Hogue, Cincinnati	Louisville, Ky.
1963	Loyola (Ill.)	George Ireland	Cincinnati	60-58(1)	Art Heyman, Duke	Louisville, Ky.
1964	UCLA	John Wooden	Duke	98-83	Walt Hazzard, UCLA	Kansas City, Mo.
1965	UCLA	John Wooden	Michigan	91-80	Bill Bradley, Princeton	Portland, Ore.
1966	Texas-El Paso	Don Haskins	Kentucky	72-65	Jerry Chambers, Utah	College Park, Md.
1967	UCLA	John Wooden	Dayton	79-64	Lew Alcindor, UCLA	Louisville, Ky.
1968	UCLA	John Wooden	N. Carolina	78-55	Lew Alcindor, UCLA	Los Angeles, Cal.
1969	UCLA	John Wooden	Purdue	92-72	Lew Alcindor, UCLA	Louisville, Ky.
1970	UCLA	John Wooden	Jacksonville	89-69	Sidney Wicks, UCLA	College Park, Md.
1971	UCLA	John Wooden	Villanova*	68-62	Howard Porter, Villanova*	Houston, Tex.
1972	UCLA	John Wooden	Florida St.	81-76	Bill Walton, UCLA	Los Angeles, Cal.
1973	UCLA	John Wooden	Memphis St.	87-66	Bill Walton, UCLA	St. Louis, Mo.
1974	N. Carolina St.	Norm Sloan	Marquette	76-64	David Thompson, No. Carolina St.	Greensboro, N.C.
1975	UCLA	John Wooden	Kentucky	92-85	Richard Washington, UCLA	San Diego, Cal.
1976	Indiana	Bob Knight	Michigan	86-68	Kent Benson, Indiana	Philadelphia, Pa.
1977	Marquette	Al McGuire	N. Carolina	67-59	Butch Lee, Marquette	Atlanta, Ga.
1978	Kentucky	Joe Hall	Duke	94-88	Jack Givens, Kentucky	St. Louis, Mo.
1979	Michigan St.	Jud Heathcote	Indiana St.	75-64	Magic Johnson, Michigan St.	Salt Lake City, Ut.
1980	Louisville	Denny Crum	UCLA*	59-54	Darrell Griffith, Louisville	Indianapolis, Ind.
1981	Indiana	Bob Knight	N. Carolina	63-50	Isiah Thomas, Indiana	Philadelphia, Pa.
1982	N. Carolina	Dean Smith	Georgetown	63-62	James Worthy, No. Carolina	New Orleans, La.
1983	N. Carolina St.	Jim Valvano	Houston	54-52	Akeem Olajuwon, Houston	Albuquerque, N.M.
1984	Georgetown	John Thompson	Houston	84-75	Patrick Ewing, Georgetown	Seattle, Wash.
1985	Villanova	Rollie Massimino	Georgetown	66-64	Ed Pinckney, Villanova	Lexington, Ky.

*Declared ineligible subsequent to the tournament. (1) Overtime.

NCAA Division I Career Scoring Leaders

Player, team	Seasons	G	FG	FT	Pts.	Avg.
Pete Maravich, Louisiana State.	1968-70	83	1387	893	3667	44.2
Austin Carr, Notre Dame	1969-71	74	1017	526	2560	34.6
Oscar Robertson, Cincinnati	1958-60	88	1052	869	2973	33.8
Calvin Murphy, Niagara	1968-70	77	947	654	2548	33.1
Dwight Lamar, SW Louisiana	1972-73	57	768	326	1862	32.7
Frank Selvy, Furman	1952-54	78	922	694	2538	32.5
Rick Mount, Purdue	1968-70	72	910	503	2323	32.3
Darrell Floyd, Furman	1954-56	71	868	545	2281	32.1
Nick Werkman, Seton Hall	1962-64	71	812	649	2273	32.0
Willie Humes, Idaho State	1970-71	48	565	380	1510	31.5
William Averitt, Pepperdine	1972-73	49	615	311	1541	31.4
Elgin Baylor, Col. Idaho, Seattle	55, 57-58	80	956	588	2500	31.3
Elvin Hayes, Houston	1966-68	93	1215	454	2884	31.0
Freeman Williams, Portland State	1975-1978	106	1369	511	3249	30.7
Larry Bird, Indiana State	1977-79	94	1154	542	2850	30.3

Wooden Award

Awarded annually to the nation's outstanding college basketball player by the U.S. Basketball Writers Assn.

1977	Marques Johnson, UCLA	1980	Darrell Griffith, Louisville
1978	Phil Ford, North Carolina	1981	Danny Ainge, Brigham Young
1979	Larry Bird, Indiana State	1982	Ralph Sampson, Virginia

1983	Ralph Sampson, Virginia
1984	Michael Jordan, North Carolina
1985	Chris Mullin, St. John's

NCAA Division I Women's Champions

Year	Champion	Coach	Final opponent	Year	Champion	Coach	Final opponent
1982	Louisiana Tech	Sonja Hogg	Cheyney	1984	USC	Linda Sharp	Tennessee
1983	USC	Linda Sharp	Louisiana Tech	1985	Old Dominion	Marianne Stanley	Georgia

NCAA Division II Champions

Year	Champion	Year	Champion	Year	Champion	Year	Champion
1966	Kentucky Wesleyan	1971	Evansville	1976	Puget Sound	1981	Florida Southern
1967	Winston-Salem	1972	Roanoke	1977	Tennessee-Chattanooga	1982	Univ. of D.C.
1968	Kentucky Wesleyan	1973	Kentucky Wesleyan	1978	Cheyney State	1983	Wright State
1969	Kentucky Wesleyan	1974	Morgan State	1979	North Alabama	1984	Central Missouri St.
1970	Philadelphia Textile	1975	Old Dominion	1980	Virginia Union	1985	Jacksonville St.

IFGA Freshwater & Saltwater All-Tackle World Records

Source: International Game Fish Association. Records confirmed to June, 1985

Saltwater Fish

Species	Weight	Where caught	Date	Angler
Albacore	88 lbs. 2 oz.	Pt. Mogan, Canary Islands	Nov. 19, 1977	Siegried Dickemann
Amberjack, greater	155 lbs. 10 oz.	Bermuda	June 24, 1981	Joseph Dawson
Amberjack, Pacific	104 lbs.	Baja, Mexico	July 4, 1984	Richard Cresswell
Barracuda, great	83 lbs.	Lagos, Nigeria	Jan. 13, 1952	K.J.W. Hackett
Barracuda, Mexican	15 lbs. 4 oz.	Zihuatanejo, México	Oct. 7, 1984	Tony Pena
Barracuda, slender	14 lbs. 10 oz.	N. Queensland, Australia	June 16, 1984	Virginia Pena
Bass, black sea	9 lbs.	Montauk, N.Y.	Oct. 10, 1983	Salvatore Vicari
Bass, European	11 lbs. 15 oz.	Pont Lorois Belz, France	July 25, 1983	Bernard Peron
Bass, giant sea	563 lbs. 8 oz.	Anacaba Island, Cal.	Aug. 20, 1968	James D. McAdam Jr.
Bass, striped	78 lbs. 8 oz.	Atlantic City, N.J.	Sept. 21, 1982	Albert McReynolds
Bluefish	31 lbs. 12 oz.	Hatteras Inlet, N.C.	Jan. 30, 1972	James M. Hussey
Bonefish	19 lbs.	Zululand, S. Africa	May 26, 1962	Brian W. Batchelor
Bonito, Atlantic	18 lbs. 14 oz.	Fayal 1., Azores	July 8, 1984	D. G. Higgs
Bonito, Pacific	23 lbs. 8 oz.	Victoria, Mahe Seychelles	Feb. 19, 1975	Anne Cochain
Cobia	110 lbs. 5 oz.	Mombasa, Kenya	Sept. 8, 1964	Eric Tinworth
Cod, Atlantic	98 lbs. 12 oz.	Isle of Shoals, N.H.	June 8, 1969	Alphonse Bielevich
Cod, Pacific	30 lbs.	Andrew Bay, Alaska	June 7, 1984	Donald Vaughn
Conger	102 lbs. 8 oz.	Devon, England	July 18, 1983	Raymond E. Street
Dolphin	87 lbs.	Papagallo Gulf, Costa Rica	Sept. 25, 1976	Manual Salazar
Drum, black	113 lbs. 1 oz.	Lewes, Del.	Sept. 15, 1975	Gerald Townsend
Drum, red	94 lbs. 2 oz.	Avon, N.C.	Nov. 7, 1984	David Deuel
Eel, African mottled	36 lbs. 1 oz.	Durban, So. Africa	June 10, 1984	Ferdie van Nooten
Flounder, southern	20 lb. 9 oz.	Nassau Sound, Fla.	Dec. 23, 1983	Larenza Mungin
Flounder, summer	22 lbs. 7 oz.	Montauk, N.Y.	Sept. 15, 1975	Charles Nappi
Halibut, Atlantic	250 lbs.	Gloucester, Mass.	July 3, 1981	Louis Sirard
Halibut, California	45 lbs.	Santa Cruz Is., Cal.	June 19, 1982	Jack Meserve
Halibut, Pacific	350 lbs.	Homer, Alaska	June 30, 1982	Vern S. Foster
Jack, crevalle	54 lbs. 7oz.	Pt. Michel, Gabon	Jan. 15, 1982	Thomas Gibson Jr.
Jack, horse-eye	24 lbs. 8 oz.	Miami, Fla.	Dec. 20, 1982	Tito Schnau
Jack, Pacific crevalle	22 lbs. 15 oz.	Salinas, Ecuador	Nov. 19, 1983	Emilio Kronfle
Jewfish	680 lbs.	Fernandina Beach, Fla.	May 20, 1961	Lynn Joyner
Kawakawa	26 lbs.	Merimbula, Australia	Jan. 26, 1980	Wally Elfring
Lingcod	46 lbs.	Hakai Pass, B.C. Canada	Aug. 31, 1983	Betty Moore
Mackerel, cero	15 lbs. 8 oz.	Key West, Fla.	Nov. 3, 1984	Jerrold Weinstock
Mackerel, king	90 lbs.	Key West, Fla.	Feb. 16, 1976	Norton Thomton
Mackeral, Spanish	12 lbs.	Ft. Pierce, Fla.	Nov. 17, 1984	John Colligar
Marlin, Atlantic blue	1,282 lbs.	St. Thomas, Virgin Islands	Aug. 6, 1977	Larry Martin
Marlin, black	1,560 lbs.	Cabo Blanco, Peru	Aug. 4, 1953	A. C. Glassell Jr.
Marlin, Pacific blue	1,376 lbs.	Kaaiwa Pt., Hawaii	May. 31, 1982	J.W. deBeaubien
Marlin, striped	455 lbs. 4 oz.	Mayor Island, New Zealand	Mar. 8, 1982	Bruce Jenkinson
Marlin, white	181 lbs. 14 oz.	Vitoria, Brazil	Dec. 8, 1979	Evandro Luiz Caser
Permit	51 lbs. 8 oz.	Lake Worth, Fla.	Apr. 28, 1978	William M. Kenney
Pollack	26 lbs.	Ile de Ouessant, France	Aug. 30, 1981	Loik La Chat
Pollock	46 lbs. 7 oz.	Brielle, N.J.	May 26, 1975	John Tomes Holton
Pompano, African	41 lbs. 8 oz.	Ft. Lauderdale, Fla.	Feb. 15, 1979	Wayne Sommers
Roosterfish	114 lbs.	La Paz, Mexico	June 1, 1960	Abe Sackheim
Runner, blue	5 lbs.	Ft. Lauderdale, Fla.	Dec. 24, 1983	Thomas Buffham
Runner, rainbow	33 lbs. 10 oz.	Clarion Is., Mexico	Mar. 14, 1976	Ralph A. Mikkelsen
Sailfish, Atlantic	128 lbs. 1 oz.	Luanda, Angola	Mar. 27, 1974	Harm Steyn
Sailfish, Pacific	221 lbs.	Santa Cruz Is., Ecuador	Feb. 12, 1947	C. W. Stewart
Seabass, white	83 lbs. 12 oz.	San Felipe, Mexico	Mar. 31, 1953	L.C. Baumgardner
Seatrout, spotted	16 lbs.	Mason's Beach, Va.	May 28, 1977	William Katko
Shark, blue	437 lbs.	Catherine Bay, N.S.W. Australia	Oct. 2, 1976	Peter Hyde
Shark, hammerhead	991 lbs.	Sarasota, Fla.	May 30, 1982	Allen Ogle
Shark, man-eater or white	2,664 lbs.	Ceduna, Australia	Apr. 21, 1959	Alfred Dean
Shark, mako	1,080 lbs.	Montauk, N.Y.	Aug. 26, 1979	James Melanson
Shark, porbeagle	465 lbs.	Cornwall, England	July 23, 1976	Jorge Potier
Shark, thresher	802 lbs.	Tutukaka, New Zealand	Feb. 8, 1981	Dianne North
Shark, tiger	1,780 lbs.	Cherry Grove, S.C.	June 14, 1964	Walter Maxwell
Skipjack, black	20 lbs. 5 oz.	Baja, Mexico	Oct. 14, 1983	Roger Torriero
Snapper, cubera	121 lbs. 8 oz.	Cameron, La.	July 5, 1982	Mike Hebert
Snook	53 lbs. 10 oz.	Costa Rica	Oct. 18, 1978	Gilbert Ponzi
Spearfish	90 lbs. 13 oz.	Madeira Island, Portugal	June 2, 1980	Joseph Larkin
Swordfish	1,182 lbs.	Iquique, Chile	May 7, 1953	L. Marron
Tanguigue	99 lbs.	Natal, So. Africa	Mar. 14, 1982	Michael J. Wilkinson
Tarpon	283 lbs.	Lake Maracaibo, Venezuela	Mar. 19, 1956	M. Salazar
Tautog	21 lbs. 8 oz.	Wachapreagee, Va.	Aug. 4, 1984	Tommy Wood
Tope	71 lbs. 10 oz.	Knysna, So. Africa	July 10, 1982	William DeWit
Trevally, bigeye	15 lbs.	Isla Coiba, Panama	Jan. 18, 1984	Sally Timms
Trevally, giant	137 lbs. 9 oz.	McKenzie St. Park, Hawaii	July 13, 1983	Roy Gushiken

Species	Weight	Where Caught	Date	Angler
Tuna, Atlantic bigeye	375 lbs. 8 oz.	Ocean City, Md.	Aug. 26, 1977	Cecil Browne
Tuna, blackfin	42 lbs.	Bermuda	June 2, 1978	Alan J. Card
Tuna, bluefin	1,496 lbs.	Aulds Cove, Nova Scotia	Oct. 26, 1979	Ken Fraser
Tuna, longtail	79 lbs. 2 oz.	Montague Is., N.S.W., Australia	Apr. 12, 1982	Tim Simpson
Tuna, Pacific bigeye	435 lbs.	Cabo Blanco, Peru	Apr. 17, 1957	Dr. Russel Lee
Tuna, skipjack	41 lbs. 12 oz.	Mauritius	Mar. 13, 1982	Bruno de Ravel
Tuna, southern bluefin	348 lbs. 5 oz.	Whakatane, New Zealand	Jan. 16, 1981	Rex Wood
Tuna, yellowfin	388 lbs. 12 oz.	San Benedicto Island, Mexico	Apr. 1, 1977	Curt Wiesenhutter
Tunny, little	27 lbs.	Key Largo, Fla.	Apr. 20, 1976	William E. Allison
Wahoo	149 lbs.	Cay Cay, Bahamas	June 15, 1962	John Pirovano
Weakfish	19 lbs. 2 oz.	Jones Beach Inlet, N.Y.	Oct. 11, 1984	Dennis Rooney
Yellowtail, California	71 lbs. 15 oz.	Alijos Rocks, Mexico	June 24, 1979	Michael Carpenter
Yellowtail, southern	114 lbs. 10 oz.	Tauranga, New Zealand	Feb. 5, 1984	Rudolf Wehrl

Freshwater Fish

Species	Weight	Where Caught	Date	Angler
Barramundi	59 lbs. 12 oz.	Pt. Stuart, Australia	Apr. 7, 1983	Andrew Davern
Bass, largemouth	22 lbs. 4 oz.	Montgomery Lake, Ga.	June 2, 1932	George W. Perry
Bass, peacock	26 lbs. 8 oz.	Matevini R., Colombia	Jan. 26, 1982	Rod Neubert
Bass, redeye	8 lbs. 3 oz.	Flint River, Ga.	Oct. 23, 1977	David A. Hubbard
Bass rock	3 lbs.	York River, Ont.	Aug. 1, 1974	Peter Gulgin
Bass, smallmouth	11 lbs. 15 oz.	Dale Hollow Lake, Ky.	July 9, 1955	David L. Hayes
Bass, spotted	9 lbs.	Perris, Lake, Ala.	Feb. 5, 1984	Jeffrey Mathews
Bass, Suwannee	3 lbs. 9 oz.	Ochlocknee R., Ga.	Oct. 6, 1984	Laverne Norton
Bass, white	5 lbs. 9 oz.	Colorado River, Tex.	Mar. 31, 1977	David Cordill
Bass, whiterock	20 lbs. 6 oz.	Savannah River, Ga.	May 26, 1978	Dan Wood
Bass, yellow	2 lbs. 4 oz.	Lake Monroe, Ind.	Mar. 27, 1977	Donald L. Stalker
Bluegill	4 lbs. 12 oz.	Ketona Lake, Ala.	Apr. 9, 1950	T.S. Hudson
Bowfin	21 lbs. 8 oz.	Florence, S.C.	Jan. 29, 1980	Robert Harmon
Buffalo, bigmouth	70 lbs. 5 oz.	Bastrop, La.	Apr. 21, 1980	Delbert Sisk
Buffalo, black	55 lbs. 8 oz.	Cherokee L., Tenn.	May 3, 1984	Edward McLain
Buffalo, smallmouth	68 lbs. 8 oz.	L. Hamilton, Ark.	May 16, 1984	Jerry Dolezal
Bullhead, brown	5 lbs. 8 oz.	Veal Pond, Ga.	May 22, 1975	Jimmy Andrews
Bullhead, yellow	4 lbs. 4 oz.	Mormon Lake, Ariz.	May 11, 1984	Emily Williams
Burbot	18 lbs. 4 oz.	Pickford, Mich.	Jan. 31, 1980	Thomas Courtemanche
Carp	57 lbs. 13 oz.	Potomac R., Wash., D.C.	June 19, 1983	David Nikolow
Catfish, blue	97 lbs.	Missouri River, S.D.	Sept. 16, 1959	E.B. Elliott
Catfish, channel	58 lbs.	Santee-Cooper Res., S.C.	July 7, 1964	W.B. Whaley
Catfish, flathead	91 lbs. 4 oz.	Lake Lewisville, Tex.	Mar. 28, 1982	Mike Rogers
Catfish, white	17 lbs. 7 oz.	Success L., Tulare, Cal.	Nov. 15, 1981	Chuck Idell
Char, Arctic	32 lbs. 9 oz.	Tree River, Canada	July 30, 1981	Jeffrey Ward
Crappie, white	5 lbs. 3 oz.	Enid Dam, Miss.	July 31, 1957	Fred L. Bright
Dolly Varden	7 lbs. 8 oz.	Kenai R., Alaska	Sept. 22, 1984	Louie Brunner
Dorado	48 lbs. 11 oz.	Corrientes, Argentina	Sept. 12, 1982	Sindo Farina
Drum, freshwater	54 lbs. 8 oz.	Nickajack Lake, Tenn.	Apr. 20, 1972	Benny E. Hull
Gar, alligator	279 lbs.	Rio Grande River, Tex.	Dec. 2, 1951	Bill Valverde
Gar, Florida	21 lbs. 3 oz.	Boca Raton, Fla.	June 3, 1981	Jeff Sabol
Gar, longnose	50 lbs. 5 oz.	Trinity River, Tex.	July 30, 1954	Townsend Miller
Gar, shortnose	4 lbs. 9 oz.	Mississippi R., Minn.	July 22, 1984	Matthew Ocel
Gar, spotted	7 lbs. 6 oz.	Cataco Creek, Ala.	Aug. 14, 1984	Linda Baker
Grayling, Arctic	5 lbs. 15 oz.	Katseyedie River, N.W.T.	Aug. 16, 1967	Jeanne P. Branson
Inconnu	38 lbs. 2 oz.	Kobuk R., Alaska	Sept. 12, 1982	Mark Feldman
Kokanee	6 lbs. 9 oz.	Priest Lake, Ida.	June 9, 1975	Jerry Verge
Muskellunge	69 lbs. 15 oz.	St. Lawrence River, N.Y.	Sept. 22, 1957	Arthur Lawton
Muskellunge, tiger	51 lbs. 3 oz.	Lac Vieux-Desert, Wis., Mich.	July 16, 1919	John Knobla
Paddlefish	76 lbs.	Table Rock L., Mo.	July 23, 1984	Lewis S. Herrill
Perch, white	4 lbs. 12 oz.	Messalonskee Lake, Me.	June 4, 1949	Mrs. Earl Small
Perch, yellow	4 lbs. 3 oz.	Bordentown, N.J.	May, 1865	Dr. C.C. Abbot
Pickerel, chain	9 lbs. 6 oz.	Homerville, Ga.	Feb. 17, 1961	Baxley McQuaig Jr.
Pike, northern	46 lbs. 2 oz.	Sacandaga Reservoir, N.Y.	Sept. 15, 1940	Peter Dubuc
Redhorse, shorthead	4 lbs. 12 oz.	Elkhart, Ind.	May 18, 1984	William Merrick
Redhorse, silver	9 lbs. 11 oz.	Winnipeg R., Manitoba, Canada	May 22, 1982	John Richards
Salmon, Atlantic	79 lbs. 2 oz.	Tana River, Norway	1928	Henrik Henriksen
Salmon, chinook	93 lbs.	Kelp Bay, Alas.	June 24, 1977	Howard C. Rider
Salmon, chum	27 lbs. 3 oz.	Raymond Cove, Alas.	June 11, 1977	Robert A. Jahnke
Salmon, coho	31 lbs.	Cowichan Bay, B.C.	Oct. 11, 1947	Mrs. Lee Hallberg
Salmon, pink	12 lbs. 9 oz.	Morse, Kenai rivers, Alas.	Aug. 17, 1974	Steven A. Lee
Salmon, sockeye	12 lbs. 8 oz.	Situk R., Alaska	June 23, 1983	Mike Boswell
Sauger	8 lbs. 12 oz.	Lake Sakakawea, N.D.	Oct. 6, 1971	Mike Fischer
Shad, American	11 lbs. 1 oz.	Delaware River, N.J.	May 5, 1984	Charles Mower
Sturgeon	468 lbs.	Benicia, Cal.	July 9, 1983	Joey Pallotta 3d
Sunfish, green	2 lbs. 2 oz.	Stockton Lake, Mo.	June 18, 1971	Paul M. Dilley
Sunfish, redbreast	1 lb. 12 oz.	Suwannee R., Fla.	May 29, 1984	Alvin Buchanan
Sunfish, redear	4 lbs. 8 oz.	Chase City, Va.	June 19, 1970	Maurice E. Ball
Tigerfish	61 lbs. 11 oz.	L. Tanganyika, Zambia	Feb. 4, 1984	Don Hunter
Tilapia	4 lbs. 5 oz.	Mittry L., Ariz.	Sept. 17, 1984	John B. Adkins
Trout, brook	14 lbs. 8 oz.	Nipigon River, Ont.	July 1916	Dr. W.J. Cook
Trout, brown	35 lbs. 15 oz.	Nahuel Huapi, Argentina	Dec. 16, 1952	Eugenio Cavaglia
Trout, bull	32 lbs.	L. Pend Oreille, Ida.	Oct. 27, 1949	N.L. Higgins
Trout, cutthroat	41 lbs.	Pyramid Lake, Nev.	Dec. 1925	J. Skimmerhorn
Trout, golden	11 lbs.	Cook's Lake, Wyo.	Aug. 5, 1948	Charles S. Reed
Trout, lake	65 lbs.	Great Bear Lake, N.W.T.	Aug. 8, 1970	Larry Daunis
Trout, rainbow	42 lbs. 2 oz.	Bell Island, Alas.	June 22, 1970	David Robert White
Trout, tiger	20 lbs. 13 oz.	Lake Michigan, Wis.	Aug. 12, 1978	Pete Friedland
Walleye	25 lbs.	Old Hickory Lake, Tenn.	Aug. 1, 1960	Mabry Harper
Warmouth	2 lbs. 2 oz.	Douglas Swamp, S.C.	May 19, 1973	Willie Singletary
Whitefish, lake	14 lbs. 6 oz.	Meaford, Ont.	May 21, 1984	Dennis Laycock
Whitefish, mountain	5 lbs. 2 oz.	Columbia R., Wash.	Nov. 30, 1983	Steven Becken
Whitefish, round	6 lbs.	Putahow R., Manitoba	June 14, 1984	Allen Ristori

National Basketball Association, 1984-85

Final Standings

Eastern Conference

Atlantic Division

Club	W	L	Pct	GB
Boston	63	19	.768	.....
Philadelphia	58	24	.707	5
New Jersey	42	40	.512	21
Washington	40	42	.488	23
New York	24	58	.293	39

Central Division

Club	W	L	Pct	GB
Milwaukee	59	23	.720	.....
Detroit	46	36	.561	13
Chicago	38	44	.463	21
Cleveland	36	46	.439	23
Atlanta	34	48	.415	25
Indiana	22	60	.268	37

Western Conference

Midwest Division

Club	W	L	Pct	GB
Denver	52	30	.634	.....
Houston	48	34	.585	4
Dallas	44	38	.537	8
San Antonio	41	41	.500	11
Utah	41	41	.500	11
Kansas City	31	51	.378	21

Pacific Division

Club	W	L	Pct	GB
L.A. Lakers	62	20	.756	.....
Portland	42	40	.512	20
Phoenix	36	46	.439	26
L.A. Clippers	31	51	.378	31
Seattle	31	51	.378	31
Golden State	22	60	.268	40

NBA Playoff Results

Eastern Division

Detroit defeated New York 3 games to 0.
Boston defeated Cleveland 3 games to 1.
Philadelphia defeated Washington 3 games to 1.
Milwaukee defeated Chicago 3 games to 1.
Philadelphia defeated Milwaukee 4 games to 0.
Boston defeated Detroit 4 games to 2.
Boston defeated Philadelphia 4 games to 1.

Western Division

L.A. Lakers defeated Pheonix 3 games to 0.
Portland defeated Dallas 3 games to 1.
Denver defeated San Antonio 3 games to 2.
Utah defeated Houston 3 games to 2.
Denver defeated Utah 4 games to 1.
L.A. Lakers defeated Portland 4 games to 1.
L.A. Lakers defeated Denver 4 games to 1.

Championship

L.A. Lakers defeated Boston 4 games to 2.

NBA Champions 1947-1985

Year	Regular season Eastern Conference	Western Conference	Playoffs Winner	Runner-up
1947	Washington	Chicago	Philadelphia	Chicago
1948	Philadelphia	St. Louis	Baltimore	Philadelphia
1949	Washington	Rochester	Minneapolis	Washington
1950	Syracuse	Minneapolis	Minneapolis	Syracuse
1951	Philadelphia	Minneapolis	Rochester	New York
1952	Syracuse	Rochester	Minneapolis	New York
1953	New York	Minneapolis	Minneapolis	New York
1954	New York	Minneapolis	Minneapolis	Syracuse
1955	Syracuse	Ft. Wayne	Syracuse	Ft. Wayne
1956	Philadelphia	Ft. Wayne	Philadelphia	Ft. Wayne
1957	Boston	St. Louis	Boston	St. Louis
1958	Boston	St. Louis	St. Louis	Boston
1959	Boston	St. Louis	Boston	Minneapolis
1960	Boston	St. Louis	Boston	St. Louis
1961	Boston	St. Louis	Boston	St. Louis
1962	Boston	Los Angeles	Boston	Los Angeles
1963	Boston	Los Angeles	Boston	Los Angeles
1964	Boston	San Francisco	Boston	San Francisco
1965	Boston	Los Angeles	Boston	Los Angeles
1966	Philadelphia	Los Angeles	Boston	Los Angeles
1967	Philadelphia	San Francisco	Philadelphia	San Francisco
1968	Philadelphia	St. Louis	Boston	Los Angeles
1969	Baltimore	Los Angeles	Boston	Los Angeles
1970	New York	Atlanta	New York	Los Angeles

Year	Atlantic	Central	Midwest	Pacific	Winner	Runner-up
1971	New York	Baltimore	Milwaukee	Los Angeles	Milwaukee	Baltimore
1972	Boston	Baltimore	Milwaukee	Los Angeles	Los Angeles	New York
1973	Boston	Baltimore	Milwaukee	Los Angeles	New York	Los Angeles
1974	Boston	Capital	Milwaukee	Los Angeles	Boston	Milwaukee
1975	Boston	Washington	Chicago	Golden State	Golden State	Washington
1976	Boston	Cleveland	Milwaukee	Golden State	Boston	Phoenix
1977	Philadelphia	Houston	Denver	Los Angeles	Portland	Philadelphia
1978	Philadelphia	San Antonio	Denver	Portland	Washington	Seattle
1979	Washington	San Antonio	Kansas City	Seattle	Seattle	Washington
1980	Boston	Atlanta	Milwaukee	Los Angeles	Los Angeles	Philadelphia
1981	Boston	Milwaukee	San Antonio	Phoenix	Boston	Houston
1982	Boston	Milwaukee	San Antonio	Los Angeles	Los Angeles	Philadelphia
1983	Philadelphia	Milwaukee	San Antonio	Los Angeles	Philadelphia	Los Angeles
1984	Boston	Milwaukee	Utah	Los Angeles	Boston	Los Angeles
1985	Boston	Milwaukee	Denver	L.A. Lakers	L.A. Lakers	Boston

Final Statistics, 1984-1985

Individual Scoring Leaders

(Minimum: 70 games played or 1400 points)

	G	Pts	Avg
King, New York	55	1809	32.9
Bird, Boston	80	2295	28.7
Jordan, Denver	82	2313	28.2
Short, Golden State	78	2186	28.0
English, Denver	81	2262	27.9
Wilkins, Atlanta	81	2217	27.4
Dantley, Utah	55	1462	26.6
Aguirre, Dallas	80	2055	25.7
Malone, Philadelphia	79	1941	24.6
Cummings, Milwaukee	79	1861	23.6
Natt, Denver	78	1817	23.3
Woolridge, Chicago	77	1767	22.9
Johnson, Kansas City	82	1876	22.9
Griffith, Utah	78	1764	22.6
Free, Cleveland	71	1597	22.5
Vandeweghe, Portland	72	1616	22.4
Mitchell, San Antonio	82	1824	22.2
Smith, L.A. Clippers	80	1767	22.1
Sampson, Houston	82	1809	22.1
Abdul-Jabbar, L.A. Lakers	79	1735	22.0

Field Goal Percentage Leaders

(Minimum: 300 FG made)

	FG	FGA	Pct
Donaldson, L.A. Clippers	351	551	.637
Gilmore, San Antonio	532	854	.623
Thorpe, Kansas City	411	685	.600
Abdul-Jabbar, L.A. Lakers	723	1207	.599
Nance, Phoenix	515	877	.587
Worthy, L.A. Lakers	610	1066	.572
McHale, Boston	605	1062	.570
Cheeks, Philadelphia	422	741	.570
Johnson, L.A. Lakers	504	899	.561
Woolridge, Chicago	679	1225	.554

Free Throw Percentage Leaders

(Minimum: 125 FT made)

	FT	FTA	Pct
Macy, Phoenix	127	140	.907
Vandeweghe, Portland	369	412	.896
Davis, Dallas	158	178	.888
Tripucka, Detroit	255	288	.885
Adams, Phoenix	250	283	.883
Bird, Boston	403	457	.882
Cheeks, Philadelphia	175	199	.879
Bridgeman, L.A. Clippers	181	206	.879
Johnson, Kansas City	325	373	.871
Green, Utah	232	267	.869

3-Pt. Field Goal Leaders

(Minimum: 25 made)

	FG	FGA	Pct
Scott, L.A. Lakers	26	60	.433
Bird, Boston	56	131	.427
Davis, Dallas	47	115	.409
Tucker, New York	29	72	.403
Ellis, Dallas	42	109	.385

Assist Leaders

(Minimum: 70 games or 400 assists)

	G	No	Avg
Thomas, Detroit	81	1123	13.9
Johnson, L.A. Lakers	77	968	12.6
Moore, San Antonio	82	816	10.0
Nixon, L.A. Clippers	81	711	8.8
Bagley, Cleveland	81	697	8.6
Richardson, New Jersey	82	669	8.2
Theus, Kansas City	82	656	8.0
Johnson, Atlanta	73	566	7.8
Green, Utah	77	597	7.8
G. Williams, Washington	79	608	7.7

Rebound Leaders

(Minimum: 70 games or 800 rebounds)

	G	Tot	Avg
Malone, Philadelphia	79	1031	13.1
Laimbeer, Detroit	82	1013	12.4
Williams, New Jersey	82	1005	12.3
Olajuwon, Houston	82	974	11.9
Eaton, Utah	82	927	11.3
Smith, Golden State	80	869	10.9
Parish, Boston	79	840	10.6
Bird, Boston	80	842	10.5
Gilmore, San Antonio	81	846	10.4
Thompson, Kansas City	82	854	10.4

Steals Leaders

(Minimum: 70 games or 125 steals)

	G	No	Avg
Richardson, New Jersey	82	243	2.96
Moore, San Antonio	82	229	2.79
Lever, Denver	82	202	2.46
Jordan, Chicago	82	196	2.39
Rivers, Atlanta	69	163	2.36
Thomas, Detroit	81	187	2.31
G. Williams, Washington	79	178	2.25
Drexler, Portland	80	177	2.21
Cheeks, Philadelphia	78	169	2.17
Conner, Golden State	79	161	2.04

Blocked Shots Leaders

(Minimum: 70 games or 100 blocked shots)

	G	No	Avg
Eaton, Utah	82	456	5.56
Olajuwon, Houston	82	220	2.68
Bowie, Portland	76	203	2.67
Cooper, Denver	80	197	2.46
Rollins, Atlanta	70	167	2.39
Hinson, Cleveland	76	173	2.28
Gilmore, San Antonio	81	173	2.14
Walton, L.A. Clippers	67	140	2.09
Lister, Milwaukee	81	167	2.06
Abdul-Jabbar, L.A. Lakers	79	162	2.05

1985 NBA Player Draft

The following are the first round picks of the National Basketball Assn.

New York—Patrick Ewing, Georgetown
Indiana—Wayman Tisdale, Oklahoma
L.A. Clippers—Benoit Benjamin, Creighton
Seattle—Xavier McDaniel, Wichita State
Atlanta—Jon Koncak, SMU
Sacramento—Joe Kleine, Arkansas
Golden State—Chris Mullin, St. John's
Dallas—Detlef Schrempf, Washington
Cleveland—*Charles Oakley, Virginia Union
Phoenix—Ed Pinckney, Villanova
Chicago—*Keith Lee, Memphis State
Washington—Kenny Green, Wake Forest

Utah—Karl Malone, Louisiana Tech
San Antonio—Alfredrick Hughes, Loyola, Chicago
Denver—Blair Rasmussen, Oregon
Dallas—Bill Wennington, St. John's
Dallas—Uwe Blab, Indiana
Detroit—Joe Dumars, McNeese State
Houston—Steve Harris, Tulsa
Boston—Sam Vincent, Michigan State
Philadelphia—Terry Catledge, South Alabama
Milwaukee—Jerry Reynolds, Louisiana Tech
L.A. Lakers—A.C. Green, Oregon State
Portland—Terry Porter, Wis.-Stevens Pt.

*Included in a trade between the 2 teams.

Individual Statistics, 1984-1985
(Over 500 Minutes Played)

Atlanta Hawks

	Min	FG%	FT%	RBs	Ast	Pts	Avg
Wilkins	3023	.451	.806	557	200	2217	27.4
Johnson	2367	.479	.798	192	566	1193	16.3
Rivers	2126	.476	.770	214	410	974	14.1
Williams	867	.439	.642	168	94	417	12.3
Wittman	1168	.531	.732	73	125	406	9.9
Levingston	2017	.527	.653	566	104	727	9.8
Willis	1785	.467	.657	522	36	765	9.3
Glenn	1126	.588	.816	81	122	518	8.6
Carr	1195	.528	.789	232	80	499	8.0
Rollins	1750	.549	.720	442	52	439	6.3
Hastings	825	.473	.778	159	46	241	3.8
Brown	814	.406	.574	223	25	195	2.8

Boston Celtics

	Min	FG%	FT%	RBs	Ast	Pts	Avg
Bird	3161	.522	.882	842	531	2295	28.7
McHale	2653	.570	.760	712	141	1565	19.8
Parish	2850	.542	.743	840	125	1394	17.6
Johnson	2976	.462	.853	317	543	1254	15.7
Ainge	2564	.529	.868	268	399	971	12.9
Maxwell	1495	.533	.831	242	102	633	11.1
Wedman	1127	.478	.764	159	94	499	6.4
Clark	562	.421	.774	69	48	169	2.7
Buckner	858	.383	.640	87	148	180	2.4

Chicago Bulls

	Min	FG%	FT%	RBs	Ast	Pts	Avg
Jordan	3144	.515	.845	534	481	2313	28.2
Woolridge	2816	.554	.785	435	135	1767	22.9
Dailey	2101	.473	.817	208	191	1262	16.0
Johnson	1659	.545	.718	437	64	743	10.0
Corzine	2062	.486	.745	422	140	701	8.5
Green	740	.432	.806	246	29	295	6.1
Greenwood	1523	.458	.713	388	78	371	6.1
Matthews	1523	.495	.694	67	354	443	5.7
Whatley	1385	.447	.791	101	381	349	5.0
Higgins	942	.441	.667	147	73	308	4.5
Ca. Jones	885	.461	.766	211	34	142	3.4
Oldham	993	.464	.680	236	31	212	3.4

Cleveland Cavaliers

	Min	FG%	FT%	RBs	Ast	Pts	Avg
Free	2249	.459	.749	211	320	1597	22.5
Hinson	2344	.503	.721	596	68	1201	15.8
Hubbard	2249	.505	.751	479	114	1201	15.8
Davis	1920	.426	.850	119	426	941	12.4
Turpin	1949	.511	.784	452	36	835	10.6
Thompson	715	.418	.849	116	58	347	10.5
Bagley	2401	.488	.749	291	697	804	9.9
Jones	769	.473	.739	171	29	342	7.8
Poquette	1656	.460	.796	473	79	532	6.7
Shelton	1244	.435	.662	267	96	367	6.4
Anderson	520	.431	.820	88	34	210	5.8
West	888	.546	.494	251	15	255	3.9

Dallas Mavericks

	Min	FG%	FT%	RBs	Ast	Pts	Avg
Aguirre	2699	.506	.759	477	249	2055	25.7
Blackman	2834	.508	.828	300	289	1598	19.7
Vincent	2543	.479	.836	704	169	1441	18.2
Perkins	2317	.471	.820	605	135	903	11.0
Davis	2539	.505	.888	193	581	825	10.1
Harper	2218	.520	.721	199	360	790	9.6
Ellis	1314	.454	.740	238	56	667	9.3
Nimphius	2010	.452	.771	408	183	500	6.1
Bryant	860	.453	.682	241	84	164	2.9

Denver Nuggets

	Min	FG%	FT%	RBs	Ast	Pts	Avg
English	2924	.518	.829	458	344	2262	27.9
Natt	2657	.546	.793	610	238	1817	23.3
Lever	2559	.430	.770	411	613	1051	12.8
Issel	1684	.459	.806	331	137	984	12.8
Cooper	2031	.472	.685	631	86	969	12.1
Evans	1437	.489	.863	119	231	816	10.1
Hanzlik	1673	.421	.756	207	210	621	7.8
Dunn	2290	.489	.724	385	153	434	5.4
Turner	1491	.466	.785	216	158	414	5.1
Schayes	542	.465	.814	144	38	199	3.6

Detroit Pistons

	Min	FG%	FT%	RBs	Ast	Pts	Avg
Thomas	3089	.458	.809	361	1123	1720	21.2
Tripucka	1675	.477	.885	218	135	1049	19.1
Laimbeer	2892	.506	.797	1013	154	1438	17.5
Long	1820	.487	.862	190	130	973	14.7
Johnson	2093	.454	.769	252	325	1051	12.8
Tyler	2004	.494	.716	423	63	950	11.6
Roundfield	1492	.467	.781	453	102	611	10.9
Benson	1401	.506	.809	324	93	478	6.6
Cureton	1642	.484	.569	419	83	496	6.1
Campbell	625	.496	.800	89	24	316	5.6

Golden State Warriors

	Min	FG%	FT%	RBs	Ast	Pts	Avg
Short	3081	.460	.817	398	234	2186	28.0
Floyd	2873	.445	.810	202	406	1598	19.5
Johnson	1565	.426	.823	396	149	875	13.3
Whitehead	2536	.510	.783	622	53	1026	13.0
Smith	2497	.530	.605	869	96	887	11.1
Conner	2258	.451	.750	246	369	640	8.1
Bratz	746	.424	.841	58	122	287	5.1
Aleksinas	1114	.478	.733	270	36	377	5.1
Wilson	1260	.460	.711	131	217	325	4.4
Plummer	702	.397	.707	134	26	250	3.8

Houston Rockets

	Min	FG%	FT%	RBs	Ast	Pts	Avg
Sampson	3086	.502	.676	853	224	1809	22.1
Olajuwon	2914	.538	.613	974	111	1692	20.6
McCray	3001	.535	.738	539	355	1183	14.4
Lloyd	2128	.526	.732	231	280	1077	13.1
Lucas	1158	.462	.798	85	318	536	11.4
Wiggins	1575	.484	.733	235	119	738	9.0
Reid	1763	.481	.698	273	171	713	8.7
Hollins	1950	.461	.794	173	417	609	7.6
Leavell	536	.421	.772	37	102	228	5.4
Micheaux	565	.580	.674	143	30	211	3.7
Petersen	714	.486	.758	147	29	190	3.2

Indiana Pacers

	Min	FG%	FT%	RBs	Ast	Pts	Avg
Kellogg	2449	.505	.760	724	244	1432	18.6
Williams	2557	.475	.657	634	252	1375	18.3
Fleming	2486	.470	.767	323	247	1126	14.1
Stipanovich	2315	.475	.798	614	199	1126	13.7
Thomas	2059	.478	.782	261	234	885	11.1
Sichting	1808	.521	.875	114	264	771	11.0
Stansbury	1278	.459	.810	114	127	526	7.1
Brown	1586	.460	.678	288	159	544	6.6
Garnett	1123	.481	.690	286	67	418	6.4
Durrant	756	.416	.706	124	80	300	5.1
Waiters	703	.447	.580	170	30	199	3.2

Kansas City Kings

	Min	FG%	FT%	RBs	Ast	Pts	Avg
Johnson	3029	.491	.871	407	273	1876	22.9
Woodson	1998	.496	.800	198	143	1329	17.0
Theus	2543	.487	.863	270	656	1341	16.4
Drew	2373	.501	.794	164	484	1075	14.9
Thorpe	1918	.600	.620	556	111	1052	12.6
Thompson	2458	.531	.721	854	130	965	11.8
Olberding	2277	.502	.832	513	243	823	10.2
Meriweather	1061	.498	.774	263	27	339	4.5
Buse	939	.404	.767	61	203	218	3.4

Los Angeles Clippers

	Min	FG%	FT%	RBs	Ast	Pts	Avg
Smith	2762	.537	.794	427	216	1767	22.1
Nixon	2894	.465	.780	218	711	1395	17.2
Johnson	2448	.452	.731	428	248	1181	16.4
Bridgeman	2042	.465	.879	230	171	1115	13.9
Donaldson	2392	.637	.749	668	48	929	11.3
Walton	1647	.521	.680	600	156	676	10.1
Cage	1610	.543	.737	392	51	533	7.1
White	1106	.516	.692	195	34	378	4.7
Gordon	682	.383	.755	61	88	259	4.1
Warrick	713	.491	.772	58	153	215	3.7
Catchings	1049	.483	.663	262	14	203	2.9

Los Angeles Lakers

	Min	FG%	FT%	RBs	Ast	Pts	Avg
Abdul-Jabbar	2630	.599	.702	622	249	1735	22.0
Johnson	2781	.561	.843	476	968	1406	18.3
Worthy	2696	.572	.776	511	201	1410	17.6
Scott	2305	.539	.820	210	244	1295	16.0
McAdoo	1254	.520	.753	295	67	690	10.5
McGee	1170	.538	.588	165	71	774	10.2
Cooper	2189	.465	.865	255	429	702	8.6
Wilkes	761	.488	.773	94	41	347	8.3
Spriggs	1292	.548	.767	227	132	500	6.7
Kupchak	716	.504	.659	184	21	306	5.3
Rambis	1617	.554	.660	528	69	430	5.2

Milwaukee Bucks

	Min	FG%	FT%	RBs	Ast	Pts	Avg
Cummings	2722	.495	.741	716	228	1861	23.6
Moncrief	2734	.483	.828	391	382	1585	21.7
Pressey	2876	.517	.758	429	543	1284	16.1
Hodges	2496	.490	.815	186	349	871	10.6
Lister	2091	.538	.588	647	127	798	9.9
Pierce	882	.537	.823	117	94	433	9.8
Thompson	942	.412	.793	158	78	453	9.2
Mokeski	1586	.478	.698	410	99	491	6.2
Grevey	1182	.448	.822	103	94	476	6.1
Davis	774	.430	.823	153	51	358	5.9
Breuer	1083	.511	.701	256	40	413	5.3
Fields	535	.440	.750	84	38	195	3.8

New Jersey Nets

	Min	FG%	FT%	RBs	Ast	Pts	Avg
Birdsong	1842	.511	.622	148	232	1155	20.6
Richardson	3127	.469	.767	457	669	1649	20.1
Williams	3182	.530	.625	1005	167	1491	18.2
Dawkins	972	.566	.711	181	45	527	13.5
Gminski	2418	.465	.841	633	158	1036	12.8
King	860	.491	.817	159	58	537	12.8
O'Koren	1119	.494	.627	166	102	438	10.2
Ransey	1689	.459	.859	130	355	724	8.9
Cook	1063	.468	.870	92	160	473	8.2
Turner	1429	.454	.859	218	108	421	5.8
McKenna	535	.455	.884	49	58	165	5.7
Johnson	800	.532	.815	185	22	107	1.6

New York Knickerbockers

	Min	FG%	FT%	RBs	Ast	Pts	Avg
King	2063	.530	.772	317	204	1809	32.9
Cummings	2069	.514	.780	518	109	997	15.8
Walker	2489	.435	.700	278	408	1103	13.5
Orr	2452	.486	.784	391	134	1007	12.7
Sparrow	2292	.492	.865	169	557	781	9.9
Tucker	1819	.483	.792	188	199	653	8.5
Carter	1279	.450	.813	95	167	548	7.9
Bannister	1404	.470	.474	330	39	509	6.8
Grunfeld	1061	.490	.740	151	105	455	6.6
Wilkins	917	.498	.541	262	16	298	5.5
Bailey	1297	.447	.676	344	39	385	5.2
Cavenall	653	.326	.564	166	19	78	1.5

Philadelphia 76ers

	Min	FG%	FT%	RBs	Ast	Pts	Avg
Malone	2957	.469	.815	1031	130	1941	24.6
Erving	2535	.494	.765	414	233	1561	20.0
Toney	2237	.492	.862	177	363	1245	17.8
Barkley	2347	.545	.733	703	155	1148	14.0
Cheeks	2616	.570	.879	217	497	1025	13.1
Jones	1633	.538	.861	297	155	600	7.5
Richardson	1531	.453	.854	155	157	443	6.0
Threatt	1304	.452	.733	99	175	446	5.4
G. Johnson	756	.407	.875	164	38	264	4.8
C. Johnson	875	.498	.735	221	33	270	4.7

Phoenix Suns

	Min	FG%	FT%	RBs	Ast	Pts	Avg
Nance	2202	.587	.709	536	159	1211	19.9
Davis	570	.450	.877	35	98	345	15.0
Edwards	1787	.501	.746	387	153	1044	14.9
Adams	2136	.520	.883	500	308	1202	14.7

	Min	FG%	FT%	RBs	Ast	Pts	Avg
Lucas	1670	.476	.750	557	145	842	13.4
Macy	2018	.485	.907	179	380	714	11.0
Foster	1318	.450	.755	80	186	696	8.8
Humphries	2062	.446	.829	164	350	703	8.8
Hulton	1761	.440	.014	132	198	624	8.4
Jones	1565	.520	.648	394	128	654	8.4
Pittman	1001	.471	.747	227	69	323	4.8
Scott	1238	.429	.716	161	127	276	3.6

Portland Trail Blazers

	Min	FG%	FT%	RBs	Ast	Pts	Avg
Vandeweghe	2502	.534	.896	228	106	1616	22.4
M. Thompson	2616	.515	.684	618	205	1451	18.4
Paxson	2253	.514	.790	222	264	1218	17.9
Drexler	2555	.494	.759	476	441	1377	17.2
Valentine	2278	.473	.793	219	522	872	11.6
Carr	1120	.523	.720	323	56	498	10.4
Bowie	2216	.537	.711	656	215	758	10.0
Colter	1462	.453	.754	150	243	556	7.1
Kersey	958	.478	.646	206	63	473	6.1
Norris	1117	.543	.665	250	47	401	5.1
B. Thompson	535	.373	.765	76	52	197	3.3

San Antonio Spurs

	Min	FG%	FT%	RBs	Ast	Pts	Avg
Mitchell	2853	.497	.777	417	151	1824	22.2
Gervin	2091	.508	.844	234	178	1524	21.2
Gilmore	2756	.623	.749	846	131	1548	19.1
Moore	2689	.457	.762	378	816	1046	12.8
Banks	2091	.586	.774	445	234	778	9.5
Robertson	1685	.498	.734	265	275	726	9.2
Paxson	1259	.509	.840	68	215	486	6.2
Iavaroni	1334	.458	.680	304	119	411	6.0
Knight	800	.441	.877	118	80	387	5.7
Cook	1288	.495	.734	314	62	323	4.5
O. Jones	888	.589	.398	238	56	245	3.7

Seattle Supersonics

	Min	FG%	FT%	RBs	Ast	Pts	Avg
Chambers	2923	.483	.832	579	209	1739	21.5
Sikma	2402	.489	.852	723	285	1259	18.5
Wood	2545	.485	.776	279	236	1203	15.0
Henderson	2648	.479	.780	190	559	1062	13.4
Sobers	1490	.446	.815	103	252	700	9.9
McCormick	1584	.557	.715	398	78	726	9.3
Vranes	2163	.463	.528	436	152	440	5.8
Sundvold	1150	.425	.814	70	206	400	5.5
Brickowski	1115	.492	.669	260	100	385	4.9
Blackwell	551	.367	.509	96	26	202	3.4
King	860	.423	.695	122	53	167	2.8

Utah Jazz

	Min	FG%	FT%	RBs	Ast	Pts	Avg
Dantley	1971	.531	.804	323	186	1462	26.6
Griffith	2776	.457	.725	344	243	1764	22.6
Bailey	2481	.490	.842	525	138	1212	15.2
Green	2431	.477	.869	189	597	1000	13.0
Eaton	2813	.449	.712	927	124	794	9.7
Wilkins	1505	.490	.763	366	81	631	8.0
Roberts	1178	.498	.824	186	87	567	7.7
Stockton	1490	.471	.736	105	415	458	5.6
Hansen	646	.489	.556	70	75	261	4.8
Kelley	1276	.477	.750	350	120	290	3.8

Washington Bullets

	Min	FG%	FT%	RBs	Ast	Pts	Avg
Williams	2960	.430	.725	195	608	1578	20.0
Ruland	1436	.569	.685	410	162	700	18.9
Malone	2613	.499	.844	206	184	1436	18.9
Robinson	1870	.471	.742	546	149	1003	16.7
Ballard	2664	.480	.795	531	208	1072	13.1
Johnson	925	.489	.750	63	143	428	9.3
McMillen	1547	.472	.830	210	52	616	8.9
Daye	1573	.512	.715	272	240	695	8.7
Mahorn	2072	.499	.683	608	121	483	6.3
Jones	667	.528	.690	184	26	174	5.6
Bradley	1232	.475	.684	134	173	358	4.9

NBA All-Defensive Team in 1985

Center: Mark Eaton, Utah; Forwards: Paul Pressey, Milwaukee & Michael Cooper, L.A. Lakers; Guards: Sidney Moncrief, Milwaukee & Maurice Cheeks, Philadelphia.

NBA Scoring Leaders

Year	Scoring champion	Pts	Avg	Year	Scoring champion	Pts	Avg
1947	Joe Fulks, Philadelphia	1,389	23.2	1967	Rick Barry, San Francisco	2,775	35.6
1948	Max Zaslofsky, Chicago	1,007	21.0	1968	Dave Bing, Detroit	2,142	27.1
1949	George Mikan, Minneapolis	1,698	28.3	1969	Elvin Hayes, San Diego	2,327	28.4
1950	George Mikan, Minneapolis	1,865	27.4	1970	Jerry West, Los Angeles	2,309	31.2
1951	George Mikan, Minneapolis	1,932	28.4	1971	Lew Alcindor, Milwaukee	2,596	31.7
1952	Paul Arizin, Philadelphia	1,674	25.4	1972	Kareem Abdul-Jabar (Alcindor), Milwaukee	2,822	34.8
1953	Neil Johnston, Philadelphia	1,564	22.3				
1954	Neil Johnston, Philadelphia	1,759	24.4	1973	Nate Archibald, Kansas City-Omaha	2,719	34.0
1955	Neil Johnston, Philadelphia	1,631	22.7	1974	Bob McAdoo, Buffalo	2,261	30.6
1956	Bob Pettit, St. Louis	1,849	25.7	1975	Bob McAdoo, Buffalo	2,831	34.5
1957	Paul Arizin, Philadelphia	1,817	25.6	1976	Bob McAdoo, Buffalo	2,427	31.1
1958	George Yardley, Detroit	2,001	27.8	1977	Pete Maravich, New Orleans	2,273	31.1
1959	Bob Pettit, St. Louis	2,105	29.2	1978	George Gervin, San Antonio	2,232	27.2
1960	Wilt Chamberlain, Philadelphia	2,707	37.9	1979	George Gervin, San Antonio	2,365	29.6
1961	Wilt Chamberlain, Philadelphia	3,033	38.4	1980	George Gervin, San Antonio	2,585	33.1
1962	Wilt Chamberlain, Philadelphia	4,029	50.4	1981	Adrian Dantley, Utah	2,452	30.7
1963	Wilt Chamberlain, San Francisco	3,586	44.8	1982	George Gervin, San Antonio	2,551	32.3
1964	Wilt Chamberlain, San Francisco	2,948	36.5	1983	Alex English, Denver	2,326	28.4
1965	Wilt Chamberlain, San Fran., Phila.	2,534	34.7	1984	Adrian Dantley, Utah	2,418	30.6
1966	Wilt Chamberlain, Philadelphia	2,649	33.5	1985	Bernard King, New York	1,809	32.9

NBA Most Valuable Player

Year	Player	Year	Player
1956	Bob Pettit, St. Louis	1971	Lew Alcindor, Milwaukee
1957	Bob Cousy, Boston	1972	Kareem Abdul-Jabbar (Alcindor), Milwaukee
1958	Bill Russell, Boston	1973	Dave Cowens, Boston
1959	Bob Russell, Boston	1974	Kareem Abdul-Jabbar, Milwaukee
1960	Wilt Chamberlain, Philadelphia	1975	Bob McAdoo, Buffalo
1961	Bill Russell, Boston	1976	Kareem Abdul-Jabbar, Los Angeles
1962	Bill Russell, Boston	1977	Kareem Abdul-Jabbar, Los Angeles
1963	Bill Russell, Boston	1978	Bill Walton, Portland
1964	Oscar Robertson, Cincinnati	1979	Moses Malone, Houston
1965	Bill Russell, Boston	1980	Kareem Abdul-Jabbar, Los Angeles
1966	Wilt Chamberlain, Philadelphia	1981	Julius Erving, Philadelphia
1967	Wilt Chamberlain, Philadelphia	1982	Moses Malone, Houston
1968	Wilt Chamberlain, Philadelphia	1983	Moses Malone, Philadelphia
1969	Wes Unseld, Baltimore	1984	Larry Bird, Boston
1970	Willis Reed, New York	1985	Larry Bird, Boston

NBA Rookie of the Year

Year	Player	Year	Player	Year	Player
1954	Don Meineke, Ft. Wayne	1965	Willis Reed, New York	1975	Keith Wilkes, Golden State
1955	Ray Felix, Baltimore	1966	Rick Barry, San Francisco	1976	Alvan Adams, Phoenix
1956	Maurice Stokes, Rochester	1967	Dave Bing, Detroit	1977	Adrian Dantley, Buffalo
1957	Tom Heinsohn, Boston	1968	Earl Monroe, Baltimore	1978	Walter Davis, Phoenix
1958	Woody Sauldsberry, Philadelphia	1969	Wes Unseld, Baltimore	1979	Phil Ford, Kansas City
1959	Elgin Baylor, Minnesota	1970	Lew Alcindor, Milwaukee	1980	Larry Bird, Boston
1960	Wilt Chamberlain, Philadelphia	1971	Dave Cowens, Boston; Geoff Petrie, Portland (tie)	1981	Darrell Griffith, Utah
1961	Oscar Robertson, Cincinnati			1982	Buck Williams, New Jersey
1962	Walt Bellamy, Chicago	1972	Sidney Wicks, Portland	1983	Terry Cummings, San Diego
1963	Terry Dischinger, Chicago	1973	Bob McAdoo, Buffalo	1984	Ralph Sampson, Houston
1964	Jerry Lucas, Cincinnati	1974	Ernie DiGregorio, Buffalo	1985	Michael Jordan, Chicago

NBA All League Team in 1985

First team	Position	Second team
Larry Bird, Boston	Forward	Terry Cummings, Milwaukee
Bernard King, New York	Forward	Ralph Sampson, Houston
Moses Malone, Philadelphia	Center	Kareem Abdul-Jabbar, L.A. Lakers
Magic Johnson, L.A. Lakers	Guard	Michael Jordan, Chicago
Isiah Thomas, Detroit	Guard	Sidney Moncrief, Milwaukee

MVP in Playoffs

Year	Player	Year	Player	Year	Player
1969	Jerry West, Los Angeles	1975	Rick Barry, Golden State	1981	Cedric Maxwell, Boston
1970	Willis Reed, New York	1976	Jo Jo White, Boston	1982	Magic Johnson, Los Angeles
1971	Lew Alcindor, Milwaukee	1977	Bill Walton, Portland	1983	Moses Malone, Philadelphia
1972	Wilt Chamberlain, Los Angeles	1978	Wes Unseld, Washington	1984	Larry Bird, Boston
1973	Willis Reed, New York	1979	Dennis Johnson, Seattle	1985	Kareem Abdul-Jabbar, L.A. Lakers
1974	John Havlicek, Boston	1980	Magic Johnson, Los Angeles		

American Basketball Association Champions, 1968-1976

	Regular season		Playoffs	
Year	Eastern division	Western division	Winner	Runner-up
1968	Pittsburgh	New Orleans	Pittsburgh	New Orleans
1969	Indiana	Oakland	Oakland	Indiana
1970	Indiana	Denver	Indiana	Los Angeles
1971	Virginia	Indiana	Utah	Kentucky
1972	Kentucky	Utah	Indiana	New York
1973	Carolina	Utah	Indiana	Kentucky
1974	New York	Utah	New York	Utah
1975	Kentucky	Denver	Kentucky	Indiana
1976		Denver	New York	Denver

Individuals in The Basketball Hall of Fame

Springfield, Mass.

Players
Arizin, Paul
Baylor, Elgin
Beckman, John
Borgmann, Bennie
Bradley, Bill
Brennan, Joseph
Barlow, Thomas
Cervi, Al
Chamberlain, Wilt
Cooper, Charles
Cousy, Bob
Davies, Bob
DeBernardi, Forrest
DeBusschere, Dave
Dehnert, Dutch
Endacott, Paul
Foster, Bud
Friedman, Max
Fulks, Joe
Gale, Lauren
Gola, Tom
Greer, Hal
Gruenig, Ace
Hagan, Cliff
Hanson, Victor
Havlicek, John
Holman, Nat
Hyatt, Chuck
Johnson, William
Jones, Sam
Krause, Moose

Kurland, Bob
Lapchick, Joe
Lucas, Jerry
Luisetti, Hank
Martin, Slater
McCracken, Branch
McCracken, Jack
Macauley, Ed
Mikan, George
Murphy, Stretch
Page, Pat
Pettit, Bob
Phillip, Andy
Pollard, Jim
Ramsey, Frank
Reed, Willis
Robertson, Oscar
Roosma, John S.
Russell, Honey
Russell, Bill
Schayes, Adolph
Schmidt, Ernest
Schommer, John
Sedran, Barney
Sharman, Bill
Steinmetz, Christian
Thompson, Cat
Thurmond, Nate
Twyman, Jack
Vandivier, Fuzzy
Wachter, Edward
West, Jerry

Wooden, John

Coaches
Auerbach, Red
Barry, Sam
Blood, Ernest
Cann, Howard
Carlson, Dr. H. C.
Carnevale, Ben
Case, Everett
Dean, Everett
Diddle, Edgar
Drake, Bruce
Gaines, Clarence
Gardner, Jack
Gill, Slats
Hickey, Edgar
Hobson, Howard
Iba, Hank
Julian, Alvin
Keaney, Frank
Keogan, George
Lambert, Ward
Litwack, Harry
Loeffler, Kenneth
Lonborg, Dutch
McCutchan, Arad
McGuire, Frank
McLendon, John
Meyer, Ray
Meanwell, Dr. W.E.

Newell, Pete
Rupp, Adolph
Sachs, Leonard
Shelton, Everett
Smith, Dean
Teague, Bertha
Wade, Margaret
Wooden, John

Referees
Enright, James
Hepbron, George
Hoyt, George
Kennedy, Matthew
Leith, Lloyd
Nucatola, John
Quigley, Ernest
Shirley, J. Dallas
Tobey, David
Walsh, David

Contributors
Abbott, Senda B.
Allen, Phog
Bee, Clair
Brown, Walter
Bunn, John
Douglas, Bob
Duer, Al O.
Fagan, Cliff

Fisher, Harry
Gottlieb, Edward
Gulick, Dr. L. H.
Harrison, Lester
Hepp, Dr. Ferenc
Hickox, Edward
Hinkle, Tony
Irish, Ned
Jones, R. W.
Kennedy, Walter
Liston, Emil
Mokray, Bill
Morgan, Ralph
Morgenweck, Frank
Naismith, Dr. James
O'Brien, John
Olsen, Harold
Podoloff, Maurice
Porter, H. V.
Reis, William
Ripley, Elmer
St. John, Lynn
Saperstein, Abe
Schabinger, Arthur
Stagg, Amos Alonzo
Steitz, Edward
Taylor, Chuck
Tower, Oswald
Trester, Arthur
Wells, Clifford
Wilke, Lou

Figure Skating Champions

U.S. Champions

World Champions

Men	Women	Year	Men	Women
Richard Button	Tenley Albright	1952	Richard Button, U.S.	Jacqueline du Bief, France
Hayes Jenkins	Tenley Albright	1953	Hayes Jenkins, U.S.	Tenley Albright, U.S.
Hayes Jenkins	Tenley Albright	1954	Hayes Jenkins, U.S.	Gundi Busch, W. Germany
Hayes Jenkins	Tenley Albright	1955	Hayes Jenkins, U.S.	Tenley Albright, U.S.
Hayes Jenkins	Tenley Albright	1956	Hayes Jenkins, U.S.	Carol Heiss, U.S.
Dave Jenkins	Carol Heiss	1957	Dave Jenkins, U.S.	Carol Heiss, U.S.
Dave Jenkins	Carol Heiss	1958	Dave Jenkins, U.S.	Carol Heiss, U.S.
Dave Jenkins	Carol Heiss	1959	Dave Jenkins, U.S.	Carol Heiss, U.S.
Dave Jenkins	Carol Heiss	1960	Alain Giletti, France	Carol Heiss, U.S.
Bradley Lord	Laurence Owen	1961	none	none
Monty Hoyt	Barbara Roles Pursley	1962	Don Jackson, Canada	Sjoukje Dijkstra, Neth.
Tommy Litz	Lorraine Hanlon	1963	Don McPherson, Canada	Sjoukje Dijkstra, Neth.
Scott Allen	Peggy Fleming	1964	Manfred Schnelldorfer, W. Germany	Sjoukje Dijkstra, Neth.
Gary Visconti	Peggy Fleming	1965	Alain Calmat, France	Petra Burka, Canada
Scott Allen	Peggy Fleming	1966	Emmerich Danzer, Austria	Peggy Fleming, U.S.
Gary Visconti	Peggy Fleming	1967	Emmerich Danzer, Austria	Peggy Fleming, U.S.
Tim Wood	Peggy Fleming	1968	Emmerich Danzer, Austria	Peggy Fleming, U.S.
Tim Wood	Janet Lynn	1969	Tim Wood, U.S.	Gabriele Seyfert, E. Germany
Tim Wood	Janet Lynn	1970	Tim Wood, U.S.	Gabriele Seyfert, E. Germany
John Misha Petkevich	Janet Lynn	1971	Ondrej Nepela, Czech.	Beatrix Schuba, Austria
Ken Shelley	Janet Lynn	1972	Ondrej Nepela, Czech.	Beatrix Schuba, Austria
Gordon McKellen Jr.	Janet Lynn	1973	Ondrej Nepela, Czech.	Karen Magnussen, Canada
Gordon McKellen Jr.	Dorothy Hamill	1974	Jan Hoffmann, E. Germany	Christine Errath, E. Germany
Gordon McKellen Jr.	Dorothy Hamill	1975	Sergei Volkov, USSR	Dianne de Leeuw, Neth.-U.S.
Terry Kubicka	Dorothy Hamill	1976	John Curry, Gt. Britain	Dorothy Hamill, U.S.
Charles Tickner	Linda Fratianne	1977	Vladimir Kovalev, USSR	Linda Fratianne, U.S.
Charles Tickner	Linda Fratianne	1978	Charles Tickner, U.S.	Anett Potzsch, E. Germany
Charles Tickner	Linda Fratianne	1979	Vladimir Kovalev, USSR	Linda Fratianne, U.S.
Charles Tickner	Linda Fratianne	1980	Jan Hoffmann, E. Germany	Anett Potzsch, E. Germany
Scott Hamilton	Elaine Zayak	1981	Scott Hamilton, U.S.	Denise Biellmann, Switzerland
Scott Hamilton	Rosalynn Sumners	1982	Scott Hamilton, U.S.	Elaine Zayak, U.S.
Scott Hamilton	Rosalynn Sumners	1983	Scott Hamilton, U.S.	Rosalynn Sumners, U.S.
Scott Hamilton	Rosalynn Sumners	1984	Scott Hamilton, U.S.	Katarina Witt, E. Germany
Brian Boitano	Tiffany Chin	1985	Aleksandr Fadeev, USSR	Katarina Witt, E. Germany

U.S. Pairs and Dancing Champions in 1985

Jill Watson and Peter Oppegard won the 1985 U.S. pairs figure skating championship in Kansas City, Mo. Judy Blumberg and Michael Seibert triumphed in ice dancing for the 5th consecutive year.

North American Squash Open in 1985

Jahangir Khan of Pakistan won the 1985 North American Open Squash championship for the second consecutive year by defeating Steve Bowditch 15-4, 15-5, 17-15. Khan received $15,000 for his victory.

Skiing in 1985

World Alpine Championships

Men

Slalom—Jonas Nilsson, Sweden.
Giant Slalom—Markus Wasmaier, W. Germany.
Combined—Pirmin Zurbriggen, Switzerland.

Women

Slalom—Perrine Pelen, France.
Giant Slalom—Diann Roffe, U.S.
Combined—Erika Hess, Switzerland.

U.S. National Alpine Championships in 1985

Copper Mountain, Col.

Men

Downhill—Brian Stemmle.
Slalom—Felix McGrath.
Giant Slalom—Tiger Shaw.
Combined—Tiger Shaw.

Women

Downhill—Holly Flanders.
Slalom—Ann Melander.
Giant Slalom—Eva Twardokens.
Combined—Eva Twardokens.

World Cup Alpine Champions

Men

1967	Jean Claude Killy, France	1974	Piero Gros, Italy	1981	Phil Mahre, U.S.
1968	Jean Claude Killy, France	1975	Gustavo Thoeni, Italy	1982	Phil Mahre, U.S.
1969	Karl Schranz, Austria	1976	Ingemar Stenmark, Sweden	1983	Phil Mahre, U.S.
1970	Karl Schranz, Austria	1977	Ingemar Stenmark, Sweden	1984	Pirmin Zurbriggen, Switzerland
1971	Gustavo Thoeni, Italy	1978	Ingemar Stenmark, Sweden	1985	Marc Girardelli, Luxembourg
1972	Gustavo Thoeni, Italy	1979	Peter Luescher, Switzerland		
1973	Gustavo Thoeni, Italy	1980	Andreas Wenzel, Liechtenstein		

Women

1967	Nancy Greene, Canada	1974	Annemarie Proell, Austria	1981	Marie-Theres Nadig, Switzerland
1968	Nancy Greene, Canada	1975	Annemarie Proell, Austria	1982	Erika Hess, Switzerland
1969	Gertrud Gabl, Austria	1976	Rose Mittermaier, W. Germany	1983	Tamara McKinney, U.S.
1970	Michele Jacot, France	1977	Lise-Marie Morerod, Switzerland	1984	Erika Hess, Switzerland
1971	Annemarie Proell, Austria	1978	Hanni Wenzel, Liechtenstein	1985	Michela Figini, Switzerland
1972	Annemarie Proell, Austria	1979	Annemarie Proell Moser, Austria		
1973	Annemarie Proell, Austria	1980	Hanni Wenzel, Liechtenstein		

Curling Champions

Source: North American Curling News

World Champions

Year	Country, skip	Year	Country, skip	Year	Country, skip
1968	Canada, Ron Northcott	1974	United States, Bud Somerville	1981	Switzerland, Jurg Tanner
1968	Canada, Ron Northcott	1975	Switzerland, Otto Danieli	1982	Canada, Al Hackner
1969	Canada, Ron Northcott	1976	United States, Bruce Roberts	1983	Canada, Ed Werenich
1970	Canada, Don Duguid	1977	Sweden, Ragnar Kamp	1984	Norway, Eigil Ramsfjell
1971	Canada, Don Duguid	1978	United States, Bob Nichols	1985	Canada, Al Hackner
1972	Canada, Crest Melesnuk	1979	Norway, Kristian Soerum		
1973	Sweden, Kjell Oscarius	1980	Canada, Rich Folk		

U.S. Men's Champions

Year	State, skip	Year	State, skip	Year	State, skip
1968	Wisconsin, Bud Somerville	1975	Washington, Ed Risling	1982	Wisconsin, Steve Brown
1969	Wisconsin, Bud Somerville	1976	Minnesota, Bruce Roberts	1983	Colorado, Don Cooper
1970	North Dakota, Art Tallackson	1977	Minnesota, Bruce Roberts	1984	Minnesota, Bruce Roberts
1971	North Dakota, Dale Dalziel	1978	Wisconsin, Bob Nichols	1985	Illinois, Tim Wright
1972	North Dakota, Bob LaBonte	1979	Minnesota, Scotty Baird		
1973	Massachusetts, Barry Blanchard	1980	Minnesota, Paul Pustover		
1974	Wisconsin, Bud Somerville	1981	Wisconsin, Somerville-Nichols		

U.S. Ladies Champions

Year	State, skip	Year	State, skip	Year	State, skip
1978	Wisconsin, Sandy Robarge	1981	Washington, Nancy Langley	1984	Minnesota, Amy Hatten
1979	Washington, Nancy Langley	1982	Illinois, Ruth Schwenker	1985	Alaska, Bev Birklid
1980	Washington, Sharon Kozai	1983	Washington, Nancy Langley		

NCAA Wrestling Champions

Year	Champion	Year	Champion	Year	Champion	Year	Champion	Year	Champion
1963	Oklahoma	1968	Oklahoma State	1973	Iowa State	1978	Iowa	1982	Iowa
1964	Oklahoma State	1969	Iowa State	1974	Oklahoma	1979	Iowa	1983	Iowa
1965	Iowa State	1970	Iowa State	1975	Iowa	1980	Iowa	1984	Iowa
1966	Oklahoma State	1971	Oklahoma State	1976	Iowa	1981	Iowa	1985	Iowa
1967	Michigan State	1972	Iowa State	1977	Iowa State				

James E. Sullivan Memorial Trophy Winners

The James E. Sullivan Memorial Trophy, named after the former president of the AAU and inaugurated in 1930, is awarded annually by the AAU to the athlete who "by his or her performance, example and influence as an amateur, has done the most during the year to advance the cause of sportmanship."

Year	Winner	Sport	Year	Winner	Sport	Year	Winner	Sport
1930	Bobby Jones	Golf	1949	Dick Button	Skating	1967	Randy Matson	Track
1931	Barney Berlinger	Track	1950	Fred Wilt	Track	1968	Debbie Meyer	Swimming
1932	Jim Bausch	Track	1951	Rev. Robert Richards	Track	1969	Bill Toomey	Track
1933	Glen Cunningham	Track	1952	Horace Ashenfelter	Track	1970	John Kinsella	Swimming
1934	Bill Bonthron	Track	1953	Dr. Sammy Lee	Diving	1971	Mark Spitz	Swimming
1935	Lawson Little	Golf	1954	Mal Whitfield	Track	1972	Frank Shorter	Track
1936	Glenn Morris	Track	1955	Harrison Dillard	Track	1973	Bill Walton	Basketball
1937	Don Budge	Tennis	1956	Patricia McCormick	Diving	1974	Rick Wohlhuter	Track
1938	Don Lash	Track	1957	Bobby Joe Morrow	Track	1975	Tim Shaw	Swimming
1939	Joe Burk	Rowing	1958	Glenn Davis	Track	1976	Bruce Jenner	Track
1940	Greg Rice	Track	1959	Parry O'Brien	Track	1977	John Naber	Swimming
1941	Leslie MacMitchell	Track	1960	Rafer Johnson	Track	1978	Tracy Caulkins	Swimming
1942	Cornelius Warmerdam	Track	1961	Wilma Rudolph Ward	Track	1979	Kurt Thomas	Gymnastics
1943	Gilbert Dodds	Track	1962	James Beatty	Track	1980	Eric Heiden	Speed Skating
1944	Ann Curtis	Swimming	1963	John Pennel	Track	1981	Carl Lewis	Track
1945	Doc Blanchard	Football	1964	Don Schollander	Swimming	1982	Mary Decker	Track
1946	Arnold Tucker	Football	1965	Bill Bradley	Basketball	1983	Edwin Moses	Track
1947	John Kelly Jr.	Rowing	1966	Jim Ryun	Track	1984	Greg Louganis	Diving
1948	Robert Mathias	Track						

Westminster Kennel Club

Year	Best-in-show	Breed	Owner
1973	Ch. Acadia Command Performance	Poodle	Mrs. Jo Ann Sering & Edward B. Jenner
1974	Ch. Gretchenhof Columbia River	German pointer	Dr. Richard Smith
1975	Ch. Sir Lancelot of Barvan	Old English sheepdog	Mr. & Mrs. Ronald Vanword
1976	Ch. Jo-Ni's Red Baron of Crofton	Lakeland terrier	Virginia Dickson
1977	Ch. Dersade Bobby's Girl	Sealyham	Dorothy Wymer
1978	Ch. Cede Higgens	Yorkshire terrier	Barbara & Charles Switzer
1979	Ch. Oak Tree's Irishtocrat	Irish water spaniel	Anne E. Snelling
1980	Ch. Sierra Cinnar	Siberian husky	Kathleen Kanzler
1981	Ch. Dhandy Favorite Woodchuck	Pug	Robert Houslohner
1982	Ch. St. Aubrey Dragonora of Elsdon	Pekingese	Anne Snelling
1983	Ch. Kabik's The Challenger	Afghan	Chris & Marguerite Terrell
1984	Ch. Seaward's Blackbeard	Newfoundland	Elinor Ayers
1985	Ch. Braeburn's Close Encounter	Scottish terrier	Sonnie Novick

Pro Rodeo Championship Standings in 1984

Event	Winner	Money won	Event	Winner	Money won
All Around	Dee Pickett, Caldwell, Ida.	$122,618	Steer Wrestling	John W. Jones Jr., Murro Bay, Cal.	$63,863
Saddle Bronc	Brad Gjermundson, Marshall, N.D.	78,151	Team Roping	(tie) Dee Pickett & Mike Beers,	
Bareback	Larry Peabody, Three Forks, Mont.	78,741		Rufus, Ore.	57,557
Bull Riding	Don Gay, Mesquite, Tex.	77,327	Steer Roping	Guy Allen, Lovington, N.M.	41,289
Calf Roping	Roy Cooper, Durant, Okla.	89,703	Women's Barrel Racing	Charmayne James, Clayton, N.M.	53,500

Pro Rodeo Cowboy All Around Champions

Year	Winner	Money won	Year	Winner	Money won
1966	Larry Mahan, Brooks, Ore.	$40,358	1976	Tom Ferguson, Miami, Okla.	$87,908
1967	Larry Mahan, Brooks, Ore.	51,996	1977	Tom Ferguson, Miami, Okla.	76,730
1968	Larry Mahan, Salem, Ore.	49,129	1978	Tom Ferguson, Miami, Okla.	103,734
1969	Larry Mahan, Brooks, Ore.	57,726	1979	Tom Ferguson, Miami, Okla.	96,272
1970	Larry Mahan, Brooks, Ore.	41,493	1980	Paul Tierney, Rapid City, S.D.	105,568
1971	Phil Lyne, George West, Tex.	49,245	1981	Jimmie Cooper, Monument, N.M.	105,862
1972	Phil Lyne, George West, Tex.	60,852	1982	Chris Lybbert, Coyote, Cal.	123,709
1973	Larry Mahan, Dallas, Tex.	64,447	1983	Roy Cooper, Durant, Okla.	153,391
1974	Tom Ferguson, Miami, Okla.	66,929	1984	Dee Pickett, Caldwell, Ida.	122,618
1975	Leo Camarillo, Oakdale, Cal.	50,300			
	Tom Ferguson, Miami, Okla.	50,300			

Intercollegiate Rowing Association Championship

Lake Onondaga, Syracuse, N.Y. (2,000 meters)

Year	Winner	Time	Year	Winner	Time	Year	Winner	Time
1968	Penn	6:15.6	1974	Wisconsin	6:33.0	1980	Navy	6:46.0
1969	Penn	6:30.4	1975	Wisconsin	6:08.2	1981	Cornell	5:57.3
1970	Washington	6:39.3	1976	California	6:31.0	1982	Cornell	5:57.5
1971	Cornell	6:06.0	1977	Cornell	6:32.4	1983	Brown	6:14.4
1972	Penn	6:22.6	1978	Syracuse	6:39.5	1984	Navy	5:54.7
1973	Wisconsin	6:21.0	1979	Brown	6:26.4	1985	Princeton	6:30.0

Professional Sports Directory

Baseball

Commissioner's Office
350 Park Ave.
New York, NY 10022

National League

National League Office
350 Park Ave.
New York, NY 10022

Atlanta Braves
PO Box 4064
Atlanta, GA 30302

Chicago Cubs
Wrigley Field
Chicago, IL 60613

Cincinnati Reds
100 Riverfront Stadium
Cincinnati, OH 45202

Houston Astros
Astrodome
Houston, TX 77001

Los Angeles Dodgers
Dodger Stadium
Los Angeles, CA 90012

Montreal Expos
PO Box 500, Station M
Montreal, Que. H1V 3P2

New York Mets
Shea Stadium
Flushing, NY 11368

Philadelphia Phillies
PO Box 7575
Philadelphia, PA 19101

Pittsburgh Pirates
Three Rivers Stadium
Pittsburgh, PA 15212

St. Louis Cardinals
Busch Stadium
St. Louis, MO 63102

San Diego Padres
PO Box 2000
San Diego, CA 92120

San Francisco Giants
Candlestick Park
San Francisco, CA 94124

American League

American League Office
350 Park Ave.
New York, NY 10022

Baltimore Orioles
Memorial Stadium
Baltimore, MD 21218

Boston Red Sox
24 Yawkey Way
Boston, MA 02215

California Angels
Anaheim Stadium
Anaheim, CA 92806

Chicago White Sox
324 W. 35th St.
Chicago, IL 60616

Cleveland Indians
Cleveland Stadium
Cleveland, OH 44114

Detroit Tigers
Tiger Stadium
Detroit, MI 48216

Kansas City Royals
Harry S. Truman Sports Complex
Kansas City, MO 64141

Milwaukee Brewers
Milwaukee County Stadium
Milwaukee, WI 53214

Minnesota Twins
501 Chicago Ave. South
Minneapolis, MN 55415

New York Yankees
Yankee Stadium
Bronx, NY 10451

Oakland A's
Oakland Coliseum
Oakland, CA 94621

Seattle Mariners
100 S. King St.
Seattle, WA 98104

Texas Rangers
1200 Copeland Rd.
Arlington, TX 76011

Toronto Blue Jays
Box 7777
Adelaide St. PO
Toronto, Ont. M5C 2K7

National Football League

League Office
410 Park Avenue
New York, NY 10022

Atlanta Falcons
Suwanee Road
Suwanee, GA 30174

Buffalo Bills
1 Bills Drive
Orchard Park, NY 14127

Chicago Bears
250 N. Washington
Lake Forest, IL 60045

Cincinnati Bengals
200 Riverfront Stadium
Cincinnati, OH 45202

Cleveland Browns
Cleveland Stadium
Cleveland, OH 44114

Dallas Cowboys
6116 North Central Expressway
Dallas, TX 75206

Denver Broncos
5700 Logan St.
Denver, CO 80216

Detroit Lions
1200 Featherstone Rd.
Pontiac, MI 48057

Green Bay Packers
1265 Lombardi Ave.
Green Bay, WI 54303

Houston Oilers
P.O. Box 1516
Houston, TX 77001

Indianapolis Colts
P.O. Box 20000
Indianapolis, IN 46220

Kansas City Chiefs
1 Arrowhead Drive
Kansas City, MO 64129

Los Angeles Raiders
332 Center St.
El Segundo, CA 90245

Los Angeles Rams
2327 W. Lincoln Ave.
Anaheim, CA 92801

Miami Dolphins
4770 Biscayne Blvd.
Miami, FL 33137

Minnesota Vikings
Hubert H. Humphrey Metrodome
500 11th Ave., So.
Minneapolis, MN 55415

New England Patriots
Sullivan Stadium
Foxboro, MA 02035

New Orleans Saints
1500 Poydras St.
New Orleans, LA 70112

New York Giants
Giants Stadium
E. Rutherford, NJ 07073

New York Jets
598 Madison Ave.
New York, NY 10022

Philadelphia Eagles
Veterans Stadium
Philadelphia, PA 19148

Pittsburgh Steelers
Three Rivers Stadium
Pittsburgh, PA 15212

St. Louis Cardinals
Busch Stadium
St. Louis, MO 63188

San Diego Chargers
P.O. Box 20666
San Diego, CA 92120

San Francisco 49ers
711 Nevada St.
Redwood City, CA 94061

Seattle Seahawks
5305 Lake Washington Blvd.
Kirkland, WA 98033

Tampa Bay Buccaneers
1 Buccaneer Place
Tampa, FL 33607

Washington Redskins
PO Box 17247
Dulles Intl. Airport
Washington, DC 20041

National Basketball Association

League Office
645 5th Ave.
New York, NY 10022

Atlanta Hawks
100 Techwood Drive NW
Atlanta, GA 30303

Boston Celtics
Boston Garden
Boston, MA 02114

Chicago Bulls
333 North Michigan Ave.
Chicago, IL 60601

Cleveland Cavaliers
2923 Statesboro Rd.
Richfield, OH 44286

Dallas Mavericks
777 Sports St.
Dallas, TX 75207

Denver Nuggets
1635 Clay St.
Denver, CO 80204

Detroit Pistons
1200 Featherstone
Pontiac, MI 48057

Golden State Warriors
Oakland Coliseum
Oakland, CA 94621

Houston Rockets
The Summit
Houston, TX 77046

Indiana Pacers
2 W. Washington St.
Indianapolis, IN 46204

Los Angeles Clippers
3939 Figueroa
Los Angeles, CA 90037

Los Angeles Lakers
PO Box 10
Inglewood, CA 90306

Milwaukee Bucks
901 North 4th St.
Milwaukee, WI 53203

New Jersey Nets
Byrne Meadowlands Arena
E. Rutherford, NJ 07073

New York Knickerbockers
4 Pennsylvania Plaza
New York, NY 10001

Philadelphia 76ers
PO Box 25040
Philadelphia, PA 19147

Phoenix Suns
2910 N. Central
Phoenix, AZ 85012

Portland Trail Blazers
700 NE Multnomah St.
Portland, OR 97232

Sacramento Kings
1515 Sports Dr.
Sacramento, CA 95834

San Antonio Spurs
P.O. Box 530
San Antonio, TX 78292

Seattle SuperSonics
419 Occidental South
Seattle, WA 98114

Utah Jazz
5505 S. 900 East
Salt Lake City, UT 84117

Washington Bullets
Capital Centre
Landover, MD 20785

National Hockey League

League Headquarters
Sun Life Bldg.
Montreal, Quebec H3B 2W2

Boston Bruins
150 Causeway St.
Boston, MA 02114

Buffalo Sabres
Memorial Auditorium
Buffalo, NY 14202

Calgary Flames
P.O. Box 1540
Calgary, Alta. T2P 3B9

Chicago Black Hawks
1800 W. Madison St.
Chicago, IL 60612

Detroit Red Wings
600 Civic Center Drive
Detroit, MI 48226

Edmonton Oilers
Northlands Coliseum
Edmonton, Alta. T5B 4M9

Hartford Whalers
One Civic Center Plaza
Hartford, CT 06103

Los Angeles Kings
PO Box 10
Inglewood, CA 90306

Minnesota North Stars
7901 Cedar Ave. S.
Bloomington, MN 55420

Montreal Canadiens
2313 St. Catherine St., West
Montreal, Québec H3H 1N2

New Jersey Devils
Byrne Meadowlands Arena
E. Rutherford, NJ 07073

New York Islanders
Nassau Coliseum
Uniondale, NY 11553

New York Rangers
4 Pennsylvania Plaza
New York, NY 10001

Philadelphia Flyers
Pattison Place
Philadelphia, PA 19148

Pittsburgh Penguins
Civic Arena
Pittsburgh, PA 15219

Quebec Nordiques
2205 Ave. du Colisee
Quebec, Que. G1L 4W7

St. Louis Blues
5700 Oakland Ave.
St. Louis, MO 63110

Toronto Maple Leafs
60 Carlton St.
Toronto, Ont. M5B 1L1

Vancouver Canucks
100 North Renfrew St.
Vancouver, B.C. V5K 3N7

Washington Capitals
Capital Centre
Landover, MD 20785

Winnipeg Jets
15-1430 Maroons Road
Winnipeg, Man. R3G 0L5

Canadian Football League

League Office
11 King St. W.
Suite 1800
Toronto, Ont. M5H 1A3

B.C. Lions
10605-135th St.
Surrey, B.C. V3T 4C8

Calgary Stampeders
McMahon Stadium
1817 Crowchild Trail N.W.
Calgary, Alta. T2M 4R6

Edmonton Eskimos
9023-111 Ave.
Edmonton, Alta T5B 0C3

Hamilton Tiger-Cats
75 Balsam Ave. N.
P.O. Box 172
Hamilton, Ont. L8N 3A2

Montreal Concordes
Olympic Stadium
P.O. Box 100, Station M
Montreal, Que. H1V 3L6

Ottawa Rough Riders
Lansdowne Park
Ottawa, Ont. K1S 2W7

Saskatchewan Roughriders
2940-10th Ave.
P.O. Box 1277
Regina, Sask. S4P 3B8

Toronto Argonauts
Exhibition Stadium
Exhibition Place
Toronto, Ont. M6K 3C3

Winnipeg Blue Bombers
1465 Maroons Rd.
Winnipeg, Man. R3G 0L6

Canadian Interuniversity Athletic Union Champions

Men

	Basketball	Football	Hockey	Soccer	Swimming, Diving	Volleyball	Wrestling
1979	St. Mary's	Acadia	Alberta	Alberta	Waterloo	Saskatchewan	O.U.A.A.
1980	Victoria	Alberta	Alberta	New Brunswick	Toronto	Manitoba	Lakehead
1981	Victoria	Acadia	Moncton	McGill	Toronto	Alberta	Guelph
1982	Victoria	British Columbia	Moncton	McGill	Calgary	Calgary	Guelph
1983	Victoria	Calgary	Saskatchewan	Laurentian	Calgary	British Columbia	Guelph
1984	Victoria	Guelph	Toronto	British Columbia	Calgary	Manitoba	Concordia
1985	Victoria	—	York	—	Calgary	Manitoba	Concordia & McMaster

Women

	Basketball	Field Hockey	Swimming, Diving	Volleyball	Gymnastics	Track & Field
1979	Laurentian	Toronto	Toronto	Saskatchewan	Alberta	—
1980	Victoria	York	Toronto	Saskatchewan	York	—
1981	Victoria	Toronto	Toronto	Saskatchewan	McMaster	Western Ont.
1982	Victoria	British Columbia	Toronto	Dalhousie	Manitoba	Western Ont.
1983	Bishop's	British Columbia	Toronto	Winnipeg	British Columbia	Western Ont.
1984	Bishop's	Victoria	Toronto	Winnipeg	York	York
1985	Victoria	—	British Columbia	Winnipeg	Alberta	Alberta & Saskatchewan

Tour de France in 1985

Bernard Hinault of France won the Tour de France, the world's most prestigious bicycle endurance race, for the 5th time on July 21, 1985. He became the third rider to win the grueling event 5 times. His time for the 3-week, 2,500-mile race was 113 hours 24 minutes 23 seconds. Greg Lemond of the United States finished second. Stephen Roche of Ireland finished third.

American Bowling Congress Championships in 1985

82d Tournament. Tulsa, Okla.

Regular Division

Individual—Glenn Harbison, Pittsburgh, Pa., 774.
All Events—Barry Asher, Anaheim, Cal., 2,033.
Doubles—Howard Higby, 718 & Clyde Gibson, both Lake Jackson, Tex., 648; aggregate 1,366.
Team—Terry's Pro Shop, Cleveland, Oh.: Curtis Childress, 615; Mike Greenwald, 653; Nick DiBlatto, 595; Jim Pencak, 678;

Larry Domzalski, 692; aggregate 3,233.

Booster Division

Team—Dr. Baur's No. 6, Milwaukee, Wis.: Doug Zahn, 524; Robert Kolz, 523; Jeff Fuggiasco, 522; Brian Karcher, 609; Ed Baur, 624; aggregate 2,802.

Other Bowling Championships in 1985

U.S. Open, Men, Venice, Fla., Feb. 3-9; Marshall Holman, Jacksonville, Ore., average 219, prize $38,000. Women, Topeka, Kan., Apr. 29-May 4; Pat Mercatanti, Yardley, Pa., average 219, prize $10,000.
National Intercollegiate Championships, Men — Tulsa, Okla., May 10, doubles: Derron Lax, Univ. of Texas & Jack Jurek, West Texas State, 1,240; singles: Jack Jurek, 653; all events: Scott Thomsen, Washington State, 2,876 (14 games).

Women — Toledo, Oh., Apr. 8, doubles: Stacey Peterson, Univ. of Florida & Rozalynd Monell, Wichita State, 1,159; singles: Rozalynd Monell, 607; all events: Michelle Mullen, Univ. of Illinois, 1,614 (8 games).
National Collegiate Team Championship — Milwaukee, Wis., May 3-5; Men: Wisconsin-LaCrosse; Women: West Texas State.

Official Records of Annual ABC Tournaments

Type of record	Holder of record	Year	Score
High team total	Ace Mitchell Shur-Hooks, Akron	1966	3,357
High team game	Falstaff Beer, San Antonio	1958	1,226
High doubles score	John Klares-Steve Nagy, Cleveland	1952	1,453
High doubles game	Tommy Hudson, Akron, Ohio-Les Zikes, Chicago	1976	558
High singles total	Mickey Higham, Kansas City, Mo.	1977	801
High all events score	Jim Godman, Lorain, Oh.	1974	2,184
High team all events	Cook County Tobacco, Chicago, Ill.	1981	9,695
High life-time pin total	Bill Doehrman, Ft. Wayne	1908-1981	109,398

Record Averages for Consecutive Tournaments

No. in row	Holder of record	Span	Games	Average
Two	Rich Wonders, Racine, Wis.	1981-82	18	229.94
Three	Jim Godman, Lorain, Oh.	1974-76	27	223.96
Four	Jim Godman, Lorain, Oh.	1974-77	36	219.44
Five	Jim Godman, Lorain, Oh.	1973-77	45	216.33
Ten	Bob Strampe, Detroit	1961-70	111	211.10

All-Time Records for League and Tournament Play

Type of record	Holder of record	Year	Score	Competition
High team total	Budweiser Beer, St. Louis	1958	3,858	League
High team game	Edwards Concrete, Moscow, Oh.	1982	1,365	League
High doubles total	Nelson Burton Jr., Billy Walden, St. Louis	1970	1,614	Tournament
High doubles game	John Cotta and Steve Larson, Manteca, Cal.	1981	600	Tournament
High individual total	Albert Brandt, Lockport, N.Y.	1939	886	League
High all events score	Paul Andrews, East Moline, Ill.	1981	2,415	Tournament

Masters Bowling Tournament Champions

Year	Winner	Runner-up	W-L	Avg
1975	Ed Ressler Jr., Allentown, Pa.	Sam Flanagan, Parkersburg, W. Va.	9-1	213
1976	Nelson Burton Jr., St. Louis	Steve Carson, Oklahoma City	7-0	220
1977	Earl Anthony, Tacoma, Wash.	Jim Godman, Lorain, Oh.	7-0	218
1978	Frank Ellenburg, Mesa, Ariz.	Earl Anthony, Tacoma, Wash.	8-1	200
1979	Doug Myers, El Toro, Cal.	Bill Spigner, Hamden, Conn.	7-1	202
1980	Neil Burton, St. Louis, Mo.	Mark Roth, North Arlington, N.J.	7-1	206
1981	Randy Lightfoot, St. Charles, Mo.	Skip Tucker, Merritt Island, Fla.	7-1	218
1982	Joe Berardi, Brooklyn, N.Y.	Ted Hannahs, Zanesville, Oh.	7-0	205
1983	Mike Lastowski, Havre de Grace, Md.	Pete Weber, St. Louis, Mo.	7-1	212
1984	Earl Anthony, Dublin, Cal.	Gil Sliker, Washington, N.J.	7-0	212
1985	Steve Wunderlich, St. Louis, Mo.	Tommy Kress, Rochester, N.Y.	7-0	210

Bowlers with 15 or More Sanctioned 300 Games

Elvin Mesger, Sullivan, Mo. ... 27	Dave Williams, Westbury, N.Y. ... 17	Tony Torrice, Wolcott, Conn. ... 15
Dave Soutar, Kansas City, Mo. ... 19	John Wilcox Jr., Shavertown, Pa. ... 16	Steve Carson ... 15
Ron Woolet, Louisville, Ky. ... 19	Ronnie Graham, Louisville, Ky. ... 15	
Dick Weber Sr., St. Louis, Mo. ... 18	Don Johnson, Las Vegas, Nev. ... 15	
George Billick, Old Forge, Pa. ... 17	Teata Semiz, Fairfield, N.J. ... 15	

Leading PBA Averages in 1984

(400 or more games in PBA tournaments)

Name	Games	Average	Name	Games	Average
Marshall Holman	1,129	213.911	Joe Berardi	833	210.598
Mark Roth	900	212.666	Rickie Sajek	1,014	210.265
Pete Weber	872	212.466	Gil Sliker	913	210.239
Brian Voss	975	210.948	Gary Skidmore	902	210.037
Mike Aulby	872	210.936	Wayne Webb	1,019	210.025
Henry Gonzalez	722	210.760	Nelson Burton, Jr.	441	209.322
Bob Handley	803	210.649	Ron Bell	523	209.258
Mark Baker	937	210.631			

PBA Leading Money Winners

Total winnings are from PBA, ABC Masters, and BPAA All-Star tournaments only, and do not include numerous other tournaments or earnings from special television shows and matches.

Year	Bowler	Dollars	Year	Bowler	Dollars	Year	Bowler	Dollars
1960	Don Carter	22,525	1969	Billy Hardwick	64,160	1978	Mark Roth	134,500
1961	Dick Weber	26,280	1970	Mike McGrath	52,049	1979	Mark Roth	124,517
1962	Don Carter	49,972	1971	Johnny Petraglia	85,065	1980	Wayne Webb	116,700
1963	Dick Weber	46,333	1972	Don Johnson	56,648	1981	Earl Anthony	164,735
1964	Bob Strampe	33,592	1973	Don McCune	69,000	1982	Earl Anthony	134,760
1965	Dick Weber	47,674	1974	Earl Anthony	99,585	1983	Earl Anthony	135,605
1966	Wayne Zahn	54,720	1975	Earl Anthony	107,585	1984	Mark Roth	158,712
1967	Dave Davis	54,165	1976	Earl Anthony	110,833			
1968	Jim Stefanich	67,377	1977	Mark Roth	105,583			

Leading PBA Averages by Year

Year	Bowler	Average	Year	Bowler	Average	Year	Bowler	Average
1962	Don Carter	212.844	1970	Nelson Burton Jr.	214.908	1978	Mark Roth	219.834
1963	Billy Hardwick	210.346	1971	Don Johnson	213.977	1979	Mark Roth	221.662
1964	Ray Bluth	210.512	1972	Don Johnson	215.290	1980	Earl Anthony	218.535
1965	Dick Weber	211.895	1973	Earl Anthony	215.799	1981	Mark Roth	216.699
1966	Wayne Zahn	208.663	1974	Earl Anthony	219.394	1982	Marshall Holman	212.844
1967	Wayne Zahn	212.342	1975	Earl Anthony	219.060	1983	Earl Anthony	216.645
1968	Jim Stefanich	211.895	1976	Mark Roth	215.970	1984	Marshall Holman	213.911
1969	Bill Hardwick	212.957	1977	Mark Roth	218.174			

Firestone Tournament of Champions

This is professional bowling's richest tournament and has been held each year since its inception in 1965, in Akron, Oh., the home of the Professional Bowlers Association.

Year	Winner	Year	Winner	Year	Winner	Year	Winner
1965	Billy Hardwick	1971	Johnny Petraglia	1976	Marshall Holman	1981	Steve Cook
1966	Wayne Zahn	1972	Mike Durbin	1977	Mike Berlin	1982	Mike Durbin
1967	Jim Stefanich	1973	Jim Godman	1978	Earl Anthony	1983	Joe Berardi
1968	Dave Davis	1974	Earl Anthony	1979	George Pappas	1984	Mike Durbin
1969	Jim Godman	1975	Dave Davis	1980	Wayne Webb	1985	Mark Williams
1970	Don Johnson						

PBA Hall of Fame

Performance				Meritorius service	
Bill Allen	Mike Durbin	Harry Smith		Eddie Elias	Joe Joseph
Glenn Allison	Buzz Fazio	Dave Soutar		Frank Esposito	Steve Nagy
Earl Anthony	Billy Hardwick	Jim Stefanich		E. A. "Bud" Fisher	Chuck Pezzano
Ray Bluth	Don Johnson	Dick Weber		Lou Frantz	Joe Richards
Nelson Burton, Jr.	Larry Laub	Billy Welu		Harry Golden	Chris Schenkel
Don Carter	Johnny Petraglia	Wayne Zahn		Ted Hoffman Jr.	Lorraine Stitzlein
Dave Davis	Dick Ritger				
	Carmen Salvino				

Women's International Bowling Congress Champions in 1985

Individual—Polly Schwarzel, Cheswick, Pa., 694.
All Events—Aleta Sill, Cocoa, Fla., 1,900.
2-Woman Team—Melody Philippson, Colfax, Ia. & Linda Graham, Des Moines, Ia., 1,246.
5-Woman Team—Don Redman Insurance, Toledo, Oh., 2,934.

Most Sanctioned 300 Games

Jeanne Maiden, Solon, Oh.	9	Toni Gilliard, Beverly, Oh.	5	Judith Seckel, Florissant, Mo.	4
Donna Adamek, Duarte, Cal.	6	Regi Jonak, St. Louis, Mo.	5	Ann Marie Pike, Cypress, Cal.	4
Letitia Johnson, Napa, Cal.	6	Pam Buckner, Reno, Nev.	5	Vicki Fischel, Denver, Col.	4
Betty Morris, Lodi, Cal.	5	Beverly Ortner, Tucson, Ariz.	4	Debbie Timberlake, Blue Springs, Mo.	4

Annual Results of Major Bowl Games

(Note: Dates indicate the year that the game was played).

Rose Bowl, Pasadena

1902 Michigan 49, Stanford 0
1916 Wash. State 14, Brown 0
1917 Oregon 14, Pennsylvania 0
1918-19 Service teams
1920 Harvard 7, Oregon 6
1921 California 28, Ohio State 0
1922 Wash. & Jeff. 0, California 0
1923 So. California 14, Penn State 3
1924 Navy 14, Washington 14
1925 Notre Dame 27, Stanford 10
1926 Alabama 20, Washington 19
1927 Alabama 7, Stanford 7
1928 Stanford 7, Pittsburgh 6
1929 Georgia Tech 8, California 7
1930 So. California 47, Pittsburgh 14
1931 Alabama 24, Wash. State 0
1932 So. California 21, Tulane 12
1933 So. California 35, Pittsburgh 0
1934 Columbia 7, Stanford 0
1935 Alabama 29, Stanford 13
1936 Stanford 7, So. Methodist 0
1937 Pittsburgh 21, Washington 0
1938 California 13, Alabama 0
1939 So. California 7, Duke 3

1940 So. California 14, Tennessee 0
1941 Stanford 21, Nebraska 13
1942 Oregon St. 20, Duke 16
     (at Durham)
1943 Georgia 9, UCLA 0
1944 So. California 29, Washington 0
1945 So. California 25, Tennessee 0
1946 Alabama 34, So. California 14
1947 Illinois 45, UCLA 14
1948 Michigan 49, So. California 0
1949 Northwestern 20, California 14
1950 Ohio State 17, California 14
1951 Michigan 14, California 6
1952 Illinois 40, Stanford 7
1953 So. California 7, Wisconsin 0
1954 Mich. State 28, UCLA 20
1955 Ohio State 20, So. California 7
1956 Mich. State 17, UCLA 14
1957 Iowa 35, Oregon St. 19
1958 Ohio State 10, Oregon 7
1959 Iowa 38, California 12
1960 Washington 44, Wisconsin 8
1961 Washington 17, Minnesota 7
1962 Minnesota 21, UCLA 3

1963 So. California 42, Wisconsin 37
1964 Illinois 17, Washington 7
1965 Michigan 34, Oregon St. 7
1966 UCLA 14, Mich. State 12
1967 Purdue 14, So. California 13
1968 Southern Cal. 14, Indiana 3
1969 Ohio State 27, Southern Cal 16
1970 Southern Cal 10, Michigan 3
1971 Stanford 27, Ohio State 17
1972 Stanford 13, Michigan 12
1973 So. California 42, Ohio State 17
1974 Ohio State 42, So. California 21
1975 So. California 18, Ohio State 17
1976 UCLA 23, Ohio State 10
1977 So. California 14, Michigan 6
1978 Washington 27, Michigan 20
1979 So. California 17, Michigan 10
1980 So. California 17, Ohio State 16
1981 Michigan 23, Washington 6
1982 Washington 28, Iowa 0
1983 UCLA 24, Michigan 14
1984 UCLA 45, Illinois 9
1985 So. California 20, Ohio State 17

Orange Bowl, Miami

1935 Bucknell 26, Miami (Fla.) 0
1936 Catholic U. 20, Mississippi 19
1937 Duquesne 13, Miss. State 12
1938 Auburn 6, Mich. State 0
1939 Tennessee 17, Oklahoma 0
1940 Georgia Tech 21, Missouri 7
1941 Miss. State 14, Georgetown 7
1942 Georgia 40, TCU 26
1943 Alabama 37, Boston Col. 21
1944 LSU 19, Texas A&M 14
1945 Tulsa 26, Georgia Tech 12
1946 Miami (Fla.) 13, Holy Cross 6
1947 Rice 8, Tennessee 0
1948 Georgia Tech 20, Kansas 14
1949 Texas 41, Georgia 28
1950 Santa Clara 21, Kentucky 13
1951 Clemson 15, Miami (Fla.) 14

1952 Georgia Tech 17, Baylor 14
1953 Alabama 61, Syracuse 6
1954 Oklahoma 7, Maryland 0
1955 Duke 34, Nebraska 7
1956 Oklahoma 20, Maryland 6
1957 Colorado 27, Clemson 21
1958 Oklahoma 48, Duke 21
1959 Oklahoma 21, Syracuse 6
1960 Georgia 14, Missouri 0
1961 Missouri 21, Navy 14
1962 LSU 25, Colorado 7
1963 Alabama 17, Oklahoma 0
1964 Nebraska 13, Auburn 7
1965 Texas 21, Alabama 17
1966 Alabama 39, Nebraska 28
1967 Florida 27, Georgia Tech 12
1968 Oklahoma 26, Tennessee 24

1969 Penn State 15, Kansas 14
1970 Penn State 10, Missouri 3
1971 Nebraska 17, Louisiana St. 12
1972 Nebraska 38, Alabama 6
1973 Nebraska 40, Notre Dame 6
1974 Penn State 16, Louisiana St. 9
1975 Notre Dame 13, Alabama 11
1976 Oklahoma 14, Michigan 6
1977 Ohio State 27, Colorado 10
1978 Arkansas 31, Oklahoma 6
1979 Oklahoma 31, Nebraska 24
1980 Oklahoma 24, Florida St. 7
1981 Oklahoma 18, Florida St. 17
1982 Clemson 22, Nebraska 15
1983 Nebraska 21, Louisiana St. 20
1984 Miami (Fla.) 31, Nebraska 30
1985 Washington 28, Oklahoma 17

Sugar Bowl, New Orleans

1935 Tulane 20, Temple 14
1936 TCU 3, LSU 2
1937 Santa Clara 21, LSU 14
1938 Santa Clara 6, LSU 0
1939 TCU 15, Carnegie Tech 7
1940 Texas A&M 14, Tulane 13
1941 Boston Col. 19, Tennessee 13
1942 Fordham 2, Missouri 0
1943 Tennessee 14, Tulsa 7
1944 Georgia Tech 20, Tulsa 18
1945 Duke 29, Alabama 26
1946 Oklahoma A&M 33, St. Mary's 13
1947 Georgia 20, No. Carolina 10
1948 Texas 27, Alabama 7
1949 Oklahoma 14, No. Carolina 6
1950 Oklahoma 35, LSU 0
1951 Kentucky 13, Oklahoma 7

1952 Maryland 28, Tennessee 13
1953 Georgia Tech. 24, Mississippi 7
1954 Georgia Tech 42, West Virginia 19
1955 Navy 21, Mississippi
1956 Georgia Tech 7, Pittsburgh 0
1957 Baylor 13, Tennessee 7
1958 Mississippi 39, Texas 7
1959 LSU 7, Clemson 0
1960 Mississippi 21, LSU 0
1961 Mississippi 14, Rice 6
1962 Alabama 10, Arkansas 3
1963 Mississippi 17, Arkansas 13
1964 Alabama 12, Mississippi 7
1965 LSU 13, Syracuse 10
1966 Missouri 20, Florida 18
1967 Alabama 34, Nebraska 7
1968 LSU 20, Wyoming 13

1969 Arkansas 16, Georgia 2
1970 Mississippi 27, Arkansas 22
1971 Tennessee 34, Air Force 13
1972 Oklahoma 40, Auburn 22
*1972 (Dec.) Oklahoma 14, Penn State 0
1973 Notre Dame 24, Alabama 23
1974 Nebraska 13, Florida 10
1975 Alabama 13, Penn State 6
1977 (Jan.) Pittsburgh 27, Georgia 3
1978 Alabama 35, Ohio State 6
1979 Alabama 14, Penn State 7
1980 Alabama 24, Arkansas 9
1981 Georgia 17, Notre Dame 10
1982 Pittsburgh 24, Georgia 20
1983 Penn State 27, Georgia 23
1984 Auburn 9, Michigan 7
1985 Nebraska 28, Louisiana St. 10
*Penn St. awarded game by forfeit

Cotton Bowl, Dallas

1937 TCU 16, Marquette 6
1938 Rice 28, Colorado 14
1939 St. Mary's 20, Texas Tech 13
1940 Clemson 6, Boston Col. 3
1941 Texas A&M 13, Fordham 12
1942 Alabama 29, Texas A&M 21
1943 Texas 14, Georgia Tech 7
1944 Randolph Field 7, Texas 7
1945 Oklahoma A&M 34, TCU 0
1946 Texas 40, Missouri 27
1947 Arkansas 0, LSU 0
1948 So. Methodist 13, Penn State 13
1949 So. Methodist 21, Oregon 13
1950 Rice 27, No. Carolina 13
1951 Tennessee 20, Texas 14
1952 Kentucky 20, TCU 7
1953 Texas 16, Tennessee 0

1954 Rice 28, Alabama 6
1955 Georgia Tech 14, Arkansas 6
1956 Mississippi 14, TCU 13
1957 TCU 28, Syracuse 27
1958 Navy 20, Rice 7
1959 TCU 0, Air Force 0
1960 Syracuse 23, Texas 14
1961 Duke 7, Arkansas 6
1962 Texas 12, Mississippi 7
1963 LSU 13, Texas 0
1964 Texas 28, Navy 6
1965 Arkansas 10, Nebraska 7
1966 LSU 14, Arkansas 7
1967 Georgia 24, So. Methodist 9
1968 Texas A&M 20, Alabama 16
1969 Texas 36, Tennessee 13

1970 Texas 21, Notre Dame 17
1971 Notre Dame 24, Texas 11
1972 Penn State 30, Texas 6
1973 Texas 17, Alabama 13
1974 Nebraska 19, Texas 3
1975 Penn State 41, Baylor 20
1976 Arkansas 31, Georgia 10
1977 Houston 30, Maryland 21
1978 Notre Dame 38, Texas 10
1979 Notre Dame 35, Houston 34
1980 Houston 17, Nebraska 14
1981 Alabama 30, Baylor 2
1982 Texas 14, Alabama 12
1983 SMU 7, Pittsburgh 3
1984 Georgia 10, Texas 9
1985 Boston Coll. 45, Houston 28

Sun Bowl, El Paso

1936 Hardin Simmons 14, New Mex. St. 14
1937 Hardin-Simmons 34, Texas Mines 6
1938 West Virginia 7, Texas Tech 6
1939 Utah 26, New Mexico 0
1940 Catholic U. 0, Arizona St. 0
1941 Western Reserve 26, Arizona St. 13
1942 Tulsa 6, Texas Tech 0
1943 2d Air Force 13, Hardin-Simmons 7
1944 Southwestern (Tex.) 7, New Mexico 0
1945 Southwestern (Tex.) 35, U. of Mex. 0
1946 New Mexico 34, Denver 24
1947 Cincinnati 38, Virginia Tech 6
1948 Miami (O.) 13, Texas Tech 12
1949 West Virginia 21, Texas Mines 12
1950 Texas Western 33, Georgetown 20
1951 West Texas St. 14, Cincinnati 13

1952 Texas Tech 25, Col. Pacific 14
1953 Col. Pacific 26, Miss. Southern 7
1954 Texas Western 37, Miss. Southern 14
1955 Texas Western 47, Florida St. 20
1956 Wyoming 21, Texas Tech 14
1957 Geo. Washington 13, Tex. Western 0
1958 Louisville 34, Drake 20
1959 Wyoming 14, Hardin-Simmons 6
1960 New Mexico St. 28, No. Texas St. 8
1961 New Mexico St. 20, Utah State 13
1962 Villanova 17, Wichita 9
1963 West Texas St. 15, Ohio U. 14
1964 Oregon 21, So. Methodist 14
1965 Georgia 7, Texas Tech 0
1966 Texas Western 13, TCU 12
1967 Wyoming 28, Florida St. 20
1968 UTex El Paso 14, Mississippi 7

1969 Auburn 34, Arizona 10
1969 (Dec.) Nebraska 45, Georgia 6
1970 Georgia Tech. 17, Texas Tech. 9
1971 LSU 33, Iowa State 15
1972 North Carolina 32, Texas Tech 28
1973 Missouri 34, Auburn 17
1974 Mississippi St. 26, No. Carolina 24
1975 Pittsburgh 33, Kansas 19
1977 (Jan.) Texas A&M 37, Florida 14
1977 (Dec.) Stanford 24, Louisiana St. 14
1978 Texas 42, Maryland 0
1979 Washington 14, Texas 7
1980 Nebraska 31, Mississippi St. 17
1981 Oklahoma 40, Houston 14
1982 North Carolina 26, Texas 10
1983 Alabama 28, SMU 7
1984 Maryland 28, Tennessee 27

Gator Bowl, Jacksonville

1946 Wake Forest 26, So. Carolina 14
1947 Oklahoma 34, N.C. State 13
1948 Maryland 20, Georgia 20
1949 Clemson 24, Missouri 23
1950 Maryland 20, Missouri 7
1951 Wyoming 20, Wash. & Lee 7
1952 Miami (Fla.) 14, Clemson 0
1953 Florida 14, Tulsa 13
1954 Texas Tech 35, Auburn 13
1955 Auburn 33, Baylor 13
1956 Vanderbilt 25, Auburn 13
1957 Georgia Tech 21, Pittsburgh 14
1958 Tennessee 3, Texas A&M 0
1959 Mississippi 7, Florida 3

1960 Arkansas 14, Georgia Tech 7
1961 Florida 13, Baylor 12
1962 Penn State 30, Georgia Tech 15
1963 Florida 17, Penn State 7
1964 No. Carolina 35, Air Force 0
1965 Florida St. 36, Oklahoma 19
1966 Georgia Tech 31, Texas Tech 21
1967 Tennessee 18, Syracuse 12
1968 Penn State 17, Florida St. 17
1969 Missouri 35, Alabama 10
1969 (Dec.) Florida 14, Tenn. 13
1971 (Jan.) Auburn 35, Mississippi 28
1972 Georgia 7, N. Carolina 3
1973 Auburn 24, Colorado 3

1973 (Dec.) Tex. Tech. 28, Tenn. 19
1974 Auburn 27, Texas 3
1975 Maryland 13, Florida 0
1976 Notre Dame 20, Penn State 9
1977 Pittsburgh 34, Clemson 3
1978 Clemson 17, Ohio State 15
1979 No. Carolina 17, Michigan 15
1980 Pittsburgh 37, So. Carolina 9
1981 No. Carolina 31, Arkansas 27
1982 Florida St. 31, West Va. 12
1983 Florida 14, Iowa 6
1984 Oklahoma St. 21, So. Carolina 14

Bluebonnet Bowl, Houston

1959 Clemson 23, TCU 7
1960 Texas 3, Alabama 3
1961 Kansas 33, Rice 7
1962 Missouri 14, Georgia Tech 10
1963 Baylor 14, LSU 7
1964 Tulsa 14, Mississippi 7
1965 Tennessee 27, Tulsa 6
1966 Texas 19, Mississippi 0
1967 Colorado 31, Miami (Fla.) 21

1968 SMU 28, Oklahoma 27
1969 Houston 36, Auburn 7
1970 Oklahoma 24, Alabama 24
1971 Colorado 29, Houston 17
1972 Tennessee 24, Louisiana St. 17
1973 Houston 47, Tulane 7
1974 N. Carolina St. 31, Houston 31
1975 Texas 38, Colorado 21
1976 Nebraska 27, Texas Tech 24

1977 USC 47, Texas A&M 28
1978 Stanford 25, Georgia 22
1979 Purdue 27, Tennessee 22
1980 No. Carolina 16, Texas 7
1981 Michigan 33, UCLA 14
1982 Arkansas 28, Florida 24
1983 Oklahoma St. 24, Baylor 14
1984 W. Virginia 31, Tex. Christian 14

Peach Bowl, Atlanta

1968 LSU 31, Florida St. 27
1969 West Virginia 14, S. Carolina 3
1970 Arizona St. 48, N. Carolina 26
1971 Mississippi 41, Georgia Tech. 18
1972 N. Carolina 49, W. Va. 13
1973 Georgia 17, Maryland 16

1974 Vanderbilt 6, Texas Tech. 6
1975 W. Virginia 13, No. Carolina St. 10
1976 Kentucky 21, North Carolina 0
1977 N. Carolina St. 24, Iowa St. 14
1978 Purdue 41, Georgia Tech. 21
1979 Baylor 24, Clemson 18

1981 (Jan.) Miami 20, Virginia Tech. 10
1981 (Dec.) West Virginia 26, Florida 6
1982 Iowa 28, Tennessee 22
1983 Florida St. 28, North Carolina 3
1984 Virginia 27, Purdue 22

Fiesta Bowl, Tempe

1971 Arizona St. 45, Florida St. 38
1972 Arizona St. 49, Missouri 35
1973 Arizona St. 28, Pittsburgh 7
1974 Okla. St. 16, Brigham Young 6
1975 Arizona St. 17, Nebraska 14

1976 Oklahoma 41, Wyoming 7
1977 Penn St. 42, Arizona St. 30
1978 UCLA 10, Arkansas 10
1979 Pittsburgh 16, Arizona 10
1980 Penn St. 31, Ohio St. 19

1981 Penn St. 26, USC 10
1983 (Jan.) Arizona St. 32, Oklahoma 21
1984 Ohio State 28, Pittsburgh 23
1985 UCLA 39, Miami 37

Liberty Bowl, Memphis

1959 Penn State 7, Alabama 0
1960 Penn State 41, Oregon 12
1961 Syracuse 15, Miami 14
1962 Oregon State 6, Villanova 0
1963 Miss. State 16, N.C. State 12
1964 Utah 32, West Virginia 6
1965 Mississippi 13, Auburn 7
1966 Miami (Fla.) 14, Va. Tech 7
1967 N.C. State 14, Georgia 7

1968 Mississippi 34, Va. Tech 17
1969 Colorado 47, Alabama 33
1970 Tulane 17, Colorado 3
1971 Tennessee 14, Arkansas 13
1972 Georgia Tech 31, Iowa State 30
1973 No. Carolina St. 31, Kansas 18
1974 Tennessee 7, Maryland 3
1975 USC 20, Texas A&M 0
1976 Alabama 36, UCLA 6

1977 Nebraska 27, N. Carolina 17
1978 Missouri 20, Louisiana St. 15
1979 Penn St. 9, Tulane 6
1980 Purdue 28, Missouri 25
1981 Ohio State 31, Navy 28
1982 Alabama 21, Illinois 15
1983 Notre Dame 19, Boston Coll. 18
1984 Auburn 21, Arkansas 15

Holiday Bowl, San Diego

1978 Navy 23, Brigham Young 16
1979 Indiana 38, Brigham Young 37
1980 Brigham Young 46, SMU 45

1981 Brigham Young 38, Wash. St. 36
1982 Ohio State 47, Brigham Young 17

1983 Brigham Young 21, Missouri 17
1984 Brigham Young 24, Michigan 17

Aloha Bowl, Honolulu

1982 Washington 21, Maryland 20

1983 Penn State 13, Washington 10

1984 SMU 27, Notre Dame 20

Florida Citrus Bowl, Orlando

1947 Catawba 31, Maryville 6	1960 (Jan.) Middle Tenn. 21,	1973 Miami (O.) 16, Florida 7
1948 Catawba 7, Marshall 0	Presbyterian 12	1974 Miami (O.) 21, Georgia 10
1949 Murray State 21, Sul Ross St. 21	1960 (Dec.) Citadel 27, Tenn. Tech 0	1975 Miami (O.) 20, South Carolina 7
1950 St. Vincent 7, Emory & Henry 6	1961 Lamar 21, Middle Tennessee 14	1976 Okla. St. 49, Brigham Young 21
1951 Morris Harvey 35, Emory & Henry 14	1962 Houston 49, Miami (O.) 21	1977 Florida St. 40, Texas Tech 17
1952 Stetson 35, Arkansas St. 20	1963 Western Ky. 27, Coast Guard 0	1978 N.C. State 30, Pittsburgh 17
1953 East Texas St. 33, Tenn. Tech 0	1964 E. Carolina 14, Massachusetts 13	1979 LSU 34, Wake Forest 10
1954 East Texas St. 7, Arkansas St. 7	1965 East Carolina 31, Maine 0	1980 Florida 35, Maryland 20
1955 Neb.-Omaha 7, Eastern Kentucky 6	1966 Morgan State 14, West Chester 6	1981 Missouri 19, Southern Miss. 17
1956 Juniata 6, Missouri Valley 6	1967 Tenn.-Martin 25, West Chester 8	1982 Auburn 33, Boston College 26
1957 West Texas St. 20, So. Miss. 13	1968 Richmond 49, Ohio U. 42	1983 Tennessee 30, Maryland 23
1958 East Texas St. 10, So. Miss. 9	1969 Toledo 56, Davidson 33	1984 Georgia 17, Florida St. 17
1958 (Dec.) East Texas St. 26, Missouri Valley 7	1970 Toledo 40, William & Mary 12	
	1971 Toledo 28, Richmond 3	
	1972 Tampa 21, Kent State 18	

Hall of Fame Classic, Birmingham

1977 Maryland 17, Minnesota 7	1980 Arkansas 34, Tulane 15	1983 W. Virginia 20, Kentucky 16
1978 Texas A&M 28, Iowa St. 12	1981 Mississippi St. 10, Kansas 0	1984 Kentucky 20, Wisconsin 19
1979 Missouri 24, So. Carolina 14	1982 Air Force 36, Vanderbilt 28	

Independence Bowl, Shreveport

1976 McNeese St. 20, Tulsa 16	1979 Syracuse 31, McNeese St. 7	1982 Wisconsin 14, Kansas St. 3
1977 Louisiana Tech 24, Louisville 14	1980 So. Miss. 16, McNeese St. 14	1983 Air Force 9, Mississippi 3
1978 E. Carolina 35, La. Tech 13	1981 Texas A&M 33, Oklahoma St. 16	1984 Air Force 23, Virginia Tech 7

California Bowl, Fresno

1981 Toledo 27, San Jose St. 25	1983 N. Illinois 20, Cal. State Fullerton 13	
1982 Fresno St. 29, Bowling Green 28	1984 Nevada-Las Vegas 30, Toledo 13	

National College Football Champions

The NCAA recognizes as unofficial national champion the team selected each year by the AP (poll of writers) and the UPI (poll of coaches). When the polls disagree both teams are listed. The AP poll originated in 1936 and the UPI poll in 1950.

1936	Minnesota	1949	Notre Dame	1961	Alabama	1973	Notre Dame, Alabama
1937	Pittsburgh	1950	Oklahoma	1962	Southern Cal.	1974	Oklahoma, So. Cal.
1938	Texas Christian	1951	Tennessee	1963	Texas	1975	Oklahoma
1939	Texas A&M	1952	Michigan State	1964	Alabama	1976	Pittsburgh
1940	Minnesota	1953	Maryland	1965	Alabama, Mich. State	1977	Notre Dame
1941	Minnesota	1954	Ohio State, UCLA	1966	Notre Dame	1978	Alabama, So. Cal.
1942	Ohio State	1955	Oklahoma	1967	Southern Cal.	1979	Alabama
1943	Notre Dame	1956	Oklahoma	1968	Ohio State	1980	Georgia
1944	Army	1957	Auburn, Ohio State	1969	Texas	1981	Clemson
1945	Army	1958	Louisiana State	1970	Nebraska, Texas	1982	Penn State
1946	Notre Dame	1959	Syracuse	1971	Nebraska,	1983	Miami (Fla.)
1947	Notre Dame	1960	Minnesota	1972	Southern Cal.	1984	Brigham Young
1948	Michigan						

College Football Teams

Division I Teams

Team	Nickname	Team colors	Conference	Coach	1984 record (W-L-T)
Air Force	Falcons	Blue & silver	Western Athletic	Fisher De Berry	8-4-0
Akron	Zips	Blue & Gold	Ohio Valley	Jim Dennison	4-7-0
Alabama	Crimson Tide	Crimson & white	Southeastern	Ray Perkins	5-6-0
Alabama State	Hornets	Black & gold	Southwestern	Jim Parker	2-9-0
Alcorn State	Braves	Purple & gold	Southwestern	Marino Casem	9-1-0
Appalachian State	Mountaineers	Black & gold	Southern	Sparky Woods	4-7-0
Arizona	Wildcats	Red & blue	Pacific Ten	Larry Smith	7-4-0
Arizona State	Sun Devils	Maroon & gold	Pacific Ten	John Cooper	5-6-0
Arkansas	Razorbacks	Cardinal & white	Southwest	Ken Hatfield	7-4-1
Arkansas State	Indians	Scarlet & black	Southland	Lawrence Lacewell	8-4-1
Army	Cadets	Black, gold, gray	1-A Eastern Ind.	Jim Young	8-3-1
Auburn	Tigers	Orange & blue	Southeastern	Pat Dye	9-4-0
Austin Peay State	Governors	Red & white	Ohio Valley	Emory Hale	7-4-0
Ball State	Cardinals	Cardinal & white	Mid-American	Paul Schudel	3-8-0
Baylor	Bears	Green & gold	Southwest	Grant Teaff	5-6-0
Bethune-Cookman	Wildcats	Maroon & gold	Mid-Eastern	Larry Little	7-3-0
Boise State	Broncos	Orange & Blue	Big Sky	Lyle Setencich	6-5-0
Boston College	Eagles	Maroon & gold	1-A Eastern Ind.	Jack Bicknell	10-2-0
Boston Univ.	Terriers	Scarlet & white	Yankee	Steve Stetson	9-3-0
Bowling Green St.	Falcons	Orange & brown	Mid-American	Denny Stolz	8-3-0
Brigham Young	Cougars	Royal blue & white	Western Athletic	LaVell Edwards	13-0-0
Brown	Bruins, Bears	Brown, cardinal, white	Ivy	John Rosenberg	4-5-0
Bucknell	Bisons	Orange & blue	1-AA Eastern Ind.	Bob Curtis	5-5-0
California	Golden Bears	Blue & gold	Pacific Ten	Joe Kapp	2-9-0
Central Michigan	Chippewas	Maroon & gold	Mid-American	Herb Deromedi	8-2-1
Cincinnati	Bearcats	Red & black	Independent	Dave Currey	2-9-0

Team	Nickname	Team colors	Conference	Coach	1984 record (W-L-T)
Citadel	Bulldogs	Blue & white	Southern	Tom Moore	7-4-0
Clemson	Tigers	Purple & orange	Atlantic Coast	Danny Ford	7-4-0
Colgate	Red Raiders	Maroon	1-AA Eastern Ind.	Fred Dunlap	5-5-0
Colorado State	Rams	Green & gold	Western Athletic	Leon Fuller	3-8-0
Colorado	Buffaloes	Silver, gold & blue	Big Eight	Bill McCartney	1-10-0
Columbia	Lions	Blue & white	Ivy	Jim Garnett	0-9-0
Connecticut	Huskies	Blue & white	Yankee	Tom Jackson	3-8-0
Cornell	Big Red	Carnelian & white	Ivy	Maxie Baughan	2-7-0
Dartmouth	Big Green	Dartmouth green & white	Ivy	Joe Yukica	2-7-0
Davidson	Wildcats	Red & black	Southern	Vic Gatto	2-8-0
Delaware	Fightin' Blue Hens	Blue & gold	1-AA Eastern Ind.	Harold Raymond	8-3-0
Delaware State	Hornets	Red & blue	Mid-Eastern	William Collick	8-2-0
Drake	Bulldogs	Blue & white	Missouri Valley	Chuck Shelton	4-7-0
Duke	Blue Devils	Royal blue & white	Atlantic Coast	Steve Sloan	2-9-0
East Carolina	Pirates	Purple & gold	1-A Southern Ind.	Art Baker	2-9-0
East Tennessee St.	Buccaneers	Blue & gold	Southern	Buddy Sasser	6-5-0
Eastern Illinois	Panthers	Blue & Gray	Mid-Continent	Al Molde	6-5-0
Eastern Kentucky	Colonels	Maroon & white	Ohio Valley	Roy Kidd	8-4-0
Eastern Michigan	Hurons	Green & white	Mid-American	Jim Harkema	2-7-2
Eastern Washington	Eagles	Red & white	Independent	Dick Zornes	7-2-1
Florida	Gators	Orange & blue	Southeastern	Galen Hall	9-1-1
Florida A&M	Rattlers	Orange & green	1-AA Southern Ind.	Rudy Hubbard	3-7-1
Florida State	Seminoles	Garnet & gold	1-A Southern Ind.	Bobby Bowden	7-3-2
Fresno State	Bulldogs	Cardinal & blue	Pacific Coast	Jim Sweeney	6-6-0
Fullerton, Cal. State	Titans	Blue, orange, white	Pacific Coast	Gene Murphy	11-1-0
Furman	Paladins	Purple & white	Southern	Dick Sheridan	8-3-0
Georgia	Bulldogs	Red & black	Southeastern	Vince Dooley	7-4-1
Georgia Southern	Eagles	Blue & white	1-AA Southern Ind.	Erskine Russell	8-3-0
Georgia Tech	Yellow Jackets	Old gold & white	Atlantic Coast	Bill Curry	6-4-1
Grambling State	Tigers	Black & gold	Southwestern	Eddie Robinson	7-4-0
Harvard	Crimson	Crimson	Ivy	Joe Restic	5-4-0
Hawaii	Rainbow Warriors	Green & white	Western Athletic	Dick Tomey	7-4-0
Holy Cross	Crusaders	Royal purple	1-AA Eastern Ind.	Rick Carter	8-3-0
Houston	Cougars	Scarlet & white	Southwest	Bill Yeoman	7-5-0
Howard	Bison	Blue & white	Mid-Eastern	Willie Jeffries	2-8-0
Idaho	Vandals	Silver & gold	Big Sky	Dennis Erickson	6-5-0
Idaho State	Bengals	Orange & black	Big Sky	Jim Koetter	5-6-0
Illinois	Fighting Illini	Orange & blue	Big Ten	Mike White	7-4-0
Illinois State	Redbirds	Red & white	Missouri Valley	Bob Otolski	5-6-0
Indiana	Fightin' Hoosiers	Cream & crimson	Big Ten	Bill Mallory	0-11-0
Indiana State	Sycamores	Blue & white	Missouri Valley	Dennis Raetz	9-3-0
Iowa	Hawkeyes	Old gold & black	Big Ten	Hayden Fry	8-4-1
Iowa State	Cyclones	Cardinal & gold	Big Eight	Jim Criner	2-7-2
Jackson State	Tigers	Blue & white	Southwestern	W.C. Gorden	4-5-1
James Madison	Dukes	Purple & gold	1-AA Southern Ind.	Joe Purzycki	6-5-0
Kansas	Jayhawks	Crimson & blue	Big Eight	Mike Gottfried	5-6-0
Kansas State	Wildcats	Purple & white	Big Eight	Jim Dickey	3-7-1
Kent State	Golden Flashes	Blue & gold	Mid-American	Dick Scesniak	4-7-0
Kentucky	Wildcats	Blue & white	Southeastern	Jerry Claiborne	9-3-0
Lafayette	Leopards	Maroon & white	1-AA Eastern Ind.	Bill Russo	5-5-0
Lamar	Cardinals	Red & white	Southland	Ken Stephens	2-9-0
Lehigh	Engineers	Brown & white	1-AA Eastern Ind.	John Whitehead	5-6-0
Long Beach, Cal. State	Forty-Niners	Brown & gold	Pacific Coast	Mike Sheppard	4-7-0
Louisiana State	Fighting Tigers	Purple & gold	Southeastern	Bill Arnsparger	8-3-1
Louisiana Tech	Bulldogs	Red & blue	Southland	A.L. Williams	10-5-0
Louisville	Cardinals	Red, black, white	1-A Southern Ind.	Howard Schnellenberger	2-9-0
Maine	Black Bears	Blue & white	Yankee	Eugene Teevens 3d	5-6-0
Marshall	Thundering Herd	Green & white	Southern	Stan Parrish	6-5-0
Maryland	Terps	Red, white, black & gold	Atlantic Coast	Bobby Ross	8-4-0
Massachusetts	Minutemen	Maroon & white	Yankee	Bob Stull	3-8-0
McNeese State	Cowboys	Blue & gold	Southland	John McCann	7-3-1
Memphis State	Tigers	Blue & gray	1-A Southern Ind.	Rey Dempsey	5-5-1
Miami (Fla.)	Hurricanes	Orange, green, white	1-A Southern Ind.	Jimmy Johnson	8-5-0
Miami (Ohio)	Redskins	Red & white	Mid-American	Tim Rose	4-7-0
Michigan	Wolverines	Maize & blue	Big Ten	Bo Schembechler	6-6-0
Michigan State	Spartans	Green & white	Big Ten	George Perles	6-6-0
Middle Tennessee St.	Blue Raiders	Blue & white	Ohio Valley	Boots Donnelly	11-3-0
Minnesota	Golden Gophers	Maroon & gold	Big Ten	Lou Holtz	4-7-0
Mississippi	Rebels	Red & blue	Southeastern	Billy Brewer	4-6-1
Mississippi State	Bulldogs	Maroon & white	Southeastern	Emory Bellard	4-7-0
Miss. Valley State	Delta Devils	Green & white	Southwestern	Archie Cooley	9-2-0
Missouri	Tigers	Old gold & black	Big Eight	Robert Widenhofer	3-7-1
Montana	Grizzlies	Copper, silver, gold	Big Sky	Larry Donovan	2-8-1
Montana State	Bobcats	Blue & gold	Big Sky	Dave Arnold	12-2-0
Morehead State	Eagles	Blue & gold	Ohio Valley	Bill Baldridge	2-9-0
Murray State	Racers	Blue & gold	Ohio Valley	Frank Beamer	9-2-0
Navy	Midshipmen	Navy blue & gold	1-A Eastern Ind.	Gary Tranquill	4-6-1
Nebraska	Cornhuskers	Scarlet & cream	Big Eight	Tom Osborne	10-2-0
Nevada-Las Vegas	Rebels	Scarlet & gray	Pacific Coast	Harvey Hyde	11-2-0
Nevada-Reno	Wolf Pack	Silver & blue	Big Sky	Chris Ault	7-4-0
New Hampshire	Wildcats	Blue & white	Yankee	Bill Bowes	9-2-0

Team	Nickname	Team colors	Conference	Coach	1984 record (W-L-T)
New Mexico	Lobos	Cherry & silver	Western Athletic	John Lee Dunn	4-8-0
New Mexico State	Aggies	Crimson & white	Pacific Coast	Fred Zechman	2-9-0
Nicholls St.	Colonels	Red & grey	Gulf Star	William Jackson	6-5-0
North Carolina	Tar Heels	Blue & white	Atlantic Coast	Dick Crum	5-5-1
North Carolina A & T	Aggies	Blue & gold	Mid-Eastern	Maurice Forte	2-8-0
North Carolina State	Wolfpack	Red & white	Atlantic Coast	Tom Reed	3-8-0
North Texas State	Mean Green, Eagles	Green & white	Southland	Corky Nelson	2-9-0
Northeast Louisiana	Indians	Maroon & gold	Southland	Pat Collins	7-4-0
Northeastern	Huskies	Red & black	1-AA Eastern Ind.	Paul Pawlak	3-7-0
Northern Arizona	Lumberjacks	Blue & gold	Big Sky	Larry Kentera	4-6-0
Northern Illinois	Huskies	Cardinal & black	Mid-American	Jerry Pettibone	4-6-1
Northern Iowa	Panthers	Purple & Old Gold	Mid-Continent	Darrell Mudra	9-2-0
Northwestern	Wildcats	Purple & white	Big Ten	Dennis Green	2-9-0
Northwestern State	Demons	Burnt orange, purple, white	Gulf Star	Sam Goodwin	7-4-0
Notre Dame	Fighting Irish	Gold & blue	Independent	Gerry Faust	7-5-0
Ohio State	Buckeyes	Scarlet & gray	Big Ten	Earle Bruce	9-3-0
Ohio Univ	Bobcats	Green & white	Mid-American	Cleve Bryant	4-6-1
Oklahoma	Sooners	Crimson & cream	Big Eight	Barry Switzer	9-2-1
Oklahoma State	Cowboys	Orange & black	Big Eight	Pat Jones	10-2-0
Oregon	Ducks	Green & yellow	Pacific Ten	Rich Brooks	6-5-0
Oregon State	Beavers	Orange & black	Pacific Ten	Dave Kragthrope	2-9-0
Pacific	Tigers	Orange & black	Pacific Coast	Bob Cope	4-7-0
Penn State	Nittany Lions	Blue & white	1-A Eastern Ind.	Joe Paterno	6-5-0
Pennsylvania	Red & Blue, Quakers	Red & blue	Ivy	Jerry Berndt	8-1-0
Pittsburgh	Panthers	Gold & blue	1-A Eastern Ind.	Serafino Fazio	3-7-1
Prairie View A & M	Panthers	Purple & gold	Southwestern	Conway Hayman	0-11-0
Princeton	Tigers	Orange & black	Ivy	Ron Rogerson	4-5-0
Purdue	Boilermakers	Old gold & black	Big Ten	Leon Bertnett	7-5-0
Rhode Island	Rams	Blue & white	Yankee	Bob Griffin	10-3-0
Rice	Owls	Blue & gray	Southwest	Watson Brown	1-10-0
Richmond	Spiders	Red & blue	1-AA Southern Ind.	Dal Shealy	8-4-0
Rutgers	Scarlet Knights	Scarlet	1-A Eastern Ind.	Dick Anderson	7-3-0
San Diego State	Aztecs	Scarlet & black	Western Athletic	Doug Scovil	4-7-1
San Jose State	Spartans	Gold & white	Pacific Coast	Claude Gilbert	6-5-0
South Carolina	Fighting Gamecocks	Garnet & black	1-A Southern Ind.	Joe Morrison	10-2-0
South Carolina State	Bulldogs	Garnet & blue	Mid-Eastern	Bill Davis	4-6-1
Southeastern La.	Lions	Green & gold	Gulf Star	Oscar Lofton	2-8-1
Southern	Jaguars	Blue & gold	Southwestern	Otis Washington	6-5-0
Southern California	Trojans	Cardinal & gold	Pacific Ten	Ted Tollner	9-3-0
Southern Illinois	Salukis	Maroon & white	Missouri Valley	Ray Dorr	3-8-0
Southern Methodist	Mustangs	Red & blue	Southwest	Bobby Collins	10-2-0
Southern Mississippi	Golden Eagles	Black & gold	1-A Southern Ind.	Jim Carmody	4-7-0
SW Missouri St	Bears	Maroon & white	Mid-Continent	Rich Johanningmeier	6-3-1
SW Texas	Bobcats	Maroon & gold	Gulf Star	John O'Hara	7-4-0
Southwestern La.	Ragin' Cajuns	Vermillion & white	Independent	Sam Robertson	6-5-0
Stanford	Cardinals	Cardinal & white	Pacific Ten	Jack Elway	5-6-0
Syracuse	Orangemen	Orange	1-A Eastern Ind.	Dick MacPherson	6-5-0
Temple	Owls	Cherry & white	1-A Eastern Ind.	Bruce Arians	6-5-0
Tennessee	Volunteers	Orange & white	Southeastern	John Majors	7-4-1
Tenn.-Chattanooga	Moccasins	Navy blue & gold	Southern	Buddy Nix	6-5-0
Tennessee State	Tigers	Blue & white	1-AA Southern Ind.	William Thomas	11-0-0
Tennessee Tech	Golden Eagles	Purple & gold	Ohio Valley	Gary Darnell	0-11-0
Texas	Longhorns	Orange & white	Southwest	Fred Akers	7-4-1
Texas-Arlington	Mavericks	Royal blue & white	Southland	Chuck Curtis	7-4-0
Texas-El Paso	Miners	Orange, white, blue	Western Athletic	Bill Yung	2-9-0
Texas A & M	Aggies	Maroon & white	Southwest	Jackie Sherrill	6-5-0
Texas Christian	Horned Frogs	Purple & white	Southwest	Jim Wacker	8-4-0
Texas Southern	Tigers	Maroon & gray	Southwestern	Lionel Taylor	5-6-0
Texas Tech	Red Raiders	Scarlet & black	Southwest	Jerry Moore	4-7-0
Toledo	Rockets	Blue & gold	Mid-American	Dan Simrell	8-2-1
Tulane	Green Wave	Olive green & sky blue	1-A Southern Ind.	Mack Brown	3-8-0
Tulsa	Golden Hurricane	Blue & gold	Missouri Valley	Don Morton	6-5-0
UCLA	Bruins	Navy blue & gold	Pacific Ten	Terry Donahue	9-3-0
Utah State	Aggies	Navy blue & white	Pacific Coast	Chris Pella	1-10-0
Utah	Utes	Crimson & white	Western Athletic	Jim Fassel	6-5-1
Vanderbilt	Commodores	Black & gold	Southeastern	George MacIntyre	5-6-0
Virginia	Cavaliers	Orange & blue	Atlantic Coast	George Welsh	8-2-2
VMI	Keydets	Red, white & yellow	Southern	Eddie Williamson	1-9-0
Virginia Tech	Gobblers, Hokies	Orange & maroon	1-A Southern Ind.	Bill Dooley	8-4-0
Wake Forest	Demon Deacons	Old gold & black	Atlantic Coast	Al Groh	6-5-0
Washington	Huskies	Purple & gold	Pacific Ten	Don James	11-1-0
Washington State	Cougars	Crimson & gray	Pacific Ten	Jim Walden	6-5-0
Weber State	Wildcats	Purple & white	Big Sky	Mike Price	5-6-0
West Texas State	Buffaloes	Maroon & white	Missouri Valley	Bill Kelly	3-8-0
West Virginia	Mountaineers	Old gold & blue	1-A Eastern Ind.	Don Nehlen	8-4-0
Western Carolina	Catamounts	Purple & gold	Southern	Bob Waters	8-3-0
Western Illinois	Leathernecks	Purple & Gold	Mid-Continent	Bruce Craddock	6-4-1
Western Kentucky	Hilltoppers	Red & white	1-AA Southern Ind.	Dave Roberts	2-9-0
Western Michigan	Broncos	Brown & gold	Mid-American	Jack Harbaugh	5-6-0
Wichita State	Shockers	Yellow & black	Missouri Valley	Ron Chismar	2-9-0
William & Mary	Indians	Green, gold, silver	1-AA Southern Ind.	Jimmye Laycock	6-5-0
Wisconsin	Badgers	Cardinal & white	Big Ten	Dave McClain	7-4-1
Wyoming	Cowboys	Brown & yellow	Western Athletic	Al Kincaid	6-6-0
Yale	Bulldogs, Elis	Yale blue & white	Ivy	Carmen Cozza	6-3-0
Youngstown St.	Penguins	Scarlet & white	Ohio Valley	Bill Narduzzi	7-4-0

College Football Coach of the Year

(Selected by the American Football Coaches Assn. & the Football Writers Assn. of America)

AFCA		FWAA		AFCA
1935	Lynn Waldorf, Northwestern	1957	Woody Hayes, Ohio St.	Woody Hayes, Ohio St.
1936	Dick Harlow, Harvard	1958	Paul Dietzel, LSU	Paul Dietzel, LSU
1937	Edward Mylin, Lafayette	1959	Ben Schwartzwalder, Syracuse	Ben Schwartzwalder, Syracuse
1938	Bill Kern, Carnegie Tech	1960	Murray Warmath, Minnesota	Murray Warmath, Minnesota
1939	Eddie Anderson, Iowa	1961	Darrell Royal, Texas	Paul "Bear" Bryant, Alabama
1940	Clark Shaughnessy, Stanford	1962	John McKay, USC	John McKay, USC
1941	Frank Leahy, Notre Dame	1963	Darrell Royal, Texas	Darrell Royal, Texas
1942	Bill Alexander, Georgia Tech	1964	Ara Parseghian, Notre Dame	Frank Broyles, Arkansas; Ara Paraseghian, Notre Dame
1943	Amos Alonzo Stagg, Pacific	1965	Duffy Daugherty, Michigan St.	Tommy Prothro, UCLA
1944	Carroll Widdoes, Ohio St.	1966	Tom Cahill, Army	Tom Cahill, Army
1945	Bo McMillin, Indiana	1967	John Pont, Indiana	John Pont, Indiana
1946	Earl "Red" Blaik, Army	1968	Woody Hayes, Ohio St.	Joe Paterno, Penn St.
1947	Fritz Crisler, Michigan	1969	Bo Schembechler, Michigan	Bo Schembechler, Michigan
1948	Bennie Oosterbaan, Michigan	1970	Alex Agase, Northwestern	Charles McClendon, LSU; Darrell Royal, Texas
1949	Bud Wilkinson, Oklahoma	1971	Bob Devaney, Nebraska	Paul "Bear" Bryant, Alabama
1950	Charlie Caldwell, Princeton	1972	John McKay, USC	John McKay, USC
1951	Chuck Taylor, Stanford	1973	Johnny Majors, Pittsburgh	Paul "Bear" Bryant, Alabama
1952	Biggie Munn, Michigan St.	1974	Grant Teaff, Baylor	Grant Teaff, Baylor
1953	Jim Tatum, Maryland	1975	Woody Hayes, Ohio St.	Frank Kush, Arizona St.
1954	Henry "Red" Sanders, UCLA	1976	Johnny Majors, Pittsburgh	Johnny Majors, Pittsburgh
1955	Duffy Daugherty, Michigan St.	1977	Lou Holtz, Arkansas	Don James, Washington
1956	Bowden Wyatt, Tennessee	1978	Joe Paterno, Penn St.	Joe Paterno, Penn St.
		1979	Earle Bruce, Ohio St.	Earle Bruce, Ohio St.
		1980	Vince Dooley, Georgia	Vince Dooley, Georgia
		1981	Danny Ford, Clemson	Danny Ford, Clemson
		1982	Joe Paterno, Penn St.	Joe Paterno, Penn St.
		1983	Howard Schnellenberger, Miami (Fla.)	Ken Hatfield, Air Force
		1984	LaVell Edwards, Brigham Young	LaVell Edwards, Brigham Young

All-Time Division 1-A Coaching Victories

Paul "Bear" Bryant	323	Dan McGugin	197	Gil Dobie	180
Amos Alonzo Stagg	314	Fielding Yost	196	Ben Schwartzwalder	178
Glenn "Pop" Warner	313	Howard Jones	194	Ralph Jordan	176
Woody Hayes	238	John Vaught	190	Frank Kush	176
Jess Neely	207	Bo Schembechler	186	Joe Paterno	176
Warren Woodson	207	John Heisman	185	Bob Neyland	173
Eddie Anderson	201	Darrell Royal	184		
Dana Bible	198	Carl Snavely	180		

All-Time Division 1-A Percentage Leaders

(Classified as Division I for last 10 years; including bowl games; ties computed as half won and half lost.)

	Years	Won	Lost	Tied	Pct	Bowl Games W	L	T
Notre Dame	96	641	186	40	.762	8	4	0
Michigan	105	655	222	31	.738	6	10	0
Alabama	90	606	213	42	.728	20	14	3
Texas	92	632	227	31	.728	15	14	2
Oklahoma	90	579	217	50	.714	16	8	1
Southern Cal	92	565	213	49	.713	21	7	0
Ohio State	95	589	233	48	.705	9	10	0
Penn State	98	593	265	40	.683	14	6	2
Tennessee	88	558	251	47	.679	12	14	0
Nebraska	95	593	271	39	.678	13	10	0
Central Michigan	84	426	217	29	.656	3	0	0
Miami (Oh.)	96	502	258	36	.653	5	1	0
Army	95	532	282	50	.645	1	0	0
Louisiana State	91	516	281	44	.640	10	13	1
Arizona State	72	385	215	21	.637	7	4	1
Georgia	91	522	296	51	.630	11	11	2
Washington	95	488	280	47	.628	7	6	1
Minnesota	101	508	301	40	.622	1	2	0
Michigan State	88	463	284	40	.614	2	3	0
Tulsa	80	427	266	26	.612	3	6	0
Bowling Green	66	331	204	47	.609	0	2	0
San Diego St.	62	348	222	27	.606	3	1	0
Pittsburgh	95	520	332	38	.606	7	9	0
Auburn	92	482	310	42	.603	9	7	1
Georgia Tech	92	499	324	40	.601	14	8	0
Stanford	78	430	278	45	.601	7	5	1
Colorado	95	483	318	32	.599	4	6	0
Boston College	86	449	297	34	.597	2	4	0

College Football Stadiums

School	Capacity	School	Capacity
Alabama, Univ. of (Bryant-Denny Stad.), University	60,000	Northern Illinois Univ. (Huskie Stad.), DeKalb	30,437
Arizona State Univ. (Sun Devil), Tempe	70,021	Northwestern Univ. (Dyche Stad.), Evanston, Ill.	49,256
Arizona, Univ. of (Arizona Stad.), Tucson	52,000	Notre Dame Stad., South Bend, Ind.	59,075
Arkansas, Univ. of (Razorback Stad.) Fayetteville.	52,055	Ohio State Univ. (Ohio Stad.), Columbus.	85,290
Auburn Univ. (Jordan Hare Stad.), Auburn, Ala.	72,169	Oklahoma State (Lewis Stad.), Stillwater	50,440
Baylor Univ. Stad., Waco, Tex.	48,500	Oklahoma, Univ. of (Owen Field), Norman	75,008
Boston Coll. (Alumni Stad.), Boston, Mass.	32,000	Oregon St. (Parker Stad.), Corvallis	40,593
Bowling Green State Univ. (Doyt Perry Field), Oh.	30,000	Oregon, Univ. of (Autzen Stad.), Eugene	41,009
Brigham Young Univ. Stad., Provo, Ut.	66,000	Penn. State Univ. (Beaver Stad.), University Park	83,770
Cal., Univ. of (Memorial Stad.), Berkeley	75,662	Penn., Univ. of (Franklin Field), Phila.	60,546
Clemson Univ. (Memorial Stad.), S.C.	79,725	Pittsburgh, Univ. of (Pitt. Stad.), Pa.	56,500
Colorado, Univ. of (Folsom Field), Boulder	51,941	Princeton (Palmer Stad.), Princeton, N.J.	45,725
Duke Univ., (Wade Stad.), Durham, N.C.	33,941	Purdue, (Ross-Ade Stad.), Lafayette, Ind.	69,250
E. Carolina Univ. (Ficklen Stad.), Greenville, N.C.	35,000	Rice Stad., Houston, Texas	70,000
Florida State, (Campbell Stad.), Tallahassee	60,519	So. Carolina, Univ. of (Williams-Brice), Columbia	72,400
Florida, Univ. of (Florida Field), Gainesville	72,000	So. Miss., Univ. of (Roberts Stad.), Hattiesburg	33,000
Georgia Tech. (Grant Field), Atlanta	58,121	Stanford Stad., Stanford, Cal.	86,055
Georgia, Univ. of (Sanford Stad.), Athens	82,122	Syracuse Univ., (Carrier Dome), N.Y.	50,000
Harvard Stad., Boston, Mass.	37,289	Tenn., Univ. of (Neyland Stad.), Knoxville	91,246
Hawaii, Univ. of (Aloha Stad.), Honolulu	50,000	Texas A. & M. Univ. (Kyle Field), College Station	72,300
Illinois, Univ. of (Memorial Stad.), Champaign	70,906	Texas Christian Univ. (Amon Carter Stad.) Ft. Worth	46,000
Indiana Univ. (Memorial Stad.), Bloomington	52,354	Texas-El Paso (Sun Bowl)	52,000
Iowa State (Jack Trice Stad.), Ames	50,000	Texas Tech. Univ. (Jones Stad.), Lubbock	47,000
Iowa, Univ. of (Kinnick Stad.), Iowa City	66,000	Texas, Univ. of (Memorial Stad.), Austin	80,000
Kansas State Univ. Stad., Manhattan	42,000	Tulsa, Univ. of (Skelly Stad.), Okla.	40,235
Kansas, Univ. of (Memorial Stad.), Lawrence	51,500	U.S. Air Force Acad. (Falcon Stad.), Col.	46,668
Kent State Univ. (Dix Stad.), Kent, Oh.	30,400	U.S. Military Academy (Michie Stad.), West Point, N.Y.	39,867
Kentucky, Univ. of (Commonwealth), Lexington	58,000	U.S. Naval Academy (Navy-Marine Corps Mem. Stad.)	
La. State Univ. (Tiger Stad.), Baton Rouge	76,869	Annapolis, Md.	30,000
Louisville, Univ. of (Cardinal Stad.), Ky.	35,500	Utah State Univ. (Romney Stad.), Logan	30,257
Maryland, Univ. of (Byrd), College Park	45,000	Utah, Univ. of (Robert Rice Stad.), Salt Lake City	35,000
Memphis State (Liberty Bowl), Tenn.	50,180	Vanderbilt Stad., Nashville	41,000
Michigan State Univ. (Spartan Stad.), E. Lansing	76,000	Virginia Tech. (Lane Stad.), Blacksburg	52,500
Michigan, Univ. of (Mich. Stad.), Ann Arbor	101,701	Virginia, Univ. of (Scott Stad.), Charlottesville	42,000
Mississippi St. Univ. (Scott Field)	41,000	Wake Forest (Groves Stad.), Winston-Salem, N.C.	31,500
Mississippi, Univ. of (Vaught-Hemingway Stad.), Univ.	41,500	Wash. State Univ. (Clarence D. Martin), Pullman	40,000
Missouri, Univ. of (Faurot Field), Columbia	62,000	Washington, Univ. of (Husky Stad.), Seattle	59,800
Nebraska, Univ. of (Memorial Stad.), Lincoln	73,650	West Va. Univ. (Mountaineer Field), Morgantown	60,686
Nevada-Las Vegas, Univ. of (Silver Bowl)	32,000	Wisconsin, Univ. of (Camp Randall), Madison	77,280
New Mexico State Univ. (Memorial Stad.), Las Cruces.	30,343	Wyoming, Univ. of (Memorial), Laramie	33,500
New Mexico, Univ. Stad., Albuquerque	30,646	Yale Bowl, New Haven, Conn.	70,896
North Carolina St. U. (Carter-Finley Stad.), Raleigh.	45,600		
North Carolina, Univ. of (Kenan Stad.), Chapel Hill	49,500		

Heisman Trophy Winners

Awarded annually to the nation's outstanding college football player.

1935	Jay Berwanger, Chicago, HB	1952	Billy Vessels, Oklahoma, HB	1969	Steve Owens, Oklahoma, RB
1936	Larry Kelley, Yale, E	1953	John Lattner, Notre Dame, HB	1970	Jim Plunkett, Stanford, QB
1937	Clinton Frank, Yale, HB	1954	Alan Ameche, Wisconsin, FB	1971	Pat Sullivan, Auburn, QB
1938	David O'Brien, Tex. Christian, QB	1955	Howard Cassady, Ohio St., HB	1972	Johnny Rodgers, Nebraska, RB-R
1939	Nile Kinnick, Iowa, HB	1956	Paul Hornung, Notre Dame, QB	1973	John Cappelletti, Penn State, RB
1940	Tom Harmon, Michigan, HB	1957	John Crow, Texas A & M, HB	1974	Archie Griffin, Ohio State, RB
1941	Bruce Smith, Minnesota, HB	1958	Pete Dawkins, Army, HB	1975	Archie Griffin, Ohio State, RB
1942	Frank Sinkwich, Georgia, HB	1959	Billy Cannon, La. State, HB	1976	Tony Dorsett, Pittsburgh, RB
1943	Angelo Bertelli, Notre Dame, QB	1960	Joe Bellino, Navy, HB	1977	Earl Campbell, Texas, RB
1944	Leslie Horvath, Ohio State, QB	1961	Ernest Davis, Syracuse, HB	1978	Billy Sims, Oklahoma, RB
1945	Felix Blanchard, Army, FB	1962	Terry Baker, Oregon State, QB	1979	Charles White, USC, RB
1946	Glenn Davis, Army, HB	1963	Roger Staubach, Navy, QB	1980	George Rogers, So. Carolina, RB
1947	John Lujack, Notre Dame, QB	1964	John Huarte, Notre Dame, QB	1981	Marcus Allen, USC, RB
1948	Doak Walker, SMU, HB	1965	Mike Garrett, USC, HB	1982	Herschel Walker, Georgia, RB
1949	Leon Hart, Notre Dame, E	1966	Steve Spurrier, Florida, QB	1983	Mike Rozier, Nebraska, RB
1950	Vic Janowicz, Ohio State, HB	1967	Gary Beban, UCLA, QB	1984	Doug Flutie, Boston College, QB
1951	Richard Kazmaier, Princeton, HB	1968	O. J. Simpson, USC, RB		

Outland Awards

Honoring the outstanding interior lineman selected by the Football Writers' Association of America.

1946	George Connor, Notre Dame, T	1959	Mike McGee, Duke, T	1972	Rich Glover, Nebraska, MG
1947	Joe Steffy, Army, G	1960	Tom Brown, Minnesota, G	1973	John Hicks, Ohio State, G
1948	Bill Fischer, Notre Dame, G	1961	Merlin Olsen, Utah State, T	1974	Randy White, Maryland, DE
1949	Ed Bagdon, Michigan St., G	1962	Bobby Bell, Minnesota, T	1975	Leroy Selmon, Oklahoma, DT
1950	Bob Gain, Kentucky, T	1963	Scott Appleton, Texas, T	1976	Ross Browner, Notre Dame, DE
1951	Jim Weatherall, Oklahoma, T	1964	Steve Delong, Tennessee, T	1977	Brad Shearer, Texas, DT
1952	Dick Modzelewski, Maryland, T	1965	Tommy Nobis, Texas, G	1978	Greg Roberts, Oklahoma, G
1953	J. D. Roberts, Oklahoma, G	1966	Loyd Phillips, Arkansas, T	1979	Jim Ritcher, No. Carolina St., C
1954	Bill Brooks, Arkansas, G	1967	Ron Yary, Southern Cal, T	1980	Mark May, Pittsburgh, OT
1955	Calvin Jones, Iowa, G	1968	Bill Stanfill, Georgia, T	1981	Dave Rimington, Nebraska, C
1956	Jim Parker, Ohio State, G	1969	Mike Reid, Penn State, DT	1982	Dave Rimington, Nebraska, C
1957	Alex Karras, Iowa, T	1970	Jim Stillwagon, Ohio State, LB	1983	Dean Steinkuhler, Nebraska, G
1958	Zeke Smith, Auburn, G	1971	Larry Jacobson, Nebraska, DT	1984	Bruce Smith, Virginia Tech, DT

College Football Conference Champions

	Atlantic Coast		Ivy League		Big Eight		Big Ten
1970	Wake Forest	1970	Dartmouth	1970	Nebraska	1970	Ohio State
1971	North Carolina	1971	Dartmouth, Cornell	1971	Nebraska	1971	Michigan
1972	North Carolina	1972	Dartmouth	1972	Nebraska	1972	Ohio State, Michigan
1973	No. Carolina St.	1973	Dartmouth	1973	Oklahoma	1973	Ohio State, Michigan
1974	Maryland	1974	Yale, Harvard	1974	Oklahoma	1974	Ohio State, Michigan
1975	Maryland	1975	Harvard	1975	Oklahoma, Nebraska	1975	Ohio State
1976	Maryland	1976	Yale, Brown	1976	Oklahoma, Colorado,	1976	Michigan, Ohio State
1977	North Carolina	1977	Yale		Oklahoma State	1977	Michigan, Ohio State
1978	Clemson	1978	Dartmouth	1977	Oklahoma	1978	Michigan St., Michigan
1979	No. Carolina St.	1979	Yales	1978	Nebraska, Oklahoma	1979	Ohio State
1980	North Carolina	1980	Yale	1979	Oklahoma	1980	Michigan
1981	Clemson	1981	Yale, Dartmouth	1980	Oklahoma	1901	Iowa, Ohio State
1982	Clemson	1982	Harvard, Dartmouth	1981	Nebraska	1982	Michigan
1983	Maryland		Penn	1982	Nebraska	1983	Illinois
1984	Maryland	1983	Harvard, Penn	1983	Nebraska	1984	Ohio State
		1984	Penn	1984	Nebraska, Oklahoma		

	Mid-America		Missouri Valley		Southeastern		Southwest
1970	Toledo	1970	Louisville	1970	Louisiana State	1970	Texas
1971	Toledo	1971	Memphis State	1971	Alabama	1971	Texas
1972	Kent State	1972	Louisville, W. Texas,	1972	Alabama	1972	Texas
1973	Miami		Drake	1973	Alabama	1973	Texas
1974	Miami	1973	No. Texas St., Tulsa	1974	Alabama	1974	Baylor
1975	Miami	1974	Tulsa	1975	Alabama	1975	Texas A&M, Texas,
1976	Ball State	1975	Tulsa	1976	Georgia		Arkansas
1977	Miami	1976	Tulsa, N. Mexico St.	1977	Alabama	1976	Houston
1978	Ball State	1977	W. Texas St.	1978	Alabama	1977	Texas
1979	Central Michigan	1978	N. Mexico St.	1979	Alabama	1978	Houston
1980	Central Michigan	1979	W. Texas St.	1980	Georgia	1979	Houston, Arkansas
1981	Toledo	1980	Tulsa, Wichita St.	1981	Georgia, Alabama	1980	Baylor
1982	Bowling Green	1981	Drake, Tulsa	1982	Georgia	1981	SMU
1983	Northern Illinois	1982	Tulsa	1983	Auburn	1982	SMU
1984	Toledo	1983	Tulsa	1984	Florida	1983	Texas
		1984	Tulsa			1984	SMU

	Pacific Ten		Southern		Western Athletic		Pacific Coast
1970	Stanford	1970	William & Mary	1970	Arizona State	1970	Long Beach State
1971	Stanford	1971	Richmond	1971	Arizona State	1972	San Diego State
1972	USC	1972	East Carolina	1972	Arizona State	1973	San Diego State
1973	USC	1973	East Carolina	1973	Arizona State, Arizona	1974	San Diego State
1974	USC	1974	VMI	1974	Brigham Young	1975	San Jose St.
1975	UCLA, Cal.	1975	Ricmond	1975	Arizona State	1976	San Diego State
1976	USC	1976	East Carolina	1976	Wyoming, Brigham Young	1977	Fresno State
1977	Washington	1977	Tenn.-Chattanooga	1977	Brigham Young, Arizona St.	1978	Utah St., San Jose St.
1978	USC	1978	Tenn.-Chattanooga,	1978	Brigham Young	1979	San Jose St.
1979	USC		Furman	1979	Brigham Young	1980	Long Beach State
1980	Washington	1979	Tenn.-Chattanooga	1980	Brigham Young	1981	San Jose State
1981	Washington	1980	Furman	1981	Brigham Young	1982	Fresno State
1982	UCLA	1981	Furman	1982	Brigham Young	1983	Cal State-Fullerton
1983	UCLA	1982	Furman	1983	Brigham Young	1984	Nevada-Las Vegas
1984	USC	1983	Furman	1984	Brigham Young		
		1984	Tenn.-Chattanooga				

Longest Division 1-A Winning Streaks

Wins	Team	Years	Ended by	Score
47	Oklahoma	1953-57	Notre Dame	7-0
39	Washington	1908-14	Oregon State	0-0
37	Yale	1890-93	Princeton	6-0
37	Yale	1887-89	Princeton	10-0
35	Toledo	1969-71	Tampa	21-0
34	Pennsylvania	1894-96	Lafayette	6-4
31	Oklahoma	1948-50	Kentucky	13-7
31	Pittsburgh	1914-18	Cleveland Naval Reserve	10-9
31	Pennsylvania	1896-98	Harvard	10-0
30	Texas	1968-70	Notre Dame	24-11
29	Michigan	1901-03	Minnesota	6-6
28	Alabama	1978-80	Mississippi State	6-3
28	Oklahoma	1973-75	Kansas	23-3
28	Michigan State	1950-53	Purdue	6-0
27	Nebraska	1901-04	Colorado	6-0
26	Cornell	1921-24	Williams	14-7
26	Michigan	1903-05	Chicago	2-0
25	Michigan	1946-49	Army	21-7
25	Army	1944-46	Notre Dame	0-0
25	Southern Cal	1931-33	Oregon State	0-0

National Football League

Final 1984 Standings

National Conference

Eastern Division

	W	L	T	Pct	Pts	Opp
Washington	11	5	0	.688	426	310
N.Y. Giants	9	7	0	.563	299	301
St. Louis	9	7	0	.563	423	345
Dallas	9	7	0	.563	308	308
Philadelphia	6	9	1	.406	275	339

Central Division

	W	L	T	Pct	Pts	Opp
Chicago	10	6	0	.625	325	248
Green Bay	8	8	0	.500	390	309
Tampa Bay	6	10	0	.375	335	380
Detroit	4	11	1	.281	283	408
Minnesota	3	13	0	.188	276	484

Western Division

	W	L	T	Pct	Pts	Opp
San Francisco	15	1	0	.938	475	227
L.A. Rams	10	6	0	.625	346	316
New Orleans	7	9	0	.438	298	361
Atlanta	4	12	0	.250	281	382

American Conference

Eastern Division

	W	L	T	Pct	Pts	Opp
Miami	14	2	0	.875	513	298
New England	9	7	0	.563	362	352
N.Y. Jets	7	9	0	.438	332	364
Indianapolis	4	12	0	.250	239	414
Buffalo	2	14	0	.125	250	454

Central Division

	W	L	T	Pct	Pts	Opp
Pittsburgh	9	7	0	.563	387	310
Cincinnati	8	8	0	.500	339	339
Cleveland	5	11	0	.313	250	297
Houston	3	13	0	.188	240	437

Western Division

	W	L	T	Pct	Pts	Opp
Denver	13	3	0	.813	353	241
Seattle	12	4	0	.750	418	282
L.A. Raiders	11	5	0	.688	371	278
Kansas City	8	8	0	.500	314	324
San Diego	7	9	0	.438	394	413

NFC playoffs—N.Y. Giants 16, L.A. Rams 13; San Francisco 21, N.Y. Giants 10; Chicago 23, Washington 19; San Francisco 23, Chicago 0.

AFC playoffs—Seattle 13, L.A. Raiders 7; Miami 31, Seattle 10; Pittsburgh 24, Denver 17; Miami 45, Pittsburgh 28.

49ers Defeat Dolphins in Super Bowl

The San Francisco 49ers won their second Super Bowl championship by defeating the Miami Dolphins 38-16 at Stanford Stadium in Palo Alto, Cal. Joe Montana of the 49ers, who passed for a Super Bowl record 331 yards, was chosen the game's most valuable player.

Score by Periods

Miami	10	6	0	0—16
San Francisco	7	21	10	0—38

Scoring

Miami—von Schamann 37 yd. field goal.
S.F.—Monroe 33 yd. pass from Montana (Wersching kick).
Miami—D. Johnson 2 yd. pass from Marino (von Schamann kick).
S.F.—Craig 8 yd. pass from Montana (Wersching kick).
S.F.—Montana 6 yd. run (Wersching kick).
S.F.—Craig 2 yd. run (Wersching kick).
Miami—von Schamann 31 yd. field goal.
Miami—von Schamann 30 yd. field goal.
S.F.—Wersching 27 yd. field goal.
S.F.—Craig 16 yd. pass from Montana (Wersching kick).

Individual Statistics

Rushing — Miami—Nathan 5-18, Bennett 3-7, Marino 1-0. San Francisco—Tyler 13-65, Montana 5-59, Craig 15-58, Harmon 5-20, Solomon 1-5, Cooper 1-4.

Passing — Miami—Marino 29-50-2-318. San Francisco—Montana 24-35-0-331.

Receiving — Miami—Nathan 10-83, Clayton 6-92, Rose 6-73, D. Johnson 3-28, Moore 2-17, Cefalo 1-14, Duper 1-11. San Francisco—Craig 8-82, D. Clark 5-72, Francis 5-60, Tyler 4-70, Monroe 1-33, Solomon 1-14.

Attendance — 84,059.

Team Statistics

	Miami	S.F.
First downs	19	31
Rushes-yards.	9-25	40-211
Passing yards.	289	326
Return yards	15	51
Passes	29-50-2	24-35-0
Sacks By	1-5	4-29
Punts	6-39	3-33
Fumbles-lost	1-0	2-2
Penalties-yards.	1-10	2-10
Time of possession	22:49	37:11

Super Bowl

Year	Winner	Loser	Site
1967	Green Bay Packers, 35	Kansas City Chiefs, 10	Los Angeles Coliseum
1968	Green Bay Packers, 33	Oakland Raiders, 14	Orange Bowl, Miami
1969	New York Jets, 16	Baltimore Colts, 7	Orange Bowl, Miami
1970	Kansas City Chiefs, 23	Minnesota Vikings, 7	Tulane Stadium, New Orleans
1971	Baltimore Colts, 16	Dallas Cowboys, 13	Orange Bowl, Miami
1972	Dallas Cowboys, 24	Miami Dolphins, 3	Tulane Stadium, New Orleans
1973	Miami Dolphins, 14	Washington Redskins, 7	Los Angeles Coliseum
1974	Miami Dolphins, 24	Minnesota Vikings, 7	Rice Stadium, Houston
1975	Pittsburgh Steelers, 16	Minnesota Vikings, 6	Tulane Stadium, New Orleans
1976	Pittsburgh Steelers, 21	Dallas Cowboys, 17	Orange Bowl, Miami
1977	Oakland Raiders, 32	Minnesota Vikings, 14	Rose Bowl, Pasadena
1978	Dallas Cowboys, 27	Denver Broncos, 10	Superdome, New Orleans
1979	Pittsburgh Steelers, 35	Dallas Cowboys, 31	Orange Bowl, Miami
1980	Pittsburgh Steelers, 31	Los Angeles Rams, 19	Rose Bowl, Pasadena
1981	Oakland Raiders, 27	Philadelphia Eagles, 10	Superdome, New Orleans
1982	San Francisco 49ers, 26	Cincinatti Bengals, 21	Silverdome, Pontiac, Mich.
1983	Washington Redskins, 27	Miami Dolphins, 17	Rose Bowl, Pasadena
1984	Los Angeles Raiders, 38	Washington Redskins, 9	Tampa Stadium
1985	San Francisco 49ers, 38	Miami Dolphins, 16	Stanford Stadium, Palo Alto, Cal.

Super Bowl MVPs

1967 Bart Starr, Green Bay	1974 Larry Csonka, Miami	1981 Jim Plunkett, Oakland
1968 Bart Starr, Green Bay	1975 Franco Harris, Pittsburgh	1982 Joe Montana, San Francisco
1969 Joe Namath, N.Y. Jets	1976 Lynn Swann, Pittsburgh	1983 John Riggins, Washington
1970 Len Dawson, Kansas City	1977 Fred Biletnikoff, Oakland	1984 Marcus Allen, L.A. Raiders
1971 Chuck Howley, Dallas	1978 Randy White, Harvey Martin, Dallas	1985 Joe Montana, San Francisco
1972 Roger Staubach, Dallas	1979 Terry Bradshaw, Pittsburgh	
1973 Jake Scott, Miami	1980 Terry Bradshaw, Pittsburgh	

National Football League Champions

Year	East Winner (W.L.T.)	West Winner (W.L.T.)	Playoff
1933	New York Giants (11-3-0)	Chicago Bears (10-2-1)	Chicago Bears 23, New York 21
1934	New York Giants (8-5-0)	Chicago Bears (13-0-0)	New York 30, Chicago Bears 13
1935	New York Giants (9-3-0)	Detroit Lions (7-3-2)	Detroit 26, New York 7
1936	Boston Redskins (7-5-0)	Green Bay Packers (10-1-1)	Green Bay 21, Boston 6
1937	Washington Redskins (8-3-0)	Chicago Bears (9-1-1)	Washington 28, Chicago Bears 21
1938	New York Giants (8-2-1)	Green Bay Packers (8-3-0)	New York 23, Green Bay 17
1939	New York Giants (9-1-1)	Green Bay Packers (9-2-0)	Green Bay 27, New York 0
1940	Washington Redskins (9-2-0)	Chicago Bears (8-3-0)	Chicago Bears 73, Washington 0
1941	New York Giants (8-3-0)	Chicago Bears (10-1-1)(a)	Chicago Bears 37, New York 9
1942	Wash. Redskins (10-1-1)	Chicago Bears (11-0-0)	Washington 14, Chicago Bears 6
1943	Wash. Redskins (6-3-1)(a)	Chicago Bears (8-1-1)	Chicago Bears, 41, Washington 21
1944	New York Giants (8-1-1)	Green Bay Packers (8-2-0)	Green Bay 14, New York 7
1945	Wash. Redskins (8-2-0)	Cleveland Rams (9-1-0)	Cleveland 15, Washington 14
1946	New York Giants (7-3-1)	Chicago Bears (8-2-1)	Chicago Bears 24, New York 14
1947	Philadelphia Eagles (8-4-0)(a)	Chicago Cardinals (9-3-0)	Chicago Cardinals 28, Philadelphia 21
1948	Philadelphia Eagles (9-2-1)	Chicago Cardinals (11-1-0)	Philadelphia 7, Chicago Cardinals 0
1949	Philadelphia Eagles (11-1-0)	Los Angeles Rams (8-2-2)	Philadelphia 14, Los Angeles 0
1950	Cleveland Browns (10-2-0)(a)	Los Angeles Rams (9-3-0)(a)	Cleveland 30, Los Angeles 28
1951	Cleveland Browns (11-1-0)	Los Angeles Rams (8-4-0)	Los Angeles 24, Cleveland 17
1952	Cleveland Browns (8-4-0)	Detroit Lions (9-3-0)(a)	Detroit 17, Cleveland 7
1953	Cleveland Browns (11-1-0)	Detroit Lions (10-2-0)	Detroit 17, Cleveland 16
1954	Cleveland Browns (9-3-0)	Detroit Lions (9-2-1)	Cleveland 56, Detroit 10
1955	Cleveland Browns (9-2-1)	Los Angeles Rams (8-3-1)	Cleveland 38, Los Angeles 14
1956	New York Giants (8-3-1)	Chicago Bears (9-2-1)	New York 47, Chicago Bears 7
1957	Cleveland Browns (9-2-1)	Detroit Lions (8-4-0)(a)	Detroit 59, Cleveland 14
1958	New York Giants (9-3-0)(a)	Baltimore Colts (9-3-0)	Baltimore 23, New York 17(b)
1959	New York Giants (10-2-0)	Baltimore Colts (9-3-0)	Baltimore 31, New York 16
1960	Philadelphia Eagles (10-2-0)	Green Bay Packers (8-4-0)	Philadelphia 17, Green Bay 13
1961	New York Giants (10-3-1)	Green Bay Packers (11-3-0)	Green Bay 37, New York 0
1962	New York Giants (12-2-0)	Green Bay Packers (13-1-0)	Green Bay 16, New York 7
1963	New York Giants (11-3-0)	Chicago Bears (11-1-2)	Chicago 14, New York 10
1964	Cleveland Browns (10-3-1)	Baltimore Colts (12-2-0)	Cleveland 27, Baltimore 0
1965	Cleveland Browns (11-3-0)	Green Bay Packers (10-3-1)(a)	Green Bay 23, Cleveland 12
1966	Dallas Cowboys (10-3-1)	Green Bay Packers (12-2-0)	Green Bay 34, Dallas 27

(a) Won divisional playoff. (b) Won at 8:15 sudden death overtime period.

Year	Conference	Division	Winner (W-L-T)	Playoff
1967	East	Century	Cleveland (9-5-0)	Dallas 52, Cleveland 14
		Capitol	Dallas (9-5-0)	
	West	Central	Green Bay (9-4-1)	Green Bay 28, Los Angeles 7
		Coastal	Los Angeles (11-1-2)(a)	Green Bay 21, Dallas 17
1968	East	Century	Cleveland (10-4-0)	Cleveland 31, Dallas 20
		Capitol	Dallas (12-2-0)	
	West	Central	Minnesota (8-6-0)	Baltimore 24, Minnesota 14
		Coastal	Baltimore (13-1-0)	Baltimore 34, Cleveland 0
1969	East	Century	Cleveland (10-3-1)	Cleveland 38, Dallas 14
		Capitol	Dallas (11-2-1)	
	West	Central	Minnesota (12-2-0)	Minnesota 23, Los Angeles 20
		Coastal	Los Angeles (11-3-0)	Minnesota 27, Cleveland 7
1970	American	Eastern	Baltimore (11-2-1)	Baltimore 17, Cincinnati 0
		Central	Cincinnati (8-6-0)	Oakland 21, Miami 14
		Western	Oakland (8-4-2)	Baltimore 27, Oakland 17
	National	Eastern	Dallas (10-4-0)	Dallas 5, Detroit 0
		Central	Minnesota (12-2-0)	San Francisco 17, Minnesota 14
		Western	San Francisco (10-3-1)	Dallas 17, San Francisco 10
1971	American	Eastern	Miami (10-3-1)	Miami 27, Kansas City 24
		Central	Cleveland (9-5-0)	Baltimore 20, Cleveland 3
		Western	Kansas City (10-3-1)	Miami 21, Baltimore 0
	National	Eastern	Dallas (11-3-0)	Dallas 20, Minnesota 12
		Central	Minnesota (11-3-0)	San Francisco 24, Washington 20
		Western	San Francisco (9-5-0)	Dallas 14, San Francisco 3
1972	American	Eastern	Miami (14-0-0)	Miami 20, Cleveland 14
		Central	Pittsburgh (11-3-0)	Pittsburgh 13, Oakland 7
		Western	Oakland (10-3-1)	Miami 21, Pittsburgh 17
	National	Eastern	Washington (11-3-0)	Washington 16, Green Bay 3
		Central	Green Bay (10-4-0)	Dallas 30, San Francisco 28
		Western	San Francisco (8-5-1)	Washington 26, Dallas 3
1973	American	Eastern	Miami (12-2-0)	Miami 34, Cincinnati 16
		Central	Cincinnati (10-4-0)	Oakland 33, Pittsburgh 14
		Western	Oakland (9-4-1)	Miami 27, Oakland 10
	National	Eastern	Dallas (10-4-0)	Dallas 27, Los Angeles 16
		Central	Minnesota (12-2-0)	Minnesota 27, Washington 20
		Western	Los Angeles (12-2-0)	Minnesota 27, Dallas 10

(continued)

Year	Conference	Division	Winner (W-L-T)	Playoff
1974	American	Eastern	Miami (11-3-0)	Oakland 28, Miami 26
		Central	Pittsburgh (10-3-1)	Pittsburgh 32, Buffalo 14
		Western	Oakland (12-2-0)	Pittsburgh 24, Oakland 13
	National	Eastern	St. Louis (10-4-0)	Minnesota 30, St. Louis 14
		Central	Minnesota (10-4-0)	Los Angeles 19, Washington 10
		Western	Los Angeles (10-4-0)	Minnesota 14, Los Angeles 10
1975	American	Eastern	Baltimore (10-4-0)	Pittsburgh 28, Baltimore 10
		Central	Pittsburgh (12-2-0)	Oakland 31, Cincinnati 28
		Western	Oakland (11-3-0)	Pittsburgh 16, Oakland 10
	National	Eastern	St. Louis (11-3-0)	Dallas 17, Minnesota 14
		Central	Minnesota (12-2-0)	Los Angeles 35, St. Louis 23
		Western	Los Angeles (12-2-0)	Dallas 37, Los Angeles 7
1976	American	Eastern	Baltimore (11-3-0)	Pittsburgh 40, Baltimore 14
		Central	Pittsburgh (10-4-0)	Oakland 24, New England 21
		Western	Oakland (13-1-0)	Oakland 24, Pittsburgh 12
	National	Eastern	Dallas (11-3-0)	Minnesota 35, Washington 20
		Central	Minnesota (11-2-1)	Los Angeles 14, Dallas 12
		Western	Los Angeles (10-3-1)	Minnesota 24, Los Angeles 13
1977	American	Eastern	Baltimore (10-4-0)	Oakland 37, Baltimore 31
		Central	Pittsburgh (9-5-0)	Denver 34, Pittsburgh 21
		Western	Denver (12-2-0)	Dallas 37, Chicago 7
	National	Eastern	Dallas (12-2-0)	Minnesota 14, Los Angeles 7
		Central	Minnesota (9-5-0)	Denver 20, Oakland 17
		Western	Los Angeles (10-4-0)	Dallas 23, Minnesota 6
1978	American	Eastern	New England (11-5-0)	Pittsburgh 33, Denver 10
		Central	Pittsburgh (14-2-0)	Houston 31, New England 14
		Western	Denver (10-6-0)	Pittsburgh 34, Houston 5
	National	Eastern	Dallas (12-4-0)	Dallas 27, Atlanta 20
		Central	Minnesota (8-7-1)	Los Angeles 34, Minnesota 10
		Western	Los Angeles (12-4-0)	Dallas 28, Los Angeles 0
1979	American	Eastern	Miami (10-6-0)	Houston 17, San Diego 14
		Central	Pittsburgh (12-4-0)	Pittsburgh 34, Miami 14
		Western	San Diego (12-4-0)	Pittsburgh 27, Houston 13
	National	Eastern	Dallas (11-5-0)	Tampa Bay 24, Philadelphia 17
		Central	Tampa Bay (10-6-0)	Los Angeles 21, Dallas 19
		Western	Los Angeles (9-7-0)	Los Angeles 9, Tampa Bay 0
1980	American	Eastern	Buffalo (11-5-0)	San Diego 20, Buffalo 14
		Central	Cleveland (11-5-0)	Oakland 14, Cleveland 12
		Western	San Diego (11-5-0)	Oakland 34, San Diego 27
	National	Eastern	Philadelphia (12-4-0)	Philadelphia 31, Minnesota 16
		Central	Minnesota (9-7-0)	Dallas 30, Atlanta 27
		Western	Atlanta (12-4-0)	Philadelphia 20, Dallas 7
1981	American	Eastern	Miami (11-4-1)	San Diego 41, Miami 38
		Central	Cincinnati (12-4-0)	Cincinnati 28, Buffalo 21
		Western	San Diego (10-6-0)	Cincinnati 27, San Diego 7
	National	Eastern	Dallas (12-4-0)	Dallas 38, Tampa Bay 0
		Central	Tampa Bay (9-7-0)	San Francisco 38, N.Y. Giants 24
		Western	San Francisco (13-3-0)	San Francisco 28, Dallas 27
1982(1)	American		L.A. Raiders (8-1-0)	
	National		Washington (8-1-0)	

AFC playoffs—Miami 28, New England 13; L.A. Raiders 27, Cleveland 10; N.Y. Jets 44, Cincinnati 17; San Diego 31, Pittsburgh 28; N.Y. Jets 17, L.A. Raiders 14; Miami 34, San Diego 13; Miami 14, N.Y. Jets 0. **NFC playoffs**—Washington 31, Detroit 7; Green Bay 41, St. Louis 16; Dallas 30, Tampa Bay 17; Minnesota 30, Atlanta 24; Washington 21, Minnesota 7; Dallas 37, Green Bay 26; Washington 31, Dallas 17.

1983	American	Eastern	Miami (12-4-0)	Seattle 27, Miami 20
		Central	Pittsburgh (10-6-0)	L.A. Raiders 38, Pittsburgh 10
		Western	L.A. Raiders (12-4-0)	L.A. Raiders 30, Seattle 14
	National	Eastern	Washington (14-2-0)	Washington 51, L.A. Rams 7
		Central	Detroit (9-7-0)	San Francisco 24, Detroit 23
		Western	San Francisico (10-6-0)	Washington 24, San Francisco 21
1984	American	Eastern	Miami (14-2-0)	Miami 31, Seattle 10
		Central	Pittsburgh (9-7-0)	Pittsburgh 24, Denver 17
		Western	Denver (13-3-0)	Miami 45, Pittsburgh 28
	National	Eastern	Washington (11-5-0)	Chicago 23, Washington 19
		Central	Chicago (10-6-0)	San Francisco 21, N.Y. Giants 10
		Western	San Francisco (15-1-0)	San Francisco 23, Chicago 0

(1) Strike-shortened season

George Halas Trophy Winners

    The Halas Trophy, named after football coach George Halas, is awarded annually to the outstanding defensive player in football in a poll conducted by Murray Olderman of Newspaper Enterprise Assn.

1966	Larry Wilson, St. Louis	1973	Alan Page, Minnesota	1980	Lester Hayes, Oakland
1967	Deacon Jones, Los Angeles	1974	Joe Greene, Pittsburgh	1981	Joe Klecko, N.Y. Jets
1968	Deacon Jones, Los Angeles	1975	Curley Culp, Houston	1982	Mark Gastineau, N.Y. Jets
1969	Dick Butkus, Chicago	1976	Jerry Sherk, Cleveland	1983	Jack Lambert, Pittsburgh
1970	Dick Butkus, Chicago	1977	Harvey Martin, Dallas	1984	Mike Haynes, L.A. Raiders
1971	Carl Eller, Minnesota	1978	Randy Gradishar, Denver		
1972	Joe Greene, Pittsburgh	1979	Lee Roy Selmon, Tampa Bay		

National Football Conference Leaders

(National Football League prior to 1970)

Passing | Pass-Receiving

Player, team	Atts	Com	YG	TD	Year	Player, team	Ct	YG	TD
Earl Morrall, Baltimore	317	182	2,909	26	1968	Clifton McNeil, San Francisco	71	944	7
Sonny Jurgensen, Washington	422	274	3,102	22	1969	Dan Abramowicz, New Orleans	73	1,015	7
John Brodie, San Francisco	378	223	2,941	24	1970	Dick Gordon, Chicago	71	1,026	13
Roger Staubach, Dallas	211	126	1,882	15	1971	Bob Tucker, Giants	59	791	4
Norm Snead, N.Y. Giants	325	196	2,307	17	1972	Harold Jackson, Philadelphia	62	1,048	4
Roger Staubach, Dallas	286	179	2,428	23	1973	Harold Carmichael, Philadelphia	67	1,116	9
Sonny Jurgensen, Washington	167	107	1,185	11	1974	Charles Young, Philadelphia	63	696	3
Fran Tarkenton, Minnesota	425	273	2,294	25	1975	Chuck Foreman, Minnesota	73	691	9
James Harris, Los Angeles	158	91	1,460	8	1976	Drew Pearson, Dallas	58	806	6
Roger Staubach, Dallas	361	210	2,620	18	1977	Ahmad Rashad, Minnesota	51	681	2
Roger Staubach, Dallas	413	231	3,190	25	1978	Rickey Young, Minnesota	88	704	5
Roger Staubach, Dallas	461	267	3,586	27	1979	Ahmad Rashad, Minnesota	80	1,156	9
Ron Jaworski, Philadelphia	451	257	3,529	27	1980	Earl Cooper, San Francisco	83	567	4
Joe Montana, San Francisco	488	311	3,565	19	1981	Dwight Clark, San Francisco	85	1,105	4
Joe Thiesmann, Washington	252	161	2,033	13	1982	Dwight Clark, San Francisco	60	913	5
Steve Bartkowski, Atlanta	423	274	3,167	22	1983	Roy Green, St. Louis	78	1,227	14
						Charlie Brown, Washington	78	1,225	8
						Earnest Gray, N.Y. Giants	78	1,139	5
Joe Montana, San Franscisco	432	279	3,630	28	1984	Art Monk, Washington	106	1,372	7

Scoring | Rushing

Player, team	TD	PAT	FG	Pts	Year	Player, team	Yds	Atts	TD
Leroy Kelly, Cleveland	20	0	0	120	1968	Leroy Kelly, Cleveland	1,239	248	16
Fred Cox, Minnesota	0	43	26	121	1969	Gale Sayers, Chicago	1,032	236	8
Fred Cox, Minnesota	0	35	30	125	1970	Larry Brown, Washington	1,125	237	5
Curt Knight, Washington	0	27	29	114	1971	John Brockington, Green Bay	1,105	216	4
Chester Marcol, Green Bay	0	29	33	128	1972	Larry Brown, Washington	1,216	285	8
David Ray, Los Angeles	0	40	30	130	1973	John Brockington, Green Bay	1,144	265	3
Chester Marcol, Green Bay	0	19	25	94	1974	Larry McCutcheon, Los Angeles	1,109	236	3
Chuck Foreman, Minnesota	22	0	0	132	1975	Jim Otis, St. Louis	1,076	269	5
Mark Moseley, Washington	0	31	22	97	1976	Walter Payton, Chicago	1,390	311	13
Walter Payton, Chicago	16	0	0	96	1977	Walter Payton, Chicago	1,852	339	14
Frank Corrall, Los Angeles	0	31	29	118	1978	Walter Payton, Chicago	1,395	333	11
Mark Moseley, Washington	0	39	25	114	1979	Walter Payton, Chicago	1,610	369	14
Ed Murray, Detroit	0	35	27	116	1980	Walter Payton, Chicago	1,460	317	15
Ed Murray, Detroit	0	46	25	121	1981	George Rogers, New Orleans	1,674	378	13
Wendell Tyler, L.A. Rams	13	0	0	78	1982	Tony Dorsett, Dallas	745	177	5
Mark Moseley, Washington	0	62	33	161	1983	Eric Dickerson, L.A. Rams	1,808	390	18
Ray Wersching, San Francisco	0	56	25	131	1984	Eric Dickerson, L.A. Rams	2,105	379	14

American Football Conference Leaders

(American Football League prior to 1970)

Passing | Pass-Receiving

Player, team	Atts	Com	YG	TD	Year	Player, team	Ct	YG	TD
Len Dawson, Kansas City	224	131	2,109	17	1968	Lance Alworth, San Diego	68	1,312	10
Greg Cook, Cincinnati	197	106	1,845	15	1969	Lance Alworth, San Diego	64	1,003	4
Daryle Lamonica, Oakland	356	179	2,516	22	1970	Marlin Briscoe, Buffalo	57	1,036	8
Bob Griese, Miami	263	145	2,089	19	1971	Fred Biletnikoff, Oakland	61	929	9
Earl Morrall, Miami	150	83	1,360	11	1972	Fred Biletnikoff, Oakland	58	802	7
Ken Stabler, Oakland	260	163	1,997	14	1973	Fred Willis, Houston	57	371	1
Ken Anderson, Cincinnati	328	213	2,667	18	1974	Lydell Mitchell, Baltimore	72	544	2
Ken Anderson, Cincinnati	377	228	3,169	21	1975	Reggie Rucker, Cleveland	60	770	3
						Lydell Mitchell, Baltimore	60	554	4
Ken Stabler, Oakland	291	194	2,737	27	1976	MacArthur Lane, Kansas City	66	686	1
Bob Griese, Miami	307	180	2,252	22	1977	Lydell Mitchell, Baltimore	71	620	4
Terry Bradshaw, Pittsburgh	368	207	2,915	28	1978	Steve Largent, Seattle	71	1,168	8
Dan Fouts, San Diego	530	332	4,082	24	1979	Joe Washington, Baltimore	82	750	3
Brian Sipe, Cleveland	554	337	4,132	30	1980	Kellen Winslow, San Diego	89	1,290	9
Ken Anderson, Cincinnati	479	300	3,754	29	1981	Kellen Winslow, San Diego	88	1,075	10
Ken Anderson, Cincinnati	309	218	2,495	12	1982	Kellen Winslow, San Diego	54	721	6
Dan Marino, Miami	296	173	2,210	20	1983	Todd Christensen, L.A. Raiders	92	1,247	12
Dan Marino, Miami	564	362	5,084	48	1984	Ozzie Newsome, Cleveland	89	1,001	5

Scoring | Rushing

Player, team	TD	PAT	FG	Pts	Year	Player, team	Yds	Atts	TD
Jim Turner, N.Y. Jets	0	43	34	145	1968	Paul Robinson, Cincinnati	1,023	238	8
Jim Turner, N.Y. Jets	0	33	32	129	1969	Dick Post, San Diego	873	182	6
Jan Stenerud, Kansas City	0	26	30	116	1970	Floyd Little, Denver	901	209	3
Garo Yepremian, Miami	0	33	28	117	1971	Floyd Little, Denver	1,133	284	6
Bobby Howfield, N.Y. Jets	0	40	27	121	1972	O.J. Simpson, Buffalo	1,251	292	6
Roy Gerela, Pittsburgh	0	36	29	123	1973	O.J. Simpson, Buffalo	2,003	332	12
Roy Gerela, Pittsburgh	0	33	20	93	1974	Otis Armstrong, Denver	1,407	263	9
O.J. Simpson, Buffalo	23	0	0	138	1975	O.J. Simpson, Buffalo	1,817	329	16
Toni Linhart, Minnesota	0	49	20	109	1976	O.J. Simpson, Buffalo	1,503	290	8
Errol Mann, Oakland	0	39	20	99	1977	Mark van Eeghen, Oakland	1,273	324	7
Pat Leahy, N.Y. Jets	0	41	22	107	1978	Earl Campbell, Houston	1,450	302	13
John Smith, New England	0	46	23	115	1979	Earl Campbell, Houston	1,697	368	19
John Smith, New England	0	51	26	129	1980	Earl Campbell, Houston	1,934	373	13
Jim Breech, Cincinnati	0	49	22	115	1981	Earl Campbell, Houston	1,376	361	10
Marcus Allen, L.A. Raiders	14	0	0	84	1982	Freeman McNeil, N.Y. Jets	786	151	6
Gary Anderson, Pittsburgh	0	38	27	119	1983	Curt Warner, Seattle	1,446	335	13
Gary Anderson, Pittsburgh	0	45	24	117	1984	Earnest Jackson, San Diego	1,179	296	8

1984 NFL Individual Leaders

National Football Conference

Passing

	Att	Comp	Pct Comp	Yards	Avg Gain	TD	Pct TD	Int	Rating Points
Montana, San Francisco	432	279	64.6	3630	8.40	28	6.5	10	102.9
Lomax, St. Louis	560	345	61.6	4614	8.24	28	5.0	16	92.5
Bartkowski, Atlanta	269	181	67.3	2158	8.02	11	4.1	10	89.7
Theismann, Washington	477	283	59.3	3391	7.11	24	5.0	13	86.6
Dickey, Green Bay	401	237	59.1	3195	7.97	25	6.2	19	85.6
Danielson, Detroit	410	252	61.5	3076	7.50	17	4.1	15	83.1
DeBerg, Tampa Bay	509	308	60.5	3554	6.98	19	3.7	18	79.3
Kemp, L.A. Rams	284	143	50.4	2021	7.12	13	4.6	7	78.7
Simms, N.Y. Giants	533	286	53.7	4044	7.59	22	4.1	18	78.1
Jaworski, Philadelphia	427	234	54.8	2754	6.45	16	3.7	14	73.5
White, Dallas	233	126	54.1	1580	6.78	11	4.7	11	71.5
Kramer, Minnesota	236	124	52.5	1678	7.11	9	3.8	10	70.6
Hogeboom, Dallas	367	195	53.1	2366	6.45	7	1.9	14	63.7
Todd, New Orleans	312	161	51.6	2178	6.98	11	3.5	19	60.6

Rushing

	Att	Yds	Avg	TD
Dickerson, L.A. Rams	379	2105	5.6	14
Payton, Chicago	381	1684	4.4	11
Wilder, Tampa Bay	407	1544	3.8	13
Riggs, Atlanta	353	1486	4.2	13
Tyler, San Francisco	246	1262	5.1	7
Riggins, Washington	327	1239	3.8	14
Dorsett, Dallas	302	1189	3.9	6
Anderson, St. Louis	289	1174	4.1	6
G. Rogers, New Orleans	239	914	3.8	2
Carpenter, N.Y. Giants	250	795	3.2	-7

Receiving

	No	Yds	Avg	TD
Monk, Washington	106	1372	12.9	7
Wilder, Tampa Bay	85	685	8.1	0
Green, St. Louis	78	1555	19.9	12
J. Jones, Detroit	77	662	8.6	5
House, Tampa Bay	76	1005	13.2	5
Craig, San Francisco	71	675	9.5	3
Anderson, St. Louis	70	611	8.7	2
Bailey, Atlanta	67	1138	17.0	6
Spagnola, Philadelphia	65	701	10.8	1
Lofton, Green Bay	62	1361	22.0	7

Scoring-Touchdowns

	TD	Rush	Pass	Pts
Dickerson, L.A. Rams	14	14	0	84
Riggins, Washington	14	14	0	84
Riggs, Atlanta	13	13	0	78
Wilder, Tampa Bay	13	13	0	78
Green, St. Louis	12	0	12	72
Mitchell, St. Louis	11	9	2	66
Payton, Chicago	11	11	0	66
Solomon, San Francisco	11	1	10	66
Craig, San Francisco	10	7	3	60

Scoring-Kicking

	XP	XPA	FG	FGA	Pts
Wersching, San Francisco	56	56	25	35	131
Moseley, Washington	48	51	24	31	120
O'Donoghue, St. Louis	48	51	23	35	117
McFadden, Philadelphia	26	27	30	37	116
Lansford, L.A. Rams	37	38	25	33	112
Septien, Dallas	33	34	23	29	102
B. Thomas, Chicago	35	37	22	28	101
Ariri, Tampa Bay	38	40	19	26	95
Andersen, New Orleans	34	34	20	27	94

Interceptions

	No	Yds	TD
Flynn, Green Bay	9	106	0
T. Lewis, Green Bay	7	151	1
Downs, Dallas	7	126	1
Ellis, Philadelphia	7	119	0
Dean, Washington	7	114	2
Haynes, N.Y. Giants	7	90	0
Watkins, Detroit	6	0	0

Kickoff Returns

	No	Yds	Avg	TD
Redden, L.A. Rams	23	530	23.0	0
Mitchell, St. Louis	35	804	23.0	0
Dar. Nelson, Minnesota	39	891	22.8	0
Anthony, New Orleans	22	490	22.3	0
Morton, Tampa Bay	38	835	22.0	0
Rodgers, Green Bay	39	843	21.6	1
Anderson, Minnesota	30	639	21.3	0
Hill, L.A. Rams	26	543	20.9	0

Punt Returns

	No	Yds	Avg	TD
Ellard, L.A. Rams	30	403	13.4	2
McLemore, San Francisco	45	521	11.6	1
Mitchell, St. Louis	38	333	8.8	0
Fields, New Orleans	27	236	8.7	0
Nelms, Washington	49	428	8.7	0
Fisher, Chicago	57	492	8.6	0
Martin, Detroit	25	210	8.4	0

Punting

	No	Yds	Avg
Hansen, New Orleans	69	3020	43.8
Coleman, Minnesota	82	3473	42.4
Scribner, Green Bay	85	3596	42.3
Horan, Philadelphia	92	3880	42.2
Giacomarro, Atlanta	68	2855	42.0

Sacks

	No		No
Dent, Chicago	17.5	Manley, Washington	13.5
Brown, Philadelphia	15.5	White, Dallas	12.5
Greer, St. Louis	14.0		

American Football Conference

Passing

	Att	Comp	Pct Comp	Yards	Avg Gain	TD	Pct TD	Int	Rating Points
Marino, Miami	564	362	64.2	5084	9.01	48	8.5	17	108.9
Eason, New England	431	259	60.1	3228	7.49	23	5.3	8	93.4
Fouts, San Diego	507	317	62.5	3740	7.38	19	3.7	17	83.4
Krieg, Seattle	480	276	57.5	3671	7.65	32	6.7	24	83.3
Anderson, Cincinnati	275	175	63.6	2107	7.66	10	3.6	12	81.0
Kenney, Kansas City	282	151	53.5	2098	7.44	15	5.3	10	80.7
Moon, Houston	450	259	57.6	3338	7.42	12	2.7	14	76.9
Elway, Denver	380	214	56.3	2598	6.84	18	4.7	15	76.8
Malone, Pittsburgh	272	147	54.0	2137	7.86	16	5.9	17	73.4
Ryan, N.Y. Jets	285	156	54.7	1939	6.80	14	4.9	14	72.0
Wilson, L.A. Raiders	282	153	54.3	2151	7.63	15	5.3	17	71.7
McDonald, Cleveland	493	271	55.0	3472	7.04	14	2.8	23	67.3
Ferguson, Buffalo	344	191	55.5	1991	5.79	12	3.5	17	63.5
Blackledge, Kansas City	294	147	50.0	1707	5.81	6	2.0	11	59.2

Rushing

	Att	Yds	Avg	TD
Jackson, San Diego	296	1179	4.0	8
Allen, L.A. Raiders	275	1168	4.2	13
Winder, Denver	296	1153	3.9	4
Bell, Buffalo	262	1100	4.2	7
McNeil, N.Y. Jets	229	1070	4.7	5
Pollard, Pittsburgh	213	851	4.0	6
C. James, New England	160	790	4.9	1
Moriarty, Houston	189	785	4.2	6
McMillan, Indianapolis	163	705	4.3	5
Heard, Kansas City	165	684	4.1	4

Receiving

	No	Yds	Avg	TD
Newsome, Cleveland	89	1001	11.2	5
Stallworth, Pittsburgh	80	1395	17.4	11
Christensen, L.A. Raiders	80	1007	12.6	7
Largent, Seattle	74	1164	15.7	12
Clayton, Miami	73	1389	19.0	18
Duper, Miami	71	1306	18.4	8
Watson, Denver	69	1170	17.0	7
Smith, Houston	69	1141	16.5	4
Franklin, Buffalo	69	862	12.5	4
Shuler, N.Y. Jets	68	782	11.5	6

Scoring-Touchdowns

	TD	Rush	Pass	Pts
Allen, L.A. Raiders	18	13	5	108
Clayton, Miami	18	0	18	108
P. Johnson, S.D.-Miami	12	12	0	72
Largent, Seattle	12	0	12	72
*Lipps, Pittsburgh	11	1	9	66
Stallworth, Pittsburgh	11	0	11	66
Kinnebrew, Cincinnati	10	9	1	60
Turner, Seattle	10	0	10	60
Jackson, San Diego	9	8	1	54
*One via return				

Scoring-Kicking

	XP	XPA	FG	FGA	Pts
Anderson, Pittsburgh	45	45	24	32	117
N. Johnson, Seattle	50	51	20	24	110
Franklin, New England	42	42	22	28	108
Lowery, Kansas City	35	35	23	33	104
Breech, Cincinnati	37	37	22	31	103
Karlis, Denver	38	41	21	28	101
Bahr, L.A. Raiders	40	42	20	27	100
Bahr, Cleveland	25	25	24	32	97
von Schamann, Miami	66	70	9	19	93
Benirschke, San Diego	41	41	17	26	92

Interceptions

	No	Yds	TD
Easley, Seattle	10	126	2
Brown, Seattle	8	179	2
Cherry, Kansas City	7	140	0
Shell, Pittsburgh	7	61	1

Kickoff Returns

	No	Yds	Avg	TD
Humphery, N.Y. Jets	22	675	30.7	1
Williams, L.A. Raiders	24	621	25.9	0
L. Anderson, Indianapolis	22	525	23.9	0
Springs, N.Y. Jets	23	521	22.7	0
Roaches, Houston	30	679	22.6	0

Punt Returns

	No	Yds	Avg	TD
Martin, Cincinnati	24	376	15.7	0
Lipps, Pittsburgh	53	656	12.4	1
Willhite, Denver	20	200	10.0	0
Fryar, New England	36	347	9.6	0
Wilson, Buffalo	33	297	9.0	1

Punting

	No	Yds	Avg
Arnold, Kansas City	98	4397	44.9
Roby, Miami	51	2281	44.7
Stark, Indianapolis	98	4383	44.7
Cox, Cleveland	74	3213	43.4
Prestridge, New England	44	1884	42.8

Sacks

	No		No
Gastineau, N.Y. Jets	22.0	J. Bryant, Seattle	14.5
Tippett, New England	18.5	Still, Kansas City	14.5
Merriweather, Pittsburgh	15.0		

American Football League

Year	Eastern Division	Western Division	Playoff
1960	Houston Oilers (10-4-0)	L. A. Chargers (10-4-0)	Houston 24, Los Angeles 16
1961	Houston Oilers (10-3-1)	San Diego Chargers (12-2-0)	Houston 10, San Diego 3
1962	Houston Oilers (11-3-0)	Dallas Texans (11-3-0)	Dallas 20, Houston 17(b)
1963	Boston Patriots (8-6-1)(a)	San Diego Chargers (11-3-0)	San Diego 51, Boston 10
1964	Buffalo Bills (12-2-0)	San Diego Chargers (8-5-1)	Buffalo 20, San Diego 7
1965	Buffalo Bills (10-3-1)	San Diego Chargers (9-2-3)	Buffalo 23, San Diego 0
1966	Buffalo Bills (9-4-1)	Kansas City Chiefs (11-2-1)	Kansas City 31, Buffalo 7
1967	Houston Oilers (9-4-1)	Oakland Raiders (13-1-0)	Oakland 40, Houston 7
1968	New York Jets (11-3-0)	Oakland Raiders (12-2-0)(a)	New York 27, Oakland 23
1969	New York Jets (10-4-0)	Oakland Raiders (12-1-1)	Kansas City 17, Oakland 7(c)

(a) won divisional playoff (b) won at 2:45 of second overtime. (c) Kansas City defeated Jets to make playoffs.

All-Time Football Records

NFL, AFL, and All-American Football Conference

(at start of 1985 season)

Leading Lifetime Rushers

Player	League	Yrs	Att	Yards	Avg	Player	League	Yrs	Att	Yards	Avg
Walter Payton	NFL	10	3,047	13,309	4.4	O.J. Anderson	NFL	6	1,690	7,364	4.4
Jim Brown	NFL	9	2,359	12,312	5.2	Leroy Kelly	NFL	10	1,727	7,274	4.2
Franco Harris	NFL	13	2,949	12,120	4.1	John Henry Johnson	NFL-AFL	13	1,571	6,803	4.3
O.J. Simpson	AFL-NFL	11	2,404	11,236	4.7	Chuck Muncie	NFL	9	1,561	6,702	4.3
John Riggins	NFL	13	2,740	10,675	3.9	Mark van Eeghen	NFL	10	1,652	6,651	4.0
Joe Perry	AAFC-NFL	16	1,929	9,723	5.0	Lawrence McCutcheon	NFL	10	1,521	6,578	4.3
Tony Dorsett	NFL	8	2,136	9,525	4.5	Mike Pruitt	NFL	9	1,593	6,540	4.1
Earl Campbell	NFL	7	2,029	8,764	4.3	Wilbert Montgomery	NFL	8	1,465	6,538	4.5
Jim Taylor	NFL	10	1,941	8,597	4.4	Lydell Mitchell	NFL	9	1,675	6,534	3.9
Larry Csonka	AFL-NFL	11	1,891	8,081	4.3	Floyd Little	AFL-NFL	9	1,641	6,323	3.8

Most Yards Gained, Season — 2,105, Eric Dickerson, Los Angeles Rams, 1984.
Most Yards Gained, Game — 275, Walter Payton, Chicago Bears vs. Minnesota Vikings, Nov. 20, 1977.
Most Games, 100 Yards or more, Season — 12, Eric Dickerson, Los Angeles Rams, 1984.
Most Games, 100 Yards or more, Career — 63, Walter Payton, Chicago Bears, 1975-84..
Most Games, 200 Yards or more, Career — 6, O.J. Simpson, Buffalo Bills, 1969-1977; San Francisco 49ers, 1978-1979.
Most Touchdowns Rushing, Career — 106, Jim Brown, Cleveland Browns, 1957-1965.
Most Touchdowns Rushing, Season — 24, John Riggins, Washington Redskins, 1983.
Most Touchdowns Rushing, Game — 6, Ernie Nevers, Chicago Cardinals vs. Chicago Bears, Nov. 8, 1929.
Most Rushing Attempts, Season — 407, James Wilder, Tampa Bay Buccaneers, 1984.
Most Rushing Attempts, Game — 43, Butch Woolfolk, N.Y. Giants vs. Philadelphia, Nov. 20, 1983; James Wilder, Tampa Bay Buccaneers vs. Pittsburgh, Sept. 30, 1984.
Longest run from Scrimmage — 99 yds., Tony Dorsett, Dallas vs. Minnesota, Jan. 3, 1983 (scored touchdown).

Leading Lifetime Passers

(Minimum 1,500 attempts)

Player	League	Yrs	Att	Comp	Yds	Pts*	Player	League	Yrs	Att	Comp	Yds	Pts*
Joe Montana	NFL	6	2,077	1,324	15,609	92.7	Joe Theismann	NFL	11	3,301	1,877	23,432	79.0
Otto Graham	AAFC-NFL	10	2,626	1,464	23,584	86.6	Johnny Unitas	NFL	18	5,186	2,830	40,239	78.2
Roger Staubach	NFL	11	2,958	1,685	22,700	83.4	Bert Jones	NFL	10	2,551	1,430	18,190	78.2
Danny White	NFL	9	1,943	1,155	14,754	82.7	Frank Ryan	NFL	13	2,133	1,090	16,042	77.6
Sonny Jurgensen	NFL	18	4,262	2,433	32,224	82.6	Bob Griese	AFL-NFL	14	3,429	1,926	25,092	77.1
Len Dawson	NFL-AFL	19	3,741	2,136	28,711	82.6	Steve Bartkowski	NFL	10	3,219	1,802	22,732	75.5
Ken Anderson	NFL	14	4,420	2,627	32,497	82.0	Ken Stabler	AFL-NFL	15	3,793	2,270	27,938	75.3
Dan Fouts	NFL	12	4,380	2,585	33,854	81.2	Norm Van Brocklin	NFL	12	2,895	1,553	23,611	75.3
Bart Starr	NFL	16	3,149	1,808	24,718	80.5	Sid Luckman	NFL	12	1,744	904	14,686	75.0
Fran Tarkenton	NFL	18	6,467	3,686	47,003	80.4	Brian Sipe	NFL	10	3,439	1,944	23,713	75.0

*Rating points based on performances in the following categories: Percentage of completions, percentage of touchdown passes, percentage of interceptions, and average gain per pass attempt.

Most Yards Gained, Season — 5,084, Dan Marino, Miami Dolphins, 1984.
Most Yards Gained, Game — 554, Norm Van Brocklin, Los Angeles Rams vs. New York Yankees, Sept. 18, 1951 (27 completions in 41 attempts).
Most Games, 300 or More Yards Passing, Career — 40, Dan Fouts, San Diego Chargers, 1973-84.
Most Touchdowns Passing, Career — 342, Fran Tarkenton, Minnesota Vikings, 1961-65; N.Y. Giants, 1967-71; Vikings, 1972-78.
Most Touchdown Passing, Season — 48, Dan Marino, Miami Dolphins, 1984.
Most Touchdown Passing, Game — 7, Sid Luckman, Chicago Bears vs. New York Giants, Nov. 14, 1943; Adrian Burk, Philadelphia Eagles vs. Washington Redskins, Oct. 17, 1954; George Blanda, Houston Oilers vs. New York Titans, Nov. 19, 1961; Y.A. Tittle, New York Giants vs. Washington Redskins, Oct. 28, 1962; Joe Kapp, Minnesota Vikings vs. Baltimore Colts, Sept. 28, 1969.
Most Passing Attempts, Season — 609, Dan Fouts, San Diego Chargers, 1981.
Most Passing Attempts, Game — 68, George Blanda, Houston Oilers vs. Buffalo Bills, Nov. 1, 1964 (37 completions).
Most Passes Completed, Season — 362, Dan Marino, Miami Dolphins, 1984.
Most Passes Completed, Game — 42, Richard Todd, N.Y. Jets vs. San Francisco 49ers, Sept. 21, 1980.
Most Consecutive Passes Completed — 20, Ken Anderson, Cincinnati vs. Houston, Jan. 2, 1983.

Leading Lifetime Receivers

Player	League	Yrs	No	Yds	Avg	Player	League	Yrs	No	Yds	Avg
Charlie Joiner	NFL	16	657	10,774	16.4	Bobby Mitchell	NFL	11	521	7,954	15.3
Charley Taylor	NFL	13	649	9,110	14.0	Billy Howton	NFL	12	503	8,459	16.8
Don Maynard	AFL-NFL	15	633	11,834	18.7	Cliff Branch	NFL	12	501	8,685	17.3
Ray Berry	NFL	13	631	9,275	14.7	Tommy McDonald	NFL	12	495	8,410	17.0
Harold Carmichael	NFL	14	590	8,985	15.2	Ahmad Rashad	NFL	10	495	6,831	13.8
Fred Biletnikoff	AFL-NFL	14	589	8,974	15.2	Drew Pearson	NFL	11	489	7,822	16.0
Harold Jackson	NFL	16	579	10,372	17.9	Don Hutson	NFL	11	488	7,991	16.4
Lionel Taylor	AFL	10	567	7,195	12.7	Jackie Smith	NFL	16	480	7,918	16.5
Steve Largent	NFL	9	545	8,772	16.1	Art Powell	AFL-NFL	10	479	8,046	16.8
Lance Alworth	AFL-NFL	11	542	10,266	18.9	Boyd Dowler	NFL	12	474	7,270	15.4

Most Yards Gained, Season — 1,746, Charley Hennigan, Houston Oilers, 1961.
Most Yards Gained, Game — 303, Jim Benton, Cleveland Rams vs. Detroit Lions, Nov. 22, 1945 (10 receptions).
Most Pass Receptions, Season — 106, Art Monk, Washington Redskins, 1984.
Most Pass Receptions, Game — 18, Tom Fears, Los Angeles Rams vs. Green Bay Packers, Dec. 3, 1950 (189 yards).
Most Consecutive Games, Pass Receptions — 127, Harold Carmichael, Philadelphia Eagles, 1972-1980.
Most Touchdown Passes, Career — 99, Don Hutson, Green Bay Packers, 1935-1945.
Most Touchdown Passes, Season — 18, Mark Clayton, Miami Dolphins, 1984.
Most Touchdown Passes, Game — 5, Bob Shaw, Chicago Cardinals vs. Baltimore Colts, Oct. 2, 1950; Kellen Winslow, San Diego vs. Oakland, Nov. 22, 1981.

Leading Lifetime Scorers

Player	League	Yrs	TD	PAT	FG	Total	Player	League	Yrs	TD	PAT	FG	Total
George Blanda	NFL-AFL	26	9	943	335	2,002	Sam Baker	NFL	15	2	428	179	977
Jan Stenerud	AFL-NFL	18	0	539	358	1,613	Lou Michaels	NFL	13	1	386	187	955*
Lou Groza	AAFC-NFL	21	1	810	264	1,608	Roy Gerela	AFL-NFL	11	0	351	184	903
Jim Turner	AFL-NFL	16	1	521	304	1,439	Bobby Walston	NFL	12	46	365	80	881
Jim Bakken	NFL	17	0	534	282	1,380	Pete Gogolak	AFL-NFL	10	0	344	173	863
Fred Cox	NFL	15	0	519	282	1,365	Errol Mann	NFL	11	0	315	177	846
Mark Moseley	NFL	14	0	426	266	1,224	Ray Wersching	NFL	12	0	319	171	832
Gino Cappelletti	AFL	11	42	350	176	1,130	Don Hutson	NFL	11	105	172	7	823
Don Cockroft	NFL	13	0	432	216	1,080	Pat Leahy	NFL	11	0	306	158	780
Garo Yepremian	AFL-NFL	14	0	444	210	1,074	*Includes safety.						
Bruce Gossett	NFL	11	0	374	219	1,031							

Most Points, Season — 176, Paul Hornung, Green Bay Packers, 1960 (15 TD's, 41 PAT's, 15 FG's).
Most Points, Game — 40, Ernie Nevers, Chicago Cardinals vs. Chicago Bears, Nov. 28, 1929 (6 TD's, 4 PAT's).
Most Touchdowns, Season — 24, John Riggins, Washington Redskins, 1984 (24 rushing).
Most Touchdowns, Game — 6, Ernie Nevers, Chicago Cardinals vs. Chicago Bears, Nov. 28, 1929 (6 rushing); Dub Jones, Cleveland Browns vs. Chicago Bears, Nov. 25, 1951 (4 rushing, 2 pass receptions); Gale Sayers, Chicago Bears vs. San Francisco 49ers, Dec. 12, 1965 (4 rushing, 1 pass reception, 1 punt return).
Most Points After Touchdown, Season — 66, Uwe von Schamann, Miami Dolphins, 1984.
Most Consecutive Points After Touchdown — 234, Tommy Davis, San Francisco 49ers, 1959-1969.
Most Field Goals, Game — 7, Jim Bakken, St. Louis Cardinals vs. Pittsburgh Steelers, Sept. 24, 1967.
Most Field Goals, Season — 35, Ali Haji-Sheikh, N.Y. Giants, 1983.
Most Field Goals Attempted, Season — 49, Bruce Gossett, Los Angeles Rams, 1966; Curt Knight, Washington Redskins, 1971.
Most Field Goals Attempted, Game — 9, Jim Bakken, St. Louis Cardinals vs. Pittsburgh Steelers, Sept. 24, 1967 (7 successful).
Most Consecutive Field Goals — 23, Mark Moseley, Washington Redskins, 1981-1982.
Most Consecutive Games, Field Goal — 31, Fred Cox, Minnesota Vikings, 1968-1970.
Longest Field Goal — 63 yds., Tom Dempsey, New Orleans Saints vs. Detroit Lions, Nov. 8, 1970.
Highest Field Goal Completion Percentage, Season (14 attempts) — 95.24 Mark Moseley, Washington Redskins, 1982 (20 FG's in 21 attempts).

Pass Interceptions

Most Passes Had Intercepted, Game — 8, Jim Hardy, Chicago Cardinals vs. Philadelphia Eagles, Sept. 24, 1950 (39 attempts)
Most Passes Had Intercepted, Season — 42, George Blanda, Houston Oilers, 1962 (418 attempts).
Most Passes Had Intercepted, Career — 277, George Blanda, Chicago Bears, 1949-1958; Houston Oilers, 1960-1966; Oakland Raiders, 1967-1975 (4,000 attempts).
Most Consecutive Passes Attempted Without Interception — 294, Bart Starr, Green Bay Packers, 1964-1965.
Most Interceptions By, Season — 14, Dick Lane, Los Angeles Rams, 1952.
Most Interceptions By, Career — 81, Paul Krause, Washington Redskins, 1964-67; Minnesota Vikings, 1968-79.
Most Consecutive Games, Passes Intercepted By — 8, Tom Morrow, Oakland Raiders, 1962 (4), 1963 (4).

Punting

Most Punts, Career — 1,083, John James, Atlanta Falcons, 1982-84.
Most Punts, Season — 114, Bob Parsons, Chicago Bears, 1981.
Highest Punting Average, Season (20 punts) — 51.40, Sam Baugh, Washington Redskins, 1940 (35 punts).
Longest Punt — 98 yds., Steve O'Neal, New York Jets vs. Denver Broncos, Sept. 21, 1969.

Kickoff Returns

Most Yardage Returning Kickoffs, Career — 6,922, Ron Smith, Chicago Bears, 1965; Atlanta Falcons, 1966-67; Los Angeles Rams, 1968-69; Chicago Bears, 1970-72; San Diego Chargers, 1973; Oakland Raiders, 1974.
Most Yardage Returning Kickoffs, Season — 1,317, Bobby Jancik, Houston Oilers, 1963.
Most Yardage Returning Kickoffs, Game — 294, Wally Triplett, Detroit Lions vs. Los Angeles Rams, Oct. 29, 1950 (4 returns).
Most Touchdowns Scored via Kickoff Returns, Career — 6, Ollie Matson, Chicago Cardinals, 1952 (2), 1954, 1956, 1958 (2); Gale Sayers, Chicago Bears, 1965, 1966 (2), 1967 (3); Travis Williams, Green Bay Packers, 1967 (4), 1969; Los Angeles Rams, 1971.
Most Touchdowns Scored via Kickoff Returns, Season — 4, Travis Williams, Green Bay Packers, 1967; Cecil Turner, Chicago Bears, 1970.
Most Touchdowns Scored via Kickoff Returns, Game — 2, Tim Brown, Philadelphia Eagles vs. Dallas Cowboys, Nov. 6, 1966; Travis Williams, Green Bay Packers vs. Cleveland Browns, Nov. 12, 1967.
Most Kickoff Returns, Career — 275, Ron Smith, Chicago Bears, 1965; Atlanta Falcons, 1966-67; Los Angeles Rams, 1968-69; Chicago Bears, 1970-72; San Diego Chargers, 1973; Oakland Raiders, 1974.
Most Kickoff Returns, Season — 60, Drew Hill, Los Angeles Rams, 1981.
Longest Kickoff Return — 106 yds., Al Carmichael, Green Bay Packers vs. Chicago Bears, October 7, 1956; Noland Smith, Kansas City vs. Denver, Dec. 17, 1967; Roy Green, St. Louis Cardinals vs. Dallas Cowboys, Oct. 21, 1979 (all scored TD).

Punt Returns

Most Yardage Returning Punts, Career — 3,008, Rick Upchurch, Denver Broncos, 1975-1983.
Most Yardage Returning Punts, Season — 666, Greg Pruitt, Los Angeles Raiders, 1983.
Most Yardage Returning Punts, Game — 207, Leroy Irvin, Los Angeles Rams vs. Atlanta Falcons, Oct. 11, 1981.
Most Touchdowns Scored via Punt Returns, Career — 8, Jack Christiansen, Detroit Lions, 1951-1958; Rick Upchurch, Denver Broncos, 1975-83.
Most Punt Returns, Career — 258, Emlen Tunnell, New York Giants, 1948-1958; Green Bay Packers, 1959-1961.
Most Punt Returns, Season — 70, Danny Reece, Tampa Bay Buccaneers, 1979.
Longest Punt Return — 98 yards, Gil LeFebvre, Cincinnati Reds vs. Brooklyn Dodgers, Dec. 3, 1933; Charles West, Minnesota Vikings vs. Washington Redskins, Nov. 3, 1968; Dennis Morgan, Dallas Cowboys vs. St. Louis Cardinals, Oct. 13, 1974 (all scored TD).

Miscellaneous Records

Most Fumbles, Season — 17, Dan Pastorini, Houston Oilers, 1973; Warren Moon, Houston Oilers, 1984.
Most Fumbles, Game — 7, Len Dawson, Kansas City Chiefs vs. San Diego Chargers, Nov. 15, 1964.
Winning Streak (Regular Season) — 17 games, Chicago Bears, 1933-34.
Most Seasons, Active Player — 26, George Blanda, Chicago Bears, 1949-1958; Houston Oilers, 1960-1966 and Oakland, 67-75.

Pro Football Hall of Fame

Canton, Ohio

Herb Adderley	Paddy Driscoll	Sam Huff	Wayne Millner	Gale Sayers
Lance Alworth	Bill Dudley	Lamar Hunt	Bobby Mitchell	Joe Schmidt
Doug Atkins	Turk Edwards	Don Hutson	Ron Mix	O.J. Simpson
Morris (Red) Badgro	Weeb Ewbank	Deacon Jones	Lenny Moore	Bart Starr
Cliff Battles	Tom Fears	Sonny Jurgensen	Marion Motley	Roger Staubach
Sammy Baugh	Ray Flaherty	Walt Kiesling	George Musso	Ernie Stautner
Chuck Bednarik	Len Ford	Frank (Bruiser) Kinard	Bronko Nagurski	Ken Strong
Bert Bell	Dr. Daniel Fortmann	Curly Lambeau	Joe Namath	Joe Stydahar
Bobby Bell	Frank Gatski	Dick (Night Train) Lane	Greasy Neale	Charlie Taylor
Raymond Berry	Bill George	Yale Lary	Ernie Nevers	Jim Taylor
Charles Bidwell	Frank Gifford	Dante Lavelli	Ray Nitschke	Jim Thorpe
George Blanda	Sid Gillman	Bobby Layne	Leo Nomellini	Y.A. Tittle
Jim Brown	Otto Graham	Tuffy Leemans	Merlin Olsen	George Trafton
Paul Brown	Red Grange	Bob Lilly	Jim Otto	Charlie Trippi
Roosevelt Brown	Forrest Gregg	Vince Lombardi	Steve Owen	Emlen Tunnell
Willie Brown	Lou Groza	Sid Luckman	Clarence (Ace) Parker	Clyde (Bulldog) Turner
Dick Butkus	Joe Guyon	Link Lyman	Jim Parker	Norm Van Brocklin
Tony Canadeo	George Halas	Tim Mara	Joe Perry	Steve Van Buren
Joe Carr	Ed Healey	Gino Marchetti	Pete Pihos	Johnny Unitas
Guy Chamberlin	Mel Hein	George Marshall	Hugh (Shorty) Ray	Paul Warfield
Jack Christiansen	Pete Henry	Ollie Matson	Dan Reeves	Bob Waterfield
Dutch Clark	Arnold Herber	George McAfee	Jim Ringo	Arnie Weinmeister
George Connor	Bill Hewitt	Mike McCormack	Andy Robustelli	Bill Willis
Jim Conzelman	Clarke Hinkle	Hugh McElhenny	Art Rooney	Larry Wilson
Willie Davis	Elroy Hirsch	John (Blood) McNally	Pete Rozelle	Alex Wojciechowicz
Art Donovan	Cal Hubbard	Mike Michalske		

1985 NFL Player Draft

The following are the first round picks of the National Football League.

Team	Player	Pos.	College	Team	Player	Pos.	College
1—Buffalo	Bruce Smith	OT	Virginia Tech	15—Kansas City	Ethan Horton	RB	North Carolina
2—Atlanta	Bill Fralic	OT	Pittsburgh	16—San Francisco	Jerry Rice	WR	Miss. Valley
3—Houston	Ray Childress	DE	Texas A&M	17—Dallas	Kevin Brooks	DE	Michigan
4—Minnesota	Chris Doleman	LB	Pittsburgh	18—St. Louis	Freddie Nunn	DE	Mississippi
5—Indianapolis	Duane Bickett	LB	USC	19—N.Y. Giants	George Adams	RB	Kentucky
6—Detroit	Lomas Brown	OT	Florida	20—Pittsburgh	Darryl Sims	DT	Wisconsin
7—Green Bay	Ken Ruettgers	OT	USC	21—L.A. Rams	Jerry Gray	S	Texas
8—Tampa Bay	Ron Holmes	DE	Washington	22—Chicago	William Perry	DT	Clemson
9—Philadelphia	Kevin Allen	OT	Indiana	23—L.A. Raiders	Jessie Hester	WR	Florida St.
10—N.Y. Jets	Al Toon	WR	Wisconsin	24—New Orleans	Alvin Toles	LB	Tennessee
11—Houston	Richard Johnson	CB	Wisconsin	25—Cincinnati	Emanuel King	LB	Alabama
12—San Diego	Jim Lachey	OG	Ohio St.	26—Denver	Steve Sewell	RB	Oklahoma
13—Cincinnati	Eddie Brown	WR	Miami	27—Miami	Lorenzo Hampton	RB	Florida
14—Buffalo	Derrick Burroughs	CB	Memphis St.	28—New England	Trevor Matich	C	BYU

NEA All-NFL Team in 1984

Chosen by team captains, player representatives, and head coaches of the 28 NFL teams in a poll conducted by Newspaper Enterprise Assn.

First team	Offense	Second team
Roy Green, St. Louis	Wide receiver	Art Monk, Philadelphia
James Lofton, Green Bay	Wide receiver	John Stallworth, Pittsburgh
Ozzie Newsome, Cleveland	Tight end	Paul Coffman, Green Bay
Anthony Munoz, Cincinnati	Tackle	Brian Holloway, New England
Keith Fahnhorst, San Francisco	Tackle	Joe Jacoby, Washington
John Hannah, New England	Guard	Randy Cross, San Francisco
Russ Grimm, Washington	Guard	Mike Munchak, Houston
Dwight Stephenson, Miami	Center	Randy Clark, St. Louis
Dan Marino, Miami	Quarterback	Joe Montana, San Francisco
Eric Dickerson, L.A. Rams	Running back	Marcus Allen, L.A. Raiders
Walter Payton, Chicago	Running back	James Wilder, Tampa Bay
Jan Stenerud, Minnesota	Placekicker	Norm Johnson, Seattle

First team	Defense	Second team
Howie Long, L.A. Raiders	End	Jacob Green, Seattle
Mark Gastineau, N.Y. Jets	End	Lee Roy Selmon, Tampa Bay
Dave Hampton, Chicago	Tackle	Gary Dunn, Pittsburgh
Randy White, Dallas	Nose tackle	Joe Nash, Seattle
E. J. Junior, St. Louis	Inside linebacker	Harry Carson, N.Y. Giants
Mike Singletary, Chicago	Inside linebacker	Steve Nelson, New England
Clay Matthews, Cleveland	Outside linebacker	Mike Merriweather, Pittsburgh
Lawrence Taylor, N.Y. Giants	Outside linebacker	Rickey Jackson, New Orleans
Mike Haynes, L.A. Raiders	Cornerback	Louis Wright, Denver
Mark Haynes, N.Y. Giants	Cornerback	Gary Green, L.A. Rams
Ken Easley, Seattle	Strong safety	Vann McElroy, L.A. Raiders
Wes Hopkins, Philadelphia	Free safety	Deron Cherry, Kansas City
Reggie Roby, Miami	Punter	Rohn Stark, Indianapolis

Bert Bell Memorial Trophy Winners

The Bert Bell Memorial Trophy, named after the former NFL commissioner, is awarded annually to the outstanding rookies in a poll conducted by Murray Olderman of Newspaper Enterprise Assn.

1964	Charlie Taylor, Washington, WR	1974	Don Woods, San Diego, RB
1965	Gale Sayers, Chicago, RB	1975	AFC: Robert Brazile, Houston, LB
1966	Tommy Nobis, Atlanta, LB		NFC: Steve Bartkowski, Atlanta, QB
1967	Mel Farr, Detroit, RB	1976	AFC: Mike Haynes, New England, CB
1968	Earl McCullouch, Detroit, WR		NFC: Sammy White, Minnesota, WR
1969	Calvin Hill, Dallas, RB	1977	Tony Dorsett, Dallas, RB
1970	Raymond Chester, Oakland, TE	1978	Earl Campbell, Houston, RB
1971	AFC: Jim Plunkett, New England, QB	1979	Ottis Anderson, St. Louis, RB
	NFC: John Brockington, Green Bay, RB	1980	Billy Sims, Detroit, RB
1972	AFC: Franco Harris, Pittsburgh, RB	1981	Lawrence Taylor, N.Y. Giants, LB
	NFC: Willie Buchanon, Green Bay, DB	1982	Marcus Allen, L.A. Raiders, RB
1973	AFC: Boobie Clark, Cincinnati, RB	1983	Eric Dickerson, L.A. Rams, RB
	NFC: Chuck Foreman, Minnesota, RB	1984	Louis Lipps, Pittsburgh, WR

Jim Thorpe Trophy Winners

The winner of the Jim Thorpe Trophy, named after the athletic great, is picked by Murray Olderman of Newspaper Enterprise Assn. in a poll of players from the 28 NFL teams. It goes to the most valuable NFL player and is the oldest and highest professional football award.

Year	Player, team	Year	Player, team
1955	Harlon Hill, Chicago Bears	1970	John Brodie, San Francisco 49ers
1956	Frank Gifford, N.Y. Giants	1971	Bob Griese, Miami Dolphins
1957	John Unitas, Baltimore Colts	1972	Larry Brown, Washington Redskins
1958	Jim Brown, Cleveland Browns	1973	O.J. Simpson, Buffalo Bills
1959	Charley Conerly, N.Y. Giants	1974	Ken Stabler, Oakland Raiders
1960	Norm Van Brocklin, Philadelphia Eagles	1975	Fran Tarkenton, Minnesota Vikings
1961	Y.A. Tittle, N.Y. Giants	1976	Bert Jones, Baltimore Colts
1962	Jim Taylor, Green Bay Packers	1977	Walter Payton, Chicago Bears
1963	(tie) Jim Brown, Cleveland Browns, and Y.A. Tittle, N.Y. Giants	1978	Earl Campbell, Houston Oilers
		1979	Earl Campbell, Houston Oilers
1964	Lenny Moore, Baltimore Colts	1980	Earl Campbell, Houston Oilers
1965	Jim Brown, Cleveland Browns	1981	Ken Anderson, Cincinnati Bengals
1966	Bart Starr, Green Bay Packers	1982	Dan Fouts, San Diego Chargers
1967	John Unitas, Baltimore Colts	1983	Joe Theismann, Washington Redskins
1968	Earl Morrall, Baltimore Colts	1984	Dan Marino, Miami Dolphins
1969	Roman Gabriel, Los Angeles Rams		

United States Football League

Final 1985 Standings

Eastern Conference

	W	L	T	Pct	Pts	Opp
Birmingham	13	5	0	.722	436	299
New Jersey	11	7	0	.611	418	377
Memphis	11	7	0	.611	428	337
Baltimore	10	7	1	.583	368	260
Tampa Bay	10	8	0	.556	405	422
Jacksonville	9	9	0	.500	407	402
Orlando	5	13	0	.278	308	481

Western Conference

	W	L	T	Pct	Pts	Opp
Oakland	13	4	1	.750	473	359
Denver	11	7	0	.611	433	389
Houston	10	8	0	.556	544	388
Arizona	8	10	0	.444	376	405
Portland	6	12	0	.333	275	422
San Antonio	5	13	0	.278	296	436
Los Angeles	3	15	0	.167	266	456

USFL Playoffs

Quarterfinals—Birmingham 22, Houston 20; Memphis 48, Denver 7; Oakland 48, Tampa Bay 27; Baltimore 20, New Jersey 17.
Semifinals—Baltimore 28, Birmingham 14; Oakland 28, Memphis 19.
Championship—Baltimore 28, Oakland 24.

1984 USFL Individual Leaders

Passing

	Att	Comp	Yards	Pct	Avg	TD	Int	Rate
Kelly, Houston	567	360	4623	63.5	8.15	39	19	97.9
Stoudt, Birmingham	444	266	3358	59.9	7.56	34	19	91.2
Hebert, Oakland	456	244	3811	53.5	8.36	30	19	86.1
Fusina, Baltimore	496	303	3496	61.1	7.05	20	14	84.0
Kelley, Memphis	260	165	2186	63.5	8.41	9	14	79.1
Williams D, Arizona	509	271	3673	53.2	7.22	21	17	76.4
Gagliano, Denver	358	205	2695	57.3	7.53	13	17	73.5
Reaves, Tampa Bay	561	314	4193	56.0	7.47	25	29	73.2
Luther, Jacksonville	400	240	2792	60.0	6.98	15	21	71.8

Scoring

	TD	FG	1XP	Pts		TD	FG	1XP	Pts
Walker, New Jersey	22	0	0	132	Franco, Jacksonville	0	24	45	117
Smith J, Birmingham	21	0	0	126	Bojovic, Oakland	0	18	57	111
Fritsch, Houston	0	21	59	122	Zendejas, Arizona	0	24	36	108
Anderson G, Tampa Bay	20	0	0	120	Miller, Birmingham	0	19	49	108*

*Includes one two-point conversion.

Rushing

	Att	Yds	Avg	TD
Walker, New Jersey	438	2411	5.5	21
Rozier, Jacksonville	320	1361	4.3	12
Johnson B, Denver	212	1261	5.9	15
Anderson G, Tampa Bay	276	1207	4.4	16
Bryant, Baltimore	238	1207	5.1	12
Cribbs, Birmingham	267	1047	3.9	7
Brown R, Arizona	229	1031	4.5	12
Bentley A, Oakland	191	1020	5.3	4
Williams J, Oakland	186	857	4.6	9
Jordan, Portland	165	817	5.0	5

Receiving

	No	Yds	Avg	TD
Johnson, Houston	103	1384	13.4	14
Harris L, Denver	101	1432	14.2	8
Smith J, Birmingham	87	1322	15.2	20
Verdin, Houston	84	1004	12.0	9
Alexis, Jacksonville	83	1118	13.5	5
Lewis, Denver	75	1207	16.1	6
Fitzkee, Baltimore	73	882	12.1	3
Anderson G, Tampa Bay	72	678	9.4	4
Crawford, Memphis	70	1057	15.1	9
Carter A, Oakland	70	1323	18.9	14

Canadian Football League

Final 1984 Standings

Eastern Division

	W	L	T	PF	PA	Pts
Toronto	9	6	1	461	361	19
Hamilton	6	9	1	353	439	13
Montreal	6	9	1	386	404	13
Ottawa	4	12	0	354	507	8

Western Division

	W	L	T	PF	PA	Pts
B.C.	12	3	1	445	281	25
Winnipeg	11	4	1	523	309	23
Edmonton	9	7	0	464	443	18
Saskatchewan	6	9	1	348	479	13
Calgary	6	10	0	314	425	12

East semifinal—Hamilton 17, Montreal 11
West semifinal—Winnipeg 55, Edmonton 20
East final—Hamilton 14, Toronto 13

West final—Winnipeg 31, B.C. 14
Championship (Grey Cup)—Winnipeg 47, Hamilton 17

Canadian Football League (Grey Cup)

Winners of Eastern and Western divisions meet in championship game for Grey Cup (donated by Governor-General Earl Grey in 1909). Canadian football features 3 downs, 110-yard field, and each team can have 12 players on field at one time.

1956	Edmonton Eskimos 50, Montreal Alouettes 27	1971	Calgary Stampeders 14, Toronto Argonauts 11
1957	Hamilton Tiger-Cats 32, Winnipeg Blue Bombers 7	1972	Hamilton Tiger-Cats 13, Saskatchewan Roughriders 10
1958	Winnipeg Blue Bombers 35, Hamilton Tiger-Cats 28	1973	Ottawa Rough Riders 22, Edmonton Eskimos 18
1959	Winnipeg Blue Bombers 21, Hamilton Tiger-Cats 7	1974	Montreal Alouettes 20, Edmonton Eskimos 7
1960	Ottawa Rough Riders 16, Edmonton Eskimos 6	1975	Edmonton Eskimos 9, Montreal Alouettes 8
1961	Winnipeg Blue Bombers 21, Hamilton Tiger-Cats 14	1976	Ottawa Rough Riders 23, Saskatchewan Roughriders 20
1962	Winnipeg Blue Bombers 28, Hamilton Tiger-Cats 27	1977	Montreal Alouettes 41, Edmonton Eskimos 6
1963	Hamilton Tiger-Cats 21, British Columbia Lions 10	1978	Edmonton Eskimos 20, Montreal Alouettes 13
1964	British Columbia Lions 34, Hamilton Tiger-Cats 24	1979	Edmonton Eskimos 17, Montreal Alouettes 9
1965	Hamilton Tiger-Cats 22, Winnipeg Blue Bombers 16	1980	Edmonton Eskimos 48, Hamilton Tiger-Cats 10
1966	Saskatchewan Roughriders 29, Ottawa Rough Riders 14	1981	Edmonton Eskimos 26, Ottawa Rough Riders 23
1967	Hamilton Tiger-Cats 24, Saskatchewan Roughriders 1	1982	Edmonton Eskimos 32, Toronto Argonauts 16
1968	Ottawa Rough Riders 24, Calgary Stampeders 21	1983	Toronto Argonauts 18, B.C. Lions 17
1969	Ottawa Rough Riders 29, Saskatchewan Roughriders 11	1984	Winnipeg Blue Bombers 47, Hamilton Tiger-Cats 17
1970	Montreal Alouettes 23, Calgary Stampeders 10		

1984 CFL Individual Leaders

Passing

	Comp	Pct Comp	Yards	TD
Brock, Hamilton	320	57.0	3966	15
Clements, Winnipeg	279	62.5	3845	29
Dewalt, B.C.	258	59.0	3613	21
Dunigan, Edmonton	220	53.3	3273	21
Paopao, Saskatchewan	260	57.3	3270	12
Barnes, Toronto	231	61.1	3128	18
Watts, Ottawa	189	52.5	3052	21
Gill, Montreal	199	53.0	2673	16
Holloway, Toronto	146	57.4	2231	16
Vavra, Calgary	161	49.6	1901	10

Rushing

	Att	Yds	Avg	TD
Reaves, Winnipeg	304	1733	5.7	14
D. Wilson, Montreal	226	1083	4.8	4
L. Cowan, Edmonton	130	759	5.8	1
Dunigan, Edmonton	89	732	8.2	9
L. Walker, Calgary	139	732	5.3	2
McCray, Ottawa	137	701	5.1	6
Ellis, Saskatchewan	141	690	4.9	8
L. Brown, Toronto	140	594	4.2	10
J.H. White, B.C.	102	523	5.1	3
Gill, Montreal	98	485	4.9	4

Pass-Receiving

	No	Yds	Avg	TD
Ellis, Saskatchewan	91	871	9.6	4
Fernandez, B.C.	89	1486	16.7	17
DiPietro, Hamilton	71	1063	15.0	5
Pearson, Toronto	71	910	12.8	5
Murphy, Winnipeg	70	1220	17.4	12
Greer, Toronto	70	1189	17.0	14
Arakgi, Montreal	67	1078	16.1	10
Poplawski, Winnipeg	67	998	14.9	3
Kelly, Edmonton	66	1310	19.8	18
R. Crawford, Hamilton	66	864	13.1	3

Scoring

	TD	Con	FG	S	Pts
Passaglia, B.C.	0	46	35	16	167
Ilesic, Toronto	0	44	30	25	159
Kennerd, Winnipeg	0	61	26	13	152
Ruoff, Hamilton	0	29	34	14	145
Hay, Calgary	0	25	33	11	135
Sweet, Montreal	0	27	33	5	131
Ridgway, Saskatchewan	0	30	28	13	127
Cutler, Edmonton	0	47	20	16	123
Dorsey, Ottawa	0	37	26	7	122

Football Stadiums

See index for major league baseball stadium seating capacity, and college football stadiums.

Name, location	Capacity	Name, location	Capacity
Alamo Stadium, San Antonio, Tex.	32,000	Liberty Bowl, Memphis, Tenn.	50,180
Anaheim Stadium, Anaheim, Cal.	69,000	Los Angeles Memorial Coliseum.	92,516
Arrowhead Stadium, Kansas City, Mo.	78,067	Louisiana Superdome, New Orleans.	71,647
Astrodome, Houston, Tex.	50,496	Mile High Stadium, Denver, Col.	75,123
Atlanta-Fulton County Stadium.	60,748	Milwaukee County Stadium.	55,958
Baltimore Memorial Stadium	60,714	Mississippi Memorial Stadium, Jackson	61,000
Buffalo War Memorial Stadium.	46,206	Oakland-Alameda County Coliseum.	54,615
Busch Memorial Stadium, St. Louis	51,392	Orange Bowl, Miami, Fla.	75,206
Candlestick Park, San Francisco, Cal.	61,185	Orlando Stadium, Orlando, Fla.	50,000
Cleveland Municipal Stadium.	80,098	Pontiac Silverdome, Mich.	80,638
Cotton Bowl, Dallas, Tex.	72,000	Portland Civic Stadium, Portland, Ore.	32,500
Franklin Field, Philadelphia, Pa.	60,546	Rich Stadium, Buffalo, N.Y.	80,290
Gator Bowl, Jacksonville, Fla.	70,000	Riverfront Stadium, Cincinnati, Oh.	59,754
Giants Stadium, E. Rutherford, N.J.	76,891	Rose Bowl, Pasadena, Cal.	106,721
Hoosier Dome, Indianapolis, Ind.	61,000	San Diego Jack Murphy Stadium, San Diego.	60,100
Hubert H. Humphrey Metrodome, Minneapolis	62,212	Shea Stadium, New York, N.Y.	60,372
John F. Kennedy Stadium, Philadelphia, Pa.	105,000	Soldier Field, Chicago, Ill.	65,790
Robert F. Kennedy Memorial Stadium, Wash., D.C.	55,363	Sugar Bowl, New Orleans, La.	80,982
Kezar Stadium, San Francisco, Cal.	59,636	Sullivan Stadium, Foxboro, Mass.	61,297
Kingdome, Seattle, Wash.	64,752	Tampa Stadium, Tampa, Fla.	74,270
Ladd Memorial Stadium, Mobile, Ala.	40,605	Texas Stadium, Dallas, Tex.	65,101
Lambeau Field, Green Bay, Wis.	56,189	Three Rivers Stadium, Pittsburgh, Pa.	59,000
Legion Field, Birmingham, Ala.	75,412	Veterans Stadium, Philadelphia, Pa.	73,484

Professional Sports Arenas

The seating capacity of sports arenas can vary depending on the event being presented. The figures below are the normal seating capacity for basketball. (*) indicates hockey seating capacity.

Name, location	Capacity	Name, location	Capacity
Arena, The, St. Louis, Mo.	20,000-*17,600	Maple Leaf Gardens, Toronto	*16,382(a)
Arizona Veteran's Memorial Coliseum, Phoenix	14,660	Market Square Arena, Indianapolis	16,825-*15,861
Baltimore Civic Center	13,043-*10,200	McNichols Arena, Denver.	17,171-*16,399
Boston Garden.	14,890-*14,451	Met. Sports Center, Bloomington, Minn.	*15,184
Buffalo Memorial Auditorium	17,900-*16,433(a)	Milwaukee Arena	11,052
Byrne Meadowlands Arena, E. Rutherford, N.J.	20,149-*19,023	Montreal Forum.	*16,074
Capital Centre, Landover, Md.	19,105-*18,130	Nassau Veterans Memorial Coliseum, Uniondale, N.Y.	*15,861
Chicago Stadium.	17,374-*17,263	Northlands Coliseum, Edmonton	*17,300-17,490(a)
Cincinnati Gardens.	11,650-*10,606	Oakland Coliseum Arena	13,335
Cobo Hall, Detroit	11,147	Olympia Stadium, Detroit	*16,673
The Coliseum, Richfield Township, Oh.	19,548	Olympic Saddledome, Calgary, Alta.	*16,520
Convention Center, San Antonio	10,146	The Omni, Atlanta	15,900
Cow Palace, San Francisco	14,500-*12,195	Pacific Coliseum, Vancouver, B.C.	*16,553
Freedom Hall, Louisville, Ky.	16,613	Pittsburgh Civic Arena	*16,033
Greensboro Coliseum	15,500-*13,280	Portland Memorial Coliseum	12,666
Halifax Metro Centre	*9,552	Quebec Coliseum	*15,434
Hartford Civic Center.	*14,800	Reunion Arena, Dallas.	17,007
HemisFair Arena, San Antonio	15,800	Riverfront Coliseum, Cincinnati	*15,794
Jefferson County Coliseum, Birmingham, Ala.	*16,753	Salt Palace, Salt Lake City	12,143-*10,594
Joe Louis Sports Arena, Detroit.	*19,275	San Diego Sports Arena	13,753-*13,039
Kemper Arena, Kansas City	16,778	Seattle Center Coliseum	14,098
Kingdome, Seattle	40,192	Silverdome, Pontiac, Mich.	22,366
Los Angeles Forum	17,505-*16,005	Spectrum, Philadelphia	17,921-*17,191
Los Angeles Sports Arena	15,501	The Summit, Houston	16,016
Louisiana Superdome	47,284	Thomas and Mack Center, Las Vegas	18,500
Madison Square Garden, New York	19,591-*17,500	Winnipeg Arena.	*15,250

(a) includes standees

Major Indoor Soccer League in 1985

Final Standings

Eastern Division

Club	W	L	Pct	GB
Baltimore	32	16	.667	—
Chicago.	28	20	.583	4
Cleveland.	27	21	.563	5
Minnesota.	24	24	.500	8
St. Louis	24	24	.500	8
Pittsburgh.	19	29	.396	13
New York(a)	11	22	.333	—

Western Division

Club	W	L	Pct	GB
San Diego	37	11	.771	—
Las Vegas	30	18	.625	7
Los Angeles	24	24	.500	13
Kansas City.	22	26	.458	15
Witchita	21	26	.447	15½
Tacoma.	17	31	.354	20
Dallas.	12	36	.250	25

(a) Discontinued operations.
Playoff Champion—San Diego Sockers.

World Track and Field Records

As of Sept. 1985

*Indicates pending record; a number of new records await confirmation. The International Amateur Atheletic Federation, the world body of track and field, recognizes only records in metric distances except for the mile.

Men's Records

Running

Event	Record	Holder	Country	Date	Where made
100 meters	9.93 s.	Calvin Smith	U.S.	July 3, 1983	Colorado Springs
200 meters	19.72 s.	Pietro Mennea	Italy	Sept. 17, 1979	Mexico City
400 meters	43.86 s.	Lee Evans	U.S.	Oct. 18, 1968	Mexico City
800 meters	1 m., 41.73 s.	Sebastian Coe	Gr. Britain	June 10, 1981	Florence, Italy
1,000 meters	2 m., 12.18 s.	Sebastian Coe	Gr. Britain	July 11, 1981	Oslo
1,500 meters	*3 m., 29.45 s.	Said Aouita	Morocco	Aug. 23, 1985	W. Berlin
1 mile	*3 m., 46.31 s.	Steve Cram	Gr. Britain	July 27, 1985	Oslo
2,000 meters	*4 m., 51.39 s.	Steve Cram	Gr. Britain	Aug. 4, 1985	Budapest
3,000 meters	7 m., 32.1 s.	Henry Rono	Kenya	June 27, 1978	Oslo
5,000 meters	*13 m., 00.40 s.	Said Aouita	Morocco	July, 1985	Oslo
10,000 meters	27 m., 13.81 s.	Fernando Mamede	Portugal	July 2, 1984	Stockholm
20,000 meters	57 m., 24.2 s.	Jos Hermens	Netherlands	May 1, 1976	Netherlands
25,000 meters	1 hr., 13 m., 55.8 s.	Toshihiko Seko	Japan	Mar. 22, 1981	New Zealand
30,000 meters	1 hr., 29 m., 18.8 s.	Toshihiko Seko	Japan	Mar. 22, 1981	New Zealand
3,000 meter stpl	8 m., 05.4 s.	Henry Rono	Kenya	May 13, 1978	Seattle

Hurdles

110 meters	12.93 s.	Renaldo Nehemiah	U.S.	Aug. 19, 1981	Zurich
400 meters	47.02 s.	Edwin Moses	U.S.	Aug. 31, 1983	Koblenz, W. Ger.

Relay Races

400 mtrs.	37.83 s.	National team (Graddy, Brown, Smith, Lewis)	U.S.	Aug. 11, 1984	Los Angeles
800 mtrs. (4×200)	1 m., 20.26 s.	USC	U.S.	May 27, 1978	Tempe, Ariz.
1,600 mtrs. (4×400)	2 m., 56.1 s.	National team (Matthews, Freeman, James, Evans)	U.S.	Oct. 20, 1968	Mexico City
3,200 mtrs. (4×800)	7 m., 03.89 s.	National team	Gr. Britain	Aug. 30, 1982	London

Field Events

High jump	*7 ft., 10¾ in.	Igor Paklin	USSR	Sept., 1985	Kobe, Japan
Long jump	29 ft., 2½ in.	Bob Beamon	U.S.	Oct. 18, 1968	Mexico City
Triple jump	*58 ft., 11½ in.	Willie Banks	U.S.	June 16, 1985	Indianapolis
Pole vault	*19 ft., 8¼ in.	Sergei Bubka	USSR	July 13, 1985	Paris
16 lb. shot put	*74 ft., 1¾ in.	Ulf Timmermann	E. Germany	Sept. 22, 1985	E. Germany
Discus throw	235 ft., 9 in.	Yuriy Dumchev	USSR	May 25, 1983	Moscow
Javelin throw	343 ft., 10 in.	Uwe Hohn	E. Germany	July 20, 1984	E. Berlin
16 lb. hammer throw	283 ft., 3 in.	Yuri Sedykh	USSR	July 3, 1984	Cork, Ireland
Decathlon	8,646 pts.	Daley Thompson	Gr. Britain	Aug. 8-9, 1984	Los Angeles

Walking

2 hours	17 mi., 881 yds.	Jose Marin	Spain	Apr. 8, 1979	Barcelona
30,000 mtrs.	2 h., 6 min., 54 s.	Ralph Kowalsky	E. Germany	Mar. 28, 1982	Berlin
50,000 mtrs.	3 hr., 41 m., 39 s.	Raul Gonzales	Mexico	May 25, 1978	Norway

Women's Records

Running

Event	Record	Holder	Country	Date	Where made
100 meters	10.76 s.	Evelyn Ashford	U.S.	Aug. 22, 1984	Zurich
			E. Germany	June 10, 1979	E. Berlin
200 meters	21.71 s.	Marita Koch	E. Germany	July 21, 1984	Potsdam
400 meters	47.99 s.	Jarmila Kratochvilova	Czech.	Aug. 10, 1983	Helsinki
800 meters	1 m., 53.28 s.	Jarmila Kratochvilova	Czech.	July 26, 1983	Munich
1,500 meters	3 m., 52.47 s.	Tatyana Kazankina	USSR	Aug. 13, 1980	Zurich
1 mile	*4 m., 16.71 s.	Mary Decker Slaney	U.S.	Aug. 21, 1985	Zurich
2,000 meters	5 m., 28.72 s.	Tatyana Kazankina	USSR	Aug. 5, 1984	Moscow
3,000 meters	8 m., 22.62 s.	Tatyana Kazankina	USSR	Aug. 26, 1984	Leningrad
5,000 meters	*14 m., 48.07 s.	Zola Budd	Gr. Britain	Aug. 26, 1985	London
10,000 meters	*30 m., 59.42 s.	Ingrid Kristiansen	Norway	July, 1985	Oslo
Marathon	*2 h., 21 m., 06 s.	Ingrid Kristiansen	Norway	Apr. 21, 1985	London

Hurdles

110 meters	12.36 s.	Grazyna Rabsztyn	Poland	June 13, 1980	Warsaw
400 meters	*53.56 s.	Sabine Busch	E. Germany	Sept. 22, 1985	E. Germany

Field Events

High jump	6 ft., 9½ in.	Ludmilla Andonova	Bulgaria	July 20, 1984	E. Germany
Shot put	73 ft., 11 in.	Natalya Lisouskaya	USSR	May 26, 1984	USSR
Long jump	*24 ft., 5 in.	Heike Drechsler	E. Germany	Sept. 22, 1985	E. Germany
Discus throw	244 ft., 7 in.	Zdena Silvaha	Czechoslovakia	Aug. 26, 1984	Prague
Javelin	245 ft., 3 in.	Tiina Lillak	Finland	June 13, 1983	Finland
Heptathlon	6,856 pts.	Sabine Paetz	E. Germany	May 5-6, 1984	Potsdam

Relay Races

Event	Record	Holder	Country	Date	Where made
400 mtrs. (4×100)	41.53 s.	National team	E. Germany	July 31, 1983	Berlin
800 mtrs. (4×200)	1 m., 28.15 s.	National team	E. Germany	Aug. 9, 1980	E. Germany
1,600 mtrs. (4×400)	3 m., 15.92 s.	National team	E. Germany	June 3, 1984	E. Germany
3,200 mtrs. (4×800)	7 m., 50.17 s.	National team	USSR.	Aug. 5, 1984	Moscow

U.S. Track and Field Indoor Records
As of Sept., 1985

*Indicates pending record; a number of new records await confirmation. The International Amateur Federation, the world body of track and field, does not recognize world indoor records.

Men's Running

Event	Record	Holder	Date	Where made
50 yards	5.22.	Stanley Floyd	Jan. 22, 1982	Los Angeles
50 meters	5.61.	James Sanford.	Feb. 20, 1981	San Diego
60 yards	6.02.	Carl Lewis	Feb. 5, 1983	Dallas
60 meters	6.54.	Houston McTear.	Jan. 7, 1978	Long Beach, Cal.
100 yards	9.54.	Harvey Glance.	Feb. 16, 1980	Houston
200 meters	20.84.	Mel Lattany.	Feb. 3, 1984	W. Germany
300 yards	29.27.	Terron Wright	Feb. 7, 1981	Bloomington, Ind.
300 meters	33.19.	Elliott Quow	Jan. 23, 1983	Boston
		Daron Council	Feb. 3, 1985	Gainesville, Fla.
400 meters	45.79.	Antonio McKay.	Feb. 11, 1984	Gainesville, Fla.
500 yards	54.4.	Lee Evans	Jan. 8, 30, 1971	Idaho and Maryland
500 meters	*1:01.24	Willie Caldwell	Mar. 9, 1985	Syracuse
600 yards	1:07.6	Marty McGrady	Feb. 27, 1970	New York City
600 meters	1:16.91.	Mark Enyeart.	Jan. 16, 1983	Sherbrooke, Canada
880 meters	*1:46.9	Johnny Gray	Feb. 15, 1985	San Diego
1,000 yards	2:04.7	Don Paige	Feb. 5, 1982	Inglewood, Cal.
1,000 meters	*2:18.88	Don Paige	Feb. 11, 1984	E. Rutherford, N.J.
1,500 meters	3:38.3	Steve Scott.	Feb. 19, 1982	San Diego
One mile.	3:51.8	Steve Scott.	Feb. 15, 1980	Los Angeles
2,000 meters	4:58.6	Steve Scott.	Feb. 7, 1981	Louisville
3,000 meters	7:44.9	Doug Padilla	Feb. 18, 1983	San Diego
		Doug Padilla	Feb. 15, 1985	San Diego
2 miles.	*8:15.3	Doug Padilla	Feb. 15, 1985	San Diego
3 miles.	12:56.6.	Alberto Salazar	Feb. 6, 1981	New York City
5,000 meters	13:20.55	Doug Padilla	Feb. 12, 1982	New York City
50-yd. hurdles.	5.92.	Renaldo Nehemiah	Jan. 29, 1982	Toronto
60-m. hurdles.	6.82.	Renaldo Nehemiah	Jan. 30, 1982	Dallas

Field Events

High jump	*7 ft. 8 1/2 in.	Jim Howard	Feb. 17, 1985	Richfield, Oh.
Pole vault	19 ft. 1/4 in.	Billy Olson	Feb. 4, 1983	Toronto
			Feb. 10, 1984	Inglewood, Cal.
Long jump.	28 ft. 10 1/4 in.	Carl Lewis	Jan. 27, 1984	New York City
Triple jump	57 ft. 1 1/2 in.	Willie Banks	Feb. 19, 1982	San Diego
Shot put	72 ft. 2 3/4 in.	George Woods	Feb. 8, 1974	Inglewood, Cal.

Women's Running

Event	Record	Holder	Date	Where made
50 yards	5.74.	Evelyn Ashford.	Feb. 18, 1983	San Diego
50 meters	6.13.	Jeannette Bolden	Feb. 21, 1981	Edmonton
60 yards	6.54.	Evelyn Ashford.	Feb. 26, 1982	New York City
60 meters	7.18.	Alice Brown.	Mar. 10, 1984	Tokyo
200 meters	23.27.	Chandra Cheeseborough.	Feb. 27, 1981	New York City
220 yards	*22.95	Valerie Brisco-Hooks.	Feb. 22, 1985	New York City
300 meters	*33.82	Angie Thacker	Feb. 23, 1985	Lincoln, Neb.
300 meters	37.50.	Diane Dixon	Feb. 19, 1983	Normal, Ill.
400 meters	*52.63	Valerie Brisco-Hooks	Feb. 9, 1985	E. Rutherford, N.J.
440 yards	*52.20	Diane Dixon	Feb. 22, 1985	New York City
500 yards	*1:02.3	Valerie Brisco-Hooks	Feb. 15, 1985	San Diego
500 meters	*1:09.75	Joetta Clark	Mar. 2, 1985	Gainesville, Fla.
600 yards	1:17.38.	Delisa Walton	Mar. 13, 1982	Cedar Falls, Ia.
600 meters	1:26.56.	Delisa Walton	Mar. 14, 1981	Pocatello, Ida.
800 meters	1:58.9	Mary Decker Slaney	Feb. 22, 1980	San Diego
880 yards	1:59.7	Mary Decker Slaney	Feb. 22, 1980	San Diego
1,000 yards	2:23.8	Mary Decker Slaney	Feb. 3, 1978	Inglewood, Cal.
1,000 meters	*2:39.28	Diana Richburg.	Jan. 13, 1985	Sherbrooke, Que.
1,500 meters	4:00.8	Mary Decker Slaney	Feb. 8, 1980	New York City
One mile.	4:20.5	Mary Decker Slaney	Feb. 19, 1982	San Diego
2,000 meters	5:51.1	Mary Decker Slaney	Feb. 5, 1982	Inglewood, Cal.
3,000 meters	8:47.3	Mary Decker Slaney	Feb. 5, 1982	Inglewood, Cal.
2 miles	9:31.7	Mary Decker Slaney	Jan. 31, 1983	Los Angeles
50-yd. hurdles.	6.37.	Deby La Plante.	Feb. 10, 1978	Toronto
50-m. hurdles.	6.85.	Candy Young.	Jan. 15, 1983	Rosemont, Ill.
60-yd. hurdles.	7.37.	Stephanie Hightower	Feb. 12, 1982	New York City
		Candy Young.	Feb. 12, 1982	New York City
60-m hurdles	7.36.	Stephanie Hightower	Feb. 25, 1983	New York City

Women's Field Events

High Jump.	6 ft. 6 3/4 in.	Colleen Rienstra	Feb. 13, 1982	Ottawa
Shot put	61 ft. 2 1/4 in.	Maren Seidler	Jan. 20, 1978	W. Germany
Long jump.	*22 ft. 3 in.	Carol Lewis	Feb. 2, 1985	Dallas, Tex.

Track and Field Events in 1985

78th Annual Millrose Games

New York, N.Y., Jan. 25, 1985

Men

60-Yd. High Hurdles—Greg Foster, World Class AC. Time—0:06.97.
400 Meters—Michael Paul, Tiger International. Time—0:47.53.
500 Yds.—Ray Armstead, Accusplit Sports. Time—0:56.36.
600 Yds.—Mark Rowe, Accusplit Sports. Time—1:10.94.
800 Meters—Edwin Koech, Atlantic Coast TC. Time—1:53.
1,000 Meters—Sammy Koskei, Kenya. Time—2:18.62.
One Mile—Eamonn Coughlan, NYAC. Time—3:53.82.
5,000 Meters—Doug Padilla, Athletics West. Time—13:38.76.
Long Jump—Carl Lewis, Santa Monica TC. 27 ft. 10¾ in.

Pole Vault—Billy Olson, Pacific Coast Club. 18 ft. 4½ in.
High Jump—Jim Howard, Pacific Coast Club. 7 ft. 8 in.

Women

60 Yds.—Jennifer Innes, Atoms TC. Time—0:06.78.
60-Yd. High Hurdles—Stephanie Hightower, Bud Light Time—0:07.51.
400 Meters—Diane Dixon, Atoms TC. Time—0:52.90.
800 Meters—Joetta Clark, Team Adidas. Time—2:05.61.
One Mile—Mary Decker. Time—4:22.01.
High Jump—Debbie Brill, Canada. 6 ft. 4¼ in.

USA/Mobil Indoor Championships

New York, N.Y., Feb. 22, 1985

Men

60 Yds.—Albert Lawrence, Bud Light. Time—0:06.16.
440 Yds.—Antonio McKay, Ga. Tech. Time—0:47.90.
600 Yds.—Elvis Forde, Atlantic Coast Club. Time—1:09.05.
1,000 Yds.—Edwin Koech, Atlantic Coast Club. Time—2:07.17.
One Mile—Sydney Maree, Athletic Attic. Time—3:54.98.
3 Miles—Doug Padilla, Athletics West. Time—12:57.15.
60-Yd. High Hurdles—Greg Foster, World Class AC. Time—0:06.85.
2-Mile Walk—Jim Heiring, Bud Light. Time—12:07.56.
35-Lb. Weight Throw—Jud Logan, NYAC. 74 ft. 7¼ in.
Shot Put—Scott Lofquist, unattached. 67 ft. 11 in.
Triple Jump—Mike Conley, U. of Arkansas. 57 ft. 1 in.
Long Jump—Mike Conley. 26 ft. 11¾ in.
Pole Vault—Doug Lytle, unattached. 18 ft. 4¾ in.

High Jump—Jim Howard, Pacific Coast Club. 7 ft. 8 in.

Women

60 Yds.—Alice Brown, World Class AC. Time—0:06.56.
220 Yds.—Valerie Brisco, Hooks World Class AC. Time—0:22.95.
440 Yds.—Diane Dixon, Atoms TC. Time—0:52.20.
880 Yds.—Christina Cojocaru, Romania. Time—2:04.15.
One Mile—Doina Melente, Romania. Time—4:37.
2 Miles—Cathy Branta, Wisconsin. Time—9:40.54.
60-Yd. Hurdles—Candy Young, Puma TC. Time— 0:07.57.
One-Mile Walk—Teresa Vaill, Island TC. Time— 6:58.70.
High Jump—Colleen Sommer, Ather TC. 6 ft. 4¾ in.
Long Jump—Carol Lewis, Univ. of Houston. 21 ft. 7½ in.
Shot Put—Bonnie Dasse, Coast Athletic. 60 ft. 6 in.

USA/Mobil Outdoor Championships

Indianapolis, Ind., June 14-15, 1985

Men

100 Meters—Kirk Baptiste, unattached.Time—0:10.11.
200 Meters—Kirk Baptiste. Time—0:20.11.
400 Meters—Mark Rowe, Accusplit. Time—0:44.87.
800 Meters—Johnny Gray, Santa Monica TC. Time—1:44.01.
1,500 Meters—Jim Spivey, Athletics West. Time—3:39.54.
5,000 Meters—Doug Padilla, Athletics West. Time—13:16.42.
10,000 Meters—Bruce Bickford, New Balance TC. Time—28:00.10.
3,000-Meter Steeplechase—Henry Marsh, Athletics West. Time—8:18.35.
110-Meter Hurdles—Roger Kingdom, New Image TC. Time—0:13.37.
400-Meter Hurdles—Andre Phillips, World Class TC. Time—0:47.67.
20-Km. Walk—Tim Lewis, NYAC. Time—1:28:26.46
High Jump—Brian Stanton, Stars & Stripes TC. 7 ft. 6½ in.
Pole Vault—Joe Dial, Athletics West. 18 ft. 9½ in.
Long Jump—Mike Conley, Bud Light Striders. 28 ft.
Triple Jump—Willie Banks, Los Angeles TC. 58 ft. 11½ in.
Discus—John Powell, Bud Light TC. 214 ft. 4 in.
Hammer—Jud Logan, NYAC. 250 ft. 2 in.
Javelin—Tom Petranoff, Athletics West. 286 ft. 1 in.

Women

100 Meters—Merlene Ottey-Page, unattached. Time—0:10.48.
200 Meters—Merlene Ottey-Page.Time—0:21.93.
400 Meters—Lillie Leatherwood, New Balance TC. Time—0:50.64.
800 Meters—Claudette Groenendaal, Athletics West. Time—1:59.48.
1,500 Meters—Diana Richburg, Gazelle Intl. Time—4:04.73.
3,000 Meters—Cathy Branta, Athletics West. Time—8:49.64.
5,000 Meters—Suzanne Girard, unattached. Time—15:47.50.
10,000-Meter Walk—Maryanne Torrellas, Abraxas TC. Time—48:36.16
100-Meter Hurdles—Rhonda Blanford, Los Angeles TC. Time—0:12.85.
400-Meter Hurdles—Judy Brown-King, Athletics West. Time—0:55.10.
High Jump—Louise Ritter, Pacific Coast Club. 6 ft. 3¼ in.
Long Jump—Carol Lewis, Santa Monica TC. 22 ft. 8½ in.
Shot Put—Ramona Pagel, unattached. 60 ft. 4½ in.
Discus—Carol Cady, Bud Light TC. 200 ft. 9 in.
Javelin—Cathy Sulinski, Millbrae Lions. 197 ft. 8 in.

NCAA Outdoor Championships

Austin, Tex. May 30-June 1, 1985

Men

100 Meters—Terry Scott, Tennessee. Time—0:10.02.
400 Meters—Roddie Haley, Arkansas. Time—0:44.70.
1,500 Meters—Abdi Bile Abdi, George Mason. Time—3:41.62.
5,000 Meters—Ed Evestone, BYU. Time—13:56.72.
110-Meter Hurdles—Henry Andrade, SMU. Time—0:13.43.
Javelin—Brian Crouser, Oregon. 281 ft.
Shot Put—John Campbell, La. Tech. 69 ft. 3 3/4 in.
Triple Jump—Mike Conley, Arkansas. 58 ft. 1 3/4 in.
Pole Vault—Joe Dial, Oklahoma St. 18 ft. 6 in.
Discus—Rick Meyer, Houston. 206 ft. 6 in.
High Jump—Thomas Ericksson, Lamar. 7 ft. 7 in.
Men's Champion—Arkansas.

Women

100 Meters—Michelle Finn, Florida St. Time—0:11.04.
400 Meters—Sherri Howard, Cal. St.-Los Angeles. Time—0:50.95.
1,500 Meters—Cathy Branta, Wisconsin. Time—4:12.65.
5,000 Meters—Sabrina Dornhoefer, Missouri. Time—15:42.22.
100-Meter Hurdles—Rhonda Blanford, Nebraska. Time—0:12.70.
High Jump—Katrena Johnson, Arizona. 6 ft. 4 1/4 in.
Triple Jump—Esmeralda Garcia, Florida St. 43 ft. 7 1/2 in.
Long Jump—Carol Lewis, Houston. 22 ft. 1 in.
Shot Put—Regina Cavanaugh, Rice. 56 ft. 7 1/2 in.
Javelin—Iris Gronfeldt, Alabama. 187 ft. 8 in.
Women's Champion—Oregon.

Toronto Star–Maple Leaf Indoor Games

Toronto, Ont., Feb. 1, 1985

Men

50 Yds.—Emmit King, New Balance T.C. **Time—0:05.35.**
50-Yd. Hurdles—Mark McKoy, Toronto. **Time—0:05.95.**
600 Meters—Fred Sowerby, Fons T.C. **Time—1:21.61.**
1,000 Meters—Earl Jones, East Mich. U. **Time—2:23.07.**
One Mile—Eamonn Coghlan, New York A.C. **Time—3:59.05.**
3,000 Meters—Sydney Maree, Athletic Attic. **Time—7:59.73.**

Women

50 Yds.—Diane Dixon, Atoms T.C. **Time—0:06.02.**
50-Yd. Hurdles—Stephanie Hightower, Bud Light T.C. **Time—0:06.50.**
600 Meters—Diane Dixon, Atoms T.C. **Time—1:31.23.**
1,5000 Meters—Brit McRoberts, Valey Royals. **Time—4:18.04.**

National Track & Field Hall of Fame

Indianapolis, Ind.

Jesse Abramson	Harrison Dillard	Bud Houser	Lon Myers	Helen Stephens
Dave Albritton	Ken Doherty	DeHart Hubbard	Parry O'Brien	James Sullivan
Horace Ashenfelter	Bill Easton	Edward Hurt	Al Oerter	Dink Templeton
Weems Baskins	James (Jumbo) Elliott	Wilbur Hutsell	Harold Osborn	John Thomas
James Bausch	Lee Evans	Bruce Jenner	Jesse Owens	Earl Thomson
Bob Beamon	Ray Ewry	Rafer Johnson	Charlie Paddock	Jim Thorpe
Percy Beard	Mae Faggs (Starr)	Hayes Jones	Mel Patton	Eddie Tolan
Dee Boeckman	Dan Ferris	Thomas Jones	Steve Prefontaine	Bill Toomey
Tom Botts	John Flanagan	Payton Jordan	Joie Ray	Forrest Towns
Ralph Boston	Dick Fosbury	John Kelley	Greg Rice	Wyomia Tyus
Bill Bowerman	Bob Giegengack	Abel Kiviat	Bob Richards	LeRoy Walker
Avery Brundage	Fortune Gordien	Alvin Kraenzlein	Betty Robinson (Schwartz)	Stella Walsh
Lee Calhoun	John Griffith	Clyde Littlefield	Ralph Rose	Cornelius Warmerdam
Alice Coachman (Davis)	Archie Hahn	Bob Mathias	Wilma Rudolph	Willye White
Harold Connolly	Brutus Hamilton	Randy Matson	Jim Ryun	Mal Whitfield
Tom Courtney	Glenn Hardin	Mildred McDaniel	Jackson Scholz	Fred Wilt
Dean Cromwell	Ted Haydon	Edith McGuire (DuVall)	Mel Sheppard	Lloyd Winter
Glenn Cunningham	Billy Hayes	Ted Meredith	Dave Sime	John Woodruff
William Curtis	Bob Hayes	Ralph Metcalfe	Robert Simpson	Dave Wottle
Willie Davenport	Ward Haylett	Billy Mills	Tommie Smith	Frank Wykoff
Glenn Davis	Ralph Higgins	Madeline Manning-Mims	Larry Snyder	Joe Yancey
Harold Davis	Harry Hillman	Bobby Morrow	Andy Stanfield	George Young
Mildred (Babe) Didrikson	Jim Hines	Michael Murphy	Les Steers	

Evolution of the World Record for the One-Mile Run

The table below shows how the world record for the one-mile has been lowered in the past 121 years.

Year	Individual, country	Time	Year	Individual, country	Time
1864	Charles Lawes, Britain	4:56	1942	Arne Andersson, Sweden	4:06.2
1865	Richard Webster, Britain	4:36.5	1942	Gunder Haegg, Sweden	4:04.6
1868	William Chinnery, Britain	4:29	1943	Arne Andersson, Sweden	4:02.6
1868	W. C. Gibbs, Britain	4:28.8	1944	Arne Andersson, Sweden	4:01.6
1874	Walter Slade, Britain	4:26	1945	Gunder Haegg, Sweden	4:01.4
1875	Walter Slade, Britain	4:24.5	1954	Roger Bannister, Britain	3:59.4
1880	Walter George, Britain	4:23.2	1954	John Landy, Australia	3:58
1882	Walter George, Britain	4:21.4	1957	Derek Ibbotson, Britain	3:57.2
1882	Walter George, Britain	4:19.4	1958	Herb Elliott, Australia	3:54.5
1884	Walter George, Britain	4:18.4	1962	Peter Snell, New Zealand	3:54.4
1894	Fred Bacon, Scotland	4:18.2	1964	Peter Snell, New Zealand	3:54.1
1895	Fred Bacon, Scotland	4:17	1965	Michel Jazy, France	3:53.6
1895	Thomas Conneff, U.S.	4:15.6	1966	Jim Ryun, U.S.	3:51.3
1911	John Paul Jones, U.S.	4:15.4	1967	Jim Ryun, U.S.	3:51.1
1913	John Paul Jones, U.S.	4:14.6	1975	Filbert Bayi, Tanzania	3:51
1915	Norman Taber, U.S.	4:12.6	1975	John Walker, New Zealand	3:49.4
1923	Paavo Nurmi, Finland	4:10.4	1979	Sebastian Coe, Britain	3:49
1931	Jules Ladoumegue, France	4:09.2	1980	Steve Ovett, Britain	3:48.8
1933	Jack Lovelock, New Zealand	4:07.6	1981	Sebastian Coe, Britain	3:48.53
1934	Glenn Cunningham, U.S.	4:06.8	1981	Steve Ovett, Britain	3:48.40
1937	Sydney Wooderson, Britain	4:06.4	1981	Sebastian Coe, Britain	3:47.33
1942	Gunder Haegg, Sweden	4:06.2	1985	Steve Cram, Britain	3:46.31

Walker Runs 100th Sub-4-Minute Mile

John Walker of New Zealand became the first athlete to run 100 sub-4-minute miles when he finished a mile race in 3 min. 54.57 seconds on Feb. 16, 1985 in Auckland, New Zealand.

American Power Boat Assn. Gold Cup Champions

Year	Boat	Driver	Year	Boat	Driver
1972	Atlas Van Lines	Bill Munsey	1979	Atlas Van Lines	Bill Muncey
1973	Miss Budweiser	Dean Chenoweth	1980	Miss Budweiser	Dean Chenoweth
1974	Pay'N Pak	George Henley	1981	Miss Budweiser	Dean Chenoweth
1975	Pay 'N Pak	George Henley	1982	Atlas Van Lines	Chip Hanauer
1976	Miss U.S.	Tom D'Eath	1983	Atlas Van Lines	Chip Hanauer
1977	Atlas Van Lines	Bill Muncey	1984	Atlas Van Lines	Chip Hanauer
1978	Atlas Van Lines	Bill Muncey	1985	Miller American	Chip Hanauer

Notable Sports Personalities

Henry Aaron, b. 1934: Milwaukee-Atlanta outfielder hit record 755 home runs; led NL 4 times.

Kareem Abdul-Jabbar, b. 1947: Milwaukee, L.A. Lakers center; MVP 6 times; leading scorer twice; playoff MVP, 1971, 1985.

Grover Cleveland Alexander, (1887-1950): pitcher won 374 NL games; pitched 16 shutouts, 1916.

Muhammad Ali, b. 1942: 3-time heavyweight champion.

Ken Anderson, b. 1949: Cinn. Bengals quarterback led AFC in passing 4 times.

Mario Andretti, b. 1940: U.S. Auto Club national champ 3 times: won Indy 500, 1969; Grand Prix champ, 1978.

Eddie Arcaro, b. 1916: jockey rode 4,779 winners including the Kentucky Derby 5 times; the Preakness and Belmont Stakes 6 times each.

Henry Armstrong, b. 1912: boxer held feather-, welter-, light-weight titles simultaneously, 1937-38.

Arthur Ashe, b. 1943: U.S. singles champ, 1968, Wimbledon champ, 1975.

Red Auerbach, b. 1917: coached Boston Celtics to 9 NBA championships.

Ernie Banks, b. 1931: Chicago Cubs slugger hit 512 NL homers; twice MVP.

Roger Bannister, b. 1929: Briton ran first sub 4-minute mile, May 6, 1954.

Rick Barry, b. 1944: NBA scoring leader, 1967; ABA, 1969.

Sammy Baugh, b. 1914: Washington Redskins quarterback held numerous records upon retirement after 16 pro seasons.

Elgin Baylor, b. 1934: L.A. Lakers forward; 1st team all-star 10 times.

Bob Beamon, b. 1946: long jumper won 1968 Olympic gold medal with record 29 ft. 2½ in.

Jean Beliveau, b. 1931: Montreal Canadiens center scored 507 goals; twice MVP.

Johnny Bench, b. 1947: Cincinnati Reds catcher; MVP twice; led league in home runs twice, RBIs 3 times.

Patty Berg, b. 1918: won over 80 golf tournaments; AP Woman Athlete-of-the-Year 3 times.

Yogi Berra, b. 1925: N.Y. Yankees catcher; MVP 3 times; played in 14 World Series.

Raymond Berry, b. 1933: Baltimore Colts receiver caught 631 passes.

Larry Bird, b. 1956: Boston Celtics forward; chosen MVP, play-off MVP, 1984.

George Blanda, b. 1927: quarterback, kicker; 26 years as active player, scoring record 2,002 points.

Wade Boggs, b. 1958: AL Batting champ, 1983, 1985.

Bjorn Borg, b. 1956: led Sweden to first Davis Cup, 1975; Wimbledon champion, 5 times.

Julius Boros, b. 1920: won U.S. Open, 1952, 1963; PGA champ, 1968.

Mike Bossy, b.1957; N.Y. Islanders right wing scored over 50 goals 8 times.

Jack Brabham, b. 1926: Grand Prix champ 3 times.

Terry Bradshaw, b. 1948; Pittsburgh Steelers quarterback led team to 4 Super Bowl titles.

George Brett, b. 1953: Kansas City Royals 3d baseman led AL in batting, 1976, 1980; MVP, 1980.

Lou Brock, b. 1939: St. Louis Cardinals outfielder stole record 118 bases, 1974; record 937 career; led NL 8 times.

Jimmy Brown, b. 1936: Cleveland Browns fullback ran for 12,312 career yards; MVP 3 times.

Paul "Bear" Bryant, (1913-1983), college football coach with record 323 victories.

Don Budge, b. 1915: won numerous amateur and pro tennis titles, "grand slam," 1938.

Maria Bueno, b. 1939: U.S. singles champ 4 times; Wimbledon champ 3 times.

Dick Butkus, b. 1942: Chicago Bears linebacker twice chosen best NFL defensive player.

Dick Button, b. 1929: figure skater won 1948, 1952 Olympic gold medals; world titlist, 1948-52.

Walter Camp, (1859-1925): Yale football player, coach, athletic director; established many rules; promoted All-America designations.

Roy Campanella, b. 1921: Brooklyn Dodgers catcher; MVP 3 times.

Earl Campbell, b. 1955: NFL running back; NFL MVP 1978-1980.

Rod Carew, b. 1945: AL infielder won 7 batting titles; MVP, 1977.

Steve Carlton, b. 1944: NL pitcher won 20 games 5 times, Cy Young award 4 times.

Billy Casper, b. 1931: PGA Player-of-the-Year 3 times; U.S. Open champ twice.

Wilt Chamberlain, b. 1936: center scored NBA career record 31,419 points; MVP 4 times.

Bobby Clarke, b. 1949: Philadelphia Flyers center led team to 2 Stanley Cup championships; MVP 3 times.

Roberto Clemente, (1934-1972): Pittsburgh Pirates outfielder won 4 batting titles; MVP, 1966.

Ty Cobb, (1886-1961): Detroit Tigers outfielder had record .367 lifetime batting average, 12 batting titles.

Sebastian Coe, b. 1956: Briton won Olympic 1,500-meter run, 1980, 1984.

Nadia Comaneci, b. 1961: Romanian gymnast won 3 gold medals, achieved 7 perfect scores, 1976 Olympics.

Maureen Connolly, (1934-1969): won tennis "grand slam," 1953; AP Woman-Athlete-of-the-Year 3 times.

Jimmy Connors, b. 1952: U.S. singles champ 5 times; Wimbledon champ twice.

James J. Corbett, (1866-1933): heavyweight champion, 1892-97; credited with being the first "scientific" boxer.

Margaret Smith Court, b. 1942: Australian won U.S. singles championship 5 times; Wimbledon champ 3 times.

Bob Cousy, b. 1928: Boston Celtics guard led team to 6 NBA championships; MVP, 1957.

Dizzy Dean, (1911-1974): colorful pitcher for St. Louis Cardinals "Gashouse Gang" in the 30s; MVP, 1934.

Jack Dempsey, (1895-1983); heavyweight champion, 1919-26.

Joe DiMaggio, b. 1914: N.Y. Yankees outfielder hit safely in record 56 consecutive games, 1941; MVP 3 times.

Leo Durocher, b. 1906: colorful manager of Dodgers, Giants, and Cubs; won 3 NL pennants.

Gertrude Ederle, b. 1906: first woman to swim English Channel, broke existing men's record, 1926.

Julius Erving, b. 1950: MVP and leading scorer in ABA 3 times; NBA MVP, 1981.

Phil Esposito, b. 1942: NHL scoring leader 5 times.

Chris Evert Lloyd, b. 1954: U.S. singles champ 6 times, Wimbledon champ 3 times.

Ray Ewry, (1873-1937): track and field star won 8 gold medals, 1900, 1904, and 1908 Olympics.

Juan Fangio, b. 1911: Argentine World Grand Prix champion 5 times.

Bob Feller, b. 1918: Cleveland Indians pitcher won 266 games; pitched 3 no-hitters, 12 one-hitters.

Peggy Fleming, b. 1948: world figure skating champion, 1966-68; gold medalist 1968 Olympics.

Whitey Ford, b. 1928: N.Y. Yankees pitcher won record 10 World Series games.

Dick Fosbury, b. 1947: high jumper won 1968 Olympic gold medal; developed the "Fosbury Flop."

Jimmy Foxx, (1907-1967): Red Sox, Athletics slugger; MVP 3 times; triple crown, 1933.

A.J. Foyt, b. 1935: won Indy 500 4 times; U.S. Auto Club champ 6 times.

Dawn Fraser, b. 1937: Australian swimmer won Olympics 100-meter freestyle 3 times.

Joe Frazier, b. 1944: heavyweight champion, 1970-73.

Lou Gehrig, (1903-1941): N.Y. Yankees 1st baseman played record 2,130 consecutive games, MVP, 1936.

George Gervin, b. 1952: leading NBA scorer, 1978-80, 1982.

Althea Gibson, b. 1927: twice U.S. and Wimbledon singles champ.

Bob Gibson, b. 1935: St. Louis Cardinals pitcher won Cy Young award twice; struck out 3,117 batters.

Frank Gifford, b. 1930: N.Y. Giants back; MVP 1956.

Dwight Gooden, b. 1964: N.Y. Mets pitcher was NL Rookie of Year, 1984; youngest 20-game winner.

Otto Graham, b. 1921: Cleveland Browns quarterback; all-pro 4 times.

Red Grange, b 1903: All-America at Univ. of Illinois; played for Chicago Bears, 1925-35.

Joe Greene, b. 1946: Pittsburgh Steelers lineman; twice NFL outstanding defensive player.

Wayne Gretzky, b. 1961: Edmonton Oilers center scored record 92 goals, 212 pts., 1982; MVP, 1980-85.

Lefty Grove, (1900-1975): pitcher won 300 AL games; 20-game winner 8 times.

Walter Hagen, (1892-1969): won PGA championship 5 times. British Open 4 times.

George Halas, (1895-1983); founder-coach of Chicago Bears; won 5 NFL championships.

Bill Hartack, b. 1932: jockey rode 5 Kentucky Derby winners.

Doug Harvey, b. 1930: Montreal Canadiens defenseman; Norris Trophy 7 times.

Bill Haughton, b. 1923: harness racing driver won Little Brown Jug 4 times, Hambletonian 4 times.

John Havlicek, b. 1940: Boston Celtics forward scored over 26,000 NBA points.

Eric Heiden, b. 1958: speed skater won 5 1980 Olympic gold medals.

Carol Heiss, b. 1940: world champion figure skater 5 consecutive years, 1956-60; won 1960 Olympic gold medal.

Rickey Henderson, b. 1958; AL outfielder stole record 130 bases, 1982.

Sonja Henie, (1912-1969): world champion figure skater, 1927-36; Olympic gold medalist, 1928, 1932, 1936.

Ben Hogan, b. 1912: won 4 U.S. Open championships, 2 PGA, 2 Masters.

Willie Hoppe, (1887-1959): won some 50 world billiard titles.

Larry Holmes, b. 1949: WBC Heavyweight Champ 1978-84.

Rogers Hornsby, (1896-1963): NL 2d baseman batted record .424 in 1924; twice won triple crown; batting leader, 1920-25.

Paul Hornung, b. 1935: Green Bay Packers runner-placekicker scored record 176 points, 1960.

Gordie Howe, b. 1928: hockey forward holds NHL career records in goals, assists, and points; NHL MVP 6 times.

Carl Hubbell, b. 1903: N.Y. Giants pitcher; 20-game winner 5 consecutive years, 1933-37.

Bobby Hull, b. 1939: NHL all-star 10 times.

Catfish Hunter, b 1946: pitched perfect game, 1968; 20-game winner 5 times.

Don Hutson, b. 1913: Green Bay Packers receiver caught NFL record 99 touchdown passes.

Reggie Jackson, b. 1946: slugger led AL in home runs 4 times; MVP, 1973; hit 5 World Series home runs, 1977.

Bruce Jenner, b. 1949: decathlon gold medalist, 1976.

Jack Johnson, (1878-1946): heavyweight champion, 1910-15.

Magic Johnson, b. 1959: NBA playoff MVP 1980, 1982.

Rafer Johnson, b. 1935: decathlon gold medalist, 1960.

Walter Johnson, (1887-1946): Washington Senators pitcher won 414 games.

Bobby Jones, (1902-1971): won "grand slam of golf" 1930; U.S. Amateur champ 5 times, U.S. Open champ 4 times.

Deacon Jones, b. 1938: L.A. Rams lineman; twice NFL outstanding defensive player.

Sonny Jurgensen, b. 1934: quarterback named all-pro 5 times; completed record 288 passes, 1967.

Duke Kahanamoku, (1890-1968): swimmer won 1912, 1920 Olympic gold medals in 100-meter freestyle.

Harmon Killebrew, b. 1936: Minnesota Twins slugger led AL in home runs 6 times.

Jean Claude Killy, b. 1943: French skier won 3 1968 Olympic gold medals.

Ralph Kiner, b. 1922: Pittsburgh Pirates slugger led NL in home runs 7 consecutive years, 1946-52.

Billie Jean King, b. 1943: U.S. singles champ 4 times; Wimbledon champ 6 times.

Olga Korbut, b. 1956: Soviet gymnast won 3 1972 Olympic gold medals.

Sandy Koufax, b. 1935: Dodgers pitcher won Cy Young award 3 times; lowest ERA in NL, 1962-66; pitched 4 no-hitters, one a perfect game.

Guy Lafleur, b. 1951: Montreal Canadiens forward led NHL in scoring 3 times; MVP, 1977, 1978.

Tom Landry, b. 1924: Dallas Cowboys head coach since 1960.

Rod Laver, b. 1938: Australian won tennis "grand slam," 1962, 1969; Wimbledon champ 4 times.

Sugar Ray Leonard, b. 1956: WBC welterweight champ, 1979-82.

Carl Lewis, b. 1961: track and field star won 4 1984 Olympic gold medals.

Vince Lombardi, (1913-1970): Green Bay Packers coach led, team to 5 NFL championships and 2 Super Bowl victories.

Joe Louis, (1914-1981): 1914: heavyweight champion, 1937-49.

Sid Luckman, b. 1916: Chicago Bears quarterback led team to 4 NFL championships; MVP, 1943.

Connie Mack, (1862-1956): Philadelphia Athletics manager, 1901-50; won 9 pennants, 5 championships.

Bill Madlock, b. 1951: NL batting leader 4 times.

Moses Malone, b. 1955: NBA center was MVP 1979, 1982, 1983.

Mickey Mantle, b. 1931: N.Y. Yankees outfielder; triple crown, 1956; 18 World Series home runs.

Alice Marble, b. 1913: U.S. singles champ 4 times.

Rocky Marciano, (1923-1969): heavyweight champion, 1952-56; retired undefeated.

Roger Maris, b. 1934: N.Y. Yankees outfielder hit record 61 home runs, 1961; MVP, 1960 and 1961.

Billy Martin, b. 1928: baseball manager led N.Y. Yankees to World Series title, 1977.

Eddie Mathews, b. 1931: Milwaukee-Atlanta 3d baseman hit 512 career home runs.

Christy Mathewson, (1880-1925): N.Y. Giants pitcher won 373 games.

Bob Mathias, b. 1930: decathlon gold medalist, 1948, 1952.

Willie Mays, b. 1931: N.Y.-S.F. Giants center fielder hit 660 home runs; twice MVP.

John McEnroe, b. 1959: U.S. singles champ, 1979-81, 1984; Wimbledon champ, 1981, 1983-84.

John McGraw, (1873-1934): N.Y. Giants manager led team to 10 pennants, 3 championships.

Debbie Meyer, b. 1952: swimmer won 200-, 400-, and 800- meter freestyle events, 1968 Olympics.

George Mikan, b. 1924: Minneapolis Lakers center selected in a 1950 AP poll as the greatest basketball player of the first half of the 20th century.

Stan Mikita, b. 1940: Chicago Black Hawks center led NHL in scoring 4 times; MVP twice.

Joe Montana, b. 1956: QB led 49ers to Super Bowl championships, 1982, 1985.

Archie Moore, b. 1913: world light-heavyweight champion, 1952-62.

Howie Morenz, (1902-1937): Montreal Canadiens forward chosen in a 1950 Canadian press poll as the outstanding hockey player of the first half of the 20th century.

Joe Morgan, b. 1943: National League MVP, 1975, 1976.

Thurman Munson, (1947-1979): N.Y. Yankees catcher; MVP, 1976.

Dale Murphy, b. 1956: Atlanta Braves outfielder chosen NL MVP 1982, 1983.

Stan Musial, b. 1920: St. Louis Cardinals star won 7 NL batting titles; MVP 3 times; NL record 3,630 hits.

Bronko Nagurski, b. 1908: Chicago Bears fullback and tackle; gained over 4,000 yds. rushing.

Joe Namath, b. 1943: quarterback led N.Y. Jets to 1969 Super Bowl title.

Martina Navratilova, b. 1956: Wimbledon champ 4 times, U.S. champ 1983, 1984.

Byron Nelson, b. 1912: won 11 consecutive golf tournaments in 1945; twice Masters and PGA titlist.

Ernie Nevers, (1903-1976): Stanford star selected the best college fullback to play between 1919-1969.

John Newcombe, b. 1943: Australian twice U.S. singles champ; Wimbledon titlist 3 times.

Jack Nicklaus, b. 1940: PGA Player-of-the-Year, 1967, 1972; leading money winner 8 times.

Chuck Noll, b. 1931: Pittsburgh Steelers coach led team to 4 Super Bowl titles.

Paavo Nurmi, (1897-1973): Finnish distance runner won 6 Olympic gold medals, 1920, 1924, 1928.

Al Oerter, b. 1936: discus thrower won gold medal at 4 consecutive Olympics, 1956-68.

Bobby Orr, b. 1948: Boston Bruins defenseman; Norris Trophy 8 times; led NHL in scoring twice, assists 5 times.

Mel Ott, (1909-1958): N.Y. Giants outfielder hit 511 home runs; led NL 6 times.

Jesse Owens, (1913-1980): track and field star won 4 1936 Olympic gold medals.

Satchel Paige, (1906-1982): pitcher starred in Negro leagues, 1924-48; entered major leagues at age 42.

Arnold Palmer, b. 1929: golf's first $1 million winner; won 4 Masters, 2 British Opens.

Jim Palmer, b. 1945: Baltimore Orioles pitcher; Cy Young award 3 times; 20-game winner 7 times.

Floyd Patterson, b. 1935: twice heavyweight champion.

Walter Payton, 1954: Chicago Bears running back has most rushing yards in NFL history; leading NFC rusher, 1976-80.

Pele, b. 1940: Brazilian soccer star scored 1,281 goals during 22-year career.

Bob Pettit, b. 1932: first NBA player to score 20,000 points; twice NBA scoring leader.

Richard Petty, b. 1937: NASCAR national champ 6 times; 7-times Daytona 500 winner.

Laffit Pincay Jr., b. 1946: leading money-winning jockey, 1970-74, 1979.

Jacques Plante, b. 1929: goalie, 7 Vezina trophies; first goalie to wear a mask in a game.

Gary Player, b. 1935: South African won the Masters, U.S. Open, PGA, and twice the British Open.

Annemarie Proell Moser, b. 1953: Austrian skier won the World Cup championship 6 times.

Willis Reed, b. 1942: N.Y. Knicks center; MVP, 1970; playoff MVP, 1970, 1973.

Jim Rice, b. 1953: Boston Red Sox outfielder led AL in home runs, 1977-78, 1983; MVP 1978.

Maurice Richard, b. 1921: Montreal Canadiens forward scored 544 regular season goals, 82 playoff goals.

Branch Rickey, (1881-1965): executive instrumental in breaking baseball's color barrier, 1947; initiated farm system, 1919.

Oscar Robertson, b. 1938: guard averaged career 25.7 points per game; record 9,887 career assist; MVP, 1964.

Brooks Robinson, b. 1937: Baltimore Orioles 3d baseman played in 4 World Series; MVP, 1964.

Frank Robinson, b. 1935: slugger MVP in both NL and AL; triple crown winner, 1966; first black manager in majors.

Jackie Robinson, (1919-1972): broke baseball's color barrier with Brooklyn Dodgers, 1947; MVP, 1949.

Larry Robinson, b. 1951: Montreal Canadiens defenseman won Norris trophy, 1977, 1980.

Sugar Ray Robinson, b. 1920: middleweight champion 5 times, welterweight champion.

Knute Rockne, (1888-1931): Notre Dame football coach, 1918-31; revolutionized game by stressing forward pass.

Pete Rose, b. 1942: won 3 NL batting titles; hit safely in 44 consecutive games, 1978; set record for most major league hits, 1985.

Wilma Rudolph, b. 1940: sprinter won 3 1960 Olympic gold medals.

Bill Russell, b. 1934: Boston Celtics center led team to 11 NBA titles; MVP 5 times; first black coach of major pro sports team.

Babe Ruth, (1895-1948): N.Y. Yankees outfielder hit 60 home runs, 1927; 714 lifetime; led AL 11 times.

Johnny Rutherford, b. 1938: auto racer won Indy 500 3 times.

Nolan Ryan, b. 1947: pitcher struck out record 383 batters, 1973; pitched record 5 no-hitters.

Gene Sarazen, b. 1902: won PGA championship 3 times, U.S. Open twice; developer of sand wedge.

Gale Sayers, b. 1943: Chicago Bears back twice led NFC in rushing.

Mike Schmidt, b. 1949: Phillies 3d baseman led NL in home runs, 1974-76, 1980-81, 1983-84; NL MVP, 1980, 1981.

Tom Seaver, b. 1944: pitcher won NL Cy Young award 3 times, won 300th major league game, 1985.

Willie Shoemaker, b. 1931: jockey rode 3 Kentucky Derby and 5 Belmont Stakes winners; leading career money winner.

Eddie Shore, b. 1902: Boston Bruins defenseman; MVP 4 times, first-team all-star 7 times.

Al Simmons, (1902-1956): AL outfielder had lifetime .334 batting average.

O.J. Simpson, b. 1947: running back rushed for 2,003 yds., 1973; AFC leading rusher 4 times.

George Sisler, (1893-1973): St. Louis Browns 1st baseman had record 257 hits, 1920; batted .340 lifetime.

Sam Snead, b. 1912: PGA and Masters champ 3 times each.

Warren Spahn, b. 1921: pitcher won 363 NL games; 20-game winner 13 times; Cy Young award, 1957.

Tris Speaker, (1885-1958): AL outfielder batted .344 over 22 seasons; hit record 793 career doubles.

Mark Spitz, b. 1950: swimmer won 7 1972 Olympic gold medals.

Amos Alonzo Stagg, (1862-1965): coached Univ. of Chicago football team for 41 years, including 5 undefeated seasons; introduced huddle, man-in-motion, and end-around play.

Willie Stargell, b. 1941: Pittsburgh Pirate slugger chosen NL, World Series MVP, 1979.

Bart Starr, b. 1934: Green Bay Packers quarterback led team to 5 NFL titles and 2 Super Bowl victories.

Roger Staubach, b. 1942: Dallas Cowboys quarterback; leading NFC passer 5 times.

Casey Stengel, (1890-1975): managed Yankees to 10 pennants, 7 championships, 1949-60.

Jackie Stewart, b. 1939: Scot auto racer retired with 27 Grand Prix victories.

John L. Sullivan, (1858-1918): last bareknuckle heavyweight champion, 1882-1892.

Fran Tarkenton, b. 1940: quarterback holds career passing records for touchdowns, completions, yardage.

Gustave Thoeni, b. 1951: Italian 4-time world alpine ski champ.

Jim Thorpe, (1888-1953): football All-America, 1911, 1912; won pentathlon and decathlon, 1912 Olympics.

Bill Tilden, (1893-1953): U.S. singles champ 7 times; played on 11 Davis Cup teams.

Y.A. Tittle, b. 1926: N.Y. Giants quarterback; MVP, 1961, 1963.

Lee Trevino, b. 1939: won the U.S. and British Open championships twice.

Bryan Trottier, b. 1956: N.Y. Islanders center led team to 4 consecutive Stanley Cup championships, 1980-83.

Gene Tunney, (1897-1978): heavyweight champion, 1926-28.

Wyomia Tyus, b. 1945: sprinter won 1964, 1968 Olympic 100-meter dash.

Johnny Unitas, b. 1933: Baltimore Colts quarterback passed for over 40,000 yds.; MVP, 1957, 1967.

Al Unser, b. 1939: Indy 500 winner, 3 times.

Bobby Unser, b. 1934: Indy 500 winner, 1968, 1981, twice U.S. Auto Club national champ.

Fernando Valenzuela, b. 1960: L.A. Dodgers pitcher won Cy Young award, 1981.

Norm Van Brocklin, b. (1926-1983): quarterback passed for game record 554 yds., 1951; MVP, 1960.

Honus Wagner, (1874-1955): Pittsburgh Pirates shortstop won 8 NL batting titles.

Bill Walton, b. 1952: led Portland Trail Blazers to NBA championship, 1977; MVP, 1978.

Tom Watson, b. 1949: golfer won British Open 5 times.

Johnny Weissmuller, (1903-1984): swimmer won 52 national championships, 5 Olympic gold medals; set 67 world records.

Jerry West, b. 1938: L.A. Lakers guard had career average 27 points per game; first team all-star 10 times.

Kathy Whitworth, b. 1939: women's golf leading money winner 8 times; first woman to earn over $300,000.

Ted Williams, b. 1918: Boston Red Sox outfielder won 6 batting titles; last major leaguer to hit over .400: .406 in 1941: .344 lifetime batting average.

Helen Wills, b. 1906: winner of 7 U.S., 8 British, 4 French women's singles titles.

John Wooden, b. 1910: coached UCLA basketball team to 10 national championships.

Mickey Wright, b. 1935: won LPGA championship 4 times, Vare Trophy 5 times; twice AP Woman-Athlete-of-the-Year.

Carl Yastrzemski, b. 1939: Boston Red Sox slugger won 3 batting titles, triple crown, 1967.

Cy Young, (1867-1955): pitcher won record 511 major league games.

Babe Didrikson Zaharias, (1914-1956): track star won 2 1932 Olympic gold medals; won numerous golf tournaments.

Polo Records

	U.S. Open			Silver Cup
1977	Retama 11, Wilson Ranch 7.		1977	Boca Raton 6, Houston 5.
1978	Abercrombie & Kent 7, Tulsa 6.		1978	Wilson Ranch 7, Ft. Lauderdale 6.
1979	Retama 6, Huisache 5.		1979	Retama 7, Willow Bend 6.
1980	Southern Hills 9, Willow Bend 6.		1980	Retama 9, Houston 8.
1981	Rolex A & K 10, Retama 9.		1981	Retama 10, Thunder 8.
1982	Retama 11, Tulsa 6.		1982	Rio Grande 10, Valdina Farms 9.
1983	Ft. Lauderdale 8; Retama 5.		1983	Tulsa 9, San Antonio 7.
1984	Retama 12, Ft. Lauderdale 9.		1984	Retama 9, Carter Ranch 7.

The World Cup

The World Cup, emblematic of International soccer supremacy, was won by Italy on July 11, 1982, with a 3-1 victory over W. Germany. It was the 3d time Italy has won the event. Colombia is scheduled to host the 1986 tournament. Winners and sites of previous World Cup play follow:

Year	Winner	Site	Year	Winner	Site
1930	Uruguay	Uruguay	1962	Brazil	Chile
1934	Italy	Italy	1966	England	England
1938	Italy	France	1970	Brazil	Mexico City
1950	Uruguay	Brazil	1974	W. Germany	W. Germany
1954	W. Germany	Switzerland	1978	Argentina	Argentina
1958	Brazil	Sweden	1982	Italy	Spain

North American Soccer League Champions

Year	Champion	Year	Champion	Year	Champion	Year	Champion
1967	Oakland Clippers (NPSL)	1971	Dallas Tornado	1976	Toronto Metros	1981	Chicago Sting
1967	Los Angeles Wolves (USA)	1972	New York Cosmos	1977	New York Cosmos	1982	New York Cosmos
1968	Atlanta Chiefs	1973	Philadelphia Atoms	1978	New York Cosmos	1983	Tulsa Roughnecks
1969	Kansas City Spurs	1974	Los Angeles Aztecs	1979	Vancouver Whitecaps	1984	Chicago Sting
1970	Rochester Lancers	1975	Tampa Bay Rowdies	1980	New York Cosmos	1985	season suspended

World Swimming Records

As of Sept., 1985

Men's Records

Freestyle

Distance	Time	Holder	Country	Where made	Date
100 Meters	0:49.24	Matt Biondi	U.S.	Mission Viejo, Cal.	Aug. 7, 1985
200 Meters	1:47.44	Michael Gross	W. Germany	Munich	July 30, 1984
400 Meters	3:47.80	Michael Gross	W. Germany	W. Germany	June 6, 1985
800 Meters	7:52.33	Vladimir Salnikov	USSR	Los Angeles	July 14, 1983
1,500 Meters	14:54.76	Vladimir Salnikov	USSR	Moscow	Feb. 22, 1983

Breaststroke

| 100 Meters | 1:01.65 | Steve Lundquist | U.S. | Los Angeles | July 9, 1984 |
| 200 Meters | 2:13.34 | Victor Davis | Canada | Los Angeles | Aug., 1984 |

Butterfly

| 100 Meters | 0:53.08 | Michael Gross | W. Germany | Los Angeles | Aug., 1984 |
| 200 Meters | 1:56.65 | Michael Gross | W. Germany | Bulgaria | Aug., 1985 |

Backstroke

| 100 Meters | 0:55.19 | Rick Carey | U.S. | Caracas | Aug. 21, 1983 |
| 200 Meters | 1:58.14 | Igor Polyanksi | USSR | E. Germany | Mar., 1985 |

Individual Medley

| 200 Meters | 2:01.42 | Alex Baumann | Canada | Los Angeles | Aug. 4, 1984 |
| 400 Meters | 4:17.41 | Alex Baumann | Canada | Los Angeles | July 30, 1984 |

Freestyle Relays

| 400 M. (4×100) | 3:19.03 | Cavanaugh, Heath, Biondi, Gaines | U.S. | Los Angeles | Aug. 2, 1984 |
| 800 M. (4×200) | 7:15.69 | Heath, Larson, Float, Hayes | U.S. | Los Angeles | Aug. 4, 1984 |

Medley Relays

| 400 M. (4×100) | 3:38.28 | Carey, Moffet, Morales, Biondi | U.S. | Tokyo | Aug. 18, 1985 |

Women's Records

Freestyle

100 Meters	0:54.79	Barbara Krause	E. Germany	Moscow	July, 1980
200 Meters	1:57.75	Kristin Otto	E. Germany	Magedeburg, E. Ger.	May 23, 1984
400 Meters	4:06.28	Tracey Wickham	Australia	W. Berlin	Aug. 24, 1978
800 Meters	8:24.62	Tracey Wickham	Australia	Edmonton, Canada	Aug. 5, 1978
1,500 Meters	16:04.49	Kim Linehan	U.S.	Ft. Lauderdale, Fla.	Aug. 19, 1979

Breaststroke

| 100 Meters | 1:08.29 | Sylvia Gerasch | E. Germany | Moscow | Aug. 23, 1984 |
| 200 Meters | 2:28.33 | Silke Hoerner | E. Germany | Leipzig | June 5, 1985 |

Butterfly

| 100 Meters | 0:57.93 | Mary T. Meagher | U.S. | Brown Deer, Wis. | Aug. 16, 1981 |
| 200 Meters | 2:05.96 | Mary T. Meagher | U.S. | Brown Deer, Wis. | Aug. 13, 1981 |

Backstroke

| 100 Meters | 1:00.59 | Ina Kleber | E. Germany | Moscow | Aug. 24, 1984 |
| 200 Meters | 2:09.91 | Cornelia Sirch | E. Germany | Ecuador | Aug. 7, 1982 |

Individual Medley

| 200 Meters | 2:10.60 | Petra Schneider | E. Germany | Gainesville, Fla. | Aug. 1, 1982 |
| 400 Meters | 4:36.10 | Petra Schneider | E. Germany | Ecuador | Aug. 1, 1982 |

Freestyle Relays

| 400 M. (4×100) | 3:42.41 | National Team (Otto, Konig, Friedrich, Meineke) | E. Germany | Moscow | Aug. 21, 1984 |

Medley Relays

| 400 M. (4×100) | 4:03.69 | National Team (Kleber, Gerasch, Geissler, Meineke) | E. Germany | Moscow | Aug. 24, 1984 |

U.S. Long Course Swimming Champions in 1985

Mission Miejo, Cal., Aug. 5-9, 1985

Men

50-Meter Freestyle—Tom Jager, Parkway. Time—0:22.63.
100-Meter Freestyle—Matt Biondi, Golden Bear. Time—0:48.95.
200-Meter Freestyle—Matt Biondi. Time—1:47.89.
400-Meter Freestyle—Matt Cetlinski, Holmes Lumber. Time—3:53.26.
800-Meter Freestyle—Dan Jorgensen, Mission Viejo. Time—7:58.71.
1,500-Meter Freestyle—Mike O'Brien, Mission Viejo. Time—15:23.34.
100-Meter Backstroke—Rick Carey, Badger. Time—0:55.94.
200-Meter Backstroke—Rick Carey. Time—2:01.64.
100-Meter Breaststroke—John Moffet, USC. Time—1:03.17.
200-Meter Breaststroke—John Moffet. Time—2:17.41.
100-Meter Butterfly—Pablo Morales, Concord Pleasant Hill. Time—0:53.35.
200-Meter Butterfly—Pablo Morales. Time—1:59.15.
200-Meter Individual Medley—Pablo Morales. Time—2:02.98.
400-Meter Individual Medley—Jeff Kostoff, Industry Hills. Time—4:22.27.
400-Meter Freestyle Relay—Holmes Lumber "A". Time—3:25.12.
800-Meter Freestyle Relay—Holmes Lumber "A". Time—7:26.36.
400-Meter Medley Relay—Concord Pleasant Hills "A". Time—3:48.33.
Team Champion—Holmes Lumber.

Women

50-Meter Freestyle—Lisa Dorman, Concord Pleasant Hill. Time—0:26.20.
100-Meter Freestyle—Carrie Steinseifer, West Valley. Time—0:56.41.
200-Meter Freestyle—Mary Wayte, Holmes Lumber. Time—2:00.56.
400-Meter Freestyle—Kim Brown, Mission Veijo. Time—4:11.74.
800-Meter Freestyle—Kim Brown. Time—8:34.94.
1,500-Meter Freestyle—Kim Brown. Time—16:20.75.
100-Meter Backstroke—Betsy Mitchell, unattached. Time—1:02.76.
200-Meter Backstroke—Andrea Hayes, Pensacola Jr. Time—2:12.65.
100-Meter Breaststroke—Jenny Hau, Mission City. Time—1:11.40.
200-Meter Breaststroke—Susan Johnson, Mission Viejo. Time—2:36.00.
100-Meter Butterfly—Mary T. Meagher, Lakeside. Time—0:59.28.
200-Meter Butterfly—Mary T. Meagher. Time—2:06.09.
200-Meter Individual Medley—Michelle Griglione, Curl. Time—2:17.42.
400-Meter Individual Medley—Erika Hansen, Germantown. Time—4:48.08.
400-Meter Freestyle Relay—Concord Pleasant Hill. Time—3:50.75.
800-Meter Freestyle Relay—Mission Viejo "A". Time—8:17.80.
400-Meter Medley Relay—Mission Viejo "A". Time—4:22.06.
Team Champion—Mission Viejo.

Trotting and Pacing Records

Source: David Carr, U.S. Trotting Assn.; records to Sept. 4, 1985

Trotting Records

Asterisk (*) denotes record was made against the clock. Times—seconds in fifths.

One mile records (mile track)

All-age — 1:53.4 — Cornstalk, Springfield, Ill., Aug. 15, 1984 & Fancy Crown, Springfield, Ill., Aug. 16, 1984.
Two-year-old — *1:55.4 — Fancy Crown, Lexington, Ky., Oct. 8, 1983.
Three-year-old — 1:53.4 — Cornstalk, Springfield, Ill., Aug. 15, 1984 & Fancy Crown, Springfield, Ill., Aug. 16, 1984.

(Half-mile track)

All-age — 1:56.4 — Nevele Pride, Saratoga Springs, N.Y., Sept. 6, 1969.
Two-year-old — 2:00 — Incredible Nevele, Delaware, Oh., Sept. 22, 1981.
Three-year-old — 1:57.1 — Fancy Crown, Delaware Oh., Sept. 20, 1984.

Pacing Records

One mile records (mile track)

All-age — *1:49.1 — Niatross, Lexington, Ky., Oct. 1, 1980.
Two-year-old — 1:52.4 — Nihilator, E. Rutherford, N.J., Aug. 16, 1984.
Three-year-old — *1:49.1 — Niatross, Lexington, Ky., Oct. 1, 1980.

(Half-mile track)

All age — 1:53.3 — It's Fritz, Louisville, Ky., Sept. 3, 1983 & Legal Notice, Delaware, Oh., Sept. 20, 1984.
Two-year-old — 1:56 — Cervantes Osborne, Delaware, Oh., Sept. 20, 1984.
Three-year-old — 1:53.3 — Legan Notice, Delaware, Oh., Sept. 20, 1984.

The Hambletonian (3-year-old trotters)

Year	Winner	Driver	Purse	Year	Winner	Driver	Purse
1948	Demon Hanover	Harrison Hoyt	$59,941	1967	Speedy Streak	Del Cameron	$122,650
1949	Miss Tilly	Fred Egan	69,791	1968	Nevele Pride	Stanley Dancer	116,190
1950	Lusty Song	Del Miller	75,209	1969	Lindy's Pride	Howard Beissinger	124,910
1951	Mainliner	Guy Crippen	95,263	1970	Timothy T	John Simpson Sr.	143,630
1952	Sharp Note	Bion Shively	87,637	1971	Speedy Crown	Howard Beissinger	128,770
1953	Helicopter	Harry Harvey	117,118	1972	Super Bowl	Stanley Dancer	119,090
1954	Newport Dream	Del Cameron	106,830	1973	Flirth	Ralph Baldwin	144,710
1955	Scott Frost	Joe O'Brien	86,863	1974	Christopher T	Bill Haughton	160,150
1956	The Intruder	Ned Bower	98,591	1975	Bonefish	Stanley Dancer	232,192
1957	Hickory Smoke	John Simpson Sr.	111,126	1976	Steve Lobell	Bill Haughton	263,524
1958	Emily's Pride	Flave Nipe	106,719	1977	Green Speed	Bill Haughton	284,131
1959	Diller Hanover	Frank Ervin	125,284	1978	Speedy Somolli	Howard Beissinger	241,280
1960	Blaze Hanover	Joe O'Brien	144,590	1979	Legend Hanover	George Sholty	300,000
1961	Harlan Dean	James Arthur	131,573	1980	Burgomeister	Bill Haughton	293,570
1962	A.C. OS Viking	Sanders Russell	116,312	1981	Shiaway St. Pat.	Ray Remmen	838,000
1963	Speedy Scot	Ralph Baldwin	115,549	1982	Speed Bowl	Tommy Haughton	875,750
1964	Ayres	John Simpson Sr.	115,281	1983	Duenna	Stanley Dancer	1,080,000
1965	Egyptian Candor	Del Cameron	122,245	1984	Historic Freight	Ben Webster	1,219,000
1966	Kerry Way	Frank Ervin	122,540	1985	Prakas	Bill O'Donnell	1,272,000

Little Brown Jug (3-year-old pacers)

Year	Winner	Driver	Purse	Year	Winner	Driver	Purse
1962	Lehigh Hanover	Stanley Dancer	$75,038	1974	Ambro Omaha	Billy Haughton	$132,630
1963	Overtrick	John Patterson Sr.	68,294	1975	Seatrain	Ben Webster	147,813
1964	Vicar Hanover	Billy Haughton	66,590	1976	Keystone Ore	Stanley Dancer	153,799
1965	Bret Hanover	Frank Ervin	71,447	1977	Gov. Skipper	John Chapman	150,000
1966	Romeo Hanover	George Sholty	74,616	1978	Happy Escort	Bill Popfinger	186,760
1967	Best of All	James Hackett	84,778	1979	Hot Hitter	Herve Filion	226,455
1968	Rum Customer	Billy Haughton	104,226	1980	Niatross	Clint Galbraith	207,000
1969	Laverne Hanover	Billy Haughton	109,731	1981	Fan Hanover(A)	Glen Garnsey	243,779
1970	Most Happy Fella	Stanley Dancer	100,110	1982	Merger	John Campbell	328,900
1971	Nansemond	Herve Filion	102,944	1983	Ralph Hanover	Ron Waples	358,800
1972	Strike Out	Keith Waples	104,916	1984	Colt Forty Six	Chris Boring	366,717
1973	Melvin's Woe	Joe O'Brien	120,000	1985	Nihilator	Bill O'Donnell	129,770(B)

(A) First filly to win the Little Brown Jug. (B) Winners share.

Leading Drivers
Races Won

Year	Driver		Year	Driver		Year	Driver		Year	Driver	
1961	Bob Farrington	201	1967	Bob Farrington	277	1973	Herve Filion	445	1979	Ron Waples	443
1962	Bob Farrington	203	1968	Herve Filion	407	1974	Herve Filion	637	1980	Herve Filion	474
1963	Donald Busse	201	1969	Herve Filion	394	1975	Daryl Buse	360	1981	Eddie Davis	404
1964	Bob Farrington	312	1970	Herve Filion	486	1976	Herve Filion	445		Herve Filion	404
1965	Bob Farrington	310	1971	Herve Filion	543	1977	Herve Filion	441	1982	Herve Filion	495
1966	Bob Farrington	283	1972	Herve Filion	605	1978	Herve Filion	423	1983	Eddie Davis	470
									1984	Michel Lachance	466

Money Won

Year	Driver	Dollars	Year	Driver	Dollars	Year	Driver	Dollars
1961	Stanley Dancer	674,723	1969	Del Insko	1,635,463	1977	Herve Filion	2,551,058
1962	Stanley Dancer	760,343	1970	Herve Filion	1,647,837	1978	Carmine Abbatiello	3,344,457
1963	Bill Haughton	790,086	1971	Herve Filion	1,915,945	1979	John Campbell	3,308,984
1964	Stanley Dancer	1,051,538	1972	Herve Filion	2,473,265	1980	John Campbell	3,732,306
1965	Bill Haughton	889,943	1973	Herve Filion	2,233,302	1981	William O'Donnell	4,065,608
1966	Stanley Dancer	1,218,403	1974	Herve Filion	3,474,315	1982	William O'Donnell	5,755,067
1967	Bill Haughton	1,305,773	1975	Carmine Abbatiello	2,275,093	1983	John Campbell	6,104,082
1968	Bill Haughton	1,654,172	1976	Herve Filion	2,241,045	1984	William O'Donnell	9,059,184

Harness Horse of the Year

(Chosen by the U.S. Trotting Assn. and the U.S. Harness Writers Assn.)

1948	Rodney	1958	Emily's Pride	1967	Nevele Pride	1976	Keystone Ore
1949	Good Time	1959	Bye Bye Byrd	1968	Nevele Pride	1977	Green Speed
1950	Proximity	1960	Adios Butler	1969	Nevele Pride	1978	Abercrombie
1951	Pronto Don	1961	Adios Butler	1970	Fresh Yankee	1979	Niatross
1952	Good Time	1962	Su Mac Lad	1971	Albatross	1980	Niatross
1953	Hi Lo's Forbes	1963	Speedy Scot	1972	Albatross	1981	Fan Hanover
1954	Stenographer	1964	Bret Hanover	1973	Sir Dalrae	1982	Cam Fella
1955	Scott Frost	1965	Bret Hanover	1974	Delmonica Hanover	1983	Cam Fella
1956	Scott Frost	1966	Bret Hanover	1975	Savior	1984	Fancy Crown
1957	Torpid						

Annual Leading Money-Winning Horses
Trotters

Year	Horse	Dollars	Year	Horse	Dollars	Year	Horse	Dollars
1961	Su Mac Lad	245,750	1969	Lindy's Pride	323,997	1977	Green Speed	584,405
1962	Duke Rodney	206,113	1970	Fresh Yankee	359,002	1978	Speedy Somolli	362,404
1963	Speedy Scot	144,403	1971	Fresh Yankee	293,960	1979	Chiola Hanover	553,058
1964	Speedy Scot	235,710	1972	Super Bowl	437,108	1980	Classical Way	350,410
1965	Dartmouth	252,348	1973	Spartan Hanover	262,023	1981	Shiaway St. Pat	480,095
1966	Noble Victory	210,696	1974	Delmonica Hanover	252,165	1982	Speed Bowl	672,084
1967	Carlisle	231,243	1975	Savoir	351,385	1983	Joie De Vie	1,007,705
1968	Nevele Pride	427,440	1976	Steve Lobell	338,770	1984	Baltic Speed	1,062,611

Pacers

Year	Horse	Dollars	Year	Horse	Dollars	Year	Horse	Dollars
1961	Adios Butler	180,250	1969	Overcall	373,150	1977	Governor Skipper	522,148
1962	Henry T. Adios	220,302	1970	Most Happy Fella	387,239	1978	Abercrombie	703,260
1963	Overtrick	208,833	1971	Albatross	558,009	1979	Hot Hitter	826,542
1964	Race Time	199,292	1972	Albatross	459,921	1980	Niatross	1,414,313
1965	Bret Hanover	341,784	1973	Sir Dalrae	307,354	1981	McKinzie Almahurst	936,418
1966	Bret Hanover	407,534	1974	Armbro Omaha	345,146	1982	Fortune Teller	1,313,175
1967	Romulus Hanover	277,636	1975	Silk Stockings	336,312	1983	Ralph Hanover	1,711,990
1968	Rum Customer	355,618	1976	Keystone Ore	539,762	1984	On The Road Again	1,751,695

Leading Money-Winning Horses

(As of Sept. 4, 1985)

Trotters				Pacers			
Savoir	$1,365,145	Sandy Bowl	$1,081,798	On The Road Again	$2,388,256	Ralph Hanover	$1,828,871
Fresh Yankee	1,294,252	Keystone Pioneer	1,071,927	Nihilator	2,149,250	Fortune Teller	1,683,639
Prakas	1,292,119	Joie De Vie	1,017,251	Cam Fella	2,041,367	McKinzie Almahurst	1,532,870
Baltic Speed	1,271,764	Green Speed	953,013	Rambling Willie	2,038,219	Guts	1,246,156
Duenna	1,131,920	Cold Comfort	931,386	Niatross	2,019,213	Albatross	1,201,470

Auto Racing

Indianapolis 500 Winners

Year	Winner	Chassis	Engine	MPH	Purse	Runner up
1950	Johnnie Parsons	Kurtis Kraft	Offenhauser	124.002(a)	$201,135	Bill Holland
1951	Lee Wallard	Kurtis Kraft	Offenhauser	126.244	207,650	Mike Nazaruk
1952	Troy Ruttman	Kuzma	Offenhauser	128.922	230,100	Jim Rathmann
1953	Bill Vukovich	Kurtis Kraft 500A	Offenhauser	128.740	246,300	Art Cross
1954	Bill Vukovich	Kurtis Kraft 500A	Offenhauser	130.840	269,375	Jim Bryan
1955	Bob Sweikert	Kurtis Kraft 500C	Offenhauser	128.209	270,400	Tony Bettenhausen
1956	Pat Flaherty	Watson	Offenhauser	128.490	282,052	Sam Hanks
1957	Sam Hanks	Epperly	Offenhauser	135.601	300,252	Jim Rathmann
1958	Jimmy Bryan	Epperly	Offenhauser	133.791	305,217	George Amick
1959	Rodger Ward	Watson	Offenhauser	135.857	338,100	Jim Rathmann
1960	Jim Rathmann	Watson	Offenhauser	138.767	369,150	Rodger Ward
1961	A.J. Foyt	Watson	Offenhauser	139.130	400,000	Eddie Sachs
1962	Rodger Ward	Watson	Offenhauser	140.293	426,152	Len Sutton
1963	Parnelli Jones	Watson	Offenhauser	143.137	494,031	Jim Clark
1964	A.J. Foyt	Watson	Offenhauser	147.350	506,625	Rodger Ward
1965	Jim Clark	Lotus	Ford	151.388	628,399	Parnelli Jones
1966	Graham Hill	Lola	Ford	144.317	691,809	Jim Clark
1967	A.J. Foyt	Coyote	Ford	151.207	737,109	Al Unser
1968	Bobby Unser	Eagle	Offenhauser	152.882	809,627	Dan Gurney
1969	Mario Andretti	Hawk	Ford	156.867	805,127	Dan Gurney
1970	Al Unser	P.J. Colt	Ford	155.749	1,000,002	Mark Donohue
1971	Al Unser	P.J. Colt	Ford	157.735	1,001,604	Peter Revson
1972	Mark Donohue	McLaren	Offenhauser	163.465	1,011,846	Al Unser
1973	Gordon Johncock	Eagle	Offenhauser	159.014(b)	1,011,846	Billy Vukovich
1974	Johnny Rutherford	McLaren	Offenhauser	158.589	1,015,686	Bobby Unser
1975	Bobby Unser	Eagle	Offenhauser	149.213(c)	1,101,322	Johnny Rutherford
1976	Johnny Rutherford	McLaren	Offenhauser	148.725(d)	1,037,775	A.J. Foyt
1977	A.J. Foyt	Coyote	Ford	161.331	1,116,807	Tom Sneva
1978	Al Unser	Lola	Cosworth	161.363	1,145,225	Tom Sneva
1979	Rick Mears	Penske	Cosworth	158.899	1,271,954	A.J. Foyt
1980	Johnny Rutherford	Chaparral	Cosworth	142.862	1,502,425	Tom Sneva
1981	Bobby Unser	Penske	Cosworth	139.085	1,609,375	Mario Andretti
1982	Gordon Johncock	Wildcat	Cosworth	162.026	2,067,475	Rick Mears
1983	Tom Sneva	March	Cosworth	162.117	2,411,450	Al Unser
1984	Rick Mears	March	Cosworth	163.621	2,795,399	Roberto Guerrero
1985	Danny Sullivan	March	Cosworth	152.982	3,261,025	Mario Andretti

(a) 345 miles. (b) 332.5 miles. (c) 435 miles. (d) 255 miles. Race record—163.621 MPH, Rick Mears, 1984.

Notable One-Mile Speed Records

Date	Driver	Car	MPH	Date	Driver	Car	MPH
1/26/06	Marriott	Stanley (Steam)	127.659	9/ 3/35	Campbell	Bluebird Special	301.13
3/16/10	Oldfield	Benz	131.724	11/19/37	Eyston	Thunderbolt 1	311.42
4/23/11	Burman	Benz	141.732	9/16/38	Eyston	Thunderbolt 1	357.5
2/12/19	DePalma	Packard	149.875	8/23/39	Cobb	Railton	368.9
4/27/20	Milton	Dusenberg	155.046	9/16/47	Cobb	Railton-Mobil	394.2
4/28/26	Parry-Thomas	Thomas Spl.	170.624	8/ 5/63	Breedlove	Spirit of America	407.45
3/29/27	Seagrave	Sunbeam	203.790	10/27/64	Arfons	Green Monster	536.71
4/22/28	Keech	White Triplex	207.552	11/15/65	Breedlove	Spirit of America	600.601
3/11/29	Seagrave	Irving-Napier	231.446	10/23/70	Gabelich	Blue Flame	622.407
2/ 5/31	Campbell	Napier-Campbell	246.086	10/9/79	Barrett	Budweiser Rocket	638.637*
2/24/32	Campbell	Napier-Campbell	253.96	10/4/83	Noble	Thrust 2	633.6
2/22/33	Campbell	Napier-Campbell	272.109		*not recognized as official by sanctioning bodies.		

World Grand Prix Champions

Year	Driver	Year	Driver	Year	Driver
1950	Nino Farina, Italy	1962	Graham Hill, England	1974	Emerson Fittipaldi, Brazil
1951	Juan Fangio, Argentina	1963	Jim Clark, Scotland	1975	Nicki Lauda, Austria
1952	Alberto Ascari, Italy	1964	John Surtees, England	1976	James Hunt, England
1953	Alberto Ascari, Italy	1965	Jim Clark, Scotland	1977	Nikki Lauda, Austria
1954	Juan Fangio, Argentina	1966	Jack Brabham, Australia	1978	Mario Andretti, U.S.
1955	Juan Fangio, Argentina	1967	Denis Hulme, New Zealand	1979	Jody Scheckter, So. Africa
1956	Juan Fangio, Argentina	1968	Graham Hill, England	1980	Alan Jones, Australia
1957	Juan Fangio, Argentina	1969	Jackie Stewart, Scotland	1981	Nelson Piquet, Brazil
1958	Mike Hawthorne, England	1970	Jochen Rindt, Austria	1982	Keke Rosberg, Finland
1959	Jack Brabham, Australia	1971	Jackie Stewart, Scotland	1983	Nelson Piquet, Brazil
1960	Jack Brabham, Australia	1972	Emerson Fittipaldi, Brazil	1984	Nicki Lauda, Austria
1961	Phil Hill, United States	1973	Jackie Stewart, Scotland	1985	Alain Prost, France

United States Auto Club National Champions

Year	Driver	Year	Driver	Year	Driver	Year	Driver
1957	Jimmy Bryan	1964	A. J. Foyt	1971	Joe Leonard	1978	Tom Sneva
1958	Tony Bettenhausen	1965	Mario Andretti	1972	Joe Leonard	1979	A. J. Foyt
1959	Rodger Ward	1966	Mario Andretti	1973	Roger McCluskey	1980	Johnny Rutherford
1960	A. J. Foyt	1967	A. J. Foyt	1974	Bobby Unser	1981	George Snider
1961	A. J. Foyt	1968	Bobby Unser	1975	A. J. Foyt	1982	George Snider
1962	Rodger Ward	1969	Mario Andretti	1976	Gordon Johncock	1983	Tom Sneva
1963	A. J. Foyt	1970	Al Unser	1977	Tom Sneva	1984	Rick Mears

Grand Prix for Formula 1 Cars in 1985

Grand Prix	Winner, car	Grand Prix	Winner, car
Austrian	Alain Prost, McLaren Porsche	French	Nelson Piquet, Brabham-BMW
Belgian	Ayrton Senna, Lotus-Renault	German	Michele Alboreto, Ferrari
Brazilian	Alain Prost, McLaren Porsche	Italian	Alain Prost, McLaren Porsche
British	Alain Prost, McLaren Porsche	Long Beach	Mario Andretti, Lola Cosworth
Canadian	Michele Alboreto, Ferrari	Meadowlands	Al Unser Jr., Lola T-900
Cleveland	Al Unser Jr., Lola T-900	Monaco	Alain Prost, McLaren Porsche
Detroit	Keke Rosberg, Williams-Honda	Portuguese	Ayrton Senna, Lotus-Renault
Dutch	Niki Lauda, McLaren Porsche	San Marino	Elio De Angelis, Lotus-Renault

Le Mans 24-Hour Race in 1985

Klaus Ludwig, John Winter, and Paolo Barilla drove their Porsche 956 turbo to victory in the 1985 Le Mans 24-hour race. They covered 3,161.94 miles at an average speed of 131.747 miles per hour.

NASCAR Racing in 1985

Winston Cup Grand National Races

Date	Race, site	Winner	Car	Average MPH
Feb. 17	Daytona 500, Daytona Beach, Fla.	Bill Elliott	Ford	172.265
Mar. 3	Carolina 500, Rockingham, N.C.	Neil Bonnett	Chevrolet	114.953
Mar. 17	Coca-Cola 500, Atlanta, Ga.	Bill Elliott	Ford	140.273
Apr. 7	Valleydale 500, Bristol, Tenn.	Dale Earnhardt	Chevrolet	81.79
Apr. 29	Northwestern Bank 400, No. Wilkesboro, N.C.	Neil Bonnett	Chevrolet	247.000
Apr. 14	Transouth 500, Darlington, S.C.	Bill Elliott	Ford	126.295
Apr. 21	Northwestern 400, N. Wilkesboro, N.C.	Neil Bonnett	Chevrolet	93.818
Apr. 28	Sovran Bank 500, Martinsville, Va.	Harry Gant	Chevrolet	72.022
May 12	Winston 500, Talladega, Ala.	Bill Elliott	Ford	186.288
May 19	Budweiser 500, Dover, Del.	Bill Elliott	Ford	123.094
May 26	World 600, Harrisburg, N.C.	Darrell Waltrip	Chevrolet	142.742
June 2	Budweiser 400, Riverside, Cal.	Terry Labonte	Chevrolet	104.276
June 9	Van Scoy Diamond Mine 500, Long Pond, Pa.	Bill Elliott	Ford	138.975
June 16	Michigan 400, Brooklyn, Mich.	Bill Elliott	Ford	144.724
July 7	Firecracker 400, Daytona Beach, Fla.	Greg Sacks	Chevrolet	158.730
July 21	Summer 500, Long Pond, Pa.	Bill Elliott	Ford	134.008
July 28	Talladega 500, Talladega, Ala.	Cale Yarborough	Ford	148.771
Aug. 11	Champion Spark Plug 400, Brooklyn, Mich.	Bill Elliott	Ford	137.430
Aug. 18	Washington 500, Monroe, Wash.	Derrick Cope	Ford	73.09
Aug. 25	Busch 500, Bristol, Tenn.	Dale Earnhardt	Ford	81.388
Sept. 1	Southern 500, Darlington, S.C.	Bill Elliott	Ford	121.255
Sept. 8	Wrangler 400, Richmond, Va.	Darrell Waltrip	Chevrolet	72.508
Sept. 15	Delaware 500, Dover, Del.	Harry Gant	Chevrolet	120.538
Sept. 22	Goody's 500, Martinsville, Va.	Dale Earnhardt	Chevrolet	70.694
Sept. 29	Holly Farms 400, N. Wilkesboro, N.C.	Harry Gant	Chevrolet	95.67
Oct. 6	Miller 500, Harrisburg, N.C.	Cale Yarborough	Ford	136.761

Daytona 500 Winners

Year	Driver, car	Avg. MPH	Year	Driver, car	Avg. MPH
1962	Fireball Roberts, Pontiac	152.529	1974	Richard Petty, Dodge (c)	140.894
1963	Tiny Lund, Ford	151.566	1975	Benny Parsons, Chevrolet	153.649
1964	Richard Petty, Plymouth	154.334	1976	David Pearson, Mercury	152.181
1965	Fred Lorenzen, Ford (a)	141.539	1977	Cale Yarborough, Chevrolet	153.218
1966	Richard Petty, Plymouth (b)	160.627	1978	Bobby Allison, Ford	159.730
1967	Mario Andretti, Ford	146.926	1979	Richard Petty, Oldsmobile	143.977
1968	Cale Yarborough, Mercury	143.251	1980	Buddy Baker, Oldsmobile	177.602
1969	Lee Roy Yarborough, Ford	160.875	1981	Richard Petty, Buick	169.651
1970	Pete Hamilton, Plymouth	149.601	1982	Bobby Allison, Buick	153.991
1971	Richard Petty, Plymouth	144.456	1983	Cale Yarborough, Pontiac	155.979
1972	A. J. Foyt, Mercury	161.550	1984	Cale Yarborough, Chevrolet	150.994
1973	Richard Petty, Dodge	157.205	1985	Bill Elliott, Ford	172.265

(a) 322.5 miles because of rain. (b) 495 miles because of rain. (c) 450 miles.

Grand National Champions (NASCAR)

Year	Driver	Year	Driver	Year	Driver	Year	Driver
1956	Buck Baker	1963	Joe Weatherly	1971	Richard Petty	1978	Cale Yarborough
1956	Buck Baker	1964	Richard Petty	1972	Richard Petty	1979	Richard Petty
1957	Buck Baker	1965	Ned Jarrett	1973	Benny Parson	1980	Dale Earnhardt
1958	Lee Petty	1966	David Pearson	1974	Richard Petty	1981	Darrell Waltrip
1959	Lee Petty	1967	Richard Petty	1975	Richard Petty	1982	Darrell Waltrip
1960	Rex White	1968	David Pearson	1976	Cale Yarborough	1983	Bobby Allison
1961	Ned Jarrett	1969	David Pearson	1977	Cale Yarborough	1984	Terry Labonte
1962	Joe Weatherly	1970	Bobby Isaac				

Boxing Champions by Classes

As of Sept., 1985 the only universally accepted title holders were in the light heavyweight and middleweight divisions. The following are the recognized champions of the World Boxing Association and the World Boxing Council.

	WBA	WBC
Heavyweight	Tony Tubbs, Cincinnati, Oh.	Pinklon Thomas, Wyncotte, Pa.
Cruiserweight (not over 195 lbs.)	Dwight Muhammad Qawi, Camden, N.J.	Alfonso Ratliff, Chicago, Ill.
Light Heavyweight (not over 175 lbs.) . . .	Michael Spinks, St. Louis, Mo.	Michael Spinks
Middleweight (not over 160 lbs.)	Marvin Hagler, Brockton, Mass.	Marvin Hagler
Jr. Middleweight (not over 154 lbs.)	Mike McCallum, New York, N.Y.	Thomas Hearns, Detroit, Mich.
Welterweight (not over 147 lbs.)	Donald Curry, Ft. Worth, Tex.	Milton McCrory, Detroit, Mich.
Jr. Welterweight (not over 140 lbs.)	Ubaldo Sacco, Argentina	Lonnie Smith, Denver, Col.
Lightweight (not over 135 lbs.)	Livingstone Bramble, Passaic, N.J.	Hector (Macho) Camacho, New York; N.Y.
Jr. Lightweight (not over 130 lbs.)	Wilfredo Gomez, Puerto Rico	Julio Cesar Chavez, Mexico
Featherweight (not over 126 lbs.)	Barry McGuigan, Ireland	Azumah Nelson, Ghana
Jr. Featherweight (not over 122 lbs.). . . .	Victor Callejas, Puerto Rico	Lupe Pintor, Mexico
Bantamweight (not over 118 lbs.)	Richard Sandoval, Los Angeles, Cal.	Miguel Lora, Colombia
Flyweight (not over 112 lbs.)	Santos Laciar, Argentina	Sot Chitalada, Thailand

Ring Champions by Years

*Abandoned title

Heavyweights

1882-1892	John L. Sullivan (a)
1892-1897	James J. Corbett (b)
1897-1899	Robert Fitzsimmons
1899-1905	James J. Jeffries (c)
1905-1906	Marvin Hart
1906-1908	Tommy Burns
1908-1915	Jack Johnson
1915-1919	Jess Willard
1919-1926	Jack Dempsey
1926-1928	Gene Tunney*
1928-1930	vacant
1930-1932	Max Schmeling
1932-1933	Jack Sharkey
1933-1934	Primo Carnera
1934-1935	Max Baer
1935-1937	James J. Braddock
1937-1949	Joe Louis*
1949-1951	Ezzard Charles
1951-1952	Joe Walcott
1952-1956	Rocky Marciano*
1956-1959	Floyd Patterson
1959-1960	Ingemar Johansson
1960-1962	Floyd Patterson
1962-1964	Sonny Liston
1964-1967	Cassius Clay* (Muhammad Ali) (d)
1970-1973	Joe Frazier
1973-1974	George Foreman
1974-1978	Muhammad Ali
1978-1979	Leon Spinks (e), Muhammad Ali*
1978	Ken Norton (WBC), Larry Holmes (WBC) (f)
1979	John Tate (WBA)
1980	Mike Weaver (WBA)
1983	Michael Dokes (WBA)
1983	Gerrie Coetzee (WBA)
1984	Tim Witherspoon (WBC); Pinklon Thomas (WBC); Greg Page (WBA)
1985	Tony Tubbs (WBA); Michael Spinks (IBF)

(a) London Prize Ring (bare knuckle champion).
(b) First Marquis of Queensberry champion.
(c) Jeffries abandoned the title (1905) and designated Marvin Hart and Jack Root as logical contenders and agreed to referee a fight between them, the winner to be declared champion. Hart defeated Root in 12 rounds (1905) and in turn was defeated by Tommy Burns (1906) who immediately laid claim to the title. Jack Johnson defeated Burns (1908) and was recognized as champion. He clinched the title by defeating Jeffries in an attempted comeback (1910).
(d) Title declared vacant by the World Boxing Assn. and other groups in 1967 after Clay's refusal to fulfill his military obligation. Joe Frazier was recognized as champion by New York, 5 other states, Mexico, and So. America. Jimmy Ellis was declared champion by the World Boxing Assn. Frazier KOd Ellis, Feb. 16, 1970.
(e) After Spinks defeated Ali, the WBC recognized Ken Norton as champion. Norton subsequently lost his title to Larry Holmes.
(f) Holmes was stripped of his WBC title in 1984. He was the International Boxing Federation champion when he lost to Michael Spinks.

Light Heavyweights

1903	Jack Root, George Gardner
1903-1905	Bob Fitzsimmons
1905-1912	Philadelphia Jack O'Brien*
1912-1916	Jack Dillon
1916-1920	Battling Levinsky
1920-1922	George Carpentier
1922-1923	Battling Siki
1923-1925	Mike McTigue
1925-1926	Paul Berlenbach
1926-1927	Jack Delaney*
1927-1929	Tommy Loughran*
1930-1934	Maxey Rosenbloom
1934-1935	Bob Olin
1935-1939	John Henry Lewis*
1939	Melio Bettina
1939-1941	Billy Conn*
1941	Anton Christoforidis (won NBA title)
1941-1948	Gus Lesnevich, Freddie Mills
1948-1950	Freddie Mills
1950-1952	Joey Maxim
1952-1960	Archie Moore
1961-1962	vacant
1962-1963	Harold Johnson
1963-1965	Willie Pastrano
1965-1966	Jose Torres
1966-1968	Dick Tiger
1968-1974	Bob Foster*, John Conteh (WBA)
1975-1977	John Conteh (WBC), Miguel Cuello (WBC), Victor Galindez (WBA)
1978	Mike Rossman (WBA), Mate Parlov (WBC), Marvin Johnson (WBC)
1979	Victor Galindez (WBA), Matthew Saad Muhammad (WBC)
1980	Eddie Mustava Muhammad (WBA)
1981	Michael Spinks (WBA), Dwight Braxton (WBC)
1983	Michael Spinks

Middleweights

1884-1891	Jack "Nonpareil" Dempsey
1891-1897	Bob Fitzsimmons*
1897-1907	Tommy Ryan*
1907-1908	Stanley Ketchel, Billy Papke
1908-1910	Stanley Ketchel
1911-1913	vacant
1913	Frank Klaus, George Chip
1914-1917	Al McCoy
1917-1920	Mike O'Dowd
1920-1923	Johnny Wilson
1923-1926	Harry Greb
1926-1931	Tiger Flowers, Mickey Walker
1931-1932	Gorilla Jones (NBA)
1932-1937	Marcel Thil
1938	Al Hostak (NBA), Solly Krieger (NBA)
1939-1940	Al Hostak (NBA)
1941-1947	Tony Zale
1947-1948	Rocky Graziano
1948	Tony Zale, Marcel Cerdan
1949-1951	Jake LaMotta
1951	Ray Robinson, Randy Turpin, Ray Robinson*

1953-1955	Carl (Bobo) Olson
1955-1957	Ray Robinson
1957	Gene Fullmer, Ray Robinson, Carmen Basilio
1958	Ray Robinson
1959	Gene Fullmer (NBA); Ray Robinson (N.Y.)
1960	Gene Fullmer (NBA); Paul Pender (New York and Mass.)
1961	Gene Fullmer (NBA); Terry Downes (New York, Mass., Europe)
1962	Gene Fullmer, Dick Tiger (NBA), Paul Pender (New York and Mass.)*
1963	Dick Tiger (universal).
1963-1965	Joey Giardello
1965-1966	Dick Tiger
1966-1967	Emile Griffith
1967	Nino Benvenuti
1967-1968	Emile Griffith
1968-1970	Nino Benvenuti
1970-1977	Carlos Monzon*
1977-1978	Rodrigo Valdez
1978-1979	Hugo Corro
1979-1980	Vito Antuofermo
1980	Alan Minter, Marvin Hagler

Welterweights

1892-1894	Mysterious Billy Smith
1894-1896	Tommy Ryan
1896	Kid McCoy*
1900	Rube Ferns, Matty Matthews
1901	Rube Ferns
1901-1904	Joe Walcott
1904-1906	Dixie Kid, Joe Walcott, Honey Mellody
1907-1911	Mike Sullivan
1911-1915	vacant
1915-1919	Ted Lewis
1919-1922	Jack Britton
1922-1926	Mickey Walker
1926	Pete Latzo
1927-1929	Joe Dundee
1929	Jackie Fields
1930	Jack Thompson, Tommy Freeman
1931	Freeman, Thompson, Lou Brouillard
1932	Jackie Fields
1933	Young Corbett, Jimmy McLarnin
1934	Barney Ross, Jimmy McLarnin
1935-1938	Barney Ross
1938-1940	Henry Armstrong
1940-1941	Fritzie Zivic
1941-1946	Fred Cochrane
1946-1946	Marty Servo*; Ray Robinson (a)
1946-1950	Ray Robinson*
1951	Johnny Bratton (NBA)
1951-1954	Kid Gavilan
1954-1955	Johnny Saxton
1955	Tony De Marco, Carmen Basilio
1956	Carmen Basilio, Johnny Saxton, Basilio
1957	Carmen Basilio*
1958-1960	Virgil Akins, Don Jordan
1960	Benny Paret
1961	Emile Griffith, Benny Paret
1962	Emile Griffith
1963	Luis Rodriguez, Emile Griffith
1964-1966	Emile Griffith*
1966-1969	Curtis Cokes
1969-1970	Jose Napoles, Billy Backus
1971-1975	Jose Napoles
1975-1976	John Stracey (WBC), Angel Espada (WBA)
1976-1979	Carlos Palomino (WBC), Jose Cuevas (WBA)
1979	Wilfredo Benitez (WBC), Sugar Ray Leonard (WBC)
1980	Roberto Duran (WBC), Thomas Hearns (WBA), Sugar Ray Leonard (WBC)
1981-1982	Sugar Ray Leonard*
1983	Donald Curry (WBA); Milton McCrory (WBC)

(a) Robinson gained the title by defeating Tommy Bell in an elimination agreed to by the NY Commission and the NBA. Both claimed Robinson waived his title when he won the middleweight crown from LaMotta in 1951.

Lightweights

1896-1899	Kid Lavigne
1899-1902	Frank Erne
1902-1908	Joe Gans
1908-1910	Battling Nelson
1910-1912	Ad Wolgast
1912-1914	Willie Ritchie
1914-1917	Freddie Welsh
1917-1925	Benny Leonard*
1925	Jimmy Goodrich, Rocky Kansas

1926-1930	Sammy Mandell
1930	Al Singer, Tony Canzoneri
1930-1933	Tony Canzoneri
1933-1935	Barney Ross*
1935-1936	Tony Canzoneri
1936-1938	Lou Ambers
1938	Henry Armstrong
1939	Lou Ambers
1940	Lew Jenkins
1941-1943	Sammy Angott
1944	S. Angott (NBA), J. Zurita (NBA)
1945-1951	Ike Williams (NBA: later universal)
1951-1952	James Carter
1952	Lauro Salas, James Carter
1953-1954	James Carter
1954	Paddy De Marco; James Carter
1955	James Carter; Bud Smith
1956	Bud Smith, Joe Brown
1956-1962	Joe Brown
1962-1965	Carlos Ortiz
1965	Ismael Laguna
1965-1968	Carlos Ortiz
1968-1969	Teo Cruz
1969-1970	Mando Ramos
1970	Ismael Laguna, Ken Buchanan (WBA)
1971	Mando Ramos (WBC), Pedro Carrasco (WBC)
1972-1979	Roberto Duran* (WBA)
1972	Pedro Carrasco, Mando Ramos, Chango Carmona, Rodolfo Gonzalez (all WBC)
1974-1976	Guts Ishimatsu (WBC)
1976-1977	Esteban De Jesus (WBC)
1979	Jim Watt (WBC), Ernesto Espana (WBA)
1980	Hilmer Kenty (WBA)
1981	Alexis Arguello (WBC), Sean O'Grady (WBA), Arturo Frias (WBA)
1982-1984	Ray Mancini (WBA)
1983	Edwin Rosario (WBC)
1984	Livingstone Bramble (WBA); Jose Luis Ramirez (WBC)
1985	Hector (Macho) Camacho (WBC)

Featherweights

1892-1900	George Dixon (disputed)
1900-1901	Terry McGovern, Young Corbett*
1901-1912	Abe Attell
1912-1923	Johnny Kilbane
1923	Eugene Criqui, Johnny Dundee
1923-1925	Johnny Dundee*
1925-1927	Kid Kaplan*
1927-1928	Benny Bass, Tony Canzoneri
1928-1929	Andre Routis
1929-1932	Battling Battalino*
1932-1934	Tommy Paul (NBA)
1933-1936	Freddie Miller
1936-1937	Petey Sarron
1937-1938	Henry Armstrong*
1938-1940	Joey Archibald (b)
1942-1948	Willie Pep
1948-1949	Sandy Saddler
1949-1950	Willie Pep
1950-1957	Sandy Saddler*
1957-1959	Hogan (Kid) Bassey
1959-1963	Davey Moore
1963-1964	Sugar Ramos
1964-1967	Vicente Saldivar*
1968-1971	Paul Rojas (WBA), Sho Saijo (WBA)
1971	Antonio Gomez (WBA), Kuniaki Shibada (WBC)
1972	Ernesto Marcel* (WBA), Clemente Sanchez* (WBC), Jose Legra (WBC)
1973	Eder Jofre (WBC)
1974	Ruben Olivares (WBA), Alexis Arguello (WBA), Bobby Chacon (WBC)
1975	Ruben Olivares (WBC), David Kotey (WBC)
1976	Danny Lopez (WBC)
1977	Rafael Ortega (WBA)
1978	Cecilio Lastra (WBA), Eusebio Pedrosa (WBA)
1980	Salvador Sanchez (WBC)
1982	Juan LaPorte (WBC)
1984	Wilfredo Gomez (WBC); Azumah Nelson (WBC)
1985	Barry McGuigan (WBA)

(b) After Petey Scalzo knocked out Archibald in an overweight match and was refused a title bout, the NBA named Scalzo champion. The NBA title succession: Scalzo, 1938-1941; Richard Lemos, 1941; Jackie Wilson, 1941-1943; Jackie Callura, 1943; Phil Terranova, 1943-1944; Sal Bartolo, 1944-1946.

History of Heavyweight Championship Bouts

*Title Changed Hands

1889—July 8—John L. Sullivan def. Jake Kilrain, 75, Richburg, Miss. Last championship bare knuckles bout.

*1892**—Sept. 7—James J. Corbett def. John L. Sullivan, 21, New Orleans. Big gloves used for first time.

1894—Jan. 25—James J. Corbett KOd Charley Mitchell, 3, Jacksonville, Fla.

*1897**—Bob Fitzsimmons def. James J. Corbett, 14, Carson City, Nev.

*1899**—June 9—James J. Jeffries def. Bob Fitzsimmons, 11, Coney Island, N.Y.

1899—Nov. 3—James J. Jeffries def. Tom Sharkey, 25, Coney Island, N.Y.

1900—May 11—James J. Jeffries KOd James J. Corbett, 23, Coney Island, N.Y.

1901—Nov. 15—James J. Jeffries KOd Gus Ruhlin, 5, San Francisco.

1902—July 25—James J. Jeffries KOd Bob Fitzsimmons, 8, San Francisco.

1903—Aug. 14—James J. Jeffries KOd James J. Corbett, 10, San Francisco.

1904—Aug. 26—James J. Jeffries KOd Jack Monroe, 2, San Francisco.

*1905**—James J. Jeffries retired, July 3—Marvin Hart KOd Jack Root, 12, Reno. Jeffries refereed and presented the title to the victor. Jack O'Brien also claimed the title.

*1906**—Feb. 23—Tommy Burns def. Marvin Hart, 20, Los Angeles.

1906—Nov. 28—Philadelphia Jack O'Brien and Tommy Burns, 20, draw, Los Angeles.

1907—May 8—Tommy Burns def. Jack O'Brien, 20, Los Angeles.

1907—July 4—Tommy Burns KOd Bill Squires, 1, Colma, Cal.

1907—Dec. 2—Tommy Burns KOd Gunner Moir, 10, London.

1908—Feb. 10—Tommy Burns KOd Jack Palmer, 4, London.

1908—March 17—Tommy Burns KOd Jem Roche, 1, Dublin.

1908—April 18—Tommy Burns KOd Jewey Smith, 5, Paris.

1908—June 13—Tommy Burns KOd Bill Squires, 8, Paris.

1908—Aug. 24—Tommy Burns KOd Bill Squires, 13, Sydney, New South Wales.

1908—Sept. 2—Tommy Burns KOd Bill Lang, 2, Melbourne, Australia.

*1908**—Dec. 26—Jack Johnson KOd Tommy Burns, 14, Sydney, Australia. Police halted contest.

1909—May 19—Jack Johnson and Jack O'Brien, 6, draw, Philadelphia.

1909—June 30—Jack Johnson and Tony Ross, 6, draw, Pittsburgh.

1909—Sept. 9—Jack Johnson and Al Kaufman, 10, draw, San Francisco.

1909—Oct. 16—Jack Johnson KOd Stanley Ketchel, 12, Colma, Cal.

1910—July 4—Jack Johnson KOd Jim Jeffries, 15, Reno, Nev. Jeffries came back from retirement.

1912—July 4—Jack Johnson def. Jim Flynn, 9, Las Vegas, N.M. Contest stopped by police.

1913—Nov. 28—Jack Johnson KOd Andre Spaul, 2, Paris.

1913—Dec. 9—Jack Johnson and Jim Johnson, 10, draw, Paris. Bout called a draw when Jack Johnson declared he had broken his arm.

1914—June 27—Jack Johnson def. Frank Moran, 20, Paris.

*1915**—April 5—Jess Willard KOd Jack Johnson, 26, Havana, Cuba.

1916—March 25—Jess Willard and Frank Moran, 10, draw, New York.

*1919**—July 4—Jack Dempsey KOd Jess Willard, Toledo, Oh. Willard failed to answer bell for 4th round.

1920—Sept. 6—Jack Dempsey KOd Billy Miske, 3, Benton Harbor, Mich.

1920—Dec. 14—Jack Dempsey KOd Bill Brennan, 12, New York.

1921—July 2—Jack Dempsey KOd George Carpentier, 4, Boyle's Thirty Acres, Jersey City, N.J. Carpentier had held the so-called white heavyweight title since July 16, 1914, in a series established in 1913, after Jack Johnson's exile in Europe late in 1912.

1923—July 4—Jack Dempsey def. Tom Gibbons, 15, Shelby, Mont.

1923—Sept. 14—Jack Dempsey KOd Luis Firpo, 2, New York.

*1926**—Sept. 23—Gene Tunney def. Jack Dempsey, 10, Philadelphia.

1927—Sept. 22—Gene Tunney def. Jack Dempsey, 10, Chicago.

1928—July 26—Gene Tunney KOd Tom Heeney, 11, New York; soon afterward he announced his retirement.

*1930**—June 12—Max Schmeling def. Jack Sharkey, 4, New York. Sharkey fouled Schmeling in a bout which was generally considered to have resulted in the election of a successor to Gene Tunney, New York.

1931—July 3—Max Schmeling KOd Young Stribling, 15, Cleveland.

*1932**—June 21—Jack Sharkey def. Max Schmeling, 15, New York.

*1933**—June 29—Primo Carnera KOd Jack Sharkey, 6, New York.

1933—Oct. 22—Primo Carnera def. Paulino Uzcudun, 15, Rome.

1934—March 1—Primo Carnera def. Tommy Loughran, 15, Miami.

*1934**—June 14—Max Baer KOd Primo Carnera, 11, New York.

*1935**—June 13—James J. Braddock def. Max Baer, 15, New York.

*1937**—June 22—Joe Louis KOd James J. Braddock, 8, Chicago.

1937—Aug. 30—Joe Louis def. Tommy Farr, 15, New York.

1938—Feb. 23—Joe Louis KOd Nathan Mann, 3, New York.

1938—April 1—Joe Louis KOd Harry Thomas, 5, New York.

1938—June 22—Joe Louis KOd Max Schmeling, 1, New York.

1939—Jan. 25—Joe Louis KOd John H. Lewis, 1, New York.

1939—April 17—Joe Louis KOd Jack Roper, 1, Los Angeles.

1939—June 28—Joe Louis KOd Tony Galento, 4, New York.

1939—Sept. 20—Joe Louis KOd Bob Pastor, 11, Detroit.

1940—February 9—Joe Louis def. Arturo Godoy, 15, New York.

1940—March 29—Joe Louis KOd Johnny Paycheck, 2, New York.

1940—June 20—Joe Louis KOd Arturo Godoy, 8, New York.

1940—Dec. 16—Joe Louis KOd Al McCoy, 6, Boston.

1941—Jan. 31—Joe Louis KOd Red Burman, 5, New York.

1941—Feb. 17—Joe Louis KOd Gus Dorzaio, 2, Philadelphia.

1941—March 21—Joe Louis KOd Abe Simon, 13, Detroit.

1941—April 8—Joe Louis KOd Tony Musto, 9, St. Louis.

1941—May 23—Joe Louis def. Buddy Baer, 7, Washington, D.C., on a disqualification.

1941—June 18—Joe Louis KOd Billy Conn, 13, New York.

1941—Sept. 29—Joe Louis KOd Lou Nova, 6, New York.

1942—Jan. 9—Joe Louis KOd Buddy Baer, 1, New York.

1942—March 27—Joe Louis KOd Abe Simon, 6, New York.

1946—June 19—Joe Louis KOd Billy Conn, 8, New York.

1946—Sept. 18—Joe Louis KOd Tami Mauriello, 1, New York.

1947—Dec. 5—Joe Louis def. Joe Walcott, 15, New York.

1948—June 25—Joe Louis KOd Joe Walcott, 11, New York.

*1949**—June 22—Following Joe Louis' retirement Ezzard Charles def. Joe Walcott, 15, Chicago, NBA recognition only.

1949—Aug. 10—Ezzard Charles KOd Gus Lesnevich, 7, New York.

1949—Oct. 14—Ezzard Charles KOd Pat Valentino, 8, San Francisco; clinched American title.

1950—Aug. 15—Ezzard Charles KOd Freddy Beshore, 14, Buffalo.

1950—Sept. 27—Ezzard Charles def. Joe Louis in latter's attempted comeback, 15, New York; universal recognition.

1950—Dec. 5—Ezzard Charles KOd Nick Barone, 11, Cincinnati.

1951—Jan. 12—Ezzard Charles KOd Lee Oma, 10, New York.

1951—March 7—Ezzard Charles def. Joe Walcott, 15, Detroit.

1951—May 30—Ezzard Charles def. Joey Maxim, light heavyweight champion, 15, Chicago.

*1951**—July 18—Joe Walcott KOd Ezzard Charles, 7, Pittsburgh.

1952—June 5—Joe Walcott def. Ezzard Charles, 15, Philadelphia.

*1952**—Sept. 23—Rocky Marciano KOd Joe Walcott, 13, Philadelphia.

1953—May 15—Rocky Marciano KOd Joe Walcott, 1, Chicago.

1953—Sept. 24—Rocky Marciano KOd Roland LaStarza, 11, New York.

1954—June 17—Rocky Marciano def. Ezzard Charles, 15, New York.

1954—Sept. 17—Rocky Marciano KOd Ezzard Charles, 8, New York.

1955—May 16—Rocky Marciano KOd Don Cockell, 9, San Francisco.

1955—Sept. 21—Rocky Marciano KOd Archie Moore, 9, New York. Marciano retired undefeated, Apr. 27, 1956.

*1956—Nov. 30—Floyd Patterson KOd Archie Moore, 5, Chicago.

1957—July 29—Floyd Patterson KOd Hurricane Jackson, 10, New York.

1957—Aug. 22—Floyd Patterson KOd Pete Rademacher, 6, Seattle.

1958—Aug. 18—Floyd Patterson KOd Roy Harris, 12, Los Angeles.

1959—May 1—Floyd Patterson KOd Brian London, 11, Indianapolis.

*1959—June 26—Ingemar Johansson KOd Floyd Patterson, 3, New York.

*1960—June 20—Floyd Patterson KOd Ingemar Johansson, 5, New York. First heavyweight in boxing history to regain title.

1961—Mar. 13—Floyd Patterson KOd Ingemar Johansson, 6, Miami Beach.

1961—Dec. 4—Floyd Patterson KOd Tom McNeeley, 4, Toronto.

.*1962—Sept. 25—Sonny Liston KOd Floyd Patterson, 1, Chicago.

1963—July 22—Sonny Liston KOd Floyd Patterson, 1, Las Vegas.

*1964—Feb. 25—Cassius Clay KOd Sonny Liston, 7, Miami Beach.

1965—May 25—Cassius Clay KOd Sonny Liston, 1, Lewiston, Maine.

1965—Nov. 11—Cassius Clay KOd Floyd Patterson, 12, Las Vegas.

1966—Mar. 29—Cassius Clay def. George Chuvalo, 15, Toronto.

1966—May 21—Cassius Clay KOd Henry Cooper, 6, London.

1966—Aug. 6—Cassius Clay KOd Brian London, 3, London.

1966—Sept. 10—Cassius Clay KOd Karl Mildenberger, 12, Frankfurt, Germany.

1966—Nov. 14—Cassius Clay KOd Cleveland Williams, 3, Houston.

1967—Feb. 6—Cassius Clay def. Ernie Terrell, 15, Houston.

1967—Mar. 22—Cassius Clay KOd Zora Folley, 7, New York. Clay was stripped of his title by the WBA and others for refusing military service.

*1970—Feb. 16—Joe Frazier KOd Jimmy Ellis, 5, New York.

1970—Nov. 18—Joe Frazier KOd Bob Foster, 2, Detroit.

1971—Mar. 8—Joe Frazier def. Cassius Clay (Muhammad Ali), 15, New York.

1972—Jan. 15—Joe Frazier KOd Terry Daniels, 4, New Orleans.

1972—May 25—Joe Frazier KOd Ron Stander, 5, Omaha.

*1973—Jan. 22—George Foreman KOd Joe Frazier, 2, Kingston, Jamaica.

1973—Sept. 1—George Foreman KOd Joe Roman, 1, Tokyo.

1974—Mar. 3—George Foreman KOd Ken Norton, 2, Caracas.

*1974—Oct. 30—Muhammad Ali KOd George Foreman, 8, Zaire.

1975—Mar. 24—Muhammad Ali KOd Chuck Wepner, 15, Cleveland.

1975—May 16—Muhammad Ali KOd Ron Lyle, 11, Las Vegas.

1975—June 30—Muhammad Ali def. Joe Bugner, 15, Malaysia.

1975—Oct. 1—Muhammad Ali KOd Joe Frazier, 14, Manila.

1976—Feb. 20—Muhammad Ali KOd Jean-Pierre Coopman, 5, San Juan.

1976—Apr. 30—Muhammad Ali def. Jimmy Young, 15, Landover, Md.

1976—May 25—Muhammad Ali KOd Richard Dunn, 5, Munich.

1976—Sept. 28—Muhammad Ali def. Ken Norton, 15, New York.

1977—May 16—Muhammad Ali def. Alfredo Evangelista, 15, Landover, Md.

1977—Sept. 29—Muhammad Ali def. Earnie Shavers, 15, New York.

*1978—Feb. 15—Leon Spinks def. Muhammad Ali, 15, Las Vegas.

*1978—Sept. 15—Muhammad Ali def. Leon Spinks, 15, New Orleans. Ali retired in 1979.

(Bouts when title changed hands only)

*1978—June 9—(WBC) Larry Holmes def. Ken Norton, 15, Las Vegas.

*1980—Mar. 31—(WBA) Mike Weaver KOd John Tate, 15, Knoxville.

*1982—Dec. 10—(WBA) Michael Dokes KOd Mike Weaver, 1, Las Vegas.

*1983—Sept. 23—(WBA) Gerrie Coetzee KOd Michael Dokes, 10, Richfield, Oh.

*1984—Mar. 10—(WBC) Tim Witherspoon def. Greg Page, 12, Las Vegas, Nev.

*1984—Aug. 31—(WBC) Pinklon Thomas def. Tim Witherspoon, 12, Las Vegas, Nev.

*1984—Dec. 2—(WBA) Greg Page KOd Gerrie Coetzee, 8, Sun City, Bophuthatswana

*1985—Apr. 29—(WBA) Tony Tubbs def. Greg Page, 15, Buffalo, N.Y.

*1985—Sept. 21—(IBF) Michael Spinks def. Larry Holmes, 15, Las Vegas, Nev.

Golf

PGA Leading Money Winners

Year	Player	Dollars	Year	Player	Dollars	Year	Player	Dollars
1946	Ben Hogan	42,556	1959	Art Wall Jr.	53,167	1972	Jack Nicklaus	320,542
1947	Jimmy Demaret	27,936	1960	Arnold Palmer	75,262	1973	Jack Nicklaus	308,362
1948	Ben Hogan	36,812	1961	Gary Player	64,540	1974	Johnny Miller	353,201
1949	Sam Snead	31,593	1962	Arnold Palmer	81,448	1975	Jack Nicklaus	323,149
1950	Sam Snead	35,758	1963	Arnold Palmer	128,230	1976	Jack Nicklaus	266,438
1951	Lloyd Mangrum	26,088	1964	Jack Nicklaus	113,284	1977	Tom Watson	310,653
1952	Julius Boros	37,032	1965	Jack Nicklaus	140,752	1978	Tom Watson	362,429
1953	Lew Worsham	34,002	1966	Billy Casper	121,944	1979	Tom Watson	462,636
1954	Bob Toski	65,819	1967	Jack Nicklaus	188,988	1980	Tom Watson	530,808
1955	Julius Boros	65,121	1968	Billy Casper	205,168	1981	Tom Kite	375,699
1956	Ted Kroll	72,835	1969	Frank Beard	175,223	1982	Craig Stadler	446,462
1957	Dick Mayer	65,835	1970	Lee Trevino	157,037	1983	Hal Sutton	426,668
1958	Arnold Palmer	42,407	1971	Jack Nicklaus	244,490	1984	Tom Watson	476,260

LPGA Leading Money Winners

Year	Winner	Dollars	Year	Winner	Dollars	Year	Winner	Dollars
1954	Patty Berg	16,011	1965	Kathy Whitworth	28,658	1976	Judy Rankin	150,734
1955	Patty Berg	16,492	1966	Kathy Whitworth	33,517	1977	Judy Rankin	122,890
1956	Marlene Hagge	20,235	1967	Kathy Whitworth	32,937	1978	Nancy Lopez	189,813
1957	Patty Berg	16,272	1968	Kathy Whitworth	48,379	1979	Nancy Lopez	215,987
1958	Beverly Hanson	12,629	1969	Carol Mann	49,152	1980	Beth Daniel	231,000
1959	Betsy Rawls	26,774	1970	Kathy Whitworth	30,235	1981	Beth Daniel	206,977
1960	Louise Suggs	16,892	1971	Kathy Whitworth	41,181	1982	JoAnne Carner	310,399
1961	Mickey Wright	22,236	1972	Kathy Whitworth	65,063	1983	JoAnne Carner	291,404
1962	Mickey Wright	21,641	1973	Kathy Whitworth	82,854	1984	Betsy King	266,771
1963	Mickey Wright	31,269	1974	JoAnne Carner	87,094			
1964	Mickey Wright	29,800	1975	Sandra Palmer	94,805			

United States Open

Year	Winner	Year	Winner	Year	Winner	Year	Winner
1901	Willie Anderson	1923	Bobby Jones*	1947	L. Worsham	1968	Lee Trevino
1902	L. Auchterlonie	1924	Cyril Walker	1948	Ben Hogan	1969	Orville Moody
1903	Willie Anderson	1925	Willie MacFarlane	1949	Cary Middlecoff	1970	Tony Jacklin
1904	Willie Anderson	1926	Bobby Jones*	1950	Ben Hogan	1971	Lee Trevino
1905	Willie Anderson	1927	Tommy Armour	1951	Ben Hogan	1972	Jack Nicklaus
1906	Alex Smith	1928	John Farrell	1952	Julius Boros	1973	Johnny Miller
1907	Alex Ross	1929	Bobby Jones*	1953	Ben Hogan	1974	Hale Irwin
1908	Fred McLeod	1930	Bobby Jones*	1954	Ed Furgol	1975	Lou Graham
1909	George Sargent	1931	Wm. Burke	1955	Jack Fleck	1976	Jerry Pate
1910	Alex Smith	1932	Gene Sarazen	1956	Cary Middlecoff	1977	Hubert Green
1911	John McDermott	1933	John Goodman*	1957	Dick Mayer	1978	Andy North
1912	John McDermott	1934	Olin Dutra	1958	Tommy Bolt	1979	Hale Irwin
1913	Francis Ouimet*	1935	Sam Parks Jr.	1959	Billy Casper	1980	Jack Nicklaus
1914	Walter Hagen	1936	Tony Manero	1960	Arnold Palmer	1981	David Graham
1915	Jerome Travers*	1937	Ralph Guldahl	1961	Gene Littler	1982	Tom Watson
1916	Chick Evans*	1938	Ralph Guldahl	1962	Jack Nicklaus	1983	Larry Nelson
1917-18	(Not played)	1939	Byron Nelson	1963	Julius Boros	1984	Fuzzy Zoeller
1919	Walter Hagen	1940	Lawson Little	1964	Ken Venturi	1985	Andy North
1920	Edward Ray	1941	Craig Wood	1965	Gary Player		
1921	Jim Barnes	1942-45	(Not played)	1966	Billy Casper		
1922	Gene Sarazen	1946	Lloyd Mangrum	1967	Jack Nicklaus		

*Amateur

U.S. Women's Open Golf Champions

Year	Winner	Year	Winner	Year	Winner	Year	Winner
1948	"Babe" Zaharias	1958	Mickey Wright	1968	Susie Maxwell Berning	1978	Hollis Stacy
1949	Louise Suggs	1959	Mickey Wright	1969	Donna Caponi	1979	Jerilyn Britz
1950	"Babe" Zaharias	1960	Betsy Rawls	1970	Donna Caponi	1980	Amy Alcott
1951	Betsy Rawls	1961	Mickey Wright	1971	JoAnne Carner	1981	Pat Bradley
1952	Louise Suggs	1962	Marie Lindstrom	1972	Susie Maxwell Berning	1982	Janet Alex
1953	Betsy Rawls	1963	Mary Mills	1973	Susie Maxwell Berning	1983	Jan Stephenson
1954	"Babe" Zaharias	1964	Mickey Wright	1974	Sandra Haynie	1984	Hollis Stacy
1955	Fay Crocker	1965	Carol Mann	1975	Sandra Palmer	1985	Kathy Baker
1956	Mrs. K. Cornelius	1966	Sandra Spuzich	1976	JoAnne Carner		
1957	Betsy Rawls	1967	Catherine Lacoste*	1977	Hollis Stacy		

*Amateur

Masters Golf Tournament Champions

Year	Winner	Year	Winner	Year	Winner	Year	Winner
1934	Horton Smith	1949	Sam Snead	1962	Arnold Palmer	1975	Jack Nicklaus
1935	Gene Sarazen	1950	Jimmy Demaret	1963	Jack Nicklaus	1976	Ray Floyd
1936	Horton Smith	1951	Ben Hogan	1964	Arnold Palmer	1977	Tom Watson
1937	Byron Nelson	1952	Sam Snead	1965	Jack Nicklaus	1978	Gary Player
1938	Henry Picard	1953	Ben Hogan	1966	Jack Nicklaus	1979	Fuzzy Zoeller
1939	Ralph Guldahl	1954	Sam Snead	1967	Gay Brewer Jr.	1980	Severiano Ballesteros
1940	Jimmy Demaret	1955	Cary Middlecoff	1968	Bob Goalby	1981	Tom Watson
1941	Craig Wood	1956	Jack Burke	1969	George Archer	1982	Craig Stadler
1942	Byron Nelson	1957	Doug Ford	1970	Billy Casper	1983	Severiano Ballesteros
1943-1945	(Not played)	1958	Arnold Palmer	1971	Charles Coody	1984	Ben Crenshaw
1946	Herman Keiser	1959	Art Wall Jr.	1972	Jack Nicklaus	1985	Bernhard Langer
1947	Jimmy Demaret	1960	Arnold Palmer	1973	Tommy Aaron		
1948	Claude Harmon	1961	Gary Player	1974	Gary Player		

Professional Golfer's Association Championships

Year	Winner	Year	Winner	Year	Winner	Year	Winner
1921	Walter Hagen	1937	Denny Shute	1954	Melvin Harbert	1970	Dave Stockton
1922	Gene Sarazen	1938	Paul Runyan	1955	Doug Ford	1971	Jack Nicklaus
1923	Gene Sarazen	1939	Henry Picard	1956	Jack Burke	1972	Gary Player
1924	Walter Hagen	1940	Byron Nelson	1957	Lionel Hebert	1973	Jack Nicklaus
1925	Walter Hagen	1941	Victor Ghezzi	1958	Dow Finsterwald	1974	Lee Trevino
1926	Walter Hagen	1942	Sam Snead	1959	Bob Rosburg	1975	Jack Nicklaus
1927	Walter Hagen	1944	Bob Hamilton	1960	Jay Hebert	1976	Dave Stockton
1928	Leo Diegel	1945	Byron Nelson	1961	Jerry Barber	1977	Lanny Wadkins
1929	Leo Diegel	1946	Ben Hogan	1962	Gary Player	1978	John Mahaffey
1930	Tommy Armour	1947	Jim Ferrier	1963	Jack Nicklaus	1979	David Graham
1931	Tom Creavy	1948	Ben Hogan	1964	Bob Nichols	1980	Jack Nicklaus
1932	Olin Dutra	1949	Sam Snead	1965	Dave Marr	1981	Larry Nelson
1933	Gene Sarazen	1950	Chandler Harper	1966	Al Geiberger	1982	Ray Floyd
1934	Paul Runyan	1951	Sam Snead	1967	Don January	1983	Hal Sutton
1935	Johnny Revolta	1952	James Turnesa	1968	Julius Boros	1984	Lee Trevino
1936	Denny Shute	1953	Walter Burkemo	1969	Ray Floyd	1985	Hubert Green

Canadian Open Golf Champions

Year	Winner	Year	Winner	Year	Winner	Year	Winner
1954	Pat Fletcher	1962	Ted Kroll	1970	Kermit Zarley	1978	Bruce Lietzke
1955	Arnold Palmer	1963	Doug Ford	1971	Lee Trevino	1979	Lee Trevino
1956	Doug Sanders	1964	Kel Nagle	1972	Gay Brewer	1980	Bob Gilder
1957	George Bayer	1965	Gene Littler	1973	Tom Weiskopf	1981	Peter Oosterhuis
1958	Wes Ellis Jr.	1966	Don Massengale	1974	Bobby Nichols	1982	Bruce Lietzke
1959	Doug Ford	1967	Billy Casper	1975	Tom Weiskopf	1983	John Cook
1960	Art Wall, Jr.	1968	Bob Charles	1976	Jerry Pate	1984	Greg Norman
1961	Jacky Cupit	1969	Tommy Aaron	1977	Lee Trevino	1985	Curtis Strange

Professional Golf Tournaments in 1985

Date	Event	Winner	Score	Prize
Jan. 13	Bob Hope Desert Classic, Palm Springs	Lanny Wadkins	*333	$90,000
Jan. 20	Phoenix Open	Calvin Peete	270	81,000
Jan. 27	Los Angeles Open	Lanny Wadkins	264	72,000
Feb. 3	Bing Crosby National Pro-Am, Pebble Beach, Cal.	Mark O'Meara	283	90,000
Feb. 10	Hawaiian Open, Honolulu	Mark O'Meara	267	90,000
Feb. 17	Isuzo-Andy Williams San Diego Open	Woody Blackburn	*269	72,000
Feb. 24	Doral-Eastern Open, Miami, Fla.	Mark McCumber	284	72,000
Mar. 3	Honda Classic, Coral Springs, Fla.	Curtis Strange	*275	90,000
Mar. 10	Bay Hill Classic, Orlando, Fla.	Fuzzy Zoeller	275	90,000
Mar. 17	U.S.F.&G. Classic, New Orleans, La.	Severiano Ballesteros	205	72,000
Mar. 24	Las Vegas Invitational	Curtis Strange	338	171,000
Mar. 31	Tournament Players Championship, Ponte Vedra, Fla.	Calvin Peete	274	162,000
Apr. 7	Greater Greensboro Open, N.C.	Joey Sindelar	285	72,000
Apr. 14	Masters Tournament, Augusta, Ga.	Bernhard Langer	282	126,000
Apr. 21	Sea Pines Heritage Classic, Hilton Head, S.C.	Bernhard Langer	273	72,000
Apr. 28	Houston Open	Ray Floyd	277	90,000
May 5	Tournament of Champions, Carlsbad, Cal.	Tom Kite	275	72,000
May 12	Byron Nelson Classic, Irving, Tex.	Bob Eastwood	272	90,000
May 19	Colonial National Tournament, Ft. Worth, Tex.	Corey Pavin	266	72,000
May 26	Memorial Tournament, Dublin, Oh.	Hale Irwin	281	100,000
June 2	Kemper Open, Bethesda, Md.	Bill Glasson	278	90,000
June 9	Westchester Classic, Harrison, N.Y.	Roger Maltbie	*275	90,000
June 16	U.S. Open, Birmingham, Mich.	Andy North	279	103,000
June 23	Atlanta Classic, Atlanta, Ga.	Wayne Levi	*273	90,000
June 30	St. Jude Memphis Classic	Hal Sutton	*279	90,000
July 7	Canadian Open, Oakville, Ont.	Curtis Strange	279	86,000
July 14	Anheuser-Busch Classic, Williamsburg, Va.	John Mahaffey	273	90,000
July 21	Quad Cities Open, Coal Valley, Ill.	Dan Forsman	267	54,000
July 28	Greater Hartford Open, Conn.	Phil Blackmar	271	72,000
Aug. 4	Western Open, Oak Brook, Ill.	Scott Verplank(1)	*279	70,000(2)
Aug. 11	PGA Championship, Denver, Col.	Hubert Green	278	125,000
Aug. 18	Buick Open, Grand Blanc, Mich.	Ken Green	268	72,000
Aug. 25	World Series of Golf, Akron, Oh.	Roger Maltbie	268	126,000
Sept. 9	Bank of Boston Classic, Sutton, Mass.	George Burns	267	72,000
Sept. 15	Greater Milwaukee Open, Wis.	Jim Thorpe	274	54,000
Sept. 22	Southwest Classic, Abilene, Tex.	Hal Sutton	*273	172,000

Women

Date	Event	Winner	Score	Prize
Jan. 27	Mazda Classic, Deerfield Beach, Fla.	Hollis Stacey	280	$30,000
Feb. 3	Elizabeth Arden Classic, Miami, Fla.	JoAnne Carner	280	30,000
Feb. 10	Sarasota Classic, Sarasota, Fla.	Patty Sheehan	278	30,000
Feb. 24	Tucson Open, Tucson, Ariz.	Amy Alcott	279	26,200
Mar. 10	Uniden Invitational, Costa Mesa, Cal.	Bonnie Lauer	277	49,500
Mar. 17	Kemper Open, Kaanapali, Ha.	Jane Blalock	287	30,000
Apr. 7	Dinah Shore Invitational, Rancho Mirage, Cal.	Alice Miller	275	55,500
Apr. 14	Kyocera Inamori Classic, San Diego, Cal.	Beth Daniel	286	26,250
Apr. 21	J & B Pro-Am, Las Vegas, Nev.	Patty Sheehan	275	30,000
May 5	Moss Creek Invitational, Hilton Head Island, S.C.	Amy Alcott	284	30,000
May 12	United Virginia Bank Classic, Suffolk, Va.	Kathy Whitworth	207	30,000
May 19	Chrysler-Plymouth Classic, Chatham, N.J.	Nancy Lopez	210	26,250
May 26	Corning Classic, Corning, N.Y.	Patti Rizzo	272	37,500
June 2	LPGA Championship, Kings Island, Oh.	Nancy Lopez	273	37,000
June 9	McDonald's Classic, Malvern, Pa.	Alice Miller	272	60,000
June 16	Rochester Invitational, Pittsford, N.Y.	Pat Bradley	280	38,250
June 23	Mayflower Classic, Indianapolis, Ind.	Alice Miller	280	37,500
June 30	Lady Keystone Open, Hershey, Pa.	Juli Inkster	209	37,000
July 7	Hall of Fame Championship, Sugar Land, Tex.	Nancy Lopez	281	45,000
July 14	U.S. Women's Open, Springfield, N.J.	Kathy Baker	280	41,900
July 21	Boston Five Classic, Danvers, Mass.	Judy Clark	280	33,750
July 28	Du Maurier Classic, Montreal, Que.,	Pat Bradley	278	41,250
Aug. 11	Henredon Classic, High Point, N.C.	Nancy Lopez	268	31,500
Aug. 19	World Championship of Women's Golf, Buford, Ga.	Amy Alcott	274	65,000
Aug. 25	National Pro-Am, Denver, Col.	Pat Bradley	284	45,000
Sept. 8	Portland Ping Championship, Portland, Ore.	Nancy Lopez	215	26,250
Sept. 15	San Jose Classic, San Jose, Cal.	Val Skinner	*209	37,500

*Won playoff. (1) Amateur; (2) Won by Jim Thorpe.

British Open Golf Champions

Year	Winner	Year	Winner	Year	Winner	Year	Winner
1925	Jim Barnes	1939	Richard Burton	1958	Peter Thomson	1972	Lee Trevino
1926	Bobby Jones	1940-45	(Not played)	1959	Gary Player	1973	Tom Weiskopf
1927	Bobby Jones	1946	Sam Snead	1960	Kel Nagle	1974	Gary Player
1928	Walter Hagen	1947	Fred Daly	1961	Arnold Palmer	1975	Tom Watson
1929	Walter Hagen	1948	Henry Cotton	1962	Arnold Palmer	1976	Johnny Miller
1930	Bobby Jones	1949	Bobby Locke	1963	Bob Charles	1977	Tom Watson
1931	Tommy Armour	1950	Bobby Locke	1964	Tony Lema	1978	Jack Nicklaus
1932	Gene Sarazen	1951	Max Faulkner	1965	Peter Thomson	1979	Seve Ballesteros
1933	Denny Shute	1952	Bobby Locke	1966	Jack Nicklaus	1980	Tom Watson
1934	Henry Cotton	1953	Ben Hogan	1967	Roberto de Vicenzo	1981	Bill Rogers
1935	Alf Perry	1954	Peter Thomson	1968	Gary Player	1982	Tom Watson
1936	Alf Padgham	1955	Peter Thomson	1969	Tony Jacklin	1983	Tom Watson
1937	T.H. Cotton	1956	Peter Thomson	1970	Jack Nicklaus	1984	Seve Ballesteros
1938	R.A. Whitcombe	1957	Bobby Locke	1971	Lee Trevino	1985	Sandy Lyle

Tennis

U.S. Open Champions

Men's Singles

Year	Champion	Final opponent	Year	Champion	Final opponent
1920	Bill Tilden	William Johnston	1953	Tony Trabert	E. Victor Seixas Jr.
1921	Bill Tilden	Wallace Johnson	1954	E. Victor Seixas Jr.	Rex Hartwig
1922	Bill Tilden	William Johnston	1955	Tony Trabert	Ken Rosewall
1923	Bill Tilden	William Johnston	1956	Ken Rosewall	Lewis Hoad
1924	Bill Tilden	William Johnston	1957	Malcolm Anderson	Ashley Cooper
1925	Bill Tilden	William Johnston	1958	Ashley Cooper	Malcolm Anderson
1926	Rene Lacoste	Jean Borotra	1959	Neale A. Fraser	Alejandro Olmedo
1927	Rene Lacoste	Bill Tilden	1960	Neale A. Fraser	Rod Laver
1928	Henri Cochet	Francis Hunter	1961	Roy Emerson	Rod Laver
1929	Bill Tilden	Francis Hunter	1962	Rod Laver	Roy Emerson
1930	John Doeg	Francis Shields	1963	Rafael Osuna	F. A. Froehling 3d
1931	H. Ellsworth Vines	George Lott	1964	Roy Emerson	Fred Stolle
1932	H. Ellsworth Vines	Henri Cochet	1965	Manuel Santana	Cliff Drysdale
1933	Fred Perry	John Crawford	1966	Fred Stolle	John Newcombe
1934	Fred Perry	Wilmer Allison	1967	John Newcombe	Clark Graebner
1935	Wilmer Allison	Sidney Wood	1968	Arthur Ashe	Tom Okker
1936	Fred Perry	Don Budge	1969	Rod Laver	Tony Roche
1937	Don Budge	Baron G. von Cramm	1970	Ken Rosewall	Tony Roche
1938	Don Budge	C. Gene Mako	1971	Stan Smith	Jan Kodes
1939	Robert Riggs	S. Welby Van Horn	1972	Ilie Nastase	Arthur Ashe
1940	Don McNeill	Robert Riggs	1973	John Newcombe	Jan Kodes
1941	Robert Riggs	F. L. Kovacs	1974	Jimmy Connors	Ken Rosewall
1942	F. R. Schroeder Jr.	Frank Parker	1975	Manuel Orantes	Jimmy Connors
1943	Joseph Hunt	Jack Kramer	1976	Jimmy Connors	Bjorn Borg
1944	Frank Parker	William Talbert	1977	Guillermo Vilas	Jimmy Connors
1945	Frank Parker	William Talbert	1978	Jimmy Connors	Bjorn Borg
1946	Jack Kramer	Thomas Brown Jr.	1979	John McEnroe	Vitas Gerulaitis
1947	Jack Kramer	Frank Parker	1980	John McEnroe	Bjorn Borg
1948	Pancho Gonzales	Eric Sturgess	1981	John McEnroe	Bjorn Borg
1949	Pancho Gonzales	F. R. Schroeder Jr.	1982	Jimmy Connors	Ivan Lendl
1950	Arthur Larsen	Herbert Flam	1983	Jimmy Connors	Ivan Lendl
1951	Frank Sedgman	E. Victor Seixas Jr.	1984	John McEnroe	Ivan Lendl
1952	Frank Sedgman	Gardnar Mulloy	1985	Ivan Lendl	John McEnroe

Men's Doubles

Year	Champions	Year	Champions
1936	Don Budge—C. Gene Mako	1961	Dennis Ralston—Chuck McKinley
1937	Baron G. von Cramm—Henner Henkel	1962	Rafael Osuna—Antonio Palafox
1938	Don Budge—C. Gene Mako	1963	Dennis Ralston—Chuck McKinley
1939	Adrian Quist—John Bromwich	1964	Dennis Ralston—Chuck McKinley
1940	Jack Kramer—Frederick Schroeder Jr.	1965	Roy Emerson—Fred Stolle
1941	Jack Kramer—Frederick Schroeder Jr.	1966	Roy Emerson—Fred Stolle
1942	Gardnar Mulloy—William Talbert	1967	John Newcombe—Tony Roche
1943	Jack Kramer—Frank Parker	1968	Robert Lutz—Stan Smith
1944	Don McNeill—Robert Falkenburg	1969	Fred Stolle—Ken Rosewall
1945	Gardnar Mulloy—William Talbert	1970	Pierre Barthes—Nicki Pilic
1946	Gardnar Mulloy—William Talbert	1971	John Newcombe—Roger Taylor
1947	Jack Kramer—Frederick Schroeder Jr.	1972	Cliff Drysdale—Roger Taylor
1948	Gardnar Mulloy—William Talbert	1973	John Newcombe—Owen Davidson
1949	John Bromwich—William Sidwell	1974	Bob Lutz—Stan Smith
1950	John Bromwich—Frank Sedgman	1975	Jimmy Connors—Ilie Nastase
1951	Frank Sedgman—Kenneth McGregor	1976	Marty Riessen—Tom Okker
1952	Mervyn Rose—E. Victor Seixas Jr.	1977	Bob Hewitt—Frew McMillan
1953	Rex Hartwig—Mervyn Rose	1978	Stan Smith—Bob Lutz
1954	E. Victor Seixas Jr.—Tony Trabert	1979	John McEnroe—Peter Fleming
1955	Kosei Kamo—Atsushi Miyagi	1980	Bob Lutz—Stan Smith
1956	Lewis Hoad—Ken Rosewall	1981	John McEnroe—Peter Fleming
1957	Ashley Cooper—Neale Fraser	1982	Kevin Curren—Steve Denton
1958	Hamilton Richardson—Alejandro Olmedo	1983	John McEnroe—Peter Fleming
1959	Neale A. Fraser—Roy Emerson	1984	Tomas Smid—John Fitzgerald
1960	Neale A. Fraser—Roy Emerson	1985	Ken Flach—Robert Seguso

Mixed Doubles

Year	Champions	Year	Champions
1961	Margaret Smith—Robert Mark	1974	Pam Teeguarden—Geoff Masters
1962	Margaret Smith—Fred Stolle	1975	Rosemary Casals—Dick Stockton
1963	Margaret Smith—Kenneth Fletcher	1976	Billie Jean King—Phil Dent
1964	Margaret Smith—John Newcombe	1977	Betty Stove—Frew McMillan
1965	Margaret Smith—Fred Stolle	1978	Betty Stove—Frew McMillan
1966	Donna Floyd Fales—Owen Davidson	1979	Greer Stevens—Bob Hewitt
1967	Billie Jean King—Owen Davidson	1980	Wendy Turnbull—Marty Riessen
1968	Mary Ann Eisel—Peter Curtis	1981	Anne Smith—Kevin Curren
1969	Margaret S. Court—Marty Riessen	1982	Anne Smith—Kevin Curren
1970	Margaret S. Court—Marty Riessen	1983	Elizabeth Sayers—John Fitzgerald
1971	Billie Jean King—Owen Davidson	1984	Manuela Maleeva—Tom Gullikson
1972	Margaret S. Court—Marty Riessen	1985	Martina Navratilova—Heinz Gunthardt
1973	Billie Jean King—Owen Davidson		

Women's Singles

Year	Champion	Final opponent	Year	Champion	Final opponent
1936	Alice Marble	Helen Jacobs	1961	Darlene Hard	Ann Haydon
1937	Anita Lizana	Pauline Betz	1962	Margaret Smith	Darlene Hard
1938	Alice Marble	Louise Brough	1963	Maria Bueno	Margaret Smith
1939	Alice Marble	Louise Brough	1964	Maria Bueno	Carole Graebner
1940	Alice Marble	Margaret Osborne	1965	Margaret Smith	Billie Jean Moffitt
1941	Sarah Palfrey Cooke	Pauline Betz	1966	Maria Bueno	Nancy Richey
1942	Pauline Betz	Jadwiga Jedrzejowska	1967	Billie Jean King	Ann Haydon Jones
1943	Pauline Betz	Nancye Wynne	1968	Virginia Wade	Billie Jean King
1944	Pauline Betz	Helen Jacobs	1969	Margaret Court	Nancy Richey
1945	Sarah P. Cooke	Helen Jacobs	1970	Margaret Court	Rosemary Casals
1946	Pauline Betz	Doris Hart	1971	Billie Jean King	Rosemary Casals
1947	Louise Brough	Margaret Osborne	1972	Billie Jean King	Kerry Melville
1948	Margaret Osborne duPont	Louise Brough	1973	Margaret Court	Evonne Goolagong
1949	Margaret Osborne duPont	Doris Hart	1974	Billie Jean King	Evonne Goolagong
1950	Margaret Osborne duPont	Doris Hart	1975	Chris Evert	Evonne Goolagong
1951	Maureen Connolly	Shirley Fry	1976	Chris Evert	Evonne Goolagong
1952	Maureen Connolly	Doris Hart	1977	Chris Evert	Wendy Turnbull
1953	Maureen Connolly	Doris Hart	1978	Chris Evert	Pam Shriver
1954	Doris Hart	Louise Brough	1979	Tracy Austin	Chris Evert Lloyd
1955	Doris Hart	Patricia Ward	1980	Chris Evert Lloyd	Hana Mandlikova
1956	Shirley Fry	Althea Gibson	1981	Tracy Austin	Martina Navratilova
1957	Althea Gibson	Louise Brough	1982	Chris Evert Lloyd	Hana Mandlikova
1958	Althea Gibson	Darlene Hard	1983	Martina Navratilova	Chris Evert Lloyd
1959	Maria Bueno	Christine Truman	1984	Martina Navratilova	Chris Evert Lloyd
1960	Darlene Hard	Maria Bueno	1985	Hana Mandlikova	Martina Navratilova

Women's Doubles

Year	Champions	Year	Champions
1939	Alice Marble—Mrs. Sarah P. Fabyan	1963	Margaret Smith—Robyn Ebbern
1940	Alice Marble—Mrs. Sarah P. Fabyan	1964	Billie Jean Moffitt—Karen Susman
1941	Mrs. S. P. Cooke—Margaret Osborne	1965	Carole C. Graebner—Nancy Richey
1942	A. Louise Brough—Margaret Osborne	1966	Maria Bueno—Nancy Richey
1943	A. Louise Brough—Margaret Osborne	1967	Rosemary Casals—Billie Jean King
1944	A. Louise Brough—Margaret Osborne	1968	Maria Bueno—Margaret S. Court
1945	A. Louise Brough—Margaret Osborne	1969	Francoise Durr—Darlene Hard
1946	A. Louise Brough—Margaret Osborne	1970	M. S. Court—Judy Tegart Dalton
1947	A. Louise Brough—Margaret Osborne	1971	Rosemary Casals—Judy Tegart Dalton
1948	A. Louise Brough—Mrs. M. O. du Pont	1972	Francoise Durr—Betty Stove
1949	A. Louise Brough—Mrs. M. O. du Pont	1973	Margaret S. Court—Virginia Wade
1950	A. Louise Brough—Mrs. M. O. du Pont	1974	Billie Jean King—Rosemary Casals
1951	Doris Hart—Shirley Fry	1975	Margaret Court—Virginia Wade
1952	Doris Hart—Shirley Fry	1976	Linky Boshoff—Ilana Kloss
1953	Doris Hart—Shirley Fry	1977	Betty Stove—Martina Navratilova
1954	Doris Hart—Shirley Fry	1978	Martina Navratilova—Billie Jean King
1955	A. Louise Brough—Mrs. M. O. du Pont	1979	Betty Stove—Wendy Turnbull
1956	A. Louise Brough—Mrs. M. O. du Pont	1980	Billie Jean King—Martina Navratilova
1957	A. Louise Brough—Mrs. M. O. du Pont	1981	Anne Smith—Kathy Jordan
1958	Darlene Hard—Jeanne Arth	1982	Rosemary Casals—Wendy Turnbull
1959	Darlene Hard—Jeanne Arth	1983	Martina Navratilova—Pam Shriver
1960	Darlene Hard—Maria Bueno	1984	Martina Navratilova—Pam Shriver
1961	Darlene Hard—Lesley Turner	1985	Claudia Kohde-Kilsch—Helena Sukova
1962	Maria Bueno—Darlene Hard		

Davis Cup Challenge Round

Year	Result	Year	Result	Year	Result
1900	United States 5, British Isles 0	1929	France 4, United States 2	1960	Australia 4, Italy 1
1901	(not played)	1930	France 4, United States 1	1961	Australia 5, Italy 0
1902	United States 3, British Isles 2	1931	France 3, Great Britain 2	1962	Australia 5, Mexico 0
1903	British Isles 4, United States 1	1932	France 3, United States 2	1963	United States 3, Australia 2
1904	British Isles 5, Belgium 0	1933	Great Britain 3, France 2	1964	Australia 3, United States 2
1905	British Isles 5, United States 0	1934	Great Britain 4, United States 1	1965	Australia 4, Spain 1
1906	British Isles 5, United States 0	1935	Great Britain 5, United States 0	1966	Australia 4, India 1
1907	Australasia 3, British Isles 2	1936	Great Britain 3, Australia 2	1967	Australia 4, Spain 1
1908	Australasia 3, United States 2	1937	United States 4, Great Britain 1	1968	United States 4, Australia 1
1909	Australasia 5, United States 0	1938	United States 3, Australia 2	1969	United States 5, Romania 0
1910	(not played)	1939	Australia 3, United States 2	1970	United States 5, W. Germany 0
1911	Australasia 5, United States 0	1940-45	(not played)	1971	United States 3, Romania 2
1912	British Isles 3, Australasia 2	1946	United States 5, Australia 0	1972	United States 3, Romania 2
1913	United States 3, British Isles 2	1947	United States 4, Australia 1	1973	Australia 5, United States 0
1914	Australasia 3, United States 2	1948	United States 5, Australia 0	1974	South Africa (default by India)
1915-18	(not played)	1949	United States 4, Australia 1	1975	Sweden 3, Czech. 2
1919	Australasia 4, British Isles 1	1950	Australia 4, United States 1	1976	Italy 4, Chile 1
1920	United States 5, Australasia 0	1951	Australia 3, United States 2	1977	Australia 3, Italy 1
1921	United States 5, Japan 0	1952	Australia 4, United States 1	1978	United States 4, Great Britain 1
1922	United States 4, Australasia 1	1953	Australia 3, United States 2	1979	United States 5, Italy 0
1923	United States 4, Australasia 1	1954	United States 3, Australia 2	1980	Czechoslovakia 4, Italy 1
1924	United States 5, Australasia 0	1955	Australia 5, United States 0	1981	United States 3, Argentina 1
1925	United States 5, France 0	1956	Australia 5, United States 0	1982	United States 3, France, 0
1926	United States 4, France 1	1957	Australia 3, United States 2	1983	Australia 3, Sweden 1
1927	France 3, United States 2	1958	United States 3, Australia 2	1984	Sweden 3, United States 0
1928	France 4, United States 1	1959	Australia 3, United States 2		

All-England Champions, Wimbledon

Men's Singles

Year	Champion	Final opponent	Year	Champion	Final opponent
1933	Jack Crawford	Ellsworth Vines	1962	Rod Laver	Martin Mulligan
1934	Fred Perry	Jack Crawford	1963	Chuck McKinley	Fred Stolle
1935	Fred Perry	Gottfried von Cramm	1964	Roy Emerson	Fred Stolle
1936	Fred Perry	Gottfried von Cramm	1965	Roy Emerson	Fred Stolle
1937	Donald Budge	Gottfried von Cramm	1966	Manuel Santana	Dennis Ralston
1938	Donald Budge	Wilfred Austin	1967	John Newcombe	Wilhelm Bungert
1939	Bobby Riggs	Elwood Cooke	1968	Rod Laver	Tony Roche
1940-45	not held		1969	Rod Laver	John Newcombe
1946	Yvon Petra	Geoff E. Brown	1970	John Newcombe	Ken Rosewall
1947	Jack Kramer	Tom P. Brown	1971	John Newcombe	Stan Smith
1948	Bob Falkenburg	John Bromwich	1972	Stan Smith	Ilie Nastase
1949	Ted Schroeder	Jaroslav Drobny	1973	Jan Kodes	Alex Metreveli
1950	Budge Patty	Fred Sedgman	1974	Jimmy Connors	Ken Rosewall
1951	Dick Savitt	Ken McGregor	1975	Arthur Ashe	Jimmy Connors
1952	Frank Sedgman	Jaroslav Drobny	1976	Bjorn Borg	Ilie Nastase
1953	Vic Seixas	Kurt Nielsen	1977	Bjorn Borg	Jimmy Connors
1954	Jaroslav Drobny	Ken Rosewall	1978	Bjorn Borg	Jimmy Connors
1955	Tony Trabert	Kurt Nielsen	1979	Bjorn Borg	Roscoe Tanner
1956	Lew Hoad	Ken Rosewall	1980	Bjorn Borg	John McEnroe
1957	Lew Hoad	Ashley Cooper	1981	John McEnroe	Bjorn Borg
1958	Ashley Cooper	Neale Fraser	1982	Jimmy Connors	John McEnroe
1959	Alex Olmedo	Rod Laver	1983	John McEnroe	Chris Lewis
1960	Neale Fraser	Rod Laver	1984	John McEnroe	Jimmy Connors
1961	Rod Laver	Chuck McKinley	1985	Boris Becker	Kevin Curren

Women's Singles

Year	Champion	Year	Champion	Year	Champion	Year	Champion
1946	Pauline Betz	1956	Shirley Fry	1966	Billie Jean King	1976	Chris Evert
1947	Margaret Osborne	1957	Althea Gibson	1967	Billie Jean King	1977	Virginia Wade
1948	Louise Brough	1958	Althea Gibson	1968	Billie Jean King	1978	Martina Navratilova
1949	Louise Brough	1959	Maria Bueno	1969	Ann Haydon-Jones	1979	Martina Navratilova
1950	Louise Brough	1960	Maria Bueno	1970	Margaret Court	1980	Evonne Goolagong
1951	Doris Hart	1961	Angela Mortimer	1971	Evonne Goolagong	1981	Chris Evert Lloyd
1952	Maureen Connolly	1962	Karen Hantze-Susman	1972	Billie Jean King	1982	Martina Navratilova
1953	Maureen Connolly	1963	Margaret Smith	1973	Billie Jean King	1983	Martina Navratilova
1954	Maureen Connolly	1964	Maria Bueno	1974	Chris Evert	1984	Martina Navratilova
1955	Louise Brough	1965	Margaret Smith	1975	Billie Jean King	1985	Martina Navratilova

French Open Champions

Year	Men	Women	Year	Men	Women
1967	Roy Emerson	Françoise Durr	1977	Guillermo Vilas	Mima Jausovec
1968	Ken Rosewall	Nancy Richey	1978	Bjorn Borg	Virginia Ruzici
1969	Rod Laver	Margaret Smith Court	1979	Bjorn Borg	Chris Evert Lloyd
1970	Jan Kodes	Margaret Smith Court	1980	Bjorn Borg	Chris Evert Lloyd
1971	Jan Kodes	Evonne Goolagong	1981	Bjorn Borg	Hana Mandlikova
1972	Andres Gimeno	Billie Jean King	1982	Mats Wilander	Martina Navratilova
1973	Ilie Nastase	Margaret Court	1983	Yannick Noah	Chris Evert Lloyd
1974	Bjorn Borg	Chris Evert	1984	Ivan Lendl	Martina Navratilova
1975	Bjorn Borg	Chris Evert	1985	Mats Wilander	Chris Evert Lloyd
1976	Adriano Panatta	Sue Barker			

Leading Tennis Money Winners in 1984

Men

John McEnroe	$1,289,109
Ivan Lendl	700,196
Jimmy Connors	544,400
Mats Wilander	441,256
Tomas Smid	394,537
Andres Gomez	344,143
Jimmy Arias	339,176

Anders Jarryd	269,162
Henrik Sundstrom	245,412
Joakim Nystrom	231,478

Women

Martina Navratilova	$2,173,556
Chris Evert Lloyd	593,135
Hana Mandlikova	470,580
Pam Shriver	454,080
Mannuela Maleeva	326,057
Helena Sukova	282,443
Wendy Turnbull	255,095
Claudia Khode-Kilsch	213,899
Barbara Potter	185,113
Zina Garrison	179,014

National Shuffleboard Championships in 1985

Lakeside, Oh. July 22-27, 1985

Men's Open — C. R. Bone, Mt. Dora, Fla.
Men's Closed — Bob Pearson, Lakeland, Fla.
Women's Open — Virginia Worden, Coldwater, Mich.
Women's Closed — Catherine McCreery, Ontario, Canada

Men's Doubles — Harold Edmondson, Upper Arlington, Oh. & Wendell Lutes, Akron, Oh.
Women's Doubles — Adele Pearson, Lakeland, Fla. & Pat Whitaker, Bradenton, Fla.

Rifle and Pistol Individual Championships in 1985

Source: National Rifle Association

National Outdoor Rifle and Pistol Championships

Pistol — Max J. Barrington, Bellingham, Wash., 2650-133X.
Civilian Pistol — Max J. Barrington, 2650-133X.
Regular Service Pistol — Thomas P. Woods, Ft. Benning, Ga., 2639-134X.
Police Pistol — John L. Firley, Coral Gables, Fla., 2611-55X.
Woman Pistol — Ruby E. Fox, Parker, Ariz., 2594-107X.
Senior Pistol — Joseph C. White, Rockville, Md., 2595-98X.
Collegiate Pistol — Stuart B. Munsch, Edgewater, Md., 2456-67X.
Smallbore Rifle Prone — Lones W. Wigger Jr., Ft. Benning, Ga., 6397-540X.
Civilian Smallbore Rifle Prone — Presley W. Kendall, Carlisle, Ky., 6392-503X.
Woman Smallbore Rifle Prone — Marsha Beasley, Arlington, Va., 6383-473X.

Senior Smallbore Rifle Prone — Joseph W. Barnes Jr., Branchville, N.J., 6374-465X.
Collegiate Smallbore Rifle Prone — Jesse J. Johnston, Wallingford, Conn., 6383-443X.
Smallbore Rifle 3-Position — Carl R. Bernosky, Gordon, Pa., 2289-30X.
Women Smallbore Rifle 3-Position — Deborah W. Lyman, Meridan, Conn., 2247-26X.
Senior Smallbore Rifle 3-Position — Robert A. Makielski, Mishawaka, Ind., 2119-17X.
Collegiate Smallbore Rifle 3-Position — Jesse J. Johnston, 2236-16X.
Junior Smallbore Rifle 3-Position — Fritz P. Borke, Loveland, Oh., 2218-21X.

U. S. NRA International Shooting Championships

English Match — Lones W. Wigger Jr., Ft. Benning, Ga., 1790.
Smallbore Free Rifle — Lones W. Wigger Jr., 3502.
Air Rifle — Matthew Suggs, Eugene, Ore., 1752.
Ladies Air Rifle — Pat K. Spurgin, Billings, Mont., 1167.
Woman Standard Rifle Prone — Deena Wigger, Ft. Benning, Ga., 1774.
Woman Standard Rifle 3-Position — Deena Wigger, 1749.

Free Pistol — Donald Hamilton, Kingston, Mass., 1672.
Air Pistol — Donald Nygord, La Crescenta, Cal., 1743.
Woman Air Pistol — Ruby Fox, Parker, Ariz., 1123.
Center Fire Pistol — Donald Nygord, 1760.
Rapid Fire Pistol — Steven Collins, Niagara Falls, N.Y., 1772.
Standard Pistol — Donald Nygord, 1816.
Woman Sport Pistol — Ruby Fox, 1737.

National Indoor Rifle and Pistol Championships

Smallbore Rifle 4-Position — Gloria K. Parmentier, Ft. Benning, Ga., 799.
Smallbore Rifle International — Lones W. Wigger Jr., Ft. Benning, Ga., 1176.
Smallbore Rifle 3-Position — Gloria K. Parmentier, 1191.
Woman Smallbore Rifle 4-Position — Gloria K. Parmentier, 799.
Woman Smallbore Rifle International — Mary L. Godlove, Ft. Benning, Ga., 1171.
Woman Smallbore Rifle 3-Position — Gloria K. Parmentier, 1191.
Conventional Pistol — Norman R. Girardin, E. Hartford, Conn., 885.
Woman Conventional Pistol — Elizabeth C. Gathright, Afton,

Va., 838.
International Free Pistol — Donald C. Nygord, La Crescenta, Cal., 559.
Woman International Free Pistol — Judith L. Kemp, Anaheim, Cal., 500.
International Standard Pistol — Donald L. Kling, Palmyra, Pa., 574.
Woman International Standard Pistol — Lori B. Kamler, Chino, Cal., 549.
Air Pistol — Donald C. Nygord, 574.
Air Rifle — Wanda R. Jewell, Redstone Arsenal, Ala., 585.
Woman Air Pistol — Judith L. Kemp, 565.
Woman Air Rifle — Ethel Ann Alves, New Castle, Del., 578.

Sports on Television

Source: Sports 1984, A.C. Nielsen Co.

	Household rating %	% Viewing Audience			
		Men	Women	Teens	Children
Football					
NFL Super Bowl XIX	46.4	50	36	8	6
ABC-NFL (Monday evening)	16.9	59	32	5	4
CBS-NFL	14.3	59	29	6	6
NBC-NFL	12.0	56	29	8	7
College bowl games	11.9	54	34	7	5
College all-star games	5.1	55	35	6	4
NCAA regular season	8.2	56	31	6	7
Baseball					
World Series	22.9	52	38	5	5
All-star game	20.1	52	34	8	6
Regular season	7.0	55	32	6	7
Horse racing					
Average all	6.9	50	44	5	1
Basketball					
NBA average	7.1	55	27	12	6
NCAA average	5.9	57	27	9	7
Bowling					
Pro tour	7.2	45	43	5	7
Auto racing	5.6	56	34	4	6
Golf	4.4	51	39	4	6
Tennis					
Wimbledon	3.9	43	42	6	8
Tournament average	3.2	41	41	9	9
Multi-sports					
ABC Wide World of Sports	11.3	46	38	7	9
CBS Sports Sunday	5.8	50	32	7	11
Sportsworld	4.9	51	33	8	8

Chess

Chess dates back to antiquity. Its exact origin is unknown. The strongest players of their time, and therefore regarded by later generations as world champions, were Francois Philidor, France; Alexandre Deschappelles, France; Alexandre Deschappelles, France; Louis de la Bourdonnais, France; Howard Staunton, England; Adolph Anderssen, Germany and Paul Morphy, United States. In 1866 Wilhelm Steinitz of Austria defeated Adolph Anderssen and claimed the title of world champion. The official world champions since the title was first used follow:

1866-1894	Wilhelm Steinitz, Austria	1937-1946	Dr. Alexander A. Alekhine,	1961-1963	Mikhail Botvinnik, USSR
1894-1921	Dr. Emanuel Lasker, Germany		France	1963-1969	Tigran Petrosian, USSR
1921-1927	Jose R. Capablanca, Cuba	1948-1957	Mikhail Botvinnik, USSR	1969-1972	Boris Spassky, USSR
1927-1935	Dr. Alexander A. Alekhine,	1957-1958	Vassily Smyslov, USSR	1972-1975	Bobby Fischer, U.S. (a)
	France	1958-1959	Mikhail Botvinnik, USSR	1975	Anatoly Karpov, USSR (b)
1935-1937	Dr. Max Euwe, Netherlands	1960-1961	Mikhail Tal, USSR		

(a) Defaulted championship after refusal to accept International Chess Federation rules for a championship match, April 1975. (b) In Feb. 1985, the International Chess Federation stopped the championship match between Karpov and Garik Kasparov, also USSR, citing exhaustion on the part of the players. The match which began Sept. 1984 ended with the score 5-3 in Karpov's favor.

United States Champions

Unofficial champions							
1857-1871	Paul Morphy	1894-1895	Albert Hodges	1957-1961	Bobby Fischer	1980-1981	(tie) Larry Evans,
1871-1876	George Mackenzie	1895-1897	Jackson Showalter	1961-1962	Larry Evans		Larry Christiansen,
1876-1880	James Mason	1897-1906	Harry Pillsbury	1962-1968	Bobby Fischer		Walter Browne
1880-1889	George Mackenzie	1906-1909	vacant	1968-1969	Larry Evans	1981-1983	(tie) Walter Browne,
1889-1890	S. Lipschutz	1909-1936	Frank Marshall	1969-1972	Samuel Reshevsky		Yasser Seirawan
1890	Jackson Showalter	1936-1944	Samuel Reshevsky	1972-1973	Robert Byrne	1983	(tie) Walter Browne
1890-1891	Max Judd	1944-1946	Arnold Denker	1973-1974	Lubomir Kavalek,		Larry Christiansen
Official champions		1946-1948	Samuel Reshevsky		John Grefe		Roman
1891-1892	Jackson Showalter	1948-1951	Herman Steiner	1974-1977	Walter Browne		Dzindzichashvili
1892-1894	S. Lipschutz	1951-1954	Larry Evans	1978-1980	Lubomir Kavalek	1984	Lev Alburt
1894	Jackson Showalter	1954-1957	Arthur Bisguier				

The America's Cup

The Australian yacht *Australia II* defeated the United States yacht *Liberty* for the fourth time in the best-of-seven series of races to win the America's Cup on Sept. 26, 1983. It was the first time that the United States had lost the America's Cup series after having successfully defended the cup against 24 challengers dating back to 1851. Businessman Alan Bond headed the victorious *Australia II* syndicate and John Bertrand was the yacht's skipper.

Competition for the America's Cup grew out of the first contest to establish a world yachting championship, one of the carnival features of the London Exposition of 1851. The race, open to all classes of yachts from all over the world, covered a 60-mile course around the Isle of Wight; the prize was a cup worth about $500, donated by the Royal Yacht Squadron of England, known as the "America's Cup" because it was first won by the United States yacht *America*. Successive efforts of British and Australian yachtsmen had failed to win the famous trophy until 1983.

Winners of the America's Cup

1851	America	1920	Resolute defeated Shamrock IV, England, (3-2)
1870	Magic defeated Cambria, England, (1-0)	1930	Enterprise defeated Shamrock V, England, (4-0)
1871	Columbia (first three races) and Sappho (last two races) defeated Livonia, England, (4-1)	1934	Rainbow defeated Endeavour, England, (4-2)
		1937	Ranger defeated Endeavour II, England, (4-0)
1876	Madeline defeated Countess of Dufferin, Canada, (2-0)	1958	Columbia defeated Sceptre, England, (4-0)
1881	Mischief defeated Atalanta, Canada, (2-0)	1962	Weatherly defeated Gretel, Australia, (4-1)
1885	Puritan defeated Genesta, England, (2-0)	1964	Constellation defeated Sovereign, England, (4-0)
1886	Mayflower defeated Galatea, England, (2-0)	1967	Intrepid defeated Dame Pattie, Australia, (4-0)
1887	Volunteer defeated Thistle, Scotland, (2-0)	1970	Intrepid defeated Gretel II, Australia, (4-1)
1893	Vigilant defeated Valkyrie II, England, (3-0)	1974	Courageous defeated Southern Cross, Australia, (4-0)
1895	Defender defeated Valkyrie III, England, (3-0)	1977	Courageous defeated Australia, Australia, (4-0)
1899	Columbia defeated Shamrock, England, (3-0)	1980	Freedom defeated Australia, Australia, (4-1)
1901	Columbia defeated Shamrock II, England, (3-0)	1983	Australia II defeated Liberty, (4-3)
1903	Reliance defeated Shamrock III, England, (3-0)		

Table Tennis in 1985

U.S. National Closed Championship

Las Vegas, Nev., Dec. 19-23, 1984

Men's Singles — Eric Boggan, Merrick, N.Y.
Women's Singles — Julia Au, San Francisco, Cal.
Men's Doubles — Scott Boggan & Perry Schwartzberg, Houston, Tex.
Women's Doubles — Diana Gee & Lisa Gee, San Carlos, Cal.
Mixed Doubles — Quang Do, Cal. & Lisa Gee.

World Championships

Goteborg, Sweden, Mar. 28-Apr. 7, 1985

Men's Singles — Jiang Jialiang.
Women's Singles — Cao Yanhua.
Men's Doubles — Mikael Appelgren & Ulf Carlsson.
Women's Doubles — Dai Lili & Geng Lijuan.

U.S. National Open Championships

Miami Beach, Fla., June 26-30, 1985

Men's Singles — Cheng Yinghua, China.
Women's Singles — Li Huifend, China.
Men's Doubles — Cheng Yinghus & Jiang Jialiang, China.
Women's Doubles — Cao Yanhua & Li Huifeng, China.

Baseball

National Baseball Hall of Fame and Museum

Cooperstown, N.Y.

Aaron, Hank	Comiskey, Charles A.	Grove, Lefty	Lloyd, Pop	Rusie, Amos
Alexander, Grover Cleveland	Conlan, Jocko	Hafey, Chick	Lopez, Al	Ruth, Babe
Alston, Walt	Connolly, Thomas H.	Haines, Jesee	Lyons, Ted	Schalk, Ray
Anson, Cap	Connor, Roger	Hamilton, Bill	Mack, Connie	Sewell, Joe
Averill, Earl	Coveleski, Stan	Harridge, Will	MacPhail, Larry	Simmons, Al
Aparicio, Luis	Crawford, Sam	Harris, Bucky	Mantle, Mickey	Sisler, George
Appling, Luke	Cronin, Joe	Hartnett, Gabby	Manush, Henry	Slaughter, Enos
Baker, Home Run	Cummings, Candy	Heilmann, Harry	Maranville, Rabbit	Snider, Duke
Bancroft, Dave	Cuyler, Kiki	Herman, Billy	Marichal, Juan	Spahn, Warren
Banks, Ernie	Dean, Dizzy	Hooper, Harry	Marquard, Rube	Spalding, Albert
Barrow, Edward G.	Delahanty, Ed	Hornsby, Rogers	Mathews, Eddie	Speaker, Tris
Beckley, Jake	Dickey, Bill	Hoyt, Waite	Mathewson, Christy	Stengel, Casey
Bell, Cool Papa	DiHigo, Martin	Hubbard, Cal	Mays, Willie	Terry, Bill
Bender, Chief	DiMaggio, Joe	Hubbell, Carl	McCarthy, Joe	Thompson, Sam
Berra, Yogi	Drysdale, Don	Huggins, Miller	McCarthy, Thomas	Tinker, Joe
Bottomley, Jim	Duffy, Hugh	Irvin, Monte	McGinnity, Joe	Traynor, Pie
Boudreau, Lou	Evans, Billy	Jackson, Travis	McGraw, John	Vance, Dazzy
Bresnahan, Roger	Evers, John	Jennings, Hugh	McKechnie, Bill	Vaughan, Arky
Brock, Lou	Ewing, Buck	Johnson, Byron	Medwick, Joe	Waddell, Rube
Brouthers, Dan	Faber, Urban	Johnson, William (Rudy)	Mize, Johnny	Wagner, Honus
Brown (Three Finger), Mordecai	Feller, Bob	Johnson, Walter	Musial, Stan	Wallace, Roderick
Bulkeley, Morgan C.	Ferrell, Rick	Joss, Addie	Nichols, Kid	Walsh, Ed.
Burkett, Jesse C.	Flick, Elmer H.	Kaline, Al	O'Rourke, James	Waner, Lloyd
Campanella, Roy	Ford, Whitey	Keefe, Timothy	Ott, Mel	Waner, Paul
Carey, Max	Foster, Andrew	Keeler, William	Paige, Satchel	Ward, John
Cartwright, Alexander	Foxx, Jimmy	Kell, George	Pennock, Herb	Weiss, George
Chadwick, Henry	Frick, Ford	Kelley, Joe	Plank, Ed	Welch, Mickey
Chance, Frank	Frisch, Frank	Kelly, George	Radbourne, Charlie	Wheat, Zach
Chandler, Happy	Galvin, Pud	Kelly, King	Reese, Pee Wee	Wilhelm, Hoyt
Charleston, Oscar	Gehrig, Lou	Killebrew, Harmon	Rice, Sam	Williams, Ted
Chesbro, John	Gehringer, Charles	Kiner, Ralph	Rickey, Branch	Wilson, Hack
Clarke, Fred	Gibson, Bob	Klein, Chuck	Rixey, Eppa	Wright, George
Clarkson, John	Gibson, Josh	Klem, Bill	Roberts, Robin	Wright, Harry
Clemente, Roberto	Giles, Warren	Koufax, Sandy	Robinson, Brooks	Wynn, Early
Cobb, Ty	Gomez, Lefty	Lajoie, Napoleon	Robinson, Frank	Yawkey, Tom
Cochrane, Mickey	Goslin, Goose	Landis, Kenesaw M.	Robinson, Jackie	Young, Cy
Collins, Eddie	Greenberg, Hank	Lemon, Bob	Robinson, Wilbert	Youngs, Ross
Collins, James	Griffith, Clark	Leonard, Buck	Roush, Edd	
Combs, Earle	Grimes, Burleigh	Lindstrom, Fred	Ruffing, Red	

All-Star Baseball Games, 1933-1985

Year	Winner	Score	Location	Year	Winner	Score	Location
1933	American	4-2	Chicago	1960	National	6-0	New York
1934	American	9-7	New York	1961	National (3)	5-4	San Francisco
1935	American	4-1	Cleveland	1961	Called-rain	1-1	Boston
1936	National	4-3	Boston	1962	National (3)	3-1	Washington
1937	American	8-3	Washington	1962	American	9-4	Chicago
1938	National	4-1	Cincinnati	1963	National	5-3	Cleveland
1939	American	3-1	New York	1964	National	7-4	New York
1940	National	4-0	St. Louis	1965	National	6-5	Minnesota
1941	American	7-5	Detroit	1966	National (3)	2-1	St. Louis
1942	American	3-1	New York	1967	National (4)	2-1	Anaheim
1943*	American	5-3	Philadelphia	1968*	National	1-0	Houston
1944*	National	7-1	Pittsburgh	1969*	National	9-3	Washington
1945	(not played)			1970*	National (2)	5-4	Cincinnati
1946	American	12-0	Boston	1971*	American	6-4	Detroit
1947	American	2-1	Chicago	1972*	National	4-3	Atlanta
1948	American	5-2	St. Louis	1973*	National	7-1	Kansas City
1949	American	11-7	New York	1974*	National	7-2	Pittsburgh
1950	National (1)	4-3	Chicago	1975*	National	6-3	Milwaukee
1951	National	8-3	Detroit	1976*	National	7-1	Philadelphia
1952	National	3-2	Philadelphia	1977*	National	7-5	New York
1953	National	5-1	Cincinnati	1978*	National	7-3	San Diego
1954	American	11-9	Cleveland	1979*	National	7-6	Seattle
1955	National (2)	6-5	Milwaukee	1980*	National	4-2	Los Angeles
1956	National	7-3	Washington	1981*	National	5-4	Cleveland
1957	American	6-5	St. Louis	1982*	National	4-1	Montreal
1958	American	4-3	Baltimore	1983*	American	13-3	Chicago
1959	National	5-4	Pittsburgh	1984*	National	3-1	San Francisco
1959	American	5-3	Los Angeles	1985*	National	6-1	Minneapolis
1960	National	5-3	Kansas City				

(1) 14 innings, (2) 12 innings, (3) 10 innings, (4) 15 innings *Night game.

Major League Pennant Winners, 1901–1985

National League

Year	Winner	Won	Lost	Pct	Manager
1901	Pittsburgh	90	49	.647	Clarke
1902	Pittsburgh	103	36	.741	Clarke
1903	Pittsburgh	91	49	.650	Clarke
1904	New York	106	47	.693	McGraw
1905	New York	105	48	.686	McGraw
1906	Chicago	116	36	.763	Chance
1907	Chicago	107	45	.704	Chance
1908	Chicago	99	55	.643	Chance
1909	Pittsburgh	110	42	.724	Clarke
1910	Chicago	104	50	.675	Chance
1911	New York	99	54	.647	McGraw
1912	New York	103	48	.682	McGraw
1913	New York	101	51	.664	McGraw
1914	Boston	94	59	.614	Stallings
1915	Philadelphia	90	62	.592	Moran
1916	Brooklyn	94	60	.610	Robinson
1917	New York	98	56	.636	McGraw
1918	Chicago	84	45	.651	Mitchell
1919	Cincinnati	96	44	.686	Moran
1920	Brooklyn	93	60	.604	Robinson
1921	New York	94	59	.614	McGraw
1922	New York	93	61	.604	McGraw
1923	New York	95	58	.621	McGraw
1924	New York	93	60	.608	McGraw
1925	Pittsburgh	89	65	.578	McKechnie
1926	St. Louis	89	65	.578	Hornsby
1927	Pittsburgh	94	60	.610	Bush
1928	St. Louis	95	59	.617	McKechnie
1929	Chicago	98	54	.645	McCarthy
1930	St. Louis	92	62	.597	Street
1931	St. Louis	101	53	.656	Street
1932	Chicago	90	64	.584	Grimm
1933	New York	91	61	.599	Terry
1934	St. Louis	95	58	.621	Frisch
1935	Chicago	100	54	.649	Grimm
1936	New York	91	62	.597	Terry
1937	New York	95	57	.625	Terry
1938	Chicago	89	63	.586	Hartnett
1939	Cincinnati	97	57	.630	McKechnie
1940	Cincinnati	100	53	.654	McKechnie
1941	Brooklyn	100	54	.649	Durocher
1942	St. Louis	106	48	.688	Southworth
1943	St. Louis	105	49	.682	Southworth
1944	St. Louis	105	49	.682	Southworth
1945	Chicago	98	56	.636	Grimm
1946	St. Louis	98	58	.628	Dyer
1947	Brooklyn	94	60	.610	Shotton
1948	Boston	91	62	.595	Southworth
1949	Brooklyn	97	57	.630	Shotton
1950	Philadelphia	91	63	.591	Sawyer
1951	New York	98	59	.624	Durocher
1952	Brooklyn	96	57	.627	Dressen
1953	Brooklyn	105	49	.682	Dressen
1954	New York	97	57	.630	Durocher
1955	Brooklyn	98	55	.641	Alston
1956	Brooklyn	93	61	.604	Alston
1957	Milwaukee	95	59	.617	Haney
1958	Milwaukee	92	62	.597	Haney
1959	Los Angeles	88	68	.564	Alston
1960	Pittsburgh	95	59	.617	Murtaugh
1961	Cincinnati	93	61	.604	Hutchinson
1962	San Francisco	103	62	.624	Dark
1963	Los Angeles	99	63	.611	Alston
1964	St. Louis	93	69	.574	Keane
1965	Los Angeles	97	65	.599	Alston
1966	Los Angeles	95	67	.586	Alston
1967	St. Louis	101	60	.627	Schoendienst
1968	St. Louis	97	65	.599	Schoendienst

American League

Year	Winner	Won	Lost	Pct	Manager
1901	Chicago	83	53	.610	Griffith
1902	Philadelphia	83	53	.610	Mack
1903	Boston	91	47	.659	Collins
1904	Boston	95	59	.617	Collins
1905	Philadelphia	92	56	.622	Mack
1906	Chicago	93	58	.616	Jones
1907	Detroit	92	58	.613	Jennings
1908	Detroit	90	63	.588	Jennings
1909	Detroit	98	54	.645	Jennings
1910	Philadelphia	102	48	.680	Mack
1911	Philadelphia	101	50	.669	Mack
1912	Boston	105	47	.691	Stahl
1913	Philadelphia	96	57	.627	Mack
1914	Philadelphia	99	53	.651	Mack
1915	Boston	101	50	.669	Carrigan
1916	Boston	91	63	.591	Carrigan
1917	Chicago	100	54	.649	Rowland
1918	Boston	75	51	.595	Barrow
1919	Chicago	88	52	.629	Gleason
1920	Cleveland	98	56	.636	Speaker
1921	New York	98	55	.641	Huggins
1922	New York	94	60	.610	Huggins
1923	New York	98	54	.645	Huggins
1924	Washington	92	62	.597	Harris
1925	Washington	96	55	.636	Harris
1926	New York	91	63	.591	Huggins
1927	New York	110	44	.714	Huggins
1928	New York	101	53	.656	Huggins
1929	Philadelphia	104	46	.693	Mack
1930	Philadelphia	102	52	.622	Mack
1931	Philadelphia	107	45	.704	Mack
1932	New York	107	47	.695	McCarthy
1933	Washington	99	53	.651	Cronin
1934	Detroit	101	53	.656	Cochrane
1935	Detroit	93	58	.616	Cochrane
1936	New York	102	51	.667	McCarthy
1937	New York	102	52	.662	McCarthy
1938	New York	99	53	.651	McCarthy
1939	New York	106	45	.702	McCarthy
1940	Detroit	90	64	.584	Baker
1941	New York	101	53	.656	McCarthy
1942	New York	103	51	.669	McCarthy
1943	New York	98	56	.636	McCarthy
1944	St. Louis	89	65	.578	Sewell
1945	Detroit	88	65	.575	O'Neill
1946	Boston	104	50	.675	Cronin
1947	New York	97	57	.630	Harris
1948	Cleveland	97	58	.626	Boudreau
1949	New York	97	57	.630	Stengel
1950	New York	98	56	.636	Stengel
1951	New York	98	56	.636	Stengel
1952	New York	95	59	.617	Stengel
1953	New York	99	52	.656	Stengel
1954	Cleveland	111	43	.721	Lopez
1955	New York	96	58	.623	Stengel
1956	New York	97	57	.630	Stengel
1957	New York	98	56	.636	Stengel
1958	New York	92	62	.597	Stengel
1959	Chicago	94	60	.610	Lopez
1960	New York	97	57	.630	Stengel
1961	New York	109	53	.673	Houk
1962	New York	96	66	.593	Houk
1963	New York	104	57	.646	Houk
1964	New York	99	63	.611	Berra
1965	Minnesota	102	60	.630	Mele
1966	Baltimore	97	63	.606	Bauer
1967	Boston	92	70	.568	Williams
1968	Detroit	103	59	.636	Smith

National League

Year	East Winner	W	L	Pct	Manager	West Winner	W	L	Pct	Manager	Playoff winner
1969	N.Y. Mets	100	62	.617	Hodges	Atlanta	93	69	.574	Harris	New York
1970	Pittsburgh	89	73	.549	Murtaugh	Cincinnati	102	60	.630	Anderson	Cincinnati
1971	Pittsburgh	97	65	.599	Murtaugh	San Francisco	90	72	.556	Fox	Pittsburgh
1972	Pittsburgh	96	59	.619	Virdon	Cincinnati	95	59	.617	Anderson	Cincinnati
1973	N.Y. Mets	82	79	.509	Berra	Cincinnati	99	63	.611	Anderson	New York
1974	Pittsburgh	88	74	.543	Murtaugh	Los Angeles	102	60	.630	Alston	Los Angeles
1975	Pittsburgh	92	69	.571	Murtaugh	Cincinnati	108	54	.667	Anderson	Cincinnati
1976	Philadelphia	101	61	.623	Ozark	Cincinnati	102	60	.630	Anderson	Cincinnati
1977	Philadelphia	101	61	.623	Ozark	Los Angeles	98	64	.605	Lasorda	Los Angeles
1978	Philadelphia	90	72	.556	Ozark	Los Angeles	95	67	.586	Lasorda	Los Angeles
1979	Pittsburgh	98	64	.605	Tanner	Cincinnati	90	71	.559	McNamara	Pittsburgh

| | | East | | | | | West | | | | |
Year	Winner	W	L	Pct	Manager	Winner	W	L	Pct	Manager	Playoff winner
1980	Philadelphia .	91	71	.562	Green	Houston	93	70	.571	Virdon	Philadelphia
1981(a)	Philadelphia .	34	21	.618	Green	Los Angeles . . .	36	21	.632	Lasorda	(c)
1981(b)	Montreal . . .	30	23	.566	Williams, Fanning	Houston	33	20	.623	Virdon	Los Angeles
1982	St. Louis . .	92	70	.568	Herzog	Atlanta	89	73	.549	Torre	St. Louis
1983	Philadelphia .	90	72	.556	Corrales, Owens	Los Angeles . . .	91	71	.562	Lasorda	Philadelphia
1984	Chicago.	96	65	.596	Frey	San Diego	92	70	.568	Williams	San Diego
1985	St. Louis . . .	101	61	.623	Herzog	Los Angeles . . .	95	67	.586	Lasorda	St. Louis

American League

| | | East | | | | | West | | | | |
Year	Winner	W	L	Pct	Manager	Winner	W	L	Pct	Manager	Playoff winner
1969	Baltimore . . .	109	53	.673	Weaver	Minnesota	97	65	.599	Martin	Baltimore
1970	Baltimore . . .	108	54	.667	Weaver	Minnesota	98	64	.605	Rigney	Baltimore
1971	Baltimore . . .	101	57	.639	Weaver	Oakland	101	60	.627	Williams	Baltimore
1972	Detroit	86	70	.551	Martin	Oakland	93	62	.600	Williams	Oakland
1973	Baltimore . . .	97	65	.599	Weaver	Oakland	94	68	.580	Williams	Oakland
1974	Baltimore . . .	91	71	.562	Weaver	Oakland	90	72	.556	Dark	Oakland
1975	Boston.	95	65	.594	Johnson	Oakland	98	64	.605	Dark	Boston
1976	New York . . .	97	62	.610	Martin	Kansas City . . .	90	72	.556	Herzog	New York
1977	New York . . .	100	62	.617	Martin	Kansas City . . .	102	60	.630	Herzog	New York
1978	New York . . .	100	63	.613	Martin, Lemon	Kansas City . . .	92	70	.568	Herzog	New York
1979	Baltimore . . .	102	57	.642	Weaver	California	88	74	.543	Fregosi	Baltimore
1980	New York . . .	103	59	.636	Howser	Kansas City . . .	97	65	.599	Frey	Kansas City
1981(a)	New York . . .	34	22	.607	Michael	Oakland	37	23	.617	Martin	(d)
1981(b)	Milwaukee . .	31	22	.585	Rodgers	Kansas City . . .	30	23	.566	Frey, Howser	New York
1982	Milwaukee . .	95	67	.586	Rodgers, Kuenn	California.	93	69	.574	Mauch	Milwaukee
1983	Baltimore . . .	98	64	.605	Altobelli	Chicago	99	63	.611	LaRussa	Baltimore
1984	Detroit	104	58	.642	Anderson	Kansas City . . .	84	78	.519	Howser	Detroit
1985	Toronto . . .	99	62	.615	Cox	Kansas City . . .	91	71	.562	Howser	Kansas City

(a) First half; (b) Second half; (c) Montreal and Los Angeles won the divisional playoffs; (d) New York and Oakland won the divisional playoffs.

Baseball Stadiums

National League

Team		Surface	Home run distances (ft.)			Seating capacity
			LF	Center	RF	
Atlanta Braves.	Atlanta-Fulton County Stadium	Natural grass	330	402	330	53,046
Chicago Cubs	Wrigley Field.	Natural grass	355	400	353	37,272
Cincinnati Reds	Riverfront Stadium	Artificial	330	404	330	52,392
Houston Astros	Astrodome	Artificial	330	400	330	45,000
Los Angeles Dodgers	Dodger Stadium	Natural grass	330	395	330	56,000
Montreal Expos	Olympic Stadium	Artificial	325	404	325	59,149
New York Mets	Shea Stadium	Natural grass	338	410	338	55,300
Philadelphia Phillies	Veterans Stadium.	Artificial	330	408	330	66,744
Pittsburgh Pirates	Three Rivers Stadium.	Artificial	335	400	335	54,429
St. Louis Cardinals	Busch Stadium	Artificial	330	414	330	50,100
San Diego Padres	San Diego Jack Murphy Stadium	Natural grass	330	405	330	58,671
San Francisco Giants	Candlestick Park	Natural grass	335	400	330	58,000

American League

Team		Surface	LF	Center	RF	Seating capacity
Baltimore Orioles	Memorial Stadium.	Natural grass	309	405	309	53,198
Boston Red Sox	Fenway Park.	Natural grass	315	420	302	33,583
California Angels	Anaheim Stadium	Natural grass	333	404	333	65,158
Chicago White Sox	Comiskey Park	Natural grass	341	401	341	44,432
Cleveland Indians	Cleveland Stadium	Natural grass	320	400	320	74,208
Detroit Tigers	Tiger Stadium.	Natural grass	340	440	325	52,806
Kansas City Royals	Royals Stadium	Artificial	330	410	330	40,625
Milwaukee Brewers	Milwaukee County Stadium	Natural grass	315	402	315	53,192
Minnesota Twins.	Hubert H. Humphrey Metrodome	Artificial	343	408	327	55,122
New York Yankees	Yankee Stadium.	Natural grass	312	417	310	57,545
Oakland A's	Oakland Coliseum	Natural grass	330	397	330	50,255
Seattle Mariners.	Kingdome	Artificial	316	410	316	59,438
Texas Rangers	Arlington Stadium	Natural grass	330	400	330	43,508
Toronto Blue Jays.	Exhibition Stadium	Artificial grass	330	400	330	43,737

The Sporting News Golden Glove Awards in 1984

National League

Keith Hernandez, New York, first base.
Ryne Sandberg, Chicago, second base.
Mike Schmidt, Philadelphia, third base.
Ozzie Smith, St. Louis, shortstop.
Dale Murphy, Atlanta, outfield.
Andre Dawson, Montreal, outfield.
Bob Dernier, Chicago, outfield.
Tony Pena, Pittsburgh, catcher.
Joaquin Andujar, St. Louis, pitcher.

American League

Eddie Murray, Baltimore, first base.
Lou Whitaker, Detroit, second base.
Buddy Bell, Texas, third base.
Alan Trammell, Detroit, shortstop.
Dwight Evans, Boston, outfield.
Dwayne Murphy, Oakland, outfield.
Dave Winfield, New York, outfield.
Lance Parrish, Detroit, catcher.
Ron Guidry, New York, pitcher.

Home Run Leaders

National League		American League	
Year	HR	Year	HR
1924 Jacques Fournier, Brooklyn	27	1924 Babe Ruth, New York	46
1925 Rogers Hornsby, St. Louis	39	1925 Bob Meusel, New York	33
1926 Hack Wilson, Chicago	21	1926 Babe Ruth, New York	47
1927 Hack Wilson, Chicago; Cy Williams, Philadelphia	30	1927 Babe Ruth, New York	60
1928 Hack Wilson, Chicago; Jim Bottomley, St. Louis	31	1928 Babe Ruth, New York	54
1929 Charles Klein, Philadelphia	43	1929 Babe Ruth, New York	46
1930 Hack Wilson, Chicago	56	1930 Babe Ruth, New York	49
1931 Charles Klein, Philadelphia	31	1931 Babe Ruth, Lou Gehrig, New York	46
1932 Charles Klein, Philadelphia, Mel Ott, New York	38	1932 Jimmy Foxx, Philadelphia	58
1933 Charles Klein, Philadelphia	28	1933 Jimmy Foxx, Philadelphia	48
1934 Collins, St. Louis; Mel Ott, New York	35	1934 Lou Gehrig, New York	49
1935 Walter Berger, Boston	34	1935 Jimmy Foxx, Philadelphia, Hank Greenberg, Detroit	36
1936 Mel Ott, New York	33	1936 Lou Gehrig, New York	49
1937 Mel Ott, New York; Joe Medwick, St. Louis	31	1937 Joe DiMaggio, New York	46
1938 Mel Ott, New York	36	1938 Hank Greenberg, Detroit	58
1939 John Mize, St. Louis	28	1939 Jimmy Foxx, Boston	35
1940 John Mize, St. Louis	43	1940 Hank Greenberg, Detroit	41
1941 Dolph Camilli, Brooklyn	34	1941 Ted Williams, Boston	37
1942 Mel Ott, New York	30	1942 Ted Williams, Boston	36
1943 Bill Nicholson, Chicago	29	1943 Rudy York, Detroit	34
1944 Bill Nicholson, Chicago	33	1944 Nick Etten, New York	22
1945 Tommy Holmes, Boston	28	1945 Vern Stephens, St. Louis	24
1946 Ralph Kiner, Pittsburgh	23	1946 Hank Greenberg, Detroit	44
1947 Ralph Kiner, Pittsburgh; John Mize, New York	51	1947 Ted Williams, Boston	32
1948 Ralph Kiner, Pittsburgh; John Mize, New York	40	1948 Joe DiMaggio, New York	39
1949 Ralph Kiner, Pittsburgh	54	1949 Ted Williams, Boston	43
1950 Ralph Kiner, Pittsburgh	47	1950 Al Rosen, Cleveland	37
1951 Ralph Kiner, Pittsburgh	42	1951 Gus Zernial, Chicago-Philadelphia	33
1952 Ralph Kiner, Pittsburgh; Hank Sauer, Chicago	37	1952 Larry Doby, Cleveland	32
1953 Ed Mathews, Milwaukee	47	1953 Al Rosen, Cleveland	43
1954 Ted Kluszewski, Cincinnati	49	1954 Larry Doby, Cleveland	32
1955 Willie Mays, New York	51	1955 Mickey Mantle, New York	37
1956 Duke Snider, Brooklyn	43	1956 Mickey Mantle, New York	52
1957 Hank Aaron, Milwaukee	44	1957 Roy Sievers, Washington	42
1958 Ernie Banks, Chicago	47	1958 Mickey Mantle, New York	42
1959 Ed Mathews, Milwaukee	46	1959 Rocky Colavito, Cleveland,	
1960 Ernie Banks, Chicago	41	Harmon Killebrew, Washington	42
1961 Orlando Cepeda, San Francisco	46	1960 Mickey Mantle, New York	40
1962 Willie Mays, San Francisco	49	1961 Roger Maris, New York	61
1963 Hank Aaron, Milwaukee		1962 Harmon Killebrew, Minnesota	48
Willie McCovey, San Francisco	44	1963 Harmon Killebrew, Minnesota	45
1964 Willie Mays, San Francisco	47	1964 Harmon Killebrew, Minnesota	49
1965 Willie Mays, San Francisco	52	1965 Tony Conigliaro, Boston	32
1966 Hank Aaron, Atlanta	44	1966 Frank Robinson, Baltimore	49
1967 Hank Aaron, Atlanta	39	1967 Carl Yastrzemski, Boston, Harmon Killebrew, Minn.	44
1968 Willie McCovey, San Francisco	36	1968 Frank Howard, Washington	44
1969 Willie McCovey, San Francisco	45	1969 Harmon Killebrew, Minnesota	49
1970 Johnny Bench, Cincinnati	45	1970 Frank Howard, Washington	44
1971 Willie Stargell, Pittsburgh	48	1971 Bill Melton, Chicago	33
1972 Johnny Bench, Cincinnati	40	1972 Dick Allen, Chicago	37
1973 Willie Stargell, Pittsburgh	44	1973 Reggie Jackson, Oakland	32
1974 Mike Schmidt, Philadelphia	36	1974 Dick Allen, Chicago	32
1975 Mike Schmidt, Philadelphia	38	1975 George Scott, Milwaukee; Reggie Jackson, Oakland	36
1976 Mike Schmidt, Philadelphia	38	1976 Graig Nettles, New York	32
1977 George Foster, Cincinnati	52	1977 Jim Rice, Boston	39
1978 George Foster, Cincinnati	40	1978 Jim Rice, Boston	46
1979 Dave Kingman, Chicago	48	1979 Gorman Thomas, Milwaukee	45
1980 Mike Schmidt, Philadelphia	48	1980 Reggie Jackson, New York; Ben Oglivie, Milwaukee	41
1981 Mike Schmidt, Philadelphia	31	1981 Bobby Grich, California; Tony Armas, Oakland; Dwight Evans, Boston; Eddie Murray, Baltimore	22
1982 Dave Kingman, New York	37	1982 Gorman Thomas, Milwaukee; Reggie Jackson, California	39
1983 Mike Schmidt, Philadelphia	40	1983 Jim Rice, Boston	39
1984 Mike Schmidt, Phil.; Dale Murphy, Atlanta	36	1984 Tony Armas, Boston	43
1985 Dale Murphy, Atlanta	37	1985 Darrell Evans, Detroit	40

All-time Major League Record (154-game Season)—60—Babe Ruth, New York Yankees (A), 1927. **(162-game Season)—61—**Roger Maris, New York Yankees, 1961.

Runs Batted In Leaders

National League		American League	
Year	RBI	Year	RBI
1951 Monte Irvin, New York	121	1951 Gus Zernial, Chicago-Philadelphia	129
1952 Hank Sauer, Chicago	121	1952 Al Rosen, Cleveland	105
1953 Roy Campanella, Brooklyn	142	1953 Al Rosen, Cleveland	145
1954 Ted Kluszewski, Cincinnati	141	1954 Larry Doby, Cleveland	126
1955 Duke Snider, Brooklyn	136	1955 Ray Boone, Detroit, Jack Jensen, Boston	116
1956 Stan Musial, St. Louis	109	1956 Mickey Mantle, New York	130
1957 Hank Aaron, Milwaukee	132	1957 Roy Sievers, Washington	114
1958 Ernie Banks, Chicago	129	1958 Jack Jensen, Boston	122
1959 Ernie Banks, Chicago	143	1959 Jack Jensen, Boston	112
1960 Hank Aaron, Milwaukee	126	1960 Roger Maris, New York	112
1961 Orlando Cepeda, San Francisco	142	1961 Roger Maris, New York	142
1962 Tommy Davis, Los Angeles	153	1962 Harmon Killebrew, Minnesota	126

Year		RBI	Year		RBI
1963	Hank Aaron, Milwaukee	130	1963	Dick Stuart, Boston	118
1964	Ken Boyer, St. Louis	119	1964	Brooks Robinson, Baltimore	118
1965	Deron Johnson, Cincinnati	130	1965	Rocky Colavito, Cleveland	108
1966	Hank Aaron, Atlanta	127	1966	Frank Robinson, Baltimore	122
1967	Orlando Cepeda, St. Louis	111	1967	Carl Yastrzemski, Boston	121
1968	Willie McCovey, San Francisco	105	1968	Ken Harrelson, Boston	109
1969	Willie McCovey, San Francisco	126	1969	Harmon Killebrew, Minnesota	140
1970	Johnny Bench, Cincinnati	148	1970	Frank Howard, Washington	126
1971	Joe Torre, St. Louis	137	1971	Harmon Killebrew, Minnesota	119
1972	Johnny Bench, Cincinnati	125	1972	Dick Allen, Chicago	113
1973	Willie Stargell, Pittsburgh	119	1973	Reggie Jackson, Oakland	117
1974	Johnny Bench, Cincinnati	129	1974	Jeff Burroughs, Texas	118
1975	Greg Luzinski, Philadelphia	120	1975	George Scott, Milwaukee	109
1976	George Foster, Cincinnati	121	1976	Lee May, Baltimore	109
1977	George Foster, Cincinnati	149	1977	Larry Hisle, Minnesota	119
1978	George Foster, Cincinnati	120	1978	Jim Rice, Boston	139
1979	Dave Winfield, San Diego	118	1979	Don Baylor, California	139
1980	Mike Schmidt, Philadelphia	121	1980	Cecil Cooper, Milwaukee	122
1981	Mike Schmidt, Philadelphia	91	1981	Eddie Murray, Baltimore	78
1982	Dale Murphy, Atlanta; Al Oliver, Montreal	109	1982	Hal McRae, Kansas City	133
1983	Dale Murphy, Atlanta	121	1983	Cecil Cooper, Milwaukee; Jim Rice, Boston	126
1984	Mike Schmidt, Phil.; Gary Carter, Montreal	106	1984	Tony Armas, Boston	123
1985	Dave Parker, Cincinnati	125	1985	Don Mattingly, New York	145

Batting Champions

	National League				American League		
Year	Player	Club	Pct.	Year	Player	Club	Pct.
1923	Rogers Hornsby	St. Louis	.384	1923	Harry Heilmann	Detroit	.403
1924	Rogers Hornsby	St. Louis	.424	1924	Babe Ruth	New York	.378
1925	Rogers Hornsby	St. Louis	.403	1925	Harry Heilmann	Detroit	.393
1926	Eugene Hargrave	Cincinnati	.353	1926	Henry Manush	Detroit	.378
1927	Paul Waner	Pittsburgh	.380	1927	Harry Heilmann	Detroit	.398
1928	Rogers Hornsby	Boston	.387	1928	Goose Goslin	Washington	.379
1929	Lefty O'Doul	Philadelphia	.398	1929	Lew Fonseca	Cleveland	.369
1930	Bill Terry	New York	.401	1930	Al Simmons	Philadelphia	.381
1931	Chick Hafey	St. Louis	.349	1931	Al Simmons	Philadelphia	.390
1932	Lefty O'Doul	Brooklyn	.368	1932	Dale Alexander	Detroit-Boston	.367
1933	Charles Klein	Philadelphia	.368	1933	Jimmy Foxx	Philadelphia	.356
1934	Paul Waner	Pittsburgh	.362	1934	Lou Gehrig	New York	.363
1935	Arky Vaughan	Pittsburgh	.385	1935	Buddy Myer	Washington	.349
1936	Paul Waner	Pittsburgh	.373	1936	Luke Appling	Chicago	.388
1937	Joe Medwick	St. Louis	.374	1937	Charlie Gehringer	Detroit	.371
1938	Ernie Lombardi	Cincinnati	.342	1938	Jimmy Foxx	Boston	.349
1939	John Mize	St. Louis	.349	1939	Joe DiMaggio	New York	.381
1940	Debs Garms	Pittsburgh	.355	1940	Joe DiMaggio	New York	.352
1941	Pete Reiser	Brooklyn	.343	1941	Ted Williams	Boston	.406
1942	Ernie Lombardi	Boston	.330	1942	Ted Williams	Boston	.356
1943	Stan Musial	St. Louis	.357	1943	Luke Appling	Chicago	.328
1944	Dixie Walker	Brooklyn	.357	1944	Lou Boudreau	Cleveland	.327
1945	Phil Cavarretta	Chicago	.355	1945	George Stirnweiss	New York	.309
1946	Stan Musial	St. Louis	.365	1946	Mickey Vernon	Washington	.353
1947	Harry Walker	Philadelphia	.363	1947	Ted Williams	Boston	.343
1948	Stan Musial	St. Louis	.376	1948	Ted Williams	Boston	.369
1949	Jackie Robinson	Brooklyn	.342	1949	George Kell	Detroit	.343
1950	Stan Musial	St. Louis	.346	1950	Billy Goodman	Boston	.354
1951	Stan Musial	St. Louis	.355	1951	Ferris Fain	Philadelphia	.344
1952	Stan Musial	St. Louis	.336	1952	Ferris Fain	Philadelphia	.327
1953	Carl Furillo	Brooklyn	.344	1953	Mickey Vernon	Washington	.337
1954	Willie Mays	New York	.345	1954	Roberto Avila	Cleveland	.341
1955	Richie Ashburn	Philadelphia	.338	1955	Al Kaline	Detroit	.340
1956	Hank Aaron	Milwaukee	.328	1956	Mickey Mantle	New York	.353
1957	Stan Musial	St. Louis	.351	1957	Ted Williams	Boston	.388
1958	Richie Ashburn	Philadelphia	.350	1958	Ted Williams	Boston	.328
1959	Hank Aaron	Milwaukee	.355	1959	Harvey Kuenn	Detroit	.353
1960	Dick Groat	Pittsburgh	.325	1960	Pete Runnels	Boston	.320
1961	Roberto Clemente	Pittsburgh	.351	1961	Norm Cash	Detroit	.361
1962	Tommy Davis	Los Angeles	.346	1962	Pete Runnels	Boston	.326
1963	Tommy Davis	Los Angeles	.326	1963	Carl Yastrzemski	Boston	.321
1964	Roberto Clemente	Pittsburgh	.339	1964	Tony Oliva	Minnesota	.323
1965	Roberto Clemente	Pittsburgh	.329	1965	Tony Oliva	Minnesota	.321
1966	Matty Alou	Pittsburgh	.342	1966	Frank Robinson	Baltimore	.316
1967	Roberto Clemente	Pittsburgh	.357	1967	Carl Yastrzemski	Boston	.326
1968	Pete Rose	Cincinnati	.335	1968	Carl Yastrzemski	Boston	.301
1969	Pete Rose	Cincinnati	.348	1969	Rod Carew	Minnesota	.332
1970	Rico Carty	Atlanta	.366	1970	Alex Johnson	California	.328
1971	Joe Torre	St. Louis	.363	1971	Tony Oliva	Minnesota	.337
1972	Billy Williams	Chicago	.333	1972	Rod Carew	Minnesota	.318
1973	Pete Rose	Cincinnati	.338	1973	Rod Carew	Minnesota	.350
1974	Ralph Garr	Atlanta	.353	1974	Rod Carew	Minnesota	.364
1975	Bill Madlock	Chicago	.354	1975	Rod Carew	Minnesota	.359
1976	Bill Madlock	Chicago	.339	1976	George Brett	Kansas City	.333
1977	Dave Parker	Pittsburgh	.338	1977	Rod Carew	Minnesota	.388
1978	Dave Parker	Pittsburgh	.334	1978	Rod Carew	Minnesota	.333
1979	Keith Hernandez	St. Louis	.344	1979	Fred Lynn	Boston	.333
1980	Bill Buckner	Chicago	.324	1980	George Brett	Kansas City	.390
1981	Bill Madlock	Pittsburgh	.341	1981	Carney Lansford	Boston	.336
1982	Al Oliver	Montreal	.331	1982	Willie Wilson	Kansas City	.332
1983	Bill Madlock	Pittsburgh	.323	1983	Wade Boggs	Boston	.361
1984	Tony Gwynn	San Diego	.351	1984	Don Mattingly	New York	.343
1985	Willie McGee	St. Louis	.353	1985	Wade Boggs	Boston	.368

National League Records in 1985

Final standings

Eastern Division

Club	W	L	Pct	GB
St. Louis	101	61	.623	—
New York	98	64	.605	3
Montreal	84	77	.522	16½
Chicago	77	84	.478	23½
Philadelphia	75	87	.463	26
Pittsburgh	57	104	.354	43½

Western Division

Club	W	L	Pct	GB
Los Angeles	95	67	.586	—
Cincinnati	89	72	.553	5½
Houston	83	79	.512	12
San Diego	83	79	.512	12
Atlanta	66	96	.407	29
San Francisco	62	100	.383	33

National League Championship Series

Los Angeles 4, St. Louis 1
Los Angeles 8, St. Louis 2
St. Louis 4, Los Angeles 2

St. Louis 12, Los Angeles 2
St. Louis 3, Los Angeles 2
St. Louis 7, Los Angeles 5

Club Batting

Club	Pct	AB	R	H	HR	SB
St. Louis	.264	5467	747	1446	87	314
Houston	.261	5582	706	1457	121	96
Los Angeles	.261	5502	682	1434	129	136
New York	.257	5549	695	1425	134	117
San Diego	.255	5507	650	1405	109	60
Cincinnati	.255	5431	677	1385	114	159
Chicago	.254	5492	686	1397	150	182
Montreal	.247	5429	633	1342	118	169
Pittsburgh	.247	5436	568	1340	80	110
Atlanta	.246	5526	632	1359	126	72
Philadelphia	.245	5477	667	1343	141	122
San Francisco	.233	5420	556	1263	115	99

Club Pitching

Club	ERA	CG	IP	H	R	BB	SO
Los Angeles	2.96	37	1465	1280	579	462	979
St. Louis	3.10	37	1464	1343	572	453	798
New York	3.11	32	1488	1306	568	515	1039
San Diego	3.40	26	1451	1399	622	443	727
Montreal	3.55	13	1457	1346	636	509	870
San Francisco	3.61	13	1448	1348	674	572	985
Houston	3.66	17	1458	1393	691	543	909
Philadelphia	3.68	24	1447	1424	673	596	899
Cincinnati	3.71	24	1451	1347	666	535	910
St. Louis	3.97	15	1445	1406	708	584	962
Chicago	4.16	20	1442	1492	729	519	820
Atlanta	4.19	9	1457	1512	781	642	776

Individual Batting

Leaders—Based on 502 plate appearances.

Player, club	Pct	AB	R	H	HR	RBI	SB
McGee, St. Louis	.353	612	114	216	10	82	56
Guerrero, Los Angeles	.320	487	99	156	33	87	12
Raines, Montreal	.320	575	115	184	11	41	70
Gwynn, San Diego	.317	622	90	197	6	46	14
Parker, Cincinnati	.312	635	88	198	34	125	5
Hernandez, New York	.309	593	87	183	10	91	3
Moreland, Chicago	.307	587	74	180	14	106	12
Sandberg, Chicago	.305	609	113	186	26	83	54
Herr, St. Louis	.302	596	97	180	8	110	31
Murphy, Atlanta	.300	616	118	185	37	111	10

Individual Pitching

Leaders—Based on 162 innings pitched.

Pitcher, club	W	L	ERA	G	IP	H	BB	SO
Gooden, New York	24	4	1.53	35	276	198	69	268
Tudor, St. Louis	21	8	1.93	36	275	209	49	169
Hershiser, Los Angeles	19	3	2.03	36	239	179	68	157
Reuschel, Pittsburgh	14	8	2.27	31	194	153	52	138
Welch, Los Angeles	14	4	2.31	23	167	141	35	96
Valenzuela, Los Angeles	17	10	2.45	35	272	211	101	208
Fernandez, New York	9	9	2.80	26	170	108	80	180
Cox, St. Louis	18	9	2.88	35	241	226	64	131
Darling, New York	16	6	2.90	36	248	214	114	167
Smith, Montreal	18	5	2.91	32	222	193	41	127

Individual Batting (at least 115 at-bats); Individual Pitching (at least 50 innings)

Atlanta Braves

Batting	Avg	AB	R	H	HR	RBI
Thompson	.302	182	17	55	0	6
Murphy	.300	616	118	185	37	111
Washington	.276	398	62	110	15	43
Oberkfell	.272	412	30	112	3	35
Horner	.267	483	61	129	27	89
Harper	.264	492	58	130	17	72
Zuvella	.253	190	16	48	0	4
Ramirez	.248	568	54	141	5	58
Chambliss	.235	170	16	40	3	21
Hubbard	.232	439	51	102	5	39
Komminsk	.227	300	52	68	4	21
Cerone	.216	282	15	61	3	25
Perry	.214	238	22	51	3	13
Benedict	.202	208	12	42	0	20

Pitching	W	L	ERA	IP	BB	SO	Sv
Forster	2	3	2.28	59	28	37	1
Mahler	17	15	3.48	266	79	107	
Garber	6	6	3.61	97	25	66	1
Smith	9	10	3.80	147	80	85	
Bedrosian	7	15	3.83	206	111	134	
Camp	4	6	3.95	127	61	49	3
Dedmon	6	3	4.08	86	49	41	
Johnson	4	4	4.10	85	24	34	
Sutter	7	7	4.48	88	29	52	23
Shields	1	2	5.16	68	32	29	
Perez	1	13	6.14	95	57	57	
Barker	2	9	6.35	73	37	47	

Chicago Cubs

Batting	Avg	AB	R	H	HR	RBI
Bosley	.328	180	25	59	7	27
Moreland	.307	587	74	180	14	106
Sandberg	.305	609	113	186	26	83
Lopes	.284	275	52	78	11	44
Durham	.282	542	58	153	21	75
Dunston	.260	250	40	65	4	18
Dernier	.254	469	63	119	1	21
Hatcher	.245	163	24	40	2	10
Speier	.243	218	16	53	4	24
Matthews	.235	298	45	70	13	40
Davis	.232	482	47	112	17	58
Cey	.232	500	64	116	22	63
Hebner	.217	120	10	26	3	22
Lake	.151	119	5	18	1	11

Pitching	W	L	ERA	IP	BB	SO	Sv
Smith	7	4	3.04	97	32	112	33
Eckersley	11	7	3.08	169	19	117	
Sanderson	5	6	3.12	121	27	80	
Sutcliffe	8	8	3.18	130	44	102	
Trout	9	7	3.39	140	63	44	
Baler	2	3	3.46	52	17	31	1
Sorensen	3	7	4.26	82	24	34	
Fontenot	6	10	4.36	154	45	70	
Ruthven	4	7	4.53	87	37	26	
Engel	1	5	5.57	51	26	29	1
Brusstar	4	3	6.05	74	36	34	4
Frazier	7	8	6.39	76	52	46	2

Cincinnati Reds

Batting	Avg	AB	R	H	HR	RBI
Perez	.328	183	25	60	0	33
Parker	.312	635	88	198	34	125
Oester	.295	526	59	155	1	34
Venable	.289	135	21	39	0	10
Krenchicki	.272	173	16	47	4	25
Rose	.264	405	60	107	2	46
Esasky	.262	413	61	108	21	66
Milner	.254	453	82	115	3	33
Redus	.252	246	51	62	6	28
Concepcion	.252	560	59	141	7	48
Davis	.246	122	26	30	8	18
Diaz	.245	237	21	58	5	31
Van Gorder	.238	151	12	36	2	24
Bell	.219	247	28	54	6	36

Pitching	W	L	ERA	IP	BB	SO	Sv
Franco	12	3	2.18	99	40	61	12
Power	8	6	2.70	80	45	42	27
Hume	3	5	3.26	80	35	50	3
Browning	20	9	3.55	261	73	155	
Soto	12	15	3.58	256	104	214	
McGaffigan	3	3	3.72	94	30	83	
Pastore	2	1	3.83	54	16	29	
Price	2	2	3.90	64	23	52	1
Tibbs	10	16	3.92	218	83	98	
Robinson	7	7	3.99	108	32	76	1
Stuper	8	5	4.55	99	37	38	

Houston Astros

Batting	Avg	AB	R	H	HR	RBI
Cruz	.300	544	69	163	9	79
Doran	.287	578	84	166	14	59
Puhl	.284	194	34	55	2	23
Ashby	.280	189	20	53	8	25
Mumphrey	.277	444	52	123	8	61
Reynolds	.272	379	43	103	4	32
Davis	.271	350	51	95	20	64
Walling	.270	345	44	93	7	45
Bass	.269	539	72	145	16	68
Garner	.268	463	65	124	6	51
Bailey	.265	332	47	88	10	45
Thon	.251	251	26	63	6	29
Pankovits	.244	172	24	42	4	14

Pitching	W	L	ERA	IP	BB	SO	Sv
Smith	9	5	2.27	79	17	40	27
Calhoun	2	5	2.54	63	24	47	4
Scott	18	8	3.29	221	80	137	
Heathcock	3	1	3.36	56	13	25	1
Knepper	15	13	3.55	241	54	131	
Dawley	5	3	3.56	81	37	48	2
Niekro	9	12	3.72	213	99	117	
Ryan	10	12	3.80	232	95	209	
DiPino	3	7	4.03	76	43	49	6
Mathis	3	5	6.04	70	27	34	1

Los Angeles Dodgers

Batting	Avg	AB	R	H	HR	RBI
Guerrero	.320	487	99	156	33	87
Scioscia	.296	429	47	127	7	53
Marshall	.293	518	72	152	28	95
Sax	.279	488	62	136	1	42
Madlock	.275	513	69	141	12	56
Cabell	.272	335	40	91	2	36
Landreaux	.268	482	70	129	12	50
Russell	.260	169	19	44	0	13
Brock	.251	438	64	110	21	66
Bailor	.246	118	8	29	0	7
Duncan	.244	562	74	137	6	39
Maldonado	.225	213	20	48	5	19
Yeager	.207	121	4	25	0	9
Anderson	.199	221	24	44	4	18

Pitching	W	L	ERA	IP	BB	SO	Sv
Hershiser	19	3	2.03	239	68	157	
Welch	14	4	2.31	167	35	96	
Valenzuela	17	10	2.45	272	101	208	
Diaz	6	3	2.61	79	18	73	
Neidenfuer	7	9	2.71	106	24	102	19
Reuss	14	10	2.92	212	58	84	
Honeycutt	8	12	3.42	142	49	67	1
Howell	4	7	3.77	86	35	85	12
Castillo	2	2	5.43	68	41	57	

Montreal Expos

Batting	Avg	AB	R	H	HR	RBI
Raines	.320	575	115	184	11	41
Webster	.274	212	32	58	11	30
Brooks	.269	605	67	163	13	100
Francona	.267	281	19	75	2	31
Law	.266	519	75	138	10	52
Wallach	.260	569	70	148	22	81
Dawson	.255	529	65	135	23	91
Washington	.249	193	24	48	1	17
Winningham	.237	312	30	74	3	21
Thompson	.224	143	10	32	0	10
Fitzgerald	.207	295	25	61	5	34
Butera	.200	120	11	24	3	12
Wohlford	.192	125	7	24	1	15

Pitching	W	L	ERA	IP	BB	SO	Sv
Burke	9	4	2.39	120	44	87	8
Youmans	4	3	2.45	77	49	54	
Hesketh	10	5	2.49	155	45	113	
Smith	18	5	2.91	222	41	127	
Reardon	2	8	3.18	87	26	67	41
Lucas	6	2	3.19	67	24	31	2
Roberge	3	3	3.44	68	22	34	2
Gullickson	14	12	3.52	181	47	68	
Palmer	7	10	3.71	135	67	106	
Schatzeder	3	5	3.80	104	31	64	
St. Claire	5	3	3.93	68	26	25	
Laskey	5	16	4.91	148	53	60	

New York Mets

Batting	Avg	AB	R	H	HR	RBI
Hernandez	.309	593	87	183	10	91
Paciorek	.284	116	14	33	1	11
Carter	.281	555	83	156	32	100
Heep	.280	271	26	76	7	42
Strawberry	.277	393	78	109	29	79
Wilson	.276	337	56	93	6	26
Backman	.273	520	77	142	1	38
Foster	.263	452	57	119	21	77
Santana	.257	529	41	136	1	29
Dykstra	.254	236	40	60	1	19
Johnson	.242	389	38	94	11	46
Bowa	.234	214	15	50	0	15
Knight	.218	271	22	59	6	36
Chapman	.174	144	16	25	0	7

Pitching	W	L	ERA	IP	BB	SO	Sv
Gooden	24	4	1.53	276	69	268	
Orosco	8	6	2.73	79	34	68	17
Fernandez	9	9	2.80	170	80	180	
McDowell	6	5	2.83	127	37	70	17
Darling	16	6	2.90	248	114	167	
Leach	3	4	2.91	55	14	30	1
Aguilera	10	7	3.24	122	37	74	
Lynch	10	8	3.44	191	27	65	
Sisk	4	5	5.30	73	40	26	2

Philadelphia Phillies

Batting	Avg	AB	R	H	HR	RBI
Aguayo	.279	165	27	46	6	21
Schmidt	.277	549	89	152	33	93
Wilson	.275	608	73	167	14	102
Stone	.265	264	36	70	3	11
Samuel	.264	663	101	175	19	74
Hayes	.263	570	76	150	13	70
G. Gross	.260	169	21	44	0	14
Schu	.252	416	54	105	7	24
Virgil	.246	426	47	105	19	55
Knicely	.242	165	17	40	5	26
Foley	.240	250	24	60	3	23
Maddox	.239	218	22	52	4	23
Russell	.218	216	22	47	9	23
Corcoran	.214	182	11	39	0	22
Jeltz	.189	196	17	37	0	12

Pitching	W	L	ERA	IP	BB	SO	Sv
Carman	9	4	2.08	86	38	87	7
Rawley	13	8	3.31	198	81	106	
Carlton	1	8	3.33	92	53	48	
K. Gross	15	13	3.41	205	81	151	
Tekulve	4	10	3.57	75	5	40	14
Hudson	8	13	3.78	193	74	122	
Denny	11	14	3.82	230	83	123	
Rucker	3	2	4.31	79	40	41	1
Andersen	3	3	4.32	73	26	50	3
Koosman	6	4	4.62	99	34	60	

Pittsburgh Pirates

Batting	Avg	AB	R	H	HR	RBI
Brown	.332	205	29	68	5	33
Orsulak	.300	397	54	119	0	21
Mazzilli	.282	117	20	33	1	9
Reynolds	.282	337	44	95	3	42
Ray	.274	594	67	163	7	70
Almon	.270	244	33	66	6	29
Morrison	.254	244	17	62	4	22
Kemp	.250	236	19	59	2	21
Pena	.249	546	53	136	10	59
Thompson	.241	402	42	97	12	61
Khalifa	.238	319	30	79	2	31
Hendrick	.230	256	23	59	2	25
Bream	.230	148	18	34	6	21
Gonzalez	.226	124	11	28	4	12
Lezcano	.207	116	16	24	3	9
Wynne	.205	337	21	69	2	18

Pitching	W	L	ERA	IP	BB	SO	Sv
Reuschel	14	8	2.27	194	52	138	1
Guante	4	6	2.72	109	40	92	5
Holland	1	4	3.45	62	21	48	5
Candelaria	2	4	3.64	54	14	47	9
Walk	2	3	3.68	58	18	40	
Robinson	5	11	3.87	95	42	65	3
Tunnell	4	10	4.01	132	57	74	
Rhoden	10	15	4.47	213	69	128	
McWilliams	7	9	4.70	126	62	52	
DeLeon	2	19	4.70	162	89	149	3
Winn	3	6	5.23	75	31	22	

St. Louis Cardinals

Batting	Avg	AB	R	H	HR	RBI
McGee	.353	612	114	216	10	82
Herr	.302	596	97	180	8	110
Cedeno	.291	296	38	86	9	49
Clark	.281	442	71	124	22	87
Landrum	.280	161	21	45	4	21
O. Smith	.276	537	70	148	6	54
Coleman	.267	636	107	170	1	40
Van Slyke	.259	424	61	110	13	55
Pendleton	.240	559	56	134	5	69
Nieto	.225	253	15	57	0	34
Porter	.221	240	30	53	10	36

Pitching	W	L	ERA	IP	BB	SO	Sv
Lahti	5	2	1.84	68	26	41	19
Tudor	21	8	1.93	275	49	169	
Dayley	4	4	2.76	65	18	62	11
Cox	18	9	2.88	241	64	131	
Horton	3	2	2.91	89	34	59	1
Andujar	21	12	3.40	269	82	112	
Campbell	5	3	3.50	64	21	41	4
Forsch	9	6	3.90	136	47	48	2
Kepshire	10	9	4.75	153	71	67	

San Diego Padres

Batting	Avg	AB	R	H	HR	RBI
Gwynn	.317	622	90	197	6	46
Templeton	.282	546	63	154	6	55
Garvey	.281	654	80	184	17	81
Flannery	.281	384	50	108	1	40
Royster	.281	249	31	70	5	24
Nettles	.261	440	66	115	15	61
Kennedy	.261	532	54	139	10	74
Martinez	.253	514	64	130	21	72
Bevacqua	.239	138	17	33	3	25
McReynolds	.234	564	61	132	15	75
Dilone	.200	130	18	26	0	7

Pitching	W	L	ERA	IP	BB	SO	Sv
Gossage	5	3	1.82	79	17	52	26
Dravecky	13	11	2.93	214	57	105	
Show	12	11	3.09	233	87	141	
Hawkins	18	8	3.15	228	65	69	
Lefferts	7	6	3.35	83	30	48	2
Hoyt	16	8	3.47	210	20	83	
Thurmond	7	11	3.97	138	44	57	2
Stoddard	1	6	4.65	60	37	42	1

San Francisco Giants

Batting	Avg	AB	R	H	HR	RBI
Brown	.271	432	50	117	16	61
C. Davis	.270	481	53	130	13	56
Youngblood	.270	230	24	62	4	24
Roenicke	.256	133	23	34	3	13
Green	.248	294	36	73	5	20
Driessen	.243	493	53	120	9	47
Gladden	.243	502	64	122	7	41
Leonard	.241	507	49	122	17	62
Uribe	.237	476	46	113	3	26
Wellman	.236	174	16	41	0	16
Trillo	.224	451	36	101	3	25
Brenly	.220	440	41	97	19	56
Trevino	.217	157	17	34	6	19
Adams	.190	121	12	23	2	10
Deer	.185	162	22	30	8	20

Pitching	W	L	ERA	IP	BB	SO	Sv
Garrelts	9	6	2.30	105	58	106	13
Krukow	8	11	3.38	194	49	150	
Minton	5	4	3.54	96	54	37	4
M. Davis	5	12	3.54	114	41	131	7
LaPoint	7	17	3.57	206	74	122	
Hammaker	5	12	3.74	170	47	100	
Gott	7	10	3.88	148	51	78	
Williams	2	4	4.19	73	35	54	
Blue	8	8	4.47	131	80	103	

Leading Pitchers, Earned-Run Average

	National League						American League			
Year	Player, club	G	IP	ERA		Year	Player, club	G	IP	ERA
1967	Phil Niekro, Atlanta	46	207	1.87		1967	Joe Horlen, Chicago	35	258	2.06
1968	Bob Gibson, St. Louis	34	305	1.12		1968	Luis Tiant, Cleveland	34	258	1.60
1969	Juan Marichal, San Francisco	37	300	2.10		1969	Dick Bosman, Washington	31	193	2.19
1970	Tom Seaver, New York	37	291	2.81		1970	Diego Segui, Oakland	47	162	2.56
1971	Tom Seaver, New York	36	286	1.76		1971	Vida Blue, Oakland	39	312	1.82
1972	Steve Carlton, Philadelphia	41	346	1.98		1972	Luis Tiant, Boston	43	179	1.91
1973	Tom Seaver, New York	36	290	2.07		1973	Jim Palmer, Baltimore	38	296	2.40
1974	Buzz Capra, Atlanta	39	217	2.28		1974	Catfish Hunter, Oakland	41	318	2.49
1975	Randy Jones, San Diego	37	285	2.24		1975	Jim Palmer, Baltimore	39	323	2.09
1976	John Denny, St. Louis	30	207	2.52		1976	Mark Fidrych, Detroit	31	250	2.34
1977	John Candelaria, Pittsburgh	33	231	2.34		1977	Frank Tanana, California	31	241	2.54
1978	Craig Swan, New York	29	207	2.43		1978	Ron Guidry, New York	35	274	1.74
1979	J. R. Richard, Houston	38	292	2.71		1979	Ron Guidry, New York	33	236	2.78
1980	Don Sutton, Los Angeles	32	212	2.21		1980	Rudy May, New York	41	175	2.47
1981	Nolan Ryan, Houston	21	149	1.69		1981	Steve McCatty, Oakland	22	186	2.32
1982	Steve Rogers, Montreal	35	277	2.40		1982	Rick Sutcliffe, Cleveland	34	216	2.96
1983	Atlee Hammaker, San Fran.	23	172	2.25		1983	Rick Honeycutt, Texas	25	174	2.42
1984	Alejandro Pena, Los Angeles	28	199	2.48		1984	Mike Boddicker, Baltimore	34	261	2.79
1985	Dwight Gooden, New York	35	276	1.53		1985	Dave Stieb, Toronto	36	265	2.48

ERA is computed by multiplying earned runs allowed by 9, then dividing by innings pitched.

Little League World Series in 1985

The team from South Korea won the 1985 Little League World Series by defeating the team from Mexicali, Mexico 7-1 at Williamsport, Pa. on Aug. 24. It was the 2d straight title for South Korea.

Most Valuable Player

Baseball Writers' Association

National League

Year	Player, team	Year	Player, team	Year	Player, team
1931	Frank Frisch, St. Louis	1950	Jim Konstanty, Philadelphia	1968	Bob Gibson, St. Louis
1932	Charles Klein, Philadelpha	1951	Roy Campanella, Brooklyn	1969	Willie McCovey, San Francisco
1933	Carl Hubbell, New York	1952	Hank Sauer, Chicago	1970	Johnny Bench, Cincinnati
1934	Dizzy Dean, St. Louis	1953	Roy Campanella, Brooklyn	1971	Joe Torre, St. Louis
1935	Gabby Hartnett, Chicago	1954	Willie Mays, New York	1972	Johnny Bench, Cincinnati
1936	Carl Hubbell, New York	1955	Roy Campanella, Brooklyn	1973	Pete Rose, Cincinnati
1937	Joe Medwick, St. Louis	1956	Don Newcombe, Brooklyn	1974	Steve Garvey, Los Angeles
1938	Ernie Lombardi, Cincinnati	1957	Henry Aaron, Milwaukee	1975	Joe Morgan, Cincinnati
1939	Bucky Walters, Cincinnati	1958	Ernie Banks, Chicago	1976	Joe Morgan, Cincinnati
1940	Frank McCormick, Cincinnati	1959	Ernie Banks, Chicago	1977	George Foster, Cincinnati
1941	Dolph Camilli, Brooklyn	1960	Dick Groat, Pittsburgh	1978	Dave Parker, Pittsburgh
1942	Mort Cooper, St. Louis	1961	Frank Robinson, Cincinnati	1979	(tie) Willie Stargell, Pittsburgh
1943	Stan Musial, St. Louis	1962	Maury Wills, Los Angeles		Keith Hernandez, St. Louis
1944	Martin Marion, St. Louis	1963	Sandy Koufax, Los Angeles	1980	Mike Schmidt, Philadelphia
1945	Phil Cavarretta, Chicago	1964	Ken Boyer, St. Louis	1981	Mike Schmidt, Philadelphia
1946	Stan Musial, St. Louis	1965	Willie Mays, San Francisco	1982	Dale Murphy, Atlanta
1947	Bob Elliott, Boston	1966	Roberto Clemente, Pittsburgh	1983	Dale Murphy, Atlanta
1948	Stan Musial, St. Louis	1967	Orlando Cepeda, St. Louis	1984	Ryne Sandberg, Chicago
1949	Jackie Robinson, Brooklyn				

American League

Year	Player, team	Year	Player, team	Year	Player, team
1931	Lefty Grove, Philadelphia	1949	Ted Williams, Boston	1967	Carl Yastrzemski, Boston
1932	Jimmy Foxx, Philadelphia	1950	Phil Rizzuto, New York	1968	Denny McLain, Detroit
1933	Jimmy Foxx, Philadelphia	1951	Yogi Berra, New York	1969	Harmon Killebrew, Minnesota
1934	Mickey Cochrane, Detroit	1952	Bobby Shantz, Philadelphia	1970	John (Boog) Powell, Baltimore
1935	Henry Greenberg, Detroit	1953	Al Rosen, Cleveland	1971	Vida Blue, Oakland
1936	Lou Gehrig, New York	1954	Yogi Berra, New York	1972	Dick Allen, Chicago
1937	Charley Gehringer, Detroit	1955	Yogi Berra, New York	1973	Reggie Jackson, Oakland
1938	Jimmy Foxx, Boston	1956	Mickey Mantle, New York	1974	Jeff Burroughs, Texas
1939	Joe DiMaggio, New York	1957	Mickey Mantle, New York	1975	Fred Lynn, Boston
1940	Hank Greenberg, Detroit	1958	Jackie Jensen, Boston	1976	Thurman Munson, New York
1941	Joe DiMaggio, New York	1959	Nellie Fox, Chicago	1977	Rod Carew, Minnesota
1942	Joe Gordon, New York	1960	Roger Maris, New York	1978	Jim Rice, Boston
1943	Spurgeon Chandler, New York	1961	Roger Maris, New York	1979	Don Baylor, California
1944	Hal Newhouser, Detroit	1962	Mickey Mantle, New York	1980	George Brett, Kansas City
1945	Hal Newhouser, Detroit	1963	Elston Howard, New York	1981	Rollie Fingers, Milwaukee
1946	Ted Williams, Boston	1964	Brooks Robinson, Baltimore	1982	Robin Yount, Milwaukee
1947	Joe DiMaggio, New York	1965	Zoilo Versalles, Minnesota	1983	Cal Ripken Jr., Baltimore
1948	Lou Boudreau, Cleveland	1966	Frank Robinson, Baltimore	1984	Willie Hernandez, Detroit

Rookie of the Year

Baseball Writers' Association

1947—Combined selection—Jackie Robinson, Brooklyn, 1b

1948—Combined selection—Alvin Dark, Boston, N.L. ss

National League

Year	Player, team	Year	Player, team	Year	Player, team
1949	Don Newcombe, Brooklyn, p	1962	Ken Hubbs, Chicago, 2b	1975	John Montefusco, S.F., p
1950	Sam Jethroe, Boston, of	1963	Pete Rose, Cincinnati, 2b	1976	(tie) Butch Metzger, San Diego, p
1951	Willie Mays, New York, of	1964	Richie Allen, Philadelphia, 3b		Pat Zachry, Cincinnati, p
1952	Joe Black, Brooklyn, p	1965	Jim Lefebvre, Los Angeles, 2b	1977	Andre Dawson, Montreal, of
1953	Jim Gilliam, Brooklyn, 2b	1966	Tommy Helms, Cincinnati, 2b	1978	Bob Horner, Atlanta, 3b
1954	Wally Moon, St. Louis, of	1967	Tom Seaver, New York, p	1979	Rick Sutcliffe, Los Angeles, p
1955	Bill Virdon, St. Louis, of	1968	Johnny Bench, Cincinnati c	1980	Steve Howe, Los Angeles, p
1956	Frank Robinson, Cincinnati, of	1969	Ted Sizemore, Los Angeles, 2b	1981	Fernando Valenzuela, Los
1957	Jack Sanford, Philadelphia, p	1970	Carl Morton, Montreal, p		Angeles, p
1958	Orlando Cepeda, S.F., 1b	1971	Earl Williams, Atlanta, c	1982	Steve Sax, Los Angeles, 2b
1959	Willie McCovey, S.F., 1b	1972	Jon Matlack, New York, p	1983	Darryl Strawberry, New York, of
1960	Frank Howard, Los Angeles, of	1973	Gary Matthews, S.F., of	1984	Dwight Gooden, New York, p
1961	Billy Williams, Chicago, of	1974	Bake McBride, St. Louis, of		

American League

Year	Player, team	Year	Player, team	Year	Player, team
1949	Roy Sievers, St. Louis, of	1962	Tom Tresh, New York, if-of	1974	Mike Hargrove, Texas, 1b
1950	Walt Dropo, Boston, 1b	1963	Gary Peters, Chicago, p	1975	Fred Lynn, Boston, of
1951	Gil McDougald, New York, 3b	1964	Tony Oliva, Minnesota, of	1976	Mark Fidrych, Detroit, p
1952	Harry Byrd, Philadelphia, p	1965	Curt Blefary, Baltimore, of	1977	Eddie Murray, Baltimore, dh
1953	Harvey Kuenn, Detroit, ss	1966	Tommie Agee, Chicago, of	1978	Lou Whitaker, Detroit, 2b
1954	Bob Grim, New York, p	1967	Rod Carew, Minnesota, 2b	1979	(tie) John Castino, Minnesota, 3b
1955	Herb Score, Cleveland, p	1968	Stan Bahnsen, New York, p		Alfredo Griffin, Toronto, ss
1956	Luis Aparicio, Chicago, ss	1969	Lou Piniella, Kansas City, of	1980	Joe Charboneau, Cleveland, of
1957	Tony Kubek, New York, if-of	1970	Thurman Munson, New York, c	1981	Dave Righetti, New York, p
1958	Albie Pearson, Washington, of	1971	Chris Chambliss, Cleveland, 1b	1982	Cal Ripken Jr., Baltimore, ss, 3b
1959	Bob Allison, Washington, of	1972	Carlton Fisk, Boston, c	1983	Ron Kittle, Chicago, of
1960	Ron Hansen, Baltimore, ss	1973	Al Bumbry, Baltimore, of	1984	Alvin Davis, Seattle, 1B
1961	Don Schwall, Boston, p				

College World Series

The Miami (Fla.) Hurricanes won the 1985 College World Series by defeating Texas 10-6 in the final game at Omaha, Neb. It was the Hurricanes second College World Series title.

American League Records in 1985

Final standings

Eastern Division

Club	W	L	Pct	GB
Toronto	99	62	.615	—
New York.	97	64	.602	2
Detroit.	84	77	.522	15
Baltimore	83	78	.516	16
Boston	81	81	.500	18½
Milwaukee	71	90	.441	28
Cleveland.	60	102	.370	39½

Western Division

Club	W	L	Pct	GB
Kansas City.	91	71	.562	—
California	90	72	.556	1
Chicago.	85	77	.525	6
Minnesota.	77	85	.475	14
Oakland.	77	85	.475	14
Seattle	74	88	.457	17
Texas	62	99	.385	28½

American League Championship Series

Toronto 6, Kansas City 1
Toronto 6, Kansas City 5
Kansas City 6, Toronto 5
Toronto 3, Kansas City 1

Kansas City 2, Toronto 0
Kansas City 5, Toronto 3
Kansas City 6, Toronto 2

Club Batting

Club	Pct	AB	R	H	HR	SB
Boston	.282	5720	800	1615	162	66
Toronto	.269	5508	759	1482	158	143
New York.	.267	5458	839	1458	176	154
Cleveland	.265	5527	729	1465	116	132
Oakland	.264	5581	757	1475	155	117
Minnesota	.264	5509	705	1453	141	68
Milwaukee	.263	5568	690	1467	101	69
Baltimore	.263	5517	818	1451	214	69
Seattle	.255	5521	719	1410	171	94
Texas	.253	5361	617	1359	129	130
Detroit	.253	5575	729	1413	202	75
Chicago.	.253	5470	736	1386	146	108
Kansas City	.252	5500	687	1384	154	128
California	.251	5442	732	1364	153	107

Club Pitching

Club	ERA	CG	IP	H	R	BB	SO
Toronto	3.29	18	1448	1312	588	484	823
Kansas City.	3.49	27	1461	1433	639	463	846
New York	3.69	25	1440	1373	660	518	907
Detroit.	3.78	31	1456	1313	688	556	943
California	3.91	22	1457	1453	703	514	767
Boston	4.06	35	1461	1487	720	540	913
Chicago.	4.07	20	1451	1411	720	569	1023
Baltimore	4.38	32	1427	1480	764	568	793
Milwaukee	4.39	34	1437	1510	802	499	777
Oakland	4.39	10	1453	1451	787	607	785
Minnesota.	4.48	41	1426	1468	782	462	767
Texas	4.56	18	1411	1479	785	501	863
Seattle	4.68	23	1432	1456	818	637	868
Cleveland	4.92	24	1421	1556	861	547	702

Individual Batting

Leaders—Based on 502 plate appearances.

Player, club	Pct	AB	R	H	HR	RBI	SB
Boggs, Boston	.368	653	107	240	8	78	2
Brett, Kansas City	.335	550	108	184	30	112	9
Mattingly, New York. . . .	.324	652	107	211	35	145	2
Henderson, New York . .	.314	547	146	172	23	72	80
Butler, Cleveland	.311	591	106	184	5	50	47
Baines, Chicago	.309	640	86	198	22	113	1
Bradley, Seattle	.300	641	100	192	26	88	22
Buckner, Boston	.299	673	89	201	16	110	18
Molitor, Milwaukee	.297	576	93	171	10	48	21
Murray, Baltimore	.297	583	111	173	31	124	5

Individual Pitching

Leaders—Based on 162 innings pitched.

Pitcher, club	W	L	ERA	G	IP	H	BB	SO
Stieb, Toronto	14	13	2.48	36	265	206	96	167
Leibrandt, Kansas City .	17	9	2.69	33	237	223	68	108
Saberhagen, Kansas City	20	6	2.87	32	235	211	38	158
Key, Toronto	14	6	3.00	35	212	188	50	85
Blyleven, Clev.-Minn. . .	17	16	3.16	37	293	264	75	206
Seaver, Chicago	16	11	3.17	35	238	223	69	134
Guidry, New York	22	6	3.27	34	259	243	42	143
Hough, Texas	14	16	3.31	34	250	198	83	141
Morris, Detroit	16	11	3.33	35	257	212	110	191
Petry, Detroit	15	13	3.36	34	238	190	81	109

Individual Batting (at least 115 at-bats); Individual Pitching (at least 50 innings)

Baltimore Orioles

Batting	Avg	AB	R	H	HR	RBI
Rayford	.306	359	55	110	18	48
Murray	.297	583	111	173	31	124
Lacy	.293	492	69	144	9	48
Wiggins	.285	298	43	85	0	21
Shelby	.283	205	28	58	7	27
Ripken.	.282	642	116	181	26	110
Young	.273	450	72	123	28	81
Lynn.	.263	448	59	118	23	68
Sheets	.262	328	43	86	17	50
Dempsey	.254	362	54	92	12	52
Dwyer	.249	233	35	58	7	36
Gross	.235	217	31	51	11	18
Roenicke	.218	225	36	49	15	43
Dauer	.202	208	25	42	2	14

Pitching	W	L	ERA	IP	BB	SO	Sv
Snell	3	2	2.69	100	30	41	5
Stewart	5	7	3.61	129	66	77	9
Dixon	8	4	3.67	162	64	108	1
Aase	10	6	3.78	88	35	67	14
Boddicker	12	17	4.07	203	89	135	
Davis	10	8	4.53	175	70	93	
McGregor	14	14	4.81	204	65	86	
Flanagan	4	5	5.13	86	28	42	
D. Martinez . . .	13	11	5.15	180	63	68	
T. Martinez	3	5	5.40	70	37	47	1

Boston Red Sox

Batting	Avg	AB	R	H	HR	RBI
Boggs	.368	653	107	240	8	78
Buckner	.299	673	89	201	16	110
Gedman	.295	498	66	147	18	80
Rice	.291	546	85	159	27	103
Hoffman	.276	279	40	77	6	34
Barrett.	.266	534	59	142	5	56
Armas	.265	385	50	102	23	64
Lyons	.264	371	52	98	5	30
Evans	.263	617	110	162	29	78
Easler	.262	568	71	149	16	74
Gutierrez	.218	275	33	60	2	21

Pitching	W	L	ERA	IP	BB	SO	Sv
Stanley	6	6	2.87	87	30	46	10
Clemens	7	5	3.29	98	37	74	
Boyd	15	13	3.70	272	67	154	
Clear	1	3	3.72	55	50	55	3
Crawford	6	5	3.76	91	28	58	12
Ojeda	9	11	4.00	157	48	102	1
Nipper	9	12	4.06	162	82	85	
Kison	5	3	4.11	92	32	56	1
Hurst	11	13	4.51	229	70	189	
Lollar	8	10	4.62	150	98	105	1
Trujillo	4	4	4.82	84	23	19	1

California Angels

Batting	Avg	AB	R	H	HR	RBI
Beniquez	.304	411	54	125	8	42
Carew	.280	443	69	124	2	39
M. Brown	.268	153	23	41	4	20
Downing	.263	520	80	137	20	85
Pettis	.257	443	67	114	1	32
Jackson	.252	460	64	116	27	85
Boone	.248	460	37	114	5	55
DeCinces	.244	427	50	104	20	78
Grich	.242	479	74	116	13	53
Jones	.231	389	66	90	21	67
Narron	.220	132	12	29	5	14
Schofield	.219	438	50	96	8	41
Howell	.197	137	19	27	5	18
Wilfong	.189	217	16	41	4	13

Pitching	W	L	ERA	IP	BB	SO	Sv
Moore	8	8	1.92	103	21	72	31
Cliburn	9	3	2.09	99	26	48	6
Clements	5	0	3.34	62	25	19	1
Witt	15	9	3.56	250	98	180	
Lugo	3	4	3.69	83	29	42	
Candelaria	7	3	3.80	71	24	53	
Sutton	15	10	3.86	226	59	107	
Romanick	14	9	4.11	195	62	64	
Slaton	6	10	4.37	148	63	60	1
McCaskill	12	12	4.70	189	64	102	

Detroit Tigers

Batting	Avg	AB	R	H	HR	RBI
Gibson	.287	581	96	167	29	97
Whitaker	.279	609	102	170	21	73
Parrish	.273	549	64	150	28	98
Lemon	.266	517	69	137	18	68
Trammell	.258	605	79	156	13	57
Garbey	.257	237	27	61	6	29
Sanchez	.248	133	19	33	6	12
Evans	.248	505	81	125	40	94
Grubb	.245	155	19	38	5	25
Herndon	.244	442	45	108	12	37
Simmons	.239	251	31	60	10	33
Brookens	.237	485	54	115	7	47
Bergman	.179	140	8	25	3	7

Pitching	W	L	ERA	IP	BB	SO	Sv
Hernandez	8	10	2.70	106	14	76	31
O'Neal	5	5	3.24	94	36	52	1
Morris	16	11	3.33	257	110	191	
Petry	15	13	3.36	238	81	109	
Terrell	15	10	3.85	229	95	130	
Tanana	12	14	4.27	215	57	159	
Scherrer	3	2	4.36	66	41	46	
Lopez	3	7	4.80	86	41	53	5
Berenguer	5	6	5.59	95	48	82	

Chicago White Sox

Batting	Avg	AB	R	H	HR	RBI
Baines	.309	640	86	198	22	113
Nichols	.273	150	23	41	2	18
Guillen	.273	491	71	134	1	33
Hulett	.268	395	52	106	5	37
Law	.259	390	62	101	4	36
Walker	.258	601	77	155	24	92
Fletcher	.256	301	38	77	2	31
Little	.250	188	35	47	2	27
Paciorek	.246	122	14	30	0	9
Salazar	.245	327	39	80	10	45
Hairston	.243	140	9	34	2	20
Fisk	.238	543	85	129	37	107
Kittle	.230	379	51	87	26	58
Boston	.228	232	20	53	3	15
Gamble	.203	148	20	30	4	20
Cruz	.197	234	28	46	0	15

Pitching	W	L	ERA	IP	BB	SO	Sv
James	8	7	2.13	110	23	88	32
Seaver	16	11	3.17	238	69	134	
Spillner	4	3	3.44	91	33	41	1
Agosto	4	3	3.58	60	23	39	1
Burns	18	11	3.96	227	79	172	
Davis	3	3	4.16	71	26	37	
Nelson	10	10	4.26	145	67	101	2
Dotson	3	4	4.47	52	17	33	
Bannister	10	14	4.87	210	100	198	

Kansas City Royals

Batting	Avg	AB	R	H	HR	RBI
Brett	.335	550	108	184	30	112
Wilson	.278	605	87	168	4	43
Orta	.267	300	32	80	4	45
McRae	.259	320	41	83	14	70
Smith	.257	448	77	115	6	41
White	.249	563	62	140	22	69
Sundberg	.245	367	38	90	10	35
Balboni	.243	600	74	146	36	88
Wathan	.234	145	11	34	1	9
Sheridan	.228	206	18	47	3	17
Iorg	.223	130	7	29	1	21
Motley	.222	383	45	85	17	49
Moreno	.221	136	21	30	3	16
L. Jones	.211	152	12	32	0	9
Concepcion	.204	314	32	64	2	20
Biancalana	.188	138	21	26	1	6

Pitching	W	L	ERA	IP	BB	SO	Sv
Quisenberry	8	9	2.37	129	16	54	37
Leibrandt	17	9	2.69	237	68	108	
Saberhagen	20	6	2.87	235	38	158	
Jackson	14	12	3.42	208	76	114	
Gubicza	14	10	4.06	177	77	99	
Beckwith	1	5	4.07	95	32	80	1
Black	10	15	4.33	205	59	122	
M. Jones	3	3	4.78	64	39	32	

Cleveland Indians

Batting	Avg	AB	R	H	HR	RBI
Butler	.311	591	106	184	5	50
Franco	.288	636	97	183	6	90
Hargrove	.285	284	31	81	1	27
Tabler	.275	404	47	111	5	59
Bernazard	.274	500	73	137	11	59
Jacoby	.274	606	72	166	20	87
Willard	.270	300	39	81	7	36
Carter	.262	489	64	128	15	59
Castillo	.245	184	27	45	11	25
Vukovich	.244	434	43	106	8	45
Thornton	.236	461	49	109	22	88

Pitching	W	L	ERA	IP	BB	SO	Sv
Easterly	4	1	3.92	98	53	58	
Reed	3	5	4.11	72	19	37	8
Ruhle	2	10	4.32	125	30	54	3
Creel	2	5	4.79	62	23	31	
Waddell	8	6	4.87	112	39	53	9
Heaton	9	17	4.90	207	80	82	
Smith	1	4	5.34	62	17	28	
Schulze	4	10	6.01	94	19	37	
Wardle	8	9	6.18	115	62	84	1
Thompson	3	8	6.30	80	48	30	5
Clark	3	4	6.32	62	34	24	2
Romero	2	3	6.58	64	38	38	

Milwaukee Brewers

Batting	Avg	AB	R	H	HR	RBI
Molitor	.297	576	93	171	10	48
Cooper	.293	631	82	185	16	99
Oglivie	.290	341	40	99	10	61
Riles	.286	448	54	128	5	45
Yount	.277	466	76	129	15	68
Simmons	.273	528	60	144	12	76
Ready	.265	181	29	48	1	21
Householder	.258	299	41	77	11	34
Gantner	.254	523	63	133	5	44
Romero	.251	251	24	63	0	21
Schroeder	.242	194	18	47	8	25
Moore	.232	349	35	81	0	31
Manning	.218	216	19	47	2	18

Pitching	W	L	ERA	IP	BB	SO	Sv
Darwin	8	18	3.80	217	65	125	2
Haas	8	8	3.84	161	25	78	
Gibson	6	7	3.90	92	49	53	11
Higuera	15	8	3.90	212	63	127	
McClure	4	1	4.31	85	30	57	3
Cocanower	6	8	4.33	116	73	44	
Burris	9	13	4.81	170	53	81	
Fingers	1	6	5.04	55	19	24	17
Vuckovich	6	10	5.51	112	48	55	

Minnesota Twins

Batting	Avg	AB	R	H	HR	RBI
Salas	.300	360	51	108	9	41
Puckett	.288	691	80	199	4	73
Hatcher	.282	444	46	125	3	49
Hrbek	.278	593	78	165	21	93
Washington	.274	135	24	37	1	14
Teufel	.260	434	58	113	10	50
Smalley	.258	388	57	100	12	45
Engle	.256	172	28	44	7	25
Gaetti	.246	560	71	138	20	64
Brunansky	.242	567	71	137	27	90
Bush	.239	234	26	56	10	35
Laudner	.238	164	16	39	7	19
Gagne	.225	293	37	66	2	23
Stenhouse	.223	179	23	40	5	21

Pitching	W	L	ERA	IP	BB	SO	Sv
Blyleven	17	16	3.16	293	75	206	
Davis	2	6	3.48	64	35	72	25
Filson	4	5	3.67	95	30	42	2
Eufamia	4	2	3.79	61	21	30	2
Viola	18	14	4.09	250	68	135	
Smithson	15	14	4.34	257	78	127	
Butcher	11	14	4.98	207	43	92	
Schrom	9	12	4.99	160	59	74	
Lysander	0	2	6.05	61	22	26	3

Seattle Mariners

Batting	Avg	AB	R	H	HR	RBI
Bradley	.300	641	100	192	26	88
Davis	.287	578	78	166	18	78
Calderon	.286	210	37	60	8	28
Presley	.275	570	71	157	28	84
Cowens	.265	452	59	120	14	69
Perconte	.264	485	60	128	2	23
Owen	.259	352	41	91	6	37
Kearney	.243	305	24	74	6	27
Henderson	.241	502	70	121	14	68
Scott	.222	185	18	41	4	23
G. Thomas	.215	484	76	104	32	87
Phelps	.207	116	18	24	9	24
Ramos	.196	168	19	33	1	15

Pitching	W	L	ERA	IP	BB	SO	Sv
Nunez	7	3	3.09	90	34	58	16
R. Thomas	7	0	3.36	93	48	70	1
Moore	17	10	3.46	247	70	155	
Vande Berg	2	1	3.72	67	31	34	3
Swift	6	10	4.77	120	48	55	
Young	12	19	4.91	218	76	136	1
Langston	7	14	5.47	126	91	72	
Barojas	0	5	5.98	52	33	27	
Wills	5	11	6.00	123	68	67	1
Beattie	5	6	7.29	70	33	45	

New York Yankees

Batting	Avg	AB	R	H	HR	RBI
Robertson	.328	125	16	41	2	17
Mattingly	.324	652	107	211	35	145
Henderson	.314	547	146	172	24	72
Hassey	.296	267	31	79	13	42
Sample	.288	139	18	40	1	15
Randolph	.276	497	75	137	5	40
Winfield	.275	633	105	174	26	114
Griffey	.274	438	68	120	10	69
Pagliarulo	.239	380	55	91	19	62
Baylor	.231	477	70	110	23	91
Wynegar	.223	309	27	69	5	32
Meacham	.218	481	70	105	1	47
Pasqua	.209	148	17	31	9	25

Pitching	W	L	ERA	IP	BB	SO	Sv
Fisher	4	4	2.38	98	29	85	14
Shirley	5	5	2.64	109	26	55	2
Righetti	12	7	2.78	107	45	92	29
Bordi	6	8	3.21	98	29	64	2
Guidry	22	6	3.27	259	42	143	
Cowley	12	6	3.95	159	85	97	
Rasmussen	3	5	3.98	101	42	63	
P. Niekro	16	12	4.09	220	120	149	
Whitson	10	8	4.88	158	43	89	

Texas Rangers

Batting	Avg	AB	R	H	HR	RBI
Tolleson	.313	323	45	101	1	18
Ward	.287	593	77	170	15	70
Slaught	.280	343	34	96	8	35
Harrah	.270	396	65	107	9	44
O'Brien	.267	573	69	153	22	92
Bannister	.262	122	17	32	1	6
Parrish	.249	346	44	86	17	51
Wilkerson	.244	360	35	88	0	22
McDowell	.239	406	63	97	18	42
Bell	.236	313	33	74	4	32
Jones	.224	134	14	30	5	23
Buechele	.219	219	22	48	6	21
G. Wright	.190	363	21	69	2	18
Walker	.174	132	14	23	5	11

Pitching	W	L	ERA	IP	BB	SO	Sv
Harris	5	4	2.47	113	43	111	11
Schmidt	7	6	3.15	85	22	46	5
Hough	14	16	3.31	250	83	141	
Welsh	2	5	4.13	76	25	31	
Rozema	3	7	4.19	88	22	42	7
Mason	8	15	4.83	179	73	92	
Noles	4	8	5.06	110	33	59	1
Hooten	5	8	5.23	124	40	62	
Stewart	0	6	5.42	81	37	64	4
Russell	3	6	7.55	62	27	44	

Oakland A's

Batting	Avg	AB	R	H	HR	RBI
Henderson	.301	193	25	58	3	31
Bochte	.295	424	48	125	14	61
Davis	.287	547	92	157	24	82
Hill	.285	393	45	112	3	48
Phillips	.280	161	23	45	4	17
Lansford	.277	401	51	111	13	46
Griffin	.270	614	75	166	2	64
Baker	.268	343	48	92	14	52
Tettleton	.251	211	23	53	3	15
Collins	.251	379	52	95	4	29
Heath	.250	436	71	109	13	55
Kingman	.238	592	66	141	30	91
Murphy	.233	523	77	122	20	59

Pitching	W	L	ERA	IP	BB	SO	Sv
Ontiveros	1	3	1.93	74	19	36	8
Howell	9	8	2.85	98	31	68	29
Langford	3	5	3.51	59	15	21	
Rijo	6	4	3.53	63	28	65	
Birtsas	10	6	4.01	141	91	94	
Atherton	4	7	4.30	104	42	77	3
Codiroli	14	14	4.46	226	78	111	
Krueger	9	10	4.52	151	69	56	
John	4	10	5.53	86	28	25	
McCatty	4	4	5.57	85	41	36	

Toronto Blue Jays

Batting	Avg	AB	R	H	HR	RBI
Iorg	.313	288	33	90	7	37
Mulliniks	.295	366	55	108	10	57
Barfield	.289	539	94	156	27	84
Fernandez	.289	564	71	163	2	51
Garcia	.282	600	70	169	8	66
Upshaw	.275	501	79	138	15	65
Bell	.275	607	87	167	28	95
Johnson	.260	369	35	96	13	66
Moseby	.259	584	92	151	18	70
Burroughs	.257	191	19	49	6	28
Oliver	.251	187	20	47	5	23
Whitt	.245	412	55	101	19	64
Matuszek	.212	151	23	32	2	15

Pitching	W	L	ERA	IP	BB	SO	Sv
Stieb	14	13	2.48	265	96	167	
Caudill	4	6	2.99	69	35	46	14
Key	14	6	3.00	212	50	85	
Lavelle	5	7	3.10	72	36	50	8
Acker	7	2	3.23	86	43	42	10
Lamp	11	0	3.32	105	27	68	2
Alexander	17	10	3.45	260	67	142	
Clancy	9	6	3.78	128	37	66	
Musselman	3	0	4.47	52	24	29	
Leal	3	6	5.75	67	24	33	

1985 World Series

First Game

St. Louis	ab	r	h	bi	Kansas City	ab	r	h	bi
McGee cf	4	0	1	0	L. Smith lf	3	0	1	0
O. Smith ss	3	0	0	0	Wilson cf	4	0	1	0
Herr 2b	4	1	1	0	Brett 3b	4	0	1	0
Clark 1b	4	0	1	0	White 2b	4	0	0	0
Landrum lf	4	1	2	0	Sundberg c	3	1	1	0
Cedeno rf	3	0	1	0	Motley rf	3	0	1	0
Worrell p	0	0	0	0	Sheridan ph	1	0	1	0
Pendleton 3b	2	1	0	0	Balboni 1b	4	0	1	1
Porter c	3	0	1	0	Biancalana ss	1	0	0	0
Tudor p	1	0	0	0	Jones ph	1	0	1	0
Van Slyke rf	2	0	0	0	Quisenberry p	0	0	0	0
					Black p	0	0	0	0
					Orta ph	1	0	0	0
					Jackson p	2	0	0	0
					McRae ph	0	0	0	0
					Concepcion ss	0	0	0	0
					Iorg ph	1	0	0	0
Totals	31	3	7	0	Totals	32	1	8	1

St. Louis . . . . 0 0 1 1 0 0 0 0 1—3
Kansas City . . . . 0 1 0 0 0 0 0 0 0—1

Game-winning RBI - Cedeno (1). DP - St. Louis, 1. LOB - St. Louis 6, Kansas City 8. 2B - Landrum, Cedeno, Sundberg, McGee, Clark, Sheridan. 3B - Jones. SB - O. Smith (1). Caught Stealing - Motley, L. Smith. S - Tudor. WP - McRae by Tudor. PB - Sundberg.

St. Louis	ip	h	r	er	bb	so
Tudor W, 1-0	6 2/3	7	1	1	2	5
Worrell S, 1	2 1/3	1	0	0	1	0
Kansas City						
Jackson L, 0-1	7	4	2	2	2	7
Quisenberry	1 2/3	3	1	1	0	2
Black	1/3	0	0	0	2	1

Attendance: 41,640.

How runs were scored—One in Royals second: Sundberg walked. Motley singled. Balboni singled scoring Sundberg.

One in Cardinals third: Pendleton walked. Porter singled. Pendleton scored on McGee's groundout.

One in Cardinals fourth: Landrum doubled. Cedeno doubled scoring Landrum.

One in Cardinals ninth: Herr singled. Clark doubled scoring Herr.

Second Game

St. Louis	ab	r	h	bi	Kansas City	ab	r	h	bi
McGee cf	4	1	1	0	L. Smith lf	4	0	2	0
O. Smith ss	4	0	0	0	Jones lf	0	0	0	0
Herr 2b	4	0	0	0	Wilson cf	4	1	2	0
J. Clark 1b	3	1	1	1	Brett 3b	4	1	1	1
Landrum lf	4	1	2	0	White 2b	3	0	3	1
Cedeno rf	3	1	0	0	Sheridan rf	4	0	0	0
Lahti p	0	0	0	0	Quisenberry p	0	0	0	0
Pendleton 3b	4	0	2	3	Sundberg c	4	0	0	0
Porter c	3	0	0	0	Balboni 1b	4	0	1	0
Cox p	2	0	0	0	Biancalana ss	1	0	0	0
Harper ph	1	0	0	0	Orta ph	1	0	0	0
Dayley p	0	0	0	0	Liebrandt p	2	0	0	0
Van Slyke rf	1	0	0	0	Motley rf	0	0	0	0
Totals	33	4	6	4	Totals	31	2	9	2

St. Louis . . . . 0 0 0 0 0 0 0 0 4—4
Kansas City . . . . 0 0 0 2 0 0 0 0 0—2

Game-winning RBI - Pendleton (1). DP - St. Louis 3. LOB - St. Louis 5, Kansas City 6. 2B - Brett, White (2), McGee, Landrum, Pendleton. SB - White (1), Wilson (1). S - Liebrandt.

St. Louis	ip	h	r	er	bb	so
Cox	7	7	2	2	3	5
Dayley W, 1-0	1	1	0	0	0	1
Lahti S, 1	1	1	0	0	0	0
Kansas City						
Leibrandt L, 0-1	8 2/3	6	4	4	2	6
Quisenberry	1/3	0	0	0	1	0

Attendance: 41,656.

How runs were scored—Two in Royals fourth: Wilson singled. Brett doubled scoring Wilson. White doubled scoring Brett.

Four in Cardinals ninth: McGee doubled. Clark singled scoring McGee. Landrum doubled. Cedeno walked. Pendleton doubled scoring Clark, Landrum, and Cedeno.

Third Game

Kansas City	ab	r	h	bi	St. Louis	ab	r	h	bi
L. Smith lf	5	0	2	2	McGee cf	4	0	1	0
Jones lf	0	0	0	0	O. Smith ss	4	1	1	0
Wilson cf	5	0	2	0	Herr 2b	3	0	1	1
Brett 3b	2	2	2	0	Clark 1b	4	0	1	1
White 2b	4	2	2	3	Van Slyke rf	4	0	0	0
Sheridan rf	5	0	0	0	Pendleton 3b	4	0	1	0
Sundberg c	2	1	1	0	Porter c	3	0	0	0
Balboni 1b	4	0	0	0	Landrum lf	3	0	1	0
Biancalana ss	5	1	2	1	Andujar p	1	0	0	0
Saberhagen p	3	0	0	0	Campbell p	0	0	0	0
					Jorgensen ph	1	0	0	0
					Horton p	0	0	0	0
					Harper ph	1	0	0	0
					Dayley p	0	0	0	0
Totals	35	6	11	6	Totals	32	1	6	1

Kansas City . . . . 0 0 0 2 2 0 2 0 0—6
St. Louis . . . . 0 0 0 0 0 1 0 0 0—1

Game-winning RBI - L. Smith (1). DP - Kansas City 1, St. Louis 1. LOB - Kansas City 11, St. Louis 5. 2B - L. Smith, White. HR - White (1). SB - Wilson (2), McGee (1). S - Saberhagen.

Kansas City	ip	h	r	er	bb	so
Saberhagen W, 1-0	9	6	1	1	1	8
St. Louis						
Andujar L, 0-1	4	9	4	4	3	3
Campbell	1	0	0	0	1	2
Horton	2	2	2	2	0	1
Dayley	2	0	0	0	2	2

Attendance: 53,634.

How runs were scored—Two in Royals fourth: Sundberg walked. Biancalana singled. L. Smith doubled scoring Sundberg and Biancalana.

Two in Royals fifth: Brett singled. White hit a home run scoring Brett.

One in Cardinals sixth: O. Smith and Herr singled. Clark singled scoring O. Smith.

Two in Royals seventh: Brett walked. White doubled scoring Brett. Biancalana singled scoring White.

Fourth Game

Kansas City	ab	r	h	bi	St. Louis	ab	r	h	bi
L. Smith lf	4	0	0	0	McGee cf	3	1	2	1
Wilson cf	4	0	1	0	O. Smith ss	2	0	0	0
Brett 3b	4	0	1	0	Herr 2b	3	0	1	0
White 2b	4	0	0	0	Clark 1b	3	0	1	0
Sundberg c	4	0	1	0	Landrum lf	4	1	1	1
Motley rf	4	0	0	0	Cedeno rf	3	0	0	0
Balboni 1b	2	0	1	0	Van Slyke rf	0	0	0	0
Biancalana ss	2	0	0	0	Pendleton 3b	3	1	1	0
McRae ph	1	0	0	0	Nieto c	1	0	0	1
Concepcion ss	0	0	0	0	Tudor p	3	0	0	0
Black p	1	0	0	0					
Wathan ph	1	0	0	0					
Beckwith p	0	0	0	0					
Jones ph	1	0	1	0					
Quisenberry p	0	0	0	0					
Totals	32	0	5	0	Totals	25	3	6	3

Kansas City . . . . 0 0 0 0 0 0 0 0 0—0
St. Louis . . . . 0 1 1 0 1 0 0 0 x—3

Game-winning RBI - Landrum (1). E - Black. DP - Kansas City 1. LOB - Kansas City 6, St. Louis 5. 2B - Herr, Jones. 3B - Pendleton. HR - Landrum (1), McGee (1). S - Nieto, O. Smith.

Kansas City	ip	h	r	er	bb	so
Black L, 0-1	5	4	3	3	3	3
Beckwith	2	1	0	0	0	3
Quisenberry	1	1	0	0	2	0
St. Louis						
Tudor W, 2-0	9	5	0	0	1	8

Wild pitch - Quisenberry.

Attendance: 56,634.

How runs were scored—One in Cardinals second: Landrum hit a home run.

One in Cardinals third: McGee hit a home run.

One in Cardinals fifth: Pendleton tripled. Pendleton scored on Nieto's sacrifice bunt.

Fifth Game

Kansas City	ab	r	h	bi	St. Louis	ab	r	h	bi
L. Smith lf	4	2	2	0	McGee cf	4	0	2	0
Jones lf	0	0	0	0	O. Smith ss	3	0	0	0
Wilson cf	5	0	2	0	Herr 2b	4	1	1	0
Brett 3b	4	0	1	0	Clark 1b	3	0	1	1
Pryor 3b	0	0	0	0	Landrum lf	4	0	1	0
White 2b	5	1	0	1	Cedeno rf	4	0	0	0
Sheridan rf	5	0	2	1	Pendleton 3b	3	0	0	0
Balboni 1b	4	0	1	0	Nieto c	4	0	0	0
Sundberg c	4	2	1	0	Forsch p	0	0	0	0
Biancalana ss	3	1	2	1	Horton p	1	0	0	0
Jackson p	4	0	0	0	Campbell p	0	0	0	0
					DeJesus ph	1	0	0	0
					Worrell p	0	0	0	0
					Harper ph	1	0	0	0
					Lahti p	0	0	0	0
Totals	38	6	11	5	Totals	32	1	5	1

Kansas City . . . . 1 3 0 0 0 0 0 1 1—6
St. Louis . . . . 1 0 0 0 0 0 0 0 0—1

Game-winning RBI - Biancalana (1). E - Jackson, Brett, O. Smith. DP - St. Louis 1. LOB - Kansas City 9, St. Louis 7. 2B - Herr, Clark, Sundberg, Sheridan. 3B - Wilson. SB - L. Smith (1).

Kansas City	ip	h	r	er	bb	so
Jackson W, 1-1	9	5	1	1	3	5
St. Louis						
Forsch L, 0-1	1 2/3	5	4	4	1	2
Horton	2	1	0	0	3	4
Campbell	1 2/3	0	0	0	0	2
Worrell	2	0	0	0	0	6
Lahti	2	5	2	1	0	1

Attendance: 53,634

How runs were scored—One in Royals first: L. Smith and Wilson singled. L. Smith scored on White's groundout.

One in Cardinals first: Herr doubled. Clark doubled scoring Herr.

Three in Royals second: Sundberg doubled. Biancalana singled scoring Sundberg. L. Smith walked. Wilson tripled scoring Biancalana and L. Smith.

One in Royals eighth: Sundberg reached first on fielder's choice. Biancalana singled. Sundberg scored on O. Smith's error.

One in Royals ninth: White reached first on fielder's choice. Sheridan doubled scoring White.

Sixth Game

St. Louis	ab	r	h	bi	Kansas City	ab	r	h	bi
O. Smith ss	3	0	0	0	L. Smith lf	4	0	1	0
McGee cf	4	0	0	0	Wilson cf	3	0	1	0
Herr 2b	4	0	0	0	Brett 3b	4	0	0	0
Clark 1b	4	0	0	0	White 2b	4	0	1	0
Landrum lf	4	0	1	0	Sheridan rf	3	0	1	0
Pendleton 3b	4	1	1	0	Motley ph	0	0	0	0
Cedeno rf	2	0	1	0	Orta ph	1	0	0	0
Van Slyke rf	0	0	0	0	Balboni 1b	3	0	2	0
Porter c	3	0	1	0	Concepcion pr	0	1	0	0
Cox p	2	0	0	0	Sundberg c	4	1	1	0
Harper ph	1	0	1	1	Biancalana ss	3	0	1	0
Lawless pr	0	0	0	0	McRae ph	0	0	0	0
Dayley p	0	0	0	0	Wathan pr	0	0	0	0
Worrell p	0	0	0	0	Leibrandt p	2	0	0	0
					Quisenberry p	0	0	0	0
Totals	31	1	5	1	D. Iorg ph	1	0	1	2
					Totals	32	2	10	2

St. Louis . . . . 0 0 0 0 0 0 1 0—1
Kansas City . . . . 0 0 0 0 0 0 0 2—2

Game-winning RBI - D. Iorg (1). DP - St. Louis, 1, Kansas City 1. LOB - St. Louis 5, Kansas City 9. 2B - L. Smith. S - Leibrandt. PB - Porter.

St. Louis	ip	h	r	er	bb	so
Cox	7	7	0	0	1	8
Dayley	1	0	0	0	1	2
Worrell L, 0-1	*1/3	3	2	2	1	0
Kansas City						
Leibrandt	7 2/3	4	1	1	2	4
Quisenberry W, 1-0	1 1/3	1	0	0	0	1

*One out when winning run scored.
Attendance: 41,628.

How runs were scored—One in Cardinals eighth: Pendleton singled. Cedeno walked. Harper singled scoring Pendleton.

Two in Royals ninth: Orta singled (controversial call). Balboni singled. Sundberg grounded into fielder's choice. Concepcion (running for Balboni) to third and Sundberg to second on Porter's passed ball. McRae intentionally walked. Iorg singled scoring Concepcion and Sundberg.

Seventh Game

St. Louis	ab	r	h	bi	Kansas City	ab	r	h	bi
O. Smith ss	4	0	1	0	L. Smith lf	3	2	1	2
McGee cf	4	0	0	0	Jones lf	1	0	0	0
Herr 2b	4	0	0	0	Wilson cf	5	1	2	1
Clark 1b	4	0	1	0	Brett 3b	5	2	4	0
Van Slyke rf	4	0	1	0	White 2b	4	1	1	1
Pendleton 3b	3	0	1	0	Sundberg c	3	1	1	1
Landrum lf	2	0	1	0	Balboni 1b	4	2	2	2
Andujar p	0	0	0	0	Motley rf	4	1	3	3
Forsch p	0	0	0	0	Biancalana ss	3	0	0	0
Braun ph	1	0	0	0	Saberhagen p	4	1	0	0
Dayley p	0	0	0	0					
Porter c	3	0	0	0					
Tudor p	1	0	0	0					
Campbell p	0	0	0	0					
Lahti p	0	0	0	0					
Horton p	0	0	0	0					
Jorgensen lf	2	0	0	0					
Totals	32	0	5	0	Totals	36	11	14	10

St. Louis . . . . 0 0 0 0 0 0 0 0 0—0
Kansas City . . . . 0 2 3 0 6 0 0 0 x—11

Game-winning RBI - Motley (1). DP - St. Louis, 2. LOB - St. Louis 5, Kansas City 7. 2B - L. Smith. HR - Motley. SB - L. Smith (2), Brett (1), Wilson (3).

St. Louis	ip	h	r	er	bb	so
Tudor L, 2-1	2 1/3	3	5	5	4	1
Campbell	1 2/3	4	1	1	1	1
Lahti	2/3	4	4	4	0	1
Horton	0	1	0	0	1	0
Andujar	0	1	1	1	0	0
Forsch	1 1/3	1	0	0	0	1
Dayley	2	0	0	0	0	0
Kansas City						
Saberhagen W, 2-0	9	5	0	0	0	2

Campbell pitched to 1 batter in the 5th; Horton pitched to 1 batter in the 5th; Andujar pitched to 2 batters in the 5th.
Attendance: 41,658.

How runs were scored—Two in Royals second: Balboni walked. Motley hit a home run.

Three in Royals third: L. Smith walked. Brett singled. L. Smith and Brett double steal. White walked. Sundberg walked scoring L. Smith. (Campbell replaced Tudor.) Balboni singled scoring Brett and White.

Six in Royals fifth: Sundberg singled. (Lahti replaced Campbell.) Balboni singled. Motley singled scoring Sundberg. L. Smith doubled scoring Balboni and Saberhagen. (Horton replaced Lahti.) Wilson singled scoring L. Smith. Brett singled. (Andujar replaced Horton.) White singled scoring Wilson. Sundberg walked. (Forsch replaced Andujar who was ejected.) Brett scored on wild pitch.

World Series MVPs

World Series Results, 1903-1985

1903 Boston AL 5, Pittsburgh NL 3	1931 St. Louis NL 4, Philadelphia AL 3	1959 Los Angeles NL 4, Chicago AL 2
1904 No series	1932 New York AL 4, Chicago NL 0	1960 Pittsburgh NL 4, New York AL 3
1905 New York NL 4, Philadelphia AL 1	1933 New York NL 4, Washington AL 1	1961 New York AL 4, Cincinnati NL 1
1906 Chicago AL 4, Chicago NL 2	1934 St. Louis NL 4, Detroit AL 3	1962 New York AL 4, San Francisco NL 3
1907 Chicago NL 4, Detroit AL 0, 1 tie	1935 Detroit AL 4, Chicago NL 2	1963 Los Angeles NL 4, New York AL 0
1908 Chicago NL 4, Detroit AL 1	1936 New York AL 4, New York NL 2	1964 St. Louis NL 4, New York AL 3
1909 Pittsburgh NL 4, Detroit AL 3	1937 New York AL 4, New York NL 1	1965 Los Angeles NL 4, Minnesota AL 3
1910 Philadelphia AL 4, Chicago NL 1	1938 New York AL 4, Chicago NL 0	1966 Baltimore AL 4, Los Angeles NL 0
1911 Philadelphia AL 4, New York NL 2	1939 New York AL 4, Cincinnati NL 0	1967 St. Louis NL 4, Boston AL 3
1912 Boston AL 4, New York NL 3, 1 tie	1940 Cincinnati NL 4, Detroit AL 3	1968 Detroit AL 4, St. Louis NL 3
1913 Philadelphia AL 4, New York NL 1	1941 New York AL 4, Brooklyn NL 1	1969 New York NL 4, Baltimore AL 1
1914 Boston NL 4, Philadelphia AL 0	1942 St. Louis NL 4, New York AL 1	1970 Baltimore AL 4, Cincinnati NL 1
1915 Boston AL 4, Philadelphia NL 1	1943 New York AL 4, St. Louis NL 1	1971 Pittsburgh NL 4, Baltimore AL 3
1916 Boston AL 4, Brooklyn NL 1	1944 St. Louis NL 4, St. Louis AL 2	1972 Oakland AL 4, Cincinnati NL 3
1917 Chicago AL 4, New York NL 2	1945 Detroit AL 4, Chicago NL 3	1973 Oakland AL 4, New York NL 3
1918 Boston AL 4, Chicago NL 2	1946 St. Louis NL 4, Boston AL 3	1974 Oakland AL 4, Los Angeles NL 1
1919 Cincinnati NL 5, Chicago AL 3	1947 New York AL 4, Brooklyn NL 3	1975 Cincinnati NL 4, Boston AL 3
1920 Cleveland AL 5, Brooklyn NL 2	1948 Cleveland AL 4, Boston NL 2	1976 Cincinnati NL 4, New York AL 0
1921 New York NL 5, New York AL 3	1949 New York AL 4, Brooklyn NL 1	1977 New York AL 4, Los Angeles NL 2
1922 New York NL 4, New York AL 0, 1 tie	1950 New York AL 4, Philadelphia NL 0	1978 New York AL 4, Los Angeles NL 2
1923 New York AL 4, New York NL 2	1951 New York AL 4, New York NL 2	1979 Pittsburgh NL 4, Baltimore AL 3
1924 Washington AL 4, New York NL 3	1952 New York AL 4, Brooklyn NL 3	1980 Philadelphia NL 4, Kansas City AL 2
1925 Pittsburgh NL 4, Washington AL 3	1953 New York AL 4, Brooklyn NL 2	1981 Los Angeles NL 4, New York AL 2
1926 St. Louis NL 4, New York AL 3	1954 New York NL 4, Cleveland AL 0	1982 St. Louis NL 4, Milwaukee AL 3
1927 New York AL 4, Pittsburgh NL 0	1955 Brooklyn NL 4, New York AL 3	1983 Baltimore AL 4, Philadelphia NL 1
1928 New York AL 4, St. Louis NL 0	1956 New York AL 4, Brooklyn NL 3	1984 Detroit AL 4, San Diego NL 1
1929 Philadelphia AL 4, Chicago NL 1	1957 Milwaukee NL 4, New York AL 3	1985 Kansas City AL 4, St. Louis NL 3
1930 Philadelphia AL 4, St. Louis NL 2	1958 New York AL 4, Milwaukee NL 3	

Major League Leaders in 1985

National League

Home Runs

Murphy, Atlanta, 37; Parker, Cincinnati, 34; Guerrero, Los Angeles, 33; Schmidt, Philadelphia, 33; Carter, New York, 32.

Runs Batted In

Parker, Cincinnati, 125; Murphy, Atlanta, 111; Herr, St. Louis, 110; Moreland, Chicago, 106; G. Wilson, Philadelphia, 102.

Stolen Bases

Coleman, St. Louis, 110; Raines, Montreal, 70; McGee, St. Louis, 56; Sandberg, Chicago, 54; Samuel, Philadelphia, 52.

Hits

McGee, St. Louis, 216; Parker, Cincinnati, 198; Gwynn, San Diego, 197; Sandberg, Chicago, 186; Murphy, Atlanta, 185.

Doubles

Parker, Cincinnati, 42; G. Wilson, Philadelphia, 39; Herr, St. Louis, 38; Wallach, Montreal, 36; Brooks, Montreal, 34; Cruz, Houston, 34; Hernandez, New York, 34.

Triples

McGee, St. Louis, 18; Raines, Montreal, 13; Samuel, Philadelphia, 13; Coleman, St. Louis, 10; Garner, Houston, 10.

Pitching (12 Decisions)

Hershiser, Los Angeles, 19-3, .864, 2.03; Gooden, New York, 24-4, .857, 1.53; Franco, Cincinnati, 12-3, .800, 2.18; B. Smith, Montreal, 18-5, .783, 2.91; Welch, Los Angeles, 14-4, .778, 2.31.

Strikeouts

Gooden, New York, 268; Soto, Cincinnati, 214; Ryan, Houston, 209; Valenzuela, Los Angeles, 207; Fernandez, New York, 180.

Saves

Reardon, Montreal, 41; Smith, Chicago, 33; Smith, Houston, 27; Power, Cincinnati, 27; Gossage, San Diego, 26.

American League

Home Runs

Evans, Detroit, 40; Fisk, Chicago, 37; Balboni, Kansas City, 36; Mattingly, New York, 35; Thomas, Seattle, 32.

Runs Batted In

Mattingly, New York, 145; Murray, Baltimore, 124; Winfield, New York, 114; Baines, Chicago, 113; Brett, Kansas City, 112.

Stolen Bases

Henderson, New York, 80; Pettis, California, 56; Butler, Cleveland, 47; Wilson, Kansas City, 43; Smith, Kansas City, 39.

Hits

Boggs, Boston, 240; Mattingly, New York, 211; Buckner, Boston, 201; Puckett, Minnesota, 199; Baines, Chicago, 198.

Doubles

Mattingly, New York, 48; Buckner, Boston, 46; Boggs, Boston, 42; Cooper, Milwaukee, 39; Brett, Kansas City, 38; Walker, Chicago, 38.

Triples

Wilson, Kansas City, 21; Butler, Cleveland, 14; Puckett, Minnesota, 13; Fernandez, Toronto, 10; Barfield, Toronto, 9; Guillen, Chicago, 9.

Pitching (12 Decisions)

Guidry, New York, 22-6, .786, 3.27; Saberhagen, Kansas City, 20-6, .769, 2.87; Cliburn, California, 9-3, .750, 2.09; Key, Toronto, 14-6, .700, 3.00; Cowley, New York, 12-6, .667, 3.95; Dixon, Baltimore, 8-4, .667, 3.67.

Strikeouts

Blyleven, Minnesota, 206; Bannister, Chicago, 197; Morris, Detroit, 191; Hurst, Boston, 189; Witt, California, 180.

Saves

Quisenberry, Kansas City, 37; James, Chicago, 32; Moore, California, 31; Hernandez, Detroit, 31; Howell, Oakland, 29; Righetti, New York, 29.

All-Time Home Run Leaders

Player	HR	Player	HR	Player	HR	Player	HR	Player	HR
Hank Aaron	755	Willie McCovey	521	Billy Williams	426	Rocky Colavito	374	Ron Santo	342
Babe Ruth	714	Ed Mathews	512	Duke Snider	407	Gil Hodges	370	John (Boog) Powell	339
Willie Mays	660	Ernie Banks	512	Dave Kingman	407	Ralph Kiner	369	Joe Adcock	336
Frank Robinson	586	Mel Ott	511	Al Kaline	399	Graig Nettles	368	George Foster	334
Harmon Killebrew	573	Lou Gehrig	493	Johnny Bench	389	Joe DiMaggio	361	Bobby Bonds	332
Mickey Mantle	536	Stan Musial	475	Frank Howard	382	John Mize	359	Hank Greenberg	331
Jimmy Foxx	534	Willie Stargell	475	Orlando Cepeda	379	Yogi Berra	358	Jim Rice	331
Reggie Jackson	530	Mike Schmidt	458	Norm Cash	377	Lee May	354	Willie Horton	325
Ted Williams	521	Carl Yastrzemski	452	Tony Perez	377	Dick Allen	351		

Cy Young Award Winners

Year	Player, club	Year	Player, club	Year	Player, club
1979	(NL) Bruce Sutter, Cubs	1981	(NL) Fernando Valenzuela, Dodgers	1983	(NL) John Denny, Phillies
	(AL) Mike Flanagan, Orioles		(AL) Rollie Fingers, Brewers		(AL) LaMarr Hoyt, White Sox
1980	(NL) Steve Carlton, Phillies	1982	(NL) Steve Carlton, Phillies	1984	(NL) Rick Sutcliffe, White Sox
	(AL) Steve Stone, Orioles		(AL) Pete Vuckovich, Brewers		(AL) Willie Hernandez, Tigers

Water Ski Champions in 1985

43d Annual National Water Ski Championships

Du Quoin, Ill., Aug. 14-18, 1985

Men's Overall—Carl Robege, Orlando, Fla., 3,272 pts.
Men's Slalom—Carl Roberge, 62½ buoys.
Men's Tricks—Cory Pickos, Eagle Lake, Fla., 10,300 pts.
Men's Jump—Mike Morgan, Lake Wales, Fla., 182 feet.
Women's Overall—Karin Roberge, Orlando, Fla., 2,882 pts.
Women's Slalom—Camille Duvall, Windermere, Fla., 55½ buoys.
Women's Tricks—Tawn Larsen, Madison, Wis., 8,110 pts.
Women's Jumping—Deena Brush, Fruitland Park, Fla., 134 feet.
Senior Men's Overall—David Benzel, Groveland, Fla., 4,045 pts.
Senior Men's Slalom—Gordon Rathbun, Rio Linda, Cal., 58 buoys.
Senior Men's Tricks—Russ Stiffler, Lake Worth, Fla., 6,840 pts.

Senior Men's Jumping—David Benzel, 142 feet.
Senior Women's Overall—Barbara Cleveland, Hawthorne, Fla., 3,205 pts.
Senior Women's Slalom—Barbara Cleveland, 46 buoys.
Senior Women's Tricks—Barbara Cleveland, 5,300 pts.
Senior Women's Jumping—Thelma Salmas, Lantana, Fla., 99 feet.
Boys' Overall—Justin Anderson, Redding, Cal., 3,193 pts.
Boys' Slalom—John Reichard, Avalon, N.J., 49 buoys.
Boys' Tricks—Russell Gay, Fredericksburg, Va., 6,770 pts.
Boys' Jumping—J. D. Wiswall, Montgomery, Ala., 139 feet.
Girl' Overall—Karrie Bowes, Lake Helen, Fla., 3,433 pts.
Girl's Slalom—Kim Laskoff, Ft. Walton Beach, Fla., 56 buoys.
Girl's Tricks—Karrie Bowes, 6,170 pts.
Girl's Jumping—Lisa Fitzgerald, Muskego, Wis., 106 feet.

26th Annual Masters Water Ski Tournament

Callaway Gardens, Ga., July 13–14

Men's Overall—Sammy Duvall, Windermere, Fla., 2,766 pts.
Men's Slalom—Andy Mapple, Great Britain, 54½ buoys.
Men's Tricks—Sammy Duvall, 8,720 pts.
Men's Jumping—Mike Hazelwood, Great Britain, 191 feet.
Women's Overall—Deena Brush, Fruitland Park, Fla., 2,684

pts.
Women's Slalom—Deena Brush, 51½ buoys.
Women's Tricks—Kristi Overton, Greenville, N.C., 6,380 pts.
Women's Jumping—Karen Morse, Great Britain, 132 feet.

Lacrosse Champions in 1985

NCAA Division I Championship—Providence, R.I., May 25: Johns Hopkins 11, Syracuse 4. **Semi-finals**—Johns Hopkins 11, Virginia 8; Syracuse 11, North Carolina 13(ot).

NCAA Division III Championship—Chestertown, Md., May 18: Hobart 15, Washington College 8.

All-Star College Game—Baltimore, Md., June 8: South 16, North 7.

National Junior College Championship—Arnold, Md., May 11: Nassau CC 14, Anne Arundel CC 9.

U.S. Club Lacrosse Association Championship—Baltimore, Md., June 9: Hofstra 21, Maryland LC 20(ot).

Women NCAA Lacrosse Championship—Philadelphia, Pa., May 19: **Division I**—New Hampshire 6, Maryland 5. **Division III**—Trenton State 7, Ursinus 4.

USILA Division I All America Team

Attack: Tim Nelson, Syracuse; Brian Wood, Johns Hopkins; Mac Ford, North Carolina.

Midfield: Del Dressel, Johns Hopkins; Brad Kotz, Syracuse; Joey Seivold, North Carolina; Leo Paytas, Pennsylvania.
Defense: John DeTommaso, Johns Hopkins; Kevin Sheehan, Syracuse; Jeff Desko, Syracuse.
Goal: Larry Quinn, Johns Hopkins.
Note: 4 midfielders selected for the 3 midfield positions.

USILA Division III All America Team

Attack: Tom Grimaldi, Hobart; Marc VanArsdale, Hobart; Mike Perkins, Cortland.
Midfield: Ricky Sowell, Washington; William Bergan, Hobart; Dave Cook, Cortland.
Defense: Daniel Whelan, Hobart; Steve Beville, Washington; Rick Young, Cortland.
Goal: Bill Pilat, Roanoke.

USILA Coach of the Year

Division I—Dom Starsia, Brown Univ.
Division III—Terry Corcoran, Washington College.
Junior College—Paul Wehrum, Herkimer County (N.Y.) CC.

NCAA Divisions I Champions

1971	Cornell	1975	Maryland	1979	Johns Hopkins	1983	Syracuse
1972	Virginia	1976	Cornell	1980	Johns Hopkins	1984	Johns Hopkins
1973	Maryland	1977	Cornell	1981	North Carolina		
1974	Johns Hopkins	1978	Johns Hopkins	1982	North Carolina		

Amateur Softball Assn. National Champions in 1985

Men's Major Fast Pitch — Pay 'n Pak, Seattle, Wash.
Women's Major Fast Pitch — Hi-Ho Brakettes, Stratford, Conn.
Men's Super Slow Pitch— Steele's Sports, Grafton, Oh.
Men's Major Slow Pitch — Blanton's, Fayetteville, N.C.
Women's Major Slow Pitch — Key Ford Mustangs, Pensacola, Fla.
Men's Class A Slow Pitch — Thompson Sporting Goods, Savannah, Ga.
Women's Class A Slow Pitch — Tuffie's, Bloomington, Minn.
Women's Class A Fast Pitch — Redding Rebels, Redding, Cal.
Men's Class A Fast Pitch — ETV Trucking, Grand Rapids, Mich.
Men's Church Slow Pitch — Hickory Hammock, Milton, Fla.
Women's Church Slow Pitch — Faith Baptist, Wichita Falls,

Tex.
Men's Major Industrial Slow Pitch — Grumman Aerospace, Bayshore, N.Y.
Men's Class A Industrial Slow Pitch — Brown and Williamson, Macon, Ga.
Women's Industrial Slow Pitch — Sheriff's Stars, Pensacola, Fla.
Men's 16-inch Slow Pitch — Hometown Touch, Chicago, Ill.
Men's Class A 16-inch Slow Pitch — Last Chance, Aberdeen, S.D.
Men's Class A Church Slow Pitch — Blessed Sacrament Catholic Church, Savannah, Ga.
Men's Modified Pitch — Piefer Pest Control, Miami, Fla.
Men's Master Slow Pitch — Budweiser, Detroit, Mich.
Women's Modified Pitch — Alibi Inn, Staten Island, N.Y.

NOVEMBER

National

Strong Economy Slows a Bit — The U.S. economic boom, a major factor in Pres. Reagan's reelection victory, appeared to be slowing down, according to figures released in November. On Nov. 2, the Labor Department reported that the unemployment rate remained at 7.3 percent. After having soared during the 1981-82 recession, the rate was one-tenth of a point lower than when Reagan took office in January 1981. Interest rates continued to edge lower; most of the major banks reduced their prime rate from 12 percent to 11.75 percent on Nov. 8. The Labor Department said, Nov. 9, that prices paid by producers for finished goods fell 0.2 percent in October. Third-quarter profits reported by U.S. corporations fell 7.3 percent, as compared with the second quarter, the Commerce Department said, Nov. 20. Economic growth of 1.9 percent was reported for the third quarter, according to the Commerce Department, Nov. 20, the slowest pace since 1982. Leading banks lowered their prime rate again, Nov. 26 and 27, to 11.50 and 11.25 percent. The Commerce Department said, Nov. 29, that the index of leading economic indicators had edged downward 0.7 percent in October.

Woman's Execution First in U.S. in 22 Years — Margie Velma Barfield, 52, who had been convicted of murdering her fiancé and who had confessed killing three other persons, including her mother, was executed by lethal injection at the state prison in Raleigh, N.C., on Nov. 2. She was the first woman to be put to death in the United States since 1962. All four of Barfield's victims had been poisoned. She was the 29th person to be executed in the United States since the resumption of executions in 1977, and the 18th to die in 1984.

Statue Honoring Vietnam Veterans Unveiled — The addition of a statue completed the Vietnam Veterans Memorial in November, and it then formally became a national monument under the jurisdiction of the National Park Service. Three days of ceremonies began in the Washington, D.C. area, Nov. 9, with the unveiling of *Three Servicemen*, a sculpture by Frederick Hart. At a distance of 80 feet, the 7-foot tall figures face the V-shaped wall of black granite inscribed with the names of 58,022 Americans killed or missing in action in Southeast Asia. A candlelight vigil was conducted at the monument, Nov. 10, and on Nov. 11, Armistice Day, Pres. Ronald Reagan dedicated the sculpture and addressed 150,000 persons.

6 CIA Employees Linked to Guerrilla Manual — Six unnamed employees of the CIA received unknown punishments for their roles in producing a manual on guerrilla warfare, it was reported, Nov. 14. The manual, which had become an issue in the presidential campaign, had discussed ways of "neutralizing" officials of Nicaragua's Sandinista government. Some critics charged that this implied assassination. The White House announced, Nov. 10, that 2 investigations had found no violation of the law, but that some persons had used bad judgment. Pres. Ronald Reagan, Nov. 10, authorized the imposition of punishment on those found to be responsible. The 6 employees were said to be mid-level in rank. Punishments were reported to include suspension without pay or letters of reprimand. One of the 6 was said to be John Kirkpatrick (a pseudonym), a contract worker who had written the manual. He reportedly was allowed to resign his contract.

$200 Billion Budget Deficits Foreseen — Officials in the Reagan administration said, Nov. 14, that the federal budget deficit for the 1986 fiscal year would be around $200 billion, some $30 billion above the previous estimate. The deficit for the current (1985) fiscal year was now being put at $210 billion, well above the $172 billion previously forecast. The rising deficits were blamed on a slowing of the economy, a drop in tax revenues, and an increase in spending by the 98th Congress in its final days. Some independent analysts had argued that the previous projections by the government, made before the election, had been too optimistic.

Treasury Announces Major Tax Revision Plan — The long-anticipated proposal for a simplified U.S. tax code was announced, Nov. 27, by Treasury Secretary Donald Regan. Although it reflected Pres. Ronald Reagan's wishes for reform without tax increases, the president did not immediately endorse it publicly. Secretary Regan insisted on the semantic distinction that the plan was the Treasury's, not the administration's. In general, the reform plan would reduce taxes on individuals and increase them on corporations. The 16 tax brackets for individuals would be replaced by only 3, with a maximum rate of 35 percent for those making more than $38,100 a year. However, many personal deductions, tax shelters, and corporate investment tax credits and rapid-depreciation provisions would be eliminated. Republican leaders in the House predicted that it would be difficult to get the plan through Congress, and that the strong support of the president would be required.

Ruckelshaus Resigns as EPA Chief — William Ruckelshaus, who in 1983 had returned to his old job as administrator of the scandal-ridden Environmental Protection Agency, said, Nov. 28, that he would resign, effective in January 1985. Ruckelshaus had been the EPA's first administrator from 1970 to 1973. During his 18-month tenure in 1983 and 1984, he had restored the morale of the agency after the resignation of its previous director, the conviction of another official, and the forced resignations of a number of other top EPA officials. The cloud of mismanagement and political manipulation of the toxic waste clean-up program cleared away during Ruckelshaus's tenure. Lee M. Thomas, assistant administrator of the EPA, was named, Nov. 29, to suc-

Reagan Reelected in a Landslide

Pres. Ronald Reagan and Vice Pres. George Bush were reelected overwhelmingly on Nov. 6. In defeating the Democratic candidates, former Vice Pres. Walter Mondale (Minn.) and Rep. Geraldine Ferraro (N.Y.), the first woman to run for vice president on a major-party ticket, Reagan and Bush carried 49 states. The Republicans won 525 electoral votes, an all-time high, and the Democrats, who carried only Minnesota and the District of Columbia, captured only 13. The Republican ticket polled 54,455,075 votes, or 59 percent, and the Democrats received 37,577,185 votes, or 41 percent. Minor party candidates won 600,000 votes, less than 1 percent of the total. The Democrats took 252 seats in the House of Representatives to 182 for the Republicans. One seat remained in doubt long after the election. The Republicans, in scoring a net gain of 14 or 15 seats in the House, appeared to have fallen short of the ideological (conserva- tive) control that they had sought. The GOP lost two seats in the Senate, but retained control, 53-47. The Democrats lost one governorship, but maintained a wide margin nationwide, 34-16. The Democrats emerged from the election in full control of 27 state legislatures, and the Republicans controlled 11. In winning, Reagan, at 73 the oldest man ever to be elected president, drew majority support from almost all demographic groups. Mondale did win among blacks, Hispanics, Jews, union members, and persons earning less than $12,500 a year. Mondale said, Nov. 7, that he had no plans for seeking any other elective office in the future, but predicted that history would deal kindly with his campaign despite its mistakes. Reagan said, Nov. 7, that the people had shown that they approved of what his administration was doing and that he would continue on the same path.

ceed Ruckelshaus. Thomas received general approval from
environmentalists and leading members of Congress, but
some expressed concern that he would not have enough personal influence to overcome the apparent lack of enthusiasm
for environmental issues within the administration.

Dole Elected Senate Majority Leader — Sen. Robert
Dole (Kan.) was elected majority leader of the U.S. Senate
by his Republican colleagues, **Nov. 28.** He succeeded Sen.
Howard Baker (Tenn.), who did not seek reelection in 1984.
Five senators entered the contest to succeed Baker, and on
the fourth ballot, with the voting narrowed to the top two
vote-getters, Dole prevailed over Sen. Ted Stevens (Alaska)
by a 28-25 margin. Sen. Alan Simpson (Wyo.) was chosen to
succeed Stevens as deputy leader, or whip. Dole said that
reducing the federal budget deficit would be the top priority
for the new Congress that would convene in January.

International

Violence Sweeps India After Gandhi's Murder — The
first week of November was a bloody time in India, with
more than a thousand persons, mostly Sikhs, being killed in
sectarian violence that followed the assassination of Prime
Minister Indira Gandhi. She had been shot by 2 of her
bodyguards, both Sikhs, as she walked in her garden Oct.
31. Mrs. Gandhi was immediately succeeded by her son
Rajiv. Army troops were sent to New Delhi, the capital, and
8 other cities, **Nov. 1,** and curfews were imposed in 30 cities.
These measures had little initial success in preventing the
killings, most of which were perpetrated by Hindus. Thousands of Sikhs were injured and up to 50,000 were left
homeless as a result of threats of violence and property destruction. The assassination was an act of vengeance growing out of the bloody government suppression of a Sikh uprising in Punjab state in June 1984, which included an
assault on the holiest Sikh shrine, the Golden Temple. Rajiv
Gandhi, a former airline pilot who had been groomed for
the succession by his mother after the death of his older
brother Sanjay in 1980, put a lighted torch to Mrs. Gandhi's
funeral pyre at an outdoor ceremony in New Delhi, **Nov. 3.**
Although Rajiv kept most of his mother's cabinet and advisers, he indicated that he would seek to eliminate inefficiency
and corruption in the nation's leadership. On **Nov. 12,** with
calm restored to the country, Gandhi was unanimously
elected president of the ruling Congress (I) Party, and on
Nov. 13, he announced that national elections would be held
in December. The Indian government said, **Nov. 15,** that
1,277 people had been killed in the violence following the
assassination.

Alleged Plot Against Honduran Leader Foiled — Agents
of the U.S. Federal Bureau of Investigation arrested 8 men,
Nov. 1, in an alleged Miami-based plot to assassinate the
president of Honduras. Other arrests were reportedly made
in Honduras the same day. At least 2 of those arrested were
said to have ties with Gen. Gustavo Alvarez Martinez, who
had been removed in March as chief of the armed forces by
President Roberto Suazo Cordova. The FBI also seized $10
million worth of cocaine, which the FBI said was to be sold
to finance the plot.

U.S.-Nicaraguan Tensions Rise — In November, Nicaragua's Sandinista regime conducted its first election since
coming to power in 1979, but this gesture toward democracy failed to avert a deepening of hostility between Nicaragua and the United States. The **Nov. 4** voting resulted in the
election as president of Daniel Ortega, who had headed the
ruling junta. Ortega, candidate of the Sandinista National
Liberation Front (FSLN), received 63 percent of the vote,
not especially overwhelming in light of the fact that some
opposition groups had boycotted the election. They had
charged, as did the Reagan administration, that the election
was not completely open and free. The FSLN won 61 of the
96 seats in the National Assembly. The U.S. government
came to believe in the first days of November that a Soviet
freighter was bound for Nicaragua with a cargo of MiG-21
combat jets. The United States warned the Soviet Union,
Nov. 6 and 7, that it would not tolerate the delivery of such
weapons. The ship docked at a Nicaraguan port, **Nov. 7,** but
reporters observing the unloading of its cargo saw no evidence that planes were aboard. Expressing the belief that the
United States would use the incident as an excuse to mount

an invasion, Nicaraguan officials began to move the country
to a war footing. The defense ministry put the armed forces
on full combat alert, **Nov. 12.** Internal political opponents of
the Sandinistas criticized U.S. moves against Nicaragua, ar-
guing that they only strengthened the hand of the hardliners in the government. A Pentagon spokesman charged,
Nov. 13, that Nicaragua had "designs" on Honduras and El
Salvador. The International Court of Justice at the Hague
voted 16-0, **Nov. 26,** to accept a suit by Nicaragua demanding that the United States end support of military activities
against Nicaragua.

Israel Adopts Wage-Price Freeze — In an effort to slow
inflation that was running at an annual rate of 900 percent,
Israel instituted a freeze on wages and prices, **Nov. 4.** Representatives of the Manufacturers Association and the Hist-
adrut, the national labor federation, had agreed to the plan 2
days earlier. Reductions in the national budget, still being
negotiated, were also a part of the plan. The government of
Prime Minister Shimon Peres said it hoped to cut the inflation rate in half by February 1985, when the freeze would
expire. Peres warned that the economy would not recover
fully because of this one action.

State of Siege Declared in Chile — Pres. Augusto Pinochet of Chile moved in November to quell the disturbances
that had recurred from time to time throughout 1984. His
cabinet resigned, **Nov. 5,** in order to permit Pinochet to reor-
ganize his government. The president announced a new cabinet, largely unchanged, **Nov. 6,** and imposed a state of siege.
It replaced the state of emergency previously in effect and
increased the government's power to make arrests and to
restrict civil liberties. Pinochet said he intended to "put an
end to the criminal increase in terrorism." The protests, the
most recent of which had begun at the end of October, had
been led by organizations of workers. The government, **Nov.
7,** forbade the head of the Roman Catholic Church's human
rights office from returning to Chile. On **Nov. 8,** it suspended publication of 6 opposition magazines. Arrests were
stepped up, with 2,000 people being detained after a raid on
one shantytown, **Nov. 10.** Bombs rocked 7 cities, **Nov. 13,**
and university students boycotted classes and held rallies to
protest the government's actions.

Lebanese-Israeli Talks Falter — Lebanon and Israel
opened talks, **Nov. 8,** in southern Lebanon in an attempt to
find a formula that would permit Israel to withdraw the rest
of its occupation force. The 2 nations were dealing with the
problem for the first time since Lebanon abrogated a previous accord with Israel on the withdrawal of Israeli troops.
The talks, held under U.N. auspices, broke off, **Nov. 10,** and
then resumed, **Nov. 15,** with the 2 sides far from an agreement. Israel was primarily concerned about protecting its
northern border after a withdrawal. Lebanon, **Nov. 26,** began to deploy troops throughout Beirut in an effort to reestablish the government's authority in the capital. The first
goal was to remove militiamen from the streets.

France, Libya in Dispute Over Chad Pullout — France
and Libya agreed in November to withdraw their military
forces from Chad. All French forces were withdrawn by
Nov. 10. Libya claimed that all of its troops were out by the
same day. After doubts arose, French President François
Mitterand and the leader of Libya, Col. Muammer el-
Qaddafi, met on Crete, **Nov. 15,** with Greek Premier Andreas Papandreou as mediator. Qadaffi reaffirmed his commitment in principle to a pullout, but he said that Libya reserved the right to defend itself in the region if threatened.
Mitterand stated publicly, **Nov. 16,** that the agreement had
not been fulfilled by Libya. France announced, **Nov. 19,** that
French reconnaissance flights over Chad would continue,
but that France would not send troops into Chad for the
present.

Egypt Fakes Murder of Libyan Exile — The Egyptian
government in November tricked the Libyan government
into boasting publicly that an exiled critic of its regime had
been murdered. Egypt said it had uncovered a plot by the
Libyan ambassador to Malta and 4 men he had hired—2
Britons and 2 Maltese—to kill Abdul Hamid Bakkoush, the
last premier of Libya under the monarchy, who had been
living in exile in Egypt since 1977. Egypt took the 4 hired
assassins into custody, then posed and photographed the
intended victim as a corpse covered with blood. The faked
photographs were sent to Libyan authorities, and on **Nov.**

16, the official Libyan press agency said that Bakkoush had been "executed" by a team established "to liquidate the enemies of the revolution." Egypt then revealed, Nov. 17, that Bakkoush was alive, and he appeared at a press conference to denounce Libyan leader Muammer el-Qaddafi as an "international criminal."

U.S., Soviet Negotiators to Meet — The United States and the Soviet Union announced, Nov. 22, that U.S. Secretary of State George Shultz and Soviet Foreign Minister Andrei Gromyko would meet in Geneva, Switzerland, in January to discuss an agenda for disarmament talks. The White House said that "the whole range of questions concerning nuclear and outer space weapons" would be open for discussion. The January meeting, if successful, would lay the groundwork for more serious discussions at a later date. Anatoly Dobrynin, Soviet ambassador to the United States, expressed interest in the U.S. proposal for "umbrella" talks that would explore all aspects of the nuclear arms race.

Western Nations Step Up Famine Relief — The United States joined other western nations in November in rushing assistance to millions of people in Africa who faced starvation as a result of a prolonged drought. The United Nations estimated, Nov. 28, that 325,000 tons of food had been pledged by foreign governments to Ethiopia during the previous 2 months. U.S. aid was valued at about $103 million. The famine was at its worst in Ethiopia, where estimates of potential deaths ran as high as 6 to 7 million. The civil conflict in Ethiopia added to the difficulties in providing aid. A U.N. report, released Oct. 29, said that 35 million Africans were threatened by food shortages in 36 countries.

General

New Orleans Fair Files for Bankruptcy — The 1984 Louisiana World Exposition filed for protection from its creditors, Nov. 6, under Chapter 11 of the U.S. bankruptcy code. The New Orleans fair had already defaulted on a $40 million loan obtained from more than 100 corporate backers. Losses for the fair were reported to be in excess of $100 million. The fair concluded its 6-month run, Nov. 11, and fair officials said they did not have enough money even to dismantle the facilities. Only 7.2 million persons attended the fair, far below the hoped-for 11 million. Construction-cost overruns and undercapitalization were also blamed for the huge deficit. A real-estate development company came to a partial rescue by working out a deal to purchase part of the fairgrounds for incorporation into a riverfront marketplace and entertainment center.

Astronauts Retrieve Wayward Satellites — An 8-day mission by the space shuttle *Discovery* in November was highlighted by the capturing of 2 stray communications satellites. *Discovery* began its second mission at Cape Canaveral, Fla., Nov. 8, after a one-day delay because of windy conditions at the launch site. The 5-person crew deployed a Canadian communications satellite, Nov. 9, and a military communications satellite, Nov. 10. On Nov. 12, the crew caught up with the first of 2 commercial communications satellites launched from the shuttle *Challenger* in February. Leaving the shuttle, astronaut Joseph Allen floated toward the Indonesian satellite, Palapa-B2, grabbed it, and used the power of the thrusters in his backpack to stop its rotation. Allen held the satellite for 90 minutes, during a complete orbit of the earth, while astronaut Dale Gardner attached grappling clamps to it, and the two men then maneuvered the satellite into the cargo bay with the help of astronaut Anna Fisher. A similar procedure was followed, Nov. 14, for the retrieval of Western Union Corporation's Westar 6. The shuttle landed at Cape Canaveral, Nov. 16.

Infant with Baboon's Heart Dies — A baby girl identified only as Baby Fae lived for almost 3 weeks with the implanted heart of a baboon, but died after her body appeared to reject her new heart. When just 12 days old, she had received the baboon's heart Oct. 26 in an operation performed at the Loma Linda University Medical Center in California. She had been born with a condition known as hypoplastic heart syndrome; the left side of her heart was much smaller than the right side. On Nov. 9, she showed the first signs of rejecting the new heart. Her doctors later reported that she had begun to recover from the rejection episode, and her death on Nov. 15 was somewhat unexpected. Dr. Leonard

Bailey, who performed the transplant, said, Nov. 16, that the knowledge gained by the experiment would some day save the lives of many children. Medical authorities elsewhere were divided on the wisdom of the operation, some saying that rejection of the heart had been a certainty.

Man Receives Artificial Heart — For the second time, a human patient underwent an operation that replaced a diseased heart with a mechanical one made of aluminum and plastic. The operation in Louisville, Ky., on Nov. 25, was performed on William Schroeder, 52, of Jasper, Ind., a retired federal worker. It took place at the Humana Heart Institute under the leadership of Dr. William DeVries, who had also headed the surgical team that had performed the first artificial-heart transplant in 1983 on Dr. Barney Clark in Salt Lake City. Clark lived for 112 days after the operation. DeVries subsequently moved his program to Louisville. The heart implanted in Schroeder's chest was a modified version of the Jarvik-7 heart given to Clark. After the Schroeder operation, which was reported to have gone "almost routinely," the patient appeared to recover more rapidly than Clark had. By Nov. 29, Shroeder was able to take a few steps.

Disasters — A typhoon that swept through the central Philippines during the first week of November claimed more than 300 lives. . . . The death toll was put at 306 in the explosion, Nov. 19, of a storage area for liquefied gas in Mexico City.

DECEMBER

National

Reagan Proposes Cuts in Budget — Pres. Ronald Reagan threw his support behind major new cuts in domestic spending in December. Faced with administration estimates that the annual federal budget deficits would exceed $200 billion in 1988, Reagan, Dec. 5, submitted to his cabinet a plan that would cut $34 billion from the 1986 budget, exclusive of defense. The Defense Department was expected to propose its own cuts at a later date. Reagan proposed to eliminate the Small Business Administration, the Job Corps, the Legal Services Corporation, rural housing programs, federal subsidies for Amtrak, dairy subsidies, and most urban mass-transit aid. Federal revenue-sharing would be allowed to expire, federal civilian employees would sustain a 5 percent pay cut, cost-of-living increases would be ended for federal retirees, and farm price-support payments and loan programs would be cut substantially. Defense Secretary Caspar Weinberger, Dec. 12, came up with $6 billion in cuts, including a freeze in military pay in the 1986 fiscal year. Displeasure within the administration concerning the size of the defense budget was apparent. David Stockman, director of the Office of Management and Budget, was known to favor cutting back on some weapons systems. The secretary of the Treasury, Donald Regan, told reporters, Dec. 12, that he favored a "pause for a year" in the military buildup.

Congressional Leaders Keep Top Jobs — Voting on congressional leadership positions in December resulted in no change among the top positions. On Dec. 3, Rep. Thomas P. (Tip) O'Neill, Jr. (Mass.) was chosen by his Democratic colleagues to serve as Speaker of the House for a sixth and last time. O'Neill had already announced that he did not plan to seek reelection to the House in 1986. Before the voting, Rep. Charles Stenholm (Tex.) abandoned an attempt to challenge O'Neill. Stenholm, a conservative, had said that he felt that O'Neill's liberal image was hurting the party at a time when the country had a popular conservative president. Rep. James Wright (Tex.) was reelected majority leader. The House Republicans also held their caucus, Dec. 3, and reelected Robert Michel (Ill.) and Trent Lott (Miss.) as minority leader and minority whip, respectively. The choice of the Democratic leader in the Senate went to a vote, Dec. 12, with the incumbent, Robert Byrd (W. Va.) prevailing over Lawton Chiles (Fla.) by 36-11. Some Democrats were said to believe that Byrd would be overmatched against Robert Dole, whom the Republicans had chosen as their new leader in November. While reelecting Byrd, the Senate Democrats also renamed Alan Cranston (Cal.) and Daniel Inouye (Haw.) as minority whip and head of the party caucus, respectively.

Economy on Steady Course — Statistics released during December provided no fuel for those who had predicted the onset of hard times in 1986. After holding fairly steady for some months, the unemployment rate fell 0.3 percent to an even 7 percent in November, the Labor Department reported, Dec. 7. An early surge in Christmas sales sent retail sales up 1.8 percent in November, the Commerce Department reported, Dec. 13. Industrial production advanced 0.4 percent in November, the Federal Reserve Board announced, Dec. 14. The Labor Department said, Dec. 14, that the index of prices paid by producers for finished goods rose 0.5 percent in November. The Commerce Department announced, Dec. 17, that the U.S. balance of payments showed a record deficit of $32.9 billion during the third quarter. The consumer price index edged upward 0.2 percent in November, the Labor Department reported, Dec. 20. The index of leading economic indicators, which had shown no clear trend in recent months, reversed itself again in November, rising 1.3 percent, the Commerce Department reported, Dec. 28.

Shuttle Flight Secrecy Imposed — The U.S. Defense Department announced, Dec. 17, that the next shuttle flight, scheduled for January, would be conducted under a veil of secrecy. The launch of the first all-military mission was to take place at Vandenberg Air Force base in California. The press was to be barred from following the countdown, and the launch time would not be made known in order to make it more difficult for the Soviet Union to track the shuttle. The Pentagon also said that news articles speculating on the secret payload would be investigated as breaches of national security. Many news organizations agreed to comply with the Pentagon's request to withhold information. The Washington Post, however, reported, Dec. 18, that a $300 million satellite carried by the shuttle would take over the task of intercepting Soviet electronic communications. The paper said that the new satellite would join several other satellites already over the Soviet Union. Defense Secretary Caspar Weinberger charged, Dec. 19, that the Post had been guilty of "the height of journalistic irresponsibility" for publishing the story. Post Executive Editor Benjamin Bradlee replied, Dec. 19, that virtually all the information in the story was already public.

Subway Gunman Stirs National Debate — A rider on a New York City subway train shot and wounded 4 teen-age boys, Dec. 22, after one of them asked him for $5. Two of the victims, all of whom were shot with a .38-caliber revolver, were wounded critically. The gunman fled from the scene. The shootings triggered a wide public debate on what action a citizen should be permitted to take in threatening situations. The incident also drew attention to the New York subway system, which had long been plagued by a high rate of crime. Sentiment, especially in New York City, appeared to run strongly in favor of the gunman. But Mayor Edward Koch and other public officials condemned the shootings and warned that vigilantism would not be tolerated. A resident of Manhattan, Bernhard Goetz, surrendered to police in Concord, N.H., Dec. 31, and said he was the gunman. Goetz was returned to New York City, and on Jan. 25 he was indicted by a grand jury for possession of unlicensed weapons. The grand jury, apparently concluding that Goetz had acted in self-defense, refused to indict him on 4 counts of attempted murder. A second grand jury, after hearing evidence not available to the first one, indicted Goetz Mar. 27, for attempted murder.

International

Labor Majority Cut in Australia Election — Prime Minister Robert Hawke retained his office in voting in Australia, Dec. 1, but his ruling Labor Party lost a few seats in the parliamentary election. Hawke had run on his record of having improved the economy, but Andrew Peacock, leader of the Liberal Party, had predicted that a reelected Labor government would increase taxes. Hawke shook up his cabinet, Dec. 11, replacing more than half of its members. Defense Minister Gordon Scholes was demoted and replaced by Kim Beazley, who had been aviation minister.

Administration Defends South African Policy — In the face of growing protests in the United States against the apartheid policies of the South African government, the Reagan administration sought to defend its approach in December. Chester Crocker, assistant secretary of state for African affairs, said, Dec. 3, that the administration's policy of "constructive engagement"—the tactic of putting quiet pressure on South Africa—had led to some reforms. His statements to the press were prompted by daily demonstrations in front of the South African embassy in Washington and at several South African consulates in the United States. The protests, begun in late November, had resulted in nearly 40 arrests by early December. Walter Fauntroy, the District of Columbia's delegate to Congress, was an organizer of the protests. Thirty-five conservatives in Congress wrote to the South African embassy, Dec. 5, warning that they would support sanctions against South Africa unless it acted quickly to end racial segregation. Bishop Desmond Tutu, a black South African who had won the 1984 Nobel Peace Prize, met with Pres. Ronald Reagan, Dec. 7. Tutu, who had criticized the president's policy toward his country, said after the meeting that the gap between them had not been closed. Reagan said his administration would carefully consider proposals that Tutu had made. Tutu accepted the Peace Prize in Oslo, Norway, on Dec. 10. On the same day, Reagan called publicly on South Africa to end "the forced removal of blacks from their communities and the detention without trial and lengthy imprisonment of black leaders." Sen. Edward Kennedy (D, Mass.) strongly criticized apartheid during a visit to South Africa, Jan. 5-13, but he was criticized there by many blacks who said he was staging a "media event" to advance his political career.

Moderate Elected in Grenada — Herbert Blaize, a former chief minister in Grenada's colonial government in the 1960s, was elected prime minister of Grenada, Dec. 3. His New National Party, a coalition of several centrist parties, won 14 of 15 seats in the Parliament. The Grenada United Labor Party, led by former Prime Minister Sir Eric Gairy, won only one seat. Blaize's victory pleased the Reagan administration, which had hoped to see Grenada return to moderate civilian rule. Gairy's eccentric leadership had led to a takeover by Marxists in 1979. The eventual rise to power of violent Marxist radicals in 1983 had prompted an invasion of the island by U.S. forces supported by neighboring Caribbean states. The outcome of the election seemed to assure that Grenada would continue to receive U.S. financial aid. Blaize was sworn in as prime minister, Dec. 4.

Hijackers Kill 2 Americans at Teheran Airport — A 6-day hijacking drama ended at the Teheran, Iran, airport, Dec. 9, when Iranian authorities captured 4 hijackers and freed 9 hostages. The rescue came after 2 Americans had been murdered and a number of other passengers beaten. Four men who spoke Arabic seized the Kuwaiti plane, Dec. 4, during a flight from Kuwait to Pakistan and forced the crew to fly to Teheran. There were 161 persons aboard. After landing, the hijackers shot Charles Hegna, an employee of the U.S. Agency for International Development, and threw him from the plane; he died on the way to the hospital. Many passengers were then freed. The hijackers announced, Dec. 5, that they had planted explosives and would blow up the plane unless Kuwait freed 17 men imprisoned for terrorist activities. Another U.S. AID official, William Stanford, was shot to death, Dec. 6. The hostages assaulted some of the passengers and shot out the windows, precluding any chance that the plane would fly again. Following the release of more hostages, only 9 remained when, on Dec. 9, Iranian security men disguised as medical and flight personnel overpowered the gunmen. The United States charged, Dec. 11, that Iran had encouraged the hijackers and had been slow to move against them. The two freed Americans said that they had seen no collusion between the Iranians and the hijackers. Iran refused, Dec. 12, to accede to a U.S. request that the hijackers be extradited.

Gorbachev is a "Hit" During British Visit — A key member of the Soviet Politburo, Michael Gorbachev, toured Britain in December and left a favorable impression with the British leaders whom he met. Gorbachev, regarded by some as next in line to succeed the ailing Konstantin Chernenko as leader of the Soviet Union, arrived, Dec. 15, accompanied by his wife Raisa. The relatively youthful and outgoing couple projected an image in sharp contrast to that provided by other Soviet leaders in recent years. In meetings with Prime Minister Margaret Thatcher and others, however, Gorba-

chev hewed to the firm Kremlin line in opposition to U.S. plans to develop space weapons. Thatcher, speaking, **Dec. 17**, of her meeting the day before, said, "I like Mr. Gorbachev—we can do business together." Although Thatcher had previously indicated concerns about U.S. space plans, it was reported that she had made clear that the Soviet Union could not split the 2 allies over the issue. Gorbachev cut short his British visit, **Dec. 21**, to attend the funeral of Soviet Defense Minister Dmitri Ustinov. Thatcher, after meeting with Pres. Ronald Reagan at Camp David, **Dec. 22**, said she supported U.S. research on a nuclear defense system in space, and added that the Soviet Union would not be able to create division between the United States and Britain.

Britain, China Sign Agreement on Hong Kong — Prime Minister Margaret Thatcher and Chinese Premier Zhao Ziyang signed an agreement in Peking, **Dec. 19**, that formally transferred the colony of Hong Kong to Chinese sovereignty in 1997. The British Parliament and Hong Kong's legislative council had already approved the draft agreement. The settlement, negotiated and announced earlier in 1984, provided for the "one country-two systems" concept under which Hong Kong would be permitted to keep its capitalist system for 50 years after 1997, when it would become a special administrative zone of China. In that year, Britain's 99-year lease is scheduled to expire.

United States Pulls Out of UNESCO — The United States followed up on its threat of December 1983 and withdrew from the United Nations Educational, Scientific, and Cultural Organization. Having served notice in 1983 that it would pull out unless significant reforms were imposed, the United States took the final step, **Dec. 19**. Assistant Secretary of State Gregory Newell said that UNESCO continued to suffer from mismanagement, excessive politicization, and "endemic hostility toward the institutions of a free society." The U.S. withdrawal became official at the end of the year. Great Britain announced, **Nov. 22**, that it would withdraw at the end of 1985 unless UNESCO changed its spending habits. Prime Minister Margaret Thatcher had said, **Nov. 20**, that the organization's leaders had been seeking "to prevent the freedom of speech and freedom of the press" in some parts of the world.

Soviet Defense Minister Ustinov Dies — Death claimed another elderly member of the Soviet Politburo, **Dec. 20**, when Defense Minister Dmitri Ustinov, 76, who had not been seen publicly for 2 months, died. Marshall Sergei Sokolow, 73, succeeded him, **Dec. 22**. No change in defense policy was anticipated. Ustinov was buried, **Dec. 24**, but Soviet Pres. Konstantin Chernenko, who was believed to be seriously ill, did not attend the outdoor ceremony in the subzero weather. Cherenenko did appear in public, **Dec. 27**, to present several medals for literature.

Rajiv Gandhi's Party Wins Indian Election — Prime Minister Rajiv Gandhi of India, in office less than 2 months, led his Congress (I) Party to a sweeping victory in elections to the national legislature in December. It appeared that the Congress (I) Party had won about 400 seats in the 542-seat lower house of Parliament. Civil unrest forced a postponement of the election in 2 states. The victory gave promise that the nation might be able to put behind it the tragedies of 1984, which included a bloody uprising by Sikhs and the assassination of Indira Gandhi, Rajiv's mother and predecessor. The Congress (I) Party had long been the dominant force in Indian politics, but its share of the popular vote—more than 50 percent—was unprecedented in the voting of **Dec. 24, 27, and 28**. Some opposition leaders were defeated. Rajiv Gandhi won his own seat overwhelmingly against a challenge by his estranged sister-in-law, Maneka Gandhi, the widow of his brother, Sanjay. At least 26 deaths were attributed to violence that accompanied the election. Gandhi and his new cabinet, including many new faces, were sworn in, **Dec. 31**. Gandhi continued to serve as foreign affairs minister.

Chemical Plant Leak Kills 2,000 in India — Toxic fumes drifted through two densely populated slum neighborhoods in the Indian city of Bhopal, **Dec. 3**, bringing death to more than 2,000 persons. The lethal gas, methyl isocyanate, leaked from a chemical plant where it was used in the manufacture of an insecticide. The plant was owned by Union Carbide India Ltd., a subsidiary of the U.S. Union Carbide Corp. The precise cause of the disaster was not immediately

known, but investigators thought that the leak may have occurred after a buildup of pressure within an underground tank containing 15 tons of liquid methyl isocyanate. The leak occurred during the night and killed many of the victims in their sleep. Others died later, and still others suffered serious damage to lungs, eyes, and other organs. The toll of injured was put at 50,000. Population in the vicinity of the plant had grown rapidly since its construction in 1977. V. P. Sathe, the Indian minister for petroleum and chemicals, charged, **Dec. 5**, that Union Carbide did not maintain the same safety standards for the plant as it did for its plant in Institute, West Virginia. A Union Carbide official denied, **Dec. 5**, that the standards were different. The government of Madhya Pradesh state filed a criminal negligence suit against Union Carbide India on **Dec. 6**. Five supervisory employees were charged with negligence. Warren Anderson, chairman of Union Carbide Corp., arrived in India, **Dec. 7**, was immediately arrested, then released and told to leave the country. The company provided money, doctors, and medical supplies to aid in the relief effort, but also faced the certainty of large lawsuits. After the government announced, **Dec. 12**, that it would restart the plant in order to neutralize the remaining gas, some 200,000 persons began to evacuate the vicinity. The Madhya Pradesh state government said, **Dec. 30**, that it would file suit in the United States against Union Carbide.

General

AMA Calls for Abolition of Boxing — The American Medical Association, **Dec. 5**, adopted a resolution calling for an end to both professional and amateur boxing. The resolution was approved overwhelmingly in a voice vote at the annual meeting of the AMA House of Delegates in Honolulu. It warned of "the dangerous effects of boxing on the health of participants." Dr. Joseph Boyle, president of the AMA, said that scientific study showed that blows sustained in boxing resulted in "both acute and long-term brain injury." He added that even short exposure to boxing could result in disabling injuries.

Russians Aim Spacecraft at Halley's Comet — The Soviet Union, **Dec. 15**, launched a spacecraft called Vega I toward a point in space where it would rendevous with Halley's Comet on March 6, 1986. The comet, returning from the void of outer space for its once-every-75-years visit to the solar system, was expected to be prominently visible to the naked eye in late 1985 and early 1986. The Vega I carried 2 television cameras and other equipment designed to obtain information on the comet. The Russians planned to launch a second spacecraft toward the comet, and the 11-nation European Space Agency and Japan also scheduled launches, but the United States planned no comparable effort because of budget limitations. However, the Soviet vehicle did carry a U.S. comet-dust detector.

Disasters — At least 100 persons were reported killed early in December when a gas explosion tore through a 9-story apartment building in Tbilisi, in the Soviet Union.

JANUARY

National

Reagan's 2d-Term Team Gets a New Look — Personnel changes within the cabinet and the White House, which had begun to occur late in 1984 after Pres. Ronald Reagan was reelected, grew quickly in January. Education Secretary T. H. Bell and William Ruckelshaus, chief of the Environmental Protection Agency, were among those who had already announced their impending departures. William Clark, a longtime friend and adviser to the president, announced, through a spokesman, **Jan. 1**, that he would retire as secretary of the Interior after serving a little more than a year. Michael Deaver, Reagan's deputy chief of staff and another old friend, was also leaving; the president announced his forthcoming departure, **Jan. 3**, with "deep regret." Reagan, on **Jan. 8**, announced a surprising exchange of jobs between James Baker, his chief of staff, and Donald Regan, the secretary of the Treasury. Both men were reported in the press to have become restless in their old jobs. With presidential counselor Edwin Meese 3d also leaving the White House,

subject to his approval as attorney general, Regan had the opportunity to take firm control of day-to-day operations there. On **Jan. 10**, Reagan announced that Energy Secretary Donald Hodel would succeed Clark at Interior; that John Herrington, the White House personnel director, would succeed Hodel; and that William Bennett, chairman of the National Endowment for the Humanities, would succeed Bell in the Education Department. Richard Darmon, an assistant to Baker in the White House, would follow Baker to the Treasury Department as deputy secretary. U.N. Ambassador Jeane Kirkpatrick met with Reagan, **Jan. 30**, and confirmed her decision to leave her position. Conservatives were outspoken in their disappointment that Reagan had not found another place in the administration for Kirkpatrick. She told The *New York Times*, **Jan. 31**, that her views had been misunderstood and distorted by 3 key administration officials, whom she did not name.

Aspin, Gray Get Key House Chairmanships — The 99th Congress convened on **Jan. 3**. Two important changes in House chairmanships were made **Jan. 4**. The Democratic caucus deposed 80-year-old Melvin Price (Ill.) as chairman of the Armed Services Committee. He was regarded by some members as too frail to continue. Ignoring the hallowed seniority system, the Democrats then chose Les Aspin (Wis.), the 7th-ranking member on the panel, to be its new chairman. Aspin had often been a critic of the Pentagon, but his key compromise in 1984 had maintained funding for the controversial MX missile for at least one more year. The Democrats chose William Gray (Pa.) to head the Budget Committee. The position was expected to make him one of the most influential blacks on Capitol Hill.

Senate GOP Leader Enters Budget Fray — Sen. Robert Dole (R, Kan.), the new Senate majority leader, plunged into the budget-deficit debate, **Jan. 3**, when he introduced a bill whose goal was to reduce federal deficits to about $100 billion by 1988. On **Jan. 2** and **3**, Budget Director David Stockman told Republican congressional leaders that projected deficits would run as high as $240 billion a year by the late 1980s. Dole and some other Republican senators indicated that they did not believe that administration proposals dealt adequately with the budget deficits. They appeared to favor freezing the costs of as many programs as possible, perhaps even cost of living increases for Social Security recipients. Sen. Barry Goldwater (R, Ariz.), chairman of the Senate Armed Services Committee, warned, **Jan. 9**, that any freeze of the military budget could seriously damage the national security. Reagan, **Jan. 9**, indicated at a press conference that he might ease his previously stated opposition to any freeze in Social Security benefits if Congress showed strong bipartisan support for such a freeze. Reagan said his goal was to hold spending in 1986 to 1985 levels, and he restated his opposition to any tax increase. Paul Volcker, the Federal Reserve chairman, said, **Jan. 15**, that a $50 billion cut in federal deficits would be the minimum required to avert an increase in interest rates. Dole warned, **Jan. 25**, that Congress would have difficulty in coming up with a deficit-reduction package unless Reagan agreed to smaller increases in defense spending. Reagan said, **Jan. 26**, that any reduction would be "very risky." But other Republican senators, including Robert Packwood (Ore.), chairman of the Finance Committee, and Mark Hatfield (Ore.), chairman of the Appropriations Committee, supported Dole. Hatfield said, **Jan. 29**, that the deficit fight required full mobilization and that Defense Secretary Caspar Weinberger could not remain a "draft dodger."

Strong 1984 Economy Painted by Numbers — Statistics released during January established that 1984 had been a very good year for the American economy. Data released on **Jan. 4** showed that sales of automobiles in the United States had risen 13.1 percent in 1984. The total of 10,358,166 cars was the highest since 1979. Some 76 percent of these were produced in the United States. The Labor Department said, **Jan. 9**, that unemployment had edged upward in December to 7.1 percent from 7.0 percent in November. The Labor Department reported, **Jan. 11**, that the prices paid by producers for finished goods rose only 1.8 percent in 1984. Continuing a trend, major banks again cut their prime rate, **Jan. 14**, this time to 10.75 percent; the rate stood at its lowest point since August 1983. The Commerce Department reported, **Jan. 17**, that construction began in 1984 on 1.74

million housing units, a 2.4 percent increase over 1983. The Department said, **Jan. 22**, that the nation's real gross national product had increased 6.8 percent in 1984, the highest rate of gain since 1951. The Labor Department said, **Jan. 23**, that the consumer price index had risen by only 4 percent in 1984, the third consecutive year of relatively low inflation. Worker productivity, a key factor in controlling inflation, rose 3.1 percent in 1983, the Labor Department reported, **Jan. 29**. On Wall Street, the Dow Jones Industrial Average closed at an all-time high of 1292.62 on **Jan. 29**. On the dark side, the Commerce Department said, **Jan. 30**, that the U.S. trade deficit stood at $123.3 billion in 1984, far above the previous record of $69.4 billion reported in 1983. The Department said, **Jan. 31**, that the index of leading economic indicators had edged downward by 0.2 percent in December.

Black Leaders and Reagan Exchange Charges — Pres. Ronald Reagan's difficulties with American blacks took a new turn in January when the president repeatedly questioned the motives of some black leaders. On **Jan. 15**, Reagan met with the Council for a Black Economic Agenda, a group of professionals that other black leaders called unrepresentative of their community. Robert Woodson, president of the group, said it had been formed to establish an alliance between blacks and the administration. In its assessment of the "State of Black America," the National Urban League said, **Jan. 16**, that blacks had felt new hope and encouragement in 1984 despite "grim" economic conditions and the administration's "deplorable" record on issues of interest to blacks. In an interview with *USA Today*, Reagan said, **Jan. 18**, that his record was much better than black leaders would admit. He said that perhaps some of the leaders were seeking to protect their positions by keeping their constituency aggrieved. John Jacob, president of the National Urban League, called Reagan's remarks insensitive and insulting. In a radio interview, **Jan. 26**, Reagan reiterated his position, adding that some leaders sought to keep blacks "stirred up." *The Washington Post* reported, **Jan. 28**, that black Republicans were unhappy because their support for Reagan had not been reflected in patronage from the administration.

Jury Finds Time Magazine Defamed Sharon — A highly publicized libel suit by former Israeli Defense Minister Ariel Sharon against *Time* magazine resulted in something of a standoff in January. A jury in federal district court in New York City found, **Jan. 16**, that a passage in an article in the magazine had defamed Sharon, and it held, **Jan. 18**, that it was false. But it held, **Jan. 24**, that *Time* had not libeled Sharon because the magazine did not have "serious doubts" as to the truth of what it had written when it was published. In its issue of Feb. 21, 1983, *Time* had reported that Sharon, then defense minister, had met with members of the Gemayel family in Lebanon following the assassination of President-elect Bashir Gemayel by unknown persons in September 1982. According to the magazine, Sharon "reportedly discussed with the Gemayels the need for the Phalangists to take revenge" for Bashir's murder. The Phalangists were a Christian military force loyal to the Gemayel family. Subsequently, Phalangists entered refugee camps in Beirut and killed hundreds of Palestinians. Contending that the story in *Time* implied that he had had foreknowledge of the massacre, Sharon sued *Time*. Although the magazine denied any such implication, the jury decided otherwise in holding that Sharon had been defamed. *Time*, in its Jan. 21, 1985 issue, renewed its contention that no role in the massacre had been implied for Sharon. *Time*, however, did acknowledge that another statement in its Feb. 21, 1983 article was incorrect—that Appendix B of an Israeli commission's report on the massacre contained further details about Sharon's visit to the Gemayel family. In making its **Jan. 24** ruling that Sharon had not been libeled, the jury was guided by the requirement of U.S. libel law that a public figure must establish that a statement, in addition to being false and defamatory, was also made with actual malice or with reckless disregard for the truth. Sharon, although forced to step down as defense minister in the aftermath of the massacre, had since become minister of industry and commerce, and his partial vindication was regarded as a step toward recovery of his public reputation in Israel.

Inaugural Parade Canceled Because of Bad Weather — Bitter cold weather, accompanied by strong winds, forced a

cancellation of the parade that was to celebrate the inauguration of Pres. Ronald Reagan. Indoor celebrations, which began **Jan. 18**, proceeded on schedule. Reagan, beginning his second term, took the oath of office twice. On Sunday, **Jan. 20**, at the White House, he and Vice. Pres. George Bush took the oaths at noon. Reagan was sworn in by Chief Justice Warren Burger. The second swearing-in ceremony was to take place on the steps of the Capitol on Monday, **Jan. 21**, but the Inaugural Committee canceled it and the parade to follow because of concern for the health of the participants and observers. Instead, Reagan took the oath inside the Capitol before nearly 1,000 invited guests. Delivering his inaugural address after the second ceremony, Reagan said that his administration had made a "new beginning" at correcting "well-intentioned errors of the past" and that the nation was "poised for greatness." On the evening of **Jan. 21**, the president and Mrs. Reagan visited each of the 9 inaugural balls.

Secret Shuttle Mission Begun — The U.S. space shuttle *Discovery* began its first secret military mission at Cape Canaveral, Fla., **Jan. 24**, lifting off at 2:50 p.m.—only 9 minutes after the launch time was disclosed. Nothing was said publicly about the orbit, payload, or length of the mission. Some news organizations reported, however, that the payload was a 5,000-pound electronic intelligence-gathering satellite that could spy on the Soviet Union. The National Aeronautics and Space Administration did say that the launch was successful and that the shuttle had obtained its intended orbit. The shuttle and its 5-man crew landed at Cape Canaveral, **Jan. 27**.

International

Soviet Missile Overflies 2 Neighbors — It was revealed in January that a Soviet cruise missile had flown over the territory of Norway and Finland on **Dec. 28**. The defense ministries of the 2 Scandinavian countries reported the overflight, **Jan. 2**, and officials of the 2 countries said, **Jan. 4**, that Soviet envoys had apologized and had said that the object was an old Soviet cruise missile used for target practice. Finnish border guards began searching for the missile, which disappeared in the vicinity of Lake Inari, near where borders of all 3 countries meet. They found it near the lake, **Jan. 30**.

Nakasone, Reagan Discuss Trade Imbalance — Pres. Ronald Reagan and Japanese Prime Minister Yasuhiro Nakasone met in Los Angeles, **Jan. 2**, to discuss ways of reducing Japan's trade surplus with the United States. In the exchange of products between the 2 countries in 1984, Japan came out ahead by about $35 billion. Such imbalances had been the source of controversy between the countries for some years and a cause of growing protectionist demands in the United States. The 2 leaders agreed to high-level negotiations that would focus on opening up specific Japanese markets to U.S. goods, especially for forest products, telecommunications, electronics, computers, and medical supplies. Nakasone, **Jan. 8**, directed his cabinet to take steps to open Japanese markets to more foreign products.

Superpowers Agree to Resume Arms Talks — Secretary of State George Shultz and Soviet Foreign Minister Andrei Gromyko met in Geneva, Switzerland, and agreed to resume negotiations on the reduction of nuclear arms. During their 2 days of meetings, **Jan. 7** and **8**, both sides made concessions. Moscow agreed to disarmament talks despite its previous refusal to do so unless the United States halted the deployment of medium-range nuclear weapons in Western Europe. The United States accepted the concept of "umbrella" talks, favored by the USSR, in which both medium-range and intercontinental nuclear weapons, plus space arms, would be discussed. Thus, the U.S. Strategic Defense Initiative, popularly known as Star Wars, would be on the table. No date was chosen at Geneva for the resumption of negotiations. Expressing his pleasure at the turn of events, Pres. Ronald Reagan, **Jan. 9**, said his ultimate goal was the "complete elimination of nuclear weapons." Gromyko, in a television interview, **Jan. 13**, said that future disarmament talks could hinge on American willingness to limit space weapons. The United States, **Jan. 18**, named Max Kampelman, a lawyer with previous experience in international negotiations, as head of its delegation at the upcoming talks.

The Soviet Union, **Jan. 26**, named Vladimir Lomeiko the head of its delegation. It was announced, **Jan. 26**, that the 2 nations would begin their formal talks March 12 in Geneva.

U.S. Rebuffs World Court on Nicaragua — The United States notified the International Court of Justice, or World Court, that it would not participate in proceedings related to Nicaragua's suit against the United States. The announcement was a bad omen for relations between the United States and the new administration of Daniel Ortega. Ortega, who had previously headed the ruling Sandinista junta, was sworn in as president, **Jan. 10**. President Fidel Castro of Cuba was among the dignitaries at the ceremony. In his inaugural speech, Ortega claimed much progress during 5 years of Sandinista rule, but warned that the intervention of the United States through its support of armed "contras" inside Nicaragua could jeopardize the revolution. The State Department announced, **Jan. 18**, its decision to boycott the World Court case in which Nicaragua charged the United States with aggression, and on the same day administration officials also announced that bilateral talks with the Sandinistas would be suspended. The United States charged that Nicaragua was using the Court for political and propaganda purposes. A visit to Nicaragua, **Jan. 23** to **25**, by the premier of Iran prompted Pres. Ronald Reagan to warn, **Jan. 24**, of a new danger to Central America from Nicaragua's ties with Iran, Libya, and the Palestine Liberation Organization.

Brazil Returning to Civilian Rule — Twenty-one years of military rule neared an end in Brazil in January as the nation's electoral college chose a civilian president. The winner, on **Jan. 15**, was Tancredo de Almeida Neves, 74, the candidate of the Democratic Alliance. He was regarded as a political moderate. He easily defeated Paulo Salim Maluf, the candidate of the dominant Social Democratic Party, who had proved to be an unpopular figure. It appeared that the military had come to trust Neves, who had reportedly given assurances that no reprisals would be taken againt members of the military linked to human-rights abuses. But Neves also drew wide support from many other sectors. Neves said he would seek to reduce Brazil's hyperinflation. Neves became ill and underwent 3 abdominal operations in March. He was unable to take the oath of office, and Vice President-elect José Sarney was sworn in, **Mar. 15**, and designated as acting president. Neves died, **Apr. 21**, from complications following the abdominal surgery. Sarney automatically became president after Neves's death.

26 Charged in Aquino's Murder — Gen. Fabian Ver, chief of staff of the Filipino armed forces, and 25 others were formally charged, **Jan. 23**, with being involved in the murder in 1983 of Filipino opposition leader Benigno Aquino. They were also charged in the death of Rolando Galman, who, like Aquino, had been shot at the Manila international airport. Ver, the chief of police for metropolitan Manila, and 6 others were named as accessories in the slayings. The prosecutor, Bernardo Fernandez, said that they knew of the plot and had sought to cover it up. Seventeen others were charged with direct involvement, and the only civilian among the 26 was charged as an accomplice. The indictments were an outgrowth of 2 reports issued in October by a government board of inquiry. On **Feb. 1**, all 26 men pleaded not guilty.

OPEC Cuts Oil Prices Amid Discord — The Organization of Petroleum Exporting Countries cut prices on most brands of its crude oil in January, and its internal squabbles threatened to weaken the future effectiveness of the cartel. Meeting in Geneva, Switzerland, nine members of OPEC approved the new pricing structure, **Jan. 30**, but three nations (Algeria, Iran, and Libya) refused to go along with the reductions and Gabon abstained from the voting. Energy conservation and competition from non-OPEC suppliers had forced the OPEC majority to act. OPEC decided to retain its output ceiling of 16 million barrels per day, which had been imposed in 1984 to deal with the oil glut on the world market.

General

College Football Champion in Dispute — The 1984 college football season ended with an unresolved debate over which team deserved to be ranked "Number 1." Brigham

Young, the only major team to go undefeated, edged Michigan, 24-17, in the relatively minor Holiday Bowl, **Dec. 21.** Many writers and fans argued that BYU (13-0) did not play as strong a schedule as other teams, and that the championship should go to Washington (11-1), which defeated Oklahoma, 28-17, in the Orange Bowl, **Jan. 1,** or to Florida (9-1-1). Polls by the Associated Press and United Press International gave the championship to BYU, but The *New York Times* put Florida first in its computer ratings. Doug Flutie, winner of the Heisman Trophy as best player of the year in college football, quarterbacked Boston College to a 45-28 victory over Houston in the Cotton Bowl, **Jan. 1.**

Hawaii to Get Biggest Telescope — The California Institute of Technology and the University of California announced, **Jan. 3,** that they would build the world's largest telescope on a 13,600-foot ridge of Mauna Kea on the island of Hawaii. The telescope, scheduled for service in 1992, would cost $85 million. Of this, $70 million would come from a grant by the W. M. Keck Foundation, and the universities would provide the rest. The 36 hexagonal mirrors, arranged in a honeycomb pattern, would be oriented by computers. With a total reflecting surface 400 inches in diameter, the telescope would have nearly 4 times the light-gathering power of the largest present telescopes, which utilize a single large mirror to gather light.

Disasters — A train derailed in eastern Ethiopia, **Jan. 13,** and plunged off a bridge into a ravine, killing at least 392 persons; relief workers put the death toll at 449. . . . A Lockheed Electra chartered from Galaxy Airlines crashed near Reno, Nev., **Jan. 21,** just after takeoff for a flight to Minneapolis, killing 68 of the 71 persons aboard.

FEBRUARY

National

U.S. Automakers Report Record Profits — Financial reports released in February showed that the American automobile industry had done its share to pace the economic recovery. Unemployment edged upward in January to 7.3 percent, the Labor Department reported, **Feb. 1.** In its economic report for 1985, released **Feb. 5,** the Reagan administration cited its achievements in increasing productivity, business investment, and total employment while reducing inflation and interest rates. The report acknowledged that unemployment, poverty, and the federal deficit were ongoing problems. Annual reports by the "Big 3" American automakers—General Motors, Ford, and Chrysler—showed by **Feb. 14,** that their total profits in 1984 stood at $9.81 billion, far above the previous high of $6.15 billion set in 1983. The Labor Department reported, **Feb. 15,** that the index of prices paid by producers for finished goods was unchanged in January. The Commerce Department said, **Feb. 21,** that the economy had grown at an annual rate of 4.9 percent during the final 3 months of 1984—a sharper rebound from the summer 1984 slowdown than had previously been estimated. At month's end, the U.S. dollar continued to post new highs against other currencies, encouraging fears that U.S. manufactures would be priced out of the world markets.

Reagan Budget Comes Under Attack — Pres. Ronald Reagan sent a $973.7 billion federal budget for the 1986 fiscal year to Congress, **Feb. 4,** and it became the center of a stormy debate. It provided for an overall increase in federal spending of only 1.5 percent, with sharp increases in defense outlays being offset by the elimination of some domestic programs and reduced funding for others. Programs that the administration sought to eliminate included the Job Corps, the Legal Services Corporation, the Small Business Administration, mass-transit subsidies, and U.S. support for passenger rail and air service. Student-aid and farm-subsidy programs faced substantial cuts, and the salaries of federal employees would be reduced by 5 percent. The projected deficit of $180 billion was significantly smaller than the $222.2 billion deficit projected for the 1985 fiscal year. The administration warned that if the spending cuts were not enacted, the annual deficits would reach new highs. Reagan, speaking to some 100 members of Congress at the White House, **Feb. 4,** said enactment of the budget would "change the course of our nation's history." After the meeting, Sen.

Robert Dole (R, Kan.), the Senate majority leader, said he would abandon his effort to write a budget with a smaller defense increase and leave the process to Sen. Pete Domenici (R, N.M.), chairman of the Budget Committee. Sen. Mark Hatfield (R, Ore.), chairman of the Appropriations Committee, called the budget a "fantasy." Defense Secretary Caspar Weinberger defended the military budget before the Senate Armed Services Committee, **Feb. 4,** only to be rebuked by Sen. William Cohen (R, Me.) for spending $640 for toilet seats that Cohen said gave "new meaning to the word 'throne.' " David Stockman, director of the Office of Management and Budget, created a furor in administration ranks, **Feb. 5,** when he told the Senate Budget Committee that the military pension system was a "scandal. . .an outrage" and that "Institutional forces in the military are more concerned about protecting their retirement benefits than they are about protecting the security of the American people." Weinberger said, **Feb. 6,** that the service of military personnel "should not be defamed." In calling for elimination of revenue sharing from the federal budget, the administration had contended that many states enjoyed relative fiscal health, but a survey by the National Governors Association, **Feb. 8,** found that most states had, at best, only small surpluses. The new Education secretary, William Bennett, created another controversy, **Feb. 11,** when he defended proposed cuts in student aid by contending that some students would just have to give up their stereos, cars, and vacations. The United States Student Association said, **Feb. 12,** that the cuts would force millions of students to end their college careers.

Senate Finally Confirms Meese — Presidential Counselor Edwin Meese 3d won confirmation from the Senate for the office of attorney general, 13 months after Pres. Ronald Reagan first nominated him for the position. Hearings on his nomination had begun in 1984, but were suspended after a court appointed an independent counsel to investigate charges that Meese had helped arrange government jobs for people who had given him financial aid. The counsel found that Meese had committed no crime, but did not comment on whether Meese's conduct was ethical. After hearings before the Judiciary Committee resumed in January 1985, Meese claimed he had met "ethical as well as legal standards" for public officials, but Sen. Joseph Biden (D, Del.) said that his conduct was "beneath the office" of attorney general. On **Feb. 5,** the committee approved the nomination 12-6. The full Senate, **Feb. 6,** gave near-unanimous approval to 3 other Cabinet nominees, William Bennett (secretary of education), Donald Hodel (secretary of the interior), and John Herrington (energy secretary). Reagan, **Feb. 8,** nominated Lt. Gen. Vernon Walters (ret.) to succeed Jeane Kirkpatrick as chief U.S. delegate to the United Nations. Walters, former deputy director of the Central Intelligence Agency, had performed diplomatic assignments for several administrations. The White House, **Feb. 21,** named Beryl Sprinkel to succeed Martin Feldstein as chairman of the president's Council of Economic Advisers. Sprinkel was a leading proponent of the monetarist school of economics, which held that government can influence the economy by its control over the amount of money in circulation. Meese finally won the approval of the Senate, **Feb. 23,** by a vote of 63 to 31, with all negative votes being cast by Democrats.

Farmers Clamor for Federal Aid — Farmers from many states, facing economic destruction because of high interest rates and lower market prices, called in February for immediate financial assistance from the federal government. Testifying before the Senate Budget Committee, **Feb. 5,** Budget Director David Stockman opposed federal bailouts for debt-ridden farmers, asserting that taxpayers should not have to refinance bad debt "willingly incurred by consenting adults who went out and bought farm land when prices were going up and thought they could get rich." Farmers had borrowed heavily in the 1970s to finance increased production, using land and equipment as collateral. The Reagan administration, **Feb. 6,** unveiled a plan to provide federal guarantees for farm loans on which bankers cut interest payments by 10 percent or more. A number of U.S. senators from farm states, believing that many farmers needed additional credit in order to begin spring planting, filibustered for a week against the nomination of Edwin Meese 3d to be attorney general. In a compromise worked out, **Feb. 23,** a vote on

Meese was allowed in return for a promise that amendments providing for financial assistance to farmers could be offered on an African famine-relief bill. This was accomplished, Feb. 27, as both houses of Congress approved proposals providing emergency loans to farmers. Ignoring Pres. Ronald Reagan's opposition, many Republicans voted for the legislation. Sen. Charles Grassley (R, Iowa) said, "I can't turn my back on the farmers without turning my back on 7 out of 10 people in my state whose jobs are directly related to agriculture." The legislation was approved as farmers and farm lobbyists from across the nation streamed into Washington. Almost the entire South Dakota state legislature—103 of 105 members—came to the Capital to plead for help.

Reagan Upbeat on Nation's Future — Celebrating his 74th birthday in style, Pres. Ronald Reagan delivered a stirring State of the Union address to a joint session of Congress, Feb. 6. Calling for "a Second American Revolution of hope and opportunity" and saying that the nation was "poised for greatness," he added that "there are no constraints on the human mind, no walls around the human spirit, no barriers to our progress except those we ourselves erect." Reagan reiterated his desire to reduce the size of government, deregulate business, build military strength, and bring greater opportunity to all sectors of society. He also called for tax reform and defended the MX missile and his Strategic Defense Initiative antimissile system. Members of the audience sang "Happy Birthday" to the president. The Democrats, in their televised response to the speech, pictured themselves as a party that recognized the need for fiscal restraint, and they acknowledged that the party needed to change its strategy if it was to regain national political leadership.

International

Opposition Leader Returns to South Korea — Kim Dae Jung, a leader of the political opposition to South Korean President Chun Doo Hwan, returned to South Korea in February after 2 years of exile in the United States. He had previously served 2½ years of a sentence for sedition in South Korea. The United States announced, Feb. 1, that Pres. Ronald Reagan had invited Chun to visit the United States. The announcement had reportedly been delayed until the South Korean government agreed not to imprison Kim. The government confirmed, Feb. 4, that Kim would not be imprisoned. Kim and his wife, accompanied by 4 Americans, including 2 members of the U.S. House of Representatives, arrived by plane in Seoul, the South Korean capital, Feb. 8. Thousands of Kim's supporters were on hand, but police and soldiers were also out in force and a melee ensued. Rep. Thomas Folietta (D, Pa.) said later that the Kims were separated from the Americans and that Kim was beaten. The United States formally protested the incident and said Kim had been put under house arrest. South Korea, after denying that anyone had been beaten, acknowledged, Feb. 9, that some force had been used. Reagan said, Feb. 11, that the incident tended to hide the fact that South Korea "has made great strides in democracy. . . ." In elections to the National Assembly, Feb. 12, in which Kim was not permitted to participate, Chun's Democratic Justice Party slipped slightly to 148 seats. The New Korea Democratic Party became the leading opposition with 67 seats. In the popular vote, the DJP led the NKDP only narrowly, 35 percent to 29 percent. The NKDP included supporters of Kim. A spokesman for the DJP acknowledged that the results showed that many people desired greater liberalization.

U.S. in Disputes With New Zealand, Australia — The 34-year-old mutual defense pact known as Anzus showed some strains in February. Australia, New Zealand, and the United States were allied by the treaty. The U.S. State Department announced, Feb. 4, that New Zealand had denied a request that a U.S. Navy destroyer be allowed to pay a port call in New Zealand. The destroyer was to participate in the Anzus exercise "Sea Eagle" scheduled for March in the South Pacific. The rejection came from the government of Prime Minister David Lange, which had been elected on an antinuclear platform. The United States had refused to say whether the ship carried nuclear arms. The United States, fearful that other allies might take similar action, canceled the "Sea Eagle" exercise and said that other responses were being considered. Anzus was dealt another shock, Feb. 5, when Prime Minister Robert Hawke of Aus-

tralia, while in Washington, announced that Australia probably would not, as previously promised, permit the United States to monitor an MX missile test from an Australian base. He said a split in his Labor Party had created the problem. Lange, Feb. 6, accused the United States of bullying tactics, and a State Department official said, Feb. 7, that the United States no longer regarded New Zealand as "a loyal and faithful ally." Lange said, Feb. 19, that the United States had canceled or altered 6 joint defense training exercises. U.S. Secretary of State George Shultz said, Feb. 19, that New Zealand had "taken a walk" from the alliance.

Vietnamese Overrun Cambodian Camps — Vietnam's offensive against Cambodians resisting Vietnamese domination of their country, which had begun in November 1984, reached a climax in March. The rebels had inflicted heavy casualties on the advancing Vietnamese troops in January and early February, but by mid-February, the invaders had captured several camps of the Khmer Rouge, a Communist group. On Feb. 15, the Vietnamese seized and burned the Khmer Rouge administrative headquarters at Phum Thmei, which also served as the capital of all 3 rebel forces, including 2 that were noncommunist. The Vietnamese also scored successes against one of the noncommunist groups, but the other, led by Prince Norodom Sihanouk, had remained relatively unscathed by the invasion. During the offensive, some 250,000 Cambodians had fled into Thailand.

U.S. Drug Agent Kidnapped in Mexico — The kidnapping in Mexico of an American employed by the U.S. Drug Enforcement Agency focused U.S. public attention on the growing violence related to drug smuggling. An eyewitness in Guadalajara, Mexico, reported that on Feb. 7, 4 men seized Enrique Camarena Salazar and forced him into a car. On the same day, a Mexican pilot and friend of Camarena, who had flown for the DEA, Alfredo Zavala Avelar, was also abducted. Francis Mullin, head of the DEA, said, Feb. 12, that Guadalajara was the "major center" for drug-trafficking gangs in Mexico. Tensions between the United States and Mexico grew, Feb. 15, when U.S. customs agents began thorough searches of Mexican cars at the border. Mexico charged that the U.S. action was not justified. John Lawn, deputy DEA administrator, said, Feb. 18, that drug bosses in Colombia had offered a $350,000 reward to anyone who kidnapped top DEA officials.

4 Poles Guilty of Priest's Murder — Four members of the Polish state security police were convicted and sentenced to prison terms in Torun, Poland, Feb. 7, in the murder of a Roman Catholic priest. The victim, Father Jerzy Popieluszko, had been an outspoken critic of the Communist government and had a devoted following. He was abducted from his car near Torun on Oct. 19, 1984, and his beaten and bound body was found in reservoir several days later. The 4 officers were later arrested and they were put on trial in January. In addition to the 3 who had carried out the crime, Col. Adam Pietruszka, their superior officer, was also brought to trial and convicted. The 4 men received terms of 14 to 25 years. The Polish public followed the trial with intense interest, believing that evidence would emerge that would implicate higher-ranking officers or members of the government. No such evidence was introduced, but the trial was believed to be a landmark in a Communist country— the first time a government had publicly prosecuted members of its internal security forces in the murder of an opponent of the regime.

Israel Begins Pullout from Lebanon — The long-awaited Israeli withdrawal from Lebanon began in February. Attacks on Israeli troops occurred more frequently in the last weeks before the withdrawal began. Responding to increased casualties, Israeli planes attacked a suspected Palestinian guerrilla base in eastern Lebanon, Feb. 10 and 11. Jeremy Levin, Beirut bureau chief for the U.S. Cable News Network, escaped from Muslim captors in eastern Lebanon, Feb. 14, after a year of solitary confinement, and was escorted to safety by Syrian soldiers. Four other Americans had been kidnapped by Islamic extremists during the past year. On Feb. 16, 2 days ahead of schedule, Israeli troops completed their withdrawal from the Sidon area in the first phase of a 3-stage pullout. Lebanese troops then occupied Sidon to the cheers of its citizens. Thousands of armed Shiite Muslims and their supporters entered the city, Feb. 18, demanding the Islamization of Lebanon. In the days following

the departure of the Israelis, there were a number of reports that persons who had "collaborated" with them had been killed.

Leaders Discuss Mideast Peace Plans — Yasir Arafat, leader of the Palestine Liberation Organization, and King Hussein of Jordan met, and the Jordanian news agency reported, **Feb. 11,** that they had decided on a "framework for common action" for a settlement of the Palestinian issue. The accord reportedly provided for an international conference on the Mideast that would include the Soviet Union. The United States and Israel had always objected to such a role for the USSR. An adviser to Egyptian President Hosni Mubarak said, **Feb. 12,** "For the first time, the PLO has unequivocally and irrevocably accepted the premise of a peaceful settlement to the Arab-Israeli conflict." But Israeli Prime Minister Shimon Peres pointed out that the accord did not reject terror or include recognition of Israel. During 2 days of talks in Washington, **Feb. 11** and **12,** King Fahd of Saudi Arabia urged Pres. Ronald Reagan to involve the United States "more vigorously" in the peace process. Reagan said he believed that direct talks between the Arabs and Israel were the best approach. An official communiqué issued **Feb. 13,** reflected a difference of opinion on the best way to proceed. Peres said, **Feb. 27,** that he was ready to meet directly with Jordan or with a Jordanian-Palestinian delegation—providing no known PLO members were included—to discuss a peace settlement. Modifying its previous position, the Reagan administration said, **Feb. 28,** that it was ready "to re-engage in the peace process" in any way that the principals thought appropriate.

South African Police Kill 18 — Killings and arrests in mid-February brought an abrupt halt to a trend toward relaxed tensions between the races in South Africa. In the previous weeks, the government of Pres. Pieter Botha had agreed to the creation of a forum in which the urban black population would have a voice, offered to free opponents of the government from jail if they renounced violence, and halted the removal of blacks from areas reserved for whites. But then, between **Feb. 18** and **21,** police killed at least 18 persons demonstrating in the community of Crossroads near Cape Town. Some 200 people were injured. Settlers were protesting what they feared would be a removal to a black township several miles further away from the city. On **Feb. 19,** police arrested 13 persons—virtually the entire top leadership of the United Democratic Front. The UDF, an umbrella organization of more than 600 anti-government groups, was committed to nonviolence, but the government charged that it was a front for the outlawed African National Congress, which favored the use of force to overthrow the government. By month's end, some 1,900 persons, including a number of members of Congress, had been arrested in the United States for demonstrating against apartheid during the past several months.

Thatcher Addresses U.S. Congress — British Prime Minister Margaret Thatcher visited Washington, **Feb. 19-21,** and on **Feb. 20** became the first British leader, since Winston Churchill in 1952, to address a joint session of Congress. Thatcher endorsed the Reagan administration's Strategic Defense Initiative—the "Star Wars" program. She said that the Soviet Union had returned to arms negotiations because of the growing military strength of the West. Thatcher endorsed U.S. efforts to reduce budget deficits, which she said affected all other countries. She condemned Americans who contributed money to the outlawed Irish Republican Army.

Reagan Seeks Ouster of Nicaragua Government — Pres. Ronald Reagan acknowledged, **Feb. 21,** that he wanted to "remove" the "present structure" of the leftist Sandinista government of Nicaragua. At a news conference, he was pressed as to his intentions on Nicaragua, especially as they related to the "contras" fighting a guerrilla war against the government. He restated his appeal to Congress to renew aid to the contras, whom he called "freedom fighters," and said that he did favor the removal of the government, which he described as Communist and totalitarian. Asked if he was seeking the overthrow of the government, he replied, "Not if the present government would turn around and say 'uncle' " to the rebels or invite them into the government. In a speech, **Feb. 22,** Secretary of State George Shultz warned that if Congress did not bankroll the rebels, Nicaragua would fall into "the endless darkness of Communist tyr-

anny" and that the United States might have to intervene directly at a later date. Gen. Paul Gorman, the retiring commander of American military forces in Central America, said, **Feb. 27,** that the contras were incapable of overthrowing the Nicaraguan government in "the foreseeable future," with or without American aid. In a peace overture, Pres. Daniel Ortega of Nicaragua, **Feb. 27,** announced an "indefinite moratorium" on the acquisition of new arms systems by his government, and he said that Nicaragua would send home 100 Cuban military advisers. White House spokesman Larry Speakes said, **Feb. 28,** that the offer was without substance and was timed to influence votes in Congress on aid to the contras.

General

Championship Chess Match Halted — The president of the International Chess Federation astonished the chess world in Moscow, **Feb. 15,** by terminating the world championship match between Anatoly Karpov, the champion, and Gary Kasparov, the challenger. The match between the 2 Russians had begun in September, and after 48 games it stood at 5 games to 3 in Karpov's favor, with 40 draws. The match, which would go to the first player to win 6 games, had set records for length and for the number of draws. The ostensible reason given for ending the match was that the players were exhausted by the long struggle. Kasparov had won the last 2 games and there was speculation that the Russian chess establishment, which reportedly preferred the champion over his more independent-minded challenger, had persuaded federation president Florencio Campomanes of the Philippines to intercede. Both the 21-year-old challenger and the 33-year-old champion said they wished to continue, to no avail. The match was rescheduled for later in the year. Kasparov was the youngest player ever to reach the championship match.

Westmoreland Drops Suit Against CBS — The libel trial involving Gen. William Westmoreland and CBS Inc. came to an abrupt end, **Feb. 18,** when Westmoreland reached an out-of-court settlement with the network. Westmoreland had commanded U.S. forces in Vietnam from 1964 to 1968. A documentary called "The Uncounted Enemy: A Vietnam Deception," which CBS had broadcast in 1982, implied that the general had conspired to deceive the government and the public about opposing troop strength. Westmoreland filed a $120 million libel suit against the network that came to trial late in 1984. After 18 weeks of testimony, and only a few days before the case was to go to the jury, Westmoreland's position appeared to be weakening. Damaging testimony came from Maj. Gen. Joseph McChristian, Westmoreland's intelligence chief in Vietnam, who said he had warned Westmoreland in 1967 that estimates of enemy troop strength were being pegged too low. Retired Col. Gains Hawkins, who had been in charge of estimates of enemy strength, testified that Westmoreland had put a "ceiling" on enemy troop figures. Hawkins said that Westmoreland had told him in substance in 1967 that high estimates of enemy strength were "politically unacceptable" and that "We had better take another look at these figures." Westmoreland was reported to be dismayed by the testimony of his former comrades. His attorney, Dan Burt, head of the Capital Legal Foundation, which was the source of much of the money for the suit, began negotiations with CBS lawyers for a settlement. In the terms, announced **Feb. 18,** Westmoreland agreed to drop his suit in return for a statement from CBS that the general, though not CBS, called an apology. CBS said that it had "never intended to assert, and does not believe, that Gen. Westmoreland was unpatriotic or disloyal in performing his duties as he saw them." It was estimated that legal expenses for both sides had totaled more than $6 million.

3d Man Receives Artificial Heart — For the third time, **Feb. 17,** a middle-aged man received a permanent artificial heart. The operation took place at Humana Hospital in Louisville, Ky., where William Schroeder was still recuperating from the operation that had given him an artificial heart in November. The latest recipient, Murray Haydon, 58, a retired auto worker, got a Jarvik-7 artificial heart in a 3½-hour operation performed by Dr. William DeVries. Doctors predicted that Haydon, who suffered from a degenerative heart disease, had a chance for a full recovery.

Disasters — An airliner crashed into a mountain near Bilbao, Spain, Feb. 19, killing all 148 persons on board. . . . An Air Mali passenger plane crashed in the Sahara near Timbuktu, Mali, Feb. 22, killing 50 persons. . . . At least 50 persons were reported to have died, Feb. 23, when a train crowded with wedding passengers caught fire in Madhya Pradesh.

MARCH

National

Economic Indicators Rise — Two computations of the index of leading economic indicators issued in March showed that the economy was on the move again after a period of uncertainty. The Commerce Department reported, Mar. 1, that the index rose 1.7 percent in January, the sharpest jump in 19 months. The Labor Department said, Mar. 8, that the unemployment rate had edged downward to 7.2 percent in February. The Commerce Department announced, Mar. 21, that the rate of economic growth was sluggish in the first quarter of 1985. The consumer price index edged upward 0.3 percent in February, the Labor Department reported, Mar. 22. The Commerce Department said, Mar. 29, that the index of leading economic indicators had risen 0.7 percent in February.

Divided Senate Committee Approves Budget — The Senate Budget Committee approved a 1986 fiscal year budget package in March, but a rewriting of its plan on the Senate floor seemed likely. Committee Chairman Pete Domenici (R, N.M.) abandoned, Mar. 4, his attempt to come up with a Republican budget-cutting plan as a result of opposition by Pres. Ronald Reagan and some Republican senators to attempts to cut the growth of military spending. Domenici then offered a package that would freeze many domestic appropriations and accept Reagan's proposed cuts or eliminations of other domestic programs. He proposed a 3 percent increase above inflation for the defense budget. The committee, Mar. 5, voted, 18-4, to hold defense spending at the rate of inflation, or slightly above, for 3 years—cutting Reagan's proposed defense outlays by $79 billion over that period. The committee, Mar. 6, rejected many of Reagan's proposals for cuts in domestic spending. The vote against Reagan's proposal to cut $6 billion from agricultural programs in 1986 was 13-9. Reagan challenged the committee to put his own budget package to a vote; it did so Mar. 13, rejecting it by a vote of 17-4. It then completed action on its own budget plan, coming up with cuts in both domestic and military outlays that would achieve savings of $55 billion in 1986. The program included elimination of cost-of-living increases for Social Security recipients and U.S. civilian and military pensioners for one year. But the 11-9 vote along party lines gave promise that the dispute would be carried to the full Senate. Reagan, complaining that cuts of domestic programs did not go far enough, and seizing on talk in the Senate of a possible tax increase, warned Mar. 13, that "I have my veto pen drawn and ready for any tax increase that Congress might even think of sending up." He dared the "tax increasers" to "Go ahead and make my day."

Congress OKs 21 More MX Missiles — The controversial MX missile—benefiting from a massive lobbying effort spearheaded by Pres. Ronald Reagan, survived critical votes in the Senate and House in March. On Mar. 4, in urging Congress to release funds for 21 MX missiles, Reagan said that without the Peacekeeper (MX) "our chances of reaching an equitable agreement with the Soviet Union to reduce significantly the size of our nuclear arsenals are substantially lowered." U.S. and Soviet arms negotiators were scheduled to meet in Geneva, Switzerland, just a few days before Congress was to vote on MX. Representatives of 90 anti-MX groups said, Mar. 4, that the missile was unnecessary and too expensive and that its continued production would increase the possibility of war with USSR. The nation's Roman Catholic bishops, Mar. 15, called on all members of Congress to vote against the MX. The Senate, on Mar. 19 and 21, handed Reagan a victory by voting 55 to 45 both times to authorize the missiles and then appropriate $1.5 billion for the construction of 21 missiles. The House gave its endorsement to the MX, Mar. 26 and 28, by narrow votes of 219 to 213 and 217 to 210. Direct appeals to House members by Max Kampelmann, the chief. U.S. arms negotiator, who returned from Geneva to lobby for the MX, were regarded as decisive in determining the outcome in the House.

Weinberger Halts Payments to Contractor — Defense Secretary Caspar Weinberger announced, Mar. 5, that he was suspending some payments to General Dynamics Corporation for 30 days pending a review of possibly improper billings by the company. He also said that Pentagon auditors would review overhead expenses billed by other major contractors, and that henceforth all contractors would be required to certify their claims under penalty of perjury. Testimony by 2 top General Dynamics executives before a U.S. House subcommittee, Feb. 28, had centered on allegations that the corporation had concealed a delay in the delivery date of a submarine to prevent a decline in General Dynamics stocks, and that the company had billed the government for $50 million dollars in frivolous and improper claims. The first allegation appeared to be supported by a tape recording of a 1977 telephone conversation between 2 executives in which they discussed the need to hold back a public announcement of a late delivery date for the submarine in order to protect the company's stock. General Dynamics announced, Mar. 25, that it would withdraw $23 million in overhead charges submitted to the government between 1979 and 1982. The Air Force said, Mar. 28, that it had temporarily suspended General Electric Company from future Pentagon contracts as a result of the company's indictment on charges it had falsified claims and lied about work on a nuclear warhead system.

Reagan Vetoes More Aid to Farmers — As he had promised to do, Pres. Ronald Reagan vetoed a bill that would have provided aid to financially strapped farmers. Congress, Mar. 5, completed action on the bill when the House 255-168 accepted a version already passed by the Senate. The bill shifted crop support payments from the fall to the spring, increased the emergency farm loan guarantee program, and allocated $100 million to banks that cut interest rates on farm loans. In vetoing the legislation, Mar. 6, Reagan criticized what he called a "massive new bailout that would add billions to the deficit." House Speaker Thomas P. O'Neill, Jr. (D, Mass.) said that the administration that had added a trillion dollars to the national debt should have been willing to pay a reasonable price to insure the survival of family-owned farms. O'Neill said that no attempt would be made in the House to override the veto. In vetoing the bill, Reagan had said that only 4 percent of the family farmers needed immediate help, but it was revealed, Mar. 10, that a new Department of Agriculture study showed that 6.3 percent of all family farms were insolvent and that an additional 7.4 percent could become insolvent.

Savings and Loans Closed in Ohio — Thousands of Ohio citizens faced the possible loss of their money in March when savings and loan institutions closed their doors. The crisis in Ohio had its origins in Fort Lauderdale, Fla., Mar. 4, when E.S.M. Government Securities Inc. ceased operations. Suspecting fraud, the U.S. Securities and Exchange Commission obtained a court order, Mar. 4, appointing a receiver for the company. E.S.M.'s customers faced losses that could run as high as $300 million. Most of them had entered into repurchase agreements, or "repros," with E.S.M. In such an exchange, the company typically borrowed money from the customer, providing government securities as collateral, and agreed to buy back the securities at a given price and time. Evidence emerged that E.S.M. had used the same securities as collateral for more than one repro agreement. E.S.M.'s collapse started a run on the Home State Savings Bank of Cincinnati, which reportedly had entered into some $600 million worth of transactions with E.S.M. Home State, which was chartered by the state of Ohio, closed Mar. 9. Estimates of its losses ranged as high as $150 million, more than the $136 million in the Ohio Deposit Guarantee Fund, which insured deposits in state savings institutions. To protect deposits at the state's other savings and loan institutions, the state legislature, Mar. 13, approved a $90 million emergency fund. A political aspect was introduced when it was learned that Marvin Warner, an owner of Home State and a financial supporter of Ohio's Gov. Richard Celeste, had closed out his personal accounts at E.S.M. early in 1985. Celeste, Mar. 15, ordered all of the

state-chartered savings and loan institutions to close for 3 days after customers who feared that they would lose their money began a run on deposits. Celeste announced, **Mar. 17,** that a plan had been worked out with federal officials under which the state institutions would obtain federal insurance and then open. The banking crisis triggered a sharp rise, **Mar. 19,** in the price of gold and an abrupt drop in the value of the dollar against foreign currencies. Several of the "thrifts" reopened, **Mar. 21,** without suffering heavy runs on their deposits. Forty-six more reopened, **Mar. 23,** with a limit of $750 imposed on withdrawals.

Brock Replaces Donovan in Cabinet — Raymond Donovan, the first sitting member of a president's Cabinet ever to be indicted, resigned as secretary of Labor, **Mar. 15.** He had taken a leave of absence in the fall of 1984 after having been indicted in New York on charges of being involved with an attempt to defraud the New York City Transit Authority. Donovan denied the accusations, which related to events that occurred before he entered the Cabinet. He resigned after a New York state judge rejected his motion to dismiss the charges and ordered him to stand trial. Pres. Reagan, **Mar. 20,** nominated William Brock, the U.S. Trade Representative and a former U.S. senator from Tennessee, to succeed Donovan. The choice of Brock, a well-regarded political moderate, was seen as an effort to improve the administration's relations with organized labor.

International

British Coal Miners Vote to End Strike — The long violent strike by British coal miners ended in March when they voted to return to work. The end of the strike, which had lasted almost a year, represented a defeat for the miners. Their principal issue—the decision by the National Coal board to shut down 20 pits that it said were "uneconomic" —was not resolved. By **Mar. 1,** more than half of the miners had already returned to work. On **Mar. 3,** the delegates to a conference of the National Union of Mineworkers voted to go back to work, and by **Mar. 5,** the strike had formally ended. Union leader Arthur Scargill, who opposed the decision, blamed the failure of the walkout on the refusal of most other unions to support it. Nearly 10,000 persons were arrested during the strike, and Prime Minister Margaret Thatcher said, **Mar. 5,** that there would be no amnesty for those who had committed "serious criminal offenses."

Japan's Auto Export Quotas Ended — Pres. Ronald Reagan announced, **Mar. 1,** that he would not ask Japan to extend voluntary export quotas for automobiles beyond the **Mar. 31** expiration date. The Japanese, while pleased by the passing of the 4-year-old quotas, were not expected to flood the United States with automobiles lest they face retaliation in the form of protectionist legislation. Reagan spoke of the "wisdom of maintaining free and fair trade for the benefit of the world's consumers." But Owen Bieber, president of the

United Auto Workers, said the action could cost the jobs of as many as 200,000 U.S. workers. The United States had a trade deficit with Japan of $37 billion in 1984. Reagan's decision came as U.S. and Japanese negotiators were seeking agreements that would open Japanese markets to various U.S. manufactures, including wood products, electronic and telecommunications equipment, and medical supplies.

Body of U.S. Drug Agent Found in Mexico — The body of Enrique Camarena Salazar, an agent of the U.S. Drug Enforcement Administration, was found in Mexico, a month after he had been abducted in Guadalajara. On **Mar. 2,** Mexican police searching for Camarena and for his pilot, Alfredo Zavala Avelar, who had also been abducted, engaged in a shootout with suspected drug traffickers at a ranch southeast of Guadalajara. The couple that owned the ranch, their two sons, and a policeman were killed. Two bodies were found on the ranch, **Mar. 6,** and they were identified as those of the 2 missing men, **Mar. 7.** John Gavin, U.S. ambassador to Mexico, said, **Mar. 7,** that the victims had been brutally beaten before they died. U.S. Secretary of State George Shultz met with Mexican Foreign Secretary Bernardo Sepulveda Amor, **Mar. 11,** amid growing tensions between the 2 countries. The United States had charged that Mexico had not made a maximum effort to track down the kidnappers and that some Mexican policemen had helped the abductors. Mexico said, **Mar. 14,** that 13 persons, including police officials and policemen, had been arrested in the murders.

Violence Mars Israeli Pullout From Lebanon — The Israeli withdrawal from southern Lebanon proceeded on schedule in March, but a number of brutal incidents added to the horror in the devastated country. As the first stage of their 3-phase withdrawal continued, the Israeli army suffered a number of casualties in attacks from Muslim opponents. Israeli, in turn, adopted what Defense Minister Yitzhak Rabin called an "iron fist" policy, which included dozens of raids on Shiite Muslin villages. On **Mar. 4,** a bomb destroyed a mosque in Marakah and killed 15 persons, including 2 guerrilla leaders. Shiites and the Lebanese government blamed Israel. A car bomb exploded in a Shiite suburb of Beirut, **Mar. 8,** killing up to 80 people and wounding 250. Israel denied responsibility for these attacks. Twelve Israelies died and 14 were wounded, **Mar. 10,** when a Lebanese driver detonated explosions in a truck near an Israeli troop convoy. Responding, Israel, **Mar. 11,** attacked the town of Zrariyah and killed at least 24 persons. The United States, **Mar. 12,** vetoed a U.N. Security Council resolution condemning Israeli policy in southern Lebanon. Protesting Pres. Amin Gemayel's alleged pro-Syrian policies, Lebanon's largest Christian militia revolted against Gemayel's leadership, **Mar. 13.** The U.S. vote in the United Nations prompted threats against Americans by Lebanese groups, and the United States said, **Mar. 14,** that it had withdrawn some nonessential personnel from its Beirut em-

---

Soviet Leader Chernenko Dies and Is Quickly Succeeded by Gorbachev

Konstantin Chernenko, president of the Soviet Union and general secretary of the Soviet Communist Party, died **Mar. 10,** in Moscow. The Central Committee, acting, **Mar. 11,** on a recommendation of the ruling Politburo, approved Mikhail Gorbachev as the new party secretary. Chernenko's death, at 73, was no surprise, because his infrequent public appearances in recent months had shown him to be in failing health. Tass, the Soviet news agency, said, **Mar. 11,** that he had died of heart failure brought on by emphysema, hepatitis, cirrhosis of the liver, and hypoxia. Chernenko's 13 months in office had been marked by a continued military buildup and a resumption of arms talks with the United States, and by ongoing domestic economic troubles. Gorbachev, the youngest member of the Politburo at 54, became the superpower's fourth leader in 3 years. Leonid Brezhnev had died in November 1982 and successor, Yuri Andropov, had died in February 1984. Gorbachev, many years younger than any of the others, projected a far more contemporary, even western-style, image. He and his wife Raisa had impressed their hosts in Great Britain in December 1984 with their outgoing personalities. Born in 1931 into a peasant family in Stavropol in the Caucasus, Gorbachev received a degree in agriculture, joined the Communist Party, and rose

in its ranks, becoming a regional party first secretary in 1970. Benefiting from close ties with Andropov and with Mikhail Suslov, the party's leading theoretician, Gorbachev joined the national secretariat and supervised the nation's agricultural policy. Despite poor grain harvests, he was named to the Politburo in 1980. When Chernenko's health failed shortly after he succeeded to power, Gorbachev assumed some of his duties. When Gorbachev succeeded Chernenko, specialists on the Soviet Union predicted that his energy and comparative youth would permit him to have a major influence on Soviet and world affairs for many years. On **Mar. 11,** he pledged to follow the policies set forth by the party and by his predecessors. He said that improvement of the economy was his most important goal, and that the Soviet Union would follow the "Leninist course of peace and peaceful coexistence" with the West. Although Pres. Ronald Reagan chose not to attend the funeral, he said, **Mar. 12,** that he would welcome the chance to meet with Gorbachev. Vice Pres. George Bush headed the U.S. delegation at funeral services for Chernenko, **Mar. 13,** in Moscow. At a meeting with Gorbachev, **Mar. 13,** Bush delivered a letter from Reagan inviting him to come to the United States. Gorbachev was noncommittal.

bassy. Israeli soldiers swept into Shiite villages in southern Lebanon, **Mar. 21**, and killed 21 "terrorists" and 2 members of a CBS camera crew. The CBS employees were Lebanese. CBS protested to Israel that the killings were "unprovoked and deliberate," but Israel said the victims had been among a group of armed men.

Mubarak Presses Peace Initiative — Egyptian Pres. Hosni Mubarak continued his search for a diplomatic solution to the Middle East crisis in March. On **Mar. 6**, he met in Egypt with King Hussein of Jordan, but the latter did not publicly endorse Mubarak's call for talks between Israel and a joint Jordanian-Palestinian delegation. Mubarak met in Washington, **Mar. 11**, with U.S. Secretary of State George Shultz and other administration officials. Meeting with Pres. Ronald Reagan, **Mar. 12**, he urged the administration to support his peace efforts and said publicly of Reagan, "No leader is more equipped to play a historic role and fulfill a sacred mission in the Middle East." Reagan restated his view that direct Arab-Israeli negotiations offered the best chance for peace. Addressing the National Press Club, **Mar. 13**, Mubarak criticized the administration's lack of initiative in the Middle East as "almost a defeatist approach." Mubarak was also disappointed by his failure to get what he had sought in additional financial aid from the United States. Hussein, **Mar. 16**, said he could do no more in behalf of the peace process unless the United States agreed to meet with a joint Jordanian-Palestinian delegation. Mubarak and Hussein met in Amman, **Mar. 18**, and then flew to Baghdad, Iraq, to express their support for Iraq in its war with Iran.

U.S.-Soviet Arms Talks Begin — Despite the death of Soviet leader Konstantin Chernenko, **Mar. 10**, disarmament talks between the United States and the Soviet Union began on schedule in Geneva, Switzerland, on **Mar. 12**. The first session lasted 2 hours and 45 minutes. At the second session, **Mar. 4**, the 2 countries agreed to divide the negotiators into subgroups that would deal with strategic nuclear weapons, intermediate-range nuclear weapons, and space weapons. The negotiators agreed that the substance of their closed-door talks would not be disclosed. In an interview on Moscow television, **Mar. 16**, Viktor Karpov, the head of the Soviet negotiating team, complained that the United States was backing away from an agreement to discuss the prevention of an arms race in space and deep cuts in nuclear arms. U.S. Secretary of State George Shultz said, **Mar. 17**, that the public criticism did not bode well for the talks.

Reagan Praises Nicaraguan Rebels — Pres. Ronald Reagan stepped up his support for guerrillas, or "contras," fighting to overthrow the leftist Sandinista regime in Nicaragua. In a speech, **Mar. 1**, to the Conservative Political Action Conference, he called the contras the "moral equal of our Founding Fathers. . . ." Pres. Daniel Ortega of Nicaragua and U.S. Secretary of State George Shultz met in Montevideo, Uruguay, **Mar. 2**, following the inauguration, **Mar. 1**, of Julio Maria Sanguinetti as president of Uruguay, but made no apparent progress in easing tensions between the two countries. Nicaraguan opponents of the Sandinista regime, showing newfound unity, met in Costa Rica, and on **Mar. 2**, called on the government to open a "national dialogue" to solve the country's problems. But first, their declaration said, there must be a general amnesty, a cease-fire, and greater freedom of expression. Americas Watch, a U.S. human rights group, asserted in a report released **Mar. 5**, that the contras had raped, kidnapped, and murdered many civilians. The report charged that the largest contra group, the Nicaraguan Democratic Force, had repeatedly executed prisoners and had resorted to terrorism. The group's report said that the Sandinistas had also committed human-rights abuses, but that their violations had declined.

Mulroney, Reagan Act on Acid Rain — Prime Minister Brian Mulroney of Canada and Pres. Ronald Reagan, meeting in Quebec, **Mar. 17**, announced the appointment of a joint team to examine the contentious issue of acid rain. For years, the Canadian government had complained that the United States was not doing enough about controlling its sources of the acid, which was believed reponsible for damage to marine and plant life in both countries. On **Mar. 18**, the leaders signed agreements involving security, trade, fishing rights, and law enforcement, but Defense Secretary Caspar Weinberger stole the spotlight when he told a television interviewer that the United States might seek to deploy defenses against cruise missiles in Canada. Canadian and U.S. officials reassured worried Canadians that the remark was hypothetical.

Iraq Repels Iranian Offensive — The war between Iraq and Iran took a new turn in mid-March when planes from each side bombed civilian-occupied areas in the other's territory. Iraq, **Mar. 17**, warned commercial airliners to avoid Iranian airspace and said it would continue to attack Iranian cities. Reagan administration officials said, **Mar. 19**, that a week-long offensive by Iran had failed, and that most of the 30,000 to 50,000 Iranians thrown into the battle had become casualties. Officials said Iran had also fired several Soviet-built surface-to-surface missiles against Baghdad, the Iraqi capital.

19 Blacks Killed by South African Police — Police, in the town of Uitenhage, opened fire on thousands of blacks in a funeral procession, **Mar. 21**, killing 19 of them. Exact circumstances of the shootings were unclear, but the blacks apparently were heading for a service for 3 persons killed in an earlier clash with police. The latter deaths occurred on the 25th anniversary of the Sharpeville massacre of 1960, when 69 blacks were shot dead by police. U.S. Secretary of State George Shultz said the killings underlined "how evil and unacceptable" apartheid was. Pres. Ronald Reagan, however, suggested that "rioting" blacks shared blame for the disaster with the police.

Russian Guard Kills U.S. Major — A U.S. Army major was shot and killed, **Mar. 25**, by a Soviet guard near a Soviet military installation in East Germany. Maj. Arthur Nicholson, Jr. was shot while observing Soviet tank sheds near Ludwigslust. The Soviet Union said he had been in a prohibited area and had ignored a warning shot. The United States rejected this explanation and called the shooting "totally unjustified." Nicholson was assigned to a military liaison in East Germany where his job was to observe military activities. In what amounted to sanctioned spying by both sides, the Russians also conducted similar observations in West Germany. Nicholson was wearing a camouflage uniform when shot.

Duarte's Party Wins El Salvador Election — The Christian Democratic Party headed by Pres. José Napoleón Duarte scored a surprising vicotry, **Mar. 31**, in elections to fill seats in the National Assembly. In the previous assembly, 2 conservative parties, including one led by Duarte's bitter rival Roberto D'Aubuisson, had held a majority of the seats. The old assembly had thwarted many of Duarte's reforms and had resisted his efforts to make peace with leftists guerrillas. In the **Mar. 31** voting, the Christian Democrats won a small majority in the 60-seat assembly despite the adoption by the previous assembly of a law that had favored the rightists by permitting them to form a coalition. Duarte pledged to continue his peace efforts and his investigation into human-rights abuses.

General

ABC Bought by Media Company — The American Broadcasting Companies was brought in March by Capital Cities Communications Inc., a company only one fourth as large. The merger was the biggest in U.S. history outside the oil industry. Rumors of possible mergers involving the television and radio networks had flourished for some time. On **Mar. 1**, the price of shares of CBS jumped after a report that Turner Broadcasting Systems Inc. was considering a hostile takeover. A conservative political organization, Fairness in Media, had already notified the Securities and Exchange Commission of its desire to take over CBS. Sen. Jesse Helms (R, N.C.) had urged his conservative followers to support the effort by buying shares of CBS. CBS sued Fairness in Media, **Feb. 14**, charging that the takeover threat was a ploy to raise contributions and harass the network. Capital Cities and ABC announced their merger, **Mar. 18**. It marked the first time that any of the nation's 3 major networks had changed hands. Capital Cities already owned television and cable TV systems, a group of business newspapers, and several daily newspapers. The new firm, to be called Capital Cities/ABC Inc., was to be headed by Thomas Murphy, the chairman of Capital Cities. Murphy said that most of the money to buy ABC would come from bank financing. The merger was subject to the approval of the Federal Communications Commission.

Patient Dies After Receiving 3 New Hearts — A 32-year-old man died in March after receiving 3 new hearts in 3 days. Already dying of heart disease, Thomas Creighton, 32, received a human heart at the University of Arizona in Tucson, **Mar. 5.** When his new heart stopped beating, Dr. Jack Copeland, leader of the surgical team, obtained an artificial heart from St. Luke's Hospital in Phoenix. The artifical heart, designed by a dentist, had not been approved by the Food and Drug Administration—unlike the Jarvik-7 heart used in the 3 previous implants. The type of artificial heart provided by Phoenix had previously been tested on 4 calves. The Phoenix heart, implanted **Mar. 6,** kept Creighton alive some 11 hours until another human heart was found and implanted, **Mar. 7.** But Creighton died, **Mar. 8,** after suffering an accumulation of fluid in the lungs. It was reported, **Mar. 13,** that the FDA had issued a mild rebuke to the University of Arizona Medical Center for using an unauthorized artificial heart.

Disasters — An earthquake in Chile, **Mar. 3,** killed at least 146 persons and injured 2,000. . . . A Bangladesh official said, **Mar. 23,** that he feared 200 persons had drowned in the capsizing of a ferry in the Burhi Ganga River near Dhaka.

APRIL

National

Reagan, GOP Senators OK Deficit Plan — The struggle in Congress to complete action on a federal budget inched forward, **Apr. 4,** when Pres. Ronald Reagan and Republican leaders in the Senate agreed on a deficit-reduction package. The administration had already rejected the budget plan approved Mar. 13 by the Senate Budget Committee. If enacted, the **Apr. 4** package would reduce deficits to less than $100 billion a year by 1988 from the current level of more than $200 billion a year. Most of the savings would come out of domestic programs, with annual cost of living adjustments (COLAs) in Social Security and other federal retirement programs being held to 2 percentage points below the inflation rate. Seventeen domestic programs would be ended immediately or phased out. Under the plan, Reagan accepted annual increases of 3 percent in military spending (above inflation) through 1988; he had sought a 6 percent real increase. In a televised address, **Apr. 24,** Reagan urged support for his budget compromise, saying the nation could not "stay on the immoral, dead-end course of deficit spending." He also promised "my certain veto of any tax increase." In the Democratic response, Senate Minority Leader Robert Byrd (D, W.Va.) charged that Reagan had "doubled the debt it took 39 presidents almost 200 years to accumulate." He said the Reagan budget ax would fall on Social Security, Medicare, farmers, families with children in college, and on nutrition programs for children. Senate Majority Leader Robert Dole (R, Kan.) unexpectedly postponed a test vote on the budget, **Apr. 25,** when it appeared that he did not have enough votes to win. The preliminary vote was taken and won by the administration plan, **Apr. 30,** but only by 50-49, as 2 Republicans joined all 47 Democrats in opposition. Before a final Senate vote, the budget resolution would be open to amendments.

Economic Statistics Are Level — Most statistics released on the U.S. economy in March showed little movement. The nation's unemployment rate stood at 7.2 percent in March, the Labor Department said, **Apr. 5;** the rate had remained between 7.0 and 7.4 percent since May 1984. The department reported, **Apr. 12,** that the index of prices paid by producers for finished goods rose 0.2 percent in March. The Commerce Department said, **Apr. 16,** that housing starts rose 16.2 percent in March. The department reported, **Apr. 18,** that the economy had grown at an annual rate of only 1.3 percent during the first 3 months of 1985. The Labor Department said, **Apr. 23,** that consumer prices rose 0.5 percent in March. The index of leading economic indicators edged downward 0.2 percent in March, the Commerce Department said, **Apr. 30.**

Disputed House Election Goes to Democrat — The protracted battle over the designation of a winning candidate in the eighth congressional district of Indiana reached a climax in April. The race between the incumbent, Frank McClos-

key, a Democrat, and his challenger, Richard McIntyre, a Republican, had been unresolved since election night, Nov. 6. At one point, the Indiana secretary of state had certified McIntyre as the winner. The Democratic majority in the House rejected the certification and ordered a recount, which was conducted by auditors from the General Accounting Office under auspices of a 3-member House Administration Committee task force. Following a series of decisions on disputed absentee ballots, with the 2 Democrats outvoting the one Republican, the task force declared McCloskey the winner, **Apr. 18,** by 4 votes out of 234,000 cast. The Republican on the task force, William Thomas (Calif.), called for a special election to settle the issue. To dramatize their objections, Republicans staged disruptive tactics from **Apr. 23** to May 1, at one point forcing the House to adjourn, **Apr. 25.** Voting mostly along partisan lines, the House, **Apr. 30,** rejected a GOP move to declare the seat vacant. On May 1, the House voted 236-190 to seat McCloskey, and the Republicans walked out of the chamber en masse.

Anniversary Revives Vietnam Memories — The approach of the 10th anniversary, **Apr. 30,** of the fall of Saigon and the end of the Vietnamese war revived the debate in the United States on the merits of U.S. involvement in the protracted conflict in Southeast Asia. Although most U.S. troops had been withdrawn from South Vietnam long before the North Vietnamese overran the country in April 1975, the outcome was widely regarded as a U.S. defeat. Ten years later, books and motion pictures on the war poured forth at a record pace. Large numbers of persons came to gaze at the Vietnam war memorial in Washington with its roster of 58,022 American dead. The influence of the war could be measured in many ways in the United States—in the number of Vietnamese refugees who lived there, and by the so-called Vietnam Syndrome, which caused many Americans to oppose involvement in what they saw as a similar quagmire developing in Central America. A *Newsweek* survey showed that a majority of Americans thought it had been a mistake to send troops to Vietnam. Pres. Ronald Reagan said, **Apr. 18,** that the United States had not lost the war on the battlefield, but that it had broken its pledge to help South Vietnam if the North violated the 1973 truce. In New York City, May 7, 25,000 veterans of the war marched past a million spectators in a long-delayed "Welcome Home" tribute.

International

Sudan's President Ousted in Military Coup — Gaafar el-Nimeiry, president of Sudan for 16 years and a survivor of several previous attempts to remove him, was overthrown by high-ranking military officers, **Apr. 6,** while abroad. Because of its large size and its position adjacent to Libya, Egypt, and the Red Sea, Sudan was regarded as being of strategic importance. The Nimeiry government had supported the United States. His Muslim regime had been plagued by a southern revolt among Christians and animists, but unrest spread throughout the country in late March following sharp increases in bread and gasoline prices. The International Monetary Fund and other creditors, including the United States, had pressured Nimeiry to impose austerity measures. Nimeiry left for the United States, **Mar. 27,** and met with Pres. Ronald Reagan, **Apr. 1,** by which time, doctors, lawyers, and others had gone on strike in Sudan. A general strike began **Apr. 3.** To forestall a coup by younger officers, Nimeiry's senior commanders, **Apr. 6,** announced that they had dismissed the president and his aides, and declared a state of emergency and martial law. Nimeiry was in Cairo when he learned of the coup. Defense Minister Gen. Abdel Rahman Siwar el-Dahab headed the new government. The new leaders persuaded Sudan's labor and professional leaders to end their strike, **Apr. 8.** John Garang, leader of the rebels in the south, said the coup leaders had "stolen victory from the masses." Gen. Dahab told foreign diplomats that Sudan would remain aligned with the West.

U.S. Presses Japan on Trade Policy — Protectionist trade policies practiced by Japan continued to be the target of U.S. pressure in April. The Senate Finance Committee, **Apr. 2,** approved a bill requiring the president to restrict Japanese imports if Japan did not widen its door to U.S.

goods within 90 days. The House, **Apr. 2**, approved, 394-19, a resolution asking Pres. Ronald Reagan to take action against Japan's trade barriers. The United States had recorded a $37 billion trade deficit with Japan in 1984. Japan, **Apr. 3**, defended its record on trade and said that the Senate bill was discriminatory because it singled out Japan. On **Apr. 9**, the Japanese govenment introduced measures to increase U.S. imports of forestry products, pharmaceuticals and medical supplies, electronic products, and telecommunications equipment. The United States and other western nations indicated that the steps did not go far enough. Japanese Prime Minister Yasuhiro Nakasone appealed to the Japanese people on television, **Apr. 9**, to buy more foreign goods. He said the disputes over trade could lead to "a very serious situation affecting the life and death of our country." He noted that Japan, which had almost no raw materials, had to rely on amicable trade relationships with other countries.

Congress Rejects Aid for Contras — Congress turned down Pres. Ronald Reagan's appeal for financial support for "contra" fighting against the leftist Sandinista regime in Nicaragua. Reagan, **Apr. 4**, modified his original appeal for military aid for the guerrillas, saying that if Congress released $14 million in aid he would use it only for food, clothing, and medicine—at least during the first 60 days. He also called for a cease-fire and mediation by the Roman Catholic Church. Reagan shifted his emphasis to humanitarian aid after being told by Republican leaders in Congress that $14 million in military aid would not be approved. House Speaker Thomas P. O'Neill, Jr. (D, Mass.), calling the contras "butchers," said that Reagan was trying to hoodwink the public with his talk of humanitarian aid. Nicaragua rejected Reagan's peace plan, saying it would not negotiate with the contras. Reagan, **Apr. 15**, launched a lobbying effort in behalf of aid for the contras, denouncing the Sandinistas for "institutionalized cruelty." But he soon ran into trouble when he claimed that Pope John Paul II and Pres. Belisario Betancur of Colombia supported U.S. military aid to the contras, only to be confronted with denials by both parties. Rejecting a compromise offered by Democrats, Reagan said, **Apr. 20**, "Any proposal that abandons over 15,000 members of a democratic resistance to Communists is not a compromise. It is a shameful surrender." Pres. Daniel Ortega of Nicaragua said, **Apr. 21**, that his government would be prepared to stop fighting the contras and let them return to Nicaragua if the United States ended its "terrorist aggression." The Nicaraguan government and an Indian contra group agreed, **Apr. 22**, to cease attacking each other. This was the first accord between the regime and any of its opponents. The U.S. Senate, **Apr. 23**, endorsed Reagan's request for aid, 53-46, after Reagan wrote a letter promising to limit the spending of the $14 million to food, clothing, and other nonlethal uses. But the House, **Apr. 23**, rejected the same resolution, 248-80. An opponent, Rep. Joseph Addabo (D, N.Y.), noted that a "press release" from the president attached to the resolution did not have the force of law. An attempt at compromise failed, and the aid proposal was killed outright, **Apr. 24**, in the House. Reagan said he was "deeply disappointed." Ortega went to Moscow, **Apr. 28**, to discuss economic assistance. He met with Soviet leader Mikhail Gorbachev, **Apr. 29**; the latter was quoted as pledging continued economic, political, and diplomatic support to Nicaragua "in its efforts to uphold its sovereignty." By voice vote, the U.S. Senate, **Apr. 29**, approved a resolution condemning Ortega's visit.

Gorbachev Proclaims Missile Moratorium — Soviet leader Mikhail Gorbachev, **Apr. 7**, announced that the USSR would cease to deploy intermediate-range nuclear missiles. He called on the United States to make a similar gesture by halting deployment of its intermediate-range missiles in Western Europe. Gorbachev said he was prepared to meet Pres. Ronald Reagan at a summit conference. He said the moratorium would last until November, and further deployment would depend "on whether the U.S. follows our example." White House spokesman Larry Speakes, **Apr. 7**, rejected a U.S. freeze, saying that the Soviet Union held a 10-1 advantage in medium-range missiles and that "prior Soviet statements of intent to establish a moratorium . . . have been followed by continued deployments." Robert McFarlane, Reagan's national security adviser, called the Soviet

offer propaganda and a political ploy on **Apr. 8**. McFarlane said, **Apr. 10**, that Reagan hoped to meet with his Soviet counterpart in the fall, perhaps at the United Nations. In Moscow, **Apr. 10**, Gorbachev met with House Speaker Thomas P. O'Neill, Jr. (D, Mass.) and 3 other members of the House. O'Neill later described Gorbachev as a "master of diplomacy" who was "hard, tough, and strong." The USSR, **Apr. 17**, signaled a willingness to suspend nuclear-weapons testing on Aug. 6, 1985, the 40th anniversary of the U.S. atomic attack on Hiroshima.

Reagan's German Itinerary Debated — Pres. Ronald Reagan's plans to visit a military cemetery in Germany in May created a storm of protest among Jewish groups and U.S. veteran's groups in April. Reagan's trip, which would include participation in the annual summit conference of major western nations and Japan—scheduled for Bonn, West Germany—would also coincide with observations of the 40th anniversary of the end of World War II in Europe. On **Mar. 21**, Reagan had ruled out a visit to the site of a concentration camp while in Germany, saying that it would reawake painful memories, and that the trip's emphasis should be on the fact that the United States and Germany were not allies. He said that "the German people have very few alive that remember even the war, and certainly none of them who were adults and participating in any way." On **Apr. 11**, it was announced that Reagan would lay a wreath in a cemetery at Bitburg for German soldiers who had fought Allied troops during 2 wars. The cemetery contained 49 graves of Hitler's elite troops, the Waffen SS. Reaction was severe: a spokesman for the American Legion said, **Apr. 12**, that honoring German dead while ignoring the victims of the Third Reich and Allied war dead "had nothing to do with reconciliation." Reagan then announced, **Apr. 16**, that he would add a concentration camp visit to his schedule. Fifty-three U.S. senators, **Apr. 17**, urged Reagan to cancel the Bitburg visit, but he was unwilling to back down on a commitment that he had made to West German Chancellor Helmut Kohl. Reagan's statement, **Apr. 18**, that German soldiers had been "victims" of the Nazis "just as surely as the victims in the concentration camps" stirred further criticism. On **Apr. 19**, Reagan presented the Congressional Gold Medal of Achievement to Elie Wiesel, the author and theologian who had been imprisoned in 2 death camps. Wiesel accepted the award with an impassioned speech in which he said of Bitburg, "That place, Mr. President, is not your place. Your place is with the victims of the SS. . . . The issue is not politics, but good and evil. And we must never confuse them." The White House announced, **Apr. 19**, that Reagan would visit the death camp at Bergen-Belsen, and Kohl said the same day that Reagan's decision to visit Bitburg showed that Reagan was "a friend of the Germans." Alfred Dregger, the leader of Kohl's party in Parliament, wrote to senators who had urged Reagan to change his plans and said that a Bitburg cancellation would insult the German people. A spokesman for Kohl said, **Apr. 24**, that U.S.-German relations would be damaged by a cancellation. On **Apr. 25**, 257 members of the U.S. House urged Kohl to relent on Bitburg, and the Senate, **Apr. 26**, passed by voice vote a resolution asking Reagan not to go. The *Washington Post* reported, **Apr. 29**, that ex-Pres. Richard Nixon had advised the administration that a cancellation would be a sign of weakness and would damage U.S. credibility. Before departing for Europe, **Apr. 30**, Reagan said what he was doing was "morally right," and he blamed the press for much of the controversy.

Albanian Leader Hoxha Dies — Enver Hoxha, first secretary of the Albanian Communist Party since 1944, died **Apr. 11**. Active in the resistance to Italian rule during World War II, Hoxha never yielded power once he attained it upon liberation. He supported Soviet leader Joseph Stalin without reservation and, after the USSR turned away from Stalinism, Hoxha broke with the USSR. He had later formed an alliance with China, only to withdraw again and lead Albania into almost total isolation. Albania, on **Apr. 12**, rejected condolences from the Soviet Union. Radio Tirana announced, **Apr. 13**, that Pres. Ramiz Alia had been chosen to succeed Hoxha as first secretary.

Lebanese Government Resigns — Lebanon's year-old national-unity government resigned, **Apr. 17**. Premier Rashid Karami and his ministers stepped down after a Shiite Mus-

lim militia seized control of West Beirut, driving out its former ally, a Sunni Muslim militia. At the request of Pres. Amin Gemayel, Karami agreed to stay on temporarily as head of a caretaker government. The government crisis occurred as Israel's control over the country was reduced as the result of its continued withdrawal. For the first time since the Israeli invasion in 1982, northern Israeli settlements were within rocket range of unoccupied southern Lebanon. The Israeli cabinet voted 18-3 on **Apr. 21** to complete the third and final stage of its withdrawal by early June. Karami, **Apr. 24**, withdrew the resignation of his cabinet after it was agreed that an army brigade would take over security duties in West Beirut. In late April, thousands of Christians in southern Lebanon fled their homes as Muslim militias continued to attack and seize their strongholds. The second stage of the Israelis' withdrawal was completed by **Apr. 29**, after they withdrew from Tyre and the Bekka Valley area.

General

Woman Says She Lied at Rape Trial — Gary Dotson, 28, was briefly freed on bail in April from a 25- to 50-year sentence for rape when his accuser recanted the testimony she had given during his trial. Cathleen Crowell Webb had testified at Dotson's trial in Illinois in 1979 that he had sexually assaulted her. Then unmarried, Ms. Crowell was 16 years old in 1977, when the assault supposedly took place. Dotson was convicted after a 3-day trial. When coming forward in 1985 to file an affidavit in Cook County Superior Court, Webb—who now lived with her husband and 2 children in New Hampshire—said her conversion to Christianity had prompted her to tell the truth. She said she had made up the story in 1977 because she feared she had become pregnant by her boyfriend at the time. She had then picked Dotson's photograph from a file of police mug shots. At a hearing in Markham, Ill., on **Apr. 11, 1985**, Judge Richard Samuels—who had presided over the original trial—reviewed the evidence and listened to Webb's new account of the 1977 events. To the stunned surprise of almost everyone present, he said he found her new testimony unreliable and announced, "Regretfully, I must let the judgment stand." Dotson's bail was revoked and he was returned to prison **Apr. 12**. His lawyer then prepared an appeal.

Sen. Garn on Shuttle Crew — Sen. Jake Garn (R, Utah) became the first "congressional observer" to ride into space, **Apr. 12**, when he was launched from Cape Canaveral, Fla., with 6 other members of the crew in the shuttle *Discovery*. Garn, a former Navy pilot who had trained for the space flight, was chairman of a Senate committee that oversaw the budget of the National Aeronautics and Space Administration. A Canadian satellite was successfully launched from the shuttle **Apr. 12**. A second satellite, built by the Hughes Aircraft Company, was launched, **Apr. 13**, but it went into a slow rotation of only about 2 revolutions a minute. Despite extraordinary efforts, including an unscheduled space walk, the crew was unable to trigger the inactive satellite into operation. The shuttle touched down safely at Cape Canaveral, **Apr. 19**, although a tire blew out when brakes locked on a landing gear.

Turner Seeks to Win Control of CBS — Ending weeks of speculation, entrepreneur Ted Turner, **Apr. 18**, launched a bid to take control of CBS Inc. Turner, the founder and owner of the Atlanta-based Turner Broadcasting System, Inc., asked CBS shareholders to sell him their shares. He proposed to merge the CBS network with his own. Turner Broadcasting operated Cable News Network, a 24-hour news and information channel. Turner offered the shareholders a package of securities that included debentures and equity in the merged company. He proposed to finance the deal by borrowing against CBS assets. He said he planned no fundamental changes at CBS, but that he hoped to improve the "quality, objectivity, and diversity" of its programming. Fairness in Media, a conservative organization that also had sought to buy CBS, applauded the move by Turner, who generally held conservative views despite a personal reputation for flamboyance. Analysts on Wall Street doubted that Turner's offer of securities rather than cash would succeed in bringing him control of the network.

2 More Receive Artificial Hearts; 1 Dies — Two more men received Jarvik-7 artifical hearts in April. In Stockholm, Sweden, **Apr. 7**, an unidentified man became the first person outside the United States to receive a permanent artificial heart. He was reported to be doing well, **Apr. 9**. The Swedish press reported that the patient was Leif Stenberg, 52, a reputed gangster who was under indictment for tax fraud. Jack Burcham, 62, received the artificial heart, **Apr. 14**, in an operation led by Dr. William DeVries, who had performed previous similar operations. On **Apr. 24**, Burcham became the second recipient to die. Two other patients were recuperating in Louisville. The Swedish patient was able to take a walk, **Apr. 25**.

Disasters — It was reported, **Apr. 9**, that a cholera epidemic in a camp for Ethiopian refugees in Somalia had taken 1,500 lives ... A fire in a psychiatric hospital in Buenos Aires, **Apr. 27**, killed 78 persons.

MAY

National

Pentagon Loses Ground in Budget Battles — The federal budget for the 1986 fiscal year began to take clear shape in Congress in May, and defense spending appeared headed for unanticipated restraints. The compromise worked out in April between Pres. Ronald Reagan and the Republican Senate leadership became a casualty on **May 2**, when the Senate voted, 51-48, to limit Pentagon outlays to 1985 levels, adjusted only for inflation. Reagan had agreed to a 3 percent "real" increase, coming down from his original request for a 6 percent increase. Twelve Republicans voted against him. Recent publicity about waste in the procurement of weapons and dishonesty among defense contractors had apparently taken its toll. The Senate, **May 8**, rejected 2 Democratic budget plans that would have included tax increases. It completed action on a budget resolution, **May 10**, but only after Pete Wilson (R, Cal.), recovering from an illness, was rushed to the Senate chamber. Vice Pres. George Bush cast a vote to break a 49-all tie. In the final package, Social Security, federal pensions, and veterans' benefits were frozen at current levels for one year, with no cost-of-living adjustments (COLAs). The budget resolution backed Reagan on some domestic cuts; 12 programs, including general revenue sharing, were eliminated, and others survived only with reduced funding. The Senate budget would reduce the 1986 deficit by more than $50 billion. However, the House Budget Committee, **May 16**, approved a 1986 budget resolution that differed sharply from the Senate version. The projected reduction in the deficit was about the same—$56 billion—but the committee rejected cuts in Social Security COLAs and the other benefits. Worse, from the administration's point of view, the committee froze military spending at 1985 levels, without even an adjustment for inflation. Among domestic programs, only revenue sharing would be killed outright. Two GOP-sponsored budget plans were rejected on the House floor, **May 22**, and the House, **May 23**, approved, 258-170, the budget resolution essentially as it had emerged from committee. Twenty-four Republicans joined the majority. A conference committee would have to resolve the considerable differences between the 2 resolutions.

Key Interest Rates Decline — Interest rates continued to fall in May amid new evidence that the economy was slowing down. The Labor Department reported, **May 3**, that unemployment held at 7.2 percent in April, still within the narrow range where it had stood for a year. The Federal Reserve Board voted, **May 17**, to cut its basic interest rate for loans to member institutions to 7.5 percent. The action, aimed at stimulating economic growth, put the discount rate at its lowest level since 1978. Two major banks immediately dropped their base lending rate on corporate loans to 10 percent from 10.5 percent. On **May 20**, the first trading day after the Fed's action, the Dow Jones Industrial Average rose 19.54 points to finish above 1,300 for the first time. Concern about an economic slowdown gained impetus, **May 21**, when the Commerce Department said that the economy had grown by only 0.7 percent during the first quarter, compared with the previous estimate of 1.3 percent, and far below the 4.3 percent growth for the fourth quarter of 1984.

The Labor Department said, May 21, that consumer prices had risen 0.4 percent in April. On May 31, the Dow Jones Industrial Average closed at an all-time high of 1,315.41.

Top Defense Contractors Punished — Leading contractors for the Pentagon who had been implicated in wrongdoing suffered judicial and administrative punishment in May. It was reported, May 10, that General Electric had agreed to pay $1 million to the government for mischarges on a space-systems contract. After admitting its guilt in another matter, GE was fined $1.04 million in a federal district court in Philadelphia, May 13, for defrauding the Air Force on a missile warhead contract. GE was also ordered to repay $800,000 obtained in the fraud. An independent federal audit revealed, May 16, that 7 contractors had submitted $109 million in questionable expense claims. The Pentagon had paid many of the claims, which covered such activities as entertainment, lobbying, and public relations. Charging "pervasive" misconduct by General Dynamics, Navy Secretary John Lehman, Jr., May 21, canceled 2 contracts with the company worth $22.5 million. Two units of the company were prohibited from getting new contracts until General Dynamics repaid $75 million in overcharges and imposed a code of ethics on its executives. Lehman fined the company $676,283 for gifts that it had presented to Adm. Hyman Rickover, former head of the Navy's nuclear submarine program, and sent a letter of censure to the retired admiral. David Lewis, chairman of General Dynamics, announced, May 22, that he would retire. It was reported, May 22, that GE had agreed to pay the government $2 million in civil penalties related to the fraud case.

Police Bomb Radicals; 11 Die, 61 Houses Burn — A violent confrontation in Philadelphia between police and a radical group ended in May with 11 deaths and the destruction of 61 row houses following an air attack by the police. Members of an anarchist group called MOVE had barricaded themselves in a house and created disturbances that had provoked complaints from neighbors. After evacuating the neighborhood, police surrounded the house, May 12, and asked the occupants to come out. After an exchange of gunfire, a state police helicopter, May 13, dropped a bomb on the house, intending to destroy a bunker on the roof. The bomb started a fire that spread and destroyed more than 2 blocks of houses and left some 300 persons homeless. The attack killed 11 persons in the MOVE house, including at least 4 children. Police Commissioner Gregore Sambor said he had ordered the bombing, but Mayor Wilson Goode said, May 15, that he accepted responsibility for the fire.

3 Members of Family Held as Spies — What appeared to be one of the most serious spy cases of the postwar era broke open in May with the arrest of 3 members of one family. It was feared that valuable secrets related to the tracking of Soviet submarines had been lost, as well as data on the capabilities of U.S. aircraft and missiles. On May 20, the FBI arrested John A. Walker, Jr., shortly after he allegedly left a shopping bag containing classified documents at a rural site in Maryland. Walker, 47, had retired as a Navy warrant officer in 1976. He had held a top secret clearance when on active duty and had served as a communications officer on Polaris submarines and at the headquarters of the Atlantic fleet in Norfolk, Va. Walker's son, Michael, 22, a seaman on the aircraft carrier *Nimitz*, was charged, May 22, after secret documents were found in his possession. The father and son were indicted for espionage in Baltimore, May 28. Government officials indicated that evidence showed that John Walker had been a spy for 15 years. Arthur Walker, 50, a retired Navy lieutenant commander and the brother of John Walker, was arrested in Virginia Beach, Va., May 29, and charged with supplying classified Navy documents for delivery to Soviet agents. He had served on several submarines and as an instructor in antisubmarine warfare. A fourth suspect in the case, Jerry Whitworth, a retired chief petty officer, was arrested June 3. John and Michael Walker entered not guilty pleas, June 4. Whitworth and Arthur Walker were indicted for spying June 17.

New MX Compromise Reached — The embattled MX was the subject of another compromise in May. The Reagan administration and Senate leaders agreed, May 23, to limit to 50 the number of the missiles that could be deployed in existing Minuteman silos. The administration had wanted to deploy 100 of the missiles. Many members of Congress, including some who had supported the MX in the past, had voiced concern that the missiles would be vulnerable in the silos, and had called for the creation of a different basing mode. The 50-missile ceiling was for one year. Under the compromise, the White House accepted a production limit of 12 missiles in the 1986 fiscal year, far below its original request for 48.

Reagan Pushes Major Tax-Law Revision — Pres. Ronald Reagan, May 28, threw the weight of his office behind a sweeping revision of the nation's tax laws. Speaking on television, he called the present tax system "unwise, unwanted, and unfair," and proposed to cut tax burdens on most individual taxpayers and close "loopholes that benefit a privileged few." Like a plan proposed by the Treasury Department in November 1984 that had not received Reagan's personal endorsement, the new "Treasury II" plan would reduce the number of personal income-tax brackets from 14 to 3. The second plan provided less reduction in taxes for individuals (7 percent) and provided a smaller increase for business (9 percent). The 3 individual rates would be 15, 25, and 35 percent. The personal exemption would rise from $1,080 to $2,000. Mortgage interest would not be deductible on a second home. The effective maximum capital-gains rate would be reduced from 20 percent to 17.5 percent. Deductions for business entertainment would be eliminated, and workers' compensation and unemployment compensation would be taxed. One of the most controversial changes would see the elimination of the deductibility of state and local taxes on federal tax returns. Rep. Daniel Rostenkowski (D, Ill.), chairman of the House Ways and Means Committee, appearing on television after Reagan, gave his tentative support, but said Congress would seek to make the plan fairer. Reagan began a series of public appearances across the nation, May 29, in support of his plan. Although he had said that it would be "revenue neutral," one analysis showed that it would decrease tax revenues.

International

U.S. Ends Trade With Nicaragua — Asserting that Nicaragua's policies and actions posed a threat to U.S. security, Pres. Ronald Reagan, May 1, ordered an embargo on trade with the Central American nation. Reagan invoked his authority under the International Emergency Economic Powers Act, which required him to declare a state of national emergency. U.S. exports to Nicaragua totaled $109.8 million in 1984, and Nicaragua sent $58.1 million in goods to the United States. A White House spokesman cited Nicaragua's "efforts to subvert its neighbors, its rapid and destabilizing military buildup, its close military and security ties to Cuba and the Soviet Union, and its imposition of communist totalitarian internal rule." Effective May 1, 1986, Reagan also terminated the U.S.-Nicaraguan treaty of friendship. Nicaragua Vice Pres. Sergio Ramirez Mercado said, May 1, that Reagan's actions were illegal and arbitrary and would bring his nation closer to nations supporting the Sandinista regime, including the Soviet Union. One hundred Cuban military advisers left Nicaragua, May 2, fulfilling a commitment made by Pres. Daniel Ortega. The governments of Mexico, Great Britain, France, Italy, and other nations voiced disapproval of the trade embargo. Pres. José Napoleón Duarte of El Salvador supported the embargo, which went into effect, May 7. José Efren Martinez Mondragon, a commander of one of the guerrilla groups fighting the Sandinistas, left his unit and went to Managua, the capital of Nicaragua, May 7. He said he had become disgusted with the atrocities being committed by the "contras."

Reagan Lays Wreath at German Cemetery — Pres. Ronald Reagan completed an eventful and dramatic trip to Europe in early May. His visits to a concentration camp site and a German cemetery monopolized public attention and overshadowed the economic summit conference of 7 major industrial democracies. The 7 leaders began their 11th annual meeting in Bonn, West Germany, May 2. In an effort to rally international support for his Strategic Defense Initiative ("Star Wars"), Reagan said, May 2, that "we don't intend to go it alone as far as deployment is concerned," and he said he would consult with U.S. allies before making decisions on deployment of the space-based antimissile program. Pres. François Mitterrand of France, by publicly opposing

research on SDI, prevented endorsement of it in the **May 4** final communiqué. Mitterrand also refused to agree to an early date for a new round of talk on liberalizing international trade; he called for a more specific agenda and guarantees that developing countries would be fully involved. As a result, the **May 4** communiqué was rather bland, with familiar pledges by the 7 leaders to fight inflation and reduce budget deficits. Events related to the 40th anniversary of the end of World War II in Europe occupied Reagan's attention next. On **May 5**, he laid a wreath from "The People of the United States of America" at an obelisk at the Bergen-Belsen concentration camp in West Germany where 60,000 persons, mostly Jews, had died during the war. Reagan declared, "Rising above all this cruelty ... beyond the anguish, the pain, and the suffering for all time, we can and must pledge, 'Never Again.' "German rabbis and survivors of the Holocaust refused to attend because of Reagan's scheduled visit later that day to the Kolmeshoehe Cemetery at Bitburg, Germany. He and West German Chancellor Helmut Kohl stood side by side at Bitburg in a demonstration of reconciliation. Mindful of the uprorar caused by the fact that the cemetery contained the graves of 49 members of the elite Nazi Waffen SS, Reagan held his visit to 8 minutes. This time his wreath read, "The President of the United States." Later, addressing Germans and U.S. military personnel at a U.S. Air Base at Bitburg, Reagan declared that lovers of freedom around the world must identify themselves with the victims of tyranny, and he said, in part, "I am a Berliner, I am a Jew in a world still threatened by anti-Semitism, I am an Afghan, and I am a prisoner of the Gulag. ..." Israeli political leaders, **May 6**, denounced Reagan for visiting Bitburg. Defense Minister Yitzhak Rabin said, referring to a statement in April, "The historic mistake of President Reagan was in equating murderers with their victims." Prime Minister Shimon Peres said, "I believe that President Reagan is a true friend of the Jewish people. ... It is precisely for this reason that we feel deep pain. ..." Traveling to Spain, **May 6**, Pres. and Mrs. Reagan dined with King Juan Carlos and Queen Sofia. After 2 days of meetings between Reagan and Premier Felipe Gonzales, officials announced, **May 7**, that the 2 governments would discuss reduction and eventual withdrawal of the 12,000 U.S. troops stationed in Spain. Gonzales told Reagan he disapproved of U.S. policy in Nicaragua. Addressing the European Parliament in Strasbourg, France, **May 8**, Reagan warned that the USSR was preparing to deploy a new multiple-warhead intercontinental ballistic missile "clearly designed" to give the Soviets a first-strike capability. Reagan met with Portuguese Premier Mario Soares in Lisbon, **May 9**.

Gorbachev Attacks U.S. Policies — Hopes for improved relations between the superpowers dimmed a bit in May when Soviet leader Mikhail Gorbachev marked the anniversary of the end of World War II by attacking the Reagan administration. Soviet Defense Minister Sergei Sokolov conceded, **May 5**, that the USSR was conducting military space research, but he said it was for peaceful purposes and in no way like U.S. research on its Strategic Defense Initiative. Speaking at a Kremlin rally, **May 8**, Gorbachev criticized U.S. support for opponents of the governments of Nicaragua and Afghanistan. Referring to Pres. Ronald Reagan's visit to a German cemetery, Gorbachev said there were "political figures ready to forget or even justify the SS cutthroats and, moreover, pay honor to them." U.S. Secretary of State George Shultz and Soviet Foreign Minister Andrei Gromyko met in Vienna, **May 14**, and Shultz said later that he was certain some progress could be made in improving relations between the 2 countries.

CIA Linked to Bombing That Killed 80 — The *Washington Post* reported, **May 12**, that a Lebanese counterterrorist unit trained by the U.S. Central Intelligence Agency was indirectly responsible for an explosion of a car bomb in a Beirut suburb, **Mar. 8**, that killed more than 80 people. The Lebanese unit reportedly hired others to detonate the bomb near the home of Sheik Mohammed Hussein Fadlallah, an anti-American Shiite Muslim cleric. Fadlallah was unhurt. The *Post* reported that the CIA had not approved of the bombing, but knew it was being planned. According to the article, the Reagan administration subsequently canceled plans to rely on proxies to launch future attacks on U.S. opponents in the area. The CIA denied, **May 13**, that it had

trained anyone to undertake the bombing. Sen. Patrick Leahy (D, Vt.), vice chairman of the Senate Select Committee on Intelligence, said, **May 12**, that committee Democrats were investigating "6 or 7" CIA covert operations, including the one in Lebanon. New violence broke out in Beirut, **May 19**, and continued for 2 weeks as Shiite Muslims battled Palestinian guerrillas over control of Palestinian refugee camps. Casualties were put at 425 dead and 1,000 wounded. The Shiites feared that a too prominent PLO presence would tempt a new Israeli military intervention. A car bomb in Christian East Beirut killed 60 people, **May 22**. Pres. Amin Gemayel was not injured, **May 29**, when his palace was bombarded.

U.S. Aims 'Radio Martí' at Cuba — The United States, **May 20**, began a new radio broadcasting service for Cuba. Radio Martí, scheduled to operate 14½ hours a day, was to bring Cuban and world news to the Caribbean island nation. Cuba denounced the broadcasts as a "barefaced provocation" and called the use of the name of Jose Martí, an independence leader, a "gross insult." In retaliation, the government of President Fidel Castro suspended an immigration agreement between the 2 countries that had been announced in December 1984, under which former political prisoners would be allowed to emigrate to the United States. The agreement had also provided that Cuba would take back 2,746 Cuban criminals and mental patients who had traveled to the United States in 1980 from the port of Mariel.

1,150 Arab Prisoners Traded for 3 Israelis — In what appeared to be a one-sided agreement, the government of Israel, **May 20**, exchanged 1,150 Arab prisoners for 3 Israeli soldiers who had been captured during the invasion of Lebanon. Israel had been negotiating for 2 years with the guerrilla faction holding the Israeli POWs, the last 3 known to be in Arab hands. The 1,150 freed Arab captives included nearly 400 who were serving life sentences in Israeli jails, many for killing Israelis. The total also included Palestinian guerrillas and many Lebanese captured during the war. Defense Minister Yitzhak Rabin said that Israel had always done whatever it could to free its soldiers or citizens. Nevertheless, many Israelis protested the exchange, especially because many hundreds of the freed prisoners were allowed to go free inside Israel and its occupied territories.

General

Brokerage Firm Admits Check Fraud — E. F. Hutton, one of the nation's largest brokerage companies, pleaded guilty, **May 2**, to 2,000 federal charges related to the manipulation of its checking accounts. The New York City company agreed to pay $2 million in fines and to pay back up to $8 million to banks it had defrauded. Under the complicated scheme, Hutton had interest-free use of up to $250 million a day that it did not in fact possess. U.S. Attorney General Edwin Meese said the prosecution of the case was a signal "to the business world that so-called white-collar crime will not be tolerated." About 25 persons were identified as organizers of the plot, and 50 employees had been given immunity from prosecution. Fifteen U.S. senators wrote Meese, **May 7**, protesting what they called the "blatant failure to find individual liability" in the case.

Sentence Commuted in Rape Case — Gov. James Thompson of Illinois commuted the sentence of Gary Dotson, who had been serving a prison sentence for the rape of a teen-age girl in 1977. In April 1985, the supposed victim, Cathleen Crowell Webb, had recanted her testimony at the trial and said she had not been raped at all. Thompson presided at a hearing of the Illinois Prisoner Review Board, **May 9-11**, that considered Dotson's petition for clemency. A former prosecutor, Thompson questioned many of the 24 witnesses, including Dotson and Webb. In commuting Dotson's sentence, **May 12**, Thompson said he had not granted a pardon because Dotson had been "proved guilty beyond reasonable doubt. ..." He noted that Dotson had already served longer than average for a convicted rapist in Illinois. Dotson and Webb embarked on a whirlwind tour of media interviews and received offers for the publication of their story.

Fire and Riots Kill 92 at Soccer Matches — Tragedies took the lives of 92 persons at soccer matches in May. Fifty-three persons died and 211 were injured at Bradford, West

Yorkshire, England, **May 11**, when a fire destroyed a grandstand during a match between 2 English teams. Locks on the rear exist of the stadium made escape difficult. The stand burned to the ground in a few minutes. Also on **May 11**, a boy died when a brick wall fell and crushed him during a riot at a match in Birmingham, England. Eighty spectators and 96 police officers were injured in the melee, and 125 persons were arrested. That incident foreshadowed a disaster in Brussels, **May 29**, just before the European Cup football (soccer) championship match between teams from Liverpool, England, and Turin, Italy. Millions of persons throughout Europe watched on television as some Liverpool fans—many of whom had been drinking—stormed into a stand containing some of the Italian fans. Thirty-eight persons were killed and more than 200 injured. Many victims were crushed by a wall that collapsed after Italians pressed against it when withdrawing from the English attack. Most of the victims were Italians. Few arrests were made. Officials ordered the game to be played for fear that a cancellation would trigger more violence. The Turin team won, 1-0. Prime Minister Margaret Thatcher declared, "Those responsible have brought shame and disgrace to the United Kingdom and to football." Thatcher, **May 30**, directed that a contribution of 250,000 pounds ($312,000) be made to the victims and their families. The Belgian government, **May 30**, banned British teams from playing in Belgium. The Union of European Football Associations, **June 2**, banned English soccer teams from European competition indefinitely.

Woman Gives Birth to Septuplets — a 30-year-old teacher who had taken a fertility drug gave birth, **May 21**, to septuplets in Orange, Cal. It was the largest multiple birth ever in the United States. The infants, born by Caesarean section to Patti Frustaci, were 12 weeks premature and weighed from 1 pound, 1 ounce to 1 pound, 13 ounces. One of the 7, a girl, was stillborn. Four boys and 2 girls were born alive. One of the boys died **May 24**. Another boy died, **June 6**, and a girl died, **June 9**.

Cyclone Kills Thousands in Bangladesh — Winds as strong as 100 miles an hour drove tidal waves onto the coast of Bangladesh, **May 25**, wreaking vast damage and claiming thousands of lives. Pres. Hossein Mohammed Ershad said, **May 28**, that 5,000 to 10,000 lives had been lost when the cyclone struck, although only 1,400 deaths had been confirmed at that point. Some 250,000 were believed to be homeless, and the government estimated, **May 28**, that 472,000 acres of land had been damaged and 140,000 head of cattle lost.

Disasters — A midair collision, **May 3**, between a Soviet airliner and a military plane in the Ukraine took the lives of about 80 persons . . . Sixty-one coal miners were killed, **May 17**, when an explosion, apparently caused by methane gas, occurred 2,640 feet below sea level on Hokkaido island . . . Two dozen tornadoes spiraling out of a 300-mile frontal system killed 90 people, **May 31**, as they plowed through a number of small town in Ontario, Pennsylvania, Ohio, and western New York.

JUNE

National

Senators Rebuff Reagan on Nominees — A Senate committee took the rare step in June of failing to approve a presidential nominee. Pres. Ronald Reagan had nominated William Bradford Reynolds, assistant attorney general for civil rights, for the higher office of associate attorney general. When hearings on the nomination opened, **June 4 and 5**, some senators criticized Reynolds on his policies in general and on his actions in several voting-rights cases. Reynolds' policies reflected the administration's strong conservative views on civil-rights matters. Liberal opposition within the committee gained moderate support when testimony by other witnesses indicated that Reynolds had not been fully candid with the committee in testimony on several occasions. Reynolds acknowledged, **June 18**, that in previous testimony he had been mistaken or unintentionally misleading. In a series of votes, **June 27**, the Senate refused to recommend Reynolds' confirmation or even send his name to the Senate floor. An angry Reagan said, "The policies he

pursued are the policies of this administration, and they will remain our policies. . . ." Reynolds was expected to continue as assistant attorney general.

U.S. Sticks to Salt II Limits — Pres. Ronald Reagan announced that the United States would stay within a restriction established by the second Strategic Arms Limitation Treaty (Salt II). Although the treaty had been signed in 1979, the U.S. Senate had never ratified it. Nonetheless, both the Soviet Union and the United States had said that they would continue to abide by its provisions. The treaty had imposed a limit of 1,200 multiple-warhead nuclear missiles. The United States would exceed this total in the autumn of 1985 when a new Trident submarine came on line. Members of the Reagan administration were sharply divided over the question of continued compliance. Defense Secretary Caspar Weinberger reportedly favored ignoring the treaty because of alleged Soviet violations. Gen. John Vessey, Jr., chairman of the Joint Chiefs of Staff, argued, on the other hand, that forsaking the treaty might lead the Soviet Union to pursue an arms buildup that the United States could not match. The U.S. Senate, **June 5**, voted 90-5 for a resolution calling on Reagan to honor Salt II. Reagan, **June 10**, followed this course, announcing that the United States would dismantle an older *Poseidon* submarine in order to maintain the missile limit. He said he was willing to "go the extra mile" to achieve meaningful arms control.

Jobless Rate Remains Level — The U.S. unemployment rate held at 7.2 percent in May, staying within the narrow range it had occupied for a year, the Labor Department reported, **June 7**. The balance of payments, the broadest measure of the nation's trade with other countries, showed a deficit of $30 billion in the first quarter, the Commerce Department reported, **June 17**. Major banks cut their prime rate from 10 percent to 9.5 percent, **June 18**, bringing the rate to its lowest level since 1978. The government's index of leading economic indicators turned upward 0.7 percent in May, the Commerce Department reported, **June 28**.

House-Senate Budget Talks Collapse — House and Senate conferees reached an impasse in their attempt to surmount differences between the budget resolutions approved by the 2 chambers. David Stockman, director of the Office of Management and Budget, **June 9**, issued a new and higher projection of the 1988 federal deficit—$175 billion, a jump of $70 billion, even if the budget compromise between the administration and the Senate became law. A Senate-House conference committee began meeting, **June 11**, in an effort to reconcile differences in the budget resolutions. Social Security and the Defense budget were the major stumbling blocks. Robert Dole (R, Kan.), the Senate majority leader, and William Gray (D, Pa.), chairman of the House Budget Committee, both suggested that higher taxes might still be necessary. The House-Senate budget conference broke up, **June 25**, and Sen. Pete Domenici (R, N.M.), chairman of the Senate Budget Committee, said Senate Republicans would not participate further unless House conferees showed a willingness to consider freezes or cuts in cost of living adjustments for Social Security and other benefit programs. In an off-the-record speech, **June 5**, that became generally known late in the month, Stockman said that because of the growing deficits a tax increase might be the only solution "consistent with fiscal sanity." He said that the administration and Congress had not "come clean" on the dimensions of the budget crisis.

Reagan's Tax Reform Plan Draws Fire — Pres. Ronald Reagan's proposal for a reform of the federal tax code was hotly debated in June, and many calls for revisions were heard. Several leading economists told the House Ways and Means Committee, **June 11**, that the proposal provided excessive benefits to the rich and would further increase budget deficits. Most of them said, however, that the plan was an improvement on the present tax code. Martin Feldstein, chariman of the Council of Economic Advisers during Reagan's first term, said the plan "has a substantial risk of losing revenue," which was "one thing the United States economy does not need—in fact, cannot stand." Patrick Buchanan, director of communications for the White House, said, **June 7**, that the Reagan plan would benefit the "traditional" family—one in which the husband worked and the wife cared for the children. He also said that high-tax states, which would be adversely affected by the plan, had a "neo-

socialist" approach to government. Gov. Mario Cuomo (D, N.Y.), **June 8,** called this description "stunningly irresponsible" and deplored the suggestion that women belonged only in the home. Treasury Secretary James Baker told the Senate Finance Committee, **June 11,** that the plan could be "revenue neutral" even if it differed from current revenue levels by up to $50 billion. The *Wall Street Journal* reported, **June 12,** that many large corporations would oppose the reform because increasing taxes on their companies would worsen the U.S. trade deficits. Union leaders, testifying before the Ways and Means Committee, **June 12,** criticized provisions taxing employer-paid health premiums and unemployment benefits. Witnesses representing capital-intensive industries said, **June 13,** that reducing tax benefits for them, as provided in the Reagan plan, would harm their industries. Oil industry representatives told the committee, **June 18,** that tax breaks for their industry that were provided by the plan must be retained if the United States was to achieve energy independence. Robert Packwood (R, Ore.), chairman of the Senate Budget Committee, said, **June 20,** that the plan would hurt the middle class, and he called on the administration to revise it. An analysis by the Congressional Budget Office, announced **June 26,** showed that Reagan's plan would significantly increase budget deficits for the rest of the century.

International

Greek Premier Wins National Election — Premier Andreas Papandreou retained power in the Greek national elections, **June 2,** by a larger margin than had been forecast. His Pan Hellenic Socialist Movement won 46 percent of the popular vote and 161 seats in the 300-member parliament. The conservative New Democracy Party, led by Constantine Mitsotakis, got 41 percent of the popular vote and 125 seats. Two communist parties received most of the rest of the votes. Mitsotakis had promised improved relations with the United States, which had been rebuked on occasion by Papandreou. The left-leaning premier had once threatened to close U.S. military bases in Greece. The 18 percent inflation rate and the growing foreign debt were other issues. But abusive language had dominated the campaign, and Papandreou hailed his victory as one of "democracy, progress, and change" over "reaction" and "authoritarianism."

6 Americans Among 13 Slain in El Salvador — Four U.S. Marines, 2 U.S. businessmen, and 7 other persons were

---

Hostages Freed by Shiite Muslims after 17-Day Ordeal

An airplane hostage drama, played out mostly in Beirut, Lebanon, riveted the attention of the world between **June 14** and **30.** The seizure by Shiite Muslim extremists of an airplane with 153 persons aboard, included 104 Americans, was a grim reminder of the 1979-81 hostage crisis in Iran. This time, however, the last of the hostages were freed after only 17 days, although one American was killed.

Trans World Airlines flight 847 took off from Athens airport, **June 14,** bound for Rome. The flight had originated in Cairo. Two hijackers boarded the plane in Athens. An accomplice failed to obtain a seat on the plane and was arrested by Greek police. Soon after the plane left the ground, the hijackers, armed with pistols and grenades, seized control and ordered the plane to fly to Beirut. Capt. John Testrake was permitted to land the Boeing 727 in Beirut only after he reported that passengers were being beaten and that a hijacker had pulled the pin on his grenade. By now, the accomplice had identified the hijackers as members of the Islamic Jihad (Holy War), a terrorist organization implicated in earlier attacks on Americans. While in Beirut, the gunmen demanded the release of 766 prisoners, mostly Shiites, whom Israeli forces had detained before and during their withdrawal from southern Lebanon. The gunmen freed 19 passengers, then ordered the plane flown to Algiers, where 21 more were freed. The plane then returned to Beirut early on **June 15,** and after landing, the captain reported that the hijackers had killed a passenger. The body of the victim, Robert Stethem, a U.S. Navy steelworker and diver, was thrown from the plane.

The hijackers were joined by about a dozen armed members of the Amal militia, a relatively moderate Shiite faction. Four men, whom the hijackers believed were U.S. military or diplomatic personnel or who had Jewish-sounding names, were removed from the plane and taken to an undisclosed place in Beirut. The plane then returned to Algiers, where more than 60 passengers and crew members were freed. Most of the Greek passengers were released after the Greek government flew the accomplice to Algiers, where he joined the other hijackers. On **June 16,** for the third time, the plane flew to Beirut, where the hijackers made public a letter signed by 32 hostages appealing to Pres. Ronald Reagan not to undertake any military action in an attempt to free them. News accounts had reported that a special U.S. antiterrorist unit had been sent to the Middle East, but U.S. officials apparently never seriously considered any attempt to free the hostages by military action. Reagan cut short a vacation, **June 16,** and returned to the White House. The Israeli government said, **June 16,** that it would consider releasing its 766 captives if the United States publicly requested it.

Nabih Berri, leader of the Amal militia and justice minister in the unstable government of Lebanon, emerged in the ambiguous role of spokesman for the Shiites and negotiator for the release of the hostages. It appeared that although the Amal held most of the hostages, the demands of the original hijackers had to be accommodated. Berri said, **June 17,** that all remaining passengers had been taken "somewhere in Beirut." He called on the United States to pressure Israel into releasing its 766 captives. By now it was believed that the original hijackers were affiliated with Hezbollah (the Party of God), a fundamentalist Shiite group backed by Iran. After Berri arranged the release of 3 passengers, **June 18,** 3 crewmen and 37 passengers—all American men—remained in captivity.

At a press conference, **June 18,** Reagan announced several steps taken to avert similar incidents. He discussed the difficulty of attempting to punish terrorists, saying that if "you just aim in the general direction and kill some people, well, then you're a terrorist too." He asserted that the United States would not give in to terrorist demands, and that he would not ask Israel to free its prisoners.

Western journalists were allowed to interview the crewmen, **June 19,** as a hijacker held a pistol to their heads. Five hostages were interviewed in Beirut, **June 20.** Allyn Conwell of Houston, chosen as spokesman by the other hostages, read a statement calling on Reagan not to attempt a rescue, and urging Israel to release its captives. Israeli Prime Minister Shimon Peres and U.S. Secretary of State George Shultz talked on the phone, **June 21,** reportedly the first high-level contact between the countries since the crisis began. Israel freed 31 prisoners, **June 24,** and said, **June 26,** that it would free more as the security situation in southern Lebanon improved. Berri demanded, **June 24,** that the United States withdraw its warships off Lebanon. The United States said, **June 25,** that if a solution were not found soon it might blockade Lebanon and try to close the Beirut airport. Vice Pres. George Bush said, **June 25,** that Israel should release its prisoners which, he said, were "being held against international law." Berri, **June 26,** released an ill passenger and proposed that the rest be moved to a western embassy in Beirut or to Damascus, Syria. The White House reported, **June 26,** that it was working closely with the Syrian government. The United States, **June 27,** demanded that 7 other Americans who had been kidnapped in Beirut during the past 15 months must also be released.

An administration official said, **June 28,** that the hostages would likely be released the next day after being taken to Damascus. Israel was to start releasing its 735 prisoners, but the United States would continue to deny any connection between Israel's action and the release of the hostages. However, Berri said, **June 29,** that the hostages would not be freed until the United States promised that it would not retaliate militarily after the release. The 39 airplane hostages were driven to Damascus, **June 30,** and, with the active involvement of the Syrian government, they were then flown to West Germany and freedom. ∎

killed, **June 19,** when they were shot while sitting at sidewalk tables at restaurants in San Salvador, the capital of El Salvador. The Marines were off-duty guards at the U.S. Embassy. Six to 10 men who leaped from a pickup truck killed the victims by firing with automatic rifles. About 15 persons were wounded. A group supporting the leftist guerilla insurrection in El Salvador claimed responsibility for the attack. Pres. Ronald Reagan, **June 20,** denounced the shootings as part of an international pattern of terrorism, and warned that "our limits have been reached." He said the administration would respond in part by seeking more military aid for El Salvador.

Bomb Suspected in Air Crash Fatal to 329 — In history's third worst aviation disaster, an Air-India Boeing 747 crashed into the Atlantic Ocean near Ireland, **June 23.** All 329 persons on board were killed. The abrupt disappearance of the plane from radar screens, plus the fact that no emergency call had been received from the plane, caused investigators to suspect that the explosion of a bomb had been responsible. The flight had originated in Toronto. The plane had stopped in Montreal and was to land in London before continuing to Bombay. Most of the passengers were of Indian descent. Less than an hour before the Air-India disaster, a bomb exploded in luggage being unloaded in Japan from another plane that had flown from Canada. Two baggage handlers at the New Tokyo International Airport were killed in the blast as they removed luggage from a Canadian Pacific Airlines Boeing 747 that had just arrived, a few minutes early, from Vancouver with 390 persons aboard. Investigators of the Air-India crash and the Tokyo bombing concentrated on Sikh extremists, including 2 Sikhs who were already being sought by the U.S. Federal Bureau of Investigation in connection with an alleged plot against Indian Prime Minister Rajiv Gandhi.

Congress Acts on South Africa — The U.S. House and a Senate committee voted for sanctions against South Africa. The Senate Foreign Relations Committee, **June 4,** approved, 16-1, a measure that would ban bank loans to the South African government and impose restrictions on computer sales and trade in nuclear technology. The bill provided for additional sanctions after 18 months if South Africa did not make "significant progess" in ending its policy of apartheid. The House, **June 5,** approved, 295-127, a bill that would ban new loans to and investments in South Africa, stop computer sales to the government, and prohibit the importation of South African gold coins. The Reagan administration, preferring to rely on persuasion, opposed the imposition of sanctions against South Africa.

Congress Votes Aid for Nicaraguan "Contras" — Both houses of Congress approved humanitarian aid for so-called contras fighting a guerilla war against the leftist Sandinista government in Nicaragua. The Senate, **June 6,** authorized, 55-42, $38 million in humanitarian aid over 2 years. Pres. Ronald Reagan praised the Senate, **June 6,** and called the contra aid issue "the transcendent moral issue of our time." The House, reversing a vote taken in April, approved, 248-184, $27 million in humanitarian aid for the contras on **June 12,** but forbade distribution by the Central Intelligence Agency or the Pentagon. In order to assure victory in the House, Reagan had given assurance that he was not trying to overthrow the Sandinistas and said he would consider trying to resume talks with the Nicaraguan government. Daniel Ortega, president of Nicaragua, said, **June 13,** in response to the vote in the House, that he would lift a moratorium on the procurement of arms that had been announced in February.

Nazi War Criminal's Remains Identified — The long search for Dr. Josef Mengele, the so-called Angel of Death, who had been wanted for the murder and torture of inmates at the Auschwitz death camp in Poland during World War II, ended in June. Forensic scientists declared that his remains had been found in a grave in São Paulo, Brazil. Mengele had been reported as living in several countries since he disappeared at the end of the war. The final bizarre chapter in the Mengele case began May 31, when West German investigators raided the home in Gunzburg, W. Germany, of Hans Sedlmeier, an employee of the Mengele family firm. Sedlmeier had reportedly boasted that he had sent money to Mengele. The investigators found photocopies of letters linking Mengele to Wolfram and Liselotte Bossert, an Austrian

couple living in São Paulo. Cooperating with investigators, the Bosserts said Mengele had come to Sao Paulo from Paraguay in 1961 and had lived with a Hungarian couple. He later became friends with the Bosserts, who said Mengele drowned in 1979 and was buried as Wolfgang Gerhard, an Austrian Nazi and friend of Mengele in Brazil who had given his identity card to Mengele. Gerhard had died in 1978. Remains now said to be Mengele's were exhumed, **June 6.** Rolf Mengele, son of Josef, said, **June 11,** that the remains were those of his father, and that he had remained silent about his father's death to protect those who had shielded him. Experts said, **June 14,** that documents found in São Paulo were in Mengele's handwriting. An international team of forensic specialists concluded, **June 21,** that the remains were those of Mengele. In the words of Lowell Levine, a consultant with the New York Police Department, "the odds are astronomical" against the skeleton not being that of Mengele. Simon Wiesenthal, a leader in the effort to track down surviving Nazi criminals, said, **June 21,** that he accepted the findings.

Gorbachev Calls for Economic Reforms — Soviet leader Mikhail Gorbachev, **June 11,** criticized his nation's economic officials, rejected the draft of the new 5-year plan, and asked for sweeping reforms to revive the economy. In a speech to leading officials, he said that the 5-year plan should focus on upgrading present facilities rather than on building new plants, and that greater emphasis should be put on improving the quality of consumer products, which he said often compared infavorably with those in other countries. Gorbachev criticized some economic managers by name for waste and incompetence, and he traced some of the economic problems to the regime of Leonid Brezhnev.

Gandhi Visits U.S. — For the first time since he became prime minister of India, Rajiv Gandhi visited the United States. The U.S. trip, **June 11-15,** was part of a 5-nation tour that included Egypt, France, Algeria, and Switzerland. Welcoming Gandhi, **June 12,** Pres. Ronald Reagan gave his support to a united India, a pointed rebuff to the Sikh separatist movement. Sikh extremists had assassinated Gandhi's mother, Prime Minister Indira Gandhi, and other Sikhs had threatened to kill Rajiv Gandhi during his U.S. visit. Gandhi reportedly told Reagan he was concerned that Pakistan would develop nuclear weapons with U.S. aid. Addressing Congress, **June 13,** he sought to meet U.S. concern about India's failure to oppose Soviet intervention in Afghanistan by calling for a political settlement that would preserve Afghan independence.

Economic Austerity Imposed in Argentina — Pres. Raúl Alfonsín of Argentina took drastic steps, **June 14,** to try to stop the inflationary spiral of the currency. Inflation had been reported at 1,010 percent for the past 12 months. Alfonsín declared a bank holiday, which remained in effect through **June 18.** He announced the creation of a new currency, the austral, which would be valued at US$1.25. The present currency, the peso, was valued at 1,000 to US$1.28. Stating that the situation made it "impossible to think of gradual methods," Alfonsín also froze wages and prices. It was anticipated that many state-employed workers would lose their jobs.

General

GM Acquires Hughes Aircraft — General Motors announced in June that it would purchase Hughes Aircraft, one of the nation's 10 largest defense contractors. In another major corporate acquisition, R. J. Reynolds Industries announced, **June 2,** that it would obtain Nabisco Brands Inc. for $4.9 billion in cash and stock. The combined firm would become the largest U.S. consumer products company. The G.M.-Hughes merger, announced **June 5,** was subject to approval by the auto company's stockholders and by the U.S. government. G.M. would acquire Hughes Aircraft from the Howard Hughes Medical Institute for cash and stock worth $5 billion. The bid surpassed offers by other companies. Hughes Aircraft, established in its original form by Howard Hughes in 1924, was a manufacturer in such high-technology areas as electronics, satellites, and missiles.

Socialite Acquitted of Trying to Kill Wife — One of the most engrossing courtroom dramas of recent years ended, **June 10,** when a jury in Providence, R. I., found Claus von

Bulow not guilty of 2 attempts to murder his wife. The prosecution had charged that von Bulow had attempted to kill Martha (Sunny) von Bulow with injections of insulin in 1979 and 1980. A jury in 1982 had found him guilty on both counts, but the verdict was later overturned on a technicality. The prosecution alleged that von Bulow wanted to be free of his wife so he could marry his mistress at the time, Alexandra Isles. Judge Corinne Grande barred testimony on another possible motive—that von Bulow would inherit a large fortune on the death of his wife. Mrs. von Bulow had been in an apparently irreversible coma since the second alleged murder attempt in 1980. Her children by an earlier marriage, Annie-Laurie Kneissl and Alexander von Auersperg, had pressed the case against their stepfather. Mrs. von Bulow's maid, Maria Schrallhammer, testified that she had found drugs, including insulin, in Mr. von Bulow's possession. Ms. Isles, a witness for the prosecution, said she had demanded that von Bulow choose between her and his wife. She said von Bulow told her in 1979 that he had watched his wife slip into a coma, but then "couldn't go through with it" and called a doctor. The defense contended that Mrs. von Bulow's comas, including a brief one in 1979, had been brought on by alcohol and drug abuse. The defense relied on medical testimony from expert witnesses who said that there had been no insulin injection.

Comatose Woman, Center of Legal Battle, Dies — Karen Ann Quinlan, who became the center of a national debate over the "right to die," died, June 11, more than 10 years after sinking into a coma. Miss Quinlan, then 21 years old and a resident of Byram Township, N.J., became comatose in 1975 after an evening in which she took tranquilizers and drank alcoholic beverages. Doctors determined that she had irreversible brain damage. She was fed by a tube and kept on a respirator. Her parents sought to have her respirator removed so that their daughter could die, but her doctors refused. Her parents sued, and the U.S. Supreme Court in 1976 upheld their request. In a new interpretation of the right of privacy, the justices held 7-0 that Miss Quinlan's interest in having the life-support system disconnected exceeded the state's interest in preserving life, so long as medical authorities saw "no reasonable possibility" that she would recover. The court thus gave force to the widespread practice of "judicious neglect," in which doctors withhold extraordinary measures to keep terminally ill patients alive. Miss Quinlan's respirator was removed but she continued to live, ultimately succumbing to pneumonia.

Shuttle Tests "Star Wars" Technology — A simple test of the Strategic Defense Initiative ("Star Wars") technology was conducted during a flight of the space shuttle *Discovery*, which was launched from Cape Canaveral, Fla., on June 17. The 7-person crew included the 98th, 99th, and 100th U.S. astronauts. Also aboard were a Saudi, Prince Sultan Salman al-Saud, and a Frenchman, Lt. Col. Patrick Baudry. The crew launched 3 communications satellites and also launched and then recovered an observatory that provided X-ray views of a "black hole" in the Milky Way. In the Star Wars test, June 21, a laser beam from earth was bounced off an 8-inch mirror mounted on the shuttle. The shuttle landed, June 24, at Edwards Air Force Base in California.

JULY

National

Forecast of Economic Growth Lowered — The Federal Reserve Board lowered its forecast of economic growth in 1985, while statistics released by the U.S. government continued to send mixed signals. The Labor Department reported, July 5, that the employment rate in June had remained at 7.2 percent for the fifth straight month. David Wyas of Data Resources Inc., said that the figures showed that "the economy still seems to be going sideways, getting neither worse nor better." The Federal Home Loan Mortgage Corp. said, July 16, that the June rate for fixed-rate mortgages fell to the lowest average level since 1979. The Federal Reserve Board, July 16, estimated real growth for 1985 at 2.75 to 3 percent, a reduction from the 3.5 to 4 percent estimate issued in February. The Commerce Department said, July 18, that the gross national product had increased at only a 1.7 percent annual rate in the second

quarter, a sharp decline from its earlier "flash" estimate of 3.1 percent. The real growth for the first quarter, as revised, was only 0.3 percent. The lower growth reports signaled that tax revenues would fall and cause a further increase in the federal budget deficit. The Dow Jones Industrial Average continued to hit all-time highs on Wall Street, closing at 1359.54 on July 19. The consumer price index edged upward 0.2 percent in June, the Labor Department reported, July 23. Treasury Secretary James Baker said, July 25, that he welcomed the moderate steady decline in the strength of the dollar against other currencies, which had occurred between April and July. The Commerce Department reported, July 30, that the U.S. trade deficit for June was $13.42 billion, the second highst ever. The index of leading economic indicators advanced 1.0 percent in June, the Commerce Department said, July 31.

Reagan Budget Shift Angers GOP Senators — The seemingly endless struggle by Congress to agree on a budget resolution for the 1986 fiscal year took a new turn in July when Pres. Ronald Reagan shifted his position on Social Security benefits. By withdrawing his support for a reduction in benefits, he angered many senators in his own party who had accepted it as part of an effort to cut the federal deficit. Reagan, July 9, offered a compromise formula to congressional leaders that provided for no new taxes and that accepted a House freeze on defense spending providing that the House accepted the Senate's higher figures on Pentagon spending authority. His proposal also provided for inflation increases in Social Security benefits each year, thus abandoning Republican senators who had pushed a one-year freeze on Social Security increases through the Senate with Reagan's reluctant support. At a meeting at the White House, July 11, some Republican senators—including some up for reelection in 1986—complained about Reagan's reversal. Alluding to Reagan's shift, Sen. Robert Dole (R, Kan.), the majority leader, accused him, July 12, of "surrendering to the deficit." The Senate-House conference committee remained deadlocked, and the House, July 16, voted 239-181 to waive the budget act, which required a binding House-Senate budget resolution that would set limits on spending bills. Speaker Thomas O'Neill (D, Mass.) said the House would pass its own appropriations bills without waiting for agreement with the Senate. The Senate Republican leadership advanced another compromise, July 25, that called for a $5-a-barrel oil import duty and the tactic of adjusting Social Security and other pension benefits every other year. Reagan rejected the compromise, July 29, on the ground that he had promised not to raise taxes or cut Social Security.

Budget Director Stockman Resigns — The White House said, July 9, that David Stockman, director of the Office of Management and Budget, would leave the administration Aug. 1, and join the investment banking firm of Salomon Brothers Inc. in New York. In his 4 years as budget director, Stockman had demonstrated a masterly understanding of the intricacies of the budget, and he was given the credit for the adoption of legislation that cut taxes and reduced spending on many domestic programs. However, his goal of reducing federal budget deficits was not attained. The White House announced, July 19, that Stockman would be succeeded by James Miller, chairman of the Federal Trade Commission.

Cancerous Growth Removed from Reagan's Intestine — Pres. Ronald Reagan underwent major intestinal surgery and a growth removed from his colon, or large intestine, proved to be cancerous. The White House had announced in June that Reagan would enter Bethesda (Md.) Navy Medical Center, July 12, for removal of a benign polyp that had been discovered in March. The polyp was removed in about an hour, but an examination with a colonoscope revealed a growth in the cecum, the upper part of the large intestine. Reagan elected to have immediate surgery, which was performed, July 13, by 5 military and civilian surgeons. During the 2 hour and 53 minute procedure, about 2 feet of the large intestine was removed, including the growth, which was about 2 inches in diameter. Before surgery began, Reagan signed letters temporarily transferring the powers of his office to Vice Pres. George Bush. The transfer of authority remained in effect for 8 hours. Doctors reported, July 14, that Reagan's recovery was "spectacular." At a press conference, July 15, Navy Capt. Dale Oiler, head of the surgical

team, said that the "villous adenoma" removed from the cecum "contained adeno carcinoma confined within the muscle of the bowel wall such that there was no evidence of spread of the cancer elsewhere." Dr. Steven Rosenberg, chief of surgery at the National Cancer Institute and another member of the surgical team, said simply, "The president has cancer." He said that there was better than a 50-50 chance that Reagan was entirely free of cancer and a "less than 50 percent" chance that cancer might recur. He said he did not believe any further treatment was needed at the present time. A debate flourished over whether Reagan should have had a full examination after doctors discovered his first benign intestinal polyp in May 1984, or in March 1985, after the discovery of the second polyp. Medical opinion was divided. The president's operation stimulated wide public discussion about colon cancer, one of the leading causes of cancer death, and doctors reported a sharp increase in inquiries. Reagan returned to the White House, July 20.

Smeal Recaptures NOW Presidency — The National Organization for Women (NOW) appeared to take a more activist turn in July, when delegates to its national convention in New Orleans returned Eleanor Smeal to the presidency. Smeal, who had served as president from 1977 to 1982, recaptured the leadership, July 21, after she challenged the reelection bid of the incumbent, Judy Goldsmith. Smeal won by a vote of 839 to 793. She argued that ratification of the Equal Rights Amendment (ERA) should continue to be a principal goal and that "large-scale mass actions" should be employed. Goldsmith preferred less confrontational tactics and said that any further push for ERA would be futile.

International

Gorbachev Shakes Up Soviet Leadership — The Supreme Soviet, the rubber-stamp parliament of the Soviet Union, named a new president and foreign minister in moves that were universally recognized as the handiwork of Mikhail Gorbachev, the new general secretary of the Communist Party. In another action that represented a victory for Gorbachev, the Central Committee of the party announced, July 1, that Grigory Romanov had resigned from the Politburo on "health grounds." It was believed that Romanov had opposed Gorbachev's election as general secretary. The Central Committee promoted Edward Shevardnadze, the Communist Party leader in Georgia, to full membership in the Politburo, July 1. In a surprise move, the Supreme Soviet, July 2, elected Andrei Gromyko, who had been foreign minister since 1957, as president of the USSR, and named Shevardnadze as his successor. Both Gromyko and Shevardnadze were regarded as allies of Gorbachev. The latter had no experience in foreign affairs. The office of president, largely ceremonial, had been vacant since the death of Konstantin Chernenko in March.

U.S.-Soviet Summit Set for November — Anatoly Dobrynin, the Soviet ambassador to the United States, met with the U.S. Secretary of State George Shultz in Washington, July 1, and it was announced, July 2, that Dobrynin had conveyed the USSR's agreement to a summit conference. The summit meeting, between Pres. Ronald Reagan and Soviet leader Mikhail Gorbachev, was scheduled for Geneva on November 19 and 20. U.S. administration officials sought to diminish speculation that the meeting might lead to a significant breakthrough in resolving the differences between the 2 countries. The second round of U.S.-Soviet arms control talks ended in Geneva, July 16. No tangible progress was reported, and each side criticized the other. The White House said that the Soviet delegates preferred not to "deal in concrete terms and with hard numbers," and the chief Soviet negotiator, Viktor Karpov, said that the United States was marking time while it pushed its military buildup. Gorbachev, in a statement issued July 29, declared a unilateral moratorium on nuclear tests, to begin Aug. 6. U.S. Secretary of State George Shultz rejected the freeze, saying it did not have any provisions for verification.

OPEC Cuts Oil Prices a Bit — Ministers representing the Organization of Petroleum Exporting Countries (OPEC) met twice in July and finally agreed on a small reduction in the prices of 2 grades of crude oil. The 13-nation cartel had cut its prices in January, but prices on the world spot markets continued to decline and had fallen below OPEC's official prices. As a result, OPEC's influence in world petroleum markets continued to decline, and oil production by OPEC nations as a group also continued to fall. A 3-day meeting of the oil ministers in Vienna ended, July 7, with no agreement on price reductions. Poorer nations opposed reductions in prices and production because of their need to maintain their oil revenues. Mexico, not a member of OPEC, dropped its prices, July 10. At the close of a 4-day meeting in Geneva, July 25, small reductions in prices were agreed to by a 10-3 vote. Saudi Arabia supported the cuts and withdrew a threat to increase production, flood the market, and drive prices down. However, Sheik Ahmed Yamani, the Saudi oil minister, said, July 31, that his country would double its production levels to the maximum allowed under OPEC production quotas.

12,000 Women Attend Kenya Meetings — Nairobi, Kenya, was the site of 2 major meetings of women in July. Some 2,200 delegates, mostly women, attended the United Nations' World Conference of Women, July 15 to 27. About 10,000 women came, July 10 to 19, from around the world for Forum '85, sponsored by nongovernmental organizations. Maureen Reagan, head of the U.S. delegation to the U.N. conference, said, July 10, that it should focus on the "unique problems of women" and avoid divisive international political issues. Nonetheless, many delegates made political statements to the conference and some used the occasion to attack U.S. policies. The delegates, July 27, unanimously approved a document that called on governments to adopt policies and programs that would improve the lot of working women, including minimum-wage laws and child day-care centers.

"State of Emergency" in South Africa — In an attempt to stem a tide of black unrest, the government of South Africa declared a state of emergency in July. The U.S. Senate voted, July 11, to impose economic sanctions on South Africa in protest against its racial policies. The Senate bill, though not as strong as one passed by the House in June, would ban loans to the government and trade in nuclear materials or technology, and it would provide harsher penalties if South Africa failed to take significant action in 18 months to reform its apartheid system. Violence had been building for a year and had resulted in up to 500 deaths, with blacks constituting almost all of the victims. Dissatisfaction with economic conditions and a lack of political rights fueled the protests. Many of those killed were black policemen and minor officials, who were perceived as "collaborators" by militant blacks. On July 20, 20,000 persons attended an emotional funeral for 4 anti-apartheid activists who had been murdered. Pres. Pieter Botha declared an indefinite state of emergency, July 20, for districts around the cities of Port Elizabeth and Johannesburg. The police and military were empowered to arrest anyone seen as a threat to public safety. In less than a week, 800 persons, mostly blacks, including priests, lawyers, labor leaders, and teachers, had been arrested. U.S. officials said, July 25, that pressure was being applied on South Africa to end the emergency. Bishop Desmond Tutu, the South African clergyman who had received the 1984 Nobel Peace Prize, offered to mediate between black activists and the government, but he was turned dow by Botha, July 29. House and Senate conferees reached agreement, July 31, on a compromise bill imposing economic sanctions.

Gandhi and Sikhs Sign Accord — Prime Minister Rajiv Gandhi of India and Harchand Singh Longowal, a moderate leader of the Sikh movement, took a bold step in July to end a troubled period in Indian history. They signed an agreement, July 24, designed to bring peace to the state of Punjab, a principal base for the Sikh religion. More than 1,000 persons had died in fighting between the army and militant Sikhs in 1984, and 2 Sikhs had assassinated Rajiv's mother, Prime Minister Indira Gandhi, in October 1984. The agreement provided for a shift in a boundary to increase the Sikh majority in Punjab. Gandhi also agreed to more lenient treatment of Sikhs arrested in recent years, and to provide more compensation for Sikhs arrested in recent years, and to provide more compensation for Sikhs injured during anti-Sikh rioting following Indira Gandhi's death. Although militant Sikhs denounced the settlement as a sellout of their aspirations for greater autonomy, a majority of Sikh leaders

reportedly approved of it at a meeting, July 26. Four weeks after signing the agreement, Longowal was assassinated, Aug. 20, while addressing his supporters at a rally in Sherpur. Two Sikhs were arrested in the shooting.

Chinese President Visits U.S. — Li Xiannian, the president of China, met with Pres. Ronald Reagan at the White House, July 23. In his first official function since major surgery, Reagan assisted his elderly guest to the podium on the South Lawn. The 2 leaders met for 30 minutes and reportedly discussed U.S. trade policies and the status of Taiwan. The 2 countries, July 23, signed a nuclear power cooperation agreement. The pact had been initialed during Reagan's visit to China in 1984, but the signing had been delayed after reports had surfaced that China was helping Pakistan develop nuclear weapons.

Ugandan President Overthrown — The turbulent history of Uganda recorded another chapter in July with the ouster of Pres. Milton Obote by a military coup. Obote's 5-year rule, punctuated with brutalities by himself and his enemies that had reportedly taken hundreds of thousands of lives, ended, July 27, when he fled to Kenya as his mutinous opponents reached the capital of Kampala. Tribal differences appeared to be at the root of the brief revolt; Obote was a member of the Langi tribe, and the rebel leader, Brig. Basilio Olara Okello, was of the Acholi tribe. The new leaders closed Uganda's borders, July 28, and suspended the constitution. Former dictator Idi Amin Dada, who had been deposed in 1979, said in Saudi Arabia, July 28, that he was ready to rescue Uganda. He was not called upon to do so, and Lt. Gen. Tito Okello (no relation to Basilio Okello) was named the country's new ruler, July 29. A commander of another rebel force that had been fighting the Obote regime declined a position on the ruling council. Widespread looting in the capital by the victorious rebels followed the change in power.

New Peru Leader Acts on Debts — Alain García Pérez was sworn in as president of Peru, July 28. He succeeded Fernando Belaunde Terry, and it marked the first time in 40 years that an elected president had succeeded another elected president in Peru. The occasion was not entirely free of political strife, however. Security was tight following a wave of bombings by leftist rebels seeking to disrupt the change of leadership. At 36 the world's youngest elected president, García led a nation heavily in debt and facing economic chaos. In a move that worried international bankers, García announced in his inaugural address that he would limit foreign debt payments to 10 percent of Peru's export earnings. Treasury Secretary James Baker, representing the United States at the inauguration, said such a solution was "counterproductive."

General

Coke Brings Back Original Formula — In one of the most abrupt reversals in the history of marketing, the Coca-Cola Company announced, July 10, that it would once again sell a soft drink using the recipe that it had used for 99 years. In April, the company had said that the original formula would no longer be available. It had conducted taste tests and found that a new, sweeter formula was preferred. The company believed that this new formula would appeal to customers who were switching to Pepsi-Cola, which was also sweeter than the original Coke. But many fans of the original protested the loss of the tangy taste they had loved so long, and sales of the new product were disappointing. The compromise response was to continue to market the new formula under the name "Coca-Cola" and to revive the old recipe under the name "Coca-Cola Classic." Coca-Cola's president, Donald Keough, said, July 11, that consumer research had failed to measure "the deep and abiding emotional attachment to the original Coca-Cola."

Rock Concert Aids Hungry Africans — a 17-hour rock concert, "Live Aid," broadcast on radio and televison to 152 countries, July 13, from London and Philadelphia, raised an estimated $70 million for the starving peoples of Africa. Footage from 7 other concerts was included, and the program also included the first live broadcast of a rock group from the Soviet Union. Dozens of popular-music performers

appeared live, including Joan Baez, David Bowie, Phil Collins, Bob Dylan, Mick Jagger, Elton John, Paul McCartney, and Tina Turner. Members of former rock groups, including The Who and Led Zeppelin, were reunited onstage. About 160,000 persons attended the concert in London and Philadelphia. Bob Geldof, an Irish rock musician, was the principal organizer of the concert. He had organized "Band Aid," a British all-star group that had recorded a famine-relief song, "Do They Know It's Christmas?" It had inspired a previous American effort, USA for Africa and its song, "We Are the World."

Disasters — More than 200 persons were killed, July 19, when a wall of mud and water burst through an earthen dam in the Dolomite Alps in Italy and poured down the Fiemme Valley, sweeping over 2 towns ... A plane crash in southeastern Colombia, during a rainstorm, killed about 80 persons, July 24 ... A land mine, possibly planted by rebels, killed 61 train passengers north of Rangoon, Burma, July 25.

AUGUST

National

Congress Approves Budget Resolution — The long congressional struggle to come up with a budget resolution acceptable to both houses ended, Aug. 1. Both the Senate (67-32) and the House (309-119) accepted a compromise conference report that called for outlays of $967.6 billion and revenues of $793.7 billion during the 1986 fiscal year, which would begin Oct. 1, 1985. The budget sought to reduce federal deficits for the next 3 years by a total of $276.2 billion, but those figures were suspect and depended in part on continued economic recovery. The resolution, approved after months of wrangling and deadlock within Congress and with the Reagan administration, terminated only one federal program, revenue sharing for state and local governments. But $137 billion was cut from Pentagon budgets, with spending authority permitted only for an increase for inflation in the first year. A number of domestic programs were trimmed back; Amtrak, once ticketed for oblivion, suffered only a 15 percent reduction. Social Security and federal retirement programs would not be touched. Pres. Ronald Reagan, Aug. 3, congratulated Congress on its effort, but warned that he would veto any spending bills that contained "excessive" levels of spending or jeopardized the national security. The Office of Management and Budget said, Aug. 8, that deficits for the next 2 years would likely exceed $200 billion a year.

Unemployment Rate Level — An immovable unemployment rate kept experts guessing as to which way the U.S. economy was headed. The Labor Department announced, Aug. 2, that the unemployment rate had stood at 7.2 percent in July for the 6th consecutive month. The *Wall Street Journal* reported, Aug. 5, that after-tax profits for more than 500 major companies declined 14 percent in the second quarter, compared with 1984. The Labor Department said, Aug. 12, that the prices paid by producers for finished goods rose 0.3 percent in July. Industrial production edged upward 0.2 percent in July, the Federal Reserve Board announced, Aug. 15. The Labor Department said, Aug. 22, that consumer prices also rose 0.2 percent in July. The U.S. Census Bureau issued a report, Aug. 27, showing that poverty in the United States had edged downward in 1984 after advancing for 5 consecutive years. The overall poverty rate was 14.4 percent, but among blacks the rate was 33.8 percent. A family of 4 was considered to be in poverty if its cash income was less than $10,609. Median family income in 1984 stood at $26,430. The Commerce Department reported, Aug. 30, that the index of leading economic indicators rose 0.4 percent in July.

Governor Survies Impeachment Vote — Gov. William Sheffield (D, Alaska) came through an investigation in July and August that scarred his reputation but ended with a decision by the state Senate not to impeach him. The Senate conducted an 11-day inquiry into the awarding of a $9.1 million contract to a firm in which one of Sheffield's political backers had a partial interest. Two lawyers prominent in the Watergate investigation, Samuel Dash and Phillip Lacovara, participated in the proceedings. Dash, employed by the Senate, said he found insufficient evidence to impeach

Sheffield, but he did find "clear and convincing evidence" that the governor had committed perjury. Sheffield's attorney, Lacovara, said that the governor's failure to remember key conversations was the result of his lack of interest in the contract. The Senate Rules Committee found, Aug. 3, that there was "substantial but not clear and convincing evidence" that an impeachable offense had been committed. The full Senate rejected the impeachment motion, Aug. 5, by a 12-8 vote.

Reagan's Skin Cancer Removed — During a news conference, Aug. 5, Pres. Ronald Reagan said that a patch of skin on his nose had been removed, July 30, and that it had been found to be cancerous. He said that the growth, a basal skin carcinoma, was usually caused by overexposure to the sun, and that his doctors expected that the condition would be cured. The discovery of the cancerous skin came less than 3 weeks after Reagan underwent major surgery for cancer of the colon.

Pentagon Cancels Antiaircraft Weapon — For the first time since the 1960s, the Pentagon scrubbed a weapon while it was still in production. On Aug. 27, Defense Secretary Caspar Weinberger announced that the Army's division air defense (DIVAD) Sergeant York gun was being dropped after flunking a series of tests earlier in 1985. Congress had been critical of the weapon and had halted outlays for purchase of more DIVADs in 1984. Ford Aerospace & Communications Corporation had delivered 65 of the weapons toward a projected total of 618. The weapon had cost $1.8 billion so far and $3 billion was still to be spent. Designed to protect infantry and tanks from low-flying aircraft, the weapon—which consisted of two 40mm guns mounted on a tank—had never performed well in simulated combat situations. Weinberger said his decision was difficult because of the Army's "very urgent need for better air defense."

Reagan's Rejects Shoe Import Quotas — Pres. Ronald Reagan advanced his reputation as a champion of free trade, Aug. 28, when he rejected advice from the U.S. International Trade Commission and said he would not impose quotas on the importation of nonrubber shoes. Imports of footwear had risen sharply in recent years and in 1984 captured 76 percent of the U.S. market. Shoe imports were only a small part of the deepening U.S. trade deficit, and Reagan's decision on shoes had been awaited as a signal of how he might deal with it. Sentiment was building in Congress for various protectionist measures. Reagan said that the prices of shoes would rise if he had imposed quotas, and that other nations might retaliate against the United States. The Footwear Industries of America, a trade group, said the decision was "callous and deplorable."

International

South African President Sticks to Policies — President Pieter Botha of South Africa disappointed those inside and beyond the borders of his country who had hoped that his government might be ready to modify its systems of racial separation. The U.S. House, Aug. 1, voted 380-48 for a Senate-House compromise conference report imposing economic sanctions on South Africa, but Senate conservatives, threatening a filibuster, prevented a vote before Congress began its August recess. Rioting in South Africa spread to the Durban area in early August, with members of the Zulu tribe fighting Asians, other blacks, and the police. More than 50 persons were killed in 4 days. Botha delivered a long-anticipated speech in Durban, Aug. 15, and rejected any thought that the apartheid system be scrapped. He said that the adoption of the principle of "one man, one vote" would "destroy white South Africa" and mean "strife, chaos, and poverty." He attributed the violence in South Africa to "barbaric communist agitators." He said, "We have never given in to outside demands and we are not going to do so now." He offered to free black nationalist leader Nelson Mandela if he would renounce violence. Botha restated his support for minor reforms offered in January that fell far short of what black leaders wanted. Bishop Desmond Tutu said, Aug. 16, that after Botha's speech that chances for peaceful change were "virtually nil." Tutu boycotted a meeting, Aug. 19, between Botha and some other church leaders that appeared to be unfruitful. After meeting with Botha, Aug. 19, the Rev. Jerry Falwell, leader of the Moral Majority in the United States, praised the South African regime and said he would seek to prevent the Senate from approving the bill on sanctions. He urged Americans to buy South African gold coins. Falwell said, Aug. 20, that Tutu was a "phony" if he presumed to speak for South African blacks. The South African government, Aug. 27, suspended trading in its currency, the rand, when it fell sharply in value. South African police, Aug. 27, arrested the Rev. Allan Boesak, founder of a multiracial coalition opposing apartheid, the day before he was to lead a demonstration.

West German Spy Scandal Breaks — West Germany suffered a serious breach in security when a top counterintelligence officer defected to East Germany. A chain of alarming events began when the secretary to the economics minister, who had clearance to handle secret documents, disappeared. The minister, Martin Bangemann, was leader of the Free Democratic Party, the junior partner in the ruling coalition, and it was believed that his secretary may have had access to highly classified information. Two more suspicious disappearances occurred, and on Aug. 19, Hans Joachim Tiedge, a top counterintelligence office, also disappeared. The East German press agency announced, Aug. 23, that he had defected. Some top German officials were criticized for having been aware of Tiedge's personal problems, including drinking and indebtedness. Tiedge knew the names of many West Germans engaged in espionage in East Germany. A secretary to West German President Richard von Weizsacker was arrested, Aug. 25, on spying charges.

Pre-Summit Tensions Rise — An increase in tensions between the superpowers appeared in part to be related to pre-summit maneuvering. The White House announced, Aug. 20, that the United States would soon test an antisatellite (ASAT) missile against a target in space for the first time. The Soviet Union had urged a moratorium on ASAT tests, but White House spokesman Larry Speakes rejected a moratorium because, he said, the Soviets had a lead in such weapons. Moscow, Aug. 21, warned that the decision could force the Soviet Union to resume its own ASAT tests. The United States charged, Aug. 21, that the Soviet Union was using a "potentially dangerous" chemical dust to track the movements of American diplomats in Moscow. The chemical, NPPD, a fine yellowish dust that glowed when exposed to ultra-violet light, was allegedly sprayed in places where Americans would pick it up on their hands and clothes. Then, Soviet intelligence supposedly followed the traces of dust they left behind to learn where they went and what Soviet citizens they met. On Aug. 22, the Soviet Union denied as "absurd" the use of a dust to track Americans.

Nigerian Government Overthrown — Maj. Gen. Mohammed Buhari, who had held power in Nigeria for 20 months after leading a military coup, was overthrown on Aug. 27. In an apparently bloodless coup, the army chief of staff, Maj. Gen. Ibrahim Babangida, took control with the support of the nation's Supreme Military Council. Buhari and his second-in-command, Maj. Gen. Tunde Idiagbon, were both removed and Buhari was believed to be under arrest. Babangida criticized his predecessor for economic mismanagement and failure to live up to promises made when he took control in 1983. Inflation and unemployment had risen sharply, and food shortages had occurred.

General

Air Crashes Take Heavy Toll — By August, 1985 had become the most tragic year in the history of commercial aviation. More than 1,400 persons had been killed in airplane crashes, surpassing the previous high of 1,299 in 1974. On Aug. 2, a Delta Lockheed L-1011 Tristar carrying 160 persons crashed while making its landing approach at Dallas-Fort Worth International Airport. The final death toll of 136 included a motorist whose car was struck by the descending plane. Just before the crash, an air traffic controller ordered the plane to decrease its speed so it would not overtake another plane using the same runway. The reduction in speed may have made the plane more subject to dangerous wind shear—a condition in which winds change speed and direction abruptly. In history's greatest tragedy involving one plane, 520 persons died, Aug. 12, when a Japan Air Lines Boeing 747 crashed into a mountain northwest of Tokyo. Four persons survived. Shortly after takeoff from To-

kyo, the Osaka-bound crew had reported that it was unable to control the plane, which then followed an erratic course until the crash. Investigators thought that the plane's vertical stabilizer had broken off. A charter jet operated by British Airtours burst into flames at Manchester airport, Aug. 22, killing 54 persons; 83 survived the accident. An engine exploded as the plane moved down the runway before takeoff; another engine exploded as passengers were being evacuated.

Baseball Strike Lasts 2 Days — Owners and players reached an agreement, Aug. 7, that ended a brief walkout by the major-league baseball players. Baseball Commissioner Peter Ueberroth, who had distanced himself from the negotiations until a final settlement was near, announced that a "tentative understanding" had been achieved. No games had been played, Aug. 6 or 7, but play resumed Aug. 8. The new accord would replace an agreement reached in 1981 after a 50-day strike. In the new agreement, players attained new objectives; no salary cap was imposed, as owners had wanted, and the owners agreed to increase substantially their contributions to the players' pension fund. The minimum player salary was raised to $60,000 from $40,000. On average, players made about $360,000 a year, up from $51,000 in 1976.

Toxic Gas Escapes in West Virginia — The leakage of toxic gas from a Union Carbide plant in West Virginia, Aug. 11, briefly sent 4 plant employees and 134 residents of the area to hospitals. The gas, aldicarb oxide, causes eye and skin irritations, and is considered more dangerous if absorbed through the skin. The plant, at Institute, also produced methyl isocyanate, a deadly gas that killed more than 2,000 persons at Bhopal, India, in 1984. The Institute plant, closed after the Indian disaster, had been reopened for only a few months after safety inspections when the Aug. 11 leakage occurred. Union Carbide was criticized for its delay, Aug. 11, in notifying authorities and the public of the leakage. Four residents of South Charleston, W. Va., were briefly hospitalized, Aug. 13, when chemicals leaked from another Union Carbide plant 5 miles from Institute. Union Carbide, Aug. 23, accepted responsibility for the Aug. 11 accident, blaming faulty equipment and violations of procedures within the plant. The company said 25 employees had not noticed that steam was escaping from leaky valves and overheating the aldicarb oxide; the condition had existed for 10 days.

Disasters — China reported, Aug. 8, that floods and rains during the summer had killed 527 people . . . The collapse of an apartment building in Bombay, Aug. 13, killed 52 persons . . . At least 110 persons were killed, Aug. 18, when a ferry capsized on the Songhua River in China.

SEPTEMBER

National

Hurricanes Menace South, East — Two hurricanes regarded as posing serious threats to human life and property struck the southern and eastern coasts of the United States in September. Although the movements of both proved to be fickle, fatalities and injuries were light thanks to highly publicized warnings and evacuations. Hurricane Elena pursued an erratic course through the Gulf of Mexico at the end of August. The worst storm in the gulf in 6 years, Elena seemed unable to choose a place to land. It made two passes at part of Florida's gulf coast, prompting the evacuation of more than one million persons. Carrying winds exceeding 100 miles an hour, Elena finally veered northwestward and crossed the Mississippi coast on Sept. 2. With receding force, the storm moved inland to Arkansas. Four deaths and damage totaling $1 billion were attributed to the storm. A second hurricane, named Gloria, was billed as one of the most dangerous of recent years, moved northward off the east coast, Sept. 26, leaving torrential rain on the outer banks of North Carolina and prompting mass evacuations from low areas as far north as New England. Unlike Elena, which had lingered in the gulf region for several days, Gloria moved swiftly and was thus less destructive than feared. Three hundred miles in width and carrying winds of 130 miles an hour, Gloria swept through the New York metropolitan area, Sept. 27; it took only a few lives, but damage

was widespread and millions of people were without power for up to several days.

Unemployment at 5-Year Low — After holding at a level of 7.2 percent for 6 months, the nation's unemployment rate finally shifted—downward—in August, the Labor Department reported, Sept. 6. The August level of 6.9 percent was the lowest since 1980, and suggested that the economy, which had appeared to be adrift for many months, finally might be gathering some momentum. The U.S. balance of payments showed a deficit of $31.8 billion in the second quarter of the year, the Commerce Department reported, Sept. 16. The figures also showed that for the first time since 1914, the United States had become a debtor nation, that is foreigners, owned more assets in the United States than vice versa. Economists and politicians argued about the significance, if any, of this statistical development. The Commerce Department reported, Sept. 30, that the index of leading economic indicators advanced for the fourth straight month in August, this time by a substantial 0.7 percent.

Reagan Acts to Boost U.S. Exports — Pres. Ronald Reagan tried to head off rising sentiment in Congress for protectionist legislation that he regarded as dangerous to U.S. interests. On Sept. 7, he announced he was taking steps to open further U.S. markets in countries that he believed were engaging in unfair trading practices. He said that under the 1974 Trade Act, official investigations would be directed at Brazil, Japan, and South Korea and their purported restrictions, respectively, on computer equipment, tobacco products, and the writing of insurance. He said he would also press negotiations to reduce or eliminate canned-fruit subsidies imposed by the European Economic Community and to increase the Japanese market for U.S. shoe and leather exports. On Sept. 11, Reagan and Republican leaders in Congress met to seek a compromise on trade legislation. Reagan warned, Sept. 17, that proposed legislation to reduce imports to the United States represented "a mindless stampede toward protectionism" that would be "a one-way trip to economic disaster." The trade imbalance between the United States and other nations was a prime factor in the decision, Sept. 22, by the officials from the United States, Britain, West Germany, France, and Japan to work together to drive down the value of the dollar relative to other currencies. This promise to intervene in the currency markets had an immediate effect as the dollar plunged more than 4 percent in value, Sept. 23, the largest one-day drop in the 12-year history of floating currency rates. Reagan, Sept. 23, announced a plan to subsidize some U.S. exports to help get them into foreign markets.

Cabinet Secretary Pressured to Resign — During September, Margaret Heckler, secretary of Health and Human Services in Pres. Ronald Reagan's cabinet, reportedly came under pressure to step down. Heckler, who presided over the largest department in the executive branch, had been criticized by some conservatives as an unsatisfactory manager and as insufficiently committed to some of the president's policies. Other conservatives praised her; Sen. Orrin Hatch (R, Utah), said she had done a "terrific job" and called maneuvering against her in the White House "pathetic and disgusting." Chief of Staff Donald Regan had reportedly been leading the effort to replace her. Heckler insisted on a meeting with the president to learn where she stood with him, and when they did meet, Sept. 30, he asked her to resign and become ambassador to Ireland. They met the press, Oct. 1, and Reagan announced that she had accepted the appointment as ambassador, which he described as a promotion.

International

South Africa Considers Concessions to Blacks — The South African government showed signs that it was ready to meet some of the demands of its black population. The shift came in the face of growing international economic pressure. Some foreign banks refused to roll over maturing loans to South Africa because of concern about the ability of the government to ride out the storm of racial unrest. Thus confronted with a serious cash-flow problem, the government, Sept. 1, halted repayments of principal on foreign loans for 4 months, although interest payments would continue. Foreseeing the prospect of having to veto a congressional bill imposing stiff sanctions on South Africa, Pres. Ronald Reagan,

Sept. 9, announced his own set of more restrained sanctions. In an executive order, he banned some computer sales and most bank loans and forbade most exports of nuclear technology. He also banned importation of South Africa gold Kruggerands, subject to the approval of U.S. trading partners. Reagan's action averted passage in the Senate of the sanctions bill; a Republican-led effort prevented an end to debate and in effect killed the bill. Pres. Pieter Botha of South Africa said he regretted Reagan's actions, though he acknowledged that the congressional bill would have been worse from his point of view. The South African black leader, Bishop Desmond Tutu, discounted the importance of Reagan's moves and called the president a racist. On **Sept. 10,** eleven Western European nations imposed trade, cultural, and military sanctions on South Africa. Botha said, **Sept. 11,** that he was ready to discuss restoring South African citizenship to nearly 10 million blacks who had lost it when nominally independent tribal homelands were created within the past few years. The South African system of apartheid, or racial separation, had contemplated the eventual concentration of all blacks in their own homelands, from which they could travel to white South Africa only to work. A committee named by Botha recommended, **Sept. 12,** the abolition of the law under which blacks were required to obtain a temporary pass to leave their homelands or township to stay or work in white areas. On **Sept. 29,** 91 South African businessmen called for the abolition of apartheid and for negotiations with "acknowledged black leaders" on sharing power.

Gorbachev, Reagan Eye Public Opinion — As their November summit meeting drew nearer, Soviet leader Mikhail Gorbachev and Pres. Ronald Reagan continued to focus on influencing world public opinion. Gorbachev granted an interview to *Time* magazine, and on **Sept. 3,** he met with 8 U.S. senators in Moscow. After the meeting, the senators described Gorbachev as a man of substance with a forceful personality. Sen. Robert Byrd (D, W. Va.), the Senate minority leader, reported that Gorbachev had said that the Soviet Union would make "radical proposals" to reduce nuclear weapons if the United States agreed to curb the "militarization of outer space." Sen. Sam Nunn (D, Ga.) said Gorbachev indicated that he might drop his demand for a total U.S. ban on its Strategic Defense Initiative (SDI, or "Star Wars") research. Gorbachev offered, **Sept. 10,** to create a European zone free of chemical weapons, but the White House rejected the proposal, saying the United States wanted a "comprehensive, verifiable ban" on chemical arms. The U.S. Air Force, **Sept. 13,** conducted a test of its antisatellite (ASAT) missile, another program to which the Soviet Union had objected. The 2-stage ASAT missile, launched from an F-15, struck and destroyed a 6-year-old U.S. research satellite orbiting at 17,500 miles an hour at an altitude of 290 miles. The F-15 had been guided by radar and the missile by heat-seeking sensors. Reagan said at a news conference, **Sept. 17,** that the United States would not negotiate a limit on SDI, nor would it ban ASAT testing because the Soviet Union was ahead in its own ASAT program. Addressing the U.N. General Assembly, **Sept. 24,** Soviet Foreign Minister Eduard Shevardnadze said that the Soviet Union was determined to reach an agreement with the United States to ban space weapons and make "truly radical reductions" in existing nuclear stockpiles. Shevardnadze and Secretary of State George Shultz met in New York for more than 4 hours, **Sept. 25,** but their conversation, while cordial, apparently did not result in any progress on substantive issues. Shevardnadze met Reagan at the White House, **Sept. 27,** and reportedly proposed a 50 percent cut in the offensive nuclear arsenals of both superpowers. Reagan said, **Sept. 28,** that he welcomed the new initiatives. The Soviet Union, **Sept. 30,** formally put its new proposal on the negotiating table at the arms talks in Geneva.

Greenpeace Scandal Rocks French Government — The French government was badly shaken when top officials were linked to the bombing in July of a ship owned by Greenpeace, the international environmental and antinuclear organization. The ship, the *Rainbow Warrior,* had been anchored in Auckland, New Zealand, prior to a protest trip into the region of the South Pacific Ocean where France was about to conduct nuclear tests. A photographer was killed by the second of 2 explosions, **July 10,** as the ship sank.

Twelve persons escaped from the ship. New Zealand officials arrested 2 persons and issued warrants for 4 others, all of whom, it turned out, were members of the French secret service. The French government began an official inquiry. The investigation, headed by Bernard Tricot, a former adviser to President Charles De Gaulle, found in August that the 6 agents had been sent to New Zealand to gather information about Greenpeace but had not been involved in the sinking. Three of the missing agents, all frogmen, turned themselves in at a Paris police headquarters. The Tricot inquiry's findings were widely rejected and ridiculed in France, New Zealand, and elsewhere. French Premier Laurent Fabius warned, **Sept. 4,** that he would not let Greenpeace dictate defense policy for France, and he said that France would fight the campaign against French nuclear testing in the Pacific. French Pres. François Mitterand visited the nuclear testing site on Mururoa atoll, **Sept. 13.** He said France would continue to test in the area as long as it was necessary. The French newspaper *Le Monde* reported, **Sept. 17,** that intelligence and military officials had not told the truth to the Tricot investigation. The paper said that a team of French military advisers, not previously mentioned publicly, had sunk the ship with the approval of the defense minister, Charles Hernu. However, the paper said it had not been able to determine whether Hernu and 2 other officials had actually ordered that the ship be sunk. Hernu said on television, **Sept. 18,** that he had ordered agents to gather information on Greenpeace, but he denied ordering the attack on the ship. Mitterand ordered Fabious to overhaul the intelligence service. Hernu resigned, **Sept. 20,** and Fabius announced, **Sept. 20,** that Adm. Pierre Lacoste, chief of the secret service, had been dismissed. Despite the accumulating evidence, the annoucement by Fabius, **Sept. 22,** that French agents had sunk the ship came as a shock. Fabius said the agents had been ordered to sabotage the ship, but he did not say who ordered them to do so, or who knew about the plan in advance. He said that the truth had been withheld from Tricot during his investigation.

Military Coup Fails in Thailand — Forces supporting Thai Premier Prem Tinsulanonda foiled an attempted coup by former military officers, **Sept. 9.** Five persons were killed and 60 were wounded during 10 hours of fighting. The dead included 2 members of an NBC television news team. Some 500 soldiers, reportedly led by former Col. Manoon Rupekachorn, seized the state radio and attacked military installations, but were unable to arouse much public support, as most the rebels had surrendered by late afternoon. Manoon surrendered and was allowed to leave for Singapore. Prem said that Manoon was freed to "avoid using drastic measures in order to maintain our unity."

Duarte's Daughter Kidnapped — The eldest daughter of President José Napoleón Duarte of El Salvador was kidnapped, **Sept. 10,** outside the New University of El Salvador in the capital, San Salvador. The kidnappers shot her 2 bodyguards, one fatally, and took her from her car. Ines Guadalupe Duarte Durán, 34, was studying public relations and advertising at the university; she owned Radio Liberty and in 1984 had managed her father's election campaign. Searching for the missing woman, police and army troops raided what they said were hideouts used by leftist rebels waging a guerrilla war against the government. Several persons were arrested and weapons and explosives were seized, but no trace of Duarte Durán was found.

Soviet KGB Agents Defect — Great Britain announced, **Sept. 12,** that Oleg Gordieyevsky, a political counselor at the Soviet embassy in London, had defected. Britain identified him as the top agent of the Soviet intelligency agency, the KGB, in Britain. Britain immediately ordered the expulsion of 25 Soviet citizens—diplomats, trade representatives, journalists, and others—who, it said, Gordieyevsky had identified as spies. The Soviet Union retaliated, **Sept. 14,** by expelling 25 Britons. On **Sept. 16,** Britain expelled 6 more Soviet citizens, and the Soviet Union responded by expelling six Britons, **Sept. 18.** There was some speculation that Gordieyevsky's decision to defect might be related to the flight of West Germans to East Germany, which had begun in August. On **Sept. 17,** it was determined that a secretary in the office of West German Chancellor Helmut Kohl had defected, along with her husband; there was concern that they were spies. Reagan administration officials reported, **Sept.**

26, that another KGB agent, a senior member of the organization, Vitaly Yurchenko, had defected; some officials reported that he had identified several U.S. CIA employees as Soviet agents.

Shiites Free American Hostage — The Rev. Benjamin Weir, an American Presbyterian missionary, was freed by his Shiite Muslim captors in Lebanon after being held for 16 months. His release came, Sept. 14, but was not confirmed until Sept. 18. Weir said at a news conference, Sept. 19, in Washington, D.C., that the Shiites had freed him "as a sign of their good intentions" and to warn Pres. Ronald Reagan that they would not release their 6 other American hostages until Kuwait freed 17 Shiite Muslim terrorists that it held. He said his captors warned of more kidnappings and of hostage executions if there was no response to their demand.

Elderly Chinese Leaders Retired — In China, a land where old age is revered, leaders of the Communist revolution have generally been permitted to hold high office as long as they wished. On Sept. 16, however, China's top leader, Deng Xiaoping, instigated the retirement of 10 (out of 24) Politburo members and 64 of some 340 members of the Central Committee. Most of those who left office were 70 or older, and many had ties to the revolutionary period. Deng had made no secret of his desire to promote, into top positions, younger and better educated people who he believed would be better able to implement his economic reforms and his more outward initiatives in foreign affairs. More than one million lesser figures in the military, civil service, and the business arena had already been replaced. The retiring Politburo members included China's vice president and the widow of premier Zhou Enlai. Some, but not all, critics of Deng's policies were removed from their posts. Despite earlier reports that he might step down, Deng 81, did not include himself among the retirees.

General

Titanic Found in Atlantic Depths — The wreckage of the ocean liner *Titanic*, which sank in 1912 and carried more than 1,500 people to their deaths, was found Sept. 1. The ship had sunk on its maiden voyage after hitting an iceberg. About one third of its passengers were rescued. The ship was found as a result of newly developed technology in lights and cameras. The technology was utilized by a joint U.S.-French search team whose American members came from the privately operated Woods Hole Oceanographic Institute in Woods Hole, Mass. Relying on color photographs and videotapes shot from unmanned submarines, the researchers reported, Sept. 2, that they had found the *Titanic* in more than 12,000 feet of water 500 miles south of Newfoundland. The exact location was not disclosed to discourage salvage attempts. The 882-foot vessel had broken in 2 and one of its 4 smokestacks was missing.

Thousands Killed in Mexican Earthquake — A powerful earthquake sent deadly shockwaves through central and southwestern Mexico, Sept. 19, taking more than 5,000 lives and causing widespread destruction. Heaviest devastation was in the capital, Mexico City. The epicenter of the quake was placed 230 miles southwest of the center of Mexico City. The quake was measured at a high of 7.8 on the Richter Scale. A second earthquake, lesser in force but still severe at 7.3 on the scale, struck some of the same areas, Sept. 20. Officials said, Sept. 20, that 250 buildings had been destroyed in Mexico City and 50 more had been damaged beyond repair. In the days after the quakes, more buildings collapsed. Rescue efforts concentrated on saving living persons trapped inside the wreckage, and thousands of people helped remove the rubble, using their hands, picks and shovels, and larger equipment where it could be employed safely. Tens of thousands of people were made homeless, and most of them had no choice but to live and sleep in the open.

Disasters — A DC-9 flown by Midwest Express crashed just after takeoff, Sept. 6, from Milwaukee's Billy Mitchell Field, killing all 31 persons on board . . . A train collision near Viseu, Portugal, had killed 54 persons and left 64 missing and feared dead, officials reported, Sept. 13.

OCTOBER

National

Toxic Spills Average 5 Per Day — More than 135 people were killed in the United States and nearly 1,500 were injured by at least 6,928 toxic-chemical accidents that occurred in the last 5 years. The total represented an average of 5 accidents per day. The data were contained in an unpublished report commissioned by the Environmental Protection Agency and made available to the *New York Times*, which reported on the findings, Oct. 3. The chemical leaks occurred in both large and small companies, mostly when the chemicals were being manufactured or stored. The EPA, which commissioned the study following the disaster in Bhopal, India, in 1984 in which 2,000 persons died, was designed to determine which substances are most frequently involved in leaks, and why.

Senate Finds New Way to Cut Deficits — The U.S. Senate came up with a new plan for eliminating the federal budget deficits. The Republican leadership in the Senate and House endorsed a proposal aimed at forcing the government to balance the budget by 1991. The plan would direct the president and Congress to cut the deficit by $36 billion a year until it disappeared. In any year that the deficit exceeded the specified level by more than 5 percent, the president would have the authority to reduce spending across the board. Support grew for the plan although it appeared to require further cuts in defense and popular domestic programs and increases in taxes. The plan was offered as an amendment to a bill to raise the government's debt ceiling to more than $2 trillion. Pres. Ronald Reagan formally endorsed the plan, Oct. 4. The debate of the amendment delayed action on the debt ceiling, and the Treasury said, Oct. 8, that it would run out of cash that night unless Congress acted on the ceiling. On Oct. 9, the Treasury borrowed $5 billion to raise the cash needed to cover checks already issued. The balanced-budget amendment won Senate approval, Oct. 9, as liberals and conservatives joined in the 75-24 majority. The House, Oct. 11, endorsed the goals of the Senate bill; without voting on a specific bill, the House went directly to a conference with the Senate.

Sales of Automobile Set a Record — The automobile industry had its biggest sales year in history, according to figures released after the end of the 1985 model year, Sept. 30. Altogether, auto companies sold 15.6 million vehicles in the United States. This surpassed the previous high set in 1978 by 300,000 units. Only 10.2 million cars and trucks were sold in the 1982 model year. Lower financing costs and cheaper gasoline contributed to the buying mood. More encouraging economic news came, Oct. 11, as the Labor Department reported that the producer price index, as indicator of future inflation trends, declined 0.6 percent in September. The Commerce Department said that retail sales had risen a strong 2.7 percent in September. The department reported, Oct. 15, that in their biggest decline in more than 2 years, business inventories fell 0.4 percent in September —usually a sign that employment will pick up as manufacturers seek to replace their stock.

International

Israelis Bomb PLO Headquarters — Israeli planes flew 1,500 miles to Tunis, Oct. 1, and bombed the headquarters of the Palestine Liberation Organization. Israel said the attack was in retaliation for the killing of 3 Israelis in Cyprus in September. The PLO had denied responsibility for those killings. The Israeli aircraft, U.S.-built F-15 fighter-bombers, refueled in midair on their way to Tunisia. A PLO spokesman said 67 persons were killed in the attack. The Israelis hit the office of PLO Chairman Yasir Arafat, who was at a PLO installation in northern Tunis at the time. The White House said that the attack was a legitimate response against terrorism. Egypt's Pres. Hosni Mubarak and Jordan's King Hussein, among other Arabs, condemned the attack. Tunisian Pres. Habib Bourguiba expressed "regret and astonishment," Oct. 2, in denouncing the U.S. defense of the strike. The White House shifted its position, Oct. 2, saying that the

raid was "understandable as an expression of self-defense" but said the bombing "cannot be condoned." An administration official was quoted as being especially troubled by the raid because the United States had taken a part in persuading Tunisia to take in the PLO after it was forced out of Lebanon in 1983. The U.N. Security Council passed a resolution, Oct. 4, condemning the raid; the vote was 14-0 with the United States abstaining.

4 Russians Kidnapped in Beirut — The endless waves of violence in Beirut finally touched the Soviet Union in October. Four of their diplomats were kidnapped and one of them murdered. The 4 men were kidnapped, Sept. 30, from 2 official cars in West Beirut. Two organizations, Oct. 1, claimed responsibility for the kidnappings. Both threatened to kill all the men unless an offensive against Tripoli, in northern Lebanon, by leftist and Communist militia backed by Syria halted. One group, the Islamic Liberation Organization, issued photographs of the Russians with guns pointed to their heads to prove that it and not other claimants held the Russians. Pres. Ronald Reagan said the Soviet Union had the right to retaliate "if they can pick out the people who are responsible." The Soviet Union said, Oct. 2, that a body found in Beirut was that of Arkady Katkov, a secretary at the Soviet Embassy, one of the kidnapped men. The Soviet Union called the murder "an atrocity which cannot be pardoned." This incident marked the first time that any Russian was taken hostage or killed in West Beirut. The Soviet Union, Oct. 3, appealed to Syria for help in winning freedom for the hostages. Syria and Sunni Muslim militia leaders agreed, Oct. 3, on a draft accord aimed at ending the fighting in Tripoli. The Soviet Union, Oct. 4, evacuated nonessential staff members and families of diplomats from its embassy in West Beirut. Syrian troops entered Tripoli, Oct. 6, to enforce a cease-fire provided by the accord. They collected heavy weapons from the militia, as required by the agreement. During the previous 3 weeks it was estimated that 500 had been killed in fighting in the area. Meanwhile, Muslim fundamentalists claimed that they had murdered an American hostage, diplomat William Buckley, but no body was produced.

Gorbachev Visits France — Pre-summit maneuvering between the leaders of the 2 superpowers continued in October. Pres. Ronald Reagan's plan to set up a pre-summit Western unity conference during his visits to the United Nations in late October hit snags in early October. Reagan hoped to meet with his major allies—Britain, France, West Germany, Canada, Italy, and Japan—while he was in New York to speak at the United Nations. France said, Oct. 1, that Pres. François Mitterrand was declining the invitation. On Oct. 2, Belgium and the Netherlands complained about not being invited. Soviet leader Mikhail Gorbachev arrived in France, Oct. 2, for his first visit to the West since taking power. His main theme in public statements was opposition to U.S. antimissile research. Defense Secretary Caspar Weinberger said, Oct. 3, that the Soviet Union had gone ahead with its own antimissile defense program even while denouncing the United States for doing the same. Gorbachev, Oct. 3, offered to make a "separate agreement" with France and Britain, which maintained their own nuclear arsenals; in the past he had insisted that these defensive weapons be included in any overall agreement between the Soviet Union and the United States. Reagan said he had no objection to separate negotiations between the other 3 countries. However, both France and Britain, Oct. 4, rejected the proposal, saying that they would not reduce their own forces until after the superpowers had reached an agreement on a reduction of nuclear forces.

Nicaragua Suspends Civil Rights — Pres. Daniel Ortega of Nicaragua announced, Oct. 15, that civil rights were being suspended because of "the brutal aggression by North America and its internal allies." He charged that some institutions, stimulated by "terrorist politics" of the United States, had sought to "sabotage the defense forces of our nation." Rights suspended included free expression, public assembly, the privacy of mails and of the home, and the

---

U.S. Planes Force Capture of 4 Palestinians After Hijacking of Italian Cruise Ship

Another hostage drama unfolded in October—this time at sea with a surprising climax. And yet another American lost his life. On Oct. 7, 4 Palestinians seized the Italian cruise ship Achille Lauro in the open sea as it approached Port Said, Egypt. Some 400 persons were aboard at the time. Most of these—about 340—were members of the crew; most of the passengers had debarked at Alexandria and were to rejoin the ship at Port Said. The hijackers, who were passengers and who indentified themselves as members of the Palestinian Liberation Front, demanded the release of 50 Palestinians held by Israel. They threatened to blow up the ship and kill their prisoners. The front was a faction that had broken away from the Palestinian Liberation Organization. The ship's captain, Gerardo de Rosa, urged in a radio broadcast that no one attempt to assault the ship.

The drama ended—or appeared to end—as abruptly as it began, when Egypt said, Oct. 9, that the hijackers had surrendered to a representative of the PLO. Egypt said the 4 men would be given safe conduct out of Egypt to an undisclosed location. Celebrations that followed the surrender ended abruptly when Italy announced that Leon Klinghoffer, a 69-year-old American confined to a wheelchair, had been shot to death and thrown overboard. His wife, Marilyn, who was traveling with him, was unharmed. Condemnation of the hijacking was universal. Israel called on Egypt to prosecute the perpetrators. The hijacking was deplored in the Arab world as an event that had hurt the Arab cause. After the men surrendered, it was reported that their original plan had been to remain on the ship undetected until it reached Ashdod, Israel, where they intended to take Israeli hostages. The latter were to be seized in reprisal for the Israeli bombing of a PLO headquarters in Tunis, Oct. 1. But it was reported that the 4 Palestinians decided to act when their weapons were discovered by the ship's crew. After their original plans fell through, it was reported that PLO Chairman Yasir Arafat sent Muhammed Abbas, leader of the PLF faction, with whom he maintained good relations, to take control of the 4 Palestinians. The whereabouts of the hijackers on the morning of Oct. 10 was unclear; Egyptian Pres. Hosni Mubarak said that he thought they were in the hands of the PLO and that they had left the country. The White House said Egypt had turned down American pleas to prosecute the 4 men. They did not, in fact, leave Egypt until that evening aboard a commercial 737 airliner bound for Tunis and presumed release to the PLO.

The Reagan administration, frustrated by its inability to act effectively against hijackers and bombers in previous incidents in the Middle East, moved effectively in this case. Reagan ordered the Egyptian plane intercepted in midair in international air space, and the action was carried out by Navy F-14 fighter jets, which forced the plane to land in Sicily. No shots were fired. Italian authorities took the hijackers into custody. Egypt, Oct. 11, condemned the interception and denied reports that it had been in collusion with the United States and Italy to allow the hijackers to be transported to Italy. Reagan said, Oct. 11, that the message of the interception to hijackers everywhere was, "You can run, but you can't hide." He added, "What we want is justice done." A public prosecutor in Italy, Oct. 11, charged the 4 hijackers with murder and kidnapping. The United States, Oct. 12, issued a warrant for the arrest of Abbas, who with another Palestinian had accompanied the hijackers on the plane that was forced to land in Italy. U.S. officials said Abbas had planned the hijacking and had a record of terrorist activities. However, Abbas and the other Palestinian left Italy and went to Yugoslavia shortly thereafter, much to the expressed irritation of U.S. officials. Mubarak stepped up his criticism of the United States, Oct. 12, calling the plane incident "piracy." In a statement issued Oct. 13, the White House said it was "incomprehensible" that Italy had let Abbas leave. The United States asked Yugoslavia to place him in custody until formal extradition proceedings began. It was reported, Oct. 14, however, that Abbas had left Yugoslavia.

Italy said, Oct. 15, that it had formally charged 2 more suspects in the hijacking. The hijackers had reportedly claimed that Klinghoffer died of a heart attack, but U.S. officials confirmed, Oct. 16, that a body washed ashore on the Syrian coast was that of the American and that he had been shot.

right to strike. The decree also strengthened the hand of the official censor.

General

Mud Slides Kill Hundreds in Puerto Rico — Hundreds of residents of a hillside shantytown north of Ponce, Puerto Rico, died, **Oct. 7,** when mud slides swept downward, burying almost everything in their path. Gov. Rafael Hernandez Colon described it as the "worst tragedy to ever strike the island." The community of Mamayes was the center of the worst devastation, with hundreds of homes destroyed, but flooding elsewhere also claimed a heavy toll. Heavy rains had soaked the soil on the hillsides and increased its weight. By **Oct. 11,** officials had put the death toll at more than 500.

Disasters — A ferry broke in half and sank in the Karnaphuli River in Bangladesh, **Oct. 5,** after hitting a trawler, and it was feared that as many as 100 people had drowned.

Population Projections, by Region and for Selected Countries: 1990 to 2025

Source: Population Division of the United Nations

(in millions)

Region and Country	1990	1995	2000	2025	Region and Country	1990	1995	2000	2025
World, total	5,248.5	5,679.3	6,127.1	8,177.1	China: Mainland	1,119.6	1,184.2	1,255.7	1,460.1
More developed[1]	1,208.5	1,242.8	1,275.7	1,396.7	Hong Kong	6.1	6.6	6.9	7.9
Less developed[1]	4,039.7	4,436.4	4,851.5	6,780.4	Japan	122.7	125.1	127.7	127.6
Africa	645.3	753.2	877.4	1,642.9	Korea, Dem. People's Rep. of	22.4	24.9	27.3	37.6
Eastern Africa[2]	189.7	224.7	266.2	531.4	Korea, Rep. of	43.8	46.8	49.5	58.6
Burundi	5.3	6.1	7.0	11.0	South Asia	1,740.2	1,909.4	2,073.7	2,770.6
Ethiopia	42.7	50.1	58.4	112.0	Eastern So. Asia[2]	440.4	480.8	519.7	684.7
Kenya	25.4	31.4	38.5	82.9	Burma	44.5	49.8	55.2	82.2
Madagascar	11.6	13.4	15.6	29.7	Indonesia	178.4	191.9	204.5	255.3
Malawi	8.3	9.8	11.7	23.2	Kampuchea	8.4	9.2	9.9	12.5
Mozambique	16.2	18.8	21.8	39.7	Laos	5.0	5.6	6.2	9.2
Rwanda	7.3	8.8	10.6	22.2	Malaysia	17.3	19.1	20.6	26.9
Somalia	5.9	6.2	7.1	13.2	Philippines	61.4	68.3	74.8	102.3
Uganda	18.8	22.5	26.8	52.3	Singapore	2.7	2.9	3.0	3.2
Tanzania	27.0	32.5	39.1	83.8	Thailand	56.2	61.1	66.1	86.3
Zambia	7.9	9.4	11.2	23.8	Vietnam	65.4	71.7	78.1	105.1
Zimbabwe	10.5	12.6	15.1	32.7	Middle So. Asia[2]	1,169.9	1,279.9	1,385.7	1,815.9
Middle Africa[2]	71.9	83.0	96.1	183.5	Afghanistan	19.3	21.7	24.2	35.9
Angola	10.0	11.5	13.2	24.5	Bangladesh	115.2	130.3	145.8	219.4
Cameroon	11.1	12.6	14.4	25.2	India	831.9	899.1	961.5	1,188.5
Cen. African Rep.	2.9	3.3	3.7	6.7	Iran	51.8	58.7	65.5	96.2
Chad	5.7	6.4	7.3	13.1	Nepal	18.5	20.7	23.0	33.9
Zaire	38.4	44.8	52.4	104.4	Pakistan	113.3	128.0	142.6	212.8
Northern Africa[2]	143.8	164.3	185.7	295.0	Sri Lanka	18.0	19.5	20.8	26.2
Algeria	26.0	30.5	35.2	57.3	Western So. Asia[2]	129.9	148.7	168.3	270.0
Egypt	52.7	58.9	65.2	97.4	Iraq	18.5	21.6	24.9	42.7
Libya	4.3	5.2	6.1	11.1	Israel	4.7	5.0	5.4	7.0
Morocco	27.6	31.9	36.3	59.9	Jordan	4.3	5.2	6.4	13.4
Sudan	24.9	28.7	32.9	55.4	Lebanon	3.0	3.3	3.6	5.2
Tunisia	8.1	8.9	9.7	13.6	Saudi Arabia	13.5	16.1	18.9	33.5
Southern Africa[2]	42.3	48.1	54.5	90.7	Syria	12.8	15.3	18.1	32.3
South Africa	36.8	41.6	46.9	76.3	Turkey	56.0	62.4	68.5	99.3
Western Africa[2]	197.6	233.1	275.0	542.4	Yemen Arab Rep.	7.5	8.6	9.9	16.5
Benin	4.7	5.4	6.4	12.2	Europe (excl. Soviet Union)	499.5	506.5	513.1	526.9
Burkina Faso[3]	8.0	9.1	10.5	19.5	Eastern Europe	115.7	118.2	121.0	131.2
Ghana	15.9	18.7	21.9	37.7	Bulgaria	9.4	9.6	9.7	10.2
Guinea	6.1	7.0	7.9	13.9	Czechoslovakia	16.0	16.3	16.8	18.8
Ivory Coast	11.5	13.4	15.6	28.1	German Dem. Rep.	16.6	16.5	16.6	16.1
Mali	9.3	10.7	12.4	21.4	Hungary	10.8	10.8	10.9	10.9
Niger	7.1	8.3	9.8	18.9	Poland	39.0	40.2	41.4	45.9
Nigeria	113.3	135.5	161.9	338.1	Romania	23.9	24.8	25.6	29.2
Senegal	7.5	8.7	10.0	18.9	Northern Europe[2]	82.6	83.0	83.4	83.6
Togo	3.4	3.9	4.6	9.0	Denmark	5.2	5.1	5.1	4.8
Latin America	453.2	501.3	550.0	786.6	Finland	4.9	5.0	5.0	4.8
Caribbean[2]	34.6	37.7	40.8	57.7	Ireland	3.8	4.0	4.2	5.2
Cuba	10.5	11.2	11.7	13.6	Norway	4.2	4.2	4.2	4.3
Dominican Rep.	7.0	7.7	8.4	12.2	Sweden	8.2	8.2	8.1	7.5
Haiti	7.5	8.6	9.9	18.3	United Kingdom	55.8	56.0	56.2	56.4
Middle America[2]	119.7	134.4	149.6	222.6	Southern Europe[2]	146.4	150.0	153.1	162.8
El Salvador	6.5	7.5	8.7	15.0	Albania	3.4	3.8	4.1	5.8
Guatemala	9.7	11.1	12.7	21.7	Greece	10.2	10.5	10.7	11.8
Honduras	5.1	6.0	7.0	13.3	Italy	57.4	57.9	58.2	56.9
Mexico	89.0	99.2	109.2	154.1	Portugal	10.4	10.7	11.0	11.9
Nicaragua	3.9	4.5	5.3	9.2	Spain	40.5	42.0	43.4	49.2
Temperate South America[2]	49.1	52.3	55.5	70.1	Yugoslavia	23.9	24.6	25.2	26.6
Argentina	32.9	35.1	37.2	47.4	Western Europe[2]	154.8	155.3	155.6	149.3
Chile	13.1	14.0	14.9	18.8	Austria	7.5	7.5	7.5	7.3
Uruguay	3.1	3.2	3.4	3.9	Belgium	9.9	9.9	9.9	9.8
Tropical South America[2]	249.8	276.9	304.1	436.3	France	55.4	56.3	57.1	58.5
Bolivia	7.3	8.4	9.7	18.3	Germany, Fed. Rep. of	60.7	60.3	59.8	53.8
Brazil	150.4	165.1	179.5	245.8	Netherlands	14.7	14.9	15.0	14.6
Colombia	31.8	34.9	38.0	51.7	Switzerland	6.2	6.0	5.9	4.9
Ecuador	10.9	12.7	14.6	25.7	Soviet Union	291.3	303.1	314.8	367.1
Paraguay	4.2	4.8	5.4	8.6	Oceania[2]	26.7	28.5	30.4	39.5
Peru	22.3	25.1	28.0	41.0	Australia	16.7	17.7	18.7	23.5
Venezuela	21.3	24.2	27.2	42.8	New Zealand	3.4	3.6	3.7	4.2
Northern America[2]	275.2	286.8	297.7	347.3	Papua New Guinea	4.2	4.8	5.3	8.2
Canada	27.1	28.3	29.4	34.4					
United States	248.0	258.3	268.1	312.7					
East Asia[2]	1,317.2	1,390.4	1,470.0	1,696.1					

(1) Regions. (2) Includes countries not shown separately. (3) Formerly Upper Volta.

U.S. District Courts—Civil and Criminal Cases: 1965 to 1983

Source: Administrative Office of the U.S. Courts, *Annual Report of the Director*.

(In thousands, except percent)

Item	1965	1970	1975	1976	1977	1978	1979	1980	1981	1982	1983
Civil cases:											
Commenced.	67.7	87.3	117.3	130.6	130.6	138.8	154.7	168.8	180.6	206.2	241.8
Cases terminated[1] . .	63.1	79.5	103.8	108.3	115.5	123.2	140.0	155.0	172.9	185.5	213.6
No court action . .	29.3	31.1	39.2	41.7	45.2	45.3	60.2	68.7	72.1	81.6	99.0
Court action, total .	33.8	48.4	64.6	66.6	70.3	77.8	79.9	86.2	100.8	103.9	114.6
Before pretrial. .	17.1	29.4	40.3	41.6	43.5	48.7	49.7	53.8	61.1	67.3	75.9
Pretrial.	9.4	11.0	15.6	16.2	17.7	19.7	20.5	22.4	28.3	25.3	27.1
Trials	7.3	8.0	8.7	8.8	9.0	9.4	9.6	10.1	11.4	11.3	11.6
Percent reaching trial	11.6	10.0	8.4	8.1	7.8	7.6	6.9	6.5	6.6	6.1	5.4
Criminal cases:											
Commenced[2]	31.6	38.1	41.1	39.1	39.8	34.6	31.5	28.0	30.4	31.6	34.7
Defendants disposed of[3]	33.7	36.4	49.2	51.6	53.2	45.9	41.2	36.6	38.1	40.5	43.3
Not convicted . . .	5.0	8.2	11.8	11.5	11.7	9.4	8.3	8.0	8.3	8.2	7.7
Dismissed	3.8	6.6	10.3	9.8	10.0	7.8	6.8	6.6	7.0	7.1	6.6
Acquitted.	1.2	1.6	1.5	1.7	1.8	1.6	1.5	1.3	1.3	1.2	1.2
Convicted.	28.8	28.2	37.4	40.1	41.5	36.5	32.9	28.6	29.9	32.3	35.6
By guilty plea[4]. .	25.9	24.1	31.8	34.0	35.3	31.1	27.3	23.1	24.3	27.4	30.5
By court or jury .	2.8	4.1	5.6	6.1	6.1	5.4	5.6	5.5	5.5	4.9	5.1
Imprisonment . .	13.7	12.4	17.3	18.5	19.6	17.4	14.6	13.2	13.7	15.9	17.9
Probation	10.8	11.4	17.9	18.2	16.1	14.5	13.5	11.1	12.2	12.7	14.1
Fine and other. .	4.3	4.4	2.2	3.4	5.8	4.6	4.9	4.4	4.0	3.7	3.6

(1) Excludes land condemnation cases. (2) Exlcudes transfers. (3) Includes DC, beginning 1975; Guam and Virgin Islands beginning 1977; Northern Mariana Islands beginning 1978; and Canal Zone, 1977 through 1982. (4) Includes nolo contendere.

U.S. District Courts—Criminal Cases Commenced and Defendants Disposed of, by Nature of Offense: 1982 to 1983

Nature of Offense	1982 Cases commenced[1]	Defendants disposed of[3]	1983 cases commenced[1]	Not convicted		Convicted[2]			Sentenced		Fine and other
				Total	Ac- quited	Total	Guilty plea[3]	By court or jury	Im- prison- ment	Proba- tion	
Total[4]	31,264	40,466	34,681	7,738	1,172	35,591	30,523	5,068	17,886	14,097	3,608
General offenses:											
Homicide.	151	172	156	36	16	117	72	45	90	8	19
Robbery	1,428	1,745	1,333	169	33	1,360	1,077	283	1,269	88	3
Assault	579	606	543	165	33	436	325	111	273	147	16
Burglary	143	174	181	30	1	173	155	18	125	48	—
Larceny—theft. . .	2,887	3,557	3,385	663	105	3,536	3,177	359	1,622	1,786	128
Embezzlement and fraud	6,780	7,976	7,661	1,338	265	7,828	6,925	903	3,054	4,565	209
Auto theft.	369	519	347	90	15	461	392	69	320	140	1
Forgery, counterfeiting . . .	2,128	2,280	2,322	387	51	2,365	2,138	227	1,309	1,047	9
Sex offenses. . . .	135	143	140	30	10	100	77	23	80	19	1
DAPCA[5]	4,192	7,981	5,024	1,674	281	7,490	5,774	1,716	5,449	1,893	148
Misc. general offenses	8,759	9,187	9,881	2,304	243	7,345	6,435	910	2,539	2,203	2,603

(1) Excludes transfers. (2) Convicted and sentenced. (3) Includes nolo contendere. (4) Includes items not shown separately. (5) All marihuana, narcotics and controlled substances prosecutions under the Drug Abuse, Prevention and Control Act.

U.S. District Courts—Trials: 1965 to 1983

A trial is defined as a contested proceeding (other than a hearing on a motion) before either court or jury in which evidence is introduced and final judgment sought.

Type of Trial	1965	1970	1975	1976	1977	1978	1979	1980	1981	1982	1983
Total	11,485	16,032	19,236	19,580	18,827	18,851	18,563	19,825	21,239	21,397	21,345
Civil trials	7,613	9,449	11,603	11,656	11,605	11,515	11,764	13,191	14,697	14,753	14,689
Nonjury.	4,459	6,078	7,903	8,098	7,792	8,236	8,348	9,254	10,047	10,074	9,712
Jury.	3,154	3,371	3,700	3,558	3,813	3,189	3,416	3,937	4,650	4,679	4,977
Criminal trials.	3,872	6,583	7,633	7,924	7,222	7,336	6,799	6,634	6,542	6,644	6,656
Nonjury.	1,143	2,357	2,726	2,773	2,661	3,344	3,132	3,216	2,962	3,076	3,003
Jury.	2,729	4,226	4,907	5,151	4,561	3,992	3,667	3,418	3,580	3,568	3,653

U.S. Courts of Appeals: 1965 to 1983

Item	1965	1970	1975	1976	1977	1978	1979	1980	1981	1982	1983
Cases commenced[1] .	6,776	11,662	16,658	18,408	19,118	18,918	20,219	23,200	26,362	27,946	29,630
Criminal	1,223	2,660	4,187	4,650	4,738	4,487	4,102	4,405	4,377	4,767	4,790
U.S. civil.	1,387	2,167	2,981	3,327	3,622	3,928	3,983	4,654	4,940	5,517	5,820
Private civil	2,677	4,834	6,511	7,077	7,358	7,234	8,237	10,200	12,074	13,267	14,429
Administrative appeals	1,106	1,522	2,290	2,515	2,564	2,382	2,922	2,950	3,800	3,118	3,069
Cases terminated[1] . .	5,771	10,699	16,000	16,246	17,784	17,714	18,928	20,887	25,066	27,984	28,660
Criminal	1,014	2,581	4,005	4,238	4,554	4,461	4,320	3,993	4,192	4,522	4,777
U.S. civil.	1,229	1,912	3,094	2,853	3,198	3,437	3,857	4,346	5,021	5,508	5,585
Private civil	2,183	4,367	6,252	6,248	6,680	6,813	7,175	8,942	11,327	13,115	13,710
Administrative appeals	1,004	1,407	1,909	2,359	2,510	2,256	2,602	2,643	3,303	3,549	3,260
Cases disposed of[2] . .	3,546	6,139	9,077	9,351	11,400	8,850	9,361	10,607	12,168	12,720	13,217
Affirmed or granted . .	2,635	4,626	6,763	6,995	7,826	6,717	7,125	8,017	9,004	9,560	10,174
Reversed or denied .	773	1,280	1,632	1,680	1,715	1,536	1,548	1,845	2,246	2,138	2,173
Other	138	233	682	676	1,859	597	688	745	918	1,022	870
Median months[3] . . .	8.0	8.2	7.4	7.1	7.0	8.0	8.1	8.9	9.3	8.9	8.6

(1) Includes original proceedings and bankruptcy appeals not shown separately. (2) After hearing or submission. Beginning 1975, data not comparable with earlier years due to changes in criteria. (3) From filing of complete record to final disposition.

U.S. Supreme Court—Cases Filed and Disposition: 1970 to 1983

Source: Office of the Clerk, Supreme Court of the United States

Action	1970	1975	1976	1977	1978	1979	1980	1981	1982	1983
Total cases on docket	4,212	4,761	4,731	4,704	4,731	4,781	5,144	5,311	5,079	5,099
Appellate cases on docket	1,903	2,352	2,324	2,341	2,383	2,509	2,749	2,935	2,710	2,688
From prior term.	325	431	452	472	434	425	527	522	545	520
Docketed during present term.	1,578	1,921	1,872	1,869	1,949	2,084	2,222	2,413	2,165	2,168
Cases acted upon	1,613	1,900	2,019	1,979	2,023	2,050	'2,234	'2,513	'2,279	'2,220
Granted review	214	244	237	224	210	199	167	203	169	140
Denied, dismissed or withdrawn	1,285	1,538	1,620	1,676	1,734	1,776	1,999	2,100	1,892	1,902
Summarily decided . . .	114	118	162	79	79	75	90	114	113	71
Cases not acted upon . .	290	452	305	362	360	459	425	422	413	468
Pauper cases on docket . . .	2,289	2,395	2,398	2,349	2,331	2,249	2,371	2,354	2,352	2,394
Cases acted upon	1,802	1,997	2,083	1,960	1,996	1,838	'2,027	'2,039	'2,013	'1,992
Granted review	41	28	30	24	27	32	17	7	10	9
Denied, dismissed or withdrawn	1,683	1,903	2,013	1,899	1,938	1,757	1,968	2,014	1,995	1,968
Summarily decided . . .	78	66	40	37	31	49	32	12	6	10
Cases not acted upon . .	487	398	315	389	335	411	344	315	339	402
Original cases on docket. . .	20	14	8	14	17	23	24	22	17	17
Cases disposed of during term.	7	7	2	3	—	1	7	6	3	5
Total cases available for argument	267	280	269	260	249	238	264	318	312	269
Cases disposed of	160	181	181	185	170	160	162	192	199	189
Cases argued	151	179	176	172	168	156	154	184	183	184
Cases dismissed or remanded without argument	9	2	5	13	2	4	8	8	16	5
Cases remaining	107	99	88	75	79	78	102	126	113	80
Cases decided by signing opinion	126	160	154	153	153	143	144	170	174	174
Causes decided by per curiam opinion	22	16	22	8	8	12	8	10	6	6
Number of signed opinions	109	138	126	129	130	130	123	141	151	151

(1) Includes cases granted review and carried over to next term, not shown separately.

Major Decisions of the U.S. Supreme Court, 1984-85

The 1984-85 Supreme Court term began October 1 and concluded July 2. The court received petitions in 4,043 cases and decided 175, a ration of one decision for every 23 petitions filed. There were 139 signed opinions, the lowest number in five years; 59 decisions came without a dissenting vote, an unusually high degree of unanimity. Among the notable actions, the Supreme Court:

Ruled, unanimously, in a summary decision, to overturn a Louisiana murder conviction, evidence for which had been obtained by police at the crime scene without a warrant. The decision reaffirmed a 1978 high court ruling requiring police to obtain a warrant before searching a murder scene. (Nov. 26)

Declined to hear a challenge to a decision dismissing a sex bias suit against a university. The predominantly female nursing faculty of the Univ. of Washington, using the idea of "comparable worth," had argued that it should be paid salaries equal to those of the faculty of other departments, which were predominantly male. (Nov. 26)

Ruled, unanimously, that the federal government need pay only the fair market value of local public property taken over for a federal project. (Dec. 4)

Ruled, 6-3, to widen the interpretation of a federal law that made it a crime to assault or rob a custodian of "mail matter, or of any money or other property of the U.S." The case concerned two men convicted under the law of attempting to rob a Secret Service agent. The defendants attempted to overturn that conviction on the ground that the law was restricted to crimes involving employees of the Postal Service. (Dec. 10)

Ruled, unanimously, that a narcotics conspiracy conviction could not be set aside merely because a jury had found the defendant guilty on some counts and acquitted him on others. (Dec. 10)

Ruled, unanimously, to reinstate the federal bank robbery conviction of a member of the Aryan Brotherhood, as secret organization of white prison inmates. This reversed an appeals court ruling that the defendant's trial had been tainted when the judge allowed testimony that the defendant was a member of the group. (Dec. 10)

Ruled, 8-0, that a defendant could not have his federal narcotics conviction overturned on the ground that he had been afraid to testify in his own behalf for fear of revealing a prior conviction. (Dec. 10)

Refused to review a federal appeals court ruling setting payment of $60 million in back pay that Northwest Airlines owed to 3,352 women flight attendants for illegal discrimination against them. (Jan. 14)

Ruled, 6-3, that public school officials could legally search students if there were "reasonable grounds" to suspect this would bring evidence of a violation of the law or school rules. The court said that the "substantial interest" of school officials in maintaining discipline must be balanced against the interest of the students in privacy. (Jan. 15)

Refused to review a ruling upholding an affirmative action plan with the goal of increasing promotions among minority corrections officers in New York State. (Jan. 7)

Ruled, unanimously, that police need not have a warrant or "probable cause" to stop and briefly detain someone suspected of involvement in a past crime in another jurisdiction. (Jan. 8)

Ruled, unanimously, that Trans World Airlines had violated a federal law by requiring pilots to retire at age 60, rather than permitting them to assume other cockpit duties. The high court held that the TWA policy violated the federal Age Discrimination in Employment Act. (Jan. 8)

Ruled, 5-4, that the federal Copyright Act of 1976 permitted a music publisher to continue earning royalties on a song after the copyright owner had terminated the contract with the publisher. (Jan. 8)

Ruled, unanimously, that federal bankruptcy law protected toxic waste polluters from civil penalties. However, the court said that the state could prosecute a bankrupt polluter for criminal contempt—in this case for not obeying an order to clean up a waste site before declaring bankruptcy —or for violation of state environmental laws. (Jan. 9)

Ruled, unanimously, that states could be held liable for unintentional discrimination against the handicapped under the federal Rehabilitation Act of 1983. A group of handicapped people had sued Tennessee under the law because of the state's reduction of some Medicaid benefits. The high court held that Congress had intended the law to protect disabled persons not only from intentional discrimination but from state officials' "thoughtlessness and indifference." (Jan. 9)

Ruled, unanimously, that the obligation to file a federal tax return on time was with the taxpayer, not his or her accountant, attorney, or whoever else might have actually prepared the return. (Jan. 9)

Ruled, unanimously, that the Internal Revenue Service could use an ordinary summons, instead of seeking a court order, to obtain information from a taxpayer during an investigation of a tax shelter involving unidentified partners. (Jan. 9)

Ruled, 5-4, that a state government could not specify how individual counties were to spend federal funds received under the Payment in Lieu of Taxes Act, which compensated counties for loss of tax revenue if they contained federal lands. (Jan. 9)

Ruled, 7-2, to overturn an appeals court ruling and approve the dismissal, in a murder case, of a potential juror who had expressed doubts about the death penalty. (Jan. 21)

Ruled, 7-2, that a criminal defendant had the right to effective counsel on appeal. (Jan. 21)

Ruled, 9-1, that the city of Memphis could be held liable for damages assessed against its chief of police, although a damage suit named only the police chief as defendant. (Jan. 21)

Ruled, 5-4, to uphold the application of federal minimum wage and overtime pay laws to state employees. In a major constitutional decision and a rare reversal of the court's own ruling, in 1976, the high court maintained that federal wage laws were binding on state and local governments. (Feb. 19)

Ruled, 8-1, that states must provide free psychiatric assistance for those pleading not guilty by reason of insanity. The court noted that 41 states had already made available "the psychiatrist's expertise." This ruling was the high court's first in years to expand the basic constitutional rights of criminal defendants. (Feb. 26)

Ruled, 5-4, to uphold the Environmental Protection Agency's authority to grant waivers from clean-water standards on toxic discharges for plants atypical of their category. (Feb. 27)

Ruled, 6-4, to allow a variation to the Miranda rule in a case involving one confession made before the suspect was told of his rights and the other made afterward. A state appeals court upset the subsequent conviction on the ground that after the first confession the "cat was sufficiently out of the bag to exert a coercive impact. . ." The high court reversed this finding. (Mar. 4)

Ruled, 5-4, to uphold the right of Oneida Indian Nation in upper New York State to sue for damages for land taken from them in 1795. (Mar. 4)

Ruled, unanimously, that passengers injured on international flights could not sue the carrier for damages unless the injury were caused by unusual or unexpected circumstances. (Mar. 4)

Ruled, 7-2, to void the $1,000 limit on spending by "PACs"—independent political action committees—to help elect presidential nominees. Deciding that the limit imposed by a 1971 law was a violation of the First Amendment guarantee of free speech, the high court noted that large spending by PACs had "a potential for corruption," but the $1,000 limit was a "fatally overbroad response." (Mar. 18)

Ruled, 7-2, to uphold the federal government's selective prosecution of draft resistors who openly showed their defiance. (Mar. 19)

Ruled, 8-1, to uphold the right of a public employee to a hearing before being fired. The high court said the worker was "entitled to oral or written notice of the charges against him, an explanation of the employer's evidence, and the opportunity to present his side of the story." (Mar. 19)

Ruled, 5-4, that workers on offshore oil drilling platforms in state waters were not covered by federal death and disability benefits, because this work was not "maritime employment," as required by the Longshoremen's and Harbor Workers' Compensation Act. (Mar. 20)

Ruled, unanimously, that an armed robbery suspect in Virginia could not be required to have surgery for removal of a bullet sought as evidence. The court deemed the surgery an unreasonable search, and as such prohibited by the Fourth Amendment. (Mar. 20)

Ruled, 8-0, that Florida police had violated the Fourth Amendment by taking a crime suspect from his house to a police station for fingerprinting, without his consent, "probable cause," or a warrant. However, the court held that this did not rule out the police's fingerprinting a suspect on the street. (Mar. 20)

Ruled, 7-2, that the Fourth Amendment protection against unreasonable seizure was not violated by a 20-minute roadside detention by police. (Mar. 20)

Ruled, 5-4, that Alabama violated the Equal Protection clause of the Constitution when granting preferential tax treatment to locally based companies in order to promote business and investment. However, the decision left open the possibility that such a tax could have another justification. (Mar. 26)

Ruled, 7-2, that federal antitrust laws did not preclude groups of truckers from forming "rate bureaus" to collectively set rates for intrastate shipments. (Mar. 27)

Automatically upheld, by a 4-4 deadlock, a federal appeals court ruling that declared unconstitutional as a violation of free speech, an Oklahoma law calling for the dismissal of any teacher advocating homosexual conduct. (Mar. 26)

Ruled, unanimously, that a defendant could not be convicted for possession of a firearm and for receiving that same firearm, despite separate federal laws against "possessing" a firearm and against a convicted felon's "receiving" a firearm. (Mar. 26)

Ruled, 6-3, that police did not have the right to shoot fleeing criminal suspects who were not armed or dangerous. (Mar 27)

Affirmed, unanimously, the CIA's right to invoke the National Security Act as the basis for withholding the identity of its information sources from public disclosure. (Apr. 16)

Affirmed, 8-0, the right of the Navaho Indian tribe to impose taxes on businesses conducted by outsiders on their land. (Apr. 16)

Ruled, unanimously, that a tax-exempt religious organization must pay the federal minimum wage to workers operating its business facilities. (Apr. 23)

Declined to hear an appeal on a ruling concerning the largest municipal-bond default in the country's history. The ruling absolved 88 municipal utilities and local governments from liability for $2.25 billion in bonds issued by the Washington Public Power Supply System. (Apr. 29)

Declined to review a ruling by a federal appeals court that the Environmental Protection Agency could order the recall of cars beyond the "useful life" category, as defined by the

Clean Air Act—five years or 50,000 miles, whichever came first. (Apr. 29)

Ruled, 6-3, to uphold the search of motor homes by police without search warrants. Since the motor homes could be easily driven away, before a warrant could be obtained, the court deemed them in the same category as cars, rather than houses. (May 13)

Refused to review an appeal by the Chicago board of education for more federal funding for its desegregation program after the government had sent the city a single payment of $20 million for this purpose. (May 20)

Ruled, 6-3, that *The Nation* magazine infringed on a copyright in 1979 by publishing without permission excerpts from a copyrighted book by former U.S. President Gerald R. Ford. *The Nation* claimed the "fair use" privilege for news reporting, since the information was by a public figure about public events of broad public concern. However, the high court said the magazine's use of material exceeded the fair use exception. (May 20)

Ruled, 5-3, to uphold the right of an attorney to advertise in a newspaper or magazine, soliciting clients on specific legal problems. The court said that legal advice was protected by the First Amendment's guarantee of freedom of speech. (May 28)

Ruled, 8-1, in two separate decisions, to rule out an exemption from federal securities law for stock sales aimed at ownership or control of a closely-held business. (May 28)

Ruled, 6-3, to affirm a federal appellate ruling striking down an Alabama law that authorized a daily one-minute period of silence in public schools for "meditation or voluntary prayer." According to the high court, the law was unconstitutional because it endorsed religion as a "favored practice." This decision came as a surprise to many, who expected the conservative court to ease Constitutional strictures between government and religion. (June 4)

Ruled, unanimously, to uphold a Massachusetts law requiring employer-sponsored health insurance plans to include mental-health care. The decision was significant because perhaps as many as 26 states had similar laws requiring that plans cover treatment for specific problems including alcoholism, neonatal care, and outpatient kidney-dialysis. (June 3)

Ruled, 8-0, to uphold an agreement between Massachusetts and Connecticut, authorizing bank mergers across state lines by New England banks but excluding banks from states outside this region. Some 15 states had authorized regional interstate bank mergers. (June 10)

Ruled, unanimously, that stock market newsletters not representing a brokerage firm or a client's stock, need not be regulated by the Securities and Exchange Commission. (June 10)

Ruled, unanimously, that an investor who traded illegally on inside information was not barred by that fact from suing the broker or corporate insider who passed on a false or misleading tip. (June 10)

Ruled, unanimously, that a business cooperative's move against an individual business was not an automatic violation of antitrust laws, the key determination being whether the action produced "predominantly anticompetitive effects." (June 11)

Ruled, 5-3, to strike down a death sentence in Mississippi, where death sentences were automatically reviewed by the state's highest court, because the prosecutor had told the jurors that the ultimate responsibility for a death penalty would not rest with them but on the state Supreme Court. (June 11)

Ruled 8-0, to re-establish the criteria that employers need meet in order to force people to retire before age 70. The court said the employer must show either that a particular age was "reasonably necessary to the normal operations of the particular business" and that "all or nearly all employees above an age lack the qualifications" or that it was "highly impractical" to test each employee for impairment by age. (June 17)

Ruled, 9-0, that the age-55 retirement rule of federal firefighters did not automatically validate similar retirement policies for state and local fire departments. (June 17)

Declined to hear an appeal by the National Association for the Advancement of Colored People (NAACP) against the continued use of its initials by the NAACP Legal Defense and Education Fund, originally the NAACP's legal arm but a separate entity for many years. In 1982, the NAACP brought suit against the fund for trademark infringement, and a federal district court backed the NAACP, but an appeals court ruled that the NAACP had waited too long to sue. (June 17)

Ruled 5-4, in two separate decisions, to reaffirm separation of church and state by voiding two programs of public aid to parochial schools. The court deemed it unconstitutional to use public funds to pay for teaching in religious schools, even if the teachers were public school teachers and the courses non-religious. (July 1)

Ruled, 8-1, to strike down a Connecticut law that an employee could not be required to work on his or her Sabbath. (June 26)

Ruled, 5-4, that a labor union could not fire a member for resigning during a strike and returning to work. The court said the National Labor Relations Act not only guaranteed an employee the right to bargain collectively, but also "the right to refrain from any or all" collective activity. (June 27)

Major Actions During the 99th Congress, 1985

The 99th Congress convened Jan. 3. Bills passed and signed and other major actions during the first three-fourths of the session included the following:

Aid to Farmers Vetoed. On Mar. 6, in his first veto of his second term in office, Pres. Reagan struck down legislation designed to give aid to farmers faced with severe liquidity problems. The bill switched crop support payments from Fall to Spring, increased the emergency farm loan guarantee program, and allocated $100 million to banks that would cut rates on farm loans. Reagan referred to the bill as a "massive new bailout that would add billions to the deficit."

MX Missiles Authorized. Pres. Reagan emerged victorious from a difficult battle on Mar. 28, when the House voted 217-210 to appropriate $1.5 billion for the production of 21 new MX missiles. The Senate had authorized the missiles on Mar. 19, 55-45, and had approved the funds on Mar. 20 by the same margin. On May 23, the Reagan administration and Senate leaders agreed to limit to 50 the number of missiles that could be deployed in existing Minuteman silos. That ceiling was set up for one year. In addition, a production limit for the missiles in the 1986 fiscal year was changed from 48 to 12.

Aid to Nicaragua Voted. Pres. Reagan agreed, Apr. 18, on a compromise proposal to postpone military aid to the Nicaraguan contras. Reagan had been advised that his request for $14 million in military aid would be met with almost certain defeat in Congress. The Senate Appropriations

Committee voted, Apr. 18, 15-13, in favor of the compromise, and sent it to the Senate floor. However, the House, in a series of votes, Apr. 23-24, rejected all forms of aid to the Nicaraguan contras. There had been agreement on limiting the funds to humanitarian aid, but Democrats insisted that the release of the funds be tied to the resumption of direct talks between the Sandinista government and the U.S. administration. There was further disagreement over how the funds would be disbursed and who would monitor a truce. In a victory for the Reagan administration, June 6, the Senate voted, 55-42, to authorize $38 million over two years in nonmilitary aid to the Nicaraguan contras. In a further action the following day, the Senate approved, by voice vote, an amendment that would prohibit the use of U.S. funds for operations against Nicaragua that would contravene international law or the charter of the Organization of American States. A compromise phrase added at the last minute allowed such operations if specifically authorized under U.S. law. The compromise plan adopted by the House, June 12, was stricter in its interpretation of "humanitarian aid" than was the Senate bill. According to the House amendment, the funds could be used for such items as food, medicine and clothing, but not for weapons, ammunition, or material that could "inflict serious bodily harm or death." The aid would not be channeled through the Central Intelligence Agency or the Pentagon. The Senate measure provided for funds to be channeled through the CIA, and could permit the purchase of helicopters or radar. Differences between the two Houses would be resolved in conference.

IRS Law Repealed. The House and Senate repealed a new Internal Revenue law requiring people who drove cars on business to keep detailed accounts of business versus personal use of the vehicles. The House approved the repeal, Apr. 2, 412-1; the Senate approved it the next day, 92-1.

Sanctions Against South Africa. On June 5, the House approved, 295-127, a package of economic sanctions against South Africa. This was designed to help force an end to South Africa's apartheid system of racial segregation. The Senate Foreign Relations Committee had approved a similar bill, June 4.

Social Security Increased. The House, Oct. 2, passed a bill guaranteeing that Social Security benefits would increase in Jan. 1986, even if inflation remained low. The House approved the Social Security bill by a 417-4 vote. A similar bill had been passed by the Senate, July 26, and the Senate was expected to accept the House version. Pres. Reagan, who had requested the legislation in July, said he was prepared to sign it.

Disability Benefits Protected. Legislation intended to prevent disabled people from being unfairly removed from the Social Security disability rolls cleared Congress, Sept. 19, and was sent to Pres. Reagan, who had indicated that he would sign it. The legislation would make it more difficult for 3.8 million disabled people on the rolls to be deprived of their benefits. It required the government to show strong proof that an individual's condition had improved sufficiently for him or her to work; it also made it easier for a person with multiple disabilities to qualify for aid; and it would allow those cut from the rolls to keep receiving benefits while they appealed the decision.

Foreign Trade Legislation. Compromise legislation affecting U.S. foreign trade was passed by the House and Senate, Oct. 9. It included both free-trade and mildly protectionist provisions. The House passed the bill by a vote of 386-1, the Senate by a voice vote. Among the provisions was an extension of duty-free treatment for many imports from 140 developing nations. In other provisions, the President was authorized to seek free-trade agreements with Israel and Canada and to negotiate wide-ranging reductions in trade barriers.

Joint Budget Resolution. After months of struggle, the Senate and House finally approved, Aug. 1, a joint budget resolution. The compromise conference report called for outlays of $967.6 billion and revenues of $793.7 billion in fiscal 1986, to begin Oct. 1, 1985. Intended to reduce federal deficits for the next three years by $276.2 billion, the resolution claimed a $55.5 billion reduction in fiscal 1986. However, many who voted for it acknowledged that those figures were dependent upon continued economic recovery and were probably unrealistic. Defense was the main area where Pres. Reagan was forced to give ground. The budget allowed military spending to rise at the rate of inflation; it included no significant changes in taxes, and no change in the cost-of-living adjustments for Social Security and federal pension benefits; further, it avoided large decreases in aid and benefits programs for the poor, the elderly, and urban residents. The House approved the resolution, 309-119; the Senate, 67-32.

Deaths, Nov. 1, 1984—Oct. 22, 1985

A

Abruzzo, Ben, 54; balloonist who crossed the Atlantic and Pacific Oceans; Albuquerque, N.M., Feb. 11.

Adams, Tom, 53; prime minister of Barbados since 1976; Bridgetown, Barbados, Mar. 11.

Addams, Dawn, 54; British-born actress who appeared in films in the 1950s; London, May 7.

Adler, Luther, 81; character actor in films and the theater; Kutztown, Pa., Dec. 8.

Aiken, George, 92; U.S. Senator from Vermont, 1941-75; Montpelier, Vt., Nov. 19.

Andrews, Edward, 70; character actor in the theater and films; Santa Monica, Cal., Mar. 8.

Aleixandre, Vicente, 86; Spanish poet who was awarded the 1977 Nobel Prize for literature; Madrid, Dec. 14.

Ankers, Evelyn, 67; actress who starred in "B" movies in the 1930s and 1940s; Hawaii, Aug. 29.

Arends, Leslie, 89; U.S. representative from Illinois, 1935-75; Naples, Fla., July 16.

B

Ashley, Laura, 60; British designer who founded the fabric and clothing empire that bears her name; Coventry, England, Sept. 17.

Bartholomew, Frank, 86; former head of the United Press International news agency; Sonoma, Cal., Mar. 26.

Bauer, Charita, 62; actress who starred on the *Guiding Light* radio and TV daytime serial for 35 years; New York, Feb. 28.

Beard, James, 81; food authority and author of numerous cookbooks; New York, Jan. 23.

Beck, Julian, 60; director who founded the Living Theater; New York, Sept. 14.

Bell, Ricky, 29; former Tampa Bay Buccaneers running back; Inglewood, Cal., Nov. 28.

Blake, Eugene Carson, 78; Protestant leader in the 1950s and 1960s; Stamford, Conn., July 31.

Blanding, Sarah G., 86; educator who headed Vassar College, 1946-64; Newtown, Pa., Mar. 3.

Boll, Heinrich, 67; West German novelist who won the 1972 Nobel Prize for Literature; Cologne, July 16.

Boyle, W.A. "Tony", 83; leader of the United Mine Workers Union 1963-72; convicted of ordering rival in UMW killed; Wilkes-Barre, Pa., May 31.

Brady, Scott, 60; actor who appeared in films and on TV; Woodland Hills, Cal., Apr. 17.

Bratteli, Trygve, 74; prime minister of Norway during the 1970s; Oslo, Nov. 20.

Brooks, Louise, 78; silent film star; Rochester, N.Y., Aug. 8.

Brown, Carter, 61; mystery novelist who authored some 270 books; Sydney, Australia, May 5.

Brynner, Yul, 65; actor who was identified with the role of the king in the musical *The King and I;* New York, Oct. 10.

Burnet, Sir Frank, 85; Australian microbiologist and virologist who shared the 1960 Nobel Prize for medicine; Melbourne, Aug. 31.

Burnham, Linden Forbes Sampson, 62; ruler of Guyana since 1964; Guyana, Aug. 6.

Burrows, Abe, 74; librettist, director, and author of numerous Broadway shows; New York, May 17.

Byrnes, John W., 71; U.S. representative from Wisconsin, 1945-73; Marshfield, Wis., Jan. 12.

C

Caldwell, Taylor, 84; prolific best-selling author, *Dear and Glorious Physician;* Greenwich, Conn., Aug. 30.

Calvino, Italo, 62; Italian novelist and short-story writer; Siena, Italy, Sept. 19.

Campbell, Kay, 80; actress who appeared in the *All My Children* daytime TV series for the past 15 years; Greenwich, Conn., May 27.

Canaday, John, 78; art critic for the *N.Y. Times,* 1959-76; New York, July 19.

Chagall, Marc, 97; Russian-born artist who was a major force in 20th-century art; St. Paul de Vence, France, Mar. 28.

Chandler, George, 86; actor who appeared in over 150 films; Los Angeles, June 10.

Charlotte, 89; ruler of Luxembourg for 45 years; Luxembourg, July 9.

Chernenko, Konstantin, 73; Soviet head of state; USSR, Mar. 10.

Claire, Ina, 92; actress who starred in the theater for 5 decades; San Francisco, Feb. 21.

Clarke, Kenny, 71; jazz drummer who helped originate be-bop; Paris, Jan. 25.

Clements, Earle, 88; governor of Kentucky, 1947-50; U.S. senator, 1950-56; Morganfield, Ky., Mar. 12.

Clinton, Larry, orchestra leader, composer and arranger during the big-band era; Green Valley, Ariz., May 2.

Colasanto, Nick, 61; actor who portrayed Coach in the *Cheers* TV sitcom; Los Angeles, Feb. 12.

Collingwood, Charles, 68; CBS News correspondent for more than 4 decades; New York, Oct. 3.

Coots, J. Fred, 87; composer of hundreds of songs, *Santa Claus is Coming to Town;* New York, Apr. 8.

Corena, Fernando, 67; Italian bass starred at the Metropolitan Opera from the 1950s through the 1970s; Lugano, Switzerland, Nov. 26.

Cowles, Jr., Gardner, 82; head of publishing empire; founded *Look* magazine; Southampton, N.Y., July 8.

Crane, Barry, 57; contract bridge expert who won more titles than anyone else in the game's history; Los Angeles, July 5.

D

Deckers, Jeanine, 52; former nun who as the "Singing Nun" had hit recording *Dominique* in th 1960s; Wavres, Belgium, Apr. 1.

Desmond, Johnny, 65; singer who was popular in the 1940s and 1950s; Los Angeles, Sept. 6.

Diamond, Selma, 64; comedy writer and actress who appeared on TV's *Night Court;* Los Angeles, May 16.

Dickenson, Vic, 78; jazz trombonist; New York, Nov. 16.

Dubuffet, Jean, 83; French painter and sculptor; Paris, May 12.

E

Ehricke, Krafft A., 67; German-born rocket pioneer and physicist; La Jolla, Cal., Dec. 11.

Eisenhower, Milton, 85; diplomat and educator; brother of the former president; Baltimore, May 2.

Elorde, Flash, 49; boxer who was the junior-lightweight champion in the 1960s; Manila, Jan. 2.

Enders, John F., 88; virologist who helped discover vaccines against polio, measles, and mumps; Waterford, Conn., Sept. 9.

Erlander, Tage F., 84; prime minister of Sweden, 1946-69; Huddinge, Sweden, June 21.

Ervin Jr., Sam, 88; U.S. senator from North Carolina, 1954-75; chaired the 1973 Senate Watergate committee; Winston-Salem, Apr. 23.

F

Faylen, Frank, 79; character actor who appeared in some 400 films; Burbank, Cal., Aug. 2.

Flory, Paul J., 75; chemist who won the 1974 Nobel Prize in chemistry; Big Sur, Cal., Sept. 9.

Foster, Phil, 72; comedian and actor who appeared on the *Laverne and Shirley* TV sitcom; Rancho Mirage, Cal., July 8.

Frazee, Jane, 67; actress who appeared in light movie musicals in the 1940s; Newport Beach, Cal., Sept. 6.

Funseth, Rod, 52; golfer who earned over $600,000 on the PGA tour; Napa, Cal., Sept. 9.

G

Gernreich, Rudi, 62; avant-garde fashion designer of the 1960s; Los Angeles, Apr. 21.

Goldman, Sylvan N., 86; businessman who invented the shopping cart; Oklahoma City, Nov. 25.

Gordon, Ruth, 88; character actress whose career spanned 70 years; Edgartown, Mass., Aug. 28.

Gould, Chester, 84; cartoonist who created the *Dick Tracy* strip; Woodstock, Ill., May 11.

Greene, Richard, 66; British actor who played Robin Hood on TV in the 1950s; London, June 1.

Guarnieri, Johnny, 67; jazz pianist; Livingston, N.J., Jan. 7.

H

Hamilton, Margaret, 82; actress who played the "Wicked Witch of the West" in film, *The Wizard of Oz;* Salisbury, Conn., May 16.

Lord Harlech (William David Ormsby Gore), 66; Britain's ambassador to the U.S. during the Kennedy and Johnson administration; Shrewsbury, England, Jan. 26.

Harris, Patricia Roberts, 60; secretary of HEW and HUD during the Carter administration; Washington, D.C., Mar. 23.

Hathaway, Henry, 86; director of over 60 Hollywood films; Los Angeles, Feb. 11.

Hauser, Gayelord, 89; pioneer health-food advocate and author, *Look Younger, Live Longer;* N. Hollywood, Cal., Dec. 26.

Haydon, Edward "Ted", 73; track and field coach; Chicago, May 3.

Hayes, Alfred, 74; novelist, poet, and screenwriter; Sherman Oaks, Cal., Aug. 14.

Hayward, Louis, 75; film actor who played swashbuckling heroes in the 1930s and 1940s; Palm Springs, Cal., Feb. 21.

Helstein, Ralph, 76; labor lawyer and trade union leader; Chicago, Feb. 14.

Hewitt, Foster, 83; sportscaster who was the voice of hockey in Canada; Toronto, Apr. 21.

Hill, Lister, 89; U.S. senator from Alabama, 1938-68; Montgomery, Ala., Dec. 20.

Himes, Chester, 75; novelist, *Cotton Comes to Harlem;* Moraira, Spain, Nov. 12.

Holt, John, 62; educator and author, *How Children Fail,* Boston, Sept. 14.

Hoxha, Enver, 76; head of the Albanian Communist Party and that nation's leader since World War II; Albania, Apr. 11.

Hudson, Rock, 59; actor who was a major star of films and TV; Los Angeles, Oct. 2.

Hutchinson, Edward, 70; U.S. representative from Michigan, 1963-77; Naples, Fla., July 22.

I

Ingersoll, Ralph, 84; journalist, author, and publisher; Miami Beach, Mar. 8.

J

Jacobs, Walter L., 88; founder of the first car rental agency which later became the Hertz Corp.; Miami, Feb. 6.

Jenner, William E., 76; U.S. senator from Indiana, 1947-59; Bedford, Ind., Mar. 9.

Jones, Jo, 73; jazz drummer who was influential in the swing era; New York, Sept. 3.

Jones, Philly Joe, 62; a leading modern jazz drummer; Philadelphia, Aug. 30.

Joy, Leatrice, 91; actress who was a leading star of silent films; New York, May 13.

K

Kelly, Charles "Commando," 64; the first enlisted man to receive the Congressional Medal of Honor in World War II; Pittsburgh, Jan. 11.

Kelly Jr., John B., 57; president of the U.S. Olympic Committee; Philadelphia, Mar. 2.

Kinard, Frank "Bruiser", 70; football player who was a charter member of the National Football Hall of Fame; Jackson, Miss., Sept. 7.

King Sr., Rev. Martin Luther, 84; religious leader and civil rights activist; father of the slain civil rights leader; Atlanta, Nov. 15.

King, Wayne, 84; saxophonist and bandleader whose waltzes made him a popular recording and radio star in the 1930s; Paradise Valley, Ariz., July 16.

Kokkinaki, Vladimir, 80; Soviet aviator who set many world records in the 1930s; Moscow, Jan. 7.

Koopmans, Tjalling C., 74; economist who won the 1975 Nobel Prize for Economic Science; New Haven, Feb. 26.

Kunkel, Bill, 48; former major league pitcher and umpire; Middletown, N.J., May 4.

Kyser, Kay, 79; band leader and radio program host in the 1940s; Chapel Hill, N.C., July 23.

L

Lang, Harold, 64; dancer who starred in several Broadway musicals; Chico, Cal., July 26.

Langer, Susanne K., 89; philosopher whose work affected thinking in psychology and the social sciences; Old Lyme, Conn., July 17.

Lawford, Peter, 61; British-born actor who appeared in some 50 films; Los Angeles, Dec. 24.

LeMaire, Charles, 88; costume designer for Broadway shows and films; won 3 Oscars; Palm Springs, Cal., June 8.

Le Roy, Hal, 71; tap dancer who appeared in clubs and the theater; Maywood, N.J., May 2.

List, Eugene, 66; concert pianist; New York, Mar. 1.

Lodge, Henry Cabot, 82; political leader served as U.S. senator, delegate to the UN, and ambassador to S. Vietnam; Beverly, Mass., Feb. 27.

London, George, 64; operatic bass-baritone; Armonk, N.Y., Mar. 24.

Long, Gillis W., 61; U.S. representative from Louisiana since 1972; Washington, D.C., Jan. 20.

M

MacInnes, Helen, 77; novelist who specialized in spy fiction; New York, Sept. 30.

Margo, 68; film actress of the 1930s and 1940s; Pacific Palisades, Cal., July 17.

Marks, Johnny, 75; songwriter best known for *Rudolph the Red-Nosed Reindeer;* New York, Sept. 3.

Marriott, J. Willard, 84; founder of the lodging and food service empire; Wolfeboro, N.H., Aug. 13.

Martin, John, 91; dance critic for the *N.Y. Times,* 1927-62; Saratoga, N.Y., May 19.

Miller, Arnold R., 62; president of the United Mine Workers of America in the 1970s; Charleston, W. Va., July 12.

Miller, Marvin, 71; actor who starred as Michael Anthony on the 1950s TV series, *The Millionaire;* Santa Monica, Cal., Feb. 8.

Mosher, Charles A., 78; U.S. representative from Ohio, 1961-77; Oberlin, Oh., Nov. 16.

Moyse, Marcel, 95; French flutest and author on flute techniques; Brattleboro, Vt., Nov. 1.

Mungo, Van Lingle, 73; pitcher for the Brooklyn Dodgers in the 1930s; Pageland, S.C., Feb. 12.

N

Naipaul, Shiva, 40; Trinidad-born author and journalist; London, Aug. 13.

Nash, Clarence, 80; the voice of Donald Duck who made over 150 cartoons and movies over 5 decades; Burbank, Cal., Feb. 20.

Nathan, Robert, 91; author who wrote some 50 books of poetry and prose, *Portrait of Jennie;* Los Angeles, May 25.

Neves, Tancredo, 75; president-elect of Brazil; Rio de Janeiro, Apr. 21.

Nolan, Lloyd, 83; character actor whose film career spanned 40 years; Los Angeles, Sept. 27.

North, John Ringling, 81; head of the Ringling Brothers and Barnum & Bailey Circus for 30 years; Brussels, Belgium, June 4.

O

O'Brien, Edmond, 69; actor who appeared in films since the 1940s; Inglewood, Cal., May 9.

O'Brien, George, 85; actor who appeared in 75 films, mostly westerns; Broken Arrow, Okla., Sept. 4.

Olson, Johnny, 75; radio and TV announcer closely associated with game shows, *The Price is Right;* Santa Monica, Cal., Oct. 12.

O'Malley, J. Pat, 80; Irish-born character actor with extensive stage and TV credits; San Juan Capistrano, Cal., Feb. 27.

Ormandy, Eugene, 85; music director of the Philadelphia Orchestra for 44 years until his retirement in 1980; Philadelphia, Mar. 12.

P

Peary, Harold, 76; actor who played The Great Gildersleeve on radio; Torrance, Cal., Mar. 30.

Peckinpah, Sam, 59; film director, *The Wild Bunch, Straw Dogs;* Inglewood, Cal., Dec. 28.

Pearce, Jan, 80; tenor who sang at the Metropolitan Opera for 27 years and whose career spanned 50 years; New York, Dec. 15.

Pelekoudas, Chris, 66; National League umpire, 1960-75; Sunnyvale, Cal., Nov. 30.

Porter, Robert Rodney, 67; British biochemist who shared the 1972 Nobel Prize for Medicine; Winchester, England, Sept. 6.

Prince, Bob, 68; broadcaster of the Pittsburgh Pirates baseball games for nearly 3 decades; Pittsburgh, June 10.

Pritikin, Nathan, 69; nutritionist and author; Albany, N.Y., Feb. 21.

Q

Quinlan, Karen Ann, 31; woman whose 10-year coma sparked debate on the definition of life and the right-to-die; Morris Plains, N.J., June 11.

R

Redgrave, Sir Michael, 77; British stage and film star; Denham, England, Mar. 21.

Richards, Harold M.S., 90; radio evangelist, "Voice of Prophecy"; Newbury Park, Cal., Apr. 24.

Richter, Dr. Charles, 85; seismologist for whom the Richter scale of earthquake magnitude was named; Pasadena, Cal., Sept. 30.

Riddle, Nelson, 64; composer and arranger who orchestrated songs for Sinatra, Ronstadt, others; Los Angeles, Oct. 5.

Rigby, Harry, 59; Broadway producer, *Sugar Babies;* New York, Jan. 17.

Robin, Leo, 89; lyricist who received 9 Oscar nominations, *Thanks for the Memory;* Los Angeles, Dec. 29.

Rock, Dr. John, 94; obstetrician and gynecologist who helped develop the first oral contraceptive in the 1950s; Peterborough, N.H., Dec. 4.

Rose, Leonard, 66; internationally reknowned cellist; White Plains, N.Y., Nov. 16.

Rothblatt, Henry B., 69; defense lawyer whose clients included 4 of the Watergate burglars; Ft. Lauderdale, Fla., Sept. 1.

Ryder, Loren L., 85; pioneer of motion picture sound technology who won 6 Oscars; Carmel, Cal., May 28.

Ryskind, Morrie, 89; comedy writer for stage and films; Washington, D.C., Aug. 24.

S

Sarkis, Elias, 60; president of Lebanon, 1976-82; Paris, June 27.

Savalas, George, 58; actor who played Detective Stavros on the *Kojak* TV series; Los Angeles, Oct. 2.

Scarne, John, 82; author of books on games and gambling; Englewood, N.J., July 7.

Scourby, Alexander, 71; actor and narrator; Boston, Feb. 23.

Sessions, Roger, 88; composer of symphonies, operas, and chamber music; Princeton, N.J., Mar. 16.

Shaughnessy, Mickey, 64; comedian and film actor; Cape May, N.J., July 23.

Sheppard, Eugenia, 80s; influential fashion columnist of the 1950s and 1960s; New York, Nov. 11.

Shepherd, Lee, 40; professional auto racer; Ardmore, Okla., Mar. 11.

Shivers, Allan, 77; governor of Texas, 1949-57; Austin, Jan. 14.

Shore, Eddie, 82; Boston Bruins defenseman who was the NHL's most valuable player 4 times; Springfield, Mass., Mar. 16.

Signoret, Simone, 64; French actress who won a 1958 Oscar as best actress for *Room at the Top;* Normandy, Sept. 30.

Sims, Zoot, 59; jazz saxophonist; New York, Mar. 23.

Sloane, Eric, 80; painter and author; New York, Mar. 6.

Smith, Kent, 78; supporting actor whose career spanned 4 decades; Los Angeles, Apr. 23.

Smith, Samantha, 13; girl who gained worldwide fame when she wrote letter about peace to Soviet leader Yuri Andropov; Auburn, Me., Aug. 26.

Sokolov, Valentin, 58; Soviet poet,

writer, and dissident; USSR, reported Nov. 8.

Sondergaard, Gale, 86; character actress who appeared in many films in the 1930s and 1940s; Woodland Hills, Cal., Aug. 14.

Spigelglass, Leonard, 76; playwright and screenwriter; Los Angeles, Feb. 14.

Springer, Axel, 73; West German publisher; W. Berlin, Sept. 22.

Stone, Louis, 74; investment analyst and financial writer; New York, Mar. 16.

Sturgeon, Theodore, 67; science fiction writer; Eugene, Ore., May 8.

Surtees, Robert, 78; Hollywood cinematographer who won 3 Academy Awards; Carmel, Cal., Jan. 5.

Sweet, Dolph, 64; actor who starred in the *Gimme a Break* TV sitcom; Tarzana, Cal., May 8.

T

Tanny, Vic, 73; physical fitness pioneer who developed aesthetically appealing health clubs in the 1930s and 1940s; Tampa, June 11.

Tebelak, John-Michael, 36; playwright and director who wrote *Godspell;* New York, Apr. 2.

Thomason, A. Mims, 74; journalist who headed UPI from 1962 to 1972; Greenwich, Conn., July 26.

V

Visser 't Hooft, Willem A., 84; Dutch theologian who headed the World Council of Churches, 1948-66; Geneva, July 4.

W

Wakefield, Dick, 64; outfielder who played for Detroit Tigers in the 1940s; Detroit, Aug. 26.

Ward, Lynd, 80; illustrator of the children's book *The Little Red Lighthouse and the Great Gray Bridge;* Reston, Va., June 28.

Wayne, Carol, 42; actress known for her numerous appearances with Johnny Carson on the *Tonight Show;* Manzanillo, Mexico, Jan. 13.

Weatherwax, Rudd, 77; Hollywood dog trainer who trained the original Lassie; Mission Hills, Cal., Feb. 25.

Weiland, Cooney, 80; hockey player and coach at Harvard Univ. for 21 years; Boston, July 3.

Welch Jr., Robert, 85; founder and patriarch of the John Birch Society; Winchester, Mass., Jan. 6.

Welles, Orson, 70; actor and director who created and starred in the film classic *Citizen Kane;* Los Angeles, Oct. 10.

White, E.B., 86; essayist and author of children's books, *Charlotte's Web;* North Brooklin, Me., Oct. 1.

Williams, Charles "Cootie", 77; trumpet player who was long associated with the Duke Ellington orchestra; New York, Sept. 15.

Woodhouse, Hedley, 74; jockey who won over 2,500 races; Franklin Square, N.Y., Dec. 29.

Woodruff, Robert W., 95; businessman who headed the Coca Cola Co. from 1923 to 1955; Atlanta, Mar. 7.

Wright, Olgivanna Lloyd, 85; collaborator and wife of Frank Lloyd Wright; Scottsdale, Ariz., Mar. 1.

XYZ

Yarbrough, LeeRoy, 46; former stock car racer; Jacksonville, Fla., Dec. 7.

Young, Stephen M., 95; U.S. senator from Ohio, 1959-71; Washington, D.C., Dec. 1.

Zaslofsky, Max, 59 basketball player who led the NBA in scoring 1947-48; New Hyde Park, N.Y., Oct. 15.

Zimbalist, Efrem, 94; Russian-born violinist; Reno, Nev., Feb. 22.

QUICK REFERENCE INDEX